THE OXFORD ENGLISH DICTIONARY

SECOND EDITION

THE OXFORD ENGLISH DICTIONARY

First Edited by

JAMES A. H. MURRAY, HENRY BRADLEY, W. A. CRAIGIE
and C. T. ONIONS

COMBINED WITH

A SUPPLEMENT TO THE OXFORD ENGLISH DICTIONARY

Edited by

R. W. BURCHFIELD

AND RESET WITH CORRECTIONS, REVISIONS
AND ADDITIONAL VOCABULARY

THE OXFORD ENGLISH DICTIONARY

SECOND EDITION

Prepared by

J. A. SIMPSON *and* E. S. C. WEINER

VOLUME XIX

Unemancipated–Wau-wau

CLARENDON PRESS · OXFORD

Oxford University Press, Great Clarendon Street, Oxford OX2 6DP
Oxford New York
Athens Auckland Bangkok Bogotá Buenos Aires Calcutta
Cape Town Chennai Dar es Salaam Delhi Florence Hong Kong Istanbul
Karachi Kuala Lumpur Madrid Melbourne Mexico City Mumbai
Nairobi Paris São Paulo Singapore Taipei Tokyo Toronto Warsaw
and associated companies in
Berlin Ibadan

Oxford is a registered trade mark of Oxford University Press

First published 1989
Reprinted 1991 (with corrections), 1998

British Library Cataloguing in Publication Data
Oxford English dictionary.—2nd ed.
1. English language—Dictionaries
I. Simpson, J. A. (John Andrew), 1953-
II. Weiner, Edmund S. C., 1950-
423
ISBN 0-19-861231-1 (vol. XIX)
ISBN 0-19-861186-2 (set)

Library of Congress Cataloging-in-Publication Data
The Oxford English dictionary.—2nd ed.
prepared by J. A. Simpson and E. S. C. Weiner
Bibliography: p.
ISBN 0-19-861231-1 (vol. XIX)
ISBN 0-19-861186-2 (set)
1. English language—Dictionaries. I. Simpson, J. A.
II. Weiner, E. S. C. III. Oxford University Press.
PE1625.087 1989
423—dc19 88-5330

Data capture by ICC, Fort Washington, Pa.
Text-processing by Oxford University Press
Typesetting by Pindar Graphics Origination, Scarborough, N. Yorks.
Manufactured in the United States of America by
World Color Book Services, Taunton, Mass.

KEY TO THE PRONUNCIATION

THE pronunciations given are those in use in the educated speech of southern England (the so-called 'Received Standard'), and the keywords given are to be understood as pronounced in such speech.

I. *Consonants*

b, d, f, k, l, m, n, p, t, v, z *have their usual English values*

g as in *go* (gəʊ)
h ... *ho!* (həʊ)
r ... *run* (rʌn), te*rr*ier ('tɛrɪə(r))
(r) ... he*r* (hɜː(r))
s ... *s*ee (siː), *s*ucce*ss* (sək'sɛs)
w ... *w*ear (wɛə(r))
hw ... *wh*en (hwɛn)
j ... *y*es (jɛs)

θ as in *th*in (θɪn), ba*th* (bɑːθ)
ð ... *th*en (ðɛn), ba*th*e (beɪð)
ʃ ... *sh*op (ʃɒp), di*sh* (dɪʃ)
tʃ ... *ch*op (tʃɒp), di*tch* (dɪtʃ)
ʒ ... vi*s*ion ('vɪʒən), dé*j*euner (deʒøne)
dʒ ... *j*u*dg*e (dʒʌdʒ)
ŋ ... si*ng*i*ng* ('sɪŋɪŋ), thi*n*k (θiŋk)
ŋg ... fi*ng*er ('fɪŋgə(r))

(FOREIGN AND NON-SOUTHERN)
ʎ as in It. serra*gl*io (ser'raʎo)
ɲ ... Fr. co*gn*ac (kɔɲak)
x ... Ger. a*ch* (ax), Sc. lo*ch* (lɒx), Sp. fri*j*oles (fri'xoles)
ç ... Ger. i*ch* (ɪç), Sc. ni*ch*t (nɪçt)
ɣ ... North Ger. sa*g*en ('zaːɣən)
c ... Afrikaans baardmanne*tj*ie ('baːrtmanəci)
ɥ ... Fr. c*u*isine (kɥizin)

Symbols in parentheses are used to denote elements that may be omitted either by individual speakers or in particular phonetic contexts: e.g. *bottle* ('bɒt(ə)l), *Mercian* ('mɜːʃ(ɪ)ən), *suit* (s(j)uːt), *impromptu* (ɪm'prɒm(p)tjuː), *father* ('fɑːðə(r)).

II. *Vowels and Diphthongs*

SHORT
ɪ as in p*i*t (pɪt), -n*e*ss, (-nɪs)
ɛ ... p*e*t (pɛt), Fr. *sept* (sɛt)
æ ... p*a*t (pæt)
ʌ ... p*u*tt (pʌt)
ɒ ... p*o*t (pɒt)
ʊ ... p*u*t (pʊt)
ə ... *a*noth*er* (ə'nʌðə(r))
(ə) ... beat*e*n ('biːt(ə)n)
i ... Fr. s*i* (si)
e ... Fr. b*é*b*é* (bebe)
a ... Fr. m*a*ri (mari)
ɑ ... Fr. b*â*timent (bɑtimɑ̃)
ɔ ... Fr. h*o*mme (ɔm)
o ... Fr. *eau* (o)
ø ... Fr. p*eu* (pø)
œ ... Fr. b*oeu*f (bœf) c*oeu*r (kœr)
u ... Fr. d*ou*ce (dus)
ʏ ... Ger. M*ü*ller ('mʏlər)
y ... Fr. d*u* (dy)

LONG
iː as in b*ea*n (biːn)
ɑː ... b*ar*n (bɑːn)
ɔː ... b*or*n (bɔːn)
uː ... b*oo*n (buːn)
ɜː ... b*ur*n (bɜːn)
eː ... Ger. Schn*ee* (ʃneː)
ɛː ... Ger. F*äh*re ('fɛːrə)
aː ... Ger. T*a*g (taːk)
oː ... Ger. S*oh*n (zoːn)
øː ... Ger. G*oe*the ('gøːtə)
yː ... Ger. gr*ü*n (gryːn)

NASAL
ɛ̃, æ̃ as in Fr. f*in* (fɛ̃, fæ̃)
ɑ̃ ... Fr. fr*an*c (frɑ̃)
ɔ̃ ... Fr. b*on* (bɔ̃)
œ̃ ... Fr. *un* (œ̃)

DIPHTHONGS, etc.
eɪ as in b*ay* (beɪ)
aɪ ... b*uy* (baɪ)
ɔɪ ... b*oy* (bɔɪ)
əʊ ... n*o* (nəʊ)
aʊ ... n*ow* (naʊ)
ɪə ... p*eer* (pɪə(r))
ɛə ... p*air* (pɛə(r))
ʊə ... t*our* (tʊə(r))
ɔə ... b*oar* (bɔə(r))

aɪə as in f*ie*ry ('faɪərɪ)
aʊə ... s*our* (saʊə(r))

The incidence of main stress is shown by a superior stress mark (') preceding the stressed syllable, and a secondary stress by an inferior stress mark (ˌ), e.g. *pronunciation* (prəˌnʌnsɪ'eɪʃ(ə)n).

For further explanation of the transcription used, see *General Explanations*, Volume I.

LIST OF ABBREVIATIONS, SIGNS, ETC.

Some abbreviations listed here in italics are also in certain cases printed in roman type, and vice versa.

a. (in Etym.)	adoption of, adopted from
a (as *a* 1850)	*ante*, 'before', 'not later than'
a.	adjective
abbrev.	abbreviation (of)
abl.	ablative
absol.	absolute, -ly
Abstr.	(in titles) *Abstract, -s*
acc.	accusative
Acct.	(in titles) *Account*
A.D.	*Anno Domini*
ad. (in Etym.)	adaptation of
Add.	Addenda
adj.	adjective
Adv.	(in titles) *Advance, -d, -s*
adv.	adverb
advb.	adverbial, -ly
Advt.	advertisement
Aeronaut.	(as label) in Aeronautics; (in titles) *Aeronautic, -al, -s*
AF., AFr.	Anglo-French
Afr.	Africa, -n
Agric.	(as label) in Agriculture; (in titles) *Agriculture, -al*
Alb.	Albanian
Amer.	American
Amer. Ind.	American Indian
Anat.	(as label) in Anatomy; (in titles) *Anatomy, -ical*
Anc.	(in titles) *Ancient*
Anglo-Ind.	Anglo-Indian
Anglo-Ir.	Anglo-Irish
Ann.	Annals
Anthrop., Anthropol.	(as label) in Anthropology; (in titles) *Anthropology, -ical*
Antiq.	(as label) in Antiquities; (in titles) *Antiquity*
aphet.	aphetic, aphetized
app.	apparently
Appl.	(in titles) *Applied*
Applic.	(in titles) *Application, -s*
appos.	appositive, -ly
Arab.	Arabic
Aram.	Aramaic
Arch.	in Architecture
arch.	archaic
Archæol.	in Archæology
Archit.	(as label) in Architecture; (in titles) *Architecture, -al*
Arm.	Armenian
assoc.	association
Astr.	in Astronomy
Astrol.	in Astrology
Astron.	(in titles) *Astronomy, -ical*
Astronaut.	(in titles) *Astronautic, -s*
attrib.	attributive, -ly
Austral.	Australian
Autobiogr.	(in titles) *Autobiography, -ical*
A.V.	Authorized Version
B.C.	Before Christ
B.C.	(in titles) British Columbia
bef.	before
Bibliogr.	(as label) in Bibliography; (in titles) *Bibliography, -ical*
Biochem.	(as label) in Biochemistry; (in titles) *Biochemistry, -ical*
Biol.	(as label) in Biology; (in titles) *Biology, -ical*
Bk.	*Book*
Bot.	(as label) in Botany; (in titles) *Botany, -ical*
Bp.	Bishop
Brit.	(in titles) *Britain, British*
Bulg.	Bulgarian

Bull.	(in titles) *Bulletin*
c (as *c* 1700)	*circa*, 'about'
c. (as 19th c.)	century
Cal.	(in titles) *Calendar*
Cambr.	(in titles) *Cambridge*
Canad.	Canadian
Cat.	Catalan
catachr.	catachrestically
Catal.	(in titles) *Catalogue*
Celt.	Celtic
Cent.	(in titles) *Century, Central*
Cent. Dict.	*Century Dictionary*
Cf., cf.	*confer*, 'compare'
Ch.	Church
Chem.	(as label) in Chemistry; (in titles) *Chemistry, -ical*
Chr.	(in titles) *Christian*
Chron.	(in titles) *Chronicle*
Chronol.	(in titles) *Chronology, -ical*
Cinemat., Cinematogr.	in Cinematography
Clin.	(in titles) *Clinical*
cl. L.	classical Latin
cogn. w.	cognate with
Col.	(in titles) *Colonel, Colony*
Coll.	(in titles) *Collection*
collect.	collective, -ly
colloq.	colloquial, -ly
comb.	combined, -ing
Comb.	Combinations
Comm.	in Commercial usage
Communic.	in Communications
comp.	compound, composition
Compan.	(in titles) *Companion*
compar.	comparative
compl.	complement
Compl.	(in titles) *Complete*
Conc.	(in titles) *Concise*
Conch.	in Conchology
concr.	concrete, -ly
Conf.	(in titles) *Conference*
Congr.	(in titles) *Congress*
conj.	conjunction
cons.	consonant
const.	construction, construed with
contr.	contrast (with)
Contrib.	(in titles) *Contribution*
Corr.	(in titles) *Correspondence*
corresp.	corresponding (to)
Cotgr.	R. Cotgrave, *Dictionarie of the French and English Tongues*
cpd.	compound
Crit.	(in titles) *Criticism, Critical*
Cryst.	in Crystallography
Cycl.	(in titles) *Cyclopædia, -ic*
Cytol.	(in titles) *Cytology, -ical*
Da.	Danish
D.A.	*Dictionary of Americanisms*
D.A.E.	*Dictionary of American English*
dat.	dative
D.C.	District of Columbia
Deb.	(in titles) *Debate, -s*
def.	definite, -ition
dem.	demonstrative
deriv.	derivative, -ation
derog.	derogatory
Descr.	(in titles) *Description, -tive*
Devel.	(in titles) *Development, -al*
Diagn.	(in titles) *Diagnosis, Diagnostic*
dial.	dialect, -al

Dict.	Dictionary; *spec.*, the *Oxford English Dictionary*
dim.	diminutive
Dis.	(in titles) *Disease*
Diss.	(in titles) *Dissertation*
D.O.S.T.	*Dictionary of the Older Scottish Tongue*
Du.	Dutch
E.	East
Eccl.	(as label) in Ecclesiastical usage; (in titles) *Ecclesiastical*
Ecol.	in Ecology
Econ.	(as label) in Economics; (in titles) *Economy, -ics*
ed.	edition
E.D.D.	*English Dialect Dictionary*
Edin.	(in titles) *Edinburgh*
Educ.	(as label) in Education; (in titles) *Education, -al*
EE.	Early English
e.g.	*exempli gratia*, 'for example'
Electr.	(as label) in Electricity; (in titles) *Electricity, -ical*
Electron.	(in titles) *Electronic, -s*
Elem.	(in titles) *Element, -ary*
ellipt.	elliptical, -ly
Embryol.	in Embryology
e.midl.	east midland (dialect)
Encycl.	(in titles) *Encyclopædia, -ic*
Eng.	England, English
Engin.	in Engineering
Ent.	in Entomology
Entomol.	(in titles) *Entomology, -logical*
erron.	erroneous, -ly
esp.	especially
Ess.	(in titles) *Essay, -s*
et al.	*et alii*, 'and others'
etc.	et cetera
Ethnol.	in Ethnology
etym.	etymology
euphem.	euphemistically
Exam.	(in titles) *Examination*
exc.	except
Exerc.	(in titles) *Exercise, -s*
Exper.	(in titles) *Experiment, -al*
Explor.	(in titles) *Exploration, -s*
f.	feminine
f. (in Etym.)	formed on
f. (in subordinate entries)	form of
F.	French
fem. (*rarely* f.)	feminine
fig.	figurative, -ly
Finn.	Finnish
fl.	*floruit*, 'flourished'
Found.	(in titles) *Foundation, -s*
Fr.	French
freq.	frequent, -ly
Fris.	Frisian
Fund.	(in titles) *Fundamental, -s*
Funk or *Funk's Stand. Dict.*	*Funk and Wagnalls Standard Dictionary*
G.	German
Gael.	Gaelic
Gaz.	(in titles) *Gazette*
gen.	genitive
gen.	general, -ly
Geogr.	(as label) in Geography; (in titles) *Geography, -ical*

Geol.	(as label) in Geology; (in titles) *Geology, -ical*
Geom.	in Geometry
Geomorphol.	in Geomorphology
Ger.	German
Gloss.	Glossary
Gmc.	Germanic
Godef.	F. Godefroy, *Dictionnaire de l'ancienne langue française*
Goth.	Gothic
Govt.	(in titles) *Government*
Gr.	Greek
Gram.	(as label) in Grammar; (in titles) *Grammar, -tical*
Gt.	Great
Heb.	Hebrew
Her.	in Heraldry
Herb.	among herbalists
Hind.	Hindustani
Hist.	(as label) in History; (in titles) *History, -ical*
hist.	historical
Histol.	(in titles) *Histology, -ical*
Hort.	in Horticulture
Househ.	(in titles) *Household*
Housek.	(in titles) *Housekeeping*
Ibid.	*Ibidem*, 'in the same book or passage'
Icel.	Icelandic
Ichthyol.	in Ichthyology
id.	*idem*, 'the same'
i.e.	*id est*, 'that is'
IE.	Indo-European
Illustr.	(in titles) *Illustration, -ted*
imit.	imitative
Immunol.	in Immunology
imp.	imperative
impers.	impersonal
impf.	imperfect
ind.	indicative
indef.	indefinite
Industr.	(in titles) *Industry, -ial*
inf.	infinitive
infl.	influenced
Inorg.	(in titles) *Inorganic*
Ins.	(in titles) *Insurance*
Inst.	(in titles) *Institute, -tion*
int.	interjection
intr.	intransitive
Introd.	(in titles) *Introduction*
Ir.	Irish
irreg.	irregular, -ly
It.	Italian
J., (J.)	(quoted from) Johnson's *Dictionary*
(Jam.)	Jamieson, *Scottish Dict.*
Jap.	Japanese
joc.	jocular, -ly
Jrnl.	(in titles) *Journal*
Jun.	(in titles) *Junior*
Knowl.	(in titles) *Knowledge*
l.	line
L.	Latin
lang.	language
Lect.	(in titles) *Lecture, -s*
Less.	(in titles) *Lesson, -s*
Let., Lett.	letter, letters
LG.	Low German
lit.	literal, -ly
Lit.	Literary
Lith.	Lithuanian
LXX	Septuagint
m.	masculine
Mag.	(in titles) *Magazine*
Magn.	(in titles) *Magnetic, -ism*
Mal.	Malay, Malayan
Man.	(in titles) *Manual*
Managem.	(in titles) *Management*
Manch.	(in titles) *Manchester*
Manuf.	in Manufacture, -ing
Mar.	(in titles) *Marine*

masc. (*rarely* m.)	masculine
Math.	(as label) in Mathematics; (in titles) *Mathematics, -al*
MDu.	Middle Dutch
ME.	Middle English
Mech.	(as label) in Mechanics; (in titles) *Mechanics, -al*
Med.	(as label) in Medicine; (in titles) *Medicine, -ical*
med.L.	medieval Latin
Mem.	(in titles) *Memoir, -s*
Metaph.	in Metaphysics
Meteorol.	(as label) in Meteorology; (in titles) *Meteorology, -ical*
MHG.	Middle High German
midl.	midland (dialect)
Mil.	in military usage
Min.	(as label) in Mineralogy; (in titles) *Ministry*
Mineral.	(in titles) *Mineralogy, -ical*
MLG.	Middle Low German
Misc.	(in titles) *Miscellany, -eous*
mod.	modern
mod.L	modern Latin
(Morris),	(quoted from) E. E. Morris's *Austral English*
Mus.	(as label) in Music; (in titles) *Music, -al; Museum*
Myst.	(in titles) *Mystery*
Mythol.	in Mythology
N.	North
n.	neuter
N. Amer.	North America, -n
N. & Q.	*Notes and Queries*
Narr.	(in titles) *Narrative*
Nat.	(in titles) *Natural*
Nat. Hist.	in Natural History
Naut.	in nautical language
N.E.	North East
N.E.D.	*New English Dictionary*, original title of the *Oxford English Dictionary* (first edition)
Neurol.	in Neurology
neut. (*rarely* n.)	neuter
NF., NFr.	Northern French
No.	Number
nom.	nominative
north.	northern (dialect)
Norw.	Norwegian
n.q.	no quotations
N.T.	New Testament
Nucl.	Nuclear
Numism.	in Numismatics
N.W.	North West
N.Z.	New Zealand
obj.	object
obl.	oblique
Obs., obs.	obsolete
Obstetr.	(in titles) *Obstetrics*
occas.	occasionally
OE.	Old English (= Anglo-Saxon)
OF., OFr.	Old French
OFris.	Old Frisian
OHG.	Old High German
OIr.	Old Irish
ON.	Old Norse
ONF.	Old Northern French
Ophthalm.	in Ophthalmology
opp.	opposed (to), the opposite (of)
Opt.	in Optics
Org.	(in titles) *Organic*
orig.	origin, -al, -ally
Ornith.	(as label) in Ornithology; (in titles) *Ornithology, -ical*
OS.	Old Saxon
OSl.	Old (Church) Slavonic
O.T.	Old Testament
Outl.	(in titles) *Outline*
Oxf.	(in titles) *Oxford*
p.	page
Palæogr.	in Palæography

Palæont.	(as label) in Palæontology; (in titles) *Palæontology, -ical*
pa. pple.	passive participle, past participle
(Partridge),	(quoted from) E. Partridge's *Dictionary of Slang and Unconventional English*
pass.	passive, -ly
pa.t.	past tense
Path.	(as label) in Pathology; (in titles) *Pathology, -ical*
perh.	perhaps
Pers.	Persian
pers.	person, -al
Petrogr.	in Petrography
Petrol.	(as label) in Petrology; (in titles) *Petrology, -ical*
(Pettman),	(quoted from) C. Pettman's *Africanderisms*
pf.	perfect
Pg.	Portuguese
Pharm.	in Pharmacology
Philol.	(as label) in Philology; (in titles) *Philology, -ical*
Philos.	(as label) in Philosophy; (in titles) *Philosophy, -ic*
phonet.	phonetic, -ally
Photogr.	(as label) in Photography; (in titles) *Photography, -ical*
phr.	phrase
Phys.	physical; (*rarely*) in Physiology
Physiol.	(as label) in Physiology; (in titles) *Physiology, -ical*
Pict.	(in titles) *Picture, Pictorial*
pl., plur.	plural
poet.	poetic, -al
Pol.	Polish
Pol.	(as label) in Politics; (in titles) *Politics, -al*
Pol. Econ.	in Political Economy
Polit.	(in titles) *Politics, -al*
pop.	popular, -ly
Porc.	(in titles) *Porcelain*
poss.	possessive
Pott.	(in titles) *Pottery*
ppl. a., pple. adj.	participial adjective
pple.	participle
Pr.	Provençal
pr.	present
Pract.	(in titles) *Practice, -al*
prec.	preceding (word or article)
pred.	predicative
pref.	prefix
pref., Pref.	preface
prep.	preposition
pres.	present
Princ.	(in titles) *Principle, -s*
priv.	privative
prob.	probably
Probl.	(in titles) *Problem*
Proc.	(in titles) *Proceedings*
pron.	pronoun
pronunc.	pronunciation
prop.	properly
Pros.	in Prosody
Prov.	Provençal
pr. pple.	present participle
Psych.	in Psychology
Psychol.	(as label) in Psychology; (in titles) *Psychology, -ical*
Publ.	(in titles) *Publications*
Q.	(in titles) *Quarterly*
quot(s).	quotation(s)
q.v.	*quod vide*, 'which see'
R.	(in titles) *Royal*
Radiol.	in Radiology
R.C.Ch.	Roman Catholic Church
Rec.	(in titles) *Record*
redupl.	reduplicating
Ref.	(in titles) *Reference*
refash.	refashioned, -ing
refl.	reflexive
Reg.	(in titles) *Register*

reg.	regular
rel.	related to
Reminisc.	(in titles) *Reminiscence, -s*
Rep.	(in titles) *Report, -s*
repr.	representative, representing
Res.	(in titles) *Research*
Rev.	(in titles) *Review*
rev.	revised
Rhet.	in Rhetoric
Rom.	Roman, -ce, -ic
Rum.	Rumanian
Russ.	Russian
S.	South
S.Afr.	South Africa, -n
sb.	substantive
sc.	*scilicet*, 'understand' or 'supply'
Sc., Scot.	Scottish
Scand.	(in titles) *Scandinavia, -n*
Sch.	(in titles) *School*
Sc. Nat. Dict.	*Scottish National Dictionary*
Scotl.	(in titles) *Scotland*
Sel.	(in titles) *Selection, -s*
Ser.	Series
sing.	singular
Sk.	(in titles) *Sketch*
Skr.	Sanskrit
Slav.	Slavonic
S.N.D.	*Scottish National Dictionary*
Soc.	(in titles) *Society*
Sociol.	(as label) in Sociology; (in titles) *Sociology, -ical*
Sp.	Spanish
Sp.	(in titles) *Speech, -es*
sp.	spelling
spec.	specifically
Spec.	(in titles) *Specimen*
St.	Saint
Stand.	(in titles) *Standard*
Stanf.	(quoted from) *Stanford Dictionary of Anglicised Words & Phrases*
str.	strong
Struct.	(in titles) *Structure, -al*
Stud.	(in titles) *Studies*
subj.	subject
subord. cl.	subordinate clause
subseq.	subsequent, -ly
subst.	substantively
suff.	suffix
superl.	superlative
Suppl.	Supplement
Surg.	(as label) in Surgery; (in titles) *Surgery, Surgical*
s.v.	*sub voce*, 'under the word'
Sw.	Swedish
s.w.	south-western (dialect)
Syd. Soc. Lex.	Sydenham Society, *Lexicon of Medicine & Allied Sciences*
syll.	syllable
Syr.	Syrian
Syst.	(in titles) *System, -atic*
Taxon.	(in titles) *Taxonomy, -ical*
techn.	technical, -ly
Technol.	(in titles) *Technology, -ical*
Telegr.	in Telegraphy
Teleph.	in Telephony
(Th.),	(quoted from) Thornton's *American Glossary*
Theatr.	in the Theatre, theatrical
Theol.	(as label) in Theology; (in titles) *Theology, -ical*
Theoret.	(in titles) *Theoretical*
Tokh.	Tokharian
tr., transl.	translated, translation
Trans.	(in titles) *Transactions*
trans.	transitive
transf.	transferred sense
Trav.	(in titles) *Travel(s)*
Treas.	(in titles) *Treasury*
Treat.	(in titles) *Treatise*
Treatm.	(in titles) *Treatment*
Trig.	in Trigonometry
Trop.	(in titles) *Tropical*
Turk.	Turkish
Typog., Typogr.	in Typography
ult.	ultimately
Univ.	(in titles) *University*
unkn.	unknown
U.S.	United States
U.S.S.R.	Union of Soviet Socialist Republics
usu.	usually
v., vb.	verb
var(r)., vars.	variant(s) of
vbl. sb.	verbal substantive
Vertebr.	(in titles) *Vertebrate, -s*
Vet.	(as label) in Veterinary Science; (in titles) *Veterinary*
Vet. Sci.	in Veterinary Science
viz.	*videlicet*, 'namely'
Voy.	(in titles) *Voyage, -s*
v.str.	strong verb
vulg.	vulgar
v.w.	weak verb
W.	Welsh; West
wd.	word
Webster	*Webster's (New International) Dictionary*
Westm.	(in titles) *Westminster*
WGmc.	West Germanic
Wks.	(in titles) *Works*
w.midl.	west midland (dialect)
WS.	West Saxon
(Y.),	(quoted from) Yule & Burnell's *Hobson-Jobson*
Yrs.	(in titles) *Years*
Zoogeogr.	in Zoogeography
Zool.	(as label) in Zoology; (in titles) *Zoology, -ical*

Signs and Other Conventions

Before a word or sense

† = obsolete
|| = not naturalized, alien
¶ = catachrestic and erroneous uses

In the listing of Forms

1 = before 1100
2 = 12th c. (1100 to 1200)
3 = 13th c. (1200 to 1300), etc.
5-7 = 15th to 17th century
20 = 20th century

In the etymologies

* indicates a word or form not actually found, but of which the existence is inferred
:— = normal development of

The printing of a word in SMALL CAPITALS indicates that further information will be found under the word so referred to.

. . indicates an omitted part of a quotation.

- (in a quotation) indicates a hyphen doubtfully present in the original; (in other text) indicates a hyphen inserted only for the sake of a line-break.

PROPRIETARY NAMES

THIS Dictionary includes some words which are or are asserted to be proprietary names or trade marks. Their inclusion does not imply that they have acquired for legal purposes a non-proprietary or general significance nor any other judgement concerning their legal status. In cases where the editorial staff have established in the records of the Patent Offices of the United Kingdom and of the United States that a word is registered as a proprietary name or trade mark this is indicated, but no judgement concerning the legal status of such words is made or implied thereby.

une'mancipated, *ppl. a.* (UN-^{1} 8.)
[1775 ASH.] **1811** F. PLOWDEN *Hist. Irel. 1801–10* II. iv. 535 The Catholics remained unemancipated. **1841** LANE *Arab. Nts.* I. 63 Unemancipated slaves..become the property of his heirs. **1875** MAINE *Hist. Inst.* vii. 223 The home-staying, unemancipated son..is preferred to the others.

une'masculated, *ppl. a.* (UN-^{1} 8.)
[1775 ASH.] **1791** COWPER *Iliad* XXIII. 474 Borne by his unemasculated steeds Of Trojan pedigree. **1888** *Pall Mall G.* 6 June 6/1 If it becomes law with its main provisions unemasculated.

unembacelled, obs. var. UNEMBEZZLED.

unem'balmed, *ppl. a.* (UN-^{1} 8.)
c **1730** WALDRON *Descr. Isle of Man* Wks. (1731) 144 A human Body, unembowelled, unembalmed. **1800** in *Spirit Pub. Jrnls.* IV. 294 Yet one shall moulder unembalmed to dust.

unem'banked, *ppl. a.* (UN-^{1} 8.)
[1775 ASH.] **1807** BRITTON *Lincoln* 547 He conjectures there may be..200,000 [acres] of commons, wastes, and unembanked salt marshes. **1894** *Daily News* 2 July 5/2 The Thames, unpurified and unembanked.

unem'barrassed, *ppl. a.* [UN-^{1} 8.]
1. Not encumbered, hampered, or impeded. (In lit. or fig. uses.)
1708 *Diss. Drunkenness* 31 Temperance, how clean and unembarassed it keeps the Senses! **1717** BERKELEY in Fraser *Life* (1871) 551 [The church of] St. Spiritus [is] very neat and unembarrassed [with ornament]. **1796** *Instr. & Reg. Cavalry* (1813) 201 The movements of the second line to conform to that of the first are free and unembarrassed. **1836** J. GILBERT *Chr. Atonem.* ix. (1852) 296 Not a single doctrine could remain unembarrassed with doubt. **1884** *Manch. Exam.* 6 Oct. 5/2 To be left to pursue an unembarrassed course in [governing] Egypt.
2. Not confused or constrained; free, at ease.
1746 YORKE in G. Harris *Life Ld. Hardwicke* (1847) II. 235 The second [ballad] is entitled, 'The Unembarrassed Countenance'. **1762** FOOTE *Liar* I. i, He is as unimbarrassed, easy, and fluent..as if he really believed what he said. **1786** *Beckford's Vathek* (1868) 73 His gait was unembarrassed and noble. **1850** THACKERAY *Pendennis* xxix, The young man was perfectly easy and unembarrassed. **1897** *Harper's Mag.* Apr. 726 Declining the unembarrassed entreaties.., I despatched my inquiries and fled.

unem'barrassedly, *adv.* (UN-^{1} 11; cf. prec.)
1873 MISS BROUGHTON *Nancy* iii, Looking frankly and unembarrassedly up into his face.

unem'barrassing, -ment: see UN-^{1} 10 and 12.

unem'battled, *ppl. a.* (UN-^{1} 8.)
1615 G. SANDYS *Trav.* 233 The walls..vnimbattald, and sheluing on the outside. **1876** T. HARDY *Ethelberta* (1890) 366 The square unembattled tower of Knollsea Church.

unem'bellished, *ppl. a.* (UN-^{1} 8.)
1630 FANSHAWE *Pastor Fido*, etc. (1648) 228 Let no darke corner of the land Be unimbellisht with one Gemme. **171.** EUSDEN in Addison *Cato* A.'s Wks. 1721 I. 266 Such energy of sense might pleasure raise, Tho' unembellish'd with the charms of phrase. *a* **1763** SHENSTONE *Past. Ode Lyttleton* 148 And Grenville..prais'd these unembellish'd woods. **1805** WORDSW. *Prelude* III. 108 Earth, nowhere unembellished by some trace Of that first Paradise whence man was driven. **1862** 'SHIRLEY' (J. Skelton) *Nugæ Crit.* ix. 416 A literal and unembellished account of the fact.

unem'bezzled, *ppl. a.* (UN-^{1} 8.)
1546 *Inv. Ch. Goods* (Surtees) 87 One chalice of sylver.. and also two bells..savely to be kept unspoiled, unembecyled, and sold. **1553** *Ibid.* 88 To..kepe unspoiled, unembacelled and solde. **1643** CHAS. I in Carte *Coll.* (1735) 165 That the houses, chattels and other estates..be saved harmless,..that so they may be found unimbezzeled. **1744** ELIZA HEYWOOD *Female Spect.* No. 3 (1748) I. 120 We should leave it as intire and unembezzled as we received it.

unem'bittered, *ppl. a.* Also 8–9 unim-. (UN-^{1} 8.)
α. *a* **1711** KEN *Hymns Evang.* Poet. Wks. 1721 I. 102 Bless'd are the Meek,..Who unimbitter'd, the injurious treat. **1748** HERVEY *Medit.* (ed. 4) II. 69 Those happy Regions, where Delights, abundant and un-imbittered flow. **1816** SCOTT *Antiq.* xvi, While the tear can drop unimbittered by any painful recollection.
β. **1744** YOUNG *Nt. Th.* VII. 296 They drink the Stream.. un-embitter'd With Doubts, Fears, fruitless Hopes. **1786** *Francis the Philanthropist* II. 92 Our parting..was however unembittered by any apprehensions. **1834** WHEWELL in Todhunter *Acc. Writ.* (1876) II. 176, I am to have them unembittered by that part of the business.

unem'bodied, *ppl. a.* Also unim-. [UN-^{1} 8.]
1. Not invested with a body; incorporeal.
1662 GLANVILL *Lux Orient.* xiii. (1682) 104 To urge, that there are..purely unembodied Spirits in the Universe. **1719** DE FOE *Crusoe* II. (Globe) 363, I am satisfied our Spirits embodied have a Converse with..the Spirits unembodied. *a* **1766** MRS. F. SHERIDAN *Nourjahad* (1767) 196 He felt as it were unimbodied, and an involuntary adjuration burst from his lips. **1848** R. I. WILBERFORCE *Incarnation* xii. 393 The natural intercourse of the mind with its unembodied Creator. **1855** MILMAN *Lat. Chr.* XIV. iii. VI. 468 Matter.. subsisted potentially only,..unembodied, immaterial.
2. Not embodied, in various senses.
1760 *Ann. Reg., Chron.* 189 The charge of pay and cloathing for the unembodied militia. **1841** MIALL in *Nonconf.* I. 17 A mere theory,..an abstract unembodied principle.

unem'bowelled, *ppl. a.* (UN-^{1} 8.)
c **1730** [see UNEMBALMED].

unem'bowered, *ppl. a.* (UN-^{1} 8.)
[1775 ASH.] **1814** WORDSW. *Excurs.* VII. 55 All unembowered And naked stood that lowly Parsonage.

unem'braceable. *a.* (UN-^{1} 7 b.)
1859 G. MEREDITH *Poet. Wks.* (1912) 92 The bride.. Scarcely faceable, Quite unembraceable!

unem'braced, *ppl. a.* (UN-^{1} 8.)
[1775 ASH.] **1792** *Elvina* II. 83 [They] took their departure, unattended,—unembraced,—unregretted. **1853** TALFOURD *Castilian* v. iii, It is hard To leave her unembraced, yet on a moment Hangs the last issue. **1867** MORRIS *Jason* x. 272 Another monster..raised aloft his crest Against her unembraced tender breast.

unem'broidered, *ppl. a.* (UN-^{1} 8.)
1649 LOVELACE *Poems* (1904) 136 Naked as their own innocence, And unimbroyder'd from Offence. **1977** A. MORICE *Scared to Death* xxv. 168 They had heard of Bernard's elopement from Helena, whose white-washed account intrigued me far less than the unembroidered version from Farndale.

unem'broiled, *ppl. a.* (UN-^{1} 8.)
1759 H. WALPOLE *Let. to Mann* 13 Sept., An opportunity of embrolling the little of Europe that remains unembroiled. **1968** P. DICKINSON *Skin Deep* v. 111 Mr Tinker reacted into ferocious melodrama, swivelling round on the unembroiled Mr Green.

unement, obs. form of OINTMENT.

une'molumented, *a.* (UN-^{1} 9.)
1810 BENTHAM *Offic. Apt. Maximized, Def. Econ.* (1830) 126 The expense..they have been at in obtaining their unemolumented seats. **1933** M. LOWRY *Ultramarine* iii. 135 'A name to conjure with.' You see, unemolumented but monumental.

une'motional, *a.* (UN-^{1} 7.)
Frequent from *c* 1880; hence also, in recent use, ***unemotionalism***, ***unemotionalness***.
1876 GEO. ELIOT *Dan. Der.* lxii, Lapidoth..thought of all that this inscription signified with an unemotional memory. **1887** MISS BRADDON *Like & Unlike* x, He was the most unemotional young man Colonel Deverill had ever encountered.
Hence **une'motionally** *adv.*
1884 *Athenæum* 12 Jan. 52/1 The aged cynic, whose ungrateful task it is to regard them unemotionally. **1894** DU MAURIER *Trilby* II. 202 He unemotionally, dispassionately, wished himself dead.

une'motioned, *a.* (UN-^{1} 9.)
1817 W. GODWIN *Mandeville* III. v. 98 The dry, sarcastic, unemotioned..way in which he detailed them [*sc.* anecdotes]. **1929** E. BOWEN *Last September* xi. 138 As a rather perplexing system of niceties, Laurence saw it;..an unemotioned kindness withering to assertion selfish or racial.

un'emperor, *v.* (UN-^{2} 6 b.)
1642 FULLER *Holy & Prof. St.* v. xviii. (1841) 427 Prince Manuel..in vain opposed this decree, alleging this to be the ready way for his father to un-emperor himself.

unem'phatic, *a.* and *sb.* (UN-^{1} 7.)
1800 *Monthly Mag.* X. 317 An emphatic syllable is long; an unemphatic syllable, short. **1836–7** SIR W. HAMILTON *Lect. Metaph.* xxi. (1859) II. 19 The participle *knowing* is too vague and unemphatic to be employed. **1874** BLACKIE *Self-Cult.* 74 The general action..languid and unemphatic.
b. As *sb.* An unstressed syllable.
1815 *Monthly Mag.* XXXIX. 118 The regular arrangement of their longs and shorts,..their emphatics and unemphatics.
So **unem'phatical** *a.* (Worcester, 1846, citing Brown), **-ically** *adv.* (Webster, 1847).

unem'pirically, *adv.* (UN-^{1} 11.)
a **1849** POE *Eureka* Wks. 1865 II. 137 This result is in the fullest keeping with that which I have reached unempirically.

unem'ploy. (UN-^{1} 12.)
1887 F. W. NEWMAN in Sieveking *Mem.* (1909) x. 241 Unless..the causes of Un-Employ be removed, we must calculate on frightful disorder. **1891** [see PTOCHOLOGY].

unem'ployable, *a.* and *sb.* (UN-^{1} 7 b.)
1887 *St. James's Gaz.* 22 Dec. 4/1 Persons who are unemployed because they are unemployable. **1900** *Q. Rev.* Jan. 174 The class of the casual labourer or the unemployable. **1909** *Chambers's Jrnl.* Nov. 728/1 Every country has its shiftless element—its 'unemployables' as they are termed by the Salvation Army. **1944** L. MUMFORD *Condition of Man* vi. 209 The artist, who was the most courted figure of the fifteenth century, became ultimately the chronic unemployable of the nineteenth century. **1979** *Daily Tel.* 22 Sept. 20 You write about the employability of school-leavers. It is farcical to suppose that this depends on whether they have been beaten at school; otherwise Germany and Japan would be nations of unemployables.
Hence **ˌunemployaˈbility**.
1921 *N.E.D.* s.v. UNEMPLOYABLE *a.* and *sb.* **1926** A. M. CARR-SAUNDERS *Eugenics* vii. 157 It is worthy of note that over half the men and over one-third of the women placed in the category of those 'verging upon unemployability' were sixty years of age or over. **1958** [see FAINÉANTISME]. **1980** J. BOYD-CARPENTER *Way of Life* xi. 131 He was also receiving what was called Unemployability Supplement, an extra allowance intended to compensate war-disabled people whose disability prevented them from earning.

unem'ployed, *ppl. a.* and *sb.* Also 7–8 unim-. [UN-^{1} 8.]
1. Not put to use; not applied to some end or purpose.
1600 SURFLET *Countrie Farme* II. iii. 205 Wherefore it behooueth that the vnimploied or fallow ground..be first well cleansed from stones. **1665** in De Foe *Plague* (1754) 53 Till their Coaches..have stood unemploy'd by the Space of five or six Days after such Service. **1748** CHESTERF. *Let.* 16 Feb., Every moment may be put to some use, and that with much more pleasure than if unemployed. **1826** KIRBY & SP. *Entomol.* III. 363 The real instrument of suction, which when unemployed is retracted within the tubulet. **1882** CHILD *Ballads* Advt. p. vii, No becoming means has been left unemployed.
2. a. Not engaged in any work or occupation; idle; *spec.* temporarily out of work.
1667 MILTON *P.L.* IV. 617 Other Creatures all day long Rove idle unimploid, and less need rest. **1677** YARRANTON *Eng. Improv.* 61 Admit there be in England and Wales a hundred thousand poor people unimployed. **1740** CIBBER *Apol.* (1756) I. 167, I remember him three times for some years unemploy'd in any theatre. **1824** MISS L. M. HAWKINS *Annaline* I. 40 Being unemployed they amused themselves and others with conjectures. **1860** RUSKIN *Unto this Last* iii. §54 The vexed question of the destinies of the unemployed workmen. **1887** [see UNEMPLOYABLE].
b. *absol.* or as *sb.*
1782 'J. H. ST. J. DE CRÈVECŒUR' *Lett. from Amer. Farmer* viii. 212 The means of procuring subsistence in Europe are limited..the manufacturer is overcharged with supernumerary hands; what then must become of the unemployed? **1817** T. BERNARD *Supply of Employment & Subsistence for Labouring Classes* 28 Our sea-coasts would swarm with adventurous fishing boats; new means of employment would be afforded to the..unemployed. **1882** *Pall Mall G.* 10 May 3/2 The genuine total abstainers among the unemployed. **1900** H. LAWSON *On Track* 108 Here I've been mooning round like an unemployed for three weeks.
c. Pertaining to, connected with, unemployed persons.
1844 STOCQUELER *Handbk. Brit. India* 49 During this interval he draws the unemployed salary of three hundred rupees per mensem. **1895** *Daily News* 19 Aug. 5/2 Twenty-four per cent. of its 10,000 members received unemployed benefits.

unem'ployment. (UN-^{1} 12.)
In common use from *c* 1895 (cf. UNEMPLOY). Also *attrib.*, as ***unemployment benefit***, ***insurance***, etc.
1888 *Science* XI. 192/1 The chief purpose of the inquiry was to ascertain..the extent of unemployment generally. **1894** *Liberal* 1 Dec. 67/2 These figures..represent the normal unemployment of the State. **1909** *R. Comm. Poor Laws* App. XIX. 78 in *Parl. Papers* (Cd. 4795) XLIV. 1 Trade Unionists have..to consider the large number of fellow workmen who are in unions which cannot afford to pay unemployment benefit. **1923** *Spectator* 13 Jan. 47/2 From the point of view of the employer unemployment insurance is not less important. **1933** *Nation* (N.Y.) 4 Jan. 13 In the interests of economy the unemployment benefits would be reduced. **1967** N. FREELING *Strike out where not Applicable* 110 Applications for a building licence, claim for unemployment benefit..—the policeman can find gold in this. **1978** S. SHELDON *Bloodline* xxxix. 347 They were listed if they had paid taxes or drawn unemployment insurance or welfare funds.

unem'poisoned, *ppl. a.* (UN-^{1} 8.)
[1775 ASH.] **1791** CHARLOTTE SMITH *Celestina* (ed. 2) II. 27 Till I..can see you, with all those delicious hopes unempoisoned.

unem'powered, *ppl. a.* (UN-^{1} 8.)
1731 A. HILL *Adv. Poets* Ep. p. vi, The Poet,.. unimpower'd to act greatly Himself, asserts his Fire in describing the Great Actions of others.

un'empt, *v. dial.* [UN-^{2} 9.] *trans.* To empty, to unload.
1798 J. JEFFERSON *Let. to J. Boucher* 19 Mar. (MS.). **1847–** in dial. glossaries (midland and western).

un'emptiable, *a.* (UN-^{1} 7 b.)
1594 HOOKER *Eccl. Pol.* II. i. §4 A drop of that vnemptiable Fountaine of wisdome. **1882** FARRAR *Early Chr.* I. 286 The unemptiable fountain of Divine wisdom.

†**un'emptible**, *a. Obs.* (Cf. prec. and EMPT *v.*)
1656 JEANES *Fuln. Christ* 229 An indeficient fullnesse, an inexhaustible fountaine, unemptible treasures.

un'emptied, *ppl. a.* (UN-^{1} 8.)
1624 MASSINGER *Renegado* III. iii, There is not a vein of mine which yet is Unemptied in his service but..should freely open. **1655** VAUGHAN *Silex Scint., Rules & Lessons* xvii, Admire his ways Who fils the world's unempty'd granaries! **1810** SOUTHEY *Kehama* XXIV. xx, Yielding to the bony hand The unemptied cup, he moved toward the Throne. **1818** BYRON *Ch. Har.* IV. lxx, An unceasing shower ..With its unemptied cloud of gentle rain. **1952** M. LASKI *Village* vi. 106 Mrs. Robinson..went, leaving Miss Evadne to stare distastefully at..the empty flower-vases, the unemptied ash-trays. **1980** J. O'FAOLAIN *No Country for Young Men* i. 20 The house was full of..smells of unemptied chamber-pots, a clutter of unassigned hats and macintoshes.

un'emulative, *a.* (UN-^{1} 7.)
1775 'J. COLLIER' *Mus. Trav.* (ed. 2) 68 The vulgar restrictions which reason imposes upon unemulative minds.

une'nabled, *ppl. a.* (UN-^{1} 8.)
1801 SOUTHEY *Thalaba* V. xxiii, No eye of mortal man, If unenabled by enchanted spell, Had pierced those fearful depths.

une'nacted, *ppl. a.* (UN-^{1} 8.)
1802–12 BENTHAM *Ration. Judic. Evid.* (1827) II. 587 Unpromulgated, and unenacted, and spurious laws. **1843** KEBLE in *Newman's Corr.* (1917) 232 The unenacted leanings and tendencies of a particular generation.

une'namelled, *ppl. a.* (UN-[1] 8.)
1851 G. A. MANTELL *Petrifact.* iii. 253 [Teeth having] an unenamelled triangular space. **1889** *Anthony's Photogr. Bull.* II. 128, I prefer the prints unenamelled.

une'namoured, *ppl. a.* (UN-[1] 8.)
[**1775** ASH.] **1791** HUDDESFORD *Salmag.* (1795) 14 There Townsend threads the pleasing maze. All who can unenamoured gaze!

†**une'narrable,** *a. Obs.* (UN-[1] 7 b and 5 b.)
1382 WYCLIF *2 Cor.* ix. 15, I do thankingis to God vpon the vnenarrable, or that may not be told, ȝifte of hym. **1382** —— *1 Pet.* i. 8 In gladnesse vnenarrable.

unen'chant, *v.* (UN-[2] 3.)
1654 GAYTON *Pleas. Notes* IV. ix. 237 Where by this time the Don is uninchanted from sleep.

unen'chanted, *ppl. a.* Also 7 uninchanted. (UN-[1] 8.)
1634 MILTON *Comus* 395 But beauty..hath need the guard Of dragon watch with uninchanted eye. *a* **1644** QUARLES *Sol. Recant.* x. 11 The rash reproving mouth of fools are arm'd Like unenchaunted serpents, if not charm'd. **1791** COWPER *Odyss.* x. 399 Amaz'd I see thee with that potion drench'd, Yet unenchanted. **1810** *Monthly Mag.* XXIX. 149 It requires ascetic virtue..to remain unenchanted by the glare.

unen'closed, *ppl. a.* Also unin-. (UN-[1] 8.)
1676 *Rector's Bk., Clayworth* (1910) 20 Such as had grounds still unenclosed. **1712** BLACKMORE *Creation* VII. 700 In the dark and undistinguish'd Space, Unfruitful, uninclos'd and wild of Face. **1776** ADAM SMITH *W.N.* I. xi. 214 In waste and uninclosed lands, any person who discovers a tin mine, may mark out its limits. **1809** PINKNEY *Trav. France* 67 Being situated in an unenclosed country. **1867** LATHAM *Black & White* p. ix, A country two-thirds of which are uninclosed. **1898** TAUNTON *Eng. Black Monks* I. 108 Unenclosed nuns doing God's work in the world.

unen'compassed, *ppl. a.* (UN-[1] 8.)
[**1775** ASH.] *a* **1822** [? SHELLEY] '*There is no work*' 16 A brain unencompassed with nerves of steel. **1848** PUSEY *Paroch. Serm.* I. viii. (1873) 152 His Own All-encompassing, Unencompassed Love.

unen'counterable, *a.* (UN-[1] 7 b.)
1590 T. FENNE *Frutes* 73 b, Philip King of Macedon having by..experience found out the unincounterable force thereof.

unen'countered, *ppl. a.* (UN-[1] 8.)
[**1775** ASH.] **1821** SCOTT *Pirate* ii, He was then most sure to wander unencountered and unobserved.

unen'couraged, *ppl. a.* (UN-[1] 8.)
[**1775** ASH.] **1854** E. FORBES in Geikie *Mem.* xv. (1861) 554 Tastes that might have speedily perished if unobserved and unencouraged.

unen'couraging, *ppl. a.* (UN-[1] 10.)
1844 STOCQUELER *Handbk. Brit. India* 277 They are, however, in an awkward and unencouraging position. **1858** POLSON *Law & L.* 105 To the junior part of the bar..Lord Kenyon was unencouraging and ungracious.

unen'croaching, *ppl. a.* (UN-[1] 10.)
a **1628** F. GREVILLE *Sidney* (1652) 208 Judicious.. Favorites of unincroaching Monarchs.

unen'cumbered, *ppl. a.* Also 8–9 unin-. (UN-[1] 8.) **a.** In pred. use and const. *with* or *by*.
α. **1722** DE FOE *Plague* (1754) 22 Such People as were unincumbred with Trades and Business. **1800** *Asiat. Ann. Reg., Hist. Ind.* 13/2 His forces now consisting of light horse only, unincumbered by artillery or heavy baggage. **1877** MRS. OLIPHANT *Makers Flor.* iv. 117 He is unincumbered by any restrictions.
β. **1727** THOMSON *Britannia* 208 Unencumber'd with the Bulk immense Of Conquest. **1822** SCOTT *Nigel* x, His address was gallant, free, and unencumbered either by pride or ceremony. **1866** GEO. ELIOT *F. Holt* iv, His small legs, unencumbered by any other drapery than his black silk stockings.
b. Without const., in predicative or attrib. use.
c **1725** SOMERVILLE *Martial's Epigr.* xlvii. 6 An estate,.. unincumber'd left, and free from debt. **1781** COWPER *Truth* 22 Heav'n's easy, artless, unincumber'd plan. **1818** SYD. SMITH *Wks.* (1867) I. 235 This seems a very spirited, unincumbered way of passing through life. **1856** KANE *Arct. Expl.* I. xvi. 188 My first impulse was to move..with an unencumbered party. **1884** SIR E. FRY in *Law Rep.* 25 *Ch. Div.* 581 Jeffery was the unencumbered lessee..of all the other plots.
Hence **unen'cumberedness.**
1891 *Atlantic Monthly* Feb. 182/2 To step jauntily along in airy unencumberedness.

unen'cumbering, *ppl. a.* (UN-[1] 10.)
[**1775** ASH.] **1824** LANDOR *Imag. Conv.* II. 330 They would lose..no graceful and unencumbering ornaments of life. **1861** SIR F. PALGRAVE *Norm. & Eng.* III. 306 The archers,..arrayed in a light and unincumbering garb.

unen'cysted, *ppl. a.* (UN-[1] 8.)
[**1775** ASH.] **1885** *Encycl. Brit.* XIX. 855/2 In rare cases sporulation has been observed in unencysted Gregarinidea.

†**un'end,** obs. var. of AN-END *adv.*
1559 *Mirr. Mag., Northumb.* xvii, Whereas the folke drew to me stil vnend.

unen'dangered, *ppl. a.* Also 7 unin-. (UN-[1] 8.)
a **1658** CLEVELAND *Rustick Rampant* Wks. (1687) 409 These Impieties being once allowed, there can be neither Peace, Society nor Government amongst Men safe and unindangered. **1746** YOUNG *Nt. Th.* IX. 1191 Un-endanger'd in health, wealth, or fame. **1814** WORDSW. *Excurs.* III. 523 See, rooted in the earth,..The unendangered myrtle.

unen'deared, *ppl. a.* (UN-[1] 8.)
1667 MILTON *P.L.* IV. 766 Not in the bought smile Of Harlots, loveless, joyless, unindeard.

unen'deavoured, *ppl. a.* (UN-[1] 8.)
1656 EARL MONM. tr. *Boccalini's Advts. fr. Parnass.* 167 Nothing was left unindeavoured, neither by himself, nor by other Princes.

unen'deavouring, *ppl. a.* (UN-[1] 10.)
1831 CARLYLE *Sart. Res.* II. iv, The as yet unendeavouring, unattaining young gentleman.

un'ended, *ppl. a.* Now *rare.* [UN-[1] 8: cf. OE. *ungeendod.*]
1. Not made to end or stop; having no limit or bounds; continued, lasting, infinite.
c **1250** *Gen. & Ex.* 3518 For if ðu it ȝernes and ȝisse, ðu tines vn-ended blisce. **1340–70** *Alex. & Dind.* 751 Bochours ben þei echon ȝour body to dismembre, & euerich pinchen his part þere paine is vnended. **1382** WYCLIF *Job* xxii. 5 For thi myche malice, and thi wickidnessis vnendid. *c* **1400** tr. *Secreta Secret., Gov. Lordsh.* 84 Thes er tho þat out soght, and disputyd..of full, of voyde, of endyd, of vnendyd. **1522** VAUS *Rudiment. Gram.* Bb ij b (Jam.), *Infinitivo modo.* Onendyt or determyt mode to nowmyr or persone. **1596** *Edw. III,* II. i. 139 Wherefore talkest thou of a period To that which craues vnended admiration?
2. Not brought to an end or conclusion; unfinished, incomplete.
1382 WYCLIF *Wisd.* iv. 5 Forsothe braunchis vnendid [1388 vnperfit] shul be to-broken. **1471** *Sc. Acts, Jas. III* (1814) II 101/1 Al materis..þat ar now opynit in þis present parliament & vnendit. **1535** STEWART *Cron. Scot.* (Rolls) II. 414 Rycht weill ȝe ken..Oure interpryiss wnendit is and done. **1591** SPARRY tr. *Cattan's Geomancie* 235 The sute shall be for unmoueable goods, and shall not last long unended. **1805** *Monthly Mag.* XX. 43 It would probably have remained unended for a long time. **1935** T. S. ELIOT *Murder in Cathedral* i. 14 Meetings unended or endless At one place or another in France.

un'ending, *ppl. a.* [UN-[1] 10.] Endless.
1661 FELTHAM *Resolves,* etc. (ed. 8) 378 When we think we have progress'd far in the un-ending Circles of laborious Science. **1729** MADDEN *Themistocles* IV. i. 50 Have I not sworn at the conscious Shrines Unending Faith to Xerxes? **1767** GOLDSM. *Vic. W.* xxix, When our bliss shall be unutterable, and still, to crown all, unending. **1813** SHELLEY *Q. Mab* II. 73 Countless and unending orbs In mazy motion intermingled. **1875** CLODD *Childhood of Religions* ii. 28 How Frost and Fire had fierce unending battle.
Hence **un'endingly** *adv.*, **un'endingness.**
1674 N. FAIRFAX *Bulk & Selv.* 165 You can no wayes.. say, This half is unbeginningly, and that unendingly. **1845** BAILEY *Festus* (ed. 2) 39 Though a thousand worlds..were elanced Each minute into life unendingly. **1881** *Brit. Q. Rev.* Oct. 499 The theory of the literal unendingness of even moral perdition.

†**unendliche,** *adv.*: see UN-[1] 3.

†**un'endly,** *a. Obs.* [UN-[1] 7: cf. ENDLY *a.*] Unending.
a **1586** SIDNEY *Arcadia* III. i, Shall..faith and loue be rewarded with mortall disdaine, bent to vnendly reuenge?

unen'dorsed, *ppl. a.* (UN-[1] 8.)
1682 SCARLETT *Exchanges* 196 When he makes his Bills.. or accepts of unendorsed Bills. **1886** *Times* 20 Aug. 9/6 Recommendations unendorsed by Government.

unen'dowed, *ppl. a.* Also 7 unin-. (UN-[1] 8.)
1647 CLARENDON *Hist. Reb.* I. §142 A man rather.. unindowed with any notable virtues, than..transported with any vitious inclinations. **1709** POPE *Jan. & May* 550 Reflect what truth was in my passion shewn, When unendow'd, I took thee for my own. **1790** [see UNCONSECRATED]. **1819** CRABBE *T. of Hall* IX. 42 That every beauty..Must be by him, if unendow'd, resign'd. **1866** GEO. ELIOT *Ess.* (1884) 348 The claims of the unendowed multitude of working men.

unen'dued, *ppl. a.* (UN-[1] 8.)
1647 CLARENDON *Hist. Reb.* v. §341 A sufficient Instance how unendued Men were with that Spirit and Courage, which was requisite. **1855** PUSEY *Doctr. Real Presence* Note I. 106 Things unendued with reason. **1862** ELLICOTT *Destiny Creature,* etc. ii. (1865) 28 Individuals that belong to lower genera unendued with foresight and reason.

unen'durable, *a.* (and *sb.*). Also 7 unin-. [UN-[1] 7 b.]
1. Incapable of enduring; †impatient *of*.
1630 *R. Johnson's Kingd. & Commw.* 79 In battell they are fearelesse,..and in service unindurable of temporizing. **1879** *Cassell's Techn. Educ.* I. 314 If it be soft, broken granite.. will prove a useless because an unendurable surface.
2. That cannot be endured; insufferable.
1801 SOUTHEY *Thalaba* XII. xviii, No eye could penetrate That unendurable excess of light. **1853** KANE *Grinnell Exp.* xxxiv. (1856) 303 The sensation most unendurable..is a pain between the eyes and over the forehead. **1880** 'OUIDA' *Moths* x, This ceaseless sense of unendurable reproach.
b. *sb.* An insufferable person.
1826 F. REYNOLDS *Life & Times* II. 84 That my friend Andrews may not be considered as one of these *unendurables*, I will yet add another short anecdote of him.
Hence **unen,dura'bility.**
1858 CARLYLE *Fredk. Gt.* v. viii, Some excessive pressure of that lisping snuffling unendurability. **1862** *Ibid.* XII. xi, Such injustices and unendurabilities.

unen'durably, *adv.* [UN-[1] 11: cf. prec.] In an unendurable manner or degree.
1832 SOUTHEY *Hist. Penins. War* III. 103 That sovereignty..would become unendurably tyrannical. **1867** AUGUSTA WILSON *Vashti* xxvii, My ardent lover would be too unendurably miserable separated from me. **1890** 'R. BOLDREWOOD' *Col. Reformer* (1891) 177 The routine life.. would be unendurably dull.

unen'during, *ppl. a.* (UN-[1] 10.)
[**1775** ASH.] **1814** WORDSW. *Excurs.* IX. 6 The stars Of azure heaven, the unenduring clouds. **1855** MILMAN *Lat. Chr.* XIV. viii. VI. 573 The architectural..conquests of Justinian were but partial and unenduring.

unener'getic, *a.* (UN-[1] 7 and 5 b.)
1805 A. KNOX *Mem.* I. 6 The cold, low, unenergetic notion of it..is really below Cicero in moral matters. **1850** THACKERAY *Pendennis* ii, He is a very good boy, rather idle and unenergetic. **1878** SEELEY *Stein* III. 532 A man of this unenergetic character..has no colour.

un'enervated, *ppl. a.* (UN-[1] 8.)
1766 in *Hansard Parl. Debates* (1813) XVI. 286 The supreme law with me shall ever be to maintain, unrelaxed and unenervated, the fundamentals of the constitution. **1854** J. S. C. ABBOTT *Napoleon* (1855) I. x. 174 We shall found a colony there unenervated by the curse of slavery.

unen'feebled, *ppl. a.* (UN-[1] 8.)
1648 HEXHAM II, *Ongekrenckt,* Vn-weakned, or Vn-enfeebled. **1814** WORDSW. *Excurs.* VII. 208 The comeliness of unenfeebled age. **1878** E. JENKINS *Haverholme* 78 The new doctrine is, that the Crown has a sacred trust..to preserve the Regal prerogative unenfeebled.

unen'forceable, *a.* (UN-[1] 7 b.)
1868 BENJAMIN *On Sales* (1884) 530 The terms of the bargain included a wager that rendered it illegal: quaere—unenforceable. **1885** *Law Times* 10 Jan. 183/1 A covenant to build or repair would be unenforceable as against an assignee even with notice.
Hence **,unenforcea'bility.**
1935 *Columbia Law Rev.* XXXV. 94 More fundamental, however, is the inherent unenforceability of any statute.. attempting to prohibit an essentially private practice where all parties concerned are desirous of avoiding the restriction. **1973** I. M. SINCLAIR *Vienna Convention on Law of Treaties* v. 131 The unenforceability of any treaty contemplating genocide or the slave trade is further assured by the fact that such a treaty would contravene the Charter of the United Nations, which prevails in the event of conflict.

unen'forced, *ppl. a.* Also 7 unin-. (UN-[1] 8.)
1607 HIERON *Wks.* I. 220, I will let you see how this doctrine ariseth kindly and vn-enforced from this scripture. **1625** K. LONG tr. *Barclay's Argenis* II. vi. 80 By a slow and uninforced inhibition of the old discipline. **1646** EARL MONM. tr. *Biondi's Civil Wars* IX. 177 The Duke of Orleans would not, unenforced, yeeld to any Pacification. **1832** MOORE *Mem.* (1854) VI. 267 Sifting both sides and leaving nothing unenforced on either. *a* **1861** SIR F. PALGRAVE *Norm. & Eng.* III. 363 A formal..submission..unenforced by the sword.
Hence **unen'forcedly** *adv.*
1617 HIERON *Wks.* II. 165 Foure points doe very kindly and vnenforcedly spring out of this place.

unen'franchised, *ppl. a.* (UN-[1] 8.)
[**1775** ASH.] **1832** A. W. FONBLANQUE *Eng. under 7 Administr.* (1837) II. 292 The identity of interest of the enfranchised, and unenfranchised. **1878** BOSW. SMITH *Carthage* 62 The long..struggle between the privileged Patricians and the unenfranchised plebeians.

unen'gaged, *ppl. a.* Also 7–8 unin-. [UN-[1] 8.]
†**1.** Unimpeded. *Obs.*$^{-1}$
1653 GAUDEN *Hierasp.* To Rdr. 2 b, From which free and un-ingaged prospect both he and they may..behold the later..changes in exterior matters of Religion.
2. Not bound or committed in any way (esp. by a pledge or promise).
a **1656** BP. HALL *Modest Offer* 2 Both the Houses of Parliament..stand yet free, and unengaged to any part. **1697** COLLIER *Ess. Mor. Subj.* I. (1703) 110 'Tis my humble Opinion, that they should keep their Inclinations unengaged. **1757** W. WILKIE *Epigon.* v. 148 The truce subsists with all the rest; are we Alone excepted, unengag'd and free?
b. *spec.* Not bound by an engagement or promise to marry; not betrothed.
1702 VANBRUGH *False Friend* III. i, His Behaviour wou'd engage any thing that were unengag'd. **1709** MRS. MANLEY *Secret Mem.* I. 217 He was handsome, he was young:..She was innocent and uningag'd. **1814** SCOTT *Wav.* lviii, An alliance, which to an unengaged person,..holds out too many charms to be lightly laid aside. **1877** SIR H. TAYLOR *Autobiog.* (1885) I. 218 He consented to our seeing more of one another on an unengaged footing.
†**3.** Not committed to a special view or opinion; unprejudiced. *Obs.*
1653 MILTON *Hirelings* Wks. 1851 V. 338 If it suffic'd..to convince..the uningag'd of other Nations in the justice of your doings. **1663** J. SPENCER *Prodigies* (1665) 401 Persons of more free and un-ingaged minds, and that use not to believe without asking themselves *why*.
4. Not hired.
1654 DOROTHY OSBORNE *Lett.* (1888) 293 He is commended to me..for a most excellent servant... I'll keep him unengaged till I hear from you. **1889** GUNTER *That Frenchman* xiii, She chances to find an unengaged cab.
5. Not occupied or busied (*in* something).
1712 POPE *Lett.* (1735) I. 187 If your Thoughts are unengaged, I shall explain myself further. **1759** JOHNSON *Rasselas* xlv, The activity of Rasselas did not leave much time unengaged. **1800** MRS. HERVEY *Mourtray Fam.* II. 78 Her companion, who wandered about..unengaged in any pursuit. **1819** CRABBE *T. of Hall* IV. 187, I took a trip, But

duty none, in a relation's ship; Thus, unengaged, I felt my spirits light.

b. Disengaged *from.*

1805 EMILY CLARK *Banks of Douro* II. 300 The first moment she was unengaged from Minette and Lady Archdale, she resolved to go and see them.

c. Not occupied or involved in fighting.

1806 A. DUNCAN *Nelson* 39 The ships..were..unengaged in the contest. **1895** A. FORBES in *Daily News* 18 Feb. 6/3 Mr. Herbert, in his redoubt in the centre of the Grivitza heights, remained unengaged until 4 p.m.

6. a. Not appropriated or allocated to a particular purpose.

a **1732** SWIFT (J.), When we have sunk the only unengaged revenues left, our incumbrances must remain perpetual.

b. Not assigned to a person.

1751 SMOLLETT *Per. Pic.* xci, Some profitable places were at that time vacant, and, as far as he knew, unengaged. **1755** JOHNSON *Let. to Richardson* 3 Feb. in *Pearson's Catal.* (1900) 44 If you have any parts of the Universal History yet unengaged I know a gentleman desirous of giving his assistance.

unen'gaging, *ppl. a.* (UN-^{1} 10.)

1749 CHESTERF. *Lett.* (1774) I. 429 Without them, your learning will be pedantry,..and your figure..awkward and unengaging. **1768–74** TUCKER *Lt. Nat.* (1834) II. 592 The one [life] is pleasant, easy, smooth, and dispatchful; the other unengaging, toilsome, stiff. **1895** KATH. SIMPSON *Yorks. Stories* 92 Too ugly and unengaging to be able to boast of a lover.

unen'gendered, *ppl. a.* (UN-^{1} 8.)

1776 S. J. PRATT *Pupil of Pleas.* (1777) I. 159 At present, this is only in embrio,..unformed, uningendered.

un-English, *a.* [UN-^{1} 7.]

1. Not English in character; lacking the qualities regarded as typically English.

1633 PRYNNE *Histrio-m.* 546 So unmanly, degenerous and un-English (if I may so speake) in their whole conversation. **1745** H. WALPOLE *Let. to H. S. Conway* 27 May, This is so un-English, or so un-heroic, that I despair of you! **1763** *Ann. Reg., Chron.* 89/2 One of the members..called the attack 'a horrid un-English act'. **1803** MACKINTOSH *Def. Peltier* Wks. 1846 III. 286 Though deserted by the un-English Government of England, they asserted their own ancient character. **1848** in *Life A. Fonblanque* (1874) 225 The un-English practice of secret voting will be resorted to. **1872** YEATS *Growth Comm.* 308 A false patriotism that thought it un-English to wear foreign fabrics.

2. Not English by occupation or possession.

1738 *Gentl. Mag.* 427/1 Such beauties..are,..save at Finedon, hardly found On English or un-English ground. **1902** *Daily Chron.* 18 July 5/4 With Delagoa Bay the only harbour still un-English passes into England's power.

un'english, *v.* (UN-^{2} 6 a.)

1745 H. WALPOLE *Lett.* (1846) II. 55, I would not for the world be so unenglished as to do otherwise. **1786** *Microcosm* (1787) 23 Having thus unenglished himself, let him get his advertisement drawn up.

un'englished, *ppl. a.* [UN-^{1} 8.] Not translated into English.

c **1546** JOYE in Gardiner *Declar.* 52 b, He layd on scriptures wryten and vnwryten, englyshed and venglyshed as thicke as hayle. **1620** BP. HALL *Hon. Marr. Clergy* III. ii. (1628) 794 We..returne his [epistle]..to the next hand; whereto I am no whit beholding for leaving it vn-Englished. **1650** FULLER *Pisgah* v. xix. 174 Such passages (which for me shall goe unenglished) being found frequent therein.

unen'graven, *ppl. a.* (UN-^{1} 8 b.)

[**1775** ASH.] **1831** CARLYLE *Sart. Res.* II. iv, I undertook to compose his Epitaph;..which however..still remains unengraven.

unen'grossed, *ppl. a.* (UN-^{1} 8.)

1681 *Lond. Gaz.* No. 1633/4 There is now published a Printed List of all such Fines as remain uningrossed.

unen'joyable, *a.* (UN-^{1} 7 b.)

a **1797** H. WALPOLE *Geo. II* (1822) I. 195 A very few years of unenjoyable power. **1850** ROBERTSON *Serm.* Ser. III. vi. (1864) 92 Life is an unenjoyable Canaan. **1869** TOZER *Highl. Turkey* I. 90 How empty and unenjoyable life would be without the range of European ideas.

unen'joyed, *ppl. a.* Also 7 unin-. (UN-^{1} 8.)

1643–5 MILTON *Divorce* II. i, A good man who finds himself consuming away in a disconsolate and uninjoy'd matrimony. **1684** T. BURNET *Theory Earth* I. 322 We cannot suppose the better [parts] to lie as desarts, uninjoy'd and uninhabited. **1757** MRS. GRIFFITH *Lett. Henry & Frances* (1767) II. 245 The pleasure..which you have suffered to pass by, unheeded, unenjoyed. **1827** POLLOK *Course T.* III. 229 The spectre..threatened..to blast it unenjoyed. **1984** H. SPURLING *Secrets of Woman's Heart* 101 She belonged to what my mother used to call the army of unenjoyed women. .. Margaret had a very unenjoyed look about her.

unen'joying, *ppl. a.* (UN-^{1} 10.)

1697 CREECH *Manilius* IV. 10 The more we have, the meaner is our Store; The unenjoying craving Wretch is poor. **1799** COLERIDGE *Ode to Duchess of Devonsh.* 18 Nor could you see The unenjoying toiler's misery. **1851** ROBERTSON *Serm.* Ser. II. 15 The shadow of our own melancholy unenjoying national character. **1866** GEO. ELIOT *F. Holt* i, When..her face looked bitter, restless, and unenjoying, like her life.

Hence **unen'joyingly** *adv.*

1844 BROWNING *Colombe's Birthday* II. 106 Hurry one's feast down unenjoyingly At the snatched breathing-intervals of work?

unen'larged, *ppl. a.* (UN-^{1} 8.)

1741 WATTS *Improvement Mind* I. xvi. 219 These unenlarged souls are in the same manner disgusted with the wonders which the microscope has discovered. **1805** FOSTER *Ess.* (1806) I. 58 Under the habitual..influence of one individual..of unenlarged views. **1844** MRS. BROWNING *Lett. R. H. Horne* (1877) II. 24 You had better leave the notice unenlarged.

unen'lightened, *ppl. a.* Also 7 unin-. [UN-^{1} 8.]

1. Not illuminated or lit up.

1662 BOYLE *Spring of Air* II. i. 22 For the Corpuscles of Light that permeate that space may be so numerous, as to leave no sensible part of it un-inlightned. **1789** *Phil. Trans.* LXXX. 8 During the time..when evidently we were turned towards the unenlightened side. **1803** *Ibid.* XCV. 152, I mentioned the probability that there existed.. unenlightened stars (if I may be allowed the expression) that have ever remained in eternal darkness. **1833–4** J. PHILLIPS *Geol.* in *Encycl. Metrop.* (1845) VI. 715/2 The Phlegrean Fields,..unenlightened either by the rising or the setting sun.

fig. **1774** *Trinket* 165 Faces unenlightened with the smile of friendship.

2. Not mentally illuminated; uninstructed.

a **1656** BP. HALL *Rev. Unrevealed* §8 A conceit, that would have sounded very strangely in the ears of our un-enlightened forefathers. **1768–74** TUCKER *Lt. Nat.* (1834) II. 638 The unenlightened Canadian takes pride in singing while tortured by his conquerors. **1797** MATHIAS *Purs. Lit.* II. 5 *note*, Such unenlightened and ignorant men as myself. **1865** M. ARNOLD *Ess. Crit.* v. 189 A strong, dogged, unenlightened opponent of the chosen people. **1882** FARRAR *Early Chr.* II. 342 Imperfect, narrow-minded and unenlightened Christians.

b. Uninformed *on* some matter.

1829 SCOTT *Anne of G.* xxxi, The old King was..still strangely unenlightened on the difference of her taste from his own.

3. Marked by lack of enlightenment.

1792 A. YOUNG *Trav. France* I. Pref. p. iv, Unenlightened practices exist, and want improvement. **1870** LOWELL *Among my Books* Ser. I. (1873) 148 Political or other doctrines which seem to us barbarous and unenlightened.

unen'lightening, *ppl. a.* (UN-^{1} 10.)

1768 PENNANT *Brit. Zool.* I. 193 Commentators, after loading whole pages with unenlightening learning, leave us ..in the dark.

unen'listed, *ppl. a.* (UN-^{1} 8.)

[**1775** ASH.] **1840** J. H. NEWMAN *Ch. of Fathers* ix. 153 Yet unenlisted in God's army.

unen'livened, *ppl. a.* (UN-^{1} 8.)

1692 ATTERBURY *Serm.* 29 May (1726) I. 31 That Majestick Plainness and Simplicity of Thought which goes through it, Unadorn'd by Words, Unenliven'd by Figures. *c* **1765** BEATTIE *Ep. to Blacklock* 57 The cautious, slow, and unenlivened eye. **1817** COLERIDGE *Biog. Lit.* (1907) I. 169 The distorting medium of his own unenlivened and stagnant understanding. **1893** LIDDON *Life Pusey* I. xiv. 330 Their intercourse was not unenlivened by differences of opinion.

unen'livening, *ppl. a.* (UN-^{1} 10.)

1774 *Trinket* 158 My ideas are more unenlivening than the desolate prospect that inspires them. **1835** A. C. DICK *Church Polity* vii. 194 [He] falls into..an unenlivening coldness of address.

une'nnobled, *ppl. a.* (UN-^{1} 8.)

[**1775** ASH.] **1830** *Westm. Rev.* Oct. 300 The..deeds of the unennobled patriot-soldier. **1863** *Q. Rev.* CXIII. 469 The unennobled inhabitants of the provinces that were to be annexed to Russia.

une'nounced, *ppl. a.* (UN-^{1} 8.)

1859 SIR W. HAMILTON *Lect.* (1877) I. xvi. 286 It remains unenounced and unknown.

unen'quired, *ppl. a.* (UN-^{1} 8 c.)

a **1818** M. G. LEWIS *W. Ind.* (1834) 367 He left their complaints unenquired into.

unen'quiring, *ppl. a.* (UN-^{1} 10.)

1813 LAMB *Play-house Mem.* Wks. 1908 I. 202, I love the unenquiring gratitude of such spectators. **1850** MARSDEN *Early Purit.* (1853) 65 He is a son of the church because he is unenquiring. **1862** M. HOPKINS *Hawaii* 373 It demands.. unenquiring condemnation and unpitying punishment.

Hence **unen'quiringly** *adv.*

1841 MYERS *Cath. Th.* III. §50. 191 They give themselves up..unenquiringly to mere traditions concerning it. **1862** M. HOPKINS *Hawaii* 350 The American missionaries.. threw themselves unenquiringly..into a crusade against the prevailing licentiousness.

unen'richableness. (UN-^{1} 7 b, 12.)

a **1816** BENTHAM *Offic. Apt. Maximized, Introd. View* (1830) 19 The French [language, with]..its scantiness, unenrichableness, and intractability.

unen'riched, *ppl. a.* Also 8 unin-. (UN-^{1} 8.)

1723 DK. WHARTON *True Briton* No. 55. II. 473 That he died un-inriched by the Plunder of his Fellow Subjects. **1786** MRS. PIOZZI *Anecd. of Johnson* Pref. 7 The great parent of African plenty,..unenriched by any extraneous waters. **18..** WORDSW. *Michael* 19 A story—unenriched with strange events. **1864** *Realm* 11 May 5 He has preferred to remain..unenriched by the events which have enriched.. others.

unen'rolled, *ppl. a.* (UN-^{1} 8.)

[**1775** ASH.] **1837** CARLYLE *Fr. Rev.* I. v. ix, Unenrolled men deposit their arms,..and receive 'nine francs.' **1881** JOWETT *Thucyd.* I. 27 The treaty allows any unenrolled cities to join either league.

unen'slave, *v.* (UN-^{2} 3.)

1644 *Prerogative Anatomized* 1 That the deceived people ..may see the necessitie..to uninslave their soules, persons and estates, from Ecclesiasticall..tyrannie.

unen'slaved, *ppl. a.* (UN-^{1} 8.)

1691 NORRIS *Refl. Cond. Hum. Life* Ep. Ded. A vj b, If I happen to bring over here and there an ingenuous and uninslaved Spirit,..I shall not think my Labour ill bestow'd. **1705** ADDISON *Remarks on Italy* 108 By Thee She sits a Sov'reign, Unenslav'd and Free.

unen'snared, *ppl. a.* (UN-^{1} 8.)

a **1711** KEN *Hymnotheo* Poet. Wks. 1721 III. 186 No Danger found them unprepar'd, They kept their Spirits un-ensnar'd. **1860** MOZLEY *Univ. Serm.* vii. (1877) 155 Free and unensnared souls.

unen'souled, *ppl. a.* (UN-^{1} 8.)

1860 PUSEY *Min. Proph.* 41 When..they were lifeless bodies, unensouled by His grace.

unen'tailed, *ppl. a.* (UN-^{1} 8.)

1713 C'TESS WINCHELSEA *Misc. Poems* 243 Your unentailed, your undivided Air, Where no Proprietor was ever known. **1784** R. BAGE *Barham Downs* II. 315 His unentailed estates are to be sold. **1827** LYTTON *Pelham* iii, The whole of his unentailed property..he bequeathed to her.

unen'tangle, *v.* Also 7 unin-. [UN-^{2} 3.] *trans.* To disentangle.

1610 DONNE *Pseudo-martyr* 226 It is impossible to.. vnentangle our consciences by any of those Rules. **1655** tr. *Sorel's Com. Hist. Francion* IV. 13 All this was intermingled ..in a more than a barbarous confusion, which was so uneasie to unintangle [etc.]. **1887** BOWEN *Æneid* VI. 29 Dædalus..of himself unentangled the woven trick of the grove.

Hence **unen'tangler.** *rare*$^{-1}$.

1610 DONNE *Pseudo-martyr* 345 The late vn-entangler of perplexities,..who vndertakes to cleare so many cases, which Nauarrus and many others left in suspence.

unen'tangled, *ppl. a.* Also 7–8 unin-. (UN-^{1} 8.)

a **1586** SIDNEY *Arcadia* III. ix, So I in simple course, and unentangled minde, Did suffer drousie lids mine eyes..to blinde. **1622** S. WARD *Christ All in All* (1627) 36 He had now nothing left but..Christ, whom hee..would now with vnlimed and vnentangled wings flye vnto. **1647** CLARENDON *Hist. Reb.* VII. §218 He was unintangled with any Acquaintance or Friends. *a* **1715** BURNET *Own Time* I. (1766) I. 124 To keep the thread of the narration in an unintangled method. **1779–81** JOHNSON *L.P., Collins*, That this man..passed always unentangled through the snares of life, it would be..temerity to affirm. **1842** J. B. FRASER *Allee Neemroo* I. 20 Its rider, shot forward from its back,.. fortunately unentangled by its harness. **1901** H. W. HOLDEN *Justif.* 96 We may be free indeed to follow the Lord.. unentangled and unembarrassed by any other will.

un'ented, *ppl. a.* [UN-^{1} 8 + late L. *ent-*, *ens*: see ENS.] Not endowed with being.

1657 REEVE *God's Plea* 241 God..out of..an unshapen un-ented Nothing hath set up..this specious and spacious Universe.

un'enterable, *a.* (UN-^{1} 7 b.)

1650 FULLER *Pisgah* 366 That mysterious place being unenterable..save [for] the high-Priest alone.

un'entered, *ppl. a.* [UN-^{1} 8.]

1. Not recorded by an entry in a book.

1482 in *Charters, etc. Edinb.* (1871) 168 Gudis..enterit in the tovnis bukis, togidder with the eschete of the sammyn quhare it beis fundin vnenterit. **1554–5** in Feuillerat *Revels Q. Mary* (1914) 169, xij elles of white & blewe sarcenet..left out vnentred in the boke of the same [masque]. **1763** *Brit. Mag.* IV. 174 The makers of cyder or perry..shall enter.. the mills,..and other places to be made use of,..under the penalty of 25*l.* for using any unentered place.

†**2.** Not initiated or introduced. *Obs.*

1548 UDALL, etc. *Erasm. Par. Luke* i. 7 A people not vtterly vntraded or vnentred in his discipline, but somwhat prepaired already. **1642** MILTON *Apol. Smect.* 45 In the Greek tongue most of them unletter'd, or unenter'd to any sound proficiency in those Attick maisters of morall wisdome.

3. *Sc. Law.* Not formally admitted.

1711 in *Nairne Peerage Evidence* (1874) 142 [They are] not to lye out themselves unentered in the superiority to their prejudice. **1868** *Act 31 & 32 Vict.* c. 101 §6 The rights and remedies competent to a superior against his vassal lying out unentered.

4. Of hounds: Not yet put into a pack.

1772 G. CARTWRIGHT *Jrnl.* 5 May (1792) I. 220 Having two couple of unentered hounds with me, I let them all loose to blood them, but the old dog following the first deer, I was not able to catch him again. **1896** *Sportsman* 10 July 4/1 In young unentered hounds the Eamont were first and Boddington second.

5. Not gone into; not penetrated.

1775 WARTON *Hist. Eng. Poetry* I. i. 20 *note*, This cavern ..remained closely shut and unentered for many ages. **1821** BYRON *Cain* II. ii, The intelligences I have seen Round our regretted and unenter'd Eden.

un'entering, *ppl. a.* (UN-^{1} 5 d and 10.)

1583 *Reg. Privy Council Scot.* III. 603 For keping of his guides and cattell unentering in the said forest. **1801** SOUTHEY *Thalaba* IX. xxxii, The evening sun Pour'd his unentering glory on the mist, And it was night below.

†**un'enterpen,** *v. Obs.*$^{-0}$ (UN-^{2} 3: see ENTERPEN *v.*)

1647 HEXHAM I. (Birds), To unenterpen a Hawke, *Een Valck ontwerren.* **1671** SKINNER s.v., The hawk unenterpenneth.

un'enterprise: see UN-^{1} 12.

un'enterprising, *ppl. a.* (UN-^{1} 10.)

Also ~~unenterprisingly~~ adv. (Webster, 1847).

1777 ROBERTSON *Hist. Amer.* II. ⁋11 A maxim under which the ignorant and unenterprising shelter themselves in every age. 1791 Burke *Th. French Aff.* Wks. VII. 29 Under a lazy and unenterprising prince. 1855 Macaulay *Hist. Eng.* xviii. IV. 235 He would not again be told that he was a timid and unenterprising commander.

unenter'tained, *ppl. a.* (un-[1] 8.)
1628 Wither *Brit. Rememb.* ii. 1647 The Mother was constrain'd To let her child depart unentertain'd. 1669 Earl Orrery *Parthen.* (1676) 737 These Generals.. afforded me Particulars, which never left me unentertained. 1754 Fielding *Voy. Lisbon* 27 July, A man must..have been..duller than Cibber is represented in the Dunciad, who could be entertained with him a little while.

unenter'taining, *ppl. a.* (un-[1] 10.)
1697 Collier *Ess. Mor. Subj.* ii. (1703) 38 If he is silent and unentertaining to a visiter, the spleen is his excuse. 1748 Melmoth *Fitzosborne Lett.* xlvii. (1749) II. 20 His conversation is unentertaining: for..all that he utters is delivered with labour and hesitation. 1796 *Hist. Ned Evans* II. 118 The ceremony of adoption being somewhat singular it may not be unentertaining to relate it. 1837 Syd. Smith *2nd Let. to Singleton* ¶21 The idea of abandoning this taxation..is not unentertaining.
Hence **unenter'taining**ly *adv.*, **-ness**.
1740 Gray *Let. to West* 25 Sept., Last post I received a very diminutive letter. It made excuses for its unentertainingness. 1847 Webster, *Unentertainingly*. 1886 Ruskin *Præterita* I. v. 146 A conceited and unentertainingly troublesome little monkey.

unen'thralled, *ppl. a.* Also 7 unin-. (un-[1] 8.)
1649 Milton *Eikon.* Pref., Wks. 1851 III. 335 It must needs be ridiculous to any judgement uninthrall'd, that they ..should in this one particular outstrip all precisianism. 1809-10 Coleridge *Friend* (1818) III. 172 Observation, unaided, but at the same time unenthralled, by partial experiment. 1851 Trench *Poems* 153, I know not any, unenthralled of sorrow.

unen'thusiastic, *a.* (un-[1] 7.)
Also, in recent use, ***unenthusiastically*** adv.
1805 A. Knox *Rem.* (1834) I. 38 There is nothing supposed here, which the..unenthusiastic Addison does not..admirably describe. 1865 Trollope *Belton Est.* xxviii, He had been calm, unenthusiastic, and reasonable.

unen'ticed, *ppl. a.* (un-[1] 8.)
[1775 Ash.] 1823 in *Spirit Pub. Jrnls.* 102 Who scorned to share it with him; unenticed By shame's imperial bait.

unen'tire, *a.* Also 7 unin-. (un-[1] 7.)
a 1618 J. Davies (Heref.) *Witte's Pilgr.* Wks. (Grosart) II. 50/2 The Elements,..in firme accord, mine ende conspire: ..Which well agrees to make me vnintire. 1702 S. Parker tr. *Cicero's De Finibus* iii. 177 Representing Vertue as Unentire and Abortive.

unen'titled, *ppl. a.* Also 8 unin-. (un-[1] 8.)
a 1768 Secker *Serm., Gal. vi. 15* (1771) V. 396 That State is undoubtedly a bad one;..unintitled to Pardon of Sin. 1832 Scott *Redgauntlet* Introd., Persons totally unentitled to..such a distinction, were presented to the unfortunate Prince. 1869 Tanner *Clin. Med.* (ed. 2) 171 A boy appropriating a nicety to which he was unentitled.

unen'tombed, *ppl. a.* (un-[1] 8.)
1697 Dryden *Æneis* vi. 508 Think'st thou thus unintomb'd to cross the Floods,..And visit, without leave, the dark abodes? 1823 J. G. Todd *Strila* 156 All gory and mangled he hung unentombed.

unentomo'logical, *a.* (un-[1] 7.)
1807 Kirby *Let.* in K. & Spence *Entomol.* (1856) App. 579 Occupied with unentomological affairs. 1817 Kirby & Sp. *Entomol.* xvi. II. 10 Unentomological observers..might easily mistake one kind of insect for another.

unen'trance, *v.* (un-[2] 3.)
1834 Sir H. Taylor *Artevelde, Elena* 278 As that common day advanced His heart was wholly unentranced.

unen'treatable, *a.* Also unin-. (un-[1] 7b.)
1561 Daus tr. *Bullinger on Apoc.* (1573) 97 Corrupt Preachers..haue..borne men in hand that God is an unintreatable Rhadamantus. 1581 J. Bell *Haddon's Answ. Osor.* 478b, The Pope..did with unentreatable bloudthyrstynes rushe upon good and godly ministers. 1611 Cotgr., *Inexorable*, inexorable, vnintreatable.

unen'treated, *ppl. a.* In 7 unin-. (un-[1] 8.)
1601 Munday & Chettle *Death Earl Huntington* ii. ii, A gallant crue Of courtly maskers.., Before whome, vnintreated, I am come. 1641 Earl Monm. tr. *Biondi's Civil Wars* i. 22 The doing of what of himself, as King, he ought unintreated to have done. *a* 1652 Brome *New Acad.* ii. ii, Will you turne Match-maker For others unintreated?

unen'trenched, *ppl. a.* (un-[1] 8.)
1641 Earl Monm. tr. *Biondi's Civil Wars* iv. 63 What doth Charles deserve, who..durst not confront him, whilst unintrench'd, hee stood ready to receive him. 1716 Pope *Iliad* II. 332 An army that lay unfortify'd and unintrench'd.

une'numerable, *a.* (un-[1] 7b.)
1895 *Westm. Gaz.* 12 June 3/1 The countless triumphs.., the unenumerable charms.

une'numerated, *ppl. a.* (un-[1] 8.)
[1775 Ash.] 1799 G. Barnes *Rights Crown of Ireland Asserted* 47 The *un-enumerated*, equally with the enumerated articles. 1887 Moloney *Forestry W. Africa* 198 Wood and timber imports... Unenumerated.

unen'venomed, *ppl. a.* (un-[1] 8.)
1767 S. Paterson *Another Trav.* II. 134 Disarm them of their stings!—that henceforward they may be all dartless unenvenomed buz. 1831 Trelawny *Adv. Younger Son* III. 322 The rejection, unenvenomed by ministers, was not offensive.

un'enviable, *a.* and *sb.* (un-[1] 7b.)
1641 Milton *Animadv.* Pref. 3 Their hopes of ascending above a lowly and unenviable pitch in this life. 1797 Mrs. A. M. Bennett *Beggar Girl* (1813) II. 205 All the unenviables of her situation recurred to her mind. 1849 Macaulay *Hist. Eng.* vi. II. 143 He now daily proved that he was well entitled to this unenviable reputation. 1885 C. E. Pascoe *Lond. of To-day* 262 The church..which has earned an unenviable notoriety in connection with..Ritualistic practices.
Hence **un'enviably** *adv.*
1854 Huxley in *Life* (1900) I. 47 One of that class unenviably distinguished in the war-time as a 'donkey frigate'.

un'envied, *ppl. a.* [un-[1] 8, 9.]
†1. Not mixed with envy. *Obs.*[-1]
1390 Gower *Conf.* I. 7 Tho was ther unenvied love, Tho was the vertu sett above And vice was put under fote.
2. Not made the object of envy; not regarded with envious feelings.
1615 Chapman *Odyss.* xvii. 285 Why thou vnenuied Swaine, Whither dost thou leade..this most nasty begger? *a* 1667 Cowley *Ess., Dangers Hon. Man*, Why you may stay, and live unenvyed here. 1725 Pope *Odyss.* xiv. 452 Let us.. here, unenvy'd, rural dainties taste. 1741 Richardson *Pamela* III. 216, I shall..injoy, unenvied, the Favour of my dear Papa and Mamma. 1831 Wordsw. *Primrose of Rock* 33 Let myriads of bright flowers, Like Thee, in field and grove Revive unenvied.
3. Not enviously desired or grudged.
1645 Symonds *Diary* (Camden) 274 My witt, That seekes no higher prise, Than in unenvyed shades to sett. 1667 Milton *P.L.* ii. 23 Mee..this loss, Thus farr at least recover'd, hath much more Establisht in a safe unenvied Throne. 1713 Berkeley in *Guard.* No. 62 ¶1 To draw a secret unenvied Pleasure from a thousand Incidents overlooked by other Men. 1816 Scott *Antiq.* xviii, Martin Waldeck..often regretted bitterly the labours and sports of his unenvied poverty. 1905 J. B. Bury *St. Patrick* ii. 17 To be a decurion..in the days of Calpurnius and his father was ..an unenvied dignity.
Hence **un'enviedly** *adv.*
1738 R. Whatley *Lett. & Applic.* vii, A Right Reverend Prelate,..unenviedly possest of one of the most eminent stations.

un'envious, *a.* (un-[1] 7.)
1656 Cowley *Pindar. Odes, 2nd Olympique* x, Fortune's free gifts as freely to impart With an Unenvious hand, and an unbounded Heart. 1746 Akenside *Hymn to Naiads* 67 You too, O Nymphs, and your unenvious aid The rural powers confess. 1754 Secker *Serm.* (1771) xi. 287 We shall be far surer of finding these upright, unenvious,.. compassionate, than others, who have not equal inducements. 1838 Lytton *Alice* v. iii, Caroline gazed with honest but not unenvious admiration at the fairy form. 1881 *Fortn. Rev.* Feb. 199 The only unenvious people in Europe.
So **un'enviously** *adv.*
1896 *Daily News* 13 June 5/6 Though the naval architects may look never so unenviously at the developement of the German fleet.

un'envying, *ppl. a.* (un-[1] 10.)
1741 Richardson *Pamela* III. 242 They all yield to her the Palm, unenvying. 1820 Shelley *Prometh. Unb.* ii. ii. 97 Delightful strains..which charm To silence the unenvying nightingales.

unen'woven, *ppl. a.* (un-[1] 8b.)
1871 Swinburne *Songs bef. Sunrise, Mentana* 83 Lycoris, with hair unenwoven.

un'epilogued, *a.* (un-[1] 9.)
1773 Goldsm. *Stoops to Conq.* Epil., And now with late repentance, Un-epilogued the Poet waits his sentence.

une'piscopal, *a.* [un-[1] 7.]
1. Not controlled by bishops; not episcopalian in character or government.
1659 Gauden *Tears Ch.* ** 2 He never set up any soveraign and unepiscopal Presbytery as an Idol or Moloch. 1863 A. Blomfield *Mem. Bp. Blomfield* I. xi. 298 The High-Church party..looked with dislike..upon any display of friendly feeling towards an un-episcopal Church.
2. Not pertaining to or befitting a bishop.
a 1661 Fuller *Worthies, Wilts.* iii. (1662) 150 If any say, this was an un-episcopal act; know, he did it not as Bishop, but as Lord Treasurer. 1716 M. Davies *Athen. Brit.* III. 34 They could not have pleas'd the Dissenters..better, than by such Un-episcopal Ravings. 1889 Gretton *Memory's Harkb.* 55 The sayings and doings of his early unepiscopal days were remembered. 1897 J. W. Clark *Barnwell* Introd. 20 The Bishop lost his temper, and used very un-episcopal language.
Hence **une'piscopally** *adv.*
1886 *Manch. Exam.* 6 Jan. 3/1 The unepiscopally explicit declaration.

un'epitaphed, *a.* (un-[1] 9.)
1827 Pollok *Course T.* iii. 434 To live unknown..: to die unpraised, Unepitaphed! 1858 M. Arnold *Merope* 779 Those dead unepitaph'd, who lie In the stone coffins at Orchomenus.

un'equable, *a.* (un-[1] 7 and 5b.)
1692 Bentley *Boyle Lect.* viii. 261 March and September ..are..the most unsettled and unequable of seasons. 1748 Hartley *Observ. Man* i. i. §3. 108 Unequable and irregular Motions of the Heart and Bowels. 1763 *Phil. Trans.* LIII. 245 The true (or unequable) motions of the Sun, Moon, and nodes. 1825 J. Nicholson *Operat. Mechanic* 45 The unequable motion of the piston moved in the common way by a crank. 1855 Faber *Growth in Holiness* xvii. 306 We are fluctuating and unequable in our very fears.
Hence **un'equably** *adv.*
1834 Mrs. Somerville *Connex. Phys. Sci.* iii. (1840) 20 As the planet moves unequably in its orbit. *a* 1849 Poe *Eureka* Wks. 1865 II. 180 We have now reached a point from which we behold the Universe as a spherical space, interspersed, unequably, with clusters.

un'equal, *sb.* [un-[1] 7, 12; cf. next.]
1. *pl.* Persons who are not on an equality with each other in respect of rank or social standing.
1600 W. Watson *Decacordon* (1602) 51 It is an act of great humility..neither to striue for the last or first word, or place taking amongst not much vnequals. 1667 Milton *P.L.* viii. 383 Among unequals what societie Can sort, what harmonie or true delight? 1768 *Woman of Honor* II. 56 Such is generally the end of that society among unequals. 1875 Poste *Gaius* i. (ed. 2) 40 The law of Persons considers men as unequals.
2. *pl.* Things that are not equal to each other in kind, magnitude, etc.
1611 W. Sclater *Key* (1629) 149 An Antithesis of things diuers;..secondly, a comparison of vnequals. *a* 1653 Gouge *Comm. Heb.* iii. 2 Unequals may be compared in quality and likeness, though not in equality. 1719 Whiston *Elem. Euclid* 6 If to Unequals you add Equals, the Wholes will be unequal. 1789 T. Taylor *Proclus* II. 17 Let a be equal to b, and add to each the unequals c, d.

un'equal, *a.* and *adv.* [un-[1] 7 and 5b: cf. the earlier unegall (uneguall) and inequal.]
1. Not equal in amount, size, quality, etc.
a. Of two or more things or persons in comparison with each other.
1565 Cooper *Thes., Calami dispares*, vnequall reedes, one smaller then an other. 1570 Billingsley *Euclid* i. post. v. 7 If to vnequall thinges ye adde equall thinges, the whole shall be vnequall. 1607 J. Davies (Heref.) *Summa Totalis* Wks. (Grosart) I. 14/2 Then, if his Will and Prayer vnequall be, How shall we equall make his Properties? 1653 Blithe *Eng. Improver Imp.* 197, I..onely advise that if your horses be unequall for height, then place the highest formost. 1693 T. Creech in *Dryden's Juvenal* xiii. (1697) 328 Ev'ry Age relates That equal Crimes have met unequal Fates. 1743 Francis tr. *Hor., Odes* i. xxxiii. 16 With sportive cruelty she binds Unequal forms, unequal minds. 1784 Astle *Orig. & Progr. Writing* 79 The Rustic capitals were bold, negligent, unequal. 1836 W. C. Taylor *Anc. Hist.* xvi. §1. 372 Tarraconensis was divided into two unequal portions by the river Iberus. 1860 Tyndall *Glac.* i. xiv. 95 Three stakes.. would, I think, move with unequal velocities. 1861 J. S. Adams *5000 Musical Terms* 104 Compositions written for both male and female voices are said to be for unequal voices.
b. With abstract sbs. in the singular.
1593 Shaks. *3 Hen. VI*, iii. ii. 159 Shee did corrupt frayle Nature..To shape my Legges of an vnequall size. 1651 Hobbes *Leviath.* i. viii. 34 The Experience of men equall in age, is not much unequall, as to the quantity. 1710 *Tatler* No. 235 ¶1 That unequal Love by which Parents distinguish their Children from each other. 1780 Cowper *Progr. Error* 560 Halting on crutches of unequal size. 1827 Jarman *Powell's Devises* II. 265 There seems to be no solid ground for treating with such unequal regard the two objects of the testator's bounty. 1838 Lytton *Calderon* i, The courtiers one by one approached the marquis, who received them with very unequal courtesy. 1908 *Animal Managem.* 185 The more unequal the balance of weight carried the greater the risk of injury.
c. Of single persons or things.
a 1677 Barrow *Math.* x. 233 That will be called unequal, which contains in it another..and some thing besides. 1829 Scott *Anne of G.* xxxv, Surely..a match with one so unequal in birth..was too monstrous to be mentioned? 1887 Bowen *Æneid* i. 475 Ill-starred youth, for Achilles unequal match in the fight.
d. Of numbers: Odd; not even.
1697 Dryden *Virg. Past.* viii. 105 Thrice bind about his thrice devoted Head,..Unequal numbers please the Gods. 1807 Robinson *Archæol. Græca* v. x. (1827) 447 The gods were supposed to be pleased with unequal numbers.
2. †a. Of things: Inadequate, insufficient. *Obs.*
1582 Bentley *Mon. Matrones* iii. 278 Continue, O God, such goodnesse towards me,..which doo here..appeale.. to accept mine vnequall thanks for the same. 1646 Sir T. Browne *Pseud. Ep.* Pref., Authority..which the privacie of our condition, and unequall abilities cannot expect. 1676 Dryden *Aurengz.* i. i. 74 Those Rebel-Sons, who dare..To sway his Empire with unequal Skill And mount a throne which none but he can fill. 1736 Gray *Statius* i. 5 From out the gazing host Young Pterelas with strength unequal drew, Labouring, the disc, and to small distance threw.
b. Not equal or adequate *to* some task, etc. (Occas. with inf. or vbl. sb.)
a 1694 Tillotson *Serm.* (1743) VII. 1991 We are very unequal to our religion, if we make a doubt of these things. 1776 Gibbon *Decl. & F.* ii. (1782) I. 60 Four of them were immediately rejected as unequal to the burden. 1802 Marian Moore *Lascelles* II. 99, I was unequal to personally opposing that dear friend. 1816 Scott *Old Mort.* xxxiii, Unequal..to arrange his own thoughts into suitable expressions. 1855 Macaulay *Hist. Eng.* xii. III. 229 Avaux had given it as his opinion that Richard Hamilton was unequal to the difficulties of the situation. 1885 'F. Anstey' *Tinted Venus* 111 Imagination was unequal to the task.
3. Exhibiting inequality in some respect; varying, variable: a. In movement or action.
1565 Cooper *Inæquabilis percussus venarum*, vnequall pulse. 1655 Culpepper, etc., *Riverius* viii. ii. 181 After an unequal Pulse, he fell into a Palpitation and an Asthma, and so died. 1715 tr. *Gregory's Astron.* (1726) I. 463 The Motion of this Body which is in its own Nature unequal, ought to be reduced to an equality. 1799 in *Spirit Pub. Jrnls.* III. 271 The gratitude of the depredator of Hibernia walked forth with unequal pace by the side of his emoluments. 1821 Scott *Kenilw.* xxxiv, Her step was not only slow, but even unequal.
b. In extent, amount, duration, etc.
1591 G. Fletcher *Russe Commw.* (Hakl. Soc.) 112 By means of an unequal partition of the people and parishes. 1593 Fale *Dialling* 40 By an unequall houre is meant the 12 part of the day whether it be short or long. 1656 Earl Monm. tr. *Boccalini's Advts. fr. Parnass.* i. xxiv. (1674) 26 Is

it not..able to make a man die for anger,..in so unequal a thirst, to drink still the same measure? **1684** EARL ROSCOM. *Ess. Transl. Verse* 234 If you will unequal Numbers try, Their Accents on odd Syllables must lie. **1815** STEPHENS in *Shaw's Gen. Zool.* IX. I. 6 Tail very long, unequal, the outer feathers the shortest: tip black. **1836** MACGILLIVRAY *Trav. Humboldt* xxi. 302 The climate..is marked by an unequal distribution of heat at different periods of the year.

spec. **1816** R. JAMESON *Char. Min.* (ed. 2) 204 Unequal tourmaline..is a nine-sided prism, having seven alternating planes on one extremity, and three on the other.

c. In surface: Uneven, undulating.

1613 PURCHAS *Pilgrimage* VIII. iii. 624 The unequall Seas, which might amaze the hearer, and amate the beholder. **1686** tr. *Chardin's Trav. Persia* 79 The Country it self is unequal; full of Hills.., Valleys and Plains. **1718** PRIOR *Solomon* II. 5 The perplexing and unequal Ways, Where Study brings Thee. **1732** MUNRO *Anat. Bones* 131 This Bone is extremely ragged and unequal. **1796** MME. D'ARBLAY *Camilla* I. 4 The parsonage-house.., beautifully situated in the unequal county of Hampshire. **1826** KIRBY & SP. *Entomol.* xlvi. IV. 270 *Unequal*, having very slight and indeterminate excavations. **1852** BAILEY *Festus* (ed. 4) 342 Shining upon it like the quiet moon Illustrating the obscure unequal earth.

d. In character, condition, quality, etc.

1703 ROWE *Fair Penit.* IV. i. 1259 With what unequal Tempers are we form'd? **1799** S. & HT. LEE *Canterb. T.* (1800) III. 147 Her spirits were often unequal from the delicate state of her health. **1811** SCOTT *Let.* in *Lockhart* (1837) II. xi. 364 The unknown author of a fine, but unequal poem, called *Albania*. **1897** GRANT DUFF *Notes from Diary* (1911) 81 No man writes above himself; but most men are very unequal.

†**4. a.** Not characterized by equal or fair treatment; inequitable, unjust, unfair. *Obs.*

1535 COVERDALE *Ezek.* xviii. 25 Are my wayes vnright, o ye house of Israel? Are not youre wayes rather vnequall? *a* **1578** LINDESAY (Pitscottie) *Chron. Scot.* (S.T.S.) I. 66 His unequall punisching of innocencie. **1606** SHAKS. *Ant. & Cl.* II. v. 101 To punnish me for what you make me do Seemes much vnequall. **1620** E. BLOUNT *Horæ Subs.* 531 It is a thing both vnequall and vniust to insnare the people with multitude of Lawes. **1647** J. TAYLOR *Lib. Proph.* Ep. Ded. 12 Yet it will be unequall to say, that he who owns this Doctrine preaches it lawfull. **1761** HUME *Hist. Eng.* I. x. 205 To lend [money] at exorbitant and unequal interest.

†**b.** Of persons: Acting, or disposed to act, unfairly or unjustly. *Obs.*

1588 GREENE *Pandosto* (1607) 15 Iealousie is an vnequall Iudge. **1605** B. JONSON *Volpone* III. ii, You are vnequall to me, and how ere Your sentence may be righteous, yet you are not. **1628** FELTHAM *Resolves* II. xxiii. 75 Few againe are so iust, as that they seeme not to some vnequall. *a* **1721** PRIOR *Ess. Opinion* Wks. 1907 II. 195 You will find him always uncertain,..an Unequal Parent and a froward Master. **1725** POPE *Odyss.* XIV. 73 Far hence is by unequal Gods remov'd That man of bounties!

transf. **1613** PURCHAS *Pilgrimage* (1614) 629 The sword, the vnequallest arbiter of equity, is now made vmpire. **1630** R. N. tr. *Camden's Hist. Eliz.* I. 111 She..admonished her, ..saying that the times were vnequall and maligne, and malice blinde. **1743** FRANCIS tr. *Hor., Odes* II. x. 4 And when you hear the tempest roar, Press not too near th' unequal shore.

5. a. In which the two sides or parties are not on equal terms, or have not equal advantage.

1552 ELYOT, *Impar certamen*, in contencion, or in gameyng, where is an vnequall matche. **1591** SHAKS. *1 Hen. VI*, V. v. 34 A poore Earles daughter is vnequall oddes, And therefore may be broke without offence. **1604** BACON *Apol.* Wks. 1879 I. 437, I doubted his words would have so unequal a passage above theirs that should charge him. **1671** MILTON *Samson* 346 Himself an Army, now unequal match To save himself against a coward arm'd At one spears length. **1748** ANSON *Voy.* III. x. 416 This was much short of her value, but the impatience of the Commodore.. prompted them to insist on so unequal a bargain. **1796** MME. D'ARBLAY *Camilla* III. 390 She had entered the world, by a sudden and most unequal marriage. **1833** HT. MARTINEAU *Cinnamon & Pearls* v. 92 The colony will not long fulfil its part in this unequal bargain. **1856** KANE *Arct. Expl.* II. xx. 205, I left my own tired dogs.., and took from them their only team in unequal exchange.

b. *esp.* (*a*) Of combats or contests.

1654 FULLER *Two Serm.* 4 The next verse presents an unequall combat between armed power..and naked Innocence. **1697** DRYDEN *Æneis* IX. 542 Or desperate should he rush and lose his life, With odds oppressed, in such unequal strife? *c* **1750** SHENSTONE *Ruin'd Abbey* 56 My pinnace..shuns Th' unequal conflict, and declines the deep. **1817** SHELLEY *Rev. Islam* VI. xiv, Then the combat grew Unequal but most horrible. **1878** DAVIDSON *Inverurie & Garioch* ix. 317 The struggle with England which ensued was necessarily an unequal one.

(*b*) Of treaties, etc.

1682 W. EVATS tr. *Grotius' Rights of War & Peace* II. xv. 184 Unequal leagues are often made, not only between the Conquerors and the Conquered..but also between people of unequal power. **1799** T. RUTHERFORTH *Inst. Nat. Law* (ed. 3) II. ix. 595 Unequal compacts, which lay the greater burden on the inferior party, are either such as diminish the sovereign power..or such as do not diminish this power. **1814** A. C. CAMPBELL tr. *Grotius' Rights of War & Peace* II. xv. 127 Unequal treaties may be made not only between the conquerors and the conquered, but also between mighty and impotent states, between whom no hostilities have ever existed. **1925** *China Yearbk.* 891 The 'most favoured nation clause'..is the basis of the intercourse between China and most foreign countries. The 'most favoured nation clause' is unilateral and is the ground for the recent agitation against 'unequal treaties'. **1962** E. SNOW *Other Side of River* (1963) iv. 38 Under the unequal treaties foreign nationals had extraterritoriality rights which enabled them to reside and do business in China while remaining accountable only to their own courts. **1973** I. M. SINCLAIR *Vienna Convention on Law of Treaties* iv. 108 The Afro-Asian majority were extremely reluctant to countenance any material departure from the texts proposed by the Commission, particularly if it could be represented that the change was designed to keep in being so-called 'unequal' treaties.

†**c.** Disproportionate, excessive. *Obs.*

1704 SWIFT *Battle of Bks.* ¶10 Which, yielding to the unequal Weight, sunk down to the very Foundation. **1717** POPE *Eloisa* 195 Unequal task! a passion to resign, For hearts so touch'd,..so lost as mine.

6. *Comb.*, as *unequal-lengthed, -lobed, -sided, -tempered, -valved*.

1853 R. S. SURTEES *Sponge's Sp. Tour* lv, The *unequal-lengthed candles of the previous night's illumination. **1851** G. A. MANTELL *Petrifact.* v. §2. 433 Two genera..which are characterised by their *unequal-lobed tail. **1725** W. HALFPENNY *Sound Building* 19 An *unequal-sided Groin. **1856** HENSLOW *Dict. Bot. Terms* 208 *Unequal-sided*, when opposite sides are not symmetrical. **1885** J. E. TAYLOR *Brit. Fossils* 243 The shells are frequently unequal-sided. **1703** MOXON *Mech. Exerc.* 169 Heavy *unequal tempered Stuff. **1822** J. PARKINSON *Outl. Oryctol.* 187 An irregular, adherent, *unequal-valved bivalve.

7. *adv.* or quasi-*adv.*

1602 SHAKS. *Ham.* II. ii. 493 (Q 1), Vnequall matcht, Pirrhus at Priam driues. **1663** GERBIER *Counsel* 50 To cause the foundation..to be..laid, without leaving any touchings, since walls new begun on them will settle more unequal than those [etc.]. **1700** S. WESLEY *Epist. Poetry* 12 Of Chaucer's Verse we scarce the Measures know, So rough the Lines, and so unequal flow. **1853** MARKHAM *Skoda's Auscult.* 266 Unequal-bubbling dull râles.

un'equalable, *a.* (UN-[1] 7 b.)

1648 BOYLE *Seraph. Love* (1659) 129 Christ.., whose love to God is questionlesse Filiall and unequalable. **1799** SOUTHEY *Lett.* (1856) I. 87 Milton and Shakspeare,..the two unequalable men. **1870** CARLYLE *New Letters* (1904) II. 263 Our welcome continues to be unsurpassable, or indeed unequallable.

une'quality. [UN-[1] 12 and 5 b.] = INEQUALITY.

1541 R. COPLAND *Guydon's Quest. Chirurg.* M iv, When it is seen that it [sc. the pulse] alyeneth to vnequalyte..the veyne ought to be stopped. **1587** GOLDING *De Mornay* ii. 20 When..wee see an equalitie of good behauior in an vnequality of degrees of people. **1623** COCKERAM II, Vnequalitie, or contrary to a thing, *anomalie*. **1720** *Temple's Ess., Govt.* Wks. I. 106 The first must overturn whenever there happens any unequality [1680 inequality] in the Balance. **1770–4** *A. Hunter's Georg. Ess.* (1803) I. 289 Hence an unequality of the crop. **1939** *Sun* (Baltimore) 21 June 1/3 Industry went into case records today to present to a Senate committee studying proposed changes in the Wagner Act fourteen specific points of 'unequality' in that statute as it stands. **1973** *Nature* 8 June p. vi/1 The tools employed include linear programming and the calculus of variations, special attention being devoted to the use of Lagrangian multipliers for unequality constraints.

un'equalized, *ppl. a.* (UN-[1] 8.)

1596 FITZ-GEFFREY *Sir F. Drake* (1881) 69 A vowed votarie to honour still, Vnequaliz'd by valours chiefest peeres. **1822** J. PARKINSON *Outl. Oryctol.* 69 The terminations of unequalized pentagons and hexagons. **1880** EARLE *Philol. Eng. Tongue* (ed. 3) §239 Its application is unequalized even within the four seas.

un'equalled, *ppl. a.* (UN-[1] 8.)

1622 FLETCHER *Sea Voy.* IV. i, Do ye like wealth, and most unequal'd beauty? **1639** SIR W. BERKELEY *Lost Lady* I. i, I will relate the story of his Unequal'd suffrings. **1667** MILTON *P.L.* IX. 983 Chiefly assur'd..of thy so true, So faithful Love unequald. **1746** FRANCIS tr. *Hor., Sat.* II. ii. 38 No; 'tis th' unequall'd beauty of its train Deludes your eye. **1794** R. J. SULIVAN *View Nat.* I. 177 Why should there be ..such unequalled heats, and such unequalled evaporation? **1841** MISS MITFORD in L'Estrange *Life* (1870) III. viii. 120 Our ancestors were rare architects. Their painted glass and their carved oak are unequalled. **1872** YEATS *Techn. Hist. Comm.* 81 Buildings which are unequalled for grandeur.

b. Const. *by*.

1769 GOLDSM. *Hist. Rome* (1786) II. 103 An act of unequalled heroism by anything that had hitherto appeared in Rome. **1796** MORSE *Amer. Geog.* II. 19 A violence and noise unequalled by the loudest cataracts. **1829** *Chapters Phys. Sci.* 64 The battering-ram..exerted a force which in some respects rendered it unequalled by our battering cannon. **1869** TOZER *Highl. Turkey* II. 124 A panorama.. unequalled..by any view in Greece.

un'equally, *adv.* [UN-[1] 11: cf. UNEQUAL *a.*]

1. In an unequal manner; not equally or evenly.

1548 ELYOT, *Inæqualiter*, vnequally. **1563** GOLDING *Cæsar* VII. (1565) 208 b, The Romanes were vnequallye matched, both in place and number. **1611** BIBLE *2 Cor.* vi. 14 Be ye not vnequally yoked together with vnbeleeuers. **1665** MANLEY *Grotius' Low C. Wars* 417 All this Region is divided, though somewhat unequally, between wild Beasts, and these Savage men. **1726** MONRO *Anat. Bones* 149 The square bone is unequally concave... Its..Edge is unequally ragged. **1776** GIBBON *Decl. & F.* i. (1782) I. 23 That great peninsula [Spain], at present so unequally divided between two sovereigns. **1831** BREWSTER *Optics* iv. 40 Rule for finding the principal focus..for a glass unequally convex. **1880** GEIKIE *Phys. Geog.* iv. 284 The rocks..are worn down unequally.

†**2.** Unfairly, unjustly. *Obs.*

1596 SPENSER *F.Q.* VII. vii. 14 Damning all Wrong.. Which any of thy creatures doe to other (Oppressing them with power, vnequally).

un'equalness. [UN-[1] 12: cf. UNEQUAL *a.*]

1. The quality of being unequal.

1550 BALE *Image Both Ch.* II. xxi. N nn iij b, As for the vnequalnesse of length in ye furlongs & cubits [etc.]. **1561** T. HOBY tr. *Castiglione's Courtyer* IV. (1577) T vij b, Bestowing promotions and honors according to the vnequalnesse of desertes. **1652** FRENCH *Yorksh. Spa* xiii. 102, I forbid much variety of meats, because of the unequalness of their concoction. **1698** ATTERBURY *Serm.* (1737) IV. 308 This unequalness in acting..will draw upon a man the suspicion of hypocrisy. **1776** *Ann. Reg.* 148 Notwithstanding the unequalness of the wind..he only missed the target three times. **1880** *Wood's Guide Steam-Engine Indicator* (title-p.), Geometrical Sketch, showing the Cause of Unequalness.

†**2.** Lack of equity; unfairness. *Obs.*

1628 tr. *Mathieu's Powerfull Favorite* 126 The vapours of his way-ward disposition, of his distrust and vnequalnesse. **1695** *Def. Vind. Deprived Bps.* 98 The very unequalness of it [*sc.* a contract] would be in Equity a strong Presumption.

une'questrian, *a.* (UN-[1] 7.)

1846 H. W. TORRENS *Rem. Milit. Hist.* 21 A remarkable proof of the unequestrian habits of the Greek.

unequi'angular, *a.* (UN-[1] 7.)

1805 R. JAMESON *Char. Min.* 41 These lateral edges are either equiangular as in the icosahedron,..[or] unequiangular as in topaz.

unequi'axed, *a.* (UN-[1] 9, 5 b.)

a **1853** PEREIRA *Polarized Light* (1854) 164 In a very large proportion of cases the axes are not all equal, and these crystals are said to be unequiaxed. **1877** LE CONTE *Elem. Geol.* (1879) 185 A plastic mass, with unequiaxed foreign particles disseminated through it.

unequi'lateral, *a.* (UN-[1] 7, 5 b.)

1662 J. BARGRAVE *Pope Alex. VII* (1867) 120, I have in my cabinet another triangular unequilateral..loadstone. **1761** *London & Environs* IV. 145 Nineteen unequilateral arches ..supported the street above.

unequi'librated, *ppl. a.* (UN-[1] 8.)

[**1775** ASH.] **1833** HERSCHEL *Ess.* (1857) 50 The..constant fluctuation of an unequilibrated ocean. **1895** W. H. HUDSON *Spencer's Philos.* 97 Remaining exposed to surrounding forces that are unequilibrated.

une'quipped, *ppl. a.* (UN-[1] 8.)

[**1775** ASH.] **1895** HARDY in *Harper's Mag.* Mar. 569 The miserable struggle in which he had been engaged thus unequipped.

un'equitable, *a.* (UN-[1] 7 and 5 b.)

1647 DIGGES *Unlawf. Taking Arms* IV. 99 Not all, but in an unequitable proportion. **1662** J. BARGRAVE *Pope Alex. VII* (1867) 82 For very fear of falling into the legate's displeasure, who they knew was averse to such unequitable designs. **1726** AMHERST *Terræ Fil.* II. App. 169 It is almost as unjust and unequitable..as it would be to act..against any such authority. **1759** STERNE *Tr. Shandy* II. xvii, A cunning contexture of dark arts and unequitable subterfuges. **1844** THIRLWALL *Greece* VIII. lxi. 101 This would seem perhaps not unequitable.

Hence **un'equitably** *adv.*

1649 [F. ROUS] *Bounds Publ. Obed.* 61 They being unequitably deriv'd upon us. **1750** SECKER *Eight Charges* (1771) 126 Any Part of it, which is illegally or unequitably seized.

†**un'equity.** *Obs. rare.* [UN-[1] 12 and 5 b.]

a. Iniquity, wickedness. **b.** Unfairness.

c **1380** WYCLIF *Wks.* (1880) 394 If it was vnequite..for to leue þe prechynge of goddis worde,..hou myche more vnequite and wronge to god & man is it [etc.]. **1382** —— *Rom.* iii. 5 If oure wickidnesse, or vnequyte, comende the riȝtwysnesse of God. **1598** FLORIO, *Inequità*, vnequitie.

un'equivalve(d), *a.* (UN-[1] 7, 9, and 5 b.)

1788 J. BARBUT *Genera Vermium* 42 The shell unequivalve, of a hard consistency. **1822** J. PARKINSON *Outl. Oryctol.* 179 A regular unequivalved, inequilateral bivalve.

une'quivocable, *a.* [irreg. f. UNEQUIVOC(AL *a.* + -ABLE.] Capable of only one interpretation; unambiguous.

1921 *Glasgow Herald* 30 Dec. 7/3 Yesterday 12 public bodies representative of the four provinces recorded in unequivocable language their conviction that the Treaty should be accepted. **1974** *Nature* 8 Feb. 397/2 Thereby providing unequivocable evidence for the former unity of the southern continents.

So **une'quivocably** *adv.*

1917 W. J. LOCKE *Red Planet* xix. 234, I knew that for his own sake he would have unequivocably declined. **1980** *Daily Tel.* 6 Sept. 9/6 In 1980 Gdansk is unequivocably Polish.

une'quivocal, *a.* (UN-[1] 7 and 5 b.)

In common use from about 1795.

1784 COWPER *Task* v. 653 In the deed, The unequivocal authentic deed, We find sound argument. **1791** NEWTE *Tour Eng. & Scot.* 236 In the Highlands..men of years..are struck with the most unequivocal proofs of depopulation. **1838** THIRLWALL *Greece* xlii. V. 213 He..aided him in several acts of unequivocal hostility against his country. **1858** SEARS *Athan.* III. v. 294 This..is here asserted by the Apostle in most unequivocal language. **1871** EARLE *Philol. Eng. Tongue* 340 An adjectival form which should be unequivocal.

Hence **une'quivocalness.**

1846 WORCESTER (citing Godwin). **1873** G. H. LEWES *Probl. Life & Mind* (Ser. 1) I. 58 The chief distinction between his [*sc.* the geometer's] probabilities and those of the physicist or biologist, lies in the greater simplicity or unequivocalness of his terms.

une'quivocally, *adv.* (UN-[1] 11.)

1794 PALEY *Evid.* I. vii, The descent of Christ from David, ..his resurrection,..are unequivocally referred to. **1800** MRS. HERVEY *Mourtray Fam.* III. 26, I hope..to receive a line from you, unequivocally to contradict it. **1844** THIRLWALL *Greece* lxvi. VIII. 467 Still the good-will of the early emperors was unequivocally manifested. **1884** EARL SELBORNE in *Law Times Rep.* 10 May 313/2 Such an intention..might have been expected to be made unequivocally clear.

une'radicable, *a.* (UN-[1] 7b and 5b.)
1818 Byron *Ch. Har.* IV. cxxvi, This uneradicable taint of sin, This boundless upas.

une'radicated, *ppl. a.* (UN-[1] 8.)
[1828–32 Webster.] 1861 J. G. Sheppard *Fall Rome* vi. 323 The uneradicated influences of heathen taste. 1871 Alabaster *Wheel of Law* 41 The believers in it.. will still have their souls contaminated with uneradicated evil.

une'ras(e)able, *a.* (UN-[1] 7b and 5b.)
1826 Mrs. Shelley *Last Man* II. 156 Now in words uneraseable.. the knowledge went forth. 1853 G. Johnston *Nat. Hist. E. Bord.* I. 233 The coloured uneraseable stain cries out for yet unavenged blood.

une'rased, *ppl. a.* (UN-[1] 8.)
1760–72 H. Brooke *Fool of Qual.* (1809) IV. 65, I discerned some unerased traces of the image.. of my God. 1821 Byron *Two Foscari* I. i, *Lor.* It is written thus. *Bar.* And will you leave it unerased?

une'rasible, *a.* (UN-[1] 7.)
1811 Shelley *St. Irvyne* i, Grief, in unerasible traces, sate deeply implanted on the front of the outcast.

une'rasing, *ppl. a.* (UN-[1] 10.)
1820 Shelley *Prometh. Unb.* III. iii. 160 Where ever lies, on unerasing waves, The image of a temple built, above.

†**unerra'bility.** (UN-[1] 12 and 5b; cf. next.)
1628 Prynne *Brief Survay* 14 Hee doeth.. likewise apply this Popish Position.. euen to iustifie the vnerrabilitie of these his Deuotions.

†**un'errable**, *a. Obs.* [UN-[1] 7b and 5b.] = INERRABLE *a.*
1616 Sheldon *Mirac. Antichrist* vii. 142 This puddle of Pope Ioane, whereout the ignominy of your vnerrable See is so liuely discouered. 1664 H. More *Myst. Iniq.* xviii. 67 The ancient Types.. already made use of by his choice who was unerrable. 1715 M. Davies *Athen. Brit.* I. Pref. 12 Those sole unerrable Records of the Holy Scriptures. 1984 *New Yorker* 12 Mar. 39/1 A submachine gun blasts at him from unerrable range.
Hence †**un'errableness.** *Obs.*
1645 Hammond *View Infallibility* (1646) 186 Concluding the truth of all their assertions from the unerrablenesse of the asserter. 1667 *Decay Chr. Piety* xvi. ¶3 The danger of presuming upon the unerrableness of a guide.

un'errancy. (UN-[1] 12 and 5b.)
1646 J. Hall *Horæ Vac.* 7 Hee takes the best course.. that narrowly heeds upon what principles both parties build.., so long as no man can challenge an unerrancy. 1891 F. G. Lee *Sinless Concept.* 66 Unerrancy belonged alone to the Church Universal.

un'erring, *vbl. sb.* (UN-[1] 13.)
1709 Strype *Ann. Ref.* 247 He was in Judgment for the unerring of General Councils.

un'erring, *ppl. a.* [UN-[1] 10 and 5b.]
1. Making no error or mistake; not going or leading astray in judgement or opinion.
*c*1660 South *Serm.* (1697) I. 254 They believed his Miracles upon the Credit of constant unerring Tradition. 1697 Dryden *Virg. Georg.* IV. 565 With sure Foresight, and with unerring Doom, He sees what is, and was, and is to come. 1732 Challoner (*title*), The Unerring Authority of the Catholic Church in matters of Faith. 1795 Southey *Joan of Arc* IV. 324, I know this vision sent From Heaven, and feel of its unerring truth. 1844 H. H. Wilson *Brit. India* I. 565 The unerring principles of political economy. 1875 Jowett *Plato* (ed. 2) I. 32 The unerring guides of ourselves and of those who were under us.
absol. 1813 Coleridge *Remorse* III. ii. 36, I breath'd to the Unerring Permitted prayers.
2. Corresponding with the utmost exactness or closeness to some standard or aim.
1665 Glanvill *Def. Van. Dogm.* 39 The unerring exactness we find in Animal formations. 1684 J. S. *Profit & Pleas. United* 166 Therefore I thought fit to lay down such Unerring Rules, as [etc.]. 1710 Prior *Examiner* 7 Sept., The Works of learned Men are weighed here by the unerring Ballance of Party. 1775 Tyrwhitt *Chaucer's Cant. T.* IV. 91 An operation, which every Ballad-monger in our days.. is known to perform with the most unerring exactness. 1819 Scott *Leg. Montrose* xiv, The Son of the Mist again led the way, with an unerring precision. 1861 Buckle *Civiliz.* (1873) II. viii. 434 We may trace with unerring certainty the steps [etc.].
3. Not going astray from the intended mark; certain, sure: **a.** Of missiles or other weapons.
1621 G. Sandys *Ovid's Met.* XII. (1626) 240 With that, th' vnerring dart.. [he] flung. 1712 *Spect.* No. 527 ¶3 Procris.. made her Husband.. a Present of an unerring Javelin. *c*1743 Francis tr. *Hor., Sec. Poem* 12 Goddess, whose unerring dart Stops the lynx, or flying hart.
b. Of aim, agents or agencies, etc.
1697 Dryden *Æneis* XII. 712 One dart he drew, And with unerring aim, and utmost vigour, threw. *c*1709 Prior *2nd Hymn Callimachus* 127 Thy unerring Hand elanc'd Another, and another Dart. 1743 Francis tr. *Hor., Odes* v. v. 9 By the unerring wrath of Jove, Unerring shall his vengeance prove. 1801 Scott *Glenfinlas* ii, How matchless was thy broad claymore, How deadly thine unerring bow! 1849 Eastwick *Dry Leaves* 46 He was considered an unerring shot. 1855 *Orr's Circ. Sci., Inorg. Nat.* 112 Occasionally striking with unerring aim at its prey.

un'erringly, *adv.* (UN-[1] 11; cf. prec.)
1645 Tombes *Anthropol.* 15 A power to interpret Scriptures unerringly. 1746 Hervey *Reflect. Flower Gard.* 76 Know, that God is unerringly wise. *a*1774 Tucker *Lt. Nat.* (1834) II. 399 It does imply an exact discernment.., so as to distinguish unerringly what lies within its compass, and what does not. 1826 Syd. Smith *Wks.* (1859) II. 104/2 They first learn it practically and unerringly. 1873 Earle *Philol. Eng. Tongue* (ed. 2) §239 Here is a distinction which is unerringly observed by the most rustic people.

un'erringness. (UN-[1] 12.)
1670 Vaughan *Rep.* (1677) 139 If any man thinks that a person.. must submit in all, or any of these, to the implyed discretion and unerringness of his Judge. 1866 Meredith *Vittoria* vii, The result corroborated his devotional belief in the unerringness of his own powerful intuition.

une'rupted, *ppl. a.* (UN-[1] 8.)
[1775 Ash.] 1802 Playfair *Illustr. Hutton. Th.* 69 A subterraneous or unerupted lava. 1833 Lyell *Princ. Geol.* III. 107 These unerupted newer Pliocene lavas of Sicily.

une'scapable, *a.* (UN-[1] 7b and 5b.)
1614 Donne *Lett.* (1651) 197 In this particular, I am under an unescapable necessity, as [etc.]. *c*1625 —— *Serm.* Wks. 1839 VI. 70 She exposes herself to an imminent and (for any thing she knew) an unescapable danger of death. 1832 L. Hunt *Redi's Bacchus in Tuscany* 135 Gall of the satiric poet, Gall from out his blackest well, Shuddering, unescapeable. 1886 W. Graham *Soc. Problem* 243 A power more subtle and all-compelling and unescapable than that of the sword.
Hence **une'scapableness**; **-ably** *adv.*
1610 Donne *Pseudo-martyr* 353 With how much curiositie and unescapablenesse their formes of Abiuration vnder oath are exhibited? 1882 *Gd. Words* Apr. 174 With a certain twinkle at the back of his eye,.. full, unescapably full of fun.

unes'chewable, *a.* (UN-[1] 7b and 5b.)
*c*1374 Chaucer *Boeth.* v. pr. i. (1868) 151 Þilke ordre procedynge by an vneschewable byndynge to-gidre. 1513 Douglas *Æneid* XI. xiv. 102 He.. schuke in hand hys oneschewabill speir. 1542 in *Harl. Misc.* (1745) IV. 509/2 Ther came a sodeyne and piteous Calamyte or Miserye vneuitable or uneschuable. 1602 Carew *Cornwall* 124b, If an vneschewable destiny had not haltered him to that aduancement. 1870 W. H. Gillespie *Being & Attributes God* (1871) IV. ii. 149 Our dread but uneschewable topic.
Hence **unes'chewably** *adv.*
*c*1374 Chaucer *Boeth.* v. pr. iii. (1868) 157 Yif þat he deme þat þei ben to comen vneschewably.

une'scorted, *ppl. a.* (UN-[1] 8.)
1774 *Trinket* 45 The chits knew I must attend them, for it was not safe to go unescorted. 1805–6 Cary *Dante, Inf.* VIII. 127 Passing the circles, unescorted, comes One. 1898 Rider Haggard *Dr. Therne* i. 13 Now, quite alone and unescorted, she was on her way to Mexico City.

une'scutcheoned, *a.* (UN-[1] 9.)
1814 Wordsw. *Excurs.* VI. 412 Their bones.., With unescutcheoned privacy interred Far from the family vault.

une'spied, *ppl. a.* (UN-[1] 8.)
*c*1374 Chaucer *Troylus* IV. 1457 It is ful hard to halten vn-espied Byfore a crepul for he kan on þe craft. 1542 Udall *Erasm. Apoph.* 81 No faulte of the bodye maye escape vnespied. 1596 Spenser *F.Q.* VI. x. 11 He.. in the couert of the wood did byde, Beholding all, yet of them vnespyde. 1653 H. Cogan tr. *Pinto's Trav.* xix. 67 He got up close to this Junk, and.. boarded her on a sudden unespied. 1697 Dryden *Æneis* IX. 786 The second shaft came swift and unespied, And pierced his hand. 1742–3 *Observ. Methodists* 8 Of all other Religions every man enjoys the free Exercise.. unquestioned and unespied. 1831 Scott *Ct. Rob.* xxvi, Nothing, however, in a palace, passes altogether unespied. 1842 Browning *Through the Metidja* ii, Through the desert.. Do I glide unespied as I ride?

une'ssayed, *ppl. a.* (UN-[1] 8.)
1642 in Clarendon *Hist. Reb.* IV. §266 They cannot leave any means unessayed for their relief. 1686 Jas. II *Sp. Edin.* 29 Apr. in *Lond. Gaz.* No. 2135/3 [He] will leave nothing unessayed that may promote a work so beneficial. 1742 *Col. Rec. Pennsylv.* IV. 601 The French, who will leave no methods unessay'd to corrupt their fidelity. 1778 Miss Burney *Evelina* lxxiv, Remains there one resource unessayed? 1855 Singleton *Virgil* II. 299 Lest aught there had been or of crime, or craft, Unhazarded or unessayed.

un'essence, *v.* [UN-[2] 4.] *trans.* To deprive of essence or essential properties.
1642 T. Case *God's Rising* (1644) 8 The Enemies of Gods truth and people would.. not un-scepter him only, but un-essence him. 1659 Revett in Lovelace *Poems* (1904) 212 While we sustain the losse that thou art gone Vn-essenc'd in the separation. 1822 Lamb *Elia* I. *Distant Correspondents*, Not only does truth, in these long intervals, unessence herself, but [etc.].

une'ssential, *a.* and *sb.* [UN-[1] 7 and 5b.]
1. Possessing no essence or substance; immaterial.
1667 Milton *P.L.* II. 439 The void profound Of unessential Night receives him next. 1727 Thomson *Summer* 81 Prime Chearer, Light!.. Without whose vesting Beauty, all were wrapt In unessential Gloom. 1768–74 Tucker *Lt. Nat.* (1834) I. 666 Ask me by what authority of history I prove that Regulus had any notion of.. the unessential nature of justice. 1827 Pollok *Course T.* III. 412 Most unsubstantial, unessential shade, Was earthly Fame.
2. Not pertaining to or affecting the essence of a matter; unimportant.
*a*1656 Bp. Hall *Beauty & Vnitie Ch.* Wks. 1837 V. 245 Neither difference of time, nor distance of place,.. nor any unessential error, can bar our interest in this Blessed Unity. 1716 Addison *Freeholder* No. 39 ¶5 Those, who differed from him in the unessential Parts of Christianity. 1748 Melmoth *Fitzosborne Lett.* (1763) 169 So far is he from thinking it unessential, that he acknowledged it as the only separation which distinguishes them from prose. 1838 Arnold *Hist. Rome* (1845) I. 166 A form.. as unessential as the crowd's acceptance of the king at an English coronation. 1873 M. Arnold *Lit. & Dogma* (1876) 166 This excludes as unessential much of the criticism which [etc.].
b. *absol.* That which is not essential.
1840 Carlyle *Heroes* iv. (1904) 139 He distinguishes what is essential, and what is not; the unessential may go very much as it will. 1841 Myers *Cath. Th.* III. §33. 120 Who is to determine.. the limit of the Unessential?
3. *sb.* An unessential thing or feature.
1828–32 Webster s.v., Forms are among the unessentials of religion. 1876 Stainer & Barrett *Dict. Mus.* 444/2 *Unessentials*, notes not forming a necessary part of the harmony. Passing, auxiliary, or ornamental notes. 1882 *Nature* XXVI. 523 A general conception.. is arrived at by abstracting the essentials and neglecting the unessentials.
Hence **une'ssentially** *adv.*
[1847 Webster.] 1856 Olmsted *Slave States* 182 With a climate so unessentially dissimiliar.

une'stablish, *v.* [UN-[2] 3.] To disestablish.
1649 Milton *Eikon.* xxvii. 215 In order to which the Parlament demanded of the King to un-establish that Prelatical Government. 1834 W. P. Wood *Let.* in Stephens *Hook* (1878) I. 261 Where we find a Church established we ought not to lend any assistance towards *un*establishing.

une'stablished, *ppl. a.* [UN-[1] 8.]
1. Not established or firmly settled.
1646 Sir T. Browne *Pseud. Ep.* 227 [A conclusion] clapt up from petitionary foundations and principles un-established. 1744 Young *Nt. Th.* VI. Pref., This great fundamental truth, unestablish'd, or unawaken'd in the minds of men. 1776 Mickle *Camoens' Lusiad* Introd. 154 A work which claims poetical merit, while its reputation is unestablished. 1873 M. Arnold *Lit. & Dogma* xi. §3. 346 A notion unestablished, not resting on observation and experience.
2. *spec.* **a.** Of churches or religious bodies: (see ESTABLISH *v.* 7).
1885 Abp. Benson in *Life* (1899) II. 496 The difference of court made no difference to the union even of an established Church, and how can it.. do so for an unestablished Church? 1887 *Pall Mall G.* 4 Oct. 1/1 Her communion embraces Churches established, unestablished, and disestablished.
b. Of employees or employment: Not included in the regular staff or establishment.
1890 *Pall Mall G.* 7 July 5/2 Sanction.. to.. increase the minimum wage to postmen (including unestablished men). 1894 *Daily News* 15 Sept. 6/3 Within the same time 'unestablished situations'.. have been given to 1,110 soldiers.

une'stablishment. (UN-[1] 12.)
1776 S. J. Pratt *Pupil of Pleas.* (1777) I. 182 Shall I once again confess to you.. my unestablishment in the maxims of thy Preceptor?

une'steemed, *ppl. a.* (UN-[1] 8.)
*c*1550 Cheke *Matt.* xiii. 57 Theer is not a propheet.. vnesteemed but in his own contree. 1561 T. Norton *Calvin's Inst.* I. 18 The Hebrue tong lay not onely vnesteemed, but almost vnknowen. 1616 Drumm. of Hawth. *Madrigals, Rose*, O Show of Showes! of vnesteemed Worth. 1852 Bailey *Festus* (ed. 4) 473 In thy voice The warning and foreknowledge unexplained, Not unesteemed. 1858 Carlyle *Fredk. Gt.* II. xii. I. 167 An unesteemed creature, who strove to make his time peaceable in this world.

†**un'estimable**, *a. Obs.* [UN-[1] 7b and 5b.]
1. = INESTIMABLE *a.* 1.
1542 Udall *Erasm. Apoph.* 172 *marg.*, A learned kyng [is] an vnestimable treasure. 1548 —— *Erasm. Par. Luke* xxiv. 188b, Beyng enkiendled with the vnestimable fyer of charytee & loue towardes mankynd. 1577 tr. *Bullinger's Decades* 210/1 Some by warre haue.. vnestimable riches with verie little losse or no dammage at all. 1628 tr. *Mathieu's Powerfull Favorite* 102 Here all the world laments the vnestimable losse of the bookes of Cornelius Tacitus.
2. = INESTIMABLE *a.* 3.
1654–66 Earl Orrery *Parthen.* (1676) 694 There can hardly be a higher evincement how unestimable most Worldly things deserve to be. *a*1670 Hacket *Abp. Williams* I. (1692) 41 None are so unestimable.. as those fickle-fancy'd men, whose friendships will hold no longer then Pliny's peaches.

une'stranged, *ppl. a.* (UN-[1] 8.)
[1775 Ash.] *a*1851 Moir *Poems, Highl. Return* viii, Four years had lapsed in absence,.. but his heart was unestranged.

†**un'ete**, *a. Obs.* [OE. **unǽte* (cf. *micel-*, *oferǽte*), f. pret. stem of *etan* to eat.] Without eating.
1387 Trevisa *Higden* (Rolls) I. 405 The men may dure longe vnete, And loueþ wel comune mete.

une'ternal, *a.* (UN-[1] 7.)
[1775 Ash.] 1862 F. Hall *Hindu Philos. Syst.* 254 That which exists, and is destroyed at a given time, is.. uneternal and perishable.

uneth(e, -ethes: see UNEATH(S *adv.*

une'therial, *a.* (UN-[1] 7.)
[1775 Ash.] 1847 Bushnell *Chr. Nurt.* II. iii. (1861) 283 This unetherial and undiffusive kind of bliss.

un'ethic, *a.* [UN-[1] 7.] = next.
1871 Tylor *Prim. Cult.* I. 370 An imagination so little in keeping with his unethic nature jars upon the reader's mind.

un'ethical, *a.* (UN-[1] 7.)
1871 Tylor *Prim. Cult.* II. 94 The savage, unethical doctrine of continuance. 1879 Spencer *Data of Ethics* xi. §68. 187 Ethics has to recognize the truth, recognized in unethical thought, that egoism comes before altruism. 1882 *Pall Mal G.* 15 July 4/2 The intermingling of so unethical a people with.. societies of European blood.
Hence **un'ethicalness.**

1886 W. S. LILLY in *Fortn. Rev.* 591 How can we predicate ethicalness or unethicalness of a thing?

Únětice (uːnjɛtiːtsiː). The Czech original of AUNJETITZ. Hence **Únětician** *a.*

1947 V. G. CHILDE *Dawn Europ. Civilization* (ed. 4) vii. 121 In the classical phase of Únětice..these [pots] are transformed by flattening out the belly into keeled mugs. *Ibid.* (*caption*) Marschwitz and early Únětice pottery. *Ibid.* x. 194 Imitations of Únětician pins and Únětician gold ornaments..show that the fourth period of the Northern Stone Age did not even begin till the Early Bronze Age was well established in Central Europe. **1977** G. CLARK *World Prehist.* (ed. 3) iv. 176 On straight radio-carbon dating the Únětice bronze industry of Czechoslovakia and adjacent parts of Germany was active by the nineteenth century B.C. *Ibid.* 180 Wealth is indicated in outstanding burials such as the Únětician one of Leubingen.

uneu'phonious, *a.* (UN-¹ 7.)

1880 BURTON *Reign Q. Anne* I. i. 36 The uneuphonious name of Godolphin has been traced..to certain words of Celtic origin.

Hence **uneu'phoniously** *adv.*

1882 *Murray's Handbk. Wiltshire, Dorsetshire & Somersetshire* (ed. 4) 261/1 On the N. bank of the most uneuphoniously named *Puddle* or *Piddle*, from which unhappily the string of villages along its banks take their names. **1939** J. SQUIRE *Water-Music* ii. 38 The mother bird (if she indeed it was) by this time screaming uneuphoniously around my head.

un-Euro'pean, *a.* (UN-¹ 7.)

1846 R. FORD *Gatherings from Spain* xv. 175 A Spanish gentleman..suspects..that you are..considering his country as Roman, African, or in a word, as un-European. **1849** EASTWICK *Dry Leaves* 81 The un-European officers might..take the lead. **1870** KINGSLEY *At Last* x, Around were..all appliances of European taste, even luxury: but in a house utterly un-European.

une'vacuated, *ppl. a.* (UN-¹ 8.)

1612 WOODALL *Surg. Mate* Wks. (1653) 201 Some cholerick matter remaineth behinde in right-gut yet unevacuated.

une'vadable, *a.* Also **-evadeable**, **-evadible**. (UN-¹ 7 b, 7, and 5 b.)

1839 DE QUINCEY *Casuistry* Wks. 1862 VII. 272 The..downright unevadable pressures of realities. **1857** TOULMIN SMITH *Parish* 367 Efficient action on this matter was formerly unevadible. **1869** ROSSETTI *Mem. Shelley* p. liv, [A] deadly, and, at last, unevadeable discovery.

uneva'nescent, *a.* (UN-¹ 7.)

1802–12 BENTHAM *Ration. Judic. Evid.* (1827) I. 597 Signs of an unevanescent and imperishable nature.

unevan'gelic, *a.* [UN-¹ 7.] = next.

1857 BADEN POWELL *Chr. without Judaism* 219 Engrafting on it an unevangelic formalism most alien from its spirit.

unevan'gelical, *a.* (UN-¹ 7.)

1648 *Eikon Bas.* xii. 103 Which..un-evangelicall Zeal is too like that of the rebuked Disciples. **1661** PRYNNE *Unbish. Tim.* (ed. 3) 81 An unevangelical, malignant, or Romish Spirit. **1710** T. GODWIN *Life Bp. Stillingfleet* 28 Their un-evangelical and destructive doctrines. **1842** MANNING *Serm.* xvii. (1848) I. 249 They are looked upon as carnal, legal, unevangelical rites. **1881** W. R. SMITH *Old Test. in Jew. Ch.* i. 7 This point of view is..unprotestant, unevangelical.

une'vangelized, *ppl. a.* (UN-¹ 8.)

[**1775** ASH.] **1813–5** *Proc. Ch. Miss. Soc.* IV. 519 If the Heathen, un-evangelized, be considered as objects of salvation. **1884** J. PARKER *Apost. Life* II. 135 The Church..would see every unevangelised country..typified in this Macedonian man.

une'vaporate, *ppl. a.* (UN-¹ 8 b.)

1864 LOWELL *Fireside Trav.* 174 Faith and Awe survive there unevaporate.

une'vaporated, *ppl. a.* (UN-¹ 8.)

1829 BENTHAM *Offic. Apt. Maximized, Militia* (1830) 6 Hostility from the small, still unevaporated, remnant of the savage race. **1890** *Nature* 11 Sept. 481/2 The natural salts..with which the unevaporated residue of water becomes saturated.

un'even, *a.* [OE. *unefen* (f. *un-* UN-¹ 7 + *efen* EVEN *a.*), = OFris. *oniovn* (WFris. *on-*, *ûneven*, NFris. *unēven*, *-īven*), MDu. and Du. *oneven*, *-effen*, MLG. *uneven*, OHG. *uneban* (MHG. and G. *uneben*), ON. and Icel. *ú-*, *ójafn* (Norw. *ujamn*, Sw. *ojemn*, Da. *ujevn*).]

1. a. Unequal; not properly corresponding or agreeing. Now *rare*.

a **900** CYNEWULF *Crist* 1460 Hu þær wæs unefen racu unc ȝemæne! *a* **1225** *Ancr. R.* 312 Ure blod..aȝean his blode þet he shedde for us were ful unefne chaunge. *a* **1340** HAMPOLE *Psalter* xlii. 1 My consciens and my ȝernynge is vneuen til þairs. **1390** GOWER *Conf.* II. 279 Thou tellest forth, Hou that hire weyhte of love unevene Is unto thin. *c* **1450** *Myrr. our Ladye* 104 Yf it were vneuen to the tother, or faylynge in eny thynge that an other had. *a* **1470** H. PARKER *Dives & Pauper* (W. de W. 1496) VII. xi. 293/1 By wyckednesse of false couetyse in the people men ben uneuen in rychesse. **1596** SPENSER *F.Q.* VI. v. 9 So forth they traueld an vneuen payre,..A saluage man matcht with a Ladie fayre. **1609** J. DAVIES (Heref.) *Holy Roode* Wks. (Grosart) I. 8/2 What diff'rence is betweene those Hymnes diuine!..They are as Fame, and Shame, no lesse vneu'n. **1669** BOYLE *Contn. New Exp.* I. (1682) 40 Two pipes of Glass very uneven in length. **1885** *Manch. Exam.* 14 July 4/5 Stands are very uneven, and the size of the plant varies from 2 in. to 3½ ft.

b. Of numbers: Odd. Also of things: Making up, or marked by, an odd number.

1577 B. GOOGE *Heresbach's Husb.* I. (1586) 35 Which Plinie accounteth to haue vneauen corners as Pease hath. **1598** FLORIO, *Disparo*, vneeuen, or od in number, vnequall. **1613** PURCHAS *Pilgrimage* (1614) 173 Nothing ought to be eaten by euen numbers, but by vneuen, wherewith God is pleased. **1615** G. SANDYS *Trav.* 78 Let rauisht Poets drinke thrice three, Of whom the vneuen Muses be Belou'd. **1728** CHAMBERS *Cycl.* s.v. *Number*, The Sum, or the Difference, of two uneven Numbers, makes an even Number. **1771** LUCKOMBE *Hist. Printing* 265 According to the folio either of an even, or uneven page. **1875** JOWETT *Plato* (ed. 2) I. 485 Then the triad or number three is uneven. **1888** JACOBI *Printers' Vocab.*, *Uneven pages*, pages with odd folios, such as 1, 3, 5, etc.

†**2.** Unequitable, unfair, unjust: **a.** Of acts, etc.

c **1380** WYCLIF *Wks.* (1880) 316 Summe ben too wel fed bi vneuene partyng of here goodis. **1398** TREVISA *Barth. De P.R.* XIX. cxxi. (1495) 922 For euen and vneuen dedes that here ben doon. **1585** ABP. SANDYS *Serm.* ii. 40 If merchaunts..doe inriche themselues by impouerishing others, through deceitfull shifts, the common wealth suffereth dammage by their vneuen dealings. **1613** J. FLETCHER *Christ's Bloody Sweat* 11 By courses indirect and lawes vn-euen, Of will and sensuall lust.

†**b.** Of persons, etc. *Obs.*

c **1400** *Apol. Loll.* 104 Þei are vnfeiþful to þer souereyns, vn euyn to þer lowar. *a* **1500** *Ratis Raving* Prol. 60 He saw..rychtwysmen and god-lyk baith, With wykyt men & wnewyne lyk scaith. **1581** J. BELL *Haddon's Answ. Osor.* III. 392 They are in this their partition, so parciall and vneuen dealers, that they will not leaue to Christ, the whole cleansing of the guilt. **1611** SPEED *Hist. Gt. Brit.* IX. xxi. 780/2 N. D. with his vneuen hand (euer ouerhard to shadow the truth). **1641** MILTON *Animadv.* 7 Sir Francis Bacon..complaines of the Bishops uneven hand over these Pamflets.

3. Diverging from a straight or exactly parallel position. (In early quots. *fig.*)

1390 GOWER *Conf.* I. 30 Thei hemself divide And stonden out of reule unevene. *Ibid.* II. 126 Among the vices..Ther is yit on..Which al this world hath set unevene. **1639** LD. DIGBY *Lett. conc. Relig.* (1651) 90 And lines many times that at first appear parallels to the eie..prove apparently uneven. **1683** MOXON *Mech. Exerc.*, *Printing* xxiv. ¶ 15 If..the sides of the Sheet lye uneven upon the Tympan-sheet. **1862** MISS BRADDON *Lady Audley* i, The windows were uneven.

4. Not smooth or level; irregular, broken, rugged.

a. Of ground, etc.

c **1275** in *O.E. Misc.* 75/88 Þe weyes beoþ vn-euene, Wiþ wepynde stefne To helle he schulle þenne. **1565** COOPER s.v. *Inæquabilis*, An open place beyng high and low, or vneuen. **1577** GOOGE tr. *Heresbach's Husb.* I. 42 b, Beastes and Poultry..with tramplyng and skraping wyll make it rugged and uneven. **1596** SHAKS. *1 Hen. IV*, II. ii. 26 Eight yards of vneuen ground, is threescore & ten miles afoot with me. **1618** J. TAYLOR (Water P.) *Penniless Pilgr.* E 4, The way so vneuen, stonie, and full of bogges. **1653** W. RAMESEY *Astrol. Restored* 91 Aquaries [governs] Hilly and uneven places. **1746** in *10th Rep. Hist. MSS. Comm.* App. I. 440 As we march'd, all the way up hill, and over very uneven Ground, our men were greatly Blown. **1774** GOLDSM. *Nat. Hist.* (1776) I. 290 In it [*sc.* the sea-bottom] we find the same uneven surface that we do upon land. **1858** HAWTHORNE *Fr. & It. Note-bks.* (1871) II. 199 On the verge and within the crater of an extinct volcano, and therefore..as uneven as the sea in a tempest.

fig. **1592** SHAKS. *Rom. & Jul.* IV. i. 5 Vneuen is the course, I like it not. *a* **1596** *Sir T. More* IV. v. 4 You see the floore of greatnesse is uneuen.

b. In general use.

1398 TREVISA *Barth. De P.R.* IV. iii. (1495) e vj b/1 The vtter partyes ben vneuyn wyth holownes sonke and had partes areyd. **1590** SPENSER *F.Q.* I. viii. 48 For one of them was like an Eagles claw,..The other like a Beares vneuen paw. **1599** HAKLUYT *Voy.* II. 162 The sorting together of Wools of seueral natures,..which causeth cloth to cockle and be uneven. **1683** MOXON *Mech. Exerc.*, *Printing* xvii. ¶ 2 [He] cuts out what may remain in the bottom of the Shanck by reason of the un-even breaking. **1712** J. JAMES tr. *Le Blond's Gardening* 140 Its Bark is somewhat rugged and uneaven. **1798** S. & HT. LEE *Canterb. T.* II. 431 The uneven writing..proved that it was sent while the young man was still fluctuating between life and death. **1810** CRABBE *Borough* xxii. 178 The sun-burnt tar..And bank-side stakes in their uneven ranks. **1855** *Poultry Chron.* III. 522/1 The upper part of the cell..being more convex; therefore, the comb is very uneven.

absol. **1796** KIRWAN *Elem. Min.* (ed. 2) I. 157 Fracture, fine or coarse splintery, which sometimes pass into the uneven of a fine grain.

c. *transf.* and *fig.* (of immaterial things, sounds, style, etc.).

OE. *unefn*, *unemn*, occurs in similar uses.

(*a*) **1596** SHAKS. *1 Hen. IV*, I. i. 50 Farre more vneuen and vnwelcome Newes Came from the North. **1603** —— *Meas. for M.* IV. iv. 3 In most vneuen and distracted manner, his actions show much like to madnesse. **1649** LOVELACE *Poems* (1864) 114 Where is a joy uneven, There never, never can be Heav'n. **1719** DE FOE *Crusoe* I. (Globe) 159 Such is the uneven State of human Life. **1763** SCRAFTON *Indostan* iii. (1770) 76 The uneven temper of the Soubah could never long retain its disguise. **1886** J. J. H. BURGESS *Shetland Sketches*, etc. i. 48 He..went away down to the house, feeling very sorrowful, and mad, and altogether uneven.

(*b*) **1608** WILLET *Hexapla Exod.* 50 The horses euill and vneuen going proceedeth of his owne lamenes.

(*c*) **1668** CULPEPPER & COLE *Barthol. Anat.* III. ix. 150 Not only with cold Air, but with any other uneven noise, passing through their Mouth into their Ears. **1731** POPE *Ep. Burlington* 143 Light quirks of Music, broken and uneven. **1811** W. R. SPENCER *Poems* Ded., His strain is weak, his voice uneven.

(*d*) **1763** J. BROWN *Poetry & Music* vi. 111 Homer is equal, large, flowing, and harmonious; Eschylus is uneven, concise, abrupt, and rugged.

(*e*) **1905** R. BROOKE *Let.* 25 Mar. (1968) 19 It's not a bad number [of a magazine], a bit uneven of course; but then you can't expect the other men to ascend to my level. **1974** *Country Life* 7 Feb. 240/2 Almost no one was more uneven, as it is politely called, than G. F. Watts.

5. *Comb.*, as ***uneven-carriaged***, ***-numbered***, ***-roofed***; **uneven-aged** *a.*, (of a group of trees) containing individuals of different ages.

1670 BROOKS *Wks.* (1867) VI. 342 A rotten heart, is a very uneven-carriaged heart. **1882** *Contemp. Rev.* Aug. 234 The 16 alternate or uneven-numbered sections in all townships. **1887** HISSEY *Holiday on Road* i. 3 Weather-stained out-buildings, lichen-laden and uneven-roofed. **1905** *Terms Forestry & Logging* (U.S. Dept. Agric. Bureau Forestry) 14 Forests in which the trees differ considerably in age..uneven-aged forest. **1953** H. L. EDLIN *Forester's Handbk.* vii. 105 Woodlands may..be..uneven-aged, with trees of various ages and therefore differing sizes.

un'even, *adv.* [OE. *unefne* (f. *un-* UN-¹ 11 b + *efne* EVEN *adv.*), = MDu. *onevene*, *-effene* (obs. Du. *oneven*), OS. *unefno*, MLG. *unevene*, *-even*, MHG. *unebene*, *-eben*.] = UNEVENLY *adv.*

c **1000** *Ags. Ps.* (Thorpe) cxl. 9 Swa unefne is eorþe þicce. *c* **1275** in *O.E. Misc.* 86/1 Weole, þu art awaried þing, vneuene constu dele. *a* **1300** *Cursor M.* 24178 Þou..folus þam þat þe wald fle, And luues all þat letthes þe, þis part vneuen es delt. **1390** GOWER *Conf.* I. 9 So stant the pes unevene parted. **1500–20** DUNBAR *Poems* lxxxi. 96 The ballance gois vnevin.

un'even, *v.* [UN-² 6 a.] To make uneven.

c **1440** *Pallad. On Husb.* x. 100 For eny thyng no beest vppon hit trede; Vneven hit they wolde, hit is to drede.

†**un'evenly**, *a. Obs.* [UN-¹ 7: cf. OE. *unefenlic* various, diverse.]

1. Incomparable.

a **1225** *Ancr. R.* 410 Þeo blisse þet he ȝerkeð ham..is unefenlich to alle worldes blissen.

2. Unequal; ill-matched.

c **1425** *Eng. Conq. Irel.* 30 Reymond & hys men—thogh they fewe wer, they wer nat feynt—with vneuenly host wenten out & assembled wyth ham. **1513** DOUGLAS *Æneid* XII. iv. 147 This ilk bargane Semyng..To be ane rycht onevynly [*v.r.* vneuinly] interprys.

3. Uneven; not level.

1683 J. REID *Scots Gard'ner* I. iii. 11 Though the ground be unevenly, yet you must hold the chain level.

un'evenly, *adv.* [UN-¹ 11.]

†**1.** Unfairly, unjustly. *Obs.*

1382 WYCLIF *Gen.* xvi. 5 And Saray seide to Abram, Vneuenlie thow dost aȝens me. *c* **1400** *Apol. Loll.* 74 Scho may sey þat Sara seid to Abraam, þu dost vneuenly aȝens me.

2. In an uneven or unequal manner; not regularly, uniformly, or smoothly.

1398 TREVISA *Barth. De P.R.* VIII. xvi. (1495) 143 b, Though it seme somtyme þat he meue vneuenly, swyfter other slower in comparison to other thynges. **1412–20** LYDG. *Chron. Troy* I. 2242 And þus sche stood in a Iupardye Of Loue and Schame, in maner of a traunce, Vn-euenly hanged in balaunce. **1557** RECORDE *Whetst.* iij b, Euen nombers vneuenly, are suche nombers as maie bee diuided into 2 equalle partes, whiche are odde nombers. **1570** BILLINGSLEY *Euclid* II. Introd. 60 In this booke are set forth the powers of lines, deuided euenly and vneuenly. **1638** RAWLEY tr. *Bacon's Life & Death* (1650) 60 The same Abundance unevenly placed, is in like manner hurtfull. **1668** H. MORE *Div. Dial.* I. xxxiv. (1713) 77 To harbour such unconceivable Notions, that lie so unevenly in every Man's Mind but your own. **1704** *Dict. Rust.* s.v. *Waggons*, Therefore the lesser the Wheel is, the heavier and more unevenly and jogging they go. **1839** DE LA BECHE *Rep. Geol. Cornwall*, etc. xi. 318 An opening between the unevenly-fractured surfaces of a fissure. **1879** R. K. DOUGLAS *Confucianism* iv. 95 A chair which..stands unevenly on its feet, is useless as a support.

†**3.** Not in equal proportion. *Obs.*⁻¹

c **1440** *Pallad. on Husb.* XII. 234 Oyldreggis watertemprid euenly..Or old vryne admyxt vneuenly With water partis too.

un'evenness. [f. UNEVEN *a.*]

1. Inequality, discrepancy, difference.

1398 TREVISA *Barth. de P.R.* IX. iii. (Tollem. MS.), Solstitium is moste uneuennesse of day and nyȝte. **1622** MALYNES *Anc. Law-Merch.* 487 Hee findeth twentie two..peeces or thereabouts, because of the vneuennesse of the sheyre. **1659** *Gentl. Calling* (1660) 18 The great unevenness that is..between Gentlemen and their Inferiors. **1884** BOWER & SCOTT *De Bary's Phaner.* 44 The subsequent various unevenness of height..arises through the growth of the cells.

2. The quality or fact of being uneven in form.

1398 TREVISA *Barth. De P.R.* IV. iii. (1495) e vj b/1 Roughnesse is not elles but an vneuynnesse in an harde thynge. *Ibid.* iv. e viij/2 Contrary humours werke contraryousnes and vneuynnesse with roughnes in the vtter parte of the body. **1560** WHITEHORNE *Arte Warre* (1588) 49 b, Also the vneuennesse of the ground saueth them, for that euery litle hillocke, or high place,..letteth the shotte thereof. **1577** B. GOOGE *Heresbach's Husb.* III. (1586) 115 His cheekebones would be euen and small, for..the vneuennes of the Cheekes will make him headstrong. **1634** SIR T. HERBERT *Trav.* 51 Hils of stupendious height and vneuennesse to ascend. *a* **1688** CUDWORTH *Immut. Mor.* (1731) 200 We plainly observe much..Unevenness and Inequality in the Lines, and Bluntness in the Angles. **1772** *Ann. Reg.*, *Nat. Hist.* 82/2 Which extreme agitation and whirling, I presume, must be owing to the unevenness of the rocky bottom. **1853** MARKHAM *Skoda's Auscult.* 3 The finger must be always used whenever, through unevenness of the surface, the pleximeter cannot be well applied. **1880** *Blackw. Mag.* Feb. 243/1 The painful unevenness of the principal roadways.

b. An instance of this; an inequality; a rough or rugged part, place, or feature.

1597 A. M. tr. *Guillemeau's Fr. Chirurg.* 12 b/2 If there remayne anye small splinter thereone, or other vnevennes. **1664** H. MORE *Myst. Iniq.* 297 To phansy one and the same

Hill for some little unevennesses in it to be more then one. **1680** *Tides* (MS. Bodl. Add. A. 202) fol. 3 In deep Rivers the surface conceales these unevennesses. **1728** CHAMBERS *Cycl.* s.v. *Filing*, The.. File.. serves to take off the Unevennesses of the Work, left by the Hammer, in Forging. **1753** *Phil. Trans.* XLVIII. 88 An horizontal thin edge, which scooped up and carried off the little unevennesses of the turfy ground. **1849** EASTWICK *Dry Leaves* 140 There was not the slightest jag or unevenness—a tolerable proof of the sharpness of the sword.

c. In various figurative uses.

1636 B. JONSON *Discoveries* Wks. (1641) 98 They would not have it run without rubs, as if that stile were more strong and manly, that stroke the eare with a kind of unevenesse. **1652** GAULE *Magastrom.* 255 Saturne was pressed with unevennesse or roughnesse, either in leaping or speaking. **1707** *Reflex. upon Ridicule* 319 The whimsical Unevenness of some People ruins the pleasure of Conversation. **1779** JOHNSON *L.P.*, *Dryden* Wks. II. 427 Such is the unevenness of his compositions, that [etc.]. **1805** *Med. Jrnl.* XIV. 395 The unevenness of disposition, the convulsive sobs and strong paroxysms of weeping. **1882** L. KEITH *Alasnam's Lady* III. 105 Di hardly noticed the unevenness of her mood.

†**3.** Unfairness, injustice. *Obs.*

a **1470** H. PARKER *Dives & Pauper* (W. de W. 1496) 293/1 Goodes of this worlde ben called rychesses of uneuenesse and of wyckednesse.

une'ventful, *a.* (UN-[1] 7.)

1800 MRS. HERVEY *Mourtray Fam.* I. 7 There is little to keep up its energy in the uneventful tenour of domestic life. **1862** *Gifts & Graces* xxv. 249 There is little to tell, for their uneventful lives are gliding on as usual. **1890** W. J. GORDON *Foundry* 167 We have said enough to show that its story has not been uneventful.

Hence **une'ventfully** *adv.*, **-fulness**.

1865 *Cornh. Mag.* Apr. 405 The two next days passed quietly and uneventfully. **1872** HOWELLS *Wedding Journ.* (1892) 192 They rattled uneventfully down.. by rail. **1878** GROSART *H. More's Poems* Introd. p. ix, The uneventfulness outwardly of the 'Life' accounts for the few facts given.

†**un'evesed**, *ppl. a. Obs.* (UN-[1] 8.)

?**14..** *Lat.-Eng. Voc.* (MS. Harl. 2257), *Intonsus*, vnclipped, vneuesed.

un'evidence. *rare*$^{-1}$. (UN-[1] 12.)

a **1676** HALE *Prim. Orig. Man.* I. i. (1677) 10 So full of unevidence and uncertainty, so full of precarious and imaginary *Postulata*.

un'evidenced, *ppl. a.* (UN-[1] 8.)

[**1775** ASH.] **1842** G. S. FABER *Prov. Lett.* (1844) II. 53 The unevidenced Popish Innovations advocated by my two opponents. **1892** J. TAIT *Mind in Matter* 234 The impression [made] on the illiterate mind by the unevidenced assertion of miracles.

un'evident, *a.* (UN-[1] 7 and 5 b.)

c **1400** *Apol. Loll.* 9 As þis consonaunt is vnknowen to þe japer, so þis fendly marchaundy is vneuident to þe feiþful peple knowend þis. **1570** LEVINS *Manip.* 69 Vneuident, *ineuidens*. **1629** H. BURTON *Truth's Triumph* 165 The actuall faith hee cals a firme and certaine, but vneuident assent. **1651** HOBBES *Leviath.* II. xxv. 134 Rash and unevident Inferences. *a* **1670** HACKET *Abp. Williams* I. (1692) 197 We conjecture at unevident things by that which is evident.

unevi'dential, *a.* (UN-[1] 7.)

1826 G. S. FABER *Diffic. Romanism* (1853) 117 Arbitrary exertion of more unevidential dogmatic authority.

†**un'evitable**, *a. Obs.* [UN-[1] 7 b and 5 b.] = INEVITABLE *a.*

1539 ELYOT *Cast. Helthe* 59 They receyue in medicine that, whiche shall ingender.. vneuitable destruction vnto al the body. **1594** J. KING *Funeral Serm.* (1599) 677 Let his dead.. corpse adde one more [instruction] vnto you of common & vnevitable mortalitie. **1621** G. SANDYS *Ovid's Met.* VI. (1626) 113 His haste th'vneuitable bowe o're-took, And through his throte the deadly arrow strook. **1656** W. MONTAGUE *Accompl. Wom.* 59 We have put on black, because mourning is unevitable, since we must needs bewaile our husbands. **1711** W. KING *Heathen Gods & Heroes* xiii. 38 [Pluto] bound them with unevitable Chains.

So †**un'evitably** *adv.*, inevitably. *Obs.*

1623 in Rushw. *Hist. Coll.* (1659) I. 142 Seeing we.. cannot but foresee and fear lest the like may.. unevitably bring such peril to your Majesties Kingdoms.

†**un'evitated**, *ppl. a. Obs.* (UN-[1] 8.)

1621 G. SANDYS *Ovid's Met.* XII. (1626) 240 With that, th'vnerring dart at Cycnus [he] flung. Th'vneuitated on his shoulder rung.

une'volved, *ppl. a.* (UN-[1] 8.)

[**1775** ASH.] **1831** LANDOR *Wks.* (1846) II. 633, I held down a branch And gathered her some blossoms... So crisp were some, they rattled unevolved. **1884** *Congregational Year Bk.* 93 Nature.. holds in her bosom, unsolved and unevolved, the problems and the germs of all the philosophies.

une'xact, *a.* [UN-[1] 7 and 5 b.] = INEXACT *a.*

1758 MACLAINE *Mosheim's Eccles. Hist.* I. 407 *note*, Dr. Mosheim's account of the time of Nestorius's death is perhaps unexact. **1776** S. J. PRATT *Pupil of Pleas.* (1777) I. 153 How is it that so scrupulous a man in point of equity is so unexact a correspondent? **1862** 'SHIRLEY' (J. Skelton) *Nugae Crit.* ii. 137 The literalness of an unpoetic intellect.. is always comparatively sterile and unexact.

So **une'xactness**, inexactness. *rare*$^{-1}$.

1677 GILPIN *Demonol.* II. ix. 389 Satan here plays upon the unexactness of the Translation.

une'xacted, *ppl. a.* (UN-[1] 8.)

1609 TOURNEUR *Funerall Poem Sir F. Vere* 23 All that I speak is unexacted, true and free. **1697** DRYDEN *Virg. Georg.* I. 196 All was common, and the fruitful Earth Was free to give her unexacted Birth.

So **une'xactedly** *adv.*

c **1642** *Observ. his Majesty's late Answer* 18 The father doth all his offices meritoriously, freely, and unexactedly.

une'xacting, *ppl. a.* (UN-[1] 10.)

1862 MILMAN in *Proc. Roy. Soc.* XI. p. xv, A seat in Parliament, independent even on generous and unexacting friendship. **1884** MRS. COOTE *Sure Harvest* 24 The most unselfish, unexacting old lady I ever knew.

une'xaggerable, *a.* (UN-[1] 7 b.)

1818 *Q. Rev.* XVIII. 41 Gongora's exaggerating and unexaggerable style.

une'xaggerated, *ppl. a.* (UN-[1] 8.)

1770 ARMSTRONG *Misc.* II. 272 In some places natural and unexaggerated representations of life are not felt. **1812** *Q. Rev.* VIII. 329 A mass of immediate evil.. of which the unexaggerated report might almost startle our belief. **1861** MILL *Repr. Govt.* (1865) 34/1 It would be.. ungenerous to offer this.. as an unexaggerated picture of the French people.

une'xaggerating, *ppl. a.* (UN-[1] 10.)

1825 LD. COCKBURN *Mem.* (1856) 332 Calm, clear, and unexaggerating, he went into all the details with precision.

une'xalted, *ppl. a.* (UN-[1] 8.)

1611 FLORIO, *Innessaltato*, vnexalted. **1648** HEXHAM II, *Ongehooght*, Vnlifted up, or Vn-exalted. **1746** YOUNG *Nt. Th.* IX. 755 Who sees it unexalted, and unaw'd? **1805** WORDSW. *Prelude* XIII. 243 Not unexalted by religious faith, Nor uninformed by books.

une'xaminable, *a.* (UN-[1] 7 b.)

1641 MILTON *Reform.* I. Wks. 1851 III. 4 The lowly, alwise, and unexaminable intention of Christ. **1890** ABP. BENSON *Let.* in *Life* (1901) 373 She had read your book carefully, and I daresay knew it (in an unexaminable sort of way).

une'xamined, *ppl. a.* (UN-[1] 8.)

1495 *Act 11 Hen. VII*, ii. §3 As often as eny suche of the seid mysdoers.. departen unexamyned and unpunysshed. **1526** *Pilgr. Perf.* (W. de W. 1531) 132 That no worde passe out vntryed, & nothynge entre vnexamyned. **1568** GRAFTON *Chron.* II. 765 Watching that no man shoulde.. passe vnserched nor vnexamined. **1620** *Southampton Court Leet Rec.* (1907) III. 582 The teachinge of a Stranger vnexamined and vnripe of yeres. **1684** T. BURNET *Theory Earth* I. 285 Those manuscripts that are yet unexamin'd in these parts of Christendom. **1747** RICHARDSON *Clarissa* (1811) II. 268 More pride and vanity than I could have thought had lain in my unexamined heart. **1779** JOHNSON *L.P.*, *Watts*. Wks. IV. 187 He has left neither corporeal nor spiritual nature unexamined. **1875** SCRIVENER *Lect. Text N. Test.* 14 To leave the great mass of copies wholly unexamined.

une'xamining, *ppl. a.* (UN-[1] 10.)

1682 in *Lond. Gaz.* No. 1714/6 A means to ferment the Factious Un-examining Vulgar into Rebellious Heats. **1748** RICHARDSON *Clarissa* (1811) IV. 213 Which concealed itself from my unexamining heart under the specious veil of humility. **1809–10** COLERIDGE *Friend* (1837) I. 163 The unexamining and boisterous youth of the world. **1835** WILLIS *Pencillings* I. 90, I passed them with the same lost unexamining.. feeling which I cannot overcome in this place.

une'xampled, *ppl. a.* [UN-[1] 8.] Having no preceding or similar example; unprecedented, unparalleled.

1610 HOLLAND *Camden's Brit.* I. 724 David King of Scots, who with his unexampled cruelty had made this country almost a wildernesse. *a* **1676** HALE *Prim. Orig. Man.* IV. iv. (1677) 325 This admirable.. production of such a Nature unexampled before. **1763** WILKES *Corr.* (1805) I. 75 Your lordship's unexampled care of his majesty's youth. **1816** J. SCOTT *Vis. Paris* (ed. 5) 176 With unexampled ability and villainy, he fashioned the people to suit his views. **1855** BAIN *Senses & Int.* III. iv. §24 This is an extreme case, but not unexampled in the history of the world.

une'xasperating, *ppl. a.* (UN-[1] 10.)

1855 MILMAN *Lat. Chr.* XIV. vii. VI. 549 The most quiet, uninsulting, unexasperating satire.

un'excavated, *ppl. a.* (UN-[1] 8.)

[**1775** ASH.] **1874** WITHROW *Catacombs* (1877) 20 Some unexcavated spaces have been observed traced in outline.

unex'ceeded, *ppl. a.* (UN-[1] 8.)

1813 T. BUSBY *Lucretius* I. I. Comm. p. xii, The comparison.. is conceived with unexceeded vigour.

unex'celled, *ppl. a.* (UN-[1] 8.)

a **1800** COWPER *Iliad* (ed. 2) v. 193 Say, Pandarus! Thy bow, thy shafts, thy fame Unrivall'd here, in Lycia unexcell'd, Where are they now? **1821** HUISH *George III*, Introd. 3 Unexcelled as a father, unshaken as a friend. **1874** H. H. COLE *Catal. Ind. Art S. Kens. Mus.* 216 The textile fabrics of India.. remain unexcelled by other countries.

unex'celling, *ppl. a.* (UN-[1] 5 d.)

1844 MRS. BROWNING *Dead Pan* xxxvii, Shame!.. To think God's song unexcelling The poor tales of our own telling.

unex'ceptable, *a.* (UN-[1] 7 b.)

1702 C. MATHER *Magn. Chr.* III. ii. 33/1 Waiting, till God might furnish him with Unexceptable Opportunities, for his .. Preaching of the Gospel.

unex'cepted, *ppl. a.* (UN-[1] 8 and 8 c.)

1614 B. JONSON *Barth. Fair* Induct., Hee that will sweare, Ieronimo, or Andronicus are the best playes, yet, shall passe vnexcepted at, heere. **1710** PRIDEAUX *Orig. Tithes* ii. 46 The Precedent doth become of unexcepted authority. **1813** CHALMERS *Posth. Wks.* (1849) VI. 172 There is no getting away from.. His ceaseless, from His unexcepted agency. **1852** BAILEY *Festus* (ed. 4) 265 Progress is nature's unexcepted law.

unex'cepting, *ppl. a.* (UN-[1] 10).

1716 M. DAVIES *Athen. Brit.* II. 410 A rising Clergyman .. seem'd to excuse that.. Prelate's Prophetick Vein, or even exempt it from his unexcepting Censure. **1870** J. BRUCE *Life of Gideon* xxii. 401 There is a general and unexcepting revival.. within his heart, even of all such graces.

unex'ceptionable, *a.* [UN-[1] 7 b.]

1. To whom, or to which, no exception can be taken; perfectly satisfactory or adequate.

a. Of persons.

1664 INGELO *Bentiv. & Ur.* VI. 276 All which I have said was done in the Presence of unexceptionable Witnesses. **1699** T. BAKER *Refl. Learn.* iii. 27 Cicero tho the most unexceptionable [authority] has not escaped their censure. **1740** CIBBER *Apol.* (1756) I. 48 Not even the Revolution.. has been able to furnish us with unexceptionable statesmen. **1796** MME. D'ARBLAY *Camilla* II. 193 She affectionately embraced the unexceptionable Lavinia. **1868** FREEMAN *Norm. Conq.* (1877) II. ix. 431 There was now no such unexceptionable rival to oppose to the Norman.

b. Of material things. (Rare before 19th c.)

1681 FLAVEL *Meth. Grace* xvi. 301 The blood of Christ..; 'tis unexceptionable blood, being.. untainted by sin. **1756–7** tr. *Keysler's Trav.* (1760) II. 425 This statue.. is in all its parts unexceptionable. **1835** BROWNING *Paracelsus* v. 455 *Fest.* This cell? *Par.* An unexceptionable vault: Good brick and stone. **1852** H. ROGERS *Ecl. Faith* 168 Questionable as was the entertainment for the mind, that for the body was unexceptionable.

c. Of character, conduct, style, taste, etc.

1697 C. LESLIE *Snake in Grass* (ed. 2) 359 And the Lives of these Seperatists were as un-exceptionable as any of the Quakers. **1716** M. DAVIES *Athen. Brit.* III. 31 His English style is unexceptionable. **1742–3** *Johnson's Debates* (1787) II. 503 The authority of this man, my Lords, cannot indeed be urged as unexceptionable and decisive. **1794** S. WILLIAMS *Vermont* 183 The most unexceptionable evidence ought to be produced. **1826** F. REYNOLDS *Life & Times* II. 126 His taste was unexceptionable, and his judgment was never sullied by prejudice. **1848** MILL *Pol. Econ.* II. xv. §1. 478 Lending his capital on unexceptionable security. **1884** *Law Rep.* 9 *App. Cases* 558, I am.. of opinion that rule 32 is unexceptionable.

2. Admitting of no exception. *rare*$^{-1}$.

1871 RUSKIN *Fors Clav.* vii. 9 That being the, alas, almost unexceptionable lot of human creatures.

Hence **unex'ceptiona,bility**.

1837 *Chambers's Jrnl.* 8 July 192 Morals of pure unexceptionability. *a* **1849** POE *Whipple*, etc., Wks. 1864 III. 388, I—with a very partial modification of the imagery .. —may elevate the passage into unexceptionability.

unex'ceptionableness. (UN-[1] 12.)

1669 H. MORE *Exp. 7 Epist.* Pref. a. vij b, If it had been accompanied with other parts of his Exposition of these Epistles that had had the like unexceptionablenesse. **1712** *H. More's Antid. Ath.* III. x. *heading*, A reflection on the unexceptionableness of these Instances for the proof of Spirits. **1753** RICHARDSON *Grandison* (1781) II. xiv. 151 My Lord.. modestly hinted at the unexceptionableness of his own character. **1823** BENTHAM *Not Paul* 229 In order to have the clearer view of the plan.., from which will be seen the unexceptionableness of it.

unex'ceptionably, *adv.* [UN-[1] 11.]

1. In an unexceptionable manner; beyond criticism or objection.

1662 H. MORE *Antidote agst. Atheism* vi. 58 Wee'l betake our selves to.. what is more unexceptionably stringent and forcing. **1718** *Free-thinker* No. 141 (1733) III. 178 It is very rare to find a Glass, that does Justice unexceptionably to Objects, in every nice Circumstance. **1740** RICHARDSON *Pamela* II. 328 It will not be an easy Task to behave unexceptionably to him. **1827** SOUTHEY *Hist. Penins. War* II. 626 The Junta of Cadiz had obtained their power unexceptionably. **1859** GEO. ELIOT *A. Bede* xvii, Let all people who hold unexceptionable opinions act unexceptionably.

2. = UNEXCEPTIONALLY *adv.*

1719 J. T. PHILLIPS tr. *Thirty-four Confer.* 89 All your Religious Women who assist at the Performances of Pagod Ceremonies, are unexceptionably great Whores. **1799** *Monthly Rev.* XXX. 507 Such is not unexceptionably the character of all treatises; such ill consequences do not obtain universally. **1806** BLOOMFIELD *Wild Flowers* 106 It has generally and almost unexceptionably appeared a subject of little promise.

unex'ceptional, *a.* [UN-[1] 7.]

1. = UNEXCEPTIONABLE *a.* 1 c.

1775 MME. D'ARBLAY *Early Diary* (1889) II. 10 She bears an unexceptional character. **1806** *Ann. Rev.* IV. 730 We.. secretly retain a higher esteem for the stimulant and unusual, than for the quotidian accuracy of regular unexceptional composition. **1877** W. S. GILBERT *Foggerty's Fairy* (1892) 62 The duty is extremely light, and the county society unexceptional.

2. Admitting of, subject to, no exception.

1844 KINGLAKE *Eothen* xxix, Declaring that the orders received from Constantinople were imperative, and unexceptional. **1883** SIR H. COTTON in *Law Rep. 24 Chan. Div.* 332, I should think that that would, almost as an unexceptional rule, be of the greatest possible advantage to the infant.

unex'ceptionally, *adv.* [UN-[1] 11.] Without exception.

1866 RUSKIN *Crown Wild Olive* (1873) 68 So completely and unexceptionally is this so, that [etc.]. **1871** W. G. WARD *Ess. Philos. Theism* (1884) I. 50 That which I have habitually and unexceptionally experienced, I regard as contingent.

†**unex'ceptioned**, *ppl. a. Obs.*$^{-1}$ [UN-[1] 8.] = UNEXCEPTIONABLE *a.* 1.

1704 T. BAKER *Act at Oxf.* II. ii. 12 A Gentleman unexception'd in Person, Temper, and Estate.

unex'ceptive, *a.* (UN-[1] 7.)
1856 *N. Brit. Rev.* XXVI. 54 An unexceptive Christian belief. **1860** I. TAYLOR *Ess.* i. 118 The Rights of Man.. are universal and unexceptive.

unex'changed, *ppl. a.* (UN-[1] 8.)
1618 in W. Foster *Eng. Factories in India* (1906) I. 8 And we compelled to leave a whole chest of ryalls and three ingotts unexchanged. **1777** BURKE *Let. to Sheriffs of Bristol* Wks. III. 143 If.. we.. contend that you may justly reserve for vengeance, those who remain unexchanged.

unex'cised, (*ppl.*) *a.*[1] [UN-[1] 8, 9.]
1. Not subjected to an Excise or tax.
c **1740** I. H. BROWNE *Pipe of Tobacco* v. 20 Come to thy poet.. And let me taste thee unexcis'd by kings. **1861** *Sat. Rev.* 23 Nov. 532 So all the benefits of a free press, unstamped, unexcised, may be altogether thrown away.
2. Not appointed to a post in the Excise.
1820 BYRON *Juan* III. xciii, All are not moralists, like Southey,.. Or Wordsworth unexcised, unhired.

unex'cised, *ppl. a.*[2] [UN-[1] 8.] Not excised or cut out.
1871 T. H. GREEN *Introd. Pathol.* 203 The inflammatory changes.. in the unexcised cornea of the opposite eye.

unex'citable, *a.* (UN-[1] 7b and 5b.)
1839 LD. CLARENDON in Maxwell *Life & Lett.* (1913) I. 155, I am of a mature age, unexcitable temperament. **1859** CORNWALLIS *New World* I. 297 He did the work simply as a means of living, and he liked it because it was dry and unexcitable. **1895** *Outing* XXVI. 432/1 During this battle royal, the other fish had darted away, and.. only the unexcitable sturgeon was to be seen.
Hence **unexcita'bility.**
1882 W. JAMES *Let.* 13 Nov. (1920) I. 215 The traditional German professor in its highest sense.. an absolute unexcitability of manner. **1885** E. G. PARRY *Suakin* ix. 215 The extreme unexcitability of temperament of these people.

unex'cited, *ppl. a.* [UN-[1] 8.]
1. Not mentally stirred or moved.
1735 LD. LYTTELTON *Lett. fr. Persian in Eng.* iii, The human brutes, who, unexcited by any rage or sense of injury, could spill the blood of others. **1850** ROBERTSON *Serm.* Ser. III. ix. (1857) 133 Remember Him pausing to weep.., unexcited, while the giddy crowd around Him were shouting 'Hosannas to the Son of David!' **1856** KANE *Arct. Expl.* I. xvii. 202 A more unexcited inspection showed us.. that their numbers were not as great.
2. Not affected by outward influence.
1746 *Phil. Trans.* XLIV. 734 There is an Endeavour by the nearest unexcited Non-electric to restore the Æquilibrium. **1839** G. BIRD *Nat. Philos.* 399 To produce upon an unexcited eye the sensation of a colour corresponding to that of the wafer. **1856** FROUDE *Hist. Eng.* II. 26 [Protestantism] sprung up spontaneously, unguided, unexcited,.. among the masses of the nation.

unex'citing, *ppl. a.* (UN-[1] 10.)
1833 J. H. NEWMAN *Arians* i. §1. 20 Judaism.. indisposed the mind for the severe and unexciting mysteries.. of the Catholic faith. **1861** MILL *Repr. Govt.* 37 Uncivilized races .. are averse to continuous labour of an unexciting kind. **1885** 'MRS. ALEXANDER' *At Bay* viii, He had.. led a quiet, busy life, humbly useful, but unexciting.
b. *spec.* of diet.
1880 BARWELL *Aneurism* v. 44 If an aneurismal patient.. have a dry, unexciting diet. **1888** P. FURNIVALL *Phys. Training* 3 Substantial, nourishing solids, with simple unexciting fluids.

unex'cluded, *ppl. a.* (UN-[1] 8.)
1780 [see UNCOUNTERBALANCED]. **1814** WORDSW. *Excurs.* v. 542 [The sun] doth dispense His beams; which, unexcluded in their fall,.. Have gently exercised a melting power.

unex'cluding, *ppl. a.* (UN-[1] 10.)
1822 LAMB *Elia* II. *Detached Th. on Bks.*, I can read almost anything. I bless my stars for a taste so catholic, so unexcluding.

unex'clusive, *a.* (UN-[1] 7.)
1831 SIR W. HAMILTON *Discuss.* (1852) 222 Muench's unexclusive views have found favor with Mayerhoff. **1862** J. MARTINEAU *Ess., Sci. Nescience & Faith* (1866) 189 To the Infinite, as unexclusive, every thing affirmative belongs.

unex'clusively, *adv.* (UN-[1] 11, 5b.)
1814 WORDSW. *Excurs.* IX. 392 From culture, unexclusively bestowed On Albion's noble Race in freedom born. **1841–2** SIR W. HAMILTON *Diss.* in *Reid's Wks.* (1846) 886/1 *note*, Mr. Stewart.. is wrong in stating, unexclusively, that Reid's writings were anterior to Kant's.

unex'clusiveness. (UN-[1] 12.)
1818 BENTHAM *Mem. & Corr.* Wks. 1843 X. 498 Though I should prefer universality on account of its simplicity and unexclusiveness. **1861** MILL *Repr. Govt.* 157 A government equally democratic in its unexclusiveness, but better organized in other important points.

unex'cogitable, *a.* (UN-[1] 7b and 5b.)
1592 R. D. *Hypnerotomachia* 81 b, Her virgineall aspects, exceedingly beautified with a comely grace and unexcogitable elegancie. **1614** RALEIGH *Hist. World* I. ii. §1. 24 Wherein can man be said to resemble his vnexcogitable power and perfectnesse? *c* **1624** CHAPMAN *Hymn Hermes* 158 Unexcogitable thoughts in act Putting.

une'xcogitated, *ppl. a.* (UN-[1] 8.)
a **1706** EVELYN *Hist. Relig.* (1850) I. 23 Moreover, this unexcogitated division would also have been illimited.

unexco'mmunicate(d, *ppl. a.* (UN-[1] 8, 8b.)
1588 UDALL *Demonstr. Discipline* (Arb.) 82 If they had not throwne out the incestuous person, he had remayned still vnexcommunicated. **1680** *Answ. Stillingfleet's Serm.* 15 Every one that dies Un-excommunicate in the Parish.

unex'corticated, *ppl. a.* (UN-[1] 8.)
1725 *Fam. Dict.* s.v. *Diahexapte*, Take Juniper-Berries unexcorticated, and Bay-berries excorticated.

†**unex'cusable,** *a. Obs.* [UN-[1] 7b and 5b.] = INEXCUSABLE *a.*: **a.** Of persons.
Chiefly in a religious or moral sense, after Rom. ii. 1 (Gr. ἀναπολόγητος, L. *inexcusabilis*).
1382 WYCLIF *Rom.* ii. 1 For which thing thou ert vnexcusable, thou ech man that demest. *a* **1425** *St. Elizabeth of Spalbeck* in *Anglia* VIII. 118/39 þou, man, arte vnexcusabil, if so quik argumentz.. stir þe not to strengthe of feith. *c* **1561** VERON *Free-will* 47 That they may.. be made unexcusable agaynst the day of iudgement. **1583** GOLDING *Calvin on Deut.* i. 4 Therefore are we too unexcusable if we cannot tell what God saith to us there. **1642** G. MOUNTAGU in *Buccleuch MSS.* (Hist. MSS. Comm.) I. 298 To leave them altogether unexcusable, [he] sent them a licence.. for their absence. **1685** BAXTER *Paraphr. N.T.* Matt. x. 17 That both Jews and Gentiles.. may.. be unexcusable in their sin.
b. Of faults, offences, etc.
1550 LATIMER *Last Serm. bef. Edw. VI*, Sermons (1580) 113 b, An irremissible sinne, an vnexcusable sinne. **1602** T. FITZHERBERT *Apol.* 12 Whereby their martyrdome was far more glorious,.. the iniury donne vnto them vnexcusable. **1659** BP. WALTON *Consid. Considered* 3 The unexcusable negligence of the Greek church. **1685** J. SCOTT *Chr. Life* II. i. 32 As gross and unexcusable a Stupidity as if [etc.].
Hence †**unex'cusableness; -ably** *adv. Obs.*
1611 COTGR., *Inexcusablement*, vnexcusably. **1647** CLARENDON *Hist. Reb.* I. §25 The Prince Electour.. had unexcusably, and directly against his Advice, incurred the Ban of the Empire in an Imperial Dyet. *a* **1660** HAMMOND *Serm.* xii. Wks. 1684 IV. 642 We will.. rip up to you the unexcusableness of the heathen ignorance in general.

unex'cused, *ppl. a.* (UN-[1] 8.)
c **1650** *Don Bellianis* 84 Get you out of my Persepolis.. unless you will here dye, unheard, and unexcused.

unex'cusing, *ppl. a.* (UN-[1] 10.)
1853 RUSKIN *Stones Ven.* II. 199 Scripture History.. sets down with unmoved and unexcusing resoluteness the virtues and errors of all men of whom it speaks. **1858** MISS MULOCK *Th. ab. Wom.* 275 With a resolute, uncompromising, unexcusing veracity.

†**unex'cussed,** *ppl. a.* (UN-[1] 8.)
1660 STANLEY *Hist. Philos.* IX. (1687) 540/1 Concerning all these, he delivered most proper Sciences, leaving nothing unexcussed.

une'xecutable, *a.* (UN-[1] 7b and 5b.)
1794 EARL MALMESBURY *Diaries & Corr.* III. 223 The instructions.. were nearly unexecutable. **1850** GROTE *Greece* II. lx. VII. 455 Though sensible of the wisdom of his advice, the generals thought it wholly unexecutable.

un'executed, *ppl. a.* (UN-[1] 8.)
1585 T. WASHINGTON tr. *Nicholay's Voy.* II. xiii. 48 b, There was no kind of.. cruelty by them left vnexecuted. **1606** SHAKS. *Ant. & Cl.* III. vii. 45 You therein.. leaue vnexecuted Your owne renowned knowledge. **1741–2** GRAY *Agrippina* 155 Why do I waste the fruitless hours In threats unexecuted? **1790** PENNANT *London* (1813) 140 A vast plan, left unexecuted on account of the unhappy times. **1850** GROTE *Greece* II. lxiv. VIII. 253 The duty remained unexecuted, and the seamen.. were left to perish unassisted. **1863** H. COX *Instit.* II. viii. 499 The Court directs the cancellation of unexecuted agreements.

un'executing, *ppl. a.* (UN-[1] 10.)
1770 *Lee's Alexander* I. i, Curse on this weak, unexecuting arm!

†**une'xemplar,** *a. Obs.* [UN-[1] 7.] = next 2.
1685 J. L. *Papist Mis-represented & Repr.* 76 If some,.. by their unexemplar lives, prove a scandal to their profession.

une'xemplary, *a.* [UN-[1] 7.]
†**1.** Unexampled, unprecedented. *Obs.*
1649 in Ellis *Orig. Lett.* Ser. II. III. 340 To give you some relation of the sad and unexemplary murther of our Soveraign. **1704** in *Lond. Gaz.* No. 4058/1 Your Majesty's unexemplary Piety. **1730** SWIFT *Vind. Ld. Carteret* Wks. 1761 III. 186 He hath in a most unexemplary manner led a regular domestic life.
2. Not exemplary; not to be taken as a model.
1699 SHAFTESB. *Inquiry conc. Virtue* I. ii. 3 Nothing horrid or unnatural, nothing unexemplary, nothing destructive of .. natural affection. **1894** *Daily News* 5 Feb. 3/3 A staunch upholder of that unexemplary husband [*sc.* George IV] in his long contest with his wife.

†**une'xempled,** obs. var. UNEXAMPLED *ppl. a.*
1611 SPEED *Hist. Gt. Brit.* IX. i. §18 His eies, which now beheld in a stranger, so strange and vnexempled kindnes. **1640–6** SIR J. CULPEPPER in Rushw. *Hist. Coll.* III. (1692) I. 35 There are some worthy Gentlemen.. that carried themselves.. with great wisdom and unexempled moderation.

une'xemplified, *ppl. a.* (UN-[1] 8.)
a **1634** CHAPMAN *Rev. for Honour* IV. i. 184 Dismiss these tyrannous instruments of death And cruelty unexemplified. **1681** OWEN *Design Impend. Judgm.* To Rdr. A 2 b, There is an unexemplified Neglect in calling the Inhabitants of it unto Repentance. **1755** JOHNSON *Dict.* Pref. C j b, It is remarkable that, in reviewing my collection, I found the word 'Sea' unexemplified.

une'xempt, *ppl. a.* [UN-[1] 8b.] = next.
1634 MILTON *Comus* 685 Scorning the unexempt condition By which all mortal frailty must subsist.

une'xempted, *ppl. a.* (UN-[1] 8.)
1636 PAGITT *Christianogr.* (ed. 2) II. 40 Ecclesiasticks were unexempted, and deposing of Kings was then undreamed of. **1643–5** MILTON *Divorce* II. xiii, How can the.. Law of God.. require an unexempted and impartiall obedience to all her decrees,.. and yet [etc.].

une'xempting, *ppl. a.* (UN-[1] 10.)
1837 CARLYLE *Fr. Rev.* I. III. iv, Is there not Calonne's.. universal, unexempting Landtax, the sheet-anchor of Finance?

un'exercise. (UN-[1] 12.)
1640 BP. REYNOLDS *Passions* xiii. 129 By reason of the volubility of the minde joyned with an infirmity and unexercise of memory.

un'exercised, *ppl. a.* [UN-[1] 8.]
1. Not employed or made use of; not put in force or practised.
c **1374** CHAUCER *Boeth.* II. pr. vii. (1868) 56 þat is to seyn, þat list þat or he wex olde, His uertue þat lay now ful stille ne sholde nat perisshe vnexcercised in gouernaunce of comune. **1526** *Pilgr. Perf.* (W. de W. 1531) 86 Let neuer ony parte of thy good day passe and scape the vnexercysed. **1562** J. SHUTE *Cambini's Turk. Wars* 19 A place wherein no filthie exercise was left unexercised. **1635** BRATHWAIT *Arcad. Pr.* 19 Their Comitiall courts like desarts, wilde and unexercised. **1671** CLARENDON *Hist. Reb.* IX. §42 The enemy left no manner of barbarous cruelty unexercised that day. **1796** MME. D'ARBLAY *Camilla* II. 278 Her judgment and penetration had been wholly unexercised. **1893** FAIRBAIRN in Selbie *Life* vii. (1914) 247 Certain faculties would remain unexercised.
2. Not taking exercise; remaining inactive; not put in motion; left unmoved or unstirred.
1562 TURNER *Baths* 6 Some other [men].. eat euell and vnholsome meates,.. and then being vnexercised.. make much euill humours. **1607** TOPSELL *Four-f. Beasts* 273 Be not afraid.. of this sluggish and vnexercised people, for.. they stir not out of the City. **1624** WOTTON *Archit.* I. 3 That it [*sc.* air] be not.. vndigested, for want of sunne, not unexercised for want of winde.
3. Of persons: Not accustomed or prepared by training or practice; untrained.
1577 tr. *Bullinger's Decades* I. iii. (1592) 24 Whereby we gather, that the scripture is difficult or obscure to the vnlearned, vnskilfull, vnexercised, and malicious.. wils. **1623** BINGHAM *Xenophon, Comp. Wars*, An vnexercised Souldier is alwaies raw, though he haue serued neuer so long. *a* **1653** GOUGE *Comm. Heb.* xii. 5 This teacheth us.. to fit and prepare ourselves for tryals. An unexercised man will not dare to enter into the list. **1702** ECHARD *Eccl. Hist.* (1710) 599 Some few.. being unprepared and unexercised, through fear and frailty, fell away. **1768–74** TUCKER *Lt. Nat.* (1834) I. 377 Unexercised in their understandings and unpractised in the ways of men. **1802** LAMB *Cooke's Rich. III*, Wks. 1908 I. 47 Breaking out into.. plaudits at its own success, like an unexercised noviciate in tricks.
transf. **1587** W. FOWLER *Wks.* (S.T.S.) I. 16 With my vnexcercised style [to] debaise suche graces.

une'xerted, *ppl. a.* (UN-[1] 8.)
1675 TRAHERNE *Chr. Ethics* 347 Without its exercise it remaineth unexerted, is wholly vain. **1708** *Brit. Apollo* No. 88. 1/2 The Faculties of the Soul lie Dormant and Unexerted. **1790** HAN. MORE *Relig. Fash. World* (1791) 181 To prevent the total stagnation of unexerted principles.

unex'haled, *ppl. a.* (UN-[1] 8.)
1703 *Phil. Trans.* XXIII. 1433 The little Water which remained unexhaled.

une'xhausted, *ppl. a.* [UN-[1] 8 and 5b.]
1. Not emptied or drained of contents.
1648 BOYLE *Seraph. Love* (1659) 87 His Plenty being so unexhausted a spring of goods. **1652** E. BENLOWES *Theoph.* VII. xc, Flouds of unebbing joyes.. Thou dost exhibit in an unexhausted bowl! **1704** *Phil. Trans.* XXV. 1786 As the Vibrations in the unexhausted Receiver were a little contracted. **1721** RAMSAY *Prospect of Plenty* 245 Neptune's unexhausted bank has store Of endless wealth. **1833–4** J. PHILLIPS *Geol.* in *Encycl. Metrop.* (1845) VI. 756/2 An unexhausted fountain of melted matter.
2. Not used up, expended, or brought to an end.
1602 LODGE *Josephus, Antiq.* VI. xiv. 149 Whatsoeuer they be that spend their many and vnexhausted labours in their seruice. **1656** COWLEY *Pindar. Odes, 2nd Olympique* vii, In the Lands of unexhausted Light. *a* **1704** T. BROWN *Mr. H. Silly* Wks. 1711 IV. 249 Thy Tenants,.. With deep and unexhausted Woe, Lament their Generous Master dead. **1827** JARMAN *Powell's Devises* II. 77 Such unexhausted interest.. belongs to the heir as real estate undisposed of. **1857** DUFFERIN *Lett. High Lat.* (ed. 3) 112 Having separated into two streams, the unexhausted torrent again recommenced its march. **1878** JEVONS *Prim. Pol. Econ.* 93 Tenant right consists in giving the tenant a right to claim the value of any unexhausted improvements.

une'xhaustible, *a.* Also 7 -able. [UN-[1] 7, 7b, 5b.] = INEXHAUSTIBLE *a.*
1656 EARL MONM. tr. *Boccalini's Advts. fr. Parnass.* I. xv. (1674) 18 His own so unexhaustible riches which he had accumulated. **1683** TRYON *Way to Health* 345 From the divine Principle.. doth arise and flow, as from an unexhaustible Fountain, all Friendly Qualities. **1690** in *Cath. Rec. Soc. Publ.* IX. 359 Ye unexhaustable purse of Gods divine providence. **1779** JOHNSON *L.P., Butler*, If unexhaustible wit could give perpetual pleasure, no eye would ever leave half-read the work of Butler.

une'xhaustion. (UN-[1] 12.)
a **1741** TULL *Horse-hoeing Husb.* (1822) 151 There unexhaustion is more effectual than dung.

une'xhibited, *ppl. a.* (UN-[1] 8.)
[**1775** ASH.] **1862** THORNBURY *Turner* I. 262 Nor can I affix a certain date to the unexhibited 'Squally Weather'.

une'xil(e)able, *a.* (UN-[1] 7b.)
1592 NASHE *Strange Newes* E iv, A thousand more such vnexileable ouer-thwart merrimentes.

une'xistence. (UN-1 12 and 5 b.)
1593 NASHE *Christ's T.* P 2 b, Some there be that fantasie phylosophicall probabilities of the Trinities vnexistence. 1623 COCKERAM I, *Vnexistence*, not being. 1828 *Blackw. Mag.* Sept. 300/1 Can it be that thou art numbered among forgotten things—unexistences! 1854 CDL. WISEMAN *Fabiola* II. viii. 179 Had he melted into unexistence?

une'xistent, *a.* (UN-1 7 and 5 b.)
1682 SIR T. BROWNE *Chr. Mor.* III. xiii. (1716) 97 A Retrograde cognition of times past..is more satisfactory than a suspended Knowledge of what is yet unexistent. 1723 BLACKMORE *Alfred* Pref. p. xlv, Only empty Phantasms, and the unexistent Creatures of human Invention. 1746 YOUNG *Nt. Th.* IX. 812 Are there..those to whom Unseen and unexistent, are the same?

une'xisting, *ppl. a.* (UN-1 10.)
1785 ANNA SEWARD *Lett.* (1811) I. 18 What you tell us is an unexisting circumstance. 1804 —— *Mem. Darwin* 33 It is surely better to recede, even at the church-porch, than to plight at it's altar the vow of unexisting love. 1834 MRS. JAMESON *Visits & Sk.* (1839) I. 138 There are those who regard..the unknown as the unexisting.

†**un'exorable,** *a. Obs.* [UN-1 7 b and 5 b.] = INEXORABLE *a.*
1577 *Fruites of Prayer* H 5 b, If God were (in a maner) vnexorable. 1608 BP. J. KING *Serm. 5 Nov.* 12 Is your malice vnexorable as the grave? Deepe and bottomles as hell? *a* 1641 BP. MOUNTAGU *Acts & Mon.* (1642) 422 They were..unexorable against malefactors for breach of the Law.
Hence †**un'exorableness.** *Obs.*
1611 FLORIO, *Inessorabilita*, vnexorablenesse.

un'exorcised, *ppl. a.* (UN-1 8.)
c 1750 SHENSTONE *Ruin'd Abbey* 174 That their dishonour'd corse..Must sleep with brutes..in marle unexorcis'd! 1854 MILMAN *Lat. Chr.* III. vii. (1864) II. 152 She is possessed by a devil, who had been swallowed in the unexorcised lettuce. 1860 FROUDE *Hist. Eng.* VI. 306 That spectre remained unexorcised in all its shadowy terror.

unex'panded, *ppl. a.* (UN-1 8.)
1664 POWER *Exp. Philos.* II. 110 The Quicksilver,..overpowring the Atmosphærical or unexpanded Ayr, falls down. 1712 BLACKMORE *Creation* VI. 290 So every fœtus bears a secret hoard, With sleeping, unexpanded issue stor'd. 1796 WITHERING *Brit. Plants* (ed. 3) III. 657 Leaves, and especially the unexpanded heads, with a good deal of woolliness. 1854 HOOKER *Himal. Jrnls.* I. vi. 163 Most of its flowers drop unexpanded from the tree. 1887 W. PHILLIPS *Brit. Discomycetes* 358 The unexpanded cups somewhat like a *Cucurbitaria*.

unex'pansive, *a.* (UN-1 7 and 5 b.)
1846 GROTE *Greece* (1862) II. 332 These bodies were close and unexpansive. 1862 T. A. TROLLOPE *Marietta* I. xv. 271 By nature an unexpansive man. 1869 LECKY *Europ. Mor.* I. 433 The Jewish religion was essentially conservative and unexpansive.

†**unex'pect,** *ppl. a.* [UN-1 8 b.] Unexpected.
1633 P. FLETCHER *Elisa* I. xl, Not unexpect thou com'st to claim thy due.

unex'pectable, *a.* (UN-1 7 b and 5 b.)
1598 BARRET *Theor. Warres* I. ii. 9 Brought through manifold daungers, and vnto vnexpectable euents. 1604 T. WRIGHT *Passions* v. §4. 289 The difficulty of obtayning that we desire..rendreth the thing desperate and consequently vnexpectable. 1664 INGELO *Bentiv. & Ur.* v. 30 The concatenation of like Successions..seems to make the end of sinning almost unexpectable. 1749 BYROM *Rem.* (1857) II. II. 489 Your brother's journey to Smithills was indeed unexpectable. 1825 BENTHAM *Offic. Apt. Maximized, Indic.* (1830) 27 One of the most unexpectable of all incidents. 1863 HAWTHORNE *Our Old Home* (1879) I. 260 Our kind friend kept bringing out one unexpected and wholly unexpectable thing after another. 1892 *Graphic* 16 Apr. 478/1 Where the unexpected, or rather unexpectable, occurred.

unex'pectant, *a.* (UN-1 7 and 5 b.)
1811 WORDSW. *Epist. to Beaumont* 209 Not unexpectant that by early day Our little Band would thrid this mountain-way. 1881 E. F. POYNTER *Among the Hills* II. 84 Abashed by the unexpectant calm that met her.

unexpec'tation. (UN-1 12 and 5 b.)
1611 FLORIO, *Innaspettatione*, vnexpectation. 1650 BP. HALL *Balm of Gilead* vii. §1 As every other evill, so this [loss] especially is aggravated by our unexpectation.

unex'pected, *ppl. a.* (UN-1 8 and 5 b.)
a 1586 SIDNEY *Arcadia* I. v, In such an unexpected mischiefe. 1597 A. M. tr. *Guillemeau's Fr. Chirurg.* 50/1 Because of vnexpected accidentes, he is blamed, disdayned and diffamed. 1634 SIR T. HERBERT *Trav.* 5 An vnexpected violent gust. 1651 HOBBES *Leviath.* II. xxviii. 162 The unexpected addition is no part of the Punishment. 1733 BERKELEY *Let.* Wks. 1871 IV. 204 This circumstance, not foreseen, occasions an unexpected delay. 1781 GIBBON *Decl. & F.* xxx. (1787) III. 147 Stilicho..suddenly repressed, by his unexpected presence, the enemy. 1825 SCOTT *Talisman* iii, His attention was suddenly caught by an unexpected apparition. 1860 MAURY *Phys. Geog.* xviii. §750 The most unexpected discovery of all.
absol. 1884 in *Littell's Living Age* April 125/2 He is very great in the art of the unexpected. 1891 BARTLETT *Fam. Quots.* (ed. 9) 701 The unexpected always happens.—A common proverb. 1892 [see UNEXPECTABLE].

unex'pectedly, *adv.* (UN-1 11, 5 b; cf. prec.)
1605 DRAYTON *Idea* li, Calling to mind..How things still unexpectedly have run, As it please the Fates. 1693 DRYDEN *Juvenal* (1697) p. xxii, A most Bountiful Present, which..came most seasonably and unexpectedly to my Relief. 1774 PENNANT *Tour Scotl. in 1772*, 283 A seat beautifully wooded, gracing most unexpectedly this almost treeless tract. 1825 SCOTT *Talisman* xxiii, Engaged in subduing the angry feelings which had been so unexpectedly awakened. 1869 TOZER *Highl. Turkey* II. 220 We found ourselves close to the beach.., on which we unexpectedly emerged.
b. With adjs. or advs.
1818 SCOTT *Rob Roy* xxvi, We took a kind farewell of this unexpectedly zealous friend. 1850 MRS. CARLYLE *Lett.* (1883) II. 123 She arrived yesterday unexpectedly early. 1877 LADY BRASSEY *Voy. Sunbeam* xviii, Rejoicing that we had..a fresh fair wind, so unexpectedly soon.

unex'pectedness. (UN-1 12 and 5 b.)
1614 TOMKIS *Albumazar* IV. ii, This man admires the vnexpectednesse Of my returne. 1654 EARL ORRERY *Parthen.* (1676) 74 You should haue lessen'd my ruine, at least of one misery, which is the suddenness and unexpectedness of it. 1725 WATTS *Logic* III. iv. §8 This will plainly prove that he describes the Unexpectedness of his Appearance. 1804–6 SYD. SMITH *Mor. Philos.* (1850) 378 The unexpectedness of the news excites..the feeling of surprise. 1893 MCCARTHY *Red Diamonds* III. 221 An adventure stranger in its ironic unexpectedness than anything which had befallen him.

unex'pecting, *ppl. a.* (UN-1 10, 5 d.)
1632 LITHGOW *Trav.* I. 7 The harmlesse innocent, vnexpecting euill, may suddenly bee surprised. 1831 JAMES *Phil. Augustus* I. ii, The cold unexpecting fixedness of his companion's features.

unex'pectingly, *adv.* (UN-1 11.)
1801 ELIZ. HELME *St. Margaret's Cave* xx, Thus unexpectingly meeting with a stranger..had the most sensible effect upon the good old man.

†**unex'pediency.** *Obs.* (UN-1 12 and 5 b.)
1607 T. SPARKE *Brotherly Persuasion* 7 Some inconuenience, and vnexpediencie in some of the things commaunded.

†**unex'pedient,** *a. Obs.* [UN-1 7 and 5 b.] = INEXPEDIENT *a.*
c 1449 PECOCK *Repr.* II. v. 163 For ellis the sacramentis of Crist weren vnleeful, vnexpedient, and vnprofitable. *c* 1520 BARCLAY *Jugurth* (1557) A ij b, Neuertheles so to do it is vnbehouefull and vnexpediente. 1583 GOLDING *Calvin on Deut.* xxiii. 134 For this kinde of speach were vnexpedient if to make images were..lawfull. 1643 QUARLES *Loyall Convert* Wks. (Grosart) I. 142/2 What is unexpedient in the one, is lawfull in the other. 1655 FULLER *Ch. Hist.* IX. ii. §25 Others did condemne the present excommunication..as unexpedient. *a* 1768 SECKER *Serm.* (1770) II. 180 For their Abuse doth not of Necessity make our Use of them unlawful, nor possibly sometimes unexpedient.

unex'peditated, *ppl. a.* (UN-1 8.)
1598 MANWOOD *Lawes Forest* xvi. 97 b, The forfaiture..onely for the keeping of Mastiues within a Forrest vnexpeditated. 1885 M. COLLINS in *Eng. Illustr. Mag.* 586/1 Some Commoners claimed a right to keep certain dogs unexpeditated.

unex'pelled, *ppl. a.* (UN-1 8.)
[1775 ASH.] 1811 BYRON *Hints fr. Hor.* 240 He.., unexpelled perhaps, retires M.A.

unex'pended, *ppl. a.* (UN-1 8.)
1571 *Act 13 Eliz.* c. 4 §9 Any Part thereof..founde to be owing and unexpended. [1775 ASH.] 1818 SCOTT *Br. Lamm.* xviii, Computing how long..the provisions which had been unexpended might furnish forth the Master's table. 1855 PUSEY *Doctr. Real Presence* Note R. 365 That which is eaten is unexpended. 1884 *Act 47 & 48 Vict.* c. 73 §5 The unexpended balances of certain votes for navy services.

unex'pensive, *a.* [UN-1 7 and 5 b.] = INEXPENSIVE *a.*
1642 MILTON *Apol. Smect.* Wks. 1851 III. 305 Providence ..hath ever bred me up in plenty, although my life hath not bin unexpensive in learning, and voyaging about. 1727 THOMSON *Britannia* 204 Then cherish this, this unexpensive power,..By lavish Nature thrust into your hand. 1770 LANGHORNE *Plutarch* (1879) I. 74/2 His sacrifices..consisting chiefly of..simple and unexpensive things. 1834 HT. MARTINEAU *Farrers* ii. 21 Mr. Farrer eschewed luxuries, except a few of the most unexpensive. 1859 MILL *Lett.* (1910) I. 233 Neither they nor the Tories wish to make elections unexpensive.
Hence **unex'pensively** *adv.*, **-ness.**
1815 JANE AUSTEN *Emma* xxv, Keeping little company, and that little unexpensively. 1825 CARLYLE *Schiller* (1845) App. 285 Add to this the unexpensiveness to me of such a town as Weimar.

†**unex'perience,** *sb. Obs.* [UN-1 12 and 5 b.] = INEXPERIENCE.
1611 FLORIO, *Imperitia*, vnskilfulnesse, vnexperience, ignorance. 1617 BP. HALL *Quo Vadis?* x, To recant that which my vn-experience hath..written in praise of the French education. 1691 HARTCLIFFE *Virtues* 61 Ignorance and Unexperience makes men bold and foolhardy. 1755 *Mem. Capt. P. Drake* I. xiii. 93 He offered to appoint me his second Lieutenant, which I declined accepting, on account of my Unexperience in maritime Affairs.

unex'perience, *v.* [UN-1 14.] *trans.* To fail to experience.
1603 HARINGTON in *Nugæ Ant.* (1804) I. 336 Nor did I..unexperience her love and kyndness on manie occasions.

unex'perienced, *ppl. a.* [UN-1 8 and 5 b.]
1. Not furnished with, or taught by, experience; not skilled or trained in this way.
1569 UNDERDOWN *Ovid's Invect. Ibis* Pref. A vj b, If you wil bear with mine vnexperienced iudgemente. 1608 WILLET *Hexapla Exod.* 273 No man will commit his..bodie to an vnexperienced physitian. 1678 OTWAY *Friendship in F.* IV. i, Her natural and unexperienc'd tenderness exceeded practis'd charms. 1751 JOHNSON *Rambler* No. 175 ¶10 Credulity is the common failing of unexperienced virtue. 1793 HOLCROFT tr. *Lavater's Physiog.* i. 16 Shades scarcely discernible to an unexperienced eye. 1822 CHISHOLM in Good *Study Med.* (1829) II. 213 Let the young and unexperienced practitioner guard himself against it. 1860 A. L. WINDSOR *Ethica* iii. 146 An unexperienced hand might have expected [etc.].
b. Const. *in.*
1599 HAKLUYT *Voy.* II. II. 138 Our English Surgeons (for the most part) be vnexperienced in hurts that come by shot. 1620 E. BLOUNT *Horæ Subs.* 85 To be vnexperienced in the first, argues much disability for the latter. 1654 tr. *Martini's Conq. China* 211 He quickly dispersed them, being wholy unexperienced in Military Discipline. 1760–72 H. BROOKE *Fool of Qual.* (1809) IV. 27 My..child here, is unexperienced in the world. 1771 SMOLLETT *Humph. Cl.* Oct. ii, Unexperienced as I am in the commerce of life.
c. *absol.* (with *the*).
1622 PEACHAM *Compl. Gent.* xvi. 200 If it be the common Law of Nature, that the learned should..instruct the ignorant, the experienced, the vnexperienced. 1665 BOYLE *Occas. Refl.* IV. xix. 125 Whatever the unexperienc'd may imagine. 1742 *Johnson's Debates* (1787) II. 100 By these arts I have known the young and unexperienced kept in suspence. 1810 CRABBE *Borough* xxiii. 87 The unexperienced and the inexpert.
2. Not known or felt by experience.
1698 NORRIS *Pract. Disc.* IV. 89 A new and altogether unexperienc'd State and way of Life. 1721 PERRY *Daggenh. Breach* 69 My Work was in a Method entirely new, and unexperienc'd by those Persons appointed to carry on the same in my Absence. 1756 *Monitor* No. 27. I. 239 The towers..gave me an unexperienced delight, as I had never seen such a place before. 1844 DISRAELI *Coningsby* IX. v, There was..no unexperienced scene or sensation of life to distract his intelligence.
Hence **unex'periencedness.**
1654 GAYTON *Pleas. Notes* I. viii. 30 Whereat he vapoured extreamely, shaking his head at the fellows unexperiencednesse. 1727 BAILEY (vol. II) s.v., *Unskilfulness.*

†**unex'perient,** *a. Obs. rare.* [UN-1 7 and 5 b.] Inexperienced.
1597 SHAKS. *Lover's Compl.* 318 The naked and concealed feind he couerd, That th'vnexperient gaue the tempter place. 1750 CARTE *Hist. Eng.* II. 638 Errors and oversights ..proceeding..from unexperient ignorance.

unex'perimented, *ppl. a.* [UN-1 8.]
†**1.** Inexperienced; unskilled. *Obs.*
1598 BARRET *Theor. Warres* I. i. 1 My selfe, and other country Gentlemen, vnexperimented in such martiall causes. 1622 R. HAWKINS *Voy. S. Sea* 152 To commend such charges to men vnexperimented in their profession. 1635 J. HAYWARD tr. *Biondi's Banish'd Virg.* 162 So ignorant and unexperimented in all wylinesse..as to discover her love.
2. Not tried, known, or ascertained by experiment.
1594 R. ASHLEY tr. *Loys le Roy* 78 b, The diligence of the auncients, who haue left nothing vnsearched, and vnexperimented. 1674 R. GODFREY *Inj. & Ab. Physic* 54, I cannot but..wonder, that any persons should be so stupidly idle, and vain, to publish unexperimented Processes. 1839 B. H. SMART *Way out of Metaph.* 51 We may..apply it to similar particulars remaining unexperimented. 1870 LOWELL *Study Wind.* 194 Whether equally so to the most distant possible heathen or not was unexperimented.

†**unex'pert,** *a. Obs.* [UN-1 7 and 5 b. Cf. MDu. *onexpert.*]
1. = INEXPERT *a.*
a 1425 tr. *Arderne's Treat. Fistula*, etc. 55 Lewed men and vnexperte men callep al þe infirmitez bredyng in þe lure emeroydez, or pilez, or fics. 1509 BARCLAY *Shyp of Folys* (1570) ¶¶ v, If ye consider the scarcenes of my wit, and my vnexpert youth. 1598 BARRET *Theor. Warres* II. i. 23 The expert souldier loth to obey the vnexpert Captaine. 1639 G. DANIEL *Ecclus.* xxxiv. 25 Ignorance is vnexpert, and the Face Of smiling Error leads to Wickedness. 1698 FRYER *Acc. E. India & P.* 269 The Men here being unexpert how far the Friendly Offices [etc.].
b. Const. *of* or *in.*
(*a*) *a* 1440 *Found. St. Bartholomew's* (E.E.T.S.) 62 Vtterly vnexpert of mannys cownsell and helpe. *c* 1520 BARCLAY *Jugurth* 32 b, Theyr felowes whiche were fereful and unexpert of suche chaunces of warre. *a* 1548 HALL *Chron., Hen. VI*, 150 b, Nor of diligence, studie, and businesse, she was not vnexperte. 1635 HEYWOOD *Hierarchy* VI. 393 A Barbarian,..Unexpert of your Greekish plenitude. *a* 1689 MRS. BEHN *Mem. Crt. K. Bantam* (1722) II. 295 A pure Celibate, and altogether unexpert of Women.
(*b*) 1526 *Pilgr. Perf.* (W. de W. 1531) 274 They that be vnexperte in suche spirituall swetnesse. 1551 ROBINSON tr. *More's Utop.* II. (1895) 121 Yf they should be al together newe and fresh and vnexperte in husbandrie. 1629 WADSWORTH *Pilgr.* 35 Wee were young and vnexpert in sea fight. 1684 J. S. *Profit & Pleas. United* 166 Such Uner[r]ing Rules, as will..perfect the unexpert therein. 1778 [W. H. MARSHALL] *Minutes Agric., Observ.* 159 A man unexpert in boxing the Compass.
c. *ellipt.* in special sense.
a 1586 SIDNEY *Arcadia* III. v, Not doubting the easie conquest of an unexpert virgin. 1623 WODROEPHE *Marrow Fr. Tongue* 322/2 If a Woman be a Virgen, shee is vnexpert.
2. Of things: Untried. *rare*-1.
c 1510 BARCLAY *Mirr. Gd. Manners* (1570) B v, When thou shalt ought do of unexpert or newe.
Hence †**unex'pertly** *adv.*, **-ness.** *Obs.*
1538 LATIMER *Rem.* (Parker Soc.) 398 If affection do reign in me, then I will not; if ignorance and unexpertness, then I cannot. 1565 COOPER, *Imperite*, vnexpertly: vnskilfully. 1598 FLORIO, *Imperitia*, vnskilfulnes, vnexpertnes. 1611 COTGR., *Imperitement*,..vnlearnedly; vnexpertly.

†**un'expiable,** *a. Obs.* [UN-1 7 b and 5 b.] = INEXPIABLE *a.* I.
1606 BP. J. KING *Serm.* Sept. 46 The fault is unexpiable; the blood of martyrdome cannot wash out this spot. 1657

TRAPP *Comm. Esther* ii. 10 This lyeth upon them as a punishment for their unexpiable guilt.

un'expiated, *ppl. a.* [UN-^{1} 8 and 5 b.] = INEXPIATED *a.*
1681 EARL ROSCOMMON *Poems* (1721) 6 The Bar.. Stain'd with the (yet unexpiated) Blood Of the brave Strafford. 1809 MALKIN *Gil Blas* x. i. ¶4 It gives me the horrors.. to think of my unexpiated murders. 1873 SYMONDS *Grk. Poets* vii. 190 Orestes.. has.. unexpiated crimes of father and of grandsire to atone for.

unex'pired, *ppl. a.* (UN-^{1} 8.)
1570 WALSINGHAM in *Wills Doctors' Comm.* (Camden) 70 All my leases, or so many of them as then shall remayne unsoulde and unexpired. 1635 QUARLES *Embl.* v. x. 281 She .. begs th' untimely date Of unexpired thraldome, to release Th' afflicted Captive. 1659 *Knaresb. Wills* (Surtees) II. 240 Yeares of a lease.. which are yet uncome and unexpired. 1778 [W. H. MARSHALL] *Minutes Agric., Observ.* 191 The unexpired term of the lease. 1859 J. LANG *Wand. India* 27 The unexpired portion of their leave having been cancelled. 1883 D. C. MURRAY *Hearts* xxiii. (1885) 189 The unexpired lease of the theatre was supposed to be worth a thousand.

unex'plainable, *a.* [UN-^{1} 7 b and 5 b.] Inexplicable.
*a*1711 KEN *Hymnotheo* Poet. Wks. 1721 III. 357 Each Plant, Worm, Mite, Pebble we behold, Strange Wonders unexplainable enfold. 1858 MRS. OLIPHANT *Laird of Norlaw* II. 88 The unconscious, unexplainable poetic elevation of the lad. 1875 WHITNEY *Life Lang.* x. 195 Facts which for the time seem unexplainable by ordinary means.
Hence **unex'plainably** *adv.*, inexplicably.
1899 SOMERVILLE & ROSS *Experiences Irish R.M.* 247 At last we came, unexplainably, into smooth water.

unex'plained, *ppl. a.* (UN-^{1} 8.)
1721 AMHURST *Terræ Filius* No. 31, All their doctrines are generally embraced whilst unexplained and unexamined. 1784 COWPER *Task* II. 58 Fires from beneath, and meteors from above, Portentous, unexampled, unexplain'd. 1842 MANNING *Serm.* (1848) 10 The great and unexplained fall of the 'sons of God'. 1879 *St. George's Hosp. Rep.* IX. 706 A rule, subject doubtless to no few unexplained exceptions.
Hence **unex'plainedly** *adv.*
1811 MISS L. M. HAWKINS *C'tess & Gertr.* II. 366 These insular situations,.. where nothing can occur unexpectedly and unexplainedly, without.. carrying an inflammable train.

unex'planatory, *a.* (UN-^{1} 7.)
1816 BENTHAM *Chrestom.* Wks. 1843 VIII. 171 The arbitrary and unexplanatory denomination given to them. 1847 C. BRONTË *J. Eyre* xxxiii, The hasty and unexplanatory reply.

†**un'expliable,** *a. Obs.* [UN-^{1} 7 b, 5 b.] = INEXPLE(A)BLE *a.*
1658 J. JONES *Ovid's Ibis* 15 The Belides sieve [may be] the unexpliable desires of the soule.

†**un'explicable,** *a. Obs.* [UN-^{1} 7 b and 5 b.]
1. = INEXPLICABLE *a.* 2.
1532 MORE *Confut. Tindale* Wks. 542/1 Which places of themselfe all olde holy doctours confesse for diffuse and almost unexplicable. 1644 DIGBY *Nat. Soul* Pref. ¶5 Later Philosophers.. haue filled their bookes.. with vnexplicable opinions, out of which no account of nature can be given. 1656 EARL MONM. tr. *Boccalini's Advts. fr. Parnass.* I. lxxvii. 100 Justice being oppressed by the unexplicable ambition of potent men. 1803 *Ann. Rev.* I. 275 What remains unexplicable in the conduct of public men is not solved by conjecture. 1815 *Monthly Mag.* XXXVIII. 111 Many hundred words obsolete, unexplicable, barbarous,.. will be dislodged.
2. = INEXPLICABLE *a.* 1.
1615 G. SANDYS *Trav.* 225 Him Minos doomes To durance, in vnexplicable roomes. *a*1624 R. CRAKANTHORP *Vigilans Dormitans* xix. (1631) 313 By most admirable and unexplicable fraud & subtilty. 1675 EVELYN *Terra* (1676) 61 Mould to entertain the Fibers, which else you will find to mat in unexplicable intanglements.
Hence †**un'explicableness.** *Obs.*
1712 *H. More's App. Antid. Ath.* 185 The unexplicableness of a Spirit's moving Maker is no greater argument [etc.].

un'explicated, *ppl. a.* (UN-^{1} 8.)
1666 BOYLE *Orig. Formes & Qual.* Pref. B 6 b, Qualities.. which have been by the Schooles either left Unexplicated, or Generally referr'd, to.. Incomprehensible Substantiall Formes. 1698 LOCKE *Let. to Molyneux* 6 Apr., To have.. unravell'd to you that which lying in the lump unexplicated in my mind I scarce yet know what it is my self.

unex'plicit(ly, *a.* and *adv.* (UN-^{1} 7, 11, 5 b.)
[1775 ASH, *Unexplicit.*] 1831 SCOTT *Ct. Rob.* xxvi, So unexplicitly expressed,.. that it was by no means easy to conceive the meaning of what he said. 1838 SIR W. HAMILTON *Logic* xvii. (1866) I. 319 Very brief and unexplicit in his treatment of this subject. 1852 JAMES *Pequinillo* II. 211 It was briefly and unexplicitly that he explained himself.

unex'ploited, *ppl. a.* (UN-^{1} 8.)
1888 *Pall Mall G.* 3 Sept. 2/1 Developing the wonderful resources of their unexploited continent.

unex'plorable, *a.* (UN-^{1} 7 b, 5 b.)
1859 T. S. HENDERSON *Life E. Henderson* 149 The guide, who regarded the region not only as unexplored, but unexplorable.

unex'plored, *ppl. a.* (UN-^{1} 8.)
1697 DRYDEN *Æneis* IV. 600 No female Arts or Aids she left untry'd, Nor Counsels unexplor'd, before she dy'd. 1700 —— *Sigism. & Guiscardo* 678 Under thy friendly Conduct will I fly To Regions unexplor'd. 1751 JOHNSON *Rambler* No. 137 ¶7 The unexplored abysses of truth. 1824 MISS L. M. HAWKINS *Annaline* III. 65 They had led him round through an unexplored country. 1884 J. GILMOUR *Mongols* xviii. 225 The spirit which prompts men to.. seek out unexplored knowledge.

unex'plosive, *a.* (UN-^{1} 7, 5 b.)
*a*1828 SIR W. CONGREVE (Worcester, 1846). 1866 [see INEXPLOSIVE *a.*] 1884 *Contemp. Rev.* Nov. 617 Guns firing solid, and therefore unexplosive, shot.

unex'portable, *a.* (UN-^{1} 7 b.)
1827 P. CUNNINGHAM *N.S. Wales* II. 103 Paper-money.. being unexportable, and consequently only available for home use.

unex'posed, *ppl. a.* [UN-^{1} 8.]
1. Not brought to light; not shown up.
1703 MRS. CENTLIVRE *Beau's Duel* II. ii, Would they take my advice, no fop.. shou'd 'scape unexposed. 1741 WATTS *Improv. Mind* I. v. §8 (1801) 55 They will endeavour.. to render it useless by their censures, rather than suffer.. the little mistakes of the author to pass unexposed. 1817 COBBETT *Taking Leave* 29 While her infamous press was revelling in unexposed falsehoods and calumnies.
2. Not rendered open, subject, or liable, *to* something.
*a*1691 BOYLE *Hist. Air* (1692) 82 A place unexposed to the moon's light. 1769 E. BANCROFT *Guiana* 17 The white inhabitants.. are unexposed to the rays of the sun near mid-day. 1814 WORDSW. *Excurs.* IV. 757 Existence unexposed To the blind walk of mortal accident. 1865 NEALE *Hymns Paradise* 10 Unexposed to change and chance.
3. *Photogr.* (See EXPOSE *v.* 3.)
1892 *Photogr. Ann.* II. 229 The principal constituent of an unexposed dry plate is silver bromide.

unex'postulating, *ppl. a.* (UN-^{1} 10.)
1819 SHELLEY *Cenci* II. ii. 150 Her mother scared and unexpostulating.

unex'poundable, *a.* (UN-^{1} 7 b.)
1611 COTGR., *Inexplicable*,.. vndisplayable, vnexpoundable. 1835 *Court Mag.* VI. 230/1 In spite of legal interdictions and unexpoundable acts of parliament. 1844 *North Brit. Rev.* I. 147 Dark sayings and unexpoundable dogmas.

unex'pounded, *ppl. a.* (UN-^{1} 8.)
1648 HEXHAM II, *Onbeduydet*, Vnexpounded. 1651 JER. TAYLOR *Serm. for Year* II. xxii. 279 When we are to choose our doctrine,.. we take that which is in the plain unexpounded words of Scripture. 1826 SCOTT *Woodst.* xiv, 'As gospel unexpounded by a steeple-man,' said the Independent.

unex'press, *a.* (UN-^{1} 7.)
1851 CARLYLE *Sterling* I. iv, The express schoolmaster is not equal to much at present—while the *unexpress*.. is so busy.

†**unex'pressable,** *a. Obs.* [UN-^{1} 7 b.] = UNEXPRESSIBLE *a.*
1548 G. WISHART tr. *Conf. Fayth* xxii, We exulte and rejoyce with a myrth unexpressable in wordes. *a*1586 SIDNEY *Arcadia* III. x, As well consorted partes to such an unexpressable [1621 unexpressible] harmonie. 1607 HIERON *Wks.* I. 468 Now she.. still beggeth with Him by sighes vnexpressable. 1652 *Eliza's Babes* 75 A felicity that fils our hearts with an unexpressable delight. 1683 E. HOOKER *Pordage's Mystic Div.* Pref. 70 To the.. unexpressabl refreshing of the.. faithful Servants of Christ. *c*1721 MRQ. TULLIBARDINE in *10th Rep. Hist. MSS. Comm.* App. I. 126 Those who find their account in unexpressable confusion.

unex'pressed, *ppl. a.* (UN-^{1} 8 and 5 b.)
1561 T. NORTON *Calvin's Inst.* I. Pref., So that he do with an vnexpressed Fayth (as they cal it) submit hys mynde to the iugement of the Church. 1611 BEAUM. & FL. *Maid's Trag.* III, And you will feel so unexprest a joy In chast embraces, that you will indeed appear another. 1659 EVELYN tr. *Gold. Bk. Chrysostome* Ep. Ded. A xj, The Ellipsis, and Defects of Verbs and Nouns unexpressed. 1676 *Life Father Sarpi* in *Brent's Counc. Trent* 8 All their regular orders continued with professions as yet unexprest. 1813 BYRON *Corsair* III. xv, His thoughts..; deep, dark, and unexprest, They bleed within.. his breast. 1876 FOX BOURNE *Locke* I. vi. 273 By its unexpressed terms all the courtiers and politicians.. were to be well bribed.
So **unex'pressedly** *adv.*
1561 T. NORTON *Calvin's Inst.* III. 173 It is not enough, if a man vnexpressedly beleue..: but he requireth an expressed acknowleging of Gods goodnesse.

unex'pressible, *a.* (and *sb.*). Now *rare* or *Obs.* [UN-^{1} 7 and 5 b.] = INEXPRESSIBLE *a.*
1621 [see UNEXPRESSABLE *a.*, quot. *a* 1586]. 1626 DONNE *Serm.* 746 That unexpressible worke of the Redemption. 1675 TRAHERNE *Chr. Ethics* 73 The first of these is occasioned by a secret and unexpressible agreement of tempers. 1731 *Hist. Litteraria* II. 267 The many, almost unexpressible, Calamities he suffered, during his Captivity. 1826 SOUTHEY *Vind. Eccl. Angl.* 177 An unexpressible, uncomparable, unimaginable stench.. filled that whole place of darkness.
b. *sb.* = INEXPRESSIBLE *sb.* 2.
1810 S. GREEN *Reformist* I. 92 No, we called 'em 'fie-for-shames', 'unexpressibles', 'inspeakables'; for 'small-clothes' has been long out of wogue.
Hence **unex'pressibleness.** Also **-i'bility.**
1649 AMBROSE *Media* iii. (1652) 56 The Infiniteness, and unexpressibleness of God's Bounty. *a*1672 STERRY *Freed. Will* (1675) 7 The unexpressibleness of the Divinity, and the Divine Vnity. 1816 BENTHAM *Chrestom.* Wks. 1843 VIII. 117 Of impracticability, in this case two causes present themselves..: viz. uncognoscibility and unexpressibility.

unex'pressibly, *adv.* Now *rare* or *Obs.* [UN-^{1} 11 and 5 b.] = INEXPRESSIBLY *adv.*
1634 BP. HALL *Char. Man* (1635) 47 Till then your condition.. is unexpressibly wofull. 1668 H. MORE *Div. Dial.* III. xvi. 411 Tumbling them down into the pit of Hell, there to be eternally and unexpressibly tormented. 1702 ECHARD *Eccl. Hist.* (1710) 598 Which meeting with a person of his age,.. must needs be unexpressibly burdensome.

unex'pressive, *a.* [UN-^{1} 7 and 5 b.]
†1. = INEXPRESSIVE *a.* 1. *Obs.*
1600 SHAKS. *A.Y.L.* III. ii. 10 Run, run Orlando, carue on euery Tree, The faire, the chaste, and vnexpressiue shee. 1629 MILTON *Hymn Nativ.* xi, Harping in loud and solemn quire, With unexpressive notes to Heav'ns new-born Heir. 1637 —— *Lycidas* 176 So Lycidas.. hears the unexpressive nuptiall Song, In the blest Kingdoms meek of joy and love.
2. = INEXPRESSIVE *a.* 2.
1755 *World* No. 150. V. 81 If the device had been a triple-crown, it would not have been unexpressive. 1816 BENTHAM *Chrestom.* 109 In so far as it simply fails of being subservient to those purposes, it is unexpressive—simply unexpressive. 1851 W. R. GREG *Creed Christendom* xv. 227 Exhausting superlatives, even to unexpressive and wearisome satiety.
So **unex'pressively** *adv.*, **-ness.**
[1846 WORCESTER, *Unexpressively.*] 1885 *Athenæum* 21 Mar. 369/2 She is distinguished from the other muses by the unexpressiveness of her name.

†**unexprimable,** *a. Obs.* [UN-^{1} 7 b and 5 b.] Inexpressible.
1632 LITHGOW *Trav.* I. 9 An infinite treasure, of vnexprimable vertues. 1727 [DORRINGTON] *Philip Quarll* 222 The two Indians.. with unexprimable Activity leapt in it.

unex'pugnable, *a.* [UN-^{1} 7 b and 5 b.] = INEXPUGNABLE *a.*
1382 WYCLIF *Ezek.* xxxii. 12 Alle thes folkis ben vnexpugnable, or mowen not be ouercomen. 1388 —— *2 Macc.* xii. 21. 1533 BELLENDEN *Livy* II. iv. (S.T.S.) I. 140 He began to edifie ane strang toure.. quhilk be municioun and straitnes of þe ground apperit Vnexpugnabil. 1608 CHAPMAN *Byron's Conspir.* Plays 1873 II. 225 Their owne strengths Are not so sure and vnexpugnable But that [etc.]. 1653 H. COGAN *Diod. Sic.* 70 Arabia is a country unexpugnable to a forraign enemy. 1831 SCOTT *Ct. Rob.* xxiv, A safe and unexpugnable barrier of the empire against the Saracens.

†**unex'puisable,** *a. Obs.* [ad. F. *inépuisable.*] Inexhaustible.
1623 LISLE *Ælfric on O. & N. Test.* Preface b 2 b, That vnexpuisable, that vnwastable light,.. which they had of old time shining.. in their sepulchers.

unex'punged, *ppl. a.* (UN-^{1} 8.)
[1775 ASH.] 1826 MALTHUS *Popul.* (ed. 6) II. 457 If the statute.. were to remain unexpunged.

un'expurgated, *ppl. a.* (UN-^{1} 8.)
1882 FARRAR *Early Chr.* II. 516 Even in the unexpurgated passages of the Amsterdam edition. 1889 HAMERTON *French & Eng.* 315 Young maids and old maids read Shakespeare in unexpurgated editions.

unex'tended, *ppl. a.* [UN-^{1} 8 and 5 b.]
1. Not extended or stretched out.
1648 HEXHAM II, *Ongereckt*,.. Vnreached, or Vnextended. 1697 CONGREVE *Mourn. Bride* III. vi, Think on to-morrow, when thou shalt be torn From these weak, struggling, unextended arms. 1712 BLACKMORE *Creation* VII. 75 See his right hand he unextended keeps. 1757 JOHNSON *Let. to C. O'Connor* 9 Apr. in *Boswell*, Of these provincial and unextended tongues, it seldom happens that more than one are understood by any one man.
2. *spec.* Having no extension.
1674 N. FAIRFAX *Bulk & Selv.* 33 Nor is All-fillingness any more unextended,.. because 'tis not thing enough to be recht out. 1678 CUDWORTH *Intell. Syst.* I. i. §20. 20 Aristotle .. did suppose Incorporeal Substance to be unextended, and as such, not to have Relation to any place. 1764 REID *Inquiry* vii. 210, I appeal to any man of common sense, whether extension can be in an unextended subject. 1803 *Monthly Mag.* XV. 322 If.. spirit be defined an active sensitive unextended formless substance. 1860 MANSEL *Proleg. Log.* (ed. 2) 49 An unextended colour is therefore a purely negative notion.
So **unex'tendedly** *adv.*, **-ness.**
1674 N. FAIRFAX *Bulk & Selv.* 16 If.. Gods eternity not be an everlasting now, and his immensity an unbounded unextendedness. 1678 CUDWORTH *Intell. Syst.* I. v. 823 Such considerations.. as tend directly to prove, that there is something unextendedly incorporeal.

unex'tenuated, *ppl. a.* (UN-^{1} 8.)
1778 JOHNSON *Shakespeare's Othello* I. iii. 80 *note*, The main, the whole, unextenuated. 1823 SOUTHEY *Hist. Penins. War* I. 237 The whole transaction was a business of pure, unmingled treachery, unprovoked, unextenuated. 1844 R. H. HORNE *New Spirit of Age* I. 150 Licentious works, which are unredeemed and unextenuated by any one sincere passion.

unex'tinct, *a.* (UN-^{1} 7 and 5 b.)
?1622 FLETCHER *Love's Cure* III. ii, Be there but one spark Of fire remaining in him unextinct, With my discourse I'll blow it to a flame. 1678 CUDWORTH *Intell. Syst.* I. iv. §18. 312 Their arcane Theology remained more or less amongst them unextinct to the last. 1820 SHELLEY *Ode to Naples* 168 Be man's high hope and unextinct desire The instrument to work thy will divine!

unex'tinguishable, *a.* [UN-^{1} 7 b and 5 b.] = INEXTINGUISHABLE *a.* **a.** Of fire or flame (also *fig.* and *transf.*).
1642 *Forerunner of Rev.* in *Select. fr. Harl. Misc.* (1793) 274 The duke's fire of his anger and fury being unextinguishable. 1654 COKAINE *Dianea* IV. 351 Perceiving

the flames unextinguishable, and defence impossible. **1762** FALCONER *Shipwr.* III. 169 There, all unquench'd by cruel fortune's ire, It glows with unextinguishable fire. **1860** PUSEY *Min. Proph.* 375 We see the arrow with the unextinguishable fire, ready to be discharged.

b. Of feelings, qualities, actions, etc.

1656 JEANES *Fuln. Christ* 156 A ground of unconquerable comfort, and unextinguishable joy. **1697** COLLIER *Ess. Mor. Subj.* II. (1709) 14, I must repeat, That this Earnestness.. is an unextinguishable Desire. **1760–72** H. BROOKE *Fool of Qual.* (1809) III. 52 The people's inseparable and unextinguishable share in the legislative power. **1815** J. CORMACK *Abol. Fem. Infanticide Guzerat* viii. 143 The ardent and unextinguishable zeal of female character. **1873** MOZLEY *Univ. Serm.* (1876) 201 The doctrine which.. declares most unextinguishable war with materialistic ideas of the Deity.

c. Of laughter. (After the Homeric ἄσβεστος γέλως, *Iliad* I. 599, *Odyss.* VIII. 326.)

1658 SIR T. BROWNE *Gard. Cyrus* ii. 42 That famous network of Vulcan, which.. caused that unextinguishable laugh in heaven. **1801** MAR. EDGEWORTH *Angelina* iii, The milliner.. burst into uncontrollable and.. unextinguishable laughter. **1842** MRS. BROWNING *Grk. Chr. Poets* iii. ¶5 That unextinguishable laughter which is the laughter of gods or poets.

Hence **unex'tinguishableness; -ably** *adv.*

a **1660** HAMMOND *Hell Torments* i. Wks. 1684 I. 615 So the Unextinguishableness of the one must be answered with the durableness of the other. **1775** JOHNSON, *Unquenchableness*, unextinguishableness. **1779** —— *L.P., Hammond*, Hammond.. was unextinguishably amorous, and his mistress inexorably cruel.

unex'tinguished, *ppl. a.* [UN-¹ 8 and 5 b.] Not extinguished, quenched, or put out: **a.** Of fire or light (also *fig.*).

1697 DRYDEN *Æneis* VI. 601 The souls whom that unhappy flame invades.. Lament too late their unextinguished fire. **1730** in Willis & Clark *Cambridge* (1886) I. 230 One of yᵉ Candles.. happen'd.. to fall down unextinguish'd. **1757** W. WILKIE *Epigoniad* VIII. 241 The seeds of fire, Which unextinguish'd glow in ev'ry pyre. **1817** SHELLEY *Rev. Islam* Ded. xiv, Two tranquil stars.. That burn from year to year with unextinguished light. **1858** HAWTHORNE *Fr. & It. Note-bks.* II. 175 The comet was already visible amid the unextinguished glow of twilight.

b. Of feelings, etc. (Cf. UNEXTINGUISHABLE *a.*)

1700 DRYDEN *Sigism. & Guisc.* 732 If thou hast remaining in thy Heart Some Sense of Love, some unextinguish'd Part Of former Kindness. **1757** W. WILKIE *Epigoniad* VII. 198 But burning still the unextinguish'd pain, The shore he left. **1800** COLERIDGE *Talleyrand to Ld. Grenville* 71 Your merit self-conscious.. keeps you up, Unextinguish'd and swoln. **1858** SEARS *Athan.* III. x. 331 There is conflict between the Holy Spirit.. and our own unextinguished selfishness.

un'extirpated, *ppl. a.* (UN-¹ 8.)

1663 BOYLE *Usef. Exp. Nat. Philos.* II. i. 10 That I might be sure there was not the least part of the spleen left unextirpated. **1792** HORSLEY *Serm.* xl. (1816) III. 221 Taking offence at the sin which remains as yet unextirpated. **1802–12** BENTHAM *Ration. Judic. Evid.* (1827) IV. 189 So long as that system of abominations remains unextirpated. **1867** PUSEY *Eleven Addresses* xi. (1908) 142 Our besetting sins, still unextirpated.

unex'torted, *ppl. a.* (UN-¹ 8.)

1711 SWIFT *Examiner* No. 25 ¶5 The free unextorted addresses sent some time before from every part of the kingdom. **1755** COWPER *To Delia* 20 The soul's affection can be only given Free, unextorted, as the grace of heaven.

unex'tractable, *a.* (UN-¹ 7 b.)

1659 FULLER *App. Inj. Innoc.* II. IV. 44 The Animadvertor now proceeds to a new Intimation of mine, utterly unextractable from my words.

unex'tracted, *ppl. a.* (UN-¹ 8.)

1630 *R. Johnson's Kingd. & Commw.* 37 Selling their Sugars unextracted from the Cane. **1879** *Pall Mall Budget* 12 Sept. 24 One passage is too characteristic of the writer to be left unextracted.

unex'travagating, *ppl. a.* (UN-¹ 10.)

1865 J. GROTE *Explor. Philos.* I. 105 It is impossible to find words un-extravagating in this respect.

†un'extricable, *a. Obs.* [UN-¹ 7 b and 5 b.] = INEXTRICABLE *a.*

1659 H. MORE *Immort. Soul.* II. ii. 126 Which supposition we shall finde involved in unextricable difficulties. *a* **1677** BARROW *Serm. Ps. cxlv.* 9 Wks. 1686 III. 402 Many times the World is rescued from confusions, and distractions unextricable by any visible wit or force.

unex'truded, *ppl. a.* (UN-¹ 8.)

[**1775** ASH.] **1808** BENTHAM *Sc. Ref.* 100 More.. there may be.. as yet lying unextruded in the womb of time.

un'eyed, *ppl. a.* [UN-¹ 8.] Unobserved, unperceived, unseen.

a **1616** FLETCHER *Wit at Sev. Weapons* II. ii, A pair of Lips, oh that we were uney'd, I could suck Sugar from 'em. **1654** E. JOHNSON *Wonder-wrkg. Provid.* 164 Many thousands uneyed of mortal man. **1820** L. HUNT *Indicator* No. 23 (1822) I. 184 The maiden.. Kept not her bloom uneyed Which now a veil must hide. **1852** BAILEY *Festus* (ed. 4) 500 Pure and mere autocracy, unchecked—Unled—uneyed—ruled with a random hand.

uneymable: see UNAIMABLE *a. Obs.*

uneyment, obs. Sc. var. OINTMENT.

un'fabled, *ppl. a.* (UN-¹ 8.)

[**1775** ASH.] **1809** SYD. SMITH *Wks.* (1859) 142 They are more amusing than plain, unfabled precept. **1853** C. BRONTE *Villette* xxvii, Not thickly, as the diamonds were scattered in the valley of Sindbad, but sparely, as those gems lie in unfabled beds.

un'fabling, *ppl. a.* (UN-¹ 10.)

1797 *The College* 33 Shall the unfabling Muse the tale pursue?

†un'fabricate, *ppl. a. Obs.* (UN-¹ 8 b.)

1630 J. TAYLOR (Water P.) *Epigr.* xxxvi. Wks. II. 266/1, I could wish man were vnfabricate, His faults he doth so much exaggerate.

un'face, *v.* [UN-² 4.] *trans.* To strip of a facing or disguise; to expose the face of.

1611 FLORIO, *Suisare*, to vnface, to disuisage. **1640** SIR J. CULPEPPER in Rushw. *Hist. Coll.* III. (1692) I. 34 Unface these, and they will prove as bad Cards as any in the Pack. **1886** *Cheshire Gloss.* 374 To 'unface sand' would be to dig away all the soil so as to expose a face of sand.

un'faceable, *a.* [UN-¹ 7 b.] **a.** (See quot. *a* 1825.) *dial.* **b.** Unattractive in features. *dial.*

a **1825** FORBY *Voc. E. Anglia*, *Unfaceable*, unreasonable; indefensible. **1899** CROCKETT *Kit Kennedy* xxxiii, I hae seen mony queer-lookin' and unfaceable ministers.

c. That cannot be faced or confronted.

1889 in *Cent. Dict.* **1966** M. RUSSELL *No Return Ticket* ix. 79 Suddenly the prospect of work was unfaceable. **1981** M. MCMULLEN *Other Shoe* (1982) xii. 111 Willett exchanged unfaceable reality for unconsciousness.

un'faceted, *ppl. a.* (UN-¹ 8.)

1893 E. A. BUTLER *Househ. Ins.* 327 A pair of simple, rounded, unfaceted eyes.

unfa'cetious, *a.* (UN-¹ 7.)

1831 [see INFICETE *a.*].

unfact ('ʌn-, older -'fækt). [UN-¹ 12.] **a.** An untruth; a fictitious or mistaken statement.

1887 *North Star* 3 Dec., The astounding statement.. was an unfact. **1890** *Cath. News* 4 Oct. 6/4 We will call this an evangelical unfact.

b. *Pol.* A fact which is officially denied or disregarded.

1954 [see UNPERSON]. **1959** *Economist* 8 Aug. 329/1 A government founded on the principle of treating as an unfact that bitter sequence of miscalculated events for which its leading members bore.. responsibility. **1967** G. STEINER *Lang. & Silence* 379 Already, under the pressure of different truths, of 'un-facts' and history rewritten, the East German language is developing its own jargon and dialect.

un'factious, *a.* (UN-¹ 7.)

1834 DE QUINCEY *Autob. Sk.* Wks. 1854 II. 220 The pure-hearted and unfactious champions of liberty. **1853** BP. S. WILBERFORCE in *Life* (1881) II. 170 Temperate, reasonable, and unfactious in their conduct.

un'fadable, *a.* (UN-¹ 7 b.)

1626 BP. HALL *Contempl. O.T.* XXI. iv, A crowne incorruptible, unfadable.

un'faded, *ppl. a.* (UN-¹ 8.)

?*a* **1550** in *Dunbar's Poems* (S.T.S.) 327 O fair sweit blossum,.. Vnfaidit bayth of cullour and vertew! **1697** DRYDEN *Æneis* XI. 101 A lovely flower, New cropt by virgin hands,.. Unfaded yet. **1782** MISS BURNEY *Cecilia* I. iii, Her cheeks.. unfaded by bad hours and continual dissipation. **1821** SHELLEY *Ginevra* 81 The flowers upon my bridal chamber strewn Will serve unfaded for my bier.

†un'fadging, *ppl. a. Obs.* [UN-¹ 10.] Not going properly; intractable.

1629 T. ADAMS *Medit. Creed* Wks. 1120 The potter may erre in framing his vessel, and so in anger dash the vnfadging clay against the walles.

un'fading, *ppl. a.* (UN-¹ 10.)

1652 BENLOWES *Theoph.* XII. xlii, Such suppling balm As might vain trophies turn to an unfading Palm. **1738** GRAY *Propertius* III. 9 Let on this head unfading flowers reside. **1816** SOUTHEY *Poet's Pilgr.* I. 216 The vallies with perpetual fruitage blest, The mountains with unfading foliage drest. **1869** RUSKIN *Q. of Air* i. §5 The real atmosphere, calm in its dominion of unfading blue.

b. In figurative use.

1665 BOYLE *Occas. Refl.* Sect. iv. iv. 73 We should.. receive unfading Honours, and uncloying Delights. **1728** RAMSAY *Bonny Kate* viii, His pleasure each moment shall blossom Unfading, gets her for his mate. **1765** TUCKER *Lt. Nat.* (1834) II. 312 He might have excited sensations, ideas, and intelligence,.. permanent, unfading, and unsatiating. **1820** SCOTT *Monast.* xxxii, By His holy Word, that unfading and unerring lamp of our paths.

Hence **un'fadingly** *adv.*, **un'fadingness.**

a **1672** STERRY *Rise, Race & Royalty Kingd. God* (1683) 211 All flourish together *unfadingly in the person of Christ. **1806** MOORE *Epist.* v. 44 That.. The rose and the stream.. Should still be before me, unfadingly bright. **1658** PHILLIPS, *Immarcescence*, *unfadingness. **1797** POLWHELE *Hist. Devonsh.* I. 160 That its use.. was known to the Phenicians will appear probable, when we consider the unfadingness of their purple. **1860** PUSEY *Min. Proph.* 91 Graces beyond nature, in their manifoldness, completeness, unfadingness.

†un'failable, *a. Obs.* [UN-¹ 7 b and 5 b.]

1. = INFALLIBLE *a.* 2 a.

c **1425** *St. Eliz. of Spalbeck* in *Anglia* VIII. 108/15 Stronge and vnfaylabil preef of hool and clene virginite. *Ibid.* 113/41 Bi an vnfaillabil clock. **1553** EDEN *Treat. New Ind.* (Arb.) 10 Moste certayne.. demonstracions of Geometrye, and vnfayleable experymentes. **1623** BP. HALL *Gt. Impostor* Wks. (1625) 509 Trust them not, till you haue tried them by that vnfaileable rule of righteousnesse. **1673** O. WALKER *Educ.* 49 [Religion] is a principle, universal, perfect, unfailable.

2. Incapable of failing; sure, reliable.

c **1450** HOLLAND *Howlat* 383 Of Scotland the wer wall,.. Our fais force to defend, and vnfalȝeable. **1553** *Short Catech. Edw. VI*, 38 b, Christ, the author, earnest and vnfailable pledge of theyr fayth. **1643** TRAPP *Comm. Gen.* xvii. 7 The sure or unfailable mercies of David. **168.** in Somers *Tracts* I. 276 That He left there one to be Heir of His Grace and Spirit, in a perpetual unfailable Succession.

Hence **†un'failableness; -ably** *adv. Obs.*

1555 EDEN *Decades W. Ind.* (Arb.) 350 By the degrees is *vnfaylably measured the hole circumference of the lande and sea. **1641** BP. HALL *Def. Humble Remonstr.* viii. 71 This is perpetually and unfailably done by us. **1624** —— *Peacemaker* Wks. (1625) 538 Euery where extolling.. the assurance and *vnfailablenesse of that comfort. **1644** —— *Serm.* Rem. Wks. (1660) 137 He takes all beleevers into the partnership of this comfortable unfailablenesse.

un'failed, *ppl. a.* (UN-¹ 8.)

1749 J. CLELAND *Mem. Woman Pleasure* II. 239 My breasts.. unfail'd in firmness. **1827** POLLOK *Course T.* v. 523 When, on the glittering dews of orient life, Shone sunshine hopes, unfailed, unperjured then.

un'failing, *ppl. a.* (and *adv.*). [UN-¹ 10.]

1. Not failing or giving way.

a **1400** *Sir Perc.* 1474 Thair scheldis were un-failande. **1648** BP. HALL *Serm.* Wks. 1808 V. 545 Hereby.. are we freed from the sense of the second death and the sting of the first, to the unfailing comfort of our souls. **1653** BLITHE *Eng. Improver Impr.* 129 An unfailing Prevention of Crows, Rooks, or Daws from Corn. **1718** POPE *Iliad* XV. 551 Some god.. Has, from my arm unfailing, struck the bow. **1798** S. & HT. LEE *Canterb. T.* II. 554 May you deserve that love, is the prayer of your unfailing friend. **1827** POLLOK *Course T.* x. 2 My God! my Father! my unfailing hope!

2. Never giving out or coming to an end; unceasing, constant, continual.

1382 WYCLIF *Ecclus.* xxiv. 6, I made in heuenus, that vnfailende liȝt shulde springe. **1435** MISYN *Fire of Love* 38 þi swetnes.., þat end art of syghing, of desire begyninge, þe ȝate of ȝernynge vnfaylinge. *c* **1450** *Myrr. our Ladye* 180 But thow in thyne vnfaylynge fayrenesse.. shuldest abyde vndepartably in his moste loued loue. **1784** COWPER *Tiroc.* 316 This fond attachment.. Maintains its hold with such unfailing sway, We feel it ev'n in age. **1832** LYTTON *Eugene A.* I. i, He found a pure and unfailing delight in watching the growth of their young minds. **1855** [J. R. LEIFCHILD] *Cornwall* 127 An unfailing bank of bituminous bullion. **1876** BANCROFT *Hist. U.S.* I. x. 29 A country.. watered by unfailing rivers.

3. Infallible, positive, certain. †Also as *adv.*

c **1400** *Sc. Trojan War* II. 273 Quharfor wnfalȝeand ar we Mayd rytht certeyn þat it shall be. **1553** WOOD tr. *Gardner's True Obed.* To Rdr. A ij b, The vndoubted truth of gods vnfailing word. **1849** MACAULAY *Hist. Eng.* vii. II. 164 The event of battles, indeed, is not an unfailing test of the abilities of a commander. **1853** KANE *Grinnell Exp.* xxix. (1856) 240 This frost-smoke is an unfailing indication of open water. **1862** A. MEADOWS *Man. Midwifery* 76 One almost unfailing test may be here mentioned, namely, chloroform.

†4. As *adv.* Without fail, unfailingly. *Obs.*

c **1425** WYNTOUN *Cron.* IX. xxi. 2146 (Cott. MS.), Off Marche þe xxv. day, Wnfaillande þat [*sc.* the Annunciation] sal be ay.

Hence **un'failingness.**

c **1630** SANDERSON *Serm.* II. 307 The stability, unchangeableness, and unfailingness of Gods counsels. *a* **1656** BP. HALL *Serm.* Wks. 1837 V. 576 We may be so much the more infallibly assured.. by how much we do more know his unfailingness, his unchangeableness.

un'failingly, *adv.* [UN-¹ 11: cf. prec.] Without fail; in all cases or circumstances.

c **1400** *Sc. Trojan War* II. 319 Fra Gregeois þat shall ay but les Be holden ay wnfalȝeandly [*v.r.* wnfenȝeandly; L. *inviolabiliter*]. **1436** *Pol. Poems* (Rolls) II. 191 God wote, we have nede, Unfayllyngly, unfeynynge, and unfeynte, That concience for slought you not atteynte. **1833** ARNOTT *Physics* (ed. 5) II. 8 If the colds of winter arrive too early, they unfailingly produce the wintry scene. **1888** H. MORTEN *Hospital Life* 26 He was.. unfailingly patient with the querulous babes.

un'fain, *a.* Now *arch.* and *dial.* [OE. *unfæȝen* (f. *un-* UN-¹ 7 + *fæȝen* FAIN *a.*), = ON. *úfeginn* (Norw. *ufegen*).] Not glad or delighted; ill-pleased, sorry; reluctant.

a **1300** *Cursor M.* 3591 Quen þai it [*sc.* eld] haue þai are vnfayn, And wald ha youthed þan again. **1338** R. BRUNNE *Chron.* (1810) 100 He seged bi þat coste þe kastelle of Tenkere... þe Courthose was vnfayn, him þenk it a trespas. *c* **1400** *Destr. Troy* 12107 All þe folke were vnfayn, & of fyn will To haue reft hir the rynke. *a* **1450** *Le Morte Arth.* 2691 They made hem Redy to that Rese, There-fore was fele folke vnfayne. **1535** STEWART *Cron. Scot.* (Rolls) II. 43 Force it wes the Romanis for till fle, And leif the feild, thocht tha war rycht vnfane. *a* **1600** *Flodden F.* xiv. in Child *Ball.* III. 355 If Lancashire and Cheshire be fled and gone, Of those tydings wee may be vnfaine.

1846 *Whistle-Binkie* II. 11 Though o' him the men were a' rede and unfain, The lasses aye leuch when they met him again. **1876** *Whitby Gloss.* **1881** *Macm. Mag.* XLIII. 234 As she told, The hearers were unfain to hear.

un'faint, *a.* (UN-¹ 7.)

1436 [see UNFAILINGLY]. **1486** *Bk. St. Albans, Her.* F j, Durable & unfaynt in his kyngys battaylle [he] shall be. **1586** FERNE *Blaz. Gentrie* 148 Dyamond [is] vnfaint and durable.

†un'fainted, *ppl. a. Obs.* (UN-¹ 8.)

c **1425** *St. Cath. of Senis* in *Anglia* VIII. 187 Alwey and wiþ vnfeyntyd herte she spake of god. *a* **1539** COVERDALE *Ghostly Ps.* cxxix. Wks. (Parker Soc.) II. 577, I wyll abyde the Lorde paciently; My soule loketh for hym unfaynted.

un'fainting, *ppl. a.* (UN-¹ 10.)

1615 G. SANDYS *Trav.* 167 And o that I could retaine the effects which it wrought, with an vnfainting perseuerance!

1691 *Andros Tracts* II. 297 With inviolate Integrity, excellent Prudence, and unfainting Diligence. **1850** S. DOBELL *Roman* vi, Thou who in thy breast didst carry The fate of worlds unfainting. **1852** BAILEY *Festus* (ed. 4) 274 Some with wings Like an unfainting rainbow.

un'faintly, *adv.* (UN-^{1} 11.)
c **1425** *St. Cath. of Senis* in *Anglia* VIII. 186/27 Vnsuffurabil labours, vnfeyntly borne. **1844** MRS. BROWNING *Catarina to Camoens* xvi, Since with saintly Watch unfaintly Out of heaven shall o'er you lean Sweetest eyes.

un'fair, *a.* [OE. *unfæȝer* (f. *un-* UN-^{1} 7 + *fæȝer* FAIR *a.*), = ON. *úfagr* (Norw. *ufager*), Goth. *unfagrs*.]

†**1. a.** Not fair or beautiful; uncomely; disfigured; ugly. *Obs.*
Beowulf 727 Him of eaȝum stod liȝȝe ȝelicost leoht unfæȝer. *c* **888** K. ÆLFRED *Boeth.* xli. §4 Sio ȝefrednes..ne mæȝ ȝefredan hwæðer he bið þe blæc þe hwit, ðe fæȝer ðe unfæȝer. **971** *Blickl. Hom.* 111 [Him] þincð his neawist laþlico & unfæȝer. *c* **1050** *Voc.* in Wr.-Wülcker 530 *Larbata*, se unfæȝera. *a* **1300** *Cursor M.* 22509 Þe sun þat es sa bright ..It sal becum þan ful vnfair, Dune and blak sum ani hair. **13..** *Gaw. & Gr. Knt.* 1572 Þe froþe femed at his mouth vnfayre bi þe wykez. *a* **1400-50** *Alexander* 4864 Rochis & rogh stanes, rokkis vnfaire. *c* **1449** PECOCK *Repr.* v. xii. 548 In oon maner of sumwhat foul or vnfair schap and in oon maner of poor and symple colour. *a* **1500** *Ratis Raving* I. 1722 Þis eild is wnfair of fassoun, And failȝes of perfectioun. **1648** HEXHAM II, *Onschoon*, Vnfaire, or Vnbeautifull.

†**b.** Wicked; evil, bad. *Obs.*
13.. *E.E. Allit. P.* B. 1801 He was corsed for his vnclannes,..Done doun of his dyngnete for dedez vnfayre. **1375** BARBOUR *Bruce* I. 123 For wnfayr thingis may fall, perfay, Als weill to-morn as ȝhisterday. *Ibid.* xv. 123 Bot I trow falsat euirmar Sall haue vnfair and euill ending.

2. Not fair or equitable; unjust: **a.** Of actions, conduct, etc.; *spec.* of (business) competition.
1713 BERKELEY *Hylas & Phil.* II. Wks. 1871 I. 319 This shifting, unfair method of yours. **1746** WESLEY *Princ. Methodist* 5 If indeed it were so abridged as to alter the Sense, this would be unfair. **1798** S. & HT. LEE *Canterb. T.* II. 98 This conclusion appeared so unfair,..that she burst into tears. **1854** E. FITZGERALD *Lett.* (1889) I. 229 There was a very unfair Review in the Athenæum. **1890** 'R. BOLDREWOOD' *Col. Reformer* (1891) 185 Riding a well-bred powerful horse, which evidently made little of his somewhat unfair weight. **1891** *Federal Reporter* (U.S.) XLIV. 278 The relief sought is based on the charge that the denomination used is untrue, is calculated to deceive the public, and operates as an unfair and fraudulent competition against the business of the complainants. **1909** H. D. NIMS *Law Unfair Business Competition* 2 Unfair competition..exists wherever unfair means are used in trade rivalry. **1931** *Economist* 17 Jan. 103/1 The only recommendation..is that which would require road hauliers to be licensed..with a view to eliminating unfair competition in the transport of goods by carriers who do not conform to decent standards of wages and hours. **1963** *Observer* 3 Nov. 33/1 'Unfair competition' is competition you cannot meet, and 'free enterprise' a condition where the Government regulations ensure that you make money. **1983** *Economist* 5 Feb. 62/1 They deplore the unfair competition between law-abiding and tax-evading firms, and the loss to the State.

b. Of persons, the mind, etc.
1724 WATERLAND *Farther Vind. Christ's Div.* ii. §15. 57 Sometimes they complain of me as very unfair to take an Advantage of an Opinion of theirs. **1736** BUTLER *Anal.* II. vi. 315 Opportunity to an unfair mind of explaining away..that evidence. **1812** SCOTT *Let. to Byron* July in *Lockhart*, I do not know the motive would make me enter into controversy with a fair or an unfair literary critic. **1855** TENNYSON *Maud* I. xiii, Who shall call me ungentle, unfair.

c. *spec.* Not paying the usual rate of wages.
1886 *Pall Mall G.* 22 Oct. 10/2 To give their printing contract..to what was known in the trade as an 'unfair house'. **1888** JACOBI *Printers' Vocab.*, *Unfair offices*, this term is applied by society hands generally to those printing offices where the existing scale of prices is not recognized.

3. Of the wind: Unfavourable.
1801 in Nicolas *Disp. Nelson* (1845) IV. 299 If the wind proved fair..they should be sent up the harbour, but if unfair, no time would have been lost. **1802** *Naval Chron.* VIII. 433 The wind being unfair at S.W.

4. Not fitting or corresponding exactly.
1869 SIR E. REED *Shipbuild.* xix. 415 That drifting unfair holes would be considered bad work. **1874** THEARLE *Naval Archit.* 58 Great precautions are..necessary to prevent unfair seams in the subsequent operations of laying the deck.

†**un'fair**, *adv. Obs.* [UN-^{1} 11 b: cf. prec.] In a rough, disorderly, or untidy manner.
a **900** *Genesis* 2063 Gripon unfæȝre under sceat werum scearpe garas. *a* **1400-50** *Alexander* 555 Cloudis clenely to-clefe, clatird vn-faire. *c* **1400** *Destr. Troy* 13891 With the remnond full rade he rixlit unfaire. *c* **1480** HENRYSON *Test. Cres.* 163 Atouir his belt his lyart lokkis lay Felterit vnfair.

un'fair, *v.* [UN-^{2} 6 a.] *trans.* To deprive of fairness or beauty.
c **1600** SHAKS. *Sonn.* v, Those howers..Will play the tirants to the very same, And that vnfaire which fairely doth excell.

un'fairly, *adv.* [UN-^{1} 11.]
1. In an unfair manner; inequitably, unjustly.
1713 BUTLER *Let. to S. Clarke* i. (1716) 8 If I have..in any respect argu'd unfairly, I assure you it was without design. *a* **1768** SECKER *Serm.* (1771) VII. xiii. 283 To use even those unfairly, who have used us so, is very bad: but to use any one unfairly, because Another hath used Us so, is..monstrously wicked. **1796** [see UNDULY 1]. **1848** KINGSLEY *Yeast* ii, Argemone..fancying herself, and not unfairly, very intellectual. **1877** HUXLEY *Physiogr.* 84 It might, therefore, not unfairly be assumed that the carbonic acid..would tend to settle down in a stratum near the ground.

2. By unfair or foul means.
1791 MRS. RADCLIFFE *Rom. Forest* v, There were strong reasons to believe he came unfairly to his end.

un'fairness. [UN-^{1} 12: cf. OE. *unfæȝernes*.] Lack of fairness or equity; injustice.
1713 BENTLEY *Remarks Disc. Free-Think.* xlv. II. 33 We may observe from this Passage..the unfairness and malignity of our Writer. **1796** MME. D'ARBLAY *Camilla* IV. 387 [They] have a certain instinctive sense of its unfairness. **1833** BURTON *Eccl. Hist.* xx. 192 The unfairness which looks for different results in the second century from those which are produced in the nineteenth. **1875** JOWETT *Plato* (ed. 2) IV. 232 He is occasionally playing both parts himself, and even charging his own arguments with unfairness.

un'faith. [UN-^{1} 12.] Lack of faith or belief, esp. in religion.
1415 HOCCLEVE *To Sir J. Oldcastle* 247 For thyn vnfeith men maken many mones. **1826** MISS MITFORD *Village* Ser. II. 272 At the end of one of her daily professions of unfaith in gipsies and their predictions. **1859** TENNYSON *Merl. & V.* 386 Faith and unfaith can ne'er be equal powers: Unfaith in aught is want of faith in all. **1870** SWINBURNE *Ess. & Stud.* (1875) 81 Another form of bastard belief, another cross-breed between faith and unfaith.

un'faithful, *a.* [UN-^{1} 7.]
1. Not having the proper religious faith; infidel, unbelieving. Also *absol.*
1382 WYCLIF *1 Cor.* vii. 12 If ony brothir haue an vnfeithful..wyf, and sche consentith for to dwelle with hym, leue he..hir not. **1388** —— *Ps.* l. 15, I schal teche wickid men thi weies; and vnfeithful men schulen be conuertid to thee. **1456** SIR G. HAYE *Law Arms* (S.T.S.) 106 Thai landis that the unfaithfull men haldis. **1534** MORE *Treat. Passion* Wks. 1341/2 Justinus..writing of our faith in his second Apologye to the vnfaithful Emperour Antonius. **1560** BIBLE (Genev.) *2 Esdras* xv. 4 For euery vnfaithful shal dye in his vnfaithfulnes. **1643-5** MILTON *Divorce* I. viii, The author of a generall divorce between the faithfull and unfaithfull seed. **1667** —— *P.L.* xii. 481 What will betide the few, His faithful, left among th' unfaithful herd, The enemies of truth? **1768-74** TUCKER *Lt. Nat.* (1834) II. 484 Whatever supernatural virtue or nutritive faculty the priest has infused into the bread, are verily..received by the unfaithful. **1800** *Asiat. Ann. Reg.*, *Misc. Tr.* 334/1 Therefore he who follows Mahommedanism and..violates this treaty, so comporting himself like the unfaithful [etc.].

†**b.** Not in accordance with faith; irreligious.
1549 *Compl. Scot.* i. 22 Mony ignorant pepil hes confermit ane ymaginet onfaythtful opinione in ther hede.

2. Not keeping good faith; acting falsely or treacherously. Also *absol.*
c **1400** *Destr. Troy* 714 Vnfaithfull freke, with þi fals cast, Þat such a lady belirt. **1530** PALSGR. 328/1 Unfaythfull of promesse, *desloyal*. **1549** CHEKE *Hurt Sedit.* Lj, Shall they not truly say the subiectes to be more vnfaithfull in disobedience, than other subiects worse ordered be. **1600** SHAKS. *A.Y.L.* IV. i. 199, I will thinke you the most patheticall breake-promise..that may bee chosen out of the grosse band of the vnfaithfull. **1620** in Foster *Eng. Factories Ind.* (1906) I. 209 Theis Pegu factors were fownde to be royotous, vitious and unfaithfull. *a* **1729** CONGREVE *Ovid's Art of Love* III. 63 The prince so far for piety renown'd, To thee, Eliza, was unfaithful found. **1803** WELLESLEY in Owen *Desp.* (1877) 331, I propose to view this transaction as the combined offence of two unfaithful servants. **1832** HT. MARTINEAU *Demerara* iii. 35, I should be unfaithful if I had ever promised either.

b. *transf.* Of things.
a **1586** SIDNEY *Arcadia* III. xii, The unfaythfull armour yeelding to the swoordes strong-guided sharpenesse. **1615** G. SANDYS *Trav.* 2 A sea tempestuous and unfaithfull, at an instant incensed with sudden gusts. **1669** DRYDEN *Tyrannic Love* I. i, I..Did first the depth of trembling Marshes sound, And fix'd my Eagles in unfaithful ground. **1726** LEONI *Alberti's Archit.* I. 35 Sea-sand..is..unfaithful in supporting great Weights. **1779** SHERIDAN *Monody on Garrick* 14 As Fancy, oft,..Has view'd by shadowy Eve's unfaithful Gloom, A weeping Cherub on a Martyr's Tomb. **1831** JAMES *Phil. Augustus* I. v, One of those people whose lips—those ever unfaithful guardians of the treasures of the heart—are peculiarly apt to murmur..unconsciously. **1842** TENNYSON *Love & Duty* 91 With quiet eyes unfaithful to the truth.

c. Not following an original, not translating or translated, faithfully; incorrect, inexact.
a **1697** AUBREY *Lives* (1898) II. 174 He was a learned man, ..but is much blamed for his unfaithfull quotations. **1724** A. COLLINS *Gr. Chr. Relig.* 163 The Septuagint seems the work both of ignorant and unfaithful Translators. **1776** MICKLE tr. *Camoens' Lusiad* Introd. 130 The unfaithful and unpoetical version [of the Lusiad] of Fanshaw. **1798** FERRIAR *Illustr. Sterne*, etc. 91 Burton has spoiled this passage by an unfaithful translation. **1855** MACAULAY *Hist. Eng.* xix. IV. 332 An unfaithful interpreter of the sense of the nation. **1864** PUSEY *Lect. Daniel* 379 To which act this writer probably alluded in his unfaithful paraphrase, 'chrism shall be removed'.

d. *spec.* Not faithful in wedlock.
1828 WEBSTER s.v., An unfaithful husband or wife. **1841** W. SPALDING *Italy & It. Isl.* II. 147 Galeotto Manfredi,..having married Francesca Bentivoglio,..not only was unfaithful to her, but treated her with cruelty.

3. Of conduct: Characterized by want of good faith; not honest or upright.
1565 COOPER s.v. *Perfidia*, To be deceiued by ones treacherie and vnfaithfull dealing. *Ibid.* s.v. *Infidus*, An vnfaithfull league that will not long be kepte. **1651** JER. TAYLOR *Serm. for Year* xxiii. 292 Lying or craftinesse, and unfaithfull usages, robs a man of the honour of his soul. **1680** OTWAY *Orphan* IV. vi, I might think with Justice most severely Of this unfaithful dealing with your Brother. **1704** TRAPP *Abra-Mulé* II. i. 451 Spies..who for hope Of a Reward, will give the Sultan notice Of such unfaithful Dealing. **1866** GEO. ELIOT *F. Holt* v, Your father..was, as I understand, a man whose walk was not unfaithful.

un'faithfully, *adv.* [UN-^{1} 11.] In an unfaithful manner; with lack of good faith.
1340-70 *Alisaunder* 239 And Philip unfaithfully þe faire coste had, Arisba in exile euer was after. **1491** *Act 7 Hen. VII*, c. 22 *Preamble*, The seid John unfeithfully and untruly suffred the bringer of the seid writing to goo at his plesure. *c* **1545** LD. MORLEY *Hyst. Massuccio* fol. 2 b, You haue been vnfaithefully, vniustly and falsely [accused]. **1579** E. K. *Spenser's Sheph. Cal.* June, Argt., He is nowe forsaken vnfaithfully. **1607-12** BACON *Ess.*, *Counsel* (Arb.) 316 The daunger of being vnfaithfullie councelled. **1679** EVERARD *Popish Plot* 5 Sir Robert most unfaithfully..discovered all to Colonel Talbot. **1722** WOLLASTON *Relig. Nat.* vi. §19 (1724) 144 He, who acts unfaithfully, acts against his promises and ingagements.

un'faithfulness. [UN-^{1} 12.]
†**1.** Lack of faith; infidelity. *Obs.*
1388 WYCLIF *2 Tim.* ii. 16 But eschewe thou vnhooli and veyn spechis, for whi tho profiten myche to vnfeithfulnesse. **1395** PURVEY *Remonstr.* (1851) 61 Unfeithful men that shulen be dampnid uttirli..if thei dien in unfeithfulnesse. **1526** *Pilgr. Perf.* (W. de W. 1531) 129 Therof foloweth somtyme infidelite or vnfaythfulnes. **1561** T. NORTON *Calvin's Inst.* I. 56 Whoso therfore wil beware of this vnfaithfulnesse, let him kepe alwayes in remembrance [etc.].

2. The quality of being unfaithful; lack of good faith or fidelity.
c **1480** HENRYSON *Test. Cres.* 570 Traisting in vther als greit vnfaithfulnes, Als vnconstant, and als vntrew of fay. **1532** in Ellis *Orig. Lett.* Ser. III. II. 251 As towchinge the onfaythfulnes..of Father Forest, I dyd wryte of unto my Lady Marcas of Penbroke. **1590** SWINBURNE *Testaments* 218 So the legataries and children of the deceased are often defrauded..by the vnfaithfulnesse of the executor. **1685** BAXTER *Paraphr. N.T.* Matt. xxv. 26-27 Unprofitableness and omission of duty, is damnable unfaithfulness in us that are but Stewards and Servants. **1737** in *10th Rep. Hist. MSS. Comm.* App. I. 493 It contains a clear Proof of the Unfaithfullness of a Person in whom Your Majesty has placed a Trust. **1752** CARTE *Hist. Eng.* III. 14 Henry was in the height of his resentment, at the unfaithfulness of his allies. **1842** J. B. FRASER *Allee Neemroo* II. 31 If you impute to me any unfaithfulness towards you, I swear that you are deceived. **1881** R. W. CHURCH *Cathedral & Univ. Serm.* v. (1892) 59 The taint..of insincerities, of treacheries, of unfaithfulnesses to light.

b. *spec.* (Cf. UNFAITHFUL *a.* 2 d.)
1848 THACKERAY *Van. Fair* lxvi, Is it unfaithfulness to my husband? I scorn it and defy anybody to prove it. **1851** FROUDE *Short Stud.* (1867) II. 191 Nor, again, was unfaithfulness..conclusively fatal against a wife.

†**unfaken**, *a.*: see UN-^{1} 2.

unfa'llacious, *a.* (UN-^{1} 7, 5 b.)
1802-12 BENTHAM *Ration. Judic. Evid.* (1827) IV. 490 Shutting the door against an article of true and unfallacious evidence.

unfa'llaciously, *adv.* (UN-^{1} 11.)
1852 BAGEHOT *Lit. Stud.* (1879) I. 69 Pope unfallaciously said, 'Once a heretic, always a heretic'.

un'fallen, *ppl. a.* [UN-^{1} 8 b. Cf. G. *ungefallen*, ON. *úfallinn* (Norw. dial. *ufallen*).]
1. Not morally fallen.
1653 H. MORE *Conject. Cabbal.* ii. 41 The natures..of the fallen and unfallen Angels, or good and bad Genii. **1679** J. C[HENEY] *Vind. Oaths & Swearing* 7 In Paradise it self,.. while man was innocent and unfallen. **1740** CHEYNE *Regimen* 129 This..must be the Constitution..of the unfallen angelical State. **1825** COLERIDGE *Aids Refl.* (1848) I. 242 We may say, that in the unfallen rational agent, the will constitutes the law. **1848** KINGSLEY *Yeast* vi, Who am I to demand her all to myself? Her, the glorious, the saintly, the unfallen!
fig. **1759** YOUNG *Conject. Orig. Composition* 60 What we mean by Blank verse, is verse unfallen, uncurst.

2. Not fallen (in literal sense).
1735 SOMERVILLE *Chase* I. 116 Fix'd as a mountain ash, that braves the bolts Of angry Jove; tho' blasted, yet unfall'n. **1878** GILDER *Poet & Master* 29 It was I who behold the sun's level light strike through the unfallen.. leaves.

Hence **un'fallenness.**
1876 W. BATHGATE *Deep Things of God* v. 79 A peerless perfect man,—albeit entirely Divine in his unfallenness.

†**un'fallible**, *a. Obs.* [UN-^{1} 7 and 5 b.] = INFALLIBLE *a.* (Common *c* 1530-1620.)
1529 MORE *Dyaloge* I. Wks. 168/2 If ye will..take a sure and vnfallyble way ye must..beleue and obey the churche. **1545** BRINKLOW *Compl.* 5 b, It is certen and vnfallible, that if we knock,..we shal be hard. **1592** R. D. *Hypnerotomachia* 82 b, Disposing my selfe to her sweete loue, with an unfallyble, obstinate, and firme resolution. **1614** LATHAM *Falconry* 68 These my friendlie admonitions, being grounded vpon the absolute truth of vnfallible experience. **1653** BLITHE *Eng. Improver Impr.* 145 A very Excellent Unfallible Remedy against Barrenness.

†**un'fallibly**, *adv. Obs.* [UN-^{1} 11 and 5 b.] = INFALLIBLY *adv.*
1542 UDALL *Erasm. Apoph.* 32 b, A feloe..who professed ..to bee hable unfallibly..to fynd out & iudge the naturall disposicion of any manne. **1567** DRANT *Horace, Ep.* I. i. C iij, The wyseman ames vnfalliblie. **1604** HIERON *Wks.* I. 547 A christian man may bee vnfallibly certaine of his saluation in his owne conscience. **1642** ROGERS *Naaman* 44 The Lord.. beholds the effecting of the one, in the other, necessarily and unfallibly.

†**un'fallid**, *a.* *Obs.*$^{-1}$ [UN-^{1} 7 and 5 b: see INFALLID *a.*] Infallible.

1624 HEYWOOD *Captives* IV. i. in Bullen *O. Pl.* IV, By these tokens, These of her childhood most unfallid signes, I knowe her for my doughter.

un'fallowed, *ppl. a.* (UN-^{1} 8.)

1607 J. CARPENTER *Plaine Mans Plough* 102 Why man..is likened to the Earth, or to the unfallowed Land. **1634** RAINBOW *Labour* (1635) 40 Let not us bee that unfallowed ground where the Divell may sowe his tares. **1708** J. PHILIPS *Cyder* I. 549 Th' unfallow'd Glebe Yearly o'ercomes the Granaries with Store Of Golden Wheat.

un'falsified, *ppl. a.* (UN-^{1} 8.)

1687 MIÈGE II. s.v., Provided the Account be true and unfalsify'd. **1855** LEWIS *Cred. Early Rom. Hist.* xiv. §2. II. 491 The current story..has descended..in a substantially unfalsified state.

un'faltering, *ppl. a.* (UN-^{1} 10.)

1727 THOMSON *Summer* 299 With unfaltering accent to conclude That This availeth nought? **1744** AKENSIDE *Pleas. Imag.* I. 163 Thro' the tossing tide of chance and pain To hold his course unfaltering. **1825** SCOTT *Betrothed* xxix, He tells me of it with..an eye composed, an unfaltering tongue. **1862** 'SHIRLEY' (J. Skelton) *Nugæ Crit.* v. 233 The confident and unfaltering witness of the strong man, who goes to the stake with..a sense of triumph in his heart.

So **un'falteringly** *adv.*

1665 BOYLE *Occas. Refl.* I. iv. 169 Unfaultringly to traverse Adversitie's rough ways. **1850** MRS. SARAH ELLIS *Pique* (1875) 269 Lady Catherine turned away, and.. unfalteringly approached the door. **1885** *Manch. Exam.* 9 Sept. 3/2 A character who is at once vividly human..and unfalteringly noble.

un'famed, *ppl. a.* (UN-^{1} 8.)

1606 SHAKS. *Tr. & Cr.* II. ii. 159 There's..none so Noble, Whose life were ill bestow'd, or death vnfam'd, Where Helen is the subiect. **1724** A. HILL *Prol. to Savage's Sir T. Overbury* p. xi, Young, and unfam'd, and but by Hope inspir'd. **1855** SINGLETON *Virgil* II. 346 Thus laid aside, unfamed here let him pass His life. **1887** HISSEY *Holiday on Road* 156 Some few whose names and deeds will dwell a little longer than the unfamed rest.

unfa'miliar, *a.* (UN-^{1} 7.)

1594 HOOKER *Eccl. Pol.* I. i. §2 The matters which we handle seeme by reason of newnesse..darke, intricate, and vnfamiliar. **1648** HERRICK *Hesper.*, *Oberons Feast* 4 Because thou prizest things that are Curious, and unfamiliar. *c* **1698** LOCKE *Cond. Underst.* §32 (1754) 127 Abstruse and unfamiliar ideas which the mind is not yet thoroughly accustomed to. **1753** WARTON *Obs. Spenser's F.Q.* 141 It must be confest that his uncouth or rather unfamiliar language has deterr'd many from perusing him. **1829** LYTTON *Devereux* III. vi, His face did not seem unfamiliar to me. **1848** DICKENS *Dombey* xlix, Looking without interest or recognition at the unfamiliar walls around her. **1891** FARRAR *Darkn. & Dawn* xli, When Onesimus recovered full consciousness he did not recognise his unfamiliar surroundings.

Hence **unfa'miliarness**.

1881 *Times* 17 May 4/6 A multitude of little changes of this kind..arouse a general sense of unfamiliarness.

unfamili'arity. (UN-^{1} 12 and 5 b.)

1755 JOHNSON *Dict.* Pref. C 2 How shall it be..recalled again..when it has once by disuse become unfamiliar, and by unfamiliarity unpleasing. **1861** MILL *Repr. Govt.* (1865) 62/2 The only serious obstacle is the unfamiliarity... But unfamiliarity is a disadvantage which..it only requires time to remove. **1880** MUIRHEAD *Gaius* IV. §16 *note*, An inaccuracy, due..to his unfamiliarity with a procedure that had become a mere matter of history.

unfa'miliarized, *ppl. a.* (UN-^{1} 8.)

1775 S. J. PRATT *Liberal Opin.* xcvii. (1783) III. 211 Whenever the eye is struck with scenes to which it is unfamiliarised. **1817** COLERIDGE *Lay Serm.* 109 The plan itself would, I suspect, startle an unfamiliarized conscience. **1847-8** DE QUINCEY *Protestantism* Wks. 1858 VIII. 163 The gay mythologic religion of Greece..; that of Egypt, more revolting to unfamiliarised sensibilities.

un'famous, *a.* [UN-^{1} 7 and 5 b.]

1. Not famous; unrenowned.

c **1384** CHAUCER *H. Fame* III. 56 Of the lettres oon or two Was molte away of euery name, So vnfamouse was wox hir fame. *a* **1560** PHAER *Æneid* x. D d 2 b, Let him dwell there, Vnfamous, free from wars, and honourlesse lead out his age. **1980** R. CONNOLLY *Sunday Kind of Woman* xxiii. 162 The former escort of a couple of unfamous film stars.

†**2.** Infamous, ill-famed. *Obs.*

c **1380** WYCLIF *Sel. Wks.* III. 357 Bi þes two unfamous lawes mai men wite whiche ben oþir. *c* **1489** CAXTON *Blanchardyn* xlviii. 186 Olde vnfamouse myschaunt, how arte thou soo folyshe..as for to wene to haue her. **1530** PALSGR. 328/1 Unfamouse, yvell named, *infame*. **1596** D. BLACK in Calderwood *Hist. Kirk Scot.* (1678) 337 To compear and answer for certain unreverent, unfamous and undecent speeches.

unfa'natical, *a.* (UN-^{1} 7.)

1826 COLERIDGE in *Lit. Rem.* (1836) III. 52 The prudential morals..that have characterized the unfanatical clergy since the Revolution in 1688. **1828** J. T. RUTT in *Burton's Diary* IV. 441 *note*, The signatures are 164, all quite unfanatical.

un'fanciable, *a.* (UN-^{1} 7 b.)

1669 EARL ORRERY *Parthen.* (1676) 796, I could not hinder myself from saying in unfanciable Transports [etc.].

un'fancied, *ppl. a.* (UN-^{1} 8.)

1655 EARL ORRERY *Parthen.* I. I. 14 So many unfancy'd joyes disclose themselves. **1771** KELLY *Clementina* v. 62 Hence with his more than crocodile complaining,..Let him teach tears of yet unfancy'd falshood. **1840** BROWNING *Sordello* I. 232 Till some growth, Unfancied yet, exuberantly clothe A surface solid now. **1922** *Daily Mail* 3 Nov. 11 By turns the favourite, Flaming Sword, and Solace, a not unfancied 9 to 1 chance, put up a challenge. **1937** E. RICKMAN *On & Off Race-course* i. 8 Horses who..are not seriously expected..to win, are said to be 'unfancied'.

un'fanciful, *a.* (UN-^{1} 7.)

1815 L. HUNT *Feast Poets*, etc. 48 There is something not inelegant or unfanciful in the conduct of Mr. Hayley's Triumphs of Temper. **1839** G. DARLEY *Beaum. & Fletcher's Wks.* (Rtldg.) p. xxiv, Ambitious fustian,.. unfanciful extravagance.

un'fankle, *v.* *Sc.* [UN-^{2} 4 b.] *trans.* To unfetter, set free.

1824 MACTAGGART *Gallovid. Encycl.* 113 The auld fowk left now closer draw, O' care their sauls unfankle.

un'fanned, *ppl. a.* (UN-^{1} 8.)

1764 GOLDSM. *Trav.* 222 Their level life is but a mouldering fire, Unquench'd by want, unfann'd by strong desire. **1816** SCOTT *Old Mort.* xxxvii, Their zeal, unfanned by persecution, died gradually away.

unfan'tastic, *a.* (UN-^{1} 7.)

1794 T. TAYLOR *Plotinus* Introd. p. xxv, Nature operates without knowledge in an unphantastic manner. **1842** LYTTON *Zanoni* 22 His wife was a daughter of quiet, sober, and unfantastic England. **1871** PALGRAVE *Lyr. Poems* 2 That unfantastic strain, Void of weak fever and self-conscious cry,..What modern hand can try?

unfan'tastical, *a.* (UN-^{1} 7.)

[**1775** ASH.] **1862** R. H. PATTERSON *Ess. Hist. & Art* 334 In any common-sense and unfantastical view of the matter.

un'farced, *ppl. a.* (UN-^{1} 8.)

1725 *Fam. Dict.* s.v. *Potage*, They may be garnish'd with farc'd or unfarc'd Lettice. **1775** ASH, *Unfarced*.., not farced, not stuffed. **1890** CHILD *Ballads* IV. 232/2 C is a briefer, that is, an unfarced, form of B.

un'farcical, *a.* (UN-^{1} 7.)

1850 L. HUNT *Autobiog.* x. II. 25 Some of these comic actors..are as unfarcical as can be imagined in their interior.

†**un'fardle**, *v.* *Obs.* [UN-^{2} 4 b.] *trans.* To unload, unburden, discharge.

1599 NASHE *Lenten Stuffe* H 3, Our Fisherman.. vnfardled to the King his whole sachel of wonders. **1706** STEVENS I, *Desenfardelar*, to unfardle, to unpack.

unfare'welled, *a.* (UN-^{1} 9.)

1704 D'URFEY *Abrad. & Panth.* i. 15 The pangs she feels To part unfarwell'd to his gloomy cells, From her lov'd Abradate.

un'faring, *ppl. a.* *Obs.* exc. *Sc.* Also *Sc.* 6 **onfarrand**, 9 **on-**, **unfarrant**. [UN-^{1} 10.] Unattractive, unpleasant. Also †**un'faringly** *adv.* *Obs.*

1513 DOUGLAS *Æneid* IX. ix. 52 Wyth drawin swerd in hand, And quhite targat, onsemly and onfarrand. **1519** HORMAN *Vulg.* 57 b, He went with an vnfaryng chere [L. *vultu abducto*]. *Ibid.*, He loked vnfaryngly [L. *truci fuit aspectu*]. *c* **1530** tr. *Erasmus' Serm. Ch. Jesus* (1901) 38 So that it, whiche a lytle to fore semed unfaryinge, waxeth amyable: whiche semed amyable, waxeth vnfarynge. **1818** HOGG *Hunt of Eildon* ii, O, man, ye're an unfarrant beast! **1887** *Suppl. Jamieson* 179 An orfarant body.

unfarme, var. UNFERME *a.* *Obs.*

un'farming, *ppl. a.* (UN-^{1} 10.)

1797 J. WHITAKER in Polwhele *Trad. & Recoll.* (1826) II. 469, I have had cares and anxieties,..that you un-farming divines can hardly conceive.

unfarrant, Sc. variant of UNFARING *ppl. a.*

un'farrowed, *ppl. a.* (UN-^{2} 4, 8.)

1842 TENNYSON *Walking to Mail* 92 We took them all, till she was left.., the Niobe of swine, And so return'd unfarrow'd to her sty.

un'fashion, *sb.* (UN-^{1} 12.)

1822 GALT *Sir A. Wylie* xxv, I have fallen in, notwithstanding the unfashion of my apparel, with some creditable acquaintance. **1876** MISS YONGE *Womankind* xiii, Sunday-schools were the fashion of one generation, then the unfashion.

un'fashion, *v.* [UN-^{2} 4.] *trans.* To undo the fashion or make of.

1569 J. SANFORD tr. *Agrippa's Van. Artes* 170 b, They rente our Sauioure Christe in peeces,..and..do facion and vnfacion him vnto what forme they liste. **1580** LUPTON *Sivqila* 23 Man..doth so disorder and unfashion himselfe, that you wyll not take hym that was laste yeare, to be hymselfe thys yeare. **1611** SPEED *Hist. Gt. Brit.* IX. ii. §10 They to curry fauour with the Normans..altogether vnfashioned themselues to imitate them. **1631** QUARLES *Samson* Wks. (Grosart) II. 149/1 Our sinfull usage does unfashion What heaven hath made, and makes a new creation.

un'fashionable, *a.* and *sb.* [UN-^{1} 7 b, 5 b.]

†**1.** Incapable of being fashioned or shaped; not admitting of a material form. *Obs.*

1563 MAN *Musculus' Commonpl.* 47 They doe sinne in that they set forth to the invisible and unfashionable God an image of an olde man with a hore beard. **1607** HIERON *Wks.* I. 236 Thou, beeing a builder, when a stone breakes or is vnfashionable, throwest it from thee.

†**2.** Badly shaped or formed. *Obs.*

1594 SHAKS. *Rich. III*, I. i. 22 Scarse halfe made vp, And that so lamely and vnfashionable, That dogges barke at me, as I halt by them. **1611** SPEED *Hist. Gt. Brit.* VI. v. §6. 58 He was of stature tall, of complexion pale and wan, of body somewhat grosse and vnfashionable. **1638** STRAFFORD *Lett.* (1739) II. 197 The Pikes short and ill-headed, their Arms unfashionable and very little good. **1663** COWLEY *Cutter Coleman St.* Pref., The slight Reparations..of an Old and unfashionable Building.

3. Of actions, conduct, etc.: Not in accordance with the prevailing fashion.

1648 BOYLE *Seraph. Love* (1659) 158 As Unfashionable as such a Profession may seem in a Gentleman not yet two and Twenty. **1693** LOCKE *Educ.* §70 All the Actions of Childishness, and unfashionable Carriage, and whatever Time and Age will of it self be sure to reform. **1759** JOHNSON *Idler* No. 48 ¶8 They give the mind an unfashionable cast. **1776** ADAM SMITH *W.N.* I. ix. (1869) I. 101 It is there [*sc.* in Holland] unfashionable not to be a man of business. **1843** BETHUNE *Sc. Fireside Stor.* 16 She had herself been bred in the country where unfashionable revels of this kind are quite common.

4. Of persons: Not following the current fashion; not living in a fashionable way.

1660 F. BROOKE tr. *Le Blanc's Trav.* 340 These unfashionable Doctors had mind on nothing but to satisfie their insatiable avarice. **1693** CONGREVE in *Dryden's Juvenal* XI. (1697) 290 Then, that Unfashionable Man am I, With me they'd starve for want of Ivory. **1704** STEELE *Tender Husb.* v. i, Let me come at the intruder on ladies' private hours—the unfashionable monster! **1766** [ANSTEY] *Bath Guide* i. 70 When Sim, unfashionable Ninny, In public calls me Cousin Jenny. **1865** DICKENS *Mut. Fr.* I. ix, They sat side by side, a hopelessly Unfashionable pair. **1890** *Spectator* 16 Aug., Far from the madding crowd of fashionable or unfashionable society.

b. *sb.* An unfashionable person.

1822 [LADY BLESSINGTON] *Magic Lantern* 19 The crowds ..tempted me to stroll into that gay *rendezvous* of fashionables, as well as unfashionables. **1831** *Westm. Rev.* XIV. 436 The fashionables are almost uniformly witty and agreeable, the unfashionables stupid and disagreeable.

Hence **un'fashionableness**.

1693 LOCKE *Educ.* §184 Natural Unfashionableness being much better than apish, affected Postures. **1884** *Contemp. Rev.* July 102 All that people will see in this latter sort of work..will be its shapelessness, *plus* its unfashionableness.

un'fashionably, *adv.* [UN-^{1} 11.] In an unfashionable manner; at variance with the prevailing fashion; so as to be unfashionable.

1621 LADY M. WROTH *Urania* 122 Assuredly more there was of this Song, or else she had with her vnframed and vnfashioned thoughts, as vnfashionably fram'd these lines. **1683** OLDHAM *Wks.* (1686) 99 That sniveling Puritan, who spite of all the mode Would be unfashionably good. *a* **1704** T. BROWN tr. *Sylvius' Death Lucretia* Wks. 1709 III. II. 84 At thy Work among thy Maids unfashionably busy. **1797** J. LAWRENCE in *Monthly Mag.* XLVIII. 490, I..am most unfashionably unacquainted with all..the great post-roads and cross-roads. **1871** *Figure Training* 50 Her waist is not only unfashionably, but..almost disproportionately large.

un'fashioned, *ppl. a.* [UN-^{1} 8.]

1. Not wrought into form or shape.

1538 ELYOT, *Ineffigiatus*, vnfacyoned, withoute good proporcyon. **1561** T. NORTON *Calvin's Inst.* I. 38 When Moses sheweth that the very vnfashioned lump [of the world] was susteined in him [*sc.* the Spirit]. **1635** DONNE *Elegy* xv. 97 Countlesse multitudes Of formlesse curses, projects unmade up, Abuses yet unfashion'd. **1669** STURMY *Mariner's Mag.* b j, Go forth, thou shapeless Embryon of my Brain, Unfashion'd as thou art. **1712** *Spect.* No. 554 ¶9 Many a good natural Genius is lost, or lies unfashioned, like a Jewel in the Mine. **1764** GOLDSM. *Trav.* 330, I see the lords of human kind pass by.., By forms unfashion'd, fresh from Nature's hand. **1848** T. AIRD *Winter Day, Evening* 24 A cloudy confluence of unfashioned light.

†**2.** Not refined or polished; not made elegant or fashionable: **a.** Of persons. *Obs.*

1606 DANIEL *Queen's Arcadia* 2509 Worthier people too, of subtler spirits, Then these vnfashion'd and vncomb'd rude swaines. **1673** DRYDEN *Marr. à la Mode* II. i, An unfashioned untravelled mere Sicilian is a *bête*. **1711** STEELE *Spect.* No. 154 ¶2 A sober modest Man was always looked upon by both Sexes as a precise unfashioned Fellow. **1821** MAR. & R. L. EDGEWORTH *Mem.* I. 75 She was a plump goodnatured unfashioned girl, with little knowledge of any sort and no accomplishments.

†**b.** Of things. *Obs.*

1630 J. TAYLOR (Water P.) *Water Cormorant* Wks. III. 6/2 That Muld-Sack for his most vnfashion'd fashions Is the fit patterne of their transformations. **1670** DRYDEN *1st Pt. Conq. Granada* III. i, There's something roughly noble there, Which, in unfashion'd Nature, looks Divine. **1695** J. EDWARDS *Perfect. Script.* 436 Illiterate, blunt, unfashion'd language.

un'fast, *a.* Now *rare*. Also 4 **unfest(e**. [OE. *unfæst* (UN-^{1} 7), = WFris. *on-*, *ûnfest*, MDu. and Du. *onvast*, MHG. *unvast*, MDa. *ufast*; OHG. *unfesti*, *-vesti* (MHG. *unveste*, G. *unfest*).]

1. Insecure.

c **888** K. ÆLFRED *Boeth.* xi. §2 For þæm þe æȝþer is unfæst, ȝe seo wyrd ȝe seo ȝesælð. *c* **897** —— *Gregory's Past. C.* 37. *a* **1300** *E.E. Psalter* xvii. 40 Þou tobreddest mi gainges under me, And mi steppes noght unfest þai be. *Ibid.* xxvi. 4 Mi faas þat are, þai are unfest and felle sare. **13..** *Prose Psalter* cviii. 23 (Dubl. MS.), Myn knowes beþ vnfast for fastyng. *c* **1584** T. MATHEW *Let.* in *Life Sir C. Hatton* (1847) 407 You be not the first, Sir,..that have found both friends unfast and neighbours unthankful. **1818** TODD, *Unfast*, not safe; not secure. **1883** R. W. DIXON *Mano* I. xiv. 45 Ah, could he but have rent shame's unfast cloak, And seen her heart.

2. Not close or tight.

1648 HEXHAM II. s.v. *Leken*, To Leake as unfast Vessels.

Hence **un'fastness**, want of firmness. *rare.*

1398 TREVISA *Barth. De P.R.* XVII. cl. (Bodl. MS.), Þat treen beþ scharp with pikes & þornes..comeþ of vnfastenes & vnsadnes of þe tre. **1616** T. ADAMS *Forest of Thorns* Wks.

(1629) 1055 Hee would haue it [*sc.* thorniness] caused by the insoliditie and vnfastnesse of the Tree.

†**un'fast**, *v. dial. Obs.* [UN-² 3.] = next.
1684 MERITON *Yorksh. Ale* Gloss. 112 To unfest is to untye or unloose.

un'fasten, *v.* Also 4 **onvestne**, 5 **onfestyn**. [UN-² 3 and 7.]
1. *trans.* **a.** To unfix; to deprive of firmness or fixity; to make loose or slack. Also *absol.*
a **1225** *Ancr. R.* 252 Al his attente is uorte unuestnen heorten & fort to binimen luue, þet halt men togederes. **1382** WYCLIF *Isaiah* xiv. 27 The Lord forsothe of ostes demede, and who shal moun vnfastnen? **1532** HERVET *Xenophon's Househ.* 55 b, Els the sonne dryinge the erthe away from the rootes of the plante, shulde lewse and vnfasten it, and so kyll it. **1597** SHAKS. *2 Hen. IV*, IV. i. 209 Plucking to vnfixe an Enemie, Hee doth vnfasten so, and shake a friend. **1698** ATTERBURY *Serm.* (1737) IV. 316 He must take care not to.. come within reach of anything that may anyways unfasten his resolutions. **1736** CARTE *Ormonde* II. 373 The design of this proposal was, first to unfasten him, and then to lay him totally aside.
b. To detach; to undo or release.
c **1440** *Promp. Parv.* 365/1 Onfestyn, *idem quod* on losyn. *a* **1586** SIDNEY *Arcadia* II. viii, He had no sooner unfastned his hold, but that a wave forcibly spoiled his weaker hand of hold. **1633** T. JAMES *Voy.* 14 We vnfastened our Ship, and came to saile. **1667** MILTON *P.L.* II. 879 Then.. every Bolt and Bar Of massie Iron or sollid Rock with ease [she] Unfast'ns. **1797** MRS. RADCLIFFE *Italian* xii, We will see whether my key cannot unfasten all the locks that hold it. **1862** MISS BRADDON *Lady Audley* vii, Lady Audley was standing unfastening her dress. *a* **1873** LYTTON in *Life & Lett.* (1883) I. 289 The man began to unfasten the boat.
fig. **1655** tr. *Sorel's Com. Hist. Francion* II. 29 She.. prayed me to come to her house as soon as I could unfasten my self from my Mistresse. **1840** BROWNING *Sordello* I. 15 Not the more Is he unfastened from the earnest eyes Because that arras fell between! **1860** WARTER *Sea-board* II. 459 Unfastening, as it were, the links that bound the people to their Parish Church.
2. *intr.* To become detached or loose; to open; *fig.* to separate.
c **1315** SHOREHAM *Poems* I. 2093 Nou lestne: ȝef þe oþer oþren so by-swykeþ, No moȝe hy nouȝt onuestne. *c* **1430** *Pilgr. Lyf Manhode* I. cxxvi. (1869) 67 The bocle holt and keepeth faste the girdel that it vnfastne nouht. **1865** SWINBURNE *Atalanta* 91 From this time.. My lips shall not unfasten till I die. **1963** [see DEPRESSURIZE *v.*].

un'fastenable, *a.* (UN-¹ 7 b.)
1880 *Blackw. Mag.* Mar. 377/1 A belt not always unfastenable in a moment.

un'fastened, *ppl. a.* (UN-¹ 8.)
1587 GOLDING *De Mornay* xxiii. 401 The Image of Serapis hung vnfastened in the ayre. **1611** SPEED *Theat. Gt. Brit.* (1614) 132/2 An Iland that removeth from place to place, as the winde forceth her spongeous and unfastened body. **1794** MRS. RADCLIFFE *Myst. Udolpho* xli, She asked the housekeeper whether she was certain no door had been left unfastened. **1861** GEO. ELIOT *Silas M.* iv, Where could he be.. on such an evening, leaving.. his door unfastened? **1897** MRS. E. L. VOYNICH *Gadfly* (1904) 69/2 The unfastened sleeve fell back, showing a series of.. scars covering the arm.

unfa'stidious, *a.* (UN-¹ 7.)
1815 JANE AUSTEN *Emma* x, So prosing—so undistinguishing and unfastidious. **1822** LAMB *Elia* I. *Decay of Beggars*, Well fare the soul of unfastidious Vincent Bourne! **1865** *Sat. Rev.* 4 Feb. 141/2 An unfastidious taste is not offended by its style.
Hence **unfa'stidiousness**.
1881 GRANT WHITE *Eng. Without & Within* 476 None the less, however, was I puzzled to account for the unfastidiousness of palate.

un'fathered, *a.*¹ [UN-¹ 9.]
1. Having no (known or acknowledged) father; illegitimate.
1597 SHAKS. *2 Hen. IV*, IV. iv. 122 The people feare me: for they doe obserue Vnfather'd Heires, and loathly Births of Nature. **1726** POPE *Odyss.* XIX. 187 Thy port asserts thee of distinguish'd race; No poor unfather'd product of disgrace. **1856** MRS. BROWNING *Aur. Leigh* VII. 327 Marian's babe, her poor unfathered child. **1874** TROLLOPE *Lady Anna* i, She would be a penniless unmarried female with a daughter, her child would be unfathered and base.
2. Unfatherly. *rare*⁻¹.
1778 LANGHORNE *Owen of Carron* XVIII. 2 And Moray, with unfather'd Eyes,.. Attends his human Sacrifice, Without the Grecian Painter's Veil.
3. Of obscure origin; unauthenticated.
1830 DE QUINCEY *Bentley* Wks. 1863 VI. 55 Unfathered rumours, rumours unacknowledged and untraceable. **1888** BRYCE *Amer. Commw.* III. ci. 419 Men are.. therefore ready to trust their own fancies or some unfathered tale.

un'fathered, *a.*² [UN-² 4, 8.] Deprived of a father; made fatherless.
a **1586** SIDNEY *Arcadia* III. xvii, Iole had her owne father killed by Hercules.. & yet ere long this.. unfathered Lady could sportfully put on the Lions skin. *c* **1600** SHAKS. *Sonn.* cxxiv, Yf my deare loue were but the childe of state, It might for fortunes basterd be vnfathered.

un'fatherlike, *a.* or *adv.* (UN-¹ 7 c.)
1610 HEYWOOD *Gold. Age* III. i, Haue not these ruthlesse and remorselesse eyes (Vn-father-like) beheld their panting hearts?

un'fatherly, *a.* [UN-¹ 7. Cf. Du. *onvaderlijk*, MHG. and G. *unväterlich*, Da. *ufaderlig*, MSw. *ofaderelik*; also OE. *unfæderlíce* adv.] Unbefitting a father.
1621 J. TAYLOR (Water P.) *Unnatural Father* Wks. (1630) 138/1 So hee performed his last vnfatherly deed vpon her. **1621** LADY M. WROTH *Urania* 209 To trie, if by his vnfatherly tortures, shee may bee wrought to leaue louing you. **1784** COWPER *Tiroc.* 866 Nature, pulling at thine heart, Condemns th' unfatherly, th' imprudent part. **1944** S. BELLOW *Dangling Man* 20 It might be considered unmanly or unfatherly to fall sick.
Hence **un'fatherliness**.
1850 L. HUNT *Autobiog.* xxv. III. 285 No hell. No unfatherliness. No monstrous exactions of assent to the incredible.

un,fathoma'bility. (UN-¹ 12; cf. next.)
1866 CARLYLE *Remin.* (1881) II. 331 To my private self his divine reflections and unfathomabilities seemed stinted.. and uncertain.

un'fathomable, *a.* [UN-¹ 7 b.]
1. *fig.* Of feelings, qualities, conditions, etc.: Incapable of being fully ascertained, explored, exhausted, etc.
1617 COLLINS *Def. Bp. Ely* II. ix. 404 Who are you then to gage hearts, which Hieremy sayes are vnfaddomable. **1663** BP. PATRICK *Parab. Pilgr.* xxvii, Thy Goodness is unfathomable, else we should have sunk long before this beyond the depth of it. **1719** YOUNG *Busiris* V. i, An earnest Of vast unfathomable woes to come. **1768–74** TUCKER *Lt. Nat.* (1834) I. 119 What their real sentiments may be I shall not pretend to guess, for they are an unfathomable sort of people. **1802–12** BENTHAM *Ration. Judic. Evid.* (1827) II. 315 Subjected to an unfathomable mass of punishment. **1850** THACKERAY *Pendennis* iv, Her eyes.. shone with tenderness and mystery unfathomable. **1891** MEREDITH *One of our Conq.* xxvi, Lady Cantor spoke to her of Dudley's unfathomable gloom.
2. Incapable of being fathomed or measured; unsoundable, immeasurable, vast:
a. Of space (esp. in depth).
a **1676** HALE *Prim. Orig. Man.* II. vii. (1677) 187 Not.. meerly by the Superficies of the Sea, but by its vast depth, which in some places is unfathomable. **1712** ADDISON *Spect.* No. 420 ¶3 Those unfathomable Depths of Ether. **1799** KIRWAN *Geol. Ess.* 479 The unfathomable abysses of the ocean. **1815** SHELLEY *Alastor* 373 On the unfathomable stream The boat moved slowly. **1851** MRS. BROWNING *Casa Guidi Wind.* I. 760 Ye may well look up surprised To those unfathomable heavens that feed Your purple hills! **1879** MISS BRADDON *Cloven Foot* iv, The long dazzling boulevards stretching into unfathomable distance before her eyes.
b. In fig. contexts. (Cf. 1.)
1640 BP. HALL *Chr. Moder.* II. §7. 47 These are indeed unfadomable depths in that Ocean, wherin we shall vainly hope to pitch our anchor. **1672** STILLINGFL. *Serm.* xii. (1673) 237 O the unfathomable Abysse of Eternity! **1712** ADDISON *Spect.* No. 309 ¶14 Sounding the unfathomable Depths of Fate, Free-will and Fore-knowledge. **1739** WESLEY *'Lo! God is here!'* v, Thou source and life of all! Thou vast, unfathomable Sea! **1820** SHELLEY *Fiordispina* 9 For thou the wonders of the depth canst know Of this unfathomable flood of hours. **1855** MACAULAY *Hist. Eng.* xxi. IV. 575 In truth the depths of this man's knavery were unfathomable. **1859** GEO. ELIOT *A. Bede* iii, An unfathomable ocean of love and beauty.
absol. **1831** CARLYLE *Sartor Res.* II. viii, Two little visual Spectra of men, hovering.. in the midst of the Unfathomable.
c. *fig.* Of the eyes.
1817 SHELLEY *Rev. Islam* VI. xxxviii, The sweet peace of joy did almost fill The depth of her unfathomable look. **1854** THACKERAY *Newcomes* xxx, Her unfathomable eyes were wells of gloom. **1882** 'OUIDA' *Maremma* I. 212 Her lustrous, unfathomable, star-like eyes.
Hence **un'fathomableness**.
1690 NORRIS *Beatitudes* (1692) 133 The Unfathomableness of the great Dispensation of Mercy. **1832** tr. *Tour Germ. Prince* II. xii. 244 The immortal secret.., the unfathomableness of which had so tormented the 'élégants' of the metropolis. **1872** GEO. ELIOT *Middlem.* III. xxiii, In Mr. Horrock there was certainly an apparent unfathomableness, which offered play to the imagination.

un'fathomably, *adv.* [UN-¹ 11; cf. prec.] To an unfathomable extent.
1695 BLACKMORE *Pr. Arth.* VII. 61 A wide mouth'd Den, ..That downward goes unfathomably deep, Beneath the subterranean Vaults. **1771** SMOLLETT *Humph. Cl.* 3 Sept., A surprising body of pure transparent water, unfathomably deep in many places. **1820** SHELLEY *Witch Atl.* xlix, The tremulous stars sparkled unfathomably. **1833** HT. MARTINEAU *Briery Creek* i. 4 His grandfather appeared to him.. unfathomably wise.

un'fathomed, *ppl. a.* [UN-¹ 8.]
1. Of unascertained depth; unsounded.
1628 FELTHAM *Resolves* II. xxvii. 85 [The river] at last.. inwaves it selfe in the vnfathom'd Ocean. **1634** MILTON *Comus* in Birch *Wks.* (1738) I. p. vii, Halfe his wast Flood the wide Atlantique fills, And halfe the slow unfadom'd Stygian Poole. **1723** MRS. CENTLIVRE *Stolen Heiress* v, Ope' earth, hide me in thy unfathom'd womb. **1757** GRAY *Elegy* xiv, Full many a gem of purest ray serene, The dark unfathom'd caves of ocean bear. **1813** SHELLEY *Q. Mab* IV. 95 The lovely silence of the unfathomed main. **1873** PROCTOR *Expanse Heav.* 302 He still saw that cloudy light which speaks of star depths as yet unfathomed.
b. In fig. context. (Cf. 2.)
1623 MIDDLETON & ROWLEY *Sp. Gipsy* III. iii, A soul drown'd deep In the unfathom'd seas of matchless sorrows. **1683** NORRIS *Passions of Saviour* 5 Sing the unfathom'd depths of love. **1755** YOUNG *Centaur* iv, The first moment man quits hold of his Creator, he drops! In distraction and ruin, how unfathomed his fall! **1817** BYRON *Manfred* I. i. 243 By thy unfathom'd gulfs of guile,.. I call upon thee! **1861** W. F. COLLIER *Hist. Eng. Lit.* 146 The unfathomed depths of the poet's mind.
2. *fig.* Not fully explored or known; unascertained; immense.
1659 T. PECKE *Parnassi Puerp.* 181 Nature in the unfathom'd Stagyrite, Compos'd a Body, abject to the sight. **1688** PRIOR *Ode* vi, Man does with dangerous Curiosity These unfathom'd Wonders try. **1784** COWPER *Task* II. 538 When in him reside Grace, knowledge, comfort—an unfathom'd store. **1809** COLERIDGE *Friend* (1865) 61 If the mere acquiescence in truth, uncomprehended and unfathomed, were sufficient. **1897** *Atlantic Monthly* LXXIX. 35 That was the thought of the unfathomed might of man.

†**un'fathomless**, *a.* (UN-¹ 5 a.)
1673 JANEWAY *Heaven on E.* 20 Oh that I might lose myself.. as a small drop in the unfathomless depth of his Love.

†**un'fatigable**, *a. Obs.* [UN-¹ 7 b and 5 b.] Indefatigable.
c **1550** *Clariodus* v. 1925 Apollo restless and unfatigabill. **1592** NASHE *P. Penilesse* F 2 b, As industrie and vnfatigable toyle rayseth meane persons.. to high thrones of authoritie. **1622** MALYNES *Anc. Law-Merch.* 84 Which cannot be done without an vnfatigable industrie. **1627** *Lisander & Cal.* IX. 184 Hee seemed so unfatigable in his armes.

unfa'tiguable, *a.* (UN-¹ 7 b.)
1799 SOUTHEY *Songs Amer. Indians, Huron's Address to Dead* iii, Those are the unfatigueable feet That traversed the forest tract. **1805** —— *Madoc* II. ix. 84 With fleet feet and unfatiguable. **1873** RUSKIN *Fors Clav.* xxxiii. 5 The waist elastic as a reed, and as unfatiguable.

unfa'tigue, *v.* [UN-² 4 b.] *refl.* To restore (oneself) from fatigue.
1734 CAREY *Chrononhotonthologos* i, Fatigu'd with the tremendous Toil of War,.. on downy Couch.. Himself he unfatigues with gentle Slumbers. **1836** B. HALL *Schloss Hainfeld* i. 14 May I trust you will induce Mrs Hall to 'unfatigue' herself.. in this Tadmore in the wilderness?

unfa'tigued, *ppl. a.* (UN-¹ 8.)
1705 J. PHILIPS *Blenheim* 39 Over dank, and dry, They journey toilsome, unfatigu'd with Length Of March. **1775** S. J. PRATT *Liberal Opin.* vi. (1783) I. 19 Celebrated for volubility of conversation, and so unfatigued a continuer, that nothing human could ever come in for a word. **1860** HOLME LEE *Leg. Fairy L.* 93 He was again standing beside me, perfectly cool and unfatigued. **1879** SPENCER *Data of Ethics* x. §65. 179 Sounds.. which yield to unfatigued ears intense pleasure.

unfa'tiguing, *ppl. a.* (UN-¹ 10.)
1808 SCOTT in *Lockhart* I. i. 20 That imperceptible and unfatiguing exercise. **1822–7** GOOD *Study Med.* (1829) III. 473 Provided the patient passes a quiet and unfatiguing life. **1865** *Pall Mall G.* 31 Aug. 3/2 To accept scanty pay for monotonous but unfatiguing work.

un'fatted, *ppl. a.* (UN-¹ 8.)
1752 J. HILL *Hist. Anim.* 486 The pheasant.. when in good condition.. is little less than a common unfatted fowl.

un'faulty, *a.* (UN-¹ 7.)
1548 UDALL, etc., *Erasm. Par. Matt.* xxi. 83 Whom because he had prouoked agaynst hym with well doynge, he made them not vnfaultye. **1587** *Mirr. Mag., Locrinus* iii, What meane I here th' unfaulty for to blame? **1628** WITHER *Brit. Rememb.* 289 b, In a Watch or Clocke When it is out of order once, or broke, The wheeles that are unfaultie move awry. **1645** MILTON *Tetrach.* 31 A Covnant therfore brought to that passe, is on the unfaulty side without injury dissolv'd. **1741** RICHARDSON *Pamela* (1824) I. xiv. 252 And glad I am that the poor unfaulty baby is so justly beloved by Mr. B——. **1855** SINGLETON *Virgil* II. 27 Be it allowed to me To pity my unfaulty friend's mishap.

un'favourable, *a.* (and *sb.*). [UN-¹ 7 b.]
1. Not favourable, in various senses: **a.** Of persons, opinions, etc.
1548 UDALL *Erasm. Par. Luke* xix. 147 The Pharisees.. thynke theimselues fortunate that they carry the deuill on theyre backes, ye roughest sitter possible and ye moste vnfauourable. **1678** SIR G. MACKENZIE *Crim. Laws Scot.* II. xxii. §i. (1699) 239 After a Crime is proved, the Pannel is most unfavourable. **1777** ROBERTSON *Hist. Amer.* II. ¶12 Talavera, at last, made.. an unfavourable report to Ferdinand and Isabella. **1779** *Mirror* No. 32, He was pleased.. to communicate his opinions. The last I found generally unfavourable both of men and things. **1835** T. MITCHELL *Acharn. of Aristoph.* 200 *note*, The insertion of a choriambus.., viewed with an unfavourable eye by Bentley and Elmsley. **1890** *Retrospect Med.* CII. 45 The prognosis was unfavourable only in severe cases.
b. Of conditions, circumstances, times, etc. Also const. *to* or *for*.
1748 *Anson's Voy.* I. viii. 77 These tempests.., though unattended by any other unfavourable circumstance, were yet rendered more mischievous to us by their inequality. **1766** SMOLLETT *Trav.* xi. I. 174, I have always found a cold and damp atmosphere the most unfavourable of any to my constitution. **1796** MME. D'ARBLAY *Camilla* III. 444 [She] thought the moment unfavourable for a tête-à-tête. **1846** MRS. A. MARSH *Father Darcy* II. xvi. 277, I must dispose of the outlaying estates in Northamptonshire, and these times are unfavourable. **1874** J. GEIKIE *Gt. Ice Age* xxiii. 302 In situations that would now be considered most unfavourable to their growth.
c. Of winds or weather.
1788 GIBBON *Decl. & F.* xli. IV. 132 An unfavourable wind detained them four days. **1789** CHARLOTTE SMITH *Ethelinde* IV. 155 A successless hunt, the morning being frosty and unfavourable. **1820** W. SCORESBY *Acc. Arctic Reg.* I. 307 The winds were mostly unfavourable. **1865** CARLYLE *Fredk. Gt.* XIX. viii. V. 581 In spite of.. the unfavorablest weather, it was.. his fixed purpose to recapture Dresden.

†**d.** Of diseases, physical injuries, etc. *Obs.*

1782 V. KNOX *Ess.* clxiii. (1819) III. 217 They were seized with an unfavourable small-pox. **1793** COWPER *Let. to J. Hill* 10 Dec., You mentioned..an unfavourable sprain that you had received. **1818** SCOTT *Hrt. Midl.* xxxiii, Her mind is totally alienated, which..is sometimes the consequence of an unfavourable confinement.

2. Of features or appearance: Ill-favoured.

1776 E. TOPHAM *Lett. Edin.* 83 The men are large and disproportioned with unfavourable, long, and saturnine countenances. **1782** A. HIGHMORE *Ramble Coast Sussex* (1873) 47 She said I did not carry an unfavourable appearance. **1825** SCOTT *Talism.* v, With all this most unfavourable exterior, there was one trait in the features of both which argued alertness and intelligence.

b. Creating a bad impression.

1817 JAS. MILL *Brit. India* II. IV. vi. 230 A procedure which bore a most unfavourable appearance.

3. *sb.* An unfavourable result.

1838 DE MORGAN *Ess. Probab.* 42 But of these 36 throws, any one of the five unfavourables of the first throw may combine with any one of the second throw.

Hence **un'favourableness.**

1764 *Phil. Trans.* LIV. 105 The best account..of my observation, however imperfect through the unfavourableness of the weather. **1842** LOUDON *Suburban Hort.* 123 The unsuitableness of the soil, the unpropitiousness of the climate, and the unfavourableness of the seasons.

un'favourably, *adv.* [UN-1 11.] In an unfavourable manner: **a.** In respect of opinion, statement, etc.

1460 *Paston Lett.* Suppl. (1901) 63 Thei reporten you unfavorabely and withoute credence, as men seyn, and some I have herd. *a* **1680** GLANVILL (J.), Bacon speaks not unfavourably of this. *a* **1768** SECKER *Serm.* (1771) V. xv. 335 There hath been..something or another that should not have been; else so many would not have judged..so unfavourably. **1816** SCOTT *Old Mort.* xv, If our summons is unfavourably received we will instantly attack. **1866** J. H. NEWMAN *Let. to Pusey* 86 That compromise of which our countrymen report so unfavourably from abroad.

b. In respect of circumstances, conditions, etc.

1833 CARLYLE *Misc.* (1840) IV. 337 A richly endowed, unfavourably situated nature. **1846** MRS. A. MARSH *Father Darcy* II. ix. 151 His tones and gestures..contrasted unfavourably with the appearance either of Catesby or Winter. **1871** A. MEADOWS *Man. Midwifery* (ed. 2) 230, I believe it..to compare very unfavourably with the death-rate of the supposed more formidable operation.

un'favoured, *ppl. a.* (UN-1 8.)

1774 GOLDSM. *Nat. Hist.* II. 251 There was a time, when these unfavoured children of Nature, were the peculiar favourites of the great. **1796** [see UNCULTIVATED *ppl. a.* 1]. **1908** WALLACE *Children Chapel* 175 This diminished the reputation and profit of the unfavored players.

un'favouring, *ppl. a.* (UN-1 10.)

1835 *Woman* II. 203 In an unfavouring soil, where many seeds are sown, we reap a full harvest of weeds. **1878** STEVENSON *Inland Voy.* 17 We still spread our canvas to the unfavouring air.

un'favourite, *a.* [UN-1 7.] Least favourite; disliked.

1934 WEBSTER, Unfavorite. **1951** N. COWARD *Star Quality* 232 *Love Child*..was my *unfavourite* play of all time. **1962** 'R. FARRE' *Time from World* xii. 152 Belloc and Chesterton,..whom I number among my unfavourite authors. **1974** N. FREELING *Dressing of Diamond* 166 Carnations..were nearly her most unfavourite flower. **1979** *Listener* 15 Nov. 668/2 Perelman did..make frequent forays to California..to report on his unfavourite city.

unfaysible, obs. f. UNFEASIBLE *a.*

un'feared, *ppl. a.* [UN-1 8.]

†**1.** Not affected by fear; undismayed. *Obs.*

1435 MISYN *Fire of Love* 100 Als þi saule criste truly has soght & vnferde & in sekynge wolde not cees. *c* **1475** *Cath. Angl.* 127/2 (A), Vn-Ferde, *vbi* hardy. **1600** FAIRFAX *Tasso* I. lii, Vnfear'd in fight, vntir'd with hurt or wound. **1611** B. JONSON *Catiline* IV. i, Though Heauen should speake, with all his wrath at once,..we should stand vpright, and vnfear'd. **1627** MAY *Lucan* II. 556 He yet vnfear'd, his anger doth retain.

2. Not regarded with fear; undreaded.

1612 *Two Noble K.* I. ii. 71 A most unbounded Tyrant, whose successes Makes heaven unfeard. **1667** MILTON *P.L.* IX. 187 Nor nocent yet, but on the grassie Herbe Fearless unfeard he slept. **1796** COLERIDGE *Destiny of Nations* 146 That..herself Unfeared by Fellow-natures, she might wait On the poor labouring man with kindly looks. **1839** BAILEY *Festus* 291 It is the thing Unfeared and unforethought which tempts, betrays. **1868** MORRIS *Earthly Par.* (1870) I. II. 597 Till death unfeared at last shall come to me.

un'fearful, *a.* [UN-1 7.] Having no fear; fearless.

1544 BETHAM *Precepts War* I. cxliii. G viij b, To chose souldyours whyche ben vnfearfull and couragious to encountre wyth theyr enemyes. *a* **1569** KINGESMYLL *Comf. Afflict.* (1585) E 6 Other notable women, that were so unfearefull to suffer moste sharpe death. **1603** BRETON *Mad World* Wks. (Grosart) II. 10/1 He..led me into his house, the doore open, as unfearefull of theeves, as vnprovided for strangers. **1784** *Unfortunate Sensibility* II. 155 Thou mayest enjoy thy full inheritance unfearful of the shafts of envy. **1850** ALISON *Hist. Eur.* (ed. 2) XIII. xc. 270 The humming-bird,..so quick in its motions, so unfearful of man. **1888** *Encycl. Brit.* XXIII. 313/2 The very fish..would glide, unfearful, between his [Thoreau's] hands.

un'fearfully, *adv.* [UN-1 11; cf. prec.] Fearlessly, resolutely.

c **1430** *Life St. Kath.* (1884) 33 þe holy seruant..was ryght nought troubled, but vnferfully sche commended þe labour of hir chyualrye vnto our lord god. **1563** GOLDING *Cæsar* (1565) 81 b, Our enemies fought stoutly and unfearfullye. **1571** —— *Calvin on Ps.* iv. 3 Unfearfully to despise whatsoever they wrought against him. **1615** G. SANDYS *Trav.* 270 The vndanted giuing or receiuing of wounds; and life so vnfearfully parted with.

un'fearing, *ppl. a.* (UN-1 10.)

1796 *Monthly Mag.* II. 615 Him would the storm-vext Adriatic surge,..The wreck of shattering worlds, Unfearing smite. **1824** MISS MITFORD *Village* Ser. I. 18 In addition to these multifarious talents, he was ready, obliging, and unfearing. **1868** LYNCH *Rivulet* CLXI. viii, Down with unfearing heart I lie, And wait sleep's healing mystery.

Hence **un'fearingly** *adv.*

1895 *Contemp. Rev.* Mar. 434 Unfearingly to allow the total severance of the bond.

unfeary, var. UNFEIRIE *a. Sc.*

†**un'feasable,** *a. Obs.* [UN-1 7 b and 5 b.] = UNFEASIBLE *a.*

1628 MEAD in Ellis *Orig. Lett.* Ser. I. III. 268 Their works seem now altogether unfeisable. **1640** SIR K. DIGBY in *Lismore Papers* Ser. II. (1888) IV. 133 All those wayes were not onely very difficult and peradventure vnfeazable [etc.]. **1673** *S'too him Bayes* 15 The bishop was a weak man, and laid an unfeisable design.

Hence †**un'feasableness;** †**un'feasably** *adv.*

1612 WOODALL *Surg. Mate* Wks. (1653) 390 To brand it with pittiful inhibitions..and *unfeasablenesse [etc.]. **1678** CUDWORTH *Intell. Syst.* 682 Those small and pitiful attempts..only showing the unfeisableness and impossibility thereof. **1638** JUNIUS *Paint. Ancients* 331 Workes..done by an unspeakable way of Art, delicatly, divinely, *unfeisably, etc. insinuate nothing els.

unfeasi'bility. (UN-1 12; cf. next.)

1655 FULLER *Hist. Cambr.* 70 The failing is not in the unfeacibility of the Design, but in the accidentall defaults of the Vndertakers. **1839** CARLYLE *Chartism* ix, The matter..can at least solace itself with hope, and die gently, convinced of unfeasibility. **1850** —— *Latter-d. Pamph.* ii. 9 Nature..taught him the futility and unfeasibility of the system followed here.

un'feasible, *a.* (UN-1 7 and 5 b.)

1527 *St. Papers Hen. VIII*, I. 247 As the discripcion..shulde be to tedious..to rede, so the explicacion therof shulde be unfaysible unto me. **1648** J. BEAUMONT *Psyche* XVIII. ccxix, But seeing this unfeasible, the sight Redoubled her compassionate sorrows weight. **1657** G. STARKEY *Helmont's Vind.* 145 This Logick would make almost all Mechanicks to be impossible, if what ever you cannot do must straight be unfecible. **1673** O. WALKER *Educ.* (1677) 37 Harshnes is discovered in..enjoying things in themselves too difficult, unfesible, unsupportable. **1804** COLEBROOKE *Husb. Bengal* 35 Circumstances that render it unfeasible to enter these fields to select the ripe plants, without damaging the rest. **1886** *Brit. Med. Jrnl.* 12 June 1142/2 The use..is doubtless charming in theory,..but, in practice, it is unfeasible.

Hence **un'feasibleness.**

1653 HOLCROFT *Procopius, Pers. Wars* II. 42 Seeing excessive undertakings ever are rewarded with unfaisibleness.

un'feasted, *ppl. a.* (UN-1 8.)

1636 HEYWOOD *Love's Mistress* I, Nor shall they part from hence with unfeasted eares. **1897** R. KEARTON *Nature & Camera* 51 The trippers had to return with..their curiosity unfeasted.

un'feastful, *a.* (UN-1 7.) †Non-festival.

a **1564** BECON *Art. Chr. Relig.* xvii, Not on yͤ feastful, nor on the vnfeastful, dayes only, but at al tymes.

un'feastly, *a.* [UN-1 7. Cf. G. *unfestlich.*] Not in festival trim.

c **1386** CHAUCER *Sqr.'s T.* 358 Hir liste nat appalled for to be Ne on the morwe vnfeestlich [*v.rr.* onfestelyche, vnfestly, etc.] for to se.

†**un'feat,** *a. Obs.*-1 [UN-1 7.] Not well disposed; unfit.

a **1533** LD. BERNERS *Gold. Bk. M. Aurel.* (1535) C c iij b, They ar vnfete to do wel: & are holly disposed to do yl.

un'feather, *v.* [UN-2 4 and 7.]

1. *trans.* To strip of feathers; to unplume.

1483 *Cath. Angl.* 124/2 To vn-Fedyr, *expennare, explumare.* **1586** J. HOOKER *Hist. Irel.* in *Holinshed* II. 116/2 He so handled the matter, that he had vnfethered him of his best friends, aids, and helps. **1603** FLORIO *Montaigne* II. x. 236, I will love him that shall trace, or vnfeather me. *a* **1639** T. CAREW *Poems* Wks. (1824) 79 Love lent thee wings to flye, so hee Unfeather'd, now must rest with mee. **1681** RYCAUT tr. *Gracian's Critick* 183 None are here of those who can..unfeather our Nests, whilst they enwrap us in the quilts. **1769** COLMAN *Oxonian in Town* I. 8 Ay, ay, we'll unfeather the whole nest in time. **1948** L. MACNEICE *Holes in Sky* 34 The foam..is a goose-quill That feathers—unfeathers—itself.

2. *intr.* To lose the feathers.

1849 J. A. CARLYLE tr. *Dante's Inf.* 202 When poor Icarus felt his loins unfeather by the heating of the wax.

un'feathered, *a.* [UN-1 9. Cf. OE. *ungefeðered*, MDu. *ongevedert*, G. *ungefiedert*, †*-federt*, older Da. *ufedret*, Sw. *ofjädrad.*]

1. Not provided or covered with feathers: **a.** Of birds, etc.

1570 LEVINS *Manip.* 50 Vnfethered, *implumis.* **1605** A. WILLET *Hexapla Gen.* Ded., I..haue brought forth my implumed and vnfeathered birds. **1653** JER. TAYLOR *Serm. for Year* I. Ep. Ded., They are like callow and unfeathered birds. **1697** DRYDEN *Virg. Georg.* IV. 745 Whose Nest some prying Churl had found, and thence, By Stealth, convey'd th' unfeather'd Innocence. **1780** COWPER *Sparrows in Trin. Coll.* 14 In hope of crumbs, Which kindly giv'n, may serve with food Convenient their unfeather'd brood. **1826** S. COOPER *First Lines Surg.* (ed. 5) 83 A roughness which is compared to the skin of an unfeathered goose. **1884** COUES *N. Amer. Birds* 86 Feathered Tracts and Unfeathered Spaces.

b. Applied generically to man.

c **1600** *Timon* V. iv. (1842) 86 A peripatetick is a two legd liuing creature, gressible, unfeathered. **1681** DRYDEN *Abs. & Achit.* I. 170 And all to leaue what with his Toil he won To that unfeather'd two-legg'd thing, a Son. **1754** WARBURTON *Bolingbroke's Philos.* i. 36 Ribaldry and ill language disgrace the *animal implume bipes*, the two-leg'd unfeathered Philosopher. **1817** BENTHAM *Parl. Reform* Introd. 213 The speeches of so many unfeathered bipeds. **1895** *Atlantic Monthly* LXXVI. 141/2 Such tastes..have been known among the unfeathered tribes.

2. Of arrows: Not fitted with feathers.

1611 COTGR., *Materas desempenné*,..an vnfeathered quarrell. **1790** *Cook's Voy.* I. 75 But..kneeling down, [he] shot an arrow, unfeathered (as they all are), near the sixth part of a mile. **1837** LYTTON *Athens* II. 122 Lycians with mantles of goat skin and unfeathered arrows of reed. **1860** MAURY *Phys. Geog.* (Low) iv. 103 The unfeathered arrows represent winds.

†**un'featly,** *adv.* (UN-1 11.)

1548 UDALL *Erasm. Pref. Par. Luke* (∴) ij b, It was a thynge not vnfeactly ne vnskilfully spoken in the prouerbes of the Grekes, that [etc.]. **1611** COTGR., *Impropremert*,..vnaptly, vnfitly, vnfeatly.

un'featured, *a.* (UN-1 9.)

1693 DRYDEN *Juvenal* x. 308 A ropy Chain of Rhumes; a Visage rough, Deform'd, Unfeatur'd, and a Skin of Buff. **1810** L. HUNT *Politics & Poetics* 30 Nightmare, horrid mass! unfeatured heap! **1856** R. A. VAUGHAN *Mystics* XIII. iii, The starless, unfeatured night. **1892** STEVENSON *Across the Plains* 226 His whole unfeatured wilderness of an existence.

†**un'featy,** *a.* (UN-1 7.) *Obs.*

a **1586** SIDNEY *Arcadia* II. ii. (1598) 100 For his part, hee neuer saw more vnfeatie [1590 unfeatlie] fellowes then great clearks were.

unfecible, obs. f. UNFEASIBLE *a.*

†**un'fect,** *a. Obs.* [UN-1 7: cf. FECT *v.*] Uninfected.

1502 ATKYNSON tr. *De Imitatione* III. xxxviii. 227 Seldome suche persones be fre and vnfecte of the venym of theyr owne sekynge.

†**un'fectual,** *a. Obs.* [UN-1 7; cf. FECTUALLY *adv.*] Uneffectual, ineffective.

1549 COVERDALE, etc. *Erasm. Par. Gal.* 11 It was..meete, that shadowes should gyue place to the truth; and the unfectuall, to that whiche was..effectuall.

un'fecundated, *ppl. a.* (UN-1 8 and 5 b.)

[**1775** ASH.] **1857** GEO. ELIOT *Amos Barton* v, An unfecundated egg, which the waves of time wash away into nonentity. **1859** *Todd's Cycl. Anat.* V. 68/1 The mass of the yolk and the germ, in their unfecundated state.

un'fed, *ppl. a.* [UN-1 8 b. Cf. MDu. *ongevoedet*, *-voet*, Du. *-voed* unfed, unnourished; ON. and Icel. *ú-*, *ófœddr* (Sw. *ofödd*, Da. *ufødt*) unborn.]

1. Not supplied or nourished with food.

a **1300** *Cursor M.* 12925 Iesus..fasted fourti dais vn-fedd. *Ibid.* 19650 Thre dais liued he þar vnfedd. **1513** DOUGLAS *Æneid* IX. vi. 71 The empty lioun, lang onfed,..Trubland the fald full of sylly schep. **1579** SPENSER *Sheph. Cal.* May 44 Shepeheards..That playen, while their flockes be vnfedde. **1641** BEST *Farm. Bks.* (Surtees) 123 Carre-swannes, that are unfedde, are usually at 2s. 6d. a peece. **1687** DRYDEN *Hind & P.* III. 195 Some sons of mine..Have sharply tax'd your converts, who unfed Have follow'd you for miracles of bread. **1737** *Gentl. Mag.* VII. 570/1, I wonder'd, why his oxen stray'd, His sheep and heifers pine'd unfed. **1853** KANE *Grinnell Exp.* xlvii. (1856) 442 Now the half-tutored, unfed Esquimaux dog would eat a goat, bones, skin, and for aught I know, horns. **1868** MORRIS *Earthly Par.* (1870) I. II. 565 Upon his perch the falcon sat Unfed.

transf. **1890** 'R. BOLDREWOOD' *Col. Reformer* xxvii, The diet..became wellnigh intolerable: the flaccid unfed meat, ..the milkless tea [etc.].

2. *fig.* Not supplied with necessary material, support, etc.

a **1625** FLETCHER & SHIRLEY *Lover's Progr.* IV. i, She that is forfeited to lust must dye, That humour being unfed. **1664** DRYDEN & HOWARD *Indian Queen* IV. ii, I shou'd..like an unfed stream run on and dye. **1697** DRYDEN *Æneis* XI. 101 A lovely Flow'r, New cropt by Virgin Hands,..Unfaded yet, but yet unfed below. **1816** BYRON *Ch. Har.* III. xliv, Even as a flame unfed, which runs to waste With its own flickering. **1883** *Jrnl. Educ.* XVIII. 148 A church unfed from the public table.

un'feeble, *a.* (UN-1 7.)

1547 SALESBURY *Dict.* C iv, *Dilesc*, unfeble. **1569** J. SANFORD tr. *Agrippa's Van. Artes* lviii. 83 b, Sinners with the faithfull had already entred into the Churche, the feeble with the unfeeble.

un'feed, *ppl. a.* [UN-1 8.] Not rewarded with, or engaged by, a fee; unpaid.

1605 SHAKS. *Lear* I. iv. 142 Then 'tis like the breath of an vnfeed Lawyer, you gaue me nothing for't. *a* **1628** DABORNE *Poor-man's Comf.* II. (1655) C 4, Now he's as speechlesse, as an unfeed Atturney. **1709** GARTH *Dispens.* (ed. 6) v. 39 Vaunt now no more the Triumph of your Skill, But, tho' unfeed, exert your Arm, and kill. **1802–12** BENTHAM *Ration. Judic. Evid.* (1827) IV. 419 But it is..the honest interest of the unfeed judge, that..the truth shall come to light. **1850** BLACKIE *Æschylus* I. 148 And why walks Grief, an unfee'd page, with thee?

un'feedable, *a.* (UN-1 7 b.)
1867 RUSKIN *Time & Tide* iii. §10 Have you considered what is to be done finally with the unfeedable mouths?

un'feeding, *ppl. a.* (UN-1 10.)
1585 ABP. SANDYS *Serm.* xviii. 316 What can..the vnfeeding pastor, the vniust iudge,..aunswere in that day but pleade guiltie? **1610** BP. HALL *Apol. Brownists* xxvii. (1627) 596 The necessary patterne of an vnteaching pastor, or an vnfeeding teacher.

unfeel: see UNFELE *a.* and UN-2 3.

un'feelable, *a.* [UN-1 7 b.]
†**1.** Unable to feel; insensible. *Obs.*
c **1400** LOVE *Bonavent. Mirr.* (1908) 243 Sche was all out of hir self and vnfelable made, as half dede. **1568** TURNER *Herbal* III. 51 The Nux methel is poyson and maketh num or vnfelable... It maketh vnfelable the head.
2. Incapable of being felt; impalpable. *rare.*
1611 COTGR., *Impalpable*, impalpable, vnfeelable. **1632** J. DOD *Ten Sermons*, etc. 269 This Christ,..in whom we behold God which is invisible, and touch him which is vnfeelable.

un'feeling, *vbl. sb.* [UN-1 13.] Lack of feeling. Also, an instance of this.
1603 FLORIO *Montaigne* II. xii. 285 Indolencie or vnfeeling of paine. **1805** *Monthly Mag.* XIX. 657 The rapacity, the selfish unfeeling, the low cunning of Odysseus. **1919** V. WOOLF *Night & Day* xxiv. 331 The chaos of the unfeelings or half-feelings of life.

un'feeling, *ppl. a.* [UN-1 10 and 5 d.]
1. Having no feeling or sensation, insensible; *fig.* not sensitive to impressions, etc.
c **1000** *Sax. Leechd.* II. 264 Yfele swilas unfelende. *a* **1300** *Cursor M.* 24426 Quen i sagh þus all thinges..Vn-feland for þair lauerd murn, Moght i me noght for-ber. *c* **1430** *Life St. Kath.* (1884) 31 For þay wot not hem self þat þay are [offended] whyl þay are bot vnfelyng matere. **1590** SHAKS. *Com. Err.* II. i. 103 Vnfeeling fools can with such wrongs dispence. **1593** —— *2 Hen. VI*, III. ii. 145 Fain would I go to chafe his palie lips,..And with my fingers feele his hand, vnfeeling. **1619** J. TAYLOR (Water P.) *Kicksey Winsey* Wks. (1630) 42/1 They must not take me for a Stupid asse, That I (vnfeeling) will let these things passe. **1760–72** H. BROOKE *Fool of Qual.* (1809) IV. 127 [He] pressed his lips to the pale and unfeeling lips. **1780** COWPER *Progr. Error* 528 So one.. Woo'd an unfeeling statue for his wife. **1846** TRENCH *Mirac.* iv. 36 When he blesses, it is men; but when he smites, it is an unfeeling tree. **1876** BLACKIE *Songs Relig. & Life* 223 All my weeping can recall her never, Back from the cold unfeeling sod!
b. Const. *of*, *to*, or with direct object.
1744 ELIZA HEYWOOD *Female Spect.* No. 3 (1748) I. 113 It is sure a pleasure which no words can paint!—No heart unfeeling it conceive! **1748** THOMSON *Cast. Indol.* II. liv, But should to fame your hearts unfeeling be,..Then hear [etc.]. **1760–72** H. BROOKE *Fool of Qual.* (1809) II. 119 They appeared so cheerful and unfeeling of their own wretchedness.
2. Devoid of kindly or tender feelings; uncompassionate, unsympathetic.
1596 SHAKS. *Merch. V.* IV. i. 63 This is no answer thou vnfeeling man, To excuse the currant of thy cruelty. **1598–9** B. JONSON *Case is Altered* v. iii, O heauen! can it be? That man should liue with such vnfeeling soules, Without or touch or conscience of religion? **1734** POPE *Ess. Man* IV. 319 The broadest mirth unfeeling Folly wears, Less pleasing far than Virtue's very tears. **1781** GIBBON *Decl. & F.* (1787) III. xxx. 167 *note*, The bloody actor is less detestable than the cool unfeeling historian. **1818** SCOTT *Rob Roy* xviii, I was neither a false lover nor an unfeeling son. **1883** FROUDE in *Mrs. Carlyle's Lett.* III. 204 John Carlyle..had been rough and unfeeling.
absol. **1742** GRAY *Prospect Eton Coll.* 94 The tender [groan] for another's pain; Th' unfeeling for his own.

un'feelingly, *adv.* (UN-1 11; cf. prec.)
c **1374** CHAUCER *Troylus* II. 19 Ek þough I speke of loue vnfelyngly, No wondir is. **1753** T. CIBBER *Lives Actors, Booth* 74 The first has been unfeelingly mouthed and ranted throughout. **1768** STERNE *Sent. Journ.*, *Dwarf*, The German turn'd his head back, look'd down upon him as Goliah did upon David—and unfeelingly resumed his posture. **1902** *Monthly Rev.* Aug. 187 'Bid your minnie good-bye, lad,' said Robin, not unfeelingly.

un'feelingness. (UN-1 12.)
1398 TREVISA *Barth. De P.R.* VI. xxv. (Tollem. MS.), Austyne sayeþ þat slep is a kyndely unfelingenesse [L. *insensibilitas*] comen to þe body and to þe soule. **1583** BABINGTON *Commandm.* (1590) 99 When wee.. headlong in vnfeelingnesse runne on. **1598** FLORIO, *Insensibilita*, sencelesnes, vnfeelingnes. **1766** MRS. CARTER *Lett.* (1809) III. 285 Surely it implies rather the want of philosophical pride and unfeelingness. **1780** *Mirror* No. 101, A warm remonstrance against the inhumanity of parents, the unfeelingness of age, and the injustice of the world. **1853** ROBERTSON *Serm.* Ser. IV. xvi. (1876) 209 Would it not be coarse unfeelingness to treat such customs with anything but respect. **1895** *Pop. Sci. Monthly* Sept. 654 The same predominance of self..is said to reappear in the.. unfeelingness of children.

un'feigned, *ppl. a.* (and *adv.*). Forms: (see FEIGN *v.*). [UN-1 8.]
1. Not feigned, pretended, or simulated; sincere, genuine, true, real.
a. *c* **1374** CHAUCER *Anel. & Arc.* 289 Verraylye yee slee me with þe peyne þat may yee see vnfeynid on myn huwe. *c* **1440** *Pallad. on Husb.* v. 194 Of vnfeyned curage [L. *sponte*] Of been therto wole come a multitude. **1494** *Act 11 Hen. VII*, c. 18 Or ellis he have such unfayned siknes, lettyng or diseas that he may not..come to do his personell attendaunce. **1526** *Pilgr. Perf.* (W. de W. 1531) 99 b, Neuer eate ne drynke out of due tyme, except..vnfayned nede compell the. **1577** GRANGE *Golden Aphrod.* Lj, Neither passed this tedious tyme..without vnfayned ioyes & vnspeakeable pleasure. **1649** BP. REYNOLDS *Hosea* ii. 68 Profession of faith, unfained, and sincere Repentance was made before Baptisme. **1712** STEELE *Spect.* No. 402 ¶2, I have an unfeigned Love of Virtue. **1778** MISS BURNEY *Evelina* lxxxii, I need not tell you what unfeigned joy accompanied our meeting. *a* **1859** MACAULAY *Hist. Eng.* xxiii. (1861) V. 82 Keppel..looked up with unfeigned admiration to a master whom he had been accustomed..to consider as the first of living men.
β. *c* **1375** *Sc. Leg. Saints* xliii. (*Cecilia*) 528 Of conscience gud & clere, & fath vnfenȝet. **1562** WINȜET *Wks.* (S.T.S.) I. 2 Ane Exhortatioun..For vnfenȝeit reformation of doctrine and maneris. **1609** HUME in *Wodrow Soc. Misc.* (1844) 585 So I wische to God that..the Prince's wrathe mycht be appeazed,..and his unfainzed favour reconcealed.
2. Of persons or the heart: Honest or sincere in feeling or action.
c **1374** CHAUCER *Troylus* II. 839, I loue oon which is most ententyf To seruen wel vnwery or vnfeyned. *c* **1400** *Rom. Rose* 7363 As it were in a pilgrimage Lyke good and hooly folk vnfeyned. **1525** LD. BERNERS *Froiss.* II. clxx. 195/2 Whan..his companyons..herde hym speke those wordes, they parceyued well howe he spake them with all his herte vnfayned. **1573** BARET *Alv.* V. 126 Your unfeined, trusty, and assured friend. **1613** W. BROWNE *Brit. Past.* I. iv. 301 Succour a seely maid, that doth implore Aide, on a bended heart, unfain'd and meeke. **1647** N. BACON *Disc. Govt. Eng.* I. iv. 16 Of fained friends, becomming unfained foes to the Britons. **1696** (*title*), Some Seasonable and Modest Thoughts..Concerning the Scots East India Company, by an unfeigned and hearty Lover of England.
†**3.** As *adv.* Without feigning; honestly. *Obs.*
1463–7 *Paston Lett.* Suppl. (1901) 81, I shal and do pray God dayly to sende you such one..that wil drede and faithfully unfeyned love you. *a* **1529** SKELTON *Ware the Hauke* 81 But the fawconer vnfayned Was much more febler brayned. **1550–3** *Decaye Eng.* in *Supplic.* (1871) 100 And then vnfayned, as we do thynke, we sholde haue corne ynough.

un'feignedly, *adv.* [UN-1 11.] In an unfeigned manner; without feigning or pretence; sincerely, honestly.
a. **1526** *Pilgr. Perf.* (W. de W. 1531) 77 b, He must subdue & meke hym selfe in very treuth vnfaynedly. **1577** tr. *Bullinger's Decades* 564 Then shall wee like true penitents vnfeignedly reuerence & dread the Lord. **1628** WITHER *Brit. Rememb.* II. 1231 And if unfainedly we practise thus He doth of safety also warrant us. **1686** HORNECK *Crucif. Jesus* xiv. 308 Both parties do unfeignedly, and without guile, or fraud, or equivocation, declare themselves willing..to perform the things agreed upon. **1763** BURKE *Corr.* (1844) I. 51, I am very unfeignedly glad to hear from you. **1825** SCOTT *Betrothed* xix, If you will speak unfeignedly, you must.. allow [etc.]. **1891** FARRAR *Darkn. & Dawn* xxiii, She rejoiced..unfeignedly at the boy's recovery.
β. **1552** ABP. HAMILTON *Catech.* (1884) 56 Quhasaevir luffis God with trew lufe unfenyetlie. **1573** *Satir. Poems Reform.* xlii. 774 Quha feiris God vnfenȝeitlie Of that sweit word will neuer Irk.

un'feignedness. [UN-1 12.] The quality of being unfeigned; sincerity, etc.
1535 COVERDALE *1 Chron.* xxx. 17, I knowe..that vnfaynednes is acceptable vnto the. **1561** T. NORTON *Calvin's Inst.* III. 299 That by prouing them yt be his he may haue a triall of their vnfainednesse. **1628** WITHER *Brit. Rememb.* v. 941 Lord, remember thou, That with unfainednesse, I beg thee, now, To keepe me alwayes mindfull of thy love. *a* **1684** LEIGHTON *Comm. 1 Peter* ii. (1693) 468 His feet strive to keep pace with his Tongue, which gives evidence of its unfainedness.

un'feigning, *ppl. a.* (UN-1 10.)
c **1400** [see UNFEIGNINGLY *adv.*]. **1436** [see UNFAILINGLY *adv.*]. **1791** COWPER *Iliad* x. 488 With unfeigning truth Simply and plainly will I utter all. **1791** —— *Odyss.* XXI. 247 He then, convinced Of their unfeigning honesty, began.

un'feigningly, *adv.* (UN-1 11.)
c **1400** *Sc. Trojan War* II. 580 Dyomed has furst sworne þe pees Wnfenȝheandly [*v.r.* wnfenȝeand] to hold. *a* **1568** *Bannatyne MS.* (Hunterian Club) 623 To yow.. Unfenyeandlie with hairtlie lufe..I me commend.

un'feirdy, *a. Sc. rare.* [UN-1 7 + *feirdy* able, active.] **a.** Awkward, clumsy. **b.** (See quot.)
c **1590** J. STEWART *Poems* (S.T.S.) II. 9/58 Than sall It pertlie occupie the place, Thocht it be framd with my vnferdie fyle. **1866** EDMONSTON *Orkney Gloss.* 136 *Unfierdy*, unwieldy, overgrown.

un'feirie, *a. Sc.* Also 6 vn-, onfery, vnfeire, 8 unfiery, 8–9 unfeary, 9 onfeirie. [UN-1 7.] Inactive; incapable of exertion.
1513 DOUGLAS *Æneid* x. xiv. 70 Thocht the violens of his sayr smart Maid hym onfery [*v.r.* vnfery]. **1535** STEWART *Cron. Scot.* (Rolls) III. 437 Cruikit he wes, ynfeire of his cors. *a* **1736** T. WHITTELL *Poems* (1815) 170 But Sawney grew weary,..Being auld, and unfeary, and fail'd of his strength. *a* **1779** GRAHAM *Writings* (1883) II. 32 The auld beast being unfiery o' the feet, she fundred. **1806** R. JAMIESON *Pop. Ball.* II. 171 Thoch auld onfeirie and lyart I'm now. **1809** SCOTT *Let.* in *Lockhart* II. vii. 263 Coursing is my only and constant amusement, and my valued pair of four-legged champions..wax old and *unfeary*.

un'fele, *a. Obs.* exc. *dial.* Forms: 1–2 unfæle (2 unn-), 3 unfeale; 2–3 unfele (vn-), 3–4 unvele (vnuele, onvele), 9 *Sc.* and *north.* onfeel, unfeil. [OE. *unfǽle*, f. *un-* UN-1 + *fǽle* good, FELE *a.*2] Bad, evil, wicked; wretched, miserable, unpleasant.
a **900** *Genesis* 723 Hit wæs þeah..menniscra morð, þæt hie to mete dædon ofet unfæle. *c* **1000** ÆLFRIC *Gloss.* in Wr.-Wülcker 108 *Satiri, uel fauni*,..unfæle men, wude-wasan, unfæle wihtu. *c* **1000** *Ags. Gosp.* Mark vi. 49 Hi wendon þæt hit unfæle [*c* **1160** un-fele] gast wære. *c* **1200** *Trin. Coll. Hom.* II. 79 Ȝif þe unfele man his wille folȝeð and..teð him to unwrenches. *c* **1205** LAY. 22018 Neh þere sæ stronde is a mære swiðe muchel; þat water is un-fæle. *a* **1250** *Owl & Night.* 1003 þat lond is grislich & vnuele. *Ibid.* 1381 He is vnvele and forbroyde. *c* **1290** *S. Eng. Leg.* I. 468/231 þe sarazins onvele weren fulle of nyþe and hete. **13..** *R. Gloucester's Chron.* (Rolls) App. G. 39 þe moder his þrote carf, þo was heo vnfele. *c* **1400** *Laud Troy Bk.* 8830 The while that he hadde his hele, Ther he sclow Gregeys as vn-vele. **1825** JAMIESON, *Onfeel*,..unpleasant, disagreeable, implying the idea of coarseness or roughness; as, 'an onfeel day', 'onfeel words', &c. Teviotd. **1894** *Northumberland Gloss.* 756.

unfe'licitous, *a.* (UN-1 7 and 5 b.)
1802–12 BENTHAM *Ration. Judic. Evid.* (1827) IV. 487 In principle, the arrangement [is]..correct, howsoever in the application misguided and unfelicitous. **1876** M. COLLINS *Midnight to Midn.* III. viii. 136 Let us predict for them premature and unfelicitous exit into the land of scoundrels.

un'felled, *ppl. a.* (UN-1 8.)
1543 *Act 35 Hen. VIII*, c. 17 §1 There shall be left standing and unfelled..twelve Standils or Storers of Oak. **1593** MARLOWE tr. *Lucan* I. 448 In vnfeld woods, and sacred groues you dwell. *c* **1611** CHAPMAN *Iliad* VI. 68 Nor, like the king of men, Let any scape unfell'd. **1839** CARLYLE *Chartism* x, Where Canadian Forests stand unfelled. **1883** *Harper's Mag.* Feb. 435/2 Couriers are out summoning..the wood-choppers to leave the half-cut tree unfelled.

un'fellied, *a.* (UN-1 9.)
1885–94 R. BRIDGES *Eros & Psyche* March xxix, Melicertes drave His chariot..with swift unfellied wheel.

un'fellow, *v.* (UN-2 6 b.)
1856 MRS. BROWNING *Aur. Leigh* v. 552 Death quite unfellows us, Sets dreadful odds betwixt the live and dead.

un'fellowed, *a.* (UN-1 9.)
1597 *Prayers in Liturg. Serv. Q. Eliz.* (Parker Soc.) 671 So shall..the faithful [be] encouraged to repose in thy unfellowed Grace. **1634** FORD *Perk. Warbeck* IV. i, The English general returns A sensible devotion from his heart ..to this unfellowed grace. **1649** ARNWAY *Tablet* 22 If it be high treason against the Allmightie, to severe so unfellow'd a Paire. **1887** MEREDITH *Ballads & P.* 104 Every second man, unfellowed, Took the strokes of two, and gave.

un'fellow-like, *a.* (UN-1 7 c.)
1608 HIERON *Defence* III. 19 An act of abasement..such as convinceth us..to be of an inferior and unfellowlike condition, with Christ at his table.

†**un'felon**, *a. Obs.* (UN-1 7.)
a **1300** *Cursor M.* 6040 þan sent drightin a litel beist, O toth es noght vnfelunest.

unfe'loniously, *adv.* (UN-1 11.)
a **1634** CHAPMAN & SHIRLEY *Chabot* III. ii, If traitorous pride..Were sentenc'd unfeloniously before, I'll burn my books.

un'felt, *ppl. a.* (UN-1 8 b. Cf. Du. *ongevoeld*, G. *ungefühlt*.)
a **1586** SIDNEY *Astr. & Stella* Sonn. xxiv, Let him, depriu'd of sweet but vnfelt ioyes,..grow in only folly rich! **1595** DANIEL *Civ. Wars* v. xcvii, Whilst Talbot..Carries his vnfelt age as if forgot. **1607** CHAPMAN *Bussy d'Ambois* III. ii, O, 'tis a subtle knave; how like the plague Unfelt he strikes into the brain of man. **1681** DRYDEN *Abs. & Achit.* I. 693 Thus, form'd by Nature, furnished out with Arts, He glides unfelt into their secret hearts. **1742** GRAY *Adversity* 8 Purple Tyrants vainly groan With pangs unfelt before, unpitied and alone. **1814** WORDSW. *Excurs.* IV. 456 Nor is its power Unfelt among the sedentary fowl That seek yon pool. **1883** PARKER *Apost. Life* II. 192 He was writhing in an unfelt and unknown agony.
absol. **1886** A. WEIR *Hist. Basis Mod. Europe* (1889) 487 Few have been destitute of some theory respecting the unseen and unfelt.
Hence †**un'feltly** *adv. Obs.*
1605 SYLVESTER *Du Bartas* II. iii. III. *Law* 107 Into his brest he blowes A banefull ayre, whose strength unfeltly flowes Through all his veins.

un'felt, *v.* (UN-2 4 b.)
1611 FLORIO, *Disfeltrāre*, to vnfelt. **1656** W. DU GARD tr. *Comenius' Gate Lat. Unl.* 135 Having unfelted the hair [the barber] partly polleth it with scisers.

un'feminine, *a.* [UN-1 7, 5 b.] Not in accordance with, or appropriate to, female character.
1757 MRS. GRIFFITH *Lett. Hen. & Frances* (1767) IV. 30, I..continue still..averse to the unfeminine Vanity of a literary Name. **1796** MME. D'ARBLAY *Camilla* III. 301 What a lesson is this to youthful females against..the false brilliancy of unfeminine popularity! **1849** MACAULAY *Hist. Eng.* vi. II. 69 She had..two brilliant eyes, the lustre of which, to men of delicate taste, seemed fierce and unfeminine. **1875** MRS. RANDOLPH *Wild Hyacinth* I. 14 Why should it be wrong and unfeminine for us to do anything except dress, and read novels, and play the piano?
Hence **un'feminineness.**
1856 MISS YONGE *Daisy Chain* I. vi, If those high purposes should..grow out into eccentricities and unfemini[ne]nesses, what a grievous pity it would be! **1876** —— *Womankind* i. 7 She becomes ridiculous..., and renders him averse to the culture to which he erroneously ascribes her unfeminineness.

unfe'minity. (UN-1 12.)
1863 COWDEN CLARKE *Shaksp. Char.* viii. 197 He has retained the two women from the remotest charge of unfeminity.

un'feminize, *v.* (UN-2 6 c.)
1886 MISS MULOCK in *Gd. Words* 313/2 These young students seem to go through the ordeal..without being

unfeminized. **1895** F. ADOLPHUS *Mem. Paris* 296 The example offered by the English is unfeminising France.

un'fence, *v.* (UN-² 4.)

a **1716** SOUTH *Serm.* (T.), Whensoever it shall please God to unfence it [*sc.* a vein or artery], and let in some sharp disease or distemper upon it.

un'fenced, *ppl. a.* [UN-¹ 8.]

1. Undefended, unprotected.

1548 ELYOT, *Immunitus*, not defended, not fortified, vnfensed. **1585** HOLINSHED *Hist. Scot.* in *Chron.* II. 408/2 Iedworth [is] a towne which after the manner of the countrie is vnwalled and vnfensed, but onelie with the strength of the inhabitants. **1646** J. HALL *Horæ Vac.* 90 When a man is in earnest, he stands upon his guard; in mirth he lies open unfenc't. **1654** tr. *Martini's Conq. China* 115 The Chineses ran all away.., leaving the whole shore unfenced to their landing. **1791** COWPER *Odyssey* XI. 316 Though puissant Heroes both, in spacious Thebes, Unfenced by towers, they could not dwell secure. **1867** MORRIS *Jason* VI. 331 For the unfenced head, Where we have been, soon rests among the dead.

2. Not provided with, or enclosed by, a fence or fences.

1608 *Presentment* in *Essex Rev.* XV. 46 The churchyard is unfensed, the windows unglazed. **1623** LISLE *Ælfric on O. & N. Test.* Ded. xviii, This three-cornerd Ile on ev'ry side, Unfens'd, undelv'd, ungardined. **1725** *Fam. Dict.* s.v. *Melonry*, These take in three Ridges, only the outermost Ridge lies to the South unfenced. **1794** MISS BERRY *Jrnl.* (1865) I. 448 The country, tho' not without trees, is.. perfectly open and unfenced and unditched. **1847** LONGF. *Evang.* I. i. 9 Orchards and cornfields Spreading afar and unfenced o'er the plain. **1885** *Law Rep.* 14 *Q.B.D.* 918 The footpath ran over an open moor and was unfenced.

b. Not provided with a ledge, guard, or the like.

1683 MOXON *Mech. Exerc.*, *Printing* xxiv. ¶11 He might draw too great a body of Inck to the unfenced sides; so that the Inck would be subject to run off. **1894** *Daily News* 4 July 3/3 Machine after machine was found thus unfenced, the workpeople being too indifferent to take the trouble of putting them on.

†**un'fencible,** *a. Sc. Obs.* In 6 -fensabil. [UN-¹ 7.] Incapable of defence.

1513 DOUGLAS *Æneid* IX. xii. 16 Lyke as ane rageand wyld tygyr onstabill Amang the febill bestis onfensabill. **1536** BELLENDEN *Cron. Scot.* (1821) I. 239 The agit and febill personis, that war left at hame as unfensabil bodyis.

†**un'fended,** *ppl. a. Obs.*⁻¹ (UN-¹ 8.)

1576 GASCOIGNE *Steele Gl.* (Arb.) 76 Some other ranne, before the greedy woolfe, And left the folde, vnfended from the fox.

un'fenestrated, *ppl. a.* (UN-¹ 8.)

1884 C. B. KELSEY *Dis. Rectum* vii. 209 A good, fresh, unfenestrated drainage-tube.

unfenȝeit(lie, obs. Sc. ff. UNFEIGNED(LY.

†**un'fere,** *sb. Obs.* [Cf. next, and ON. *úfœ́ra* fem., *úfœ́ri* neut., a state of trouble or difficulty.] Infirmity, weakness.

a **1300** *Cursor M.* 3556 Sir ysaac þat dughti man, Vnfere and eld a-pon him ran.

†**un'fere,** *a. Obs.* Also 3-4 **unfer**, 3 **onver**, **-viere**, **vnueren**. [OE. *unfére* (= ON. and Icel. *ú-*, *ófœ́rr*, Norw. *uf*ø*r*, MSw. and Sw. *ofö*r): see UN-¹ 7 and FERE *a.*] Infirm, weak, unfit for or incapable of exertion. Also *absol.*

a **1060** *O.E. Chron.* (MS. C) an. 1055, Tremerig se Wylsca biscop.. wæs Æþelstanes biscopes ȝespelia syððan he unfere wæs. *c* **1205** LAY. 6780 þa iwærð þe king vn-fere [*c* **1275** on-ver]. *Ibid.* 11079 þa iwærð his fader vnueren [*c* **1275** onviere]. *c* **1250** *Gen. & Ex.* 2810 In hise bosum he dede his hond, Quit and al unfer he it fond. *a* **1300** *Cursor M.* 3507 His fader þat old was and vnfere. **13..** *Ibid.* 13262 (Gött.), þe vnfer fast tille him þai soght. *c* **1325** *Metr. Hom.* (MS. Ashm. 42) fol. 158b, A man vnfere þat nouther might speke ne here. *c* **1400** *Destr. Troy* 1357 Childer.. of chere febill, Wyth olde ffolke vnfere. *Ibid.* 13618, I am febyll and vnfere, fallyn into elde.

Hence †**un'fereness**, infirmity. *Obs.*

a **1300** *Cursor M.* 20744 He on hir bere laid his hand, þarof vnfernes son he fand.

†**unferme** (also 6 -farme), obs. var. UNFIRM *a.*

c **1450** tr. *De Imitatione* III. lxiv. 149 In þe þerfore I sette all my tribulacion,.. for I finde all vnferme & vnstable, what euere I beholde oute of þe. **1483** CAXTON *Gold. Leg.* 84/1 Theuangelyste was not so unferme but that he myght gete for hys syght that saynt andrewe gate for hym so lyghtly. *a* **1542** WYATT in *Anglia* XIX. 427, I..fele my bonis consume and wax vnfarme By dayly rage.

unfer'mentable, *a.* (UN-¹ 7b.)

1844 H. STEPHENS *Bk. Farm* II. 131 Filling the paunch with unfermentable matter.

unfer'mented, *ppl. a.* (UN-¹ 8 and 5b.)

1663 BOYLE *Usef. Exp. Nat. Philos.* II. ii. 40 The volatile salt of unfermented urine. **1731** ARBUTHNOT *Aliments* v. (1735) 123 All such Vegetables must be unfermented, for Fermentation changes their Nature. **1799** G. SMITH *Laboratory* I. 430 To make the wine keep unfermented. **1834** *Brit. Husb.* I. 250 (L.U.K.), The effect of unfermented dung on..crops. **1886** AXON *Ann. Manchester* 217 An unfermented wine for sacramental use.

un'fertile, *a.* and *sb.* (UN-¹ 7 and 5b.)

1596 *Edward III*, I. ii. 151 The ground.. Seemes barrayne, sere, vnfertill. **1620** MARKHAM *Farew. Husb.* (1625) 24 That barren and unfertile earth,.. which is overrunne only with whinnes. **1661** J. CHILDREY *Brit. Bacon.* 51 These unfertile beds do intersect each other. **1792** *Resid. France* (1797) I. 121 Unfertile, neglected vallies and hills. **1818** COLEBROOKE *Import Colonial Corn* 104 The permanent improvement of poor and unfertile land. **1865** W. G. PALGRAVE *Arabia* II. 244 A not unfertile strip of coast. *fig.* **1616** R. C. *Times' Whistle* (1871) 110 The abortive issue of my vnfertile braine. **1667** *Decay Chr. Piety* xix. ¶12 Peace is not.. such a sapless unfertile thing. **1866** WHIPPLE *Char. & Charac. Men* 54 The thought.. would not come into that unfertile brain.

b. *sb.* An unfertile egg.

1891 *Bazaar* 20 Feb. 269/3 Purchasers should always make sure that unfertiles will be replaced before giving their orders. *Ibid.*, I returned the unfertiles carriage paid.

Hence **un'fertileness, unfer'tility.**

1611 COTGR., *Infecondité*,.. vnfertilnesse, vnfruitfulnesse. **1888** *19th Cent.* June 834 The unfertility of the soil. **1899** MARY KINGSLEY *W. African Stud.* xi. 279 The unfertility of the greater part of their country.

un'fertilized, *ppl. a.* (UN-¹ 8.)

[**1775** ASH.] **1893** TUCKEY *Amphioxus* 37 A nucleus.. in the unfertilized [eggs].. was always quite plainly to be seen.

un'fervency. (UN-¹ 12.)

1787 J. BROWN in Mackenzie *Life* (1918) 285, I see.. such unfervency, and unconcern,.. in all that I have done.

unfery, obs. f. UNFEIRIE *a. Sc.*

†**un'fest,** *v. Obs.* [UN-² 4b + *fest* FAST *v.*¹] *trans.* To unfasten; to untie.

a **1225** *Ancr. R.* 218 He.. makeð him swuðe sterne,.. uorte uonden ȝete ȝif he muhte hire luue touward him unuesten. *c* **1330** R. BRUNNE *Chron. Wace* (Rolls) 651 Loke þy schip be vnfest, & þy folk be al prest. **1790** GROSE *Prov. Gloss.*, *Unfest*, to untie.

un'festival, *a.* (UN-¹ 7.)

1603 HOLLAND *Plutarch* 599 But a sacrifice, where no god is present,.. is profane, unfestivall, impious.

un'festive, *a.* (UN-¹ 7.)

1844 THACKERAY *Greenwich Whitebait* Wks. 1899 XIII. 615 Sudden gusts of genius unknown in the quiet unfestive state.

un'festly: see UNFEASTLY *a.*

un'fetched, *ppl. a.* (UN-¹ 8c.)

c **1611** CHAPMAN *Iliad* XIX. 196 Our friends by Hector slaine,.. lie vnfetch [*sic*] off. **1616** J. LANE *Contn. Sqr.'s T.* x. 430 Distroienge all and some, that stood in 's way, nor left hee one vnfetchd vp.

unfete: see UNFEAT *a. Obs.*

un'fetid, *a.* (UN-¹ 7.)

1754 *Phil. Trans.* XLVIII. 829 Which must therefore be the effect of unfetid putrefaction.

un'fetter, *v.* [UN-² 4b. Cf. G. *entfesseln.*] To free from fetters; to remove the fetters from.

1362 LANGL. *P. Pl.* A. III. 134 Heo ȝeueþ þe Iayler Gold and grotes.. To vn-Fetere þe False. *c* **1400** *Gamelyn* 613 The shirreue unfetered him right sone anone. *c* **1412** HOCCLEVE *De Reg. Princ.* 2399 To prison he gooth; he gette no bettre, Til his mainpernour his arrest vnfettre. **1485** CAXTON *Paris & V.* (1868) 81 He sayd to the freres that they shold unfeter the doulphyn. **1598** FLORIO, *Scatenare*, to vnchaine, to vnfetter, to vnshakle. **1611** COTGR., *Destraver*, to vnshackle, vngyue, vnfetter. **1748** SMOLLETT *R. Random* xxvii, Captain Oakum.. ordered the fellow to be unfettered. **1799** COLERIDGE *Devil's Thoughts* xi, He saw the same Turnkey unfetter a man, With but little expedition.

b. In fig. contexts or uses.

c **1374** CHAUCER *Troylus* II. 1216 She.. gan hire herte vnfettre Out of disdaygns prison but a lyte. *a* **1470** HARDING *Chron.* CXI. vii, Fyftye batayls and syx he smote, Somtyme the worse, and somtyme had the better;.. Lyke as fortune his cause leste vnfeter. **1627** SANDERSON *Serm.* I. 280 As for whatsoever other hank thou mayst think thou hast over him,.. he can.. easily unfetter himself from them all. **1671** WOODHEAD *St. Teresa* I. xx. 136 Whom she desires to see unfettered from the prison of this life. **1766** BLACKSTONE *Comm.* II. 345 The transcendent power of parliament is called in.. to unfetter an estate. **1830** HERSCHEL *Study Nat. Phil.* 8 It unfetters the mind from prejudices of every kind. *c* **1860** FABER *Hymn, Desire of God* v, And the langour of love captive hearts can unfetter.

Hence **un'fettering** *vbl. sb.* and *ppl. a.*

a **1653** BINNING *Serm.* (1845) 189 To bring along a Deliverer unto your spirits, for the.. unfettering of them from the chains of fleshly lusts. **1824** MISS L. M. HAWKINS *Mem.*, etc. I. 257 Too much of the spirit of John Knox, or something equally unfettering. **1854** J. B. PATON in *Life* iii. (1914) 33 Those words which should for ever consecrate us to His unfettering service.

un'fettered, *ppl. a.* [UN-¹ 8: cf. Sw. *ofjettrad.*] Not confined or restrained by fetters. Chiefly in fig. use: Unrestrained, unrestricted.

1601 DONNE *Progr. Soul* I. xviii, To an unfetterd soules quick nimble hast Are falling stars, and hearts thoughts, but slow pac'd. **1697** DRYDEN *Æneis* Ded., Ess. (ed. Ker) II. 220 Now, if a Muse cannot run when she is unfettered, it is a sign she has but little speed. **1748** SMOLLETT *R. Random* xxiv, One of my fellow captives who was unfettered. **1787** BURNS *Let. to Moore* 15 Feb., The unfettered wild flight of native genius. **1855** PRESCOTT *Philip II*, II. i. (1857) 193 A people accustomed from infancy to the unfettered exercise of their faculties. **1879** FROUDE *Cæsar* x. 117 He was left unfettered to act at his own discretion.

b. Const. *by.*

1800 *Asiat. Ann. Reg., Chron.* 14/1 He took a new estate, unfettered by conditions, and subject only to the quit rents. **1850** TENNYSON *In Mem.* xxvii, I envy not the beast that takes His license.. Unfetter'd by the sense of crime.

un'feudal, *a.* (UN-¹ 7.)

c **1815** JANE AUSTEN *Persuas.* xv, Feelings.. too strict to suit the unfeudal tone of the present day.

un'feudalize, *v.* (UN-² 6c.)

1837 CARLYLE *Fr. Rev.* II. v. v, The Austrian Kaiser answers that his German Princes.. cannot be unfeudalised.

un'feudalized, *ppl. a.* (UN-¹ 8.)

1801 HELEN M. WILLIAMS *Sk. Fr. Rep.* I. vi. 57 The lavish produce of the earth unfeudalized, and untythed. **1874** *Act 37 & 38 Vict.* c. 94 §9 A personal right to land under an unfeudalized conveyance.

un'feued, *ppl. a. Sc.* (UN-¹ 8.)

1819 *Aberdeen Jrnl.* 20 Jan. (Jam.), The unfeued and unproductive property. **1871** W. ALEXANDER *Johnny Gibb* xliv, Half-a-dozen acres of the unfeued land.

un'fevered, *ppl. a.* (UN-¹ 8.)

1864 SIR A. DE VERE *Tr. & Cr.* 4 Had I been worthy of the love you gave,.. My bed had been unfever'd as my grave.

†**unfew,** *a.*: see UN-¹ 3.

unfezable, var. UNFEASABLE *a. Obs.*

un'fibrous, *a.* (UN-¹ 7.)

1768–74 TUCKER *Lt. Nat.* (1834) I. 395 That small mixture of unfibrous matter, which may serve as an integument.

un'fickle, *a.* (UN-¹ 7.)

1802 MARIAN MOORE *Lascelles* II. 233 Frank, ingenuous, and unfickle in his behaviour.

unfic'titious, *a.* (UN-¹ 7.)

1836 *Todd's Cycl. Anat.* I. 799/2 Scott's touching picture.. has had many unfictitious counterparts. **1858** CARLYLE *Fred. Gt.* IV. xiii, For work is of an extremely unfictitious nature.

un'fiery, *a.* (UN-¹ 7.)

c **1611** CHAPMAN *Iliad* VII. 84 But you are earth and water all, which.. Have framed your faint unfiery spirits.

un'fight, *v.* (UN-² 3.)

1720 T. GORDON *Humourist* I. 3 Fighting Battles and unfighting them in the same Paper.

un'fighting, *ppl. a.* (UN-¹ 10.)

1678 RYMER *Trag. Last Age* 27 The Spectators were some sort of feminine unfighting fellows. *a* **1704** T. BROWN *Wks.* (1720) IV. 37 Their General gone, the rest like Lightning fly, A cheap unfighting Herd. **1747** in *Gentl. Mag.* XVII. 234 Descants upon unfighting captains at sea.

†**un'figurate,** *a. Obs.* (UN-¹ 7.)

a **1752** R. ERSKINE in Fisher *Mem.* (1765) 115 Christ is the second Adam, the real unfigurate head of the human body.

un'figurative, *a.* (UN-¹ 7.)

1780 BENTHAM *Princ. Legisl.* x. §4 The sense it bears on these occasions may be styled its literal or unfigurative sense. **1871** MACDUFF *Macduff Mem. Patmos* xxi. 287 St. Peter's unfigurative Epistle.

un'figured, (*ppl.*) *a.* [UN-¹ 8 and 9.]

1. Not expressed in, or employing, figurative speech.

1577 tr. *Bullinger's Decades* IV. i. 534/2 The vnfigured and vnrecouered promises.. in the Psalmes. **1783** BLAIR *Lect.* I. xv. 317 What we call the moral, is the unfigured sense or meaning of the Allegory. **1827** G. S. FABER *Sacr. Cal. Prophecy* (1844) I. 8 The unfigured language of highly cultivated nations. **1904** DOWDEN *Browning* 68 A plain, unfigured and uncoloured style.

2. Not marked with a numerical figure or figures.

1596 NASHE *Saffron Walden* F 2b, Hee.. in halfe a quire of paper.. hath left the Pages vnfigured. **1873** H. C. BANISTER *Music* 62 It is understood that the unfigured notes bear Triads. *Ibid.* 287 All the Unfigured Basses.

3. Not including figures of persons, etc.

1624 WOTTON *Elem. Archit.* 96 In vnfigured paintings the noblest is, the imitation of Marbles, and of Architecture it selfe.

b. Not (yet) depicted by a figure.

1822 J. PARKINSON *Oryctology* 244 *Nautilus*, an unfigured species deeply umbilicated. **1869** D. G. ELLIOT (*title*), The new and heretofore unfigured Species of the Birds of North America.

4. *Logic.* Of a syllogism: Not belonging to one of the usual figures.

1838 SIR W. HAMILTON *Logic* App. (1860) IV. 350 The Unfigured Syllogism, or that in which the terms compared do not stand to each other in the reciprocal relation of subject and predicate. **1864** BOWEN *Logic* viii. 244 Reducing all Mediate Inference to what he calls the Unfigured Syllogism.

un'filamentous, *a.* (UN-¹ 7.)

1831 R. KNOX *Cloquet's Anat.* 472 The white and unfilamentous cord.. behind the rest of the nerve.

un'filched, *ppl. a.* (UN-¹ 8.)

1818 BYRON *Juan* I. clxv, Nothing so dear as an unfilch'd good name!

un'filed, *ppl. a.*¹ *Obs.* exc. *dial.* [UN-¹ 8 + FILE *v.*²] Undefiled; unfouled.

c **1200** *Trin. Coll. Hom.* 133 Ure drihten him shop of eorðe þat was unfiled. *a* **1300** *E.E. Psalter* xvii. 33 Mi God unfiled es his wai. *a* **1340** HAMPOLE *Psalter* xvii. 35 God þat beltid me wiþ vertu, & sett vnfiled my way. **1435** MISYN *Fire of Love* 44 Faynres of þi mynde.. sall make þe beloued if it to lufe of hym onely þou kepe vnfilyd. *a* **1470** HARDING *Chron.* CXXVI. iii, Clothes and meate and beddyng newe vnfiled, Wyne also and ale she gaue. **1513** DOUGLAS *Æneid* II. ii. 153

Be the hie goddis abuife,..And by the faith wnfilit,..Gif it with mortale folkis ma fundin be. **1583–4** *Burgh Rec. Edinb.* (1882) IV. 321 That thai keip the said nichtbouris quheitt.. vnfylet. **1791–** in *Eng. Dial. Dict.*

un'filed, *ppl. a.*^{2} [UN-^{1} 8 + FILE *v.*^{1}] Not reduced or smoothed by filing; *fig.* unpolished, rude.

1590 SPENSER *F.Q.* III. vii. 30 He was all armd in rugged steele vnfilde, As in the smoky forge it was compilde. **1633** WITHER *Juvenilia, Sat. King* 342 Pardon me, and daigne a gracious eye On this my rude unfil'd Apologie. **1641** W. CARTWRIGHT *Royal Slave* Epil., The unfil'd Author.. Fears yet he may miscarry. **1774** W. MASON *Heroic Postscript to Chambers* 12 Each glittering orb the sacred features bore Of George.., Unfil'd, unsweated, all of sterling weight.

un'filed, *ppl. a.*^{3} [UN-^{1} 8 + FILE *v.*^{3}] Not arranged in or as in a file; not placed on a file.

1571 CAMPION *Hist. Irel.* v. (1633) 15 Of this people therefore severally by themselves I must intreate. Yet none otherwise then as they stand unfiled. **1864** TREVELYAN *Compet. Wallah* (1866) 36 Codes and translations of codes, and letters of every size and age, filed and unfiled.

un'filial, *a.* (UN-^{1} 7.)

Also ***unfilially*** adv. (Webster 1864), ***unfilialness***.

1611 SHAKS. *Wint. T.* IV. iv. 417 You offer him.. a wrong Something vnfilliall. **1648** BOYLE *Seraphic Love* (1659) 121 To preserve them from the Contagion of Sinne, or Cure them of the unfilial habitudes of it. **1756** FOOTE *Eng. fr. Paris* II, Ungrateful, unfilial wretch! so soon to trample on his ashes. **1803** WORDSW. *'When I have borne'* 8 Verily, in the bottom of my heart, Of those unfilial fears I am ashamed. **1880** MOULE *Chinese Stories* v. 78, I charged him with unfilial conduct in compelling his mother.. to connive at idolatry.

†**un'filing**, *ppl. a.* (UN-^{1} 10 + FILE *v.*^{2})

a **1400** *New Test.* (Paues) 1 Peter iii. 4 (p. 215), þat þat is hydde wiþ-inne in mans herte.. in vnfilynge reste (of here body & soule).

un'fill, *v.* [UN-^{2} 3. Cf. obs. Flem. *ontvullen.*] *trans.* † **a.** To stop, break off. *Obs.* **b.** To empty.

1486 *Bk. St. Albans, Hunting* e vj b, To fulfill or vnfill eche maner of chaas The hunt euermoore in his mowth that worde he haas. **1607** TOURNEUR *Rev. Trag.* II. ii, Thy veines are sweld with lust, this shall unfill 'em. **1611** COTGR., *Desemplir*, to emptie, or vnfill.

un'fillable, *a.* Now *rare.* (UN-^{1} 7 b.)

a **1340** HAMPOLE *Psalter* c. 7 Wiþ proude eghe & vnfilabil [L. *insatiabili*] hert. **1382** WYCLIF *Prov.* xxvii. 20 Helle and perdiciour neuere ben fulfild; and the eȝen of men vnfillable. **1456** SIR G. HAYE *Law Arms* (S.T.S.) 27 Ane unfillable gredy appetite. *c* **1475** *Cath. Angl.* 130/2 VnFylabylle, *insaciabilis.* *c* **1610** *Women Saints* 178 Ouergoing that vnsatiable greedynes of euill, with vnfillable desire of goodnes. **1890** *Brit. Med. Jrnl.* 2 Aug. 293 Places which had hitherto seemed unfillable by the pigmies of our later days.

un'filled, *ppl. a.* [UN-^{1} 8, 8 c. Cf. OE. *unȝefylled*, Du. *ongevuld*, G. *unausgefüllt.*]

1. Not filled; not made full.

1584 COGAN *Haven Health* ccxiv. 201 That it were better to eate fine meates first, and grosser meates afterward, if perchaunce any corner were left vnfilled. **1601** SHAKS. *Twel. N.* II. iii. 7 A false conclusion: I hate it as an vnfill'd Canne. **1646** CRASHAW *Sospetto d'Herode* xlii, A cursed Feast, Which Harpyes, with leane Famine feed upon, Unfill'd for ever. **1755** JOHNSON, *Unstuffed*, unfilled, unfurnished. **1837** CARLYLE *Fr. Rev.* I. VII. i, Our mouths, unfilled with bread, are to be shut, under penalties? **1893** *Spectator* 15 Apr. 471/1 The Colonies.. possess great properties in their unfilled lands.

b. With *up.*

c **1640** J. SMYTH *Lives Berkeleys* (1883) II. 380 Hee.. being within less then his length of an old Colepit unfilled up. **1817** J. SCOTT *Paris Revisit.* (ed. 4) 105 That their capacities.. did not seem to be improved,—that much of them remained unfilled up.

†**2.** Unfulfilled. *Obs.*

c **1400** *Apol. Loll.* 34 So is no man worþi to mak a letter or title of his to go by vnfillid. **1651** BAXTER *Inf. Bapt.* 296 Those to whom that Promise is yet unfilled.

un'filleted, *ppl. a.* (UN-^{1} 8.)

[**1775** ASH.] **1802** COLERIDGE *Picture* 158 The hand Holds loosely its small handful of wild-flowers, Unfilleted, and of unequal lengths. **1868** SWINBURNE *Ess. & Stud.* (1875) 363 The heavy straying flakes of unfilleted hair.

†**unfilling(like**, (*ppl.*) *a.* *Obs.* [UN-^{1} 10, 7 c.] Insatiable.

a **1300** *E.E. Psalter* c. 6 With proud egh and un-fillandlike [*v.r.* un-filland] hert.

un'film, *v.* (UN-^{2} 4 b.)

1839 BAILEY *Festus* 16, I will.. unfilm them, That so thou mayst not dally with the blind. **1871** PALGRAVE *Lyr. Poems* 115 The callow bird unfilm'd his fervent eyes.

un'filtered, *ppl. a.* (UN-^{1} 8, 9.)

[**1775** ASH.] **1896** *Pop. Sci. Monthly* April 857 The resulting unfiltered stream of bacteria. **1976** 'O. BLEECK' *No Questions Asked* iv. 48 Spivey produced a pack of unfiltered Camels, lit one. **1980** M. GORDON *Company of Women* (1981) II. v. 227 They both smoked unfiltered cigarettes.

un'findable, *a.* (UN-^{1} 7 b.)

1791 BENTHAM *Mem. & Corr.* Wks. 1843 X. 248 Hampstead is the road you must take, as the other would be unfindable. **1859** GREEN *Lett.* (1901) 32 Lady of my dream, unfindable among human flesh and blood. **1895** *Athenæum* 17 Aug. 224/3 [A book] not unfindable, scarce though it be.

un'fine, *a.* (UN-^{1} 7; cf. MDu. *onfijn*, MHG. *unvin*, G. *unfein*, Da. *ufin.*)

c **1400** MAUNDEV. (Roxb.) 149 Pissemyres.. disseuerez þe fyne gold fra þe vnfyne. **1566** DRANT *Horace, Sat.* II. iii. G j b, If one.. drincke nothing but vinaiger, vntastie and vnfyne. **1687** MONTAGUE & PRIOR *Hind & P. Transv.* 26 Thou hast brought us Wine, Sour to my tast, and to my Eyes unfine. *a* **1700** B. E. *Dict. Cant. Crew, Foul Wine*, when it stinks; also when unfine. **1762** H. WALPOLE *Let. to Montagu* 8 June, The birth-day was far from being such a show; empty and unfine as possible. **1793** SIR J. DINELY *Methods to get Husbands* 7 Your convenient legs, younger than mine, Can nimbly travel in weather unfine.

†**un'fined**, *ppl. a.* *Obs.* [UN-^{1} 8 + FINE *v.*^{3}] Unrefined, unpurified.

a **1500** *Colkelbie Sow* III. 857 (Bannatyne MS.), So long as it lay on the ground, It was vnfynit as fruct nevirmoir found. **1606** W. CRASHAW *Rom. Forgeries* 33 This is new and vnfined wine put into this old vessell. **1611** COTGR., *Balluque*, gold ore, or gold vnfined. **1628** FELTHAM *Resolves* I. lxxxix. 83 In drinking the Wine, that is yet vnfined.

un'fingered, (*ppl.*) *a.* [UN-^{1} 8 and 9. Cf. (in sense 2) older Flem. *ongevingert.*]

1. Not provided with fingers.

1603 J. DAVIES (Heref.) *Extasie* Wks. (Grosart) I. 91/1 Not haire, but golden wire drawne like the Twist The Spider spins with her vnfing'red fist.

2. Not touched with the fingers; unhandled.

1811 W. R. SPENCER *Poems* 190 When sighs of seraph lovers Breathe upon th' unfinger'd wire. **1889** BARRIE *Window in Thrums* 173 The few shillings.. remained unfingered.

†**un'finified**, *ppl. a.* *Obs.* (UN-^{1} 8.)

1609 W. M. *Man in Moone* (1849) 26 No friend to the barber it should seeme by his rusticall, overgrowne, and unfinified beard.

un'finish. [UN-^{1} 12.] Want of finish; unfinished state.

1831 FR. A. KEMBLE *Rec. Girlhood* (1878) III. 26 Found the stage in a state of unfinish. **1875** PITT-RIVERS *Evol. Culture* (1906) 34 A celt.. somewhat rougher, and showing evidence of unfinish.

un'finishable, *a.* (UN-^{1} 7 b.)

a **1739** JARVIS *Quix.* I. I. i, He commended in his author the concluding his book with a promise of that unfinishable adventure. **1835** MOTLEY *Corr.* (1889) I. iii. 59, I thought.. of strange, unfinished, unfinishable buildings. **1878** T. SINCLAIR *Mount* 166 Faust.. ever remains a torso unfinishable.

un'finished, *ppl. a.* (UN-^{1} 8.)

1553 in Feuillerat *Revels Q. Mary* (1914) 150 The same.. surseased and were lefte of vnfynysshed. **1590** SHAKS. *Com. Err.* III. ii. 173 The chaine vnfinish'd made me stay thus long. **1671** MILTON *Samson* 1027 That inward gifts Were left for hast unfinish't. **1714** R. FIDDES *Pract. Disc.* I. 144 We haue so great a work lying unfinish'd upon our hands. **1797** S. & HT. LEE *Canterb. T.* (1799) I. 373 The recital he was about to make remained unfinished. **1865** DICKENS *Mut. Fr.* II. i, Here, another unfinished street already in ruins. **1887** BOWEN *Æneid* IV. 77 She.. Speaks, then leaves unfinished the speech already begun.

Hence **un'finishedness**.

1887 *Pall Mall G.* 22 Jan. 4/1 There is an appearance of hurry and unfinishedness about some [pictures].

un'finishing, *vbl. sb.* (UN-^{1} 13.)

1642 MILTON *Apol. Smect.* §8 Their noble deeds, the unfinishing whereof already surpasses what others before them have left enacted.

un'fired, *ppl. a.* [UN-^{1} 8.]

1. Not set on fire; unignited.

1590 SIR J. SMYTH *Disc. Weapons* 18 b, With the powder next vnto the bullets vnfired. **1623** MASSINGER *Bondman* IV. ii, *Marullo.* We'll right ourselves... *Gracculo.* And not leave One house unfired. **1664** EVELYN *Sylva* 102 It is continually to be fed with short and fitting wood, that no part remains unfir'd. **1756** *Demi-Rep* 14 Chaste as unfired coals they seem. **1781** *Phil. Trans.* LXXI. 248 No less than 40 large grains of unfired powder were driven through the screen. **1849** JAMES *Woodman* ix, The abbey itself was still unfired. *fig.* **1729** T. COOKE *Tales*, etc. 24 The human Brute, who view'd her Charms unfir'd. *a* **1788** EARL NUGENT *Ep. Visct. Cornbury* 154 Such gifts she to the happy few imparts,.. To heads unfir'd by youth's tumultuous rage.

2. Not subjected or exposed to fire.

1791 COWPER *Iliad* XXIII. 1092 Then, last, Achilles in the circus placed A pond'rous spear and cauldron yet unfired. **1888** *Archaeol.* LI. I. 52 These un-fired bricks lasted perfectly well.

3. Of a gun: Not discharged by firing.

1892 GREENER *Breech-Loader* 200 If one barrel is fired repeatedly without discharging the other, it is advisable to take out the unfired cartridge occasionally. **1902** *Daily Chron.* 16 Apr. 7/6 The starboard gun remained unfired.

un'firm, *a.* [UN-^{1} 7 and 5 b; cf. INFIRM *a.* and the earlier form UNFERME.]

1. Of a loose or soft consistency; incompact.

1592 SHAKS. *Rom. & Jul.* v. iii. 6 The Churchyard.. Being loose, vnfirme with digging vp of Graues. **1625** K. LONG tr. *Barclay's Argenis* II. ii. 71 Further onward the water very deepe, and the ground unfirm. **1683** TRYON *Way to Health* 95 What is the reason that most Veal is so unfirm and like a Jelly? **1726** LEONI *Alberti's Archit.* II. 117 b, When the banks of a River are unfirm, its channel will be stopt up with shelves. **1866** J. B. ROSE tr. *Ovid's Met.* 1 Unfirm the earth, unbuoyant was the wave.

†**2.** Unsteady, flighty. *Obs.*

1601 SHAKS. *Twel. N.* II. iv. 34 Our fancies are more giddie and vnfirme.. Then womens are.

†**3.** Weak; wanting in strength or power; feeble, infirm, invalid. *Obs.*

1616 SURFL. & MARKH. *Country Farme* III. ix. 345 A subiect of a more feeble and vnfirme nature than the graft it selfe. **1660** JER. TAYLOR *Ductor* III. v. rule viii. §8 For without it, it [*sc.* marriage] is not only inauspicious and unlucky, but illegal, unfirm and insufficient.

4. Not firmly placed or planted; insecure; unstable, unsteady; liable to slip or fall.

1697 DRYDEN *Æneis* x. 397 Now take the time, while staggering yet they stand With feet unfirm. **1761** EARL PEMBROKE *Milit. Equitation* (1778) 58 Depend upon it those people are not only ignorant and unfeeling, but also very unfirm in their seat. **1771** MRS. GRIFFITH *Hist. Lady Barton* III. 20 His supplicating eye.. may change my unfirm purpose. **1809** *Susan* I. 176 Our best resolutions are, however, unfirm.

un'firmamented, *ppl. a.* (UN-^{1} 8.)

1843 CARLYLE *Past & Pr.* III. viii, Burying itself.. in the waste unfirmamented seas. **1865** MRS. WHITNEY *Gayworthys* xliii, He had touched unfirmamented space.

un'firmly, *adv.* (UN-^{1} 11, 5 b. Cf. UNFIRM *a.*)

1633 FORD *Broken H.* IV. ii, Like tempest-threatened trees, unfirmly rooted. **1822–7** GOOD *Study Med.* (1829) II. 418 The child walks unfirmly, as though stepping over a threshold.

un'firmness. (UN-^{1} 12, 5 b; cf. INFIRMNESS.)

1566 *Act 8 Eliz.* c. 8 §1 Fenne Groundes, because of their rottennesse, unfirmnes, moysture and wateryshnes [etc.]. **1828** WEBSTER.

un'fishable, *a.* (UN-^{1} 7 b.)

1873 G. C. DAVIES *Mount. & Mere* ii. 8 The other side was so shallow and muddy that it was unfishable. **1891** A. LANG *Angling Sk.* 98 The loch is almost unfishable.

un'fished, *ppl. a.* (UN-^{1} 8.)

1863 JOHNS *Home Walks* 47 The main reason why unfished waters are most productive, is that they are then more plentifully stocked. **1883** in N. Okoshi *Fisheries Japan* 26 In his unfortunate country [*sc.* Ireland] they had at present over 2500 miles of unfished coast.

un'fishlike, *a.* (UN-^{1} 7 c.)

1874 WOOD *Nat. Hist.* 621 A creature so unfishlike that its real position.. was long undecided.

un'fist, *v.* [UN-^{2} 4 b.] *trans.* To unhand.

1692 [J. SMITH] *Scarron.* 85 You goodman Brandy-face, unfist her; How durst you keep my wife?—your sister.

un'fit, *a.* (and *adv.*). [UN-^{1} 7 and 5 b.]

1. a. Of things: Not fit, proper, or suitable *for* some purpose or end. †Also const. *to* (a person).

In quot. 1709 app. 'badly fitting'.

1548 UDALL, etc. *Erasm. Par. John* i. 11 b, For there is no tyme nor place vnfit or vnconuenient for to learne those thynges whiche pertayne to euerlastynge welth. **1584** in *Cath. Rec. Soc. Publ.* V. 82 The Earle.. gave the poore man many.. opprobrious wordes, unfytte and unseemely for a man of that howse and blod. *a* **1658** LOVELACE *Poems* (1904) 191 He that dares this, nothing to him's unfit. **1697** DRYDEN *Virg. Georg.* IV. 190 Lord of few Acres, and those barren too; Unfit for Sheep or Vines, and more unfit to sow. **1709** *Lond. Gaz.* No. 4551/4 He wears.. a brown Drugget Coat and Wastecoat.. very unfit for him. **1785** COWPER *Let. to Newton* 19 Mar., The sideboard-table.. was equally unfit for my purpose. **1812** CRABBE *Tales* xiii. 351 Those duties were to her unfit, Nor would her spirit to her tasks submit. **1827** FARADAY *Chem. Manip.* v. (1842) 151 Mortars of wood, marble, or iron, are unfit for ordinary laboratory service. **1884** THOMPSON *Tumours of Bladder* 71 In cases considered temporarily unfit for operation through exhaustion, etc.

b. Without prepositional const.

1545 ASCHAM *Toxoph.* (Arb.) 118 An vnfit and staffysh bow. *a* **1586** SIDNEY *Arcadia* II. xxix, Because of the unfit election she had made. **1604** E. G[RIMSTONE] *D'Acosta's Hist. Indies* VI. xiv. 460 Although these buildings were great, yet were they commonly ill appoynted and vnfit. **1661** RUST *Origen's Opin.* 78 If old age it self can make the Soul quit her unfit tenement. **1711** in *Nairne Peerage Evidence* (1874) 133 Rendered the same unfit and in human probability impossible. **1863** HAWTHORNE *Our Old Home* (1879) 317 The anxious fidelity with which they discharged their unfit office.

c. Const. with inf. (active or passive).

a **1586** SIDNEY *Arcadia* I. xiii, A place for pleasantnes, not unfitte to flatter solitarinesse. **1611** COTGR., *Imbuvable*, vndrinkable; vnfit to be drunke of. **1651** HOBBES *Leviath.* II. xxix. 173 There be other [diseases], not so great; which neverthelesse are not unfit to be observed. **1697** [see 1 a]. **1710** LADY M. W. MONTAGU *Let. to Mr. W. Montagu* Aug., There are a thousand things, not ill in themselves, which custom makes unfit to be done. **1879** HARLAN *Eyesight* viii. 117 The flame.. is never steady, and is unfit to read by.

2. a. Of persons (or other agents): Not fitted, suited, or adapted for some end or action. Also *Comb.* (in ***unfit-like***) and *absol.*

1551 T. WILSON *Logike* D j, We see many dull wittes for lernyng, and muche vnfit that waie. **1577** tr. *Bullinger's Decades* (1592) 510 To giue an vnfitte man orders,.. is that kind of sin which we doe call anothers sin. **1782** J. BROWN *Nat. & Rev. Relig.* II. i. (1796) 105 In propagating the gospel by so unfit-like instruments. **1818** CRUISE *Digest* (ed. 2) III. 128 A person unknown and unfit.. may happen to have the same, under an estate of inheritance. **1882** *Nonconf. & Indep.* 10 Oct. 986/1 The survival of the unfittest, instead of the fittest.

b. Const. *to* (chiefly with inf.) or *for.*

(*a*) **1586** T. B. *La Primaud. Fr. Acad.* (1589) 111 It maketh him good for nothing,.. slothfull, and unfit to every good thing. **1630** PRYNNE *Anti-Armin.* 136 This makes them.. open rebels against God, vnfit to take his word or name within their lips. **1645** MILTON *Colast.* Wks. 1851 IV. 349 The unfittest man that could bee to offer at a comment upon Job. **1747** H. WALPOLE *Lett.* (1846) II. 201, I am the unfittest person in the world to give you any satisfaction on this head. **1816** BYRON *Ch. Har.* III. xii, But soon he knew himself the most unfit Of men to herd with Man. **1863** H. COX *Instit.* I. vii. 91 Men who are morally or intellectually unfit to be jurors.

(*b*) **1594** SHAKS. *Rich. III*, I. ii. 109 *Rich.* He was fitter for that place then earth. *An.* And thou vnfit for any place, but hell. **1660** R. COKE *Power & Subj.* 73 Being of all mortal men the most unfit for a Churchman. **1697** DRYDEN *Virg. Georg.* III. 102 Then release the Cow, Unfit for Love, and for the lab'ring Plough. **1736** BERKELEY *Disc.* Wks. 1871 III. 413 Monsters, utterly unfit for human society. **1855** MACAULAY *Hist. Eng.* xv. III. 584 In order that one man might fill a post for which he was unfit. **1880** DIXON *Windsor* IV. i. 2 He was a man unfit for such a trust.

3. Not physically fit.

Usually const. *for* or with infinitive.

1665 in *Verney Mem.* (1907) II. 251, I grow every day more unfit for such a Jorney. *a* **1718** PRIOR *Amaryllis* 24 The furious heat forbids the reaper's toil. Both beast and men for work are now unfit. **1798** S. & HT. LEE *Canterb. T.* II. 428 The Marquis was very unfit for a journey when he left Naples. **1856** KANE *Arct. Expl.* II. i. 26, I am myself so disabled..as to be entirely unfit..to do any work.

4. As *adv.* Unfitly.

1653 J. TAYLOR (Water P.) *Cert. Trav. uncert. Journ.* 8 Sometimes the wits and tongues do, most unfit, Travell, when tongues do run before the wit.

5. As *sb.* A person whose mental or physical health falls below a desired standard.

1912 *Q. Rev.* Apr. 496 The statistics..showing the enormous number of 'unfits', made clear the havoc wrought by the modern city. **1925** *Scribner's Mag.* July 7/2 By cutting off the reproduction of these social unfits,..we can go so far.

un'fit, *v.* [UN-^{2} 6.] *trans.* To render unfit; to disqualify.

1611 FLORIO, *Disadattare*, to vnfit, to disorder. **1665** BOYLE *Occas. Refl.* II. x. (1848) 128, I..esteem'd sickness more formidable for its unfitting me to learn. **1690** NORRIS *Beatitudes* (1692) 80 Consider again, How much causless.. Anger unfits us for all the Parts of Divine Worship. **1779** *Mirror* No. 16, It may disqualify the mind for the more active..scenes of life, and unfit it for the enjoyments of ordinary society. **1847** HELPS *Friends in C.* (1851) I. 36 To have erred in one branch of our duties does not unfit us for all the rest. **1898** 'MERRIMAN' *Roden's Corner* vi. 57 Those whose birth and education unfit them for such pursuits.

un'fitly, *adv.* [UN-^{1} 11.] In an unfit or unsuitable manner; unfittingly, inappropriately.

1561 T. NORTON tr. *Calvin's Inst.* I. xiii. 37b, Least if I bryng foorth any thyng vnfittly, it shuld geue occasion..to the malicious to cauill. **1632** MASSINGER & FIELD *Fatal Dowry* III. i, Wherein hath Charalois Unfitly so demean'd himself? **1676** JAS. COOKE *Marrow Chirurg.* I. III. vii. 590 There are chaps of the Lips and other parts, which if neglected or unfitly dressed, may turn Cancerous. **1788** GIBBON *Decl. & F.* lx. VI. 128 Their military talents were unfitly recompensed by the lucrative offices of judges and treasurers. **1807** G. CHALMERS *Caledonia* I. III. vii. 393 It is, however, unfitly interpolated, by the editor, as a continuation of the *Chronicon Pictorum*.

b. In the phr. ***not unfitly***.

1586 T. B. *La Primaud. Fr. Acad.* I. 160 The answer also of an Egyptian was not unfitlie made to one that asked him what he caried there folded. **1615** CROOKE *Body of Man* 541 Thence also they are not vnfitly called by a Poet..The leaues of the Eye. **1695** J. EDWARDS *Perfect. Script.* 236 They..are not unfitly translated *aprons.* **1710** BERKELEY *Princ. Hum. Knowl.* §108 The steady consistent methods of nature may not unfitly be styled the Language of its Author. **1853** RUSKIN *Stones Ven.* II. vi. 215 The three architectures may..not unfitly receive their names from those nations by whom they were carried to the highest perfection.

un'fitness. [UN-^{1} 12.]

1. Want of fitness (in various senses).

a **1586** SIDNEY *Arcadia* III. xxiv, Having impatiently borne the delay of the nights unfitnesse, this morning he gat up. **1624** in Ellis *Orig. Lett.* Ser. I. III. 173, I represented to her the unfitnesse of the seventh article. **1643-5** MILTON *Divorce* I. i, What greater..unfitnes of mind then that which hinders ever the solace..of the married couple. **1736** BUTLER *Anal.* I. iii. 69 A Proof from Fact..which is deduced from..the Fitness and Unfitness of Actions. **1750** tr. *Leonardus' Mirr. Stones* 31 A bad commixture..sometimes happens..from the unfitness of the place, which gives a diversity to stones. **1824** SOUTHEY *Sir T. More* (1831) II. 94 There is a natural unfitness in distant dominion. **1863** COX *Instit.* III. iii. 636 The rule..has no respect to the fitness or unfitness of the persons.

b. Const. *for*, or *to* with inf.

1619 in Foster *Eng. Factories India* (1906) I. 70 The unfitnesse of those comodityes for the Dabulleers. **1631** GOUGE *God's Arrows* III. §22. 223 Mans unworthinesse and unfitnesse to appeare in Gods sight. **1750** SECKER *Eight Charges* (1771) 124, I have too much Cause, in every Thing, to be sensible of my own Unfitness to direct. **1811** *Regul. & Orders Army* 283 The Causes of their unfitness for further Military Service. **1885** *Manch. Exam.* 18 Mar. 5/2 There was..evidence of his unfitness to take care of himself.

2. With pl. An instance of lack of fitness.

1645 MILTON *Tetrach.* Wks. 1851 IV. 193 Law..cannot make equal those inequalities, it cannot make fit those unfitnesses. **1674** N. FAIRFAX *Bulk & Selv.* 32 If they could be brought in without other unfitnesses.

un'fitted, *ppl. a.* [UN-^{1} 8.]

1. Not adapted or suited; unfit.

1592 in Ellis *Orig. Lett.* Ser. III. IV. 109, I am come upp raggedlie suted and clothed, unfittedst to geve duetiefull attendance on Royall presence. *a* **1625** FLETCHER *Hum. Lieut.* II. iv, How yet unripe we were, unblown, unharden'd, Unfitted for such fatal ends. **1794** S. WILLIAMS *Vermont* 351 Such a code is wholly unfitted to the uncorrupted state of the people. **1809** KENDALL *Trav.* I. i. 7 A scene, that was not unfitted to leave on the mind a..respectful impression. **1873** SYMONDS *Grk. Poets* x. 340 Unfitted, perhaps, by temperament for the most impassioned lyrics, Tennyson delights in minutely finished pictures.

2. Not provided with something suitable.

1606 CHAPMAN *Gentl. Usher* IV. iv, If it be nothing but the jarre Of your unfitted fancie that procures Your wilfull coynesse.

3. Not fitted up or out; not properly furnished.

1708 *Lond. Gaz.* No. 4414/3 Some [ships] in the Peer are yet unfitted. **1908** *Animal Managem.* 269 If for military reasons long journeys have to be made in unfitted trucks.

4. Not adjusted by fitting.

1895 *Pall Mall G.* 1 Feb. 5/2 Nations that have not arrived at the artificial prettiness of finely-fitted dress had best be content with the natural beauty of unfitted.

Hence **un'fittedness.**

1654 GAYTON *Pleas. Notes* III. v. 94 The Actors were privately to be tried upon the Stage, that upon the insufficiency of the persons, or unfittednesse, the men might be chang'd. **1870** HALES *Longer Eng. Poems* 112 This sense of his unfittedness to perform as yet a poet's high duties.

un'fitting, *ppl. a.* [UN-^{1} 10, 5 d.] Not fitting or suitable; unbecoming, improper.

Apparent earlier examples, when verifiable, have proved to be errors for *unsitting*. Cf. the note to FITTING *ppl. a.*

1590 GREENE *Orl. Fur.* I. i. 220 Least little brooking these vnfitting braues, My cholar ouer-slip the law of Armes. **1631** WEEVER *Anc. Funeral Mon.* 318 These Canons did not continue long at Otteham, the scituation of the place being vnfitting. **1656** EARL MONM. tr. *Boccalini's Advts. fr. Parnass.* II. lxviii. (1674) 221 A thing which..is altogether unfitting to be named. **1687** in *Magd. Coll. & Jas. II* (O.H.S.) 103 He was unfitting by reason of his Immorality. **1771** BURKE *Prosecut. Libels* Wks. 1842 II. 493 This is an unfitting, it is a dangerous, state of things. **1853** ABP. THOMSON *Laws Th.* (ed. 3) Pref. p. v, Some account of the exact position which this work pretends to occupy..may not be an unfitting introduction to its pages.

b. Const. *for*, or with direct object.

1591 *1st Pt. Troub. Raigne K. John* (1611) Bjb, These thoughts are farre vnfitting Fauconbridge. *a* **1593** MARLOWE *Ovid's Elegies* III. i. 40 Small doores vnfitting for large houses are. **1603** FLORIO *Montaigne* I. xxxix. 125 Qualities mis-seeming his place, and unfitting his calling. **1660** R. COKE *Power & Subj.* 71 Lest..the seamen should be forgetful, and unfitting for naval warfare. **1849** ROCK *Ch. of Fathers* I. v. (1903) I. 293 What so unfitting the solemnity of soul..at a burial service?

Hence **un'fittingness.**

1861 *Macm. Mag.* June 134 Colour or form which represents an unfittingness would be likely to become itself an unfittingness.

un'fittingly, *adv.* (UN-^{1} 11.)

1637 ABP. LAUD *Sp. Star-Chamber* 14 June 24 That clause being unfittingly expressed, we thought fit to passe it over. **1656** W. MONTAGUE *Accompl. Wom.* 101 It were to be ill advised..to be so unfittingly pitifull to insolence or detraction. **1828** SCOTT *F.M. Perth* xiii, Men who have matched unfittingly become careless in the choice of those whom they love.

un'fitty, *a.* Now *dial.* [UN-^{1} 7.] Unfit.

1613 WITHERS *Juvenilia, Abuses* I. x, For, 'tis a shame to speake How wonderfull vnfitty and how weake This ignorance makes most of vs. **1837-** in s.w. glossaries (s.v. *Unvitty*).

un'fix, *v.* [UN-^{2} 3 and 7.]

1. *trans.* To undo from a fixed state or position; to unfasten, loosen.

1597 SHAKS. *2 Hen. IV*, IV. i. 208 Plucking to vnfixe an Enemie, Hee doth vnfasten so, and shake a friend. **1605** —— *Macb.* I. iii. 135 That suggestion, Whose horrid Image doth vnfixe my Heire. **1775** ASH, *Unfix*,..to loosen, to make less fast. **1804** J. GRAHAME *Sabbath* 554 Storms that loudly threaten to unfix Islands. **1854** H. MILLER *Sch. & Schm.* (1858) 438 Unfixing the haulser from the stem, and bringing it aft to the stern, we commenced hauling.

b. *spec.* in military use.

1802 JAMES *Milit. Dict.*, *To unfix*, in a military sense, to take off, as Unfix Bayonet, on which the soldier disengages the bayonet from his piece, and returns it to the scabbard. **1813** *Examiner* 10 May 303/2 Two men lost their bayonets, whilst in the act of unfixing them. **1859** F. A. GRIFFITHS *Artill. Man.* (1862) 13 Unfix Swords (or bayonets).

2. *fig.* To unsettle; to render uncertain or doubtful.

1650 R. STAPYLTON *Strada's Low C. Wars* I. 6 Neither gold,..nor the noise of War,..could any way unfix his mind. **1663** J. SPENCER *Prodigies* (1665) 211 Now one Negative instance will appear..of far more force to unfix a pretending Rule, then two Affirmative to establish it. **1802** PALEY *Nat. Theol.* xxvi. Wks. (1834) 548/2 By unfixing those motives which promote exertion, or by relaxing those habits which engender patient industry. **1849** MACAULAY *Hist. Eng.* viii. II. 322 The shock which had overturned his early prejudices had at the same time unfixed all his opinions.

3. *intr.* To become unfixed; to lose fixity.

1844 HOOD *Forge* II. 417 But the ruthless talons refuse to unfix. **1863** READE *Hard Cash* II. 57 As the blood escaped, his eye unfixed, and the pupils contracted and dilated.

un'fixable, *a.* (UN-^{1} 7 b.)

1831 T. HOPE *Ess. Orig. Man* I. 26 The fleeting perceptions of that fugitive and unfixable present. **1832** COLERIDGE *Self-knowledge* 7 Dark fluxion, all unfixable by thought.

un'fixed, *ppl. a.* [UN-^{1} 8.]

1. Not fixed in a definite place or position; unfastened, loose, free.

1598 SYLVESTER *Du Bartas* II. ii. IV. *Columnes* 131 The Criticall and double-sexed Seven, The Number of th' unfixed Fires of Heav'n. **1660** JER. TAYLOR *Ductor* I. iii. rule i. §5 It is like a fire-stick, which..being gently mov'd gives a volatile and unfixed light. **1721** RAMSAY *Morning Interview* 93 Her unfix'd eyes with various turnings range. **1787** JEFFERSON *Writ.* (1859) II. 99 The Count of Vergennes has ..had a very severe attack of what is deemed an unfixed gout. **1805** LOUDON *Improv. Hot-Houses* 65 A stripe of cloth ..is left unfixed at top. **1837** DICKENS *Pickw.* iii, There was a low cinder fire in a rusty unfixed grate. **1844** *Regul. & Ord. Army* 260 All Guards are to parade, with shouldered Arms, and unfixed Bayonets.

†b. Of persons: Not restricted by office to one or a special place. *Obs.*

1661 *Papers on Alter. Prayer-bk.* 10 Generall unfixed Bishops, like the Evangelists or Apostles,..and the fixed Bishops of Parochial Churches. **1685** BAXTER *Paraphr. N.T.* 1 Tim. iii. 7 The Ministeriall Work was..Indefinite, by Itinerant, or unfixed Men.

2. *fig.* a. Unsettled, uncertain, undetermined; fluctuating, variable.

1654 Z. COKE *Logick* Pref., To guid the intricate and perplexed thoughts of the unfixed people through the great Labyrinth of Time. **1697** J. POTTER *Antiq. Greece* I. ix. (1715) 48 It appears to have been unfix'd and arbitrary. **1763** JOHNSON 21 July in *Boswell*, He is totally unfixed in his principles, and wants to puzzle other people. **1826** E. IRVING *Babylon* I. III. 197 Which..doth exactly determine the time of this trumpet which otherwise would have been unfixed. **1862** ANSTED *Channel Isl.* III. xix. (ed. 2) 440 The orthography is not only unfixed, but..is varied.

absol. **1844** MRS. BROWNING *Vis. Poets* clix, The tones.. throbbed betwixt The incomplete and the unfixed.

b. Unstable; lacking permanency.

1669 BOYLE *Notes Atmospheres* in *Contn. New Exp.* I. 196 The weights themselves..are commonly made of Brass (a Metal very unfixt).

†3. Not properly fitted. *Obs.*$^{-1}$

1643 CHAS. I in *Tregaskis' Catal.* (1907) 6 So many recovered men of that Regiment as are able to march, divers of whom have unfixed muskets.

Hence **un'fixedness.**

1668 J. CORBET *Sec. Disc. Relig. Eng.* §xix. 44 Christianity it self would be much endangered in a state of Ataxy and unfixedness. **1707** NORRIS *Treat. Humility* ii. 53 The unfixedness and dissipation of his spirit. **1754** EDWARDS *Freed. Will* III. v. 174 There is a vast Indistinctness and Unfixedness in..very many of the Terms. **1840** MILL *Ess.* (1859) 65 That entire unfixedness in the social position of individuals.

un'fixing, *ppl. a.* (UN-^{1} 10.)

1810 CRABBE *Borough* III. 38 Who sought a readier way the heart to move Than by faint dalliance of unfixing love.

un'fixity. (UN-^{1} 12.)

1856 BAGEHOT *Biog. Studies* (1880) 19 A certain unfixity of opinion.

un'flagged, *ppl. a.* (UN-^{1} 8 and FLAG *v.*^{1})

1608 HEYWOOD *Lucrece* v. vii, Yet grow our lofty plumes unflagg'd with blood.

un'flagging, *ppl. a.* (UN-^{1} 10.)

1715 SOUTH *Serm.* IV. i. 4 With a continued, unflagging Vigor of Expression. **1860** FROUDE *Hist. Eng.* VI. 395 A purpose..which he pursued with unflagging energy. **1891** E. PEACOCK *N. Brendon* II. 347 Her unflagging spirits were a great consolation.

So **un'flaggingly** *adv.*

1858 *Lit. Churchman* 15 May 186/2 A hundred pages, in which the 'view' of this writer is unflaggingly pursued. **1883** *Contemp. Rev.* Sept. 331 Forces that are constantly and unflaggingly at work.

†unflain, *ppl. a. Obs.* [UN-^{1} 8 b.] = UNFLEAD *ppl. a.*

c **1320** *Sir Tristr.* 468 ȝond lip a best vnflayn, Atire it as þou wold. **1486** *Bk. St. Albans* e iij, Ye shall vndo hym vnflayne when he shall be dight.

un'flaky, *a.* (UN-^{1} 7.)

1675 HAN. WOOLLEY *Gentlew. Comp.* 162 Green ginger;.. the better sort is unfleaky.

un'flame, *v.* (UN-^{2} 4.)

1635 QUARLES *Embl.* III. Prol. 22 Where neither..doubt afflicts, nor baser fear Unflames your courage in pursuit.

un'flaming, *ppl. a.* (UN-^{1} 10.)

1644 NYE *Gunnery* xlvi. (1647) II. 24 Dispart your peece with a lighted and unflaming wax candle.

un'flanked, *ppl. a.* (UN-^{1} 8.)

1553 BRENDE *Q. Curtius* III. 25 It was the thing that he doubted moste, that they..should inuade the open side of his battaile whiche lay vnflancked towardes them. **1756** HOME *Douglas* III. iii. 40 Water-wafted armies, whose chief strength Lies in firm foot, unflank'd with warlike horse. **1870** *Milit. Engineering* I. v. 333 The points selected for assault should be, if possible, unflanked parts of the work.

un'flappable, *a. colloq.* [UN-^{1} 7 b.] Not subject to nervous excitement or anxiety; imperturbable.

1958 *Observer* 27 July 11/1 Six months ago even the unflappable Mr. Macmillan had his doubts and sometimes asked in bewilderment what he was doing wrong. **1963** *Times* 27 May 4/5 The Stowe captain looked a neat and unflappable batsman, and his 41 out of 62 was the yard-stick of his value to the team. **1973** 'B. MATHER' *Snowline* iv. 47 He was a senior policeman, and as such deemed to be unflappable. **1980** L. BIRNBACH et al. *Official Preppy Handbk.* 34/2 Charm is the Preppy's suit of armor, the facade of unflappable gentility. **1984** *Listener* 20-27 Dec. 48/1 In other economic areas Japan appears equally unflappable, and with reason.

Hence **unflappa'bility; un'flappably** *adv.*

1959 *Economist* 30 May 823/2 The Prime Minister..has no doubt been reflecting on the virtues of the legend of unflappability. **1965** C. FREMLIN *Jealous One* xxi. 169 The confident unflappability of the one who doesn't actually have to make the journey. **1966** *Guardian* 19 Aug. 8/6 An omission unflappably repaired by the BBC's music library. **1971** *Ibid.* 9 Sept. 9/6 Catering apparently unflappably for whole houses full of actors. **1982** J. ELLIOTT *Country of her Dreams* i. 14 Nicholas..had been roped in..as nanny to the British delegation..for his unflappability.

un'flattened, *ppl. a.* (UN-^{1} 8.)
[**1775** ASH.] **1884** McLAREN *Spinning* 178 Four feet of yarn in its natural state unrubbed and unflattened.

un'flatterable, *a.* (UN-^{1} 7 b.)
1640 D. CAWDREY *Commission for Assise* (1641) 9 Such as Chrysippus would have all earthly Judges: Incorrupt, unflatterable. **1647** TRAPP *Comm. Matt.* xxii. 16 He was *inadulabilis*, unflatterable.

un'flattered, *ppl. a.* (UN-^{1} 8.)
1634 HABINGTON *Castara* I. (Arb.) 47 Time mocks our youth; and..brings us to unflattered age. *Ibid.* II. 76 Retir'd like Princes from the noise of men, To breath a while unflatter'd. **1742** YOUNG *Nt. Th.* II. 631 In vaults, thin courts of poor unflatter'd kings. **1789** T. TWINING *Aristotle's Treat. Poetry* 352 The unsoftened and unflattered character of Achilles. **1845** DARWIN in F. Darwin *Life* (1887) I. 333 At which I ought to be much flattered and unflattered.

un'flattering, *ppl. a.* (UN-^{1} 10.)
1581 SIDNEY *Apol. Poetrie* (Arb.) 62 They that delight in Poesie it selfe, should..looke themselues in an vnflattering Glasse of reason. **1651** SHERBURNE *Salmacis* 283 The Neighbouring Lake,..In whose unflattering Mirrour, every Morn, She Counsell takes how best her self t'adorn. **1704** NORRIS *Ideal World* II. iii. 257 A faithful and unflattering representation of his beloved object. **1823** BYRON *Juan* IX. x, To you the unflattering Muse deigns to inscribe Truths, that you will not read in the Gazettes. **1873** H. ROGERS *Orig. Bible* ii. (1875) 96 A plan so unflattering to man's self-righteousness.
So **un'flatteringly** *adv.*
1874 *Fortn. Rev.* Feb. 246 Our most popular poet..unflatteringly compares them to 'broken lights'.

un'flawed, *ppl. a.* (UN-^{1} 8.)
1665 HOOKE *Microgr.* 97 A very solid and unflaw'd piece of cleer white Marble. **1817** SCOTT *Harold* VI. vii, Firm was that faith,—as diamond stone Pure and unflaw'd. **1856** RUSKIN *Mod. Paint.* IV. v. ix. §7 Furnishing light, broad, and unflawed pieces to serve for slates upon the roof.

†**un'flead,** *ppl. a. Obs.* [UN-^{1} 8 + *flea* FLAY *v.*] Not flayed or skinned.
1580 BLUNDEVIL *Horsemanship* III. 32 b, Two sheepes-heads vnfleade. **1647** HERRICK *Noble Numb., Thanksgiving for House* 22 A little Byn, Which keeps my little loafe of Bread Unchipt, unflead. **1654** GAYTON *Pleas. Notes* III. x. 142 Such a beardlesse boy as the unflead goatheard.

unflechand: see UNFLICHING *ppl. a. Obs.*

un'flecked, *ppl. a.* (UN-^{1} 8.)
1865 J. THOMSON *Sunday up River* VI. iii, White-robed, my own white dove un-flecked. **1883** STEVENSON *Silverado Sq.* 4 Although the upper sky was still unflecked with vapour.

un'fledge, *v.* (UN-^{2} 4.)
1598 FLORIO, *Spennacchiare*,..to vnfeather, to vnfledge, to vnplume. **1809** MALKIN *Gil Blas* x. x. ¶33 For fear he should unfledge me, by taking away my livery.

†**un'fledge,** *a. Obs.* [UN-^{1} 7.] = next.
1581 NEWTON tr. *Seneca's Plays* Pref., Mine I confess to be an unfledge nestling, unhable to flye. **1603** HOLLAND *Plutarch's Mor.* 570 The nightingales instruct their yoong birds in song, insomuch as those which be taken unfledge out of the nest,..never afterwards sing so well.

un'fledged, *ppl. a.* Also 7–8 unfletch'd, 7 unfletcht. [UN-^{1} 8.]
1. Not yet furnished or covered with feathers; callow; unfeathered. Also in fig. context.
1611 SHAKS. *Cymb.* III. iii. 27 We poore vnfledg'd Haue neuer wing'd from view o' th' nest. **1717** *Poem Birthday K. George*, Now boldly dare, With unfletch'd Wings, Nobly to soar. **1752** FOOTE *Taste* I. i, This superannuated Beldame gapes for flattery, like a nest of unfledg'd crows for food. **1821** SCOTT *Kenilw.* ix, The two-legged and unfledged species called mankind. **1890** *Science-Gossip* XXVI. 19/2, Two unfledged birds lying dead at the base of the wall.
b. *poet.* Of an arrow: = UNFEATHERED *a.* 2.
1752 YOUNG *Brothers* II. i, Nor can he feather there his unfledg'd shaft But from ambition's wing.
2. Of things: Not fully developed; still in a crude or imperfect state.
1615 BRATHWAIT *Strappado* (1878) 50 You that..betake to worser parts Your vnfledg'd fancies. **1649** G. DANIEL *Trinarch., Hen. V*, xxxvii, Vnfledg'd Witt Imp't from the ragged Sarcill Chaucer drop't. **1790** SIR J. REYNOLDS in Leslie & Taylor *Life & Times* (1865) II. x. 592 Newly hatched, unfledged opinions. **1851** MRS. BROWNING *Casa Guidi Wind.* II. 270 Alas, poor people, of an unfledged will!
3. Of persons: Immature, inexperienced, undeveloped in knowledge, etc.
1602 SHAKS. *Ham.* I. iii. 65 But doe not dull thy palme, with entertainment Of each vnhatch't, vnfledg'd Comrade. **1669** DRYDEN *Prol. to Wild Gallant reviv'd* 14 By such degrees, while knowledge he did want, Our unfletch'd Author writ a Wild Gallant. **1712** ADDISON *Spect.* No. 305 ¶15 This Society of unfledged Statesmen. **1769** *Junius Lett.* xxv. (1788) 159 The unfledged race of ensigns, who infest our streets. **1824** DOYLE in Fitz-Patrick *Life* (1880) I. 314 To stare with wonder..at what appears strange only because it is unknown to some unfledged traveller or essayist.
4. Pertaining to, characteristic of, youth and inexperience.
1611 SHAKS. *Wint. T.* I. ii. 78 In those vnfledg'd dayes, was my Wife a Girle. **1760–72** H. BROOKE *Fool of Qual.* (1809) III. 134, I am but as a bird from the nest, and this is the first of my unfledged excursions. **1809** MALKIN *Gil Blas* x. x. ¶42 My unfledged youth might lead him to take me for some graceless little truant. **1881** *World* 28 Dec., She has lost the innocence of unfledged girlhood.

un'fleece, *v.* (UN-^{2} 4.)
1609 DEKKER *Ravens Alm.* D 2 The Clergie..shall haue thin cheekes, for euerie body shall fleece or rather vnfleece them.

un'fleeced, *ppl. a.* (UN-^{1} 8.)
c **1825** MOORE *Country Dance & Quad.* 98 Yet unfleeced by funding blockheads, Happy John Bull..had..'Money in both pockets'.

un'fleeting, *ppl. a.* (UN-^{1} 10.)
a **1640** JACKSON *Creed* x. iii. §1 The original controversy..plainly propounded in constant or unfleeting terms. **1811** W. R. SPENCER *Poems* 49 Painting,..whose magic-gifted hand Can..raise unfleeting visions of the past.

un'flenched, *ppl. a.* (UN-^{1} 8.)
1820 SCORESBY *Acc. Arctic Reg.* II. 32 Leaving one ship with..two whales and a half unflenched.

un'flesh, *v.* [UN-^{2} 4.] *trans.* To strip of flesh. Hence **un'fleshing** *vbl. sb.*
1598 FLORIO, *Scarnare*, to vnflesh, to pare the flesh from the bones. **1611** *Ibid.*, *Scarnatura*, any vnfleshing. **1683** E. HOOKER *Pordage's Mystic Div.* Pref. 25 When the inexorable Messenger..shal come..and uncloath and unflesh him too. **1894** BARING-GOULD *Deserts S. France* I. 190 A body had been deliberately unfleshed before it was laid in its last habitation.

un'fleshed, *ppl. a.*^{1} [UN-^{1} 8 + FLESH *v.*] Not yet stimulated by tasting flesh; *fig.*, untried, inexperienced, new. Also *absol.*
1542 UDALL *Erasm. Apoph.* 280, I wil never present an hoste unto ye high capitaine of Roome..unfleashed on their enemies. **1611** SPEED *Theat. Gt. Brit.* 125/1 Some..who (like unflesht souldiers) gaue ouer their enterprise without further hope. **1635–56** COWLEY *Davideis* III. 499 With some less Foe thy unflesht valour try. **1692** DRYDEN *Cleomenes* V. ii, As a generous, unfleshed hound, that hears From far the hunters' horn and cheerful cry. **1748** RICHARDSON *Clarissa* VII. 409, I am no unfleshed novice; this [duel] is a sport, that ..I love as well as my food. **1833** LYTTON *Godolphin* 8 Percy's heart was full of enterprise and the unfleshed valour of inexperience. **1895** MEREDITH *Amazing Marriage* ix, Customary phrases of the unfleshed in folly.

un'fleshed, *ppl. a.*^{2} [f. UNFLESH *v.*, or UN-^{1} 8.]
a. Stripped of flesh. **b.** Not covered with flesh.
1607 W. BARKSTED *Mirrha* D 4 b, Nor let the dead repine, ..let the vnflesht thronges..be glad. **1795** SOUTHEY *Vis. Maid Orleans* I. 99 Behold this skull, These eyeless sockets, and these unflesh'd jaws. **1864** LOWELL *Fireside Trav., At Sea*, May it be long before Professor Owen is comforted with the sight of his unfleshed vertebræ.

un'fleshly, *a.* (UN-^{1} 7.)
1834 J. H. NEWMAN in *Brit. Mag.* Aug. 156 Our ample choir of holiest souls Are followers of the unfleshly seraphim. **1855** PUSEY *Doctr. Real Presence* 335 For if some unfleshly quality of a body be opposed to us, surely..it will not have blood. **1861** READE *Cloister & H.* l, Those unfleshly eyes, with which they say the very air is thronged.
Hence **un'fleshliness.**
a **1859** DE QUINCEY *Posth. Wks.* (1891) I. 186 Without the idea of holiness and unfleshliness, eternity..cannot sustain itself.

un'fleshy, *a.* (UN-^{1} 7.)
1612 J. DAVIES (Heref.) *Muse's Sacr.* Wks. (Grosart) II. 13/1 At gastly Deaths vnfleshy feet.

†**un'flet,** *ppl. a. Obs.*$^{-1}$ (UN-^{1} 8 b + FLEET *v.*^{2})
1688 R. HOLME *Armoury* III. 335/1 Dairy People..make ..Flet and unflet Milk Cheese.

unfletch'd, obs. var. UNFLEDGED.

†**un'flexible,** *a. Obs.* [UN-^{1} 7 and 5 b.] = INFLEXIBLE *a.*
a **1586** SIDNEY *Arcadia* III. xv, Falsly accounting an unflexible anger, a couragious constancie. **1611** SPEED *Hist. Gt. Brit.* IX. viii. §44. 498 Seeing the Pope vnflexible, and vnsensible of so many Christians calamitie. **1677** GILPIN *Demonol.* (1867) 152 Some spirits are unfixed and volatile... Others are tenacious and unflexible.

†**un'fliching,** *ppl. a. Obs.* [UN-^{1} 10.] Unflinching.
a **1340** HAMPOLE *Psalter* ii. 9 þou sall gouern þaim..in stabile and vnflichand [*v.r.* unflechande] rightwisnes.

un'flickering, *ppl. a.* (UN-^{1} 10.)
1856 MRS. BROWNING *Aur. Leigh* III. 173 With fixed unflickering outline of dead heat. **1884** *Pall Mall G.* 23 June 16/2 A steady and unflickering light.

un'flinching, *ppl. a.* (UN-^{1} 10.)
1728 MORGAN *Algiers* II. v. 315 The Valour and Resolution of the unflinching Knights. **1814** SCOTT *Lord of Isles* VI. xxvi, Unflinching foot 'gainst foot was set. **1846** MRS. A. MARSH *Father Darcy* II. ix. 145 A fresh element of resolute, unflinching, persevering determination. **1882** *Macm. Mag.* XLV. 372 Yet he is..determinedly persevering, unflinching as a foe.
Hence **un'flinchingly** *adv.*
1833 COLERIDGE *Table-t.* 5 Feb., Oh! for a great man.. who could..unflinchingly put it into act! **1879** CHR. G. ROSSETTI *Seek & F.* 236 The more unflinchingly we abide by this truth, the keener will our spiritual faculty become.

un'floatable, *a.* (UN-^{1} 7 b.)
1880 'MARK TWAIN' *Tramp Abr.* I. 231 The floating of iron cable-chains and other unfloatable things. **1884** LD. BLACKBURN in *Law Rep.* 9 *App. Cases* 409 That natural impediment renders the stream at that spot practically unfloatable.

un'flock, *v.* (UN-^{2} 6 b.)
1611 FLORIO, *Disgreggiáre*, to scatter, to vnflocke. **1778** H. BROOKE *Contending Brothers* V. vi, It were pity that birds of such a feather should be unflock'd.

un'floor, *v.* (UN-^{2} 4.)
1589 PUTTENHAM *Arte Eng. Poesie* III. xix. (Arb.) 230 They beate downe the walles, they vnfloored the loftes, they vntiled it. **1611** COTGR., *Desplanché*,..vnfloored, or, whose floore is taken vp.

un'floored, *ppl. a.* (UN-^{1} 8.)
1816 in Hone *Every-day Bk.* (1825) I. 572 The upper story is unfloored. **1897** *Daily News* 26 Nov. 8/5 A tiny unfloored, corrugated iron shanty.

un'floured, *ppl. a.* (UN-^{1} 8.)
[**1775** ASH.] **1795** in *Spirit Pub. Jrnls.* IV. 229 With surly face and head unflour'd.

un'flourished, *ppl. a.* (UN-^{1} 8.)
1486 *Bk. St. Albans, Her.* a j b, Adam the begynnyng of man kynde was as a stokke vnsprayde and vnfloreshed.

un'flourishing, *ppl. a.* (UN-^{1} 10.)
1782 BAKER *Biog. Dramatica* III. 92 The Edinburgh theatre, at that time in no unflourishing condition.

un'flower, *v.* (UN-^{2} 4.)
1610 G. FLETCHER *Christ's Vict.* I. lxxxv, Bring..all your silver flaskets,..That I may soone unflow'r your fragrant baskets, To strowe the fields with odours.

un'flowered, *ppl. a.* (UN-^{1} 8.)
1648 HEXHAM II, *Ongebloemt*, vnflowred, or without Flowers. **1775** ASH, *Unflowered*.., not flowered, not ornamented with flowers.

un'flown, *ppl. a.* (UN-^{1} 8 b.)
[**1775** ASH.] **1791** COWPER *Iliad* IV. 137 He chose a dart Unflown, full-fledged. **1969** *Guardian* 13 Feb. 1/8 The backlog of unflown flights was, of course, appalling.
b. *absol.*
1913 A. E. BERRIMAN *Aviation* p. xxi, Today, the great unflown is divided into two camps... 'I should love to go up.'.. 'Not I, at any price.'

un'fluctuating, *ppl. a.* (UN-^{1} 10.)
1723 BLACKMORE *Alfred* IV. 129 In the Steerage they preside, And, tho' in Storms, unfluctuating guide The agitated State. **1823** DE QUINCEY *Lett. Educ.* i. 1 That you had the priceless blessing of unfluctuating health. **1858** NORTON *Topics* 243 The tax must be..unfluctuating in amount. **1896** *N. Amer. Rev.* Dec. 743 A sound unfluctuating currency.

un'fluent, *a.* (UN-^{1} 7.)
1605 SYLVESTER *Du Bartas* I. vi. 29 Poure vpon my faint vn-fluent tongue The sweetest hunnie of th' Hyantian Fount. **1659** O. WALKER *Instruct. Oratory* 25 The first making the language dull and slow; the other,..abrupt, and unfluent.

un'flurried, *ppl. a.* (UN-^{1} 8.)
1854 CDL. WISEMAN *Fabiola* (1855) 287 She completed, unflurried, the preparations for supper.

un'flush, *v.* (UN-^{2} 7.)
1866 M. ARNOLD *Thyrsis* xvii, The west unflushes, the high stars grow bright.

un'flushed, *ppl. a.*^{1} [UN-^{1} 8 + FLUSH *v.*^{1} 2.] Of game: Not driven up.
1769 *Stratford Jubilee* I. i, There will be rare poaching for experienced sportsmen among unflush'd game.

un'flushed, *ppl. a.*^{2} [UN-^{1} 8 + FLUSH *v.*^{2}] Not flushed in colour.
[**1775** ASH.] **1860** LD. LYTTON *Lucile* II. i. §16. 4 That pale cheek for ever by passion unflush'd. **1868** H. BUSHNELL *Moral Uses Dark Th.* (1869) 217 We see it in a laying out of white, unflushed by mortal sympathy.

un'fluted, *ppl. a.* (UN-^{1} 8.)
[**1775** ASH.] **1843** *Civil Eng. & Arch. Jrnl.* VI. 270/2 The columns are unfluted. **1854** tr. *Hettner's Athens & Peloponnese* 46 Pieces of friezes,..and unfluted drums of pillars.

un'flutterable, *a.* (UN-^{1} 7 b.)
1871 MRS. WHITNEY *Real Folks* viii, The quiet, unflutterable gray bonnet calmly horizontal.

un'fluxile, *a.* (UN-^{1} 7.)
1757 tr. *Henckel's Pyritol.* 349 Crude, unmetallic, unfluxile earth.

un'foaled, *ppl. a.* (UN-^{1} 8.)
1863 MISS BRADDON *Aurora Floyd* xiii, Winning future Derbys..with colts that are as yet unfoaled.

un'foed, *a.* (UN-^{1} 9.)
1586 WARNER *Alb. Eng.* III. xviii, Augustus..was Emperour alone; In whose unfoed Monarchie our comon health was known.

un'foiled, *ppl. a.*^{1} [UN-^{1} 8 + FOIL *v.*^{1}]
†**1.** Not injured, marred, or impaired. *Obs.*
1579–80 NORTH *Plutarch* (1595) 242 When the golden and vnfoiled age remained yet whole..at Rome. *a* **1640** JACKSON *Creed* x. viii. §3 The Naturalist..hunts after the truth with fresh unfoiled scent. **1691** RAY *Creation* II. (1692) 22 To let in [to the eye] the Light and Colors unfoiled and unsophisticated by any inward Tincture.
2. Not overcome, beaten, or baffled.

1587 T. HUGHES *Misfort. Arthur* v. i. 31 For had impatient ire indu'rde abuse,.. I mought haue liu'd in forreine coastes vnfoilde. **1600** SIR F. VERE *Comm.* 93 Their footmen (which were old trained souldiers, and to that day unfoiled in the field). **1672** TEMPLE *Ess., Govt.* Wks. 1720 I. 107 The usurped Powers..thought themselves secure in the Strength of an unfoiled Army of above Sixty Thousand Men.

†un'foiled, *ppl. a.*^{2} *Obs.* [UN-^{1} 8 + FOIL *v.*^{3}] Unploughed.

1611 COTGR., *Terre vierge*, ground that is whole or vnfoyled; good ground that was neuer plowed.

unfoiled, *ppl. a.*^{3} [UN-^{1} 8 + FOIL *v.*^{4}] Not coated or backed with foil.

1640 in Entick *London* (1766) II. 165 Glass-plates, or sights for looking-glasses, unfoiled. **1731** *Phil. Trans.* XXXVII. 155 The second Speculum may have a Part unfoil'd. **1761** *Ibid.* LII. 561 By reflexion from the unfoiled part of the speculum.

un'fold, *v.*^{1} Forms: 1 unfealdan, 3 unuolden, 3–6 un-, vnfolde (5 onfolde), 4– unfold (4–7 vn-), 6–7 vnfould; 5 *north.* vnfald(e, 6, 8 *Sc.* unfauld. [OE. *unfealdan* (f. *un-* UN-^{1} + *fealdan* FOLD *v.*^{1}), = MDu. and Du. *ontvouden, -vouwen* (eastern MDu. *-volden, -valden*), G. *entfalten.*]

1. *trans.* To open or unwrap the folds of; to spread open; to expand; to straighten out.

c **890** WÆRFERTH tr. *Gregory's Dial.* 333 þa boc..unlysan & unfealdan. *c* **1000** *Ags. Gosp.* Luke iv. 17 Sona swa he þa boc unfeold, þa funde he [etc.]. *c* **1205** LAY. 10544 Æuere his writen he vnfeold þer he forð ferde. **13..** *Coer de L.* 4809 Hys baner anon was unfolde, The Sarezynes anon gan behold. **1338** R. BRUNNE *Chron.* (1810) 284 Bot if þe bulle vnfolden were red among vs here, ȝour hote salle be holden. **1377** LANGL. *P. Pl.* B. XVII. 176 Þe paume hath powere..to vnfolde þe folden fuste. *a* **1400–50** *Alexander* 3027 Bald bernes on bent banars vnfaldis. *c* **1450** LOVELICH *Grail* xxxvi. 462 Whanne this body he hadde beholde, Anon the clothes he dyde on-folde. **1530** PALSGR. 767/2, I unfolde any thyng that is folded up togyder, *Je desployе. Ibid.*, Unfolde this clothe. *a* **1553** UDALL *Roister D.* III. iv, No lesse..Than this letter purporteth, which ye haue vnfolde. **1663** DAVENANT *Siege of Rhodes* Wks. (1672) 8 Sweeter then Buds unfolded in a Shower. **1697** DRYDEN *Æneis* VI. 393 Strife, that shakes Her hissing tresses, and unfolds her snakes. **1743** FRANCIS tr. *Hor., Odes* IV. xv. 5 Phœbus..warn'd me..Not to unfold my little sail. **1784** COWPER *Task* IV. 153 The pattern grows, the well-depicted flow'r..Unfolds its bosom. **1828** SCOTT *F.M. Perth* xix, Come now,..unfold your arms from about my patient. **1841** T. R. JONES *Anim. Kingd.* 399 One of the snails unfolds from the right side of its neck..a wide sacculus.

b. *transf.* or *fig.*

1390 GOWER *Conf.* II. 24 For I ne mai my wit unfolde To find o word of that I mene. **1603** KNOLLES *Hist. Turks* (1621) 540 Unfolding his troupes (that standing there, they might at more libertie use their swords). **1633** G. HERBERT *Temple, Dawning* 3 Unfold thy forehead gather'd into frowns. **1744** AKENSIDE *Pleas. Imag.* I. 73 Till in time..What he admired and loved, his vital smile Unfolded into being. **1839** THIRLWALL *Greece* VI. 253 As these thoughts had been nourished and unfolded in himself by the recent change in his fortunes.

c. To open (the eyes or lips); to open (a gate, etc.) upon hinges.

a **1325** in Horstm. *Altengl. Leg.* (1878) 144 Adam his eiȝen vnfeld; & seþþen his sone he biheld. **1620** SHELTON *Quix.* I. IV. xix. 518 He would not once vnfold his lips, vntill he might see what would be the period of his disgrace. **1667** MILTON *P.L.* IV. 381 Hell shall unfould..her widest Gates. **1801** SOUTHEY *Thalaba* VI. xvi, The gates of iron, by no human arm Unfolded, turning on their hinges slow. **1896** DE VINNE *Moxon's Mech. Exerc.* 410 He..unfolded the frisket and tympan.

d. *refl.* (Also in fig. use.)

1779 *Mirror* No. 22, Her voice seemed to unfold itself in singing, to suit every musical expression. **1821** SHELLEY *Epipsych.* 480 An atom of th' Eternal, whose own smile Unfolds itself. **1891** FARRAR *Darkn. & Dawn* xxxv, The whole world had turned..to thorns; would some new rosebud now unfold itself among them?

2. To disclose or reveal by statement or exposition; to explain or make clear.

a **1050** *Liber Scintill.* xxxviii. (1889) 140 ðeþancu unrihtwisnysse [hi] unfealdað. *a* **1225** *Ancr. R.* 100 Þis is a cruel word... Hit is bilepped & bihud, ac ich hit wulle unuolden. *a* **1250** *Prov. Ælfred* 659 Al he bi-fulit his frend, þen he him vnfoldit. **13..** *E.E. Allit P.* B 1563 Calle hem alle to my cort.., Vnfolde hem alle þis ferly þat is bifallen here. **1426** LYDG. *De Guil. Pilgr.* 10962 At the grete Iugement Wher tassyses shal be holde, Al couert falsenesse to vnfolde. *c* **1475** *Partenay* 5124 The holy fader wondred on that he told, Off tho merueles that ther [he] gan vnfold. **1595** *Locrine* I. i. 83, I will vnto you all vnfold Our royall mind and resolute intent. **1658** FLECKNOE *Epigr. & Enigm. Char.* 1 Clearly unfolding and explicating the notions of her minde. **1693** *Humours Town* 38, I will only unfold it to you as the nature of the thing is. **1782** PRIESTLEY *Matt. & Spir.* I. Pref. p. xxxii, His system is..perhaps the same..if he would distinctly unfold it. **1817** JAS. MILL *Brit. India* II. v. ix. 689 In a speech..[he] unfolded the causes and extent of the national calamities. **1875** JOWETT *Plato* (ed. 2) IV. 239 The brethren whose mysteries I am about to unfold to you are far more ingenious.

refl. **1602** SHAKS. *Ham.* I. i. 2 Nay answer me: Stand & vnfold your selfe. **1637** B. JONSON *Sad Sheph.* II. v, What riddle is this? unfold your selfe, deare Robin. **1831** CARLYLE *Sart. Res.* II. v, The self-secluded unfolds himself in..free, glowing words.

3. To disclose or lay open to the view; to display. Also *fig.*

c **1374** CHAUCER *Boeth.* IV. met. v. (1868) 132 Whi þat boetes þe sterre vnfoldiþ his ouer swift arisynges. **1590** SHAKS. *Mids. N.* I. i. 146 Briefe as the lightning in the collied night, That (in a spleene) vnfolds both heauen and earth. **1713** BLACKMORE *Creation* I. 430 The hollow vales their smiling pride unfold. **1812** S. ROGERS *Columbus* XII. 32 To other eyes shall Mexico unfold Her feathered tapestries, and roofs of gold. **1872** JENKINSON *Guide Eng. Lakes* (1879) 91 When the steep part of the journey is accomplished a lovely prospect is unfolded.

refl. **1837** W. IRVING *Capt. Bonneville* III. 76 From this lofty eminence, a vast and magnificent prospect unfolds itself.

4. a. To unwrap; to take out of something folded.

1553 BRENDE *Q. Curtius* 190 Vnfolding his wound,..[he] shewed his legge vnto them. **1827** SCOTT *Chron. Canongate* v, Then was unfolded, out of many a little scrap of paper, the reserved sum of fifteen shillings.

b. To release, let go.

In Beaum. & Fl. *Faithf. Shepherdess* II, 'vnfould' is an error for 'infold' or 'enfold': see note to UN-^{1} 5 b.

1633 P. FLETCHER *Purple Isl.* XII. xlviii, These suppliant hands..Will never let thee loose, will never more unfold thee.

5. *intr.* To open (up or out); to spread out or expand; to become patent or plain, etc.

(*a*) *c* **1350** *Libeaus Desc.* 2091 As he set þus in halle, Out of þe stone walle A window faire unfelde. **1697** DRYDEN *Æneis* X. 1 The Gates of Heav'n unfold; Jove summons all The Gods to Council. **1715** POPE *Iliad* IV. 1 And now Olympus' shining gates unfold. **1725** —— *Odyss.* IX. 533 Seest thou these lids that now unfold in vain? **1746** FRANCIS tr. *Horace, Epist.* I. xviii. 122 Ears, that unfold to every Tale, Intrusted Secrets ill conceal. **1828** SCOTT *F.M. Perth* xix, But the fingers do unfold. **1887** BOWEN *Æneid* III. 94 The gates unfold of the shrine.

(*b*) *c* **1586** C'TESS PEMBROKE *Ps.* (1823) LXXXI. i, Let joyfull songes to god unfold. **1601** SHAKS. *Twel. N.* I. ii. 19 Mine owne escape vnfoldeth to my hope. **1725** POPE *Odyss.* XII. 240 Now all at once tremendous scenes unfold. **1759** ROBERTSON *Hist. Scot.* II. Wks. 1813 I. 139 The queen's scheme began gradually to unfold. **1833** TENNYSON *Eleanore* v, I see thy beauty gradually unfold. **1858** SEARS *Athan.* III. i. 256 A system of infinite truth, which is to unfold through the ages.

(*c*) *a* **1649** CRASHAW *Carmen Deo Nostro, To C'tess of Denbigh*, Unfold at length, unfold fair flowre. **1813** SCOTT *Rokeby* VI. i, That morning sun has three times seen The flowers unfold on Rokeby green. **1862** THACKERAY *Philip* xvi, The pony-chaise unfolded into a noble barouche. **1875** BENNETT & DYER tr. *Sachs' Bot.* 175 The position of the leaves in the lateral buds before unfolding.

un'fold, *v.*^{2} [UN-^{2} 4 b + FOLD *v.*^{2}] *trans.* To release (sheep) from a fold or folds.

1530 PALSGR. 768/1 It is tyme to unfolde our shepe. *a* **1613** OVERBURY *A Wife*, etc. (1638) 172 She dares goe alone and unfold sheepe i'th'night. **1781** COWPER *Retirem.* 397 The boy, who..Unfolds his flock.

†un'foldable, *a. Obs.* [UN-^{1} 7 b.] Incapable of being unfolded.

1611 COTGR., *Inexplicable*, inexplicable, vnfouldable. *a* **1641** BP. MOUNTAGU *Acts & Mon.* (1642) 420 The sense is marred, intricate, unfoldable.

un'folded, *ppl. a.*^{1} [UN-^{1} 8 + FOLD *v.*^{1}] Not folded or arranged in folds.

1683 MOXON *Mech. Exerc., Printing* xxii. ¶ 10 Folding in the un-folded corners. **1695** *Lond. Gaz.* No. 3047/4 Part of them is Unfolded, so as to be useful to all Gentlemen and others conversant in the Mechanicks. **1860** DICKENS *Uncomm. Trav.* ix, A pretty large prayerbook in an unfolded pocket-handkerchief.

un'folded, *ppl. a.*^{2} [UN-^{1} 8 + FOLD *v.*^{2}] Not enclosed in a (sheep) fold.

1589 GREENE *Menaphon* (Arb.) 44 So long we..forget our labours, that both our flockes shall be vnfolded. **1641** BEST *Farm. Bks.* (Surtees) 14 Men cannot leave their sheepe unfolded soe longe as there is any corne in the field. **1832** J. BREE *St. Herbert's Isle* 81 Th' unfolded flocks that o'er them bleat. **1856** MRS. BROWNING *Aur. Leigh* II. 602 A lamb's small shadow.., Unfed, unfolded!

un'folded, *ppl. a.*^{3} [f. UNFOLD *v.*^{1}] Opened out or up; *fig.* displayed, revealed.

1602 FULBECKE *Pandects* 29 Though the parties will, doe appeare in a secret will,..yet consent is onely verified in an expresse & vnfolded wil. **1629** H. BURTON *Truth's Triumph* 212 Euery beleeuer must haue..a cleare, explicite, and vnfolded faith in Christ. **1697** CONGREVE *Mourn. Bride* II. v, The iron gates..are still wide stretch'd..And staring on us with unfolded leaves. **1784** COWPER *Task* VI. 280 From shop to shop Wandering, and littering with unfolded silks The polished counter. **1820** SHELLEY *Liberty* iv, Like unfolded flowers beneath the sea.

un'folder. [f. UNFOLD *v.*^{1}] One who, or that which, unfolds, in various senses of the word.

1611 COTGR., *Expliqueur*, an explicator, vnfolder, explainer. **1651** BAXTER *Inf. Bapt.* 240 Himself was an accurate unfolder of truth. **1728** THEOBALD *Double Falsehood* I. ii, Is your Father yet moved in the Suit, who must be the prime Unfolder of this Business? **1797** *Monthly Mag.* III. 264 Both copyists and unfolders [of papyrus rolls] are injudiciously paid by the month. **1845** TRENCH *Huls. Lect.* vii. 115 The unfolder of all the nobler and higher life of the world. **1871** MACDUFF *Mem. Patmos* ix. 119 The sudden appearance..of the Unfolder of the roll.

un'folding, *vbl. sb.* [f. UNFOLD *v.*^{1}] The action of the verb, in various senses.

1483 *Cath. Angl.* 121/1 An vn Foldynge, *explicio, deuolucio.* **1538** ELYOT, *Replicatio*, a replycation or vn-foldynge of a thynge. **1599** MINSHEU *Span. Gram.* 80 The farther unfolding of this language. **1615** HIERON *Wks.* I. 653 Death..is (as it were) the vnfolding of the net, or the breaking open of the prison doore. **1646** P. BULKELEY *Gospel Covt.* I. 121 The time of unfolding [of the blessings] is not yet come. **1760–72** H. BROOKE *Fool of Qual.* (1809) IV. 45 The growth and unfolding of any common vegetable from.. the seed. **1794** MRS. RADCLIFFE *Myst. Udolpho* i, He watched the unfolding of her infant character with anxious fondness. **1843** MANNING *Serm.* I. 276 The springing or unfolding of a stately tree. **1873** TRISTRAM *Moab* ii. 26 The sudden unfolding [to view] of the Dead Sea basin.

un'folding, *ppl. a.*^{1} [f. UNFOLD *v.*^{1} 5.] That unfolds, discloses, or develops.

1762 FALCONER *Shipwr.* II. 285 The sailors..Attend th' unfolding brails at his command. **1798** S. & HT. LEE *Canterb. T.* II. 355 The gay delights of unfolding nature. **1814** WORDSW. *Excurs.* VI. 855 It was the season of unfolding leaves. **1862** 'SHIRLEY' (J. Skelton) *Nugæ Crit.* ii. 107 The unfolding acts of a great drama.

un'folding, *ppl. a.*^{2} [f. UNFOLD *v.*^{2}]

1. Indicating the time for unfolding sheep.

1603 SHAKS. *Meas. for M.* IV. ii. 218 Looke, th' vnfolding Starre calles vp the Shepheard.

2. Coming out of the fold.

1821 CLARE *Vill. Minstr.* I. 13 Raising the bleatings of unfolding sheep.

un'foldment. [f. UNFOLD *v.*^{1}] The process of unfolding.

1850 D. THOMAS *Crisis of Being* iv. 64 Matter is..the unfoldment of ideas. **1884** *Christian World* 11 Sept. 688/2 All that is asked..is your co-operation..in its unfoldment.

un'foldress. [f. UNFOLDER.] A female unfolder.

1577 STANYHURST *Descr. Ireland* Ep. Ded. in *Holinshed* I. 1 b/1 The learned haue..adiudged an hystorie to be..the vnfoldresse of treacherie.

un'foldure. [f. UNFOLD *v.*^{1}] Unfolding.

1837 C. LOFFT *Self-formation* I. 254 The relaxation and expansion and gentle unfoldure of the mind.

un'foliaged, *ppl. a.* (UN-^{1} 8.)

1795 ANNA SEWARD *Lett.* (1811) IV. 91 The pale unfoliaged ruins of Castle Dinas Bran. **1804** —— *Mem. Darwin* 123 There, indeed, we see rocks piled on rocks, unfoliaged and frowning. *a* **1843** SOUTHEY *Comm.-pl. Bk.* (1851) IV. 86 The ash is still unfoliaged.

un'foliated, *ppl. a.* (UN-^{1} 8.)

1859 A. NESBITT in *Archaeol.* XXXIX. 105 Two segmental unfoliated arches, on which rests a circle, also unfoliated. *a* **1878** SCOTT *Lect. Archit.* (1879) I. 176 The use..of moulded unfoliated capitals.

un'followed, *ppl. a.* (UN-^{1} 8.)

1508 [see UNACCUSED *ppl. a.*]. **1596** DANETT tr. *Comines* VIII. vi. 332 The Estradiots..forsooke their men of armes, who by means thereof were vnfollowed. **1630** J. TAYLOR (Water P.) *Trav.* Ded., I shall hereafter sacrifice whole Hecatombs..at the shrine of your vnfellowed and vnfollowed vertues. **1826** *Q. Rev.* XXXIV. 75 This example remained unfollowed by England for almost a century. **1864** E. SARGENT *Peculiar* I. 121 We will allow Peculiar Institution to quit this room free and unfollowed.

un'fool, *v.* (UN-^{2} 6 b.)

1598 SHAKS. *Merry W.* IV. ii. 120, I, but if it proue true (Mr. Page) haue you any way then to vnfoole me againe. **1632** STRAFFORD in *Life* (1892) 301 The sooner wee vnfoole ourselues of this errore, the sooner wee shall learne to know our selues. **1635** QUARLES *Embl.* II. iii. 5 Will no plump fee Bribe thy false fists..T'unfool whom thou hast fool'd?

un'foolish, *a.* (UN-^{1} 7.)

1603 FLORIO *Montaigne* 561, I daylie heare fooles utter unfoolish wordes. **1885** *Sat. Rev.* 3 Jan. 12/2 The foolisher sort of a very unfoolish people.

un'foot, *v.* [UN-^{2} 4.] *trans.* To wash or wear away the foot of.

1758 BORLASE *Nat. Hist. Cornw.* 66 Vast masses of cliff, which the sea has unfooted. *Ibid.* 109 The contiguous strata have been unfooted..many times.

un'footed, *ppl. a.* [UN-^{1} 8.] Not trodden by the feet (of man); untraversed.

1818 KEATS *Endym.* I. 77 Some unfooted plains Where fed the herds of Pan. **1839** BAILEY *Festus* 338 And oft, at night, ..We would breathe ourselves amid unfooted snows. **1895** MEREDITH *Amazing Marriage* xxx, Calamity hung around, with the future an unfooted wilderness.

†un'footsore, *a. Sc. Obs.* (UN-^{1} 7.)

c **1480** HENRYSON *Fables, Two Mice* 15 Ane tyme quhen scho wes full and vnfute sair. *c* **1500** *Priests of Peblis* 5 Thrie Preists..sat richt soft and vnfutesair.

un'foraged, *ppl. a.* (UN-^{1} 8 + FORAGE *v.* 1.)

a **1649** DRUMM. OF HAWTH. *Hist. Jas. IV*, Wks. (1711) 75 By fighting in England, he kept his own Country unforaged.

unfor'bade, *ppl. a.* (UN-^{1} 8 b.)

1844 MRS. BROWNING *Vis. Poets* ccxlii, Nor know I if the man who prayed Rose up accepted, unforbade.

unfor'bearance. (UN-^{1} 12.)

1699 SHAFTESB. *Char.* (1711) II. 150 The Injurys we do our-selves, by Excess and Unforbearance.

unfor'bearing, *ppl. a.* (UN-^{1} 10.)

1820 T. MITCHELL *Aristoph.* I. 113 A ranting, storming, unforbearing fellow.

unfor'bid, *ppl. a.* [UN-^{1} 8 b.] = next.

1667 MILTON *P.L.* VII. 94 If unforbid thou maist unfould What wee..aske. **1827** POLLOK *Course T.* VIII. 350 He.. took all joys, Forbid and unforbid, as impulse urged. **1869** LOWELL *Winter Evening Hymn to Fire* vii, Nicotia..We worship, unforbid of thee.

unfor'bidden, *ppl. a.* (UN-^{1} 8 b.)

1535 COVERDALE *Acts* xxviii. 31 Teachinge those thinges ..with all boldnesse, vnforbydden. **1611** FLORIO, *Inuietato*, vnforbidden. **1648** HEXHAM II, *Ongeboden*,..Vnforbidden.

1819 Shelley *Cenci* iv. iv. 29 All was prepared by unforbidden means Which we must pay so dearly, having done. **1861** Geo. Eliot *Silas M.* x, To..take up his old quarters unforbidden, and swagger as usual.

Hence **unfor'biddenly** *adv.*, **-ness**.

1665 Boyle *Occas. Refl.* v. ix. 179 This unforbiddenness they think sufficient to evince, that the Sumptuousness..is not absolutely..Sinful. **1860** Ellicott *Life Our Lord* viii. 387 When..love..may hereafter unforbiddenly direct itself to the ascended Lord.

† **unfor'boden**, obs. var. unforbidden *ppl. a.* Cf. MDu. and Du. *onverboden*, MHG. and G. *unverboten*.

1534 Tindale *Acts* xxviii. 31 Teachynge those thinges.. with all confidence, vnforboden.

un'forced, *ppl. a.* [UN-^{1} 8.]

1. Not compelled or constrained.

1598 Sylvester *Du Bartas* ii. ii. *Colonies* 513 Being fed.. With wholesome Fruits of an un-forced soyl. **1624** Heywood *Gunaik.* v. 231 Artimesia..unforced and uncompeld followed the expedition of Xerxes against Greece. **1697** Dryden *Æneis* xi. 654 Why thus, unforced, should we so tamely yield? **1741** Richardson *Pamela* III. 248 He will judge us according to the unforced and unbyassed Use we make of that Light. **1805** Wordsw. *To the Daisy* 52 Unforced by wind or wave To quit the Ship for which he died. **1884** *19th Cent.* Mar. 436 The unforced zeal and docility of the horse.

b. Of plants: Not produced out of season.

1868 *Daily News* 8 July, Some of the fuchsias..would have borne comparison with any unforced flowers of their class.

2. Not pushed beyond the natural limits; not produced by exertion or effort; easy, natural.

1604 Shaks. *Oth.* ii. i. 239 This granted (as it is a most pregnant and vnforc'd position) who stands so eminent..as Cassio do's? **1665** J. Spencer *Vulg. Proph.* 52 All the great Prophets..delivered themselves in a natural and unforc'd order of words. **1717** Addison tr. *Ovid's Met.* iii. Notes, Wks. 1721 I. 242 This is one of Ovid's finished stories. The transition to it is proper and unforced. **1790** Paley *Horæ Paul.* xii. §2 Here we have a fair unforced example of coincidence. **1850** Irving *Goldsmith* i. 17 The unforced humour, blending so happily with good feeling and good sense. **1883** D. C. Murray *Hearts* ix, His objections..were unforced and genuine.

3. Requiring or involving no physical exertion.

1643 Denham *Cooper's H.* 42 With such an easie and unforc't ascent. **1765** Sterne *Tr. Shandy* viii. xix, By an unforced compression..of his cap with the thumb and the two forefingers.

Hence **un'forcedly** *adv.*; **un'forcedness**.

1632 G. Sandys *Ovid's Met.* xiii. Notes 451 This may vnforcedly admit of the former interpretation. **1664** H. More *Myst. Iniq.* 261 The naturalness and unforcedness of this Imbibition shall be made good. **1696** M. Henry *Life P. Henry* iv. Wks. 1853 II. 647/1 Such a distribution as the matter did most easily and unforcedly fall into.

un'forcible, *a.* [UN-^{1} 7.]

1. Lacking force or power.

1597 Hooker *Eccl. Pol.* v. lxv. §9 Wee cannot thinke that the signe which our new baptized foreheads did there receiue, is either vnfit or vnforcible. **1754** A. Murphy *Gray's Inn Jrnl.* No. 90, Pieces..unforcible in Sentiment, and destitute of Character.

2. Incapable of being forced or enforced.

1611 Cotgr., *Inforçable*, vnforcible, vnexpugnable, impregnable. **1649** Milton *Tenure Kings* 39, I wish them.. not to compell unforcible things in Religion especially.

un'forcibly, *adv.* (UN-^{1} 11.)

1831 Scott *Ct. Rob.* v, So I did express myself,..and, as I trust, not altogether unforcibly. *c* **1890** A. Murdoch *Yoshiwara Episode* 8 Which..illustrates not unforcibly what a glorious thing the..system is for the capitalist.

un'fordable, *a.* (UN-^{1} 7b and 5b.)

1611 Florio, *Inguazzabile*, vnwadable, vnfoordable. **1649** Taylor *Gt. Exemp.* ii. §21 When he is to pass a sudden or unfordable flood. **1732** Lediard *Sethos* II. vii. 58 Their excursions..over unfordable rivers. **1834** Pringle *Afr. Sk.* 187 A very heavy rain..swells the river to an unfordable size. **1868** *Rep. U.S. Commissioner Agric.* (1869) 351 Many of the unfordable streams are still crossed by flat-boat ferries.

fig. *a* **1641** Bp. Mountagu *Acts & Mon.* (1642) 25 Many deep hidden mysteries, and unfordable.

Hence **un'fordableness**.

1652 Heylyn *Cosmogr.* ii. 193 The unfordablenesse of the River.

un'forded, *ppl. a.* (UN-^{1} 8.)

1697 Dryden *Virg. Georg.* iii. 396 He..contemns Unruly Torrents, and unfoorded Streams.

unfore'boded, *ppl. a.* (UN-^{1} 8.)

1818 Colebrooke *Import Colonial Corn* 58 In the event of ultimate failure of accustomed supplies not unforeboded. **1863** B. Taylor *H. Thurston* III. 284 A power,..as welcome as it was unforeboded, had usurped her life.

unfore'boding, *ppl. a.* (UN-^{1} 10.)

1725 Pope *Odyss.* ii. 212 Unnumber'd birds glide through the aërial way, Vagrants of air, and unforeboding stray. **1863** Mrs. Oliphant *Chron. Carl.* I. *Salem Ch.* xvi. 146 She could see the half-awakened girl starting up,..unforeboding of evil.

unfore'gone, *ppl. a.* (UN-^{1} 8b.)

1844 Mrs. Browning *Vis. Poets* cxlii, The life lay coiled unforegone Up in the awful eyes alone.

un'foreign, *a.* (UN-^{1} 7.)

1718 Quincy *Compl. Disp.* 36 The Amalgamation of Metals..[is] not unforeign to this Head.

unfore'knowable, *a.* (UN-^{1} 7b.)

1678 Cudworth *Intell. Syst.* i. v. 710 Predictions of Future Events, otherwise unforeknowable to men. **1697** J. Sergeant *Solid Philos.* 447 These, and a thousand other Unforeknowable Mischances.

unfore'known, *ppl. a.* (UN-^{1} 7b.)

1667 Milton *P.L.* iii. 119 Foreknowledge had no influence on their fault, Which had no less prov'd certain unforeknown. *a* **1680** Charnock *Attrib. God* (1834) I. 561 No man can certainly prove that anything is unforeknown to him. **1882** Armstrong *Garl. fr. Greece* 95 Nor unforeknown it comes.

unfo'rensic, *a.* (UN-^{1} 7.)

1858 Carlyle *Fredk. Gt.* viii. iv. II. 323 Fancy the hurry-scurry, the unforensic attitudes and pleadings! **1883** *Edin. Rev.* Jan. 245 The turn of his mind did not lead him astray into unforensic rhetoric.

unfore'see, *v.* [UN-^{1} 14.] To fail to foresee.

a **1670** Hacket *Abp. Williams* (1693) I. 171 The Lord Keeper did not unforesee how far this Cord might be drawn.

unfore'seeable, *a.* (UN-^{1} 7b.)

Also, in recent use, ***unfore'seeableness***, ***-ably***.

1672 South *Serm.* (1717) V. 300 By such unlikely and unforeseeable Ways does Providence sometimes bring about its great Designs. **1802–12** Bentham *Ration. Judic. Evid.* (1827) I. 205 The suddenly put and unforeseeable question. **1877** Morley *Crit. Misc.* Ser. ii. 377 The source of continual and unforeseeable improvements.

unfore'seeing, *ppl. a.* (UN-^{1} 10, 5d.)

1602 Daniel *Cleopatra* i. Fiiij, My vnforeseeing weakenesse must intoome My Countries fame and glory with my fall. **1690** Child *Disc. Trade* Pref. A7b, May we not think that some..People in the World may be as un-foreseeing as this Gentleman pretends to be? **1755** *Man* No. 4. 3 An indulgent but unforeseeing parent. **1801** Southey *Thalaba* iv. xv, Later years..teach me to regret Youth's unforeseeing indolence. **1886** Swinburne *Misc.* 130 The unforeseeing security of a charmed and confident happiness.

absol. **1855** Singleton *Virgil* I. 94 Ne'er storm of rain Hath to the unforeseeing scathful proved.

b. Const. with object.

1871 M. Collins *Marq. & Merch.* II. iv. 112 Amy, unforeseeing anything of this sort, had been doing what she thought was her duty.

Hence **unfore'seeingly** *adv.*

1611 Florio, *Improuistamente*, vnprouidedly, suddainely, vnforeseeingly. **1832** Chalmers *Pol. Econ.* iii. 96 This sum ..might have been imprudently or unforeseeingly vested in the manufacture of luxuries.

unfore'seen, *ppl. a.* (UN-^{1} 8b. Cf. MDu. *onvoresien*, Du. *onvoorzien*; MHG. *unvorsên*.)

1651 Hobbes *Leviath.* iv. xliv. 334 By reasoning from the un-foreseen mischances. **1667** Milton *P.L.* ii. 821 Through dire change Befalln us unforeseen, unthought of. **1725** Berkeley *Proposal* Wks. 1871 III. 228 Unforeseen difficulties may arise. **1778** Earl Carlisle in Jesse *Selwyn & Contemp.* (1844) III. 302 In case nothing unforeseen happens. **1836** W. Irving *Astoria* III. 132 Unless some unforeseen contingency should render a modification necessary. **1875** Whitney *Life Lang.* vii. 127 The unforeseen consequence of an external addition.

Hence **unfore'seenly** *adv.*, **-ness**.

1853 G. J. Cayley *Las Alforjas* I. 104 A peasant appeared unforeseenly, and offered to carry me across. **1897** *Daily News* 21 Sept. 4/7 The 'unforeseenness' of the cycle is its worst reproach in towns.

unfore'shortened, *ppl. a.* (UN-^{1} 8.)

1846 Worcester (citing Godwin). **1866** Herschel *Familiar Lect. Sci.* v. §19. 194 So as to be seen unforeshortened from the star.

un'foreskinned, (*ppl.*) *a.* (UN-^{1} 9 or UN-^{2} 4.)

1671 Milton *Samson* 1100 The glory of Prowess..won by a Philistine From the unforeskinn'd race.

unfore'stalled, *ppl. a.* (UN-^{1} 8.)

1657 J. Howe in H. Rogers *Life* (1836) 74 They shall meet with unforestalled judgments. **1658** Osborne *Adv. Son* Wks. (1673) 178 Unforestalled by a like custom.

un'forested, *ppl. a.*^{1} [UN-^{1} 8.] Not covered with forest; not included in a deer-forest.

1885 *Pall Mall G.* 11 Mar 4/2 One class of incident..on unforested ground when in quest of deer. **1897** *Outing* XXIX. 357/2 The snowskate..is better adapted to an unforested, or partially forested, hilly country.

un'forested, *ppl. a.*^{2} [UN-^{2} 6b, 8.] Deprived of forest, or of the status of a forest; deforested.

1502 Arnolde *Chron.* (1811) 19 That alle the wareyn of Stanes wyth the apertinaunce be unwareyned and vnforested for euermore. **1881** C. Morrison *Hist. School Geog.* ii. 58 Sherwood Forest in Notts,..now almost unforested.

unfore'thought, *ppl. a.* (UN-^{1} 8b, c.)

1601 Daniel *Civ. Wars* vi. vii, This unfore-thought-on accident confounds All their dessignes. **1839** [see unfeared *ppl. a.* 2].

unfore'told, *ppl. a.* (UN-^{1} 8b.)

1846 Worcester (citing *Ec. Rev.*). **1853** Ruskin *Stones Ven.* II. iv. §71 A silence has followed them, not unforetold.

unfore'warned, *ppl. a.* (UN-^{1} 8.)

1651 Cleveland *Poems* 38 The Devill sure such language did atchieve, To cheat our un-fore-warned Grandam Eve. **1667** Milton *P.L.* v. 245 This let him know, Least..he pretend Surprisal, unadmonisht, unforewarnd. **1814** Wordsw. *Excurs.* vii. 685 All unforewarned, The household lost their pride and soul's delight.

un'forfeit, *a.* [UN-^{1} 7.] Unforfeited.

1631 Chapman *Cæsar & Pompey* i. ii. 156 That most strangely Would put..powers (Unforfeit by my fault) in others' wills. **1742** Young *Nt. Th.* iii. 96 This group Of bright ideas, flow'rs of Paradise, As yet unforfeit!

un'forfeitable, *a.* (UN-^{1} 7b.)

1648 Nethersole *Problems* i. 3 Their rights ought..to be ..unforfeitable. *a* **1754** Carte *Hist. Engl.* (1755) IV. 62 Conveying an actual right..unforfeitable by any act of their father. **1874** W. R. Greg *Rocks Ahead* 45 Short of declaring this peasant's farm inalienable,..unforfeitable for any negligence,..—how is he to keep it?

un'forfeited, *ppl. a.* (UN-^{1} 8.)

1596 Shaks. *Merch. V.* ii. vi. 7 To keepe obliged faith vnforfaited. **1663** Cowley *Verses Sev. Occas.*, *To Royal Society* 3 All that Human Knowledge which has bin Unforfeited by Mans rebellious Sin.

un'forgeable, *a.* (UN-^{1} 7b.)

1837 Lockhart *Scott* III. x. 332 Stamped with the unforgeable seal of truth and nature. **1889** *Pall Mall G.* 30 Dec. 2/3 There is..no difficulty in the way of making a practically unforgeable note.

un'forged, *ppl. a.* [UN-^{1} 8.]

1. Not fashioned at the forge.

c **1374** Chaucer *Former Age* 49 Vnforged was the hawberke and the plate.

2. Not forged or counterfeit; genuine.

1610 Bp. Carleton *Jurisd.* 102 You dare not auouch them to be vnforged. **1628** Ford *Lover's Mel.* iii, A letter printed From my vnforg'd relation. **1804** *Europ. Mag.* XLV. 367/2 We have as much reason to doubt the existence of any unforged manuscript upon this subject.

unfor'getful, *a.* (UN-^{1} 7.) Also **-ness** (UN-^{1} 12).

1632 Lithgow *Trav.* vi. 285 A grateful and vnforgetfull Frier. **1850** Blackie *Æschylus* I. 111 For vengeance unforgetful, From their graves they call. **1888** Mackey *Life Bp. Forbes* ix. 76 The bishop's unforgetfulness of those to whom honour is due.

unfor'gettable, *a.* Also **-getable**. (UN-^{1} 7b.)

1806 *Ann. Rev.* IV. 608 The unforgettable scenes of this fine poem. **1856** Emerson *Eng. Traits* i. 5 Wisdom, wit, and indignation that are unforgetable. **1873** M. Arnold *Lit. & Dogma* (1876) 173 In single sentences, which have their ineffaceable and unforgettable stamp.

Hence **unfor'gettably** *adv.*

1871 Carlyle in Mrs. Carlyle *Lett.* (1883) II. 242 Jean's look unforgettably sad and grand. **1899** Mackail *Life Morris* I. 213 The powerful..face impressed itself unforgettably even on those who saw it but once.

unfor'getting, *ppl. a.* (UN-^{1} 10.)

1777 Potter *Æschylus, Prom. Bd.* 33 The triple Fates and unforgetting furies. **1867** Howells *Ital. Journ.* 95 The latest witness of God's unforgetting justice.

unfor'giv(e)able, *a.* (UN-^{1} 7b.)

Sometimes spec. with *sin*, in allusion to Matt. xii. 31.

1548 R. Hutten *Sum of Diuinitie* H3b, Euerye persecution of the Gospell is not to be iudged synne unforgyueable. **1550** Latimer *Last Serm. bef. Edw. VI*, Wks. (Parker Soc.) I. 250 This sin it was that he thought to be unforgiveable. **1832** Southey *Hist. Penins. War* III. 195 Bad as his conduct was, it would be his own fault if he made it unforgiveable. **1851** Carlyle *Sterling* i. vii, This is what it would have been the unforgivable sin to swerve from and desert. **1885** *Manch. Exam.* 17 June 4/7 The circumstances ..ought to stamp it as an unforgivable offence.

Hence **unfor'giv(e)ably** *adv.*

1890 *Pall Mall G.* 15 May 2/3 All these books sin unforgiveably against the scientific sense. **1897** 'Mrs. Rayner' *Type-writer Girl* xxi. 243, I have never acted.. grossly and unforgivably wrong.

unfor'given, *ppl. a.* [UN-^{1} 8b. Cf. (in sense 2) OE. *unforȝifen*, MDu. *onvergeven*.]

† **1.** *Sc.* Without any remission. *Obs.*

1425 *Sc. Acts Jas. I* (1814) II. 12/1 Ande quha sa..be fundyn fautyfe sal pay ane vnlaw..vnforgevin. **1442** *Extr. Aberdeen Rec.* (1844) I. 7 The said Master Jhon sal pay to kyrk werk xl s. vnforgiffin. **1510** *Ibid.* 81 Ane amerciament of viii s. vnforgiven. *a* **1578** Lindesay (Pitscottie) *Chron. Scot.* (S.T.S.) II. 242 Nane sould eit flesche on frydayes..vnder the paine of xx poundis on forgivin for the first fault. **1622** *Extr. Aberdeen Rec.* (1848) II. 378 The counsallour..sall pay for ilk dayis absence..twelff schillingis, money vnforgiwen.

2. Not forgiven. Also *absol.*

1565 Harding *Confut. Apol. Ch. Eng.* v. vii. 251b, That temporall satisfaction, which after the sacrament of penaunce is left vnforgeuen. **1737** Chesterf. *Epitaph Q. Charlotte* 18 To her own offspring mercy she denied, And unforgiving, unforgiven died. **1796** Mme. D'Arblay *Camilla* V. 409 To present herself..undemanded and unforgiven at Etherington, she thought impossible. **1819** Shelley *Cenci* iv. i. 89 As she shall die unshrived and unforgiven. **1845** Bailey *Festus* (ed. 2) 226 And thou wilt then be wretcheder than I;—The unforgiving than the unforgiven.

unfor'giveness. [UN-^{1} 12.]

= unforgivingness.

1611 Florio, *Imperdonanza*, vnforgiuenesse. **1748** Richardson *Clarissa* VII. 118 They are sufficiently cleared from every imputation of unforgiveness. **1797** Mrs. A. M. Bennett *Beggar Girl* (1813) I. 65 He became notorious for ingratitude to his friends, and unforgiveness of his enemies. **1829** *Westm. Rev.* XI. 276 Adding at that fearful moment the expression of his unforgiveness and his hate. **1870** T. Erskine *Unconditional Freeness Gospel* vii. 153 We cannot have confidence in any one who, we think, regards us with unforgiveness.

unfor'giver. (UN-¹ 12.)
1748 RICHARDSON *Clarissa* (1811) VII. 26, I hope, however, that these unforgivers..were always good, dutiful, passive children to their parents.

unfor'giving, *ppl. a.* (UN-¹ 10.)
1713 ROWE *Jane Shore* IV, Accursed Jealousy! O merciless, wild and unforgiving Fiend! **1784** COWPER *Task* II. 247 Chatham..Secur'd it by an unforgiving frown. **1828** SCOTT *F.M. Perth* xi, I have brought the vengeance of an unforgiving devil upon this helpless creature. **1880** 'OUIDA' *Moths* II. 165 We are an unforgiving race.
absol. **1819** SHELLEY *Cenci* V. iii. 105 Canst Thou forgive even the unforgiving? **1845** [see UNFORGIVEN 2].
Hence **unfor'givingness.**
1748 RICHARDSON *Clarissa* VII. xlvii. 184 That cruelty and unforgivingness, which..have no example. **1850** L. HUNT *Autobiog.* II. xi. 55 An extraordinary mixture of..good nature with unforgivingness. **1887** MARY BURT *Browning's Women* 52 Unforgivingness beyond a certain limit is a base crime.

unfor'got, *ppl. a.* [UN-¹ 8 b.] = next.
1653 J. TAYLOR (Water P.) *Cert. Trav. Uncert. Journey* 15 But to them all my thanks is unforgot. *a* **1847** ELIZA COOK *Old Barn* iv, Delight that is still unforgot. **1870** MORRIS *Earthly Par.* III. IV. 372 Many a tale yet unforgot.

unfor'gotten, *ppl. a.* (UN-¹ 8 b. Cf. MDu. and Du. *onvergeten*, MHG. *unvergezzen*, G. *unvergessen*.)
1813 BYRON *Giaour* 103 Clime of the unforgotten brave! *a* **1822** SHELLEY *Triumph Life* 209 The great, the unforgotten,—they who wore Mitres and helms and crowns. **1850** HAWTHORNE *Scarlet L.* xviii, The foe that would win over again his unforgotten triumph.

un'fork, *v.* [UN-² 5, 6 b.]
1. *trans.* To remove from a fork.
1598 FLORIO, *Disforcare*, to vnforke. **1611** *Ibid.*, *Sforcinato*, vnforked, vnhooked.
2. To make straight or plain.
1654 Z. COKE *Logick* (aj), It unforks Oracles, making them Toothless. **1657** TOMLINSON *Renou's Disp.* Pref., Their Enigmatical expressions unforked and unvailed.

†**unfor'latit,** *ppl. a. Sc. Obs.* [UN-¹ 8 + MDu. *verlaeten* to draw off, rack (wine).] Not drawn off from one vessel into another.
1513 DOUGLAS *Æneid* v. Prol. 53 Bot my propyne..[is] Vnforlatit, not jawyn fra tun to tun. *Ibid.* Direction 90 Onforlatyt, new from the berry run.

†**unfor'let,** *ppl. a. Sc. Obs.* [UN-¹ 8 b. Cf. OE. *unforlǣten*.] Not abandoned or given up.
1513 DOUGLAS *Æneid* XI. xi. 16 Ne this luf, suythly, is nocht cummin of new,..Bot of ald kyndnes lang tyme vnforleyt.

unfor'lorn, *ppl. a.* [UN-¹ 8 b. Cf. OFris. *onforloren* (unforfeited), MDu. and Du. *onverloren*, MHG. *unverlorn* (G. *-loren*), older Da. *uforloren*.] **a.** Not lost. **b.** Not bereft (*of*).
1567 *Gude & Godlie B.* (S.T.S.) 146 Zit keipit scho hir madinheid vnforlorne. **1635** J. HAYWARD tr. *Biondi's Banish'd Virg.* 13 Yet was hee alive, and as yet unforlorne of either sense or memory.

†**un'form,** obs. var. INFORM *a.* or UNFORMED *ppl. a.*
?*a* **1400** in *MS. Lincoln A i 17* fol. 276 b, Whilom when a man was noghte, Bothe vnfourme and vn forthe broghte.

un'form, *v.*¹ [UN-² 4.] *trans.* To divest of (a special) form; to make formless. Also *absol.*
1621 G. SANDYS *Ovid's Met.* II. (1626) 35 How great our act! how is our powre display'd! Vnform'd a Woman, and a Goddesse made. **1704** *Hymn Victory* xvi, He never form'd a proper Scheme, But they unform'd it all again. *a* **1822** SHELLEY in Medwin *Life* II. 169 It was easier to form, than unform or reform. **1876** GLADSTONE in *Contemp. Rev.* June 12 It has formed Christian nations; or at least, has not unformed them. **1882** *Pall Mall G.* 14 June 5/1 It unforms his style, and produces scrappy..sentences.

un'form, *v.*² [UN-² 5.] *trans.* To rouse (a hare) from its form.
a **1773** in Ruddiman *Coll. Pieces* (1773) 277 Such with the beagle rise, at dusky morn,..Unfourm the hare close squatted in her bush.

un'formal, *a.* [UN-¹ 7, 5 b.] = INFORMAL I.
c **1449** PECOCK *Repr.* I. ii. 9 Thei schulden not be..so ruyde and vnformal and boistose in resonyng. **1597** MORLEY *Introd. Mus.* 81 Your fift, sixt, and seuenth notes be wilde and vnformall, for that vnformall skipping is condemned in this kinde of singing. **1661** CAMPION *Counterpoint* 109 This passage from the flat to the sharp would be unformal. **1678** SIR G. MACKENZIE *Crim. Laws Scot.* II. xxiii. §4 (1699) 249 Often times they return unformal verdicts. **1799** H. MITCHELL *Scotticisms* 87 The contract was unformal.
b. = INFORMAL *a.* I b.
1825 CATH. STANLEY *Jrnl.* in *Mem.* (1879) 211 The unpunctual [people] are easy, good-tempered, unfussy,..unformal. **1858** M. PATTISON *Ess.* (1889) II. 328 The rude independence of character, which was generated by that free and unformal life.
Hence **un'formally** *adv.*
1597 MORLEY *Mus.* 86 Your seuenth and eighth notes, wherein you fal..so vnformallie to B fa ♮ mi backe againe.

un'formalized, *ppl. a.* (UN-¹ 8 a *c.*)
1853 C. BRONTE *Villette* xix, He listened so kindly, so teachably; unformalized by scruples.

un'formed, *ppl. a.*¹ [UN-¹ 8 and 5 b. Cf. MDu. *ongeformet*, *-vormet* (Du. *-vormd*), MHG. *ungeformet* (G. *-formt*), NFris. *ünfuaremd*.]
1. Not formed or fashioned into a regular shape; not invested with any definite form.
a **1340** HAMPOLE *Psalter* xxxii. 9 þai ere fourmyd of vnfourmyd matere. **1382** WYCLIF *Deut.* xxvii. 6 Thow shalt bild there up an auter..of stonus vnfourmed and vnpolishid. **1599** DANIEL *Musoph.* 951 Who..knows..What words in th' yet unformed Occident, May come refin'd with th' accents that are ours? **1621** G. SANDYS *Ovid's Met.* xv. 406 [He] sees Their bodies limme-lesse: these vnformed things In time put forth their feet, and after, wings. **1651** HOBBES *Leviath.* I. xii. 55 The unformed matter of the World, was a God, by the name of Chaos. **1712** ADDISON *Spect.* No. 309 ¶2 His Passage through the Regions of unformed Matter. **1825** *Bull-baiting* II. in *Houlston Tr.* I. No. 28. 6 His head so torn and mangled, that it appeared nothing but a frightful unformed mass of blood. **1855** *Poultry Chron.* III. 571/1 Those amateurs who, like myself, prefer..the breast small and unformed. **1877** CAIRD *Philos. Kant* II. i. 203 While matter altogether unformed is a mere abstraction.
b. *transf.* Of immaterial things: Not brought to a definite or properly developed state; crude.
1689 *Andros Tracts* II. 195 They would..endeavour to prevent what ill effects an Unform'd Tumult might produce. **1736** BUTLER *Anal.* I. v. 86 Mankind is left, by Nature, an unformed, unfinished Creature. **1774** REID *Aristotle's Logic* vi. §2 (1788) 144 Every science is in an unformed state until its first principles are ascertained. **1857** BUCKLE *Civiliz.* I. xiv. 832 The chemical department of mineralogy is in an unformed and indeed anarchical condition. **1880** SAYCE *Introd. Sci. Lang.* viii. II. 188 The rude and unformed Bushman and the polished Finnic [language].
c. *fig.* Of persons (or the mind): Not developed by education or training; unpolished.
1711 ADDISON *Spect.* No. 66 ¶2 You can't imagine how unformed a Creature it is. She comes to my Hands just as Nature left her. **1798** S. & HT. LEE *Canterb. T.* II. 12 On [him],..in the helplessness of an unformed mind, his sister threw herself. **1856** MISS YONGE *Daisy Chain* I. xx, Ethel was very queer and unformed, and could do nothing by herself. **1894** MRS. H. WARD *Marcella* I. 104 Very clever in some ways—and very unformed—childish almost—in others.
2. Not formed or made; uncreated.
a **1325** *Prose Psalter* (1891) 194 Vnfourmed is þe fader, vnfourmed is þe sone, vnformed is þe holi gost. *c* **1400** *Pilgr. Sowle* (Caxton, 1483) v. xiv. 107 God hymself is nature vnformed and vnwrought that yeueth nature fourmed to euery creature. **1611** COTGR., *Informé*,..also, vnformed, vnmade, vnfashioned. **1757** in *10th Rep. Hist. MSS. Comm.* App. I. 313 If the New Ministry yet unformed, should subsist. **1794** R. J. SULIVAN *View Nat.* IV. 99 Would it not sound strangely to talk of a self-existent house, an uncaused pyramid, an unformed statue? *a* **1824** BYRON *Heav. & Earth* I. iii, He broke forth Into the dawn, which lighted not the yet Unform'd forefather of mankind. **1855** *Poultry Chron.* III. 195/2 Lime..is especially necessary for making the as yet unformed bones.
†**3.** ***unformed stars*** (or ***signs***): (see quots.). *Obs.*
1590 T. HOOD *Use Celestial Globe* 34 b, The vnformed starres about the Scorpion. **1638** CHILMEAD tr. *Hues' Treat. Globes* (1889) 53 This Constellation hath..three unformed ..Starres. **1700** MOXON *Math. Dict.*, *Unformed Signs*, such are those that are called Nebulous or Cloudy, scarce to be seen by the bare Eye or Instrument. **1764** J. FERGUSON *Lect.* 185 Those stars which lie between the figures of those imaginary animals, and could not be brought within the compass of any of them, were called unformed stars. **1810** VINCE *Elem. Astron.* 269.

†**un'formed,** *ppl. a.*² [UN-¹ 8.] = UNINFORMED *ppl. a.*
c **1400** *Destr. Troy* 760 Lest þe day vs be-daghe..And I vnformet in faith how I fare shall.

un'formidable, *a.* (UN-¹ 7 b and 5 b.)
1667 *Decay Chr. Piety* xi. ¶2 A guilt which nothing but our too familiar acquaintance with it could make unformidable. **1846** M'GEE *Gallery Irish Writers* 163 It was no unformidable degree of success which could call Clarendon against him. **1898** BODLEY *France* II. III. v. 235 When a minister thus retains his portfolio, it is because he is unformidable.

un'formulated, *ppl. a.* (UN-¹ 8.)
1866 *Spect.* 14 Apr. 406/1 The trustful, free, unformulated attitude of mind. **1899** MACKAIL *Life Morris* II. 115 The ambiguities of an unformulated creed.

unfor'saken, *ppl. a.* (UN-¹ 8 b.)
1648 HEXHAM II, *Onbegeven*, Vnforsaken. **1654** HAMMOND *Fundam.* viii. Wks. 1674 I. 290 Any sort of sins continued in or unforsaken. **1857** J. H. NEWMAN *Serm. Var. Occas.* vi. 100 Hearts polluted with mortal, unforsaken sin. **1864** PUSEY *Lect. Daniel* viii. 495 He..did not enter into a relation to His creature, only, of His own accord, Himself unforsaken, to end it.

unfor'saking, *ppl. a.* (UN-¹ 10.)
1862 MRS. NORTON *Lady of La Garaye* Ded. 74 Towards thee their thoughts shall roam, Whose unforsaking faith time hath not riven.

unfor'sook, *ppl. a.* (UN-¹ 8 b.)
1838 MRS. BROWNING *Seaside Walk* v, Absent friends and memories unforsook.

unfor'sworn, *ppl. a.* (UN-¹ 8 b.)
1636 MASSINGER *Gt. Dk. Florence* v. ii, *Cozimo*. You all conspire To force our mercy from us. *Charomonte*. Which giv'n up To after-times preserves you unforsworne.

†**unforthbrought:** see UNFORM *a.*

†**unfor'thinking,** *sb.* and *ppl. a. Obs.* (UN-¹ 12, 10.)
1483 *Cath. Angl.* 139/1 An vn Forthynkynge, *jnpenitencia. Ibid.*, Vn Forthynkynge, *jnpenitens*.

un'fortified, *ppl. a.* (UN-¹ 8.)
1525 LD. BERNERS *Froiss.* II. clxx. 484 The lorde of the Towre was sore blamed..that he had lefte that place vnfortifyed and vnprouyded. **1607** TOPSELL *Four-f. Beasts* 467 The which Beare..finding the den vnfortified..entred into the same. **1709** POPE *Ess. Crit.* 434 While their weak heads, like towns unfortify'd, 'Twixt sense and nonsense daily change their side. **1775** BURKE *Sp. Concil. Amer.* Wks. III. 64 Pouring down upon your unfortified frontiers a fierce and irresistible cavalry. **1849** GROTE *Greece* II. xlvii. (1862) IV. 170 Samos remained..unfortified, deprived of its fleet.
fig. **1602** SHAKS. *Ham.* I. ii. 96 It shewes..A Heart vnfortified, a Minde impatient. **1646** HAMMOND *Sinnes* 18 The will will be taken unfortified, and so..won to consent. **1705** COLLIER *Ess. Mor. Subj.* III. *Pain* 14 Persons of the tenderest Age, of the most unfortified Sex,..encountered the Fury of wild Beasts. **1802–12** BENTHAM *Ration. Judic. Evid.* (1827) V. 659 A mere pecuniary interest, unfortified by any admixture of sympathy. **1885** *Manch. Exam.* 4 Feb. 5/2 This opinion,..unfortified by legal sanction.

un'fortify, *v.* (UN-² 3.)
1574 HELLOWES tr. *Gueuara's Fam. Ep.* (1577) 272, I commaund you..to discamp your camp, and to vnfortifie Tordisillas. **1603** FLORIO *Montaigne* II. xv. 359 A peaceable time will require we shall vnfortifie them [*sc.* our houses].

†**un'fortunable,** *a. Obs.* [UN-¹ 7 b, 5 b.] Unfortunate.
1509 BARCLAY *Shyp of Folys* (1570) 223 Which seeth and feeleth..That all his dedes are much unfortunable. **1567** PAYNELL tr. *Treas. Amadis of Gaule* 77 This manner of doing ..is so unfortunable, and so farre out of reason. **1715** H. CAREY *Contrivances* (1729) 27 The Gentleman of this House, who was so unfortunable as to be kill'd by Thieves.

†**un'fortunacy.** *Obs.* [UN-¹ 12, 5 b.] Lack of good fortune; an unfortunate occurrence.
a **1575** tr. *Pol. Verg. Eng. Hist.* (Camden Soc. 29) 124 The rumor was spred that the same was doone by therles assent, ..but in dede yt was the unfortunacy of king Henry. *a* **1662** HEYLYN *Laud* II. (1671) 312 The King he tacitly upbraids with the unfortunacies of his Reign by Deaths and Plagues.

un'fortunate, *a.* and *sb.* [UN-¹ 7 and 5 b.]
A. *adj.* **1. a.** Of persons, etc.: Not favoured by fortune; meeting with bad fortune; suffering mishap or mischance; unlucky.
For examples of the superlative in *-est* see (*b*).
1530 PALSGR. 328/1 Unfortunate,..*malfortuné*. **1553** BRENDE *Q. Curtius* IV. 55 b, I haue learned to be vnfortunate, and it is often tymes a comforte of a mans calamitie to knowe his misshapp. **1577** tr. *Bullinger's Decades* 254 Hee was of all the Jewishe kinges..in his lyfe the most vnfortunate. **1652** *Nicholas Papers* (Camden) 315 He hath been not only unfortunate in most of his counsels but incompatible in business. **1680** *Charac. Town-Miss* (Hindley III) 5 She shall ..fall a Sniveling and call herself the most unfortunate of Women. **1769** ROBERTSON *Chas. V*, II. Wks. 1813 VI. 81 It was late next morning before the fate of the unfortunate prince was known. **1804–6** SYD. SMITH *Mor. Philos.* (1850) 218 You travel for twenty or five-and-twenty miles over one of the most unfortunate, desolate countries under heaven. **1885** 'MRS. ALEXANDER' *Valerie's Fate* vi, The unfortunate gentleman was well known... What a blow his death will be to..his partner!
absol. **1675** DRYDEN *Aurengz.* v. (1676) 72 Envious death will shun th'unfortunate. **1712** POPE *Lett.* (1735) I. 177 The Unfortunate of all People are the most unfit to be left alone. **1781** GIBBON *Decl. & F.* xxvii. (1787) III. 7 He was taught, by cruel experience, that every gate is shut against the unfortunate. **1825** SCOTT *Talism.* xx, To have doomed the unfortunate to death might have been severity, but had a show of justice.
(*b*) **1622** R. HAWKINS *Voy. S. Sea* 2 The *Revenge*, which was ever the vnfortunatest Ship the late Queenes Maiestie had. **1639** S. DU VERGER tr. *Camus' Admir. Events* 35 Tearming himselfe the unfortunatest of all lovers. **1840** DICKENS *Old C. Shop* xxix, I remember the time when he was the unluckiest and unfortunatest of men.
†**b.** Const. *of*. *Obs.*⁻¹
1611 SPEED *England*, *Wales* II. vii, The Townes for commerce,..two of them vnfortunate of their former greatnes.
c. In specific uses: (see quots.).
1785 GROSE *Dict. Vulg. T.*, *Unfortunate gentlemen*, the horse guards, who thus named themselves in Germany. **1792** *Observer* 24 June 3/1 The great number of unfortunate young women, who nightly parade the streets of this immense metropolis, for the horrid purpose of.. prostitution of their persons. **1796** —— *Unfortunate women*, prostitutes. **1827** HARE *Guesses* Ser. I. (1847) 154 As a strumpet is become an unfortunate female. **1883** MISS BETHAM-EDWARDS *Disarmed* xxxviii, Alice Ashe, seamstress, unmarried, 'unfortunate'.
2. Marked by, or associated with, misfortune or mishap; disastrous, inauspicious. Also, in weaker sense: Untoward, unlucky, regrettable.
a **1548** HALL *Chron.*, *Hen. VI*, 178 What number of noble men haue ben..executed sith that vnfortunate day. **1560** DAUS tr. *Sleidane's Comm.* 404 b, But after chaunced a time more vnfortunate. **1600** HAKLUYT *Voy.* III. 318 They put themselues to sea, and with so slender victuals, that the end of their interprise became vnluckly and vnfortunate. **1626** D'EWES in Ellis *Orig. Lett.* Ser. I. III. 218 By reason of suspicion of irregularitie upon the unfortunate killing of a man some few yeares since. **1671** MILTON *Samson* 747 In some part to recompense My rash but more unfortunate misdeed. **1779** *Mirror* No. 33, But for this unfortunate weakness, Mr. Gold..would make one of the best of husbands. **1846** MRS. A. MARSH *Father Darcy* II. xxi. 354 Would not some link of connexion with this 'unfortunate business', as he styled it, be detected? **1885** 'MRS. ALEXANDER' *At Bay* iii, Is it not unfortunate?..my father

can not return till to-morrow. 1890 *Retrospect Med.* CII. 103 The word 'massage' seems rather an unfortunate one to apply to the procedure.

B. *sb.* **1.** One who is unfortunate; an unfortunate person.

1683 T. HOY *Agathocles* 23 But of the brave Unfortunates was none Whose glorious Suff'rings Philocles out-shone. 1697 BURGHOPE *Disc. Relig. Assemb.* 87 Out of pity to those unfortunates that are design'd for that place [*sc.* hell]. 1776 S. J. PRATT *Pupil of Pleas.* (1777) I. 206 You..appeared only in the light of a person..not allied to the parent of that dear unfortunate. 1801 *Monthly Mag.* II. 131 You will not be able to avoid pitying these unfortunates when they inform you that their souls are mortal. 1875 WHITNEY *Life Lang.* i. 2 These unfortunates are wont to be trained and taught by those who speak.

2. A fallen woman; a prostitute.

1803 G. COLMAN *John Bull* II. ii. 20 *Frank.* Where is the reparation to the unfortunate he has deserted? *Shuffleton*... A great many unfortunates sport a stilish carriage. 1844 HOOD *Bridge of Sighs* i, One more Unfortunate..Gone to her death! 1866 ROGERS *Agric. & Prices* I. v. 118 Unfortunates committed to prison were in evil case.

3. *Irish.* An idiot.

1881 *Folk Lore Rec.* IV. 113 Do you see that 'innocent' or 'unfortunate' or 'object'?

†**un'fortunate**, *v. Obs.* [UN-^{2} 6 a.] *trans.* To make unfortunate or unlucky.

1602 CAREW *Cornwall* 101 b, By his dreery influence, [he] unfortunateth any birth that shal then casually befall. 1653 W. RAMESEY *Astrol. Restored* 317 An Eclipse of the Sun.. unfortunateth the Sea and the affairs thereof.

Hence †**un'fortunating** *ppl. a.*

1647 LILLY *Chr. Astrol.* xxii. 131 If the unfortunating Planet be in the seventh.

un'fortunately, *adv.* [f. UNFORTUNATE *a.*] **a.** In an unfortunate manner; unhappily, unluckily.

1548 ELYOT, *Infœliciter*, vnhappily, vnfortunately. 1560 DAUS tr. *Sleidane's Comm.* 282 b, The death of kinge Fraunces chaunced unfortunately for studentes. 1621 LADY M. WROTH *Urania* 536 Shee was..the vnfortunateliest married, and vnhappiest wife this Countrey had. 1651 HOBBES *Leviath.* 390 Sidney Godolphin, who..was unfortunately slain in the..late Civill warre. 1700 DRYDEN *Sigism. & Guiscardo* 630 She..Ev'n kept her Count'nance, when the Lid remov'd Disclosed the Heart, unfortunately lov'd. 1710 STEELE *Tatler* No. 204 ¶4 We use Words of Respect sometimes very unfortunately. 1936 R. LEHMANN *Weather in Streets* I. ii. 36 Etty had not married—not even unfortunately.

b. In parenthetic or detached use.

1706 E. WARD *Wooden World Diss.* (1708) 37 He might unfortunately have grown up to be a Pedant. 1779 *Mirror* No. 10, Unfortunately for us, we found with our friend a number of his jovial companions. 1827 FARADAY *Chem. Manip.* xviii. 472 Unfortunately this evil increases with the heat. 1874 J. GEIKIE *Gt. Ice Age* xiv. 183 These relics, unfortunately, have almost invariably been lost or mislaid.

un'fortunateness. (UN-^{1} 12 and 5 b.)

1561 T. HOBY tr. *Castiglione's Courtyer* IV. (1577) X ij b, Although it putteth them in afflictions, daungers, trauels, and..unfortunatenesse. 1608 T. MORTON *Preamb. Encounter* 123 The vnfortunatenesse of this his declamatorie calumniation. 1654 GAYTON *Pleas. Notes* II. xxv. 285 O the unfortunatenesse of this adventure! 1697 COLLIER *Ess. Mor. Subj.* I. 205 To play upon the Indigence..of another; and take an advantage from the Unfortunateness of his Condition. 1867 BP. WILBERFORCE *Let.* in *Life* (1882) III. 217, I cannot agree as to the unfortunateness of the language.

un'fortune. Now *arch.* [UN-^{1} 12, 5 b. Cf. WANFORTUNE.] Misfortune, mischance; bad luck.

c 1470 *Gol. & Gaw.* 1225 Quhan on-fortone quhelmys the quheil, thair gais grace by. 1483 CAXTON *Cato* g iij, Thys felawe mocqued..suche one now late of his unfortune and myserye. *a* 1533 LD. BERNERS *Gold. Bk. M. Aurel.* (1546) Ff iv, The calme seson moste sure, is the vigile of the more vnfortune. 1647 HEXHAM I. s.v., An unfortune that cold not be avoided. 1888 STEVENSON *Black Arrow* 164 What unfortune [ye have had], ye have noways deserved.

un'fortuned, *a. rare.* [UN-^{1} 9.] Connected with, visited by, misfortune.

c 1403 LYDG. *Temple of Glas* 389 Þuruȝ þe cruelte Of old Saturne, my fadur vnfortuned. 1909 R. BRIDGES *Virgil's Æneid* VI. 618 Sitteth and to eternity shall sit Unfortun'd Theseus.

unfossi'liferous, *a.* (UN-^{1} 7.)

1836 T. THOMSON *Min., Geol.*, etc. II. 193 The unfossiliferous stratified formations. 1882 GEIKIE *Geol. Sk.* 292 The rocks of Scotland are, as a whole, unfossiliferous.

un'fossilized, *ppl. a.* (UN-^{1} 8.)

1846 WORCESTER (citing *Qu. Rev.*). 1848 OWEN in *Times* 14 Nov. 9/1 The carcase of such reptiles..in a recent or unfossilized state. 1887 MOLONEY *Forestry W. Africa* 127 Newer resins (unfossilized).

un'fostered, *ppl. a.* (UN-^{1} 8.)

1744 ARMSTRONG *Preserv. Health* II. 170 No youth of genius whose neglected bloom Unfoster'd sickens in the barren shade. 1847 C. BRONTË *J. Eyre* xiv, I was..partial to the unfledged, unfostered and unlucky.

un'fothered, *ppl. a. Sc.* [UN-^{1} 8.] Not foddered.

1725 RAMSAY *Gentle Sheph.* II. i, Like the pack-horse that's unfother'd And burden'd, [they] will tumble down faint.

un'fought, *ppl. a.* [UN-^{1} 8 b, 8 c; cf. next.]

1. Of persons: Not fought *with* or *for*.

1523 LD. BERNERS *Froiss.* I. xviii. 25 He toke mede and money of the Scottis, to thentent they myght departe pryuely by nyght, vnfoughte withall. 1586 J. HOOKER *Hist. Irel.* 148/1 in *Holinshed* II, Thinking it should be too great a dishonour vnto him to be bearded with a traitor, and to let him depart vnfought withall. 1619 FLETCHER, etc. *Knt. Malta* I. iii, Mountferrat should perceive my Sister had A Brother would not live to see her dye Unfought for. 1659 B. HARRIS *Parival's Iron Age* 211 Prince Rupert..might have gone away unfought with but that such counsell was too cold for so hot a stomach. [1822 SCOTT *Halidon Hall* I. ii. 9 If we leave it Unfought withal, it squares not with our honour.]

b. Not encountered in fight; without fighting.

1596 *Edward III*, III. iii. 139 These English faine would spend the time in words, That, night approching, they might escape vnfought. 1697 DRYDEN *Æneis* IX. 159 For fly they cannot, and, constrained to stay, Must yield unfought, a base inglorious prey.

2. Of battles, etc.: Not fought; uncontested.

1669 EARL ORRERY *Parthen.* (1676) 738 How many Battels ..had been unfought? 1807 WORDSW. *White Doe* III. 217 We yield (and can it be?) an unfought field! 1820 PRAED *Eve of Battle* 68 Anticipation fires his brain With fights unfought. 1898 *Westm. Gaz.* 6 June 2/2 We think that the constituency ought not to go unfought.

un'foughten, *ppl. a.* Now *arch.* [UN-^{1} 8 b. Cf. MDu. and Du. *ongevochten*, MHG. *ungevohten* (without fighting).] = prec.

1475 *Bk. Noblesse* (Roxb.) 47 Youre gret adversarie of Fraunce..fled and voided unfoughten at the said jorney of Senlis. *c* 1500 *Three Kings Sons* 89 In-asmoche as we haue ben so long vnfoughten with. ? 15.. *Battle of Otterburn* xli. in Child *Ball.* III. 297 If that I weynde..onfowghten awaye, He wolde me call but a kowarde knyght. *a* 1575 tr. *Pol. Verg. Eng. Hist.* (Camden No. 29) 140 He had sufferyd them..to passe by him unfoughten withal. 1811 SCOTT *Don Roderick* III. viii, But thou—unfoughten wilt thou yield to Fate? 1867 MORRIS *Jason* IX. 369 Soothly, have we no will to fight with thee If we may pass unfoughten.

un'foulable, *a.* (UN-^{1} 7 b.)

1862 *Catal. Internat. Exhib.* II. No. 2796, Unfoulable anchor. 1884 *Health Exhib. Catal.* 82/1 Treated with our patent unfoulable enamel.

un'fouled, *ppl. a.*^{1} [UN-^{1} 8 + FOUL *v.*^{1}] Not made foul or impure; undefiled.

c 1380 WYCLIF *Sel. Wks.* III. 388 Seynt Jame seis, For þis is a clene religioun,..to kepe a mon unfoulid fro þis worlde. *a* 1425 *Cursor M.* 19504 (Trin.), God him kepte..His hondes vnfouled of monnes blood. *a* 1470 HARDING *Chron.* LXXII. vii, Hir wyfehode..Afore that tyme euer was kept vnfouled. 1653 H. MORE *Antid. Ath.* II. xii. §3 Light and Colours unfoul'd and unsophisticated by any inward tincture. 1916 G. FRANKAU *Poet. Wks.* (1923) II. 3 The Killer-men of Valhalla looked up from the banquet-board At the unfouled breach of his rifle. 1929 D. H. LAWRENCE *Pansies* 74 The soul's first passion is for sheer life Entering in showers of truth, unfouled by lies.

†**un'fouled**, *ppl. a.*^{2} *Sc. Obs.* [UN-^{1} 8 + FOUL *v.*^{2}] Unexhausted.

1535 W. STEWART *Cron. Scot.* (Rolls) II. 412 Kenethus than..maid efter thame till go The freschest men [that] onfowllit wer in feild.

un'found, *ppl. a.* [UN-^{1} 8 b, 8 c. Cf. ON. *úfundinn*, older Da. *ufunden*, Du. *ongevonden*.] Not found; undiscovered. Also with *out*.

1584 LYLY *Campaspe* V. ii, Content to lyue vnknowne, and die vnfounde. 1644 QUARLES *Barnabas & B.* (1651) 211 Being lost, hee seekes himselfe unfound, or findes himselfe unknowne. 1678 DRYDEN & LEE *Œdipus* I. i, But for the Murderer's self, unfound by Man, Find him ye Pow'rs Cœlestial and Infernal. 1721 RAMSAY *Content* 316 More than seventy years..I've sought this court, till now unfound by me. 1818 BYRON *Ch. Har.* IV. cxxiv, Unfound the boon, unslaked the thirst. 1895 RIDER HAGGARD *Heart of World* xi, Our eyes might behold the greatest of these cities, sought for many generations but as yet unfound.

(*b*) 1621 G. SANDYS *Ovid's Met.* II. (1626) 28 To farthest Earth affrighted Nilus fled; And there conceal'd his yet vnfound-out head.

un'found, *v.* (UN-^{2} 3.)

c 1430 *Pilgr. Lyf Manhode* III. viii. (1869) 139 To a king it is thing reprouable..to vnfounde foundaciouns that hise auncestres hauen founded.

un'founded, *ppl. a.*^{1} [UN-^{1} 8 + FOUND *v.*^{1}] Having no foundation or basis; chiefly *fig.*, groundless, unwarranted.

1648 HEXHAM II, *Ongegrondet*, Vngrounded, or Vnfounded. 1667 MILTON *P.L.* II. 829, I..one for all My self expose, with lonely steps to tread Th' unfounded deep. 1785 BURKE *Nabob of Arcot* Wks. IV. 282 These debts..[he] at one stroke expunged..as utterly irrecoverable; he might have added, as utterly unfounded. 1828 LYTTON *Pelham* I. xxxiv, I advance a claim not altogether new and unfounded. 1855 *Orr's Circ. Sci., Inorg. Nat.* 129 Vague speculations and unfounded theories concerning the origin of things. 1883 *Law Rep.* 11 *Q.B.D.* 593 The imputation..was altogether unfounded and absurd.

Hence **un'foundedly** *adv.*

1820 SCOTT *Monast.* xxvi, I should wish to know the author..of all these suspicions, so unfoundedly urged against me. 1883 *Law Times Rep.* XLIX. 251/1 Bringing a civil action, however unfoundedly.

†**un'founded**, *ppl. a.*^{2} *Obs.* [UN-^{1} 8 + FOUND *v.*^{3}] Not numbered or powerless.

14.. *Sege Jerusalem* (E.E.T.S.) 35/618 Þei wynnen vp whyȝtly þe walles to kepe, Fresche vnfounded folke.

un'foxed, *ppl. a.* [UN-^{1} 8.] Sober.

1622 J. TAYLOR (Water P.) *Farewell to the Tower Bottles* A 2 b, Yet alwayes 'twas my chance in Bacchus spight, To come into the Tower, vnfox'd vpright.

un'fractured, *ppl. a.* (UN-^{1} 8.)

1742 *De Foe's Tour Gt. Brit.* (ed. 3) I. 262 Its huge Bulk lies unfractur'd. *a* 1845 S. SMITH in S. Holland *Mem. Sydney Smith* (1855) I. xi. 387 To him..I owe unfractured integrity of limb. 1927 E. V. GORDON *Introd. Old Norse* 254 The *e* of verbs of the fourth and fifth conjs. remained unfractured. 1946 F. E. ZEUNER *Dating Past* ix. 286 The (fractured or unfractured) raw material is not directly shaped into the tool. 1982 W. J. WALSH *R. K. Narayan* ii. 29 A coherent and unfractured psyche.

un'fragrant, *a.* (UN-^{1} 7, 5 b.)

1858 HAWTHORNE *Fr. & It. Note-bks.* (1871) II. 211 Children..exceedingly unfragrant, but very courteous and gentle. 1880 RUSKIN *Bible Amiens* i. (1884) 4 Extensive plains of useful and not unfragrant peat.

un'fragrantly, *adv.* (UN-^{1} 11.)

1883 *Harper's Mag.* June 121/1 It fumed not unfragrantly.

†**un'fraisted**, *ppl. a. Obs.* [UN-^{1} 8.] Untried, inexperienced.

? *a* 1400 *Morte Arth.* 2736 Bot I ame bot a fawntkyne, vn-fraystede in armes. *Ibid.* 2861.

†**un'frame**, *sb.*: see UN-^{1} 3.

un'frame, *v.* [UN-^{2} 3.]

†**1.** *trans.* To distress, trouble. *Obs.*$^{-1}$

c 1250 *Gen. & Ex.* 1213 Wintres forð-wexen on ysaac, And ysmael was him vn-swac; Often it gan ysaac un-framen.

2. To take to pieces; to destroy. Also *fig.*

a 1548 HALL *Chron., Hen. V*, 46 All the bridges wer by his enemies broken and unframed. 1603 J. DAVIES (Heref.) *Microcosmos* Wks. (Grosart) I. 83/2 The Pynns, the Tenons, Beams, Bolts,..All which they marke when they doe it vnframe. 1621 SANDERSON *Serm.* I. 179 The curse of God.. gnaweth asunder the pins and the joynts of the building, till it have unframed it, and resolved it into a ruinous heap. *a* 1716 SOUTH *Serm.* (1744) VIII. v. 129 Sin has unframed the fabrick of the whole man.

†**b.** To undo. *Obs.*

1567 TURBERV. *Epit.*, etc. 82 b, Those two agreed with common voyce my bondage to vnframe.

3. To dislocate; to throw into confusion or disorder, to distract.

1574 HELLOWES *Gueuara's Fam. Ep.* (1584) 109 You are much offended by manie slaunderers that deprave your doings, and unframe your attempts. 1603 J. DAVIES (Heref.) *Microcosmos* Wks. (Grosart) I. 55/1 Disastrous Richard second of that name,..Who did the forme of this State quite vnframe. 1668 OWEN *Mortif. Sin* ii. (ed. 3) 14 It unframes our Spirit; and thence is called the sin that so easily besets us. 1727 [DORRINGTON] *Philip Quarll* 87 This unexpected but lucky Adventure, like a sudden Surprize, unfram'd his Reason.

un'fram(e)able, *a.* (UN-^{1} 7 b.)

1594 HOOKER *Eccl. Pol.* I. xvi. §6 The cause of..their disposition so vnframeable vnto societies wherein they liue. 1597 *Ibid.* v. ix. §1 The matter which he hath to worke on is vnframable.

un'fram(e)ableness. (UN-^{1} 12.)

1648 SANDERSON *Serm.* (1653) 9 The unframableness of our nature, to the doing of anything that is good.

un'framed, *ppl. a.* [UN-^{1} 8.]

1. Not formed or moulded, unfashioned.

1548 UDALL, etc. *Erasm. Par. John* vi. 37 b, He fourmeth and fasshyoneth the rude and vnframed witte with certayne principles. 1591 SAVILE *Tacitus, Agricola* 238 To compose, though in rude and vnframed speech, a memory of our late thraldome. 1621 G. SANDYS *Ovid's Met.* I. (1626) 1 The Sea, the Earth, al-couering Heauen vnfram'd, One face had Nature, which they Chaos nam'd.

2. Not set or enclosed in a frame.

1718 POPE *Lett.* (1737) 201 He lugg'd out the tatter'd fragments of an unframed picture. 1885 HOWELLS *Silas Lapham* (1891) I. 13 A large warped, unframed photograph.

un'franchised, *ppl. a.* (UN-^{1} 8.)

1648 HEXHAM II, *Onbevrijdt*, Vnfreed, or Vnfranchized. [1775 ASH.] 1832 A. W. FONBLANQUE *Eng. under 7 Administr.* (1837) II. 284 The honest elector will only derive from his suffrage a share..which his unfranchised neighbour will also enjoy. 1847 GROTE *Greece* II. xxxi. IV. 217 The memorable partnership..between Kleisthenês and the unfranchised multitude.

†**un'frangible**, *a. Obs.* (UN-^{1} 7 and 5 b.)

1601 DOLMAN *La Primaud. Fr. Acad.* (1618) III. 847 Iron, be it neuer so thin, is made vnfrangible by blowes. 1654 JER. TAYLOR *Real Pres.* 198 That body of Christ which is in heaven..being whole and impassible, and unfrangible.

un'frank, *a.* (UN-^{1} 7.)

1861 C. W. S. BROOKS *Silver Cord* xxvi, Impertinent curiosity, and..unfrank conversation.

un'frankable, *a.* (UN-^{1} 7 b.)

1819 SOUTHEY *Lett.* (1856) III. 106 The next question is how to transport them.., for they are of an unfrankable shape and texture.

un'franked, *ppl. a.* (UN-^{1} 8. Cf. G. *unfrankiert*, Da. *ufrankeret*, Sw. *ofrankerad*.)

a 1765 D. MALLET *Let.* in *Pearson's Catal.* No. 81 (1900) 50 My last letter was franked by Mr. Nugent. Perhaps that was the cause of its miscarriage. I therefore send this unfranked. 1809 SIR G. JACKSON *Diaries & Lett.* (1873) I. 3, I wondered..that a letter—and unfranked one, too—should follow me. 1843 CARLYLE *Past & Pr.* III. xv, Heavy Packets, most of them unfranked.

unfra'ternal, *a.* (UN-^{1} 7.)

1865 CARLYLE *Fredk. Gt.* XX. v, A not unfraternal or unpatriotic procedure. 1879 FARRAR *St. Paul* I. 447 To them..he never utters one single disrespectful or unfraternal word.

un'fraudulent, *a.* (UN-^{1} 7.)
1590 SWINBURNE *Testaments* 237 To take of the goods.. by the lawful & vnfraudulent gift of the testator.

†**un'fraught**, *sb. Obs.*$^{-1}$ [UN-^{1} 12.] Want of cargo or freight.
1436 *Libel Eng. Policy* in *Pol. Poems* (Rolls) II. 191 And now so fele shippes thys yeres there were, That moche losse for unfraught [*v.r.* unfreyght] they bare.

un'fraught, *ppl. a.* (UN-^{1} 8 b.)
1587 TURBERV. *Trag. T.* (1837) 16 With manly minde, and mouth unfraught of feare. **1605** BACON *Adv. Learn.* II. To the King §12 Mindes emptie & vnfraught with matter. **1650** ASHMOLE *Chym. Collect.* Prol. 15 Such Vagrants doubtless are empty and unfraught. **1709** *Brit. Apollo* II. No. 53. 2/1 Men of narrow Intellects are Unfraught with..Noble Ideas.

†**un'fraught**, *v. Obs.* [UN-^{2} 3.] *trans.* To unload, discharge.
1559 *Mirr. Mag.* (1563) X ij, Suffiseth nowe this playnt.. Whereof my hart his bottome hath vnfraught. **1633** P. FLETCHER *Purple Isl.* VI. xix, Then thou deare swain, thy heav'nly load unfraught. **1773** J. ROSS *Fratricide* I. 413 (MS.), Meantime, unfraughting thus returning love, He to his Mother runs.

†**un'frayed**, *ppl. a. Sc. Obs.* [UN-^{1} 8.] Undaunted.
1536 BELLENDEN *Cron. Scot.* (1541) 142b/2 Thir men.. went, with vnfrayit curage, to ye wallis. **1680** in *Proc. Soc. Antiq. Scot.* XLV. 249 Beliving in the sufficencie of a Saviour..quherby ye may stand unfraid befor his tribunall.

†**un'frayned**, *ppl. a. Obs.*$^{-1}$ [UN-^{1} 8.] Unasked.
a **1275** *Ancr. R.* 338 Schrift ouh to beon willes, þet is, willeliche, iureined [*MS. C.* vnfreined].

†**un'fredeable**, *a. Obs.* [UN-^{1} 7 b + FREDE *v.*] Insensible; without feeling.
c **1450** in *Alphita* (Anecd. Oxon.) 123 *note*, A fishe þat..yf fissher put his honde upon hit hit makeþ his honde onfredeabile.

un'free, *a.* [ME. *unfre* (UN-^{1} 7), = MDu. *onvri* (Du. *onvrij*), OHG. *unfrî* (MHG. *unvrî*, G. *unfrei*), WFris. *on-*, *ûnfrij*, MDa. and Da. *ufri*, MSw. and Sw. *ofri*.]
†**1.** Ignoble, base. *Obs.*$^{-1}$
c **1320** *Sir Tristr.* 2727 Þou slouȝ his breþer þre In fiȝt: Vrgan and morgan vn-fre And moraunt, þe noble kniȝt.
2. Characterized by want of freedom.
13.. *E.E. Allit. P.* B 1129 So if folk be defowled by vnfre chaunce,..he may polyce hym at þe prest, by penaunce taken. **1568** GRAFTON *Chron.* II. 120 The election beyng vnfree,..eche of them almost of necessitie must hate the other. **1849** KEMBLE *Saxons in Eng.* I. 203 Serfs by reason of unfree birth. **1882-3** *Schaff's Encycl. Relig. Knowl.* 2206 The State..must be invested with all power over industry, which thus may be called practically unfree.
†**3.** Not at liberty *to* do something. *Obs.*
c **1380** WYCLIF *Wks.* (1880) 284 ȝif lordis myȝte ȝeue here heritage to clerkis..þei were vnfree to helpe here soulis.
4. Not possessed of personal liberty; destitute of freedom.
c **1380** WYCLIF *Sel. Wks.* I. 363 And so, as myche as in hem is, þei have maad Crist unfree. **1587** GOLDING *De Mornay* xii. 207 If it be demaunded why God created man free, and not vnfree. **1602** J. DAVIES (Heref.) *Mirum in Modum* Wks. (Grosart) I. 28/1 Better vnfree (saist thou) then be so ill, But 'tis not ill at libertie to bee.
1849 KEMBLE *Saxons in Eng.* I. 203 The children..of parents who are both unfree, or..of one unfree parent. **1865** KINGSLEY *Hereward* xx, All the folk, free and unfree, man and woman, were out on the streets. **1882** WEEDEN *Soc. Law Labor* 40 The savage is the most unfree man in the world.
absol. **1864** KINGSLEY *Roman & T.* 54 The custom of chiefs choosing..their companions-in-arms, from among the most valiant of the unfree. **1874** GREEN *Short Hist.* i. §2 (1882) 13 A slave class, a class of the unfree.
5. Not holding the position of a free or privileged member of a corporation. *Obs.* or *arch.*
1442 *Extr. Aberd. Rec.* (1844) I. 8 Item, that al the communytie, alsweile vnfree as free men, be sworne to rise ..in the defence of the toune. **1459-60** *Cal. Anc. Rec. Dublin* (1889) 303 Thay be put out of ther franches and ymad unfre. **1574** in *10th Rep. Hist. MSS. Comm.* App. V. 423 None of the inhabitance of Galway, free or onfree, yonge or old. **1608** in Gross *Gild Merch.* (1890) I. 150 *note*, Anie Englishe borne subiect beinge vnfree or no member of this ffellowshippe. **1687** LUTTRELL *Brief Rel.* (1857) I. 407 The lord mayor might drink to one as sherif free or unfree of the citty. **1717** in J. J. Vernon *Par. & Kirk Hawick* (1900) 205 Payd..for the bells tolling at the buriall of every unfree person within the said toun.
6. Not free of duty, tax, or impost; not exempt from commercial restrictions.
1678 SIR G. MACKENZIE *Crim. Laws Scot.* I. xxvi. §ii. (1699) 130 The Customers Officers were about to poynd some unfree goods. **1684** *Lond. Gaz.* No. 1916/1 No such Clause or Provision as makes Free Goods to become Unfree when Laden and taken in Unfree Ships.

unfree, *v.* [UN-^{2} 6 a.] *trans.* To make unfree; to deprive of freedom.
c **1380** WYCLIF *Sel. Wks.* III. 431 Also oblishyng of men unfreeþ hem to God.

un'freed, *ppl. a.* (UN-^{1} 8.)
1565 *Reg. Privy Council Scot.* I. 423 How lang that evir the said Thomas remanit in Ingland unfred or put to libertie. **1648** HEXHAM II, *Onbevrijdt*, Vnfreed, or Vnfranchized. **1715** POPE *Iliad* II. 213 Shall beauteous Helen still remain unfreed? **1852** M. ARNOLD *Summer Night* 50 Death in their prison reaches them Unfreed, having seen nothing, still unblest. **1873** W. MORRIS *Love is Enough* 127 Few folk as friends shall unfreed Pharamond meet.

un'freedom. (UN-^{1} 12.)
c **1380** WYCLIF *Wks.* (1880) 286 Þe moste vnfredom is vnfredom of synne, for þat makiþ a man seruaunt..to þe fend. **1884** *Athenæum* 12 Apr. 465/3 Slavery as distinct from unfreedom died out very early [in England].

†**un'freeholder.** *Sc. Obs.* (UN-^{1} 12.)
1507 *Extr. Aberd. Rec.* (1844) I. 436 [Selling of ale] be fre folkis, and..be vnfrehaldaris.

†**un'freely**, *a. Obs.* [UN-^{1} 7.] Not beautiful.
a **1300** *Cursor M.* 8082 Þair muthes wide, þair eien brade, Vn-freli was þair face made! *c* **1450** HOLLAND *Howlate* 56 Quhy is..My forme and my fetherem vnfrely, but feir? *Ibid.* 851. *a* **1568** STEWART in *Bannatyne MS.* (Hunter. Club) 397/35 Fast vnfrely fowll ffobbis, And bubillis full lyk.

un'freeman. Now *arch.* [f. UNFREE *a.* 5.] One who is not a freeman of a corporation.
1445 in *Charters*, etc. *Edinb.* (1871) 67 Of strangearis and of vnfremen. **1480** *Newcastle Merch. Vent.* (Surtees) I. 3 The ackit [= act] of collarying of an unfremans gudes. **1511** *Burgh Rec. Edinb.* (1869) I. 134 Pakkis of lint..brocht to the samyn be vnfreemen and strayngeris. **1584** in *10th Rep. Hist. MSS. Comm.* App. V. 433 Any goodes that apertayned to unfreemen (as it is termed). **1627** in Irving *Hist. Dumbarton.* (1860) 476 Gif ony freeman byis the same..for the use and behoof of an unfreeman..or w^t unfreemanis moneyis to the unfreemanis behoof. **1707** *Lond. Gaz.* No. 4306/1 The Duties to be paid by the Unfreemen Importers of Coals into the Port..of Great Yarmouth. **1788** *Faculty Decisions* II. 30-1 (E.D.D.), That the three saddlers should be discharged to pack and peel with unfreemen. **1824** SCOTT *Redgauntlet* ch. x, I am not a person to pack or peel with Jacobites, and such unfreemen as poor Redgauntlet. **1876** GRANT *Burgh Sch. Scot.* 141 The supplying of instruction to the son and daughter of every burgess and unfreeman.

†**un'freeness.** *Obs.* (UN-^{1} 12.)
1648 HEXHAM II, *Onvryigheydt*, Vnfreenesse, or Subjection. **1657** THURLOE in *State Papers* (1742) VI. 281 The three great men professinge their great unfreenes to act, ..sayd, that [etc.].

un'freeze, *v.* [UN-^{2} 3 and 7.]
1. *trans.* To cause to thaw.
1584 HUDSON *Du Bartas' Judith* IV. 196 Loues firy dart Could neuer vnfriese the frost of her chast hart. **1598** FLORIO, *Disghiacciare*, to vnfreese, to thaw. **1651** OGILBY *Æsop* (1665) 11 Such Trumpeters would blood turn'd Ice unfreeze. **1879** MISS BIRD *Lady's Life Rocky Mount.* I. 280 Eggs, butter, milk,..have to be unfrozen.
b. *fig. spec.* (in recent use) to make (assets, credits, etc.) realizable; to remove restrictions or rigid control from.
1637 N. WHITING *Albino & Bellama* 36 Such quickning heat..That thawd his voyce, and did unfreeze his tongue. **1670** BROOKS *London's Lament.* 41 God by fiery tryals will unfreeze the frozen graces of his people. **1862** THORNBURY *Turner* II. 125 At an age when..he could not unfreeze himself into hospitality. **1933** *Kalends* (Williams & Wilkins Co.) May, Among other horrors..of our present adventure into fiscal delirium tremens, we discover the rise and growth of the monstrous verb, *unfreeze*. **1940** *Sun* (Baltimore) 3 Dec. 1/6 Great Britain and..Spain signed an agreement today designed to 'unfreeze' Spanish funds blocked in London. **1948** DYLAN THOMAS *Let.* 17 Nov. (1966) 323, I have already borrowed in advance from my fee..in order to unfreeze my Bank account. **1948** *Time* 22 Nov. 58/3 Thanks to improved domestic production of newsprint, circulation would be unfrozen Jan. 1. **1957** *Economist* 28 Sept. 1006/1 If Britain were to unfreeze the Egyptian working sterling account..President Nasser would be willing to discuss diplomatic relations. **1974** *Guardian* 23 Jan. 10/1 Building projects..were due to be unfrozen early this year. **1983** *Time* 20 June 6/1 The [EEC] leaders agreed..to unfreeze the aid package for Israel, blocked..after the Israeli invasion of Lebanon.
2. *intr.* To become thawed. Also *fig.*
1662 J. DAVIES tr. *Olearius' Voy. Ambass.* 64 The cold having..pierc'd to the Centre of the earth, it must have leasure to unfreeze. **1746** W. HORSLEY *Fool* (1748) I. 234, I wish he would put off his Amour to the ensuing May, when the Virgin Heart unfreezes. **1918** *Scotsman* 6 Apr. 7/2 Their enthusiasms were reached only by tact and wise consideration... The atmosphere unfroze; and even the hotel people became polite and gentle. **1958** *Times* 11 Nov. 8/1 Members of his [*sc.* de Gaulle's] staff point out that he never expected educated Muslim opinion to 'unfreeze' all at once. **1968** K. O'HARA *Bird-Cage* xiii. 99 A small Scotch to his hand, a steak quietly unfreezing in the kitchen. **1981** P. VANSITTART *Death of Robin Hood* III. iii. 143 She slowly unfroze, motioning him to the damson ottoman.

un'freezing, *ppl. a.* (UN-^{1} 10.)
1775 T. SMITH *Jrnl.* (1849) 279 It has been a wonder of a winter, so moderate and unfreezing. **1897** *Outing* XXIX. 555 Ghastly in its shroud of snow and the blackness of unfreezing waters about it.

†**unfreight**, *sb.*: see UNFRAUGHT *sb.*

un'freight, *v.* (UN-^{2} 3.)
1580 H. GIFFORD *Gilloflowers* 36 Unfraight the shippe of all unlawfull wares.

un'freighted, *ppl. a.* (UN-^{1} 8.)
[**1775** ASH.] **1854** PATMORE *Angel in Ho.* I. viii. 5 [I] Breathed with a heart unfreighted.

†**unfreme**: see UN-^{1} 3.

un-French, *a.* (UN-^{1} 7.)
1803 *Lett. Miss Riversdale* II. 249 Madame de Sainval.. prides herself much upon being so *un*french as to admit it. **1830** MISS MITFORD *Our Village* Ser. IV. 74 A step..so un-French, so un-English. **1850** N. HAWTHORNE *Amer. Note-bks.* (1883) 380 This poor little Frenchman,..eating our most un-French victuals. **1878** E. FITZGERALD *Lett.* (1889) I. 423 Alfred [de Musset] appears to me a fine Fellow, very un-French in some respects.

un-French, *v.* [UN-^{2} 6 a.] *trans.* To translate from French.
1605 GAYWOOD in *Sylvester's Du Bartas* Pref. Sonn., Whom..loue to Heau'n and vs, Mou'd to vn-French his learned labours thus.

un'frenchified, *ppl. a.* (UN-^{1} 8.)
1784 P. OLIVER in *T. Hutchinson's Diary* (1886) II. 400 Be sure, return unfrenchified in thought, word, and deed. **1833** T. HOOK *Love & Pride*, *Marquess* vii, Following the extremely unfrenchified fashion.

un'frenchify, *v.* (UN-^{2} 6 c.)
1598 FLORIO, *Sfranciosato*,..vnfrenchifide. **1814** *Edin. Rev.* Sept. 297 We are glad..to have the assistance of a Parisian..to help to unfrenchify them.

un'frenzied, *ppl. a.* (UN-^{1} 8.)
1805 in *Spirit Pub. Jrnls.* IX. 243 In thy calmer and unfrenzied hour.

un'frequency. Now *rare* or *Obs.* (UN-^{1} 12, 5 b.)
1611 COTGR., *Infrequence*, vnfrequencie, solitarinesse. **1662** GLANVILL *Lux Orient.* 133 This may be the reason of the unfrequency of their appearance. **1753** MISS COLLIER *Art Torment.* 224 The frequency of corporal punishments, and the unfrequency of rewarding men. **1802-12** BENTHAM *Ration. Judic. Evid.* (1827) V. 708 The comparative unfrequency of criminative perjury. **1834** *Good's Study Med.* (ed. 4) IV. 397 A point, however, of less importance, from the unfrequency of their occurrence.

un'frequent, *a.* [UN-^{1} 7 and 5 b.]
1. = INFREQUENT *a.* 3.
1611 FLORIO, *Infrequente*, vnfrequent, seld, not frequent. **1712** STEELE *Spect.* No. 472 ⁋1 This Misfortune is so very great and unfrequent, that one would think, an Establishment for all the Poor under it might be easily accomplished. **1793** COLERIDGE *Songs of Pixies* iii, Beneath whose foliage pale Fann'd by the unfrequent gale We shield us from the Tyrant's mid-day rage. **1824** MISS MITFORD *Village* Ser. I. 246 In those unfrequent frosts which destroy all vegetation. **1866** HOWELLS *Venet. Life* v. 63 The blond, unfrequent beauty of the German aliens.
b. With preceding negative.
1665 BOYLE *Occas. Refl.* II. xiii. 230 As Deliriums and Phrensies are not unfrequent in Feavers. **1749** J. MASON *Numbers in Poet. Compositions* 57 This is a peculiar close, but not unfrequent in Milton. **1831** SCOTT *Ct. Rob.* vii, A personage not so unfrequent in the streets of Constantinople as to excite any particular notice. **1871** MILL *Pol. Econ.* (ed. 7) 200 There is, however, a not unfrequent case, in which the purpose of the borrower is different.
†**2.** = INFREQUENT *a.* 2. *Obs.*$^{-1}$
1618 ROWLANDS *Sacred Mem.* 24 This place is solitary, vnfrequent; We are belated.

unfre'quent, *v.* [UN-^{1} 14 or UN-^{2} 3.] *trans.* To refrain or cease from frequenting.
1598 FLORIO, *Disconuersare*, to vnfrequent, not to conuerse together. *Ibid.*, *Sconuersare*, to disaccompanie, to vnfrequent. **1708** J. PHILIPS *Cyder* I. 404 Glad to shun his hostile Gripe, They quit their Thefts, and unfrequent the Fields.

unfre'quented, *ppl. a.* (UN-^{1} 8.)
1588 SHAKS. *Tit. A.* II. i. 115 The Forrest walkes are wide and spacious, And many vnfrequented plots there are. **1653** H. COGAN tr. *Pinto's Trav.* xlviii. 277 Not one appearing in the streets for the space of ten days, during which time all places were unfrequented. **1701** NORRIS *Ideal World* I. viii. 452 The straight and single, however unfrequented path of truth. **1779** FORREST *Voy. N. Guinea* 154 During our stay here we found the islands unfrequented. **1817** J. SCOTT *Paris Revisit.* (ed. 4) 275 Going round..by one of the more unfrequented walks, running through the woods. **1878** HUXLEY *Physiogr.* 189 There are no doubt many slight disturbances, in unfrequented districts.
Hence **unfre'quentedness.**
1654 EARL ORRERY *Parthen.* (1676) 79 A Grove, whose unfrequentedness was fit for my melancholly. **1680** H. MORE *Apocal. Apoc.* 160 There would be a great deadness of Trade,..and so great unfrequentedness..would seize his principal Seat. **1727** A. HAMILTON *New Acc. E. Ind.* I. i. 5 The Unfrequentedness of the Coast between the Cape of Good Hope and Natal.

unfre'quenting, *vbl. sb.* (UN-^{1} 12.)
1620 *Southampton Court Leet Rec.* (1907) III. 578 We fynde the vnfrequentinge therof doth breed a murmer.

unfre'quenting, *ppl. a.* [UN-^{1} 10.]
†Unfrequented.
1607 ROWLANDS *Famous Hist.* 46 Terry, Guy and Osile wanting guide, Did stay about the unfrequenting Wood.

un'frequently, *adv.* (UN-^{1} 11 and 5 b. Usually with preceding negative.)
1646 SIR T. BROWNE *Pseud. Ep.* 7 They like Judas desire death, and not unfrequently pursue it. **1674** BOYLE *Excell. Theol.* 196 'Tis not unfrequently so [prejudiced] by those, that mention him with an *Encomium*. **1794** R. J. SULIVAN *View Nat.* I. 397 Systematic philosophy..is not unfrequently involved in difficulty. **1845** LINDLEY *Sch. Bot.* iv. (1858) 35 Flowers white, unfrequently pink. **1893** *Law Times* XCV. 56/1 Negotiations..not unfrequently fall through on some point of disagreement.

†**un'fret**, *v.*^{1} *Obs.*$^{-1}$ [UN-^{2} 3 + FRET *v.*^{3}] *trans.* To unbind, untie.
1496 *Bk. St. Albans, Fishing* h j b, Unfrette hym thenne and lete hym drye in an hous roof in the smoke.

† **un'fret**, *v.*² *Obs.* [UN-² 3 + FRET *v.*¹] *trans.* To make smooth; to unknit.

1594 GREENE & LODGE *Looking Gl.* III. i, To Ioppa will I flee, And for a while to Tharsus shape my course, Vntill the Lord vnfret His angry browes. **1601** CHESTER *Love's Mart.* xcix, O happie time since I with Nature met, My unmelodious Discord I vnfret.

un'fretted, *ppl. a.* [UN-¹ 8.]

1. Not eaten or worn away; unimpaired.

1577 STANYHURST *Hist. Irel.* 91/1 in *Holinshed* I, At night againe he founde the Paper vnfretted, and musing thereof he beganne to poare on the writing. **1663** BOYLE *Usef. Exp. Nat. Philos.* II. iii. 84 Shewing that the shell was..eaten away,..but the thin skin..continu'd altogether unfretted. **1894** MRS. A. WEBSTER *Mother & Dau.* (1895) 30 She sees this [feature] fair, and that unfretted still.

2. Not vexed or worried.

1870 E. PEACOCK *Ralf Skirl.* III. 47 When his mind was sufficiently unfretted. **1893** *Atlantic Monthly* Feb. 283 He is ..unfretted by the cares of housekeeping.

un'friable, *a.* (UN-¹ 7 b.)

1802 PALEY *Nat. Theol.* viii. (1819) 105 The elastic and unfriable nature of cartilage.

un'friend, *sb.* (and *a.*). Forms: (see UN-¹ and FRIEND *sb.*). [ME. *unfreond*, *-frend*, = WFris. *on-*, *ûnfrjeon*, MDu. *onvrient* (Du. *-vriend*), MLG. *unvrund*, MHG. *unvriunt* (G. *unfreund*).]

1. One who is not a friend or on friendly terms; an enemy. In early use chiefly *Sc.* (sometimes in predicate without article), and in the 19th cent. app. revived by Scott.

c **1275** LAY. 5632 We sollen..slean houre onfrendes and wenden after Brenne. *Ibid.* 17612 Wend to oure onfreondes and drif heom of londe. *c* **1425** WYNTOUN *Cron.* VIII. xxvi. 3890 For he doutit þe gret mycht Off his vnfreyndis, and þare slycht. *a* **1475** ASHBY *Dicta Philos.* 885 Showe to al maner freindis grete honnour..And pardon freendes & vnfreendes errour. **1581** MULCASTER *Positions* xxxix. (1887) 213 Socrates..uniustely condemned by the furie of the people, and persuasion of his vnfreindes. **1600** W. WATSON *Decacordon* (1602) 125 Some night Crowes, or other vnfriends or backe friends that may be set on to incense against him. **1663** *Lauderdale Papers* (Camden) I. 127 His unfriends here had taken pains to procure..copies of the books. **1814** SCOTT *Wav.* xv, He is a very unquiet neighbour to his un-friends. **1835** GEN. P. THOMPSON *Exerc.* (1842) III. 158 With this reservation, there must be no unfriends. **1877** STUBBS *Med. & Mod. Hist.* (1886) 110, I am ready to stick to my friends and vote against my un-friends.

b. Const. *of*, *to*.

1513 DOUGLAS *Æneid* IX. vi. 111 The day lycht, quhilk is to ws onfrend, Approchis neyr. *c* **1600** W. FOWLER *Wks.* (S.T.S.) I. 241/30 Thow, o atropos, vnfreind to hir, and to to freind to me. **1626** in Rushw. *Hist. Coll.* (1659) I. 253 That one near the Crown of England should..become an unfriend to our State. **1692** *Scotch Presbyterian Eloquence* (1738) 47 This Way will render us more formidable to our Enemies, and Unfriends to our Way. **1819** SCOTT *Leg. Montrose* vi, They are but unfriends to each other. **1888** *Spectator* 22 Dec. 1804 Mr. Courtney, certainly no unfriend of the Parnellites.

2. One who is not a member of the Society of Friends. Also *attrib.*

1828 SOUTHEY *Ep. to A. Cunningham* 387 From such a barber, O unfriend Darton! was that portrait made. **1846** W. E. FORSTER in T.W. Reid *Life* (1888) I. 186 To make their movement a national one by adding the names of unfriend ladies to their committee.

un'friend, *v.* (UN-² 6 b.)

1659 FULLER *App. Inj. Innoc.* III. xxxj b, I hope, Sir, that we are not mutually Unfriended by this Difference which hath happened betwixt us.

un'friended, *a.* [UN-¹ 9.] Not provided with friends; friendless.

1513 MORE *Rich. III* (1883) 55 In how much she is now in the more beggerly condicion, vnfrended and worne out of acquaintance. **1554** ASCHAM in Whitaker *Richmondshire* (1823) I. 275 That [time] when I, unfreinded and unknowne, came first to your lordshipp. **1601** SHAKS. *Twel. N.* III. iii. 10 A stranger, Vnguided, and vnfriended. **1656** JEANES *Mixt. Schol. Div.* 5 And how should they, who were but..poor unfriended persons, escape..so potent..a malice. **1735** POPE *Let.* Wks. 1751 IX. 195 He will be a friend and benefactor..to your un-friended, un-benefited Nation. **1772** *Test Filial Duty* II. 2 [I] cannot think that I am unfriended, unheeded. **1842** ROGERS *Burke's Wks.* Introd. I. 10 Barry (afterwards the well known painter, then an unfriended son of genius). **1875** HOWELLS *Foregone Concl.* 209 A man more than ordinarily orphaned and unfriended.

absol. **1804** W. L. BOWLES *Spir. Discov.* III. 120 Who stood a guardian angel in distress To the unfriended.

b. Const. *of*.

1589 WARNER *Alb. Eng.* Prose Addit. 159 Fly Trayterous Æneas, fly vnfolowed and vnfriended of Elisa. **1725** POPE *Odyssey* IV. 631 Still on this desert Isle my fleet is moor'd; Unfriended of the gales. **1868** LANIER *Jacquerie* v. 18 That blade flew up..And left Lord Raoul unfriended of his weapon.

Hence **un'friendedness**.

1821 *Tales Landlord, Fair Witch of Glas Llyn* III. 325 This sublime unfriendedness.

† **un'friendfully**, *adv. Obs.*⁻¹ (UN-¹ 11.)

1513 DOUGLAS *Æneid* VI. i. 135 Hard fortoun has..The Troianis..persewit vnfreindfully [**1533** vnfrendly].

un'friend-like, *a.* (UN-¹ 7 c.)

1797 LAMB *Let. to Coleridge* 7 April, I did not expect so long, so unfriend-like a silence.

un'friendlily, *adv.* (UN-¹ 11.)

1864 W. J. LINTON *Claribel* II. ii, Your harsh words Unfriendlily apparel'd.

un'friendliness. (UN-¹ 12; cf. next.)

a **1684** LEIGHTON *Comm. 1 Pet.* ii. 11 (1693) 351 But by the troubles, and unfriendliness of the World he gains this. *a* **1768** SECKER *Serm.* (1771) V. iv. 71 Every Day we see those ..return monstrous Acts of Injustice for slight Instances of Neglect or Unfriendliness. **1790** MME. D'ARBLAY *Diary* 20 May, I never diminished from the frank unfriendliness to the cause with which I began. **1861** GEO. ELIOT *Silas M.* ix, Not because of any unfriendliness, but because..courtesy is not a growth of such homes.

un'friendly, *a.* [UN-¹ 7. Cf. WFris. *on-*, *ûnfrjeonlik*, MDu. *onvriendelijc* (Du. *-lijk*), MHG. *unvriuntlîch* (G. *unfreundlich*).]

1. Not characteristic of a friend or friends; exhibiting dislike or hostility.

1425 *Rolls of Parlt.* IV. 274/1 Þis delaye, of which were like to growe unease and unfrendely love betwene me and my said Cousyn. *a* **1513** FABYAN *Chron.* (1516) VII. 134/1 They mette with vnfrendely countenaunce, &..departyd with lytle loue or charyte. *a* **1548** HALL *Chron., Edw. IV*, 229 The French kyng..knewe by his espials..the vnfrendly departyng of the Duke of Burgoyn. **1663** BP. PATRICK *Parab. Pilgr.* xxxvii, Nor have you given me cause to be less your Friend than heretofore; unless it be by this unfriendly jealousie. **1757** FOOTE *Author* II, It was, d'ye see, a very unfriendly thing to make love to Becky in my absence. **1837** DE QUINCEY *Lake Poets, Coleridge*, Discoverers who would make a more unfriendly use of the discovery. **1898** *Westm. Gaz.* 21 Jan. 2/2 We are very much afraid that this would be looked upon by other countries as an 'unfriendly act'.

2. Not having the qualities or disposition of a friend; *esp.* unfavourably disposed, inimical, hostile.

1483 *Cath. Angl.* 142/2 Vn Frendly, *inhumanus, inimicus.* **1553** ASCHAM *Germany* Wks. (1904) 127, I am not so vnaduised..nor you so vnfrendly to looke for so much from me. **1579** HARVEY *Letter-bk.* (Camden) 58 To his very unfrendly frende that procurid yᵉ edition of his slender and extemporall devises. *a* **1616** BEAUM. & FL. *Wit at Sev. Weapons* v. i, Sure some unfriendly Messenger Is imploy'd betwixt you. **1629** in Foster *Eng. Factories India* (1909) III. 358 Our unfriendlie neighbours the Dutch. **1794** S. WILLIAMS *Vermont* 170 The Indians became unfriendly. **1836** THIRLWALL *Greece* III. 379 They put forward some of their partizans, who were not so notoriously unfriendly to him. **1884** CHURCH *Bacon* 18 His unsympathetic and suspicious, but probably not unfriendly relative.

3. Not propitious or favourable (*for* or *to*).

1513 BRADSHAW *Lyfe St. Werburge* II. 1047 By fortune vnfrendly..Both horse and man fell to grounde sodendly. **1608** SHAKS. *Per.* III. i. 58 No light, no fire; the unfriendly elements Forgot thee utterly. **1707** *Curios. in Husb. & Gard.* 41 The Wind that blows from thence..is always unfriendly to Vegetation. **1784** *Phil. Trans.* LXXIV. 468 It must be supposed to have arisen from some unfriendly mixture in the tin, probably from Arsenic. **1805** DICKSON *Pract. Agric.* I. 406 It frequently happens that..a coarse, unfriendly, stiff soil, is brought up. **1815** JANE AUSTEN *Emma* xvi, The atmosphere in that unsettled state..which is..the most unfriendly for exercise. **1845** WHATELY in *Encycl. Metrop.* (1845) I. 225/1 Qualities unfriendly to each other are rarely combined.

un'friendly, *adv.* Now *rare.* [UN-¹ 11.] In an unfriendly manner.

a **900** *Genesis* 2689 Þu us leanast nu, unfreondlice fremena þancast. **1483** *Cath. Angl.* 142/2 Vn Frendly,..*inhumane, inhumaniter.* **1548** ELYOT, *Insequor*,..to speake vnfrendly agaynst one. **1553** [see UNFRIENDFULLY]. **1570** G. HARVEY *Letter-bk.* (Camden) 3, I delaied thus unfrendly. **1722** WOLLASTON *Relig. Nat.* vi. §15 To covet to obtain what is another man's by just means, and with his consent,..has nothing surely that looks unfriendly upon truth, or is blameable, in it. **1757** W. THOMPSON *R.N. Advoc.* 46 [This] I leave to be determined by the..Wisdom of the Contracting Coopers that undermine one another unfriendly.

un'friendship. Now *arch.* [UN-¹ 12. Cf. MDu. *onvrientscap* (Du. *onvriendschap*), MLG. *unvruntschap*, OHG. *unvriuntscap* (G. *unfreundschaft*).] Unfriendliness; enmity.

a **1340** HAMPOLE *Psalter* xl. 10 In signe þat crist did til him nane vnfrendschip. *a* **1400-50** *Alexander* 2722 And if þou wirke þaim all þe wa & wrak at þou may, þe mare vnfryndschip þarfore fall sall þe neuire. **1549** COVERDALE, etc. *Erasm. Par. Jas.* iv. 36 A Christian, if he assaye to haue frendshyp agayne with the worlde, doeth vtterly receaue vnfrendshyp with God. **1666** *Despautere's Gram. Instit.* D 8 b (Jam.), *Inimicitiæ*, unfriendship. **1819** SCOTT *Ivanhoe* i, An act of unfriendship to my sovereign person and royal wardrobe. **1897** LD. E. HAMILTON *Outlaws of Marches* xi, The auld unfriendship betwixt the twa houses.

† **un'fright**, *a. Obs. rare*⁻¹. [UN-¹ 7. Cf. AFFRIGHT *ppl. a.* and OE. *unforht.*] Unafraid.

c **1250** *Gen. & Ex.* 3713 Burȝes stronge and folc v(n)friȝt, stalwurði to weren here riȝt.

un'frighted, *ppl. a.* (UN-¹ 8.)

1611 B. JONSON *Catiline* v. vi, If..he alone, In so great feare of all men, stand vn-frighted. **1624** QUARLES *Job* xvii. 54 Who euer heard the voyce Of th' angry heauens, vnfrighted at the noyse? ? *c* **1730** RAMSAY *Thimble* 53 Could you unfrighted view hell's dismal shore? **1840** BROWNING *Sordello* VI. 629 To the soft small unfrighted bee.

un'frightened, *ppl. a.* (UN-¹ 8.)

1675 CROWNE *Calisto* Prol. A. 4 b, These beautious Nymphs unfrightned too,..Their innocent delights pursue. **1835** W. IRVING *Tour Prairies* 259 He..fired, but without effect: the deer remained unfrightened. **1885** PENNELL *Fishing* (1889) 417 He then..renews his attentions to the still unfrightened fish above.

Hence **un'frightenedness**.

1858 FABER *Foot of Cross* 138 The manifest unfrightenedness of a creature who has for the moment forgotten Him.

un'frightful, *a.* (UN-¹ 7.)

1837 CARLYLE *Fr. Rev.* I. VII. iv, Not unfrightful it must have been; ludicro-terrific, and most unmanageable.

un'fringed, (*ppl.*) *a.*¹ [UN-¹ 8, 9 + FRINGED *ppl. a.*] Not fringed; unadorned.

1646 JENKYN *Remora* 30 Plain and unfringed reformations ..are poor, dry, dull things to such.

† **un'fringed**, *ppl. a.*² *Obs.*⁻¹ [UN-¹ 8 + (IN)FRINGE *v.*] Not infringed.

1751 ELIZA HEYWOOD *Betsy Thoughtless* II. 234 She.. thought it the privilege of youth to do whatever it listed, provided the rules of virtue were unfringed.

† **unfrith**: see UN-¹ 3.

un'frizzled, *ppl. a.* (UN-¹ 8.)

1611 COTGR., *Drap d'or ras*, smooth, or unfrizeled cloth of Gold. **1765** STERNE *Tr. Shandy* VII. xxxviii, She had better have gone with it [= her hair] unfrizled.

un'frock, *v.* [UN-² 4. Cf. F. *défroquer*, and UNGOWN *v.*]

1. *trans.* To strip (an ecclesiastic) of his frock as a sign of degradation; hence, to deprive of priestly function or office. Also **un'frocking** *vbl. sb.*

The second quotation is the only source for the common attribution of the term to Queen Elizabeth.

1644 MILTON *Areop.* 30 It is not the unfrocking of a Priest ..that will make us a happy Nation. ? *a* **1750** *Forged Letter Q. Eliz.* in *Ann. Reg., Char.* (1761) 15/1 If you do not forthwith fulfil your engagement, by ——, I will immediately unfrock you. **1817** T. L. PEACOCK *Melincourt* I. 10 He took especial care that this..should not reach the ears of his bishop, who would infallibly have unfrocked him. **1857** TROLLOPE *Barchester T.* III. xvii. 296 Clergymen have been unfrocked for less than what you have been guilty of. **1884** *Nonconf. & Indep.* 22 May 505/3 Mr. Justice Stephen truly remarked, there was no power to unfrock him.

refl. **1822** *Q. Rev.* XXVIII. 41 Who had been first a Dominican friar, then, having unfrocked himself, a gardener. **1855** L. HUNT *Old Court Suburb* I. 150 Who had also been a prelate, but had unfrocked himself to become a statesman.

absol. **1808** E. S. BARRETT *Miss-led General* 85 He had unfrocked, that is, given over the cure of souls in this world.

2. *transf.* To unmask or expose.

1876 BANCROFT *Hist. U.S.* VI. xxix. 74 Spain had the monkish Calderon... There no poet like Molière unfrocked hypocrisy.

Hence **un'frocked** *ppl. a.*

1794 MATTHIAS *Purs. Lit.* (1798) 44, I love no atheist French Bishops, nor unfrocked grammarians in England. **1861** PEARSON *Early & Mid. Ages* 357 The unfrocked priest would of course be amenable to lay tribunals in future. **1880** DIXON *Windsor* III. xxiv. 245 On the unfrocked priest attempting flight, he..locked him in the Tower.

† **un'frockify**, *v.* [UN-² 6 c.] = UNFROCK *v.*

1694 MOTTEUX *Rabelais* v. xxvii. 134 In Germany they pull down Monasteries and *unfrockifie* the Monks.

† **unfrome**, var. *unfreme*: see UN-¹ 3.

un'fronted, *ppl. a.* [UN-¹ 8.] Not faced or confronted.

1615 BRATHWAIT *Strappado* 25 Hence Sergeants walk vnfronted (though they know it).

un'frost, *v.* [UN-² 4 b.] *trans.* To thaw.

1611 FLORIO, *Disghiacciáre*, to vnfrost, to thaw. **1853** KANE *Grinnell Exp.* xxxii. (1856) 275 We celebrated it by an extra dinner, a plum-cake unfrosted for the occasion.

un'frosted, *ppl. a.* (UN-¹ 8.)

[**1775** ASH.] **1886** C. SCOTT *Sheep-farming* 45 The relative value of frosted and unfrosted turnips in the feeding of sheep. **1887** W. WESTALL *Her Two Millions* xxi, The lightness of his hair..as yet unfrosted with white.

un'frowardly, *adv.* (UN-¹ 11.)

1859 TENNYSON *Pelleas & Ettarre* 612 Hath the great heart of knighthood in thee fail'd So far thou canst not bide, unfrowardly, A fall from him?

un'frowning, *ppl. a.* (UN-¹ 10.)

1830 W. TAYLOR *Hist. Surv. Germ. Poetry* III. 5 O Jove, Canst thou, unfrowning, view his perfidy? **1888** A. S. WILSON *Lyric Hopeless Love* 123 Enough one solitary ray From thine unfrowning sky.

un'froze, var. of next.

1705 J. PHILIPS *Blenheim* 234 The Memphian Soldiery That swell'd the Erythræan Wave, when Wall'd The unfroze Waters marvellously stood. **1774** GOLDSM. *Nat. Hist.* (1776) I. 178 The ice..grown more bulky, by freezing, than the water, which remains unfroze.

un'frozen, *ppl. a.*¹ [UN-¹ 8 b. Cf. Norw. *ufrosen*, Sw. *ufrusen*, MDu. (once) *ongevroren*.] Not frozen; not congealed by frost.

1596 DALRYMPLE tr. *Leslie's Hist. Scot.* (S.T.S.) I. 31 Thair fatt..freises nocht frahand..bot certane dayes remanes vn-frossin lyke oyle. **1598** FLORIO, *Ingelido*, not frozen, vnfrozen. **1656** tr. *Hobbes' Elem. Philos.* xxviii. 354 The Wine which remains unfrozen in the midst will be very strong. *a* **1691** BOYLE *Hist. Air* (1692) 154 They..were obligated to dig about six foot deep in the ice, before they could come at unfrozen water. **1766** REID *Wks.* (1846) I. 45/1 The unfrozen water soon came to the temperature of the room. **1817** KIRBY & SP. *Entomol.* II. 451 Remaining unfrozen though exposed to the severest cold. **1860**

TYNDALL *Glac.* II. xxiv. 360 The water..which has been carried down from the névé unfrozen.

un'frozen, *ppl. a.*[2] [f. UNFREEZE *v.*] Released from frost; thawed.

1633 P. FLETCHER *Purple Isl.* VI. lxviii, The flowres that.. in the Spring..Peep out again from their unfrozen tombe.

un'fructed, *a. Her.* [UN-[1] 9.] Not furnished with fruit.

1688 R. HOLME *Armoury* II. 83/1 The branch is not to be so termed (unfructed, or without fruit) except it be thus made, and consist of nine leaves. *c* **1828** BERRY *Encycl. Her.* I. Gloss. s.v., Slips of laurel, bay, and the like, consist of three leaves, the sprig of five leaves, and the branch, being unfructed, of nine leaves.

† **un'fructful,** obs. var. UNFRUITFUL *a.*

1549 COVERDALE, etc. *Erasm. Par. Eph.* v. 11 b, To doe fruictefull honeste offices of godlines,..and from henceforth be ashamed to haue adoe with the vnfructefull workes of darkenesse.

un'fructify, *v.* [UN-[2] 6 c.] *trans.* To render unfruitful.

1628 R. HOBART *Edw. II*, cclxiii, So may we see how God unfructifies A fruitfull land for mens impieties.

un'fructifying, *ppl. a.* (UN-[1] 10.)

1827 MONTGOMERY *Pelican Isl.* IV. 55 While in the womb of earth their embryos tarried, Unfructifying, yet imperishable.

unfructu'osity. (UN-[1] 12 and 5 b; cf. next.)

1884 *Manch. Exam.* 29 Mar. 4/8 The intellectual unfructuosity of the Royal stock.

un'fructuous, *a.* [UN-[1] 7 and 5 b.]

† **1.** Producing no fruit; unfruitful. *Obs.*

1382 WYCLIF *Exod.* xxiii. 26 Ne thi loond shal be vnfructuous, ne bareyn. —— *Job* xxiv. 20 Be he not in recording, but be to-trede as a tree vnfructuous. *c* **1400** *Pilgr. Sowle* (Caxton, 1483) IV. ii. 58 The trees..were bycomen wylde and vnfructuous.

2. *fig.* = UNFRUITFUL *a.* 2. Now *rare.*

c **1380** WYCLIF *Sel. Wks.* III. 29 My mouþ..þat bifore was filid þoru unfructuouse jangelingis. *c* **1430** LYDG. *Min. Poems* (Percy Soc.) 258 Ryot and dronkenesse, Unfructuous talkyng, intemperat diete. *c* **1450** tr. *De Imitatione* III. ii. 65 Speke..þou, my lorde god, euerlastyng trouþe; lest I dye & be made unfructuouse. **1513** DOUGLAS *Æneid* IV. Prol. 19 Ȝour frute is bot vnfructuus fantasy. **1588** A. KING tr. *Canisius' Catech.* 135 Be ȝe nocht partakers of the vnfruictuous warkis of wickitnes. **1828** SCOTT *Jrnl.* 27 Feb., We had a final and totally unfructuous meeting. **1904** R. BRIDGES *Demeter* III. 954 Unfructuous night Stifles her essence in her truthless heart.

Hence **un'fructuously** *adv.*

1827 SCOTT *Jrnl.* 6 May, Wrought again at Hoffmann—unfructuously I fear.

un'frugal, *a.* (UN-[1] 7 and 5 b.)

? **1629** T. CRAUFURD *Hist. Univ. Edinb.* (1808) 113 He was not given to the cares of the world, though not unfrugal. **1720** *Humourist* Ded. p. xvi, They will..restore us again to our unfrugal and unfortunate Ravings. **1780** BENTHAM *Princ. Legisl.* xvii. §19 This punishment, it is evident, is in an eminent degree unfrugal. **1826** *Art of Brewing* (ed. 2) 29 Some..brewers adopt the following dangerous and unfrugal practice. **1846** LANDOR *Imag. Conv.* Wks. II. 113/1 Ladies who have been unfrugal of their favours.

un'fruitful, *a.* [UN-[1] 7. In early use after L. *infructuosus, infecundus.*]

1. Not producing offspring; barren.

1388 WYCLIF *Exod.* xxiii. 26 Neithir a womman vnfruytful, neither bareyn, schal be in thi lond. **1535** COVERDALE *Judg.* xiii. 2 His wife was vnfrutefull & bare him no children. **1577** B. GOOGE *Heresbach's Husb.* iv. (1586) 169 The vnfruitfull.., and the otherwise faultie, ought cheefely to be fatted. **1650** BULWER *Anthropomet.* 233 They cur'd themselves, but became unfruitful and impotent. **1735** BERKELEY *Querist* §208 So many unhappy and unfruitful marriages.

2. *fig.* Not productive of good results; unprofitable, unremunerative.

a **1400** *New Test.* (Paues) Eph. v. 11 þe vnfruytful werkes of darkenesse. *c* **1430** *Life St. Kath.* (1884) 47 What euer we do to oure goddes me thinkeþ hit is bot veyn and vnfruytfull. **1526** *Pilgr. Perf.* (W. de W. 1531) 76 b, The communycacyon was not onely vnfruytfull, but also moche euyll. **1593** SHAKS. *Lucr.* 344 But in the midst of his unfruitful prayer,..Even there he starts. **1634** SIR T. HERBERT *Trav.* 29 Conditions dishonourable and vnfruitfull. *a* **1718** PARNELL *Donne's 3rd Sat. Versified* 4 To laugh or weep at sins might idly show Unheedful passion, or unfruitful woe. **1780** *Mirror* No. 72, The cold unfruitful virtues of monkish solitude. **1821** SCOTT *Pirate* x, It was a time of idle and unfruitful laughter. **1869** J. MARTINEAU *Ess.* II. 250 This hint has not been permitted to remain unfruitful.

absol. **1781** COWPER *Truth* 500 She may..leave to mercy ..The worthless and unfruitful of mankind.

3. Of trees: Not bearing fruit. Also *fig.*

1531 TINDALE *Exp. 1 John* (1537) 94 He y[t] is cut from y[e] vynestocke..can not but abyde vnfruteful. **1846** J. BAXTER *Libr. Pract. Agric.* (ed. 4) II. 177 The substratum ought to be dry,..otherwise trees planted will be liable to become.. unhealthy and unfruitful.

4. Of ground or seasons: Not yielding fruit or crops; unfertile, unproductive.

1545 BRINKLOW *Compl.* 14 Moory ground, as is vnfruteful for corne or pasture. **1585** T. WASHINGTON tr. *Nicholay's Voy.* III. xxi. 110 Manye desartes, sandye, wythered, vnfruitefull. **1615** G. SANDYS *Trav.* 1 A hill not vnfruitfull in Olives. **1653** W. RAMESEY *Astrol. Restored* 228 The year shall be unseasonable,..unfruitful or scarce. *Ibid.* 284. **1712** BLACKMORE *Creation* II. 197 Should but the sun his duty once forget,..Unfruitful earth her wretched fate would mourn. **1782** MARTYN *Geog. Mag.* I. iii. I. 201 Mountains and rocks, interspersed with unfruitful plains. **1820** WORDSW. *River Duddon* v, Unfruitful solitudes, that seem to upbraid The sun in heaven.

fig. *a* **1586** SIDNEY *Arcadia* II. xxix, She..besought him, not to cast his love in so unfruitfull a place.

un'fruitfully, *adv.* (UN-[1] 11; cf. prec.)

c **1450** tr. *De Imitatione* I. x. 11 We speke muche of suche þinges as we loue or desire... But allas! ofte tymes veinly & unfruytfully. **1529** *Supplic. Hen. VIII* (1871) 42 To lyue both wickedly towardes God, and also vnfruitefully towardes the worlde. **1583** MELBANCKE *Philotimus* M j b, Senior Mondaldo which neuer mispent time vnfruitfully. **1654-66** EARL ORRERY *Parthen.* (1676) 568 Civilities were not unfruitfully placed. **1833** S. HOOLE *Discourses* xiii. 171 We shall..praise him—not tremblingly and unfruitfully,..but joyfully and profitably.

un'fruitfulness. (UN-[1] 12; cf. prec.)

1565 COOPER *Thesaurus, Infœcunditas*,..barrainenesse: vnfruitefulnesse. **1577** B. GOOGE *Heresbach's Husb.* IV. (1586) 158 The little Pullets, or Hennes,..both for their vnfruitfulnesse, and other causes. **1615** BP. HALL *Contempl., O.T.* XI. v, The unfruitfulness of Hannah. **16..** MIDDLETON, etc. *Old Law* II. i, We judge Dotage complete then, as unfruitfulness In women at threescore. **1707** MORTIMER *Husb.* 527 The great Point to be taken care of about Fruit Trees, which is the Unfruitfulness of them. **1764** H. WALPOLE *Otranto* i, I divorce her from this hour. Too long has she cursed me by her unfruitfulness. **1850** R. I. WILBERFORCE *Holy Baptism* 35 It is unreasonable..to complain of that unfruitfulness [of baptism] which results from their own neglect. **1873** B. STEWART *Conserv. Force* v. 140 The unfruitfulness of the earlier views.

† **un'fruiting,** *ppl. a.* [UN-[1] 10.] Barren.

a **1300** *Cursor M.* 12257 A commament nu mak i here, ..þat þe vnfruitand þair frutes find.

† **un'fruitous,** *a. Obs.* [UN-[1] 7.] = UNFRUCTUOUS *a.*

1382 WYCLIF *Eph.* v. 11 Vnfruytouse workes of derknessis. —— *Tit.* iii. 14 Oure men lerne for to be bifore in good werkis,..that thei be not vnfruytouse.

un'frustrable, *a.* (UN-[1] 7 b and 5 b.)

1714 R. FIDDES *Pract. Disc.* II. 239 Here is a fix'd and unfrustrable reward secur'd. **1791** W. JAY in *Autobiog.* (1855) vii. 74 Immutable in his nature, unfrustrable in his designs. **1832** BP. LAW *Charge to Clergy* (R.), An irresistible, or, what the schoolmen have called, an unfrustrable power.

So **un'frustrably** *adv.* (UN-[1] 11.)

1654 OWEN *Doctr. Saint's Persev.* xii. 274 Those cloudy expressions of 'irresistibly' and 'unfrustrably'. **1754** EDWARDS *Freed. Will* II. xii. 123 Such Means, as shall unfrustrably produce the End.

un'fuelled, (*ppl.*) *a.* (UN-[1] 8, 9.)

1687 *Death's Vis.* viii, But Let me Gaze on..That Boyling Ocean of Unfuel'd Fire. **1801** SOUTHEY *Thalaba* II. ii, Before them in the vault, Blazing unfuel'd..., Ten magic flames arose. **1817** COLERIDGE *Lay Serm.* 61 It must be Seraphs..that can burn unfuelled and self-fed. *Ibid.* 102 Ill-fed, ill-clothed, and unfuelled winters.

unful'filled, *ppl. a.* (UN-[1] 8.)

1382 WYCLIF *Rom.* ix. 6 Sothli not that the word of God hath falle down, or failide vnfulfillid. **1526** *Pilgr. Perf.* (W. de W. 1531) 187 b, Than one iote or lettre of y[e] lawe of God sholde be vnfulfylled or founde vntrue. **1548** UDALL *Erasm. Par. Luke* iii. 34 b, To the entente that he would leaue no one poynte of humilitee or of righteousnesse vnfulfilled. **1610** HEALEY *St. Aug. Citie of God* XVII. ii. 621 No part of the earthly promise was left vnfulfilled. **1676** GLANVILL *Ess. Philos. & Relig.* i. 26 Had Authority prevail'd here,.. Seneca's Prophesie had been an unfulfil'd Prediction. **1796** MME. D'ARBLAY *Camilla* V. 459 Thou art come,..thy task unfulfilled, thy peace unearned. **1821** SHELLEY *Adonais* xlv, The inheritors of unfulfilled renown Rose from their thrones. **1879** B. TAYLOR *Germ. Lit.* 275 The promise of loftier development was not left unfulfilled.

unful'filling, *ppl. a.* (UN-[1] 10.)

1821 SHELLEY *Hellas* 973 Alas! for Liberty! If numbers, wealth, or unfulfilling years, Or fate, can quell the free!

un'full, *a.* (UN-[1] 7.)

c **1450** *Mirk's Festial* 80 And fore bycause þat þylke nombyr may not be vnfulle, hit ys nedfull to chese on of þes men. **1598** SYLVESTER *Du Bartas* II. i. *Handycrafts* 540 Th' un-full Harmony Of uneven Hammers, beating diversly.

un'fulled, *ppl. a.* (UN-[1] 8.)

1467 *Rolls of Parlt.* V. 621 That noo persone..carie..by yonde the See, any Wollen Yerne, nor untoked and unfulled Cloth. *Ibid.*, To bie rawe Clothes, untoked and unfulled. *c* **1550** CHEKE *Matt.* ix. 16 No man doth lai on a patch of an vnfulled ragg on an old garment.

un'fully, *adv.* (UN-[1] 11.)

c **1449** PECOCK *Repr.* v. xv. 564 It is no nede forto seie ther of eny thing vnperfitli and vnfully..here.

† **un'fulyeit,** *ppl. a. Sc. Obs.* [UN-[1] 8.] Not exhausted or worn out.

1508 DUNBAR *Tua Mariit Wemen* 62 Birdis..ilk ȝeir.. fangis thame ane fresche feyr, vnfulȝeit, and constant. **1535** STEWART *Cron. Scot.* (Rolls) I. 71 We ar all fresche vnfulȝeit into feild.

un'fumed, *ppl. a.* (UN-[1] 8.)

1667 MILTON *P.L.* v. 349 She..strews the ground With Rose and Odours from the shrub unfum'd. **1891** *Anthony's Photogr. Bull.* IV. 117 It is often advisable to print..on unfumed paper.

unfunda'mental, *a.* (UN-[1] 7.)

1638 CHILLINGWORTH *Relig. Prot.* I. ii. §155. 114 This assertion..is neither a Fundamentall nor Vnfundamentall point of Faith. *a* **1711** KEN *Hymnotheo* Poet. Wks. 1721 III. 236 How tenderly God treats all Hearts sincere, Who tow'rds Mistakes unfundamental veer.

un'funded, *ppl. a.* (UN-[1] 8.)

[**1775** ASH.] **1776** ADAM SMITH *W.N.* v. iii. II. 539 What is called the unfunded debt of Great Britain, is contracted in the former of those two ways. **1812** *Examiner* 4 May 285/1 The Unfunded Debt, up to the 5th of January 1812, amounted to fifty two millions. **1879** F. HITCHMAN *Public Life Beaconsfield* I. vii. 415 That notable device for swelling the unfunded debt of the country.

un'funny, *a.* (UN-[1] 7.)

1858 HOGG *Life Shelley* I. 318 The application was ..'haud illepidum', not unfunny. **1892** *Nation* (N.Y.) 30 June 489/1 It is most lugubriously unfunny.

Hence **un'funnily** *adv.*; **un'funniness.**

1927 *Daily Mirror* 10 Dec. 4/1, I saw quite a lot of Mark Twain, and my chief astonishment was his regular unfunniness. **1958** N. MARSH *Singing in Shrouds* (1959) viii. 160 Could he hit quite such an all-time-low for unfunniness, do you suppose? **1963** V. NABOKOV *Gift* iv. 221 A student who unfunnily plays the fool. **1973** *Daily Tel.* 16 Mar. 14/4 The amiable progress began..at Harwich, which Mr Cutforth..unfunnily commended for being pleasant and rather empty. **1980** *Times Lit. Suppl.* 21 Nov. 1342/5 For me, it had all the wearisome unfunniness of back numbers of *Punch* perused in the dentist's waiting-room.

un'fur, *v.* (UN-[2] 4.)

1598 FLORIO, *Spellicciare*, to vnskin, to vnfur. **1655** MOUFET & BENNET *Health's Improv.* (1746) 295 To stir up Appetite, to unfur the Tongue and relish the Mouth.

un'furbelowed, *ppl. a.* (UN-[1] 8.)

1772 *Test Filial Duty* II. 64 My ruffles are short, and my aprons unfurbellowed.

un'furbished, *ppl. a.* (UN-[1] 8.)

[**1775** ASH.] **1829** SCOTT *Anne of G.* iii, Near these, but.. unfurbished and neglected, hung a helmet.

un'furl, *v.* [UN-[2] 3.]

1. *trans.* To open or spread out (a flag or sail) to the wind.

1641 MILTON *Reform.* II. 69 Such poor drifts to..ingage the unattainted Honour of English Knighthood, to unfurle the streaming Red Crosse. **1667** —— *P.L.* I. 535 A Cherube tall: Who forthwith from the glittering Staff unfurld Th' Imperial Ensign. **1717** PRIOR *Alma* I. 489 Antonius fled from Actium's Coast,..His Sails by Cupid's Hand unfurl'd. **1795** in *Naval Chron.* III. 117 The royal standard was unfurled in the barge. **1836** W. IRVING *Astoria* I. 87 They saw the sails unfurled, and that it was getting under way. **1860** TYNDALL *Glac.* I. xvi. 105, I took the glorious banner thus unfurled as a sign of hope.

b. *transf.* and *fig.*

1678 *Poor Robin's True Char. Scold* 4 When once her Flag of Defiance, the Tippet, is unfurl'd, she cares not a straw for Constable. **1711** ADDISON *Spect.* No. 102 ¶4 The next Motion is that of unfurling the Fan, in which are comprehended several little Flirts and Vibrations. **1796** *Mod. Gulliver* 226, I once more unfurled my umbrella, and away we went. **1840** DICKENS *Old C. Shop* xvii, Codlin pitched the temple,..hastily unfurling the drapery and concealing Short therewith. **1884** *Harper's Mag.* Dec. 117/1 He takes the fan out, and unfurls it.

2. *intr.* To open to the wind.

1813 BYRON *Corsair* I. xvi, As marks his eye..the sails unfurling fast. **1854** PATMORE *Angel in Ho., Betrothal* 119 As to the breeze a flag unfurls My spirit expanded.

Hence **un'furled** *ppl. a.*, **un'furling** *vbl. sb.*

1647 N. WARD *Simple Cobler* 54, I am resolved to display my unfurled soule in your face. **1780** *Mirror* No. 102, The art which the ladies..used in the unfurling of their fans.

un'furlable, *a.* (UN-[1] 7 b.)

1845 E. WARBURTON *Crescent & Cross* I. 188 The Arabs.. reel with the staggering boat, and look fearfully up to the unfurlable sails.

un'furnish, *v.* [UN-[2] 4.]

1. *trans.* To divest (a place, etc.) of men or other means of defence. Also const. *of.*

1580 HOLLYBAND *Treas. Fr. Tong, Se Desgarnir de son armée*,..to vnfurnish. **1591** HARINGTON *Orl. Fur.* XXXI. xlix, Renaldo had six hundred men and more,..Though at this need his Princes turn to furnish, He soon agreed his own towns to unfurnish. **1600** E. BLOUNT tr. *Conestaggio* VII. 225 He desired first to see the issue, before he woulde bee vnfurnished of his forces. **1686** PARR *Life Usher* 58 He was now forced to unfurnish this, as well as others, of its Souldiers and Ammunition. **1829** SIR W. NAPIER *Penins. War* VI. iii. II. 157 English troops should, without unfurnishing Lisbon, co-operate for the relief of Oporto.

† **b.** To make clear *of*; to depopulate. *Obs.*

1603 KNOLLES *Hist. Turks* (1621) 292 Europe is unfurnished of the Turks, busied in the Caramanian warre. **1614** MARKHAM *Cheap Husb.* I. viii. 50 This Pestilence.. hath vtterly vnfurnished whole Countries.

2. To divest of furnishings or furniture; to dismantle.

1598 FLORIO, *Sfornire*.., to vnfurnish, to disaray, to deface. **1598** W. PHILLIP tr. *Linschoten* 66/2 All their ships are brought into the riuer, and vnfurnished of tacklings. *a* **1638** MEDE *Wks.* (1672) 174 When men account them the most religious to God-ward who do or would unfurnish the House of God most. **1662** J. DAVIES tr. *Mandelslo's Trav.* 108 His predecessour makes way for him,..unfurnishes the Palace, and leaves him only the Guards and the bare walls. **1707** *Lond. Gaz.* No. 4377/1 His Excellency dispatch'd Orders to Rome to forbid his House being unfurnish'd. **1886** P. FITZGERALD in *Art Jrnl.* 324/1 Among the incidents of a flitting, or of unfurnishing a house.

† **3.** To divest or deprive *of* something. *Obs.*

1611 SHAKS. *Wint. T.* v. i. 123 Thy speeches Will bring me to consider that, which may Vnfurnish me of Reason. *a* **1642** SIR W. MONSON *Naval Tracts* v. (1703) 489/1 This will.. unfurnish them of all Materials to fit out Fleets. **1664** T.

MUN *Eng. Treas.* 112 To unfurnish the poor Prince of his provision.

†**b.** *spec.* To divest (a tree) of foliage. *Obs.*$^{-1}$

1712 J. JAMES tr. *Le Blond's Gardening* 47 To raise..the Palisade itself,..would certainly unfurnish it at Foot.

un'furnished, *ppl. a.* [UN-^{1} 8.]

1. Not furnished, in various senses; unprovided, unequipped, unprepared.

(*a*) **1549** CHEKE *Hurt Sedit.* (1569) F ij, Exeter..being in the middest of Rebelles, vnuittailed, vnfurnished, vnprepared, for so long a siege. **1592** SHAKS. *Rom. & Jul.* IV. ii. 10 Go, be gone, we shall be much vnfurnisht for this time. **1599** —— *Hen. V,* I. ii. 148 The Scot, on his vnfurnisht Kingdome, Came pouring like the Tyde into a breach. **1601** W. T. *Ld. Remy's Civ. Considerations* ix. *heading,* Ambassadours of Princes ought not to shew themselues bashfull and vnfurnished. **1638** T. VERNEY in *V. Papers* (Camden) 197, I need not putt downe tooles for euery trades-man, for I beleeue you will not send them unfurnished. **1734** WATERLAND *Doctr. Holy Trin.* vii. 396 [New servants] who..may be unfurnished for the Employ, or not well affected to his Person and Government. **1822** SHELLEY *Chas. I,* II. 266 We want money, and my mind misgives me That for so great an enterprise, as yet, We are unfurnished. **1860** FROUDE *Hist. Eng.* V. 183 As the treasury was unfurnished, the lords..raised money by every possible shift.

(*b*) **1697** COLLIER *Ess. Mor. Subj.* I. (1703) 25 What though our Minds were poor, and unfurnished at first. **1731** FIELDING *Grub St. Op.* I. ii, Whatever Nature hath done for him in another way, she hath left his head unfurnish'd. **1784** COWPER *Task* IV. 209 All the tricks That idleness has ever yet contriv'd To fill the void of an unfurnish'd brain. **1817** COLERIDGE *Biogr. Lit.* xvii. (1907) II. 43 An unfurnished or confused understanding.

b. Const. *of* or *with.*

(*a*) **1541** *Act 33 Hen. VIII,* c. 9 §2 Other cities..remaine and be vnfurnished of artificers and craftes men before rehersed. **1625** HART *Anat. Ur.* Ded. A iv, Some nations vnfurnished of frankincense, offer vp milke..to their gods. **1707** NORRIS *Treat. Humility* Pref. 3 So that..he may not be unfurnished of a competent consideration of the matter in hand. **1802** LAMB *J. Woodvil* I, Nor am I so unfurnish'd, as you think, Of practicable schemes.

(*b*) **1611** in *Essex Rev.* (1906) XV. 155 The sayd place is very muche hindred and unfurnyshed with a convenient Schole howse. **1691** T. H[ALE] *Acc. New Invent.* 41 England being never to be supposed unfurnished with Lead, as bearing it within its own Bowels. **1791** COWPER *Iliad* XVII. 173 Chieftain of excelling form, But all unfurnish'd with a warrior's heart! **1833** CHALMERS *Const. Man* v. (1835) I. 211 Because he is so unfurnished with the ideas of justice.

2. Of houses or apartments: Not provided with furniture, *spec.* not furnished by the landlord or person letting; requiring to be furnished by the tenant or occupant.

1581 ANNE ASKEW in Nicolas *Hatton's Life & T.* (1847) 223 This short warning and my unfurnished house, do ill agree. **1593** SHAKS. *Rich. II,* I. ii. 68 Alacke, and what shall good old Yorke there see But empty lodgings, and vnfurnish'd walles. **1680** *Lond. Gaz.* No. 1553/4 A Fair House to be Lett Furnished or Unfurnished. **1769** *Phil. Trans.* LIX. 181 An unfurnished room of the Hospital. **1824** MISS L. M. HAWKINS *Annaline* II. 268[He] pays for ships and houses,..the latter he would let if he could either furnished or unfurnished. **1885** [W. H. WHITE] *M. Rutherford's Deliv.* i. (1892) 11 McKay..had unfurnished apartments.

fig. **1663** BUTLER *Hud.* I. i. 162 Such [cobwebs] as take Lodgings in a Head That's to be lett unfurnished.

b. Not fitted up; devoid of the usual fittings, tackle, etc.

1608 SYLVESTER *Du Bartas* II. iv. *Schisme* 298 Chariots, unfurnisht and unharnest. **1623** *State Papers, Col., East Indies* (1878) 202 They utterly refuse unfurnished ships.

c. Destitute of foliage; defective in flesh.

1712 J. JAMES tr. *Le Blond's Gardening* 151 If the Plant be crooked,..mishapen.., or very much unfurnish'd. **1893** *Kennel Gaz.* Aug. 217/3 The latter [dog] is also smart but quite unfurnished, and his feet are not good.

Hence **un'furnishedness.**

1647 BOYLE in Birch *Life* (1744) 82 Trying such experiments, as the unfurnishedness of the place..will permit me.

†**un'furniture.** *Obs.* [UN-^{1} 12 + FURNITURE 2.] Lack of intellectual equipment.

1640 REYNOLDS *Passion* xxxvii. 481 [His] hesitancy and slownesse of resolution in matter of Learning proceeded not from any emptines or unfurniture. *Ibid.* xxxix.

un'furnitured, *a.* (UN-^{1} 9.)

? **1879** LOWELL *To W. L. Garrison* i, The place was dark, unfurnitured, and mean.

un'furred, (*ppl.*) *a.* [UN-^{1} 8, 9.]

1. Not lined or trimmed with fur.

a **1450** *Knt. de la Tour* (1868) 165 She clothed her in a cote hardy vnfurred, the whiche satte right streite upon her.

2. Not having or provided with fur.

1830 MISS MITFORD *Village* Ser. IV. 80 The unfurred, unfeathered animals, who walk on two legs,..and are called rational. **1906** *Westm. Gaz.* 8 June 8/1 Unfledged birds, and un-furred baby mice.

un'furrowable, *a.* (UN-^{1} 7 b.)

1860 RUSKIN *Unto this Last* (1862) 167 Their desert kingdoms, bound with unfurrowable rock, and swept by unarrested sand.

un'furrowed, *ppl. a.* (UN-^{1} 8.)

1566 DRANT *Horace, Sat.* iii. B 3 b, In feildes vnforowde frute is none, for brakes all over growes. *a* **1700** KEN *Hymnotheo* Poet. Wks. 1721 I. 67 The Wheels kiss lightly the unfurrow'd Air. **1721** RAMSAY *Content* 303 Unfurrow'd was her brow, her cheeks were smooth. **1791** COWPER *Odyss.* IX. 140 The unseeded and unfurrow'd soil. **1823** BYRON *Island* II. xi, The unreap'd harvest of unfurrow'd fields. **1859** GEO. ELIOT *A. Bede* xii, Such young unfurrowed souls roll to meet each other like two velvet peaches.

un'furthersome, *a. Sc.* (UN-^{1} 7.)

c **1820** HOGG *Tales & Sk.* (1836) II. 131 The snow had been accumulating all day, so as to render walking very unfurthersome. **1864** CARLYLE *Fredk. Gt.* IV. v. (1872) I. 310 Tearing off..his own full-bottom wig,..finding it unfurthersome for actual business in battle.

un'fused, *ppl. a.* (UN-^{1} 8.)

[**1775** ASH.] **1796** KIRWAN *Elem. Min.* (ed. 2) I. 396 Shorls, which are fusible at 95°, are ejected [from volcanos], unfused, and unaltered. **1875** WHITNEY *Life Lang.* vii. 123 As *donner-ai,* 'I shall give', when compared with..'I have to give', its unfused equivalent.

un'fused, *a.* (UN-^{1} 9.)

1885 *Science* V. 74/2 Three unfuzed shells..were fired from the eighty-pounder.

un'fusible, *a.* (UN-^{1} 7 and 5 b.)

1758 REID tr. *Macquer's Chym.* I. 6 Earth, in general, with regard to its properties, may be distributed into *fusible,* and *unfusible.*

un'fussy, *a.* (UN-^{1} 7.)

1823 H. FROUDE *Let.* 12 Aug. in G. Battiscombe *John Keble* (1963) iv. 75 The unfussy way in which he [*sc.* Keble] goes on, and the complete indifference which he seems to feel to the opinions of people. **1825** CATH. STANLEY *Jrnl.* in *Mem.* (1879) 211 The unpunctual are easy, good-tempered, unfussy. **1862** H. R. REYNOLDS in *Life* vii. (1898) 185 The annual meeting will be made as quiet and unfussy as possible.

Hence **un'fussily** *adv.*; **un'fussiness.**

1960 *Guardian* 29 Oct. 5/6 The film..becomes what, unfussily, it tries to be: a genuine human document. **1968** D. E. ALLEN *British Tastes* iv. 95 The Welsh unfussiness about social class. **1977** K. BENTON *Red Hen Conspiracy* viii. 50 She handled the little car well, unfussily.

un'gag, *v.* (UN-^{2} 4 b.)

1705 ELSTOB in Hearne *Collect.* (O.H.S.) I. 109 Then he ungagg'd him. **1719** DE FOE *Crusoe* II. (Globe) 580 Having ..ungagg'd their Mouths. **1890** C. MARTYN *W. Phillips* 303 Here lips were ungagged when they were padlocked elsewhere for thirty years.

un'gaged, *ppl. a.* [UN-^{1} 8.] †Unentangled, free.

1617 CAMPION *Wks.* (1909) 181 Shall my wounds onely weepe, and hee vngaged goe?

un'gagged, *ppl. a.* (UN-^{1} 8.)

1863 W. PHILLIPS *Speeches* viii. 226 They must be free and ungagged. **1887** *Pall Mall G.* 8 July 4/1 A free, public, ungagged meeting.

†**un'gain,** *sb. Obs.*$^{-1}$ [UN-^{1} 12 + GAIN *sb.*^{1} Cf. ON. *úgagn* (MSw. and Sw. *ogagn,* MDa. *ugavn*), Norw. dial. *ugjegna.*] Detriment, harm.

13.. *St. Cristofer* 251 in Horstm. *Altengl. Leg.* (1881) 457 þere rynnes bysyde þis heghe mountayne A water, þat turnes to mekill vngayne.

un'gain, *a.* Now chiefly *dial.* [UN-^{1} 7 + GAIN *a.* Cf. ON. *úgegn* unreasonable, obstinate, MSw. *ogēn* unsuitable, unpleasant.]

1. Of ways: Not plain or direct.

a **1400** *Bone Florence* 1421 The lady seyde, We ryde ylle, Thes gates they are ungayne. **1426** AUDELAY *Poems* (Percy Soc.) 14 Therof the pepul wold be fayne, Fore to cum home aȝayne, That hath goon gatis ungayne, for defaute of lyȝt. **1613** BEAUM. & FL. *Cupid's Rev.* IV. i, Though she take th' ungain'st weas she can, I'll ne'er ha't fro' you. **1824** [CARR] *Craven Gloss.* 119 *Vngain,* round about, indirect. **1854** MISS BAKER *Northampt. Gloss.* s.v., An indirect roundabout road is an ungain one.

†**2.** Unsparing, severe; rough. *Obs.*

c **1400** *Destr. Troy* 1332 Ercules..Gird gomes vnto grounde with vngayn strokes. *c* **1425** WYNTOUN *Cron.* I. xi. 952 Thare reueris ragis for na rayne, Na muffis for na wedderis vngayne.

3. Unpleasant, disagreeable.

a **1425** *Cursor M.* 22751 (Trin.), Alas what shal þe synful say? vngeyn [*earlier MSS.* ungainand] þenne shal be his gamen. **1795** H. WALPOLE *Let. to Miss Berry* 28 Aug., The assemblage was not so ungain as I expected, for..there were several I knew. **1851** PALGRAVE *Normandy & Eng.* I. 312 The ungain character of Raoul Torta..has been clearly chronicled.

4. Awkward, inconvenient, troublesome, difficult. †*at ungain,* inconveniently.

c **1460** *Towneley Myst.* ii. 379 Bot this cors I wold were hid, For som man myght com at vngayn. **1553** BALE *Gardiner's De Vera Obed.* C iij b, Left hande mater is vngayne, and wicked what soo euer proceedeth of the fleshe. **1635** QUARLES *Embl.* I. xiii, How backward! how preposterous is the motion Of our ungain devotion! **1763** WESLEY *Compend. Nat. Philos.* (1784) I. II. i. § 2. 206 The joints by which they bend are nearly in the middle,..and the large bulk which they are to support, makes their flexure ungain. **1764** *Museum Rust.* II. 84 As they are ungain to empty on the cloth,..they are not much used. **1782** MISS BURNEY *Cecilia* IX. vi, But, Sir, that was but an ungain business..t'other morning. **1823–** in dialect glossaries. **1837** MARRYAT *Dog Fiend* iii, The ungain temper of his brute companion. **1893** P. H. EMERSON *Lagoon* xxxii. 168 Are you all alone in that wherry?..isn't she ongain for the bridges?

5. Unskilled, incompetent; good-for-nothing.

1658 W. BURTON *Itin. Anton.* 229 Peutingers Military Tables, which the noble Mark Velser set forth, but corruptly (for how could it be otherwise after so long time, and so ungain Transcribers?). **1834** BECKFORD *Italy* II. 93 One of the most ungain, conceited professors of the art of murdering I ever met with. **1851** BORROW *Lavengro* III. 374 For fear that he should turn out what is generally termed ungain, my father determined to send him to sea.

6. = UNGAINLY *a.* 1.

1709 MRS. MANLEY *Secret Mem.* (1720) III. 269 She look'd wholesome, ungain, and country. *Ibid.* IV. 72 What we see of her now is nothing but an old slatternly, ungain Thing. **1779** G. KEATE *Sk. fr. Nat.* (ed. 2) II. 66, I was..a pupil of the famous Marcel of Paris, though no one who now views my curved and ungain figure, would suppose it. **1835** BECKFORD *Recoll.* 108 One of the most ungain hobble-dehoys I ever met with. **1844** *P. Parley's Ann.* V. 306 He is the most ungain and foolish loitering bird in our domain.

Comb. **1834** J. J. HALLS *Life H. Salt* I. i. 15 A tall, thin, and somewhat ungain-looking young man.

b. Of movement, bearing, etc.

1757 [E. PERRONET] *Mitre* I. xxxi, What ungain postures of defence, As void of manliness as sense! **1776** MME. D'ARBLAY *Let.* 2 Dec. in *Early Diary,* She..has a carriage the most ungain that ever was seen. **1820** L. HUNT *Indicator* No. 64 (1822) II. 95 Walking in the most ungain manner upon its hind legs. **1824** *Examiner* 1 Feb. 71/1 The position on her knees is ungain.

un'gainable, *a.* (UN-^{1} 7 b.)

1661 PIERCE *Serm. 29 May* 35 The better protected your Peace will be from the ungainable enemies of each extream.

†**un'gainand,** *ppl. a. north.* and *Sc. Obs.* [UN-^{1} 10.] Inappropriate, unbecoming, unsuitable.

a **1300** *Cursor M.* 12404 Quen iesus him sagh sa bese be Abute þis ilk vngainand tre. *Ibid.* 17248 For for to serue lauerds tuin It es vngainand to be-gin. **1493** in Laing *Abbey of Lindores* (1876) 181 Gyff thar be ony vnganand persons resett in the burgh..that thair persons..be removit the tovne. **1533** BELLENDEN *Livy* IV. v. (S.T.S.) II. 66 þai faucht in place richt vnganand to batell, and mare vnganand to fle. **1562** WINȜET *Wks.* (S.T.S.) II. 59 It is weray iniust and vnganand, that we,..for the self veritie of the quheit, mot cheis the errour of fitches.

un'gained, *ppl. a.* (UN-^{1} 8.)

1606 SHAKS. *Tr. & Cr.* I. ii. 315 Men prize the thing vngain'd, more then it is. **1860** FROUDE *Hist. Eng.* V. 389 Thus it is that patriots and..reformers show in fairest colours when their cause is ungained.

†**un'gainful,** *a.*^{1} *Obs.*$^{-0}$ = UNGAIN *a.* 4.

1565 COOPER *Thesaurus, Incommodus,*..hurtfull: noysome: vngaynefull; unhandsome.

un'gainful, *a.*^{2} (UN-^{1} 7.)

1599 DANIEL *Musoph.* 2 Fond man,..that thus dost spend ..In an ungainful art thy dearest days. **1647** BP. HALL *Account* Wks. 1808 I. p. xxxii, Sir Robert Drury,..hearing my errand, dissuaded me from so ungainful a change. **1803** A. SWANSTON *Serm. & Lect.* II. 231 Their conduct may be accounted for when they perform unfashionable or ungainful duties. **1849** ALFORD *Grk. Test.* I. Prol. 45 Those who carried on the by no means despised or ungainful business of fishermen.

†**un'gainfully,** *adv.*^{1} *Obs.* [Cf. UNGAINFUL *a.*^{1}] With discomfort; severely.

c **1320** *Antichrist* 564 (MS. Cott. Vesp. A III), Ungainfulli þan sal þai quak, þat alle þe erth it sal do scak.

un'gainfully, *adv.*^{2} [f. UNGAINFUL *a.*^{2}] Unprofitably.

1593 NASHE *Christ's T.* Wks. (Grosart) IV. 93 Wherefore you Pilgrims,..vngainefully you consume good houres. **1611** COTGR., *Incommodement,*..vngainefully, vnprofitably.

un'gaining, *ppl. a.* (UN-^{1} 10.)

c **1630** H. R. *Mythomystes* 24 All vngaining Sciences, that conduce not to worldly profit. **1801** *Monthly Mag.* XII. 579 The porcelain-makers of Paris..saunter in ungaining idleness.

un'gain-like, *a.* [f. UNGAIN *a.*] Unsuitable.

1796 MME. D'ARBLAY *Camilla* IV. 166 It's ungain-like to speak for one's self.

un'gainliness. (UN-^{1} 12; cf next.)

1755 JOHNSON s.v. *Clumsiness.* **1848** L. HUNT *Town* iv. I. 182 There is an ungainliness in the lines we have just quoted. **1870** DICKENS *E. Drood* ix, His ungainliness gave him enough of the air of his simile to set Rosa off laughing.

un'gainly, *a.* [UN-^{1} 7. Cf. Norw. dial. *ugjegnleg* vexatious, obstinate.]

1. Awkward, clumsy, ungraceful.

1611 COTGR., *Saugrenu,* vntoward, vngainely, ill-fauoured. *a* **1700** B. E. *Dict. Cant. Crew, Blunderbuss,* a Dunce, an unganely Fellow. **1709** STEELE *Tatler* No. 193 ¶3 Persons..so very aukward and ungainly, that it is impossible to believe the Audience will bear them. **1752** MRS. DELANY in *Life & Corr.* (1861) III. 79 Her person is fine, her arms a little ungainly, and her voice disagreeable. **1814** SCOTT *Wav.* xxix, At length the tall ungainly figure and ungracious visage of Ebenezer presented themselves. **1878** E. JENKINS *Haverholme* 44 A man..with a slow delivery, ungainly gestures, an affected manner and accent.

†**2.** Unsuitable, improper. *Obs.*$^{-1}$

a **1660** HAMMOND *Serm.* (1664) xiii. 217 Their Misusing of their knowledge to ungainly ends, as either ambition, superstition [etc.].

un'gainly, *adv.* [Cf. prec. and UNGAIN *a.*]

†**1.** Threateningly, terribly. *Obs.*$^{-1}$

a **1200** *St. Marher.* 9 He..ȝeonede mid his wide geneow uppon hire ungeinliche.

†**2.** Improperly, unduly; unsuitably. *Obs.*

c **1400** *Destr. Troy* 9333 Oure godys, oure gold [are] vngaynly dispendit. *c* **1460** *Towneley Myst.* xvi. 160 Thus shuld ye not thrett vs, vngaynly to bete vs. **1548** ELYOT, *Incommodé,*..vngaynely,..vnhansomely, vneasyly.

3. In an ungainly manner; awkwardly, clumsily, ungracefully.

a **1661** FULLER *Worthies, Cambridge.* I. (1662) 150 A Camel passeth in the Latine proverb, either for gibbous and distorted, or for one that undertaketh a thing awkely or ungeenly. **1705** VANBURGH *Confed.* I. iii, Why dost thou stare, and look so ungainly; Don't I speak to be understood? **1854** MISS BAKER *Northampt. Gloss., Skrauming*, spreading widely, stretching out the arms ungainly. **1896** *Westm. Gaz.* 9 May 2/1 Mr. Record-Breaker..waddles ungainly by, and is lost in the crowd.

un'gainness. [f. UNGAIN *a.*] Ungainliness.
1727 BAILEY (vol. II), *Ungainness*,..Awkwardness. **1896** *Midl. Herald* 28 May (E.D.D.), Their [*sc.* cattle] lovely ungainness when at play.

ungain'said, *ppl. a.* (UN-[1] 8.)
1587 GOLDING *De Mornay* xv. 263 With consent of all the wyse men of olde tyme vngeinesaid of any. **1610** HOLLAND *Camden's Brit.* I. 365 The sirname of *Doctor Irrefragabilis*, that is, the Doctor ungainsaid, as hee that could not bee gain-said. **1641** MILTON *Animadv.* §I. 11 The Pope may as well boast his ungainsaid authority.

ungain'sayable, *a.* (UN-[1] 7 b.)
1618 *Barnevelt's Apol.* G 3 The hypothesis makes the proposition of an ungainsayable truth. **1634** JACKSON *Creed* VII. iv. §3 Many matters of fact..of which there can be no ungainsayable proof or demonstration. **1718** BP. HUTCHINSON *Witchcraft* 95 A Book that was Ungainsayable. **1890** GEN. BOOTH in *Daily News* 18 Nov. 6/5 In the first place the facts were ungainsayable.
Hence **ungain'sayably** *adv.*
Cf. the earlier UNGAINSAYABLY.
1637 *Declar. Pfaltzgrave's Faith* 35 Out of which vngainesayably followes, that also wee ought to haue no Images. **1702** C. MATHER *Magn. Chr.* III. III. (1852) 551, I wish that the ministers..may be as ungainsayably importunate..as Mr. Eliot was.

ungain'saying, *ppl. a.* (UN-[1] 10.)
1681 J. SCOTT *Chr. Life* I. iii. 89 A full and ungainsaying Judgment.

un'gainsome, *a.* **-somely,** *adv.* (UN-[1] 7, 11.)
1655 GURNALL *Chr. in Arm.* I. (1669) 497/1 They know not how to handle them [*sc.* tools], they go ungainsomly about the work, and cut all into Chips. **1832** LYTTON *Eugene A.* II. vi, 'Tis so ungainsome, and be d——d to it.

ungallant (-'lænt, older 'ʌn-), *a.* (UN-[1] 7.)
a. **1710** SHAFTESB. *Charac.* (1711) I. 312 Nor is there any thing ungalante in the manner of thus questioning the Lady-Fancys. **1762** H. WALPOLE *Vertue's Anecd. Paint.* (1765) II. 128 Vandyck..was so ungalant as to dispute with her on the price of her picture.
β. **1731** GAY *Let. to Swift* 27 Apr., All my fear is, that you will give up me for her, which, after my ungallant declaration, would be very ungenerous. **1829** LYTTON *Devereux* I. i, It must not be supposed that Sir William Devereux was an ungallant man. **1863** 'OUIDA' *Held in Bondage* viii, True enough!.. It is an ungallant admission. *absol.* **1808** ELEANOR SLEATH *Bristol Heiress* V. 282 His behaviour was..a little upon the ungallant.
Hence **ungallantness.**
1859 JEPHSON & REEVE *Brittany* 176 On my making him aware of his ungallantness.

ungallantly, *adv.* (UN-[1] 11: cf. prec.)
1835 MARRYAT *Olla Podr.* xv, The doctor..ungallantly told his wife she might remain all night. **1865** TRISTRAM *Land of Israel* iv. 68 They had seen us indignantly chide one of our lads for ungallantly threatening them with the stick.

un'gallantry. (UN-[1] 12.)
1723 *Briton* No. 7 (1724) 29 That I in a private capacity may atone for the Ungallantry of my Brethren. **1891** *Pall Mall G.* 29 Oct. 2/1 Such ungallantry, while there were partners sitting out, being considered most reprehensible.

un'galled, *ppl. a.* (UN-[1] 8.)
1590 SHAKS. *Com. Err.* III. i. 102 Supposed by the common rowt Against your yet vngalled estimation. **1602** —— *Ham.* III. ii. 283 Why let the strucken Deere go weepe, The Hart vngalled play? **1621** G. SANDYS *Ovid's Met.* III. (1626) 45 Cadmus..a Hecfer saw, by no man tended, Her neck vngall'd with groning seruitude. **1818** SCOTT *Hrt. Midl.* li, Her conscience was ungalled. **1868** GEO. ELIOT *Sp. Gipsy* 15 Men With limbs ungalled by armour.

un'galling, *ppl. a.* (UN-[1] 10.)
1744 ELIZA HEYWOOD *Female Spect.* IV. (1748) I. 208 Follies..exposed in the ungalling satire of genteel comedy!

un'gamboling, *ppl. a.* (UN-[1] 10.)
1788 H. WALPOLE *Let. to Mrs. H. More* 22 Sept., Your *gambols*, as you call them, after the most ungamboling peeress in christendom.

†**un'gang,** *v. Sc. Obs.* [f. *un-* UM- + GANG *v.*] *trans.* To surpass, go beyond.
1768 ROSS *Helenore* II. 85 For it ungangs me sair gin at the last, To gang together binna found the best.

un'gangrened, *ppl. a.* (UN-[1] 8.)
1753 N. TORRIANO *Gangr. Sore Throat* 81 Those..think that by cutting,..they can more easily separate the gangrened from the ungangrened Parts.

un'garbed, *ppl. a.* (UN-[1] 8.)
1848 BAILEY *Festus* (ed. 3) 199 A pure, cold..rayonnance As is the moon's of naked light, ungarbed In circumspheral air.

un'garbished, *ppl. a.* (UN-[1] 8 and GARBAGE *v.*)
1641 S. SMITH *Herring Buss Trade* 18 To sell them at sea ungarbished, salted or unsalted.

un'garbled, *ppl. a.* [UN-[1] 8.]
1. Not garbled, cleansed, or sifted; not selected or sorted out.
1439 *Rolls of Parlt.* V. 32/1, Uppon peyne of forfaiture of the said Spiceries so yfound ungarbeled and unclensyd. **1483** *Act 1 Rich. III*, c. xi. §1 They will not suffre any garbelyng of theym to be made but sell good and bad at so excessyf price togedyr ungarbeled. **1614** *St. Papers., Col., E. Indies* (1862) 294, 20 bags of ungarbled pepper. **1649** *Jrnl. Ho. Commons* VI. 304/1 An Act for Liberty to transport Spices ungarbled, was this Day read the Third time. **1859** R. F. BURTON *Centr. Afr.* in *Jrnl. Geog. Soc.* XXIX. 37 At the end of the rains..[the copal] is usually carried ungarbled to Zanzibar. *c* **1870** *Townend & Co.'s Circular Col. & For. Produce* s.v. *Coffee*, Mocha Coffee, ungarbled.
2. Of a fact or statement: Not mutilated or misrepresented.
1721 AMHERST *Terræ Fil.* No. 41 (1726) 213 Some future unprostituted, ungarbled history of a rebellion. **1810** BENTHAM *Packing* (1821) 116 A jury of the original, the constitutional, the ungarbled, the uncorrupted stamp. **1834** H. N. COLERIDGE *Grk. Poets* (ed. 2) 141 It is not without parallel in the ungarbled writings of greater wits than Zoilus.

un'gardened, (*ppl.*) *a.* (UN-[1] 8, 9.)
1623 [see UNFENCED 2]. **1928** 'BRENT OF BIN BIN' *Up Country* ix. 139 Shy, ungardened, but industrious and dependable, he's worked his sentence out without moral mishap. **1981** *Times Lit. Suppl.* 8 May 520/1 There were too ..the un-gardened gardens, the unapologetic messes, too sodden in winter..for any caller to beat a path to their owners' doors.

un'garlanded, (*ppl.*) *a.* (UN-[1] 8, 9.)
1828 WORDSW. *Triad* 108 The ringlets of that head Why are they ungarlanded?

un'garment, *v.* (UN-[2] 4.)
1805 SOUTHEY *Madoc in Wales* I. v. 73 They.. Ungarmented my limbs, and in a net..They laid and left me.

un'garmented, *ppl. a.* (UN-[1] 8.)
1798 SOUTHEY *Joan of Arc* (ed. 2) IV. I. 245 And round her limbs ungarmented, the fire Curl'd its fierce flakes. **1818** SHELLEY *Rosal. & Helen* 477 'Tis..houseless Want in frozen ways Wandering ungarmented. **1866** J. B. ROSE tr. *Ovid's Met.* 73 Now tell..that thou hast viewed Dian ungarmented.

un'garnered, *ppl. a.* (UN-[1] 8.)
1850 TENNYSON *In Mem.* lxxii, Thro' clouds that drench the morning star, And whirl the ungarner'd sheaf afar. **1883** GOODE *Fish. Indust. U.S.A.* 10 Where the harvest of the sea is still, for the most part, ungarnered.

un'garnish, *v.* (UN-[2] 4.)
1530 PALSGR. 768/1, I ungarnysshe, *je desgarnis*... Me thynke my cupborde is ungarnisshed nowe I wante my salte celler. **1598** FLORIO, *Sfregiare*, to vngarnish, to vndeck, to disadorne. **1848** DICKENS *Dombey* iii, When the funeral was over, Mr. Dombey ordered the furniture to be covered up.. and the rooms to be ungarnished.

un'garnished, *ppl. a.* (UN-[1] 8.)
13.. *E.E. Allit. P.* B. 137 The gome was vngarnyst with god men to dele. *c* **1400** *Pilgr. Sowle* (Caxton, 1483) v. i. 74 How durst ony wyght trowen..that he wold leuen his regne ..vngarnysed of his werkes. *a* **1548** HALL *Chron., Edw. IV*, 249 b, Thei shall..deplore, and lament their vngarnished estate, and naked condicion. **1591** SYLVESTER *Du Bartas* I. i. 291 A Heav'n..Un-garnished, un-gilt with Stars apparent. **1621** QUARLES *Div. Poems, Esther* viii, May my vngarnisht Quill presume so much, To glorifie it selfe. **1641** MILTON *Animadv.* §4. 38 He that now for haste snatches up a plain ungarnish't present as a thanke-offering to thee. **1705** WATTS *Lyrick Poems* II. (1743) 144 Beauteous she lies;.. Ungarnish'd; yet not blushing. **1800** WORDSW. *Michael* 19 A story..ungarnished with events. *a* **1847** ELIZA COOK *Christmas Song of Poor Man* ii, Some scrap, ungarnished, cold and scant. **1876** FOX BOURNE *Locke* II. xi. 189 Plain, ungarnished words were certainly the best.

un'garrisoned, *ppl. a.* (UN-[1] 8.)
1660 MARVELL *Corr.* Wks. (Grosart) II. 18, I..hope to see your Town once more ungarrisond. *a* **1701** MAUNDRELL *Journ. Jerus.* (1721) 48 On the north side it has an old Turkish ungarrison'd Castle. **1813** *Edin. Rev.* XXI. 193 The frontiers were unguarded,..the forts dismantled or ungarrisoned. **1865** W. G. PALGRAVE *Arabia* II. 289 It is crowned by an old castle and tower.., now ungarrisoned.

un'garter, *v.* (UN-[2] 4 b.)
1594 NASHE *Unfort. Trav.* Wks. (Grosart) V. 98 He that had then vngartered mee, might haue pluckt out my heart at my hams. **1607** MARKHAM *Cavel.* IV. (1617) 9 Which as soone as he doth, you shall immediately vngarter his legges. **1753** A. MURPHY *Gray's Inn Jrnl.* No. 31, Ungartering my Stockings, and pulling off my Wig. **1886** *Pall Mall G.* 2 Dec. 6 A native unbraceleting or ungartering himself.
Hence **un'gartering** *vbl. sb.*
1785 G. A. BELLAMY *Apology* (ed. 3) II. 15 He loved his good fat capon;..and *ungartering*, as he called it.

un'gartered, (*ppl.*) *a.* [UN-[1] 8, 9.]
1. Not tied with or wearing a garter.
1591 SHAKS. *Two Gentl.* II. i. 79 When you chidde at Sir Protheus, for going vngarter'd. **1607** *Puritan* II. i. 233 A man that would..go vngarterd, vnbuttend, nay, sir Reuerence, vntrust, to Morning Prayer. **1647** R. STAPYLTON *Juvenal* 68 Trebius, oblig'd, has that for which he must Break's sleep, and run ungarter'd and untrust. **1749** FIELDING *Tom Jones* IV. viii, Catching hold of her ungartered stocking. **1823** S. ROGERS *Italy* I. viii. 50 Gliding on, he comes Slip-shod, ungartered. **1828** LYTTON *Pelham.* I. xxiv, Thornton.. lounged idly in a chair, with one ungartered leg thrown over the elbow.
2. Not invested with the Order of the Garter.
1845 DISRAELI *Sybil* IV. xiv, Ireland was not yet governed by the Duke of Fitz-Aquitaine, and the Earl de Mowbray was still ungartered.

un-'Gasconated, *ppl. a.* (UN-[2] 8.)
1658 R. BAKER tr. *Balzac's Lett.* I. iv. 102 You may..teach them to speak good French, now you are perfectly Vn-Gasconated.

un'gathered, *ppl. a.* [UN-[1] 8. Cf. Du. *ongegaderd, -gegaard.*]
1. Not gathered or brought together; uncollected.
1461 *Rolls of Parlt.* V. 495/1 Youre dettes remaynyng ungadered. **1481** *Coventry Leet Bk.* 478 þer rested behynde vngadered..of þe seide hole some xiij li. ix s. vj d. **1525** LD. BERNERS *Froiss.* II. cxvi. 332 A great parte of that money as than nat payde and vngadered. **1590** H. BARROW in *Confer.* i. 9 They being as yet vngathered to Christ. **1625** CHAS. I *Sp.* in Rushw. *Hist. Coll.* (1659) I. 177 Your love to me..you expressed by a Grant of Two Subsidies yet ungathered. **1851** *Buried City of East, Nineveh* vi. 93 Finding..the bundle of faggots for the evening fire yet ungathered. **1873** PROCTOR *Expanse Heav.* 191 Enormous quantities of as yet ungathered materials.
b. *spec.* (See quot.)
1888 JACOBI *Printers' Vocab., Ungathered*, books delivered to binders in sheets, i.e. not gathered into books.
2. Of flowers, etc.: Not gathered or culled; unpicked, unharvested.
1592 DANIEL *Compl. Rosamond* I 3 b, Th' vngathred Rose, defended with the thornes. **1600** SURFLET *Countrie Farme* II. lxv. 412 If at this time there be found euer a combe vngathered and not pluckt away,..you must not therefore kill the Bees. **1697** DRYDEN *Virg. Past.* I. 51 We wonder'd.. For whom so late th' ungather'd Apples hung. **1825** SCOTT *Talism.* xix, Is it not hard that..I should be doomed to see fade before me ungathered such a rich harvest of glory to God? **1850** TENNYSON *In Mem.* civ, This holly by the cottage-eave, To night, ungather'd, shall it stand. **1896** *Daily News* 4 Sept. 7/5 The barleys which are still ungathered will, it is feared, be spoilt for malting purposes.
3. Not drawn together.
1615 G. SANDYS *Trav.* 63 Ouer all when they goe abroad they weare gownes..vngathered in the shoulders. **1690** C. NESSE *O. & N. Test.* I. 104 As a web of cloth is rolled up, only a little left at the end ungathered.

un'gaudy, *a.* (UN-[1] 7.)
1795 SOUTHEY *Let. to G. C. Bedford* 29 Nov., The violet is ungaudy in the appearance. *a* **1834** COLERIDGE *To Thelwall* Poet. Wks. 1912 II. 1090 Ungaudy flowers that chastest odours breathe.

un'gauged, *ppl. a.* (UN-[1] 8.)
1745 YOUNG *Nt. Th.* VIII. 671 A cask Unbroach'd by just authority, ungaug'd By temperance, by reason unrefin'd. **1872** GEO. ELIOT *Middlem.* iii, Dorothea..had looked deep into the ungauged reservoir of Mr. Casaubon's mind. **1881** M. A. LEWIS *2 Pretty G.* III. 207 There may be ungauged depths behind our chatter, and ungauged vanity behind your silence.

un'gauntlet, *v.* (UN-[2] 4.)
1846 LANDOR *Imag. Conv.* Wks. I. 144/2 The kings..ran against the chalice of poison,..by which their own hands were..ungauntleted, undirked, and paralysed.

un'gauntleted, (*ppl.*) *a.* (UN-[1] 8, 9.)
1800 COLERIDGE *Talleyrand to Ld. Grenville* 12 I'm no Jacobin foul,..That your Lordship's ungauntleted fingers need fear An infection! *a* **1876** M. COLLINS *Th. in Garden* (1880) II. 266 [He] offers his ungauntleted hand in knightly fashion to his old opponent.

un'gayed, *ppl. a.* (UN-[1] 8.)
1670 EACHARD *Cont. Clergy* 7 Getting by heart three or four leaves of ungay'd nonsense.

un'gazed, *ppl. a.* (UN-[1] 8 c.)
1818 MRS. SHELLEY *Frankenst.* xix, I lived ungazed at and unmolested. **1820** SHELLEY *Prometh. Unb.* II. iv. 5 The meridian sun, Ungazed-upon and shapeless. **1902** F. THOMPSON in *Academy* 12 Apr. 378/1 Ophir he saw, her long-ungazed at gold.

unga'zetted, *ppl. a.* (UN-[1] 8.)
1825 T. HOOK *Sayings* Ser. II. II. 352 An ungazetted commandery of Poyais.

un'gear, *v.* [UN-[2] 3, 4 b.]
1. *trans.* To unharness. Now *dial.* and *N. Amer.*
c **1611** CHAPMAN *Iliad* XI. 536 And Nestor's squire, Eurymedon, the horses did ungear. [**1775** ASH, *Ungear*,..to unharness, to deliver from the gears.] **1825** BROCKETT *N.C. Words* s.v., Ungear the yoke. **1828** *Trial of W. Dyon & Son at York Assizes* II, I was ungeering the horses. **1846** T. L. MCKENNEY *Mem.* I. vii. 157 Wading into the stream, we ungeared the obstinate animal, and led him out. **1854** MISS BAKER *Northampt. Gloss., Ungear*, to unharness; restricted to husbandry horses. **1878** J. H. BEADLE *Western Wilds* xv. 237 At 2 p.m. we..ungeared the mules, and crawled under the wagon for shade. **1975** E. WIGGINTON *Foxfire 3* 235 When I come in at night I'd put m' mules up an' ungear 'em.
2. To disconnect the gearing of. Also *fig.*
1828 *Craven Gloss.* s.v., A mill is also said to be *ungeared*, when the water is turned off or the machinery displaced. **1852** MORFIT *Tanning & Currying* (1853) 118 The necessity of ungearing the pinion. **1931** GALSWORTHY *Maid in Waiting* xxii. 188 He'll almost certainly get up against something now he's back. If he does it will ungear him in no time.

un'geared, *ppl. a.* (UN-[1] 8.)
15.. *Christ's Kirk* 167 Bot quhair thair gobbis wes vngeird They gat vpoun the gammis. **1588** *Wills & Inv. N.C.* (Surtees 1860) 329, vj geared yockes 4[s], iiij yockes, ungeared, 6[d], v geard forkes, 20[d], ij forkes, vngeared, 6[d].

†**'unged,** *a. Her. Obs.* [Irreg. f. L. *ung-uis* or *ung-ula* hoof.] Represented with the hoofs of a different tincture from the animal itself.
1562 LEGH *Armory* (1597) 51 b, He bereth Or, a Hart tripping Geules. If you should haue occasion to tel of his hornes, you should saie, he were attyred, and so likewise of the Bucke, and they are both vnged.

un'gelatinizable, *a.* (UN-[1] 7 b.)
1809 *Phil. Trans.* XCIX. 338 Ungelatinizable oxide of animal substance. **1884** *Encycl. Brit.* XVII. 675/1 Gelatin.. is converted into an ungelatinizable modification.

un'gelded, un'gelt, *ppl. a.* (UN-[1] 8, 8 b.)
α. **1398** TREVISA *Barth. De P.R.* v. xxiii. (Bodl. MS.), Malis haue strenger senewes..þanne femalis.., and vngelded haue strenger þanne gelded. **1598** FLORIO s.v. *Integro.*
β. **1573** TUSSER *Husb.* (1878) 82 Ungelt of the best [sows] keepe a couple for store. **1607** MARKHAM *Cavel.* I. (1617) 68 The longer that a Colt goes vngelt, the thicker and fatter his head will growe. **1651** HOWELL *Venice* 124 What are their soldiers but..a multitude of unghelt Eunuchs? **1725** *Fam. Dict.* s.v. *Sow*, The Male [swine] ungelt being call'd a Boar.

un'gendering, *ppl. a.* (UN-[1] 10.)
1706 DE FOE *Jure Div.* XI. 260 The Froth of Envy! Vain ungendring Cloud, To beat the Minds of Fools, and move the Crowd.

un'general, *v. rare.* [UN-[2] 6, 6 b.]
1. *trans.* To deprive of the rank of general.
a **1657** LOVEDAY *Lett.* (1663) 80 My Lord F. his house (retir'd thither to a private life since he ungenerall'd himself).
†**2.** To free from generality or vagueness. *Obs.*
a **1661** FULLER *Worthies, Wales* IV. (1662) 8, I doe not despair,..that having gained better intelligence,..these persons may be Un-general'd, and impaled in their particular Counties.

un'generalized, *ppl. a.* (UN-[1] 8.)
1843 MILL *Logic* II. iii. §3 A number of..unexpressed, ungeneralized analogies.

un'generate, *ppl. a.* [UN-[1] 8 b.] = next.
1546 LANGLEY tr. *Pol. Verg. de Invent.* I. iii. 5 They which contende that the worlde was vngenerate. *a* **1618** SYLVESTER *Mysterie of Myst., Holy-Ghost* 2 The Comforter, ay Uncreate, Unmade, Unborne, Ungenerate.

un'generated, *ppl. a.* (UN-[1] 8 and 5 b.)
1614 RALEIGH *Hist. World* I. iv. §1. 66 He foresaw..that Millions of soules must haue beene vngenerated, and haue had no being, if the first number..had abode thereon for euer. **1738** WARBURTON *Div. Legat.* App. 52 He must needs have made it ungenerated. **1861** STANLEY *East. Ch.* iii. 99 Ask a man how many oboli, he answers by dogmatising on generated and ungenerated being.

un'generative, *a.* (UN-[1] 7.)
1733 THEOBALD *Shakspere's Meas. for M.* III. ii. 104 He is a motion ungenerative [1623 generatiue] that's infallible. **1854** MAURICE *Mor. & Met. Philos.* (ed. 2) vi. §17 Justinian existed..to declare that the Greek Church and the Greek Empire were withered and ungenerative stocks.

ungene'rosity. (UN-[1] 12; cf. next.)
1757 MRS. GRIFFITH *Lett. Henry & Frances* (1767) II. 91, I..take it very unkindly that you will not recollect yourself a little, before you treat me with so much ingratitude and ungenerosity. **1886** STEVENSON *Kidnapped* xxiv, I could open my mouth upon neither [subject] without black ungenerosity.

un'generous, *a.* [UN-[1] 7 and 5 b.]
1. Not generous or large-minded; illiberal:
a. Of actions, conduct, etc.
1641 MILTON *Ch. Govt.* II. iii, To start back..from the mixture of any ungenerous and unbeseeming motion. **1699** BENTLEY *Phalaris* 213, I will not say, how ungenerous a design this is, to leave his Sicilian Prince in the lurch. **1748** SMOLLETT *R. Random* xli, I recounted to him the ungenerous usage I had met with from Potion. **1796** MME. D'ARBLAY *Camilla* V. 514 The sense that now breaks in upon me of ungenerous..doubt. **1842** W. C. TAYLOR *Anc. Hist.* xvii. §9 (ed. 3) 552 An ungenerous attack on the memory of the late emperor. **1882** MISS BRADDON *Mt. Royal* II. ix. 168 She had never harboured an ungenerous thought.
b. Of persons, disposition, etc. Also *absol.*
a **1704** T. BROWN *Eng. Sat.* Wks. 1730 I. 25 His ungenerous Father-in-law..discreetly hang'd himself. **1753** MISS COLLIER *Art Torment.* II. iii. (1757) 141 Bent upon defeating the purposes of ungenerous friends or relations. **1798** S. & HT. LEE *Canterb. T.* II. 350 The Duke too, though not a tender parent, had never been an unkind or ungenerous one. **1850** MRS. BROWNING *Sonn. fr. Portuguese* ix, Givers of such gifts as mine are, must Be counted with the ungenerous. **1874** MOZLEY *Univ. Serm.* ix. (1876) 195 An ungenerous temper may be easily fostered under the guise of generous condescension.
†**2.** Inferior or poor in quality. *Obs.*$^{-1}$
1744 *Phil. Trans.* XLIII. 163 A small armed Loadstone.. which, being reputed but of an ungenerous Nature, took up ..barely 2 Ounces.
Hence **un'generousness.**
1757 MRS. GRIFFITH *Lett. Henry & Frances* (1767) I. 94 The poverty of my nature, and ungenerousness of my principles. **1892** R. W. CHURCH *Cathedral & Univ. Serm.* 61 The ungenerousnesses of the generous, the injustices of the just.

un'generously, *adv.* (UN-[1] 11; cf. prec.)
1722 WODROW *Corr.* (1843) II. 676 People very ungenerously take more liberty with him when he is not to answer for himself. **1775** SHERIDAN *Rivals* III. ii, I am ever ungenerously fretful. **1830** D'ISRAELI *Chas. I*, III. iii. 29 Charles..felt that the Commons had ungenerously used him. **1855** MACAULAY *Hist. Eng.* xvi. III. 718 Halifax, who had..been ungenerously and ungratefully persecuted by the Whigs. **1895** *Daily News* 29 May 3/6 [The horse] running ungenerously towards the finish, he was headed in the last few strides by Boxer.

un'genial, *a.* [UN-[1] 7.]
1. Not favourable to growth or development. Also const. *to.*
1726 THOMSON *Winter* 718 Those sullen seas, That wash th' ungenial pole, will rest no more. **1796** W. H. MARSHALL *W. England* II. 100 The frequency of rain..renders West Devonshire,..in a wet season, ungenial to Agriculture. **1829** SOUTHEY *Sir T. More* II. 142 No plants will thrive in a cold and meagre soil, ungenial to their nature. **1856** EMERSON *Eng. Traits, Land* ¶1 Art..transforms a rude,..ungenial land into a paradise of comfort and plenty.
fig. **1768** [W. DONALDSON] *Life Sir B. Sapskull* II. i. 7 The citizen from the ungenial atmosphere of Watling-Street.
b. Of weather: Cold or wet: raw.
1815 JANE AUSTEN *Emma* I, I did not quite like your looks on Tuesday, but it was an ungenial morning. **1885** *Manch. Exam.* 14 May 5/1 The ungenial weather has compelled the outdoor part of the programme to be abandoned.
2. Not agreeable or pleasant (*to* one).
1796 MME. D'ARBLAY *Camilla* V. 243 She declined the excursion, as..ungenial to her feelings. **1822** LAMB *Elia* I. *Praise of Chimney-sweepers*, The rake..curses the ungenial fume, as he passeth. **1857** DUFFERIN *Lett. High Lat.* (ed. 3) 401 Henceforth, the words..can convey no cold or ungenial associations to my ears.
b. Not congenial or suited *to* the genius of.
1871 EARLE *Philol. Eng. Tongue* 145 We must regard this ..as being a creation of the English speech-genius. To the Danish it is ungenial.
3. Not cheerful, jovial, or kindly.
1796 MME. D'ARBLAY *Camilla* V. 38 [I] appeared to you too rigorous, too ungenial. **1867** LD. HOUGHTON in Brodrick, etc. *Ess. Reform* 48 An ungenial German, ignorant of our language and offensive to our manners. **1870** LOWELL *Among Bks.* Ser. I. 237 The Puritans had their faults. They were narrow, ungenial. **1889** GRETTON *Memory's Harkb.* 25 He was of somewhat ungenial, crusty temperament.
Hence **ungeni'ality.**
1859 G. WILSON *Mem. E. Forbes* iv. (1861) 109 A deep, quiet enthusiasm..which his ungeniality of nature could not prevent being contagious.

un'genially, *adv.* (UN-[1] 11; cf. prec.)
1814 F. BURNEY *Let.* 4 Sept. (1978) VII. 457 O drive, as fast as you can, this W[illia]m L[ocke] who has broken so ungenially upon your happiness, from your mind. **1858** CARLYLE *Fredk. Gt.* x. iii. II. 609 The Crown-Prince reports to Papa, in a satirical vein, not ungenially. **1889** SWINBURNE *Study Jonson* 85 He shows himself ungenially observant and contemptuously studious of his models.

un'genitured, *a.* (UN-[1] 9.)
1603 SHAKS. *Meas. for M.* III. ii. 184 This vngenitur'd Agent will vn-people the Prouince with Continencie.

ungen'teel, *a.* Also 7 ungenteile, -iel, 7–8 ungentile. [UN-[1] 7 and 5 b.] Not genteel: **a.** Of manners, habits, employments, etc.
α. **1633** PRYNNE *Histrio-m.* Ep. Ded., Yet I hope I shall finde no such ungenteile, discourteous entertainment. **1642** FULLER *Holy & Prof. St.* V. xiv. 413 Drinking is..a most ungentile quality, fit to be banished to rogues and rags. **1691** E. RAWSON in *Andros Tracts* I. 68 The Buffoonry and Railery of such ungentiel Pens. **1711** J. GREENWOOD *Eng. Gram.* 110 It is counted ungentile and rude to say, Thou dost so and so.
β. **1683** MOXON *Mech. Exerc., Printing* xii. ¶1 Some Letter-Cutters..scorn to use a Forge, as accounting it.. Ungenteel for themselves to officiate at. **1716** M. DAVIES *Athen. Brit.* I. 180 Bale bestows another ungenteel Sarcasm upon this great Armach. **1778** EARL MALMESBURY *Diaries & Corr.* I. 211 His person was awkward, and his dress ungenteel. **1811** *Sporting Mag.* XXXVIII. 93 It is considered ungenteel to cut the pastry. **1898** WATTS-DUNTON *Aylwin* IV. ii, Have I not often told you the reason why I..missed my high vocation in ungenteel comedy?
b. Of persons.
1676 SHADWELL *Libertine* II, Thou art the most ungenteel Knight alive: use your Ladies civilly, for shame. **1712** *Spect.* No. 404 ¶6 Iras is ugly and ungenteel, but has Wit and good Sense. **1749** FIELDING *Tom Jones* I. x, [The half-pay officer] was not ungenteel, nor entirely void of Wit. **1813** JANE AUSTEN *Lett.* (1884) II. 172 She is a large, ungenteel woman, with self-satisfied and would-be elegant manners. **1844** THACKERAY *Barry Lyndon* ix, With this sum of money..we were enabled to make no ungenteel figure.
Hence **ungen'teelness.**
1706 STEVENS I, *Desalino*,..sluttishness, ungenteelness. **1723** *Briton* No. 11 (1724) 50 Philander discovers some Ungenteelnesses in his Manner and Behaviour. **1727** *Art of Speaking in Publick* 81 The indecency and ungenteelness of clamour and noise.

ungen'teelly, *adv.* Also 7 ungenti(le)ly. (UN-[1] 11; cf. prec.)
1666 PEPYS *Diary* 6 Aug., My Lord..did treat her thereupon very rudely and ungenteely. **1673** BP. S. PARKER *Reproof Reh. Transp.* 452 You might have done very honestly, but yet very ungentily. **1709** STRYPE *Ann. Ref.* I. 505 And further, very ungenteely,..Dorman..charged his Adversary with no less than Eighty Two Lyes. **1825** WATERTON *Wand. S. Amer.* I. ii. (1879) 132 Parson Evans, the Welshman, was treated most ungenteelly by an enraged spirit. **1875** W. ALEXANDER *Ain Folk* 115 After you felt that you had been ungenteelly treated.

†**ungentilesse.** *Obs.* (UN-[1] 12.)
1390 GOWER *Conf.* II. 30 Wher was ther evere such a knyht, That so thurgh his ungentilesce..Ayein his trowthe brak his stevene?

ungen'tilify, *v.* (UN-[2] 6 c.)
1614 in Birch *Crt. & Times Jas. I* (1848) I. 299 It is propounded that all these should be disarmed or ungentilified, unless they will give twenty or thirty pounds for confirmation of their gentry.

ungen'tility. (UN-[1] 12 and 5 b.)
1822 LAMB *Old Actors* Wks. 1908 I. 849 Miss Pope, a gentlewoman ever, to the verge of ungentility. **1871** W. ALEXANDER *Johnny Gibb* xxxii, At the *ungentility* of which saying Miss Birse looked shocked.

un'gentilize, *v.* (UN-[2] 6 c.)
1637 W. SALTONSTALL *Eusebius' Constantine* 36 Such as had beene ungentiliz'd, and degraded from their Gentility.

un'gentle, *a.* Forms: see UN-[1] and GENTLE *a.* [UN-[1] 7.]
†**1.** Of persons, their birth, family, etc.: Not gentle or belonging to a family of position; not distinguished by birth. Also *absol.* *Obs.*
c **1374** CHAUCER *Boeth.* II. pr. iv. (1868) 41 Som man haþ grete rycchesse, but he is ashamed of hys vngentil lynage. **1387** TREVISA *Higden* (Rolls) III. 415 [He] putte adoun meny gentil men, and putte ungentil men in here stede. *c* **1440** *Promp. Parv.* 365/1 On-gentylle of kynne, *ignobilis, degener*. *Ibid.* 365/2 On-gentyl be fadyr, and moder, *ybridus*. **1486** *Bk. St. Albans, Her.* A j, How gentilmen shall be knowyn from vngentill men. *a* **1533** LD. BERNERS *Gold. Bk. M. Aurel.* (1546) H viij, But for all he was not called vngentyll, nor infamed, nor traytour. **1594** R. ASHLEY tr. *Loys le Roy* 56 b, Of noble, and vnnoble, of gentlemen, and vngentle. **1648** HEYLIN *Relat. & Observ.* I. 23 Gentle or ungentle, I write to all. **1688** R. HOLME *Armoury* III. 68/2 The Ungentle is bound..to keep silence whilst a Gentleman speaks.
2. Of persons: Not possessing the attributes or characteristics of good birth; unchivalrous; discourteous, unmannerly. Now somewhat *arch.*
1411–2 HOCCLEVE *De Reg. Princ.* 3300 He dredde hym.. The peple hym wolde han for a proude man deemed, And vngentil. *c* **1450** CAPGRAVE *Life St. Aug.* 44, I aspied wel þat I must chere men þat cam on-to me with mete and drynk, for if I ded not, I schuld be hald on-gentil. **1562** LEGH *Armory* Pref. ¶iv, The second sort are vngentle gentlemen. **1593** MARLOWE *Edw. II*, IV. ii, Sith the vngentle king Of Fraunce refuseth to giue aide of armes To this distressed Queene his sister heere. **1653** J. TAYLOR (Water P.) *Short Relat. Long Journ.* (1859) 22 Quoth I, I doubt I must bee necessitated to take up my lodging in the field: to which the said ungentle gentlewoman..gave me a finall answer, that I might if I would. **1688** SHADWELL *Sqr. Alsatia* II, Belfond, thou art the most ungentle Knight alive. **1829** CUNNINGHAM *Brit. Paint.* I. 344 They aided him in the resolution..of making his escape from such crushing patronage and ungentle company. **1872** TENNYSON *Gareth & Lynette* 738 Too well I know thee, ay—The most ungentle knight in Arthur's hall.
transf. **1398** TREVISA *Barth. De P.R.* XII. xxxvii. (Tollem. MS.), The lapwynke is ungentel [1535 most filthy] and unclene.
b. *absol.* and as *sb.*
1562 LEGH *Armory* Pref. ¶iij b, I beseche your honours, to dayne to be patrones of this my woorke, against the middle finger poyntinges of the vngentiles. *Ibid.*, The first wherof are gentel vngentile.
c. Not appropriate to or befitting one of gentle birth or breeding.
1565 JEWEL *Reply Harding* (1611) 160 This seemeth to be a very simple argument, and a grosse vngentle opinion of the simplicity of the people. **1590** SPENSER *F.Q.* III. i. 67 For nothing would she lenger there be stayd, Where so loose life, and so vngentle trade Was vsd of Knights and Ladies seeming gent. **1642** MILTON *Apol. Smect.* Wks. 1851 III. 270 Whereof not to be sensible,..argues both a grosse and shallow judgement, and withall an ungentle, and swainish breast. **1823** SCOTT *Quentin D.* x, According to the rules of woodcraft, he held it ungentle to interfere with the game attacked by another hunter. **1861** MEREDITH *Evan Harrington* xxx, They had seen her ungentle training in a dozen little instances.
3. Not gentle in action; rough, harsh, unkind, violent: **a.** Of persons or disposition.
1509 FISHER *Funeral Serm. C'tess Richmond* Wks. (1876) 307 Were not she an vnkinde and vngentyl moder? **1561** T. NORTON *Calvin's Inst.* III. 202 The judge that threatneth that he wil be vnappeasable to them that be to rigorous and ungentle. **1628** WITHER *Brit. Rememb.* II. 1835 To travell farre, and finde Those prove ungentle, whom you hoped, kinde. **1693** DRYDEN *Ovid's Met.* I. 876 Her Head to her ungentle Keeper bow'd, She strove to speak. **1763** G. COLMAN *Posth. Lett.* (1820) 256 Pray hint this to him, but let him not be ungentle with Sterne. **1837** HT. MARTINEAU *Soc. in America* III. 117 Men are ungentle, tyrannical. **1849** MACAULAY *Hist. Eng.* vi. II. 47 His temper, naturally ungentle, had been exasperated by his domestic vexations. **1872** CALVERLEY *Fly Leaves* (1903) 7 She had gone from the ken of ungentle men!
b. *fig.* Of things.
1551 ROBINSON tr. *More's Utopia* I. (1895) 62 Moyses lawe, thoughe it were vngentle and sharpe,..punnyshed thefte by the purse, and not wyth deathe. **1596** SHAKS. *1 Hen. IV*, V. i. 13 You haue..made vs doffe our easie Robes of Peace, To crush our old limbes in vngentle Steele. *a* **1649** CRASHAW *Carmen Deo Nostro, Mary Magd.* xxvii, Such Teares the suffring Rose that's vext With ungentle flames does shed. **1812** BYRON *Ch. Har.* I. xxiii, Vain are the pleasaunces on earth supplied; Swept into wrecks anon by Time's ungentle tide!
c. Of actions, language, etc.
1603 DEKKER & CHETTLE *Grissil* 2022 Why must my babes beare this vngentle doome? **1649** JER. TAYLOR *Gt. Exemp.* Disc. iii. §15 When two seas meet, the billows contest in ungentle embraces. **1726** POPE *Odyss.* XVII. 548 His shoulder-blade receiv'd th' ungentle shock. **1779** *Mirror* No. 43 ¶2 Every better feeling, warm and vivid; every ungentle one, repressed or overcome. **1846** KEBLE *Lyra Innoc.* (1873) 180 Jesus in His babes abiding Shames our cold ungentle ways. **1890** DOYLE *White Company* xxviii, Taken aback at this ungentle speech,..Alleyne stood [etc.].

†**un'gentled,** *ppl. a.* (UN-[2] 6 a, 8.)
? **1584** SIDNEY *Disc. Def. Earl of Leicester* Misc. Wks. (1829) 269 Even of charity sake he should..not leave him not only ungentled, but fatherless.

†**un'gentlefy,** *v.* (UN-[2] 6 c.)
1595 R. JOHNSON *Maroccus Extaticus* 10 The state of gentlemen that have ungentlefied..themselves by buying and selling.

un'gentleman, *v.* [UN-^{2} 6 b.] *trans.* To deprive of the standing or character of a gentleman. Also *refl.*

1671 F. PHILIPPS *Reg. Necess.* 204 A man disenabled, or ungentleman'd by reason of his Fathers attainder of Treason. **1713** *Gentl. Instructed* III. vi. (ed. 5) 419 Some tell me home-breeding will ungentleman him. **1719** DE FOE *Serious Refl.* ii. 58 The minute he does that, he ungentlemans himself. **1752** CHESTERF. *Let.* Misc. Wks. 1777 II. 558, I..am persuaded, that you do not give into this *cochonnerie*, which ungentlemans every body.

un'gentlemanlike, *a.* and *adv.* [UN-^{1} 7 c.]

A. *adj.* **1.** Of character, actions, etc.: Not befitting or natural to a gentleman.

1592 NASHE *Four Lett. Confuted* H I b, Neither was I..pincht with any vngentleman-like want, when I inuented Pierce Pennilesse. **1652** WADSWORTH tr. *Sandoval's Civ. Wars Spain* 363 Hee was mightily condemned by all that saw or heard of that ungentleman-like action. **1728** *Lett. fr. Fog's Jrnl.* 21 Dec. 1/1, I cannot conceive the Cause from whence that base, that unworthy, that Un-Gentleman-like Quality [*sc.* avarice] should arise. **1800** MAR. EDGEWORTH *Limerick Gloves* iv, Complaining of the ungenerous and ungentleman-like behaviour in the grocer. **1884** *Macm. Mag.* Nov. 12/2 Work just as dirty, and tricks just as ungentleman-like.

2. Not resembling a gentleman.

1718 *Free-thinker* No. 126, The most Illiberal, Ungentlemanlike, Members of Society. **1749** CHESTERF. *Lett.* 15 May (1774) I. cl. 413 They come home, the unimproved, illiberal, and ungentleman-like creatures, that one daily sees them. **1814** JANE AUSTEN *Mansfield Park* xli, Ungentlemanlike as he looked.

B. *adv.* Not after the fashion of a gentleman.

1664 PEPYS *Diary* 14 July, My Lord Chancellor..said that I did most ungentlemanlike with him. **1687** SETTLE *Refl. Dryden* 74 Do not deal so unnaturally and ungentleman like, to treat so honourable a man..so rudely. **1823** SCOTT *Quentin D.* xxiii, How unkingly, unknightly, ignobly, ungentleman-like, he hath conducted himself towards us.

Hence **un'gentlemanlikeness.**

1848 J. H. NEWMAN *Loss & Gain* I. iv. (1853) 201, I have behaved quite rudely to the Puseyites sometimes, and then been ashamed of my ungentlemanlikeness.

un'gentlemanliness. (UN-^{1} 12: cf. next.)

1828 *Q. Rev.* XXXVIII. 560 A charge of bigotry, intolerance, calumny, and ungentlemanliness. **1877** MISS YONGE *Cameos* III. xxxii. 329 The ungentlemanliness of the Tudor.

un'gentlemanly, *a.* (UN-^{1} 7.)

1562 LEGH *Armory* 122 There are nyne rebatings of armes, which for nyne sondry vngentilmanly dedes done, are resembled as hereafter followeth. **1614** B. JONSON *Barth. Fair* I. iii, What an vnmercifull companion art thou to quit thy lodging at such vngentlemanly houres! **1684** OTWAY *Atheist* v, It is an opportunity I should make no ungentlemanly use of. **1741** RICHARDSON *Pamela* (ed. 3) I. 84, I can stoop to the ordinariest Work of your Scullions, sooner than bear such ungentlemanly Imputations. **1825** T. HOOK *Sayings* Ser. II. III. 303 This letter produced an abusive, vulgar, and ungentlemanly answer. **1881** W. G. WARD *Ess. Philos. Theism* (1884) II. 286 They thought it thoroughly ungentlemanly so to speak in the presence of ladies.

Hence **un'gentelmanly** *v.*

1834 MEDWIN *Angler in Wales* II. 117 There were some ungentlemanlying themselves, by giving it against the horse.

un'gentlemanly, *adv.* (UN-^{1} 11.)

1572 BOSSEWELL *Armorie* 12 b, The rebatinge of Armes for diverse vngentle deedes vngentlemanly donne. **1603** HOLLAND *Plutarch's Mor.* 179 They..so defraud and cousin them ungentlemanly of their parents love. **1713** S. SEWALL *Diary* 24 Apr., [She] said Mr. Alford had done ungentlemanly by her. **1819** *Metropolis* II. 207 He speaks ungentlemanly loud, as all sailors do.

†**un'gentlemanny,** *a.* *Sc. Obs.* [UN-^{1} 7.] = UNGENTLEMANLY *a.*

1667 SIR R. MORAY in *Lauderdale Papers* (1885) II. 42 How ungentlemanny a thing it is to use a lady rudely. **1770** BP. FORBES *Jrnl.* (1886) 315 No man dare say he has ever been guilty of a dirty or ungentlemanny Action.

un'gentleness. [UN-^{1} 12.]

†**1.** Lack of good breeding or manners; discourtesy; boorishness. *Obs.*

1387-8 T. USK *Test. Love* II. ii (Skeat) l. 132 And therfore, he that wol ben gentil, he mot daunten his flesshe fro vyces that causen ungentilnesse. **1470-85** MALORY *Arthur* VIII. xxxviii. 332 For your curtosy and gentilnes I shewed you vngentilnesse, & that now me repenteth. *a* **1533** LD. BERNERS *Gold. Bk. M. Aurel.* II. xv. (1536) 150 The whiche forgettynge is as straunge to be in him that serueth, as vngentilnes in the ladye that is serued. *a* **1577** SIR T. SMITH *Commw. Eng.* (1609) 131 It is taken for vngentlenes and dishonor,..if any gentleman doe take an other gentlemans seruant [etc.]. **1600** SHAKS. *A.Y.L.* v. ii. 83 You haue done me much vngentlenesse, To shew the letter that I writ to you.

2. Meanness of birth. *rare*$^{-0}$.

1552 HULOET, Vngentlenes of bloude, *ignobilitas*.

3. Harshness, roughness, unkindness.

1548 PATTEN *Exped. Scotl.* Pref. d ij, It was too muche vngentlenes and inhumanitie sure in suche a case too be shewed. **1598** FLORIO, *Inhumanita*, inhumanitie, vngentlenes. **1623** COCKERAM II, *Vngentlenes*, inclemencie. **1716-20** *Lett. fr. Mist's Jrnl.* (1722) I. 231 There runs through the Male Line an odd Ungentleness of Temper. **1871** SMILES *Charac.* ix. (1876) 240 Their own crossgrained ungentleness. **1889** F. C. KOLBE *Minnie Caldwell* iv. 30 Whatever ungentleness or unkindness she had shown.., had proceeded from thoughtlessness, not ungenerosity.

un'gentlewomanlike, *a.* (UN-^{1} 7 c.)

1789 ANNA SEWARD *Lett.* (1811) II. 295 Vulgarisms, of most ungentlewomanlike choice, and most unscholar-like frequency.

un'gently, *adv.* [UN-^{1} 11.] In an ungentle manner; unkindly; roughly; discourteously, rudely.

c **1440** *Jacob's Well* 200, I seyde of hym vnkyndely, vndewly, vngentylly, vnwysely, folyly, & perylously. **1483** *Vulgaria abs Terentio* 25 Thow hast seruyd me vngentilly. **1523** [COVERDALE] *Old God* (1534) D j, It shall make the sorye..to see that Paule..was so vnkyndly and vngentily entreated. **1575** VAUTROLLIER *Luther on Ep. Gal.* 210 Paule handleth you very vngentely, he calleth you foolish,..and disobedient to the truth. **1621** BP. MOUNTAGU *Diatribæ* 25 In this poynt you are to be taxed deeply, for dealing vngently and vnthankfully with your much admired..Joseph Scaliger. **1655** tr. *Sorel's Com. Hist. Francion* IV. 23 It was not by these people alone that I was..so ungently intreated. **1822** LAMB *Gentle Giantess* Wds. 1909 I. 269, I have seen these shy gownsmen..ungently neglecting the delicacies of her polished converse. **1860** RUSKIN *Unto this Last* i. (1896) 12 The servant who, gently treated, is ungrateful, treated ungently, will be revengeful.

un'genuine, *a. rare.* (UN-^{1} 7 and 5 b.)

1665 J. WEBB *Stone-Heng* (1725) 178 Making ungenuine and false Translations. **1698** JER. COLLIER *Immor. Stage* i. 18 His best Plays are almost alwaies Modest... His Amphitrio, excepting the ungenuine Addition, is such. **1883** *Schaff's Encycl. Relig. Knowl.* 2400 The writings that had been declared ungenuine.

Hence **un'genuineness.**

1848 FR. A. KEMBLE *Rec. Later Life* (1882) III. 328 There is an element of ungenuineness about her. **1866** FELTON *Anc. & Mod. Gr.* I. v. 84 Internal evidence of ungenuineness or genuineness, founded on mere style.

ungeo'graphical, *a.* (UN-^{1} 7.)

1702 C. MATHER *Magn. Chr.* I. i. (1852) 41, I would not quote any words of Lactantius,..because of their being so ungeographical. **1873** W. CORY *Lett. & Jrnls.* (1897) 301 They say things wildly ungeographical.

ungeo'metric, *a.* [UN-^{1} 7.] = next.

1789 [see UNARITHMETIC *a.*].

ungeo'metrical, *a.* (UN-^{1} 7.)

1570 BILLINGSLEY *Euclid* XII. prop. xviii. 385 A notable Error, which among..vngeometricall Masters and Doctors hath..been vpholden. *a* **1696** SCARBURGH *Euclide* (1705) 13 Of all our late Transformers of Euclide, He is the most Ungeometrical in Demonstration. **1788** T. TAYLOR *Proclus* p. cvii, The testimony of the first mathematicians..against the unlawfulness of this ungeometrical invasion.

Hence **ungeo'metricalness.**

1690 LEYBOURN *Curs. Math.* 771 For they that object against Him an Ungeometricalness in the Hypothesis, have not yet solv'd his Problem.

un-'German, *a.* (UN-^{1} 7.)

1830 CARLYLE *Richter Again* Ess. 1840 II. 298 Even the Un-German part of the public. **1855** GEO. ELIOT in Cross *Life* (1885) I. 374 Lessing's 'Laocoon'—the most un-German of all the German books that I have ever read.

un'germanism. (UN-^{1} 12.)

1858 CARLYLE *Fredk. Gt.* VI. v. II. 61 Friedrich Wilhelm ..snorting contempt on 'Ungermanism (*Undeutschkeit*)'.

un'germinated, *ppl. a.* (UN-^{1} 8.)

1899 J. R. GREEN *Soluble Ferments* ii. 19 The diastase..of ungerminated grain.

un'get, *v.* [UN-^{2} 3.]

1. *trans.* To cause to be unbegotten.

1775 SHERIDAN *Rivals* II. i, I'll disown you. I'll disinherit you, I'll unget you! **1788** COLMAN *Ways & Means* III. 47 I'll disclaim him, I'll discard him,..I'll unget him,..That's disinherit him.

2. To give up possession of.

1893 *Daily News* 14 July 2/7 Having got the conviction, how was he to unget it?

unget-'at-able, *a.* (UN-^{1} 7 b.)

1862 H. MARRYAT *Year in Sweden* II. 204 The lusus more usually refers to some ungetatable new fashion. **1886** W. J. TUCKER *E. Europe* 2 The country swarms with quiet, retired, remote, cheap, and un-get-at-able towns. **1897** *Outing* XXX. 271/1, I always have the feeling..that we do not know him at all. He seems so unget-at-able.

un'gettable, *a.* (UN-^{1} 7 b.)

1554 *Extr. Aberd. Reg.* (1844) I. 282 [If the sum is] vngettable of his office, thai oblissis thame..to releiff him therof.

un'ghostly, *a.* [UN-^{1} 7. Cf. (in sense 1) MDu. *ongeestelijc*, MHG. and G. *ungeistlich*.]

1. Unspiritual.

1526 TINDALE *1 Tim.* iv. 7 Cast awaye ungostly and olde wyves fables. **1535** in *Lett. Suppress. Monast.* (Camden) 78 The mayntenans of the busshope and his ungostly spirituall officers. **1565** STAPLETON *Fortr. Faith* 94 Martin Luther the first preacher of this vnghostely ghospell. **1822** T. L. PEACOCK *Maid Marian* 219 The abbot of Rubygill picked up the..arrow..with a very unghostly malediction on the sender. **1864** CARLYLE *Fredk. Gt.* XVII. ii. IV. 524 Whom the Pompadour has brought with her as henchman, or *un*ghostly counsellor.

2. Not belonging to a ghost.

1888 *Daily Tel.* 26 Jan. (Cassell's), A most unghostly-looking pair of boots.

un'ghostly, *adv. rare*$^{-1}$. [UN-^{1} 11. Cf. prec. 1.] † Unspiritually.

a **1400-50** *Alexander* 4430 Ȝoure grete garisons of gold vngastly ȝe spende In bigging of burgis & bilding of toures.

unȝoun, -ȝown(e, obs. Sc. ff. ONION.

un'gibbet, *v.* (UN-^{2} 3.)

1747 W. HORSLEY *Fool* (1748) II. 195 When..you become a sincere Penitent,..you shall be fairly ungibbetted again, and exposed to the Public View.

un'giddy, *a.* (UN-^{1} 7.)

1615 BRATHWAIT *Strappado* (1878) 158 If I had liu'd in Phaeton his daies, When with vngiddy course he rul'd the Sun. **1904** E. NESBIT *Phœnix & Carpet* ii. 28 When..they were ungiddy enough to look about them, they were out of doors.

un'gifted, (*ppl.*) *a.* [UN-^{1} 8, 9.]

1. Having no spiritual or intellectual gifts.

1637 LD. WARISTON *Diary* (S.H.S.) 276 Thou knouest thy servant,..hou ungifted, unfit, unready. **1655** tr. *Sorel's Com. Hist. Francion* x. 16 We ought not to believe such an ungifted Prophet as he is. **1712** ARBUTHNOT *Hist. John Bull* II. i. 7 A hot-headed, ungifted, unedifying Preacher. **1850** ROBERTSON *Serm.* Ser. III. iii. Introd. (1857) 33 The Eternal Word spoke..to those who were uninspired and ungifted. **1891** FARRAR *Darkn. & Dawn* xvi, While he was still young and beautiful, and not ungifted.

b. Not gifted *with* something.

1831 PALMERSTON in Francis *Opinions & Policy* (1852) 176 The conduct of a child ungifted with reason. **1861** BERESF. HOPE *Eng. Cathedr. 19th C.* ii. 41 The man ungifted with architectural tact.

2. Having received no gifts; giftless.

a **1631** DONNE *Lett.* (1639) A 4 b, Pure Virtue; an ungifted Deity..without Oblation, Altar, or Temple. **1791** COWPER *Odyss.* xv. 258 He..will himself enforce Thy longer stay, That thou may'st not depart Ungifted. **1822** MILMAN *Mart. Antioch* 19 The sad priests of all our Gods do sit Round their cold altars and ungifted shrines. **1887** BOWEN *Æneid* v. 304 This festival day None of the number around me shall go ungifted away.

Hence **un'giftedness.**

1646 MAYNE *Serm. agst. False Proph.* 35 The ungiftednes of the persons, who have drawn this reproofe upon us.

†**un'gig,** *v. Obs.*$^{-1}$ [UN-^{2} 3 + GIG *v.*^{1} (?).] *trans.* To unravel, extricate.

1686 F. SPENCE tr. *Euvremont's Misc.* Pref. C 3 In a Comedy nothing is so unmercifully insupportable as to ungigg or explicate the Intrigue by a Miracle.

un'gild, *v.* (UN-^{2} 4.) Also **un'gilding** *vbl. sb.* (also *attrib*).

1611 COTGR., *Dedorer*, to vngild. **1641** MILTON *Animadv.* Wks. 1851 III. 238 By all this wee may conjecture, how little wee neede feare that the unguilding of our Prelates will prove the woodening of our Priests. **1651** STANLEY *Poems* 209 Night began to ungild the skies. **1743** YOUNG *Nt. Th.* v. 174 Vice sinks in her allurements, is ungilt, And looks, like other objects, black by night. **1873** SPON *Workshop Rec.* Ser. I. 205/2 Iron and steel articles are ungilt..by dipping them into [etc.]. *Ibid.*, Removing the gold from articles..which cannot be submitted to the ungilding bath.

un'gildated, *ppl. a.* (UN-^{1} 8 a.)

1890 GROSS *Gild Merch.* I. 49 Ungildated merchants could purchase..exemption from the many restrictions.

un'gilded, *ppl. a.* [UN-^{1} 8.] = next.

1674 DRYDEN *Prol. at Opening of New House* 7 You, who each Day can Theatres behold, Like Nero's Palace, shining all with Gold, Our mean ungilded Stage will scorn, we fear. **1688** *Lond. Gaz.* No. 2329/4 A good Quantity of all sorts of Pictures, and Frames gilded and ungilded. **1815** KIRBY & SP. *Entomol.* iii. (1816) I. 67 Terms..not strictly applicable to ungilded pupæ. **1872** HOLMES *Poet Breakf.-t.* ii, A.. chamber..obliged to content itself with ungilded daylight.

un'gilt, *ppl. a.* (UN-^{1} 8 b. Cf. ON. and Icel. *ú-, ógylldr.*)

1444 *Test. Ebor.* (Surtees) II. 112, I wil y^t William my sone haue..vj sponis gilt, a dosen vngilt. **1497** *Naval Acc. Hen. VII* (1896) 98 Halberdes gilt in a chest, l; Halberdes vngilt in the same Chest, xx. **1532-3** *Act 24 Hen. VIII*, c. 13 It shall be lefull for him to weare..a horne tipped or flewed with siluer, gilte or vngilte. **1591** SYLVESTER *Du Bartas* I. i. 291 A Heav'n..Un-garnished, un-gilt with Stars apparent. **1692** *Lond. Gaz.* No. 2806/4 A large gilt Plate for the Bread and a large Cup ungilt. **1812** *Monthly Rev.* LXVII. 529 They..forbad any other than..gondolas unvarnished, ungilt, undecorated. **1866** G. STEPHENS *Runic Mon.* I. 183 The staves are carved on the ungilt back.

†**un'gilt,** *v. Obs. rare.* [UN-^{2} 4.] = UNGILD *v.*

a **1533** LD. BERNERS *Golden Bk. M. Aurel.* Prol. (1536) A ij b, Bycause that there was none yll that did vngylt it. **1580** HOLLYBAND *Treas. Fr. Tong, Desdorer*, to vngilt.

ungiltyf, obs. variant of UNGUILTY *a.* 1.

un'ginned, *ppl. a.* (UN-^{1} 8 + GIN *v.*^{2} 2.)

a **1858** in Homans *Cycl. Comm.* 436/2 An acre of ground will produce about 600 lbs. of unginned cotton.

un'gird, *v.* [UN-^{2} 4, 4 b. Cf. MDu. *on(t)gorden* (Du. *ont-*), OHG. *ingurten, -curten* (MHG. *engürten*, G. *entgürten*).]

1. *trans.* and *refl.* To divest of, or free from, a girdle or girth.

In OE. (quot. *c* 900) also with instr. (of the thing) as well as acc. (of the person).

c **900** tr. *Baeda's Hist.* III. xiv. (1890) 196 Se cyning þonne ..ongyrde hine þa his sweorde & sealde his þegne. *c* **1000** ÆLFRIC *Saints' Lives* XXX. 409 Se casere..het hine ungyrdan and bewæpnian. **14..** in Wr.-Wülcker 578 *Discingo*, to ungyrd. **1530** PALSGR. 768/1, I ungyrde a horse. **1548** UDALL, etc. *Erasm. Par. John* xxi. 117 For thou vngirdedst or gyrdest thy self at thyne owne wil and pleasure. **1568** GRAFTON *Chron.* II. 391 As he stoode at the Barre, the Lord Neuel was commaunded..to vngyrde him. **1601** HOLLAND *Pliny* II. 301 Let the man come,..and after he hath ungirt himselfe, gird her about the middle with his owne girdle. **1611** BIBLE *Gen.* xxiv. 32 The man..vngirded his camels. *fig.* **1593** NASHE *Christ's T.* E iv b, The resplendent.. buildings of your Temple, (like a Drum), shal be vngirt & vnbraced. **1825** MACAULAY *Ess., Milton* (1897) 5 The sportive exercises for which the genius of Milton ungirds itself.

2. To release, or take off, by undoing a belt or girth.

1485 CAXTON *Chas. Gt.* 158 Rychard..descended fro hys hors for to vngyrde and lose hys sadle. **1623** BP. HALL *Contempl., O.T.* XIX. iii, Was not this he that advised Benhadad, not to boast in the putting on his armour, as in the ungirding it. **1641** J. JACKSON *True Evang. T.* I. 63 How many..in the hot sun-shine of prosperity have ungirt and cast off that cloake. **1810** SCOTT *Lady of L.* VI. xxii, When mourns thy tribe thy battles done,.. Thy sword ungirt ere set of sun! **1848** BP. A. JOLLY *Observ. Sunday Services* (ed. 4) 293 We must..never ungird our armour.

fig. **1601** SHAKS. *Twel. N.* IV. i. 15, I prethee now vngird thy strangenes, and tell me.

Hence **un'girding** *vbl. sb.*

1639 J. CORBET (*title*), The Ungirding of the Scottish Armour: or, an Answer to the Informations [etc.].

un'girded, † un'gird, *ppl. a.* [UN-[1] 8 or UN-[2] 8.] = UNGIRT *ppl. a.*

1382 WYCLIF *1 Kings* xx. 11 Ne glorye euenly the gird as the vngird. **1387** TREVISA *Higden* (Rolls) VIII. 213 þe abbot and þe chanouns of Osenay..com barefoot and barelegged and ungerd [*v.r.* ungurd] þorugh Londoun. *c* **1449** PECOCK *Repr.* II. i. 135 That a man wole were a girdel, or that he wole go vngerd. **1490** CAXTON *Eneydos* xxiv. 89 [She was] alle vngyrde, and vpon her knees, as a vassall that doeth homage to his lorde. **1523** FITZHERB. *Surv.* 31 b, He shalbe vngirde and his heed vncouered. **1565** COOPER, *Recinctus*, vngirded. **1865** W. G. PALGRAVE *Arabia* II. 42 His attendants caught up their swords where they lay ungirded for prayer. **1867** AUGUSTA WILSON *Vashti* xxx, Her white merino *robe de chambre* was partially ungirded.

un'girdle, *v.* [UN-[2] 4, 4 b.] = UNGIRD *v.*

1618 BOLTON *Florus* II. iv. 132 For Æmilius having the victory, ungirdled them in the Capitoll. **1629** J. MAXWELL tr. *Herodian* (1635) 141, I command my souldiers to ungirdle you; and divest you of all Military Attire.

un'girdled, *ppl. a.* (UN-[1] 8 or UN-[2] 8.)

1611 FLORIO, *Discinto*, vngirt, vngirdled. **1834** LYTTON *Pompeii* I. iii, Loosening to a yet more luxurious ease his ungirdled tunic. **1867** MYERS *St. Paul* (1908) 23 Oceans ungirdled of the ocean-stream. **1887** BOWEN *Æneid* IV. 518 One foot all unsandalled, her robe ungirdled, she stands.

un'girlish, *a.* (UN-[1] 7.)

1850 LYNCH *Theoph. Trinal* v. 80 Are not..these last lines a little ungirlish? **1863** [MISS M. ROBERTS] *Denise* I. 92 Her new acquaintances thought her odd and ungirlish.

un'girt, *ppl. a.* [UN-[1] 8 b or f. UNGIRD *v.* Cf. OFris. *un-, ongert*, MDu. *ongegort* (Du. *-gord*), MHG. (and G.) *ungegürtet*.]

1. Not girded or wearing a girdle; having the girdle or belt undone, slackened, or removed.

1297 R. GLOUC. (Rolls) 10826 Vn-hosed & bareuot & vn-gurt al so. **13..** *Coer de L.* 4153 Out com the wardayn Orgayl, And an hundryd knyghtes.., Barefoot, ungyrt, withouten hood. *c* **1380** *Sir Ferumb.* 1943 Bar-fot þou most go, Al open-her, & eke oungerte. *c* **1400** *Gamelyn* 215 Barfoot and vngirt Gamelyn In came. **1550** THOMAS *Ital. Gram., Discinto*, vngyrte. **1586** FERNE *Blaz. Gentrie* 109 The idle and sluggish person..goeth loose and vngirt. **1604** *Littleton's Tenures* C 2 b, When the Tenaunt shall make Homage to his Lord, he shall be vngirt, and his head vncouered. *a* **1658** CLEVELAND *Old Gill* vi, She has always the Squirt, She is loose and ungirt. **1700** J. TYRRELL *Hist. Eng.* II. 835 Prince Lewis coming Barefoot and Ungirt from his own Pavillion. *a* **1822** SHELLEY *Fragm. Elegy Death Adonis* 18 Aphrodite..is wandering through the woods, 'Wildered, ungirt, unsandalled. **1850** ROSSETTI *Blessed Damozel* ii, Her robe, ungirt from clasp to hem.

† b. In proverbial use. *Obs.*

1596 SPENSER *F.Q.* IV. v. 18 Fie on the man, that did it first inuent, To shame vs all with this, 'Vngirt vnblest'. **1635** QUARLES *Embl.* III. xiii, Am I a fitting Guest.. With hands and face unwash'd, ungirt, unblest? **1690** C. NESSE *O. & N. Test.* I. 451 Here, if ever, doth that proverb Ungirt, Unblest, hold true.

2. *fig.* **a.** Deprived or destitute *of* something.

c **1412** HOCCLEVE *De Reg. Princ.* 3653 Dignite had ben vnlaced And vngirt of honour, nad vertu be.

b. Not drawn together; left loose or incompact; not braced up for action.

1579 SPENSER *Sheph. Cal.* Ep. Ded., What in most English wryters vseth to be loose, and as it were vngyrt, in this Authour is..strongly trussed vp together. **1644** MILTON *Divorce* (ed. 2) Pref. A 4 b, Let him bethink him withall how he will soder up the shifting flaws of his ungirt permissions. **1670** *Devout Commun.* (1688) 27 If I go with a loose, ungirt spirit, I cannot instantly entertain my Lord. **1878** EMERSON *Sov. Ethics* Wks. (Bohn) III. 381 Our later generation appears ungirt, frivolous, compared with the religions of the..Calvinistic age.

† un'girt, *v. Obs.* [UN-[2] 4 b.] = UNGIRD *v.*

1598 FLORIO, *Discingere*,..to vnguirt. **1612** R. DABORNE *Christian turn'd Turke* 1275 The Muffty..girds his sword: then sweares him on the Mahomet's head, vngirts his sword [etc.]. **1661** MORGAN *Sph. Gentry* IV. i. 5 He ungirteth himself of his Sword, and..to God offereth it there.

un'girth, *v.* [UN-[2] 4 b.] *trans.* To free from a girth; to release or remove by undoing a girth.

1580 HOLLYBAND *Treas. Fr. Tong, Descengler vn cheval*, to vngirth a horse. **1760–72** H. BROOKE *Fool of Qual.* (1792) IV. 180 Two knavish wags came, and, ungirthing his saddle, supported it on either hand. **1787** W. TAYLOR *Scots Poems* 100 You hear, an e'en ungirth their laigen. **1820** SCOTT *Monast.* ix, Ye may ungirth your horses,..and dismiss.

un'girthed, (*ppl.*) *a.* [UN-[1] 8, 9.] Not provided with, or secured by, a girth. Also *fig.*

1628 FELTHAM *Resolves* II. ix. 24 Many times, honest Industry spends a man more, then the vngirthed Solaces of a sensuall Libertine. **1813** SCOTT *Rokeby* VI. *note*, The major ..clapped the saddle, ungirthed as it was, upon his horse. **1901** *Westm. Gaz.* 13 Aug. 8/2 If..there had been a saddle thrown upon the pony, it was ungirthed.

un'give, *v.* [UN-[2] 7, 3. Cf. obs. Flem. *ontgheven* to fail, Du. (*zich*)*ontgeven* to yield, desist.]

1. *intr.* To give way, to relax; to lose tenacity or firmness. Now *dial.*

1523 FITZHERB. *Husb.* §25 Make it in greatter hey-cockes, and to stande so one nyght or more, that it maye vngiue and sweate. **1655** FULLER *Ch. Hist.* II. ii. §40 That Religion which is rather suddenly parched up, then seasonably ripened, doth commonly ungive afterwards. **1670** EVELYN in *Phil. Trans.* V. 1063 When the wheels will not turn round because of the clay and over-much moisture, it is a signe, that 'tis not fit for cultivation, until it ungive, and be dry. *c* **1700** in *Bell's Anc. Poems* (1857) 19 Who thinks that love doth live In beauty's tempting show, Shall find his hopes ungive, And melt in reason's thaw. **1854** MISS BAKER *Northampt. Gloss.* 369 Gingerbread losing its crispness, and salt or any other substance relaxing from the humidity of the atmosphere, are said to ungive. **1881–** in *Eng. Dial. Dict.* s.v. (Lancs., Chesh., Leics., Bedford, Hants).

† 2. *trans.* To relax; to yield or give up. *Obs.*

1645 LIGHTFOOT *Comm. Acts* vi. 104 It is a daring that deserves castigation in him,..that hee should..deny the puritie of the Greeke text, before hee will ungive any thing of his owne groundlesse opinion. **1655** FULLER *Hist. Cambr.* 118 He was over-frozen, in his Northern Rigour, and could not be thaw'd, to ungive any thing of the rigidnesse of his Discipline.

un'given, *ppl. a.* [UN-[1] 8 b. Cf. ON. and Icel. *ú-, ógefinn* (MSw. *ogivin*), MDu. *ongegeven*, MHG. *ungegeben*.]

† 1. Not given in marriage. *Obs.*

c **1330** R. BRUNNE *Chron. Wace* (Rolls) 6545 Gentil damysels vngyuen, þat able to mennes companye were þryuen.

2. Not given or bestowed as a gift; not imparted.

1511 *Acc. Ld. High Treas. Scot.* IV. 253 To hald in un-gewin the Kingis goune..quhilk the King ordanit to be gewin. **1542** UDALL *Erasm. Apoph.* 230 b, Fortune leaft nothyng vngeuen to hym. *a* **1586** SIDNEY *Arcadia* III. viii, Philanax himselfe could haue wished the blow vngiuen, when he saw him fal. **1600** SIR R. CECIL *Lett.* (Camden) 62, I beleeve that office wilbe for a while vngeuen. **1662** H. HIBBERT *Body Divinity* I. 172 Sometimes men take offence ungiven. **1713** MRS. CENTLIVRE *Wonder* II. i, What proof remains ungiven of his love? **1768–74** TUCKER *Lt. Nat.* (1834) I. 63 Neither let him harbour such an overweening conceit of his own ungiven strength. **1818** COLEBROOKE *Obligations* 48 By the Hindu law, whatever has been given by mistake, must be considered as ungiven.

3. a. Not given *over*; unsurrendered.

a **1670** SPALDING *Troub. Chas. I* (1850) I. 272 It [*sc.* the castle] wes not long on-givin over.

b. Unaddicted *to* something.

1876 *Whitby Gloss.* 206. **1897** *Westm. Gaz.* 2 Mar. 2/1 Silent of speech, morose of nature, not ungiven to beer.

un'giving, *ppl. a.* (UN-[1] 10.)

1682 DRYDEN *Epil. Unhappy Favourite* 8 Courtiers living on the Rents Of the three last ungiving Parliaments. **1692** DRYDEN *Cleomenes* III. ii, In vain at shrines the ungiving suppliant stands. **1737** HERVEY *Mem.* (1848) xxviii. II. 251 The costive nature of the King's ungiving spirit. **1829** LAMB *Gypsy's Malison* 14 So sang a wither'd Beldam.., And bann'd the ungiving door.

un'glaciated, *ppl. a.* (UN-[1] 8.)

1883 *Science* I. 270/2 The average production..is nearly twice as large in the glaciated as in the unglaciated portion.

un'glad, *a.* [OE. *unglæd* (UN-[1] 7 + GLAD *a.*) = ON. *úglaðr* (MSw. *ogladh*, Norw. and Da. *uglad*).] Not glad or joyful; unhappy, sorry.

c **888** K. ÆLFRED *Boeth.* vi, þon wyrð heo swiðe hraðe ungladu, þeah heo ær gladu wære on to locienne. **13..** *Guy Warw.* (A.) 1554 Now haþ Gij miche sorwe made, For his felawes he is vnglade. *c* **1350** *Will. Palerne* 2106 He..goþ to þemperour of grece vnglad at his herte. **1390** GOWER *Conf.* III. 370, I..sih my colour fade, Myn yhen dymme and al unglade. *c* **1412** HOCCLEVE *De Reg. Princ.* 4081 At the last, Men þinke shullen þei to mochil haue had, And of þis worldys muk be ful vnglad. **1470–85** MALORY *Arthur* X. iii. 499 Whanne this crye was made many knyghtes were gladde and many were vngladde. **1536** BELLENDEN *Cron. Scot.* (1821) II. 128 The Scottis wer not unglaid thairof. **1620** SHELTON *Quix.* II. x. 60 Don Quixote..beheld with vnglad ..eyes her that Sancho call'd Queene and Lady. **1648** HEXHAM II, *Onblijde*, Vnglad, Vnjoyfull. **1819** LAMB *Sonn., Work* 8 Sabbathless Satan! he who his unglad Task ever plies mid rotatory burnings. **1873** DIXON *Two Queens* IX. iv. II. 119 Max had been as loth to let him go, as he had been unglad to see him come.

† un'glad, *v. Obs.* [UN-[2] 6 a. Cf. ON. *úgleðja*.] *trans.* To afflict, distress.

1390 GOWER *Conf.* II. 317 O thou, which alle love ungladest, And art ensample of alle untrewe. *c* **1430** *Syr Gener.* (Roxb.) 9202 The first assaute that euer thei made, Gwynan thei gan to vnglade.

un'gladdened, *ppl. a.* (UN-[1] 8.)

a **1851** MOIR *Lament of Selim* i, The soul Of him whose days ungladden'd roll On, month by month. **1861** J. G. SHEPPARD *Fall Rome* iii. 148 A howling wilderness, ungladdened by the sight of 'Flocks, or herds'.

† un'gladly, *a. Obs.*[−1] [UN-[1] 7; cf. OE. *unglædlic* morose.] Of the eyes: Dull.

c **1450** *Bk. Hawking* in *Rel. Ant.* I. 301 At his eyen thu mayst perceve [it], for his eyen woll be derke, and ungladly.

un'gladly, *adv.* [UN-[1] 11.] Without gladness (†or brightness.)

a **1225** *Ancr. R.* 338 Hwon ich hit do,..oðer ich hit do ungledliche,..oðer lete wel þerof. **1486** *Bk. St. Albans, Hawking* C iv b, When yowre hawke is encombred in the bowillis..hir Eighen will be derke and she will looke ungladli. **1902** *Westm. Gaz.* 25 Jan. 1/3 Men and women who know their Asia and are now returning to it ungladly.

un'gladness. [UN-[1] 12.] Want of gladness (†or good spirits).

a **1300** *Cursor M.* 15545 Time sal cum þat yee Sal yur vngladnes þat es nu haf turnd in to gle. *c* **1450** *Bk. Hawking* in *Rel. Ant.* I. 304 A man may knowe by the ungladnesse after the chear that he maketh. [**1486** *Bk. St. Albans, Hawking* C iv, A man may knaw by the chere and vngladnes of an hawke this infirmyte.]

un'gladsome, *a.* (UN-[1] 7.)

1558 PHAER *Æneid* III. I j, Than hauen at Drepanus I tooke, in that vngladsome shore [L. *illætabilis ora*].

un'glamoured, *ppl. a.* (UN-[1] 8.)

1891 T. HARDY *Tess* x, However terrestrial and lumpy their appearance just now to the mean unglamoured eye.

un'glazed, *ppl. a.* [UN-[1] 8. Cf. (in sense 2) MDu. *ongeglaset*.]

1. Not glazed or having a smooth shining surface.

1599 A. M. tr. *Gabelhouer's Bk. Physicke* 43/2 Combure it to poulder in an vnglazede pot. **1612** WOODALL *Surg. Mate* Wks. (1653) 211 Put these into an earthen pan unglazed. **1694** SALMON *Bate's Dispens.* (1713) 497/2 Lemery heats an unglazed Pot or Crucible red hot. **1744** BERKELEY in Fraser *Life* (1871) viii. 300 Tar-water is best made in glazed earthen vessels;..it is finer and clearer when so made than if in unglazed crocks. **1799** G. SMITH *Laboratory* I. 95 Then take an unglazed pot, or a large crucible. **1844** NOAD *Electricity* (ed. 2) 160 These porous jars..are now composed of the thinnest unglazed biscuit ware. **1874** H. H. COLE *Catal. Ind. Art S. Kens. Mus.* 208 Made of common red clay, unglazed.

2. Not filled in with glass; lacking glass windows.

1608 *Presentment* in *Essex Rev.* XV. 46 The churchyard is unfensed, the windows unglazed. *a* **1721** PRIOR *Down-Hall* xxxvii, O now a low ruin'd white Shed I discern, Untyl'd and unglaz'd; I believe 'tis a Barn. **1816** *Q. Rev.* XVI. 346 Unglazed windows, balconies, and lattices,—shops without windows. **1882** LYTTON *Str. Story* I. 215 The cornice of the ceiling rested on pilasters, within which the compartments were formed into open unglazed arches.

† 'ungle. *Obs.* [ad. F. *ongle* (cf. ONGLE) or L. *ungula* UNGULA.]

1. A claw, nail, or hoof.

1480 CAXTON *Myrr.* II. iv. 70 The gryffons wylde.. whiche easily bere a man away..whan he may sease hym with his clawes and vngles. **1491** —— *Vitas Patr.* (W. de W. 1495) I. xlviii. 93/2 The ungles or nayles of his fete and hondes weren merueyllously longe. **1566** ADLINGTON *Apuleius* 39 We fleade of the skinne..of the beare..and kept his ungles whole. **1657** TOMLINSON *Renou's Disp.* 457 It hath bifidous ungles like a Goat.

2. A hooked instrument of torture.

1483 CAXTON *Gold. Leg.* 122/2 The tormentes of the pryson, the naylles, the vngles, the streynynge combes of yron.

3. A morbid growth in the eye; = UNGULA 2.

1590 BARROUGH *Meth. Physick* I. xxxvi. (1596) 59 Somtime..another,vngle ariseth in the other corner [of the eye].

4. *Geom.* = UNGULA 4.

1669 WALLIS in Rigaud *Corr. Sci. Men* (1841) II. 508 He proceeds to a sum of squares to find the solid ungula, or the moment of that plane; and so to the sums of cubes, to find the moment of that ungle, and so on.

un'gleaned, *ppl. a.* (UN-[1] 8.)

[**1775** ASH.] **1858** in *Homans' Cycl. Commerce* 1775/1 Scarce a field [has been] left ungleaned. **1869** RUSKIN *Q. of Air* §157 Remnants of tradition..which remain ungleaned.

'ungled, *ppl. a. Her.* [f. UNGLE. Cf. F. *onglé*.] = UNGULED.

1675 WOOD *Life* (O.H.S.) II. 311 A lyon rampant sable ungled and lang'd gules. **1684** *List Military* 11 Vnicorn passant, argent, armed, ungled. **1722** A. NISBET *Syst. Her.* I. 333 A stag..attired and ungled, Or. **1892** *Daily Tel.* 12 July 5/1 A cock..armed or 'ungled'.

† unglee. *Obs.*[−1] [UN-[1] 12.] Sadness.

a **1300** *Cursor M.* 24120 (Edin.), Bot for na bod þat he me mad, Ne moht he min vngle ma [= make] glad.

un'glittering, *ppl. a.* (UN-[1] 10.)

1813 *Monthly Rev.* LXX. 458 The unglittering dilation of their stanzas. **1868** GEO. ELIOT *Sp. Gipsy* I. 54 The time of sweet serenity When colour glows unglittering.

un'globe, *v.* (UN-[2] 3.)

1611 FLORIO, *Disglobare*, to vnglobe, to make vnround. **1855** PATMORE *Angel in Ho.* II. Prol. 3 The beast [*sc.* the hedge-hog], Found stock-still..And feigning so to be deceased,..Unglobed himself.

un'gloomed, *ppl. a.* (UN-[1] 8.)

1737 GREEN *Spleen* 700 With look ungloom'd by guile, And wearing Virtue's livery-smile.

un'glorified, *ppl. a.* (UN-[1] 8.)

a **1395** HYLTON *Scala Perf.* I. xliii. (MS. Bodl.), þe resoun was maad cleer and briȝt..as parfytli as a soule in a bodi vnglorifyed myȝte haue. **1533** MORE *Answ. Frith* Wks. 839/1 But I am sure glorified or vnglorified, yf hee sayed it hee is able to dooe it. **1597** HOOKER *Eccl. Pol.* v. xliii. §3. 90 Least God should be any way vnglorified, the greatest part of our dayly seruice they know consisteth..in much varietie of Psalms and Hymnes. **1653** W. RAMESEY *Astrol. Restored* 10 So long as we carry this earthy Tabernacle about us unchanged and unglorified. **1876** MRS. OLIPHANT *Curate in Charge* II. ii. 34 The triumphant sunshine..leaving not an inch even of the common high road unglorified.

un'glorify, *v.* (UN-² 6 c.)
a **1740** WATTS *Remnants of Time*, etc. §21 Forbid it, O my God, that ever I should be so unhappy as to unglorify..my Saviour, or my Sanctifier. **1751** R. SHIRRA in *Remains* (1850) 75 The Word should as it were unglorify himself. **1873** BROWNING *Red Cott. Nt.-cap* III. 145 Unglossed was shrubbery, unglorified Each copse, so wealthy once.

un'glorious, *a.* Now *rare.* [UN-¹ 7 and 5 b. Cf. MDu. *onglorioos.*] = INGLORIOUS *a.*
In earliest quots. rendering L. *inglorius.*
1382 WYCLIF *Job* xii. 19 He bringeth the prestis of hem vnglorious, and the beste men of wrshipe he supplauntith. —— *Isaiah* lii. 14 So vnglorious shal ben among men his siȝte. *c* **1400** *The Brut* ccxxvii. 298 þe same vnglorious Philip wiþdrowe him, wiþ þe residue of al his peple. *c* **1450** *Myrr. our Ladye* 183 Tho aungels,..made vngloryous for thyr wyckednes, felle from glory. **1663** COWLEY *Ess. in Verse & Pr.*, *Virg. Georg.* 46 In the next place, let Woods and Rivers be My quiet, though unglorious destiny. **1744** ARMSTRONG *Preserv. Health* III. 13 Needlessly to brave Unglorious dangers. **1882** FROUDE *Carlyle* II. 153 Something should be found..neither unglorious nor unprofitable.

un'glory, *v.* [UN-² 4.] To deprive of glory.
1626 LAUD *Serm. Ps. lxxiv. 22*, 16 Wee must not looke that God should Arise to help vs, if wee arise to oppose and vnglorie him. **1655** SHIRLEY *Politician* III. i, The triumph he Expected..Will be unglories in our sudden match.

un'gloss, *v.* (UN-² 4.)
1873 [see UNGLORIFY *v.*].

un'glossaried, *a.* (UN-¹ 9.)
1887 W. BEATTY-KINGSTON *Music & Manners* II. 341 Why has he been thus branded, dateless and unglossaried. **1894** J. R. C. HALL *Anglo-Saxon Dict.* Pref., I do not profess to have searched unglossaried matter.

un'glossed, *ppl. a.*¹ (UN-¹ 8 and GLOSS *v.*¹)
1866 MORRIS *Ayenbite* Pref., Editors have left the word unglossed.

un'glossed, *ppl. a.*² (UN-¹ 8 and GLOSS *v.*²)
1802 H. MARTIN *Helen of Glenross* III. 293 Her errors you saw unveiled, unglossed. **1862** MRS. H. WOOD *Channings* xxiv, Tell me..the simple truth, unglossed over.

un'glossing, *ppl. a.* (UN-¹ 10.)
1827 LAMB in Hone *Table-bk.* I. 488 The honest unglossing pages of the homely Newgate Ordinary.

un'glossy, *a.* (UN-¹ 7.)
1822 GOOD *Stud. Med.* IV. 693 A dull or unglossy white diffused over the body. **1854** H. MILLER *Sch. & Schm.* xxi. 438 The dull, unglossy coat given..by the agencies of friction and water.

un'glove, *v.* [UN-² 4 and 7.]
1. *trans.* To divest of a glove or gloves.
c **1430** *Pilgr. Lyf Manhode* IV. xliii. (1869) 196 Weel þou wost þe name of þe gloouen... A fool þou were whan þou vnglooeuedest þee of hem. **1611** FLORIO, *Disguantare*, to vngloue. **1624** MASSINGER *Parl. Love* II. iii, See, I dare touch this hand, And without adoration unglove it. *a* **1625** FLETCHER & SHIRLEY *Lover's Progress* II. i, *Cla.* 'Tis said you can tell fortunes to come. *Lan.* Yes Mistris and what's past, Unglove your hand. **1823** SCOTT *Quentin D.* xii, The King, ungloving his right hand, courteously handed the Countess Isabelle and her kinswoman to their apartment. **1861** *Eng. Wom. Dom. Mag.* III. 142 He laid the hand which he had ungloved upon his heart.
2. *intr.* To remove a glove or gloves. Also *fig.*
1797 MRS. A. M. BENNETT *Beggar Girl* (1813) IV. 212 The earl, on every occasion a complete courtier, got out to unglove to Mrs. Woudbe. **1855** LYNCH *Rivulet* LXVI. iii, The covered buds ungloving Seem with offered hand to greet.
Hence **un'gloving** *vbl. sb.*
1818 KEATS *To Lady at Vauxhall* 4 Snared by the ungloving of thine hand. **1873** T. W. HIGGINSON *Oldport Days* v. 129 The turning of her head, the ungloving of her hand.

un'gloved, *ppl. a.* (UN-¹ 8.)
1626 BACON *New Atl.* (1650) 26 Holding forth his Hand ungloved, and in Posture of Blessing. **1626** BRETON *Fantastickes* Wks. (Grosart) II. 8/1 It is now March,..and the faire hands must not be vngloued. **1802** COLERIDGE *Lett.* (1895) 417, I..would shake hands with them ungloved. **1844** W. IRVING in *Life & Lett.* (1866) III. 359 On one hand is a black glove; the other hand, ungloved, is small. **1888** A. K. GREEN *Behind Closed Doors* v, She had laid her ungloved hand upon his arm.

un'glozed, *ppl. a.* (UN-¹ 8.)
1377 LANGL. *P. Pl.* B. IV. 145 Late ȝowre confessoure, sire Kynge, construe þis vnglosed.

un'glue, *v.* [UN-² 3 and 7.]
1. *trans.* To free from the binding or adhesive effect of glue; to detach or make loose in this way.
1548 ELYOT, *Reglutino*,..to vnglewe. **1598** FLORIO, *Sgommare*, to vngum, to vnplaister, to vnglue. **1686** AGLIONBY *Painting Illustr.* i. 29 Being Vexed at the Suns ungluing some Pictures of his. **1703** R. NEVE *City & C. Purchaser* 277 To prevent..Brick-walls from Ungluing the Joynts of the Pannels. **1718** OZELL tr. *Tournefort's Voy.* I. 130 Their Strings or Filaments separate..in parcels, as if they had been glued together at first, and now were unglued. **1859** MORLEY *Mem. Bartholomew Fair* i. 12 There was a young man..whose head stuck to his left hand. He was unglued at St. Bartholomew's establishment. **1872** T. HARDY *Under Greenw. Tree* I. v, That there instrument [a fiddle] will be unglued and spoilt in ten minutes.
b. *transf.* To open (the eyes) after sleep.
1606 DEKKER *Seuen Deadly Sinnes* Wks. (Grosart) II. 31 Another..arriu'de at one of the Gates, before any Porters eyes were vnglewd. **1682** N. O. *Boileau's Lutrin* IV. 207 But yet the Noise that had unglew'd their eyes Could not perswade the Sluggish Chanons rise. **1728** SWIFT *Jrnl. of Mod. Lady* 42 She stretches, gapes, unglues her eyes, And asks if it be time to rise.
c. *fig.* To detach, separate, dissolve.
1619 HIERON *Wks.* I. 641 Happy were it for vs if the meditation of this point..were able to vnglue and vntwist our affections, which are so neerely tyed vnto it. **1649** BP. HALL *Cases Consc.* IV. ii. (1654) 307 Heresie and Infidelitie, which are enough to unglew all naturall and civill relations betwixt father and son. **1675** HOBBES *Odyssey* (1677) 130 Your death.., for which Age shall prepare you, and your soul unglew Insensibly. **1831** SYD. SMITH in Lady Holland *Mem.* (1855) II. 314 Where is it to end? Are all political agglutinations to be unglued? **1897** HALL CAINE *Christian* IV. iii, Unless we unglue ourselves from the vanities which imperil our existence.
2. *intr.* To lose cohesion; to become detached.
1693 EVELYN *De la Quint. Compl. Gard.* II. 112 Otherwise they are apt to unglue, that is, to separate cleverly from the part where they are Graffed, in great Storms of Wind. **1703** R. NEVE *City & C. Purchaser* 29 When ever the Joints shall happen to unglue.
Hence **un'gluing** *vbl. sb.*
1591 PERCIVALL *Sp. Dict.*, *Desengrudamiento*, vngluing. **1623** COCKERAM I, *Reglutination*, an vngluing. **1703** R. NEVE *City & C. Purchaser* 277 Yet neither of these ways will prevent their ungluing in some Houses.

un'glued, *ppl. a.* [UN-¹ 8.] Having no glue; unstuck. Also *fig.*: in a confused or incoherent state or condition. Normally preceded by *come* or *become.*
1694 STRYPE *Mem. Cranmer* II. xv. 206 They had Leaves put in as Additions to the Book, some glewed, and some unglewed. **1870** CROWN PRINCESS OF PRUSSIA *Let.* 15 Feb. in R. Fulford *Your Dear Letter* (1971) 261 All the woodwork comes unglued and the tilestones all cracked and bent. **1922** M. A. VON ARNIM *Enchanted April* xx. 322 Now that Mrs. Fisher too had at last come unglued,—Rose protested at the expression, and Lotty retorted that it was in Keats. **1971** *Wall St. Jrnl.* 13 Aug. 1/5 Already-negotiated agreements may come unglued. **1980** A. COPPEL *Hastings Conspiracy* xxviii. 181 What's gone wrong? You wouldn't be here if something weren't coming unglued.

un'glutinate, *v.* [UN-² 3.] = UNGLUE *v.* 1 c.
1683 PETTUS *Ess. Metallick Words* s.v. *Load-stone*, To be kept from..moist places, which do unglutinate, and so destroyes or subdues their Virtues.

un'glutted, *ppl. a.* (UN-¹ 8.)
1813 BYRON *Corsair* II. viii, For Seyd's unglutted eye Would doom him ever dying—ne'er to die! **1847** LYTTON *Lucretia* II. viii, The two inheritors of a revenge unglutted by the grave. **1897** RHOSCOMYL *White Rose Arno* 46 His eyes all hell with unglutted murder.

†**ungly**, erroneous f. UGLY *a.* and *adv.*
c **1400** *Apol. Loll.* 55 But wo is þe..biginning of þis þus gret iuel, I drede ungly to sey. *a* **1513** FABYAN *Chron.* v. cix. 83 Such an vngly nombre of multytude of monkes.

un'gnawed, *ppl. a.* (UN-¹ 8.)
1836 F. MAHONY *Rel. Father Prout* (1859) 376 Thy MSS. have come down to us..ungnawed by the tooth of Time. **1881** DARWIN *Veg. Mould* 80 Ungnawed petioles had not become more decayed near the base than elsewhere.

un'gnawn, *ppl. a.* (UN-¹ 8 b.)
a **1560** PHAER *Æneid* VIII. Y 3 To thee he trembling shooke, and left his bones begonne ungnawn. **1648** HEXHAM II, *Ongeknaeght*, Vngnawne. **1775** ASH, *Ungnawn.*

†**un'gnede**, *a. Obs.* [UN-¹ 7: cf. OE. *ungnīeðe.*] Unsparing, liberal.
a **1300** *Cursor M.* 9933 þat castel brightnes sua vngnede, Oueral þat curt on lenght and brede. *a* **1400** *Pistill of Susan* 276 Grete god,..of gyftes vngnede.

ungnement, obs. form of OINTMENT.

†**un'go**, *v. Obs.*⁻¹ [UN-² 7. Cf. MDu. *ontgaen* (Du. *-gaan*), LG. *und-*, *untgân*, MHG. *ent-*, *engân* (G. *entgehen*), to escape, fail, etc.] *intr.* To pass away, perish.
c **1450** *Hymns Virgin* (1867) 121 They schalle se heuyn vngo, And þe erthe schall also.

un'goaded, *ppl. a.* (UN-¹ 8.)
[**1775** ASH.] **1817** LADY MORGAN *France* VI. (1818) II. 130 Ungoaded by the necessities of a cŏmmercial existence. **1873** W. CORY *Lett. & Jrnls.* (1897) 313 A..creaking wheel turned by an ungoaded, tall, lean ox.

un'god, *v.* [UN-² 6 b. Cf. Du. *ontgoden*, G. *entgöttern.*] To deprive of the qualities or position of deity; to undeify. (Common *c* 1640–1740.)
1627 WREN *Serm. bef. King* 17 Feb. 33 All slight and unawful Expressions. Vngodding him no lesse..then does rash and unadvised blasphemie. **1655** GURNAL *Chr. in Arm.* II. 61 Though men cannot come to pull God out of his throne, and un-god him. **1677** [see UNCHRISTED *ppl. a.*]. **1708** O. DYKES *Eng. Prov. & Refl.* (1709) 243 Attempting saucily to rival, to insult, or to ungod his Creator. *a* **1750** T. GORDON *Another Cordial* (1751) II. 203 The Jew crucifies his Saviour, the Socinian and Mahometan ungod him. *a* **1834** COLERIDGE in *Lit. Rem.* (1839) IV. 224 A consistent Socinianism..in ungodding the Saviour must deify cats and dogs. **1892** *Gospel Watchman* Dec. 191/1 God..will be dethroned and ungodded before it shall come to pass.
refl. **1672** VILLIERS (Dk. Buckhm.) *Rehearsal* IV. ii, For fair Parthenope, Gods would, themselves, un-god themselves to see. **1685** J. SCOTT *Chr. Life* II. vii. §1 Which would be to destroy his own Being, and un-god himself.
Hence **un'godding** *vbl. sb.*
1656 BEAKE in *Burton's Diary* (1828) I. 59 It is a crime that deposes the majesty of God himself,..the ungodding of God. **1678** CUDWORTH *Intell. Syst.* I. iv. §20. 381 His Ungodding of the Sun, Moon and Stars. **1716** M. DAVIES *Athen. Brit.* II. 407 What a horror the Primitive Christians had of the Notions, of Ungodding our Saviour.

†**un'godded**, *ppl. a. Obs.* [UN-¹ 8: see GOD *v.* 2.] Not spiritually united with God.
1579 W. WILKINSON *Confut. Fam. Love* B iij b, They are ..vnrenewed, vngodded, vnsent. **1660** H. MORE *Myst. Godl.* VI. xii. 248 What the ungodded or unilluminated men ..preach and teach. **1687** DRYDEN *Hind & P.* III. 742 Thus men ungodded may to places rise.

un'goddess, *v.* [UN-² 6 b.] *trans.* To deprive of the status of a goddess.
1760 MURPHY *Way to Keep Him* I. i, They whisk about the Town,..as if they were treated at home like so many Goddesses, though every body knows possession has ungoddessed them all long ago. **1797** MRS. A. M. BENNETT *Beggar Girl* (1813) III. 290 Fortune..was at this moment most unmercifully ungoddessed. **1837** CARLYLE *Fr. Rev.* III. v. iv, What articulate words poor Mrs. Momoro..uttered, when she had become ungoddessed again.

†**un'goderly**, *a. Obs.* [UN-¹ 7; the second element is obscure.] Squalid, filthy.
13.. *E.E. Allit. P.* B. 145 þow art a gome vngoderly in þat goun febele. *Ibid.* 1092 [Christ] nolde neuer towche Oȝt þat was vngoderly oþer ordure was inne.

un'godlike, *a.* (UN-¹ 7 c.)
a **1652** J. SMITH *Sel. Disc.* viii. (1660) 364 But alas, such an ungodlike Religion as this can never be owned by God. **1684** T. BURNET *Theory Earth* I. 165 This, I confess, seems to me..a way of working very un-God-like. **1729** W. REEVE *Serm.* 149 The pleasures at God's right hand must be tasteless to an ungodlike filthy spirit. **1854** P. FAIRBAIRN *Typol. Script.* (ed. 2) I. II. ii. 218 How cheering to know this ungod-like state of disorder and confusion is not to be perpetual. **1869** GLADSTONE *Juv. Mundi* vii. 211 It did not assign to deity that most ungodlike quality, respect of persons.

un'godlily, *adv.* (UN-¹ 11.)
1583 J. FIELD *Godly Exhort.* C j b, Being thus vngodlilie assembled, to so vnholy a spectacle. **1645** PAGITT *Heresiogr.* (1647) 66 Ungodlily alledging the..Scriptures. **1674** *Govt. Tongue* 114 'Tis but an ill essay of that reverence and godly fear, to use that very gospel so irreverently and ungodlily as men now do. **1860** PUSEY *Min. Proph.* 413 Israel..slaying ungodlily Him who was by nature His Begotten Son.

un'godliness. (UN-¹ 12: cf. next.)
1526 TINDALE *Rom.* i. 18 For the wrath of god of heven apereth agaynst all vngodlynes and vnrightewesnes. *Ibid.* xi. 26. **1555** EDEN *Decades W. Ind.* (Arb.) 58 He dyd not keepe silence of so wicked an vngodlynesse. **1642** L. HUGHES (*title*), Certain Grievances: or, the Popish Errors and Ungodlinesse of the Service-book plainly laid open. **1671** BARROW *Duty & Reward Charity* 21 Performing such acts, is a good sign of true Piety; and omitting them, is a certain argument of ungodliness. **1742** YOUNG *Nt. Th.* III. 165 Oh! the curst ungodliness of zeal! **1865** C. J. VAUGHAN *Plain Words* x. (1866) 183 The recollection of His love in contrast with our ungodliness.

un'godly, *a.* [UN-¹ 7. Cf. MDu. *ongodelijc* (Du. *ongoddelijk*), MHG. *ungötlich* (G. *ungöttlich*), (M)Da. *ugudelig.* MSw. *ogudhlik* (Sw. *ogudlig*).]
1. Of persons: Not fearing or reverencing God; irreligious, impious, wicked.
1526 TINDALE *Rom.* v. 6 Christ dyed for vs which were vngodly. **1587** GOLDING *De Mornay* xx. 358 There is also a certeine Religion,..and the vngodlyest man that is cannot scape from it. *a* **1613** OVERBURY *A Wife*, etc. (1614) H 4 b, The charitable man dreames of building Churches, but starts to thinke the vngodly Courtier will pull them down again. **1653** HOLCROFT *Procopius, Pers. Wars* II. 48 His son succeeding him, being the ungodlyest man living. **1698** NORRIS *Pract. Disc.* IV. 180 Which justifies a certain English Phrase..wherein we use to call a Man of a Wicked Life, an Vngodly Man. **1731** WATERLAND *Script. Vind.* II. 100 Shimei was an ungodly wretch. **1849** JAMES *Woodman* ii, The admission into her own private chamber of such very ungodly personages as Mars and Venus.
absol. **1526** TINDALE *1 Pet.* iv. 18 Yf the righteous scasly be saved: where shall the vngodly and the sinner appere? **1535** COVERDALE *Zeph.* iii. 5 But the vngodly will not lerne to be aszshamed. **1631** GOUGE *God's Arrows* I. §12. 17 Of the godlies exemption from the ungodlies destruction. **1738** WESLEY *Ps.* I. iv, But no Success th' Ungodly find. **1825** J. NEAL *Bro. Jonathan* I. 24 While he was rebuking the ungodly. **1847** S. AUSTIN *Ranke's Hist. Ref.* III. 385 He did not doubt that the ungodly, as well as the pious, partook of the body and blood of Christ.
transf. **1595** SHAKS. *John* III. i. 109 Let not the howres of this vngodly day Weare out the daies in Peace.
b. Of the stomach: Gluttonous, greedy.
c **1746** J. COLLIER (Tim Bobbin) *Goose* 78 You must not Pamper your ungodly Belly. **1746** AINSWORTH (ed. 2) I, An ungodly gut, *venter improbus.* **1828** [CARR] *Craven Gloss.*, *Ungodly*, insatiable, or squeamish and nice; used of the stomach or guts.
2. Of actions, etc.: Not in accordance with the will or law of God.
1526 [see UNGODLY *adv.*]. **1555** EDEN *Decades* (Arb.) 109 They sayde it was vngodly to feyght ageynst any, not beinge prouoked. **1577** GOOGE *Heresbach's Husb.* 15 Let hym in no

wyse suffer them..to vse filthy or vngodly speache. **1617** WOODALL *Surg. Mate* Pref., Wks. (1639) 6 Wherefore it were a very ungodly thing..to forbid a Surgeon to learne all, or any thing that concerneth his calling. **1671** MILTON *Samson* 898 Gods unable To acquit themselves and prosecute their foes But by ungodly deeds. **1851** LONGFELLOW *Gold. Leg.* IV. *Refectory*, Were Peter Damian still upon earth, To be shocked by such ungodly mirth. **1864** PUSEY *Lect. Daniel* i. (1876) 3 The moral law..strongly condemned forgery even when not ungodly.

3. *colloq.* Outrageous, dreadful.

1887 STEVENSON *Merry Men, Olalla*, The wind['s]..ungodly and unintermittent uproar, would not suffer me to sleep.

un'godly, *adv.* *Obs.* exc. *arch.* [UN-[1] 11. Cf. MDu. *ongod(e)like* (Du. *ongoddelijk*), MHG. *ungöttlich*, MSw. *ogud(e)like* (Sw. *ogudligt*).] = UNGODLILY *adv.* (Common in 16th c.)

1526 TINDALE *Jude* 15 To rebuke..all their vngodly dedes, which they have vngodly committed. [Also in later versions.] **1533** FRITH *Judgm. Tracy* Pref., But this I dare boldly professe, that his godly sayinges are vngodly handled. **1564** *Brief Exam.* A iij, All true Godly men, may Godly vse those rites, which wicked men haue abused, howesoeuer vngodly. **1606** G. WOODCOCK *Hist. Ivstine* Ii 2, Leontius..being made Emperor, ruled most vngodly eleuen years.

un'godmothered, *a.* (UN-[1] 9.)

?**1714** *Widow of Watling Street* I. i, You Half Christened Katomites—ungodmothered varlets.

†**un'goingable**, *a.* *Obs.*[−1] [UN-[1] 7 b.] Impossible to traverse.

1482 *Monk of Evesham* (Arb.) 39 Sothly to owre semyng the lengthe of thys fyrste place afore seyde was on goyngable.

ungold, *v.* (UN-[2] 4.)

1637 N. WHITING *Albino & Bellama* 28 Saturne's exilde, Jove awes this massie Ball, And now the Iron age un-goldeth all.

ungon, obs. var. ONION.

un'gone, *ppl. a.* [UN-[1] 8 b.]

1. Not (yet) gone or departed. †*to keep ungone* (Sc.), to keep from going.

c **1475** *Rauf Coilȝear* 661 ȝit was the King in the hall, And mony gude man with all, Vngane to the meit. **1597** in *Archpriest Controv.* (Camden) I. 2 Mr. Gwyn tould me that fissher was vngone at his comyng from London. **1638** SIR E. STANHOPE in *Strafford's Lett.* (1739) II. 239 A Letter..to intreat me to meet him the next Day, and if he were ungone, to bring my Son John with me. **1657** *Rec. Burgh Lanark* (1893) 160 To keip their prenteissis, servands, and childrin ungone avaiging on the Lordes day. **1824–77** in dialect glossaries (Yks., Linc.).

†**2.** Untraversed. *Obs.*[−0]

1611 FLORIO, *Inuio sentiere*, an vngone, vntroden or vncouth path.

un'good, *a.* Now *rare.* [OE. *ungód* (UN-[1] 7), = MDu. *ongoet* (older Du. *ongoed*), MLG. *ungût* (LG. *ungôd*), OHG., MHG. *unguot* (G. *ungut*), ON. *úgóðr* (Norw. dial. *ugod*).] **a.** Not good; evil, bad; wicked.

c **1000** *Sax. Leechd.* III. 184 Seldan he bið eald, ungodan deaðe he swylt. *Ibid.* 188. *c* **1200** ORMIN 16739 Forrþi þatt teȝȝre dede iss all Unngod & all unnclene. *Ibid.* 17056. *a* **1300** *E.E. Psalter* i. 1 In strete of sinfulle noght he stode, Ne sat in setel of storme un-gode. *c* **1305** *Judas Iscariot* 22 in *E.E.P.* (1862) 107 Loþ hem was..a bern to norischie, so liþer and vngod. **1390** GOWER *Conf.* I. 20 The vice of hem that ben ungoode Is no reproef unto the goode. *c* **1445** PECOCK *Donet* 37 Þat þing whiche resoun knowiþ..to be bad, or vngood. *c* **1485** *Digby Myst.* (1882) IV. 675 His synows..Are brokyn sonder by payns vngude!

(*b*) In mod. use.

1904 C. N. & A. M. WILLIAMSON *Princess Passes* xii, You have been so good to us; don't be ungood now. **1949** 'G. ORWELL' *Nineteen Eighty-Four* I. 53 If you have a word like 'good', what need is there for a word like 'bad'? 'Ungood' will do just as well—better, because it's an exact opposite, which the other is not. **1964** W. GOLDING *Spire* viii. 150 Jocelin found the capstone ungood to look at.

b. *absol.* or as *sb.*

a **1250** *Owl & Night.* 129 Al so hit is þi þan vngode þat is icumen of fule brode. *Ibid.* 1364 Vor nys a worlde þing so god þat ne may do sum vngod. *a* **1568** in *Bannatyne MS.* (Hunter. Cl.) 203/86 Vngud and gud sall fair,..Bot richteous gud..lestis for euir mair. **1885** L. OLIPHANT *Sympneumata* 248 For universal good, and for suppression of the ungood.

†**un'goodlihead.** *Obs.*[−1] [UN-[1] 12: cf. next.] Lack of goodness.

1430–40 LYDG. *Bochas* VI. iii. (1554) 150 b, She her cours gan varye..To shewe her malice and ungoodlyhed.

†**un'goodly**, *a.* *Obs.* [UN-[1] 7. Cf. MDu. *ongoedelijc-* (Du. *ongoedelijk*), MLG. *ungûtlik*, *-gôtlik*, MHG. *unguotlich*, *-güetlich* (G. *ungütlich*).]

1. Lacking goodness; bad, wicked: **a.** Of persons.

1390 GOWER *Conf.* I. 293 He is that ilke ungoodlieste Which many a lusti love hath twinned. *Ibid.* II. 338 Ha, thou ungoodlich ypocrite. **1432** *Paston Lett.* I. 32 The whiche lak or defaulte mighte be caused by ungodly or unvertuous men. **1472** *Coventry Leet Bk.* 374 Wher ther be diuers and many vagabundes, and vngoodly & ille disposed persones. **1553** BECON *Reliques of Rome* (1563) 159 This is y[e] goodly Godlye Catholyke doctrine wherwith the vngoodly vngodly Papists infecte the mindes of such Christians as are simple.

b. Of actions, language, etc.

1390 GOWER *Conf.* II. 333 Which thing, mi Sone, I thee forbede, For it is an ungoodly dede. **1412–20** LYDG. *Chron. Troy* III. 3352 Epistrophus..Rebuked hym in vngoodly wyse. **1455** T. BECKINGTON *Corr.* (Rolls) II. 342 That I sholde haue vttered and seid vngoodly langage touchynge yor noble persone. **1530** in W. H. Turner *Select. Rec. Oxford* (1880) 84 For his ungoodly maner so then usid to the comyssarie [he] did send hym to prison.

2. Uncomely; unhandsome.

1495 *Trevisa's Barth. De P.R.* v. xiii. 42 Yf the nose lackyth, all y[e] other dele of y[e] face is y[e] more vngoodly & vnsemely. **1519** HORMAN *Vulg.* 14 b, No man that..hath a mahayme or a blemmysshe, that maketh hym vngoodly, shall take orders. **1549** COVERDALE, etc. *Erasm. Par. I Cor.* 34 Suche [parts] as seme vngoodly, to them ioyne we some comly vesture.

†**un'goodly**, *adv.* *Obs.* [UN-[1] 11. Cf. MDu. (and obs. Du.) *ongoedelike*, MLG. *ungûtliken*, *-gôtliken*, MHG. *unguotlîche*, *-güetlîche.*]

1. In an uncomely manner. *rare.*

a **1300** *Cursor M.* 18404 Þar come ouerthuert A wreche man, vngodli gert, On his schuldres a croice he bar.

2. Badly, wrongly, improperly; roughly or rudely.

c **1380** WYCLIF *Wks.* (1880) 339 And þus is þat man contrite of synne, þat he vngodeli to god haþ don. **1426** LYDG. *De Guil. Pilgr.* 3952, I..ful vngoodly spoke now, Wher-off I repente sore. **1450** *Paston Lett.* I. 158 He tolde H. his part how that he levid ungoodly in puttyng awey of his wyff, and kept an other. **1475** *Bk. Noblesse* (Roxb.) 5 That noble and trew knight,..ayenst all manhode ungoodely entretid, died in prison. **1526** TINDALE *Matt.* xxii. 6 The remnaunt toke his servauntes and entreated them vngoodly and slewe them. **1545** ASCHAM *Toxoph.* (Arb.) 50 Good thinges ungoodlye vsed, are not good.

un'gored, *ppl. a.*[1] [UN-[1] 8.] Unpierced.

1604 SHAKS. *Ham.* v. ii. 261 (Q. 2), I..will no reconcilement, Till..I haue a voyce and president of peace To [keep] my name vngord [**1623** vngorg'd]. **1647** HEXHAM I, Vngored, *ondoorsteken.*

†**un'gored**, *ppl. a.*[2] [UN-[1] 8.] Unbloodied.

1605 SYLVESTER *Du Bartas* II. iii. *Vacation* 288 Yet one might behold Bright swords and shields, and plumed helms of gold Un goard with bloud.

un'gorge, *v.* (UN-[2] 3.)

1601 CHETTLE & MUNDAY *Death Earl Huntington* v. ii. L j b, But when thou dost vngorge thee, grant me this, Thou power those poysons on the head of Iohn.

un'gorged, *ppl. a.* (UN-[1] 8.)

[**1623**: see UNGORED[1].] **1700** DRYDEN *Theod. & Hon.* 213 The Hell-hounds, as ungorg'd with Flesh and Blood, Pursue their Prey. **1743** FRANCIS tr. *Hor.*, *Odes* III. iv. 79 On Tityus' liver shall the vulture feed With rage ungorged.

un'gorgeous, *a.* (UN-[1] 7.)

1837 CARLYLE *Fr. Rev.* II. IV. viii, The ignominious Royal Procession..sweeps along there, in most *un*gorgeous pall.

un'gospel, *a.* [UN-[1] 12 b.] Unevangelical.

1649 H. LAWRENCE *Some Consid.*, etc. 75 Can that Ordinance be legall, and servile, and ungospell? **1653** PRYNNE *Gospel-plea* 33 Which ungospell practises I wish they would first reforme.

un'gospel, *v.* (UN-[2] 6 b.)

1847 H. BUSHNELL *Chr. Nurt.* II. vii. (1861) 376 Confessing shortcomings and defeats..enough to ungospel all the gospel promises.

un'gospelized, *ppl. a.* (UN-[1] 8.)

1706 *Acc. Soc. Propag. Gospel* 57 They had addressed the Remoter ungospelized Plantations. **1721** S. SEWALL *Diary* 16 Feb., The Money for Gospellizing ungospellized places.

un'gospelled, *a.* (UN-[1] 9.)

1674 N. FAIRFAX *Bulk & Selv.* 8 That thread-bare Question, which did so much gravel the ungospel'd world. **1902** SKRINE *Pastor Agnorum* 193 The sick that need the physician, the ungospelled poor.

un'gospel-like, *a.* (UN-[1] 7 c.)

1574 *Life 70th Abp. Canterb.* Pref. E 4 That so the open mouth off the Lewde Papist might bee stopped from..the approuing of suche vngospellike legends. **1641** MILTON *Ch. Govt.* II. iii, The..tyranny of an undue, unlawfull and ungospellike jurisdiction. **1674** PENN *Urim & Thummim* (title-p.), The opposite plea of Samuel Grevill..in his ungospel-like discourse.

un'got, *ppl. a.* Also 5 vnget. [UN-[1] 8 b.]

1. Not acquired, obtained, or won.

c **1400** *Sege Jerus.* (E.E.T.S.) 68/1169 Ay wer þe ȝates vnget till two ȝeres ende: So longe þey souȝt hit by sege, or þey þe cite hadde. **1601** DANIEL *Civ. Wars* VI. xlvii, Whilst Sommerset with maine endeuour lay To get his giuen but vngot gouernment. **1611** COTGR., *Vuarisons*,..corne, grasse ..standing, or vncut, vngot.

2. Unbegot.

1603 SHAKS. *Meas. for M.* v. i. 141 Your Substitute, Who is as free from touch, or soyle with her As she from one vngot.

un'gotten, *ppl. a.* Also 5 vngettyn, -getyn. [UN-[1] 8 b.]

1. Unbegotten.

1435 MISYN *Fire of Love* 14 For nouþer þe substanc of þe sone som-tyme vngetyn myȝt be called,..with-oute an onely gettyn sone of þe self. **1470–85** MALORY *Arthur* VI. i. 571 He that shal sytte there is vnborne and vngoten. **1548** PATTEN *Exped. Scotl.* A vij, Astyages..was..admonished y[t] he shoulde be ouercommen by a nephew of hys as yet then vngotten & vnborne. **1599** SHAKS. *Hen. V*, I. ii. 288 And some are yet vngotten and vnborne, That shal haue cause to curse the Dolphins scorne.

2. Not acquired, obtained, or won.

a **1548** HALL *Chron.*, *Hen. VI*, 107 b, The Frenchemen..seyng the strong fortres was ungotten,..fetched a compasse about. **1600** PALFREYMAN *Baldwin's Mor. Philos.* 135 b, They that indeuour to get theyr husbandes or wiues by deceipts & charmes, may lightly get them, but better vngotten. **1628** FELTHAM *Resolves* I. xlviii. 45 Let her wander, in a wearied sollicitude, after vngotten plenty. **1775** ASH, *Ungotten*,..not gotten, not gained. **1876** GEO. ELIOT *Dan. Der.* xxiii, To carry the map of an ungotten estate in your pocket is a poor sort of copyhold. **1883** GRESLEY *Gloss. Coal-m.* 197 Solid or ungotten coal forming the roof of a roadway.

un'governable, *a.* (and *sb.*). [UN-[1] 7 b.] That cannot be governed; uncontrollable. **a.** Of persons (or animals).

1673 [R. LEIGH] *Transp. Reh.* 112 Such ungovernable cattle as conscientious savages. **1680** DRYDEN *Ovid's Ep.* Pref. (ad fin.), So wild and ungovernable a poet cannot be translated literally. **1725** DE FOE *Voy. round World* (1840) 312 The fellows were so rude, so ungovernable and unbounded in their hunting after gold. **1768** BOSWELL *Corsica* ii. (ed. 2) 135 A lawless and ungovernable rabble of banditti. **1829** SCOTT *Anne of G.* xxv, The abbess..will have an ungovernable penitent under her charge. **1849** MACAULAY *Hist. Eng.* v. I. 592 These animals..became ungovernable as soon as they heard a gun fired. **1855** *Ibid.* xvii. IV. 101 The fiercest and most ungovernable part of the ..population.

sb. **1810** BYRON *Let. to H. Drury* 3 May, I have been with ..governors and ungovernables.

b. Of temper, passion, etc.

1676 HALE *Contempl.* I. 341 Men pretending to greatness of wit and learning, but in truth of haughty and ungovernable spirits. **1741** RICHARDSON *Pamela* II. 36 This strange wayward Heart of mine, that I never found so ungovernable and awkward before. **1781** GIBBON *Decl. & F.* xxxi. (1787) III. 251 The ungovernable spirit of a Barbarian host, impatient of peace or discipline. **1843** BETHUNE *Sc. Fireside Stor.* 100 He fell into a most ungovernable passion. **1876** T. HARDY *Ethelberta* (1890) 400 As if by an ungovernable impulse, Ethelberta broke into laughter also.

c. Of things.

1773 COOK *Voy. S. Pole* II. ii. (1777) I. 205 Having unshipped the rudder, which rendered her vngovernable. **1839** FR. A. KEMBLE *Resid. in Georgia* (1863) 58 The stiff and ungovernable hair. **1852** HAWTHORNE *True Stories* iii. (1879) 22 That..ungovernable wonder the wind.

Hence **un,governa'bility, un'governableness.**

1673 *Lady's Calling* I. ii. §13 The ungovernableness of a woman. **1701** COLLIER *M. Aurel.* (1726) 96 You'd best murther your general, and add villany to your ungovernableness. **1751** ELIZA HEYWOOD *Betsy Thoughtless* I. 103 Lamenting the ungovernableness of youth. **1853** RUSKIN *Stones Ven.* II. App. 393 The ungovernableness of its colour (changing in the furnace). **1882** *Pall Mall G.* 20 June 2/1 As much an illustration of misgovernment as of our ungovernableness. **1968** *Economist* 18 May 3/1 [Mr Wilson's] going might merely contribute to Britain's drift towards ungovernability. **1977** *Financial Times* 1 Apr. 22/8 Beyond the immediate question of the invasion perhaps the most serious problem is what has been termed Zaire's fundamental ungovernability. **1983** *Guardian Weekly* 16 Jan. 9/3 Now comes the threat the Germans call 'ungovernability'.

un'governably, *adv.* (UN-[1] 11; cf. prec.)

1682 NORRIS *Hierocles* 134 Demeaning themselves ungovernably in all fortunes. **1764** GOLDSM. *Trav.* 314 Heavens! how unlike their Belgic sires of old! Rough, poor, content, ungovernably bold. **1810** CRABBE *Borough* iii. 42 Accuse me not that I..think the passions,..Strong as they are, ungovernably strong. **1855** MACAULAY *Hist. Eng.* xix. IV. 357 He had..been turned out of office in a way which had made him ungovernably ferocious. **1882** M. DODDS *Genesis* 195 A nature..whose passions raged ungovernably.

un'governed, *ppl. a.*[1] [UN-[1] 8.] Not brought under government or control; uncontrolled:

a. Of disposition, feelings, actions, etc.

1591 SHAKS. *Two Gentl.* IV. i. 45 Some of vs are Gentlemen, Such as the fury of vngouern'd youth Thrust from the company of awfull men. **1622** MISSELDEN *Free Trade* 73 It now remaineth briefely to show the Too Loose Vse thereof, by Vngouerned Trade. **1667** MILTON *P.L.* XI. 514 When themselves they vilifi'd To serve ungovern'd appetite. **1712** STEELE *Spect.* No. 290 ¶1 The ungoverned Passions of such as are enamoured of each other. **1781** GIBBON *Decl. & F.* xviii. (1787) II. 95 Unable to withstand the ungoverned fury of the populace. **1839** FR. A. KEMBLE *Resid. in Georgia* (1863) 14 The furious and ungoverned execration which all reference to the possibility..draws down upon those who suggest it. **1846** MRS. A. MARSH *Father Darcy* II. x. 165 There was..something so violent and ungoverned in her temper and feelings.

b. Of persons, animals, or things.

1594 SHAKS. *Rich. III*, IV. iv. 392 Thou.., Vngouern'd youth. **1606** CHAPMAN *Gentl. Usher* IV. iii, For mad men, By paynes vngouernd, have no sense of payne. **1628** in Foster *Eng. Factories India* (1909) III. 198 Our people for the most part being heedlesse, ungoverned, without discipline and order. **1719** DE FOE *Crusoe* I. (Globe) 348, I knew they were a Parcel of refractory, ungovern'd Villains. **1725** POPE *Odyss.* VIII. 199 Ill bear the brave a rude ungovern'd tongue. **1791** COWPER *Iliad* XXIII. 585 Thrown..From his seat,..his ungovern'd steeds have roam'd away. **1827** POLLOK *Course T.* v. 1052 The Tartar hordes, that roamed.., Ungoverned, southward to the wondrous Wall.

†**un'governed**, *ppl. a.*[2] [UN-[2] 6 b.] Deprived of the position of governor.

1654 GAYTON *Pleas. Notes* IV. 230 Ungovern'd, Uncardinall'd, Unlorded, Outed of all his hopes.

un'governing, *ppl. a.* (UN-[1] 10.)

1823 J. F. COOPER *Pioneers* xxxi, The ungoverning feeling that caused the violence of the youth had passed away.

un'gown, *v.* [UN-² 4.] **a.** *refl.* To deprive (oneself) of a gown. **b.** *trans.* = UNFROCK *v.*
1789 COWPER *Let. to Lady Hesketh* 31 Jan., I had a thousand times rather be as poor as all poets are, than you should ungown youself to prevent it. **1895** *Westm. Gaz.* 30 Jan. 5/3 She said he had gone out cursing her and then assisted in God's house, but she had no wish to ungown him.

un'gowned, *ppl. a.* (UN-¹ 8.)
1611 SPEED *Hist. Gt. Brit.* IX. ix. §59 To whose importunity the proud Legate would not condiscend, vnlesse all the Bishops.., vngowned and vnshod, should humbly craue absolution. **1721** AMHERST *Terræ Fil.* No. 50. 267 Sure of being mobb'd and insulted by whole crowds of the gown'd and ungown'd rabble. **1827** POLLOK *Course T.* VIII. 69 Ungowned, unbeneficed, Uncorpulent.

un'grace. (UN-¹ 12. Cf. WANGRACE¹.)
1430–40 LYDG. *Bochas* v. xxii. (1554) 137b, Ungrace and youth made hym for to erre. **1871** JOWETT *Plato* I. 512 Ungrace and love are always at war with one another.

un'graced, *ppl. a.*¹ (UN-¹ 8.)
1595 DANIEL *Civ. Wars* IV. iv, Can England see the best that shee can boast, Ly thus vngract, undeckt, and almost lost? **1603** DRAYTON *Bar. Wars* IV. lxii, Merit goes vnregarded and vngrac'd. *a* **1618** SYLVESTER *Du Bartas* II. Ded. to Essex 14 Daign [thou] to grace my yet vngraced Muse. **1735** THOMSON *Liberty* I. 265 Unadorn'd your hills; Ungrac'd your lakes. **1769** CHURCHILL *Rosciad* 884 To epithets [he] allots emphatic state, Whilst principals, ungrac'd, like lacqueys wait. **1867** JEAN INGELOW *Story of Doom*, etc. 52 Her eyes..looked One moment in the ungraced lover's face. **1889** SKRINE *Mem. Thring* 42 The plain, ungraced, ungifted nature, without destiny or distinction.
b. Const. *by* or *with*.
1768 *Woman of Honor* I. 60 A woman of honor though ungraced with a coronet in her family. **1781** COWPER *Table-T.* 378 Courage, ungrac'd by these, affronts the skies. **1862** H. AIDÉ *Carr of Carrlyon* II. 165, I see..all the deformity ungraced by anything save love.

un'graced, *ppl. a.*² [UN-² 4, 8.] Deprived or stripped *of* something.
1602 MARSTON *Antonio's Rev.* I. ii, Poore Maria must appeare ungrac't Of the bright fulgor of gloss'd majestie.

un'graceful, *a.* (UN-¹ 7.)
1667 MILTON *P.L.* VIII. 218 Nor are thy lips ungraceful, Sire of men, Nor tongue ineloquent. *a* **1732** T. BOSTON *Crook in Lot* (1805) 11 The cause of the uneasy and ungraceful walking of the lame. **1751** EARL ORRERY *Remarks Swift* (1752) 111 These real ornaments, like his hair, were thin and ungraceful. **1821** SCOTT *Kenilw.* xiv, His stature low, his limbs stout, his bearing ungraceful. **1849** MACAULAY *Hist. Eng.* iii. I. 356 The front, though ungraceful, was lofty and richly adorned. **1871** KENNEDY *Lat. Gram.* 467 In Versus Elegiacus a final trisyllable is rare and ungraceful.

un'gracefully, *adv.* (UN-¹ 11: cf. prec.)
1661 COWLEY *Cromwell* Wks. (1669) 74 This Man was wanton and merry (unwittily and ungracefully merry) with our sufferings. **1711** STEELE *Spect.* No. 151 ⁋7 He has been ..ungracefully noisy at such a Time. **1748** CHESTERF. *Lett.* (1774) I. 299, I shall judge of your parts by your speaking gracefully or ungracefully. **1827** LYTTON *Pelham* xiv, In person, Vincent was short and ungracefully formed. **1868** BROWNING *Ring & Bk.* v. 914 Men say I battled ungracefully enough.

un'gracefulness. (UN-¹ 12; cf. prec.)
1658 PHILLIPS, *Inconcinnity*, Ungracefulness. **1673** *Lady's Call.* I. i. ⁋11 Whether it were from the ungracefulness of the thing,.. I shall not determin. **1782** SIR J. REYNOLDS *Disc.* xi. (1825) 75/1 The child..appeared to observe only the ungracefulness of the persons represented. **1835** LYTTON *Rienzi* II. iii, Habituated to the ungracefulness of an unlettered pride. **1867** RUSKIN *Time & Tide* xix. §115, I cannot help what taint of ungracefulness you..may feel that I incur in speaking..of myself.

un'gracious, *a.* [UN-¹ 7 and 5b. Cf. (in sense 5) MDu. *ongracioos*.]
†**1. a.** Of persons: Devoid of spiritual grace; graceless, reprobate, wicked. *Obs.*
In ME. also const. with inf. (quot. 1362).
a **1225** *Ancr. R.* 368 þauh clennesse..beoð ȝeouen of grace, vngraciuse stondeð þer to-ȝeines. *c* **1330** R. BRUNNE *Chron.* (1810) 103 þris þat alle mot se þe light on Roberd toke, Vngracious man was he, þris he it forsoke. **1362** LANGL. *P. Pl.* A. x. 206 False folke..Vn-Gracios to gete loue or eni good elles. *c* **1420** LYDG. *Assembly of Gods* 754 He seyde he shuld haue..With Vyce to do a myghty strong batayll; Of vngracious gastes he bryngeth a long tayll. **1461** *Paston Lett.* II. 59 Ther is an ongracious felaschip of hem and a fals. **1523** LD. BERNERS *Froiss.* I. clxxxii. 217 These myscheuous peple chose hym that was moost vngracyoust of all other. *Ibid.*, Ther were a certayne of the same vngracyous peple bytwene Parys and Noyon. **1579** LODGE *Defence of Poetry* 19 The Angels haue sinned in heauen,..emong yᵉ holy apostles vngratious Iudas. *a* **1638** MEDE *Wks.* (1672) 203 Let him..take heed of familiar and friendly converse with lewd, prophane and ungracious company. **1693** DRYDEN *Juvenal* x. 545 To the Gods alone Our future Offspring, and our Wives are known; Th'audacious Strumpet, and ungracious Son. **1771** FOOTE *Maid of B.* I, Well, you ungracious young dog, and what is become of the poor wench? **1793** BURKE *Conduct Minority* Wks. 1842 I. 623 The consequences are most logically..drawn from the premises..by that wicked and ungracious faction.
transf. **1820** SOUTHEY *Wesley* II. 256 At baptism, it was customary not to dip the right arm,..that he might strike a more deadly and ungracious blow therewith.
†**b.** Of actions, conduct, etc.: Characterized by gracelessness, or wickedness. *Obs.*
1415 SIR T. GREY in *43rd Rep. Dep. Kpr. Rec.* 582 This vngracius and mescheffus gouernaunz. *c* **1485** *Digby Myst.* (1882) IV. 649 Cruell Iewes! what mad yow so bold To commyt þis Crym most vngraciose? *a* **1548** HALL *Chron.*, *Hen. VI*, 104 Inquisicion was made of the authors of this ungracious conjuracion. **1593** SHAKS. *Rich. II*, II. iii. 88 That word Grace, In an vngracious mouth, is but prophane. **1634** SIR T. HERBERT *Trav.* 70 Their sonnes vngracious life opposed their best contentments. **1683** D'URFEY in *Roxb. Ball.* (1888) V. 246 Let Perkin his ungracious errour see, And Toney 'scape no more the Triple-Tree.
†**2.** Unfortunate, unlucky, unfavourable. *Obs.*
1387 TREVISA *Higden* (Rolls) IV. 289 He was most ungracious in homeliche þinges, and happy in oþer þinges. **1398** —— *Barth. De P.R.* XII. xxxvii. (Bodl. MS.), Amonge dyuynours here [*sc.* owls'] voice is vngracious. **1445–50** METHAM *Wks.* 152 The .xv. day ys noght spedeful to be-gynne ony werke vp-on, for yt ys ongracyus. **1515** *Scottish Field* 349 in *Chetham Misc.* (1856) II, They had gotten them a ground Most ungracious of other Upon the toppe of a high hill. *c* **1550** CHEKE *Let.* in *Athenæum* 28 Aug. (1909) 237/3 Until I be mended of my ungracious disease. **1600** HOLLAND *Livy* II. xlix. 78 Then set they forward on their journey,.. taking the ungracious and unluckie way,..untill at length they came to the river Cremera. *a* **1634** CHAPMAN *Rev. for Honour* I. i. 42 To give the noble weasand, Which has the steel defied, to th' hanging mercy Of the ungracious cord.
†**3. a.** Rude; unmannerly. *Obs.*
1534 MORE *Comf. agst. Trib.* II. Wks. 1187/1 Her husband said also that it were lytle synne..to choppe of that vnhappye head of hers, that caryed suche an vngracious tong therin. *c* **1550** *Vertuous Scholehous* Bijb, Thou vsest vngracious wordes, cursest thy good husbande. **1601** SHAKS. *Twel. N.* IV. i. 51 Vngracious wretch, Fit for the Mountaines,..Where manners nere were preach'd. **1606** —— *Tr. & Cr.* I. i. 92 Peace you vngracious Clamors, peace rude sounds.
†**b.** Of low birth and manners. *Obs.*⁻¹
1584 LODGE *Alarum agst. Vsurers* (Hunter. Cl.) 23 Doeth the Weesell loue the Cockatrice? Or gentle borne, such as bee vngratious?
4. a. Not held in favour; unacceptable; disliked.
1598 FLORIO, *Sgrato*, vngratious, nothing acceptable. **1671** CLARENDON *Hist. Reb.* XI. §149 Prince Rupert, at that time, was generally very ungracious in England. **1761** HUME *Hist. Eng.* III. l. 95 Abbot's principle of liberty, and his opposition to Buckingham, had always rendered him very ungracious at court.
b. Unpleasant and unappreciated.
1807 *Med. Jrnl.* XVII. 317 However ungracious the task is, I conceive it necessary to correct mistake. **1844** H. H. WILSON *Brit. India* II. 115 The ungracious duties inseparable from his office. **1884** *L'pool Mercury* 21 June 5/3 It is an ungracious duty to preach saving habits when times are bad.
5. a. Ungraceful, unattractive.
1647 CLARENDON *Hist. Reb.* IV. §122 His Person, and manner of Speaking, were ungratious enough. **1695** DRYDEN *Du Fresnoy's Art Painting* 23 Show no parts which are ungracious to the Sight, as all fore-shortnings usually are. **1762–71** H. WALPOLE *Vertue's Anecd. Paint.* (1786) I. 181 It was difficult to ascertain the period when one ungracious form jostled out another. **1775** T. SHERIDAN *Art Reading* I. 4 The best scholars often..disgraced beautiful composition by an ungracious delivery. **1807** SIR R. WILSON *Jrnl.* 7 May in *Life*, A religion so ungentlemanlike mean and ungracious that I would sooner be a pagan.
b. *ungracious living* (opp. GRACIOUS *a.* 2c).
1958 *Spectator* 4 July 13/2 He had gone straight to a bodge-you-up builder for a slab of ungracious living. **1976** R. RENDELL *Demon in my View* i. 11 The houses were warrens... Ungracious living was evinced by a row of doorbells, seven in an eight-roomed house.
6. Lacking in condescension, courtesy, or affability: **a.** Of actions.
1745 H. WALPOLE *Lett.* (1846) II. 78 An ungracious parallel between the mercenary views of..the regiment-factors,..with the disinterested behaviour of my Lord Kildare, was drawn. **1780** *Mirror* No. 103, An overture of mine towards a reconciliation.., which met with a very ungracious reception. **1844** KINGLAKE *Eothen* xii, Whilst the amber is at your lips, there is nothing ungracious in your remaining silent. **1868** DICKENS *Lett.* (1880) II. 400 Refusal on my part would be too ungracious. **1890** *Lancet* 29 Nov. 1151 It would be ungracious to conclude without expressing my gratitude to our distinguished colleagues.
b. Of persons. Also *fig.* of a country.
1752 YOUNG *Brothers* III. i, Nor in my brother let it pass for virtue, That, as he is, ungracious he would seem. **1819** SHELLEY *Cyclops* 117 Ah! no; they live in an ungracious land. **1849** MACAULAY *Hist. Eng.* v. I. 654 The meek and affable duchess turned out an ungracious and haughty queen. **1864** TENNYSON *Aylmer's Field* 247 Take it,..tho' his gift; For I am more ungracious ev'n than you, I care not for it either.

un'graciously, *adv.* [UN-¹ 11; cf. prec.]
†**1.** With ill fortune; unfortunately, unhappily.
c **1330** R. BRUNNE *Chron.* (1810) 223 To Chestrefeld ilkon þei com vngratiously. þe kyng did þam spie.., assailed þam in þe toun. **1387** TREVISA *Higden* (Rolls) VI. 193 Eiþer of hem hadde hymself so ungraciousliche, þat me woste nevere wheþer of hem hadde worse spede. **1533** FRITH *Judgem. upon Tracy* Wks. (1573) 81/2 And verely the iudgement of this cause came out of season, & euer vngraciously vnto our Canonistes. **1578** *Chr. Prayers* in *Priv. Prayers* (Parker Soc.) 454 We have learned of thee, how ungraciously [L. *infeliciter*] we be born of the first Adam.
†**b.** Injuriously, severely. *Obs.*
c **1450** HOLLAND *Howlat* 840 He cryid: 'Allace,.. I am vngraciously gorrit, baith guttis and gall!' *c* **1520** SKELTON *Magnyf.* 2270 Some rybbys of the motton be so ranke That they wyll fyre one vngracyously in the flanke.
†**2.** Gracelessly: wickedly, wrongfully. *Obs.*
1377 LANGL. *P. Pl.* B. xv. 129 þis þat with gyle was geten, vngraciouslich is spended. *a* **1400** *Partonope* 6432 'Allas,' þoȝte he, 'howe vn-gracyously To my loue haue I gouerned me!' *c* **1520** SKELTON *Magnyf.* 2295 And so vngracyously thy dayes thou hast spent, That thou arte not worthy to loke God in the face. **1581** NOWELL & DAY in *Confer.* I. (1584) F ij, Hee hath most vngratiously broken the vowe made to God in Baptisme. **1645** GATAKER *God's Eye on Israel* 44 Tho they ungratiously and ungratefully..demand of him, wherein he had loved them.
3. Not with a good grace; not pleasantly or agreeably.
1664 JER. TAYLOR *Diss. from Popery* ii. §4. 99 That a wicked person..can ease and take off the punishment..by any external good work done ungraciously, is a piece of new Divinity. **1823** GRACE KENNEDY *Father Clement* i. 18 Permission was always so unwillingly and so ungraciously given, that it was a penance to ask it. **1849** MACAULAY *Hist. Eng.* ii. I. 227 The treasurer..was induced..to become, unwillingly indeed and ungraciously, an agent in those transactions. **1894** H. NISBET *Bush Girl's Rom.* 95 'I'll do that also,' grumbled Timothy, somewhat ungraciously.
4. Unbecomingly; with lack of manners, discourteously.
1736 WARBURTON *Alliance* I. v. 51 They are,..I know not why, ungraciously ashamed of their Pedigree. **1791** BOSWELL *Johnson* (1904) II. 627 *note*, It were to be wished, that he..had not followed the example of Dr. Adam Smith in ungraciously attacking his venerable *Alma Mater*, Oxford. **1829** SCOTT *Anne of G.* xxix, His 'fleecy care' seemed actually to be under the influence of his music, instead of being ungraciously insensible to its melody.

un'graciousness. [UN-¹ 12; cf. prec.]
†**1.** Gracelessness, reprobacy, wickedness. *Obs.*
1509 BARCLAY *Shyp of Folys* (1570) 219 Yet trouble thou not by thy vngraciousnes Suche as are good and liue in righteousnes. **1571** GOLDING *Calvin on Ps.* Ep. Ded. 3 The verye welsprings of all error, hipocrisie, and ungraciousnes. **1612** BRINSLEY *Lud. Lit.* xxiv. (1627) 268 Who cannot indure to see sluggishnesse or idlenesse in any, much lesse any ungraciousnesse. **1658** T. WALL *Charact. Enemies Ch.* 34 Dost thou see a man,..in contempt of goodness, to be a graduate in ungraciousness. **1742** RICHARDSON *Pamela* IV. 353 Can those Persons be surpris'd at the Ungraciousness of their Children?
†**2.** Unfortunate or wretched state. *Obs.*⁻¹
1578 J. STOCKWOOD *Serm. 24 Aug.* 89 Complaintes of the vngraciousnesse and vnhappinesse of schollers.
3. Lack of courtesy or pleasantness.
1836 KEBLE *Let.* in Liddon *Pusey* (1893) I. 428 It was a great piece of ungraciousness, my not telling you sooner how much I am obliged to you. **1864** TENNYSON *Aylmer's F.* 245 O pardon me, I seem to be ungraciousness itself. **1884** *Contemp. Rev.* July 150 To surrender the hand of a woman ..after a great deal of hesitation and ungraciousness.

ungra'dated, *ppl. a.* (UN-¹ 8.)
1859 RUSKIN *Two Paths* App. v. 270 Colour ungradated is wholly valueless.

un'graded, *ppl. a.* [UN-¹ 8.]
1. Not laid out with or in proper gradients.
1845 S. JUDD *Margaret* I. vi. 33 The roads rough, ungraded, and divided by parallel lines of green grass. **1879** MISS BIRD *Lady's Life in Rocky Mount.* 219 Golden City.. is ungraded, with here and there a piece of wooden sidewalk. **1885** *Atlantic Monthly* April 467/1 These roadways, ungraded, unsewered, and unpaved.
2. Not classified by grades.
1884 *Pall Mall G.* 14 Aug. 11/1 Sales have been made of ungraded wheat..at 75 c.

†**un'graduate**, *v. Obs.* [UN-² 4.] *trans.* To degrade.
1633 T. ADAMS *Exp. 2 Peter* iii. 3 Alas, that man should degenerate and ungraduate himselfe to a childe.

un'graduated, *ppl. a.* [UN-¹ 8.]
1. That has not graduated; having no University degree.
1783 H. WALPOLE *Let. to Earl Strafford* 12 Sept., I am glad at least that they have ungraduated assessors. **1802–12** BENTHAM *Ration. Judic. Evid.* (1827) V. 120 Your learned brethren, and their ungraduated fellow-practisers, the barristers of the present time. **1867** SEEBOHM *Oxford Reformers* 6 Another Oxford Student,..yet ungraduated in divinity, not even in deacon's orders.
2. Not graded or regularly arranged.
1841 MYERS *Cath. Th.* III. §4. 11 So ungraduated an estimate of Duty as this. **1899** *Allbutt's Syst. Med.* VII. 363 These [limbs] being..raised and set down in a brusque and characteristically ungraduated fashion.

un'graft, *v.* (UN-² 3.)
1600 SURFLET *Countrie Farme* III. v. 432 You must also take graftes and graft them in other plum trees,..and not to vngraft siences to transplant them.

†**un'graft**, obs. var. of next.
1598 SYLVESTER *Du Bartas* II. i. I *Eden* 525 A plenteous Orchard planted rare With un-graft Trees.

un'grafted, *ppl. a.* (UN-¹ 8.)
1657 AUSTEN *Fruit Trees* II. 175 Fruit trees that are ungrafted (wild trees). **1766** *Compl. Farmer* s.v. *Fence*, If they have proceeded from apple-kernels, they may remain ungrafted. **1795** *Phil. Trans.* LXXXV. 293 The bearing branches of some old ungrafted pear-trees. **1905** HAGGARD *Gard. Year* 235 An ungrafted bush of..the common stock.

†**un'grained**, *a. Obs.*⁻¹ [UN-¹ 9.] Seedless.
c **1440** *Palladius on Husb.* III. 1121 Vngreyned grape in high iocundite Me may suppe of.

†**un'grained**, *ppl. a.*¹ *Obs.* [UN-¹ 8.] Not dyed in grain.
1502 ARNOLDE *Chron.* (1811) 193 The Subside of Cloth as wel in greine as vngreyned.

un'grained, *ppl. a.*[2] [UN-[1] 8.] Not reduced to separate grains.
1884 E. F. KNIGHT *Cruise Falcon* I. xv. 266 When the maize arrived..we found it was ungrained.

un'graining, *vbl. sb.* [UN-[2] 4, 8.] (See quot.)
1839 URE *Dict. Arts* 613 *Ungraining* [of gilt work] consists in rubbing the whole work with shave-grass, to remove any granular appearance.

†**un'graith**, *a. Obs.* [UN-[1] 7. Cf. ON. *úgreiðr* (Norw. *ugreid*).] **a.** Unready. **b.** Not straightforward; perverse.
a **1310** in Wright *Lyric P.* xxxvi. 99 Vol of merci thou art ay, al ungreythe icham to the to go. *a* **1400** *Pistill of Susan* 293 Vmbeloke ȝou, lordes; suche lawes ben leiþ;..Aȝein to þe ȝild-halle, ȝe gomes vngreiþ.

un'graithed, *ppl. a. Obs.* exc. *dial.* (UN-[1] 8.)
c **1290** *Beket* 2200 in *S. Eng. Leg.* I. 169 þat bodi..Al ongreiþet [*v.r.* ungreithed] to leggen it in [the grave] heo heiȝeden bliue. **1876** *Whitby Gloss.* 206/1 *Ungraith'd*, not yet furnished or equipped; unadorned.

†**un'graithly**, *adv. Obs.* Also 4 vngretli, 5 vngraidly. [UN-[1] 11.] Badly, improperly.
a **1300** *Cursor M.* 24504 On him mi hefd i scock, and said, Vngretli, leif sun, er þou graid! *c* **1400** *Destr. Troy* 7615 As folis, þat folily hade..Myche gold & goodes vngraidly dispendit. *c* **1460** *Towneley Myst.* x. 341, I that thus haue vngrathly gone, And vntruly taken apon Mary, that dere darlyng. *Ibid.* xxvii. 100.

un'grammared, *a.* (UN-[1] 9.)
1837 FR. A. KEMBLE *Rec. Later Life* (1882) I. 119 Uncultivated men, unlettered, and ungrammared.

ungra'mmatic, *a.* [UN-[1] 7.] = next.
1806 ANNA SEWARD *Lett.* (1811) VI. 258 All modes of phraseology within the limits of the immodest, the disgusting, and the ungrammatic. **1850** BROWNING *Christmas Eve* XXII. 30 Fourthly, the English is ungrammatic.

ungra'mmatical, *a.* [UN-[1] 7 and 5 b.]
1. a. Not in accordance with the rules of grammar.
1654 JER. TAYLOR *Real Pres.* §5. 88 [To] expound it in a sense which suffers a violence and a most unnatural, ungrammatical torture. **1679** DRYDEN *Troil. & Cress.* Pref. ¶1 Of those [words] which we understand, some are ungrammatical, others coarse. **1749** CHESTERF. *Let.* 5 Dec., His diction was not only inelegant, but frequently ungrammatical, always vulgar. **1821** LAMB *Elia* I. *Mrs. Battle on Whist*, She called it an ungrammatical game. **1848** THACKERAY *Van. Fair* xxxii, French..of a very ungrammatical sort. **1883** *Law Rep.* 11 *Q.B. Div.* 614 A defining section, confused and ungrammatical.
b. Not observing the rules of grammar.
1859 *Habits of Gd. Society* iii. 155, I am wondering whether everybody arranges his wardrobe as our ungrammatical nurses used to do ours. **1871** EARLE *Philol. Eng. Tongue* 412 So they (the ungrammatical people) made a plural *this-e*.
2. At variance with correct rule or method.
1851 RUSKIN *Mod. Paint.* I. II. II. ii. §12 Some really ungrammatical and false picture of the old masters. **1903** G. BALDWIN BROWN *Arts Early Eng.* II. viii. 327 The enrichment of the wall surfaces..is..in parts quite ungrammatical.
Hence **,ungrammati'cality; ungra'mmaticalness.**
1698 *Christ Exalted* §xi. 9 Omitting several Blunders of Ungrammaticalness. **1803** *Gentl. Mag.* LXXIII. I. 145 To vindicate the dialect of London..from the imputation of vulgarisms and ungrammaticalness. **1961** *Word* XVII. 6 On the other hand, sentences which are not universally rejected do not show ungrammaticality either total, or to a significant degree. **1967** R. W. LANGACKER *Language & its Structure* II. iv. 94 It is important not to confuse ungrammaticalness with excessive complexity that makes a sentence difficult or impossible to use. **1969** D. T. LANGENDOEN *Study of Syntax* ii. 8 Ungrammaticality arises not when there is merely internal contradiction within a linguistic object, but when it is felt that the object possesses some gross deformity in comparison with sentences in the language. **1975** *Language* LI. 579 The two sources of ungrammaticality in written texts are slips of the pen..and deliberate breaches of grammar.

ungra'mmatically, *adv.* (UN-[1] 11.)
1727 BOYER *Dict. Royal* II. **1737** *Gentl. Mag.* VII. 13/2 As A. P. has very weakly, as well as unliterally and ungrammatically translated. **1763** BP. LOWTH *Introd. Eng. Gram.* 32 *note*, Some Writers have used *Ye*, as the Objective Case.., very improperly and ungrammatically. **1860** HUXLEY in *Life* (1900) I. 214 Some of the..articles being absolutely ungrammatically written.

un'grantable, *a.* (UN-[1] 7 b.)
1784 R. BAGE *Barham Downs* II. 258 'You shall be allowed to give and grant it, out of your own free will.'.. 'Ungrantable,' says Sir George. **1794** LD. MACARTNEY *Wks.* (1807) II. 326 A court artifice to elude an ungrantable demand.

un'granted, *ppl. a.* (UN-[1] 8.)
1570 LEVINS *Manip.* 50 Vngranted, *inconcessus*. **1660** BONDE *Scut. Reg., Hist. Phaeton* 12 He wisht..His suites ungranted. **1697** DRYDEN *Æneis* IX. 377 This only from your goodness let me gain; (And, this ungranted, all rewards are vain). **1828** P. CUNNINGHAM *N.S. Wales* (ed. 3) II. 333 The local administration..having the sole disposal of the ungranted lands. **1870** MORRIS *Earthly Par.* IV. IV. 385 He some day might..turn away from that ungranted kiss.

un'grapple, *v.* (UN-[2] 4 b.)
1611 COTGR., *Desagrafer*, to vnclaspe, vngraple, vnhaspe. *a* **1642** SIR W. MONSON *Naval Tracts* II. (1704) 246/2 Our Barks were forc'd to ungraple and fall off. **1653** URQUHART *Rabelais* I. xlii. 188 The Monk going about to ungrapple his vizor, let go his hold of the bridle.
Hence **un'grappler**.
1891 C. E. NORTON tr. *Dante, Hell* xxii. 119 The heat was a sudden ungrappler.

un'grasp, *v.* (UN-[2] 3.)
1621 BP. MOUNTAGU *Diatribæ* 328 He might have knowne ..yt Popes vse neuer to vngraspe what they haue griped. *a* **1784** C. DUNSTER in Chambers *Illustr. Worcester* (1820) 555 Have I not seen at thy command, Avarice herself ungrasp her hand?

un'graspable, *a.* (UN-[1] 7 b.)
1741 RICHARDSON *Pamela* I. Introd. p. xxvi, A beautiful Girl of Sixteen, who..had not, yet, reach'd ungraspable Roundness. **1822** POLLOK in D. Pollok *Life* (1843) 129 The ungraspable spectres of the night. **1853** CDL. WISEMAN *Ess.* II. 305 Of all slippery phrases in controversy, a metaphorical one is the most ungraspable. **1880** 'MARK TWAIN' *Tramp Abroad* I. 168 How ungraspable is the fact that real men ever did fight in real armour.

un'grasped, *ppl. a.* (UN-[1] 8.)
1743 YOUNG *Nt. Th.* IV. 241 Its value vast, ungraspt by minds create. **1897** MATHER *Ruskin* (ed. 5) p. xvii, Even though the truth burdening the style remains vague and is ungrasped by the reader.

un'grasping, *ppl. a.* (UN-[1] 10.)
1855 FABER *Growth in Holiness* viii. 128 Humility..makes us unanxious, ungrasping,..and calm.

un'grassed, (*ppl.*) *a.* [UN-[1] 8, 9.] Not sown with grass.
1934 in WEBSTER. **1947** *Sun* (Baltimore) 26 June 10/3 The visitors saw evidence of erosion in corn fields and former timberland, steep embankments along roadsides and ungrassed drainage ditches. **1974** R. ADAMS *Shardik* xlii. 339 At a little distance were four or five mounds of newly-turned earth, ungrassed and strewn with a few flowers.

†**un'grate**, *a.* and *sb. Obs.* [UN-[1] 7 and 5 b.]
1. Unpleasant, disagreeable; = INGRATE *a.* 1.
1550 CROWLEY *Inform. & Petit.* 469 To passe ouer the days of theyr youth in vngrate seruitude. **1646** R. BAILLIE *Lett.* (Bann. Cl.) II. 364 It's a marvell to me if these men should allwayes prosper, their wayes are so impious, unjust, ungrate, and every way hatefull. **1656** *Artif. Handsom.* 46 Impertinent and ungrate must that superstition be.
2. a. Ungrateful; = INGRATE *a.* 3. (In later use chiefly *Sc.*)
a **1548** HALL *Chron., Hen. VII*, 12 Kyng Henry..thought it..necessary..to forgett the vngrate offence agaynst the duke of Briteyne commytted. *Ibid.* 26 b, So vngrate people were they to their soueraigne lorde. **1561** T. HOBY tr. *Castiglione's Courtyer* I. (1577) C vi, To discouer the deceytes of an ungrate woman, who..neuer agreeth hir tong wyth hyr minde. **1606** MARSTON *Sophonisba* II. ii, But, Carthage, fie! It cannot be ungrate, faithlesse through feare. **1697** G. KEITH *2nd Narr. Proc. Turner's Hall* 6 Judge.. whether they be not a very ungrate People. **1720** A. PETRIE *Rules Good Deportm.* (1877) 24 It is rude and ungrate to leave a House..without your taking Leave of the Master and Mistress. **1767** MESTON *Poems* 196 Ye Muses, who were never yet ungrate, When you your benefactors deed relate.
arch. **1922** JOYCE *Ulysses* 394 The men of the island, seeing no help was toward as the ungrate women were all of one mind, made a wherry raft.
b. *sb.* An ungrateful person; an ingrate.
c **1400** *Destr. Troy* 13944 þan he..told hym full tyte, þat Telagon he was, His son,..þat þou gate on þi gamyn, as vngrate felle. **1596** DALRYMPLE tr. *Leslie's Hist. Scot.* I. 122 A murthirer, a dum, or vngrate to his parents. **1689** *Gt. Bastard, Protector of Little One* 5 It was indeed the true Motive that induc'd this Vngrate to ruin them. **1720–1** *Lett. fr. Mist's Jrnl.* (1722) II. 118 The Sweetness of my Lips, which that Ungrate too oft has praised.

un'grateful, *a.* [UN-[1] 7 and 5 b.]
1. Not feeling or displaying gratitude.
1553 BRENDE *Q. Curtius* x. 216 The Macedons.. confessyng them selues bothe wicked and vngrateful for depriuyng him of anye name wherof he was worthye. **1587** *Mirr. for Mag., Albanact* lxii, If you ungratefull mindes doe beare, What meaneth death to let mee linger here. **1621** in Foster *Eng. Factories Ind.* (1906) I. 354 Such base ungratfull slaves they bee. **1697** DRYDEN *Æneis* IV. 529 All, symptoms of a base ungrateful mind, So foul, that which is worse, 'tis hard to find. **1740** RICHARDSON *Pamela* II. 356 If it was, I must be the ungratefullest Person in the World, because I am the most obliged Person in it. **1813** SCOTT *Rokeby* IV. xx, Ungrateful to God's clemency, That spared me penitential time. **1875** JOWETT *Plato* (ed. 2) III. 206 That I am ungrateful I wholly deny.
absol. **1675** DRYDEN *Aurengz.* IV. (1676) 64 Th' ungrateful does a more ungrateful find. **1690** *The Great Scanderbeg* 82 The Ungrateful despises my flame with a cruel obstinacy. **1829** LYTTON *Devereux* I. i, He could not persuade his lips to repeat a sarcasm hurting even the dead or the ungrateful.
spec. **1785** GROSE *Dict. Vulgar T.*, *Ungrateful man*, a parson, who at least once a week abuses his best benefactor, i.e. the devil.
b. Of actions, etc.: Displaying lack of gratitude.
a **1586** SIDNEY *Arcadia* III. iv, By ungratefull scorning the ornaments of Nature, am I now piping in a shadow? **1641** PRYNNE *Antipathie* 9 O perfidious, ungratefull Councell and swasion of this Prelate. **1700** PRIOR *Carm. Sec.* xxxv, Nor let the Muses, with ungrateful Pride, The Sources of their Treasure hide. **1799** *Med. Jrnl.* I. 220 Asserting, that contemporary writers received his works with an ungrateful silence. **1825** SCOTT *Betrothed* xix, These sentiments..I have combated..as being..ungrateful to you.
c. *transf.* Of soil, trees, etc.: Not responding to cultivation.
1681 DRYDEN *Abs. & Achit.* I. 12 A soil ungrateful to the Tiller's care. **1732** POPE *Ess. Man* II. 181 As fruits, ungrateful to the planter's care, On savage stocks inserted, learn to bear. **1788** GIBBON *Decl. & F.* l. V. 178 Their ungrateful soil refused the labours of agriculture. **1842** BORROW *Bible in Spain* xxiii, The land is ungrateful and barren. **1864** TREVELYAN *Compet. Wallah* (1866) 288 The labourers in this ungrateful vineyard.
2. Unpleasant, disagreeable, distasteful.
1596 DAVIES *Orchestra* 19 [To] tell..How she illudes.. Th'vngratefull loue which other Lords began. **1641** *Vind. Smectymnuus* iii. 53 It is in his power to save himselfe and us this ungrateful labour. **1691** HARTCLIFFE *Virtues* 178 For a Man to praise or dispraise himself is ungrateful, and quickly cloyes the hearer. **1753** HANWAY *Trav.* (1762) v. lxxi. I. 320 Monopolies..are generally ungrateful to the people of a free state. **1776** GIBBON *Decl. & F.* xii. I. 325 The ungrateful rumour reached his ears. **1836** J. GILBERT *Chr. Atonem.* ix. (1852) 281 Even the kindness.., though not ungrateful, will not excite the proper working of esteem.
b. Of taste or smell, or of things in respect of these.
1597 GERARDE *Herbal* I. xxviii. 34 These roots haue a strong..smell, and somewhat an vngratefull taste. **1612** WOODALL *Surg. Mate* Wks. (1653) 307 Laudanum is best to be taken in a Pill, because of his ungrateful tast. **1663** BP. PATRICK *Parab. Pilgr.* xxviii, Good wine which..is rendred ..acid and ungrateful to our palate. *a* **1682** SIR T. BROWNE *Tracts* (1683) 12 That which we now have is of an ungrateful odour. **1725** SLOANE *Jamaica* II. 17 The Nuts.. are then tosted,..and made into an ungrateful drink. **1753** HANWAY *Trav.* v. lx. (1762) I. 279 The reeds through which we passed sent forth an ungrateful stench. **1846** MRS. A. MARSH *Father Darcy* II. ii. 69 There he sat—endeavouring to touch the ungrateful food. **1897** *Allbutt's Syst. Med.* III. 465 By which certain foods are recognised, consciously or not, as grateful or ungrateful.
c. Of sounds.
1659 O. WALKER *Instruct. Oratory* 24 Too many Consonants or Vowells comming together are to be avoided, as causing an ungrateful sound. **1690** C. NESSE *O. & N. Test.* I. 16 Some sounds..are very harsh and ungrateful. **1759** GOLDSM. *Polite Learn.* ii, It was the poet who harmonized the ungrateful accents of his native dialect. **1850** TENNYSON *In Mem.* xxxviii. 12 Then are these songs I sing of thee Not all ungrateful to thine ear.

un'gratefully, *adv.* [UN-[1] 11 and 5 b.]
1. Harshly, unpleasantly, disagreeably.
1581 SIDNEY *Apol. Poetrie* (Arb.) 42 Telling of a man, whose beloued Lambe was vngratefullie taken from his bosome. **1693** DRYDEN *Juvenal* (1697) p. lxxxi, It tickles aukwardly with a kind of pain;..we are pleas'd ungratefully, and, if I may say so, against our liking. **1698** HEARNE *Duct. Hist.* (1714) I. 385 Cæsar..returned to Rome and triumphed, though a little ungratefully to some of Pompey's friends. **1712** ARBUTHNOT *John Bull* II. v, The musick.. sounded more ungratefully in her ears than the noise of a screech-owl.
†**2.** Without due return or gratitude. *Obs.*[−1]
1593 NASHE *Christ's T.* P 1 b, Vngratefully hath God giuen thee long peace and plenty, since..thy peace and plentie hath begotte more sinnes then warre euer hearde of.
3. With lack of gratitude.
a **1625** FLETCHER *Hum. Lieutenant* III. vi, I am not greedy of your lives and fortunes, Nor do I gape ungratefully to swallow ye. **1692** WASHINGTON tr. *Milton's Def. Pop.* M.'s Wks. 1738 I. 537 Yet these very men did a great part of the People ungratefully desert in the midst of their undertaking. **1737** in *10th Rep. Hist. MSS. Comm.* App. I. 493 A Person in whom your Majesty has placed a Trust and who has so Ungratefully abused that Trust. **1798** PENNANT *Hindoostan* II. 47 He continued in employ till 1754, when he was ungratefully superseded. **1856** *N. Brit. Rev.* XXVI. 195 Having been coldly and (as he thought) ungratefully treated by the Whig leaders.

un'gratefulness. [UN-[1] 12 and 5 b.]
1. = INGRATITUDE 1.
1581 SIDNEY *Apol. Poetrie* (Arb.) 20 They goe very neer to vngratefulnes, to seek to deface that which..hath been the first light-giuer to ignorance. **1599** SANDYS *Europæ Spec.* (1632) 247 Those graces and blessings, which vngratefulnesse would not acknowledge. **1631** GOUGE *God's Arrows* I. §20. 27 O the ungratefulnesse of the wicked in the world! **1734** CHALKLEY *Jrnl.* Wks. (1766) 271 A Youth.. went out hastily..as I was showing the Ungratefulness of the first [*sc.* disobedience], much more of the last. **1896** *Cincinnati* (Ohio) *Sunday Sch. Jrnl.* Apr. 237/1 The ungratefulness of people to those who have helped them.
2. Unpleasantness; disagreeableness. *rare.*
a **1680** GLANVILL in *Disc., Serm., & Rem.* (1681) 338 He (considering the ungratefulness of the Message..) diverts another way, and flees towards Tarshish. *a* **1688** CUDWORTH *Immut. Mor.* (1731) 54 The Gratefulness and Ungratefulness of Tastes and Smells.

†**un'grately**, *adv. Obs.* [UN-[1] 11 and 5 b.] Ungratefully.
1548 ELYOT, *Ingratè*, vngrately, vnthankefully. *c* **1614** SIR W. MURE *Dido & Æneas* II. 412 A woman..My mariage most vngrately hath disdain'd.

un'gratified, *ppl. a.* (UN-[1] 8.)
1613 FLETCHER, etc. *Hon. Man's Fort.* I. i, By the justice now Of thine own rule,..I should turn thee away ungratified For all thy former kindness. **1728** ELIZA HEYWOOD tr. *Mme. de Gomez's Belle A.* (1732) II. 17 That Request being refused, he made his escape privately, resolving that the Queen should not be long ungratified. **1779** JOHNSON *L.P., Waller* Wks. II. 269 The poem of Davis, which..seldom leaves the ear ungratified. **1821** BYRON *Sardanap.* I. ii. 582 Leaving thy subjects' eyes ungratified. **1865** TREVELYAN *Cawnpore* 67 No whim ungratified, every propensity cherished and pampered. **1894** H. NISBET *Bush Girl's Rom.* 263 He had not a wish left ungratified.

un'gratifying, *ppl. a.* (UN-¹ 10.)
1697 COLLIER *Ess. Mor. Subj.* III. (1703) 115 Envy is of all others the most ungratifying and disconsolate passion. 1885 *Law Times* 3 Jan. 172/2 It will not be ungratifying to have the statute more authoritatively expounded.

†**un'gratitude.** *Obs.* [UN-¹ 12 and 5b.] Ingratitude; ungratefulness.
a 1548 HALL *Chron., Edw. IV*, 249b, That the sequele thereof, maie rather turne..to an vngratitude, than to a rewarde. *Ibid., Rich. III*, 34b, All these vngratitudes and vndeserued vnkindnes I..suffered pacientelie. 1621 LADY M. WROTH *Urania* 29, I..neuer could be wonne to thinke of harming him, whose vngratitude I beleeu'd sufficiently would one day burden him. 1685 J. FRASER *Let.* in *Academy* 21 Oct. (1876) 408/2 The Princess..giving a Reprimand for their ungratitud, dismissed them.

†**un'grave,** *a. Obs.* (UN-¹ 7.)
1609 J. DAVIES (Heref.) *Holy Roode* Wks. (Grosart) I. 7/1 Now thinke..thou seest those hounds of hell,..With vngraue gate, to runne doe him compell. 1642 in Clarendon *Hist. Reb.* v. §276 Sure,..the Penner of that Declaration inserted that ungrave and insolent expression,..without the consent..of both Houses. *a* 1674 CLARENDON *Surv. Leviath.* 73 A very bold and ungrave wresting of Scripture.

un'grave, *v.* [UN-² 5.] *trans.* To take out of the grave; to disinter.
1664 J. WILSON *Commenius* II. i, I scorn to raze Thy monument, or to ungrave thy dust. 1788 MICKLE *Eskdale Braes* ix, As the spectres, ungrav'd, glide along. 1849 ROCK *Ch. of Fathers* II. vi. 179 *note*, The unknown bishop whose body was as late as A.D. 1827, ungraved in Durham cathedral. 1866 R. MORRIS *Ayenb.* 61 *margin*, The beast Hyane, who ungraves dead men's bodies and eats them.

un'graved, *ppl. a.* [UN-¹ 8.] Unburied.
a 1547 SURREY *Æneid* IV. 832 His realme, nor life desired may he brooke; But fall before his time, ungraved amid the sandes. 1635 PAGITT *Christianogr.* I. 131 After his death..he was ungraved and kept above ground 5 yeares.

un'gravelled, *ppl. a.* (UN-¹ 8.)
1611 W. AUSTIN *Paneg. Verses* 3 in Coryat *Crudities*, To him that farre and neere hath traueld, Gone & retourned, his wit ungraveld. 1616 [see UNDASHED *ppl. a.* 1].

un'gravelly, *a.* (UN-¹ 7.)
1655 MOUFET & BENNET *Health's Improv.* 213 The most clear, transparent, thin-skind, ungravelly [apples].

un'gravely, *adv.* (UN-¹ 11.)
1607 SHAKS. *Cor.* II. iii. 233 His present portance, Which most gibingly, vngrauely, he did fashion After the inueterate Hate he beares you. 1698 *Christ Exalted* Ep. A4 The Doctor, whom you have very ungravely treated, as an Heterodox wild Monster.

un'graven, *ppl. a.* Also 4 vngraue. [UN-¹ 8b. Cf. (M)Du. *ongegraven* unburied, undug.]
1. Not engraved or carved.
1377 LANGL. *P. Pl.* B. IV. 130 That..Rome-renneres [take]..no siluer ouer see,..Noyther graue ne vngraue. 1611 FLORIO, *Inscolpito*, vncarued, vngrauen. 1651 STANLEY *Poems* 169 The oaks that most obdurate are Shall..by themselves ungraven wear My verse upon their leaves and rind. 1855 M. ARNOLD *Balder Dead* II. 165 Young men who died Too soon for fame, with white ungraven shields.
†2. Unburied, uninterred. *Obs.*
c 1400 *Laud Troy Bk.* 11104 Kyng Priamus Thought.. Where he myght saue Ector his sone Vngrauen with-oute corrupcione. *c* 1425 WYNTOUN *Cron.* v. x. 2590 Mony a day Vngraiffin [*v.r.* vngrawyn] outwith þe erd he lay.

ungrayhair, *v.* (UN-² 4.)
1639 FULLER *Holy War* III. xxix. 160 Whilest his old wife plucked out his black hairs.., his young one ungray-haired him.

un'graze, *v.* [UN-² 4.] *trans.* To render unfit for grazing.
1661 FELTHAM *Resolves* (ed. 8) II. xlvi. 273 No crowded throngs need fill our Law-Tribunals; nor armed Troops ungraze our fruitful fields.

un'grease, *v.* (UN-² 4.)
1611 COTGR., *Desgraisser*, to vnfatten; vngrease. 1799 G. SMITH *Laboratory* I. 436 To ungrease Wine in less than twenty-four hours.

un'greased, *ppl. a.* (UN-¹ 8.)
c 1440 *Jacob's Well* 260 As a carte-qweel, drye & vngrecyd, cryeth lowdest of oþere qwelys. 1663 BOYLE *Usef. Exp. Nat. Philos.* II. v. xiv. 250 The grating of an ungreased cartwheele upon the axle-tree. 1668 SHADWELL *Sullen Lovers* IV, What a vile noise he makes, worse than..a coach-wheel ungreas'd. 1783 LATHAM *Gen. Syn.* IV. 687 Having a creaking harsh kind of note, somewhat like..an ungreased axle-tree. *a* 1894 STEVENSON *Lay Morals*, etc. (1911) 247 A creaking of ungreased axles had been heard.

un'greasing, *vbl. sb.* (UN-² 4, 8.)
1883 R. HALDANE *Workshop Receipts* Ser. II. 321/1 The cleansing or separation of the peritoneal membrane, a portion only of which has been removed by the 'ungreasing' at the slaughter-house.

†**un'great,** *a. Obs.* In 6 *Sc.* ongrit. [UN-¹ 7.] Small.
1549 *Compl. Scotl.* xiv. 113 And als it vas as ongrit blythnes to sa mony..tounis quhilkis hed randrit them..to Annibal.

un-'Grecian, *a.* (UN-¹ 7.)
1799 F. BURNEY *Let. a* 19 Nov. (1973) IV. 359 William there may see Noses to his mind—& if difficult already, make himself 10 times more so with every ungrecian one he sees. 1847 LEITCH tr. *C. O. Müller's Anc. Art* §206. 171 The reliefs on sarcophagi..did not come into general use until this period, through the influence of un-Grecian ideas. 1859 E. MASSON *Winer's Gram. N.T. Diction* I. Introd. 14 Peculiarities manifestly derived from an un-Grecian source.

un'greeable, *a. Obs.* exc. *dial.* [UN-¹ 7b.] Disagreeable.
1550 *Chaucer's Boethius* I. met. i. 220b, Myne vnpytous lyfe draweth alonge vngreable dwellinges [L. *ingratas moras*]. 1580 E. KNIGHT *Trial Truth* 4b, This doctrine is so vngreeable vnto the children of pride, as [etc.]. 1886 CUNLIFFE *Rochdale Gloss.* 94 *Ungreeable*, disagreeable.

†**un'greeing,** *ppl. a. Obs.* [UN-¹ 10.] Unfitting.
1560 J. HEYWOOD *Seneca's Thyestes* Translatour to Bk., Though thou slender volume be, Vngreeyng gyfte for state of honour guest.

un-'Greek, *sb.* and *a.* [UN-¹ 12 and 7. Cf. (in sense 1) Du. *Ongriek*, G. *Ungrieche* (Luther), older Da. *Ugræke*.]
A. *sb.* One who is not a Greek. *rare.*
1535 COVERDALE *Rom.* i. 14, I am detter both to the Grekes, and to the vngrekes.
B. *adj.* Not Greek in character; not in accordance with Greek ideas or habits.
1846 KEIGHTLEY *Notes Virg.* 332 Supplying..a totally un-Latin *secundum*, in Greek a κατά, which is for the most part quite as un-Greek. 1853 WHEWELL *Grotius* III. 221 The slaughter of the Thebans, who had surrendered, was an un-Greek massacre. 1871 JOWETT *Plato* II. 38 One of the most remarkable conceptions of the Republic [of Plato], because un-Greek in character.

un'green, *a.* (UN-¹ 7: cf. OE. *ungréne*, Du. *ongroen*, MHG. *ungrüene*.)
c 1400 *Rom. Rose* 4749 May devoide of al delite With seer braunches, blossoms vngrene. 1838 MRS. E. B. BROWNING *Seraphim* II. 32, I see her vales, ungreen Where steps of man have been!

un'greenable, *a.* (UN-¹ 7b.)
1882 [see GREENABLE *a.*].

un'greeted, *ppl. a.* (UN-¹ 8. Cf. OE. *unȝegrét*, MDu. *ongegroetet*, MHG. *ungegrüezet*.)
1611 FLORIO, *Insalutato*, vnsaluted, vngreeted. 1648 HEXHAM II, *Ongegroetet*, Vnsaluted, or Vngreeted. *a* 1849 POE *Angel of Odd* Wks. 1864 IV. 285 My premeditated rudeness in passing her by ungreeted. 1877 TALMAGE *Serm.* 322 This Young Man was not ungreeted when he came back.

un'greeting, *ppl. a.* (UN-¹ 10.)
1855 M. ARNOLD *Haworth Churchyard* 142 Faces ungreeting and cold.

ungre'garious, *a.* (UN-¹ 7.)
1829 SOUTHEY in *Corr. w. C. Bowles* (1881) 173 Which would infallibly have made me a Beguine,..if I was not a most ungregarious animal. 1884 AUGUSTA WILSON *Vashti* xi, They appeared as gravely silent and ungregarious as Sphinxes.

†**ungrete**: see UN-¹ 3.

ungretli, obs. var. UNGRAITHLY *adv.*

†**un'grieffulness.** *Obs.*⁻¹ (UN-¹ 12.)
1553 GRIMALDE *Cicero's Offices* III. (1558) 118 As they who measure thyngs meete to bee desired eyther by pleasure or ungrieffulnes.

un'grieve, *v.* (UN-² 4b.)
1589 WARNER *Alb. Eng.* VI. xxix. 129 For you were boote es then to gesse how to vngreeue my smart.

un'grieved, *ppl. a.* (UN-¹ 8.)
1676 HOBBES *Iliad* I. 397 Ay me, (said Thetis) would you could here rest Unhurt, ungriev'd. 1837 VERLANDER *Vestal*, etc. 74 And joy'st thou in the life unliv'd?..the griefs ungriev'd?

un'grieving, *ppl. a.* (UN-¹ 10.)
1837 PRAED *Drachenfels* 142 If the blinded tribes..Could but have caught one bright brief glance Of that ungrieving countenance.

†**un'grieving,** *pres. pple. Sc. Obs.* [UN-¹ 5d.] Without grieving, distressing, or injuring.
c 1375 *Sc. Leg. Saints* xxxiii. (*George*) 517 Vngrewand hyme mare þan he Had drunkyne pyment & clarre. 1456 SIR G. HAYE *Law Arms* (S.T.S.) 162 How may than a man do till othir sik dissait, ungrevand God?

†**un'gright,** *ppl. a. Obs.* [UN-¹ 8b: see GRUTCH *v.*] Ungrudgingly; readily.
c 1400 *Destr. Troy* 8868 Priam..grauntid vngright with a good chere. *a* 1400-50 *Bk. Curtasye* 751 in *Babees Bk.*, Þo Coke assayes þe mete vngryȝt.

un'grindable, *a.* (UN-¹ 7b.)
1840 CARLYLE in A. H. Stirling *Life Stirling* (1912) iii. 50 Windmills..to grind..sunbeams, or some other entirely ungrindable substance.

†**ungrith**: see UN-¹ 3.

un'grizzled, *ppl. a.* (UN-¹ 8.)
1858 MOTLEY *Corr.* (1889) I. 311 Having thick, brown, ungrizzled hair and beard.

un'groaning, *ppl. a.* (UN-¹ 10.)
1821 BYRON *Sardanap.* I. ii. 265 Enough For me, if I can ..glide Ungroaning to the tomb.

un'groomed, *ppl. a.* (UN-¹ 8.)
1829 G. GRIFFIN *Collegians* I. x. 216 Close behind..on that long-backed, ungroomed creature..rides the crafty Ulysses of the assemblage. 1864 SALA in *Daily Tel.* 26 Feb., Their horses as ungroomed, and their hair as unkempt as usual.

un'gropable, *a.* (UN-¹ 7b.)
1558 PHAER *Æneid* VI. Riij b, Through his hands he flies Like wind vngropable, or dreames.

un'ground, *ppl. a.* [UN-¹ 8b.]
1. Not ground in a mill; not crushed or reduced to powder.
1488 *Acta Dom. Conc.* (1839) 98/2 Half a boll of malt vngrond, price xs. 1623 FLETCHER & ROWLEY *Maid in Mill* v. ii, Shall the sayls of my love stand still? Shall the grists of my hopes be unground? 1631 GOUGE *God's Arrows* II. §24. 163 Some of them did eate the corne as it was unground. 1722 DE FOE *Col. Jack* (1840) 300 A hundred sacks of unground malt. 1760 *Ann. Reg., Chron.* 192/2 A duty of 1d. ½..shall be paid on every bushel of malt, whether ground or unground, which [etc.]. 1805 DICKSON *Pract. Agric.* I. 211 The trials which Dr. Hunter made with ground and unground bones. 1882 *U.S. Rep. Prec. Met.* 603 The mill is then stopped, [and] the water drained off from the unground sand and mercury.
2. Not sharpened, smoothed, or worn down by grinding.
1611 COTGR. s.v. *Morfil*, The edge side of a new and vnground knife. 1793 *Phil. Trans.* LXXXIII. 92 The swinging level.., fixed to the tube of the telescope,..is unground. 1865 TYLOR *Early Hist. Man.* viii. 193 The finding of hundreds of unground implements. 1893 *Athenæum* 25 Mar. 382/2 The palæolithic or unground stage of the implement-maker's art.

un'groundable, *a.*; **-ably,** *adv.* (UN-¹ 7b, 11.)
1395 PURVEY *Remonstr.* (1851) 84 The noveltees of this Innocent,..that ben ungroundable and unlicli to be sothe. *c* 1449 PECOCK *Repr.* I. xviii. 104 Rather he schal be schamed that he hath it bifore so vngroundabili holde, and withoute suficient evidence thereto.

un'grounded, *ppl. a.* [UN-¹ 8. Cf. MDu. *ongegrondet*, *-gront* (Du. *-grond*), G. *ungegründet*, Da. *ugrundet*, Sw. *ogrundad*.]
1. Not based or established *in* something.
c 1380 WYCLIF *Wks.* (1880) 38 Euyle lawis vngroundid in holy writt & reson. *c* 1380 —— *Sel. Wks.* III. 351 Þus love ungroundid in God..mut nedis faile. 1426 AUDELAY *Poems* (Percy Soc.) 25 ȝe beth ungroundid in grace.
2. Having no real basis or justification; unfounded, groundless.
c 1380 WYCLIF *Wks.* (1880) 337 If he had not couetise of worldly goodis..he shuld..leue al siche rownyng þat is ungrundid. 1597 HOOKER *Eccl. Pol.* v. lxii. §16 A few men's new, ungrounded, and as yet unapproved imagination. 1629 H. BURTON *Truth's Triumph* 291 Humane deuices, and labyrinths of vngrounded distinctions. 1672 NEWTON in *Phil. Trans.* VII. 5084, I shall refer him to my former Letter, by which that conjecture will appear to be ungrounded. 1728 R. MORRIS *Ess. Anc. Archit.* 70 The Executions of their own ungrounded Fancies. 1782 PRIESTLEY *Corrupt. Christianity* I. I. 30 Nothing can appear..more ungrounded. 1863 E. V. NEALE *Anal. Th. & Nat.* 58 Thus the whole operation appears either useless or ungrounded.
3. Of persons: Not properly instructed or informed (*in* something).
c 1449 PECOCK *Repr.* Prol. 3 Therfore to ech such vngroundid and vnredy and ouer hasti vndirnymer and blamer y seie [etc.]. 1581 MULCASTER *Positions* iii. 11 It is a sufficient argument..of an vngrounded learner, if his error be in speeche. 1646 P. BULKELEY *Gospel Covt.* II. 111 If any be ignorant and ungrounded in the doctrine of grace. 1670 BAXTER *Cure Ch. Div.* 168 The pitiful case of the ignorant and ungrounded, and troubled sort of religious persons.

un'groundedly, *adv.* [UN-¹ 11.] Without any ground or basis.
1550 BALE *Apol.* 84b, That putteth he in here, vngroundedly, doubtfully, hypocritically, and vtterly agaynst hymselfe. 1593 NASHE *Strange Newes* Bj, They that are vngroundedly offended at any thing in 'Pierce Pennilesse'. 1624 BEDELL *Lett.* iii. 59 Many things there be in Poperie..to my conceit weakely and vngroundedly affirmed. 1692 RAY *Disc.* III. ix. 343 The event shews how ungroundedly and erroneously. [Also in recent use.]

un'groundedness. [UN-¹ 12.] The quality or state of being ungrounded: **a.** Of persons.
1628 BP. HALL *Old Relig.* Ded. ¶8b, The cause..was, their vngroundednes in the points of Catechisme. 1652 GAULE *Magastrom.* 28 Away, then, with that excuse, from the folly, errour, and ungroundedness of the artsmen!
b. Of opinions, statements, etc.
1637 BASTWICK *Litany* III. 7 Besides the impiety, vanity, and ungroundednes of it, let us looke..into the needlesnesse and unprofitablenes of it. 1688 STEELE *Old Age* 284 The folly and ungroundedness of this Imagination, is obvious. 1804 *Ann. Rev.* II. 296 We mention this..to expose the utter ungroundedness of the writer's speculation.

un'grouped, *ppl. a.* (UN-¹ 8.)
[1775 ASH.] 1853 RUSKIN *Stones Ven.* II. vii. §8. 238 That palace;..its capitals are all different and ungrouped.

un'grow, *v.* (UN-² 7.)
1598 FLORIO, *Discrescere*,..to vngrow, to diminish, to wane. 1648 HEXHAM II, *Onwassen*, To Vngrowe, to Waxe lesse.

un'grown, *ppl. a.* [UN-¹ 8b.] Not yet grown up or fully grown; immature.
1592 SHAKS. *Ven. & Ad.* 526 No fisher but the ungrown fry forbears. 1596 —— *1 Hen. IV*, v. iv. 23 With lustier maintenance then I did looke for Of such an vngrowne Warriour. 1633 P. FLETCHER *Purple Isl.* VI. iv, A narrow compasse best my ungrown Muse impounds. 1880 MISS BROUGHTON *Sec. Th.* I. i, The Squire; his half-grown daughters..; [and] his ungrown son.

'ungrown-up, *ppl. a.* and *sb.* [UN-^{1} 8c, 12.]

A. *adj.* Not grown-up; immature.

1937 *Mind* XLVI. 515 He may feel anxiety in the face of the infantile threats of his ungrown-up super-ego. **1945** A. L. ROWSE *Eng. Spirit* xxxiii. 229 There was something curiously unadult, ungrown-up about him. **1960** C. STORR *Marianne & Mark* x. 116 She thought this a very ungrown-up thing to do. **1980** J. LEES-MILNE *Harold Nicolson* xi. 201 To some extent he..remained ungrown-up in that his code of social behaviour was what he had imbibed from his.. parents and schoolmasters.

B. *sb.* An ungrown-up person. *rare.*

1946 J. LEES-MILNE *Diary* 22 Feb. (1983) 21 J. just the same sweet ungrown-up he always will be.

un'grubbed, *ppl. a.* (UN-^{1} 8.)

c **1374** CHAUCER *Former Age* 14 Vn-koruen and vn-grobbed lay the vyne.

un'grudged, *ppl. a.* (UN-^{1} 8.)

a **1631** DONNE *Div. Poems, Cross* 31 For when that Crosse ungrudg'd, unto you stickes, Then are you to your selfe, a Crucifixe. **1822** LAMB *Elia* I. *Decay of Beggars*, Theirs were the only rates..ungrudged in the assessment. **1877** BLACKIE *Wise Men* 345 Loved and lover grow, By mutual breathing in of excellence, Ungrudged, unstinted.

un'grudging, *ppl. a.* (UN-^{1} 10.)

1768–74 TUCKER *Lt. Nat.* (1834) II. 218 Such perfect ungrudging resistance both of pleasure and pain..being impracticable. **1823** LAMB *Elia* I. *Decay of Beggars*, Cheap monument of no ungrudging hand. **1890** *Science-Gossip* XXVI. 178/2 The provisions gathered by their sisters with ungrudging generosity.

Hence **un'grudgingness**.

1885 J. MARTINEAU *Types Ethic. Th.* I. I. 58 Plato speaks of the world as the product of the divine ungrudgingness.

un'grudgingly, *adv.* (UN-^{1} 11.)

Common from *c* 1860.

a **1631** DONNE *Elegies* xi. 67 Receive from him that doome ungrudgingly, Because he is the mouth of Destiny. **1822** LAMB *Elia* I. *Roast Pig*, I am one of those, who freely and ungrudgingly impart a share..to a friend. *a* **1862** BUCKLE *Misc. Wks.* (1872) I. 15 Let that honour be paid freely, ungrudgingly, and with an open and bounteous heart. **1887** *Spectator* 15 Oct. 1392 His gifts and graces must be ungrudgingly admitted.

ungtment, obs. form of OINTMENT.

ungual ('ʌŋgwəl), *a.* and *sb.* [f. L. *ungu-is* nail, claw + -AL^1. Cf. UNGUEAL *a.*]

A. *adj.* **1.** *Anat.* **a.** Pertaining to, connected with, a nail or claw; esp. ***ungual phalanx***, the terminal bone in the digits of the hand or foot.

1834 ROGET *Anim. & Veg. Phys.* I. 405 To the last joint, which is often termed the *ungual bone*, there is usually attached either a nail, a claw, or a hoof. **1836** *Penny Cycl.* V. 22/2 An external thick condyle, with which the ungual phalanx is articulated. **1898** A. S. PACKARD *Entomol.* 101 The ungual joint is wanting in the weevil Anoplus.

b. ***ungual bone***, a lachrymal bone.

1888 *Cassell's Encycl. Dict.* s.v. *Lachrymal.*

2. *Path.* Affecting the nail.

1872 T. BRYANT *Pract. Surg.* 450 Ungual exostosis..is a bony outgrowth from the extreme phalanx of the great toe.

B. *sb.* An ungual phalanx, claw, or bone.

In recent use.

unguaran'teed, *ppl. a.* (UN-^{1} 8.)

1855 MILMAN *Lat. Chr.* XIV. i. VI. 396 The faith and hope unguaranteed by any earthly mediator. **1864** SMILES *G. & R. Stephenson* 305 Stephenson..avoided holding unguaranteed railway shares.

un'guard, *v.* [UN-^{2} 4.]

1. *trans.* To strip of a guard or edging.

1598 FLORIO, *Disfrangiare*, to vnfringe,..to vngard.

2. To deprive of a guard or defence; to lay open to attack.

1745 FIELDING *Tom Jones* v. v, Some well-chosen presents from the philosopher so softened and unguarded the girl's heart, that a favourable opportunity became irresistible. **1801** IRELAND *Nuptiæ Sacræ* 128 Every man, by degrees, will unguard the virtue of his house, hitherto sacred. **1847** LYTTON *Lucretia* 64 She accepted the intimacy held out to her, not to unguard herself, but to lay open her opponent.

b. *Whist*, etc. To expose (a high card) to the risk of loss by discarding a lower and protecting card.

1862 'CAVENDISH' *Whist* (1864) 95 Trick v.—*a* unguards his queen of spades. **1887** MCINTOSH *Mod. Whist* 81 It is better to blank an ace than unguard king or queen.

un'guardable, *a.* (UN-^{1} 7b.)

1690 *Def. Dr. G. Walker* 14 Yet this boldly asserted impregnable Fortress hath an unguardable Breach.

un'guarded, *ppl. a.* [UN-^{1} 8.]

1. Not furnished with, or protected by, a guard; left undefended or open to attack, spoliation, etc.

a **1593** MARLOWE *Ovid's Elegies* III. iv. 26 Few loue what others haue vnguarded left. **1626** MEAD in Ellis *Orig. Lett.* Ser. I. III. 250, I hear some of opinion that the Duke likes not so unguarded a place. **1697** DRYDEN *Æneis* XII. 817 He views the unguarded city from afar, In careless quiet, and secure of war. **1741–2** GRAY *Agrippina* 5 Alone, unguarded and without a lictor. **1781** GIBBON *Decl. & F.* xxxi. III. 193 His troops..occupied the unguarded passes of the Apennine. **1824** MISS L. M. HAWKINS *Annaline* III. 40 [He] made off and left the door unguarded. **1869** TOZER *Highl. Turkey* I. 208 We used to ride..through the country unarmed and unguarded. **1885** *Manch. Exam.* 13 Jan. 5/3 A small body..entered the town by an unguarded gate.

b. In fig. contexts.

1673 [R. LEIGH] *Transp. Reh.* 39 This is Momba's and De Groot's doings, to leave this passage open and ungarded. *a* **1704** T. BROWN *Sat. agst. Woman* Wks. 1730 I. 56 Thus all the unguarded passes of his mind she'll try.

c. *transf.* In chess or card-playing: Not protected by other pieces or cards.

1808 *Hoyle's Game of Chess* 46 *note*, Your knight will then defend your king's pawn, otherwise unguarded. **1862** 'CAVENDISH' *Whist* (1864) 95 Queen singly guarded may make a trick, but the ten of clubs unguarded cannot.

2. Not on one's guard; not taking heed or exercising caution. Chiefly *fig.*

1640 FLETCHER, etc. *Coronat.* IV. i. ad fin., I..have not A thought so much unguarded, as to be won From my truth, and innocence. **1697** DRYDEN *Æneis* XII. 1058 Rais'd on the Stretch, young Turnus aims a blow, Full on the Helm of his unguarded Foe. *a* **1763** W. KING *Polit. & Lit. Anecd.* (1819) 44 Sir Robert [Walpole] was frequently very unguarded in his expressions. **1796** MME. D'ARBLAY *Camilla* IV. 185 The unsuspicious frankness of an unguarded, because innocent nature. **1840** LADY LYTTELTON *Corr.* (1912) 298 Such a new thing for her to dare to be unguarded in conversation with anybody. **1881** JOWETT *Thucyd.* I. 186 The general who.. never loses an opportunity of striking at an unguarded foe.

b. Of times: Characterized by the absence of guard or caution.

1680 OTWAY *Orphan* I, I'll yet possess her love, Wait on and watch her loose unguarded hours. **1776** GIBBON *Decl. & F.* xii. I. 336 An active enemy..must, in the end, discover some feeble spot or some unguarded moment. **1855** MACAULAY *Hist. Eng.* xv. III. 596 It is highly probable that his mother..took a fatal advantage of some unguarded hour, when he was irritated by finding his advice slighted.

c. Of expressions, actions, etc.: Incautious, imprudent; careless.

1714 S. OCKLEY in *Lett. Lit. Men* (Camden) 350 If a person should..upon the account of an unguarded expression..suffer a capital sentence. **1751** EARL ORRERY *Remarks Swift* ix. (1752) 114 A picture..drawn in too loose a garment, and too unguarded a posture. **1827** LYTTON *Falkland* 37, I have watched feeling in its unguarded sallies. **1835** —— *Rienzi* x. vii, Their gestures were vehement and unguarded. **1849** MACAULAY *Hist. Eng.* vii. II. 163 Every unguarded word uttered by him was noted down.

3. Not protected, screened, or fenced off, by some arrangement or device.

1771 LUCKOMBE *Hist. Print.* 240, *d, f, l*, when they stand with their beaks unguarded,..run as great a hazard [of being broken]. **1784** COWPER *Task* IV. 469 Ev'ry twentieth pace Conducts th' unguarded nose to such a whiff Of stale debauch. **1844** NOAD *Electricity* (ed. 2) 80 Decomposing water by current alone, and with unguarded poles. **1872** HOWELLS *Wedding Journ.* (1892) 177 The road.., next the precipice, is unguarded by any sort of parapet. **1900** *Westm. Gaz.* 2 May 6/3 Dust or gas..ignited by an unguarded lamp.

Hence **un'guardedness**.

1818 T. BROWN *Brighton* III. i. 38 So also does he argue with ability, when unguardedness does not break in upon him. **1825–9** MRS. SHERWOOD *Lady of Manor* IV. xxvii. 282 That sort of unguardedness which consists in supposing all around one to be well-intentioned. **1887** *Women's Union Jrnl.* 15 Dec. 94 A moment of optical unguardedness, when ..eve-glasses lay on a table before him.

un'guardedly, *adv.* [UN-^{1} 11.] In an unguarded manner; incautiously, uncircumspectly.

1713 BERKELEY *Guard.* No. 3 ¶ 1 Whatever Clergymen, in Disputes against each other, have unguardedly uttered. **1746** WESLEY *Princ. Methodist* 40 But how little did I profit by begging your Excuse, suppose I had spoken a Word unguardedly? *a* **1813** in J. Thomson *Lect. Inflam.* 477 The same spunge having been unguardedly used for different sores. **1886** *Manch. Exam.* 19 Oct. 5/5 The Bishop spoke unguardedly and without due premeditation.

'ungueal, var. of UNGUAL *a.* I.

1835–6 *Todd's Cycl. Anat.* I. 289/2 The ultimate or ungueal phalanges. **1851** MANTELL *Petrifactions* ii. §3. 116 The ungueal or claw-bones are large and strong.

unguent ('ʌŋgwənt), *sb.* Also 5 vngwent, 6–7 vnguent. [ad. L. *unguent-um*, f. *unguĕre* to anoint. Cf. F. *onguent*, It., Sp., Pg. *unguento.*] An ointment or salve.

c **1440** *Pallad. on Husb.* IV. 147 Or madifie hit so in oil lauryne, Let drie hem, sowe hem, vp by oon assent They wol, and haue odour like her vnguent. **1448–9** J. METHAM *Amoryus & Cleopes* 1500 For had not a bene that precyus vngwent, He had be slayn and on pecys rente. **1563** T. GALE *Antidot.* II. 7 Unto whiche I haue also added no smal number of vnguents. **1624** HEYWOOD *Gunaik.* III. 131 Forgetting the Physitions with all their drugges, unguents, and emplasters. **1656** J. SMITH *Pract. Physick* 66 Unguents for scaldings must be made so that they stick not too fast. **1720** POPE *Iliad* XXIII. 229 Celestial Venus hover'd o'er his head, And roseate unguents, heav'nly fragrance! shed. **1778** LIGHTFOOT *Flora Scot.* II. 618 The buds yield a yellow resinous unguent. **1857** MAURICE *Ep. St. John* x. 162 Oils and unguents in the East had a virtue which we do not commonly attach to them. **1887** BOWEN *Æneid* III. 280 Bared and anointed shoulders with glistening unguent stream.

attrib. **1894** *Daily News* 13 Dec. 8 A small unguent bottle, only slightly damaged, was in this part of the building.

b. *fig.* or in fig. context.

1596 FITZ-GEFFREY *Sir F. Drake* (1881) 19 Soules sweet Emplastrum, unguent of the eyes. *a* **1625** FLETCHER & MASS. *Elder Bro.* v. i, Your festred reputation, which no Balm or gentle Unguent could ever make way to. *a* **1683** OWEN *Two Discourses Holy Spirit* (1693) 62 An Unction, an Unguent from the Holy One. **1838** JAMES *Louis XIV*, I. 257 There was no unguent which made the wheels of their foreign policy move so rapidly as gold.

c. *spec.* (See quot.)

1867 *Ure's Dict. Arts* (ed. 6) III. 971 *Unguents*, the name given by engineers to the greases applied to the bearing parts of machinery.

'unguent, *v.* [f. prec. Cf. L. *unguent-āre*, It. *-are.*] *trans.* To treat with an unguent; to anoint.

1656 S. HOLLAND *Zara* (1719) 42 When they found their Ears unguented with warm water. **1657** TOMLINSON *Renou's Disp.* 689 A Medick should be Unguented, that is, Perfumed. **1819** *Metropolis* III. 194 Brushing, perfuming, unguenting, and twisting about the hair. **1918** A. QUILLER-COUCH *Foe-Farrell* xvi. 273 'I under-stand,' said I, looking up from my business of unguenting the stoker, who was not badly burnt.

'unguent, *a. rare.* [f. UNGUENT *sb.* or *v.*] Of a person: emollient in manner, unctuous.

1931 BELLOC *Cranmer* ii. 30 He shrank, withdrew, was suave and unguent.

unguen'tarian. *rare.* [-IAN.] = UNGUENTARY *sb.* I.

1657 TOMLINSON *Renou's Disp.* 123 Plaisters..bought in unguentarians shops. **1894** *Yellow Bk.* I. 81 The admirable unguentarians of Bond Street.

‖**unguen'tarium.** *Archæol.* [L. *unguentārium* (*vās*), f. *unguent-um* UNGUENT *sb.*] A vessel for holding ointment; an unguentary.

1859 R. HUNT *Guide Mus. Pract. Geol.* (ed. 2) 85 Vases, bowls, lamps, unguentaria, amphoræ. **1888** *Pall Mall G.* 22 Aug. 5/2 Besides the unguentaria, there are..specimens of the early Phœnician glass.

'unguentary, *sb.* and *a.* Now *rare.* [ad. L. *unguentārius, -a, -um* (adj. and sb.), f. *unguentum* ointment. Cf. It. and Sp. *unguentario*, OF. *ung-, onguentaire.*]

A. *sb.* **1.** A maker of or dealer in (perfumed) ointment; a perfumer.

1382 WYCLIF *Exod.* xxx. 25 An oynement maad with the werk of ungwentarye [1388 a makere of oynement]. **1483** CAXTON *Gold. Leg.* 64b/2 He shal also take your doughters and make them his unguentaryes. **1609** BIBLE (Douay) *Exod.* xxx. 25 Thou shalt make the holie oile of unction, an ointment compounded by the arte of an unguentarie. **1684** tr. *Agrippa's Van. Arts* xc. 313 In stead of Alchymists, Cacochymists;..in stead of Unguentaries, Victuallers.

2. = UNGUENTARIUM.

1911 *Sotheby's Sale Catal. Egypt. Antiq.* 87 An Unguentary, shaped as a Gazelle with its legs tied together.

B. *adj.* Adapted for use in, suitable for, having connexion with, ointments.

1657 TOMLINSON *Renou's Disp.* 273 Which Hippocrates calls myrepsicum, that is, unguentary, from its suavity. **1846** WORCESTER (citing *Gent. Mag.*). **1891** *Cent. Dict.*, *Unguentary vase*, a small vase for unguents.

unguen'tiferous, *a.* [See UNGUENT *sb.* and -(I)FEROUS. Cf. It. *unguentifero.*] Producing ointment.

1844 T. MEYRICK *Fam. St. Richard*, etc. 95 The saints who are called 'Elæophori' or 'unguentiferous'.

'unguentous, *a. rare.* [f. UNGUENT *sb.* + -OUS.]

1. Smeared with ointment; greasy.

1654 GAYTON *Pleas. Notes* III. ii. 73 His bed was full of holes, so that the Flocks broke through the breaches, and stuck all about his fulsome and unguentous Body.

2. Of the nature of ointment.

1684 tr. *Bonet's Merc. Compit.* XIX. 833 Unguentous things hinder transpiration. **1819** *Metropolis* III. 151 His unguentous compound has not hindered a spoke from being put into his wheel.

†**unguenty.** *Obs.*$^{-1}$ (See quot.)

c **1720** W. GIBSON *Farrier's Dispens.* XV. (1734) 284 *Unguentum Album*, called by the common people, Unguenty.

un'guerdoned, *ppl. a.* Now *poet.* (UN-^{1} 8.)

1433 *Rolls of Parlt.* IV. 424/2 Suche as have so served and be unguerdonned. *c* **1477** CAXTON *Jason* 47b, As your trewe louer and humble seruaunt vnguerdonned I shal goe withdrawe me into som deserte. **1611** COTGR., *Inguerdonné*, vnguerdoned, vnrecompenced. **1813** SCOTT *Rokeby* VI. xii, Unguerdon'd, I would give with joy The father's arms to fold his boy. **1855** SINGLETON *Virgil* II. 25 No one of this company By me unguerdoned shall depart.

un'guessable, *a.* (UN-^{1} 7b.)

1832 MISS MITFORD *Our Village* Ser. v. 278 An old bonnet,..so twisted..that its pristine shape was unguessable. **1865** *Dublin Univ. Mag.* I. 266 There are passages..the meaning whereof..is to me unknowable, unguessable. [Common in recent use.]

un'guessed, *ppl. a.* [UN-^{1} 8 and 8c.]

†**1.** Unexpected, unlooked-for. *Obs.*

c **1400** *Comm. Luke* (MS. Bodl. 143) i. 7 God ordeyned þat ioon was born of fadir & modir of old age,..þat bi vngessid birþe of child a graciousere ȝifte shulde enfourme hem.

2. Not solved or known by guessing.

1590 SPENSER *F.Q.* I. ix. 7 For whither he through fatall deepe foresight Me hither sent, for cause to me vnghest, Or [etc.]. **1805** SCOTT *Last Minstrel* v. xvii, But cause of terror, all unguess'd, Was fluttering in her gentle breast. **1837** LYTTON *Athens* I. 50 The frequent operation of causes unrecognised, unforeseen, unguest. **1900** *Pilot* 22 Sept. 358/2 An explanation of its mysterious and once unseen and unguessed processes.

b. Not guessed *at*, not dreamt *of*.

1746 ELIZA HEYWOOD *Female Spect.* No. 22 (1748) IV. 203 By what unseen, unguessed at means, are frequently the greatest events brought about! **1838** LYTTON *Zicci* xiv, Art thou some itinerant mountebank, or some unguest-of-friend? **1876** Miss Yonge *Womankind* xiii, The best endeavours..are often frustrated by some unguessed-at peril.

un'guestlike, *a.* or *adv.* (UN-^{1} 7 c or 11 b.)
1645 Milton *Tetrach.* Wks. 1851 IV. 207 He cast his eye unlawfully and unguestlike upon Herodias.., the wife of Philip.

'unguical, *a. rare.* [f. L. *unguic-ulus* (see next) + -AL^1.] = UNGUAL *a.* 1.
1833 Sir C. Bell *Hand* (1834) 106 These unguical bones, or bones of the claws.

†'unguicle. *Bot. Obs.* [ad. L. *unguiculus*, dim. of *unguis* nail, claw.] A part of a leaf or petal resembling a nail or claw.
1657 Tomlinson *Renou's Disp.* 375 Medlers, which are of a moderate magnitude, with late heads, discreted with five unguicles or leafes. **1796** H. Hunter tr. *St.-Pierre's Stud. Nat.* (1799) II. 95 The unguicle..is always clearer [in colour] than that of the rest of the petal.

un'guicular, *a. rare.* [f. as prec. + -AR.] = UNGUAL *a.* 1.
1826 Kirby & Sp. *Entomol.* III. xxxii. 307 The last or unguicular joint..is on both sides fringed with long hairs.

unguiculate (ʌŋ'gwɪkjʊlət), *a.* and *sb.* [ad. mod.L. *unguiculāt-us* (Ray, 1693), f. L. *unguiculus* UNGUICLE. Cf. F. *ung-*, *onguiculé*.]
1. *Bot.* Of petals: Having an unguis or claw.
1802 R. Hall *Elem. Bot.* 193 *Unguiculate*,..clawed. **1830** Lindley *Nat. Syst. Bot.* 34 Their..many-celled fruit, and unguiculate petals. **1861** Bentley *Man. Bot.* 454 Petals..imbricate, generally unequal and unguiculate.
2. *Zool.*, etc. Ending in, assuming the form of, a nail or claw: **a.** Of the limbs of animals.
1826 Kirby & Sp. *Entomol.* III. xxx. 138 Those of the former..resemble the second class of unguiculate prolegs, except in the defect of claws. **1852** Dana *Crust.* I. 252 Tarsus not unguiculate. **1881** Mivart *Cat* 472 Their digits are also unguiculate and never sheathed in horny hoofs.
b. Of other organs or parts.
1826 Kirby & Sp. *Entomol.* III. xxviii. 30 Mandibles cheliform or unguiculate. **1851** S. P. Woodward *Mollusca* 102 The operculum is described as..Claw-shaped, or unguiculate. **1872** Coues *N. Amer. Birds* 25 A bill is..unguiculate (clawed), when strongly epignathous.
3. *Zool.* Of quadrupeds: Furnished with nails or claws; belonging to the order *Unguiculata*.
1839 Hallam *Hist. Lit.* IV. viii. §16 Quadrupeds he [*sc.* Ray] was the first to divide into ungulate and unguiculate, hoofed and clawed. *a* **1847** *Todd's Cycl. Anat.* III. 843/2 In all unguiculate Mammalia the tarsal bones are well developed. **1877** Coues *Fur Anim.* iv. 117 Causing the feet to appear slender.., though they are relatively stouter than in many unguiculate animals.
b. *sb.* An unguiculate quadruped.
1840 *Cuvier's Anim. Kingd.* 42 Among the unguiculates the first is Man. *a* **1847** *Todd's Cycl. Anat.* III. 236/2 Those Unguiculates which have the front teeth trenchant.

un'guiculated, *ppl. a.* [f. as prec. + -ED.]
1. = prec. 2.
1752 J. Hill *Hist. Anim.* 110 The Lacerta,..with five unguiculated toes to each foot. **1819** Samouelle *Entomol. Compend.* 192 *Antennæ* moniliform,..*maxillæ* unguiculated. **1841** *Penny Cycl.* XXI. 424/1 The external jaw-feet are..sometimes unguiculated at the end. **1861** Hulme tr. *Moquin-Tandon* II. III. i. 69 The toes free, flat, and unguiculated.
2. = prec. 3.
1834 M'Murtrie *Cuvier's Anim. Kingd.* 224 As the Marsupialia..are parallel to the other unguiculated Mammalia. **1851** G. F. Richardson *Geol.* 336 Rodentia (or Gnawers).—Form a natural order of unguiculated animals.

'unguicule. *rare*$^{-1}$. [ad. L. *unguicul-us.*] A finger-nail.
1694 Motteux *Rabelais* v. xx, Your Taciturnity..discovers that..you have..scalptiz'd your heads with frequent applications of your Unguicules. [Not in Fr. original.]

un'guidable, *a.* (UN-^{1} 7 b.)
1822 Bewick *Mem.* 6 My father began by telling him that I was so very unguidable that he could not manage me. **1896** *Westm. Gaz.* 12 May 4/1 [The vessel,] in the absence of much wind, was almost unguidable.

un'guidably, *adv.* (UN-^{1} 11.)
1837 Carlyle *Fr. Rev.* I. II. vi, Beautiful invention; mounting heavenward, so beautifully,—so unguidably!

un'guided, *ppl. a.* [UN-^{1} 8.] Not guided in a particular path or direction; left to take one's own course or way.
1585 Abp. Sandys *Serm.* xix. 341 The ship cannot keepe hir right course vnguided but will fall vpon euerie sande. **1633** Fletcher & Shirley *Night-Walker* IV. i, *Ha.* The world's a Labyrinth, where unguided men Walk up and down to find their weariness. **1674** Boyle *Grounds Corpusc. Philos.* 3 The material parts being able by their own unguided motions, to cast themselves into such a system. **1726** Pope *Odyss.* xx. 441 Unguided hence my trembling steps I bend. **1801** Southey *Thalaba* I. xviii, Not by Heaven unseen, Nor in unguided wanderings, hast thou reach'd This secret place. **1856** Kane *Arct. Expl.* II. xxi. 211 The dogs speed from hut to hut, almost unguided by their drivers. **1891** T. Hardy *Tess* ii, An unguided ramble into its recesses in bad weather.
b. *fig.* Of action, conduct, etc.: Undirected, uncontrolled.
1597 Shaks. *2 Hen. IV*, IV. iv. 59 Th' vnguided Dayes, And rotten Times, that you shall looke vpon. **1651** Hobbes *Leviath.* I. viii. 37 Passions unguided, are for the most part meere Madnesse. **1711** Steele *Spect.* No. 167 ¶1 The unhappy Force of an Imagination, unguided by the Check of Reason and Judgment. **1760–72** H. Brooke *Fool of Qual.* (1809) III. 136 He..has left his own household unchastened and unguided. **1856** Froude *Hist. Eng.* II. 26 It [Protestantism] sprung up spontaneously, unguided, unexcited,..among the masses of the nation. *a* **1880** Geo. Eliot *Leaves fr. Note-bk.*, *Ess.* (1884) 364 They are not left to their own unguided rashness, or their own unguided pusillanimity.
Hence **un'guidedly** *adv.*
1660 tr. *Amyraldus' Treat. conc. Relig.* II. i. 153 To discharge all his actions at randome, and permit his natural appetites to run unguidedly at a venture. **1885** E. F. Byrrne *Entangled* I. xi, Her tongue spoke strangely and unguidedly.

un'guiferous, *a. rare*$^{-1}$. [f. L. *ungui-s* nail, claw + -FEROUS.] Bearing nails or claws.
1826 Kirby & Sp. *Entomol.* III. 137 The remaining description of unguiferous prolegs..are those of certain *Diptera*.

'unguiform, *a.* [f. as prec. + -FORM.] Having the form of a nail or claw; claw-shaped.
1726 Monro *Anat. Bones* 137 These unguiform Bones compose the anterior internal Parts of the Orbites. **1815** Kirby & Sp. *Entomol.* iv. (1816) I. 140 Armed with two unguiform mandibles. **1843** Humphreys *Brit. Butterflies* 36 With simple claws furnished with an unguiform appendage. **1866** R. Tate *Brit. Mollusks* iv. 83 The shell..is unguiform.

un'guilded, *a.* (UN-^{1} 9.)
1858 J. S. Brewer *Mon. Francisc.* Pref. p. xvii, For the unguilded population who resided in the suburbs..there were no such advantages.

un'guileful, *a.* (UN-^{1} 7.)
1630 I. Craven *Gods Tribunall* (1631) 33 In the day when an vnguilefull Israelite shall not faile of a Testimoniall.

'unguilite. *Geol.* [f. L. *ungui-s* nail + -LITE.] Gompholite.
1799 Kirwan *Geol. Ess.* 246 It alternates with unguilite (Nagel fluhe) in Swisserland..and in Bavaria.

un'guillotined, *ppl. a.* (UN-^{1} 8.)
1837 Carlyle *Fr. Rev.* I. II. viii, There too an unruly Linguet, still unguillotined,..can emit his hoarse wailings.

†un'guiltihead. *Obs.* = UNGUILTINESS.
a **1470** H. Parker *Dives & Pauper* (1493) IV. xix. N vij b/1 The prest moste take hede whether his vngiltyede is openly knowen or is in doute.

un'guiltily, *adv.* (UN-^{1} 11.)
a **1634** Chapman *Alphonsus* I. Plays 1873 III. 211 Thus am I wrong'd, God knows, unguiltily. **1861** Trench *Comm. Ep. Churches Asia* 119 All of us, by careless walking,..are in danger of unconsciously, but not unguiltily, being the same. **1891** Meredith *One of our Conq.* xxvi, Unguiltily tainted, in herself she was innocent.

un'guiltiness. (UN-^{1} 12.)
1535 Coverdale *Job* vi. 29 Be indifferent iudges, and considre myne vngyltinesse. **1571** Golding *Calvin on Ps.* xvii. 1 It is lawfull for us to protest our ungiltynesse before God. *a* **1634** Chapman *Alphonsus* v. 60 Great Emperor,..Your Conscience knows my hearts unguiltiness. *a* **1680** Butler *Rem.* (1759) I. 301 Their approved Liberty of Conscience, and Unguiltiness of Faith.

†un'guiltless, *a. Obs.*$^{-1}$ (UN-^{1} 15.)
c **1320** *Sir Tristr.* 2144 Vngiltles er ȝe In swiche a sclaunder brouȝt.

un'guilty, *a.* Forms: (see UN-^{1} 4 c and GUILTY *a.*). [UN-^{1} 7.]
1. Not guilty; guiltless; innocent: **a.** Of persons.
c 893 [see below]. *c* **1374** Chaucer *Troylus* III. 1018 Is þis an honour to þi deite That folk vngiltyf [*v.r.* ongilti] suffren here Iniure? **1388** Wyclif *Num.* xiv. 18 Doynge awei wickidnesse and trespassis, and leeuynge no man vngilti. *c* **1440** *Jacob's Well* 22 Fleeth hem, ȝif ȝe be vngylty, & leuyth hem, ȝif ȝe be gilty. **1558** Phaer *Æneid* II. C iv b, Whom by a treason false the Greekes..Ungiltie did condempne. **1599** Breton *Miseries Manillia* Wks. (Grosart) II. 46/1 The Lord of lordes dooth knowe this tale to bee untrue, And her unguiltie. *a* **1634** Chapman *Alphonsus* v. i. 220, I kill'd thy father, therefore let me die, But save the life of this unguilty Empress. **1736** Thomson *Liberty* IV. 330 Rare to be seen, unguilty cities rise, Cities of brothers form'd. **1816** *Monthly Mag.* XLII. 430 Thou sea,..Receive for ever in thy dark abyss The unguilty Melicertes. **1860** Trench *Serm. Westm. Abb.* v. 53 The clothing..could only have been obtained at the cost of..the life of one unguilty.
absol. *c* **893** K. Ælfred *Oros.* IV. vii. 184 Ac hit God wræc on him..þæt hie mid hiera cucum onguldon þæt hie ungyltiȝe cwealdon. **13..** *Prose Psalter* ix. 30 (Dubl. MS.), He sitteþ in waytynges wyþ ryche men in preuytes þat he slee þe vngylty. **1553** Latimer *Serm. Lord's Prayer* vi. (1562) 46 And so we acknowledge our selues to be offenders. For the vngilty nedeth no pardon. **1612** Woodall *Surg. Mate* Wks. (1653) 146 The guilty and unguilty are censured both alike by the common sort. **1703** *Secr. Policy of Jansenists* 24 That I may not asperse the unguilty.
b. Of the hands, mind, blood, etc.
13.. *Prose Psalter* cv. 35 And hij..shadde blode nouȝt filed [*v.r.* vngilty blode]. **1382** Wyclif *Gen.* xxxvii. 22 Kepe ȝe ȝoure hondes vngilti. **1595** Daniel *Civ. Wars* I. xc, Stay here thy foote, thy yet vnguilty foote. **1605** —— *Philotas* III. i, With th' assured Chear Of my unguilty Conscience. **1633** Ford *Broken H.* II. iii, Time can never On the white table of unguilty faith Write counterfeit dishonour. **1740** Richardson *Pamela* I. 230 Surrendering up my Life, spotless and unguilty, to that merciful Being who gave it.
c. Of an animal. *rare*$^{-1}$.
1600 *Maides Metam.* I. in Bullen *O. Pl.* (1882) I. 109 And, hauing slaine it, rip his panting breast, And take the heart of the vnguiltie beast.
2. Guiltless or innocent *of* something.
c **1440** *Jacob's Well* 89 He of Baldac cryed, 'late be! late be! he is vngylti of þat mannys deth!' **1535** Coverdale *Matt.* xxvii. 24, I am vngiltie of yᵉ bloude of this righteous man. **1577** Grange *Golden Aphrod.* E iij b, Sith I vnguiltie am thereof, I wil not seeke the same T'excuse. **1606** Chapman *M. D'Olive* Plays 1873 I. 224 Keepe your cullour stiffe, vnguiltie of passion or disgrace. **1820** Hogg *Tales & Sk.* (1837) III. 96 He is as unguilty of the whole affair, as the child that is not after being born.
†b. Undeserving *of*. *Obs.*$^{-1}$
1596 W. Smith *Chloris* (1877) 21 With patience bearing loues captiuitie, Themselues vnguiltie of his wrath alleaging.
†3. Not involving guilt. *Obs.*
a **1586** Sidney *Arcadia* III. x, This outward glosse, intitled Beautie, which it pleaseth you to lay to my (as I thinke) vnguiltie charge. **1662** J. Chandler *Van Helmont's Oriat.* 213 That now and then, the digestion beares the unguilty fault of the expulsive faculty.

'unguinal, *a. Anat.* [Irreg. f. L. *ungui-s* nail, claw.] = UNGUAL *a.*
1860 Mayne *Expos. Lex.* s.v. **1870** Gillmore tr. *Figuier's Reptiles & Birds* ii. 59 A spur or nail..in which the anatomist discovered the elements of an unguinal phalanx.

†'unguinous, *a. Obs.* [ad. L. *unguinōsus*, f. *unguin-*, *unguen* ointment.] Greasy, oily.
1601 Holland *Pliny* II. 174 The powder entreth into those unguinous or oleous plasters which the Greeks call Liparas. **1603** —— *Plutarch's Mor.* 675 The tortch staves made of them..are so fattie and unguinous.

‖unguis ('ʌŋgwɪs). Pl. ungues (-iːz). [L. *unguis* nail, claw, etc.]
†1. = UNGULA 2. *Obs.*
1693 [see UNGULA 2]. **1728** Chambers *Cycl.* s.v. *Pannus*, The Pannus is an Excrescence..less hard and membranous than the Unguis.
2. *Bot.* The narrow part of a petal, by which it is attached to the receptacle.
1728 Chambers *Cycl.* s.v., In preparing of Medicines, the *Ungues*..are pull'd off the Flowers. **1760** J. Lee *Introd. Bot.* I. iii. (1765) 7 Each Petal consists of *Unguis*, a Claw, which is the lower Part fastened to the Base. **1830** Lindley *Nat. Syst. Bot.* 284 The inner segments of the perianthium being petaloid, with the stamens proceeding from the top of their ungues. **1879** A. Gray *Struct. Bot.* vi. §4. 245 The expanded portion of a petal..is the *Lamina* or Blade; any much contracted base is the *Unguis* or Claw.
†3. A claw-shaped obstetrical instrument. *Obs.*$^{-1}$
1752 Smellie *Midwif.* Introd. p. xii, [Hippocrates] directs us to introduce the hand,..dividing the parts with an *unguis* fixed on the great finger.
4. *Zool.*, etc. A nail or claw.
c **1790** *Encycl. Brit.* (ed. 3) VI. 680/1 Tarsus, or foot..Unguis, or claw. **1819** Macleay *Horæ Entomol.* I. 66 The size of their tarsi and ungues, and their comparatively small pectus. **1840** *Cuvier's Anim. Kingd.* 526 *Dasyus*..has the ungues of the two fore-feet..bifid, the others entire. **1884** Coues *N. Amer. Birds* 102 There it is always terminated by a hard, horny, unguis or 'nail', more or less distinct.

†ungul, anglicized f. next (in sense 4).
1670 *Phil. Trans.* V. 2006 He shews the Center of Gravity of all Arches of Circles, with their Superficial Vnguls.

‖ungula ('ʌŋgjʊlə). [L. *ungula* claw, hoof, f. *unguis* nail, UNGUIS.]
†1. = ONYCHA, ONYX 2. *Obs.*
1382 Wyclif *Ecclus.* xxiv. 21 [15], Galban, and vngula, and gutta [**1388** vngula, and gumme].
†2. A morbid growth in the eye; = ONYX 3, PTERYGIUM 2 a. *Obs.*
c **1400** *Lanfranc's Cirurg.* 19 Vngula is a þing, þat bigynneþ bi þe nose & goiþ over þe iȝe til he keuere al þe iȝe. **1597** A. M. tr. *Guillemeau's Fr. Chirurg.* c ij b/1 When we desire to cut of[f] an Vngula. *Ibid.* c ij b/2 An Eye, in the which is an Vngula. **1693** tr. *Blancard's Phys. Dict.* (ed. 2), *Pterygium*,..a membranous Excrescence above the horny Tunicle of the Eye, called *Unguis* and *Ungula*.
†3. = UNGUIS 3. *Obs.*$^{-0}$
1693 tr. *Blancard's Phys. Dict.* (ed. 2), *Ungula*, a sort of hooked Instrument to draw a dead Fœtus out of the Womb.
4. *Geom.* (See quots.)
1710 J. Harris *Lex. Techn.* II, *Ungula*, in Geometry, is the Section of a Cylinder cut off by a Plane, which passes obliquely thro' the Plane of the Basse, and part of the Cylindric Surface. **1824–5** *Encycl. Metrop.* (1845) I. 362/1 A spherical wedge or ungula is that portion of the solid sphere, which is included between the same great semicircles, and has the lune for its base. **1843** *Penny Cycl.* XXV. 514/2 The hoof of a horse looks like the part of a cone which is separated from the part containing the vertex by an oblique plane. Hence such a solid is called an ungula.

‖Ungulata (ʌŋgjʊ'leɪtə), *sb. pl.* [L. *ungulāta*, neut. pl. of *ungulātus*: see next.] The order or division of ungulate or hoofed animals.
1839 *Penny Cycl.* XIV. 352/2 The *Ungulata*, comprising the *Belluæ* and *Pecora*. **1872** Mivart *Elem. Anat.* 43 The spinous processes may be very much more prolonged, as in the Ungulata. **1891** W. H. Flower *Horse* i. 11 The group *Ungulata*, discarded by Linnæus, Cuvier, and others,..has been resuscitated of late years.

ungulate ('ʌŋgjʊlət), *a.* and *sb.* [ad. L. *ungulāt-us*, f. *ungula* hoof.]
1. Having the form of a hoof; hoof-shaped.
1802 R. Hall *Elem. Bot.* 193 Ungulate, or Hoof-shaped, *ungulatus*. **1858** W. Clark *Van der Hoeven's Zool.* II. 634

Feet tridactylous, with all the toes insistent, ungulate. **1888** G. ALLEN in *Longm. Mag.* July 303 The slender and delicate ungulate feet of the gazelles and the chamois.

2. Of quadrupeds: Having hoofs.

The classification was introduced by Ray (1693).

1839 G. ROBERTS *Dict. Geol.* s.v., An ungulate quadruped. **1872** DARWIN *Orig. Spec.* (ed. 6) vii. 179 The competition.. must be between giraffe and giraffe, and not with the other ungulate animals. *Ibid.* xi. 302 The existing horse and certain older ungulate forms. **1875** C. C. BLAKE *Zool.* 32 The odd-toed division of ungulate Mammalia.

b. *sb.* An ungulate animal.

1842 BRANDE *Dict. Sci.*, etc. 1274/2. **1854** OWEN in *Orr's Circ. Sci., Org. Nat.* I. 236 In the odd-toed or 'perissodactyle' ungulates. **1894** LYDEKKER *Roy. Nat. Hist.* II. 152 In all the Ungulates the limbs have entirely ceased to be used as organs of prehension.

So **'ungulated** *a. rare.*

1822 GOOD *Study Med.* I. 174 Generally speaking, the tenderest food is that of the gallinaceous birds: then that of the ungulated quadrupeds. **1891** W. H. FLOWER *Horse* i. 11 The ungulated or hoofed animals, and the unguiculated.

unguled ('ʌŋgjuːld), *a. Her.* [f. L. *ungul-a* claw, hoof. Cf. UNGLED.] Of animals: Having the hoofs or claws of a different tincture from the body.

1572 BOSSEWELL *Armorie* II. 100 Two demye hyppotames, sable, armed and vnguled. **1610** GUILLIM *Heraldry* III. xiv. 130 He beareth Argent, a Stagge Tripping Proper, Armed and Vnguled. *a* **1695** WOOD *Surv. Oxford* (O.H.S.) III. 143 A lyon rampant sable, collered or, unguled and langed gules. **1728** CHAMBERS *Cycl.* s.v. *Unicorn*, An Unicorn seiant sable, armed and unguled, Or. **1763** *Brit. Mag.* IV. 238 Two bucks, proper, attired, and unguled, or. **1864** BOUTELL *Her. Hist. & Pop.* xvii. (ed. 3) 280 Two bulls arg.,.. armed unguled, collared and chained. *Ibid.* xxi. 366 An ox gu., armed and unguled or.

'unguligrade, *a. Zool.* [ad. mod.L. *unguligradus*, f. L. *ungula* claw + *-gradus* walking. Cf. F. *ongulograde.*] Walking on the tips of the digits.

1869 HUXLEY *Introd. Classif.* 146 *Unguligrade*, those animals which walk on the tips of the digits only, which are always hoofed. **1881** MIVART *Cat* 472 The Carnivora also are always digitigrade or plantigrade, never unguligrade.

ungulite ('ʌŋgjʊlaɪt). *Palæont.* [f. L. *ungul-a*, UNGULA + -ITE[1].] A Palæozoic brachiopod, the obolus. ***ungulite grit***: see OBOLITE.

1850 ANSTED *Elem. Geol., Min.*, etc. §980 A sandstone, or grit, distinguished by a remarkable fossil (the *Ungulite*) unknown in Western Europe. *Ibid.* Index, Ungulite grit. **1859** MURCHISON *Siluria* (ed. 3) xiv. 374 The little horny brachiopod, the Obolus or Ungulite, is so much more abundant than any other fossil, as to have induced Pander to give to the rock the name of Ungulite grit.

un'gull, *v.* (UN-[2] 6 b.)

1652 BENLOWES *Theoph.* x. xxvi, Fawn, and betray, and Treasons self outdare,.. But I'l ungull thy Minions.

'ungulous, *a.* [f. UNGULA.] Pertaining to or resembling a hoof; ungulate. (Webster, 1879.)

un'gum, *v.* [UN-[2] 4 b. Cf. Du. *ontgommen.*] *trans.* To free from gum or from being gummed; *spec.* in the preparation of silk.

1598 FLORIO, *Sgommare*, to vngum, to vnplaister, to vnglue. **1839** URE *Dict. Arts* 142 As soon as the whole [of the silk] is completely ungummed, they [*sc.* the hanks] are taken out. **1901** B. PAIN *Another Englishwoman's Love-Lett.* xxv. 111, I kiss the label.. until it comes ungummed.

Hence **un'gumming** *vbl. sb.*

1839 URE *Dict. Arts* 142 For the first [method of scouring silk], or the ungumming. **1883** R. HALDANE *Workshop Receipts* Ser. II. 39/1 Two operations are necessary [in silk-bleaching], 'ungumming' (*dégommage*) and 'boiling'.

un'gummed, *ppl. a.*[1] [UN-[1] 8. Cf. Du. *ongegomd.*] Not smeared or treated with gum; free from gumming.

[**1775** ASH.] **1799** G. SMITH *Laboratory* II. 80 An ungummed paper will stick very close to the top of your tongue. **1891** KIPLING *City Dreadf. N.* 95 He now takes up an ungummed *chupatti* and fits it carefully all round.

un'gummed, *ppl. a.*[2] [f. UNGUM *v.*] Freed from gum; detached from being gummed.

1839 URE *Dict. Arts* 142 Into bags of coarse canvass.. about 25 lbs. or 35 lbs. of ungummed silk are enclosed.

un'gutted, *ppl. a.* (UN-[1] 8.)

1712 in J. J. Vernon *Par. & Kirk Hawick* (1900) 99 Thinking they [*sc.* herring] would spile if lying ungutted until ye Monday.

un'gyve, *v.* [UN-[2] 4 b.] *trans.* To free from gyves or fetters. Also *fig.*

1531 ELYOT *Gov.* II. vi, He.. commaunded hym to be ungyued and sette at libertie. **1569** NEWTON *Cicero's Olde Age* 4, I haue knowen a great maignie.. who were well pleased to be ungiued, loosed, and deliuered out of the yoke of their sensuall lustes. **1610** HEALEY *St. Aug. Citie of God* 310 Our intellect being ungived from the body, if it want the light of God's truth, it must needes lament and languish. **1831** CARLYLE *Sart. Res.* II. ix, My mind's eyes were now unsealed, and its hands ungyved.

un'gyved, *ppl. a.* [UN-[1] 8.] Not gyved or fettered; free.

1607 MARSTON *What you Will* II. i, Think'st thou a libertine, an vngiu'd breast Skornes not the shacklesse of thy enuious clogges? *c* **1850** LOWELL *Without & Within* vii, I envy him the ungyved prance By which his freezing feet he warms. **1892** 'M. FIELD' *Sight & Song* 40 Intent upon her work, as though It were full liberty ungyved to go.

unhabil, obs. Sc. var. UNABLE *a.*

†**un'habile**, *a. Obs.* [UN-[1] 7 and 5 b.] = INHABILE *a.*, UNABLE *a.*

1539 ELYOT in Ellis *Orig. Lett.* Ser. I. II. 117 Nowe althowgh very unmeete and unhabile, I have servyd the King .. truely and faithfully. **1567** *Sc. Acts, Mary* (1814) II. 573/1 Decerning thairfore.. his posteritie to be fra thine furth unhabile to bruik offices.. within this Realme. **1660** JER. TAYLOR *Ductor* III. ii. rule 2 § 14 The offending person is bound in Conscience not to accept a benefice.. to which by that censure he is made unhabile and unapt.

un'habit, *v.* [UN-[2] 4 b.] *trans.* To free from a habit; to disaccustom.

1650 FULLER *Pisgah* II. i. 64 So hard it is to unhabit mens mouths from old ill customs.

†**un'habit**, *ppl. a. Sc. Obs.* [UN-[1] 8 b.] Uninhabited.

1580 *Reg. Privy Council Scot.* III. 304 The said hous.. remanis unhabite be him.

un'habitable, *a.* Now *rare.* [UN-[1] 7 b and 5 b.] Uninhabitable. (Common *c* 1550–1690.)

1382 WYCLIF *Jer.* ii. 6 Wher is the Lord, that.. ladde vs ouer by desert, by the lond vnhabitable? **1388** —— *Jer.* vi. 8 Lest.. Y sette thee forsakun, a loond vnhabitable [**1382** vndwellable]. *a* **1485** FORTESCUE *Wks.* (1869) 486 He.. made Babyloyne unhabitable. **1527** in Hakluyt *Voy.* (1599) I. 219 The.. opinion, that vnder the line Equinoctiall for much heate the land was vnhabitable. **1555** EDEN *Decades* (Arb.) 297 That opinion.. touching the vnhabitable clime vnder the poles. **1615** G. SANDYS *Trav.* 90 Next vnto this stands Rhodes,.. once couered with the sea, or at least an vnhabitable marish. *a* **1652** J. SMITH *Sel. Disc.* ix. 452 The soul of a wicked man becomes a very unhabitable and incommodious place to itself. **1702** C. MATHER *Magn. Chr.* I. v. (1852) 76 They that have made Britain more unhabitable than the Torrid Zone. **1733** SWIFT *On Poetry* 181 So Geographers in Afric-Maps.. o'er unhabitable Downs Place Elephants for want of Towns. **1887** *Spectator* 15 Oct. 1381 The whole deep Northern fringe.. is unhabitable and uninhabited except by a few savages.

Hence **un'habitableness**.

1661 BOYLE *Physiol. Ess.* (1669) 27 The Unhabitableness of the Torrid Zone. **1668** H. MORE *Div. Dial.* III. xxxiv. I. 523 *marg.*, Difficulties touching the Habitableness or Unhabitableness of the Planets.

†**un'habitated**, *ppl. a. Obs.*[−0] [UN-[1] 8.] = next.

1648 HEXHAM II, *Een Onbewoont landt*, a land or country Vnhabitated.

†**un'habited**, *ppl. a. Obs.* [UN-[1] 8 and 5 b.] Uninhabited. (Freq. *c* 1500–1625.)

1490 CAXTON *Eneydos* xxii. 81 Goyng by longe wayes, dystroied, deserte & vnhabyted. **1491** —— *Vitas Patr.* (W. de W. 1495) III. i. 317 b/2 We arryued a londe in a contree unhabyted. **1553** EDEN *Treat. New Ind.* (Arb.) 39 When Vesputius had entered into the Iland, he founde it rude and vnhabited. **1585** T. WASHINGTON tr. *Nicholay's Voy.* II. xi. 45 b, The promontory is ful of ruines vnhabited. **1640** J. RUTTER *2nd Pt. Cid* III. i. 19 Ile seek some place unhabited by women. **1656** HEYLIN *Surv. France* 75 She will rather choose to leave her fine house unhabited.

unha'bitual, *a.* (UN-[1] 7.)

1864 LOWELL *Fireside Trav.* 60 A deacon.. drinking in, with unhabitual ears, a song.. with a dash of libertinism. **1895** J. RAE *Life A. Smith* xx. 324 Smith's outbreak of very unhabitual irritation with Strahan.

unha'bituate, *ppl. a.* [UN-[1] 8 b.] = next.

1815 MILMAN *Fazio* (1821) 28 This cataract of courtesy O'erwhelms my weak and unhabituate ears.

unha'bituated, *ppl. a.* (UN-[1] 8.)

[**1775** ASH.] **1796** MME. D'ARBLAY *Camilla* I. 227 Delighted to give, but unhabituated to any other exertion. **1834** COOPER *Good's Study Med.* (ed. 4) I. 632 Strangers, unhabituated to the climate and its diseases, suffer from remittents. **1898** P. MANSON *Trop. Diseases* iv. 89 A full dose of the drug which in the unhabituated would produce profound.. narcosis.

unhable, obs. var. UNABLE *a.* and *v.*

un'hacked, *ppl. a.*[1] [UN-[1] 8 + HACK *v.*[1] Cf. MDu. *ongehact*, Sw. *ohackad.*] Not hacked or cut.

1595 SHAKS. *John* II. i. 254 With vnhack'd swords, and Helmets all vnbruis'd. **1606** —— *Ant. & Cl.* II. vi. 38 To part with vnhackt edges, and beare backe Our Targes vndinted.

un'hacked, *ppl. a.*[2] [UN-[1] 8, 9 + HACK *sb.*[3] or *v.*[3]]

1. Not employed as a literary hack.

1778 *Heroic Ep. Unfort. Monarch* 2 A plain bard,.. Unhack'd, unplac'd, amongst the venal quire.

2. Not made common or hackneyed.

1894 BARING-GOULD *Deserts S. France* I. Pref. p. vii, It is a country unhacked by ordinary tourists.

un'hackled, *ppl. a.* (UN-[1] 8.)

1853 HICKIE *Aristoph.* (1872) II. 424 My flax which I have left at home unhackled.

un'hackneyed, *ppl. a.* [UN-[1] 8.]

1. Not habituated by long practice; inexperienced. Const. *in.*

1759 STERNE *Tr. Shandy* I. xi, In plain truth, he was a man unhackneyed and unpractised in the world. **1785** G. A. BELLAMY *Apology* III. 94, I was then unhackneyed in the villainies of mankind. **1814** SCOTT *Wav.* xxxii, He had a sort of naiveté and openness of demeanour, that seemed to belong to one unhackneyed in the ways of intrigue.

absol. **1796** MME. D'ARBLAY *Camilla* III. 112 Public amusements, to the young and unhackneyed, give entertainment without requiring exertion.

2. Not rendered commonplace or stale by frequent use or contact.

1824 MISS MITFORD *Village* Ser. I. 93 Her English was racy, unhackneyed, proper to the thought to a degree that only original thinking could give. **1856** G. BRIMLEY *Ess.* (1858) 236 To open to her almost untried and certainly unhacknied regions of beauty. **1880** *Academy* 27 Nov. 390/1 His [picture].. shows a research after unhackneyed effects.

Hence **un'hackneyedness**.

1884 SAINTSBURY in Ward *Eng. Poets* III. 218 There is almost always something novel in his dressing up of his images and a suggestive unhackneyedness in their expression.

un'had, *ppl. a. rare.* [UN-[1] 8 b.] Unobtained.

1421 HOCCLEVE *Jereslaus' Wife* 111 With this addicion, þat he nat shal Wirke, my Conseil and assent vnhad. *c* **1449** PECOCK *Repr.* II. xi. 212 That the hool profite of remembring .. be not lost and vnhad. **1876** *Whitby Gloss.* 206 *Unhad*, not yet obtained.

†**unhadien**, *v.*: see UN-[2] 2.

un'haft, *v.* (UN-[2] 4.)

1582 STANYHURST *Æneis* I. (Arb.) 21 The oars are cleene splintred, the helme is from ruther vnhafted. **1598** FLORIO, *Smanicare*,.. to vnhaft, to vnhilt, to vnhandle. **1611** COTGR., *Desmanchement*, an vnhafting.

un'hafted, (*ppl.*) *a.* (UN-[1] 8, 9.)

1894 BARING-GOULD *Deserts S. France* I. 145 Their rude stone axes,.. unhafted.

unhail, *a.*: see UNHALE *a.*

un'hailed, *ppl. a.* (UN-[1] 8.)

1715 ROWE *Lady Jane Grey* IV. i, Thro' a staring ghastly looking crowd, Unhail'd, unbless'd, with heavy heart he went. **1828** ALFORD in *Life* (1873) 31 Disappointment, and unhail'd success. **1832** TENNYSON *Lady of Shalott* 21 Unhail'd The shallop flitteth silken-sail'd. **1896** KIPLING *Seven Seas* 7 'Twixt seas unsailed and shores unhailed.

unhailsum, obs. Sc. var. UNWHOLESOME.

un'hair, *v.* [UN-[2] 4 and 7. Cf. MDu. and Du. *ontharen*, MHG. *enthâren.*]

1. *trans.* To deprive (the head, etc.) of hair.

1382 WYCLIF *Ezek.* xxix. 18 Eche heed maad ballid, and eche shuldre is vnheerid. **1598** FLORIO, *Disparuccare*, to pull off ones haire or perawig, to vnhaire. **1606** SHAKS. *Ant. & Cl.* II. v. 64 Ile vnhaire thy head, Thou shalt be whipt with Wyer. **1849** J. A. CARLYLE tr. *Dante's Inf.* 393 Even if thou unhair me, I will not tell thee who I am.

b. *Tanning.* To remove the hair from (a skin) by special processes.

1845 G. DODD *Brit. Manuf.* Ser. v. 182 The hide is then spread out on the beam, and 'unhaired', that is, scraped with a knife till the hair is removed. **1880** *Times* 27 Sept. 12/6 The cost of unhairing, fleshing, and scudding all kinds of skins.

2. *intr.* To lose the hair; to become free of hair.

1843 in Morfit *Tanning & Currying* (1853) 177 So that they [*sc.* the hides] may unhair without tainting. **1883** R. HALDANE *Workshop Rec.* Ser. II. 370/1 The hide is said to unhair in 24 hours.

Hence **un'haired** *ppl. a.*

1852 MORFIT *Tanning & Currying* (1853) 20 The softened and unhaired skins. **1881** MORGAN *Contrib. N. Amer. Ethnol.* 127 Screens of willow matting or unhaired skins.

un'haired, *a.* [UN-[1] 9.] Hairless, beardless.

Suggested by Theobald (1733), and formally possible, but cf. UNHEARD *ppl. a.* 2.

1595 SHAKS. *John* v. ii. 133 This vn-heard [*Th.* unhair'd] sawcinesse and boyish Troopes, The King doth smile at.

un'hairing, *vbl. sb. Tanning.* [f. UNHAIR *v.* 1 b.] The process of removing the hair from skins. Also *attrib.*

1842 *Penny Mag.* 28 May 212/1 The operations of 'fleshing', of 'unhairing' and of 'graining' are.. nearly alike in their general appearance. **1851-4** TOMLINSON *Arts & Manuf.* II. 30/1 A curved two-handled iron scraper, called the unhairing knife. **1897** C. T. DAVIS *Manuf. Leather* (ed. 2) 331 The goat-skins.. then go on to the unhairing machine .. or to the unhairing beams.

un'hairy, *a.* (UN-[1] 7.)

1576 NEWTON *Lemnie's Complex.* 42 b, In their other partes their skinne is smothe and vnhayrye, because moysture is aboue heate.

un'hale, *a. rare.* [UN-[1] 7. See HAIL *a.*, HALE *a.* 3.] †**a.** Unsalutary. *Obs.* **b.** Not hale or healthy.

a. **1483** *Gower's Conf.* (Caxton) I. 2122 [He] yaf suche counseyle Towarde his kyng, which was vnheyle.

b. **1653** E. WATERHOUSE *Apol. Learn.* 74 No more then it follows that a wasted man must get a child unhail, because he him-self is consumptive. **1828-32** WEBSTER, *Unhale*, a., unsound;.. not healthy.

unhale, obs. variant of UNWHOLE *a.*; dial. var. UNHELE *v.*

unhalesom, Sc. var. UNWHOLESOME.

un'hallow, *v.* [UN-[2] 3. Cf. G. *ent-*, Du. *ontheiligen*, ON. *úhelga* (Sw. *ohelga*, older Da. *uhelge*).] *trans.* To deprive of a holy or sacred character; to profane. (Common *c* 1575–1660.)

1535 COVERDALE *Isaiah* lvi. 2 He that taketh hede, yᵗ he vnhalowe not the Sabbath. —— *Zeph.* iii. 4 Hir prestes vnhalowe the Sanctuary. **1571** GOLDING *Calvin on Ps.* l. 8

Defylements that unhalowe the servis of God. **1628** WITHER *Brit. Rememb.* III. 1898 That I, for ever, may those paths refuse Which may unhallow, or pervert my Muse. **1645** MILTON *Tetrach.* Wks. 1851 IV. 192 Nothing more unhallows a man,..then a habit of wrath and perturbation. **1694** F. BRAGGE *Disc. Parables* xiv. 462 Pride, and vainglory, and self-esteem,..unhallow'd everything else that was good in him. **1821** LAMB *Elia* I. *Grace before Meat*, A sense of the co-presence of circumstances which unhallow the blessing. **1860** TRENCH *Serm. Westm. Abb.* xxix. 331 In a world where so much is ever seeking to unhallow our spirits, to render them common and profane.

un'hallowed, *ppl. a.* [OE. *unhālᵹod* (and *unᵹehālᵹod*), f. UN-[1] 8 + HALLOWED *ppl. a.*]

1. Not formally hallowed or consecrated; left secular or profane.

c **1000** *Sax. Leechd.* I. 380 Nim eall swa fela dropena.. unhalᵹodes eles. **1297** R. GLOUC. (Rolls) 7156 Ac vor þe chirche vn-halewed was, þeruore him was wo; He þoȝt lete it halwy. **1303** R. BRUNNE *Handl. Synne* 8609 Ȝyf þyng vnhalewed were forgete, þat yn holy cherche were lete, Or halewed þyng yn ouþer stede lay. *c* **1380** WYCLIF *Wks.* (1880) 69 þei wolen suffre an auter vnhalwedid [*sic*], or a chirche or a chirche ȝerde suspendid. *c* **1440** *Jacob's Well* 16 þey..þat..beryn awey, or stelyn holy cherche good out of ony oþer place vnhalwyd. **1532** MORE *Confut. Tindale* Wks. 375/1 Nowe wyll not Tyndal sette a strawe the more by the annoyntyng with holye oyle, then by smeryng with vnhalowed butter. **1587** in T. Norton *Calvin's Inst.* IV. xix. 492 *margin*, Men vnhallowed and vnconsecrated. **1797** S. & HT. LEE *Canterb. T.* (1799) I. 311 Let us beware how we deem that spot unhallowed which receives the ashes of the good! **1805** SOUTHEY *Madoc* I. xv, This night, Thy father's body..shall be..cast aside In some unhallowed pit, with foul disgrace.

2. Not having a hallowed or sacred character; unholy, impious, wicked: **a.** Of actions.

1591 *Troub. Raigne K. John* xii. 88 His quarrell is vnhallowed, false, and wrong. **1626** JACKSON *Creed* VIII. xi. § 1 To adventure upon the pretended mysteries of some unhallowed art. **1656** MILTON *Lett. State* Wks. 1851 VIII. 361 That unhallow'd villany nefariously attempted upon the Person of our Agent. **1725** POPE *Odyss.* XII. 468 Six guilty days my wretched mates employ In impious feasting, and unhallow'd joy. **1813** SCOTT *Rokeby* VI. xviii, What ruth can Denzil claim from him, Whose thoughtless youth he led astray, And damn'd to this unhallow'd way? **1846** MRS. A. MARSH *Father Darcy* II. xvi. 271 She..felt her heart shudder with unhallowed pleasure, as she thought of the dreadful day of reckoning.

b. Of persons, the hands, tongue, etc.

1588 SHAKS. *Tit. A.* V. iii. 14 Away Inhumaine Dogge, Vnhallowed Slaue. **1603** DRAYTON *Bar. Wars* V. xxxv, Vile traytors, hold of your vnhallowed hands. **1663** BP. PATRICK *Parab. Pilgr.* xvii, He cares not for being extolled by such unhallowed mouths. **1703** ROWE *Ulysses* I. i, The rude unhallow'd Railer's Tongue. **1765** GOLDSM. *Hermit* xxiv, Forgive a stranger rude,..Whose feet unhallow'd thus intrude Where Heaven and you reside. **1827** DISRAELI *V. Grey* VI. i. 272 Ye most unhallowed rogues.

c. Of places or things.

1588 SHAKS. *Tit. A.* II. iii. 210 Why dost not..helpe me out, From this vnhallow'd and blood-stained Hole? **1634** MILTON *Comus* 757, I had not thought to have unlockt my lips In this unhallow'd air. **1651** HOBBES *Leviath.* IV. xliv. 339 Wherein every thing..(except the unhallowed Spittle of the Priest) hath some set form of Exorcisme. **1853** KINGSLEY *Hypatia* i, He had entered the unhallowed precincts, where devils still lingered about their ancient shrines.

Hence **un'hallowedness.**

1899 MRS. E. KENNARD *Morals Midlands* 399 It has shown me the unhallowedness of love that is not lawful.

un'hallowing, *vbl. sb.* [f. UNHALLOW *v.*] The action of making unhallowed.

c **1554** BRADFORD *Hurt of Hearing Mass* (1580) C v, The prophanation and vnhallowyng, bothe of bodie and soule. **1571** GOLDING *Calvin on Ps.* lxxiv. 1 Beholding the horrible unhalowing of the Temple. **1645** USSHER *Body Div.* (1647) 242 The unhallowing or prophaneing of the Sabbath. *a* **1859** DE QUINCEY in Hogg *De Q. & Friends* (1895) 89 A sort of desecration and unhallowing analogous to the profanation of a temple.

unhallow-washed, *ppl. a.* [UN-[1] 8.] Not sprinkled with holy water.

1614 SYLVESTER *Parl. Vertues Royall* 196 When, by misheed or by mis-hap, hee coms Un-hallow-washt into the Sacred Rooms.

un'haloed, *a.* (UN-[1] 9.)

1823 J. WILSON *Trials Marg. Lyndsay* xxxix, The evening sun sank..and left the sky open..to an unhaloed moon.

un'halsed, *ppl. a. Sc.* [UN-[1] 8 + HALSE *v.*[1] 3. Cf. ON. *úheilsaðr* (MSw. *ohelsadh*, MDa. *uhelset*).] Not greeted or saluted.

1513 DOUGLAS *Æneid* IX. v. 141 Now hir I leif onhalsyt as I ryde. **1821** SCOTT *Pirate* xxi, It shall never be said that my kinswoman sat in her bower unhalsed.

un'halter, *v.* (UN-[2] 4 b. Cf. MDu. *onthalteren.*)

1584 PEELE *Arraignm. Paris* IV. ii, I do know a cast..that we would help t'unhalter them as fast. **1598** FLORIO, *Scapestrato*, vnbridled, vnhaltred, disintangled. **1611** COTGR., *Deschevestrer*, to vnhalter, or take off the halter from. **1816** J. WILSON *City of Plague* 287 Unhalter yon poor wretch—he must be carried Back to his prison.

un'halting, *ppl. a.* (UN-[1] 10.)

1832 L. HUNT *Poems* Pref. p. xlv, An unhalting and consistent narrative. **1852** ROCK *Ch. of Fathers* I. viii. III. 54 Holding..the true Catholic belief in the Eucharist, with a faith that was unhalting.

un'hammered, *ppl. a.* (UN-[1] 8.)

[**1775** ASH.] **1861** SIR W. FAIRBAIRN *Iron* 214 These results give a mean of 27·246 tons for the unhammered.. steel.

un'hamper, *v.*[1] [UN-[2] 5.] *trans.* To let out of a cage or hamper.

1620 SHELTON *Quix.* II. xvii. 105 Ech of them striuing to get as farre from the Cart as they could, before the Lyons should be vnhampered.

un'hamper, *v.*[2] [UN-[2] 3.] *trans.* To disengage; to set free, release.

1648 J. BEAUMONT *Psyche* XX. xxxvi, Now all her Passions unhamper'd were, And every Bond to Libertie relented. **1675** WORTHINGTON *Self-Resignation* I. vi. 39 His mind is unhampered, disentangled, and set loose. **1831** LAMB *Hercules Pacificatus* 111 The varlets, glad to be unhamper'd, Made each a leg,—then fairly scamper'd.

un'hampered, *ppl. a.* [UN-[1] 8.] Unclogged, unimpeded. (Common from *c* 1850.)

a **1699** J. BEAUMONT *Psyche* IX. lxxxix, Their free unhamper'd Contemplations towre Up to the crest of their divine desires. **1724** E. ERSKINE *Serm.* Wks. (1791) 118 A full, free, and unhampered offer. **1882** BRYCE *Manitoba* 23 He would start unhampered by old conditions and preexisting enactments.

†**un'hanced,** *ppl. a.* [UN-[1] 8.] Not raised or lifted up.

1582 STANYHURST *Æneis*, etc. (Arb.) 126 Therefor in houre iudicial The vngodlye shal vnhaunst remayne.

un'hand, *v.* [UN-[2] 4 b.] *trans.* To take the hand off; to release from one's grasp; to let go. Chiefly *arch.* in the imperative phrase ***unhand me!***

1602 SHAKS. *Ham.* I. iv. 84 Vnhand me Gentlemen: By Heau'n, Ile make a Ghost of him that lets me. **1655** tr. *Sorel's Com. Hist. Francion* VII. 22, I desire them to unhand me. **1687** MRS. BEHN *Lucky Chance* v, Unhand me, false deceiver, let me loose! **1748** RICHARDSON *Clarissa* (1811) II. 358 Unhand me this moment, or I will cry out for help. **1801** MAR. EDGEWORTH *Moral T.*, *Angelina* iv, Unhand my Angelina, or I shall die! **1860** SALA *Baddington Peerage* I. vii. 132 The surgeon unhanded his assistant, looking at him with a vexed and puzzled air.

fig. **1880** LANIER *Sunrise* 77 'Tis here thou canst unhand thy heart And breathe it free.

un'handcuffed, *ppl. a.* (UN-[1] 8.)

1861 GEN. P. THOMPSON *Audi Alt. Part.* III. clxii. 178 They might as well say, allow men to go un-handcuffed, and [etc.]. **1894** *Daily News* 8 Dec. 7/1 The prisoner..was seen sitting..unhandcuffed.

un'handicapped, *ppl. a.* (UN-[1] 8.)

1879 MEREDITH *Egoist* xxxvi, How was he to compete with these unhandicapped men?

un'handily, *adv.* (UN-[1] 11.)

1706 STEVENS I, *Inabilmente*, unaptly, unhandily. **1775** ASH, *Unhandily*.., aukwardly. **1865** CARLYLE *Fredk. Gr.* XII. vi. IV. 163 St. Agnes Day falls but unhandily this year; and I think the Fair will..not be held. **1896** DE VINNE *Moxon's Mech. Exerc.*, *Printing* 421 The signature was put unhandily in the center of the line.

un'handiness. [UN-[1] 12.]

1. Awkwardness, inexpertness.

1706 STEVENS I, *Inhabilidad*, Inhability, Unhandiness, Incapacity. **1862** MISS YONGE *C'tess Kate* iii, Whether it were from the difference of height, or from Kate's innate unhandiness. **1889** *The Voice* (N.Y.) 19 Sept., From whom communications would be accepted,..if only some one would help their unhandiness with the pen.

2. Unmanageableness.

1883 *Harper's Mag.* Aug. 449/1 The sloop rig..is so dangerous as to demand large crews to control its unhandiness. **1897** MARY KINGSLEY *W. Africa* 609 It was highly dangerous,..because of the violent storms..and the unhandiness of the native craft.

un'handled, *ppl. a.* [UN-[1] 8. Cf. MDu. *ongehandelt*, OHG. *ungehandelôt*, MDa. *uhandlet* (not negotiated).]

1. Of horses, etc.: Not broken in; untamed.

1558 *N. Co. Wills* (Surtees 1912) 12 My yong blacke hambling gelding unhandlyd. **1596** SHAKS. *Merch. V.* V. i. 72 A wilde and wanton heard Or race of youthful and vnhandled colts. **1639** T. DE GRAY *Expert Farrier* 302 Horses unhandled, to wit, in their youth. **1812** *Sporting Mag.* XXXIX. 68 Every description of horse, or mule, whether previously broke or unhandled. **1902** KIPLING *The Islanders* 21 Sons of the sheltered city—unmade, unhandled, unmeet—Ye pushed them raw to the battle.

2. Not dealt with or treated of.

1613 SHAKS. *Hen. VIII*, III. ii. 58 Cardinall Campeius.. Ha's left the cause o' th' King vnhandled. **1657** TOMLINSON *Renou's Disp.* 79 The extraction of oyles is yet unhandled.

b. Untried, unemployed.

1826 GALT *Last of Lairds* xi. 103 There's no a claw..the whilk Caption will leave unhandled.

3. Not touched with the hand. Also *fig.*

a **1657** R. LOVEDAY *Lett.* (1663) 218 Those [delights] that ..after an advantagious intermission return fresh and unhandled to the senses. **1745** ELIZA HEYWOOD *Female Spect.* No. 17 (1748) III. 258 The plumb unhandled lost its bloom. **1794** COLERIDGE *Lett.* (1895) 59, I, too, possessed the tender irritableness of unhandled sensibility.

un'handselled, *ppl. a.* (UN-[1] 8.)

1837 EMERSON *Addr. Amer. Schol.* Wks. (Bohn) II. 182 Out of unhandselled savage nature..come at last Alfred and Shakespeare. *a* **1862** THOREAU *Maine W.* i. (1864) 70 Here was no man's garden, but the unhandselled globe.

un'handsome, *a.* (and *adv.*) [UN-[1] 7. Cf. WFris. *on-*, *ûnhânsum* inexpert, unmanageable, Du. and Flem. *onhandzaam* (earlier *-saem*) intractable, unusable, older Da. *uhandsøm.*]

1. Not handsome, elegant, or graceful; faulty in appearance, form, or structure, plain, uncomely.

1530 PALSGR. 328/1 Unhansome,..*mausade.* **1579** E. K. *Gloss to Spenser's Sheph. Cal.* Nov. 51 Not comed, that is rude and vnhansome. **1589** HORSEY *Trav.* (Hakl. Soc.) App. 343, I was placed in an howse verie unhandsom [and] unholsoom. **1648** J. BEAUMONT *Psyche* XVI. clxxxix, Who ever thought the Rose or Lilie stood Guilty of course unhandsom Nakednesse, Because they never put on borrowed Hood? **1695** *Phil. Trans.* XIX. 152 This was formerly no unhandsom Structure, being built in the form of our Churches. **1781** P. BECKFORD *Hunting* (1802) 49, I could tell you that I have seen very good sport with very unhandsome packs. **1789** GIBBON *Autobiogr.* (1854) 43 A narrow, gloomy street, the most unfrequented of an unhandsome town. **1819** SCOTT *Ivanhoe* xiv, Both dressed in the ancient Saxon garb,..not unhandsome in itself. **1866** R. TATE *Brit. Mollusks* iv. 142 *Helix rotundata* is provided with not an unhandsome shell. **1895** SIR G. PARKER *Trail of Sword* viii, A large unhandsome house.

b. Of persons, their features, etc.

a **1586** SIDNEY *Arcadia* II. xix, I was glad I had done so good a deede for a Gentlewoman not unhandsome. **1631** A. TOWNSHEND *Albion's Tri.* 22, I was as loath to be brought vpon the Stage as an vnhansom Man is to see himselfe in a great Glasse. **1653** R. SANDERS *Physiogn.* 144 Socrates was the most nasty and unhandsom of all men living. **1709** MRS. MANLEY *Secret Mem.* (1720) II. 215 This spruce, affected, not unhandsome Lawyer had maid the Overture of his fair Person to Corinna. **1787** W. THOMSON tr. *Hist. Gt. Brit.* III. I. 121 Being generally well-shaped, and not unhandsome. **1826** *Q. Rev.* XXXIV. 331 It was hard to say whether he was more dunce or dwarf, more unlearned or unhandsome. **1887** ANNE ELLIOT *Old Man's Favour* II. i, A dark, unhandsome ..face.

c. As *adv.* Unhandsomely.

1596 SPENSER *F.Q.* V. xii. 38 Such were these Hags, and so vnhandsome drest.

†**2.** Unhandy, inconvenient, ill-adapted. *Obs.*

1548 UDALL, etc. *Erasm. Par. John* ix. 67 The night (perdy) is unhansome to woorke in. **1567** PALFREYMAN *Baldwin's Mor. Philos.* To Rdr., If I should haue ioyned the said number of sentences to the whole sum of this treatise, it should..haue seemed..the more vnhandsome of the reader to be carried. **1608** TOPSELL *Serpents* 270 These kindes of Spyders haue..shorter feete, and more vnhandsome to worke or finish any Webbes in their Loomes. **1690** NESSE *O. & N. Test.* I. 451 A loose, discinct, and diffluent mind is unready, unnimble, unhandy, and unhandsome for Gods service.

†**3.** Inexpert, unskilful. *Obs.*[-1]

1604 SHAKS. *Oth.* III. iv. 151, I was (vnhandsome Warrior, as I am) Arraigning his vnkindnesse with my soule.

4. Unfitting, unbecoming, unseemly; discourteous, mean.

1645 CHAS. I in Ellis *Orig. Lett.* Ser. I. III. 317 The treuth is, that his unhansom quitting the Castell and Forte of Bristol, hath inforced me to put him off those Commands. **1658** in *Verney Mem.* (1907) II. 83 Let mee conjure you not to doe a thing soe unhandsom, soe unmanly. **1729** FRANKLIN *Ess.* Wks. 1840 II. 18 It is barbarously unhandsome that one should be the butt of the company. **1799** DUNDAS in Owen *Wellesley's Desp.* (1877) 700 It was an unhandsome proceeding upon their part. **1810** *Sporting Mag.* XXXVI. 234 What he thought unhandsome conduct on the part of the plaintiff. **1856** G. WILSON *Gateways Knowl.* (1859) 96 To employ one's tongue..to speak against itself is but unhandsome treatment of it.

b. Of expressions, language, etc.

1647 CLARENDON *Hist. Reb.* V. § 263 To countenance those unhandsome expressions..they had found a new way of exprobration. **1656** HOBBES *Six Lessons* Wks. 1845 VII. 331, I leave it to your consideration to whom belong..the unhandsome attributes you so often give me. **1704** *Lond. Gaz.* No. 3987/2 Their Commander, having used some unhandsome Expressions, was detained. **1732** NEAL *Hist. Purit.* I. 187 It was reported that some of the warmer Puritans had turned the Habits into ridicule, and given unhandsome language to them that wore them. **1814** JANE AUSTEN *Mansfield Park* xxi, Lest it should betray her into any observations seemingly unhandsome.

c. Not generous or liberal.

1800 MRS. HERVEY *Mourtray Fam.* III. 109 I'll take her without a sixpence; which, let me tell you, I think no unhandsome offer.

†**5.** Unfortunate; unhappy. *Obs.*

1633 FLETCHER & SHIRLEY *Night-Walker* I. i, I know she loves him..Beyond the Indies in his mouldy Cabinets, But 'tis her unhandsome fate. **1657** W. COLES *Adam in Eden* To Rdr., Sundry unhandsome dysasters have happened to the ruine of many.

†**6.** Unpleasant, nasty. *Obs.*

1660 JER. TAYLOR *Ductor* I. v. rule 8 § 28 Like unhandsome and ill-tasted physick, it is against nature in the taking and in its operating.

un'handsomely, *adv.* [UN-[1] 11; cf. prec.]

†**1.** Not dexterously or cleverly; unskilfully. *Obs.*

1545 ASCHAM *Toxoph.* I. (Arb.) 89 And so the more strongе man not vsed to shote, shootes moost vnhansumlye. **1611** COTGR., *Faire le mibaudichon*, to doe a thing foolishly, or ill-fauouredly; vnhandsomely to goe about it. **1638** JUNIUS *Paint. Ancients* 100 The boy..did delight..to make oxen, horses, and men likewise, and..did it not unhandsomly.

2. Ungracefully, inelegantly.

1565 COOPER s.v. *Incompositus*, The verses runne vnhandsomely. *a* **1586** SIDNEY *Arcadia* I. xvii, About his middle he had..a long cloake of silke, which as unhandsomely, as it needes must, became the wearer. **1632** MASSINGER & FIELD *Fatal Dowry* IV. i, What fouler object in the world than to see a young, fair, handsome beauty unhandsomely dighted? **1670** OWEN *Disc.* vi. (1760) 82 A Man may have a Garment that may fit very ill, very unhandsomely, about him. **1705** COLLIER *Ess. Mor. Subj.* III. *Pain* 13 The Roman Gladiators..chose rather to receive a Cut than avoid it unhandsomely.

†**3.** Unfitly; inappropriately, awkwardly. *Obs.*

1548 ELYOT, *Incommodé*,..vngaynely,..vnhandsomely, vn-easyly. **1573** BARET *Alv.* I. 96 Verie Incommodiouslie, verie vnhandsomelie. **1649** JER. TAYLOR *Apol. Liturgy* §92 This was not unhandsomely intimated by the word sometimes used by..the Greek church. **1651** C. CARTWRIGHT *Cert. Relig.* I. 290 These things do but very unhandsomely hang together. **1680** H. MORE *Apocal. Apoc.* 192 Lacqueyes..in querpo, which sutes not unhandsomly with the word σώματα, bodies.

4. Unfittingly, unbecomingly; illiberally, meanly.

1650 R. STAPYLTON *Strada's Low C. Wars* IV. 79 His Majesty..thought it best to do that, while his authoritie was intire, which perhaps necessity might unhandsomely inforce him to. **1668** DRYDEN *Tyrannic Love* IV. i, He raves, sir, and, to cover my disdain, Unhandsomely would his denial feign. **1700** in *Pennsylv. Hist. Soc. Mem.* IX. 4 A bill..opposed and voted out—I think, very unhandsomely. **1709** STRYPE *Ann. Ref.* iv. 82 Dering..had charged him with neglect of religion, and unhandsomely and untruly told him [etc.]. **1839** HALLAM *Hist. Lit.* III. ii. §61 This story Franklin, rather unhandsomely, appropriated to himself. **1855** MACAULAY *Hist. Eng.* xvii. IV. 55 He had poor relations; and the government..had most unhandsomely left them to his care.

b. Discourteously, rudely; without due respect or consideration.

1662 PEPYS *Diary* 5 Nov., My Lady Batten..complained ..of my wife's speaking unhandsomely of her. **1707** NORRIS *Treat. Humility* vi. 250 To know when he is handsomely or unhandsomely treated. **1759** STERNE *Tr. Shandy* I. xii, Bruised and mis-shapened with the blows which..some others have so unhandsomely given me in the dark. *a* **1781** R. WATSON *Philip II*, III. (1793) I. 378 They complained that their masters were rather used unhandsomely. **1817** KIRBY & SP. *Entomol.* xix. II. 170 They seize her, keep her in confinement, and treat her very unhandsomely.

un'handsomeness. [UN-[1] 12.]

†**1.** Unhandiness; inconvenience. *Obs.*

1550 THOMAS, *Malageuolezza*, vnhandsomnesse, or difficultee. **1577** B. GOOGE *Heresbach's Husb.* II. (1586) 83 b, Such Uines as are ioyned with Trees, for the vnhandsomenesse, can not be thus handled.

2. Inelegance, uncomeliness, plainness.

a **1586** SIDNEY *Arcadia* II. xxii, The sweetnes of her countenance did give such a grace to what she did, that it did make hansome the unhansomnes. **1606** DEKKER *Sev. Sins* I. (Arb.) 11 Couered with two or three threed-bare Carpets.. to hide the vnhandsomnes of the Carpenters worke. **1658** *Whole Duty Man* xiii. §7 First, for infirmities, be they either of body or mind, the deformity and unhandsomness of the one, or the weakness and folly of the other [etc.]. **1675** G. R. tr. *Le Grand's Man without Passion* 168 You carry nothing of less use about you then that which you employ to hide your unhandsomeness. **1873** MISS BROUGHTON *Nancy* I. 6 We reach our nadir of unhandsomeness in Ton Ton.

3. Unbecomingness; unfittingness.

1598 FLORIO, *Sgratia*, a disgrace, a gracelesnes or vnhandsomnes. **1611** COTGR., *Inconvenance*, a misbecomming, vnhandsomenesse, vnfitnesse, vnseemelinesse. **1653** JER. TAYLOR *Serm. for Year, Winter* ii. 26 Then we shall see things as they are, the evill circumstances and the crooked intentions, the adherent unhandsomenesse and the direct crimes. **1664** INGELO *Bentiv. & Ur.* VI. 350 When they Consider that Unhandsomness which will never cease to attend their unjust Prosperities. **1774** ADAM SMITH in Thomson *Life Cullen* (1832) I. 475 Bating the unhandsomeness of the practice,..in what manner does the public suffer by it? **1871** *Routledge's Ev. Boy's Ann.* June 338 The unhandsomeness of breakfasting upon one's offspring.

un'handsoming, *vbl. sb.* (UN-[2] 6 a, 8.)

1592 NASHE *P. Penilesse* B iv b, Any thing that is said or doone to the vnhandsoming of their ambition, is straight wrested to the name of treason. **1593** G. HARVEY *Pierce's Super.* 180 Vnhandsoming of diuinityship, absurdifying of phrases.

un'handy, *a.* [UN-[1] 7. Cf. WFris. *on-, ûnhandich*, Du. *onhandig*, LG. *unhandig*, Da. *uhændig*, Norw. *uhendig*, Sw. *ohändig*.]

1. Not easy to handle or manage; inconvenient, awkward, clumsy.

1664 ETHEREDGE *Love in Tub* II. iii, If she be not as kind as fair, But peevish and unhandy, Leave her. **1719** DE FOE *Crusoe* II. (Globe) 422 They took in Pieces all my clumsy unhandy Things. **1775** R. CHANDLER *Trav. Asia M.* (1825) I. 68 Our boat carried a large unhandy sail. **1778** [W. H. MARSHALL] *Minutes Agric., Digest* 47 Their being worked double made them unhandy. **1816** J. WILSON *City of Plague* II. v. 114 These swords are ugly and unhandy things. **1871** *Routledge's Ev. Boy's Ann.* Feb. 91 The very size and nature of the rig of many of the Spanish ships rendered them unwieldy and 'unhandy', as sailors call it. **1876** *N. Amer. Rev.* CXXIII. 32 An unhandy arrangement, which detracts from the value of the work.

2. Not skilful in using the hands; lacking in dexterity.

1669 SHADWELL *Royal Shepherd* I. i, O fie, Urania! how unhandy art thou! Sir, let me practise my little skill in surgery Upon you. **1726** SWIFT *Gulliver* III. ii, Yet in the common actions and behaviour of life, I have not seen a more clumsy, awkward, and unhandy people. **1798** W. HUTTON *Life* 6 Being hurt at seeing the nurse unhandy, she would do the work herself. **1850** GROTE *Greece* II. lx. (1862) V. 288 The Akarnanian darters..were for this reason unhandy with their missiles. **1876** TREVELYAN *Macaulay* (1883) I. 123 He was unhandy to a degree quite unexampled in the experience of all who knew him.

fig. **1683** KENNETT *Erasm. on Folly* 32 Wise men were so awkward and unhandy in the ordering of publick affairs.

un'hang, *v.* [UN-[2] 3. Cf. Du. *onthangen*.]

1. *trans.* To take down from a hanging position.

1399 LANGL. *Rich. Redeles* III. 293 For ho so þus leued his lyff to the ende..My3te seie þat he sawe..þat heuene were vnhonge out of þe hookis. *c* **1430** *Pilgr. Lyf Manhode* I. cxxiv. (1869) 66 From thennes the scauberk she vnheeng and brouhte it. *c* **1532** DU WES *Introd. Fr.* in *Palsgr.* 941 To unhange, *despendre*. **1598** FLORIO, *Disimpiccare*, to vnhang. **1614** W. BROWNE *Sheph. Pipe* I. B 2 b, Wicked Swaines, that beare me spight,..Of my fold will draw the pegges,..Or vnhang my Weathers bell. **1630** J. TAYLOR (Water P.) *Trav.* Wks. III. 82/1, I pray the let vs make hast, and put the Waggon vnder the Gibbet, to see if we can vnhang and saue him. **1722** DE FOE *Col. Jack* v, They unhanged a small copper, and brought it off. **1769** *Lloyd's Even. Post* Sept.–Oct. 319/2 A Butcher's wife..was endeavouring to unhang a joint of meat. **1856** SMETHAM in Beardmore *Smetham* (1906) 26 Unhanging a Turner from the wall of a distant room, he brought it to the table. **1888** A. NUTT *Holy Grail* 40 No knight should..unhang the shield till Galahad should come.

fig. **1616** HIERON *Wks.* II. 24 It was not inough..for our Sauiour to take them off, & (as it were) to vnhang them from the world, unlesse He did also fixe them other-where.

b. *Naut.* To remove (a rudder) from its fastening.

1600 HAKLUYT *Voy.* III. 552 Their cables do oftentimes breake, and their ruthers are vnhanged,..by reason the shippes doe ride but in little water. **1691** T. H[ALE] *Acc. New Invent.* 49 They were forced to unhang the Rudder, and new hang it again. **1772–84** *Cook's Voy.* (1790) III. 796 We..found the Tamar lying between the island and the main, having unhung her rudder. **1799** *Naval Chron.* II. 568 The rudder of the Isis was unhung.

c. To divest of hangings. *rare*[−0].

1719 BOYER *Dict. Royal* II, To Unhang a Room, *détendre la Tapisserie d'une Chambre*.

2. To undo the hanging of (a person).

1829 SOUTHEY *Pilgrim to Compostella* III. 54 So, with all honours that might be, They gently unhang'd Pierre. **1837** HAWTHORNE *Twice-told T.* (1851) I. vii. 134 And hanging the nigger wouldn't unhang the old gentleman!

un'hanged, *ppl. a.* [UN-[1] 8. Cf. Sw. *ohängd*.] Not (yet) executed by hanging. (Cf. UNHUNG *ppl. a.* 2.)

c **1440** *York Myst.* xxxii. 186 þou on-hanged harlott, hark what I saie. **1525** LD. BERNERS *Froiss.* II. ccxviii. [ccxiv.] 674 It is pytie these vnthriftes be vnhanged or drowned, for tellyng of suche lies. **1596** SHAKS. *1 Hen. IV*, II. iv. 144 There liues not three good men vnhang'd in England. **1786** BURNS *Twa Dogs* 228 They..Pore owre the devil's pictur'd beuks;..An' cheat like ony unhanged blackguard. **1821** SCOTT *Kenilw.* v, Some evil fortune dogs the heels of that unhanged rogue Lambourne. **1848** THACKERAY *Van. Fair* li, We may abuse a man as much as we like, and call him the greatest rascal unhanged—but do we wish to hang him therefore? **1899** T. M. ELLIS *Cat's-eye Rings* 78 Through this unhanged fiend..my mother was one day..murdered.

transf. **1834** *Tait's Mag.* I. 54/1 The advent of the Whigs to power..has been a decided godsend to the trading advocates of unhanged abuses.

un'hanging, *vbl. sb.* [UN-[1] 13.] Omission of hanging (a gate).

a **1500** *Bk. of Brome* (1886) 166 3e shall enquere 3ef yer is ony mane yat hath no3te hangyd his fal-3ates,..the whiche on-hangyng hath be noyans to hys neybur.

un'hangingly, *adv.* [UN-[1] 11.]

† Disconnectedly.

c **1449** PECOCK *Repr.* IV. iv. 441 For elles this clausul.. hadde be seid vnpertynently and vnhangingli fro the materis of the clausulis folewing and afore going.

†**un'hap,** *sb. Obs.* [UN-[1] 12. Cf. ON. *úhapp* (Icel. *óhapp*, Norw. dial. *uhapp*), and WANHAP.]

1. Misfortune, mishap.

a **1225** *Ancr. R.* 180 Mislikunge wiðuten—ase sicnesse, meseise, scheome, vnhep. *c* **1325** *Body & Soul* 257 in *Map's Poems* (Camden) 343 What eyleth the, thou grimli gaast? That me thus breidest of myn unhap. *c* **1384** CHAUCER *H. Fame* 89 [To] shelde hem fro pouerte and shonde And fro vnhappe and eche disese. **1412–20** LYDG. *Chron. Troy* III. 5099 For of þe cite, sothly, and þe toun, His vnhap were endeles ruyne. *c* **1440** *Gesta Rom.* xxxiii. 129, I have thorow vnhappe slayn a man. *c* **1489** CAXTON *Sonnes of Aymon* i. 38 Your sone is ded by grete unhappe. **1523** LD. BERNERS *Froiss.* I. 521 This was the ende of yuan, or Owen, of Wales, ..slayne by great vnhap and treason. *a* **1586** SIDNEY *Arcadia* II. xvi, Sometime to visit that place, where first she was so happy as to see the cause of her vnhap.

2. With pl. A misfortune or mishap.

c **1230** *Hali Meid.* 29 Ne mei na worldlich unhap bireauen ham hare weole. *a* **1250** *Owl & Night.* 1267 Naueþ mon no sikerhede þat he ne may wene & adrede þat sum vnhap neih him beo. **13..** *E.E. Allit. P.* B. 892 þay wern wakned..Of on þe vglokest vnhap þat euer on erd suffred. **1390** GOWER *Conf.* II. 36 Thei..to the god for helpe criden Of suche unhappes as betyden. *c* **1440** *York Myst.* xviii. 152 That no myscheue on hym betyde, Nor none vnhappe. **1559** *Mirr. Mag.* (1562) A a vj, Al which unhappes that they were not foreseene, I was in fault.

3. *attrib.* or as *adj.* = UNHAPPY *a.*

1509 HAWES *Past. Pleas.* (Percy Soc.) 82 Now all my desteny Unhap and happy, upon you doth growe. *Ibid.* 137 This unhap love had his mynde so broken.

†**un'hap,** *v. Obs.*[−1] [f. prec.] *intr.* To bring misfortune.

c **1560** A. SCOTT *Poems* xxxiv. 123 Quhair [*v.r.* For] hurdome ay vnhappis With quenry, canis, and coppis.

unhap'ly, obs. var. UNHAPPILY *adv.*

†**un'happen,** *a. Obs.* [UN-[1] 7: cf. ON. *heppinn* fortunate, Norw. *uheppen* unfortunate; and see UNHEPPEN *a.*] Unfortunate, miserable, wretched.

13.. *E.E. Allit. P.* B. 573 And al was for þis ilk euel, þat vn-happen glette. **13..** *St. Erkenwolde* 198 in Horstm. *Altengl. Leg.* (1881) 270 One þe vnhapnest hathel þat euer one erthe 3ode. **1535** STEWART *Cron. Scot.* (Rolls) I. 528 Than da by da tha waittit on thair tyme, For to commit that curst vnhappin cryme.

un'happen, *v.* [UN-[1] 14 or UN-[2] 7.] *intr.* Of an event, etc.: to be reversed; to become as though it had never occurred. Also *trans.*, to cause not to happen or to have happened.

1805 *Ann. Rev.* III. 270 The past cannot unhappen. **1876** MRS. WHITNEY *Sights & Ins.* II. xxxiii. 628 Had I been letting things happen that couldn't unhappen any more, ever? **1975** I. MURDOCH *Word Child* 135 All these things did happen. Keeping them secret isn't going to unhappen them. **1980** —— *Nuns & Soldiers* iii. 187 It's..so unreal. All this can unhappen. You can unhappen it just by saying we won't speak of it again.

un'happily, *adv.* [UN-[1] 11. Cf. ON. *úheppiliga* (Norw. dial. *uheppelege*).]

1. Unfortunately, unluckily; by misfortune or mischance; regrettably.

c **1374** CHAUCER *Troylus* v. 937 But he was slayn.. Vnhappyly at Thebes al to raþe. *c* **1400** *Destr. Troy* 7104 þen vnhappely hys hest he hastid to do, þat angart hym after angardly sore. *c* **1430** *Syr Gener.* (Roxb.) 7351 Jewel vnhappelie hidre did hir bring, For now he hath an euel ending. **1558** in Feuillerat *Revels Q. Mary* (1914) 251, I ame not able to ryde..by reason of a strayn which I have vnhappelie mett with. **1576** LAMBARDE *Peramb. Kent* 138 b, I delyver suche only as lying in my waye doe offer them selues, and suche as..I haue not vnhappily lighted vpon. **1609** DANIEL *Civ. Wars* IV. lvii, Worc'ster (who had escap'd vnhappily His death in battel) on a Scaffold dies. **1647** CLARENDON *Hist. Reb.* I. §51 That War in which the King was so unhappyly engaged against Spain. **1738** in *Nairne Peerage Evidence* (1874) 42 Whereas John Nairne..was unhappily seduced..to join in the rebellion.

b. Used parenthetically or in loose construction.

a **1586** SIDNEY *Arcadia* III. xxviii, She saw, as he lifted up his armes.., about one of them, unhappily, tied a garter. **1603** SHAKS. *Meas. for M.* I. ii. 160 *Lucio.* With childe, perhaps? *Claudio.* Vnhappely, euen so. **1649** *Bounds Publ. Obed.* 2 The first Treatise, in which (and the unhappilier, to give foundation to practicable errors) they..mistake principles. **1697** BENTLEY *Phal.* (1699) 109 He had unhappily forgot it, when he writ this Epistle. **1728** *Col. Rec. Pennsylv.* III. 327 By being unhappily in the Company of those who committed it. **1796** MME. D'ARBLAY *Camilla* III. 388 But to all that was thus most fascinating to others, she joined unhappily all that was most dangerous for her-self. **1849** MACAULAY *Hist. Eng.* iv. I. 460 Unhappily the splendid qualities of John Churchill were mingled with alloy of the most sordid kind. **1890** *Retrospect Med.* CII. 340 But when this is unhappily not to be accomplished, a partial removal has obviously prolonged life.

2. With evil fortune or mischance; evilly, miserably, wretchedly.

c **1375** *Sc. Leg. Saints* xxxiv. (*Pelagia*) 179, I..þat has nocht anerly my-selfe Sonkyne in syne vnhapely. **1390** GOWER *Conf.* I. 54 And ate laste unhappely This Hert his oghne houndes slowhe. **1412–20** LYDG. *Chron. Troy* IV. 1489 Achilles axeþ how it is Amonge Grekis, & clerly how it stood...'Certis,' quod he, 'ful vnhappily'. **1509** BARCLAY *Shyp of Folys* (1570) 20 But these lewde caitifs.., liuing vnhappily, In shame they liue, and wretchedly they dye. **1596** in *10th Rep. Hist. MSS. Comm.* App. I. 76 At the last maist unnaturally and unhappilie..fell out the lamentable slauchter of the saidis vmquhill James Stirling. **1605** SHAKS. *Lear* I. ii. 157, I promise you, the effects he writes of, succeede vnhappily. *a* **1658** LOVELACE *Poems* (1904) 134 Ah Victory! unhap'ly wonne, Weeping and Red is set the Sun. **1667** MILTON *P.L.* x. 917, I..unweeting have offended, Unhappilie deceav'd. **1779** WARNER in Jesse *Selwyn & Contemp.* (1844) IV. 300 The giddy girl who married unhappily. **1781** COWPER *Charity* 632 If, unhappily deceiv'd, I dream, And prove too weak for so divine a theme.

b. Unsuccessfully.

1533 BELLENDEN *Livy* I. xv. (S.T.S.) I. 86 þe Sabynis faucht vnhappely in þis last battall. **1654** tr. *Martini's Conq. China* 55 So as if any fought unhappily,..the Governors hardly ever escaped alive. **1831** SCOTT *Ct. Rob.* xiii, One of those simple persons who manage so unhappily what they mean for civilities, that those to whom they are addressed receive them frequently in another sense.

†**3.** Mischievously, maliciously. *Obs.*

1509 HAWES *Past. Pleas.* XVIII. (Percy Soc.) 85 What man on live can use suche governaunce..but right pryvely Behinde his backe some sayth unhappely? **1549** CHALONER *Erasm. on Folly* G iij, They thynke unhappeliest in their herts, whan they speake smotheliest with their toungs. **1660** J. S. *Andromana* III. iii, I know you always talk'd unhappily, And if your heart dare do what's ill, I know it can well teach your tongue excuses.

†**b.** Unfavourably. *Obs.*[−1]

1613 SHAKS. *Hen. VIII*, I. iv. 89 You are a Churchman, or Ile tell you Cardinall, I should iudge now vnhappily.

†**4.** Unpleasantly near the truth; shrewdly. *Obs.*

1577–82 BRETON *Toyes Idle Head* Wks. (Grosart) I. 33/2 The iust occasion why, God knowes: and I, perhappes, can gesse vnhappily. **1584** LYLY *Campaspe* V. iv, *Alex.* Think you not, Hephestion, that she wold faine be commaunded? *Hep.* I am no thought catcher, but I gesse vnhappily. **1602** SHAKS. *Ham.* IV. v. 13 Which..Indeed would make one thinke there would be thought, Though nothing sure, yet much vnhappily.

†**5.** Unfitly; unskilfully. *Obs.*

1602 BRETON *Wonders worth Hearing* To Rdr., A few odde Wonders, that being vnhappily set downe, might passe away a little idle time to looke on. **1704** SWIFT *T. Tub* Pref., My genius being conceived to lie not unhappily that way. **1726** —— *Gulliver* III. iv, On the contrary, I never knew a soil so unhappily cultivated.

6. Without happiness or pleasure.

1687 MIÈGE *Gt. Fr. Dict.* II, He lives very unhappily with her, *il vit fort mal avec elle.* **1814** JANE AUSTEN *Mansfield Park* ii, Fanny..grew up there not unhappily among her cousins. **1848** THACKERAY *Van. Fair* xxxvi, A village.. where little Rawdon passed the first months of his life, not unhappily, with a numerous family of foster-brothers.

un'happiness. [UN-¹ 12.]

1. Misfortune, mishap, ill luck.

1470–85 MALORY *Arthur* VII. vii. 221 Vnhappely he hath donne this day thorou myshappe; ..and other dedes he dyde beforne ryght meruleyllous and thorou vnhappynes. **1509** HAWES *Past. Pleas.* XVI. (Percy Soc.) 70 Now have I tolde you all the veray trouthe Of my wofull chaunce and great unhappynesse. **1561** T. NORTON *Calvin's Inst.* II. iii. 17 b, Whose feete are swyfte to shedde bloude, in whose wayes ys sorrowe and vnhappynesse. **1621** WITHER *Motto, Nec Habeo* C 1 b, I haue not that vnhappinesse, to be A Rich Mans Sonne. **1651** HOBBES *Gov. & Soc.* Ep. Ded., Yet the naturall right of Preservation..will not admit it to be a Vice, though it confesse it to be an Unhappinesse. *a* **1701** MAUNDRELL *Journ. Jerus.* 17 March 1697, It was our unhappiness to have ..a very violent storm of Thunder, and Rain. **1753** CIBBER *Lives Poets* I. 18 Lamenting the unhappiness of a fluctuating language, that buries in its ruins even genius itself. **1872** TENNYSON *Gareth & Lynette* 1204, I..here lie thrown by whom I know not, all thro' mere unhappiness—Device and sorcery and unhappiness.

b. Unfavourable character.

1704 *Collect. Voy.* (Churchill) III. 659/2 The Unhappiness of the Climate.

†**2.** Evil, wrong-doing, mischief. *Obs.*

c **1485** *Digby Myst.* (1882) II. 627 Thys traytour..That doth this vnhappynes a-gayns all! **1526** *Pilgr. Perf.* (W. de W. 1531) 242 b, Manasses was as the pyt and synke of all fylth & synne and vnhappynesse. **1548** UDALL, etc. *Erasm. Par. John* vii. 57 Readye to be hiered to do all unhappinesse. **1606** HOLLAND *Sueton.* 156 *margin*, Such as would play Bo-peepe and hide themselves when they had done some unhappinesse. *a* **1625** FLETCHER *Love's Pilgrimage* II. ii, A wild boy, That for the fruits of his unhappiness, Is faign to seek the wars.

3. The condition of being unhappy in mind.

1722 WOLLASTON *Relig. Nat.* vi. (1724) 143 No doubt there is to every wrong and vitious act a suitable degree of unhappiness and punishment annext. **1791** BOSWELL *Johnson* an. 1758, As easy and pleasant a state of existence, as constitutional unhappiness ever permitted him to enjoy. **1842** A. COMBE *Physiol. Digestion* (ed. 4) 201 Hence..too often arise indifference and unhappiness between those whom Nature has formed..to suit each other. **1861** MILL *Utilit.* ii. 10 By unhappiness is intended, pain and the privation of pleasure. **1895** ROSA BAUGHAN *Palmistry* 27 A star on Venus means unhappiness caused by love.

un'happy, *a.* [UN-¹ 7.]

1. Of persons (or animals): Causing misfortune or trouble (to oneself or others); objectionable or miserable on this account.

To some extent passing into sense 2.

a **1300** *Cursor M.* 3637 Ful lath me ware, þat he þat blissing fra þe bare, Vnhappi wreche has he ben ai. *c* **1375** *Sc. Leg. Saints* xxxvi. (*Baptista*) 736 For cowaitise a man, vnhappy & wnwyse, dalf vpe his graf be nichtirtale. **1470–85** MALORY *Arthur* VII. vii. 221 He is an vnhappy knaue, and vnhappely he hath donne this day thorou myshappe. *c* **1489** CAXTON *Sonnes of Aymon* viii. 194 Lete vs goo assaylle thise vnhappy folke of the kynge Charlemagne. *c* **1518** SKELTON *Magnyf.* 1374, I haue brought Vnto Magnyfycence a full vngracyous sorte, For all hokes vnhappy to me haue resorte. **1585** T. WASHINGTON tr. *Nicholay's Voy.* I. xix. 22 b, An vnhappie souldier of Prouence..declared vnto the Turkes the weakest places of the castle. **1607** G. WILKINS *Miseries Enforced Marriage* K 1, I am sure they are greater sinners, That made this match, and were vnhappy men, For they caus'd all, and may heauen pardon them. *a* **1614** FLETCHER *Valentinian* v. ii, *Lici.* He is poyson'd... *Lyci.* Who? *Lici.* The wretch Aretus, That most unhappy villain. **1624** DARCIE tr. *Du Moulin's Heraclitus* vi. 41 There is nothing more hard to find in this world than a good woman, a good Mule, and a good Goat, being three vnhappie beasts. **1770** HARRIS in *Priv. Lett. Ld. Malmesbury* (1870) I. 192 He was an unhappy sot, and last week shot himself through the head. **1828** SCOTT *F.M. Perth* x, These unhappy Highland clans are again breaking into general commotion.

†**b.** *Sc.* Ill-natured; bad-tempered. *Obs.*⁻¹

1756 MRS. CALDERWOOD in *Coltness Collect.* (Maitl. Cl.) 127 Indeed he was so unhappy, (which signifies ill-nature in Scots,) that she durst never ask anything at him he was not pleased to tell her.

2. Of persons: Unfortunate, unlucky, ill-fated; miserable in lot or circumstances. Also, in later use, wretched in mind.

1375 BARBOUR *Bruce* III. 291 Bot he the mar be wnhappy, He sall eschew it in party. *c* **1400** *Destr. Troy* 2689 A! nobill Troye, þe noy þat neghis þe at hond!.. A! vnhappy hegh kyng, what hardship is to the! *c* **1440** *Promp. Parv.* 365/2 On-happy, *infortunatus, infelix.* **1470–85** MALORY *Arthur* VI. x. 198 Who that vseth peramours shalle be vnhappy, and all thyng is vnhappy that is aboute hem. **1523** FITZHERB. *Husb.* §144 He is an vnhappy man or woman, that..woll chose the worst parte. **1587** GOLDING *De Mornay* xvi. 295 The most parte..come to this point, that man is the most vnhappiest of liuing wights. **1600** J. PORY tr. *Leo's Africa* II. 70 This unhappie king beeing utterly driuen to dispayre,.. in the night time road foorth of the citie. **1655** FULLER *Ch. Hist.* III. vi. §40. 86 Endless it were to reckon up the indignities offered unto these Jews... A people equally unhappy at feasts, and at frays. **1726** SWIFT *Gulliver* II. viii, The seamen might conjecture some unhappy mortal to be shut up in the box. **1794** MRS. RADCLIFFE *Myst. Udolpho* xxvii, Some unhappy person, who, having been plundered by his banditti, was brought hither a captive. **1849** MACAULAY *Hist. Eng.* iv. I. 432 In the midst of this splendour,..the unhappy woman gave herself up to an agony of grief. **1900** *Longm. Mag.* Mar. 450 He fully agreed that her mother must not be made unhappy.

absol. **1647** COWLEY *Mistr., Sleep* iv, Thou scorn'st th' Unhappy; and the Happy, Thee. **1762** STERNE *Tr. Shandy* v. i, Pity the unhappy, said a devout, venerable, hoary-headed man. **1839** CARLYLE *Chartism* viii, A tear at least is due to the unhappy.

b. Const. *in* (some respect).

1604 SHAKS. *Oth.* III. iv. 102 Sure, there's some wonder in this Handkerchiefe, I am most vnhappy in the losse of it. **1634** SIR T. HERBERT *Trav.* 221 Vnhappiest in this, that their owne Nation forgot them quite. **1711** ADDISON *Spect.* No. 164 ¶1 Constantia was..very unhappy in a Father, who ..took delight in nothing but his Money. **1770** HARRIS in *Priv. Lett. Ld. Malmesbury* (1870) I. 201 They have been unhappy in another fire at Wilton.

c. Unsuccessful; apt to make mistakes.

1651 WITTIE tr. *Primrose's Pop. Err.* I. 45, I have observed that no man is more unhappy than those physicians, that note their medicines out of books. **1662** STILLINGFL. *Orig. Sacræ* I. iii. §9 He is as unhappy a person in Philology, as any that have pretended so much acquaintance with it. **1711** MRS. LONG *Let. to Swift* 18 Nov., That I may clear my meanings, which are always far from offending my friends, however unhappy I may be in my expressions.

d. Of places: Subject to, suffering from, misfortunes or evils.

1591 SPENSER *Ruins Time* 146 Seemes, that that gentle Riuer..From my vnhappie neighborhood farre fled. **1667** MILTON *P.L.* I. 268 Wherefore..call [we] them not to share with us their part In this unhappy Mansion? **1697** DRYDEN *Virg. Georg.* II. 308 And such a country could Acerræ boast, Till Clanius overflowed the unhappy coast. *Ibid.* IV. 751 Th' unhappy Climes, where Spring was never known. **1846** MRS. A. MARSH *Father Darcy* II. iv. 92 You!—have you ventured to our unhappy house? **1849** MACAULAY *Hist. Eng.* iv. I. 498 The bands which oppressed and wasted these unhappy districts.

3. Of things: Associated with, bringing about or causing, misfortune or mishap; disastrous.

c **1386** CHAUCER *Man of Law's T.* 204 Infortunat ascendent tortuous,..O fieble Moone, vnhappy been thy paas. **1390** GOWER *Conf.* I. 236 Sche tok out thilke unhappi scherte. *Ibid.* 326 At thilke unhappi freisshe welle. **1420–2** LYDG. *Thebes* I. 821 Of whom the weddyng..Vnhappy was and passing odious, Infortuned and vngracious. **1470–85** MALORY *Arthur* II. xviii. 97 Thenne Balyn smote hym ageyne with that vnhappy swerd. **1523** LD. BERNERS *Froiss.* I. cccxl. 216/2 This vnhappy wether for the englisshmen fell well for them in the cyte. **1607** *Peele's Jests* 14 The Gentleman was..disturbed in thought at this unhappy accident. **1652** HOWELL *Giraffi's Rev. Naples* II. 142 An unhappy Bullet came and killed one of the principall of the Black-coats that was in Arms. **1711** ADDISON *Spect.* No. 125 ¶7 It is very unhappy for a Man to be born in such a stormy and tempestuous Season. **1796** MME. D'ARBLAY *Camilla* III. 18, I am shocked to find you informed of this unhappy transaction. **1837** LOCKHART *Scott* III. iii. 110 His friend was aware that he had an unhappy propensity to drinking. **1891** FARRAR *Darkn. & Dawn* lxiii, An unhappy and accidental collision between the jealous cohorts led to a battle.

b. Inauspicious; foreboding evil.

1533 BELLENDEN *Livy* I. viii. (S.T.S.) I. 47 Numa schewe in his Calendar sic dayis as wer happy and sic dayis as war unhappy. **1590** SPENSER *F.Q.* II. vi. 44 Death is for wretches borne vnder vnhappie starre. **1638** RAWLEY tr. *Bacon's Life & Death* (1650) 11 The Black-Bird is reported to be..one of the longest livers: An unhappy Bird, and a good singer. **1814** SOUTHEY *Roderick* VI. 90 The spurious race Whom in unhappy hour Favila's wife Brought forth for Spain.

c. Infelicitous; unsuccessful.

1719 SWIFT *To Yng. Clergyman* Wks. 1755 II. II. 3 Neither is it rare to observe among excellent..divines a certain un-gracious manner, or an unhappy tone of voice. **1779** JOHNSON *L.P., Rochester* Wks. II. 199 His imitation of Horace on Lucilius is not inelegant or unhappy.

4. Of conditions: Marked by misfortune or mishap; miserable, wretched.

1390 GOWER *Conf.* III. 59 Helas, that evere was I bore, That his unhappi destine So wofulli comth in be me! **1484** CAXTON *Fables of Æsop* II. viii, In the vnhappy and Infortunat tyme men ought not to be despayred. **1509** HAWES *Past. Pleas.* XVI. (Percy Soc.) 68 Sayeng to him, my chance and desteny Of al other is the moste unhappy. **1585** T. WASHINGTON tr. *Nicholay's Voy.* I. xv. 16 The end of his moste vnhappye life. *Ibid.* IV. xxvii. 146 Through hunger [he] was..to die an vnhappie death. **1600** BRETON *Pasquil's Madcappe* D 3 b, If they be met with in their going home, I can not pitty their vnhappy speede. **1712** BLACKMORE *Creation* III. 325 You oft declaim on man's unhappy fate. **1794** MRS. RADCLIFFE *Myst. Udolpho* xxx, Her mind deeply impressed with the unhappy fate of this object, she forgot all her faults. **1838** FR. A. KEMBLE *Resid. in Georgia* (1863) 13, I have never been among them to judge what faculties their unhappy social position leaves to them un-impaired. **1878** BROWNING *La Saisiaz* 30 Life thus owned unhappy, is there supplemental happiness..in life to come?

†**5.** Causing or involving trouble or mischief; objectionable, evil; naughty. *Obs.*

1474 *Paston Lett.* III. 121 Wherffor I sende yow herwith yowr rynge, and the onhappy muskeball. **1529** MORE *Dyaloge* IV. Wks. 259/2 Moreouer the vnhappy dedes of yᵗ sect must nedes be imputed to the sect selfe. **1585** T. WASHINGTON tr. *Nicholay's Voy.* III. xvii. 102 They are also full of diuers vnhappy vices. *a* **1618** RALEIGH *Rem.* (1664) 110 The world..never gave you but an unhappy welcome —a hurtful entertainment. **1678** CUDWORTH *Intell. Syst.* 420 It seems to be but like to Womens frighting of Children from doing unhappy tricks.

†**b.** Unfavourable, poor. *Obs.*

1765 *Museum Rust.* IV. xxviii. 125 A very proper grass to cultivate on such unhappy soils, where hardly any other grass..will grow at all.

6. *Comb.*, as ***unhappy-faced, -happy, -looking, -witted*** adjs.

1591 SPENSER *M. Hubberd* 49 For both were craftie and vnhappie witted. *a* **1618** SYLVESTER *Funeral Elegie Dr. Hill's Wife* 185 (Her first and last) unhappy-happy Boy, Which cost her life. **1863** W. C. BALDWIN *Afr. Hunting* ix. 378 An odd unhappy looking springbuck or two. **1876** GEO. ELIOT *Dan. Der.* xxviii, That unhappy-faced woman.

†**un'happy,** *v. Obs.* [UN-² 6 a.] *trans.* To make unhappy or unfortunate.

1593 SHAKS. *Rich. II,* III. i. 10 You haue mis-led a Prince, ..A happie Gentleman in Blood, and Lineaments, By you vnhappied, and disfigur'd cleane. **1605** SYLVESTER tr. *Paradox agst. Libertie* 410 In our selues doth rest That which vnhappieth vs, and that which makes vs blest. **1653** E. LLOYD *Let.* 28 July (MS. Ashmole), I admire you..should for any By-end vnhappie your selfe and stepdame your children.

un'harassed, *ppl. a.* (UN-¹ 8.)

[**1775** ASH.] **1796** P. L. COURTIER *Pleas. Solitude* (1802) 58 The solitary haunt, by foe unharassed more! **1883** 'ANNIE THOMAS' *Mod. Housewife* 30 'We must retrench!' we said.., and in those unharassed days we said it cheerfully enough.

†**un'harborough,** *v. Obs.* [UN-² 5.] = next.

1611 FLORIO, *Disalbergare,* to dislodge, to vnharborough.

un'harbour, *v.* [UN-² 5.] *trans.* To dislodge (a deer) from covert or shelter.

1576 TURBERV. *Venerie* 100 An Hart and a Bucke [are] likewise reared, rowsed, and vnharbored. **1582** STANYHURST IV. (Arb.) 100 The heard deare dooth stray from mounten vnharbourd. **1686** R. BLOME *Gentl. Recreat.* II. 83/1 Your Hounds should not all be uncoupled until the Hart is un-harboured by the Harbourer. **1721** *Phil. Trans.* XXXI. 167 After you unharbour a Moose, he will run a Course of 20, or 30 miles, before he..comes to a Bay. **1797** *Sporting Mag.* IX. 264 Mr. Sturt's stag hounds unharboured a hind at Maggot-Hill Wood. **1823** SCOTT *Quentin D.* ix, To the devil with the discourse, for the boar is unharboured. **1856** STONEHENGE *Brit. Rural Sports* 109 The regular pack being held at hand.., ready to be laid on when the hart or hind is 'unharboured'.

b. *transf.* and *fig.*

1593 *Sidney's Arcadia* III. (1922) II. 29 Your compassion makes me open my hart to you, and leave unharboured mine owne thoughts. **1647** N. WARD *Simple Cobler* 44, I am sure ..it was never storyed that *Salus Populi* began with *Majestas Imperii,* unlesse *Majestas Imperii* first unharbour'd it, and hunted it to a stand. **1768** FOOTE *Devil* I, Advance! now let us unharbour the rascal! **1771** R. CUMBERLAND *West Indian* II. vi, I'll unlodge him, I'll unharbour him, I warrant. **1824** SCOTT *St. Ronan's* iv, Clara..is a little wilful; and I believe your ladyship must take the task of unharbouring her into your own hands.

Hence **un'harbouring** *vbl. sb.*

1591 R. TURNBULL *Exp. St. James* 102 These..house themselues by the vnharbouring..of the poore. **1686** R. BLOME *Gentl. Recreat.* II. 83/1 The Chase of the Hart or Stag; and first the Vnharbouring him. **1897** D. H. MADDEN *Diary W. Silence* 30 The rest of the company made ready to assist at the unharbouring of the hart.

un'harboured, *a.* [UN-¹ 8.]

1. Having no shelter or refuge.

c **1450** *Cov. Myst.* (Shaks. Soc.) 403 Ye had no pete on seke nor lame... Unherborwed men ye servyd the same.

2. Affording no shelter; wild.

1634 MILTON *Comus* 423 She that has that..May trace huge Forests, and unharbour'd Heaths.

†**un'hard,** *a. Obs.* [UN-¹ 7. Cf. ON. *úharðr,* obs. Flem. *onherd,* OHG. *unherti.*] Soft.

a **1300** *Cursor M.* 24502 Quen i sa moght kis þat suete, þe vnharder was mi harm. **1552** HULOET, Vnharde, *edurum.* **1570** LEVINS *Manip.* 31 Unhard, *mollis.*

un'harden, *v.* (UN-² 6 a.)

1552 HULOET, Vnharden, *eduro.* **1611** FLORIO, *Discallire,* to suple, to vnharden. **1879** BROWNING *Ivan Ivanovitch* 243 Ivan Ivanovitch, 'Tis you unharden me.

un'hardened, *ppl. a.* (UN-¹ 8.)

fig. **1590** SHAKS. *Mids. N.* I. i. 35 Messengers Of strong preuailment in vnhardned youth. **1608** H. CLAPHAM *Errour Right Hand* A 4 If thine heart be vn-hardned, it will easily ioyne with mee. **1619** [see UNHATCHED²]. **1747** RICHARDSON *Clarissa* (1811) II. 26 After you have heard what your friends shall further urge in his behalf, unhardened by clandestine correspondencies. **1792** MME. D'ARBLAY *Diary* V. 390 The few unhardened in crimes. **1821** SOUTHEY in *Life A. Bell* (1844) III. 630 Preserving his heart the while unstained and unhardened. **1846** LANDOR *Imag. Conv.* Wks. I. 249/2 The studious, the enthusiastic, the unhardened in politics.

lit. **1835–6** *Todd's Cycl. Anat.* I. 349/1 An intermediate layer of unhardened epiderm. **1884** F. J. BRITTEN *Watch & Clockm.* 6 Unhardened springs do not accelerate.

un'hardiness. (UN-¹ 12.)

1611 FLORIO, *Sbaldanza,* vnboldnesse, vnhardinesse. **1893** *Mod. Rev.* April 252 A hundred generations of unhardiness and want of power.

†**un'hardle,** *v. Obs.*⁻¹ [UN-².

The second element is app. f. OF. *hardel* m. or *hardelle* f., either in the sense of 'troop, company', or of 'cord, leash' (cf. F. *harde* leash for hounds). In the former case the sense is 'to break up, disperse'; in the latter, 'to unleash, uncouple'. Either meaning is suitable to the context.]

13.. *Gaw. & Gr. Knt.* 1697 Hunteres vnhardeled bi a holt syde, Rocheres roungen bi rys, for rurde of her hornes.

un'hardy, *a.* (UN-¹ 7.)

1377 LANGL. *P. Pl.* B. Prol. 180 [They] helden hem vn-hardy and here conseille feble. *c* **1386** CHAUCER *Reeve's T.* 4208, I wil arise, and auntre it by my fayth: Vnhardy is vn-seely, thus men sayth. **1430–40** LYDG. *Bochas* IV. viii. (1554)

105 Nother heauenly gods nor fortune blind of syght Wer both vnhardy tattempt agein his might. **1539** TAVERNER *Erasm. Prov.* (1545) 79 With sluggers or unhardy persons, it is alwayes holy daye. **1611** SPEED *Hist. Gt. Brit.* IX. xi. §5. 555/1 Neither yet was he vnhardie in Arms. **1671** MILTON *P.R.* III. 243 The wisest, unexperienc't, will be ever.. Irresolute, unhardy, unadventrous.

un'harmed, *ppl. a.* (UN-[1] 8.)
1340-70 *Alex. & Dind.* 227 And y bi-hote ȝou her vnharmed to leue. *c* **1400** *Beryn* 1804 Howe shuld o sely lombe, a-mong wolvis weld, And scapen vn-i-harmyd? **1456** SIR G. HAYE *Law Arms* (S.T.S.) 164 He sall seurly cum and gang un-harmyt of me or ony of myn. **1513** DOUGLAS *Æneid* I. Prol. 51 Thocht I offend, onhermit is thine fame. **1582** STANYHURST *Æneis* II. (Arb.) 64 Wasd for this (moother) that mee throgh danger vnharmed You led? **1667** DRYDEN & DAVENANT *Tempest* II. (1670) 25 *Prosp.* No courage can resist 'em. *Hip.* How then have you, Sir, Liv'd so long unharm'd among them? **1687** [see next]. **1791** COWPER *Odyss.* v. 197, I will also give New raiment for thy limbs, and will dispatch Winds after thee to waft thee home unharm'd. **1855** MACAULAY *Hist. Eng.* xiii. III. 327 Here he might possibly have remained unharmed and harmless, had not an event.. made his enemies implacable. **1886** HALL CAINE *Son of Hagar* III. vi, What a mercy we're safe and unharmed.

un'harmful, *a.* (UN-[1] 7.)
1538 ELYOT, *Innocuus*, vnharmefull, he that doth none harme. **1548** UDALL, etc. *Erasm. Par. John* i. 9 b, This is he .. whose vnharmefull blood defended the children of Israel. **1594** CAREW *Tasso* (1881) 87 That hungry teene of gold, and thirst withall Of mine vnharmefull blood. **1615** CHAPMAN *Odyss.* II. 138 And.. hold unharmful on your wished way. **1687** DRYDEN *Hind & P.* I. 299 Themselves unharmful, let them live unharm'd, Their jaws disabl'd, and their claws disarm'd. **1855** SINGLETON *Virgil* I. 162 Often have malignant stepdames.. mingled drugs and not unharmful spells.

un'harmfully, *adv.* (UN-[1] 11.)
1888 *Contemp. Rev.* Nov. 676 To grapple unharmed and unharmfully with the very deepest problems of our being.

un'harming, *ppl. a.* (UN-[1] 10.)
1795 SOUTHEY *Joan of Arc* VII. 162 Again he thrust the spear; At once Dunois on his broad buckler met The unharming stroke. **1835** LYTTON *Rienzi* X. iv, Dangerous tools they were, but without the workman they may rust unharming. **1852** KINGSLEY *Andromeda* 149 A fiery rainfall, unharming, Sparkled and gleamed.

unhar'monic, *a.* (UN-[1] 7 and 5 b.)
1694 PEPYS *Let.* in *Academy* 9 Aug. (1890) 110/1 There is a decent and not unharmonick playnesse in it. **1810** S. GREEN *Reformist* II. 20 The unharmonic squalling of a ballad-singer.

unhar'monious, *a.* [UN-[1] 7 and 5 b.]
1. Not sounding in harmony; unmelodious.
a **1634** CHAPMAN *Rev. for Honour* II. i. 224 These sounds are unharmonious. **1727** SWIFT *Let. Eng. Tongue* Wks. 1755 II. I. 188 Such harsh unharmonious sounds, that none but a northern ear could endure. **1753** R. CLAYTON *Jrnl. fr. Cairo to Mt. Sinai* 4 The noisy sonnets of our Eastern friends, who.. designed these their unharmonious vociferations as a compliment. **1832** G. DOWNES *Lett. Cont. Countries* I. 139 Some country-seats, one of which bears the unharmonious name, Gutsch. **1859** R. F. BURTON *Centr. Afr.* in *Jrnl. Geog. Soc.* XXIX. 266 An unharmonious chorus of collective voices.
b. Not yielding or producing harmonious sounds.
1742 YOUNG *Nt. Th.* III. 89 Transfixt by fate,.. How from the summit of the grove she fell, And left it unharmonious! **1784** COWPER *Task* III. 734 Wholesome airs,.. And groves, if unharmonious, yet secure From clamour. *a* **1861** T. WOOLNER *My Beautiful Lady, Night* i, What trite old folly unharmonious sages.. write.. Of sin original and growing crime!
2. Not exhibiting harmony or agreement.
1667 MILTON *P.L.* XI. 51 Those pure immortal Elements that know No gross, no unharmoneous mixture foule. **1796** MRS. M. ROBINSON *Angelina* I. 125 Pardon me.. for the impertinence of supposing that your enlightened mind can for a moment be unharmonious. **1805** LOUDON *Improv. Hot-Houses* 38 Walls and flues covered with white plaster, the raw glare of which.. has a harsh and unharmonious effect. **1846** GROTE *Greece* IX. (1862) II. 246 The distinct and un-harmonious elements of which the population.. was made up. **1876** BERNSTEIN *Five Senses* 120 The cause of the harmonious or unharmonious relation between colours.

unhar'moniously, *adv.* (UN-[1] 11; cf. prec.)
[**1775** ASH.] **1783** BLAIR *Lect.* I. xix. 393 [There is] little beauty in the construction of his sentences, which are frequently suffered to drag unharmoniously. **1856** FROUDE *Hist. Eng.* I. 262 Factions nearly equal in number, though unharmoniously composed.

un'harmonize, *v.* (UN-[2] 6 c.)
1797 MRS. A. M. BENNETT *Beggar Girl* (1813) III. 67 It was not in the power of sir Jacob or his companion entirely to unharmonise her mind.

un'harmonized, *ppl. a.* (UN-[1] 8.)
[**1775** ASH.] **1803** MARY CHARLTON *Wife & Mistress* III. 144 This promised interview was now the only circumstance she looked forward to, ere she quitted this unharmonized society. **1873** SYMONDS *Grk. Poets* xii. 417 Fragments of primitive.. superstition unharmonized with the serene element of the Hellenic spirit.

un'harmonizing, *ppl. a.* (UN-[1] 10.)
1851 W. R. GREG *Creed of Christendom* xi. 152 Those single, unharmonizing discrepant texts. **1865** PUSEY *Truth Eng. Ch.* 42 The Holy Synod approved the letter.. as.. in no wise unharmonizing with the inspired Scriptures.

un'harmony. (UN-[1] 12, 5 b.)
1832 GEN. THOMPSON *Exerc.* (1842) 101 A marvellous blunder,.. which.. caused all ancient music to flounder in a mass of unharmony. **1866** R. CHAMBERS *Ess.* Ser. II. 189 That unharmony of opinion which so often makes social life uncomfortable.

un'harness, *v.* [UN-[2] 4, 4 b. Cf. Du. and Flem. *ontharnassen* to disarm ('exarmare', Kilian).]
1. *trans.* To divest of armour. Also *fig.*
c **1435** *Torr. Portugal* 302 Blythe then wase that lady jent, For to on-harnes Torrent. **1549** COVERDALE, etc. *Erasm. Par. Col.* ii. 6 Then declared he them freely and playnly to be ouer-commen and vnharnysed, when.. he caryed vs about as it were in a triumphe. **1552** HULOET, Vnharnayes *exarmo*. **1802** JAMES *Milit. Dict.*, *Unharnessed*, disarmed, divested of armour or weapons of offence.
2. To free (horses, etc.) from harness; to unyoke. Also *fig.* and (in recent use) *absol.*
1611 COTGR., *Desharnacher*, to vnharnesse, or vntrap; to take off the furniture from a horse. **1643-5** MILTON *Divorce* II. xxi, When two unfortunately met are by the Canon forc't to draw in that yoke.. till death unharnesse 'em. **1697** DRYDEN *Virg. Past.* II. 96 The sweating steers, unharnessed from the yoke, Bring, as in triumph, back the crooked plough. **1746** *Phil. Trans.* XLIV. 296 The Carter drove him home; but, as soon as he had unharnessed him, the poor Creature.. dropp'd down dead immediately. **1799** *Hull Advertiser* 2 Feb. 2/4 A number of respectable inhabitants unharnessed the cattle from his carriage. **1852** GROTE *Greece* II. lxxi. IX. 203 Xenophon unharnessing a waggon-bullock .., immediately offered sacrifice. **1894** *Westm. Gaz.* 10 June 5/1 He had to leave off helping to unharness the horse.
Hence **un'harnessing** *vbl. sb.*
1856 LEVER *Martins of Cro' M.* xv, Grooming, and shoeing, and unharnessing went on with.. noise and merriment.

un'harnessed, *ppl. a.*[1] [UN-[1] 8.]
†**1.** Not ornamented or trimmed. *Obs.*
1488 *Acc. Ld. High Treas. Scot.* I. 83 A belt of crammassy hernessit with gold and braid;.. a belt of gold vnharnessit.
2. Not provided with or wearing armour.
a **1513** FABYAN *Chron.* VII. 308 Kynge Rycharde,.. with a fewe accompanyed & vnharnaysed, shulde comme to yᵉ Frenshe Kynges tent. **1562** PILKINGTON *Expos. Abdyas* 55, 300 naked men unharnessed,.. vanquished them all. **1586** HOOKER *Conq. Irel.* I. xliii. 28/1 in *Holinshed*, As in combates in England, so they being vnharnessed, did fight with their swords or weapons in the open sight of the people. **1721** RAMSAY *Poems* 397 *Ungeard*, naked, not clad, unharness'd.
3. Not fitted with, or put into, harness.
1608 SYLVESTER *Du Bartas* II. iv. *Schisme* 298 Chariots, unfurnisht and unharnest. **1697** DRYDEN *Æneis* IX. 425 Unharnessed chariots stand along the shore. **1791** COWPER *Iliad* II. 950 Beside the chariots stood the unharness'd steeds Cropping the lotus.
b. Not adapted for industrial use.
1903 KIPLING *5 Nations* 57 Watching unharnessed rapids wasting fifty thousand head an hour.

un'harnessed, *ppl. a.*[2] [f. UNHARNESS *v.*]
1. Released from harness.
1676 HOBBES *Iliad* 212 The horses, that me brought, unharnessed Attend me at the foot of Ida hill. **1725** POPE *Odyss.* VI. 103 The mules unharness'd range beside the main. **1859** DICKENS *Holly Tree* i. (1899) 31, I had the honour of leading one of the unharnessed post-horses.
fig. **1867** MACGREGOR *Voy. Alone* ii. 29, I reclined unharnessed in the cabin, reading intently.
2. Divested of armour.
1664 BUTLER *Hud.* II. II. 49 Where now arriv'd, and half unharnest, To carry on the work in earnest, He stopp'd.

un'harped, *ppl. a.* (UN-[1] 8.)
1859 F. K. HARFORD *Martyrs of Lyons & V.* 26 Song unharp'd on Seraph's golden strings.

un'harried, *ppl. a.* (UN-[1] 8.)
1871 FREEMAN *Norm. Conq.* xvii. IV. 80 The coast.. remained unharried by either friends or enemies. **1889** *Daily News* 10 Apr. 5/1 You will leave his nest unharried.

un'harrowed, *ppl. a.* (UN-[1] 8.)
1573 TUSSER *Husb.* (1878) 88 Not onely thy peason, but also thy beanes, Unharrowed die, being buried in clay. *a* **1722** LISLE *Husb.* (1752) 118 Let the furrows lie unharrowed for some time. **1778** [W. H. MARSHALL] *Minutes Agric., Observ.* 103 A belt across the middle [of the field], left experimentally unharrowed.

un'harvested, *ppl. a.* [UN-[1] 8.]
1. From which no harvest is taken.
1867 MORRIS *Jason* II. 731 In what strange wain Hast thou crossed o'er the green and restless plain Unharvested of any? **1868** *Rep. U.S. Commissioner Agric.* (1869) 428 The method .. of turning the hogs into an unharvested field when commencing to fatten. **1879** BUTCHER & LANG *Odyssey* 77 The perilous gulfs of the unharvested sea.
2. Not reaped or brought in.
1874 J. W. LONG *Amer. Wild-fowl* xvi. 198 They feed upon the previous season's waste and unharvested grain.

un'hasp, *v.* [UN-[2] 4 b.] *trans.* To free from a hasp or catch; to unfasten; *fig.* to disclose.
13.. *E.E. Allit. P.* B. 688 Me bos.. alle myn atlyng to abraham vn-haspe bilyue. **1598** *Mucedorus* Epil. 22 Enuie, spit thy gall;.. Vnhaspe the Wicket where all periureds roost. **1615** J. TAYLOR (Water P.) *Urania* i, Eternall God, which.. at the doomefull day will once vnhaspe Th' acusing booke of Subiects and of Kings. **1810** SCOTT *Lady of L.* VI. xii, While bolt and chain he backward roll'd, And made the bar unhasp its hold. **1895** *Chamb. Jrnl.* XII. 781/1 Old Hird unhasped the door in the corner.

un'hasped, *ppl. a.* (UN-[1] 8.)
1856 HAWTHORNE *Snow Image*, etc. (1879) 221 By some accident, it had been left unhasped. **1894** BARING-GOULD *Kitty Alone* II. 35, I will leave the door of my stores open —unhasped.

un'haste. (UN-[1] 12.)
1879 DESHLER *Afternoons w. Poets* 8 'Cultivate the virtue of patience,' he replied with imperturbable unhaste. **1893** BLISS CARMAN *Low Tide on Grand Pré* 54 The noiseless secret Of Eternity's unhaste.

un'hasted, *ppl. a.* (UN-[1] 8.)
1854 S. DOBELL *Balder* iii. 13 The un-hasted life That plods with equal step the wonted way.

un'hasting, *ppl. a.* (UN-[1] 10.)
Also, in recent use, ***unhastingness***.
1839 CARLYLE *Chartism* iv, Perseverance, unhasting unresting diligence,.. characterise this people. **1872** MORLEY *Voltaire* 287 That grave and unhasting dignity, which is the life of history. **1891** W. TUCKWELL *Tongues in Trees* 151 Unhasting yet unresting chroniclers of fleeting time.

un'hasty, *a.* (UN-[1] 7.)
1590 SPENSER *F.Q.* I. iii. 4 One day nigh wearie of the yrkesome way, From her vnhastie beast she did alight. **1651** JER. TAYLOR *Serm. for Year* II. xv. 192 He is a perfect man .. who hath.. so unhasty and wary a spirit, as that he decrees upon no act before he hath considered maturely.

un'hat, *v.* (UN-[2] 4, 7.)
1611 FLORIO, *Disberettare*, to vncap, to vnhat. **1879** H. SPENCER *Ceremonial Inst.* vi. 134 Unhatting on the knees when the host is carried by, occurs still in Catholic countries. **1883** *Academy* 30 June 460/1 To the latter we must often unhat as to the oldest of acquaintances.

un'hatched, *ppl. a.*[1] (UN-[1] 8 + HATCH *v.*[1])
1601 HOLLAND *Pliny* I. 298 Whiles the chick is unhatched and within the egge. **1794** MORSE *Amer. Geog.* 169 The young cuckow.. immediately sets about clearing the nest of the young sparrows, and the remaining unhatched eggs. **1854** BADHAM *Halieut.* 186 Many [tunny-fish].. drop their unhatched posterity about, wherever they may happen to reside. **1872** DARWIN *Orig. Spec.* (ed. 6) iv. 68 The hard tip to the beak of unhatched birds, used for breaking the egg.
fig. **1602** SHAKS. *Ham.* I. iii. 65 But doe not dull thy palme, with entertainment Of each vnhatch't, vnfledg'd Comrade. **1635** PAGITT *Christianog.* 223 Papall Indulgences were then unhatched. *a* **1639** T. CAREW *Poems* Wks. (1824) 85 Though niggard Time left much unhatch'd by deeds.

†**un'hatched,** *ppl. a.*[2] *Obs.* [UN-[1] 8 + HATCH *v.*[2]] Unhacked; unstained.
1601 SHAKS. *Twel. N.* III. iv. 257 *Vio.* I pray you sir what is he? *To.* He is knight dubb'd with vnhatch'd Rapier. **1619** FLETCHER *Knt. Malta* II. v, Tender, and full of fears our blushing Sex is, Unhardned with relentless thoughts; unhatcht With bloud, and bloudy practice.

un'hatted, *a.* (UN-[1] 9.)
1832 MISS MITFORD *Village* Ser. v. 197 Frederick of Prussia's unhatted soldier. **1847** HELPS *Friends in C.* I. ii. 31 A great, unhatted, uncravated, bearded man. **1893** *Westm. Gaz.* 22 Apr. 2/3 He was unhatted, but he leant forward with a graceful bow.
b. *spec.* (See HAT *sb.* 3.)
1880 *Sat. Rev.* 25 Dec. 808/1 Bembo.. in his pleasant, unregenerate, because still unhatted, days.

un'haunted, *ppl. a.* [UN-[1] 8.]
†**1.** Not practised or used. *Obs.*[−1]
1533 BELLENDEN *Livy* III. (S.T.S.) I. 298 Nocht knawand .. quhy þe thing (þat was sa mony ȝeris afore vnhantit and out of consuetude) was brocht agane in vse.
2. Not frequented; lonely, solitary.
1568-9 *Act 11 Eliz.* in Bolton *Stat. Irel.* (1621) 369 Enormities that have followed of the disordered trade of aliens to creekes and unhaunted portes. **1581** J. BELL *Haddon's Answ. Osor.* 349 b, Nor were they sojourning then in yᵉ Cities, or Townes. But coucht close.. in unhaunted woodes and fennes. **1617** CAMPION *Wks.* (1909) 181 We both will sit in some vnhaunted shade. **1659** W. CHAMBERLAYNE *Pharonnida* IV. 94 Like beauteous flowers, which vainly waste the scent Of odors in unhanted desarts.
3. Not haunted *by* (or *of*) something.
1818 COBBETT *Pol. Reg.* XXXIII. 162 [They] can lay their heads on their pillows unhaunted by the apprehension of seeing him no more. **1819** KEATS *Indolence* ii, Unhaunted quite of all but—nothingness. **1866** HOWELLS *Venet. Life* ii. 21 Unhaunted by any pang for the decay that afterwards saddened me.., I glided on.
Hence **un'hauntedness.**
1611 FLORIO, *Infrequenza*, vnhauntednesse.

un'haunting, *vbl. sb.* (UN-[1] 13.)
1538 ELYOT, *Insolentia*, seldomnes of vse in any thynge, vnhauntynge of a place.

†**un'having,** *vbl. sb. Obs.*[−1] (UN-[1] 13.)
c **1449** PECOCK *Repr.* I. xvi. 89 For harme which y haue knowen come bi defaut and the vnhauying and the vnknowing of this.. consideracioun.

un'hazarded, *ppl. a.* (UN-[1] 8.)
1588 HOWARD in Laughton *State Papers Defeat Armada* (1894) I. 288 There shall be nothing either neglected or unhazarded, that may work their overthrow. **1649** MILTON *Eikon.* v. Wks. 1851 III. 376 He.. hath himselfe left nothing unhazzarded to keep three [kingdoms]. **1671** —— *Samson* 809 Here I should still enjoy thee day and night, Whole to my self, unhazarded abroad. **1855** [see UNESSAYED].

un'hazarding, *ppl. a.* (UN-[1] 10.)
1807 SOUTHEY *Espriella's Lett.* III. 75 Their habits of patient and unhazarding industry ensure success.

un'hazardous, *a.* (UN-[1] 7.)
1682 DRYDEN *Dk. Guise* Epist. A ij b, 'Tis enough, my Lord, that your own Part was neither obscure in it, nor unhazardous. **1802-12** BENTHAM *Ration. Judic. Evid.* (1827) II. 227 It is in the honest and unhazardous task of recollection that he employs himself. **1891** T. HARDY *Tess*

xiii, The fact.. lent Tess's.. position, by its fearsomeness, a far higher fascination than it would have exercised if unhazardous.

un'head, *v.* [UN-² 4. Cf. MDu. *onthoveden*, *onthoofden* (also Du.), MLG. *enthoveden*, MHG. *enthoubeten*, *-houpten* (G. *enthaupten*).]

1. *trans.* To behead (a person).

c **1375** *Sc. Leg. Saints* i. (*Peter*) 377 For, lo, as I vnhevdyt wes,.. þe thrid day, as I sad to þe, I am resine. *Ibid.* xxxi. (*Eugenia*) 432 Scho.. gert þe lord þe ȝerle ta, &.. At hyr tysinge gert hyme vnhed. *a* **1704** T. BROWN *Wks.* (1720) II. 260 You.. did not only dare to uncrown, but to unhead a Monarch. *a* **1734** NORTH *Exam.* III. vii. §98 (1740) 580 Legs and Arms lay scattered about, Heads undressed, and Bodies unheaded.

2. To deprive or divest of a head, top, or end.

1611 FLORIO, *Scapezzare*, to vntop, to vnhead, to shred or lop trees on the top. **1725** *Fam. Dict.* s.v. *Verjuice*, And when you have a mind to have your Verjuice you must un-head the Barrel, and you will find it very good. **1778** W. PRYCE *Min. Cornub.* 98 They often meet with a Cross-Gossan, which.. unheads and breaks off the continuity of the Lode they work upon. **1843** TIZARD *Brewing* 473 When steam is not to be had, stinking casks need unheading.

un'headed, *a.* [UN-¹ 9.] Destitute or devoid of a head or heading, in various senses.

(*a*) **1586** J. HOOKER *Hist. Irel.* 94/1 in *Holinshed* II, The most part of those arrowes, which were shot ouer the walles, were vnheaded. **1600** J. PORY tr. *Leo's Africa* Introd. 36 A kinde of small slender dartes or pikes, some whereof are headed with some kinde mettall, the residue being unheaded.

(*b*) **1608** TOPSELL *Serpents* 609 This monster.. nor man nor dragon is.., But man unlegged, and snake unheaded.

(*c*) **1607** *Puritaine Widdow* v. iv. 8 Such is the blind besotting in the state of an vnheaded woman thats a widdow. **1673** TEMPLE *Obs. United Prov.* Wks. 1720 I. 16 The People were enraged, but awed and unheaded.

(*d*) **1908** KIPLING *Lett. of Travel* (1920) 153 Even unheaded clippings from them [*sc.* various newspapers] declared their origin. **1970** R. JEFFRIES *Dead Man's Bluff* xix. 189 How did you know which hotel to come to today?.. The letter was written on unheaded notepaper.

† **un'heal.** *Obs.* [OE. *unhǽlu*, *-o*, *unhǽl* (UN-¹ 12 + HEAL *sb.*), = OHG. *unhailî*, *-heilî* fem. Cf. MDu. (rare) and Du. *onheil*, MLG. *unheil*, OHG. *unhail*, *unheil* (also MHG., G.), Goth. *unhaili* neut.] Want of health or soundness; infirmity, trouble, misfortune.

c **700** *Laws of Ine* §56 ðif mon hwelcne ceap ȝebyȝeð, & he þonne onfinde him hwelce unhælo on [etc.]. *c* **893** K. ÆLFRED *Oros.* IV. iv. 164 þa ðe þær on unhæle wæran. *c* **950** *Lindisf. Gosp.* Matt. iv. 23 Hælend.. hælde all unhælo & all untrymnise in folce. *c* **1000** *Rule of Chrodegang* vii, þæt nan ne beo aspelod.. butan hwa for unhæle.. ne maȝe. *c* **1200** *Trin. Coll. Hom.* 33 Ðos word sede þe engel.. naht for englen unhele þe habbeð eche hele, ac far mannen unhele. *a* **1225** *Leg. Kath.* 1064 He.. healde halte & houerede, & euch un-heale. *a* **1300** *Cursor M.* 8137 Mikel on him he had vn-hele, Thritti yere had ben mesel. *c* **1386** CHAUCER *Doctor's T.* 116 Saue Enuye allone That sory is of oother mennes wele And glad is of his sorwe and his vnheele. *c* **1450** HOLLAND *Houlate* 254 It neidis nocht to renewe all myn vnhele.

unheal, var. UNHELE *v.*

un'healable, *a.* [UN-¹ 7 b.] Incapable of being healed; incurable.

1382 WYCLIF *Ecclus.* xxviii. 30 Lest parauenture.. thi fallyng be vnheleable in to the deth. —— *Isaiah* xiv. 6 The Lord to-brosede the staf of vnpitous men.. with an vnheleable plage. **1611** COTGR., *Incurable*,.. vnhealeable. *a* **1661** FULLER *Worthies*, *Warwick.* III. (1662) 125 He in his Youth was afflicted with an unhealable Sprain in his Hip. **1795** COLERIDGE *Let. to Southey* 135 Of innovation they see dreadful and unhealable consequence. **1862** THACKERAY *Philip* xx, In the midst of feuds unhealable. **1891** F. W. NEWMAN *J. H. Newman* p. vi, A most painful breach, through mere religious creed, broke on me.., and was unhealable.

absol. **1837** CARLYLE *Fr. Rev.* II. v. xii, Lafayette indites his emphatic Letter.. against Jacobinism; which.. will not heal the unhealable.

un'healed, *ppl. a.* (UN-¹ 8. Cf. NFris. *unhialed*, Du. *ongeheeld*, MHG. *ungeheilet*, G. *-heilt.*)

a **1225** *Ancr. R.* 328 Forði he iwende awei unhealed.. ut of þe temple. **1398** TREVISA *Barth. De P.R.* VII. liv. (Bodl. MS.), But if he leue one [hemorrhoid] vnheled it is perile. *a* **1425** tr. *Arderne's Treat. Fistula*, etc. 44 If þe fynger.. of any man haue be long vnheled of vnwise cure. **1500–20** DUNBAR *Poems* xc. 22 Off tuenty woundis, and ane be left unhelit Quhat awalis the leiching of the laif? **1573** BARET *Alv.* V. 142 Unhealed, vncured. **1647** HEXHAM I, Vnhealed, *ongenesen.* **1795** HELEN M. WILLIAMS *Lett. on France* I. 251 Whom the tyrants had dragged to prison, while the wounds were yet unhealed, which he had received in defending his country. **1846** TRENCH *Mirac.* xxxi. (1862) 444 Their condemnation was.. that, being unhealed, they counted themselves whole. **1884** R. W. CHURCH *Bacon* vi. 154 The wounds of Ireland were unhealed.

† **un'healful**, *a. Obs.* [UN-¹ 7.] Unwholesome.

c **1400** tr. *Secreta Secret.*, *Gov. Lordsh.* 79 þay ar vnhelfull, as þes stondyng waters. *Ibid.*, Waters.. hote and vnhelfull.

un'health. [UN-¹ 12: cf. UNHEAL.] Want of health; weak or poor health.

c **1000** *Ags. Gosp.* Luke v. 31 Ne beþurfon læces þa ðe hale synd, ac þa ðe unhælþe habbaþ. *a* **1050** *Liber Scintill.* xxviii. (1889) 107 Maneȝa.. menn þurh win lichaman un-hælþe mæste togæderetugan. *a* **1200** *Moral Ode* 323 Ac þer nis hunger ne þurst ne deð, ne vnhelþe ne elde. *a* **1250** *Prov. Ælfred* 113 in *O.E. Misc.* 108 þenne cumeþ elde, and vn-helþe. **1551** PARRY in *Macm. Mag.* XLV. 454 Her Grace's unhealth hath made it [her hand] weaker, and so unsteady. **1826** COLERIDGE in D. Campbell *Life* (1894) 267 *note*, I am at present sadly below even my par of health, or rather unhealth. **1853** KINGSLEY *Misc.* I. 316 The spokesman.. of all the unrest and unhealth of sensitive young men for many a year after.

un'healthful, *a.* [UN-¹ 7.]

1. = UNHEALTHY *a.* 1.

1580 SIDNEY *Ps.* XXII. i, My God,.. from me why is thy presence taken? Soe farre from seeing mine unhealthfull eyes. **1600** SURFLET *Countrie Farme* I. xv. 95 They be small, alwaies leane, vnhealthfull, and their flesh of small relish. **1683** TRYON *Way to Health* 202 These latter sort of People.. are certainly the most unhealthful men in the World. ? **1737** BOLINGBROKE *Study Hist.* vii, Charles the second: an unhealthful youth. **1768–74** TUCKER *Lt. Nat.* (1834) II. 81 Many come into the world maimed, weakly, and unhealthful.

absol. **1660** R. COKE *Power & Subj.* 164 That you may never in the same manner judge rich and poor,.. the healthful and unhealthful.

b. Of life, growth, etc.

1595 in Ellis *Orig. Lett.* Ser. III. IV. 124 In my declyninge and unhealthfull yeres. **1612** T. TAYLOR *Comm. Titus* i. 13 Of an vnhealthfull.. and painfull life men are so weary, as they would seeke for death. **1786** ABERCROMBIE *Gard. Assist.* 247 Any plants of an infirm, unhealthful, stunted.. growth. **1831** WILLIS *Poem Brown University* 88 Unhealthful fires burn constant in his eye. **1895** *Atlantic Monthly* Mar. 340 The bark peels away in strips, leaving them in white un-healthful nakedness.

2. = UNHEALTHY *a.* 2.

1598 FLORIO, *Insalubre*, vnholsome, vnhealthfull. **1653** W. RAMESEY *Astrol. Restored* 303 The Winter following will be very unhealthful and obnoxious to all creatures. **1683** DRYDEN *Life Plutarch* in *P.'s Lives* I. 5 Being also expos'd to the winds which blew from that quarter, the town was perpetually unhealthful. **1756** C. LUCAS *Ess. Waters* I. 36 All countries where stagnant waters abound must be unhealthful. **1784** COWPER *Task* IV. 363 The unhealthful East, That breathes the spleen, and searches ev'ry bone Of the infirm. **1841** MYERS *Cath. Th.* III. §50. 193 Such Rest.. is sweeter far than any which unhealthful indolence.. can supply. **1865** MRS. WHITNEY *Gayworthys* xxiii, There was truly something in the air that had made the place unhealthful to her.

un'healthfully, *adv.* (UN-¹ 11.)

1677 MIÈGE II. s.v., To live somewhere unhealthfully. **1846** WORCESTER.

un'healthfulness. [UN-¹ 12.] Unhealthiness:

a. Of persons.

1589 PUTTENHAM *Eng. Poesie* I. viii. (Arb.) 33 Horace.. was thought meete.. to be Secretarie of estate,.. which neuerthelesse he refused for his vnhealthfulnesse sake. **1611** COTGR., *Indisposition*,.. vnhealthfulnesse. *a* **1676** WHITELOCKE *Memorials* (1732) 378 Which occasioned sir Thomas Widdrington to.. excuse himself.. because of his unhealthfulness. **1727** BAILEY (vol. II), *Sickliness*, Unhealthfulness.

b. Of places, climate, etc.

1598 FLORIO, *Insalubrita*, vnhealthfulnes. **1626** BACON *Sylva* §786 *margin*, Experiment Solitary, touching the Healthfulnesse or Vnhealthfulnesse of the Southern wind. **1677** in *Misc. Cur.* (1708) III. 246 The Town lying in a bottom,.. the Air may be infected, and contribute to its unhealthfulness. **1757** J. H. GROSE *Voy. E. Indies* 48 Bombay, in fact, had long born an infamous character for unhealthfulness. **1802** *Naval Chron.* VIII. 147 The unhealthfulness of Madagascar. **1897** BRYCE *Impress. S. Africa* 2 Its unhealthfulness is a factor of prime importance.

un'healthily, *adv.* (UN-¹ 11.)

1644 MILTON *Divorce* (ed. 2) Pref. A 2, Which.. puffs up unhealthily a certaine big face of pretended learning. **1673** KIRKMAN *Unlucky Citizen* x. 171 She.. lived poor and unhealthily, wanting and miserably. **1807** SIR R. WILSON in *Life* (1862) II. 302 His face was very pale and unhealthily full. **1876** MISS YONGE *Womankind* xxxi, When a child is dressed cumbrously or unhealthily because it is the fashion.

un'healthiness. [UN-¹ 11.] The quality or condition of being unhealthy: **a.** Of persons, etc.

1634 SIR T. HERBERT *Trav.* 25 Doubtlesse their too much farcinating.. acted rather their vnhealthinesse. **1727** BAILEY (vol. II), *Unhealthiness*.., sickliness, unhealthful Quality or Condition. **1789** W. BUCHAN *Dom. Med.* (1790) 7 One great source of the diseases of children is, the unhealthiness of parents. **1828–32** WEBSTER s.v., The unhealthiness of trees or other plants. **1851** HAWTHORNE *Twice-told T.* I. vi. 107 A certain unhealthiness in the mind of the boy.

b. Of places, climate, etc.

1666 SANCROFT *Lex Ignea* 51 To scatter the Cloud of the last years unhealthiness. **1697** DAMPIER *Voy.* I. 224 Whether it was the badness of the Water, or the unhealthiness of the Town was the cause of it we did not know. **1773** *Cook's Voy.* III. xi. III. 728 In less than a week, we were sensible of the unhealthiness of the climate. **1871** NAPHEYS *Prev. & Cure Dis.* I. viii. 205 Hence the unhealthiness of brilliantly lighted apartments. **1898** *Jrnl. Sch. Geog.* (U.S.) Oct. 300 The chief.. cause of the unhealthiness of the city.

un'healthsome, *a.* Now *rare.* [UN-¹ 7.]

The spelling with *-same* in quots. 1597–9 is due to the Dutch origin of the translations (after Du. *-saem*).

1. Unwholesome.

1544 BETHAM *Precepts War* II. xxxviii. K vij, To make the water noysome and vnhealthsome to thyne enemies. **1599** A. M. tr. *Gabelhouer's Bk. Physicke* 378/1 Experience also hath taught the same to defende any man from vn-healthsame ayre. **1621** *Henryson's Fables* (1832) 50 Un-healthsome meat is of ane sairie Mouse. *a* **1860** J. YOUNGER *Autobiog.* (1881) 130 No corn in these years was substantial; all meal black 'mattened' and unhealthsome.

2. Unhealthy.

1597 A. M. tr. *Guillemeau's Fr. Chirurg.* 23/1 In aged persons, and in those which are vnhealthsame of bodye. *Ibid.* 52/1 Those which.. have binn badlye nourished, we call vnhealthsame poeple.

Hence **un'healthsomeness.** ? *Obs.*

1613 PURCHAS *Pilgrimage* (1614) 688 The aire is vnholesome. But what vnhealthsomenesse can there be found, where God is found?

un'healthy, *a.* [UN-¹ 7.]

1. a. Of persons, etc.: Not possessed of good health; weak or sickly in health. **b.** *Path.* Not in a sound or healthy condition; diseased, morbid. Also *absol.*

1611 COTGR., *Mal-sain*,.. sicklie, crazie, vnhealthie. **1813** J. THOMSON *Lect. Inflam.* 424 When they exceed this, and take on a growing disposition, they are then unhealthy. **1825** T. HOOK *Sayings* Ser. II. II. 61 A watering-place, one of the most fashionable resorts for the idle and unhealthy. **1862** A. MEADOWS *Man. Midwifery* v. ii. 181 They are apt to take on afterwards unhealthy inflammation. **1877** W. ROBERTS *Spontaneous Generation* 22 We know that when a wound becomes unhealthy, as surgeons term it, the discharges become offensive.

2. a. Of places, climate, etc.: Prejudicial or hurtful to health; insalubrious; unwholesome.

1595 in Hakluyt *Voy.* (1600) III. 587 The towne was situated in a waterie soile,.. very vnhealthy as any place in the Indies. **1616** W. BROWNE *Brit. Past.* II. i. 785 Then mists from marishes,.. From standing pooles and fens were following Unhealthy fogs. **1739** LABELYE *Piers Westm. Bridge* 72 The opposite Shore,.. cover'd with unhealthy Ooze and Filth. **1740** in *10th Rep. Hist. MSS. Comm.* App. I. 275 That very unhealthy and dangerous climate. **1806** *Med. Jrnl.* XV. 17 It was now the most unhealthy season of the year. **1827** SCOTT *Chron. Canongate* iv, There never was a trade so unhealthy yet, but men would fight to get wark at it. **1884** in Cawston *Street Improv. London* (1893) 108 We bought shops and warehouses on just the same terms as we bought unhealthy dwellings.

b. *Mil. slang.* Dangerous.

1915 A. D. GILLESPIE *Lett. from Flanders* (1916) 266 All this place is 'out of bounds' to the troops, for it must be an unhealthy corner when shells are falling. **1930** E. RAYMOND *Jesting Army* I. vi. 93 The Gully Ravine.. was now 'unhealthy': it was being sprinkled with shrapnel bullets.

3. *fig.* (See HEALTHY *a.* 3.)

1821 LAMB *Elia* I. *Imperfect Sympathies*, I do feel the differences of mankind, national or individual, to an unhealthy excess. **1849** W. S. MAYO *Kaloolah* v. (1850) 39 He had set himself.. against what his good sense led him to pronounce an unhealthy.. excitement.

4. *Comb.*, as ***unhealthy-looking*** adj.

1890 L. C. D'OYLE *Notches* 98 We steamed away again, through a swampy and unhealthy-looking country. **1890** *Retrospect Med.* CII. 318 The skin is usually described as dusky,.. unhealthy looking, or yellowish.

un'hear, *v. rare.* [UN-¹ 14.] *trans.* To hear not; to refuse to hear.

a **1300** *Cursor M.* 28793 Certes vr lauerd.. for na riche man to here, Vn-hers he pouer man praier. **1604** J. FRASER *Offer maid to Gentilman of Qualitie* 182 Many of ws hes done weal worse hauing condemned the kirk the spouse of Iesvs Christ vnhard hir, following the first that hes accused hir and praised him self. **1953** DYLAN THOMAS *Let.* 22 June (1966) 408 The woman next to me was stonedeaf so I spoke to her all the way more.. and more wildly.., and she unheard all my delirium with a smile.

un'hearable, *a.* (UN-¹ 7 b.)

1483 *Cath. Angl.* 184/1 Vn-Hereabylle, *in-audibilis.* **1841** T. CARLYLE *Let.* 19 July in T. Wemyss Reid *Life Lord Houghton* (1890) I. vi. 267 Drawing.. things unspeakable into things unhearable.

b. *absol.*

1931 R. CAMPBELL *Georgiad* I. 10 With the Unhearable their ears we'll din.

un'heard, *ppl. a.* [UN-¹ 8. Cf. NFris. *unhiard*, ON. and Icel. *ú-*, *óheyrðr* (Sw. *ohörd*, Da. *uhørt*); also OE. *unȝehéred* (in sense 2), MDu. *ongehoort* (Du. *-hoord*), MLG. *ungehôrt*, OHG. *ungehôret* (MHG. *-hôrt*, *-hœrt*, G. *-hört*).]

1. Not caught or apprehended by the sense of hearing; not heard.

a **1300** *Cursor M.* 25182 Or ai vm-quil vr bon es right, Bot vnherd thoru vr aun plight. *c* **1450** *Myrr. our Ladye* 51 He that wyttyngly leuyth oughte of these holy houres vnsayde & vnharde.. he synneth deadly. *Ibid.* 294 The prayer.. may not be vnherde. **1595** SHAKS. *John* IV. ii. 137 But if you be a-feard to heare the worst, Then let the worst vn-heard, fall on your head. **1616** W. BROWNE *Brit. Past.* II. i. 789 Clamour grew dumb, unheard was shepheard's song, And silence girt the woods. **1667** MILTON *P.L.* I. 395 Their childrens cries unheard, that past through fire. *Ibid.* III. 645 He drew not nigh unheard. **1742** YOUNG *Nt. Th.* III. 337 To see what we have seen? Hear, till unheard, the same old slabber'd tale? **1796** MME. D'ARBLAY *Camilla* V. 66 The energy of Melmond made her approach unheard. **1842** J. WILSON *Chr. North* I. 89 Not unheard, although scarcely noticed, was the cry of the curlew. **1894** MRS. DYAN *Man's Keeping* (1899) 143 Craving.. for the sound of the long-unheard familiar tones.

b. Of persons: Not heard in self-defence or entreaty; not listened to.

1595 DANIEL *Civ. Wars* III. xxii, Neuer shall this poore breath of mine consent That he.. Should here be iudgd vnheard, and vnaraignd. **1606** SHAKS. *Ant. & Cl.* III. xii. 24 This if shee performe, She shall not sue vnheard. **1607** —— *Cor.* v. i. 43. **1655** in *Verney Mem.* (1907) I. 538, I will not condemn you unheard. **1718** PRIOR *Solomon* II. 720 Un-heard the injur'd Orphans now complain. **1760** [see UNCONVICTED]. **1805** SCOTT *Last Minstrel* v. xxiii, Unheard he prays;—the death-pang's o'er! Richard of Musgrave breathes no more.

2. Not before heard of; unknown, new, strange.

c **1375** *Sc. Leg. Saints* I. (*Catherine*) 845 With wnhard pane Sa fellounly scho sall be slaane. **1382** WYCLIF *Esther* xvi. 13 For Mardoche.. with newe maner and vnherd engynes ful out askide [Haman] in to deth. **1459** *Rolls of Parlt.* V. 346/1 His fals and traiterous ymaginations,..compassed by the most unherd meanes. **1535** COVERDALE *2 Macc.* iv. 13 The Heithenish & straunge conuersacion, brought in thorow the vngracious and vnherde wickednesse of Iason. **1586** A. DAY *Eng. Secretary* I. (1625) 23 A huge wonder, of the vn-heard secrets neuer before reported of. **1658** COKAINE *Trappolin* IV. ii, Some unheard malady Vnknown unto the world before. **1677** YARRANTON *Eng. Improv.* 7 Notwithstanding all these strange, and unheard Inconveniences, yet they will not quit their Station. **1746** FRANCIS tr. *Horace, Art of Poetry* 68 A new-discover'd Theme.., unheard in ancient Times. **1813** SHELLEY *Q. Mab* VII. 165 Humbly He came,.. His name unheard, Save by the rabble of His native town.

b. More usually with *of.* (Common from *c* 1600.)

Hence, in recent use, ***unheard-of-ness.***

1592 GREENE *Groat's W. Wit* (1617) 35 If wofull experience may moeue you (Gentlemen) to beware, or vnheard of wretchednes intreat you to take heed. **1615** G. SANDYS *Trav.* 145 Inflicting vnheard-of tortures on the patient Christians. **1699** BENTLEY *Phalaris* 170 The Phrase was then so new and unheard of, that it puzzled a whole City. **1752** in *10th Rep. Hist. MSS. Comm.* App. I. 308 An Arminian who governed with unheard of Despotism. **1790** BURKE *Fr. Rev.* 20 This new, and hitherto unheard-of bill of rights. **1848** THACKERAY *Van. Fair* lxvii, She tended him through a series of unheard-of illnesses. **1891** FARRAR *Darkn. & Dawn* xv, From the first he broke out into unheard-of extravagance.

un'hearing, *ppl. a.* (UN-[1] 10.)

1785 BURKE *Sp. Fox's E. Indian Bill* Wks. IV. 41 The cries of India are given to seas and winds to be blown about..over a remote and unhearing ocean. **1828** *Lights & Shades* II. 106 My own close, unhearing, unseeing condition. **1894** *Outing* XXIV. 461/2 The inexorable mandate..resounded in our unhearing ears.

un'hearse, *v.* (UN-[2] 5. The exact sense is doubtful.)

1596 SPENSER *F.Q.* V. iii. 37 He..from him reft his shield, and it renuerst,..And himselfe baffuld, and his armes vnherst.

un'hearsed, *ppl. a.* (UN-[1] 8.)

1809 LAMB *To a River,* etc. ii, In thy channel,..Deep immersed, and unhearsed, Lies young Edward's corse. **1813** HOGG *Queen's Wake* Concl. xxxviii, The Border chiefs, that long had been In sepulchres unhearsed and green.

un'heart, *v.* [UN-[2] 4. Cf. MDu. *ontherten,* MHG. and G. *entherzen.*] *trans.* To deprive of heart; to dishearten. Also **un'hearted** *ppl. a.*

1593 *Pass. Morrice* (1876) 76 My..sences gon, my bodie haue vnharted: so that I liue aliue, as being dead. **1607** SHAKS. *Cor.* V. i. 49 Yet to bite his lip, And humme at good Cominius, much vnhearts mee. **1650** *Let. Cens. & Redargution Lilburne* Verses, Which scorn the Son of Noble Jonathan, As a desponding, poore unhearted man. **1830** CARLYLE *Richter & De Stael* Ess. 1840 II. 431 It is probable she knows only the French (un-souled and un-hearted) Shakspeare.

†**un'heart's-ease.** *Obs.* (UN-[1] 12.)

1470 *Paston Lett.* II. 405 Wretyn with onhertes ease the Monday next aftir Relike Sonday. *c* **1530** LD. BERNERS *Arth. Lyt. Bryt.* (1814) 70 It is a great shame for you..thus to suffre payne and vnhertes ease.

un'heartsome, *a. Sc.* and *north.* (UN-[1] 7.)

1637 RUTHERFORD *Lett.* I. clxxix. (1664) 347 It is an unheartsom thing to see our Father & mother agree so ill. **1752** E. ERSKINE *Serm.* Wks. 1871 III. 440 A melancholy unheartsome habitation would this be. **1876** *Whitby Gloss.* 206/2 *Unheartsome,*..without affection. **1897** CROCKETT *Lochinvar* xxi, An uncanny and unheartsome journey.

un'hearty, *a.* [UN-[1] 7.]

†**1.** Faint-hearted, spiritless. *Obs.*

c **1440** *Promp. Parv.* 237/2 Hertles, or vnherty, *vecors.* *c* **1482** J. KAY tr. *Caoursin's Siege of Rhodes* ¶ 12 They had not..to fyghte wyth men of Asea..couwerdes and unherty as women.

2. Not hearty or cordial.

1583 MELBANCKE *Philotimus* X ij b, I..salute thy ingratitude with an vnhartie greeting. **1621** *First & Second Bk. Discipl.* 11 Such as embraced the true religion..were not onely unheartie friends, but..great hinderers. **1784** J. BROWN *Hist. Brit. Ch.* (1823) II. v. 188 Most of the English either declined serving in the invasion, or were very unhearty in it.

3. *Sc.* Listless, dispirited; in poor condition.

a **1698** J. FRASER *Mem.* (1738) 136, I..lost my Assurance, Peace, and Strength, and became very unhearty and indisposed. **1825** JAMIESON *Suppl.*

un'heated, *ppl. a.* (UN-[1] 8.)

a **1691** BOYLE (J.), Neither salts, nor the distilled spirits of them can penetrate the narrow pores of unheated glass. **1768** STERNE *Sent. Journ.* I. 78 Submitting the offer, and themselves with it, to be sifted..by an unheated mind. **1843** *Civil Eng. & Arch. Jrnl.* VI. 304/1 A blast of atmospheric air, in the natural or unheated state. **1883** *World's Cycl. Sci.* 15 As attraction is weak in the gases of the Earth's atmosphere—comparatively unheated.

un'heaven, *v.* (UN-[2] 5.)

1609 J. DAVIES (Heref.) *Holy Roode* Wks. (Grosart) I. 28/1 Vnheau'n your selues, ye holy Cherubins, And giue attendance on your Lord, in Earth. **1659** GAUDEN *Tears Ch.* II. xxxviii. 242 How should all men..be..unsainted, unheavened,..if these men might not have their wills. **1844** L. HUNT *Our Cottage* 97 Heav'n..held us flimsy triflers—gnats i' the sun—Made but for play, and so to die, unheav'n'd.

un'heavenly, *a.* (UN-[1] 7.)

1752 LAW *Spirit of Love* I. (1766) 21 To remove every Thing that is unheavenly, gross, dark, from every Part of this fallen World. **1823** MOORE *Loves of Angels* Introd. 61 Still fair and glorious, he but shone Among those youths th' un-heavenliest one. **1893** J. PULSFORD *Loyalty to Christ* II. 230 He feels that he is very unheavenly, very unworthy.

un'hedged, (*ppl.*) *a.* (UN-[1] 8, 9.)

1648 HEXHAM II, *Onbeheymt,* Vnhedged, or Vnfenced. **1743** YOUNG *Nt. Th.* V. 741 Our needful knowledge, like our needful food, Unhedg'd, lyes open in life's common field. **1855** LEWES *Goethe* I. 98 The botanist despairs of flowers on the unhedged plains of France. **1868** MORRIS *Earthly Par.* (1870) I. I. 345 The fair abode..o'erlooked, across the road, Unhedged green meads.

un'heed, *v.* [UN-[1] 14.] *trans.* To pay no heed to, to disregard. (Cf. UNHEEDING *ppl. a.* 2 *b.*)

1847 *Illustr. Lond. News* 17 July 39/2 The girl..began to unheed his solicitations. **1856** J. PULSFORD *Jesus Revealing Heart of God* (ed. 2) 19 He unheeds the charges brought against him.

un'heeded, *ppl. a.* (UN-[1] 8.)

1611 COTGR., *Improuueu,* vnprouided for,..vnheeded, vnthought vpon. **1660** BOYLE *New Exp. Phys. Mech.* xxxviii. 320 Whether it were due to any unheeded accident, or to the exsuction of the Air. **1736** GRAY *Statius* i. 21 He..scornful flung th' unheeded weight Aloof. **1748** *Anson's Voy.* III. v. 336 A good meal was neither an uncommon nor an unheeded article. **1817** SHELLEY *Prometh. Unb.* II. iv. 26 Pain, whose unheeded and familiar speech Is howling. **1864** PUSEY *Lect. Daniel* (1876) 326 Only one or two raised an unheeded doubt.

b. In predicative use.

1682 CREECH *Lucretius* IV. 126 The fleeting Images, Unseen,..unheeded, cease. **1709** PRIOR *Henry & Emma* 666 Succeeding Years their happy Race shall run; And Age unheeded by Delight come on. **1783** CRABBE *Village* I. 293 His drooping patient,..long unheeded, knows remonstrance vain. **1824** MISS L. M. HAWKINS *Annaline* II. 221 [She] left them when she found that her warning to take rest passed unheeded. **1875** JOWETT *Plato* (ed. 2) I. 33 He cannot let the thought..pass away unheeded and unexamined.

Hence **un'heededly** *adv.*

1818 BYRON *Ch. Har.* IV. lxiii, And such the frenzy,..that, beneath the fray, An earthquake reel'd unheededly away! **1821** SHELLEY *Epipsych.* 421 Day, and Storm, and Calm,.. Treading each other's heels, unheededly.

un'heedful, *a.* [UN-[1] 7.] Heedless.

1570 LEVINS *Manip.* 186 Vnheedful, *incautus.* **1591** SHAKS. *Two Gentl.* II. vi. 11 Vn-heedfull vowes may heedfully be broken. **1631** HEYLIN *St. George* 28 Some secret venome, which the unheedfull Reader may swallow unawares. **1740** CIBBER *Apol.* (1756) I. 175 He so often lost the value of them by an unheedful confidence. **1782** ELIZ. BLOWER *Geo. Bateman* II. 171 The glassman, unheedful of his threats, picked up the half-crown. **1804** J. GRAHAME *Sabbath* 25 The toil-worn horse,..Unheedful of the pasture. **1842** TENNYSON *Gardener's Dau.* 261 As once we met Unheedful, tho' beneath a whispering rain [etc.].

So **un'heedfully** *adv.*; **un'heedfulness.**

1591 SHAKS. *Two Gentl.* I. ii. 3 Would'st thou then counsaile me to fall in loue? *Luc.* I Madam, so you stumble not *vnheedfully. **1586** W. WEBBE *Eng. Poetrie* (Arb.) 91 Such errours doo happen..by *vnheedefulnes, when one escapeth them by negligence. **1603** BRETON *Packet Mad Lett.* II. lxxxv, I know you..therefore doe thus kindly touch the hurt of vnheedfulnesse.

†**un'heedily,** *adv.* [UN-[1] 11.] Heedlessly.

1596 SPENSER *F.Q.* IV. x. 13 Whose manner was all passengers to stay,..Through which some lost great hope vnheedily. **1603** FLORIO *Montaigne* II. xxxv. 428 Beseeching her, that she wold not so vnheedily loose her self. **1629** H. BURTON *Truth's Triumph* 301 If vnheedily thou hast fallen vpon the same rockes. **1720-1** *Lett. fr. Mist's Jrnl.* (1722) II. 270 Anything that has the Name of it deceives them, who unheedily take the Title for the Reality.

†**un'heediness.** *Obs.* [UN-[1] 12.] Unheedfulness, heedlessness.

1486 *Lichfield Gild Ord.* (1920) 21 That the seid summe.. by vnhedynes, blame, and neglygens of kepers..ys now diminysshed. **1576** NEWTON *Lemnie's Complex.* 23 b, Them y[e] be phlegmatick, they helpe forward, to slouth,.. sleapines, rechlesse vnheedynes. **1607** R. WILKINSON *Serm. at Whitehall* 9 She sailes not, but by sounding, lest by her vnheedines she runne her selfe aground. *a* **1641** BP. MOUNTAGU *Acts & Mon.* (1642) 276 The wicked practices ..whereto, through un-heedinesse the two young men had given great fomentation.

un'heeding, *ppl. a.* [UN-[1] 10, 5 d.]

1. Not giving heed; heedless, inattentive.

pred. **1737** GLOVER *Leonidas* VI. (1810) 111 Some torn deer, which..Had roam'd, unheeding, in the secret shade. **1816** BYRON *Parisina* x, All silent and unheeding now, With downcast eyes and knitting brow. **1848** MRS. GASKELL *Mary Barton* ix, He sat down by the fire in his wet things, unheeding.

attrib. **1791** COWPER *Iliad* XVI. 424 Lambs, which haply some unheeding swain Hath left to roam at large the mountains wild. **1817** SHELLEY *Rev. Islam* III. x, These words had fallen on my unheeding ear. **1872** BLACK *Adv. Phaeton* xxvi. 355 Groups of unheeding trees and streams.

2. Const. *of,* or with direct object.

(*a*) **1795** *Fate of Sedley* II. 198, I ramble over the country unheeding of the storm. **1840** T. HOOK *Fitzherbert* II. vi. 153 To pull the rose unheeding of the thorn.

(*b*) **1798** SOUTHEY *Joan of Arc* (ed. 2) I. I. 124, I sat in silence,..unheeding and unseeing all Around me. **1835** LYTTON *Rienzi* I. iii, Waving his hand to the smith, and unheeding his brandished weapon. **1892** GUNTER *Miss Dividends* xi, Then, unheeding his proffered aid, Erma descends from the carriage.

Hence **un'heedingly** *adv.,* heedlessly.

1787 *William of Normandy* II. 126 All the secrets..I unheedingly trusted him with. **1834** LYTTON *Pilgr. Rhine* xix, He passed..unheedingly.

un'heedy, *a.* Now *rare.* [UN-[1] 7.] Unheedful.

1579 E. K. *Gloss to Spenser's Shepherd's Cal.* April 26 His præsumptuous and vnheedie hardinesse. **1590** SHAKS. *Mids. N.* I. i. 235 Nor hath loues minde of any iudgement taste: Wings and no eyes, figure, vnheedy haste. **1631** MILTON *Epit. Marchioness Winchester* 38 So have I seen som tender slip..Pluck't up by som unheedy swain. **1656** HOBBES *Six Lessons* Wks. 1845 VII. 222 So much is un-heedy learning a hinderance to the knowledge of the truth. **1787** *William of Normandy* II. 9 He again set off for his unheedy voyage. **1919** R. BRIDGES in W. Caröe *Tom Tower* (1923) 112 Nor 'mong them was a single person..so void of scruple and unheedy.

†**un'heer,** *a. dial. Obs.* [? OE. *unhéore, -hére,* etc., fierce.] (See quot.)

1691 RAY *N. Co. Words* (ed. 2) 78 *Unheer,* adj., impatient. [Hence in Bailey (1721), etc.]

‖**unheimlich** (ʊn'haɪmlɪç), *a.* [Ger.] Uncanny, weird.

c **1877** W. JAMES in R. B. Perry *Thought & Character of W. James* (1935) I. xxix. 499 To human nature there is something uncanny, *unheimlich,* in the notion of a universe stripped so stark naked [as pure phenomenalism would have it]. **1900** G. BELL *Let.* 9 Apr. (1927) I. v. 81 But it is very strange—'unheimlich', some silly German said and it's not as silly as it sounds at first. **1945** B. RUSSELL *Let.* 20 Feb. in *Autobiogr.* (1969) III. i. 41 The new ways on the Campus make it strange and *unheimlich* to me.

unheind, var. UNHEND *a. Obs.*

un'heired, *ppl. a.* (UN-[2] 4 and 8.)

c **1611** CHAPMAN *Iliad* V. 25 If the God..Had not (in.. pittie of his Sire, To leaue him vtterly vnheird) giuen safe passe to his feet.

un'held, *ppl. a.* (UN-[1] 8 b: cf. UNHOLDEN.)

1612 WARNER *Alb. Eng.* XI. lxv. 279 If amorous Hopes, or Hopes vnheld to him from me had past. **1827** POLLOK *Course T.* V. 661 Forgetful, she leaves him [*sc.* her infant] a while unheld.

unhele, *sb.;* see UNHEAL.

un'hele, *v. Obs.* exc. *dial.* Forms: 1 unhelan, 2-3 unhelen, 4-6 vnhele, 4-6, 9 *dial.,* unhele (4 oun-), 6 *Sc.* vnheild-, 6-7 vnheale, 7-8, 9 *dial.,* unheal, 8 unheel, 9 *dial.* unhale. [OE. *unhelan* (UN-[2] 3 + HELE *v.*): cf. MDu. *onthelen,* MHG. *enthelen,* and UNHILL *v.*]

1. *trans.* To uncover (something) so as to display or make visible; hence *fig.,* to discover, reveal, make patent or known. Also *refl.*

c **1000** *Ags. Gosp.* Luke xii. 2 Nis nan þing oferheled, þe ne beo unheled. *c* **1200** *Trin. Coll. Hom.* 77 Seinte poul.. minegeð us..þat we..cumen festliche to ure saule leche and unhelen him ure saule wundes. *a* **1225** *Ancr. R.* 150 Al so god dede þet wule adeaden forworpeð hire rinde, þet is, unheleð hire. *c* **1330** *Arth. & Merl.* 2689 (Kölbing), þe king.. ladde him fram & gan his priuete vnhele, & bad, þat he it schuld hele. **1387** TREVISA *Higden* (Rolls) VIII. 161 Here he is i-hud, but he is unheled. **1483** CAXTON *Gold. Leg.* 249/1 Netheles the body of saynt laurence was discouerd and unheled by ygnorance. **1530** TINDALE *Practice Prelates* H vij, Thou shalt not vnhele ye secretes of thy brothers wyffe. **1590** SPENSER *F.Q.* II. xii. 64 Then suddeinly both would themselues vnhele.

2. To uncover so as to leave open or exposed; to strip of covering or (freq.) roofing material.

a **1225** *Ancr. R.* 58 Auh þe dom is ful strong upon ham þet unhelieð þene put. **1387** TREVISA *Higden* (Rolls) I. 367 þere was a welle in þat lond..alle wey i-heled; and ȝif it were vnheled, þe welle wexe and adrenche al þe lond. **1393** LANGL. *P. Pl.* C. xx. 301 Yf hus hous be vnheled and reyne on hus bedde. *c* **1440** *Pallad. on Husb.* II. 56 Yet wol this werk the roote..Vnhele or kerue, and cold hit after quelle. **1501** DOUGLAS *Pal. Hon.* II. xlv, I kneillit law, and vnheildit my heid. **1551** *Southampton Court Leet Rec.* (1905) I. 28 Robarde foster hathe vnhellyde partte off thomas cupers housse. **1604** MARSTON *Malcontent* II. iii. D ij b, Would I were forcde To burne my fathers Tombe, vnheale [*v.r.* vnhill] his bones..., rather than this. **1610** G. FLETCHER *Christ's Tri.* II. ix, Thear should the Swallowe see..the grave vn-heale his face, To let the living from his bowels creepe. **1730** BUDGEN *Passage of Hurricane fr. Bexhill* 9 Mr John Collier had..the ridging of the house unheeled. **1741** *Phil. Trans.* XLI. 852 It presently unhealed the House we were in. **1848-** in *Eng. Dial. Dict.* s.v. *Unheal* (Wilts, Dorset, Som., Devon). **1891** T. HARDY *Tess* xlvii, They were busily 'unhaling' the rick, that is, stripping off the thatch.

†**b.** In pa. pple. Of the head: Uncovered. *Obs.*

1377 LANGL. *P. Pl.* B. XIV. 232 He goth to cold beddynge, And his heued vn-heled vn-esiliche i-wrye. *a* **1400-50** *Alexander* 3450 Hire hede vn-helid was on hiȝe & hild all in trissis.

Hence **un'heler; un'heling** *vbl. sb.*

c **1430** *Pilgr. Lyf Manhode* III. xvii. (1869) 144 This hand is an vnmakere of howses, and an *vnhelere and brekere of cofres. **1398** TREVISA *Barth. De P.R.* V. xxvii. (Bodl. MS.), In acutis [febribus] *vnheling and puttinge oute of bare armes is tokene of deeþ. **1640** in *Archæol. Cant.* (1902) XXV. 8 His mother being then in distress, by reason of the unhealing of her house by the late severe time.

un'helm, *v.* [UN-[2] 4, 7. Cf. Du. *onthelmen.*]

1. *refl.* and *trans.* To divest (oneself or another) of a helmet.

refl. *c* **1400** *Pilgr. Sowle* (Caxton, 1483) IV. xxxviii. 66 This knyght..vnhelmed hym, and come before the kynge. *c* **1468** in *Archaeol.* (1846) XXXI. 338 Then the Duke unhelmed hyme, and..chargid pece in paine of deth. **1587** HOLINSHED *Chron.* (ed. 2) III. 825/1 When the iusts were doone, the king & all the other vnhelmed them, & rode about the tilt. **1632** J. Hayward tr. *Biondi's Eromena* 100 Striving to unhelme himself.., he taking his brothers hand, would needs kisse it. **1801** Strutt *Sports & Past.* III. i. 124 The laws of the tournament permitted any one of the combatants to unhelm himself at pleasure. **1866** Lawrence *Sans Merci* xli, The five kings..unhelmed themselves to quench their thirst.

trans. **1470–85** Malory *Arthur* x. lxxxvi. 565 Thenne they vnarmed them. And whanne syre Launcelot was vnhelmed, sir Tristram and syr Palomydes knewe hym. **1525** Ld. Berners *Froiss.* II. clxviii. 468 Eche of them strake other on their helmes... With y^t ataynt the lorde of saynt Pye was vnhelmed. **1587** Hughes *Misfort. Arthur* v. i, Vnhealme his luckelesse head, set bare his face. **1819** Scott *Ivanhoe* xii, The marshals..unhelmed him by cutting the laces of his casque. **1848** Lytton *Harold* xii. ix, They unhelmed another corpse.

2. *intr.* To take off one's own helmet.

1865 J. M. Ludlow *Epics Mid. Ages* II. 228 Nor will she let William in till he has unhelmed.

un'helmed, (*ppl.*) *a.*[1] [f. prec., or f. UN-[1] 9 + HELM *sb.*[1]] **a.** Divested of a helmet. **b.** Not covered by, or not wearing, a helmet.

[**1775** Ash.] **1795** Southey *Joan of Arc* v. 26 The Maid, her brows in reverence vnhelm'd,..Knelt to his prayer. **1805** —— *Madoc in Azt.* xxii. 5 The victors,..With unhelm'd heads, reclining on their shields. **1834** Beckford *Italy* II. 317 Here,..bare-headed and unhelmed, kneel the figures [etc.]. **1868** Morris *Earthly Par.* (1870) I. I. 20 By his side unhelmed, but armed, stood one.

un'helmed, (*ppl.*) *a.*[2] [UN-[1] 8, 9 + HELM *sb.*[2] or *v.*[2]] Unguided, ungoverned.

1628 Feltham *Resolves* II. xxiv. 78 As if hee were an imperfect Prince, that leaueth an vnhelmed State. **1794** Coleridge *Relig. Musings* 126 Embattling Interests on each other rush With unhelmed rage.

un'helmet, *v.* [UN-[2] 4.] = UNHELM *v.*

1823 Scott *Quentin* xv, He was compelled to dismount,.. and unhelmet himself.

un'helmeted, *a.* (UN-[1] 9.)

1823 Scott *Quentin D.* xxii, His head was unhelmeted, but he wore the rest of his ponderous and bright armour. **1870** Ruskin *Lect. Art* vi. 153 Next you have Athena, again unhelmeted and crowned with leaves.

†**un'help,** *sb. Obs.* [UN-[1] 12. Cf. MLG. *unhulpe* disadvantage.] Absence of help; hindrance.

c **1449** Pecock *Repr.* I. xviii. 108 Manie lettis and manye vnhelpis and manye lackis of helpis. **1483** *Cath. Angl.* 182/2 Vn Helpe, *irrefugium.* **1598** Florio, *Disaiuto*, hinderance, vnhelpe, let.

un'help, *v.* [UN-[2] 3. Cf. MDu. *onthelpen*, MLG. *enthelpen.*] *trans.* To deprive of help; to hinder.

1598 Florio, *Disaiutare*, to vnhelpe, to hinder, to disfauour. **1845** T. W. Coit *Puritanism* 118 They would help him, if thereby they might unhelp Churchmen.

un'helpable, *a.* (UN-[1] 7 b.)

1886 *Illustr. Lond. News* 5 June 597/3 The most unhelpable creature possible.

un'helped, *ppl. a.* (UN-[1] 8.)

1388 Wyclif *Wisd.* xii. 5 Fadris and modris, autours of soulis vnhelpid. **1598** Drayton *Heroic Ep.* 6 That poore king, of al these hopes preuented, Vnhard, vnhelp'd. **1720** Pope *Iliad* xvii. 580 Unhelp'd we stand, unequal to engage The force of Hector. *a* **1784** T. Adam *Poor Man's Guide* (1788) 13 Your case is as much unhelped as if there was not one promise there. **1853** Ruskin *Stones Ven.* III. ii. 53 Let him consider..how many living souls may have been left uncomforted and unhelped by him. **1888** Bryce *Amer. Commw.* II. 531 Nor will the opposite party always accept the proffered help..; sometimes it hopes to win unhelped.

un'helpful, *a.* [UN-[1] 7.]

1. Unable to help; not rendering help.

1593 Shaks. *2 Hen. VI*, III. i. 218 Euen so my selfe bewayles good Glosters case With sad vnhelpefull teares, and with dimn'd eyes. **1643–5** Milton *Divorce* II. xvii, A blamelesse creature,..to whose ease you cannot adde the tithe of one small atome, but by letting alone your unhelpfull surgery. **1856** Miss Yonge *Daisy Chain* I. xvii, Standing unhelpful, when the others were busy bringing in the benches. **1880** Swinburne *Stud. Shaks.* 62 As yet the one contemporary book..remains..inaccessible and unhelpful to students.

2. Helpless, shiftless. Also *absol.*

1855 I. Taylor *Restor. Belief* (1856) 290 The luckless, the unhelpful, the feeble,..receive such help as their several cases call for.

Hence **un'helpfully** *adv.*; **un'helpfulness.**

1626 Bp. Hall *Contempl., O.T.* xxi. v, To take vengeance ..for this cold unhelpfulnesse to his distressed Church. **1889** in *Cent. Dict.* **1971** *Daily Tel.* 21 Apr. 12/3 The situations are promising, but the play becomes unhelpfully confusing.

un'helping, *ppl. a.* (UN-[1] 10.)

1604 E. Hake (*title*), Of Golds Kingdome and this Unhelping Age. **1645** W. Jenkyn *Stil-Destroyer* 35 View them as usefull and efficacious, not as idle and unhelping. **1861** [Mrs. A. J. Penny] *Romance Dull Life* xiii. 98 Others of the family came in with kind words and offered help... Poor Constance, alone, sat silent and unhelping.

†**un'helpless,** *a. Obs.*[-1] [UN-[1] 5 a.] Helpless.

1681 Crowne *Hen. VI*, IV. 45 Whilst I with as unhelpless tears bewail The good Man's injuries.

†**un'helply,** *a. Obs.*[-1] [UN-[1] 7. Cf. Da. *uhjelpelig*, Sw. *ohjelplig* irremediable; Norw. *uhjelpelig* unserviceable.] Unhelpful.

1408 tr. *Vegetius' Art War* (MS. Digby 233) fol. 216/2 Al þat is helpliche to hym is vnhelpliche to þe.

un'hemmed, *ppl. a.* [UN-[1] 8.]

1. Unconfined, unrestrained.

a **1400–50** *Alexander* 2835 For-þi hoo with þi hatness & þi vn-hemmyd wittes, Avale of þi vanyte.

2. Not furnished with a hem.

1561 in *Inuentaires de la Royne Descosse* (Bannatyne Club) 24 Aucht serviottis of vnhemmit great lyning. **1611** Florio, *Inorlato*,..vnhemmed. **1889** *Daily News* 13 July 3/3 The new little Redfern capes..with their triple row of unhemmed cloth.

†**un'hend,** *a.*, *sb.*, and *adv.* [UN-[1] 7.]

1. Of persons: Discourteous, impolite; ungentle, rude, rough.

c **1205** Lay. 28826 Ne durste nauere nan vn-hende þas kinges hus isechen. *a* **1300** *Cursor M.* 9023 Bot mistru nan ..þat i Thinc sai o womman wilani, If i sua did i war vn-hind [*v.r.* vnhend]. *Ibid.* 28426 Gains godd i haue bene vn-hende, þat i wit-halden ha my tende. *c* **1330** R. Brunne *Chron. Wace* (Rolls) 16022 But longe er hit was brought til ende, He was slayn wyþ folk vnhende. *c* **1380** *Sir Ferumbras* 1965 þar-after schalt þow wende..And take þe kyng þat is ounhende. *a* **1450** *Le Morte Arth.* 1081 Off foo ne frend, the sothe to say, So vn-hend of thewis is ther none.

absol. *c* **1460** *Towneley Myst.* xx. 642 My comforth from care may ye sone wyn, If ye happely may hent that vnheynde.

2. Of acts, words, etc.: Unfitting, improper.

c **1205** Lay. 13265 þe frume wes vnhende & al swa wes þe ænde. *c* **1225** *Ancr. R.* 204 Mid luue speche, cos, unhende gropunges, þet beoð heaued sunnen. *a* **1300** *Cursor M.* 27734 Vnheind talking, o dede vtrage,..Hurtes grett, and sclander and tene. ?*c* **1400** *Emare* 445 The old qwene spakke wordus unhende. *c* **1425** *Cast. Persev.* 2030 in *Macro Pl.* 138 þis day ȝe dyth a good defens! Whyl Mankynde is in good entent, His þoutis arn vn-hende.

b. *sb.* Trouble, mischief.

1377 Langl. *P. Pl.* B. xx. 185 'Sire euel-ytauȝte elde,' quod I, 'vnhende go with the!'

3. *adv.* Improperly; unfaithfully.

1338 R. Brunne *Chron.* (1810) 259 ȝe sette a certeyn þing, at ȝour boþe assent,..þou brak þat certeynte wikkedly & vnhende.

†**un'hendly,** *adv. Obs.* [UN-[1] 11.] Discourteously, rudely, roughly; improperly.

a **1225** *Leg. Kath.* 2117 He..het, on hat heorte, unhende-liche neomen hire. **1297** R. Glouc. (Rolls) 8540 He it vorsok vnhendeliche & in vaire manere none. *c* **1350** *Will. Palerne* 492 Now witterly ich am vn-wis..þus vn-hendly & hard mi herte to blame. *c* **1400** *Destr. Troy* 6729 He hurlet forth vnhyndly, harmyt full mony.

unhenge, obs. f. UNHINGE *v.*

un'hent, *pa. pple.* [UN-[1] 8 b.] Untaken.

c **1350** *Will. Palerne* 1671, I kan bi no coyntyse knowe nouȝ þe best, how ȝe mowe un-hent or harmles a-scape.

un'heppen, *a. north. dial.* [UN-[1] 7 + dial. *heppen* tidy, handy, a. ON. *heppinn* (Norw. *heppen*) lucky, dexterous. Cf. Norw. *uheppen.*] **a.** Untidy, slatternly. **b.** Ungainly, etc.

1790 Grose *Prov. Gloss.*, *Unheppen*, slatternly. **1824** [Carr] *Craven Gloss.* 119 *Unheppen*, unbecoming, uncomfortable, indecent, untidy. **1855–** in *Eng. Dial. Dict.* (Yks., Linc.). **1880** Tennyson *Village Wife* xvi, An' Lucy wur läame o' one leg,..Straänge an' unheppen Miss Lucy!

un'heralded, *ppl. a.* (UN-[1] 8.)

1845 Neale *Euphratean Angels* iv. in *Seatonian Poems* (1864) 7 Yet not unheralded by fear, The End of all things shall draw near. **1871** Macduff *Mem. Patmos* xxiii. 315 A prey to the disquieting thought of the unheralded foot-fall. [Freq. in recent use.]

un'herd, *v.* [UN-[2] 5, 6 b, 7.]

1. *trans.* To disperse or separate (cattle, etc.) from a herd.

1611 Florio, *Smandrare*, to let out of the fold or pen, to vnherd, to scatter cattle. *a* **1641** Suckling *Brennoralt* I. i, When I had..at length unhearded the proud Deer, The Currs have snatch'd him up.

2. *intr.* To break away from the common herd.

1661 Boyle *Style of Script.* (1675) 175 The..title of a wit, which they hope to acquire by unherding and keeping out of the road.

un'herded, *ppl. a.* (UN-[1] 8.)

[**1775** Ash.] **1891** in C. Roberts *Adrift in America* 241 It is my opinion, after experience.., that unherded sheep do much better than those which are closely looked after.

unhe'reditary, *a.* (UN-[1] 7.)

1823 Lamb *Elia* II. *Child Angel*, As if to explore its path in those its unhereditary palaces. **1848** J. O'Donovan tr. *Four Masters* III. 2299 Countless numbers..were buried in strange places and unhereditary churches.

un'heritable, *a.* [UN-[1] 7 b.]

†1. Incapable of being heirs. *Obs.*[-1]

1553 in Holinshed *Chron.* (1577) II. 1717/1 Thereby you [are] iustly made illegitimate and vnheritable to the Crowne Imperiall of thys Realme.

2. Uninheritable.

[**1775** Ash.] *a* **1854** H. Reed *Lect. Brit. Poets* (1857) 384 The glory of Shakspeare's name began and ended with himself, his own unheritable self.

†**un'herited,** *ppl. a. Obs.* [UN-[1] 8.] Uninherited.

1542 *Test. Ebor.* (Surtees) VI. 128 An erle or an erles sone and heyre,..his landes beinge unherited. *Ibid.*, A knyghte havinge his lands unherited.

†**un'herly,** *a. Obs.*[-1] [repr. OE. *unhéorlic*, *unhíerlic* (*-hýrlic*), fierce, savage, dismal.] Repulsive.

c **1325** *Metr. Hom.* 129 Riht als leper mas bodi Ugli, and lathe, and unherly.

unhe'roic, *a.* and *sb.* (UN-[1] 7.)

1732 Ld. Peterborow *Let.* in *Pope's Wks.* (1751) VIII. 164 If the translator of Homer find fault with this unheroic disposition. **1745** [see UN-ENGLISH *a.* 1]. **1840** Carlyle *Heroes* v. (1904) 177 Hollow Formulism, gross Benthamism, and other unheroic atheistic Insincerity. **1881** P. Brooks *Candle of Lord* 169 The heroic moments in all of our most unheroic lives.

absol. and *sb.* **1843** Carlyle *Past & Pr.* IV. i, The Unheroic of such volumes. *Ibid.*, An Alexandrian Library of Unheroics.

unhe'roical, *a.* [UN-[1] 7.] = prec.

1635–56 Cowley *Davideis* III. Note 1, I call it Nobe..; for (methinks) Nob is too unheroical a Name. **1718** J. Trapp tr. *Virgil* (1735) I. Pref. p. xlix, Nor can I forbear thinking.. that the Figure which Vulcan makes..is a little improper, and unheroical.

unhe'roically, *adv.* (UN-[1] 11.)

1834 Beckford *Italy* I. 39 We procured comfortable though not magnificent apartments, and slept most unheroically sound. **1876** Emerson *Lett. & Soc. Aims* i. 63 The brains are so marred, so imperfectly formed, unheroically.

un'heroism. (UN-[1] 12.)

1845 Carlyle *Cromwell* (1871) I. 72 Search not for the secret of Heroic Ages..among their falsities, their greedy quackeries and *un*heroisms! **1871** J. S. Brewer *Eng. Stud.* (1881) 267 Shakspeare in his unheroism and in his realism was exhibiting..the growing tendency of his own age.

†**unhersumness:** see UN-[1] 3.

unhese, obs. f. UNEASE.

un'hesitating, *ppl. a.* (UN-[1] 10.)

1753 Francis *Constantine* IV. 48 Answer me: speak; un-hesitating speak. **1823** Scott *Quentin D.* xxiii, I, who have the advantage of your unhesitating devotion, have done you foul and ungrateful wrong. **1862** 'Shirley' (J. Skelton) *Nugæ Crit.* vii. 295 He can discover..little or nothing that can command his clear and unhesitating assent.

Hence **un'hesitatingness.**

1876 Meredith *Beauch. Career* xl, Unhesitatingness was the warrior virtue of her desire.

un'hesitatingly, *adv.* [UN-[1] 11.] Without hesitation; confidently; promptly.

1829 S. H. Cassan *Lives Bps. Bath & Wells* 15 *note*, Such alienations have been unhesitatingly made. **1853** Kane *Grinnell Exp.* xliii. (1856) 396 They [snowbirds] alight on the decks, and come unhesitatingly to our very feet. **1877** Mrs. Oliphant *Makers Flor.* iv. 103 All the critics..take his opinion unhesitatingly on this point.

un'hewed, *ppl. a.* [UN-[1] 8. Cf. MHG. *ungehouwet.*] = next.

1382 Wyclif *Josh.* viii. 31 Thanne Josue bilde vp..an auter of stonus vnhewid, the whiche yren hath not towchid. **1612** Drayton *Poly-olb.* ix. 421 With a bended knee On th' un-hew'd altar laid. **1644** Bulwer *Chiron.* 5 If Man were disarmed of this native weapon..the expression of his Tongue would be very weake and unhewed.

un'hewn, *ppl. a.* [UN-[1] 8 b. Cf. MDu. *on-*, MHG. *ungehouwen*, ON. *úhǫgginn* (MDa. *u-*, Sw. *ohuggen*).]

1. Not hacked or cut with weapons.

a **1400–50** *Alexander* 1945 Besely we shapid Out of þe handis vn-hewyn of oure hatill fais.

2. Not hewn or cut into shape; not fashioned or shaped by hewing.

1382 Wyclif *Josh.* viii. 31 (MS. Douce 369), An auter of stones vnhewen þe whiche eiren haþ not touchid. **1651** Hobbes *Leviath.* IV. xlv. 359 A Stone unhewn has been set up for Neptune. **1797** Mrs. Radcliffe *Italian* xviii, The walls, of unhewn marble, were high and strengthened by bastions. **1804** *Ann. Rev.* II. 191 An unhewn log of wood.. decorated with red feathers. **1857** Dufferin *Lett. High Lat.* (ed. 3) 309 This fringe of unhewn timber that lined the beach. **1887** Bowen *Æneid* III. 688 Pantagia's harbour, a gorge in the unhewn stone.

b. *fig.* Unpolished, rough, rugged.

1659 Pell *Impr. Sea* 44 Ignorant, knotty, illiterate, and unhewn Sailors. **1667** Montague & Prior *Hind & P. Transv.* Wks. 1907 II. 18, I hate such a rough unhewen Fellow as Milton. **1703** Mrs. Centlivre *Beau's Duel* IV. i I hope the world will distinguish the difference between a rough, unhewn soldier, and a polish'd Gentleman. **1850** Marsden *Early Purit.* iii. 71 Cartwright is described as unhewn and awkward.

unheyle, obs. var. UNHALE *a.*

unheynd, var. UNHEND *a. Obs.*

un'hid, *ppl. a.* [UN-[1] 8 b.] Not hid; unconcealed.

a **1300** *Cursor M.* 26617 O sin þat opin es and kid Tak open penance and vn-hid. *a* **1400–50** *Alexander* 3437 Bot ȝour harmes were vnhid I held noȝt myne athis. *c* **1430** *Pilgr. Lyf Manhode* I. xxxv. (1869) 22 It is bettere the keyes..ben hid than unhyd. **1648** Hexham II, *Ongeborgen*, Vnhid, or Vncovered.

un'hidden, *ppl. a.* (UN-¹ 8 b.)
1599 SHAKS. *Hen. V*, I. i. 86 The seueralls and vnhidden passages Of his true Titles to some certaine Dukedomes. **1829** H. MILLER in *Sch. & Schm.* xx. (1858) 439 All around we saw extended the complete sphere,—unhidden above from Orion to the Pole. **1868** MORRIS *Earthly Par.* I. I. 379 All unhidden once again they saw That peerless beauty.

un'hide, *v.* [UN-² 3.] *trans.* To make unhidden; to lay open; to disclose, reveal.
a **1300** *Cursor M.* 7230 Drunkennes oft mai bitide Dos man his consail to vn-hide. *c* **1375** *Sc. Leg. Saints* i. (*Peter*) 283 For dowt his craft vnhid suld be, He kest his bukis in þe se. *c* **1400** *Rom. Rose* 2168 If that ye wole so long abide Tyl I this Romance may vnhide. *c* **1420** *Anturs of Arth.* 328 (Douce MS.) Þe wyndes, þe weders, þe welkene vnhides; Þene vnclosed þe cloudes. **1535** STEWART *Cron. Scot.* (Rolls) III. 431 Quhen tha saw him nakit and wnhid, With bludie woundis.., tha..weipit full soir. **1580** HOLLYBAND *Treas. Fr. Tong, Descacher*, to vnhide. **1631** P. FLETCHER *Piscatory Eclog.* v. xiv, If thou desir'st my help, unhide the sore. **1676** HOBBES *Iliad* 59 Whilst in stooping he his flank un-hides, Agenor quickly his advantage spyes. **1880** J. NICOL *Poems & Songs* 126 To thee the sea her secret oft unhides.

un'hideable, *a.* (UN-¹ 7 b.)
1606 SYLVESTER *Du Bartas* II. iv. II. *Magnificence* 1256 A light so bright, set in such eminence (Un-hideable by envious Arrogance, Under the Bushell of black Ignorance).

un'hidebound, *a.* (UN-¹ 7.)
1667 MILTON *P.L.* x. 601 Which here..all too little seems To stuff this Maw, this vast unhide-bound Corps.

un'hided, *ppl. a.*¹ [UN-¹ 8.] Of land: Not divided into hides.
1867 *Chronicle* 10 Aug. 470/1 At 120 acres the hide..only one-tenth of England would be left unhided. But..the real proportion of hided to unhided land was only as 1 to 2.

un'hided, *ppl. a.*² [UN-² 4, 8.] Deprived of hide; skinned.
a **1658** LOVELACE *Poems* (1904) 179 Is not this finer far Then walk un-hided, when that every Stone Has knock'd acquaintance with your Ankle bone?

un'high, *a. rare.* [UN-¹ 7, after OE. *unhéah, -héh.*] Wanting in height.
1838 LONGF. *The Grave* ii, Thy house..is unhigh and low [*orig.* unheh and lah]. *Ibid.*, The heel-ways are low, The side-ways unhigh [*orig.* unheȝe].

†**un'hight**, *v. Obs.* [UN-² 3.] *trans.* To deprive of grace or beauty.
1387 TREVISA *Higden* (Rolls) I. 11 Ȝif I..vnhiȝte [L. *decolorarem*] so noble a matire with grisbaitinge. **1398** —— *Barth. De P.R.* IX. xxv. (Tollem. MS.), Nyȝte schulde nouȝt be all unhyȝte [L. *indecora*] by absence of þe sonne.

†**un'highted**, *ppl. a. Obs.*⁻¹ [UN-¹ 8.] Not invested with beauty.
1629 T. ADAMS *Med. Creed* Wks. 1138 Through the chinkes of an vnhighted flesh, we may read a neglected soule.

†**un'hightness.** *Obs.* [UN-¹ 12.] Impairment; uncomeliness.
1398 TREVISA *Barth. De P.R.* VII. iii. (Bodl. MS.), Þe heed [suffereth] in heere þereof with..vnhiȝtenes þat phisicians clepen furfurisca. *Ibid.* VII. xvii, Suche an vn-hiȝtenes in þe yȝe comeþ of blood.

unhi'larious, *a.* (UN-¹ 7.)
1879 F. W. ROBINSON *Coward Consc.* I. iv, He laughed in an odd, unhilarious fashion.

†**un'hill**, *v. Obs.* [UN-² 3 + HILL *v.*¹]
1. = UNHELE *v.* 1.
c **1200** *Trin. Coll. Hom.* 69 Synnes on dede and on speche unhileð hem seluen. *c* **1250** *Gen. & Ex.* 1912 If he saȝ hise breðere mis-faren, His fader he it gan vn-hillen & baren. *a* **1300** *Cursor M.* 26585 Noght wit wordes fayr and slight Agh þou for to plane þi plight, þat mai þi derf dedis dill, Bot openli þou þam vnhill. **13..** *E.E. Allit. P.* B. 1628 Goddes gost is þe geuen.., & þou vnhyles vch hidde þat heuen kyng myntes. **1388** WYCLIF *Ecclus.* xlvii. 16 He was fillid with wisdom,..and his soule vnhilide the erthe. **1482** CAXTON *Trevisa's Higden* 369 Here he is hyd, but he is vnhyled, for name dureth euermore.
2. = UNHELE *v.* 2. Also *refl.*
a **1250** *Ancr. R.* 58 (Trin. MS.), [If anyone] unhulede þe put & beast fel þerin. *a* **1300** *E.E. Psalter* xxviii. 9 Vn-hil thickenesses sal he swa. *a* **1340** HAMPOLE *Psalter* cxviii. 18 Vnhil myn eghen & i sall bihalde wondirthyngis of þi laghe. *a* **1375** *Joseph Arim.* 515 Þer weoren hedes vn-huled, helmes vphaunset. **1388** WYCLIF *2 Sam.* vi. 20 The kyng of Israel.. vnhilynge hym silf bifor the handmaidis. *c* **1440** *Promp. Parv.* 364/2 Oncuryn, or on-hyllyn, *detego, discooperio.* **1604** [see UNHELE *v.* 2.] **1611** COTGR., *Descouvrir*, to vncouer, vnhill, denude.
b. In pa. pple. = UNHELE *v.* 2 b.
13.. *Gosp. Nicod.* 169 His heued vnhyld, on knese he kneled. *c* **1400** *Gamelyn* 87 His howses were vnhiled; and ful yuel dight. **1470–85** MALORY *Arthur* XIV. iii. 644 A passynge old man..; his sholders were naked & vnhylled.
3. To remove (a covering).
1388 WYCLIF *Ruth* iii. 4 Thou schalt..vnhile the cloth, with which he is hiled.

unhind, var. UNHEND *a. Obs.*

un'hinderable, *a.* (UN-¹ 7 b.)
1678 CUDWORTH *Intell. Syst.* 429 God made..the whole World it self Perfect and Vnhinderable. **1894** *Advance* (Chicago) 1 Mar., Nothing could be more natural or more unhinderable.

un'hinderably, *adv.* (UN-¹ 11.)
1678 CUDWORTH *Intell. Syst.* 482 Because all things are by him Connected together, and proceed from him unhinderably.

un'hindered, *ppl. a.* (UN-¹ 8. Cf. MDu. *ongehindert, ongehendert* (Du. *ongehinderd*), MHG. (MLG., G.) *ungehindert*, MSw. *ohindraper, ohindrat*, etc. (Sw. *ohindrad*), MDa. (Da.) *uhindret.*)
1615 T. ADAMS *Blacke Devill* 30 The vnhindred force of the wind. **1703** CLARKE *Evid. Nat. & Rev. Relig.* II. iv. (1738) 260 Virtue,..with all its full Effects and Consequences unhindered. **1839** ALFORD in *Life* (1873) 11 Flowing in one full, unhindered stream. **1856** R. A. VAUGHAN *Mystics* I. 361 The unhindered service of the state of glory.

un'hindering, *ppl. a.* (UN-¹ 10.)
1839 BAILEY *Festus* 28 In her [*sc.* Fiction's] loving and unhindering lap Voluptuously lulled, we dream.

un'hinge, *v.* [UN-² 3.]
1. *trans.* To take (a door, etc.) off the hinges; to remove the hinges from; to open in this way.
1616 A. RICH *Cabinet* 96 A house, whose chambers are full of cobwebbes; the dores vnhindged. **1634** W. WOOD *New Eng. Prosp.* (1865) 106 Our hogges having found a way to unhindge their barne doores. **1644** QUARLES *Sheph. Orac.* x, The arme that shall unhenge Th' incestuous gates of Sodom. **1674** *Jackson's Recantation* A 2, I..perswaded my self that the Machinations of my Brain were able to un-hinge the Poles. **1775** MRS. DELANY *Life & Corr.* Ser. II. (1862) II. 108 That may still be done, and yᵉ box none the worse for it, or you may unhinge it and keep it in the top.
fig. **1633** G. HERBERT *Temple, Sunday* vii, As Samson bore the doores away, Christs hands, though nail'd, wrought our salvation, And did unhinge that day.
b. *transf.* To unlock, unclose, open.
1624 QUARLES *Job* xv. 16 Would any..try a fall with Angels, and preuaile? Or with a Hymne, vnhinge the strongest Iayle? **1865** A. J. MUNBY *Verses New & Old* 185, I will not once..Unhinge my jaws to speak again.
2. To unsettle, unbalance, or disorder (the mind, brain, etc.).
1612 SHELTON *Quix.* II. xlvi. 303 The powerfull force of Loue Oft doth vnhindge the soule. **1663–70** SOUTH *Serm.* (1715) IV. 306 Why should I then unhinge my Brains? **1690** NESSE *O. & N. Test.* I. 60 Until another bad bargain happen ..to unhinge his spirit again. **1764** H. WALPOLE *Otranto* iv, Theodore..has unhinged the soul of Manfred. **1793** *Friendly Address to Poor* 13 These plays..serve only to unhinge and disorder their minds. **1867** BAKER *Nile Trib.* xii. (1872) 215 The nerves of Mahomet were completely unhinged. **1885** *Law Times* 7 Feb. 270/2 Study..had unhinged the deceased's mind.
b. With personal object. Also in weaker sense: To upset.
1631 MABBE *Celestina* xvii. (1894) 254 The Blockhead hath swallowed the bayte; hee hath let her unhinge him. **1681** H. MORE *Postscr. Glanvill's Sadducismus* 50 The Soul of Samuel might indeed have..so unhinged her, that she had been fit for nothing. **1719** DE FOE *Crusoe* II. (Globe) 320 One Blow from unforeseen Providence unhing'd me at once. **1782** MISS BURNEY *Cecilia* IV. vi, The effort..has unhinged me for a fortnight! **1855** BAIN *Senses & Int.* III. iii. §13 Some constitutions are rendered more alert and active by excitement, others are unhinged. **1888** MISS BRADDON *Fatal Three* I. v, The very mention of sickness..had unhinged him.
c. To unsettle (opinions, etc.), to render uncertain or doubtful. Also with personal object.
1719 DE FOE *Crusoe* II. (Globe) 320 But in the Middle of all this Felicity, one Blow from unforeseen Providence unhing'd me at once; and..drove me [etc.]. **1770** PRIESTLEY in *Phil. Trans.* LX. 197 The following experiments..quite unhinged me again, and left me as much at a loss as ever. **1782** —— *Matt. & Spir.* I. p. xxviii, When persons' minds are unhinged with respect to their opinions. **1831** BLAKEY *Free-will* 28 Calculated..to unhinge our opinions on matters highly important to our interests. **1856** DOVE *Logic Chr. Faith* VI. §4. 352 Does any such fact unhinge our moral convictions?
3. To deprive of stability or fixity; to throw into confusion or disorder.
1664 LYTTELTON in *Hatton Corr.* (Camden) 37 Which wee doubt will unhinge all that trade we thought soe well settled. **1674** N. FAIRFAX *Bulk & Selv.* 149 Our bounded wills not being of strength enough to unhinge Gods unbounded power. **1709** T. ROBINSON *Vind. Mosaick Syst.* Introd. 5 To entertain such..Ideas of God..would certainly unhinge the Foundation of all Religion. **1760** *Ann. Reg., Hist. War* 15/2 Any motion of his threatened to shake and unhinge the whole scheme of his defence. **1796** MRS. M. ROBINSON *Angelina* I. 2 The extravagance of sordid connections..have so unhinged my finances. **1886** *Daily News* 10 Dec. 2/4 The supplies are coming in very irregularly and unhinge the trade.
b. *esp.* To unsettle (some established order of things).
1679 *Hist. Jetzer* Pref. A j b, That Principle which obliges them to unhinge, and overturn all Government. **1688** LUTTRELL *Brief Rel.* (1857) I. 468 Restoring things to their old legall foundation, which hath been the work of some years past to unhinge. **1718** *Free-thinker* No. 42. 306 The Luxury of a Nation does likewise unhinge the Publick Peace and Tranquillity. **1788** JEFFERSON *Writ.* (1859) II. 372 The old system is unhinged, and no new one hung in its place. **1812** *Examiner* 24 Aug. 533/2 Wages that unhinged all that order in society.
4. To detach, separate, or dislodge *from* something. †Also const. *of.*
1655 FULLER *Ch. Hist.* XI. xvii. 145 These unhinge the day off from any Divine Right. **1680** C. NESSE *Church Hist.* 463 Thus God by this providence unhing'd him of his Romish religion. **1713** BLACKMORE *Creation* I. 233 And hills unhing'd from their deep roots depart. **1764** *Mem. G. Psalmanazar* 14 Some other avocations..unhinged me from my method oftener than I wished. **1788** WESLEY *Wks.* (1872) VI. 447 Whenever the mind is unhinged from God. **1861** GEO. ELIOT *Silas M.* ii, Minds that have been unhinged from their old faith and love.
Hence **un'hinging** *vbl. sb.*
1661 FELTHAM *Resolves* (ed. 8) I. iii. 181 The unhindging of the whole frame of Government. **1678** *Yng. Man's Call.* 72 The unhinging of the whole man from things of nobler worth toward God. *a* **1704** T. BROWN *Wks.* (1709) III. II. 97 It portends..the unhinging of his Polish Majesty, or the beating of Prince Eugene out of Italy. **1850** HT. MARTINEAU *Hist. Peace* II. v. vi. 313 The unhinging of society. **1886** *Athenæum* 4 Dec. 742/1 The outcome of an entire unhinging of his system caused by physical fear.

un'hinged, *ppl. a.* [f. prec.]
1. Thrown into confusion; unsettled, disordered.
1719 DE FOE *Crusoe* II. (Globe) 509, I might by my loose and unhing'd Circumstances be the fitter to embrace a Proposal for Trade. **1778** PRINGLE *Gunnery* 23 The unhinged state of this part of the mixed mathematics. **1835** MARRYAT *Olla Podr.* i. 5 Society is unhinged, and every one is afraid to offer an opinion. **1811** CHALMERS *Let.* in *Life* (1851) I. 243 The moral constitution of our nature is unhinged. **1895** J. A. NOBLE in *Contemp. Rev.* Apr. 490 A person whose intellectual, moral, or emotional sanity was unhinged.
b. *spec.* Of persons or the mind.
1732 J. WHALEY *Poems* 213 Shall the Mind lie unhing'd by each mad flight? **1757** FOOTE *Author* I, Last winter..I cou'd have made as good a speech upon any subject,..but I am all unhinged, all. **1811** LAMB *Shaks. Trag.* Wks. 1908 I. 131 Tokens of an unhinged mind. **1836** MARRYAT *Japhet* xxx, I never felt more nervous or more unhinged.
2. Deprived of hinges; taken off the hinges.
1824 W. IRVING *T. Trav.* I. 14 An unhinged window-shutter. **1824** GALT *Rothelan* II. IV. iv. 130 Bearing the corpse of a man on an unhinged door.

un'hingement. [f. as prec.] The act of unhinging; the fact of being or becoming unhinged.
1817 CHALMERS *Astron. Disc.* vii. 251 A melancholy unhingement in the constitution of man. **1857** J. HAMILTON *Less. fr. Gt. Biog.* 203 The disciples were beginning to recover from..the unhingement of old hopes. **1886** SYMONDS *Renaiss. It.* VII. viii. 130 The unhingement of his reason.

un'hinted, *ppl. a.* (UN-¹ 8.)
1889 C. C. R. *Up for Season* 16 New novels unprinted, new scandals unhinted Before.

un'hipped, *a.* (UN-¹ 9.)
1847 L. HUNT *Men, Women, & B.* I. xiv. 278 The most melancholy, hipped, unhipped generation, that ever walked.

un'hired, *ppl. a.* (UN-¹ 8. Cf. older Du. *ongehuurt* (Du. *ongehuurd*), Sw. *ohyrd.*)
1617 MORYSON *Itin.* To Rdr., I wrote at leasure, giuing (like a free and vnhired workeman) much time to pleasure. **1653** MILTON *Hirelings* Wks. 1851 V. 348 And who unhir'd will be so hardy as to say, that [etc.]? **1821** SCOTT *Kenilw.* iv, There..is thy morning wage—thou shalt not say thou hast been my guide unhired. **1852** MUNDY *Antipodes* (1857) 203 There were..three hundred of them unhired at the Immigrant Dépôt.

unhi'storic, *a.* (UN-¹ 7; cf. next.)
1862 'SHIRLEY' (J. Skelton) *Nugæ Crit.* iii. 177 Only a rash and unhistoric mind can affirm that [etc.]. **1874** WITHROW *Catacombs of Rome* (1877) 535 A new, unscriptural, and unhistoric method.

unhi'storical, *a.* [UN-¹ 7.]
1. Not in accordance with history.
1611 SPEED *Hist. Gt. Brit.* IX. viii. §9 So partiall and vnhistoricall is the report of one,..who faines [etc.]. **1830** *Gentl. Mag.* C. II. 139 It is perfectly unhistorical to suppose that [etc.]. **1852** BUNSEN *Hippolytus & Age* II. 160 The notion of a merely historical revelation by written records is as unhistorical as it is unintellectual. **1877** J. NORTHCOTE *Catacombs* I. v. 89 The thoroughly unhistorical way in which these few subjects are dealt with.
b. Not versed in history.
1865 W. G. PALGRAVE *Arabia* II. 22 Perhaps the unhistorical prophet had in mind some confused idea [etc.].
2. Not possessed of a historical character; not having actually occurred.
1848 JAS. SMITH *Voy. & Shipwr. Paul* 252 Such circumstances..are unhistorical, and are..omitted by the Evangelist who wrote historically. **1882** FARRAR *Early Chr.* II. 13 The supposed fact is unhistorical, but the remark shows [etc.].
So **unhi'storically** *adv.*
Also, in recent use, ***unhistoricalness.***
1846 GEO. ELIOT tr. *Strauss's Life of Jesus* I. II. i. 310 We might..be led to the supposition that the words *for the remission of sins*..was commonly used in relation to Christian baptism, and was thence transferred unhistorically to that of John. **1887** *Athenæum* 13 Aug. 206/3 We have unhistorically applied the word 'German' as the designation of one particular language of the group.

unhistri'onic, *a.* (UN-¹ 7.)
1837 CARLYLE *Fr. Rev.* III. vi. vi, 'What is passing?' repeats Collot, in the unhistrionic Cambyses' vein.

un'hit, *ppl. a.* (UN-¹ 8 b.)
1513 DOUGLAS *Æneid* VI. xiv. 87 Quha wald the, gret Cato, leif vnhit? **1595** RALEIGH *Discov. Guiana* (1596) 97 The woods are so thicke..as a mouse cannot sitte in a boate vnhit from the banke. **1601** B. JONSON *Poetaster* To Rdr. 26 Whilst I, at whom they shot, sit here shot-free, And as vn-

hurt of enuy, as vnhit. **1889** 'MARK TWAIN' *Yankee* xiii, They all looked unhit, and said they didn't know.

un'hitch, *v.* [UN-[2] 4 b.]

1. *trans.* To detach (*from* a practice).

1622 MABBE tr. *Aleman's Guzman d'Alf.* I. i. i. 10 From which terrible griping..nothing can vn-hitch them but deaths flesh-hooke.

2. To detach (a horse, etc.) by undoing a fastening: **a.** From a vehicle, plough, or the like.

1706 STEVENS I, *Destravar*, to unhitch. **1862** B. TAYLOR *Home & Abroad* Ser. II. II. iv. 91 While the younger children unhitched and watered the horses. **1884** J. GILMOUR *Mongols* i. 2 My Chinese carter,..unhitching his two mules [from the cart], went off and left me in the encampment. *absol.* **1887** I. R. *Lady's Ranche Life Montana* 150 So he helped me to unhitch, and I led the horses, while he dragged the buggy across.

b. From something to which its head is tied.

1883 *Harper's Mag.* Aug. 386/2, I went out and unhitched the horse, and drove straight home.

3. To detach or unfasten (a thing).

1876 WHYTE MELVILLE *Katerfelto* xxviii. 315 He unhitched his bridle from the garden palings. **1891** COTES *2 Girls on Barge* 27 With silent alacrity I unhitched the lamp. **1901** *Westm. Gaz.* 24 Oct. 7/3 A detachment of the men unhitched the long ladders.

un'hive, *v.* [UN-[2] 5.] *trans.* To turn out of a hive.

1729 MADDEN *Themistocles* I. i. 2 These armed Millions, that, like some vast Swarm,..unhiv'd have left their Home To seek new Seats of Empire. **1736** NEAL *Hist. Purit.* III. Pref. p. ix, Having unhived a numerous swarm of labouring bees. **1879** BROWNING *Ivan Ivanovitch* 71 Fancies, swarms that stung like bees unhived.

un'hoard, *v.* [UN-[2] 5.] *trans.* To take or bring out of a hoard.

1667 MILTON *P.L.* IV. 188 As a Thief bent to unhoord the cash Of some rich Burgher. **1721** AMHURST *Terræ Fil.* No. 12 (1726) 60 Every old hunks and miser unhoarded his dear treasure. **1797** *Monthly Rev.* XXIII. 569 Much coin has been reimported, and much unhoarded.

un'hoarded, *ppl. a.* (UN-[1] 8.)

a **1683** OLDHAM *Rem.* (1684) 99 His unconfin'd unhoarded Store Was still the vast Exchequer of the poor.

un'hoarding, *ppl. a.* (UN-[1] 10.)

1695 LOCKE *Further Consid. Value Money* 54 They would still be..greater losers than their unhoarding Neighbours.

un'hobble, *v.* (UN-[2] 4 b.)

1881 *Chequered Career* 335 Unhobble the spare horses. **1887** W. S. S. TYRWHITT *New Chum in Queensland Bush* ix. 179 The horses are now un-hobbled, saddled and bridled.

un'hoed, *ppl. a.* (UN-[1] 8.)

1733 TULL *Horse-hoeing Husb.* (Dublin ed.) 72 A Hoed Plant of Corn will have Twenty or Thirty Stalks,..where an unho'd Plant..will have only Two or Three Stalks. **1872** *Pall Mall G.* 22 Aug. 5 His roots cannot be left un-hoed,..or his corn uncut.

un'hogged, *ppl. a.* (UN-[1] 8.)

1886 KIPLING *Departm. Ditties*, etc. (1899) 100 With your mane unhogged and flowing.

†**un'hold**, *a.* (and *sb.*). *Obs.* [OE. *unhold* (f. UN-[1] 7 + HOLD *a.*), = MDu. *onhout*, Flem. (Kilian) *onhoud*, OS., OHG., G. *unhold*, MLG., MHG. *unholt*; MSw. *ohulder* (*ohwl*, *ohull*), MDa. *uhuld*.]

1. Unfaithful; disloyal; false.

c **1000** ÆLFRIC *Hom.* II. 556 Se unholda ðeowa wearð ða aworpen on þam yttrum þeostrum. *c* **1395** *Plowman's Tale* 473 Hir servaunts be to hem unhold, But they can doublin hir rentall To bigge hem castels.

2. Of persons: Exhibiting dislike or hostility; unfriendly, hostile.

c **900** tr. *Bæda's Hist.* II. xii. (1890) 132 Swa..he him þa sætunge þa ȝewearonode þæs unholdan cyninges [*L. regis sibi infesti*]. *c* **1050** *O.E. Chron.* an. 1040 (Tiberius B. i), Him wæs þa unhold eall þæt his ær ȝyrnde. *c* **1320** *Sir Tristr.* 936 Marke schuld ȝeld vnhold..þre hundred pounde of gold.

b. Of events: Troublesome, disastrous.

a **1310** in Wright *Lyric P.* iv. 24 He mai..sore ben fered on folde, Lest he to harmes helde, ant happes hente unholde.

3. *absol.* or as *sb.* An enemy or foe.

a **1200** *Moral Ode* 36 (Lamb. MS.), Monies monnes sare iswinc habbeð oft unholde. *a* **1225** *Ancr. R.* 222 Vnholde uor-ureten þe strencðe of his soule, & he hit nout nuste.

†**un'holden**, *ppl. a.* [UN-[1] 8 b. Cf. MDu. and Du. *ongehouden* (dial. *ongeholden*, *-halden*), MLG. *ungeholden*, MHG. and G. *ungehalten*.]

a. = UNBEHOLDEN 1. **b.** Not kept; unobserved.

c **1380** WYCLIF *Serm.* Sel. Wks. I. 309 Here it semeþ þat þes prestis ben moche unholden to seculer lordis. *a* **1425** *Cursor M.* 18736 (Trin.), Þe lawe he helde wondir wel Vnholden lafte he neuer a del.

unhole, obs. f. UNWHOLE *a.*

un'holily, *adv.* (UN-[1] 7. Cf. UNHOLY *a.*)

1561 T. NORTON *Calvin's Inst.* III. 221 So is it vnlawfull that it be vnholily profaned by the vncleannesse of the inhabitantes. **1619** W. SCLATER *Exp. 1 Thess.* 439 Men of corrupt mindes,..if they be elected,..shall be saued, how euer holily, or vnholily they liue. **1647** J. VICARS *Coleman-st. Conclave Visited* B ij b, The sad..breach, which is..most unholily made by..Sectaries. **1754** EDWARDS *Freed. Will* IV. ii, It is impossible for Him to act unrighteously and unholily. **1898** *Advance* (Chicago) 16 June 808/2 Before their imaginations were unholily stirred by these pages.

un'holiness. [UN-[1] 12.]

1. The quality of being unholy; lack of holiness or sanctity.

1534 MORE *Treat. Passion* ii. Wks. 1311/2 The vyces of vicious folke in Christes church, can not lette, but that hys catholike church..is for their vnholynes, his holy catholyke churche. **1597** HOOKER *Eccl. Pol.* v. lxxiv. §2 She is not..in respect of any vnholinesse forbidden entrance into the Church. **1645** MILTON *Tetrach.* 36 Where an unfit mariage administers continual cause of hatred and distemper, there ..cannot choose but much unholines abide. **1675** BROOKS *Gold. Key* Wks. 1867 V. 195 Adam's holiness was as natural ..to him as any way of unholiness can be natural..to us. **1845** CORRIE in *Encycl. Metrop.* II. 880/1 All that blindness of heart, all that unholiness of affections,..which issue in overt acts of sin. **1871** FARRAR *Witn. Hist.* i. 11 Let us.. beware that in us unholiness do not cloud the spiritual eye.

2. Applied to the Pope: cf. HOLINESS 2.

1682 G. TOPHAM *Rome's Tradit.* 204 No sooner did the news of that bloody Butchery arrive his Unholiness [Gregory XIII], but [etc.].

unholl, obs. f. UNWHOLE *a.*

un'hollow, *a.* (UN-[1] 7.)

1548 UDALL, etc. *Erasm. Par. John* 117 b, The sepulchre ..was cut out of an whole sound vnholow rocke of stone. **1611** FLORIO, *Inuacuo*, vnempty, vnhollow.

un'hollowed, *ppl. a.* (UN-[1] 8.)

1609 DOULAND *Ornith. Microl.* 22 Make it hollow in the middle, leauing the ends of it vnhollowed. **1913** R. HARRIS *Boanerges* xxxi. 301 The hollow oak is higher in sanctity than the unhollowed tree.

un'holpen, *ppl. a.* Now *arch.* [UN-[1] 8 b. Cf. MDu. (and Du.) *ongeholpen*, MHG. *ungeholfen*; Sw. *ohulpen*.] = UNHELPED *ppl. a.*

1382 WYCLIF *1 Esdras* ix. 11 But for the multitude is gret, and the time winter, and wee moun not vnholpen stonde. **1390** GOWER *Conf.* II. 189 'The lif is suete', and that he kepeth, So that the feith unholpe slepeth. *c* **1440** *Gesta Rom.* 121 (Add. MS.), She will leve none vnholpen that crieth to her hertly. **1485** CAXTON *Chas. Gt.* (1881) 174 God forbede ..that I leue hym vnholpen. **1545** BRINKLOW *Lament.* 88 Ye ..leaue..the presoned vnholpen. **1568** T. HOWELL *Arb. Amitie* (1879) 70 Thou hast the forme that cut the wound, of my vnholpen paine. **1608** DOD & CLEAVER *Expos. Prov.* xi–xii. 183 Neuer any was left unholpen, that sought help at his hand. **1864** SWINBURNE *Atalanta* 1674 These shall lie Dead, unbeloved, unholpen. **1870** MORRIS *Earthly Par.* III. IV. 224 The maddening fear that burned Round his unholpen heart.

un'holy, *a.* and *sb.* [OE. *unhálig* (f. *un-* UN-[1] 7 + *hálig* HOLY *a.*), = NFris. *unhilleg*; older Fl. (Kilian) *onheyligh*, MDu. *onheilich* (rare), Du. *onheilig*; ON. *úheilagr* (MDa. and Da. *uhellig*, Sw. *ohelig*).]

1. Not holy; impious, profane, wicked: **a.** Of persons.

c **1000** *Lambeth Ps.* xlii. 1 Toscead intingan minne of unhaliȝre þeode. **1362** LANGL. *P. Pl.* A. Prol. 3 In Habite of an Hermite vn-holy of werkes. **1526** TINDALE *2 Tim.* iii. 2 The men shalbe..vnthankfull, vnholy, churlisshe. **1607** SHAKS. *Cor.* v. vi. 119 Will you be put in minde of his blinde Fortune..by this vnholy Braggart? **1685** BAXTER *Paraphr. N.T.* Matt. xxv. 26 To confess God's holy Government, and yet to be unholy, is to be self condemning. **1738** WESLEY *Ps.* v. ii, In Souls unholy and unclean Thou never canst delight. **1817** SHELLEY *Rev. Islam* x. xlvii, Unholy men, Feasting like fiends upon the infidel dead. **1833** CARLYLE *Misc.* (1857) III. 287 To lodge the whole unholy Brotherhood..in separate cells of the Bastille!

absol. **1526** TINDALE *1 Tim.* i. 10 The lawe is..geven..to synners, to vnholy and vnclean. **1667** MILTON *P.L.* XI. 106 Hast thee, and..drive out the sinful Pair, From hallowd ground th' unholie. **1873** SYMONDS *Grk. Poets* vii. 192 The idea of Nemesis quelling the insolent and smiting the unholy.

b. Of acts, things, etc.

1382 WYCLIF *2 Tim.* ii. 16 Schonye thou vnhooli and veyn spechis. **1390** GOWER *Conf.* II. 363 (MS. A), If he pourchace By wey of thefte unholy thing. **1526** TINDALE *Heb.* x. 29 He..which..counteth the bloud off the testament as an vnholy thynge. **1591** SHAKS. *Two Gent.* IV. iii. 30 To keepe me from a most vnholy match. **1632** MILTON *L'Allegro* 4 In Stygian Cave forlorn 'Mongst horrid shapes, and shreiks, and sights unholy. **1653** JER. TAYLOR *Serm. for Year* iv. 50 If things that are lawfull may yet be unholy in this sense; much more are unlawfull things most unholy in all senses. **1717** POPE *Eloisa to Abelard* 224 Far other dreams my erring soul employ, Far other raptures, of un-holy joy. **1791** COWPER *Odyss.* XXII. 479 Unholy is the voice Of loud thanksgiving over slaughter'd men. **1842** MANNING *Serm.* x. (1848) I. 135 Cultivation of mind, refinement,..are often found in men of the unholiest passions. **1885** 'MRS. ALEXANDER' *Valerie's Fate* v, There is nothing so awful, so unholy as a mere marriage of expediency.

2. *colloq.* Awful, dreadful. (Cf. UNGODLY *a.* 3.)

1842 DICKENS *Let.* 24 Dec. (1974) III. 401, I am reminded of my promise to see to the Pantomime, and am called out at this unholy hour. **1865** —— *Mut. Fr.* IV. iii, An unholy glare ..shone in the eyes of Mr. Wegg. **1883** D. C. MURRAY *Hearts* xxxiv. (1885) 288 He had arrived..at a rather unholy sort of hour. **1899** E. PHILLPOTTS *Human Boy* 35 Trelawny had called him an 'unholy bounder'.

3. *sb.* An unholy person or thing.

1831 CARLYLE *Sart. Res.* III. xi, How many other Unholies has your covering Art made holy, besides this Arabian Whinstone! **1837** —— *Fr. Rev.* I. I. ii, All Phenomena of the spiritual kind: Dignities, Authorities, Holies, Unholies!

un'holy, *v.* [UN-[2] 3.] *trans.* To make unholy. Hence **un'holied** *ppl. a.*

a **1555** PHILPOT in Coverdale *Lett. Mart.* (1564) 238 You haue bene sanctifyed and made pure through the truth, take hede you be not vnholied and defyled. **1603** DRAYTON *Bar. Wars* I. vi, Thou shouldst to them haue layd the Holy Word, And not thy hand to the unholyed Sword. **1649** HEYLIN *Relat. & Observ.* II. To Rdr., O wretched unholied men! What are they that thus commit Burglary in the Sanctum Sanctorum of Gods Providence?

un'homed, *ppl. a.* (UN-[1] 8 and UN-[2] 8.)

1839 BAILEY *Festus* xxvii. 334 [The day] shall shew itself With all its little tyrannous..deeds, Unhomed and clear. **1884** *Advance* (Chicago) 13 Mar., In no state of the Union are there more un-homed young men.

un'homelike, *a.* (UN-[1] 7 c.)

1852 MUNDY *Antipodes* (1857) 194 The untidy and unhomelike look of the half-cleared fields. **1886** *Athenæum* 8 May 621/2 The same large room with the dreadful shadows and unhomelike furniture.

un'homelikeness. (UN-[1] 12.)

1858 HAWTHORNE *Fr. & It. Note-bks.* (1872) I. 57 The ugliness, shabbiness, unhome-likeness of a Roman Street. **1869** JOS. BUTLER, etc. *Women's Work* i. 10 The unhomelikeness of the abodes of the richest single men..is pitiable.

un'homeliness. (UN-[1] 12; cf. next.)

c **1440** *Relig. Pieces fr. Thornton MS.* (1914) 12 Ypocrisy and vnhamlynes, and oþer [sins] þat ofte ere sene amanges prowde men. **1879** MISS KEARY *Doubting Heart* III. 120 Such signs..only seemed to bring out more prominently the stately unhomeliness of the place.

un'homely, *a.* (UN-[1] 7.)

1871 *Athenæum* 4 Mar. 280 Everything in the picture is neglected and unhomely and coarse. **1882** *Pall Mall G.* 31 Aug. 4 He does not chafe..because the hotels are so unhomely. **1892** STEVENSON *Across the Plains* 185 This unhomely, rugged turret-top of submarine sierras.

un'homish, *a.* (UN-[1] 7.)

1858 MRS. GORE *Heckington* viii, The unhomeish home of her aunt. **1880** T. HODGKIN *Italy & Inv.* I. I. v. 298 Nor drinks he, wandering, from un-homish streams.

unhomoge'neity. (UN-[1] 12.)

1862 E. B. DENISON in *Guardian* No. 882, The founder.. and his advocates declare that porosity and unhomogeneity are unavoidable [in bells].

unhomo'geneous, *a.* (UN-[1] 7.)

1828 HERSCHEL in *Encycl. Metrop.* (1845) IV. 449 Bodies of unhomogeneous density. **1865** W. G. PALGRAVE *Arabia* I. 369 Without taking into account healthier but unhomogeneous admixtures. **1899** *Speaker* 11 Nov. 134/1 The native races of Africa are at present utterly unhomogeneous.

†**un'hone.** *Obs.*[-1] [UN-[1] 12 + HONE *sb.*[2]] Absence of delay; haste.

a **1400–50** *Alexander* 5530 And he vnhurt with mikill vn-home [*read* -hoine] he to his ost wynes.

un'honest, *a. Obs.* exc. *arch.* or *dial.* [UN-[1] 7 and 5 b.]

In senses 2 and 3 very common in the 16th cent.

1. a. Physically or morally objectionable, offensive, or unpleasant; indecent, filthy, vile.

13.. *K. Alis.* 6472 Bothe byfore and eke byhynde, They haveth clothyng unhonest. *a* **1350** *St. Philip & Jas.* 21 in Horstm. *Altengl. Leg.* (1881) 52 Blastes out of his mouth he blew, þat war so euyl and vn-honeste, þai destryd oft both man and beste. **1526** *Pilgr. Perf.* (W. de W. 1531) 283 The membres of our body that be moost vnhonest and moost rebellynge to our reason. **1542** UDALL *Erasm. Apoph.* 152 b, Whatsoever thyng wer not of it self unhonest, he affermed not to bee unhoneste in open presence. **1633** P. FLETCHER *Purple Isl.* VIII. xx, His shamefull parts, that shunne the hated light, Were naked left; (ah foul unhonest sight!).

b. Uncomely, unhandsome.

1382 WYCLIF *1 Cor.* xii. 23 And tho membris that ben vnhonest, han more honeste. **1398** TREVISA *Barth. De P.R.* v. lxvi. (Bodl. MS.), If a man is withoute heed heere, he is yholde þe more vnhoneste.

c. Unseemly, unbecoming, improper.

a **1400–50** *Bk. Curtasye* 96 in *Babees Bk.*, While þou holdes mete in mouthe, be war To drynke, þat is an [vn]honest char. **1502** ARNOLDE *Chron.* (1811) 277 Item that the bookis and vestmentis bien broken and vnhonest for dyuine seruice. **1542** UDALL *Erasm. Apoph.* 89 b, It was not a thyng unhonest for one to carrye a gammonde of bakon in his hande. **1568** GRAFTON *Chron.* II. 234 They dayly chaunged there apparel, sometime long and wide, and at another tyme, cutted short.., and altogether vnsemely and vnhonest.

2. Of actions, language, etc.: **a.** Morally unfitting or unbecoming; unseemly, immodest, lewd.

13.. *E.E. Allit. P.* B. 579 Alle illez he hates..; But non nuyez hym..As harlottrye vnhonest, heþyng of seluen. *c* **1380** WYCLIF *Sel. Wks.* III. 29, I dreede to telle holy wordis wiþ my foule mouþ, fillid wiþ unhoneste wordis. **1456** SIR G. HAYE *Law Arms* (S.T.S.) 142 Thair undertaking was in the begynnyng unhonest, unlefull. *c* **1475** *Babees Bk.* 99 Whenne yee er sette, take noone vnhoneste tale. **1502** *Ord. Crysten Men* (W. de W. 1506) IV. xvi. T ij, Yf in songes vnhonest, & tryfylles, & talkynges of langage, he swereth god. **1598** GRENEWEY *Tacitus, Ann.* IV. xii. (1622) 107 Domitius Afer..laid to her charge that she lead an vnhonest life with Furnius. **1607** DEKKER *Jests to make you Merry* Wks. (Grosart) II. 302 To this vnhonest pleasure, is begot a companion repentance. **1645** USSHER *Body Div.* 279 This commandement [is] broken by..taking delight in hearing unhonest things.

b. Dishonourable, discreditable.

c **1400** *Apol. Loll.* 100 A wowe is..vnwise, wan it is only about temporal þingis, or vnhonest, or vnprofitable to soule hele. *c* **1440** *Alph. Tales* 41 What profettis þi frenship vnto me, when þu desyris me for to do for þe þat þing þat is vnhoneste? *a* **1470** *Dives & Pauper* (W. de W. 1496) IV. xviii.

181/2 The suget shal not..do ony thyng unryghtfull & unhonest. **1540** CROMWELL in Merriman *Life & Lett.* (1902) II. 254 There is daunger of vnhonest condicions or of Discontentement at departing. **1587** FLEMING *Contn. Holinshed* III. 1384/1 My case is hard, but yet am I not so desperat as to reuenge it vpon my selfe, which must needs be the euent of so vnhonest and vnpossible an enterprise. **1614** RALEIGH *Hist. World* III. x. §5. 116 He brought an vnhonest message to his owne Countrimen. **1649** CANNE *Snare Broken* 14 An oath is unlawfull when..we promise any thing that is unjust or unhonest. **1825** BROCKETT *N.C. Words*, *Unhonest*, dishonourable, dishonest. Stated in Todd's John. to be obsolete; but it is not so in the North.

3. Of persons: **a.** Not honourable, respectable, or of good repute; acting in a dishonourable or discreditable manner. Also *absol.*

1382 WYCLIF *Ecclus.* xxxvii. 13 With the dredful trete [not] of bataile,..with the vnhonest, of honeste. **1388** —— *Prov.* xxv. 8 Whanne thou hast maad thi frend vnhonest. *c* **1400** tr. *Secreta Secret., Gov. Lordsh.* 64 Kepe þy most noble saule hegh,..þat ys geuyn to þe, noght to be maad vnhonest by þe, but to be enhyed and glorifyed. *a* **1548** HALL *Chron., Hen. IV*, 16b, This false father in lawe, this untrew, unhonest and perjured persone. **1586** A. DAY *Eng. Secretary* I. (1625) 32 These and such like, as confounders of all ciuility,..are confirmed to be vnhonest. **1610** HEALEY *St. Aug. Citie of God* 462 Some ambitious unhonest fellow. **1624** BURTON *Anat. Mel.* (ed. 2) III. ii. 442 Of a majesticall presence, but peradventure imperious, vnhonest, selfewill'd.

b. Bad or immoral in character or conduct; disreputable.

c **1422** HOCCLEVE *Min. Poems* 218/63 To goode wommen that it be no shame, Al thogh þat thow vnhonest wommen blame. **1456** SIR G. HAYE *Law Arms* (S.T.S.) 190 Gif a man fyndis ane unhonest foule creature hafand conversacioun with his wyf. **1536** CROMWELL in Merriman *Life & Lett.* (1902) II. 28 They shall not geve theymself to drinking and ryote sitting all daye at Tables or cardes playng..and specially with vnhonest and vnthryftye persons. **1574** HELLOWES *Gueuara's Fam. Ep.* (1577) 60 All which were in their liues very vnhonest, and in their gouernement very offensiue. **1621** BURTON *Anat. Mel.* I. ii. IV. i, If a Nurse be mishapen, vnchast, vnhonest, impudent, drunke,..the child..will be so too. **1640-1** *Kirkcudbr. War-Comm. Min. Bk.* (1855) 35 George cryit—Unhonest Beoche and adulterous Beoche.

4. Dishonest (in respect of dealings with others).

a. Of actions, gain, etc. (Also *dial.* as *adv.*)

1583 FULKE *Def. Tr. Script.* iii. (1843) 195 This scornful replier..is so accustomed to false and unhonest dealing. **1607** MARKHAM *Cavel.* III. (1617) 35 To give a false colour to their owne knowledges,..or..to get vnhonest polling pence to their own purses. **1628** FELTHAM *Resolves* II. xxxv. 109 Vnworthines is euer the end of vnhonest Deceit. *a* **1670** SPALDING *Troub. Chas. I* (1850) I. 109 The purchess of there bischoprikis be brybes, thair vnhonest dealling in civill barganes. **1730** *St. Trials* I. 315 The Earl as well abusing the King's Favours,..as bearing unhonest Friendship, in Conference with Sir Thomas concerning that Imployment. **1901** 'ZACK' *Dunstable Weir* 48 What wud it feel like to come by the money unhonest?

b. Of persons.

1545 ASCHAM *Toxoph.* (Arb.) 20 Honest fletchers and bowyers do not so, and they that be vnhonest, oughte..to amende them selues. *a* **1586** SIDNEY *Arcadia* II. xv, The old man..folowed his suite with all maner of vnhonest seruants, large promises [etc.]. **1603** BRETON *Dial. Pith & Pleas.* Wks. (Grosart) II. 13/2 How vnhonest is that labourer, who will not worke for his wages? **1645** in J. Wilson *Annals of Hawick* (1850) 65 In calling of him..ane runnigat beggar,..and ane false unhonest thief. **1825-** in dial. glossaries (N. Cy., Yorks., Lancs., Linc.).

un'honestly, *adv.* ? *Obs.* [UN-[1] 11, 5b.]

1. In an unbecoming manner; indecorously.

c **1380** WYCLIF *Sel. Wks.* II. 193 Trowe we not þat Crist dide here dispitously or unhonestly, spittynge in þis mannis face? *c* **1400** MAUNDEV. (Roxb.) xxvi. 123 When þai hafe eten, þai wype þaire hend on þaire clathez vnhonestly. **1502** ARNOLDE *Chron.* (1811) 278 Item that the chircheyard is vnhon[e]stly kepte.

2. With dishonour; disgracefully; discreditably, dishonourably; dishonestly.

1382 WYCLIF *2 Macc.* ix. 1 In the same tyme Antiochus turnyde aȝein vnonestly [L. *inhoneste*] fro Perse. *c* **1449** PECOCK *Repr.* 325 As into this point, that he therbi be iust or uniust,..doing honestli or doing vnhonestli. **1535** COVERDALE *Ecclus.* x. 34 Who so ordreth himself vnhonestly in riches, how moch more shal he behaue himself vnhonestly in pouerte? **1598** R. BERNARD tr. *Terence, Adelphos* II. i, I my selfe am very vnhonestly dealt withall. **1628** FELTHAM *Resolves* II. ii. 5 As I would neuer doe any thing vnhonestly, so I would neuer feare the immateriall wind of censure, when it is done. **1648** HEXHAM II, *Oneerbaerlick*, Vnhonestly, Dishonestly, or Impudently. **1721** STRYPE *Eccl. Mem.* II. 388 Most unhonestly slandering old Writings.

3. Indecently, immorally.

1382 WYCLIF *2 Sam.* xiii. 2 The which for she was a mayde, hard to hym it semede, that eny thing vnhonestly [L. *inhoneste*] he shulde do with hir. *c* **1400** *Pilgr. Sowle* (Caxton, 1483) III. x. 56 These it ben that so horrybly stynken,..for they haue liued ful vnhonestly in fowle lustes. **1486** *Rec. St. Mary at Hill* (1905) 12 Yf the same preest so chosen vnhonestly behave hym. **1535** COVERDALE *Prov.* xii. 4 She that behaueth herself vnhonestly, is a corrupcion in his bones. **1597** BEARD *Theatre God's Judgem.* (1612) 400 His Proctors wife, with whom..he acquainted himselfe ouer familiarly and vnhonestly. **1609** BIBLE (Douay) *2 Sam.* xiii. 2.

un'honesty. *Obs.* exc. *dial.* [UN-[1] 12, 5b.] Absence or lack of honesty (esp. in obsolete senses of that word).

c **1425** WYNTOUN *Cron.* IV. xxv. 2356 Þat nane suld se Spot, fylth na vnhoneste Behind him in his doun falling. *a* **1470** *Dives & Pauper* (W. de W. 1496) VIII. vi. 328/2 The bac-byter hath more lykynge to speke of other mennes defautes & of theyr unhonestes & synne. **1526** TINDALE *2 Cor.* iv. 1 We..have cast from vs the clokes of vnhonestie. **1586** A. DAY *Eng. Secretary* II. (1625) 22 Where Gentilitie is not all onely spotted, but in a manner couered and debased already with vnhonesty. **1600** BRETON *Strange Fort. Two Princes* Wks. (Grosart) II. 4/1 Vnthankefulnesse is so neare to vnhonestie, as to auoid the touch of both. **1647** HEXHAM I, Vnhonesty or dishonesty, *ouneerbaerheyt*. **1871** W. ALEXANDER *Johnny Gibb* viii. 51 Sic creaturs [ye are] wi' oonhonesty.

†**un'honour,** *v. Obs.*[−1] [UN-[2] 3.] *trans.* To dishonour.

1382 WYCLIF *John* viii. 49, I honoure my fadir, and ȝe han vnhonourid me.

†**un'honourable,** *a. Obs.* [UN-[1] 7.]

1. Not honourable; not deserving of honour.

a **1400-50** *Alexander* 2950 Sen þis vse is here vnhonourable, here I þam leue. **1456** SIR G. HAYE *Law Arms* (S.T.S.) 280 He war a wikkit man of lyf, a tyran and unhonourable. **1548** GESTE *Pr. Masse* 117 Why then shuld..thee presence therof cause to honour his Godhed in the same, ther otherwyse unhonourable. **1599** SANDYS *Europæ Spec.* (1632) 209 To trace out an unhonourable and fruitlesse life. **1635** [GLAPTHORNE] *Lady Mother* III. ii. in Bullen *O. Pl.* (1883) II. 161 We are noe peasants or unhonorable To be affronted with indignities.

2. Dishonourable, discreditable.

1540 SIR T. WYATT *Let. to Cromwell* 5 April, If it were so the King's pleasure, I would make him such company as should not be unhonourable to the King. **1595** DANIEL *Civ. Wars* II. xxiv, Th' vnhonourable meanes of safety, bade Danger accept, what Maiesty withstood. **1621** in Foster *Eng. Factories Ind.* (1906) I. 274 Unhonnorable action by breatch of his word and cowle.

†**un'honourably,** *adv. Obs.* [UN-[1] 11.] Dishonourably, discreditably.

1553 ASCHAM *Germany* Wks. (1904) 159 Libertie in speakyng should be so mingled with..discretion, as no great person should be vnhonorably spoken vpon. **1560** PILKINGTON *Expos. Aggeus* (1562) 133 Mahomet..made him glad with money to bye peace unhonorably. **1589** PUTTENHAM *Eng. Poesie* II. xi[i]. (Arb.) 116 Dishonored be he, who meanes vnhonorably.

un'honoured, *ppl. a.* (UN-[1] 8.)

a **1513** FABYAN *Chron.* VII. (1516) 103/1 The holye seruyce of God [was] lefte, and holye Churche vnworshyppyd & vnhonouryd, with many great enormyties. **1633** P. FLETCHER *To my honoured Cousin W. R.* vii, Here among th' unhonour'd willows shade. **1697** DRYDEN *Æneis* XI. 314 The rest, unhonoured, and without a name, Are cast a common heap to feed the flame. **1718** PRIOR *Solomon* III. 176 Unhonor'd from the Board The Crystal Urn, when broken, is thrown by. **1751** GRAY *Elegy* xxiv, Mindful of th' unhonour'd Dead. **1849** RUSKIN *Sev. Lamps* vi. §3. 166 Those comfortless and unhonoured dwellings. **1891** FARRAR *Darkn. & Dawn* xxxvi, The site of her sepulchre was left unhonoured and no mound was raised above her ashes.

un'hood, *v.* [UN-[2] 4.] *trans.* To divest (*spec.* a hawk) of a hood or similar covering. Also *absol.*

(*a*) **1575** TURBERV. *Falconrie* 79 At the ende of three dayes you may unhood hir and feede hir unhooded. **1652** FULLER *Holy & Prof. St.* v. xviii. 488 Like Hawks when they are first unhooded, and newly restored to the light. **1667** DRYDEN *Sir Martin Mar-all* v. iii, He's an ill Falconer that will unhood before the quarry be in sight. **1742** SOMERVILLE *Field Sports* 10 Falcner, take care,..And slily stalk; unhood thy Falcon bold. **1852** R. F. BURTON *Falconry Valley Indus* vi. 65 The falconer unhoods her, places her upon the perch. (*b*) **1601** HOLLAND *Pliny* I. 221 Perceiving after that he was unhooded that he served as a stalion to his own dam. **1608** SYLVESTER *Du Bartas, Job Triumphant* 615, I will not hide..[Leviathan's] Strength, nor seemly Symmetries. Who shall unhood him? **1629** MASSINGER *Picture* III. v, Enter servants with Mathias..blindfolded. *Acanthe*... I'll anon unhood him. **1797** MRS. RADCLIFFE *Italian* xii, [In] one of the lonely aisles..he unhooded the lamp. **1853** ROCK *Ch. of Fathers* III. x. 491 Among all that sea of heads, there is not one but is bared and unhooded. **1887** BROWNING *Parleyings, Apollo & Fates* 121 Unhook wings, unhood brows! Dost hearken?

transf. **1603** FLORIO *Montaigne* II. xii. 334 Some people..who tooke pleasure to vnhood the end of their yard, and to cut off the fore-skin.

b. *fig.* or in fig. context.

1648 BOYLE *Seraph. Love* (1660) 11 As it has hitherto been my not unprosperous task to unhood your soul, I shall now..shew her game to fly at. *c* **1681** HICKERINGILL *Trimmer* Wks. 1716 I. 356, I am forc'd to bring him to light, and unhood him, sometimes by some (otherwise unwelcome) Periphrasis. **1824** *New Monthly Mag.* X. 306 Thou unhood'st the stars, Shew'st their bright eyes. **1848** BOKER *Calaynos* III. iii, They two can put their restless heads together, Unhood their thoughts at every whim that flies. **1869** BLACKMORE *Lorna D.* xii, Tom Faggus himself was a quarry for the law, if ever it should be unhooded.

un'hooded, *ppl. a.* [UN-[1] 8 or UN-[2] 8: cf. prec.] Not wearing, divested of, a hood. Also *fig.*

1575 [see UNHOOD *v.* (*a*)]. **1614** LATHAM *Falconry* 32 Many of them will be more gentle..when they are vnhooded, then when they are hooded. **1730** RAMSAY *Fables, Lure* 63 [He] loos'd the falcon frae his hand. Unhooded, up she sprang with birr. **1795** SOUTHEY *Joan of Arc* VII. 140 A rude coat of mail Unhosed, unhooded, as of lowly line He wore. **1798** BLOOMFIELD *Farmer's Boy, Autumn* v. 269 In earliest hours of dark unhooded morn. **1848** LYTTON *Harold* IX. i, On a perch..sate his favourite Norway falcon, unhooded. **1868** ADAH I. MENKEN *Infelicia* 129 In the great strength of thy unhooded soul, pray for my weakness.

un'hoodwink, *v.* (UN-[2] 4.)

a **1608** DEE *Relat. Spir.* I. (1659) 393 Least peradventure God unhood-wink and make open the sight of Satan. **1682** HICKERINGILL *Black Non-Conformist* Introd. C, The Popish methods of old, but not practicable now, people are generally unhoodwinkt. **1691** tr. *Emiliane's Frauds Rom. Monks* (ed. 3) 242 There is scarcely any way left to disabuse and unhoodwink them.

un'hoodwinked, *ppl. a.* (UN-[1] 8.)

1657 W. BRAYNE in Thurloe *Coll. St. Papers* (1742) VI. 211 They haveing bin unadvisedly brought unhudwinckt through the fortifications of our harbour. **1904** KIPLING *Traffics & Discoveries* 38 Let Zeus adjudge your landward kin,..But ye the unhoodwinked waves shall test.

un'hoof, *v.* (UN-[2] 3.)

1530 PALSGR. 768/1, I unhooffe a horse, I pull of his hooffe, *je dessole. Ibid.*, And you unhoofe this hors agaynst wynter, he is utterly marred. **1598** FLORIO, *Disonghiare*, to vn-naile, or to vnhoofe.

un'hoofed, *ppl. a.* (UN-[1] 8.)

1709 SHAFTESB. *Charac.* (1711) II. 301 Ask not merely, Why Man is naked, why unhoof'd, why slower-footed than the Beasts?

un'hook, *v.* [UN-[2] 4b.]

1. *trans.* To detach from a hook; to disengage or unfasten in this way. Also *refl.* See also HOOK *v.* 5b.

1611 COTGR., *Desaccrocher*, to vnhooke. **1662** J. BARGRAVE *Pope Alex. VII*, etc. (1867) 136 To break a fall, they will hang by the horns, and, when they have taken breath, they unhook themselves and take another leap. **1825** J. NICHOLSON *Operat. Mechanic* 132 If the wind should blow against the back sides of the said sails..the said bars or rods will be unhooked and set at liberty. **1856** LEVER *Martins of Cro' M.* 147 In an instant she had unhooked the heavy chain. **1878** T. HARDY *Ret. Native* v. viii, Venn unhooked the lantern and leaped down. **1892** [see UNHOOKER].

fig. **1640** C. HARVEY *Synagogue, Ch.-gate* iii, Unhook'd from him, we quickly turn aside. **1669** BARROW in Rigaud *Corr. Sci. Men* (1841) II. 70 My mind being indeed unhooked from these things. **1672** MARVELL *Reh. Transp.* I. 324 Striving to unhook himself hence, p. 152 of his Second Book, swallows it deeper. **1966** *Guardian* 17 June 22/8 Girls who have been in trouble over drugs have been helped to stay 'unhooked'. **1977** B. GARFIELD *Recoil* xxxiii. 328 We..made a junkie out of her... I'll just get her unhooked.

2. To take out the hooks of (a dress). Also with personal object.

1840 COCKTON *Val. Vox* xiii, The ladies [began] to unhook their dresses behind, in order to enjoy another small glass of gin. **1898** *Longm. Mag.* Aug. 366 She..remarked that..I must have my frock unhooked and be tried on. I submitted silently to be unhooked.

3. To disengage from a curved position.

1865 DICKENS *Mut. Fr.* II. i, As she said it, she unhooked her arm.

Hence **un'hooker**.

1892 *Labour Commission* Gloss., *Unhookers*, old men or boys who stand on the plank connecting a ship with the dock and unhook the coal when it is in a stable position on the back of the men who carry it.

un'hooked, *ppl. a.* (UN-[1] 8.)

1600 in Hakluyt *Voy.* III. 671 What more nimble spirits, Apter to byte at such vnhooked baytes, Gaine by our losse. **1897** *Outing* XXX. 220/2 Another instance will give an idea of how high an unhooked bass can leap when frightened.

un'hool, *v. Sc.* [UN-[2] 5.] To disembody.

1722 RAMSAY *Three Bonnets* IV. 19 A stalwart ghaist Whase stern and angry looks amaist Unhool'd their sauls.

unhool, obs. f. UNWHOLE *a.*

un'hoop, *v.* (UN-[2] 4. Cf. Du. *onthoepen.*)

1611 DONNE *Paneg. Verses* 36 in Coryate *Crudities*, When Merchants do unhoope Voluminous barrels. **1657** DAVENANT *Entertainment at Rutland House* 43 Let the sour Cynick live coopt; Let him quake in his thrid-bare Cloak Till he find his old Tub unhoopt. **1711** ADDISON *Spect.* No. 127 ¶10 To Unhoop the Fair Sex, and cure this fashionable Tympany that is got among them.

un'hoopable, *a.* (UN-[1] 7b.)

1672 MARVELL *Reh. Transp.* I. 246 Instead of assuming your unhoopable jurisdiction, they are..satisfied with the abundance of their power. **1673** [R. LEIGH] *Transp. Reh.* 23 The unhoopable Tun of Heidelberg.

un'hooped, *ppl. a.* (UN-[1] 8.)

1861 DICKENS *Gt. Expect.* i, Like an unhooped cask upon a pole.

†**unhope.** *Obs.* exc. *poet.* [UN-[1] 12. Cf. MDu. *onthope*, and WANHOPE *sb.*] Lack of hope; despair.

a **1225** *Ancren R.* 8 Þet ȝe muhten sone uallen..in desperaunce, þet is, in unhope. *a* **1240** *Sawles Warde* in *O.E. Hom.* I. 251 Ant tis ilke unhope is ham meast pine. **1477** EARL RIVERS (Caxton) *Dictes* H iv, Take not vnhope of that, that thou maist not amende. **1895-6** HARDY *Poems of Past & Present* (1902) 214 But death will not appal One who, past doubtings all, Waits in unhope.

un'hoped, *ppl. a.* [UN-[1] 8. Cf. MDu. *ongehopet*, MDu. and Du. *-hoopt.*]

†**1. a.** Unexpected, unforeseen. *Obs.*

c **1374** CHAUCER *Boeth.* IV. pr. vi. (1876) 108 What so euere þou mayst sen þat is don in this world vnhoped, or vnwenyd. **1382** WYCLIF *Wisd.* xvii. 14 Forsothe to them sodeyn and vnhopid drede ouercam. *a* **1575** tr. *Pol. Verg. Eng. Hist.* (Camden 36) 185 [He was] amazed at this unhoped danger. **1697** DRYDEN *Æneis* x. 99 Did God, or Man, your Fav'rite Son advise, With War unhop'd the Latians to surprise?

†**b.** Unconceived, unimagined. *Obs.*

1435 MISYN *Fire of Love* 15 Treuly it is not of gods vnpower þat he may not þe tech hym-self als he is in hym-self, bot for hys vnhopyd worþines.

2. Not anticipated with hope or desire; not hoped for. (Cf. 3.)

1382 WYCLIF *Wisd.* v. 2 Thei..shulmerueilen in the sodeynesse of the vnhopid helthe. **1561** T. NORTON *Calvin's Inst.* I. 19 Paul,..from a cruell and bloody enemy conuerted to a new man, with sodaine and vnhoped change. *a* **1586** SIDNEY *Arcadia* IV. (1629) 426 His other prisoners..he found increased by this vnhoped meanes. **1593** SHAKS. *3 Hen. VI*, III. iii. 172 What are thy Newes?..*Margaret.* Mine such, as fill my heart with vnhop'd ioyes. **1660** DRYDEN *Astræa Redux* 140 The Prince of Peace would..confer A Gift un-hop'd without the price of war. **1697** —— *Æneis* v. 262 Chance aids their daring with unhop'd success. **1721** RAMSAY *Love's Cure* i, He spies A ship, which gives unhop'd surprise. **1728** ELIZA HEYWOOD tr. *Mme. de Gomez's Belle A.* (1732) II. 175 Kerme, who waited her Answer,..was so much transported at the unhoped Compliance of it, that [etc.]. **1820** L. HUNT *Indicator* No. 31 (1822) I. 245 What unhoped courage reanimates me!

b. In quasi-adverbial construction: Unexpectedly, beyond expectation.

1667 MILTON *P.L.* x. 348 To Hell he now return'd, And ..unhop't Met who to meet him came, his Ofspring dear. **1734** THOMSON *Liberty* III. 453 The power resign'd, And all unhop'd the commonwealth restor'd, Amaz'd the public. **1791** COWPER *Odyssey* v. 491 Though Jove hath given me to behold, Unhop'd, the land again. **1810** SCOTT *Lady of L.* v. xvii, He falter'd thanks to Heaven for life, Redeem'd, unhoped, from desperate strife. **1830** W. TAYLOR *Hist. Surv. Germ. Poetry* II. 328 Like sons who meet unhop'd a father.

3. Not hoped (†or looked) *for*.

1598 R. BERNARD tr. *Terence, Andriæ* III. iv, I was the cause of the marriage that shall be made to day, euen quite vnhoped for of the old man. **1622** FLETCHER *Love's Cure* I. ii, A Temple..where I may give thanks For this unhop'd for blessing. **1697** DRYDEN *Æneis* IX. 939 Suddenly th' unhop'd for News was brought. **1725** POPE *Odyss.* v. 525 When ..These eyes at last behold the unhoped-for coast. **1749** FIELDING *Tom Jones* XVI. vi, Blifil having obtained this unhoped for acquiescence. **1825** SCOTT *Betrothed* Concl., Her unhoped-for union with Damian. **1857** DUFFERIN *Lett. High Lat.* (ed. 3) 406 These unhoped-for circumstances opened a new field to our explorations.

un'hopedly, *adv.* (UN-¹ 11.)

1611 FLORIO, *Insperatamente*, vnhopedly. **1831** HOWITT *Seasons* 123 Was it that some faint pilgrim came Unhopedly to thee?

un'hopeful, *a.* [UN-¹ 7.]

1. Not affording grounds for hope; unpromising.

c **1450** *Mirour Saluacioun* 2871 For both thire sonnes tholed she the vnhopfulle bitternesse. **1599** SHAKS. *Much Ado* II. i. 392 And Benedick is not the vnhopefullest husband that I know. **1646** G. DANIEL *Poems* Wks. (Grosart) I. 73 More valewing encrease From this vnhopefull Impe, then all the Store Hee had beside. **1663** BOYLE *Usef. Exp. Nat. Philos.* II. iii. 67 The unhopefullest season of the year, the winter solstice. **1785** JEFFERSON *Corr.* Wks. 1859 I. 406 The lethargic character of their ambassador here gives a very unhopeful aspect to a treaty on this ground. **1858** H. BUSHNELL *Nat. & Supernat.* vi. (1864) 183 There is nothing in it unhopeful, nothing to accuse. **1890** *Spectator* 7 June, The chance of reading the great Minister a lesson in humility seemed not unhopeful.

2. Not feeling hope; despondent.

1850 *Westm. Rev.* April 64 The fear which the mass, if uneducated and unhopeful, will always feel. **1858** CARLYLE *Fredk. Gt.* II. xiv. I. 180 Jobst tried..to do some governing; but finding all very anarchic, grew unhopeful.

Hence **un'hopefulness**.

[**1737** BAILEY.] **1868** H. BUSHNELL *Mor. Uses Dark Th.* (1869) 346 They become, in this way, a kind of mystery of unhopefulness.

un'hopefully, *adv.* (UN-¹ 11; cf. prec.)

1840 LOWELL *Moon* 13 The sea..lay unhopefully alone, And lived but in an aimless seeking. **1861** *Sat. Rev.* 21 Dec. 639 Measuring its force and danger..more unhopefully than many of his contemporaries.

un'hoping, *ppl. a.* (UN-¹ 10.)

a **1628** F. GREVIL *Wks.* (1870) IV. 267 In which unhoping time you must resolue [etc.]. **1738** G. LILLO *Marina* II. i, Or Jove restore to my unhoping eyes What his vindictive hand hath taken from me. **1866** CARLYLE *Remin.* (1881) II. 172, I was Thomas the Doubter, the unhoping. **1892** *Nation* (N.Y.) 28 Apr. 322/2 The latest of these unhoping encomiums on greatness deferred.

b. As pple. with object. (UN-¹ 5 d.)

1748 RICHARDSON *Clarissa* (1811) III. 40 Unhoping..the success of their schemes in Solmes's behalf.

un'hopingly, *adv.* [UN-¹ 11.] Inconceivably.

1435 MISYN *Fire of Love* 36 þat heet treuly sensibily swete smellynge vnhopingly [L. *inestimabiliter*], I was besy vnto þe ..takynge of heuenly sounde.

un'hopped, *ppl. a.* (UN-¹ 8. See HOPPED *ppl. a.*, and cf. G. *ungehopft.*)

1725 *Fam. Dict.* s.v. *Malt Liquor*, Hopp'd and unhopp'd Drinks. *Ibid.*, Unhopp'd Liquor. **1799** W. TOOKE *View of Russian Empire* I. 362 Brown beer and metheglin are more in use than..busa or white unhopped wheat-beer.

unho'rizoned, *ppl. a.* (UN-¹ 8.)

1811 MISS L. M. HAWKINS *C'tess & Gertr.* II. 121 The unhorizoned charity of him who bid us pray. **1888** LIGHTHALL *Yng. Seigneur* 122 A vista ocean-like and unhorizoned.

un'horned, *a.* (UN-¹ 9. Cf. Du. *ongehoorned*; older Da. *uhornet.*)

1570 LEVINS *Manip.* 50 Vnhorned, *incornis.* **1607** TOPSELL *Four-f. Beasts* 233 There are two kindes of Goates,..the vnhorned are best for breed. **1621** G. SANDYS *Ovid's Met.* IV. (1626) 66 Thou 'rt seene in heauen;..And, when vnhorn'd, thou hast a Virgins face. **1648** HEXHAM II, *Ongehoornt*, Vnhorned, or without hornes.

un'horse, *v.* [UN-² 3. Cf. MDu. *ontorsen.*]

1. *trans.* To throw or drag (a person) from his horse, esp. in battle. Also in fig. context.

1390 GOWER *Conf.* I. 368 He..smot him with a dethes wounde, That he unhorsed fell to grounde. **1412-20** LYDG. *Chron. Troy* IV. 2077 Menelay..to Troilus faste gan hym spede Fully avysed to vnhorsen hym anon. **1448-9** METHAM *Amoryus & Cleopes* 933 Qwat ys he yon,..that thus fersly iustyth to-day; That no knyght hym onhors may? **1530** PALSGR. 768/1, I unhorse a man by feates of armes in the felde, *Je rue jus.* **1563** GOLDING *Cæsar* 39 b, If any of them were sore wounded or vnhorsed, theis garded him about. **1607** CHAPMAN *Bussy d'Ambois* IV. i, He turn'd wild lightning in the lackeys' hands, Who, through their sudden violent twitch unhors'd him. **1668** R. STEELE *Husbandman's Calling* vi. (1672) 159 Neither wouldst thou be ridden at the Devil's pleasure if thou didst understand thyself: unhorse Satan quickly from off thy soul. **1724** DE FOE *Mem. Cavalier* (1840) 277 Ireton..was unhorsed and taken prisoner. **1756** tr. *Keysler's Trav.* I. 29 A large quantity of armour,..some for unhorsing an antagonist in a turnament. **1820** SCOTT *Monast.* xxiv, To me it is recommended, because it..unhorses the lazy monks that have ridden us so long, and spur-galled us so hard. **1843** JAMES *Forest Days* xx, And so you unhorsed the traitor, but could neither kill nor take him?

b. *fig.* To dislodge, overthrow, discomfit, nonplus.

1577 *F. de L'isle's Legendarie* G vij, The Duke of Guise and his partakers..without the policie of the Queene mother,..had at the same instant bene quite vnhorsed. **1602** J. RHODES *Answ. to Romish Rime* 519 So did all of Rome beside, Untill they grew to their full pride; And were of late unhorst agayne. **1656** EARL MONM. tr. *Boccalini's Advts. fr. Parnass.* I. lxxviii. (1674) 106 The trick of un-horsing people ..by meer Words. **1680** C. NESSE *Church-Hist.* 280 The scruple..about his marriage became the occasion of unhorsing the Pope in England. **1825** SCOTT *Talism.* xxvi, Thou hast unhorsed me with that very word. **1845** DISRAELI *Sybil* (1863) 207 She did not deign even to notice the unhappy cavalier whom she had thus as it were un-horsed.

c. In passive: To be thrown from a horse.

1583 MELBANCKE *Philotimus* X j b, He that rides with one girth, may feare to be vnhorst. *a* **1713** ELLWOOD *Autobiography* (1714) 72 It if [*sc.* the knife] should have been found..under my coat when I came to be Unhorsed. **1748** *Anson's Voy.* II. xii. 263 His horse..turning round suddenly rode off with his master, who was very near being unhorsed in the surprize. **1802** JAMES *Milit. Dict.*, *Unhorsed*, thrown from the saddle; dismounted.

†**2.** To help (one) to dismount. *Obs.*

1530 PALSGR. 768/1, I unhorse a man, I sette hym bysyde his horse, *je desmonte. Ibid.*, Helpe to unhorse these ladyes.

b. *intr.* To dismount.

1633 QUARLES in P. Fletcher *Poet. Wks.* (1909) II. 284 I lasht through thick and thinne, Dispatch'd my businesse, and return'd agen; I call'd the second time; unhors'd, went in.

3. To deprive of a horse. *rare.*

1465 *Paston Lett.* II. 178 But I trow to gyte Dorlet ayen hys hors or els Mr Phylyp ys lyke to be unhorssyd ons, and we lyve all. **1651** in *Crawford Proclam.* (1910) II. 58 All tories not joining the army within 14 days to be unhorsed and counted traitors. **1837** W. IRVING *Capt. Bonneville* xii, A whip and a rope were left..by the robbers, as a taunt to the simpletons they had unhorsed.

4. To unharness the horses from (a carriage, etc.).

1654 EARL MONM. tr. *Bentivoglio's Wars Flanders* 385 Coming to their Batteries they unhorst some of their Peeces. **1784** COWPER *Task* VI. 701 Others..unhorse The gilded equipage,..turning loose His steeds. **1829** SIR W. NAPIER *Penins. War* VI. iii, The artillery was unhorsed.

Hence **un'horsement**; **un'horsing** *vbl. sb.*

1603 BP. HALL *Serm.* v. 13 If you ever therefore look to see ..the unhorseing and confusion of that strumpet of Rome. **1884** TRAILL *New Lucian* 52 It was a moral un-horsement of the most dishonouring kind.

un'hose, *v.* [UN-² 4. Cf. Flem. (Kilian) *onthosen.*] *trans.* To strip or divest of hose. Also *fig.* Hence **un'hosing** *vbl. sb.*

1483 CAXTON *Gold. Leg.* 161 b/2 Peter is as moche to saye as knowynge or unhosyng,..and therfore he was sayd unhosyng for he unhosed and dyd of his wyll fro his feet. *c* **1489** —— *Sonnes of Aymon* xvi. 371 Whan mawgis had taken all this, he..vnhosed him. *c* **1532** DU WES in *Palsgr.* 942 To unhose, *deschausser.* **1598** FLORIO, *Scalciatura*, an vnshoing, vnhosing, vnbreeching. **1611** COTGR., *Deschausser*,..to vnhose, or draw off hosen.

un'hosed, *ppl. a.* [UN-¹ 8.] Not wearing hose.

1297 R. GLOUC. (Rolls) 10826 And hii..To him come at gloucetre..Vn-hosed & bareuot & vngurt al so. **1594** R. ASHLEY tr. *Loys le Roy* 27 Without clothing, vnhosed, and vnshood. **1795** [see UNHOODED].

un'hospitable, *a.* [UN-¹ 7 b, 5 b.]

= INHOSPITABLE *a.* **a.** Of places.

1601 SHAKS. *Twel. N.* III. iii. 11 Being skillesse in these parts: which to a stranger..often proue Rough, and vnhospitable. **1612** WEBSTER *White Devil* v. iii. 45 They have ..divorst friends, and made great houses unhospitable. **1687** DRYDEN *Hind & P.* III. 612 No neighbouring Dorp, no lodging to be found, But bleaky plains, and bare unhospitable ground. **1703** ROWE *Ulysses* I. i, You..from th'unhospitable Dwelling drive Safety and friendly Peace. **1740** CHEYNE *Regimen* 106 Our Earth has,..unfruitful Climates, unhospitable and uninhabited Regions. **1808** FORSYTH *Beauties Scotl.* V. 472 A cluster of unhospitable rocks.

b. Of persons.

a **1625** FLETCHER *Fair Maid Inn* II. i, *Serv.* Shall we kill him? *Alber.* No, I'll not be so unhospitable. **1641** J. SHUTE *Sarah & Hagar* (1649) 116 James and John..call'd for fire from heaven upon those unhospitable Samaritans. **1708** ROWE *Royal Convert* v. i, The Britons then shall join their Arms with yours, To drive out these unhospitable Guests. **1722** DE FOE *Plague* (1754) 163 They would be loth to have it remembered..how unhospitable, and how unkind they were. **1842** J. B. FRASER *Allee Neemroo* II. 289 The young man, unwilling to be rash or unhospitable. **1864** TROLLOPE *Can you forgive her?* xii, It cannot perhaps fairly be said that George Vavasor was an unhospitable man.

c. Of actions, character, etc.

1625 K. LONG tr. *Barclay's Argenis* IV. ii. 237 To renounce your hospitality, were superfluous, when you have done first, by offering vnhospitable iniury. **1682** MRS. BEHN *City Heiress* 50 What Recompence can I make for so unhospitable usage? **1727** SWIFT *State Irel.* Wks. 1755 V. II. 168, I think it a little unhospitable..that..guests [etc.]. **1750** G. HUGHES *Barbados* 93 He lies concealed..till the next prey calls him forth to repeat his unhospitable talents. **1760** *Ann. Reg.*, *Chron.* 66/1 The unhospitable custom of giving vails to servants.

Hence **un'hospitableness.**

1681 J. KETTLEWELL *Meas. Chr. Obed.* II. iv. 165 The Law against uncharitableness.., against unhospitableness.

†**un'hospital**, *a. Obs.* [UN-¹ 7, 5 b.] Inhospitable.

1570 LEVINS *Manip.* 15 Vnhospitall, *inhospitus.* *a* **1586** SIDNEY *Arcadia* I. ii, A civill warre..hath..disfigured the face of nature, and made it so unhospitall as now you have found it. **1615** G. SANDYS *Trav.* 39 First called Axenus, which signifieth vnhospitall: by reason of the coldnesse thereof, and inhumanity of the bordering Nations. *a* **1639** W. WHATELEY *Prototypes* I. xix. (1640) 174 Hee was hospital in that unhospitall citie.

†**unhospi'tality.** *Obs.* [UN-¹ 12, 5 b.] Inhospitality.

1388 WYCLIF *Wisd.* xix. 13 Thei suffriden iustli,..for thei ordeyneden more abhomynable vnospitalite.

un'hostile, *a.* (UN-¹ 7.)

1705 J. PHILLIPS *Blenheim* 163 Of Pain impatient, the high prancing Steeds..Spurn their dismounted Riders; they expire Indignant, by unhostile Wounds destroy'd. **1825** R. WILSON *Sk. Hist. Hawick* 214 A House of Commons, formed of such materials,..would be unhostile to the security of property.

un'house (ʌn'haʊz), *v.* [UN-² 5. Cf. MDu. *onthusen*, WFl. *onthuizen*, MHG. *enthûsen.*] *trans.* To turn out of a house, habitation, or abode; to make houseless or homeless.

a **1375** *Joseph Arim.* 455 þei come bi tholomers tentes, vnhoused hem sone, Token holliche his stor. **1598** SYLVESTER *Du Bartas* II. ii. *Colonies* 154 So one People doth pursue another; And scarce the second hath a first un-housed, Before a third him thence again have roused. **1633** P. FLETCHER *Purple Isl.* VII. i, Thirsil up starting from his fearlesse bed,..Unhous'd his bleating flock. **1643** [ANGIER] *Lanc. Vall. Achor* 8 If they peeped out of the houses, they were unhoused. **1759** SARAH FIELDING *C'tess of Dellwyn* II. 147 He was at once unwived, unhoused, and undone. **1795** MACNEILL *Scotland's Scaith* III. vi, What a change, unhoused and beggared, Starving. **1821** CLARE *Vill. Minstr.* I. 72 Unhous'd from beds of ling The fluskering pheasant took to wing. **1885** *Manch. Exam.* 13 July 5/5 Only 150 persons will be for the present unhoused.

refl. **1599** NASHE *Lenten Stuffe* 38 When he vn-househ him, or hath cast off his shel, he..lookes as red as a Fox. **1606** J. RAYNOLDS *Dolarneys' Prim.* (1880) 123 The drowsie vapours, takes their sable flyghts, And bright Aurora, doth her selfe vnhouse. **1854** MILLER *Sch. & Schm.* xiii, We had very nearly unhoused ourselves ere our work was finished.

b. *fig.* or in fig. context.

1594 DANIEL *Cleopatra* (Bang) 1323, I must myselfe force open wide a dore To let out life, and to vnhouse my spirit. **1625** MILTON *Death Fair Infant* 21 He..all unwares with his cold-kind embrace Unhous'd thy Virgin Soul from her fair biding place. **1690** C. NESSE *O. & N. Test.* I. 122 He that hath God for his house..can never be unhoused. **1727** DE FOE *Hist. Appar.* v. (1840) 45 Souls which have been encased in flesh, but being unhoused are now moving about. *a* **1814** *Sulieman* II. iii. in *New Brit. Theatre* II. 26 But for wine..This shatter'd shell of body had unhous'd Long since my soul.

Hence **un'housing** *vbl. sb.*

In mod. use also *attrib.*, as ***unhousing scheme.***

1809 R. LANGFORD *Introd. Trade* 72 Unhousing, Wharfage and Shipping, £2 2*s.* 1*d.* **1886** *Pall Mall G.* 22 Sept. 6/1 This scheme..will take five years to complete, so that the unhousing will be gradual.

un'housed, *ppl. a.*¹ [UN-¹ 8. Cf. MDu. *ongehuset*, MLG. *ungehuset*, MHG. *-hûset.*]

1. Not provided with, not lodged in, a house; homeless.

1604 SHAKS. *Oth.* I. ii. 26, I would not my vnhoused free condition Put into Circumscription, and Confine, For the Seas worth. **1623** MIDDLETON *More Dissemblers* IV. i, Th' unhous'd race of fortune-tellers. **1649** OGILBY *Virgil's Georgics* III. 370 Lybian Shepherds..unhous'd Cattel through vast Desarts lead. **1709** POPE *Lett.* (1735) I. 86 The faithful Dog,..Unfed, unhous'd, neglected, [lay] on the Clay. **1743** FRANCIS tr. *Hor., Odes* IV. xiv. 44 Whom unhoused Scythians fear, unconquer'd Spain obeys. **1830** CROLY *Geo. IV*, 283 Unhoused beggary, and the hideousness of civil bloodshed, combined and shaped themselves into a colossal power. **1860** LONGF. *Wayside Inn, K. Olaf* XVII. v, Every warlike Dane..Left..Unhoused the cattle. **1867** LEWES *Hist. Philos.* (ed. 3) II. 210 Their tottering architecture would have sheltered none whom Spinoza's visionary fabric left unhoused.

2. Not occupied by houses.

1582 STANYHURST *Æneis* IV. (Arb.) 96 Heere ye sit embayed with Moors, with Syrtis vnhowsed [L. *inhospita Syrtis*]. **1611** COTGR., *Place*, a plaine and vnhoused ground.

un'housed, *ppl. a.*^{2} [f. UNHOUSE *v.*] Deprived of house or dwelling. Also *absol.*

1621 SANDYS *Ovid's Met.* IV. (1626) 77 The gates still open stand..And as all Riuers run into the Deep: So all vnhoused Soules doe thither creep. **1886** *Pall Mall G.* 22 Sept. 6/1 This is a sufficient accommodation for the unhoused in this improvement.

un'housed, *ppl. a.*^{3} [UN-^{1} 8: see HOUSE *v.*^{2}] Not covered with a house or housing.

1560 [see HOUSED *ppl. a.*^{2}].

un'houseled, *ppl. a.* [UN-^{1} 8.] Not having had the Eucharist administered.

1532 MORE *Confut. Tindale* Wks. 377/2 Yet thynketh Tyndall that..the people were as good vnhowseled as howseled. **1602** SHAKS. *Ham.* I. v. 77 Cut off euen in the Blossomes of my Sinne, Vnhouzzled, disappointed, vnnaneld. **1819** SCOTT *Ivanhoe* xxx, Me..they suffer to die like the houseless dog on yonder common, unshriven and unhouseled. **1826** SOUTHEY *Vind. Eccl. Angl.* 500 He died, unhouselled, in his sins. **1865** E. BURRITT *Walk to Land's End* 334 The articulate plaint of some unhouseled spirit moaning for admission.

un'housewife. (UN-^{1} 12 b.)

1823 J. WELSH in *Love Lett.* (1909) I. 199 These 'reddings-up'..to my unhousewife perceptions..produce no other effects than confusion, discomfort, and dirt.

†un'hovable, *a. Obs. rare*$^{-0}$. [UN-^{1} 7 b. Cf. UNBEHOVABLE *a.*] Unfitting.

1570 LEVINS *Manip.* 3 Vnhouable, *impertinens.*

†un'hove. *Obs. rare*$^{-1}$. [UN-^{1} 12 + HOVE *sb.*^{2}, probably after ON. *úhóf.*] Lack of moderation.

a **1300** *Cursor M.* 28222 My breth [= anger] it wald be til vnhoue þat many man was won to droue.

†un'hoven, *ppl. a. Sc. Obs.* [UN-^{1} 8 b: see HEAVE *v.* 3.] Unbaptized.

c **1375** *Sc. Leg. Saints* xxxiv. (*Pelagia*) 115 He..byd þam þat vnhowine ware, þat þai suld ga þar gat but mare. **1456** SIR G. HAYE *Law Arms* (S.T.S.) 204 Him behufit to be slayne or ellis to leve the barne unhovin.

un'hover, *v.* [UN-^{2} 5: see HOVER *sb.* 3.] *trans.* To dislodge from a hiding-place.

1827 *Sporting Mag.* XX. 104 Mr. Treby's harriers, assisted by his..terriers, unhovered an otter.

unhue, *v.*: see WANHUE *v. Obs.*

un'hulled, *ppl. a.*^{1} [UN-^{1} 8.]

1. Not furnished with a hull or husk.

1597 GERARDE *Herbal* I. xlviii. 68 These naked Otes..in Northfolke and Southfolke..are called unhulled and naked Otes. *a* **1722** LISLE *Husb.* (1752) 126 Seeds will not grow unhulled, or extra cotyledones.

2. Not freed from husk.

1883 *Pall Mall G.* 27 Sept. 11/1 Sand and unhulled paddy are mixed with their morning and evening rice.

un'hulled, *ppl. a.*^{2} [UN-^{2} 4, 8.] Having the hull or husk removed.

1656 J. SMITH *Pract. Physick* 84 Take the decoction of unhulled Barley. **1658** BROWNE *Gard. Cyrus* iii. 131 If Barley unhulled would grow.

un'human, *a.* [UN-^{1} 7, 5 b.]

1. Inhuman, inhumane, unmerciful, cruel: **a.** Of actions, etc.

α. **1549** *Compl. Scot.* xiv. 119 Ther for ȝe hef committit ane onhumain act. **1605** *London Prodigal* III. ii. 185 That were vnchristian, and an vnhumane part. **1622** in Foster *Eng. Factories Ind.* (1908) II. 18 They..have..committed such unhumaine acts in murtheringe all they take. *a* **1660** *Contemp. Hist. Irel.* (Ir. Archæol. Soc.) I. 251 Unnaturall lust and unhumane crueltie.

β. **1646** HAMMOND *Tracts* Pref., Not only the most unchristian but unhuman practices. *a* **1716** SOUTH *Serm.* (1744) XI. ii. 39 Their insatiable avarice, and their unhuman and remorseless cruelty. **1796** MRS. M. ROBINSON *Angelina* III. 373 Against parental authority so unhuman, nature has some plea. **1871** BLACKIE *Four Phases* i. 36 A one-sided, unhuman, unworthy and altogether false assertion.

b. Of persons.

1611 SPEED *Hist. Gt. Brit.* VI. xxxv. §5. 136 He was flaied alive by direction of this vnhumane King. **1663** SOUTH *Serm.* (1717) V. 101 Bleeding and dying at the Feet of Bloody, Unhuman Miscreants. **1700** RYCAUT *Hist. Turks* 333/2 That insolent and unhumane Robber. **1749** FIELDING *Tom Jones* VI. xi, All agreed that he was sent away pennyless ..from the house of his unhuman father.

2. Not limited by human qualities or conditions; superhuman.

1782 MME. D'ARBLAY *Let.* 6 Apr., [They] are neither plunged in the depths of misery, nor exalted to unhuman happiness. **1855** CDL. WISEMAN *Fabiola* I. ix. 49 Converted ..by some means, so unhuman, so divine, as we shall never ..forecast. **1856** R. A. VAUGHAN *Mystics* (1860) I. 100 This divorce between the virtues of daily life and certain other virtues which are unhuman. **1874** H. ROGERS *Orig. Bible* ii. 70 An argument for the unhuman character of the project.

3. Not pertaining to mankind.

1861 W. JAMES *Let.* Sept. (1920) I. 38, I have noticed fleeting shades of expression on her face..*unhuman*, ghoul-like, fiendish-cunning. **1885** G. ALLEN *Darwin* vii. 120 These curious and almost unhuman-looking objects [*sc.* palæolithic implements]. **1885** R. L. & F. STEVENSON *Dynamiter* 153 'How is this?' he cried, in a sharp, unhuman voice. 'Am I blind?'

Hence **un'humanness.**

1885 L. OLIPHANT *Sympneumata* 275 The stamp of unhumanness which clings to the acts and operations of success.

un'human, *v.* [UN-^{2} 6 a.] *trans.* To make unhuman.

1648 EARL WESTMORELD. *Otia Sacra* 129 And yet (as if unhuman'd) we By no means with each other can agree.

un'humanize, *v.* [UN-^{2} 6 c.]

1. *trans.* To deprive of human virtues; to render inhuman or callous.

1752 YOUNG *Brothers* III. i, Thy heart, how dead to every call of nature! Unson'd! unbrother'd! nay, unhumaniz'd! **1755** *Man* No. 24. 3 A life consisting entirely of..sensual delights, unhumanises the soul. **1807** J. BARLOW *Columb.* VI. 398 How long, deluding phantom, wilt thou blind, Mislead, debase, unhumanize mankind? **1852** HAWTHORNE *Blithedale Rom.* xviii, That cold tendency..appeared to have gone far towards unhumanizing my heart. **1860** I. TAYLOR *Spir. Hebrew Poetry* (1873) 124 The work of slaughter did not unhumanize those who effected it.

2. To deprive of human qualities.

1800 *Monthly Mag.* X. 319 By endeavouring to sublimate his Jesus into a Jehovah, he unhumanizes the most lovely of characters.

Hence **un'humanized** *ppl. a.*

c **1780** PORTEUS *Serm.* (1799) II. vi. 140 Purity is ridiculed and set at nought, as a sour, unsocial, unhumanized virtue. **1805** FOSTER *Ess.* (1806) I. 207 The firmness..is accompanied..in a mere man of the world, with an unhumanized repulsive hardness. **1815** KIRBY & SP. *Entomol.* xiv. (1816) I. 434 The most ignorant and unhumanized of their race.

un'humanly, *adv.* (UN-^{1} 11, 5 b.)

1586 *Reg. Privy Council Scot.* IV. 118 The said Jonnett.. maist cruellie and unhumanlie invadit and persewit hir. **1663** SOUTH *Serm.* (1717) V. 55 Charles I,..Unhumanly Imprison'd, and at length Barbarously Murder'd. **1868** H. BUSHNELL *Mor. Uses Dark Th.* (1869) 305 Acting in a style of frenzy so unhumanly foul and malign.

un'humble, *a.* (UN-^{1} 7.)

1611 FLORIO, *Dishumile*, vnhumble, high minded. **1642** DAVENANT *Unfort. Lovers* Epil., An unhumble Epilogue. **1842** PUSEY *Crisis Eng. Ch.* 13 A Communion,..in this country, schismatic, and acting in a very unhumble and schismatic spirit. **1882** W. MORRIS in Mackail *Life* (1899) II. 77, I hope I am not quite unhumble.

Hence **un'humbleness.**

a **1732** T. BOSTON *Crook in Lot* (1805) 117 Their condition will be brought to the lowest pass, but the unhumbleness of their spirits will remain.

un'humbled, *ppl. a.* (UN-^{1} 8.)

1604 HIERON *Wks.* I. 498 The sawcines of an ignorant and vnhumbled heart. **1657** BAXTER *Agst. Quakers* 8 What an unhumbled people these are. **1671** MILTON *P.R.* III. 429 Unhumbl'd, unrepentant, unreform'd. **1704** *Faction Displ.* x, Uncheck'd by Fear, unhumbled by Disgrace. **1808** HAN. MORE *Cœlebs* xxiv. II. 3 A critical spirit..being a symptom of an unhumbled mind. **1846** G. S. FABER *Lett. Tractar. Secess.* 65 Or did he come to it in the unhumbled position of a modern Socinian..? **1904** P. FOUNTAIN *Gt. North-West* xxiv. 294 A flag..floating over its unhumbled sons.

absol. *a* **1732** T. BOSTON *Crook in Lot* (1805) 101 The removal of the cross is not a means to humble the unhumbled. *a* **1838** C. NEAT *Serm.* (1839) 129 The worldly-minded, the unhumbled, the prayerless.

Hence **un'humbledness.**

c **1670** O. HEYWOOD *Diaries*, etc. (1881) II. 326 The unhumbledness and impenitency of most under open scandalls. **1737** J. WILLISON *Afflicted Man's Comp.* (1744) 46 It imports much Impenitency and Unhumbledness for sin.

unhu'miliated, *ppl. a.* (UN-^{1} 8.)

1856 RUSKIN *Mod. Paint.* IV. 248 Precipices..gathered after every fall into darker frowns and unhumiliated threatening.

un'humorous, *a.* (UN-^{1} 7.)

1881 *Athenæum* 17 Dec. 810/3 To treat the most dreadful of all crimes as a slight misdemeanour is..essentially unhumorous.

un'humorously, *adv.* (UN-^{1} 11.)

1768 *Woman of Honor* III. 229 Mrs. Arnold used, not quite unhumorously, to say [etc.].

un'hung, *ppl. a.* [UN-^{1} 8 b.]

1. Not furnished with hangings.

1648 HEXHAM II, *Ongehangen*, Vnhung, or, not Hanged with hangings or tapistry. **1666** PEPYS *Diary* 2 Mar., [Sir P. Warwick] shewed me his house, which is yet all unhung, but will be a very noble house indeed.

2. Of persons: Not (yet) executed by hanging. (Cf. UNHANGED *ppl. a.*)

[**1775** ASH, *Unhung*,..not hanged.] **1840** DICKENS *Old C. Shop* lxvi, One of the greatest scoundrels unhung. **1875** W. S. GILBERT *Tom Cobb* II, To look upon you as the coolest scamp unhung. **1892** ZANGWILL *Childr. Ghetto* I. 206 The Emperor let the man go unhung.

b. Not hung up (for exhibition).

1880 *Pall Mall G.* 28 Aug. 6/1 It is said that much good work [in painting] will remain unhung for want of room.

transf. **1906** *Macm. Mag.* Feb. 302 Declaiming excitedly because some fragile painter is unhung at the Academy.

unhung, pa. pple. of UNHANG *v.*

unh-unh ('ʌ̃ʌ̃), *int.* Expressing negation or denial.

1951 J. CORNISH *Provincials* 38 'I guess no one'd buy *here.*' 'Unh-unh.' Gloom flooded back. **1963** M. MCCARTHY *Group* xi. 255 'I should think he would step in as a doctor,' Polly said mildly. Gus shook his head. 'Unh-unh,' he said. 'That's what they have to watch out for.' **1977** *New Yorker* 20 June 31/2 Unh-unh, I don't feel like it.

un'hunted, *ppl. a.* [UN-^{1} 8.]

1. Not hunted in; not searched by hunting.

1572 BOSSEWELL *Armorie* II. 94 A great Parke..that had remained vnhunted, duringe the time of foure mens ages. **1811** MISS L. M. HAWKINS *C'tess & Gertr.* 59 No part of England, but the extreme northern counties, was 'unhunted' in this search. **1883** R. BRIDGES *Prometh.* 1078 Skirting wide The unhunted forest. **1899** F. V. KIRBY *Sport Africa* xi. 118 In comparatively unknown and unhunted districts.

2. Not hunted or chased.

1648 HEXHAM II, *Ongejaeght*, Vnhunted, or Vnchased. **1809** CAMPBELL *Gert. Wyom.* I. iii, The wild-deer arched his neck from glades, and then Unhunted sought his woods. *a* **1822** SHELLEY *Fragm.*, *'When soft Winds'* 4 Bold as an unhunted fawn.

un'huntsmanlike, *a.* (UN-^{1} 7 c.)

1607 MARKHAM *Cavel.* III. (1617) 9 When..I haue vn-Huntsman-like ridden in amongst the Dogges.

un'hurdled, *a.* (UN-^{1} 9.)

a **1711** KEN *Ded.* Poet. Wks. 1721 I. 4 My Flock stray on the unhurdled Wild.

un'hurled, *ppl. a.* (UN-^{1} 8.)

[**1775** ASH.] **1798** W. TAYLOR in Robberds *Mem.* (1843) I. 219 Not yet the great retributress has closed The book of fate—her unhurled lightnings glow.

un'hurried, *ppl. a.* (UN-^{1} 8.)

1768–74 TUCKER *Lt. Nat.* (1834) II. 547 There is a virtue in keeping one's self..unhurried in dangers or alluring pursuits. **1859** RUSKIN *Two Paths* i. 47 The noble person.. deals with them in unalarmed intelligence and unhurried strength. **1876** MRS. WHITNEY *Sights & Ins.* II. xxvi. 540 It was built into ourselves, by our unhurried possession of it in restful hours. **1881** A. A. KNOX *New Playground* (1883) 9 Eight hours of bed, and an unhurried breakfast.

So **un'hurriedly** *adv.*

1880 P. GILLMORE *On Duty* 349, I..then, unhurriedly, rode through the station.

un'hurrying, *ppl. a.* (UN-^{1} 10.)

1768–74 TUCKER *Lt. Nat.* (1834) II. 537 Continual unhurrying activity in pursuit of some end. **1918** *Glasgow Herald* 15 May 5/2 Through all this..blaze of conflict the old Vindictive, still unhurrying, was walking the lighted waters towards the entrance. **1928** *Daily Express* 13 July 10/2 Others..detect something fine and typical of the national character in the mild and unhurrying dignity of this annual contest. **1972** P. D. JAMES *Unsuitable Job for Woman* iii. 107 Benskin arrived, unhurrying, imperturbable.

un'hurt, *ppl. a.* (UN-^{1} 8 b.)

a **1225** *Juliana* 31 þe worldes wealdent þat wiste sein iuhan ..unhurt iþe ueat of wallinde eoli. **1387** TREVISA *Higden* (Rolls) VII. 165 Sche passed unhert nyne brennynge cultres. *c* **1440** *Destr. Troy* 1264 His shafte all-to sheuerit, the shalke was unhurt. *c* **1440** *Alph. Tales* 25 If þine arme com vp vnhurte. *c* **1460** *Oseney Reg.* 144 And I and myne heyres that howse schall kepe vn-hurt, that hit be not..apeyred by owr vse. **1565** COOPER *Thesaurus, Indistrictus*,..vnhurte: without scarre. **1597** A. M. tr. *Guillemeau's Fr. Chirurg.* 9 b/2 With the shott of a gunne, the first table was vnhurte. **1601** [see UNHIT]. **1647** CLARENDON *Hist. Reb.* II. §7 They believed there [were]..no Persons of what Quality soever unconcerned and..unhurt in them [*sc.* matters of religion]. **1676** HOBBES *Iliad* I. 397 Would you could here rest Unhurt, ungriev'd. **1718** PRIOR *Pict. Seneca Dying* 11 While unhurt, divine Jordain, Thy Work and Seneca's remain. **1755** YOUNG *Centaur* iv, His happiness is of so strong a constitution, that it can stand real calamities unhurt. **1818** [S. WESTON] *La Scava* 27 A statue of Venus,..the legs and arms are broke, the nose unhurt. **1894** D. CAMPBELL *Coleridge* i. 12 [He] escaped unhurt from the fray.

un'hurted, *ppl. a.* [UN-^{1} 8.] *Obs.* or *dial.* = prec.

1483 CAXTON *Gold. Leg.* 432/2 They had oute of the quarrye the forsayd ten men the whyche were founde unhurted. **1742** T. DE LA MAYNE *Love & Honour* 102 With Them familiar grown, unhurted dwell In unmolested Truce.

un'hurtful, *a.* (UN-^{1} 7.)

1549 COVERDALE, etc. *Erasm. Par. 1 Cor.* 15 In vnhurtefull manners, playne, pure, and without all counterfaictyng. **1570** DRANT *Serm.* G vij, That..the Wolfe [might] become an vnhurtfull neighbour to the Lambe. **1603** SHAKS. *Meas. for M.* III. ii. 175 You imagine me to vnhurtfull an opposite. *a* **1680** BUTLER *Charac., Humorist*, A Humorist is..some out-lying Whimsie of Bedlam, that being tame and unhurtful is suffered to go at Liberty. **1712** BLACKMORE *Creation* IV. 175 Whence shoots..the falling star, And flames unhurtful hovering dance in air? **1753** RICHARDSON *Grandison* (1781) III. ix. 62 All that is wished for..is, that she may be made unhurtful. *a* **1806** H. K. WHITE *Poems* (1837) 136 When happy Superstition, gabbling eld, Holds her unhurtful gambols.

Hence **un'hurtfully** *adv.*, **un'hurtfulness.**

1549 COVERDALE, etc. *Erasm. Par. 1 Cor.* vi. 15 b, Your vnhurtefulnes shal condemne theyr vnclennes. **1725** POPE *Let. to Swift* 14 Sept., To laugh at others as innocently and as unhurtfully as at ourselves.

un'hurting, *ppl. a.* (UN-^{1} 10, 5 d.)

1613 W. BROWNE *Brit. Past.* I. iv. 74 As if she in her kinde (vnhurting elfe) Did bid me take such lodging as her selfe. **1814** *Monthly Mag.* XXXVII. 146 While the evening shower retires, Kindle thy unhurting fires. **1822** BEDDOES *Bride's Trag.* IV. i, Because I fold Mine arms like any man unhurt, unhurting.

†b. *Sc.* With object: Without violating.

1581 *Rec. Burgh Lanark* (1893) 84 Hie being chossing hie may, unhurtand his aith, refuis the samyn offece.

un'husbanded, *ppl. a.* [UN-^{1} 8.]

1. Not improved by husbandry; untilled, uncultivated: **a.** Of ground.

1538 ELYOT, *Incultus*, a place vnhusbanded or vntilled. **1601** R. JOHNSON *Kingd. & Commw.* (1603) 184 No foot of land is left vnhusbanded. **1628** ROBSON *News fr. Aleppo* 13 The vnhusbanded plaines, for many miles together blame their stupidity. **1654** EARL MONM. tr. *Bentivoglio's Wars Flanders* 134 Other little islands..are almost nameless, as being almost unhusbanded. **1894** *Pall Mall G.* 1 Nov. 2/3 Dwellers for the more part in remote, unhusbanded districts.

b. Of plants or trees.

1615 G. SANDYS *Trav.* II. 116 A desert producing here and there a few vnhusbanded Palmes. **1616** W. BROWNE *Brit. Past.* II. v. 341, I have beheld A widow vine,.. Unhusbanded, neglected, all forlorne. **1620** BRINSLEY *Virgil* 43/2 The great brambles vnhusbanded (or vntrimmed, or not cut) but wilde. **1888** DOUGHTY *Arabia Deserta* II. 184, I went..to dig up off-sets of unhusbanded young palms.

2. Not provided with a husband.

[**1775** ASH.] **1797** SOUTHEY *Eng. Ecl., Hannah* 19 She bore unhusbanded a mother's pains. **1879** MEREDITH *Egoist* xxxii, He considered himself to have been too lenient to the wine of an unhusbanded hostess.

†**un'husbanding**, *vbl. sb.* *Obs.*$^{-1}$ [UN-^{1} 13.] Lack of husbandry.

c **1440** *Pallad. on Husb.* I. 284 Vnhusbondynge vndoth fertilite.

un'husbandly, *adv.* (UN-^{1} 11.)

1607 NORDEN *Surv. Dial.* v. 239, I see the hedges lye very vnhusbandly: a true note of few good husbands.

un'hushed, *ppl. a.* (UN-^{1} 8.)

1813 BYRON *Corsair* I. xiv, Still must each action to my bosom suit, My heart unhush'd, although my lips were mute!

un'husk, *v.* [UN-^{2} 5.]

1. *trans.* To divest of husk or shell; †to clean (a fish) of spines.

1598 FLORIO, *Diliscare*, to vnhuske or clense fish from bones. **1602** DOLMAN *La Primaud. Fr. Acad.* (1618) III. 812 It must bee beaten in a morter, to vnhuske it. **1665–6** *Phil. Trans.* I. 202, I have sown a little French Barley and Rice seed and am thinking on a way of un-husking them. *a* **1693** *Urquhart's Rabelais* III. xviii. 145 The Bean is not seen till.. it be unhuskt. **1808–14** A. WILSON in *Poems & Lit. Prose* (1876) I. 288 Unhusking the seed from the burr in a twinkling. **1884** R. WALKER *Five Threes* 79 The nuts..are then split open with an axe (not unhusked).

2. *fig.* To strip of a covering or disguise; to lay open, expose.

1596 NASHE *Saffron-Walden* S iv, I would we might know her, and see her vnhu[s]kt and naked once. **1607** TOURNEUR *Rev. Trag.* I. i, He began By policy to open and unhusk me About the time and common rumour. **1610** HEALEY *St. Aug. Citie of God* 390 All the good wee doe, comes from God, by whose pardon wee are unhusked of the old man, sinne. **1892** *Sat. Rev.* 17 Dec. 719/1 The 'Comic Spirit' may puzzle him. .. You have got but to unhusk and unshell it, and there it is.

Hence **un'husking** *vbl. sb.*

1706 PHILLIPS (ed. Kersey), *Decortication*,..the peeling, or unhusking of Roots, Seeds, Fruits, &c. **1756** T. BIRCH *Hist. Royal Soc.* II. 78 The way used by them for the unhusking of rice.

un'husked, *ppl. a.*^{1} [UN-^{1} 8.] Not divested of the husk.

1769 E. BANCROFT *Guiana* 61 Resembling unhusked coffee-berries. **1787** JEFFERSON *Writ.* (1859) II. 196 To furnish you with some of the Piedmont rice, unhusked. **1859** R. F. BURTON in *Jrnl. Geog. Soc.* XXIX. 365 Upon journeys the African boils his holcus unhusked in an earthen basin. **1888** J. Q. BITTINGER *Hist. Haverhill* (N.H.) 360 The unhusked corn was piled in a heap,..and the huskers..sat around the fire on the floor.

un'husked, *ppl. a.*^{2} [f. UNHUSK *v.*] Stripped of, taken out of, the husk.

1597 BP. HALL *Sat.* III. i, Could no vnhusked Akorne leaue the tree, But there was chalenge made whose it might bee. **1661** LOVELL *Hist. Anim. & Min.* 440 The diet of the sick..: sparing, as unhusked barley, hydromel. **1708** OCKLEY *Saracens* I. 250 That sort of Provision..is either Barley, Rice, or Wheat, sodden and unhusk'd.

unhy'gienic, *a.* (UN-^{1} 7.)

1883 *Jrnl. Educ.* XVIII. 83 Unhygienic conditions in or about the building. **1897** *Allbutt's Syst. Med.* II. 315 When the heat is intense,..the surroundings unhygienic.

unhy'gienically, *adv.* (UN-^{1} 11.)

1861 J. H. BENNET *Winter Medit.* I. viii. (1875) 209 A densely populated city,..badly drained, and unhygienically built. **1897** *Daily News* 17 Sept. 6/7 Skirts will continue.. dangerously and unhygienically to trail upon the ground.

un'hymned, *ppl. a.* (UN-^{1} 8.)

1851 MEREDITH *Poems, Pastorals* vii, All the flowers are falling! Falling unhymned.

unhynde, var. UNHEND *a. Obs.*

un'hyphenated, *ppl. a.* [UN-^{1} 8.] **1.** Not joined by a hyphen; not written with a hyphen.

1934 in WEBSTER. **1960** *Amer. Speech* XXXV. 215 The authors seem to be unsure whether some forms occur as nicknames or as generic epithets... Some unhyphenated terms comprising two words have only the first capitalized. **1980** *Washington Post* 25 Apr. (Weekend Section) 4 [Noel Hume's]..double barreled name goes unhyphenated because such things are regulated by law as well as custom in his native Britain.

2. Not employing a hyphenated term (such as *French-Canadian*) in describing one's political or cultural allegiance. Of such allegiance, etc.: not divided. Cf. HYPHENATED *a.* 2. *N. Amer.*

1970 L. B. PEARSON *Words & Occasions* 229, I am a Canadian who speaks English. There are millions [of others] who speak French... Others..have an ancestral language which they use. But we are all, or should be, Canadians—and unhyphenated with pride in our nation and its citizenship. **1973** *Saturday Night* (Toronto) Oct. 17/2 Many Canadians..were interpreting his One Canada to be on a par with the call for unhyphenated Canadianism. **1981** *Washington Post* 30 Jan. A15 Unhyphenated Democrats, at least those brave enough to acknowledge their political heritage, have a brand-new patron saint.

unhypochon'driacous, *a.* (UN-^{1} 7.)

1683 E. HOOKER *Pref. Pordage's Mystic Div.* 13 All the name I desire is an honest good Fellow;.. Unhypochondriacous, or toucht with the yellow.

unhypo'critical, *a.* (UN-^{1} 7.)

1854 GEO. ELIOT tr. *Feuerbach's Essence Christianity* 310 The unhypocritical, honest acknowledgment of sensual life is the acknowledgment of sensual pleasure. **1862** CARLYLE *Fredk. Gt.* XI. iii. III. 61 My shrill Princess,..of a highly unhypocritical nature.

unhy'pothecated, *ppl. a.* (UN-^{1} 8.)

1802 *Guineas an Incumbrance* 73 The unhypothecated part of the income tax. **1897** *Westm. Gaz.* 2 Oct. 6/3 The unhypothecated portion of the revenue.

unhy'sterical, *a.* (UN-^{1} 7.)

1886 GURNEY, etc. *Phantasms of Living* II. 323 Accounts of..apparitions at death from educated and unhysterical witnesses.

uni ('ju:nɪ). Chiefly *Austral.* and *N.Z.* Also Uni. Colloq. abbrev. of UNIVERSITY *sb.* 1. Also *attrib.* and *Comb.* Cf. UNIV.

1898 *Bulletin* (Sydney) 17 Dec. (Red Page), The only classical idioms I have found..are *rotter*, *i.e.*, an adept in learning anything; and *panem agere*, Sydney Uni. slang for 'doing a loaf'. **1913** *Lincoln* (Nebraska) *Daily News* 28 Feb. 1/7 (*heading*) Uni. men depart to judge debates. **1929** K. S. PRICHARD *Coonardoo* 163 Stay in Perth, go to the uni, be a lawyer or doctor, or something? **1962** A. SEYMOUR *One Day of Year* 103, I think I might ditch my course. Leave Uni. **1966** 'L. LANE' *ABZ of Scouse* 112 *Uni-type*, a university student. **1975** M. BRADBURY *History Man* x. 169 All the girls at the uni, what she calls the uni, in her set talk about separating. **1984** *Metro* (Auckland) Mar. 15/2 The poor fool who sat the exam and got potted has been threatened with having his own accreditation cancelled and may be banned from sitting the exam for another two years—when he planned to go to uni in this year.

uni- ('ju:nɪ), repr. L. *ūni-* combining form of *ūnus* one, a single, forming the first element in a number of words with the sense 'having, composed or consisting of, characterized by, etc., one (thing specified by the second element)'. The Latin prefix *ūni-* (before a vowel *ūn-*) was employed before or during the classical period in only a few terms, as *ūnicolor*, *ūnigena*, *ūnimanus*, *ūniversus*, *ūnanimus*, *ūnoculus* adjs.; *ūniversitās*, *ūnanimitās* sbs. In the post-classical and later language the prefix had a more extensive use, although the recorded instances are not very numerous; they are chiefly adjectival forms, as *ūnicalamus*, *ūnicaulis*, *ūnicornis*, *ūniformis*, *ūnigenitus*, *ūnijugus*, *ūniversālis*, *ūnivocus*, etc., *ūnanimis*. The earliest appearance of the element in English is naturally in words directly adopted from French or Latin, as UNANIMITY, UNICORN, UNIFORM *a.*, UNISON, UNIVERSAL *a.*, UNIVERSE, UNIVERSITY, etc. In more general use it first appears in words adapted from Latin compounds or modelled on these, as *univocate* (1432–50), *univocal* (1541), *unigenit* (*a* 1568); but it was not until the 17th c. that the prefix obtained much currency, when in addition to normal combs. as *unicolorate*, *unicornous*, *uniparous*, *unireme*, *univalve*, etc., such occasional formations as *unifoil*, *unifold*, *unipresence*, *unipresent* were coined on analogy with other numerical prefixes. In the 18th c. a comparatively small number of new compounds were adapted or formed, as *uniangulate*, *unicapsular*, *unigenous*, *unilocular*, *unisoil*, etc. In the 19th c. the element came to be freely employed in the formation of scientific and technical terms, especially in *Bot.* and *Zool.*, freq. after mod.L. formations as *unicapsularis*, *-cellularis*, *-foliatus*, *-labiatus*, *-lobatus*, *-nervatus*, *-nervus*, *-ovulatus*, *-sexus*, or adapted from F. terms as *unicursal*, *-cuspidé*, *-lobé*, *-nerve*. The second element in these compounds is thus naturally of Latin origin, but after the prefix had acquired a more extensive use it was not infrequently combined with English forms or words, and has been used occasionally in place of the Greek equivalent MONO-. (The use with English participial forms in *-ed* was not fully established until the 19th c.)

In scientific works the prefix is sometimes represented by the Arabic numeral, as *1-bracteate*, etc.

The older and more important combinations will be found in this Dict. in their alphabetical place as main words.

1. Forming adjectives with the general sense 'having, provided with, composed or consisting of, or characterized by one (thing specified or connoted by the second element)'. Many of these compounds are self-explanatory or are sufficiently explained by the quots., and in such cases no definition is added. **uni'algal** *Bot.* (see quot. 1914); **uni'angulate** *Bot.*; **uniare'agerous** [-GEROUS] *Conch.*, having a single 'area'; **uniar'ticulate** *Ent.* and *Zool.*, having a single joint; **uniau'riculate(d** *Zool.*, having a single auricle or auriculate process; **uni'basal**, **uni'bracteate**, **-'bracteolate**; **uni'central** (see quots. and cf. *monocentric* MONO- 1); **,uniconso'nantal**; **uni'corneal** *Zool.*, of an ocellus: having a single cornea; **uni'costate** *Bot.* and *Zool.*, having one rib; **unicui'rassed**, = *unipeltate*; **uni'cuspid** *Zool.* = *unicuspidate* s.v. UNI- 1 a; **uni'cuspidate**, ending in one cusp or point; **uni'dentate(d** *Zool.* and *Bot.*, having a single tooth-like serration; **uniden'ticulate** *Zool.* and *Bot.*, having but one denticulation; **unidi'mensional**, of one dimension; **unie'quivalent**, = UNIVALENT *a.*; **'unifaced**, of a coin (see quot.); **uni'facial**, (*a*) *Zool.*; (*b*) *Archæol.*, of a flint tool, etc.: (worked) on one side only; cf. BIFACIAL *a.*; also *absol.* as *sb.*; **uni'flagellate** *Zool.*, of an infusorian: having but one flagellum; **uni'florate**, **-'flowered**, = UNIFLOROUS *a.*; **uni'foliate**, **-'foliolate**, of leaves, etc.: consisting of one leaflet; of plants: characterized by or bearing leaves of this kind; **uni'globular**, consisting of a single globular part; in quot. *absol.*; **uni'guttulate**, marked with one drop-like spot; **uni'jugate** *Bot.*; **uni'lamellar**, **uni'laminar**, having one lamella, lamina, or layer; **uni'linear**, (*a*) *Math.*, affecting or involving but one line (see quot. 1851); (*b*) of an evolution, a theory, etc.: having a single line of development or progression; **uni'lobar**, **-'lobate**, **-lobed**; **uni'lobular** *Path.*, of cirrhosis: characterized by hypertrophy of single lobules; hypertrophic; **uni'macular**, marked with a single spot; **uni'medial**, coming through a single medium; **unimodular** *Math.*, having a determinant whose value is 1; **uni'multiplex**; **uni'muscular** *Zool.*; **uni'nervate**, **-nerved**; **uni'ovular**, **-'ovulate** = MONOVULAR *a.*; **uni'peltate** *Zool.* (see 2); **uni'potent** *Med.* and *Biol.*, of a cell: capable of giving rise to only one type of cell or tissue; **uni'radiate(d**; **unira'mose**, **-'ramous**, having or consisting of single ramus or branch; **,uniseg'mental**; **uni'septate** *Bot.*; **'unisexed**, consisting of members of one sex; **uniso'cietary**, consisting of or characterized by one society or social order; **uni'spiculate**, having but one spicule; **unispi'nose**, having or bearing one spine; **uni'sulcate**, having one groove or furrow; **unitele'graphic**, pertaining to a telegraph capable of being used by only one person at a time; **uniten'tacular**; **uni'ternary** *Cryst.* (see quot.); **unitu'berculate**; **uniun'guiculate**, having one unguis or claw; **uni'vallate** *Archæol.*, having a single encircling rampart; cf. MULTIVALLATE *a.*; **uni'variant** *Physical Chem.*, of a chemical system: having one degree of freedom (cf. FREEDOM 10b); **uni'variate** *Statistics*, involving or having one variate or variable; **uni'vocalized**, converted into a single voiced sound.

Various terms having little or no real currency have appeared in Dicts., etc., as *unicarinated*, *-lineated* (1840), *uniclinal* (1879), *unicarinate*, *-foliar* (1888), *uniforate*, *-foveate*, *-lamellate*, *-laminate*, *-loculate*, *-sepalous*, *-serrate*, *-serrulate*, *-spiral* (1891); etc.

1914 G. M. SMITH in *Trans. Wisconsin Acad.* XVII. 1173 According to the usage of some authors, a pure culture is one that contains only one algal species; others under-stand it to be a culture of single algal species that is also free from other organisms... To differentiate between the two I propose the term **unialgal culture* to designate one which contains but a single species of alga, but which may contain other organisms. **1946** E. G. PRINGSHEIM *Pure Cultures of Algae* vi. 79 The separation of the purification process into two stages, the first involving the preparation of unialgal or species-pure cultures, the second that of bacteria-free or absolutely pure cultures, is very helpful. **1979** *Nature* 27 Sept. 300/2 This infective filtrate caused the destruction of cultures of four unialgal strains of *M*[*icromonas*] *pusilla*. **1777** S. ROBSON *Brit. Flora* 4 **Uniangulate*, having one angle, as in Stinking Sedge. **1850** W. KING *Permian Fossils* 142 Genus *Ismenia*. Diagnosis.—*Uni-areagerous... *Area*, both halves oblique to the hinge-margin, and to each other. **1819** SAMOUELLE *Entomol. Compend.* 99 Legs bifid, the last joint of the four anterior pairs..*uniarticulate. **1856** W. CLARK *Van der Hoeven's Zool.* I. 300 Tarsi uniarticulate, with single arcuate claw. **1835** KIRBY *Hab. & Inst. Anim.* II. xxii. 416 The *Cæcilia*, or blind serpent, too, is almost *uniauriculate. **1859** AGASSIZ *Ess. Classification* 338 Gasteropoda (Uniauriculate animals). Membranous heart with one auricle. **1839** *Penny Cycl.* XIV. 335/2 M. de Blainville divides the genus into three sections..; 2, consisting of *uniauriculated species (*Malleus normalis*). **1890** *Amer. Naturalist* May 406 *Unibasal pectoral and ventral fins. **1870** HOOKER *Stud. Flora* 387 Bog Asphodel,.. pedicel *1-bracteate. *Ibid.*, Eriocauloneæ... Flowers minute..in involucrate heads, *1-bracteolate. **1864** SPENCER *Biol.* I. §50. 137 Central development may be distinguished into **unicentral* and *multicentral*, according as the product of the original germ develops symmetrically round one centre, or..in subordination to many centres. **1875** DOWDEN *Shakespere* 61 Assured that the organism is living, he fearlessly lets it develope itself in its proper mode, unicentral (as Macbeth) or multicentral (as King Lear). **1902** *Brit. Med. Jrnl.* No. 2154. 908 Cancers either started from one centre (unicentral or monocentral) or from many centres (multicentral or plurocentral). **1948** D. DIRINGER *Alphabet* ii. 60 The phonograms were bi-consonantal..or *uni-consonantal. **1884** SEDGWICK & HEATHCOTE tr. *Claus' Zool.* 538 The *unicorneal ocelli are principally present in larval life. **1849** BALFOUR *Man. Bot.* 72 Reticulated Venation. I. *Unicostate... A single rib or costa in the middle (midrib). **1852** DANA *Crust.* I. 335 Hand..faintly uni-costate towards lower part. **1842** *Penny Cycl.* XXIII. 82/1 *Unicuirassed Stomapods. **1894** GOULD *Dict. Med.* 1572/1 *Unicuspid. **1948** A. L. RAND *Mammals Eastern Rockies* 54 The skull when viewed from the side appears to hold only 3 unicuspid teeth. **1977** *Lancet* 17 Sept. 610/2 Surgical exploration..revealed a unicuspid aortic valve with a 'horseshoe' appearance. **1883** FLOWER in *Encycl. Brit.* XV. 403/2 The *unicuspidate upper and lower front incisors. **1819** SAMOUELLE *Entomol. Compend.* 222 Antennæ with their internal base *unidentate. **1833** HOOKER in *Smith's Eng. Flora* V. I. 124 The lower [lobes of the leaves].. frequently unidentate. **1856** W. CLARK *Van der Hoeven's Zool.* I. 357 Mandibles small, narrow, unidentate or edentulous. **1822** J. PARKINSON *Outl. Oryctol.* 201 *Ancilla olivula*: *unidentated at the base. **1828** STARK *Elem. Nat. Hist.* II. 266 Mandibles small, depressed, pointed and entire, or unidentated in the internal side. **1887** *Trans. Royal Soc. Edin.* XXXII. 637 Radula, two rows of teeth. 1 and 2, lateral teeth; 3, median tridenticulate; 5 and 4, central *unidenticulate. **1883** *C. S. Peirce's Studies in Logic* 156 Analogous reasoning would obviously apply to any portion of an *unidimensional continuum. **1867** *Chambers' Encycl.* IX. 537/1 Monad or *Uniequivalent Elements (or Monads), one atom of which in combination is equivalent to..one atom of hydrogen. **1877** JEWITT *Half-hrs. among Eng. Antiq.* 139 Many of the early coins are *unifaced, i.e. one side is plain, while the other bears the device. **1846** DANA *Zooph.* IV. (1848) 65 A species, which usually has polyps only on one surface,—*unifacial. **1951** *N. & Q. Anthropol.* (ed. 6) IV. 345 The distinction between tools made on cores and tools made on flakes or blades should be noted, and also that between tools flaked on both faces (so-called bifacials) and those flaked or retouched on one side only (unifacials). **1957** *Jrnl. R. Anthropol. Inst.* Jan. 119 A wide range of choppers and chopping tools, core, flake, bifacial and unifacial, is still in use. **1981** *Science* 4 Sept. 1115/2 Simple unifacial tools. **1881** CARPENTER *Microscope* (ed. 6) xi. §419 Their simple *uniflagellate Monad (*Monas Dallingeri*). **1860** MAYNE *Expos. Lex.* 1310 *Uniflorus*, Bot., having or bearing one flower: *uniflorate. **1845–50** MRS. LINCOLN *Lect. Bot.* App. 27 Pl. VII, Scape naked, *uni-flowered. Flower drooping, spathaceous. **1849** CRAIG s.v., *Unifoliate. **1881** *Jrnl. Linn. Soc.* XVIII. 291 These apparently unifoliate stems are long petioles. **1866** *Treas. Bot.* 1191/2 *Unifoliate*, **Unifoliolate*, when a compound leaf consists of one leaflet only; as in the orange-tree. **1872** OLIVER *Elem. Bot.* II. 130 Common Barberry,..with fascicled unifoliolate leaves. **1875** BENNETT & DYER tr. *Sachs' Bot.* 823 As in Duchesne's unifoliolate Strawberry. **1891** *Geol. Jrnl.* XLVII. 6 The structure of the zoæcia and of the dorsal surface is the same as in those with shorter nodes, so that we seem to have a series from the *uniglobular. **1887** W. PHILLIPS *Brit. Discomycetes* 13 Sporidia elliptic, obtuse, *uniguttulate. **1849** BALFOUR *Man. Bot.* 79 When a pinnate leaf has one pair of leaflets, it is **unijugate*. **1861** BENTLEY *Man. Bot.* 168 The leaflets..are arranged along the sides of the rachis or common petiole in pairs, and according to their number, the leaf is said to be unijugate or one-paired,..bijugate, etc. **1875** BENNETT & DYER tr. *Sachs' Bot.* 315 A vein..is formed from the base towards the apex, dividing the *unilamellar lamina into right and left halves. **1876** VAN DUYN tr. *Wagner's Gen. Pathol.* 466 In epithelial regeneration with *unilaminar epithelium. **1851** SYLVESTER in *Lond.* etc. *Phil. Mag.* Feb. 128 Accordingly this may be termed *unilinear-intersection contact, or more briefly, unilinear contact. **1910** *Athenæum* 12 Mar. 299 A worldwide unilinear evolution. **1939** *Mind* XLVIII. 369 It is an order in which the thoughts in the chains of reasoning are *not* linked in a unilinear, but in a 'global' fashion. **1974** tr. *Wertheim's Evolution & Revolution* i. 22 In Soviet Russia during the twenties..the issue of unilinear evolution also came in for serious discussion. **1870** ROLLESTON *Anim. Life* 29 Both the liver and the pulmonary organs [of the common ringed snake] are *unilobar, the left lung being merely represented by a rudimentary structure. **1839–47** *Todd's Cycl. Anat.* III. 310/1 In the Potoroo the left lung is *unilobate. **1851** G. F. RICHARDSON *Geol.* 286 In the strata anterior to the lias, almost all the fishes had heterocercal or *unilobed tails. **1897** *Allbutt's Syst. Med.* IV. 170 In a less common variety [of cirrhosis of the liver] a finer network of new fibrous tissue tends to surround individual lobules (*unilobular). **1859** *Todd's Cycl. Anat.* V. [134]/1 The germinal vesicle is *unimacular in general in the small-yolked ova. **1802–12** BENTHAM *Ration. Judic. Evid.* (1827) III. 438 Constitutive of so many modifications or species of unoriginal evidence, we have *unimedial, bimedial, trimedial and so forth: in a word, multimedial evidence. **1852** J. J. SYLVESTER in *Cambr. & Dublin Math. Jrnl.* VII. 52 The linear-transformations are supposed to be always taken such that the modulus..is unity; or, as it may be phrased, the transformations are *uni-modular. **1866** BRANDE & COX *Dict. Sci.*, etc. II. 378/1 The determinant formed from the coefficients..is called the modulus of transformation, and when D is equal to unity the transformations are said to be *unimodular*. **1973** L. J. TASSIE *Physics Elementary Particles* xi. 136 The group *SU*(3) is the group of all unimodular unitary 3 × 3 matrices. **1816** T. L. PEACOCK *Headlong Hall* ix, These thousand images, indeed, were but one; and yet the one was a thousand, a sort of *uni-multiplex phantasma. **1835** KIRBY *Hab. & Inst. Anim.* I. viii. 237 The second [order of molluscans] is *Unimuscular, having only one such [attaching] muscle with one impression. **1875** BLAKE *Zool.* 241 If there be but one muscular impression on a valve, then it belongs to monomyary or unimuscular bivalve. **1866** *Treas. Bot.* 1191/2 **Uninervate*,..one-ribbed. **1891** *Nature* XLIII. 454/1 The linear, *uninerved leaves characteristic of the.. genus *Asterophyllites*. **1904** *Brit. Med. Jrnl.* 17 Dec. 1644 A chapter is devoted to this subject [i.e. polysomatous terata] under the subheadings of *uniovular twins. **1948** 'M. INNES' *Night of Errors* ix. 102 The two men were uncommonly like each other—a most striking family resemblance. But then I suppose they were what are called uniovular twins—or triplets, I should say. **1965** J. POLLITT *Depression & its Treatment* vii. 91 Kallman..showed that 96 per cent of uniovular twins of manic-depressive partners were similarly affected. **1979** G. BOURNE *Pregnancy* (rev. ed.) xxx. 448 These babies will be identical, or uniovular twins since they have exactly the same genetic structure and the same chromosomes. **1857** A. GRAY *First Less. Bot.* (1866) 235 **Uniovulate*, having only one ovule. **1845** *Encycl. Metrop.* XXV. 2 This genus [Squilla] belongs to the *Unipeltate family of the Stomapodous order. **1974** *Brit. Jrnl. Haematol.* XXVI. 605 Stem cells are assayed by quantifying their progeny. In techniques measuring cells of one lineage this measurement reflects the number of *unipotent stem cells. **1979** *Nature* 18 Jan. 177/1 Such a cell is unipotent and exclusively committed to maturation along the erythroid pathway. **1887** SOLLAS in *Encycl. Brit.* XXII. 416/2 Monaxon *Uniradiate Type (stylus).—By the suppression of one of the rays of an oxea, an acuate spicule or stylus results. **1828–32** WEBSTER (citing *Encyc.*), **Uniradiated*, having one ray. **1888** ROLLESTON & JACKSON *Anim. Life* 532 The first antenna is primitively *uniramose. **1890** *Microsc. Sci.* XXX. 109 Six pairs of (thoracic) appendages.., of which the first are long, slender, and uniramose. **1877** HUXLEY *Anat. Inv. Anim.* vi. 283 Entirely destitute of appendages, except a shorter anterior, *uniramous..pair of oar-like organs. **1955** *Uni-segmental [see *multi-segmental* s.v. MULTI- 1 b]. **1977** *Word 1972* XXVIII. 183 The data discussed there share with these data the fact of unisegmental modification. **1866** *Treas. Bot.* 1192/1 **Uniseptate*, having but one septum or partition. **1875** COOKE *Fungi* 40 In other..species they [i.e. spores] are uniseptate. **1856** *Putnam's Mag.* Oct. 390/2 Besides, in England a bar-maid was highly respectable. How precious must she be in this *uni-sexed fair! [= California]. **1885** L. OLIPHANT *Sympneumata* 286 The wise and sanguine..infer, both from the suffering and the capacities of present human nature, a future of new order in a *uni-societary world. **1900** *Proc. Zool. Soc.* 20 Feb. 138 Skeleton forming a rather regular reticulum of *unispiculate fibres. **1828** STARK *Elem. Nat. Hist.* II. 168 The Shrimp. Thorax behind, and on each side of the rostrum *unispinose. **1852** DANA *Crust.* I. 414 Emargination uni-spinose. **1819** SAMOUELLE *Entomol. Compend.* 181 Thorax with a gibbous protuberance, *uni-sulcate above. **1853** URE *Dict. Arts* I. 626 According to this improved plan of working, the wire of communication.. may be considered as a public word road, or an omnitelegraphic way; whereas, in contradistinction, the conductor, as heretofore used, may be considered a private word road, or a *unitelegraphic way. **1889** *Amer. Nat.* XXIII. 597 Microcampana is not the only *unitentacular Medusa found in the prolific waters of our Pacific coast. **1816** R. JAMESON *Char. Min.* (ed. 2) 212 A crystal is named ..*Uniternary, when there is one by one row, the other by three rows. **1852** DANA *Crust.* I. 122 Post-medial region with a small tubercle; intestinal *uni-tuberculate. **1856** W. CLARK *Van der Hoeven's Zool.* I. 303 *Gyropus Nitzsch.*—Tarsi *uniunguiculate. **1950** *Archaeol. Jrnl. 1948* CV. 56 The first *univallate enclosure on Eddisbury Hill was preceded by a palisade structure. **1979** L. LAING *Celtic Britain* ii. 56 The simple univallate hillforts were in some cases given further ramparts. **1899** *Univariant [see INVARIANT *a.* b]. **1940** GLASSTONE *Text-bk. Physical Chem.* vi. 467 When two phases are in equilibrium..the conditions must correspond to a point on one of the lines..in Fig. 99: only temperature *or* pressure need be arbitrarily fixed..in order to define the system, and the latter has one degree of freedom, i.e., it is univariant. **1978** P. W. ATKINS *Physical Chem.* vii. 181 The system is univariant when two phases are present; there is only one degree of freedom. **1928** *Biometrika* XXA. 32 Various writers struggled with the problems that arise when samples are taken from *uni-variate and bi-variate populations. **1938** *Brit. Jrnl. Psychol.* XXIX. 451 (*heading*) The influence of univariate selection on factorial analysis of ability. **1973** *Nature* 16 Mar. 210/3 The wealth of mathematical forms with which we can express the frequency or probability distributions of univariate theory. **1876** DOUSE *Grimm's Law* App. 206 Our own familiarity with *univocalized consonants.

b. Prefixed to a sb. and forming a compound used attrib., as ***uni-direction***, ***-face***, ***-pivot***, ***-rhyme***, ***-soil***.

1778 [W. H. MARSHALL] *Minutes Agric., Digest* 18 A Unisoil Farm requires fewer Implements than a Polysoil Farm. **1859** E. WILLIAMS in *Cambrian Jrnl.* March 12 Four-lined unirhyme stanzas, of five or six syllables in a line. **1888** BOTTONE *Electr. Instr. Making* (ed. 2) 103 The uni-direction current machine. **1897** W. C. HAZLITT *Suppl. Coinage Europ. Continent* 17 A silver uniface bracteate of Otho I. **1900** *Engineering Mag.* XIX. 740 In some instances the engines are only uni-direction. **1911** H. M. HOBART *Dict. Electr. Engin.* II. 591/1 (*heading*) Unipivot measuring instrument. *Ibid.*, The chief advantage of the unipivot instrument is that, owing to the fact that the moving system is supported on a single jewel, it may be entirely lifted off when the instrument is out of use. **1940** *Chambers's Techn. Dict.* 878/1 *Unipivot instrument*, an instrument whose moving-coil system is balanced on a single pivot passing through its centre of gravity. **1944** *Antiquity* XVIII. 217 Amid the amazing expressions of the goldsmith's art which Scandanavia..produced between the late 4th and mid-5th centuries, perhaps the most interesting is the bracteates, the pendent uniface medallions. **1977** *Signature* May/June 34/4 By October 1914 watermarked paper was produced and used. This had a uniface surface, as did the first issue. **1977** *Gramophone* Aug. 377 (Advt.), A unique system of magnetic stabilization on the unipivot bearings.

2. Forming sbs., as **uni'axifer**; **'unicell** *Bot.*, a unicellular plant (Jackson *Gloss. Bot. Terms*, 1900); **ˌunidimensio'nality**; **ˌuni'linearism**; **uni'peltate** (see quot.); **uni'stylist** [L. *stylus*] (see quot.); †**'unitrine** [L. *trīn-us*], a unity in trinity (*obs.*); **uni'trinity**, unity in trinity; **'unitrope** (see quot.).

1869 *Student* II. 12 They [*sc.* polymerous leaves] will be *uniaxifers, biaxifers, etc.; multiaxifers, according as their meriphylls [= the space between two nodes of a leaf] are arranged along a single axis, or an axis ramified two, three, or more times. **1953** C. E. BAZELL *Linguistic Form* 3 *Unidimensionality. There is only one dimension of succession. **1975** *Human Relations* XXVIII. 795 Another factor is the unidimensionality of the approach. **1964** P. WORSLEY in I. L. Horowitz *New Sociol.* 374 It will certainly have to eschew *unilinearism and the West-European ethnocentrism of nineteenth-century schemas. **1842** BRANDE *Dict. Sci.*, etc. 1275 *Unipeltates, [Cuvier's] *Unipeltata*, the name of a family of Stomapodous Crustaceans, comprehending those in which the carapace is composed of a single shield-like plate. *a* **1849** POE *Marginalia* cxlii, He is as thorough a *unistylist as Cardinal Chigi, who boasted that he wrote with the same pen for a half a century. **1605** TIMME *Quersit.* II. ii. 108 It hath pleased the omnipotent Creator to manifest & showe himselfe a *Unitrine or Triune. **1775** ADAIR *Amer. Ind.* 127 Her belief of the *uni-trinity, and tri-unity of the deity. **1910** A. B. BASSET *Treat. Geom. Surfaces* 25 The reciprocal polar of a unode is called a *unitrope.

†**uniable**, *a.* *Obs.*⁻¹ (Meaning obscure.)

a **1450** *Ten Comm. of Love* (MS. Fairfax 16, fol. 185 b), Consider that my conning is disable To write to you the figure vniable.

†**'unial**, *a.* *Obs.*⁻¹ [f. UNI- + -AL¹. Cf. OF. *uniel*, *unial* in Godef. *Compl.*] United into one.

1613 SHERLEY *Trav. Persia* 4 Those Countries, limitting vpon the King of Spaines vniall parts.

Uniat, Uniate ('juːnɪæt, -ət). [ad. Russ. *uniyat*, f. *uniya* union (spec. the united Greek and Roman Catholic Churches), f. L. *ūni-*, *ūnus* one.] A Russian, Polish, or other member of that part of the Greek Church which, while retaining its own liturgy, acknowledges the supremacy of the Pope and is in communion with the Roman Catholic Church; a United Greek.

1833 R. PINKERTON *Russia* 82 The inroads of the Uniats among the members of the Greek Church. **1863** EDWARDS *Polish Captivity* II. 61 As a Uniate he acknowledges the authority of the Pope. **1883** BERESF. HOPE *Worship & Order* 127 The restoration of the uniates to Eastern communion.

b. *attrib.* or as *adj.* Of, adhering or pertaining to, or denominating the United Greek Church.

1855 *Pict. Chr. Heroism* 37 The Greek-uniat curé of Jansff. **1885** *Ch. Quarterly Rev.* Apr. 162 In Russia, the once powerful Uniat Church has declined. **1905** *Times* 22 Sept. 7 The much persecuted Uniate or Greek Catholic creed.

uniaxal (juːnɪ'æksəl), *a.* [f. UNI- 1 + AXAL *a.*] = UNIAXIAL *a.* Hence **uni'axally** *adv.*

1829 *Nat. Philos., Polaris. Light* vii. 24 (L.U.K.), The whole system of rings will appear to be like the uniaxal system. **1866** B. STEWART *Heat* §43 Crystals that are optically uniaxal. **1881** GLAZEBROOK in *Phil. Trans.* CLXXIII. 595 The Surface of a Uniaxal Crystal.

uniaxial (juːnɪ'æksɪəl), *a.* [f. UNI- 1 + AXIAL *a.*]

1. *Optics* and *Crystall.* Having one optical axis.

1827–8 HERSCHEL in *Encycl. Metrop.* (1845) IV. 520 When the two axes coalesce, or the crystal becomes uniaxial, the lemniscates become circles. *a* **1853** PEREIRA *Polarized Light* (1854) 176 The crystal possesses the singular property of being uniaxial for violet light and biaxial for red. **1888** RUTLEY *Rock-Forming Min.* 37 Uniaxial crystals.

2. *Bot.* and *Zool.* = MONAXIAL *a.*

1879 ROSSITER *Dict. Sci.*, *Uniaxial development*: in all vertebrate animals, some molluscs and annulosa; in some of exogens, endogens, algæ, and fungi.

3. Characterized by one axis of alignment or action.

1965 E. B. ATKINSON in P. D. Ritchie *Physics of Plastics* v. 250 The cube is subjected to a simple tensile stress normal to the *x* faces,..i.e. a state of simple uniaxial tension exists. **1969** W. R. R. PARK *Plastics Film Technol.* ii. 28 Uniaxial orientation takes place during the drawing of a filament. Here the polymer chains are aligned in one direction. **1982** *Jrnl. de Physique: Lettres* XLIII. 585 The dynamics of an amorphous polystyrene..melt is studied..during stress relaxation following a uniaxial deformation.

Hence **uni'axially** *adv.*

1909 in WEBSTER. **1969** *Jrnl. Appl. Physics* XL. 1301 The coercive force for a pair of identical interacting uniaxially anisotropic dipoles of arbitrary bond angle is calculated. **1979** *Nature* 15 Mar. 222/2 The entire assembly would then be hot-pressed, either uniaxially or isostatically, at a temperature of 1,200–1,300°C.

uniber, error or mispr. for UMBER *sb.*¹ 4.

1824 MEYRICK *Ant. Armour* II. 99 The war helmet.. shews the intermediate form of the uniber. **1844** JAMES *Agincourt* I. 77 Shields, and pallets and unibers.

†**unible**, *a.* *Obs. rare.* [ad. med.L. *ūnibilis* (Dief.), f. L. *ūnīre* to UNITE. So Sp. and Pr. *unible*, It. *unibile*.] Capable of being united; unitable.

1559 UDALL tr. *Geminus' Anat.* 3/1 A father, by whose grace we haue receaued a nature..vnible to the glorified bodie of his sonne Christ. **1683** BAXTER *Dying Thoughts* 22 Either Souls are partible substances or not. If not partible, how are they unible?

unic, obs. f. UNIQUE *a.* and *sb.*

† **unical**, *a.* *Obs. rare.* [f. L. *ūnic-us* UNIQUE *a.* + -AL[1].] Forming or consisting of one only; alone of its kind, unique.

1598 Sylvester *Du Bartas* II. i. II. *Impost.* 651 A body.. differing little from th' One unicall,..the onely-beeing Beeing. **1650** Charleton *Paradoxes* Prol. 26 The form or Essence of Verity, is unicall, single, and devoid of all Alterity.

Hence † **unically** *adv.*, entirely, undividedly.

1689 G. Harvey *Curing Dis. by Expect.* v. 33 If..your confidence is so unically fixed on the Virtues of Steel.

uni'cameral, *a.* [f. UNI- 1 + CAMERAL *a.*] Having, consisting of, or characterized by one legislative chamber.

1853 F. Lieber *Civil Liberty & Self-Govt.* xxiv. 242 As a feature of Gallican liberty, must be mentioned here the unicameral system. **1890** *Century Mag.* Feb. 506/1 Georgia, Pennsylvania and New Hampshire abandoned the unicameral system after a short trial of it. **1894** Morley in *Daily News* 28 June 7/4 There is very little chance of our being..what is called unicameral.

Hence **uni'cameralism**, the system of having only one legislative chamber. **uni'cameralist**, **uni'camerist**, an advocate of a unicameral system.

1888 Earl of Pembroke in *Univ. Rev.* I. 101 The ideal of the unicamerists seems to me to be quite out of the region of practical politics. **1893** *Westm. Gaz.* 14 Feb. 1/3 Of course, I, as a Democrat, do not care for the two Chambers. I am a unicameralist. **1924** *Fortn. Rev.* Oct. 742 With rare unanimity the civilized world has rejected the nostrum of unicameralism, and has decided that two legislative chambers are..necessary to a modern democracy. **1957** A. C. Breckenridge *One House for Two* i. 4 Unicameralism at best simply became a thing of historical interest.

uni'capsular, *a.* *Bot.* [ad. mod.L. *ūnicapsulār-is* (whence F. *unicapsulaire*): see UNI- and CAPSULAR *a.*] Of a pericarp: Having a single capsule. Of a plant: Characterized by a pericarp of this kind.

Also *Zool.* = MONOCYTTARIAN *a.* (*Cent. Dict.* 1891).

1720 P. Blair *Bot. Ess.* ii. 52 Therefore Papaver is only an Unicapsular Plant. **1760** Lee *Botany* I. xv. 38 In respect to external Division, the Pericarpium is either..Unicapsular, ..as in Lychnis [etc.]. **1793** Martyn *Lang. Bot.* s.v., A Unicapsular pericarp.

'unicelled, *a.* [UNI- 1.] Unicellular.

1877 Le Conte *Elem. Geol.* (1879) 154 The beautiful siliceous shells of diatoms (uni-celled plants).

unicellular (juːnɪˈsɛljʊlə(r)), *a.* (and *sb.*). *Biol.* [ad. mod.L. *ūnicellulār-is* (whence also F. *unicellulaire*): see UNI- and CELLULAR *a.*]

1. Composed or consisting of, having, a single cell; said esp. of the organisms belonging to the primary divisions of the animal and vegetable kingdoms.

Also in recent use as *sb.*

1858 Carpenter *Veg. Phys.* §35 The minute unicellular plants, known by the name of Diatomaceæ. **1875** Darwin *Insectiv. Pl.* xiv. 329 All the leaves contained unicellular and other Algæ. **1892** Mivart *Ess. & Crit.* II. 437 The distinction between unicellular and multicellular animals.

2. Characterized by the formation or presence of a single cell or cells.

1863 Dana *Man. Geol.* 747 Plants in passing from the unicellular state by growth lose in power. **1892** J. Tait *Mind in Matter* (ed. 3) 58 In the animal world colonies are the next approach of unicellular to multicellular organisation.

unicellu'larity. [a. F. *unicellularité*, or f. prec. + -ITY.] Unicellular condition or formation.

1896 G. W. Field tr. *Hertwig's Zool.* 21 The unicellularity of the lowest animals.

† **uniceptor** (ˈjuːnɪˌsɛptɔː(r)). *Immunol. Obs.* [f. UNI- 2 + RE)CEPTOR.] In Ehrlich's theory of immunization, a receptor having only one combining or haptophoric group of atoms, by which it unites with the immunizing body but not with the complement. Cf. AMBOCEPTOR.

1902 *Jrnl. Exper. Med.* VI. 281 According to the manner of action he distinguishes 'uniceptors' and 'amboceptors'. **1910** in *Lippincott's New Med. Dict.*

unicist (ˈjuːnɪsɪst). [f. L. *ūnic-us* one + -IST.]

1. A believer in the unicity of the Godhead.

1807 Coleridge in *Lit. Rem.* (1839) IV. 291 As understood by the modern Unicists. **1832** —— *Table-t.* 4 Apr., The schoolmen would perhaps have called you Unicists: but your proper name is Psilanthropists.

2. *Med.* An advocate or adherent of the theory of unicity. Also *attrib.*

1890 Billings *Nat. Med. Dict.* II. 720. **1901** J. Ewing in *Jrnl. Exper. Med.* V. 483 Inclined to accept the unicist theory.

unicity (juːˈnɪsɪtɪ). [ad. med.L. **ūnicitās* (whence F. *unicité*, It. *unicitá*, Sp. *unicidad*), or f. L. *ūnic-us* one, unique: see -ITY.]

1. The fact of being or consisting of one in number or kind; oneness.

1691 J. Howe *Wks.* (1834) 147/2 The most unquestionable unity or unicity of the Godhead. **1694** R. Burthogge *Reason & Nat. Spirits* 166 Composition is Unity, but simplicity is Unicity. **1817** Coleridge '*Blessed are ye that sow*' 55 For Unity or Unition, and indistinguishable Unicity or Oneness, are incompatible terms. **1849** Alford *Grk. Testament* I. 608 The καινότης of this commandment consists in its simplicity and (so to speak) unicity. **1880** C. I. Black *Proselytes of Ishmael* 301 What our so-called Unitarians teach is..the Unicity of the Godhead.

b. *Med.* The theory that syphilis is caused by only one kind of venereal virus.

1861 Bumstead *Ven. Dis.* 349 Some explanation..of what was called by its discoverer [Ricord] the 'unicity' of syphilis.

2. The fact or quality of being unique; unique nature or character.

1859 *Todd's Cycl. Anat.* V. 106/1 Bernard then goes on to prove, by the method of elimination, the unicity and propriety of this property of the pancreatic secretion. **1887** Saintsbury *Hist. Elizab. Lit.* 91 Which..gives The Faerie Queene its unique unicity, if such a conceit may be pardoned.

unick, obs. f. UNIQUE *a.*

uniclinal (juːnɪˈklaɪnəl), *a.* *Geol.* [f. UNI- + Gr. κλιν- (see CLINO-) + -AL[1].] Characterized by a uniform angle of dip; formed by uniformly dipping strata; = *homoclinal* adj. s.v. HOMOCLINE. (In quot. 1884 = MONOCLINAL *a.* b.)

1846 Darwin *Geol. Obs. S. Amer.* vii. 197 The masses having these different inclinations, are separated from each other by parallel vertical faults.., often giving rise to separate, parallel, uniclinal ridges. **1884** A. J. Jukes-Browne *Student's Handbk. Physical Geol.* 342 When a set of horizontal beds is suddenly bent up or down into a sharp curve, and then continued horizontally at a higher or lower level, the flexure is called a monoclinal or uniclinal curve. **1921** A. W. Grabau *Textbk. Geol.* I. xxii. 733 Thus a series of uniclinal ridges is produced, facing the center of the original anticline. **1937** Wooldridge & Morgan *Physical Basis Geogr.* xii. 159 This general process of asymmetrical development [of valleys] is called uniclinal shifting. [*Note*] The word 'uniclinal'..is preferable to 'monoclinal', since the asymmetrical development of valleys bears no necessary relation to 'monoclines'. **1970** R. J. Small *Study of Landforms* xi. 402 Glacial streams which happen to be superimposed on to the slopes above a col will undergo 'uniclinal' shifting along the ice-rock contact towards the centre of the col. **1975** *New Oxf. Atlas* 106 Newer sediments ..with gentle or moderate uniclinal dips.

'unicode. [UNI- 2.] A telegraphic code in which one word or set of letters represents a sentence or phrase; a telegram or message in this.

1886 '*Unicode*': *The Universal Telegraphic Phrase-Book* Pref. p. iii, The 'Unicode' aims at..a low price. *Ibid.* p. v, The 'Unicode' word 'Obumbro'. **1897** *Westm. Gaz.* 20 Jan. 6/3 [He] gave evidence as to sending a unicode to both [persons]. **1899** *Daily News* 23 Dec. 5/3 The dispatch of messages in 'Unicode'.

uni'color, *a.* [L.; cf. F. *unicolore.*] Of a single uniform colour. Chiefly *Nat. Hist.*

1781 Pennant *Hist. Quadrup.* II. 482 Unicolor Shrew of an uniform dusky cinereous color. **1811** Shaw *Gen. Zool.* VIII. 538 Unicolor Lory, *Psittacus unicolor.*

uni'colorate, *a. rare.* [f. L. *ūnicolor* + -ATE[2].] Unicoloured, unicolorous.

1657 Tomlinson *Renou's Disp.* 302 Its flowers like Peasebloom, but lesser, unicolorate and purpureous. **1826** Kirby & Sp. *Entomol.* IV. xlvi. 291 Unicolorate (*Unicolor*), when a surface is of one colour. **1837** Richardson *Fauna Bor.-Amer.* IV. 14 Cymindis Unicolor. Unicolorate Cymindis.

unicolorous (juːnɪˈkʌlərəs), *a.* Also 7, 9 unicolourous. [f. L. *ūnicolor* + -OUS.] Having only one colour; uniform in colour. Chiefly *Ent.*

1657 Tomlinson *Renou's Disp.* 197 Two unicolourous juices mixed together. **1843** Humphreys *Brit. Moths* II. 66 The wings rounded, destitute of markings, and unicolorous. **1894** *Naturalist* 226 All unicolorous black, instead of having the typical red elytra.

uni'colour, *a.* [Cf. UNICOLOR.] = prec.

1860 *Proc. Zool. Soc.* 51 The fur of all parts of the body.. is unicolour, and of a lightish cinnamon-brown.

uni'coloured, *a.* [UNI- 1.] Unicolorous.

1811 Pinkerton *Petral.* II. 121 Others are spotted in infinite variety; and others, though rarely, are unicoloured. **1821** Meyrick & C. H. Smith *Costume Orig. Inhab.* 24 The uni-coloured robe of sky-blue. **1890** *Sat. Rev.* 5 Apr. 413/2 The uni-coloured thread that runs throughout my motley history.

unicorn (ˈjuːnɪkɔːn). Forms: 3-7 uni-, 4-6 uny-, 4-7 vni-, vnycorne (6 inny-, ine-; *Sc.* 5 iny-, owni-, 6 wnicorne); 4-5 vny-, 4-6 vni-, 5 unycorn, 5- unicorn (5-6 vnykorn, 6 vnykhorn). [a. AF., OF. (mod.F.) *unicorne* (= Pg. *unicorne*, Pg. and Sp. *unicornio*, It. *unicorno*), or directly ad. their source L. *ūnicorn-*, *ūnicornis* having one horn (also in late Lat. as sb.), f. *ūn-us* UNI- + *cornu* horn. Cf. late L. *ūnicornuus*, med.L. *unicornus*, -(*i*)*um* sbs., from the same source.

The word was corrupted in OF. to *licorne* (the usual form in mod.F.), *lincorne*, etc., It. *liocorno*, Pg. (*a*)*licorne*, etc.]

I. 1. A fabulous and legendary animal usually regarded as having the body of a horse with a single horn projecting from its forehead (cf. 2 *note*); the monoceros of the ancients.

The unicorn has at various times been identified or confused with the rhinoceros, with various species of antelope, or with other animals having a horn (or horns) or horn-like projection from the head. According to Pliny (*Nat. Hist.* VIII. xxi. §31) it had a body resembling that of a horse, the head of a deer, the feet of an elephant, and the tail of a lion, with one black horn projecting 'two cubits' from the middle of the forehead.

The horn of this animal was reputed to possess medicinal or magical properties, esp. as an antidote to or preventive of poison: see UNICORN'S HORN.

a **1225** *Ancr. R.* 120 Mon wroð is wulf, oðer leun, oðer unicorne. **13..** *K. Alis.* 6710 (Bodl. MS.), ȝitt þou shalt habbe sex hundreþ Rinoceros..And two hundreþ vnicornes. *c* **1315** Shoreham *Poems* v. 113 Of hyre barme hyt was god game, þer-inne þe vnicorn weks tame þat er þan was so wylde. **1387** Trevisa *Higden* (Rolls) I. 159 þere beeþ also..vnycornes [L. *rhinoceros*], camels, pardes [etc.]. **1423** Jas. I *Kingis Q.* clv, The lufare vnicorne, That voidis venym with his euoure horne. *c* **1511** *1st Eng. Bk. Amer.* (Arb.) p. xxxiii/2 These vnicornes slee many Lyons, and the Lyon sleeth the vnicorne with subtylnes. **1590** Spenser *F.Q.* II. v. 10 Like as a Lyon, whose imperiall powre A prowd rebellious Vnicorne defies. **1609** Dekker *Gull's Horn-bk.* ii. 12 The Unicorne, whose horne is worth halfe a City. **1657** Trapp *Comm. Job* xxxix. 9 This is the..Unicorn... A very fierce and strong creature it is; and now adayes very rare, but anciently more common. **1735** Johnson *Lobo's Abyssinia, Descr.* ii. 51 In the Province of Agaus, has been seen the Unicorn, that Beast so much talk'd of, and so little known. **1801** *Monthly Rev.* XXXV. 351 On the probability of the existence of an Unicorn. **1843** De Quincey *Ceylon* Wks. 1859 XII. 8 The whole traditionary character of the unicorn as the antagonist..of the lion. **1895** J. G. Millais *Breath fr. Veldt* 133 Any one who has seen a wild sable antelope galloping cannot fail to be struck by its resemblance to the unicorn.

b. Used in ME. versions of the OT. to render the Vulgate *ūnicornis* or *rhīnocerōs* (Gr. μονόκερως) as translations of Heb. *r'em* (also *rēym*), and retained in various later versions (but translated by 'wild-ox' in the Revised Bible). See REEM.

a **1300** *E.E. Psalter* xxi. 22 (xxii. 21), Sauf me fra mouth of lioun es, And fra hornes of vnicornes mi mekenes. [Also versions *a* 1340-1611.] **1382** Wyclif *Numb.* xxiii. 22 Whos strengthe is lijk to an vnycorn. [Also versions 1388-1611.] *c* **1580** Sidney *Psalms* xxii. xiii, Show to heare me, By aiding, when fierce Vnicornes come neere me. **1639** Sir W. Mure *Ps.* xxii, Wks. (S.T.S.) II. 89 From the hornes of vnicornes Thine eare (Lord) found I have. **1696** Tate & Brady *Ps.* xxix. 6 They..leap, like Hinds that bounding go, Or Unicorns in youthful play.

c. In fig. or allusive use.

In quot. 1607 = 'a cuckold'.

1509 Barclay *Shyp of Folys* 212 [Let] James of Scotlande ..haue the forwarde, haue ye no disdayne Nor indignation, for neuer kynge was borne, That of ought of warre can shewe the vnycorne. **1592** G. Harvey *Four Lett.* 52 The only Vnicorne of the Muses. **1607** Dekker *Northw. Hoe* IV. Fj b, Fetherstone..it seemes makes her husband a vnicorne. **1826** Galt *Last of Lairds* vi. 53 Bridle the unicorn o' your impatience.

† **d.** Horn reputed to be that of the unicorn prepared as an embellishment or ornament. *Obs.*

a **1533** Ld. Berners *Gold. Bk. M. Aurel.* (1559) Y ij b, It was of wood Libanus, and round about garnished with unicorne. **1599** Peele *David & Bethsabe* H ij, Shee that in chaines of pearle and vnicorne, Leads at her traine the ancient golden world.

2. A figure, picture, or representation of this animal, esp. in *Her.* either as a charge or more usually as a supporter of the Royal Arms of Great Britain (or Scotland).

Usually depicted heraldically as having the head, neck, and body of a horse, the legs of a deer and the tail of a lion, with a straight and spirally twisted horn growing out of the forehead.

c **1400** *Emaré* 164 The fayr mayden her by-forn Was portrayed an vnykorn, Wyth hys horn so hye. **1488** *Acc. Ld. High Treas. Scot.* I. 85 A couering..browdin with thrissillis and a vnicorne. **1549** in Gage *Hengrave* (1822) 127, iij cuppes with a cover chased, with unicorns on the top. **1610** Guillim *Heraldry* VI. vii. 280 Supported by a Lion..and an Vnicorne Luna, gorged with a Crowne. **1766** in Seton *Law Her. Scotland* (1863) 442 His Majesty's royal coat-of-arms supported on the right side by a unicorn with an imperial crown over the head. **1789** Mrs. Piozzi *Journ. France*, etc. II. 221 The family crest, a unicorn, made in white marble. **1813** *Gentl. Mag.* LXXXIII. 37/2 With supporters (lion and unicorn) of the Royal arms. **1875** W. McIlwraith *Guide Wigtownshire* 55 Here is an escutcheon bearing two unicorns and a lion rampant and the crown.

3. *Sc.* The specific designation of one of the pursuivants of the court of the Lyon King of Arms. See PURSUIVANT 1.

1445 *Exchequer Rolls Scot.* V. 204 Quia Unicorn signifer regis illam terram habuit ex concessione regis. **1473-4** *Acc. Ld. High Treas. Scot.* I. 52 Item gevin to Vnicorne herald, ..to his expensis, x li. **1546** *Ibid.* IX. 33 To Petir Thomson, alias Unicorne pursevant. **1636** *Reg. Privy Council Scot.* Ser. II. VI. 605 The deceased George Wast, Unicorn pursuivant. **1662** *Ibid.* Ser. III. I. 259 Leyes..was charged by William Malcolm, Unicorn pursuivant, to compear this day. **1742** Nisbet *Syst. Heraldry* II. IV. xvi. 171 As for Pursevants, they are also for most Part locally denominate, Unicorn only excepted. **1863** Seton *Law Her. Scotland* 38 As in the case of the Heralds, the Pursuivants are also six in number, and bear the names of Kintyre, Dingwall, Carrick, Bute, Ormond, and Unicorn.

4. A Scottish gold coin current in the 15th and 16th centuries at the value of 18 shillings Scots; so called from the figure of the unicorn stamped upon its obverse. Also ***half unicorn***. Now *Hist.*

1487 *Exchequer Rolls Scot.* IX. 549 In denariis aureis vocatis unicornys. **1500-20** Dunbar *Poems* lxvi. 78 Vpon the heid of it is hecht Bayth unicornis, and crownis of wecht. **1538** *Aberd. Reg.* XVI. (Jam.), Ane vnicorn gud & sufficient gold. **1845** Lindsay *Coinage Scot.* 137 The Unicorns generally weigh about fifty-eight grains,..the half Unicorns in proportion. **1887** E. BURNS *Coinage Scotl.* II. 151 The coinages of unicorns that took place under James V.

†**b.** Used *attrib.* as the designation of a weight, equivalent to about one-eighth of an ounce troy.

1506 *Extr. Aberdeen Reg.* (1844) I. 434 Ane corss of gold, weyand half ane unce, and half ane unicorn weicht. **1560** *St. Giles Charters* (1859) p. xlvii, Foure vnce, ane half, and ane vnicorne weicht of gold.

5. *Astr.* A southern constellation lying between Canis Minor and Canis Major.

This constellation was noted by Hevelius in his *Prodromus Astron.* (1690) pp. 118, 294, under the name of *Monoceros*.

1771 *Encycl. Brit.* I. 487/2 Hevelius's Constellations made out of the unformed Stars [include]..*Monocerus*, The Unicorn. **1868** LOCKYER *Guillemin's Heavens* (ed. 3) 382 The northern half of the Milky Way extends..to the Unicorn at the altitude of and near the belt of Orion.

6. A carriage, coach, etc., drawn by three horses, two abreast and one leader; hence usually, a team of three horses so arranged. (Cf. 11 b.)

1785 GROSE *Dict. Vulgar T.*, *Unicorn*, a coach drawn by three horses. **1800** MAR. EDGEWORTH *Belinda* xvi, She drove in her unicorn to Oakly-park. **1866** FREEMAN in *Life & Lett.* (1895) I. 342, I would put on the children's pony..in front of my two, so as to make an unicorn. **1889** *Evening News* 28 Aug 3/2 Their demands of 24*s.* for a single horse, 28*s.* for a pair, and 30*s.* for a 'unicorn'.

transf. **1860** R. F. BURTON *Centr. Afr.* xiii. II. 38 We crossed as usual on a 'unicorn' of negroids, the upper part of the body supported by two men, and the feet resting upon the shoulders of a third. **1887** *Cyclists' Tour. Cl. Gaz.* May 215/1 The unicorn..is made up of a[n]..ordinary bicycle front-wheel coupled to a..sociable.

b. Quasi-*adv.*

1859 *Habits of Gd. Society* v. 200 You will seldom be called upon to drive tandem, unicorn, or four in hand. **1863** MISS BRADDON *Aurora Floyd* v, There were more lofty accomplishments than driving unicorn or shooting..game.

II. †**7.** The one-horned rhinoceros. *Obs.*

1398 TREVISA *Barth. De P.R.* XIV. ix. (Bodl. MS.), [In] þat londe [*sc.* Ethiopia] beþ..þe rynocerota þat is þe vnicorne, a beste wiþ oon horne. *a* **1700** EVELYN *Diary* 22 Oct. 1684, I went..to see the Rhinoceros, or Unicorn, being the first that I suppose was ever brought into England.

8. As the name of a fish, shell, etc., having a projecting horn or horn-like process, or regarded as resembling the fabulous unicorn in some other respect. Cf. MONOCEROS 2 and 4.

A few examples other than those illustrated here are recorded in American Dicts. from 1891 onwards.

†**a.** (See quot.) *Obs.*

1668 CHARLETON *Onomast.* 123 *Monoceros Clusii*, the little Vnicorn, or Sawfish.

b. The narwhal or sea-unicorn.

Named also *unicorn-fish*, *-whale*, and abbrev. UNIE.

1694 *Marten's Voy. Spitzbergen* in *Acc. Sev. Late Voy.* II. 126 The Unicorn is but seldom seen in these parts. **1745** tr. *Egede's Descr. Greenland* 76 Among the different Kinds of Whales, some reckon the Unicorn, as they commonly call him,..but his right Name is Nar-Whale. **1823** W. SCORESBY *Jrnl.* 39 Here we saw a considerable number of 'unicorns' (narwals).

c. A unicorn-shell. (See 11.)

c **1711** PETIVER *Gazophyl.* VI. liii, Grass girdled Indian Unicorn, Cat. 263. A beautiful Shell and rarely met with.

9. *Zool.* A species having one horn.

1822 J. PARKINSON *Outl. Oryctol.* 312 There appear to be three existing species of rhinoceroses:—1. That of India: a unicorn;..—2. That of the Cape: a bicorn.

III. 10. *attrib.* and *Comb.*, as ***unicorn bone*** (i.e. horn), ***horse***, ***-ivory***; ***-crested***, ***-like*** adjs.

1477 EARL RIVERS (Caxton) *Dictes* D iv, Ther is summe contre that a litil yuory or vnycorne bone is bought for a grete somme of gold. **1838** *Penny Cycl.* XII. 306/1 The..Onager, figured..with a unicorn-like horn in the midst of its forehead. **1843** *Ibid.* XXVI. 3 Strabo..refers to Unicorn horses with the heads of deer. **1853** R. S. SURTEES *Sponge's Sp. Tour* xlix, The unicorn-crested gates, with tea-caddy looking lodges. **1856** KANE *Arct. Expl.* II. xiv. 141 The natives carried no arms but the long knife and their unicorn-ivory lances.

11. Special combs., chiefly in the names of animals, birds, fishes, plants, etc., which are characterized by a long projecting horn-like process or spine regarded as resembling the horn of the unicorn: **unicorn acanthurus** (see quot. and UNICORN-FISH *c*); **unicorn auk** (see quot.); **unicorn-bird**, the horned screamer, *Palamedea cornuta*; **unicorn file-fish** (see quot.); †**unicorn guard** *Fencing*, a guard in which the sword is advanced well to the front of the fencer; **unicorn hawk (-moth)**, **hornbill** (see quots.); **unicorn-moth**, the North American moth, *Cœlodasys unicornis*; **unicorn narwhal**, = sense 8 b; **unicorn-plant** *U.S.*, a name for various North American plants, esp. *Martynia proboscidea*, the capsule of which terminates in two horn-like spines; **unicorn-root** *U.S.* (see quots.); **unicorn-shell**, a marine gasteropod having a horn-like lip projecting from the shell, now esp. one belonging to the genus *Monoceros*; **unicorn whale**, = sense 8 b.

1803 SHAW *Gen. Zool.* IV. 374 *Unicorn Acanthurus. *Acanthurus Unicornis*... From the front proceeds a strong, conical, horn-shaped process. **1884** COUES *North Amer. Birds* 805 *Ceratorhina monocerata*. *Unicorn Auk. Horn-bill Auk. **1681** GREW *Musæum* I. §iv. ii. 65 The *Unicorne Bird [is]..Horned on his Forehead (with some likeness) as the Unicorne is pictur'd. **1863** BATES *Nat. Amazon* I. 277 The Curicáca..was soon joined by a unicorn bird..; whose harsh screams [etc.]. **1804** SHAW *Gen. Zool.* V. II. 399 *Unicorn File-fish. *Balistes Monoceros*... Immediately over the head..is a very strong..spine of considerable length. **1617** J. SWETNAM *Sch. Sci. Defence* 126 An other very sure and dangerous guard at the Backe-sword, called the *Vnicorne guard, or the fore-hand guard. **1711** WYLDE *Eng. Master Defence* 23 The Medium Unicorn or Center Guard, is made thus. **1832** J. RENNIE *Consp. Butterfl. & M.* 24 The *Unicorn Hawk (*Sphinx Convolvuli*, Linnæus) appears in September. **1834** T. BROWN *Butterflies & Moths* I. 96 Two fine males of the *Sphinx Convolvuli* (Unicorn Hawk-moth). **1811** SHAW *Gen. Zool.* VIII. II *Unicorn Hornbill. [*Buceros Monoceros*.].. The casque is prolonged in front into a kind of horn. **1891** *Cent. Dict.* s.v., Larva of *Unicorn-moth. **1813** BINGLEY *Anim. Biog.* (ed. 4) II. 1 The *Unicorn Narwal, or Sea Unicorn. **1796** MORSE *Amer. Geog.* I. 189 *Unicorn [plant] (*Aletris farinosa*). **1845–50** MRS. LINCOLN *Lect. Bot.* II. 110/1 *Helonias diœcia*, scape leafy... Unicorn plant. **1847** DARLINGTON *Amer. Weeds*, etc. (1860) 222 *M. proboscidea*..Long-beaked Martynia. Unicorn Plant. **1891** H. HERMAN *His Angel* 6 Woodbine, unicorn plant, and wild currant surged all about it. **1846** A. WOOD *Class-bk. Bot.* (1850) 559 *Helonias dioica*, Ph. (*Veratrum luteum*. Linn.) *Unicorn Root. **1847** WEBSTER, *Unicorn-root*, a popular name of two plants, viz. *Chamælirium Carolinianum* [= *Helonias dioica*], to which this name was first applied, and *Aletris farinosa*..; both used in medicine. **1891** *Cent. Dict.*, *Unicorn-root*, the blazing star, *Aletris farinosa*. *c* **1711** PETIVER *Gazophyl.* VI. lv, A *Unicorn Shell with Bugle Twirls. *Ibid.* VIII. lxxv, Small Unicorn-shell, with rugged Twirls and Waves between. **1888** *Cassell's Encycl. Dict.*, *Monoceros*,..Unicorn-shell; a genus of prosobranchiate gasteropods..peculiar to the west coast of America. **1668** CHARLETON *Onomast.* 168 *Balæna Monoceros*, *Vnicornu Marinum*,..the *Vnicorn Whale. **1694** *Acc. Sev. Late Voy.* p. xix, The Monoceros or Unicorn Whale. **1858** BAIRD *Cycl. Nat. Sci.* 199/1 The..unicorn whale, *Monodon Monoceros*, has no teeth in the lower jaw.

b. Attrib. in sense 6, as ***unicorn carman***, ***fashion***, ***omnibus*** (attrib.), ***team***.

1856 MORTON *Cycl. Agric.* II. 726 A unicorn team is two abreast and one in front. **1877** 'C. BEDE' *Figaro at Hastings* 47 Some [wagonettes] with four horses, some with three (unicorn fashion). **1884** 'R. BOLDREWOOD' *Melb. Mem.* i. 14 Frank Liardet is driving his unicorn omnibus team from the lonely beach. **1898** *Westm. Gaz.* 6 Sept. 1/3 A 'unicorn carman'..means 'one who drives three horses'.

†**12.** Passing into *adj.* Made a unicorn or cuckold (cf. sense 1 c above). *Obs.*$^{-1}$

1603 DEKKER *Wonderfull Yeare* E 4 The vnicorne cobler being ouer head and eares in sleepe.

unicorn-fish. [Cf. UNICORN 8 b.] The narwhal or sea-unicorn, *Monodon monoceros*.

1688 R. HOLME *Armory* IV. vii. (Roxb.) 324/1 For his Supporters he beareth a vnicorne fish, Argent, the fish or taile part, Azure: Horne, Hoofes, and finns, Or. **1752** J. HILL *Hist. Anim.* 314 Monodon. The Unicorn-fish, or Narwal. **1773** *Gentl. Mag.* XLIII. 220 The Jackulator Fish, the Unicorn Fish, the Trumpet Fish. **1812** J. WALKER *Ess. Nat. Hist.* 527 *Monodon Monoceros*. Linn... Scot. Unicorn Fish. **1860** WRAXALL *Life in Sea* i. 12 The Narwhal, or Unicorn-fish, attains a length of twenty or twenty-five feet.

b. (See quots.)

1876 GOODE *Fishes of Bermudas* 17 The Bahama Unicorn-Fish is *Alutera scripta*. **1900** *Nature* 21 June 182/2 An example of the rare unicorn-fish (*Lophotes cepedianus*) from the Cape of Good Hope.

c. One or other of various fishes belonging to the genus *Acanthurus*. (Webster, 1911.)

uni'cornic, *a. rare.* [f. prec. + -IC.] Resembling, having the form of, a unicorn.

1881 R. BROWN *Unicorn* 14 A unicornic animal frequently appears in archaic art. **1885** —— in *Academy* 28 Nov. 363/2 The familiar conventional unicornic representation.

uni'cornous, *a. rare.* [f. L. *ūnicorn-is* (see UNICORN) + -OUS.] Having but one horn.

1646 SIR T. BROWNE *Pseud. Ep.* v. xix. 261 The Rhinoceros, the Indian Asse, and the Unicornous Beetles. [Hence in Blount, Phillips, Bailey, etc.]

unicorn's horn. Also †unicorn horn. [See UNICORN 1.]

1. A horn regarded as or alleged to be obtained from the legendary unicorn, but in reality that of the rhinoceros, narwhal, or other animal, freq. mounted or made into a drinking cup and employed as a preventive of or charm against poison.

α. **1451** *Lincoln Diocese Doc.* (1914) 51 A ryng of vnicorn horne. **1555** *Reg. Gild Co. Chr. York* (1872) 207, I give to Sir Thomas Chaloner, knyghte, my unicorn horne. *c* **1650** *Invent. Goods Chas. I* in Pegge *Curalia* (1806) IV. 122 An unicorn horn.

β. **1549** THOMAS *Hist. Italie* 80 b, Two fayre vnicornes hornes. **1564** BULLEYN *Dial. agst. Pest.* 74 A pece of a Unicornes horne, good against poison. **1603** LODGE *Treat. Plague* Wks. (Hunter. Cl.) IV. 61 The horne of that beast which..the simple sorte [call] vnicornes horne. **1687** *Lond. Gaz.* No. 2227/4 There will be exposed to Sale.. considerable quantities of Drugs, Colours, and Unicorns Horns. **1728** CHAMBERS *Cycl.* s.v., What ordinarily passes among us for Unicorn's Horn,..we are assured by Pereyra ..to be the Tooth of a large Fish of the Whale Kind. **1838** PRESCOTT *Ferd. & Is.* I. vii. 383 He is said to have kept a reputed unicorn's horn always on his table.

b. Narwhal's horn.

1856 KANE *Arct. Expl.* I. 412 A shaft of unicorn's horn.

†**2.** The material of this powdered or prepared as a drug and used medicinally, esp. as an antidote against poison. *Obs.*

1590 E. WEBBE *Trav.* (Arb.) 35 Some lewde Gunners.. gaue me poyson in drinke..; his Phisition..gaue me speadely Unicorns horne to drinke. **1631** JORDEN *Nat. Bathes* vii. (1632) 44 This volatill salt..is commonly very Diaphoreticke: & this it is which makes our..supposed Vnicornes horne to be in such esteeme. **1698** *New Descr. Moscovy* 21 Likewise some use the Powder to Antedote Poison, as the Vnicorns horne; this I hold to be the same with the Morse.

3. *Bot.* (See quot.)

1864 *Chambers's Encycl.* VI. 393 The root of *Helonias dioica* is used..as an anthelmintic... The plant..is called Starwort and Blazing Star, also Unicorn's Horn. [Cf. *unicorn-plant*, *-root* s.v. UNICORN 11.]

‖**unicum** ('juːnɪkəm). [L., neut. sing. of *ūnic-us* UNIQUE *a.* So in G. and Du.] A unique example, specimen, or thing.

1885 *Daily Tel.* 14 July 5/3 Some picture, work of art, or old book, which is represented to him as being a 'unicum'. **1892** MRS. J. P. MORGAN tr. *Rubinstein's Conv. on Music* 26 The symphony in G minor (this *unicum* of symphonic-lyric).

unicursal (juːnɪ'kɜːsəl), *a.* and *sb. Math.* [f. UNI- 1 + L. *cursus* course: see -AL[1].] **a.** *adj.* Having, traversing, or being on one course or path. **b.** *sb.* A unicursal curve.

1866 CAYLEY in *Proc. London Math. Soc.* April, A unicursal curve is nothing else than a curve with a deficiency D = 0. **1871** —— *Math. Papers* (1895) VIII. 388 On the Transformation of Unicursal Surfaces. **1873** G. SALMON *Higher Plane Curves* ii. 29 If the coordinates can be expressed as rational functions of a parameter the curve has the maximum number of double points. Curves of this sort are called unicursal curves.

Hence **unicur'sality**; **uni'cursally** *adv.*

1887 *Amer. Jrnl. Math.* X. 24 In the unicursality-equation a cusp plays the role of an ordinary double-point. **1892** W. W. R. BALL *Math. Recreat.* 124 A figure is described unicursally when the whole of it is traversed in one route.

unicycle ('juːnɪsaɪk(ə)l). orig. *U.S.* [f. UNI- 2 + CYCLE, after *bicycle*, *tricycle*.] A vehicle or conveyance having only one wheel; esp. a monocycle used by acrobats or for gymnastic displays.

1869 *The Velocipede* (N.Y.) April 76 Hemmings' Unicycle or 'Flying Yankee Velocipede'. **1884** KNIGHT *Dict. Mech.* Suppl. 913/1 *Unicycle*, a one-wheeled vehicle for propulsion by foot-power. **1897** *Wheelist Ann.* 15 It's all been so slow at Slochester Park, That of fun or of frolic I've not seen a spark, Until yesterday week, when we had a rare treat: The first *rocking-horse* and *unicycle* meet. **1978** J. IRVING *World according to Garp* vi. 123 There's no *tradition* of bears on unicycles here. *Ibid.* 127 The sullen animal unicycling in the lunatic's left-behind clothes. *Ibid.* 128 Even his one talent, unicycling, was irretrievable. **1980** *Radio Times* 23–29 Feb. 10/1 He rejects the 'pure' dumbshow of performers like Marcel Marceau, preferring to mix..verbal humour, video, the odd spot of unicycling, and mask work.

Hence as *v. intr.*, to ride on a unicycle; **'unicycling** *vbl. sb.*; **'unicyclist**, one who rides a unicycle.

1881 *Sells Bros. Show-Bill*, Celebrated Russian Bicyclists, Unicyclists, and Roller Skaters.

uni'deaed, *a.* Also unidea'd. [UN-[1] 9.] Not furnished with an idea.

1752 JOHNSON in *Boswell* (1904) I. 166 Leaving his social friends, to go and sit with a set of wretched un-idea'd girls. **1822** SCOTT *Peveril* xxvii, A silly scrupulous unidea'd Puritan. **1888** *Jrnl. Educ.* May 242 The un-idea'd vulgarity of the lower middle classes.

uni'deal, *a.* [UN-[1] 7.]

†**1.** Of sounds or words: Expressing or conveying no idea. *Obs.*

1751 JOHNSON *Rambler* No. 184 ¶12 However we amuse ourselves with unideal sounds. **1792** W. ROBERTS *Looker-On* No. 23 (1794) I. 324 A language..rich in the unideal terms of a raving philosophy.

†**2.** Destitute of, lacking in, ideas. *Obs.*

1751 JOHNSON *Rambler* No. 135 ¶9 A short relief from the tediousness of unideal vacancy. **1801** *Phil. Trans.* XCI. 91 Un-ideal operations conducted without principle, purpose, or regularity.

3. Having or following no ideal.

1760 D. WEBB *Beauties of Painting* iv. 68 Those servile and unideal painters. **1856** EMERSON *Eng. Traits, Lit.* Wks. (Bohn) II. 113 The scholars have become un-ideal. They parry earnest speech with banter and levity. **1867** F. HARRISON *Choice of Bks.* (1886) 110 To be fierce is to be un-ideal, to be unideal is to be sanguinary.

4. Not marked by idealism; having no ideal character or features, etc.

1838 E. FITZGERALD *Let.* 8 June (1979) 26 The best painter of the unideal Christ is, I think, Rembrandt. **1846** RUSKIN *Mod. Paint.* II. III. xiii. §2 Unideal works of art.. represent actual existing things. **1873** SPENCER *Stud. Sociol.* ix. (1877) 222 Instead of our practice being unideal, the ideas which guide it verge on the romantic. **1877** L. MORRIS *Epic Hades* III. 276 The bare And unideal aspect of the fields Which Spring not yet had kissed.

uni'dealism, -ist. (UN-[1] 12.)

Also, in recent use, *unidealistic* adj.

1870 J. GROTE *Exam. Utilit. Phil.* xvii. 273 Utilitarianism may be..either of an idealist or unidealist type. **1888** W. S. LILLY *Right & Wrong* (1890) iv. 121 The singular unidealism..of the English mind in respect of eternal and divine things.

uni'dentified, *ppl. a.* [UN-[1] 8.] That has not been identified; of which the identity has not been established; esp. as ***unidentified (flying) object***: cf. UFO.)

1860 R. NOEL in *Vac. Tour.* 467 The site of a town or village unidentified presented itself within incredibly short distances. **1867** LATHAM *Black & White* 68 Of these graves 138,901 will be nameless and unidentified. **1950** *Chambers's*

Jrnl. Nov. 668/1 Project Saucer revealed that it had analysed 375 incidents of 'unidentified flying objects'. **1954** 'R. CRANE' *Hero's Walk* v. 81 Five unidentified objects were discovered last night..flying..in the direction of Earth. **1966** *New Scientist* 14 Apr. 87/1 Community after community observed unidentified flying objects. There were the inevitable sightings by police. **1976** L. DEIGHTON *Twinkle, twinkle, Little Spy* i. 11 The strictly infra dig. pastime of looking for unidentified flying objects, or what the sci-fi freaks call ufology.

un,idio'matic, *a.* (UN-[1] 7.)
a **1822** SHELLEY *Pr. Wks.* (1888) I. 395 The clear, and exact, but unidiomatic phrases of their native language. **1855** PUSEY *Doctr. Real Presence* 153 The interpretation of Bellarmin is inconsistent and unidiomatic. **1891** DRIVER *Introd. Lit. O. Test.* 445 An author who..translated the Aramaic idiom..into unidiomatic Hebrew.

unidi'rectional, *a.* [f. UNI- 1 + DIRECTIONAL *a.*] Having or being motion in one direction; operating or functional in one direction only.
1883 *Knowledge* 13 July 25/2 Intermittent, unidirectional currents in the brushes. **1894** *Athenæum* 9 June 745/3 Note on the Possibility of obtaining a Unidirectional Current to Earth from the Mains of an Alternating Current System. **1946** *Nature* 9 Nov. 674/2 The simplified apparatus was.. actuated by unidirectional air flow. **1955** O. G. SUTTON *Sci. of Flight* 36 The effect is to give an additional but unidirectional motion to the molecules of air. **1961** A. NISBETT *Technique Sound Studio* i. 23 Cardioids—sometimes called unidirectional microphones—have a heart-shaped response. **1962** Y. MALKIEL in Householder & Saporta *Probl. Lexicogr.* 13 The kernel of Howell's ..*Lexicon tetraglotton* (1660) is a unidirectional dictionary providing for the translation of each English entry into French, Italian, and Spanish. **1971** I. G. GASS et al. *Understanding Earth* xiii. 174/2 The uni-directional flow of rivers is complicated by the development of meanders. **1975** *Sci. Amer.* Mar. 36/1 For years psychologists have been concerned with the effectiveness of unidirectional modes of communication such as highway signs, books, lectures and television programs. **1983** *Trans. Philol. Soc.* 6 The impression that [linguistic] evolution is neat, continual and unidirectional is a mirage. **1984** *What Video?* Aug. 59/1, 1·5 in. electronic viewfinder, unidirectional mike *but* it is heavy.
Hence **,unidirectio'nality; unidi'rectionally** *adv.*
1958 W. D. KINGERY *Ceramic Fabrication Processes* viii. 70/2 A much more suitable method is to apply pressure from all sides instead of unidirectionally. **1960** A. C. SPAULDING in Dole & Carneiro *Essays in Science of Culture* 454 Unidirectionality of formal changes through time is simply the idea of cultural evolution. **1968** *Science* 21 June 1365/3 The unidirectionality observation..may be placed in correspondence with certain findings concerning functional neuroanatomy of OKN [*sc.* optokinetic nystagmus]. **1970** *Proc. I.E.E.E.* Aug. 1252/1 Unidirectionality increases transducer conversion efficiency by 3 dB. **1976** *Nature* 10 June 516/1 Replication..proceeds either unidirectionally or bidirectionally away from this site. **1980** *English World-Wide* I. 1. 16 If there was initially unresolved conflict at the level of decision-making this lack of unidirectionality can be expected to re-emerge at the implementation stage.

un'idle, *a.* [UN-[1] 7.] Busy, industrious.
a **1586** SIDNEY *Astr. & Stella* Sonn. xxvi. (Qo.[2]), For me, I doe Nature vnydle know. **1604** MARSTON *Malcontent* v. iii, Is he not a pretty dapper unydle gallant?

†uni'dolatrize, *v. Obs.*[−1] (UN-[2] 6 c.)
1659 FULLER *App. Inj. Innoc.* I. 55 The Animadvertor.. endeavouring to un-idolatrize the Brittains as much as he could.

uni'dolatrous, *a.* (UN-[1] 7.)
1841 WISEMAN *Remarks on Lett. Palmer* 6 To substitute an idolatrous, for an unidolatrous, worship. **1881** *19th Cent.* No. 49. 502 The two religions..were both nominally monotheistic, and both unidolatrous.

unie ('juːnɪ), abbrev. of UNICORN 8 b.
1874 A. H. MARKHAM *Whaling Cruise Baffin's B.* 137 A couple of narwhals, or as they are called by the whalers, 'unies' (unicorn abbreviated). **1878** —— *Gt. Frozen Sea* v. 67 Another source of amusement..was chasing 'unies'.

unie, *v.*: see UNY *v.*

unific (jʊ'nɪfɪk), *a.* [ad. L. type *ūnificus*: see UNI- and -FIC.] That unifies or unites; producing unity.
1788 T. TAYLOR *Proclus* I. 118 A power collective of divisible natures, and unific of such as are multiplied. **1841** *Fraser's Mag.* XXIII. 130 The centre of unific power is the invisible. **1861** *Q. Rev.* CX. 394 That so-called unific principle..by which we are impelled to reduce all that we see and hear to unity. **1877** FARRAR *Days of Youth* xi. 105 The unific rectitude of a manly life.

unification (juːnɪfɪ'keɪʃən). [f. UNIFY *v.* (see -ATION), or a. F. *unification*, It. *unificazione*.]
1. The action or process of unifying or uniting; reduction to unity or to a uniform system; the result of this.
1851 GALLENGA *Italy* II. i. 25 The unification of Italy would thus be gradual and pacific. **1865** LECKY *Ration.* I. 231 A process of transformation or unification of religious ideas. **1880** E. KIRKE *Garfield* 46 The recent movement for the unification and preservation of nations.
2. *Comb.* **Unification Church**, an evangelistic religious and political organization (see quot. 1973) founded in 1954 in Korea by Sun Myung Moon, and subsequently known as a cult religion in the U.S. and elsewhere. Its adherents are sometimes contemptuously called *Moonies.*
1973 *Time* 15 Oct. 129/3 By 1954 he had founded the Holy Spirit Association for the Unification of World Christianity—known more simply as the Unification Church. **1975** *Americana Ann.* 481/1 A..group in Korea, called the Unification Church, claiming Christian origins and suggesting Messianic status for its leader, the Rev. Sun.. Moon, engaged in evangelistic work in the United States. **1976** *Daily Colonist* (Victoria, B.C.) 18 Mar. 7/2 The fringe religious groups include..Unification Church, [etc.]. **1979** *Minutes Gen. Synod House of Bishops* 3 May 4 The Archbishop of York made a statement..relating to the Unification Church.
Hence **unifi'cationist** *sb.* and *a.*; **'unificator**, a unifier; **unifi'catory** *a.*, tending to unify.
1870 *Contemp. Rev.* XV. 400 The people..proclaimed them in anticipation the 'unificators' of Italy. *a* **1897** W. WALLACE *Lect.* (1898) 84 The monistic, if that means the unificatory, instinct is irresistible. **1909-** Unificationist *sb.* and *a.* [listed in *N.E.D.* (1926) as having 'had some slight currency in recent use']. **1932** W. T. STACE *Theory of Knowl.* vii. 156 The other chief logical character of unificatory constructions is that they..are simply serviceable fictions. **1971** A. KIRK-GREENE in J. Spencer *Eng. Lang. W. Afr.* 143 In Nigeria, Hausa..played the same unificatory role until its use was forbidden..during the 1939–45 war.

unified ('juːnɪfaɪd), *ppl. a.* [f. UNIFY *v.* + -ED[1].]
1. a. That is or has been made into one from separate parts; united, combined, consolidated.
1862 F. HALL *Hindu Philos. Syst.* 178 The residual part.. he is to consider as unified. **1882** *Standard* 30 Dec. 2/2 The Unified Debt fell about 18*l.* **1883** *Fortn. Rev.* July 107 After the whole metropolis is under a unified authority.
b. Used absolutely or as *sb.*
1883 *Pall Mall G.* 30 Nov. 5/2 Egyptian Unifieds continued to rise yesterday. **1884** *Academy* 2 Aug. 74/1 Unification is pleasant to the unifier only, not to the unified.
2. Special collocation. ***unified (field) theory*** (Physics): a field theory that describes two or more of the four interactions (orig. gravitation and electromagnetism) previously described by separate theories.
1935 E. A. MILNE *Relativity, Gravitation & World-Structure* i. 13 This view is in violent opposition to the demand for a 'unified field theory', a demand for further geometrical modification of the space used so as to be able to employ these modifications in describing electro-magnetic phenomena. **1959** *Listener* 26 Mar. 544/2 The first unified field theory was produced not by Einstein but by Hermann Weyl, in 1918. **1979** *New Scientist* 1 Mar. 667/2 QCD is a particularly favoured theory because it is very similar to the 'field theories' of the other forces in nature, and this would be a great help in formulating 'GUTs', the grand unified theories of the strong, weak and electromagnetic forces which currently challenge theorists. **1983** *Nature* 27 Jan. 285/2 Minimal SU(5), one of the simplest of the 'grand unified theories', or GUTs, which links all the non-gravitational forces.

unifier ('juːnɪfaɪə(r)). [f. as prec. + -ER.] One who or that which unifies or unites; one who advocates unification in administration.
1867 SPENCER *First Princ.* II. iii. §51 (ed. 2) 171 The derivative data needed by Philosophy as the unifier of Science. **1881** *Echo* 2 Feb. 1/6 The Great Victor Emmanuel, the liberator and unifier of Italy.

unifilar (juːnɪ'faɪlə(r)), *a.* [f. UNI- 1 + L. *fīl-us* thread: see -AR[1].] Of a magnetometer or other magnetic instrument: Having or suspended by a single thread or fibre.
1856 KANE *Arct. Expl.* I. xiv. 153 We had a good unifilar [magnetometer]. **1873** J. C. MAXWELL *Electr. & Magn.* II. 119 The Unifilar Declinometer. **1879** THOMSON & TAIT *Nat. Phil.* I. I. §435 In the unifilar torsion-balance.

unifilarly (juːnɪ'faɪləlɪ, -'fɪləlɪ), *adv. Biochem.* [f. as UNIFILAR *a.* + -LY[2].] In a single strand of a DNA duplex.
1974 *Nature* 13 Sept. 156/2 The unifilarly substituted chromatids fluoresced more brightly than the bifilarly substituted sister chromatids. **1980** *European Jrnl. Cell Biol.* XXII. 552 Unifilarly-substituted DNA.

uni'floral, *a.* [UNI- 1.] = UNIFLOROUS *a.*
1849 CRAIG. **1861** BENTLEY *Man. Bot.* 212 A series of single-flowered axes (unifloral) arranged in the form of a raceme.

uniflorous (juːnɪ'flɔərəs), *a. Bot.* [f. mod.L. *ūniflōr-us* (f. L. *ūn-us* UNI- + *flōr-*, *flōs* flower) + -OUS. Cf. F. *uniflore* (1753), Pg. *unifloro.*] Having or bearing only one flower.
1760 [see MULTIFLOROUS *a.*]. **1800** *Asiatic Ann. Reg.* 299/1 The hermaphrodite calyx is sometimes biflorous,.. sometimes uniflorous. **1881** *Jrnl. Linn. Soc.* XVIII. 353 Distinguished..by its unifoliate uniflorous stem.

uniflow ('juːnɪfləʊ), *a.* Also **una-** (now *rare*). [f. UNI- 2 + FLOW *sb.*[1]] Involving flow in one direction only; *spec.* applied to: (*a*) a type of reciprocating steam engine in which the steam in the cylinder flows in one direction from inlet(s) to outlet; (*b*) scavenging in an internal-combustion engine in which there is a similar flow of waste gases in the cylinder. Also *ellipt.*, a uniflow steam engine.
1912 tr. *J. Stumpf's Una-Flow Steam-Engine* i. 1 Unaflow engines..may be made with a single expansion stage. **1913** G. F. GEBHARDT *Steam Power Plant Engin.* (ed. 4) ix. 379 A 20 × 30, 200 horse-power Nordberg uniflow engine using very wet steam. **1942** L. B. CHAPMAN *Marine Power Plan* (ed. 2) v. 127 The unaflow engine has been widely used for stationary work in both Europe and the United States. **1949** C. W. CHAPMAN *Mod. High-Speed Oil Engines* I. xi. 95 There are three main systems employed: cross scavenging, loop scavenging and uniflow scavenging. **1963** H. W. DICKINSON *Short Hist. Steam Engine* (ed. 2) viii. 156 The uniflow engine is a gallant attempt on the part of the reciprocating engine-makers to hold the field against the advance of the turbo-alternator and the electrical drive. **1963** R. R. A. HIGHAM *Handbk. Papermaking* vii. 184 Contraflow vat. This vat is similar in construction to the uniflow type. **1971** G. WATKINS *Textile Mill Engine* II. 74 The gearing of the waterwheel was destroyed by grit in a flood, and the uniflow then drove the whole until the mill was closed. **1981** BURGHARDT & KINGSLEY *Marine Diesels* iv. 62 Figure 4–8(d), illustrating an opposed piston engine, is another method of uniflow scavenging.

†'unifoil. *Obs.*[−0] [f. UNI- + FOIL *sb.*[1]] The plant one-blade, *Smilacina bifolia.*
1688 R. HOLME *Armoury* II. 58/1 He beareth Argent, an Unifoile Vert... Vnifoile or Vnfall. This is an Herb that never hath more then one leaf from a Root,..it is also called one blade. [Hence in Berry *Encycl. Her.* (*c* 1828), Elvin (1889), and in some recent Dicts. as a bearing in Heraldry.]

uniform ('juːnɪfɔːm), *sb.* [f. the adj. Cf. F., It., Sp., and Pg. *uniforme*, Du., G., Sw., and Da. *uniform* in sense 2.]
†I. 1. ***in uniform***, in one body or flock. *Obs.*
1623 LISLE *Ælfric on O. & N. Test.* Ded. p. ix, Our sheepe shall feare no Wolfe, or suddaine storme; But goe and come all safe in vniforme.
II. 2. a. A distinctive dress of uniform cut, materials, and colour worn by all the members of a particular naval, military, or other force to which it is recognized as properly belonging and peculiar.
1748 in *Jrnl. Archæol. Soc.* (1847) II. 79 That no commission-officer or midshipmen do presume to wear any other uniform than what properly belongs to his rank. **1760** *Cautions & Adv. to Officers of Army* 123 You are..to consider what is to be furnished out of this last Sum, and that is your Regimentals or Uniform. **1802** JAMES *Milit. Dict.* s.v., Scarlet is the national uniform of the British army. *Ibid.*, Generally speaking each [corps] has an uniform within itself, yet this uniform, strictly considered, is a regimental. **1837** DICKENS *Pickw.* iv, Colonel Bulder, in full military uniform, on horseback. **1879** *Cassell's Techn. Educ.* III. 363 Insisting that none shall fight who do not wear the uniform of one of the armies engaged.
fig. **1768–74** TUCKER *Lt. Nat.* (1834) II. 121 Passion so commonly marches under the colours and in the uniform of reason,..that [etc.].
b. A distinctive uniform dress worn by the members of any civilian body or association of persons.
1837 DICKENS *Pickw.* ii, The proposed uniform, sir, of the Pickwick Club. **1885** 'MRS. ALEXANDER' *At Bay* i, A good-looking boy in the polytechnique uniform. **1897** HALL CAINE *Christian* x, The girls were nearly all nurses, and they wore their nurse's uniform.
c. A single suit of this kind. †Also *pl.*, the separate garments composing this.
1783 *Ann. Reg., Chron.* 193/2 Such flag officers, however, as were provided with the uniforms were permitted to wear the same. **1814** SCOTT *Wav.* xvii, He had laid aside the Highland dress for the time, to put on an old blue and red uniform. **1834** MARRYAT *P. Simple* xxxviii, That is the reason why my uniforms are so shabby. I spoilt them then.
d. *transf.* The customary dress or mode of appearance characteristic of persons of a certain age, class, or lifestyle.
1930 G. B. SHAW *Apple Cart* I. 13 (*Pointing to his blouse.*) *Boanerges.* The uniform of Labor, your Royal Highness. **1967** *Listener* 17 Aug. 197/3 One day one had one's hair flopping down one's back, short skirts which barely cleared the knee. (Ironically that's the uniform of grown-ups nowadays, isn't it?) **1976** 'D. FLETCHER' *Don't whistle 'Macbeth'* 37 The discreet beads, the silver bracelet,..court shoes..were identical with the uniform of hundreds of women..of the middle class.
3. a. A person wearing a uniform. *rare.*
1786 MME. D'ARBLAY *Diary* Oct., I opened the eating-room door,..but saw to my surprise a party of uniforms. **1900** J. K. JEROME *Three Men on Bummel* ix. 208, I believe there is a heavy fine for joking with any German uniform. **1970** G. JACKSON *Let.* 24 Mar. in *Soledad Brother* (1971) 189 If a uniform denied some small request, we would take it to the counselor.
b. Short for *uniform branch* (see below).
1978 F. BRANSTON *Sergeant Ritchie's Conscience* i. 13 'Spoken to the Chief?' he said... 'Uniform have done that,' guessed Ritchie.
4. *attrib.* **a.** In the sense 'pertaining to, forming (part of) a uniform', as ***uniform case, clothes, coat.***
In some instances not clearly distinguishable from the adj. Cf. UNIFORM *a.* 2 c.
1807 P. GASS *Jrnl.* 188 We got a canoe from the natives, for which we gave an officer's uniform coat. **1825** in J. A. Heraud *Voy. Midshipm.* (1837) x. 179 Buy your..uniform clothes (two jackets and one coat) in London. **1852** THACKERAY *Esmond* II. xiii, An officer in a green uniform coat. **1889** HISSEY *Tour in Phaeton* 399 We pack our personal belongings in tin uniform cases.
b. In the sense 'wearing uniform; uniformed'; *spec.* in the police force, distinguished from the plain-clothes section, esp. in ***uniform branch.***
1895 *Westm. Gaz.* 1 Jan. 4/3 Several uniform policemen watched the prosecutor and prisoners. **1938** F. D. SHARPE *Sharpe of Flying Squad* i. 15, I don't wish to detract from the valuable work carried out by the Uniform Section..but.. the Flying Squad plays a leading part in this work. **1970** P. LAURIE *Scotland Yard* ii. 51 The school also provides instructors to train uniform officers. **1972** *Police Rev.* 17 Nov. 1509/1, I would like to express my gratitude..for the efforts of both the C.I.D. and the uniform branch to deal

with crime. **1980** P. G. WINSLOW *Counsellor Heart* ii. 41 Uniform Branch have had complaints of noise... Late parties.

uniform ('juːnɪfɔːm), *a.* Also 6 vnifourme, 6–8 uniforme. [a. F. *uniforme* (14th c. in Godef., = It., Sp., Pg. *uniforme*), or ad. L. *ūniform-is*: see UNI- and FORM.]

I. Of things in respect to their own qualities or constitution.

1. Of one form, character, or kind; having, maintaining, occurring in or under, the same form always; that is or remains the same in different places, at different times, or under varying circumstances; exhibiting no difference, diversity, or variation.

1540 PALSGR. *Acolastus* A ij, One selfe and vniforme maner of teachynge of all those Grammaticalle ensygnementes. **1555** WATREMAN *Fardle Facions* I. v. 72 The ordre of Mariage emong the Egiptians is not vniforme. **1601** HOLLAND *Pliny* I. 161 This impression, that maketh either the foresaid uniforme likenesse, or confusion and varietie. **1662** *Extr. St. Papers Friends* Ser. II. (1911) 150 Wee would be glad that all our Subjects could be brought to agree in a uniforme Worship of God. **1710** PRIDEAUX *Orig. Tithes* ii. 127 From whence else should they have such a Uniform Usage but by a Uniform Tradition from them? **1780** BENTHAM *Princ. Legisl.* xiv. §1 It is lost time to seek for an uniform base of agreement upon so essential an object. **1818** SCOTT *Br. Lamm.* xi, According to a uniform custom in remote places in Scotland. **1869** F. W. NEWMAN *Misc.* 224 A uniform franchise through the whole federation would have followed. **1891** *Law Times* XCII. 124/1 In Ireland the practice in this respect..was not uniform.

absol. **1606** SYLVESTER *Du Bartas* II. iv. II. *Magnif.* 1335 Cause of all Causes, Ocean of all Good,..The Uni-form, which gives all forms their Beeing.

b. Of persons (or personifications), their disposition, etc. Hence, exhibiting or preserving uniformity or consistency in respect of conduct or opinion; consistent.

1551 CRANMER *Answ. to Gardiner* I. 14 The churche of Rome..sheweth her selfe alway vniforme and consonaunt, to confound all the doctrine of Christe. **1647** H. MORE *Phil. Poems* II. lxxii, If he will his own fortunes overturn It cannot well be holp, we must be uniform. **1692** DRYDEN *St. Euremont's Ess.* 339 There is a man so uniform as to having nothing of Inequality and contrariety in his Actions. **1748** RICHARDSON *Clarissa* i. I. 3 Every-body pities you. So steady so uniform in your conduct. **1799** WELLINGTON in Gurw. *Desp.* (1834) I. 16 Of this uniform disposition abundant proofs have been afforded by each of the allies. **1822** SCOTT *Peveril* xlviii, For Buckingham's sins,..he is the regular and uniform sponsor.

†**c.** Of consent: Unanimous. *Obs.*

1559 in Strype *Ann. Ref.* viii. (1709) 116 We..have with one uniform consent set forth this short declaration. **1620** BRENT tr. *Sarpi's Counc. Trent* VIII. 745 An vniforme consent of Doctors.

d. Of clothing or dress: Of the same pattern, colour, and material amongst a number or body of persons.

Merging into an attrib. use of UNIFORM *sb.* (sense 4).

1746 in *Jrnl. Archaeol. Soc.* (1847) II. 77 That a uniform dress is useful and necessary for the commissioned officers. **1768** *Ann. Reg., Chron.* 63/1 The lappels and cuffs of the military uniform frocks, appointed to be worn by the lieutenants of his Majesty's fleet. **1783** *Ibid.* 193/2 The uniform clothing..worn by the flag officers. **1890** *Harper's Mag.* Feb. 333 The practice of clothing soldiers, by regiments, in one uniform dress.

2. Having or presenting the same appearance or aspect; exhibiting no, or little, diversity in respect of form, design, or dimensions; hence, having a plain, unbroken, or undiversified surface or exterior.

In the 17th–18th centuries freq. of buildings, etc.

a **1550** LELAND *Itin.* (1768) I. 107 The Chirch of S. Mary is excellent, newe, and uniforme yn work. **1621** in Kempe *Losely MSS.* (1836) 456 The church of St. Treguse ys..a very good one, were it uniforme. **1632** MASSINGER & FIELD *Fatal Dowry* III. i, All else about you, cap-a-pie, So uniform in spite of handsomeness, Shews such a bold contempt of comeliness. **1696** WHISTON *Theory of Earth* II. 115 Every such state of external Nature was even, uniform, and regular. **1723** CHAMBERS tr. *Le Clerc's Treat. Arch.* I. 59 Columns..ought not to have any Flutings; for..plain uniform Columns carry..a better appearance. **1756** NUGENT *Gr. Tour, Nethèrl.* I. 299 The street called La Rue Royale, is one of the longest, straightest, and most uniform in Europe. **1784** COWPER *Task* VI. 178 All this uniform, uncolour'd scene, Shall be dismantled of its fleecy load. **1859** DARWIN *Orig. Spec.* iii. 73 The face of nature remains uniform for long periods of time. **1884** BOWER & SCOTT *De Bary's Phaner.* 110 The thickening mass is either uniform or pitted.

As *adv.* **1630** *R. Johnson's Kingd. & Commw.* 132 Paris..is the greater, the uniformer built, and stronglier situate.

†**b.** *Bot.* Of flowers: (see quots.). *Obs.*

1693 *Phil. Trans.* XVII. 929 Such as have a Uniform Flower, as Senna, or such as have a difform or Papilionaceous Flower. **1704** J. HARRIS *Lex. Techn.* I, *Uniform Flowers* of Plants, the Botanists call such as are all round of the same Figure; or whose fore and back part, and whose right and left parts are exactly alike.

c. Of material things or colour.

In this group the sense sometimes becomes narrowed down to 'not mixed or blended'.

1756 BURKE *On the Sublime & Beautiful* III. xxvii, Nor..is the power of black as black, or of white as white, so strong as when each stands uniform and distinguished. **1764** HARMER *Observ.* iv. §27. 192 This mingled wine stands in opposition to new wine, which is, to the eye, an uniform liquor. **1823** SCOTT *Quentin D.* ii, His jerkin, hose, and cloak, were of a dark uniform colour. **1845** *Florist's Jrnl.* 261 Few gardens could boast an uniform luxuriant green among the plants. *c* **1860** FARADAY *Forces Nat.* 67 This piece of glass..being perfectly uniform in its internal structure.

3. Of motion, dimensions, etc.: Free from fluctuation or variation in respect of quantity or amount.

1559 W. CUNNINGHAM *Cosmogr. Glasse* 10 The sterres kepe one vniforme distance in mouing. **1597** HOOKER *Eccl. Pol.* v. lxix. §2 The heauens..keepe in their motions vniforme celeritie. **1656** tr. *Hobbes' Elem. Philos.* III. xv. 156 Uniform [motion] is that by which equal Lines are alwayes transmitted in equal times. **1764** *Museum Rust.* IV. 58 We should find it in an uniform progression of encrease. **1796** WITHERING *Brit. Plants* (ed. 3) III. 879 Branches of a uniform breadth. **1860** MAURY *Phys. Geog.* (Low) xxii. §883 The flow of heat from the sun is held to be uniform. **1879** THOMSON & TAIT *Nat. Phil.* I. I. §20 Velocity..may be uniform, *i.e.* the same at every instant; or it may be variable.

II. Of things of the same class in respect of each other, or of one thing in relation to another or others of the same class.

4. Of the same form, character, or kind as another or others; agreeing or according with one another, conforming to one standard, rule, or pattern; alike, similar.

1548 W. THOMAS in Strype *Eccl. Mem.* (1721) II. App. v. 71 So because we have no neighbour of uniform religion, I determine we can find no friend, whose amity is to be trusted. **1594** HOOKER *Eccl. Pol.* IV. xiii. §2 The only doubt is about the manner of their unity; how far churches are bound to be uniform in their ceremonies. **1637** SALTONSTALL *Eusebius' Constantine* 77 Thus the Emperours Edict discovered the Dens and uniforme Cages of these Heretickes. **1660** R. COKE *Power & Subj.* 222 The ceremonies of Edward's Reformation were more uniform than before. **1702** *Engl. Theophrast.* 263 Things Past, Present, and to Come, are strangely Uniform and of a Colour. **1762** KAMES *Elem. Crit.* (1833) 481 When two figures are composed of similar parts, they are said to be uniform. **1794** MRS. RADCLIFFE *Myst. Udolpho* xvi, My answers on the subject have been uniform. **1867** SMILES *Huguenots Eng.* i. 6 The copies sold having been compared with each other, were found to be exactly uniform. **1878** BRISTOWE *Th. & Pract. Med.* (ed. 2) 534 The symptoms of rupture of the heart are far from uniform.

†**b.** Of buildings. *Obs.*

1549 W. THOMAS *Hist. Italy* 207 Buildynges on bothe sides so fayre and vniforme. **1617** MORYSON *Itin.* III. 66 The houses are most of bricke,..and so vniforme, as if they had all beene built at a time, and by the same workemen. **1684** BURNET tr. *More's Utopia* 73 Their Buildings are good, and are so uniform, that a whole side of a Street looks like one House. **1700** in Picton *L'pool Munic. Rec.* (1883) I. 291 Y^e buildings be handsome & uniform.

†**c.** Of persons. *Obs.*

In quot. referring to Matt. xxii. 11–13.

a **1626** BP. ANDREWES *Pattern Cath. Doctr.* (1630) 210 He that was not uniforme was punished.

†**d.** In agreement with, accordant *to*, something.

a **1586** SIDNEY *Arcadia* II. xii, So divers be the Elements disposed In this weake worke, that it can never be Made uniforme to any state reposed. **1669** in Willis & Clark *Cambridge* (1886) II. 557 Three outward dore cases shalbe arched..with freestone vniforme to the windowes. **1702** H. DODWELL *Apol.* §19, I have shewn it agreeable to the severest Reasoning..to make his Death uniform to the rest of his Life.

uniform ('juːnɪfɔːm), *v.* [f. the adj. or sb. Cf. Sp. and Pg. *uniformar*, It. *uniformarsi*.]

1. *trans.* To make conformable *to*.

In a parody of pedantic language.

a **1586** SIDNEY *Wanstead Play* in *Arcadia* (1629) 622 Thus must I vniform my speech to your obtuse conceptions.

2. To make or render (a number of persons or things) uniform or alike; to bring or reduce to uniformity.

In later quots. with suggestion of sense 3.

c **1681** HICKERINGILL *Trimmer* iii. Wks. 1716 I. 372 We'll uniform you all, and make you all alike. **1708** T. WARD *Eng. Ref.* I. (1710) 64 To..Uniform the Multitude In Prayer, and joyn the jarring crowd. **1870** LOWELL *Study Wind.* (1871) 258 The more than Protean travesties which words underwent before they were uniformed by Johnson and Walker. **1887** *Harper's Mag.* July 280 It is a human device to uniform people into friends and enemies.

3. To dress in, put into, uniform. Cf. UNIFORMED *a.*, UNIFORMING *vbl. sb.* orig. *U.S.*

1861 O. W. NORTON *Let.* 8 June in *Army Lett.* (1903) 12 We are to be uniformed and equipped immediately. **1888** *Long Branch* (New Jersey) *News* 7 Apr., In our spirit of imitation do we not go too far when we talk of uniforming the shop girls in the big dry goods store. **1894** *Outing* XXIV. 78/2 Hull persisted in uniforming the militia after his own sweet will.

†**uni'formable**, *a. Obs. rare.* [f. L. *ūniform-is* UNIFORM *a.* + -ABLE.] Uniform.

1632 LITHGOW *Trav.* x. 474 Vniformable no; some of your Priests giue the Sacrament onely in Bread..; some in Wine without Bread, and some in both. **1653** BLITHE *Eng. Improver Impr.* 155 As easie..to cast or lot out thy Wood into an Artificiall uniformable plot, as to do it rudely or confusedly.

uni'formal, *a.* [f. as prec. + -AL[1].] Uniform, in various senses.

1573 [implied in next]. **1598** FLORIO, *Simbolo*,..an vniformall consent of sundry opinions. *a* **1608** DEE *Relat. Spir.* I. (1659) 4 All things shall be brought into an uniformal order. **1645** HERRICK *Descr. Woman* 11 Her comly nose with vniformall grace Like purest white stands in the middle place.

1848 BAILEY *Festus* (ed. 3) 206 One arrayed in white And one in uniformal black. **1888** D. MAGUIRE *Art Massage* ii. (ed. 4) 18 A uniformal friction on those parts of the body which are irregularly formed.

Hence **uni'formally** *adv. rare.*

1573 BARET *Alv.* s.v. C, [The letter C] shoulde haue his proper sownd and euer to keepe the same vniformally in speaking, nor waueringly. **1603** FLORIO *Montaigne* III. ii. 491, I will present my selfe..every where vniformallie. **1624** GATAKER *Transubst.* 48 These being..uniformally recounted by three Evangelists.

uniformali'zation. [f. next + -ATION.] The action of making or fact of being made uniform.

1805 *Ann. Rev.* III. 255 The uniformalization of tenures.

uni'formalize, *v. rare.* [f. UNIFORMAL *a.* + -IZE.] *trans.* To make uniform; to reduce to a uniform system.

1805 *Ann. Rev.* III. 294 It is desirable to uniformalize the circulating medium of both countries. **1830** W. TAYLOR *Hist. Surv. Germ. Poetry* I. 161 By uniformalizing coins, weights, and measures.

unifor'mation. *rare.* [f. UNIFORM *a.* + -ATION.] The action of making uniform; reduction to uniformity.

1895 *Dublin Rev.* April 335 Not through the blunting, checking, or uniformation of thinking.

'uniformed, *a.* [f. UNIFORM *sb.* 2 + -ED.] Dressed in or wearing uniform. (Freq. *c* 1880–.) *spec.* of police officers: see UNIFORM *sb.* 4 b.

1813 LADY LYTTELTON *Corr.* 12 Dec., Wednesday we dine at Count Romanzoff's—full-dressed, long-trained, uniformed. **1840** GEN. P. THOMPSON *Exerc.* (1842) V. 53 A uniformed agent of the law. **1895** MEREDITH *Amazing Marriage* xliii, A foreign army or tag-rag of uniformed rascals. **1922** *Rep. Tax Cases 1913–21* VII. 176 Detective officers receive the same rates of pay as uniformed officers. **1945** *Law Rep. King's Bench Div.* 420 When they saw the uniformed officer they hurried in the opposite direction. **1973** 'E. PETERS' *City of Gold & Shadows* v. 81 Sergeant Comstock, of the uniformed branch..came from a long line of native fishermen.

fig. and *transf.* **1864** LOWELL *Fireside Trav.* 154 We..come out uniformed..with habits of thinking and doing cut on one pattern. **1892** *Nation* (N.Y.) 3 Mar. 176/1 The book is handsomely uniformed in Confederate gray.

uni'forming, *vbl. sb.* [f. UNIFORM *v.*]

1. The action of making or fact of being made uniform in some respect. *rare*$^{-1}$.

1700–1 GOUGH *Hist. Myddle* (1875) 115 The Twelvth Peiw..Was a supernumerary Peiw at the uniforming of the seates.

2. The action of clothing in or providing with uniform or a uniform dress.

1891 *Harper's Mag.* March 647/1 In the uniforming of a community set apart for an unworldly purpose. **1897** *Daily News* 4 May 9/2 The uniforming of troops.

uniformist ('juːnɪˌfɔːmɪst). [f. UNIFORM *a.* + -IST.] An advocate of or believer in uniformity or a uniform system, esp. in respect of religious doctrine or observance.

1885 R. W. DIXON *Hist. Ch. Eng.* III. 465 He was..as staunch a Uniformist now, as..he had been a Nonconformist. **1891** *Athenæum* 15 Aug. 214/3 A strict uniformist with regard to the phonetics of Latin.

uniformitarian (ˌjuːnɪfɔːmɪ'tɛərɪən), *sb.* and *adj.* [f. UNIFORMIT-Y + *-arian*.]

A. *sb.* **1.** *Geol.* One who maintains or accepts the theory that geological processes and phenomena have always been and still are due to causes or forces operating continuously and with uniformity. (Opposed to CATASTROPHIST or CONVULSIONIST.)

1840 WHEWELL *Philos. Induct. Sciences* I. p. xxxvi, The Catastrophist constructs Theories, the Uniformitarian demolishes them. **1860** HUXLEY *Darwiniana* Coll. Ess. 1893 II. 65 The most philosophical uniformitarian of the present day. **1891** SIR R. BALL *Ice Age* 173 It places the ice-sheet..at the disposal of the geological uniformitarian.

2. An advocate of uniformity; a uniformist. *rare.*

1890 GILDERSLEEVE *Ess. & Stud.* 214 The Procrustean work of a miserable uniformitarian.

B. *adj.* **1.** *Geol.* Of or pertaining to, characteristic of or held by, uniformitarians.

1840 WHEWELL *Philos. Induct. Sci.* II. 135 The uniformitarian doctrine on this subject rests on most unstable foundations. **1869** HUXLEY in *Scientific Opinion* 21 April 464/3 The influence of uniformitarian views has been ..favourable to the progress of sound geology. **1884** H. SPENCER in *Contemp. Rev.* July 25 The leading expositor of the uniformitarian theory in Geology.

b. In accordance with the theory of the uniformitarians; proceeding from geological uniformity.

1869 HUXLEY in *Scientific Opinion* April 487/1 All these irregular..catastrophes would be the result of an absolutely uniformitarian action.

c. Of persons: Holding or adhering to the theory or doctrines of the uniformitarians.

1864 BOWEN *Logic* ix. 301 The speculations of those whom Dr. Whewell calls the uniformitarian school of geologists. **1895** *Q. Rev.* April 386 The most influential uniformitarian geologist of our age.

2. Of or pertaining to, advocating or practising, uniformity in something.

1897 *Daily News* 12 July 6/3 The Puritanism of the intolerant, uniformitarian Presbyterians.

uniformitarianism (juːnɪfɔːmɪˈtɛərɪənɪz(ə)m). *Geol.* [f. prec. + -ISM.] The principles or doctrines held by the uniformitarian school of geologists; the theory of uniformity of action in the forces and processes of inorganic nature. (Opposed to CATASTROPHISM or CONVULSIONISM.)

1865 T. MARSDEN *Sacr. Steps Creation* 113 One is induced to ask, whether Uniformitarianism be mere Proselytism in the garb of Philosophy. **1894** *Nature* 26 July 290/1 The natural though exaggerated reaction into scientific uniformitarianism.

uniformity (juːnɪˈfɔːmɪtɪ). Forms: 5 vniformite, 6 -ete, 6–7 -itie, 7 -ity, uniformitie, 7– -ity. [a. F. *uniformité* (14th c., = It. *uniformità*, Sp. *uniformidad*, Pg. *-dade*), or ad. L. *ūniformitāt-*, *ūniformitās*, f. *ūniformis* UNIFORM *a.*: see -ITY. So also Du. *uniformiteit*, G. *uniformität*.] The quality of being uniform.

1. The fact or condition of having the same form or character as another or others; conformity amongst several things, parts, etc., to one form or character.

1432–50 tr. *Higden* (Rolls) III. 215 Zenon, whiche put euery synne to be of vniformite, so that he scholde synne as moche that did steyle chaffe as the man stelenge golde. **1513** DOUGLAS *Æneid* IX. iv. 39 To thir tua was a will in vnite, A lust, and mynd in vniformete. **1611** CORYAT *Crudities* 23 Such is the vniformity of almost al the houses of the same streete..that they are made alike both in proportion of workmanship and matter. **1614** RALEIGH *Hist. World* II. 543 The consent of those that have written thereof, being nothing neare to uniformity. **1630** *R. Johnson's Kingd. & Commw.* 132 Its attributes of a Winding river, and the five Bridges, sorting forsooth to uniformitie of streets. **1701** NORRIS *Ideal World* I. ii. 50 Whence should arise this specific uniformity in the natures of man..if not that they are all cast in one mould? **1756** BURKE *Subl. & B.* II. ix, Succession and uniformity of parts are what constitute the artificial infinite. **1815** J. SMITH *Panorama Sci. & Art* II. 601 Various differences in the depth, extent, or want of uniformity of the gravelly or clayey strata. **1854** *Poultry Chron.* II. 149/1 Quality, purity, beauty of plumage, and uniformity [in fowls].

b. Conformity to (or compliance with) one standard of opinion, practice, or procedure, esp. in respect of religion or religious observance.

Act of Uniformity, in *Eng. Hist.*, one or other of three Acts regulating public worship, passed in 1549 (21 Jan.), 1559, and 1662 respectively, which prescribed the use and acceptance of the Books of Common Prayer published in those years; esp. the Act (13 & 14 Charles II, c. 4) passed 19 May 1662, which also required the 'assent and consent' of the clergy to everything contained in the Book of Common Prayer; etc.

1549 *Act 2 & 3 Edw. VI*, c. 1 (*title*), An Acte for the Unyformytie of Service and Admynistracion of the Sacramentes throughout the Realme. **1552** ABP. HAMILTON *Catech.* Pref., To keip vniformitie and concord in setting furth to ye people the doctrine. **1611** BIBLE *Transl. Pref.* ¶13 When the father of their Church..findeth so great fault with them for their oddes and iarring; we hope the children haue no great cause to vaunt of their vniformitie. **1651** BAXTER *Inf. Bapt.* 147 His treatise against Uniformity. **1670** in Somers *Tracts* I. 21 All Uniformity (or Colour of it) was distasteful to the Independents. **1708** J. CHAMBERLAYNE *St. Gt. Brit.* I. III. i. (1710) 155 He must carry with him.. Letters Testimonial..from..Three..Reverend Divines, who..can give a good Account of his Vertue, Uniformity, and Learning. **1830** D'ISRAELI *Chas. I*, III. v. 63 Lord Bacon considered that uniformity in religion was absolutely necessary. **1871** C. DAVIES *Metric Syst.* III. 79 Its adoption was therefore a great and important advance toward uniformity.

Comb. **1647** *Case Kingd.* 10 Till Vniformity-mongers be pointed at as the only Enemies of a State.

c. With *a* or *an*.

1560 DAUS tr. *Sleidane's Comm.* 125b, Therfore is an vniformitie to be sought for, that maye be grounded vpon the sure foundation of Scripture. **1641** MILTON *Reform.* II. 17 This distinction of honour will bring forth a seemly and graceful uniformity over all the kingdom. **1705** NELSON *Fest. & Fasts* i. (ed. 3) 19 The great Council of Nice ordained there should be a constant uniformity in this Case. **1874** GREEN *Short Hist.* iii. §3. 125 An uniformity of weights and measures was ordered to be enforced throughout the realm.

2. The condition of having, occurring in, or maintaining only one form or character; resemblance to or agreement with itself at all times or on all occasions; regularity in action or occurrence. Freq. const. *of*.

1577 HARRISON *England* II. iii. (1877) I. 73 For vniformitie of building, orderlie compaction, and regiment, the towne of Cambridge exceedeth that of Oxford..by manie a fold. **1739** BUTLER *Serm.* Wks. 1874 II. 217 There is a wonderful uniformity in the conduct of Providence. **1802** PALEY *Nat. Theol.* xxv. 482 Of the unity of the Deity, the proof is, the uniformity of plan observable in the universe. **1863** KINGLAKE *Crimea* I. 64 That branch of industry which seeks to give uniformity and mechanic action to bodies of men. **1875** JOWETT *Plato* (ed. 2) IV. 415 Genius is of all ages, and there is perhaps more uniformity in excellence than in mediocrity.

b. *spec.* in *Geol.* Cf. UNIFORMITARIAN(ISM.

1837 WHEWELL *Hist. Induct. Sci.* III. 609 The progress of physical geology will be better understood by attending to the doctrine of uniformity. **1869** HUXLEY in *Scientific Opinion* 28 Apr. 487/1 It is very conceivable that catastrophes may be part and parcel of uniformity.

3. The condition of having the parts similar in appearance; presentation of one regular or unvaried form on this account; similarity of appearance, design, structure, style, etc.; freedom from or lack of variety, diversity, or irregularity.

Regarded as either an artistic virtue or defect.

1625 BACON *Ess.* (Arb.) 547 Houses are built to Liue in, and not to Looke on: Therefore let Vse bee preferred before Vniformitie. **1642** FULLER *Holy & Prof. St.* III. vii. 168 Uniformity also much pleaseth the eye. **1686** PLOT *Staffordsh.* 360 The beauty of a structure..did not consist, as now, in uniformity; but in the greatest variety the Artist could possibly shew. **1753** HOGARTH *Anal. Beauty* iv. 22 Variety is more pleasing than uniformity, where the same end is answer'd by both. **1778** SHERIDAN *Camp* II. iii, The tents are all ranged in a straight line; now,..is there not a horrid uniformity in their infinite vista of canvas? no curve, no break. **1842** MRS. BROWNING *Bk. Poets* ii. Wks. (1904) 635/1 There is a difference between uniformity and monotony, and he [Marlowe] found it.

b. Unvaried or wearisome sameness; monotony, esp. *of* life.

1707 *Curios. in Husb. & Gard.* 64 Custom and Uniformity ..soon make the best Things seem dull and insipid. **1751** JOHNSON *Rambler* No. 167 ¶6 The uniformity of life must be sometimes diversified. **1819** SCOTT *Leg. Montrose* xvii, Men to whom the late uniformity of their military life had rendered any change of society an interesting novelty. **1860** W. COLLINS *Wom. White* I. W. H.'s Narr. viii, The dull uniformity of life at Limmeridge.

4. With *a* and pl. A particular instance of this condition; a uniform feature, law, etc.

1665 J. SPENCER *Prodigies* (ed. 2) 104 All kind of pretty Equalities and Uniformities, especially between Signs and Events. **1733** BERKELEY *Th. Vision Vind.* §67 We must not, for the sake of uniformities or analogies, depart from truth and fact. **1864** BOWEN *Logic* xii. 412 Simple uniformities, such as are comprehended in a General Fact, may be merely accidental. **1867** BAKER *Nile Trib.* iii. 63, I measured the depth of some of the wells, and found a uniformity of forty feet.

uniformize (ˈjuːnɪfɔːmaɪz), *v.* [f. UNIFORM *a.* + -IZE. Cf. F. *uniformiser*, Pg. *-izar*, med.L. *ūniformisāre*.] **1.** *trans.* To make uniform; to reduce to a uniform system. *rare.*

1866 [implied at *uniformized* below]. **1889** *Nature* Oct. 563 The formation of..an International Commission to fix units and uniformize methods.

2. *Math.* To transform (an equation or expression) so that each variable is expressed as a single-valued function of a new parameter; to parameterize.

1899 *Phil. Trans. R. Soc.* A. CXCII. 1 The only automorphic functions known hitherto which have been applied to uniformise forms whose genus is greater than unity, are [etc.]. **1940** E. T. BELL *Devel. Math.* xxi. 474 The circle $x^2 + y^2 = 1$ is uniformized by $x = \sin t$, $y = \cos t$. **1972** M. KLINE *Math. Thought* xxxix. 938 The parametric equations (11) or (12) are said to uniformize the algebraic equation (10).

Hence **'uniformized** *ppl. a.*; **'uniformizing** *vbl. sb.* and *ppl. a.*; **,uniformi'zation**.

1866 G. STEPHENS *Runic Mon.* I. p. xiii, To translate the oldest runic inscriptions..into a modern uniformized 'Icelandic'. **1899** *Phil. Trans. R. Soc.* A. CXCII. 1 Comparatively little of the published work on automorphic functions..has been written in connexion with the uniformisation of algebraic forms. *Ibid.* 2 The analytical connexion between the uniformising variable *t* and the variables *u*, *z*, of the algebraic form. **1933** E. SAPIR in *Encycl. Social Sci.* IX. 160/2 Language acts as a socializing and uniformizing force. **1954** HODGE & PEDOE *Methods Algebraic Geom.* III. xvi. 112 A necessary and sufficient condition that *P* be a simple point of *V* is that there exist a set of uniformising parameters at *P*. **1972** M. KLINE *Math. Thought* xxxix. 938 Clebsch's results on the uniformization of curves of genus 1 by means of elliptic functions of a parameter made it possible to establish for such curves remarkable properties about points of inflection, [etc.].

'uniformless, *a.* [f. UNIFORM *sb.* + -LESS.] Lacking or not wearing uniform.

1863 W. H. RUSSELL *My Diary North & S.* I. 308 Great long-bearded fellows in flannel shirts and slouched hats, uniformless.

'uniformly, *adv.* Also 6–7 vni-, 7 uniformely. [f. UNIFORM *a.* + -LY².] In a uniform manner; with uniformity.

1. With or in conformity to one form or standard on the part of several; in the same way as others or another; without diversity of one from another.

In later use merging into sense 3, from which it is not always clearly distinct.

1549 W. THOMAS *Hist. Italy* 74b, The one syde [of the street] is built of harde stone, all vniformely with faire glasen wyndowes. **1559** BP. C. SCOT in Strype *Ann. Ref.* (1709) I. II. App. x. 27 Common prayers, and the holie sacraments uniformly mynystred. **1617** MORYSON *Itin.* I. 182 The houses are vniformely, and very fairely built of free-stone. **1748** *Anson's Voy.* III. vii. 360 A hundred..were uniformly drest in the regimentals of the marines. **1847** C. BRONTE *J. Eyre* v, They were uniformly dressed in brown stuff frocks.

2. With uniformity in degree, quantity, or extent; in or with the same relative proportion; equally, equably.

1577 HARRISON *England* II. vi. (1877) I. 156 They giue it gentle heats..till it be drie, and in the meane while they turne it often, that it may be vniformelie dried. **1609** DOULAND *Ornithoparcus' Microl.* 78 A Consonance is a mixture of two Sounds falling into the eares vniformely. **1656** HOBBES *Six Lessons* Wks. 1845 VII. 282 Two movents, one uniform, the other uniformly accelerated. **1743** W. EMERSON *Fluxions* 109 The Space..would be uniformly discribed in a given Time. **1773** COOK *First Voyage* III. vi. III. 632 Their skins were so uniformly covered with dirt, that it was very difficult to ascertain their true colour. **1815** J. SMITH *Panorama Sci. & Art* II. 654 It is advisable to make the soil uniformly deep in every part. **1869** TYNDALL in *Fortn. Rev.* 1 Feb. 244 If..the plate be wedge-shaped, thickening gradually and uniformly from edge to back.

3. In a manner that is always the same; without variation or alteration; at all times or in every case alike; invariably.

1682 NORRIS *Hierocles* 11 By Law is understood the power of God as it always acts uniformly. **1736** BUTLER *Anal.* I. ii. Wks. 1874 I. 38 We find the consequences, which we were beforehand informed of, uniformly to follow. **1776** GIBBON *Decl. & F.* xiii. I. 375 The calm dignity which he uniformly affected. **1825** SCOTT *Talism.* xxvi, When once noticed, it uniformly made a strong impression on the spectator. **1863** E. V. NEALE *Anal. Th. & Nat.* 249 The judgments of our propositions are uniformly made by the verb 'to be'. **1891** *Law Times* XCII. 124/1 Since 1846 the Chancellorship has been uniformly held by Irish barristers.

b. Qualifying adjectives or adverbs.

1769 ROBERTSON *Chas. V*, XI. Wks. 1813 III. 329 An administration uniformly equitable and moderate. **1827** J. IVIMEY *Pilgr. 19th Cent.* iii. 59 'Was he uniformly successful in trade?'.. 'I cannot say that he was always successful; he was uniformly honourable.' **1842** J. WILSON *Chr. North* I. 245 Life has gone uniformly well with him. **1898** 'MERRIMAN' *Roden's Corner* x, The result has been uniformly satisfactory.

'uniformness. [f. as prec.] Uniformity.

1579 W. WILKINSON *Confut. Fam. Love* Bij, That we might serue euen so the onely liuing God in..vniformenes of hart. **1581** MULCASTER *Positions* xlv. 296 The great varietie in teaching, which is now generally vsed, maye be reduced to some vniformnesse. **1710** BERKELEY *Princ. Hum. Knowl.* I. §105. 151 Rules grounded on the Analogy, and Uniformness observ'd in the Production of Natural Effects.

unify (ˈjuːnɪfaɪ), *v.* [ad. med.L. *unificāre*, f. L. *ūni-* UNI-: see -FY. So F. *unifier* (14th c.), It. *unificare*, Sp. *unificar*.] *trans.* To make, form into, or cause to become one; to combine (two or more) *in* one; to join (one or more) *to* or *with* another or others so as to form one whole or unit; to unite, consolidate.

Rare in 18th c. (see the *ppl. a.*); frequent in recent use.

1502 *Ord. Crysten Men* (W. de W. 1506) I. vii. Giv, Yᵉ holy goost vnyeth & vnyfyeth al these membres of the holy chyrche in one. **1509** HAWES *Joyf. Med.* 6 Two tytles in one thou dydst well vnyfye. **1654** W. MONTAGU *Dev. Ess.* II. viii. 156 Let then all the pretenders to peace, procure to simplifie and unifie their desires by this single address to the will and order of God. **1656** BLOUNT *Glossogr.*, *Unifie*,..to joyn or make one, as mariage doth Husband and Wife. [Hence in later Dicts.] **1802** COLERIDGE *Lett.* (1895) 404 A poet's heart and intellect should be..intimately combined and unified with the great appearances of nature. **1853** LYNCH *Self-Improv.* 3 Religion will..unify and glorify all his studies. **1884** *Manch. Exam.* 26 Mar. 5/1 The great effect of successive Reform Bills has been to unify the nation.

absol. **1817** COLERIDGE *Biog. Lit.* xiii. (1882) 144 It.. dissipates, in order to re-create; or..at all events, it struggles to idealize and to unify. **1888** *Classical Rev.* Oct. 256/1 These Homeridæ..worked continuously.., adding and unifying, and so they produced the epics.

Hence **'unifying** *vbl. sb.*

1681 BAXTER *Acc. Sherlocke* vi. 209 Distinguishing between the Unifying of the Society, and the uniting a single Member to that Society.

'unifying, *ppl. a.* [f. prec. + -ING².] That unifies.

1681 BAXTER *Acc. Sherlocke* iv. 184 The Church hath its true, proper, specifying and unifying, that is, constitutive Government. **1751** HARRIS *Hermes* III. iv. (1765) 363 No where is this collecting and (if I may be allowed the expression) this unifying Power more conspicuous. **1775** —— *Philos. Arrangem.* vii. 137 By virtue..of this combining, this unifying Comprehension. **1840** DE QUINCEY *Style* iv. (1860) 298 This great unifying event. **1881** MIVART *Cat* 376 The organ and vehicle of such unifying activity.

u'nigenist, *a.* [f. UNI-, after MONOGENIST.] Of or pertaining to monogeny; monogenistic.

1896 A. H. KEANE *Ethnology* vii. 156 Another argument in support of the unigenist doctrine against polygenist views.

†**unigenit**, *a. Obs.*⁻¹ [ad. eccl. L. *ūnigenit-us*. Cf. OF. *unigenit*.] Only begotten.

*a*1568 in *Bannatyne MS.* (Hunter. Club) 107/5 O vnigeneit Sone to God of micht!

uni'geniture. [f. as prec. + -URE.]

1. *Theol.* The fact of being the only-begotten Son.

1659 PEARSON *Creed* 278 Unigeniture being the foundation of his singular love. *Ibid.* 279 As primogeniture consisteth in prelation, so unigeniture in exclusion. **1691** E. TAYLOR *Behmen's Theos. Philos.* 369 The intire Will, and Divine Unigeniture.

2. The fact of being an only child; the practice of having only one child.

1887 *Edin. Rev.* Oct. 304 The Norman peasantry who secure the advantages of primogeniture by unigeniture.

†**u'nigenous**, *a. Geol. Obs.*⁻¹ [f. UNI- + Gr. γέν-ος kind, origin: see -OUS.] Of uniform structure. (Cf. MONOGENOUS *a.* 4.)

1799 KIRWAN *Geol. Ess.* 214 The unigenous limestone mountains of Carniola.

unig'nited, *ppl. a.* (UN-¹ 8.)

1773 *Phil. Trans.* LXIV. 27 The dark and unignited state of the great internal globe of the sun. **1784** *Ibid.* LXXV. 194 A very dense fume of unignited particles arises. **1856**

FROUDE *Hist. Eng.* I. 28 Like a train of gunpowder, the isolated grains of which have..no effect on each other, while they remain unignited.

unihoded, *ppl. a.*: see UN-^{1} 3.

ˈunijunction. *Electronics.* Also **uni-junction.** [UNI- 1 b.] A negative-resistance device consisting of a rectifying *p–n* junction in the middle of a length of semiconducting material that has an ohmic contact at each end, used as a switching element.

1957 *Automatic Control* Feb. 24 The silicon unijunction transistor has characteristics resembling a neon light; it can be wired to a capacitor and a resistor to yield an oscillator. **1962** SIMPSON & RICHARDS *Physical Princ. Junction Transistors* viii. 192 A device whose regenerative property is obtained in a somewhat different manner..is the unijunction transistor or double-based diode. **1981** NASHELSKY & BOYLESTAD *Devices* vii. 291 Recent interest in the unijunction transistor (UJT) has, like that for the SCR, been increasing at an exponential rate.

uniˈlabiate, *a.* [ad. mod.L. *ūnilabiāt-us*: see UNI- and LABIATE *a.*] (See quots.) Also **uniˈlabiated** *a.*

1731 BAILEY (ed. 2) II, *Unilabiated*, having but one lip, spoken of flowers. [Hence in Ash (1775), etc.] **1826** KIRBY & SP. *Entomol.* IV. 38 Some spiracles, however, are unilabiate, or have only one lip. **1847** ROYLE *Mat. Med.* 614 Corolla with outer limb 3-parted, the interior unilabiate.

uniˈlateral, *a.* [ad. mod.L. *ūnilaterāl-is*, or f. UNI- + LATERAL *a.* Cf. F. *unilatéral* (1804), Sp. and Pg. *unilateral*, It. *-ale*.]

I. 1. a. *Bot.* Of a raceme or panicle: Having the flowers on one side of the peduncle. Also, of a cyme: Having a branch or axis on one side only.

1802 R. HALL *Elem. Bot.* 156 One-sided, or Unilateral, *unilateralis*, applied to a raceme with all the flowers inserted on one side. **1853** G. JOHNSTON *Nat. Hist. E. Bord.* I. 218 A coarse but productive species, distinguished readily by its unilateral panicle.

b. *Bot.* and *Zool.* Arranged or produced on one side of an axis or surface; directed or turned towards one side.

1870 HOOKER *Stud. Flora* 275 Disk hypogynous unilateral. **1876** tr. *Wagner's Gen. Pathol.* 118 The genital pores are unilateral. **1879** *Hardwicke's Science-Gossip* XV. 203/2 Its flowers are unilateral, as those of the forget-me-not.

c. Of car-parking: restricted to one side of the street.

1945 *Rep. Watch Comm. Oxf. City Council* 7 June, The Council desired to preserve the effect of the war-time Orders..relating to unilateral parking in King Edward Street. **1954** *Highway Engin. Terms* (*B.S.I.*) 57 *Unilateral waiting* (*prohibition of*), a system under which vehicles are prohibited from waiting on one side of a carriageway. The side may be fixed or alternated. **1959** *Listener* 14 May 841/2 Or, if it is unilateral parking, that you go to the side where parking is allowed.

2. a. Of or pertaining to, occurring on or affecting, one side of an organ or part.

unilateral horse-shoe (see quot. 1843).

1843 YOUATT *Horse* (ed. 3) xxi. 424 The Unilateral, or one side nailed shoe. *Ibid.*, The unilateral shoe has this great advantage. **1877** M. FOSTER *Physiol.* III. vi. 456 The loss of voluntary movement which follows upon a unilateral section of the medulla. **1880** BASTIAN *Brain* iii. 57 The unilateral influence of Light.

b. *Path.* and *Med.* Affecting or developed on only one side of the body at the same time.

1876 DUHRING *Dis. Skin* 225 Zoster is almost invariably unilateral. **1879** P. SMITH *Glaucoma* 5 Hence the bilateral character of chronic glaucoma, and the unilateral acute attacks. **1893** A. S. ECCLES *Sciatica* 7 In the more common form, viz., unilateral sciatica.

c. *Phonetics.* Uttered or produced with the glottis open on one side only.

1867 ALEX. MELVILLE BELL *Visible Speech* 59 Uni-lateral formations. When the breath issues by only one side aperture in forming any 'divided' consonant, the modifier [etc.]. **1887** ELLIS in *Encycl. Brit.* XXII. 387/1 Voiced form or buzz of unilateral Welsh *ll*.

3. *Math.* (See latter quot.)

1884 SYLVESTER *Coll. Math. Papers* (1912) IV. 152 A unilateral simple equation. *Ibid.* 225 The Quadratic Equation of a form which I call unilateral, because the quaternion coefficients in it are supposed all to lie on the same side of the unknown quantity.

II. 4. a. Performed or undertaken by or on the part of one side; made, enjoyed, shared in, felt, etc., by only one person or party.

1802 W. WINDHAM *Let.* in *Windham Papers* II. 200 This communication..is in this way..unilateral, in which I may speak to you, without hearing anything in return. **1836** TURNBULL *Stubbes' Anat. Abuses* Pref. p. x, That the Editor may not be accused of an unilateral predilection for his *protegé*. **1885** *Times* 6 May 9 It is time to make him understand..that our relations with him cannot continue to be of this unilateral character.

b. *Law.* Made or entered upon by one party, esp. without reciprocal obligation on the part of another or others; binding or imposed upon one party only.

1802–12 BENTHAM *Ration. Judic. Evid.* (1827) II. 495 In the case of an unilateral deed, the scribe may be the party himself. **1826** G. J. BELL *Comm. Laws Scotl.* I. 334 Unilateral obligations and bonds. *a* **1859** AUSTIN *Jurispr.* (1879) I. 324 The promise..is, in the language of the jurists, a convention unilateral. **1875** POSTE *Gaius* III. 362 A unilateral Disposition is one made by a solitary principal disposer.

c. Of succession: Of or from one side or parent.

1881 *Times* 17 Jan. 4 Men may contract for reciprocal rights of cross or unilateral succession.

d. ***unilateral disarmament***, disarmament (in recent use, *spec.* of nuclear weapons) by one state, irrespective of whether others take similar action. Also ***unilateral disarmer***.

1929 *Times* 15 Nov. 14/3 Lord Salisbury agreed that unilateral disarmament had probably reached its limits. **1935** C. R. ATTLEE in *Hansard Commons* 22 May 375, I want to recall to the House what our position is as a party on the question of defence... We do not stand for unilateral disarmament. **1960** [see DISARMER b]. **1969** PLANO & OLTON *Internat. Relations Dict.* 237 By demonstrating peaceful intentions rather than merely talking about them, unilateral disarmament theorists believe, one side could put the arms-race cycle into reverse by evoking reciprocation of its disarmament initiatives. **1980** *Observer* 14 Sept. 11 To adopt the unilateral disarmament option would be akin to behaving like a virgin in a brothel. **1980** *Times* 17 Nov. 15/3 Mr Foot..is a unilateral disarmer. **1984** S. TOWNSEND *Growing Pains A. Mole* 90 Went back to Pandora's and watched the Labour Party Conference vote for unilateral disarmament... If elected the Labour Party would chuck all their nuclear weapons away.

5. a. Dealing or concerned with, relating to, only one side of a subject; one-sided.

1830 *Edin. Rev.* LI. 531 The results of this uni-lateral.. mode of proceeding. **1838** SIR W. HAMILTON *Logic* xxx. (1866) II. 111 The unilateral and incompetent reasoning which I have here supposed in the case of time. **1873** MORLEY *Rousseau* II. 145 This is a unilateral view of the social contract, and omits the element of reciprocity.

b. *Logic.* (See quot.)

1864 BOWEN *Logic* vi. 170 In some cases, the Restriction ..and the Integration may be bilateral.., as affecting both Subject and Predicate;..or unilateral,..as affecting either the Subject only,..or the Predicate only.

Hence **unilateˈrality**, the quality or character of being unilateral.

1844 DELANE in Dasent *Life & Corr.* (1908) I. 46 Unilaterality (there's a long word for you) is an essential ingredient in a printer's happiness. **1887** ELLIS in *Encycl. Brit.* XXII. 387/1 This unilaterality [of click] is insisted on by Salesbury. **1899** *Allbutt's Syst. Med.* VIII. 622 True zoster of the face characterized by unilaterality.

uniˈlateralism. [-ISM.] = *unilaterality* s.v. UNILATERAL *a.*; *spec.* (*a*) = *unilateral disarmament* s.v. UNILATERAL *a.* 4 d; (*b*) *U.S.*, the pursuit of a foreign policy without allies or irrespective of their views.

1926 *Public Opinion* 30 Apr. 434/2 We must..surmount national and social unilateralism in the domain of the spirit. **1935** *Punch* 25 Sept. 354/2 Laugh heartily when politicians talk about 'unilateralism'. **1959** *Manch. Guardian* 20 July 6/2 He said that unilateralism would take Britain out of N.A.T.O. **1964** GOULD & KOLB *Dict. Social Sci.* 357/1 *Unilateralism* is now used to mean 'no alliances' while *isolationism* is more often used to mean an attitude of withdrawal. **1968** N. NICOLSON in H. Nicolson *Diaries* III. 385 The policy of unilateral renunciation by Britain of the atomic bomb had been advocated by Bevan... The Labour Party Conference had voted..for unilateralism. **1979** H. KISSINGER *White House Years* xxiv. 1089 From an early hostility to the American alliance with Japan..the Chinese leaders soon came..to view it as a guarantee of America's continued interest in the Western Pacific and a rein on Japanese unilateralism. **1984** *New Statesman* 16 Nov. 10/1 After the Labour defeat at the General Election, the installation of Cruise missiles and a seemingly unequivocal Labour commitment to unilateralism, many CND activists are looking at the shape and direction CND needs to take in order to win the political debate on disarmament.

uniˈlateralist, *sb.* and *a.* [-IST.] **A.** *sb.* One who favours or adopts a policy of unilateral disarmament.

1927 *Daily Tel.* 14 Mar. 9/7 The lack of foresight on the part of the 'Unilateralists'..led..to the..postponement of Germany's entry into the League. **1959** *Guardian* 15 Oct. 10/4 Defeats among unilateralists were matched by defeats among believers in the 'great deterrent'. **1960** [see *multilateralist* adj. and sb. s.v. MULTILATERAL *a.*]. **1980** *Times Lit. Suppl.* 14 Nov. 1277/2 For Bevan was emphatically no fellow-traveller, no isolationist, no unilateralist and certainly no pacifist.

B. *adj.* Of or pertaining to unilateral disarmament, or to unilateralists or their activities.

1959 *Manch. Guardian* 20 July 6/2 There is..little danger that it [*sc.* the Labour Party conference] will go along the unilateralist road. **1960** *News Chron.* 20 Sept. 6/1 By insisting that this country should abandon nuclear weapons and any alliance that possesses them, Mr. Cousins is taking up a unilateralist position. **1963** *Ann. Reg. 1962* 22 Mr Gaitskell's recapture of Labour Party defence policy from the hands of the Campaign for Nuclear Disarmament..had left him exposed as the chief target for unilateralist retaliation.

ˌunilateraliˈzation. *Electronics.* [f. UNILATERAL *a.* + -IZATION.] Neutralization (sense 1 d), esp. of resistive as well as reactive feedback. So **uniˈlateralized** *ppl. a.*

1954 *IRE Trans. Circuit Theory* May 23/1 (*caption*) Lossless unilateralization. *Ibid.*, Suppose..that a number of active devices are to be placed in cascade, each being unilateralized with lossless coupling in order to avoid the problem of wave reflection back through the chain. **1962** [see NEUTRALIZATION 1 d]. **1974** HARVEY & BOHLMAN *Stereo F.M. Radio Handbk.* v. 99 The winding direction of L_7 is such that signals at the lower end of this coil are in antiphase with the signals at the lower end of L_4. In this way the stage is unilateralized. **1981** E. OXNER in A. D. Evans *Designing with Field-Effect Transistors* iv. 144 The advantages of neutralization and unilateralization are that input and output are effectively isolated from each other and maximum stable gain results.

uniˈlaterally, *adv.* [f. UNILATERAL *a.* + -LY^2.] In a unilateral manner: **a.** *Bot.*, *Zool.*, and *Path.* On one side or surface only.

1830 LINDLEY *Nat. Syst. Bot.* 162 Flowers..often arranged unilaterally along the divisions of the cymes. **1852** DANA *Crust.* II. 1297 With several setæ at apex, which are unilaterally setulose. **1875** BENNETT & DYER *Sachs' Bot.* 463 The descending portions..joining others lower down either unilaterally or on both sides.

b. In respect of one side only; by means of or on the part of one side or party; one-sidedly.

1858 GLADSTONE *Homer* II. 297 But then such representations in Homer are not perseveringly, much less are they unilaterally, developed. **1875** POSTE *Gaius* I. Introd. (ed. 2) 8 A judgment..may be unilaterally penal, that is, may impoverish the defendant without enriching the plaintiff.

† uniliche, *a.* and *sb. Obs.* [OE. *unȝelíc* (see UN-^{1} 7 and YLIKE *a.*), = MDu. *ongelijc* (Du. *ongelijk*, WFris. *on-*, *ungelyk*), MLG. *ungelîk* (LG. *unglîk*), OHG. *ungalîh* (MHG. *ungelîch*, *unglich*, G. *ungleich*), ON. *úglíkr*.]

A. *adj.* Unlike; not of the same kind or condition; different; *spec.* incomparable, superior.

c **888** K. ÆLFRED *Boeth.* xxxiii. §5 Ealle ȝesceafta þu ȝesceope him ȝelice, & eac on sumum ðingum unȝelice. **971** *Blickl. Hom.* 97 þonne is unȝelic be þon ecan life. *a* **1100** in Napier *O.E. Glosses* I. 2325 *Dispari sexu*, unȝelicum [*Brussels MS.* unilicum] hade. *a* **1200** *Moral Ode* 360 (Trin. MS.), þar ben wuniinges fele elch oðer uniliche. *a* **1225** *Juliana* 60 An godd al mihti, al oðer unilich. *c* **1400** *R. Gloucester's Chron.* (Rolls) 815/268 He was..swiþe riche; Of richesse to fore alle oþere he was vniliche.

B. *sb.* = UNILIKE (q.v., quot. *a* 1250).

† uniliche, *adv. Obs.* [OE. *unȝelíce* (cf. prec.) differently, = OS. *ungilîko*, OHG. *ungelîcho*, etc.] Incomparably.

c **1290** *St. Brendan* 143 in *S. Eng. Leg.* I. 223 Fairere hi beoþ þan ȝoure scheep, & grettere vnyliche. *a* **1400** *R. Gloucester's Chron.* (Rolls) 786/58 Ac þe oþer were strengore, & richore oniliche.

† unilike. *Obs. rare.* [OE. *unȝelíca*, = MDu. *ongelike*: cf. UNILICHE *a.*] One different from, or superior to, another.

c **1000** ÆLFRIC *Saints' Lives* vii. 28 Ic hæbbe oðerne lufiend, þinne unȝelican on æðelborennysse. *a* **1250** *Owl & Night.* 806 (Cott.), þu seist þat þu canst fele wike Ac euer ich am þin unilike [*Jesus MS.* vnyliche].

uniˈlineal, *a.* [f. UNI- 1 + LINEAL *a.*]

1. *Anthropol.* Of or relating to a kinship system in which group membership, inheritance, etc., are established through either the father's or the mother's lineage. Opp. MULTILINEAL *a.*

1935 A. R. RADCLIFFE-BROWN *Structure & Function Primitive Society* (1952) ii. 36 The problem..of the nature and function of the unilineal transmission of rights. **1947** *Advancem. of Sci.* IV. 219/1 This leads to the emergence of more stable groupings of kin according to a principle of unilineal affiliation. **1957** V. W. TURNER *Schism & Continuity in Afr. Soc.* x. 291 Nor is their polity one consisting of homologous unilineal descent groups. **1963** *Brit. Jrnl. Sociol.* XIV. 24 Both [patrilineal and matrilineal] kinds of lineage system are described as *unilineal*. **1964** GOULD & KOLB *Dict. Social Sci.* 367/1 In a double unilineal system, while both parents are severally members of the same group as their child, he has kinsmen..who are not members of either of his unilineal groups. **1976** *Times Lit. Suppl.* 6 Aug. 992/1 Positive marriage rules which established alliance relations between unilineal descent groups.

2. Of a theory, progress, etc.: that adheres to one line of development, *spec.* that of uniform stages in the evolution of culture.

1957 G. CLARK *Archaeol. & Society* (ed. 3) vi. 173 Those who believed in the unilineal progress of culture. **1962** M. S. ZENGEL in J. A. Fishman *Readings Sociol. of Lang.* (1968) 298 It can be said that the 100 word list shows no more validity for this type of unilineal study than the 200 word list. **1968** *Encycl. Brit.* IX. 519/2 In the second half of the nineteenth century a belief in unilineal social evolution and the passage of all peoples through successive and similar stages of development was generally held by anthropologists and was not limited to them. **1980** *Times Lit. Suppl.* 15 Aug. 911/5 Hallpike seems to be a unilineal evolutionist for one kind of cognitive operation (that studied by developmental psychology), and a permissive relativist in the sphere of practical wisdom.

Hence **uniˈlinealism**, adherence to unilineal views; **uniˈlineally** *adv.*, in a unilineal manner.

1947 *Advancem. of Sci.* IV. 219/2 Factors tending to produce both unilineal transmission of rights and status and groups of unilineally related kin. **1957** K. A. WITTFOGEL *Oriental Despotism* ix. 371 (*caption*) The spread of a 'Marxist-Leninist' neo-unilinealism. **1964** GOULD & KOLB *Dict. Social Sci.* 367/1 A kind of discrete..descent group which in certain respects resembles a unilineally constructed group. **1984** *Times Lit. Suppl.* 16 Mar. 279/1 Soviet Marxism, as it crystallized during the Stalin period, had a clear and sharp outline, with its theory of a single dominant historical highway... This celebrated unilinealism is easy to attack.

uniˈlingual, *a.* (*sb.*) [See UNI- 1 and LINGUAL *a.*, and cf. F. *unilingue*.] **1.** Pertaining to one language only; knowing or employing only one language.

Hence, in recent use, ***unilingualism***.

1866 VISCT. STRANGFORD *Select.* (1869) II. 18 In Crete, one of the most primitive and unilingual parts of the Levant. **1886** *Standard* 8 Oct. 5 A good linguist has a pull..over his unilingual contemporary. **1894** *Educat. Rev.* VII. 190 The unilingual method..advocated by pedagogical writers.

2. *absol.* as *sb.* = MONOGLOT *sb. rare.*

1956 *Publ. Amer. Dial. Soc.* XXVI. 9 A monolingual (also called a monoglot or a unilingual) is a person who knows only one language. **1976** *Word 1971* XXVII. 382 Swedish was usually spoken to unilinguals.

uni'literal, *a.* [See UNI- 1 and LITERAL *a.*]

1. *Math.* (See quot.)

1817 COLEBROOKE *Algebra*, etc. 185 Equation uniliteral, or involving a single unknown quantity.

2. Involving the use of, or consisting of, only one letter.

1828–32 WEBSTER. **1863** TOWNSEND *Mod. Geom.* I. 2 The latter or uniliteral notation is generally the more convenient. **1892** C. TAYLOR *Witness of Hermas* 86 Examples of the uniliteral acrostic abound in the Sibylline Oracles.

uni'llumed, *ppl. a.* (UN-[1] 8.)

1796 COLERIDGE *Destiny of Nations* 161 Her full eye, now bright, now unillumed. **1869** TYNDALL in *Fortn. Rev.* 1 Feb. 143 The unillumed blackness of space.

uni'lluminated, *ppl. a.* [UN-[1] 8.]

1. Not spiritually or mentally enlightened.

1579 W. WILKINSON *Confut. Fam. Love* Biij b, H. N. sayth of all preachers without his Familie, that they are vnilluminated. **1639** W. SCLATER *Worthy Commun.* 23 Thus surely may your dull Capernaites, and unilluminated men imagine. **1660** H. MORE *Myst. Godl.* VI. xii. 248 What the ungodded or unilluminated men..bring forth. **1798** *Brit. Critic* XI. 47 The hazard of being reputed the disciples of a very *unilluminated* school. **1858** H. BUSHNELL *Serm. New Life* 100 The unilluminated and superficial speculations of our times. **1882** FARRAR *Early Chr.* I. 454 To the eyes of the unilluminated heart the region in which Faith lives and moves is a dark cavern.

2. Not illuminated or lighted up. Also *fig.*

1824 DE QUINCEY *Analects fr. Richter* Wks. 1860 XIV. 137, I saw the Form which still lightened as before, but left all around it unilluminated. **1874** tr. *Lommel's Light* 15 The back unilluminated surface of the body.

uni'lluminating, *ppl. a.* (UN-[1] 10.)

1882 A. AINGER *C. Lamb* 70 The very unilluminating notes of Johnson or Malone.

uni'llumined, *ppl. a.* (UN-[1] 8.)

[**1775** ASH.] **1826** LAMB *Elia* II. *Pop. Fallacies* xv, Our ancestors..wintering in caves and unillumined fastnesses. **1892** 'M. FIELD' *Sight & Song* 54 A solid disc of unillumined brown.

uni'llusory, *a.* (UN-[1] 7.)

1853 LYTTON *My Novel* III. xxii, Always scrutinizing the domestic felicity..through a pair of cold unillusory barnacles.

un'illustrated, *ppl. a.* (UN-[1] 8.)

[**1775** ASH.] **1828** WEBSTER (citing Good). **1879** *Cassell's Techn. Educ.* II. 275/1 Better than the most impressive verbal description, unillustrated. **1883** *American* VII. 9 Heavy, unillustrated English magazines.

uni'llustrative, *a.* (UN-[1] 7.)

1803 GODWIN *Chaucer* II. xliii. 282 It may not..prove.. unillustrative of the history..of England. **1867** *Fortn. Rev.* Oct. 377 Certain lights, not unillustrative as well of the one side as of the other.

uni'llustrious, *a.* (UN-[1] 7.)

1885 D. HANNAY in *Mag. Art* Sept. 448/1 A long and unillustrious line of successors. **1897** W. WATSON *Year of Shame, To Sultan*, It merged thee with the unillustrious herd.

uni'locular (juːnɪ-), *a.* [f. UNI- + LOCULAR *a.* Cf. mod.L. *ūniloculāris* and F. *uniloculaire* (1771).] Having, consisting of, characterized by only one loculus (in various senses); one-celled.

1753 *Chambers' Cycl.* Suppl. *App.*, *Unilocular*, in botany, is applied to a capsule having but one cell. **1762** *Phil. Trans.* LIII. 83 An oblong, oval striated unilocular seedvessel. **1815** W. WOOD *Gen. Conchol.* p. lx, The Paper Nautilus, the Cowries, the Olives, etc. are unilocular shells. **1860** PIRRIE *Surg.* 607 The unilocular cystic tumour. **1867** J. HOGG *Microsc.* II. ii. 376 The Polythalamia or Multilocular Rhizopods, in their earliest state are unilocular. **1899** *Allbutt's Syst. Med.* VIII. 634 A vesicle of H[erpes] Zoster at its height is a unilocular cavity.

Hence **unilocu'larity**, unilocular character or formation.

1819 LINDLEY tr. *Richard's Observ. Fruits & Seeds* 11 Unilocularity (provided there be no abortion) always establishes the unity of fruit. **1839** A. GRAY *Lett.* (1893) I. 150 The unilocularity of the anthers.

un'imaged, (*ppl.*) *a.* (UN-[1] 8, 9.)

1648 HEXHAM II, *Ongebeeldt*, Vn-imaged, without Figure or Image. **1775** ASH, *Unimaged*,.. not imaged, not formed in the imagination. **1841** CLOUGH *Poems* (1862) 17 The bare conscience of the better thing Unfelt, unseen, unimaged. **1860** PUSEY *Min. Proph.* 153 Their great forefathers.. worshipped the un-imaged Self-existing God.

uni'maginable, *a.* and *sb.* [UN-[1] 7 b, 5 b.]

1. *adj.* Incapable of being imagined; inconceivable, incomprehensible.

1611 COTGR., *Inimaginable*, vnimaginable, vnconceiuable. *a* **1631** DONNE *Serm.* I. (1634) 30 Miserable, unexpressible, unimaginable, macerable condition, where [etc.]. **1655** H. MORE *App. Antid.* vii. 377 It is utterly unimaginable, but that there should be a Triangular distance in the midst of them. **1746** HERVEY *Medit.*, *Refl. Flower Garden* 42 With what un-imaginable Complacency, does Justice rest satisfied! **1821** SCOTT *Kenilw.* vi, I shall thank him more for the love that has created such an unimaginable paradise, than for all the wonders it contains! **1878** P. BAYNE *Purit. Rev.* i. 7 To believe in an unseen and unimaginable Spirit.

2. *sb. pl.* = INEXPRESSIBLE *sb.* 2.

1833 T. HAMILTON *Men & Manners* (1843) 391 The men ..rejoiced in snuff-coloured waistcoats and unimaginables.

Hence **uni'maginableness**.

1659 H. MORE *Immort. Soul* I. vi. 37 The unimaginableness of Points and smallest Particles. **1871** W. G. WARD *Philos. Theism* (1884) I. 17 That the unimaginableness of a proposition is incompatible with its truth.

uni'maginably, *adv.* (UN-[1] 11; cf. prec.)

1666 BOYLE *Orig. Forms & Qual.* II. ix. 395 It appear'd a ..heap of Corpuscles..unimaginably small. *a* **1672** STERRY *2nd Posth. Vol.* 331 The Righteousness..of God in Christ.. unimaginably outshineth ten thousand Suns. **1734** WATTS *Reliq. Juv.* 191 And thus..we unimaginably slide into a cordial Defence of the Cause. **1857** HAWTHORNE *Eng. Note-bks.* (1870) II. 432 Hues..indescribably beautiful, and unimaginably, unless one can conceive of the colours of the rainbow [etc.]. **1883** *Harper's Mag.* June 115/2 Unimaginably frightful shapes.

uni'maginary, *a.* (UN-[1] 7.)

1608 D. PRICE *Chr. Warre* 27 God ouercame more gloriously for you by a weake, small vnimaginarie, Characterical armie. **1828** MACKINTOSH *Sp.* Wks. 1846 III. 490 One of their not unimaginary grievances.

uni'maginative, *a.* (UN-[1] 7.) Also *absol.*

1802 WORDSW. *Excurs.* II. 24 Ranging through the tamer ground Of these our unimaginative days. **1831** SCOTT *Ct. Rob.* xvii, Nor shall Anna Comnena, the soul of wit and genius, be chained to such an unimaginative log as yonder half barbarian. **1898** *Fortn. Rev.* LXIV. 300 To the un-imaginative, all imaginative work must inevitably present a closed door.

Hence **uni'maginatively** *adv.*, **-ness.**

1850 *N. Brit. Rev.* XII. 320 Not contented with such a stretch of unimaginativeness. **1883** *Cornh. Mag.* April 456 The Roman, more unimaginatively, held to the bare fact of change.

uni'magine, *v.* (UN-[2] 3.)

a **1670** RUST *Disc. Truth* (1682) 170 He may as easily unimagine that Imagination.

uni'magined, *ppl. a.* and *adv.* (UN-[1] 8.)

a **1548** HALL *Chron.*, *Hen. VI*, 103 A thyng discended from heauen, of theim vnsought, vnimagined and not deuised. **1649** LOVELACE *Poems* (1904) 69 The unimagin'd Woes..of the Hierarchy. **1736** BUTLER *Anal.* I. i. 20 A latent and..an unimagined unknown power of perceiving sensible objects. **1754** FRANCIS *Constantine* III. 36 What uninvented, unimagin'd Tortures Have I to dread? **1846** TRENCH *Mirac.* xvii. 276 His walking over the sea must have been altogether unimagined by them. **1884** CHURCH *Bacon* viii. 187 That hitherto unimagined empire of man over the powers and forces that encompassed him.

†**b.** *adv.* Unexpectedly. *Obs.*⁻¹

1614 W. B. *Philosopher's Banquet* (ed. 2) 254 When, vnimagined, the wench demaunded of him,..whether he [etc.].

unim'bued, *ppl. a.* (UN-[1] 8.)

[**1775** ASH.] **1813** SHELLEY *Q. Mab* v. 152 A weak and inexperienced boy,..unimbued With pure desire and universal love. **1880** TROLLOPE *Life of Cicero* I. 202 He was ..altogether unimbued with the humanity..of his brother.

unimer ('juːnɪmə(r)). *Chem.* [f. UNI- 2 + -MER.] One of the single molecules (usu. macro-molecules) that go to make up a multimeric aggregation. Cf. MULTIMER.

1967 *Chimia* XXI. 53/1 Methods to determine the association of macromolecules and to calculate the molecular weight of the unimer..are discussed. **1972** [see MULTIMER]. **1976** [see POLYMOLECULAR *a.* d].

†**uni'mete**, *sb. Obs.* [OE. *unȝemet*: see UN-[1] 12 and IMET.] Immoderation, excess.

c **888** K. ÆLFRED *Boeth.* xl. §3 He ne mæȝ nauþres unȝemet adrioȝan. *c* **1000** *Sax. Leechd.* II. 106 Þonne ȝeweaxeð on innan unȝemet wætan. *a* **1225** *Ancr. R.* 74 Urom soð hit slit te uals; vt of god into vuel, & from mesure into unimete.

†**uni'mete**, *adv. Obs.* [OE. *unȝemete*, dat. of *unȝemet*: see prec.] Immoderately, excessively.

Beowulf 2420 Him wæs ȝeomor sefa,..wyrd unȝemete neah. *Ibid.* 2721 Þeȝn unȝemete till. *c* **1000** *Ags. Ps.* (Thorpe) cxv. 2 Ic sylfa cwæð..þæt wæron ealle menn unȝemete lease. *c* **1205** LAY. 7393 Sixti scipen heo makeden vnimete [*c* **1275** onimete] muchele. *a* **1225** *Leg. Kath.* 738 Stoden on an half þeos meistres so monie, & unimete modi. **1300–1400** *R. Gloucester's Chron.* (Rolls) App. A. 15 Þe wynd..schouueþ & þrast þat al þe erþe quakiȝeþ & schakeþ onymete.

†**uni'mete**, *a. Obs.* [OE. *unȝemǽte*: see UN-[1] 7 and IMETE *a.*] Immeasurable, vast; immoderate, excessive.

a **1122** *O.E. Chron.* an. 1115 (Laud MS.), Ðises ȝeares wæs swa strang winter..& wearð þurh þæt unȝemæte orf cwealm. *c* **1175** *Lamb. Hom.* 101 Unimete festen and to michel forhefednesse..macað þene mon un-halne. *c* **1205** LAY. 4964 Þe ferde wes swa muchel þat heo wes vnimete [*c* **1275** onimete]. *a* **1225** *Ancr. R.* 40 Þo þi swete blisfule sune underueng ðe in his vnimete blisse. *c* **1275** *Sinners Beware* 50 in *O.E. Misc.* 73 Chele and hete, And hunger vnymete.

Hence †**uni'metely** *adv.*, immeasurably. *Obs.*

a **1225** *Ancr. R.* 398 Ne schal neuer heorte þenchen swuch seluhðe, þet ich nulle ȝiuen more uor þine luue, vnimeteliche and vnendliche more. *a* **1240** *Wohunge* in *O.E. Hom.* I. 281 Swa unimeteliche þu swanc and swa sare þat reade blod þu swattes.

un'imitable, *a.* ? *Obs.* (UN-[1] 7 b, 5 b.)

Very common in 17th century.

1581 SIDNEY *Apol. Poetrie* (Arb.) 46 As the vnimitable Pindar often did. **1622** F. MARKHAM *Bk. Warr* Ep. Ded. A 3 b, As by his owne vnimitable pen is protested. **1683** KENNETT *Erasm. on Folly* 48 As they [*sc.* bees] give a model of in their unimitable Combs. **1695** J. EDWARDS *Perfect. Script.* Ded., You bore the..insults of the enemy with unimitable bravery. **1773** JOHNSON in *Shakespeare's Wks.* V. 508 But Falstaff unimitated, unimitable Falstaff, how shall I describe thee?

So †**un'imitably** *adv. Obs.*

1622 PEACHAM *Compl. Gent.* x. 91 His sweetnesse and facilitie in a verse, vnimitably excellent. **1670** WALTON *Lives, Donne* 80 His fancy was unimitably high, equalled only by his great wit.

un'imitated, *ppl. a.* (UN-[1] 8.)

c **1610** *Women Saints* 185, I beseeche..you women doe not leaue this example vnimitated. *a* **1670** HACKET in Plume *Life* (1865) 171 The..perpetual sobriety of the primitive Christians began to be unimitated. **1773** [see UNIMITABLE *a.*]. **1837** CARLYLE *Fr. Rev.* I. III. viii, An excellent new-idea, which, in these coming years, shall not remain unimitated.

un'imitating, *ppl. a.* (UN-[1] 10.)

1748 RICHARDSON *Clarissa* (1811) VIII. 331 A spiteful, perverse, unimitating thing.

un'imitative, *a.* (UN-[1] 7.)

1807 ANNA SEWARD *Lett.* (1811) VI. 334 The original unimitative compositions of James H. **1849** RUSKIN *Sev. Lamps* iv. §2. 95 The Doric capital was unimitative. **1883** *Pall Mall G.* 8 Sept. 2/1 Among us unimitative but not unappreciative Britons.

uni'mmediate, *a.*, **-ly**, *adv.* (UN-[1] 7, 11.)

1802–12 BENTHAM *Ration. Judic. Evid.* (1827) III. 362 In an unimmediate, though, for efficacy, not too remote way. **1816** —— *Chrestom.* Wks. 1843 VIII. 91 Instruments of all kinds, whether applied immediately or unimmediately to use.

uni'mmergible, *a.* [UN-[1] 7.] Insubmergible.

1806 L. LUKIN (*title*), The Invention, Principles of Construction, and Uses of Unimmergible Boats. **1809** *Naval Chron.* XXI. 299 To make it..unimmergible,..casks ..were ranged along. **1823** *Blackw. Mag.* XIV. 303 They met with an unimmergible buoyancy in this case.

uni'mmersed, *ppl. a.* (UN-[1] 8.)

[**1775** ASH.] **1835** I. TAYLOR *Spir. Despot.* iv. 408 These good souls will not eat the Lord's loaf in company with the unclean and unimmersed commonalty of professed Christians. **1885** PENNELL *Fishing* 267 The effect of refraction kept the unimmersed portion of the fly fisher's figure practically out of sight.

un'immolated, *ppl. a.* (UN-[1] 8.)

1855 PUSEY *Doctr. Real Presence* Note I. 115 We too shall be able to receive Him wholly in ourselves continually immolated unimmolated for us.

uni'mmortal, *a.* (UN-[1] 7.)

1667 MILTON *P.L.* x. 611 They both betook them several wayes, Both to destroy, or unimmortal make All kinds. **1876** FARRAR *Marlb. Serm.* i. (1877) 5 Their unimmortal but sinless destiny being accomplished.

uni'mmortalize, *v.* (UN-[2] 6 c.)

1839 BAILEY *Festus* 336 They have well-nigh unimmortalized myself.

uni'mmortalized, *ppl. a.* (UN-[1] 8 *a* *c.*)

[**1775** ASH.] **1839** BAILEY *Festus* 10 But The shadowy giant alway thinned away, And I was fated unimmortalized.

uni'mmured, *ppl. a.* [UN-[1] 8.] †Unwalled. (See IMMURE *v.* 1.)

1615 G. SANDYS *Trav.* 155 The Iewes..began to reedifie the same [temple]; which yet was vnimmured for three-score and three yeares after.

unimodal (juːnɪ'məʊdəl), *a.* [f. UNI- + MODE *sb.* + -AL[1].] Of a frequency curve or distribution: having one mode (MODE *sb.* 7 c). Of a phenomenon or property: described by such a distribution.

1923 *Biometrika* XIV. 339 The distribution according to size of family..would be represented by one of the unimodal curves of the Pearson types. **1932** J. S. HUXLEY *Probl. Relative Growth* VII. i. 210 The frequency-curve for female body-length is unimodal. **1975** *Sci. Amer.* Feb. 70/2 The unimodal solar-day rhythms of organisms geared to the 24-hour solar day.

Hence **unimo'dality**, the property or quality of being unimodal.

1934 in WEBSTER. **1967** *Ann. Math. Statistics* XXXVIII. 1296 (*heading*) A note on the unimodality of distribution functions of class *L*. **1978** *Nature* 3 Aug. 504/1 The switch from bimodality to unimodality (that is convergence of two peaks into one) is what is expected for X-chromosome inactivation.

ˌunimo'lecular, *a. Chem.* [f. UNI- 1 + MOLECULAR *a.*] **a.** [ad. F. *unimoléculaire* (J. H. Van 't Hoff *Études Dynam. Chim.* (1884) 8).] In chemical kinetics: having or pertaining to a molecularity of one; involving the fragmentation or internal transformation of a single molecule in the rate-determining step of a reaction (rather than the collision of a pair of molecules); in quot. 1901, first-order (see ORDER *sb.* 10 f). Cf. MONOMOLECULAR *a.* b.

1901 *Jrnl. Chem. Soc.* LXXX. II. 647 The reaction between ferric salts and metallic iodides is unimolecular for the iron salt and bimolecular for the iodide. **1946** [see BIMOLECULAR *a.*]. **1972** R. A. JACKSON *Mechanism* i. 5 Unimolecular reactions occur as a result of reorganization of the bonds within a molecule, with or without rupture into fragments. **1978** P. W. ATKINS *Physical Chem.* xxvi. 863 Most reactions can be broken down into a sequence of steps that involve either a unimolecular reaction, in which a single molecule shakes itself apart or into a new configuration, or a bimolecular reaction.

b. = MONOMOLECULAR *a.* c.

1925 *Proc. R. Soc.* A. CIX. 303 Unimolecular films are thus to be anticipated in those cases in which the surface of the adsorbate is not very active, *e.g.*, on diamond. **1942** S. BRUNAUER *Adsorption of Gases & Vapours* I. i. 6 When a surface can take up only one layer of adsorbed gas the adsorption is called *unimolecular*. [*Note*] I. Langmuir [proposing the concept in 1917] used the term *monomolecular*. However since this is a term of mixed Greek and Latin derivation the use of the term unimolecular is preferable. **1978** K. J. LAIDLER *Physical Chem. with Biol. Applic.* xi. 462 Ammonia molecules are rather strongly attached to such a surface, which may become completely covered by a unimolecular layer.

Hence **unimo'lecularly** *adv.*

1901 *Jrnl. Chem. Soc.* LXXX. II. 647 Strontium and calcium iodides act unimolecularly. **1935** *Jrnl. Chem. Physics* III. 112 Suppose we have a non-linear molecule of *n* atoms decomposing unimolecularly. **1974** GILL & WILLIS *Pericyclic Reactions* vi. 203 Both 2,5-dihydrofuran and 1,4-cyclohexadiene are decomposed unimolecularly into hydrogen and respectively furan and benzene.

unim'pairable, *a.* (UN-^{1} 7 b.)

1627 HAKEWILL *Apol.* (1630) 288 It is unimpareable like the light..of the sunne. **1647** CLARENDON *Contempl. Ps.* Tracts (1727) 504 From that unimpairable stock of thy mercies..blot out our offences. **1653** H. MORE *Conject. Cabbal.* (1713) 175 It being the lowest degree and shadow of Being; and not only immoveable, but undiminishable and unimpairable.

unim'paired, *ppl. a.* (UN-^{1} 8.)

Before 1760 somewhat *rare*; in freq. use from *c* 1790.

1583 GOLDING *Calvin on Deut.* 41 b, In such wise as God may holde still his right vnempayred. **1628** LE GRYS tr. *Barclay's Argenis* 122 To him will I restore what they rob'd thee of, as I finde by them yet vnempayred. **1738** G. LILLO *Marina* II. ii, My youth yet unimpair'd By riot or disease. **1772** *Junius' Lett.* Ded. (1788) 7 When you leave the unimpaired, hereditary freehold to Your children. **1816** BYRON *Ch. Har.* III. v, Shapes which dwell Still unimpair'd, though old, in the soul's haunted cell. **1855** MACAULAY *Hist. Eng.* xx. IV. 532 She..repeated her part of the office with unimpaired memory. **1860** MOTLEY *Netherl.* ii. I. 51 He had preserved the most unimpaired good-humour.

unim'paradised, *ppl. a.* (UN-^{2} 5, 8.)

1601 W. PARRY *Trav. Sir A. Sherley* (1863) 4 A scruple.. whether Man were (for transgression) ever unimparadized or no.

unim'parted, *ppl. a.* (UN-^{1} 8.)

1655 (*title*), Natura Exenterata,..Whereunto are annexed, Many Rare, hitherto un-imparted Inventions. **1791** COWPER *Iliad* XI. 924 But brave Achilles shuts His virtues close, an unimparted store. **1824** SCOTT *St. Ronan's* xvi, That the knowledge which is unimparted is necessarily a barren talent.

unim'passionate, *a.* (UN-^{1} 7.)

1845 MOZLEY *Ess.* (1878) II. 119 In proportion to the extent to which such a view obtains, worship must become necessarily unimpassionate and unadoring.

unim'passioned, *ppl. a.* (UN-^{1} 8.)

1744 THOMSON *Autumn* (ed. 4) 1070 Fancy then..Will.. Correct her Pencil to the purest Truth Of Nature, or, the unimpassion'd Shades Forsaking, raise it to the human Mind. **1778** MISS BURNEY *Evelina* xxiii, The cool eye of unimpassioned philosophy. **1802** COLERIDGE *Dejection* ii, A stifled, drowsy, unimpassion'd grief. **1876** T. HARDY *Ethelberta* xxvii, She would not go out of her way at a beck from a man whose interest was so unimpassioned.

unimpeacha'bility. (UN-^{1} 12; cf. next.)

1830 R. CHAMBERS *Life Jas. I*, I. iv. 119 Nations..too much disposed..to question the unimpeachability of their sovereigns. **1881** SALA in *Illustr. Lond. News* 19 Feb. 171 The unimpeachability of the arrangements.

unim'peachable, *a.* (UN-^{1} 7 b.)

1784 COWPER *Task* IV. 676 Merchants, unimpeachable of sin Against the charities of domestic life. **1794** BURKE *Sp. Acts Uniformity* Wks. 1842 II. 465 The unimpeachable integrity and piety of many of the promoters of this petition. **1830** MISS MITFORD *Village* Ser. IV. 189 He could..take Harry's dinner to the same place with unimpeachable honesty. **1848** DICKENS *Dombey* iv, Seeing what time it is by the unimpeachable chronometer. **1864** BOWEN *Logic* xii. 392 The testimony of one unimpeachable witness.

Hence **unim'peachableness.** Also **unim'peach-ably** *adv.*

1817 GODWIN *Mandev.* III. 188 The insinuations they threw out against the *unimpeachableness of his motives. **1866** GEO. ELIOT *F. Holt* iv, Mrs. Holt was not given to tears; she was much sustained by conscious unimpeachableness. **1821** LAMB *Confess. Delamore* Wks. 1908 I. 266 For more than five centuries, the current of our blood hath flowed *unimpeachably. **1883** *Manch. Exam.* 22 Dec. 5 The jury were aided by a luminous and unimpeachably fair summing up.

unim'peached, *ppl. a.* [UN-^{1} 8.]

†**1.** Not impeded or hindered. *Obs.*

c **1430** *Pilgr. Lyf Manhode* II. xcvi. (1869) 110 With hire cordes she withheeld me, of which j was not unenpeched.

2. Not assailed, accused, or called in question.

1583 GOLDING *Calvin on Deut.* xxxix. 235 Let vs glorifie him, and beware yᵗ he remaine vnimpeached in his Maiestie. *c* **1611** CHAPMAN *Iliad* IX. 383 Many fair Achive princesses of unimpeached life. **1702** ROWE *Tamerl.* IV. i, While yet my Regal State stood unimpeach'd. **1790** COWPER *Let. to Bagot* 22 June, A person of most unimpeached veracity. **1823** BYRON *Siege Cor.* vii, When unimpeached for traitorous crime..He glittered thro' the Carnival. **1869** [see UNIMPLICATE]. **1871** JOWETT *Plato* IV. 158 The public and unimpeached use of anything for a year.

un'imped, *ppl. a.* (UN-^{1} 8 + IMP *v.* 8.)

1603 DRAYTON *To Maiestie K. Jas.* A 3, Our early Muse.. Of her own strength which boldly thus presumes, That's yet vnimpt with any borowed plumes.

unim'peded, *ppl. a.* (UN-^{1} 8.)

1760 D. MALLET in Derrick *Lett.* (1767) II. 23 Much more so as..your access to them [is] unimpeded. **1795** SOUTHEY *Vis. Maid of Orleans* I. 79 Through the roof..The moonbeams enter'd..With unimpeded light. **1861** MILL *Repr. Govt.* 52 Whatever invigorates the faculties,..creates an increased desire for their more unimpeded exercise. **1878** BOSW. SMITH *Carthage* 388 It gave them an unimpeded landing, and a second base of operations in Africa.

Hence **unim'pededly** *adv.*

Also, in recent use, *unimpededness.*

1846 POE *A. C. Mowatt* Wks. 1864 III. 43 The mere instruments by which she may effectively and unimpededly lay bare to the audience the movements of her own passionate heart.

unim'pedible, *a.* (UN-^{1} 7.)

1677 GALE *Crt. Gentiles* III. II. 515 Where-ever there is passive Power there is impedibilitie: There is nothing ἀνεμπόδιστος, unimpedible, but God.

unim'perative, *a.* (UN-^{1} 7.)

1817 BENTHAM *Parl. Reform* Introd. 102 A mere exercise of the unimperative faculty of deputation.

unim'perious, *a.* (UN-^{1} 7.)

[**1775** ASH.] **1792** J. RICHARDSON *Fugitive* IV. iii, The merits of your most unimperious sex.

unim'pinging, *ppl. a.* (UN-^{1} 10.)

1800 COLERIDGE *Lett.* (1895) 326 Alfoxden would make two houses sufficiently divided for unimpinging independence.

un'implicate, *ppl. a.* [UN-^{1} 8 b.] = next.

1869 BROWNING *Ring & Bk.* XI. 1287 She, unimpeached of crime, unimplicate In folly.

un'implicated, *ppl. a.* (UN-^{1} 8.)

1822–7 GOOD *Study Med.* (1829) IV. 687 The sound parts remain unimplicated in the action. **1857** DE QUINCEY in 'H. A. Page' *Life* (1877) II. xvii. 56 The boy was quite unimplicated in any part of the case.

unim'plicit, *a.* (UN-^{1} 7.)

1673 MILTON *True Relig.* 16 Which must needs conduce much..to the general confirmation of unimplicit truth.

unim'plored, *ppl. a.* (UN-^{1} 8.)

1667 MILTON *P.L.* IX. 22 If answerable style I can obtaine Of my Celestial Patroness, who deignes Her nightly visitation unimplor'd. *a* **1711** KEN *Hymnarium* Poet. Wks. 1721 II. 85 To Sinners thou..Grace unimplor'd benignly dost impart. **1746** YOUNG *Nt. Th.* IX. 904 We feel A sudden succour, un-implor'd, un-thought. **1806** JOHN HOGG *Poems* 31 [She was] Impatient to perform her offer made To Zara, unimplor'd. **1842** WORDSW. *Eccles. Sonn.* III. xxix, If sorrow for thy sin be dead, Guilt unrepented, pardon unimplored.

unim'portance. (UN-^{1} 12.)

1751 JOHNSON *Rambler* No. 146 ⁋5 By such arts..does every man endeavour to conceal his own unimportance from himself. **1775** S. J. PRATT *Liberal Opin.* v. (1783) I. 15 The eye of a child converts every trifle into an object of entertainment, and every pretty unimportance, is esteemed a joyful acquisition. **1823** LAMB *Wks.* (1908) I. 286 The unimportance of the subject. **1879** R. K. DOUGLAS *Confucianism* iii. 66 To the succeeding millions of China it has been a matter of unimportance.

unim'portant, *a.* [UN-^{1} 7.]

1. Unassuming, modest. *rare*$^{-1}$.

1727 POPE *Let. to Swift* 8 Mar., A free, unimportant, natural, easy manner; diverting others just as we diverted ourselves.

2. Of no importance or moment.

1750 CHESTERF. *Let.* 1 Nov., Ransacking..the minute and unimportant parts of remote and fabulous times. **1798** S. & HT. LEE *Canterb. T.* II. 465 He was too unimportant to act on [the passions]..of any one around him. **1841** MIALL in *Nonconf.* I. 1 The ends they sought appeared too unimportant to justify the cost. **1869** FREEMAN *Norm. Conq.* xi. III. 53 Esegar and Bondig play not unimportant parts in the great struggles of the year.

Comb. **1841** CARLYLE *Heroes* iv. (1904) 129 There was not a more entirely unimportant-looking pair of people.

unim'ported, *ppl. a.* (UN-^{1} 8.)

[**1775** ASH.] **1784** R. BAGE *Barham Downs* II. 88 Two bottles of unimported wine.

†**unim'porting**, *ppl. a.* [UN-^{1} 10.] = UNIMPORTANT *a.* 2.

c **1625** BP. HALL *St. Paul's Combat* Wks. 1634 II. 449 If it be only matter of rite, or of unimporting consequence. **1642** FULLER *Holy & Prof. St.* III. xx. 206 Such Divines, who in unimporting controversies extract the probablest opinions from all Professions. **1658** T. WALL *Charact. Enemies Ch.* 40 Things of unimporting consequence.

unim'portunate, *a.* (UN-^{1} 7.)

1755 YOUNG *Centaur* iii. Wks. 1757 IV. 174 These are the men, who..rush headlong into..even unimportunate temptations. **1824** LANDOR *Imag. Conv.* I. 299 The demon of Socrates, not always unimportunate, followed Euripides.

unimportuned, *ppl. a.* (UN-^{1} 8.)

? **1611–2** DONNE *Let. to Lady Carey* 23 Who ever ran To danger unimportun'd. *a* **1631** —— *Paradoxes* (1652) 27 To run into Death unimportuned is to run into the first condemned Desperateness. **1849** C. BRONTË *Shirley* xiii, [They] were suffered to keep details to themselves, unimportuned by the curiosity of their listeners.

unimpor'tunely, *adv.* (UN-^{1} 11.)

1657 EARL MONM. tr. *Paruta's Pol. Disc.* 42 Rather..to dissemble their injuries and suspitions, then by unimportunely revenging the one and assertaining the other, put their affairs in greater danger.

unim'posed, *ppl. a.* (UN-^{1} 8.)

1642 MILTON *Apol. Smect.* 50 The very act of prayer and thanksgiving with those free and unimpos'd expressions..is the greatest decency that can be imagin'd. **1677** GILPIN *Demonol.* II. iv. 249 From the toleration of a private Opinion of some Doctors and unimposed, it obtained at last a Canon to make it Authentick, Publick Doctrine.

So **unim'posedly** *adv.*

1647 BOYLE in Birch *Life* (1744) 80 The gallantry..of their own principles will carry them on unimposedly to do much more.

unim'posing, *ppl. a.* [UN-^{1} 10.]

†**1.** Not burdensome or oppressive. *Obs.*$^{-1}$

1736 THOMSON *Liberty* v. 626 Beauteous Order reigns, Manly Submission, unimposing Toil.

2. Unimpressive.

1809 C. SIMEON in W. Carus *Life* (1847) 272 The slow unimposing voice. **1854** MILMAN *Lat. Christianity* VII. ii. III. 169 A grey haired man..of small unimposing stature. **1871** EARLE *Philol. Eng. Tongue* 421 A feature..unimposing in its appearance.

So **unim'posingly** *adv.*

1880 MISS BIRD *Japan* I. 15 The British Consulate, imposingly ugly;..the Union Church,..unimposingly so.

unim'pounded, *ppl. a.* (UN-^{1} 8.)

1866 HOWELLS *Venetian Life* 5, I do not say that these cells are calculated to enamour the unimpounded spectator with prison-life.

unim'powered, *ppl. a.* (UN-^{1} 8.)

1731 A. HILL *Adv. Poets* Epist. p. vi, The Poet.. unimpower'd to act greatly Himself, asserts his Fire in describing the Great Actions of others.

unim'pregnate, *ppl. a.* [UN-^{1} 8 b.] = next.

1834 LD. HOUGHTON *Mem. Tour Greece* 140 Dumb forms, unimpregnate with vital emotion. **1849** LOWELL *Biglow P.* Ser. I. Poet. Wks. (1912) 226/2 Lads, unimpregnate with the more sublimated punctiliousness of Walton.

unim'pregnated, *ppl. a.* [UN-^{1} 8.]

1. Not rendered pregnant.

1744 *Phil. Trans.* XLIII. 83 Nor can we conceive any Use of them while the Uterus is unimpregnated at any time. **1793** M. BAILLIE *Morb. Anat.* 269 The uterus in such cases is considerably larger than the unimpregnated size. **1862** A. MEADOWS *Man. Midwifery* 52 The nerve-tubules in the unimpregnated state. **1877** HUXLEY *Anat. Inv. Anim.* vii. 446 The unimpregnated, apterous, caterpillar-like females of the Lepidopterous genera Psyche and Solenobia.

b. Not fructified or made prolific.

1800 *Med. Jrnl.* III. 160 The remark, that a similar liquor had been found in unimpregnated eggs. **1842** J. BURNET *Reynold's Disc.* 33 Many young men of genius have disappeared like unimpregnated blossoms, flowery but fruitless.

2. Not impregnated (*with* some matter).

1772–3 T. PERCIVAL *Ess.* (1777) I. 59 An ounce and a half of Jamaica Rum, which was..unimpregnated with any astringent matter from the cask. **1790** *Phil. Trans.* LXXX. 372 A thick white turbid liquor, which was rendered clear by addition of unimpregnated oil of vitriol.

unim'pressed, *ppl. a.* [UN-^{1} 8.]

†**1.** Not subjected to restraint. *Obs.*$^{-1}$

1743 YOUNG *Nt. Th.* v. 122 Thoughts uncontroul'd, and unimpress'd, the births Of pure election.

2. Not affected by feelings of respect or awe.

1861 [F. W. ROBINSON] *Under the Spell* I. 300 He did not mind her being 'un-impressed' by the knowledge that her father was only his tutor. **1896** MRS. CAFFYN *Quaker Grandmother* 110 Mossy did this sort of thing remarkably well. But Miriam was quite unimpressed.

3. Not bearing an impression.

1868 HERSCHEL in *People's Mag.* Jan. 63 Do the same with one side of the unimpressed square, and then apply the one square to the other,..the impression being between them.

unimpressi'bility. (UN-^{1} 12; cf. next.)

1854 YONGE tr. *Athenæus* III. 966 When he found he could make no impression on the coldness and unimpressibility of the stone. **1889** SKRINE *Mem. Thring* 124 Heartiness in his own belief, and iron unimpressibility against the noise and flourishes of an enemy.

unim'pressible, *a.* (UN-^{1} 7.)

1828 L. HUNT *Byron & Contemp.* 26 She..was.. absolutely unimpressible in that respect. **1856** KANE *Arct. Expl.* I. ii. 24 As stolid and unimpressible as one of our own Indians. **1878** BOSW. SMITH *Carthage* 44 The African was so unimpressible, and the Phœnician was so little disposed..to assimilate himself to his surroundings.

Hence **unim'pressibleness.**

1830 ARNOLD *Let.* in Stanley *Life* (1858) I. 223 Thorough careless unimpressibleness beats one all to pieces.

unim,pressiona'bility. (UN-^{1} 12; cf. next.)

1862 F. W. ROBINSON *Female Life in Prison* I. 80 This strange apathetic indifference, this unimpressionability.

unim'pressionable, *a.* (UN-^{1} 7 b.)
1847 C. BRONTE *J. Eyre* xxi, Unimpressionable natures are not so soon softened. **1850** THACKERAY *Pendennis* xv, Ah! what mad desires dashing up against some rock of obstruction or indifference, and flung back again from the unimpressionable granite! **1884** E. YATES *Recoll.* II. 201 [He] was..as unimpressionable as an oyster.

unim'pressive, *a.* (UN-^{1} 7.)
1796 GISBORNE *Walks Forest* (ed. 2) vi. 121 Does Truth, disclosed from heaven,..her sacred shafts behold Bound unimpressive from the callous heart? **1828** P. CUNNINGHAM *N.S. Wales* (ed. 3) II. 314 The slovenly and unimpressive manner in which the witness is sworn. **1880** C. WICKSTEED in *S. Brooke's Life & Lett.* (1917) I. 330 Look at the men who pass into the shades of our theology—impassive, unimpressive shades!
Hence **unim'pressively, -ness.**
1827 HARE *Guesses* Ser. I. 107 The accuracy and unimpressiveness of Algebraic characters. **1832** J. S. MILL *Let.* 29 May (1910) I. 30 The opinions I have put forth in these different articles..are expressed so coldly and unimpressively that I can scarcely bear to look back upon such poor stuff. **1860** GEO. ELIOT in Cross *Life* (1885) II. 221 The variety is in some degree a cause of comparative unimpressiveness.

unim'prison, *v.* (UN-^{2} 3.)
1817 COLERIDGE *Biog. Lit.* (1882) 263 No fly unimprisoned from a child's hand, could more buoyantly enjoy its element.

unim'prisonable, *a.* (UN-^{1} 7 b.)
1649 MILTON *Eikon.* 148 To imprison and confine by force..those two most unimprisonable things, our Prayers and that Divine Spirit of utterance that moves them.

unim'prisoned, *ppl. a.* [UN-^{1} 8 and UN-^{2} 8.]
a. Not imprisoned. **b.** Released from prison.
1659 W. CHAMBERLAYNE *Pharonnida* I. 75 Her unimprisond Soul disrob'd of all Terrestrial thoughts. **1809–14** WORDSW. *Excurs.* IV. 106 The unimprisoned Mind May yet have scope to range among her own. **1820** BENTHAM *Liberty of Press* Wks. 1843 II. 283/1 To live unhanged, unsabred, unimprisoned. **1837** CARLYLE *Fr. Rev.* III. I. iv, That the King's Friends in Prison would burst out, and, joined by the unimprisoned, ride roughshod over us all.

unim'prisoning, *ppl. a.* (UN-^{2} 3, 8.)
1820 E. IRVING in Froude *Carlyle* (1882) I. 86 Now it will be like the unimprisoning of a bird to come and let me have free talk.

unim'propriate, *ppl. a.* (UN-^{1} 8.)
1655 FULLER *Waltham Abbey* 8 An Abby and a Parsonage unimpropriate in the same place, are as inconsistent together, as good woods and an Iron Mill.

unimprova'bility. (UN-^{1} 12; cf. next.)
1814 H. C. ROBINSON *Diary* 28 May (1967) 34 The doctor's favourite opinion of the unimprovability of mankind met with no opposition from the Lambs. **1861** *Gd. Words* 432 The Boeotian dulness and unimprovability of the fatuous German king.

unim'provable, *a.* (UN-^{1} 7 b.)
a **1660** HAMMOND *Serm.* Wks. 1684 IV. 577 The principal faculty which is irrecoverably wanting in such, and by all teaching irreparable and unimproveable, is the power of numbring. *a* **1683** OLDHAM *Art of Poetry* Wks. (1684) II. 14 At first dash, as if before 'twere known, [he] Embarques you in the middle of the Plot And what is unimprovable leaves out. **1785** G. A. BELLAMY *Apol.* (ed. 3) III. 52 The 'Squire, however, remained totally unimprovable. **1790** *Act 30 Geo. III*, c. 50 To sell or alienate Fee Farm, and other unimproveable Rents. **1822** SCOTT *Nigel* xv, You show an absolute and unimprovable acquaintance with..mankind in general. **1847** GROTE *Greece* xxiv. III. 548 A people the most unprincipled and unimproveable of all.
Hence **unim'provableness.**
1654 HAMMOND *Fundam.* xvi. 174 This must be imputed ..to their ignorance and unimprovableness in matters of knowledge.

unim'proved, *ppl. a.*^{1} [UN-^{1} 8.]
1. Not made better; not raised in quality.
1665 BOYLE *Occas. Refl.* I. ii. 163 Flowers (which, unimprov'd by Art, delight but whilst they are..fresh). *c* **1695** J. MILLER *Descr. New York* (1843) 41 The whole country, improved or unimproved, to belong to the King. **1764** GOLDSM. *Trav.* 230 From sire to son Unalter'd, unimprov'd the manners run. **1794** S. WILLIAMS *Vermont* 134 Man in the most simple, rude and unimproved state. **1858** GREENER *Gunnery* 4 This range being quite equal..to that of the late unimproved rifles. **1890** 'R. BOLDREWOOD' *Col. Reformer* (1891) 247 A cheap unimproved property.
2. Not turned to use; not taken advantage of.
1781 COWPER *Truth* 524 He that scorns the noon-day beam, perverse, Shall find the blessing, unimprov'd, a curse. **1820** W. JAY *Prayers* 110 Those privileges, which, unimproved, will only augment our guilt. **1850** GROTE *Greece* lxi. VII. 533 They preferred leaving their victory unimproved, to the hazard of a general battle.
3. Not medically bettered.
1879 *St. George's Hosp. Rep.* IX. 466 One case was discharged 'unimproved',..but the others were all benefited.

†**unim'proved,** *ppl. a.*^{2} *Obs.*$^{-1}$ [UN-^{1} + IMPROVE *v.*^{1}] Unreproved, uncensured.
1602 SHAKS. *Ham.* I. i. 96 Young Fortinbras Of vnimproued Mettle, hot and full.

unim'provement. (UN-^{1} 12.)
1757 MRS. GRIFFITH *Lett. Henry & Frances* (1767) I. 80 The visto of some absurd fellows unimprovement.

unim'proving, *ppl. a.* (UN-^{1} 10.)
1747 *Mem. Nutrebian Crt.* I. 206 While Gen Haragen was indulged in play, and idle unimproving amusements. **1788** V. KNOX *Winter Even.* lii. (1790) 378 If the idle were to lay aside such unimproving works. **1823** KEBLE *Serm.* iii. (1848) 48 It might be no unimproving exercise of self-denial, to men of refined judgments. **1883** *Academy* 15 Sept. 175/2 Many unimproving anecdotes of his proceedings still linger along the Spanish Main.

unim'pugnable, *a.* (UN-^{1} 7 b.)
1832 MRS. GORE *Fair of May Fair* III. 278 His judgment was invaluable,..and unimpugnable at Lloyd's. **1857** DICKENS *Dorrit* II. xxxii, Solely supported by his unimpugnable calculations.

unim'pugned, *ppl. a.* (UN-^{1} 8.)
[**1775** ASH.] **1838** JAMES *Louis XIV*, I. 247 That all the arbitrary acts of his predecessor..should remain as unimpugned precedents in case of necessity. *a* **1857** R. A. VAUGHAN *Ess. & Rem.* (1858) I. 37 Thus did Origen.. attempt to retain the justice of God unimpugned.

unim'pulsive, *a.* (UN-^{1} 7.)
[**1775** ASH.] **1856** LEVER *Martins of Cro' M.* xiv. 138 The most suspectful, unimpulsive, and ungenerously-disposed of all natures, an old lawyer. **1886** RUSKIN *Præterita* I. iv. 112 The steady pains of her unimpulsive practice.
Hence **unim'pulsiveness.**
1860 TROLLOPE *Framley P.* xxv, Such a degree of unimpulsiveness as this.

unim'puted, *ppl. a.* (UN-^{1} 8.)
1723 POPE *Let. to Blount* 27 June, You must look on this as the first day I've been myself, and pass over the mad interval un-imputed to me.

uni'naugurated, *ppl. a.* (UN-^{1} 8.)
1823 SCOTT *Quentin D.* Introd., An immense *assiêtte* of spinage, not smoothed into a uniform surface, as by our uninaugurated cooks upon your side of the water.

unin'carnate, *a.* (UN-^{1} 7.)
1687 *Death's Vision* 182 Blind to the World of Unincarnate Hosts! **1716** HUME *Sacr. Succession* 159 What God..perform'd by heavenly un-incarnate angels. **1827** POLLOK *Course T.* v. 575 The spirits unincarnate. **1860** FABER *Bethlehem* 90 The unincarnate Saviour redeemed millions before His actual Incarnation.
So **unin'carnated** *ppl. a.*
1859 W. ANDERSON *Disc.* (1860) 146 The idea of the Unincarnated Eternal One.

unin'censed, *ppl. a.* (UN-^{1} 8.)
1594 CAREW *Huarte's Exam. Wits* x. 139 The flegmaticke vnincensed, haue their braine very cold and moist. *a* **1800** COWPER *Iliad* (ed. 2) v. 899 Jove! see'st thou, unincensed, these deeds of Mars? **1885** SWINBURNE *Stud. Victor Hugo* (1886) 84 The aspect of babies when unvexed and unincensed by any cross accident.

un'inchoative, *a.* (UN-^{1} 7.)
1649 J. ELLISTONE tr. *Behmen's Epist.* 106 The soule (which ariseth..out of the Eternall un-inchoative Nature). **1691** E. TAYLOR *Behmen's Theos. Philos.* 367 What God is in his Eternal uninchoative Generation.

uninci'dental, *a.* [UN-^{1} 7.] Not marked by any incident.
1772 *Theatrical Biogr.* I. 147 [Parsons'] memoirs would be too unincidental, and consequently too unentertaining for a place here. **1853** WILBERFORCE in *Life* (1881) II. 194 The dead level plains of times of fat quietness and un-incidental ease.

unin'cited, *ppl. a.* (UN-^{1} 8.)
1648 HEXHAM II, *Ongehisset*, Vn-incited, or Vnsummoned. **1809–14** WORDSW. *Excurs.* v. 597 And unincited by a wish to look Into high objects farther than they may.

unin'clinable, *a.* (UN-^{1} 7 b.)
1640 WALTON *Life of Donne* in *D.'s Eighty Serm.* Pref., The King..perswaded M. Donne to enter into the Ministery, to which he appeared (and was) uninclinable. **1656** HOBBES *Liberty, Necess., & Chance* 9 Seeing that mans heart without the grace of God, is uninclinable to good.

unin'clined, *ppl. a.* (UN-^{1} 8.)
1729 LAW *Serious C.* xvi. 291 They who..render themselves..uninclin'd to observe rules and hours of devotion. **1740** RICHARDSON *Pamela* II. 10 In which..you take Notice of my being uninclin'd to marry.

unin'clining, *ppl. a.* (UN-^{1} 10.)
1794 T. TAYLOR *Pausanias' Descr. Greece* III. 294 Of pure and uncontaminated order, and of unInclining power.

unin'cluded, *ppl. a.* (UN-^{1} 8.)
1775 R. CHANDLER *Trav. Greece* (1825) II. 299 Lombardi was..unincluded in the general amnesty. **1802–12** BENTHAM *Ration. Judic. Evid.* (1827) III. 474 If any one of the possible modes of transcription were left unincluded in the penal consequences. **1855** W. H. MILL *Applic. Panth. Princ.* (1861) 234 Those who believe St. James the Just to be unincluded in the number of the twelve.

unin'clusive, *a.* (UN-^{1} 7.)
1864 PUSEY *Lect. Daniel* viii. 468 The word 'until'..is to be understood ideally of an unending, unclosed, uninclusive term.

unincon'venienced, *ppl. a.* (UN-^{1} 8.)
1829 *Encycl. Metrop.* (1845) VI. 291/1 Casemates.. unInconvenienced by smoke.

unin'corporate, *a.* [UN-^{1} 7.]
1. Unembodied.
1821 BYRON *Sardanap.* IV. i, If there be indeed A shore where mind survives, 'twill be as mind, All unincorporate. **1866** GROTE *Exam. Utilit. Phil.* iv. (1870) 62 He is writing as a true utilitarian about happiness in that unindividual, unincorporate, abstract notion of it.
2. = next 2.
1880 *Act 43 & 44 Vict.* c. 42 §7 Where the employer is a body of persons corporate or unincorporate.

unin'corporated, *ppl. a.* [UN-^{1} 8.]
1. Not incorporated or united *with*.
1715 ATTERBURY *Serm.* (1737) III. 128 They have continued unmixed, unincorporated with any of the nations ..amidst whom they dwelt.
2. Not formed into a corporation.
1818 HALLAM *Mid. Ages* (1819) I. 443 The arrangement of twenty-one trading companies had still left several kinds of artisans unincorporated. *Ibid.* III. 167 The representation of unchartered, or at least unincorporated boroughs. **1884** *St. James's Gaz.* 10 May 5/1 The regulation of proceedings brought against unincorporated clubs.

unin'creasable, *a.* (UN-^{1} 7 b.)
1648 BOYLE *Seraph. Love* i. (1659) 8 An..almost unincreaseable Elevation, and vastnesse of affection. **1698** NORRIS *Pract. Disc.* IV. 296 The Blessed God, whose Perfect and Unincreaseable Happiness makes him utterly uncapable of..such a Love. **1872** RUSKIN *Fors Clav.* xvi. 12 These..are your wealth, for ever—unincreasable. **1872** BAGEHOT *Physics & Pol.* 54 The unincreasable land being occupied.

unin'creased, *ppl. a.* (UN-^{1} 8.)
[**1775** ASH.] **1824** MISS MITFORD *Village* Ser. I. 273 There it stands,..unincreased and undiminished by a single brick. **1890** *Retrospect Med.* CII. 140 Even with the urine unincreased..there is a large drain upon the liquids.

unin'creasing, *ppl. a.* (UN-^{1} 10.)
1587 GOLDING *De Mornay* vi. 72 To be short, he calleth him ye myndly speech,..vncorruptible, vnincreasing, vndecreasing,..and first beknowne after God.

unin'crusted, *ppl. a.* (UN-^{1} 8.)
1880 SWINBURNE *Stud. Shaks.* 157 Unincrusted with any flake of dirt.

un'incubated, *ppl. a.* (UN-^{1} 8.)
1859 DARWIN *Orig. Spec.* vii. 217 Those first laid would have to be left for some time unincubated. **1891** *Science-Gossip* XXVII. 8 A nest..which contained four eggs unincubated.

unin'debted, *ppl. a.* (UN-^{1} 8.)
1672 DRYDEN *Assignation* v. iv, So you shall still be innocent, and I Die blessed, and unindebted for my being. **1759** *Ann. Reg., Hist. War* 41/2 Unindebted to family or connections. **1781** COWPER *Table-t.* 525 Give me the line.. That, like some cottage beauty, strikes the heart, Quite unindebted to the tricks of art. **1846** SIR W. HAMILTON *Diss.* in *Reid's Wks.* 891 Neither ignorant of, nor unindebted to, their writings. **1882** SAINTSBURY *Hist. French Lit.* III. vii. 380 He was..probably not unindebted to Descartes for the force and vigour of his reasonings.
Hence **unin'debtedness.**
1866 *Times* 4 Jan. 8/4 If they shall have paid off their present debt, they will enjoy a confidence far stronger than that from simple unindebtedness.

unin'dented, *ppl. a.* [UN-^{1} 8.]
1. Not marked with indentations.
1750 G. HUGHES *Barbados* 133 Two unindented Seams crossing one another at Right Angles. **1828** LYTTON *Pelham* III. v, The rest of the countenance was perfectly smooth and unindented. **1863** TYNDALL *Heat* v. 160 The border finally becomes unindented.
2. Of type: Set up without indention.
1903 *Athenæum* 17 Jan. 78/2 Printed either in fourteen unindented lines, or with only the final couplet indented.
3. Not indentured.
1881 STEVENSON *Not I & other Poems* (1898) 7 The pamphlet..Was planned and printed by A printer unindented.

un'indexed, *ppl. a.* (UN-^{1} 8.)
1832 PALGRAVE *Eng. Commw.* II. 124 These most valuable records..are still unindexed. **1856** RUSKIN *Mod. Paint.* IV. v. ii. §17 Over all this unindexed and immeasurable mass of treasure.

un'indicated, *ppl. a.* (UN-^{1} 8.)
[**1775** ASH.] **1825** COLERIDGE *Aids Refl.* 148 *note*, The unprotrusive and unindicated convolutes of the Brain, that secrete honesty and common-sense. **1904** E. GOSSE *Jer. Taylor* iii. 103 No temptation..is allowed to pass unindicated or unreproved.

unin'dictable, *a.* (UN-^{1} 7 b.)
1861 WYNTER *Soc. Bees* 29 The various hydro-carbons.. escape in the form of thin unindictable vapour, of a highly obnoxious character. **1870** LOWELL *Among my Bks.* Ser. I. 127 The unindictable Powers of Darkness.

unin'dicted, *ppl. a.* (UN-^{1} 8.)
[**1775** ASH.] **1806** in *Spirit Pub. Jrnls.* X. 311 By unindicted thieves, alas! purloin'd. **1978** *N.Y. Times* 30 Mar. B13/6 [He] had been named by a grand jury as an unindicted co-conspirator in a series of allegedly illegal break-ins. **1979** *N.Y. Rev. Bks.* 8 Feb. 8/1 The publishers of this chaotically dull..work of angry, apologetic confusion, should be named unindicted co-conspirators in this sinister effort to get those few left who read to switch to television.

unin'difference. [UN-^{1} 12.] = next.
1665 EVER *Tryals per Pais* ix. 106 Where there is no unindifference or default in the Sheriff. **1824** BARNEWALL & CRESSWELL *Rep.* II. 104 The panel of talés having been quashed..on the ground of the unindifference of the sheriff.

unin'differency. Now *arch.* [UN-^{1} 12 + INDIFFERENCY I.] Lack of impartiality.
1578 WHETSTONE *1st Pt. Promos & Cass.* IV. ii, Such grace woulde mee, with vnindifferencie tuch, To pardon him, that dyd commit a Rape. **1625** tr. *Boccaccio's Decam.* II. 26 His successe proved answerable to his hope, no unindifferencie

appearing in their purposes. **1665** Ever *Tryals per Pais* ix. 106 In respect of the cause of unindifferency, or default of the Sheriff or other Officer that made the Return. **1844** *Judgm. Ld. Denman in O'Connell* v. *Queen* 7 Unindifferency or misconduct on the part of the sheriff.

unin'different, *a.* [UN-[1] 7.]

†**1.** Unequal, unfavourable. *Obs.*[−1]

1565 Golding *Cæsar* 209 When he saw howe thencounter was in an vnindifferent place..[he] sent to..his Lieuetenant.

2. a. Of persons: Not impartial or fair-minded; prejudiced. Now *arch.*

1571 Golding *Calvin on Ps.* xli. 3 The miserable man whom cruel and unindifferent persons surmise to bee forlorne. **1611** A. Munday *Brief Chron.* A8, This vertuous ..man, knowing Death to be an vnindifferent Executor. **1673** O. Walker *Educ.* 204 Unindifferent are those who are pre-ingaged. **1852** *Fraser's Mag.* March 246/1 He may consequently be supposed, to use the language of the law, 'to stand unindifferent as he stands unsworn'.

†**b.** Of actions, etc.: Lacking in impartiality or fairness. *Obs.*

1583 Golding *Calvin on Deut.* xxxix. 231 Such vnindifferent dealing shall alwayes be taken for theft before God. **1600** Tate in Gutch *Coll. Cur.* I. 7 It may justly be thought unindifferent to nominate his own country for the place. **1602** Warner *Alb. Eng.* Epit. 378 Stomacking..the vnindifferent sharing of the Nordaine Bootie.

3. Not indifferent; concerned, interested.

1813 Lamb *Play-ho Mem.* Wks. 1908 I. 202 Those honest, hearty, well-pleased, unindifferent mortals above.

So **unin'differently** *adv.*, unfairly.

1608 Hieron *Defence* II. 126 He..maie easely perceyve.. how unindifferently and unequally he sorteth us and Cochlæus togither.

un'indigent, *a.* (UN-[1] 7.)

1830 T. Taylor *Argts. Celsus* 63 A corporeal worship cannot even be paid to these, because they are naturally unindigent.

unin'dignant, *a.* (UN-[1] 7.)

1789 Anna Seward *Lett.* (1811) II. 299 A well-informed woman..will at once find these volumes..too vulgar for her unindignant endurance. **1800** G. Wakefield in *Mem.* (1804) II. 425 With unindignant apathy pass by Of Antijacobins the filthy stye?

unindi'vidual, *a.* (UN-[1] 7.)

1812 Coleridge in *Lit. Rem.* (1836) I. 351 In the abstract and, as it were, unindividual nature of the idea, self, or soul. **1892** *Pall Mall G.* 27 Apr. 2/3 A patient, thoughtful pianist, ..but almost altogether unindividual.

unindi'vidualized, *ppl. a.* (UN-[1] 8.)

1844 Poe in *Columbian Lady's & Gentleman's Mag.* Aug. 69/2 Man thus divested *would be* God—would be unindividualized. **1864** W. Shedd *Hist. Chr. Doctrine* II. 81 Original sin is the product of human will as yet unindividualized in Adam. **1882** Traill *Sterne* iv. 42 A completely colourless and unindividualized figure.

unin'ductive, *a.* (UN-[1] 7.)

1855 Baden Powell *Ess.* 58 The 'catastrophic' hypothesis seems of an essentially unindüctive nature.

unin'dulged, *ppl. a.* (UN-[1] 8.)

[**1775** Ash.] **1820** T. Mitchell *Aristoph.* I. p. lxxviii, To leave nothing unindulged, which could contribute to their gratification. **1847** *Ainsworth's Mag.* XII. 42 A luxury almost unindulged since she had been in England.

unin'dulgent, *a.* (UN-[1] 8.)

1743 Francis tr. *Horace, Odes* II. xvi, To Me, not unindulgent Fate Bestow'd a rural, calm Retreat.

unin'dustrious, *a.* (UN-[1] 7, 5 b.)

1599 Daniel *Musoph.* Wks. (1602) C iii b, So farre beyond the ordinarie course, That other vnindustrious Ages ran. **1612** Donne *Lett.* (1651) 122, I have [not] been.. unindustrious in attempting that [*i.e.* to do good]. **1667** *Decay of Chr. Piety* xiii. ¶1 We cannot think it so sluggish or unindustrious an agent. **1693** W. Freke *Sel. Ess.* xxxiv. 216 It were..an unindustrious encroaching on the publick property to attain it. **1883** *Century Mag.* XXVI. 805 Hardly an industry, perhaps, or at any rate an unindustrious one. **1887** Rider Haggard *Jess* xxi, That intelligent but unindustrious race.

So **unin'dustriously** *adv.*

1648 Boyle *Seraph. Love* xvii. (1659) 115 Ev'n the Socinians..are not a little, or un-industriously sollicitous.

uni'nebriating, *ppl. a.* (UN-[1] 10.)

a **1861** T. Winthrop *Life in Open Air* xii. (1863) 96 Toasting each other in the uninebriating flow of our beverages.

unineme ('juːnɪniːm), *a. Cytology.* [f. UNI- I + Gr. νῆμα thread.] Of a chromatid: having (as usual) just one duplex of DNA.

1963 *Proc. Nat. Acad. Sci.* XLIX. 794 Autoradiographic experiments..have yielded results conformable to a polyneme rather than a unineme structure of the chromosome. **1972** *Proc. R. Soc.* B. CLXXXI. 21 Most cytologists refused (and some still refuse) to accept the simplest and most direct deduction from Taylor's classical labelling experiment, namely that a chromatid, prior to replication, is unineme. **1981** *Chromosoma* LXXXII. 1 The unineme concept is supported by genetical data.

Hence **uni'nemic** *a.*, in the same sense; **'uninemy**, the state of having one duplex of DNA per chromatid.

1970 *Cold Spring Harbor Symp. Quantitative Biol.* XXXV. 533/1 The current usage of the hybrid word *uninemic* is, etymologically, quite incorrect. **1972** *Proc. R. Soc.* B. CLXXXI. 26 Another line of evidence for 'uninemy' ..was provided a few years ago by Miller. **1980** *Tsitologiya* XXII. 83 Chromosomes are uninemic, i.e. each chromonema consists of a single DNA molecule (or a single chain of linked DNA molecules) whose ends are located in telomeres. **1981** *Chromosome* LXXXII. 1 (*heading*) Evidence for the uninemy of eukaryotic chromatids.

unin'fected, *ppl. a.* [UN-[1] 8.]

1. Not infected or tainted with sedition, heresy, vice, or the like. Also const. *by, with.*

1628 Le Grys tr. *Barclay's Argenis* 88 What dost thou stay for? Till there be nothing vninfected in Sicily. Art thou afraid to disturbe their scarce ripe preparations? **1678** Cudworth *Intell. Syst.* I. iv. §36. 553 Neither was Plotinus himself..altogether uninfected with this Phantastick Conceit. *a* **1715** Burnett *Own Time* II. xiii. (1897) I. 535 By this means..all the outed ministers would be..kept from going round the uninfected parts of the kingdom. **1777** Robertson *Hist. Amer.* I. (1778) I. 8 Preserving them a separate people uninfected by idolatry. **1795** V. Knox *Spir. Despotism* §29 As influence increases, the jealousy and vigilance of the uninfected part of the community should increase in proportion.

2. *spec.* Not infected with disease, poison, etc.

1625 K. Long tr. *Barclay's Argenis* II. xv. 111 Let us see, quoth hee, whether the Bracelet be uninfected. **1684** J. S. *Profit & Pleas. United* 16 Separating the infected, from the uninfected [cattle]. **1744** Armstrong *Preserv. Health* III. 31 Serene he bears the peevish eastern blast, And uninfected breathes the mortal South. **1813** J. Thomson *Lect. Inflam.* 485 If pains be taken to prevent intercourse between the infected and uninfected. **1890** *Retrospect Med.* CII. 292 The risk of leaving untreated a clot in the immediate neighbourhood of very virulent septic matter in the hope that it may remain uninfected.

unin'fectious, *a.* (UN-[1] 7.)

1744 Birch *Life Boyle* 32 If he were given to any vice himself, he was careful..to render it uninfectious.

unin'feft, *pa. pple.* (UN-[1] 8 b.)

1869 R. Campbell *Austin's Jurispr.* I. 392 A. infeft can enforce his right against a persona in general; A. uninfeft, only against certas personas.

unin'fested, *ppl. a.* (UN-[1] 8.)

1670 Milton *Hist. Eng.* VI. 244 Nor was Devonshire and Cornwall uninfested on the shore. **1787** *Generous Attachment* IV. 81 The haunts uninfested by the voice of man.

un'infiniteness. (UN-[1] 12.)

1656 [? J. Sergeant] tr. *T. White's Peripat. Inst.* 230 Science..is only restrain'd by uninfinitenesse of the number of the objects.

unin'flamed, *ppl. a.* [UN-[1] 8.]

1. Not set on fire.

1626 Bacon *Sylva* §602 When any of those..Bodies come to bee Inflamed then they gather a much greater Heat, than others have un-inflamed. **1663** J. Spencer *Prodigies* 15 The more gross and uninflamed parts must sometimes needs interrupt our sight of that fire. **1743** Young *Nt. Th.* IV. 647 Rise odours sweet from incense uninflam'd? **1794** R. J. Sulivan *View Nat.* II. 163 That this inflammable body of coal should have remained uninflamed..seems highly improbable.

2. *fig.* Not emotionally warmed or excited.

1714 Young *Force of Relig.* II. 199 Oh! let thy thought o'er our past converse rove, And show one moment un-inflam'd with love! **1846** Landor *Imag. Conv.* Wks. I. 204/2 You enunciate even these sentences,..the most seditious, uninflamed, unwarmed. **1876** Lowell *Among my Bks.* Ser. II. 235 So hard is it to escape..uninflamed by the tumult of partisanship which besets the doors.

3. *Path.* Not affected by inflammation.

1793 J. Hunter *Treat. Blood*, etc. (1794) 280 The uninflamed ear dried clear and transparent. **1813** Thomson *Lect. Inflam.* 75 That the circulation is slower in inflamed than in uninflamed arteries. **1866** Aitken *Pract. Med.* II. 911 Dry, imbricated scales..resting upon a perfectly uninflamed surface.

uninflamma'bility. (UN-[1] 12; cf. next.)

1826 Henry *Elem. Chem.* II. 553 The second class..are distinguished..by their uninflammability. **1843** *Civil Eng. & Arch. Jrnl.* VI. 210/2 To test their uninflammability, Mr. Nash had a bonfire..lighted on the roof.

unin'flammable, *a.* (UN-[1] 7 b.)

1666 Boyle *Orig. Forms & Qual.* II. v. 325 To produce, out of two uninflammable Bodies, a third, that would be easily inflammable. **1674** —— *Grounds Corpusc. Philos.* 25 Sulphur..abounds with an acid and uninflammable salt. **1756** C. Lucas *Ess. Waters* I. 52 Water is an uninflammable fluid. **1826** Henry *Elem. Chem.* I. 234 That one measure of hydrogen and oxygen gases..was rendered un-inflammable by eight additional measures of hydrogen. **1897** F. J. Burgoyne *Library Construct.* 22 Some uninflammable non-conductor.

fig. *a* **1797** H. Walpole *Geo. II* (1847) III. iv. 97 Uninflammable as the times were, they carried a great mixture of superstition.

unin'flated, *ppl. a.* (UN-[1] 8.)

[**1775** Ash.] **1861** *Times* 22 Oct., He is perfectly modest, unassuming, and uninflated.

unin'flected, *ppl. a.* [UN-[1] 8.]

1. Not bent or deflected.

1713 Derham *Phys. Theol.* I. i. 13 An uninflected Ray [of light]. **1843** Griffith in *Trans. Linnæan Soc.* XIX. 198 The ordinary and uninflected membrane of the sac.

2. Not possessed of inflections.

1875 Whitney *Life Lang.* vii. 133 The original indefiniteness of uninflected languages.

Hence **unin'flectedness.**

1875 Whitney *Life Lang.* xii. 239 The line which separates utter uninflectedness from a rude agglutination.

unin'flicted, *ppl. a.* (UN-[1] 8.)

1757 W. Wilkie *Epigon.* v. 151 While uninflicted hangs the fatal stroke.

un'influenceable, *a.* (UN-[1] 7 b.)

1734 Bolingbroke *On Parties* Ded. p. xii, The uninfluenc'd and uninfluenceable Freedom of Elections.

un'influenced, *ppl. a.* [UN-[1] 8.] Not influenced or affected (*by* something).

1734 [see prec.]. **1748** *Anson's Voy.* III. vii. 363 Cool and uninfluenced by what they had drank. **1773** J. Allen *Serm. at St. Mary's, Oxford* 18 The unprejudiced, uninfluenced members of the holy Catholic Church. **1853** Kane *Grinnell Exp.* xii. (1856) 86 The pack seems as yet uninfluenced. **1880** Disraeli *Endym.* xliii, Lord Roehampton..will not.. be uninfluenced by the circumstances.

un'influencing, *ppl. a.* (UN-[1] 10.)

1813–21 Bentham *Wks.* (1843) VIII. 209 Uninfluential or uninfluencing circumstances.

un'influencive, *a.* (UN-[1] 7.)

1816 Coleridge *Statesm. Man.* App. 32 A few, on whose convictions it will not be uninfluencive to know, that [etc.].

uninflu'ential, *a.* (UN-[1] 7.)

1661 Glanvill *Van. Dogm.* 191 Causes in our account the most palpable, may possibly be but uninfluential attendants. **1815** Wordsw. *Prose Wks.* (1876) II. 123 Those pretended treasures of antiquity..have been wholly uninfluential upon the literature of the Country. **1840** Gen. P. Thompson *Exerc.* (1842) V. 67 It is intimated in some far from uninfluential journals. **1882** Farrar *Early Chr.* I. 206 Would a writer so..powerful..have remained uninfluential and unknown?

Hence **uninflu͵enti'ality.**

1880 J. Cairns *Let.* in MacEwen *Life* (1895) 701 There has been a stronger tendency..to put the broader side..into visible uninfluentiality.

unin'formative, *a.* (UN-[1] 7.)

1837 C. Lofft *Self-formation* I. 129 The child is driven to learn everything from books..uninformative upon points of doubt.

unin'formed, *ppl. a.* [UN-[1] 8.]

1. Not informed, instructed, or enlightened on some matter or in some respect.

1597 Sir R. Cecil in Ellis *Orig. Lett.* Ser. I. III. 45 His being a King not of many yeares..may happilie leave him uninformed of that course. **1644** Milton *Bucer on Div.* To Parlt. B 2 b, I..was not un-inform'd that divers..men testify'd their daily approbation of the book. **1667** —— *P.L.* VIII. 486 Guided by his voice, nor uninformed Of nuptial Sanctitie and marriage Rites. **1725** Pope *Odyss.* VIII. 533 Who by Phœbus uninform'd, could..sing so well the woe? **1794** S. Williams *Vermont* 156 The uninformed spectator is struck with horror. **1796** Mme. D'Arblay *Camilla* IV. 328 She was uninformed he had propagated it. **1854** J. S. C. Abbott *Napoleon* (1855) I. xxvii. 436 Uninformed as to its contents. **1854** *Poultry Chron.* I. 260/2 Persons..totally uninformed on the subject.

absol. **1815** J. Cormack *Abol. Fem. Infanticide Guzerat* i. 5 This is a position, which the uninformed and the un-intelligent alone will dispute. **1892** *Temple Bar* Oct. 185 Notwithstanding the abstract nature of his studies, Mr. Hopkins was a charming companion, even to the uninformed.

2. Uninstructed, uneducated, ignorant.

1647 Clarendon *Hist. Reb.* II. §98 They..obtained Proselytes of weak uninformed Ladies. **1745** Fielding *Tom Jones* VI. ii, So great a politician..must surely..find out what passes in the rude uninformed mind of a girl. **1791** Newte *Tour Eng. & Scot.* 372 Uninformed and credulous minds readily discover a similitude. **1825** Coleridge *Aids Refl.* 169 Even though the uninformed Heathens should not perish.

b. Marked by lack of enlightenment, information, or knowledge.

1796 Gisborne *Walks Forest* (ed. 2) i. 14 Him uninform'd attachment to his chief..arranged Beneath Rebellion's standard. **1817** J. Scott *Paris Revisit.* (ed. 4) 114 In the vagueness of uninformed speculation. **1891** *Daily News* 5 Nov. 2/5 The bankers pledged themselves..with blind and uninformed confidence.

3. Not animated, enlivened, or inspired.

1709 Swift *Vind. Bickerstaff* Wks. 1755 II. I. 172 If an uninformed carcase walks still about. **1711** Steele *Spect.* No. 33 ¶12 Without this irradiating Power..her most perfect Features are Uninform'd and Dead. **1803** Wordsw. *Yew-Trees* 19 A growth Of..fibres serpentine upcoiling, and inveterately convolved,—Nor uninformed with Phantasy, and looks That threaten the profane.

†**4.** Unimproved by art. *Obs.*

1748 Foote *Knights* I. Wks. 1799 I. 61 A raw boarding-school girl..with a mind unpolished, a figure uninformed.

unin'forming, *ppl. a.* (UN-[1] 10.)

1709 Mrs. Manley *Secret Mem.* (1720) II. 199 An Absence of Mind, and an uninforming Faculty. **1764** Goldsm. *Hist. Eng. in Lett.* (1772) II. 222 It would be.. uninforming to relate all the preparations. **1812** Combe *Syntax, Picturesque* 11, The mangled post thus long had stood, An un-informing piece of wood. **1901** C. A. Scott *Evang. Doctrine* ii. 28 The name of 'Protestant' is popular, accidental and uninforming.

unin'fringeable, *a.* (UN-[1] 7. Cf. *uninfringible* there.)

1743 H. Walpole *Lett.* (1903) I. 368 Upon conditions uninfringeable, I will give you one [*sc.* a commission].

unin'fringed, *ppl. a.* (UN-[1] 8.)

1610 Healey *St. Aug. Citie of God* 784 Yet this doth not barre them [*i.e.* the Romans] the name of a people..as long as they beare this our last definition vnin-fringed. **1663** Boyle *Usef. Exp. Nat. Philos.* II. ii. 60 Whether their strength be that way more uninfringed..then if they [*sc.*

poisons] were taken in at the mouth. **1736** Franklin *Ess.* Wks. 1840 II. 281 Let us be vigilant to preserve them un-infringed, and free from encroachments. **1791** Cowper *Iliad* III. 128 He..insures The compact, to both parties, uninfringed. **1852** M. Arnold *Human Life* 4, I haue kept uninfringed my nature's law. **1871** Geo. Eliot *Middlem.* xxxvii, Here was a question of ties which left them un-infringed.

unin'genious, *a.* [un-[1] 7.]
†**1.** = uningenuous *a. Obs.*
1638 Chillingw. *Relig. Prot.* I. iv. §53. 220 Full of un-ingenious dealing with your adversary. **1656** Heylyn *Extraneus Vapulans* 20 Of Mr. Noye..(besides those un-ingenious passages of him which are still left standing) he telleth us also [etc.].
2. Lacking in ingenuity.
1769 Burke *Obs. Late St. Nation* 8 These uningenious paradoxes and reveries without imagination. **1787** Bentham *Def. Usury* xiii. 183 The wounded pride of the uningenious herd. **1888** Doughty *Arabia Deserta* I. 244 Little cups.. made, for the uningenious Arabs, in the West.

uninge'nuity. [un-[1] 12.] † Disingenuousness.
1650 J. Weekes *Truth's Confl.* ii. 34 With as much disparagement and uningenuity, as likely can be in so many words. **1672** Clarendon *Ess.* Tracts (1727) 264 This un-ingenuity is still practised,..contrary to truth.

†**unin'genuous,** *a. Obs.* [un-[1] 7.]
1. Not frank, candid, or open; disingenuous.
1638 Chillingw. *Relig. Prot.* Answ. to Pref. 6 If beginings be ominous..D. Potter hath cause to look for great store of uningenuous dealing from you. **1670** Clarendon *Ess.* Tracts (1727) 189 The grossest and most uningenuous importunities of the most worthless men.
2. Ignoble, servile.
1660 Jer. Taylor *Ductor* III. ii. rule 9 §5 It is..an uningenuous subjection, to pay tribute for our meat and drink.
Hence †**unin'genuousness.** *Obs.*
1644 Hammond *Vind. Christ's Reprehending Peter* 72, I cannot guesse what could be further added to prove the injustice and uningenuousnesse..of this answer.

†**unin'genuously,** *adv. Obs.* [un-[1] 11.] Disingenuously.
1656 Hobbes *Lib., Necess., & Chance* 4 To bring [such] arguments..is to deale uningenuously and fraudulently with his Readers. **1796** Mme. D'Arblay *Camilla* III. 394 A conquest, unduly, unfairly, and uningenuously obtained.

unin'grafted, *ppl. a.* (un-[1] 8.)
1830 Gen. P. Thompson *Exerc.* (1842) I. 289 [France] attempted..to make terms with uningrafted royalty. **1834** J. Brown *Lett. Sanctif.* i. 204 It is folly to look for good fruit on an uningrafted tree.

†**unin'habit,** *ppl. a. Sc. Obs.* [un-[1] 8b.] Uninhabited.
c **1460** in *Bann. Cl. Misc.* (1855) III. 36 To seke void landis and unenhabyte.

unin'habitable, *a.* (un-[1] 7b. Cf. unhabitable.)
1448 *Extr. Aberd. Reg.* (1844) I. 401 The balyheis sal..tak doune the durris..of thaim [*sc.* houses], and mak thaim uninhabitable. **1574** Golding *Marlorat's Apocalips* 299 The countrie of Sichimie..is desert and vninhabitable by reason of extreme cold. **1610** Shaks. *Temp.* II. i. 37 Though this Island seeme to be..Vninhabitable, and almost inaccessible. **1662** J. Davies tr. *Mandelslo's Trav.* 281 They would needs know of him..how he came to that uninhabitable place. **1774** Pennant *Tour Scotl. in 1772*, 174 The far greater part of the country being uninhabitable by reason of the..mountains. **1837** Whewell *Hist. Induct. Sci.* I. 155 It was supposed that the space between the tropical circles must be uninhabitable from heat. **1884** *Law Times* 27 Sept. 359/2 The Manor House..being so dilapidated as to be almost uninhabitable.
Hence **unin'habitableness.**
1669 Stillingfl. *Serm.* ix. (1673) 166 The opinion of the Ancients concerning the uninhabitableness of the torrid Zone. **1676** *Doctrine of Devils* 194 The Uninhabitableness of the middle Zone. **1839** Fr. A. Kemble *Rec. Later Life* I. 255 Eight dwelling houses, all in different states and stages of uninhabitableness.

unin'habited, *ppl. a.* (un-[1] 8. Cf. unhabited.)
1571 Golding *Calvin on Ps.* lxv. 12 The same fatnesse spreadeth itselfe even into the uninhabited countries. **1647** Cowley *Mistr.*, *Welcome* iii, Hast thou not found each womans breast..Either by Savages possest, Or wild, and uninhabited? **1670** R. Coke *Disc. Trade* 10 The Country too becomes thin and uninhabited. **1711** Addison *Spect.* No. 26 ¶4 The present War had filled the Church with many of these uninhabited Monuments. **1794** Mrs. Radcliffe *Myst. Udolpho* xxxv, This chateau was uninhabited when St. Aubert and his daughter were in the neighbourhood. **1824** Miss L. M. Hawkins *Annaline* III. 193 The imposing stillness pervading these almost uninhabited regions. **1866** Geo. Eliot *F. Holt* i, We have been too poor to keep servants for uninhabited rooms.
Hence **unin'habitedness.**
1727 Bailey (vol. II), *Wildness*,..uninhabitedness. **1884** *Chr. World* 12 June 434/4 The solitary uninhabitedness.. was something awful in its impressiveness.

uninherita'bility. (un-[1] 12.)
1812 Coleridge in Southey *Omniana* II. 7 A most determined believer in the uninheritability of sin.

unin'heritable, *a.* [un-[1] 7b.] † Incapable of inheriting.
1611 Speed *Hist. Gt. Brit.* IX. xvi. 671/1 [They allege] that the said Richard was finally for treason attainted, and adiudged vninheritable. **1780** M. Madan *Thelyphthora* II. 13 If women..were not lawful wives in God's sight, then.. the issue must be illegitimate, and, if so, uninheritable.

unin'hibited, *ppl. a.* [un-[1] 8.] Not inhibited; unrestrained.
1880 W. James *Feeling of Effort* 24 The motor idea,.. uninhibited by remote associations,..discharges by the preappointed mechanism into the right muscles. **1929** B. Russell *Marriage & Morals* x. 111, I think that uninhibited civilised people, whether men or women, are generally polygamous in their instincts. **1949** M. Mead *Male & Female* xii. 263 'Why,' asks the uninhibited American child of 1949, 'does no one ever go to the bathroom in a book?' **1956** P. H. Johnson *Last Resort* xlv. 293 He coughed once or twice, blew his nose with an uninhibited trumpeting. **1971** S. Hill *Strange Meeting* II. 147 Hilliard stood, pitying them their lack of privacy..yet envying them too, their carefully ordered life and clear uninhibited friendships and enmities. **1980** A. N. Wilson *Healing Art* xvi. 194 In the States..he was being, according to his own lights, uninhibited.
Hence **unin'hibitedly** *adv.*
1959 *Times* 10 Jan. 7/6 An informal folk concert in which the audience uninhibitedly join. **1966** L. Ó Broin *Dublin Castle & 1916 Rising* vi. 47 Birrell was accustomed to express himself thus uninhibitedly to Nathan about personalities. **1976** *New Society* 22 Jan. 147/1 If, as a child, things don't go your way and you're miserable, you can make the point by screaming, kicking or flinging your food on the floor. Adolescents and adults cannot show their unhappiness so uninhibitedly.

unin'humed, *ppl. a.* (un-[1] 8.)
1621 G. Sandys *Ovid's Met.* VII. (1626) 142 Dead corps, without the Dues of funerall, They weakly beare:..Or vn-inhum'd they lye. **1791** Cowper *Odyss.* XI. 84 Leave me not undeplored Nor uninhumed. **1835** *Oriental Ann.* 215 Thousands of carcasses..would not then lie uninhumed, scattering pestilence over the land.

uni'nitiate, *ppl. a.* [un-[1] 8b.] = next.
1801 Southey *Thalaba* v. xxxvi, That, led by me, Feet uninitiate tread Your threshold, this atones! **1853** Kingsley *Hypatia* viii, The uninitiate vulgar..who revile such interpretations. **1874** Withrow *Catacombs* (1877) 532 The sacred mysteries hidden from the uninitiate and the unworthy.

uni'nitiated, *ppl. a.* (un-[1] 8.) Also *absol.*
1678 Cudworth *Intell. Syst.* I. v. 637 The Prophane and Un-initiated in the Mysteries. **1800** Whiter *Etymol. Magnum* 174 The uninitiated reader will perhaps be astonished. **1816** Bentham *Chrestom.* 55 Those.. formularies, so appalling to every as yet uninitiated, and more particularly to the uninitiated juvenile eye. **1842** Dickens *Amer. Notes* i, What seemed to the uninitiated a serious journey. **1885** *Athenæum* 19 Dec. 800/2 One uninitiated in the mysteries of Scottish genealogies.

uniniti'ation. (un-[1] 12.)
1834 H. O'Brien *Round Towers* 303 Nor was it but on the plea of ignorance and un-initiation that he did ultimately obtain pardon. **1873** Mrs. Whitney *Other Girls* xv, She left no lee-way for uninitiation.

unin'jectable, *a.* (un-[1] 7b.)
1830 R. Knox *Béclard's Anat.* 178 The sum of the capillary blood vessels, and their proportion to the solid and uninjectable substance.

un'injurable, *a.* (un-[1] 7b.)
1846 Mrs. Gore *Eng. Char.* I. 310 His soda-water..being uninjurable by street rumbling.

un'injured, *ppl. a.* (un-[1] 8.)
1578 R. L. in Whetstone *Promos & Cass.* A iij, I hould my paynes wel satisfyed, and Maister Whetston uninjured. **1634** Milton *Comus* 403 [To] let a single helpless maiden pass Uninjur'd. **1693** Prior *To Dr. Sherlock* 57 Untouch'd thy Tomb, uninjur'd be thy Dust. **1725** Pope *Odyss.* XI. 477 Heroes who uninjur'd stood Amidst a war of spears. **1797** Nelson in Nicolas *Disp.* (1845) II. 346 To put me on board the first uninjured Ship of the Line. *a* **1821** V. Knox *Serm.* Wks. 1824 VI. 171 Their own bosoms will be calm and serene, uninjured and uninjurious. **1884** *Fortn. Rev.* Jan. 50 The Indian tribes..uninjured by and uninjuring Western culture.

un'injuring, *ppl. a.* (un-[1] 10, 5d.)
1820 Milman *Fall of Jerusalem* 42 The pines..From their proud heads shake off the uninjuring tempest. **1884** [see prec.].

unin'jurious, *a.* (un-[1] 7.)
1809 Coleridge *Friend* 155 The uninjurious and useful privileges of our English Nobility. *a* **1821** [see uninjured]. **1866** Pusey *Mirac. Prayer* 32 A concentration of rain or its absence, uninjurious at other times, would ruin seed-time or harvest.
Hence **unin'juriousness.**
1860 Pusey *Min. Proph.* 374 Yea, foolishness itself is cloked under the name of uninjuriousness.

unin'juriously, *adv.* (un-[1] 11.)
1881 Sir W. Thomson in *Times* 2 Sept. 4/1 The charging [of a Faure cell] may be done uninjuriously, and with good dynamical economy [etc.].

un'inked, *ppl. a.* (un-[1] 8.)
1637 Rutherford *Lett.* (1664) 290 What is harder then.. to have blanks & uninked paper for assurance of Christ in real fruition or possession?

un'inn, *v.* [un-[2] 7.] *intr.* To leave an inn.
1602 Warner *Alb. Eng.* XII. lxxv. 312 The Gentle woman, hearing this, vn-Inn'd by day did peepe.

un'innocence. (un-[1] 12.)
1593 Nashe *Christ's T.* Fij b, Thou shalt be my vninnocence, and whole summe of delinquishment.

uni'noculated, *ppl. a.* (un-[1] 8.)
[**1775** Ash.] **1818** *Monthly Rev.* LXXXVII. 131 Mr. Koster..observes that the cow-pox was extensively contagious..among the uninoculated inhabitants. **1898** P. Manson *Trop. Diseases* 151 Afterwards the originally healthy and uninoculated mice also succumbed.

uni'nodal (ju:nɪ-), *a.* [See uni- 1 and nodal *a.*] Having one node or nodal point.
1839 Lindley *Introd. Bot.* 160 The cyme of Monocotyledons appears to be typically uninodal. **1880** *Nature* XXI. 427 Long oscillations..due to uninodal waves. **1894** *Athenæum* 17 Feb. 216/3 Some Properties of the Uninodal Quartic and Quintic having a Triple Point.

uni'nominal (ju:nɪ-), *a.* [a. F. *uninominal* (1878): see uni- 1 and nominal *a.*]
1. Based on the principle of one member being separately elected by each constituency.
1881 *Times* 12 Mar. 11 At present..the Chamber of Deputies is elected by what is called..the uninominal method of voting. **1884** *Pall Mall G.* 8 Nov. 1 The proposed uniformity of uninominal electoral districts.
2. Having or involving one name, *spec.* in *Nat. Hist.*
188. [see *plurinominal* pluri-].

unin'quired, *ppl. a.* (un-[1] 8c.)
1725 De Foe *Voy. round World* (1840) 224 Infinitely more [wealth] lay uninquired after, than had yet been known. **1826** Scott *Woodst.* xxviii, Some unhappy mistake, the grounds of which shall remain..uninquired into.

unin'quiring, *ppl. a.* (un-[1] 10.)
1804 *Ann. Rev.* II. 68 The uninquiring and contented ignorance with which he has beheld every thing. **1833** L. Ritchie *Wand. by Loire* 8 Wandering..through a foreign town, ignorant and uninquiring, without a plan. **1863** Whittier *Countess* 83 There..The native dweller..keeps, in uninquiring trust, The old, dull round of things.

unin'quisitive, *a.* (un-[1] 7.)
1609 Daniel *Civ. Wars* VI. xxxv, Go loose the links of that soule-binding chaine; Inlarge this vninquisitiue Beliefe. *a* **1639** Wotton *Reliq.* (1651) 154 Of those..have I many times heard (not uninquisitive, I acknowledg..) how [etc.]. **1796** Horsley *Serm.* xi. (1816) I. 236 Their uninquisitive temper keeps them in a total ignorance about secondary causes. **1815** L. Hunt *Feast Poets* 34 So contented and uninquisitive had every body become. **1848** Thackeray *Van. Fair* xii, Mrs. Sedley was of so easy and uninquisitive a nature, that she wasn't even jealous. **1872** Tulloch *Ration. Theol.* I. 290 Uninquisitive, unreflecting faith.

unin'scribed, *ppl. a.* (un-[1] 8.)
1704 Pope *Windsor For.* 320 Make sacred Charles's tomb for ever known (Obscure the place, and un-inscrib'd the stone). **1837** Lytton *Athens* I. 325 Altars uninscribed to a particular god. **1859** G. Wilson *Mem. E. Forbes* vi. (1861) 173 The whole of the uninscribed leaves of the book.

unin'spected, *ppl. a.* (un-[1] 8.)
[**1775** Ash.] **1858** in *Sat. Rev.* 27 Nov. 531/1 Those schools,..'whether Church or Dissenting,..inspected or uninspected'. **1895** *Westm. Gaz.* 11 Oct. 2/2 Any change that gave us uninspected drinking clubs for inspected public-houses.

unin'spired, *ppl. a.* (un-[1] 8.)
1690 Locke *Hum. Und.* IV. xix. §11 All the truths..that men uninspired are enlightened with. **1707** E. Chishull (*title*), The great Danger and Mistake of all new uninspired Prophecies relating to the End of the World. **1715** Pope *Iliad* II. 220 Ulysses heard, nor uninspir'd obey'd. **1746** Young *Nt. Th.* IX. 439 No mortal, un-inspir'd, Has ever yet conceiv'd..How kind is God. **1831** Campbell *Lines on Poland* 5 A theme for uninspired lips too strong. **1846** J. E. Ryland *Life Foster* I. 3 Vivacity was merely physical and uninspired by sentiment. **1900** *Ch. Q. Rev.* Apr. 110 As though..Paul [were] on a level with any uninspired writer.

unin'spiring, *ppl. a.* (un-[1] 10.)
Also, in recent use, ***uninspiringly***.
1815 J. Scott *Vis. Paris* 24 Monotonous in its character, and uninspiring in its tendency. **1859** Jephson & Reeve *Brittany* 268 The uninspiring region of railroads and metropolitan industry. **1896** *Harper's Mag.* XCIII. 17/2 Gazing..over the uninspiring chimney-pots of New York, at the equally uninspiring Long Island station.

unin'stalled, *ppl. a.* (un-[1] 8.)
[**1775** Ash.] *a* **1856** H. Miller *Cruise Betsey* 353 The minister of Allness—uninstalled at the time in his new dwelling.

un'instigated, *ppl. a.* (un-[1] 8.)
[**1775** Ash.] **1846** Poe *Criticism* Wks. 1865 III. 22 A voluntary, that is to say, an uninstigated notice of the book.

un'instituted, *ppl. a.* (un-[1] 8.)
1702 C. Mather *Magn. Chr.* II. vii. (1852) 144 Certain confessedly unscriptural and uninstituted rites. **1742** J. Willison *Balm of Gilead* iv. Wks. (1852) 404/2 Many are warping towards popery.., observing uninstituted festivals.

unin'structed, *ppl. a.* [un-[1] 8.]
1. Not instructed or informed; unenlightened, ignorant. Also const. *in*, or with clause.
1598 Florio, *Inerudito*,..vntaught, vninstructed. **1660** Jer. Taylor *Ductor* II. iii. rule 10 §12 By uninstructed is only meant such who have not heard, or could not learn. **1665** Boyle *Occas. Refl.* III. xx. 131 These are utterly uninstructed in the Laws. **1690** Dryden *Don Sebast.* III. i, That Fool intrudes,..uninstructed how to stem the tide. **1744** Harris *Three Treat.* Wks. (1841) 3 Not even what we do intentionally, if it proceed from mere will and uninstructed instinct. **1785** Reid *Intell. Powers* II. xx. 326 The most uninstructed peasant. **1806** A. Hunter *Culina* (ed. 3) 268 Women uninstructed in cookery and the management of a family. **1875** E. White *Life in Christ* v. xxviii. 491 To build a credulous assent..on the authority of the uninstructed multitude.

absol. **1662** JER. TAYLOR *Fides Formata* (1663) 167 Faith.., if it be not followed,..damns deeper than the Hell of the Infidels and uninstructed.

2. Not furnished with instructions.

1892 *Spectator* 21 May 699/1 Its delegates will enter the Convention 'uninstructed'.

Hence **unin'structedness**.

1833 MONTGOMERY *Lect. Poetry* 333 That perpetual thraldom of uninstructedness (if I may coin such a negative). **1871** JOWETT *Plato* I. 170 These base fears and confidences originate in ignorance and uninstructedness.

unin'structing, *ppl. a.* [UN-¹ 10.] = next.

?**1630** H. R. *Mythomystes* 45 Our common uninstructing fabulous rimes. **1642** MILTON *Apol. Smect.* 30 That Lordly and uninstructing jurisdiction which properly makes the Pope Antichrist. **1762** MILLS *Syst. Pract. Husb.* I. 441 The little differences in their methods may not be un-instructing.

unin'structive, *a.* (UN-¹ 7.)

1666 BOYLE *Orig. Forms & Qual.* II. vii. 369 That the present Discourse shall not be uninstructive to You. **1695** LOCKE *Hum. Und.* II. xx. §18 (ed. 3) 123 Pain from captious uninstructive wrangling. **1764** REID *Inquiry* vi. §15. 172 Facts less vague and uninstructive. **1839** DE LA BECHE *Rep. Geol. Cornwall*, etc. ii. 29 The sections near the Start Point are..particularly uninstructive. **1849** MACAULAY *Hist. Eng.* vi. II. 104 His character was remarkable, and his history not uninstructive.

So **unin'structively** *adv.*

1816 *Edin. Rev.* Sept. 182 No great man has been..more uninstructively commended.

un'insulate, *v.* [UN-² 3.] *trans.* To deprive of insulation.

1844 NOAD *Electricity* (ed. 2) 17 Let the metallic plate be replaced, and uninsulated by touching it with the finger. **1866** R. M. FERGUSON *Electr.* 54 When an insulated body is charged by being uninsulated.

un'insulated, *ppl. a.* (UN-¹ 8.)

1794 *Phil. Trans.* LXXXIV. 266 The insulated and un-insulated parts of my high pointed rod. **1839** G. BIRD *Nat. Philos.* 204 Holding beneath and parallel to it..a second disc of metal, but uninsulated. **1884** C. G. W. LOCK *Workshop Receipts* Ser. III. 116/1 Uninsulated German silver wire.

unin'sulted, *ppl. a.* (UN-¹ 8.)

1747 CARTE *Hist. Eng.* I. 288 The Danes..left no part of the coast of England un-insulted. **1832** L. HUNT *Poems* Pref. p. xlv, The hearth of an uninsulted poverty.

unin'sulting, *ppl. a.* (UN-¹ 10.)

1855 MILMAN *Lat. Chr.* XIV. vii. VI. 549 The most quiet, uninsulting, unexasperating satire.

unin'surable, *a.* (UN-¹ 7 b.)

1864 T. S. WILLIAMS & SIMMONDS *Eng. Commerc. Corr.* 275 That vessel however being an American..was almost uninsurable here. **1884** *Law Times Rep.* LI. 248 The life..is..uninsurable by reason of the assumed state of his health.

Hence **uninsura'bility**.

Also, in recent use (1903), *uninsurableness*.

1884 *Law Times Rep.* LI. 244/2 Written opinions..as to the insurability or uninsurability of the life of..Harvey.

unin'sured, *ppl. a.* (UN-¹ 8.)

1799 *Hull Advertiser* 16 Nov. 3/3 The tenant, who..will be a considerable sufferer, is uninsured. **1853** R. S. SURTEES *Sponge's Sp. Tour* lxix, Farmer Slyfield's stack-yard was fired.., and all its uninsured contents destroyed. **1891** C. JAMES *Rom. Rigmarole* 154 My boots..were in London; and my life was uninsured.

uninte'llective, *a.* (UN-¹ 7.)

1837 C. LOFFT *Self-formation* I. 36 Scholarship without talent is..a mass of unintellective confusion—a mere chaos.

uninte'llectual, *a.* [UN-¹ 7.]

†**1.** Not endowed with intellect; unintelligent.

a **1676** HALE *Prim. Orig. Man.* IV. viii. (1677) 373 The rest of Mankind, or the unintellectual Creatures.

2. a. Not intellectually developed; dull.

1819 KEATS *Lines to Fanny* 14 My muse..Unintellectual, yet divine to me. **1872** LIDDON *Elem. Relig.* i. 13 They thought that the apostles had been unintellectual persons.

b. Not characterized by the presence of intellect.

1837 HALLAM *Hist. Lit.* I. viii. §3 A sound..not unpleasing to all.., but monotonous, unintellectual. **1846** POE *A.C. Mowatt* Wks. 1865 III. 43 The forehead is..by no means an unintellectual one. **1856** *N. Brit. Rev.* XXVI. 129 It has become the fashion to decry such pleasures..as unintellectual.

Hence **uninte'llectualism, unintellectu'ality**.

Also *unintellectually* adv. (Webster, 1847).

1850 *Tait's Mag.* XVII. 735/1 The very same characteristics of inertia, unintellectuality, and uncombiningness. **1880** W. L. COURTNEY in E. Abbott *Hellenica* 254 That theory of unintellectualism with which Epicurus started.

unin'telligence. (UN-¹ 12; cf. next.)

1634 BP. HALL *Contempl.*, *N.T.* IV. iv, His un-intelligence, was not more strange then his mis-construction. **1829** CARLYLE *Misc.* (1840) II. 228 From afar I heard say, that Unintelligibility was but the result of Unintelligence. **1891** ETHEL GLAZEBROOK *Dower of Earth* II. xv. 236 The general moroseness and unintelligence of the English race.

unin'telligent, *a.* [UN-¹ 7.]

1. Having no knowledge or understanding *of* something. *rare.*

1609 B. JONSON *Sil. Wom.* IV. iii. 572 My mistris is not altogether vn-intelligent of these things. **1611** SHAKS. *Wint. T.* I. i. 16 That your Sences (vn-intelligent of our insufficience) may..as little accuse vs. **1850** CARLYLE *Latter-d. Pamph.* iv. 23 With China, or some distant country, too unintelligent of us and too unintelligible to us.

2. Devoid of intelligence.

1664 H. MORE *Myst. Iniq.* xiii. 45 The Sun is..an Inanimate and unintelligent masse of flammeous matter. **1701** NORRIS *Ideal World* I. vi. 342 So we must suppose God..as an unintelligent being, and also in the production of truth acting as an unintelligent agent. **1788** REID *Active Powers* IV. ix. 627 If this be so, what is unintelligent may be the cause of what is intelligent. **1802** PALEY *Nat. Theol.* ii. §2 By the application of an unintelligent impulse to a mechanism previously arranged..the corn is ground. **1864** PUSEY *Lect. Daniel* viii. 554 Time,..the most spiritual of the unintelligent creatures of God.

3. Deficient in intelligence or intellect; dull, stupid. Also *absol.*

a **1676** HALE *Ep. to Son* (1684) 13 A sort of brain-sick, melancholy, unintelligent persons. **1703** MOXON *Mech. Exerc.* 95 Its use is..well known (even to the most unintelligent). **1791** COWPER *Odyss.* VI. 234 Neither base by birth thou seem'st, Nor unintelligent. **1815** [see UNINFORMED *ppl. a.* 1 *absol.*]. **1861** OLMSTED *Journ. & Expl. Cotton Kingd.* I. 44 Most of the company were of a very poor appearance, rude and unintelligent.

b. Marked by lack of intelligence.

1860 W. COLLINS *Wom. White* II. 267 My servant..is really attached to me, in his unintelligent way. **1869** TOZER *Highl. Turkey* I. 302 [A man] with..an unintelligent expression of countenance.

†**4.** Unintelligible. *Obs.*

1683 MOXON *Mech. Exerc.*, *Printing* xxii. ¶5 That I may be the less unintelligent to the Reader. **1756** MRS. CALDERWOOD in *Coltness Collect.* (Maitl. Club) 190 He was obliged then to have recourse to 'calling grace', and severall other unintelligent things.

unin'telligently, *adv.* (UN-¹ 11; cf. prec.)

1754 EDWARDS *Freed. Will* II. xiii. 134 Liable to act un-intelligently and unreasonably. **1836** J. GILBERT *Chr. Atonem.* iv. 119 The doctrine..has been charged with exhibiting the Divine Being as implacable, most unintelligently. **1889** JESSOPP *Coming of Friars* v. 224 They knew how to..go through the services though unintelligently.

unintelligi'bility. (UN-¹ 12; cf. next.)

1665 GLANVILL *Scepsis Sci.* iv. 17 To credit the unintelligibility..of this union and motion. **1719** *T. Burnet's Theory Earth* (ed. 4) I. vii. 107 If we have truly prov'd..the Impossibility or Unintelligibility of it in all other ways. **1806–7** J. BERESFORD *Miseries Hum. Life* IV. i, Their own ruin..must obviously be the direct consequence of their unintelligibility. **1866** FELTON *Anc. & Mod. Gr.* II. ii. 288 Lycophron, chiefly famous for his unintelligibility.

unin'telligible, *a.* and *sb.* [UN-¹ 7.]

1. Not intelligible; incapable of being understood. Also *absol.*

1616 BULLOKAR *Eng. Expos.*, *Vnintelligible*, which cannot be vnderstood. **1647** COWLEY *Mistr.*, *Womens Superstit.* i, Or I'm a very Dunce, or Womankind Is a most unintelligible thing. **1684** T. BURNET *Theory Earth* I. 259 The trajection..is to me, I confess, unintelligible. **1717** BERKELEY *Tour Italy* Wks. 1871 IV. 527 The ruins above ground are pretty unintelligible. **1796** MME. D'ARBLAY *Camilla* V. 516 This is..so incredible—so unintelligible! **1834** LAMB *Wks.* (1908) I. 454 Coleridge..had the tact of making the unintelligible seem plain. **1871** JOWETT *Plato* I. 26 He made an unintelligible attempt to hide his perplexity.

b. Of language, statements, etc., or persons in respect of such.

1651 HOBBES *Leviath.* I. xii. 53 Men..choose rather to confesse he is Incomprehensible,.. than to..confesse their definition to be unintelligible. **1683** *Brit. Spec.* 40 Their Records also were preserved in the Greek Tongue and Characters..unintelligible by the Vulgar. **1703** DE FOE *More Reform.* 41 To b' Unintelligible is a Crime. **1765** JOHNSON *Shakespeare's Plays* I. p. lxviii, Homer has fewer passages unintelligible than Chaucer. **1841** LANE *Arab. Nts.* I. 113 Where, taking a little of its water, she pronounced over it some unintelligible words. **1884** *Solicitors' Jrnl.* 8 Nov. 29/2 The prisoner..having an impediment in his speech, which made him unintelligible and unable to read it.

c. *sb.* An unintelligible thing.

1838 SOUTHEY *Doctor* cxlix. V. 176 As two negatives make an affirmative, it might be found that two unintelligibles make a meaning.

†**2.** Unintelligent. *Obs.*⁻¹

1694 R. FRANCK *North. Mem.* 121 Nor has it any Claim or Title from the Lough Minever, as superstitiously surmiz'd by the unintelligible Inhabitant.

unin'telligibleness. [UN-¹ 12, or f. prec.]

†**1.** Lack of understanding. *Obs.*⁻¹

1616 DONNE *Serm.* V. 466 God shall suffer him to settle..in an insensibleness and an unintelligibleness..of his own Condition.

2. The quality or fact of being unintelligible; unintelligibility.

1678 ALLESTREE *Lively Oracles* viii. §14. 201 We ordinarily have so much candor, as to impute their unintelligibleness to our own ignorance. **1736** BUTLER *Anal.* II. vii. 347 The obscurity or unintelligibleness of one part of a prophecy. **1754** EDWARDS *Freed. Will* II. ii. 38 The Thing in Question seems to be forgotten, or kept out of Sight, in a Darkness and Unintelligibleness of Speech. **1832** H. MELVILL in *Preacher* III. 222/1 If it is unintelligible, it is the unintelligibleness of the Scriptures, and not of the commentator. **1877** E. R. CONDER *Basis Faith* ii. 69 The supposed unintelligibleness..of the doctrine.

unin'telligibly, *adv.* (UN-¹ 11.)

1664 POWER *Exp. Philos.* Pref. 11 Motion may be both invisibly and unintelligibly slow, as well as swift. **1713** BERKELEY *Hylas & Phil.* II. (1725) 70 You talk unintelligibly, instead of forming a reasonable Hypothesis. **1794** MRS. RADCLIFFE *Myst. Udolpho* xxx, He..hurried unintelligibly over some lines, and..offered her a pen. **1808** L. MURRAY *Eng. Gram.* I. 413 The second occasion of our being apt to write unintelligibly. **1892** [see UNDISCOVERABLY].

unin'tended, *ppl. a.* (UN-¹ 8.)

1649 MILTON *Eikon.* xix. 173 By any pretentions in the Parlament, which are now prov'd false, and unintended. **1670** EACHARD *Cont. Clergy* 78 The ridiculous, senseless, and unintended use, which many of them make of concordances. **1740** CIBBER *Apol.* 117 The first unintended Favour. **1796** MME. D'ARBLAY *Camilla* I. 233 The youthful group was much diverted with this unintended exhibition. **1835** MILL *Diss. & Disc.* (1859) I. 153 The unintended good or evil which has followed from our actions. **1884** *Manch. Exam.* 4 Nov. 6/1 The debate very nearly suffered an unintended collapse.

So **unin'tendedly** *adv.*

1782 PAINE *Let. Abbé Raynel* (1791) 43 This declaration..has led me unintendedly into a train of metaphysical reasoning. **1818** BENTHAM *Ch. Eng.* Introd. 34 The intimation thus..unintendedly afforded.

unin'tentional, *a.* [UN-¹ 7.]

1. Not done with, not arising from, intention.

Given by Johnson (1755) as employed by Boyle.

1782 V. KNOX *Ess.* I. 120 The infirmity of human nature which causes unintentional lapses in the duties of friendship. **1803** SYD. SMITH *Wks.* (1859) I. 28 A very unintentional encouragement to offences. **1883** J. GILMOUR *Mongols* xxiii. 285 The accused admitted the charge, but pleaded that it was unintentional.

2. Not acting with intention.

1838 JAMES *Robber* v, He had been an unintentional, and even an unwilling witness to [it]. **1851** KITTO *Hist. Palestine* v. iii. 125 Six cities,..to any one of which the unintentional man-slayer might hasten.

Hence **unintentio'nality**.

1780 BENTHAM *Princ. Legisl.* (1823) II. xiii. 8 In the case of unintentionality: where he intends not to engage..in the act. *a* **1859** AUSTIN *Jurispr.* (1863) II. xx. 110 Unintentionality, and innocence of intention, seem both to be included.

unin'tentionally, *adv.* (UN-¹ 11.)

1769 PENNANT *Brit. Zool.* III. 71 A spear..with which he afterwards committed parricide, unintentionally,..on his father Ulysses. **1849** MACAULAY *Hist. Eng.* x. II. 574 Those who..had unintentionally done him a great service. **1874** H. R. REYNOLDS *John Bapt.* i. §6. 55 He unintentionally revealed the forgery.

unin'tentioned, *ppl. a.* (UN-¹ 8.)

1851 MRS. BROWNING *Casa Guidi Wind.* II. 11 As little children take up a high strain With unintentioned voices.

unin'tentness. (UN-¹ 12.)

1670 CLARENDON *Contempl. Ps.* Tracts (1727) 651 There is not a greater obstruction to devotion than the unintentness upon the action they are at.

uninter'cepted, *ppl. a.* (UN-¹ 8.)

1646 EARL MONM. tr. *Biondi's Civil Wars* VII. 92 She had not time enough to keep the secret undiscover'd, and him unintercepted. **1814** R. HALL *Wks.* (1832) I. 288 The light..becomes stronger and clearer by an unintercepted converse with its object.

†**un'interessed**, *ppl. a. Obs.* Also 8 -est. [UN-¹ 8.] = UNINTERESTED *ppl. a.* 1 and 2.

1647 DIGGES *Unlawf. Taking Arms* IV. 158 None can be named, who are uninteressed in the decision. **1688** NORRIS *Theory Love* I. v. 58 Although there cannot be a pure and uninteressed Malice. **1702** tr. *Le Clerc's Prim. Fathers* 153 This is rather a Panegyrick than an uninterest History.

Hence †**un'interessedness**. *Obs.*

1702 *Eng. Theophrast.* 360 'Tis the Motive only that gives Merit to our Actions, and Uninteressedness that makes them perfect.

un'interest. (UN-¹ 12.)

1890 *Tablet* 5 July 19 A few notes concerning the great antiquity of the..church..may not be of uninterest.

un'interested, *ppl. a.* [UN-¹ 8.]

†**1.** Unbiassed, impartial. *Obs.*

a **1646** J. GREGORY *Posthuma*, *Episc. Puerorum* (1649) 107 By this uninterested disguis, the more to justifie the Celebrations. **1660** R. COKE *Power & Subj.* 49 Nor do I think that any uninterested casuist will deny [etc.].

†**2.** Free from motives of personal interest; disinterested. *Obs.*

1661 (*title*), A Relation of the business..concerning Bedford Levell,..by a person uninterested. **1704** N. N. tr. *Boccalini's Advts. fr. Parnass.* III. 191 What think you of uninterested Men, who value the Publick Good beyond their own private Interest? **1767** COWPER *Let.* Wks. 1837 XV. 17 You know me to be an uninterested person.

3. Unconcerned, indifferent. In this sense *disinterested* is increasingly common in informal use, though widely regarded as incorrect: see DISINTERESTED *ppl. a.* 1.

1771 *Ann. Reg.* II. 253/1 He is no cold, uninterested, and uninteresting advocate for the cause he espouses. **1774** *Trinket* 54 In this amiable society can my heart be uninterested? **1823** BYRON *Juan* x. lxxiii, In the same quaint, Uninterested tone. **1850** THACKERAY *Pendennis* lvii, An almost silent but not uninterested spectator. **1980** G. GREENE *Dr Fischer* iv. 28, I wouldn't say that—he was totally uninterested in both of us. **1981** *London Rev. Bks.* 19 Nov.–2 Dec. 21 Classical historiography was on the whole uninterested in local provincial history. **1982** D. FRASER *Alanbrooke* iii. 53 He gave, at that time and later, a certain impression of being uninterested in people except at an agreeably superficial level, absorbed only in practical or professional pursuits.

Hence **un'interestedly** *adv.*, **-ness**.

1691 T. H[ALE] *Acc. New Invent.* 55 As to that Uninterestedness so pretended to by them. **1891** H.

HERMAN *His Angel* 108 He looked upon the..crowds.. uninterestedly.

un'interesting, *ppl. a.* (UN-¹ 10.)
1769 BURKE *Observ. State of Nation* ¶4 Uninteresting barren truths which generate no conclusion. **1782** MISS BURNEY *Cecilia* VII. ix, Too much occupied..to..listen to such uninteresting discourse. **1840** HOOD *Up Rhine* 43 The banks of the Lower Rhine are of a very uninteresting character. **1869** TOZER *Highl. Turkey* II. 176 Writers, whose pages are..extremely uninteresting.

Hence **un'interestingness.** Also **un'interestingly** *adv.*
1793 W. ROBERTS *Looker-on* No. 82 My days pass serenely, but *uninterestingly. **1896** BLACK *Briseis* xvii, I'm sick of blue skies—skies that are monotonously and uninterestingly blue. **1794** *European Mag.* XXVI. 344 The *uninterestingness of genealogical detail. **1854** FABER *Growth in Holiness* viii. (1872) 129 The momentary dulness and uninterestingness of the things of God.

uninter'mediate, *a.* (UN-¹ 7.)
1863 LD. LYTTON *Ring of Amasis* II. 232 His nerves..had forced into his service a new unintermediate sense.

uninter'mission. (UN-¹ 12.)
1681 BP. S. PARKER *Demonstr. Law of Nat.* 134 The continuation and unintermission of his Pain had tired out his Patience.

†**uninter'missive,** *a. Obs.* (UN-¹ 7.)
1610 E. SKORY *Extract fr. Hist. Hen. IV of France* 5 Anxieties caused by vn-intermissiue infidelities. **1645** QUARLES *New Distemper* Wks. (Grosart) I. 150/2 The unintermissive continuance [of Episcopal government] for so many Ages. **1655** EARL ORRERY *Parthen.* II. III. 293 His first stroakes were so vnintermissiue and briske.

Hence †**uninter'missively** *adv.*, **-ness.** *Obs.*
1655 EARL ORRERY *Parthen.* I. I. 3 Perceiveing the unintermissiuenes of his melancholy. **1656** *Ibid.* III. IV. 295 That admirable equalitie which this fair Princess had so unintermissively practised.

uninter'mitted, *ppl. a.* (UN-¹ 8.)
1611 COTGR., *Suyte*,..a succession, continuance, or vnintermitted course of things. **1651** T. STANLEY *Poems, Moschus* 48 The hoarse frogs unintermitted groan. **1738** *Gentl. Mag.* VIII. 581/2 His Application was unintermitted, his Head clear. **1751** JOHNSON *Rambler* No. 108 ¶1 Some scorched with unintermitted heat. **1812** SHELLEY in Dowden *Life* (1887) I. 218 My desire is ardent and unintermitted. **1884** CHURCH *Bacon* ix. 220 Easy and unstudied as his writing seems, it was..the result of unintermitted trouble.

Hence **uninter'mittedly** *adv.*
a **1693** URQUHART *Rabelais* III. xvii. 140 A pair of Yarn Windles, which she nine times unintermittedly veered, and frisked about. **1861** MILL *Utilit.* v. 81 Unless the machinery ..is kept unintermittedly in active play. **1863** W. PHILLIPS *Speeches* iii. 51 This heart of mine which beats so unintermittedly in the bosom.

uninter'mittent, *a.* (UN-¹ 7.)
1850 J. H. NEWMAN *Diffic. Anglic.* 130 Which has been in unintermittent traditionary error. **1883** J. GILMOUR *Mongols* 261 The unintermittent feasting lasts about a week.

Hence **uninter'mittently** *adv.*
1875 *Wonders of Phys. World* I. iii. 100 Their ruins crumble unintermittently.

uninter'mitting, *ppl. a.* (UN-¹ 10.)
1661 FELTHAM *Resolves*, etc. 384 To procure an unintermitting joy..is beyond a Solomon. **1709** MRS. MANLEY *Secret Mem.* (1720) IV. 195 In answer to her unintermitting Reproaches. **1777** ROBERTSON *Hist. Amer.* v. (1778) II. 117 All were ready to sink under the toils of unintermitting service. *a* **1818** M. G. LEWIS *Jrnl. W. Ind.* (1834) 4 The flashes of lightning were..unintermitting. **1890** *Retrospect Med.* CII. 368 The continuous roar..is..unintermitting.

Hence **uninter'mittingness.**
1866 MRS. RITCHIE *Village on Cliff* xiv, His talk was a wonder of ingenuity and unintermittingness.

uninter'mittingly, *adv.* (UN-¹ 11; cf. prec.)
1782 *Ann. Reg., Hist.* 85/2 An infinite number of rockets were unintermittingly thrown. **1809** PINKNEY *Trav. France* 164 The attention of the French Government is now unintermittingly occupied. **1885** J. PAYN *Talk of Town* I. 103 He now resolved to cultivate it [*i.e.* his father's favour] un-intermittingly, and at any sacrifice.

uninter'mixed, *ppl. a.* (UN-¹ 8).
1595 DANIEL *Civ. Wars* I. vi, Vnintermixt with fiction's fantasies, I versify the truth. **1618** SIR S. D'EWES *Autobiog.* (1845) I. 110 An eternal and unintermixed happiness. **1630** DRUMM. OF HAWTH. *Hymn of Fairest Faire* 189 Those Bodies faire and greate Which faint not in their Course,.. Vnintermixt, which no disorder proue. **1720** WELTON *Suffer. Son of God* II. xxvii. 714 In Him, Alone, whose Love and Friendship is Pure, and un-intermixed.

unin'terpolated, *ppl. a.* (UN-¹ 8.)
1790 PORSON *Lett. to Travis* 277 [They] think that *authenticæ* means no more than genuine, uninterpolated. **1818** G. S. FABER *Horæ Mosaicæ* I. 350 It is found impossible to ascribe the uninterpolated Pentateuch to any author save Moses.

uninter'posing, *ppl. a.* (UN-¹ 10.)
1749 MELMOTH *Fitzosborne Lett.* xlviii. II. 13 To prove, that the supreme being remains an uninterposing spectator of what is transacted upon this theatre of the world.

unin'terpretable, *a.* (UN-¹ 7b.)
1625 PURCHAS *Pilgrims* II. 1456 Through the virtue of an uninterpretable name. **1729** G. ADAMS tr. *Sophocles, Antig.* IV. i. II. 56 An unknown Voice of Birds crying with an ill Fury, uninterpretable. **1879** THOMSON & TAIT *Nat. Phil.* I. I. §385 Many formulae are at present obscure and uninterpretable. **1884** *Pop. Sci. Monthly* XXIV. 822 Figures of men and animals and uninterpretable signs.

unin'terpreted, *ppl. a.* [UN-¹ 8.] That has not been interpreted. *spec.* in *Logic*, applied to a calculus, formula, or symbol that has no meaning assigned to the symbol(s) independently of the calculus.
1662 HIBBERT *Body of Divinity* I. 218 Amen. It is..an Hebrew word,..and..remaines uninterpreted. *a* **1768** SECKER *Serm.* (1771) V. vii. 139 Combinations of several Words may come to have Meanings very different from what the Terms,..uninterpreted by Practice, would lead one to apprehend. **1848** E. A. LEATHAM *Charmione* (1858) II. 22 Attributing that uninterpreted gladness to..the sights and sounds of a spiritual world. **1895** *Educat. Rev.* Nov. 352 Unsorted and uninterpreted fragments. **1898** A. N. WHITEHEAD *Universal Algebra* i. 5 When the marks and their rules of arrangement are such as appear likely to receive an interpretation..then the art of arranging such marks may be called..an uninterpreted calculus. **1947** H. REICHENBACH *Elem. Symbolic Logic* 165 The uninterpreted formula, regarded only as an aggregate of symbols equipped with certain structural properties. **1963** H. WANG *Survey Math. Logic* ii. 29 It is more correct to call the sentence-like expressions of Q statement schemata..because the symbols for predicate, functions, and individuals are uninterpreted.

unin'terred, *ppl. a.* (UN-¹ 8.)
1648 *Hunting of Fox* 17 Left uninter'd for the Fox and other beasts to prey upon. *a* **1684** LEIGHTON *Com. 1 Pet.* iii. 19 Rotting above ground, as carcases uninterred. **1720** POPE *Iliad* XXII. 474 Unwept, unhonour'd, uninterr'd he lies! **1827** POLLOK *Course T.* VI. 258 By him lay the uninterred corpse. **1837** LYTTON *Athens* II. 161 Leaving the remainder uninterred he invited all..to examine the scene of contest.

unin'terrogable, *a.*, **-ated,** *ppl. a.* (UN-¹ 7b, 8.)
1802-12 BENTHAM *Ration. Judic. Evid.* (1827) II. 295 His own ready-written and uninterrogable testimony. *Ibid.* I. 450 The mass of sworn but uninterrogated deposition called an affidavit. **1803** MARY CHARLTON *Wife & Mistress* III. 174 No one will question me upon the dark subject.., and un-interrogated, how could I endure to mention it!

uninte'rrupt, *ppl. a. Sc.* [UN-¹ 8b.] = next.
1776 C. KEITH *Farmer's Ha'* lxiii, O here are joys uninterrup', Far hence is pleasure's gangrene cup.

uninte'rrupted, *ppl. a.* and *adv.* [UN-¹ 8.]
1. Not interrupted or broken in respect of continuity or sequence; unintermittent, continuous.
1602 WARNER *Alb. Eng.* XIII. lxxvi. 316 The euer mouing heauens vninterrupted rounde. **1647** CLARENDON *Hist. Reb.* I. §5 The uninterrupted pleasures..of twenty-two years Peace. **1709** ADDISON *Tatler* No. 192 ¶6 An uninterrupted Friendship and Felicity. **1781** GIBBON *Decl. & F.* xxxi. III. 195 The uninterrupted succession of senators. **1849** COBDEN *Speeches* 29 An interval of several years of uninterrupted peace. **1880** MCCARTHY *Our Times* xl. III. 223 His career was one of uninterrupted success.
b. Not broken in surface; having no intervals between the parts.
1791 NEWTE *Tour Eng. & Scot.* 58 The cascade..falls.. in one uninterrupted sheet. **1822** J. PARKINSON *Outl. Oryctol.* 159 The margin [of the shell is]..uninterrupted and reflected. **1866** *Treas. Bot.* 1191/2 *Uninterrupted*, consisting of regularly increasing or diminishing parts, or of parts all of the same size.
2. Not disturbed or broken into; not interrupted *by* something.
1657 CROMWELL *Sp.* in Somers *Tracts* (1811) VI. 367 A more free exercise, more uninterrupted by any hand of power. **1728** ELIZA HEYWOOD tr. *Mme. de Gomez's Belle A.* (1732) II. 63 The rest of our Voyage was..uninterrupted by the least cross Accident whatever. **1796** MME. D'ARBLAY *Camilla* V. 202 Mr. Tyrold would not suffer this scene to be long uninterrupted. **1854** *Poultry Chron.* II. 194/2 An uninterrupted day of rest. **1873** B. HARTE *Fiddletown* 7 The dwellings were..uninterrupted by shops.
3. *adv.* Without interruption; unhindered.
1677 YARRANTON *Eng. Improv.* 3 That the Smacks and small Vessels may..fetch in Provisions and Naval Stores uninterrupted.

uninte'rruptedly, *adv.* [UN-¹ 11; cf. prec.] Without interruption or break; continuously, connectedly.
1665 SIR T. HERBERT *Trav.* (1677) 203 Where the Mountain uninterruptedly runs as far as Mergiana. *a* **1691** BOYLE *Hist. Air* (1692) 7 Having not the leisure to prosecute this discourse uninterruptedly. **1794** *Phil. Trans.* LXXXV. 39 In which case the following particles would exert their force uninterruptedly. **1826** F. REYNOLDS *Life & Times* II. 183 From that time..our intimacy has continued.. uninterruptedly. **1875** JOWETT *Plato* (ed. 2) III. 4 That the Republic was written uninterruptedly and by a continuous effort.

uninte'rruptedness. (f. UNINTERRUPTED.)
1665 J. SERJEANT *Sure Footing* 106 The ever-continuance or uninterruptedness of Tradition. **1671** FLAVEL *Fount. Life* ii. 4 The Perpetuity and uninterruptedness thereof. **1791** WASHINGTON *Let.* Writ. 1892 XII. 46 My return to this place is sooner than I expected, owing to the uninterruptedness of my journey. **1834** J. W. CROKER in *C. Papers* 11 June, The musicians..spoiled that uninterruptedness (what a word) which was so beautiful yesterday. **1876** CARPENTER in *Contemp. Rev.* Jan., The Scientific Theist..looks at the uninterruptedness of this order [in Nature] as the highest evidence of its original perfection.

uninte'rruptible, *a.* (UN-¹ 7.)
a **1683** SIDNEY *Disc. Govt.* III. xxx. (1704) 361 An uninterruptible Line of Descent. **1984** *Sunday Tel.* 22 July 13/8 He no longer discusses. He just gives uninterruptible lectures.

uninte'rruptibleness. (UN-¹ 12.)
1654 OWEN *Doctr. Saints' Persev.* Pref. Rdr. B j b, The uninterruptibleness of any Act of God.

uninte'rrupting, *ppl. a.* (UN-¹ 10.)
1809 W. TAYLOR in Robberds *Mem.* (1843) II. 364 My imagination is rapidly learning..to exult in the uninterrupting character of rural scenery.

uninte'rruption. (UN-¹ 12.)
1647 CLARENDON *Hist. Reb.* III. §65 To have Questioned ..the Seditious Riots..before the uninterruption and security had confirmed the People in all three. **1740** CHEYNE *Regimen* 47 To allow Time and Uninterruption from the natural Powers. **1744** WALDRON *Descr. Isle of Man* (ed. 2) 106 That Uninterruption and Solitude of the Sea, gave the Mermen..frequent Opportunities of visiting the Shore. **1808** G. EDWARDS *Pract. Plan* iii. 20 The enlargement and uninterruption of commerce.

uninter'spersed, *ppl. a.* (UN-¹ 8.)
1887 BROWNING *Parleyings, Apollo & Fates*, Is age..so uninterspersed with good?

un'interviewed, *ppl. a.* (UN-¹ 8.)
1886 PHELPS *Burglars in Paradise* viii, The hitherto uninterviewed American citizen.

uninthralled, -intitled, etc.: see UNEN-.

unin'timidated, *ppl. a.* (UN-¹ 8.)
1764 *Museum Rust.* II. lxxviii. 275 If I find your *Museum* that unintimidated receptacle which I hope it will appear to be. **1815** WRAXALL *Hist. Mem.* I. 361 Unintimidated by the clamours of Sir Fletcher's adherents. *a* **1849** H. COLERIDGE *Ess.* (1851) II. 60 The unbought, unintimidated suffrage of fame. **1876** BANCROFT *Hist. U.S.* III. xx. 305 Unintimidated by the prophecy.

unin'toxicating, *ppl. a.* (UN-¹ 10.)
1773 *Observ. State Poor* 57 This unintoxicating beverage. **1844** H. G. ROBINSON *Odes of Horace* I. xvii, Here shalt thou quaff..The unintoxicating bowl Of Lesbian. **1876** TYNDALL *Fragm. Sci.* (1879) II. xii. 256 Unintoxicating grape-juice is converted into intoxicating wine.

un'intricated, *ppl. a.* (UN-¹ 8.)
a **1660** HAMMOND *Serm.* Wks. 1683 IV. 502 The fair open Campania of even, clear, unintricated designs.

unin'triguing, *ppl. a.* (UN-¹ 10.)
1755 *Monitor* No. 9. I. 72 The plain, disinterested, unintriguing man. **1771** H. WALPOLE *Vertue's Anecd. Paint.* IV. 5 In truth he was..a modest unintriguing man.

unintro'duced, *ppl. a.* (UN-¹ 8.)
1743 YOUNG *Nt. Th.* v. 89 Think not un-introduc'd I forc'd my way. **1813** *Examiner* 19 Apr. 250/1 The romping, ungainly, unintroduced girl of seventeen. **1897** MARY KINGSLEY *W. Africa* 6 When I have arrived..in a steamer or canoe, unexpected, unintroduced, or turned up equally unheralded out of the bush.

unin'troitive, *a.* (UN-¹ 7.)
1819 COLERIDGE in *Lit. Rem.* (1836) II. 239 And then again, still unintroitive, [Banquo] addresses the witches.

unintro'mitted, *ppl. a.* (UN-¹ 8.)
1563 *Reg. Privy Council Scot.* I. 246 To..keip the samyn [corn]..upoun the grund of the saidis landis, unintromittit with be ather of the saidis parteis.

unin'truding, *ppl. a.* (UN-¹ 10.)
1796 MME. D'ARBLAY *Camilla* III. 300 She is there almost every night; only being unintruding, she is unnoticed.

unin'tuitive, *a.* (UN-¹ 7.)
1842 SIR W. HAMILTON *Diss.* in *Reid's Wks.* 767 The unintuitive judgments.

uni'nuclear (juːnɪ-), *a.* [UNI- 1.] Having, or characterized by, one nucleus.
1882 VINES tr. *Sachs' Bot.* 946 Treub..has observed the division of the nucleus..and finds that it takes place in the manner described..for uninuclear cells. **1896** *Allbutt's Syst. Med.* I. 71 In the boundary zone away from the cocci the uninuclear form [of leucocyte] predominated.

So **uni'nucleate, uni'nucleated** *adjs.*
1885 E. RAY LANKESTER in *Encycl. Brit.* XIX. 862/1 Young uninucleate individual which has emerged from the cyst within the Tadpole, and will now multiply its nuclei. **1898** *Allbutt's Syst. Med.* V. 636 There are present in the blood numerous large uninucleated cells.

uni'nured, *ppl. a.* (UN-¹ 8.)
a **1708** J. PHILIPS *Fall of Chloe's Jordan* 100 Protected mice The race exiguous, uninured to wet, Their mansions quit. *a* **1800** COWPER *Odyss.* (ed. 2) XXI. 182 Fatiguing, first, his hands Too delicate and uninured to toil. **1856** ALFORD *Quebec Chapel Serm.* III. 128 Uninured to the selfishness of this wicked world. **1880** SWINBURNE *Stud. Shaks.* 18 An incongruity..imperceptible to eyes uninured to the use of their spectacles.

unin'vadable, *a.* (UN-¹ 7b.)
a **1711** KEN *Hymns Evang.* Poet. Wks. 1721 I. 32 Spreading a glorious Evangelick Light, And uninvadeable by ghostly Night. *a* **1806** ELIZ. CARTER in *Mem.* (1808) I. 36 My heart, which I thought so secure and so uninvadable.

unin'vaded, *ppl. a.* (UN-¹ 8.)
[**1571-2** *Reg. Privy Council Scot.* II. 125 To be unhurt, unharmit, un-molestit invadit and in ony wayis persewit.] **1647** CLARENDON *Hist. Reb.* II. §7 They believed there was no part of their Civil Government uninvaded by them. **1748** RICHARDSON *Clarissa* (1881) III. 165, I expect to be uninvaded in my retirements. **1769** SIR J. REYNOLDS *Disc.* ii. (1778) 36 Of this I shall speak with such latitude, as may leave the province of the professor uninvaded. **1830** TENNYSON *Kraken* 3 His ancient, dreamless, uninvaded sleep The Kraken sleepeth. **1885** O. CRAWFURD *Woman's*

Reputation i, Our old England indeed, uninvaded by modern ideas.

unin'validated, *ppl. a.* (UN-[1] 8.)
1813 *Monthly Mag.* XXXV. 217 The fact remains uninvalidated.

unin'veigled, *ppl. a.* (UN-[1] 8.)
1687 tr. *Sallust* (1692) 38 Nor did he leave uninveigl'd the very Thieves and Robbers.

unin'vented, *ppl. a.* (UN-[1] 8.)
1611 Beaum. & Fl. *King & No King* IV. ad fin., If that happen Then I..shall pull a heap Of strange yet uninvented sin upon me. **1667** Milton *P.L.* VI. 470 Not uninvented that, which thou aright Beleivst so main to our success. **1680** Otway *Orphan* v, Rack me..with all your choicest torments,..and pains yet uninvented. **1754** [see unimagined]. **1875** Jevons *Money* xxi. 283 It has grown spontaneously, uninvented, unauthorized by the legislature.

unin'ventful, *a.* (UN-[1] 7.)
1856 Ruskin *Mod. Paint.* III. IV. xviii. §13 The harsh outline and..uninventful blankness of the design.

unin'ventive, *a.* (UN-[1] 7.)
1776 Mickle tr. *Camoens' Lusiad* Dissert. 164/1 A most servile uninventive imitation of the sixth Eneid. **1783** Blair *Lect.* I. 349 Nature..appears, to his uninventive genius, exhausted by those who have gone before him. **1816** *Q. Rev.* XV. 71 One is of a dry and uninventive faculty. **1855** Milman *Lat. Chr.* XIV. iii. VI. 447 The inert and uninventive disciple of the Western philosophy.

Hence **unin'ventively** (Webster, 1847), **-ness.**
1863 *Sat. Rev.* 14 March 335/2 The very grotesqueness and uninventiveness..which distinguished the illuminations of Tuesday.

unin'verted, *ppl. a.* (UN-[1] 8.)
1745 Young *Nt. Th.* VIII. 1161 He follows nature (not like thee), and shews us An uninverted system of a man. **1865** J. Hullah *Transition Period of Music* 217 There are..no less than six perfect cadences, in the direct or uninverted form.

unin'vested, *ppl. a.* (UN-[1] 8.)
[**1775** Ash.] **1802-12** Bentham *Ration. Judic. Evid.* (1827) V. 218 A man..uninvested with any coercive power. **1816** Scott *Old Mort.* xxii, Supposing the insurgents were to march onward and leave it [*sc.* a stronghold] uninvested. **1833** J. Burke (*title*), A Genealogical and Heraldic History of The Commoners..uninvested with Heritable Honours.

unin'vestigable, *a.* (UN-[1] 7 b, 5 b.)
a **1677** Barrow *Serm.* Wks. 1686 III. 464 We (to whom God's judgments are inscrutable, and his ways uninvestigable). **1691** Ray *Creation* I. (1692) 2 The Number of them being uninvestigable by us. **1768-74** Tucker *Lt. Nat.* (1834) I. 582 Brought about by the courses of fortune dependent upon one another, to us accidental and uninvestigable. **1858** H. Bushnell *Serm. New Life* 31 The manner of the fact is uninvestigable and mysterious. **1866** —— *Vicar. Sacr.* II. iv. 179 God is.., in some sense uninvestigable by us, both finite and subject.

unin'vestigated, *ppl. a.* (UN-[1] 8.)
1816 Scott *Bl. Dwarf* iv, I am unwilling to leave a matter uninvestigated which [etc.]. **1862** Miller *Elem. Chem., Org.* (ed. 2) iii. §4. 244 It yields a liquid..the nature of which, however, is at present uninvestigated.

unin'vestigating, *ppl. a.* (UN-[1] 10.)
1802 *Noble Wanderers* I. 246 The secret of his heart was too visible to escape the uninvestigating eye.

unin'vidious, *a.* (UN-[1] 7.)
1822 Lamb *Elia* I. *Decay of Beggars*, Theirs were the only rates uninvidious in the levy. **1865** F. Oakeley *Hist. Notes* 3 Unpretending, uninvidious, and sufficient for the purpose.

unin'vidiously, *adv.* (UN-[1] 11.)
1678 Cudworth *Intell. Syst.* I. iii. 117 Intellectual Love ..having an Infinite overflowing Fulnes and Fecundity, dispenses it self Uninvidiously.

unin'vite, *v.* [UN-[2] 3 or UN-[1] 14.] *trans.* To cancel or omit the invitation of (a person).
1665 Pepys *Diary* 26 Nov., So I made them uninvite their guests. **1873** Mrs. Whitney *Other Girls* xviii, Without letting him answer, she turned..and sprang up the rugged stairway... But she had not uninvited him, after all.

unin'vited, *ppl. a.* (UN-[1] 8.)
1631 Massinger *Emperor East* IV. v, Thou uninvited guest,..I charge thee, leave me! **1665** Boyle *Occas. Refl.* IV. xvii. 112 The great Advantage..of freeing themselves from uninvited Companions. **1702** Vanbrugh *False Friend* III. ii, That thought comes uninvited. Then, like an uninvited guest, let it be treated: Begone intruder. **1796** Mme. D'Arblay *Camilla* IV. 183 [There] he had spend the night, though uninvited by its agitated owner. **1840** Hood *Up Rhine* 241 Uninvited and unannounced, an unceremonious visitor stepped boldly into the room. **1882** Mayne Reid in *N. York Tribune* 21 June, All uninvited people would be looked upon as intruders.

Hence **unin'vitedly** *adv.*
1669 Earl Orrery *Parthen.* III. v. 11 Uninvitedly I came to participate in their Glory. **1828** E. W. Hamilton *Diary* 12 May (1972) I. 272 The Government..could not fail to take heed of information tendered to them uninvitedly.

unin'viting, *ppl. a.* (UN-[1] 10.)
1686 Plot *Staffordsh.* 301 That a man should thus long after such uninviting things. **1690** Boyle *Chr. Virtuoso* I. 102 That such Unlikely Men should so Succesfully preach so Uninviting a Doctrine. **1777** Robertson *Hist. Amer.* VI. (1778) II. 151 He found every where the same uninviting country. **1821** Lamb *Elia* I. *Old Benchers I.T.*, His look was uninviting. **1894** Mrs. Dyan *Man's Keeping* (1899) 60 The outside looked formidable and uninviting.
Comb. **1880** Beale *Slight Ailm.* 172 Half a dozen unripe and very uninviting-looking apples.

unin'voked, *ppl. a.* (UN-[1] 8.)
1718 Rowe tr. *Lucan* I. 125 Let Phœbus dwell Still uninvok'd in Cyrrha's mystick cell. **1809-14** Wordsw. *Excurs.* III. 753 The powers of song I left not uninvoked. **1849** Grote *Greece* II. xlvii. VI. 123 That the god would help them, invoked or uninvoked.

unin'volved, *ppl. a.* (UN-[1] 8.)
1793 V. Knox *Lett. Yng. Noblem.* xxvii, So long as you preserve your own finances uninvolved. **1853** Ruskin *Stones Ven.* II. 207 Loveliness of simple design and grace of uninvolved proportion.

‖**unio** ('juːnɪəʊ). *Zool.* Pl. unios (‖uniones). [L. *ūnio* a single large pearl (Pliny). Cf. UNION *sb.*[2]] A genus of freshwater bivalves typical of the family *Unionidæ*; a mussel belonging to this or a related genus, esp. one yielding pearls; a river-mussel, pearl-mussel.
1824 *Encycl. Brit.* Suppl. V. 581/1 The second [family], *Uniodæ* [sic], will embrace Unio,..Anodonta, and Iridina. **1834** Griffith tr. *Cuvier* XII. 387 Pearls..are more especially produced by the thick bivalve shells, such as the *uniones*. *Ibid.* 401 There is nothing to induce us to mention the Unio here, except [etc.]. **1851** S. P. Woodward *Mollusca* 41 Some of the unios thicken their umbones enormously. **1899** *Nature* 15 June 151/2 The washing out of loose pearls from the unios.
b. *attrib.* and *Comb.*, as ***unio-fisher, mollusc, -shaped***; **unio-beds** (see quot. 1888).
1861 P. P. Carpenter in *Rep. Smithsonian Instit. 1860*, 259 *Unio*-shaped shells. *Ibid.* 263 The musk-rats..being nature's great Unio-fishers. **1882** *Proc. Berw. Nat. Club* IX. 506 Birds..picking up the large Unio molluscs in rivers. **1888** *Cassell's Encycl. Dict.*, *Unio-beds*,..certain beds in the Purbeck, characterized by the occurrence of species of Unio. **1897** *Quart. Jrnl. Geol. Soc.* Index 400/2 Unio-bed on Notowasaga River (Canada).

uni'ocular, *a.* [See UNI- and OCULAR *a.*, and cf. med.L. *ūnioculus*.] **a.** *fig.* Characterized by the use of one eye. **b.** Of or pertaining to, affecting, one eye. Cf. MONOCULAR *a.*
a. 1830 *Edin. Rev.* LI. 531 The results of this unilateral, uni-ocular mode of proceeding.
b. 1890 *Lancet* 28 June 1416/1 In two [cases] there was occasional lateral nystagmus; one uniocular. *a* **1901** F. W. H. Myers *Human Personality* (1903) I. 479 Cases, where ciliary spasm..led to uniocular diplopia.

'unioid, *a.* *Zool.* [f. UNI-O + -OID. Cf. UNIONOID *a.*] Resembling or shaped like (that of) a unio.
1861 P. P. Carpenter in *Rep. Smithsonian Instit. 1860*, 268 Shells, with two Unioid teeth in each valve.

union ('juːnɪən), *sb.*[1] Also 5-6 vnyon, 5-7 vnion. [a. F. *union* (12-13th c., = Sp. *union*, Pg. *união*, It. *unione*), ad. L. *ūniōn-em*, *ūnio* the number one, unity, uniting, etc., f. *ūnus* one.]
I. 1. The action of joining or uniting one thing to another or others, or two or more things together, so as to form one whole or complete body; the state or condition of being so joined or united; combination, conjunction: **a.** In non-physical sense or of abstract things.
hypostatic union: see HYPOSTATIC *a.* 1.
1432-50 tr. *Higden* (Rolls) V. 9 He ordeynede that water scholde be mixte with wyne in the chalice, to betoken the union of the churche un to Criste. *c* **1450** *Myrr. Our Ladye* 208 Conuenyently are deuoute weldockes lykened vnto fayre trees, wherof the route ys suche vnyon of tow hartes. *Ibid.* 229 By whiche knyttynge..the godhed was vnyed vnto the manhed, and the very manhed vnto the godhed... And in this moste acceptable vnyon [etc.]. **1538** Starkey *England* 41 The vnyon and coniunctyon of the body and soule togyddur. **1560** tr. *Fisher's Godly Treat. Prayer* F 5 b, The very true and sincere delectation, whiche groweth by a certayne vnion and perfect agreement..of our soules with almightie God. **1627** Sir J. Finch in *Parl. Hist.* (1807) II. 224/2 This union of hearts, sir, is a greatness beyond that of the kingdom to which you are heir. **1651** Hobbes *Leviath.* II. xviii. 92 The strength of an Army [consisteth] in the union of their strength under one Command. **1667** Milton *P.L.* IX. 966 Adam, from whose deare side I boast me sprung, And gladly of our Union heare thee speak, One Heart, one Soul in both. **1728** Chambers *Cycl.* s.v. *Hypostatical*, The Union of the human Nature with the Divine. **1800** *Med. Jrnl.* IV. 334 By the union and investigation of several data, the truth may at last be discovered. **1841** Miall in *Nonconf.* I. 1 The union of church and state. **1873** Freeman *Comp. Politics* ii. 49 The union of Roman and Teutonic elements.
b. Of persons or countries with reference to joint action or policy. Cf. 3.
1608 W. Wilkes *Sec. Memento for Magistrates* 59 Compleat union is of better consequence to the furtherance of religion. **1687** A. Lovell tr. *Thevenot's Trav.* I. 78 The Janizaries swore the same Union with the Spahis. **1711** Dk. Marlborough in *10th Rep. Hist. MSS. Comm.* App. I. 144, I haue no other views then what tend to the firmest union with his Lordship. **1817** Shelley *Rev. Islam* IX. xviii, The cold sneers of calumny were vain, The union of the free with discord's brand to stain.
c. In physical sense; *spec.* in *Surg.*, the growing together of the parts of a broken bone, lips of a wound, etc., in the process of healing.
1631 H. C[rooke] *Expl. Instrum. Chirurg.* 13 To hold the lips of the wound..together till the vnion be perfected. **1704** J. Harris *Lex. Techn.* I. s.v., The Union of Atoms, or Particles which touch in a Plain: as in the Chrystallization of Salts, and other like Bodies. **1767** Gooch *Treat. Wounds* I. 152 The time generally allowed for the union of wounds. **1815** J. Smith *Panorama Sci. & Art* II. 341 This affinity or union, is always..of a chemical nature, for it is attended with the grand characteristic of chemical union, viz. it destroys the identity of the ingredients. **1842** Loudon *Suburban Hort.* 287 To fit the scion to the stock in such a manner that the union of their inner barks..may be as close as possible. **1860** Tyndall *Glac.* I. vii. 54 The moraine.. formed by the union of the lateral moraines.
d. With *a* and pl. An instance or occasion of this. (Rarely in physical sense, see (*b*).)
In some instances not clearly separable from 7.
1570 Levins *Manip.* 166 An Vnion, *vnio*. *c* **1600** Shaks. *Sonn.* viii. 6 If the true concord of well tuned sounds, By vnions married, do offend thine eare. *a* **1653** Binning *Serm.* Wks. (1735) 8/2 There was an Union made already in his first Moulding. **1679** South *Serm.* 167 The same [object] luckily hapning upon another [mind] of a Disposition.. framed for it, is..greedily clasped into the nearest Unions and Embraces. **1781** Cowper *Charity* 122 While providence enjoins to ev'ry soul An union with the vast terraqueous whole. **1871** J. Bradbury *Trav. Amer.* 331 A colony having an union of interest, and of course an union of action. **1871** Jowett *Plato* III. 363 There is a union of qualities in him such as I have never seen in any other.
(*b*) **1826** S. Cooper *First Lines Surg.* (ed. 5) 281 In some instances [of compound fracture], only a partial union follows. **1842** Loudon *Suburban Hort.* 281 Instances frequently occur of the inner bark of the scion being placed out of contact with that of the stock, and a union nevertheless ensues.
e. Without article, in prec. senses.
† ***at union***, in union, united.
c **1483** H. Baradoun in *Pol., Rel. & L. Poems* 289 Hertis ease & I be not at vnion. **1526** *Pilgr. Perf.* (W. de W. 1531) 284 b, In that all sweetenesse and vnyon of loue and grace is signifyed. **1625** Bacon *Ess.*, *Friendship* (Arb.) 173 For in Bodies, Vnion strengthneth and cherisheth any Naturall Action;..And euen so is it of Minds. **1651** Hobbes *Govt. & Soc.* v. §7. 79 This submission of the wills of all those men to the will of one man, or one Counsell, is then made, when each one of them obligeth himself by contract to every one of the rest,..this is called union. **1675** R. Burthogge *Causa Dei* 39 The Soul in state of Union to the Body. **1738** R. Grey *Meth. Hebrew* p. v, The Line of Union called *Maccaph*. **1789** Belsham *Ess.* II. xli. 526 Persecution, said Mr. Fox, is a bond of union. **1800** tr. *Lagrange's Chem.* II. 114 Nitric solutions of mercury and silver..are themselves decomposed at the moment of union. **1847** Mrs. A. Kerr tr. *Ranke's Hist. Servia* 117 The league of independent chiefs ..was on the closest terms of union with both these parties. **1849** Lever *Con Cregan* xi, While a sharp wound in my neck ..had just begun that process called 'union'. *a* **1881** A. Barratt *Phys. Metempiric* (1883) p. xxv, The feeling of real invisible union among the spirits of all the universe.
f. Sexual conjunction; copulation. *rare.*
1728 Chambers *Cycl.* s.v. *Univocal*, Animals..produced by Univocal Generation, that is, by the sole Union or Copulation of a Male and Female of the same Species. **1799** *Med. Jrnl.* II. 321 A female rabbit..and..a buck..were allowed to caress each other whilst absolute union was prevented. **1960** C. Winick *Dict. Anthropol.* 554/2 *Ritual union*, sexual intercourse on special occasions, as part of a ceremonial.
2. a. The uniting together of the different sections, parties, or individuals of a nation, people, or other body so as to produce general agreement or concord; the condition resulting from this; absence of dissension, discord, or difference in opinion or doctrine; unity.
c **1460** *Brut* II. 508 This Frederike..was long Emperoure, & differred for to be crowned at Rome because of þe Scisme; but after þat vnion was had, he was crowned with Emperial Diademe. *c* **1460** G. Ashby *Dicta Philos.* 703 That kyng that maketh his Region To be obedient to his iuste lawe, That reigne peasibly in an vnyon. **1525** Ld. Berners *Froiss.* II. ccxxxiii. 301 b/1 The vnyon of the churche I desyre, and I haue taken great payne therin. **1539** Cromwell in Merriman *Life & Lett.* (1902) II. 230 Ye shal..bring a very vnion..bitwene all them there & conduce them to suche a knott as there shalbe perfite vnion amonges them without striffe. **1647** Clarendon *Hist. Reb.* I. §10 The Union, Peace and Plenty of the Kingdom. **1683** Temple *Mem.* Wks. 1720 I. 480, I, that never had any thing so much at heart as the Union of my Country. **1828** Scott *F.M. Perth* xiii, Have I not thanks to pay to God, who has restored union to my family? **1841** Borrow *Zincali* I. iii. II. 271 However some of the Gitános may complain that there is no longer union to be found amongst them, there is [etc.]. **1849** Macaulay *Hist. Eng.* i. I. 160 They were so far from being disposed to purchase union by concession that they objected to concession chiefly because it tended to produce union.
b. *Painting.* Agreement or harmony in respect of colour, design, etc.
1704 J. Harris *Lex. Techn.* I, *Union* (a Term among Painters) is the mutual Agreeableness and Sympathy of the Colours in a Piece of Painting. **1728** Chambers *Cycl.*, *Harmony*,..in the Ordonnance,..signifies the Union, or Connection between the Figures, with Respect to the Subject of the Piece. **1770** Sir J. Reynolds *Disc.* iii. (1778) 83 A figure..though deviating from beauty, may still have a certain union of the various parts.
c. *Horsem.* (See quots.)
1753 *Chambers's Cycl.* Suppl. s.v. *Unite*, A horse is said to *unite*, or walk in union, when, a galloping, the hind quarters follow and keep time with the fore. **1884** E. L. Anderson *Mod. Horsem.* 110 That state of collection that we have styled the union. That is, the forces of the two extremities must be united as closely as is consistent with the maintenance of the pace.
3. a. *Scots Law.* The uniting into one tenantry of lands or tenements not lying contiguous. ***charter*** or ***clause of union*** (see quot. 1765-8).
1503 *Sc. Acts, Jas. V* (1814) II. 246 Anent landis..quhilk ..ar anext or vnit in ane halding or barony þat nochtwithstanding þe said anexation or vnion [etc.]. **1542** *Acc. Ld. High Treas. Scotl.* VIII. 117 The forfaltouris and unionis

maid in the last parliament. **1578** *Reg. Privy Council Scot.* II. 693 Erectionis of baroniis, unionis or burghis in barony. **1693** Stair *Instit.* ii. ii. §44. 221 The whole Lands lying contiguous are naturally Unite, and needs no Union. **1751** McDowall *Inst. Laws Scot.* ii. iii. I. 567 The union or erection into a barony of lands, lying in different shires. **1765–8** Erskine *Inst. Law Scotl.* ii. iii. §45 By a charter of union, i.e. by a charter in which the sovereign dispenses with the necessity of taking a separate seisin upon every discontiguous tenement. **1838** W. Bell *Dict. Law Scot.* 1020 The object of a charter, or clause of union.

b. *Eccl.* The uniting or combination of two or more churches or benefices into one. (Cf. UNITION a.)

1529 *Act 21 Hen. VIII*, c. 13 §11 If any person..procure..any Licence or Licences, Union, Toleration or Dispensation, to receive and take any mo Benefices with Cure than is above limited. **1537** tr. *Latimer's Serm. bef. Convoc.* D j b, Some brought forth canonizations, some expectations, some pluralities and unions. **1545** *Act 37 Hen. VIII*, c. 21 A Unyon or Consolidacion of two Churches in one, or of a Churche and Chappell in one. **1607** Cowel *Interpr.*, *Vnion*,..is a combining or consolidation of two Churches in one, which is done by the consent of the Bishop, the Patron, and the Incumbent. **1665** *Act 17 Chas. II*, c. 3 ¶3 The said Union shall take effect for every such Church or Chappell. **1713** E. Gibson *Eccl. Law* 920 By the union, the two churches are become so much one, that a second benefice may be taken. **1796** Pegge *Anonym.* (1809) 444 Consolidation, or the union of divers places in the person of one man, is a great obstacle to justice and equity. **1860** *Act 23–24 Vict.* c. 142 §2 An Union of Two or more contiguous Benefices with one another.

4. The action of uniting, or the state or fact of being united, into one political body; esp. formation or incorporation into a single state, kingdom, or political entity, usually with one central legislature.

a. In general use.

1547 J. Harrison (*title*), An Exhortacion to the Scottes to conforme themselfes to the..godly Union betweene the two Realmes of Englande & Scotland. **1603** Bacon *Briefe Discourse* B ij, And..leauing violent Vnions [of countries]: wee will consider onelye naturall Vnions. **1672** Petty *Pol. Anat.* (1691) 35 Why was there ever a Union between England and Wales? **1729** T. Innes *Crit. Ess.* (1879) 67 That the Picts continued in possession..till their union in one kingdom with the Scots. **1754** Franklin *Plan of Union* Wks. 1887 II. 351 The said commissioners..came to an unanimous resolution: That a union of the colonies is absolutely necessary for their preservation. **1848** W. H. Kelly tr. *L. Blanc's Hist. Ten Y.* I. 268 To the Belgians France could offer, as the price of a fraternal union, the substitution [etc.]. **1855** Motley *Dutch Rep.* v. i. (1906) III. 95 Early in January, 1577, the celebrated 'Union of Brussels' was formed. **1888** *Encycl. Brit.* XXIII. 741/2 This success of the struggle for union gave the United States a date for the political..existence of the nation.

b. *Eng. Hist.* The uniting of the English and Scottish crowns in 1603, or parliaments in 1707; or of the parliaments of Great Britain and Ireland, dating from 1 Jan. 1801. (With *the* and capital.)

(*a*) **1603** Bacon (*title*), A Briefe Discovrse, tovching the Happie Vnion of..England, and Scotland. **1604** *Proclam. Jas. I*, 20 Oct., The blessed Union, or rather reuniting of..England and Scotland, vnder one Imperiall crowne. *a* **1700** Evelyn *Diary* 25 Feb. 1671, Came to visit me one of the Lords Commissioners of Scotland for the Union. **1707** Hearne *Collect.* (O.H.S.) II. 10 This day being the beginning of the Union of England with Scotland. **1712** Z. Haig in J. Russell *Haigs* (1881) xii. 344 Prosperity to Scotland, and No Union! **1827** Hallam *Const. Hist.* xvii. II. 696 The union closes the story of the Scots constitution. **1864** Burton *Scot Abr.* I. 121 Scotland did not fully recover from the ruin of that conflict until the Union made her secure.

(*b*) **1798** *The Union* (ed. 4) 15 As..the Protestants become the majority of our people upon the establishment of the Union. **1829** Scott *Wav.* Gen. Pref., Miss Edgeworth..may be truly said to have done more towards completing the Union, than [etc.]. **1880** *Encycl. Brit.* XIII. 271 Carried in great measure by the same corrupt means as the constitution of '82 had been worked by, the Union earned no gratitude.

5. The joining of one person to another in matrimony; an instance or occasion of this, a marriage.

1595 Shaks. *John* ii. ii. 446 This vnion shall do more than batterie can To our fast-closed gates. **1678** E. Cooke (*title*), Love's Triumph,—or, The Royal Union: A Tragedy. **1751** Johnson *Rambler* No. 167 ¶2 The happy event of a union in which caprice and selfishness had so little part. **1778** Miss Burney *Evelina* lxxix, He was himself of opinion, the sooner the union took place, the better. **1826** Miss Mitford in L'Estrange *Life* (1870) II. xi. 239 The immediate union of the Princess Constance..to Don Pedro. **1841** Thackeray *Gt. Hoggarty Diam.* viii, Her grandfather had been at the first very much averse to our union. **1879** Farrar *St. Paul* II. 69 He pronounced against any voluntary dissolution of unions already existing between Pagans and Christians.

II. †**6. a.** The quality of being one in number; oneness; the fact or condition of consisting of, involving, or being restricted to, one person or thing only. *Obs.*

In quots. 1548 and *a* 1564 with reference to the partaking of the Communion by the priest only.

a **1513** Fabyan *Chron.* vii. ccxliv. 286 An other erronyous opynyon concernynge the vnyon of the Trynytie. **1548** Geste *Pr. Masse* K viii, Thee prieste masse, whyche is rather an vnion then a communion. *a* **1564** Becon *Display. Popish Mass* Wks. II. 50 Ye call it a Communion, which is a partaking of many together; but ye might right well call it an vnion. For no man eateth and drinketh of the bread and wyne but you alone. **1564** Harding *Answ. Jewel* 81 For euery multitude..contineweth one. And that whereof it is one, and is kepte in vnion or onenesse, it is necessary that it be one, elles [etc.]. **1652** Benlowes *Theoph.* viii. xxvii, Thus Holy, Holy, Holy's nam'd, to show A Ternion we in Union know.

†**b.** = MONAD *a.* 1 b. *Obs.*⁻¹

1565 B. Googe tr. *Palingenius' Zodiac* vii. U iij, As from the Union [L. *monas*] fyrst eche other number springs.

†**c.** A unique example. *Obs.*⁻¹

1657 J. Watts *Vind. Ch. Eng.* 48 But an Union, one such text, I mean, in all the Bible.

7. a. That which is united or combined into one; a body formed by uniting one thing to another or others, or several things together; a combination or compound.

1660 Jer. Taylor *Worthy Commun.* Introd. 10 My purpose is..to gather together into an union al these several portions of truth. **1696** Stanhope *Chr. Pattern* (1711) 2 What is a man the better for entring into the sublime mysteries of the Trinity, and being able to dispute nicely upon that adorable Union? **1807** J. E. Smith *Phys. Bot.* 212 Carbonic acid gas, (which was formerly called fixed air, and is an union of oxygen and carbon).

b. A number, group, or body of persons or states joined or associated together for some common purpose or action; an association, league, or society; in later use esp. = TRADE UNION.

(*a*) **1660** Jer. Taylor *Ductor* iii. iv. rule x. §11 He is not to be reckoned as a Brother, or a relative in our religious friendship and union. **1736** Butler *Anal.* i. iii. 83 To separate from their adversaries, and to form an union among themselves. **1762** Falconer *Shipwr.* ii. 409 [The] sagacious statesman..darts around his penetrating eyes, Where Dangers grow and hostile unions rise. **1832** Gen. P. Thompson *Exerc.* (1842) II. 236 Once more to the Political Unions,..don't endure it [*sc.* slavery]; but hold together like burrs. **1903** *Science* (N.Y.) 5 June 892/2 The International Union of the American Republics, popularly known as the Pan-American Union.

(*b*) **1833** *2nd Rep. Factory Com.* D 2. 39 Our spinners..said they had no fault to find.., but the union obliged them to turn out. **1848** Mrs. Gaskell *M. Barton* viii, Block-printers is going to strike; they'n gotten a bang-up Union, as won't let 'em be put upon. **1878** Jevons *Prim. Pol. Econ.* 65 It is certain that the increase of wages is not confined to those trades which have unions.

c. *spec.* A number of states or provinces united together or incorporated into one legislative confederacy; a confederation or federation; esp. the United States of America.

Sometimes in American use restricted to the Northern States which adhered to the Union in contradistinction to the eleven Southern States whose attempted secession from it led to the Civil War of 1861–5.

1775 Jefferson *Let.* Writ. 1892 I. 491 So as to bring the Canadians into our Union. **1792** Belknap *Hist. New Hampsh.* III. 257 An important branch of the American union. **1817** J. Bradbury *Trav. Amer.* 277 The separation of the States west of the Alleghanies from the Union. **1865** Lowell *Wks.* (1890) V. 258 The South will come back to the Union. **1909** in R. H. Brand *Union of S. Africa* 142 The words 'the Union' shall be taken to mean the Union of South Africa as constituted under this Act.

d. A number of parishes united or incorporated together under one Board of Guardians for the administration of the poor laws; an area or sub-district so formed and administered.

1834 *Act 4–5 Will. IV*, c. 76 §26 Such Parishes shall thereupon be deemed a Union for such Purpose. **1837** McCulloch *Acc. Brit. Empire* II. 639 The operation of Gilbert's Act in the unions formed under it. **1862** Gladstone *Sp.* in *Times* 29 Dec. 9/5 The bulk of the cotton manufacture was carried on in a region comprised within 27 Unions.

e. A textile fabric composed of two or more different materials woven together, esp. one containing cotton and linen, or cotton and some other material as wool, silk, or jute. Freq. *pl.*, kinds or varieties of goods or fabrics so woven, union-cloths.

1844 G. Dodd *Textile Manuf.* v. 167 A mixture of flax and cotton called 'union'. **1851** Mayhew *Lond. Labour* I. 378/1 Then we had an Irish linen, an imitation, you know, a kind of 'Union', which we call double twist. **1893** *Photogr. Ann.* 284 Two or three yards of 'union', or white window blind material.

pl. **1851** Mayhew *Lond. Labour* I. 376/2 Linen of good quality used to be extensively hawked, but from 1820 to 1825, or later..the hawkers got to deal in an inferior quality, 'unions' (a mixture of linen and cotton) glazed and stiffened. **1879** *Cassell's Techn. Educ.* IV. 387/2 A real Scotch carpet is all wool, but fabrics similar in appearance are made with cotton warps and worsted wefts, in which case they are called 'unions'. **1890** *Textile News* 20 Oct. (List Manufacturers), Manufacturer of black and coloured unions.

f. *India*, *Pakistan*, and *Bangladesh*. A local administrative unit comprising several rural villages. Freq. *attrib.*

1885 *Bengal Local Self-Govt. Act.* ii. §38 in *Acts of Lieutenant-Governor of Bengal in Council* (1886) 38 The Lieutenant-Governor may, by order in writing, constitute any village or group of villages into a Union; and may prescribe for such Union the number of members of which the Union Committee shall consist. **1959** *Pakistan Q.* Winter 14/2 Basic Democracy creates institutions at the Union, Tehsil, Divisional and Provincial levels... At the Union level the Panchayat or Council, has roughly ten elected and five nominated (non-official) members. **1964** R. W. Gable in Inayatullah *District Admin. W. Pakistan* i. 15 Basic Democracies are characterized by a four-tier structure of councils... The councils operate, in ascending order, at the level of unions, or groups of villages; *tehsils* (in West Pakistan) and *thanas* (in East Pakistan); districts; and divisions. In urban areas there are Town Committees and Union Committees in place of Union Councils. **1977** *Bangladesh Times* 19 Jan. 1/8 Elections in 229 unions will be held today (Wednesday) in 18 districts of the country.

g. *Math.* The set that comprises all the elements (and no others) contained in any of two or more given sets; also, the operation of forming such a set.

1941, 1968 [see INTERSECTION 3 b]. **1970** O. Dopping *Computers & Data Processing* i. 28 The formation of the union is analogous to a logical addition... The union $X \cup Y$ (also written $X + Y$ and spoken as 'X union Y') comprises all elements which are elements in set X, set Y, or both. **1972** *Computer Jrnl.* XV. 195/1 The character set handled by most of the systems programs is practically the union of all the characters available on the various devices.

8. *Brewing.* One of a series of casks or vats used in the Union or Burton system of cleansing beer.

1876 *Encycl. Brit.* IV. 275/2 When beer is cleansed..it is necessary to keep the casks or Unions full to the bung. **1897** W. J. Sykes *Brewing* 448 When a set of unions are cleansed, the swan-necks are first removed.

III. 9. That which unites or connects one thing to another; *techn.*, a device for connecting the ends of pipes or tubes, or for attaching a pipe to some other part; a coupling, pipe-coupling.

1850 [see *union joint* in sense 12]. **1863** *Appleby's Handbk. Mach. & Iron Work* 59 Wrought-iron Wrenches for Hose Unions. **1864** *Riddel & Co.'s Catal.*, Steam and Valve Cocks. Brass Unions. **1889** *Daily News* 11 Feb. 4/7 Makers of cocks, taps, unions, and bar fittings are fairly busy.

IV. 10. In elliptical senses. **a.** = UNION FLAG or UNION JACK, either as (*a*) a separate flag (also †*great union*), or (*b*) as inserted in the upper inner canton of the ensign; freq. in phr. ***union down*** or ***downwards***, indicating an inverted position, with the union as if in the lower inner canton, when the flag is hoisted or flown on a vessel as a signal of distress or mourning.

(*a*) **1769** Falconer *Dict. Marine* (1780) s.v. *Jack*, In the British Navy the jack is..a small union flag..; but in merchant-ships this union is bordered with a red field. **1812** *Ann. Reg., Gen. Hist.* 110 The proud old British Union floated triumphantly over it. **1849** C. Sturt *Exped. Centr. Australia* I. 20 Some young ladies of the colony..had worked a silken union to present to Mr. Eyre. **1865** *N. & Q.* 18 Feb. 136/1 His majesty is depicted stepping from a barge with the Union hoisted at the stern.

(*b*) **1804** *Naval Chron.* XII. 144 The colours..were hoisted Union downwards. **1830** Campbell *Dict. Mil. Sci.* s.v. *Colours*, The Red Cross of St. George in a White Field, with the Union in the Upper Canton. **1883** *Harper's Mag.* Jan. 321/1 The American flag..was by mistake hoisted 'union down'.

b. Short for *Union House*, *workhouse* (sense 12).

1843 Neale *Ball. & Songs for People* 16 We never built the unions Wherein they starve the poor. **1874** T. Hardy *Far fr. Mad. Crowd* xxx, I wonder sometimes if I am doomed to die in the Union.

c. (With capital.) The name at various Universities (orig. at Oxford and Cambridge) of a general club and debating society usually open to all members, or all undergraduates, of the University; also, the buildings or offices of such.

Originally short for *Union Society* or *Union Club.* Also used attrib., as ***Union audience***, ***rhetoric***, ***speech***.

1835 *Rep. Committee Oxford Union Soc.* 2 The Treasurer of the Union. **1853** Thackeray *Eng. Hum.*, *Congreve* (1858) 58 Before the passing of the Reform Bill, there existed at Cambridge a certain debating club, called the 'Union'. **1883** *Oxford Univ. Mag.* 24 Jan. 7/1 No more eloquent speech has been heard in the Union during the last three years. **1891** *Cal. St. Andrews Univ.* 315 The scheme for instituting a Students' Union in the University of St. Andrews. *Ibid.* 316 The general management of the Union.

V. Attrib. and comb., passing into adj.

11. a. In senses 4 b and 7 c, with the sense 'of or belonging to, promoting or advocating, adhering to or supporting (a particular) legislative union', as (*a*) ***union arms***, ***colours***, ***-maker***, ***parliament***; esp. (*b*) in American use (see 7 c note), as ***Union Army***, ***banner***, ***league***, ***man***, ***planter***, etc.

(*a*) **1707** *Lond. Gaz.* No. 4374/1 On Two opposite Corners were the Union Arms. *Ibid.*, The Norton Galley hoisted the Union Colours. **1771** Smollett *Humph. Cl.* To Phillips 8 Aug., During a sitting of the union parliament [at Edinburgh, 1707]. **1811** *Gen. Reg. & Orders of Army* 13 The first Standard, Guidon, or Colour of Regiments, which is the Union Colour. **1846** A. Amos *Gt. Oyer of Poison.* 4 The union-maker, King James.

(*b*) **1863** Bright *Sp. Amer.* 26 Mar. 127 Not Union planters only, but Secession planters began to bring in the produce. **1863** Hawthorne *Our Old Home* (1883) I. 23 The latest is now a gallant general under the Union banner. **1866** 'F. Kirkland' *Bk. Anecdotes* 376 Colonel Bailey..[believed] that their capture or destruction would involve the destruction of the Union army. **1872** De Vere *Americanisms* 280 The Union-men..or Federals..fought for the Union against rebellion. *Ibid.* 289 Loyal Leagues, as well as Union Leagues, were formed all over the country. **1931** E. O'Neill *Homecoming* i, in *Mourning becomes Electra* (1932) 27 He wears the uniform of an artillery captain in the Union Army. **1973** A. Dundes *Mother Wit* 562 The Union Army..was ostensibly fighting in part to end slavery.

b. In general and miscellaneous use, as ***union-band***, ***canopy***, ***vowel***, etc.

1723 E. Fenton *Mariamne* iii. vi, Such as good spirits are suppos'd to sing O'er saints, while death dissolves the union-band. **1785** [R. Graves] *Eugenius* II. xxxi. 188 A great many variegated roses..called union roses (as they unite the party distinctions of York and Lancaster). **1824** T. FENBY *Mulberry Tree* iii, The tree, Which love's union-canopy made. **1879** WHITNEY *Sanskrit Gram.* 78 All the simple vowels come to assume in certain cases the aspect of union-vowels, or insertions between root or stem and ending of inflection or of derivation.

c. In sense 7 b, as ***union baron, -basher, -card, dues, hours, house, -jobber, negotiator, pay, scale, ticket; union-bashing, -busting*** (also as *pres. pple.*), ***-smashing*** vbl. sbs.

1974 *Socialist Worker* 26 Oct. 11/5 There is a need for links with the other unions in the entertainment industry and beyond, not just Media Conferences where Labour MPs and *union barons spout and TV directors nod approvingly. **1977** *Times* 14 Sept. 1/1 Voices in the Conservative Party arguing moderation rather than '*union bashing' in its approach to the closed shop... Sir Keith Joseph had been depicted as an 'enthusiastic *union basher'. **1980** *Illustr. London News* Mar. 19/3 It [*sc.* the Employment Bill] is not revolutionary, it is not union-bashing, but it imposes some legal restraints on secondary strike activity and provides some stimulus to union democracy. **1913** J. LONDON *Valley of Moon* 198 They're all *union-bustin' to beat the band. **1947** *Sun* (Baltimore) 26 June 1/7 Union-busting act. **1874** *Rep. Proc. Internat. Typographical Union N. Amer.* 84 The International Typographical Union shall issue..a card, with appropriate designs, to be called the '*Union Card'. **1977** 'W. HAGGARD' *Poison People* iv. 141 There's..an efficient Trade Union... You'll need a Union card. **1977** *Undercurrents* June–July 11/4 Being an anarchist I don't take dole nor can I afford *union dues. **1945** *Union hours [see *social disease* s.v. SOCIAL *a.* 12]. **1937** F. M. FORD *Let.* 27 Mar. (1965) 277 Doing what I can to persuade any publishers.. [to have] their printing done by *union houses. **1841** *Penny Cycl.* XXI. 411/1 The many dishonest abstractions of their [Pension Societies'] funds, of which the mere *Union jobbers are so often guilty. **1964** *Mod. Law Rev.* XXVIII. iii. 274 The local *union negotiator (shop steward and the like, who is so vital to the operation of collective bargaining) will..usually be an employee. **1914** D. H. LAWRENCE *Widowing of Mrs. Holroyd* iii. 75 Well, if he's badly hurt, there'll be the *Union-pay, and sick-pay—we shall manage. **1976** *Honolulu Star-Bull.* 21 Dec. D-2/6 The artists will be paid *union scale, and the Kennedy Center is donating the space, he added. **1897** *Westm. Gaz.* 30 Aug. 1/3 A general policy of *union-smashing. **1891** A. FRENCH *Otto the Knight* 19, I went to two or three cities, but I couldn't get work, having no *union ticket. **1908** KIPLING *Lett. of Travel* (1920) 167 It is difficult to get skilled labour into here?.. Even if he has his Union ticket? **1948** Union ticket [see ANTE *v.*].

d. In sense 7 e, as ***union cloth, cord (braid), damask, diaper, goods***, etc.; also (of garments), 'made of union cloth or fabric'.

1862 *Catal. Internat. Exhib., Brit.* II. No. 3995, Woollen and union cloths. **1867** *Ure's Dict. Arts* (ed. 6) III. 971 *Union goods*, cloths of a mixed character, as of flax and jute, or cotton and jute. **1868** *Chambers' Encycl.* X. 268/1 Many of the names used in the all-wool class are retained in this [*sc.* fabrics composed of wool and cotton], with the addition of the word 'union', as union merino, union shalloon, union damask, &c. **1882** CAULFEILD & SAWARD *Dict. Needlew.* 507 *Union cord*, a round white cord, made for stay-laces,.. composed of both linen and cotton thread. *Ibid.*, Union Cord Braid, Union Diaper. **1896** *Godey's Mag.* Feb. 218/2 Union undergarments of silk or wool.

e. In senses 7 d, 10 b, as ***union boy, man.***

1846 (*title*), The Union and Parish Officer's Pocket Almanac and Guide. **1859** J. H. STEGGALL *Hist. Suffolk Man* i. 29, I was worse than any union boy with his hair polled. **1871** 'M. LEGRAND' *Cambr. Freshm.* 303 He's out o' the Union... The Union men break the stones on the roads.

12. Special combs.: **union bow** *Archery*, a bow made of two or more pieces united together; a backed or back bow (*Cent. Dict.* 1891); **union catalogue**, a catalogue of the combined holdings of several libraries; **union dye**, a dye that will satisfactorily dye the two materials of a union cloth, esp. cotton and wool, at the same time; so **union dyeing** *vbl. sb.*; **union-grass**, one or other of the grasses belonging to the genus *Uniola* (ibid.); **Union House**, the poorhouse or workhouse of a Poor Law union (cf. senses 7 d and 10 b, and *Union workhouse*); **union-joint** (see quots. and sense 9); **union list**, a union catalogue, esp. one giving details of periodical holdings in several libraries; **union nut**, (*a*) a nut used with a screw to unite one part to another; (*b*) the Australian timber-tree *Bosistoa sapindiformis*, or its wood; **union pear** (see quot.); **union-pump** (see quot.); **union purchases**, a method of cargo-handling (see quots.); **union-room** *Brewing*, the room containing the unions or cleansing vats; **union-rustic**, a British night-moth, *Apamea connexa* (*Encycl. Dict.* 1888); **union screw** (see quot. and *union joint*); **union shop** orig. *U.S.*, a shop, factory, trade, etc., in which employees must belong to or join a trade union; a post-entry closed shop (see POST-ENTRY *a.*); **union suit**, †(*a*) ? a set of mirrors; (*b*) chiefly *N. Amer.*, a one-piece under-garment reaching to the ankles; = COMBINATION 9; **union system** *Brewing* (see quots. and sense 8); **union-wide** *a.*, that involves or encompasses the whole of a trade union (movement); **Union workhouse**, = *Union House*. See also UNION FLAG, JACK.

1897 *Libr. Jrnl.* Sept. 437 One of the latest examples of co-operative library work is the *union catalog of medical literature recently completed in Denver. **1982** *Papers Dict. Soc. N. Amer. 1979* 83 Most union catalogs are made up from individual libraries' catalog cards and are created by dispensing with the subject element in the individual library catalogs. **1909** OWENS & STANDAGE *Dyeing & Cleaning Textile Fabrics* 36 *Union dyes are..of more general adaptation to the renovating of garments than any other class of dyewares. **1963** A. J. HALL *Student's Textbk. Textile Sci.* iv. 191 Union dyes are a mixture of direct cotton dyes and neutral dyeing acid wool dyes. **1909** OWENS & STANDAGE *Dyeing & Cleaning Textile Fabrics* 38 Full directions are given later for *union dyeing. **1974** N. G. & T. E. HARRIES *Textiles* vi. 517 Two variations of piece dyeing are union dyeing and cross dyeing. **1847** ALB. SMITH *Chr. Tadpole* xlvi, 'Anything new at the *Union House to-day, Mr. Mole?' **1893** *Daily News* 10 April 5/4 The Prince's inscription in the Dunmow Union House visitors' book. **1850** WEALE *Dict. Terms* 493 **Union screws* or *joints*,..the brass unions for connecting the elastic bore-pipe of the tender to the feed-pipe of the [locomotive] engine. **1867** J. HOGG *Microsc.* I. ii. 107 A finer [adjustment] is secured by a well made union-joint. **1885** *Libr. Jrnl.* X. 370 A *union list of periodicals in these libraries. **1968** *Bodl. Libr. Rec.* VIII. 63 Union list of serials in the science area, Oxford. **1978** *Amer. N. & Q.* XVII. 9/1, I am initiating a union list of 19th century photographically illustrated books in library collections throughout the country. **1838** *Civil Eng. & Arch. Jrnl.* I. 133/1 It..is attached to a ferrule by a *union nut and screw, and can be as easily removed. **1889** MAIDEN *Useful Pl.* 387 *Bosistoa sapindiformis*, Union Nut. **1731** MILLER *Gard. Dict.* 6 U, The *Union Pear; otherwise call'd Dr. Uvedale's St. Germain. This is a very large long Pear, of a deep green Colour. **1860** J. HOGG *Fruit Man.* 217. **1875** KNIGHT *Dict. Mech.* 2681/2 **Union-pump*,..one in which the engine and pump are united in the same frame. **1926** B. CUNNINGHAM *Cargo Handling at Ports* (ed. 2) v. 46 The principle of using the double line with a single hook for the combined process of lifting and slewing, called in this country [*sc.* Great Britain] the *Union Purchase. **1961** *B.S.I. News* Mar. 13/1 Greater safety for stevedores handling cargo by the union purchase method (the operation of two ships' derricks in tandem). **1886** 'BICKERDYKE' *Cur. Ale & Beer* 339 The *union-room..[at Allsopp's] contains 1,424 unions, which can cleanse 230,688 gallons at one time. **1850** WEALE *Dict. Terms* 494 The feed-pipe is likewise attached to the lower end of the pump by a large *union screw. **1904** *McClure's Mag.* Feb. 370/1 Many stores, restaurants, and saloons display placards in their windows advertising the fact that they are strictly *union shops. **1937** F. M. FORD *Let.* 27 Mar. (1965) 276, I will..ask the publisher..whether or not the Riverside Press, which prints this book, is or is not a union shop. **1977** *Time* 7 Mar. 28/2 The section permits states to ban the so-called union shop, which requires new employees to join unions. **1714** *Lond. Gaz.* No. 5214/3 All sorts of Coach Glasses, Chimney Glasses, Sconces, Dressing Glasses, *Union Suits, Dressing Boxes, swinging Glasses [etc.]. **1892** *Ladies' Home Jrnl.* Sept. 29/3 *Yes*, you will say to yourself, I know all about *union suits*, but *do* you? **1948** W. FAULKNER *Intruder in Dust* vii. 147 The sagging fences..by nightfall would be gaudy with drying overalls..and unionsuits. **1967** E. S. TURNER *Taking Cure* xii. 187 Smedley..urged the wearing of merino union suits for both adults and children. **1876** *Encycl. Brit.* IV. 275/2 There are three modes of cleansing—..2*d*, by running the beer into casks, and then allowing the yeast to work out through the bung holes; and 3*d*, on what is called the *Union, or Burton system, which is the second plan with some improvements. **1886** 'BICKERDYKE' *Cur. Ale & Beer* 333 When the fermentation has almost ceased, the beer is put into smaller vessels..and the froth either works over the side or is skimmed off or, as in the 'union' system at Burton, works up through pipes. **1937** *Nation* 14 Aug. 165/1 Assuming..*unionwide participation. **1981** *N.Y. Times* 24 Mar. 14B/4 The operators also gave up a unionwide arbitration review board. **1851** KINGSLEY *Yeast* xii, As he went on, talking wildly to himself, he passed the *Union Workhouse. **1863** FAWCETT *Pol. Econ.* iv. iv. 581 The inmates of the union-workhouse are subject to certain restraints.

Hence **ˈunional** *a.*, of or pertaining to union or a union (esp. of countries); **ˈunioned** *a.*, joined in union; **ˈunioner** *U.S.*, an adherent of the Union during the American Civil War.

1889 *Scott. Leader* 18 Apr. 6 If the Unionist has destroyed both the national and *unional sentiment in the Irish. **1905** *Q. Rev.* July 273 The Unional flag had been hauled down. **1787** J. BARLOW *Vision of Columbus* vi. 191 Great Washington arose in view, And *union'd flags his stately steps pursue. **1880** TOURGEE *Fool's Err.* vii. 31 The old *Unioner's report in regard to the doughty colonel.

ˈunion, *sb.*² Now *arch.* Also 4 vniune. [ad. L. *ūniōn-em*, *ūnio* UNIO: cf. ONION *sb.* 7.

So called (acc. to Pliny *Nat. Hist.* ix. xxxv. §56) because no two are exactly alike.]

A pearl of large size, good quality, and great value, esp. one which is supposed to occur singly.

Freq. in 17th c., esp. in allusion to or echoes of the story related of Cleopatra: see Pliny *loc. cit.* §59. The following early instance is prob. of AF. origin: *c* **1305** *Land Cokayne* 89 Þer is saphir and vniune, Carbuncle and astiune.

1592 *Soliman & Pers.* ii. i, Then they play, and when she hath lost her gold, Erastus pointed to her chaine, and then she said: I, were it Cleopatraes vnion. **1599** HAKLUYT *Voy.* II. 5 Precious unions and costly spyces. **1635** HEYWOOD *Hierarchy* vii. 419 A Pendant Vnion to adorne her Eare, Rarer no Queene was euer seene to weare. **1694** MOTTEUX *Rabelais* iv. iv. 19 Between whose Septenary Links.. Rubies, Emeralds,..and Unions were alternatively set in. *a* **1700** EVELYN *Diary* 21 Feb. 1645, The other Union, that Cleopatra was about to dissolve and drink up.

fig. *a* **1672** P. STERRY *Posth. Wks.* (*c* 1680) II. 227 Pearls are called Unions, because they are ever found alone: a Saint's Pearl is his Union for a contrary Reason, because he is never found alone in his Spiritual Being or Beauty.

b. *attrib.* with *pearl*. Also *transf.*

1656 BLOUNT *Glossogr.* s.v., Union Pearls..are the best sort of Pearl. [Hence in Phillips, Bailey, etc.] **1885** R. F. BURTON *Arab. Nts.* (1887) III. 67 This damsel, the mistress of moons, the union pearl.

†ˈunion, *v. Obs. rare.* Also 5 unyon. [f. UNION *sb.*¹] *trans.* To unite.

a **1470** HARDING *Chron.* ccxli. *heading*, The kynges tytle to all his londes, briefely reported, with a monicion to vnion Scotlande and Englande. **1475** *Bk. Noblesse* (Roxb.) 23 The countee of Mayne by Maryage was unyoned to the erledom of Angew.

‖**Union Corse** (ynjɔ̃ kɔrs). [Fr., lit. 'Corsican union'.] A criminal organization controlled by Corsicans, operating in France and elsewhere. Cf. next.

1963 I. FLEMING *On Her Majesty's Secret Service* v. 51 'The Union Corse', more deadly and perhaps even older than the Unione Siciliano, the Mafia..it controlled most organised crime throughout metropolitan France and her colonies. **1973** *Times* 21 May 14/3 A key figure was a former model..said to have been living with an Union Corse racketeer..before his death in a gun battle with Mexican police. **1978** W. GARNER *Möbius Trip* (1979) iii. 80 His signet ring featured the Moor's head and eagle of the official Union Corse.

‖**Unione Siciliana** (uniˈone sitʃiliˈana). Also (*erron.*) **Unione Siciliano**, etc. [It., lit. 'Sicilian union'.] A criminal organization controlled by Sicilians, operating in Italy and the United States.

Similar but not equivalent to the Mafia. The Union's roots in the U.S. were apparently as a mutual protection society amongst early Sicilian immigrants.

1924 *Chicago Daily Tribune* 13 Nov. 5/5 At [Merlo's] death he was chairman of the board of the Unione Siciliana, with hundreds of thousands of members. **1924** *Chicago Herald Examiner* 13 Nov. 3/1 A guard also was maintained at the wake for Michael Merlo, head of the Unione Siciliano society. **1930** F. D. PASLEY *Al Capone* (1931) v. 231 Lombardo fell in his tracks, two dumdum bullets in his brain, the third president of the Unione Sicilione to die by the gun. **1956** C. COCKBURN *Discord of Trumpets* xvi. 218 He had recently been elected the President of the Unione Siciliano, a slightly mysterious, partially criminal society, which certainly had its roots in the Mafia. **1970** P. GEDDES *November Wind* iv. 35 The Trust..came into existence when the Mafia and *L'Unione Siciliana* were both on the slide.

Union flag. [UNION *sb.*¹ 4 b, 7 c.] **a.** The national flag or ensign, formerly of Great Britain, in later use (from 1801) of the United Kingdom of Great Britain and Ireland, formed by combining the crosses of St. George, St. Andrew, and St. Patrick, retaining the blue ground of the banner of St. Andrew. See UNION JACK, and UNION *sb.*¹ 10 a.

This flag was introduced to symbolize the union of the crowns of England and Scotland and was formed by surmounting the cross saltire of St. Andrew by the cross of St. George; the cross saltire of St. Patrick was added on the union of the parliaments of Great Britain and Ireland, when the whole flag was blazoned by Royal Proclamation (*Lond. Gaz.* 1 Jan. 1801), as follows: Azure, the Crosses saltires of St. Andrew and St. Patrick Quarterly per Saltire, counterchanged Argent and Gules; the latter fimbriated of the Second, surmounted by the Cross of St. George of the Third, fimbriated as the Saltire.

1634 in Rymer *Fœdera* (1732) XIX. 549/1 None shall from henceforth presume to carry the Union Flag in the main Top or other part of their Ships, that is Saint George his Cross and Saint Andrews Cross joined together,..but that the same Union Flag be still reserved as an Ornament proper for our own Ships, and Ships in our immediate Service and Pay, and none other. **1681** in *English Hist. Rev.* Jan. (1911) 50 [An article forbidding] privateers to wear our Union flagg and jack. **1696** *Lond. Gaz.* No. 3190/3 Leaving the Command of the Fleet with my Lord Berkeley, who.. has put up the Union Flag on Board the Britannia. **1724** C. JOHNSON *Hist. Pirates* 153 One of them struck the Union Flag on the Top of the Castle. **1769** [see UNION¹ 10 a]. **1829** MARRYAT *F. Mildmay* viii, A union flag is displayed at the mizen peak. **1844** *Regul. & Ord. Army* 48 The Union Flag or Jack being the distinctive flag or mark of an Admiral of the Fleet, when displayed at the main-top-gallant-mast-head. **1865** *N. & Q.* 11 March 208/2 The incorporation of the red saltier of St. Patrick into the Union Flag.

b. The flag of the federated colonies or provinces of the American Union.

1776 *Pennsylv. Even. Post* 28 May 266/2 The Union Flag of the American States waved upon the Capitol.

Unionic (juːnɪˈɒnɪk), *a.* [f. UNION *sb.*¹ + -IC.] Of or pertaining to, characteristic of, a Union or University Union Society; frequenting or debating at the Union.

1855 *Househ. Words* 30 June 521, I breakfasted with jovial undergraduates... I heard old talk..of Unionic speakers eloquent. **1865** *Pall Mall G.* 13 April 10/1 The characteristics of Unionic eloquence. **1884** J. PAYN *Lit. Recoll.* 54 In Mr. Lewis's classification of his fellow-students, it was that of 'the Unionic Cantab.'

unionid (ˈjuːnɪəʊnɪd). *Zool.* [a. mod.L. *Unionid-æ* (see def.), f. L. *unio* UNIO: see -ID³.] A member of the *Unionidæ*, a large family of bivalve molluscs typified by the genus *Unio* of freshwater mussels; a unio.

1861 P. P. CARPENTER in *Rep. Smithsonian Instit. 1860*, 263 The extreme forms of the Unionids.

uni'oniform, *a. Zool.* [f. mod.L. *Unio* UNIO: see -(I)FORM.] Belonging to or resembling the *Unionidæ*; unionoid.

1868 R. TATE *App. to Woodward's Mollusca* 71 *Anthracosia* differs from *Unio*, to which genus the majority of the Unioniform shells have been referred.

unionism ('juːnjənɪz(ə)m). [f. UNION *sb.*¹ + -ISM.] **a.** The principle or policy of union; combination in union as a system of social organization; advocacy of this. Also *ellipt.* for TRADE(S) UNIONISM.

1845 MIALL in *Nonconf.* V. 173 The gravest objections against congregational unionism. **1869** J. STIRLING *Trade Unionism* 21 To the unionist himself, the results of Unionism are no less hurtful. **1884** *Brit. Alm. & Comp.* 67 The growth of unionism among farm labourers. **1904** W. T. MILLS *Struggle for Existence* (ed. 8) xxxv. 487 The New Unionism of recent years has been continuously enlarging the number of those to be included. **1976** F. ZWEIG *New Acquisitive Society* I. v. 65 White-collar unionism has grown over the last two or three decades much faster than manual workers' unionism. **1978** S. BRILL *Teamsters* vii. 279 The appeal of unionism diminished, especially in the eyes of younger workers.

b. *U.S.* Advocacy of, attachment or adherence to, a legislative union between states.

1864 LOWELL *McClellan or Lincoln?* Pr. Wks. 1890 V. 157 The somewhat light Unionism of Mr. Pendleton. **1865** — *Reconstruct.* Ibid. 222 We do not mean to say that there is any very large amount of even latent Unionism at the South. **1883** *American* VI. 92 The obstinate Unionism of the mountaineer farmers.

c. Loyalty to or advocacy of the principles, views, or programme of the Unionist party of Great Britain and Ireland; the political tenets characteristic of a Unionist.

1886 *Sat. Rev.* 5 June 763/2 Unionism has to deal with an enemy perfectly unscrupulous. **1889** MRS. BUXTON in O'Brien *Life Parnell* (1898) I. 220 We talked a little about Home Rule and the future of Ireland—my Unionism getting very shaky.

unionist ('juːnjənɪst), *sb.* and *a.* [f. as prec. + -IST. Cf. F. *unioniste.*]

A. *sb.* **1.** An adherent of or believer in unionism as a political principle or system of organization; esp. one who advocates or supports the formation or maintenance of some particular legislative union.

Usually with initial capital in particularized sense.

1799 *Monthly Rev.* XXX. 337 [Duigenan] is particularly severe in his criticisms on Lord Minto, a Brother Unionist. **1851** GALLENGA *Italy* 41 Nothing..has been more fatal to the cause of Italian federation than a departure from the views of the Unionists. **1887** MAHAFFY & GILMAN *Alexander's Empire* xxx. 286 There was a large nationalist party..violently opposed to the unionists,..constantly asserting the right of every Greek state to legislate for itself. **1890** HATTON *By Order of Czar* II. i, [He] was above all things an Imperial Unionist, and would defend to the death the merest scrap of soil over which the flag had ever floated.

b. *U.S.* A supporter or advocate of the Federal Union of the United States of America; esp. one who during the Civil War of 1861–5 was opposed to Secession.

1830 D. WEBSTER *1st Sp. on Foot's Res.* Wks. 1851 III. 259, I am a unionist, and, in this sense, a national republican. **1862** MOTLEY *Corr.* (1889) II. 94 The anti-slavery men became the Unionists, the slaveholders the Destructionists. **1883** *American* VII. 149 A Texas 'Unionist' is going to sue the United States for the value of his slaves.

c. *British Politics.* A member of the political party which advocated or supported maintenance of the parliamentary Union between Great Britain and Ireland; an opponent of Home Rule.

This party was formed in 1886 by the coalition of the Conservatives with those Liberals (Liberal Unionists: see LIBERAL *a.* 5) who were opposed to Gladstonian Home Rule. While the chief tenet of this party was the maintenance of the Union, its general policy and principles gradually became identified with those of the Conservative party. The name remained the official designation of the alliance of Liberal Unionists and Conservatives until 15 January 1922, when the Irish Free State was established. The title is retained, however, by loyalist parties in N. Ireland (the official *Unionist*, *Ulster*, and *Democratic Unionist* Parties, etc.); also in the full name of the Conservative (and Unionist) Party, and in the Scottish Unionist Association (see quot. 1982 of the adj. 1 b).

1886 LD. R. CHURCHILL *Sp. at Manch.* 3 March, Do you not think that such a party might be formed which might combine all that is best of the politics of the Tory, the Whig, or the Liberal?.. Might we not call it the party of the Union? Members of that party might be known as Unionists. **1886** in *Pall Mall G.* 6 July 14/1 The opinion.. that..the Liberal Unionists are coming to signal grief... The Unionists have, indeed, pulled the chestnuts out of the fire for Lord Salisbury. **1893** *Times* 25 Apr. 11/1 A representative company of British Unionists to meet the Unionists of Ireland. **1953** *Times* 23 Oct. 8/6 The Unionists were returned to power again in the general election in Northern Ireland. **1964** G. D. M. BLOCK *Source Book of Conservatism* 67 In Ulster and Scotland 'Unionist' has entirely carried the day, but in the Southern Kingdom the 'new term' of Conservative has survived as an official name of the Party. **1974** *Times* 18 Feb. 14/8 Opposed to them are three loyalist groups: the Rev Ian Paisley's Democratic Unionists, Mr William Craig's Vanguard Unionists, and Mr Harry West's Ulster Unionists.

2. A member of a trade-union; a TRADE UNIONIST.

1834 *John Bull* 13 July 219/1 The cases on the Crown side were principally Unionists, charged with administering unlawful oaths. **1854** H. MILLER *Sch. & Schm.* xv. 327 The life of my friend was..pitched on a..higher tone than that of most of his brother unionists. **1879** T. H. S. ESCOTT *England* I. 282 The charges of conspiracy and violence brought against unionists and unionism.

3. One who desires or advocates the union of churches or congregations. Cf. REUNIONIST.

1852 NEWLAND *Lect. Tractar.* 165 We are Tractarians or Unionists or whatever you may please to call us. **1866** G. TALBOT in E. Purcell *Life A. P. de Lisle* (1900) I. xv. 408, I think that the sympathy of the Unionists for the Greek Schism is a proof of want of sincerity. **1869** *Union Review* 311 The Unionist, whether he be a Roman or an Anglican.

B. *attrib.* passing into *adj.* **1.** Of or pertaining to, advocating or supporting, a legislative union, esp. that between Great Britain and Ireland.

1816 SCOTT *Bl. Dwarf* xii, The Unionist courtiers, that have bought and sold old Scotland. **1848** DAUNT *Recoll. O'Connell* I. ii. 16, I spoke in reply to a Unionist effusion of Emerson Tennent's. **1863** DICEY *Federal St.* II. 187 The *Atlantic Monthly*..is..staunchly Unionist, and more or less anti-slavery. **1888** A. J. BALFOUR in *Times* 2 Oct. 10/1 The union of the Unionist party.

b. Of or belonging to the Unionists or Unionist Party. (Cf. A. 1 c.)

1885 *Cork Constitution* 1 Dec. 3/2 (*heading*) Unionist meeting. **1886** *Pall Mall G.* 3 July 4/1 The utter failure of the Unionist attack..at Stockton. **1890** RIDER HAGGARD *Beatrice* xviii, He knew the head Unionist whip very well. **1897** H. TENNYSON *Tennyson* II. 412 The large Unionist meetings throughout Great Britain. **1955** *Times* 16 May 3/5 The fact that Sinn Fein has put forward candidates for West Belfast, Mid-Ulster, and Fermanagh and South Tyrone may mean that a Unionist gain will be recorded. **1965** *Times* 6 Mar. 6/2 The Scottish Conservatives set the seal on their reorganization plans by approving a new constitution today. .. The title of the organization is to be changed from the Scottish Unionist Association to the Scottish Conservative and Unionist Association. **1974** *Times* 5 Sept. 2/5 Mr Brian Faulkner..launched his own political group yesterday. It is ..called the Unionist Party of Northern Ireland. **1982** R. ROSE *Understanding United Kingdom* iii. 68 The Conservative Party officially styles itself the Conservative and Unionist Party. *Ibid.* 69 In Scotland, the party is organized separately. Its modern foundation dates from amalgamation in 1912 of Scottish Conservatives and the Liberal Unionist Association under the name of the Scottish Unionist Association.

2. Of or belonging to trade-unionism or trade-unionists.

1879 H. SPENCER *Data of Ethics* xii. §78. 211 The unionist principle that the better workers must not discredit the worse by exceeding them in efficiency. **1884** *Pall Mall G.* 11 Sept. 3/1 The success of the unionist movement.

unio'nistic, *a.* [f. UNIONIST *sb.* + -IC.] Of or relating to, characteristic of, unionists; advocating, promoting, or favourable to union or unionism.

1860 WORCESTER (citing Schaff). **1867** LD. ACTON *Lett.* (1906) 346 The Bishop of Mentz..has written a pamphlet decidedly unionistic. **1882–3** *Schaff's Encycl. Relig. Knowl.* II. 1683 When the unionistic measures of Bucer were being discussed. **1884** *American* VIII. 6 For this reason the simply unionistic feeling burned in the northwest.

'unionite. *Min.* [Named by Silliman from its locality, *Unionville*, Pennsylvania.] = ZOISITE.

1849 B. SILLIMAN in *Amer. Jrnl. Sci. & Arts* Ser. II. VIII. 384 Unionite..in general appearance..somewhat resembles scapolite or spodumene. **1855** *Orr's Circ. Sci., Geol.*, etc. 521 Antitomus Felspar, Soda Spodumene, Unionite.

unionize ('juːnjənaɪz), *v.* [f. UNION *sb.*¹ + -IZE.] **1. a.** *trans.* To form into a union. *rare*⁻¹.

1841 R. OASTLER *Fleet Papers* I. No. 23. 182 The breaking up of the old local, domestic, family system of self-government, by unionizing and centralizing society.

b. *esp.* To bring under trade-union rules or principles; to cause (persons) to become members of a trade-union.

Freq. since *c* 1900.

1890 *Columbus* (Ohio) *Dispatch* 18 Nov., It has been decided by the Trades Council to take radical measures..to unionize all work in the building trades. **1903** *Liberty Review* July 16 The servants have been unionised under the rules of the..Federation.

2. *intr.* To become unionized; to join or constitute a trade union.

1969 *Computers & Humanities* IV. 95 It would be especially inappropriate in this context to get into the question of whether scholar/teachers should unionize or professionalize. **1974** J. WHITE tr. *Poulantzas's Fascism & Dictatorship* VI. iv. 292 The agricultural proletariat unionized in massive numbers. **1978** J. L. HENSLEY *Killing in Gold* viii. 99 There is a new breed of school-teachers... They unionize, they strike.

Hence **unioni'zation**; **'unionized** *ppl. a.*¹; **'unionizing** *vbl. sb.*

1896 *Proc. Internat. Typogr. Union* 30/2, I am sure there would be little to gain in its unionization. **1900** *Amer. Review of Reviews* XXI. 651 This year [*sc.* 1900] the strikes were notably successful—New England papers reporting that nearly every 'unionized' town in that section has now the eight-hour workday for..building trades workmen. **1918** *World's Work* XXXV. 486 The issue of the strike being once more unionization. **1920** A. C. PIGOU *Econ. of Welfare* III. iv. 388 The facts..do not warrant us in supposing that local non-governmental Boards would fail if tried on the less completely unionised soil of the Continent. **1947** J. BERTRAM *Shadow of War* I. iii. 26 Under the reorganised National Government of 1946, the voluntary unionisation of labour in China is legalised in the country as a whole for the first time. **1957** W. H. WHYTE *Organization Man* 42 The employers..resisted unionization. **1978** S. BRILL *Teamsters* v. 159 He was..emphasizing the benefits of unionization. **1980** *Times* 23 Jan. 10/6 We should also ask whether big, bureaucratic, hierarchical, highly unionized, cumbersome and cautious local government machines are the best instruments for delivering social services. **1984** *Guardian* 5 Nov. 6/5 Mr Mondale's day started early yesterday with church in Memphis, just as it began on Saturday among unionised car workers outside Detroit.

unionized (ʌn'aɪənaɪzd), *ppl. a.*² Also un-ionized. [UN-¹ 8.] Not ionized.

1900 B. D. JACKSON *Gloss. Bot. Terms* 283/1 *Unionized*, when the molecules are undivided. (J. F. Clark). **1915** *Chem. Abstr.* IX. 1412 Thus HX and YOH (un-ionized) may unite to form HX.YOH. **1962** D. H. CALAM in A. Pirie *Lens Metabolism Rel. Cataract* 439 At the low pH employed, only strongly acidic groups remain charged, most of the carboxyl groups are unionized. **1973** *Sci. Amer.* Apr. 57/1 Later neutral, or un-ionized, sodium was also found to be a constituent of the interstellar medium.

Union Jack. [f. UNION *sb.*¹ + JACK *sb.*³] Originally and properly, a small British union flag flown as the jack of a ship; in later and more general use extended to any size or adaptation of the union flag (even when not used as a jack), and regarded as the national ensign. See UNION FLAG a and UNION *sb.*¹ 10 a.

Written either with capitals or small initials.

1674 *Lond. Gaz.* No. 924/1 To Charge..His Subjects.., That from henceforth they do not presume to wear His Majesties Jack (commonly called, The Union Jack) in any of their Ships or Vessels, without particular Warrant. **1694**, **1702** [see JACK *sb.*³]. **1801** *Union Magazine* Jan. 52 The Royal Union standard was hoisted on the Tower;..the Union Jack on the Parade. **1822** *Admiralty Order* in *Lond. Gaz.* No. 17871. 1893/1 We..authorize all His Majesty's subjects to hoist the Union Jack at the top-mast-head.., or at the fore-top-mast-head.., as a signal for a pilot. **1883** MRS. BISHOP *Golden Chersonese* 222 Everything was 'ship-shape',..a union jack over the desk, from which the liturgy was read, and a tiger-skin [etc.].

b. A figure or representation of this. Also *attrib.*

1848 ALBERT SMITH *Chr. Tadpole* xxiv. 220 Quite unexpectedly they all produced union-jack pocket-handkerchiefs, at the same moment. **1856** MISS YONGE *Daisy Chain* I. xix, Harry used to write his name all over his —see—and draw union-jacks on it. **1886** *Pall Mall G.* 3 July 4/1 In Sunderland the Liberals have all taken to wear Union Jacks in their buttonholes.

Hence (with reference to the use of the union jack as a national flag) **Union 'Jackery**, **Union 'Jackist**, **'Jackite**. *nonce-words.*

1886 *Pall Mall G.* 3 July 4/1 At Nottingham,..the Tory party is locally known as the Union Jackists. **1896** *Spectator* 7 March 342 The national outbursts of 'Union-Jackery' in the courts and music-halls. **1901** *Daily Chron.* 2 Dec. 10/2 Men who no doubt call themselves patriotic Union-Jackites and Big Englanders.

'unionoid, *a.* and *sb. Zool.* [f. mod.L. *Union*-UNIO.] **a.** *adj.* Of or belonging to the *Unionidæ*; unioniform. **b.** *sb.* A unionid (*Cent. Dict.* 1891).

1879 H. A. NICHOLSON *Palæont.* (ed. 2) I. 492 Unionoid Bivalves, with thick shells.

union pipes, *sb. pl.* [? ad. Ir. *píob uilleann*, f. *píob* pipe + *uilleann*, gen. sing. of *uille* elbow.] A form of bagpipes in which the wind-bag is inflated by bellows worked by the elbow; Irish bagpipes.

1851–61 MAYHEW *Lond. Labour* III. 163/1 The union pipes are the old Irish pipes improved. **1877** R. BELL *Early Ballads*, etc. 441 We first heard it sung in Malhamdale, Yorkshire, by..an old Dales'-minstrel, who accompanied himself on the union-pipes.

unipa'rental, *a. Biol.* [UNI- I.] Of, pertaining to, or derived from, one parent.

1900 K. PEARSON *Grammar of Sci.* (ed. 2) xi. 469 The algebraical discussion of this problem..involves no further assumptions than those already made for uniparental inheritance. **1963** E. MAYR *Animal Species & Evolution* ii. 27 Clandestine sexuality appears to be rather common among so-called asexual organisms. The expression 'uniparental reproduction' is being used increasingly, instead of 'asexual reproduction', to overcome this and other difficulties. **1975** *Nature* 29 May 401/2 This indicates that streptomycin resistance was transmitted in a non-Mendelian, uniparental way [in tobacco hybrids].

uni'parient, *a.* [See UNI- and PARIENT *a.*] = next 1.

1822–7 GOOD *Study Med.* (1829) V. 227 [These signs] belong as frequently to the uniparient as to the multiparient, and hence are unentitled to attention. **1859** *Todd's Cycl. Anat.* V. 560/2 In Man, although generally uniparient, two or more follicles may..become matured about the same time.

uniparous (juː'nɪpərəs), *a.* [f. mod.L. *ūniparus* (whence F. *unipare*, It. *uniparo*, Sp. *uniparo*): see UNI- and -PAROUS.]

1. Bearing or producing one at a birth; characterized by this kind of parturition.

1646 SIR T. BROWNE *Pseud. Ep.* VI. vi. 298 For animals multifidous..there are but two that are uniparous, that is, Men and Elephants. **1662** PETTY *Treat. Taxes & Contrib.* xii. 58 'Tis also the second choice out of the young of multiparous Cattle taken in *specie*,..or else a Composition in Money for the Uniparous. **1744** MONRO *Compar. Anat.* 37 Those of the uniparous Kind have them placed between the posterior Extremities. **1787** *Phil. Trans.* LXXVII. 358

The females of the human species, though most commonly uniparous. **1839–47** *Todd's Cycl. Anat.* III. 315 The oviducts are shorter..in the uniparous Kangaroo,..than in the multiparous Opossums. **1856** GRINDON *Life* iv. (1875) 41 Rousseau ingeniously urges..that woman is a uniparous animal. **1859** OWEN *Lect. Classif. Mammalia* 56 The mastodons, megatheria,..and diprotodons, are uniparous.

2. *Bot.* Of a cyme: Having only one axis or branch; developing a single axis at each branching.

1839 LINDLEY *Introd. Bot.* (ed. 3) 160 [An] axis of uniparous, that is one-peduncled, cymes. **1878** M. T. MASTERS *Henfrey's Bot.* 318 The inflorescence..is probably a uniparous scorpioid cyme. **1887** BENTLEY *Man. Bot.* (ed. 5) 215 The terms *helicoid* and *scorpioid* are thus used by us indifferently to indicate the same form of *unilateral, monochasial*, or *uniparous cyme*.

unipartite (juːnɪˈpɑːtaɪt), *a.* *Math.* [See UNI- and PARTITE *a.*] Consisting of or involving a single part.

1870 CAYLEY *Math. Papers* (1893) VI. 464 The quantic is unipartite, bipartite, tripartite, etc., according as the number of sets [of variables] is one, two, three, etc. **1890** *Nature* 20 Feb. 380/2 In the theory of the single system [of equations] the conceptions and symbolism..are based upon the properties of single integral numbers and their partitions into single integral parts. In this sense the former theory may be regarded as being unipartite.

uniped (ˈjuːnɪpɛd), *sb.* and *a.* Also **-pede** (-piːd). [f. UNI- + L. *ped-*, *pēs* foot.]

A. *sb.* A person having only one foot (or leg); a one-footed creature.

1801 SOUTHEY *Thalaba* iv. 218 *note*, There is said to be a nation of one legged men, and one of these unipeds is represented in a print, lying on his back, under the shade of his own great foot. **1846** *Blackw. Mag.* LX. 227 To wake up ten minutes afterwards an unsuffering uniped. **1863** C. M. SMITH *Dead Lock* 248 In all diseases of the toes, the liabilities of the uniped are but as five to ten compared with those of his two-legged brethren.

fig. **1897** *Contemp. Rev.* Oct. 536 The greater sort will escape one-sidedness by inventing some outlet for themselves, but the average will present us with an endless variety of quaint queer unipeds.

B. *adj.* Having only one foot (or leg); one-footed.

1835 KIRBY *Hab. & Inst. Anim.* II. 125 [These] Molluscans..are the only instance of a *unipede* structure in creation. **1866** R. CHAMBERS *Ess.* Ser. II. 206 An auctioneer ..who..sells off pots and pans, and small uniped tables.

uniˈpersonal, *a.* [See UNI- and PERSONAL *a.* Cf. F. *unipersonnel* (in sense 2), Pg. *unipessonal.*]

1. a. Consisting of a single person or individual.

c **1810** COLERIDGE in *Lit. Rem.* (1838) III. 220 If there be a functionary of divine institution, synodical or unipersonal, who with the name of the 'Church' has the right [etc.].

b. Having, or existing as, one person.

Cf. TRI-PERSONAL *a.* and PERSON 7 a.

1869 *Contemp. Rev.* XII. 450 The God of the Bible is neither unipersonal nor tripersonal in that sense of person. **1901** R. C. MOBERLY *Atonem. & Person.* viii. 172 [Not] one of them [*sc.* analogies]..go far towards enabling unipersonal man to enter into the consciousness of Tripersonality.

2. *Gram.* Of a verb: = IMPERSONAL *a.* 1. *rare.*

1843 G. CRANE *Princ. Lang.* v. 207 Verbs, which thus express action without a definitely conceived subject, are called *impersonal*, or perhaps more properly *unipersonal*, verbs. **1860** WORCESTER (citing Wells). [Hence in Webster (1864) and later Dicts.]

Hence **uniˈpersonalist,** a believer in the unipersonality of the Deity (1846 Worcester, citing Faber); **uniperso'nality,** existence in one person.

1859 J. MARTINEAU *Ess. & Addr.* (1891) II. 389 If we set up as our essential a doctrine, like that of the Unipersonality of God. **1884** —— in *Life* (1902) II. viii. 70.

uniˈpetalous, *a.* *Bot.* *rare*$^{-1}$. [ad. mod.L. *unipetal-us* (whence F. *unipétalé*): see UNI- and PETALOUS *a.*] (See quot.)

1849 J. H. BALFOUR *Man. Bot.* 178 A corolla rarely consists of one petal, and when this occurs..it depends on the abortion or non-development of others. Such a corolla is *unipetalous*.., a term quite distinct from monopetalous.

uˈniphonous, *a.* *rare*$^{-1}$. [f. UNI- 1, after MONO-, POLYPHONOUS *adjs.*] Producing only one kind of note.

1832 *Westm. Rev.* Nov. (Cassell's), That uniphonous instrument the drum.

uniˈplanar, *a.* [See UNI- and PLANAR *a.*]

1. *Geom.* Having or characterized by coincident planes. ***uniplanar node*** (or ***point***), a form of node or conical point in which the tangent cone has become a pair of coincident planes; a unode.

1866 BRANDE & COX *Dict. Sci.*, etc. II. 675 When this cone breaks up into two planes, the node is termed a biplanar node, and when these planes coincide, a uniplanar node. **1869** [see UNIPLANE]. **1889** *Cent. Dict.* s.v. *Dyadic*, *Uniplanar diadic*, a planar diadic in which the plane of the antecedents coincides with that of the consequents.

2. *Mech.* Of motion: Lying or taking place in, confined to, one plane; of or pertaining to such motion.

1882 MINCHIN (*title*), Uniplanar Kinematics of Solids and Fluids. *Ibid.* 1 By uniplanar motion, or one-plane motion, is understood in the following pages motion which takes place in one plane or parallel to one plane.

ˈuniplane, *a.* and *sb.* [UNI-.] **a.** *adj.* Forming or lying in one plane. **b.** *sb.* (See quot. 1869.)

1843 *Civil Eng. & Arch. Jrnl.* VI. 218/2 A pneumatic machine for casting, and a uniplane machine for composing. **1869** CAYLEY *Math. Papers* (1893) VI. 361 U..is a uniplanar-node, where the quadric cone becomes a coincident plane-pair; say, the plane is the uniplane.

ˈuniplicate, *a.* *rare*$^{-0}$. [f. UNI- 1, after MULTIPLICATE *a.*] Having but one fold.

1840 SMART; and in later Dicts.

unipod (ˈjuːnɪpɒd). *Photogr.* [f. UNI-, after TRIPOD *sb.* 4.] A one-legged support for a camera. Cf. MONOPODE *sb.*

1935 *Camera* Feb. 361/2 The Unipod. Pocket models, which extend to 4ft. 3 ins. and 5 feet... This real aid to steadiness should meet with a universal sale. **1937** L. C. PELTIER in Fraprie & Jordan *Photographic Hints & Gadgets* 40 (*title*) Unipod made from flexible steel tape measure. **1951** G. H. SEWELL *Amat. Film-Making* (ed. 2) iii. 34 An alternative to the tripod is the 'unipod'. That is a single stick or rod, with a screw at the top for fixing the camera. **1979** *Mod. Photogr.* (N.Y.) Oct. 60/1 (Advt.), Now that you've steadied your camera on a conventional unipod, what are you going to do about your arms?

uniˈpolar, *a.* (and *sb.*). [See UNI- and POLAR *a.* Cf. F. *unipolaire.*]

1. *Electr.* **a.** Produced by, proceeding from, one magnetic pole; exhibiting one kind of polarity. ***unipolar induction***: electrical induction in which a continuous direct current is produced in a conductor joining a magnetic pole and equator by the rotation of either the conductor or the magnet. Cf. HOMOPOLAR *a.* 2.

1812 SIR H. DAVY *Chem. Philos.* 168 There are substances that are imperfect conductors which are capable of receiving only one kind of electricity..and which M. Ehrman..has named unipolar bodies. **1873** J. C. MAXWELL *Electr. & Magn.* II. 7 The property produced by magnetism in transparent bodies of twisting the plane of polarization of the incident light, is, like magnetism itself, a unipolar property. **1881** *Nature* XXIII. 616 To illustrate unipolar conductivity. *Ibid.* XXIV. 570 Whether it be not possible entirely to separate one from the other, and to produce what may be called a unipolar discharge. **1884** S. P. THOMPSON *Dynamo-Electric Machinery* ix. 176 The same fundamental idea has been worked upon by Messrs. Siemens and Halske, who have produced a so-called 'unipolar' machine. [*Note*] This sounds like a *lucus a non lucendo*, for the machine has two poles. But the name is derived from the term 'unipolar induction', which Continental electricians give to the induction of currents by a process of 'continuous cutting'. **1888** *Encycl. Brit.* XXIII. 330/1 The so-called 'unipolar' induction supposed to be due to the rotation of the earth. **1982** *Astrophysical Jrnl.* CCLXII. 87 A potential drop $\sim 10^{19}$ volts is generated by the unipolar induction of a rotating accretion disk surrounding the black hole.

b. Of apparatus: Having, or operating by means of, one magnetic pole; involving, or operating by means of, unipolar induction. Also *ellipt.*

1876 *Nature* XIV. 263/2 A unipolar magnetic needle. *Ibid.*, The space through which a subsidiary magnet must be moved in order to restore the unipolar to its original position. **1883** *Daily News* 10 Sept. 2/2 The remarkable machine of Messrs. Siemens and Halske, called the unipolar machine. **1884** *Health Exhib. Catal.* 79/2 A true unipolar continuous current dynamo. **1884** [see prec. sense]. **1920** *Whittaker's Electr. Engineer's Pocket-bk.* (ed. 4) 139 Unipolar machines have not been able to compete with heteropolar types. **1940, 1973** [see INDUCTOR 3 b]. **1975** *Nature* 6 Feb. 416/2 The satellite Io acts as a unipolar inductor and a source of constant e.m.f. across the Io flux tube as it moves through the Jupiter magnetic field. **1975** A. SHADOWITZ *Electromagnetic Field* xi. 410 A unipolar generator (or motor) differs from a homopolar generator (or motor) in that the rotating disk or cylinder is also a uniform magnet.

2. *Biol.* **a.** Of nerve-cells: Having one pole or fibrous prolongation; connected to the nerve-fibre by a single fibrous process.

1859 *Todd's Cycl. Anat.* V. 436/2 Those [ganglionic corpuscles] from which one tube proceeds are termed unipolar. **1873** A. FLINT *Physiol. Man, Nerv. Syst.* i. 46 Unipolar cells exist in some of the lower orders of animals. **1880** BASTIAN *Brain* ii. 48 Unipolar nerve cells..are alleged to exist in the ganglia on the spinal nerves and elsewhere.

b. (See quot.)

1878 F. J. BELL tr. *Gegenbaur's Comp. Anat.* 597 If the rete remains broken up, then it is known as a diffuse, unipolar, or monocentric rete mirabile.

3. *Electronics.* Of a transistor or similar device: involving conduction by charge carriers of a single polarity.

1952 W. SHOCKLEY in *Proc. IRE* XL. 1313/1 In order to distinguish between the more conventional transistors and the analog types, we propose to use the words *bipolar* and *unipolar*. *Ibid.* 1365/2 In a 'field-effect' transistor, the current flow is carried by one type of carrier only... For this reason the name 'unipolar transistors' is proposed. **1973** *Sci. Amer.* Aug. 48/2 Most integrated circuits produced in the 1960's were of the bipolar type, but production of the newer unipolar type is growing rapidly. **1981** J. C. SPROTT *Introd. Mod. Electronics* viii. 169 The bipolar transistor is so named because current is carried simultaneously by charges of both polarities (electrons and holes) rather than by a single species, as in the FET which is an example of a unipolar device.

4. *Psychol.* Of a psychiatric disorder: characterized by depressive but not manic episodes.

1965 *Acta Psychiatrica Scandinavica* Suppl. No. 180. 87 We..have assumed that 'middle age depressions' according to Stenbäck and 'unipolar depressions' according to Leonhard are merely different terms, which..cover the same nosographic entity. **1982** DONLON & ROCKWELL *Psychiatric Disorders* v. 76 Unipolar disorders are much more common than bipolar.

Hence **ˌunipoˈlarity,** the condition or character of being unipolar. (Cf. F. *unipolarité.*)

1888 *Philos. Mag.* Ser. v. XXVI. 129 We do not believe that Ohm ever observed the phenomenon of unipolarity in strong sulphuric acid with [etc.].

unipole (ˈjuːnɪpəʊl). *Radio.* [f. UNI- 2 + POLE *sb.*[2]] = MONOPOLE[3] 2. Also *attrib.* or as *adj.*

1950 H. P. WILLIAMS *Antenna Theory & Design* II. v. 226 Fig. 5.13 (*b*) shows a folded unipole antenna which is suitable for mounting in an attic. **1958** *Engineering* 31 Jan. 157/3 It works into groundplane folded unipole aerials on top of 80 ft. masts. **1973** *Electronics Lett.* IX. 300/2 The input impedance of a coaxially fed short unipole can be brought to resonance by encasing the antenna in a slab of high-permittivity dielectric material.

uˈniporous, *a.* [UNI- 1. Cf. POLYPOROUS *a.*] (See quot.)

1888 DAWSON *Geol. Hist. Plants* 160 Wood-cells elsewhere called discigerous tissue, and to which I applied the terms uniporous and multiporous.

†uniˈpresence. *Obs.*$^{-1}$ [f. UNI- + PRESENCE, after OMNIPRESENCE.] The fact, on the part of a number, of being present in one place. So **†uniˈpresent** *a.* *Obs.*$^{-1}$

1619 LUSHINGTON *Recant. Serm.* (1659) 77 The unipresence, or local union of body; 'in one place'. *Ibid.* 96 They were unanimous and unipresent.

unique (juːˈniːk), *a.* and *sb.* Also 7 unick(e, 7–8 unic. [a. F. *unique* (†*unic* masc.), ad. L. *ūnic-us* (whence also Sp., Pg., It. *unico*) single, sole, alone of its kind, f. *ūnus* one. In early use also directly ad. L. *ūnicus*, and stressed on the first syllable.]

Regarded by Todd (1818) as 'an affected and useless term of modern times'.

A. *adj.* **1.** Of which there is only one; one and no other; single, sole, solitary.

1602 DOLMAN *La Primaud. Fr. Acad.* (1618) III. 639 Engendring one eternitie, and by an alone vnique action never disturbed, his linage full of understanding. *c* **1645** HOWELL *Lett.* II. xliv, He hath lost..his unic Son in the very flower of his age. **1677** GALE *Crt. Gentiles* IV. I. ii. 53 Divines, who make..right Reason the unic Criterion or Rule of moral Virtue.

1818 TODD, *Unique*, adj.,..sole;..without another of the same kind known to exist. **1861** PALEY *Æschylus, Prometh.* (ed. 2) 39 The student will notice the unique example of στιχομυθία. **1873** HAMERTON *Intell. Life* III. iii. 87 A man.. who made Latin scholarship his unique intellectual purpose. **1882** FARRAR *Early Chr.* II. 476 St. John instantly leaves the subject..to which he has made this unique and passing allusion.

2. a. That is or forms the only one of its kind; having no like or equal; standing alone in comparison with others, freq. by reason of superior excellence; unequalled, unparalleled, unrivalled.

In this sense readopted from French at the end of the 18th c. and regarded as a foreign word down to the middle of the 19th, from which date it has been in very common use, with a tendency to take the wider meaning of 'uncommon, unusual, remarkable'.

The usage in the comparative and superlative, and with advs. as *absolutely, most, quite, thoroughly, totally*, etc., has been objected to as tautological.

1618 W. BARCLAY *Well at King-horne* A vij, This is a soueraigne and vnicke remedie for that disease in Women. **1794** R. J. SULIVAN *View Nat.* I. 3 A concentrated, and an unique aggregation of almost all the wonders of the natural world. **1809** R. K. PORTER *Trav. Sk. Russia & Sweden* (1813) I. xxv. 285 As it was thoroughly *unique*, I cannot forbear presenting you with so singular a curiosity. **1842** J. P. COLLIER *Armin's Nest Ninn.* Introd., A relic..not only *unique* in itself, but unprecedented in its kind. **1866** LIDDON *Bamp. Lect.* v. (1867) 368 [Christ's] relationship to the Father..is absolutely unique. **1871** B. TAYLOR *Faust* (1875) II. II. i. 84 A thing so totally unique The great collectors would go far to seek. **1885** *Harper's Mag.* April 703/1 When ..these summer guests found themselves defrauded of their uniquest recreations. **1908** K. GRAHAME *Wind in Willows* viii. 168 'Toad Hall,' said the Toad proudly, 'is an eligible self-contained gentleman's residence, very unique.' **1912** CHESTERTON *Manalive* I. iii. 86 Diana Duke..began putting away the tea things. But it was not before Inglewood had seen an instantaneous picture so unique that he might well have snapshotted it. **1939** *Country Life* 11 Feb. p. xviii/2 (Advt.), Almost the most unique residential site along the south coast. **1960** [see DIQUAT]. **1980** *Verbatim* Autumn 15/2 A high-ranking state Alcoholic Beverage Commission official said Friday that Wednesday's retroactive renewal and transfer of the beverage permit of the rural Bloomington Liars' Lodge by the Monroe County Alcoholic Beverage Board was 'unique but not uncommon'.

b. Of persons.

1808 FOSTER *Contrib. Eclectic Rev.* (1844) I. 233 [Sir T. More] is a person so *unique* in the records of statesmen, that [etc.]. **1871** BLACKIE *Four Phases* 15 Such a unique mortal.. no man can describe. **1885** MABEL COLLINS *Prettiest Woman* xi, He believed this woman whom he loved to be unique. **1934** G. B. SHAW *On Rocks* II. 262 You don't appreciate him. He is absolutely unique. **1938** [see CHEF D'ÉCOLE].

c. *absol.* with *the*: (see quots.).

1767 *Phil. Trans.* LVIII. 26 All these are examples of the *unique*; that is, of quantities in a state that is..exclusive of all others. **1849** C. BRONTË *Shirley* xxiii, She felt that Rose Yorke was a peculiar child—one of the unique.

†**3.** Formed or consisting of one or a single thing. *Obs.*—¹

a **1631** DONNE *Lett.* (1651) 163 A Mathematique point, which is the most indivisible and unique thing which art can present.

B. *sb.* **1. a.** A thing of which there is only one example, copy, or specimen; esp., in early use, a coin or medal of this class.

1714 R. THORESBY *Diary* 23 June, My Lord showed me some unics and other valuable curiosities. **1730** A. GORDON *Maffei's Amphith.* 47 It..may be an Unic, for what we know as yet. **1774** *Gentl. Mag.* XLIV. 8 A coin, which I have reason to think is a Unic. **1826** DISRAELI *V. Grey* II. viii, Mr. Vivian Grey had promised his Lordship, who was a collector of medals, an unique which had never yet been heard of. **1872** O. W. HOLMES *Poet Breakf.-t.* iii. 89 A unique, sir, and there is a pleasure in exclusive possession.

†**b.** Something of which only one is possessed by a person or persons. *Obs. rare.*

1783 H. WALPOLE *Let. to C'tess Upper Ossory* 20 June, Lady Pembroke having lent them a servant besides their own unique. **1806** SURR *Winter in Lond.* III. 170 This Belcher girdle was not old; but being an *unique*, it had been ..constantly in use.

2. a. A thing, fact, or circumstance which by reason of exceptional or special qualities stands alone and is without equal or parallel in its kind.

1768 *Phil. Trans.* LVIII. 215 When I presented this map to the Academy..it was looked upon as an Unique. **1781** *Gentl. Mag.* LI. 280/2 The dedication [of a volume of Sermons] being an *unique* in its kind. **1794** PALEY *Evid.* II. ix. iii. ad fin., The propagation of Christianity..is an *unique* in the history of the species. **1835** *Tait's Mag.* II. 651 It is..an *unique* in English biography. **1838** DE QUINCEY *Lamb* Wks. 1858 IX. 156 Of Lamb's writings..some were so memorably beautiful as to be uniques in their class. **1844** *N. Brit. Rev.* I. 124 A conflict, that stands out from all shadow of parallelism—a wild originality—a terrible unique.

b. A person of this class.

1758 *Case of Authors Stated* 14 He presumes, that he, this *Unic*, must therefore appear in the same stupendous Magnitude to every body else. **1782** COWPER *Let.* Nov., Wks. (1876) 121 He is a man much to my taste, and quite an unique in this country. **1802** MRS. E. PARSONS *Myst. Visit* IV. 145, I trust that he though very good, is not an unique. **1813** *Examiner* 22 Feb. 122/2 Those..charms of manner, which constitute an *unique.* **1866** ALGER *Solit. Nat. & Man* II. 65 The peculiar endowment in which he so far surpasses others as to be an insulated unique.

u'niquely, *adv.* [f. prec. + -LY².]

1. Exclusively, solely; only.

1820 T. MITCHELL *Aristoph.* I. 13 It is a picture uniquely Greek, to have a person of his rank in life giving such a debtor and creditor account of his intellectual pleasures as Dicæopolis does. **1893** SALTUS *Mme. Sapphira* 182 She had married him uniquely to go into society. **1893** *Nation* (N.Y.) 28 Sept. 220/1 That distinction he can still boast to be his uniquely.

b. By itself alone; separately.

1885 LEUDESDORF *Cremona's Proj. Geom.* 43 Therefore D_1 must coincide with D', since the three points $A'B'C'$ determine uniquely the fourth point which forms with them a harmonic range.

2. To a unique degree or extent; so as to be unique; singularly, especially, pre-eminently.

1846 DARWIN in *Life & Lett.* (1887) I. 345, I sent you a uniquely laudatory epistle. **1881** H. W. NICHOLSON *From Sword to Share* vii. 41 The climate is simply and uniquely perfect. **1886** W. J. TUCKER *E. Europe* 310 The uniquely-shaped and quaintly-coloured furniture.

u'niqueness. [f. as prec. + -NESS.] The fact or condition of being unique or unequalled; unique quality or character; an instance of this; a unique fact or circumstance.

1820 COLERIDGE *Lett., Convers., &c.* I. 152 The contra-distinction between the Shakespearian and the Greek Drama, and its still remaining uniqueness. **1874** H. R. REYNOLDS *John Bapt.* i. §1. 4 So a great man loses something of his sublimity and uniqueness as we come close to him. **1880** BERTHA THOMAS *Violin-Player* II. x. 231 The novelty, the uniqueness of the scene. **1897** D. W. FORREST *Christ of Hist. & Exper.* v. 205 The uniquenesses of Christ are manifold and indubitable.

u'niquity. [Irreg. f. UNIQUE *a.* + -ITY, prob. after *antiquity.*] = prec. (Cf. UNICITY 2.)

Also, in recent use (1917), = a unique book.

1789 H. WALPOLE *Let.* 20 July, As rarities, a collector would give ten times more for them: and *uniquity* will make them valued more than the charming poetry. **1793** —— *Let.* 17 Sept., I lament that the summer is over; not because of its uniquity, but because you two made it so delightful to me. **1862** B. TAYLOR *Home & Abr.* Ser. II. 399 The originality, the uniquity, of the place. **1886** E. RANDOLPH *Mostly Fools* II. i. 16 The idea..is unique, and uniquity, if I may permit myself the expression, is what we must aim at. **1898** *Atlantic Monthly* LXXXII. 495/1 The lateness..of the bird's appearance, together with what a certain scholarly friend of mine would have called his 'uniquity'.

unireme ('ju:nɪri:m). [f. UNI- + L. *rēm-us* oar, after *bi-*, *quadri-*, *trireme*, etc.] An ancient vessel or galley having one bank of oars.

1699 J. POTTER *Antiq. Greece* III. xiv. II. 135 [A ship] betwixt an Vnireme, and Bireme, consisting of a Bank, and a half. **1799** CHARNOCK in *Naval Chron.* I. 134 The Uniremes..had only one row of oars. **1900** *Athenæum* 18 Aug. 221/3 The thing shown is meant for a unireme.

un-'Irish, *a.* (UN-¹ 7.)

1829 G. GRIFFIN *Collegians* III. xli. 225 Suicide is a very un-Irish crime. **1842** LOVER *Handy Andy* ix, The youth endeavoured to become un-Irish in everything. **1854** GRACE GREENWOOD *Haps & Mishaps* 108 An awkward effort at enjoyment and amusement, un-Irish and lamentable in the extreme.

un-'Irishly, *adv.* (UN-¹ 11.)

1830 MOORE *Mem.* (1854) VI. 135 They wisely and un-Irishly chose the money.

†**un'irked**, *ppl. a. Sc. Obs.* (UN-¹ 8.)

1513 DOUGLAS *Æneid* XIII. xi. 35 The Eneadanis all of his menȝe Ithandly and onyrkyt luiffit haue I. **1533** BELLENDEN *Livy* IV. xiv. (S.T.S.) II. 99 Horsmen..fresche and vnirkit of lauboure.

un'iron, *v.* (UN-² 4 and 4 b.)

1611 FLORIO, *Disferrare*, to vniron, to vnshooe a horse. *Ibid.*, *Sferrare*, to vniron, to free or deliuer from out irons or bondes. [**1863** SALA *Captain Dangerous* II. i. 18 Captain Handsell had me unironed.]

un'ironed, *ppl. a.* (UN-¹ 8.)

c **1430** *Pilgr. Lyf Manhode* I. cviii. (1869) 57 A burdoun yrened weyeth more than thilke that is vnyrened. **1788** HOLCROFT tr. *Baron Trenck* (1886) II. 21, I was thus left four days in peace, unironed. **1880** *New Virgin.* I. 57 Unironed shirts and coats.

uni'rradiated, *ppl. a.* (UN-¹ 8.)

1806 SYMMONS *Life of Milton* 544 (Jod.), A mind not unirradiated with the golden visions of fancy. **1816** COLERIDGE *Lay Serm.* (Bohn) 342 The understanding.. unirradiated by the reason and the spirit. **1955** *Radiation Res.* II. 364 When both haploid cells were unirradiated, zygote formation occurred in about 95% of the pairs. **1978** *Jrnl. R. Soc. Med.* LXXI. 670 Patients with grade III astrocytoma who were irradiated had greater 1-5 year survival rates than those unirradiated.

un'irrigated, *ppl. a.* (UN-¹ 8.)

1876 'MARK TWAIN' *Tom Sawyer* iv. 44 When he emerged from the towel, he was not yet satisfactory, for the clean territory stopped short at his chin... Below..there was a dark expanse of unirrigated soil. **1878** BROWNING *Poets Croisic* 83 Our Academic clodpoles must be dense Indeed to stand unirrigated still. **1883** *Standard* 31 Aug. 4/6 The unirrigated tracts between the head waters of the..rivers.

un'irritant, *a.* (UN-¹ 7.)

1822-7 GOOD *Study Med.* (1829) V. 120 We should employ the unirritant tonics.

un'irritated, *ppl. a.* (UN-¹ 8.)

1649 EARL MONM. tr. *Senault's Use Passions* (1671) 83 Bulls..do little unirritated. **1793** T. BEDDOES *Lett. Darwin* 71, I do not understand why in an irritable state of the body, the iris should be un-irritated.

un'irritatedly, *adv.* (UN-¹ 11.)

1869 BROWNING *Lett.* Ser. II. (1907) I. 34 Yours unirritatedly, R. B.

u'nirritating, *ppl. a.* (UN-¹ 10.)

Also *unirritatingly* (Webster, 1847).

1797 ABERNETHY *Surg. Ess.* 98 The abscess at last became ..un-irritating to the constitution. **1839-47** *Todd's Cycl. Anat.* III. 613/2 The smooth and unirritating condition of the inner surface of the deserted shell. **1896** MRS. CAFFYN *Quaker Grandmother* 20 Sin is a chastener that conduces to unirritating niceness.

†**uni'rrooted**, *ppl. a. Obs.* [f. UN-¹ 8 c + *y-rooted*, pa. pple. of ROOT *v.*² Cf. UNROOTED *ppl. a.*] Not rooted out or eradicated.

1600 TOURNEUR *Transf. Metam.* lviii, Not hable to endure His heart should knowledge of such harme immure An houre, and th' wrong rest vnirrooted out.

uniselector ('ju:nɪsɪlɛktə(r)). *Teleph.* and *Electr.* [f. UNI- 2 + SELECTOR.] A selector (sense c(*b*)) which has a wiper free to rotate about an axis but not to move along it.

1930 *Gloss. Terms Telegraphs & Telephones* (*B.S.I.*) 27 Uniselector. **1938** C. W. WILMAN *Automatic Telephony* (ed. 2) iii. 20 Single-motion switches are commonly termed uniselectors, lineswitches being known as subscribers' uniselectors. **1956** G. A. MONTGOMERIE *Digital Calculating Machines* ix. 181 The other major component of interest to us is the stepping switch or uniselector. **1971** J. H. SMITH *Digital Logic* i. 4 An electronic telephone exchange uses static switching, but..a conventional exchange..uses relays and uniselectors consisting entirely of moving parts.

uniserial (ju:nɪ'sɪərɪəl), *a.* Chiefly *Bot.*, *Zool.*, etc. [See UNI- and SERIAL *a.*] Arranged in, consisting of, one series or row; characterized by this kind of form or arrangement.

1839 *Proc. Berw. Nat. Club* I. 198 Suckers uniserial. **1859** *Todd's Cycl. Anat.* V. 290/1 In those genera in which these processes form a single line the gills are said to be uniserial. **1872** H. A. NICHOLSON *Palæont.* 325 The teeth are conical and uniserial.

uniseriate (ju:nɪ'sɪərɪət), *a. Bot.* and *Zool.* [See UNI- and SERIATE *a.*] = prec.

1846 DANA *Zooph.* (1848) 215 With cellules interruptedly uniseriate, and occasionally biseriate. **1872** H. C. WOOD *Fresh-w. Algæ* 68 Cells uni-seriate. **1887** W. PHILLIPS *Brit. Discomycetes* 243 Sporidia uniseriate.

Hence **uni'seriately** *adv.*

1848 DANA *Zoo.* 133 Upper margin uniseriately tuberculate.

'unisex, *a.* and *sb.* [f. UNI- + SEX *sb.*] **A.** *adj.* Of, pertaining to, or characterized by a style (of dress, appearance, etc.) that is designed or suitable for either sex; not peculiar to one sex, sexually indeterminate or neutral.

1968 *Life* 21 June 87 With-it young couples..are finding that looking alike is good fashion as well as good fun. The unisex trend was launched by..the teen-agers. **1968** *Manch. Guardian Weekly* 21 Nov. 4 Greenwich Village..has just spawned the world's 'first unisex boutique for men and women from 16 to 25'. **1969** *New Yorker* 5 Apr. 99/1 Unisex metallic trouser suits. **1969** *Daily Tel.* 6 June 17 Unisex fashions have literally gone to children's heads, with look-alike brother and sister haircuts. **1970** P. CARLON *Death by Demonstration* vi. 71 A lot of the men..were friendly with her on a strictly unisex level. I mean there was nothing in the slightest degree like romantic attraction. **1972** *Sat. Rev.* (U.S.) 1 July 47/1 'How clean,' 'how Spartan,' 'how unisex' the Chinese appeared to be. **1976** J. I. M. STEWART *Memorial Service* xv. 262 A sexuality quite as strong as Anna's moved beneath the androgynous or 'unisex' persona she had created for herself. **1980** *Times Lit. Suppl.* 21 Mar. 320/1 A group of student actors, all with cropped hair, sallow cheeks and dressed in unisex denims, are warming up in front of a packed house.

B. *sb.* A condition or phase during which people of both sexes appear to be indistinguishable in dress and outward behaviour.

1969 *Sunday Mail* (Brisbane) 11 May 24/8 It's unisex where men and women have abandoned the old 'vive la difference' school of thought in dressing and added a fillip to the old guessing game of 'is it a he or a she?' **1972** *Nature* 28 Jan. 234/2 It could be pertinent to recall that, at the time these results were obtained, the adolescent trend towards unisex was strongly under way. **1976** T. SHARPE *Wilt* i. 5 Eva Wilt was too easily influenced..to be allowed out with a woman who believed that..unisex was here to stay.

unisexual (ju:nɪ'sɛksju:əl), *a.* [ad. mod.L. *unisexual-is* (F. *unisexuel* (1812), Pg. *unisexual*): see UNI- and SEXUAL *a.*]

1. Of one sex; having the essential generative or reproductive organs of one or other sex developed or present in individuals: **a.** *Bot.* Of flowers: In which either the stamens or pistils are absent or suppressed. Also, of plants: Characterized by flowers of this kind; = DICLINOUS *a.*

1802 R. HALL *Elem. Bot.* 193 *Unisexual*,..having one sex. **1828** STARK *Elem. Nat. Hist.* II. 461 The last three classes [of plants]..have the flowers thus disposed, and are hence named unisexual. **1839** LINDLEY *Sch. Bot.* 16 In particular species the stamens are found in one flower, and the pistil in another..; such plants are called unisexual. **1854** S. THOMSON *Wild Fl.* 62 These unisexual blossoms being either the production of the same individual plant, or of separate individuals of the same species. **1872** OLIVER *Elem. Bot.* II. 169 Burnet Sanguisorb,..with..unisexual flowers.

Comb. **1877** *Nature* 26 April 548/1 A unisexual-flowering plant.

b. *Zool.* Of animals or their organs.

In *Ent.* of certain agamic broods of *Aphides*: consisting of the female sex only (*Cent. Dict.* 1891).

1830 R. KNOX *Béclard's Anat.* 29 The organs of generation present all the varieties, unisexual, without copulation, hermaphrodite [etc.]. **1861** HULME tr. *Moquin-Tandon* II. I. 47 In a great number of animals the sexes are separated and placed on distinct individuals: these are said to be unisexual. **1877** DARWIN *Forms of Fl.* Introd. 2 The males and females of ordinary unisexual animals.

2. Pertaining or restricted to one sex; *U.S.* esp. of colleges or schools.

1885 L. OLIPHANT *Sympneumata* 182 The relationship of person which would maintain in a painful activity the currents of the decaying unisexual layers of either frame. **1886** *Century Mag.* June 326/1 One final provincialism of the mind there is, which a unisexual college certainly never would have any power to eradicate. **1904** *Daily Chron.* 14 Oct. 6 The present unjust system of unisexual punishments.

3. = UNISEX *a.*

1970 *Sunday Times* 29 Nov. 29/2 Adolescents of both genders strode along..with books and long flaxen unisexual hair. **1978** C. SYKES in R. Buckle *U & Non-U Revisited* 52 By the 1960s unisexual umbrellas were commonplace in Germany.

Hence **uni'sexually** *adv.*

1891 *Cent. Dict.* s.v., Animals unisexually developed. **1901** *Nature* 10 Jan. 252/1 Not that spontaneous variations are always inherited unisexually.

unisexu'ality. *Bot.* and *Zool.* [f. prec. + -ITY.]

a. The state or condition of being unisexual.

1830 LINDLEY *Nat. Syst. Bot.* 155 The unisexuality of the flowers of both genera. **1877** HUXLEY *Anat. Inv. Anim.* i. 67 There is some reason to suspect..that unisexuality is the result of the abortion of the organs of the other sex, in males and females respectively. **1898** *Pop. Sci. Monthly* July 298 Asexuality passes through bisexuality into unisexuality.

b. In sense of UNISEXUAL *a.* 3.

1971 *Daily Tel.* 13 Aug. 9/2 If he meant anything serious at all in his comedy..it can only have been the tedium arising from such coy and quaint treatments of unisexuality. **1973** *Ibid.* 25 Sept. 18 The notion of a blatant unisexuality such as she implies is not the aim of these anti-discrimination laws—or of the majority of feminists.

uni'silicate. *Min.* [UNI-².] (See quot. from Dana.) Also *attrib.*

1879 RUTLEY *Stud. Rocks* x. 140 In chemical composition the garnets are essentially unisilicates of different sesquioxides and protoxides. **1879** DANA *Man. Min.* (ed. 3) 242 In the Unisilicates, one molecule of silicon is combined with two of an element in the protoxide state..; or with two-thirds of a molecule in the sesquioxide state. *Ibid.*, Among the species referred to the Unisilicates there are some that vary from the unisilicate ratio.

u'nisolated, *ppl. a.* (UN-[1] 8.)
1886 *Jrnl. R. Microsc. Soc.* VI. 47 The unisolated hyoid muscles of the frog.

unison (ˈjuːnɪsən, -zən), *sb.* and *a.* Also 6 unisonne, vnisone, unizon (vnisson), 7 unisone. [a. OF. *unison* (Oresme), later and mod.F. *unisson* (16th c.), or ad. late L. *unison-us* (whence It., Sp., and Pg. *unisono* (also as *sb.*), It. †*unissono*, Sp. *unison*) of the same sound as something else, f. L. *ūni-* UNI- and *sonus* SOUND *sb.*[3]]
The apparently early example in the *York Mystery Plays* xxv. 262 is probably a scribal error for 'vrysoune' (= orison).

A. *sb.* **1.** *Mus.* and *Acoustics.* **a.** A sound or note of the same pitch as another; also loosely, a note taken as a starting-point from which intervals are reckoned. Now *rare*, or taken as *transf.* from b.
1574 F. KETR. *A. Le Roy's Instr. Lute* 17 You must..haue recourse to an other stryng, that maketh the vnisson with that. **1609** DOULAND *Ornithoparcus' Microl.* 17 An Vnison is..a Voyce so qualified, that it neither tendeth to depth nor to height. **1660** BOYLE *New Experiments Phys. Mech.* 211 A string tun'd (as Musicians speak..) to an Unison with it. **1694** HOLDER *Harmony* iv. 54 By Unison is meant, sometimes the Habitude or Ration of Equality of two Notes compared together, being of the very same Tune. Sometimes (as here) for the given single Note to which the Distance, or the Rations of other Intervals are compared. **1728** CHAMBERS *Cycl.* s.v. *Interval*, Unisons, 'tis plain, cannot possibly have any Variety. **1881** *Nature* XXIV. 358 When the higher note has reached a point about half-way between unison and the octave note.
transf. **1677** *Phil. Trans.* XVIII. 840 Not the whole of that other string doth thus tremble, but the several parts severally, according as they are Unisons to the whole.
fig. **1760–72** H. BROOKE *Fool of Qual.* (1792) I. 181 The muscles of Harry's expressive countenance, like an equally-tuned instrument, uttered unisons to every word he heard.

b. Identity in pitch of two or more sounds or notes; the agreement or consonance of the sounds of two or more bodies vibrating at equal rates; the relation of two notes of the same pitch reckoned as one of the musical 'intervals'.
1575 GASCOIGNE *Weedes* Wks. 1907 I. 381 At Musickes sacred sounde, my fansies eft begonne, In concordes, discordes, notes and cliffes, in tunes of unisonne. **1596** BATHE *Brief Introd. Skill of Song* C, A concord is diuided into an Vnizon, Third, Fift, Sixt [etc.]. **1626** BACON *Sylva* §103 The Diapason or Eight in Music is the sweetest Concord; insomuch as it is in effect an Unison. **1694** [see a]. **1728** CHAMBERS *Cycl.* s.v. *Octave*, The most simple Perception the Soul can have of true Sounds, is that of Unison. **1749** J. MASON *Numbers in Poet. Comp.* 21 Those [metrical] Feet..are in Proportion of the Unison in Musick. .. And they are said to answer to the Unison. **1806** CALLCOTT *Mus. Gram.* II. i. 90 The Unison,..although it cannot properly be reckoned an Interval, is always considered as such. **1873** BANISTER *Music* §103 Two, or more, perfect 5ths, perfect 8ves, or perfect unisons, are forbidden between the same two parts. **1896** W. G. WOOLCOMBE *Pract. Work Physics* III. Pref., The nearest approach to unison between two musical notes.

c. A combination of melodies at the same pitch (or, loosely, one or more octaves apart) in different parts, i.e. performed by different voices or instruments. Also in fig. context.
In quot. 1730 used loosely for each of such melodies (in this case on different sets of strings of the same instrument: cf. *unison string* in 5).
[**1724** *Short Explic. For. Wds. in Mus. Bks.*, *Unissono*, a Unison... This word is also used when in Symphonies of Songs Two Violins both play the same Thing, or the Violin and Song, or the Bass and Song, &c.] **1730** in *Abridgm. Specif. Patents, Music* (1871) 1 A new invented harpsichord upon which (having only two sets of strings) may be performed either one or two unisons, or two unisons & one octave together. **1795** MASON *Ch. Music* i. 82 Every ear felt the stupendous effect both of unison and harmony. **1799** KOLLMANN *Ess. Mus. Composition* iii. 18 In Unisons, or passages where all instruments play the same melody, though in different Octaves. **1855** PUSEY *Doctr. Real Presence* 721 When the Holy Spirit..swept over the discordant strings of human tongues and thoughts..and blended all their varying notes into one holy unison of truth. **1869** OUSELEY *Counterp.* xiv. 83 When the number of parts exceeds four, unisons may be used.

d. In the phrase *in* (..) *unison* (in sense b or c).
1616 W. BROWNE *Brit. Past.* II. ii. 546 Not suffering her shrill waters, as they run, Tun'd with a whistling gale in unison. **1749** J. MASON *Numbers in Poet. Comp.* 21 Two Strings of equal Length (supposing their respective Tensions and Thickness to be equal) being put in Motion, will be in Unison, or give exactly one and the same Sound. **1765** STERNE *Tr. Shandy* VII. xliii, The nymphs joined in unison, and their swains an octave below them. **1795** MASON *Ch. Music* iii. 208 What old Calvin meant to be sung in unison, they chose should be performed in counter-point, or in four parts. **1856** MRS. C. CLARKE tr. *Berlioz' Instrument.* 32 To violoncellos..is ordinarily given the part of the double bass, which they double in the octave above or in unison. **1873** HALE *In His Name* vi. 58 As the three voices, in strict unison, closed the little song.
transf. **1828** SCOTT *F.M. Perth* xxvii, The cry from the numberless boats..rose in wild unison up to the Tom-an-Lonach. **1876** HOLLAND *Seven Oaks* xi. 149 'Not at all,' was responded almost in unison.

e. *ellipt.* for 'unison string' (see 5).
1820 *Q. Mus. Mag.* II. 306 He tried the octaves, and found them..all flat..; the unisons, generally speaking, were in tune. **1889** [see *unison-tuning* in 5].

2. A single unvaried tone; a monotone. ? *Obs.*
1609 DOULAND *Ornithoparcus' Microl.* 26 The prayers.. are read in an Vnison. **1742** POPE *Dunc.* IV. 612 Lost was the Nation's Sense, nor could be found, While the long solemn Unison [*sc.* a yawn] went round.

3. A union or combination of concordant sounds; a united and unanimous declaration or utterance.
1806 WORDSW. '*Loud is the Vale*' 3 A mighty unison of streams! Of all her Voices, One! **1871** PALGRAVE *Lyr. Poems* 135 That cry has been heard By a nation's unison swelled.

4. *fig.* **a.** Something perfectly agreeing or consonant with another; an utterance or expression of perfect agreement or assent; something that responds sympathetically as a string tuned to a corresponding note. Now *rare* or *Obs.*
1650 BULWER *Anthropomet.* 63 A forehead which keeps its natural magnitude is one of the Unisons of the face. **1658** GURNALL *Chr. in Arm.* II. 205 Adam indeed had such a righteousnesse made to his hand, his heart and the Law were unisons. **1702** C. MATHER *Magn. Chr.* III. III. (1852) 539 He thought that ministers and market-men were not unisons. **1796** ELIZA HAMILTON *Lett. Hindoo Rajah* (1811) II. 218 The tender sigh..in vibrating on the ears of Miss Ardent, seemed to touch some pleasant unison, that over-spread her countenance with a smile. **1812** COLERIDGE in *Lit. Rem.* (1836) I. 375 To make the intellectual faith a fair analogon or unison of the vital faith.

b. Exact or perfect agreement, concord, or harmony; harmonious combination or union.
1654 WHITLOCK *Zootomia* 454 Physitians..are at Discord the best, but at Unisons the worst; for they do all so disagree [etc.]. **1674** PLAYFORD *Skill Mus.* A 5, Friendship the Vnison of well tun'd Hearts. **1744** THOMSON *Summer* (ed. 5) 1375 Social Friends, Attun'd to happy Unison of Soul,.. Now call'd abroad enjoy the falling Day. **1796** MME. D'ARBLAY *Camilla* I. 4 This exemplary couple was bound to each other by the most perfect unison of character. **1819** KEATS *Vis. Hyperion* I. 418 Nor could my eyes And ears act with that unison of sense Which marries sweet sound with the grace of form. **1858** SEARS *Athan.* ix. 77 Thence life and health spread through our animal frames, restoring them to a unison with divine laws. **1871** FARRAR *Witn. Hist.* v. 183 That beautiful unison of noble manhood, stainless womanhood, joyous infancy, and uncontaminated youth.

†**c.** *at unison* (also *at..unisons*), = next. *Obs.*
1665 GLANVILL *Scepsis Sci.* xiii. 76 Reason and Faith are at perfect Unisons. **1772** *Test Filial Duty* II. 173 The sensations of friendship have not enough of fire in them, to warm the heart into that proper temperature, requisite to render it at unison with the delirium of lovers. *Ibid.* 238 Set all my affections at unison.

d. *in unison*, in agreement or harmony, concordant, consonant, harmonious. Freq. *in unison with.*
1780 COWPER *Parrot* 36 Each character in ev'ry part Sustain'd with so much grace and art, And both in unison. **1782** V. KNOX *Ess.* xxviii. ¶8 It is the more tranquil style which is most frequently in unison with our minds. **1815** JANE AUSTEN *Emma* xli, It was all in unison; words, conduct, discretion and indiscretion told the same story. **1836** W. IRVING *Astoria* I. 287 A mode of redress perfectly in unison with the character of the man. **1860** PUSEY *Min. Proph.* 26 Dumb inanimate nature seems to rejoice and to be in unison with our sense of joy. **1879** FARRAR *St. Paul* I. 312 When such allies were in unison..it was easy to strike a deadly blow at the Nazarenes.

5. *attrib.*: **unison stop**, (*a*) in an organ, a stop of the same pitch as the diapasons; (*b*) in a harpsichord (see quot. 1896); **unison string**, in a pianoforte or other instrument, a string tuned to the same pitch as another (or, loosely, to a pitch an octave higher); **unison tune**, a tune to be sung in unison, as distinct from harmony or 'parts'; **unison-tuning**, the tuning of strings (of a pianoforte, etc.) in unison.
1840 *Penny Cycl.* XVI. 493/1 Trumpet and Oboe stops, being what are called *unison stops,..take their lengths from the open diapason. **1896** A. J. HIPKINS *Pianoforte* 122 *Unison Stop*, properly the second foundation register in a harpsichord; the shorter of the unison strings in a double keyboard one, and sounding on the lower keyboard only. **1685** BOYLE *Effects Motion* vii. 80 A certain impulse of Air, made by one of the *Unison-strings of a musical Instrument, may suffice to produce a visible motion in another. **1732** BERKELEY *Alciphr.* III. §4, I feel an affection in my soul, like the trembling of one lute, upon striking the unison strings of another. **1896** [see *unison stop* above]. **1869** *Pall Mall G.* 7 July 12/2 Mr. John Goss, Mr. E. J. Hopkins, and Mr. J. Baptiste Calkin have composed *unison tunes for this volume. **1889** BRINSMEAD *Hist. Pianoforte* 186 The same plan as that for learning the *unison-tuning may be adopted for the octave, but care must be taken that the unison of the note is tuned afterwards.

B. *adj.* †**1.** Sounding at once or together. *Obs.*[−1]
1582 STANYHURST *Æneis* III. (Arb.) 73 Thus God Apollo cryed; but wee with an vnison outcrye..demaunded, what place God Phœbus apoincted.

†**b.** *fig.* United and consenting, as the pronouncement of a number of persons; expressing complete agreement; unanimous, concordant, consonant, harmonious. *Obs.*
1650 W. CHARLETON *Paradoxes* Prol. f 4 b, By the unisone vote of the multitude. **1651** H. L'ESTRANGE *Answ. Mrq. Worcester* 51 Is the Church of Rome so unison, so all of a piece, as to afford no jarres? *a* **1662** HEYLYN *Laud* II. (1671) 447 The first branch [of a Bill] was carried in the Negative by..an Unison-consent in the Lords then present. **1760–2** GOLDSM. *Cit. W.* xxx, I only beg you'll endeavour to make your souls unison with mine.

†**c.** Concordant or consonant *to* something. *Obs.*
1710 R. WARD *Life H. More* 234 Some Circumstances.., or Particulars of his Writings, are not so unison to my Slower Faculties. **1760–72** H. BROOKE *Fool of Qual.* (1792) V. 10 This doctrine sounded unison to the secret feelings of our young Englishman.

†**d.** Like-sounding; equivalent. *Obs.*[−1]
1759 STERNE *Tr. Shandy* I. xix, Tristram!—Melancholy dissyllable of sound! which, to his ears, was unison to Nincompoop.

2. *Mus.* and *Acoustics.* Identical in pitch; singing, sounding, etc., in unison; unisonal, unisonous. Now *rare* or *Obs.*
1614 JACKSON *Creed* III. xviii. §4 As a string, though untouched, and unable to begin motion of itself, will yet raise it selfe to an vnison voice. **1622** PEACHAM *Compl. Gent.* xi. 104 Two Lutes of equall size being laid vpon a Table, and tuned Vnison, or alike in..any..string; the one stricken, the other untouched shall answer it. **1667** MILTON *P.L.* VII. 599 All sounds on Fret by String or Golden Wire Temper'd soft Tunings, intermixt with Voice Choral or Unison. **1694** HOLDER *Harmony* iv. 51 The Unison Concord..is no Space or Interval, but an Identity of Tune. **1721** A. MALCOLM *Treat. Mus.* 580 When Two Voices sing together one Song, 'tis more agreeable that they be 8ve than *unison* with one another, in every Note. **1893** S. GEE *Auscult. & Percussion* (ed. 4) I. iii. 69 A unison vibration, convibration, or consonance of the wall is required to the production of tone.

unisonal (juːˈnɪsənəl), *a. Mus.* [f. prec. + -AL[1].] = UNISONOUS *a.* 1.
1728 R. NORTH *Mem. Music* (1846) 66 All was plain-song, that is counterpoint unisonall. **1865** *Reader* 19 Aug. 214 The unisonal female-voice choruses. **1882** *Amer. Missionary* Mar. 70 Their general style is recitative and chorus, though a few are pure solos or unisonal measures. **1898** *Record* 4 Nov. 1084/2 In spite of one's own loving reverence for unisonal singing.
Hence **u'nisonally** *adv.*, in unison.
1882 *Standard* 20 Feb., A passage of broken quavers.. given out unisonally by the full orchestra. **1887** *Ch. Times* 4 March (Cassell's), Tenors and basses burst in unisonally.

u'nisonance. *rare.* [ad. L. type **unisonantia* (whence Sp. and Pg. *unisonancia*), f. med.L. *unison-us*: see UNISON.] Agreement or identity of sounds (see quots.).
1728 CHAMBERS *Cycl.* s.v. *Concord*, Unisonance, then, being the Relation of Equality between the Tunes of two Sounds, all Unisons are Concords, and in the first Degree. *Ibid.* s.v. *Unison*, What constitutes Unisonance, is the Equality of the Number of Vibrations of the two sonorous Bodies in equal Times. [Hence in Webster (1828–32), etc.]

unisonant (juːˈnɪsənənt), *a.* [f. L. *ūni-* UNI- + *sonant-*, *sonans* (see SONANT *a.*), after *dissonant*, etc. Cf. F. *unissonant.*] Of the same pitch or sound; unisonal, unisonous. Also in fig. context.
1801 BUSBY *Dict. Mus.*, *Unisonus*, or *Unisonant*, an epithet applied to those sounds which are..in unison with each other. **1834** MRS. SOMERVILLE *Connex. Phys. Sci.* xvii. (1836) 168 If two bottles be..tuned by filling them with such a quantity of water as will render them unisonant with two tuning-forks which differ in pitch. **1886** LINSKILL *Haven under Hill* II. ix. 115 The mystic, moving, unisonant harmony that was stirring and breaking upon her own soul.

†**uniso'neity.** *Obs.*[−1] [f. as next + -(E)ITY.] A state of agreement or concord; unanimity.
1663 WATERHOUSE *Fortesc. Illustr.* 414 The Lawes of Nations do affirm the nature of it [*sc.* marriage] to a Vnisoneity, as appears in the Digest.

unisonous (juːˈnɪsənəs), *a.* [f. late L. *unison-us* (see UNISON) + -OUS.]
1. *Mus.* Of the same pitch for the different voices or instruments; composed, performed, or rendered in unison or in octaves, and not in parts; unisonal.
1781 WARTON *Hist. Eng. Poetry* III. 171 These apt notes [to sing the Psalms with] were about forty tunes, of one part only, and in one unisonous key. **1789** BURNEY *Hist. Mus.* III. 389 Nothing now but syllabic and unisonous psalmody was authorised in the Church. **1818** *Blackw. Mag.* III. 65 The Psalms being set to simple or unisonous melodies, to render them fit for public service. **1867** *Contemp. Rev.* IV. 190 Their deadness took the form of a drawling unisonous singing of the old tunes. **1894** *Times* 11 June 9/5 The player's left hand..was audibly less at home than the right in the unisonous finale.
2. Exhibiting agreement, concord, or sameness of character or nature; concordant.
1812 SHELLEY *Let. to Miss Hitchener* 29 Jan., Minds unisonous in reason and feeling. **1851** GALLENGA *Italy* II. xii. 415 The patriots are uniform, methodical in their transactions, unisonous in their demands. **1858** GLADSTONE *Homer* I. 34 The voice of the Homeric poems is in this respect..unisonous,..and not multiform.

†**unisound.** *Obs. rare.* [Alteration of UNISON *sb.*: see UNI- and SOUND *sb.*[3]] A unison.
1763 *Ann. Reg., Misc.* 192/2 By dividing the musical notes into six, as nature directs, the unisound will fall on the seventh note. *Ibid.* 193/1 [The notes] *i, j, s, d*, are likewise unisounds to *f, z, t*, alike.

†**'unisounding,** *ppl. a. Obs.*[−1] [See UNI-.] Having only one sound.
1620 H. FITZ-GEOFFERY *Certain Elegies* A 8 b, Fennor, with his Vnisounding Eare word.

un'issued, *ppl. a.* (UN-[1] 8.)
1667 *10th Rep. Hist. MSS. Comm.* App. V. 57 He may be recompenced..out of the pay of the said Sir James Midleton unissued. **1703** *Lond. Gaz.* No. 3890/3 Several of the Debentures..do remain still unissued. **1898** *Daily News* 12 Oct. 9/3 A large block of unissued shares.

unit ('juːnɪt), *sb.* (and *a.*). Also 6–8 **unite**. [f. L. *ūn-us* one; the ending was probably suggested by *digit* and *composit(e*.

Introduced by Dee, who thus draws attention to the form in his *Math. Pref.* (1570) *iij *marg.*, Note the worde, Vnit, to expresse the Greke Monas, and not Vnitie: as we haue all, commonly, till now, vsed.]

1. a. *Math.* A single magnitude or number regarded as an undivided whole and as the ultimate base of all number; *spec.* in *Arithmetic*, the least whole number; the numeral 'one', represented by the figure 1. Cf. UNITY 1 b.

α. **1570** DEE *Math. Pref.* *iij, Number, we define, to be, a certayne Mathematicall Summe, of Vnits. And, an Vnit, is that thing Mathematicall, Indiuisible, by participation of some likenes of whose property, any thing, which is in deede, or is counted One, may reasonably be called One. **1575** RECORDE *Gr. Artes* Y iij b, An Improper Fraction,.. that is to saye, a fraction in forme, which in dede is greater than an Unit. **1654** J. EYRE *Exact Surveyor* 12 In the ordinary use of this [Decimal] Chain, for measuring and plotting, you may take onely notice of Units and Primes. **1669** STURMY *Mariner's Mag.* VII. xxxiv. 51 The Characteristick of any Logarithme must consist of an Unit less than the given Number consisteth of Digits or Places. **1728** CHAMBERS *Cycl.* s.v. *Number*, Cardinal Numbers [are] those which express the Quantity of Units; as, 1, 2, &c. **1794** CUNN *Doctr. Fractions* 62 Repetends that begin at the same place, whether at Units, Primes, Seconds. **1832** HOOD *Ode to J. Hume* i, Units, Tens, Hundreds, Thousands, Millions. **1838** DE MORGAN *Ess. Probab.* 33 Write down as many numbers, reckoning downwards, as there are units in the number. **1875** *Encycl. Brit.* II. 527/1 [In arithmetical notation] the figure placed furthest to the right has the same significance as when it stands alone, *i.e.* it represents units.

β. **1588** A. KING tr. *Canisius' Catech.* i ij, Compte..swa mony epactis as yair is vnites in ye golden nombre. **1597** BLUNDEVIL *Exerc.* (ed. 2) I. vii. 12 Such [numbers] as cannot bee divided but that there will remaine some odde unite, those are called Primes. **1669** W. SIMPSON *Hydrol. Chym.* 226 The great variety the number seven doth produce by the various transposition of its unites. **1679** MOXON *Math. Dict.* 162 An Unite is the beginning of Number, and..receiveth no division in Numbers, even as a Point in Magnitudes. **1726** LEONI *Alberti's Archit.* II. 89/1 If, as some affirm, the unite be no number, but only the source of all others.

†**b.** Without article: = UNITY 1 b. *Obs.*

1717 *Phil. Trans.* XXX. 618 The Logarithm of Unite is nothing; and..the nearer any Number is to Unite, the nearer will its Logarithm be to 0. **1823** JEFFERSON *Writ.* (1830) IV. 364 In the proportion of a million at least to unit.

c. Any determinate quantity, dimension, or magnitude adopted as a basis or standard of measurement for other quantities of the same kind and in terms of which their magnitude is calculated or expressed.

A large number of special units adopted in technical and scientific use are recorded in some Dicts.

1738 CHAMBERS *Cycl.* s.v. *Degree*, Thus, a Degree, as being the integer or unite, is denoted by °. **1816** PLAYFAIR *Nat. Phil.* II. 209 Hitherto, the distance of the Sun from the Earth has served as the unit, by which we have measured all other distances in the planetary system. **1825** JEFFERSON *Autobiog.* Wks. 1859 I. 52 The necessity of establishing a standard of value with us, and of the adoption of a money Unit. **1854** RONALDS & RICHARDSON *Chem. Technol.* (ed. 2) I. 253 The loss of heat from these sources has been estimated ..at about 7 units of heat per hour per square foot. **1867** NOAD *Text. Bk. Electricity* 201 The unit of a current conveys a unit of electricity through the circuit in a unit of time. **1870** F. L. POPE *Electric Tel.* iii. (1872) 25 The ohm is a unit of resistance, in the same manner that an inch is a unit of length, or a pound a unit of weight. **1886** RUSKIN *Præterita* I. 323 Musical people..have not yet fixed their unit of time. *Comb.* **1892** *Nation* (N.Y.) 15 Dec. 459/1 The hopeful earnestness with which Mr. Norman offers his unit-of-weight system as a panacea for the cure of all financial ills.

(*b*) *spec.* one kilowatt-hour, as the unit used in measuring and charging for mains electricity; also, the unit used for metered telephone calls.

1891 *Minutes of Proc. Inst. Civil Engineers* CVI. 16 Fuel used..has..fallen from 12 lbs. to 7·9 lbs. per unit generated. **1926–7** *Army & Navy Stores Catal.* 344/3 Electric radiators... Two bars..consumes 2 units per hour when full-on. **1961** *Which?* Dec. 334/1 Local and trunk calls are divided into 2*d.* 'units', the amount of the time you get for your 2*d.* depending on the distance. **1972** *Daily Tel.* (Colour Suppl.) 12 May 15/1 Food freezers are inexpensive to run, using about 2 units of electricity for each cubic foot per week.

d. A substance adopted as a standard by which the specific gravity of various bodies is estimated.

1829 *Chapters Phys. Sci.* 169 As water is taken as the unit for solids and liquids, so is atmospheric air for gases. **1869** GILL *Chem. for Sch.* xxii. 274 Dalton..adopted it [*sc.* hydrogen] as the unit or standard of atomic weight.

e. (See quots. and REPEAT *sb.* 4 b.)

1855 R. N. WORNUM *Anal. Ornament* 18 Units of repetition, or repeats of irregular shapes, arranged diagonally. *Ibid.* 19 As it is in this case the group that is repeated, the group of figures becomes the pattern or unit of repetition.

f. ***unit of account***, a monetary unit in which accounts are kept; *spec.* in the European Economic Community (see quots. 1977 and 1982).

1882 R. BITHELL *Counting-House Dict.* 311 *Unit of Account*, the unit of value in which accounts are kept. It may, or may not, coincide with any coin in circulation... The Anglo-Saxon unit of account was the shilling..but no coin called a *shilling* was issued before the reign of Henry VII. **1959** A. H. ROBERTSON *European Institutions* ii. 42 After offsetting these balances (measured in 'units of account' equivalent to the gold value of the U.S. dollar) against each other, Members are left with a credit or debit account *vis-à-vis* the [European Payments] Union. **1973** *Physics Bull.* Apr. 207/1 The four year allocation for direct research work amounts to 157·2 million units of account (UA, equal to the predevaluation US dollar, ie about £65m). **1977** *Times* 6 Dec. (Europa Suppl.) p. iii/6 *Units of account*, embryonic European currency used as a device for calculating the EEC budget, fixing farm prices and in certain transactions with non-Community countries. The value of the *unit of account* in national currencies depends on the purpose for which it is being used. **1982** J. PHILLIPS *Dict. Trading Terms* 67 The unit of account is now equivalent to a group, or 'basket' of fixed amounts of European currencies, and is described as a 'basket unit of account'.

g. A basic measure of educational attainment credited to a student for completing the number of hours of study assigned to one section of an academic course. Cf. CREDIT *sb.* 13 d. *U.S.*

1894 *Univ. of Chicago Weekly* 4 Oct. 4/1 The system of majors and minors, units and flunks, is harder to understand than any other 'credit' method in operation among educational institutions. **1930** A. FLEXNER *Universities* II. 47 When a college catalogue states that fifteen units of high school work are required for matriculation, a unit, as defined by the College Entrance Examination Board, represents one year's study in any one subject in a high school. **1945** C. V. GOOD *Dict. Educ.* 436/1 *Unit*..(3) a basic measure used in calculating the amount of credit to be assigned to any particular course or the number of graduation credits earned by a pupil or student in completing a course..(*a*) in secondary education, one *unit* equals approximately 120 hours of classroom or laboratory work in a given subject ..(*b*) in higher education,..one *unit* may equal 1 hour of class or laboratory work per week during one term, semester, or school year. **1974** *Aiken* (S. Carolina) *Standard* 18 Apr. 4-c/3 Their required 18 units of study. **1981** D. ROWNTREE *Dict. Educ.* 335 *Unit*... 3 (US) In high school, one hour in class per day of a subject (for five days a week over the academic year) counts as one course unit of that subject.

h. The standard unit of quantity by which bread and petrol were rationed during and immediately after the war of 1939–45; a coupon of this value.

1939 *Punch* 18 Oct. 439 (*caption*), I can't move on—I've used up all my units. **1946** [see B. U. s.v. B III. b]. **1948** *Daily Tel.* 26 Oct. 5 Nine Hundred Petrol Units were stolen from an office at Swanley, Kent. **1963** S. COOPER in Sissons & French *Age of Austerity* ii. 41 The Bread Unit represented seven ounces of bread... A large loaf..would require four Units, one pound of flour three Units.

2. a. A single individual or thing regarded as a member of a group or number of things or individuals, or discriminated from these as having a separate existence; one of the separate parts or members of which a complex whole or aggregate is composed or into which it may be analysed.

1642 H. MORE *Song of Soul* II. I. ii. 55 In number, measure, weight, he all things made; Each unite he dissevers by his Art. **1690** LOCKE *Hum. Und.* II. xii. §6. 74 Which collective Ideas of several Substances thus put together, are as much each of them one single Idea, as that of a Man, or an Unite. **1716** M. DAVIES *Athen. Brit.* II. To Rdr. 13 Some few Despicable Unadditionable Units or Unitarians. **1739** HUME *Hum. Nat.* I. II. ii, 'Tis evident, that existence in itself belongs only to unity, and is never applicable to number, but on account of the unites, of which the number is composed. **1817** SCOTT *Rob Roy* xxxi, The unit of that life..was for ever withdrawn from the sum of human existence. **1856** MERIVALE *Rom. Emp.* xl. IV. 459 Our history becomes a review of the affairs of a vast unit, the aggregate of a multitude of smaller members. **1872** H. C. BASTIAN *Begin. Life* I. 216 Before a nucleus is evolved.., the simple living unit (*plastide*) is able to assimilate nutritive material and grow.

b. That division or section of a collective body or whole which is regarded as the lowest or least to have a distinctive existence; such a division or group of individuals considered as a basis of formation or administration.

1847 GROTE *Greece* II. xxviii. IV. 68 The village is a fraction, but the city is an unit. **1861** MAINE *Anc. Law* v. 126 The unit of ancient society was the Family. **1888** BRYCE *Amer. Commw.* II. 224 The county remained the practically important unit of local administration, the unit to which the various functions of government were aggregated.

c. In military or naval use.

1876 VOYLE & STEVENSON *Milit. Dict.* 446/1 In military organization, the term unit is applied to that single portion upon which any part of an army, regiment, &c. is formed. Thus a company is the unit of a regiment; a battery, that of a brigade of artillery. **1893** *Infantry Drill* p. xxiii, [A] Battalion [is] the unit of infantry. **1899** *Times* 14 Oct. 9 A waterproof bag which is left at the base..on a unit going into action.

d. A group of buildings, wards, etc., in a hospital; *spec.* one equipped to provide a particular type of health care.

1893 D. GALTON *Healthy Hospitals* xiii. 229 Separation of the ward unit has been the principal feature of modern hospital construction in Germany and..the United States. **1911** W. OSLER in *Lancet* 28 Jan. 212/1 There might be, as at Berlin and Vienna, two or three medical and the same number of surgical units. **1927** J. E. STONE *Hospital Organization & Management* xiv. 287 The operating theatre unit is a very important part of a hospital. **1955** R. F. BRIDGMAN *Rural Hospital* ii. 70 With the rural hospital as a base, mobile health-units may be organized, through which modern medical techniques can be taken to the villages in sparsely populated countries with poor communications. **1965** *Nursing Times* 5 Feb. p. vi/1 (Advt.), Plastic Surgery and Burns Unit..Regional Thoracic Surgical Unit. **1976** *Amer. Speech* 1973 XLVIII. 195 The inhalation therapist, for example, supplies hospital floors, or units, with oxygen masks and in emergencies is summoned to start and operate O_2 tents 'oxygen tents'.

e. A piece of (esp. storage) furniture or equipment which may be fitted with other pieces to form a larger system, or which is itself composed of smaller complementary parts. Freq. *attrib.* Also *transf.* (see also *unit audio*, *construction*, sense 3 c below).

1912 L. WEAVER *House & its Equipment* 44 The unit system of bookcases, by which they are built up of sections of standard size, and are thus capable of indefinite expansion. **1930** *N.Y. Times* 10 Aug. v. 14/4 He [*sc.* Franz Schuster] has developed a kind of 'unit' furniture. He reduces the shapes of chest and cabinet to their fundamental forms and by standardizing their measurements permits the combination of parts by the manufacturer. **1937** [see *kitchen unit* s.v. KITCHEN *sb.* 5 c]. **1944** J. VAN DRUTEN *Voice of Turtle* I. 3 The kitchen has an icebox, stove and sink in a combined unit in the left wall. **1958** *Engineering* 7 Mar. 320/2 The cooking unit..is mounted on top of a storage cupboard with a sliding serving shelf. **1974** *Gramophone* Nov. 1009 The connoisseur takes pride in choosing separate units. **1978** [see RECLINER 2]. **1981** M. E. ATKINS *Palimpsest* ix. 92 I'm going to..start with the kitchen. I'll have units all round, a new sink and cooker.

f. An accommodation unit in a larger building or group of buildings, esp. in a block of flats or a motel. *U.S.*, *Austral.*, and *N.Z.*

1932 F. L. WRIGHT *Autobiogr.* II. 223, I lingered in Los Angeles aided by my son Lloyd working on the new unit-block system. **1937** *Tourist Court Jrnl.* Oct. 6/2 Being separate units each cottage is assured of ample ventilation.. through the windows on each side. **1953** *Hotel Monthly* Nov. 27/1 Additional units will be added to the Kahler Ranchotel. **1963** D. B. HUGHES *Expendable Man* ii. 46 No one was waiting for him at the motel. No one stopped him at the door of his unit. **1971** 'A. BLAISDELL' *Practice to Deceive* i. 2 She lived in one unit of a triplex. **1973** *Sun-Herald* (Sydney) 26 Aug. 103/1 We live in a unit in a delinquency-prone inner area. **1980** 'D. SHANNON' *Felony Files* x. 230 It was a pleasant, unpretentious furnished apartment in a six-unit place.

g. = *film unit* s.v. FILM *sb.* 7 c.

1959 E. H. CLEMENTS *High Tension* i. 13 The hectic urgency of everyone else in the unit. **1962** L. DAVIDSON *Rose of Tibet* i. 26 Location work would have finished in Calcutta and..the unit would have moved up into the foothills of Everest.

3. *attrib.*, passing into *adj.*, with the general meaning 'of, pertaining or equivalent to, (that of) a unit; produced or caused by a unit; consisting of, containing, or forming a unit or units'.

a. In sense 1 c, chiefly in *Electr.*, as ***unit coil***, ***current***, ***force***, ***jar***, ***measure***, ***pole***, etc.

1839 NOAD *Electricity* i. 31 A very useful little electrical instrument..for registering the exact quantity of electricity given to a Leyden phial from the machine; it is called the unit jar. **1842** BRANDE *Dict. Sci.*, *Unit jar*..announce[s] by its repeated discharges, which may be counted, the number of them which have passed into the larger jar. **1844** NOAD *Electricity* (ed. 2) 53 The value of the unit measure. **1866** R. M. FERGUSON *Electr.* 17 A magnetic needle of unit size and strength. **1867** NOAD *Text Bk. Electricity* 201 A circuit of unit resistance. *Ibid.*, The unit current flowing through a conductor unit of length will exert the unit force on the unit pole at the unit distance. **1867** BRANDE & COX *Dict. Sci.*, etc. III. 899/1 *Unit coil*,..a standard measure used by electricians for expressing the amount of resistance experienced in a given electrical circuit. **1873** J. C. MAXWELL *Electr. & Magn.* II. 3 The unit-pole is a pole which points north, and is such that, when placed at unit distance from another unit-pole, it repels it with unit of force. **1876** P. G. TAIT *Rec. Adv. Phys. Sci.* (ed. 2) xiv. 357 Unit force is..that force which, whatever be its source, produces unit momentum in unit of time. **1884** KNIGHT *Dict. Mech.* Suppl. 913/2 *Unit and safety valve*, one exposing 1 square inch to the force of the steam.

b. In general use.

1896 R. G. MOULTON *Lit. Study Bible* xi. 258 These Unit Proverbs exhibit two varieties. **1897** *Daily News* 9 Feb. 3/4 Was the scheme to be organized on brigade, battalion, or unit lines? *Ibid.*, The unit system of organization. **1898** *Engineering Mag.* XVI. 104 A plant of a certain size may be run by a unit-body of men. **1898** SIR W. CROOKES in *Daily News* 8 Sept. 6/1 The consumption of wheat per head of the population (unit consumption) was over 6 bushels per annum.

c. Special Combinations. **unit audio**, a sound reproduction system which comprises separate matching parts; **unit cell** *Cryst.*, the smallest structural unit having the overall symmetry of a crystal, which by repetition in three dimensions gives the entire lattice; **unit character** *Genetics*, a character inherited according to Mendelian laws, esp. one controlled by a single pair of alleles; also, †the alleles themselves (see quot. 1966); **unit construction**, modular construction, esp. of buildings (cf. MODULAR *a.* 1 b); **unit cost** *Accounting*, the cost of manufacturing or otherwise processing one unit of production; **unit factor** *Genetics* = GENE[1] (cf. FACTOR *sb.* 7 b); now *hist.*; **unit-holder**, one who holds securities in a unit trust; **unit-linked** *a.*, of a life assurance policy (see quot. 1979); **unit load**, a package of goods arranged for shipment, etc., as a single unit (esp. on a pallet) to facilitate handling; **unit matrix** *Math.* = *identity matrix* s.v. IDENTITY 10; **unit membrane** *Biol.*, any lipoprotein membrane composed of two electron-dense layers enclosing a less dense layer, found enclosing many cells and cell organelles; **unit price**, the price at which a single unit of a commodity is sold; **unit pricing** (see quot. 1970); **unit train** *N. Amer.*, a train allocated to transport a single commodity (i.e. coal or grain) at special rates between two points; **unit trust**, an investment group investing combined contributions from many persons in various securities and paying them dividends in proportion to their holdings.

1966 *Hi-Fi News* Nov. 592/3 '*Unit audio' is the name given to a new range of matching equipment... Two loudspeakers, a tuner-amplifier, an amplifier and a tape recorder..are available. **1976** *Gramophone* Nov. 880/1 People without expert knowledge will generally find it easier to buy a 'unit audio' system made up from matching units from the same manufacturer. **1915** W. H. & W. L. Bragg *X-Rays & Crystal Structure* viii. 116 Only calcium and carbon atoms are shown in their places in the *unit cell of the structure. **1930** G. P. Thomson *Wave Mech. Free Electrons* iii. 40 Each unit cell of a crystal lattice contains the same amount of matter similarly arranged. **1966** C. R. Tottle *Sci. Engin. Materials* iii. 50 In many cases it is convenient to avoid drawing the complete crystal lattice extended over many unit cells, and merely to draw the unit cell itself. **1977** A. Hallam *Planet Earth* 114 All crystalline substances have lattices built of one of these types of unit cell. **1902** Bateson & Saunders *Rep. Evol. Comm. R. Soc.* I. 126 The purity of the germ-cells, and their inability to transmit both of the antagonistic characters, is the central fact proved by Mendel's work. We thus reach the conception of *unit-characters existing in antagonistic pairs. Such characters we propose to call allelomorphs. **1903** *Biometrika* II. 286 Mendel was the first to systematically analyse the differential characters of a race or species into a series of unit-characters, each of which might..be inherited independently of the others. **1915** T. H. Morgan et al. *Mechanism of Mendelian Heredity* ix. 210 So much misunderstanding has arisen amongst geneticists themselves through the careless use of the term 'unit character' that the term deserves the disrepute into which it is falling. **1945** M. F. Glaessner *Princ. Micropalaeontol.* v. 79 The numerical values of morphological features (unit characters) plotted against numbers of specimens in which the progressive values occur, tend to arrange themselves in a regular curve. **1966** E. A. Carlson *Gene* ii. 13 The unit-character [of Bateson] combined the 'differentiating character' used by Mendel with the 'formative element' which he assumed to represent it in the germ cell. **1921** *Conquest* May 291/2 Houses built on the '*Unit' construction system... The concrete blocks are made of a standard size, the dimensions of windows and door openings being made multiples of the block size. **1959** *Motor Manual* (ed. 36) v. 3 The body now forms the main structure of the car... This form of construction is now known by a variety of names, including 'integral construction', 'unit construction' and 'chassisless construction'. **1964** *McCall's Sewing* ii. 33/1 *Unit construction*, organisation of sewing procedure so that an entire garment section is completed before it is joined to another. **1914** E. H. Jones *Unit Construction Costs from New Smelter* 1498 These *unit costs ..represent delays in material shipments.., delayed plans, ..labor troubles, [etc.]. **1962** *Listener* 17 May 835/1 Wages and unit costs rise faster than ever. **1978** J. Kellock *Elements of Accounting* iii. 66 The stock valuation..is calculated by taking a physical stock count of the stock on hand at the end of the period and multiplying each item by the appropriate unit of cost... Unit cost is the cost of purchasing or manufacturing identifiable units of stock. **1911** *Unit factor [see gene[1]]. **1926** J. S. Huxley *Ess. Pop. Sci.* 9 Inheritance takes place by means of separable units, generally known as unit-factors or genes. **1966** E. A. Carlson *Gene* iv. 26 When unit-character was changed to 'unit-factor' or to 'factor' alone, Castle no longer dissociated the transmitting agent from its effect on a character. **1965** M. Naylor *Your Money* 87 One great advantage of unit trusts is that *unit-holders can buy or sell at any time, and get the 'true' value of their investment. **1969** *Daily Tel.* 8 Feb. 6/3 A unit trust management pays capital gains tax at 30 p.c. for either long- or short-term gains, irrespective of the tax position of the individual unitholder. **1969** *Times* 30 Apr. 28/3 Nearly every time we open the paper we read of the attractions of Unit Trusts and *Unit-linked life assurance policies. **1979** F. E. Perry *Dict. Banking* 258/2 *Unit-linked policy*, a type of life assurance policy where a part of the premium is invested on behalf of the assured in a unit trust. **1939** *Steel* 12 June 54/1 *(caption)* *Unit load of four edgewise-wound copper coils on pallet handled by fork truck. **1945** D. L. Beattie *Unit Load Materials Handling* I. 9 Once the unit load is established for a material, there is every reason to expect that this unit load may be standardized. **1970** *Times* 2 June (Container Suppl.) p. i/1 The British Transport Docks Board has a nationwide network of nine well equipped ports, providing some of the most advanced facilities for unit-load handling. **1862** *Unit-matrix [see premultiplication]. **1972** M. Kline *Math. Thought* xxxiii. 807 The product of a matrix and its inverse is the unit matrix, denoted by *I*. **1959** J. D. Robertson in E. M. Crook *Structure & Function Subcellular Components* (Biochem. Soc. Symposium XVI) 33 Perhaps the gap substance or the character of the *unit membrane surfaces here is different. **1970** Ambrose & Easty *Cell Biol.* v. 173 The chloroplast, like all plastids, is bounded by a double unit membrane. **1934** Webster, *Unit price. **1953** [see field *sb.* 15 f]. **1977** P. Way *Super-Celeste* I. 45 Whoever sold a plane here would sell it to NATO through the 1990s. Sell here and the unit price would come down. **1970** *Wall St. Jrnl.* 17 June 40/4 Mr. Alldredge..told the meeting that '*unit pricing', or the marking of all packaged commodities with the price per unit weight, 'would be frighteningly expensive'. **1971** *Guardian* 3 June 2/6 Unit pricing, a new system under which large supermarkets have to indicate the cost of food items by measure, completed its first day here [*sc.* in New York]. **1967** *Times Rev. Industry* Apr. 47/2 *Unit trains working on the principles now applied in the Great Lakes coal trade would discharge coal through ground hoppers without uncoupling. **1979** *Sci. Amer.* Jan. 29/1 *(caption)* Coal-carrying 'unit' trains have been developed to move coal expeditiously at low cost, usually between one mine and one customer, which is most often an electric utility. The trains shuttle back and forth without being uncoupled, acting much like a conveyor belt. **1936** *Economist* 18 Apr. 135/2 Three new trusts with different degrees of flexibility have recently appeared, which extend the activities of the *unit trust movement into new fields. **1958** *Spectator* 18 July 108/1 All unit trusts have this much in common: investments..are deposited with a bank or insurance company, acting as trustee, who issues participation certificates (called units) in exchange. **1980** *Times* 5 Jan. 18 Most of the unit trusts managed not to lose too much money for unit holders last year.

4. As *adj.* Having the distinct or individual existence of a unit; individual.

1870 J. H. Newman *Gram. Assent* I. i. 7 All things in the exterior world are unit and individual;..the mind contemplates these unit realities as they exist. *a* **1881** A. Barratt *Phys. Metempiric* (1883) 115 If the unit minds were parts or modes of this absolute mind.

unit, variant of unite *sb.*

unitable (juːˈnaɪtəb(ə)l), *a.* [f. unit-e *v.* + -able.] That can be united; capable of union.

1653 H. More *Antid. Ath.* (1662) 151 The Plantal faculty of the Soul whereby she is unitable to this terrestrial body. **1659** —— *Immort. Soul* III. xiv. 481 That Order of immaterial Creatures which we call Souls, vitally unitable with the Matter. **1678** Cudworth *Intell. Syst.* 565 Such Beings or Spirits Incorporeal..are Vitally Unitable to Bodies. **1707** *Vulpone* 22 The Offer of the Scots to Unite the Nations in such things as they are Unitable. **1854** Owen in *Orr's Circ. Sci., Org. Nat.* I. 166 When fractured, the broken parts..are not unitable..from within.

Hence **unitaˈbility**.

1863 tr. *Dorner's Person of Christ* III. 280 The real unitability of the divine and human.

†**uˈnitage.** *Obs.*⁻¹ [f. as prec. + -age.] The action of uniting; union.

1641 *Dial. Rattlehead & Roundh.* 4 You can find no means to conjoyn an vnity? *Rattleh.* Only perversnesse in the vnitage of your circular opinions.

unital (ˈjuːnɪtəl), *a.* [f. unit or unit-y + -al[1].] That unites; causing or producing unity or union; of the nature of a unit; unitary.

1860 W. J. C. Muir *Pagan or Chr.* 82 The nave grandly predominates over the aisles, without there being any unital element common to both. **1882** J. B. Stallo *Concepts & The. Mod. Physics* 20 In nature there is a great unital, continuous and everlasting process of development. **1894** *Forum* March 34 To give to each one-tenth of its capital stock..a single director, is open to the objection that it prevents unital control.

unitard (ˈjuːnɪtɑːd). orig. *U.S.* Also **Unitard, unitards.** [f. uni- + leo)tard.] A tight-fitting one-piece garment of stretchable fabric which covers the body from neck to feet, worn by gymnasts, dancers, and as a fashion garment. (Formerly a proprietary name in the U.S.) Cf. *cat-suit* s.v. cat *sb.*[1] 18.

1961 *Official Gaz.* (U.S. Patent Office) 5 Dec. TM15/1 Danskin Inc., New York... Unitard. For one piece form-fitting integral neck-to-ankle..garment, with sleeves, for gymnastics, and dance use. **1978** *Newsweek* 13 Feb. 68/3 Danskin now offers 75 styles for men, women and children, including..a one-piece neck-to-toe 'Unitard'. **1978** *Washington Post* 11 Dec. B8/2 Stan Fowler..had cut, dyed and sewn together the pieces of his 'milliskin unitard' to get the Spiderman look of bright blue and red from head to toe. **1979** *N.Y. Times* 2 Feb. C16 One woman, dressed in unitards and a wide gold sash, bounces dull-eyed in the center of the rooms. **1984** *Times* 14 Feb. 9/2 Unitards—one-piece suits with built-in leg interest like stripey panels at the calf.

Unitarian (juːnɪˈtɛərɪən), *sb.* and *a.* [Partly, in theol. use, f. mod.L. *unitari-us* (1656: f. L. *ūnitās* unity) + -an, partly f. unit-y *sb.* + *-arian*. So F. *unitarien* a. and sb. Cf. unitary *a.*]

A. *sb.* **1.** *Theol.* **a.** One who affirms the unipersonality of the Godhead, especially as opposed to an orthodox Trinitarian; *spec.* a member or adherent of a Christian religious body or sect holding this doctrine.

1687 [? S. Nye] *Brief Hist. Unitarians* 109 The Polonian Unitarians were..zealous.., the Unitarians of Transylvania were more moderate. *Ibid.* 117 The Unitarians, vulgarly called Socinians. **1697** Stillingfl. *Disc. Trinity* 22 Our Vnitarians own the Ebionites as their Predecessors. **1705** T. Emlyn *Vind. Worship Christ* 1/1 Mr. B. flatters himself upon this head, as tho he had quite baffled the Cause of the Unitarians. **1782** Priestley *Corrupt. Chr.* I. i. 8 Eusebius [had] prejudice against the unitarians of his own time. **1787** Hawkins *Life Johnson* (ed. 2) 233 In his religious principles he [Dr. E. Barker] professed himself an unitarian. **1813** J. Adams *Wks.* (1856) X. 50 The dissenters of all denominations in England, and, especially, the Unitarians, are cowed. **1837** Ht. Martineau *Soc. Amer.* III. 279 The Unitarians, the religious body with which I am best acquainted. **1889** *Ch. Q. Rev.* April 35 We may roughly state these three conceptions [of Christianity] as (1) the Unitarian, which conceives of Christ as an exhalted human teacher merely; (2) the Protestant,..(3) the Catholic.

b. In wider use, as applied to any non-Christian monotheist, esp. a Muslim.

1708 Ockley *Saracens* 227 Abu Obeidah sent Abdo'llah Ebn Kort with an Express to Omar..begging his Prayers and some fresh Recruits of Vnitarians (a Title they glory in, reckoning themselves the only Asserters of the Unity of the Deity). **1788** Gibbon *Decl. & F.* lix. VI. 105 His preachers ..called aloud on the unitarians, manfully to stand up against the Christian idolaters. **1819** W. J. Fox *Lect.* iv. Wks. 1865 I. 211 Five different classes of Unitarians, who are out of the pale of Christianity. **1909** G. K. Chesterton *Orthodoxy* viii. 249 The real Unitarians who with scimitar in hand have laid waste the world.

2. One who believes in or favours some theory or system based upon unity: **a.** *Philos.* (See quot. and monist). *rare.*

1836–7 Sir W. Hamilton *Metaph.* xvi. (1859) I. 295 The Realists or Substantialists are again divided into Dualists, and into Unitarians or Monists, according as they are, or are not, contented with the testimony of consciousness to the ultimate duplicity of subject and object in perception.

b. In miscellaneous uses.

1847 Emerson *Poems, Blight* 27 The old men studied magic in the flower..And an omnipotence in chemistry, Preferring things to names, for these were men, Were unitarians of the united world. **1865** Mansfield *Salts* 254 A compound, which even by the unitarians, must be called a double salt. **1904** *Brit. Med. Jrnl.* 10 Sept. 572 In this toxin-antitoxin discussion there has been a tendency to ascribe to us the position of 'unitarians' in contradistinction to the 'pluralists'.

c. An advocate of national or political unity; one who supports the union of several states into one confederation under a central government.

1832 *Ann. Reg. 1831 Hist.* xv. 464/2 The Unitarians were dispossessed of the government of that province [*sc.* Entre-rios, Argentina], and the preponderance of Buenos Ayres restored. **1862** *Times* 9 April, Garibaldi..said all great Italians had been unitarians. **1865** *Cornh. Mag.* Aug. 249 As a unitarian and partisan of centralization he hurled anathemas at all autonomous cities and provinces. **1882–3** in *Schaff's Encycl. Relig. Knowl.* III. 2422/2 There is also a political party in Buenos Ayres..devoted to centralization in government, called Unitarians.

d. A critic who ascribes the *Iliad* and the *Odyssey* to the same author. Opp. separatist *sb.* 1 f. Cf. chorizontes *sb. pl.*

1959 *Times Lit. Suppl.* 13 Mar. 138/4 Any Unitarian must depend very largely on demonstrating some recognizable pattern or design in the Homeric poems as evidence of single authorship. **1976** [see separatist *sb.* 1 f].

B. *adj.* **1.** *Theol.* **a.** Of or pertaining to, connected with, the Unitarians or their doctrines; of the nature of, characteristic of, Unitarianism.

1687 [? S. Nye] *Brief Hist. Unitarians* 36 The Unitarian Doctrine has been reduced so low by the Persecutions of Rome [etc.]. **1691** W. Nicholls *Answ. Naked Gospel* 101 Whilst Faustus kept close in Italy, the Unitarian Cause was carried on by others. **1705** Emlyn (*title*), Vindication of the Worship of the Lord Jesus Christ on Unitarian Principles. **1782** Priestley *Corrupt. Chr.* I. i. 8 What could this be but the proper unitarian doctrine? **1819** M. Stuart *Lett. to W. E. Channing* 144 The younger preachers of Unitarian sentiments. **1824** Longf. in *Life* (1891) I. v. 52 Our little Unitarian Society at Bowdoin. **1889** *Ch. Q. Rev.* April 35 The Unitarian conception of our Lord's Person and Office.

b. Of persons: Accepting, professing, or advocating the doctrines of Unitarianism; belonging to a religious body or sect of Unitarians.

1691 W. Nicholls *Answ. Naked Gospel* 96 The most remarkable of this sort of Unitarian Hereticks. ? **1765** [W. Hopkins] *Attempt* (title-p.), A Friendly Dialogue between a common Unitarian Christian and an Athanasian. **1793** Kippis *Biog. Brit.* (ed. 2) V. 596 Dr. Bennet..laid himself open to the strictures both of Trinitarian and Unitarian Divines. **1815** W. J. Fox *Serm.* 38 The general character of Unitarian professors and converts. **1876** Fox Bourne *Locke* II. xii. 240 Thomas Firmin..the excellent unitarian merchant.

c. In wider use (see A. 1 b).

1780 Wesley *Hymn, 'Sun of unclouded righteousness'* iii, Stretch out thy arm, thou triune God, The Unitarian fiend expel, And chase his doctrine back to hell.

2. Of or pertaining to, involving, based or founded upon, characterized by, unity (in various senses); unitary: **a.** *Philos.* Monistic. *rare.*

1836–7 Sir W. Hamilton *Metaph.* xxiii. (1859) II. 78 He would..be forced to admit one or other of the unitarian conclusions of materialism or idealism.

b. Of systems, theories, etc.

1845 Lowell *Lett.* (1894) I. 102 My system is fully as unitarian as your own. **1875** *Encycl. Brit.* I. 460/2 These two theories, the one dualistic, the other unitarian, strangely foreshadow the discoveries of modern dynamics. **1893** *19th Cent.* Aug. 249 Under the unitarian system we no longer divide the molecule.

c. Advocating, promoting, or directed towards national unity, union, or centralization in government or administration.

1865 *Morn. Star* 10 Feb., The King of Unitarian Italy. **1877** *Academy* 10 Nov. 1/1 The unitarian movement of twenty years later differed..from the revolution which enthroned the triumvirate at Rome.

d. Applied to the theory that the *Iliad* and the *Odyssey* are the work of a single person. Cf. *Homeric question* s.v. Homeric *a.*, and sense A. 2 d above.

1865 M. Pattison in *North British Rev.* June 277 Even on the more special question of the origin of the Homeric poems,..we may safely say that no scholar will again find himself able to embrace the unitarian hypothesis.

Unitarianism (juːnɪˈtɛərɪənɪz(ə)m). [f. prec. + -ism. So F. *unitarianisme*.]

1. *Theol.* Belief in or affirmation of the unity of God; esp. the tenets, principles, or views of the Unitarians; Unitarian doctrine or beliefs.

1698 F. B. *Modest Censure* 22 The Missionary Fathers have not more ways..of gaining Converts in China,..than these men have of winning over people to Unitarianism.

1792 (*title*), Reasons for Unitarianism; or the Primitive Christian Doctrine... By a Welsh Freeholder. **1815** W. J. Fox *Serm.* 39 The success of Unitarianism speaks in its favour. **1874** Huxley in *Sci. & Cult.* (1881) 94 That hypothesis respecting the Divine nature which is termed Unitarianism by its friends and Socinianism by its foes. **1876** Gladstone in *Contemp. Rev.* June 17 Considerable changes seem to have taken place in the scheme of Unitarianism.

transf. **1823** Coleridge *Table-t.* 1 Jan., The Turks have no church; religion and state are one; hence there is.. no mutual support. This is the very essence of their Unitarianism.

2. a. *Philos.* = monism 1. **b.** Any unitarian or unitary system or theory.

1891– in recent Dicts.

Uni'tarianize, *v.* [f. as prec. + -ize.]

a. *trans.* To make Unitarian. **b.** *intr.* To become Unitarian; to adopt Unitarianism. Hence **Uni'tarianized** *ppl. a.*

1846 Worcester (citing *Ec. Rev.*). **1893** J. Martineau in *Life* (1902) II. 191 For its support it depends on a people long Unitarianised.

'unitarist. [f. unitar-y + -ist.] An advocate of a unitary system of government; *spec.* a supporter of the unity of Italy.

Also, in recent use (1910), ***unitarism***.

1862 *Parthenon* 26 July 398 Was Cavour, up to the time of the treaty of Villafranca, 'Unitarist' or Federalist? **1882** *Contemp. Rev.* Sept. 465 The Constitutional Monarchists of Italy are naturally Unitarists.

unitary ('ju:nɪtərɪ), *a.* [f. unit *sb.* or unit-y[1] + -ary[1]. Cf. F. *unitaire* sb. and a., It. *unitario* sb., f. mod.L. *unitari-us* Unitarian.]

1. *Crystallography.* (See quot.)

1816 R. Jameson *Char. Min.* (ed. 2) 211 A crystal is named Unitary, when it experiences only a single decrement by one row.

2. a. Of or pertaining to, characterized by, based upon, or directed towards, unity.

1847 *Tait's Mag.* XIV. 560 The parcelled and the associative systems... With the latter the economies of unitary habitation.. might be obtained. **1871** Lowell *Study Wind.* (1886) 221 The national and unitary tendencies of the people. **1893** *Contemp. Rev.* 799 The unitary movement in the latter country [*sc.* Italy].

b. *Philos.* Of or pertaining to, proceeding from, involving, unity of being or existence. Also *absol.*

a **1842** Channing *Perfect Life* (1888) 64 Man loves the Universal, the Unchangeable, the Unitary. **1885** J. Martineau *Types Eth. Th.* I. 86 Every attempt at unitary deduction of a universe by predicamental logic. **1893** C. B. Upton *Bases Relig. Belief* 298 A unity of substance which.. connects every part with the unitary life of the whole.

3. a. Of the nature of a unit; having the separate existence or individual character of a unit. Of sounds: Simple, uncompounded.

1861 Lowell *E Pluribus Unum* Pr. Wks. 1890 V. 49 The United States are not a German Confederation, but a unitary and indivisible nation. **1875** Whitney *Life Lang.* iv. 56 We have altered their original unitary sounds. **1881** Huxley in *Nature* XXIV. 345 An indivisible unitary archæus dominating.. the parts of the organism.

b. *Philos.* Of being or personality.

1865 J. Grote *Explor. Philos.* I. 88 Whether.. we are to be considered as having a locally distributable, or on the other hand concentrated and unitary, feeling self. **1886** *Encycl. Brit.* XXI. 379/1 Indirect proofs of a universe of pure and unitary Being. *a* **1901** F. W. H. Myers *Human Personality* (1903) I. p. xxvi, Each man is at once profoundly unitary and almost infinitely composite.

c. Serving as a unit of measurement or calculation.

1889 *Sci. Amer.* LX. 304/1 A wind pressure of 1,200 pounds for the same unitary distance is allowed for.

4. a. Of or pertaining to a unit or units; esp. in *Chem.*, and *spec.* as denominating a theory or system in which the molecules of all bodies are regarded as units.

1865 Mansfield *Salts* 137 The unitary theory of the substitution of the two halves of the hydrogen of water. **1867** Bloxam *Chem.* Index 675 Unitary definitions, 256. **1880** Clemenshaw *Wurtz' Atomic Theory* 84 This was at that time—perhaps improperly—called the unitary system.

b. Of an alphabet, etc.: Consisting or composed of single letters or symbols for each sound.

1874 Ellis *Eng. Pronunciation* IV. 1338 His 'unitary' arrangement. *Ibid.* 1339 Professor Whitney's Unitary Alphabet.

c. *Arith.* A modification of the 'rule of three,' by which, the value, extent, etc., of one unit being first determined, that of any number is found by multiplication.

1877 J. Hamblin Smith *Arithmetic* 164 The Unitary Method.. is rapidly displacing the Rule of Three. **1908** Hall & Stevens *School Arith.* 135 The process is known as Reduction to the Unit, or the Unitary Method.

d. *Math.* and *Physics.* Applied to mathematical entities that in some specific way are described by or related to a ***unitary matrix***, one which when multiplied by the transpose of its complex conjugate gives the unit matrix; ***unitary group***, the group of all square unitary matrices of a given size; ***unitary symmetry***, the symmetry of a unimodular unitary group as used to relate the properties of different subatomic particles.

1908 H. Hilton *Introd. Theory Groups Finite Order* iii. 16 The substitution A is called.. unitary if $A\bar{A}' = 1$. **1935** P. A. M. Dirac *Princ. Quantum Mech.* (ed. 2) v. 111 We can now see that a unitary transformation transforms observables into observables. **1937** *Physical Rev.* LI. 109/2 The representations of the four-dimensional unitary group will characterize the multiplet systems. **1941** Birkhoff & MacLane *Survey Mod. Algebra* ix. 255 One may adopt the properties of linearity, skew-symmetry, and positiveness as the postulates for an inner product.. in an abstract vector space over the complex numbers; the space is then called a unitary space. *Ibid.*, A linear transformation T of the space is unitary if it preserves lengths $|\xi T| = |\xi|$. **1961** M. Gell-Mann in Gell-Mann & Ne'eman *Eightfold Way* (1964) i. 12 We attempt.. to treat the eight known baryons as a supermultiplet, degenerate in the limit of a certain symmetry but split into isotopic spin multiplets by a symmetry-breaking term... The symmetry is called unitary symmetry and corresponds to the 'unitary group' in three dimensions in the same way that charge independence corresponds to the 'unitary group' in two dimensions. **1969** [see Lie]. **1975** *Physics Bull.* Apr. 176/2 Strong interactions among nucleons are invariant under a group of unitary symmetry transformation which changes protons into neutrons and vice versa—the group SU(2). **1979** Cheng & O'Neill *Elementary Particle Physics* xiii. 275 The mathematical groups on which elementary particle physicists have concentrated most of their attention are.. continuous groups described by matrices U that are unitary: $U^{\dagger}U = 1$.

5. Forming a unit *with* something.

1868 Lowell *Among my Bks.* Ser. I. Wks. 1890 III. 26 [Shakespeare] seems in some strange way unitary with human nature itself.

6. Special collocations: ***unitary taxation*** (U.S.), a system of taxation by which a company or business is taxed on a proportion of its worldwide earnings, and not just on those made within the jurisdiction of the taxation authority (i.e. a State government); also ***unitary tax***.

1977 *Washington Post* 14 Aug. A8/4 Brown is moving to alleviate concerns of multinational companies over the state's 'unitary tax'. **1979** *Economist* 7 July 91/2 Unitary taxation (purists call it combined or consolidated income reporting).. hits a company not on profits made in a given state but on a percentage of the parent's total (multi-state or world-wide) income. **1984** *Miami Herald* 6 Apr. 22A/3 When the governor crawfishes out of his ill-advised unitary tax (his great tax-reform promise), the greedy ones might try to increase property taxes again.

Hence **'unitarily** *adv.*, in a unitary manner; **'unitariness, uni'tarity**, the property of being unitary.

1865 J. Grote *Moral Ideals* (1876) 27 [Must not] the plant.. have.. a sort of feeling to the extent of its unitariness of organization? **1924** *N.E.D.* s.v. *Unitary a.*, Unitarily. **1932** *Amer. Jrnl. Math.* LIV. 149 Similar unitary matrices are.. always unitarily equivalent. **1959** *Nuovo Cimento* XIII. 354 The unitarity of the S-matrix implies that it can be written in terms of a hermitian matrix A in the form $S =$ [etc.]. **1969** *Nature* 24 May 720/1 SU_2 and SU_3.. are simple unitary symmetries in which the unitarity ensures that a set of possibilities has unit probability. **1979** J. C. Polkinghorne *Particle Play* vi. 88 S-matrix theory played a valuable role in highlighting certain general properties (unitarity, crossing, analyticity) which are important aspects of relativistic quantum mechanics.

unite ('ju:naɪt, ju:'naɪt), *sb. Numism.* Also **unit.** [f. pa. pple. of unite *v.* Cf. unity[2].

Named in allusion to the Union of the Crowns under James I, coins of the original issue bearing on the obverse the inscription *Faciam eos in gentem unam* (Ezek. xxxvii. 22). The β-form is prob. due to asimilation with unit. *sb.*]

An English gold coin first issued by James I in 1604, originally current at the value of 20 shillings, and raised in 1611 to 22 shillings. Cf. broad *sb.* 4, broad-piece, and Jacobus.

Different issues of this coin were denominated the *laurel* (laurel *sb.* 4) and the *sceptre* (sceptre *sb.* 3) after the distinguishing feature of each, and these terms were also used attrib. with *unite.*

α. **1604** *Proclam. Coynes* 16 Nov., One piece of Gold of the value of Twentie shillings sterling, to be called The Vnite, stamped on the one side with our Picture formerly vsed, with this Stile [etc.]. **1611** *Proclam. Alteration Prices of Gold* 23 Nov., The piece of Gold called the Vnite [to be current] at xxij.s. **1612** R. Ricart *Maire of Bristowe's Kal.* (Camden) 65 In which purse were 100 vnites of gould, amountinge to the summe of 110[li]. **1726** S. M. Leake *Nummi Brit. Hist.* 90 A Pound weight of Crown Gold 22 Carracts fine, and two Carracts Allay into 41 l, by Tale, to wit, into Unites at 20 s. **1763** [see broad *sb.* 4]. **1898** Gertr. B. Rawlings *Story Brit. Coinage* 77 A triple unite was also coined, but at the Oxford mint only.

β. **1736** Folkes *Gold Coins* 6, 2 Ja. I. Sovereign or Units, vulgarly called Scepters. **1853** Humphreys *Coin-Coll. Man.* II. 471 The principal gold coins in the early part of the reign [of Charles I] were—the unit, or broad-piece (20 shillings), with its half and quarter.

†**b.** As the name proposed for certain silver coins (see quots.). *Obs.*

1691 Locke *Lower. Interest* Wks. 1714 II. 79 He proposes that his Silver Vnite.. should go for 75 Pence. **1695** Lowndes *Rep. Ess. Amend. Silver Coins* 62 One Piece which may be called the Sceptre or the Silver-Unite.

†**unite,** *pa. pple.* and *ppl. a. Obs.* [ad. late L. *ūnīt-us* (whence also It. *unito*, Sp. and Pg. *unido*, F. *uni*), pa. pple. of L. *ūnīre*: see the vb.] Combined or formed into one; conjoint, united. (Latterly *Sc.*)

1422 Yonge tr. *Secreta Secret.* 143 By lewte and trowthe and feyth the Pepill byth vnyette [*sic*], Citteis fulfillid, and mayntenyd lordshuppis. **1460** *Rolls of Parlt.* V. 381/2 Londes and Tenementes.. that were unyte or annexed to the same Duchie. **1542** Hen. VIII *Declar. Scots* in *Compl. Scot.* 199 Two or mo of one astate might be rulers in one countrie vnite as this Isle is. *a* **1548** Hall *Chron., Hen. IV*, 2 By the whiche mariage.. the redde Rose was vnite and joyned with the white Rose. **1605** *Play of Stucley* 1508 in Simpson *Sch. Shaks.* (1878) I. 219 That Spain and Portingale shall be unite. **1647** H. More *Song of Soul* II. App. lxxxiii, A cluster of small starres unite These Meteors some do deem. **1693** Stair *Inst.* II. ii. §18. 201 When Lands are rightly Unite or Erected in Barronies. **1721** Wodrow *Corr.* (1843) II. 595 The body of the ministers are joint and unite.

b. In attributive use.

1613 Heywood *Silver Age* III. i, My charm, Which gods and devils gave unite consent To be infract. **1632** Lithgow *Trav.* IV. 133 [He] reduced all the Empire of Greece, to a vnite tranquilitie. **1675** R. Fleming *Short Acc. Doctr. Rom. Ch.* 2 A continual visibility of the Church, as an unite body.

unite (ju:'naɪt), *v.* Also 5–6 **unyte.** [f. *ūnīt-*, ppl. stem of post-Aug. L. *ūnīre*, to join together, make one, f. *ūnus* one. Cf. une *v.*, uny *v.*]

1. *trans.* To combine or join (one or more things) *to* or *with* another or others, to bring or put together (separate or divided things), so as to form one connected or contiguous whole; to form or incorporate into one body or mass; to make or cause to be one: **a.** In non-physical connexion or union.

In early examples used as pa. t. and pa. pple. active without final *-d*: cf. prec.

1432–50 tr. *Higden* (Rolls) VI. 289 Egberte prevaylynge in that batelle, unyte to his realme the realmes of the marches. **1513** Douglas *Æneis* x. Prol. 26 Set our natur God hes to hym vnyte. **1560** Daus tr. *Sleidane's Comm.* 16 That he take no counsel to vnite Thempire to his house and posteritie. *c* **1630** Milton *At a Solemn Music* 27 Till God ere long To his celestial consort us unite, To live with him. **1651** Hobbes *Leviath.* II. xix. 96 Where the publique and private interest are most closely united. **1728** Chambers *Cycl.* s.v. *General*, By retaining only those Qualities, and uniting them into one Idea, they have another, more general Idea. **1781** Gibbon *Decl. & F.* xxviii. III. 73 A wealthy and noble senator, who united the sacred characters of pontiff and augur, with the civil dignities of proconsul of Africa. **1825** Scott *Betrothed* xix, Before the *fiançailles* had united his troth with that of Eveline Berenger. **1839** Murchison *Silur. Syst.* I. xxvi. 333, I attribute the discrepancy to my having united observations made on both flanks of the river. **1882** Mrs. Pitman *Mission L. Greece & Pal.* 174 The strongest wish of the Cretans is that they should be united to Greece.

absol. **1713** Blackmore *Creation* VII. 273 The mind.. does distinguish here, and there unite.

refl. **1818** Scott *Hrt. Midl.* xviii, Here our story unites itself with that part of the narrative which [etc.].

b. In physical connexion or union.

In quot. 1602 in figurative context.

1597 Shaks. *2 Hen. IV*, IV. i. 222 Our Peace will (like a broken Limbe vnited) Grow stronger. **1602** Marston *Antonio's Rev.* v. i, Be gratious, observation, to our sceane, For now the plot unites his scattred limbes. *a* **1700** Evelyn *Diary* 23 May 1645, The whole Chapell.. and roofe are full of precious stones united with the mouldings. **1738** Gray *Tasso* 61 The parent sun's warm powers.. In one rich mass unite the precious store. **1788** Sir J. Reynolds *Disc.* (1789) 22 Much smoothness, and uniting the colours, is apt to produce heaviness. **1800** tr. *Lagrange's Chem.* II. 46 A salt which crystallizes in small needles united together. **1846** Brittan tr. *Malgaigne's Man. Oper. Surg.* 244 Sanson made his incision.., and united the wound from before backwards. **1867** Pitt-Rivers *Evol. Culture* (1906) 67 A.. breast-piece of armour.. composed of seals' teeth, set like scales, and united with string.

refl. **1788** Lemprière *Classical Dict.* s.v. *Cælus*, Saturn.. deprived his father of the organs of generation, as he was going to unite himself to Terra.

c. To combine or amalgamate into one body; to bring together or consolidate (an army).

1591 Shaks. *1 Hen. VI*, IV. I. 164 Vnite Your Troopes of horsemen, with his Bands of foote. **1599** Hakluyt *Voy.* II. 69 The English and French, with forces and mindes vnited, sayled ouer into Africa. **1647** Clarendon *Hist. Reb.* VIII. §153 All those forces.. being united with Manchester. *Ibid.*, The King.. not believing that the enemy could be so soon united. **1802** James *Milit. Dict.* s.v. *Battle*, You should unite all your force, examine the advantage of the ground [etc.]. **1840** Thirlwall *Greece* VII. 369 [If] the forces of Greece.. had been united and well directed.

d. To join or clasp (hands), esp. in the marriage ceremony. (Cf. 2 b.)

1602 Shaks. *Ham.* III. ii. 170 Since.. Hymen did our hands Vnite comutuall, in most sacred Bands. **1817** Shelley *Rev. Islam* v. xlviii, Now unite Thine hand with mine. **1820** Scott *Monast.* xxxvii, A house of the village, where next day their hands were united by the Protestant preacher.

e. *Horsem.* To cause (a horse) to move with the hind- and fore-quarters in union or agreement. (Cf. 5 d, union *sb.*[1] 2 c, and F. *unir.*)

1884 E. L. Anderson *Mod. Horsem.* 110 To unite a horse at a walk, the rider will press his legs against the sides of the animal, and, carrying back the forces of the forehand, prevent an increase of the speed by a corresponding operation of the hand.

2. To make one in feeling or thought; to cause to agree; to combine or join (persons) together in action or interest, or for some special purpose.

1547 J. Harrison *Exhort. Scottes* h iv b, Remember (I besech you..) how that by this calling of vs into this vnitie, .. he woulde also vnite & ioyne vs in one religion. **1565** Cooper *Thesaurus* s.v. *Vnitas, In vnitatem venire*, Plin., to be vnited:.. to be no more at variance. **1593** Shaks. *2 Hen. VI*, I. i. 23 If Simpathy of Loue vnite our thoughts. **1599** [see 1 c]. **1647** Clarendon *Hist. Reb.* VIII. §84 A general who might unite all those northern counties in his service. **1649** *Nicholas Papers* (Camden) 155 The meanes to unite the heartes of all the sober Royalysts. **1709** PRIDEAUX *Lett.* (Camden) 202 His interest with the northern protestants may be of great use to unite them with the Church of England. **1791** COWPER *Odyss.* XXIV. 567 Let mutual amity ..Unite them, and let wealth and peace abound. **1817** SHELLEY *Rev. Islam* XII. xxiii, The fond and long embrace which did their hearts unite. **1857** BUCKLE *Civiliz.* I. xii. 661 Men of all tastes..were on this point united as by a common bond.

refl. **1594** HOOKER *Eccl. Pol.* I. x. §1 This was the cause of mens vniting themselues at the first in politique societies. **1648** MILTON *Ps.* lxxxiii. 19 Themselves against thee they unite And in firm union bind. **1706** PHILLIPS (ed. Kersey) s.v. *Province*, Provinces..that made a firm Alliance...by which they united themselves, so as never to be divided.

b. To join (persons) in marriage. Also *refl.*

1728 CHAMBERS *Cycl.*, *Marriage*, a..Contract, by which a Man is join'd and united to a Woman. **1871** R. ELLIS tr. *Catullus* lxiv. 21 Then did a father agree Peleus with Thetis unite him. **1882** MISS BRADDON *Mt. Royal* II. vi. 119 She wants to see the two people she loves best on earth united.

3. Of persons (or things): To have, possess, or exhibit (qualities, etc.) in union or combination; to combine (features usually regarded as distinct).

1796 H. HUNTER tr. *St.-Pierre's Stud. Nat.* I. 52 We shall seek that [specific character] of each plant.. in it's grain, which, as being the principle, must unite every thing proper for it's expansion. **1798** FERRIAR *Illustr. Sterne*, etc. ii. 38 A specimen of D'Aubigné's style, which unites the severe and the ludicrous. **1824** *Encycl. Brit. Suppl.* II. 111/1 Uniting in himself all the vices of..a Barbary despot. **1864** BRYCE *Holy Rom. Emp.* xii. (1875) 195 The Emperor..was also the East Frankish King, uniting in himself, to use the legal phrase, two wholly distinct 'persons'. **1871** FREEMAN *Norm. Conq.* xviii. IV. 143 The sons of Ealdgyth united the blood of the two greatest houses in England.

4. *intr.* Of persons, personifications, states, etc.: To enter into association, alliance, combination, or union; to join together or *with* others for some common purpose; to combine *in* some action or *to* do something; to act in concert or agreement.

1613 SHAKS. *Hen. VIII*, III. ii. 1 If you will now vnite in your Complaints,..the Cardinall Cannot stand vnder them. **1670** CLARENDON *Hist. Reb.* XIII. §58 The Presbyterians of Lancashire..nobody imagined to be..unwilling to unite and join with the royal party. **1749** FIELDING *Tom Jones* VIII. xiv, All united at last, to drive out that king. **1787** WASHINGTON *Lett.* Writ. 1891 XI. 183 Is it best for the States to unite or not to unite? **1847** MRS. A. KERR tr. *Ranke's Hist. Servia* 22 Now it was necessary that all should unite in direct conflict against a common enemy. **1890** *Retrospect Med.* CII. 343 Teachers and text-books have all united in impressing upon us the necessity of the greatest care in handling tar.

b. Of hearts or minds: To become one in feeling or sentiment. *poet.* or *rhet.*

1766 FORDYCE *Serm. Yng. Wom.* (1767) II. x. 101 With mind only can mind unite. **1781** COWPER *Ep. Lady Austen* 32 When minds, that never met before, Shall meet, unite, and part no more. **1817** SHELLEY *Rev. Islam* VI. xxxix, Few were the living hearts which could unite Like ours.

c. To join in marriage *with* another.

1755 JOHNSON, *To Join*, v.n.,..to unite with in marriage. **1866–7** BARING-GOULD *Curious Myths* (1872) 216 A man.. unites with a woman of the underground race.

5. To form one material whole or body; to become one; to be joined together, or *to* or *with* others; to combine physically; to coalesce; *spec.* in *Chem.*, to combine by chemical affinity or attraction.

1667 MILTON *P.L.* XII. 382 From my Loynes Thou shalt proceed, and from thy Womb the Son Of God most High; So God with man unites. **1690** LOCKE *Hum. Und.* II. xxiii. §26 Let but a sharp cold come, and they unite, they consolidate, these little atoms cohere. **1716** POPE *Iliad* V. 375 Where to the hip the inserted thigh unites. **1794** R. P. KNIGHT *Landscape* I. 194 To lead..the prying sight To where component parts may best unite. **1826** S. COOPER *First Lines Surg.* (ed. 5) 292 When not too severely contused, they will be found to live and unite to the surrounding parts. **1835** J. DUNCAN *Beetles* (Nat. Lib.) 213 There are two broad stripes..on each wing-case, which unite behind. **1871** A. MEADOWS *Man. Midwifery* (ed. 2) 54 The tubes.. sometimes remaining throughout single, but at other times dividing and uniting again.

(*b*) **1800** tr. *Lagrange's Chem.* I. 303 They form together a triple salt,..which proves that they exercise a reciprocal attraction, in virtue of which they unite. **1807** T. THOMSON *Chem.* (ed. 3) II. 103 In this way it [water] unites to lime. **1867** BLOXAM *Chem.* 1 Chemical attraction is the force which causes different kinds of matter to unite, in order to form a new kind of matter.

b. Of naval or military forces, etc.: To form one combined or conjoint body.

a **1700** EVELYN *Diary* 5 May 1692, The Eastern wind so constantly blowing, gave our fleete time to unite. **1748** *Anson's Voy.* I. vii. 75 The time drew near, when the squadron would be separated never to unite again.

c. Of immaterial things or in non-physical connexion.

1795 in Cruise *Digest* (1818) III. 228 Their heirship is *unitas juris*: the whole body of the coheirs, however numerous, must unite to constitute the heir. **1809** COLERIDGE *Friend* 142 The nature of the Earth and the nature of the Mind unite to make the contrary impossible. **1822** BYRON *Vis. Judgem.* lxvi, The next world; where unite All the costumes since Adam's.

d. *Horsem.* (See quot. and cf. 1 e above.)

1753 *Chambers' Cycl.* Suppl. s.v., A horse is said to *unite*, or walk in union, when, in galloping, the hind quarters follow and keep time with the fore.

u'nited, *ppl. a.* [f. prec.]

1. Put or joined together; combined, connected, made one. (Cf. also sense 4.)

1552 HULOET, Vnited, *vnitus*. **1663** BP. PATRICK *Parab. Pilgr.* xiii, They will teach those united hearts the greatest Love. **1671** MILTON *Samson* 1110 [They] durst not with thir whole united powers In fight withstand me. **1706** PRIOR *Ode to Queen* xiii, Unmov'd the Two united Chiefs abide. **1796** WITHERING *Brit. Plants* (ed. 3) I. 340 Anthers 5, narrow, united. **1804** *Gazetteer Scot.* (1806) 541 The united streams of the Dochart and Lochy. **1839** T. MITCHELL *Frogs of Aristoph.* p. xcviii, A poem at least of equal length with the Iliad and Odyssey united. **1865–6** CAYLEY *Math. Papers* (1893) VI. 9 If two points of a unicursal curve have an (*a*, *a*′) correspondence, the number of united points is = *a* + *a*′.

2. a. Of, belonging to, or produced by two or more persons, agents, or things in union or combination; conjoint, joint.

a **1586** SIDNEY *Arcadia* II. xxvi, Their united rage was now growne..to a crossing one of another. **1647** CLARENDON *Hist. Reb.* VIII. §235 They could not..support the war any longer against the united power of the rebels. **1697** DRYDEN *Virg., Georg.* IV. 242 All, with united Force, combine to drive The lazy Drones from the laborious Hive. **1797** MRS. RADCLIFFE *Italian* ix, With sudden strength, he burst from their united hold. **1820** R. PEEL in *Croker Papers* (1884) I. 177 The united voice of King, Lords, and Commons. **1847** MRS. A. KERR tr. *Ranke's Hist. Servia* 257 The united consent of all Europe would have been the most desirable. **1856** KANE *Arct. Expl.* I. xxiii. 300 Our united estimate assigned to it an elevation of from 2500 to 3000 feet. **1871** JOWETT *Plato* II. 174 Incapable of united action by reason of sedition.

b. Constituted or formed by, resulting from, the union of two or more parts or sections.

Freq. in the titles of churches, societies, etc., formed by the union or reunion of bodies or sections which had seceded or were formerly separate, e.g. United Free Church of Scotland, United Methodist Free Church, United Secession Church: cf. 4.

1697 DRYDEN *Æneis* IV. 145 One common kingdom, one united line. **1833** JAS. DAVIDSON *Brit. & Rom. Rem. Axminster* 25 Where, forming a junction with its fellow ['trackway'], the united road leads through the town. **1835** [T. JACKSON] *Man. Sects & Heresies* 112 In 1829 the two bodies were rejoined under the name of the United Secession Church. **1847** MRS. A. KERR tr. *Ranke's Hist. Servia* 284 The united army took up its position close by the mouths of the Morawa.

c. *Bot.* Of a flower (see quot. 1829).

1807 J. E. SMITH *Phys. Bot.* 396 In this genus the Pistil of the united flower scarcely produces seed. **1829** T. CASTLE *Introd. Bot.* 92 When the stamens and pistils are both, as usual, in one flower, it is called perfect or united.

d. *Horsem.* (See UNITE *v.* 1 e and 5 d.)

1884 E. L. ANDERSON *Mod. Horsem.* 139 When the horse will continue the united trot without the aid of the reins. *Ibid.*, The horse will be practised in keeping the united form at the walk.

†**3.** Forming or conferring union. *Obs.*$^{-1}$

1598 SHAKS. *Merry W.* IV. vi. 51 That you'l procure the Vicar To stay for me at Church... And in the lawfull name of marrying, To giue our hearts vnited ceremony.

4. a. Special collocations in the names of states, corporate bodies, or persons allied, associated, or joined together in a union or confederation.

United Brethren, the Moravians; ***United Colonies***, †(*a*) the four colonies which formed the New England Confederation (see CONFEDERATION 2); (*b*) the thirteen North American colonies which revolted against Great Britain and formed the original Republic of N. America (see UNION *sb.*[1] 3 c and 7 c, and cf. UNITED STATES 1 *b*); ***United Empire Loyalist***: see LOYALIST; ***United Front***, a common alliance of political groups; *spec.* in Communism: (*a*) = POPULAR FRONT; (*b*) in Chinese communism, an alliance with the Kuomintang; subsequently, a coalition of several parties in a Communist government; also *transf.*; ***United Greek***, a member of the United Greek Church (see quot. 1863), a Uniat; ***United Irishman***, a member of the Society of United Irishmen, a political association, originally formed to promote union between Protestants and Catholics, which became a separatist secret society and took part in organizing the rebellion of 1798; ***United Presbyterian***: (see PRESBYTERIAN *a.* 1 c); ***United Provinces***, the seven northern provinces of the Netherlands, allied together principally by the Union of Utrecht in 1579, and subsequently developing into the kingdom of Holland (cf. UNITED STATES 1 a).

1586 *Acts Privy Counc.* (N.S.) 190 The knowen subjectes ..of the Unyted Provinces. **1617** MORYSON *Itin.* III. 92 The States of the vnited Provinces. **1643** in Winthrop *New Eng.* (1826) II. 101 They..do..conclude that they all be..called by the name of the United Colonies of New England. **1677** W. HUBBARD *Narrative* (1865) II. 252 The Commissioners of our United Colonyes. **1702** C. MATHER *Magnalia* IV. iv. 177 It had not been so long before the Names of Presbyterian and Congregational, had been melted down into that One of United Brethren. **1775** *Pennsylv. Even. Post* 21 Dec. 587/1 Captain Coit, in an armed schooner of the United Colonies, lately chased a transport. **1777** R. WATSON *Philip II*, XXIV. II. 406 Although this event gave great satisfaction to the people subject to the Spanish government, it was not likely to produce any change in the sentiments, or conduct of their neighbours in the United Provinces. **1791** in W. Tone *Autobiog.* (1826) I. 368 We have agreed to form an association to be called 'The Society of United Irishmen'. **1799** J. ADAMS *Wks.* (1854) IX. 4 He is doubtless a United Irishman. **1837** LOVER *Rory O'More* I. x. 214 An extended palm which..exchanged with him the grip of the United Irishman. **1849** ROCK *Ch. of Fathers* I. ii. I. 90 The United or orthodox Greeks. **1863** *Chambers' Encycl.* V. 88/1 The United Greek Church comprehends those Christians who, while they..observe the general discipline of the Greek Church,..are yet united with the Church of Rome. *Ibid.*, The United Greeks. **1934** A. WERTH *France in Ferment* xiii. 277 The rank and file of the United Front and of Bergery's Front Commun are merely unhappy and disgruntled people. **1935** B. RUSSELL *Relig. & Sci.* ii. 42 The wars of religion made a 'united front' desirable. **1937** E. SNOW *Red Star over China* III. iii. 101 The building up of a United Front, such as has been advocated by the Communist Party ever since 1932. **1943** J. T. PRATT *War & Politics in China* XV. 264 Ch'iang Kai Shek ..sternly rejected the overtures of the Shensi communists who naively proposed to enter the united front as the equal allies of the Kuomintang. **1954** *Round Table* Dec. 46 United Front leaders in East Bengal. **1958** J. CANNAN *And be Villain* i. 6 That blasted Primrose will have arrived..and the old witch herself will be there... I'll have a united front to cope with. **1971** J. J. TAYLOR in D. J. Dwyer *China Now* (1974) xxii. 412 Mao's insistence on the development of an armed capability..is a reflection of the history and the experience of the Chinese Communist Party, most notably the failure in 1927 of the First United Front with the KMT and the marked Communist success with the Second United Front between 1937 and 1945. **1980** S. J. BURKI *Pakistan under Bhutto* ii. 22 The Muslim League was squarely beaten in Bengal by the United Front.

b. United Kingdom, the kingdom of Great Britain, (after the union with Ireland in 1801) of Great Britain and Ireland, or esp. (after the formation of the Irish Free State in 1921) of Great Britain and Northern Ireland. Abbrev. *U.K.*

1737 *Gentl. Mag.* VII. 609/1, I have more Reason to oppose it, than any Man in this House, nay perhaps than any Man in the United Kingdom. **1800** *Act 39 & 40 Geo. III*, c. 67. 359 The said Kingdoms of Great Britain and Ireland shall..be united into one Kingdom, by the name of The United Kingdom of Great Britain and Ireland. **1832** *Act 2 & 3 Will. IV*, c. 75 §1 That part of the United Kingdom called Great Britain, and..that part of the United Kingdom called Ireland.

c. *United Irishism*, the views or principles of the United Irishmen.

1800 W. DRENNAN in *Microscope* March 134 He fears that political and religious schism, that White-Boyism,.. Catholicism, United-Irishism may..change into Patriotism. **1844** P. HARWOOD *Hist. Irish Reb.* 120 Munster was..the only province of Ireland not deeply leavened with Defenderism or United Irishism.

d. United Nations: in the war of 1939–45, the Allied nations who united against the Axis powers; hence, an international peace-seeking organization of these and many other States, founded by charter in 1945 (in full, ***United Nations Organization***), with a permanent headquarters in New York; abbrev. *U.N.* s.v. U 4 a; cf. LEAGUE OF NATIONS; *Security Council* s.v. SECURITY 12 e; TRUSTEESHIP 2 b.

1942 *Daily Tel.* 28 Jan. 3/3 But at any rate it will be long enough for Japan to inflict..losses upon all of the United Nations who have..possessions in the Far East. **1942** H. A. WALLACE in *N.Y. Times* 9 Nov. 19/7 The first article in the international law of the future is undoubtedly the United Nations' Charter. **1944** [see *Security Council* s.v. SECURITY 12 e]. **1946** A. BOYD (*title*) The United Nations Organisation handbook. **1953** R. NIEBUHR *Christian Realism & Polit. Probl.* (1954) ii. 25 The necessarily minimal constitutional structure which we have embodied in the United Nations. **1958** *Times* 7 Aug. 7/5 It emphasizes..the case for creating a permanent United Nations police force, including an increased number of United Nations observers. **1974** P. GORE-BOOTH *With Great Truth & Respect* 141 Mrs Eleanor Roosevelt came to propose that the organization be called 'The United Nations'... I put forward a motion to the effect that we accept Mrs Roosevelt's proposal subject to a committee of jurists being satisfied that the term 'United Nations' presented no legal difficulty. **1980** *Jrnl. R. Soc. Arts* July 501/2 The *inter-governmental* component of world conservation is represented by the United Nations Environment Programme (UNEP).

u'nitedly, *adv.* [f. UNITED *ppl. a.* + -LY[2].] In a united manner; so as to be united; in union or combination, together; with agreement or concurrence of thought or action on the part of several.

1603 FLORIO *Montaigne* I. xxvii. 93 Our mindes haue jumped so vnitedly together. **1641** LD. DIGBY *Parl. Sp.* 9 Feb. 7 All the Vertue of this House, how unitedly soever collected. **1697** *State Philadelph. Soc.* 8 Though they meet ..to implore the good Spirit of God Unitedly. **1762** tr. *Busching's Syst. Geog.* V. 491 Both unitedly pay eighty-six rixdollars. **1788** *Trifler* No. 16. 214 The various pleasures and inconveniences of which..we had unitedly participated. **1835** *Fraser's Mag.* XI. 494 Our possession of power, and our belief in the truth of our own religious professions, cannot, even when taken unitedly, justify us. **1865** PUSEY *Truth Eng. Ch.* 6 To resist unitedly an inroad upon our common faith.

u'nitedness. [f. as prec. + -NESS.] The state or quality of being united; union.

1636 DRUMM. OF HAWTH. *Fam. Ep.* Wks. (1711) 151 So harmonious an Unitedness, as hath so long continued between us. **1652** BENLOWES *Theoph.* VIII. xlv, Be ever-ever-ever blest, ô Trine! Ever Unitednesse divine! **1679** KING in *Spirit of Popery* 37 Harmony and Unitedness in things. **1864** PUSEY *Lect. Daniel* viii. 498 The assurance of a deathless unbroken unitedness with God. **1894** G. GRIFFITH tr. *Fouard's St. Paul* xii. 296 An act of thanksgiving for the spirit of unitedness now restored among them.

United States.

1. The proper name or distinctive title of a confederacy, federation, or union of States.

In later use freq. construed as a singular.

a. The kingdom or republic of Holland, = the United Provinces (UNITED *ppl. a.* 4). Also *attrib.* Now *rare* or *Hist.*

1617 MORYSON *Itin.* III. 94 The Territory of Utrecht is also associated under the same United States. *c* **1622**

FLETCHER & MASSINGER *Barnavelt* v. iii, in Bullen *O. Pl.* II. 306 Do you hold the United States so tame to feare him? **1665** MANLEY *Grotius' Low C. Wars* 929 By the publick and private colloquies of the United States people. **1779** HERVEY *Nav. Hist.* II. 168 The United States, overwhelmed with the expence of the war,..were extremely desirous of an accommodation.

b. The Republic of North America. Abbrev. *U.S.* or *U.S.A.* (Cf. STATE *sb.* 31 c, d, and *United Colonies* UNITED *ppl. a.* 4 a.)

1776 *Jrnls. Continental Congress* (1906) VI. 865 Resolved, that the inhabitants of Canada, captivated by the United States..be released and sent home. **1781** J. ADAMS *Fam. Lett.* (1876) 403 You will never have peace while the Britons have a company of soldiers at liberty within the United States. **1781–8** in Bryce *Amer. Commw.* (1888) I. 569 The style of this Confederacy shall be, 'The United States of America'. **1812** EARL OF LIVERPOOL in *Examiner* 11 May 292/2 The United States had assumed a very warlike attitude. *a* **1817** T. DWIGHT *Trav. New Eng.*, etc. (1821) I. 18 The United States have been regarded by this class of men as fair game. **1888** *Encycl. Brit.* XXIII. 759/1 The United States..was anxious to establish what Great Britain was not disposed to grant.

attrib. **1819** G. FLAGG *Let.* 12 June in *Trans. Illinois State Hist. Soc. 1910* (1912) XV. 165 They settle on united States land. **1840** (*title*), United States Digest. **1843** *Penny Cycl.* XXVI. 13/2 The officers of the United States navy. **1875** JEVONS *Money* xix. 246 The United States government.

c. In other applications (see quots.).

1864 *Chambers's Encycl.* VI. 734 New Granada (since 1858 the official designation has been The Granadian Confederation, and since 1862, The United States of Colombia). **1890** *Hazell's Annual* 64/2 That the provinces of Brazil, united by federation, compose the United States of Brazil.

2. The form of English spoken in the United States of North America or regarded as distinctly American. *to talk United States*, to use strong language, to express oneself forcibly.

1891 E. ROPER *Track & Trail* ix. 134 Most of the ladies spoke decided 'United States'; one was 'Dutch',..and one ..had a decided British accent. **1898** HAMBLEN *Gen. Manager's Story* x. 134 If he made any disparaging comments..I vowed to myself that I'd talk United States to him if I lost my job by it.

Hence **United-'Statesian** *a.*, of or belonging to the United States of America; *sb.*, an inhabitant or citizen of the United States.

Also ***United Statesman*** (1850), and, in recent use, ***United Stateser***.

1892 *N. & Q.* 8th Ser. II. 146/2 To an outsider, say a Frenchman or a United-Statesian. **1897** *Westm. Gaz.* 26 Aug. 3/3 The secret of the American or rather United-Statesian race.

†**u'nitely**, *adv. Obs.* [f. UNITE *ppl. a.* + -LY².] Unitedly.

1602 LD. MOUNTJOY *Let.* in Moryson *Itin.* (1617) II. 213 The Lyst of the Forces here in Ireland, being vnitely considered. **1614** CORNWALLIS in Gutch *Coll. Cur.* I. 164 That we might all unitely..cast ourselves at his Majesty's feet. **1677** GALE *Crt. Gentiles* IV. 247 Unitie..hath all numbers in it singularly and unitely.

†**u'nitement**. *Obs.*⁻¹ [f. UNITE *v.* + -MENT.] The fact or condition of being united; union.

1631–2 N. FERRAR *Story Bks. Little Gidding* (1899) 169 The hope of better serving God and the firmer unitment [*sic*] unto him.

†**u'niteness**. *Obs.* [f. as prec. + -NESS.] Unitedness.

1639 LD. DIGBY, etc. *Lett. conc. Relig.* (1651) 132 Conformity and uniteness of minde. **1684** J. RENWICK in *Biogr. Presbyt.* (1827) II. 261 The Uniteness of my Heart unto you.

uniter (juːˈnaɪtə(r)). [f. UNITE *v.* + -ER¹. Cf. UNITOR and It. *unitore.*] One who or that which unites; a uniting agency or quality.

1587 GOLDING *De Mornay* vi. 79 The Vniter, and the thing Vnited. **1605** BACON *Adv. Learn.* I. vii. §1 Uniters of states and cities. **1633** T. ADAMS *Exp. 2 Peter* i. 7 Friendship is a great uniter. **1700** J. BROME *Trav. Eng.* 199 James.. became the Happy Uniter of the two Crowns. **1724** SWIFT *Drapier's Lett.* iv, Money..hath..been the great uniter of a most divided people. **1746** HERVEY *Medit. Flower Garden* 29 The Ocean is the grand Vehicle of Trade, and the Uniter of distant Nations. **1840** CARLYLE *Heroes* iv, The Priest.. presides over the worship of the people; is the Uniter of them with the Unseen Holy. **1852** LYNCH *Lett. Scattered* (1872) 299 How could we love God the bereaver, if He were not the uniter also?

†**u'niterable**, *a. Obs.*⁻¹ [UN-¹ 7 b.] That cannot be repeated.

1682 SIR T. BROWNE *Chr. Mor.* III. §23 To play away an uniterable life.

Uniterm (ˈjuːnɪtɜːm). *Library Science.* Also †**unit term**. [f. UNI- 2 or UNIT *sb.* (and *a.*) + TERM *sb.*] The name for a system of indexing whereby each of a series of documents is accessible through an alphabetical index of subject headings; a keyword which forms one of these subject headings.

1952 M. TAUBE in *Amer. Documentation* III. 213/2 The basic ideas of unit terms as a substitute for standard indexing for subject headings and logical combination and order as a substitute for..alphabetic cross-reference structures. **1953** —— et al. *Studies in Compar. Indexing* I. 5 We have used the name 'coordinate indexing' for this general method and the more specific name 'Uniterm System' to designate a particular manual application of coordinate indexing. **1961** T. LANDAU *Encycl. Librarianship* (ed. 2) 100/1 Co-ordinate indexing..is based on the conception of the Uniterm... In the Uniterm system each book..or other item is numbered as it is received and..it is possible to gain an approximate idea of the date of any currently-published item from its serial number. The title, salient contents, etc.,..are then analysed into fundamental terms usually of one word each. These constitute the Uniterms. **1976** *Gloss. Documentation Terms* (*B.S.I.*) 70 *Uniterm*, originally a single word selected from, and characterizing a part of the subject matter of, a document, for use in a co-ordinate indexing system. Now loosely used as a synonym for keyword or descriptor.

uniting (juːˈnaɪtɪŋ), *vbl. sb.* [f. UNITE *v.* + -ING¹.] The action of the verb; union; an instance or occasion of this.

1548 ELYOT, *Vnitas*, vnitee, vnityng or ioygnyng of two thynges or mo together. **1559** *Fabyan's Chron.* 567/2 The vnitinge of the twoo houses of Yorke and Lancaster. **1581** T. ROGERS *St. Aug. Praiers* xvi. (1597) 66 That vnspeakable.. vniting togither of thy Godhead and manhood in one person. **1615** CROOKE *Body of Man* 379 These vnitings are not alwayes after one manner. **1651** HOBBES *Leviath.* II. xxii. 122 All uniting of strength by private men. **1712** J. JAMES tr. *Le Blond's Gardening* 172 Cavities or Stones..hinders their uniting with the Ground. **1778** in Picton *L'pool Munic. Rec.* (1886) II. 211 A Bill..for the uniting the kingdom of Ireland with this kingdom. **1841** LANE *Arab. Nts.* I. 125 The uniting of two persons in marriage.

attrib. **1713** BERKELEY in *Guardian* 5 Aug., That benevolent uniting instinct implanted in human nature. **1714** in *Jrnl. Friends Hist. Soc.* (1918) 29 Truth..broke through for our..comfort, soe 'twas an Uniting time.

b. The place where two or more things unite or join. *rare*⁻¹.

1728 R. MORRIS *Ess. Anc. Archit.* 81 The Joint is..apt to discover the Grains of each Wood at the uniting.

u'niting, *ppl. a.* [f. as prec.] That unites or joins.

a **1635** SIBBES *Confer. Christ & Mary* (1656) 92 That Spirit of God..is a uniting spirit. *a* **1653** BINNING *Serm.* Wks. (1735) 11/2 Christ is the uniting Principle. **1713** BLACKMORE *Creation* VI. 420 The sportive flood..with uniting tides..wanton clasps the intercepted soil. **1817** SHELLEY *Rev. Islam* II. xlvi, Then..shall all the kinds Of evil, catch from our uniting minds The spark which must consume them. **1826** HENRY *Elem. Chem.* I. 192 When the uniting wire was perpendicularly opposite to the north pole of the suspended needle. **1895** *Athenæum* 6 July 8/3 A book of impressions without any uniting idea.

Hence **u'nitingly** *adv.*

1728 R. MORRIS *Ess. Anc. Archit.* p. iv, Inroads daily made..unitingly conspire, to destroy..its Beauties.

unition (juːˈnɪʃən). Also 6 unycion. [ad. late L. *ūnītiōn-*, *ūnītio*, n. of action f. L. *ūnīre*: see UNITE *v.* Cf. OF. *unition*, *unicion*, It. *unizione*.] The action of uniting; the fact or condition of being united; union, conjunction, junction.

†**a.** Of ecclesiastical benefices. *Obs.*

1511–2 *Act 3 Hen. VIII*, c. 17 §14 The appropriacion, unycion, or consolidacione of the same Patronage..to the seid Abbot & Convent. **1564** PARKER *Corr.* (Parker Soc.) 214 This is to require you, if upon the understanding of the matter ye shall see cause to give out such an unition [of a benefice and a chapel], to grant it. **1587** HARRISON *England* II. i. (1877) I. 21 The vnition of two [livings] in one man.

†**b.** Of material substances or bodies. *Obs.*

1543 TRAHERON *Vigo's Chirurg.* III. i. vi. 93 The curation ..is accomplisshed..by vnition, or coniunction of seperated or soundred partes. **1587** HARRISON *Desc. Brit.* in Holinshed *Chron.* I. 78/1 After whose vnition with the aforesaid water, they run on as one till they meet with the Clothie. **1613** M. RIDLEY *Magn. Bodies* 78 To cause these Magneticall bodies to..turne away, to the end that they may better..dispose themselues to a conuenient and naturall vnition. *c* **1644** W. CHAMBERLAYNE *Pharon.* II. iii. 255 Death's large gripe did take Whole troops.., and in 's march prevents The unition of unrallied regiments. **1699** *Phil. Trans.* XXI. 140 This Unition of Bones at their articulations. **1738** BRACKEN *Farriery Impr.* (1757) II. 244 Motion hinders Unition in Wounds.

c. Of abstract things, persons, etc., in non-physical or ideal union.

1584 *Leycesters Commonw.* 24 By this breach wyth Fraunce, we stand alone..wythout anie great vnition or friendship abrode. **1629** H. BURTON *Truth's Triumph* 106 That is the most singular..vnity, which consists not by vnition, but existeth by eternity. *a* **1680** GLANVILL *Sadducismus* I. (1681) 174 The unition of Spirit with Matter. **1709** T. ROBINSON *Vind. Mosaick Syst.* 21 The Seminal Forms being by a vital Unition conjoined to their Material Vehicles or Bodies. **1733** WATTS *Philos. Ess.* III. (1734) 85 The Union or rather Unition of a particular Soul and particular Body. **1816** [see UNICITY]. **1871** W. H. GILLESPIE *Argt. Being & Attrib. God* IV. iii. (ed. 5) 159 The attributes, whose unition yields us this Holiness. **1873** B. GREGORY *Holy Catholic Ch.* xvi. 187 The ultimate unition and universal inclusiveness of the Church.

d. Of man and (*to* or *with*) the Deity. Now *rare.*

Sometimes distinguished from *union* (see quot. 1681).

1635 JACKSON *Creed* VIII. 79 This part of the nature wounded..was first to bee perfectly cured, and throughly purified by personall unition to the Sonne of God. **1681** FLAVEL *Method of Grace* v. 94 There must be an unition before there can be a union with Christ. Unition is to be conceived efficiently as the work of God's spirit, joyning the believer to Christ; and union is to be conceived formally, the joyning itself of the persons together. **1782** J. BROWN *Nat. & Rev. Relig.* III. ii. 232 Christ..signified his unition of his people into one mystical body with himself. **1784** —— *Hist. Brit. Ch.* (1823) I. 343 Their regeneration and spiritual unition to him. **1845** BAILEY *Festus* (ed. 2) 323 The summit-flower of all created life Is its unition with Divinity.

'**unitism**. *rare*⁻¹. [f. UNIT *sb.* + -ISM.] = MONISM 1 b.

1850 W. SMITH *Conf. Faith* I. in *Thorndale* (1857) 488 He [*sc.* Seckendorf] would coin the term *Unitism* as a simple opposite to the generally received *Dualism*.

uni'tistic, *a.* [f. UNITY: see -IST and -IC.] Of or pertaining to, believing in, a theory of unity.

1888 T. K. CHEYNE in *Jewish Q. Rev.* Oct. 77 A unitistic critic. *Ibid.* 82 From a decided separatist [he] became as decided a maintainer of the unitistic view of the Book of Zechariah.

unitive (ˈjuːnɪtɪv), *a.* [ad. late L. *ūnītīv-us* (Quicherat), f. L. *ūnīt-*, ppl. stem of *ūnīre*: see UNITE *v.* and -IVE. Cf. F. *unitive*, *-if*, (15th c.), Sp., Pg., and It. *unitivo*.]

1. Having the property or effect of uniting; serving to unite or cause union; characterized by or involving union.

Freq. *c* 1643–*c* 1670, esp. in the writings of H. More.

1526 *Pilgr. Perf.* (W. de W. 1531) 285 b, For loue..is unityue, that is to saye, it disposeth and draweth all thynges that it ruleth, to peace & vnite. **1647** H. MORE *Song of Soul* Notes 136/2 The unitive power of the Intellect. **1660** JER. TAYLOR *Ductor* II. i. rule i. §33 That all laws which are commonly called Natural are most reasonable, they are perfective of Nature, unitive of Societies. **1678** CUDWORTH *Intell. Syst.* 162 The ground of magical fascination is one vital unitive principle in the universe.

a **1834** COLERIDGE in *Lit. Rem.* (1839) IV. 26 Christ, the head, and by his Spirit the bond, or unitive *copula* of all. **1845** J. H. NEWMAN *Ess. Developm.* 337 The very nature of a true philosophy relatively to other systems is to be polemical, eclectic, unitive. **1893** PATMORE *Relig. Poetæ* 99 Genius consists wholly in the possession of the divine faculty of synthetic or unitive apprehension.

†**b.** Of a person. *Obs. rare*⁻¹.

1651 H. MORE *Second Lash* in *Enthus. Tri.*, etc. (1656) 195 Thou art so unitive a soul, Phil,..that thou wouldst not stick to match chalk and cheese together.

c. *Anat.* Of fibres: (see quots.).

1875 HAYDEN *Dis. Heart* 31 Luton describes the fibres of the ventricles [of the heart] as common and proper. The former are the 'unitive' fibres of Gerdy. *Ibid.* 32 The posterior 'unitive' fibres pass from the posterior segments of the auriculo-ventricular zones..to the right edge of the heart.

2. Having the quality or attribute of uniting spiritually to the Deity.

a **1659** ROUS *Heav. Univ.* (1702) 160 Until that I shall arrive to the unitive union of the Father. **1675** O. WALKER *Paraphr. St. Paul* 94 The institution of the unitiue vertue of the Sacrifices. **1855** PUSEY *Doctrine of Real Presence* 312 This introduction [of the body of Christ under these species]..is not an action bringing (adductive of) the Body of Christ, nor simply unitive. **1855** BAILEY *Mystic*, etc. 58 That blessed secret, unitive and divine,..which us Ones with the heavens. **1879** L. SHEPHERD tr. *Guéranger's Liturg. Year* I. 389 This unitive power of the Eucharist.

b. *spec.* in ***unitive life, way***, etc., applied to the third and final stage of spiritual advancement.

1649 JER. TAYLOR *Gt. Exemp.* Disc. i. §9 All the eminencies and spirituall riches of the unitive life. *Ibid.* Disc. iii. §26 Concerning the very same thing which the old Divines call the unitive Way. **1687** NORRIS *Coll. Misc.* (1699) 341 Seraphic love, and this with Contemplation, makes up that which the Mystic Divines stile the Unitive way of Religion. **1716** M. DAVIES *Athen. Brit.* I. 237 The Purgative, Illuminative and Unitive Conditions of the Mind. **1749** LAVINGTON *Enthus. Meth. & Papists* (1754) 146 By the purgative and illuminating Way, she attains to the Unitive. **1830** *For. Rev. & Cont. Misc.* V. 318 The purgative, illuminative, and unitive stages of devotion. **1848** BAILEY *Festus* (ed. 3) 208 The soul..Lay lulled in glory, and in unitive Life with divinity. **1899** W. R. INGE *Chr. Mysticism* i. 10 Strictly, the unitive road (*via*) leads to the contemplative life (*vita*).

Hence '**unitively** *adv.*; '**unitiveness**.

1664 H. MORE *Myst. Iniq.* 322 The consideration of the collectiveness and unitiveness of..[these] types. **1678** CUDWORTH *Intell. Syst.* 307 Jupiter who conteineth the Vniverse, and All things within himself, Vnitively and Intellectually. *Ibid.* 582 The First of these is sometimes said to be..'All things Vnitively,' The Second..'All things Intellectually.' **1812–29** COLERIDGE in *Lit. Rem.* (1838) III. 147 The corrupt will cannot..be unitively subordinated to the reason. **1865** NEALE *Hymns Paradise* 68 Whom, embracing unitively, Thou shalt love with perfect will.

uniti'zation. [f. next + -ATION.] **1.** The joint development of a petroleum source which straddles territory controlled by several companies.

1930 *Handbk. Unitization of Oil Pools* (Mid-Continent Oil & Gas Assoc.) i. 15 The term 'Unitization' refers to the practice of unifying the ownership and control of an actual or prospective oil or gas pool by the issuance or assignment of units or undivided interests in the entire area with provision for development and operation by an agent, trustee or committee representing all holders of undivided interests therein. **1938** D. HAGER *Practical Oil Geol.* (ed. 5) ix. 263 The ideal is for one oil concern to own a whole field and to unitize the leases so that property owners are allowed a royalty on all the oil produced in proportion to their property holdings. *Ibid.*, Unitization as an ideal is fine for the oil producer. **1952** *South Western Reporter* (U.S.) CCXLIX. 917/1 Respondents suggest that the conclusion we have reached will discourage the making of unitization agreements. **1977** *Internat. & Compar. Law Q.* XXVI. 353 Discussions are already under way between Norway and the United Kingdom on the unitisation of the Statfjord oil and gas field.

2. The packaging of cargo into unit loads (see UNIT *sb.* (and *a.*) 3 c); = PALLETIZATION.

1953 *Times* 20 Jan. 2/5 Addresses will be given on ..'Packaging and air freight', and 'Packaging and unitization'. **1967** D. WILSON *Use of Expendable Pallets* 1 Since most modern handling systems of unit loads are based around the fork-lift truck there has to be a common denominator of any method of unitisation i.e. that it is capable of being lifted and moved by fork-lift truck. **1981** E. CORLETT *Revolution Merchant Shipping* 12/1 Militating against the spread of container unitisation was the lack of infra-structure.

3. Conversion of an investment trust to a unit trust (see UNIT *sb.* (and *a.*) 3 c).

1974 *Daily Tel.* 10 Aug. 17/4 The cost of unitisation 'would be high'. **1982** *Observer* 7 Feb. 20/1 Fleming..may well find that unitisation cannot be avoided in respect of some of the trusts.

ˈunitize, *v.* [f. UNIT *sb.* + -IZE.] **1.** *trans.* To form into a unit; to unite or make one.

1849 [implied in *unitizing ppl. a.* below]. **1860** WORCESTER (citing *Ch. Reg.*). **1893** J. PULSFORD *Loyalty to Christ* II. 320 [Christ] is the head of every principality and power..to subdue all things to Himself, and to unitise highest and lowest. **1939** D. HAGER *Fund. Petroleum Industry* ix. 201 The new drilling outfits are unitized, i.e., the various sections are mounted on single steel frames which are enclosed in steel cases to protect the workers from the machinery. **1962** *Engineering* 21 Sept. 369 As much as possible of each engine has been 'unitized'.

2. *techn.* In the senses of: **a.** UNITIZATION 1.

1938 D. HAGER *Pract. Oil Geol.* (ed. 5) ix. 263 The ideal is for one oil concern to own a whole field and to unitize the leases.

b. UNITIZATION 2.

1962 [see CONTAINERIZE *v.*]. **1968** *Globe & Mail* (Toronto) 13 Feb. B1/8 The parcel was not drilled, but was unitized into one of the Rainbow pools and is producing revenue prorated to the company's share of the pool's reserves. **1973** (*title*) Packing for profit 1: the economic advantages of unitising break-bulk cargo.

c. UNITIZATION 3. Also *intr.* or *absol.*

1978 *Daily Tel.* 4 Feb. 21/1 With the current average discount on investment trust shares running at around 30 p.c. there is considerable pressure from the private shareholder to unitise the trusts, which would mean a payout at the full value of the underlying investments. **1982** *Sunday Times* 7 Feb. 54/1 Robert Fleming..promised to take the question of unitising seriously.

So **ˈunitized, ˈunitizing** *ppl. adjs.*

1849 SEARS *Regeneration* III. xii. (1859) 239 The governing and unitizing principle of all endeavour. **1873** *Contemp. Rev.* XXI. 269 The rapid immediate advance of unitized societies. **1947** *Sun* (Baltimore) 23 Aug. 7 You must see the Nash '600' to realize how far into the future this big car takes you..with..girder-strong unitized body and frame. **1950** *Nucleonics* May 15/2 The fitting of unitized furniture into the laboratory is a critical consideration which must be applied to the dimensioning of all of the rooms. **1961** *Times* 22 Feb. 11/6 In the United States mechanized and 'unitized' general cargo handling is racing ahead. **1964** *Economist* 26 Sept. 1243/1 The roads have..introduced..unitised trains made up of wagons carrying one product to one customer. **1970** R. P. LOVELAND *Photomicrography* I. iii. 121 Unitized construction allows change of body tube between binocular and monocular for photomicrography. **1978** *N.Y. Times* 29 Mar. D10/5 The Institute of Mental Health, a unitized psychiatric hospital, requires a clinical psychologist PhD.

†uˈnitor. *Obs.*$^{-1}$ [f. UNITE *v.* + -OR.] = UNITER.

1602 WARNER *Albion's England* XIV. 339 Seauenth Henry, the Vnitor of those Flowers that long dissented.

ˈunitude. *nonce-word.* [f. UNI- or UNIT, after *multitude*: see -TUDE.] The character of being one.

1851 SPENCER *Soc. Stat.* 18 It hints that the first principle of a code for the right ruling of humanity in its state of multitude, is to be found in humanity in its state of unitude.

unity[1] (ˈjuːnɪtɪ). Forms: 4-6 **vnite, vnyte,** 4-7 **unite,** 5-6 **unyte;** 4 **vnitee, vnytee,** 6 **unitee;** 5 **vnytie,** 6 **unytie,** 5-6 **vnytye, vnitye,** 5-7 **vnitie,** 6-7 **unitie, vnity** (7 **vnitty**), 7- **unity.** [a. AF. *unite*, OF. *unite, uniteit* (*c* 1200), F. *unité* (= Sp. *unidad*, Pg. *unidade*, It. *unità*), or ad. L. *ūnitāt-, ūnitās* oneness, sameness, agreement, f. *ūn-us* one: see -ITY.]

I. 1. The fact, quality, or condition of being, comprising, or consisting of one in number; oneness, singleness. Freq. of the Deity, and in early use in the phr. ***in unity.***

Used *spec.* in *Philos.* and *Metaph.* to express the negation of multiplicity of being or existence; individuality, identity (see Baldwin *Dict. Philos. & Psychol.*).

a **1300** *Cursor M.* 6342 Þis wandes takens persons thre, And an-fald godd in vnite. *c* **1325** *Spec. Gy Warw.* 429 Wid þe fader, and wid þe sone, And wid þe holi gost in vnite. *c* **1380** WYCLIF *Serm.* Sel. Wks. I. 383 Two passen fro unyte. **1398** TREVISA *Barth. De P.R.* XIX. cxvi. (1495) 921 The one and vnyte of nombre..: therby is fygure and lyknesse of the vnyte of our lorde god. *c* **1532** DU WES *Introd. Fr.* in *Palsgr.* 1023 The blessed Trinite thre persones in unite. **1594** HOOKER *Eccl. Pol.* I. ii. §2 Our God is one, or rather very oneness, and meere unitie. **1606** SHAKS. *Tr. & Cr.* v. ii. 141 If there be rule in vnitie it selfe, This is not she. **1621** T. BEDFORD *Sin unto Death* 6 The singular number doth not alwayes imply an individuall vnitie. **1690** LOCKE *Hum. Und.* II. vi. §1 Amongst all the Ideas we have,..there is none more simple than that of Unity, or One. **1725** WATTS *Logic* (1736) 245 The Unity and Spirituality of the Godhead. **1766** BLACKSTONE *Comm.* II. 433 The notion of an unity of person between the husband and wife. **1844** KINGSLEY *Lett.* (1878) I. 117 Perfect unity in extreme multiplicity. **1864** BOWEN *Logic* ix. 292 A question often involves a real duplicity under a seeming unity. *a* **1881** A. BARRATT *Phys. Metempiric* (1883) 106 *A priori* a spacial principle of unity seems as reasonable as a temporal.

b. *Math.* The condition of the unit or number one; the numeral one regarded abstractly as the basis of number in reckoning or calculation.

1570 BILLINGSLEY *Euclid* VII. i. 184 Vnitie is that, whereby euery thing that is, is sayd to be on. **1657** HOBBES *Absurd Geom.* 2 The excess of the rising proportion above subtriple is the same which unity hath to the six times the number of termes after 0. **1709-29** V. MANDEY *Syst. Math., Arith.* 6 Unity measures every number by the number itself; so 1 measures 7 by 7. **1831** BREWSTER *Optics* iv. 28 Take 1 part or unity from the same scale. **1869** J. H. SMITH *Elem. Algebra* 50 The quotient is unity when the Dividend and the Divisor are equal. **1885** WATSON & BURBURY *Math. Th. Electr. & Magn.* I. 232 Taking unity as the combining number for hydrogen.

c. A quantity, magnitude, or substance regarded as equivalent to the number one in calculation, measurement, or comparison.

1728 CHAMBERS *Cycl.*, *Measure*, in Geometry, any certain Quantity assumed as one, or Unity, to which the Ratio of other..Quantities is express'd. **1797** *Encycl. Brit.* (ed. 3) XVII. 659/1 The most convenient way..would be to consider the weight of the standard as unity. **1801** *Monthly Rev.* XXXV. 525 The ten millionth part of the..distance..was taken as the unity of measure. **1816** PLAYFAIR *Nat. Phil.* II. 287 If the mass of Jupiter be supposed unity. **1836** BRANDE *Chem.* (ed. 4) 220 Others adopt oxygen as unity, in which case hydrogen becomes one-eighth of that unit. **1880** HAUGHTON *Phys. Geog.* iii. 138 If we call the Gulf Stream unity, we may form an approximate estimate of the other four systems of circulation.

2. An instance of this: **†a.** = UNIT *sb.* 1. *Obs.*

c **1425** *Craft Nombrynge* (E.E.T.S.) 22 Reken ten for on vnite. *Ibid.* 28 Loke how mony vnityes ben in þe nounbre þat comes of þe multiplicacioun of þe 2 digittes. **1543** RECORDE *Arith.* 119 b, In that place of vnities dothe appere only 7. **1587** FLEMING *Contn. Holinshed* III. 1490/2 The residue.. being multiplied by vnities, doo make vp the complet number of three score and twelue. **1630** WINGATE *Arith.* I. i. 15 The Integers, or intire Vnities. **1669** STURMY *Mariner's Mag.* III. ii. 129 Because the Angle CAB is a Right Angle,.. I therefore only put an Unity before the second Term. **1837** WHEWELL *Hist. Induct. Sci.* I. 250 His objections to geometry and arithmetic are founded on abstract cavils concerning the nature of points, letters, unities.

b. One separate or single thing, quality, etc.; something which is complete or entire in itself, or is regarded as such.

1587 GOLDING *De Mornay* ii. 16 The foresayd most single and alonly One, abyding still one in it selfe, bringeth foorth all the other vnities. **1598** MARSTON *Sco. Villanie* I. iv. (1599) 187 Sylenus now is old, I wonder, I, He doth not hate his triple venerie... Me thinkes a vnitie were competent. *a* **1600** EDMONDS *Observ. Cæsar's Comm.* 38 The life and strength of a multitude consisteth in vnities. **1681** *Whole Duty Nations* 7 He himself is the prime Unity and Universality. **1828** CARLYLE *Misc.* (1840) I. 319 The clear view of it as an indivisible Unity. **1847** EMERSON *Repr. Men, Swedenborg* ¶17 The unities of each organ are so many little organs, homogeneous with their compound. **1889** MIVART *Orig. Hum. Reason* 46 They are apprehensions of abstract qualities grouped round a unity.

II. 3. The quality or condition of being one in mind, feeling, opinion, purpose, or action; harmonious combination together of the various parties or sections (*of* the Church, a state, etc.) into one body; concord or harmony amongst several persons or between two or more.

In the usage with *a* (†*an*) the meaning tends to become concrete (see (*b*)).

c **1325** *Poem temp. Edw. II* (Percy) xxii, Among men of religioun Is non unite. *c* **1380** WYCLIF *Serm.* Sel. Wks. II. 226 Þis unite shulden men have bi þe lore of Jesus Crist, and þanne shulden þei be of o wille. *c* **1425** WYNTOUN *Cron.* IX. viii. 942 That tyme at Bulone..Wes a tretis of vnyte Betuix þe Franche and Inglismen. **1460** CAPGRAVE *Chron.* (Rolls) 294 Be this mene was the unite of the Cherch lettid. **1560** DAUS tr. *Sleidane's Comm.* 123 The Germains within them selues shold..come to some vnitie & concord. **1590** GREENE *Never too late* (1600) 42 Vnitie is the essence of amitie. **1606** SHAKS. *Tr. & Cr.* I. iii. 100 The vnity and married calme of States. **1647** TRAPP *Comm. Rom.* xv. 6 (1656) 652 It is recorded to the high commendation of the Church of Scotland, that for this 90 years and upwards they have kept unity. **1738** WESLEY *Ps.* CXXXIII. i, When Brethren all in One agree; Who knows the Joys of Unity! **1776** PAINE *Com. Sense* 49 'Tis not in numbers but in unity that our great strength lies. **1830** D'ISRAELI *Chas. I*, III. v. 62 Laud.. contemplated establishing unity by uniformity. **1854** MILMAN *Lat. Chr.* IV. iv. II. 99 No sooner has Anglo-Saxon Britain become one (no doubt her religious unity must have contributed..to her national unity) than [etc.]. **1878** STUBBS *Const. Hist.* III. xviii. 221 The king's death at once broke up the unity of the Court.

(*b*) **1460** CAPGRAVE *Chron.* (Rolls) 120 Edgare..mad a very unite of all the vii. kyngdammes. *a* **1466** *Hist. Coll. Cit. Lond.* (Camden) 116 The same yere..the general conselle was endyd, and a unyte made in Hooly Chyrche, and oo pope chosynne. *a* **1500** *Bale's Chron.* in *Six Town Chron.* (1911) 145 The king..and divers lordes..agreed and ther made a full unyte and peas betwene the dukes of york and somerset. **1577** HOLINSHED *Chron.* I. 286/2 Diuerse offers were made on both partes..for an vnitie to haue beene had betwixte the two Princes.

b. Freq. in adverbial phr. ***at*** or †***in unity,*** in agreement, concord, or harmony; at one.

c **1374** CHAUCER *Troylus* III. 29 Ye holden regne and hous in vnite. **1390** GOWER *Conf.* III. 194 So schal I live in unite With every man. *c* **1430** LYDG. *Lyke thyn Audience* i, Yf yow wilt lyffe in pease and vnite. *c* **1450** BURGH *Secrees* 1520 These Sustrys Cheyned in parfight vnyte, departe may not by natural resoun. **1535** COVERDALE *Ps.* cxxi, Ierusalem is buylded as a cite, that is at vnitie in it self. *a* **1619** FOTHERBY *Atheom.* II. x. §4 (1622) 308 An Vnity is alwayes at vnitie with it selfe, and neuer varieth from it selfe. **1662** PLAYFORD *Skill Mus.* I. v. 18 To guide his Voyce in unity to the sound of the Instrument. **1671** BAXTER *Holiness* lxiv. 18 It plainly sheweth that they are very much at unity in the main. **1714** in *Jrnl. Friends Hist. Soc.* (1918) 27 Leaving our family and friends in great love and Unity. **1768** STERNE *Sent. Journ.*, *Dwarf*, The old French officer would have set me at unity with myself. **1825** *Q. Rev.* XXXII. 369 No Italian city or state was at unity in itself. **1871** JOWETT *Plato* I. 56 The bad ..are never at unity with one another or with themselves.

c. Agreement or accord between things.

1393 LANGL. *P. Pl.* C. IV. 338 As adiectif and substantyf vnite asken, Acordaunce in kynde, in cas and in numbre. *Ibid.* 398. **1593** SHAKS. *Lucr.* 1558 These contraries such unity do hold, Only to flatter fools and make them bold. **1611** —— *Wint. T.* v. ii. 35 There is such vnitie in the proofes.

†d. Agreement or concurrence *with* something.

1760 J. WOOLMAN *Journal* vii. (1900) 146 Some Friends.. expressed their willingness to have it read; which being done, many expressed their unity with the proposal.

4. The fact of forming or being united into one body or whole; union (of two or more persons or things, or of one *with* another); rarely, physical union or connexion; †conjunction of two or more things.

1387 TREVISA *Higden* (Rolls) V. 9 By tokene þe onynge and þe unite of Crist and of holy chirche. **1472-3** *Rolls of Parlt.* VI. 23/1 Entierly desiryng..the unyte of the nobles and other his subgettes. **1483** CAXTON *Gold. Leg.* 255 b/2 The unyte and assemble of the flesshe of oure lord and of oure lady. **1565** ALLEN *Defence Purg.* xvii. 283 Which forme of argument serued the Arians against the consubstantiall vnitye of God the father, and his son our sauiour. **1578** TIMME *Calvin on Gen.* 76 Herein we see a true image of our unitie with the Son of God. **1597** A. M. tr. *Guillemeau's Fr. Chirurg.* 11/2 The synnuish filamentes which have a vnitye and fastening with the Pericranium. **1611** TOURNEUR *Ath. Trag.* I. ii, The unitie of Families is a worke of loue and charitie. **1651** HOBBES *Leviath.* II. xvii. 87 This is more than consent, or concord; It is a reall Unitie of them all, in one and the same Person. **1796** BURKE *Regic. Peace* i. 43 In this unity and indivisibility of possession are sunk ten..wealthy provinces. **1801** HAMILTON *Wks.* (1886) VII. 186 They have approved the unity of the legislative power in one branch. **1871** R. W. DALE *Commandm.* i. 23 That our Lord claimed for himself a mysterious unity with the Father. **1880** J. CAIRD *Philos. Relig.* v. 157 The unity of subject and object ..is implied in every act of thought.

†b. A meeting or assembly of people. *Obs.*$^{-1}$

a **1470** HARDING *Chron.* CLXXXVII. ii, In cytees al he helde wel vnitees, Great iustes ay, and ioyous tournementes.

c. A body formed by union, esp. ***the Unity of the*** (Moravian) ***Brethren.*** In later quots. *ellipt.*

1780 LA TROBE tr. *Cranz's Hist. Brethren* 67 Twenty-four ministers of the Unity of the Brethren. *Ibid.* 353 Every actual member of the Unity that is desirous of taking the benefit of this act. **1814** WM. BROWN *Hist. Propag. Christianity* II. 124 This, by the synods of the Brethren's church, is vested solely in the Elders' Conference of the Unity. **1865** J. GILL *Banished Count* xxv. 262 The affairs of the Unity called the Count..to the Continent.

5. The quality or fact of being one body or whole, esp. as made up of two or more parts; an undivided whole, as distinct from its parts.

1390 GOWER *Conf.* I. 37 If a man were Mad al togedre of o matiere Withouten interrupcioun, Ther scholde no corrupcioun Engendre upon that unite. **1398** TREVISA *Barth. De P.R.* v. ii. (Bodl. MS.), Yf the vertu is ilette..þe vnyte & ioynyng of alle þe body to falleþ. **1533** GAU *Richt Vay* (S.T.S.) 57 He is wordine man and sua is spousit with the halie chrissine kirk in to ane body the quhilk vnite S. Paul..callis ane greit halie secreit thing [etc.]. **1583** MELBANCKE *Philotimus* P iv b, The coniunction of manye in an vniforme vnitie. **1813** SHELLEY *Q. Mab* IV. 144 Every grain Is sentient both in unity and part. **1850** ROBERTSON *Serm.* Ser. III. iv. (1857) 57 In proportion as you rise from lower to higher life, the parts are more distinctly developed, while yet the unity becomes more entire. **1875** JOWETT *Plato* (ed. 2) V. 69 [Plato] does not insist, as in the Protagoras, on the unity of the virtues.

†6. The quality of being of one kind; uniformity of substance or appearance. *Obs.*

1638 JUNIUS *Paint. Ancients* 119 To vary the unitie of a stone by inserting such spots into the crust as were not by nature.

7. As a literary or artistic quality:

a. Agreement of the various parts of which something is composed so as to form a whole which exhibits singleness of design or effect; combination or arrangement which produces this, or the effect so produced.

1712 ADDISON *Spect.* No. 267 ¶3 Aristotle himself allows, that Homer has nothing to boast of as to the Unity of his Fable. **1756** J. WARTON *Ess. Pope* I. iii. 101 Horace observed a strict method, and unity of design, in his epistle to the Pisones. **1783** BLAIR *Lect.* I. 216 The second quality of a well-arranged sentence, which I termed its Unity. **1808** L. MURRAY *Eng. Gram.* I. 430 But most of all, in a single sentence, is required the strictest unity. **1864** PUSEY *Lect. Daniel* i. 11 Amid apparent want of unity on the surface of the Book, there is a real unity in the whole, resting on the unity of the plan of the writer. **1874** R. TYRWHITT *Sketch. Club* 272 Unity in a picture is the sympathy of its groups or parts.

b. One or other of the three principles of the Aristotelian canon of dramatic composition as adopted and expanded by the French classical dramatists, according to which a play should consist of one main action, represented as occurring at one time (i.e. one day) and in one place. Also in loose application.

1668 DRYDEN *Ess. Dram. Poesy* Ess. (Ker) I. 38 The famous Rules, which the French call *Des Trois Unitez*, or, the Three Unities, which ought to be observed in every regular play. [**1682** SHEFFIELD (Dk. Buckhm.) *Ess. Poetry* 12 The Unites of Action, Time, and Place.] **1712** ADDISON *Spect.* No. 267 ¶2 Homer to preserve the Unity of his Action hastens into the Midst of Things. **1789** BELSHAM *Ess.* I. ii. 18 The diction of these plays is lofty,..the unities strictly preserved. **1816** SCOTT *Old Mort.* xxxvii, It is fortunate for tale-tellers that they are not tied down like theatrical writers to the unities of time and place. **1859** TROLLOPE *Bertrams* xvi, Two years..; it is a terrible gap in a story, but in these days the unities are not much considered. **1878** O. W. HOLMES *Motley* iv. 24 A series of incidents..flung together with no more regard to the unities than [etc.].

transf. **1821** LAMB *Elia* I. *My Relations*, Nature hath her unities, which not every critic can penetrate.

c. *transf.* (See quot.)

1861 WHYTE MELVILLE *Good for Nothing* xvi, Those functionaries in white hats and red waistcoats, who with singular attention to 'the unities,' adopt the very colours of the Post-office Directory and Court Guide.

8. Freedom from or absence of diversity or variety; unvaried nature *of* (some quality or thing).

Not always clearly distinct from sense 1.

1802 PALEY *Nat. Theol.* xx. (1819) 314 What we have first to notice is unity of purpose under variety of expedients. **1824** MISS MITFORD in L'Estrange *Life* (1870) II. ix. 176 ['Our Village'] is..a series of sketches..with some story intermixed, and connected by unity of locality, and of purpose. **1841** MYERS *Cath. Th.* III. §48. 184 Amidst all this variety, what unity of spirit and of aim is there in the Bible! **1884** F. TEMPLE *Relat. Relig. & Sci.* vi. 164 The unity of plan..pervading any great class of animals..seems to point to unity of ancestry.

b. Singleness of aim, purpose, or action.

1836 HOR. SMITH *Tin Trump.* I. 5 There is a simplicity and unity in despotism which is not without its advantages. **1848** W. H. KELLY tr. *L. Blanc's Hist. Ten Y.* II. 176 The grand principle of unity in power. **1866** GEO. ELIOT *F. Holt* i, She had thought that the possession of this child would give unity to her life.

9. *Law.* (See quots.)

1607 COWELL *Interpr.*, *Vnitie of possession*,..in the Ciuill lawe,..a ioynt possession of two rights by seuerall titles. **1691** BLOUNT *Law. Dict.* s.v. *Possession*, If the Lord purchase the Tenancy held by Heriot service, the Heriot is extinct by Unity of Possession. **1766** BLACKSTONE *Comm.* II. 180 The properties of a joint estate are derived from it's unity, which is fourfold; the unity of interest, the unity of title, the unity of time, and the unity of possession. **1818** CRUISE *Digest* (ed. 2) III. 104 It was held clearly that this common was extinguished by the unity of possession. **1858** LD. ST. LEONARDS *Handy-bk. Prop. Law* xxv. 189 Unity of possession—that is, where the land and the right exercised over it are in the same person.

† **'unity²**, obs. var. of or error for UNITE *sb.*

1604 in Rymer *Fœdera* (1715) XVI. 605/2 One Peece of Gold.., to be called The Unitie. **1643** BAKER *Chron., Jas. I*, 147 Ordayning the peice called the Vnity..to bee currant now for two and twenty.

Univ ('ju:nɪv), colloq. abbrev. of UNIVERSITY *sb.* 1; *spec.* University College (Oxford, etc.) Cf. UNI.

1896 F. W. MAITLAND *Let.* 6 Dec. (1965) 153 We have several good MSS at the Univ. Lib. **1903** FARMER & HENLEY *Slang* VII. 256/1 *Univ*, *subs.* (Oxford University), University College. **1950** M. MARPLES *University Slang* 131 *Oxford colleges*... *University*: always *Univ* nowadays, but apparently *Varsity* during the second half of the last century.

univalent (ju:nɪ'veɪlənt, ju:'nɪvələnt), *a.* and *sb.* *Chem.* [f. UNI- + L. *valent-em*, pr. pple. of *valēre* to be worth.] **A.** *adj.* **1.** Having a valency of one; having the combining power of one atom of hydrogen or other radical.

Also, in recent Dicts. (1891-), *univalence*, *univalency*.

1869 *Eng. Mech.* 19 Nov. 222/1 A univalent body can only join its single atom to a single atom of a univalent body. **1872** WATTS *Dict. Chem.* VI. 243 Chlorine is univalent in argentic chloride. **1893** *19th Cent.* Aug. 249 Each atom of potassium ..is univalent, and has the same valency as one atom of hydrogen.

2. *Cytology.* (ju:'nɪvələnt). [ad. mod.L. *univalens* (introduced in Ger. by O. Hertwig 1890, in *Arch. f. mikrosk. Anat.* XXXVI. 6).] Of a chromosome: remaining unpaired during meiosis. Cf. MONOVALENT *a.* 3.

1898 *Zool. Jahrb.* (Abt. für Anat.) XII. 79 The chromosomes of the 1st reduction division are univalent, when they occur in the normal number. **1916** *Jrnl. Morphol.* XXVII. 226, I believe he [*sc.* Haecker] is wrong in thinking that the 'univalent' chromosomes making up these 'bivalents' are to be considered as members of homologous chromosome pairs. **1971** *Nature* 19 Feb. 570/2 Many authors have reported that the behaviour of univalent chromosomes at meiosis is irregular. **1981** *Jrnl. Cell Biol.* LXXXVIII. 281 During meiosis I in males of the mole cricket *Neocurtilla* (*Gryllotalpa*) *hexadactyla*, the univalent X_1 chromosome and the heteromorphic X_2Y chromosome pair segregate nonrandomly.

3. *Immunol.* = MONOVALENT *a.* 2 b.

1939 *Bacteriol. Rev.* III. 76 If Hooker and Boyd now believe antibody to be univalent they must abandon the entire basis for these and other of their calculations. **1940** *Jrnl. Exper. Med.* LXXI. 271 Antibody is referred to as low grade, incomplete, imperfect, or 'univalent' in instances in which it is incapable by itself of precipitating with added antigen. **1977** M. W. STEWARD in Glynn & Steward *Immunochemistry* vii. 245 There are several reports which show the reduction in neutralization of both animal viruses ..and bacteriophages..when univalent antibodies have been used.

B. *sb.* *Cytology.* (ju:'nɪvələnt). A univalent chromosome.

1912 *Jrnl. Exper. Zool.* XIII. 350 In the first division the X- and Y-chromosomes divide as separate univalents. **1921** *Ann. Bot.* XXXV. 173 These chromosomes were of two types, as revealed during meiosis, fourteen being bivalents and twenty-one univalents. **1971** *Nature* 19 Feb. 570/2 In the triploid species *Leucopogon juniperinus* univalents are close to the poles at metaphase, but..they are not in the same plane as the spindle on which the bivalents are positioned.

univalve ('ju:nɪvælv), *a.* and *sb.* *Nat. Hist.* [See UNI- and VALVE *sb.*¹ Cf. F. *univalve* (1752), It. and Pg. *univalve*, It. and Sp. *univalvo*, mod.L. *univalvis*.]

A. *adj.* **a.** *Conch.* Of molluscs: Having a shell consisting of one valve. Of shells: Composed of a single valve or piece.

1661 LOVELL *Hist. Anim. & Min.* A 7 b, Fishes, which.. are, turbinate,..bivalve,..or univalve. **1752** J. HILL *Hist. Anim.* 115 The first [series of shellfish] containing those formed of only one piece; this I shall call the simple ones; others have called them univalve ones. **1774** *Phil. Trans.* LXV. 46 The smallest univalve or testaceous animal of any such kind. **1816** W. SMITH *Strata Ident.* 27 Bivalve shells [are] most common to the thick beds; univalve to the thin. **1851** G. F. RICHARDSON *Geol.* viii. 230 When they have a shell it is thin, fragile, and univalve. **1872** W. S. SYMONDS *Rec. Rocks* vi. 181 A univalve mollusk.

b. *Ent.* Having one valve.

Also in recent use in *Zool.* and *Bot.*

1826 SAMOUELLE *Direct. Collect.* 54 Proboscis [of *Diptera*] (rarely wanting) univalve.

B. *sb.* *Conch.* A univalve mollusc or shell.

1668 WILKINS *Real Char.* 129 Venus Shell..being of near affinity to the Univalvs. **1683** *Phil. Trans.* XIV. 507 Distinction of shells into Univalves, Bivalves, and Turbinated. **1755** *Gentl. Mag.* XXV. 32/2 When a shell, therefore, is found to be a Univalve. **1785** *Phil. Trans.* LXXV. 342 The univalves..have the intestine reflected back. **1832** LYELL *Princ. Geol.* II. 110 Aquatic univalves usually attach their eggs to leaves and sticks. **1854** KINGSLEY *Lett.* (1878) I. 411 The crevices of the highest rocks..have their peculiar little univalves. **1879** tr. *Sempter's Anim. Life* 41 Animals..as low in the scale as the Amphibia or Univalves.

Hence **uni'valved**, **uni'valvular** *adjs.*, *Bot.* having or consisting of one valve.

Also, in recent Dicts. (1891-), *univalvate*.

1823 CRABB *Technol. Dict.*, **Univalved*,..one-valved; an epithet for a pericarp. **1857** A. GRAY *First Less. Bot.* (1866) 235 *Univalved*, a pod of only one piece after dehiscence. **1793** MARTYN *Lang. Bot.*, *Folliculus*,..a follicle, a *univalvular pericarp. **1830** LINDLEY *Nat. Syst. Bot.* 294 Those species of Panicum whose outer flower is univalvular. **1849** BALFOUR *Man. Bot.* §530 The pericarp becomes divided into different pieces, which are denominated valves, the fruit being univalvular, bivalvular,..&c. according as there are one, two, or many valves.

universal (ju:nɪ'vɜ:səl), *a.* (*adv.*) and *sb.* Forms: α. 4-5 vni-, 5 unyuersel, 4 universiel (-uersele). β. 4-5 uny-, 5-6 vnyuersal, 5 -all, 4-7 vniuersal (5 -ale, -versale), 6-7 -all, vniversal(l, 5-6 universalle, 6 -ersalle, 6-7 uniuersal(l; 4, 6- universal. See also VARSAL *a.* and VERSAL *a.* [a. OF. *universel*, *universal* (12-13th c.; F. *universel*, = It. *universale*, Sp. and Pg. *universal*), or ad. L. *ūniversāl-is* (post-Aug.), f. *ūniversus*: see UNIVERSE and -AL¹. The sb. occurs in OF. *universal* (1372), in F. (17th c.) in pl. *universaux* universals (see B. 1), F. *universel* (16th c.) the universe, It. *universale*.

Early examples in verse exhibit stressing on the second or fourth syllable.]

A. *adj.* **1. a.** Extending over, comprehending, or including the whole of something specified or implied; prevalent over all.

Contexts in which the reference is to the whole of a particular community are numerous, esp. in groups b and c.

Freq. the adj. develops a more or less specialized sense, as in *universal grammar*, *root*, *succession*; see also 14.

*c***1374** CHAUCER *Boeth.* v. pr. iv. (1868) 165 Resoun surmounteth ymaginacioun and comprehendeþ by an vniuersel lokynge þe commune spece þat is in þe singuler peces. *c***1386** —— *Pars. T.* ¶292 His contricioun...shal been vniuersal [*Camb. MS.* vnyuersel] and total, this is to seyn, a man shal be verray repentaunt for alle hise synnes. **1390** GOWER *Conf.* III. 77 Ther felle wondres many on Of terre-mote universiel. **1398** TREVISA *Barth. de P.R.* (W. de W. 1495) II. xii. 39 By an vnyuersall excellence the hygher angellis ben areryd aboue a subieccion. **1555** EDEN *Decades* (Arb.) 45 Of the vniuersall carde and newe worlde. *Ibid.* 211 After my vniuersall description of the historie of the Indies. **1557** RECORDE *Whetst.* Rr iij b, These rootes therefore bee called vniuersalle rootes, because thei are the rootes..of the whole compounde nomber. **1597** BLUNDEVIL *Exerc.* III. I. xv. (ed. 2) 150 The Moone..cannot shadow all the Earth, and therefore the Eclipse of the Sunne cannot be vniuersall. **1630** J. TAYLOR (Water P.) *Jack a Lent* Wks. 118/1 The knauery of the Baker is vniuersal, in Asia, Europa, Afrike, and America. **1647** CLARENDON *Hist. Reb.* I. §32 The loudest and most universal rejoycing over the whole Kingdom. **1697** DRYDEN *Æneis* VIII. 194 What further force can stay The victor troops from universal sway? **1736** BUTLER *Anal.* II. vi, As neither the iewish nor christian Revelation have been universal. **1751** HARRIS *Hermes* Wks. (1841) 120 How few, then, must be those who know grammar universal; that grammar which..only respects those principles that are essential to them all? **1765-8** ERSKINE *Inst. Law Scot.* III. viii. §1 This kind of succession is called universal; and may be defined, the right of an heir or executor to enter upon the estate which belonged to a person deceased at the time of his death. **1784** COWPER *Task* IV. 204 The slope of faces.. Relax'd into an universal grin. **1822** BYRON *Vis. Judgem.* xxvii, The gate flew Asunder, and the flashing of its hinges Flung over space an universal hue Of many-colour'd flame. **1860** TYNDALL *Glac.* I. i. 226 This is now the universal belief. **1891** FARRAR *Darkn. & Dawn* xxiv, The day was kept as a universal holiday.

b. Affecting or involving the whole of something specified or implied; *spec.* in *Path.* (see quot. 1876).

*c***1412** HOCCLEVE *De Reg. Princ.* 2295 Gretter cheerte He hadde of the profet vniuersel Than of hym self. *a***1425** tr. *Arderne's Treat. Fistula*, etc. 64 Without dout it schal cure perfitely, vniuersale purgacions goyng afore. *a***1475** ASHBY *Active Policy* 772 The vniuersal And the comyn wele of this Region. **1542** BOORDE *Dyetary* xxxvi. (1870) 297 They the whiche haue the Palsye, vnyuersall or pertyculer, must beware of anger. **1560** DAUS tr. *Sleidane's Comm.* 108 The Emperour doth establyshe a vniuersall peace throughout Germany. **1611** SHAKS. *Wint. T.* v. ii. 100 If all the world could haue seen't, the Woe had beene vniuersall. **1656** EARL MONM. tr. *Boccalini's Advts. fr. Parnass.* II. vi. (1674) 140 In Germany, and in universal concerns, there appears but one only Commonwealth.., but many in particulars. **1697** DRYDEN *Virg. Georg.* III. 827 At length [Tisiphone] strikes an Universal Blow; To Death at once whole Herds of Cattle go. **1734** POPE *Ess. Man.* IV. 114 God sends not ill; if rightly understood, Or partial Ill is universal Good. **1754** SHERLOCK *Disc.* (1759) I. 11 Are you alone exempt from this common, this universal Blindness? **1826** DISRAELI *V. Grey* VI. i, The battle was general, the overthrow universal. **1876** DUHRING *Dis. Skin* 52 When an eruption involves the whole surface, it is said to be universal. **1878** BROWNING *La Saisiaz* 44 What a preferable state were universal happiness?

c. Proceeding from the whole body or number; committed, given, made, etc., by all without exception of the persons to whom there is reference or allusion.

1586 DAY *Eng. Secretary* II. (1625) 41 The vniuersall sentence of the whole boord. **1611** CORYAT *Crudities* 627 The vniuersall suffrage of all the learned. **1663** BP. PATRICK *Parab. Pilgr.* xxxviii, His title and claim unto our universal obedience. **1687** A. LOVELL tr. *Thevenot's Trav.* II. 30 Baron ..discharged that Office [of Consul] with honour and universal Approbation. **1701** SWIFT *Contests Nobles & Comm.* v, For a house of commons to lose the universal favour of the numbers they represent. *a***1800** COWPER *Odyss.* (ed. 2) xxiv. 598 Forefathers, whose exploits Have shared so long, such universal praise. **1844** H. H. WILSON *Brit. India* III. 432 An almost universal insurrection of the Bhils. **1871** FREEMAN *Norm. Conq.* xvii. IV. 91 The English visitors were the objects of universal attention, of universal admiration. **1871** JOWETT *Plato* II. 185 The universal voice of mankind is saying that [etc.].

†**d.** Applied to the whole body. *Obs.*⁻¹

1725 *Fam. Dict.* s.v. *Fomentation*, A Bath is universal, and therefore never made use of to Horses, because of their large Size.

2. a. Qualifying (in senses 1 and 1 a) agent-nouns, personal designations, or titles; freq. in ***universal bishop***, esp. (now *Hist.*) as a title assumed by or given to some of the Popes.

*c***1380** *Antecrist* in Todd *Three Treat. Wyclif* 118 Oo bischop þat wole be clepid vnyuersal bischop. **1483** CAXTON *Cato* a ij b, God is the unyuersal commaunder of alle our production. **1552** ABP. HAMILTON *Catech.* (1884) 38 The universal Lord of all this world. **1582** T. W[ILCOX] *B. de Loque's Disc. Ch.* 73 Saint Peter was not an vniuersall Apostle, nor a soueraigne and high bishoppe ouer all the Churche. **1606** SHAKS. *Ant. & Cl.* III. xiii. 71 To heare frome me you had..put your selfe vnder his shrowd, the vniuersal Landlord [*sc.* Julius Cæsar]. **1632** LITHGOW *Trav.* x. 474 Boniface the third obtained of Phocas..to be called vniuersall Bishop. **1667** MILTON *P.L.* III. 317 Here shalt [thou] Reigne Both God and Man,..Anointed universal King. **1728** CHAMBERS *Cycl.* s.v. *Oecumenical*, Supposing the Title *Oecumenic* to imply Universal Bishop, or Bishop of all the World. **1784** COWPER *Task* VI. 449 The universal Father's love. **1818** SHELLEY *Homer's Hymn to Earth* I O universal Mother, who dost keep From everlasting thy foundations deep! **1876** FREEMAN *Norm. Conq.* xxiv. V. 391 He became universal landlord, but he did not cease to be universal ruler.

b. In legal use (*spec.* in *Scots Law*): Of or in respect of the whole estate or property.

1669 in W. M. Morison *Dict. Decis.* (1807) 16167 His executor and universal legatar. **1702** *London Gazette* No. 3806. 6 His Majesty has..appointed the Prince of Frise to be his Universal Heir. **1765-8** ERSKINE *Inst. Law Scot.* III. ix. §6 Where a settlement is made by the deceased of the whole or the *universitas* of his moveable estate, the person gratified is called universal legatee. **1790** in *Nairne Peerage Evidence* (1874) 99 The said Marg^t Mercer to be my sole executor and universal intromitter.

c. *Scots Law.* Succeeding to an estate by a universal, as distinct from a singular, title.

1681 STAIR *Inst.* xxvi. 92 Heirs in Law are called Universal Successors,..[because] they do wholly represent the defunct. **1838** BELL *Dict. Law Scot.* 951 In this sense the two terms of *singular successor* and *universal successor* are opposed to each other.

3. a. Of or pertaining to the universe in general or all things in it; existing or occurring everywhere or in all things; occas., of or belonging to all nature. Chiefly *poet.* or *rhet.*

1390 GOWER *Conf.* III. 91 Yit withouten eny forme Was that matiere universal, Which hihte ylem. **1637** MILTON *Lycidas* 60 Her inchanting son Whom Universal nature did lament. **1643** SWAN *Spec. Mundi* (ed. 2) 213 These things.. are but in particular seas,..where a generall and universall cause may be much hindered. **1731** BOLINGBROKE *Let. to Swift* 2 Aug., The first epistle, which considers man.. relatively to the whole system of universal being. **1738** GRAY *Propertius* III. v. 18 That first, eternal, universal Cause. **1819** SHELLEY *Peter Bell 3rd* v. viii, On the universal sky. **1823** S. ROGERS *Italy*, *St. Mark's Place* 165 Subtle, invisible, And universal as the air. **1848** R. I. WILBERFORCE *Doctr.*

Incarnation xi. (1852) 267 The Universal Mind which pervades all things.

b. *poet.* as an epithet of Pan.

1667 MILTON *P.L.* IV. 266 While Universal Pan Knit with the Graces and the Hours in dance Led on th' Eternal Spring. **1809** WORDSW. '*O'er the wide earth*' 3 A Godhead, like the universal Pan. **1820** SHELLEY *Witch Atlas* ix, And universal Pan, 'tis said, was there.

c. Of language, etc.: Adopted, (intended to be) used, understood, etc., everywhere or by all nations; freq. = Latin.

1652 URQUHART *Jewel* 24 Bringing all these words within the systeme of a Language, which.. may.. be intituled The Universal Tongue. **1653** —— *Logopandect.* 13 So can there be no Universal Language but this I am about to divulge unto the world. *Ibid.*, The Universal Alphabet therefore must be first conceived. **1668** WILKINS *Real Char.* 13 A Real universal Character. **1756** MRS. CALDERWOOD in *Coltness Collect.* 131 The universall language so much wished for. **1793** MARTYN *Lang. Bot.* Pref. p. xiii, The advantage which is derived from speaking and writing one universal language. **1818** HAZLITT *Eng. Poets* i. 2 Poetry is the universal language which the heart holds with nature and itself. **1836** (*title*), Universal Character; or, Manner of Writing intelligible to the Inhabitants of every Country. **1885, 1890** [see VOLAPÜK].

d. *Mil.* Of stores: (see quot.).

1876 VOYLE & STEVENSON *Milit. Dict.* 446/2 *Universal*.. is applied to certain stores of a general pattern, such as the saddlery and harness now in use in the army.

†**4.** Not going into details or particulars; general. *Obs.*$^{-1}$

c **1430** *Lanfranc's Cirurg.* 5 (MS. Addit.), Chap. j of broken bonys an vniuersel word.

†**5. a.** Of a council: General, œcumenical (see COUNCIL 2). *Obs. rare.*

1432-50 tr. *Higden* (Rolls) V. 241 A cownsayle universalle of vj^{c} and xxx^{ti} bischoppes hade at Calcedonia.

†**b.** Made up of, inclusive of, all. *Obs.*$^{-1}$

1585 T. WASHINGTON tr. *Nicholay's Voy.* II. vi. 36 Many fair fountaines, which after a long.. course do come altogether into an vniuersall flood [Fr. *vn vniuersel fleuve*].

†**6.** Of persons: Preserving the same attitude *to* all. *Obs.*$^{-1}$

c **1450** in Aungier *Syon* (1840) 269 The presidente.. owethe to be unyuersal to al and not parcial.

7. Of the church: Of, belonging to, or including all persons; consisting of the whole body of Christians; = CATHOLIC *a.* 5.

1483 CAXTON *Cato* b ij, Our moder chyrche unyuersall. **1509** *Paternoster, Ave & Creed* (W. de W.) a iij, I trowe in y^{e} holy goost, holy chirche Unyversall [etc.]. **1552** ABP. HAMILTON *Catech.* (1884) 3 The haly spreit quhilk is ane daily techeour and governour of the hail universal kirk. **1620** T. GRANGER *Div. Logike* 227 Euen the vniuersall Church may erre. **1645** USSHER *Body Div.* (1647) 187 The Catholick Church, that is, God's whole or universall Assembly. **1663-70** SOUTH *Serm.* (1715) IV. 281 The Universal Christian Church. **1807** J. CROOK (*title*), The Universal Church; an Essay on Nature, as the Universal Basis of Truth, Perfection, and Salvation. **1893** LIDDON, etc. *Life Pusey* I. 417 The Ancient Fathers.. bring the thought of particular Churches into community with the thought of the Universal Church when outwardly united.

8. Constituting or forming, existing or regarded as, a complete whole; entire, whole.

a. Of the world, earth, etc.

Common in 16th c.; now somewhat *rare*. See VARSAL *a.* 1.

1470-85 MALORY *Arthur* v. i. 160 That noble empyre whiche domyneth vpon the vnyuersal world. **1480** CAXTON *Myrr.* Prol. 4 b, The situacion.. of the firmament, and how the vnyuersal erthe hangeth in the myddle of the same. **1513** DOUGLAS *Æneid* VI. xii. 10 By his power mydlit is our all This meikle body clepit vniuersall. **1527** R. THORNE in Hakluyt *Voy.* (1589) 253 This Card, though little, conteineth the vniuersall whole world. **1649** QUARLES *Virgin Widow* II. i, 'Twas for nothing in the universal world but for killing a rich Patient. **1667** MILTON *P.L.* v. 154 Thine this universal Frame, Thus wondrous fair. [Hence in Blackmore *Creation* v. 657, Cowper *Retirement* 90.] *Ibid.* VII. 257 With joy and shout The hollow Universal Orb they fill'd. **1823** W. FAUX *Mem. Days* 212, I would live no where else in all the universal world. **1859** DARWIN in *Life & Lett.* (1887) II. 169 Now I care not what the universal world says.

b. In general use.

1502 ATKYNSON tr. *De Imitatione* IV. xviii. (1893) 282 All the vniuersall people prayse the. **1559** W. CUNNINGHAM *Cosmogr. Glasse* 48 At midde day through the vniuersal yere. **1585** T. WASHINGTON tr. *Nicholay's Voy.* III. iii. 73 b, Their order vniuersall is distributed in tenths. **1603** DANIEL *Def. Ryme* G 3 b, Euery Rymer in this vniuersall Iland. **1615** G. SANDYS *Trav.* 113 Neither cement nor wood was imploied thorowout the vniuersall fabricke. **1667** MILTON *P.L.* I. 541 The universal Host upsent A shout that tore Hells Concave. **1830-1860** in Thornton *Amer. Gloss.* (1912) s.v., The Universal Yankee nation. **1871** BLACKIE *Four Phases* i. 27 The political importance.. had been blazoned forth before universal Greece.

9. a. Of persons: Instructed or learned in all or many subjects; having an extensive knowledge or experience; widely accomplished; interested in or devoted to a great variety of subjects; having a wide range of interests or activities. Also of the mind or disposition.

1520 *Caxton's Chron. Eng.* IV. 32 b/2 He [Adrian] was an vnyuersall man almost in all scyences. **1540** J. HEYWOOD *Four P.P.* B ij, Why be ye so vniuersall, That ye can do what so euer ye shall. **1631** WEEVER *Anc. Funeral Mon.* 383 One William West, a Canon of Saint Pauls,.. a good companion, a man vniuersall, affable, and curteous. **1679** DRYDEN *Pref. to Troylus & Cress.* ad fin., Shakspeare had an universal mind. *a* **1700** EVELYN *Diary* 5 Mar. 1673, This gentleman is a very excellent and universal scholar. *Ibid.* 19 July 1691, I never knew a man of a more universal and generous spirit. *a* **1715** BURNET *Own Time* II. x. (1897) I. 427 He was.. very universal in all other learning. **1749** SMOLLETT *Gil Blas* XI. v, He sets up for an universal man, because he has a small tincture of every science. **1829** LYTTON *Devereux* II. vi, Don Saltero is a universal genius. **1833** COLERIDGE *Table-t.* 17 Feb., Shakspeare is universal, and in fact has no manner. **1841** D'ISRAELI *Amen. Lit.* III. 178 With a universal mind Rawleigh was eager after universal knowledge.

b. Not limited or restricted to any particular branch or class of work, etc. †***attorney universal***, an Attorney-General (*obs.*); ***universal maid***, a maid of all work, a general servant; ***Universal Aunts***, the name of a company incorporated in 1922 and based in London, which provides domestic assistance to its clients through a staff of professional helpers; hence ***Universal Aunt***, a member of the organization; usually *transf.* Cf. AUNT 1 b. Similarly ***Universal Uncle.***

1637 J. BASTWICK (*title*), The Answer.. to the Information of Sir John Bancks, Knight, Atturney universall. **1770** R. WESTON (*title*), The Universal Botanist and Nurseryman, etc. **1840** THACKERAY *Shabby-genteel Story* iii, She had been in the kitchen helping Becky, the universal maid. **1922** *Certificate of Incorporation No. 185,178* (Department of Trade) 20 Oct., I hereby certify that Universal Aunts, Limited is this day incorporated under the Companies Acts.. and that the Company is Limited... Registrar of Joint Stock Companies. **1923** *Westm. Gaz.* 10 Jan. 7/6 Associations such as 'Universal Aunts' and 'Useful Women' who supply workers for.. social work. **1929** M. ALLINGHAM *Mystery Mile* iii. 38 He's really a sort of 'Universal Aunt', isn't he? 'Your adventures undertaken for a small fee.' **1931** —— *Look to Lady* iii. 42, I am.. a sort of universal uncle, a policeman's friend and master-crook's factotum. **1937** A. THIRKELL *Summer Half* viii. 229 The universal uncle went down to dinner. **1961** *Listener* 12 Oct. 576/1 His role of cultural Universal Uncle. **1978** M. DICKENS *Open Book* iv. 33 There was a domestic agency in Knightsbridge called Universal Aunts—now in Chelsea—which was famous for doing things that real aunts ought to be doing, like meeting small boys from India at the boat train and taking them across London to their train for school.

c. Embracing or covering all (or a great variety of) subjects, branches of knowledge, etc. Also ***universal decimal classification***, a form of decimal library classification (see DECIMAL *a.* 1 a).

1638 R. BAKER tr. *Balzac's Lett.* (vol. II) 39 His knowledge is so universal, and comprehends such an infinite number of things that one cannot touch upon any point where he is not ready for you. **1688-9** (*title*), The Universal Intelligence. **1690** LOCKE *Hum. Und.* IV. iii. §28 For wherever we want that, we are utterly uncapable of universal and certain Knowledge. **1786** (*title*), The Fashionable Magazine,.. being a Compleat Universal Repository of Taste, Elegance, and Novelty for both Sexes. **1821** A. JAMIESON (*title*), Universal Science, or the Cabinet of Nature and Art. **1841** [see sense 9 a]. **1861-5** (*title*), Beeton's Dictionary of Universal Information. **1882-4** (*title*), Universal Instructor; or, Self-Culture for All. **1930** [see DECIMAL *a.* 1 a]. **1949** *College & Research Libraries* Oct. 333 The Universal Decimal Classification (U.D.C.). This last was the name given to the 'Brussels expansion' of the *Decimal Classification and Relative Index* of Melvil Dewey. **1958** *B.S.I. News* Sept. 12/1 The B.S.I., with the support of ASLIB and the Library Association, is arranging a series of one-day discussions on universal decimal classification.

†**10.** With pl. sbs. All, every one, regarded collectively as a body or whole. *Obs. rare.*

1530-1 *Act 22 Hen. VIII*, c. 14 His lyberall and free habytations resortes and passages to and fro the vniuersall places of this realme. **1563** *Homilies* II. *The Sacrament* II. 458 b, Wherfore, let vs all vniuersall and singuler, beholde our owne maners and lyues, to amend them.

11. a. *Logic.* Applicable to, extending or relating to, involving, the whole of a class or genus, or all the individuals or species forming it; *spec.* of a proposition: Predicable of each of the things denoted by the subject. Opposed to *particular*.

1551 T. WILSON *Logike* G viii, The first proposition must be vniuersall euer, or els it is not good. **1606** BRYSKETT *Civ. Life* 124 That sense is busied about things particular, and.. onely things vniuersall are knowne. **1650** HOBBES *Hum. Nat.* v. 50 The appellations that be universal, and common to many things, are not always given to all the particulars. **1697** tr. *Burgersdicius' Logic* I. xvii. 66 Cause efficient is divided into universal and particular. Universal is that which concurrs with other causes. **1725** WATTS *Logic* (1726) 36 This sort of universal Ideas, which may either be considered as a Genus, or a Species, is call'd Subaltern. *Ibid.* 147 An universal Proposition is when the Subject is taken according to the whole of its Extension. **1842** ABP. THOMSON *Laws Th.* 64 As to Quantity, judgments are either Universal, Particular, or Singular. **1885** J. MARTINEAU *Types Eth. Th.* I. I. ii. §8. 201 What is there 'universal' in this geometrical equation?

b. Applicable to, operative or valid in, all cases. Of a law or rule (cf. GENERAL *a.* 5 b).

1583 MELBANCKE *Philotimus* R j b, Yet the vniuersallest Axiomes haue their cautions. **1651** HOBBES *Leviathan* II. xxvi. 148 Naturall Lawes being Eternall, and Universall, are all Divine. **1667** SPRAT *Hist. R. Soc.* 247 A universal Standard, or measure of Magnitudes, by the help of a Pendulum. **1687** P. AYRES *Lyric Poems* (1906) 309 This Universal Remedy, To hope and live. **1728** CHAMBERS *Cycl.* s.v. *General*, A *General* Rule, *q.d.* an universal Rule. **1747** WESLEY *Prim. Physick* (1762) p. xxvii, It comes the nearest an Universal Medecine. **1839** DICKENS *Nickleby* ix, As there is no reason to suppose that she was a solitary exception to a universal rule. **1884** tr. *Lotze's Metaph.* 117 The validity of Universal laws. **1890** 'R. BOLDREWOOD' *Col. Reformer* (1891) 317 Compelled to employ that only universal solvent, a cash payment.

†**12.** Of motion or action: Constant, continual, perpetual. *Obs. rare.*

1588 SHAKS. *L.L.L.* IV. iii. 305 Why, vniuersall plodding poysons vp The nimble spirits in the arteries. **1604** E. G[RIMSTONE] *D'Acosta's Hist. Indies* III. vi. 137 [The comet] mooved daily with an vniversal motion, from East to Weast.

13. Of implements, machines or their parts, etc.: Adjustable to all conditions or requirements; not restricted to one fixed type of operation, but capable of variety of work; adapted to various purposes, sizes, forms, etc.

Freq. ***universal joint***, a joint or coupling which permits of free movement in any direction of the parts joined, *spec.* one which does this in such a way that one of the connected parts conveys rotary action to the other.

A number of other instances in purely technical use are recorded in Knight's *Dict. Mech.* (1875) and *Suppl.* (1884), and recent Dicts. (1891–).

1676 HOOKE *Helioscopes* 14 The Universal Joynt for all these manner of operations. **1688** HOLME *Armoury* III. 373 Pendant Dials.., commonly called Equinoctial or Universal Dials, are most used by Sea-Men and Travellers. **1700** MOXON *Math. Instr.* s.v., [The] Universal Equinoctial Dial ..finds the Latitude and Hour of the day and most propositions on the Globe. **1815** J. SMITH *Panorama Sci. & Art* I. 111 The stop and fence of the universal plough. **1825** J. NICHOLSON *Operat. Mechanic* 324 On the end, *n*, of the spindle P,.. is screwed occasionally an universal chuck for holding any kind of work which is to be turned. **1829** *Nat. Philos., Mechanics* II. xiii. 62 (L.U.K.), Hooke's universal joint is a very simple and effectual method of transferring rotation from one axis to another. **1881** RAYMOND *Mining Gloss.*, *Universal train*, a roll train having adjustable horizontal and vertical rolls, so as to produce sections of various sizes. **1888** JACOBI *Printers' Vocab.*, *Universal machine*, a jobbing platen machine—for steam or treadle.

14. Special collocations: **universal arithmetic**, † **mathematics**, algebra; **universal donor** *Med.*, a person whose blood is group O (so called because before the discovery of other blood group systems group O blood was thought to be compatible with that of any individual); **Universal Product Code** *N. Amer.* (see quot. 1979); **Universal Provider**, the name of a well-known general store formerly trading in London; freq. with small initials and *transf.*; **universal quantifier** *Logic* [tr. G. *allgemeiner quantificator* (Łukasiewicz & Tarski 1930, in *Sprawozdania z Posiedzeń Towarżystwa naukowego Warszawskiego* (Wydział III) XXIII. 44)], a quantifier referring to all the members of a universe or class; **universal set** *Logic* and *Math.* = UNIVERSE 2 d; **universal suffrage**, a suffrage extending to the whole of a community, esp. one in virtue of which all persons (formerly all male persons) over a certain age, except lunatics, aliens, and criminals, have the right to vote for representatives to a legislative (usually parliamentary) assembly; hence ***universal suffragist***; **universal time**, Greenwich time calculated from midnight at the Greenwich meridian (rather than from noon, as formerly); **universal umbel** (see quot.).

1720 RAPHSON, etc. (*title*), *Universal Arithmetick: or, a Treatise of Arithmetical Composition and Resolution. Translated from the Latin [of Newton's *Arithmetica Universalis* (1707)]. **1826** *Encycl. Metrop.* (1845) I. 524/2 The title *Universal Arithmetic* very inadequately expresses the nature, objects, and extent of this department of Analysis. **1922** G. KEYNES *Blood Transfusion* iv. 72 Individuals of Groups I and IV have therefore been named 'universal recipients' and '*universal donors' respectively. **1976** EDINGTON & GILLES *Path. in Tropics* (ed. 2) 480 Universal donor group O blood should not therefore be employed for transfusing A or B recipients without prior investigation. **1673** J. KERSEY *Algebra* b 3, The learned Works of which [they].. proclaim their rare Talents in *Universal Mathematicks. **1752** (*title*), The Elements of Universal Mathematics, or Algebra; to which is added, a Specimen of a Commentary on Sir Isaac Newton's Universal Arithmetic. **1974** *Consumer Reports* (U.S.) May 364/2 A computer.. knows the package code (the grocery industry has agreed on a *universal product code). **1979** *Hammond Almanac 1980* 761/2 *Universal Product Code*, a pattern of lines and numbers by which information about a product may be encoded for automatic scanning by a device ..that records its price for charging the consumer as well as its stock numbers, inventory, etc. **1884** *List of Subscribers* (London & Globe Telephone Co.), *Whiteley, W.*, *Universal Provider, Westbourne Grove, W. **1903** BEERBOHM *Around Theatres* (1924) I. 461 As a curate he has to offer that consolation of which he is universal provider. **1953** *Guardian* 11 Sept. 6/5 To our children we will always be a kind of Universal Provider, vague of face but soft of bosom. **1962** *Sunday Express* 23 Dec. 2/4 The world-famous 'Universal Provider'. Anything from a flea to an elephant.. Whiteley boasted he could provide. [**1845** *Encycl. Metrop.* I. 207/1 When the subject of a Proposition is a common Term, the universal signs ('all, no, every') are used.] **1936** *Amer. Jrnl. Math.* LVIII. 353 Then..$(x)P$ and $(\exists x)P$ are propositions of elementary number theory, where (x) and $(\exists x)$ are respectively the *universal and existential quantifiers. **1940**, etc. [see QUANTIFIER 1 a]. **1961** J. E. WHITESITT *Boolean Algebra* iii. 60 $\forall x$ is called the universal quantifier of the variable *x* and is usually read 'for all *x*' or 'for every *x*'. **1980** E. P. LYNCH *Applied Symbolic Logic* i. 11 The universal quantifiers are 'all', 'for every', 'for all', and so on. [**1910** WHITEHEAD & RUSSELL *Principia Mathematica* I. i. 30 The class determined by a function which is always true is called the universal class, and is represented by V.] **1959** *Universal set [see *solution set* s.v. SOLUTION *sb.* 12]. **1975** I.

STEWART *Concepts Mod. Math.* iv. 57 In any particular problem, the sets one is concerned with often lie inside some reasonably small universal set. **1706** DE FOE *Jure Div.* v. 3 The Land divided, Right to rule divides, And *universal Suffrage then provides. **1798** [see SUFFRAGE 10 b]. **1817** COBBETT *Pol. Reg.* XXXII. 226 That, as to Universal Suffrage, you cannot help calling it universal impracticability. **1857** D. P[USELEY] *Rise Australia*, etc. 69 Even absolutism with its attendants evils would..be preferable to universal suffrage. **1822** *Blackw. Mag.* XII. 156 If they come back *Universal Suffragists. **1834** MAR. EDGEWORTH *Helen* xxxv, It is curious that..Louisa Castlefort, should be obliged..to..turn ultra liberale, or an universal suffragist. **1882** *Monthly Notices R. Astron. Soc.* XLII. 205 (*heading*) *Universal time and the selection of a prime meridian. *Ibid.*, The American Meteorological Society further considered it desirable that in the future a universal time reckoned from the meridian 180° from that of Greenwich should be generally introduced. **1969** *Times* 24 June 4/7 The object rose above the eastern horizon at 2.49 a.m., universal time. **1760** J. LEE *Introd. Bot.* I. viii (1765) 17 The Umbel that bears the Umbellula on its Footstalks, is called an *universal Umbel.

15. Quasi-*adv.*

a. Universally; in all places. **b.** With universal power. *rare.*

1524 in *Acta Parlt. Scotl.* (1875) XII. 40/2 Þat Justice Airis be halden universale throu oute þe Ralme. **1759** MASON *Caractacus* 86 What, if Cæsar aims To lord it universal o'er the world.

16. *absol.* with *the.* **a.** The whole of, all of (something expressed or implied); *spec.* in *Logic* and *Philos.*, the whole class or genus, as distinct from the individuals comprising it.

c **1374** CHAUCER *Boeth.* v. pr. iv. (1868) 165 For resoun is she þat diffinisseþ þe vniuersel of hir conseite ryȝt þus. **1551** T. WILSON *Logike* I i b, From the vniuersall to the particular, the argument goeth well. **1818** COLERIDGE *Friend* (ed. 2) I. 269 The ideas of the Necessary and the Universal. **1865** MOZLEY *Mirac.* ii. 46 The universal as a law and the universal as a proposition are wholly distinct. **1871** JOWETT *Plato* I. 265 Tell me what virtue is in the universal.

†**b.** *by* or *in the universal*, in respect of, or with reference to, the whole class; in general terms; generally. *Obs.*

1552 LATIMER *Serm.* (1562) 127 Suche a maner of speakyng is vsed in the scripture, to speake by the vniuersall: meaning a great numbre, but yet not all: only those that be giltie. **1628** SPENCER *Logick* 206 Both of these distinct formes are one, and the same thing in the generall, or vniversall.

†**c.** The whole community; the people in general. *Obs.*

1676 in *Brent's Counc. Trent* p. lxx, Which hath produced ..a most intense desire of the conservation of their good Servant, and in the universal a more glorious fame to see.. so singular a favour.

†**17.** *in universal*: **a.** As a body or whole; collectively. **b.** In respect of every thing or part; entirely, wholly. *Obs.*

1387-8 T. USK *Test. Love* II. xiii. (Skeat) l. 70 At the ginninge of the worlde, every thing by him-selfe was good; and in universal they weren right good. **1615** in *Buccleuch MSS.* (Hist. MSS. Comm.) I. 168 The Spaniard interdicteth Trade to the East Indies in universal, and the Hollanders but to a part.

B. *sb.* **1. a.** *Logic* and *Philos.* That which is predicated or asserted of all the individuals or species of a class or genus, or of many things which are regarded as forming a class; an abstract or general concept regarded either as having an absolute, mental, or nominal existence; a universal proposition; a general term, notion, or idea. Chiefly in *pl.* and opposed to *particulars* or *singulars*.

In mediæval Scholastic philosophy the nature of universals gave rise to the great controversy which resulted in the division of the Schoolmen into Realists, Nominalists, and Conceptualists, according to their respective theories.

sing. **1553** EDEN *Treat. New Ind.* (Arb.) 9 A perticuler proueth no vniuersall. **1692** BENTLEY *Boyle Lect.* 141 It is merely a notional and imaginary thing, an abstract universal, which is properly nothing, a conception of our own making. **1697** tr. *Burgersdicius' Logic.* I. i. 3 A universal is that which is apt..to be predicated of many things, as *man, horse, plant,* &c. **1728** CHAMBERS *Cycl.* s.v. *Predicable*, Thus Animal is an Universal, with regard to Man and Beast. **1751** *Phil. Trans.* XLVII. 314 The business of natural philosophy is..to note down facts,..and..to collect their proper universal, by a fair..induction. *Ibid.* A new collection of constant and similar facts affords an higher universal.

pl. **1606** BRYSKETT *Civ. Life* 124 As the hand is apt to take hold of all instruments; so is this power or facultie apt to apprehend the formes of all things, from whence grow the vniuersals. *a* **1676** HALE *Prim. Orig. Man.* (1677) 28 For Universals are but Notions and *Entia Rationis*. **1725** WATTS *Logic* (1726) 36 Some of these Universals are Genus's, if compared with less common Natures. **1794** BURKE *On Petition of Unitarians* Wks. 1842 II. 474 No rational man ever did govern himself, by abstractions and universals. **1837** HALLAM *Hist. Lit.* I. iii. §67 The long controversies between the Realists and Nominalists concerning the nature of universals. **1860** ABP. THOMSON *Laws Th.* (ed. 5) §62 Universals..or those general properties which many things share alike, and which are acquired by the mind only by abstracting from the things that exhibit them. **1889** MIVART *Orig. Hum. Reason* 43 General ideas, or 'universals', only arise in our mind after we have experienced corresponding groups of sense-impressions.

†**b.** *pl.* Items of general information or news.

1650 HOWELL *Lett.* III. 3 This Letter runs upon Universalls, because I know your Lordship hath..a spacious understanding, which comprehends the whole world.

†**c.** Abstract magnitude or volume. *Obs.*

1674 N. FAIRFAX *Bulk & Selv.* 66 Universal, or boak, as taken in the Mathematicks.

2. That which is universal; esp. one who or that which is universally powerful, potent, current, etc.

1556 OLDE *Antichrist* 49 For that cause this honour ought to be graunted to the bishop of Constantinople, that he maye be called the universall of all prelates and the bishop of bishoppes. **1709** MRS. MANLEY *Secret Mem.* (1720) III. 122 Omnipotent Gold has a Power so extensive, that we presume we are not guilty of Hyperbole..in representing it, as the grand Universal. **1855** MILMAN *Lat. Chr.* XIV. vii. VI. 528 The primitive word for 'father' is so nearly an universal, that [etc.].

†**3.** The universe. *Obs.* (common 1600–1625).

1569 J. SANFORD tr. *Agrippa's Van. Artes* 65 b, It is no lesse folie to saye that, in the universall, is but one worlde alone. **1591** SPARRY tr. *Cattan's Geomancie* 23 So the Earth ..resteth in the middle of the whole vniuersall. **1613** CHAPMAN *Rev. Bussy d' Ambois* III. iv. 72 Hee that striues t'inuert The Vniuersals course with his poore way. **1628** FELTHAM *Resolves* II. lviii. 168 There is a secret chaine in Nature, which drawes the Vniversall to revenge a vice.

†**4.** A medicament or remedy affecting the whole body or system. *Obs.*

1656 J. SMITH *Pract. Physick* 119 Gallen commends a Bath after Universals. **1694** SALMON *Bate's Dispens.* Pref. A 4 b, Russel's Powder,..that Fam'd Universal, which for these twenty-five Years last past has obtain'd a general Reputation..in a manner through the whole World. *Ibid.* I. xvii. 793/2 If it be used for a Gonorrhœa,..Universals ought to be premised, that the Body may be cleansed as much as may be.

5. An artificial language invented for universal use by H. Molenaar; also known as PAN-ROMAN. Cf. sense 3 c of the adj.

1907, etc. [see PAN-ROMAN, PANROMAN]. **1928** O. JESPERSEN *International Lang.* 40 Among numerous systems of the same type, but not worked out to the same extent as Neutral, I shall here mention only H. Molenaar's *Universal* (1906). **1947** [see NEUTRAL *sb.* 5].

6. *Linguistics.* Any of the fundamental rules or features proposed as universal attributes of natural languages (see quots.).

1948 B. W. & E. G. AGINSKY in *Word* IV. 109 What are the universals of language?.. All languages employ sound sequences in which may be discerned a limited number of recurring types of speech-sound segments. These..are meaningless.., but enter into the meaningful units of form, the morphemes. All languages employ such morphemes in sequences. **1964** KATZ & POSTAL *Integrated Theory of Linguistic Descriptions* 160 A formal universal is a specification of the form of a statement in a linguistic description, while a substantive universal is a concept or set of concepts out of which particular statements in a linguistic description are constructed. **1965** N. CHOMSKY *Aspects of Theory of Syntax* i. 28 The study of linguistic universals is the study of the properties of any generative grammar for a natural language. *Ibid.*, It is useful to classify linguistic universals as *formal* or *substantive*. A theory of substantive universals claims that items of a particular kind in any language must be drawn from a fixed class of items. **1972** HARTMANN & STORK *Dict. Lang. & Linguistics* 245/2 Examples of universals are the conventional character of language.., the duality of transmission and reception, the presence of names and deictic elements. A distinction is sometimes made between *substantive universals*, i.e. features of sound substance such as the phonological elements..and *formal universals* which are made explicit by the linguist in the form of grammatical rules. **1973** *Language* XL. 178 It seems to be a language universal that productive inflectional morphemes are not only very short, but also employ a reduced inventory of phonemes.

‖**univer'salia**, *sb. pl.* ? *Obs.* [L., neut. pl. of *ūniversālis*: see prec.] An official letter or proclamation issued by one in authority to all the states or nobles of Poland, esp. one convening the national diet. Also erron. as *sing.* (quot. 1772).

1708 *Lond. Gaz.* No. 4429/7 The Grand General has.. publish'd his Universalia, to exhort the Confederate Estates to continue firm in their Adherence to each other. **1763** *Brit. Mag.* IV. 551 The Primate..dispatches his universalia to the several provinces. **1772** *Hartford Merc.* Suppl. 18 Sept. 4/1 General Haddick is going to publish an Universalia.

univer'salian, *a. rare.* [f. UNIVERSAL *a.* + -IAN.] Universalist, universalistic. Also *spec.* = UNIVERSALISTIC *a.* 1.

1837 W. JENKINS *Ohio Gazetteer* 357 It has..three houses for public worship (methodist, presbyterian, and universalian). **1852** J. REYNOLDS *Hist. Illinois* 327 He is one of the Universalian Baptists. **1853** E. G. HOLLAND *Mem. J. Badger* xi. (1854) 205 [Calvinism's] bold premises were the foundation of the plea of its opposite extreme,—the Universalian statement.

uni'versalism. [f. as prec. Cf. F. *universalisme.*]

1. The fact or quality of being concerned with or interested in all or a great variety of subjects; universality of knowledge.

c **1827** COLERIDGE in *Blackw. Mag.* (1882) CXXXI. 119 The all-meaningness and thin-blown bladdery universalisms of the lectures. **1838** *New Monthly Mag.* LIV. 132 The full-blown facility of modern universalism. **1877** MORLEY *Crit. Misc.* Ser. II. 247 That weak kind of universalism which nullifies some otherwise good men.

2. *Theol.* The beliefs or special views held by the Universalists; the doctrine of universal salvation or redemption.

1805 J. SPAULDING (*title*), Universalism Confounds and Destroys Itself. **1840** G. S. FABER *Christ's Disc. Capernaum* 224 A tremendously wide and long enduring Apostasy..is ..rhetorically spoken of in terms which literally import Universalism. **1864** J. DONALDSON *Crit. Hist. Chr. Lit. & Doctr.* I. 37 Heathen Christianity..proclaimed all men alike in God's sight. Paul was the preacher of this universalism. **1871** MOZLEY *Univ. Serm.* v. (1876) 112 The waves of universalism..cannot possibly shake the seat of distributed power and government.

3. The fact or condition of being universal in character or scope; universality.

1835 *Leigh Hunt's London Jrnl.* 11 July 221/1 What (if we might take the liberty to coin a word) we would call the universalism of the Homeric poetry. **1840** T. GORDON tr. *Menzel's Germ. Lit.* III. 288 Poetical Universalism.—Herder. **1882** *Athenæum* 14 Oct. 490/1 It is, indeed, somewhat doubtful whether the religion of Rome did not approach universalism almost as much as Islam. **1883** FAIRBAIRN *City of God* III. i. 230 This is..the universalism of Jesus Himself... He belongs to humanity, not to Israel. *Ibid.* 240 The universalism of the person has its counterpart in the universalism of the words.

b. *spec.* in *Sociol.* and *Econ.*, contrasted with PARTICULARISM 5 b and REGIONALISM 1.

1939 T. PARSONS in *Social Forces* May 462/2 The fact that the central focus of the professional rôle lies in a technical competence gives a very great importance to universalism in the institutional pattern governing it. **1947** —— *Weber's Theory Social & Econ. Organization* 72 Ethical universalism, the insistence on treatment of all men by the same generalized, impersonal standards. **1955** *Bull. Atomic Sci.* Apr. 142 The humanitarian theme of the two preceding centuries certainly persisted, but universalism yielded step by step to national particularism.

uni'versalist, *sb.* and *a.* [f. as prec. + -IST. Cf. F. *universaliste*, G. *universalist.*]

A. *sb.* **1. a.** *Theol.* One who believes or maintains the doctrine that redemption or election is extended to the whole of mankind and not confined to a part of it; *spec.* in *U.S.*, a member of a sect or Church holding this doctrine.

1626 tr. *Parallel* A ij, The error of the Vniuersalists is too vniuersally dispread. **1648** O. HOWE (*title*), The Vniversalist examined and convicted, destitute of plaine Sayings of Scripture. **1684** BURNET *Trav.* i. (1750) 58 Some Assertors both in Geneva and Switzerland, who denied the Imputation of Adam's Sin, and asserted the Universality of Christ's Death, together with a sufficient Grace given to all Men... These came to be called Universalists. **1728** CHAMBERS *Cycl.* s.v., The Arminians are particularly denominated Universalists. **1773** WESLEY *Wks.* (1872) X. 425 Bishop Ridley, Hooper, and Latimer..were firm Universalists. **1805** J. SPAULDING *Universalism* 150 These Universalists pretend to be the foremost in extolling the grace of God. **1853** BP. S. WILBERFORCE *Let.* in *Life* (1881) II. 211 That you therefore do..revive the old doctrine of the Universalists. **1861** *Contrib. Eccl. Hist. Connecticut* 278 Attempts..to gather a congregation of Universalists for public worship.

b. *transf.* One who believes in the brotherhood of all men in a manner not subject to national allegiances.

1944 [see REGIONALIST]. **1952** V. GOLLANCZ *My Dear Timothy* xii. 110 A universalist is a person for whom nations don't exist, only persons. **1955** *Times* 25 Aug. 7/2 It seemed unfair to call him an expatriate, for he was a true universalist. It is as a man who loves his fellow men..that Mr. MacDonald has succeeded in being a one-man civilizing factor in this territory.

†**2.** A believer in or maintainer of the universality of the Roman Catholic Church. *Obs.*⁻¹

1644 FEATLY *Roma Ruens* 29 To this poynt I earnestly desire particular satisfaction, which I have not yet received from any Roman Catholike, or universalist (as they would be called).

3. One who in respect of a specified thing acts with universality or uniformity. *rare.*

1677 GILPIN *Demonol.* III. xx. 172 A true Christian should be a perfect Universalist, he should be universally against all Sin, and universally for All Duty.

†**4.** One who uses universals or universal propositions. *Obs.*⁻¹

1680 BAXTER *Answ. Stillingfl.* Pref. A 3 Universallists, that can prove me to be an Ass, because I am an Animal.

5. a. One who is supposed to have, or pretends to, a knowledge of all things; a person who is devoted to many subjects or sciences, as opposed to a *specialist*; a universal scholar.

1713 BENTLEY *Freethinking* iii. 11 A modern Free-thinker is an Universalist in Speculation: any Proposition whatsoever he's ready to decide. **1800** in *Spirit Pub. Jrnls.* IV. 154 All subjects were alike to this universalist. **1830** S. H. CASSAN *Bps. Bath & Wells* II. 172 He was an Universalist in the best sense of the word; and not a smatterer in various sciences. **1881** *Nature* XXIV. 356 The gold of a universalist is apt to shrink down into dross when tested in the crucible of a specialist.

b. One who has many occupations, interests, etc.

1801 *Sporting Mag.* XVIII. 104 You'll find I'm an universalist; i.e. a *Professor* of all trades.

6. One who regards something as a whole and not from one particular point of view.

1892 E. C. STEDMAN *Nat. Poetry* iv. 142 The best critic, then, is the universalist, who sees the excellence of either phase of expression according as it is natural to one's race and period.

B. *adj.* Universalistic.

1819 *Universalist Mag.* 21 Aug. 32/3 Pastor of the First Independent Church of Christ, called Universalist, in Philadelphia. **1859** ALLIBONE *Dict. Eng. Lit.* I. 109 Ballon, Rev. Hosea,..a prominent Universalist minister. **1877** J. E.

Carpenter tr. *Tiele's Hist. Relig.* 89 The universalist monotheism of the Gospel, which has entirely broken down the bounds of nationality.

universa'listic, *a.* [f. prec. + -ic.]

1. *Theol.* Of or pertaining to, characteristic of, Universalism or the Universalists.

1847 R. W. Hamilton *Rewards & Punishm.* vii. 389 A strong defence of the universalistic doctrine. **1887** E. Johnson *Antiqua Mater* 219 The Gnostics, sharing the universalistic aspirations of the time.

2. Of, pertaining or extending to, including or affecting, the whole of something, esp. the whole of mankind; inclined to be universal in scope or character. Also *transf.*

Universalistic Hedonism, Utilitarianism.

1872 *Contemp. Rev.* XIX. 664 A..syncretion of Egoistic and Universalistic Hedonism. **1878** Morley *Diderot* II. 207 Holbach is a universalistic and not an egoistic Hedonist. **1882** *Athenæum* 11 Feb. 184/1 The universalistic tendencies of the great empires. **1886** *Encycl. Brit* XX. 370/1 Universalistic religious communities: Islâm, Buddhism, Christianity.

universality (juːnɪvɜːˈsælɪtɪ). [a. F. *universalité*, OF. *universaliteit* (14th c.; = It. *universalità*, Sp. *-idad*, Pg. *-idade*), or ad. late L. *ūniversālitās* (Boethius), f. L. *ūniversālis*: see universal *a.* and -ity.]

I. 1. The fact or quality of extending over, existing in, or belonging to the whole (of something expressed in or implied by the context); esp. extension, occurrence, prevalence, or diffusion throughout the whole world, everywhere, or in all things.

c **1374** Chaucer *Boeth.* v. pr. v. (1868) 169 þat is..þat resoun lokeþ and comprehendiþ by resoun of vniuersalite [L. *in ratione universitatis*], boþe þat þat is sensible and þat þat is ymaginable. **1587** Golding *De Mornay* 351 All men knowe, that cheefly Auerrhoes vrgeth the eternitie of the World, and the vniuersalitie of one onely Mynd. **1589** Puttenham *Eng. Poesie* I. ix. (Arb.) 38 The Nobilitie and dignitie of the Art considered aswell by vniuersalitie as antiquitie. **1624** H. Mason *Art of Lying* ii. 25 Persons claimeth..Universality, Antiquity, and Consent, for this..vpstart fancie of their owne. **1686** *Caldwell Papers* (Maitl. Cl.) I. 168 The French language, being, because of its universalitie, so very necessarie for converse. **1707** Mortimer *Husb.* 501 The Planting of Fruit-Trees;..and the Advantages of it, which consist..in the Universality of it, there being hardly any Soil, but one sort..or other may be raised on them. **1760–72** H. Brooke *Fool of Qual.* (1809) IV. 78 God..cannot depart from..that universality of essence, by and in which alone all essences subsist. **1811** Pinkerton *Petral.* p. xxxvi, Experiments more and more evince the universality of iron. **1879** Farrar *St. Paul* II. 266 He has shown the universality of guilt, and the universality of grace.

b. Of a church or religion, esp. Roman Catholicism: Extension to the whole world or all men.

Freq. in 17th cent.; now *rare* or *Obs.*

? **1559** A. P. tr. *Vincent of Lirins' Golden Treatise* (title-p.), The antiquitie, and vniuersalitie, of the Catholicke Religion. **1574** Whitgift *Def. Aunsw.* ii. 106 This strengthneth the Papistes vniversalitie. **1608** Willet *Hexapla Exod.* 551 Vniuersalitie and multitude..is no good rule to know the right church..by. **1691** Sir T. P. Blount *Ess.* 90 That thing call'd *Vniversality*, is so slight an Evidence of Truth, that even Truth it self is asham'd of it. **1728** Chambers *Cycl.* s.v., The Catholicks assert the Universality of their Church, both as to Time, and Persons. **1730** J. Denne (*title*), Want of Universality no just Objection to the Truth of the Christian Religion. **1874** Green *Short Hist.* ix. §1 He dismissed with contempt the accepted test of universality.

†c. Of persons with reference to power or authority (see universal *a.* 2). *Obs.*

1620 T. Granger *Div. Logike* 228 Gregory pronounced the same of Iohn Patriarch of constantinople affecting vniuersalitie. **1661** Morgan *Sph. Gentry* iii. vii. 67 The pope, who hath usurped the Universality, will have his triple Crown, to signifie his dominion over the Universe.

2. The fact or quality of extending or applying to, affecting or prevailing among, all the members of a class of persons or things; relation to or inclusion of all individuals, cases, or instances.

1577 Harrison *England* ii. xix. (1877) i. 307 If a man may presentlie giue a ghesse at the vniuersalitie of this euill. **1634** *T. Norton's Calvin's Inst.* Table of Contents, The universality of the promises of salvation maketh nothing against the doctrine of the predestination of the reprobate. **1695** J. Edwards *Perfect. Script.* 342 The universality of the slaughter. **1764** Harmer *Observ.* ii. §17. 75 The tents of the Arabs are with great universality black. **1771** Sir J. Reynolds *Disc.* iv. (1778) 113 He might have seen it in an instance or two; and he mistook accident for universality. **1829** Gen. P. Thompson *Exerc.* (1842) I. 132 Closely connected with the universality of suffrage, is the opportunity of its frequent exercise. **1873** Holland *A. Bonnic.* ix. 162 The universality of the influence which they [*sc.* religious revivals] exert during the time of their highest activity.

b. Of laws, etc., esp. with reference to validity.

1712 Berkeley *Pass. Obed.* Wks. 1871 III. 138 The universality of this mathematical rule. **1747** *Gentl. Mag.* 120/2 That we are not sure of the universality of this law. **1855** Brewster *Newton* I. xiii. 381 Every new comet, every new planet,..proclaims the universality of Newton's philosophy. **1874** Carpenter *Ment. Phys.* ii. xvi. 634 The universality of the Law of Gravitation.

†3. The study or contemplation of things from a general point of view. *Obs. rare.*

1605 Bacon *Adv. Learn.* i. v. §5 Another error..is, that after the distribution of particular arts and sciences, men haue abandoned vniuersalitie, or *Philosophia prima*. *Ibid.* ii. To the King §6 If any man think philosophy and universality to be idle studies, he doth not consider that all professions are from thence served and supplied.

4. The quality or character of extending to or comprehending all or (more usually) a great variety of subjects; unbounded or very great versatility *of* (mind, genius, etc.).

1765 H. Walpole *Vertue's Anecd. Paint.* III. 11 The following [pictures] by Streater..show the universality of his talent. **1818–9** Lady Morgan *Autobiog.* (1859) 203 His gigantic labours..indicate the universality of the highest order of mind. **1824** Miss Mitford *Village* Ser. i. 17 A man..of that peculiar universality of genius which forms..a handy fellow. **1871** 'M. Legrand' *Cambr. Freshm.* 112 The universality of my friend's mind.

b. Capacity for, knowledge of, interest in, all or many things or pursuits; width or extensiveness of understanding, knowledge, or sympathy.

1831 Carlyle *Sart. Res.* ii. iv, Whereby..the vague universality of a Man shall find himself ready-moulded into a specific Craftsman. **1855** Hawthorne *Eng. Note-bks.* (1870) I. 375 Perhaps there may be a universality in his face. **1856** R. A. Vaughan *Mystics* I. 7 One quality in Gower I have always especially liked,—his universality. **1862** *Macm. Mag.* 240 The universality of the heart, which enables them to feel for, and make allowances for all. **1900** E. Holmes *What is Poetry?* 65 Universality, not individuality, is of the essence of the poet's genius.

c. The fact of knowing everybody or a large number of persons; extensiveness *of* (acquaintance).

1791 Paine *Rights of Man* 89 By the universality of his acquaintance. **1838** Ticknor in *Life*, etc. (1876) II. ix. 182 He added, that he himself had never seen him so as to know him..; a curious fact, considering Roger's own universality.

II. 5. The entire or whole body or number, the whole, *of* the people, a nation, mankind, etc., regarded collectively; also, the bulk or mass *of* the people. Now *arch.* (Cf. university 2.)

1561 T. Norton *Calvin's Inst.* i. 7 Shall the whole vniuersalitie of the world be without this prerogatiue? **1588** *Copy of a Letter* in *Harl. Misc.* (1809) II. 82 The universality of the people through the realm. **1655** *Theophania* 77 The vast frame of the world may be shaken, and the universality of nature suffer a change. **1673** *Essex Papers* (Camden) I. 65 Ye Universallity of their Clergie,..& all their Merchants. **1680** H. More *Apocal. Apoc.* 163 One mighty City..consisting of the Universality of Cities considered as one. **1709** Strype *Ann. Reformation* ii. 72 So averse did the universality of the nation stand against popery. **1737** L. Clarke *Hist. Bible* vi. 356/1 Innumerable Acclamations..by the Universality of the People. **1874** Green *Short Hist.* iv. §5. 203 The consent of the prelates, earls, barons, and universality of the realm.

†b. The whole world; the universe. *Obs. rare.*

a **1586** Sidney *Arcadia* iii. x, What madd furie can ever so enveagle any conceipte, as to see our mortall..selves to have a reason, and that this universalitie (whereof we are but the lest pieces) should be utterly devoide thereof? **1593** Q. Eliz. *Boeth.* iii. pr. xii. 72 That God was he that ruld the vniuersalitie by the raynes of goodnes.

†c. The whole people or state; the people in general. *Obs.*

1614 Raleigh *Hist. World* v. iii. 496 The Common happinesse of the vniuersalitie. **1644** [H. Parker] *Jus Populi* 18 The Parliament differs many wayes from the rude bulk of the universality. **1675** *Machiavelli's Prince* xvii. Exorbitant mercy has an ill effect upon the whole universality.

†d. The whole subject; a matter or subject regarded generally or as a whole. *Obs.*$^{-1}$

1726 Leoni *Alberti's Archit.* II. 5/1, I shall speak first of those wherein this particular Art is most concerned; and as for the others, which relate to the universality, they shall serve by way of epilogue.

6. *pl.* Something which extends to all the members of a class; a general statement or description, a generality. *Obs.*

a **1591** H. Smith *Sinful Man* (1592) A 5 To the Heathen hee shewed vniuersalities and antiquities. **1608** D. T[uvill] *Ess. Pol. & Mor.* 9 Simple men; who..beeing vnable to iudge, or conceiue of vniuersalities, suffer themselues..to be wholly guided by their externall sense. **1629** H. Burton *Truth's Triumph* 210 The deceitful man loueth to walke in vniuersalities or generalities. **1647** Jer. Taylor *Lib. Proph.* ix. 162 If you can..determine those great questions which consist much in universalities, then also you may determine the particulars.

†b. A universal medicine or remedy; a panacea. *Obs.*$^{-1}$

1756 Toldervy *Hist. 2 Orphans* IV. 126 Men who..poyson you with universalities, medicines that are generally ineffectual, and of whose formations they are quite unacquainted.

†7. A collective whole or body, as distinct from one of the parts of which it is composed. (Cf. 5.)

1622 Breton *Strange News* C 3 b, Neare the chiefe Citie of Nullibi, in an vniuersalitie, in stead of an Vniuersitie,..there was a deepe student in the secrets of Nature. **1642** *View Print. Book int. Observat.* 8 Kingdome or *Regnum* denotes an universalitie or body collected. [**1875** Poste *Gaius* ii. com. (ed. 2) 290 As single things can be bequeathed, so can a universality.]

†8. Something which exists everywhere or in all things: a universal being. *Obs.*$^{-1}$

1681 *Whole Duty Nations* 7 He himself is the prime Unity and Universality.

ˌuniversa'lizable, *a.* Chiefly *Philos.* [f. universalize *v.* + -able.] That can be made or rendered universal; capable of universal application.

1952 A. E. Duncan-Jones *Butler's Moral Philos.* viii. 171 In order that he shall be said to make a moral judgement, his attitude must be 'universalisable'. **1955** *Proc. Aristotelian Soc.* LV. 170 If too few details are included in the maxims, it will be difficult to find *any* that will be universalisable at all. **1977** P. Baelz *Ethics & Belief* ii. 18 Reasons are impersonal, or inter-personal. They are logically impartial, or universalizable. **1982** *Times Lit. Suppl.* 24 Dec. 1423/4 That a moral imperative should be universalizable seems to be at the heart of what we understand when we understand it as a *moral* imperative.

Also **uniˌversaliza'bility**; **ˌuniversa'lizably** *adv.*

1952 A. E. Duncan-Jones *Butler's Moral Philos.* viii. 173 What we are calling the universalisability of his attitude consists in his being disposed..to respond in an equivalent way to people and situations of a given kind, should he come to consider them. **1954** W. D. Ross *Kant's Theory of Ethics* 33 But the man who tells the lie may well retort to Kant 'Why should the test of universalizability be applied to my act regarded in this very abstract way, simply as a lie?' **1963** R. M. Hare *Freedom & Reason* vi. 91 This argument would break down if 'ought' were not being used both universalizably and prescriptively. **1982** *Times Lit. Suppl.* 2 July 713/1 'Ought'..commits one to universalizability, in the sense that if I say you ought to do *A*, I implicitly affirm that everyone ought to do *A* in identical circumstances.

universali'zation. [f. next + -ation.] The action of the verb; the fact or process of becoming universal.

1798 *Monthly Rev.* XXVI. 538 A language already so general must, for that very reason, tend to universalization. **1840** G. S. Faber *Christ's Disc. Capernaum* 225 [A] sentence, which..would have changed this Apparent Universalization into Real Generalization. **1886** W. Graham *Social Problem* 13 A universalisation of the practice [of striking] over the entire field of labour.

universalize (juːnɪˈvɜːsəlaɪz), *v.* [f. universal *a.* + -ize. Cf. F. *universaliser*, It. *-izzare*, Pg. *-isar*.]

1. *trans.* To make or render universal; to give a universal character to; to extend to all the members of a class; to apply or appropriate to a class of things, as distinct from the individuals composing it.

1642 H. More *Song of Soul* ii. ii. iii. 7 Can souls that be thus universalis'd, Begot into the life of God e're dy? **1664** —— *Apology* 552, I do not speak of the English Church,..but of..the Reformed Churches in General—so Universalized were my thoughts in that Meditation. **1840** L. Hunt *Seer* 73/1 Their ideal of a face, let them try to universalise it as they can, is a French one. **1855** Milman *Lat. Chr.* xiv. iii. VI. 463 The conception by the senses is confused,..till abstracted, analysed, at once universalised and individualised by the intelligence. **1876** L. Stephen *Eng. Th. 18th C.* I. 323 We must, then, universalize our terms.

absol. *a* **1853** Robertson *Lect.* ii. (1858) 185 It is thus that the poets universalize and unite. **1871** Fraser *Life Berkeley* iii. 77 We cannot even perceive without universalizing.

†2. To imbue with general (in contrast to specific) properties. *Obs.*$^{-1}$

1676 *Princ. Chymists Lond.* 59 Salts distilled from the Soots of Chymnies, arising from different Woods, notwithstanding their Alteration by the Ambient Air, and their being (by that Medium) in some measure Universallized.

3. To make of universal application; to bring into universal use.

1809 *Crit. Rev.* XVI. 499 He must universalize in his empire the given religion which he prefers. **1829** Bentham *Justice & Cod. Petit.* 102 In the case of circuit business this source of misdecision is purposely established and universalised. **1845** Maurice *Mor. Philos.* in *Encycl. Metrop.* II. 603/1 To universalize the system of Plato. **1891** [F. C. S. Schiller] *Riddles Sphinx* 183 If the law of evolution could be really and completely universalized.

b. To extend or spread over the whole expanse.

1813 Jefferson *Writ.* (1830) IV. 186 To complete and universalize the desolation of the globe. **1875** W. R. Greg *Misc. Ess.* vi. (1882) 144 Our sewerage system shall be universalized and perfected.

Hence **uni'versalized** *ppl. a.*; **uni'versalizing** *vbl. sb.* and *ppl. a.* Also **uni'versalizer**, one who makes universal.

1651 H. More *Second Lash* in *Enthus. Tri.*, etc. (1656) 179 A free divine *universalized spirit is worth all. **1691** Norris *Pract. Disc.* 64 The unselfish universalized nature of God. **1871** R. H. Hutton *Ess.* I. 169 The fourth gospel is essentially a universalised Judaism. **1895** W. M. Ramsay *St. Paul* xvi. §3. 375 A distinct step towards the Universalised Church. **1853** E. G. Holland *Mem. J. Badger* xviii. (1854) 372 The active theological minds..may fall under two general classifications which..we may call the centralizers and *universalizers. **1811** Bentham *Panopt. Corr.* Wks. 1843 XI. 161 An engine for the *universalising of Protestantism. **1891** [F. C. S. Schiller] *Riddles Sphinx* 183 The first case will evidently not bear universalizing. **1836** G. S. Faber *Prim. Doctr. Election* ii. iii. 306 The attentive reader..will readily perceive their palpably *universalising tenor. **1851** *Fraser's Mag.* XLIII. 150 A kind of vagabondizing, universalizing philanthropy.

†uni'versaller. *Obs.*$^{-1}$ [f. universal *a.* + -er^{1}.] One who believes that something is universal; a universalist.

1626 W. Fenner *Hid. Manna* (1652) 44 Thou that are an Universaller of Grace.

universally (juːnɪˈvɜːsəlɪ), *adv.* Also 4 **vniuersalliche, 5 vniuerselly, 6 -allye, -allie.** [f. as prec. + -LY².] In a universal manner.

1. In every case or instance.

1398 TREVISA *Barth. De P.R.* XVI. ii. (Bodl. MS.), Grauel ..also..haþ vniuersalliche kinde of druynge and of clensinge. **1530** PALSGR. Introd. p. xvii, That thyng happeneth in the soundyng of thre of theyr vowelles onely, ..and that nat universally, but onely so often as [etc.]. **1544** *Exhort.* in *Priv. Prayers* (1851) 565 Universally in all our affairs, whatsoever shall befall unto us. **1613** PURCHAS *Pilgrimage* (1614) 130 The fat and bloud being vniuersally forbidden them for food. **1625** N. CARPENTER *Geogr. Del.* I. iii. 66 This proportion is not to be taken vniuersally, but commonly for the most part. **1755** MAGENS *Insurances* II. 189 All Insurances on expected Gains [etc.]..are universally forbid. **1781** GIBBON *Decl. & F.* xxxviii. (1787) III. 588 Under the empire of Charlemagne, murder was universally punished with death. **1809** COLERIDGE *Friend* 28 Such a Rule, if it were universally established, would encourage the arrogant. **1871** MOZLEY *Univ. Serm.* vi. (1876) 122 It would not be true..to say that use was universally accompanied by beauty.

2. So as to include every individual of a group or number; without exception of any.

c **1412** HOCCLEVE *De Reg. Princ.* 2454, I wolde that the hye degree Of Chiualrie vniuersally Bare vp his hede. **1496** *Act 12 Hen. VII*, c. 6 Wollen Clothe,..by making wherof..the pover pepull have moste universally their leving. **1561** T. NORTON *Calvin's Inst.* III. 210 Not one or two of them, but all the Scholemen vniuersallye. **1590** GREENE *Never too late* (1600) 9 Women are vniuersally *mala necessaria*, wheresoeuer they be eyther bred or brought vp. **1618** BOLTON *Florus* (1636) 141 Spaine never had a disposition to rise universally against us. **1662** STILLINGFL. *Orig. Sacræ* III. i. §11 It is hardly conceivable..how mankind should universally agree in some common sentiments. **1709** STEELE *Tatler* No. 46 ¶1 The Zealots..fell universally into this Emperor's Policies. **1798** S. & HT. LEE *Canterb. T.* II. 133 A splendid entertainment, to which the English strangers were universally invited. **1847** G. HARRIS *Life Ld. Hardwicke* II. 33 The whole nation was universally against it. **1869** TOZER *Highl. Turkey* II. 308 They are almost universally malevolent.

3. With extension to every part of a definite whole; in every part or place; everywhere.

c **1430** HOCCLEVE *Min. Poems* 46 The sonne, of whom hir light Shee [*sc.* the moon] takith, & it vniuerselly Yeueth vn-to the world whan it is nyght. **1577** HOLINSHED *Chron.* II. 362/1 Murreyn of cattel beganne..so vniuersally in all places, that no towne nor village escaped free. **1664** H. MORE *Myst. Iniq.* xvi. 58 Which implies that the Church has a right..to be universally spred over the face of the Earth. **1664** H. POWER *Exp. Philos.* I. 61 They are universally diffused throughout all Bodies in the World. **1750** tr. *Leonardus' Mirr. Stones* p. ix, An age when Superstition universally prevailed. **1796** H. HUNTER tr. *St.-Pierre's Stud. Nat.* V. 188 The opinion..is universally propagated over all the Nations. **1846** *J. Baxter's Libr. Pract. Agric.* (ed. 4) I. 15 It is an element universally present in nature. **1871** C. DAVIES *Metric Syst.* III. 275 We have universally the Winchester bushel. **1872** RAYMOND *Statist. Mines & Mining* 15 Universally distributed through the vein.

†**4.** So as to affect the whole or every part of something expressed or implied; all over. *Obs.*

c **1485** *Digby Myst.* (1882) IV. 1357 He suffered patiently.. To be woundid vniuersally with scowrges, nayles, & spere. **1580** BLUNDEVIL *Horsemanship* III. 72 If he be vexed with an ague, or with anie other disease, vniuersallie hurting his bodie. **1734** tr. *Rollin's Anc. Hist.* (1827) IX. 154 The whole city continued universally in flames. **1758** J. S. *Le Dran's Observ. Surg.* (1771) 36 The Child seemed to be universally swelled. **1793** *Minstrel* II. 159 The storm..universally chilled her frame. **1805** EMILY CLARK *Banks of Douro* II. 280 She trembled so universally, that Lucy gave her some.. water to drink.

†**b.** Inclusively, all together. *Obs.*⁻¹

1673 CAVE *Prim. Chr.* III. i. 221 Himself, family, and house [were] universally burnt to ashes.

5. *Logic* and *Metaph.* In relation to all the members of a class or genus; in the manner of a universal proposition or concept (see UNIVERSAL *a.* 11).

1551 T. WILSON *Logike* G vi b, The argument is euermore made from the generall, to the kynde vniuersally. **1620** T. GRANGER *Div. Logike* II. vi, The predicate is in the Subiect vniuersally, that is, in euery subiect of the same kind. **1678** CUDWORTH *Intell. Syst.* 67 The Essences of singular Bodies ..being Abstracted from those Bodies themselves, are consider'd Universally. **1697** tr. *Burgersdicius' Logic* I. xxxi. 122 The enunciation universally first is only that in which the predicate agrees or convenes with the subject. **1725** WATTS *Logic* II. ii. (1726) 152 Mankind..generally have an Inclination to magnify their Ideas, and to talk roundly and *universally* concerning any thing they speak of. **1825** WHATELY *Logic* in *Encycl. Metrop.* (1845) I. 200/1 The term 'necessary to life' is affirmed of food, but not universally; for it is not said of every kind of food.

b. In relation to, in respect of, all the things or subjects of the same class or kind.

1660 BOYLE *New Exp. Phys. Mech.* Pref. p. xiii, Being almost universally a Linguist. **1741** KAMES *Decis. Crt. Sess. 1730–52* (1799) 37 The defender's possession of the estate subjected him universally to the predecessor's debts.

6. With respect to every individual of a class; by, among, to, etc., all the persons concerned.

1647 CLARENDON *Hist. Reb.* II. §51 Which was a design willingly heard, and universally grateful. **1667** MILTON *P.L.* IX. 542 Thy Celestial Beautie.., there best beheld Where universally admir'd. **1726** SWIFT *Gulliver* II. vii, I could not avoid reflecting how universally this talent was spread, of drawing lectures in morality..from the quarrels we raise with nature. **1765** *Museum Rust.* IV. 344 Rye is generally (nay universally, I think) allowed to be a better bearer than wheat. **1804** *Med. Jrnl.* XII. 397 As to my third assertion, its truth is so universally known, that all proof is unnecessary. **1838** DE MORGAN *Ess. Probab.* 167 These tables..are almost universally used by the assurance offices. **1875** W. S. HAYWARD *Love agst. World* 5 He was universally respected in the county.

7. With adjs. or pa. pples. (Sometimes hyphened.)

1656 COWLEY *Praise of Pindar* Notes iv, The Fabulous, but universally received Tradition. **1675** OWEN *Indwelling Sin* v. (1732) 43 The constant keeping of the Soul in an universally holy Frame. *a* **1700** EVELYN *Diary* 13 July 1654, We all din'd at that..universally-curious Dr. Wilkin's. **1818** COBBETT *Pol. Reg.* XXXIII. 180 The chief reason of this universally evil effect. **1869** DUNKIN *Midn. Sky* 8 The universally-known seven stars in Ursa Major. **1890** *Science-Gossip* XXVI. 30/1 The universally received opinion.

uni'versalness. [f. as prec. + -NESS.] The quality of being universal; universality.

1561 T. NORTON *Calvin's Instit.* III. 310 The vniuersalnesse of yᵉ promise. **1587** GOLDING *De Mornay* Pref. xxx, The vniuersalnesse of this consent. **1642** H. MORE *Song of Soul* II. I. ii. 46 They'll object Gainst th' universalnesse of this clear notion. *a* **1680** CHARNOCK *Attrib. God* (1834) I. 56 The universalness of his knowledge. **1880** SCHAFF *Person of Christ* 158 The universalness of his character and mission. **1888** *Longm. Mag.* July 255 The apparent universalness of what is presented to them in quantity.

†**uni'versalty.** *Obs.*⁻¹ [f. UNIVERSAL *a.* + -TY¹.] Universality.

1567 MAPLET *Gr. Forest* 29 Not onely intending an Aegemonie which we onely promised and is but the chiefest part, but an vniuersaltie which is ye whole.

univer'sanimous, *a. nonce-wd.* [Irreg. f. L. *ūnivers-us* universal + *animus* mind.] Universally or completely unanimous.

1862 LOWELL *Biglow P.* Ser. II. ii. ¶2 Though the learned are not agreed as to the particular dialect employed by Theocritus, they are universanimous..as to its rusticity.

univer'sarian. *rare*⁻¹. [Cf. next and -ARIAN.] One who belongs to the universe in respect of knowledge (see quot.).

1880 *Times* (weekly ed.) 16 April, If a mind open to new ideas, no matter whence they come, is to be termed 'cosmopolite', then every thinking being must be a universarian.

uni'versary, *sb.* and *a. rare.* [f. L. *ūnivers-us* UNIVERSAL *a.* or *ūnivers-um* UNIVERSE *sb.*]

†**A.** *sb.* The whole body or number *of* something. *Obs.*⁻¹

a **1604** HANMER *Chron. Ireland* (1633) 205 He injoyned the collegiat Vicars of Kilkenny to celebrate the universary and aniversary of the reverend fathers his predecessors.

B. *adj.* Of or pertaining to, open to, all.

1816 in *N. & Q.* 9th Ser. XII. (1903) 365/2 This first Stone of the Royal Universary Infirmary for Children.

universe (ˈjuːnɪvɜːs). Also 5 **vniuerse, 6 -uers, 7 univers.** [a. F. *univers* (12th c.; = Sp., Pg., It. *universo*), ad. L. *ūniversum* sb., the whole world, orig. neut. sing. of *ūniversus* all taken collectively, universal, f. *ūnus* UNI- and *versus*, pa. pple. of *vertĕre* to turn.]

†**1.** *in universe*, universally, of universal application. *Obs.*⁻¹

c **1374** CHAUCER *Troylus* III. 36 Ye folk a lawe han sette in vniuerse; And þis know I by hem þat loueres be, þat whoso stryueth with ȝow hath þe worse.

2. a. The whole of created or existing things regarded collectively; all things (including the earth, the heavens, and all the phenomena of space) considered as constituting a systematic whole, esp. as created or existing by Divine power; the whole world or creation; the cosmos.

1589 PUTTENHAM *Eng. Poesie* II. xi. (Arb.) 111 The Roundell or spheare..for his ample capacitie doth resemble the world or vniuers. **1596** SPENSER *Hymn Heav. Beauty* 31 Looke on the frame Of this wyde vniuerse, and therein reed The endlesse kinds of creatures. **1611** B. JONSON *Catiline* I. i, O for a clap of thunder now, as loud As to be heard throughout the universe, To tell the world the fact. **1656** COWLEY *Davideis* I. 800 Dull Earth with its own Weight did downwards pierce To the fixt Navel of the Universe. **1738** SWIFT *Pol. Conversat.* 63, I wou'dn't touch a Man's Flesh for the Universe. **1796** H. HUNTER tr. *St.-Pierre's Stud. Nat.* I. 149 That active power of Nature which fills the Universe. **1817** BYRON *Manfred* II. ii. 111 She had..The quest of hidden knowledge, and a mind To comprehend the universe. **1843** *Penny Cycl.* XXVI. 18/1 *Theory of the Universe*,..what is known of the general arrangement of planets, stars, etc. and of their connexion with one another. **1871** MORLEY *Carlyle* in *Crit. Misc.* Ser. I. 216 The same sense of the puniness of man in the centre of a cruel and frowning universe.

b. With *a* and pl. Also const. *of* (something).

1667 MILTON *P.L.* II. 622 A Universe of death, which God by curse Created evil. **1805** WORDSW. *Prelude* XIV. 160 To..substitute a universe of death For that which moves with light and life informed. **1837** CARLYLE *Fr. Rev.* I. I. ii, To Newton and to Newton's Dog Diamond, what a different pair of Universes! **1872** MOZLEY *Mirac.* (ed. 3) Pref. p. xxvi, These two schools of minds live indeed in different universes.

c. *transf.* and *fig.*

less universe (quot. 1674) = MICROCOSM I.

1674 MILTON *P.R.* IV. 459 As..harmless, if not wholsom, as a sneeze To mans less universe. **1728** CHAMBERS *Cycl.* s.v. *University*, They are call'd Universities, or Universal Schools, by reason the four Faculties are supposed to make the World or Universe of Study. **1821** SHELLEY *Epipsych.* 589 Into the height of Love's rare Universe. **1847** J. KIRK *Cloud Dispelled* iv. 67 His conduct is false, and will be denounced as such by the universe of mind. *a* **1854** H. REED *Lect. Brit. Poets* ii. (1857) 62 To trace the associations between the universe of sense and the spiritual life within us. **1871** E. F. BURR *Ad. Fidem* xv. 299 A universe of light and color—a universe of sound.

d. ***universe of discourse***: the totality of entities under consideration; all those that the terms of a proposition may refer to. Also *absol.*, and (as *universe*) in *Statistics*, = POPULATION² 2 d.

1849 A. DE MORGAN in *Trans. Cambridge Philos. Soc.* VIII. 380 By not dwelling upon this power of making what we may properly (inventing a new technical name) call the universe of a proposition, or of a name, matter of express definition, all rules remaining the same, writers on logic deprive themselves of much useful illustrations. *Ibid.*, Let the universe in question be 'man': then *Briton* and *alien* are simple contraries. **1881** J. VENN *Symbolic Logic* vi. 128 We must be supposed to know the nature and limits of the universe of discourse with which we are concerned... If we are talking of ordinary phenomena we must know whether we refer to them without limit of time and space. **1896** 'L. CARROLL' *Symbolic Logic* I. II. iii. 14 The Genus, of which [the] Terms [of a Proposition] are Species, is called its 'Universe of Discourse'. **1898** A. N. WHITEHEAD *Treat. Universal Algebra* I. II. v. 110 If we extend the Universe of self-evident propositions either by some natural or conventional definition, we may extend the conception of conversion. **1911** G. U. YULE *Introd. Theory Statistics* ii. 17 For actual work on any given subject, no term is required to denote the material to which the work is so confined... But for theoretical purposes some term is almost essential to avoid circumlocution. The expression the *universe of discourse*, or simply the *universe*, used in this sense by writers on logic, may be adopted. **1939** A. E. TRELOAR *Elements Statistical Reasoning* i. 8 Such a type of selective sampling from this universe is wholly impossible. **1967** G. WILLS in Wills & Yearsley *Handbk. Management Technol.* 191 Numbers of calls made by sales representatives is a meaningless item of statistics unless it can be related to..the total universe of outlets which can handle such a product. **1972** *Science* 23 June 1306/2 The universe of discourse is severely restricted in this jargon. **1975** *Brit. Jrnl. Sociol.* XXVI. 37 The universe from which the sample was drawn was all Royal Navy officers stationed in England.

3. a. The world or earth, esp. as the place of abode of mankind or as the scene of human activities.

1630 *R. Johnson's Kingd. & Commw.* 134 Such a bridge, that without exception, it may worthily be accounted the admirablest Monument, and firmest erected Collosseum (in that kinde) of all the Vniverse. **1687** T. BROWN *Saints in Uproar* Wks. 1720 I. 89 No People in the Universe know better. **1704** (*title*), The Present State of the Universe. **1765** BLACKSTONE *Comm.* I. 6 A land, perhaps the only one in the universe, in which political or civil liberty is the very end and scope of the constitution. **1791** HAMPSON *Mem. J. Wesley* III. 96 [Wesley] took the universe for his parish. **1820** SHELLEY *Prometh. Unb.* IV. 339 Who all our green and azure universe Threatenedst to muffle round with black destruction.

b. *transf.* The inhabitants of the earth; mankind in general.

1742 *Johnson's Debates* (1787) II. 222 The decline of that power which has so long intimidated the universe. *Ibid.* 230 That wisdom..which..the greatest part of the universe will remember with gratitude. **1774** GOLDSM. *Retal.* 31 Here lies our good Edmund,..Who, born for the universe,..to party gave up what was meant for mankind. **1843** CARLYLE *Past & Pr.* III. viii, 'Go to,..thou shalt pay due debt!' shouts the Universe to them.

Hence **'universeful**, as many or as much as the universe will hold.

1891 J. ORR *Chr. View of God & World* (1893) 374 A whole universeful of other spiritual beings.

universitarian (juːnɪvɜːsɪˈtɛərɪən), *a.* [f. as next + *-arian.*] Of or pertaining to, characteristic of, obtaining in, a university.

1834 F. MAHONY in *Fraser's Mag.* X. 317/1 Awfully ludicrous were the dying convulsions of the old universitarian system. **1858** *Almae Matres* 44 No wars between privileges collegiate and universitarian. **1872** MRS. OLIPHANT *Mem. Montalembert* II. 44 The desire that this universitarian teaching should be above reproach.

Hence **universi'tarianism**, the educational method or system characteristic of or prevailing in a university; advocacy of or preference for this.

1889 *Jrnl. Educ.* 1 Sept. 479/1 At the risk of being accused of classicism, or universitarianism, I must confess that I do believe in a certain amount of classical work.

uni'versitary, *a. rare.* [f. UNIVERSIT-Y + -ARY¹. Cf. F. *universitaire* (1835).] Of the nature of, having the character of, a university.

1889 *Cath. News.* 26 Oct. 5 The half-ecclesiastical, half-universitary French College of Tunis.

‖**uni'versitas.** *Scots Law.* [L.: see next.] The whole (of an estate or inheritance).

1765–8 [see UNIVERSAL *a.* 2 b]. **1838** W. BELL *Dict. Law Scot.* 467 Things, in their nature heritable, may become moveable by being made part of a moveable *universitas.* **1888** LD. MACNAGHTEN in *Law Rep. Ho. Lords* XIII. 383 The legacies are to be paid out of the universitas of the testator's estate.

university (juːnɪˈvɜːsɪtɪ), *sb.* Forms: 6 **vniuersite, 5 -versite, 5–6 -uersitee, 4–5 vnyuersite(e, 5–6 -uersyte(e; 5–7 vniuersitie** (6 *Sc.* **wni-**), **6 -tye, vnyuersytye, -tie, 7 vniuersity, -versity, 6–7 universitie, 7- university.** See also VARSITY, VERSITY. [a. AF. *université, universeté, univercyté*, OF. *universitei, universiteit, université* (13th c.; mod.F. *université*, = Pr.

universitat, It. *università*, Sp. *universidad*, Pg. *-idade*; also in sense 1 MDu. *universitet*, MDu. and Du. *universiteit*, MG., MLG. *universitête*, MHG. *universitêt*, G. *universität*, Dan., Sw. *universitet*):—L. *ūniversitāt-*, *ūniversitās*, (1) the whole, entire number, universe, (2) in later and mediæval Latin (chiefly in legal use), a society, company, corporation, or community regarded collectively; f. L. *ūniversus* (see UNIVERSE).]

I. 1. a. The whole body of teachers and scholars engaged, at a particular place, in giving and receiving instruction in the higher branches of learning; such persons associated together as a society or corporate body, with definite organization and acknowledged powers and privileges (esp. that of conferring degrees), and forming an institution for the promotion of education in the higher or more important branches of learning; also, the colleges, buildings, etc., belonging to such a body. In recent use, const. without article: ***at*** (or ***to***) ***university***, etc.

Sometimes, especially in former use, synonymous with *college*: see COLLEGE *sb.* 4c.

c **1300** *St. Edmund* in *S. Eng. Leg.* I. 438/256 So þat he bigan at Oxenford of diuinite, So noble alosed þer nas non in al þe vniuersite. *Ibid.* 439/278 He bigan so deope desputi of þe trinite, þat gret wonder me hadde þurf al þe vniuersite. *c* **1384** ? WYCLIF *Wks.* (1880) 157 Heþene mennus lawis and worldly clerkis statutis ben red in vnyuersitees. *c* **1400** *Rom. Rose* 6769 At Parys..he had..The accorde of the vniuersite, And of the puple as semeth me. *c* **1425-** [see COLLEGE *sb.* 4]. *c* **1450** *Godstow Reg.* 438 The house..that Robert of Staunton held of the vnyuersite of Oxenford. **1509** FISHER *Funeral Serm. C'tess Richmond* Wks. (1876) 301 The studyentes of bothe the vnyuersytees. **1579** W. WILKINSON *Confut. Fam. Love* 40 They labour to put out the eyes of this land (the Vniuersityes I meane). **1644** MILTON *Educ.* 3 This place should be at once both School and University. **1661** LAMPLUGH in *Extr. St. Papers Friends* Ser. II. (1911) 126 University, Town and Country are far more active and vigilant then before. **1702** LUTTRELL *Brief Rel.* (1857) V. 145 A patent..for founding an university.., to be called king Williams university. **1725** BAILEY *Erasm. Colloq.* (1733) 259 Are you going to Louvain to see the University? **1785** J. ADAMS *Wks.* (1854) IX. 530 He is anxious to study some time at your university [= Harvard College] before he begins the study of law. **1840** CARLYLE *Heroes* v. (1858) 305 Universities are a notable, respectable product of the modern ages. **1856** STANLEY *Sinai & Pal.* x. 364 The great Jewish university which rendered Tiberias for three centuries the metropolis of the race. **1868** M. PATTISON *Academ. Org.* 46 The university of the chancellor, masters, and scholars, is one corporation, and each of the colleges distinct and independent societies. **1959** *Listener* 22 Jan. 153/2 Is the son of a miner working-class, suppose he has gone to university. *Ibid.* 5 Mar. 405/2 At school or at university. **1968** *New Society* 22 Aug. 266/2 'He's at university' (very widely used) is certainly non-U.

b. *fig.* and *transf.* Also in phr. ***the university of life***, the experiences of life, considered as a means of instruction. Cf. *the school of hard knocks* s.v. SCHOOL *sb.*[1] 4b.

1595 *Locrine* III. iii, I think you were broght vp in the vniuersitie of bridewell; you haue your rhetorick so ready at your toongs end. **1607** HIERON *Wks.* I. 386 To be admitted into that great vniuersitie, where He, which is the doctour of the chaire, Christ Iesus, will [etc.]. **1615** (*title*), A Catalogue or Table of all the Arts and Sciences read and taught in this University of London. **1652** BENLOWES *Theoph.* II. xiii, Man,..by infusion wise;..Chanc'llor install'd of Eden's University. *c* **1852** J. GIBSON in *Biog.* (1911) iii. 28 He looked upon Rome as the great University of Sculpture. **1863** MISS BRADDON *Aurora Floyd* xxxi, In the London universities of crime. **1890** 'R. BOLDREWOOD' *Col. Reformer* (1891) 215 None of these young gentlemen was absolutely necessary at that ovine university [= a sheep-station.] **1959** A. GLYN *I can take it All* i. 12 A revolting cliché like 'educated in the University of Life'. **1972** [see LIFE *sb.* 12d]. **1978** P. HILL *Enthusiast* iii. 25 Bob..had the chance to educate him in the real world of people, in the university of life.

c. ***University of the Air***: †(*a*) *Aeronaut.* (see quot. 1931); (*b*) an organization which provides a course of (higher) education partly through radio and television broadcasts; *spec.* an early name for the Open University (see OPEN *a.* 22c).

1931 *Civil & Milit. Gazette* (Lahore) 4 Nov. 2/3 To meet the demand for trained and competent personnel..the College of Aeronautical Engineering has been formed—the University of the Air. **1959** *Twentieth Cent.* Nov. 369 Any government that was determined could give us a University of the Air tomorrow. **1963** *Glasgow Herald* 9 Sept. 1/1 Mr Wilson..suggested the broadcasting time for the 'university of the air' could be obtained by allocation of the fourth television channel... There could also be appropriate radio facilities. **1969** *Radio Times* 27 Nov. 12 Originally named 'the University of the Air', the Open University offers an exciting new opportunity for adults throughout the country to study for degree qualifications through the media of integrated television, radio and specially-designed correspondence courses. **1984** *Listener* 10 May 7/2 When the idea of a university of the air was first floated, sceptics abounded.

†2. a. The whole body, aggregate, or number *of* creatures, persons, things, etc.; = UNIVERSALITY 5.

1382 WYCLIF *Tobit* viii. 19 That the vnyuersite of Jentilis knowe, for thou art God alone in al erthe. ? **1402** QUIXLEY in *Yorksh. Archæol. Jrnl.* (1908) XX. 50 To all þe worldes vniversitie This balade be ensample and myrrour. *c* **1449** PECOCK *Repr.* II. xvi. 243 In al the hool vnyuersite of thingis and of beingis. **1494** *Hylton's Scala Perf.* II. xlvi. (W. de W.), Al thise gracyous knowynges felid in a soule of the vnyuersitee of al creatures. *c* **1510** MORE *Picus* Wks. 18/2 If any part of the whole vniuersitye of creatures were destroyed. **1563** MAN *Musculus' Commonpl.* 29b, All that compasse of the whole vniversitie of thinges and times. **1581** W. FULKE in *Confer.* III. (1584) O ivb, The vniuersitie of faithfull doeth pray. **1604** T. WRIGHT *Passions* VI. 304 The vniversity of Beastes, foules, and fish. **1659** H. THORNDIKE *Wks.* (1846) II. 483 If in all Scripture..a Church signify the university of Christians. **1677** GALE *Crt. Gentiles* IV. 180 The Communitie or Universitie of the Multitude. [**1862** G. LONG tr. *Th. M. Aurelius Anton.* p. lxxvi, The gods will do whatever is best and consistent with the university of things.]

fig. **1382** WYCLIF *Jas.* iii. 6 Oure tunge is fijr, the vniuersite of wickidnesse [L. *universitas iniquitatis*]. **1526** *Pilgr. Perf.* (W. de W. 1531) 76b, Ye tonge is but a small thynge,..but it is (sayth the sayd apostle) the vniuersite of all euyls.

†b. Without const. The whole of something; all things, etc.; universal nature. *Obs.*

c **1374** CHAUCER *Boeth.* v. pr. iv. (1868) 165 þe eye of intelligence is heyȝer for it sourmounteþ þe envirounynge of þe vniuersite and lookeþ ouer þat by pure subtilite of þouȝt. **1382** WYCLIF *2 Macc.* xiv. 35 Thou, Lord of vnyuersitee, or of alle creatures. **1387-8** T. USK *Test. Love.* I. ix. (Skeat) l. 46 Man is mad of al the foure elementes. Al universitee is rekened in him alone. **1432-50** tr. *Higden* (Rolls) II. 205 For God knowethe how euery thynge awe to be create, and how he scholde dispose the pulcritude of the vniversite in hit. **1502** *Ord. Crysten Men* (W. de W. 1506) I. iv. D iij, By the nombre of seuen..vnyuersyte to vs is sygnyfyed. **1610** HEALEY *St. Aug. Citie of God* 314 Where ever they live, they may finde a god the governor and father of all university.

†c. The universe; = UNIVERSALITY 5b. *Obs.*

1494 *Hylton's Scala Perf.* II. xlvi. (W. de W.), Our lorde Jhesu maker & keper of al this fayr vnyuersitee. **1591** SYLVESTER *Du Bartas* I. i. (1641) 5/1 In Six dayes [God] formed..All things contain'd in th' Universitie. **1598** T. BASTARD *Chrestoleros* (1880) 6 Man is a little world and beares the face And picture of the Vniuersitie. *a* **1619** FOTHERBY *Atheom.* II. x. §1 (1622) 299 This Vnity: which they make the onely cause of the whole vniuersity. **1642** H. MORE *Song of Soul* I. ii. 13 Physis is the great womb From whence all things in th' University Yclad in divers forms do gaily bloom.

†d. The whole people; = UNIVERSALITY 5c.

1677 GALE *Crt. Gentiles* III. I. v. 181 That the first invention..of Laws may be committed to prudent men; and yet the..confirmation of them appertain to the universitie or common multitude.

e. *Law.* (See quot. 1832.)

1832 AUSTIN *Jurisprudence* II. p. xli, Such universities of rights and duties (or such complex aggregates of rights and duties) as arise by universal succession. **1861** MAINE *Anc. Law* 178 Without this fact there is no university of rights and duties.

†3. ***your university***, the collective whole of the members of a body, group, or company of persons specifically addressed in some formal or official document. Also pl. in Sc. use. *Obs.*

Chiefly in renderings of the common phrase *Noverit universitas vestra.*

c **1400** *Brut* cli. 163 To alle Cristen peple..Iohn, by the grace of God, kyng of Engeland, gretyng to ȝour vniuersite. **1416** *Munim. de Melros* (Bann. Cl.) 539 Wit yhoure vniuersite þat [etc.]. **1500** *Cartular. St. Nicholai Aberdon.* (New Spald. Cl.) I. 76 Till all ande sindry.., gretinge in gode euirlesting. ȝoure vniuersiteis sall wit ws..till hafe consentit [etc.]. **1543** *Test. Ebor.* (Surtees) VI. 161 Knowe your universitie, that I..do make my last will of certayne my landes. *c* **1596** in *Abstr. Protocols Town Clerks of Glasgow* (1897) V. Pref. 16 To all and sindry..gretyng... Wittis your universiteis that [etc.].

†4. a. A body or company of persons associated together for some purpose. *Obs.*[−1]

1471 CAXTON *Recuyell* (Sommer) 617 Hit is leefful þ[a]t an vnyuersite answere not alway to one maister.

†b. A body or class of persons regarded collectively; esp. an aggregate of persons forming a corporate body or society, a corporation. *Obs.*

1607 COWELL *Interpr.*, *Vniversitie*, is by the Ciuill lawe any bodie politicke, or corporation. **1643** PRYNNE *Sov. Power Parl.* App. 159 Although kings doe die, the people in the mean time (as niether any other Universitie) never dyeth. **1678** SIR G. MACKENZIE *Crim. Laws Scot.* I. i. §7 (1699) 11 A collective Body of People, or university, such as a Burgh or Incorporation. [**1755** MAGENS *Insurances* II. 40 The Prior and Consuls..of the University of the Shippers and Merchants..of this City of Seville. **1776** A. SMITH *W.N.* I. x. I. 148 All such incorporations [of trades] were antiently called universities. *Ibid.*, The university of smiths, the university of tailors, &c. **1843** *Penny Cycl.* XXVI. 22/2 The universities or corporate bodies at Rome.]

II. †5. Extension to the whole (*of* something); = Universality 1. *Obs. rare.*

1553 ASCHAM in *Lett. Lit. Men* (Camden) 18 My trust is ye will not judge me unconstant, for this universitie in choice of my living. **1677** GALE *Crt. Gentiles* III. II. iv. 270 Al perfection importes some kind of universitie. *Ibid.* 271 Now God having the whole of essence in himself must necessarily have an universitie of perfection.

III. *attrib.* and *Comb.* (in sense 1).

6. a. Simple attrib., passing into adj. use (rarely with hyphen): Of, pertaining or belonging to, characteristic of, prevailing or obtained at, a university or universities, as ***university campus***, ***course***, ***court***, ***education***, ***entrance***, ***grant***, ***learning***, ***lecture***, ***library***, ***oath***, ***town***, etc.; ***university-level*** adj.

1379 *Rolls of Parlt.* III. 69/1 Son College appellez Mokel Universite Hall en Oxenford. **1589** R. HARVEY *Pl. Perc.* (1590) 17 He will..praise him, that he is not infected with ..Vniuersitie learning. **1602** *2nd Pt. Return Parnass.* IV. v. 1806 Few of the university pen plaies well. **1606** DEKKER *News fr. Hell* F 3b, Ibis Homere, that hath laine sick seuenteen yeers together of the Vniuersitie plague, (watching and want). **1623** W. L'ISLE *Sax. Treat. conc. Old & New Test.* f. e 3, I meane ere long to let the world know what is more remaining; as more I have seene both in our Universitie Libraries, and that of Sir Robert Cotton. *a* **1628** F. GREVIL *Sidney* (1652) 199 Lest..she might be constrained to..labour the compassing of disorderly ends, by a Mechanicall kinde of University Canvasse. *a* **1700** EVELYN *Diary* 5 Mar. 1673, University lectures and erudition. **1708** J. CHAMBERLAYNE *St. Gt. Brit.* I. III. (1710) 302 [The] University Library [Cambridge]. **1721** SWIFT *Let. to Young Gentleman* 26 You cannot but have already observed, what a violent Run there is among too many weak People against University Education. **1726** R. NEWTON (*title*), University Education; or, an Explication and Amendment of the Statute which [etc.]. **1783** *Encycl. Brit.* (ed. 2) X. 8753/2 The jurisdiction of the university-courts in criminal matters. **1823** J. S. MILL in *Morning Chron.* 8 Feb. 3/1 The violation of the University oath, in every case where its observance interferes in the slightest degree with the convenience of the swearer, is a complete proof that the ceremony of swearing affords no security whatever for veracity in any other case. **1857** C. M. YONGE *Dynevor Terrace* I. v. 68 Fitzjocelyn was twenty-one, and had nearly finished his university education. **1868** *Rep. U.S. Commissioner Agric.* (1869) 140 Students enter upon the university course with a certain preparation. **1871** J. PLACE (*title*), University Tests, and their Abolition, Considered in a Letter [etc.]. **1872** O. W. HOLMES *Poet at Breakfast-Table* 23 The soil of the University town is divided into patches of sandy and of clayey ground. **1895** RASHDALL *Univ. of Europe* II. II. 325 Another essential qualification for a University town..is facility of access. **1919** *Treasury Minute* 14 July in *Rep. University Grants Comm.* 2 in *Parl. Papers* (1921) XI. 362 The Chancellor of the Exchequer states..that he proposes to appoint a Standing Committee..to enquire into the financial needs of University Education... He proposes that the Committee should be known as 'The University Grants Committee'. **1939** University campus [see CAMPUS]. **1957** *Encycl. Brit.* VIII. 941/2 The relationship between the G.C.E. and university entrance qualifications had in the early 1950s reached only a temporary definition. **1962** E. SNOW *Other Side of River* (1963) xxx. 226 Among full-term university-level students 283,000 were engineers. **1974** N. FREELING *Dressing of Diamond* 149 A university education served this much purpose..that emotional problems always got placed at the level of intellectual argument. **1982** H. R. LANE tr. *M. Vargas Llosa's Aunt Julia & Scriptwriter* xv. 266, I had a sudden inspiration and headed..for the university campus. **1982** 'J. ROSS' *Death's Head* xiii. 75 Mrs Knostig's work is financed by a university grant. **1983** *Chron. Higher Educ.* 19 Oct. 1 More and more university libraries are charging fees for interlibrary loans.

b. That is (or has been) a member of a university; educated or studying at a university, as ***university chum***, ***man***, ***student***, etc.

1580 SPENSER *Three Proper Lett.* Wks. (1912) 619/1 Some learned, and well aduized Uniuersitie man. **1641** R. BROOKE *Eng. Episc.* II. vii. 111 They thinke the wayes of Gods Spirit are free, and not tied to a University man. **1706** PHILLIPS (ed. Kersey), *Servitour*,..a poor University-Scholar that attends others for his Maintenance. **1755** *Man* No. 13. 4 An university chum of mine. **1868** M. PATTISON *Academ. Org.* 2 Even University men themselves betray..an impression that something should be done. **1914** G. B. SHAW *Misalliance* p. lxv, An office boy of fifteen is often more of a man than a university student of twenty. **1981** A. EDWARDS *Sonya* iii. 45 Putting his school in the hands of a young university student who had become his assistant.

c. With the names of officials, etc., attached to or connected with a university, as ***university auditor***, ***don***, ***lecturer***, ***librarian***, ***orator*** (see ORATOR 5), ***preacher***, ***professor***, ***register***, ***staff***, ***teacher***, etc.

1589 NASHE in Greene *Menaphon* (1610) A ivb, That royall erection of Trinitie Colledge, which the Vniuersity Orator..aptly termed *Colonia deducta.* **1614** J. CHAMBERLAIN in *Crt. & Times Jas. I* (1848) I. 305 The University Orator, Nethersole,..is taxed for calling the prince *Jacobissime Carole.* **1631** MILTON (*title*), On the University Carrier who sicken'd in the time of his vacancy. *a* **1700** EVELYN *Diary* 10 July 1669, The *Terræ filius* (the Universitie Buffoone). **1708** J. CHAMBERLAYNE *St. Gt. Brit.* I. III. (1710) 298 The Custos Archivorum, or University-Register. **1800** *Cambr. Univ. Cal.* 6 University Officers [include] Chancellor,..High Steward,..Vice-Chancellor [etc.]. **1882** *Addenda Corpus Stat. Univ. Oxon.* 882/2 The University Auditor appointed under the provisions of the Statute. **1893** *Glasgow Univ. Calendar* 19 Lecturers, Demonstrators, or University Assistants. **1907** G. B. SHAW *Major Barbara* II. 236 This love of the common people may please an earl's granddaughter and a university professor. *Ibid.* III. 277 How can you succeed in business when you are willing to pay all that money to a University don who is obviously not worth a junior clerk's wages! **1948** M. LASKI *Tory Heaven* iv. 54 The White Paper analysing the origins and opinions of University staffs appalled the whole nation. **1954** M. BERESFORD *Lost Villages* viii. 266, I went north in April 1948 to become a University teacher. **1971** HALSEY & TROW *Brit. Academics* xv. 413 We see the results in their university teacher children. **1977** *Times* 19 Sept. 3/4, 10,000 more students..with a reduction in the unit cost per student ..is effectively increasing university dons' teaching loads. **1977** M. KENYON *Rapist* iv. 42 Miss Hitchcock, a university professor, arrived in Ireland only yesterday.

d. With past or pres. pples., chiefly in locative combs., as ***university-bred***, ***-educated***, ***-taught***, ***-trained***; ***-going*** adjs.; also with vbl. sbs., as ***university teaching***.

1846 LD. CAMPBELL *Chancellors* cxxi. (1857) VI. 2 The common-place progress of a high-born, university-bred barrister. **1879** J. C. MORISON *Gibbon* 11 The two greatest historians..were not university-bred men. **1898** *Edin. Rev.* Jan. 121 The university-going class among the Roman Catholic community. **1923** R. MACAULAY *Told by Idiot* I. 44 No creature was ever more solemn, more earnest,..than the university-educated young female of the eighties. **1962** C. L. BARBER in F. Behre *Contrib. Eng. Syntax* 21 Those countries where a great deal of university-teaching is carried out in English. **1981** J. Halkin *Fatal Odds* iii. 49 Well-heeled families, university-educated.

7. Special combs., as **university cap**, the academical cap worn by the members of a university, a square cap or 'mortar-board'; **university chair**, the chair or office of a university professor; **University Chest**, at Oxford and Cambridge, the funds of the university, or the office which receives and administers these; **university college** = COLLEGE *sb.* 4 d, *spec.* one which is not or was not empowered to grant degrees (see also quot. 1981); **university extension**: (see EXTENSION 9 g); **university member**, a member of the House of Commons representing a university or a group of universities (university seats were abolished in Britain in 1948); **university sermon**, a sermon preached before the members of a university, usually by a specially nominated or appointed person.

1772 Nugent *Hist. Fr. Gerund* I. 73 Heads stuck in *university-caps. **1831** Carlyle *Sart. Res.* iii. x, They sometimes invert the hat, and wear it brim uppermost, like a University-cap. **1883** *N. & Q.* 15 Dec. 469/1 The University or 'Trencher' Cap. **1711** Shaftesb. *Charac.* III. 287 He finds these Subjects..appropriated to the School, the *University-Chair, or Pulpit. **1717** E. Miller *Acc. Univ. Camb.* 177 Neither the Vice-chancellor.., or the *University Chest, get one Farthing of Money by it. **1870** *Addenda Corpus Stat. Univ. Oxon.* ii. 800 The Curators of the University Chest. **1838**, etc. *University college [see COLLEGE *sb.* 4 d]. **1954** *Times* 1 July 9/6 University College of North Staffordshire..is the only university college empowered to grant degrees. **1981** D. Rowntree *Dict. Educ.* 335 *University colleges.* 1. The name formerly given to the UK civic universities which, when first set up, did not have the power to grant their own degrees and usually granted those of London University instead. The last such (Leicester) became autonomous in 1957. 2. In addition, Oxford, Cambridge, Durham and London each has a college named University College, and it is also the name of the independent university at Buckingham. **1867** *Hansard Commons* 18 June 29, I share the opinion of my hon. Friend the Member for Birmingham, that we are already overstocked with *University Members. **1949** A. P. Herbert in *Punch* 27 Apr. 453/3 Mr. Haddock, by the way, complains rather bitterly that the University Members are being flung out of Parliament in the sacred name of 'One-Man-One-Vote'. **1979** J. Adam Smith *John Buchan & his World* 80 Buchan was delighted, especially because a university member could sit fairly loose to party. **1827** *Oxford Guide* 56 In the Long Vacation there are no *University sermons.

Hence †**uni'versity** *v.*, to provide or endow with a university; **uni'versityless** *a.*, having no university; **uni'versityship**, the state or condition of being a university; status as a university.

1682 *Loyal Satirist* in Somers *Tracts* (1812) VII. 69 Pembroke may be visited, and Manchester *universitied. **1655** Fuller *Hist. Camb.* 21 As for Scotland, it was *University-less till [etc.]. *Ibid.* 35 The *University-ship of Cambridge, is to be accounted from her original constitution.

†**u'nivocacy.** *Obs.*$^{-1}$ [f. post-cl. L. *ūnivoc-us* (see next) + -ACY.] Univocal quality; oneness or sameness of character.

1658 Sir T. Browne *Gard. Cyrus* 135 The Æquivocall production of things under undiscerned principles, makes a large part of generation, though they seem to hold a wide univocacy in their set and certain Originals.

univocal (juː'nɪvəkəl), *a.* and *sb.* Also 6 vnyuocal(le. [f. post-cl. L. *ūnivoc-us* having one meaning (f. L. *ūni-* UNI- + *vōc-*, *vōx* VOICE *sb.*) + -AL^1. So It., Sp., Pg. *univoco*, F. *univoque* (see UNIVOQUE).]

A. *adj.* **1.** †**a.** Of symptoms, signs, etc.: Indicative of, signifying, or denoting one thing; certain or unmistakable in significance. Chiefly *Med. Obs.*

1541 Copland *Guydon's Quest. Chirurg.* Q iij b, Fyrste than in procedynge..to the knowlege of the vnyuocal sygnes. *Ibid.*, The sygnes of lepry aswel equyuocalles as vnyuocalles. **1706** Phillips (ed. Kersey), *Univocal Signs* (in Surgery) are certain Accidents or Signs of the Fracture of the Scull,..distinguish'd from others termed Equivocal. **1738** Warburton *Div. Legat.* I. 5 No less illustrious, but more univocal Marks of Truth, that God hath been pleased to impress upon his Dispensations. **1783** Pott *Chirurg. Wks.* II. 405 Though this be one symptom,..yet it is not an univocal or infallible one.

b. Of terms, etc.: Having only one proper meaning or signification; admitting or capable of a single interpretation or explanation; of which the meaning is unmistakable; unambiguous.

Opposed to EQUIVOCAL *a.* 2. Now esp. in *Logic*.

1656 [? J. Sergeant] tr. *T. White's Peripat. Inst.* 285 The same name would signifie God and a Creature, in the same signification, and would be univocall. **1661** Morgan *Sph. Gentry* I. vi. 88 The crown and horn are in the sacred scripture univocal expressions of glory and dignity. **1671** Baxter *Holiness* xxviii. 9 It is but Analogically called either *Holiness* or *Morality*, and not in a proper or univocal sense. **1725** Watts *Logic* I. iv. §6 Univocal words are such as signify but one idea, or at least but one sort of thing. **1774** Reid *Aristotle's Logic* i. §3. 4 An explication of what is meant by univocal words, what by equivocal. **1843** Mill *Logic* I. ii. §8 A name is univocal, or applied univocally with respect to all things of which it can be predicated in the same sense. **1865** Grote *Plato* I. xvii. 500 The different significations of the same word: the univocal and the equivocal. **1892** *Tablet* 28 May 848 Declaring in terms which are simply univocal [etc.].

†**c.** *Mus.* (See quot.) *Obs. rare*$^{-0}$.

1801 Busby *Dict. Mus.*, *Univocal*, the epithet applied by Ptolemy to the octave and its replicates. [Hence in some later Dicts.]

†**2.** Uniform, homogeneous; not exhibiting variation or deviation; confined to one kind or nature.

Freq. in the latter half of the 17th c., esp. in the writings of Jeremy Taylor; in some instances it is difficult to determine the precise sense.

1615 Crooke *Body of Man* 28 A dead or mortified part.. may not be called a part but equiuocally, because it hath not an vniuocall forme with the whole. **1647** Jer. Taylor *Lib. Proph.* xiii. 201 When the actions and perswasions of a sect ..are univocall. **1653** —— *Serm. for Year* I. xx. 255 The joyes of religion are not univocal but productive of.. præternatural pleasures. **1662** J. Chandler *Van Helmont's Oriat.* 156 So, from the univocall, simple, and homogeneall immortall minde, should so many properties and inclinations of men badly be fetched. **1727** Warburton *Tracts* (1789) 87 But Truth..is of much cooler Contemplation; as paying its Court to the Understanding only, by affording a regular View of its simple univocal Original.

†**3.** Of or belonging to, characteristic of, things of the same name or species; esp. in ***univocal generation***, normal or regular generation between male and female members of the same species. *Obs.*

1638 Jackson *Creed* ix. viii. §3 He which is as truly the Son of God..must needs be as absolutely eternal as the Deity,..otherwise the generation should be equivocal and imperfect, not univocal. **1660** R. Coke *Justice Vind.* 6 Creatures..generated and produced from univocal generation or production, that is, from the coition of male and female of the same species. **1708** *Brit. Apollo* No. 2. 2/1 Generation is Univocal: That is, a Species can be no otherwise naturally formed than by a seminal Production. **1748** *Phil. Trans.* XLV. 656 Thus do these Principles..never deviate further than is consistent with univocal Generation. **1822** J. Fleming *Philos. Zool.* I. 23 A process which is termed Univocal or Regular Generation.

†**b.** Of actions, causes, etc. *Obs.*

a **1640** J. Ball *Answ. to Can* (1642) I. 132 That which is spoken of causes univocall, necessary and proper. **1669** Flavel *Husb. Spiritualized* viii. 76 Grace in it self..cannot be the proper univocal cause of any evil effect. **1697** tr. *Burgersdicius' Logic* I. viii. 27 Action univocal is that by which the action produces an effect of its own species; action æquivocal, of a diverse.

†**4.** Made, uttered, etc., with or as if with one voice. Of consent, etc.: Unanimous. *Obs.*

1615 J. Stephens *Satyr. Ess.* 242 Hee..is never free of the Company..till hee hath drunke out his Apprentise-hood among the grand Masters; and then with an vnivocall consent, hee may commend his Wares. *a* **1734** North *Lives* III. 114 They bellowed and roared with univocal noise, not only in the city but all over England. *a* **1734** —— *Exam.* III. vii. §61 (1740) 548 It was their univocal Declaration, that [etc.].

B. *sb.* A univocal term or word.

1728 Chambers *Cycl.* s.v., Univocals..are defined by Aristotle to be those Things whose Name is common, and the Reason corresponding to the Name..the same. **1788** T. Taylor *Proclus* I. p. ii, If infinite men, horses, and a multitude of other univocals, are produced in an infinite time. **1822-7** *Good's Study Med.* (1829) I. 407 Regius, arquatus, aurigo, are not indeed univocals, but very clearly equivalents.

univo'cality. [f. UNIVOCAL *a.* + -ITY.] The state or condition of being univocal (sense 1 b).

1934 *Theology* XXIX. 342 The Scotists, for whom analogy of being gives way to univocality of being. **1959** *Analysis* XX. 7 Calling them by one name because of three features that they all lack (predicative meaning, ascriptive force, and univocality). **1977** E. von Glasersfeld in D. M. Rumbaugh *Language Learning by Chimpanzee* v. 125 It is unlikely that this univocality will be preserved when more correlators and conceptual lexigram classes are added.

u'nivocally, *adv.* [f. UNIVOCAL *a.* + -LY^2.]

1. So as to mean only one thing or species; in one and the same sense; with one meaning or signification; hence, unmistakably, unambiguously.

1593 T. Bell *Motives Romish Faith* (1605) 110 If matrimony be a sacrament properly and vnivocally so called. **1626** Jackson *Creed* viii. viii. §2 The generall definition..of a servant is univocally the same, (1) in legall servants, (2) in servants to sin [etc.]. **1638** Chillingw. *Relig. Prot.* I. vi. §42. 363 You have not set down cleerely and univocally what you mean by it. **1677** Gale *Crt. Gentiles* III. II. iii. 248 That nothing can predicate univocally of God and the Creature is most evident. **1728** Chambers *Cycl.* s.v. *Predicable*, A Predicable is a Nature which may be predicated univocally of all things to which it is common. *c* **1790** Reid *Let.* Wks. 1846 I. 75/2 The same word may be applied to different things in three ways:..Univocally, when the things are species of the same genus [etc.]. **1842** Sir W. Hamilton in *Reid's Wks.* (1846) I. 205/2 If the names..were to be employed univocally—*i.e.*, to denote always things the same or similar. **1874** *Contemp. Rev.* XXIV. 788 As if every tyro in theology did not know that not even 'being' could be predicated univocally of God and of any creature.

†**2.** By members of the same species; regularly, normally. (Cf. UNIVOCAL *a.* 3.) *Obs.*

a **1676** Hale *Prim. Orig. Man.* II. ix. (1677) 207 Animals which are perfect and univocally generated. **1704** Ray *Creation* (ed. 4) II. 372 All Creatures are generated Univocally by Parents of their own kind. **1728** Chambers *Cycl.* s.v. *Equivocation*, The Moderns..hold that all Animals, nay and Vegetables too, are Univocally produced.

3. With one voice; unanimously.

1671 J. Webster *Metallogr.* xviii. 255 Therefore the.. Secretaries of this Philosophy do univocally testifie, that [etc.]. **1862** *Temple Bar Mag.* VI. 171 All bellowed out univocally that the sole object..was to drive dull care away.

†**u'nivocalness.** *Obs.*$^{-1}$ [-NESS.] = UNIVOCATION.

1697 J. Sergeant *Solid Philos.* 26 The Univocalness which I assert to the word (Cogniton) and (Notion) is such a one as is taken from their Radix (Nosco).

†**u'nivocate,** *a. Obs.*$^{-1}$ [f. post-cl. L. *ūnivoc-us* UNIVOCAL *a.*: see -ATE^2.] Of one sound or pronunciation.

1432-50 tr. *Higden* (Rolls) II. 161 The langage of Normannes is oon and vniuocate [L. *univoca*] allemoste amonge theyme [*sc.* Englishmen] alle.

†**univocation.** *Obs. rare.* [ad. late L. *ūnivocātiōn-*, *ūnivocātio* (Quicherat), noun of action f. **ūnivocāre* (see UNIVOCAL *a.*). Cf. F. *univocation*, Sp. *univocacion*, Pg. *univocação*, It. *univocazione*.] Oneness or identity of name or meaning.

a **1610** G. Fletcher *Israel Redux* (1677) 13 This univocation of Tartar Cities with those of Israel..doth plainly shew that the Israelitish People have been there. **1693** South *Animadv. Sherlock's Bk.* (ed. 2) 242 Since no one Thing can agree both to God and the Creature, by a perfect Univocation. **1728** Chambers *Cycl.* s.v., The School-men have long disputed about the Univocation of Being.

uni'voltine, *sb.* and *a.* [ad. F. *univoltin*, *-tain*, f. *uni-* UNI- + It. *volta* turn, time.] **a.** *sb.* One of a breed of silkworms which produces a single brood in a year. **b.** *adj.* Having but one brood each year.

1874 J. Geoghegan *Parl. Rep. Silk in India* 118 That this insect [*sc.* a silkworm] has quite changed its period of existence.., and from a multivoltine become a uniovoltine [*sic*]. **1883** G. Watt *Econ. Prod. India* III. 66 In Upper India and in Kashmir the univoltine worms are those usually reared. **1892** *Chambers's Encycl.* IX. 453/1 The *B[ombyx] mori* is univoltine or annual.

†**univoque,** *a. Obs.*$^{-1}$ In 6 vnyuoke. [a. F. *univoque*: see UNIVOCAL *a.*] = UNIVOCAL *a.* 1 a.

1541 R. Copland *Guydon's Quest. Chirurg.* Q ij, They.. shulde ryght dylygently beholde theym & considre the vnyuoke sygnes and equyuokes also. And nat for one onely token gyue theyr sentences, but by many conuenaunces, and specyally vnyuokes.

†**uni'ware,** *adv. Obs.* In 4 vn-, onywar, oniwar. [UN-^{1} 11 b and 7: cf. UNAWARE and UNWARE.] Unaware, unawares; esp. in phr. ***on uniware*** = at unaware(s).

1297 R. Glouc. (Rolls) 1966-7 þis prince al an onywar [*v.rr.* al vn ywar, al in on oniwar] toward hom drou. Hii come aȝen him onywar [*v.r.* on oniwar] & slowen him al vor noȝt. *Ibid.* 2927, 3261, 3501, 4328, etc.

†**uni'wares,** *adv. Obs.*$^{-1}$ In 3 unȝewares. [f. as prec. + -S^1. Cf. UNAWARES, UNWARES.] Unawares.

a **1200** *Vices & Virtues* 19 Spedeð ȝeu, forðan ȝure ændedai neihȝeð, and cumð unȝewares al swa þief be nihte.

†**un'jacobitize,** *v.* [UN-^{2} 6 c.] *trans.* To detach from the Jacobite cause.

1719 Ozell tr. *Misson's Mem.* 138 Now their Castles in the Air being overturn'd, they begin to be Unjacobitiz'd.

un'jaded, *ppl. a.* (UN-^{1} 8.)

[**1775** Ash.] **1779** J. Moore *View Soc. Fr.* (1789) I. iii. 23 My head undisturbed with wine, and my spirits unjaded by play. **1876** Miss Yonge *Womankind* xix, The freshness of her unjaded mind. **1880** J. Nichol *Byron* 71 A public taste as yet unjaded by..imaginative descriptions of foreign scenery.

un'jagged, *a.* (UN-^{1} 9.)

1728 Bradley *Dict. Bot.* s.v. *Jacobæa*, This unjagged Ragwort hath..Leaves lying next the Root, not jagged or divided at all.

un'jailed, *pa. pple.* (UN-^{2} 5, 8.)

1630 J. Taylor (Water P.) *World's Eighth Wonder* Wks. II. 62 For Eolus..With winds vniayled came at vnawares, And greeneface'd Neptune with defiance dares.

un'jarring, *ppl. a.* (UN-^{1} 10.)

1624 T. Adams *The Temple* 31 God who..hath put vs in the right & vniarring harmony of truth. **1651** H. L'Estrange *Answ. Mrq. Worcester* 52 A grave Author hath cull'd out..303 oppositions amongst the Marquis his unjarring Catholiques. **1880** S. Lanier *Poems* (1884) 8 The wave-serrate sea-rim sinks unjarring, unreeling.

un'jaundiced, *ppl. a.* (UN-^{1} 8.)

[**1775** Ash.] **1792** Cowper *Lines to Darwin* v, But we.. Can gaze on even Darwin's wit With an unjaundic'd eye. **1804** Collins *Scripscrap.* 161 Men of Merit and Sense.. Behold its Promotion with unjaundic'd Eyes. **1879** Mallock *Is Life Worth Living?* 19 To the unjaundiced eye nothing is more clear than that happiness [etc.].

un'jaunty, *a.* [UN-^{1} 7.] † Ungenteel.

1671 Mrs. Behn *Forc'd Marriage* II. ii, 'Tis the most unjanty humour that ever I saw; I, I, he is my rival. **1687** Settle *Refl. Dryden* 41 It being something Drydenish, Illnatured and unjauntee.., to fair well, and cry Roastmeat, especially to a Husbands face.

un'jealous, *a.* (UN-^{1} 7.)
Also, in recent use, *unjealously* adv.
1673 Clarendon *Relig. & Policy* x. (1811) II. 706 The gentle and unjealous temper of the King. **1789** E. Darwin *Bot. Gard.* II. 8 And three unjealous husbands wed the dame. **1824** Miss Mitford *Village* Ser. I. 121 A pure and unjealous delight that made its own happiness. **1850** L. Hunt *Autobiog.* II. x. 23 The poet, though not unjealous of his dignity. **1876** S. Lanier *Poems, Clover* 2 My large unjealous Loves.

un'jealoused, *ppl. a.* (UN-^{1} 8.)
1710 T. Blackwell *Schema Sacra* Pref. p. ii, Incorporating himself with an unjealoused Creature.

un'jesting, *ppl. a.* (UN-^{1} 10.)
1885 Ruskin *Pleas. Eng.* 108 The unjesting Lombards. **1894** *Athenæum* 23 June 800/1 Until one longs for a dull, unjesting page or two.

†**un'jesuited,** *ppl. a. Obs.* [UN-^{1} 8.] Not influenced by Jesuits.
1659 Gauden *Tears Ch.* III. xxiv. 346 If the unjesuited Papists could have found in their hearts..to apply to that Reformation of Religion [etc.]. **1716** M. Davies *Athen. Brit.* III. *Diss. Drama* 8 The said Servant left most of the Estate to the Un-Jesuited Knight's Lady.

un'jewish, *a.* (UN-^{1} 7.)
1822 *Monthly Mag.* LIII. 125 No other Protestant nation ..keeps the sabbath in so unjewish and unscriptural a manner. **1892** Zangwill *Childr. Ghetto* I. 208 Keeping a dog is an un-Jewish trait.

un'jobed, *ppl. a.* [UN-^{1} 8.] Not reproved.
1732 J. Whaley *Poems* 165, I with gracious Furlo bless'd Unjob'd can Sport and Play.

un'jogging, *ppl. a.* (UN-^{1} 10.)
1748 A. Hill in Mrs. Barbauld *Life Richardson* (1804) I. 129 The unjogging slide of something..that paces their lame understanding smoothly on.

un'join, *v.* Now *rare.* [UN-^{2} 3.]
1. *trans.* To detach from being joined; to disjoin, sever, separate.
1340 *Ayenb.* 107 He him uestneþ zuo ine god þet no þing ne may him to parti ne onioyni. *c* **1374** Chaucer *Boeth.* v. pr. iii. (1868) 159 It byhoueþ..þat þe lynage of mankynde..ben departed and vnioyned from hys welle and faylen of hys bygynnynge. **1400** *Destr. Troy* 939 Jason..gyrd of his hede, Vnioynis the Jamnys þat iuste were to-gedur. **1538** Elyot, *Disiungo*, to vnioyne, to separate. **1583** Golding *Calvin on Deut.* xxi. 127 Euen by vnioyning the thinges that God had ioyned. **1603** J. Davies (Heref.) *Microcosmos* 107 It glues together states, that Warres vnioin'd. **1878** T. Hardy *Ret. Native* I. iii, When folks are just married 'tis as well to look glad o't, since looking sorry won't unjoin 'em.
b. *intr.* To become unjointed or detached.
a **1533** Ld. Berners *Gold. Bk. M. Aurel.* (1536) T iv, My sinewes dry..: the ioyntes vnioyne asonder, and mi spirites are troubled.
2. *trans.* To separate the parts of; to take apart. Also *fig.*, to undo.
1340–70 *Alisaunder* 294 Stones stirred they þo & stightlich layde On hur engines full gist to ungome [*read* unjoine] þe walles. **1377** Langl. *P. Pl.* B. xviii. 255 But ihesus rise to lyue,..conforte al his kynne.., And al þe iuwen ioye vnioignen & vnlouken. *c* **1430** *Pilgr. Lyf Manhode* II. cxlviii. (1869) 135 In Iacob and Esau thou hast seyn the figure: I sawede hem and vnioyned hem.
†**3.** *intr.* To rejoin, make answer. *Obs.*
c **1400** *Destr. Troy* 824 Than Jason vnioynid to the gentill speche:—Lord, and it like you, longe am I here!
Hence **un'joining** *vbl. sb.*
1589 Puttenham *Eng. Poesie* III. xi. (Arb.) 173 This alteration is sometimes by..ioyning or vnioyning of sillables. **1598** Florio, *Diuulsione*, a diuulsion, vnioyning, cutting.

un'joined, *ppl. a.* (UN-^{1} 8.)
1538 Elyot, *Incompactum*, vnioyned, or yll ioyned. **1595** Daniel *Civ. Wars* II. xci, Nor my teares without thine are fullie teares, For thus vnioyn'd, sorrow but halfe appeares. *a* **1600** Hooker *Eccl. Pol.* VII. xxi. §2 In respect of them, who being as yet unjoined unto this conspiracy, may be haply somewhat stayed. **1615** Markham *Eng. Housewife* II. iv. 111 Gather the butter together into one intire lumpe and body, leauing no peeces thereof seuerall or vnioyned.

un'joint, *v.* [UN-^{2} 3.]
1. *trans.* To sever the joints of; to disjoint, to dislocate.
1390 Gower *Conf.* II. 10, I wolde I were unjoynted Of every lime. *a* **1547** Surrey in *Tottel's Misc.* (Arb.) 17 Vnhappy hand, it had been happy time for me, If.. vnioynted hadst thou be. **1561** T. Norton *Calvin's Inst.* II. 115 Like to the partes of a house vnioynted and fallen downe. **1579** Spenser *Sheph. Cal.* Mar. 52 Thilke same vnhappye Ewe..vnioynted both her bones. **1609** Holland *Amm. Marcell.* 161 This old Ram, being unjoynted and taken in pieces, for easier carriage. **1646** Fuller *Wounded Consc.* 101 In case his Leg be set, he flings, flounces, and flies out, unjoynting it again. **1723** *Pres. St. Russia* I. 63 The Houses..are wholly made of Timber notched in on the four Corners, which they can unjoint in a few Hours. **1762** *Phil. Trans.* LII. 509 Hence it proceeded up the nave..to the pulpit, which it unjointed. *a* **1878** W. Carleton *Farm Ballads* (1893) 84 The mechanic Had well-nigh unjointed the stove-pipe. **1903** A. Adams *Log Cowboy* xi, The steer's leg had been unjointed in swinging him around.
†**b.** To carve (*spec.* a curlew or bittern). *Obs.*
c **1470** *Hors, Shepe & G.* (Roxb.) 33 A curlew unioynted. **1508** W. de Worde *Bk. Keruynge* B j b, Vnioint that bytture. [Hence in later works.] **1821** G. Lamb *Catullus* I. 139 Let me see a fowl unjointed, When your table next is spread.
2. *fig.* To sever, separate, disunite.
1561 Norton & Sackv. *Gorboduc* I. i, Eche chaunge of course vnioynts the whole estate. **1577** Hanmer *Anc. Eccl. Hist.* 239 In as much as the subtletye of sophisters, fonde quirckes,..seuered also, and as it were vnioynted the membres of Christ. **1612** Donne *Progr. Soule, 2nd Anniv.* 133 None can these lines or quantities unjoynt, And say this is a line, or this a point. **1624** Middleton *Game at Chess* IV. ii, Hast thou..Unjointed the fair frame of peace? **1671** Milton *Samson* 177, I hear the sound of words, thir sense the air Dissolves unjointed e're it reach my ear.
3. *intr.* To come asunder.
1826 *Acc. Loss Wesleyan Missionaries* (ed. 2) 18 The wreck began to unjoint.
Hence **un'jointed** (also 6 **vnioynte**) *ppl. a.*
1541 R. Copland *Guydon's Quest. Chirurg.* L iv b, To stay and conpryme the places dissolued, and confort the natural heate of the membre vnioynte. **1561** T. Norton *Calvin's Inst.* I. 54 In a ruine they sought for an vpright building, and for strong ioyntes in an vnioynted ouerthrow. **1591** Florio *2nd Fruites* 129 Shee is some what crooke backt, shee hath one shoulder vnioynted. **1614** Raleigh *Hist. World* Pref. A j, The unioynted and scattered frame of our English affaires.

un'jointed, *a.* [UN-^{1} 9.]
1. *fig.* Lacking due connexion or cohesion; unconnected, incoherent.
1588 Fraunce *Lawiers Log.* Ded. ¶4 Neyther himselfe can well understand his unjoynted discourse, nor the hearers conceave his uncohærent jangling. **1596** Shaks. *1 Hen. IV*, I. iii. 65 This bald, vnioynted Chat of his. *a* **1610** Healey tr. *Theophrastus* (1636) 37 Their tedious unjoynted tales. **1687** *Reflect. Hind. & Panther* 35 To renew the old way of fighting with Sand-bags, the true Emblem of his unjoynted, incoherent Stuff.
2. Not furnished with, or connected by, joints.
1681 Grew *Musæum* I. ii. 161 Upon his Shoulders he hath two immovable or unjoynted Horns. **1774** *Phil. Trans.* LXV. 7 The columns..are of the simple, or unjointed species. **1826** Kirby & Sp. *Entomol.* III. 520 A short, tapering, unjointed bristle. **1854** Owen in *Orr's Circ. Sci., Org. Nat.* I. 183 They may be simple, unjointed, firm, bony spines. **1877** Huxley *Anat. Inv. Anim.* vii. 399 Two minute unjointed styles.

un'jointing, *vbl. sb.* [f. UNJOINT *v.*] The action of disjointing or dislocating.
1598 Florio, *Dislogatione*, an vniointing of any lim or joint. **1603** —— *Montaigne* II. xxxi. 410 These spraines, and vnjoyntings of lims. **1639** Fuller *Holy War* v. xxx. 284 The cause, first of the unjoynting, and then of the finall ruine.. of many worthy States.

un'jolly, *a.* (UN-^{1} 7.)
1791–3 *Spirit Public Jrnls.* (1799) I. 419 In dusty schools forlorn, Amongst..books unjolly. **1856** Whewell in *Life* (1881) 458, I look at this prospect with horror. Besides, the mere sitting so long will be 'awfully unjolly'.

un'jolted, *ppl. a.* (UN-^{1} 8.)
1777 Sheridan *Trip Scarb.* Prol., The cramm'd glutton snores, unjolted, home.

un'jostled, *ppl. a.* (UN-^{1} 8.)
1831 Scott *Ct. Rob.* ix, Do you feel that I have not left you unjostled by my advance to these squadrons of yours?

un'journalized, *ppl. a.* (UN-^{1} 8 *a c.*)
1843 Moore *Mem.* (1856) VII. 359 Much of late has been left unjournalised by me.

†**un'journeyed,** *ppl. a. Sc. Obs.*$^{-1}$ [UN-^{1} + JOURNEY *v.* 6.] Not adjourned.
1542 in *Origines Par. Scotiæ* (1854) II. I. 310 [To go and come to the King] vnarrestit, vniornait, vncallit, vnpersewit.

un'jovially, *adv.* (UN-^{1} 11.)
1607 Middleton *Phœnix* II. ii, Lady—what, so unjovially departed?

un'joyed, *ppl. a.* (UN-^{1} 8.)
1837 Verlander *Vestal*, etc. 74 And joy'st thou in..the joys unjoy'd? the griefs ungriev'd?

un'joyful, *a.* (UN-^{1} 7.)
1340–70 *Alisaunder* 1161 Menne..wer..By iustes unioyfull iugged too death. *c* **1374** Chaucer *Boeth.* II. pr. v. (1868) 47 Certys þilke þinges..shullen ben vnioyeful to þe. **1709** Steele *Tatler* No. 16 ⁋2 This unjoyful Set of People, who are always Enemies to those in Possession of the good Opinion of the Company. **1837** Carlyle *Fr. Rev.* III. I. viii, A squalid unjoyful Figure. **1868** Lynch *Rivulet* CLII. ii, Not with unjoyful care Nor with unpraiseful prayer We live below.

un'joyfully, *adv.* (UN-^{1} 11; cf. prec.)
1553 Bale *Vocacyon* Pref. 4 By his Regall power..was I.. confirmed and not all vnioyfully receiued of ye people. **1831** James *Phil. Augustus* III. iii, There were but two beings.. to whom that peal sounded unjoyfully.

un'joyous, *a.* (UN-^{1} 7.)
Also, in recent use (1891–), *unjoyously* adv.
1645 Milton *Tetrach.* 62 It must needs bee both unjoyous and injurious to any perceaving person so detain'd. **1712** Steele *Spect.* No. 406 ⁋8 The wat'ry Length of these unjoyous Moors. **1797** *Monthly Mag.* III. 536/1 The aspect of the new moon was only unjoyous to those who owed money. **1829** Lytton *Devereux* II. ii, A coarse, yet not unjoyous, spirit of reckless debauchery. **1857** Hawthorne *Eng. Note-bks.* (1870) II. 216 All looking unjoyous, and as if they had no home nor parents' love.

un'judge, *v.* [UN-^{2} 6 b.] *trans.* To deprive of the office of judge.
1633 T. Adams *Exp. 2 Peter* ii. 9 If he be not at leisure to do this, it is time to unjudge him.

un'judged, *ppl. a.* (UN-^{1} 8.)
1647 Hexham I, Vnjudged, *ongeoordeelt*. **1709** Shaftesb. *Charac.* (1711) II. 424 Never can the Form be of real force where it is uncontemplated, unjudg'd of, unexamin'd. **1718** Prior *Solomon* II. 722 Causes unjudg'd disgrace the loaded File. **1837** Carlyle *Fr. Rev.* I. v. ix, The morning has worn itself into noon: and he is still unjudged! **1859** Gen. P. Thompson *Audi Alt.* lxxxvii. II. 57 The American colonel who is claiming his millions of dollars..for some unjudged complaint.

un'judge-like, *a.* (UN-^{1} 7 c.)
1644 Milton *Divorce* II. xi. (ed. 2) 53 What more un-Judge-like, more un-Magistrate-like, and in warre more un-commander-like? **1792** Wolcot (P. Pindar) *Ode Ld. Lonsdale* 114 While Erskine..Tears to un-judgelike grins, the hanging Graces.

un'judging, *ppl. a.* (UN-^{1} 10.)
1679 J. Goodman *Penit. Pard.* I. iii. (1713) 65 Those strong, but unjudging faculties,..have an inclination to such things. **1712** Blackmore *Creation* III. 644 You may.. with a different cant the unjudging ear amuse.

un'judicable, *a.* (UN-^{1} 7 b.)
1678 Cudworth *Intell. Syst.* 897 These Sovereign Legislative Powers, may be said to be Absolute also,..as being..Un-Judicable or Un-Censurable by any Humane Court.

unju'dicial, *a.* (UN-^{1} 7, 5 b.)
1599 *Warn. Faire Wom.* I. 34 You have..Some odd ends of old jests scrap'd up together, To tickle shallow unjudicial ears. **1867** *Sat. Rev.* 6 Apr. 436/2 A vigour which almost reaches vehemence, but which is never unscholarlike or unjudicial. **1894** *Daily News* 15 June 3/3 Infusing into it a very unjudicial amount of sentiment and passion.

unju'dicially, *adv.* (UN-^{1} 11, 5 b; cf. prec.)
a **1628** F. Grevil *Sidney* xv. (1652) 198 Not truly active, but rather passive vaine, to imprison and release unjudicially. **1884** *Spectator* 16 Feb. 210/2 Afraid of having the law which they have interpreted so passionately and unjudicially, reviewed in a really judicial spirit.

unju'dicious, *a.* ? *Obs.* (UN-^{1} 7, 5 b.)
1614 Sylvester *Bethulia's Rescue* III. 459 O! unjudicious Judges, will you thus Give Law to God? *a* **1624** Bp. M. Smith *Serm.* (1632) 71 Feare not vniudicious and impudent iudgement of the multitude. *a* **1674** Milton *Hist. Eng.* III. Wks. 1851 V. 100 Prosperous to win a field; but to know the end and reason of winning, unjudicious and unwise. **1725** *Fam. Dict.* s.v. *Lucatellus*, The Sanders is a very unjudicious Ingredient, since it cannot answer any End as a Balsamick. **1776** Mickle tr. *Camoens' Lusiad* 139 *note*, An unjudicious mixture of sacred and profane mythology and history.

un'juiced, *ppl. a.* [UN-^{2} 4, 8.] Deprived of juice; squeezed out.
a **1652** Brome *City Wit* IV. i, Every man lov'd his Fortune, squeez'd it, and when it was unjuic'd, farewell kind heart.

un'juicy, *a.* (UN-^{1} 7.)
1712 Blackmore *Creation* VII. 418 From unjuicy limbs without a root..leafy branches shoot.

un'jumpable, *a.* (UN-^{1} 7 b.)
1886 *Horse & Hound* 4 Dec. 742 A fine fox..ran..by the side of the unjumpable bottom.

un'just, *a.* [UN-^{1} 7, 5 b; cf. Du. *onjuist*.]
1. a. Of persons: Not acting justly or fairly; not observing the principles of justice or fair dealing. Also const. *to*.
1382 Wyclif *Heb.* vi. 10 Sothli God is not vniust, that he forȝete ȝoure workis. **1549** Cheke *Hurt Sedit.* (1569) D iij b, Shall they be thought not vniust, who..misvse and waste the same vngodlye? **1568** Grafton *Chron.* II. 400 An vniust and unprofitable Prince. **1603** Shaks. *Meas. for M.* v. i. 302 The Duke's vniust, Thus to retort your manifest Appeale. **1664** in *Verney Mem.* (1907) II. 208 You would bee very unjust to your sonne. **1729** Butler *Serm.* Wks. 1874 II. 16 [Men] are as often unjust to themselves as to others. **1781** Cowper *Expost.* 56 He saw his people..avaricious, arrogant, unjust. **1841** Lane *Arab. Nts.* I. 74 In the beginning of his reign [he was] an unjust monarch. **1876** J. Parker *Paracl.* II. xix. 354 To compare the universal with the limited is to be unjust to both.
absol. **1382** Wyclif *1 Pet.* iii. 18 Crist oonys dyede for oure synnes, he iust for vniuste. **1593** Shaks. *Lucrece* 285 Foul hope and..fond mistrust; Both which, as servitors to the unjust, So cross him [etc.]. **1667** Milton *P.L.* XI. 455 Th' unjust the just hath slain, For envie. **1781** Cowper *Expost.* 268 Cry to the proud, the cruel, and unjust. **1847** Emerson *Repr. Men, Plato*, False opinion respecting the just and unjust.
b. Of actions, etc.: Not in accordance with justice or fairness. Phr. ***unjust enrichment***: see quots.
c **1400** *Destr. Troy* 12965 This Forsenes..prayet, þat he might ryde..To Ioyne with Engest for his vniust werkes. **1549** *Compl. Scot.* 2 [They] intendit ane oniust veyr.. contrar our realme. *a* **1586** Sidney *Astr. & Stella* v. x, I lay then to thy charge vniustest tyrannie. **1611** Bible *Prov.* xxviii. 8 By vsurie and vniust gaine. **1697** Dryden *Virg. Past.* I. 93 Are we condemned by fate's unjust decree, No more..our homes to see? **1766** Kames *Princ. Equity* (1767) 6 An action that we ought not to do is termed unjust; and the omission of what we ought to do is also termed unjust. **1858** J. B. Norton *Topics* 156 Every case of annexation has been most manifestly unjust. **1890** *Retrospect Med.* CII. 399 It would be unjust not to refer..to the excellent results obtained by Pawlik and Byrne. **1942** *Law Rep.* 4 July 135 It is clear that any civilised system of law is bound to provide remedies for cases of what has been called unjust enrichment or unjust benefit, that is, to prevent a man from retaining the money of..another which it is against conscience that he should keep. **1962** A. Turner *Law of Trade Secrets* IV. iv. 346 The term 'unjust enrichment' refers to the use to which a disclosure is put. **1973** *N.Y. Law Jrnl.* 24 July 12/3 The defendants..have counterclaimed for $7,500, in damages for unjust enrichment.
absol. **1659** Rushworth *Hist. Coll.* I. Ep. Ded., The Law ..puts a Difference betwixt Good and Evil, betwixt Just and

Unjust. 1733 Pope *Ess. Man* III. 269 So drives Self-love, thro' just and thro' unjust, To one Man's pow'r.

2. Not upright or free from wrong-doing; faithless, dishonest. Also const. *of* or *to*. Now *rare*.

c 1500 *Communycacyon* (W. de W.) B ij, But lorde though I haue ben uniuste..I hope to rube awaye the ruste With repentaunce and grace of the. 1526 Tindale *Luke* xvi. 8 The lorde commended the uniust stewarde because he had done wysly. *a* 1593 Marlowe *Massacre Paris* II. v. 686 Thou trothles and vniust, what lines are these? 1603 Knolles *Hist. Turks* (1621) 958 Their king accounted unjust of his word; who [etc.]. 1651 Hobbes *Leviath.* I. xv. 71 When a Covenant is made, then to break it is Unjust. 1766 Goldsm. *Vicar* xxxi, Else nothing could have ever made me unjust to my promise. 1857 Trollope *Barchester T.* xxxix, Mr. Plomacy was not quite happy in his mind, for he thought of the unjust steward.

†**3.** Improper; incorrect. *Obs.*

a 1533 Ld. Berners *Gold. Bk. M. Aurel.* (1546) Q vj b, They..leaue the iuste trauayle, and take vniuste idelnesse. 1586 A. Day *Eng. Secretary* II. (1625) 98 Would they not thinke you, straight proclaime against vs the vniust name of Christians. 1613 Purchas *Pilgrimage* II. viii. 143 Beda giveth an uniust interpretation of their name. 1713 Steele *Guard.* No. 17 ¶ 1 The unjust taste they have who affect that way of pleasure.

†**4.** Irregular; inexact; inaccurate. *Obs.*

1602 J. Davies (Heref.) *Mirum in Modum* Wks. (Grosart) I. 22/2 The Sea through vaines and Arteries of the Earth, Creeps through her Corpes,..And then returnes with windings most vniust. 1612 W. Colson *Gen. Tresury* 246 Because of the vniust fractions in the said table..the said proofe will be found somewhat vniust, but tollerable.

un'justice. [un-¹ 7, 5 b.]

1. = injustice. *Obs.* exc. *Sc.*

1532 More *Confut. Tindale* Wks. 579/2 An occasion to lay the weght of their iust damnacion, to the vniustice of gods eternal ordinaunce. 1569 Underdown *Ovid's Invect. Ibis* E iiij, Pausanias therefore much moued with the kings vniustice,..slewe hym. 1626 R. Harris *Hezekiah's Recovery* (1630) 4 He intimated that Ingratitude was a kinde of Vnjustice. 1687 Stanley *Hist. Philos.* (ed. 2) XIII. 933/1 His unjust deeds will come to the ears of the avengers of Unjustice. 1704 J. Gibbs *Sev. Divine Treat.* (ed. 3) 103 All the Infidelity and Unjustice of Unbelievers. 1871 W. Alexander *Johnny Gibb* xvii, To dee 'im nae oonjustice, we sall suppose that he only deliver't the laird's orders.

†**2.** (See quot. and justice *sb.* 8.) *Obs.*⁻¹

a 1661 Fuller *Worthies, Essex* I. (1662) 323 Rose Allin.., who being in her Calling,..was intercepted by Iustice, or rather un-justice Tyrrell, who with a Candle most cruelly burnt her wrists.

un'justifiable, *a.* (un-¹ 7 b, 5 b.)

In very frequent use from *c* 1760.

1641 Clarendon *Hist. Reb.* I. §117 Their unjustifiable designs and pretences. 1674 *Essex Papers* (Camden) 262 Being resolved never to doe any Thing unjustifyable. 1716 Hearne *Collect.* (O.H.S.) V. 324 An intolerable and unjustifyable Injury. 1748 Hartley *Observ. Man* II. ii. §34. 171 They did nothing unjustifiable. 1849 Macaulay *Hist. Eng.* vii. II. 178 That even..Russell had gone to unjustifiable lengths against the government. 1879 Trollope *Cousin Henry* xi, They had been hard words—quite unjustifiable unless [etc.].

Hence **un'justifiableness.**

1653 Manton *Exp. James* ii. 24 The unjustifiableness of that faith which is without works. 1728 R. Morris *Ess. Anc. Archit.* 91 The Unjustifiableness of Proceedings of this nature. 1745 J. Marchant *Expos. Gen.* xix. 66/2 The Unjustifiableness of the Means dissecrates the Means. 1853 Ruskin *Stones Ven.* III. i. §14. 9 In proportion to the unjustifiableness of its introduction, was the extravagance of the form it assumed.

un'justifiably, *adv.* (un-¹ 11.)

[1755 Johnson.] 1758 Secker *Serm. 5 Nov.* (1771) 355 Censuring the legal Constitution of any Government, because they, who rebel against it, behave unjustifiably. 1796 Morse *Amer. Geog.* I. 116 That part of Florida which they had cruelly and unjustifiably seized three years before. 1834 James *J. Marston Hall* xxi, That liberty of which they have been most unjustifiably deprived. 1883 Ruskin in *Westm. Gaz.* 8 Aug., My friends flatter me unkindly and unjustifiably.

un'justified, *ppl. a.* [un-¹ 8.]

†**1.** Not brought to justice; not punished or executed. *Obs.*

c 1340 Hampole *Pr. Consc.* 5871 At þat day..loverds alswa [shall give account] of þair meigne þe whilk þai lete uniustifyed be. 1564 *Reg. Privy Council Scot.* I. 306 He wald haif sauffit the sone of ane theif, being his tennent, unjustifiit, allegeand [him]..to be his awin. 1596 Dalrymple tr. *Leslie's Hist. Scot.* II. 202 Gif it be won, nocht ane in the castel, except the king sal chaip vniustifiet.

2. a. Not brought into a state of justification.

1651 Baxter *Inf. Bapt.* 308 If they have not *Jus in re*, then they are still unpardoned, and unjustified. 1661 *Papers Alter. Prayer-bk.* 104 Those that by living in open sin, do shew themselves to be unjustifyed. 1701 Beverley *Glory of Grace* 51 Let him be Unjustifyed still. 1828 Webster (citing J. M. Mason).

b. Not cleared from a charge or imputation.

1678 Dryden *All for Love* IV. iv, I go Unjustifi'd, for ever from your sight.

3. a. Not made exact or accurate.

1671–2 T. Marshall in Hart *Notes Cent. Typogr. Oxf.* 166, I haue examined yᵉ unjustifyed Paragon Greek matrices.

b. With type not adjusted to fill up the line or produce an even margin.

1961 Webster, *Unjustified*,..of a line of type: not adjusted properly to fill the measure. 1963 *Times* 6 Mar. 9/6 The *Oklahoma City Times* published its regular editions today with type set entirely by computer... 'Unjustified' perforated tape, such as might be made by a reporter working on a special tape-producing typewriter, is fed into the computer, which cuts a perforated tape. 1971 *Sci. Amer.* Aug. 116/2 This 300-page book, with..its text in unjustified typescript, indexes the work of the center. 1980 C. Burke *Printing Poetry* iii. 32 Some..of the problems in a prose setting can be obviated by setting it 'ragged right', that is by leaving the right-hand margin unjustified.

4. Not proved to be right or proper; unwarranted.

In frequent use from *c* 1885.

1685 Boyle *Enq. Notion Nat.* iv. 97 The boldness of these unjustified paradoxes. 1849 Cobden *Speeches* 27, I hope I may not be considered as unjustified by precedent. 1885 *Law Times* 23 May 62/1 The plaintiff's conduct..was unjustified.

un'justify, *v.* (un-² 6 c.)

1646 Hammond *Tracts* 31 In the same proportion that any such act of sin doth unjustify, it doth unsanctify also. 1654 Warren *Unbelievers* 250 No following sin shall unjustifie him.

un'justly, *adv.* [un-¹ 11, 5 b.]

1. In an unjust manner; contrary to the principles of justice.

1382 Wyclif *1 Pet.* ii. 19 If for conscience of God ony man suffrith sorewes,..suffringe vniustly. 1529 More *Suppl. Souls* Wks. 291/1 He concludeth..who that iustlye punishe a priest by the temporal law, is vniustly troubled agayn in the spirituall law. *a* 1557 in *Tottel's Misc.* (Arb.) 141 Here lieth vnhappy Harpelus,..By Phillida vniustly thus Murdred with false disdaine. 1604 Rowlands *Looke to it* 8 Suff'ring the Iust vniustly be oppreſt. 1651 Hobbes *Leviath.* II. xxii. 122 It is evident enough, that they have done unjustly. 1722 Wollaston *Relig. Nat.* vi. (1724) 138 Even the desire of obtaining any thing unjustly is evil. 1783 Hailes *Antiq. Chr. Ch.* iv. 79 Rutilius..was unjustly banished. 1860 Pusey *Min. Proph.* 314 To judge unjustly, absolving the guilty, condemning the innocent. 1891 Farrar *Darkn. & Dawn* lxvi, Unjustly suspected of a disloyal intention.

†**2.** Improperly; incorrectly. *Obs.*

1612 Selden *Illustr. Drayton's Poly-olb.* iv. 73 This accompt..White of Basingstoke (although ayming to be accurat) uniustly followes. 1755 *Phil. Trans.* XLIX. 222 Whose upper surface is strictly a horizontal plane, and not convex,..as is always, tho' very unjustly, painted.

un'justness. [un-¹ 12.] Injustice.

c 1449 Pecock *Repr.* I. xviii. 106 The vniustnes of iuging which is ȝouun upon me y knowe better than the vniustnes of iugingis doon vpon othere. 1586 A. Day *Eng. Secretary* I. (1625) 67 The indignity, vniustnesse, wickednesse,..that thereof ensueth. 1599 Crompton *Mansion of Magnan.* L 1 b, The vniustnesse of this man to his Lord. 1622 Mabbe tr. *Aleman's Guzman d' Alf.* II. 9 He shall therein..giue me iust cause to suspect the vniustnesse of his intent. 1670 Penn *Truth Rescued* 62 The Unreasonableness and Unjustness of such Arbitrary Proceedings. 1757 Mrs. Griffith *Lett. Hen. & Frances* (1767) I. 48, I interdict you..from the unjustness of any satyr against our sex. 1879 C. Geikie *Eng. Reform.* xix. 330 The unjustness of a wholesale confiscation. 1887 L. Oliphant *Episodes* 211 The unjustness of my suspicions.

†**unk,** *pron. Obs.* In 3 unc (*Orm.* unnc), unke. [OE. *unc*, dat. and acc. of *wit* we two, = NFris. *unk*, *onk*, OS. *unc*; Goth. *ugkis* (also acc. *ugk*); ON. *okkr*.] Us two, both of us.

c 1200 Ormin Ded. 27 Unnc birrþ baþe þannkenn Crist þatt itt iss brohht till ende. *c* 1205 Lay. 23626 For þi hit is betere bi-twixen unke seoluen to-dælen and to-dihten þis kine-lond mid fihte. *a* 1225 *Leg. Kath.* 1515 Swa þe cnotte is icnut bituhhen unc tweien. *a* 1275 *Prov. Alfred* 583 Mine daȝis arren nei done, and we sulen unc to-delen.

unk (ʌŋk), *sb.* Also **unkie, unky.** Colloq. or nursery abbrevs. of uncle *sb.*

1907 A. Bennett *Grim Smile of Five Towns* 21 'You carry me down-stairs, unky?' the little nephew suggested. 1957 W. Faulkner *Town* iii. 65 'We need a grindstone,' Gowan said. 'Unk Noon,' Top said. 'We'll take the gun like we're going rabbit hunting,' Gowan said. So they did: As far as Uncle Noon Gatewood's blacksmith shop on the edge of town. 1959 N. Marsh *False Scent* (1960) ii. 50 It's so hard to explain, Unky. 1971 A. Diment *Think Inc.* ii. 19 Didn't you realise you should come home..and tell Unkie Rupert all about it? 1977 C. McCullough *Thorn Birds* xvii. 408 There's been tons of male influence for your children with the Unks around.

unkaimed, -kamed: see uncombed.

unkard(ness, dial varr. unked(ness.

Cf. *unkward* in Skinner (1671) s.v., and dial. *unkert*.

1727 Bailey (vol. II), *Unkardness*, Solitariness, Loathsomeness. 1787 Grose *Prov. Gloss.*, *Unkard*, awkward. 1788 W. H. Marshall *Yorksh.* II. Gloss. s.v., A servant is *unkard* on his first going to a fresh servitude. 1855–91 in Whitby and Gloucester glossaries.

un'keamed, obs. variant of unkembed.

1600 J. Lane *Tom Tel Troth* 369 Pyning Enuie..With..withered face, and with vnkeamed haire. 1697 *View Penal Laws* 260, 2000 Tods of unkeamed Wool.

'unked, 'unkid, *a.* Now *dial.* Forms: α. 4–5 vnkid (4 -kidd, 5 -kidde), vnkyd (4 -kydd, 6 -kydde), vnkud, 8–9 unkid. β. 4 vnkede, 5– unked, 8–9 unket. [ME. *un-kidd*, f. un-¹ + pa. pple. of kithe *v.* Cf. unco, uncouth, unkard, unketh, and unquod *adjs.*]

1. Not made known or revealed; unknown, unfamiliar, strange.

a 1300 *Cursor M.* 6920 He-self has berid him and hidd In a priue sted vn-kydd. *c* 1375 *Sc. Leg. Saints* xxxi. (*Eugenia*) 90 Oure treutht to þaim wes vnkid. *a* 1400 *R. Gloucester's Chron.* (Rolls) 7247 þre kinges were of engelond of vnkunde [*MS. C.* vnkede] sede. *c* 1465 *Eng. Chron.* (Camden, 1856) 2 Not onli for deuocion, but also forto se the newe and unkid solennite. 1540 Hyrde tr. *Vives' Instr. Chr. Wom.* (1541) 47 The women were taken with an unked kynd of franzy. 1583 *Abstract of Acts, Canons, etc. temp. Q. Eliz.* 70 A phisition..must not minister after any vnked maner, but [etc.]. 1825 Brockett *N.C. Words*, *Unket*, *Unkid*, strange, unusual. 1894–6 in Northumb. and Warw. glossaries.

2. Awkward or troublesome through being unfamiliar or unknown.

1634 C. Butler *Eng. Gram.* Pref., So powerful is the tyrant custom..that..this little change..will seem to some harsh and unked at first. 1810 S. Green *Reformist* I. 89, I, who never has handled a needle, will make but an unked kind of business of it. 1815 Mrs. Pilkington *Celebrity* I. 131 It is but an unked kind of way for a stranger to find.

b. Causing awkwardness or unpleasantness.

1860 Hughes *T. Brown at Oxf.* xviii, I hopes as you don't think I be any ways unked 'bout this here quire-singin'.

3. Unfamiliarly lone or dreary; lonely, dismal, forbiddingly dull.

1706 Phillips (ed. Kersey), *Unked*,..Solitary, Lonely. 1727 Hearne *Diary* 11 Nov., W[hi]ch way (a strangely unked, solitary walk) I had never went..before. 1790 Cowper *Let. to Mrs. Throckmorton* 21 Mar., Weston is sadly unked without you. 1825 Jennings *Observ. Dial. W. Eng.* 148 Late at night a rawd along All droo a unket ood. 1869 Blackmore *Lorna D.* xiii, The place was unkid and lonesome, and the rolling clouds very desolate.

b. Of persons: Feeling lonely, dull, or depressed.

1760 Miss Talbot *Let. to Mrs. E. Carter* 8 May, Mr. Okey gone to his apprenticeship, and I a little *unkit* for want of my scholar. 1795 H. Walpole *Let. to Miss Berry* 2 Sept., I am very unked without you. 1854 Miss Baker *Northampt. Gloss.* s.v., Old people suffering from the loss of friends will frequently say they feel very unkid.

4. Disagreeable, unpleasant, unnatural, eerie.

1800 *Gentl. Mag.* Feb. 107 [In Oxon.] every thing that is unfortunate, or unlucky, or not as it could be wished, is *unked*. 1864 Chr. G. Rossetti *Jessie Cameron* v, By her hut ..they would not pass at night, Lest they should hear an unked strain Or see an unked sight. 1884 *Standard* 6 Sept. 2/1 The..lapping of the waters evoke[s] a weird feeling that is somewhat, as the West Country people called it, *unked*.

Hence **'unkedness.** *rare.*

1796 Charlotte Smith *Marchmont* I. 232 The unketness of the place. 1838 Lady Lyttelton *Lett.* (1873) 235, I.. had a wretched unkedness of a morning at the Inn. 1905 *Eng. Dial. Dict.* s.v.

unked: see uncked *a. Obs.*

un'keeled, *ppl. a.* [un-¹ 8.]

1. Not sailed upon; not traversed by ships.

1807 J. Barlow *Columb.* I. 526 Their waves unkeel'd, their havens unexplored.

2. Not furnished with a keel.

a 1844 Campbell *Napoleon & Brit. Sailor* 35 A wherry.. uncompass'd, and unkeel'd. 1870 Hooker *Stud. Flora* (1884) 289 The glabrous unkeeled sepals.

un'kembed, *ppl. a.* Now *rare.* Forms: α. 4, 6–7 **vnkemd** (7 unkem'd), 5 **vnkemmyde**, 6 *Sc.* **vnkemmit**, 6–7 **vnkemmed** (9 un-). β. 5 **vnkembyd**, 6 **-keembd**, 7 **-kembed, -kemb'd, -kembd.** [un-¹ 8. Cf. ON. *úkembdr*, MHG. *ungekembet*.] Uncombed, unkempt.

1390 Gower *Conf.* III. 260 Hire her hangende unkemd aboute. 1483 *Cath. Angl.* 202/1 Vn kembyd,..*jmcomptus*, *impexus*. 1542 Udall *Erasm. Apoph.* 80 b, He brought theim foorth vnkembed & vnpiked, without cotes. 1565 Golding *Ovid's Met.* I. (1590) 16 Hir haire unkemd about hir necke downe flaring. 1627 May *Lucan* VI. 585 Laden she is with long vnkemmed haires. 1693 Dryden *Juvenal* III. 121 His once unkem'd, and horrid Locks. 1697 *View Penal Laws* 267, 1000 Tods of unkemb'd Wool. 1824 Carr *Craven Gloss.*, *Unkemmed*, [1828 *Unkemb'd*,] uncombed. 1860 Kay-Shuttleworth *Scarsdale* II. 28 Ungroomed, and unkemmed strings of 'gals'.

fig. 1577 tr. *Bullinger's Decades* I. i. 13/1 In these plaine and simple, not darke and vnkemmed books, is comprehended the ful doctrine of godlynes.

un'kempt, *ppl. a.* [un-¹ 8 b: cf. prec. and older Flem. *ongekempt*.]

1. Of hair, etc.: Uncombed.

1742 Shenstone *Schoolmistr.* ii, Oft-times [they]..For Hair unkempt..are sorely shent. 1825 Ld. Cockburn *Mem.* (1856) 268 The burr in the throat,..the unkempt locks. 1843 Carlyle *Past & Pr.* III. x, It is forever indispensable for a man to fight: now with Necessity,..tangled Forests, unkempt Cotton.

b. Having the hair uncombed or dishevelled.

1748 Thomson *Cast. Indol.* I. lxi, Unkempt, and rough, of squalid face and mein. 1812 Byron *Ch. Har.* I. xvii, Though shent with Egypt's plague, unkempt, unwashed. 1877 Black *Green Past.* xlv, Tall, uncouth, unkempt fellows.. seated on a bench smoking.

transf. 1864 Miss Braddon *Doctor's Wife* i, The horse had a rakish, unkempt look about the head and mane.

c. Neglected; not cared for; untrimmed; rough.

1867 D. G. Mitchell *Rural Stud.* 1 A wild, unkempt, slatternly farm. 1879 Dixon *Windsor* II. xx. 207 Their filthy habits and unkempt attire.

fig. 1861 J. Brown *Horæ Subs.* Ser. II. 370 In that formidable and unkempt nature..lay the delicacy..of a gentleman.

†**2.** *fig.* Of language: Inelegant, unrefined; rude. (Cf. incompt *a.*, uncombed *ppl. a.* 2.) *Obs.*

1579 Spenser *Sheph. Cal.* Nov. 51 To well I wote..howe my rymes bene rugged and vnkempt. 1590 —— *F.Q.* III. x. 29 Thy offers base I greatly loth, And eke thy words vncourteous and vnkempt. 1606 N. Baxter *Sidney's*

Ourania D 2 Our Spokes beene blunt, .. Vnable in Mysteries to know the sooth; Vnkempt, vnpolished, ignorant, lewde.

Hence **un'kemptness**.

1876 *World* V. 16 Untidyness and unkemptness [of a garden]. **1900** *Scribner's Mag.* Sept. 297/2 The foul unkemptness of the natives.

un'kenned, *ppl. a.* Chiefly *Sc.* and *north.* Now *arch.* or *dial.* [UN-¹ 8. Cf. NFris. *ünkänd*, Norw. *ukjend*, Da. *ukendt*, Sw. *okänd*, Du. *ongekend*. See also UNKENT *ppl. a.*]

1. Unknown; strange.

a **1300** *Cursor M.* 28474 Wit womman knaun and vnkend. *c* **1375** *Sc. Leg. Saints* xvi. (*Magdalene*) 891, I ame scho .. þat here þe thretty vintir ay til al men has vnkennyt bene. *c* **1400** tr. *Secreta Secret., Gov. Lordsh.* 84, I aiugyd þat þey [*sc.* secrets] sholde noght be vnkennyd to þy worthy myghtynesse. *a* **1440** *Sir Eglam.* 843 A grype .. Hur yonge sone awey .. bare Yn-to a cuntre unkende. *c* **1475** *Rauf Coilȝear* 247, I am wonder wa to cum quhair I am vnkend. **1535** STEWART *Cron. Scot.* (Rolls) II. 115 Quhat movit thame it is wnkend to me. **1591** SYLVESTER *Du Bartas* I. iii. 1160 Let me .. among the Great un-kend, My rest of dayes in the Calm Countrey end. **1632** J. HAYWARD tr. *Biondi's Eromena* 193 Both of us altogether unkend and quite forgotten. **1721** RAMSAY *Keitha* 37 Ye unkend pow'rs wha water haunt or air. **1785** BURNS *To W. Simpson* vii, She lay like some unkend-of isle. **1814** SCOTT *Wav.* xviii, For the .. trouble which he had .. to an unkenn'd degree.

2. Undescried, unperceived; unexplored.

1592 DANIEL *Compl. Rosamond* 422 Witnesse the world, wherein is nothing rifer, Then miseries vnken'd before they come. *a* **1680** BUTLER *Rem.* (1759) I. 417 No Ship in the Day time, can pass unken'd. **1747** [G. RIDLEY] *Psyche* xxiv. in *Museum* III. 88 Unkenn'd of her, he raught the embroider'd Bank. **1890** Æ. PRINCE *Palomide* 25 Deep in trackless, unkenned ways.

Hence **un'kennedness**.

1896 FLORA A. STEEL *Face of Waters* I. vi, There was a strange unkennedness about their would-be familiarity.

un'kennel, *v.* [UN-² 5.]

1. *trans.* To dislodge (a fox) from its hole; to start. Also in fig. context, and *absol.*

1576 TURBERV. *Venerie* 100 An Hart or a Bucke is flayed, .. an Hare started, and a Fox vnkennelled. **1598** SHAKS. *Merry W.* III. iii. 172 Ascend my Chambers ..: Ile warrant wee'le vnkennell the Fox. **1632** B. JONSON *Magn. Lady* I. i, Your fox there, Unkennell'd with a choleric, ghastly aspect, .. Would run their fears to any hole of shelter. **1679** C. NESSE *Antichrist* 105 The great fox that hath so long spoild the vines of Christs vineyard shall be unkennel'd. **1703** (*title*), The Fox with his Fire-Brand unkennell'd and Insnar'd. **1753** FOOTE *Eng. in Paris* I. i, Did I tell you what a Chace she carry'd me last Christmas Eve? We unkennel'd at ——. **1825** *Eng. Life* I. 216 We unkennelled Reynard capitally. **1852** MISS YONGE *Cameos* I. xxvii. 221 Vowing he would unkennel the young fox, .. John sent his troops into Scotland.

b. *intr.* To come out of a hole or lair.

c **1760** in T. C. Croker *Pop. Songs Irel.* (1839) 223 Ten minutes past nine was the time o' the day, When Reynard unkennelled. *c* **1820** S. ROGERS *Italy, Banditti* 59 He comes slowly forth, Unkennelling.

2. *fig.* To force or drive out from a place or position; to dislodge; to bring to light.

1612 WEBSTER *White Devil* v. i, I'le unkennell one example more for thee. **1630** J. TAYLOR (Water P.) *Jack a Lent* Wks. (1630) 116/2 The wet Fishmongers .. vnkennell the salt Eeles from their brinie Ambuscadoes. **1670** COTTON *Espernon* I. IV. 149 Hunting, and every where unkennelling the Savoyards, .. who had possess'd themselves of most of the best Cities of Provence. **1743** YOUNG *Nt. Th.* v. 969 A precious pack of votaries Unkennell'd from the prisons. **1749** FIELDING *Tom Jones* XV. v, Where is she? .. I'll unkennel her this instant. Shew me her chamber. **1809** SOUTHEY *Lett.* (1856) II. 131, I am in want of the 'Annual Letters from Paraguay'; .. by that time; if they are in England, I may hope to unkennel them. **1818** MOORE *Fudge Fam. Paris* VI. 25 Lucky the dog that first unkennels Traitors and Luddites now-a-days. **1839** *Times* 10 June, It is their interest to unkennel this knavery.

refl. **1602** SHAKS. *Ham.* III. ii. 86 If his occulted guilt Do not it selfe vnkennell in one speech, It is a damned Ghost that we haue seene.

3. To let (hounds) out of a kennel. Also *fig.* and in fig. context.

1607 DEKKER *Wh. Babylon* C 4, Shee shall bee torne, Euen ioynt from ioynt: to haue her baited wel, .. wee will vnkennell hell. **1628** WITHER *Brit. Rememb.* Pref. 157, I can unkennell such an eager packe Of deep-mouth'd Hounds. **1840** KEIGHTLEY *Hist. Roman Empire* I. iii. 63 The baleful pack of informers was unkennelled, and their victims .. were hunted to death. **1861** DIXON *Pers. Hist. Bacon* vi. § 1 Blount .. unkennels .. a pack of needy ruffians eager for any service.

Hence **un'kennelled** *ppl. a.*¹; **un'kennelling** *vbl. sb.*

1589 WARNER *Alb. Eng.* VI. xxxiii. 144 Like *vnkenneld Cerberus the crooked Tyrant swore. *a* **1653** G. DANIEL *Idyll., Landskip* 7 Vnkennell'd Fury (deep-mouth'd) rings Liberty lodg'd; and Chas'd it quite away. **1687** DRYDEN *Hind. & P.* I. 152 Thou first Apostate to Divinity, Unkennel'd range in thy Polonian Plains. **1700** S. PARKER *Six Philos. Ess.* 48 The poor unkennell'd Fryars .. are ready to bear me out in my Assertion. **1600** J. B. (*title*), A Toile for Two-legged Foxes, wherein their noisome properties, their hunting and *vnkenelling, .. is liuelie discouered. **1602** *2nd Pt. Return Parnass.* II. v. 829 What sir, do you meane at the vnkennelling, vntapezing, or earthing of the Fox?

un'kennelled, *ppl. a.*² [UN-¹ 8.] Not provided with a kennel.

1838 ELIZA COOK *Old Pincher* ix, Unkennelled and chainless, yet truly he served.

un'kenning, *ppl. a.* *Sc. rare.* [UN-¹ 10.] Unknowing, ignorant.

c **1375** *Sc. Leg. Saints* xl. (*Ninian*) 98 Fore scorne it ware gret to se þe thechure [= teacher] suld vnkennand be. **1788** J. MACAULAY *Poems* 130 Unkenning how to carp or mourn, Their joy to spoil. *a* **1870** in Rogers *Scottish Minstrel* 488/2 Unkennin' o', uncarin' for, cauld care or crosses stern.

un'kent, *ppl. a.* Chiefly *north.* and *Sc.* [UN-¹ 8 b.]

†1. Undirected, untaught. *Obs.*—⁰

1570 LEVINS *Manip.* 67 Vnkent, untaught, *incorrectus*.

2. Unknown. (Cf. UNKENNED *ppl. a.* 1.)

1579 SPENSER *Sheph. Cal.* To his Bk. i, Goe little booke: thy selfe present, As child whose parent is vnkent. **1613** W. BROWNE *Brit. Past.* I. i, I .. sought [not] for bay, .. But as a Swaine unkent fed on the plaines. **1647** TRAPP *Comm., 1 John* iii. 1 Princes unknown are unrespected; Unkent, unkist, as the Northern Proverb hath it. **1790** A. SHIRREFS *Poems* 174 Unkent to a', .. Ae night I bade the cruel place adieu. **1807-** in dialect use (*Eng. Dial. Dict.*).

un'kept, *ppl. a.* Also 4 *north.* **unkepide**, 5 (*Sc.* 6) **unkepit**; etc. [UN-¹ 8, 8 b.]

1. Not attended to; not tended or looked after; neglected.

c **1340** HAMPOLE *Prose Tr.* 28 If þou .. latis þame [*sc.* the feet] spill for defaute of kepynge—unarayede, unkepide, and noghte tente to as þam aughte for to be,—thou pleses Hym noghte. *c* **1440** *Pallad. on Husb.* XII. 57 Lond vnkept and insolent. *c* **1450** *St. Cuthbert* (Surtees) 514 Sho hir childe saw vnkepyd, And wante þat he was wonte to haue. **1469** *Cal. Anc. Rec. Dublin* (1889) 336 That they goo to noon other labore and lewe the gye rope unkepit. **1600** SHAKS. *A.Y.L.* I. i. 9 He keepes me rustically at home, or (to speak more properly) staies me heere at home vnkept. **1611** FLORIO, *Incustodito*, vnkept, not looked vnto.

b. Unguarded, undefended.

c **1400** *Destr. Troy* 1085 The kyng had no knawlache .. Of the folke so furse, .. For-þi vnkeppit were þe costes all þe kythe ouer. **1611** FLORIO, *Suadata*, open, vnkept, free for all men.

2. Not observed or obeyed; disregarded.

c **1380** WYCLIF *Wks.* (1880) 38 Certis þei .. maken hem .. to leue holy writt vnstudied, vnknoud & vnkept. *c* **1440** *Jacob's Well* 154 He .. is for-sworn, for truthe vnkept & othe brokyn is all on. **1513** DOUGLAS *Æneid* IV. x. 61 Allace! vnkeipit is the trew cunnand. **1594** HOOKER *Eccl. Pol.* IV. xiv. § 5 Many things generally kept heretofore, are now .. vnkept and abolished euerywhere. **1623** SANDERSON *Serm.* (1632) 151 Lawes .. are farre better vnmade, then vnkept.

3. Not stored up.

1842 TENNYSON *Will Waterproof* 97 Whether the vintage, yet unkept, Had relish fiery-new.

†**unker**, *pron. Obs.* [OE. *uncer* (gen. of *wit* we two), = OHG. *unker*, *uncher*, OS. *unkero*, Goth. **ugkara*, ON. *okkarr* (Icel. *okkar*).] Of us two.

In quot. *a* 1300 apparently for *inker* 'of you two'.

c **1205** LAY. 23665 And whaðer unker þe geð abake: .. beo he in ælche londe iqueðe for ane sconde. *a* **1250** *Owl & Night.* 151 Hwy neltu fleon into [þe] bare and schewi hweþer vnker beo Of brihtur hewe of fayrur bleo. *a* **1300** *Havelok* 1882 Roberd! William! hware ar ye? Gripeth eyþer unker a god tre.

†'**unker**, *poss. a. Obs.* [OE. *uncer* (cf. prec.), = OS. *unka*, ON. *okkarr*.] Belonging to us two.

c **1200** ORMIN Ded. 80 Þe33 shulenn lætenn hæþeli3 Off unnkerr swinnc, lef broþerr. *c* **1205** LAY. 8891 Ilæst ich habbe þe .. al þet ich þe bi-hehte bi-foren vnkere cnihten. *a* **1250** *Owl & N.* 1689 Ah hit wes vnker uoreward .. þat we [etc.].

un'kerchiefed, *a.* (UN-¹ 9.)

[**1775** ASH.] **1781** COWPER *Truth* 137 With bony and unkerchief'd neck. **1812** CARY *Dante, Purg.* XXIII. 95 [Lest] The unblushing dames .. bare Unkerchief'd bosoms to the common gaze. *a* **1851** MOIR *Poems, Highl. Ret.* xi, Before him she reclined In half unkerchief'd loveliness.

un'kernelled, *a.* (UN-¹ 9.)

1673 BP. S. PARKER *Reproof Reh. Transp.* 189 An empty and unkernel'd shell. **1827** POLLOK *Course T.* IX. 972 Nor failed [Satan] to misadvise his .. faith, by false unkerneled promises.

unkert, unket, dial. varr. UNKARD, UNKED *a.*

†**unketh**, *a. Obs.* Also 3-4 **onekeþ**, 4-5 **unkythe**. [var. ME. *uncoth*: see UNCOUTH *a.* and cf. UNKED.] Unknown, strange.

a **1275** *Prov. Ælfred* 535 in *O.E. Misc.* 133 Elde cumid to tune, mid fele unkeþe costes. **1297** R. GLOUC. (Rolls) 6758 Mid lute onekeþ folc to engelond he drou. *c* **1400** *Destr. Troy* 3325 Weikenes of wemen may not wele stryve, .. And nomely in an unkythe lond nedys hom so. *c* **1510** *Lytell Geste Robyn Hode* 24 (W. de W.), To dine I have no lust, Till I have some bold Baron, Or some unketh guest. **1577** HOLINSHED *Chron., Hist. Scotland* I. 297/1 Many strange wonders and vnketh sightes were seene in the dayes of this Alexander the thyrde.

Hence †'**unkethness**. *Obs.*

1564 HAWARD tr. *Eutropius* x. 108 This unkethenesse of passinge greate good fortune, and successe in his affairs.

unkeuer(e, obs. variants of UNCOVER *v.*

un'kevel, *v.* [UN-² 4 b.] *trans.* To ungag.

c **1300** *Havelok* 601 He stirten boþe up to the knaue, .. Vnkeueleden him, and swiþe unbounden.

un'key, *v.* (UN-² 4; cf. KEY *v.*)

1751 LABELYE *Westm. Bridge* 22 Upon unkeying any one of the Arches the whole Bridge would fall. **1828** SPEARMAN *Brit. Gunner* (ed. 2) 183 [No. 3] keys and unkeys the left hand cap-square of the gun-carriage. **1840** *Civil Eng. & Arch. Jrnl.* III. 402/1 The labour .. of removing the wheels from the axles, which in the keying and unkeying is known to be very troublesome. **1859** F. A. GRIFFITHS *Artill. Man.* (ed. 8) 179 No. 1 attends to the pawls and commands, keys, and unkeys keep chain.

un'kicked, *ppl. a.* (UN-¹ 8.)

1732 LADY MARY MONTAGU & LD. HERVEY *Verses to Pope* 69 If .. Unwhipt, unblanketed, unkick'd, unslain, That wretched little carcase you retain.

unkid, var. of UNKED *a.*

unkilla'bility. (UN-¹ 12; cf. next.)

1835 LADY LYTTON *Diary* in L. Devey *Life* (1887) 102 My nature must be a happy mixture of asbestos, cast iron, and feline unkillability.

un'killable, *a.* (UN-¹ 7 b.)

1878 P. BAYNE *Purit. Rev.* x. 409 Of all the unkillable lies .. this is perhaps the most toughly immortal. **1885** *Daily News* 14 July 2 The chickens are so hardy as to be unkillable by the ordinary diseases.

un'killed, *ppl. a.* (UN-¹ 8.)

1535 STEWART *Cron. Scot.* (Rolls) I. 586 All his men .. That levand war on lyfe that tyme vnkeild. **1547** *Homilies* I. *Obedience* I. N i b, Take away Kynges, Princes, Rulers, .. no man shall slepe in his awne house or bed vnkylled. **1608** *Yorksh. Trag.* I. ix. 215, I repent now that one is left unkill'd; My brat at nurse. **1662** HIBBERT *Body Divinity* I. 197 If he sees a snake unkilled, he fears a mischief. **1707** MORTIMER *Husb.* 45 Leave no Weeds or Turfs of Grass unkilled or unbroke with your Harrows. **1802** H. MARTIN *Helen of Glenross* I. 146 Scream ladies; for our pistols are fired, and we unkilled. **1842** THACKERAY *Sultan Stork* Wks. 1898 IV. 738 Nor of the latter did there remain any unkilled (if I may coin such a word). **1901** G. DOUGLAS *Ho. w. Green Shutters* 264, I have let him get away unkilled.

un'killing, *ppl. a.* (UN-¹ 10.)

1651 W. JANE *Εικων Ακλαστος* 171 The instruments of Rebells are harmles, and vnkilling.

un'kilned, *ppl. a.* (UN-¹ 8.)

1658 tr. *Porta's Nat. Magic* VI. vii. 183 Fill an earthern pot with unkill'd lime. **1890** GEN. BOOTH *Darkest England* Pref., If the bricks were merely unkilned clay.

un'kind, *a.* [UN-¹ 7. Cf. OE. *uncynde*, *unȝecynde* (ME. *unicunde* UN-¹ 3), Norw. *ukyndt*.]

†1. Strange, foreign. *Obs.*

c **1250** *Gen. & Ex.* 2302 Iosep .. hem .. taȝte wel, And hu he sulden hem best leden, Quene he comen in vnkinde ðeden. **1297** R. GLOUC. (Rolls) 7247 Vor þre kinges were of engelond of vnkunde [*v.r.* vnkynde] sede. *a* **1400** *Northern Passion* 1554 (Camb. MS.), A vnkynd man sone gan þai mete.

2. a. Of the weather or climate: Not mild or pleasant; ungenial. Now *dial.* or *arch.*

a **1300** *Frag. Pop. Sci.* (Wright) 168 He ne mai nevere thanne come bote the weder uncunde beo. *c* **1325** *Poem temp. Edw. II* (Percy Soc.) lxxvi, Wederyng .. Cold & unkynde. *c* **1330** R. BRUNNE *Chron. Wace* (Rolls) 16541 Al þe folk wyþ tempest vnkynde Were slayn. **1580** LYLY *Euphues* (Arb.) 465 So vnkinde a yeare it hath beene in England, that [etc.]. **1733** TULL *Horse-Hoeing Husb.* xii. 145 Favourable Years will cure the Smut, as *unkind* ones will cause it. **1775** JOHNSON *West. Isl.* Wks. X. 488 The climate is unkind and the ground penurious. **1813** C. MARSHALL *Gardening* (ed. 5) xviii. 294 A fourth bed .. would be a greater advantage as to size, especially if the weather is unkind. **1876, 1881** in Surrey and Radnor glossaries (s.v. *Kind*).

†b. Physically unnatural; contrary to the usual course of nature. *Obs.*

1435 *Cov. Leet Bk.* 181 Yif he be necligent & mysrule his Iron, that he wirkithe, be onkynd hetes or elles in oder maner. *c* **1440** *Promp. Parv.* 365/2 On-kyynd, or nowȝt after cowrs of kynde, *innaturalis*. **1546** PHAER *Bk. Children* (1553) X ij b, A soueraine medycyne for burning and scaldyng, and all vnkynde heates. **1601** HOLLAND *Pliny* II. 167 They doe quench and allay thirst, and coole unkind heat. **1603** J. DAVIES (Heref.) *Microcosmos* 53 That by their service that fire might not vade, Which vnkind coldnesse else might overlade.

c. Naturally bad or hurtful; unfavourable or unsuitable; untoward. Also const. *for* or *to*. Now *dial.* (esp. of soil).

c **1425** LYDGATE *Assem. Gods* 1023 Sensualyte .. sewe the felde with hys vnkynde seede. *c* **1450** LOVELICH *Grail* xxxvi. 595 That beste wolde .. ony man qwelle that there-offen ete, it is so vnkynde, And þerto so hot. **1541** R. COPLAND *Galyen's Terap.* 2 A iv b, Whiche is .. commune to the curatyons of vnkynde humoures. **1609** C. BUTLER *Fem. Mon.* ii. B 8 b, The East-wind being cold .. is verie vnkind for Bees. **1682** W. HEWER *Let. to Pepys* 13 May, A very unfortunate and unkinde disaster. **1762** MILLS *Pract. Husb.* I. 19 The blue, white, and red clay, if strong, are all unkind. **1767** A. YOUNG *Farmer's Lett. to People* 16 The constitutions .. of several countries in Europe, which are unkind to the cultivation of the earth. **1877-** in dialect glossaries, etc. (*Eng. Dial. Dict.*). **1879** MISS JACKSON *Shropshire Word-bk.* 169 *Gall*, .. a stiff, wet, 'unkind' place in plough-land.

d. Of animals: Not thriving or naturally tending to do so. Now *dial.*

1814 G. HANGER *To all Sportsmen* 13 Whenever a horse looks unkind in his coat. **1834** SOUTHEY *Doctor* cxliv, If ever he attempts to fatten an unkind beast.

e. *dial.* (See quot.)

1866 BROGDEN *Linc. Gloss.* 216 *Unkind*, rough or crooked. These poles are very unkind.

†3. a. Lacking in natural gratitude or willingness to acknowledge benefits; ungrateful. *Obs.*

c **1290** *S. Eng. Leg.* I. 204/156 Ȝwane þov hast boþe bodi and soule iȝyuen us bi þine liue, Saunt faille we ne beoth nouȝt so onkuynde þat we it nellez ȝelde þe bliue. **1338** R.

BRUNNE *Chron.* (1810) 62 Malcolme..ȝit on Inglond ran, þe kyng had him auanced, he was an vnkynd man. **1377** LANGL. *P. Pl.* B. v. 437 ȝif any man..helpeth me at nede, I am vnkynde aȝein his curteisye. **1422** YONGE tr. *Secreta Secret.* 205 He is an onkynde man that denyeth hym to haue recevid a good dede. *c* **1450** *Mirk's Festial* 26 þat scho was vnkynde to hym þat suffred so moche for hur. **1509** BARCLAY *Shyp of Folys* (1570) 85 These vnkinde caytiues will scantly him honour. **1576** LAMBARDE *Peramb. Kent* 276 Whiche.. inestimable benefites..if any man..acknowledge not, he is to to vnkinde. **1649** J. TAYLOR (Water P.) *Western Voy.* 6 The Redeemer of unkinde mankinde.

absol. **1382** WYCLIF *Wisd.* xvi. 29 The hope of the vnkinde as cold ijs shal flowen. **1526** TINDALE *Luke* vi. 35 He is kynde vnto the vnkynde.

†**b.** Lacking in filial affection or respect; undutiful. *Obs.*

a **1300** *Cursor M.* 28270 Vn-kynd i was..Gayn fader & moder. **1303** R. BRUNNE *Handl. Synne* 1072 ȝyf þou euer.. On fadyr or modyr leydest þyn hand,..swyche a chylde ys kalled vnkynde. **1380** *Lay Folks Catech.* (Lamb. MS.) 710 Vnkende men..helpe not here eldrys as þey schuld do. **1595** DANIEL *Civ. Wars* I. lxxxix, O! whither dost thou tend my vnkind sonne? What mischiefe dost thou go about to bring To..Thy mother countrey?

†**c.** Devoid of natural goodness; vile, bad, wicked, villainous. *Obs.*

1297 R. GLOUC. (Rolls) 2379 þere he kudde wat he was vnkunde ssrewe & quoynte. **13..** *Guy Warw.* (A.) 4382 þou me hast bitreyd,..þou fel treytour, vnkinde blod. **1377** LANGL. *P. Pl.* B. v. 276 Thow art an vnkynde creature; I can þe nouȝte assoille, Til þow make restitucioun. **1430–40** LYDG. *Bochas* VIII. xxv. (1494) E iij b/2, Late men beware euer of vnkynde blode. *c* **1460** *Towneley Myst.* xxiv. 192 Then noy vs nomore of this noyse; you carles vnkynde, who bad you call me? **1529** S. FISH *Supplic. Beggers* (1871) 4 Let vs then compare the nombre of this vnkind idell sort, vnto the nombre of the laye people. **1590** SPENSER *F.Q.* III. ii. 43 For they, how euer shamefull and vnkind, Yet did possesse their horrible intent. **1602** *2nd Pt. Return fr. Parnass.* IV. ii. 1705 Thou slimie sprighted vnkinde Saracen.

†**d.** Of a worse kind; degenerate. *Obs.*

1340 *Ayenb.* 188 þe zone ssel by ylich þe uader oþer he is onkende be zaynte peter. **1398** TREVISA *Barth. De P.R.* XII. xxvi. (Tollem. MS.), þe lenger he lyueþ þe more he scheweþ þat his owen kynde is unkynde. **14..** *Voc.* in Wr.-Wülcker 577/41 *Degener*, vnkynde. **1483** *Cath. Angl.* 203/1 To be vn Kynde, or to go oute of kynde, *degenerare.*

†**e.** Uncharitable, ungenerous. *Obs.*

1303 R. BRUNNE *Handl. Synne* 6788 For ful comunly shalt þou fynde Ofte ryche men vnkynde. **1377** LANGL. *P. Pl.* B. x. 29 þilke þat god moste gyueth, leste good þei deleth, And moste vnkynde to þe comune þat moste catel weldeth. *Ibid.* XI. 206 Euery man helpe other,..And be we nouȝte vnkynde of owre catel ne of owre kunnynge neyther.

†**4.** Of actions: Contrary to nature, unnatural, *esp.* unnaturally bad or wicked. *Obs.*

c **1250** *Gen. & Ex.* 449 Bigamie is unkinde ðing, On engleis tale, twie-wifing. **1297** R. GLOUC. (Rolls) 852 Many kundemen of þis lond mid king leir hulde also, Vor þe vnkunde [*v.r.* vnkynde] suikedom þat is doȝtren adde ido. *c* **1320** *Sir Tristr.* 2758 Vnkinde were ous to kis As kenne. **1377** LANGL. *P. Pl.* B. XIII. 356 þorw coueityse and vnkynde desyrynge. *c* **1480** HENRYSON *Fables, Trial of Fox* 809 Fy! Couetice, vnkynd and venemous. **1592** GREENE *Philomela* Wks. (Grosart) XI. 131 If such vnlawfull lust, such vnkinde desires,..procures so great losse. **1606** SYLVESTER *Du Bartas* II. iv. I. *Tropheis* 1232 Cowardly treason,..Un-kinde Rebellion. **1656** COWLEY *Davideis* III. 204 Their too much Wealth, vast, and unkind does grow.

†**5.** Unnaturally cruel, severe, or hostile. *Obs.*

1340–70 *Alex. & Dind.* 540 Vn-kinde kiþe ȝe ȝou to kille ȝour children. *a* **1375** *Joseph Arim.* 242 He tolde hem..of heore fadres bi-fore þat he fond vn-kuynde. *c* **1400** *Brut* 245 Wiþ sir Andrew of Herkela, þat is callede þe vnkynde out-putter. *c* **1440** *Gesta Rom.* lxvii. 306 (Harl. MS.), My fadir is so vnkynde, þat he woll not pay my raunsom for me. **1513** DOUGLAS *Æneid* I. i. 44 Full deip ingravin in hir breist vnkynd [was] The jugement of Paris. **1635** R. JOHNSON *Hist. Tom a Lincolne* (1828) 117 Making thyselfe vnkinde and monstrous in murthering of thy mother. **1659** HAMMOND *On Ps.* cxxxvii. 7 When our unkind neighbours the Edumæans were so forward to joyne their hands with our enemies.

6. Lacking in kindness or kindly feeling; acting harshly or ungently to others. Also *absol.*

1362 LANGL. *P. Pl.* A. I. 166 Beo no men hardore þen þei,..Vn-kuynde to heore kun and to alle cristene. **1393** *Ibid.* C. xx. 216 Beo unkynde to þyn emcrystene, and..The holy-gost huyreþ þe nat. **1509** FISHER *Funeral Serm. C'tess Richmond* Wks. (1876) 307 Were not she an vnkinde & vngentyl moder? **1523** FITZHERB. *Husb.* §11 His neyghbours be vnkynde, if they wyll not lende this yonge housbande parte of this sede. *a* **1550** in *Early XVI Cent. Lyrics* lxv. 71 The turtle doue is not vnkinde to him that loues her so. **1602** SHAKS. *Ham.* III. i. 101 To the Noble minde, Rich gifts wax poore, when giuers proue vnkinde. **1645** in *Verney Mem.* (1904) I. 422 Censured by the world to be the most unkind and unnatural brother. **1675** DRYDEN *Aurengz.* I. i. 428 That Man..Has been to you unkind, to me unjust. **1738** WESLEY *Ps.* v. iii, The Hearts unkind, and Hearts untrue, Are both abhor'd by Thee. **1796** MRS. J. WEST *Gossip's Story* II. 169 She tried to recal the dear unkind by tears, and soft complaints. **1820** SHELLEY *Hymn Mercury* lii, What mean you to do With me, you unkind God?

transf. **1802** WORDSW. *'Bright Flower'* 15 Thou wouldst teach him how to find..A hope for times that are unkind. **1875** MORRIS *Æneid* XII. 144 Thee only..I love of all who e'er have come Into the unkind bed of Jove from out a Latin home. **1885** R. BRIDGES *Eros & Psyche* Apr. xxiv, Ascending many a mile Over the long brown slopes and crags unkind.

b. Of actions, speech, etc.: Characterized by want of kindness.

c **1400** *Destr. Troy* 1452 What myschefe befell, þere no cause was to ken but vnkynd wordes. *c* **1586** C'TESS PEMBROKE *Ps.* (1823) LV. iii, Then I would have borne with patient cheere An unkind part from whom I know unkind. **1596** SPENSER *F.Q.* VI. xi. 24 In charge of one..who with vnkind disdaine..her did much molest. **1601** SHAKS. *Jul. C.* III. ii. 187 This was the most vnkindest cut of all. **1647** CLARENDON *Hist. Reb.* I. (1702) I. 6 The abrupt, and unkind breaking off the Two first Parliaments. **1710** STEELE *Tatler* No. 246 ¶1 The Word Imperfection would not carry an unkinder Idea than the Word Humanity. **1796** MME. D'ARBLAY *Camilla* III. 432 If she persisted in such unkind and unnatural conduct. **1810** LAMB *Wks.* (1908) I. 78 This was the unkindest blow of all. **1891** FARRAR *Darkn. & Dawn* xxx, A mistress who never addressed to them an unkind word.

†**un'kindfully,** *adv. Obs.* (UN-¹ 11.)

c **1500** *Communycacyon* (W. de W.) C j, Without cause ofte thou arte wrothe Unto thy frendes unkyndfully.

†**un'kindhead.** *Obs.* [f. UNKIND *a.*] Unnatural conduct; ingratitude; baseness.

1297 R. GLOUC. (Rolls) 765 þis leir..plainede of þe unkundhede [*v.rr.* vnkuinde-, vnkyndehede] of is doȝter gornorille. *Ibid.* 2392, etc. **1303** R. BRUNNE *Handl. Synne* 5093 Yn sum man, vnkyndehede ys so rank þat [etc.]. *Ibid.* 6508 þarfore..spende weyl þyn owne þyng, þat þou fal nat yn auaryce: Of vnkyndhede hyt cumþ, þat vyce.

unkind'hearted, *a.* (UN-¹ 9.)

1759 STERNE *Tr. Shandy* I. x, He was not an unkind-hearted man, and every case was more pressing..than the last.

un'kindled, *ppl. a.* (UN-¹ 8.)

a **1513** FABYAN *Chron.* VII. 648 In this yere began a grudge to growe.., but it was keept vnkyndelyd duryng yᵉ lyfe of yᵉ duke. **1535** COVERDALE *Job* xx. 26 An vnkyndled fyre shal consume him. **1717** POPE *Iliad* XI. 239 The unkindled lightning in his hand he [*sc.* Jove] took. **1742** YOUNG *Nt. Th.* I. 111 They live! they greatly live a life on earth Unkindl'd, unconceiv'd. **1809** COLERIDGE *Friend* 161 My feelings..and imagination did not remain unkindled in this general conflagration. **1865** DICKENS *Mut. Fr.* I. xiii, The unkindled lamp stood on the table.

Hence **un'kindledness.**

1869 ABP. BENSON in *Life* (1901) 116 The yellow wax lights on the Altar stood in their irrational, legal, unkindledness.

un'kindliness. (UN-¹ 12; cf. UNKINDLY *a.*)

c **1470** HENRY *Wallace* IX. 347 We fand nane in that art, That proffryt ws sic wnkyndlynes. **1587** GOLDING *De Mornay* xvii. 308 His wrath..cannot bee kindled against nature.., but against the faultinesse and vnkindlynesse that are in nature. **1627** HAKEWILL *Apol.* II. §3. 133 The vnkindlinesse of the weather now..hurtfull to the fruites. **1668** H. MORE *Div. Dial.* II. ix. 223 The..unkindliness of the Season. **1763** MILLS *Pract. Husb.* I. 206 The uncommon ..unkindliness of the soil. **1797** LAMB *Let. to Coleridge* 7 Apr., Clear from the imputation of unkindliness (a word, by which I mean the diminutive of unkindness). **1859** TENNYSON *Merlin & V.* 735 Kill'd with inutterable unkindliness.

un'kindling, *ppl. a.* (UN-¹ 10.)

1818 MILMAN *Samor* II. 108 As summer meteor,.. Waning into the dull unkindling air.

un'kindly, *a.* [repr. OE. *ungecyndelic*, or in later use f. UN-¹ 7 + KINDLY *a.*]

†**1. a.** Morally unnatural; unnaturally wicked or vile. *Obs.*

a **1225** *Ancr. R.* 116 Vor hondlunge, oðer eni velunge bitweone mon & ancre is..unkundelich þincg. *a* **1300** *Cursor M.* 27966 Vnkindli sin and sodomite, Austin cals al suilk delite. **1418** *26 Pol. Poems* xiv. 84 Vnkyndely synne and shameles haunted. *a* **1450** *Knt. de la Tour* (1868) 102 The deuell slow all, for as moche as they vsed unkindely werke. **1590** SPENSER *F.Q.* II. x. 9 Their owne mother..gan abhorre her broods vnkindly crime. **1614** SYLVESTER *Little Bartas* 905 Besides th' unkindly slaughter Of his owne Selfe, by his owne Sons soon after.

†**b.** Unnatural in respect of relations or dealings with others. *Obs.*

1456–70 in *Acta Parlt. Scotl.* (1875) XII. 27/1 Thynkand it onkyndle tyll thole ane nominatioun of lardschipe of sic ane man. *a* **1513** FABYAN *Chron.* VII. 642 After this vnkyndly warre had duryd by the space of vi. monethes. **1591** *Troub. Raigne K. John* (1611) 68 Vnkindly rage, more rough than northern wind, To clip the beautie of so sweete a flower! **1605** SYLVESTER *Du Bartas, Sonn. Late Peace* iv, War's unkindly quarrels. **1647** N. WARD *Simple Cobler* 15 How unseasonable and unkindely it is, to interturbe the State and Church with these Amalekitish onsets.

†**2.** Unnatural in respect of physical qualities or actions. *Obs.*

a **1300** in *E.E.P.* (1862) 10/104 þe þing þat bodi no flesse naþ non..vnkundlich þing ded sal don. *c* **1375** *Cursor M.* 26253 (Fairf.), þe man þat mengis wiþ vnkindeli best his flesshe luste to fulfille. **1390** GOWER *Conf.* I. 264 Thilke unkendeli peines Thurgh whiche Envie is fyred ay. *a* **1500** *Flower & Leaf* 413 Salades, which they made hem ete, For to refresh their greet unkindly hete. **1555** WATREMAN *Fardle Facions* 324 Lest therby the vnkindlie couplings against kinde, passe also at lengthe vnto men. **1611** GUILLIM *Heraldry* III. xxv. 179 The shape of the Leopard bewraieth his vnkindly birth. **1639** T. DE GREY *Expert Farrier* II. xxi. (1656) 628 Unkindly and unnatural heats given him by most violent and intemperate riding.

b. Of weather, soil, etc.: Unnaturally bleak or cold; unfavourable to growth or comfort, inclement.

14.. in *Tundale's Vis.* (1843) 154 Mych of oure welth hase wastud awey With grete darthe..And unkyndly wedurs. **1535** W. STEWART *Cron. Scot.* (Rolls) III. 43 In..Hungar and cald, and wnkyndlie distres. **1579** SPENSER *Sheph. Cal.* Jan. 26 My life bloud friesing with vnkindly cold. **1652** GAULE *Magastrom.* 332 We had not a more unkindly summer, for many yeeres, in respect of extraordinary cold. *a* **1684** LEIGHTON *Wks.* (1835) I. 109 A tender plant in a strange unkindly soil. **1763** MILLS *Pract. Husb.* I. 188 The land continued unkindly and sour. **1775** *Phil. Trans.* LXVI. 282 The summers are often so unkindly, that their wheat is blighted while in ear. **1850** ROBERTSON *Serm.* Ser. III. iii. (1857) 36* The unkindly climate of their birth. *a* **1864** HAWTHORNE *Amer. Note-bks.* (1868) I. 282 Besides the bleak, unkindly air.

c. Not answering to its (or their) proper kind; not properly conditioned, developed, or thriving. Now *dial.* or *arch.*

c **1400** *Destr. Troy* 8523 Ho was vnkyndly to knaw of hir kyd frendis, So disfigurt of face & febill of hew. **1587** GOLDING *De Mornay* xvii. 313 In vs only there is such an vnkindly and Bastardly Nature, that [etc.]. **1601** HOLLAND *Pliny* I. 225 Kine, Buls, and Oxen are not to be despised as unkindly, although they looke but illfavouredly. **1616** BRETON *Invective agst. Treason* Wks. (Grosart) I. 4/1 [To] make theyr bread, of an vnkindly Branne; which seeming Wheate, is but a Hellish weede, sown by the Devill. **1790** *Trans. Soc. Arts* VIII. 32 [These] Peas..ripen later, and become so unkindly that the pods..never fill. *c* **1813** MRS. SHERWOOD *Stories Ch. Catech.* xxxiv. 357 Lopping off..a dead leaf, or unkindly branch. **1887–8** in Cheshire and Somerset glossaries (applied to plants or animals).

†**d.** Prejudicial to health; not developing in a natural healthy manner. *Obs.*

a **1649** DRUMM. OF HAWTH. *Hist. Jas. V*, Wks. (1711) 114 He was troubled by an unkindly Medicine. **1667** MILTON *P.L.* IX. 1050 Grosser sleep Bred of unkindly fumes. **1797** UNDERWOOD *Disorders Childhood* II. 117 An oozing of blood from the part, after an unkindly separation of the cord. **1822–7** GOOD *Study Med.* (1829) IV. 99 The exciting causes [of madness]..are..unkindly child-bed [etc.]. *Ibid.* V. 583 It [*sc.* opium] proved a cordial to him through the whole of this tedious affection, without a single unkindly concomitant.

†**3.** Not of the same kind; strange. *Obs.*

1560 ROLLAND *Seven Sages* 23 Vnkyndlie Captanes ouir-thrawis And commoun welth doun drawis. **1591** SYLVESTER *Du Bartas* I. v. 765 Th' infamous Bird that layes His Bastard Egges within the nests of other, To have them hatcht by an unkindely Mother.

†**4. a.** Lacking natural affection. **b.** Cruel, malicious. *Obs.*

1590 SPENSER *F.Q.* I. i. 26 To see th' vnkindly Impes.. Deuoure their dam. **1591** —— *Tears Muses* 15 Her loued Twinnes,..whom her vnkindly foes The fatall Sisters, did for spight destroy.

5. Devoid of kindness; unkind.

1805–6 CARY *Dante, Inf.* XXI. 97, I to my leader's side adhered, mine eyes..bent On their unkindly visage. **1827** SCOTT *Surg. Dau.* vii, He was conscious of unkindly, if not hostile feelings towards his old companion. **1862** LYTTON *Str. Story* 132 That gentle heart could not bear one unkindlier shade between itself and what it loved.

un'kindly, *adv.* [repr. OE. *ungecyndelíce*, or in later use f. UN-¹ 11 + KINDLY *adv.*]

†**1. a.** With unnatural immorality or impropriety. *Obs.*

a **1225** *Ancr. R.* 50 Ne of tollinde lokunges, ne lates, þæt summe,..weilawei! unkundeliche makieð. *a* **1300** *Cursor M.* 28495 Wit womman seke vmquile haue i And vnkyndeli don licheri. *c* **1386** CHAUCER *Pardoner's T.* 485 Lo how þat dronken loth vnkyndely Lay by his doughtres two vnwityngly. *c* **1400** *Destr. Troy* 13820 Now full hard..is þi hegh lust, þat þou couetus vnkyndly to couple with me. **1579** [see UNKINGLY *adv.*]. **1602** WARNER *Alb. Eng.* XIII. lxxvi. 315 Vnkindly though Nature it is defaced so in some, As that by often sinning Sinne an habette doth become.

†**b.** With unnatural enmity, harshness, or cruelty. *Obs.*

c **1300** *Beket* (Percy Soc.) 1540 The Kyng..sende him word that him thoȝte..That hi wolde him so moche misdo uncundeliche and wouȝ. **1535** COVERDALE *2 Macc.* xv. 2 O do not so cruelly and vnkyndly [1611 barbarously], but halowe yᵉ Sabbath daye. **1547** J. HARRISON *Exhort. Scottes* h j b, That you..should thus vnkindly, vnnaturally, and vnchristenly bathe youre swoordes in eche others blode. **1598** SYLVESTER *Du Bartas* II. i. IV. *Handy-crafts* 7 Envious Cain His (better) Brother doth vnkindly brain. **1605** *Ibid.* iii. IV. *Captains* 833 Lo there, another valiant Champion..His onely Daughter doth unkindly kill.

†**c.** Contrary to right feeling or conduct; improperly; ungratefully. *Obs.*

1380 *Lay Folk's Catech.* (L.) 952 [To] be euer sory..for he haþ greuyd god so vnkendely. **1393** LANGL. *P. Pl.* C. IV. 264 Vnkyndely þow, conscience, consaileddest hym þennes, To lete so hus lordshup for a lytel moneye. *c* **1440** *Promp. Parv.* 365/2 On-kyndely yn herte, *ingratanter, acaride.* **1470–1** *Rolls of Parlt.* VI. 233/1 Unnaturelly, unkyndly and truly entendyng his destruccion. **1567** *Gude & Godlie B.* (S.T.S.) 65 Lat nocht my hart vnkyndlie depart, From the rycht lufe of thy mercie. **1588** SHAKS. *Titus* v. iii. 104 Lastly, [I was] my selfe vnkindly banished.

†**2.** Unsuitably. *Obs. rare.*

c **1300** *Havelok* 1250 Goldeborw.. wende she were bi-swike, þat she were yeuen un-kyndelike. **1362** LANGL. *P. Pl.* A. x. 177 Summe..For Coueitise of Catel vnkuyndeliche beoþ maried.

†**b.** Contrary to the usual course of nature; at variance with natural conditions. *Obs.*

1390 GOWER *Conf.* I. 292 Unkindeliche he was transformed, That he which erst a man was formed Into a womman was forschape. **1426** LYDG. *De Guil. Pilgr.* 3530 But ye wolden..Tourne vnkyndely my wyn In-to blood, folk for to drynke. **1541** R. COPLAND *Gaylen's Terap.* 2 Bj, There must be had delyberacyon, to knowe yf all the party dyscoloured and hardened vnkyndly ought to be cut. **1615** W. LAWSON *Country Housew. Gard.* (1626) 8 Who did euer know a tree so vnkindly splat, come to age? **1667** MILTON *P.L.* III. 456 All th' unaccomplisht works of Natures hand, Abortive, monstrous, or unkindly mixt,..fleet hither. **1703** ROWE *Fair Penit.* I. i, You mourn unkindly by your self, And rob me of my Partnership of Sadness. **1766** *Compl. Farmer* s.v. *Malt*, The malt..appears shrivelled, and often is unkindly hard.

c. Badly, unsuccessfully.

1763 MILLS *Pract. Husb.* III. 128 Kiln-drying is apt to make wheat grind unkindly. **1811** *Self Instructor* 516 Umber is..very greasy, and mixes unkindly with water-colours. **1887** *Daily News* 21 July 2/4 Fanfare remained a staunch favourite to the end. He, however, ran very unkindly.

3. In an unkind or unkindly manner; with marked want of kindness.

c **1384** CHAUCER *H. Fame* I. 295 How he betrayed hir allas, And lefte hir ful vnkyndely. **14..** *Sir Beues* (C.) 1448 That he tolde me not, when he went, Iwysse, he dud onkyndely, verament. *c* **1489** CAXTON *Sonnes of Aymon* xvii. 397 The whiche Reynawde kepeth..for his prysoner not vnkyndely. **1590** SHAKS. *Mids. N.* III. ii. 183 But why vnkindly didst thou leaue me so? **1603** KNOLLES *Hist. Turks* (1621) 114 Vnkindly to cast him off that had so honorably vsed him in like extremitie. **1695** LD. PRESTON *Boeth.* II. 55 She hath looked unkindly upon thee. **1768** STERNE *Sent. Journ.*, *Snuff-box*, I treated him most unkindly; and from no provocations. **1828** SCOTT *F.M. Perth* x, 'You will not deal so unkindly with us, cousin,' replied the gentle Monarch. **1889** B. WHITBY *Awakening Mary Fenwick* II. 45 Don't haul me over the coals so unkindly.

Comb. **1605** SYLVESTER *Du Bartas* II. iii. II. *Fathers* 480 Among them all..you shall not finde Such an example, where (unkindly-kinde) Father and Son so mutually agree. *a* **1699** J. BEAUMONT *Psyche* XII. v, Nor could unkindly-courteous He resist The huging of his Spouse's seeming Friend.

4. With dissatisfaction or resentment.

Freq. in the phrase *to take* (..) *unkindly*.

1562 GRESHAM in Burgon *Life* (1839) I. 448 Assewring yow, I doo take it very unkindelye at your handes. **1607** SHAKS. *Timon* III. vi. 39, I hope it remaines not vnkindely with your Lordship, that I return'd you an empty Messenger. **1635** *Argt. Pastoral of Florimene* 6 Florimene desires Dorine not to take it unkindly, if [etc.]. **1725** DE FOE *Voy. round World* (1840) 91 Nothing to be had but for ready money; which our men took so unkindly,..that [etc.]. **1771** *Junius Lett.* l. (1788) 270 The only letter I ever addressed to the King was..unkindly received.

un'kindness. [UN-^{1} 12.]

†**1.** Unnatural conduct; absence of natural affection or consideration for others. *Obs.*

a **1300** *Cursor M.* 13018 þis herod..vnkendnes kidd ful rjf, He reft his broþer philipp his wijf. **1362** LANGL. *P. Pl.* A. III. 280 Vnkuyndenesse is Comaundour and kuyndenesse is Banescht. **1380** *Lay Folks Catech.* (L.) 938 Yf he kepe hem [*sc.* the commandments] not he doþ to god more vnkendenesse þan ony broþer may do to anoþer. *c* **1400** *Beryn* 1354 He cursid his grete vnkyndnes To foreȝit his modir. **1477** *Rolls of Parlt.* VI. 173/1 The grett offences, unkyndnesse and mysbehavyngs, that..Nevell hath doon. *a* **1513** FABYAN *Chron.* I. xv. (1811) 15 The vnkyndenesse of his ii. doughters, consyderynge theyr wordes to hym before spoken and sworne. **1570** *Homilies* II. *Wilful Rebellion* I. (1640) 282 So farre doth their unkindnesse, unnaturalnesse, wickednesse..excell anything..that can be expressed.

†**b.** Uncharitableness; niggardliness. *Obs.*

1377 LANGL. *P. Pl.* B. XVII. 263 Diues deyed dampned for his vnkyndenesse Of his mete & his moneye to men that it neded.

†**2.** Ingratitude, unthankfulness. *Obs.*

1340 HAMPOLE *Pr. Consc.* 5587 Agayne þam sal Crist allege sone,..and reherce his benefices,..To reprove þam of þair unkyndenes. **1380** *Lay Folks Catech.* (L.) 946 Yf we with-stond þat lord þat made vs..we do þe most vnkendenesse þat may be wroȝt. *c* **1450** *Mirk's Festial* 113 Saynt Barnard yn Cristys person makyth gret waymentacyon for þe vnkyndnesse þat he sethe yn men. **1483** CAXTON *Gold. Leg.* 362/2 We receyue dayly many bienfaites of this cyte and it sholde be a grete unkyndnesse to us yf we socoured it not in this grete nede. **1531** ELYOT *Gov.* II. xiii, The most damnable vice..is ingratitude, commenly called unkyndnesse. **1585** ABP. SANDYS *Serm.* 189 After that God had thus set forth his great goodnesse towardes them, hee chargeth them with their great vnkindenesse towards him. **1605** SHAKS. *Lear* III. ii. 16, I taxe not you, you Elements with vnkindnesse. I neuer gave you Kingdome, call'd you Children.

†**b.** A flock (of ravens). *Obs.*$^{-0}$

c **1452** in *Trans. Philol. Soc. 1907–10*, III. 52 Vnkyndenys of rauynnys. **1486** *Bk. St. Albans* f vj.

3. The fact of being unkind; unkind action or treatment.

c **1374** CHAUCER *Anel. & Arc.* 292 My self I mourdre with my prevy thoght For sorowe and routhe of your vnkyndnesse. **1390** GOWER *Conf.* II. 299 This Emperour al that he tolde Hath herd, and thilke unkindenesse He seide he wolde himself redresse. *c* **1491** *Chast. Goddes Chyld.* 12 Trouth fynde they nowhere but wronges detraccyons and un-kyndenes. **1535** COVERDALE *2 Macc.* xiv. 30 When Machabeus sawe that Nicanor beganne to be churlish vnto him..he perceaued that soch vnkyndnes came not of good. **1594** R. WILSON *Coblers Proph.* III. iii, Know you not, vnkindnes kills a woman? **1621** J. TAYLOR (Water P.) *Unnat. Father* Wks. (1630) 136/2 Ruing his vnkindnesse to his Wife. **1651** HOBBES *Leviath.* I. vi. 27 Some Weep for the losse of Friends; Others for their unkindnesse. **1742** GRAY *Eton* 76 The stings of Falshood those shall try, And hard Unkindness' alter'd eye. **1784** COWPER *Task* VI. 627 Attachment..proof alike Against unkindness, absence, and neglect. **1825** SCOTT *Talism.* xx, Eloquent in urging her own defence, the Queen was far more so in pressing upon Richard the charge of unkindness. **1882** 'OUIDA' *Maremma* I. 69 Joconda feared no scorn and unkindness on the score of her birth.

b. An instance of this: an unkind action.

1505 in *Mem. Hen. VII* (Rolls) 266 The whiche the kynge ..takithe for a grete onkyndnes. **1555** BRADFORD *Let.* in Foxe *A. & M.* (1583) 1661/1 All those vnkyndnesses, rudenes, &c., whereof you accuse your selfe. **1606** SHAKS. *Ant. & Cl.* I. ii. 138 Why then we kill all our Women. We see how mortall an vnkindnesse is to them. **1660** *Trial Regic.* 133, I hope he will think it no unkindnesse in me. **1809–14** WORDSW. *Excurs.* VI. 776 Her uncharitable acts, I trust, And harsh unkindnesses are all forgiven. **1860** EMILY EDEN *Semi-attached Couple* xiii, A series of small unkindnesses is very offensive indeed.

4. Unkindly feeling; ill-will, enmity, hostility. Now *rare* or *Obs.*

c **1400** *Destr. Troy* 144 With a course of vnkyndnes he caste in his thoghte, The freike vpon faire wise ferke out of lyue. **1465** in *10th Rep. Hist. Mss. Comm.* App. V. 302 The tyme of thar unkyndnesse other warre with the citie. **1562** *Child Marr.* 203 By which did growe an vnkindnes betwene them. **1588** *Marprel. Epist.* (Arb.) 38 Because the gamesters ..wan all his monie at trey trip [he] tooke such vnkindenes at the alehouse that [etc.]. **1624** CAPT. SMITH *Virginia* III. 52 This bred some vnkindnesse betweene our two Captaines. **1658** JER. TAYLOR *Let.* in *12th Rep. Hist. MSS. Comm.* App. V. 5 If ever you have..heard of any overtures of unkindnesse betweene them. *a* **1700** EVELYN *Diary* 24 Apr. 1692, Unkindness betweene the Queene and her sister. **1823** SCOTT *Quentin D.* vii, I will bestow another to wash away unkindness. **1825** —— *Betrothed* xviii, He died when we were in unkindness with each other.

†**5.** Unnatural character or quality. *Obs.*

1502 *Ord. Crysten Men* (W. de W. 1506) I. vii. F iv b, By this artycle we sholde knowe the mysery & ryght unkyndenesse of humanyne condycyon. *a* **1513** FABYAN *Chron.* v. cxxiv. 104 Whan the Embassade..had shewyd yᵉ vnkyndnesse of this warre with the ieopardyes that myght ensue of yᵉ same.

un'kindred, *a.* (UN-^{1} 7.)

1700 SHIPPEN *Hymn to Sun* x, in Rowe *Amb. Step-Mother* III. ii, Conscious of superior birth [It] Despises this unkindred earth. **1804** EUGENIA DE ACTON *Tale without Title* III. 75 Their souls, unkindred, can never understand our language. **1865** *Spectator* 14 Jan. 42 Not quite unkindred to this fact is the other.

un'kindredly, *a.* (UN-^{1} 7.)

1748 RICHARDSON *Clarissa* (1811) VI. 381 What an implacable..set of wretches are those of her unkindredly kin.

†**un'kindship.** *Obs.* [UN-^{1} 12.] Unkindness.

1390 GOWER *Conf.* I. 263 As he which thurgh unkindeschipe Envieth every felaschipe.

un'king, *v.* [UN-^{2} 6 b. Cf. MDu. *ontconingen*, Du. *ontkoningen*, G. *entkönigen*.]

1. *trans.* To deprive of the position of king; to depose from sovereignty. (Common in 17th c.)

1578 *Paradise Dainty Devices* L ij, Such toile do thei sustain, That often tymes God thei wishe, to be unkyngde again. **1602** MARSTON *Ant. & Mel.* IV, That very word Unkings me quite, makes me vile passions slave. **1684** E. PELLING *Serm. 30 Jan.* 20 They may crown them or unking them as they think fit. **1711** *Pol. Ballads* (1860) II. 100 These men do design To un-king the Queen and keep out the Right Line. **1784** COWPER in Hayley *Life* (1809) II. 158 Government therefore is bound to interfere, and to un-king these tyrants. **1815** *Q. Rev.* XIII. 489 Having..escaped unhanged when they were unkinged, they started up again to perform the part of princes in the new revolutionary drama. **1870** LOWELL *Study Wind.* (1871) 216 Some passion which the churchyard smothered while the Stuarts were yet unkinged.

fig. **1638** SUCKLING *Aglaura* I. i, There was with me fresh Rebellion, And reason was almost unking'd agen. **1731** *Gentl. Mag.* I. 168 The comic muse Unkings your Cupid, or obstructs his views. **1818** MILMAN *Samor* v. 463 Thou.. hast unking'd Thy stately soul within the wreathing arms Of that fair Saxon.

absol. **1644** MAXWELL *Prerog. Chr. Kings* 3 [That] the Pope..by this indirect power..may King and unking at his pleasure. **1646** BP. MAXWELL *Burd. Issach.* 18 Every individual Person is..to punish, to dethrone, to un-King, to kill, &c.

b. *refl.* To divest (oneself) of royal status or character; to abdicate.

1647 N. WARD *Simple Cobler* 54, I would honour their very heeles, that would..teach me..to king it better, when they saw me unkinging myselfe and kingdome. **1689** *Advantages of Present Settlement* 22 If a king..ruine his people..he so far Unkings himself. **1700** J. TYRRELL *Hist. Eng.* II. 794 [King John] thereby..Unking'd himself. **1859** J. MARSHALL *Hist. Scott. Eccl. & Civ. Affairs* 290 Charles's concessions had been in vain. He had unkinged himself.

2. To deprive (a country) of a king.

1647 *Old Ballads* (Percy Soc.) 86 They may thus..Unking our state, un-church us too. **1820** BYRON *Mar. Fal.* v. i. 437 A wife's dishonour unking'd Rome for ever. **1883** *Harper's Mag.* June 139/1 An empire, unkinged to-night, sees to-morrow a new king.

un'kingdomed, *ppl. a.* (UN-^{2} 8.)

1611 SPEED *Hist. Gt. Brit.* IX. vi. 463 Hee was not vnking'd, though vnkingdom'd. **1917** J. B. CABELL *Cream of Jest* (1923) xix. 109 The Stuarts or the Valois or the Cæsars, or other dynasties long since unkingdomed.

un'kinged, *ppl. a.*^{1} [f. UNKING *v.*] Deprived of the position or authority of king; deposed from kingship. Also *absol.*

1593 SHAKS. *Rich. II*, IV. i. 220 God saue King Henry, vn-King'd Richard sayes. **1611** [see prec.]. **1818** MILMAN *Samor* XI. 196 Then gaz'd the unking'd, then cried out the fallen. **1837** CARLYLE *Fr. Rev.* I. i. iv, There must thou enter, naked, all unking'd. **1845** FORD *Handbk. Spain* II. 947 Ferdinand..dismissed,..a prisoner and unkinged.

un'kinged, *ppl. a.*^{2} [UN-^{1} 8.] Not raised to the dignity of king.

1855 BAILEY *Mystic, Spir. Leg.* 82 Fair thorn, as yet unkinged, Unsanctified by woes of brow divine.

un'kinger. [f. UNKING *v.*] One who deposes a king.

1656 S. H. *Gold. Law* 24 It unking'd him, and King'd his unkingers in point of Power.

un'kinglike, *a.* (UN-^{1} 7 c.)

1611 SHAKS. *Cymb.* III. v. 7 For our selfe To shew lesse Soueraignty then they, must needs Appeare vn-Kinglike. **1892** TENNYSON *Akbar's Dream* 60 To drive A people from their ancient fold of Faith, And wall them up perforce in mine—unwise, Unkinglike.

un'kingly, *a.* [UN-^{1} 7. Cf. ON. *úkonunglígr.*]

1. Unbecoming to a king; not in accordance with the position or character of a king.

1600 HEYWOOD *2nd Pt. Edw. IV*, Wks. 1874 I. 100 Edward of England, these are vnkingly words. **1658** OSBORNE *Q. Eliz.* 12 An Art lost in these latter times, or thought unkingly. *a* **1661** HOLYDAY *Persius* (1673) 310 When cruel lust..moves..fierce kings To act unworthy and unkingly things. **1702** ROWE *Tamerl.* I. i, With most unkingly baseness, H' has ta'en the advantage of their absent arms. **1765** BURKE *Tracts on Popery Laws* Wks. 1812 V. 250 [Louis XIV] had recourse..to an unkingly denial of the fact which made against him. **1853** TRENCH *Proverbs* 41 He was about, in somewhat unsoldierly and unkingly fashion, immediately to retire. **1880** SHORTHOUSE *J. Inglesant* xii, To introduce Popery..by ways the most unkingly and perfidious.

2. Unlike a king.

1718 POPE *Iliad* XIV. 90 What shameful words (unkingly as thou art) Fall from that trembling tongue and timorous heart?

un'kingly, *adv.* [UN-^{1} 11. Cf. ON. *úkonungliga*, MHG. *unkünecliche.*] In an unkingly manner; unlike a king.

1412–20 LYDG. *Chron. Troy* I. 3770 He vnkyngly of verray malys souȝt Ageynes vs firste occasioun. **1579** STUBBES *Gaping Gulf* C 5 Rychard [II]..fell amourous most unkindlye and vnkingly with a french girle but eyght yeeres of age.

†**un'kingship.** *Obs.*$^{-1}$ (UN-^{1} 12.)

a **1700** EVELYN *Diary* 30 May 1649, Un-kingship was proclaim'd, and his Majesty's statues thrown down.

un'kink, *v.* [UN-^{2} 3, 7.] **a.** *trans.* To take the kinks out of, to smooth, to straighten. **b.** *intr.* To lose the kinks, become straight. Also *fig.*

1891 KIPLING & BALESTIER in *Cent. Mag.* Dec. 193/1 Tarvin got himself out of the cart, unfolding his long stiffened legs..and unkinking his muscles one by one. **1947** *Daily Progress* (Charlottesville, Va.) 20 Mar. 8 Designed to un-kink highways. **1947** J. STEINBECK *Wayward Bus* ii. 18 Unkinking the cable behind him on the ground. **1972** C. SHORT *Blue-Eyed Boy* viii. 82 Gradually my soul began to unkink. **1980** J. MCNEIL *Spy Game* xiv. 138 The road unkinked and far ahead Corrigan was hopping past a goods van.

un'kinlike, *a.* (UN-^{1} 7 c.)

1869 BLACKMORE *Lorna D.* xi, It would be a sad and unkinlike thing for you to despise our dwelling-house.

†**un'kinsman.** *Obs.*$^{-1}$ (UN-^{1} 12.)

1606 SYLVESTER *Du Bartas* II. iv. *Tropheis* 1216 With an un-kinsman's kisse (un-loving Lover) The Brother shall his Sister's shame discover.

un'kirsened, *ppl. a. dial.* [UN-^{1} 8.] Unchristened.

a **1779** GRAHAM *Writings* (1883) II. 136 A cock, a cat, or some unkirsen'd creature. **1824** J. TELFER *Border Ball.* 65 It was unkirsent blood. **1873–** in *Eng. Dial. Dict.* s.v.

un'kiss, *v.* (UN-^{2} 3.)

1562 A. BROOKE *Romeus & Jul.* 843 A thousand times she kist, and him vnkist agayne. **1593** SHAKS. *Rich. II*, V. i. 74 Let me vnkisse the Oath 'twixt thee, and me. **1634** FORD *Perk. Warbeck* V. iii, That man, that shall vnkisse This sacred print next. **1653** W. HEMINGS *Fatal Contract* III. ii, With this kiss..Unkiss the kiss that seal'd it on thy lips.

un'kissed, *ppl. a.* Also 4–7 unkist, etc. [UN-^{1} 8. Cf. Du. *ongekust*, Sw. *okysst.*] Not kissed; without being kissed.

1390 GOWER *Conf.* II. 92 Ofte he goth to bedde unkist. *a* **1400** *Hymns Virg.* (1867) 80 We schulen go vnkist boþe at þe dore & at þe gate. *a* **1542** WYATT '*What should I say?*' 28 And thus betraide, Or that I wiste Farewell, unkiste! *a* **1592** GREENE *Jas. IV*, I. ii, I cannot abide a full cup unkissed. **1852** WHITTIER *April* 11 Round the boles of the pine-wood the ground-laurel creeps, Unkissed of the sun-shine. **1870** MORRIS *Earthly Par.* III. IV. 53 She sighed as those sweet sounds did fall From her unkissed lips.

†**b.** In the phrase *unknown* (*unknowe* or *uncouth*), *unkissed*. *Obs.*

1374 CHAUCER *Troylus* I. 809 Vnknowe vnkyst and lost þat is vn-sought. **1401** *Pol. Poems* (Rolls) II. 59 On old Englis it is said, unkissid is unknowun. **1562** J. HEYWOOD *Prov. & Epigr.* (1867) 148 Unknowen vnkist, and beyng knowen I weene, Thou art neuer kist, where thou mayst be seene. **1579** E. K. *Ded. to Spenser's Sheph. Cal.* §1 Our new Poete, who for that he is vncouthe (as said Chaucer) is vnkist, and vnknown to most men, is regarded but of few. *c* **1592** NASHE *Mar-Martine* xxii, Thou caytif kerne, vncouth thou art, vnkist thou eke sal bee. **1624** BP. MOUNTAGU *Immed. Addr.* 119, I would gladly see and know, by what warrant I on Earth so vncouth and therefore vnkist,..can say unto them, Holy Peter, blessed Paul, pray for mee. *a* **1697** AUBREY *Lives* (1898) II. 254 He..ransackt the MSS. of the church of Hereford (there were a great many that lay uncouth and unkiss). [**1897** V. HUNT (*title*), Unkist, Unkind!]

†**un'kithe,** *v.* *Obs.*$^{-1}$ [UN-^{2} 3.] *intr.* To disappear, vanish.

a **1300** *Cursor M.* 11438 Fra þai come þar als suith, þe stern it hid and can vnkyth.

un'knave, *v.* (UN-^{2} 6 b.)

1746 W. HORSLEY *Fool* (1748) II. 9 By pursuing their Master's Instructions, [they] make it their Business to unknave him.

un'kneaded, *ppl. a.* (UN-¹ 8.)
c **1631** T. CAREW *Elegy Death Donne* 4 Why yet dare we not trust Though with unkneaded dowe-bakt prose thy dust.

un'knelled, *ppl. a.* (UN-¹ 8.)
a **1770** CHATTERTON *Battle of Hastings* II. 556 And sowles unknelled hover'd oer the bloude. **1818** BYRON *Ch. Har.* IV. clxxix, Without a grave, unknell'd, uncoffin'd, and unknown.

un'knight, *v.* [UN-² 6 b.] *trans.* To divest of knighthood; to depose from the rank of knight. Hence **un'knighting** *vbl. sb.*
1623 in Birch *Crt. & Times Jas. I* (1848) II. 439 Francis Mitchell, that was unknighted the last parliament. *a* **1661** FULLER *Worthies, Yorks.* III. (1662) 207 Another author unknighteth him, allowing him only a plain Esquire. **1844** *P. Parley's Ann.* V. 251 By St. George, I will unknight thee. **1856** DORAN *Knights* xxx. 489 Knights, irregularly made so, were unknighted with little ceremony. *Ibid.* 490 There are fewer examples of unknighting in this country than in France.

un'knighted, *ppl. a.* [UN-¹ 8.] Not raised to the rank of knight; not invested with knighthood.
1631 in Birch *Crt. & Times Chas. I* (1848) II. 99 Ere long they will bring all the unknighted lords into play. *a* **1661** FULLER *Worthies, Camb.* I. (1662) 168 Indeed, I..cannot believe that he was Un-knighted so long. **1892** *Verney Mem.* I. 205 Mr. Badnage..remained unknighted.

un'knightlike, *adv.* (UN-¹ 7 c.)
1872 TENNYSON *Gareth & Lynette* 1122 Forth that other sprang, And, all unknight-like, writhed his wiry arms Around him.

un'knightly, *a.* [UN-¹ 7.]
1. Not appropriate to a knight or to knighthood.
c **1412** HOCCLEVE *De Reg. Princ.* 2286 Of suche vnknyghtly trikkes he nat roghte. **1423** JAS. I *Kingis Q.* lv, The crueltee of that vnknyghtly dede. **1586** FERNE *Blaz. Gentry* 161 Lewes..had so vnknightlye a regarde..of Armes, that [etc.]. **1611** GUILLIM *Heraldry* II. vi. 56 Base and vnknightly actions and qualities, deserue a base and vnknightly chastisement. **1664** BUTLER *Hud.* II. I. 832, I here..free you from th' Unknightly Jail. **1704** D'URFEY *Tales. Abradatus & P.* I. 12 The dire reward that did belong To him that Acted such unknightly wrong. **1828** SCOTT *F.M. Perth* viii, The unknightly advantage which yonder rascal had taken of his stumbling horse. **1860** GEN. P. THOMPSON *Audi Alt. Part.* III. cxlii. 123 A foreign force..threatening to sack, unless unknightly and degrading terms were complied with.
2. Unlike a knight; not having the qualities of a knight.
1596 SPENSER *F.Q.* VI. iii. 35 Vnknightly Knight,..Loe I defie thee. **1813** BYRON *Ch. Har.* Pref., Add., It has been stated, that..he is very unknightly, as the times of the Knights were times of Love, Honour, and so forth. **1842** TENNYSON *Morte d'Arth.* 120 Ah,..untrue, Unknightly, traitor-hearted!

un'knightly, *adv.* [UN-¹ 11.] In an unknightly manner.
a **1586** SIDNEY *Arcadia* III. xviii, They helde playe against the rest, though the two brothers unknightly helped them. **1859** TENNYSON *Geraint & Enid* 723 The brute Earl..unknightly with flat hand, however lightly, smote her on the cheek.

un'knit, *v.* [OE. *uncnyttan* (UN-² 4 b).]
1. *trans.* To untie or undo (a knot or something tied).
c **1000** *Ags. Gosp.* Luke iii. 16 þæs ic ne eom wyrþe þæt ic hys sceo-þwangc uncnytte. *c* **1200** *Trin. Coll. Hom.* 137 Ich nam noht ne forðen wurðe þat ich un-cnutte his sho þuong. **1387** TREVISA *Higden* (Rolls) II. 43 So þat þe more wynd he wol haue, he wil vnknette þe mo knottes. *c* **1430** *Syr Gener.* (Roxb.) 7091 Hir kerchef lift vp wold he Hir visage there forto see; Tho thoght he hir kerchefe to vnknyt. **1530** PALSGR. 768/1 Unknyt my gyrdell, I praye you. **1547** in *Leland's Collect.* (1774) IV. 321 Then tooke he the said Rope, and..tyed himselfe by the Right Legg,..and after..unknet the Knot, and came downe again. **1615** G. SANDYS *Trav.* 66 Tying on her silken buskins with knots easily not vnknit. **1675** HOBBES *Odyssey* (1677) 147 Binde me you must upright, both hand and foot, And so as I may not the knot unknit.
b. In figurative contexts (with *knot* or *bond*).
a **1225** *Leg. Kath.* 1150 Ich habbe uncnut summe of þeos cnotti cnotten. *c* **1374** CHAUCER *Boeth.* v. pr. iii. (1868) 154 þat som men wenen þat þei mowen assoilen & vnknytten þe knot of þis questioun. **1387-8** T. USK *Test. Love* III. vi. (Skeat) l. 129 Thilke falsheed..hath unknit the bond of understanding reson bytwene wil and the herte. *c* **1407** LYDG. *Reson & Sens.* 3202 Wher so as her [*sc.* Venus's] sort was set, The knot never was vnknet. *c* **1430** *Life St. Kath.* (1884) 44, I haue spoused me to hym in a bonde þat neuer schal be vnknytte. **1561** NORTON & SACKV. *Gorboduc* IV. ii, Whan thus I sawe the knot of loue unknitte. **1596** SHAKS. *1 Hen. IV*, v. i. 15 Will you againe vnknit This churlish knot of all-abhorred Warre? **1850** W. R. WILLIAMS *Religious Progress* IV. (1854) 82 Demoralization that unknits the bonds of obligation.
†**c.** To ungird (oneself). *Obs.*⁻¹
a **1500** in *Three 15th Cent. Chron.* (Camden) 111 Ther he shall unknyte hym, and his swerde..shall offer to God and to Holy Churche moste devowtly.
d. To disjoint, disunite; to unclasp. *rare.*
1580 HOLLYBAND *Treas. Fr. Tong* s.v. *Desnouer*, To vnknitte a bone, to put out of ioynte. **1582** STANYHURST *Æneis* II. (Arb.) 58 Thee ioyncturs vnknit, with an horribil hurring Pat fals thee turret. **1726** LEONI *Alberti's Archit.* I. 15 Rain..loosens and unknits all the Nerves of the Building. **1856** RUSKIN *Mod. Paint.* III. IV. xviii. Concl. 339 If again petty jealousies..prevail to unknit their hands from the armoured grasp.
e. To smooth out. *rare*⁻¹.
1596 SHAKS. *Tam. Shr.* v. ii. 136 Fie, fie, vnknit that threatning vnkinde brow.
2. *fig.* **a.** To disperse, dissolve, undo, destroy; to relax or weaken. Also *absol.*
1377 LANGL. *P. Pl.* B. XVIII. 213 So god..suffred to be solde to see þe sorwe of deyinge, The which vnknitteth al kare & comsynge is of reste. *c* **1412** HOCCLEVE *De Reg. Princ.* 2564 Al-thogh a kyng haue habundance of myght In his land, at his lust knytte & vnknytte. *a* **1500** *Ragman Roll* 151 in Hazl. *E.P.P.* I. 76 Weyr he unknytte, al this worldes rychesse Ne myghte noghte yow two knyttyn in feir. **1551** T. WILSON *Logike* 3 Logike is bound..to knit true argumentes and unknit false. **1592** LYLY *Gallathea* III. i, I feele my thoughts vnknit. **1642** CHAS. I *Let. to both Ho. Parl.* 7 Ambitious spirits, that may disjoynt and unknit his Majesty and this House. **1655** VAUGHAN *Silex Scint.*, *Match* ii, Shut out all distractions That may unknit My heart. *c* **1837** WORDSW. '*Ah why*' 5 Where for ages they have lain..With life's best sinews more and more unknit.
b. To separate, sever, detach.
1388 WYCLIF *Job* vi. 17 Thei schulen be vnknyt fro her place. *a* **1395** HYLTON *Scala Perf.* I. xii. (MS. Bodl. 592), þis spirit wole vnknytte and vndo ih'u fro þe soule: & þerfore it is not of god. *c* **1412** HOCCLEVE *De Reg. Princ.* 1658 þanne is to hem an helle hire mariage, þanne þei desyren for to be vnknyt.
3. *intr.* To become unknit, in various senses.
1574 HELLOWES *Gueuara's Fam. Ep.* (1577) 187 It is a sore that neuer openeth, and a bonde that neuer vnknitteth. **1609** C. BUTLER *Fem. Mon.* v. F 3 b, Then may you bid them farewel: for presentlie they begin to vnknit, and to be gone. **1677** *Gov. Venice* 6 The private Magistrates are as it were the Nerves and Bones..; and the Council of Ten are the ligaments, hindring the parts from unknitting. **1748** THOMSON *Cast. Indol.* I. xxiii. For whomsoe'er the villain takes in hand, Their joints unknit, their sinews melt apace. **1870** *Pall Mall G.* 10 Dec. 12 The lady's eyebrows unknit, and wintry smiles break from the grey eyes.
Hence **un'knitting** *vbl. sb.*
1382 WYCLIF *Nahum* ii. 10 Herte feylynge, and vnknytynge of smale knees. **1545** *Act 37 Hen. VIII*, c. 21 §2 Without any dissolucion, undoinge, unknittinge, or repeale of them. **1611** COTGR., *Desnouement*, an vntying, vnknitting, vnbinding (of knots).

un'knit, *ppl. a.* [UN-¹ 8 b.] Not knit together or closely united.
1607 MARKHAM *Cavel.* I. xviii. 73 His ioynts being tender and vnknit. *a* **1625** FLETCHER *Fair Maid of Inn* III. i, The petty brawls..shall, like tender unknit joynts, Fasten again together of themselves. **1809-14** WORDSW. *Excurs.* III. 914 Let us..Leave this unknit Republic to the scourge Of her own passions. **1860** MOTLEY *Netherl.* vii. (1868) I. 465 A loose, disordered and unknit state needs no shaking, but propping.

un'knitting, *ppl. a.* (UN-¹ 10.)
1587 GOLDING *De Mornay* x. 165 [Aristotle] sayth that the knitting parts,..the bones, the skin, the sinewes,..may be made of the mixing togither of the elements, and that the vnknitting parts, as the Head, the Leg, the Arme,..cannot.

un'knock, *v.* (UN-² 3.)
1680 MOXON *Mech. Exerc.* xii. 203 Its Office is to knock and unknock the Wedge in the Puppets.

un'knot, *v.* (UN-² 3. Cf. G. *entknoten.*)
1598 FLORIO, *Sgroppare*, to vntie, to vnknot. **1623** COCKERAM II, Not to be vnknotted, *inenodable.* **1866** MISS A. CARY *Ball. & Lyrics* 54, I saw my Charley The..shawl from his neck Unknot, with a quick, wise cunning. **1891** *Daily News* 8 July 4/8 The man..who hoards string, unknotting it ..from parcels.
refl. **1880** *Daily News* 27 Nov. 2/8 This remarkable worm ..has the power of unknotting himself.

un'knotted, *ppl. a.* (UN-¹ 8.)
1642 H. MORE *Song of Soul* To Rdr., All homogeneall, simple, single,..unknotted, uncocted. **1744** MRS. DELANY *Life & Corr.* (1861) II. 291 You ask me how many pounds of thread I have got for you; do you mean knotted or unknotted? **1756** DYER *Fleece* III. 58 Even, unknotted, twine will praise your skill. **1892** YEATS *C'tess Kathleen* III. 51 The green things love unknotted hearts and minds.

un'knotty, *a.* (UN-¹ 7.)
1621 G. SANDYS *Ovid's Met.* x. (1626) 198 Vnknottie Firre, the solace-shading Planes, Rough Chestnuts. **1622** MABBE tr. *Aleman's Guzman d'Alf.* II. 348 The wooll of the Matresses..[was] kept vnknotty, and soft.

un'know, *v.*¹ [UN-¹ 14.]
1. *trans.* Not to know (something); to fail to recognize or perceive. Also *absol.*
c **1380** WYCLIF *Serm.* Sel. Wks. I. 160 þou art maister in Israel, and 3it þou unknowist þes þingis. **1382** —— *1 Cor.* xiv. 38 If ony man vnknowith, he schal be vnknowen. *c* **1400** *Apol. Loll.* 61 þoo þat vnknawen þe ri3twisnes of God. *c* **1532** DU WES *Introd. Fr.* in *Palsgr.* 942 To unknowe, *descognoistre.* **1646** SIR T. BROWNE *Pseud. Ep.* 41, I hardly beleeve, he hath from elder times unknowne the verticity of the loadstone. **1709** MRS. MANLEY *Secret Mem.* (1720) III. 252 [He] is obliged to turn his Eyes, as if to unknow, or at least must take no notice of it here. **1871** SWINBURNE *Hertha* 19 Love or unlove me, Unknow me or know.
†**2.** To be ignorant *that*, etc. Also *intr.* with *of.*
1382 WYCLIF *1 Cor.* x. 1, I nyle 3ou for to vnknowe, for [**1388** that] alle oure fadris weren vndir cloude. [Also *1 Kings* xxii. 3, *Rom.* i. 13.] *a* **1400** *Pauline Ep.* (Powell) 2 Cor. i. 8 We wil not 3ou to vnknowe, breþere, of oure tribulacyoun. **1709** MRS. MANLEY *Secret Mem.* (1720) II. 58 Sure these seem to unknow that there is a certain Portion of Misery..allotted to all Men.

un'know, *v.*² [UN-² 3.] *trans.* To cease to know, to forget (what one has known). Also *absol.*
a **1586** SIDNEY *Arcadia* III. v, She..rather wished to unknowe what she knewe, then to burden her hart with more hopeles knowledge. **1627** S. WARD *Happiness of Practice* 31 Such..shall soone vnknow that which they know [to be good]. **1697** J. SERGEANT *Solid Philos.* b 2, His Method of Unknowing all that Nature had taught him. **1782** PAINE *Let. Abbé Raynel* (1791) 50 There is no possibility..of the mind *un*knowing any thing it already knows. **1859** I. TAYLOR *Logic in Theol.* 270 Unless I might unknow what I have come to know. **1865** J. GROTE *Explor. Philos.* I. 243 We have got to unsee and unknow much further back than this, if [etc.].

unknow, variant of UNKNOWE *ppl. a. Obs.*

unknowa'bility. (UN-¹ 12; cf. next.)
1863 MILL *Lett.* (1910) I. 272 The doctrine of unknowability. **1871** R. H. HUTTON *Ess.* I. 28 The unknowability of the primal Cause.

un'knowable, *a.* and *sb.* (UN-¹ 7 b.)
c **1374** CHAUCER *Boeth.* III. met. vii. (1886) 47 Liggeth thanne stille al owtrely vnknowable, ne fame ne maketh yow nat knowe. **1456** SIR G. HAY *Bk. Knighthood* Wks. (S.T.S.) II. 16 The quhilkis ar unknawable till..unworthy personis. **1653** H. MORE *Antid. Ath.* I. iv. §3 He is a very Novice in Speculation that does not acknowledge that to be unknowable. **1678** CUDWORTH *Intell. Syst.* I. iv. §31. 471 There is something of God Vnknowable and Incomprehensible by all Mortals. **1740** CHEYNE *Regimen* 35 If we drop both substances, as unknown and unknowable Things at present. **1754** EDWARDS *Freed. Will* II. xii. 119 If there be any Truth which is absolutely without Evidence, that Truth is absolutely unknowable. **1818** F. HALL *Trav. Canada & U.S.* 28 Indeed privacy..seems quite unknown, and unknowable to the Americans. **1873** MORLEY *Rousseau* II. 90 Men..will be thankful not to waste life in guessing evil about unknowable trifles.
b. *absol.* (with *the*). That which cannot be known. (Common from *c* 1860.)
1823 *Monthly Rev.* CI. 447 Here, again, the author professes to know the unknowable. **1867** LEWES *Hist. Philos.* I. p. cxv, We always hope that the Unknown is not also the Unknowable.
c. As *sb.* An unknowable thing.
1725 WATTS *Logic* I. vi. §1 To distinguish well between Knowables and Unknowables. **1733** —— *Philos. Ess.* I. xii, In every Age..there will be some Unknowables and Insolvables. **1874** B. P. BROWNE *Philos. H. Spencer* ii. 41 (Stand.), Mr. Spencer's argument proves an unexplainable, not an unknowable.
Hence **un'knowableness.**
1664 N. INGELO *Bentiv. & Ur.* II. VI. 367 The unknowableness of the manner of this Union. **1697** J. SERGEANT *Solid Philos.* 301 The Unknowableness of Real Essences. **1856** RUSKIN *Mod. Paint.* IV. 81 The great religious painters rejoiced in that kind of unknowableness. **1886** JANE LEE *Faust* p. xxxiii, The unknowableness of the nature of things.

†**un'knowe** (also 5–6 **-know,** 6 *Sc.* **-knaw**), obs. variants of UNKNOWN *ppl. a.*
For the phrase *unknowe, unkissed*, see UNKISSED *ppl. a.*
1340-70 *Alex. & Dind.* 382 We holden hit a vertu..Among þe men of our march mercy vnknowe. *c* **1350** *Lybeaus Disc.* 71 Than may ye wete a rowe, 'The fayre unknowe', Sertes so hatte he. **1387** TREVISA *Higden* (Rolls) I. 87 þan were þe Parthi as it were..vnknowe amonge men of the est londes. **1430-40** LYDG. *Bochas* VIII. xiv. (1558) 9 b, A knight vnknowe angelyke of vysage. *c* **1440** *Gesta Rom.* i. 2 (Harl. MS.), þat she euer pursuyd for my deth, þat is vnknowe to me. **1513** DOUGLAS *Æneid* VI. ii. 52 Virgyne, na kynd of pane may rise Vnknaw to me.
So †**un'knowed** *ppl. a. Obs.*
c **1380** *Sir Ferumb.* 3847 If þar comeþ any ounknowed man. *c* **1380** [see UNKEPT *ppl. a.* 2].

un'knowing, *vbl. sb.* [UN-¹ 13.] Ignorance. Revived in mod. use, esp. in phr. ***cloud of unknowing*** (after quot. *a* 1400).
1340 HAMPOLE *Pr. Consc.* 194 In myrknes of unknawyng þai gang. *Ibid.* 5741 Ne mene þou noght Of my freyle, unknawynges of thoght. *c* **1380** WYCLIF *Sel. Wks.* I. 159 So Nichodeme..for þis unknowinge..axide þis questioun. *a* **1400** (*title*) þe clowde of vnknowyng. *c* **1449** PECOCK *Repr.* I. xvi. 89 The vnhauyng and the vnknowing of this..consideracioun. *c* **1450** LOVELICH *Grail* lii. 775 That I haue don be vnknowenge, Of for3evenesse I preye 3ow. **1556** OLDE *Antichrist* 127 b, What other thing shal we cal this, but the most grosse unknowing of God? **1629** A. BAKER *Commentary on Cloud* (1924) II. iii. 355 This cloud of unknowing..is but the self-same knowledge and sight of God which I and others do usually term the light, sight and knowledge that we have by our faith. **1911** E. UNDERHILL *Mysticism* II. vii. 415 Reason finds itself, in a very actual sense, 'in the dark'—immersed in the Cloud of Unknowing. **1939** T. S. ELIOT *Family Reunion* II. ii. 110 Accident is design And design is accident In a cloud of unknowing. **1957** *Oxf. Dict. Christian Church* 402/2 This [progressive deification of man] is to be obtained by a process of 'unknowing', in which the soul leaves behind the perceptions of the senses as well as the reasoning of the intellect. **1976** H. MONTEFIORE in *Christian Believing* 154 Even in granting as much as this to doctrine and dogma, I have to enter into the cloud of unknowing and assert the Church's apophatic tradition. **1984** *Daily Tel.* 9 Feb. 16/5 This is one of those incidents which cloud the mind with mystery, forming, as we brood on it, a positive cloud of unknowing. **1984** *Sunday Tel.* 8 July 18/4 Ideally, the fearful void of unknowing should be filled by the ballast of faith.

un'knowing, *ppl. a.* [UN-¹ 10, 5 d.]
1. Not knowing; not possessed of knowledge; uninformed, ignorant.
c **1315** SHOREHAM v. 148 Al one-knowynge þa3 hy were, Hy makede ioye. **1386** *Rolls of Parlt.* III. 225/2 Owre lyge Lordes comaundement to symple and unknouuing men. **1435** MISYN *Fire of Love* 48 Bot þies ar vnknawand, for vertew of contemplatife þai knaw not. **1538** G. BROWNE in Ware *Hist. Coll.* (1681) 3 The People of this Nation be zealous, yet blind and unknowing. **1612-3** C. BROOKE *Elegy*

Poems (1872) 175 Those baser mindes, vnknowing, sensuall, rude. **1649** Bp. Hall *Cases Consc.* vi. (1654) 45 The matter may be intricated by passing through many perhaps unknowing hands. **1725** Pope *Odyss.* xx. 56 Man on frail unknowing man relies. **1760–72** H. Brooke *Fool of Qual.* (1809) IV. 27 My..child..is unexperienced in the world, quite unknowing and unknown. **1845** Hirst *Com. Mammoth*, etc. 89 Winds that pilfer from unknowing flowers Their balmy breaths. **1871** H. Macmillan *True Vine* vi. 249 It..does what it does in simple, perfect, unknowing dependence upon the will of God.

absol. **1718** J. Chamberlayne *Nieuwentijdt's Relig. Philos.* p. xx, [They] pass amongst the Unknowing for great Mathematicians. **1833** Disraeli *Cont. Flem.* i. i, Our instructors are the unknowing and the dead. **1876** *Nature* 2 Nov. 17/1 Undated..works..may be palmed off on the unknowing as the genuine product of the current year.

2. Without knowledge, ignorant, *of* something.

In frequent use from *c* 1700.

a **1300** *Cursor M.* 28313 O godds godes..haue i ben vnknauand. *c* **1400** *26 Pol. Poems* 149 All that lyuen..Shall dye, vnknowyng of her day. *a* **1450** *Knt. de la Tour* (1868) 159 That is gret pite..to be vncunnynge and vnknowynge of hym selff. **1542** Udall *Erasm. Apoph.* 16 The residue wer vnknowyng of this thyng. **1691** Wood *Ath. Oxon.* I. 587 [He was] simple, and unknowing of matters of State. **1740** Richardson *Pamela* II. 270 She had found out a Match for me,..and had..brought me into the Lady's Company, unknowing of her Design. **1844** [see 2c]. **1869** Freeman *Norm. Conq.* III. xii. 242 He laid his hand on the chest, while still unknowing of all that was in it.

b. With direct object.

1382 Wyclif *Gal.* iv. 8 ȝe, vnknowynge God, seruyden to hem that weren not goddis. **1460** Capgrave *Chron.* 110 Sche went onknowyng hir tyme fro Seynt Petirs onto Lateran. *c* **1500** *Melusine* v. 27 He..rode apas vnknowing the way. **1760–2** Goldsm. *Cit. W.* xxii, Mankind wanders, unknowing his way, from morning till evening. **1830** Tennyson *Grasshopper* i. 16 Unknowing fear, Undreading loss, A gallant cavalier. **1847** T. D'Arcy McGee *Art MacMurrogh* p. x, When, unknowing facts, they [*sc.* historians] lay down suppositions in their place.

c. With objective clause.

c **1425** *St. Elizabeth* in *Anglia* VIII. 147 Not vnknowynge þat oure lorde couerde þe naked of oure firste fader and moder after hir falle. *c* **1465** *Eng. Chron.* (Camden, 1856) 62 Unknowyng the said peple wherfore it was. **1542** Udall *Erasm. Apoph.* 182 b, Thou art not unknowyng that we are now conquerours. **1697** Dryden *Æneis* vi. 236 Æneas went Sad from the cave,..Unknowing whom the sacred Sibyl meant. **1748** Richardson *Clarissa* (1811) III. i. 2 They were all working for me,..unknowing that they did so. **1820** Scott *Monast.* xxv, Driven by calamity, and unknowing where my course is bound. **1844** Kinglake *Eothen* xii, Unknowing of all geography, unknowing where he was, or whither he might go.

d. With inf. (alone or preceded by *how*, etc.).

1666 Dryden *Ann. Mirab.* xcvi, The Kingly beast..slowly moves, unknowing to give place. **1697** —— *Virg. Georg.* iv. 126 Unknowing how to fly, And obstinately bent to win or dye. **1700** —— *Wife of Bath's T.* 100 Lest surpriz'd, unknowing what to say, Thou damn thy self. **1746** Francis tr. *Horace, Art of Poetry* 51 In one grand Whole unknowing to unite Those different Parts. **1771** Goldsm. *Hist. Eng.* II. 204 Unknowing whether to ascribe their misfortunes to..sorcery, or to a celestial influence. **1801** Southey *Thalaba* v. 170 Unknowing whitherward to bend his way, He stood. **1812** J. Henry *Camp. agst. Quebec* 46 The huge animal..seemed unknowing which way to run.

†**3.** In absolute construction. *Obs.*

1451 *Paston Lett.* I. 198 He thought that ye and James Gresham had do it un malyce,..your moders unknowyng. **1483** *Vulgaria abs Terentio* 20 He hyde nott fro me that..odyr doo, vnknowynge theire faders. *c* **1500** *Melusine* xxiv. 171 They came & lodged them a leghe nygh to the Calyphes oost, vnknowyng the paynemes of it.

4. As quasi-*adv.* = unknowingly *adv.*

1392 Wyclif *Acts* xvii. 23 Therfore which thing ȝe vnknowynge worschipen, this thing I schewe to ȝou. **1470–85** Malory *Arthur* x. lxxix. 554 There syr Tristram vnknowyng smote doune kyng Arthur. **1721** Amherst *Terræ Fil.* (1726) 101 See..what mischiefs ye might do unknowing. **1743** Francis tr. *Hor., Odes* v. iii. 6 Have I swallow'd the gore of a viper unknowing? **1852** Kingsley *Andromeda* 250 From afar, unknowing, I marked thee.

5. Unknown *to* (a person). Chiefly in absolute const., = without the knowledge of. *Obs.* exc. *dial.*

c **1400** *Destr. Troy* 11318, I..neuer comynd in þis case vnknowing to you. **1462** *Paston Lett.* II. 119 It is not on knowyng to you that [etc.]. **1513** Bradshaw *St. Werburge* i. 2677 A seruaunt..pryuely hydde it,..Vnknowynge to Werburge. **1577** Grange *Golden Aphrod.* I iv b, He..sodenly departed (vnknowing to the Ladies). **1617** Collins *Def. Bp. Ely* (1628) 302 When he praied for his children, vnknowing to them. **1643** E. Symmons *Loyal Subjects Belief* Ep. Ded., Unknowing, I beleeve, to them in particular, some others did intend [etc.]. **1886–91** in Somerset and Devon glossaries.

Hence **un'knowingness**.

1493 *Festivall* 23 b/1 Vnknowyngnesse shalle not exscuse you at yᵉ day of dome. **1872** H. Bushnell *Serm. Living Subj.* 211 The unknowingness, the innocence, the sweet simplicity of childhood.

un'knowingly, *adv.* [un-¹ 11: cf. prec.] Without knowledge, ignorantly; unintentionally. Also const. *to* (a person).

1340 *Ayenb.* 175 Huanne me zeneȝeþ wytindeliche, me zeneȝeþ more ynoȝ þanne onknawyndliche. *c* **1440** *Promp. Parv.* 366/1 On-knowyngly, *ignoranter.* *a* **1500** *Ratis Raving* i. 904 Better to be styll Than say vnknawandly ther tyll. **1641** Sir E. Dering *Sp. on Relig.* 22 Nov. 70, I speake it not unknowingly. **1697** *Dryden's Virg. Past.* Preface (1721) I. 97 The Roman Historian..falls, unknowingly, into a Verse not unworthy Virgil himself. **1709** Shaftesb. *Charac.* (1711) II. 89 An Eye..fails not to shut together, of its own accord, unknowingly to us. **1768–74** Tucker *Lt. Nat.* (1834) I. 595 Made unknowingly to work out the advantage of fellow-creatures, whereof we have not the least knowledge. **1807** Wordsw. *White Doe* ii. 100 Leaning on a lance Which he had grasped unknowingly. **1871** Freeman *Hist. Ess.* Ser. i. iii. 213 Nations and parties learn to shape themselves unknowingly.

†**un'knowledge.** *Obs.* [un-¹ 12.]

1. Unacknowledgement.

a **1300** *Cursor M.* 27833 O couaitise..cums..fals wittnesing, Vnknaulage, manath, and lesing.

2. Absence or want of knowledge; ignorance. ***your unknowledge***, unknown to you.

c **1450** *Cov. Myst.* (Shaks. Soc.) 121 For unknowlage he is desesyd. **1470** *Paston Lett.* II. 393, I have betyn the mater for yow, your onknowleche, as I told hyr. **1483** *Sc. Acts, Jas. III* (1814) II. 166 At thay may not excuse thame of the vnknawlege of thir articlis. **1593** Nashe *Christ's T.* F ij b, Your pretence of vnknowledge or ignorance.

un'knowledgeable, *a.* [un-¹ 7 b.]

1. Unknowable. *rare.*

1920 C. M. Grieve in *Northern Numbers* 69 The barrier..Lifts sheerly..To the unknowledgeable skies. **1926** W. de la Mare *Connoisseur* 303 Such facts were strange, and, as you might say almost unknowledgeable.

2. Not knowledgeable; uninformed.

1969 *Islander* (Victoria, B.C.) 9 Nov. 7/2 Many unknowledgeable people find their way into the mountains. **1974** H. L. Foster *Ribbin', Jivin', & Playin' Dozens* iv. 128 By using the inversion process blacks were able to take advantage of the unknowledgeable white opponents.

†**un'knowledged**, *ppl. a.* [un-¹ 8.] Unacknowledged.

c **1445** Pecock *Donet* 96 þat no svnne be left bihinde for vnknowen and vnknowlechid. **1598** *Mucedorus* v. ii. 104 Condemne not..My rude behauiour, so compeld by Nature, That manners stood vnknowledged. **1603** B. Jonson *The Satyr* Wks. (Rtldg.) 537/2 For which bounty to us lent, Of him unknowledg'd, or unsent, We prepared this compliment.

†**un'knowledging.** *Obs.* [un-¹ 12.] Ignorance. ***unknowledging to*** without the knowledge of.

1357 *Lay Folks Catech.* 73 Nane sal excuse tham Thurgh unknalechyng for to kun tham. ?**1530** in Ellis *Orig. Lett.* Ser. iii. II. 229 The sayd Dean,..vnknowlegyng to..the surveyor of Hampton Corte,..hathe..dygyd uppe by the rootts xxxv. of my..ffeyrest elmes.

un'known, *ppl. a.*¹ and *sb.* [un-¹ 8 b. Cf. OE. *unȝecnawen.*]

A. *adj.* **1.** Not known; strange, unfamiliar:

a. Of places.

13.. *Cursor M.* 1170 (Gött.), I sal be flemed for mi sinne, In vnknaun land to duell ine. **13..** *E.E. Allit. P.* B. 1679 He ..carfully is out-kast to contre vnknawen. *a* **1440** *Sir Eglam.* 917 As sche were of an unknowen londe. **1586** T. B. *La Primaud. Fr. Acad.* i. 71 As if he should undertake to..walke through unknowen places without a guide. **1638** in *Verney Mem.* (1907) I. 90 Some unknown place in the world. **1697** Dryden *Virg. Georg.* iii. 532 So vast a Space Of Wilds unknown..Allures their Eyes. **1790** Cowper *Odyss.* xxiv. 344 The fishes of the unknown deep. **1844** H. H. Wilson *Brit. India* II. 402 The armies..beheld countries previously unknown. **1853** M. Arnold *Scholar Gypsy* xiv, Where o'er thy unknown grave..white flowering nettles wave.

b. Of persons.

unknown God: see quot. 1526. ***unknown soldier*** or ***warrior***, an unidentified soldier whose tomb symbolizes that of all those killed in battle: see warrior 2 a.

For the phrase ***unknown, unkissed***, see unkissed.

13.. *Cursor M.* 12131 (Gött.), Ani man, vnknauen or cuth. **1382** Wyclif *1 Cor.* xiv. 38 Forsothe if ony man vnknowith, he schal be vnknowen [Vulg. *ignorabitur*]. *c* **1386** Chaucer *Friar's T.* 99, I am vnknowen as in this contree. *c* **1440** *Alph. Tales* 175 Ane vnknowen man sittand on a hors. *c* **1449** Pecock *Repr.* 53 He schal be vnknowen of God forto be eny of hise. **1526** Tyndale *Acts* xvii. 23, I founde an aultre wher in was written: vnto the vnknowen god. **1555** Eden *Decades* (Arb.) 49 It had byn better for hym to haue byn obscure and vnknowen. **1607** E. Topsell *Four-footed Beasts* 96 The Arabians sacrifice a camell to the vnknowne god. **1622** J. Taylor (Water P.) *Sir G. Nonsence* To Nobody, The narration of the Vnknowne Knight. **1676** Ray *Corr.* (1848) 123 An unknown person, who sent me a letter without a name. **1718** *Free-thinker* No. 4. 25 The Discourse ..turned upon the Unknown Fair. **1797** S. & H. Lee *Canterb. T.* (1799) I. 364 To Lothaire the lord of St. Aubert was personally unknown. **1846** Mrs. A. Marsh *Father Darcy* II. x. 164 Mr. Keyes..was a man quite unknown about town. *c* **1848** M. M. Sherwood *Last Days of Boosy* (ed. 2) 152 The child..addressed the fearful name..as I had taught him to do to the to him unknown God who made the heavens. **1885** 'Mrs. Alexander' *At Bay* iv, Unknown, doubtful Americans, neither rich nor highly-placed are beyond the pale. **1920** *Times* 11 Nov. 14/1 The Unknown Warrior..was brought to London by night... He lay..awaiting burial today in the Abbey among the greatest of his race. *Ibid.* 12 Nov. 13/1 The body of the Unknown Warrior ..was buried in Westminster Abbey yesterday, the King being chief mourner. **1942** E. Waugh *Put out More Flags* i. 36 Rupert Brooke, Old Bill, the Unknown Soldier—thus three fond women saw him. **1947** E. M. Forster in *Harper's Mag.* July 9/2, I add the proviso 'if all goes well' because success lies on the knees of an unknown God. **1970** *Times* 3 June 5/6 Princess Margaret drove today to Mount Avala to lay a wreath of red poppies on the tomb of the unknown soldier. **1980** I. Murdoch *Nuns & Soldiers* i. 42 The soldiers at the Unknown Warrior's grave in Warsaw.

c. Of things or facts.

unknown quantity, orig. a term of algebra (see quots. 1676, 1728, and cf. quantity 12); also freq. in figurative use.

c **1330** R. Brunne *Chron. Wace* (Rolls) 2757 [They] caste þer armes of, þe vnknowen, And armede hem eft wyþ here owen. *c* **1374** Chaucer *Former Age* 6 Onknowyn was þe quyerne and ek the melle. *c* **1450** *Myrr. our Ladye* 158 Then oure lady..was sturred in her harte wyth vnspecable & vnknowen gladnesse. **1509** Fisher *Wks.* (1876) 297 It is not vnknowen how studyously she procured Iustyce to be admynystred. **1568** Grafton *Chron.* II. 180 A man of vnknowen or low birth. **1622** S. Ward *Life of Faith* (1627) 51 Death is the knownest and vnknownest thing in the world. **1669** Sturmy *Mariner's Mag.* iv. i. 138 Many times the Ship is carried away by unknown Currents. **1676** Glanvill *Ess.* iii. 15 The degree of Composition in the unknown Quantity of the Æquation. **1728** Chambers *Cycl.* s.v. *Equation*, The Root of an Equation, is the Value of the unknown Quantity in the Equation. *a* **1768** Secker *Serm.* (1770) IV. xviii. 387 Their having a real, though unknown, Subserviency to valuable Ends. **1827** Faraday *Chem. Manip.* xv. 389 As the whole volume of gas introduced is unknown, and the specific gravity is as yet unknown. **1865** W. Bagehot in *Fortn. Rev.* 15 May 21 The first election of Mr. Lincoln..was government by an unknown quantity. **1883** [see quantity 12]. **1885** 'Mrs. Alexander' *At Bay* vi, For some reasons unknown very little was said of the occurrence in the newspapers. **1951** *Sport* 30 Mar.–5 Apr. 6/3 Mel Ford, the Aberavon prop who gets a 'cap' is an unknown quantity in the North. **1973** *Times* 16 Apr. 14/2 Unless some formula is found for substantial alternative investments for Arab oil money it will continue to be an unknown quantity on the world money market.

d. Const. *to* (*unto*, †*till*) or †*of* (= by).

1340 Hampole *Pr. Consc.* 7694 Na thyng..tylle him unknawen es. **1399** Langl. *Rich. Redeles* iii. 263 It is not vnknowen to kunnynge leodis. **1486** *Paston Lett.* III. 328 What pleasur ye maie do to the Kings Grace..is not to you unknowen. **1578** Lyte *Dodoens* 5 Straunge herbes.. vnknowen of the common people. ?**1600** C. Percy in *Shaksp. Cent. Of Praise* 38 Anything..that may bee unknown unto you. **1670** Pettus *Fodinæ Reg.* 11 That Mine, which was afterward discovered..in that Countie (as yet unknown to the Societie). **1738** Gay *Propertius* iii. 65 Happy the youth, and not unknown to Fame. **1823** H. J. Brooke *Introd. Crystallogr.* 231 A crystal whose primary form is unknown to us. **1866** Geo. Eliot *F. Holt* Introd. 16 These things are often unknown to the world.

e. With *of.* (Cf. know *v.* 18 b.)

1606 G. Woodcock *Lives Emperors* in *Hist. Ivstine* G g 2 When nature did hatch such euils as were vnknowne of to the whole world. **1839** Mary Howitt *Boy of Southern Isle* i. xx, Some unknown-of isle. **1864** Pusey *Lect. Daniel* ii. 94 It is..one strange, unknown-of, God, whom he shall recognise.

2. In absolute const.: Without it being known (*to* one), without the knowledge *of* (some one).

1390 Gower *Conf.* II. 169 Diane his dowhter he begat Unknowen of his wif Juno. **1423** Jas. I *Kingis Q.* xlv, Bewailling myn infortune.., Vnknawin how or quhat was best to doon. *c* **1450** *Mirk's Festial* 207 Scho..was þer þrytte ȝere vnknowon of all men wythout mete oþir drynke. **1483** Caxton *G. de la Tour* I j, Two prestes unknowen of her cam wher as she was alone. **1523** Ld. Berners *Froiss.* I. 74 The kyng..was ther unknowen of his ennemyes. **1590** Shaks. *Com. Err.* iv. ii. 48 Thus he vnknowne to me should be in debt. **1606** —— *Ant. & Cl.* ii. vii. 84 Being done vnknowne, I should haue found it afterwards well done. **1672** Wiseman *Wounds* i. viii. 74 The Patient, unknown to me, pursued his intention. **1761** Mrs. F. Sheridan *Sidney Bidulph* III. 106 He stole, unknown to anybody, on board a ship. **1820** Keats *Isabella* xi, All close they met,..Unknown of any, free from whispering tale. **1823** Southey *Hist. Penins. War* I. 77 An agent..was employed to negociate it unknown to the Spanish embassador. **1898** 'Merriman' *Roden's Corner* iii, The terrible distress..going on unknown to us in our very midst.

†**3. a.** Ignorant (*of*), unskilled *in*. *Obs.*

a **1300** *Cursor M.* 11809 þis herods..[was] O carles costes al til vnknauin. *c* **1475** *Rauf Coilȝear* 127 Sen ellis thow art vnknawin, To mak me Lord of my awin. **1653** W. Ramesey *Astrol. Restored* 3 We see thereby the folly of such..gain-sayers of what they are altogether unknown in.

†**b.** Not recognizing, owning, acknowledging, or confessing. *Obs.*

a **1300** *Cursor M.* 18796 Of vn-man-hede es it draun, To be again god dede vn-knaun. *Ibid.* 28288 Ic ha made vous oft vn-right, And halden þam efter my might, þe gode vous ic am vn-knaun. *c* **1375** *Ibid.* 26666 (Fairf.), þat is þou art vnknawen of ani man synnis bot þine awen.

B. *sb.* **1.** An unknown person: **a.** With *the.*

the Great Unknown (quot. 1825), the author of the Waverley Novels.

1597 in Salusbury & Chester *Poems* (1914) 79 To the Honorable minded vnknowne, the Name-lesse wisheth.. perpetuall happines. **1652** Loveday *Hymen's Præludia* 8 The faire Unknowne found enough in his Noble looks to claime respect. **17..** Watts *Hymn*, '*Who dares*' iv, When shall we see the Great Unknown, And in his presence stand? **1774** *Trinket* 70 The charming unknown turned his eyes on me. **1825** R. Wilson *Sk. Hist. Hawick* 51 The powerfully superior mind of the Great Unknown. **1834** Dickens *Sk. Boz, Boarding-ho.* i, The distinguished unknown who condescends to play the 'swell' in the pantomime.

b. With *an, this*, etc., or pl.

1611 Shaks. *Cymb.* iv. iv. 43, I am asham'd To looke vpon the holy Sunne,..remaining So long a poore vnknowne. **1686** tr. *Agiatis or Civ. Wars Lacedemonians* 71 To unite her self to that Unknown, whom she prefers before me. **1709** Mrs. Manley *Secret Mem.* (1720) IV. 140 I'll never run after the Cant of a Letter from an unknown again. *a* **1774** Goldsm. tr. *Scarron's Com. Romance* (1775) II. 160 He immediately recollected his unknown by her person. **1839** W. Irving *Wolfert's R.* (1855) 45, I have only to find out this amiable Unknown, to wed her, and be happy! **1902** Eliz. Banks *Newspaper Girl* 214 Looking at the bodies of the unfortunate unknowns.

2. a. With *the*: That which is unknown.

1656 Stanley *Hist. Philos.* viii. (1687) 433/2 From which proceedeth Opinion..to the false and unknown. **1759** B. Porteus *Death* 300 When my Soul starting from the dark unknown Casts back a wishful look. **1816** Chalmers *Let.* in *Life* (1851) II. 65 Running into the dark unknown of legal perplexities. **1876** T. Hardy *Ethelberta* xxxv, Losing the indefinite interest of the unknown, it acquired the charm of a riddle.

b. An unknown state or condition. More widely, an unknown thing; an unknown factor (merging with *fig.* use of sense 3).
1837 CARLYLE *Fr. Rev.* I. IV. i, A new omnipotent Unknown of Democracy was coming into being. **1878** E. DICKINSON *Poems* (1955) III. 849 Let my first Knowing be of thee With morning's warming Light And my first Fearing, lest Unknowns Engulph thee in the night. **1947** H. S. SHELTON in Dewar & Shelton *Is Evolution Proved?* xi. 319 We cannot, therefore, correlate all these unknowns and say what variations result from what changes. **1948** R. SPILLER et al. *Literary Hist. U.S.* 1159 Sensitivity to spiritual unknowns. **1964** M. GOWING *Britain & Atomic Energy 1939–1945* i. 36 He acknowledged the unknowns in the situation.

3. *Math.* An unknown quantity.
1817 H. T. COLEBROOKE *Algebra*, etc. 63 The demonstration is by resolution of a quadratic equation involving several unknown. **1890** A. MARSHALL *Princ. Economics* p. xi, His equations are neither more nor less in number than his unknowns.

†**unknown**, *ppl. a.*[2] *Obs.*[−1] [var. of *on-*, *aknown*: see ACKNOW *v.* 4 d.] In a state of acknowledgement or confession.
a **1300** *Cursor M.* 26094 þe toþer pont es scrift o muth To mak to preistes vr costes cuth; Of al vr plight to be vnknaun, Wit will to bete þat we ha schaun.

un'knownly, *adv. rare.* [f. UNKNOWN *ppl. a.*[1]] In an unknown manner; mysteriously.
1611 FLORIO, *Isconosciutamente*, vnknowenly. **1644** QUARLES *Sheph. Orac.* vi, Just then it open'd; and th' enclosed Grain Unknownly vanisht; and then, clos'd again.

un'knownness. [f. UNKNOWN *a.*] The quality of being unknown.
1619 W. SCLATER *Exp. 1 Thess.* (1630) 398 The vnknownnesse, and suddennesse of Christs comming. **1675** tr. *Camden's Hist. Eliz.* (ed. 3) II. 252 They stood in no Fear at all of Pirates, by reason of..the Unknownness of that Sea. **1864** N. HAWTHORNE *S. Felton* (1883) 383 Soon they would all drop away,..all leaving him in blessed unknownness to adopt new temporary relations. **1899** *Outlook* 15 Apr. 364/2 Her studies..appeal by the very unknownness to English readers.

un'knownst, dial. var. (see -ST) of UNKNOWN *ppl. a.* 2 (*c*).
1805 E. CAVANAGH *Let.* 4 Oct. in Londonderry & Hyde *Russ. Jrnls. M. & C. Wilmot* (1934) II. 185 An Army, God knows, might live *unknownst* in the House! **1837** LOVER *Handy Andy* iii, By the powers! I'll pop in a ball *onknownst* to him. **1887** HALL CAINE *Deemster* xxiii, It'll be unknownst to the law as we are..innocent.

unko, var. UNCO *a.*

'unk-unks, *sb. pl. U.S. slang.* [duplication of the first three letters of the word *unknown* + *pl.* ending *-s.*] A condition resulting from fear of or apprehension about the unknown; unknown factors.
1970 *Time* 9 Mar. 63 Lately the industry has suffered a succession of blows:..As a result, aerospacemen have come down with a severe case of what they call the 'unk-unks'—the 'unknown unknowns'. **1970** *Guardian Weekly* 1 Aug. 24 'Unk Unks'..are the villains favoured by Lockheed to explain the extraordinary series of financial disasters that has led it to the verge of bankruptcy.

unkunning, -yng, varr. UNCUNNING *Obs.*

unkward: see UNKARD *a.*

unky: see UNK *sb.*

unkyt, ME. var. UNCUT.

un'labelled, *ppl. a.* Also unlabeled. [UN-[1] 8.] Not labelled. (In *Biol.* and *Chem.*: cf. LABELLED *a.* d.)
1844 KINGLAKE *Eothen* xii. 175 A little while you are free, and unlabelled, like the ground that you compass; but Civilization is coming. **1890** W. J. GORDON *Foundry* 166 The reels are turned over, and their unlabelled ends exposed. **1935** [see LABEL *v.* 2]. **1981** *Jrnl. Gen. Microbiol.* CXXVI. 97 Catechol methyltransferase..was localized immunocytochemically in the yeast *Candida tropicalis* by the unlabelled antibody enzyme method.

un'labiate, *a.* (UN-[1] 7.)
1835–6 *Todd's Cycl. Anat.* I. 265/2 Two unlabiate and edentate mandibles.

unla'borious, *a.* (UN-[1] 7.)
1644 MILTON *Areop.* (Arb.) 54 The Parlament, whose command perhaps made all things seem easie and unlaborious to them. **1750** MRS. CARTER *Johnson's Rambler* No. 44 ¶7 Does she [*sc.* Religion] lead her votaries through flowery paths, and bid them pass an unlaborious life? **1809** *Edin. Rev.* XIV. 4 The simple and unlaborious plenty which reigned among the scattered inhabitants. **1863** LD. LYTTON *Ring Amasis* I. 260 Those wandering but not unlaborious days.
Hence **unla'boriousness**.
1642 J. CARYL *Wks. of Ephesus Expl.* 21 Unlaboriousnesse ..is the buriall of our workes.

un'laboured, *ppl. a.* [UN-[1] 8.]
†**1.** Not cultivated by study. *Obs.*
c **1450** BURGH *Secrees* 1516 These Sevene Sustryn..The nyne musys blame shal in maneere, That they vnlabouryd stant on my partye.
2. Of land: Unworked, untilled, uncultivated.
1473 *Reg. Cupar Abbey* I. 201 Gif thar be ony..that levis ony his land..onlaboryt. *a* **1513** FABYAN *Chron.* VII. ccxix. 241 He destroyed the lande..in suche wyse, that .ix. yeres after..the lande laye vnlabored and vntylled. **1586** T. B. *La Primaud. Fr. Acad.* I. 166 Good ground becommeth unfruitfull,..the more it is left unlaboured. **1684** T. BURNET *Theory Earth* I. 243 Seeing it..had a soil so fruitful, a new unlabour'd soil. **1708** J. PHILIPS *Cyder* I. 115 Let thy Ground Not lye unlabour'd. **1804** *Europ. Mag.* XLV. 60/2 Gallia mourns..Unpeopled cities, and unlabour'd plains.
3. Not obtained or brought about by labour; *esp.* attained or accomplished in an easy or natural manner; spontaneous.
1631 SIR W. CORNWALLIS *Disc. Seneca* L16b, When goodnes was vnlabored excellency. **1697** DRYDEN *Virg. Past.* IV. 33 Unlabour'd Harvests shall the Fields adorn. **1797** *Monthly Mag.* III. 538 Of the translation itself we shall only observe, that it is natural and unlaboured. **1853** RUSKIN *Stones Ven.* II. viii. 369 Their perfect, pure, unlaboured naturalism. **1882** *Homiletic Monthly* July 599 Such inspirational and unlabored success was built on a firm basis of general study.
†**4.** Left unapproached or uninfluenced. *Obs.*[−1]
1644 LAUD *Wks.* (1854) IV. 147 The judge at Chester (altogether unknown to me and unlaboured by me) did say [etc.].
5. Not subjected to, free from, labour.
1598 GRENEWEY *Tacitus, Descr. Germanie* ii. 261 Horses, which are..maintained in those woods.., white, vnbacked, or vnlaboured. **1765** BEATTIE *Judgm. Paris* 514 The bower of bliss..be thine, Unlabour'd ease, and leisure's careless dream.

un'labouring, *ppl. a.* (UN-[1] 10.)
1619 SIR J. SEMPIL *Sacrilege Handled* 57 Paul had..onely to iustifie, that he and Barnabas might live vnlabouring, as well as other Apostles. **1791** COWPER *Odyss.* XXI. 488 A bard Unlabouring strains the chord to a new lyre. **1795** COLERIDGE *To Jos. Cottle* 18 Ere aught of perilous ascent you meet, A mead of mildest charm delays th' unlabouring feet. **1810** T. L. PEACOCK *Genius of Thames* 77 Where Lechlade sees thy current strong First waft the unlaboring bark along.

un'lace, *v.* [UN-[2] 3.]
1. *trans.* To undo the lace or laces of (a piece of armour, clothing, etc.); to unfasten, or loosen in this manner.
13.. *Coer de L.* 3171 A knyght hys armes gan unlace. **1388** WYCLIF *Mark* i. 7 Y am not worthi to..unlace his schoone. *c* **1400** *Beryn* 2426 He vnlacyd his mantell. **1470–85** MALORY *Arthur* I. xxiii. 69 He vnlaced his helme and gate hym wynde. **1590** C'TESS PEMBROKE *Antonie* 1593 His armor he vnlaste, and cast it of. **1652** C. B. STAPYLTON *Herodian* 129 His Purple Coat he 'gins for to Unlace. *c* **1696** PRIOR *Love Disarmed* 12 Her Boddice half way She unlac'd. **1731** SWIFT *Poems, Nymph going to Bed* 24 The lovely goddess Unlaces next her steel-rib'd bodice. *a* **1861** T. WOOLNER *My Beautiful Lady, Night* x, I wonder whether She now her braided opulent hair unlace. **1885** *Law Rep. 15 Q.B.D.* 360 The belts..could be removed from the shafting altogether by being unrivetted or unlaced. **1888** J. PAYN *Myst. Mirbridge* viii, She instantly busied herself..in unlacing her boots.
b. In fig. context, or *transf.*
c **1400** *Beryn* 67 [He] pryuelich vnlasid his both eyen liddes, And lokid hir in the visage. *c* **1422** HOCCLEVE *Min. Poems* 224/231 The feruence Of loue..Was qweynt, & loues knotte was vnlaced. **1593** G. HARVEY *Pierce's Super.* 69 Thou mightest haue knowen him, that can Vnbutton thy vanity, and Vnlase thy folly. *a* **1699** J. BEAUMONT *Psyche* XVI. xvii, Unlace my nerves, and try My finest tenderest membranes to unpin.
c. *Naut.* (See quot. 1769.) Also *absol.*
1669 STURMY *Mariner's Mag.* I. ii. 16 The Wind blows a fresh Gale... Unlease your Bonnets. **1769** FALCONER *Dict. Marine* (1780), *Délacer la bonnette*, to unlace or take off the bonnet from the foot of a sail. **1777** COOK *Second Voyage* III. ii. II. 18 [To] unlace that part of the sail from the yard which is between the tack and mast-head. **1886** R. C. LESLIE *Sea-painter's Log* iii. 41 With bonnet-pieces..made to unlace instead of reef.
2. To free or relieve (a person, the body, etc.) by undoing a lace or laces. Also *refl.* and *absol.*
c **1350** *Will. Palerne* 3200 þe quen kauȝt a knif & komli hire-selue william & his worþi fere swiftli vn-laced out of þe hidous hidus. *a* **1400** *Sir Perc.* 786 Gawayne doun lyghte, Unlacede the rede knyghte. *c* **1440** *York Myst.* xxxi. 42 My lorde, vn-lase you to lye, Here schall none come for to crye. *a* **1524** W. CORNYSHE in *Early XVI Cent. Lyrics* lxii. 45 Ther wyth reuyued sche, and her smalle wast ful fast vnlast. *a* **1586** SIDNEY *Arcadia* II. xii, She lay for dead, till I helpt with vnlasing her. **1648** HERRICK *Hesper.* (title), Upon Julia's unlacing her self. *c* **1680** *Roxb. Ball.* (1891) VII. 459 Do no less, then undress, and unlace, all a-pace. **1725** *Fam. Dict.* s.v. *Swoon*, To make him lie on his Back, to unbutton or unlace. **1889** *Spectator* 9 Nov. 635/1 Showin' their tongues Or unlacin' their lungs, For divle one symptom the docther disparages.
transf. *c* **1440** *Pallad. on Husb.* VII. 26 If al the lond attonys rody grete, Enclyne, and thonke vnlaced so for hete. **1762** STERNE *Tr. Shandy* VI. xi, As if he had snatched the occasion of unlacing himself with a few more frolicsome strokes at vice, than the straitness of the pulpit allowed.
†**3.** To cut up or carve (in later use *spec.* a rabbit); to cut off in carving. *Obs.*
13.. *Gaw. & Gr. Knt.* 1606 A wyȝe þat was wys vpon wod craftez, To vnlace þis bor lufly bigynnez. *c* **1460** J. RUSSELL *Bk. Nurture* 410 Furst, vn-lace þe whynges, þe legges þan in sight. *c* **1486** *Bk. St. Albans* F vij b, A Cony vnlaceedde. **1508** W. DE WORDE *Bk. Keruynge* A j b, Vnlace that cony. **1618** BRETON *Court & Country* Wks. (Grosart) II. 13/1 A Trencher must not be laid, nor a..Capon carued, nor a Rabbet vnlaced out of order. *a* **1661** HOLYDAY *Juvenal* (1673) 78 'Tis no small difference, with what gesture men Of art vnlace a hare and spoil a hen. **1687** J. SHIRLEY *Accomp. Ladies Rich Closet Rarities.* 52 In unlacing a Coney, Turn the belly upwards, cutting the belly-pieces from the kidneys. **1771** MRS. HAYWOOD *New Present for Maid* 269 To unlace a Rabbit.
†**4.** To disentangle, unravel. *Obs.*[−1]
c **1374** CHAUCER *Boeth.* III. pr. xii. (1868) 105 Scornest þou me..þat hast so wouen me wiþ þi resouns, þe house of didalus so entrelaced, þat it is vnable to ben vnlaced.
†**5.** *fig.* **a.** To undo or destroy; to deprive *of* something. *Obs.*
c **1412** HOCCLEVE *De Reg. Princ.* 2456 Of his honour, vntrouthe a knyght vnlaceth. *Ibid.* 3652 Dignite had ben vnlaced And vngirt of honour. **1577** GRANGE *Golden Aphrod.*, etc. Q j b, Milesian maydes, your steppes I mean to trace, And as Lucrecia did, my lyfe for to vnlace. **1604** SHAKS. *Oth.* II. iii. 194 What's the matter That you vnlace your reputation thus.
†**b.** To disclose, reveal. *Obs.*
1567 PAINTER *Pal. Pleas.* II. xiii. (1890) II. 301, I purpose, then, to vnlace the dissolute lyues of three Amorouse Dames. **1577** GRANGE *Golden Aphrod.*, etc. R iv b, Wherefore if my penne were able, well might I here vnlace my loyaltie. **1582** STANYHURST *Æneis* Ded. (Arb.) 7 Yt may bee..I shal bee occasioned..too vnlace more of theese mysteries.
†**c.** To relax or loosen; to set free. *Obs.*
1610 G. FLETCHER *Christ's Tri.* II. xlii, An intire embrace That no satietie can ere unlace. **1639** FULLER *Holy War* II. iv. 48 These Hospitallers afterwards getting wealth, unlaced themselves from the strictnesse of their first Institution.
6. To strip of lace.
1598 FLORIO, *Disfrangiare*, to vnfringe, to vnlase.

un'laced, *ppl. a.* [f. prec. or UN-[1] 8.]
1. a. Having a lace or laces undone or slackened. **b.** Not laced; with lace(s) unfastened.
1447 BOKENHAM *Seyntys* (Roxb.) 277 Whan the gospel shulde be Red..evere ryht up stude she Wyth sleyvs unlaced. *a* **1529** SKELTON *E. Rummyng* 133 Some wenches come vnlased, Some huswyues come vnbrased. **1582** STANYHURST *Æneis* IV. (Arb.) 113 Her self..standing neere the halloed altars, Naked in her oane foote, with frock vnlaced aparralyd. **1601** HOLLAND *Pliny* II. 308 Women.. with their haire hanging loose about their eares, vngirt, vnlaced, and vnbraced. **1827** POLLOCK *Course T.* VIII. 91 Unscutcheoned all,..Unlaced, uncoroneted, unbestarred. **1871** *Figure Training* 79, I had never..been suffered to remain unlaced one instant longer than was absolutely necessary.
†**2.** Cut up, carved. *Obs.*[−1]
1602 *2nd Pt. Return Parnass.* IV. i. 1526 Sometimes a messe of stewd broth will do well, and an vnlac'd Rabbet is best of all.

unlach, obs. Sc. variant of UNLAW.

†**un'lackable**, *a. Obs.* [UN-[1] 7 b.] Indispensable.
c **1449** PECOCK *Repr.* I. ix. 44 Thilk leernyng..is necessarie and vnlackeable to Cristen men.

†**un'lackably**, *adv. Obs.* [UN-[1] 11.] Indispensably.
1449 PECOCK *Repr.* I. vii. 35 Ellis he were not vnlackeabli necessarie to Cristen men.

un'lackeyed, *ppl. a.* (UN-[1] 8.)
1784 COWPER *Task* II. 652 To her who, frugal only that her thrift May feed excesses she can ill afford, Is hackney'd home unlacquey'd.

un'lacquered, *ppl. a.* (UN-[1] 8.)
[**1775** ASH, *Unlackered*, not lackered.] **1833** CARLYLE *Misc.* (1872) V. 124 The brow of brass, behold how it has got all unlacquered.

un'lade, *v.* [UN-[2] 4. Cf. OE. *onhladan*, OHG. *intladen*, MHG., MLG., G. *entladen*, MDu. and Du. *ontladen.*] To unload.
1. *trans.* To take a load off (a horse, cart, etc.).
1398 TREVISA *Barth. De P.R.* XVIII. xxviii. (Bodl. MS.), þei leyeþ..þe stikkes and wood bitwene his legges and þies and drawiþ hem home..and vnladeþ and dischargeþ hym þanne. *c* **1489** CAXTON *Sonnes of Aymon* iii. 103 Thenne they vnladed theyr somers & theyr cartes. **1494** *Cov. Leet Bk.* 557 To drive his Cart laden with Otes into þe Croschepyng & there to vnlade the seid Cart. **1622** FLETCHER *Span. Cur.* II. i, I have the mony ready, and I am weary... Pray ye Sir, unlade me. **1695** CONGREVE *Mourn. Muse Alexis* 6 Thither, let all th' industrious Bees repair, Unlade their Thighs, and leave their Hony there. **1760–72** H. BROOKE *Fool of Qual.* (1809) III. 64 Some arose, and unladed two asses of the creels..they carried.
fig. *a* **1592** T. WATSON *Tears of Fancie* xlii, Vnlade me of the burthen..enuious fates..Haue heapt vpon me.
b. To take the cargo out of (a ship). Also in fig. context.
c **1489** CAXTON *Sonnes of Aymon* 525 As they vnladed the ship. **1555** EDEN *Decades* (Arb.) 240 The port..is so.. commodious to defraight or vnlade shyppes, as [etc.]. **1586** B. YOUNG *Guazzo's Civ. Conv.* IV. 194 b, If you thinke.. your stomacke will not serue you to vnlade all the ship, let me helpe you. **1642** MILTON *Apol. Smect.* 36 He must cut out large docks and creeks into his text to unlade the foolish frigate of his unseasonable autorities. **1693** *Lond. Gaz.* No. 2838/2 They are now Unlading her, but the Goods are very much Dammified. **1781** GIBBON *Decl. & F.* xxiv. (1787) II. 443 Fourscore vessels were gradually unladen. **1864** TENNYSON *En. Ard.* 812 He..help'd At lading and unlading the tall barks. **1871** KINGSLEY *At Last* ii, Along the beach a market.., with canoes drawn up to be unladen.
refl. **1666** DRYDEN *Ann. Mirab.* ccc, The vent'rous Merchant..Shall here unlade him, and depart no more. **1860** GEO. ELIOT *Mill on Floss* I. xii, Where the black ships unlade themselves of their burthens.
c. To unburthen or relieve by the removal or discharge of something. Chiefly *fig.* and const. *of.*
1581 J. BELL *Haddon's Answ. Osor.* 263 b, To unlade you of some cholericke humours. *c* **1600** CHALKHILL *Thealma & Cl.* (1683) 127 Cattel gan to low Homewards t'unlade their

milky bags. **1688** *Pulpit-Sayings* 29 When a Man unlades himself of all his Sins. **1703** Rowe *Fair Penit.* I. i, Let me unlade my Breast. **1898** Watts-Dunton *Aylwin* VII. iii, Unlading the mind of the trash previously called knowledge.

2. To discharge (a cargo, etc.) from a ship.

1427–8 *Rec. St. Mary at Hill* 68 For cariage of ij lode fro Cambregges key, ladyng & vnladyng, xiiij d. **1542–3** *Act 34 & 35 Hen. VIII*, c. 9 §4 That no persone..doo caste or unlade out of any..ship..Balast rubbishe gravell or any other wracke. **1590** Webbe *Trav.* (Arb.) 19 We vnladed our bourthen at Narre. **1612** in *10th Rep. Hist. MSS. Comm.* App. V. 467 Goodes to be discharged, unladen, or brought in. **1661** Godolphin *View Admir. Jurisd.* Introd. b 3 b, A Lighter, or Skiff, or the Ships Boat into which part of the Cargo is unladen for the lightning of the Ship. **1722** De Foe *Plague* (1754) 246 They would not suffer them..to unlade their Goods upon any Terms whatever. **1725** Pope *Odyss.* XVI. 375 They moor the vessel and unlade the stores. *a* **1864** Hawthorne *Amer. Note-bk.* (1868) I. 164 Huge trunks and bandboxes [were] unladed and laded. **1884** *Harper's Mag.* June 52/1 All cargoes must be unladed between sunrise and sunset.

b. To discharge or get rid of; to put off or lay down (a burden, etc.); to unpack or bring forth. Chiefly *fig.*

1591 Spenser *Daphn.* lxx, There will I..the huge burden of my cares vnlade. **1599** Chapman *Humorous Days Mirth* F 4 b, Forth and vnlade the poyson of thy tongue. **1639** J. Shirley *Maid's Rev.* II. i. D 3, Ere you let fall words of welcome, Let me unlade a treasure in your eare. **1812** Crabbe *Tales, Arabella* 283 When all inquiries had been duly made, Came the kind friend her burthen to unlade. **1821** Lamb *Elia* I. *Imperfect Sympathies*, He..unlades his stock of ideas in perfect order.

3. *absol.* To discharge a cargo or cargoes.

1547 *Privy Council Acts* (1890) II. 466 If he unladed there, he might cary the vytayles a good wey after by the river. **1568** Grafton *Chron.* II. 567 The ships..were forced to vnlade at Douer. **1666** *Lond. Gaz.* No. 69/2 A large Swede ..is likewise arrived with Deales, and is to unlade in this Harbor. **1774** E. Jacob *Faversham* 15 Where the great Vessels used to unlade. **1796** Morse *Amer. Geog.* II. 24 Large ships may..lade and unlade close to the ware houses. **1863** Susan Warner *Old Helmet* xxxv, At Tonga she was detained a week and more, unlading and taking in stores. **1879** Farrar *St. Paul* II. 405 The wharfs where the barges ..were accustomed to unlade.

b. To discharge a burden, contents, etc. Also *fig.*

1629 Massinger *Picture* IV. ii, You may safer run vpon The mouth of a cannon, when it is vnlading. **1717** Bullock *Wom. a Riddle* I. i, What adventure is this you are so full of? come, unlade, unlade. **1862** Goulburn *Pers. Relig.* III. viii. (1873) 226 While caravans were unlading or making up their complement of passengers.

†**4.** *trans.* To discharge (a fire-arm). In quot. *fig.*

1649 G. Daniel *Trinarch., Rich. II*, ccxliii, Thus over-charg'd & yet vnwilling to Vnlade Himselfe by the first Match that came.

Hence **un'lading** *ppl. a.*

1607 Chapman *Bussy d' Ambois* III. ii. 38 I'll..so thump his liver, That, like a huge unlading Argosy, He shall confess all.

un'laden, *ppl. a.* [un-¹ 8 b.] Unloaded.

?**1802** Forster *Arabian Nights* (1839) 393/1, I was returning from Balsora with my camels unladen, which I had conducted thither with goods to be embarked for India. **1820** Shelley *Witch Atl.* lxviii, The wizard-maiden..with an eye serene and heart unladen. **1849** Eastwick *Dry Leaves* 70 Send no camels unladen, if you have wherewith to lade them. **1930** *Road Traffic Act 20 Geo. V* 24 in *Parl. Papers 1929–30* IV. 140 The weight unladen of any vehicle shall be taken to be the weight of the vehicle..exclusive of the weight of water, fuel or accumulators used for the purpose of propulsion. **1959** *Motor Manual* (ed. 36) xiii. 270 'Unladen weight' is open to all sorts of interpretation and may bear little relation to what the caravan weighs when it eventually comes to the customer.

un'lading, *vbl. sb.* [f. unlade *v.*] The action of unloading or discharging.

1428–9 *Rec. St. Mary at Hill* 70 Also paid..for þe caryage & ladyng & vnladyng, ix d. **1627** J. Taylor (Water P.) *Navy of Land Ships* Wks. (1630) 82/1 The often returnes, lading and vnlading of this ship. **1691** *Lond. Gaz.* No. 2656/2 That no such..Vessel shall be above Ten days in Unlading. **1726** Leoni *Alberti's Archit.* I. 75 b, For the more easy unlading of the Shipping. **1818** *Sporting Mag.* II. 161 Hogarth has already given the picture of the unlading of a stage coach. **1849** Eastwick *Dry Leaves* 210 Affording great facilities for the unlading or shipment of cargoes.

b. *attrib.*, as ***unlading place, port, time.***

1611 Florio, *Sbarco*,..[an] vnlading place for ships. **1681** *Cal. Treas. Bks.* 7 The books of the unlading port. **1755** Magens *Insurances* I. 48 The customary unlading Places in that Port. **1884** J. Parker *Apost. Life* III. 61 We must have landing places, and unlading times,..in life.

un'ladyfied, *ppl. a.* (un-² 6 c.)

1612 N. Field *Wom. a Weathercock* v. ii, Know That I am married to this gentleman... What ease I find being unladified!

un'ladylike, *a.* (un-¹ 7 c.)

1824 Miss Mitford *Village* Ser. I. 229 A very discreditable and unladylike partiality, of which I am quite ashamed. **1856** Whyte-Melville *Kate Coventry* i. 4 She said it was improper and unladylike, and even unfeminine.

unlage, obs. variant of unlaw.

un'laid, *ppl. a.* and *sb.* [un-¹ 8 b. Cf. ON. *úlagðr*; also Du. *ongelegd*, G. *ungelegt* (of eggs).]

1. a. Not laid, placed, or set.

1468–9 *Paston Lett.* Suppl. (1901) 124 The lenger that it [*sc.* the roof-tile] lythe unleyd the wers it wyll be. **1570** Levins *Manip.* 197 Vnlayd, *non positus.* **1597** Hooker *Eccl. Pol.* v. lvi. §5 The first foundation of the world being as yet vnlayd. **1656** Osborne *Adv. Son* Lett., Wks. 1722 I. B 5, The severest Curse remaining in the custody of Fortune, yet unlaid upon me. **1872** *Daily News* 12 Aug., The spot where the final stone of the great structure yet hung unlaid.

b. ? Laid out (as a corpse); laid in the grave.

c **1635** B. Jonson *Underwoods, Petition Chas. I*, Parts of me they judg'd decay'd; But we last out still unlay'd.

c. Of a hedge: (see lay *v.*¹ 6 b).

1868 *Rep. U.S. Commissioner Agric.* (1869) 255 If..the shoots are cut toward the bottom growth of the wood as downward in an unlaid one, or against the leaning direction of the layers in a laid hedge.

d. Of a woman with whom no one has had, or a particular person has not had, sexual intercourse. *slang.*

1962 'E. McBain' *Like Love* (1964) iv. 56 What it all meant was: 1. Gaspipe. 2. Sober. 3. Unlaid. **1977** *Sunday Times* 27 Mar. 42/2 A thousand places visited and not absorbed, a thousand paperbacks unread, a thousand unlaid airhostesses.

2. Of spirits: Not laid by exorcism.

1611 Shaks. *Cymb.* IV. ii. 278 *Guid.* Ghost vnlaid forbeare thee. *Arui.* Nothing ill come neere thee. **1634** Milton *Comus* 434 No evil thing that walks by night,..Blew meager Hag, or stubborn unlaid ghost,..Hath hurtfull power o're true virginity. **1780** Burke *Œcon. Reform* Wks. III. 297 Ghosts of unlaid accountants, haunt the houses. **1806** Moore *Epist.* VIII. i, Pagan spirits, by the Pope unlaid. **1831** Wordsw. '*The forest huge*' 11 The feudal Warrior-chief, a Ghost unlaid, Hath still his castle. **1888** (*title*), Unlaid Ghost: a Study in Metempsychosis.

3. Not laid *open*, *out*, etc.

1608 Shaks. *Per.* I. ii. 89 How many worthy princes' bloods were shed, To keep his bed of blackness unlaid ope. **1674** N. Fairfax *Bulk & Selv.* 62 Though they be unlaid out in themselves, they may be laid out by body laid in.

4. Not covered or plated *with* something.

1648 Hexham II, *Ongebleckt*, Vnlaid with plates of Lettine.

5. In technical uses, e.g. of a rope (see lay *v.* 37), of paper (see laid *ppl. a.*), etc.

In recent dicts.

6. *sb.* A blanket made from untarred wool. *Sc.*

a **1869** J. Younger *Autobiog.* (1881) iv. 38 He rolled up his pipes, bag and all, in the blankets above him..—which bag imparted that election-dinner stain to her best white unlaids.

un'lame, *a.* [un-¹ 7.] † Wholly free.

a **1300** *Cursor M.* 21045 [John] was o lust vn-lame.

un'lamed, *ppl. a.* (un-¹ 8. Cf. MLG. *ungelemt.*)

c **1470** *Gol. & Gaw.* 442 Sauand my senyeoury fra subiectioun, And my lordscip vn-lamyt, withoutin legiance. **1839** Carlyle *Chartism* iii. (1840) 23 His unlamed right-hand,..is not this defined to be 'the sceptre of our Planet'?

unla'mented, *ppl. a.* (un-¹ 8.)

1595 Daniel *Civ. Wars* I. xx, A tyrant loth'd,..Poysoned he dies, disgrac'd, and vnlamented. **1626** Massinger *Rom. Actor* v. ii, Such as governed only by their will,.. unlamented fall. **1647** Clarendon *Hist. Reb.* I. §115 He died unlamented by any, bitterly mentioned by most. **1717** Pope *Elegy Unfort. Lady* 43 Thus unlamented pass the proud away. **1818** Shelley *Rosal. & Helen* 231, I watched..My husband's unlamented tomb. **1896** *Pop. Sci. Jrnl.* L. 277 The old systems that lie unlamented in their graves.

unlam'pooned, *ppl. a.* (un-¹ 8).

[**1775** Ash.] **1828** Southey *To A. Cunningham* 36 Extend those laws Till every chimney its own smoke consume, And give thenceforth thy dinners unlampoon'd.

un'lanced, *ppl. a.* (un-¹ 8.)

1593 G. Harvey *Pierce's Super.* 26 Where..the filthiest corruption of abhominable villany [may] passe vnlaunced. **1643** Fuller *Serm.* 27 Mar. 7 Sometimes Chirurgions leave their ulcers unlaunch't [*sic*].

†**unland,** *sb. Sc. Obs.* [un-¹ 12. Cf. OE. *unland*, ON. *úland*, WFris. *onlân*, *unlân*, MDu. *onlant* (Du. *onland*), MLG. *unlant*, LG. and G. *unland.*] Unarable land.

1573–4 *Reg. Mag. Sig. Scot.* 577/2 Terras arabiles *lie corneland*, terras non arabiles *lie unland.* **1611** *Ibid.* 250/2 Cum..parca, pratis, wardis (*lie unland* seu *tedderingis*) et silvis apud idem.

un'land, *v.* [un-² 4.] *trans.* To deprive of land.

a **1661** Fuller *Worthies, Monmouth.* IV. (1662) 51 But one Bishop..more unlanded Llandaff in one, than all his Predecessors endowed it in four hundred years.

un'landed, *a.* [un-¹ 9.] Not possessed of land.

1488 *Sc. Acts, Jas. IV* (1814) II. 207/1 The gudis movabill belanging to the pure vnlandit folkis. **1530** *Extr. Aberd. Reg.* (1844) I. 138 Ilk gentilman landit ij^c lib., ilk gentilman vnlandit ij^c markis. **1581** Mulcaster *Positions* xxxix. 199 Either rich or poore: landed or vnlanded. **1633** Ford *Love's Sacr.* IV. i, The sallow-colour'd brat Of some unlanded bankrupt. **1668** Sedley *Mulberry Gard.* III. ii, Give your estate where you please, so you will but settle your affection upon me,..and the like artillery of unlanded lovers. **1884** *Pall Mall G.* 2 April 2/1 The rights of the unlanded millions.

un'landmarked, *a.* (un-¹ 9.)

1870 Lowell *Among my Bks.* Ser. I. 124 The unlandmarked deep of speculation.

un'languaged, *a.* [un-¹ 9.]

1. Not gifted with speech.

1654 Davenant in Earl Monm. *Bentivoglio's Warrs Flanders* b 1 b, The ceaseless nature of your Kindness then, Still ready to inform un-languag'd Men, Deserves less Praise [etc.]. **1850** H. Bushnell *God in Christ* i. 11 There is no difficulty in perceiving how our two unlanguaged men will proceed.

2. Not expressed in articulate speech.

1846–8 Lowell *Biglow P.* Ser. I. ii. Introd. Let., The unlanguaged prattlings of infants. **1860** Faber *Bethlehem* 100 To what numberless unlanguaged and unsung Magnificats did not all this give rise.

un'lanterned, *ppl. a.* (un-¹ 8.)

1826 Lamb *Elia* II. *Pop. Fallacies* xv, It has a sombre cast, ..derived from the tradition of those unlantern'd nights.

un'lap, *v.* Now *rare.* [un-² 4.]

1. *trans.* To uncover by withdrawing a cloth or the like. Also *refl.* and *fig.*

13.. *E.E. Allit. P.* A. 214 As schorne golde schyr her fax þenne schon. On schylderez þat leghe vnlapped lyȝte. *c* **1440** *York Myst.* xxx. 256 Vnlappe yow belyve wher ye lye. **1656** Baxter *Reformed Pastor* 369 If a cripple do but unlap his sores. **1664** Mrs. Hutchinson *Mem. Col. Hutchinson* (1806) 441 Satisfied with this, they did not unlap the body. **1809** Mar. Edgeworth *Manœuvring* xv, The influence of her.. prettiness, joined to the power of my mother's irresistible address have almost lapped me in elysium... But..I unlapped myself. **1886–** in dial. glossaries, etc. (Yks., Lancs., Chesh.)

2. To unfold; to spread open. Also *intr.*

a **1400–50** *Alexander* 1932 þire princes, sone as þe pistill was put þam in hand,..Vn-lappis liȝtly þe lefe & þe line redes. **1501** Douglas *Pal. Hon.* Prol. 37 The dasy and the maryguld vnlappit, Quhilks all the nicht lay with their leuis happit. **1586** W. Travers *Supplic. Privy Council* (1612) 23 Tapestrie which,..being vnlapt and laid open, sheweth plainely to the eye all the worke that is in it.

3. To detach in a strip or flap.

1834–6 *Encycl. Metrop.* (1845) VIII. 103/2 A curve traced by the extremity of the thread *FC*, unlapped from the circumference. *Ibid.*, Let the acting face of the tooth *b* be formed by unlapping a thread from its circumference.

Hence **un'lapping** *vbl. sb.*

1839 Ure *Dict. Arts*, etc. 233 In the course of the lapping and unlapping of such a length of webs.

un'lapsed, *ppl. a.* (un-¹ 8.)

1668 H. More *Div. Dial.* IV. vii. 26 His Dominion..over Angels, whether lapsed or unlapsed. **1740** Cheyne *Regimen* 297 Unlapsed, tried and purified angelical Hierarchies.

un'larded, *ppl. a.* (un-¹ 8.)

1748 Chesterf. *Lett.* 22 Feb., Speak the language.. purely, and unlarded with any other.

un'large, *a.* [un-¹ 7.] † Not generous in giving.

1483 *Cath. Angl.* 208/2 Vn Large, *illeberalis.*

unla'scivious, *a.* (un-¹ 7.)

1593 Nashe *Strange Newes* E 3 There is no other unlascivious use or end of poetry but to..magnifie vertue.

un'lash, *v.* [un-² 4 b.]

1. *trans.* To detach or release by undoing a lashing.

1748 Smollett *R. Random* xxvi, Our hammocks..were immediately unlashed. **1850** R. G. Cumming *Hunter's Life S. Afr.* (1902) 102/2 Returning to the waggons, I commenced to unlash from the side of one of these a shovel. **1862** *Catal. Internat. Exhib.* II. No. 2659, Improved systems of unlashing..ships' boats. **1879** Farrar *St. Paul* IX. xliii. II. 379 They began to unlash the boat and lower her into the sea.

2. To undo or untie (a lashing).

1853 Sir H. Douglas *Milit. Bridges* (ed. 3) 67 Nos. 1 and 3 unlash the [Pontoon] Lashings. **1870** *Milit. Engineering* 347 At the word *Unlash*, each man stoops down, and casts off the lashing in front of him.

un'lashed, *ppl. a.* [un-¹ 8.] Not scourged.

1761 Churchill *Rosciad* 500 Actors, unlash'd themselves, may lash mankind.

†**un'last,** *v. Obs.*⁻¹ [un-¹ 14.] *intr.* To fail to last. (A misunderstanding of L. *indurare.*)

a **1300** *E.E. Psalter* lxxxix. 6 It wites als gresse areli at dai; ..At euen doun es it broght, Un-lastes, and welkes, and gas to noght.

un'lasting, *ppl. a.* (un-¹ 10.)

1585 Abp. Sandys *Serm.* ix. 146 Mans life is as vnlasting as a flower. **1790** A. Wilson *Epist. to A. Clarke* Poet. Wks. (1846) 48 Struggling hard for base unlasting pelf.

un'latch, *v.* [un-² 3.]

1. *trans.* To undo the latch or catch of (a door, etc.); to unfasten in this way.

1642 H. More *Song of Soul* I. I. 60 Then stiller whispering winds dark visions unlatch. **1697** Dryden *Æneis* VI. 704 Mean time my worthy wife..The door unlatch'd. **1822** Byron *Werner* IV. i. 434 Who..Unlatch'd the door of death for thee. **1873** Miss Broughton *Nancy* I. 54 Unlatching the gate in the fence. **1890** *Anthony's Photogr. Bull.* III. 200 The bellows is closed up, it is now allowed to fall open, when unlatched, by a catch on the side and top.

b. *intr.* To become, or admit of being, thus unfastened.

1871 B. Taylor *Faust* (1875) I. I. ii. 12 The gate of gold no more unlatches. **1875** Blackmore *A. Lorraine* xviii, The gate at this end unlatches.

2. *trans.* To unlace (shoes). Cf. latchet 1 c.

1880 L. Wallace *Ben-Hur* 253 Another unlatched Ben-Hur's Roman shoes.

un'latched, *ppl. a.* [un-¹ 8.] Not fastened by a latch.

1888 *Daily News* 5 Dec. 7/5 An unlatched window. **1901** *Munsey's Mag.* XXV. 435/1 [He] had left the flat door unlatched.

†**un'lated**, *ppl. a. Sc. Obs.* [UN-^{1} 8.] Undisciplined.
a **1449** in Bower *Fordun's Scotichron.* (1759) II. 376 The unlatit woman the licht man will lait.

un'lathed, *ppl. a.* (UN-^{1} 8.)
1854 H. MILLER *Sch. & Schm.* (1858) 44 A mud floor below, and an unlathed roof above.

un-'Latin, *a.* [UN-^{1} 7.] †**a.** = next. *Obs.*$^{-1}$
1675 T. TULLY *Let. to Baxter* 2 Only I beg your leave to English it for the sake of your un-latine Readers.
b. Not true to the character of the Latin language or of Latins.
1846 [see UN-GREEK *a.*] **1858** J. A. SYMONDS *Let.* 28 Nov. (1967) I. 173 After the Greek paper came.. Latin prose from [Sir Francis] Bacon—a queer and Un Latin piece. **1932** *Times Lit. Suppl.* 21 Jan. 37/3 In one of these [Catalan] poems he writes:..'I know not what thou wouldst say to me..': certainly an un-Latin vagueness.

†**un'latined**, *a. Obs.* [UN-^{1} 9.] Not acquainted with Latin.
1550 HARINGTON tr. *Cicero's Bk. Friendship* (1562) Pref. A iij b, How so euer it [*sc.* this translation] shalbe lyked of the learned, I hope it shalbe allowed of the vnlatined. **1570** DEE *Math. Pref.* A iij b, Being vnlatined people, and not Vniuersitie Scholers.

un'latinize, *v.* (UN-^{2} 6 c.)
1836 *Penny Cycl.* V. 325 Published.. by Conrad Aslacus (we cannot unlatinize Gassendi's name). **1847** DE MORGAN *Arith. Bks.* p. viii, Why the unlatinizing process should.. be practised by the learned only.

un'latticed, *ppl. a.* (UN-^{1} 8.)
1820 SCOTT *Abbot* ix, An unlatticed aperture gave him the view of the demolished garden.

unlauch, obs. Sc. form of UNLAW.

un'laudable, *a.* (UN-^{1} 7 b. Cf. ILLAUDABLE.)
1550 THOMAS *Ital. Dict., Dispregeuole*, shamefull or vnlaudable. **1673** *Lady's Call.* II. i. §12 Some very unlaudable qualities of a woman. **1826** *Q. Rev.* XXXIV. 451 Playing small games,.. an innocent and not unlaudable pastime.
Hence **un'laudableness**.
1744 [GARRICK] *Essay on Acting* 26 A farther Confirmation of the Unlaudableness of such Proceedings.

un'laugh, *v.* (UN-^{1} 3.)
1532 MORE *Confut. Tindale* Wks. 684/1 Tindall must of reason gyue vs leaue to laugh at hys proude inuented folye. And I shall find hym fower suerties.. that at what tyme hereafter he proue himselfe a true prophete, I shall vppon reasonable warning onlaughe agayn it al. **1637** J. WILLIAMS *Holy Table* 153 You must unlaugh again this foolish Laughter.

†**un'laught**, *ppl. a. Obs.*$^{-1}$ [UN-^{1} 8 b + *laght*, obs. pa. pple. of LATCH *v.*^{1}] Unseized, untaken.
c **1400** *Destr. Troy* 3237 The Troiens.. Lefte noght vnlaght þat lykyng was in.

†**un'laughter-mild**, *a. Obs.*$^{-1}$ [UN-^{1} 7: cf. ON. *hlátr-mildr*, Da. *lattermild*, prone to laugh.] Not given to laughter or mirth.
a **1300** *Cursor M.* 3283 Had he noght rested bot a thrau, O maidens sagh he cum on raw; þe formast was vnlaghter milde, Hir semed na wight to be wilde.

un'launched, *ppl. a.* (UN-^{1} 8.)
[**1775** ASH.] **1810** BYRON *Occas. P., Nurse's Dole* 3 The good ship Argo.. still unlaunch'd from Grecian docks. **1863** P. BARRY *Dockyard Econ.* 128 To allow the unlaunched ship to remain and rot.

un'laurelled, *ppl. a.* (UN-^{1} 8.)
1812 BYRON *Ch. Har.* I. xci, Thus unlaurel'd to descend in vain, By all forgotten. **1856** MERIVALE *Rom. Emp.* xliii. V. 63 The Marcomanni.. had kept Tiberius himself at bay, and sent him back unlaurelled across the Danube.

un'laving, *ppl. a.* (UN-^{1} 10.)
1834 LYTTON *Pompeii* I. vii, Those who took only the cold bath.. withdrew into that graceful.. building.. to shame the unlaving posterity of the south.

un'lavish, *a.* (UN-^{1} 7.)
1728 THOMSON *Spring* 733 Unlavish Wisdom never works in vain.

un'lavished, *ppl. a.* (UN-^{1} 8.)
1743 SHENSTONE *Elegies* xx. 12 He blam'd.. My time, unlavish'd in pursuit of pow'r.

'unlaw, *sb.* [OE. *unlagu* (UN-^{1} 12), = ON. *úlög* (pl.), Icel. *ólög*, Norw. *ulag*, Sw. *olag*, MDa. *ulog* (Da. *ulov*).]
1. Illegal action; illegality.
After the early 14th cent. only in occasional Sc. use, but revived by recent writers.
1008 *Laws Ethelred* (Lieberm.) I. 236 þæt man rihta laȝe up-arære & ælce unlaȝa ȝeorne afylle. *a* **1200** in Kemble *Cod. Dipl.* IV. 195 Ich nelle suððen ðat man hym eny unlawe beode. **1297** R. GLOUC. (Rolls) 9705 ȝuf.. eni man made is apel, ȝuf me dude him vnlawe. *a* **1300** *Cursor M.* 19196 þe lauerd þat bidd þe man wit-stand, Vnlau it es to tell in land. **1303** R. BRUNNE *Handl. Synne* 8795 ȝyf þou dedyst euer þat vnlawe, A man oute of holy cherche to drawe. **1318** *Sc. Acts Parlt.* (1844) I. 471 Torth & noun raysoun quod dicitur wrang et unlaw. **14..** *Ibid.* 347/2 Bot þai hald na court of lyfe and lym bot of jniur and vnreson þat is to say wrang and vnlaw. **1609** SKENE *Reg. Maj., Stat. Robt. I*, 23 Sa lang as he or his preloquutour defends tort and non reason, that is, wrang and vnlach (that is to haue done na iniurie, nor vnreason agains the Law). **1871** FREEMAN *Norm. Conq.* xxi. IV. 620 This state of things was what our fathers called *unlaw*. **1876** *Ibid.* xxii. V. 52. **1881** PUSEY (*title*), Unlaw in Judgements of the Judicial Committee of Privy Council. **1883** BP. E. H. BROWNE *Serm. Reading Congress* 15 The conflict between law and unlaw, between Christianity and irreligion.
†**b.** An evil custom or habit. *Obs.*$^{-1}$
a **1225** *Juliana* 72 Bireowseð ower sunnen,.. leaueð ower unlahen.
†**2.** *Sc.* A fine or amercement; a penalty. *Obs.*
1424 *Sc. Acts, Jas. I* (1814) II. 5/1 Quha sa euer be conuickit.., he sall pay xl. s. for þe vnlaw. **1459** in *Laing Charters* (1899) 37 Syndry unlawis amerciamentis and all uther fautis. **1496** *Acta Dom. Conc.* II. 2 Ane unlaw of xl s. **1541** *Rec. Elgin* (1903) I. 65 The baxstaris for thair falt salbe punist.. with viii s. of vnlaw. **1613** in *Northern N. & Q.* I. 74 Under the payne of ane vnlaw of ane pound Fleymis. **1678** SIR G. MACKENZIE *Crim. Laws Scot.* I. xix. §15 The Unlaw to be ten Pound. **1732** J. LOUTHIAN *Form of Process* 273 Fines, Amerciaments, or Unlaws inflicted upon Offenders,.. are sometimes ordained wholly to be paid to the King. **1767** in Craig & Laing *Hawick Tradition* (1898) 243 [He] is not worth the King's unlaw, being on the Parish Roll or Poors List.

unlaw, *v.* [f. prec., or UN-^{2} 3, 7.]
†**1.** *trans.* (also *absol.*) To fine, amerce. *Sc. Obs.*
14.. in *Sc. Acts Parlt.* (1844) I. 710/2 Item.. to his [*sc.* the justice's] clerk for jlk man vnlawit or sald, ij s. **1491** [see the vbl. sb.]. **1508** *Reg. Privy Seal Scotl.* I. 244/2 That nane of ȝow presume to call, geif sentence, unlaw,.. the said Johnne. **1564** *Reg. Privy Council Scot.* I. 307 [He] wes unlawit in the soum.. of ane thowsand markis. **1613** in R. M. Fergusson *A. Hume* (1899) 199 The counsall.. have.. unlawit the said Adam.. for his said offence. **1678** SIR G. MACKENZIE *Crim. Laws Scot.* II. xiii. §3 A Barron may unlaw for Absence, for ten Pounds. **1710** in J. J. Vernon *Par. & Kirk Hawick* (1900) 203 [They] were each of them.. fyned and onlawed in egregious ryotts. **1732** J. LOUTHIAN *Form of Process* 295 The several Sheriff Deputes,.. if any be absent,.. are unlawed in 100 Merks each.
†**b.** *intr.* To pay a fine. *Obs.*$^{-1}$
1692 in W. Hector *Judic. Rec. Renfrew* (1876) 54 Ilk ane o' them ought to unlaw to the Pror.-Fiscal.
2. *trans.* To annul (a law). Also *refl. rare.*
1644 MILTON *Areop.* (Arb.) 76 That also.. no law can possibly permit, that intends not to unlaw it self. **1654** CROMWELL *Sp.* 12 Sept. (Carlyle), Of what assurance is a Law to prevent so great an evil, if it lie in the same Legislature to unlaw it again?
Hence **un'lawing** *vbl. sb.*
1491 *Acta Dom. Audit.* (1839) 164/1 þe vnlawing of þe said alexr. blare. **1511** *Reg. Privy Seal Scotl.* I. 351/2 That thai desist.. fra all.. unlawing, forfaltin and proceding agains the said David. **1651** N. BACON *Disc. Govt. Eng.* II. xxvii. 213 The King hath a power of Lawing, and Unlawing in Christs kingdome.

un'lawed, *ppl. a.* [UN-^{1} 8.]
1. (See LAW *v.* 3, EXPEDITATE *v.*)
1598 MANWOOD *Laws Forest* xvi. 92 The owners.. are to be amerced 3s. for the keeping of such Dogges vnlawed. **1659** *Termes de la Ley* 163 b/2 A privilege to keep Doggs within the Forrest unlawed without punishment. **1685** BRADY *Hist. Eng.* App. 142 (tr. *Charter of Forests*), He whose Dog at such time shall be found unlawed. **1913** *Contemp. Rev.* Oct. 560 It was considered a great honour to be allowed to keep unlawed dogs for pleasure of the chase.
2. Exempt from law.
1880 *Mem. J. Legge* 291 Miracle is not an unlawed interference.

un'lawful, *a.* and *adv.* [UN-^{1} 7, 11 b.]
1. Contrary to law; prohibited by law; illegal.
a **1300** *Cursor M.* 29516 þat cursing tald vn-laghful es þat ordir wantes and right-settnes O lagh. **1398** TREVISA *Barth. De P.R.* IX. xxvi. (Bodl. MS.), It was iholde vnlawefulle to goo more wey one þe seturdaie. *c* **1430** *Syr Gener.* (Roxb.) 3024 Here ye thes vnlawful reasouns Mi lord the Soudon seith vs among. **1475** *Cov. Leet Bk.* 418 Vnlaufull & hurtfull ordenaunces made by the seid dyers. *Ibid.*, Vnlaufull othes and wrytynges. **1515** in W. H. Turner *Select. Rec. Oxford* (1880) 13 William Flemynge usith.. unlawfull mesures, that is to seye, an unlawfull yerde. **1581** [see next]. *a* **1613** OVERBURY *A Wife*, etc. (1614) B 4 b, Some lawfull things to be auoyded are, When they occasion of vnlawfull be. **1652** NEEDHAM tr. *Selden's Mare Cl.* 449 Anie other prohibited places and unlawful Ports whatsoever, in the Kingdoms of Denmark, Sweden, and Norway. **1667–8** MARVELL *Corr.* Wks. (Grosart) II. 239 The unlawfull meetings of Papists and Non-conformists. **1805** SOUTHEY *Madoc in W.* xv. 131 Becket did excommunicate thy sire For his unlawful marriage. **1891** FARRAR *Darkn. & Dawn* liv. A fresh edict.. which declared Christianity to be an unlawful religion.
b. ***unlawful assembly***: (see quots. 1581, 1841).
1485 *Rolls of Parlt.* VI. 287/2 Maintenance, Imbracerie, Riotts, or unlawfull Assemblie. **1549** *Act Edw. IV*, c. 5 (*heading*), An Acte for the punyshment of Unlawfull Assemblyes. **1581** LAMBARDE *Eiren.* I. xix. 175 An Vnlawful Assembly is, ye company of three persons (or more) gathered togither to doe.. an vnlawfull acte. **1651** HOBBES *Leviath.* II. xxii. 123 It is not a set number that makes the Assembly Unlawfull, but such a number [etc.]. **1664** *Act 16 Chas. II*, c. iv. 9 Every person who shall.. suffer any such Conventicle, unlawfull Assembly or Meeteing aforesaid to be held in his or her House. **1714** *Act Geo. I*, c. 5. 5 Any such unlawful, riotous, and tumultuous Assembly. **1841** *Penny Cycl.* XX. 17/1 It is an unlawful assembly when great numbers of people meet together with such circumstances of behaviour as to raise the fears of their fellow-subjects, and to endanger the public peace.
c. Of offspring: Illegitimate.
1606 SHAKS. *Ant. & Cl.* III. vi. 7 All the vnlawfull issue, that their Lust Since then hath made betweene them. **1833** DISRAELI *Cont. Flem.* I. i, The unlawful children of ignorance and expediency.
2. Not permissible; contrary to moral standards or spiritual principles.
? *c* **1475** *Knight Curtesy* 120 (Ritson), The knight.. Which with your lady was talkinge Of love unlawfull pryvely. **1526** *Pilgr. Perf.* (W. de W. 1531) 45 They profyte moche in yᵉ refreynynge.. of vnlawfull pleasures. **1590** SHAKS. *Com. Err.* V. i. 51 Hath not else his eye Stray'd his affection in vnlawfull loue? **1601** —— *All's Well* III. v. 73 May be the amorous Count solicites her In the vnlawfull purpose. **1641** J. JACKSON *True Evang. T.* III. 206 That Anabaptisticall.. tenet.. that all warres were utterly unlawfull under the Gospel. **1751** JOHNSON *Rambler* No. 178 ¶4 The allurements of unlawful pleasure. **1827** LYTTON *Falkland* 81 How fearful, how selfish, how degrading, is unlawful love! **1849** MACAULAY *Hist. Eng.* vii. II. 244 He cannot be accused of having deviated from the path of right in search.. of unlawful pleasure.
3. Of persons: Not obeying the law; acting or ruling illegally.
1429 *Rolls of Parlt.* IV. 344/1 Unlaweful hunters of Forestes, Parkes or Warennes. ? **1536** ANNE BOLEYN in *Harl. Misc.* (1809) III. 62 Mine offence being so lawfully proved, your Grace is at liberty.. to execute worthy punishment on me as an unlawful wife. **1581** *Satir. Poems Reform.* xliv. 319 Moyses forbad ȝou to giue the nichbouris vyf To the vnlauchful husbandis cumpanie. **1603** SHAKS. *Meas. for M.* IV. ii. 16, I haue beene an vnlawfull bawd. **1643** PRYNNE *Sov. Power Parl.* I. (ed. 2) 49 These Lawes.. are the Acts of the.. Courts themselves, which are lawfull; not of the usurping King, who is unlawfull. **1859** DICKENS *T. Two Cities* II. i, The unlawful opener of a letter was put to death.
4. Contrary to rule; irregular.
1729 T. COOKE *Tales*, etc. 208 The same Word in the Greek and Latin likewise has unlawful Degrees of Comparison. **1836** J. R. MAJOR *Guide Grk. Trag.* 117 In Iambic verse it is unlawful to divide the anapæst between two words.
†**5.** As *adv.* = next. *Obs.*
1477 in *Surtees Misc.* (1890) 27 William Bacon holdes ij dogges unlawefull.

un'lawfully, *adv.* [UN-^{1} 11.]
1. In an unlawful manner; illegally.
a **1310** in Wright *Lyric P.* xvi. 53 That he wolde.. Me lede to my lyves ende, unlahfulliche in lyhte. **1393** LANGL. *P. Pl.* C. IV. 290 As þe sauter sheweþ by suche as ȝeuen mede, þat vnlaufulliche lyuen, hauen large honden. **1414** *Rolls of Parlt.* IV. 57/1 The processe of myn outelawery was unlawfully made. **1456** SIR G. HAYE *Law Arms* (S.T.S.) 134 Injure or violence unlauchfully usurpit. **1549** CHEKE *Hurt Sedit.* (1569) D iij b, If their goodes.. shall vnlawfully and vnorderly.. be spoyled. **1653** *Urquhart's Logopandecteision* H iij b, Unlawfully-acquired goods. **1685** BAXTER *Paraphr. N.T.*, Mark i. 44 The unlawfully called and bad priests. **1710** *Act 9 Anne* c. 16 If any Person.. shall unlawfully attempt to kill, or shall unlawfully assault.. one of the most Honourable Privy Council. **1824** MACKINTOSH *Sp. Ho. Comm.* 1 June, Wks. 1846 III. 401 Whether a British subject has been lawfully or unlawfully condemned to death. **1844** KINGLAKE *Eothen* xxv, The Mahometan authorities.. were conscious of having acted unlawfully.
2. Illegitimately.
1552 ELYOT, *Illegitimi*, vnlaufully begotten, bastardes. **1596** DALRYMPLE tr. *Leslie's Hist. Scot.* (S.T.S.) I. 132 Athir Bastardis, or vnlawfollie gottin and borne. **1603** SHAKS. *Meas. for M.* III. i. 196 Rather.. then my sonne should be vnlawfullie borne. **1711** ADDISON *Spect.* No. 203 What Part I, being unlawfully born, may claim of the Man's Affection who begot me. **1755** JOHNSON, *Illegitimate*, unlawfully begotten; not begotten in wedlock.

un'lawfulness. [UN-^{1} 12.]
†**1.** Unlawful (or disloyal) conduct. *Obs.*
c **1500** *Melusine* i. 14 Ye ne oughte to retche ne care more of the vnlawfulness [F. *desleaulté*] & falshed of oure fader. **1531** TINDALE *Exp. 1 John* (1537) 53 That the Englyshe calleth here vnryghteousnesse the Greke called Anomia, vnlawfulnesse or breakynge yᵉ lawe. **1613** PURCHAS *Pilgrimage* (1614) 28 The Formall part of sinne, being nothing else but a deformitie.. and vnlawfulnesse in our naturall condition.
2. The quality of being unlawful; illegality.
1593 *Sidney's Arcadia* III. (1922) II. 48 Now that love.. had awaked her spirits, and perchance the very unlawfulnes of it had a litle blowne the coale. **1631** GOUGE *God's Arrows* I. §18. 25 That shewes the frailty of the person, not the unlawfulnesse of the action. **1673** S. DUGARD (*title*), Marriages of Cousin Germans, Vindicated from the Censures of Unlawfullnesse and Inexpediency. **1720** WODROW *Corr.* (1843) II. 522 The treatise I sent you of the Unlawfulness of Limited Episcopacy is answered. *a* **1779** WARBURTON *Alliance* II. Wks. 1788 IV. 190 The unlawfulness of tithes,.. the unlawfulness of oaths. **1824** MACKINTOSH *Sp. Ho. Comm.* 1 June, Wks. 1846 III. 415 The unlawfulness and nullity of the proceedings. **1874** MOTLEY *Barneveld* II. xviii. 86 Doctors ever wanting to prove the unlawfulness of law which interferes with the purposes of a despot.
b. Illegitimacy. (Todd. 1818.)

un'lawlearned, *a.* (UN-^{1} 9.)
1810 BENTHAM *Offic. Apt. Maximized, Def. Econ.* (1830) 23 To a plain and unlaw-learned understanding, they cannot both be good.

un'lawlike, *a.* (UN-^{1} 7 c.)
1649 MILTON *Eikon.* vi. 53 A remedy so slender and unlawlike.

unlawly, *adv.*: see UN-^{1} 3.

†**un'lawty**. *Sc. Obs.* [UN-^{1} 12.] Disloyalty, unfaithfulness.
1456 SIR G. HAYE *Law Arms* (S.T.S.) 172 Of this wrechit disobeysaunce cummys untreuth and unlautee. *a* **1568** in *Bannatyne MS.* (Hunterian Cl.) 766/32 Go follow thame, quha list vnlawty leir.

un'lawyered, *a.* (UN-[1] 9.)
1602 MIDDLETON *Phœnix* IV. i, One quiet, suffering, and unlawyer'd man.

un'lawyer-like, *a.* (UN-[1] 7 c.)
1869 TAYLOR & DUBOURG *New Men & Old Acres* III. 53 Everything hurried through in the most unlawyer-like manner. **1874** LISLE CARR *J. Gwynne* I. iii. 84 Nor were these talents much marred by those unlawyer-like attributes.

†**unlay**, *sb. Sc. Obs.* [UN-[1] 12 + LAY *sb.*] = UNLAW *sb.* 2.
1503 *Sc. Acts, Jas. IV* (1814) II. 242/2 At þat be ane punt of dittay in tyme to cum, and at þe vnlay þerof be x li. *Ibid.*, Item, as anent þe vnlay of þe grene wod.

un'lay, *v.* [UN-[2] 3.] *trans.* To untwist (a rope) into separate strands.
1726 SHELVOCKE *Voy. round World* 436 Till we could unlay our best cable to make more. **1748** *Anson's Voy.* II. ii. 135 We were..obliged to unlay a cable to work into running rigging. **1831** JANE PORTER *Sir E. Seaward's Narr.* I. 123, I also took thence a piece of rope, which I unlaid. *c* **1860** H. STUART *Seaman's Catech.* 28 Unlay the other two strands.

unlay'holdable, *a.* (UN-[1] 7 b.)
1860 W. W. READE *Liberty Hall* I. xv. 304 The Proctor caught Maidlow..in one of those trivial unlayholdable offences.

un'leached, *ppl. a.* (UN-[1] 8.)
1804 in J. Roberts *Penn. Farmer* 111 Are leeched or unleeched ashes most beneficial as manure? **1847** WEBSTER s.v., Unleached ashes. **1884** L. F. ALLEN *New Amer. Farm Bk.* 81 Eight bushels of unleached wood ashes. **1898** *Jrnl. Sch. Geog.* (U.S.) Oct. 288 Unleacht samples of many rocks.

unlead, *dial.*: see UNLEDE *a.*

un'lead, *v.* [UN-[2] 4 + LEAD *sb.*] *trans.* To divest or strip of lead.
1591 PERCIVALL *Sp. Dict.*, *Desplomado*, liuely, vnleaded. **1611** FLORIO, *Spiombare*, to vnleade. *a* **1661** FULLER *Worthies, Norwich* II. (1662) 275 A very fair structure, but lately unleaded, and new covered with tyle. **1801** CARTER *Cathedral Ch. Durham* 5 The Galilee was unleaded, and its demolition was determined on.

un'leaded, *ppl. a.* [UN-[1] 8.]
1. Not weighted, covered, or furnished with lead.
1611 in *Essex Rev.* XV. 47 The church is unleaded and unshingled. **1648** HEXHAM II, *Ongeloot*, Vnleaded, or Vnplumbt. **1909** *Westm. Gaz.* 28 Aug. 2/2 The motion of the death-curtain, hanging free and unleaded from its headrope, would be inconceivably graceful.
2. *Printing.* Not spaced with leads; 'solid'.
1902 *Westm. Gaz.* 23 May 7/1 Tucked away in an unleaded telegram..is an item which may possess some significance.
3. Of petrol, etc.: without added lead. Also *ellipt.*
1965 *Oil & Gas Jrnl.* 20 Dec. 26/1 The industry association will make a study next year of the cost of producing unleaded gasoline. **1970** *Daily Tel.* 14 Oct. 11/8 While a change to unleaded petrol reduces exhaust emission and engine deposits..it necessitates a reduction in the compression ratios to cope with lower octane fuels. **1981** J. D. MACDONALD *Free Fall in Crimson* iv. 38 He pulled up to the pump... He took six and four-tenths gallons of unleaded, which came to eight sixty-four.

un'leaf *v.* [UN-[2] 4.] *trans.* = UNLEAVE *v.*
1598 FLORIO, *Sfogliare*,..to vnleafe. **1611** COTGR., *Despamper*, to vnleafe,..pull the leaues off a Vine, &c. **1811** H. G. KNIGHT *Phrosyne* 40 Stern Winter..Unleafs the forest, and unchains the wind.

un'leafed, *ppl. a.* (UN-[1] 8.)
1848 LOWELL *Vision of Sir Launfal* II. Prelude 7 The chill wind..carried a shiver..From the unleafed boughs and pastures bare.

†**un'league**, *v. Obs.*[−1] (UN-[2] 3.)
c **1645** HOWELL *Lett.* (1650) II. 107 Monsieur dela Chatre ligu'd you, let him then unligue [F. *desligue*] you.

†**un'leaguer**, *v. Obs.*[−1] [UN-[2] 3.] *trans.* To cause (an army or leader) to abandon an investment.
1592 GREENE *Conny Catch.* II. A 2, Though I can-not as he [*sc.* Scævola]..attempt to vnleager Porsenna; yet [etc.].

un'leakable, *a.* (UN-[1] 7 c.)
1902 *C. Baker's Catal. Microscopes*, etc. 34 A Solid [Glass] Trough..practically unleakable.

un'leal, *a.* Now *arch.* [UN-[1] 7.] Unfaithful, disloyal, dishonest, false.
a **1300** *Cursor M.* 13173 Wit him-self he wex ful wrath, ..þat men suld hald him for vn-lele. *Ibid.* 25167 Vr praier es vn-lele And askes gains vr saul hele. *c* **1375** *Sc. Leg. Saints* vii. (*Jacob*) 456 Sa þat na lele man suld forfare amange vnlele þat wekit ware. **1393** LANGL. *P. Pl.* C. XIV. 69 Boþe louye and lene þe leelle and þe vnleelle. *c* **1430** in *Pol., Rel., & L. Poems* (1903) 203 þou lyuest a letcherouse lijf vnleel. **1456** SIR G. HAYE *Law Arms* (S.T.S.) 30 Untrewe and unlele to thair soveraynis lordis. **1528** LYNDESAY *Dreme* 313 Sum part thair was of vnleill Lauboraris. *c* **1560** A. SCOTT *Poems* (S.T.S.) xxiii. 25 Hir fenȝeit wordis fals,..And als the luik vnleill Of hir bricht fair ene twane. **1848** LYTTON *Harold* I. i, Words so unleal and foul. *Ibid.* XII. v, I hold it..disgrace to barter words with a knight unleal.

†**un'lean**, *a. Obs.*[−1] (UN-[1] 7.)
c **1440** *Pallad. on Husb.* I. 96 But se thyn ayer be feir, and lond vnlene.

un'leared, *ppl. a. Obs.* exc. *dial.* [OE. *unlǣred* (UN-[1] 8), = ON. *úlærðr* (Icel. *ólærðr*, MSw. *olärdher*, Sw. *olärd*, Da. *ulærd*). Cf. OE. *unȝelǣred*, MDu. *ongeleert*, etc.] Unlearned, untaught; ignorant.
c **1200** ORMIN 17117 þatt doþ uss tunnderrstanndenn wel þatt he wass ȝet unnlæredd Off þatt. *a* **1300** *Cursor M.* 13884 Qua herd euer man sua spell, Man vnlerd o boken lare. **1340** HAMPOLE *Pr. C.* 5947 þam þat er unlered men. **1390** GOWER *Conf.* I. 11 Suche as stode of trowthe unliered. *a* **1425** *Cursor M.* 22454 (Trin.), Hidur is good þat þei drawe,..And here wel þat I shal sey þat he wende not vnlered awey. **1552** ABP. HAMILTON *Catech.* (1884) 26 Thai that ar..unleirit in haly writ. **1876** *Whitby Gloss.* 206 *Unlared*, or *Unlear'd*, unlearned.

un'learn, *v.* [UN-[2] 3. Cf. MDu. *ont-*, *onleren*, older Fl. *ontleeren*, MLG. and G. *entleren.*]
1. *trans.* To discard from knowledge or memory; to give up knowledge of (something).
In very frequent use from *c* 1630.
c **1450** tr. *De Imitatione* I. xi. 12 Withstonde þyne inclinacion & unlerne euel custom. **1547** BALDWIN *Mor. Philos.* (1551) Niij, The best kynde of learnynge is to vnlearne our euyls. **1575** VAUTROLLIER *Luther on Ep. Gal.* 188 It is to vs no lesse labour to vnlearne and forget the same. **1612** BRINSLEY *Lud. Lit.* (1627) 9 Those things which are hurtfull,..they must bee taught to vnlearne againe. **1686** W. DE BRITAINE *Hum. Prud.* i. 2 The most necessary learning for mans life, is to unlearn that which is nought and vain. **1779** *Mirror* No. 12, As they have learned many foreign, so have they unlearned some of the..best understood home phrases. **1813** SHELLEY *Q. Mab* III. 6 Thou hast given A boon which I will not resign, and taught A lesson not to be unlearned. **1866** BRYCE *Holy Rom. Emp.* xviii. 363 The habits of centuries were not to be unlearnt in a few years.
b. *absol.*, or const. with inf.
1530 PALSGR. 768/2 It is a payne to lerne thynges, but a man may unlerne by goyng a huntyng. **1584** LYLY *Campaspe* II. ii, *Alex.* How should one learn to be content? *Diog.* Vnlearn to couet. **1631** P. FLETCHER *Piscatory Eclog.* III. xi, How canst unlearn by learning to forget it? **1649** F. ROBERTS *Clavis Bibl.* 351 In these I learn to shun sin, I unlearn to blush at repentance for offences. **1799** *Monthly Rev.* XXX. 120 According to an axiom founded on daily experience, to unlearn and forget are very difficult. **1823** *Monthly Mag.* LVI. 125 It is..long since the Romans have unlearned to conquer. **1868** LOWELL *Parting of the Ways* 59 That way lies Youth, and Wisdom,..For only by unlearning Wisdom comes.
2. To unteach.
1664 POWER *Exp. Philos.* Pref. 7 [The microscope] wil ocularly evince and unlearn them their opinions. **1802–12** BENTHAM *Ration. Judic. Evid.* (1827) V. 495 Legal learning ..can never have unlearnt a man the difference between three and one and a half. **1863** SUSAN WARNER *Old Helmet* v, I must unlearn you a little of your kindness. **1893** *Harper's Mag.* Dec. 61/2 He's jest said what I've been a-learnin' 'im. .. But he's got to be unlearned.
Hence **un'learning** *vbl. sb.*
1713 STEELE *Englishm.* No. 7. 46 Art is only the unlearning of what is unnatural. **1873** E. H. THOMPSON *Baron de Rendy* ii. 43 A school for the unlearning of every Christian..feeling of compassion.

unlearna'bility. (UN-[1] 12.)
1777 H. WALPOLE *Corr.* (1846) V. 473 The pleasure of correcting my awkwardness and unlearnability.

un'learnable, *a.* (UN-[1] 7 b.)
1846 WORCESTER (citing *Ed. Rev.*).

un'learned, *ppl. a.* [UN-[1] 8. Cf. UNLEARED *ppl. a.* and OHG. *ungelirnêt* (MHG. *-lërnet*, *-lehrnt*, G. *-lernt*).]
1. Not possessed of learning; uninstructed; untaught; ignorant.
c **1400** MAUNDEV. (1839) xvii. 184 How it semethe to symple men unlerned, that [etc.]. *c* **1420** *Wycliffite Bible* (1850) I. 67/2 Bothe of the lerned man and vnlerned. **14..** *Lat. & Eng. Prov.* (MS. Douce 52) fol. 27 Better is a chylde vnborne þen vnlerned. **1537** in *Bury Wills* (Camden) 131 Because I am rude and vnlernyd, and know not the scriptur. **1582** N. T. (Rhem.) *Luke* x. 21 *margin*, The humble vnlearned Catholike knoweth Christ better than the proud learned Heretike. **1651** HOBBES *Leviath.* II. xxix. 169 These three opinions..proceeded chiefly from the tongues, and pens of unlearned Divines. **1699** BENTLEY *Phal.* 331 Andronicus's name was prefix'd to it by a Modern and a very Unlearned Hand. **1765** *Museum Rust.* IV. 450, I will now.. give a free translation of it for the sake of your unlearned readers. **1854** WHITTIER *Maud Muller* 79 She wedded a man unlearned and poor. **1875** JOWETT *Plato* (ed. 2) I. 198 But if you were not wise you were unlearned.
b. *spec.* (See quots.)
1643 BAKER *Chron.* (1653) 236 Another Parliament.., named the unlearned Parliament, either for the unlearnednesse of the persons, or for their malice to learned men. **1878** STUBBS *Const. Hist.* III. xx. 401 The year 1404, when Henry IV stirred up strife by excluding lawyers from his 'unlearned parliament' [at Coventry].
2. *absol.* Those who have no learning.
c **1500** *Babees Bk.*, etc. (1868) 23/126 In þi dysch sette not þi spone,..os vn-lernyd done. **1549** OLDE *Erasm. Par. Ephesians* Prol. to Rdr. C ii, To seke the edification of the playne vnlearned. **1578** BIBLE (Geneva) Pref. to Christian Reader, I haue so done for the vnlearneds sake. **1656** STANLEY *Hist. Philos.* v. 50 He useth variety of names, that his work may not easily be understood by the unlearned. **1712** ADDISON *Spect.* No. 457 ¶4 An Account of the Works of the Unlearned. **1746** FRANCIS tr. *Horace, Art of Poetry* 644 With all the Horrours of a desperate Muse The Learned and Unlearned he pursues. **1886** *Fortn. Rev.* Oct. 508 We must acknowledge, too, that experts know better than the unlearned.
3. Not skilled or versed *in* something.
1565 COOPER *Thesaurus* s.v. *Rudis*, Vnlearned in the Greeke tongue. *c* **1600** SHAKS. *Sonn.* cxxxviii, Some vntuterd youth, Vnlearned in the worlds false subtilties. **1607** —— *Timon* IV. iii. 56, I know thee well: But in thy Fortunes am vnlearn'd, and strange. **1725** POPE *Odyss.* IX. 150 Unlearn'd in all th' industrious arts of toil. **1833** TENNYSON *To J. S.* v, Alas! In grief I am not all unlearn'd. **1885** 'MRS. ALEXANDER' *At Bay* viii, Unlearned in the world's lore which was so familiar to himself!
4. Characterized by want of learning; pertaining to the unlearned class.
1526 TINDALE *2 Tim.* ii. 23 Folisshe and vnlearned questions. **1589** *Marprel. Epit.* D iij b, His booke is a carnall and vnlearned booke. **1604** HERRING *Def. Caveat* (title-p.), That unlearned and dangerous opinion. *c* **1657** COWLEY *Ode Dr. Harvey* v, A barb'rous Wars unlearned Rage. **1785** BURKE *Sp. Nabob Arcot* Wks. IV. 316 The unlearned and vulgar passion of admiration. **1844** STANLEY *Arnold* (1858) II. 146 An unlearned familiarity with the Scriptures. **1875** WHITNEY *Life Lang.* x. 187 The unlearned speech of the lower orders.
5. Not acquired by learning. (Cf. UNLEARNT.)
1534 LD. BERNERS *Gold. Bk. M. Aurel.* (1546) C v, That there shulde be nothyng vnlerned of hym, he aboue all sciences sette his mynd to Cosmography. **1607** MARKHAM *Cavel.* III. i. 4 My first Arte were better vnlearned then for want of this latter to doe euill by misimployment. **1611** SHAKS. *Cymb.* IV. ii. 178 'Tis wonder That an inuisible instinct should frame them To Royalty vnlearn'd, Honor vntaught. **1644** MILTON *Educ.* 3 Mispending our prime youth..in learning meere words or such things chiefly, as were better unlearnt.

un'learnedly, *adv.* (UN-[1] 11; cf. prec.)
1532 MORE *Confut. Barnes* VIII. Wks. 786/2 He shall speake very vnlernedly. **1578** LYTE *Dodoens* V. lxvi. 631 It is fondly and vnlearnedly named in Englishe, Dittany. **1651** BAXTER *Inf. Bapt.* 239 Some..unlearnedly and boldly scold about..unprofitable matters. **1689** W. A. *Herbert's Account Examined* 3 He very unlearnedly clogs the Definition of a Dispensing Power. **1834** BECKFORD *Italy* II. 226 He.. entered minutely and not unlearnedly into the ancient jurisprudence..of his country.

un'learnedness. [UN-[1] 12.] The condition of being unlearned; want of learning; ignorance.
1562 TURNER *Baths* 1 b, The vnlearnednes..of the Physiciones. **1581** W. CLARKE in *Confer.* IV. (1584) F f j, The errour and vnlearnednesse of your distinction appeareth. **1643** [see UNLEARNED 1 b]. **1674** W. ALLEN *Danger Enthus.* 18 Your Leaders manifest a strange degree of Unlearnedness in the things of the Gospel, when [etc.]. **1721** BAILEY, *Illiterateness*, Unlearnedness.

un'learnt, *ppl. a.* [UN-[1] 8 b.] = UNLEARNED 5.
1879 FARRAR *St. Paul* I. v. I. 97 The inference that the gift of unlearnt languages was designed to help the Apostles in their future preaching.

un'leased, *ppl. a.* [UN-[1] 8.] **a.** Not held or let on lease. **b.** Not having a lease.
1716 *Lond. Gaz.* No. 5467/3 Lands unleased. **1801** *Farmer's Mag.* Apr. 143 Landlords..compelling their unleased tenantry to sell below market-price. **1906** *Daily Chron.* 30 Aug. 3/3 The proceeds derived from ordinary Crown lands unsold or unleased.

un'leash, *v.* [UN-[2] 4 b.] *trans.* To free from a leash; to set free in order to pursue or attack. Chiefly *fig.*
1671 PHILLIPS (ed. 3), *To unleash*,..to let go the dogs after the Game. **1821** SHELLEY *Hellas* 357 Like beasts When earthquake is unleashed. **1854** J. S. C. ABBOTT *Napoleon* (1855) I. xxvi. 418 The bloodhounds of war were unleashed and England had unleashed them. **1868** GEO. ELIOT *Sp. Gipsy* 48 With power to check all rage until it turned To ordered force, unleashed on chosen prey.

un'least, *a. rare*[−1]. (UN-[1] 7.)
c **1440** *Pallad. on Husb.* I. 487 Another craft vnlest is: Fro floor to floor to chaunge hit ofte, his fest is.

†**un'least**, obs. var. *unlest* UNLESS *adv.*
1574 J. DEE in *Lett. Lit. Men* (Camden) 34 Unleast your honor had putte your helping hand. **1601** YARRINGTON *Two Lament. Trag.* III. ii. in Bullen *O. Pl.* IV, I nam'd not God, unleast twere with an othe.

un'leave, *v.* [UN-[2] 4; cf. UNLEAF *v.*] **a.** *trans.* To strip of leaves. Hence **un'leaving** *vbl. sb.*
1589 PUTTENHAM *Eng. Poesie* III. xxv. (Arb.) 309 The good gardiner..vnleaues his boughes to let in the sunne. **1598** SYLVESTER *Du Bartas* II. i. IV. *Handie-crafts* 136 Somtimes they do the far-spread Gourd unleave. **1611** COTGR., *Effueillement*, an vnleauing. **1648** HEXHAM II, *Ontbladeren*, to Vnleave, or, to Take away the Leaves.
b. *intr.* To lose or shed leaves. *rare.*
1880 G. M. HOPKINS *Poems* (1967) 88 Margaret, are you grieving Over Goldengrove unleaving?

un'leaved, *ppl. a.*[1] [Cf. prec.] Stripped of leaves.
1598 SYLVESTER *Du Bartas* II. i. I. *Eden* 122 Amorous Myrtles and immortall Bays Never un-leav'd. **1610** G. FLETCHER *Christ's Vict.* II. lix. Ode 25 See, see the flowers.. How they all unleaved die. **1624** HEYWOOD *Gunaik.* IV. 171 Behold how this lettice now unleaved looketh. **1870** ROSSETTI *Poems, Ho. Life* v, Nor quite unleaved [is] our songless grove.

un'leaved, *ppl. a.*[2] [UN-[1] 8.] Not furnished with leaves.
1501 DOUGLAS *Pal. Hon.* I. iii, Muskane treis.., Combust, barrant, vnblomit and vnleift. **1770** LANGHORNE *Plutarch* III. 38 Unleav'd, unhonour'd e'en with bark, See this sad tree, the gibbet of Alcæus!

un'leavened, *ppl. a.* (UN-[1] 8.)
1530 TINDALE *Exod.* xii. 17 See that ye kepe you to vnleuended [*sic*] breed. **1594** HOOKER *Eccl. Politie* IV. §10 The vse of vnleauened bread in that sacrament. **1611** BIBLE *Exod.* xii. 39 They baked vnleauened cakes of the dough. —— *Lev.* ii. 4 Vnleauened wafers. **1702** L'ESTRANGE *Josephus* III. vi. 64 Twelve Loaves of Unleavened Bread. **1737** CHALLONER *Cath. Chr. Instr.* (1753) 59 Unleavened Bread is an Emblem or Symbol of Sincerity and Truth. **1822–7** GOOD *Study Med.* (1829) I. 212 Toasted bread, and unleavened biscuits. **1867** LADY HERBERT *Cradle L.* vii. 191 Soft unleavened cakes and some excellent coffee,.. completed our repast.
absol. *c***1550** CHEKE *Matt.* xxvi. 17 Yᵉ first dai of yᵉ vnlevened cam yᵉ discipils to Jesus.
fig. **1611** BIBLE *1 Cor.* v. 7 Purge out therefore the olde leauen, that ye may be a new lumpe, as ye are vnleauened. **1814** BYRON *Lara* II. iv, Now rose the unleaven'd hatred of his heart. **1829** LYTTON *Disowned* xiv, He is..giving the very goods..to that..starving stripling! No, Warner, no! even this mass is not unleavened.

un'lectured, *ppl. a.* [UN-[1] 8.] Not lectured to or upon.
1593 G. HARVEY *Pierce's Super.* 190 [He] is a prowd man, if he contemne expert artisans,..howsoeuer Vnlectured in Schooles, or Vnlettered in bookes. **1743** YOUNG *Nt. Th.* v. 513 Hast thou ever..study'd the philosophy of tears? (A science, yet, unlectur'd in our schools!)

un'led, *ppl. a.* [UN-[1] 8b. Cf. ON. *úleiddr*.]
1. Not led; unconducted, unguided.
1615 G. SANDYS *Trav.* 66, I haue seene but few go away vnled from the Embassadors table. **1693** DRYDEN *Ovid's Met.* XIII. *Acis & Gal.* 52 Here on the midst he sate; his Flocks, unled, Their Shepherd follow'd. **1758** *Monthly Rev.* 503 Already reckoning captives yet unled. **1817** JEFFERSON *Writ.* (1830) IV. 305 The people [were] not only unled by their leaders, but in opposition to them. **1859** TENNYSON *Geraint & Enid* 577 His gentle charger following him unled.
2. *dial.* Of a crop: Not carried in.
1569 *Richmond Wills* (Surtees) 219 Tathe ledd and unledd.
3. *Sc.* Not carried out or prosecuted.
1586 in *Bk. Univ. Kirk Scotl.* (1839) 298 We hold the said proces and sentence as unled, undecydit or pronuncit.

†**un'lede,** *sb.*[1] *Obs.* [UN-[1] 4b + LEDE *sb.*] A foreign or hostile people.
*c***1205** LAY. 4982 Heo comen to his neode to driuen vt þa vnleoden. *a***1300** *Cursor M.* 7641 Wit þat vnled [*v.rr.* unlede, folke] son dauid mete, And wightli wan o þam his dete.

†**unlede,** *a.* and *sb.*[2] Forms: 1 unlǽde, 3 vnlede (-ledde), oun-, 4 onlede; 7 unleed, -lead, 9 unlete. [OE. *unlǽd(e* (UN-[1] 7), = Goth. *unlêds* (or *unlêþs*) poor.]
1. *adj.* Unhappy, miserable; wicked, evil; dreadful.
*a***1250** *Owl & Night.* 976 Solde euch mon wonie & grede, Riȝt suich hi weren unlede. *c***1275** *Sinners Beware* 72 in *O.E. Misc.* 74 To donne he beoþ swete. Þy vs is eþ-gete Helle þat is vnlede. *c***1315** SHOREHAM I. 588 Ounde and wreþe and coueytyng, Sleuþe and lestes on-lede. *a***1400** *St. Alexius* (Trin.) 333 Ofte hy him bete and burste, Þo vnlede fode.
2. *sb.* A vile or detestable person or thing.
*c***1315** SHOREHAM IV. 235 Þe ferste pryns hys prede, þat ledeþ þane flok, Þat of alle oþere onlede Hys rote and eke stok. **1677** NICOLSON in *Trans. Royal Soc. Lit.* (1870) IX. 321 *Unlead*, outlaw. **1691** RAY *N.C. Words* 138 *Unleed* or *Unlead*,..any crawling venomous creature; as a Toad, etc. It's sometimes ascribed to Man, and there it denotes a sly wicked fellow,..the very pest of Society. **1829** BROCKETT *N.C. Gloss.* (ed. 2) 315 *Unletes*, displacers or destroyers of the farmer's produce.

†**un'leeful,** *a. Obs.* [UN-[1] 7.] Not permissible or allowable; illicit.
*c***1374** CHAUCER *Boeth.* v. pr. iii. (1868) 154 Þe whiche þinge to trowen on god I deme it felonie and vnleueful. *c***1386** —— *Pars. T.* ¶ 593 The wounde shal nat departe from his hous whil he vseth swich vnleueful [*v. rr.* vnlefful, vnlieful] sweryng. **1449** [see next]. *c***1491** *Chast. Goddes Chyld.* 25 Her rest was full short by cause it was..unlefull. **1529** MORE *Dyaloge* I. Wks. 157/2 The thinges nowe forbeden vs, and therfore to vs vnleful. **1547** BOORDE *Brev. Health* xxvii. 16b, Desyre to eate rawe and unlefull thynges, as women with chylde doth. **1567** *Reg. Privy Council Scot.* I. 524 That pretendit and unlefull mariage.
Hence †**un'leefulness.** *Obs.*
1382 WYCLIF *Wisd.* xiv. 8 The maumet..is cursid,..and he that made it, for he forsothe wroȝte vnleefulnesse. *c***1449** PECOCK *Repr.* II. i. 136 Ech such doable thing..is in it silf neither leeful neither vnleeful, in eny of the ij. no seid maners of propre taking leefulnes and vnleefulnes. *c***1475** *Cath. Angl.* 212/1 (A.), To do Vnlefulnesse, *illicebrare.*

†**un'leefully,** *adv. Obs.* [UN-[1] 11: cf. prec.] Illicitly; improperly.
*c***1375** *Sc. Leg. Saints* x. (*Matthew*) 384 How dar þu þane ..fra þi lorde tak hyre to þe, vnlefully to wedyte be? **1386** *Rolls of Parlt.* III. 226/1 Any..wronge suggestion, by which owre lige Lorde hath ybe unleeffullich enfourmed. *c***1400** *Apol. Loll.* 110 Al bi power of bischopis name þat þei chalang unlefuly to hem wiþ out þe kirk. **1456** SIR G. HAYE *Law Arms* (S.T.S.) 288 He suld nocht..unlefully trete him.

†**un'leeped,** *ppl. a. Sc. Obs.* [UN-[1] 8 + *leep* to boil slightly.] Uncooked, raw.
*a***1568** in *Bannatyne MS.* (Hunter Cl.) 385/4 Ane grit gyre carling..That levit vpoun christiane menis flesche and rewth heidis vnleipit.

†**un'leesable,** *a. Obs.* [UN-[1] 7b.] Incapable of being lost.
1647 TRAPP *Comm. Matt.* vii. 26 Saving grace is unleesable, though it may be impaired in the degrees.

†**un'leese,** *v. Obs. rare.* [OE. *un-*, *onlíesan* (= MHG. *entlœsen*, MG. *entlôsin*, MLG. *entlosen*, G. *entlösen*): see UN-[2] 9 and LEESE *v.*[2]] *trans.* To unfasten, undo, open.
1377 LANGL. *P. Pl.* B. Prol. 213 Seriauntz..nouȝt for loue of owre lorde vnlese here lippes onis.

un'leesome, *a. Sc.* [UN-[1] 7.] = UNLEEFUL *a.*
*c***1375** *Sc. Leg. Saints* x. (*Matthew*) 10 Lewy, þat as a tollare þare wes sate, Vnlessume wynnynge for to get. **1500–20** DUNBAR *Poems* xvii. 16 Thir merchantis takis vnlesum win. **1552** LYNDESAY *Monarche* 5104 And sum, for thare vnleifsum actis, Ar rent and rewin apone the ractis. **1600** HAMILTON in *Cath. Tractates* (S.T.S.) 235 How mony young wemen..hes murtherit the fruict of thair auin wombes, some be vnlisome drinkis. **1864** LATTO *Tam. Bodkin* x. 92 The loons that had received the unleisum stoutherie. *Ibid.* xvii. 170 The unleisome possession o' the game.
So **un'leesomely** *adv.* ? *Obs.*
*c***1400** *Sc. Trojan War* II. 1103 [To] lat of hyr virgynite The closoures vnlefsomely [L. *illicite*] To be broken. **1528** LYNDESAY *Dreme* 230 Vnleifsumlie thay vsit propertie. *a***1578** LINDESAY (Pitscottie) *Chron. Scot.* (S.T.S.) II. 207 Putting hand in the quenis grace vnlesomelie..but athir law or ressoune.

un'leeze, *v. dial.* [UN-[2] 9 + *leeze* to arrange (threads).] *trans.* To unravel.
1889 H. JOHNSTON *Glenbuckie* iv, The hank she had left me to unleeze was truly a tangled one.

un'left, *ppl. a.* (UN-[1] 8b.)
*c***1611** CHAPMAN *Iliad* II. 615 Yet were his men unleft Without a chief. **1634** FORD *Perk. Warbeck* v. iii, Your father ..Would blush on your behalf, and wish his country Unleft. **1659** *Nicholas Papers* (Camden) IV. 179 All malladies and goutes vnleft behynde at Bathe.

un'leg, *v.* (UN-[2] 4.)
1598 FLORIO, *Sgambare*, to vnleg. **1654** GAYTON *Pleas. Notes* III. v. 100 That is to say, with three hard words, unmule, un-leg and un-able, Alanso Lopez.

un'legacied, *ppl. a.* (UN-[1] 8.)
1556 *Wills & Inv. N.C.* (Surtees, 1835) 149, I will that my said sonne..shall have..of my goods..on hundreth pounds and the rest vnlegased to be parted betwix barbare and hym. **1846** WORCESTER (citing *Q. Rev.*).

un'legal, *a.* (UN-[1] 7, 5b.)
1643 PRYNNE *Open. Gt. Seal* 29 The unlegall wilfull absence of the..Lord Keeper from the Parliament. *a***1810** TANNAHILL *Poems* (1846) 68 Selfish, mean, unlegal deeds. **1899** *Westm. Gaz.* 10 July 3/1 The illegal—or let us say the unlegal—interference of the English Government.

un'legalized, *ppl. a.* (UN-[1] 8.)
1830 BENTHAM *Offic. Apt. Maximized, Further Extr. Const. Codex* (1830) 23 Accustomed, though unlegalized profit in every shape. **1860** FROUDE *Hist. Eng.* VI. 267 He hated lies—legalized or unlegalized.

un'legally, *adv.* (UN-[1] 11.)
1888 *Pall Mall G.* 3 April 3/1 If such a delicate matter as extradition were left to be dealt with unlegally.

un'legate, *v.* [UN-[2] 6b.] *trans.* To deprive of the office of legate.
*a***1548** HALL *Chron., Hen. VI*, 111 Sone after, the bishop of Rome..vnlegated hym, and set another in his stede. **1651** N. BACON *Disc. Govt. Eng.* II. xvii. 150 The Cardinall is Un-Legated, and that Power conferred upon the Arch-Bishop of Canterbury.

†**unlegated,** *ppl. a. Obs.* [UN-[1] 8.] Not left by will.
1562–3 *N.C. Wills* (Surtees) II. 38 My goodes unlegated I doe give to my brother.

un'legged, *a.* (UN-[1] 9.)
1608 TOPSELL *Serpents* 609 This monster..nor man nor dragon is.., But man unlegged, and snake unheaded.

†**un'legible,** *a.* [UN-[1] 7, 5b.] Illegible.
1611 SPEED *Hist. Gt. Brit.* x. i. §57. 892/2 The letter was ..somewhat vnlegible. **1655** EARL ORRERY *Parthen.* I. VI. 150 Perceiveing my joy in my Face, it inflam'd to such a degree, that for a good while his choller was unleagible in any thing else. **1671** WOOD *Life* (O.H.S.) II. 226 The base and unlegible hand of the translator.

un'legislative, *a.* (UN-[1] 7.)
1791 BENTHAM *Panopt.* II. Postscr. 165 More unlegislative minuteness, more unthrifty fixation.

†**unle'gitimate,** *a. Obs.* [UN-[1] 7, 5b.] Illegitimate.
1655 EARL ORRERY *Parthen.* I. VII. 347 Shee persever'd in a Passion which tended to..a more vnlegittimate end.

†**unle'gitimate,** *ppl. a. Sc. Obs.* [UN-[1] 8b.] Not legitimated.
1516 *Reg. Mag. Sig. Scot.* 23/1 Borne bastard and unlegittimate be ony mariage.

†**unle'gitimate,** *v. Obs.* [UN-[2] 6a.] *trans.* To make illegitimate.
1606 MARSTON *Parasit.* II. C4b, I will vnlegittimate the issue.

un'leisured, *a.* (UN-[1] 9.)
*a***1586** SIDNEY *Arcadia* II. xxv, But her vnleasured thoughtes ran not ouer the ten first wordes. **1644** MILTON *Areop.* (Arb.) 56 Unlesse he carry all his considerat diligence ..to the hasty view of an unleasur'd licencer.
Hence **un'leisuredness.**
1661 BOYLE *Style of Script.* To Rdr., The Unleisurednesse, and Rellish of the Unsetl'dnesse of the Wandering Author.

†**un'leke,** *v. Obs.* [UN-[2] 3 + *leke* (cf. *leke*, ME. pa. t. of LOUK *v.*[1]).] *trans.* To unlock (a door).
*c***1380** *Sir Ferumbras* 1264 Floripe hure drow to anoþer parr, & þar an dore ounlekes þat drow to þe putte ward, & doun in the pyt sche strekes.

†**un'length.** *Obs.*[−1] [UN-[1] 3, 12.] Shortness.
*a***1250** *Owl & Night.* 752 Hwy atwitestu me myne vnstrengþe & myne vngrete & myn vnlengþe.

un'lent, *ppl. a.* (UN-[1] 8b.)
[**1775** ASH.] **1887** *Daily News* 11 June 2/1 Much depends ..upon the amount of the unlent surplus of money.

unlered: see UNLEARED *ppl. a.*

unless (ən'lɛs), *prep. phr.*, *prep.*, *conj.*, and *sb.* Forms: α. 5 of lasse, oo lesse, o less, oless(e, *Sc.* oles, 9 *Sc.* aless. β. 5 vpon less. γ. 5 in lasse, yn las, 5 in less (9 *dial.* inless), 6 inlesse. δ. 5 on lasse, 5–6 onlesse, 6 oon-, oneles, -lez, 5–7 onles, 9 *dial.* onless. ε. 5 vnlasse, 6– 7 vn-, unlesse, 6 vnles, 6– unless. [f. LESS *a.* 7, with the preps. *of*, *in*, *upon*, and *on*; the last of these by want of stress has been assimilated in form to the prefix UN-[1]. Cf. LESS *conj.*, also UNLEAST, UNLEST.]
†**1.** *prep. phr.* On a less or lower condition, requirement, footing, etc., *than* (what is specified).
With preceding negative, expressed or implied.
*c***1400** MAUNDEV. (1919) xxi. 122 But þat may not be vpon less þan wee mowe falle toward heuene. *Ibid.* (Roxb.) xxv, 118 [see LESS *a.* 7c]. **1475** *Rolls of Parlt.* VI. 127/1 His Land, which many persones..fere to take.., olesse then they myght be made verrey sure of payment. *a***1500** in C. Trice-Martin *Chanc. Proc. 15th C.* (1904) 5 Robert wil not suffre hym to be laten to baile on lasse than he will make..a generall acquytaunce.
2. Except, if..not: †**a.** With retention of *than* (cf. prec.), but without a negative. *Obs.*
1431 *Acts. Privy Counc.* IV. 96 It shulde be entendede unto, namely, olesse þan before þᵗ men can se..þᵉ meenes.. of ferþer conduyt of þᵉ werre. *c***1449** PECOCK *Repr.* III. xvi. 386 Alle hise successouris ben..excludid for euer, in lasse thanne the same good be ȝouun aȝen. **1467** in *Eng. Gilds* (1870) 408 Vppon peyn of euery man so failynge, vnlesse then he haue a sufficient depute, of xl.*d.* **1530** TINDALE *Gen., Prol. Use Script.* Av, Inlesse then we entend to be ydle disputers, and braulers aboute vayne wordes.
†**b.** Followed by *that*. *Obs.*
1440 in *Wars Eng. in France* (1864) II. 458 The kyng conceyueth wele that onlesse that it like him so to tendre the said duc he [etc.]. **1470–85** MALORY *Arthur* I. x. 47 Onlesse that our kyng haue more chyualry,..he shal be ouer-come. **1529** WOLSEY in Cavendish *Life* (1825) II. 261 Onles that yow..do helpe & releve me therin. **1534** in Leadam *Star Chamber Cases* (Selden) II. 211 [They] cowde not..sell so myche..onelez that they wold sell so reasonable a pennyworthe. **1596** SPENSER *F.Q.* VI. iii. 39 Ne would I gladly combate with mine host,..Vnlesse that I were thereunto enforst.
c. With omission of conjunction before the subordinate clause, and thus passing into *conj.* (Cf. 4.) Freq. in phr. ***unless and until.***
1509 FISHER *Serm.* Wks. (1876) 277 There is no man.. oneles he haue it by reuelacyon that knoweth certaynly [etc.]. **1542** *Lam. & Piteous Treat.* in *Harl. Misc.* (1745) IV. 505/2 It was a verey daungerous and ieoperdous Thinge,.. inlesse they had been..weryd by longe Soiouryinge. **1563** *Mirr. Mag., Blacksmith* lxviii, For one [talent] is to much, onles it be well spent. **1607** in *Eng. Gilds* (1870) 442 Margory Davies..wold not remove her habitacion onles she might haue a way..to passe [etc.]. **1662** STILLINGFL. *Orig. Sacræ* II. iii. §5 Will God condemn them for that, which it was impossible they should have, unless God gave it them? **1710** SWIFT *Jrnl. to Stella* 8 Oct., I was at a loss to-day for a dinner, unless I would have gone a great way. **1752** YOUNG *Brothers* I. i, Dominion, and the princess, both are lost, Unless you gain the king. **1820** SOUTHEY *Wesley* II. 211 No person was admitted to this rank, unless he were thought competent by the preachers of the circuit. **1877** RUSKIN *Fors Clav.* lxxx. VII. 234, I am never angry with anybody unless they deserve it. **1937** D. JONES in *Le Maître Phonétique* Apr.–June (Suppl.), We should as a rule stick to that pronunciation unless and until we find another native whose speech we have reason to think is more characteristic. **1956** A. WILSON *Anglo-Saxon Attitudes* II. ii. 335 Mother and son had both arrived with the fixed determination of not leaving unless and until either of the two women..should have paid handsomely to secure their departure. **1983** *Times* 1 Feb. 15/1 Unless and until the government also proposes the abolition..of the GLC, the savings in public money are likely to be minimal.
d. Followed by a prepositional or participial clause without verb, or by *when*, *where*, etc.
1548–9 (Mar.) *Bk. Com. Prayer, Offices, Bapt. Priv. Ho.*, [That] the people..defer not the Baptisme of infantes.. onlesse vp on a greate & reasonable cause. **1610** FLETCHER *Faithful Sheph.* v. v, [Let] not wine, Unless in sacrifice, or rites divine, Be ever known of Shepherd. **1681** DRYDEN *Abs. & Achit.* I. 590 Nor ever was he known..[to] Curse, unless against the Government. **1721** BRADLEY *Philos. Acc. Wks. Nat.* 77 We had no Frost or Snow.., unless in the most Inland Parts. **1749** FIELDING *Tom Jones* XVII. ix, Jones passed above twenty-four melancholy hours by himself, unless when relieved by the company of Partridge. **1789** CHARLOTTE SMITH *Ethelinde* (1814) II. 147 But I dare not shew them, unless to you. **1818** SCOTT *Rob Roy* v, A beautiful horse, jet black, unless where he was flecked by spots of..foam. **1897** MARY KINGSLEY *W. Africa* 439 They never wear clothes unless compelled to.
3. *prep.* **a.** Except, but.

1531–2 *Act 23 Hen. VIII*, c. 1 That no suertye be taken onles suche as maye dyspende..yerly..xxvi.s. viii.d. **1563** HILL *Art Garden.* II. lxiv. (1574) 132 The floures..ought then to be gathered..vnlesse the Lilly..and Rose. **1600** HEYWOOD *If you know not me* Wks. 1874 I. 205 All forbeare this place, vnlesse the Princess. **1683** D. A. *Art Converse* 117 They say nothing unless a meer *yes sir* or *no Madam*. **1709** T. ROBINSON *Nat. Hist. Westmoreld.* viii. 53 Inconsistent..with the Nature of Lead, Copper, Coal, or any other Mineral, unless Iron. **1796** MORSE *Amer. Geog.* II. 33 Unless the Swedish part,..the Laplanders can be said to be under no regular government. **1886** *Pall Mall G.* 4 Aug. 1/2 He did not believe that he would ever obtain anything..unless a species of elevated poor-law system of government.

†**b.** Without; but for. *Obs.*

1536 *St. Papers Hen. VIII* (1830) I. 469 Soo that, unles the most infinite mercy of God, both bodyes and soules shuld perishe togither. **1796** MRS. J. WEST *Gossip's Story* I. 190 You instilled into my infant soul principles, which, unless my own fault, must insure my present and future happiness.

†**4.** *conj.* **a.** Lest. *Obs.*

1508 FISHER 7 *Penit. Ps.* cii. Wks. (1876) 142, I fere..oneles I shall fall agayne amonge those theues. **1543** BECON *Invect. agst. Swearing* E iiij b, I feare vnlesse we shall be redy ..to runne hedlong into hell fyre. *a* **1592** GREENE *Alphonsus* I. i, Presume not, villaine, further for to go, Vnles you do at length the same repent.

†**b.** But that. *Obs.*$^{-1}$

1608 in *Harl. Misc.* (1744) I. 181 A Flea shall not frisk forth, unless they comment upon her.

5. *sb.* An utterance or instance of the word; a reservation, proviso.

1861 DICKENS in *Pall Mall G.* 24 Sept. (1891) 3/2 Let us have no unlesses, sir. **1904** HICHENS *Woman with Fan* vii, There's very often an unless hanging about, like a man at a street corner.

un'lessened, *ppl. a.* (UN-[1] 8.)

1736 BUTLER *Anal.* I. i. 31 This active power..remains unlessened. **1842** J. B. FRASER *Allee Neemroo* II. 99 His uneasiness remained unlessened and unaltered. **1891** C. M. *J. Mitford's Lett. & Remin.* 163 His love for me remained unlessened.

un'lessoned, *ppl. a.* (UN-[1] 8.)

c **1550** WALKER *Dice-Play* D v b, Pety figgers, and vnlessoned laddes. **1596** SHAKS. *Merch. V.* III. ii. 161 An vnlessoned girle, vnschool'd, vnpractiz'd. **1807** J. BARLOW *Columb.* v. 673 To Fame's hard school the warm disciples came, To learn sage Liberty's unlesson'd lore. **1882** *Century Mag.* XXIV. 658/1 That unlessoned insight which comes of loving them.

†**un'lest,** obs. var. UNLESS. (Cf. UNLEAST.)

1535 in *Lett. Suppress. Monast.* (Camden) 91 The dean wolde not resign unto hym, unleste he wolde leffe hym other possessions. **1583** STUBBES *Anat. Abus.* II. C 8 b, May subiects..rise against their prince? No, at no hand, vnlest they will purchase to themselues eternall damnation. **1599** THYNNE *Animadv.* (1875) 19 Difference of armes semethe a difference of famelyes, vnleste you canne prove that..they altered their armes vppone somme iuste occasione.

un'let, *ppl. a.* Also 5 unlate, 6 unletton. (UN-[1] 8 b; cf. LET *ppl. a.*)

1453 *Paston Lett.* Suppl. (1901) 49, I know not oon rode unlate, but alle ocupyed to your profyghte. **1537** in *Lett. Suppress. Monast.* (Camden) 163 The house..wiche was unlet at the tyme of owre repare thether. **1545** *Act 37 Hen. VIII*, c. 12 §16 Hawles of Craftes.., soo long as they bee keapte unletton. **1769** GRAY in *Corr. G. & Nicholls* (1843) 93, I believe all that are unlet will be cheap as the time approaches. **1866** GEO. ELIOT *F. Holt* ii, Having three farms unlet. **1885** *Law Times* 28 Mar. 384/2 In the present day, when unlet land is becoming so common.

un'lettable, *a.* (UN-[1] 7 b.)

In frequent use from *c* 1895.

1882 *Ch. Times* XX. 21, I fear to find myself with a[n]..unlettable glebe on my hands. **1893** DK. ARGYLL *Unseen Found Soc.* x. 305 Farms which have been unlettable.

†**un'letted,** *ppl. a.* [UN-[1] 8. Cf. MLG. *ungeletted*, etc.] Unhindered.

a **1500** *Chaucer's Dreme* 1831 A bird song full low and softely,..Unletted of every wight. *a* **1553** BECON *Jewel of Joy* Wks. 1564 II. 35 The holye scripture requireth of us..an vnletted perseueraunce in the vaye of Godlines.

†**un'letten,** *ppl. a. Sc. Obs.* [UN-[1] 8 b.] Not let or allowed.

1574 *Sc. Acts Jas. VI* (1814) III. 87 That all..vagaboundis..be committit in ward in the commoun presoun;..thair to be kepit vnlettin to libertie,..quhill thay [etc.].

un'lettered, *a.* [UN-[1] 9. Cf. MDu. *ongelettert*, Du. *ongeletterd*.]

1. Not instructed in letters; not possessed of book-learning.

c **1340** HAMPOLE *Prose Tr.* 32 Anoþer mane..unletterede may noght so redyly hafe at his hand Haly Writt. **1387** TREVISA *Higden* (Rolls) VII. 181 A man forsoþe..þat was unlettred, but ful myghty in money. *c* **1440** *Alph. Tales* 468 When þe abbott Pambo was vnletterd, he went vnto a man þat was letterd [etc.]. **1544** LELAND *N. Y. Gift* in *Itin.* (1768) I. p. xix, The Italians..counte..al other nations to be barbarus and onletterid saving their owne. **1593** [see UNLECTURED *ppl. a.*]. **1624** GATAKER *Transubst.* 156 As children or unlettered persons, when they looke on bookes, know not the power of the letter. **1642** MILTON *Apol. Smect.* 36 Such a lost construction, as no man either letter'd or unletter'd will be able to piece up. **1747** WESLEY *Prim. Physick* (1762) p. xxiv, Easy to be applied by plain unlettered Men. **1781** COWPER *Conversat.* 12 As alphabets in ivory employ..the yet unletter'd boy. **1817** CHALMERS *Disc. Chr. Revel.* ii. 86 The mind of an ordinary and unlettered peasant. **1867** AUGUSTA WILSON *Vashti* xxv, Sturdy but unlettered mechanics.

absol. **1751** JOHNSON *Rambler* No. 180 ¶2 The unlettered and unenlightened. **1812** G. CHALMERS *Dom. Econ. Gt. Brit.* Pref. 14 That the learned are sometimes too confident, and the unlettered always too credulous. **1861** STANLEY *East. Ch.* viii. (1869) 273 Sacred pictures..are the Bibles of the unlettered.

b. Pertaining to, characterized by, ignorance of letters.

1588 SHAKS. *L.L.L.* IV. ii. 18 After his..vnpolished, vneducated,..or rather, vnlettered..fashion. **1697** COLLIER *Ess. Mor. Subj.* II. (1703) 99 Books..give a more universal insight into things, than can be learned from unlettered observation. **1763** J. BROWN *Poetry & Music* iv. 36 Savages ..in their present unlettered State of Ignorance and Simplicity. **1807** G. CHALMERS *Caledonia* I. III. vii. 423 An upright stone still forms the unlettered memorial of his odious end. **1820** HAZLITT *Lett. Dram. Lit.* 186 They were learned men in an unlettered age. *a* **1864** HAWTHORNE *Amer. Note-bks.* (1879) I. 142 His conversation has much strong, unlettered sense.

2. Not expressed in, or marked with, letters.

1633 P. FLETCHER *Poet. Misc., Asclepiads* 1 Unletter'd Word, which never eare could heare. **1782** [T. MAUDE] *Verbeia* 37 This unlettered tomb is in a mutilated state.

Hence †**un'letteredly** *adv.*, **un'letteredness**.

c **1440** *Promp. Parv.* 366/1 On-letterydly, *illiterate.* **1653** E. WATERHOUSE *Apol. Learn.* 120 Ignorance and unletteredenesse ill becomes any man who bears the Image of God. **1890** BP. HOBHOUSE *Churchw. Acc.* (Somerset) p. xxiii, The entire unletteredness of the community.

unleueful, variant of UNLEEFUL *a. Obs.*

†**un'levable,** *a. Obs.* [UN-[1] 7 b.] Unbelieving, incredulous.

1382 WYCLIF *Ecclus.* xvi. 29 Be thou not vnleeuable to the wrd of hym. **14..** *Voc.* in Wr-Wülcker 589/23 *Incredulus*, unlefable.

†**un'leveful,** *a. Obs.*$^{-1}$ [UN-[1] 7: cf. UNBELIEFFUL *a.* and OE. *unȝeléafful*.] = prec.

1382 WYCLIF *Ecclus.* xxiii. 33 In the lawe of the heȝest she was vnleeueful.

un'level, *a.* (UN-[1] 7; cf. ILLEVEL *a.*)

1571 DIGGES *Pantom.* I. xii. D iij b, How vneuen or vnleuell so euer the ground bee. **1644** QUARLES *Sheph. Orac.* iii, All things were unlevel, And rude disorder crept into our State. **1683** MOXON *Mech. Exerc., Printing* xxiv. 338 The small un-level lying of every Sheet..makes each Sheet incline to the lowest side of the Heap. **1771** *Ann. Reg., Usef. Projects* 109/2 That unlevel pastures may be ploughed down without any injury. **1817–8** COBBETT *Resid. U.S.* (1822) 286 A place situated..upon high and unlevel lands. **1873** E. SPON *Workshop Receipts* Ser. I. 36/1 Should the cloth have got unlevel.

un'level, *v.* [UN-[2] 6 a.] *trans.* To make uneven; to divest of levelness.

a **1586** SIDNEY *Arcadia* III. xi, [The] place..was so plaine, as there was scarcely any bush, or hillock, either to unlevell, or shadowe it. **1624** QUARLES *Div. Poems, Job* xix. 10 His Lunatick affections doe vnleuell, What Heauen created by iust Waight and Measure. **1648** HERRICK *Hesper., To the Fever* 8 Come thou not neere that Filme so finely spred, Where no one piece is yet unlevelled. **1703** [R. NEVE] *City & C. Purchaser* 189 There are as many places that seem to be unlevel'd, as there are level'd. **1834** SOUTHEY *Doctor* xlvi. (1862) 109 In 1723 the church floor and church-yard, which had both been unlevelled by Death's levelling course, were levelled anew.

un'levelled, *ppl. a.* [UN-[1] 8.] Not made level; not reduced to a level condition.

1622 DRAYTON *Poly-olb.* xxiii. 184 Where Cheshire..with Lancashire doth lie Along th' unlevel'd shores. **1730** TICKELL *Kensington Garden* 30 Where all unlevell'd the gay Garden lies. **1854** DORA GREENWOOD *Haps & Mishaps Tour Eur.* 30 The grandeur of its yet unlevelled walls and towers.

†**unleventhe,** obs. variant of ELEVENTH *a.*

13.. *Coer de L.* 2455 The unleventhe day they saylyd in tempest.

un'levied, *ppl. a.* (UN-[1] 8.)

1450 *Rolls of Parlt.* V. 211/1 The Subsidie..is yit unlevied and unpaied. **1540** *Act 32 Hen. VIII*, c. 5 The residue of the said dett..remayning unlevied or unreceyvid by the said former execution. **1569** *Lanc. Wills* (Chetham Soc. 1884) 31 Fyve hundrethe marks..or so muche therof as shalbe then unlevyed. **1634** *Ir. Act 10 Chas. I*, Sess. III. c. 7 §2 [= quot. 1540]. **1864** *Morn. Star* 2 Feb., Arrears of unlevied poor rates.

un'levigated, *ppl. a.* (UN-[1] 8.)

1768 R. DOSSIE *Elaboratory* 290 The cinnabar should be procured..in an unlevigated state.

†**un'leving,** *ppl. a. Obs.* [UN-[1] 10.] Unbelieving.

a **1300** *Cursor M.* 20852 Þe apostlis þat all wide war spred, ..til our lagh þe vnleuand led. **1382** WYCLIF *Isaiah* xxi. 1 [He] that vnleeuende [1388 vnfeithful] is, vnfeithfully doth.

†**un'lewty.** *Obs.* [UN-[1] 12.] Disloyalty.

a **1300** *Cursor M.* 7135 Þat was mikel vnleute, To tell hir husband priuete. **13..** *Gaw. & Gr. Knt.* 2499 Þat he laȝt for his vnleute at þe leudes hondes, for blame. **1456** SIR G. HAYE *Law Arms* (S.T.S.) 25 The thrid part of the sternis was obumbrit with mirknes of unleautee. *a* **1470** HARDING *Chron.* CXIII. xiv, Through theyr vnlewtee [the Scots] Crowned Gilryke a Dane.

un'liable, *a.* (UN-[1] 7 b.)

1624 QUARLES *Div. Poems, Job* xvi. 32 How can I.., Vnliable to danger, flatter any? **1664** H. MORE *Myst. Iniq.* Pref. 1 *margin*, This Idea..is..unliable to any uncivil construction. **1679** PULLER *Moderat. Ch. Eng.* v. 88 No where judging of them as unliable to error. **1710** NORRIS *Chr. Prud.* vii. 297 Things that..are not so unliable to Disorder and abuse.

un'libbed, *ppl. a.* (UN-[1] 8.)

1607 TOPSELL *Four-f. Beasts* 324 They vse to geld them in March..: afterward being well nourished, they [*sc.* gelded horses] are no lesse strong..then other vnlibbed.

un'liberal, *a. rare*$^{-0}$. (UN-[1] 7.)

1570 LEVINS *Manip.* 15 Vnliberall, *illiberalis.* **1611** FLORIO, *Inliberale*, vnliberall, sparing.

un'liberalized, *ppl. a.* (UN-[1] 8 a *c.*)

1793 J. WILLIAMS *Mem. W. Hastings* 40 Are there any so unliberalized as to insist, that..the calumniated should only be allowed a passport to Peace from Death?

un'liberated, *ppl. a.* (UN-[1] 8.)

1837 *Penny Cycl.* VIII. 411/1 The removal of pressure upon the nerves, produced by the advancing and unliberated tooth. **1865** *Reader* 14 Oct. 430/2 The irregular weapons of a still unliberated press. **1970** *Time* 31 Aug. 18 Unliberated honorifics like 'Mrs.' and 'Miss' are replaced by the noncommittal 'Ms.'. **1971** S. BERMAN *Underground Guide to College of your Choice* 144 Most chicks are still unliberated and the virginity index is still quite high. **1975** *Listener* 9 Oct. 486/4 Ann is..the unliberated woman striving for acceptance in a permissive world. **1981** J. SUTHERLAND *Bestsellers* vii. 85 The unliberated condition of woman—incarcerated, flagellated, degraded, violated—was celebrated time and again.

unli'bidinous, *a.* (UN-[1] 7.)

1667 MILTON *P.L.* v. 449 But in those hearts Love unlibidinous reign'd.

un'licensed, *ppl. a.* [UN-[1] 8.]

1. Of persons, etc.: **a.** Not authorized by a formal license to carry on some occupation, industry, etc.

1634 in *10th Rep. Hist. MSS. Commission* App. IV. 428, 100 unlicensed alehowsses. **1643** [see 2 a]. **1746** FRANCIS tr. *Horace, Epist.* II. i. 154 A doubtful Drug unlicens'd Doctors fear. **1845** MCCULLOCH *Taxation* II. x, A fine..rigorously exacted from unlicensed dealers. **1855** MACAULAY *Hist. Eng.* xx. IV. 417 With great difficulty and after long search the most important of all the unlicensed presses was discovered.

b. Not furnished with authority, sanction, or formal permission to do something.

1608 SHAKS. *Per.* I. iii. 17 Why, as it were unlicens'd of your loves, He would depart, I'll give some light unto you. **1685** BAXTER *Paraphr. N.T.* To Rdr. A 3 b, The Papists restraint of the Laity unlicensed, from reading it translated in a known Tongue. **1725** POPE *Odyss.* XIII. 175 To warn the thoughtless self-confiding train No more unlicens'd thus to brave the main. **1795** SOUTHEY *Joan of Arc* IV. 414 Did she upon thy parting steps bestow Her free-will blessing, or hast thou set forth..unlicensed and unblest?

2. a. Of books, etc.: Published without licence.

1643 *Order* in *Milton's Areop.* (Arb.) 27 All unlicensed Printing Presses, and all Presses any way imployed in the printing of scandalous or unlicensed Papers. **1644** MILTON *Areop.* (Arb.) 53 All scandalous and unlicenc't books. **1647** (*title*), An Ordinance against unlicensed or scandalous Pamphlets.

b. Not authorized or sanctioned.

1649 JER. TAYLOR *Apol. Liturgy* §135 Many such cases will occurre in..unlicenc'd prayers. *a* **1704** T. BROWN *Dial. Dead, Reas. Oaths* Wks. 1720 IV. 184 Is any..of the good People of Doctors Commons [turned] to unlicens'd Marriages? **1728** POPE *Dunciad* IV. 228 For Attic Phrase in Plato let them seek, I poach in Suidas for unlicens'd Greek. **1819** SCOTT *Leg. Montrose* Introd., No less would our sexton ..have held it an unlicensed intrusion. **1856** FROUDE *Hist. Eng.* II. 193 The clergy had promised to abstain..from unlicensed legislation.

3. Free from requiring a licence.

1644 MILTON (*title*), Areopagitica: a Speech..For the Liberty of Vnlicenc'd Printing, To the Parlament of England. **1863** H. COX *Instit.* I. ix. 146 This act was kept in force..until 1694, when..it expired. The liberty of unlicensed printing dates from that period.

4. Unregulated, lawless. *rare*$^{-1}$.

1828 TYTLER *Hist. Scot.* I. 183 This prelate..with much personal risk, owing to the unlicensed state of the country, ..travelled with his suit..as far as Kirkcudbright.

unli'centious, *ppl. a.* (UN-[1] 7.)

1768–74 TUCKER *Lt. Nat.* (1834) II. 415 The exercise of sober, unlicentious freedom of thought.

un'lichened, *ppl. a.* (UN-[1] 8.)

1843 RUSKIN *Mod. Paint.* I. 239 Unlichened, dead, desolated rock.

un'lickable, *a.* (UN-[1] 7 b.)

1845 D'ISRAELI *Sybil* v. vii, One of the most unlicked and unlickable cubs that ever entered society.

un'licked, *ppl. a.* [UN-[1] 8. Cf. Du. *ongelikt*, G. *ungeleckt*.]

1. Not licked into shape. (See LICK *v.* 4.) Chiefly *fig.*, esp. with *cub* (or *whelp*).

1593 SHAKS. *3 Hen. VI*, III. ii. 161 Like to..an vn-lick'd Beare-whelpe, That carryes no impression like the Damme. *c* **1618** MORYSON *Itin.* IV. (1903) 1 Being drawne to the writing hereof..out of a naturall affection to give all the members to this my unlicked whelpe. **1687** DRYDEN *Hind & P.* I. 36 The bloudy Bear, an Independent beast, Unlick'd to form, in groans her hate express'd. **1687** [see CUB *sb.* 3]. **1728** VANBR. & CIB. *Prov. Husb.* II. i, The Son is an unlick'd Whelp, about sixteen. ? **1795** COLERIDGE *After a Walk bef. Supper* 30 A little ape with huge she-bear..: An unlicked mass the one— the other An antic huge. **1845** [see prec.]. **1871** BESANT & RICE *Ready-money Mort.* x, You know, Polly, what an unlicked cub I was when I married you.

b. *fig.* Not reduced to form or order; unfinished, unpolished, rude or crude.

1661 BOYLE *Style of Script.* 185 Confus'd Notions, and Abortive or Unlick'd Conceptions. **1682** DRYDEN *Abs. & Achit.* II. 502 But thou in Clumsy verse, unlickt, unpointed, Hast shamefully defi'd the Lord's Anointed. **1758** WESLEY *Wks.* (1872) II. 457, I rode back..to put the society there (an unlicked mass) into some form. **1773** MME. D'ARBLAY *Early Diary* Oct., I saw..the appearance of unlicked nature in all his motions. **1835** LAMB *Elia* II. Pref., My late friend's writings..are..a sort of unlicked, incondite things.

2. Not licked.

1861 L. L. NOBLE *Icebergs* 296 Poor Pussy,..a creature of backbone and ribs, coated with fur unlicked and scorched. **1895** R. W. CHAMBERS *King in Yellow, Str. Four Winds* i, [The cat's] purple tongue travelled over every unlicked spot ..[of] the saucer.

un'lid, *v.* Also 3 unlide. [UN-² 4. Cf. OE. *unhlidian.*] *trans.* To remove the lid from; to uncover.

a **1250** *Ancr. R.* 58 *note* (Trin. MS.), þe dom is ful grureful & strong o þa þet unliden ham þe put. **1693** R. LYDE *Retaking a Ship* 17, I answered, *alle abau*, for I don't want your help, and then they..unlid the Scuttle and went down. **1821** CLARE *Vill. Minstr.* I. 116 The pitmen often..'neath many a loosen'd block, Unlid coffins in the rock. **1853** C. BRONTE *Villette* xiii, Not a paper but was glanced over, not a little box but was unlidded.

un'lidded, *ppl. a.* [UN-¹ 8.] Not furnished or covered with a lid.

1819 KEATS *Song Four Faeries* 86 My bare unlidded eyes. **1868** BROWNING *Ring & Bk.* III. 1366 If, with the midday blaze of truth above, The unlidded eye of God awake. **1897** MARY KINGSLEY *W. Africa* 208 These pots..are unglazed, unlidded bowls.

†**un'lief**, *a. Obs.* [OE. *unléof* (UN-¹ 7), = MDu. (Du.) *onlief*, OHG. *unliup, unleub*, MHG. *unliep* (G. *unlieb*), ON. *úljúfr*, Goth. *unliubs*.] Not dear or valued; disliked, distasteful, unpleasant.

c **1200** *Trin. Coll. Hom.* 189 Ðe lichame..and þe gost.. fliten and winnen bitwenen hem, þat al þat is on unlef and unqueme, hit is þat oðer iqueme. *c* **1400** *Destr. Troy* 2949 Therfore saintes to seche and to sere halowes,..it ledis vnto laithnes and vnlefe werkes. **1430–40** LYDG. *Bochas* I. i. (1544) 2 Theyr..unware mischief..It was to them ful uncouth and unlefe. ? *a* **1500** *Chester Pl.* (Shaks. Soc.) I. 42 To all men thou shalbe unleffe,..And over all sette at naughte. **1513** DOUGLAS *Æneid* XII. xiii. 48 Sustenand thus ..euery stres, baith lesum and onleif. *a* **1596** SIR T. CHALONER in *Harington's Nugæ Ant.* (1804) II. 379 Nat so unleef, that I shold wysh To be thy Trojan wyfe.

un'lifelike, *a.* (UN-¹ 7 c.)

1818 HOGG *Brownie of Bodsbeck* II. iv. 75, I see the chaps are living, an' no that unlife-like, as a body may say. **1881** *Athenæum* 19 Nov. 664/3 The Highland characters of his present story are not unlifelike.

un'liftable, *a.* (UN-¹ 7 b.)

[**1775** ASH.] **1818** *Art Preserv. Feet* 93 Facts..not of sufficient importance to form the basis of a huge unliftable quarto. **1854** FERRIER *Inst. Metaph.* 59 Suppose he were to call the latter the unliftable, the imponderable without any qualification.

un'lifted, *ppl. a.* (UN-¹ 8.)

[**1775** ASH.] **1815** BYRON *Destr. Sennacherib* v, The tents were all silent,..The lances unlifted. **1882** AINGER *Lamb* v. 94 The cloud of domestic anxiety was still unlifted.

un'lifting, *ppl. a.* (UN-¹ 10.)

1845 MRS. NORTON *Child of Islands* 131 Veiling dear eyes ..With an unlifting veil.

un'ligable, *a. rare*⁻¹. [UN-¹ 7 b.] Incapable of being bound.

1653 R. BAILLIE *Dissuas. Vind.* (1655) 70 Remember what you assert of unligable Proteus.

un'light, *a.*¹ [UN-¹ 7 + LIGHT *a.*¹ Cf. ON. *úléttr* (MSw. *olätter*), MHG. *unlîhte*.] Not light (in weight or feeling); heavy.

c **1320** *Sir Tristr.* 419 He toke his lod vnliȝt. *Ibid.* 1039 A launce vn-liȝt. *c* **1440** *Ipomydon* 472 He..takith hys leue with hert vnlyght. **1480–1** J. WATTON *Spec. Xristiani* 46 A temple..With walles and pylers here onlyght.

un'light, *a.*² *rare*⁻⁰. [UN-¹ 7 + LIGHT *a.*²] Not bright or clear; dark, obscure.

1570 LEVINS *Manip.* 119 Vnlight, *obscurus*.

un'light, *v.* Now *s.w. dial.* [UN-² 9. Cf. dial. *onlight* (1825–).] *intr.* To alight, dismount.

1623 COCKERAM I, *Degresse*, to vnlight from a Horse. **1796** MRS. M. ROBINSON *Angelina* II. 174 I'm sure you hadn't no companion when you unlighted. **1847** HALLIWELL. **1886–** in Glouc., Som., and Devon glossaries, etc.

†**un'light**, *ppl. a.*¹ *Obs.*⁻¹ [UN-¹ 8 b + LIGHT *v.*¹ 6.] Not dismounted.

c **1400** *Destr. Troy* 3446 He raght to the reynes of þe riche qwene,..And led hir vnlight into a large halle.

†**un'light**, *ppl. a.*² *Obs.* [UN-¹ 8 b.] = next 1.

a **1500** *Three 15th Cent. Chron.* (Camden) 104 The torches unlight met hym at the steyre foote..., and so went byfore hym unlyght to the chirche. **1591** SYLVESTER *Du Bartas* I. ii. 670 As lighted Candles doe th' unlight inflame.

un'lighted, *ppl. a.* [UN-¹ 8.]

1. Not lighted; not set on fire; unkindled.

169. *Ad Populum Phaleræ* ii, Ask him but whence unlighted Candles came? **1718** PRIOR *Solomon* III. 708 The sacred Wood, which on the Altar lay, Untouch'd, unlighted glows. **1863** THORNBURY *True as Steel* III. 16 The cannonier, rising, unlighted linstock in hand. **1883** D. C. MURRAY *Hearts* xxxiv, With his unlighted pipe between his teeth.

2. Not lighted up or illuminated; not furnished with light. Also *fig.*

[**1775** ASH, *Unlighted*,..not directed by light.] **1825** T. HOOK *Sayings* Ser. II. III. 102 The countenance of..Fanny, was the only one unlighted by smiles and happiness. **1855** ARNOLD *Balder Dead* II. 213 Ye..gave me nine unlighted realms to rule. **1886** C. E. PASCOE *London of To-day* (ed. 3) 254 A cell..unlighted except by the door.

un'lightened, *ppl. a.* [UN-¹ 8.]

†**1.** Unenlightened. *Obs.*

1587 GOLDING *De Mornay* xxii. 389 Princes vnlightened by God, are so desirous of vainglorie. **1627** HAKEWILL *Apol.* 35 Onely this part of [Christendom]..remaines.. vnlightned, in the darkenes of ignorance.

2. Not lighted up; unbrightened; †unlighted.

1637–50 ROW *Hist. Kirk* (Maitland Cl.) I. 113 A glorious altar sett vp, with..two unlightned candles, and two basins. **1659** W. CHAMBERLAYNE *Pharonnida* III. ii. 19 Whilst she did remain Unlightened with a beam of comfort. **1852** BAILEY *Festus* (ed. 4) 42 Some seem to live, Whose hearts are like those unlightened stars Of the first darkness. **1896** *Westm. Gaz.* 2 May 2/2 Sombre gloom, unlightened save for the red staves of the inverted halberds.

un'lightsome, *a.* (UN-¹ 7.)

1592 R. D. *Hypnerotomachia* 17 This dark vnlightsome place. **1594** CHAPMAN *Shadow of Night* 30 When vnlightsome, vast, and indigest, The formelesse matter of this world did lye. **1667** MILTON *P.L.* VII. 355 Of Celestial Bodies first the Sun A mightie Spheare he fram'd, unlightsom first. **1686** J. S[ERGEANT] *Hist. Monast. Convent.* 167 The place of Election is very unlightsom, as having but a few Lights.

un'lignified, *ppl. a.* (UN-¹ 8.)

1875 BENNETT & DYER tr. *Sachs' Bot.* 100 An unlignified gelatinous thickening-mass. **1878** MASTERS *Henfrey's Elem. Bot.* (ed. 3) 414 The cell-walls consist of unlignified cellulose.

un'like, *a.* and *sb.* Forms: 3–4 un-, vnlich, 4 -liche (-lichy, 5 onliche), -leche; 3 unnlic, 4 vnlic, -lijc, 4–5 vnlyk, 5–6 vnlyke (6 -leke), 3– unlike. [ME. *unlich(e, unlik(e* (UN-¹ 7), corresponding to OE. *unȝelic* UNILICHE *a.* Cf. OFris. (NFris.) *unlik*, obs. Du. *onlijk*, MLG. (LG.) *unlîk*, ON. *úlíkr* (Icel. *ólíkur*, MSw. *oliker, olika*, Sw. *olik, olika*, MDa. *ulig, ulige*, Da. and Norw. *ulig*, Norw. *ulik*).]

1. Not like or resembling, different from, dissimilar to (some other person or thing).

c **1200** ORMIN 16859 Forr all þatt follc let tatt he wass Unnlic all oþerr lede. *a* **1225** *Juliana* 14 Ich am iweddet to an ..þe is unlich him. **1390** GOWER *Conf.* III. 64 He was unlich all othre there. **1553** ASCHAM *Germany* ℙ 14 He thought it his most honor to be vnlykest such for his gentlenes, which were misliked..for their crueltie. **1596** SHAKS. *Merch. V.* II. ix. 56 How much [thou art] vnlike my hopes and my deseruings! **1634** SIR T. HERBERT *Trav.* 183 [The banana] giues a most delicious..rellish, not much vnlike our choicest Peares. **1676** GLANVILL *Ess.* vi. 30 Those, whose Genius and Ways are so unlike him. **1725** POPE *Odyss.* IX. 221 A form enormous! far unlike the race Of human birth, in stature. **1750** tr. *Leonardus' Mirr. Stones* 112 Some jaspers are not much unlike red porphyry. **1829** JAS. MILL *Hum. Mind* (1869) II. 252 As unlike to any of those..as the sensation of white is unlike the sensations of the seven prismatic colours. **1875** JOWETT *Plato* (ed. 2) I. 401 The philosopher has notions of good and evil unlike those of other men.

b. Const. *to*; also (quot. 1873) *from*.

1340–70 *Alex. & Dind.* 271 Oure lif & oure lawe vnlich is to ȝoure. *c* **1400** *Rom. Rose* 6360 Vnlyk is my word to my dede. *c* **1450** *Myrr. our Ladye* 224 How vnlyke worldely worshyp is vnto gostly ioye. **1531** ELYOT *Gov.* II. xiv, This maner of flatery is mooste unlyke to that whiche is communely used. **1556** OLDE *Antichrist* 116 b, Two heades .., farre unlyke the one to the other. **1670** BAXTER *Cure Ch. Div.* 238 You would shew yourselves much..unliker to Satan the accuser. **1825** SCOTT *Betrothed* xiv, Their very saints are unlike to the saints of any Christian country. **1873** PATER *Stud. Hist. Renaiss.* 80 They were of a spirit as unlike as possible from that of Lorenzo. **1876** GLADSTONE *Glean.* (1879) II. 271 He was very unlike to any other man.

2. Not like each other; different, dissimilar.

c **1250** *Gen. & Ex.* 1726 Ðoȝ him boren ðes ones bles Vnlike maniȝe and likeles. *c* **1380** *Antechrist* in Todd *Three Treat. Wyclif* (1851) 150 Loke Cristis copborde, and hers; and þei ben ful unlichy. **1565** STAPLETON tr. *Bede's Hist. Ch. Eng.* 25b, The parties there wer farre vnleke of condition. **1605** BACON *Adv. Learn.* II. xxiii. §29 The unlikest in the worlde; the one being fierce..; the other solemn. **1641** MILTON *Ch. Govt.* I. iv. 13 There can be no possible imitation of Lording over their brethren in regard of their persons altogether unlike. **1704** J. HARRIS *Lex. Techn.* I. s.v., Unlike Quantities and Signs in Algebra. **1807** CRABBE *Par. Reg.* II. 283 How fair these names, how much unlike they look. **1842** FRANCIS *Dict. Arts, Unlike quantities*, in algebra, are such as are expressed by different letters, or different roots or powers of the same letter. **1889** GRETTON *Memory's Harkb.* 125 We may take together two other Judges,..as unlike as the bear and the innate gentleman.

absol. **1831** CARLYLE *Sart. Res.* II. v, This approximation of the Like and Unlike. *Ibid.*, In this case of the Like-Unlike.

b. *sb. pl.* Dissimilar things or persons.

1612 W. SCLATER *Sick Souls Salve* 1 He amplifies it in a comparison of unlikes. *a* **1626** —— *Comm. Malachy* (1650) 66 It is handled in a plenary comparison of unlikes. **1857** J. PULSFORD *Quiet Hours* 43 Like can reach like, and act upon it, in a way that unlikes cannot.

3. †**a.** Differing from others of the kind; incomparable; unusual. *Obs.*

1390 GOWER *Conf.* II. 275 Bot certes such usure unliche It falleth more unto the riche. **14..** *R. Gloucester's Chron.* (MS. Digby 205) fol. 26 He was in his lyue euer ryȝt ryche Of richesse before al oþer he was vnliche.

b. Differing from, dissimilar to, the thing or person in question. Also *absol.*

c **1374** CHAUCER *Boeth.* IV. vi. (1868) 138 Ne it ne is nat an vnlyke miracle to hem þat ne knowen it nat. **1542** UDALL *Erasm. Apoph.* 5 Nor a muche vnlyke aunswere dyd Wylliam, late archebishop of Canterbury,..gyue vnto me. **1595** DANIEL *Civ. Wars* V. lxxxii, He saw prepard, against his side, Both vnlike fortune, and vnequall force. **1667** MILTON *P.L.* VI. 517 Part hidd'n veins diggd up (nor hath this Earth Entrails unlike) of Mineral and Stone. **1847** HELPS *Friends in C.* Ser. I. I. ix. 166 Not only like likes like, but unlike likes unlike. **1865** SWINBURNE *Atalanta* 620 A god Faultless; whom I that love not, being unlike, Fear, and give honour. **1877** E. R. CONDER *Bas. Faith* ii. 81 Awaiting the presence of unlike atoms to call them forth in turn.

c. *sb.* A person differing from another or others.

13.. *Sir Beues* (A.) 1099 Her is..min vnliche, Brademond king, þat is so riche. [Cf. UNILICHE *sb.*]

1875 JOWETT *Plato* (ed 2) III. 219 The just does not desire more than his like but more than his unlike. **1896** *Pop. Sci. Monthly* Feb. 494 As long as it remains a stranger and an unlike.

4. Presenting points of difference or dissimilarity; not uniform or even; unequal.

c **1375** *Cursor M.* 7917 (Fairf.), þer was wonande þat was vn-like ij men a pouer and a rike. **1387** TREVISA *Higden* (Rolls) VI. 289 Þere was unleche noumbre of array of knyȝtes, for aȝenst an hondred..come a þowsand. **1535** COVERDALE *Ecclus.* xxvi. 7 Whan an vnlike pare of oxen must drawe together. *c* **1550** H. LLOYD *Treasury of Health* b 5 If the water do appeare vnlike of substance. **1642** J. EATON *Honey-c. Free Justif.* 261 That unlike likenesse betweene Adam and Christ, which the Apostle speaks of, Rom. 5. **1645** MILTON *Tetrach.* 9 Where the different sexe in most resembling unlikenes, and most unlike resemblance, cannot but please best.

5. Unlikely, improbable. Now *dial.* or *arch.*

a. With subordinate clause.

c **1400** *Destr. Troy.* 565 The perlouse pointtes þat passe you behoues, Hit is vnlike any lede with his liffe pas. **1400–10** CLANVOWE *Cuckow & Night.* ix, Hit is vnlyk for to be That eny herte shulde slepy be [etc.]. **1535** CROMWELL in Merriman *Life & Lett.* (1902) I. 413 It is not vnlike but that the saide Duke hathe ben deceyued. **1577** HANMER *Anc. Eccl. Hist.* (1663) 235 Neither is it unlike, but that these circumstances might be. **1610** HEALEY *St. Aug. Citie of God, Vives' Comm.* VIII. xi. 317 It is vnlike that so sharpe a wit.. found not the difference and multitude of things. **1729** T. INNES *Crit. Essay* (1879) 230 In process of time..it is not unlike there might come..new colonies from Spain. **1795** SOUTHEY *Joan of Arc* III. 401 Whether so [it is] not unlike Heaven might vouchsafe its gracious miracle. *a* **1905** in *Eng. Dial. Dict.* (Yks., Warw.).

b. With inf.

1400–10 [see a]. **1538** HENRY VIII in *Wyatt's Wks.* (1816) II. 498 Unjust..demands, and unlike to proceed out of a willing heart to conclude. **1584** R. SCOT *Discov. Witchcr.* III. xviii. 54 Being through age unlike to live one whole yeare. **1626** in Rushw. *Hist. Coll.* (1659) I. 286 He thought the Match very unlike to be effected. **1655** EARL ORRERY *Parthen.* I. I. 26 This Arabian was not altogether unlike to escape unpunished. **1665** BOYLE *Occas. Refl.* I. iii. 168 Blessings, that I do not so much as know of, and which consequently I am very unlike particularly to acknowledge.

†**c.** Without likelihood *of* something. *Obs.*⁻¹

1559 *Mirr. Mag., Fall R. Tresilian* xiv, Thus all went to wracke vnlyke of remedie.

un'like, *adv.* Forms: 4–5 vnliche, 4 onlyche; 4–7 vnlike (5 -lyk, 6 -lyke), 7, 9 unlike. [UN-¹ 11 b. Cf. UNILICHE *adv.*]

†**1. a.** Unevenly, unequally; in a higher or lower degree. *Obs.*

a **1300** *Fragm. Seven Sins* 55 in *E.E.P.* (1862) 20 Worldis wel fallip vnliche, and noȝt euch man ilich. **1390** GOWER *Conf.* III. 89 Theologie in such a wise Of hih science and hih aprise Above alle othre stant unlike. *c* **1425** WYNTOUN *Cron.* VIII. xvi. 2594 Na man..euer couþ tell..A maire commendable memore, As þai did of þis pure kinrik, In þat batall bodin vnlike.

†**b.** Incomparably. *Obs.*

14.. *R. Gloucester's Chron.* (MS. Digby 205) fol. 19 b, Cloten hadde most riȝte to þis kyngeryche But þe oþere were strenger & rycher vnliche [*v.r.* onlyche]. *c* **1425** *Cursor M.* 5325 (Trin.), Þe kyng lete write lettres ȝare To gider alle ..þe beste in þat londe vnliche.

2. †**a.** Differently, diversely. Also const. *to*.

1526 *Pilgr. Perf.* (W. de W. 1531) 5 Whiche the Romayns vsed, but vnlyke to vs. **1552** HULOET, Vnlyke or in a diuers fashyon, *dissimiliter*. **1595** in *Cath. Rec. Soc. Publ.* V. 350 Some tyme yt pleaseth God to reveale his wille..by dreames, as He did to Joseph, Pharo, and others, and here not unlike to His designed martyr.

b. In a manner differing from (that of a specified person).

1593 SHAKS. *2 Hen. VI*, I. i. 189 Oft haue I seene the haughty Cardinall..demeane himselfe Vnlike the Ruler of a Common-weale. **1619** SIR A. GORGES tr. *Bacon's De Sap. Vet.* 82 This Loue..directing his pace..by that which it perceaues neerest, not vnlike blind men that goe by feeling. **1634** SIR T. HERBERT *Trav.* 14 A little haire before, bauld else-where, not vnlike occasion. **1818** SCOTT *Br. Lamm.* xxi, The Master has treated me unlike a gentleman. **1841** W. SPALDING *Italy & It. Isl.* II. 387 They stand apart from all the others, because, unlike these, they applied [etc.].

†**3.** Improbably; unlikely. *Obs.*

a **1548** HALL *Chron., Hen. V*, 67 b, Some say that he was therto stirred..by the dolphyn (and not vnlike). **1596** SPENSER *F.Q.* V. v. 38 And, though (vnlike) they should for euer last, Yet in my truthes assurance I rest fixed fast.

†**un'like**, *v.*[1] *Obs. rare.* [UN-[1] 14.] **a.** *intr.* To become displeased. **b.** *trans.* To displease.

c **1275** LAY. 3266 Leir king was wel ipaid and eft onlikede. *c* **1380** WYCLIF *Sel. Wks.* II. 267 He haþ sorwe of þe synne, bi resoun þat it unlikiþ God.

un'like, *v.*[2] *rare.* [UN-[2] 7.] *intr.* To give up liking; to cease to like.

1761 MRS. F. SHERIDAN *Sidney Bidulph* I. 183 My heart is not in a disposition to love... I cannot compel it to like and unlike, and like anew at pleasure.

un'lik(e)able, *a.* (UN-[1] 7 b.)

1841 L. HUNT *Seer* II. (1864) 1 Without trying to render it unlikeable from its inferiority. **1888** *Athenæum* 31 March 396/1 There are touches about her that..make her unlikable.

un'liked, *ppl. a.* (UN-[1] 8, 8 c.)

1561 B. GOOGE *Palingenius' Zodiac Life* I. A j b, Not worse vnliked now shal I be, yf that thou wylt me blesse. **1620** BP. HALL *Hon. Marr. Clergy* I. xxvii. (1628) 769 That more vnliked epistle which Ignatius wrote to Saint John. **1641** (*title*), An Aprovd Answer to the partiall and unlikt of Lord Digbies Speech to the Bill of Attainder.

un'likelihood. [UN-[1] 12. Cf. UNLIKELY *a.*, and MDa. *uligelighed.*]

†**1.** Unlikeness, dissimilarity, discrepancy. *Obs.*

1483 CAXTON *Gold. Leg.* 273/1, I fond myself right fer fro the in a Regyon of unlykelyhode [L. *dissimilitudinis*]. **1550** THOMAS *Ital. Dict.*, *Disaguaglianza*, vnseemelinesse, vnlikelyhoode, or the difference that is betwene the comparison of one thyng to an other. **1564** *Brief Exam.* 20 b, Euery man..may see a great vnlikelyhood betwixt those tymes and ours. **1613** PURCHAS *Pilgrimage* (1614) 573 By which likenesse in name great confusion and vnlikelihoods haue happened in Historie.

2. The state or fact of being unlikely; improbability.

1548 UDALL, etc. *Erasm. Par. John* xix. 109 So muche vnlikelyhoode was it, that the felowship of punishement should defyle hym. **1598** R. BERNARD tr. *Terence, Andria* II. ii, Hauing gathered by sundrie signes and coniectures the vnlikelihood of the marriage. **1646** EARL MONM. tr. *Biondi's Civil Wars* IX. 199 By the Unlikelyhood and Impossibility that he should escape the hands of a Crafty..Uncle. **1695** J. EDWARDS *Perfect. Script.* 238 There was no unlikelihood of the thing. **1767** MRS. DELANY *Life & Corr.* Ser. II. (1862) I. 116 Knowing the unlikelihood of your being to return to us. **1794** PALEY *Evid.* II. viii, The extreme unlikelihood that such men should engage in such a measure. **1860** MISS YONGE *Stokesley Secr.* xii, The exceeding unlikelihood of a girl like Elizabeth committing..a theft. **1877** FREEMAN *Norm. Conq.* I. vi. 462 Statements which have no inherent unlikelihood in them.

b. With *a* and pl. An improbable occurrence, fact, statement, etc.

a **1550** LELAND *Itin.* (1769) II. 35 Dyvers Brethren dyed.., and by a great vnlykelihod al the Landes descendid to.. the Yonggest of the Brethren. **1561** DAUS tr. *Bullinger on Apoc.* (1573) 2, I will shew the lykelyhodes and the vnlykelyhodes. **1647** JER. TAYLOR *Lib. Proph.* ii. 41 The rarest mixture..of unlikelihoods that I have observed. **1682** LUTTRELL *Brief Rel.* (1857) I. 188 By the severall contradictions and unlikelyhoods in his evidence. **1738** G. LILLO *Marina* III. ii, What strange unlikelihood assaults my mind! **1814** SOUTHEY *Roderick* XII. 14, I will believe that we have days in store Of hope,.. Yea, maugre all unlikelihoods, ..of peace. **1862** LEVER *Barrington* xv, He hesitated how to measure an unlikelyhood.

un'likeliness. [UN-[1] 12. Cf. prec. and next.]

†**1.** Unsuitableness. *Obs.*

c **1374** CHAUCER *Troylus* I. 16 For I þat god of loues seruantz serue Ne dar to loue for myn vnlikelynesse.

†**2.** Unseemliness, unbecomingness. *Obs.*

1456 SIR G. HAYE *Law Arms* (S.T.S.) 190 Nevertheles and he saw..him mak grete repaire till his hous, and unlyklynes, he mycht mak him..exhortacioun to nocht mak sik unlikly repaire. **1685** H. MORE *Paralip. Prophet.* xxxiv. 306 What unlikeliness or Indecorum is it, that Proclamation be made who he is, that shall..[open] the Book?

†**3.** Dissimilarity, discrepancy. *Obs.*

1561 T. NORTON *Calvin's Inst.* II. 143 It shall be sufficient that we wey the wordes of one of them, to attain the meaning of them both. Albeit, there is some vnlikelinesse betwene them. **1604** T. WRIGHT *Passions* v. iv. 189 Likelinesse or vnlikelinesse are also relatives, and consequently belong to this same predicament. *c* **1620** BP. HALL *Contempl.*, *N.T.* II. ii, Neither was there more unlikeliness in their disposition and cariage, than similitude in their function. **1730** BAILEY (fol.), *Dissimilitude*, unlikeliness.

4. Unlikelihood, improbability.

1614 RALEIGH *Hist. World* III. vii. §4. 82 Whether Themistocles perceiued much vnlikelinesse of good successe [etc.]. **1690** LOCKE *Human Understanding* IV. xv. §2. 332 There being degrees herein, from the very neighbourhood of Certainty and Evidence, quite down to Improbability and Unlikeliness. **1841** GEN. P. THOMPSON *Exerc.* (1842) VI. 160 The unlikeliness that he should get what he asked for. **1881** SAINTSBURY *Dryden* 72 The unlikeliness of his ever having been a very fervent Roundhead.

un'likely, *a.* (and *sb.*). [UN-[1] 7. Cf. ON. *úlíkligr* (Icel. *ólíklegur*, MSw. *olikliker*, Sw. *olikli*g, MDa. *uligelig*, Norw. *ulikleg*).]

1. Not likely to occur or come to pass; improbable in respect of occurrence.

1375 BARBOUR *Bruce* IX. 670 He oft full vnlikly thing Brocht rycht weill to full gud ending. **1488** *Cely Papers* (Camden) 169 They of Bruges sayth all schall be well schorttly but hytt ys onlyckly. **1513** DOUGLAS *Æneid* XI. viii. 119 Tyme.. Reducit hes full mony onlikly thyng To bettir fyne than was thair begynning. *a* **1533** LD. BERNERS *Gold. Bk. M. Aurel.* xxxvi. (1536) R ii, The more yll they vtter, the more vnlykely is the redres therof ageyn. *c* **1580** *Bugbears* I. ii. 121 Why is it a thing vnpossyble or vnlikelie that sprites wil deall withe gold? **1642** D. ROGERS *Naaman* 200 Thus Papists conceiue it an unlikelyer thing, that [etc.]. **1692** BENTLEY *Boyle Lect.* 218 Which makes it..more improbable, that they should interfere..even in the last and unlikeliest instance. **1861** PALEY *Æschylus* (ed. 2) *Supplices* 979 *note*, However, κᾆωρα is an unlikely crasis.

b. Not likely to be true or correct; improbable in respect of fact.

1592 SHAKS. *Ven. & Ad.* 989 The one doth flatter thee in thoughts unlikely, In likely thoughts the other kills thee quickly. **1613** PURCHAS *Pilgrimage* (1614) 595 Josephus and Eusebius thinke them to bee the Israelites, which is vnlikely. **1673** DRYDEN *Marr. à la Mode* III. i, They tell, for news, such unlikely stories! **1712** J. JAMES tr. *Le Blond's Gardening* 141 An Opinion very unlikely, to believe Trees have their Male and Female. **1780** *Mirror* No. 73, If this..be the effect of habit, which is not unlikely. **1871** FREEMAN *Norm. Conq.* IV. xviii. 231 The presence of Matilda..at such a time is in itself unlikely.

c. Not likely, in various implications.

1535 COVERDALE *Ecclus.* xi. 6 Many tyrauntes haue bene fayne to syt downe vpon the earth, & ye vnlickly hath worne ye crowne. **1593** *Sidney's Arcadia* IV. ¶1 That by unlikeliest meanes greatest matters may come to conclusion. **1622** DONNE *Serm.* 25 A farre vnlikelier sort of people, then any of these. **1656** COWLEY *Davideis* IV. 828 Nor would ill Fate that meant me to surprise, Come cloath'd in so unlikely a Disguise. **1694** ATTERBURY *Serm. Isaiah lx.* 22 14 This..was an Unlikely way of gaining Proselytes. **1749** LAVINGTON *Enthus. Meth. & Papists* II. (1754) 129 He cures Diseases.. with unlikely Remedies. **1774** G. WHITE *Selborne* lxi, A succession [of swifts] still haunts the same unlikely roofs. **1847** C. BRONTË *J. Eyre* xxxiv, That a poor lad was come, at that unlikely time, to fetch Mr. Rivers. **1855** A. J. MORRIS *Words for Heart & Life* iii. 52 God is in the habit of employing unlikely instruments. **1898** 'MERRIMAN' *Roden's Corner* ii, Cases where brilliant men have failed and unlikely ones have covered themselves with..glory.

Comb. **1858** FABER *Spir. Confer.* (1870) 131 Those vices of which the unlikeliest-looking souls are often the likeliest to be guilty.

d. *sb.* An unlikely person.

1867 LATHAM *Black & White* 98 He goes round with his ..papers, dealing one to each passenger likely or unlikely (because the unlikelies would be offended if omitted).

2. With complement: **a.** With *to* and inf. (active or passive).

1395 PURVEY *Remonstr.* (1851) 84 The noueltees of this Innocent ben vnlicli to be sothe. **1412-20** LYDG. *Chron. Troy* IV. 23 Vnlikly [it was] euere vs to han had victorie. *c* **1450** *Mirk's Festial* 140 Ierusalem..was þe strengest cyte yn all þe world, and vnlykly forto haue ben wonon. **1611** FLORIO, *Inaccadeuole*, vnlikely to chance or befall. **1658** OSBORNE *Adv. Son* Wks. (1673) 112 The not unlikeliest to know Truth. **1711** STEELE *Spect.* No. 143 ¶1 It will be much more unlikely for us to be well-pleased. **1764** *Museum Rust.* IV. 11 Salt-petre Bay, which is not unlikely to have been so denominated from salt-petre there. **1842** LOUDON *Suburban Hort.* 377 They are the most unlikely to become fruit-buds. **1890** 'R. BOLDREWOOD' *Col. Reformer* (1891) 216 He was as unlikely as Grahame to take..to the improvement of the common people.

b. With *that* and clause.

1412-20 LYDG. *Chron. Troy* IV. 3243 For now, allas! vnlikly is þat we Shal euere wynne..þis cite. **1722** WOLLASTON *Relig. Nat.* v. (1724) 82 Make him understand how unlikely a thing it is, that they should be placed there only to adorn..a canopy over our heads. **1855** *Orr's Circ. Sci., Inorg. Nat.* 226 It is not unlikely that the gas thus formed occupies the place of water. **1884** THOMPSON *Tumours of Bladder* 55 It is not unlikely that some of these may be congenital.

†**3.** Unsuitable, unsuited; not fit or proper. *Obs.*

c **1386** CHAUCER *Merch. T.* 936 That whan I considere youre beautee, And ther with al the vnlikly elde of me, I may nat certes..Forbere to been out of youre compaignye. *c* **1440** CAPGRAVE *Life St. Kath.* III. 782 His clothis to his woordis arn ful onlykly. **1470-85** MALORY *Arthur* II. viii. 84 Thou art a boystous man and an vnlykely to telle of suche dedes. **1571** *Southampton Court Leet Rec.* (1905) I. 77 Such as arre..unlyklye and unmeete men to serve for that poorpose. **1588** *Nottingham Rec.* LV. 221 Yt ys an onlykelye house for suche one to dwelle there.

b. Unseemly, unbecoming; not acceptable or agreeable; objectionable, distasteful. *Obs.* exc. *dial.*

1456 [see UNLIKELINESS 2]. *c* **1470** HENRY *Wallace* II. 263 On a caar wnlikly thai him cast. *a* **1586** SIDNEY *Arcadia* II. ii. (1912) 153 For a very unlikely envie she hath stumbled upon, against the Princesses..beautie. **1590** *Serpent of Devis.* B j/2 The most unlikely person and the most wretch that in any countrye might be found. **1725** RAMSAY *Gentle Sheph.* I. i. 24 Yet I am tall, and as weel built as thee, Nor mair unlikely to a lass's eye. **1889** *N.W. Linc. Gloss.* 586 *Unlikely*, bad, displeasing.

†**c.** Unpromising; poor in quality or condition.

1560 ROLLAND *Seven Sages* 46 This auld tre..fra the ȝoung takis all substance and air;..Sa the ȝoung plant is sa vnliklie maid. *a* **1648** LD. HERBERT *Hen. VIII* (1683) 522 That Forests..should be driven once in the year, and unlikely Tits in them to be killed.

un'likely, *adv.* [UN-[1] 11: cf. prec. and MSw. *oliklika.*] Improbably.

c **1449** PECOCK *Repr.* III. xiii. 361 The oon bifore seid epistle putt and ascryued vnlikeli to Constantyn. **1641** MILTON *Ch. Govt.* I. vii. 40 [He] may fall not unlikely sometimes..into an uncouth opinion. **1716** POPE *Lett.* (1737) I. 146 The pleasures..must undoubtedly be of a nobler kind, and (not unlikely) may proceed from the discoveries each shall communicate to another, of God and of nature. **1830** SOUTHEY in *Corr. w. C. Bowles* (1881) 199 This provides also (most unlikely) in case of his half-craziness again becoming whole-craziness. **1867** FREEMAN *Norm. Conq.* I. v. 298 The church..may, not unlikely, have been raised..to commemorate the event.

†**un'liken**, *v.* *Obs.* [UN-[2] 6 a. Cf. MDu. *ontliken.*] *trans.* To dissemble.

1382 WYCLIF *1 Kings* xiv. 5 Whanne she was comen yn, and hadde vnlikned hire self to be that she was.

un'likenable, *a.* (UN-[1] 7 b.)

1845 BAILEY *Festus* (ed. 2) 46 The earth..Is not so like the unlikenable One As thou.

un'likeness. [UN-[1] 12.]

†**1.** Strangeness. *Obs.*

c **1230** *Hali Meid.* 13, I þis world þat is icleopet lond of unlicnesse. *a* **1380** *St. Augustin* 224 in Horstm. *Altengl. Leg.* (1878) 65/2, I fond fro þe þat fer I was, As in a kyngdam of vnlikenes.

2. The quality of being unlike; want of likeness or resemblance; dissimilarity.

c **1380** WYCLIF *Serm.* Sel. Wks. II. 227 For noo drede licknesse of breþeren causiþ love among hem, and unliknesse is cause of discord. **1398** TREVISA *Barth. De P.R.* II. xii. (1495) c j/1 No violence of tyrannye bendyth theym to oppresse..the nether angellis. Therefore Denys sayth that they vse theyr lordshypp wyth vnlyknesse of tyrannye. **1533** MORE *Debell. Salem* Wks. 998/2 The causes that he laieth of dyssimilitude & vnlikenes, be twene the witnesses. **1548** UDALL *Erasmus Par. Matt.* v. 37 The unlikenes of manners declareth and argueth a bastarde. **1634** CANNE *Necess. Separ.* (1849) 89 Mark..what they speak here, touching their likeness and unlikeness with the papists. **1645** MILTON *Tetrach.* 9 Where the different sexe in most resembling unlikenes, and most unlike resemblance cannot but please best. **1709** *Brit. Apollo* II. Supernum. No. 1. 2/1 We meet with some Characters of Unlikeness in this Similitude. **1772** WESLEY *Jrnl.* 11 Feb. (1827) III. 440 For..unlikeness to all the world beside,..the writer is without a rival! **1846** TRENCH *Mirac.* xxv. (1862) 359 There are..points of unlikeness in the two miracles. **1853** KINGSLEY *Hypatia* xxi, It was..strange in its utter unlikeness to any teaching.. which he had ever heard before. **1875** WHITNEY *Life Lang.* ix. 173 We know of no other way in which this likeness in unlikeness can be brought about.

b. With *a* and pl. An instance of dissimilarity or want of resemblance.

1662 SOUTH *Serm.* (1679) 116 As great an unlikeness, as between St. Pauls a Cathedral, and St. Pauls a Stable. **1667** *Phil. Trans.* II. 611 These two unlikenesses I mention together. **1718** *Freethinker* No. 155 (1733) 240 Such Unlikenesses as, by their Subtility, escape the Observation of Judgments less acute. **1746** W. HORSLEY *Fool* (1748) I. 33 They are the Beau and the Belle; and, if I may be understood in thus speaking, are a similar Unlikeness. **1828** SOUTHEY *Epist. to A. Cunningham* 370, I recognise all these unlikenesses, Spurious abominations though they be. **1879** SIR G. CAMPBELL *Black & White* 22 The likenesses are much more numerous and much more prominent than the unlikenesses.

3. A bad or poor likeness.

1729 T. COOKE *Tales, &c.* 127 His ample Shield..On which th' Unlikeness of the Greek appears. **1843** LONGF. in *Life* (1891) II. 4 In the next number is an *un*-likeness of me, ..in a morning-gown.

†**un'likening**, *ppl. a.* *Obs.*[−1] [UN-[1] 10.] Differing.

c **1430** *Pilgr. Lyf Manhode* I. cxxxii. (1869) 70 These ben thinges gretliche unliknynge and discordinge.

un'liking, *vbl. sb.* [UN-[1] 13.] Want of liking; dislike; †dissatisfaction.

1398 TREVISA *Barth. De P.R.* v. xxxvi. (Bodl. MS.), þe making of þe hert..is þe..wel of meuyng and liking [and] of alle vnliking. *c* **1400** *Cato's Morals* in *Cursor M.* App. iv. 242 Quen þou has of þi þing þorou hap vnliking..behalde þou on oþer men. **1876** MRS. WHITNEY *Sights & Ins.* II. xxiii. 512 A gradual liking that was at first almost unliking. **1886** D. C. MURRAY *First Person Sing.* xxv, Angela had..a genuine unliking for O'Rourke.

†**un'liking**, *ppl. a.* *Obs.* [UN-[1] 10.] Unpleasant, disagreeable.

1393 LANGL. *P. Pl.* C. VIII. 23 Ich hadde leuere..lacke men, and lykne hem in vnlykynge manere, þan al þat euere Marc made. *a* **1470** H. PARKER *Dives & Pauper* (W. de W. 1496) XII. v. 213/1 Yf one corde..in the harpe be broke,.. all the songe..shall be vnlykynge to all that here it. *?a* **1500** *Chester Pl.* (Shaks. Soc.) I. 83 Lorde, I muste doe thy byddinge, Though yt be to me unlikinge. *c* **1520** SKELTON *Magnyf.* 1958, I am lowsy and vnlykynge and full of scurffe. **1570** LEVINS *Manip.* 137 Vnliking, *displicitus.*

un'limb, *v.* [UN-[2] 4.] *trans.* To dismember.

1694 MOTTEUX *Rabelais* IV. liii. 208 Batter 'em, burst 'em, quarter 'em, unlimb 'em,..these wicked Heretics. **1869** J. CONINGTON *Horace, Sat.* (1874) 17 Still The bard remains, unlimb him as you will.

un'limber, *a.* (UN-[1] 7.)

a **1639** WOTTON *Charac. F. di Medici* in *Reliq.* (1651) 364 To which temper more septentrionall unlimber Nations have not yet bent themselves.

un'limber, *v.* [UN-[2] 5.]

1. *Mil.* To free (a gun) from the limber, by detaching and withdrawing this, preparatory to bringing the gun into action.

1802 JAMES *Milit. Dict.* s.v. *Limber*, A two-wheel carriage ..taken off..; which is called unlimbering the guns. **1839** F. A. GRIFFITHS *Artill. Man.* 93 Square can only be formed when..both guns and waggons are unlimbered. **1879** C. R. LOW *Jrnl. General Abbott* ii. 146 Abbott..unlimbered the 24-pounder howitzer.

fig. **1864** TREVELYAN *Compet. Wallah* (1866) 272 Then are the 'English name', and the 'development of the resources of India', unlimbered, and trundled out to overawe the.. magistrates.

b. *absol.* To perform the operation of detaching and withdrawing the limber.

1828 Spearman *Brit. Gunner* (ed. 2) 177 Unlimbering, or Coming into Action. **1875** Clery *Min. Tact.* xi. 136 A H. A. battery..unlimbered and came into action.

transf. **1888** *Harper's Mag.* Sept. 555/1 A travelling band which [was]..in the second-class car, and which good-naturedly unlimbered at the stations.

2. To detach and withdraw the front-wheels of (a boat-carriage).

1853 Douglas *Milit. Bridges* (ed. 3) 92 To launch the bateau, the carriage is placed with the pole towards the river, and unlimbered: by this means an inclined plane is formed.

un'lime, *v.* [un-² 3. Cf. Flem. *ontlijmen* 'deglutinare' (Kilian), G. *entleimen.*]

†**1.** *trans.* To detach, dissever. *Obs.*⁻¹

1225 *Ancr. R.* 256 Þet he wot ful wel: & for þi he is umbe ..uorte unlimen ou mid wreððe. [**1648** Hexham ii, *Ontlijmen*, to Vnglue, or to Vnlime.]

2. To free (dressed hides) from lime.

1885 *Harper's Mag.* Jan. 275/2 This washing in warm water is a preparation for 'drenching', the first process of unliming. **1888** *Pop. Sci. Monthly* Dec. 287 The process of unliming hides and skins.

un'limed, *ppl. a.* [un-¹ 8. Cf. Du. *ongelijmd*, G. *ungeleimt.*]

1. Not smeared or clogged with bird-lime. In quots. *fig.*

1622 S. Ward *Christ All in All* (1627) 36 Christ, whom hee longed to bee with, and would now with vnlimed and vnentangled wings flye vnto. *a* **1672** Sterry *Freed. Will* (1675) 137 It keeps these wings unlimed..by the filth or guilt of fleshly lusts.

2. Not dressed or treated with lime.

1756 F. Home *Exper. Bleaching* 215 This makes limed cloth easily distinguishable from unlimed. **1801** *Farmer's Mag.* Nov. 478 As the grain must have lain in the ground for two years, and none was observed in the unlimed part.

un'limitable, *a.* [un-¹ 7 b, 5 b.] Incapable of being limited; illimitable.

In frequent use from *c* 1610 to *c* 1650.

1604 Marston *Malcontent* i. vi, O vnlimitable impudencie! **1690** Locke *Govt.* i. ii. (1694) 9 An Absolute, Arbitrary, Unlimited, and Unlimitable Power. **1716** M. Davies *Athen. Brit.* iii. *Diss. Drama* 33 In talking so much ..of other People's unlimitable Liberty of Thinking and Worshipping.

un'limited, *ppl. a.* [un-¹ 8.]

1. Not limited or restricted in amount, extent, or degree: **a.** Of power or authority, a rule, etc.

c **1445** Pecock *Donet* 129 Which gouernaunce in it silf is vnlimited and vnassigned to eny special tyme. *a* **1586** Sidney *Arcadia* iii. i. (1912) 355 It must be an unlimited Monarchy. *Ibid.* xx. 472, I know thy power is not unlimited. **1644** Hunton *Vind. Treat. Monarchy* v. 45 That the Power of the Monarch in this Frame is not unlimited. **1690** [see prec.]. **1717** Lady M. W. Montagu *Let. to C'tess of Bristol* 1 April, The unlimited power of these fellows. **1777** Cook *Third Voyage* ii. xi. (1784) I. 406 The power of the king is unlimited. *a* **1850** Calhoun *Wks.* (1874) III. 234 Money is not only the sinew of war, but of politics, over which..it exercises almost unlimited control. *Ibid.* VI. 133 A government of unlimited powers.

b. In other applications.

a **1586** Sidney *Arcadia* iii. iv. (1912) 371 All such, whom ..youth-like mindes did fill with unlimited desires. **1602** Marston *Antonio's Rev.* iii. ii, The curse of Heaven raines In plagues unlimited through all his daies. **1647** Clarendon *Hist. Reb.* i. §18 The expences of the Court..[were] vast, and unlimited by the old good rules of economy. *a* **1704** T. Brown *Praise Drunken.* Wks. 1730 I. 35 Their highest excellency consists in having their will unlimited by any superior power. **1782** Priestley *Corrupt. Chr.* I. ii. 158 The absolute and unlimited declarations of the divine mercy. **1846** Mrs. Marsh *Father Darcy* II. 149 My confidence in his talents and energy is unlimited. **1878** Jevons *Prim. Pol. Econ.* 19 We never want an unlimited quantity of anything.

transf. **1837** Carlyle *Fr. Rev.* iii. ii. vi, So violent.. are the Limited Patriots and the Unlimited.

2. Not limited in number.

1665 Sir T. Herbert *Trav.* (1677) 308 Four Wives the Law tolerates, Concubines are unlimited.

3. *Math.* (See quots.)

1704 J. Harris *Lex. Techn.* I. s.v., Unlimited Problem.. is such a Problem in Mathematicks, as is capable of Infinite Solutions. **1843** *Penny Cycl.* XXVI. 31/1 *Unlimited*,..is frequently used by mathematical writers, in the same manner as *Indefinite*, to avoid the entrance of the word *Infinite*. It is also used to describe a problem which may have an infinite number of answers, and which is called an unlimited problem.

4. Of a hydroplane: having no limit placed on its engine capacity. Also *absol.* as *sb. U.S.*

[**1953** W. A. Shrader *Fifty Yrs. of Flight* 54 Fifth Annual All-American Air Races are held at Miami, Fla. In the free-for-all unlimited engine displacement race, James Wedell is the winner.] **1956** *Rudder* Apr. 40/2 A dozen open regattas for unlimited inboard hydroplanes have been scheduled. **1959** *Yearbk. Amer. Power Boat Assoc.* 165 Unlimited Hydroplanes shall be designated by the prefix letter 'U'. **1962** *New Yorker* 29 Sept. 102/2 The sleek-shaped unlimiteds, gaily painted like some archaic 'flying circus'. **1972** *Collier's Encycl. Year Bk. 1971* 521 Unlimiteds, those manta-ray shaped thunderboats that have over 200 mph on straightaways. **1976** *World Bk. Year Bk.* 218 The national championship series for unlimited hydroplanes consisted of 10 races with $350,000 in purses.

un'limitedly, *adv.* [un-¹ 11: cf. prec.] Without limitation.

1611 Florio, *Sterminatamente*,..infinitely, vnlimitedly. *a* **1639** W. Whateley *Prototypes* ii. xxvi. (1640) 81 It is an easie thing for inferiours to obey their Governours..a little too unlimitedly. *a* **1680** Corbet *Non-conf. Plea* (1683) 19 The said promise must be understood either unlimitedly, or with limitation. *a* **1716** Blackall *Wks.* (1723) I. 226 If this had been express'd as universally and unlimitedly. **1796** Burney *Mem. Metastasio* I. 238 A great..prince, who deigns to be so unlimitedly my protector. **1836** *New Monthly Mag.* XLVIII. 409 His Grace is unlimitedly hospitable. **1891** Meredith *One of our Conq.* III. xix. 171 He feels the publishers pouring their gallons through it unlimitedly.

un'limitedness. [un-¹ 12.] The fact of being unlimited; absence of limitation.

1641 Falkland in Marriott *Life & Times* (1908) 204 This unlimitednesse and independence is onely in spirituall things. *a* **1664** M. Frank *Serm.* (1672) 421 The unlimittednesse of His power. **1710** A. B. *Answ. to Argts. in Bp. Oxford's Sp. Resistance* 13 The unlimitedness of our Obedience. **1796** Lamb *Lett.* (1888) I. 41 Omnipresence is an attribute the very essence of which is unlimitedness. **1904** A. C. Fraser *Biog. Philos.* ii. 60 It was impossible to believe either space or time limited: it was equally impossible to understand their unlimitedness.

un'line, *v.*¹ [un-² 4.]

1. *trans.* To divest (a garment, etc.) of lining.

1606 J. Davies (Heref.) *Bien Venu* Wks. (Grosart) I. 6/2 Two Kings thus met, make Kingdomes richly thriue, Though it vnlines their Purse with wearing much. **1611** Cotgr., *Desdoubler*, to vnlyne; or take the lynings out of a garment.

2. *intr.* To separate as a lining.

1848 Lindley *Introd. Bot.* (ed. 4) I. 331 They all pass out of each other (*désemboîtent*); they all unline.

un'line, *v.*² (un-² 4 b + line *v.*³)

1598 Marston *Sco. Villanie* i. iv, To morrow doth Luxurio promise me, He will vnline himselfe from bitchery.

un'lineal, *a.* (un-¹ 7.)

1593 Nashe *Strange Newes* H 4, The vnlineall vsurper of iudgement from all his true owners. **1605** Shaks. *Macb.* iii. i. 63 They..put a barren Scepter in my Gripe, Thence to be wrencht with an vnlineall Hand. **1832** [R. Cattermole] *Beckett*, etc. 170 The Men of England..From her last Despot wrung The sceptre,..to grace A wiser not unlineal race. **1884** *N. & Q.* 6 Oct. 264 The ancient manor house.. has long since passed into unlineal hands.

un'lined, *ppl. a.*¹ [un-¹ 8 + line *v.*¹] Not furnished with a lining.

In very frequent use from *c* 1890.

1521 in *Test. Ebor.* (Surtees) VI. 4 My unlynded gowne. *a* **1599** Spenser *F.Q.* vii. vii. 29 Dight In a thin silken cassock coloured greene, That was vnlyned all. **1630** J. Taylor (Water P.) *Trav.* Wks. iii. 89/1 The men..are clad in thin buckeram, vnlined. **1655** tr. *Sorel's Com. Hist. Francion* xi. 19 Although it was not unfashionable to have a Cloak unlined as was theirs. **1861** *Eng. Wom. Dom. Mag.* III. 118/2 Stiff muslin petticoats..are very suitable for wearing with..unlined silk dresses. **1878** March. Dufferin *Canad. Jrnl.* (1891) 408 Our A.D.C.'s unlined suit of tussore silk.

un'lined, *ppl. a.*² [un-¹ 8 + line *v.*² Cf. Du. *ongelijnd.*] Not marked with lines.

1865 Mrs. Whitney *Gayworthys* I. 6 Round fair face, unlined by any perplexity. **1885** Whittier *Pr. Wks.* (1889) II. 316 The faces represented are not so unlined and ruddy.

un'lingering, *ppl. a.* (un-¹ 10.)

1849 De Quincey *English Mail Coach* Wks. 1862 IV. 322 By the word 'sudden' [Cæsar] means 'unlingering'. **1887** Bowen *Æneid* i. 655 Armed with his royal mission of the chief unlingering speeds.

unlin'guistic, *a.* [f. un-¹ 7 a + linguistic *a.*] Not related to linguistics.

1960 [see stance *sb.*² 1 e]. **1962** Y. Olsson in F. Behre *Contrib. Eng. Syntax* 98 Unlinguistic speculations.

un'lining, *vbl. sb.* [un-¹ 13.] (See quots.)

1848 Lindley *Introd. Bot.* (ed. 4) I. 332 Here we have a succession of true unlinings; but in Crucifers..the large stamens offer an example of simple unlining in the full meaning of the word, since they present a separation into two parts only. **1862** M. C. Cooke *Man. Bot. Terms* 87 *Unlining*, a separation of parts originally united.

un'link, *v.* [un-² 4 b.]

1. *trans.* **a.** To undo the links of (a chain, etc.). Also *refl.*, *fig.*, and in fig. context.

1600 Shaks. *A.Y.L.* iv. iii. 112 About his necke A greene and guilded snake had wreath'd it selfe..: but sodainly Seeing Orlando, it vnlink'd it selfe. **1635** Quarles *Embl.* v. ix. 7, I cannot mount till thou unlink my chaine. *a* **1670** Rust *Disc. Truth* (1682) 185 It will unlink and break that chain and method of Gods Decrees. **1822–56** De Quincey *Confess.* (1862) 154 Those fatally tortuous paths of which the windings can never be unlinked. **1890** Talmage *From Manger to Throne* 639 The chain of the most tremendous natural law is unlinked.

b. To detach, set free, by undoing or unfastening a link or chain. Also *refl.*, *absol.*, and *fig.*

1655 R. Crab in *Harl. Misc.* (1809) IV. 483 Those that will not unlink themselves from the world. *a* **1680** Charnock *Attrib. God* (1834) II. 395 He doth..correct those actions, that unlink the mutual assistance between man and man. **1688** R. Holme *Armoury* iii. xix. (Roxb.) 153/1 March to your horses. Vnlink your horses. Fasten your links. **1796** *Instr. & Reg. Cavalry* (1813) 235 The men move up to their horses, and unlink. *Ibid.*, Unlink Horses! **1802** J. Baillie *2nd Pt. Ethwald* iv. iii, (*Stage direction.* The chiefs instantly let go hands...) *Her.* Ha! have I then so suddenly unlink'd you? **1849** H. Mayo *Pop. Superst.* (1851) 79 The attention..is unlinked from the other faculties.

2. *intr.* To lose connexion; to part; to become relaxed.

1641 Milton *Ch. Govt.* i. v. 15 To make a King a type, we say is an abusive and unskilful speech... Therefore your typical chaine of King and Priest must unlink. **1786** W. Gilpin in *Mrs. Delany's Life & Corr.* (1862) III. 372 We travelled amicably, arm in arm,..we had not one occasion to unlink. **1806** H. Siddons *Maid, Wife, & Widow* III. 44 He felt her arms unlink, and saw that a convulsive fit had put an end to all her recollections.

un'linked, *ppl. a.* [un-¹ 8.] Not linked, connected, or united.

1813 Shelley *Q. Mab* vi. 170 Whilst, to the eye of shipwrecked mariner,..All seems unlinked contingency and chance. *a* **1857** R. A. Vaughan *Mystics* (1860) II. viii. ii. 37 So his life is a series of starts; his actions..unlinked, unharmonized.

un'liquefied, *ppl. a.* (un-¹ 8.)

1705 Addison *Italy* 237 These huge unwieldy Lumps [of lava]..remain'd in the melted Matter rigid and unliquify'd. **1857** Spencer *Progress* (1864) 285 Yet the gas remained unliquified!

un'liquid, *a.* [un-¹ 7.]

1. (See liquid *a.* 1.)

1547 Boorde *Brev. Health* cxcvi. 68 b, Take gargarices lyquide and unliquyde. **1611** Cotgr. s.v. *Pot*, Small vessels wherein..liquors, and sometimes vnliquid things, are kept.

2. (See liquid *a.* 6.)

1818 Colebrooke *Obligations* 195 Though evidently due, it is unliquid, so long as the precise amount of it is unascertained. **1865** Carlyle *Fredk. Gt.* vi. vi. (1873) II. 188 [She] had left considerable properties;..but all was rather in an unliquid state, not so much as her Will was to be had.

un'liquidate, *a.* [un-¹ 7.] = next.

1818 Colebrooke *Obligations* 194 Unliquidate damages for non-performance of an agreement.

un'liquidated, *ppl. a.* [un-¹ 8.]

1. Not cleared off or paid.

1765 *Ann. Reg., Chron.* 155/1 They will likewise forfeit all pretensions on their unliquidated papers. **1788** Cowper *Let.* Wks. 1837 XV. 206 The accounts of a large estate unliquidated many years. **1812** G. Chalmers *Dom. Econ. Gt. Brit.* 180 Every war leaves many unliquidated claims. **1883** *Fortn. Rev.* July 104 There will still remain a considerable debt unliquidated.

2. Not made clear or distinct; indefinite.

1780 Bentham *Princ. Legisl.* iii. §10 The best ideas..of such pains..are altogether unliquidated in point of quality. **1818** —— *Ch. Eng., Catech. Exam.* 254 An unliquidated number of instances.

un'liquidating, *ppl. a.* (un-¹ 10.)

1824 Byron *Juan* xvi. xcix, The Sinking Fund's unfathomable sea, That most unliquidating liquid, leaves The debt unsunk.

un'liquored, *ppl. a.* (un-¹ 8.)

1642 Milton *Apol. Smect.* 10, I doubt me whether the very sobernesse of such a one, like an unlicour'd Silenus, were not stark drunk. *a* **1658** Cleveland *Inund. Trent* 60 We whose unliquor'd Hides will turn no wet.

†**unlisible,** *a. Obs.*⁻¹ [un-¹ 7.] Unlawful.

c **1412** Hoccleve *De Reg. Princ.* 3357 Hir spiritis benigne ..Thoghten þat craft vnlusty and alenge, And forbaar it; þei knewe it vnlisible [*v.r.* vnlesible].

un'list, *v.* (un-² 3.)

1793 Pearce *Hartford Bridge* ii. iii, I told him a bargan was a bargan, and that I defied him to unlist me!

un'listed, *ppl. a.* [un-¹ 8.]

1. Not placed on a list.

1644 *God appearing for Parl.* 5 (D.), The names of many are yet unlisted.

2. *spec.* **a.** *Stock Exchange.* Formerly designating securities not dealt in on the Stock Exchange; also (*N. Amer.*), those sold over the counter (see over-the-counter *adv.* (*a.*) b); now in ***unlisted securities market***, a market for securities in small companies admitted for trading on the Stock Exchange but not bound to comply with the rules for listed securities.

1905 *Daily Chron.* 28 Apr. 4/4 Some of the most important securities..are 'unlisted,' and therefore not dealt in on the Stock Exchange. **1921, 1929** [see over-the-counter *adv.* (*a.*)]. **1979** *Times* 13 Dec. 17/5 A new Unlisted Securities Market (USM) has been proposed which will provide a half way house between a private company and an official listing. **1983** *Sunday Tel.* 10 Apr. 22/6 The Unlisted Securities Market (U.S.M.) is now an established part of The Stock Exchange London.

b. Of a telephone (number): = ex-directory *a.* Chiefly *U.S.*

1937 R. Chandler in *Dime Detective Mag.* Nov. 48/2 Willie Peters..did a sideline selling unlisted telephone numbers bribed from maids and chauffeurs. **1942** E. S. Gardner *Case of Careless Kitten* xiv. 137 Mason's unlisted telephone was ringing as he opened the door of his apartment. **1974** 'J. le Carré' *Tinker Tailor Soldier Spy* xi. 84 A belly-ache from Brixton..about the misuse of unlisted Circus telephones for private calls. **1980** G. V. Higgins *Kennedy for Defense* v. 48 Gretchen doesn't give out the unlisted number. If I had a call, it was from somebody important.

un'listened, *ppl. a.* (un-¹ 8, 8 c.)

1787 Burns *Death R. Dundas* 31 Hark, injur'd Want recounts th' unlisten'd tale! **1793** Wordsw. *Descr. Sketches* 119 The thicket, where th' unlisten'd stock-dove coos. **1864** Pusey *Lect. Daniel* iii. 105 Noah was the unlistened-to preacher of righteousness during those 120 years. **1876** Mrs. Whitney *Sights & Ins.* II. 104 One..knows by some fine, unlistened sound,..the nearness of a large body to the touch.

un'listening, *ppl. a.* (UN-[1] 10.)
1736 THOMSON *Liberty* IV. 45 Unlistening, barbarous Force, to whom the sword Is reason, honour, law. **1823** PRAED *Troubadour* I. 215 Brought back from their unlistening sleep. **1839** CARLYLE *Chartism* v, Unlistening multitudes see not but that it is all right. **1897** *Outing* XXX. 450/2 Little Josef talked away to unlistening ears.

un'listy, *a.* ? *Obs.* [UN-[1] 7. Cf. OHG. *unlistîg, -îk*, and Yorks. dialect *unlisting.*] Indisposed to action; inert; listless.
c **1425** *Orolog. Sapient.* i. in *Anglia* X 334/21 þe wrecchede sowle sodenlye is chaungete, and is madc as scke & vnlistyc. *c* **1440** *Promp. Parv.* 366/1 On-lysty, or lystles, *deses.* **1597** *Guistard & Sismond* C 3, He waxed all vnlisty and also somnolent. *a* **1894** in *Northumberland Gloss.* 756 *Unlisty*, listless.

un'lit, *ppl. a.* (UN-[1] 8 b.)
1852 M. ARNOLD *Youth of Nature* 102 The vastness,..the gloom Of the unlit gulf of himself. **1855** BROWNING *Statue & Bust* 247 The unlit lamp and the ungirt loin.

un'literal, *a.* (UN-[1] 7.)
1851 G. S. FABER *Many Mansions* 368 The completely unliteral freedom of the Latin Vulgate. **1857** E. FITZGERALD *Lett.* (1889) I. 249 Not only..unliteral, but I doubt unoriental, in its form and Expression.

un'literally, *adv.* (UN-[1] 11.)
1737 *Gentl. Mag.* VII. 13/2 As A.P. has..unliterally and ungrammatically translated.

un'literalness. (UN-[1] 12.)
1836 NEWMAN in Liddon *Life Pusey* (1893) I. xvii. 422, I ..do not like diffusive translations; unliteralness is no more diffusive than the contrary.

un'literary, *a.* (UN-[1] 7.)
In frequent use from *c* 1880.
1820 LAMB *Austral. Poetry* Wks. 1908 I. 251 To go and administer tedious justice in inauspicious unliterary Thiefland. **1868** HOOK in Stephens *Life* (1878) II. 482 Here we are very unliterary. **1885** HOWELLS *Silas Lapham* (1891) I. 235 Her talk was very unliterary.
Hence **un'literariness.**
1961 C. S. LEWIS *Experiment in Criticism* viii. 76 His very unliterariness saves him from confusing the two [*sc.* art and knowledge].

†un'literate, *a.* [UN-[1] 7, 5 b.] **a.** Illiterate.
a **1548** HALL *Chron., Hen. IV,* 11 These monasticall persones, lerned and vnliterate. **1688** W. SCOT *Hist. Fam. Scot* p. v, An unliterate Souldier.
b. Unliterary; not interested in reading or literature. Also *absol.*
1950 M. MEAD *Male & Female* xiii. 271 The Gesell norms used by the reading mother or the neighbourhood gossip of the unliterate. **1960** *Guardian* 13 June 5/2 The innumerate humanist and the unliterate scientist were equally inadequate.

un'litten, *ppl. a.* (UN-[1] 8 b.)
1875 MYERS *Poems* 106 Unlitten dawn of day.

un'littered, *ppl. a.* (UN-[1] 8.)
1762 MISS TALBOT *Lett.* (1809) III. 10 Comfort yourself when you sit in your littered room, that..you can sit in it with an unlittered mind. **1855** SINGLETON *Virgil* I. 159 He ..persevering lies mid flinty stones On an unlittered couch.

†un'little, *a. Obs.* [OE. *unlýtel* (UN-[1] 7); ON. *úlítill.*] Not little.
c **1200** ORMIN 726 þat wass till all þe childess kinn Wurrþshipe, & tatt unnlitell. *Ibid.* 16065, I þe ȝife forr þiss mahht Fe mikell & unnlitell.

unli'turgical, *a.* (UN-[1] 7.)
1868 SPROTT *Book Com. Order* p. lxii, Sentiments..more unliturgical than those of the reformers.

un'liturgize, *v.* (UN-[2] 6 c.)
1659 GAUDEN *Tears Ch.* IV. xxii. 609 These were..to Directorize, to Unliturgize, to Catechize..their Brethren.

un'live, *v.* [UN-[2] 3, 4.]
†1. *trans.* To deprive of life. *Obs.*
1593 SHAKS. *Lucr.* 1754 If in the child the father's image lies, Where shall I live now Lucrece is unlived? *c* **1600** CHALKHILL *Thealma & Cl.* 131 Happy had it been, if my stern fate Had..un-liv'd me then. **1621** QUARLES *Div. Poems, Esther* Introd., These braue Ioynt-tenants that suruiu'd To see a little world of men vnliu'd. **1635** [GLAPTHORNE] *Lady Mother* v. ii, in Bullen *O. Pl.* (1883) II. 188 But..suppose he did unlive Thurston in faire duell? **1702** *Burlesque Lestrange's Quevedo* 244 A Plot that may himself unlive.
2. To reverse, undo, or annul (past life or experience.)
1614 BP. HALL *Char. Virtues & Vices* I. 249 As if he desired to vnliue his youth. **1661** GLANVILL *Van. Dogm.* 72 We must unlive our former lives. **1688** NORRIS *Love* II. i. 68 To unravel the prejudices of our youth, and..unlive our former life. *a* **1716** SOUTH *Serm.* (1744) VII. v. 92 Many entertain principles which they defy by their practices, and unlive all that they have believed. **1850** S. DOBELL *Roman* vii, Years are unlived! **1879** *Churchman* I. 16 Not in our power is it to unlive the past.
Hence **un'living** *vbl. sb.*
1599 NASHE *Lenten Stuffe* K iv b, Nor liuest thou [= a herring] by the vnlyuing or euiscerating of others, as most fishes do.

un'liv(e)able, *a.* [UN-[1] 7 b.]
1. That cannot be lived.
1869 E. HATCH in *Mem.* (1890) 48 Stoicism did but show them how to live an unliveable life.
2. Incapable of being lived in. Also with *in.*
1834 M. EDGEWORTH *Tour in Connemara* (1950) i. 43 The want of window curtains..gave the whole an unfinished unlivable appearance. **1898** E. F. BENSON *Money Market* ii, He saw no reason for making his own rooms unlivable-in. **1899** *Contemp. Rev.* Dec. 848 Rural theft makes parts of Sardinia unlivable.

un'lived, *ppl. a.*[1] [UN-[2] 8.] Deprived of life.
1642 H. MORE *Song of Soul* II. i. I. 15 The hidden might And root of motion, unliv'd, unbeen'd they leave In their vain thoughts.

un'lived, *ppl. a.*[2] [UN-[1] 8.] **a.** Not really or fully lived.
1867 J. THOMSON *Two Lovers* (1881) 116 He loathed his unlived life, his unspent force.
b. [UN-[1] 8 c.] With *-in.* Uninhabited; unused by the inhabitants.
1931 H. NICOLSON *Diary* 28 Jan. (1966) 67 The room has an unlived-in appearance. **1943** D. WELCH *Jrnl.* 15 June (1952) 74 There is the feeling about the whole place of utter solitude, stealth, the ghostly, unlived-in, fascinating feeling of week-end houses. **1975** *New Yorker* 29 Dec. 22/1 Any room..has an unlived-in corner. **1979** J. GARDNER *Nostradamus Traitor* xxiii. 95 The vestibule led to the main room, large and uninviting....The place looked unlived-in.

un'lively, *a.* [UN-[1] 7. Cf. ON. *úlífligr.*]
†1. Unliving, lifeless. *Obs.*[−1]
1563 MAN *Musculus' Commonpl.* 43 b, What honor is that to God..to worshippe the dead and unlively shapes as Gods.
2. Not lively, animated, or bright; dull.
1608 WILLET *Hexapla Exod.* 340 Dead and vnliuely colours. **1615** G. SANDYS *Trav.* 114 These [medals] now cut, seeme lame..and vnliuely counterfets. **1723** GAY in *Lett. C'tess Suffolk* (1824) I. 120 This is no unlively picture of a damsel who might please. **1866** *Athenæum* No. 1999. 235/1 Their hopes are not unlively. **1894** *Daily News* 27 July 5/3 This list was considerably thinned before the long, unlively debate concluded.
Hence **un'liveliness.**
1643 MILTON *Divorce* I. 8 All the unlivelines and naturall sloth which is really unfit for conversation.

un'lively, *adv.* (UN-[1] 11.)
1641 LD. DIGBY *Parl. Sp.* 9 Feb. 14 As dully, as faintly, as unlively, as in Language these Actions..have beene expressed.

un'liver, *v.* ? *Obs.* [UN-[2] 9 + LIVER *v.*] *trans.* To discharge (a ship or cargo). Also *absol.*
1637 in Foster *Eng. Factories India* (1912) 10 Haveing unlivered our shipp. **1638** *Ibid.* 54 Begann to unliver. **1805** SIR C. ROBINSON *Admiralty Rep.* VI. 232 That notice was given to the master.., before the whole cargo was unlivered.

un'liveried, *ppl. a.* (UN-[1] 8.)
1823 H. RAVELIN *Lucubrations* 303 A train of liveried and unliveried domestics.

un'livery. *Law.* [Cf. prec. and LIVERY *sb.* 6.] Discharge of a ship or cargo. (Cf. quot. 1867.)
1805 SIR C. ROBINSON *Admiralty Rep.* VI. 232 A commission of unlivery was taken out by the captor on the same day. **1811** SIR WM. SCOTT *Dodson's Rep.* I. 50 Charges attending the execution of the commission of unlivery and appraisement. **1867** SMYTH *Sailor's Word-bk.* 707 Expenses of unlivery and appraisement are a charge in the first instance against the captors of a prize, to be afterwards apportioned by them ratably against the cargo.

un'living, *ppl. a.* [UN-[1] 10. Cf. OE. *unlifiȝende* and *unlibbende*, OHG. *unlëbende*, MDu. *onlevende*, MSw. *olivande.*] Not living or alive; lifeless.
1561 tr. *Calvin's 4 Serm. Idol.* i. B ij b, An vnliuing creature. **1594** SOUTHWELL *M. Magd. Funeral T.* 68 Her heart [seemed but] the cophin of an vnliuing soule. **1611** FLORIO, *Inuiuente*, vnliuing. **1741** in Richardson *Pamela* I. p. xxxvii, Sweet Pamela!.. Thou dear, unliving, yet immortal, Shade! **1809** CAMPBELL *Gert. Wyom.* II. ii, Past those settlers' haunts the eye might roam, Where earth's unliving silence all would seem. **1855** M. ARNOLD *Balder Dead* III. 299 Entreat All living and unliving things to weep For Balder.
Hence **un'livingness.**
1914 D. H. LAWRENCE *Prussian Officer* 80 The sick man lay as if dead... Miss Louisa was heavy-hearted under the load of unlivingness. **1928** [see *rubber-necked* s.v. RUBBER *sb.*[1] 13 c].

un'load, *v.* [UN-[2] 3. Cf. UNLADE *v.*]
1. a. *trans.* To take off, remove (something carried or conveyed); to discharge (a cargo).
1523 FITZHERB. *Husb.* §29 Benes..bounden..are the more redyer to lode and vnlode. **1600–1** in Willis & Clark *Cambridge* (1886) II. 483 Payd to diuerse labourers for.. vnloadinge great tymber. **1643** BAKER *Chron., Eliz.* 91 The wealth of an East-Indian Caraque was lately unloden. **1722** DE FOE *Plague* (1756) 175 The Man caus'd the Goods to be unloaden and lay'd at the Door. **1817** J. SCOTT *Paris Revisit.* (ed. 4) 31 The canal here.. admitting large vessels to.. unload their cargoes. **1884** *Macm. Mag.* Oct. 426/2 One.. green brig..was unloading shaddocks from Naxos.
b. *fig.* To discharge, give vent to (feelings); to communicate or transfer *to* another. Also with *on.*
1593 SHAKS. *2 Hen. VI,* I. i. 76 To you Duke Humfrey must vnload his greefe. *a* **1656** HALES *Gold. Rem.* (1688) 159 An Excuse to unlode your faults upon the Devil. **1697** DRYDEN *Æneis* XII. 1165 Reclined upon my breast, thy grief unload. **1775** SMOLLETT *Quixote* II. 296 Now..you may unrip, and unload, all that lies on your sorrowful heart. **1816** SCOTT *Antiq.* xxii, He unloaded his discontent in such grumblings. **1887** B. HARTE *Millionaire & Devil's Ford* 158 He might unload his gossip because Mamie wouldn't have him. **1904** *Minneapolis Times* 28 June 6 Dr. Dowie has landed in New York and unloaded an interview in praise of President Roosevelt. **1976** J. I. M. STEWART *Memorial Service* v. 66 This was probably why he unloaded on me these useless gobbets of information. **1978** 'S. WOODS' *Exit Murderer* 160 If we succeed in identifying Mr. X I shall unload the whole thing on them [*sc.* the police].
c. To discharge or pour (a liquid). *rare.*
1603 DRAYTON *Bar. Wars* VI. xxiv, When som brook..By swelling waters..shouldreth downe his mownd, And from his course dooth quite himselfe vnloade. *c* **1630** RISDON *Surv. Devon* §42 The river Tale..unloadeth itself into the river Otter. **1891** A. WELCKER *Wild West* 68 He unloaded the other bottle of gin into himself.
2. a. *absol.* To perform the operation of unloading.
1587 FLEMING *Contn. Holinshed* III. 1544/2 Sheluers.. pulled downe the courts as soone as they came to the place where it was needfull to vnlode. **1614** GORGES *Lucan* VII. 269 Those streames..spread their springs abroad, And in Timavas flood vnlode. **1635** J. TAYLOR (Water P.) *Very Old Man* B 2, The Harrow, Mattock,..Goad, And Whip, and how to Load, and to Vnload. **1710** SWIFT *Poems, Atlas* 6 The pedlar overpress'd Unloads upon a stall to rest. **1855** *Poultry Chron.* II. 500/1 One of the company's collecting-carts had just arrived, and was unloading.
(*b*) *fig.*: *esp.*, to confide in someone, to divulge information, etc. Also with *on.*
1885 HOWELLS *Silas Lapham* (1891) I. 83, I was loaded up with a partner that..couldn't do anything, and I un-loaded; that's all. **1904** W. H. SMITH *Promoters* i. 8 I'm so full of it that I shall burst if I don't unload. **1972** 'J. GODEY' *Three Worlds of Johnny Handsome* (1973) ii. 27 If you get along with your cell partner, you usually unload. I did the same with him. **1978** 'D. KYLE' *Black Camelot* xii. 135 'What's the problem with this German? Why won't he unload?'.. 'He thinks once he comes through..we'll knock him off because he knows too much.' **1984** *Miami Herald* 30 Mar. 3 B/1 Your letter exhibits a great deal of bottled rage. I strongly suggest that you unload on a counselor.
b. *Naut.* Of vessels: To discharge cargo.
1799 *Hull Advertiser* 4 May 2/2 The Wasp has come into Leith harbour to unload. **1865** MILTON & W. B. CHEADLE *N.-W. Passage* vi, Whilst it [*sc.* a barge] was unloading.
3. a. *trans.* (and *refl.*). To free, relieve, or divest of a load or burden; to clear of something heavy or bulky.
1591 H. SMITH *Exam. Vsurie* 3 When hee hath loden himselfe like a cart, he shall be vnloden like a cart againe. **1648** T. GAGE *West Ind.* xvii. 114 The Indians helped one another to unload and load the mule. **1697** DRYDEN *Virg. Georg.* II. 554 Besides thy daily pain T' unload the Branches, or the Leaves to thin. **1751** LABELYE *Westm. Bridge* 81 The Commissioners..moved the Board..to unload the said Pier. **1828** STARK *Elem. Nat. Hist.* I. 145 He is trained to lie down when he receives his load and to be unloaded. **1894** S. FISKE *Holiday Stories* (1900) 28 Unload yourself and pull up a chair.
b. To relieve by evacuation. Chiefly *Med.*
1653 J. TAYLOR (Water P.) *Cert. Trav. Uncert. Journ.* 21 If to unloade your Bellies, Nature drive ye. **1764** GRAINGER *Sugar Cane* IV. 124 With sempre vive Unload their bowels. **1822** GOOD *Study Med.* III. 437 Brisk purging..unloads the infarcted viscera. **1875** H. C. WOOD *Therap.* (1879) 441 Tartar emetic is rarely used simply to unload the stomach.
c. To relieve (the heart, etc.) by utterance.
1720 MISS VANHOMRIGH in *Swift's Lett.* (1766) II. 289, I must..unload my heart, and tell you all its griefs. **1808** SCOTT *Marmion* IV. xviii, By that strong emotion press'd, Which prompts us to unload our breast, Even when discovery's pain. **1816** J. WILSON *City of Plague* I. iii. 40 If thou cam'st hither to unload thy soul, Kneel down.
d. To relieve (one) *of* something burdensome.
a **1721** SHEFFIELD (Dk. Buckhm.) *Wks.* (1723) II. 207 Antony..having a secret satisfaction in being unloaded of such a friend; who was..sometimes troublesome. **1776** *Ann. Reg., Char.* 49/2 When America is better peopled,..the plains unloaded of their vast forests and cultivated. **1902** *Westm. Gaz.* 15 Oct. 1/2 A very sagacious tendency to unload himself of mansions rather than to take on new ones.
4. To discharge the cargo from (a vessel).
1599 E. WRIGHT *Voy. Earl Cumbld.* 19 in *Cert. Err. Navig.*, Thre of the greatest..were vnloden of their.. marchandise. **1671** *New Jersey Archives* (1880) I. 64 Wheras a certain Vessell or Ship hath..bine unloaden & loaden contrary to an Act of Parliament. **1748** *Anson's Voy.* II. v. 173 To assist him in unloading the Sloop. **1836** W. IRVING *Astoria* II. 197 Here it was necessary to unload the canoes. **1885** W. H. WHITE *M. Rutherford's Deliv.* iii, 'Guffy'..got drunk, unloaded barges [etc.].
5. †a. To discharge, fire off (artillery, etc.). *Obs.*
1625 MASSINGER *New Way* v. i, [I can now] Unload my great artillery, and shake..the walls. **1712** BLACKMORE *Creation* IV. 444 The powder which destructive guns explode, And by its force their hollow wombs unload. **1755** JOHNSON, *Discharge*,..to unload a gun.
b. To withdraw the charge from (a fire-arm, cartridge, etc.).
1709 STEELE *Tatler* No. 82 ¶8 A Pistol which he knew he had unloaded the Night before. **1734** in *10th Rep. Hist. MSS. Comm.* App. I. 192 His instructions..concerning unloading the Artillery. **1855** KINGSLEY *Westw. Ho!* xxi, 'You took care to flood the powder?' 'Ay, ay, sir, and to unload the ordnance too.'
6. a. *Stock Exchange.* To get rid of, dispose of, sell out (stock, etc.).
1870 J. K. MEDBERY *Men & Mysteries Wall St.* 138 To unload, is to sell out a stock which has been carried for some time. **1876** 'E. PINTO' *Ye outside Fools!* 359 Bulls rush in to aid their philanthropic game of *Unloading*, as we term it, their expensive wares. **1893** *Nation* (N.Y.) 21 Sept. 204/2 The American passion for speculation—that is, for getting hold of something to be unloaded rapidly on somebody else.
absol. **1888** *Daily News* 16 Feb. 6/2 New York...'Bears' selling freely, and 'bulls' unloading, combined to depress values.

b. *transf.* To sell or dispose of (anything); to get rid of by sale; *esp.* to dispose profitably of something that is unwanted or that constitutes an embarrassment. Also with *on.*

1884 *Boston Jrnl.* 15 Mar. 2/3 There is a flavor of reviving an excitement in order to unload oil lands. **1901** MERWIN & WEBSTER *Calumet 'K'* ii. 30 They're going to make a mighty good try at unloading it on him and making him pay for it. **1929** D. HAMMETT *Dain Curse* v. 40 That dinge of yours—Rhino Tingley—was picked up in a hock shop last night trying to unload some jewelry. **1946** *Time* 25 Mar. 82/3 Many a landlord..has already unloaded a building, at a fat price, on his tenants. **1976** 'M. DELVING' *China Expert* v. 56 Tashjian..had only the day before unloaded an extremely dubious Han tomb figurine on an unsuspecting dealer.

c. To get rid of (a person).

1973 E.-J. BAHR *Nice Neighbourhood* xiii. 139 John wasn't about to be any problem when she had everything set up and wanted to unload him. **1982** C. WATSON *Whatever's been going on at Mumblesby?* xvi. 150 Cork-Bradden's main object was to 'unload' the woman on to me, in order to placate his wife.

Hence **un'loader**, one who or that which unloads.

1611 FLORIO, *Scarcatore*, a discharger, an vnloder. **1880** J. W. HILL *Guide Agric. Implements* 469 An efficient Sack Lifter, Loader, Unloader, and Shooter. **1898** *Allbutt's Syst. Med.* V. 24 As in the case of unloaders of grain-ships.

un'loaded, *ppl. a.*[1] (UN-[1] 8.)

1648 HEXHAM II, *Ongeladen*, Vnloaded. **1753** *Stewart's Trial* 273 The unloaded gun. **1800** *Asiat. Ann. Reg., Misc. Tr.* 245/1 Water..sufficient to give passage to large unloaded boats. **1840** *Civil Eng. & Arch. Jrnl.* III. 89/2 This..would only be what M. Pambour properly calls the 'unloaded friction'. **1871** 'M. LEGRAND' *Cambr. Freshm.* 181 Shooting with unloaded pistols. **1899** *Allbutt's Syst. Med.* VIII. 11 Holding out the poker or even the unloaded hand at arm's length.

transf. **1890** 'R. BOLDREWOOD' *Miner's Right* (1899) 83 You're armed, of course?' I touched my left hip significantly... 'Too long in the country to travel unloaded.'

un'loaded, *ppl. a.*[2] (f. UNLOAD *v.*)

1807 J. BARLOW *Columb.* IV. 367 As from unloaded waves, the rising sand Swell'd into light.

†**un'loaden**, *ppl. a. Obs.* [UN-[1] 8 b.] = UNLOADED *ppl. a.*[1]

1599 HAKLUYT *Voy.* II. 132 No man wil iudge their fare good, or their bodies vnloden of stripes.

un'loaden, *v. Obs.* exc. *dial.* [UN-[2] 3.] *trans.* = UNLOAD *v.*

1567 DRANT *Horace, Ep.* xiii. E iij, If that my booke be burthenouse, shift the of it be tyme, Least thou asslyke vnloden the with greater note of cryme. **1663** BP. PATRICK *Parab. Pilgr.* xxxi, They..unloadned themselves of the passions which they felt in their hearts.

un'loading, *vbl. sb.* [f. UNLOAD *v.*] The action of the verb, in various senses.

a **1522** W. LILY *Gram.* (1549) D iij b, Verbes of..lodyng or vnlodyng, will haue an ablatiue case. **1587** FLEMING *Contn. Holinshed* III. 1544/2 To loose..the tackle of euerie court immediatlie before the vnloding or sheluing thereof. **1612** in *10th Rep. Hist. MSS. Comm.* App. V. 467 The unlodeing or bringeinge in of any..merchandize. **1748** *Anson's Voy.* II. xiii. 269 We compleated the unloading of the Carmelo. **1829** LYTTON *Disowned* xvi, The wallet of diurnal anecdote was full, and craved unloading. **1868** GARROD *Mat. Med.* 399 Purgatives..cause..an unloading of the large and small intestines.

attrib. **1755** MAGENS *Insurances* I. 46 The usual unloading Place on the Weser. **1875** KNIGHT *Dict. Mech.* 2683/1 *Unloading machine*, an apparatus for removing freight from boats, cars, or wagons.

un'loath, *a.* (UN-[1] 7.)

a **1850** ROSSETTI *Dante & Circle* I. (1874) 199 To mine arms I took her tenderly: With no rebuke the beauty laughed unloth.

un'loathfulness. (UN-[1] 12.)

a **1470** H. PARKER *Dives & Pauper* (Pynson, 1493) VI. xv, Swete Iesu cryste what is thy gylt That thou thus for me arte spylt, floure of vnlothfulnes?

un'loathingly, *adv.* (UN-[1] 11.)

1836 E. HOWARD *R. Reefer* xlix, My mind looked not unloathingly on..suicide.

un'loathly, *adv.* (UN-[1] 11.)

1844 MRS. BROWNING *Drama of Exile* 2079 Softly and unlothly..We will draw you soothly Toward the Heavenly people.

un'loathsome, *a.* (UN-[1] 7.)

In quote 1583 misused for 'loathsome' (UN-[1] 15).

c **1440** *Promp. Parv.* 366/1 On-lothesum. **1583** MELBANCKE *Philotimus* H j, Shee had not neede to sleepe, that wakes a quicke corse, lest her heauie drowsines breede vnlothsome dreames, or sodeyne startinge affright her sleapinge. **1611** FLORIO, *Inschisoso*, vncoy, vnnice, vnloathsome.

unloca'lizable, *a.* (UN-[1] 7 b.)

1868 SPENCER *Princ. Psychol.* (1870) I. 253 Unlocalizable feelings.

un'localized, *ppl. a.* (UN-[1] 8.)

1823 LAMB *Elia* II. *Sydney's Sonn.*, They are not rich in words only, in vague and unlocalised feelings. **1881** FAIRBAIRN *Stud. Life Christ* xii. 211 The incident could find a place in his history only as unlocalized.

un'locally, *adv.* (UN-[1] 11.)

1602 WARNER *Alb. Eng.* XIII. lxxviii. 321 Superessentiall Being, Selfe-suffising,..Locall vnlocally each wheare, Super-substantiall.

unlo'cated, *ppl. a.* (UN-[1] 8.)

1776 JEFFERSON *Writ.* (ed. Ford) II. 80 The idea of Congress selling out unlocated lands has been sometimes dropped. **1828–32** WEBSTER, *Unlocated*, not placed; not fixed in a place. 2. In America, unlocated lands are such new and wild lands as have not been..designated by marks, limits or boundaries. **1876** BANCROFT *Hist. U.S.* III. xlviii. 346 The duties on trade and the unlocated lands. **1902** *Academy* 23 Aug. 200/2 He was coo-eeing to some party of unlocated climbers in the cloud-enveloped heights.

un'lock, *v.* [UN-[2] 3: cf. UNLOUK *v.*]

1. *trans.* To undo the lock of (a door, chest, etc.) by turning the key; to make capable of opening by this means. Also in fig. context.

c **1400** *Langland's P. Pl.* B. XII. 112 (Wright), Which is the cofre of Cristes tresor And clerkes kepe the keyes, To unloken it at hir likyng. **14..** *Sir Beues* (M.) 4119, I rede, that ye on-lok the yate. **1426** LYDG. *De Guil. Pilgr.* 23934, I cam after..and she gan vnlokke a chest. **1530** PALSGR. 768/2, I unlocke a dore or cofer. **1560** DAUS tr. *Sleidane's Comm.* 327 Yet hath he keyes wherwith to unlock yͤ same [*sc.* city-gates]. **1612** DONNE *Progr. Soule, 2nd Anniv.* 156 Yet Death must usher, and unlocke the doore. **1690** BERLU (*title*), Treasury of Drugs Unlock'd. **1754** GRAY *Progr. Poesy* 92 This can unlock the gates of Joy. **1794** MRS. RADCLIFFE *Myst. Udolpho* xxvi, That leads to the inner court, which I don't choose to unlock. **1812** BYRON *Ch. Har.* I. xviii, The bard..Who to the awe-struck world un-lock'd Elysium's gates. **1847** C. BRONTE *J. Eyre* xvii, I knelt down at and unlocked a trunk.

absol. **1768** FOOTE *Devil* I. Wks. 1799 III. 247 Unlock, Mrs. Minx! your minion is discovered.

2. To set free by undoing a lock; chiefly *fig.*, to allow to flow or come forth; to make open to all.

c **1400** *Gamelyn* 417 He vnlokked gamelyn both hondes and feete. *c* **1412** HOCCLEVE *De Reg. Princ.* 1047 Sone, if oght in þin herte elles be loke, Vnlokke it blyue! com of; what seist þou? **1697** DRYDEN *Virg. Georg.* II. 245 For thee my tuneful Accents will I raise,..Once more unlock for thee the sacred Spring. **1708** PHILIPS *Cyder* II. 60 When the kind early Dew Unlocks th' embosom'd Odors. *a* **1764** LLOYD *Shakespeare* Poet. Wks. 1774 I. 77 Translation has unlock'd the store, And spread abroad the Grecian lore. **1820** SHELLEY *Prometh. Unb.* III. i. 74 Let hell unlock Its mounded oceans of tempestuous fire. **1884** *Times* (weekly ed.) 19 Sept. 6/1 Capital, whether public or private, is so very hard to unlock.

b. To give or obtain access to; to bring to light; to display.

1593 SHAKS. *Lucrece* 16 He the night before..Vnlockt the treasure of his happie state. **1596** —— *Merch. V.* II. ix. 52 Giue me a key for this, And instantly vnlocke my fortunes here. **1649** JER. TAYLOR *Gt. Exemp.* II. xii. 46 Jesus unlock't the secrets of her heart, and let in his grace. **1722** WOLLASTON *Relig. Nat.* v. 101 The future actions of free agents are at once all unlocked, and exposed to His view. **1809–14** WORDSW. *Excurs.* IV. 570 These hoards of truth you can unlock at will.

3. *fig.* To cause to open or unclose.

1531 TINDALE *Exp. 1 John* (1537) 5 The doctryne..is the keye, that..locketh and unlocketh the conscience of all synners. **1634** MILTON *Comus* 852 She can unlock The clasping charm, and thaw the numming spell. **1662** J. DAVIES tr. *Olearius' Voy. Ambass.* 214 The small Presents..un-lock'd the man's breast, and drew out the whole secret. **1792** WORDSW. *Descrip. Sketches* 627 Mournful measures..Unlocking bleeding Thought's 'memorial cell'. **1822** BYRON *Werner* I. i. 306 Wine he shall have; if that unlock him not, I shall not sleep. **1859** GEO. ELIOT *A. Bede* xlv, I know you have a key to unlock hearts.

b. To explain, provide a key to (something obscure).

1636 K. LONG tr. *Barclay* (title-p.), Argenis, or the Loves of Polyarchus and Argenis,..with a Key Præfixed to vnlock the whole Story. **1690** T. BURNET *Theory Earth* III. 21 Such a key as this.., that does so easily unlock this hard passage, and makes it intelligible. **1879** S. C. BARTLETT *Egypt to Pal.* iii. 51 To unlock and read a tongue of which..not even the nature of the language was known.

4. To open, or cause to open, by physical action; to cause to separate or part.

c **1586** C'TESS PEMBROKE *Ps.* (1823) LI. vii, Unlock my lipps, shut up with sinnfull shame. **1637** COWLEY *Sylva, Verses on Virgin*, The breath gives sparing kisses, nor with powre Unlocks the Virgin bosome of the Flowre. **1694** SALMON *Bate's Dispens.* 269/1 That sulphurous Tincture is better able to unlock, or open the Bodies of the Ingredients. **1707** MORTIMER *Husb.* 56 [Clay-lands] hardning with the Sun and Wind, till they are unlocked by industry. **1775** SHERIDAN *Rivals* IV. ii, Unlock your jaws, sirrah. **1802** J. BAILLIE *2nd Pt. Ethwald* II. v, A brawny ruffian, whose firm clenched gripe No struggles can unlock. **1860** TYNDALL *Glac.* I. x. 65 The discharge seemed to unlock the clouds above us.

b. To undo or unfasten by some mechanical operation, or by force.

1606 SHAKS. *Tr. & Cr.* V. vi. 29, I like thy armour well, Ile frush it and vnlocke the riuets all. **1683** MOXON *Mech. Exerc., Printing* xxii. §16 He must Vn-lock and Loosen the Form. **1704** J. HARRIS *Lex. Techn.*, *Detents*, in a Clock, are those stops, which..lock and unlock the Clock in striking. **1757** W. WILKIE *Epigon.* II. 43 The hero..His mail unlock'd; and loos'd the golden chains. **1847** *Infantry Man.* (1854) 109 The sword is..unlocked by the thumb and forefinger. **1892** A. OLDFIELD *Man. Typog.* viii, Some compositors seem to drive up quoins as if they thought the form would never have to be unlocked again.

c. To free from being fixed or immovable.

1735 ARBUTHNOT *Aliments* 97 The Power of a Lixivium..to unlock the Salts that are entangled in the viscid Juices. **1798** WORDSW. *Anecd. for Fathers* 53 Then did the boy his tongue unlock. **1819** SCOTT *Noble Moringer* xxxii, Nor golden meed nor garment gay, unlocks his heavy tongue. **1902** *Brit. Med. Jrnl.* 12 Apr. 879 At first he could unlock the knee easily.

5. *intr.* To become unlocked.

1470–85 MALORY *Arthur* XI. i. 571 When he came to the chamber..the dores of yron vnlocked and vnbolted. **1748** RICHARDSON *Clarissa* (1811) IV. 396, I heard her lady's door..unbar, unbolt, unlock, and open. **1804** *Europ. Mag.* XLV. 13/1 They had but just time to make this arrangement, when the door unlocked.

Hence **un'locked** *ppl. a.*[1]; **unlocker.**

1649 tr. *Warn. Jac. Beem* xxv. 17 Onely the holy spirit is the opener and unlocker. **1890** 'R. BOLDREWOOD' *Col. Reformer* (1891) 399 Once more the unlocked earth receives the plough.

un'locked, *ppl. a.*[2] [UN-[1] 8, 8 c. Cf. ON. *úlokaðr.*] Not locked (up).

1603 HOLLAND *Plutarch's Mor.* 165 Letting all ly unfortified, unbard, and unlockt. *a* **1740** TICKELL *Fragm. on Hunting* 139 Unlock'd in covers let her freely run To range thy courts. **1813** SCOTT *Trierm.* III. xviii, Unbarr'd, unlock'd, unwatch'd, a port Led to the Castle's outer court. **1858** MRS. CARLYLE *Lett.* (1883) II. 366 The only drawer which is unlocked. **1887** S. CUMBERLAND *Queen's Highway*, etc. 63 The unlocked-up land does not appear to tempt the independent purchaser.

un'locking, *vbl. sb.* [f. UNLOCK *v.*] The action of the verb, in various senses.

[**1719** BOYER *Dict. Royal* II, Unlocking, *ouverture, l'action d'ouvrir.*] **1825** J. NICHOLSON *Operat. Mechanic* 509 The scape-wheel teeth..[being] under-cut for the purpose of avoiding friction..and for safe unlocking. **1890** *Retrospect Med.* CII. 128 The sudden unlocking of abnormal metabolic processes.

attrib. **1850** CHUBB *Locks & Keys* 25 An unlocking notch in the outer edge of the slider. **1884** F. J. BRITTEN *Watch & Clockm.* 276 Unlocking Resistance..[is] the resistance opposed to unlocking..by the draw of the locking faces.

unloco'motive, *a.* (UN-[1] 7.)

1828 SCOTT in Lockhart *Life* (1839) VII. 154, I am getting very unlocomotive. **1863** LD. LYTTON *Ring of Amasis* I. 206 Where these ponderous locomotives of an unlocomotive age used to lurk harnessed.

un'lodge, *v.* [UN-[2] 5, 7.]

1. *trans.* To dislodge; to drive out of a lodging or resting-place.

1560 WHITEHORNE *Ord. Souldiours* (1588) 36 b, He vnlodgeth thee, and thou arte constrained to issue out of thy fortresse. **1576** TURBERV. *Venerie* 37 When the houndes haue unlodged the harte. **1672** T. VENN *Milit. Observ.* 181 The Ensigne hath..a Guard ever about it,..neither is it to be disimbogued, or unlodged, without a special Guard. **1703** S. PARKER tr. *Eusebius' Eccl. Hist.* VI. 96 The Gentiles in Alexandria..unlodg'd him from House to House. **1796** *Hist. Ned Evans* I. 9 Groping into the kitchen, [he] discovered Molly in her covert, whom he quickly unlodged.

2. *intr.* To leave one's lodging.

1560 WHITEHORNE *Ord. Souldiours* (1588) 36 b, Thou shalt be constrained of some necessitie to vnlodge, and come to fight the field. **1608** D. T[UVILL] *Ess. Pol. & Mor.* 19 Beeing constrained one day to vnlodge somwhat in hast, and to leaue a certaine sick friend.

un'lodged, *ppl. a.* (UN-[1] 8.)

1634 T. CAREW *Cœlum Brit.* 10 Now that those heavenly Mansions are to be voyd, you that shall hereafter be found unlodged, will become inexcusable.

un'lofty, *a.* (UN-[1] 7.)

1790 ANNA SEWARD *Lett.* (1811) II. 384 [They] wore their dark hair in reverse curls upon their naturally unlofty foreheads. **1869** *Temple Bar Mag.* July 458 Tennyson's feminine, unlofty way of looking at things.

un'logic. (UN-[1] 12.)

1843 CARLYLE *Past & Pr.* III. v, The most Conservative English People..is driven alike by its Logic and its Unlogic..to be wholly a Reforming People.

un'logical, *a.* [UN-[1] 7, 5 b.] Illogical; not involving logic. Hence **un'logically** *adv.*

a **1661** FULLER *Worthies, Kent* II. (1662) 65 All heartily laughed at his unlogical Reason. **1720–1** *Lett. fr. Mist's Jrnl.* (1722) II. 174 That pert and unlogical Writer. **1748** RICHARDSON *Clarissa* II. 40 An un-learned, un-logical girl. **1829** SCOTT *Jrnl.* 27 Jan., If [my reflections]..are unlogical. **1867** ATWATER *Logic* 189 Unlogical is counterfeit thought. **1897** W. M. URBAN *Hist. Princ. Suff. Reason* iv. 45 Sufficient Reason he speaks of as a metalogical truth..which functions unlogically in space, time, causality and motivation. **1922** tr. *Wittgenstein's Tractatus* 43 We cannot think anything unlogical, for otherwise we should have to think unlogically.

†**un'loke**, *pa. pple. Obs.*[−1] [UN-[1] 8 b + *loke*, p.p. of LOUK *v.*] Unfastened.

c **1400** *Gamelyn* 438 þou shalt stond vp by the post as þou were hond fast, And I schal leue hem [*sc.* the fetters] vn-loke þat away þou may hem cast.

un'lonely, *a.* [UN-[1] 7 a.] Not lonely. Also *absol.*

1952 J. STEINBECK *East of Eden* 396 The poison of loneliness and the gnawing envy of the unlonely. **1967** H. W. SUTHERLAND *Magnie* iv. 63 A man should sleep with his wife in winter. It's warm—unlonely. **1971** P. SCOTT *Towers of Silence* III. iv. 197, I am not unlonely.

un'longed, *ppl. a.* (UN-[1] 8 c.)

1849 C. BRONTE *Shirley* xviii, A gentle human form,..unknown, unloved, but not unlonged-for.

un'look, *v.* (UN-[2] 3.)

1748 RICHARDSON *Clarissa* V. 135 He..now turn'd his eyes towards me, then from me, as if he would unlook his own looks.

un'looked, *ppl. a.* [UN-[1] 8, 8 c.]

1. †**a.** Not attended to; neglected. *Obs.*

a **1300** *St. Gregory* 1064 in *Archiv Stud. neu. Spr.* LVII. 70 ȝe witeþ wel hit may nout longe holye churche vnloked be.

b. Not looked *at*, *on*, *to*, etc.; unregarded, unheeded, unexamined.

1563 NOWEL *Serm. bef. Queen* (1853) 226 Such errors or heresy ought not..to be unlooked unto. **1581** W. S. *Compend. or Briefe Exam.* 3 Theyr husbandry unlookte to at home. **1615** G. SANDYS *Trav.* Ded., Leauing no securitie saue..vnlookt on pouertie. **1654** C. WASE *Gratius' Cyneget*, Pref. 7 The occasion that a polite and classical Poet..should have been so long unlook'd into,..and unsought for in our Land. **1856** R. A. VAUGHAN *Mystics* I. 214 The wares lay unlooked at and untouched.

2. Not looked *for*; unexpected, unanticipated. (In predicative use sometimes quasi-*adv.*)

1535 COVERDALE *Wisd.* xi. 7 Thou gauest vnto thine awne a plenteous water vnloked for. **1544** BETHAM *Precepts War* II. xli. K viij b, When they be wythout watch,..then sodaynlye, and vnloked for, rushe vppon them. **1615** G. SANDYS *Trav.* 112 The vnlookt-for assault of Achillas. **1672** T. VENN *Milit. Observ.* 192 He shall see them [*sc.* sentinels] changed at due time, and shall now and then visit them unlook'd for. **1725** POPE *Odyss.* XXII. 164 Oh curst event! and oh unlook'd-for aid! **1837** J. D. LANG *New S. Wales* I. p. v, The causes..producing so unlooked-for and so unfortunate a result. **1878** BOSW. SMITH *Carthage* 30 Elated by an unlooked-for victory.

†**b.** Without prep., = prec. *Obs.*

1553 T. WILSON *Rhet.* 74 Thei..shal bee able to abashe a righte worthy man,..through the sodein quip & vnloked frumpe geuen. **1594** SHAKS. *Rich. III*, I. iii. 214 God, I pray him, That none of you may liue his naturall age, But by some vnlook'd accident cut off. **1618** J. TAYLOR (Water P.) *Penniless Pilg.* C 2 b, This vnlook'd pleasure, was to me such pleasure, That [etc.].

Hence **un'lookedforness.** *rare*$^{-1}$.

a **1586** SIDNEY *Arcadia* III. xvi, The unlookedfornesse of his comming.

un'loop, *v.* (UN-² 3, 4 b.)

1599 NASHE *Lenten Stuffe* G iij, Which made her at breake of day..to vnloope her luket or casement. **1840** BROWNING *Sordello* III. 759 Slouch bonnet, unloop mantle, careless go Alone..Through Venice.

un'looped, *ppl. a.* (UN-¹ 8.)

1716 GAY *Trivia* I. 197 While you with hat unloop'd, the fury dread Of spouts high streaming. **1850** ALLINGHAM *Poems, Pilot's Dau.* ii, [Locks] unbraided, and unloop'd. **1855** BROWNING *Saul* III. 4 The tent was unlooped.

un'loosable, *a.* [UN-¹ 7 b.] Incapable of being loosened.

a **1425** tr. *Arderne's Treat. Fistula* 29 Bounden wiþ tuo knottis or þre vnlouseable. *c* **1550** COVERDALE *Fruitful Lessons* (1593) O iij, [He] dooth..snare himselfe with vnlowsable bands. *a* **1564** BECON *Art. Chr. Relig.* Wks. 1564 II. 128 The simbole..of that vnloseable bargaine, whiche they call the Communion.

un'loosably, *adv.* [UN-¹ 11.] †Indissolubly.

c **1445** PECOCK *Donet* 214 More wo is to me þat þei ben vnlosabli lettid..from þe laboure of meditacioun.

un'loose, *v.* [UN-² 9. Cf. UNLEESE *v.*]

1. *trans.* To relax, slacken the tension or firmness of (some part of the body, one's grasp or hold, etc.).

1362 LANGL. *P. Pl.* A. Prol. 87 Seriauns..Not for loue of vr lord vnloseþ heore lippes ones. **1377** *Ibid.* B. XVII. 139 þe fader was fyrst, as a fyst with o fynger foldynge, Tyl hym loued and lest to vnlosen his fynger. **1545** RAYNALD *Byrth Mankynde* 89 By that the body is opened, vnlosed, and resolued. **1564** *Child-Marriages* 200 And so, vnlosinge handes, they kissed. **1606** SHAKS. *Tr. & Cr.* III. iii. 223 The weake wanton Cupid Shall from your necke vnloose his amorous fould. **1661** CHILDREY *Brit. Baconica* 143 The Salmon..takes his tail in his mouth, and with all his force unloosing his circle on a sudden.. he mounteth up. **1727** GAY *Begg. Op.* I. xiii, My hand, my heart,..is so riveted to thine that I cannot unloose my hold. **1790** MRS. A. M. JOHNSON *Monmouth* III. 152 Her hands were clasped about his neck, which could not be unloosed without the greatest violence. **1834** L. RITCHIE *Wand. by Seine* 35 He found it impossible to unloose her arms from his neck. **1853** MISS YONGE *Heir of Redclyffe* xii, Saying 'Good night..,' [she] unloosed her embrace.

fig. **1757** MRS. GRIFFITH *Lett. Henry & Frances* (1767) II. 47 Providence has wisely ordered, that disappointments.. should, by degrees, unloose the hold we take of this dim spot.

2. To set free from bonds, harness, etc.; to release from confinement. Also *fig.* and *refl.*

1393 LANGL. *P. Pl.* C. II. 198 þat is þe lok of loue þat vnloseþ grace [B. I. 200 lateth oute my grace]. *a* **1400** in *Engl. Studien* XXXII. 19 þou, lady, vnlose me of þo bondes þat I wrot with myn owyn hondes. **1512** COLET *Serm. Convoc.* C iv b, Vnlouse your selfe frome the worldly bondage. **1593** SHAKS. *2 Hen. VI*, v. i. 88 Then Yorke vnloose thy long imprisoned thoughts. **1655** tr. *Sorel's Com. Hist. Francion* III. 67 After she had unloosed and well washed me. **1664** JER. TAYLOR *Dissuas. Popery* I. iii. §1. 159 You can as well be dispenc'd with for that Perjury as the other; and you cannot be tied so fast, but the Pope can unloose you. *a* **1711** KEN *Psyche* Poet. Wks. 1721 IV. 299 The Soul..seem'd from Flesh unloos'd To..spatiate unconfin'd. **1777** SHERIDAN *Trip Scarb.* v. ii, Unloose my lord there, you scoundrel! **1856** KANE *Arct. Expl.* I. xxiii. 288 They were obliged to unloose the dogs and drive them forward alone. **1872** HOLLAND *Marb. Proph.* 10 [To] unloose a soul from purgatorial bonds.

absol. **1851** HT. MARTINEAU *Hist. Peace* (1858) 144/1 The function of that new spirit was not to bind but to unloose.

b. To set free for action; to bring into play.

1735 THOMSON *Liberty* II. 59 When mysterious Superstition came,..Then tyrant Power the righteous scourge unloos'd. **1828** LYTTON *Pelham* II. iv, How wonderfully..your city dignities unloose the tongue. **1831** SCOTT *Cast. Dang.* v, Having unloosed his repartee to this extent.

3. To undo, untie, unfasten (a knot, belt, band, bundle, etc.). Also in fig. context.

1526 TINDALE *Luke* iii. 16 Whose shue latchet I am nott worthy to vnloose. **1551** T. WILSON *Logike* P v, To confute, is nothyng els but..to vnlose by reason, thynges knit together by craft. **1577** GOOGE tr. *Heresbach's Husb.* 39 Then the bundels vnloosed and dryed in the Sunne, are beaten with beetelles. **1608** D. PRICE *Chr. Warre* 1 The Ænigma is disclosed, the knot vnloosed. **1669** EARL ORRERY *Parthen.* III. VII. 200 The Gallies..grappled so strongly, that nothing but Victory was able to unloose them. **1760** STERNE *Tr. Shandy* III. viii, Dr. Slop must have had three fifths of Job's patience..to have unloosed them [*sc.* knots]. **1765** BLACKSTONE *Comm.* I. 358 To unloose those bands, by which he is connected to his natural prince. **1821** SCOTT *Kenilw.* xxxviii, There are other means of disengaging such ties, without unloosing the cords of life. **1847** F. W. NEWMAN *Hist. Hebrew Monarchy* viii. 272 To unloose the covering from his loins. **1860** TYNDALL *Glac.* I. xxii. 155, I now unloosed my scrip.

fig. **1668** H. MORE *Div. Dial.* I. 93 These Experiments indeed strike very strongly on the..senses, but there is a subtile Reason that presently unlooses all again. **1710** R. WARD *Life H. More* 116 Nothing can unloose the Sophistries of the selfish Animal Life, but [etc.]. **1820** SHELLEY *Prometh. Unb.* II. iii. 96 The Eternal..Must unloose..The snake-like Doom coiled underneath his throne By that alone.

4. To detach, so as to get rid of or remove.

a **1470** H. PARKER *Dives & Pauper* (W. de W. 1496) vi. Int. 26/1 Unlouse soo thy richesses from the, that [etc.]. **1555** EDEN *Decades W. Ind.* (Arb.) 214 At which tyme they vnlose the stones, & ryse vppe at their pleasure. **1593** SHAKS. *Lucr.* 136 That which they possess They scatter and unloose it from their bond. **1748** HERVEY *Medit.* (ed. 4) I. 214 Those beneficent Hands, which were..stretched out to unloose the heavy Burthens.

5. *intr.* To become loose or unfastened. *rare.*

1594 CAREW *Huarte's Exam. Wits* 321 The creature easily vnlooseth, because the same was moist and watry. **1697** COLLIER *Ess. Mor. Subj.* I. 143 Without this Virtue, the publick Union must unloose.

Hence **un'looser; un'loosing** *vbl. sb.*

1860 MISS MULOCK *Domest. Stories* (1862) 152 Thus let us think of thee, O Death; gentle *unlooser of life's burthen. **1611** FLORIO, *Dislegamenti*, *vnloosings, vnbindings. **1831** A. W. FONBLANQUE *Eng. under 7 Administr.* (1837) II. 80 The unloosing of Anti-Christ and Satan. **1866** J. H. NEWMAN *Lett. to Pusey* 37 The knot of Eve's disobedience received its unloosing through the obedience of Mary.

un'loosed, *ppl. a.*¹ [f. prec.] Made loose, relaxed; let loose.

1382 WYCLIF *Ecclus.* xxv. 32 Feble hondis and vnloosid knees. **1552** HULOET, Vnlowsed, *discinctus*. **1839** DARWIN *Voy. Nat.* xxi. 603 The strife of the unloosed elements. **1884** *Pall Mall G.* 6 May 1/1 All around him rages the unloosed flood of Moslem fanaticism.

un'loosed, *ppl. a.*² [UN-¹ 8.] Not loosened.

c **1430** *York Memo. Bk.* (Surtees, 1912) I. 194 Pro la vaumpedyng xij parium ocrearum lowsed a retro, xiij *d.* ob. .. Et pro xij paribus unlowsed retro x *d.* ob. **1435** MISYN *Fire of Love* 91 þe knot vnlousyd of drawynge frenschyp sal comforth heuynes of bodily sondyrynge.

un'loosen, *v.* [UN-² 9.] *trans.* = UNLOOSE *v.*

c **1450** *Cov. Myst.* (Shaks. Soc.) 252 There xul ȝe ffyndyn ..An asse tyed.. Unlosne þat asse, and brynge it to me. **1586** D. ROWLAND *Lazarillo* II. (1672) M 6, A Cord fastened about my foot, which..was tied to a great Chest..which though I could, I would not unloosen. **1610** MARKHAM *Masterp.* II. xliv. 294 Forget not..to vnloosen the list and to take it away. **1650** EARL MONM. tr. *Senault's Man bec. Guilty* 335 God..would..teach us that accidents might be unloosened from their substance. **1782** V. KNOX *Ess.* ii. I. 11 Fix them [*sc.* religious principles] deeply in your bosom, and let them go with you unloosened and unaltered to the grave. *c* **1845** J. T. GOODSIR in *Ch. Scot. Pulpit* I. 248 Whose power ..unloosened the dumb tongue of conscience. **1863** P. BARRY *Dockyard Econ.* 189 Ankle chains..riveted together, ..never to be unloosened night nor day.

Hence **un'loosening** *vbl. sb.*

1867 E. S. PURCELL in *Ess. Relig. & Lit.* Ser. II. 476 Everything tends..to the unloosening of all bonds between society and the Church.

un'loosing, *ppl. a.* (UN-¹ 10.)

1593 Q. ELIZ. *Boeth.* III. met. ii. 46 Nature..strains with vnlosing Knot [L. *irresoluto nexu*] eche thing.

un'lopped, *ppl. a.* (UN-¹ 8.)

1573 TUSSER *Husb.* (1878) 78 In lopping,..for feare of mishap, one bough stay vnlopped, to cherish the sap. **1620** BRINSLEY tr. *Virgil* 54 The hills vnlopt lift vp their voices with ioy. **1683** J. REID *Scots Gard.* (1907) 120 Forrest-trees ..with high bodies, and unlopt heads. *a* **1722** LISLE *Husb.* (1757) 359 Those [trees] he had planted with their heads unlopped. **1849** JAMES *Woodman* vii, The dry unlopped shoots, and withered leaves. **1853** M. ARNOLD *Sohrab & Rustum* 409 An unlopp'd trunk it was, and huge.

un'lord, *v.* [UN-² 6 b.] *trans.* (and *refl.*) To deprive of the rank of lord.

1572 in Neal *Hist. Purit.* (1732) I. 288 Because..we would have Bishops unlorded. **1648** PRYNNE *Plea for Lords* 1 The treasonable..designe..to..unlord the Lords. **1669** SHADWELL *Royal Shepherdess* III. i, Those wild desires, That made me..then Unlord my Confident. **1714** ATTERBURY in Beeching *Life* ix. (1909) 261 Furnishing the Reverend Bench with such Members as few Churchmen will pity or regret, when they shall be unlorded. **1828** CAROLINE FRY *Scripture Reader's Guide* ii. 20 He would incline to unlord himself again, and return to his companions in the cellar. **1875** TENNYSON *Q. Mary* IV. ii, We had to dis-archbishop and unlord, And make you simple Cranmer once again.

fig. **1656** S. WINTER *Serm.* 42 The Papists..make void and unlord the second commandment. **1662** GURNALL *Chr. in Arm.* III. xviii. 171 Ye have made void..the Commandment ..ἠκυρώσατε, you have unlorded it.

Hence **un'lording** *vbl. sb.*

1649 MILTON *Eikon.* vi. 52 The unlording of Bishops, and expelling them the House.

un'lorded, *ppl. a.* [UN-¹ 8.]

1. Not having the rank of a lord.

1641 MILTON *Reform.* I. 22 He that will mould a modern Bishop into a primitive, must yeeld him to be elected by the popular voyce, undiocest, unrevenu'd, unlorded. **1808** BENTHAM *Sc. Reform.* 43 For doing Sheriff's work, we should be reduced to men as yet unlorded.

2. Not owned by, or subject to, a lord.

1803 MOORE *To Miss Moore* 54 While Peace..Walks o'er the free unlorded soil.

un'lordly, *a.* (UN-¹ 7.)

1575 CHURCHYARD *Chippes* 40 b, The discourage and infamye of this vnlordly enterpryse. **1626** MIDDLETON *Anything for Quiet Life* v. i, The lord Beaufort's most unlordly breach Of promise to him. **1641** MILTON *Reform.* II. 86 The Pastorlike and Apostolick imitation of meeke and unlordly Discipline. **1832** L. HUNT *Gentle Armour* II. 9 A knight unknown, Who..to mortal fight defies Three lordly knights for most unlordly calumnies.

un'lordly, *adv.* (UN-¹ 11.)

? *a* **1400** *Morte Arth.* 1267 Saise to syr Lucius, to vn-lordly he wyrkez, Thus letherly agaynes law to lede my pople.

un'losable, *a.* (UN-¹ 7 b.)

1647 TRAPP *Comm. Rev.* iii. 11 Not that crown of eternall life (for that is unloosable). **1662** BOYLE *Examen* ii. 11 For they think Motion..an unlooseable Property, congenit to Matter. **1690** C. NESSE *O. & N. Test.* I. 272 Special saving grace..is certainly unloseable. **1882** *Lit. World* (U.S.A.) 14 Jan. 15 It keeps them clean, smooth, in order,..unlosable.

†**unlossed,** *ppl. a. Sc. Obs.*$^{-1}$ [UN-¹ 8 + LOSS *v.*] Not unloaded; undischarged.

1580 *Reg. Privy Council Scot.* III. 331 Merchandis that preissis the said schip to transport thair lynt..unloissit furth of the realme.

un'lost, *ppl. a.* (UN-¹ 8 b.)

1513 DOUGLAS *Æneid* v. ii. 80 Allace! was it nocht lefull, thow vnlost, The boundis of Itail..to haue socht. **1612** R. DABORNE *Chr. turn'd Turke* 2 Heer's 400 Crownes vnlost yet. **1624** QUARLES *Div. Poems, Job* xvi. 10 It is an influence.. vnlost by death. **1746** YOUNG *Nt. Th.* IX. 1071 An Eden, this! a Paradise unlost! **1818** COLEBROOKE *Obligations* 88 An assurance of a ship lost or unlost. **1892** LD. LYTTON *King Poppy* Epil. 57 A few illusions that, unlost, endure.

un'lotted, *ppl. a.* (UN-¹ 8.)

1758 J. BLAKE *Mar. Syst.* 25 Unless he finds another unlotted man to serve for him.

†**un'louk,** *v. Obs.* [OE. *unlúcan*, *onlúcan* (UN-² 3), = WFris. *ont-*, *ûntluke*, OS. *antlûkan* (MDu. *ontluken*, Du. *ontluiken*, MLG. *entluken*), OHG. *antlûhhan*, *in(t)luchan* (MHG. *entlûchen*).]

1. *trans.* To undo or open (a gate, door, etc.); to unlock.

c **1000** *Rule of Chrodegang* x, þæt he preosta gatu.. alyfedum tidum luce & unluce. *c* **1175** *Lamb. Hom.* 127 þet is þet loc þe ðe deofel ne con unlucan. *c* **1275** *Pains Hell* 9 in *O.E. Misc.* 147 Hwo haueþ helle dure vnloke þat þu ert of pyne ibroke. **13..** *Sir Beues* (A.) 3152 Hii vn-lek þe ȝate at þe frome. **1377** LANGL. *P. Pl.* B. XII. 112 Clerkes kepe þe keyes, To vnlouken it at her lykynge. *c* **1420** *Chron. Vilod.* 4510 When all þe ȝates of þe castell weron unloke.

absol. **1377** LANGL. *P. Pl.* B. XVIII. 313 Efte þe liȝte bad vnlouke, & Lucifer answered, What lorde artow?

transf. **1390** GOWER *Conf.* I. 293 So that his lippes ben unloke And his corage is al tobroke. *c* **1450** *Cov. Myst.* (Shaks. Soc.) 28 Oure fflescly eyn byn al vnlokyn, Nakyd for synne ouresylf we se.

2. *fig.* **a.** To unfold, expound, declare.

13.. *K. Alis.* 69 (Laud MS.), Ac whi ich habbe hem þus vnleke, ȝee shullen me after her speke. *c* **1315** SHOREHAM I. 1504 Nou ich wolle ondo þys eft By þe wey of mystyke;.. Nou lestlich schel ich on-louke þys. **1390** GOWER *Conf.* I. 25 That swevene hath Daniel unloke.

b. To evolve or extract.

c **1320** *Cast. Love* 77 [Who] con þat muchel of luitel unlouken,..Alle poyntes he fynde may Of vre be-leeue.

c. To dissolve, destroy.

1377 LANGL. *P. Pl.* B. XVIII. 255 But ihesus rise to lyue,.. And conforte al his kynne,..And al þe iuwen ioye vnioignen & vnlouken.

d. To set free, make open way for.

14.. *Langland's P. Pl.* C. II. 198 þat is þe lok of loue þat vnloseþ [*MS. F.* vnlowketh] grace.

3. *intr.* To open; to go asunder.

c **1315** SHOREHAM *Poems* v. 178 Ine flom iordanes syche He was ycrystned, þe heuene onleake. *c* **1350** *Lybeaus Disc.* 1816 That deys began to schake,..The rof abone unlek,.. As hyt wolde asonder.

un'lovable, un'loveable, *a.*¹ (UN-¹ 7 b.)

1570 LEVINS *Manip.* 4 Vnloueable, *inamicabilis*. **1858** CARLYLE *Fredk. Gt.* IV. viii. I. 465 His masters, though rigorous, were not unlovable to him. **1894** LD. WOLSELEY *Life Marlborough* I. 173 An essentially worldly and vnlovable woman.

un'love, *sb.* [UN-¹ 12.] Absence of love.

1611 FLORIO, *Disamore*, the contrary of loue, vnloue, hate. **1860** PUSEY *Min. Proph.* 541 He now forbids every sort of unlove. **1865** —— *Truth Eng. Ch.* 58 Souls purified..from passion..and all unlove. *Ibid.* 65.

un'love, *v.* [UN-² 3.] *trans.* To cease to love (a person, etc.).

Sometimes possibly 'not to love': see UN-¹ 14.

c **1374** CHAUCER *Troylus* v. 1698, I ne kan..withinne myn herte fynde To vnlouen yow. **1575** PETERSON tr. *Della Casa's Galateo* 8 Ynough to cause men,..if they did loue vs, to vnloue vs againe. **1640** FULLER *Joseph's Coat* 122 How then shall I unlove the world, which hath been my bosome Darling so long? **1712** STEELE *Spect.* No. 310 ¶1 They bid me love him, and I cannot unlove him. **1847** C. BRONTE *J. Eyre* xviii, I have told you..that I had learnt to love Mr. Rochester: I could not unlove him now. **1855** BROWNING *In a Balcony* 582 Remember, I..Would..Do all but just unlove him.

absol. **1561** T. HOBY tr. *Castiglione's Courtyer* II. (1577) H iv, More apt to brawling and chyding,..that love and vnlove al at a time. **1635** J. HAYWARD tr. *Biondi's Banish'd Virg.* 10 If we returne not to our former state of freedome, and unlove againe. **1859** MRS. STOWE *Minister's Wooing* xxv, We never know how we love till we try to unlove. **1881** EMMA J. WORBOISE *Sissie* xv, I am sure one cannot unlove, just because one's esteem is lessened!

†un'lov(e)able, *a.*² *Obs.* [UN-¹ 7 b.] Not to be praised or commended.

c **1450** HOLLAND *Howlat* 227 The Sparrowe..Lyand in lichory, laith, vnloveable. *Ibid.* 917 With vnloveable latis nocht till allow.

un'loved, *ppl. a.* [UN-¹ 8.]

1. Not loved; not held in affection; unrequited with love.

a **1395** HYLTON *Scala Perf.* II. xiv. (MS. Bodl. 592), Vnresonabli he werkiþ þᵗ loueþ not þe souereyn good.. vnsouȝt & vnloued. **14..** in *Rel. Ant.* I. 71 Wo worth love unlovyd! **1503** HAWES *Examp. Virt.* I. xv, Loue neuer vnloued for that is payne. **1590** SHAKS. *Mids. N.* III. ii. 234 Miserable most, to loue vnlou'd. **1645** MILTON *Tetrach.* 9 A neglected and unlov'd race, the fruits of a delusive marriage. **1671** MRS. BEHN *Forc'd Marriage* v. iii, The embraces of an unlov'd maid. *a* **1718** PARNELL *Hesiod* 253 Here Hesiod lies: ..Unlov'd, unloving, 'twas his fate to bleed. **1821** SHELLEY *To Night* iii, Lingering like an unloved guest. **1891** FARRAR *Darkn. & Dawn* xviii, The void of an unloved heart.

2. Not pursued or felt as love.

1606 SHAKS. *Ant. & Cl.* III. vi. 53 You..haue preuented The ostentation of our loue; which left vnshewne, Is often left vnlou'd.

un'loveliness. (UN-¹ 12; cf. next.)

a **1586** SIDNEY *Arcadia* II. xv, The old man..folowed his suite with..each thing..that might help to countervaile his owne unlovelines. **1628** PRYNNE (*title*), The Vnlouelinesse of Love-Lockes. **1681** FLAVEL *Meth. Grace* xii. 250 [It] excludes all unloveliness and distastefulness from Jesus. **1873** M. ARNOLD *Lit. & Dogma* ix. 298 Pulverising alike the historic churches in their beauty and the dissenting sects in their unloveliness. **1892** *Welsh Rev.* I. 754 This incarnation of ingratitude and unloveliness.

un'lovely, *a.* [UN-¹ 7.]

1. Not evoking feelings of love or affection; unattractive, unpleasant, repellent.

1377 LANGL. *P. Pl.* B. XII. 244 For þe pekok..is.. vnlouelich of ledene. *Ibid.* xv. 114 ȝowre wordes..aren ful vnlouelich. *a* **1586** SIDNEY *Arcadia* III. xii, Both [were] wearie of so unlovely embracements. **1670** BAXTER *Cure Ch. Div.* Pref. II. § 6 They are agreed in the assumption, that their neighbour is unlovely. **1742** YOUNG *Nt. Th.* III. 403 By passionately loving life, we make Lov'd life unlovely. **1817** [W. BELOE] *Sexagenarian* I. 35 This unlovely branch of writing [*sc.* satire]. **1889** *Times* 3 Dec. 9/3 This very unlovely quarrel.

2. Unattractive or unpleasing in appearance; unhandsome; ugly.

1393 LANGL. *P. Pl.* C. IX. 262 Ac let hure be vnloueliche, vnlofsom a bedde [etc.]. *c* **1450** LOVELICH *Merlin* 6447 A ful old man..that onlovely was of face & lere. **1513** DOUGLAS *Æneid* VI. vii. 33 The wofull pule, with wattir wnluffly. **1598** R. HAYDOCKE tr. *Lomazzo* II. 133 A discontented woman.. will seeme yl-favored and vnloouely. **1647** TORSHELL *Designe disp. Bible* 7 He that looks upon an unlovely thing, with the eye of love, thinks it lovely. **1734** THOMSON *Liberty* IV. 6 Unlovely forms Of little pomp. **1820** SHELLEY *Sensit. Pl.* II. 42 Gnawing worms, And things of obscene and unlovely forms. **1895** P. HEMINGWAY *Out of Egypt* II. 156 The town of Port Said is unlovely.

†un'lovely, *adv. Obs.* (UN-¹ 11; cf. prec.)

1377 LANGL. *P. Pl.* B. V. 363 Is non so hungri hounde.. Durst lape of þe leuynges, so vnlouely þei smauȝte. **14..** *Langland's P. Pl.* C. XI. 271 (Camb. Univ. MS.), þei lyue here lif vnlouely til deth hem departe. **1613** PURCHAS *Pilgrimage* (1614) 607 The father maketh hatefull loue to the daughter, and the brother is vnlouely louing to the sister.

un'loverlike, *a.* (UN-¹ 7 c.)

1797 JANE AUSTEN *Sense & Sens.* xxxix, Shocked at so unlover-like a speech. **1830** MISS MITFORD *Village* Ser. IV. 19 This unlover-like parting occurred..one fine afternoon. **1893** K. SIMPSON *Yorksh. Stories* 278 Oliver had been cold and unloverlike during the last three weeks.

un'lovesome, *a.* (*adv.*). *Obs.* or *Sc.* (UN-¹ 7.)

13.. *K. Alis.* 6423 The face of heom is playn, and hard,.. Unlossom is that kynrede. **1393** [see UNLOVELY *a.* 2]. *c* **1420** *Chron. Vilod.* 4333 He was an vnlofsom page. **1513** DOUGLAS *Æneid* VIII. Prol. 119 With a luik vnlufsum he lent me sik wordis. **1721**, **1813–25** in Sc. glossaries, etc. (in forms *unlussum, unlo'e-, unluesome*).

†b. As *adv.*

c **1480** HENRYSON *Bludy Serk* 61 Vnlusum was his likame dicht, His sark was all bludy.

un'loving, *vbl. sb.* (UN-¹ 13.)

a **1533** LD. BERNERS *Gold. Bk. M. Aurel.* (1546) Nn viij b, The vnlouyng of women, and the vnkyndnesse of men, which are vices committed of malyce.

un'loving, *ppl. a.* (UN-¹ 10, 5 d.)

1529 MORE *Suppl. Souls* Wks. 326/2 In holye scripture yᵉ father is not accompted for vnlouing and cruel, that beateth his childe. **1597** SALUSBURY *Poems* (1914) 75, I loue, inforst by loues vnlouing charmes, My loue is pure. **1645** MILTON *Tetrach.* 4 To lead a wearisom life of unloving and unquiet conversation with one who neither affects nor is affected. *a* **1718** [see UNLOVED 1]. **1757** MRS. GRIFFITH *Lett. Henry & Frances* (1767) III. 38 The cool, unloving stoic Tenets, that ..are sure to risk nothing for their Friends. **1840** BROWNING *Sordello* VI. 596 A Power above you still,..Which thus you can Love, tho' unloving all conceived by man. **1868** MISS YONGE *Cameos* (1877) I. xv. 116 It was an unloving marriage; but he was much respected and beloved.

un'lovingly, *adv.* (UN-¹ 11; cf. prec.)

1512 in Ellis *Orig. Lett.* Ser. II. I. 197 Thowȝ..the Kings Grace [be]..unlovingli oon sum partise served. **1583** BABINGTON *Commandm.* (1590) 264 Vnaduisedly, & I feare vnlouingly we speake what wee list. **1866** B. NORTH *Ourselves* 3 If I seem..to speak unlovingly.

un'lovingness. (UN-¹ 12; cf. prec.)

1598 FLORIO, *Disamoreuolezza*, vnkindnes, vnlouingness. *a* **1639** W. WHATELEY *Prototypes* I. xix. (1640) 193 A kind of heate and unlovingnesse against the doer of them. *a* **1652** BROME *Eng. Moor* II. iii, Unlovingness of nature, Forgetfulness of blood. **1840** L. HUNT *Seer* I. 83/2 To continue to love every thing which unlovingness has not had a hand in altering. **1868** PUSEY *Serm. Pharisaism* 7 His lack of humility engendered his unlovingness.

un'loyal, *a.* (UN-¹ 7.)

1594 in *Liturg. Serv. Q. Eliz.* (1847) 661 Her most unloyal, desperate, and rebellious Subjects. **1600** HOLLAND *Livy* IX. xxvi. 332 The Romaines found all unloyall unto them. **1741** S. A. LAVAL *Hist. Reform.* IV. VIII. 992 Any undutiful or unloyal Word.

un'loyalty. (UN-¹ 12.)

1560 DAUS tr. *Sleidane's Comm.* 311 What ende..doe you loke of this obstinacy and vnloyaultie?

un'lubricated, *ppl. a.* (UN-¹ 8).

[**1775** ASH.] **1879** *Cassell's Techn. Educ.* I. 66 The tallow melted, leaving the rifle unlubricated.

un'lucent, *a.* (UN-¹ 7.)

1819 KEATS *Song Four Fairies* 61 Before the stains Of the mountain soil they take, And thee too unlucent make. **1837** CARLYLE *Fr. Rev.* II. v. iii, A combustion most fierce, but *un*-lucent.

un'lucid, *a.* (UN-¹ 7.)

1858 CARLYLE *Fredk. Gt.* VII. ix. II. 287 Rebuke which can still be read in growling, unlucid phraseology.

un'luck. (UN-¹ 12. Cf. WFris. *onlok, ûnlok*, MLG. *unlucke*, LG. *unlük*, ON. *úlukka*, etc.; and WANLUCK.)

[The following instance is of foreign origin:—**1556** *Aurelio & Isabell* N 7, The fortune that unto her ennemys makes to seake the onlockes.]

1795 E. WYNNE *Diary* 16 Jan. (1937) II. ii. 12 This feast has great many misfortunes we have every day more unluck. **1838** *Cruikshank's Comic Almanack* I. 142 Last Friday was a notable instance of my unluck. **1891** ATKINSON *Moorland Par.* 94 That bad management..might have something to do with the unluck of his stock.

†un'luckful, *a. Obs.*⁻¹ [UN-¹ 7.] Bringing ill-luck.

1542 UDALL *Erasm. Apoph.* 338 Why settest thou thy delite in three the most vnluckefull beastes of yᵉ worlde?

un'luckily, *adv.* [UN-¹ 11. Cf. ON. *úlukkuliga.*]

1. Unfortunately, unhappily.

Usually in parenthetic or loose construction.

1530 PALSGR. 840/1 Onluckely, *de grant malheur.* *a* **1586** SIDNEY *Arcadia* III. ii, Blind Fortune hating sharpe-sighted inventions, made them unluckily to be killed. **1638** SIR T. HERBERT *Trav.* (ed. 2) 92 Darab..most unluckily denyes, and goes on to levy men to support the rebellion. **1673** [R. LEIGH] *Transp. Reh.* 128 Unluckily..there has happen'd a prodigious conjunction. **1766** GOLDSM. *Vicar* xxviii, Unluckily all our money had been laid out..in provisions. **1825** J. NEAL *Bro. Jonathan* III. 404 Unluckily for him, the order for pursuit was given too early. **1871** FREEMAN *Norm. Conq.* IV. xvii. 74 Of the state of things..we unluckily hear nothing.

b. With verbs of happening, succeeding, etc.

c **1550** *Vertuous Scholehous* H 6 b, Man feareth that it [*sc.* matrimony] myght succede vnluckely. **1592** SHAKS. *Rom. & Jul.* III. iv. 1 Things haue falne out..vnluckily. **1607** —— *Timon* III. ii. 51 How vnluckily it hapned, that [etc.]. **1711** SWIFT *Let. to Abp. King* 8 Mar., Nothing could happen so unluckily..as Mr. Harley's death. **1819** SHELLEY *Cenci* V. i. 12 It has turned out unluckily.

†2. Unsuccessfully, badly. *Obs. rare.*

a **1586** SIDNEY *Arcadia* I. xvi, Urania, whom a rich knight ..had unluckely defended. **1638** JUNIUS *Paint. Ancients* 305 A certain Painter,..who painted cockes most unluckily, gave his boy great charge, to chase the true cockes away from his picture. **1665** BOYLE *Occas. Refl.* IV. xx, Many of those young Ladies..are so unluckily Bred,..that [etc.].

un'luckiness. [UN-¹ 12: cf. next.]

1. Want of luck; unlucky character or fortune.

1561 T. HOBY tr. *Castiglione's Courtyer* IV. U vij b, You haue better declared the vnluckinesse of yonge men, then the happynesse of olde menn. **1638** SIR T. HERBERT *Trav.* (ed. 2) 227 Black..they call..a type of hell, and unluckinesse. **1673** KIRKMAN *Unlucky Citizen* A 5 b, Although I had been unlucky, yet I my own self caused that unluckyness. **1734** MRS. DELANY *Life & Corr.* (1861) I. 452 A piece of unluckiness of yours which has disappointed and mortified me. **1835** *Wilson's Tales Borders* I. 65/1 The luckiness or unluckiness of a First Foot. **1897** E. W. B. NICHOLSON *Golspie* 67 A belief in the unluckiness of Friday.

2. Tendency to mischief.

1760–72 H. BROOKE *Fool of Qual.* (1809) I. 163 Ned.. would not willingly have exchanged his unluckiness for the heirship of an estate. *Ibid.* 174 Ned's natural unluckiness.

†un'luckly, *a. Obs.* [UN-¹ 7. Cf. Sw. *olycklig*, Da. *ulykkelig*, Norw. *ulukkeleg*; MHG. *unge-*, G. *unglücklich.*] = UNLUCKY *a.*

1585 GREENE *Planetom.* B 1 b, A peeuish Parent, whose celestial (but infortunate) impression ioyned with a perpetuall vnluckly irradiation, breedeth both in mens mindes and bodies..haplesse passions. **1600** HAKLUYT *Voy.* III. 318 The end of their interprise became vnluckly and vnfortunate. **1678** MOXON *Mech. Exerc.* iv. 73 A negligent or un-luckly knock with the Mallet.

un'lucky, *a.* [UN-¹ 7. Cf. WFris. *on-, ûnlokkich*, MLG. *unluckich.*]

1. Having an unfortunate character or issue; marked by misfortune or failure.

1530 PALSGR. 328/2 Unluckye, *meschant.* *a* **1548** HALL *Chron., Hen. VI*, 138 b, Accomptyng to hym their euil chaunce & vnluckey fortune. **1563** *Mirr. Mag., Somerset* xxxi, My life I lost in that vnlucky place. **1588** SHAKS. *Tit. A.* II. iii. 251 Brought hither in a most vnluckie houre. **1609** ROWLANDS *Dr. Merrie-man* (1627) C 1 b, One..brake his Arme, And did complaine vnto a Friend Of his vnlucky harme. **1676** HOBBES *Iliad* I. 200 To put an end to this un-lucky strife. **1712** ADDISON *Spect.* No. 271 ¶4 This unlucky Accident happened to me in a Company of Ladies. **1829** LYTTON *Disowned* 79 It was the unluckiest step we ever made to admit him into the bosom of our family. **1855** MACAULAY *Hist. Eng.* xvi. III. 721 The year which was closing had certainly been unlucky.

2. Boding or involving misfortune; ill-omened, inauspicious.

a **1547** SURREY *Æneid* II. 1026 Th' unlucky figure of Creusaes ghost. **1568** GRAFTON *Chron.* II. 382 The Scottes ..thought John an unluckie name for a King. **1617** MORYSON *Itin.* I. 61 The King and the Queen,..while sometimes they thought Munday, sometimes Friday, to be vnlucky daies, had lost many faire winds. **1686** tr. *Chardin's Trav. Persia* 19 Nor do I know what unlucky star brought him to Constantinople. **1700** ROWE *Amb. Step-Moth.* III. i, Why do you urge my Father's fatal Power to curse you with a sad unlucky Bride. **1843** PRESCOTT *Mexico* (1850) I. 105 On the arrival of the five 'unlucky' days..they abandoned themselves to despair.

3. Having ill-luck; meeting with misfortune or mishap.

1552 HULOET, Vnluckye, to be, or haue yll lucke, *exauspicor.* **1560** DAUS tr. *Sleidane's Comm.* 29 b, You muste haue respecte also that this newe Empire..be not made vn-lucky and vnfortunate. **1627** J. TAYLOR (Water P.) *Navy of Land Ships* Wks. (1630) 79/1 Some Ships..are so vnlucky, that they neuer make a good voyage. **1673** *S'too him Bayes* 4 Thou are the unluckyest disputant in the world. **1807** CRABBE *Par. Reg.* I. 705 The unlucky peasant heard the stranger's cry. **1896** HOWELLS *Impressions & Exp.* 239 A pair of grim old ladies, who..lived..aloof from their unluckier sisters.

4. Bringing ill-luck; causing mishap or harm; mischievous, malicious.

a **1586** SIDNEY *Arcadia* I. xi, By an unluckye blow the poore Philoxenus fell dead at his feete. **1598** R. BERNARD tr. *Terence, Phormio* II. ii, Are you vnluckie varlot so ready to doe euerie thing against me? **1712** ADDISON *Spect.* No. 343 ¶9 An unlucky Cock-Sparrow that..had before made great depredations upon our Commonwealth. **1727** [DORRINGTON] *Philip Quarll* (1816) 72 These unlucky instruments, which were intended for destruction, shall be employed for..preservation. **1768–74** TUCKER *Lt. Nat.* (1834) I. 571 Schoolmasters may not be displeased at unlucky tricks played by their lads. **1875–** in many dialect glossaries (*Eng. Dial. Dict.*).

b. Of a horse: Bad-tempered, vicious.

1707 MORTIMER *Husb.* 151 If he [*sc.* the stallion] be unlucky and mad.

5. Of an unfortunate or regrettable nature; not entitled to commendation.

1628 FELTHAM *Resolves* II. l. 146 In some vnlucky dispositions, there is such an enuious kinde of Pride. **1671** tr. *Charente's Let. Customs Mauritania* 18 There would be much greater [plenty], if it was not for the unlucky custom of those people to bury their Gold. **1746** FRANCIS tr. *Horace, Epist.* I. i. 137 If some unlucky Barber notch my Hair. **1815** SCOTT *Guy M.* i, Mannering resolved..to halt for the night ..unless he could procure a guide to this unlucky village of Kippletringan.

un'lucrative, *a.* (UN-¹ 7.)

1771–2 *Ess. fr. Batchelor* (1773) II. 135 An unlucrative and perillous profession. **1839** CARLYLE *Chartism* viii, The unlucrative fishing of ambergris.

†un'lude. *Obs.*⁻¹ [UN-¹ 4 b + LUDE¹. Cf. ON. *úhljóð.*] An unpleasant noise.

a **1275** *Prov. Ælfred* 689 in *O.E. Misc.* 138 He wole maken fule luden; he wole grennen,..and hewere [= ever] faren mid vnluden.

un'lull, *v.* (UN-² 3.)

1743 *Humours of Whist* 40 They love Opera's, say they, because they lull the Passions.., and yet..afterwards they fall to gaming, and very often pay for unlulling them again.

un'luminous, *a.* (UN-¹ 7.)

1773 *Gentl. Mag.* XLIII. 238 Hell's unluminous domains. **1837** CARLYLE *Fr. Rev.* II. v. iii, A tragical combustion, long smoking and smouldering unluminous. **1872** HOWELLS *Wedd. Journ.* v, The dense unluminous shadows of the moonshine.

†un'lust, *sb. Obs.* [OE. *unlust* (UN-¹ 12), = MDu. (Du.) *onlust*, MLG. *unlust*, OHG., MHG., G. *unlust* (Sw. *olust*), Goth. *unlustu-s* disinclination, displeasure, dislike. Cf. also ON. *úlyst* (Da. *ulyst*).]

1. Absence of pleasure; distress, weariness.

a **1000** *Sal. & Sat.* 268 (Gr.), Se fuȝel..wylleð hine on ð am wite, wunað unlustum. *c* **1440** *Jacob's Well* 116 No lyif of sweete deuocyoun ne gostly gladnesse is in ȝou, but dedly heuynes, & angwysch, & vnlust.

2. Want of appetite; nausea.

c **1000** *Sax. Leechd.* II. 158 Læcedomas wiþ unluste & wlætan þe of maȝan cymð. *c* **1230** *Hali Meid.* 35 Hwat mete se þi mahe hokerliche underfeð; þat is, wið unlust. **1561** HOLLYBUSH *Hom. Apoth.* 22 In all hys meates lette a litle saffron be put:..but it causeth vnluste in the stomacke.

3. Disinclination to be active or bestir oneself; slothfulness, laziness, idleness.

c **1000** ÆLFRIC *Hom.* II. 556 He þolað neadunge þeostra þurh wrace, se þe ær lustlice forbær his unlustes þeostra. *c* **1200** ORMIN 2623 Forr unnlusst & forrswundennleȝȝc Iss Drihhtin swiþe unncweme. *a* **1300** *Body & Soul* in *Map's Poems* (Camden) 336 Gloterie and lecherie, prude and wicke coveytise,..And in unlust for to lye. *c* **1386** CHAUCER *Pars. T.* ¶680 He dooth all thyng..with ydelnesse and vnlust. *a* **1470** H. PARKER *Dives & Pauper* (W. de W. 1496) VII. xxiii. 311/2 Goodes of holy chirche..ben gyuen to helpe of the poore &..not to selle them ayen to ryche men to maynten them in unlust & in bodely ease.

b. Disinclination (for something). Const. *of*, *to* (with inf.), *towards*.

1390 GOWER *Conf.* III. 291 For unlust of that aventure Ther was noman which tok tonsure. **1530** TINDALE *Prol. Epist. Romans* A ij b, We fynde in oure silves vnlust and tediousnes to do good. **1535** COVERDALE *Isaiah* xliii. 22 Thou haddest an vnlust towarde me, o Israel.

4. Evil desire or inclination. (UN-[1] 4 b.)

a **1225** *Ancr. R.* 288 (MS. B), Hwon þe heorte draheð to hire unlust [F. *a son mal desir*].

5. Unpleasantness, repulsiveness.

a **1529** SKELTON *El. Rummyng* 148 Theyr tresses untrust, All full of vnlust.

† **un'lust**, *v. Obs.* (UN-[2] 6 b.)

1683 *Argt. for Union* 38 It sounded more decently..to pray in the Churches words,..then to use those of an eminent Dissenter, Lord un-lust us.

† **un'lusthead.** *Obs.* [UN-[1] 12.] = UNLUST *sb.* 3.

1340 *Ayenb.* 31 Þet uerþe heaued..is onlusthede. *Ibid.* 163 Þe zenne of sleawþe and of onlosthede.

† **un'lustily**, *adv. Obs.* [UN-[1] 11. Cf. MHG. *unlusticlichen*, MDa. *onlustelijc*, MSw. *olustelika*.] Slothfully, idly; weakly; unwillingly.

c **1360** *Song of Mercy* 143 in *E.E.P.* (1862) 122 Vnlustily vr lyf we lede. *a* **1470** TIPTOFT *Tulle on Friendsh.* (Caxton, 1481) b iv, That is the cause..that they that be right wys ben moest sory for the thynges whiche be doen unrihtwisly and they that ben stronge for thynges doen unlustely. **1598** FLORIO, *Suogliatamente*,..sadly, vnlustily, without taste.

† **un'lustiness.** *Obs.* [UN-[1] 12: see UNLUSTY.]

1. Lack of health and strength; physical weakness or debility. *Obs.*

1486 *Bk. St. Albans, Hawking* b vi b, A medecyne that an hawke shall not lie in mew for unlustynese. **1547** BOORDE *Brev. Health* xlix. 15 [Gaping] doth come of unlustines or els for lake of slepe. **1596** BARROUGH *Meth. Physick* VIII. 470 When..the wearinesse or the vnlustinesse of the sinewes is to be asswaged. **1620** VENNER *Via Recta* Introd. 4 Vnlustinesse of the limmes.

2. Lack of cheerfulness or readiness; dullness; disinclination.

a **1470** H. PARKER *Dives & Pauper* (W. de W. 1496) I. lix. 101/2 Melodye was ordeyned in holy chirche..to put awaye heuynesse & unlustynesse. **1502** *Ord. Crysten Men* (W. de W. 1506) IV. xxx. 350 By unlustynes in dyffaylynge without desyre to do well. **1583** GOLDING *Calvin on Deut.* x. 54 Wee see what vnlustinesse is in vs when God commaundith vs any thing.

un'lustrous, *a.* (UN-[1] 7.)

1709 ROWE *Shakspere's Cymb.* I. vii. 127 An Eye, Base and unlustrious [*sic*; 1623 illustrious] as the smoaky Light That's fed with stinking Tallow. **1790** ANNA SEWARD *Lett.* (1811) II. 378 How dim and unlustrous is Mr. Merry's muse! **1863** W. LANCASTER *Praeterita* 70 Sweet unlustrous eyes.

un'lusty, *a. Obs.* exc. *dial.* [UN-[1] 7. Cf. MDu. *onlustich* (Du. *onlustig*), MLG. *unlustich*, MHG. *unlustic* (G. *unlustig*), ON. *úlystugr*, older Da. *ulystig*, MSw. *olustogher* (Sw. *olustig*).]

1. Indisposed to activity or exertion; slothful, lazy; dull, listless. Also const. *to* with inf.

c **1230** *Hali Meid.* 43 And te oðre þat halden ham vnforgult & cleane, beon ase sikere unlustie & wlecche, liueð i godes luue wiðuten euch heate of þe hali gast. *a* **1240** *Lofsong* in *O.E. Hom.* I. 205 Touel spac and slow to godd, ȝemeleas and unlusti. **1340** *Ayenb.* 170 To þe sleauolle and to þe onlosti þet byeþ slacke to godes service. **1390** GOWER *Conf.* I. 203 Thus his yonge unlusti lif He dryveth forth. *c* **1450** *Mankind* 538 in *Macro Plays* 20 Thys londe ys so harde, yt makyth wn-lusty & yrke. **1504** C'TESS RICHMOND tr. *De Imitatione* IV. xii. (1893) 276 If thou haue nat that grace whan thou woldest but fele thy selfe drye and vnlusty. **1519** HORMAN *Vulg.* 48 My mynde..when it is cloudy wether..is vnlusty. **1560** PILKINGTON *Exp. Aggeus* B vi *marg.*, Eate not so that it make ye unlustie to serue God. **1617** HIERON *Wks.* (1620) II. 273 Dauid..went on in a kinde of dull, and heauy, and vnlusty manner with them [*sc.* holy services].

b. *dial.* 'Unwieldly; very fat.'

1881–2 in Cornwall glossaries.

2. Lacking in bodily vigour; deficient in health and strength; weak, feeble.

1400–10 CLANVOWE *Cuckoo & Night.* viii, Thogh I be old and vnlusty. **1577** B. GOOGE *Heresbach's Husb.* 127* The Cowe should..haue but short pasture, and the Bull his belly full: so shall neyther she be too fat, nor he vnlusty. *a* **1624** BP. SMITH *Serm.* (1632) 249 Infants..borne lame or vnlusty.

b. Of land: Not in good heart.

1573–80 TUSSER *Husb.* (1878) 50 If land be vnlustie, the crop is not great.

3. Having an unattractive or ill-favoured look.

c **1400** *Destr. Troy* 8035 All wan was the weghe.., With lamentacion & langour vnlusty to se. **1430–40** LYDG. *Bochas* I. i. (1554) 2 b, By..great labours, They were unlusty and ugly of their cheres. *a* **1529** SKELTON *P. Sparowe* 915 His gummes rusty Are full vnlusty.

4. Undesirable, objectionable, unpleasant.

c **1412** HOCCLEVE *De Reg. Princ.* 3356 They often hadde gret cause hem to venge, But hir spiritis..pesible Thoghten þat craft vnlusty and alenge. *c* **1445** PECOCK *Donet* 24 Forto þus do and procede..wolde be ouer longe and tediose and vnlusty to þe heerers.

un'lute, *v.* [UN-[2] 4.] *trans.* To remove the lute from (a vessel, etc.).

1661 BOYLE *Sceptical Chym.* I. 68 Upon the unluting the vessels, it infected the Room with a scarce supportable stink. **1662** MERRETT tr. *Neri's Art of Glass* lxxiii, Unlute the Chrysibles. **1758** REID tr. *Macquer's Chym.* i. 226 Let the vessels cool, unlute them. **1839** URE *Dict. Arts* 10 The adopter tube is then unluted, and is slid into its junction pipe.

un'luted, *ppl. a.* (UN-[1] 8.)

1663 BOYLE *Usef. Exp. Nat. Philos.* II. App. 318 A calcining pot unluted. **1877** TEALE *Dangers to Health* Pl. v, Unluted joints leaking under the floor.

unlu'xuriant, *a.* (UN-[1] 7.)

1723 *Historical Rev.* VIII. 43 A fruitful, yet unluxuriant and agreeable Imagination. **1805** WORDSW. *Prelude* VIII. 161 The unluxuriant produce of a life Intent on little but substantial needs.

unlu'xurious, *a.* (UN-[1] 7.)

1700 PHILIPS *Pastorals* i. 7 In unluxurious times of yore. **1795** COLERIDGE *Plot Discov.* 50 The enlightened and unluxurious ancients. **1853** MISS YONGE *Heir of Redclyffe* xxiii, Unpretending, unluxurious chairs. **1868** W. R. GREG *Lit. & Soc. Judgm.* 357 A comparatively humble and un-luxurious home.

unly'canthropize, *v.* (UN-[2] 6 c; cf. LYCANTHROPE.)

1660 HOWELL *Parly of Beasts* 114 She is ready to unlycanthropize you from this Wolfish shape to your former condition.

un'lyrical, *a.* (UN-[1] 7.)

1833 MILL *Diss. & Disc.* (1859) I. 85 The genius of Wordsworth is essentially un-lyrical.

un'lyrically, *adv.* (UN-[1] 11.)

1891 *Athenæum* 3 Oct. 445/2 The assemblage of trochee words..keeps the rhythm unlyrically staccato.

unma'cadamized, *ppl. a.* (UN-[1] 8.)

1840 HOOD *Kilmansegg, Accident* xvi, So she gathered the awful sense Of the street in its past unmacadamiz'd tense. **1852** SMEDLEY *L. Arundel* xxxii. 238 Flinty hearts, unmacadamised by the smallest grain of pity. **1879** E. WALFORD *Londoniana* I. 40 Along roads rugged, rutty, and un-macadamized.

un'mackly, *a.* and *adv. north. dial.* [UN-[1] 7, 11: see MACK *a.* and MACKLY *adv.*] Unshapely; ill-favoured(ly).

? *a* **1600** *Sir Cawline* xxx. (Percy Folio MS.), Vpon his squier [= neck] fiue heads he bare, Vnmackley made was hee. **1811–76** in northern glossaries.

† **un'maculat**, *ppl. a. Sc. Obs.* [UN-[1] 8 b, 5 b.] Immaculate.

1535 STEWART *Cron. Scot.* (Rolls) II. 158 His awin ladie vnmaculat and clene. **1607** *Melrose Regality Rec.* (1914) 35 The judge..ordanis him to redelyver..the said obligatioun unmaculat, uncuttit.

un'mad, *a.* (UN-[1] 7.)

1570 FOXE *A. & M.* (ed. 2) III. 2134/1 Old and yong, blind and lame, madde and vnmadde. **1694** ECHARD *Plautus* 61 She's th' only unmad Person o' my Family.

un'maddened, *ppl. a.* (UN-[1] 8.)

1797 COLERIDGE *Osorio* III. i. 22 What sense unmadden'd, might bear up against The rushing of your congregated wings? **1868** E. R. SILL *Poems, Hermitage* xx, Unmaddened by the babble of vain men.

un'made, *ppl. a.* [UN-[1] 8 b, 5 d.]

1. a. Not (yet) made, in senses of the verb.

c **1250** *Gen. & Ex.* 671 Babel, ðat tur, bi-lef un-mad. **1375** BARBOUR *Bruce* IV. 608 He..thoucht to leif the fyre vnmaid. *c* **1400** *Pilgr. Sowle* (Caxton, 1483) v. i. 74 God..maketh as many werkes as better ben made than vnmade. *c* **1489** CAXTON *Sonnes of Aymon* xx. 445 Thys cave sheweth not that it hathe be vnmade this hundred yeres passed. **1526** *Pilgr. Perf.* (W. de W. 1531) 81 Whiche..lefte the lettre .O. that he was in makynge halfe vnmade. **1592** SHAKS. *Rom. & Jul.* III. iii. 70 Taking the measure of an vn-made graue. **1623** SANDERSON *Serm.* (1632) 151 Lawes..are farre better vnmade, then vnkept. **1680** SIR J. FOULIS *Acc. Bk.* (S.H.S.) 165 To [blank] davison for 4 duz[n] unmade pens. **1704** *Lond. Gaz.* No. 3981/4 With new fine Holland Shifts and Hankerchiefs unmade. **1716** *Wodrow Corr.* (1843) II. 132 Whatever of cloth, made or unmade, linen yarn or woollen. **1807** CRABBE *Par. Reg.* III. 180, I die,..My mind unsettled, and my will unmade. **1828** *Lights & Shades* I. 286 A halfclothed mother seated on the corner of an unmade bed. **1885** C. E. PASCOE *Lond. of To-day* 315 The plain unmade satin scarf.

b. *spec.* Untrained. (Cf. MADE *ppl. a.* 6.)

1856 H. DIXON *Post & Paddock* i. 4 The largest market in the world for unmade hunters and carriage-horses.

2. Existing without having been made; uncreated but existent.

c **1350** *Athanasian Creed* in *MS. Bodl. 425* fol. 69 b, Bot on unmade and on mikel is he. **1434** MISYN *Mending Life* 122 O sweit light..þat is my makar vn-made, liȝt þe face..of my Inward eyn with clernes vn-made. *c* **1449** PECOCK *Repr.* II. xvi. 242 Thei..helden that al the bodili heuen..was vnmaad, and was euer withoute bigynnyng of tyme. **1563** MAN *Musculus' Commonpl.* 373, I doe fynde generally two Natures, one not made, the other made. Wee call that unmade (*non factam*), which belongeth unto God. **1678** CUDWORTH *Intell. Syst.* Pref., The Latter asserted an Unmade Mind, whereas the Former Generated all Mind..out of those Qualified Atoms. **1682** NORRIS *Hierocles* Pref. 23 Unmade, Self-existent, independent Deities. **1720** WATERLAND *Eight Serm.* 239 If He existed before anything was made, He must..be unmade, and therefore eternal. **1827** POLLOK *Course T.* VI. 630 Maker, Upholder, Governor of all! Thyself unmade, ungoverned, unupheld! **1884** *Congregat. Year Bk.* 93 His world is a world without design, atoms are the unmade makers of all things.

3. † **a.** *Sc.* (with complement). *Obs.*

1456 [see UN-[1] 5 d (*b*).] **1596** DALRYMPLE tr. *Leslie's Hist. Scot.* (S.T.S.) II. 436 Quhat chancet on Pasche day..suld not be vnmaid mentioune of.

b. With advs. Not made *out*, *up*, etc.

1600 HAKLUYT *Voy.* III. 87 A Pinnesse..which was caryed in pieces, and vnmade vp. *a* **1631** DONNE *Elegy* xv. 97 Countless multitudes Of formlesse curses, projects unmade up. *a* **1680** BUTLER *Charac., Pedant* (1908) 136 He wears his little Learning, unmade-up, put it on, before it was half finished. **1707** MORTIMER *Husb.* 379 Where the rows and brush lie longer unbound or unmade up. **1833** LAMB *Let. to Cary* in *Final Mem.* viii, I think we scarce left anything unmadeout. **1936** D. POWELL *Turn, Magic Wheel* II. 133 Their decently un-made-up little wives. **1960** *News Chron.* 12 Oct. 3/2 Her unmade-up face smiling. **1971** J. TURNER *Stone Dormitory* vi. 63 He went on along the unmade-up road. **1978** R. HILL *Pinch of Snuff* iv. 42 He was roused from the unmade-up spare bed by Ellie pulling his hair.

† **un'maggled**, *ppl. a. Obs.*[−1] [UN-[1] 8.] Unmangled.

c **1470** *Gol. & Gaw.* 720 Wes nane forssy on fold, that wes feghtand, Wnmaglit [*edd.* -manglit] and marrit.

un'magic, *v.* [UN-[2] 6.] *trans.* To disenchant.

1650 H. MORE *Observ.* in *Enthus. Tri.*, etc. (1656) L 2 b, Poor Galen's Antichrist, though one Purge of his Might so un-magick thee as make thee wise.

un'magistrate, *v.* (UN-[2] 6 b.)

1649 MILTON *Tenure Kings* (ed. 2) 55 If this Parlament..might..take all power..out of his hand, which in effect is to unmagistrate him.

un'magistrate-like, *a.* (UN-[1] 7 c.)

1644 MILTON *Divorce* (ed. 2) II. xi. 53 What more un-Judge-like, more un-Magistrate-like, and in warre more un-commander-like?

unmag'nanimous, *a.* (UN-[1] 7.)

1856 DE QUINCEY *Confess.* Wks. I. 206 *note*, A man so unmagnanimous as Napoleon. **1877** OWEN *Wellesley's Desp.* p. xl, The indirect and unmagnanimous revenge..galled him to the quick.

unmag'netic, *a.* (UN-[1] 7.)

1805 *Phil. Trans.* XCV. 283 Such substances as may be sublimed with facility, will gradually quit the oxide,..leaving it unmagnetic, as at first. **1844** NOAD *Electricity* (ed. 2) 425 An unmagnetic needle, placed within a close helix, formed by the wire of the circuit. **1860** O. W. HOLMES *Prof. Breakf.-t.* i, A new clean unmagnetic word.

unmag'netical, *a.* [UN-[1] 7.] = prec.

1815 J. SMITH *Panorama Sci. & Art* II. 177 If an unmagnetical bar be struck with a hammer. **1832** *Nat. Philos., Magnetism* iv. 34 (L.U.K.), Unmagnetical iron or steel.

un'magnetized, *ppl. a.* (UN-[1] 8.)

1834 MRS. SOMERVILLE *Connex. Phys. Sci.* xxix. (1836) 321 An unmagnetised iron bar. **1873** J. C. MAXWELL *Electr. & Magn.* III. vi. II. 76 In the un-magnetized state of ordinary iron.

un'magnify, *v.* (UN-[2] 3.)

1747 E. POSTON *Pratler* I. 38 Whenever we think..that we understand the Nature and Ways of God, what do we in Reality, but unmagnify him, or..disrobe him of his Honour and Glory?

† **un'maht.** *Obs.*[−1] [UN-[1] 12.] One not possessed of any power or means.

a **1300** *Prov. Hendyng* in *Rel. Ant.* I. 114 Moni mon mid a lutel ahte ȝeveth is dohter an un-mahte, Ant lutel is the bettre.

un'maid, *v.* (UN-[2] 6 b.)

1638 N. WHITING *Albino & Bellama* 3527 Is't not said Spirits have power a damsel to un-maid? **1922** JOYCE *Ulysses* 386 She was there unmaided.

† **un'maiden**, *sb. Obs.*[−1] (UN-[1] 12.)

a **1380** *Langland's P. Pl.* A. x. 193 (Vernon MS.), Bote Maydens and vn-Maydens clene ow save.

un'maiden, *v.* [UN-[2] 6 b. Cf. Du. *ontmaagden*, G. *entmägden*.] *trans.* To deprive of maidenhood; to deflower.

1579 NORTHBROOKE *Dicing* 68 b, Through this dauncing many maidens haue beene vnmaidened. **1612** DRAYTON *Poly-olb.* vii. 47 Least by the Sylvans..She might unmaidned goe unto her soveraigne flood. **1660** J. S. *Andromana* II. v, Sturdy Hercules, When he unmaiden'd fifty in one night. *a* **1693** *Urquhart's Rabelais* III. xii. (1694) 96 He unmaiden'd his Sister Juno. [**1876** *Whitby Gloss.*, *Unmaiden'd*, married.]

refl. **1592** WARNER *Alb. Eng.* VIII. xli. 179 Think not Lord Cliffords daughter will vn-maiden her for pay.

Hence **un'maidening** *vbl. sb.*

a **1693** *Urquhart's Rabelais* III. vi. 58 The unmaidning or depucelating of a hundred Virgins.

un'maidenlike, *a.* (UN-^{1} 7 c.)

1876 SWINBURNE *Erectheus* 364 Not moved of mine own will, Unmaidenlike.

un'maidenly, *a.* (UN-^{1} 7.)

1634 BP. HALL *Contempl., N.T.* IV. iv, [These] wanton gesticulations of a virgin..could be no other than riggish and unmaidenly. **1828** SCOTT *F.M. Perth* xxv, Such tokens of intimacy..are uncomely and unmaidenly. **1848** MRS. GASKELL *Mary Barton* xv, The whisperings of her womanly nature..caused her to shrink from any unmaidenly action. **1866** G. MACDONALD *Ann. Q. Neighb.* xxxii, At least do not put your character in question by going in this unmaidenly fashion.

Hence **un'maidenliness.**

1874 *Fortn. Rev.* Feb. 239 What the poet thinks of the unmaidenliness of Lynette. **1879** MEREDITH *Egoist* xxi, You, father! you have driven me to unmaidenliness.

un'mail, *v.* [UN-^{2} 4. Cf. MDu. *ontmaelgeren, -mailleren.*] *trans.* To break or detach the links of (a mail-coat).

?*a* **1412** LYDG. *Two Merch.* 668 How many a man hath Fortune assayled..Her habiriownys of steel also vnmayled. *c* **1489** CAXTON *Sonnes of Aymon* iii. 79 Ye sholde haue seen ..many a good haubergen vnmayled. **1611** COTGR., *Desmaillé*, vnmailed; vnlinked; vndone..as a coat of maile.

Hence **un'mailing** *vbl. sb.*

1591 PERCIVALL, *Desmalladura*, vnmailing. **1611** COTGR., *Desmaillure*, an vnmailing; an vndoing..of maile.

un'mailable, *a. U.S.* (UN-^{1} 7 b.)

1875 *U.S. Official Post Guide* 23 (Flügel), Such matter must be forwarded to the Dead Letters Office, marked as 'unmailable.'

un'mailed, *ppl. a.* [UN-^{1} 8.] Not covered or protected by mail.

1806 *Ann. Rev.* IV. 562 The brother of Biorn with his mail; Herbert unmailed. **1807** WORDSW. *White Doe* I. 765 With breast unmailed, unweaponed hand.

un'maimable, *a.* (UN-^{1} 7 b.)

1565 GOLDING *Ovid's Met.* XII. (1587) 155 When Ceny had sufficiently giuen Latreus leaue too smyght His flesh which was vnmaymeable.

un'maimed, *ppl. a.* (UN-^{1} 8.)

1470–85 MALORY *Arthur* x. lix. 515, I shalle be with yow ..yf I be vnslayne or vnmaymed. **1595** MARKHAM *Sir R. Grinvile* clxxi, They..to theyr Generall brought His mangled carkasse, but vnmaimed minde. **1614** T. GODWIN *Rom. Antiq.* II. §ii. 5. 40 He was to be..of a life vnspotted, and a body vnmaimed. **1630** DRUMM. OF HAWTH. *Flowres Sion* xxiv. 8 His spight yet so cannot her all throw downe, But that some Statue..Yet lurkes vnmaym'd within her weeping walles. **1715** POPE *Iliad* Pref. E 2, It is the first grand Duty of an Interpreter to give his Author entire and unmaim'd. *c* **1810** J. BAILLIE *2nd Part Ethwald* I. ii, Standing erect, Unmaim'd and vigorous.

†**un'main.** *Obs.*$^{-1}$ [UN-^{1} 12. Cf. OHG. *unmagen*, ON. *úmegin, úmegn* (Icel. *ómegin*, MSw. *omäghin*, Norw. dial. *umegje, umeie*); also OE. *unmæȝness.*] Want of strength.

1338 R. BRUNNE *Chron.* (1810) 55 Þof I had stombled þorgh myn vnmayn, He suld haf..reised me agayn.

unmain'tainable, *a.* (UN-^{1} 7 b.)

1625 DONNE *Serm.* 657 They have bound themselves not to recede from those doctrines, how unmaintenable so-ever they be in themselves. **1701** NORRIS *Ideal World* I. vi. 352 The defence of so desperate and unmaintainable a breach. *a* **1832** BENTHAM *Levelling Syst.* Wks. 1843 I. 362 The good expected..would be altogether unattainable—at least unmaintainable for two instants together. **1853** GROTE *Greece* XI. 499 That the festivals..were unmaintainable during such a war. **1883** *Law Times* 22 Dec. 135/1 The society..was..an illegal society..and the action was consequently unmaintainable.

unmain'tained, *ppl. a.* (UN-^{1} 8.)

1691 BAXTER *Nat. Ch.* xv. 72 A Life of unmaintained poverty, and censure. **1885** *Pall Mall G.* 1 July 6/1 Hence we have crime un-noticed, discipline unmaintained.

un'makable, *a.* (UN-^{1} 7 b.)

1674 GREW *Disc. Mixture* iii. §13 No Principle is made by the fire: all Principles being unalterable; and therefore unmakable. **1701** —— *Cosm. Sacr.* I. iii. 13. **1939** W. FORTESCUE *There's Rosemary* l. 282 The designer had drawn a lovely but unmakeable model which had only one side. **1974** E. BRAWLEY *Rap* (1975) I. xi. 183 He knew escape was impossible, an unmakable caper. **1979** *Country Life* 4 Oct. 1127/2 Seven No Trumps was unmakeable.

un'make, *v.* [UN-^{2} 3. Cf. MDu. (Du.) *ontmaken*, OHG. *in(t)mahhôn* (G. *entmachen*).]

1. *trans.* To reverse or undo the making of (some thing or object); to reduce again to an unmade condition.

1426 LYDG. *De Guil. Pilgr.* 11270 He made [nets], & hem vnmade ageyn. *c* **1430** *Pilgr. Lyf Manhode* I. lxiii. (1869) 38 It is a iewell that was..maad..of my fader with oute smytinge of strok... For noyse and strokes maken it nouht, but tobreken it and vnmaken it. **1641** MILTON *Ch. Govt.* vi, So that Prelaty..must be forc't to dissolve and unmake her own pyramidal figure. **1690** T. BURNET *Theory Earth* II. 132 God does not make or unmake things, to try experiments. **1750** JOHNSON *Rambler* No. 74 ¶11 She compels them to alter their work, then to unmake it. **1857** EMERSON *Ode to Beauty* 99 Dread Power!..if God thou be, Unmake me quite, or give thyself to me. **1868** MORRIS *Earthly Par.* (1870) I. I. 339 And now thou knowest in how short a space The God that made the world can unmake thee.

absol. **1426** LYDG. *De Guil. Pilgr.* 11416 And thogh that I make & vnmake, Blame me nat. **1821** BYRON *Cain* I. i. 142 But, if he made us—he cannot unmake.

b. With immaterial object.

1377 LANGL. *P. Pl.* B. xv. 236 Matrimoigne for monye [they] maken & vnmaken. **1513** DOUGLAS *Æneid* VI. ix. 199 Sum vtheris..That lawis maid and wnmaid, as thaim list. *a* **1536** TINDALE in Marbeck *Bk. of Notes* (1581) 746 Who can suffer them.., for their owne profites, to make and vnmake lawes..? **1639** FULLER *Holy War* II. xvii. 67 God will not unmake his miracles by making them common. **1802–12** BENTHAM *Ration. Judic. Evid.* (1827) V. 266 When a statute..has been unmade by the authority that made it. **1822** BYRON *Juan* VI. lx, In perfect innocence she then unmade Her toilet, which cost little. **1860** GEN. P. THOMPSON *Audi Alt. Part.* III. cxxiv. 77 The study of what has made and unmade military successes.

absol. **1604** SHAKS. *Oth.* II. iii. 352 His Soule is so enfetter'd to her Loue, That she may make, vnmake, do what she list. **1848** BAILEY *Festus* (ed. 3) 17 Then comes the feeling which unmakes, undoes. **1876** MRS. WHITNEY *Sights & Ins.* II. 401 Perhaps the very first thing we see that wisdom do, is to unmake and separate, and seem to break and mix yet more.

2. a. To deprive of a particular rank or station; to depose.

1554 BALE *Declar. Bonner's Articles* xix. 68 He is wonte to make kinges, and to vnmake them again at his plesure. **1567** JEWEL *Def. Apol.* 418 Saieinge withal, Hee had Power to make Emperours, and to vnmake them. **1651** N. BACON *Disc. Govt. Eng.* II. xiv. 129 An English King hath power.. to make and unmake Members [of Parliament] as he shal please. **1670** G. H. *Hist. Cardinals* I. III. 70 They made and unmade Popes at their pleasure. **1736** THOMSON *Liberty* IV. 879 He mark'd the Barons of excessive sway, At pleasure making and unmaking kings. **1808** MITFORD *Hist. Greece* IV. 353 He made and unmade there what kings he pleased. **1894** LD. WOLSELEY *Life Marlborough* I. 178 Her authority was such, that she could make and unmake ministers.

b. To deprive of a certain character or quality; to alter in nature. Also with compl.

1616 B. JONSON *Epigr.* lv, At once thou mak'st me happie, and vnmak'st. **1669** DRYDEN *Tyrannic Love* III. i, You are so pure—That in the act 'twould change the impiety. Heaven would unmake it sin! **1709** *Tatler* No. 66 ¶4 To make our Patient any Thing better, we must unmake him what he is. **1710** SHAFTESB. *Charac.* (1711) I. 308 That which we fondly make our Happiness at one time, we may as readily un-make again at another. **1856** MRS. BROWNING *Aur. Leigh* IX. 200, I take her as God made her, and as men Must fail to unmake her. **1858** HAWTHORNE *Fr. & It. Note-bks.* (1871) II. 8 Her modest attitude..is partly what unmakes her as the heathen Goddess, and softens her into woman.

3. *fig.* To undo; to ruin or destroy; to bring to nothing.

1605 SHAKS. *Macb.* I. vii. 54 They haue made themselues, and that their fitnesse now Do's vnmake you. **1652** BENLOWES *Theoph.* III. lxxxix, Sure, Thou to guilt, Which would unmake thy creatures, wilt Be just. **1674** N. FAIRFAX *Bulk & Selv.* 189 To mistrust boundless wisdom, to contrive so, that it might have better been contrived, is to unmake its boundlesness. **1867** FELTON *Anc. & Mod. Gr.* II. i. 264 If the great powers are going to make a permanent European state out of Turkey, they must unmake the Turk. **1870** EMERSON *Soc. & Solit.* vii. 135 The machine unmakes the man.

4. To annul a decision of (the mind).

1897 MARY KINGSLEY *W. Africa* 4 When you have made up your mind to go to West Africa the very best thing you can do is to get it unmade again.

Hence **un'making** *vbl. sb.*

1591 PERCIVALL, *Deshazimiento*, vndooing, vnmaking. *a* **1676** HALE *Prim. Orig. Man.* III. i. (1677) 254 Though he seems to admit Eternal Vicissitudes of such Making, and Unmaking, and Restitutions of the inferior World. **1867** H. BUSHNELL *Moral Uses Dark Th.* 285 A general unmaking of the world by transgression. **1871** SMILES *Charac.* xi. 324 A wife may be the making or the unmaking of the best of men.

un'maker. [UN-^{1} 12, or f. prec.] One who unmakes.

c **1430** *Pilgr. Lyf Manhode* III. xvii. (1869) 144 This hand is an vnmakere of howses. **1684** BAXTER *Par. Congreg.* 40 The Magistrate may command men how to do their office-work, and yet neither be the maker nor unmaker of the office. **1862** MRS. CROSLAND *Mrs. Blake* II. 47 That the soldier is rather an 'unmaker' and instrument of destruction than anything else. **1893** W. WATSON *Lachrymæ Mus.* 26 Unmaker of all, and renewer, The Lord of Death.

unma'licious, *a.* (UN-^{1} 7.)

1649 JER. TAYLOR *Gt. Exemp.* II. viii. 68 An unconfirmed, unresolved, unmalicious habite. **1663** COWLEY *Verses, Ode Cowley's Book* iv, As when a seat in Heaven Is to an unmalicious Sinner given. **1795** T. WRIGHT *Autobiog.* (1864) 17 The sudden little unmalicious quarrel. **1866–7** CARLYLE *E. Irving* in *Remin.* (1881) I. 145 A most quizzing, merry, entertaining, guileless, and unmalicious man. **1886** RUSKIN *Præterita* I. 382 His subtle,..unmalicious sarcasm.

unma'lignant, *a.* (UN-^{1} 7.)

1841 L. HUNT *Seer* (1864) 47 Nature has a beautiful way of reconciling all necessities that are unmalignant.

un,mallea'bility. (UN-^{1} 12; cf. next.)

[**1828–32** WEBSTER.] **1875** MAINE *Hist. Inst.* ii. 62 The great unmalleability of all bodies of law. **1887** RUSKIN *Præterita* II. i. 13 The density and unmalleability of the world.

un'malleable, *a.* (UN-^{1} 7 b.)

1609 G. BENSON *Serm. 7 Mar.* 55 Be perswaded, let not your hearts be vnmalleable. **1665** J. SPENCER *Prodigies* (ed. 2) 341 To grow (like Iron often heated and quench'd) churlish and unmalleable by the hammer of the Divine threatnings. **1779** JOHNSON *L.P., Dryden* Wks. II. 395 After this he did not often bring upon his anvil such stubborn and unmalleable thoughts. **1795** *Phil. Trans.* LXXXV. 341 Hard unmalleable iron. **1838** HAWTHORNE *Amer. Note-bks.* (1883) 166 A man of unmalleable habits. **1890** *Spectator* 19 July 79/2 The large masses of rather unmalleable human material which he contrives to collect together.

Hence **un'malleableness.**

1644 R. CHALFONT *Serm.* 10 May 8 The hardnesse and unmalleablenesse of heart.

un'maltable, *a.* (UN-^{1} 7 b.)

1778 [W. H. MARSHALL] *Minutes Agric., Digest* 43 To feed cart-horses on unmaltable barley.

un'malted, *ppl. a.* (UN-^{1} 8.)

1651 R. CHILD in *Hartlib's Legacy* (1655) 141 Beer may be made of Wheat, Barley, Pease, &c. unmalted. **1707** MORTIMER *Husb.* 267 The part of the Corn which it passeth not, will remain unmalted, the rest will be perfect Malt. **1790** LUCKOMBE *Eng. Gazetteer* I. p. xviii, Thirty-four millions of bushels of barley unmalted. **1830** M. DONOVAN *Dom. Econ.* I. 143 The comparative analyses of malted and unmalted barley. **1884** *Law Rep. 27 Chanc. Div.* 497 The gelatinization or conversion of unmalted grain.

un'man, *sb. rare.* [UN-^{1} 12, 4 b. Cf. OE. *unmann*, Du. *onman*, MLG., MHG. *unman.*]

a. One below the status of a man. **b.** A monster.

a **1400** *Minor Poems fr. Vernon MS.* 336/295 Þou seidest I scholde ben holden an vn-mon. *a* **1641** in *Vox Borealis* C 1 b (Old adage), Waters shall waxe, and Woods shall waine, And unman shall be Man, and Man shall be naine. **1879** G. MACDONALD *Sir Gibbie* xxi, He was on the wild hill, with miles on miles of cover! Here the unman could not catch him.

un'man, *v.* [UN-^{2} 6 b. Cf. MDu. (Du.) *ontmannen*, MHG. (G.) *entmannen.*]

1. *trans.* To deprive of the attributes of a man; to remove from the category of men.

1598 MARSTON *Sco. Villanie* II. vii. (1599) 204 Why, sower Satyrist, Canst thou vnman him? here I dare insist And soothly say, he is a perfect soule. **1643** TUCKNEY *Balm of G.* 40 It is..the cruell man (saith Solomon) that troubles his owne flesh; nay the Apostle un-manneth him that hates it. **1681** BAXTER *Acc. Sherlocke* vi. 212 Every Humanist that useth..gawdy fashions, is not thereby unchristened, unchurched, or unman'd. **1711** G. HICKES *Two Treat. Chr. Priesth.* (ed. 3) I. p. ccx, We cannot suppose that infinite Goodness would bind us..to such strict unalterable Duties, as unman us in this World. **1751** R. SHIRRA in *Rem.* (1850) 86 The first [Ebion] ungods him; the other [Marcion] unmans him. **1884** BROWNING *Feristah, Family* 77, I may put forth angel's plumage, once unmanned, but not before.

2. To reduce below the level of man; to degrade, brutalize. Also *refl.*

1637 A. STAFFORD *Vind. Fem. Glory* (1860) p. xxii, Hee that is not tender..unmanneth himselfe, and is but best a Monster..in humane shape. **1660** tr. *Amyraldus' Treat. conc. Relig.* I. vii. 106 They whom barbarisme ha's unman'd in all other things. **1701** W. WOTTON *Hist. Rome* 246 Habits of Vice unman Men's minds.

3. To deprive of manly courage or fortitude; to make weak or effeminate.

c **1600** CHALKHILL *Thealma & Clearchus* 846 They heard they had unmann'd themselves by ease. **1605** SHAKS. *Macb.* III. iv. 73 What? quite vnmann'd in folly... Fie for shame. *a* **1628** F. GREVIL *Poems, Hum. Learn.* xlii, Engines that did un-man the mindes of men. **1673** HICKERINGILL *Greg. F. Greyb.* 318 Impressions of fear that mollifie and unman vulgar and narrow spirits. **1715** ADDISON *Drummer* III. i, That dear Woman! the sight of her unmans me. **1736** A. HILL *Zara* V. I. 64 Tears!.. The first which ever yet unmann'd my Eyes! **1780** *Mirror* No. 90, This blow, for a time, unmanned me quite. **1847** PRESCOTT *Peru* I. 441 For a moment the overwhelming conviction of it unmanned him. **1883** *Manch. Exam.* 24 Nov. 5/1 Thirty or forty years of such treatment is enough to unman any people.

absol. **1811** BYRON *Euthanasia* vi, And women's tears, produced at will, Deceive in life, unman in death.

4. To divest of the character of a grown man. Also *intr.* (for *refl.*).

1672 PENN *Spir. Truth Vind.* 23 As he is unmanned, that is, again become a little Child. **1889** *Harper's Mag.* Jan. 191/2 But find where children haunt, and there unman, And with them laugh and play.

5. To deprive of virility; to emasculate.

1684–9 A. G. in *Plutarch's Morals* (1718) IV. 334 Because the Samians had saved the Children of the Greeks from being unmann'd [*tr.* 1603 from eviration]. **1885** E. CLODD *Myths & Dreams* 36 Gæa..provided Cronus..with an iron sickle, wherewith he unmanned Uranus.

6. To denude (a vessel or fleet) of men.

1687 MIÉGE *Gt. Fr. Dict.* II. s.v., To unman a Ship, *desarmer un Vaisseau.* **1696** in *London Gaz.* No. 3250/1 After the Fleet has been Manned, it hath been in a great Measure Unmanned again by Desertion. **1796** NELSON in Nicolas *Disp.* (1846) VII. p. xxxiv, If the Admiral had small Vessels, he could not venture to unman his Fleet.

7. *fig.* To deprive (oneself) *of* something.

1694 R. FRANCK *North. Mem.* Ded. p. xv, Let me admonish the more Ingenious Artist to be mindful of Experience, lest peradventure he slide into the slippery Tract of an Author, so unman himself of practical Demonstration.

Hence **un'manning** *vbl. sb.* and *ppl. a.*; **un'manningly** *adv.*

1610 HEALEY *St. Aug. Citie of God* VII. xxiv. 285 Here they feare not the vn-manning of them-selues. **1624** MIDDLETON *Game at Chess* I. i, I never give absolution To any crime of that unmanning nature. **1831** COLERIDGE *Table-t.* 12 Sept., The most wretched and unmanning reluctance and shrinking from action. **1886** STEVENSON *Dr. Jekyll* 58 A place for sufferings and terrors so unmanning. **1947** DYLAN THOMAS in *Horizon* Dec. 302 For who unmanningly haunts the mountain caverned eaves.

un'manacle, *v.* [UN-^{2} 4 b.] *trans.* To free from manacles. Also *fig.*

1582 STANYHURST *Æneis* II. (Arb.) 48 This sayd, my yooncker..Too stars vp mounting both his hands vnmannacled [L. *exutasvinclis*], aunswer'd. *c* **1629** DONNE *Serm* (1640) 601 We shall see the Church emancipated, enfranchised, unfettered, unmanacled. **1638** MAYNE *Lucian* (1664) 24 Stretch forth thy right hand: unmanacle him Vulcan, and nail him. **1833** TENNYSON *Two Voices* 236 This anguish fleeting hence, Unmanacled from bonds of sense. **1866** NEALE *Sequences & Hymns* 153 While..they unmanacled cold hands and numbed feet. **1889** G. SMITH *St. Paul at Sea* ii, Caesar and slave alike must be Unmanacled by me.

Hence **un'manacling** *vbl. sb.*

1635 A. STAFFORD *Fem. Glory* 208 That Death to the just is no other than..the unmanacling of the Soule.

un'manacled, *ppl. a.* (UN-^{1} 8.)

1726 C. PITT *Vida's Art of Poetry* III. 63 The lurking faults and errors you may see, When the words run unmanacled and free. **1781** COWPER *Table-t.* 589 Language,..warm As ecstasy, unmanacled by form. **1805** SOUTHEY *Madoc in W.* v. 28 Thus their limbs Unmanacled display'd the truest forms Of strength and beauty. *a* **1849** POE *Loss of Breath* Wks. 1864 IV. 308 His extreme infirmity..had obtained him the privilege of remaining unmanacled.

un'manageable, *a.* [UN-^{1} 7 b.]

1. Incapable of being governed or controlled: **a.** Of persons or their disposition.

1632 B. JONSON *Magn. Lady* I. i, My humour being as stubborn as the rest, And as unmanageable. **1665** GLANVILL *Def. Van. Dogm.* p. x, They..are rendred unmanageable by any Authority but that of Absolute Dominion. **1728** MORGAN *Algiers* II. v. 316 That tough, lofty, unmanageable Monarch [*sc.* Henry VIII]. **1791** BENTHAM *Panopt.* I. 39 As to safe custody and good order, four [prisoners] is not such a number as can well be deemed unmanageable. **1804** ABERNETHY *Surg. Obs.* 186 [During] the greater part of the delirium he had been very unmanageable. **1887** *Spectator* 25 June 854/2 The rise of soldiers who might be unmanageable or too successful.

b. Of animals. (Also in fig. context.)

1678 MRS. BEHN *Sir P. Fancy* I. i, [The fops] of the Town are the most unmanageable beasts in nature. **1681** R. L'ESTRANGE *Tully's Offices* 45 Horses..grown Fierce, and Unmenageable, by being chaf'd. **1712** WATERLAND *Serm.* Wks. 1823 VIII. 383 When they grow impatient of the curb ..they do but show..how much more unruly and unmanageable they had been without it. **1823** SCOTT *Quentin D.* ix, Each fresh gambade of his unmanageable horse. **1855** *Poultry Chron.* II. 611/1 She [*sc.* a hen] was rather conceited, unmanageable, and very touchy about interference. **1878** BOSW. SMITH *Carthage* 314 The elephants..became unmanageable.

c. Of things.

1794 PALEY *Evid.* I. II. ii. §3 Convulsions..are amongst the..most uncertain and unmanageable applications to the human frame. **1898** 'MERRIMAN' *Roden's Corner* xxi, When human affairs suddenly appear to become unmanageable.

2. Incapable of being properly or conveniently handled or manipulated.

1658 PHILLIPS, *Immanity*,..such a hugenesse as renders a thing unmanageable. **1779** *Phil. Trans.* LXIX. 422 It required an index of an unmanageable length. **1805** in Nicolas *Disp. Nelson* (1846) VII. 166 So that the Ship was entirely unmanageable. **1822** J. FLINT *Lett. Amer.* 75 Travellers..ought not to adopt large boxes, which..are comparatively unmanageable on every occasion. **1885** *Manch. Exam.* 17 Jan. 5/4 A great, awkward, unmanageable goods train.

transf. **1827** SCOTT *Two Drovers* i, The hill rung with the discordant attempts of the Saxon upon the unmanageable monosyllable. **1855** *Poultry Chron.* III. 335/1 Irish [oats] are unmanageable and comparatively neglected.

Hence **un'manageably** *adv.*

1805 FOSTER *Ess.* (1806) I. 185 If even one of the four [horses] were unmanageably perverse, while the three were obedient. **1860** FROUDE *Hist. Eng.* VI. 329 Meantime, Philip ..was becoming unmanageably impatient.

un'manageableness. (UN-^{1} 12, or f. prec.)

Also, in recent use, *unmanageability*.

1664 INGELO *Bentiv. & Ur.* VI. 182 The unmanageableness of their Horses. **1701** COLLIER *M. Anton.* (1726) 11 Their unmanageableness ruins their health. **1748** RICHARDSON *Clarissa* VII. 244 Thy servant gives me a dreadful account of thy raving unmanageableness. **1862** A. MEADOWS *Man. Midwifery* 239 Instead of a state of stupor, there is a restless unmanageableness approaching to maniacal excitement. **1877** 'H. A. PAGE' *De Quincy* I. 42 Inveterate unmanageableness, under home supervision and French tutors.

un'managed, *ppl. a.* [UN-^{1} 8.]

1. Not controlled or regulated.

1603 DRAYTON *Bar. Wars* I. i, A strong nation, whose vnmanag'd might Them from their naturall Soueraigne did diuide. **1646** HAMMOND *Tracts* 22 Mounted on an unmanaged or tender-mouth'd horse. **1673** O. WALKER *Educ.* ii. 22 Indiscreet, impertinent, unmenaged servants. **1746** FRANCIS tr. *Hor.*, *Sat.* II. ii. 11 Pursue the Chace: th' unmanaged Courser rein. **1848** T. AIRD *Christian Bride* III. vi, The abandoned chariots with unmanaged steeds Roll mad about.

b. Of language: Unrestrained, outspoken.

1771 BURKE *Corr.* (1844) I. 323 Your lordship's criminal accusations, so heavy in the matter and unmanaged in the epithets. **1791** —— *Th. French Aff.* Wks. VII. 63 The Prussian ministers in foreign courts have..talked the most democratick language with regard to France, and in the most unmanaged terms.

†**2.** Unlaboured, uncultivated. *Obs.*$^{-1}$

1634 W. WOOD *New Eng. Prosp.* (1865) 52 The folly..of such as would venture into so rude and unmanaged a countrey, without..much provisions.

un'manful, *a.* (UN-^{1} 7.)

1858 CARLYLE *Fredk. Gt.* III. xix. I. 368 He..suffered a good deal.., not at all in a dishonest or unmanful manner.

un'manfully, *adv.* (UN-^{1} 11.)

c **1400** *Destr. Troy* 10426 *heading*, Menon þe Kyng, by Achilles vnmonfully slayn. **1664** ETHEREDGE *Love in Tub* I. ii, Now have I most unmanfully fallen foul upon some Woman. **1670** MILTON *Hist. Eng.* VI. 305 They dy'd not unmanfully,..turning oft upon thir Enemies. **1711** STEELE *Spect.* No. 133 ¶2 When a Poor-spirited Creature.. bemoaned himself unmanfully, he rebuked him. [**1843** CARLYLE *Past & Pr.* III. ii, It was the terror..of doing.. unvirtuously, which was their word for un*man*fully.]

un'mangled, *ppl. a.* (UN-^{1} 8.)

For correct reading in *Gol. & Gaw.* 720, see UNMAGGLED.

1557 CHEKE in T. Hoby *Castiglione's Courtyer* (1561) 235 Our own tung shold be written cleane and pure, vnmixt and vnmangeled with borowing of other tunges. **1587** HOLINSHED *Hist. Eng.* (ed. 2) III. 298/2 From whome Grafton hath deriued his words; sense for sense vnmangled (as he found the same written). **1885** MEREDITH *Diana* i, Let her escape unmangled, it will pass in the record that she did once publicly run.

†**un'manhead.** *Obs.* [UN-^{1} 12. Cf. OHG. *unmanaheit*, MHG. *unmanheit*.] Unmanliness; unmanly conduct.

a **1300** *Cursor M.* 18795 Naman es he dos na man-hede, And of vn-man-hede es it draun, To be again god dede vn-knaun. **1387** TREVISA *Higden* (Rolls) V. 227 [The Romans] chargede þe Britouns to leve of unmanhede. *c* **1400** MAUNDEV. (Roxb.) xxxii. 145 It ware grete harme and grete vn-mannhede to grefe swilk folk.

†**un'manhood.** *Obs.*$^{-1}$ (UN-^{1} 12.)

c **1374** CHAUCER *Troylus* I. 824 Sothe hym seyde pandarus, þat for to slen hym self myghte he nat wynne But bothe doon vn-manhode and a synne.

†**un'maniable**, *a.* *Obs.*$^{-1}$ [UN-^{1} 7 b.] Unmanageable.

a **1618** RALEIGH *Lett.* (1651) 127 The lesser [ship]..is yare, whereas the greater is slow, unmanyable, and ever full of encumber.

un'manifest, *a.* (UN-^{1} 7.)

1535 W. STEWART *Cron. Scot.* (Rolls) III. 555 Trowand sic thing wnmanifest. **1687** STANLEY *Hist. Philos.* (ed. 2) XII. 782/1 It is therefore unmanifest, whether it really hath these qualities. **1760** LAW *Spir. Prayer* II. 49 Nature..is the manifestation of all that in God, which was before unmanifest. **1864** JEAN INGELOW *Poems* 22 Like the dead to sight unmanifest, They are, and they are not.

un'manifested, *ppl. a.* (UN-^{1} 8.)

1683 TRYON *Way to Health* 432 [In] all things and Creatures, in which the divine Principle does predominate, the poysonous wrathful Tree of Life lies hid and unmanifested. **1856** R. A. VAUGHAN *Mystics* II. VIII. viii. 84 The divine One, the unmanifested Subject, seeking an object. **1871** R. H. HUTTON *Theol. Ess.* I. 112 We yet have ..an inextinguishable faith in His perfection even as unmanifested.

†**un'mankled**, obs. Sc. f. UNMANACLED.

1729 RAMSAY *Sec. Answ. to Somerville* 22 My muse.. loves..to frisk..Unmankl'd, o'er poetic ground.

un'manlike, *a.* and *adv.* [UN-^{1} 7 c, 11 b.]

1. Below the level of manly conduct towards others; brutally harsh or cruel; inhuman.

1579 J. STUBBES *Gaping Gulf* E vij, That barbarous vn-manlike, and treasonable victory vpon the noble Admirall. *a* **1586** SIDNEY *Arcadia* I. xii, The unman-like cruelty of mankind. **1633** FORD *'Tis Pity* IV. iii, And wud you..kill her in your rage too? O 'twere most vn-manlike.

2. Inappropriate to a man or men.

a **1586** SIDNEY *Arcadia* II. xviii, It was the voice of a man, though it were a verie unmanlike voice. **1638** MAYNE *Lucian* (1664) A 4 Rude, un-manlike Raylings; which concluded in a Civil Warre. **1660** T. PIERCE *Inq. Nat. Sin* vi. §20. 122 As if he were proud of such an unmanlike tergiversation.

3. = UNMANLY *a.*

a **1586** SIDNEY *Arcadia* II. xviii, Never was there man that could..with a more unmanlike braverie use his tongue to her disgrace. **1619** A. NEWMAN *Pleas. Vis.* (1840) 2 He with vnmanlike Curiousnesse was dect. **1692** WASHINGTON tr. *Milton's Def. Pop.* vii, 'Tis most justly so ordered..that you your self should live in a scandalous most unmanlike slavery at home.

4. Unnaturally licentious or debasing.

1752 FIELDING *Amelia* I. iv, Having got possession of a man who was committed for certain unmanlike practices, not fit to be named.

5. *adv.* In a manner unlike that of a man.

1611 HEYWOOD *Gold. Age* I. i, Their God-like Issue thriue, Whilst I vn-man-like must destroy my babes. **1881** D. C. MURRAY *Joseph's Coat* xxvii, [He] snuffled unmanlike through his tears.

un'manlily, *adv.* (UN-^{1} 11.)

1795 MARY WOLLSTONECR. *Lett. to Imlay* 10 Feb., Yesterday he very unmanlily exulted over me.

un'manliness. (UN-^{1} 12, or f. next.)

1603 HOLLAND *Plutarch's Mor.* 93 Temperance was thought to be a cloke of effeminate unmanlinesse. **1675** *Charac. Town-Gallant* (Hindley) II. 5 Impudence he calls Boon Assurance, and unmanliness, the Genteel Negligence. **1785** WILKINS *Bhagvat* ii. 28 Yield not thus to unmanliness. **1848** KINGSLEY *Yeast* ii, You and yours make piety a synonym for unmanliness. **1861** MILL *Repr. Govt.* iii. 63 We rightly ascribe this sort of contentment to mere unmanliness and want of spirit.

un'manly, *a.* [UN-^{1} 7. Cf. MDu. *onmanlijc* (Du. *-lijk*), MHG. *unman-*, *unmenlîch* (G. *unmännlich*), ON. *úmannlig-r* (MSw. *omanliker*).]

1. Dishonourable or degrading to a man.

c **1475** *Cath. Angl.* 227/2 vn-Manly,..*inhumanus*. **1593** SHAKS. *3 Hen. VI*, I. i. 186 Be thou a prey vnto the House of Yorke..for this vnmanly deed. **1603** DEKKER *Wonderfull Yeare* Wks. (Grosart) I. 108 Now..thou..basely descendest into bruitish & vnmanly passions. **1697** DRYDEN *Æneis* II. 810 Why this unmanly rage? **1706** S. CLARKE *Attrib.* (ed. 2) 10 All mocking and scoffing at Religion..is the most unmanly and unreasonable thing in the World. **1782** MISS BURNEY *Cecilia* V. vii, [To] be guilty of.. unmanly cruelty. **1817** COLERIDGE *Zapolya* II. I. i, Your servants..Offer'd gross insults, in unmanly sort, To our village maidens. **1855** MACAULAY *Hist. Eng.* xiii. III. 310 Hatred, which showed itself by unmanly outrages to defenceless captives.

2. Not manly; unbefitting (or unlike) a man in respect of fortitude or energy; weak-tempered, effeminate.

a **1547** SURREY *Æneid* IV. 276 That Paris now, with his unmanly sorte, With mitred hats..His rape enjoyth. **1565** COOPER *Thesaurus* s.v. *Infractus*, A softe and vnmanly fourme of speakyng. **1602** SHAKS. *Ham.* I. ii. 94 'Tis vn-manly greefe, It shewes a will most incorrect to Heauen. **1682** FLAVEL *Fear* Ded., An unmanly and unchristian faintness. **1743** FRANCIS tr. *Hor.*, *Odes* V. x. 17 Thy vile, vn-manly wailings. **1796** MME. D'ARBLAY *Camilla* IV. 122 An unmanly fop. **1812** BYRON *Ch. Har.* I. xii, Others sate and wept, And to the reckless gales unmanly moaning kept. **1835** THIRLWALL *Greece* I. 339 Unmanly and pernicious luxury.

un'manly, *adv.* Now *rare.* [UN-^{1} 11. Cf. Du. *onmanlijk*, ON. *úmannliga* (MSw. *omanlika*).]

1. Dishonourably; treacherously.

c **1400** *Destr. Troy* 13785 [A] kyng..By the myrmydons vnmonly murtherit to dethe. *c* **1465** *Eng. Chron.* (Camden, 1856) 50 He was traitorly and vnmanli slayn, and cast in to a pit. **1626** R. PEEKE *Three to One* B 3, Some of our Men were vnfortunately and vnmanly surprised.

2. Inhumanely; with unmanly cruelty or unkindness.

c **1475** *Cath. Angl.* 227/2 Vn-Manly, *inhumaniter*. **1594** *Selimus* 1513 Shall he thus unmanly be misus'd? **1658** CLEVELAND *Rustic Ramp.* Wks. (1687) 464 A Dominion so unmanly cruel. **1673** HICKERINGILL *Greg. F. Greyb.* 46 If he had not so unmanly..play'd upon the dead. **1717** MRS. CENTLIVRE *Cruel Gift* IV, Unmanly dost thou urge my Father's faults. **1824** T. FENBY *Last Sad Scene* viii, This was all for him who hath, Untimely and unmanly, left me.

3. With unmanly weakness.

1579–80 NORTH *Plutarch* (1595) 908 So he tooke his banishment vnmanly. **1603** HOLLAND *Plutarch's Mor.* 61 We ought not to heare the reprehensions..of Philosophers recklessly.., nor yet unmanly.

un'manned, *ppl. a.*^{1} [UN-^{1} 8.]

1. Not furnished with men or with a crew (cf. MAN *v.* 1).

1544 BETHAM *Precepts War* II. li. L iij, That he leaue not his campe vndefenced and vnmanned. **1592** KYD *Sp. Trag.* IV. iv. 211 Set me with him—Vpon the maine mast of a.. ship vnmand. **1670** MILTON *Hist. Eng.* I. 5 Not put to death, but turn'd out to Sea in a Ship unmann'd. **1726** POPE *Iliad* XXII. 469 See, if already their deserted towers Are left unmann'd. **1830** MARRYAT *King's Own* xlvi, One of the unmanned oars. **1844** KINGLAKE *Eothen* vi, Four of the craft ..had been left unmanned. **1895** MARG. STOKES *Three Months in France* 230 The phantom ship, sail-less, rudderless, and unmanned. **1906** *Nature* 8 Nov. 35/2 The machines he made and launched were all 'unmanned'. **1907** *Ibid.* 4 Apr. 538/2 During the course of the last few years very rapid strides have been made in investigating the upper air by means of manned and unmanned balloons. **1946** *Congressional Digest* May 154/2 'Drone' aircraft—they are unmanned, radio controlled. **1954** *Economist* 11 Sept. 3/2 The manned fighter is surrendering some of its duties to wingless, almost tailless, unmanned missiles. **1962** F. I. ORDWAY et al. *Basic Astronautics* xiii. 552 Unmanned satellites and guided missiles. **1969** *Listener* 20 Feb. 232/2 The pictures you brought back from the Moon were not as good as those taken on an unmanned flight. **1972** *Guardian* 22 Feb. 2/4 The unmanned Soviet moon probe Luna 20 made a soft landing on the moon's surface last night. **1977** *R.A.F. News* 11–24 May 3/4 The RAF was watching the developments concerning Cruise missiles and other unmanned systems... If unmanned vehicles could be developed to take on some of the roles of air power this would be welcomed.

fig. **1602** MARSTON *Antonio's Rev.* I. v, Native heate So prodigally flow'd t' exterior parts, That inner citadell was left unmand. **1675** DRYDEN *Aurengz.* IV. i, To guard that Breach [I] did all my Forces guide And left unmann'd the quiet Senses side.

2. a. Devoid of a man; empty.

1602 WARNER *Alb. Eng.* XII. lxix. 291 At first she feares, but lastly findes the Armor was vn-man'd.

b. Unsupported by men; unassisted.

c **1620** [FLETCHER & MASS.] *Trag. Barnavelt* IV. i. in Bullen *O. Pl.* (1883) II. 271 Make haste, he is yet unmand: we may come time enough To enter with him. **1642** FULLER *Holy & Prof. St.* Pref. §5 Nor let it render the modestie of this book suspected, because it presumes to appear in company unmann'd by any Patron.

c. Unoccupied by men; unpeopled.

1680 C. NESSE *Church Hist.* 230 They left it [*sc.* the land] unmann'd thrice in the year. **1764** GOLDSM. *Trav.* 142 Nought remain'd..But towns unmann'd, and lords without a slave.

3. Not trained or broken in; *spec.* of a hawk.

1592 SHAKS. *Rom. & Jul.* III. ii. 14 Come ciuill night,.. Hood my vnman'd blood bayting in my Cheekes, With thy Blacke mantle. **1611** COTGR. s.v. *Acheter*, Buy a house made, and a wife vnmand. **1623** J. TAYLOR (Water P.) *Discov. by Sea* Wks. (1630) 28/2 Like a wild Kestrell or vnmand Hawke. *a* **1637** B. JONSON *Sad Sheph.* III. iii, No colt is so unbroken, Or hawk yet half so haggard or unmann'd.

un'manned, *ppl. a.*² [f. UNMAN *v.*] Deprived of courage; made weak or timid.

1694 F. BRAGGE *Disc. Parables* ix. 317 Imaginary dangers terrifie their unmanned souls.

un'manner, *v. rare*⁻¹. (UN-² 6 b).

1613–8 DANIEL *Coll. Hist. Eng.* Wks (Grosart) V. 140 Those softnings of Luxury and Idlenesse which vnmanners them.

un'mannered, *ppl. a.* [UN-¹ 8.]

†**1.** Not duly regulated or moderated. *Obs.*⁻¹

1435 MISYN *Fire of Love* 94 Lufe forsoth of kynsmen, if it be vn-manerd, fleschly affeccione it is cald [= called], .. and if it be manerd, kyndely it is calde.

2. Of persons: Not possessed of good manners; unmannerly, rude.

1594 SHAKS. *Rich. III*, I. ii. 39 Vnmanner'd Dogge, Stand'st thou when I commaund. **1610** FLETCHER *Faithf. Sheph.* II. i, I fear I am too much unmanner'd, far too rude. **1693** DRYDEN *Juvenal* VI. 543 No Pray'r can bend her, no Excuse appease. Th' unmanner'd Malefactor is arraign'd. **1745** J. MASON *Self-Knowl.* I. ix, He is not only ignorant and unmanner'd, but unsufferably vain. **1824** SCOTT *St. Ronan's* xxxi, This awkward, ill-dressed, unmannered dowdy. **1879** MEREDITH *Egoist* xix, He knew scholars to be an unmannered species.

transf. **1854** S. DOBELL *Balder* i. 5 Thou grim wall, Hemming her in with thine unmannered rock.

3. Of conduct: Characterized by want of manners.

1760–72 H. BROOKE *Fool of Qual.* (1809) IV. 103 He gazed at Louisa with .. an unmannered intenseness. **1772** *Ess. fr. Batchelor* (1773) II. 146 His superior abilities .. were never exerted with unmannered insolence. **1836** *Lyra Apost.* 27 A ready prey, as though in absent mood They calmly move, nor hear the unmannered mirth. **1871** B. TAYLOR *Faust* (1875) II. III. 176 In most unmannered anger ye Have conjured hither pictures of the shapes of dread.

4. Free from artificial manners.

1813 LAMB *Reynolds* Wks. 1908 I. 190 The plain unmannered old Nobility of the .. Plays of Shakspeare.

Hence **un'manneredly** *adv.*

1894 KIPLING in *My First Bk.* 92 All my verses .. came without invitation, unmanneredly, in the nature of things.

†**un'manneredly**, *a. Obs.* [UN-¹ 7.] Unmannerly.

1792 W. ROBERTS *Looker-On* iv. 30 In flying from two unmanneredly catchpoles, you ran full against me. *Ibid.* xxx. 238 In your unmanneredly haste to interrupt us.

un'mannerliness. [f. next.] The condition or fact of being unmannerly.

1580 HOLLYBAND *Treas. Fr. Tong, Incivilité*, vnmanerlines, vncurtesie. **1598** HAKLUYT *Voy.* I. 586 Moreouer he noteth much vnmanerlinesse of eating and drinking at bankets. *c* **1629** DONNE *Serm.* Wks. 1839 V. 16 It were un-mannerliness to hold you longer in the Entry. **1647** H. MORE *Song of Soul* Ded. A 2 b, What a piece of Unmannerlinesse and Incivility it would be held to seem wiser then them. **1699** LOCKE *Educ.* (ed. 4) 263 A sort of Unmannerliness very apt to grow up with young People. *a* **1782** BP. NEWTON *Wks.* II. 681 The unmannerliness and unruliness of some of his subjects.

un'mannerly, *a.* [UN-¹ 7. Cf. WFris. *ûn-*, *onmenearlijk*, MDu. *onmanierlijc*, G. *unmanierlich*; Da. *umanerlig*, Sw. *omanerlig.*]

1. Of persons: Devoid of manners; impolite; behaving rudely or discourteously.

1388 WYCLIF *Rom.* i. 31 Thei ben .. vnwise, vnmanerli, withouten loue. **1575** R. B. *Appius & Virg.* in Hazl. *Dodsley* IV. 121 Have ye heard such an unmannerly villain? **1591** SHAKS. *Two Gent.* III. i. 393 An vnmannerly slaue, that will thrust himselfe into secrets. *a* **1616** BEAUM. & FL. *Wit at Sev. Weapons* IV. i, Fall back, .. you unmannerly puppy. **1653** R. SANDERS *Physiogn.* 58 A rustick, unmannerly, dull person. **1730** FIELDING *Rape upon Rape* IV. iv, The Fright which that unmannerly Friend of yours occasioned. **1833** HT. MARTINEAU *Brooke Farm* ii. 19 Billy was not fit to go into a gentleman's family, he was so unmannerly. **1885** 'MRS. ALEXANDER' *Valerie's Fate* iv, I fear you must think me very unmannerly, very rude.

transf. **1827** POLLOK *Course T.* III. 570 Comets rude, That should unmannerly and lawless drive Athwart the path of Earth.

2. Of actions, conduct, speech, etc.: Showing want of manners.

c **1425** in *Anglia* VIII. 139 Vnsem and vnmanerly berynge of body. *Ibid.* 194, I wole make an ende of myn vnmanerly wordes. *c* **1510** MORE *Picus* Wks. 15/1 The company of the court .. (as it is their vnmanerly maner) descanted therof. **1581** J. BELL *Haddon's Answ. Osor.* 262 b, If there were any reason in all these your unmannerly tauntes. **1617** WOODALL *Surg. Mate* Pref. (1639) B, Comparisons being odious and unmannerly amongst good men. **1699** BENTLEY *Phal.* 122 Breaking his unmannerly Jests upon his own mistakes. **1722** DE FOE *Relig. Courtsh.* I. i. (1840) 29 That's the unmannerliest thing in the World. **1756** WASHINGTON *Let. to Dinwiddie* 24 Nov., I am very sorry any expression in my letter should be deemed unmannerly. **1846** TRENCH *Mirac.* xxx. 425 These ill-timed and unmannerly clamors. **1884** *Manch. Exam.* 27 Nov. 5/2 The opposition to Mr. Caine was singularly unmannerly.

un'mannerly, *adv.* [UN-¹ 11.]

1. In an unmannerly fashion; with lack of good manners; impolitely.

13.. *Gaw. & Gr. Knt.* 2339 Be not so gryndel; No mon here vn-manerly þe mys-boden habbe[z]. **1460** CAPGRAVE *Chron.* (Rolls) 145 Thei .. treted the ladies onmanerly. **1509** BARCLAY *Shyp of Folys* (1570) 192 In praying thou bokest vnmanerly, Spuing vp thy prayers .. vndeuoutly. **1594** CAREW *Huarte's Exam. Wits* 210 If .. so they should deliuer vs their opinion .. we would hold them importunate and vnmannerly brought vp. **1625** K. LONG tr. *Barclay's Argenis* v. xviii. 394 He, out of good manners, came close to him, .. that the King might not be unmannerly left alone in the midst of the roome. **1682** C. IRVINE *Hist. Scot. Nomencl.* Ded. *iij b, They would easily excuse him .. that must, with the croud, unmannerly approach your Highness. **1832** J. J. BLUNT *Reform. in Eng.* 209 The Reformers .. did not unmannerly reject those Offices of the Church. **1859** TENNYSON *Guinevere* 314 If I seem To vex an ear too sad to listen to me, Unmannerly, with prattling.

†**2.** Improperly, immoderately. *Obs.*⁻¹

1435 MISYN *Fire of Love* 53 Fraward men þer ar, þat þer wyffis for þer bewte vnmanerly lufys.

unmanning, *vbl. sb.* and *ppl. a.*: see UNMAN *v.*

un'mannish, *a.* (UN-¹ 7.)

a **1894** STEVENSON *St. Ives* iii, There was something wild and unmannish in his smile.

un'mantle, *v.* [UN-² 4, 7. Cf. Du. *ontmantelen*, G. *entmanteln*, *-mänteln.*]

1. *trans.* To divest of a mantle or covering.

1598 FLORIO, *Smantellare*, to vnmantle, to vncloke. *c* **1645** HOWELL *Lett.* (1650) I. 26 They unmantled him of a new plush cloke. **1745** H. WALPOLE *Lett.* (1846) II. 86 The new-born babe was shown in a .. cradle .. under a canopy; .. the governess advanced to unmantle it. *a* **1800** COWPER *Odyss.* (ed. 2) x. 215 Obedient from the ground, Their folded brows unmantling, all arose, And with admiring eyes .. the stag survey'd. **1821** SCOTT *Kenilw.* vii, The Earl .. affected to resist when she strove to take his cloak from him. 'Nay,' she said, 'but I will unmantle you'.

fig. **1660** C. SOUTHAICK *Fames Genius* (1863) 23 Not to unmantle self and subtilty, But the true Portraicture of honesty.

b. *intr.* To take off one's mantle.

1822 A. CUNNINGHAM *Tradit. Tales* I. 239 Unmantling as she spoke, [she] turned back to the Towers of Haddon the fairest face that ever left them.

2. *trans.* To dismantle, unfurnish.

1828 SCOTT *Tapestried Chamber* ad fin., Lord Woodville [went] to command the Tapestried Chamber to be unmantled, and the door built up.

un'mantled, *ppl. a.* [UN-¹ 8.] Not mantled or covered.

[**1775** ASH.] **1800** CAMPBELL *Ode to Winter* iii, Shuddering Want's unmantled bed. **1818** BYRON *Ch. Har.* IV. cxlviii, Her unmantled neck, and bosom white and bare.

†**un'manuable**, *a. Obs.*⁻¹ [UN-¹ 7 b.] Unmanageable.

1633 T. JAMES *Voy.* 116 Our sailes froze in lumps to the yards, vnmanuable.

unmanu'facturable, *a.* (UN-¹ 7 b.)

1784 *Phil. Trans.* LXXIV. 468 Whence it should seem, that neither .. tend much to render gold unmanufacturable.

unmanu'factured, *ppl. a.* (UN-¹ 8.)

[**1775** ASH.] **1796** MORSE *Amer. Geog.* II. 608 Unmanufactured as well as prepared flax. **1841** W. SPALDING *Italy & It. Isl.* III. 385 There are exported, in the unmanufactured state, about 5,508,000 lbs. **1879** *Cassell's Techn. Educ.* II. 114 Unmanufactured cork is admitted into England duty free.

unmanu'mitted, *ppl. a.* (UN-¹ 8.)

1661 HICKERINGILL *Jamaica* 30 The Petticoat Sex (through the rigour of their masters unmanumitted). **1880** MUIRHEAD *Gaius* Dig. 540 Women who had been remancipated .., but were still un-manumitted.

unma'nurable, *a.* [UN-¹ 7 b.] †Uncultivable.

1610 HOLLAND *Camden's Brit.* I. 799 [Land] rough and as it were un-manurable. **1707** SLOANE *Jamaica* I. p. vii, The quantity of Acres are ..: Manurable 6,100,000; Unmanurable 100,000.

unma'nured, *ppl. a.* [UN-¹ 8.]

†**1.** Of land: Uncultivated, untilled. *Obs.*

In frequent use from *c* 1590 to *c* 1640.

1570 FOXE *A. & M.* (ed. 2) I. 222/2 The prouince lay waste and vnmanured. **1578** LYTE *Dodoens* 257 All rough and unmanured places. **1632** W. LITHGOW *Trav.* III. 85, I could not find a foote of ground vnmanured. *c* **1694** DRYDEN *Let. to J. Dennis* ¶4 It looks like a vast tract of land newly discover'd: the soil is wonderfully fruitful, but unmanur'd. **1721** RAMSAY *Prospect of Plenty* 222 To let braid tracts of land lie unmanur'd.

b. *fig.* or in fig. contexts.

1594 *Selimus* 381 It argueth an unmanured wit. *a* **1631** DONNE *Heroical Epist.* 36 Thy body is a naturall Paradise, In whose selfe, unmanur'd, all pleasure lies. **1663** COWLEY *On Orinda's Poems* ii, 'Twere shame .. if in thee A Spirit so rich .. Should unmanur'd, or barren lye. **1700** T. BROWN *Amusem. Ser. & Com.* 69 Gallantry .. which was formerly so well Cultivated, .. is at present Desolate, Unmanur'd and Abandoned!

2. Not supplied with manure.

[**1828–32** WEBSTER.] **1849** JOHNSTON *Exp. Agric.* 105 The unmanured [crop] might have ripened its seed while the manured was still growing. **1868** *Rep. U.S. Commissioner Agric.* (1869) 419 The average product of unmanured American soil.

un'mapped, *ppl. a.* (UN-¹ 8.)

1805 *Ann. Rev.* III. 13 Both travellers have .. rivers unmapped to navigate. **1857** THOREAU *Maine W.* i. (1869) 87 The country is virtually unmapped. **1876** GEO. ELIOT *Dan. Der.* III. xxiv, There is a great deal of unmapped country within us.

un'marching, *ppl. a.* (UN-¹ 10.)

1837 CARLYLE *Fr. Rev.* II. v. vii, To all which our poor Legislative, tied up by an unmarching Constitution, can oppose nothing.

un'maritime, *a.* (UN-¹ 7.)

1817 G. S. FABER *Eight Dissert.* (1845) II. 230 The thoroughly unmaritime Empire of Rome.

un'marked, *ppl. a.* [UN-¹ 8. Cf. ON. *úmarkaðr*; also ON. *úmerktr* (MSw. *omärkter*, Sw. *omärkt*, older Da. *umærket*.)]

1. a. Having received no mark or impress; left without a mark; having no distinguishing or identificatory mark.

14.. *Sir Beues* (M.) 160/3111 None went vnmarked away, That Beuys hyt wyth Morglay. **1480** *Cely Papers* (Camden) 53, [1093] felles qwherof be iiij^c xlvj Cottysowlde on-markyd and the rembnant .. be markyd w^t an O. *a* **1578** LINDESAY *Chron. Scot.* (S.T.S.) II. 320 Nane wald resawe thame [*sc.* pennies] nathir marcat nor onmarcat. **1651** BAXTER *Inf. Bapt.* 199 You may know such a man's Flock of Sheep by the mark; when yet perhaps some may be unmarkt. **1705** *Lond. Gaz.* No. 4104/4 Stoln .., 2 Sweet-meat Spoons, forked, unmarked. *c* **1790** IMISON *Sch. Arts* II. 762 That the magnet .. may rest with its marked end on the unmarked end of A. **1872** M. S. DE VERE *Americanisms* 211 The name of *Maverick*, used in Texas to designate an unmarked yearling. **1936** M. MITCHELL *Gone with Wind* xxx. 502 The thousands in unmarked graves who would never come home. **1960** 'E. MCBAIN' *Give Boys Great Big Hand* (1962) v. 42 The unmarked police sedan pulled to the curb. **1967** L. HUGHES *Panther & Lash* 65 They buried Lumumba In an unmarked grave. But he needs no marker —For air is his grave. **1975** *New Yorker* 2 June 101/1 The two patrolmen had driven in their unmarked car to the west end of the Mercer Island Floating Bridge. **1979** C. MCCARRY *Better Angels* III. iii. 208 He had flown in from Paris .. in his own unmarked plane.

Comb. **1895** *Daily News* 25 Mar. 8/6 The attempt to unite the unmarked iron firms has not been abandoned.

b. Not marked off or out, not distinguished or characterized (*by* something).

1791 F. BURNEY *Jrnl.* Dec. (1972) I. 103 Our visit to Mrs. Montagu turned out very unmarked; I met my good Mrs. & Miss ord, & a little chat with them was all my entertainment. **1815** *Monthly Rev.* LXXVI. 455 Virgil's characters are mostly cold, unmarked, and not attaching. **1824** SCOTT *St. Ronan's* xi, Men .. whose spirit and courage lie hidden .. under an unmarked or a plain exterior. **1882** FARRAR *Early Chr.* II. 482 Compositions so short .. and so unmarked by special features.

c. Of a linguistic construction, form, etc.: not marked (see MARKED *ppl. a.* 1 c).

1933, etc. [see MARKED *ppl. a.* 1 c]. **1964** C. BARBER *Present-Day Eng.* iv. 105 *Author* .. can be used of both men and women; this is called the *unmarked* member of the pair [*author*: *authoress*]. **1978** *Sci. Amer.* Nov. 95/1 In the case of 'wide' and 'narrow', 'wide' is the unmarked word: asking 'How wide is the road?' does not suggest that the road is wide, but asking 'How narrow is the road?' does suggest that the road is narrow. **1980** *Amer. Speech* LV. 88 Features of an unmarked register may be imported into a marked one, but not vice versa.

2. Unnoticed, unobserved.

1533 MORE *Debell. Salem* Wks. 1026/2 Here was himselfe faine .. to begyle the reader vppon the readyng of the place, and make hym passe ouer his faute for the while vnmarked. **1583** BABINGTON *Commandm.* (1590) 251 Sathan breedeth by his vnmarked creeping into our affections a misliking of such a man or woman. **1628** SIR S. D'EWES *Jrnl.* (1783) 42 Hee passed quietlie unmarked .. out of the saied hall. **1667** MILTON *P.L.* x. 441 He through the midst unmarkt .. past. **1744** AKENSIDE *Pleas. Imag.* II. 184 Oft the hours From morn to eve have stol'n unmark'd away. **1821** SCOTT *Kenilw.* xiii, Like one who has suddenly recognized some mighty hero .. in the person of an unknown and unmarked stranger. **1850** TENNYSON *In Mem.* xcviii, Let her great Danube rolling fair Enwind her isles, unmark'd of me.

un'marketable, *a.* (UN-¹ 7 b.)

Hence, in recent use, ***unmarketability***, ***-ableness***.

1654 in *Manchester Crt. Leet Rec.* (1887) IV. 112 Roger Royle of Eccles for sellinge vnmarkettable Beefe. **1776** *Ann. Reg., Chron.* 139/2 A parcel of hops .. badly cured, and, on that account, unmarketable. **1800** G. G. STONESTREET *Portentous Globe* 33 Their trade would be rendered unprofitable—their shares unmarketable. **1861** GEO. ELIOT *Silas M.* iv, His own ill-favoured person, which was unmarketable, escaped without injury. **1885** SIR W. V. FIELD in *Law Times' Rep.* LII. 654/1 So as to render the property unmarketable.

un'marred, *ppl. a.* (UN-¹ 8.)

a **1200** *St. Marher.* 10 þe edle meiden allunge unmerred wiðuten euereuch weom wende ut of his wombe. **13..** *E.E. Allit. P.* B. 867 Maydenez vnmard for alle men ȝette. [*c* **1470** *Gol. & Gaw.* 720 Wes nane .. Wnmaglit and marrit.] **1596** SPENSER *F.Q.* VI. x. 7 His siluer waues did softly tumble downe, Vnmard with ragged mosse or filthy mud. **1744** YOUNG *Nt. Th.* VII. 301 Their good is good entire, unmixt, unmarr'd. **1827** POLLOK *Course T.* VII. 585 Unmarred, unfaded work of Deity. **1851** SIR F. PALGRAVE *Norm. & Eng.* I. 473 The spirit and talent which, unmarred by fate, might [etc.]. **1871** MACDUFF *Mem. Patmos* xix. 263 In the fellowship of unmarred and unbroken communion.

un'marriable, *a.* (UN-¹ 7 b.)

1542 UDALL *Erasm. Apoph.* 177 b, Cleopatra .. beeyng yet a young damysell vnmariable. **1611** COTGR., *Immariable*, vnmarriable. **1643** MILTON *Divorce* 36 Parted from each other, as two persons unconjunctive, and unmariable together.

un'marriageable, *a.* (UN-¹ 7 b.)

[**1775** ASH.] **1787** W. THOMSON tr. *A. Cunningham's Hist. Gt. Brit.* I. 121 Their women are seldom married young; and are indeed long unmarriageable. **1841** EMERSON *Method Nature* (1844) 14 He was hurled into being as .. the mediator betwixt two else unmarriageable facts. **1856** S. DOBELL *Lyrics War Times, German Legion*, I could kneel down by thee, And o'er thy chill unmarriageable rest Cry [etc.].

un'married, *ppl. a.* [UN-¹ 8.]

1. a. Of persons: Not married; unwedded.

1297 R. Glouc. (Rolls) 737 Þe gode cordeile vnmaried was so. *c* **1400** Maundev. (1839) xix. 209 Wommen that ben un-maryed, thei han Tokenes on hire Hedes. *a* **1450** Lovelich *Grail* lv. 50 Wedded weren.. Alle his bretheryn except on.. that tho was vn-maryed. **1491** *Act 7 Hen. VII*, c. 20 §6 If.. Elizabeth dye unmaryed. *a* **1540** Barnes *Wks.* (1573) 364/2 This thing dyd Paphnutius, though that hee hym selfe was vnmaryed. **1591** *Knaresb. Wills* (Surtees) I. 187 All my children bothe maryed and unmaried. **1607–12** Bacon *Ess., Marriage & Single Life* (Arb.) 266 Vnmarryed Men are best Frendes. **1653** H. Cogan *Diod. Sic.* iv. xxii. 152 He lived all his life time unmarried. **1728** Young *Love Fame* vi. 79 Unmarry'd Abra puts on formal airs. **1779** *Mirror* No. 12, The two eldest of my unmarried daughters. **1834** *Rep. Poor Laws* 196 in *Parl. Papers* XXVII. 200 An unmarried mother has voluntarily placed herself in the situation of a widow. **1834** Wellington *Let. to Miss J.* 24 Oct., The Duke is not in the habit of visiting young unmarried ladies. **1875** Ruskin *Fors Clav.* V. lvi. 235 Every unmarried woman should have enough left her by her father to keep herself, and a pet dog. **1933** D. C. E. Peel *Life's Enchanted Cup* i. 9 People did not look upon unmarried mothers with so lenient an eye as they came to do during the war. **1965** Hall & Howes *Church in Social Work* ii. 50 Unmarried fathers and 'other men in moral difficulty'. **1972** *Guardian* 15 Nov. 9/1 One [letter] suggests that if unmarried mums were only encouraged to keep their babies, this sort of thing couldn't happen. **1983** J. Gardner *Elephants in Attic* iv. 29 In the thirties unmarried mums were not the 'in' thing.

transf. **1611** Shaks. *Wint. T.* iv. iv. 123 Pale Prime-roses, That dye vnmarried, ere they can behold Bright Phœbus in his strength. **1771** *Encycl. Brit.* I. 651/2 [The insect] flies from flower to flower till it arrives at the unmarried female.

b. *absol.* and as *sb.*

1557 N.T. (Geneva) *1 Cor.* vii. 8, I say vnto the vnmaried, and widowes, it is good [etc.]. **1619** Fletcher *Knt. Malta* v. i, Husband, Wife, There is some holy mystery in those names That sure the unmarried cannot understand. **1728** Eliza Heywood tr. *Mme. de Gomez's Belle A.* (1732) II. 147 Neither did the Night want its Charms both to the married and the unmarried. **1819** *Metropolis* I. 71 We had a very bad turn out of British females, mostly dowagers and elderly unmarrieds. **1871** A. Meadows *Man. Midwifery* (ed. 2) ii. 59 In the case of the unmarried, he may.. cast a slur upon a spotless character.

2. Lived free from marriage.

1648 Hexham ii, *Een eeloosen Staet*, an Unmarried State. **1747** Francis tr. *Horace, Epist.* i. i. 125 How happy then is an unmarried Life! **1755** Johnson, *Celibacy*, single life; unmarried state. **1930** R. Lehmann *Note in Music* iv. 157 He carried on the splendid tradition of unmarried fatherhood. **1962** *Sunday Express* 30 Dec. 19/5 The problems of unmarried motherhood. **1980** C. Fremlin *With No Crying* i. 6 Friends.. passionately defending her right to unmarried motherhood.

un'marry, *v.* [un-[2] 3, 7.]

1. *trans.* (and *refl.*). To dissolve the marriage of; to free from the marriage-tie; to divorce.

1530 Palsgr. 768/2, I can unmary my selfe by ronnyng away. **1588** Parke tr. *Mendoza's Hist. China* 401 He doth vnmarry them, and setteth her at libertie that she may marry with an other. **1637** Shirley *Gamester* i. i, Yes, I did marry you;.. I would there were a parson to unmarry us! **1680** Baxter *Answ. Stillingfl.* xii. 20 As he that marrieth Persons may not.. unmarry them again, save for Adultery. **1760–72** H. Brooke *Fool of Qual.* (1809) II. 59 If he does not first unmarry himself, I will never see him any more. **1857** Dickens *Dorrit* ii. viii, They are fast married, and can't be unmarried. **1881** Besant & Rice *Chapl. of Fleet* II. 177 Nothing can unmarry you now.

absol. **1708** O. Dykes *Eng. Prov. & Refl.* 7 In fine, an After-Thought cannot unmarry; it cannot set a broken Leg.

b. To put away, to divorce (a wife).

1645 Milton *Tetrach.* 49 Is it imaginable there should bee among these.. a law giving permissions laxative to unmarry a wife and marry a lust? **1797** Mrs. A. M. Bennett *Beggar Girl* (1813) III. 177 Though he did not live with her, he could not unmarry her.

2. *intr.* To free oneself from marriage.

1635 J. Hayward tr. *Biondi's Banish'd Virg.* 172 Having left her father, and unmarried and remarried againe at her pleasure. **1652** J. Wright tr. *Camus' Nat. Paradox* x. 244, I marry without injoying my wife, I unmarry, I marry again. **1769** in *Priv. Lett. Ld. Malmesbury* (1870) I. 172 We are unmarrying among the great; the Duke of Grafton's divorce was finished this morning. **1839** J. Rogers *Antipopopr.* xvi. §3. 332 Thus people may neither marry nor unmarry without priorly obtaining permission from the priesthood. **1895** *How to get Married* 86 Actors marry and unmarry *ad libitum* in a disgraceful way.

un'marrying, *ppl. a.* (un-[1] 10.)

1846 H. G. Robinson *Odes of Horace* ii. xv, The unmarrying [L. *cælebs*] plane [will] o'erwhelm Shortly with its growth the elm. **1848** Lady Lyttelton *Corr.* (1912) 385 An unmarrying old young lady.

un'marshalled, *ppl. a.* (un-[1] 8.)

1767 Lewis *Statius* xii. 906 Ev'ry Plain To Combate sends a rude, unmarshall'd Train.

un'martial, *a.* (un-[1] 7.)

1611 Speed *Hist. Gt. Brit.* vi. xxii. §4. 109 [They] consumed their times in banquetting, and vnmartiall disports. **1797** *Monthly Mag.* III. 306 The effect of the whole is so dry and unmartial as to do little credit to the musical taste of Louis the XVIth. **1880** L. Wallace *Ben-Hur* 520 This most unmartial figure.

†**un'martial**, *v. Obs.*[−1] (un-[2] 6 a.)

1654 Gayton *Pleas. Notes* iv. ii. 180 To unmartiall the whole man, and leave him without steel or iron upon him, is as if you should pare the nailes of a Lyon.

un'martyr, *v.* (un-[2] 6 b.)

1646 Prynne *Canterb. Doome* Ep. Ded. a 2, The setting forth of this History of his Tryall, will soon Un-martyr, Un-saint, Uncrown this Arch-Imposter. **1655** Fuller *Ch. Hist.* ii. iv. §36 Scotus.. was made a Martyr after his Death... But since Baronius hath unmartyred him.

un'martyred, *ppl. a.* (un-[1] 8.)

c **1580** Munday *View Sundry Examples* (Shaks. Soc.) 88 Beaten.. so that from the crown of the hed to the soles of the feet, was left no member unmartired. *a* **1633** W. Austin *Medit.* (1635) 112 They.. left not a peece of him unmartyred, till they had killed him. **1908** Rider Haggard *Ghost Kings* i. 7 Should he return.. not only unmartyred but a palpable failure..?

un'marvellous, *a.* (un-[1] 7.)

1790 Wolcot (P. Pindar) *Ode Jas. Bruce* iv, Thy soul delights in wonder, pomp, and bustle; Mine in th' unmarvellous and placid scene. **1855** Maurice *Learn. & Work.* iv. 107 This Hope.. may.. shrink into a very obvious, intelligible, unmarvellous quality.

†**un'masculate.** *v. Obs.*[−1] [un-[2] 3.] *trans.* To emasculate.

1639 Fuller *Holy War* 255 The sinnes of the South unmasculate Northern bodies.

un'masculine, *a.* (un-[1] 7.)

1649 Milton *Tenure Kings* 5 The unmasculine Rhetorick of any puling Priest or Chaplain. **1829** Lamb *Lett.* (1886) II. 304 My whole heart is faint, and my whole head is sick.. at this damned canting, unmasculine age!

un'mask, *v.* [un-[2] 4, 7. Cf. Du. *ont-*, G. *entmasken*.]

1. *trans.* To free (the face) from a mask or vizard; to remove a mask or covering from. Also in fig. context.

1602 Shaks. *Ham.* i. iii. 37 The chariest Maid is Prodigall enough, If she vnmaske her beauty to the Moone. **1626** T. H[awkins] *Caussin's Holy Crt.* 134 An heresy discouered, is a face unmasked, take away the vizard, you disarme her. **1665** Sir T. Herbert *Trav.* (1677) 154 The Bridge.. was.. full of Women,.. many of which.. in a fair deportment un-masqued their faces. **1728** Eliza Heywood tr. *Mme. de Gomez's Belle A.* (1732) II. 24 The Demand I am about to make.. is to follow my Example, and immediately be all unmask'd. **1841** Emerson *Lect. on Times* (1844) 72 To-day is a king in disguise... Let us unmask the king as he passes. **1876** J. Saunders *Lion in Path* xxxvii, We must unmask you, pretty Mistress Preston.

refl. **1825** Scott *Talism.* x, Putting his hand to his chin, and withdrawing it with the action of one who unmasks himself.

b. To remove like a mask.

1624 G. Raleigh in Farr *Sel. P. Jas. I* (1847) 242 Our tender muse hath labored as she could; Her sable vaile she must of force unmaske.

2. *fig.* To divest of a specious appearance or show; to disclose the true character of; to bring into the light; to make plain or obvious.

1593 Shaks. *Lucr.* 1602 Vnmaske.. this moodie heauinesse, And tell thy griefe. **1611** Speed *Theat. Gt. Brit.* i. xlii. 81/2 Since the true God hath vnmasked the errors of those times by the truth of his word. **1646** Gataker *Mistake Removed* 39 Which yet the whole drift of his discours will easily un-maske. **1672** Wilkins *Nat. Relig.* 44 Time.. doth by degrees discover & unmask the fallacy of ungrounded perswasions. **1704** Norris *Ideal World* ii. iii. 257 Could we but unmask nature, and strip it of all those false ornaments wherewith our prejudiced imagination has cloathed it. **1798** *Monthly Mag.* VI. 552 In unmasking the popular heathenism, and in revealing the immortality of the soul. **1844** Thirlwall *Greece* VIII. 241 The accuser.. unmasked their conspiracy with Apelles. **1869** Mozley *Univ. Serm.* ii. (1876) 43 That judicial mission which was to unmask false goodness.

b. With personal object. Also *refl.*

a **1586** Sidney *Arcadia* ii. xxiii, Zelmane thought-sicke, unmaskes her selfe. **1640** Sir W. Mure *Counter-Buff* 125 Now thy piece I must anatomize... The frontespiece un-maskes an hypocrite. **1668** Temple *Let. to Ld. Arlington* Wks. 1720 II. 97 They must now suddenly unmask them-selves in one way or other, no farther Pretences being left. **1718** *Free-thinker* No. 75. 140 The Person.. lives under a perpetual Apprehension of being unmasked. **1797** Mrs. Radcliffe *Italian* ix, 'The hypocrite!' said he to himself..; 'but I will unmask him'. **1819** Crabbe *T. of Hall* xii. 296 No sooner was it [*sc.* her hand in marriage] ask'd Than she the lovely Jezebel unmask'd. **1872** Morley *Voltaire* i. 4 Christian charity feels constrained to unmask a demon from the depths of the pit.

3. *absol.* To take off one's mask. Also in fig. context (quot. 1683).

1603 Shaks. *Meas. for M.* v. i. 206 My husband bids me, now I will vnmaske, This is that face.. Which once [etc.]. **1611** Chapman *May-Day* v. 74 *Quint.* O no, you must not vnmaske. *Innoc.* No, no, Ile kisse her with my maske and all. **1683** Kennett *Erasm. on Folly* 2 At the first sight of me, you all unmasque, and appear in more lively colours. **1728** Fielding *Lov. in Sev. Masques* iv. iii, Unmasque then. If I like your Face no better than your Principles, Madam; I will immediately take my Leave of both. **1756** tr. *Keysler's Trav.* I. 349 A female bed-fellow, who never unmasks till she comes into the bed-chamber. **1818** Lady Morgan *Autobiog.* (1859) 299, I was obliged to unmask from the heat, and soon got a crowd about me.

b. *fig.* To display one's true character.

1602 Bacon *Julius Cæsar* Mor. & Hist. Wks. (Bohn) 502 Though this was ever his scheme, and at last put in execution, yet he did not unmask. **1745** Young *Nt. Th.* viii. 224 Their treach'rous blessings, at the day of need, Like other faithless friends, unmask, and sting.

4. *trans. Mil.* **a.** To reveal the presence of (a gun or battery) by opening fire.

1747 *Gentl. Mag.* 450 The besieged unmask'd 4 batteries. **1812** *Examiner* 31 Aug. 549/2 He unmasked a battery of forty pieces of cannon. **1884** *Manch. Exam.* 9 Sept. 8/4 The Chinese, unmasking a mountain gun, fired on the Bayard.

b. To make patent; to show plainly.

1816 Sir H. Douglas *Milit. Bridges* iv. 110 The other divisions.. hastened their march as soon as the movement was unmasked. **1879** Low *Afghan War* 100 With a view of making the Afghan commandant.. unmask his force.

5. *intr.* To emerge into view.

1858 *Merc. Marine Mag.* V. 227 Two Obelisks.. on the strand.. will.. unmask.

Hence **un'masking** *ppl. a.*

1807 J. Barlow *Columb.* vi. 568 Gates guides the onset.. And tells the unmasking batteries when to roar.

un'masked, *ppl. a.* (un-[1] 8.)

1590 Greene *Never too late* (1600) 14 The maids in Rome durst not looke at Venus Temple till they were thirtie, nor went they vnmasked till they were married. **1628** Feltham *Resolves* ii. viii. 18 Diseased eyes indure not an vnmasked Sunne. ? **1630** H. R. *Mythomystes*, A 3, To lay downe a naked & vnmasked Trueth. **1679** in *Lond. Gaz.* No. 1406/1 The unmasked Boldness of such as durst openly.. assemble themselves together, to Kill.. the Primate. **1740** H. Walpole *Corr.* (1820) I. 45, I have found a little unmasqued moment to write to you. **1784** Cowper *Task* ii. 695 They.. in th' end, disclose a face That would have shock'd credulity herself, Unmask'd. **1811** Scott *Don Roderick* ii. xli, He saw her hideous face, and loved the fiend unmask'd. **1855** Pusey *Doctr. Real Presence* 717 An universal suppression of the truths.. and the unmasked substitution of falsehood.

un'masker. [f. unmask *v.*] One who unmasks.

1644 Milton *Areop.* 7 The great unmasker of the Trentine Councel. **1697** Locke *2nd Vind. Reason. Chr.* 183 The Unmasker smartly convinces me of no small Blunder in these words. **1833** Carlyle *Misc.* (1840) IV. 404 'Far from being modest,' says this Unmasker, 'he brags beyond expression'. **1850** L. Hunt *Autobiog.* v. 98 [They] stood side by side in my imagination as unmaskers of venerable appearance. **1884** *Manch. Exam.* 9 May 5/5 The first unmasker of the forgery.

un'masking, *vbl. sb.* [f. as prec.] The action of divesting of a mask. Chiefly *fig.*

a **1586** Sidney *Arcadia* iii. xxiii, Her unmasking of Cecropias fruitlesse sophistrie. **1602** J. H[all] (*title*), The Un-masking of the Politique Atheist. **1641** Milton *Reform.* i. 8 The unmasking of Hypocrites. **1741** Richardson *Pamela* IV. 233 Because of her Freedoms when mask'd; her Un-masking, and her Handkerchief. **1861** Trench *Comm. Ep. Churches Asia* 87 An unmasking of them that said they were Apostles and were not. **1895** *Athenæum* 17 Aug. 218/3 Mr. Meredith's pitiless unmaskings of folly.

un'massacred, *ppl. a.* (un-[1] 8.)

1608–9 Middleton *Widow* iii. i, Would you let him 'scape unmassacred?

un'massed, *ppl. a.* (un-[2] 6 b, 8.)

1847 *Athenæum* April 393/1 The inside.. of the building.. is minutely decorated everywhere, but certainly is not dismembered or unmassed anywhere.

un'massy, *a.* (un-[1] 7.)

1665 Sir G. Mackenzie *Moral Essay* 52 So unmassie a reputation, that, when it is hammered out [etc.].

un'mast, *v.* [un-[2] 4. Cf. Du. *ont-*, G. *entmasten*.] *trans.* To divest of a mast.

1611 Florio, *Disarborare*,.. to unmast a ship. **1668** *Lond. Gaz.* No. 238/1 The same Tempest.. unmasting several others [*sc.* ships]. **1698** T. Froger *Voy.* 17 We also began to unmast the Fruitful Pink to turn it into a Bomb-Galley.

un'masted, *ppl. a.* (un-[1] 8.)

[**1775** Ash.] **1804** J. Larwood *Gun Boat* 12 An unruddered, unmasted, unordonanced existence.

un'master, *v.* (un-[2] 3.)

1593–4 Sylvester *Profit Imprisonm.* Wks. (Grosart) II. 56/2 Small the honour is to be acknowledg'd King And Monark of the World, one's self un-mastering.

un'masterable, *a.* (un-[1] 7 b.)

1617 Daniel *Coll. Hist. Eng.* (1626) 114 By this violence, thinking to quaile the heart of a most vnmaisterable King. **1625** Jackson *Creed* v. xxxv. §6 An unexpected instinct or unmasterable impulsion. **1646** Sir T. Browne *Pseud. Ep.* iv. ii. 201 The Faetor whereof may discover it self by sweat.., as being unmasterable by the naturall heat of man.

un'mastered, *ppl. a.* (un-[1] 8.)

1561 Norton & Sackv. *Gorboduc* ii. ii, Great is the daunger of vnmaistred might. **1593** *Sidney's Arcadia* iv. Wks. 1922 II. 107 The unmastred vertu of Pyrocles. **1602** Shaks. *Ham.* i. iii. 32 If with too credent eare you list his Songs;.. or your chast Treasure open To his vnmastred importunity. **1700** Dryden *Sp. Ajax*, etc. 595 He.. cannot his unmaster'd Grief sustain, But yields to Rage. **1793** *Minstrel* II. 194 To appropriate to her own use these evidently unmastered treasures. **1800** Coleridge *Piccolom.* iv. vii, Nature.., like the emancipated force of fire, Unmastered scorches.. Their fine-spun webs. **1870** Bryant *Iliad* v. I. 145 Lest, taking flight, they range Unmastered when they hear thy voice no more.

†**un'masterly**, *adv. Obs.*[−1] [un-[1] 11.] Without being supervised.

1684 H. More *Answer* Pref. b 4 b. To act at pleasure, prosperously, freely and unmasterly.

un'masticated, *ppl. a.* (un-[1] 8.)

1815 J. Smith *Panorama Sci. & Art* II. 643 The unmasticated part contributes nothing to their nourishment. **1896** *Allbutt's Syst. Med.* I. 396 Masses of unmasticated food.

†**un'match**, *a.* (un-[1] 7.)

1570 Levins *Manip.* 38 Vnmatche, *inequalis*.

un'matchable, *a.* [un-[1] 7 b.]

1. Incapable of being matched or equalled; incomparable, matchless. Also const. *by*.

In very common use from *c* 1590 to *c* 1660.
1544 BETHAM *Precepts War* I. lxxxix. E vj, The renoume of that capitayne..is vnmatcheable. **1587** A. DAY *Daphnis & Chloe* (1890) 16 Loue, the..Soueraigne of their vnmachcable bcwtics. **1649** BAXTER *Saint's R.* II. v. §3. 218 Those divine unmatchable Psalms. **1683** *Brit. Spec.* 277 With un-matchable Valor, and Extraordinary Hazard of his Princely Person. *c* **1799** *Villario* III. iii. in *New Brit. Theatre* II. 165 It is the mind that is unmatchable By aught on earth. **1856** RUSKIN *Mod. Paint.* IV. v. xvii. §51 Of such landscape ..he has expressed the power in..a central and unmatchable way. **1881** TENNYSON *Cup* I. i, The brows and eyes Of Venus: face and form unmatchable!

b. Incapable of being compared *to* others.
1611 SPEED *Hist. Gt. Brit.* VI. 45 These Britaines, although..vnmatchable to them in educated ciuility, yet [etc.].

c. To which nothing properly matching can be found. (See MATCH *v.* 9b.)
1809 SIR G. JACKSON in *Diaries & Lett.* (1873) I. 3 A scrap of riband..unmatchable in Bath. **1852** MISS SEWELL *Experience of Life* xiv. (1858) 95, I was especially directed to match some unmatchable silk.

2. Incapable of being matched together.
1643 MILTON *Divorce* 18 He forbids all unmatchable and unmingling natures to consort. **1645** —— *Tetrach.* 48 His law tells us he joynes not unmachable things.

Hence **un'matchableness.**
1627 BP. HALL *Epist.* IV. ii. 340 In the presumption of his vnmatchablenesse. **1676** *Doctrine of Devils* 182 The Unmatchableness of his Antagonist being considered.

un'matchably, *adv.* (f. prec., or UN-^{1} 11.)
1603 LD. HERBERT *Corr.* in *Life* (1886) 335 As knowing that his worthy disposition that began it of himself, will continue it as undeservedly as he did unmatchably enter into it. **1609** W. M. *Man in Moon* G 2 b, Seeing therefore it is such an inestimable iewell, how warily are you to keep it?.. so vnmatchably allied, how much are you to make of it? **1882** *Harper's Mag.* LXV. 548 The unmatchably pale bright yellow-white of the grain fields.

un'matched, *ppl. a.* [UN-^{1} 8.]
1. Not matched or equalled; matchless; unrivalled.
1581 SIDNEY *Apol. Poetrie* (Arb.) 26 Though we get not so vnmatched a praise as the Etimologie of his names wil grant. **1621** G. SANDYS *Ovid's Met.* VI. (1626) 109 Antigone, who stroue For vnmatcht beautie with the wife of Ioue. **1637** J. RUTTER *1st Pt. Cid* V. iii. 27 It were better that his unmatch'd valour Should get him victory. **1678** DRYDEN *All for Love* IV. i, Your unmatch'd desert. **1780** BURKE *Sp. Bristol* Wks. 1792 II. 313 Refusing to commit this act of un-matched turpitude. **1812** COMBE *Syntax, Picturesque* XXIV. 89 Shakespeare, immortal Bard sublime! Unmatch'd within the realms of time! *a* **1845** HOOD *Lamia* i. 40 Let such an unmatched vision still shine on. **1878** SYMONDS *Sonn. M. Angelo* lix, Nay, nor the unmatched phœnix lives anew, Unless she burn.
absol. **1632** R. ALLEN in Lithgow *Trav.* B 3 b, This thy second Pilgrimage of Minde,..in Methode, Phrase, and Stile, May match the most vnmatched in this Ile.

b. Const. *by*; *at*, *for*, *in*, or *of*.
1592 DANIEL *Compl. Rosamond* xxiv, Vnmatch'd by sword, [he] was vanquisht by a glaunce. **1602** WARNER *Alb. Eng.* XII. lxxiii. 304 Fertile grounds, vnmatch't for fruits. **1700** ROWE *Amb. Step-Moth.* II. ii, Long time unmatcht in War the Hero shone. **1789** BURNS *Whistle* iv, Unmatch'd at the bottle, unconquer'd in war. **1810** SCOTT *Lady of L.* I. vii, Two dogs..Unmatch'd for courage. **1868** MORRIS *Earthly Par.* I. II. 629 This is the man, unmatched of heart and limb.

2. Not provided with something equal or alike.
1645 MILTON *Tetrach.* 19 When love findes it self utterly unmatcht, and justly vanishes. **1824** GALT *Rothelan* III. 132 A mean abode,..with old-fashioned unmatched chairs.

Hence **un'matchedness.**
c **1611** CHAPMAN *Iliad* Pref. A 3 b, His cleare vnmatchednesse in all manner of learning.

†un'matchless, *a.* *Obs.*$^{-1}$ [UN-^{1} 5 a.] Unmatchable, matchless.
1657 F. COCKIN *Div. Blossomes* 49 Those rare unmatchlesse sweets.

unmate, early ME. variant of UNMEET *a.*

un'mate, *v.* (UN-^{2} 3.)
1891 C. E. NORTON *Dante's Hell* xxx. 164 The heavy hydropsy which..so unmates the members that the face corresponds not with the belly.

un'mated, *ppl. a.* (UN-^{1} 8.)
1614 GORGES *Lucan* II. 53 Nothing at all these horrid facts Sylla's vnmated minde distracts. **1633** FORD *'Tis Pity* V. i, Here like a Turtle, (mew'd vp in a Cage,) Vnmated, I conuerse with Ayre and walls. **1850** BLACKIE *Æschylus* II. 236 She in unmated grief to moan Is left alone. **1891** *Anthony's Photogr. Bull.* IV. 380 To immortalize the smiling eyes, which in repose are..unmated.

unma'terial, *a.* [UN-^{1} 7, 5 b.] Immaterial.
1398 TREVISA *Barth. De P.R.* (1495) II. ii. 27 In somoche he is the more perfyte in contemplacyon of spirytuell and vnmateriall thynges. **1587** GOLDING *De Mornay* xiv. 239 An vnmateriall substance, which hath being of it selfe. **1599** DANIEL *Musoph.* 940 Should we this ornament of glory then, As th' unmaterial fruits of shades, neglect. **1602** WARNER *Alb. Eng.* XIII. lxxix. 326 Vnpassiue, vnmateriall, vncompounded, Infinite. **1883** ROSSETTI in *Athenæum* 15 Dec. 776/2 The scholar who constantly lives an inward and unmaterial life.

unma'ternal, *a.* (UN-^{1} 7.)
1821 SHELLEY *Epipsych.* 18 Thy panting, wounded breast Stains with dear blood its unmaternal nest! **1885** tr. *A. Monad's Life & Lett.* 17 You only wished to try me, and not seriously to give me such unmaternal advice.

unmathe'matical, *a.* (UN-^{1} 7.)
1720 PRIOR in *Q. Rev.* Jan. (1913) 115 All the cross unmathematical devils upon earth first put it together. **1784** R. BAGE *Barham Downs* I. 230 One unmathematical passion however, Avarice,..had got fast hold of me. **1804–6** SYD. SMITH *Mor. Philos.* (1850) 395 Any immoral, irreligious or unmathematical track of thought.

unmathe'matically, *adv.* (UN-^{1} 11.)
1644 in Halliwell *Lett. Sci. Subj.* 80 Mr. Warner's papers ..are..most unmathematically divided between the sequestrators and creditors.

un'mating, *ppl. a.* (UN-^{1} 10.)
1855 M. ARNOLD *To Marguerite* 32 Or, if not quite alone, yet they Which touch thee are unmating things.

unma'triculated, *ppl. a.* (UN-^{1} 8.)
1644 MILTON *Educ.* 2 Instead of beginning with Arts most easie,..they present their young unmatriculated novices at first comming with the most intellective abstractions of Logick and metaphysicks. **1884** *Manch. Exam.* 27 Nov. 5/4 Matriculated and unmatriculated students.

unmatri'monial, *a.* (UN-^{1} 7.)
1572 tr. *Buchanan's Detectioun* F iij b, Within VIII. Dayis, scho finischit that unmatrimoniall Matrimonie.

un'matronlike, *a.* (UN-^{1} 7 c.)
1748 RICHARDSON *Clarissa* V. 256 The behaviour of the unmatron-like jilt, whom thou broughtest to betray me.

†un'mattered, *a.* *Obs.*$^{-1}$ [UN-^{1} 9.] Immaterial.
1646 J. HALL *Poems* I. 30 Let men desire, like those above Un-matter'd forms, wee'l onely love.

unma'tured, *ppl. a.* (UN-^{1} 8.)
1741 W. WHITEHEAD *Danger of Writing Verse* 23 That, unmatur'd by years, My easy numbers pleas'd your partial ears. **1836** F. MAHONY *Rel. Father Prout* (1859) 374 Whatever might have been crude and unmatured in his juvenile lucubrations.

†un'maw, *v.* *Obs.*$^{-1}$ [UN-^{2} 3.] *trans.* To empty of knowledge.
1631 MABBE *Celestina* xvii. 175 With my..inticing termes,..I will quite unmaw him, and draw from him all that hee..knowes.

†unmawe, *a.* *Obs. rare.* In 4 on-, oun-. [OE. *unmaȝa* a poor or helpless person.] Helpless.
c **1380** *Sir Ferumb.* 2658 He hew of heuedes, armes, & haunde of þe Sarasyns þat were on-mawe. *Ibid.* 2766 Hwich þe Sarazyns þat were ounmawe angryde in euery syde.

un'maze, *v.* [UN-^{2} 3.] *trans.* To free from amazement or confusion.
1647 R. STAPYLTON *Juvenal* 149 This new man Tully.. Set guards, where e're the line of danger ran, Unmaz'd us, and took pains for all the town.

un'meaning, *ppl. a.* [UN-^{1} 10.]
1. a. Of features, etc.: Expressionless, vacant, unintelligent.
1704 STEELE *Lying Lover* III. i, Poor stupid insipid Lady Fad,..with that unmeaning Face of hers. **1760** DODD *Hymn Good-Nat.* Poems (1767) 3 Daughter of Folly; whose unmeaning front Wears the soft simper of perpetual smiles! **1815** SCOTT *Guy M.* ix, Bertram turned a stupified and unmeaning eye on the messenger. **1836** KINGSLEY *Lett.* (1878) I. 34 The old man spoke in his dreams and muttered with unmeaning visage and fixed eye.

b. Of persons: Having no serious aim or purpose.
1746 ELIZA HEYWOOD *Female Spect.* No. 24 (1748) IV. 305 Being a fool, [she] was thoughtless, giddy, and unmeaning. **1812** MISS MITFORD in L'Estrange *Life* (1870) I. 172 Peace be to them, sweet simpletons! as unmeaning.. as their own dinner-bells. **1846** MRS. GORE *Eng. Char.* I. 40 The vapid, unmeaning, unconnected Lady P——.

2. Having no meaning or significance; meaningless: **a.** Of actions, conduct, etc.
1728 ELIZA HEYWOOD tr. *Mme. de Gomez's Belle A.* (1732) II. 228 Turning the Effect of his Admiration into the Appearance of an unmeaning Gallantry. **1776** MICKLE *Camoen's Lusiad* p. lxxvii, Unmeaning slaughter.. comprise[s] the whole history of his regency. **1825** T. HOOK *Sayings* Ser. II. III. 320 Full of grimace, affectation, and unmeaning levity. **1869** J. MARTINEAU *Ess.* II. 229 The tendency..is not an unmeaning accident.

b. Of words, utterances, etc.
1709 POPE *Essay on Criticism* 355 At the..only couplet fraught With some unmeaning thing they call a thought. **1727** BOYER *Dict. Royal* II. s.v., Unmeaning Words. **1771** T. PERCIVAL *Ess.* (1777) I. 6 [They] conceal their own ignorance..by unmeaning terms and pompous phrases. **1855** MACAULAY *Hist. Eng.* xv. III. 559 That several neighbouring nations..thought this most unmeaning of all names worth borrowing. **1875** FORTNUM *Maiolica* xi. 109 The unmeaning designs of the oriental porcelain.
absol. **1870** DISRAELI *Lothair* lxxvii, I do not believe in the unmeaning.

3. Uttering nothing significant.
1743 W. WHITEHEAD *Ep. Ann Boleyn* 90 Each distant Hint that hung On broken Sounds of an unmeaning Tongue.

un'meaningly, *adv.* (UN-^{1} 11; cf. prec.)
1775 ASH, *Nonsensically*, unmeaningly, foolishly. **1808** *Sketches of Character* (1813) I. 133 Look at the soft soul—how unmeaningly she stares at the Band. **1870** LOWELL *Study Wind., Gt. Publ. Char.*, Those threads of gossamer, the nearest approach to nothing unmeaningly prolonged.

un'meaningness. (UN-^{1} 12.)
1796 MME. D'ARBLAY *Camilla* II. 13 She perceived her two little sprigs..under the feet of Indiana, who with apparent unmeaningness..had trampled upon them both. **1825** COLERIDGE *Aids Refl.* 391 The utter emptiness and unmeaningness of the vaunted Mechanico-corpuscular Philosophy. **1864** PUSEY *Lect. Daniel* iv. 189 The unmeaningnesses, which they have brought into the prophecy, cannot be its meaning.

un'meant, *ppl. a.* [UN-^{1} 8 b.] Not meant or intended.
a **1634** CHAPMAN *Revenge for Honour* V. ii, Howere you're pleas'd to mock me..with these impertinent, unmeant discourses, I cannot..give them the least credit. **1697** DRYDEN *Æneis* x. 561 The flying Spear was after Ilus sent, But Rhœtus hapen'd on a Death unmeant. **1738** G. LILLO *Marina* II. i, I who cou'd not bear The unmeant rivalship of sweet Marina. **1820** SHELLEY *Prometh. Unb.* III. iv. 151 That ..hollow talk Which makes the heart..question that unmeant hypocrisy. **1891** E. KINGLAKE *Australian at Home* 71 It is the short sighted gentleman..on whom the ball finds its unmeant mark as a rule.

b. Const. *by* and with complement.
c **1700** CONGREVE *To Cynthia* Wks. 1730 III. 291 Curse on that Word so ready to be spoke, For through my Lips, unmeant by me, it broke. **1745** YOUNG *Nt. Th.* VIII. 682 Can man..strike out A self-wrought happiness unmeant by him Who made us? **1848** BAILEY *Festus* (ed. 3) 211 These mysteries Unmeant by Heaven to be cleared up on earth.

un'measurable, *a.*, *sb.*, and *adv.* ? *Obs.* [UN-^{1} 7 b, 5 b, 12, and 11 b.]
1. Incapable of being measured on account of great size, extent, or amount; immense, vast:
a. Of material things, dimensions, time, etc.
c **1386** CHAUCER *Man of Law's T.* 934 O Golias, vnmesurable of lengthe. **1513** DOUGLAS *Æneid* VI. vi. 71 Cerberus,..Vnmesurable in his cave quhar he lay. *a* **1541** WYATT in *Tottel's Misc.* (Arb.) 70 Lyke vnto these vnmesurable mountaines, So is my painefull life, the burden of yre. **1585** T. WASHINGTON tr. *Nicholay's Voy.* II. iii. 33 The walles..are made of grauen stone..of length and bignesse vnmeasurable. **1610** HEALEY *St. Aug. Citie of God* III. xxxi. 152 A most huge and vnmesurable cloud. **1691** NORRIS *Pract. Disc.* 243 Truth and Falshood..are removed from each other by an unmeasurable distance. **1754** EDWARDS *Freed. Will* IV. viii. 240 Unlimited and Unmeasureable Periods of Time. **1774** J. BRYANT *Mythol.* I. 398 The tower..was of an unmeasurable height.

b. Of actions, qualities, feelings, etc.
1377 LANGL. *P. Pl.* B. xv. 69 (W.), Ye moeven materes unmesurable [*v.rr.* vn-, inmesurables] To tellen of the Trinite. *c* **1450** *Merlin* xx. 329 He..yaf hym soche a stroke with the brasen betell so vn-mesurable, that [etc.]. **1542** BECON *News Heaven* H iij b, Your ioy can not be expressed, your gladnes is vnmeasurable. **1588** in *Harl. Misc.* (1808) I. 143 An unmeasurable deep despair. **1648** SANDERSON *Serm.*, *Ad Aul.* (1681) II. 242 We..shall have an unmeasurable reward ..for the good we have done. *a* **1677** BARROW *Serm.* Wks. 1716 I. 345 He did by unmeasurable communications of divine virtue assist his humanity. **17..** WATTS *Hymns*, *'Come, dearest Lord'* ii, The Heighth, and Breadth, and Length, Of thine unmeasurable Grace. **1760–72** H. BROOKE *Fool of Qual.* (1809) II. 120 This..parade of sanctity gave him..unmeasurable credit.

c. Used with reference to God.
1535 COVERDALE *Baruch* iii. 25 Greate is he,..hye and vnmeasurable. **1551** VERON *Godly Saiyngs* E viii, Touchinge his godheade, and vnmeasurable substaunce. **1581** MARBECK *Bk. of Notes* 126 The same one man is locall..as touching his manhood, which is also God unmeasurable from the Father.

2. Immoderate, inordinate, unbounded:
a. Of persons (or other agents).
1388 WYCLIF *Prov.* xv. 4 The tunge which is vnmesurable, schal defoule the spirit. *c* **1400** *Pilgr. Sowle* (Caxton, 1483) III. ix. 55 These haue ben so vnmesurable in their expensys. *c* **1450** *Mirour Saluacioun* 3936 Nabal.. made to hym kyng Dauid his vnmesurable enemy. *c* **1520** BARCLAY *Jugurth* xxvii. 37 b, Their myndes were greatly immoderate and vnmeasurable in their desyre to ouercome thestates. **1597** BRETON *Auspicante Jehoua* Wks. (Grosart) II. 6/2 So great and vnmeasurable a sinner. **1629** J. MAXWELL tr. *Herodian* 155 An vnmeasurable Louer of Money. **1667** SOUTH *Serm.* (1697) 32 He..shall find [sin].. an Unmeasurable Exactor.

b. Of desires or the gratification of these.
c **1386** CHAUCER *Pars. T.* ¶818 Glotonye is vnmesurable Appetit to ete or to drynke. **1388** WYCLIF *1 Pet.* iv. 3 Whiche walkiden..in myche drinking of wyn, in vnmesurable etyngis and drynkyngis. **1422** YONG tr. *Secreta Secret.* 194 Hit is dedly syn whan that concupiscens is so vnmesurable that [etc.]. **1482** *Monk of Evesham* xxi. (Arb.) 49 Y was.. ageyne bonde yn to luste and custome of the same sinne, that was yn mine owne onmeserabulle taking and appetite. **1583** BABINGTON *Commandm.* 176 So euil an example of vnmeasurable sotting in bed. **1594** T. B. *La Primaud. Fr. Acad.* II. 269 Other carnall pleasures.., especially when they are excessiue and vnmeasurable. *a* **1648** LD. HERBERT *Hen. VIII* (1683) 220 His Cardinal['s]..unmeasurable Ambition and Covetousness. **1788** JEFFERSON *Writ.* (1859) II. 371 The unmeasurable ambition of the Emperor.

c. In miscellaneous applications.
c **1425** in *Anglia* VIII. 139/11 Vnmesurabil laghter or vnsem and vnmanerly berynge of body. **1461** *Rolls of Parlt.* V. 493/2 The inordynat and unmesurable Enditementz and Presentementz..of Felonye. **1535** COVERDALE *Ecclus.* xxxvii. 30 Glotony commeth at the last to an vnmeasurable heate. **1592** TIMME *Ten Eng. Lepers* H 2 Through unmeasurable abstinence, the moysture of the bodie is dried up. **1638** PENKETHMAN *Artach.* K j, Great Tempests, unmeasurable Windes and Raines. **1674** TEMPLE *Let. to Ld. Treas.* Wks. 1720 II. 311 The unmeasurable Burden of their Taxes. **1709** SWIFT *Adv. Relig.* Wks. 1755 II. I. 97 The lustre of that most noble family..which the unmeasurable profusion of ancestors..had too much eclipsed.

3. Not admitting of measurement; immensurable.
1652 *Zeal Examined* Add. §9. 40 Which rendered the true Church unmeasureable by any outward Formes. **1714** *Barrow's Euclid* Pref. p. ii, Both measurable and unmeasurable Magnitudes.

b. *sb.* An immensurable thing.

1652 BENLOWES *Theoph.* v. lxxxvi, Can measures such Unmeasurables hold? Can time Infinity unfold?

4. *adv.* = UNMEASURABLY *adv.*

c **1440** *Alph. Tales* 343 When he saw any yong monk lagh vnmesurable. *c* **1445** PECOCK *Donet* 85 God is.. vnmesurable greet in goostly greetnes. **1586** T. B. *La Primaud. Fr. Acad.* I. 671 So that great heede is to be taken, that none grow to be unmeasurable great. **1650** BULWER *Anthropomet.* 202 An huge unmeasurable great Ring.

Hence †**un'measurableness.** *Obs.*

1533 FRITH *Book Answ. More's Lett.* H ij, Shewynge the vnmeasurablenes of his Godhead. **1571** GOLDING *Calvin on Ps.* xxxix. 3 To give himself the brydle to anye unmeasurablenesse of greefe. **1634** T. JOHNSON *Parey's Chirurg. Wks.* XXI. i. 776 The unmeasurablenesse of the manifest.. qualities whereof they [*sc.* poisons] consist. **1656** JEANES *Fuln. Christ* 204 The unmeasurablenesse of his affection unto us. **1724** WELTON *Chr. Faith & Pract.* 185 His judgments are as the great deep for their obscurity and unmeasurableness.

un'measurably, *adv.* [UN-^{1} 11.]

†**1.** Without measure or moderation; immoderately, unrestrainedly. *Obs.*

a **1420** *Wycliffite Bible* Ecclus. xi. 10 *margin*, If thou suest, in sekinge richessis vnmesurably, thou schalt not take. *a* **1450** *Knt. de la Tour* 53 Other that be.. enflamed unmesurably like wolues. **1542-5** BRINKLOW *Lament.* 9 b, Ye abvse your riches,.. for ye spende vnmeasurably. **1561** HOLLYBUSH *Hom. Apoth.* 40 Eating and drinking vnmeasurably. **1631** ANCHORAN *Comenius' Gate Tongues* 190 To laugh aloud and vnmeasurably. **1679** *Hist. Jetzer* 17 He.. frets and fumes unmeasurably. *a* **1693** LUDLOW *Mem.* (1698) II. 624 The Court.. grew unmeasurably insolent. **1722** WOLLASTON *Relig. Nat.* v. xviii. (1724) 111 Opposite parties make a merit of blackening their adversaries.. undeservedly and unmeasurably.

2. To an immeasurable extent or degree; excessively, extremely.

1513 *Henry V* (1911) 132 Famyne.. vnmeasurably raigned amongest them. *c* **1530** LD. BERNERS *Arth. Lyt. Bryt.* (1814) 336 Hys spere.. was so long & byg so vnmesurably, y^{t} [etc.]. **1624** BP. HALL *Peace Maker* in *Var. Treat.* (1627) 538 Grace sensibly imperfect, sinne vnmeasurably sinfull. *a* **1670** RUST *Disc. Truth* (1682) 180 A Soul unmeasurably breathing after the Embraces of Truth. **1704** NORRIS *Ideal World* II. xii. 510 'Tis not to be imagined .. how unmeasurably the powers of that soul must needs be illuminated. *a* **1797** H. WALPOLE *Mem. Geo. II* (1847) I. vi. 186 He was.. unmeasurably obstinate. **1828** LD. GRENVILLE *Sink. Fund* 1 Unmeasurably more beneficial to mankind, are those qualities. **1866** AIRY *Pop. Astron.* i. 37 That the distance.. is unmeasurably small, compared with the distances of the stars.

†**un'measurate**, *a.* *Obs.* [UN-^{1} 7.] = UNMEASURED *ppl. a.* (Cf. IMMENSURATE *a.*)

1557 *Primer, Crede*, Euen as there be not thre vncreat nor thre vnmeasurate, but one vncreat and one vnmeasurate.

un'measure. [UN-^{1} 12.]

†**1.** Lack of measure; excess. *Obs.*

a **1300** *Cursor M.* 15543 Til vnmesur mismai yow noght. *c* **1440** *Jacob's Well* 303 So wast hath manye expensys and costys.. in vnmesure & werkys, bareyn wyth-oute fruyte. **1598** FLORIO, *Dismisura*, an vnmeasure, out of measure.

2. An improper or illegal measure.

1820 BENTHAM *Lib. Press* Wks. 1843 II. 283/2 The last, though not the least, of all their fears is—lest un-measures, which.. have already been taken.. for the extinction of all power of controul [etc.].

un'measured, *ppl. a.* [UN-^{1} 8.]

1. Not limited or known by measurement; immense in size, extent, or amount.

1398 TREVISA *Barth. De P.R.* x. iv. (Bodl. MS.), Fuyre.. is icleped vnmesured, for his vertu.. encreseþ wiþoute eende. **1585** T. WASHINGTON tr. *Nicholay's Voy.* II. iii. 33 The stature of a woman.. of bignes vnmeasured. *c* **1611** CHAPMAN *Iliad* II. 78 So from the ships and tents the army's store Troop'd to these princes.. along th' unmeasur'd shore. **1646** CRASHAW *Sospetto d'Herode* xxii, That the unmeasur'd God so low should sinke, As Pris'ner in a few poore Rags to lye. **1718** PRIOR *Solomon* I. 640 This ample azure Sky,.. With Stars unnumber'd, and unmeasur'd Light. **1794** R. J. SULIVAN *View Nat.* I. 320 Of an unmeasured fluid, we can only reason by conjecture. **1810** SCOTT *Lady of Lake* II. xxxi, When.. Such startler cast his glance below, And saw unmeasured depth around. **1870** MORRIS *Earthly Par.* III. IV. 2 Pale stars.. make heaven so vast That earth.. Seems shrunken 'neath the grey unmeasured height.

absol. **1844** MRS. BROWNING *Drama of Exile* 1710 As the thunder roars deep in the Unmeasured.

b. Of feelings, qualities, etc.

1435 MISYN *Fire of Love* 6 In þe flaume vnmesurde of lufe. *c* **1450** *Mirour Saluacioun* 3008 Gods vnmesured bountee. **1618** in Foster *Eng. Factories Ind.* (1906) I. 22, I have stroven.. with their tricks of unmeasured greatenes. **1692** PRIOR *Ode Imit. Hor.* iii, Distracted Lewis can descry Only a long unmeasur'd Ruin nigh. **1793** SMEATON *Edystone L.* §179 The unmeasured violence of the sea. **1856** FROUDE *Hist. Eng.* I. 116 Wolsey.. combined practical sagacity with an unmeasured power of hoping. **1864** SKEAT *Uhland's Poems* 151 All men are rivals in unmeasured wo.

2. Not doled *out* by measure. *rare*$^{-1}$.

1667 MILTON *P.L.* v. 399 Our Nourisher from whom All perfet good unmeasur'd out, descends.

3. Not subjected to measure; not composed of measured syllables.

1715 POPE *Iliad* IV. 298 Unmix'd, unmeasured, are thy goblets crown'd. **1728** CHAMBERS *Cycl.* s.v. *Poetry*, These, in a Discourse that has no poetical Feet or Measures, do yet .. make it a kind of unmeasured Poetry. **1808** L. MURRAY *Gram.* I. 84 In regard to unmeasured quantities and qualities, the degrees of more and less.. may be expressed intelligibly. *a* **1822** SHELLEY *Def. Poetry, Essays & Lett.* (1840) 9 It is necessary.. to determine the distinction between measured and unmeasured language. **1863** HAWTHORNE *Our Old Home* II. 175 His delightful prose, his unmeasured poetry.

4. Immoderate, unrestrained.

1820 HAZLITT *Lect. Dram. Lit.* 106 His pride and unmeasured pretensions. **1839** HALLAM *Hist. Lit.* II. 287 The unmeasured eulogies he bestows upon him. **1884** JEBB in *Fortn. Rev.* 1 Apr. 434 The habitual use of unmeasured language [in criticism].

Hence **un'measuredly** *adv.*, **-edness.**

1435 MISYN *Fire of Love* 75 No marevayle þof I.. vnmesurdnes of þat endles swetnes to ȝow may not opyn. **1602** MARSTON *Ant. & Mel.* III. Wks. 1856 I. 43 This vengeance .. will lengthen out My daies unmeasuredly. **1864** G. GILFILLAN in *Lett. & Jrnls.* (1892) 373, I intend considering .. the energy—the unmeasuredness—of their life.

†**un'measurely**, *a.* and *adv.* *Obs.* (UN-^{1} 7, 11.)

a **1300** *Cursor M.* 27047 Quen þai vn-mesurli ar radd Efter rising to fall egain. **1513** DOUGLAS *Æneid* XII. xii. 33 Twa of sik statur, onmysurly of hycht.

unme'chanic, *a.* (UN-^{1} 7.)

1687 *Death's Vision* vii, Magnetic Virtues.. Which Unmechanic seem'd and sprung from Laws Of some strange Forreign System. **1789** [see UNMETAPHYSIC *a.*]. **1800** COLERIDGE in C. K. Paul *W. Godwin* (1876) II. i. 3 His taste acts so as to appear like the unmechanic simplicity of an instinct.

unme'chanical, *a.* (UN-^{1} 7.)

1674 BOYLE *Grounds Corpusc. Philos.* 13 The like unmechanical principles and agents. **1693** *Phil. Trans.* XVII. 660 Deep Pools, which could never have been searched by these unmechanical people. **1794** G. ADAMS *Nat. & Exp. Philos.* III. xxiv. 21 It is absurd in philosophers to use unmechanical principles, where mechanical ones will answer the purpose. **1825** J. NICHOLSON *Operat. Mechanic* 368 This unmechanical and desultory mode of operation. **1845** FORD *Handbk. Spain* II. 853 The unmechanical Spaniards still work their mines.. as the.. Iberians did. **1865** MRS. WHITNEY *Gayworthys* xxvii, Unscrupulous, even doubting thoughts, they might be; yet real, unmechanical.

unme'chanically, *adv.* (UN-^{1} 11.)

1833 G. S. FABER *Recapit. Apostasy* 80 It does not therefore follow, that one of the two names is incapable of producing that number, when calculated unmechanically or with wisdom.

un'mechanize, *v.* (UN-^{2} 6 c.)

1687 *Death's Vision* ii, When these soft Bellows [*sc.* the lungs] too, Shall all Unmechaniz'd, and all Unactive grow. **1760** STERNE *Tr. Shandy* IV. xix, What one misfortune or disaster in the book of embryotic evils, that could unmechanize thy frame,.. has not fallen upon thy head!

un'mechanized, *ppl. a.* (UN-^{1} 8.)

1802 PALEY *Nat. Theol.* ii. §4 If nothing had been before us but an unorganized, unmechanized substance, without mark or indication of contrivance. *a* **1930** D. H. LAWRENCE *Last Poems* (1932) 180 But oh, men, men still unmechanised, .. what are you going to do, entangled among all the engines? **1937** B. H. L. HART *Europe in Arms* xxii. 296 The enemy is not only taken unaware but is himself unmechanized. **1973** R. LANE FOX *Alexander the Great* iv. 79 An agricultural and unmechanized world.

un'meddled, *ppl. a.* [UN-^{1} 8.]

†**1.** Unmixed. *Obs.*

c **1380** WYCLIF *Sel. Wks.* II. 320 Love of Crist is not, but ȝif it be cleer, unmedlid wiþ errours. *c* **1449** PECOCK *Repr.* I. x. 49 Euen as grammer and dyuynyte ben ij. dyuerse.. kunnyngis, and therfore ben vnmedlid. **1555** WATREMAN *Fardle Facions* II. iv. I ij, The wisedome, and vnmedled puritie of Language. **1595** SOUTHWELL *Poems*, '*Times goe by Turnes*,' Unmeddled joyes heere to no man befall.

2. Not meddled or interfered *with*. Also without prep.

1535 COVERDALE *Judith* xii. 11 That a woman shulde so laugh a man to scorne, that she were come from him vnmedled withall. **1573** *Reg. Privy Council Scot.* III. 292 [The corn] to remane unmedlit or disponit upoun be ony. **1602** CAREW *Cornwall* 105 [The flood-gate] is opened and closed for sixe dayes in the whole, continuing.. other ten dayes vnmedled withall. **1641** BEST *Farm. Bks.* (Surtees) 68 Yow are to lette the water in the tubbe stande all night unmedled with. **1690** W. WALKER *Idiomat. Anglo-Lat.* 269 He left it as he found it,—untoucht; unmedled withall. **1884** SIR C. BOWEN in *Law Times Rep.* LI. 531/1 To have the enjoyment of his goods and chattels unmeddled with by others. **1898** *Wide World Mag.* Oct. 90/2 This might lie long unmeddled with by the common crowd of the deeps.

un'meddlesome, *a.* (UN-^{1} 7.)

1852 DAVIES & VAUGHAN *Republic Plato* VIII. 550 He hears the quiet and unmeddlesome called simpletons. **1853** W. CORY *Lett. & Jrnls.* (1897) 59 Goodford is laconic, prudent, unmeddlesome.

un'meddling, *ppl. a.* (UN-^{1} 10.)

1765 CHESTERF. *Lett.* (1774) II. 486 She is.. a tender mother; and an unmeddling Queen. **1774** 'J. COLLIER' *Mus. Trav.* App. 4 A contented, unmeddling man. **1793** JEFFERSON *Writ.* (1859) IV. 16 Unmeddling with the affairs of other nations, we [etc.].

Hence **un'meddlingly** (Webster, 1847), **-ness.**

a **1656** B. HALL *Serm. 1 Pet. i. 17* Rem. Wks. (1660) 202 Here must be an ἀπραγμοσύνη, an unmeddlingness with these worldly concernments.

un'mediated, *ppl. a.* (UN-^{1} 8.)

1648 HEXHAM II, *Ongemiddelt*, Vnmediated. **1850** J. MARTINEAU *Misc.* (1852) 225 This unmediated dualism follows the Evangelical into his theory as to the State of each individual soul before God. **1881** G. MACDONALD *Mary Marston* xlviii, In a woman's love there is more of the specially divine element than in a man's—namely, the original, the unmediated.

un'mediatized, *ppl. a.* (UN-^{1} 8.)

1839 LIEBER *Man. Pol. Ethics* I. 358 Wherever all power that can be obtained, is undivided, unmodified and unmediatised.

un'medical, *a.* (UN-^{1} 7.)

1809 MALKIN *Gil Blas* IX. viii. ¶7 Fancying in his unmedical head that physicians cured fevers. **1840** DICKENS *Sk. Loving Couples* 34 The medical gentleman.. was observed to laugh and wink, and look as unmedical as might be. **1888** E. W. BENSON in *Life Dean Lake* (1901) 293 All his habits are so vigorous and unmedical that he is most difficult, even for doctors.

un'medicative. *a.* (UN-^{1} 7.)

1836 CARLYLE in Froude *Life in London* (1884) I. 84 London has been like a course of mercury to body and mind; hard enough, but not un-medicative.

un'medicinable, *a.* [UN-^{1} 7 b, 5 b.]

1. Incurable.

1575 GASCOIGNE *Glasse of Govt.* V. iii, The misgovernment of a mans children.. is unto the wysest mynde an unmedicinable wounde. **1624** HEYWOOD *Gunaik.* III. 160 To give date unto.. thy violent and unmedicinable torture.

b. Refusing medical treatment.

c **1611** CHAPMAN *Iliad* XVI. 24 But these [chiefs].. physicians can recure, Thou yet unmed'cinable still, though thy wound all endure.

2. Incapable of effecting a cure.

1606 CHAPMAN *Gent. Usher* IV. ii, Away with this unmedcinable balme Of worded breath. **1614** LATHAM *Falconry* 116 As it is a thing very medicinable,.. being rightly giuen; so also, it is as vnmedicinable and hurtfull if .. otherwise vsed.

un'meditated, *ppl. a.* (UN-^{1} 8.)

1624 HEYWOOD *Gunaik.* I. 45 [They] left nothing unmeditated that might stirre up men to the adoration of the divine powers. **1667** MILTON *P.L.* v. 149 To praise Thir Maker, in fit strains pronounc't or sung Unmeditated. **1790** PALEY *Horæ Paul.* vii. §5 The intimations upon the subject preserve among themselves.. a consistency certainly unmeditated. *a* **1797** H. WALPOLE *Mem. Geo. II* (1847) I. vi. 174 His wit.. was constant and unmeditated.

un'meditative, *a.* (UN-^{1} 7.)

1831 *Examiner* 12 June 370/1 The inert, unobserving unmeditative mass. **1842** G. S. FABER *Prov. Lett.* (1844) I. 229 This sentence reads well: and, with the unmeditative, will probably tell well. **1866** CARLYLE *Remin.* (1881) II. 330 A man.. given to meditation, and much contemptuous of the unmeditative world.

†**un'meedful**, *a.* *Obs.* [UN-^{1} 7.] Undeserving of reward.

c **1400** *Cursor M.* 28772 (Cott. Galba), Els vnmedeful es þe dede, And makes to þe doer no mede. **1435** MISYN *Fire of Love* 93 Þa trespas fowll þerfore þat say þat all owr dedys inwarde or vtward ar meydfull or vnmedefull.

†**un'meedy**, *a.* [UN-^{1} 7.] Unrewarded.

a **1300** *Cursor M.* 28772 Elles vn-medi sal it be, Scathel and wrangwise als to þe.

un'meek, *a.* [UN-^{1} 7. Cf. ON. *úmjúk-r.*]

1. Not meek or gentle; †unkind, harsh, cruel.

c **1200** ORMIN 9880 Hæþenndom.. Iss harrd & starrc all allse stan, Unnmeoc & all unnmilde. *a* **1300** *Cursor M.* 14616 Wit þaa vn-meke þar was he mett, And son wit þam he was vmsett. ? *a* **1366** CHAUCER *Rom. Rose* 590 And she to me was nought vnmeke, Ne of hir answer daungerous. *c* **1374** —— *Boeth.* IV. met. vii. (1886) 115 He.. as it is sayd hath put an vnmeke lord [as] foddre to his crwel hors. *c* **1449** PECOCK *Repr.* I. xvii. 96 The ȝifte which he wol ȝeue into the resoun or vndirstonding of vnmeke men. **1483** *Cath. Angl.* 233/1 Vn Meke, *vbi* felle. **1509** BARCLAY *Shyp of Folys* 8 Do nat Poetis revyle.. all suche as ar vnmeke, Prowde, Couetous? **1595** W. I. *Two Disc. F. Guicciardin* A j b, Old fooles, yong maids,.. Daunsing their roundes with Sathans dam vnmeeke. *a* **1653** BINNING *Serm.* (1845) 527 An unmeek spirit.. troubles itself and annoys others. **1819** KEATS *Ode Indolence* iii, The last, whom I love more, the more of blame Is heap'd upon her, maiden most unmeek.

†**2.** Unsupple, stiff. *Obs.*$^{-1}$

a **1275** *Prov. Ælfred* 538 Elde.. makit him wel vnmeke, & binimit him is miȝte.

un'meekened, *ppl. a.* (UN-^{1} 8.)

1612 T. TAYLOR *Comm. Titus* iii. 2 Rather then by an vnmeekned and vnsubdued stomacke, [to] hurt both themselues and others.

un'meekly, *adv.* (UN-^{1} 11. Cf. ON. *úmjúkliga.*)

c **1380** WYCLIF *Sel. Wks.* II. 44 Þat he speke neiþer unmekeli to terre men for to fiȝte, ne [etc.]. *a* **1400** *Cursor M.* 27763 (Cott. Galba), Slewth oft samnes sorow strang, And þat vnmekely lastand lang.

un'meekness. (UN-^{1} 12.)

c **1440** *Jacob's Well* 266 Whil vnmekenesse is in þin herte, it faryth as þe see. **1509** BARCLAY *Shyp of Folys* 198 b, This rauenyng sort.. Be theyr vnmekenes the pore oft maketh bare. **1828** E. IRVING *Last Days* 255 Unwillingness to obey, or unmeekness or ungentleness in obedience.

un'meet, *a.* [OE. *unmǣte* (UN-^{1} 7 + MEET *a.*). Cf. OHG. *unmâzi* (MHG. *unmâze, unmǣze*) and UNIMETE *a.*]

†**1. a.** Immoderate or excessive in amount. *Obs.*

c **900** tr. *Bæda's Hist.* v. xii. (1890) 422 Ond ealle.. mid unmæte eȝe ȝeslæȝene weron & utfluȝon. *c* **1175** *Lamb. Hom.* 103 Ȝifernesse.. maceð þan men muchele untrumnesse and to deþe bringeð mid unmete drunche. *c* **1200** *Vices & Virtues* 19 Ðar is chiueringe of toðen for ðe unmate chele. *a* **1300** *Cursor M.* 23035 Þat drednes sal be sua vn-mete, Þat it mai all sli plightes bete. *a* **1310** in Wright

Lyric P. iv. 23 This wilde wille went a-wai, with mone and mournyng muchel un-mete.

†**b.** Excessive in size; immense, huge. *Obs.*

c **900** tr. *Bæda's Hist.* v. xiii. (1890) 438 þa teah he forð boc .. unmættre micelnisse. *a* **1300** *Cursor M.* 16566 For to ber it [*sc.* a tree] vte o þe kirk þai fand it ful vn-mete. **13..** *Gaw. & Gr. Knt.* 208 He hade .. an ax in his oþer [hand], a hoge & vn-mete. *c* **1350** *Lybeaus Disc.* 1629 Another helm hym was brought, And a schaft unmete. *a* **1400-50** *Alexander* 143 þen metis he furthe to Messadon full vn-mete gatis. **14..** *Sir Beues* (C.) 2537 Ascopard hys staffe onmeete Smot after hym a strok gret. *c* **1475** *Partenay* 5775 Hys panche as a pipe hug and comerous;.. Off hir unmete hugenesse is gret meruaill.

†**2.** Unequal; unevenly matched. *Obs.*

a **1300** *Cursor M.* 9362 Als rose and thron ar tua vnmete; And tuix þam fair a-cord es nan. **13..** *E.E. Allit. P.* A. 759 My makelez lambe .. Me ches to hys make, al-þaȝ vn-mete Sum tyme semed þat assemble. **1390** GOWER *Conf.* II. 121 Thou wost nothing of my desese, Hou thou and I be now unmete. *c* **1400** *Destr. Troy* 1324 But vnmete was the Macche at þe mene tyme: The Grekes were grym [etc.]. **1513** DOUGLAS *Æneid* II. xi. 76 Litle Iulus .. With wnmeit paiss his fader fast followand. *a* **1548** HALL *Chron., Hen. V*, 76 b, Their numbre was but small .. and far vnmete to compare with halfe the power of his puissaunt armie. **1563** *Mirr. Mag.* Induct. xxviii, We passed on with steppes and pace vnmete. ?*a* **1760** in Child *Ballads* IV. 165/1 Four he killd and five did wound, That was an unmeet marrow!

†**b.** Lacking in equality; inferior. *Obs. rare.*

1390 GOWER *Conf.* III. 260 Sche .. thoghte hirself unmete And the lest worth of wommen alle. *a* **1547** SURREY in *Tottel's Misc.* (Arb.) 219 He bowed at her feete, In humble wise as who would say I am to farre vnmete.

†**c.** Superior. *Obs. rare.*

1390 GOWER *Conf.* I. 163 This Galathee .. Above alle othre was unmete Of beaute. *Ibid.* II. 199 The thridde maister scholde mete, Which, as thei seiden, was unmete Above hem alle, and couthe most.

†**d.** As *adv.* Unequally. *Obs.*$^{-1}$

1515 *Scottish Field* 188 in *Chetham Misc.* (1856) II, They were numbered nyne hundreth,.. And they were x thousand .. upon the other partie; Full unmette were they matched.

†**3.** Not closely united; remote. *Obs.*

1390 GOWER *Conf.* I. 316 Fro merci thei ben al unmeete, And thus ben thei the worste of alle Of hem whiche unto wraththe falle. *a* **1500** *Flower & Leaf* 17 As I lay in my bed, sleep ful unmete Was unto me.

4. Unfitting, unsuitable, unbecoming, improper.

Common *c* 1535-1675, and in 19th cent.

a **1529** SKELTON *Replyc.* 49 With baudy wordes vnmete Your tonges were to flete. *a* **1602** W. PERKINS *Cases Consc.* (1619) 6 Inconuenience is when the thing or action is done in vnmeete circumstances. **1649** BP. HALL *Cases Consc.* IV. vi. 450 Such a marriage is very unmeet. **1675** HOBBES *Odyss.* 27 While they contending were with words unmeet. **1790** COWPER *Iliad* I. 145 It were much unmeet that I alone .. should want due recompense. **1814** SCOTT *Lord of Isles* V. vii, With unaccustom'd ears, A language much unmeet he hears. **1850** NEALE *Med. Hymns* (1867) 138 It is not for man's devices Here to pry with gaze unmeet. **1885-94** R. BRIDGES *Eros & Psyche* June xxiv, [There] were noises at the door .. Such as .. now seem'd most unmeet to be.

b. Const. *for*, or *to* with inf. (Cf. next.)

1541 *Act 33 Hen. VIII*, c. 21 §7 Soo allso were it unmete and daungerous to the suretye of our .. Kynge .. to be construed by any lawe [etc.]. *c* **1555** HARPSFIELD *Divorce Hen. VIII* (Camden) 97 This kind of reason is .. far unmeet for .. these learned men. **1583** STUBBES *Anat. Abus.* II. D 6, It is very vnmeete to feede forren nations, and our owne country famish at home. *a* **1683** OWEN *Two Disc. Holy Spirit* (1693) 54 That which some oppose as unmeet for him, and beneath his Glory. *a* **1703** BURKITT *On N.T.* Mark iv. 2 Christ thought .. a ship no unmeet place to preach in. **1807** WORDSW. *White Doe* I. 312 Why mention other thoughts unmeet For vision so composed and sweet? **1867** G. MACDONALD *Poems* 48 Trailing loose their white attire For the sapphire-floor unmeet. **1868** MORRIS *Earthly Par.* I. I. 353 He rose and spoke in humble words, unmeet For a great King.

5. Unfit or unsuited for some end or purpose; incompetent: **a.** With *for*.

c **1522** SKELTON *Why nat to Courte* 32 Age is a page For the courte full vnmete. **1577** B. GOOGE *Heresbach's Husb.* III. 126 b, The olde that be barraine, or vnmeete for breeding. **1626** GOUGE *Serm. Dignity Chivalry* §2 They were too meane and unmeet persons for a function so high. **1647** N. BACON *Disc. Govt. Eng.* I. xlvii. 129 The more Baron, the lesse Bishop, and more unmeet for the service of Rome. **1676** ROW *Contn. Blair's Autobiog.* xi. (1848) 326 Mr. Blair was now infirm and unmeet for travel. **1855** TENNYSON *Maud* I. IV. x, Ah Maud, you milkwhite fawn, you are all unmeet for a wife. **1863** CONINGTON tr. *Hor., Odes* II. xix. 27 [They] Deem'd thee belike for war's rough game Unmeet.

b. With †*to* (prep.), or *to* with inf.

a **1513** FABYAN *Chron.* v. cxl. 125 They chase a man of lowe byrth & vnmete to that rome. **1533** SIR T. MORE *Lett. Impugn. J. Fryth* liv, Fryth is an vnmete mayster to teche vs what we shold praye. **1535** COVERDALE *Tit.* i. 16 For so moch as they are .. dishobedient, and vnmete to all good workes. **1600** HOLLAND *Livy* 596 They supposed, that they would .. bee farre unmeet to contrive a conspiracie. **1642** H. MORE *Min. Poems* Wks. (Grosart) 177/1 Such surface skill's Unmeet to measure the profounder quill. **1670** BAXTER *Cure Ch. Div.* 372 In those cases where violent restraint .. is necessary, the Pastor is the unmeetest person to meddle in it. **1808** SCOTT *Marm.* VI. xiii, To each one whom he lists, howe'er Unmeet to be the owner's peer. **1846** KEBLE *Lyra Innoc.* 235 Behold me, Lord, a worthless Gibeonite, Unmeet to bear one burthen in thy sight.

c. Without const.

1535 COVERDALE *Job* xxxvii. 19 Teach vs what we shal saye vnto him, for we are vnmeete because of darcknes. **1557** *Act 4 & 5 Phil. & Mary* c. 3 §1 The same Disability .. notwithstanding, the same unable and unmeet Persons .. have also been released. **1598** GRENEWEY *Tacitus, Ann.* XIII. vi. 187 Neither did that [practice] long continue, because the lot fell oft vpon the vnmeetest. **1706** PRIOR *Ode to Queen* xxxv, That Muse desires .. the lowest Place; Who tho' unmeet, yet touch'd the trembling String. **1825** SCOTT *Betrothed* xii, He were rather an unmeet counsellor in that which we now treat of. **1844** IS. WILLIAMS *Baptistery* III. ii, Then like the Leper stand and pray aloof,—Like the Centurion deem thyself unmeet.

un'meetable, *a.* (UN-^{1} 7 b.)

1837 T. HOOK *Jack Brag* i, As light of darkness, fire of water, or any other two unmeetable opposites.

†**un'meetly**, *a. Obs. rare.* [UN-^{1} 7. Cf. OE. *unmǣtlíc*, OHG. (MHG.) *unmâzlich*.]

1. = UNMEET *a.* 1 b.

a **1400-50** *Alexander* 321 A mouthe as a mastis hunde, vnmetely to shaw.

2. = UNMEET *a.* 4.

1534 MORE *Treat. Passion* Wks. 1316/1 Peter .. thought it in hys mynde vnmetely that hys lorde and mayster shoulde weshe his feete.

un'meetly, *adv.* [UN-^{1} 11. Cf. prec., and ON. *úmátaliga*, OHG. *unmâzlîche* (MHG. *unmǣzlîche*).]

†**1.** Immoderately, excessively. *Obs.*$^{-1}$

a **1300** *Cursor M.* 27763 O suernes cums care to strang And þat vnmetele lastand lang.

2. Unfitly, unbecomingly.

1596 SPENSER *F.Q.* VI. vi. 16 A faire Mayden .. Vpon a mangy iade vnmeetely set. **1611** COTGR., *Induëment*, .. vnmeetly, vnfitly. **1826** SCOTT *Woodst.* xxviii, A benevolent smile .. accorded not unmeetly with his glistening eyes. **1864** NEALE *Seatonian Poems* 108 Tell, nor unrashly nor unmeetly, how God came from Teman.

un'meetness. [f. UNMEET *a.* Cf. OE. *unmǣtness* immenseness.] Unfitness, unsuitableness.

1573 BARET *Alv.* F 796 Unaptnesse or vnmeeteness, .. *ineptia*. **1586** W. WEBB *Eng. Poetrie* (Arb.) 88 In a Satyr greate heede is to be taken .. of the vnmeetnesse or inconuenience of the matter. **1633** BP. HALL *Hard Texts* 228 As there is a disproportion in the legges of a lame man, .. so there is much unmeetness in a fooles parable. **1645** MILTON *Tetrach.* 66 A perpetuall unmeetnes and unwillingnesse to all the duties of helpe. *a* **1683** OWEN *True Nat. Gosp. Ch.* (1689) 164 The unmeetness of the People to be lead under this Spiritual Rule. **1827** *Q. Rev.* XXXVI. 36 The unmeetness of the parties being a satisfactory ground of divorce. **1868** WHITTIER *Among the Hills* 312 Love has naught to do With meetness or unmeetness.

un'mellow, *a.* (UN-^{1} 7.)

1787 *Generous Attachment* IV. 172 You .. shall proclaim the unsavoury news; pert unmellow children shall bear it about. **1863** W. LANCASTER *Praeterita* 44 Gray the mask Of twilight, and the bleak unmellow speed Of blindness on the visage of fresh hills.

un'mellowed, *ppl. a.* (UN-^{1} 8.)

1573 GASCOIGNE *Hearbes* Wks. 1907 I. 327 The brall Which raging youth .. Did whilome breede in mine unmellowed brayne. **1591** LYLY *Endym.* III. i, Whose vnmellowed conceits promise rype counsell. **1607** ROWLANDS *Fam. Hist.* 7 In Nature's green unmellowed years Cupid tormenteth Guy. **1743** FRANCIS tr. *Hor., Odes* II. v. 12 The crude, unmellow'd grape. **1781** COWPER *Truth* 492 If the youth, unmellow'd yet by time, Bore on his branch .. Fruits of a blighted size. **1829** LYTTON *Devereux* III. v, These rare scents that make an Araby of this unmellowed clime. **1841** GRESLEY *For. Arden* xv. 167 They drew nearer to the ruins, unmellowed by age.

unme'lodic, *a.* (UN-^{1} 7.)

1849 *Edin. Rev.* July 54 In primitive music we find a preponderance of those ordinary intervals which characterise speech, and which are unmelodic.

unme'lodious, *a.* (UN-^{1} 7.)

1665 SIR T. HERBERT *Trav.* (1677) 173 The unmelodious noise of the braying mules. **1748** THOMSON *Cast. Indol.* II. lxxxi, Of barking dogs the bitter throng Makes them renew their unmelodious moan. **1777** POTTER *Æschylus, Persians* 512 Rude strains, that unmelodious flow. **1808** SCOTT *Marm.* VI. Introd., If unmelodious was the song, It was a hearty note. **1871** DARWIN *Desc. Man* II. xiii. II. 55 Even the unmelodious sparrow has learnt to sing like a linnet.

So **unme'lodiously** *adv.*, **-ness** (Webster, 1847).

1846 WORCESTER (citing Dr. Allen). **1858** CARLYLE *Fredk. Gt.* v. i. I. 529 An English Parliament jangling and debating unmelodiously. **1867** MORRIS *Jason* IV. 102 Nor toiled the heroes unmelodiously.

un'melodized, *ppl. a.* (UN-^{1} 8.)

1771 LANGHORNE *Fables Flora* xi. 22 Unlike to living sounds it came, Unmix'd, unmelodis'd with breath.

†**un'melt**, *ppl. a.* [UN-^{1} 8 b.] = next.

a **1642** SUCKLING *Fragm. Aurea* (1646) 29 The other fair hand .. whose perfect white .. shew'd like unmelt snow unto the sight.

un'melted, *ppl. a.* (UN-^{1} 8.)

1549 *Compl. Scot.* vi. 59 The snau .. remanis langar on-meltit, be rason that it fallis aye in cald vedthir. **1611** SPEED *Theat. Gt. Brit.* 111/1 The snow .. lasteth long vnmelted vnder those .. high hils. **1657** G. THORNLEY *Daphnis & Chloe* 114 The snow lay unmelted. **1713** SALMON *Bate's Dispens.* (ed. 4) 438/2 Unmelted Antimony in fine Pouder. **1796** KIRWAN *Elem. Min.* (ed. 2) I. 448 It is found .. on gneiss unaltered, on sandstone unmelted. **1833-4** J. PHILLIPS *Geol.* in *Encycl. Metrop.* (1845) VI. 738/1 The houses .. which have been enveloped in liquid lava, remained unmelted by it. **1892** M. DODS *Gosp. John* II. xiv. 223 A lens of ice will .. itself unmelted .. fire the tinder to which it transmits its rays.

un'melting, *ppl. a.* (UN-^{1} 10.)

1743 FRANCIS tr. *Hor., Odes* II. ix. 5 Nor on Armenia's frozen Plain The loitring Snow unmelting lies. **1798** *Monthly Mag.* V. 208 To yon pale zone Where drifts the unmelting snow. **1896** E. RIDLEY in *Class. Rev.* XI. 271/2 Parched by cruel suns, Or palled by snows unmelting.

†**un'member**, *v.* [UN-^{2} 4.] *trans.* To deprive of membership. Also **un'membering** *vbl. sb.*

a **1658** DURHAM *Comm. Revelation* II. iii. (1680) 73 This unmembering or unchurching of a Person. **1683** T. HUNT *Def. Charter Lond.* 41 Every mans particular consent was necessary to make him a member of any society, and so it is to unmember him. **1847** WEBSTER.

un'memorable, *a.* (UN-^{1} 7 b, 5 b.)

1598 FLORIO, *Immemorabile*, vnmemorable, not worth the remembrance, forgetfull. **1607** TOPSELL *Four-f. Beasts* 142 Such was the vnmemorable vanity of the Heathens in theyr goddes and sacrifices. **1858** CARLYLE *Fredk. Gt.* v. iii. I. 559 If a few things memorable are to be remembered, millions of things unmemorable must first be .. forgotten! **1885** DIXON *Hist. Ch. Eng.* III. 229 A not unmemorable duel.

absol. **1879** F. HARRISON *Choice of Bks.* i. (1886) 9 The memoirs of the unmemorable, and lives of those who never really lived at all.

un'memoried, *ppl. a.* (UN-^{1} 8.)

1830 JAMES *De L'Orme* xi, The mountains .. in the same .. forms that they had presented unmemoried centuries ago. **1879** R. BRIDGES *Shorter Poems* II. (1912) 263, Flowers that fade, Within whose magic tents Rich hues have marriage made With sweet unmemoried scents.

un'menaced, *ppl. a.* (UN-^{1} 8.)

[**1775** ASH.] **1821** BYRON *Sardanap.* I. ii. 640 Here we are still unmenaced. **1837** LYTTON *Athens* I. 212 When Sparta was unmenaced he was lukewarm.

un'mendable, *a.* (UN-^{1} 7 b.)

1584 MELVILLE in *Cal. Sc. Papers* (1913) VII. 175, I assured hym .. matters wer able to fall out to her unmendable miscontentement. **1760** MRS. F. SHERIDAN *Sidney Bidulph* lxi. (1796) V. 178 The wheel was unmendable. **1822** T. G. WAINEWRIGHT *Ess. & Crit.* (1880) 281 An unmendable slit. **1855** [J. R. LEIFCHILD] *Cornwall* 76 That vase, .. which one puff of wind .. would dash down into innumerable and unmendable fragments! **1877** M. ARNOLD *Last Ess.* Pref. p. xii, They dream of patching up things unmendable.

un'mended, *ppl. a.* (UN-^{1} 8.)

[**1775** ASH.] **1880** *West Cornwall Gloss.* 62 *Voyder*, .. a large basket for holding unmended linen. **1888** MISS BRADDON *Fatal Three* I. iv, The wardrobe-woman left her clothes unmended.

†**un'menged**, *ppl. a. Obs.* [UN-^{1} 8 + MENG *v.* Cf. OE. *un(ȝe)menged*, MDu. *on-*, MHG. *ungemenget*, etc., older Da. *umængt*.] Unmixed.

1562 TURNER *Baths* 6 They drink .. excessively wyne, and that unmenged.

un'menseful, *a. Sc.* and *dial.* (UN-^{1} 7.)

1801 *Marvellous Love-Story* II. 31 Hauld your tongue, ye unmenseful brute! **1818-** in dialect glossaries, etc. (Sc., Yks., Lancs., Linc.). **1898** LD. E. HAMILTON *Mawkin* xx. 268 The daft unmensefu' things!

unmensken, *v.*: see UN-^{2} 2.

un'mensurable, *a.* (UN-^{1} 7 b.)

1513 DOUGLAS *Æneid* x. Prol. 93 Consider quhou he [*sc.* God] is onmensurabyll; Him, as he is, to knaw thou art not abyll. **1683** CAVE *Ecclesiastici, Athanasius* 47 This he cryes out upon as .. an unmensurable madness.

unmentiona'bility. [UN-^{1} 12.]

a. = next b.

1840 *New Monthly Mag.* LX. 373 One whose unmentionabilites are not worth a thought.

b. The fact of (some things') being unmentionable.

1909 G. B. SHAW in *Three Plays by Brieux* (1911) p. xv, Their imitators assumed that unmentionability was an end in itself. *c* **1925** D. H. LAWRENCE *Virgin & Gipsy* (1930) i. 12 The children were brought up in this atmosphere of cunning self-sanctification and of unmentionability.

un'mentionable, *a.* and *sb.* [UN-^{1} 7 b.]

a. That cannot or should not be mentioned.

1837 CARLYLE *Fr. Rev.* I. I. iii, The .. whole posthumous hope of Jesuitism now hangs by the apron of this same unmentionable Woman. **1852** MRS. STOWE *Uncle Tom's C.* xiii, Rows of shining tin, suggestive of unmentionable good things to the appetite. **1875** JOWETT *Plato* (ed. 2) V. 422 If any citizen be found guilty of any great or unmentionable wrong.

absol. **1848** MRS. CARLYLE in *New Lett. & Mem.* (1903) I. 242 Her tendency towards the unmentionable is too strong for me to stay it.

b. *sb. pl.* Trousers. (Cf. INEXPRESSIBLE B. 2.) Also, underpants, and (chiefly *joc.*) underwear, esp. women's.

1823 *London Mag.* Oct. 433/2 Liston, in a pair of *unmentionables* coming half-way down his legs. **1830** in Thornton *Amer. Gloss.* (1912) I. 478 The waist bands of his unmentionables. **1836-7** DICKENS *Sk. Boz, Shabby-Genteel People*, The knees of the unmentionables .. began to get alarmingly white. **1883** S. C. HALL *Retrospect* II. 318 The priest's unmentionables drying on a hedge. **1910** O. JOHNSON *Varmint* 221 Each [boy] was required to don upper and lower unmentionables. **1930** *Amer. Speech* V. 497 Silk nighties, panties, and undies in general .. these articles were consistently grouped in the common speech as 'unmentionables'. **1972** *Daily News-Miner* (Fairbanks, Alaska) 3 Nov. 1/7 The Russians .. 'd buy up perfume, wrist watches and ladies' unmentionables. **1974** *Times* 5 Jan. 10/6

Fear of being ambulanced away to a place where nurses will ..snigger at your frayed unmentionables.

c. *sb.* A person or thing not to be mentioned (by name). Chiefly *pl.*

1928 *Public Opinion* 8 June 547/3 If you pinched a penny of his pay you passed beyond the pale, you became an unmentionable, you ceased to be a comrade. **1939** F. THOMPSON *Lark Rise* iii. 51 Those parts of the human body then known as 'the unmentionables'. **1975** *Nature* 17 Jan. 149/3 The lowest grade, dirty, wet mixtures of plastic, paper and other organic unmentionables could at least provide heat, if distilled in a pyrolysis plant set up on a wasteplex site. **1976** *Sat. Rev.* (U.S.) 30 Oct. 24/2 *Feijoada*, a Brazilian mix of rice, beans, and pork unmentionables. **1981** *Times* 6 Mar. 6/5 Already the unmentionables have been mentioned and the unpublishables published in the main..weeklies. **1982** 'P. LORAINE' *Sea-Change* III. vii. 168 The whole plan was based upon unmentionables.

Hence **un'mentionableness; un'mentionably** *adv.*

1870 MISS BROUGHTON *Red as Rose* I. 157 At the rate of purity at which we are advancing, 'legs' will soon walk off into the limbo of silence and unmentionableness. **1879** W. COLLINS *Rogue's Life* ii, He asserted, with an unmentionably vulgar oath, his resolution to turn me out of doors.

un'mentioned, *ppl. a.* (UN-¹ 8, 8 c.)

1545 RAYNALD *Byrth Mankynde* (1552) 5 Muskles of the body left apart and vnmencioned of. **1612** T. WILSON *Chr. Dict.* 146 Melchisedech['s]..Parents..be vnmentioned in the holy Story. **1661** BOYLE *Style of Script.* 187 Barabbas his Name is signally Recorded in Scripture, whereas the Penitent Thief is left Unmention'd. **1709** ADDISON *Tatler* No. 102 ¶1 There was not a single Accomplishment unmentioned. **1831** SCOTT *Ct. Rob.* viii, And now let this singular person remain for a time unmentioned. **1879** LUBBOCK *Sci. Lect.* vi. 173 Stonehenge..is unmentioned by any..Roman writer.

†**un'menyied,** *ppl. a.* *Sc. Obs.* [UN-¹ 8: see MANYIE *v.*] Unmaimed.

1500–20 DUNBAR *Poems* ix. 155, I ask thy Passioun in me so to habound, Quhill nocht vnmenȝeit be in me ane member.

un'mercantile, *a.* (UN-¹ 7.)

1783 BURKE *Rep. Aff. India* Wks. XI. 166 The false principles of this unmercantile transaction. **1848** MILL *Pol. Econ.* III. xii. §3. II. 58 An improvident and unmercantile mode of conducting business.

un'mercenary, *a.* (UN-¹ 7.)

1643 PRYNNE *Sov. Power Parl.* I. Pref. (ed. 2) A ij b, The cordiallest Endevours of a reall unmercenary Philo-pater. **1692** ATTERBURY *Serm.* (1726) I. 19 Praise is a generous and unmercenary Principle. **1702** S. PARKER tr. *Cicero's De Finibus* II. 135 An Inbred and Unmercenary Goodness of Temper. **1891** MEREDITH *One of our Conq.* xxix, She was all impulse; a shifty piece of unmercenary stratagem occasionally directing it.

Hence **un'mercenariness.**

1863 *N. & Q.* 3rd Ser. IV. 301 The genus 'he-flirt,' a race which is unhappily increased by the unmercenariness of mothers and chaperones.

†**un'merchandable,** obs. var. of next.

1670 J. SMITH *Eng. Improv. Reviv'd* 264 Vending any unmerchandable Ware..at lower Rates.

un'merchantable, *a.* (UN-¹ 7 b.)

1602 CAREW *Cornwall* 105 b, They feed on salt vnmarchantable Pilchard. **1722** *Lond. Gaz.* No. 6042/6 Wines..corrupt, or unmerchantable. **1763** *Brit. Mag.* IV. 174 Damaged and unmerchantable wines. **1818** COLEBROOKE *Import Colonial Corn* 9 A permission to dispose of his goods..before they are..rendered unmerchantable by decay. **1896** *Law Times Rep.* LXXIII. 649/1 So damaged by water as to be un-merchantable as dates.

un'merchantlike, *a.* (UN-¹ 7 c.)

1622 E. MISSELDEN *Free Trade* 100 The one taketh aduantage of our vn-merchant-like courses.

†**un'merciable,** *a.* [UN-¹ 7.] Unmerciful.

1382 WYCLIF *Jer.* l. 42 Cruel thei ben and vnmerciable. *c* **1412** HOCCLEVE *De Reg. Princ.* 3330 Where as our werkes moste ben avowed, The vnmerciable schal be disallowed. **1450** *Rolls of Parlt.* V. 212/1 Arraied in fourme of werre, with..unmerciable forboden wepons. **1509** BARCLAY *Shyp of Folys* 150 Alas mad Fole and man vnmerciable.

†**un'mercied,** *a.* [UN-¹ 9.] Merciless.

c **1600** DRAYTON *Miseries Q. Margaret* xl, The Irish,.. with sword and fire, Vnmercied hauocke of the English made.

un'merciful, *a.* [UN-¹ 7.] Merciless.

1. Of persons: Having or exhibiting no mercy.

1481 CAXTON *Reynard* (Arb.) 37 He was alway to hem vnmercyful. *a* **1548** HALL *Chron., Hen. VI*, 167 b, The vnmercifull pagans and cruel Turkes. **1584** CONSTABLE *Sonn.* VII. vii, Seeke with humble prayer Meanes how to mooue th' unmercifullest fayre. **1631** *High Commission Cases* (Camden) 231 Though he be unmercifull to us olde men, yet we are..mercifull to him. **1667** *Decay Chr. Piety* viii. ¶47 There are indeed no such unmerciful exactors as our own lusts. **1711** SWIFT *Jrnl. Stella* 7 June, Why this same Stella is so unmerciful a writer, she has hardly left any room for Dingley. *a* **1770** CHATTERTON *Battle of Hastings* 427 A wight unmercifull. **1825** J. NEAL *Bro. Jonathan* III. 250 Any female..unmerciful to those who had gone astray.

transf. *a* **1586** SIDNEY *Arcadia* I. xiii, The unmercifull Sea deprived me of my company.

absol. **1795** SOUTHEY *Joan of Arc* I. 445 Will not God In sunder smite the unmerciful, and break The sceptre of the wicked?

2. Of actions, etc.: Devoid of the quality of mercy.

1549 *Compl. Scot* i. 23 The..distructione of oure nobil barrons..be cruel ande onmercyful slauthyr. **1582** STANYHURST *Æneis* I. (Arb.) 18 Shee bears..that sept vnmerciful hatred. **1621** J. TAYLOR (Water P.) *Unnat. Father* Wks. (1630) 140/2 Weeping teares of pitilesse pity, and vnmercifull mercy. **1677** WYCHERLEY *Pl. Dealer* IV. i, When a Lover's hopes Are dead,.. Life is unmerciful. **1758** JOHNSON *Idler* No. 14 ¶10 Some stop might be put to this unmerciful prosecution. **1778** MISS BURNEY *Evelina* lxi, Her un-merciful propensity to satire. **1846** MRS. A. MARSH *Father Darcy* II. x. 170 He had resolved..upon a course of the most unmerciful policy.

3. Unsparing; excessive in amount, etc.

1706 E. WARD *Wooden World Diss.* (1708) 69 Knock'd down by an unmerciful Bowl of Punch or two. **1710** STEELE *Tatler* No. 207 ¶2 There was no enduring that this Fop should outshine us all at this unmerciful Rate. **1811** A. CLARKE *Kneeling* Wks. 1837 XI. 340 In addition to the injury I sustained by his unmerciful prayer, I had the following reproof. **1835** T. MITCHELL *Acharn. of Aristoph.* App. 252 *note*, Explain them he accordingly does at the same unmerciful length as he does every other topic.

Hence †**un'mercifulhead.** *Obs.*

c **1440** *Jacob's Well* 256 Ryȝtwysnesse may noȝt helpe þe.. in þin vnkyndenesse, in þin vnmercyfulhed.

un'mercifully, *adv.* [UN-¹ 11.]

1. Without mercy; mercilessly.

1548 ELYOT, *Immisericorditer*, without pitee, vnmercifully. **1596** SPENSER *F.Q.* v. vii. 31 The Amazon.. dealt her blowes vnmercifully sore. **1653** H. COGAN tr. *Pinto's Trav.* liii. 209 He caused [them]..to be unmercifully butchered. **1711** STEELE *Spect.* No. 145 ¶2 He went on unmercifully to Triumph over my Ignorance. **1766** HAMILTON *Vesuvius* in *Phil. Trans.* LVII. 197, I saw it.. unmercifully destroy a poor man's vineyard. **1818** SCOTT *Rob Roy* xxii, The laws concerning debt, in most countries, are..unmercifully severe. **1860** FROUDE *Hist. Eng.* V. 119 A change in the relations between the peasantry and the owners of the soil..was attempted harshly and unmercifully.

2. Unsparingly, excessively. Now *dial.*

1686 F. SPENCE tr. *St. Euvremont's Misc.* Pref. C 3, In a Comedy nothing is so unmercifully insupportable as to.. explicate the Intrigue by a Miracle. **1716** HEARNE *Collect.* (O.H.S.) V. 331 He steals unmercifully, and..without Acknowledgment. **1794** C. PIGOT *Female Jockey Club* 139 If surprised by the sight of a black lobster, she screams unmercifully. **1854** MISS BAKER *Northampt. Gloss.* 369 It's unmercifully bad.

un'mercifulness. [UN-¹ 12.] The quality of being unmerciful; mercilessness.

1545 ASCHAM *Toxoph.* (Arb.) 81 Made drunke with the frutes of the flesh, as infidelitie,..oppression, vnmercifulnesse. **1565** CECIL *Let.* in Strype *Ann. Ref.* xliv. (1709) 444 To sharpen their tongues against the idols..of.. malice, and unmercifulness. **1649** F. ROBERTS *Clavis Bibl.* 423 Babylon being devoted to destruction for her unmercifulnesse to the Jewes. **1682** *Sec. Plea Nonconform.* 63 If Justices are not merciful, they have the Countenance of the Law, for Un-mercifulness. **1722** WOLLASTON *Relig. Nat.* vi. 141 Injustice, unmercifulness, and cruelty are wrong. **1864** PUSEY *Lect. Daniel* 524 That common sin of conquerors, unmercifulness and oppression.

†**un'merciless,** *a.* [UN-¹ 5 a.] Unmerciful.

1545 JOYE *Exp. Dan.* vi. 86 b, Now ye see..their deceites, vnmercieles murther, and ingratitude. **1554** F. YAXLEY in Ellis *Orig. Lett.* Ser. III. III. 313, I was so tormented..in the unmercelesse seas. **1570** GOOGE *Pop. Kingd.* IV. 45 b, Seeking Christ to kill, [Herod] Destroyde the little infants yong, a beast vnmercilesse. **1614** JACKSON *Creed* III. 199 The Egyptians consciousnesse of their vnmercilesse practises against poore Israel.

†**un'mercy.** *Obs.* [UN-¹ 12.] Lack of mercy; unmercifulness.

c **1380** WYCLIF *Wks.* (1880) 72 Wiþ-drawynge goddis word..for ensaumple of pride, coueitise, wraþþe, vnmercy. *c* **1400** *Found. St. Bartholomew's* (1923) 41 Our synnes askyng the vnmercy of oure Lordys ire. *c* **1407** LYDG. *Reson & Sens.* 6651 Daunger sholde exiled be, Vnmercy also.

un'merged, *ppl. a.* (UN-¹ 8.)

1818 CRUISE *Digest* (ed. 2) II. 481 The estate for life of the joint tenant having the fee, is distinct from, and unmerged in, his greater estate.

un'meritable *a.* [UN-¹ 7 b.]

1. Unable to claim merit.

1594 SHAKS. *Rich. III*, III. vii. 155 Your loue deserues my thankes, but my desert Vnmeritable, shunnes your high request. **1601** —— *Jul. C.* IV. i. 12 This is a slight vnmeritable man, Meet to be sent on Errands. **1797** LD. THURLOW in *Cowper's Wks.* (1836) III. 212 Cowper's distemper persuades him that he is unmeritable and unacceptable to God. **1884** CHILD *Ballads* II. 393/1 An Italian ballad, a slight and unmeritable thing. **1885** SWINBURNE *Misc.* (1886) 137 He was content to rely on his ..simplicity alone; with a result sometimes merely trivial and unmeritable.

†**2.** Unmerited, undeserved. *Obs.*

1635 J. HAYWARD tr. *Biondi's Banish'd Virg.* 22 You..are ..come to undoe me with your unmeritable favours. **1666** EARL ORRERY in *St. Lett.* (1743) II. 93 Those unmeritable expressions of your grace's kindness.

un'merited, *ppl. a.* (UN-¹ 8.)

1648 HEXHAM II, *Onbedient*, Vndeserved, or Vnmerited. **1667** MILTON *P.L.* XII. 278 Favour unmerited by me, who sought Forbidd'n knowledge. **1711** *Spect.* No. 77 ¶5 Those Nods of Approbation which I never bestow unmerited. **1740** RICHARDSON *Pamela* (1824) I. 157 This, sir,..is all goodness unmerited on my side. **1808** WORDSW. *White Doe* II. 525 The excess Of an unmerited distress. **1889** in *Retrospect Med.* CII. 33 Years ago I remember getting a good deal of quite unmerited credit.

Hence **un'meritedness.**

1648 BOYLE *Seraph. Love* (1659) 70 The freenesse or unmeritednesse of God's love. *a* **1680** CHARNOCK *Attrib. God* (1834) II. 437 The unmeritedness of them doth enhance this.

un'meritedly, *adv.* (UN-¹ 11. Cf. prec.)

1791 ELIZA CLARKE *Sword* II. 90 The Regard which you have so unmeritedly shown for me. **1806** SCOTT *Let.* in *Lockhart* (1837) II. 88 Any prepossession which my literary reputation may, however unmeritedly, have created in my favour. **1840** *New Monthly Mag.* LX. 369 A word thus unmeritedly sent to Coventry.

un'meriting, *ppl. a.* (UN-¹ 10, 5 d.)

Also *absol.*, and with object.

1594 *Zepheria* xix, No no Zepheria, fame is too rich a prize My all vnmeriting lines for to attend on. **1607** SHAKS. *Cor.* II. i. 47 A brace of vnmeriting, proud, violent, testie Magistrates. **1795** *Fate of Sedley* I. 135 Why should we conceal our affections, when they are not improperly placed upon the unmeriting? **1827** POLLOK *Course T.* IX. 926 Unmeriting alike reward or blame. **1828** PUSEY *Hist. Enq.* I. 83 To charge heresy upon unmeriting and orthodox men.

†**un'meritingly,** *adv.* *Obs.* [UN-¹ 11.] Undeservedly.

1621 LADY M. WROTH *Urania* 399 Bee sure you mistake him not, or vnmeritingly condemne him.

unmeri'torious, *a.* (UN-¹ 7.)

[**1775** ASH.] **1855** FABER *Growth in Holiness* xiv. 233 There are a variety of unmeritorious occupations. **1862** CARLYLE *Fredk. Gt.* XII. xii. III. 374 You may buy them [*sc.* votes].. by preferments and appointments of the un-meritorious man.

So **unmeri'toriously** *adv.*

1840 DE QUINCEY *Essenes, Suppl. Note* Wks. 1857 VII. 299 Josephus..most unmeritoriously found himself.. translated into the meridian sunshine of court favour.

un'merry, *a.* (OE. *unmyrȝe*: see UN-¹ 7.)

a **1000** *Gloss.* in Wr.-Wülcker 211 *Collidium*, unmyrȝe pleȝa. *c* **1250** *Owl & Night.* 346 Ne beo þe song ne so murie þat he ne sal þinche vnmurie If he ilesteþ ouer vn-wille. *c* **1384** CHAUCER *H. Fame* 74 There slepeth ay this god [*sc.* Sleep] unmerie. *c* **1430** *Syr Gener.* (Roxb.) 9022 To Amanewel that was slaw Into the Citie forto burie, For him was Amalek vnmerie. **1530** PALSGR. 328/2 Unmery, *triste*. **1582** T. WATSON *Centurie of Love* lxxxv, Cares rowd with vowes the ship vnmery minde.

un'mesh, *v.* [UN-² 4 b.] *trans.* To undo the meshes of; to free from meshes.

c **1822** T. L. BEDDOES *Poems, Alfarabi* 138 Hands of eternal stone, that would unmesh And fray this starry company of orbs. **1856** RUSKIN *Mod. Paint.* III. IV. iv. §16 They had gone back to their daily work, thinking still their business lay net-wards, unmeshed from the literal rope and drag. **1891** C. E. NORTON *Dante's Purgat.* xxi. 136, I see the net which snares you here, and how it is unmeshed.

un'mesmerized, *ppl. a.* (UN-¹ 8 a c.)

1889 J. M. ROBERTSON *Christ & Krishna* xii. 61 Sufficient to indicate to any student unmesmerised by religion that a nature myth underlies every case.

un'met, *ppl. a.*¹ (UN-¹ 8 b: cf. MEET *v.*)

1603 B. JONSON *Sejanus* v. i, Winds lose their strength, when they do empty fly, Unmet of woods or buildings. **1641** EARL MONM. tr. *Biondi's Civil Wars* IV. 42 Had Warwick been of this opinion, succour had not come unmet withall. **1798** *Monthly Mag.* V. 367 Back to the desert-air Unmet shall he repair. **1818** COLEBROOKE *Import. Colonial Corn* 108 Yet are his productions not unthreatened nor unmet by dangerous rivalship. **1868** MORRIS *Earthly Par.* I. II. 662 While through this poor land range the heathen men, Unmet of any but my King. **1962** *Guardian* 13 July 10/4 Housing needs often make unmet demands. **1969** *Listener* 6 Feb. 172/3 There remains a massive unmet need for advice and aid from legally trained people. **1980** *Times Lit. Suppl.* 6 June 652/2 The particular need of the rapidly growing sectors, unmet by the traditional capital market, was to be of significance.

†**un'met,** *ppl. a.*² *Obs.*⁻¹ [UN-¹ 8: cf. METE *v.*¹] Unmeasured.

1482 in *Charters, etc. Edinb.* (1871) 168 Of ilk laid vnmet i obl.

un'metalled, *ppl. a.* (UN-¹ 8.)

1843 in T. J. Dyke *Addr. Public Medicine* (1885) 2 The unmetalled and unchannelled highways and streets. **1862** PATTERSON *Ess. Hist. & Art* 211 The continuation of this road..is unmetalled. **1897** *Trans. Roy. Hist. Soc.* XI. 72 The balks..seem to be..unmetalled roadways.

unme'tallic, *a.* (UN-¹ 7.)

1757 tr. *Henckel's Pyritol.* (title-p.), Its Iron, Copper, Unmetallic Earth, Sulphur [etc.]. **1796** KIRWAN *Elem. Min.* (ed. 2) I. 487 Metallic substances..held in solution by any unmetallic acid. **1841** BRANDE *Man. Chem.* 210 Heat is thrown off much more quickly from the unmetallic than from the metallic surface. **1864** BOWEN *Logic* vi. 154 All infusible things are unmetallic.

un'metallized, *ppl. a.* (UN-¹ 8.)

1796 KIRWAN *Elem. Min.* (ed. 2) II. 90 Some unmetallic or unmetallized substance. **1805** *Phil. Trans.* XCV. 169 An unmetallized portion of that [ore].

unmeta'morphosed, *ppl. a.* (UN-¹ 8.)

1600 TOURNEUR *Transf. Metam.* xvi, If any rest unmetamorphosed. **1787** *Generous Attachment* IV. 35 Many.. affect for a time the rank of Captain, but I continue unmetamorphosed. **1849** OWEN *Parthenogenesis* 39 Such unmetamorphosed germ-masses. **1880** CARPENTER in *Jrnl. Linn. Soc.* XV. 214 Unmetamorphosed embryonic basals.

unmeta'phorical, *a.* (UN-¹ 7.)

1746 J. WESLEY *Let.* 25 June (1982) II. 199 In as plain and unmetaphorical words as the nature of the thing would bear. **1767** STERNE *Tr. Shandy* IX. xiii, I am got..into a cold unmetaphorical vein of infamous writing. **1831** CARLYLE

Sart. Res. I. xi, An unmetaphorical style you shall in vain seek for.

Hence **unmeta'phorically** *adv.*

1829 G. GRIFFIN *Collegians* II. xxiv. 193 Sitting down to her, unmetaphorically, bitter draught with the meekest resignation. **1932** H. H. PRICE *Perception* i. 13 This assumption when openly and unmetaphorically stated, is.. extraordinary. **1963** R. M. HARE *Freedom & Reason* xi. 210 Prepositions expressed in terms of them [*sc.* metaphors] are, when put unmetaphorically, true.

unmeta'physic, *a.* [UN-^{1} 7.] = next.

1789 H. WALPOLE *Let. to Mrs. H. More* 4 Nov., My head is as un-mechanic as it is.. un-metaphysic, un-commercial.

unmeta'physical, *a.* (UN-^{1} 7.)

1691 NORRIS *Pract. Disc.* 301 A notion of God so very natural, that even the Jews as gross and unmetaphysical as they were, could not but imbrace it. **1701** —— *Ideal World* I. vi. 323 A blunt unmetaphysical Roman. **1825** COLERIDGE *Aids Refl.* 252 The unmetaphysical tribes of New Holland. **1871** FRASER *Life Berkeley* ii. 44 The book was too far in advance of an unmetaphysical generation to draw general attention.

un'meted, *ppl. a.* [UN-^{1} 8.] Unmeasured.

1838 MRS. BROWNING *Isobel's Child* iii, Its mother's smile, Full of love's unmeted weight. **1853** C. BRONTE *Villette* xli, Surely those near me must have felt some little of the anxiety I felt, in degree so unmeted.

un'metered, (*ppl.*) *a.* [UN-^{1} 8, 9.] Not measured by means of a meter; not provided with a meter.

1909 in WEBSTER. **1967** *Guardian* 13 Sept. 8/3 It is quite untrue that airport taxis are unmetered... The tariff is clearly displayed inside the cab on the taximeter. **1977** C. BRANDRETH *Parking Law* 57 Any unmetered spaces are provided for loading and unloading and picking up and setting down passengers. **1980** *Blair & Ketchum's Country Jrnl.* Oct. 111/2 A 1975 report on metropolitan area water usage and 'unmetered water'—quantities leaked, used to flush mains or extinguish fires, or consumed free by public facilities.

†**un'meth,** *adv.* [Cf. next, and *unimeað* s.v. UN-^{1} 3.] Immoderately, extremely.

a **1225** *Ancr. R.* 50 Vor aȝein kunde hit is, & unmeð swuc [*v.r.* sullich, selli] wunder, þet te deade totie. *a* **1225** *Juliana* 4 Maximian þe modi keiser.. wið unmeð muchel hird & unduhti duheðe.

†**un'methe,** *sb. Obs.* [OE. *unmǽþ* (UN-^{1} 12 + METHE *sb.*).] Immoderation; excess; fault.

a **1100** in Assmann *Ags. Hom.* 162 þa discipulas.. wæron on heora modȝeþance swiðlice afyrhte and ȝedrefede, swa hit nan unmæþ næs. *a* **1250** *Owl & Night.* 352 Eurich þing may lesen his godhede Mid unmeþe and ouerdede. *a* **1300** *Florice & Bl.* (Camb. MS.) 675 Min is þe guld and þe unmeþ, þat þu for me schalt þolie deþ.

†**un'methe,** *a. Obs.* [Cf. prec. and METHE *a.*] Unequal; unfair; ungentle.

c **1250** *Owl & N.* 1618 (Jesus MS.), þarfore þe is wel unmeþe, For þhah þu ligge ded & clinge þi deþ nys nouht to none þinge. *a* **1300** *Cursor M.* 11815 þat caitif vn-meth and vn-meke Nu bigines he to seke. *c* **1325** *Spec. Gy Warw.* 615 Swich a fiht is vnmeþ, For aȝein þe kinde hit geþ.

unmethlich, -ship: see UN-^{1} 3.

unme'thodical, *a.* (UN-^{1} 7.)

1601 CORNWALLIS *Ess.* II. l. Nn7, They are unmethodicall, hardly to be caught by one forme, any in truth wil do it. *c* **1720** W. GIBSON *Diet Horses* xi. (1731) 165 The.. Instructions.. are so obscure and un-methodical, that it is not an easy matter to follow them. **1862** LYTTON *Str. Story* II. 62 When I saw her.. smoothing his papers (in which he was apt to be unmethodical). **1869** ROGERS *Smith's Wealth N.* I. Pref. p. xxiv, The resources and defects of vast but un-methodical learning. **1872** LIDDON *Elem. Relig.* i. 28 Its form is of necessity unmethodical: it is, if you will, anti-scholastic.

So **unme'thodically** *adv.*

1632 MASSINGER & FIELD *Fatal Dowry* IV. i, What fouler obiect in the world, then to see.. a hopefull Cheualier vn-methodically appointed in the externall ornaments of nature?

un'methodized, *ppl. a.* [UN-^{1} 8.]

1. Not reduced to method.

a **1677** J. HARRINGTON *Grounds & Reasons* Wks. (1700) 12 Tho the Understandings of most men seem to agree in som general maxims, but unpolish'd, unnumber'd and unmethodiz'd. **1734** HERVEY *Mem. Geo. II* (1848) I. 400 The loose, unmethodized, and often incoherent manner, in which it is put together. **1834** SIR H. TAYLOR *Artevelde* II. v. ii, What is earth? A huge congestion of unmethodised matter.

2. Not become Methodist.

1751 LAVINGTON *Enthus. Meth. & Papists* III. (1754) 236 Hence they justly contemn.. all the Unmethodized, as of a mean and reprobate Way.

un'methodizing, *vbl. sb.* (UN-^{2} 6 c, 8.)

1818 COLERIDGE in *Encycl. Metrop.* (1845) I. Introd. 4 To the utter confusion and *unmethodising* of the science of the human mind.

un'metrical, *a.* (UN-^{1} 7.)

1791 BOSWELL *Johnson* Dec. 1784, Discoursing vehemently on the unmetrical effect of such a lapse. **1856** MASSON *Ess. Biog. & Crit.* 412 The art of producing, by means of articulate language, metrical or unmetrical, a fictitious concrete. **1885** *Athenæum* 17 Jan. 84/2 A kind of unmetrical narrative so poetic in motive.. as [etc.].

un'mew, *v.* (UN-^{2} 5; cf. MEW *v.*^{2})

1818 KEATS *Endym.* I. 132 Let a portion of ethereal dew Fall on my head, and presently unmew My soul.

unmi'caceous, *a.* (UN-^{1} 7.)

1833-4 *Encycl. Metrop.* (1845) VI. 758/1 A felspathic quartzose rock, of rather dubious character, which may be called.. unmicaceous granite.

un'midwifed, *a.* (UN-^{1} 9.)

1747 *Gentl. Mag.* 242 Her uberous store, To these, parturient Earth unmidwif'd yields.

†**un'might.** *Obs.* [OE. *unmiht, -meht* (UN-^{1} 12), = WFris. *on-, ûnmacht*, MDu. (Du.) *onmacht*, MLG. *unmacht* (LG. *unmagt*), OHG. (MHG.) *unmaht* (G. *unmacht*), Goth. *unmaht-s*; cf. also ON. *úmáttr*, MDa. *umagt*.] Want of might or strength; weakness, feebleness.

c **897** K. ÆLFRED *Gregory's Past. C.* xxxii. 208 Đonne hie onȝietað hiera unbældo & hiera unmihte, hie weorðað oft ormode. *c* **1200** *Vices & Virtues* 129 For þan euel to done nis non strencþe, ac is unmihte. *a* **1290** *Becket* 1408 in *S. Eng. Leg.* I. 146 For mine sunnes and for mine onmiȝte, þat I ne may hire wardi nouȝt. *c* **1330** R. BRUNNE *Chron. Wace* (Rolls) 15564 An heuinesse, a gret vnmight, On Cadwalyn gan to lepe. *c* **1375** *Sc. Leg. Saints* xxxii. (*Justin*) 205 þe vnmycht of my compere, þat to spede had na powere. *c* **1400** *Pilgr. Sowle* (Caxton, 1483) v. xiv. 108 In hym is feblesse and grete vnmyght. **1429** *Rolls of Parlt.* IV. 343 Grete myght on that o syde, and unmyght on that other.

†**un'mightful,** *a. Obs.* [UN-^{1} 7.]

a. Unable. **b.** Impossible.

1340-70 *Alex. & Dind.* 762 þei beþ vn-mihtful y-mad, men for to wisse. *c* **1460** *Towneley Myst.* x. 141 No word, lady, that I the bryng, Is vnmyghtfull to heuen kyng.

†**un'might(i)ly,** *advs.* *Obs.*$^{-0}$ [UN-^{1} 11.] Weakly, ineffectually.

c **1440** *Promp. Parv.* 366/1 On-myghtly [*Winch. MS.* on-myhtyly], *inpotenter*.

†**un'mightiness.** *Obs.*$^{-1}$ [UN-^{1} 12.] Impotence.

14.. in *Anglia* VIII. 124 Dredynge leste þat houge wonderynge of merueylles shulde.. arrecte goddes dedys to vnmyghtynes.

un'mighty, *a.* Now *arch.* [OE. *unmihtiȝ* (UN-^{1} 7), = OFris. *un-, onmachtich*, WFris. *on-, ûnmachtig*, MDu. *onmachtich* (Du. *-ig*), MLG. *unmechtich*, OHG. *unmahtîg, -îk* (MHG. *unmehtec, -ic*, G. *unmächtich*), Goth. *unmahteig-s*: cf. also ON. *úmáttig-r*, MDa. *umægtug*, early mod.Da. *umægtig*.] Devoid of might or strength; weak, feeble, powerless, impotent.

c **888** K. ÆLFRED *Boeth.* xxix. §1 Ælc ȝesceadwis man mæȝ witan þæt hi bioð full earme & ful unmihtiȝe. *c* **1200** *Trin. Coll. Hom.* 35 He bicom unmihti & wreche & unhol. *a* **1310** in Wright *Lyric P.* iv. 22 Middel-end for mon wes mad, un-mihti aren is meste mede. *c* **1374** CHAUCER *Boeth.* IV. pr. ii. (1868) 114 Nedes goode folk moten ben myȝty, and shrewes feble and vnmyȝty. **1402** *J. Upland* (Skeat) §63 He coude not make his rule so good as an-other did his, (.. and so were he unmighty and not god). *c* **1450** tr. *De Imitatione* II. viii. 49 Whan þe grace of god.. goþ away, þan shal he be poure & unmiȝty. **1483** CAXTON *Gold. Leg.* C ij b, He was.. so feble and so unmyghty that hys dysciples susteyned.. hym in goyng to chirche. **1545** RAYNALD *Byrth Mankynde* 79 Yf the matryce be vnmighty and weakened. **1611** FLORIO, *Impoderoso*, vnmightie, vnpowerfull. **1876** MORRIS *Sigurd* II. 97 Myself a little fragment amidst it all I saw,.. unmighty as the tempest-driven straw.

absol. *c* **1400** *Apol. Loll.* 30 It is necesari to hem to visit þe sek, to pray for þe vnmiȝti. **1549** ALLEN *Jude's Par. Rev.* 33 Both masters and seruauntes,.. hyghe and lowe, myghtie and vnmyghtie. **1587** GOLDING *De Mornay* Ep. Ded., The welbeloued Sonne of God.. must stande for all:.. the mightie for the vnmightie.

b. Const. *to*, usually with inf.

c **1000** ÆLFRIC *Saints' Lives* x. 257 Hwi come þu mid wæpnum.. to anum mædene unmihtiȝum to wiȝe. *a* **1240** *Sawles Warde* in *O.E. Hom.* I. 257 Nu is riht þenne þat we demen us seolf eauer unmihtie to werien ant to witen us.. wið ute godes helpe. *a* **1300** *Cursor M.* 6706 Qua smites vte his thains eie, And mas him vn-mighti for-to seie. *a* **1340** HAMPOLE *Psalter* cvi. 12 þai ware vnmyghty to stande agayn vicys. **1390** GOWER *Conf.* II. 177 Thei with-oute lyves chiere Unmyhti ben to se or hiere. **1422** YONG tr. *Secreta Secret.* 235 Who-so hath the paas litill and swyfte, he is suspeccious, of euyl will, on-myghty to werkys.

†**un'mild,** *a. Obs.* [OE. *unmilde* (UN-^{1} 7), = MDu. *onmilde* (obs. Du. *onmild*), OHG. *unmilti* (MHG. *unmilte, unmilde*, G. *unmild*), ON. *úmild-r* (MSw. *omilder*, Sw. *omild*, MDa., Da., and Norw. *umild*), Goth. *unmild-s* unkind.]

1. Not mild or gentle; harsh, rough, unkind.

c **900** tr. *Bæda's Hist.* II. ii. (1890) 100 ᵹif he þonne is unmilde & oferhyȝdiȝ, þonne is þæt cuð þæt he nis of Gode. *c* **1200** ORMIN 9880 Hæþenn lif & hæþenn follkess herrte Iss harrd & starrc all allse stan, Unnmeoc & all unnmilde. *a* **1250** *Owl & Night.* 61 Ich wot þat þu art unmilde Wiþ hom þat ne muȝe from þe schilde. *a* **1290** *Beket* 1460 in *S. Eng. Leg.* I. 148 Ovt of Engelonde he let heom driue:.. muche was he on-milde! *a* **1340** HAMPOLE *Psalter* cxlvi. 6 Synful men þat ere sharpe and vnmyld and contrary. **1398** TREVISA *Barth. De P.R.* XII. x. (Bodl. MS.), þe crowe.. is a iangelingge brid vnmylde [L. *impia*], and greuous to men. **1412-20** LYDG. *Chron. Troy* I. 281 Bolys ful vnmylde, with brasen feet, ramegous and wylde. **1482** *Monk of Evesham* l. (Arb.) 100 Sche was only to her cosynis ryghte gastful and on mylde. **1526** *Pilgr. Perf.* (W. de W. 1531) 113 b, Eschewe the occasyons of testynes or hastynes, and other vnmylde behauour. **1558** PHAER *Æneid* IV. K iij, Some Tigres thee did nurse, and gaue to thee their milke unmild. **1611** FLORIO, *Immite*, vnmilde, cruel.

2. Harsh of taste.

1566 DRANT *Horace, Sat.* III. G j, Eatinge most bitter rootes and leaves, unmilde unto the taste.

Hence †**un'mildness.** *Obs.*

1570 DRANT *Two Serm.* I viij, Mildnes to some is oft tymes vnmildnes and crueltie to many other. **1611** FLORIO, *Immitezza*, vnmildenesse, cruelty. **1644** MILTON *Divorce* (ed. 2) II. vii. 46 The unmildnesse of Evangelick grace shall turn servant to declare the grace and mildnesse of the rigorous Law.

un'mildewed, *ppl. a.* (UN-^{1} 8.)

[**1775** ASH.] *a* **1814** A. BECKET *Genii* i. in *New Brit. Theatre* I. 518 Kind Power, Still give the gold rod of our fields Unmildew'd.

un'militarily, *adv.* (UN-^{1} 11.)

a **1856** in Strang *Glasgow & Clubs* 585 A prisoner, who most unmilitarily occupied the front of the saddle.

un'military, *a.* [UN-^{1} 7.]

1. Not in accordance with military practice or conforming to military standards.

1777 W. DALRYMPLE *Trav. Sp. & Port.* cxliii, The king has a large.. army, which had better be reduced, than continue in its present unmilitary state. **1806** *Ann. Rev.* IV. 246 Defence—the very word is unmilitary. **1826** SCOTT *Woodst.* xii, We must not hazard the whole troops in one sortie—that were unmilitary. **1861** GEN. P. THOMPSON *Audi Alt. Part.* III. clxxiv. 206 It is simply unmilitary babble, that would talk of the difficulty of doing what is wanted, when once the military superiority is decided.

2. Not belonging to, or connected with, the military profession.

1802-12 BENTHAM *Ration. Judic. Evid.* (1827) V. 663 Suppose two persons in office, military and unmilitary. **1883** *American* VI. 233 [This] may be objected to in un-military quarters.

un'milked, *ppl. a.* (UN-^{1} 8.)

1648 HEXHAM II, *Ongemolcken*, Vnmilked. **1725** POPE *Odyss.* IX. 318 The ewes.. with distended thighs Unmilked lay bleating. **1891** HARDY *Tess* xxiv, Five unmilked cows chanced to stand apart from the general herd.

un'milled, *ppl. a.* (UN-^{1} 8.)

1555 *Richmond. Wills* (Surtees) 86 Item ij webbe un-milled... Item xiiij peces of cloth. *c* **1600** *Transcript W. Riding Sessions Rolls* (1888) 160 Duas pecias panni lanei.. vocat. vnmylned Karsey. **1726** LEAKE *Hist. Acc. Eng. Money* 121 A Cutter,.. which some have call'd the Unmill'd Guinea. **1783** COOK *First Voy.* III. xiv. III. 766 There are two kinds of coin here, of the same denomination, milled and unmilled.

†**un'mind,** *a. Obs.*$^{-1}$ [UN-^{1} 7.] Unmindful.

a **1300** *Cursor M.* 1572 þai left þe lede of þar lau, þat es, o settnes and o kind Wit-vtun mensk þai ar [*Gött.* were] vn-mind.

un'mind, *v.* [UN-^{2} 3.] *trans.* To reverse the views of.

1859 J. TAYLOR *Logic in Theol.* 239 The attempt to un-mind the Christian world at that time was impracticable.

un'minded, *ppl. a.* [UN-^{1} 8.]

†**1.** Unmentioned; not borne in mind. *Obs.*

a **1513** FABYAN *Chron.* I. xxii. 17 This also is vnmynded of wryters.. for rudenesse of his dedes, that clerkes lyst nat to spende any tyme in wrytynge of suche dedes. **1590** SPENSER *Muiopot.* Ep. Ded., Which taketh glory.. to spend it selfe in honouring you: not so much for your great bounty to my self, which yet may not be vnminded;.. as for [etc.].

2. Unheeded, unregarded.

1562 J. HEYWOOD *Prov. & Epig.* (1867) 17 Unminded, vnmoned, go make your mone. **1596** SHAKS. *1 Hen. IV*, IV. iii. 59 When he was.. A poore vnminded Out-law, sneaking home. *a* **1625** BEAUM. & FL. *Laws of Candy* v. i, Where was your gratitude, who in your Coffers Hoarded the rustic treasure which was due To my unminded Father? **1667** MILTON *P.L.* x. 332 Hee, after Eve seduc't, unminded slunk Into the Wood fast by. **1710** *Brit. Apollo* No. 61. 3/1 Sable Night unminded past away. **1846** LANDOR *Imag. Conv.* Wks. I. 390/1 Even grandmothers ere now have been unminded by their own grandchildren.

b. Left unnoticed, overlooked.

1698 *Christ Exalted* §99 It is not to be unminded how the Rebuker slides off the three first Conditions.

un'mindful, *a.* [UN-^{1} 7.] Not mindful; careless, heedless: **a.** Const. *of.*

1382 WYCLIF *Ecclus.* xxxvii. 6 Be thou not vnmyndeful of hym in thi werkis. **1500-20** DUNBAR *Poems* xiii. 47 Religious men.. ar vnmyndfull of thair professioun. **1555** EDEN *Decades* (Arb.) 56 Owre predicessoures were not vtterlye vnmyndefull of these benefites. **1631** GOUGE *God's Arrows* II. Ep. Ded., Can I then be unmindfull of her? **1663** BP. PATRICK *Parab. Pilgr.* xxx, When you find them so un-mindful of themselves. **1706** E. WARD *Wooden World Diss.* (1708) 16 One so sollicitous about other Men's Healths, cannot be unmindful of his own. **1760-2** GOLDSM. *Cit. W.* lix, Every person was willing to save himself, unmindful of others. **1821** SHELLEY *Epipsych.* 302 At her silver voice came Death and Life, Unmindful each of their accustomed strife. **1874** J. BALDW. BROWN *Higher Life* p. viii, Unmindful of the large blessing which intellectual culture and political activity bring in their train.

b. With inf. or clause.

1615 SIR W. MURE *Misc. Poems* xiv. 10 Heiping wp treassour wnmyndfull quho lent it. **1652** GAULE *Magastrom.* 323 He caused Cassius Longinus.. to be slain; unmindfull that Chærea (the man that did the deed) was so called. **1697** DRYDEN *Virg. Past.* VIII. 125 She seeks the weedy Pools,.. Careless of Night, unmindful to return. *a* **1750** A. HILL *Picture of Love* 173 Unmindful, that of old they veil'd his face.

c. Attrib. or without const. *rare.*

1594 SHAKS. *Rich. III*, IV. iv. 446 Dull vnmindfull Villaine, Why stay'st thou here? **1598** FLORIO, *Smemorato*, .. a forgetfull, obliuious, or vnmindfull man. **1608** BEAUM.

& Fl. *Four Plays in One* Wks. 1912 X. 359 Hear me,..And take my wrongs into thy hands, thou justice Done by unmindful man, unmerciful. **1796** Scott *Wild Huntsman* xxxix, His courser rooted to the ground, The quickening spur unmindful bears.

Hence **un'mindfulness**; also **un'mindfully** *adv.* (1755 Scott, and later Dicts.).

1567 Allen *Def. Priesthood* Pref., Loue of sinne,..and vnmyndfulnes of saluation. **1631** Mabbe *Celestina* xii. 132 Of my much mindfulnesse for this nights meeting, and your much unmindfulnesse and extreme carelesnesse. *a* **1680** Charnock *Attrib. God* (1834) I. 507 Why should we forget it? yea, what a shame is our unmindfulness of it.

†**un'minding**, *vbl. sb. Obs.* [un-^{1} 13.] The action of forgetting or disregarding.

1382 Wyclif *Wisd.* xiv. 26 And alle thingus ben mengd togidere,..the vnmynding [L. *immemoratio*] of the goodes of the Lord,..the vnordeynyng of leccherie and of vnclennesse. **1602–9** A. Munday tr. *Palmerin of Eng.* I. (1639) A 5 b, Pleasant passages through the grassy groves, would be an occasion of the vnminding her former fits. *a* **1684** Leighton *Comm. 1 Pet.* v. 8 The fumes..cast us into a deep sleep; a secure unminding of God and of ourselves.

un'mined, *ppl. a.* (un-^{1} 8.)

a **1849** Poe *E. B. Browning* Wks. 1865 III. 404 The reader will suffer the most valuable ore to remain unmined to all eternity, before [etc.]. **1895** *Chambers's Jrnl.* XII. 629/1 The coal in the country still unmined.

un'mineralized, *ppl. a.* (un-^{1} 8.)

1843 *Penny Cycl.* XXVII. 112/1 The mineralized hot springs and the unmineralized.

un'minglable, *a.* (un-^{1} 7 b.)

1661 Boyle *Scept. Chem.* iv. 231 The Property of Oyle.. of being unminglable with the Water. *Ibid.* 257 Divers and unminglable oyles.

un'mingle, *v.* (un-^{2} 3, 7.)

1594 T. B. *La Primaud. Fr. Acad.* ii. 155 This facultie of the fantasie..changeth and rechangeth, mingleth and vnmingleth, so that it cutteth asunder and seweth vp againe as it listeth. **1626** Bacon *Sylva* §14 It will unmingle the Wine from the Water; the Wine ascending and..the Water descending. **1646** Gataker *Mistake Removed* 39 To unmingle things that Antichrist hath confounded and put together.

un'mingled, *ppl. a.* (un-^{1} 8.)

1548 Elyot, *Impromiscuus*, vnmyngled, not confuse. **1577** tr. *Bullinger's Decades* iv. i. 559/2 The doctrine of Faith.. ought to bee reteined vnmingled, and vncorrupte in the Churche. **1626** Bacon *Sylva* §396 Springs on the Tops of High-Hills..are most pure and vnmingled. **1665** Boyle *Refl.* v. vii, Two or three unmingled Liveries, whose single Colours are bright. **1725** Pope *Odyss.* ix. 238 Vessels of unmingled wine. **1746** Hervey *Medit.* (1748) 38 Where Imagination dreams of unmingled Sweets. **1818** Scott *Hrt. Midl.* xix, She looked up with anxious surprise, not unmingled with a cast of horror. **1875** Jowett *Plato* (ed. 2) III. 252 He to whom is given the cup of unmingled ill.

un'mingling, *ppl. a.* (un-^{1} 10.)

1643 [see unmatchable *a.* 2]. **1855** Milman *Lat. Chr.* xiv. iii. VI. 463 Into this separate immaterial and unmingling world.

un'minished, *ppl. a.* (un-^{1} 8.)

1533 More *Answ. Poysoned Bk.* Wks. 1096/1 By hys ascendyng vp wyth hys body hole and vnminished. **1583** Golding *Calvin on Deut.* xxxvi. 215 That he must be so obeyed, as his whole right be reserued to him unminished. **1848** Pusey *Paroch. Serm.* (1852) I. 121 One Everlasting, Unminished, Unchanging Joy. **1854** S. Dobell *Balder* xxiii. 102 He walks, Hale and unminished, to and fro. **1870** Swinburne *Ess. & Stud.* (1875) 142 For him the sleepless wellsprings of Cephisus are yet unminished and unfrozen.

un'minister, *v.* (un-^{2} 6 b.)

1636 Prynne *Unbish. Tim.* (1661) 80 They..Un-church most Protestant Churches in forein parts, and Un-minister their Ministers. **1676** Row *Contn. Blair's Autobiog.* ix. (1848) 138 They did not unminister him, and therefore did not quarrel his preaching or praying in public.

un'ministered, *ppl. a.* and *a.* [un-^{1} 8, 9.]

1. Not administered (to a person).

1532 More *Confut. Tindale* Wks. 377/1 It were as good to leaue the sacramentes vnministred vnto him as ministred. **1545** Coverdale *Def. Chr. Man* Wks. (Parker Soc.) II. 473 Therefore must so great a sacrament in no wise be left unministered.

2. Destitute of a minister.

1657 W. Fenner *2nd Pt. Christ's Alarm* 97 Any Parish that is unchurched and unministred.

unmini'sterial, *ppl. a.* (un-^{1} 7.)

1727 Pope, etc. *Art of Sinking* 118 Used in the praise and dispraise of ministerial and unministerial persons. **1735** Hervey *Mem. Geo. II* (1848) I. 492 One of the most impolitic unministerial acts I ever knew him guilty of. **1816** Coleridge *Lett.* (1895) 660 The plain, unministerial..spirit of your writings. **1863** Edith J. May *Stronges of Netherstronge* 115 The perplexed minister recollected his office in time to repress a very unministerial reply.

un'minted, *ppl. a.* (un-^{1} 8. Cf. Da. *umyntet.*)

1611 Speed *Hist. Gt. Brit.* ix. xxiv. 164 [She] caused the value of fortie thousand Angels in Bullion, vnminted,..to be sent. **1636** Pagitt *Christianogr.* (ed. 2) ii. 40 The Treasury of merits was unminted. **1739** G. Ogle *Gualtherus & Griselda* 87 Virtue, in low, is an unminted Mine. **1845** Petrie *Round Towers Irel.* 215 The precious metals were used as a circulating medium in large unminted pieces. **1881** Duffield *Don Quixote* II. 402 To rail on the lightness of women,..their unminted promises.

un'minuted, *ppl. a.* (un-^{1} 8.)

[**1775** Ash.] **1778** [W. H. Marshall] *Minutes Agric., Observ.* 136 From the above Minutes, as well as from repeated, unminuted Observations, I am clearly of opinion [etc.]. **1824** Bentham *Bk. Fallacies* Wks. 1843 II. 465/2 From speeches—spoken and unminuted speeches.

un'miracled, *ppl. a.* (un-^{2} 6 b, 8.)

1609 F. Grevil *Mustapha* iv. iv, That our great lord may see Vnmiracled his owne humanitie.

unmi'raculous, *a.* (un-^{1} 7.)

1746 Young *Nt. Th.* ix. 1262 Miracles..can not more amaze the mind, Than this, call'd unmiraculous survey. **1858** Carlyle *Fredk. Gt.* ix. viii. II. 476 The phantom becomes reasonably unmiraculous again. **1882** Seeley *Nat. Relig.* 254 The unmiraculous part of the Christian tradition.

un'mired, *ppl. a.* (un-^{1} 8.)

c **1586** C'tess Pembroke *Ps.* lxix. vi, Gratious God,.. Keepe me safe unsunck, un-myred, Safe from flowing foes retyred.

un'mirthful, *a.* (un-^{1} 7.)

1815 Jane Austen *Emma* xvi, Difficulties..enough to occupy her in most unmirthful reflections. **1835** Lytton *Rienzi* i. iv, None saw that the unmirthful flash [of wit] was the token of the coming storm.

un'mirthfully, *adv.* (un-^{1} 11.)

1894 Wilkins & Vivian *Green Bay Tree* vii, 'Oh! come now,' exclaimed Coryton, laughing unmirthfully.

un'miry, *a.* (un-^{1} 7.)

1716 Gay *Trivia* iii. 187 There may'st thou pass with safe unmiry feet, Where the rais'd pavement leads athwart the street.

unmis'carrying, *ppl. a.* (un-^{1} 10.)

1657 Trapp *Comm. Ps.* cxx. 1 The unmiscarrying return of prayer should bee carefully observed.

un'mischievous, *a.* (un-^{1} 7.)

1821 Lamb *Elia* i. *Quakers' Meeting*, Nothing-plotting, nought-caballing, unmischievous synod! **1848** R. W. Hamilton *Sabbath* v. 170 Though overtrading is a solecism, not unmischievous is the unrequired extension of stock.

un'miscible, *a.* (un-^{1} 7.)

[**1775** Ash.] **1883** R. Haldane *Workshop Receipts* Ser. ii. 441/2 Oil and water are unmiscible.

unmis'giving, *ppl. a.* (un-^{1} 10.)

1693 Howe *Carnality Relig. Contention* Wks. 1724 II. 211 An high and unmisgiving Confidence, and expectation to be saved! **1832** L. Hunt *Poems* Pref. p. xi, A small and unambitious, yet unmisgiving and happy production. **1863** Cowden Clarke *Shaks. Char.* i. 6 He has an unmisgiving confidence in his own powers. **1867** Lewes *Hist. Philos.* (ed. 3) II. 24 Discussing, with ardour and unmisgiving ingenuity, topics..necessarily beyond all possible demonstration.

unmis'givingly, *adv.* (un-^{1} 11; cf. prec.)

1842 Mrs. Browning *Bk. Poets* iv. §6 As it is a fault in the Greek lyrist to leave his buoyancy..too unmisgivingly and entirely for the right reverence of Unity in Beauty. **1861** Earle *Glouc. Fragm.* 40 Much in the same way as..one..is unhesitatingly and unmisgivingly pronounced 'a saint in glory'.

unmis'guided, *ppl. a.* (un-^{1} 8.)

1830 W. Taylor *Hist. Surv. Germ. Poetry* I. 91 Unmisguided by ecclesiastic missionaries and monastic institutions.

unmisin'terpretable, *a.* (un-^{1} 7 b.)

a **1631** Donne *Serm.* 589 This usefull and unmisinterpretable Confession which we speak of.

un'missable, *a.* [un-^{1} 7 b.] That cannot or should not be missed.

1934 in Webster. **1972** *Guardian* 18 Mar. 10/2 Radio 4's unmissable 'Word in Edgeways'. **1978** *Times* 28 Aug. 8/8 William Randolph Hearst's fairy castle..is an unmissable monument to random acquisitiveness. **1980** *Daily Tel.* 23 Aug. 10 One act in the 'unmissable' category at the Edinburgh festival must surely be the Prvimaj Pirot Workers Culture Art Band from..Yugoslavia. **1983** *Observer* (Colour Suppl.) 13 Mar. 32/3 One unmissable part of her daily routine.

un'missed, *ppl. a.* (un-^{1} 8.)

a **1400** *Relig. Pieces fr. Thornton MS.* (1914) 105/255 Thay menskede the with manhede, with mytir vn-myste. *c* **1520** Barclay *Jugurth* (1557) 8 The right kayes..nyghtly were delyuered vnto Hiempsall..soo myght they nat be vnmyssed the space of a nyght. **1621** G. Sandys *Ovid's Met.* iv. (1626) 68 Then Thisbe..slipping forth, vnmissed of her guard, Comes maskt to Ninus tomb. **1757** Gray *Let. to Mason* 28 Sept., Why should he not steal away, unmarked and unmissed till the hurry of passions in those..was a little abated? **1791** Cowper *Iliad* xvi. 652 Thy allies..Perish, unaided and unmiss'd by thee. **1819** Scott *Ivanhoe* vi, Of comfort there was little, and, being unknown, it was unmissed. **1835** *Court Mag.* VI. 59/1 He's only fit for the dunghill, where he would rot among other offal, unmissed.

un'missionized, *ppl. a.* (un-^{1} 8.)

1860 Tylor *Anahuac* xii. 325 Various tribes of Red Men in Hudson's Bay Territory, as yet unmissionized.

un'mist, *v.* (un-^{2} 4.)

1611 Florio, *Disinebbiare*, to vnmist, to vnfog. **1675** G. R. tr. *Le Grand's Man without Passion* 21 They are not very far distant from the Truth, and by a little light brought in to unmist them, they may easily pass for Articles of our Faith.

unmi'stakable, *a.* (un-^{1} 7 b.)

In common use from *c* 1855.

1666 Tillotson *Rule of Faith* i. iii. §9. 31 Unmistakeable, indefectible Oral Tradition. *a* **1834** Coleridge *Biogr. Lit.* (1847) I. 305 In Nature..there are unmistakeable foretokens of Evil. **1840** Hood *Up Rhine* 242 The unmistakeable Roman features of the Centurion. **1860** Tyndall *Glac.* 390 The veins..cutting each other at an unmistakeable angle.

Hence ˌ**unmistaka'bility; unmi'stakableness.**

1866 Grosart in *Lismore Papers* Introd. 13 The frankness and unmistakableness with which facts are given. **1923** J. M. Murry *Pencillings* 13 It matters only if another writer should arise who..will take advantage of some of Henry James's explorations and use them in order to increase his own unmistakability. **1972** *Daily Tel.* (Colour Suppl.) 19 May 41/3 One thing all [these villages] possess, and Torremolinos-rampant does not, is unmistakeability.

unmi'stakably, *adv.* (un-^{1} 11; cf. prec.)

1854 tr. *Hettner's Athens* 51 Architectural fragments, unmistakably of very ancient origin. **1894** Sala *London up to date* xxiii. 347 A cleanly-shaven fellow with..an unmistakably horsey look about the eyes and lips.

unmi'staken, *ppl. a.* (un-^{2} 8 b.)

1768–74 Tucker *Lt. Nat.* II. 523 That obedience which is ..the genuine product of an unmistaken sanctity.

unmi'stakingly, *adv.* (un-^{1} 11.)

1870 Rock *Textile Fabrics* p. xxx, The affection shown by ..all our nobility..for cloth of gold in their garments, was unmistakingly set forth in so many of their likenesses.

un'mistressed, *a.* (un-^{1} 9.)

1867 *Chamb. Jrnl.* 21 Dec. 801 The unmistressed labouresses [*sc.* servants] sat in a smaller room.

unmis'trusted, *a.* (un-^{1} 8.)

1600 Tourneur *Transf. Metam.* xxv, Worlde's trustlesse trust, soule's unmistrusted fall. **1621** Lady M. Wroth *Urania* 393 In stead of loue, to giue me frownes;..and all vnlook'd for, or, vnmistrusted; it wounds my very soule.

unmis'trustful, *a.* (un-^{1} 7.)

1768–74 Tucker *Lt. Nat.* II. 606 A prospect of futurity and unmistrustful hope in the divine goodness.

unmis'trusting, *ppl. a.* (un-^{1} 10.)

c **1598** Deloney *Thomas of Reading* xiv, The vnmistrusting man thinking no euill, went to the doore. **1762** Sterne *Tr. Shandy* vi. xxix, An unmistrusting ignorance of the plies..of the heart of woman. **1787** Burns *Highland Tour* Aug. (Friday), Kind openheartedness, mixed with unmistrusting simplicity.

†**unmithe**: see un-^{1} 3.

un'mitigable, *a.* (un-^{1} 7 b.)

1610 Shaks. *Temp.* i. ii. 276 Her most vnmittigable rage. **1628** Bp. Hall *Serm. bef. Chas. I*, 100 The desperate man.. pierceth his owne heart with a deepe, irremediable, vnmittigable, killing sorrow. **1646** —— *Devout Soul* xii. 42 The un-pitiable, interminable, unmitigable tortures of those ..never-dying souls. **1805** Foster *Ess.* (1806) I. 174 The great Cause..assumed in his administrations an unmitigable urgency. **1862** Lytton *Str. Story* II. 172 A remembrance of unrelaxed, unmitigable indignation.

un'mitigably, *adv.* (un-^{1} 11.)

1868 Browning *Ring & Bk.* iv. 768 Practising,.. Unmitigably from the very first, The finer vengeance.

un'mitigated, *ppl. a.* [un-^{1} 8.]

1. Not softened in respect of severity or intensity.

1599 Shaks. *Much Ado* iv. i. 308 With publike accusation, ..vnmittigated rancour. **1814** J. Austen *Mansfield Park* ix, The unmitigated glare of day. **1833** L. Ritchie *Wand. by Loire* 26 [It] is not an unmitigated evil. **1856** Kane *Arct. Expl.* I. xxv. 328 [He] fell sick with the unmitigated fatigue. **1873** Symonds *Gk. Poets* v. 129 Supreme art lends solemnity and grandeur to the expression of unmitigated passion.

2. Not modified or toned down; absolute.

1840 Mill *Diss. & Disc.* (1859) I. 428 Still more unmitigated savages, the wild Indians. **1849** C. Bronte *Shirley* vii, Caroline 'was glad to see them' (an unmitigated fib). **1860** *All Year Round* No. 72. 511 In very plain speech, I look on him as an unmitigated humbug. **1871** L. Stephen *Playgr. Eur.* iv. 311 A slope of hard, blue, unmitigated ice.

Hence **un'mitigatedly** *adv.*

1851 in C. Martyn *W. Phillips* (1890) 242 Of all the institutions of slavery on the face of the earth, there are none so unmitigatedly bad..as [that]..in the United States. **1865** *Ch. Times* 11 Mar. 76/3 The unmitigatedly gloomy manner in which funerals are now conducted. **1884** *Manch. Exam.* 27 Dec. 3/5 Nor is it unmitigatedly depressing, though far from cheerful.

un'mitre, *v.* (un-^{2} 4.)

1598 Florio, *Dimitriare*, to vnmitre. **1644** Milton *Areop.* (Arb.) 67 The unmitring of a Bishop. **1675** Penn *Eng. Pres. Interest* 53 [He] hop't..to inculcate that Doctrine which should un-Mitre the Pope.

un'mitred, *ppl. a.* (un-^{1} 8.)

1688 R. Holme *Armory* iv. xi. (Roxb.) 442/2 The Metropolitan..standing vnmittered..saith (the other Bishops standing vnmittered) this prayer. **1848** Lytton *Harold* ii. ii, Nor misdeem me, that I, humble, unmitred priest, should be thus bold. **1856** Masson *Ess. Biog. & Crit.* 43 Such an archbishop, mitred or unmitred, as England has never seen.

un'mittened, *ppl. a.* (un-^{1} 8.)

1853 Kane *Grinnell Exp.* xxxvi. (1856) 325 [It] gave..a warm impression to the un-mittened hand.

un'mix, *v.* [un-^{2} 3.] **a.** *trans.*

1558 Warde tr. *Alexis' Secr.* 7 After you haue wel vnmixed, and purged it from the saied Honnie wyth hote water. **1661** Cotterell tr. *Calprenède's Cassandra* ii. i.

(1676) 120 The eye of the mind lost itself in the care of unmixing them. *a* **1693** *Urquhart's Rabelais* III. lii. 421 How would you unmix them? **1973** *Sci. Amer.* Apr. 115/2 That is why it is easy to mix cream into a cup of coffee but difficult to unmix the two.

b. *intr.*

1968 *Physical Rev. Lett.* XX. 318/1 These particles will phase 'unmix' causing the appearance of a third wave, 'the echo'. **1971** I. G. GASS et al. *Understanding Earth* i. 18/1 A high temperature feldspar..frequently 'unmixes' if cooled slowly to form a crystal composed of discrete blebs or laminae of two compositionally different feldspars. **1980** *Phil. Mag.* A. XLI. 637 For situations in which a true thermodynamic equilibrium can be attained, the equilibrating species unmix, producing a heterogeneous composition.

un'mixable, *a.* (UN-1 7 b.)

1759 SARAH FIELDING *C'tess of Dellwyn* II. 142 Two things so very unmixable in their Natures as Truth and Falsehood. **1844** W. H. MILL *Serm. Tempt. Christ* Notes 161 Therefore things in themselves unmixable are mingled.

Hence **un'mixableness**.

1881 WHITNEY *Mixt. Lang.* 7 The unmixableness of grammar.

un'mixed, *ppl. a.* (UN-1 8.)

1526 *Pilgr. Perf.* (W. de W. 1531) 280 b, Myne odour..is as the pure balme vnmixt. **1573** TUSSER *Husb.* (1878) 111 Yet may a good huswife..haue mixt and vnmixt at hir pleasure. **1607** TOPSELL *Four-f. Beasts* 292 The Sarmatican kinde of horsses is..very fit for running, vnmixt, hauing a wel set body. **1667** MILTON *P.L.* VI. 742 Thy Saints unmixt, and from th' impure Farr separate. **1709** PRIOR *Henry & Emma* 172 Great Heav'n, bestow Our Cup of Love unmix'd. **1753** HANWAY *Trav.* I. III. li. 234 If mankind cannot think so abstractedly as a pure effort of unmixed reason implies. **1805** R. W. DICKSON *Pract. Agric.* II. 1124 The Lowland or Fifeshire breed of cattle is rarely met with in an unmixed state. **1889** S. WALPOLE *Life Ld. J. Russell* II. 26 Lord John could not derive unmixed comfort from [such] a victory.

b. Const. *with* or †*from*.

1602 SHAKS. *Ham.* I. v. 104 Thy Commandment all alone shall liue Within the Booke and Volume of my Braine, Vnmixt with baser matter. **1660** SHARROCK *Vegetables* 29 There grew..wild Oates unmixt from any other weeds. **1725** POPE *Odyss.* IV. 767 Joys ever-young, unmix'd with pain or fear. **1816** BYRON *Prisoner Chillon* 185 But these were horrors—this was woe Unmix'd with such. **1861** PALEY *Æschylus* (ed. 2) *Supplices* 1054 *note*, The better part, though not unmixed with evil.

Hence **un'mixedness**.

1612 T. WILSON *Chr. Dict.*, Puritie sig[nifieth] Vnmixednesse with sinne. **1681** DODWELL *Sanchoniathon's Phoenic. Hist.* 87 The particular conveniences they enjoyed, above others,..and their unmixedness with the Prophane Vulgar.

un'mixedly, *adv.* (UN-1 11: cf. prec.)

1642 W. PRICE *Serm.* 1 Our meaning is not that they are unmixtly such, we onely denominate them from their chiefe scope. **1682** INGELO *Bentiv. & Ur.* (ed. 4) I. II. 60 Since nothing is unmixedly pure in this world. **1748** RICHARDSON *Clarissa* (1811) V. ii. 12 How pleasing..to look back upon the happy days I gave her; though mine would doubtless have been more unmixedly so [etc.]. **1833** *Q. Rev.* XLIX. 375 There is nothing..so unmixedly pathetic. **1867** M. ARNOLD *Celtic Lit.* 89 The genius and the literature were purely and unmixedly German.

un'mixing, *vbl. sb.* [UN-2 8.] The process by which the components of a mixture separate.

1929 *Amer. Mineralogist* XIV. 235 Pentlandite is supposed to be one of the components of the 'unmixing' of a solid solution of (Fe, Ni)S. **1934** *Proc. Nat. Acad. Sci.* XX. 452 This is evidently the reason for unmixing of a solid solution (in mineralogical parlance) or the formation of a segregate phase (in metallographic parlance). **1950** [see SOLVUS]. **1974** *Nature* 9 Aug. 480/1 To avoid any appreciable unmixing occurring on cooling, the sample was rapidly removed from the hot furnace into a water-cooled brass jacket.

un'moan, *v.* (UN-1 14.)

1790 J. WILLIAMS *Shrove Tuesday*, etc. 32 They..pierc'd him as he flew: The Gods unmoan'd him as he bled—Hell yawning gulp'd its due.

un'moaned, *ppl. a.* (UN-1 8.)

1562 [see UNMINDED 2]. **1594** SHAKS. *Rich. III*, II. ii. 64 Our fatherlesse distresse was left vnmoan'd. **1622** WITHER *Philarete* M 4 Yet I..must perish nay-theless,..Vnmoaned I must dye.

†**unmoar**, obs. var. UNMOOR *v.*

1750 BLANCKLEY *Nav. Expositor* s.v., When a Ship or Vessel that Rides at two Anchors begins to get them up in order to Sail, she is Unmoaring.

†**un'moble**, *a.* and *sb.* [UN-1 7 (5 b), 12. Cf. MDu. *onmeubel*, *-moebel*, etc.] = UNMOVABLE.

1377 LANGL. *P. Pl.* B. III. 267 Moebles and vnmoebles [*v.r.* vnmebles], and al þat þow myȝte fynde. *c* **1380** WYCLIF *Wks.* (1880) 12 3if þei coueiten..þe housis, þat ben goodis vnmeble of here neiȝeboris, as londis or rentis. **1429** *Wills & Inv. N.C.* (Surtees) 80 All remenant and residewe of my goods moblez and vnmoblez. **1456** SIR G. HAYE *Law Arms* (S.T.S.) 261 Gif a man had tane possession of ony gude moble or unmoble. **1594** CAREW *Tasso* (1881) 110 If you also prisonment refuse, And fetters fly, as waight vnmoble fro.

†**un'moblety.** *Obs.*$^{-1}$ [UN-1 12.] = UNMOVABLETY.

a **1400** *Pauline Ep.* (Powell) Heb. vi. 17 In whiche thyng god wilande to schewe..þe vnmoebilte of his counseil.

un'mocked, *ppl. a.* (UN-1 8.)

1648 HEXHAM II, *Onbegeckt*, Vnmocked, or not Flouted. **1817** MOORE *Lalla R.*, *Fire-Worshippers* II. 251 Here we may bleed, unmock'd by hymns Of Moslem triumph. **1904** *Westm. Gaz.* 2 Apr. 2/2 You'll hear a voice..Aspire a moment, pause, and die—Unmocked of Echo.

un'mockingly, *adv.* (UN-1 11.)

1872 TENNYSON *Gareth & Lynette* 286 Unmockingly the mocker ending here Turn'd to the right.

un'modelled, *ppl. a.* (UN-1 11.)

1875 RUSKIN *Fors Clav.* xlix. V. 4 Not in my model colony only, but as best it can be managed in any unmodelled place or way. **1895** *Westm. Gaz.* 6 Dec. 3/1 The unmodelled homes of the poor.

†**un'moderate**, *a.* *Obs.* [UN-1 7, 5 b.] Immoderate.

1398 TREVISA *Barth. De P.R.* XI. ii. (Bodl. MS.), 3if þe winde is contrarie and vnmoderat, þanne he bringeþ peril. *Ibid.* XIII. xxvi, Vnmoderat heete greueþ fysche. **1539** ELYOT *Cast. Helthe* 64 If the fluxe be vnmoderate, it engendreth myscheuous diseases. **1584** FENNER *Def. Ministers* (1587) 59 Vnlesse he thinke the..persons..were so vnlearned, vnmoderate, and vngodlie. **1617** MINSHEU, *Un-moderate*,.. immoderate.

†**un'moderately**, *adv.* *Obs.* (UN-1 11, 5 b.)

1528 PAYNELL *Salerne's Regim.* Y iv, Wyne vnmoderately taken..febleth the eies and syght. **1548** ELYOT s.v. *Cibus*, To eate vnmoderately. **1647** HEXHAM I, Vnmoderately, *onmatelick*.

unmoderly, obs. Sc. f. UNMOTHERLY *adv.*

un'modern, *a.* (UN-1 7.)

1757 MRS. GRIFFITH *Lett. Henry & Frances* (1767) III. 116 Like an unmodern Critic, let me first commend, before I find Fault. **1876** *N. Amer. Rev.* CXXIII. 182 His style is unmodern. **1889** SKRINE *Mem. Thring* 69 His language, so unmodern and so expressive.

un'modernize, *v.* (UN-2 6 c (*b*).)

1818 KEATS *Lett.* (1848) I. 133, I shall have it bound in Gothique—a nice sombre binding; it will go a little way to unmodernize. **1834** LAMB in *N. & Q.* Ser. VI. IV. 223/1 'Ween', and 'wist',..are antiquated frippery, and unmodernize a poem rather than give it an antique air.

un'modernized, *ppl. a.* (UN-1 8.)

[**1775** ASH.] *c* **1815** JANE AUSTEN *Persuas.* v, The mansion of the squire,..substantial and unmodernized. **1883** *Harper's Mag.* Mar. 533/2 That, too, had been left unmodernized.

†**un'modest**, *a.* *Obs.* [UN-1 7, 5 b.] Immodest.

1565 COOPER *Thesaurus* s.v. *Immodestus*, A saucie and vnmodest kinde of iestyng. *a* **1586** SIDNEY *Arcadia* II. xxiii, This breaking of my harte..will make you (I hope) think I was not altogether unmodest. **1632** SHERWOOD, Unmodest, *immodeste*.

†**un'modestly**, *adv.* (UN-1 11, 5 b.)

1580 HOLLYBAND *Treas. Fr. Tong*, *Intemperément*, vntemperately, vnmodestly. **1632** SHERWOOD s.v.

†**un'modesty.** (UN-1 12.)

1647 HEXHAM I, Vnmodestie, *ongeschicktheyd*.

un'modifiable, *a.* (UN-1 7 b.)

1825 COLERIDGE *Lit. Rem.* (1836) II. 353 Reason theoretical and practical,..unapproachable and unmodifiable by the animal basis. **1860** GEO. ELIOT *Mill on Fl.* I. v, Some of her most unmodifiable characters. **1883** F. GALTON *Inq. Hum. Faculty* 156 They remain unmodified and unmodifiable.

Hence **un'modifiableness**.

1876 GEO. ELIOT *Dan. Der.* lviii, A nature not of brutish unmodifiableness.

un'modified, *ppl. a.* (UN-1 8.)

1792 BURKE *Let. to Sir H. Langrishe* Wks. VI. 308 An universal unmodified capacity, to which the fanaticks pretend. **1823** H. J. BROOKE *Introd. Crystallogr.* 251 The *o*, by which we have proposed to denote the unmodified angles or edges. **1841** MYERS *Cath. Th.* III. §30. 106 Our Lord everywhere exhibited a form of Truth unmodified by Individuality. **1871** DARWIN *Desc. Man* II. xiii. II. 67 We have seen that some birds..rattle their unmodified feathers together.

un'modish, *a.* [UN-1 7, 5 b.] Unfashionable.

c **1665** C'TESS WARWICK in C. F. Smith *Life*, etc. (1901) 327 To be so unmodish as..to walk in the straight and holy path. **1672** J. PHILLIPS *Montelion's Predict.* 4 To offer more Reasons..would be absurd and unmodish. **1716** LADY M. W. MONTAGU *Toilet* 21 At Chapel..Who..appears at those unmodish Hours But Ancient Matrons? **1728** MORGAN *Algiers* I. Pref. p. i, [I am] so impoliticly unmodish, that I never can speak one thing when I mean another. *a* **1974** R. CROSSMAN *Diaries* (1977) III. 225 Of all the places which are not exactly with-it that dreary part of South London is the worst, brand new and yet unpopular and unmodish.

un'modulated, *ppl. a.* (UN-1 8, 5 b.)

1815 JANE AUSTEN *Emma* iv, The uncouthness of a voice ..wholly unmodulated. **1861** [MRS. A. J. PENNY] *Romance Dull Life* xx. 150 He answered with a short and unmodulated monosyllable. **1866** LIVINGSTONE *Last Jrnls.* (1873) I. xi. 292 A low unmodulated guttural drawl.

un'moist, *a.* (UN-1 7.)

1611 FLORIO, *Inhumido*, vnmoist, dry, saplesse. **1708** J. PHILIPS *Cyder* I. 333 With heavy Bulk Volatile Hermes, fluid and unmoist, Mounts on the Wings of Air. *Ibid.* II. 159 The Dew..left unmoist His execrable Glebe. **1825** COLERIDGE *Poet. Wks.* (1912) II. 1111 With unmoist Lip and wreathless Brow I stroll. **1855** SINGLETON *Virgil* II. 287 Jaws, unmoist with blood.

un'moisted, *ppl. a.* [UN-1 8.] = next.

1492 RYMAN in *Archiv Stud. neu. Spr.* LXXXIX. 185 Beholde, the yerde of Aaron Vnmoysted bare a floure.

un'moistened, *ppl. a.* (UN-1 8.)

a **1625** FLETCHER *Nice Valour* II. i, Mayst thou dye with an unmoist'ned eye. **1708** J. PHILIPS *Cyder* II. 400 The Muses still require Humid Regalement, nor will aught avail Imploring Phœbus, with unmoisten'd Lips. **1735** SOMERVILLE *Chase* I. 176 The drooping Pack..loll their unmoisten'd Tongues. *c* **1830** BRYANT *Murdered Traveller* 28 They..marked his grave with nameless stones, Unmoistened by a tear. **1844** NOAD *Electr.* (ed. 2) 416 If the brass conducting tubes..are grasped..with the unmoistened hands.

†**unmo'lest**, *ppl. a.* *Obs.* [UN-1 8 b.] = next.

c **1560** A. SCOTT *Poems* (S.T.S.) vii. 6 Thairfoir go,..And lat me leif thus vnmolest. **1773** J. ROSS *Fratricide* III. 1000 (MS.), He sees his Brother's sacrificial fire To Heaven ascending unmolest and bright!

unmo'lested, *ppl. a.* (UN-1 8.)

1531 *Reg. Privy Seal Scot.* II. 134/2 The saidis personis.. to be unattechit,..unmolestit, and untrublit. **1603** KNOLLES *Hist. Turks* (1621) 25 King Baldwin..liued for a season vnmolested by his enemies. **1689** BOYLE *Martyrd. Theodora* xii. 246 The unmolested Exercise of a Religion, that [etc.]. **1740** CIBBER *Apol.* viii. 164 Continuing to act with as little Authority, unmolested. **1772** PRIESTLEY *Inst. Relig.* (1782) II. 26 They..suffered them to live unmolested. **1812** BYRON *Ch. Har.* II. lxxxvi, Where the gray stones and unmolested grass Ages, but not oblivion, feebly brave. **1884** SIR W. B. BRETT in *Law Times Rep.* LI. 530/1 He has a perfect right..to have his person unmolested by the negligence of another man's servant.

Hence **unmo'lestedly** *adv.*

1641 LD. DIGBY *Parl. Sp.* 19 Jan. 21 To let them injoy unmolestedly, what belongs unto them. **1665** BOYLE *Occas. Refl.* VI. ix, The Devil sometimes do's unmolestedly suffer us to write well. **1839** LADY LYTTON *Cheveley* viii, They unmolestedly went to..dinners for six months. **1879** FARRAR *St. Paul* II. 510 Teaching the things concerning the Lord Jesus Christ with all confidence unmolestedly.

unmo'lesting, *ppl. a.* (UN-1 10.)

c **1792** WOLCOT (P. Pindar) *Old Simon* viii, Sweetly she slept..In good old Simon's unmolesting arms. **1891** *Daily News* 30 Dec. 5/1 Living their quiet useful lives, unmolesting and unmolested.

un'mollified, *ppl. a.* (UN-1 8.)

1628 FELTHAM *Resolves* I. lxxv. 68 So still he rests vnmollified, for all this raine and haile. **1760–72** H. BROOKE *Fool of Qual.* (1809) I. 156 The..crude element of earth, unmollified by the fluidity of water and light. **1934** W. S. CHURCHILL *Marlborough* II. xxiv. 531 Slangenberg, unmollified, objected even to receiving the order of his own Government from the Commander-in-Chief under whom he was to serve. **1968** *Punch* 12 June 853/1 Animals not allowed, said the hatchet manageress. Good God, woman, this is our last night in England. She was unmollified.

un'molten, *ppl. a.* [UN-1 8 b.] Unmelted.

1525 in Lindsay *Coinage Scot.* (1845) 232 The gold.. beand bocht for vii. Li. the unce unmoltyn. **1555** EDEN *Decades* (Arb.) 164 The snowe lyinge contynually vnmolten. **1613** PURCHAS *Pilgrimage* VI. i. 464 Old Atlas..hath alwayes on his..high toppes vnmolten snow. **1844** MRS. BROWNING *Drama of Exile* 399 The unmolten lightnings vein it motionless.

un'momentary, *a.* [UN-1 7, 5 b.]

†**1.** Of no moment; unimportant. *Obs.*

1624 HEYWOOD *Gunaik.* II. 69 Whence soever shee had that name bestowed upon her, it was neither idle nor unmomentarie. **1635** —— *Hierarchy* I. 27 Such childish and vnmomentary grounds These Atheists build vpon.

2. Not occupying a moment of time. *rare*$^{-1}$.

1635 HEYWOOD *Hierarchy* VII. 439 From heav'n to earth he can descend, and bee Aboue and here in space vnmomentarie.

unmo'mentous, *a.* (UN-1 7, 5 b.)

1824 CAMPBELL *Theodric* 168 How our fates from unmomentous things May rise! **1858** CARLYLE *Fredk. Gt.* III. v. I. 229 There is lastly a still more unmomentous Margraf, only son of said Unmomentous and his said Spouse.

un'monarch, *v.* (UN-2 6 b. Cf. UNKING *v.*)

1667 KATH. PHILIPS *Poems* 2 As we unmonarch'd were for want of thee. **1681** SIR J. TYRRELL (*title*), Patriarcha non Monarcha. The Patriarch Unmonarch'd..; in which The falseness of those Opinions that would make Monarchy *Jure Divino* are laid open. **1746** W. HORSLEY *Fool* (1748) II. 2 [They] take great Pains to unmonarch me, and constitute themselves in my Stead. **1818** J. HASSELL *Rides & Walks* II. 123 The dignity and sarcasm..so far unmonarched his most Christian majesty, that he burst into a violent fit of passion.

Hence **un'monarched** *ppl. a.*

c **1844** LOWELL *To the Past* iv, The eternal sorrow In their unmonarched eyes. **1868** HEAVYSEGE *Jezebel* I. 218 Thou didst discrown Thyself. Unmonarched man!

unmo'nastic, *a.* (UN-1 7.)

1849 I. TAYLOR *Loyola & Jes.* I. vii. 151 Their unmonastic habit..afforded ground enough for such imputations. **1869** TOZER *Highl. Turkey* I. 93 My tumbler..was engraved with most unmonastic Cupids.

un'moneyed, *ppl. a.* (UN-1 8.)

1677 W. HUGHES *Man of Sin* II. viii. 129 What Rich Bargains of Popish Pardons may be had..both by the Monyed and Unmonyed Chapmen too. **1742** SHENSTONE *Schoolmistr.* xxxiii, Apples with cabbage-net y-cover'd o'er, Galling full sore th' unmoney'd wight, are seen. **1822** *Liberal* I. 210 Their sympathy with the natural unmonied faculties of poets in general. **1868** R. LYTTON *Chron. & Char.* II. 230 This pauper Priest..from thankless doors drave forth The messenger unmonied and amazed.

†**un'monished**, *ppl. a. Obs.* (UN-¹ 8.)
1596 LODGE *Prosopopeia* Wks. (Hunter. Cl.) III. 47 O turn vnto me, whom..no man seeketh vnmonished, and no man findeth vnpurged.

un'monkish, *a.* (UN-¹ 7.)
1851 CARLYLE *Sterling* I. iv. 45 A singular condition of Schools and High-schools, which have come down..from the monkish ages into this highly unmonkish one.

un'monkly, *a.* (UN-¹ 7.)
1833 *Fraser's Mag.* VIII. 323 He..shook hands in a cordial and quite unmonkly manner.

unmo'nopolized, *ppl. a.* (UN-¹ 8.)
[**1775** ASH.] **1879** H. GEORGE *Progr. & Pov.* III. vi, New countries where land is yet unmonopolized. **1898** *Westm. Gaz.* 21 Jan. 3/2 The profits that would accrue from unmonopolised sale.

unmo'nopolizing, *vbl. sb.* (UN-² 8.)
1641 MILTON *Reform.* II. 85 The unappropriating, and unmonopolizing the rewards of learning and industry, from the greasie clutch of ignorance.

unmo'nopolizing, *ppl. a.* (UN-¹ 10.)
1875 *Encycl. Brit.* I. 216/1 The disinterested and unmonopolising side of æsthetic pleasure.

un'monumented, *ppl. a.* (UN-¹ 8.)
1865 E. BURRITT *Walk to Land's End* 13 [They] lay long in unmonumented..graves.

un'moor, *v. Naut.* [UN-² 4 b.]
1. *trans.* To free from moorings; *spec.* 'to reduce (a ship) to the state of riding by a single anchor and cable' (Falconer).
1497 *Naval Acc. Henry VII* (1896) 229 The Remoovyng & Vnmoryng ye said Ship. **1681** *Lond. Gaz.* No. 1663/4 They lye Unmored, and ride single, and intend to Sail this Afternoon. **1704** *Ibid.* No. 3981/3 All the Ships..are unmoor'd, and will sail with the next Opportunity. **1725** POPE *Odyss.* IV. 786 With sails we wing the masts,..Unmoor the fleet, and rush into the sea. **1800** *Hull Pilotage Act* 14 The pilot..shall be paid for unmooring..such ship. **1828** SCOTT *F.M. Perth* xxiv, They seated themselves in the boat and unmoored it from the pier. **1882** 'OUIDA' *Maremma* I. 135 She found her boat safe, and unmoored it and rowed backward.
transf. **1866** BRIGHT *Sp.* (1876) 177 They would unmoor the island from its fastenings in the deep.
2. *intr.* To cast off moorings. (Cf. UNMOAR.)
1611 COTGR., *Demarer*, to vnmoore; to loosen a ship thats moored,..and put out to sea. **1693** *Lond. Gaz.* No. 2935/4 Sir Francis Wheeler made the Signal for the Ships to Unmoore. **1745** P. THOMAS *Jrnl. Anson's Voy.* 117 The next Morning we unmoor'd..and at Six weigh'd. **1778** J. ADAMS *Diary* 14 Feb., Wks. 1851 III. 95 At daybreak, orders were given to unmoor. **1840** R. H. DANA *Bef. Mast* xvii. 46 She unmoored and warped down into the bight, from which she got under weigh. **1887** BOWEN *Æneid* III. 639 Fly! and unmoor forthwith from his coasts.
Hence **un'mooring** *vbl. sb.*
1497 *Naval Acc. Hen. VII* (1896) 252 The vnmoryng of the seid Ship in Portesmouth haven after her comyng owte of Scoteland. **1710** *Lond. Gaz.* No. 4720/3 The Lancaster fired a Gun as a Signal for Unmooring. **1899** F. T. BULLEN *Way Navy* 25, I had..been endeavouring to secure some snap-shots of the fo'castle during the evolution of unmooring.

un'moored, *ppl. a.* (UN-¹ 8.)
1683 in *L'pool Munic. Rec.* (1883) I. 308 Noe shipp shall lye upon the strand unmoored.

un'mopped, *ppl. a.* (UN-¹ 8.)
[**1775** ASH.] **1848** B. D. WALSH *Aristoph., Clouds* I. i, Dusty, unmopped, reclining at my ease.

un'moral, *a.* [UN-¹ 7, 5 b.] Non-moral; not influenced by, or connected with, moral considerations. (Common from *c* 1860.)
1841 MYERS *Cath. Th.* IV. §13. 254 The disorganisation and imperfection of the unmoral part of the universe. **1855** [MISS COBBE] *Ess. Intuitive Mor.* 17 These beings are unmoral, and neither virtuous nor vicious. **1871** TYLOR *Prim. Cult.* II. 326 The lower animism is not immoral, it is unmoral.

unmo'rality. (UN-¹ 12, 5 b.)
1866 LOWELL *Biglow P.* Ser. II. Introd., That half-conscious *un*-morality which I had noticed as the recoil in gross natures from a puritanism that [etc.]. **1879** W. H. MALLOCK *Is Life Worth Living?* iii. 44 The condition of the completest personal un-morality.

un'moralize, *v.* (UN-² 6 c. Cf. IMMORALIZE *v.*)
1640 BASTWICK *Ld. Bps.* viii. H 3 They doe unmoralize the 4th Commandement, as concerning the Sabbath day for Christians: they allow profane Sports thereon. **1693** NORRIS *Pract. Disc.* (1711) III. 109 Contributing..to the unmoralizing and debauching the Age.

un'moralized, *ppl. a.* [f. prec., or UN-¹ 8.] Deprived, or devoid, of morality.
1668 H. MORE *Div. Dial.* IV. xiv. II. 58 Sensuality..makes holy things..hard and tedious to such unmoralized minds. **1690** J. NORRIS *Beatitudes* iv. (1694) 106 There being but few so wretchedly wicked and unmoraliz'd as [etc.]. *a* **1866** J. GROTE *Exam. Utilit. Phil.* xii. (1870) 185 The difference between the moralized and unmoralized, the better and the worse, human nature. **1886** *New Princeton Rev.* Mar. 180 There are no cabinets of unmoralised or half-moralised conceptions, serving as illustrations of the evolution hypothesis.

un'moralizing, *ppl. a.* (UN-¹ 10.)
1889 *Atlantic Monthly* Nov. 701/2 He was primarily the artist, impersonal, unmoralizing.

un'moralness. (UN-¹ 12.)
1642 D. ROGERS *Naaman* 554 Their opinion about the unmoralnesse of the Sabbath.

un'mordanted, *ppl. a.* (UN-¹ 8.)
1838 T. THOMSON *Chem. Org. Bodies* 394 When printed on unmordanted cotton and washed..in hot water. **1876** MORRIS in Mackail *Life* (1899) I. 315 The wool was unmordanted.

†**un'morrised**, *ppl. a.* [UN-¹ 8.] Not prepared for morris-dancing.
a **1625** FLETCHER *Women Pleas'd* IV. i, What a devil ails this fellow..Thus to appear before me too, unmorris'd?

un'morrowing, *ppl. a.* (UN-¹ 10.)
1855 BAILEY *Mystic*, etc. 154 She laid her down, and.. slept the long unmorrowing sleep.

un'mortal, *a.* (UN-¹ 7, 5 b.)
1538 ELYOT, *Immortalis*, vnmortall, that lyueth euer. **1608** WILLET *Hexapla Exod.* 75 The soule being unmortall. **1935** DYLAN THOMAS in *New Verse* Aug.–Sept. 2 My man of leaves and the bronze root, mortal, unmortal.

†**un'mortalize**, *v. Obs.* [UN-² 6 c.] *trans.* To put to death.
1593 NASHE *Christ's T.* 19 b, Man, woman, chylde, he shall vnmortalize and mangle. [**1623** COCKERAM II, *To Kill*, ..Vnmortalize, Inage.]

un'mortared, *ppl. a.* (UN-¹ 8.)
a **1656** BP. HALL *Christ Mystical* Wks. (1714) II. 348 Some loose Stones perhaps that lye unmortered upon the Battlements. **1664** EVELYN *Sylva* xxxii. 112 The Haw-thorn well plash'd..is a better..Fence then unmorter'd walls. **1860** TRISTRAM *Gt. Sahara* viii. 124 An empty watercourse, built up of unmortared stone. **1895** *Blackw. Mag.* Nov. 642/1 A carefully mown piece of turf enclosed by an unmortared wall.

un'mortgage, *v.* (UN-² 3.)
1637 HEYWOOD *Royall King* IV. iv, Sir, since you did vnmorgage all your meanes, It came into my thoughts.

un'mortgaged, *ppl. a.* (UN-¹ 8.)
1638 QUARLES *Hieroglyph.* x. vi, His quick-nos'd armie.. Must now prepare To chase the tim'rous Hare About his yet unmorgag'd grounds. **1676** D'URFEY *Mme. Fickle* v. ii, I have 200*l.* a year, I've my Lands free and unmorgag'd. **1705** ADDISON *Italy* 210 There is scarce a single Gabel unmortgag'd. **1776** ADAM SMITH *W.N.* v. iii. (1904) II. 583 The only considerable branch of the public revenue which yet remains unmortgaged. **1828** [G. C. LEWIS] tr. *Böckh's Publ. Econ. Athens* II. 247 Cleon..was so deeply involved in debt, that nothing he had was unmortgaged. **1881** *Law Rep. Ch. Div.* XV. 59 The unmortgaged portion [of the estate].

†**unmor'tificate**, *ppl. a. Obs.* (UN-¹ 8 b, 5 b.)
c **1450** tr. *De Imitatione* 126, I desire to cleve to hevenly þinges, but fleshly þinges & unmortificate passions depressen me.

un'mortified, *ppl. a.* [UN-¹ 8, 5 b.]
1. Not spiritually mortified or subdued:
a. Of passions, desires, etc.
c **1450** tr. *De Imitatione* I. iii. 5 What lettiþ þe more..þan þin unmortified affeccion of herte? **1612** T. TAYLOR *Comm. Titus* ii. 12 These lusts are fitter for the course of nature vnmortified. **1671** WOODHEAD *St. Teresa* II. xii. 101 Their passions are unmortified. *a* **1695** Z. CRADOCK *Serm. Charity* (1740) 18 His yet unmortified Lusts and Passions. **1748** HARTLEY *Observ. Man* II. iv. §4. 415 He finds many unmortified Desires..in his best Words and Actions. **1857** SUSANNA WINKWORTH tr. *Life Tauler* 390 He who wishes to ..subdue such an unmortified nature.
b. Of persons (or the heart).
1526 *Pilgr. Perf.* (W. de W. 1531) 160 Yᵉ unmortified herte hath not the housholde of yᵉ soule in suche peace. **1641** MILTON *Animadv.* 57 Unconfessing and unmortify'd sinners. **1691** HARTCLIFFE *Virtues* 210 As thou wouldst not demonstrate thy self to be a rash and unmortified Person. **1748** RICHARDSON *Clarissa* (1811) III. xxi. 127 By his soul (the unmortified creature swore,)..he was now in earnest in his good resolutions. *Ibid.* 166 An unmortified libertine. **1894** HEDLEY *Retreat* xviii. 207 No one can be relaxed, unmortified, and lazy, and at the same time desire to love God with..a whole heart.
2. *Sc. Law.* Not disposed of by mortification.
1467 *Sc. Acts, Jas. III* (1814) II. 90 Þe soume..to be Raisit of all lordis,..and vþeris quhatsumeuer hafand land vtouth burgh vnmortifijt.
3. Not affected by gangrene.
1732 MONRO *Anat.* (ed. 2) 18 An unmortified Part..can have Nerves.., and yet enjoy no Sensation.
Hence **un'mortifiedness**.
1643 T. GOODWIN *Trial Christian's Growth* II. iii. (1651) 73 This argues much unmortifyednesse, though it run not out into acts. *a* **1677** MANTON *Disc. Peace* Wks. 1871 II. 66 The more men increase in grace..the more they know their emptiness, unmortifiedness, and manifold sins. **1727** *Biog. Presbyt.* (1827) I. 338, I have seen some..become fearful Examples of Apostacy, in Covetousness and Unmortifiedness.

un'mortised, *ppl. a.*¹ (UN-¹ 8 + MORTISED *ppl. a.*)
1678 MOXON *Mech. Exerc.* vi. 103 This Square Peece hath a square wide Mortess in it..to screw against that part of the Wooden Peece un-mortessed at the Top,..stiff against the fore-side of the un-mortessed Peece.

un'mortised, *ppl. a.*² (UN-² 8 + MORTISE *v.*¹)
1748 RICHARDSON *Clarissa* (1811) VI. 304 An old broken-bottomed cane couch,..unmortised by the failing of one of its worm-eaten legs. **1859** TENNYSON *Merlin & V.* 402 The wrist is parted from the hand that waved, The feet unmortised from their ankle-bones Who paced it, ages back.

unmo'saic, *a.* (UN-¹ 7 + MOSAIC *a.*²)
1644 MILTON *Divorce* (ed. 2) II. ix. 50 By this reckning Moses should bee most unmosaick, that is, most illegal, not to say most unnaturall. **1868** W. SMITH *Book of Moses* p. v, The Separatist Theory..breaks up the whole Pentateuch into un-Mosaic fragments.

unmossed, *ppl. a.* (UN-¹ 8.)
1863 LOWELL *Memoriae Positum* I. 14 Bleaker than un-mossed stone.

un'motheaten, *ppl. a.* (UN-¹ 8 b.)
1574 HELLOWES *Gueuara's Fam. Ep.* (1577) 56, I doe craue, from hencefoorth you keepe your letter vnmoatheaten.

un'mothered, *ppl. a.* [UN-¹ 8 and UN-² 8.]
1. Deprived of motherly feelings.
1607 TOURNEUR *Rev. Trag.* II. i, I e'en quake to proceed, my spirit turns edge, I fear me she's unmother'd.
2. Deprived or destitute of a mother.
1847 H. BUSHNELL *Chr. Nurt.* iii. (1861) 65 The young go forth untended, or unmothered. **1856** MRS. BROWNING *Aur. Leigh* I. 95 Nursing me, Unmothered little child of four years old. **1876** SWINBURNE *Erechtheus* 1057 Thralls of no man's blood, Unchilded and unmothered.

un'motherly, *a.* (UN-¹ 7.)
Also, in recent use, ***unmotherliness***.
1593 *Sidney's Arcadia* IV. (1629) 413 Well hath my mother reuenged vpon me my vnmotherly hating of thee. **1622** E. CLINTON *C'tess Lincoln's Nursery* 13 They argue vnmotherly affection, idlenesse, desire to haue liberty. **1825** COLERIDGE *Aids Refl.* 357 To asperse my friend's wife for unmotherly conduct in taking an infant six months old to a crowded theatre. **1850** BLACKIE *Æschylus* I. 120 My mother most unmotherly, her own children With godless hate pursuing.

un'motherly, *adv.* [UN-¹ 11.] Unkindly.
c **1425** WYNTOUN *Cron.* II. viii. 702 Thai at coyme to spy þat lande, þai dressit wnmodyrly; For sum of þaim þai slew richt þar. **1456** SIR G. HAYE *Law Arms* (S.T.S.) 30 [They] bitterly and unmoderly will bakbyte behynd bakkis.

un'motived, *ppl. a.* (UN-¹ 8.)
1794 COLERIDGE *Lett.* (1895) 59 Your gossip with the commanding officer seems so totally useless and unmotived. **1830** W. TAYLOR *Hist. Surv. Germ. Poetry* I. 286 The sentiments of the personages..[are] often superfluous and un-motived. **1885** *Pall Mall G.* 2 Oct. 5/1 Looking back, we begin to understand actions which seemed dreamily unmotived.

un'mould, *v.* [UN-² 3, 5, 7.]
1. a. *trans.* To destroy the mould or form of.
1611 COTGR., *Demouler*, to vnmould; breake the mould,.. spoyle the frame, of. **1634** MILTON *Comus* 529 His baneful cup..Whose pleasing poison The visage quite transforms of him that drinks,..unmoulding reasons mintage Character'd in the face. [**1745** WARTON *Pleas. Melancholy* 89 That charmed cup, which Reason's mintage fair Unmoulds.] **1797** COLERIDGE *Dungeon* 18 So he lies Circled with evil, till his very soul Unmoulds its essence. **1826** [see DISLIMN *v.* 1].
b. To take out of a mould. Also *absol.*
c **1900** *Century Cook Bk.* 493 (Cent. Suppl.), To unmold creams. *Ibid.*, The unmolding of creams requires great care. **1971** *Daily Tel.* 15 July 15/2 The no-cooking puddings.. can await your pleasure in the freezer..; but do remember not to unmould them until the moment of service. **1972** *Ibid.* 28 Dec. 11/3 Unmould, and dust with sifted icing sugar and serve with orange sauce. **1977** *Lancashire Life* Mar. 111/2 Pour into a suitable mould and chill or leave to set. Unmould onto lettuce leaves and serve with mayonnaise. **1982** L. CHAMBERLAIN *Food & Cooking of Russia* (1983) 265 Refrigerate for a few hours. Unmould on to a serving plate.
2. *intr.* or *absol.* To lose form or shape.
1834 DE QUINCEY *Autob. Sk.* Wks. 1854 II. 223 The restless elements of opinion..mould themselves eternally, ..and finally unmould and 'dislimn'.

un'moulded, *ppl. a.* [UN-¹ 8.] Not moulded or shaped.
1620 SHELTON *Quix.* II. xlv. 294 Without thee I am dull, vnmolded, and confused. **1636** PAGITT *Christianogr.* (ed. 2) II. 40 Their Masse was then unmoulded: Transubstantiation unbaked. **1852** TENNYSON *Ode Death Wellington* 233 Peace, his triumph will be sung By some yet unmoulded tongue. **1853** RUSKIN *Stones Ven.* II. vi. 229 Plain openings in the walls studiously simple, and unmoulded at the sides. **1875** *Carpentry & Join.* 41 A plain unmoulded strip.

un'mouldered, *ppl. a.* (UN-¹ 8.)
[**1775** ASH.] **1843** POE *Premature Burial* Wks. 1864 I. 327 It was the skeleton of his wife in her yet unmouldered shroud.

un'mouldering, *ppl. a.* (UN-¹ 10.)
1821 BRYANT *Ages* xvii, Deeds, engraved On fame's unmouldering pillar.

un'mouldy, *a.* (UN-¹ 7.)
1654 GAYTON *Pleas. Notes* I. v. 17 A piece of the Groaning Cake,..which she kept religiously..full forty good yeares unmouldy, and unmouse-eaten.

†**un'mouled**, *ppl. a. Obs.*⁻¹ [UN-¹ 8.] Not grown mouldy.
c **1450** CAPGRAVE *Life St. Gilbert* 75 Ther was bred kept sextene ȝere aftir his deth, on-corupte, onmouled, whech he blessed.

un'mounded, *ppl. a.* (UN-¹ 8.)
a **1661** HOLYDAY *Juvenal* VI. (1673) 91 Nor men Fear'd lest their..fruits should be a prey To theives, and gardens all unmounded lay. **1661** FELTHAM *Resolves* II. lxv. 326 By Nature, he may be..of a good soyl; yet, if he lyes unmounded, he shall be sure to be alwayes low.

un'mount, *v.* [UN-^{2} 5, 8.]
1. *trans.* To unfix and take down or remove.
a **1680** BUTLER *Rem.* (1759) I. 23 Others conceiv'd it much more fit T' unmount the Tube, and open it. **1885** C. G. W. LOCK *Workshop Receipts* Ser. IV. 397/1 If the print be a mounted one, it is by no means necessary to unmount it previously to treatment.
2. To dismount. Also *intr.*
1787 *Generous Attachment* II. 131, I immediately unmounted, and giving my horse his liberty, wandered about the country. **1892** *Schoolmaster* 26 Mar. 519/2 The German Emperor has had to unmount his high horse, and abandon the..Education Bill.

un'mountable, *a.* (UN-^{1} 7 b.)
1549 *Compl. Scot.* xi. 98 That place stude betuix tua strait montanis inhabitabil and onmontabil. **1603** KNOLLES *Hist. Turks* (1621) 938 Hauing left the fennes of Meotis, and the vnmountable shores of the Blacke sea. *a* **1608** SIR F. VERE *Comm.* (1657) 11 Being reared of a good height with earth, and then with gabions set therevpon of six foot high, made almost unmountable.

un'mounted, *ppl. a.* [UN-^{1} 8.]
1. a. Of cannon: Not placed on carriages.
1627 *Taking St. Esprit* in *Harl. Misc.* (Malh.) III. 550 Twelve pieces unmounted in her hold. **1690** J. MACKENZIE *Siege London-Derry* 7/2 [We] found..most of the Guns unmounted for want of Carriages. **1790** BEATSON *Nav. & Mil. Mem.* I. 325 In the fort were four guns mounted, and as many unmounted. **1909** G. M. TREVELYAN *Garibaldi* 243 The carts that carried the yet unmounted cannon.
b. Not fixed up for use or display; not provided with a mount or mounts.
1888 *Encycl. Dict.* **1890** *Science-Gossip* XXVI. 144/1 Wanted, good unmounted material, also foreign butterflies and shells. **1891** *Anthony's Photogr. Bull.* IV. 235 To use unmounted slides it is necessary to have auxiliary carriers. **1892** *Photogr. Ann.* II. 57 We had also in our album a lot of other unmounted prints.
2. Not provided with, or riding on, a horse or horses.
1592 NASHE *Four Lett. Confut.* H 2, Thy excellent out-cast selfe that liu'dst at Cambridge vnmounted. **1630** CAPT. SMITH *Trav. & Adv.* vi. 10 Captain Smith..was not long un-mounted, for there was choice enough of horses. **1688** *Lond. Gaz.* No. 2380/2 A good part of the Cavalry will remain unmounted. **1828** WEBSTER s.v., Unmounted dragoons. **1831** JAMES *Phil. Augustus* III. x, All the most beautiful horses..were led..by the pages and squire, unmounted. **1900** *Westm. Gaz.* 3 Feb. 6/1 The number of mounted and un-mounted troops.

un'mourned, *ppl. a.* (UN-^{1} 8.)
1650 VAUGHAN *Olor Iscanus, Tristium* III. iii. 51 Unpittied, and unmourn'd for, my sad head..goes friendless to the dead. **1721** SOUTHERNE *Spartan Dame* IV. i, Oh! let me here..Sink down..Into my grave, unmention'd and unmourn'd. **1813** BYRON *Corsair* II. xiv, Still he goes unmourn'd, returns unsought. *a* **1851** MOIR *Poems, Leg. St. Rosalie* v, Down to the dreary caverns of the grave Pass'd,.. Unmark'd, un-mourn'd, the beauteous and the brave.

un'mouse-eaten, *ppl. a.* (UN-^{1} 8 d.)
1654 [see UNMOULDY].

un'mouthable, *a.* (UN-^{1} 7 b.)
1842 MIALL in *Nonconf.* II. 809 A barbarous and unmouthable jargon.

un'mouthpieced, *a.* (UN-^{1} 9.)
1836–48 B. D. WALSH *Aristoph., Acharnians* II. vi, Though we've lost all conception Of such matters, and are deaf And un-mouthpieced.

un'movable, *a.* and *sb.* [UN-^{1} 7 b, 5 b.]
1. = IMMOVABLE *a.* 1. Now *rare.*
1382 WYCLIF *Exod.* xv. 16 Be thei maad vnmouable as a stoon. *c* **1400** MAUNDEV. (1919) xiii. 67 It is clept the dede see for it..is euere vnmeuable. *c* **1440** *Alphabet of Tales* 447 Hur handis hang vp in þe ayre vnmovable. *a* **1548** HALL *Chron., Edw. IV*, 192 b, He was set in the..stable throne, and vnmoueable chaire, of the croune of his realme. **1594** T. B. *La Primaud. Fr. Acad.* II. 11 Aristotle also..sheweth that he knew God vnder the name of the first mouer, who was perpetual and vnmoueable. **1626** GOUGE *Serm. Dignity Chivalry* §15 Like the unmoveable mountaines. *a* **1676** HALE *Prim. Orig. Man.* I. vi. (1677) 123 If we should suppose the Circle *ABC* to move about a fixed unmoveable Center at *D.* **1776** MICKLE *Camoens' Lusiad* p. xxxvii, They remained unmoveable on the shore till the fleet..evanished from their sight. **1870** LOWELL *Among my Bks.* Ser. I. (1873) 129 Some man whose brain rests on a still more unmovable basis. **1874** W. HUMPHREY in *Ess. Relig. & Lit.* Ser. III. 361 The unmoved and unmovable Prime Mover of the ever-moving universe of creatures.
b. *sb.* Something immovable.
1876 MRS. WHITNEY *Sights & Ins.* xx, We groped and peered under unmovables and pulled about everything that could be moved.
2. = IMMOVABLE *a.* 2.
1388 WYCLIF *Heb.* vi. 18 God..puttide betwixe an ooth, that bi twey thingis vnmeuable, bi whiche it is impossible that God lie, we han strengeste solace. *c* **1425** in *Anglia* X. 380/35 Vnmouabil tranquillite and reste of soule. **1502** *Ord. Crysten Men* (W. de W. 1506) I. vii. Fib, Sythen that Iustyce vnmeuable requyreth suche payne. **1599** SANDYS *Europæ Spec.* (1632) 111 Having their ground on the unmovable principles of true wisedome and vertue. **1638** JUNIUS *Paint. Ancients* 28 A sad unmoveable countenance. **1650** BAXTER *Saints' R.* III. vii. 383 They that are sure to receive the un-moveable Kingdom must yet serve God with reverence and godly fear. **1691** NORRIS *Pract. Disc.* 248 This was ever..an unmoveable Objection.
b. = IMMOVABLE *a.* 2 b.
1382 WYCLIF *Col.* i. 23 Stable, and vnmouable fro the hope of the gospel. **1445** in *Anglia* XXVIII. 259 Onmevable thou owist not endure, whan benygne preyers be offrid. *a* **1542** WYATT in *Tottel's Misc.* (Arb.) 70 Wilde beastes in them, fierce loue in me is fed. Vnmoueable am I: and they stedfast. **1570** T. WILSON *Demosth. Orat., Life* 129 Who helde out with a stomacke vpright and vnmoooueable, in all the..stormes of fortune. *a* **1624** BP. M. SMITH *Serm.* (1632) 34 Fabricius..remained..vndauntable, and vnmoveable. **1683** TEMPLE *Mem.* Wks. 1720 I. 399 The Prince was unmoveable in the Point of not leaving his Allies. **1748** RICHARDSON *Clarissa* (1811) I. 154 Ungrateful girl, and unmovable as ungrateful! **1856** MISS WARNER *Hills Shatemuc* xl, She begged to be allowed to stay..; but Elizabeth was unmoveable.
†**3.** Of property: = IMMOVABLE *a.* 3. (Cf. MOVABLE *a.* 4.)
c **1375** *Sc. Leg. Saints* xliv. (*Lucy*) 90 þane sawyt þai..þare gudis unmowable sone. *c* **1449** PECOCK *Repr.* I. x. 49 The endewing of preestis bi rentis and bi vnmoueable possessiouns. **1467–8** *Rolls of Parlt.* V. 593/1 The Londes and Tenementes, Goodes and Catalles, meovable and unmeovable. **1535** COVERDALE *Judith* viii. 7 Hyr husbande also had lefte her..greate vnmoueable possessions and many catell. **1565** *Wills & Inv. N.C.* (Surtees) 235 Executrix and mynyster of all my goods mewable and vnmewable. *c* **1618** MORYSON *Itin.* IV. (1903) 155 In..Italy the father dying intestate, the brothers diuide his mouable and vnmouable goods.
†**b.** *sb. pl.* Immovable goods. *Obs.*
1536 in *Lett. Suppress. Monast.* (Camden) 146 We.. submytt owr selfes and our monasterye, with all the moveables and unmovables therof, unto your majesties accustomede grace. **1562** J. HEYWOOD *Prov. & Epigr.* (1867) 148 Mouables, vnmouables, lande or farme, Thou hast not one grotes woorth, of good or goodnes. *a* **1577** SIR T. SMITH *Commw. Eng.* (1609) 121 Touching marriage and the right in moueables and vnmoueables which commeth thereby.

un'movableness. (UN-^{1} 12, 5 b.)
1382 WYCLIF *Heb.* vi. 17 God willinge for to schewe..the vnmouablenesse, or sadnesse, of his conseil. **1398** TREVISA *Barth. De P.R.* VI. xxiv. (Bodl. MS.), Slepe is a kindelich vnmeuablenes and helpe of þe wittes. **1611** COTGR. *Immobilité*,..firmenesse, assuredenesse, unmouablenesse. **1629** H. BURTON *Truth's Triumph* 264 A most stedfast vnmoueablenesse of faith. **1655** EARL ORRERY *Parthen.* II. VI. 550 She..by that Posture, and hir unmoveableness in it, by degrees took root. **1818** RANKEN *Hist. France* IV. 43 This unmoveablenesse was not the effect of pride. **1885** *In Mem. J. L. Aikman* 38 He was..surefooted with a central unmovableness.

†**un'movablety.** *Obs. rare.* [UN-^{1} 12.] Unmovableness.
c **1374** CHAUCER *Boeth.* IV. pr. vi. (1886) 106 It is constreynyd in to symplicite, þat is to seyn in to vnmoeuablete, and it cesith..to fletyn diuersely. *c* **1400** *Lanfranc's Cirurg.* 140 Vnmouablete of alle þe membris outcept þe lacertis of þe brest.

un'movably, *adv.* (UN-^{1} 11, 5 b.)
c **1400** *Found. St. Bartholomew's* (1923) 13 Those thyngis ..[given] to the chirche vnmoueably & stedfastly to beholde. *c* **1440** *Gesta Rom.* lvi. 240 (Harl. MS.), He that.. wolle not..leeve synne,..but lithe stille in synnys vnmevably. *c* **1460** *Oseney Reg.* 161 And þat, as þenne markyng whas i-sette by boundes i-sett.., Surely and vnmevabely hit be keped. **1513** DOUGLAS *Æneid* IV. i. 33 Fix[i]t in my mynd unmovably, That [etc.]. *a* **1555** R. TAYLOR in Coverdale *Lett. Mart.* (1564) 177 But God be praysed,..I am vn-moueably setled vpon the rocke. *a* **1619** FOTHERBY *Atheom.* I. iv. §4 (1622) 23 A radicall.. conclusion, vnmoueably grounded in the heart of a man. **1683** *Apol. Prot. France* vi. 75 The greatest Protectors of the holy See, to which they have always unmoveably held. **1743** J. ELLIS *Knowl. Div. Th.* 372 So the evil Angels are as unmoveably determined still to adhere to that which is Evil.

un'moved, *ppl. a.* [UN-^{1} 8, 5 b.]
1. Not moved by emotion or excitement; unaffected, undisturbed; collected, calm.
c **1375** *Sc. Leg. Saints* xxxvii. (*Vincencius*) 397 His thocht wes vnmowit ay, Sa ferme wes he in cristis fay. **1561** T. NORTON *Calvin's Inst.* I. 2 They which in his absence did stand assured and vnmoued. *a* **1586** SIDNEY *Arcadia* I. i, Holding his head up full of unmoved majestie. **1647** CLARENDON *Hist. Reb.* I. §44 When he found the Duke unmoved by all the considerations and arguments..he had offered. **1697** DRYDEN *Æneis* v. 526 My soul is still the same, Unmoved with fear, and moved with martial fame. **1720** SWIFT *Fates Clergym.* Wks. 1755 II. II. 26 Only Corusodes was silent and unmoved. **1796** MME. D'ARBLAY *Camilla* IV. 326 Edgar could not hear unmoved the dialogue which ensued. **1830** TENNYSON *Poems* 39 If so be if from doubt at length, Truth may stand forth unmoved of change. **1831** JAMES *Philip Augustus* III. vii, The chilling unmoved glance of her large dark eye. **1885** 'MRS. ALEXANDER' *At Bay* v, The unmoved composure of the practised detectives.
†**b.** Unprovoked. *Obs.*$^{-1}$
1634 SIR T. HERBERT *Trav.* 212 The Mannatee or Cow-fish..is..a gentle fish vnmoued, and some say affects the visage of a man.
2. Not moved in position; unstirred; remaining fixed or steady.
c **1440** *Promp. Parv.* 366/1 On-mevyd, *immotus.* **1513** DOUGLAS *Æneid* VII. v. 131 His sycht vnmovyt to the erd dyd he prent. **1628** MAY *Virg. Georg.* II. 51 Therefore no windes ..orethrow Those Trees; for many yeares unmov'd they grow. **1697** DRYDEN *Virg. Past.* x. 45 Unmoved, and with dejected eyes, he mourned. **1744** BERKELEY *Siris* §1 The vessel must stand close covered and unmoved three days. *a* **1795** PHILIDOR *Studies of Chess* (1817) 99 An un-moved Rook. **1841** JAMES *Brigand* ix, The heavy vapours hung unmoved around the peaks. **1887** *Field* 15 Oct. 603/2 The unmoved ground..is very dry a few inches from the surface.
3. (See MOVE *v.* 5 b.)
1843 R. J. GRAVES *Syst. Clin. Med.* xiv. 153 He told me he passed the night in great torture, and that the bowels were still unmoved.
Hence **un'movedness**.
1628 FELTHAM *Resolves* II. xix. 61 They set him almost in the Throne of a Deitie; ascend him to an vnmouednesse. **1687** BOYLE *Martyrd. Theodora* xi. 120 All the unmov'dness of mind, she us'd to be Mistress of.

un'movedly, *adv.* (UN-^{1} 11; cf. prec.)
1611 BEAUM. & FL. *Philaster* I. i, If you intreat, I will unmov'dly hear. **1689** POPPLE tr. *Locke's 1st Let. Toleration* 17 Then they can bear most patiently, and unmovedly, the Contagion of Idolatry. **1846** LANDOR *Imag. Conv.* Wks. II. 250/2 Quietly and unmovedly as she was standing. **1883** MYERS *Ess., Mod.* (1885) 44 Through all the perils of the siege they sat unmovedly,..perfecting the new constitution.

un'moving, *ppl. a.* [UN-^{1} 10.]
1. Not moving; devoid of motion.
c **1425** WYNTOUN *Cron.* II. xii. 1178 þan gert he stand Baith sone and mone, still vnmovand As wer þe space all of a day. **1594** *Selimus* 1442 All those moving and un-moving eyes. **1598** FLORIO, *Stella fissa*, a fixed, vnmouing starre. **1610** HEALEY *St. Aug. Citie of God* XIV. ix. 510 The eternall beatitude shall haue both ioye and loue,..firme, and vnmoouing. **1705** CHEYNE *Philos. Princ.* I. (1715) 186 Without this Impulse, they had continued unactive, unmoving Heaps of Matter. **1804** J. GRAHAME *Sabbath* 10 Calmness seems thron'd on yon unmoving cloud. *a* **1834** COLERIDGE *Shaks. Notes* (1849) 35 Succession of time and unmoving eternity. **1900** *Scribner's Mag.* Sept. 289 Everywhere were vast ghostly figures unmoving in the moonlight.
2. Unaffecting; stirring no feeling.
1698 NORRIS *Pract. Disc.* IV. 54 How flat and insipid, how dead and unmoving must all Discourse of it be to him! **1971** S. HILL *Strange Meeting* 188 We have had a pep talk from the Brigadier, and last week, a pep letter came round to all officers and N.C.O.'s—entirely unmoving.

un'movingly, *adv.* (UN-^{1} 11.)
[**1775** ASH.] **1831** JAMES *Phil. Augustus* III. iv, Her eyes were fixed unmovingly on the ground.

un'mowed, *ppl. a.* [UN-^{1} 8.] = next.
1763 MILLS *Pract. Husb.* III. 325 [He] ordered a small part of a meadow..to be left unmowed till the seeds were fit for gathering.

un'mown, *ppl. a.* (UN-^{1} 8 b.)
1549 *Compl. Scot.* vi. 66 Ane onmauen medou. **1557** TUSSER *100 Points Husb.* xcii, Doune with thy hedlondes,.. leaue neuer a dalop, vnmoune or had out. **1616** W. BROWNE *Brit. Past.* II. iii. 1086 As a meade in July, which unmowne Beares in an equall height each bent and stem. **1648** HEXHAM II, *Ongemaeyt*, Vnmowne, or Vnreapt. **1809** BYRON *Bards & Rev.* 636 Let..beer undrawn, and beards unmown, display Your holy reverence for the Sabbath-day. **1820** SHELLEY *Hymn Merc.* xii, Oxen..pastured in the flowering unmown meadows. **1830** TENNYSON *Arab. Nts.* 29 Deep inlay Of braided blooms unmown.

un'mudded, *ppl. a.* (UN-^{1} 8.)
1780 *Phil. Trans.* LXXI. 450 All the unwashed and unmudded trees that I measured. **1809** W. BLAKE *Descr. Catal.* 1 Clear [water-]colours un-mudded by oil.

un'muddied, *ppl. a.* (UN-^{1} 8.)
1654 WHITLOCK *Zootomia* 159 Who I hope in fine, to the un-muddied judgement, it will appeare meant the Literate.

un'muddled, *ppl. a.* (UN-^{1} 8.)
1840 HOWITT *Visits Remark. Places* Ser. I. 233 The Thames, there unmuddled by commerce,..flowing free and pure.

un'muffle, *v.* [UN-^{2} 4.]
1. *trans.* (and *refl.*). To divest of something which muffles or conceals the face.
1611 COTGR., *Desaffubler*, to vnmuffle, vnhood, vnhoodwinke. **1629** DAVENANT *Albovine* IV. i, Were my lean Iaws unmuffled you should see me mump. *a* **1652** BROME *Queen & Concubine* IV. iv, Take off his false beard;..And let the woman be unmuffled. **1768–74** TUCKER *Lt. Nat.* (1834) I. 442 He muffled up my head all round, as with the hood of a great-coat... In this guise he held me some time... He then unmuffled and let me go. **1838** LYTTON *Alice* VII. iv, The rest..unmuffled themselves of cloaks. **1851** HAWTHORNE *Twice-told T.* II. i. 21 'Villain, unmuffle yourself!' cried he.
fig. and in fig. context. **1652** BENLOWES *Theoph.* XI. lxxii, Unmuffle, ye dim clouds, and disinherit From black usurping mists his spirit. **1685** LD. HALIFAX *Char. Trimmer* (1688) 28 'Twill be worth his pains to see if he [*sc.* a papist] can unmuffle himself from the Mask of Infallibility. **1886** W. ALEXANDER *St. Aug. Holiday*, etc. 137 And darkness was unmuffled, and was ripp'd Like crape from heaven's jewell'd hilt.
b. To remove the muffling of (a drum).
1828–32 WEBSTER.
2. *intr.* To remove or cast off a muffling.
1634 MILTON *Comus* 331 Unmuffle ye faint stars, and thou fair Moon,..Stoop thy pale visage through an amber cloud. **1830** tr. *Aristoph., Birds* 941 Pisthetærus. What means this? What muffling is this? *Prometheus.* After a while I will unmuffle.

un'mule, *v.* (UN-^{2} 3.)
1654 GAYTON *Pleas. Notes* III. v. 100 With three hard words, [to] un-mule, un-leg, and unable, Alanso Lopez.

un'mullioned, *ppl. a.* (UN-^{1} 8.)
1859 JEPHSON *Brittany* ii. 15 The large unmullioned windows of the aisles.

un'multipliable, *a.* (UN-^{1} 7 b.)
1628 JACKSON *Creed* VI. I. iii. §5 His incomprehensible being, who is..most truly one, because indivisible and unmultipliable.

un'multiplied, *ppl. a.* (UN-^{1} 8.)
1570 BILLINGSLEY *Euclid* 128 b, The one remayning vnmultiplied, and the other being certaine times multiplied, shall be greater then it. **1817** H. T. COLEBROOKE *Algebra*,

etc. 211 Now the coefficient of the root is the unmultiplied (or original) coefficient of the square unknown term.

Hence **un'multipliedly** *adv.*

1678 CUDWORTH *Intell. Syst.* I. v. 776 It is indivisibly and unmultipliedly and illocally there.

un'mummied, *ppl. a.* (UN-¹ 8.)

1822 BYRON *Vis. Judgem.* xi, As the mere million's base unmummied clay.

un'munched, *ppl. a.* (UN-¹ 8.)

1870 DICKENS *E. Drood* xii, Even Durdles pauses..and looks at him, with an un-munched something in his cheek.

unmu'nitioned, *ppl. a.* (UN-¹ 8.)

1626 R. PEEKE *Three to One* C iv b, Cales..was held Poore, Vnmand, and Vnmunitioned.

un'murdered, *ppl. a.* (UN-¹ 8.)

1586 J. MUSH in J. Morris *Troub. Cath. Forefathers* III. (1877) 363 Not one Catholic priest but judged as a traitor or able to escape unmurthered. *a* **1652** BROME *Damoiselle* IV. ii, How know I..that I haue a Son By thee unmurther'd. *a* **1683** OLDHAM *Poems & Transl.* (1684) 47 Poor I am only left unmurder'd yet. **1746** YOUNG *Nt. Th.* IX. 1797 How unlike The lot of man! how few of human race By their own mud unmurder'd!

un'murmured, *ppl. a.* (UN-¹ 8.)

a **1625** FLETCHER *Nice Valour* IV. i, That if my anger chance let fall a stroke,..Yet it may pass unmurmur'd, undisputed.

un'murmuring, *ppl. a.* (UN-¹ 10.)

1784 R. BAGE *Barham Downs* II. 33 Poverty is the natural parent of..unmurmuring obedience. **1801** SOUTHEY *Thalaba* X. xxvii, I am cut off from all the ties of life, Unmurmuring. **1882** FARRAR *Early Chr.* I. 170 Then come fresh exhortations to unmurmuring hospitality.

un'murmuringly, *adv.* (UN-¹ 11.)

1845 F. E. PAGET *Tales Village Childr.* Ser. II. 142 The thoughts..which best enabled him to submit unmurmuringly. **1861** *Court Life at Naples* II. 119 When we are punished for our sins by pain..it should be borne unmurmuringly.

un-'Murrayed, *a.* [UN-¹ 9.] Not described in Murray's Guide.

1873 BROWNING *Red Cott. Nt.-cap* I. 20 Meek, hitherto un-Murrayed bathing-place, Best loved of sea-coast-nook-ful Normandy!

un'muscled, *ppl. a.* (UN-¹ 8.)

1748 RICHARDSON *Clarissa* (1811) VI. 362 Distended their parched mouths!—sunk their unmuscled cheeks!—dropt their under jaws!

un'muscular, *a.* (UN-¹ 7.)

1825 CARLYLE *Schiller* III. 234 [Schiller] was..unmuscular and lean. **1861** READE *Cloister & H.* lii, Shallow women, that have neither read nor suffered, have an unmuscular barbarity of their own.

un'muse-like, *a.* (UN-¹ 7 c.)

1754 A. MURPHY *Gray's Inn Jrnl.* No. 88, An unmuse-like Poem.

un'musical, *a.* [UN-¹ 7.]

1. Of sounds: Not of a musical nature; unmelodious, harsh.

1607 SHAKS. *Cor.* IV. v. 64 A name vnmusicall to the Volcians eares. *a* **1637** B. JONSON *Rules Tavern Acad.* ix, Let argument bear no unmusical sound. **1718** LADY M. W. MONTAGU *Let. to C'tess Bristol* 10 Apr., Their pipes..are no unmusical instruments. **1753** CIBBER *Lives Poets* I. 18 His stile..is equally unmusical and obsolete with Chaucer's. **1801** BUSBY *Dict. Mus.*, *Unmusical*, an epithet applied..to whatever is not absolutely harmonious, melodious, or agreeable to a cultivated ear. **1855** *Poultry Chron.* III. 500/2 At this time..its not unmusical cry is heard. **1880** MᶜCARTHY *Own Times* xlviii. IV. 22 His voice was singularly un-musical and harsh.

2. Of persons: Not musically gifted; not appreciative of music. Also *absol.*

1634 CARTWRIGHT *Ordinary* II. iii, I'll..Give organs to every parish..; And so root out th' unmusical elect. **1861** tr. *Mendelssohn's Lett. Italy* 69 The Papal singers..are almost all unmusical, and do not execute even the most established pieces in tune. **1896** *Westm. Gaz.* 2 June 2/3 The unmusical admired her singing, the musical her acting.

3. Not based on musical principles.

1786 T. TWINING in *Recreat. & Stud.* (1882) 132 All this is unmusical criticism, and goes upon the false notion of the words..being principal.

Hence **un'musicalness; unmusi'cality.**

1678 CUDWORTH *Intell. Syst.* I. v. 759 Matter..perpetually remains, and all other things whatsoever are but ..passions and affections..thereof, as musicalness and unmusicalness. **1873** C. M. YONGE *Pillars of House* I. x. 201 Geraldine resembled Fulbert in unmusicalness. **1890–** Unmusicality [listed in *N.E.D.* (1924) as 'in recent use']. **1922** *Daily Mail* 10 Nov. 7 She had been painfully struck by ..'the unmusicalness' of the bells of public clocks. **1946** *Penguin Music Mag.* Dec. 14 Our vaunted choral singing is really the proof of our fundamental unmusicality, because any amateur can sing in a chorus. **1963** *Times* 17 May 18/6 Beethoven (whom to admit disliking is still tantamount to an admission of unmusicality). **1984** *Listener* 12 Jan. 28/3 Their unmusicality demands public exposure.

un'musically, *adv.* (UN-¹ 11, 5 b.)

1609 DEKKER *Gull's Horn-bk.* I, I make a scuruy noise, and..my tunes sound vnmusically. **1631** —— *Match me in London* 111, The song..did to your eare Vnmusically sound. **1710** NORRIS *Chr. Prud.* vi. 172 Let the Ear be unmusically disposed, the sweetest Sounds..will give it no Entertainment. **1843** CARLYLE *Past & Pr.* III. i, The Honourable Member complains unmusically. **1896** *Advance* (Chicago) 6 Feb. 197/1 The sublime..thoughts which the eloquent preacher has not..unmusically expressed here.

un'mustered, *ppl. a.* (UN-¹ 8.)

1581 SIDNEY *Apol. Poetrie* (Arb.) 56 Therefore, though Cato misliked his vn-mustered person, hee misliked not his worke.

†**un'mutable,** *a. Obs.* [UN-¹ 7 b, 5 b.] Immutable.

1414 BRAMPTON *Penit. Ps.* (Percy Soc.) 38 Thou art unmutable be kynd! There is no changyng foundyn in the! **1429** *Pol. Poems* (Rolls) II. 145 Prince excelent, be..liberal of courage, unmutable. **1491** CAXTON *Vitas Patr.* (W. de W. 1495) II. 272/2 We have one unmutable rule in fastyng. **1548** UDALL *Erasm. Par. Luke* 165 b, Leat that bee dooen, whyche thy wyll beyng vnmutable hath determined. **1550** COVERDALE *Spir. Perle* viii. (1588) 93 His vnmutable truthe, wherby he doth faithfully performe all his promises.

unmu'tated, *ppl. a.* (UN-¹ 8.)

1888 SWEET *Hist. Eng. Sounds* 129 In other words it..shows the unmutated *eo.*

un'mutilated, *ppl. a.* (UN-¹ 8.)

[**1775** ASH.] **1790** PENNANT *London* 105 The brazier..buried it unmutilated, and shewed to them some broken pieces of brass in tokens of his obedience. **1825** SCOTT *Betrothed* Concl., It was an unmutilated, unspotted, and beautifully formed hand. **1860** F. MAHONY *Rel. Father Prout* 376 Thy MSS. have come down to us unmutilated by pumice-stone of palimpsestic monk. **1865** F. G. LEE *Direct. Anglic.* 44 As the unmutilated rubric directs.

un'mutual, *a.* (UN-¹ 7, 5 b.)

1593 *Tell-Troth's N.Y. Gift* A 3, What is the cause of so many housholde breaches..but vnnaturall disagreementes by vnmutuall contractes?

un'muzzle, *v.* [UN-² 4 b.] *trans.* To free (a dog, etc.) from a muzzle; to remove the muzzle from. Also *fig.*

1600 SHAKS. *A.Y.L.* I. ii. 74 *Cel.* How proue you that in the great heape of your knowledge? *Ros.* I marry, now unmuzzle your wisedome. **1639** T. DE GRAY *Expert Farrier* 280 Put a muzell upon his mouth..and the next morning unmusell him. **1645** QUARLES *Sol. Recant.* VI. 5 Why Did that corrected Twilight of his eye Vnmussle darknesse, and with morning light Redeeme the day from new baptized night? **1791** BURKE *Let. to Memb. Nat. Assemb.* Wks. VI. 43 The hell-hounds of war, on all sides, will be uncoupled and unmuzzled. **1854** EMERSON *Soc. Aims* Wks. (Bohn) III. 181 Beware of unmuzzling a valetudinarian. **1891** *Daily News* 22 Jan. 3/7 Her dog was muzzled. They un-muzzled him when they got home.

Hence **un'muzzling** *vbl. sb.*

1760–72 H. BROOKE *Fool of Qual.* (1809) III. 37 A licentious unmuzzling from all restraint. **1898** *Daily News* 2 Dec. 5/1 The unmuzzling of London dogs.

un'muzzled, *ppl. a.* [UN-¹ 8 or f. prec.] Not muzzled; freed from a muzzle.

1601 SHAKS. *Twel. N.* III. i. 130 Haue you not set mine Honor at the stake, And baited it with all th' vnmuzled thoughts That tyrannous heart can think? **1604** *Nottingham Rec.* IV. 275 Kepyng a banddog vnmusselled. **1669** *N. Riding Rec.* VI. 138 A weaver presented for keeping a mastiff unmusled. **1811** W. R. SPENCER *Poems* 40 When Pestilence was rife, And all her friends unmuzzled rush'd on life. **1891** *Daily News* 22 Jan. 3/7 His dog..was unmuzzled. Plaintiff's dog was also unmuzzled.

unmy'sterious, *a.* (UN-¹ 7.)

1746 YOUNG *Nt. Th.* IX. 825 Shall God be less miraculous, than what His hand has form'd? Shall mysteries descend From unmysterious? **1846** MRS. GORE *Eng. Char.* Introd., Lord Chancellors have become unmysterious as haberdashers. **1862** SPENCER *First Princ.* I. v. §28 (1875) 100 The disappearance of those positive dogmas by which the mystery was made unmysterious.

un'mystery, *v.* (UN-² 6 b.)

a **1661** FULLER *Worthies, Hereford* II. (1662) 40 He hath unmysteried the mysterie of Heraldry.

un'mystical, *a.* (UN-¹ 7.)

1862 MAURICE *Mod. Philos.* ii. §18. 45 He..is ready to quote..from the most unmystical authors, such as Cicero and Terence. **1899** INGE *Chr. Mysticism* 278 We cannot be surprised that the unmystical Eighteenth Century declared [etc.].

un'mystified, *ppl. a.* (UN-¹ 8.)

1844 KINGLAKE *Eothen* (1845) 106 A promontory, bare and unmystified by the gloom of surrounding groves.

†**un'nack,** *v. Obs.*⁻¹ [UN-² 3 + *nack* NOCK *v.* (?).] *trans.* To disarrange.

1649 G. DANIEL *Trinarch., Rich. II,* cxciv, Soe wee vnnack the Ballance, where the Spring Beats truly, to enforce another Thing.

un'nail, *v.* [UN-² 3. Cf. MDu. *ontnaghelen* (Du. *-nagelen*), OHG. *innagalen* (G. *entnageln*).]

1. *trans.* To undo or unfasten in structure by the extraction or removal of nails.

1470–85 MALORY *Arthur* II. xviii. 97 Their hawberkes vnnailled that naked they were on euery sydc. **1523** LD. BERNERS *Froiss.* I. ccccxii. 718 They made all yᵉ bridge to be vnnayled, redy to be broken downe. **1595** *Caxton's Blanchardyn* B ij, Vnnayling his armor.., he sent him to carry newes of Blanchardines valure. **1704** tr. *I. le Fevre's Memoir* 87 The Almoner..caus'd the Coffin to be unnail'd again. **1884** STEVENSON in *St. James's Gaz.* 10 Apr. (1899) 4/2 If we do possess these opposite gifts, we must unnail the scaffolding.

2. To free (artillery) from being spiked.

1562 WHITEHORNE *Ord. Souldiours* 34 The speediest way to vnnaile them, is firste to charge againe all such peses of artillerie, with smaller bullettes then their ordinarie.

3. To detach or unfasten from something by the removal of nails.

1598 ROWLANDS *Betraying of Christ* 55 Hands and feet they carefull did vn-naile, Letting the body downe. **1668** EVELYN tr. *Freart's Idea Perf. Paint.* 51 At the foot..stands the B. Virgin,..whiles Joseph of Arimathea and Nicodemus un-nail our Lord. **1683** MOXON *Mech. Exerc., Printing* xxiv. ¶3 He cannot alter the position of the Rounce without un-nailing and nailing the Girts again. **1797** *Trans. Soc. Arts* XV. 256 This is done by unnailing from the board a part on each side. **1846** LANDOR *Exam. Shaks.* Wks. II. 273/2 Having..unnailed from our chapels, many dozens of decent saints. **1858** GLENNY *Gard. Every day Bk.* 19/1 We must think it no trouble to unnail even large branches.

absol. **1683** MOXON *Mech. Exerc., Printing* xxiv. 278 The Press-man, without nailing or un-nailing, Sets the Rounce to what Position he will.

Hence **un'nailing** *vbl. sb.*

1622 MABBE tr. *Aleman's Guzman d'Alf.* II. 258 Even to the vnnayling from heaven, of the Sunne, and the Moone. **1756** NUGENT *Gr. Tour, France* IV. 99 A picture of the un-nailing from the cross,..which is greatly admired.

un'nailed, *ppl. a.* (UN-¹ 8.)

1625 K. LONG tr. *Barclay's Argenis* I. i. 13 Two plankes artificially closed, but left unnayled. **1748** *Anson's Voy.* II. iii. 143 The scuttle of the fore-castle..happened to be unnailed. *Ibid.*, The unnailed scuttle. **1829** H. HAWTHORN *Visit Babylon* 7 The unnailed branches of the honeysuckle. **1896** *Rural World* 4 Jan. 5/3 Leave the..nectarine trees unnailed to keep the blossoms as backward as possible.

†**un'nait,** *a.* and *adv. Obs.* [UN-¹ 7, 11 b + NAIT *a.* Cf. ON. *úneyt-r* useless, incapable.] Useless, unprofitable, vain.

a **1250** *Ancr. R.* 130 Siggeð þet ȝe beoð unnute [*Trin. MS.* unneite] þrelles. *a* **1300** *Cursor M.* 23566 If þai a-noþer heuen wroght, It war vnnait and al for noght. *a* **1340** HAMPOLE *Psalter* xxviii. 7 þa þat..gas agayn til besynes of þe warld & vnnayte thynge. *c* **1380** WYCLIF *Sel. Wks.* III. 29 Folk þat haþ foule lippis, foulid wiþ vein speche and unnayt. *c* **1400** *Rule St. Benet* (Prose) 9 Wicke þohtis do oway..; and gete yure muþes fra unait wordis.

b. As *adv.* Unprofitably, vainly.

a **1300** *Cursor M.* 5976 'Do wai,' þai said, 'þou speckes vnnait'.

Hence †**un'naitlike** *adv.*, **-ness, -ship.** *Obs.*

a **1300** *E.E. Psalter* xxxviii. 15 Vnnaitlike to-droued ilke man is. *Ibid.* xl. 6 Vnnaitnes Spake he, his hert samened to him wicnes. *a* **1300** *Cursor M.* 10135 For-þi rede i þaim þat yee here..And leue your vnnaitschip a quile.

un'naked, *ppl. a.* (UN-¹ 8.)

1628 *Robin Goodfellow* II. (Percy Soc.) 40 Then..lay I them in the doore, naked or unnaked I care not whether.

un'nam(e)able, *a.* (UN-¹ 7 b.)

In frequent use from *c* 1840.

1610 HEALY *St. Aug. Citie of God* 354 God is celestiall, ineffable, and un-name-able. **1652** GAULE *Magastrom.* 270 Invisible and unnameable powers and persons. **1824** MISS MITFORD *Village* Ser. I. 234 Oh the saltings, the picklings,.. the unnamed and unnameable confectionery doings over which she presided! **1874** LISLE CARR *J. Gwynne* I. iv. 120 Her lustrous eyes wide distended with unnamable horror.

absol. **1818** MILMAN *Samor* XI. 387 Th' Unnameable, he fix'd On his flint pedestal.

Hence **unnamea'bility.**

1862 CARLYLE *Fredk. Gt.* XIV. v. III. 695 The Reich..will go ever deeper into anarchies and unnameabilities.

un'named, *ppl. a.* [UN-¹ 8. Cf. OFris. *unnamed, onnamd*, MDu. *ongenaemt* (Du. *-naamd*).]

1. Not mentioned or specified by name.

1509 BARCLAY *Ship of Folys* 162 They shall vnnamyd my shyppis haue in cure. **1526** R. WHYTFORD *Martiloge* (1893) 65 A woman vnnamed, with her two chylder twyndles. **1599** DALLAM in *Early Voy. Levant* (Hakl. Soc.) 81, I have not time now to wryte them, but of force muste leave them un-named untill a time of better Leasur. *c* **1620** FLETCHER *False One* II. ii, Cæsar's angry, And our design to please him lost and perish'd; Be glad thou art unnam'd. **1667** MILTON *P.L.* x. 595 Stil at Hels dark threshold to have sate watch, Unnam'd, undreaded. **1728** RAMSAY *Archers diverting themselves* 136 Dear nymphs unnam'd, lay not the blame On us. **1798** S. & HT. LEE *Canterb. T.* II. 86 [She] left unnamed, and unprovided for, the young woman she had raised so far above her condition. **1836** [MRS. MAITLAND] *Lett. fr. Madras* (1843) 4 A number of hitherto un-named gentlemen, who sit down to eat and drink. **1866** MEREDITH *Vittoria* xlv, Throwing the burden..on some unnamed third person.

2. Not provided with a name; nameless.

1611 DONNE *Anat. World* 35 As a child kept from the font, thou unnam'd had'st laid. **1667** MILTON *P.L.* XII. 140 From Hamath Northward to the Desert South (Things by thir names I call, though yet unnam'd). **1848** BAILEY *Festus* (ed. 3) 219 All terms are relative expressing bound, But Deity, interminable being, Hath ever therefore been unnamed. **1868** MORRIS *Earthly Par.* I. I. 338 Robe..Inwrought with flowers of unnamed colours bright. **1876** SMILES *Sc. Natur.* x. 202 Among the plants, were a great number unnamed.

absol. **1840** CARLYLE *Heroes* i. ¶13 The Highest Being reveals himself in man. This body, these faculties, this life of ours, is it not all as a vesture for that Unnamed?

b. *unnamed bone*, the innominate bone (INNOMINATE *a.* 3).

1845 *Encycl. Metrop.* VII. 329/1 [The sides] of the Hip-girdle [are]..formed..by the pair of Unnamed..bones, each consisting..of three pieces whilst the bird is young, but becoming consolidated early. *Ibid.*, Of the Unnamed bone.

un'napkined, *ppl. a.* (UN-¹ 8.)

1607 BEAUM. & FL. *Woman-Hater* I. iii, An un-napkin'd Lawyers greasie fist.

un'napped, *ppl. a.* (UN-[1] 8.)
1619 FLETCHER *Knt. Malta* I. i, Did I attempt her with a thread-bare name, un-napt with meritorious actions. **1620** SHELTON *Quix.* II. xxxviii. 248 Countesse Trifaldi.., clad all in finest vn-napped Bayes. **1884** *Imp. Dict.* IV. 509/3 Unnapped cloth.

†**un'nath**, *v. Obs.*[-1] [UN-[1] 3; cf. NATHE.] *trans.* To take the nave or naves off.
1637 N. WHITING *Albino & Bellama* 1304 Methinks I see the sun.. Unnath his car, and throw his whipstaff by.

un'nation, *v.* (UN-[2] 6 b.)
1646 W. PRICE *Mans Delinquencie* 39 Wee have deserved to be un-nation'd, un-Church'd by a Bill of divorce from heaven.

un'national, *a.* (UN-[1] 7.)
1753 HANWAY *Trav.* I. I. viii. 54 Of the partial and un-national manner in which the trade was managed. **1763** WILKES *Corr.* (1805) I. 227 Three known, hackneyed tools of that very minister, who were.. to pursue the same system, the same unnational measures. **1834** G. CROLY *Butler's Anal.* p. xxvi, The rash and unnational peace of Utrecht. **1865** W. G. PALGRAVE *Arabia* II. 366 Their easy-going, un-national, indistinctive character.

un'native, *a.* (UN-[1] 7.)
1712 BLACKMORE *Creation* VII. 413 British Gibbons.. makes that tree unnative charms assume. **1734** THOMSON *Liberty* I. 336 Against depressing skies,.. How could thy spirits hold? where vigour find, Forced fruits to tear from their unnative soil?

un'native, *v.* (UN-[2] 6 b.)
1855 MRS. GASKELL *North & S.* xli, Frederick had written ..a pretty vehement letter, containing his renunciation of England as his country; he wished he could unnative himself.

un'natural, *a.* (*sb.*) [UN-[1] 7, 5 b.]
1. Not in accordance or conformity with the physical nature of persons or animals.
a **1425** tr. *Arderne's Treat. Fistula*, etc. 60 Also in þe veynez ar gendred vnnaturale humours. *Ibid.* 68 [It] doþ away wicked colour & vnnatural, and it restoreþ natural colour. **1541** R. COPLAND *Guydon's Quest. Chirurg.* Bj, He ought to knowe the vnnaturall thynges, that is yͤ meate, the drynke, &c. **1597** A. M. tr. *Guillemeau's Fr. Chirurg.* 1 b/1 *Physiologia*..wherin is to be..noted on the seaven vnnaturalle thinges. **1614** LATHAM *Falconry* I. xiii. 48 Which is vnnaturall, and therfore must needs be vnwholsome [for the hawk]. **1617** WOODALL *Surg. Mate* Wks. (1639) 301 After extraction of unnaturall things, forced into the wound. **1774** GOLDSM. *Nat. Hist.* (1776) IV. 71 The Black Rat..is..possessed of all the voracious and unnatural appetites of the former. **1805** *Med. Jrnl.* XIV. 246 The mother..was very solicitous about her on account of this, her unnatural situation, as she always thought it. **1846** MRS. A. MARSH *Father Darcy* II. xi. 179 The tones of their voice sounded..hollow, hoarse, and unnatural. **1890** *Retrospect Med.* CII. 236 The unnatural state occasioned by the presence of sugar.
2. Not in accordance or agreement with the usual course of nature. Also *absol.*
a **1513** FABYAN *Chron.* ci. (1533) 42/1 Berynge in mynde the vnnaturall deth of her parentes. **1605** SHAKS. *Macb.* II. iv. 10 'Tis vnnaturall, Euen like the deed that's done. **1653** W. RAMESEY *Astrol. Restored* 250 There shall be..unnatural Dews and Rains. **1722** WOLLASTON *Relig. Nat.* i. 13 Nothing can interfere with any proposition that is true, but it must likewise interfere with nature,..and consequently be unnatural, or wrong in nature. **1814** SCOTT *Lord of Isles* v. xv, Faintly the moon's pale beams supply That ruddy light's unnatural dye. **1846** TRENCH *Mirac.* 15 The miracle is not thus unnatural, while the unnatural, the contrary to order, is of itself the ungodly. **1854** KINGSLEY *Misc.* (1859) I. 85 Unnatural weather, so that a fourteen days' voyage takes forty days.
b. Abnormal; monstrous.
1516 *Reg. Privy Seal Scotl.* I. 431/2 The said Johne is be the hand of God dum and defe and unnaturale. **1632** LITHGOW *Trav.* II. 52 Which vnnaturall Childe being brought, I was amazed..to behold the deformity of Nature.
c. Devoid of natural qualities or characteristics; artificial.
1746 FRANCIS tr. *Horace, Epist.* I. x. 28 Among your Columns, rich with various Dyes, Unnatural Woods with aukward Art arise. **1827** STEUART *Planter's G.* (1828) 7 Whatever there was of unnatural or formal,..is now banished from the English garden. **1828** LYTTON *Pelham* III. iii, Hence, you perceive all people timid, stiff, unnatural, and ill at ease.
3. At variance with natural feeling or moral standards; excessively cruel or wicked.
1529 MORE *Suppl. Souls* Wks. 314/2 In this thei shew their affeccion much more vnnatural & abhominable [etc.]. **1571** *Act 13 Eliz.* c. 2 §1 Moste wycked and unnatural Rebellyon hathe ensued. **1612** DRAYTON *Poly-olb.* xi. 178 The vnnatural'st deed that e're was done by man. **1642** D. ROGERS *Naaman* To Rdr. §2 Even an unnaturall cruelty. **1732** *Col. Rec. Pennsylv.* III. 497 A final Period was to be putt to all such unnatural Differences. *a* **1800** COWPER *Odyss.* (ed. 2) II. 175 To thrust the mother forth, Who gave me birth.., were a deed Unnat'ral and impossible to me. **1828** SCOTT *Tapestr. Chamb.* ad fin., In yon fatal apartment incest and unnatural murder were committed. **1864** KINGSLEY *Rom. & T.* i. 4 They tar them on to the unnatural fight.
b. Of persons: Devoid of natural feeling; acting at variance with the dictates of nature.
1552 HULOET, Vnnaturall to parentes, *bactri, bactriani.* **1579** GOSSON *Sch. Abuse* (Arb.) 66 Iupiter,..though hee were a cruell tyrant, an vnnaturall childe,..by Poets is made the king of gods. **1611** SHAKS. *Wint. T.* II. iii. 113 A most vn-worthy, and vnnatural Lord Can doe no more. **1685** in P. Wright *New Bk. Martyrs* (1784) 804/1 As vnnatural as children that seek the ruin of their parents. **1819** SCOTT *Ivanhoe* xxix, The messengers of Jehovah's wrath to the unnatural child, who thinks of a stranger's captivity before a parent's. **1836** THIRLWALL *Greece* III. xix. 97 It would be impolitic in the Athenians..to countenance the revolt of an unnatural colony. **1871** JOWETT *Plato* II. 408 Then he is a parricide, and a cruel unnatural son to an aged parent.
†**4.** Illegitimate; having no natural right or claim. *Obs.*
c **1550** BALE *K. Johan* (Camden) 4 *K.I.* They are thy chylderne, thou oughtest to say them good. *Y.* Nay, bastardes they are, unnaturall by the rood. **1570** *Homily agst. Rebellion* ¶ I It may seeme more then maruell, that anye subictes woulde..holde with vnnaturall forraigne vsurpers.
5. At variance with what is natural, usual, or to be expected; unusual, strange.
a **1586** SIDNEY *Arcadia* I. i, They ranne unto him, and pulling him backe,..by force stickled that unnatural fray. **1647** CLARENDON *Hist. Reb.* II. §104 With some cloudiness (which was not unnatural) and trouble in his countenance, he desired his Majesty to give him leave to Travel. **1668** DRYDEN *Dram. Poesy* Ess. (ed. Ker) I. 72 It is unnatural for any one in a gust of passion to speak long together. **1729** BUTLER *Serm.* (1848) 34 Since such an action is utterly disproportionate to the nature of man, it is in the strictest and most proper sense unnatural. **1780** *Mirror* No. 100, An unnatural violence done to the work of his favourite poet. **1849** MACAULAY *Hist. Eng.* v. I. 533 What seemed to his associates to be his unnatural recklessness and audacity. **1850** BAYNES *Analytic* 13 Unnatural, indirect or irregular predication..was..that, to wit, in which the species was predicated of the genus.
b. *sb.* An unnatural thing or state.
1682 SIR T. BROWNE *Chr. Mor.* III. §20 No practice being able to naturalize such unnaturals or make a man rest content not to be himself.

un'naturalism. (UN-[1] 12.)
1754 WARBURTON *Bolingbroke's Philos.* ii. 67 Which, however, they were ready to distinguish..from the Unnaturalism (if we may so term it) of ranker Atheism. **1840** T. GORDON tr. *W. Menzel's Ger. Lit.* I. 35 The writings of [our nation]..have a tinge of supernaturalism or unnaturalism; something strange, ghost-like, and ill-suited for this world. **1889** *Harper's Mag.* Nov. 963/1 French naturalism is better at its worst than French unnaturalism at its best.

un'naturalist. *nonce-wd.* [See UNNATURAL *a.* 3 b.] One devoid of natural feeling.
1835 SOUTHEY *Doctor* interchap. xiii, Me, a poor unit of humanity, to be treated like a polypus under the scissors of an experimental naturalist, or unnaturalist.

unnatu'rality. *rare.* [UN-[1] 12.]
1. Unnatural feeling or conduct.
a **1548** HALL *Chron., Hen. VIII*, 229 b, What vnkyndnes and vnnaturalitie may we impute to you. **1691** Z. HAIG in J. Russell *Haigs* (1881) xi. 324 If I had had any such unnaturality lodged in my breast.
2. *Sc.* Imbecility, weak-mindedness.
1823 GALT *Entail* lii, He has a because o' his ain for keeping his thumb on Watty's unnaturality.

un'naturalizable, *a.* (UN-[1] 7 b.)
1833 LYTTON *Eng. & English* IV. ix. 394 Its minute details of alien and un-naturalizable mythology are carefully preserved.

un'naturalize, *v.* [UN-[2] 6 c *b.*]
1. *trans.* and *refl.* To deprive of natural character; to make unnatural in disposition.
a **1613** OVERBURY *A Wife* (1630) M vj, Religion is commonly his pretence of discontent, though he can be of all religions; therefore truely of none. Thus by vnnaturalizing himselfe [etc.]. **1625** LAUD *Serm.* Wks. 1847 I. 69 In all that large discourse..Saint Paul..conceives at full how corruption can unnaturalize nature itself. **1651** JANE *Image Unbr.* 62 Rebellion hath not vnnaturalized them. *a* **1656** HALES *Gold. Rem.* I. (1673) 145 Here he strives, as it were, to un-naturalize himself, and lay by his natural sweetness of disposition. **1894** *Daily News* 5 Oct. 6/5 None the less do they feel the sad influence of the mixed education that has.. unnaturalised them.
2. To divest of the status or privileges of a native-born subject.
1698 J. COLLIER *Immor. Stage* vi. (1730) 157 Any Roman who turn'd Actor was..to be..as it were disincorporated, and unnaturalized. **1754** A. MURPHY *Gray's Inn Jrnl.* No. 84, Mr. Arne..will apply for a private Bill to unnaturalize him, that he may then enjoy the Privileges of an Englishman. **1817** *Parl. Deb.* 1830 This petitioner prayed to be unnaturalized, or to be brought to trial.
3. To make unnatural or artificial. Also *absol.*
1741 RICHARDSON *Pamela* (1824) I. 6 It may disguise the facts,..and unnaturalize the incidents. **1767** *Ann. Reg., Ess.* 196/2 If they should thus endeavour to unnaturalize their singing, they would render it harsh. **1839** DARLEY *Beaum. & Fletcher's Wks.* I. Introd. p. xxv, Our poets..idealise farther than he; that is, they unnaturalise, often making beautiful chimeras of their virtuous characters.
Hence **un'naturalizing** *vbl. sb.*
1647 N. WARD *Simple Cobler* 47 Such usurpations by Rulers, are the unnaturallizings of nature, disfranchisements of Freedome.

un'naturalized, *ppl. a.* (UN-[1] 8.)
1611 COTGR., *Morte-main*,..the..estate left by.. vnnaturalized strangers, and vnaffranchized villaines. **1621** BRATHWAIT *Nat. Embassie* Ded., Nature..thinks she can mend her selfe by being adorned with vnnaturalized ornaments. **1652** EVELYN *St. France* 37 The goods of strangers dying in France, most inhospitably escheat to the King; putting..no difference between them, and Bastards unnaturalized. **1828–32** WEBSTER, *Unnaturalized*, a.,..not made a citizen by authority. [Freq. in recent use (1914–), of aliens.]

un'naturally, *adv.* [UN-[1] 11.]
1. In a manner at variance with normal human nature; with unnatural depravity, wickedness, or want of feeling.
c **1485** *Digby Myst.* (1882) IV. 537 Was his..gudnese owt of thy mynd So vn-naturallye? **1540** *Act 32 Hen. VIII*, c. 24 §1 Knightis of Sainct Johnes..have unnaturally.. maynteynid the usurped powre..of the Bishop of Rome. **1562** J. HEYWOOD *Prov. & Epigr.* (1867) 96 Alas mother what is the why, That ye draw from vs vnnaturally? **1610** HOLLAND *Camden's Brit.* 465 The yong man..most unnaturally waged war against his owne father. **1634** SIR T. HERBERT *Trav.* 30 He..had most vnnaturally..caused his elder Brother..[to] be murdred. **1719** DE FOE *Crusoe* II. (Globe) 361 They had acted..unnaturally by their Countrymen.
2. In a manner differing from what is natural or normal; abnormally.
1611 FLORIO, *Distortione*, a turning awry vnnaturally. **1614** LATHAM *Falconry* I. viii. 31 The fire..pierceth into the bodie, and heateth it most vnnaturallie. **1668** DRYDEN *Dram. Poesy* Ess. (ed. Ker) I. 95 Where you see both the clauses are placed unnaturally, that is, contrary to the common way of speaking. **1721** SOUTHERNE *Fate Capua* IV. i, It was a task unnaturally impos'd. **1848** W. H. KELLY tr. *L. Blanc's Hist. Ten Y.* II. 283 Words of malediction not unnaturally marked his parting adieus. **1878** BRISTOWE *Th. & Pract. Med.* (ed. 2) 850 The former may attain the bulk of a bullock's kidney, and the latter is usually unnaturally small.

un'naturalness. [f. UNNATURAL *a.*]
1. Unnatural conduct or disposition.
1537 CROMWELL in Merriman *Life & Lett.* (1902) II. 86 Promysing hym..forgeuenes..of his most shamefull ingratitude, vnnaturalnes, conspiracie against his honour. **1550** W. LYNNE tr. *Carion's Cron.* 36 Thys cruell dede declareth the vnnaturalnesse of the Barbarous nation. **1643** TRAPP *Comm. Gen.* ix. 25 Their parents also through their unnaturalness are compell'd to curse them. **1689** D. GRANVILLE *Lett.* (Surtees No. 37) 97, I am not..guilty in the lest-wise of..injustice and unnaturallness to my fellow-subjects. **1703** QUICK *Dec. Wife's Sister* 26 A Prodigy of Baseness, Unnaturalness and Ungratefulness. **1758** JORTIN *Erasmus* I. 547 Burnet hath retracted his mistake that this Lord..sat in judgment upon his daughter, which would have impeached him of great unnaturalness.
2. Unnatural character.
1605 B. JONSON *Volpone* III. v, That the unnaturalness.. of the act..would sure enrage him. **1633** T. JAMES *Voy.* 77 This vnnaturalnesse of the season did torment our men. **1664** INGELO *Bentiv. & Ur.* VI. 349 The Unnaturalness of such Disobedience will appear yet farther. **1859** GEO. ELIOT *A. Bede* xliii, The unnaturalness of her crime. **1865** PUSEY *Truth Eng. Ch.* 12 The unnaturalness and strangeness of the facts. **1884** *Spectator* 4 Oct. 1302/1 The unnaturalness of the situations in which he acts a part.
3. Want of natural grace or ease.
? **1803** DOROTHY WORDSWORTH *Recoll. Tour* (1875) 49 The unnaturalness of a modern garden. **1870** LOWELL *Study Wind.* 205 What we call unnaturalness always has its spring in a man's thinking too much about himself. **1876** A. SIDGWICK *Gr. Prose* §107 He will..be saved from falling into many unnaturalnesses of expression.

un'nature, *sb.* (UN-[1] 12. Cf. G. *unnatur*, Du. *onnatuur.*)
1843 CARLYLE *Past & Pr.* III. i. 193 *Un*nature, what we call Chaos, holds nothing in it but vacuities, devouring gulfs. **1858** H. BUSHNELL *Nat. & Supernat.* ii. (1864) 46 So as to be rather unnature, after all, than nature.

un'nature, *v.* (UN-[2] 6 b. Cf. MDu. *onnaturen.*) Also **un'naturing** *ppl. a.*
a **1586** SIDNEY *Arcadia* III. x, A right heavenly Nature indeed, as it were unnaturing them, doth so bridle them. *a* **1628** F. GREVIL *Inquis. Fame & Hon.* xix, To be nothing to subsistence is A fatall, and unnaturing award. **1640** REYNOLDS *Passions* xv. 141 He can hardly so unnature him-selfe, as still to feed on those vanities. **1865** *Reader* 11 March 286/1 Dr. Manning seems to have unnatured himself.

un'nautical, *a.* (UN-[1] 7.)
1852 MUNDY *Antipodes* (1857) 185 His great rough hands fumbling the small tapes into all sorts of un-nautical knots.

unnaviga'bility. (UN-[1] 12, 5 b; cf. next.)
1835 *Edin. Rev.* LX. 460 We must leave the demonstration of its unnavigability to repose with the.. demonstrations of the permeability of the Polar Sea. **1884** LD. HARRIS in *Nat. Rev.* March 125 Frustrated by the unnavigability of its upper waters.

un'navigable, *a.* [UN-[1] 7 b, 5 b.]
1. Incapable of being sailed on or over; not admitting of navigation.
1579–80 NORTH *Plutarch* (1595) 1 Deepe drye sands without water, full of foule ill fauoured venimous beasts, or much mudde vnnauigable. **1604** E. G[RIMSTONE] *D'Acosta's Hist. Indies* I. xxii. 72 The sea was made unnavigable, through the aboundance of banckes, rockes. **1616** HEALEY *Theophrastus* To the Reader, In Winter, the Seas were lockt vp;..vtterly vnnauigable. **1697** DRYDEN *Æneis* VI. 341 There th' unnavigable Lake extends. **1719** DE FOE *Crusoe* II. (Globe) 595 An unnavigable Ocean, where Ship never sail'd. **1798** S. & HT. LEE *Canterb. T.* II. 440 A river,—wholly unnavigable from its rude course and stony bed. **1836** W. IRVING *Astoria* I. 181 The men returned, therefore, in despair, and declared the river unnavigable. **1898** F. T. BULLEN in *Nat. Rev.* Aug. 856 The unnavigable coast of Palawan.
b. *fig.* or in fig. context.
1656 COWLEY *Pindar. Odes, Praise of P.* i, Pindars un-navigable Song Like a swoln Flood from some steep Mountain pours along. **1688** PRIOR *Ode on Exod. iii. 14* ii, Yet cease to hope thy short-liv'd Bark shall ride Down spreading Fate's unnavigable Tide. **1693** DRYDEN *Juvenal* x. 13 Some who the depths of Eloquence have found, In that

unnavigable Stream were Drown'd. **1768–74** TUCKER *Lt. Nat.* (1834) I. 610 Nor would the unnavigable gulph utterly exclude his hopes.

c. Adverse to navigation.

a **1641** BP. MOUNTAGU *Acts & Mon.* (1642) 253 He puts to Sea..at an unseasonable, and unnavigable time of the yeare.

2. Of a vessel: Incapable of being navigated.

1755 MAGENS *Insurances* II. 139 When a Ship insured is become unnavigable.

un'navigated, *ppl. a.* (UN-[1] 8.)

[**1775** ASH.] **1777** COOK *Voy.* I. Introd. p. xxvi, To traverse a far greater space of sea, till then unnavigated. *a* **1796** ADML. FORBES in Cook *Voy.* (1842) I. p. xix, They have discovered seas unnavigated and unknown before.

†**unne,** *v. Obs.* Forms: *Inf.* 1 unnan, 3 unnen. *Pres. indic.* 1 ann, onn, 1, 3 an, 3 on (also 3 unne, unnest), *pl.* 1 unnon, 3 unnen (unneð). *Pres. subj.* 1, 3 unne (3 hunne). *Pa. t.* 1, 3 uþe, uðe (3 ouþe); *pl.* 1 uþon, uðon, 3 uðen. *Pa. pple.* 3 i-unnen, unen, unned. Cf. I-UNNE *v.* [OE. *unnan,* = OS. *unnan,* OHG. *unnan, unnen* (MHG. *unnen*), MDu. *onnen,* ON. *unna* (Icel., Norw., Swed. *unna,* Da. *unde*), one of the class of preterite-present verbs. The stem *ann-* is the base of Goth. *anst-s,* OE. *ést* ESTE *sb.*]

1. *trans.* To grant, allow, give (freely).

In OE. construed with the genitive.

Beowulf 1225 Ic þe an tela sincȝestreona. *a* **900** *O.E. Chron.* an. 755 (Parker MS.), þa ȝebead he him hiera aȝenne dom feos & londes, ȝif hie him þæs rices uþon. *c* **1000** *Ags. Ps.* (Thorpe) cxxxi. 4 ðif ic minum eaȝum unne slæpes. *a* **1122** *O.E. Chron.* an. 1041 (Laud MS.), Eall folc ȝeceas Eadward to cynge..healde þa hwile þe him God unne. *c* **1205** LAY. 14851 Habbe alc god mon his rihte, ȝif godd hit an. *a* **1225** *Ancr. R.* 90 Ase quite ase ȝe beoð..weren alle þe oðre, ure Louerd hit vðe. *c* **1275** *Sinners Beware* 272 in *O.E. Misc.* 81 Loke, seyde god nuþe, Hwat ich for ou ouþe.

2. To wish or like (one) to have (something).

c **893** K. ÆLFRED *Oros.* III. i. 98 Næs na for þæm þe hie him æniȝra goda uþen. *c* **1000** *Ags. Psalter* (Thorpe) xxxix. 17 Ondrædon him þa þe me yfeles unnon. *c* **1200** *Trin. Coll. Hom.* 79 Ne wile [he]..naðemore haten him þe..him iuel unnen. *a* **1225** *Leg. Kath.* 2344 Beoð bliðe, ich bisehe ow, Ȝef ȝe me blisse unnen. *a* **1310** in Wright *Lyric P.* xi. 40 Ich unne hire wel ant heo me wo; Ycham hire frend ant heo my fo. *c* **1320** *Sir Tristrem* 1928 Meriadok was a man þat tristrem trowed ay; Miche gode he him an.

3. To grant, permit, or allow *that.* Also const. with inf.

Beowulf 2874 Hwæðre him God uðe,..þæt he hyne sylfne ȝewræc. *c* **897** K. ÆLFRED *Gregory's Past. C.* 349 Ðæt is ðæt hwa..him unne ðæt he to ryhte ȝecierre. *c* **950** *Lindisf. Gosp.* Matt., Int. 4 Ic onn [L. *opto*] ðæt in crist ðu ȝetreowfæstniȝ. *a* **1200** *Moral Ode* 314 Ac drihte crist..of alle vre gultes unne us come bote. *a* **1225** *Ancr. R.* 380 Ȝe nowen nout unnen þet eni vuel word kome of ou. *a* **1250** *Gen. & Ex.* 2249 God hunne him eði modes ben, And sende me min childre agen. **1258** *Charter Hen. III,* We willen and unnen þæt þæt vre rædesmen..habbeþ idon..be stedefæst.

ellipt. a **1250** *Owl & Night.* 1739 Ich an [*v.r.* vnne] wel, cwað the niȝtegale.

Hence †'**unnung** *vbl. sb. Obs.*

a **1225** *Ancren R.* 282 Ondes salue, ich seide, þet was feolaulich luue, and god vnnunge: & god wil, þer ase mihte of dede wonteð.

†**un'nealed,** *ppl. a. Obs.* (UN-[1] 8.)

1563 HYLL *Art Garden.* (1574) 72 An earthen pot, not glased, or rather vnnealed. **1745** *Phil. Trans.* XLIII. 506 Hollow Balls, made of unnealed glass. **1789** E. DARWIN *Bot. Gard.* I. 203 Thus the slight wound ingraved on glass unneal'd Runs in white lines along the lucid field.

†**un'near,** *prep.* and *adv. Obs.* (UN-[1] 11 b.)

1612 J. DAVIES (Heref.) *Muse's Sacr.* Wks. (Grosart) II. 51/1 Where the Earth was couer'd with her Floud, now Citties stand, vneere the Oceans Brim. **1648** HEXHAM II, *On-na-by,* vnneere.

un'neared, *ppl. a.* (UN-[1] 8.)

1852 M. ARNOLD *Empedocles on Etna* II. 294 [The stars] renew..Night after night your courses, In echoing unnear'd silence.

un'neat, *a.* (UN-[1] 7.)

1648 HEXHAM II, *Ongekuyst,* Vnneate, Foule, or Filthy. **1849** D. J. BROWNE *Amer. Poultry Yard* (1855) 71 The white of their plumage is not brilliant, and is sure to be un-neat in the places where they are usually kept. **1866** MISS MULOCK *Noble Life* xii, A letter, so unlike Helen's, so un-neat, blurred and blotted.

Hence **un'neatness.**

1844 N. PATERSON *Manse Gard.* 91 A great degree of unneatness in the mode of training. *a* **1864** HAWTHORNE *Dr. Grimshawe* vi, The sordidness and unneatness of the apartment.

†**unneath,** reduced f. UNDERNEATH *prep.*

1654 VILVAIN *Epit. Ess.* VII. lxx, A noble Pair..ly here unneath one stone. *a* **1718** PARNELL *Fairy Tale* xvi, Where by the back the youth he hung To spraul unneath the roof. *c* **1750** SHENSTONE *Ruin'd Abbey* 174 That their dishonour'd corse..Must sleep with brutes their vassals, on the field Unneath some path. **1847** HALLIWELL, *Unneath,* beneath. *Somerset.*

un'nebulous, *a.* (UN-[1] 7.)

1845 tr. *Humboldt's Cosmos* I. 161 The latter ring..is a mixture of unnebulous stars.

†**un'necessaire,** *a. Obs.*[−1] [UN-[1] 7.] Unnecessary.

c **1440** *Pallad. on Husb.* v. 78 Vnnecessaire Is hym to plaunte yf he be wel ysowe.

un'necessarily, *adv.* [UN-[1] 11.] Without necessity; needlessly.

1594 HOOKER *Eccl. Pol.* II. iv. §2, I hope wee shall not seeme altogether vnnecessarily to doubt of the soundnesse of their opinion. **1610** SHAKS. *Temp.* II. i. 260 There be..Lords, that can prate As amply, and vnnecessarily As this Gonzallo. **1691** T. H[ALE] *Acc. New Invent.* 94 Excess of thickness is not only unnecessarily paid for, but it makes the Sheet worse. **1712** *Spect.* No. 283 ¶6 Sums which they have spent unnecessarily. **1786** COWPER *Let.* Wks. 1837 XV. 184 Again I remind you, though perhaps unnecessarily, of the two volumes. **1833** T. HOOK *Parson's Dau.* I. viii, You..unnecessarily agitate yourself. **1879** *Cassell's Techn. Educ.* I. 312/2 Such furniture is unnecessarily heavy and clumsy.

un'necessariness. (UN-[1] 12.)

1628 BP. HALL *Old Relig.* 117 An opinion of the vnnecessarinesse of deuotion in these holy businesses. **1685** BOYLE *Enq. Notion Nat.* v. 124 The unnecessariness of such a nature as is pretended. **1720** SIR J. STEWART in *Wodrow Corr.* (1843) II. 489 *note,* The unnecessariness of oaths, as being no security to a government. **1810** COLERIDGE *Lit. Rem.* (1838) III. 337, I should confine my grounds of opposition to the article thus stated to its unnecessariness. **1845** R. BALMER *Lect. & Disc.* II. 307 To demonstrate the unnecessariness of the miraculous gifts of the Spirit.

†**unnece'ssariously,** *adv. Obs.*[−1] (UN-[1] 11.)

1798 *Lit. Mem. Living Authors* I. 283 The extravagant price at which a Work so unnecessariously sumptuous must be sold.

un'necessary, *a.* and *sb.* [UN-[1] 7, 12.]

1. Not necessary or requisite; needless.

1548 UDALL, etc. *Erasm. Par. John* xxi. 117 b, This vnnecessarie care that Peter had of another mans death [etc.]. **1596** *Edward III,* III. i. 7 To lay aside vnnecessary soothing. **1623** BINGHAM *Xenophon* 49 To leaue behind vs our vnnecessarie stuffe, and to take with vs only such as..we stand in need of. **1655** EARL ORRERY *Parthen.* I. I. 81 If any thing could make me offended with Artabanes, 'twould be this unnecessary interceding. **1726** SWIFT *Gulliver* II. vii, That a prince..should, from a nice, unnecessary scruple,..let slip an opportunity..that [etc.]. **1791** MRS. RADCLIFFE *Rom. Forest* i, This was a very unnecessary caution to La Motte. **1823** SCOTT *Quentin D.* Introd., Ringing the dinner-bell—a most unnecessary ceremony for assembling three persons. **1898** 'MERRIMAN' *Roden's Corner* iii, A generation ..much addicted to unnecessary haste.

b. With indefinite subject (*it,* etc.), and usually const. *to* with inf.

1597 HOOKER *Eccl. Pol.* v. lxviii. §2 The greatest part of the common multitude..who thinke it either vnmeet or vnnecessary to put them euen man by man. **1612** JAS. I. in Ellis *Orig. Lett.* Ser. I. III. 104 To bidde a running man goe faster, quhiche is both unnecessarie and injuriouse. **1757** W. PITT in *10th Rep. Hist. MSS. Comm.* App. I. 214 His Majesty judges it unnecessary to send you particular Orders. **1771** *Junius Lett.* liv. (1788) 300 It is unnecessary to pursue the argument any farther. **1845** MCCULLOCH *Taxation* II. v. 201 This would be inconsistent alike with the objects and limits of this work, and it would, besides, be wholly unnecessary. **1869** TANNER *Clin. Med.* (ed. 2) 10 It is almost unnecessary to say that mediate percussion must be employed.

c. *sb. pl.* Unnecessary things.

1559 AYLMER *Harborowe* Pj, Vnfitting superfluitie in apparel, dyet, and other vnnecessaries. **1618** FLETCHER *Loyal Subject* II. v, It contains nothing But rubbish from the other rooms and unnecessaries. **1691** NORRIS *Pract. Disc.* 113 Not to burthen my Discourse or your Patience with Unnecessaries. **1748** RICHARDSON *Clarissa* (1811) IV. 184 Wanting nothing but unnecessaries. **1839** MARRYAT *Diary Amer.* Ser. I. II. 161 Very pretty did its little tiny black feet look, relieved by these expensive unnecessaries. **1881** *Q. Rev.* Jan. 51 Nowhere are the unnecessaries of life..sold at such extravagant prices as in San Francisco.

†**2.** Not requiring much. *Obs.*[−1]

1605 SHAKS. *Lear* II. iv. 157 Age is unnecessary: on my knees I begge, That you'l vouchsafe me Rayment, Bed, and Food.

unne'cessitated, *ppl. a.* (UN-[1] 8.)

1635 JACKSON *Creed* VIII. v. §5 All other habitual sinnes or vices are not acquired but by many unnecessitated vicious acts. **1650** EARL MONM. tr. *Senault's Man bec. Guilty* 376 To expose himselfe voluntarily to dangers unnecessitated. **1712** BLACKMORE *Creation* VII. 480 From all compulsion free, Unforc'd, and unnecessitated, we Ourselves determine. **1813** SHELLEY *Q. Mab* VI. 172 No atom of this turbulence fulfils A vague and unnecessitated task. **1904** *Brit. Med. Jrnl.* 17 Sept. 692 The category of..unnecessitated motives, which the normal man predicates of part of his mental processes.

unne'cessitating, *ppl. a.* (UN-[1] 10.)

1738 WARBURTON *Div. Legat.* I. 48 The unnecessitating Command of an intelligent Superior.

unne'cessity. (UN-[1] 12.)

1672 SIR T. BROWNE *Let. Friend* §9 So that to be carried 'sextâ cervice' to the grave, was but a civil unnecessity.

†**unnedd,** *ppl. a.*: see UN-[1] 3.

un'needed, *ppl. a.* (UN-[1] 8.)

[**1775** ASH.] **1844** R. CHAMBERS *Vestiges Nat. Hist. Creation* 112 Blood circulating in particular vessels,..which are unneeded by mammifers. **1868** E. PEACOCK *Myrc's Instr.* 67 A piece of advice..not entirely unneeded in these days.

un'needful, *a.* [UN-[1] 7.]

1. Unnecessary; not required.

c **1380** WYCLIF *Sel. Wks.* II. 58 So shal cloþis be more unnedeful þan þei weren in staat of innocence. *c* **1450** *Myrr. our Ladye* 227 Her eyne..were neuer lyfte vp to beholde eny vnnedeful thinge. **1543** RECORDE *Arithm.* 119 b, I iudge that good reason, for many are vnnedefull, where one wyll serue. **1597** J. KING *On Jonas* (1618) 281 The matter of all their vowes vnneedefull, in some vnlawfull, in some vnpossible. **1624** CAPT. SMITH *Virginia* I. 2 Which vnneedfull Southerly course..occasioned them..much sicknesse. **1677** *Lond. Gaz.* No. 1170/3 Since your Majesty will see what I write..it is unneedful that I should repeat it. **1768** [W. DONALDSON] *Life Sir B. Sapskull* I. iii. 29 Mere negative qualifications totally unneedful in the education of a polite gentleman. **1905** *Athenæum* 30 Sept. 431/1 The editor has..also (a rarer thing in editors) refrained from doing what was unneedful.

2. Not standing in need *of* something.

1876 MRS. H. WOOD *Parkwater* (1879) 258 The heart has a language of its own, unneedful of common syllables.

So **un'needfully** *adv.,* unnecessarily.

1642 MILTON *Apol. Smect.* 2 Yet those I intreat who have found the leasure to reade that name,..unworthily defam'd, would be so good..as to heare the same person not unneedfully defended.

un'needy, *a.* (UN-[1] 7.) Also *absol.*

c **1440** *Jacob's Well* 108 Whethir þi neyȝboure..be syke or hool, nedy or vnnedy. **1477** RIVERS *Dictes* (1877) 27 b, Som simple folkes yeue to the vnnedy, and refuse hit to thoos that haue nede. **1550** BALDWIN *Mor. Philos.* Qib, To the vnneady a man to make hys dole, Is lyke the ministring of playsters to the whole.

unne'glected, *ppl. a.* (UN-[1] 8.)

a **1652** BROME *Novella* II. ii, My profit in this too is unneglected.

un'negligent, *a.* (UN-[1] 7, 15.)

1597 *Return fr. Parnass.* IV. i. 1250 You are the moste unnegligent Sexton that ever came these forty years.

unne'gotiable, *a.* (UN-[1] 7 b.)

[**1775** ASH.] **1893** F. F. MOORE *I forbid Banns* xli, Discoveries of an interesting but unnegotiable nature.

un'neighboured, *ppl. a.* (UN-[1] 8.)

1657 H. KING *Woes of Esay* 8 Making a dearth Of all inhabitants, until they stand Unneighbour'd, as unblest. **1704** D'URFEY *Night Adventures* 180 Homely, unneighbour'd, and alone. *a* **1800** COWPER *Odyss.* (ed. 2) VI. 9 An unneighbour'd isle, And far from all resort of busy man. **1804** SYMMONS *Milton* (1810) 79 A crowd of beauties, unneighboured by a thought, a line,..which we can be desirous of changing.

un'neighbourly, *a.* (UN-[1] 7.)

1583 BABINGTON *Commandm.* (1590) 372 Haue you not often refused of a meere pinching and an vnneighbourlie mind euen in small matters? **1601** J. WHEELER *Treat. Comm.* 43 The proud, vnneighbourly..Proscriptions of the Dutchesse of Parma. **1657** PIERCE *Div. Philanthr.* Ded. 1 The late un-Neighbourly usage which I have publickly received. **1705** SIR J. PACKINGTON in Hearne *Collections* (O.H.S.) I. 125 Unneighbourly Proceedings against your own Tenants. **1768–74** TUCKER *Lt. Nat.* (1834) II. 307 These things are unneighbourly or unnatural, if we consider only their present effect upon the party suffering by them. **1807** G. CHALMERS *Caledonia* I. 397 The cause of this unneighbourly irruption into Cumberland. **1895** *Westm. Gaz.* 18 June 5/1 He could not conceive conduct worse and more unneighbourly.

Hence **un'neighbourliness.**

1653 BP. WEBBE *Pract. Quiet.* (1657) 155 Causing barrennesse of all goodnesse where there is that unquiet unneighbourliness. **1865** MEREDITH *R. Fleming* iv, The yeoman's pride struggled..to vindicate his unneighbourliness.

un'neighbourly, *adv.* (UN-[1] 11.)

1549 SIR W. PAGET in Strype *Eccl. Mem.* (1721) II. xix. 156 The French have..dealt on this side very unfriendly and unneighbourly towards us. **1595** SHAKS. *John* v. ii. 39 Where these two Christian Armies might combine The bloud of malice, in a vaine of league, And not to spend it so vnneighbourly.

†**unneod, -neomelich**: see UN-[1] 3.

†**un'nervate,** *a. Obs.*[−1] [UN-[1] 7.] Nerveless, feeble.

1725 W. BROOME *Notes Pope's Odyss.* II. 107 Scaliger calls them fine and lively in Musæus, but abject, unnervate, and unharmonious in Homer.

un'nerve, *v.* [UN-[2] 3. Cf. Du. *ont-,* G. *entnerven.*]

1. *trans.* To destroy the strength of; to render physically weak. Also *fig.*

1621 G. SANDYS *Ovid's Met.* II. (1626) 26 Pale sudden feare vn-nerves his quaking thighs. **1697** ADDISON *Ess. Georgics* ¶8 in Dryden's *Virgil,* The Precepts..are often so minute..that they weaken and un-nerve his Verse. **1725** POPE *Odyss.* XV. 448, When a length of years unnerves the strong, Apollo comes. **1792** S. ROGERS *Pleas. Mem.* II. 111 The spectre Poverty unnerv'd his frame. **1836** J. GILBERT *Chr. Atonem.* ix. (1852) 271 The sight of mercy so transcendent..has unnerved the power of determined obduracy. **1850** MERIVALE *Rom. Emp.* xxi. II. 453 This consciousness..unnerved his arm for the execution of the Herculean task. **1870** BRYANT *Iliad* v. I. 175 The weariness of toil unnerves thy frame.

2. To deprive (the mind, etc., or a person) of firmness or courage; to render incapable of acting with ordinary firmness or energy.

1704 *Moderat. Display'd* v, A Modern Coward Principle design'd To stifle Justice, and unnerve the Mind. **1725** POPE *Odyss.* XII. 245 Fear seiz'd the mighty, and unnerv'd the brave. **1780** COWPER *Progr. Err.* 272 'Tis not alone the grape's enticing juice Unnerves the moral pow'rs, and mars their use. **1791** NEWTE *Tour Eng. & Scot.* 57 The horrid and incessant din..unnerves and overcomes the heart. **1844** TALFOURD *Athenian Captive* I. i, To speak of mortal sickness, and unnerve A soul of noble essence. **1878** BOSW. SMITH *Carthage* 125 The fear which it seems to have inspired completely unnerved the Romans.

Hence **un'nerving** *ppl. a.*; **un'nervingly** *adv.*

1722 Hamilton *Wallace* v. (1816) 73 And sure while Scotia's enemies remain, Unnerving love should ever sue in vain. **1744** P. Whitehead *Gymnasiad* III. 53 He, alas! had felt th' unnerving Blow. **1821** Clare *Vill. Minstr.* (1823) I. 7 The mystic tribes of night's unnerving breeze. **1894** Crockett *Raiders* 354, I had that sense of being hunted, which comes so quickly and is so unnerving. **1962** I. Murdoch *Unofficial Rose* xxxiii. 313 There was something unfocussed, something a little unnervingly fragmentary, in his present apprehension of Lindsay. **1976** T. Heald *Let Sleeping Dogs Die* i. 10 Parkinson had been unnervingly friendly.

un'nerved, *ppl. a.* [See prec.] Rendered nerveless or weak; unmanned.

1602 Shaks. *Ham.* II. ii. 496 With the whiffe and winde of his fell Sword Th' vnnerued Father fals. **1659** W. Chamberlayne *Pharonnida* III. i. 398 Whilst her brother stands Unnerved with grief. **1718** Rowe tr. *Lucan* 33 Then Sons forsook their Sires un-nerv'd and old. **1781** Cowper *Retirem.* 677 A mind unnerv'd, or indispos'd to bear The weight of subjects worthiest of her care. **1855** Macaulay *Hist. Eng.* xx. IV. 429 Her recent efforts..had left her spent and unnerved. **1894** S. Fiske *Holiday Stories* (1900) 83 The situation was becoming terribly strained... Tom had given way under it, and was completely unnerved.

unnes, variant of UNEATHS *adv. Obs.*

un'nest, *v.* (UN-^{2} 5. Cf. Du. *ontnesten.*) Chiefly *fig.* (In first quot. *intr.*)

c **1374** Chaucer *Troylus* IV. 305 O soule, lurkynge in þis wo, vnneste; Fle forth out of myn herte. *c* **1532** Du Wes *Introd. Fr.* in *Palsgr.* 941 To unneste, *deniser.* *c* **1600** Chalkhill *Thealma & Cl.* (1683) 120 Alexis rising, thanks his prudent care And as his Father lov'd him; all prepare T'unnest these Pyrates. ? **1658** J. M. in Cleveland *Wks.* (1687) 283 The Presbyterian he did un-nest, With the whole Kennel o' th' two-footed Beast. **1679** J. Somerville *Mem. Somerville* (1815) I. 222 The queen..encourages the souldiers..to unnest from that hold the ancient enemies of ther countrey. **1790** A. Wilson *To J. Kennedy* Poet. Wks. (1846) 16 As..seeming doubts when told oft take to wing, Permit me here some miseries to unnest, That long have harbour'd in my labouring breast. **1879** H. W. Warren *Recr. Astron.* iv. 58 The earth on its softly-spinning axle never jars enough to unnest a bird or wake a child.

Hence **un'nested** *ppl. a.*

1860 Patmore *Faithf. for Ever* I. i, No more the unnested blackbird's shriek Startled the light-leaved wood.

un'nestle, *v.* (UN-^{2} 3 + NESTLE *v.*^{1} Cf. Du. *ontnestelen.*) Chiefly *fig.*

c **1430** *Pilgr. Lyf Manhode* II. cix. (1869) 116 He vnnestleth the hye briddes, and overthroweth here feedinges. **1592** Bacon *Confer. Pleasure* (1870) 20 Leste anie man should think her intent was to unnestle ill neyghbors. **1658** Evelyn *Fr. Gard.* (1675) 101 There is a Green-Worm which devours the young shoots.., and those are very hard to un-nestle. **1694** Motteux *Rabelais* v. ix. 43 Murther all the Kings..in the world,..unnestle the Angels from their Cock-loft.

Hence **un'nestling** *vbl. sb.*

1653 Urquhart *Rabelais* I. xxiv. 113 Unnestling of sparrowes, taking of quailes, and fishing for frogs.

unnet, var. UNNUT *a. Obs.*

unnet (uncompelled): UN-^{1} 3.

unneth(s, etc., varr. UNEATH(S.

un'netted, *ppl. a.* (UN-^{1} 8.)

1833 Tennyson *Blackbird* 7 The unnetted black-hearts ripen dark..against the garden wall. **1860** 'Ouida' *Tricotrin* I. 20 Like the bloom to an unnetted peach.

un'neutral, *a.* (UN-^{1} 7.)

1782 Earl Malmesbury *Diaries & Corr.* (1844) I. 486 It is in vain to remind her how..very unneutral her Armed Neutrality is. **1895** T. A. Walker *Man. Public Internat. Law* IV. ii. 165 A neutral Government is in general responsible in respect of the unneutral employment of its territories and territorial waters. **1949** W. S. Churchill *2nd World War* II. II. xx. 358 The transfer to Great Britain of fifty American warships was a decidedly unneutral act by the United States. *a* **1974** R. Crossman *Diaries* (1976) II. 366 Most of the gains we made by the July measures would have been upset by an unneutral policy.

un'neutralized, *ppl. a.* (UN-^{1} 8.)

1758 *Elaboratory laid Open* 136 A redundant portion of a[n] unneutralized acid. **1771** T. Percival *Ess.* (1777) I. 31 If they remain unneutralised in the first passages, they will powerfully promote putrefaction. **1848** A. S. Taylor *Poisons* 202 The action of sulphuric acid in an unneutralized or imperfectly neutralized condition. **1881** Tyndall *Ess. Floating Matter* 90 Two [shades] containing strong turnip-infusion and hay-infusion unneutralized.

†**un'nevened**, *ppl. a. Obs.* [UN-^{1} 8. Cf. ON. *únefnd-r*, Da. *unævnt.*] Unnamed.

13.. *E.E. Allit. P.* B. 727 Þat nas neuer þyn note, vnneuened hit worþe, Þat art so gaynly a god & of goste mylde!

†**un'newsed**, *ppl. a. Obs.*$^{-1}$ (UN-^{1} 8.)

1644 Quarles *Sheph. Orac.* x, Nuncius never uses To come unnews'd.

un'niche, *v.* (UN-^{2} 5.)

1771 *Ess. fr. Batchelor* (1773) I. 30 It is my ambition to un-nich Saint Charles, and place him in his proper rank.

un'nicher. (UN-^{2} 8.)

1823 D'Israeli *Cur. Lit.* Ser. II. I. 344 The learned De Launoi had successfully attacked the legends of saints, and was called the *Denicheur de Saints*—the 'Unnicher of Saints'.

un'nicked, *ppl. a.* (UN-^{1} 8.)

c **1480** *Test. Ebor.* (Surtees) III. 253, xij shaffe of clense arros un nykt. *Ibid.*, xxxj shaffe of childre ware, clenst and un nyked.

un'niggard, *a.* (UN-^{1} 7.)

1591 Sylvester *Du Bartas* I. iv. 375 That sumptuous Canapy, The which th' unniggard hand of Majesty Poudred so thick with Shields so shining cleer.

un'niggardly, *a.* (UN-^{1} 7.)

1768–74 Tucker *Lt. Nat.* (1834) I. 614 Wherein there appears..no spark of arbitrary or inequitable disposition, but unreserved and unniggardly goodness.

un'night, *v.* (UN-^{2} 3, 7.)

1594 *Zepheria* iv, The summe of life that Chaos did vnnight. **1598** Florio, *Disanottare*, to vnnight, to wax day.

un'nimbed, *a.* (UN-^{1} 9.)

1880 *Smith's Dict. Chr. Antiq.* II. 1400/2 On the tomb.. she is unnimbed, while the Holy Child has the nimbus.

un'nimble, *a.* (UN-^{1} 7.)

1566 Drant *Horace, Med. Morall* A ij, When unnimble age Hath refte them of their warke. **1607** Markham *Cavel.* II. 48 A horse that is sloathfull or vnnimble in turning. **1681** Rycaut tr. *Gracian's Critick* 76 These..sluggishly moved their unnimble legs. **1703** Thoresby *Let. to Ray* (E.D.S.), *Clunter*, an unnimble stumbler.

Hence **un'nimbleness**.

1607 Markham *Cavel.* II. 177 Some horses,..out of vn-nimblenesse,..are..more apt to turne vpon one hand then vpon another.

un'nimbly, *adv.* (UN-^{1} 11; cf. prec.)

1607 Markham *Cavel.* II. 126 Which hee dooing at the first slouenlie, and vnnimbly, you shal..beat him about the buttocks. **1631** A. Townshend *Albion's Tri.* B, What mak's me so vnnimbly ryse, That did descend so fleete? **1665** Brathwait *Comment Two Tales* 170 Like another Omphada, she had unnimbly rushed down upon her four Quarters. **1704** *Dict. Rust.* s.v. *Rules buying Horses*, To tread unnimbly, shews a false Pace, that never continues.

†**'unning**, *vbl. sb. Obs.*$^{-1}$ [app. f. UNNE *v.*; but perh. for *inning*, f. ON. *inna* to relate, tell.] Indication, sign.

13.. *E.E. Allit. P.* C. 213 He ossed hym by vnnynges þat þay vnder-nomen, Þat he was flawen fro þe face of frelych dryȝtyn.

un'nipped, *ppl. a.* (UN-^{1} 8.)

[**1775** Ash.] **1855** Browning *Lover's Quarrel* xx, Then.. We can stand apart, Heart dispense with heart In the sun, with the flowers unnipped.

un'nitrogenized, *ppl. a.* (UN-^{1} 8 a (*c*).)

1869 Tanner *Clin. Med.* (ed. 2) 149 The nitrogenized and unnitrogenized substances.

unnitt, variant of UNNUT *a. Obs.*

†**unno'bility.** *Obs.*$^{-1}$ (UN-^{1} 12.)

a **1400** *Pauline Ep.* (Powell) 2 Cor. vi. 8 In alle þing gife we vsself as goddys mynystris,..thurgh glorye and vnnobylyte [L. *ignobilitatem*]; thurgh ylle fame and good fame.

un'noble, *a.* (and *sb.*) Now *rare*. [UN-^{1} 7. Cf. IGNOBLE *a.*]

1. Not noble or distinguished by rank or birth.

1382 Wyclif *1 Sam.* ii. 30 Who so euere honourith me, Y shal glorifie hym; forsothe who dispisen me, shulen be vn-noble. —— *1 Cor.* iv. 10. **1489** Caxton *Faytes of A.* I. x. 29 The noble men bare a garment vnlyke to them that were vnnoble. **1545** Brinklow *Compl.* 38 b, No noble or vnnoble man shall retayne any of the kyngs subiectys withowt lauful wagys. **1571** Golding *Calvin on Ps.* xlvii. 5 He setting all the world asyde, had adopted to himself a feawe unnoble persons. **1607** Cowell *Interpr.* s.v. *Corruption of blood*, If he were noble, or a gentleman before, he and his children are made vnnoble and vngentle in respect of the father. **1660** Waterhouse *Arms & Arm.* 179 They must be contented to stand included under the base and unnoble state of people. **1832** S. Austin tr. *Tour Germ. Prince* III. iv. 80 It is an almost universal weakness of the unnoble in England to parade an acquaintance with the noble. **1855** Singleton *Virgil* II. 478 Other unwedded maids In Latium be, and in Laurentine fields, Nor they unnoble in their pedigree.

b. *absol.* (chiefly pl.) or as *sb.*

1382 Wyclif *Isaiah* iii. 5 Ther shal striue the child aȝen the old man, and the vnnoble aȝen the noble. *c* **1400** *Apol. Loll.* 43 Noiþer..of pore to be maad riche, ne gloriouse of þe vnnoble. *a* **1513** Fabyan *Chron.* II. xxxix. 27 Artogayle.. imaginyd causes agayne his nobles to put theym from theyr ..dignyties, and in theyr places to sette & ordeyne vnnoble. **1581** Pettie tr. *Guazzo's Civ. Conv.* II. (1586) 92 Hee which despiseth the vnnoble, despiseth his first Fathers. **1602** Fulbecke *1st Pt. Parall.* Introd. 3 The noble and vn-noble were put to death. **1688** R. Holme *Armoury* III. 69/1 It is the Duty of the unnoble to Honor and Salute a Gentleman. *sb.* **1563** Foxe *A. & M.* 70 b/1 He had followers of his doltish religion, both of the nobles, and vnnobles of Rome.

†**2. a.** Of or pertaining to one who is not of noble birth or rank. *Obs.*

c **1520** [see UNNOBLENESS]. **1561** T. Hoby tr. *Castiglione's Courtyer* III. Hh ij b, So glorious a soule, that deserued.. renowme after death, as in lief it dwelled in an vnnoble body. *a* **1586** Sidney *Arcadia* II. ii, The perfections are such in the partie I love, as the feeling of them cannot come into any unnoble hart.

†**b.** Of things: Undistinguished, unnoted, common, mean. *Obs.*

1382 Wyclif *1 Cor.* i. 28 God chees the vnnoble thingis [L. *ignobilia*] and dispisable thingis of the world. **1589** Cooper *Admon.* 199 The..unnoble thinges of the worlde.. God hath chosen. **1590** Burrough *Meth. Physick* 211 The bloud being driuen backe from the vnnoble members, it rusheth vp to the principal members. **1612** Drayton *Poly-olb.* v. 332 Since, holy Dauid's seat; which of especiall grace Doth lend that nobler name, to this vnnobler place. **1631** Widdowes *Nat. Philos.* 51 The more un-noble senses are Tasting, and Smelling.

3. Not noble in disposition; ignoble, mean, base: **a.** Of persons.

1566 Gascoigne, etc. *Jocasta* II. i, So, woulde the Gods, that in this noble realme Shoulde never long unnoble tyrant reigne. **1616** Breton *Good & Bad* Wks. (Grosart) II. 6/2 An vnnoble man is the griefe of Reason, when the title of honour is put vpon the subiect of disgrace. **1641** Earl Cork *Diary* in *Lismore Papers* Ser. I. (1886) V. 195 Papers concerning the vnnoble Earle of Middlesex.

transf. **1607** Topsell *Four-f. Beasts* 321 Neither is there any Horsse, swift or slow, noble, or vnnoble, that can be guided without these [reins].

b. Of actions, character, etc.

1606 Shaks. *Ant. & Cl.* III. xi. 50, I haue offended Reputation, A most vnnoble swerueing. **1628** Ford *Lover's Mel.* II. ii, My affections..are pure, Without all mixture of un-noble thoughts. **1680** *Life Edw. II*, in *Select. Harl. Misc.* (1793) 37 If Lancaster had been of so unnoble a disposition. **1855** Singleton *Virgil* I. 152 Him, likewise,.. If now..he fails, Conceal at home; nor his unnoble eld Forgive.

Hence **un'nobleness**.

c **1400** *New Test.* (Paues) 2 Cor. vi. 8 þoroȝ worschupe & vnnobelnesse, þoroȝ diffamynge & good loos. *c* **1520** Barclay *Jugurth* (1557) 75 b, The lownes and vnnoblenes of Marius encreased to hym fauour specially of the commentie which were come of vnnoble bloude, as he was. **1569** J. Sanford tr. *Agrippa's Van. Artes* 127 b, That they whiche had not slayne some enimie, shoulde go girte with a halter in reproche of vnnoblenes. **1618** Fletcher *Loyal Subj.* I. iii, You made this Vow, and whose unnobleness, Indeed forgetfulness of good— *Ar.* No more.

un'noble, *v.* (UN-^{2} 6 a.)

1605 Heywood *If you know not me* F 3 b, The treasons of the father being noble, Vn-nobles all your children. **1656** Jeanes *Mixt. Schol. Div.* 119 A foul incongruity..is it for us ..to unnoble, and pollute that flesh.

†**unnoblety.** *Obs.*$^{-1}$ [UN-^{1} 12.] = prec.

a **1400** *Pauline Ep.* (Powell) 2 Cor. xi. 21 Aftyr þe vn-noblete I seye; as we hadde be syke in þis partye.

†**un'nobley.** *Obs.* [UN-^{1} 12.] Low estate.

1382 Wyclif *1 Cor.* xv. 43 It is sowun in vnnobley, it schal ryse in glorie. —— *2 Cor.* vi. 8 By glorie and vnnobley; by yuel fame and good fame.

un'nobly, *adv.* (UN-^{1} 11. Cf. IGNOBLY *adv.*)

1618 Fletcher *Loyal Subj.* v. vi, You do the most unnobly to be angry. *a* **1628** F. Grevil *Alaham* II. iii, True hearts, to doe vnnobly, haue no spirit. ? **1648** H. King *Elegy Lucas & Lisle* 314 Which..Shall..enhearse this blood unnobly spilt.

un'nock, *v. rare*$^{-0}$. (UN-^{2} 3; cf. NOCK *v.*)

1530 Palsgr. 768/2, I unnocke a shafte, *je descosche. Ibid.*, Who hath unnocked my shafte?

†**un'nome**, *pa. pple. Obs.* [UN-^{1} 8 b; cf. NIM *v.*] Untaken.

1297 R. Glouc. (Rolls) 11872 Ȝut he percede þe ost,..& aliue & vn-nome of scapede among echon. **13..** *Guy Warw.* (A.) 5154 Alle þai ben ded oþer ouer-come: Þer bileued non vn-nome.

un'nooked, *ppl. a.* [UN-^{1} 8.] Having no nooks or corners.

1602 Marston *Antonio's Rev.* IV. iii, With innocent upreared armes to Heaven: With my unnookt simplicitie.

un'nose, *v.* (UN-^{2} 4.)

Hence **un'nosed** *ppl. a.*

1598 Florio, *Snasato*, without a nose, vn-nosed. **1603** —— *Montaigne* II. vi. 219 That is now called to vn-nose himselfe. **1620** Shelton *Quix.* II. xiv. 89 Quoth the vn-nosed Squire. **1738** *Common Sense* II. 106 The persons who remain behind un-nos'd will immediately..clap on their original Noses. **1742** Jarvis *Quix.* II. I. xiv, 'Indeed am I,' answered the unnosed squire.

un'notable, *a.* and *sb.* (UN-^{1} 7 b, 12.)

1528 Paynell *Salerne's Regim.* O ij b, Fyshe..bred in shalowe & vnnotable waters. **1611** Florio, *Innotabile*, vnnoteable, not to be noted. **1831** Carlyle *Sart. Res.* II. v, Nay, who knows..but Blumine herself might have aforetime noted the so unnotable. **1837** —— *Fr. Rev.* II. IV. vi, Unnotable hum of sweet human gossip rises from this Village.

b. *sb.* One who is not notable.

1861 H. S. Cunningham *Wheat & Tares* 324 If you get anybody else better worth having to dinner, I'll come in my sedan..along with the other unnotables.

un'notched, *ppl. a.* [UN-^{1} 8.]

†**1.** Not cut or trimmed. (Cf. NOTCH *v.* 1, OCHE *v.*) *Obs.*$^{-1}$

1557 *Tottel's Misc.* (Arb.) 159 All ruff of heare, my nayles vnnocht, as to such semeth best, That wander by theyr wittes.

2. Not marked with a notch; unnicked.

[**1775** Ash.] **1811** Miss L. Hawkins *C'tess & Gertr.* IV. 5 The un-notched paling, the walls capt with straw and stone. **1844** Noad *Electricity* (ed. 2) 392 Provided the intersecting curves proceeding from A abut upon the notched surface of the knife, and those from B upon the un-notched side. **1883** *Encycl. Brit.* XVI. 648/2 Reptant Azygobranchia with..the lip of the shell unnotched.

un'noted, *a.* [UN-^{1} 9.] Characterized by absence of musical notes.

1866 Meredith *Vittoria* xxiv, A song of three notes and a sort of unnoted clanging chorus.

un'noted, *ppl. a.* [UN-^{1} 8.]

1. Not noticed or observed; unmarked.

1563 GOLDINGE *Cæsar* III. (1565) 74 b, Bycause the thing was done in yᵉ sight of Cesar and all his army, insomuch that no dede..could escape vnnoted. **1600** *Bodenham's Belvedere* (1875) 59 Gnats are vnnoted where-soe're they flie But Eagles gaz'd vpon with euery eye. *c* **1620** FLETCHER *False One* I. i, I'le be admitted for a wanton tale To some most private Cabinets, when your Priest-hood..Shall wait without unnoted. **1725** POPE *Odyss.* I. 177 Where the free guest, unnoted, might relate, If haply conscious, of his Father's fate. **1742** YOUNG *Nt. Th.* II. 274 Unnoted, [conscience] notes each moment misapply'd. **1813** BYRON *Corsair* I. xvii, Secure, unnoted, Conrad's prow pass'd by. **1894** MRS. DYAN *Man's Keeping* (1899) 135 Unnoted by him, that vision had faded much of late.

2. Not specially noted or observed; undistinguished, obscure.

1592 *Soliman & Pers.* I. ii. 73 Sweet Perseda, vnnoted though I be, Thy beauty yet shall make me knowne ere night. **1621** G. SANDYS *Ovid's Met.* IX. (1626) 191 Phæstus ..fostered One, Lydgus, of vn-noted parents bred. **1725** POPE *Odyss.* V. 402 Un-wept, un-noted, and for ever dead! **1789** BURNS *Let. to Lady Constable* 16 Dec., Only to add so many units more to the unnoted crowd that followed their leaders. **1860** ELLICOTT *Life Our Lord* ii. 67 The devout.. Simeon..saw perchance before him no more than two unnoted worshippers. **1883** MYERS *Ess., Mod., Mazzini* (1885) 69 It has run its fair course unnoted, and in silence passed away.

† un'noteful, *a. Obs.* [UN-¹ 7.] Unprofitable; useless.

a **1300** *E.E. Psalter* lii. 4 Alle helded þai, sammen ai Vn-noteful maked ere þai. *a* **1395** HYLTON *Scala Perf.* II. xxxvii. (W. de W. 1494), All men are before oure lorde as noughte, & as vnnotefull and nought they are acounted to hym.

un'noteworthy, *a.* (UN-¹ 7.)

1881 SAINTSBURY *Dryden* ii. 24 It is not unnoteworthy that Lady Elizabeth was five and twenty.

un'noticeable, *a.* (UN-¹ 7 b.)

1775 ADAIR *Amer. Ind.* 287 They were afraid of being imprisoned,..even for things unnoticeable in the eye of the law. **1810** WORDSW. *Prose Wks.* (1876) II. 304 A light vapour unnoticeable but by a shepherd. **1859** GEO. ELIOT *A. Bede* x, A long-neglected and unnoticeable rent in the.. bed-curtain.

Hence **un'noticeableness; un'noticeably** *adv.*

1872 GEO. ELIOT *Middlem.* IV. VIII. lxxx. 285 She would make as quietly and unnoticeably as possible her second attempt to see and save Rosamond. **1883** *Harper's Mag.* Sept. 566/1 Unnoticeableness..is..the character..of the dwellings. **1885** 'E. GARRETT' *At Any Cost* xv, One seal was broken! So cleanly, too, that she almost thought it might be mended unnoticeably.

un'noticed, *ppl. a.* (UN-¹ 8.)

In common use from *c* 1750.

1720 PR. JAMES in *10th Rep. Hist. MSS. Comm.* App. I. 91 To repose yourselves for some time somwhere in France where your usuall prudence will make you unnoticed. **1762** STERNE *Tr. Shandy* VI. v, There are a thousand unnoticed openings,..which [etc.]. **1819** SCOTT *Leg. Montrose* xix, The strife..had been unnoticed by the stragglers around. **1891** FARRAR *Darkn. & Dawn* xxx, It was that little unnoticed impulse of natural kindness..which saved her fortunes.

absol. **1841** CARLYLE *Heroes* ii. (1904) 77 See, the unnoticed becomes world-notable, the small has grown world-great.

un'noticing, *ppl. a.* (UN-¹ 5 d, 10.)

(*a*) **1782** ELIZ. BLOWER *Geo. Bateman* II. 42 Unnoticing the looks of surprize. **1796** MME. D'ARBLAY *Camilla* III. 78 She was thus employed, unnoticing the passage of time, when Mrs. Arlbery tapped at her door. **1904** SLADEN *Lovers Japan* II. ix, They rode..through the delicious avenues of Shiba, unnoticing the temples.

(*b*) **1821** SCOTT *Pirate* i, He..lived as one of the family, unnoticed and unnoticing. *a* **1873** LYTTON *Parisians* X. ii, Lemercier stopped a gentleman who was about to pass him unnoticing.

un'notified, *ppl. a.* (UN-¹ 8.)

[**1775** ASH.] **1802-12** BENTHAM *Ration. Judic. Evid.* (1827) II. 508 The keeping of the rule of action..in one immense and unorganic mass, undistributed, and consequently unnotified. **1871** *Standard* 27 Jan., It would be hypocrisy.. to gloss over this odious outrage of the un-notified bombardment of Paris.

un'notify, *v.* (UN-² 3.)

1757 H. WALPOLE *Let. to Mann* 3 July, I notified to you the settlement of the ministry, and, contrary to late custom, have not to unnotify it again.

un'noting, *ppl. a.* (UN-¹ 10.)

1868 MORRIS *Earthly Par.* I. I. 405 Her dizzied eyes.. wandered from unnoting face to face.

un'nourishable, *a.* (UN-¹ 7 b.)

1607 TOPSELL *Four-f. Beasts* 719 Their flesh is not good for meate, but is bitter and vnnourishable.

un'nourished, *ppl. a.* (UN-¹ 8.)

a **1617** DANIEL *To Sir T. Egerton* 96 Having not this skill how to contend, Th' unnourish'd strife would quickly make an end. **1896** *N. Amer. Rev.* CLXIII. 715 As only the unnourished tree can battle.

un'nourishing, *ppl. a.* (UN-¹ 10.)

1605 CHAPMAN *All Fools* I. i. 185 A gentlewoman: But her unnurishing dowry must be tolde Out of her beauty. **1640** BP. REYNOLDS *Passions* xx, The minde being mollified and puffed up with windie and unnourishing comfort. **1826** LAMB *Elia* II. *Pop. Fallacies* xii, The aliment of this poor babe was thin, unnourishing. **1860** PUSEY *Min. Proph.* 216 Which..sold to the poor only what, although unnourishing, was wholesome!

un'nourishment. (UN-¹ 12.)

1662 J. CHANDLER *Van Helmont's Oriat.* 24 A sickness, which the Rabbins call Binsica: which properly, is an unnourishment, or pining away of the Organ of the phantasie.

† un'noyand, -ing, *ppl. a. Obs.*⁻¹ [UN-¹ 10.] Not causing offence or annoyance; harmless. Also **† un'noyandness.** *Obs.*

a **1340** HAMPOLE *Psalter* vii. 5 Deme me lord..eftere myn vnnoyandnes abouen me. *Ibid.* xl. 13 Me sothly for vn-noyandnes thou vptoke. *a* **1400** *Relig. Pieces fr. Thornton MS.* 61 The noyeand [creatures] þou made vs for to chasty, The vnnoyeand to sustayne vs and fede. *c* **1475** *Cath. Angl.* (MS. A) 256/1 Vn Noying, *jnnocens* [etc.].

† un'noyed, *ppl. a. Obs.*⁻¹ [UN-¹ 8.] Not disturbed.

a **1470** HARDING *Chem.* LXXXVII. xii, The Christen faith in thy lande [is] distroyed, That with the peace shuld haue be kept vnnoyed.

† un'noyous, *a. Obs.*⁻⁰ [UN-¹ 7.] = UNNOYAND *ppl. a.*

1483 *Cath. Angl.* 256/1 Vn Noyovs, *jnnocens*...*innocuus.*

un'numberable, *a.* [UN-¹ 7 b, 5 b.] Incapable of being numbered; innumerable.

a **1340** HAMPOLE *Psalter* xxxviii. 6 How fa my dayes ere here, and how vnnoumberabil in heuen. **1382** WYCLIF *Exod.* x. 14 A brennynge wynd reride vp locustes, the whiche.. seeten in alle the coostis of Egipciens vnnoumbrable. *c* **1440** *Gesta Rom.* lvii. 241 (Harl. MS.), Thorow this pryde bethe vnnumberable peple infecte and dede. **1513** DOUGLAS *Æneid* VI. xi. 53 The flude Lethe..About the quhilk peple vn-nomerable..fleis fast. **1756** MRS. CALDERWOOD in *Coltness Collect.* (Maitl. Cl.) 144 The unnumberable wind-milns through Holland. **1774** tr. *Helvetius' Child of Nature* I. 53 Unnumberable are the unfortunate he has relieved. **1852** BAILEY *Festus* (ed. 5) 173 With starry globes unnumberable, suns, Planets and moons.

un'numbered, *ppl. a.* [UN-¹ 8, 5 b.]

1. Not numbered or reckoned up; uncounted.

c **1375** *Sc. Leg. Saints* xli. (*Agnes*) 224 þe gret Ioy in hewine þat he saw, þat vnnovmerit mycht be. **1434** MISYN *Mending of Life* 126 God truly is infinit of gretnes,..of swetnes vn-nowmbyrde. **1480** CAXTON *Chron. Eng.* ccxxxii. 249 Ther were take many knyȝtes and squyers and other men that were vnnombred. **1601** SHAKS. *Jul. C.* III. i. 63 The Skies are painted with vnnumbred sparkes. **1656** COWLEY *Davideis* I. 749 Of Numbers too th' unnumbred wealth he showes. **1725** POPE *Odyss.* II. 212 Unnumber'd Birds glide thro' the aërial way. **1746** HERVEY *Medit., Refl. on Flower-Garden* 4 Prodigious Theatre!.. Where..Worlds un-numbered roll at large! **1844** KINGLAKE *Eothen* xi, The fleas of all nations were there:—Asiatic hordes unnumbered. **1891** FARRAR *Darkn. & Dawn* lvi, To represent these un-numbered agonies as a festival of expiation.

2. Not included in an enumeration; not marked or provided with a number.

a **1533** LD. BERNERS *Gold. Bk. M. Aurel.* (1546) H vij b, The .ix. Epiphanes of the Egiptiens was vnnoumbred and putte downe. **1654** LD. HATTON in *Nicholas Papers* (Camden) II. 147, I have receaved yours (unnumbred) of the 8th of Dec. *a* **1667** [see UNMETHODIZED 1]. **1816** WILSON *City of Plague* II. iii. 94 He for his lust, Unnumber'd lies.

† un'numerable, *a. Obs.* [UN-¹ 7 b, 5 b.] Innumerable.

c **1400** *Brut* 316 Men founden vnnumerable multitudes of hem [*sc.* sparrows] dede in feldes. *c* **1440** *Alph. Tales* 485 He was deseyvid be a fend þat promysid hym to gyff hym..ane vnnumerable porcion of gude. **1536** in *Songs, Carols,* etc. (E.E.T.S.) 162 At þe Towr..þer was shott vnnumerable many gonnes. **1567** GOLDING *Ovid's Met.* VIII. (1593) 186 So winding waies Unnumerable Dædalus within his worke convays. **1611** COTGR., *Innombrable*, innumerable, vnnumerable.

Hence **† un'numerableness.** Also **† un'numerably** *adv.*

1565 COOPER *Thesaurus, Innumerabilitas*, *vnnumerable-nesse: passyng all number. *c* **1440** *Promp. Parv.* 366/1 *On-numerably, *innumerabiliter.* **1611** COTGR., *Innumerablement*, innumerably, vnnumerably.

un'nun, *v.* (UN-² 6 b.)

1611 FLORIO, *Smonacato*, vnmonked, vnnunned, hauing cast of the orders of religion. **1638** N. WHITING *Albino & Bellama* 4217 Albino..to the church did haste T' un-nun Bellama. **1639** FULLER *Holy War* V. vi. 238 Many did quickly unnunne and disfriar themselves.

un'nursed, *ppl. a.* (UN-¹ 8.)

[**1775** ASH.] **1875** RUSKIN *Fors Clav.* lv. 204 Sternly to forbid cat-nursing, till no child is left unnursed.

un'nurtured, *ppl. a.* (UN-¹ 8, 5 b.)

a **1548** HALL *Chron., Hen. V,* 42 b, The presumptuous saiynges..of the vnnurtered and vnmanerly byshop. **1567** GOLDING *Ovid's Met.* V. (1593) 126 These unnurtred damsels overcome began to fall a scolding. **1623** BINGHAM *Xenophon* 40 He esteemed him that was no circumventer, to be vn-nurtured and to want education. **1647** CLARENDON *Hist. Reb.* VII. §387 [To] impose upon Men unnurtur'd, and unacquainted with any Knowledge or Science. **1822** SCOTT *Peveril* xxvii, [I] never saw so unnurtured a cub. **1861** GEO. ELIOT *Silas M.* i, Pale-faced weavers, whose unnurtured souls have been..fluttering forsaken in the twilight.

† un'nut, un'net, *sb. Obs.* Also 1 unnyt (-nit). [OE. *unnyt* (cf. next and NUT *sb.*²), = WFris. *on-, ûnnut*, NFris. *unnatt* useless person, LG. *unnütte* useless thing, MDu. *onnut*, MHG. and G. (now chiefly dial.) *unnutz* damage, loss, harm, ON. *únytja* waste, Sw. *onytta*, Da. *unytte* uselessness.] That which is useless or worthless; idleness, vanity; wrong-doing.

c **888** K. ÆLFRED *Boeth.* xxxv. §1 Eall þæt yfel & þæt unnet þe he ær on his mode hæfde. *c* **965** *Canons Edgar* §28 We lærað þæt man æt ciric-wæccan..æniȝ unnit þar ne dreoȝe. *c* **1000** *Ags. Ps.* (Thorpe) xxx. 6 þu hatodest..þa þe unnyt worhton. *c* **1175** *Lamb. Hom.* 153 Swa deð þe douel ine þe monnes eȝen, if ho boð opene to bihalden idel and unnet. *a* **1225** *Ancr. R.* 352 He isihð & ihereð oðerhwule unnut. *c* **1230** *Hali Meid.* 17 ȝif ȝe þrafter þenne speken togedere folliche, & talkeð of unnet.

† un'nut, un'net, *a. Obs.* Forms: α. 1-2 unnyt, 2-3 unnut. β. 1-4 unnet. γ. 3 unnitt. [OE. *unnyt* (f. *un-* UN-¹ 7 + *nyt* NUT *a.*), = OFris. *un-, onnet*, WFris. *on-, ûnnut, ûnnutte*, NFris. *unnatt*, MDu. *onnutte, onnut* (Du. *onnut*), MLG. *unnutte*, LG. *unnüt*, OHG. *unnuzzi, -nuzze* (MHG. *unnütze, -nutze*, G. *-nütz*), Goth. *unnuts.*] Useless, worthless, unprofitable, vain.

α. *Beowulf* 413 Secgað sæliðend, þæt þes sele stande..idel & unnyt. *c* **1000** *Ags. Gosp.* xxv. 30 Wurpað þone unnyttan þeowan on þa uttran þystru. *c* **1200** *Trin. Coll. Hom.* 129 Al þat folc þat þurh unnutte speche..turneð fro gode. *c* **1250** *Prayer Our Lady* 3 in *O.E. Misc.* 192 Vnnut lif to longe ich lede.

β. *a* **1000** *Boeth. Metr.* x. 17 Is ðæt unnet ȝelp. *a* **1200** *Moral Ode* 5 Vnnet lif ich habbe iled. *a* **1225** *Ancr. R.* 82 Idel is & unnet al þet god ne cumeð of. *c* **1330** *Arth. & Merl.* 1254 (Kölbing), þis men hadde wonder gret, Him to sle, it were vnnet.

γ. *c* **1200** ORMIN 4921 Icc amm an allforrwurrþenn þeoww & all unnitt & idel. *Ibid.* 15127 Acc þatt wass all..Unnitt & idell dede.

unnu'tritious, *a.* (UN-¹ 7, 5 b.)

1846 WORCESTER (citing *Ed. Rev.*). **1855** SINGLETON *Virgil* I. 342 An unnutritious food, Berries and stony cornels, boughs purvey. **1861** H. MACMILLAN *Footn. Page Nat.* 100 Miserable and un-nutritious diet.

un'nutritive, *a.* (UN-¹ 7, 5 b.)

[**1775** ASH.] **1829** CARLYLE *Misc.* (1840) II. 50 Germans, who..have in fact nothing else to live on but that highly unnutritive victual.

un'oath, *v.* (UN-² 3.)

1675 W. PENN *England's Pres. Interest* d 2 b, Q. Elizabeth ..calls back Protestancy, ordains a new Oath, to un-Oath Q. Marys Oath.

† uno'bedience. *Obs.* [UN-¹ 12, 5 b.] Disobedience.

c **1380** WYCLIF *Sel. Wks.* II. 357 þat were fendis obedience, and unobedience to God. *c* **1440** *Jacob's Well* 71 þe thrydde cornere of pride..is vnbuxumnes, vnobedyens. *Ibid.* 72. *a* **1470** H. PARKER *Dives & Pauper* (W. de W. 1496) x. vi. 247/2 They felle in open unobedyence.

uno'bedient, *ppl. a.* (UN-¹ 7, 5 b.)

1382 WYCLIF *Titus* i. 10 Ther ben manye vnobedient, and veyn spekeris. *a* **1425** tr. *Arderne's Treat. Fistula*, etc. 15 þe pacient is waike of herte or vnobedient for to persew his cure. *c* **1440** *Jacob's Well* 71 Who-so were vnobedyent to his fadyr & modyr. *Ibid.*, It is perylous to be vnobedyent to þi souerayn. **1509** BARCLAY *Shyp of Folys* (1570) 56 O man presumpteous and vnobedient. **1571** GOLDING *Calvin on Ps.* To Rdr. 7 If they had not bin vtterlye vnobedient too all good counsel. **1614** W. B. *Philosopher's Banquet* (ed. 2) 81 The Wall-nut is vnobedient to Digestion, and much hinders egestion. **1641** MILTON *Reform.* II. 50 Pepin, not unobedient to the Popes call,..frees him out of danger. **1801** SOUTHEY *Thalaba* VIII. x, But unobedient to that well-known voice, His eye was seeking it.

† uno'beisance. *Obs. rare.* [UN-¹ 12, 5 b.] Disobedience.

1382 WYCLIF *Esther* xvi. 24 And so be he don awei, that ..[he] be in to euer mor, for exsaumple of dispising and vnobeisaunce. *c* **1420** *Wycliffite Bible* Pref. Ep. (1850) I. 63/2 Redy to vndurȝoke al vnbuxumnesse [*v.r.* vn-obeisaunce].

† uno'beisant, *a. Obs.* [UN-¹ 7, 5 b.] Disobedient.

1382 WYCLIF *Prov.* xxix. 21 Who delicatli fro childhed nurshith his seruaunt, afterward shal feelen hym vnobeisaunt. *c* **1400** tr. *Secreta Secret., Gov. Lordsh.* 115 He þat hauys greet eghen ys enuyous.., sleuthful, and vnobeyssant.

† uno'beishing, *ppl. a. Obs.* [UN-¹ 10.] Disobedient.

1382 WYCLIF *1 Kings* xiii. 26 He..was vn-obeshynge to the mouth of God.

† uno'bey, *v. Obs.*⁻¹ [UN-¹ 14.] *intr.* To be disobedient.

c **1445** PECOCK *Donet* 208 O lord,..how myȝt I be so boolde, so vnkinde,..forto vnobeie to þee?

uno'beyed, *ppl. a.* (UN-¹ 8.)

1595 DANIEL *Civ. Wars* II. liii, Poorely prouided, poorely followed, Vncourted, vnrespected, vnobayd. **1667** MILTON *P.L.* v. 667 He resolv'd..[to] leave Unworshipt, unobey'd the Throne supream. **1772** *Ann. Reg., Hist. Eur.* 61/2 The standing order..had not only been unobeyed, but.. outrageously insulted.

uno'beying, *ppl. a.* (UN-¹ 10.)

1796 COLERIDGE *Destiny of Nations* 66 The Laplander beholds the far-off Sun Dart his slant beam on unobeying snows.

unob'jected, *ppl. a.* (UN-¹ 8.)

17.. ATTERBURY (J.), What will he leave un-objected to Luther, when he makes it his crime that he defied the devil? **1823** SCOTT *Quentin D.* xxxv, [They] heard from the mouth of Charles of Burgundy, unobjected to by that of Louis, .. that [etc.].

unob'jectible, *a.* [UN-[1] 7.] = next.
1748 RICHARDSON *Clarissa* III. 13 Nor will I ask for your favour, but as upon full proof I shall appear to deserve it: Fortune, alliances unobjectible!

unob'jectionable, *a.* (UN-[1] 7b.)
In common use from *c* 1800.
1793 A. GEDDES *Addr. to Public* 3 A New Translation, that should be unobjectionable to my brethren of the R. Catholic communion. **1794** PALEY *Evid.* III. vi. ¶5 There are few cases in which .. we cannot suppose something more perfect, and more unobjectionable, than what we see. **1819** G. S. FABER *Dispensations* (1823) II. 152 A safe and unobjectionable medium through which to prove the divine legation of Moses. **1882** MISS BRADDON *Mt. Royal* II. iv. 66 His conduct was unobjectionable.
Hence **unob'jectionableness**; **unob'jectionably** *adv.*
1828–32 WEBSTER s.v., Unobjectionably. *a* **1849** POE *E. B. Browning* Wks. 1865 III. 411 The former poem is purely imaginative; the latter is unobjectionably because unobtrusively suggestive of a moral. **1878** W. WALKER *Life Bp. Gleig* vii. 299 The Canonical unobjectionableness of the Bishop-elect.

unob'jective, *a.* (UN-[1] 7.)
1855 MILMAN *Lat. Chr.* XIV. x. VI. 613 Allegory in itself is far too unobjective for art.

uno'bligatory, *a.* (UN-[1] 7.)
1802–12 BENTHAM *Ration. Judic. Evid.* (1827) IV. 539 In causes non-criminal, obligatory at one stage, unobligatory at another. **1851** W. R. GREG *Creed Christendom* xiv. 208 If investigation shows the miracles of the Bible to be .. unobligatory upon our belief.

uno'bliged, *ppl. a.* [UN-[1] 8.]
1. Of persons: Not bound or constrained to do something.
1648 HEXHAM II, *Ongehouden*, Vnbound, Vnobliged. **1658** EARL MONM. tr. *Paruta's Wars Cyprus* 163 Unobliged thereunto, he had readily assisted, the first year of this war. **1682** SCARLETT *Exchanges* 154 A prudent .. Drawer will judge himself unobliged to make any Bills, but such as make the Value to be received of the Remitter.
2. Not made obligatory or necessary.
1855 FABER *Growth in Holiness* v. 79 Look at the phenomena of the Incarnation, what were they? Helplessness, unnecessary and unobliged suffering.

uno'bliging, *ppl. a.* (UN-[1] 10.)
[**1847** WEBSTER.] **1891** H. HERMAN *His Angel* 16 An uncivil, unobliging, ugly young brute.

uno'bligingness. [UN-[1] 12.] †Absence of obligatoriness.
1646 HAMMOND *Tracts* 63 You see the unobligingnesse of that interdict.

uno'bliterable, *a.* (UN-[1] 7b.)
1662 J. CHANDLER *Van Helmont's Oriat.* 263 The unobliterable or undefaceable substance of the soul.

uno'bliteratable, *a.* (UN-[1] 7b.)
1865 W. H. GILLESPIE *Argt. Being & Attrib. God* (1906) 253 The relation which does exist, and the existence of which is unobliteratable.

uno'bliterated, *ppl. a.* (UN-[1] 8.)
1644 [H. PARKER] *Jus Populi* 43 Whilst [in the times of Adam] the neare relation of blood was fresh, and unobliterated. **1680** H. DODWELL *Two Lett.* (1691) 68 Those unobliterated impressions of Conscience and Modesty. **1738** G. LILLO *Marina* III. ii, Some traces there .., yet unobliterated, Of my long dead .. Pericles. **1835** LYTTON *Rienzi* x. viii, There was a red stain upon the pavement, unobliterated. **1894** *Daily News* 10 Mar. 3/4 The letter-carrier would either appropriate the stamp .. or he would deliver it unobliterated.

unob'noxious, *a.* [UN-[1] 7, 5b.]
1. Not exposed or liable *to* something. Also *ellipt.*
?**1609** DONNE *Elegy on Lady Marckham* 35 For, graves our trophies are, and both deaths dust. So, unobnoxious now, she hath buried both. **1667** MILTON *P.L.* VI. 404 In fight they stood Unwearied, unobnoxious to be pain'd By wound. **1704** NORRIS *Ideal World* II. iii. 125 But neither the matter, nor yet the form of this division, .. are un-obnoxious to just exception. **1809–14** WORDSW. *Excurs.* v. 868 Some, apart, In quarters unobnoxious to such chance. **1862** F. HALL *Hindu Philos. Syst.* 50 The soul is immutable, and unobnoxious to error.
2. Not objectionable or offensive.
1678 *Lively Oracles* vii. §9 (1684) 308 Surely the meanest unobnoxious laic .. might .. be trusted with the reading of those sacred books. **1802** H. MARTIN *Helen of Glenross* I. 201 Mr. Mulgrave, unobnoxious to any party, was advised to remain. **1858** *Times* 3 Dec. 8/6 The Roman Catholic priests are lowly, zealous men... We want the same class of men for our unobnoxious Christianity [in China].

unob'scured, *ppl. a.* (UN-[1] 8.)
1646 J. HALL *To Stanley* 4 But thou At first appearance dost display A bright and unobscured day. **1667** MILTON *P.L.* II. 265 How oft amidst Thick clouds and dark doth Heav'ns all-ruling Sire Choose to reside, his Glory unobscur'd. **1748** THOMSON *Cast. Indol.* II. lviii, O who can speak the vigorous joys of health! Unclogged the body, unobscured the mind. **1764** *Phil. Trans.* LIV. 146 The unobscured part of the Sun. **1849** HERSCHEL *Outlines of Astronomy* x. 332 The cone of the shadow .. permits their occultations to be completely observed both at ingress and egress, unobscured. **1879** *St. George's Hosp. Rep.* IX. 180 Gradual and progressive cough, unobscured by other symptoms.

unob'sequious, *a.* (UN-[1] 7.)
[**1775** ASH.] **1810** BENTHAM *Packing* (1821) 203 Unobsequious Jurors dropped: or, in the .. familiar phrase, cut.

unob'sequiousness. (UN-[1] 12, 5b.)
1661 BOYLE *Style of Script.* 169 Their Succeeders .. are afterwards bold to mis-name all Unobsequiousnesse to their Incogitancy, Presumption. **1810** BENTHAM *Packing* x. §1 Unobsequiousness found unavoidable by a veteran Advocate.

unob'servable, *a.* [UN-[1] 7b, 5b.]
1. Incapable of being observed; imperceptible, unnoticeable.
1651 HOBBES *Leviath.* II. xxix. 169 Which accidents .. are not supernaturall, but onely .. unobservable. **1664** BOYLE *Exp. touching Colours* 114 Little and Singly Unobservable Images of the Lucid Body. *a* **1715** SOUTH *Serm.* IV. 163 Such small, such contemptible, and almost unobservable Hints have sometimes unraveled .. the deepest-laid Villanies. **1895** BARING-GOULD *Noémi* xiii, He had to beware of putting his hand on fire that was unobservable by daylight.
†2. Undeserving of notice or remark. *Obs.*
1665 J. WEBB *Stone-Heng* (1725) 16 It is not unobservable, that these Stones seem to have been .. more entire, than when Mr. Jones made his Survey. **1675** M. CLIFFORD *Hum. Reason* 40 It is not unobservable, that the Unity of the Church of God is compared [etc.].
3. *sb. pl.* Things which cannot be observed.
1944 *Mind* LIII. 227 It is not at all certain that there are not highly respected scientific hypotheses which allege the existence of unobservables. **1980** *Times Lit. Suppl.* 17 Oct. 1181/2 The logical positivists held that for a sentence to be meaningful it must be capable of experiential verification. In consequence they had a central problem with discourse about unobservables... Their standard line of solution was some kind of definitional reduction of unobservables to observables.
Hence ˌ**unobserva'bility**.
1944 *Mind* LIII. 224 The positivist principle .. does not tell us anything at all about the observability or unobservability of the facts stated in P. **1979** *Amer. Pol. Sci. Rev.* Mar. 164/2 Unobservability is one reason .. for the relative unfamiliarity of political things.

unob'servance. (UN-[1] 12, 5b.)
1654 WHITLOCK *Zootomia* 419 The two first require the more serious inquiry into, for the universality of their Power (and yet generall unobservance of it). **1681** J. KETTLEWELL *Meas. Chr. Obed.* II. iv. 166 The Law .. against irreverence, against unobservance, against disobedience. **1788** D. GILSON *Serm. Pract. Subj.* xiii. 381 We are awakened .. to lament our own unobservance and ingratitude. **1844** SOUTHEY *Life A. Bell* I. 182 The various instances of neglect .. on the part of the schoolmaster and ushers, and their unobservance of those rules [etc.]. **1893** F. F. MOORE *Gray Eye or So* I. 180 Nodding himself into a condition of unobservance.

unob'servant, *a.* [UN-[1] 7, 5b.]
†1. Unattentive in service. *Obs.*[−0]
1611 COTGR., *Inofficieux*, vnofficious, vnobseruant, vnseruiceable.
2. Not observant; not taking notice.
1661 GLANVILL *Van. Dogm.* xxiv. 247 The unobservant Multitude may have some general confus'd apprehensions of [etc.]. **1775** ASH, *Disobedient*, .. unobservant of lawful authority. **1782** V. KNOX *Ess.* xc. (1819) II. 173 An unexperienced and unobservant man. **1816** SOUTHEY *Poet's Pilgr.* I. 34 No unobservant travellers they, but well Of what they there had learnt they knew to tell. **1825** SCOTT *Talism.* iv, [This] fear .. made her behave with indifference, as if unobservant of his presence. **1888** F. HUME *Mme. Midas* I. v, Vandeloup looked idly at all this beauty with an unobservant eye.
absol. **1898** 'MERRIMAN' *Roden's Corner* iv, The unobservant may pass it by without distinguishing it.
Hence **unob'servantly** *adv.*
[**1847** WEBSTER.] **1868** MRS. WHITNEY *P. Strong* xvii, I have not read the new style of novel and magazine writing unobservantly.

unob'served, *ppl. a.* [UN-[1] 8.] Not observed; unperceived, unnoticed.
1612 COTTA (*title*), The Unobserved Dangers .. of ignorant and unconsiderate Practisers of Physicke in Englande. **1624** MASSINGER *Renegado* v. ii, You shall find, If any look of mine be unobserved, I am not ignorant of a mistress' power. **1673** TEMPLE *Obs. United Prov.* Wks. 1720 I. 46 Most National Customs are the Effect of some unseen, or unobserved natural Causes, or Necessities. **1741** CHESTERF. *Let.* 25 July, This quick and unobserved observation is of infinite advantage in life. **1796** MME. D'ARBLAY *Camilla* III. 322 This was not unobserved by Edgar. **1836** MARRYAT *Midsh. Easy* xxxix, Finding themselves unobserved, .. they dropped gently alongside one of the double-masted latteen vessels. **1864** BOWEN *Logic* x. 343 By detecting hitherto unobserved similarities and conjunctions in time.
b. In complementary (quasi-adverbial) const.: Without being observed.
a **1616** BEAUM. & FL. *Cust. Country* II. i, He had liv'd unobserv'd By any man of mark. **1671** MILTON *P.R.* IV. 638 Hee unobserv'd Home to his Mothers house private return'd. **1709** STEELE *Tatler* No. 57 Many .. live in the constant Practice of baser Methods unobserved. **1796** MME. D'ARBLAY *Camilla* V. 4 He was now waiting but to speak to her unobserved. **1827** FARADAY *Chem. Manip.* xiii. 285 The crucible furnace .. where the heat is not so liable to rise unobserved as in a close furnace. **1891** MARIE A. BROWN tr. *Runeberg's Nadeschda* 35 The gentle maiden had .. stolen unobserved among the group.

unob'servedly, *adv.* (UN-[1] 11; cf. prec.)
1656 EARL ORRERY *Parthen.* III. I. 12 Nicomedes the more unobservedly to gaze on his new Conqueror, had retir'd himself into the throng. **1702** BP. PATRICK *Comm. Judg.* xvi. 1 He went thither secretly and unobservedly, in the dusk of the evening. **1795** *Phil. Trans.* LXXXV. 174 A single instrument, having an excess of light, in which the irradiation may unobservedly extend further than in weaker telescopes. **1861** WRIGHT *Ess. Archæol.* vii. 107 Great numbers of .. tumuli have been destroyed unobservedly in the various processes of agriculture. **1884** *Manch. Exam.* 20 Aug. 5/1 A train came upon him unobservedly, and the poor fellow was literally cut to pieces.

unob'server. (UN-[1] 12.)
1713 *Guardian* No. 60, How unheeded must the general character of it be, when given by one of these serene unobservers.

unob'serving, *ppl. a.* (UN-[1] 10.)
1690 T. BURNET *Theory Earth* II. 41 Those [prophecies] that concern the end of the world are of this latter sort to unobserving men. **1749** FIELDING *Tom Jones* VIII. xii, There are people who find an inconvenience in this unobserving temper of mankind. **1792** CHARLOTTE SMITH *Desmond* I. 142 An unobserving or disinterested spectator of what was passing. **1815** *Zeluca* III. 106 Wholly unobserving of the earnest conversation of her companions. **1818** SCOTT *Br. Lamm.* xxxii, To an eye so unobserving as that of Bucklaw.

un'obstinate, *a.* (UN-[1] 7, 5b.)
1656 [? J. SERGEANT] tr. *T. White's Peripat. Inst.* Auth. Design a 7, This the Order, and Brevity, and the invincible firmnesse, surely of some Consequences will obtain of an unobstinate person. **1665** J. SERGEANT *Sure Footing* 40 As is easy to be evinc't against an unobstinate Adversary. *a* **1859** DE QUINCEY *Posth. Wks.* (1891) I. 63 They were a plastic, yielding, unobstinate race.

unob'struct, *v.* (UN-[2] 3.)
1659 W. CHAMBERLAYNE *Pharonnida* III. v. 339 Which carelesse pride did unobstruct the way, Through which to liberty love's progress lay.

unob'structed, *ppl. a.* (UN-[1] 8.)
1659 W. CHAMBERLAYNE *Pharonnida* III. iv. 361 Anger, like unobstructed love, breaks forth In flaming haste. *Ibid.* III. v. 516. *a* **1711** KEN *Hymnarium* Poet. Wks. 1721 II. 137 From thence o'er the celestial Vast, Eyes unobstructed cast. **1748** MELMOTH *Fitzosborne Lett.* lxi. (1749) II. 117 Much caution is necessary to give a fine taste its full and unobstructed effect. **1808** MRS. C. KEMBLE *Day after Wedding* 6 You hope to glide along the stream of life, unobstructed by the shoals of misfortune. **1859** PARKINSON *Optics* (1866) 245 The eye having an unobstructed view through the hole.
Hence **unob'structedly** *adv.*
[**1847** WEBSTER.] **1867** H. MACMILLAN in *Macm. Mag.* No. 99. 259/2 The sun to shine down unobstructedly. **1897** *Outing* XXX. 139/2 A huge triangle that led unobstructedly into the wide mouth of this baggy apex.

unob'structive, *a.* (UN-[1] 7.)
1712 BLACKMORE *Creation* II. 307 Why should he halt at either station? why Not forward run in unobstructive sky? **1855** *Poultry Chron.* III. 442/2 The unobstructive nature of the coops to the opportunity of inspection by spectators.

unob'tainable, *a.* (UN-[1] 7b, 5b.)
[**1775** ASH.] **1860** FROUDE *Hist. Eng.* V. 129 Her own consent would have been unobtainable. **1876** 'OUIDA' *Winter City* vii, Seeking some unobtainable enamel. **1930** [see NUMBER *sb.* 4f]. **1961** E. WAUGH *Unconditional Surrender* II. iv. 96 When they tried to ring him up they were told the number was 'unobtainable'. **1968** P. GEDDES *High Game* v. 58 He .. retreated to telephone... A misconnection to Guildford, two unobtainable signals and nine minutes later he had finally made it. **1976** 'K. ROYCE' *Bastillo* vi. 82 He .. rang Todashi... He got the unobtainable tone.

unob'tained, *ppl. a.* (UN-[1] 8.)
1594 HOOKER *Eccl. Pol.* I. xi. §3 As the will doth now worke vpon that obiect by desire, which is as it were a motion towards the end as yet vnobtayned. **1742** YOUNG *Nt. Th.* II. 503 Wisdom, .. What is she, but the means of happiness? That unobtain'd, than folly more a fool.

unob'trusive, *a.* (UN-[1] 7, 5b.)
In common use from *c* 1800.
1743 YOUNG *Nt. Th.* IV. 625 Ye Quietists, .. who mildly make An unobtrusive tender of your hearts. **1790** HAN. MORE *Relig. Fash. World* (1791) 131 Those secret habits of self-controul, those interior and unobtrusive virtues. **1828** MACKINTOSH *Char. Canning* Wks. 1846 II. 457 His manner was simple and unobtrusive; his language always quite familiar. **1840** DICKENS *Old C. Shop* xiv, I trace the same current now, flowing through all his quiet and unobtrusive proceedings. **1890** 'L. FALCONER' *Mlle. Ixe* vi, Captain Leslie kept unobtrusive, but attentive watch.
Hence **unob'trusiveness.**
1797 JANE AUSTEN *Sense & Sens.* xlvi, She saw only an emotion .. in its unobtrusiveness entitled to praise. **1826** DISRAELI *V. Grey* III. viii, He is an object of observation from his very unobtrusiveness. **1879** *Cassell's Techn. Educ.* II. 152/2 All walls, however decorated, .. must retire even behind the furniture by their unobtrusiveness.

unob'trusively, *adv.* (UN-[1] 11, 5b.)
1796 MME. D'ARBLAY *Camilla* I. 358 The most unobtrusively gay .. of almost any young creature I ever beheld. **1852** W. COLLINS *Basil* II. i, He was dressed as unobtrusively as possible, entirely in black. **1884** C. T. SAUNDERS in *Law Times* 25 Oct. 412/2 The abolition of primogeniture was .. unobtrusively proposed.

un'obvious, *a.* (UN-[1] 7.)
Frequently used by Boyle and Jer. Bentham.
1643 PRYNNE *Popish R. Favourite* 36 Some more speciall passages in Popish writers, .. which because then unobvious and unknown to most, I had an intention to have published. **1661** BOYLE *Style of Script.* 45 Though some unobvious Stars of that bright sphære cannot be discerned without the help of a Telescope. **1676** GLANVILL *Ess.* iii. 44 The knowledge and application of some unobvious and unheeded Properties and Laws of natural things. **1718** *Freethinker* (1733) No. 155. 240 It is able to perceive the

unobvious Distinctions between things, which bear a very near Resemblance to one another. **1798** T. GREEN *Diary Lover of Lit.* (1810) 109 Its efficient cause, therefore, must not be sought..in any unobvious qualities. **1845** MILL *Ess.* II. 183 To trace back this philanthropic movement..to its small and unobvious beginnings. **1890** *Spectator* 25 Oct., Mr. Orger's amendment..would appear to be as unobvious ..as need be.

uno'ccasional, *a.* (UN-^{1} 7.)
1724 WELTON *Chr. Faith & Pract.* 232 Scripture, the only rule to guide and direct a true unoccasional conscience by.

uno'ccasioned, *ppl. a.* (UN-^{1} 8.)
1586 *Cyuile & Vncyuile Life* (1868) 80 You might haue gathered, that vnoccasioned, or not contryued, no man will resort vnto your Town house. **1747** WARBURTON *Shakespeare's Wks.* VIII. 360 *note,* This observation seems strangely abrupt and unoccasioned.

un'occupancy. (UN-^{1} 12.)
1833 T. HOOK *Parson's Dau.* I. i, The tear-like drippings from its various windows..during the several years of its unoccupancy.

un'occupied, *ppl. a.* [UN-^{1} 8.]
1. Not occupied or engaged in some work or pursuit; idle.
c **1380** WYCLIF *Wks.* (1880) 191 First men ordeyned..to putte awey ydelnesse & to be not vnoccupied in goode manere for þe tyme. *c* **1440** *Jacob's Well* 231 þou þat syttest stylle here in cherch, vnocupyed & thynkest on þi muk. *c* **1490** CAXTON *Rule St. Benet* 132 Lete theym be assigned to other occupacyons to doo, so that they be neuer vnoccupied in vertu. *c* **1529** CAPON in Ellis *Orig. Lett.* Ser. I. I. 190 So that your workemen shall not be un occupyed for wante of stone. **1555** EDEN *Decades* (Arb.) 137 A valiente mynde can not rest in one place or bee vnoccupyed. **1573** TUSSER *Husb.* (1878) 118 Prouide of thine owne to haue all things at hand, least worke and the workman vnoccupide stand. **1647** HEXHAM I, Vnoccupied, or doing nothing, *onbesich.* **1751** JOHNSON *Rambler* No. 141 ¶2 Acting when his imagination was unoccupied, and his judgment unsettled. **1780** BURKE *Œcon. Reform* Wks. III. 324 The council, or committees of council, were never a moment unoccupied, with affairs of trade. **1827** LYTTON *Falkland* 22, I am unoccupied by a single pursuit. **1898** 'MERRIMAN' *Roden's Corner* xvii, She led a blameless, unoccupied, and apparently purposeless life.
2. Not put to use; left unemployed. (In later use only of time.)
1448–9 METHAM *Amoryus & Cl.* 2210 Tyme on-ocupyid, qwan folk haue lytyl to do. **1486** *Bk. St. Albans* B vj, Tho saame lewnes þou shalt fastyn slackely as a bowstryng vnocupyede. **1523** [COVERDALE] *Old God* (1534) Bj, The sword..beynge through dust & longe beynge unoccupied, ..defiled with ruste. **1561** T. HOBY tr. *Castiglione's Courtyer* IV. (1577) Tv, They..fell into decay and loste theyr puissaunce and brightnesse, lyke yron vnoccupied. **1796** MME. D'ARBLAY *Camilla* V. 354 Her time..hung not upon her unoccupied. **1829** SCOTT *Anne of G.* xxv, As if desirous that the hour should arrive which would put an end to a day unoccupied.
3. Of ground, etc.: Not occupied by inhabitants or indwellers; not put to use in this way; not frequented or filled up; empty.
c **1425** WYNTOUN *Cron.* IV. xix. 1780 Thare wes vnoccupiit ..A land beȝond ane arme of the se. **1560** BIBLE *Judges* v. 6 The hye wayes were vnoccupied, and the trauelers walked through bywayes. **1573** TUSSER *Husb.* (1878) 15 No dwellers, what profiteth house for to stand? What goodnes, vnoccupied, bringeth the land? **1691** RAY *Creation* I. (1692) 189 Doubtless, if we shall discover further to the very North-pole, we shall find all that Tract not to be vain, useless, or unoccupied. **1784** COWPER *Task* v. 557 The word That, finding an interminable space Unoccupied, has fill'd the void so well. **1807** *Europ. Mag.* LII. 111/1 This part of Lancashire is..highly cultivated, not an inch of ground lies waste and unoccupied. **1884** in A. Cawston *Street Improv. London* (1893) 115 There are always a very large number of unoccupied houses even in towns where the building trade is very active.
b. Not taken up or appropriated.
1701 GREW *Cosmol.* II. iii. 43 The Phancy hath full Power to create them in the Sensories themselves, then unoccupy'd by External Impressions. **1830** MISS MITFORD *Village* Ser. IV. 107 She could not have chosen an occupation more completely unoccupied, or more loudly called for. **1832** *Westm. Rev.* Oct. 353 Cadences..highly favourable for leaving the ear unoccupied for any measure which may follow.
c. *spec.* Designating that part of France not held under German military occupation during the war of 1939–45. Cf. OCCUPIED *ppl. a.*
1940 *New Statesman* 19 Oct. 380 A Jewish friend (who recently returned from unoccupied France to his home in Paris) told me that he liked the English immensely. **1942** MRS. BELLOC LOWNDES *Let.* 3 July (1971) 230, I hear dreadful accounts of France—all old people and delicate people, are dying—especially..in the unoccupied districts. **1978** A. PRICE *'44 Vintage* xviii. 210 A chateau south of the Loire..in the Vichy zone of unoccupied France.

u'nocular (juːn-), *a.* [f. L. *ūnocul-us* one-eyed + -AR. Cf. UNIOCULAR *a.*] One-eyed.
1864 DE MORGAN in Graves *Life Sir W. Hamilton* (1889) III. 613 Accordingly I have always been strictly unocular.

unode ('juːn-). *Geom.* A uniplanar node.
1869 CAYLEY *Math. Papers* (1893) VI. 362 If there is a unode, then this may be and is taken to be at *D*, and its uniplane may be taken to be $X = 0$. *Ibid.*, There is never, besides the unode, any other node.

†**un'odorable,** *a.* [UN-^{1} 7 b.] Incapable of being smelled.
1674 GREW *Disc. Mixture* iii. §17 As in any fixed unodorable or untastable Body.

†**uno'fearned,** *ppl. a. Obs.* [UN-^{1} 8 + OF-EARN *v.*] Undeserved.
c **1200** *Vices & Virtues* 3 Asolkenesse..me haueð ofte idon eten oðermannes sare swink all un-of-earned. *Ibid.* 51, 59.

uno'ffendable, *a.* (UN-^{1} 7 b.)
1839 LADY LYTTON *Cheveley* (ed. 2) II. i. 12 The most obsequious civility and unoffendable good-humour.

uno'ffended, *ppl. a.* (UN-^{1} 8.)
1481 *Cov. Leet Bk.* 494 That, his highnes vnoffended, we here..may procede amonges our-self to the determinacion therin. **1598** FLORIO, *Inoffeso,* vnoffended, vntoucht, vnwrongd. **1633** BP. HALL *Occas. Medit.* lii. 124 The Bee stings..when she is provoked; these draw blood, unoffended, and sting for their owne pleasure. **1673** [R. LEIGH] *Transp. Reh.* 84 Reverence..might perhaps occasion more sport then a man..could brook unoffended. **1749** JOHNSON *Irene* v. ii, This gen'ral calm Is sure the smile of unoffended heav'n. **1782** V. KNOX *Ess.* c. (1819) II. 218 It is the common people,..unoffended and unoffending, who chiefly suffer in the evil consequences. **1809** MALKIN *Gil Blas* VII. v. ¶4 They, with unoffended nostrils, were engaged in general conversation, though they dined individually.
Hence **uno'ffendedly** *adv.*
1856 RUSKIN *Mod. Paint.* IV. v. xx. §28 They were both of them..to behold unoffendedly all that was upon the earth.

uno'ffending, *ppl. a.* (UN-^{1} 10, 5 b.)
1569 *Reg. Privy Council Scot.* I. 668, I..sall keip gude rewle and quietnes unoffending aganis the lawis or makand troubill. *a* **1600** *Grim the Collier of Croydon* (1662) 9 Some will count it Vertue in a woman Still to be bound to unoffending Silence. *a* **1625** BEAUM. & FL. *Laws of Candy* II. i, My prayers pull daily blessings on thy head, My unoffending child. **1703** POPE *Statius' Thebais* I. 771 Yet why must unoffending Argos feel The vengeance due to this unlucky steel? **1796** MME. D'ARBLAY *Camilla* III. 403 How should I rejoice..to rescue this one poor unoffending.. animal from such tyranny! **1828** SCOTT *F.M. Perth* xix, Who ..could have thought of harming a creature so simple, and so unoffending? **1876** BANCROFT *Hist. U.S.* II. xxx. 253 The councillors were famed for their unoffending respectability.

†**uno'ffensed,** *ppl. a. Obs.*$^{-1}$ [UN-^{1} 8.] Unoffended.
c **1440** *Pallad. on Husb.* I. 32 The contrey men colourid wel vchoone, Their wittis cleer and vnoffensid sight.

†**uno'ffensive,** *a. Obs.* (UN-^{1} 7, 5 b.)
1612 R. DABORNE *Christian turn'd Turke* 214 [Nature] sent him to the world, All vnoffensiue, vnarm'd. **1642** VICARS *God in Mount* 66 Coming onely in a fair and unoffensive manner. **1674** J. FELL *Hammond* Wks. I. 14 Notwithstanding his unoffensive and cautious return to those ill laid demands. **1768** *Woman of Honor* II. 158 That modest unoffensive turn you gave to your non-acceptance.
So **uno'ffensively** *adv.*
1606 BP. W. BARLOW *Serm.* 21 Sept., Ep. Ded. A j b, Discussing the point sincerely and, I trust, vnoffensiuely.

un'offered, *ppl. a.* (UN-^{1} 8, 8 c.)
1526 *Pilgr. Perf.* (W. de W. 1531) 103 Leuynge in hym nothynge vnoffred for vs, but in all partes he suffered payne for our synne. *a* **1586** SIDNEY *Arcadia* III. xxiii, I know too well their cunning (who leave no mony unoffered that may buy mine honour). **1642** CHAS. I *Declar. Intentions Brainford* 7 Unfought with, and unoffered at,..to march away. **1658** *Whole Duty of Man* iii. §18 Though the gift be already at the Altar, it must rather be left there unoffered, than [etc.]. **1736** WEBSTED *Wks.* (1787) 477 To the end they might do so, no methods were left untried, no motives unoffered. **1747** P. FRANCIS tr. *Horace, Ep.* I. xiii. 4 If he ask'd to read th' unoffer'd Lay. **1848** BUCKLEY *Iliad* 5 Neither on account of a vow unperformed, nor of a hecatomb unoffered.

un'officed, *ppl. a.* (UN-^{1} 8 or UN-^{2} 8.)
1657 BP. H. KING *Elegy* Poems (1664) 3 The now unoffic'd Servants crack their Staves.

un'officered, *ppl. a.* (UN-^{1} 8.)
1655 EARL ORRERY *Parthen.* I. VIII. 450 This treachery.. brought a world of confusion in those vn-officer'd Troopes. **1754** P. H. *Hiberniad* iii. 25 Raw, unofficer'd..Militias. **1782** PENNANT *Journ. Chest. to London* 50 A..band of mountaineers, undisciplined, unofficered, and half-armed. **1852** GROTE *Greece* II. lxx. IX. 115 The unofficered Grecian army.

un'officerlike, *a.* (UN-^{1} 7 c.)
1803 NELSON in Nicolas *Disp.* (1845) V. 206 Such conduct is highly reprehensible and unofficerlike. **1831** TRELAWNY *Adv. Younger Son* vii, It's unofficer-like to get drunk before sunset. **1871** *Routledge's Ev. Boy's Ann.* Nov. 695 The unofficer-like want of method in these signals.

uno'fficial, *a.* and *sb.* [UN-^{1} 7, 5 b, 12.]
1. Of things: Not having an official character or stamp.
unofficial strike: one not endorsed by the relevant union.
1798 *Monthly Rev.* XXVI. 511 Impertinent and unofficial as it seems, it may have been intended to intimate [etc.]. **1866** GEO. ELIOT *F. Holt* Introd. 3 His sheep-dog following with a heedless unofficial air as of a beadle in undress. **1884** HUXLEY in *Life* (1900) II. 80, I wrote to Evans an unofficial letter. **1946** 'G. ORWELL' in *Partisan Rev.* Summer 321 There is resentment against long hours and bad working conditions, which has shown itself in a series of 'unofficial' strikes. **1955** *Times* 24 June 4/3 The Minister of Labour could not deal with unofficial strikes in the normal way. That was a matter for the union concerned to re-establish its authority over its own members. **1972** *Guardian* 24 Nov. 10/1 Lower-paid hospital workers are resorting to a series of unofficial strikes.
2. a. Of persons: Not holding an official position; not acting in an official capacity; spec. *unofficial member* = *private member* s.v. PRIVATE *a.* 2 c.
1829 GEN. P. THOMPSON *Exerc.* (1842) I. 124 Unofficial philosophers must be content to classify appearances as they rise. **1869** J. MARTINEAU *Ess.* II. 97 The theories of these unofficial masters of philosophy. **1879** *Tablet* 31 May 709/1 An unofficial member. **1893** ERSKINE MAY *Law of Parl.* (ed. 10) viii. 245 The relative precedence of government business, and business in charge of unofficial members,..is prescribed by the standing orders. **1970** A. P. HERBERT *In Dark* iii. 74 There spoke, besides two long-suffering Ministers, 14 private (or 'unofficial') members—12 against and 2 in favour.
b. *sb.* One who is not an official.
1887 *Pall Mall G.* 29 July 4/1 We have a letter this morning from St. Petersburg, the writer of which is a leader among the 'unofficials'.

uno'fficially, *adv.* (UN-^{1} 11; cf. prec.)
1830 COBBETT *Hist. Geo. IV*, iii. §139 He did it unofficially, in letters to Lord Grey. **1860** FROUDE *Hist. Eng.* VI. 275 The two Houses of Parliament were invited to be present unofficially at Whitehall.

uno'fficious, *a.* (UN-^{1} 7, 5 b.)
1611 FLORIO, *Inficioso,* vnofficious, negligent. **1645** MILTON *Tetrach.* 81 Thus all occasions..are not unofficious to administer somthing which may conduce to explain..the assertion of this book. **1807** *Ann. Rev.* V. 171 The editor.. deserves public thanks for the unostentatious, unofficious propriety, with which his laudable task is performed.
Hence **uno'fficiousness.**
1611 COTGR., *Inofficiosité,* vnofficiousnesse, vnrespectiuenesse, or want of due respect.

†**unof'served,** *ppl. a. Obs.* [UN-^{1} 8.] = UNDESERVED *ppl. a.* I.
a **1200** *St. Marher.* 16 Hwet so ich am, þurh godes grace ich hit do ant am wilȝeoue unofservet. *a* **1240** *Lofsong* in *O.E. Hom.* I. 215 Deorwurðe drihten, þu..dest us al þet þu dest þurh þine swete grace al unofserued. **1297** R. GLOUC. (Rolls) 1256 Mi mede þer of is þat he me wole driue of is lond vnofserued iwis.

un'oft, *adv.* (UN-^{1} 11 b; cf. next.)
1864 SIR J. K. JAMES *Tasso* x. xx, Since not Unoft it happens that the wise and strong Carve for themselves the best and happiest lot.

un'often, *adv.* [UN-^{1} 11 b.] Infrequently; seldom. (Only with negatives.)
1741 HARRIS *Three Treat.* II. (1765) 194 The Man of Gallantry not unoften has been found to think after the same manner. **1835** LYTTON *Rienzi* I. iii, Nor was it unoften that the mere presence of a noble sufficed to scatter whole crowds. **1864** J. BROWN *Jeems* 15 You get more patient,.. and not unoften you come to a stand-still.

un'oil, *v.* (UN-^{2} 3.)
1693 *Dryden's Juvenal* viii. (1697) 205 A tight Maid, e're he for Wine can ask, Guesses his Meaning, and unoils the Flask.

un'oiled, *ppl. a.* (UN-^{1} 8.)
1728 YOUNG *Love Fame* VI. 138 His wounded ears complaints eternal fill, As unoil'd hinges, querelously shrill. *c* **1799** J. FOSTER in *Life & Corr.* (1846) I. 97 The creak of unoiled wheels. **1851** H. D. WOLFF *Pict. Span. Life* 134 The chain again clanks, unoiled hinges creak. **1884** MCLAREN *Spinning* (ed. 2) 70 Much dust can be shaken out of the wool when it is unoiled.

un'oily, *a.* (UN-^{1} 7.)
1674 GREW *Anat. Trunks* II. iv. §17 A third sort of Gum, is that which is Unoylie. **1682** —— *Disc. Mixture* App. §1 Oyls..easily mingleable with any unoyly Liquor.

un'old, *a.* (UN-^{1} 7.)
c **1440** *Pallad. on Husb.* IV. 9 The trunkes sadde, in humor that abounde, Vnolde, vnrende.

un'old, *v.* (UN-^{2} 6 a.)
1608 SYLVESTER *Du Bartas* II. iv. *Schisme* 697 There ripes the rare cheer-cheek Myrobalan, Minde-gladding Fruit, that can un-old a Man.

un'ominously, *adv.* (UN-^{1} 11.)
1849 *Brand's Pop. Antiq.* I. 38 The sun would not shine unominously on the day on which the saint was burnt.

†**un'oning,** *vbl. sb. Obs.* [UN-^{2} 3, 8.] Disunion, discord.
1340 *Ayenb.* 65 þe uerste is strif, þe oþer chidinge,..þe zixte þreapinge, þe zeuende vnonynge.

un'oped, *ppl. a. poet.* [UN-^{1} 8.] = UNOPENED *ppl. a.*
1815 SCOTT *Guy M.* xx, The close-press'd leaves unoped for many an age. [Cf. Crabbe *Library* 147.]

un'openable, *a.* (UN-^{1} 7 b.)
1832 MISS MITFORD *Village* Ser. v. 36 Trying to lift the lid of the unopenable chest.

un'opened, *ppl. a.* [UN-^{1} 8. Cf. Du. *ongeopened.*]
1. Not opened; left, or remaining, closed or shut: **a.** Of letters, books, etc.
1600 E. BLOUNT tr. *Conestaggio* 74 This Letter.. remained still with them vnopened. **1700** FARQUHAR *Constant Couple* I. i, Angelica, send it [*sc.* a letter] back unopened! say you? **1711** LADY M. W. MONTAGU *Let. to W. Montagu* 26 Feb., If you write, be not displeased if I send it back unopened. **1766** *Parlt. Deb.* (1813) XVI. 303 [They] went to statute books before unopened,.. and there made the amazing, astonishing discovery. **1836** H. COLERIDGE *Northern Worthies* (1852) I. 43 A sealed and unopened epistle. **1865** DICKENS *Mut. Fr.* I. iii, A book..unopened on

a shelf. **1888** JACOBI *Printer's Vocab.*, *Unopened edges*, applied to books the edges of which have not been opened.

b. In other applications.

1627 MAY *Lucan* III. D 7, Before the yet vnopen'd doore he stay'd. **1742** YOUNG *Nt. Th.* II. 468 Like bales unopen'd to the sun. **1796** WITHERING *Brit. Plants* (ed. 3) III. 689 Unopened flowers nodding. **1843** R. J. GRAVES *Syst. Clin. Med.* ix. 102, I have frequently directed the blister to be left unopened. **1884** in A. Cawston *Street Improv. London* (1893) 117 The consequences of leaving *culs de sac* even of a respectable kind unopened.

2. Not opened up for use.

1756 P. BROWNE *Jamaica* 13 Every settler inclined to reserve some unopened land. **1858** LD. ST. LEONARDS *Handy-bk. Prop. Law* xxiii. 179 If you were to sell part of your estate, reserving the unopened mines with a right of entry. **1890** HALLETT *1000 Miles on Elephant* 434 [To] throw open for British commerce the most magnificent, unopened, and available market in the world.

un'opening, *ppl. a.* (UN-^{1} 10.)

1732 POPE *Ep. Bathurst* 194 Benighted wanderers.. Curse the sav'd candle, and unop'ning door. **1852** M. ARNOLD *Empedocles* II. 359 Still Thought and Mind Will hurry us.. Over the unallied unopening Earth.

un'operable, *a.* (UN-^{1} 7 b, 5 b.)

1652 ASHMOLE *Theat. Chem.* Prol. 9 They wrought unoperable Workes.

un'operated, *ppl. a.* (UN-^{1} 8.) Not having been operated (on: *spec.* in *Med.*).

1802 *Noble Wanderers* I. 37 Native energy.. which, unoperated upon by adversity,.. remains an inactive principle in the mind. **1932** J. S. HUXLEY *Probl. Relative Growth* IV. iv. 126 The effect of regeneration on the normal growth of neighbouring unoperated structures. **1975** *Year Bk. Ear, Nose & Throat* 119 Increased uptake in the unoperated ear.

un'operating, *ppl. a.* (UN-^{1} 10.)

1719 WATERLAND *Vind. Christ's Div.* 158 The perfect Nativity.. of the Word: who had been, as it were, quiescent or un-operating from all Eternity, till [etc.]. **1768–74** TUCKER *Lt. Nat.* (1834) I. 507 Neither is it practicable.. for us to frame an idea of such unoperating nature.

†**un'operative**, *a. Obs.* (UN-^{1} 7, 5 b.)

1641 MILTON *Reform.* II. 48 For if the life of Christ be hid to this world, much more is his Scepter unoperative, but in spirituall things. **1685** SOUTH *Serm.* (1727) I. 389 It.. imports no more than an idle unoperative.. desire of the end, without any consideration of.. the means. **1756** BURKE *Subl. & B.* IV. xxiv, There lie the qualities of beauty either dead or unoperative. **1783** —— *Rep. Ind. Com.* Wks. II. 22 By which measure this provision of the Act has proved as unoperative as all the rest. **1818** BENTHAM *Ch. Eng.*, *Catech. Exam.* 248 Mere unoperative existence.

uno'perculate, *a.*, **-ated**, *ppl. a.* (UN-^{1} 7, 8, 5 b.)

1847 WEBSTER, *Unoperculated*, having no cover or operculum. **1884** *Imp. Dict.* IV. 510/2 *Unoperculate.*

uno'pinionated, *ppl. a.* (UN-^{1} 8.)

[**1775** ASH.] **1824** MEDWIN *Conversat. Ld. Byron* II. 140 No man was more unopinionated.

†**un'opportune**, *a. Obs.* (UN-^{1} 7, 5 b.)

1787 BENTHAM *Def. Usury* x. 99 The anti-jewish side of it found no unopportune support in a passage of Aristotle. **1802** MRS. J. WEST *Infidel Father* III. 235 Your excusing yourself from that unopportune engagement.

†**un'opportunely**, *adv. Obs.* (UN-^{1} 11, 5 b.)

1657 EARL MONM. tr. *Paruta's Pol. Disc.* 37 They sent their Fleet to regain Sicily; but the counsel was too late and unopportunely taken. **1766** COLMAN & GARRICK *Clandestine Marriage* II. 37, I have broke in upon you a little unopportunely, I believe.

uno'pposable, *a.* (UN-^{1} 7 b.)

1667 WATERHOUSE *Fire Lond.* 60 Illiterate men Apostoliz'd and made by him unopposable. **1802–12** BENTHAM *Ration. Judic. Evid.* (1827) IV. 151 The application is either opposable or unopposable.

uno'pposed, *ppl. a.* (UN-^{1} 8.)

1659 W. CHAMBERLAYNE *Pharon.* V. ii. 345 Impetuous rage, like whirlwinds unopposed. **1672** DRYDEN *Conq. Granada* IV. i, The people, like a headlong torrent goe;.. But, unoppos'd, they either loose their force, Or [etc.]. **1780** BURKE *Sp. at Bristol* Wks. III. 415 For what end was that bill to linger beyond the usual period of an unoppos'd measure? **1794** MRS. RADCLIFFE *Myst. Udolpho* xxxviii, His talents for play.. were generally successful when unopposed by the tricks of villany. **1841** ELPHINSTONE *Hist. India* I. 507 The Mahometans pursued their success unopposed. **1859** G. WILSON *Mem. E. Forbes* ii. 45 Thus, unopposed but unencouraged, he laboured at Natural History. **1899** MACKAIL *W. Morris* I. 336 An unopposed candidate. *ellipt.* **1893** *Daily News* 3 May 5/7 The Unopposed Committee of the House of Commons.

un'opposite, *a.* (UN-^{1} 7.)

1802–12 BENTHAM *Ration. Judic. Evid* (1827) I. 499 In point of affections, let the witness be, with reference to each party, altogether unopposite;.. equally a friend to both.

uno'ppressed, *ppl. a.* (UN-^{1} 8.)

a **1572** KNOX *Hist. Ref.* Wks. 1846 I. 357 As alsua the said town mycht.. brooke thair ancient lawis and liberteis unoppressed by men of wear. **1659** W. CHAMBERLAYNE *Pharon.* IV. ii. 445 Harmless nature, living unopprest With surfeits. *Ibid.* 453 Fair virgins.. unopprest By dark suspicion. **1709** *Brit. Apollo* II. No. 10. 3/2 Your.. Spirits, Unopprest, Glide freely on. **1781** COWPER *Table-T.* 272 The soul emancipated, 'unoppressed,.. Learns much.

uno'ppressive, *a.* (UN-^{1} 7, 5 b.)

1648 W. ASHHURST *Reasons agst. Agreement* 13 They are to have nothing but in an unoppressive way. **1782–3** W. F. MARTYN *Geog. Mag.* I. 355 [The Gentoo laws] are unoppressive. **1790** BURKE *Fr. Rev.* 53 You would have had an unoppressive but a productive revenue. **1874** RUSKIN *Fors Clav.* xl. IV. 78 What was an act of distressing servitude has become an unoppressive act of love.

uno'ppressively, *adv.* (UN-^{1} 11.)

1656 EARL ORRERY *Parthen.* III. III. 152 A negative obedience is the farthest it [*sc.* paternal right] can unoppressively extend it self.

un'opulence. (UN-^{1} 12.)

1796 *Monthly Mag.* II. 467 The unopulence of the pastor. **1830** BENTHAM *Offic. Apt. Maximized, Further Extr. Const. Code* 11 But the proposed system—does it not hold up to view unopulence as an efficient cause of aptitude?

un'opulent, *a.* (UN-^{1} 7, 5 b.)

a **1816** BENTHAM *Offic. Apt. Maximized, Introd. View* (1830) 11 Unopulent classes excluded, and thus injured. **1829** *Westm. Rev.* Oct. 472 The poor (i.e. the unopulent, not the absolutely poor).

unora'torial, *a.* (UN-^{1} 7.)

1753 N. TORRIANO *Gangr. Sore Throat* Pref., However un-oratorial my Expression.

†**unor'dain**, *a. Obs.*$^{-1}$ [f. UN-^{1} 7 + *ordeyne* ORDENE *a.*] Not observing order or rule. So †**unor'dainly** *adv. Obs.*$^{-1}$

a **1400** *Pauline Ep.* (Powell) Rom. i. 31 Þei [being].. vnwise, unordeyne [L. *incompositos*], withoute affeccioun. ? *a* **1400** *Spec. Vitæ* (MS. Bodl. 446) fol. 126 b, A man þat wedded es Shuld.. no dede vnordeynly wirke Agayne þe sacrament of holy kirke.

unor'dain, *v.* (UN-^{2} 3.)

c **1440** *Wycliffite Bible* (1850) IV. 438 Ne he vnordeynede vs of sum veyn speche feynynge, that vs ouerturne fro the sothfastnesse of the gospel. **1709** J. JOHNSON *Clergym. Vade M.* II. p. lxxi, Tho' Bishops ordain, they cannot unordain.

unor'dained, *ppl. a.* [UN-^{1} 8.]

†**1.** Not regulated or controlled. *Obs.*$^{-1}$

c **1340** HAMPOLE *Prose Tr.* 13 Þe delyte þat has noghte of vnordaynde styrrynge, and mekely has styrrynge in Criste.

2. Not ecclesiastically ordained.

1653 BAXTER *Chr. Concord* 84 They are bound to choose a man unordained to this work. *a* **1691** —— in Calamy *Life* vii. (1702) 131 There is a Duty in such a Case of Necessity, even on Persons unordain'd. **1804** *Ann. Rev.* II. 208 The distinction between ordained and unordained preachers. **1865** S. WILBERFORCE in R. G. Wilberforce *Life* (1882) III. 166 Brotherhoods of unordained men not in Holy Orders.

3. Not appointed or decreed.

1815 WORDSW. *Ode* 63 Be it not unordained that solemn rites.. Shall be performed at pregnant intervals.

unor'daining, *vbl. sb.* (UN-^{1} 13.)

In quot. rendering L. *inordinatio* disorder.

1382 WYCLIF *Wisd.* xiv. 26 The defouling of soules,.. the vnordeynyng of leccherie and of vnclennesse.

un'order, *v.* [UN-^{2} 3.] *trans.* To recall an order for (something); to countermand.

c **1440** *Alph. Tales* 402 He garte take Formosius oute off his grafe & vnordurd all þat he had giffen ordurs to. **1782** MISS BURNEY *Cecilia* VIII. iii, I think I must *un*order the tea.. if I am to be responsible for any mischief from your drinking it. **1803** NELSON in Nicolas *Disp.* (1845) V. 65 If Lord Keith or any other man is to have her, I must un-order all these things. **1843** F. E. PAGET *Pageant* 94 Mrs. Sawderley was not permitted to unorder her dress.

un'ordered, *ppl. a.*^{1} [UN-^{1} 8.]

†**1.** Not belonging to a religious order; not properly ordained. *Obs.*

c **1386** CHAUCER *Parson's T.* ¶ 85 Thow shalt considere.. whiether thou be.. wedded or sengle, ordered or unordred,.. clerk or seculeer. **1588** ALLEN *Admon.* 32 Creatinge.. new, hungrie, base, and vnordered Preistes. **1607** T. ROGERS *39 Art.* (1625) 200 They be vnordered Apostates, pretended, and sacrilegious ministers.

2. a. Not put in order; unarranged.

1477 NORTON *Ord. Alch.* (MS. Ashm. 1464) Proem, Of all the bookes vnordered of Alchimy The effectes be heere sett owt orderlie. **1504** ATKYNSON tr. *De Imitatione* III. xliii. 231 God.. that lefte nothynge vnordred in all the worlde. **1549** CHEKE *Hurt. Sedit.* (1569) G i b, What is vnordred plentie, but a wastfull spoyle? **1826** MRS. SHELLEY *Last Man* III. 200 The consequence of their journey in their present unordered and chiefless array. **1877** MORLEY *Crit. Misc.* Ser. II. 183 This was not a mere casual reflection.. taking a solitary.. position among those various and unordered ideas.

b. *Linguistics.* Of rules: not requiring to be applied in a particular order.

1968 *Language* XLIV. 696 Unordered disjunctive sets [of rules] are abbreviated by variables. **1970** *Canadian Jrnl. Linguistics* XV. 97 These rules are considered unordered; the initial numbers are inserted merely for reference. **1979** *Trans. Philol. Soc.* 106 The type of phonological theory which allows the maximum simultaneity of application of rules is the so-called 'unordered rule hypothesis'.

†**3.** Not observing due order; disorderly. *Obs.*

1572 ABP. PARKER *Corr.* (Parker Soc.) 403 [To] inquire of such unordered persons papistically set, not coming to prayers according to the laws. **1582** STANYHURST *Æneis* I. (Arb.) 22 Dare ye.. Too raise such raks iaks on seas, and danger vnorderd? **1611** A. STAFFORD *Niobe* 191 To satisfie the vnordred appetites of the body, and vnlawfull desires of the soule.

4. Not ordered or commanded.

1891 *Cent. Dict.* **1906** *Westm. Gaz.* 23 May 4/1 The gay tweeds.. remain unordered.

†**un'ordered**, *ppl. a.*^{2} *Obs.*$^{-1}$ [UN-^{2} 6 b.] Disordered.

1621 in Foster *Eng. Factories Ind.* I. (1906) 242 Their shipping rent, battered, and much unordered.

un'orderly, *a.* Now *rare.* [UN-^{1} 7, 5 b.]

1. Not in conformity with good order; irregular in respect of action or conduct.

1483 *Acta Dom. Audit.* 142*/2 The wrangwis and vnordourly leding of a processe apoune þe said land. **1561** T. NORTON *Calvin's Inst.* I. xi. 26 b, The fountaine of al this whole mischiefe is an vnorderly counterfaiting. **1587** HOLINSHED *Chron.* (ed. 2) III. 1254/1 Although it be somewhat.. vnorderlie to treat of vnorderlie officers vnder such an vnorderlie king as Richard the third was. **1601** J. WHEELER *Treat. Comm.* 107 The vnorderlie settinge foorth and publishing of the Emperors Mandate. **1642** *Coll. Rights & Priv. Parl.* 7 How unorderly were it for the satisfying of men, to runne into his displeasure. **1800** COLERIDGE *Piccolom.* IV. vii. 214 The Emperor perpetrated.. deeds most unorderly.

b. In stronger sense: Disorderly.

1583 GOLDING *Calvin on Deut.* clxxxv. 1147 Wee see why God hath pronounced that.. they be.. destitute of vnderstanding when their lyfe is loose and vnorderly. **1626** L. OWEN *Running Register* 16 The Englishmens dissolute liuing, and vnorderly behauiour in the said Seminarie. **1761** *Ann. Reg.*, *Chron.* 235/2 Small parties of the unorderly, undisciplined mob.

2. Not observing due order or arrangement; disordered, confused.

1578 THYNNE in *Animadv.* (1865) p. lix, To desplay my Inwarde mynde, whiche.. thus entreth into his vnorderly discourse. **1588** FRAUNCE *Lawiers Log.* I. ii. 7 b, Thereby to giue sentence of methodicall proceeding or vnorderly confusion. **1609** R. BARNERD *Faithf. Sheph.* 83 An vnorderly heaping vp of things together confounds memory. **1656** HOBBES *Liberty, Necess., & Chance* 143 After much unorderly discourse he comes in with This is the doctrine [etc.].

un'orderly, *adv.* [UN-^{1} 11.]

1. Not in good order; not according to a fixed order or arrangement; irregularly.

c **1470** HENRY *Wallace* x. 685 Wallace has seyn the Scottis wnordourly Folow the chas. **1547** RECORDE *Judic. Ur.* 9 Nothynge done unorderly cann be well understanded of the reders. **1578** BANISTER *Hist. Man* I. 7 These bones are perforated, here, and there, vnorderly, with a sort of smal holes. **1603** FLORIO *Montaigne* III. viii. 558 Shee seemeth faultie and vnprofitable, being ill placed and vnorderly disposed. **1637–50** ROW *Hist. Kirk* (Wodrow Soc.) 46 Whatever member of the Assemblie does speak unorderlie, and without leave asked.. of the Moderator.

2. Not in an orderly or well-regulated manner; irregularly, improperly.

1471 *Act. Audit.* (1839) 16/1 The lordis.. deliuers þat þe processis of þe breif of Richt.. is vnlachfully and vnorderly procedit. **1559** AYLMER *Harborowe* G 4 b, Paule mente to bridle them.. if they had prophecied vnorderly. **1596** *Southampton Court Leet Rec.* (1906) II. 315 So that such disobedient and lawlesse persons may not live so unorderly. **1610** DONNE *Pseudo-martyr* 387 They make Conuenticles against bishopps, and accuse them vnorderly, and against the forme of Canons. *a* **1653** BINNING *Usef. Case Consc.* (1693) 17 Paul would have as much distance kept with a brother walking unorderly, as a pagan.

†**un'ordinal**, *a. Obs.* [UN-^{1} 7.] Not reduced to order; unregulated.

c **1380** WYCLIF *Serm.* Sel. Wks. I. 2 Þat þere was a myche void place stablid betwene hem, derke and unordynel, þat lettid dampned men to come to hem. *Ibid.* III. 128 Riȝt as pride.. is unordynel wille of a monnis owene hyenesse, so envye.. is unordynel wille of mon to his neghtbore.

un'ordinarily, *adv.* (UN-^{1} 11; cf. next.)

1574 *Brieff Disc. Troub. Franckford* 79 For that we had proceaded vnordinarilie, that is.. contrary to the olde discipline.

un'ordinary, *a.* (UN-^{1} 7, 5 b.)

1547 EDW. VI *Jrnl.* in *Lit. Rem.* (Roxb.) II. 213 Order was taken for al his servauntes.. and the ordinary and unordinary were appointed. **1574** *Brieff Disc. Troub. Franckford* 79 They made cauillation at the manner off doinge off things as an vnordinary manner. **1610** HEALEY *St. Aug. Citie of God* 646 A proper phrase to the Greeke tongue, but vnordinary in the Latine. **1690** LOCKE *Hum. Und.* III. xi. §20, I do not know how they can be excused from Murther, who kill monstrous Births (as we call them) because of an unordinary shape. **1730** T. BOSTON *Mem.* App. 45 A man of unordinary application to business. **1909** A. BLACKWOOD *Jimbo* i, A supreme ignorance of unordinary children.

†**un'ordinate**, *a. Obs.* [UN-^{1} 7, 5 b.] = INORDINATE *a.* (in various senses).

c **1375** in *Rel. Ant.* I. 39 Unordynate love of worldly things. **1398** TREVISA *Barth. De P.R.* v. xxiii. (Bodl. MS.), An vnordinat voice and horrible þat gladeþ not noþer comforteþ. *c* **1425** *St. Mary of Oignies* I. vi. in *Anglia* VIII. 139/10 Ydel worde or vnordynat lokynge or vnhonest hauynge of body. *c* **1491** *Chast. Goddes Chyld.* 22 This feuer tercian comyth somtyme of an unordynate hete. **1561** T. HOBY tr. *Castiglione's Courtyer* II. (1577) I viij, Our Courtier ought not to professe to be a glutton nor a dronkerd, nor riotous & vnordinate in any yll condition. **1591** HARINGTON *Orl. Fur.* VIII. Notes 63 The vncomely and carelesse actes that dishonest or vnordinat loue do prouoke euen the noblest vnto. **1610** S. RID *Martin Mark-all* H 1, A iust punishment for their presumptuous and vnordinate proceedings.

†**un'ordinately**, *adv. Obs.* (UN-^{1} 11, 5 b.)

c **1380** WYCLIF *Sel. Wks.* III. 38 Ech body forȝetiþ him while þer þouȝt is bounden to love ony creature unordynatli. *c* **1425** *St. Mary of Oignies* I. v. in *Anglia* VIII. 138/16 Pronounsynge many wordes vnordynatly. *c* **1440** *Jacob's Well* 161 Whanne a man delyth wyth his wyif vnordynatly &

vnkyndely. **1545** RAYNALD *Byrth Mankynde* 137 The sowar maye vnordinatly strewe.. the seade on the earth. **1550** T. HOBY *Trav.* (1902) 57 Yf a mann drink unordinatlie of yt, yt makethe him dronke.

un'ordnanced, *ppl. a.* (UN-¹ 8.)
1804 LARWOOD *No Gun Boats* 12 Better to give all than suffer their Gun Boats to remain in even an unruddered, unmasted, unordonanced existence.

un'organed, *ppl. a.* [UN-² 4, 8 + ORGAN *sb.*¹ 5.] Organically dissolved.
1624 QUARLES *Job* xix. 51 But man (vnorgan'd by the hand of Death) Dyes not, is but transplanted from beneath, Into a fairer soyle.

unor'ganic, *a.* (UN-¹ 7 and 5 b.)
[**1775** ASH.] **1802–12** BENTHAM *Ration. Judic. Evid.* (1827) II. 508 The keeping of the rule of action.. in one immense and unorganic mass.

un'organizable, *a.* (UN-¹ 7 b, 5 b.)
1868 R. H. QUICK *Ess. Educ. Reform.* viii. 222 To cram the mind with isolated, or as Mr. Spencer calls them, unorganizable facts. **1902** *Encycl. Brit.* (ed. 10) XXXI. 515/2 The floor is covered by dead or dying unorganizable materials, without any layer of regenerative cells.

un'organized, *ppl. a.* [UN-¹ 8, 5 b.]
1. Not brought into an organic state.
1690 LOCKE *Hum. Und.* II. xxx. §5 An uniform, unorganized body, consisting.. all of similar parts. **1746** BERKELEY in Fraser *Life* (1871) viii. 316 To me it seems that stones are vegetables unorganized. **1794** R. J. SULIVAN *View Nat.* I. 467 If we find causes of uncertainty in regard to organized beings, how many more must we find in regard to unorganized beings. **1829** T. CASTLE *Introd. Bot.* 225 That the epidermis is a fine, transparent, unorganized pellicle. **1899** *Allbutt's Syst. Med.* VI. 189 Ordinary unorganised or partly organised polypoid thrombi.
2. Not formed into an orderly or regulated whole.
1836 H. COLERIDGE *North. Worthies* (1852) I. 16 Confiding in the unorganised valour of the English nation.. he.. opposed a standing army. **1860** FROUDE *Hist. Eng.* V. 213 The sustained fire.. threw their dense and unorganized masses into rapid confusion.
Hence **un'organizedness.**
1664 H. MORE *Apology* 486 Which makes me.. seem to allow of the Unorganizedness of the Æthereal Vehicle of the Soul.

unori'ental, *a.* (UN-¹ 7.)
1820 BYRON *Juan* III. xxviii, A most unoriental roar of laughter. **1862** THORNBURY *Turner* I. 194 The Jerusalem is very unoriental.

uno'riginal, *a.* and *sb.* [UN-¹ 7, 12.]
1. Having no origin; uncreated.
1667 MILTON *P.L.* x. 477 Plung'd in the womb Of unoriginal Night and Chaos wilde.
2. a. Not original; derivative; second-hand.
1774 GERARD *Ess. Genius* 42 Nothing appears in it uncommon or new; every thing is trite and unoriginal. **1802–12** BENTHAM *Ration. Judic. Evid.* (1827) I. 57 The evidence may be termed unoriginal in so far as the narrating witness.. speaks of some other person and not of himself. *a* **1849** POE *Diddling* Wks. 1865 IV. 269 He would return a purse.. upon discovering that he had obtained it by an unoriginal diddle. **1897** W. P. KER *Epic & Rom.* 329 The 'Song of Roland' is comparatively late and unoriginal.
b. *sb.* One who lacks originality.
1847 MEDWIN *Life Shelley* II. 203 A cold, selfish, mathematical unoriginal, like Hobbes.
Hence **uno'riginally** *adv.*
1934 in WEBSTER. **1963** V. NABOKOV *Gift* v. 297 'And so I'll never see him again,' he told himself, unoriginally. **1964** *Archivum Linguisticum* XVI. 15 Several handbooks discuss our problem either too cursorily or too unoriginally to invite analysis.

unorigi'nality. (UN-¹ 12.)
1798 LAMB *Let.* in *Final Mem.* iv. 32, I love to anticipate charges of unoriginality. **1802–12** BENTHAM *Ration. Judic. Evid.* (1827) III. 434 The quality of unoriginality seems applicable to an article of evidence in either of two cases. *a* **1849** POE *Longf.*, etc., Wks. 1865 III. 360 Of the unoriginality of the thesis we have already spoken.

uno'riginate, *a.* and *sb.* [UN-¹ 7, 12, 5 b.]
= next.
1719 J. JACKSON *Let. to Auth. True Doctr. Trinity* 216 Self-existent being the same as unoriginate, is (you think) merely a Negative Character. **1755** AMORY *Mem.* (1769) 183 One spirit possessed of all possible perfections, self-existent, unoriginate, the first cause of the universe. **1855** PUSEY *Doctr. Real Presence* 236 For God is unoriginate, and not generate. **1872** LIDDON *Elem. Relig.* ii. 53 A supreme all-producing Cause, Itself uncaused, unoriginate.
b. As *sb.* An unoriginated being.
1724 WATERLAND *Athan. Creed* 145 That.. neither the Son nor Holy Ghost have any share in these Titles or Characters, to make Three Unoriginates. **1875** *Encycl. Brit.* II. 537/2 Arius denied of Christ that He was.. part of the Unoriginate.
Hence **uno'riginately** *adv.*, **-ness.**
1720 WATERLAND *Eight Serm.* Pref., It is only saying that he is so emphatically, or unoriginately. **1723** —— *Second Vind.* 125 It was to admit of a higher and a lower Sense of the Word God; the higher supposed to have nothing above the other but Self-existence, or Unoriginateness.

uno'riginated, *ppl. a.* (UN-¹ 8.)
1696 PAYNE *Let. to Bp. of R——* 15 The Father is the only self-existent, unoriginated Being. **1712** S. CLARKE *Script. Doct. Holy Trinity* II. 243 The Father (or First Person) Alone is Self-existent, Underived, Unoriginated, Independent. **1797** *Encycl. Brit.* (ed. 3) X. 730 Any two unoriginated powers acting upon one another at right angles. **1838** MRS. BROWNING *Measure* i, God, the Creator, with a pulseless hand Of unoriginated power, hath weighed The dust of earth. **1867** H. MACMILLAN *Bible Teach.* i. (1870) 16 The force of gravitation, which is not a mere mechanical agency, unoriginated and uncontrolled.
Hence **uno'riginatedness.**
1862 F. HALL *Hindu Philos. Syst.* 160 The unoriginatedness of souls.

unorigi'nation. (UN-¹ 12.)
1755 AMORY *Mem.* (1769) I. 50 [To] worship three distinct conscious beings, of coordinate powers, equal independency and unorigination.

uno'riginative, *a.* (UN-¹ 7.)
1874 SAYCE *Compar. Philol.* iii. 114 Unlike the Aryans they [*sc.* the Etruscans] were unoriginative and receptive.

† un'orn, *a. Obs.* [OE. *unorne*, f. *un-* UN-¹ 7 + *orne* unusual, excessive (?).]
1. Of persons: Plain (in manners or appearance); humble, simple; mean, wretched.
c **1000** *Battle of Maldon* 256 Dunnere þa cwæð,.. unorne ceorl ofer eall clypode. *c* **1200** ORMIN 4884 Forr Godess Sune.. Warrþ an unnorne & wrecche mann. *a* **1225** *Ancr. R.* 424 Ancre þet naueð nout neih hond hire uode, beoð bisie two wummen,.. and þeo beo ful unorne, oðer of feir elde. *a* **1250** *Owl & Night.* 1492 If hire louerd is forwurþe & vnorne at bedde and at borde. *a* **1300** *K. Horn* 330 Ne spek ihc noȝt wiþ horn, Nis he noȝt so unorn; Horn is fairer þane beo he. *c* **1400** *Laud Troy Bk.* 7485 Episcropus that schrewe vnorne Might not his word performe. *a* **1470** H. PARKER *Dives & Pauper* (W. de W. 1496) IV. xxvii. 195/1 Suche ye shall be.., feble, unourne, & loth to the syght.
transf. *c* **1412** HOCCLEVE *De Reg. Princ.* 876 Now age vnourne a-wey putteþ fauour, þat floury youþe in his seson conquerde.
2. Of things: Poor or inferior in quality, amount, or appearance.
c **1175** *Lamb. Hom.* 85 Þenne he brohte hine uppen his werue, þet is unorne mare, þet bitacned ure unorne fleis. *c* **1200** ORMIN 828, I þe wesste þær he wass Hiss fode wass unnorne. *a* **1225** *Ancr. R.* 108 Uorto leren ancren þet heo ne gruchie neuermore uor none mete, ne uor none drunche, ne beo hit neuer so unorne. *a* **1250** *Owl & Night.* 317 Mi stefne is bold & nouht vnorne. **1398** TREVISA *Barth. De P.R.* v. xiii. (Tollem. MS.), Yf þe nose lakkeþ, all þe toþer del of þe face is þe more unhorne and unsemely.
Hence **† un'ornly** *adv. Obs.*
c **1200** ORMIN 3750 Þatt te birrþ aȝȝ.. lætenn swiþe unnorneliȝ & litell off þe sellfenn. *Ibid.* 4858. *c* **1300** *Havelok* 1941 Me wore leuere i wore lame, Þanne men dide him ani shame,.. or onne handes leyde, Vn-ornelike.

unorna'mental, *a.* (UN-¹ 7.)
1747 G. WEST *Resurrect.* 355 The simple, unaffected, unornamental and unostentatious Manner, in which they deliver Truths so important. **1829** COBBETT *Eng. Gard.* v. §198 Borage.. is by no means unornamental in a flower-garden. **1834** *Gentl. Mag.* CIV. I. 34 Two small arches of massy and unornamental stone-work.
Hence **unorna'mentally** *adv.*
1889 *Times* 27 Dec. 11 These cans.. are used ingeniously, if unornamentally, as building materials in the repair of roofs.

unorna'mented, *ppl. a.* (UN-¹ 8.)
1697 COLLIER *Ess. Mor. Subj.* I. (1703) 236 'Tis more reputable.. to prefer a homely, unornamented liberty to a splendid servitude. **1740** CIBBER *Apol.* xiv. 273 Nature, in her plain Dress, and unornamented. **1798** *Brit. Critic* XI. 31 A plain unornamented folio. **1831** JAMES *Phil. Augustus* III. iii, One of those plain and unornamented suits [of armour]. **1878** LECKY *Eng. in 18th C.* II. ix. 532 So in the pulpit they affect the most unornamented simplicity.

uno'rthodox, *a.* (UN-¹ 7, 5 b.)
1657 W. RAND tr. *Gassendi's Life Peiresc* I. 127 That he might not any longer persist in an un-orthodox Religion. *a* **1661** HOLYDAY *Juvenal* (1673) 24 There's a parity of reason for these unorthodox philosophers. **1737** *Gentl. Mag.* VII. 15/1 His Doctrine may seem Un-orthodox and Paradoxical to many. **1830** LYELL *Princ. Geol.* I. 48 Buffon was invited by the College.. to send in an explanation.. of his unorthodox opinions. **1863** MRS. WOOD *Verner's Pride* xlix, If he were a respectable ghost he'd confine himself to the churchyard, and not walk in unorthodox places. **1882** FARRAR *Early Chr.* II. 533 To throw any doubt upon it was to brave the charge of being arrogant or unorthodox.
Hence **un'orthodoxly** *adv.*
1934 WEBSTER, *Unorthodoxly*. **1969** *Daily Tel.* 25 Apr. 21/3 Everything seemed to be right, both in this unorthodoxly proportioned work itself and in the expounding of it. **1977** A. WILSON *Strange Ride R. Kipling* vi. 285 The loves in the village world.. are enjoyed precariously and unorthodoxly.

un'orthodoxy. (UN-¹ 12.)
a **1704** T. BROWN *Laconics* Wks. 1711 IV. 7 Calvin made Roast-meat of Servetus at Geneva, for his Unorthodoxy. **1860** FROUDE *Hist. Eng.* VI. 130 If they dreaded a Spanish sovereign, they hated unorthodoxy more. **1879** M. PATTISON *Milton* 118 Insinuations of unorthodoxy such as are ever rife in clerical controversy.

unortho'graphically, *adv.* (UN-¹ 11.)
1687 J. BARNES *Hist. Edw. III*, 568 Whose Names I had rather omit, than set them down, as I find them, unorthographically.

un'ossified, *ppl. a.* (UN-¹ 8.)
1726 MONRO *Anat.* 59 The Separation of the unossified Parts. **1778** *Encycl. Brit.* (ed. 2) I. 344/2 A portion of the cranium then [*sc.* in new-born infants] unossified. **1828** RYAN *Man. Midwifery* 12 Owing to its bones being separate and unossified. **1878** A. H. GREEN, etc. *Coal* iv. 122 The occipital condyles appear to have been similarly unossified.

uno'stensible, *a.* (UN-¹ 7, 5 b.)
[**1775** ASH.] **1851** MERIVALE *Rom. Emp.* xxv. III. 121 The real though unostensible leader of the republic.

unosten'tatious, *a.* (UN-¹ 7.)
1747 [see UNORNAMENTAL *a.*]. **1782** V. KNOX *Ess.* iii. (1819) I. 18 They induce idleness.. not to neglect the reality as attainable only by a painful and unostentatious application. **1825** SCOTT *Betrothed* xi, Hugo de Lacy was, on most occasions, plain and unostentatious. **1874** GREEN *Short Hist.* vii. §1 His personal habits were simple and unostentatious.
Hence **unosten'tatiousness.**
1846 WORCESTER (citing Allen). **1901** *Chambers's Jrnl.* Apr. 234/2 A pattern of unostentatiousness.

unosten'tatiously, *adv.* (UN-¹ 11; cf. prec.)
1795 V. KNOX *Chr. Phil.* §39 I. 281 He is silently and unostentatiously happy. **1844** H. H. WILSON *Brit. India* II. 228 The preparations were conducted as unostentatiously as possible. **1891** DRIVER *Introd. Lit. O.T.* 428 How a religious spirit may be carried unostentatiously into the conduct of daily life.

† unout'speakable, *a. Obs.* [UN-¹ 7 b.] Unutterable.
1535 COVERDALE *2 Cor.* ix. 15 Thanks be vnto God for his vnoutspeakeable gifte. *a* **1564** BECON *Policy War* Wks. 1564 I. 129 What was ye cause of that theyr greuous miserye and vnoutspeakable calamite?

† un'oven, *v. Obs.* (UN-² 5.)
1611 FLORIO, *Disfornáre*, to vnfurnace, to vnouen. **1653** URQUHART *Rabelais* I. xxii. 95 Gargantua.. played.. at unoven the iron.

unover'clouded, *ppl. a.* (UN-¹ 8.)
a **1658** LOVELACE *Lucasta Posth.* (1659) 71 I'm un-ore-clowded too! free from the mist!

unover'comable, *a.* (UN-¹ 7 b.)
c **1445** PECOCK *Donet* 160 Þat þe peple were.. so obstynat and so vnouercomable and vnaȝendressabli hardid. **1508** DUNBAR *Poems* vii. 44 Welcum thou campioun, in feght wnourcumable.

unover'come, *ppl. a.* (UN-¹ 8 b.)
OE. *unofercumen* occurs as a gloss on L. *indigestus*.
c **1375** *Sc. Leg. Saints* xxii. (*Laurence*) 374 Thane decius.. Þame commawndit.. to dyng hym fast; bot vnourcumyne he can ay last. **1382** WYCLIF *Judith* Prol., The vnouercomen of alle men she ouercam, and the vnouerpassable she ouerpassede. **1434** MISYN *Mending Life* 123 Truly þen is luf vnouercomyn qwhen with no nodyr desyr it may be ouercomyn. *c* **1520** BARCLAY *Jugurth* (1557) 33 b, Ye vnouercome of your ennemies, maisters, and emperours, ouer the most part of the worlde. **1579–80** NORTH *Plutarch* (1676) 507 Though now they lead me bound, yet do I remain free unovercome. *c* **1611** CHAPMAN *Iliad* XVI. 92 O would to Jove.. That not.. any one of all the Greeks.. might live unovercome.

unover'leaped, *ppl. a.* (UN-¹ 8.)
1849 M. ARNOLD *To Republican Friend, contn.* 7 This Earth, whereon we dream, Is.. o'ershadow'd by the high Uno'erleap'd Mountains of Necessity.

unover'passable, *a.* (See UNOVERCOME *ppl. a.*, quot. 1382.)

unover'taken, *ppl. a.* (UN-¹ 8 b.)
1629 T. ADAMS *Serm.* Wks. 984 The sunne is vpon his backe, behind him, and his shadow is still vn-ouertaken before him.

unover'thrown, *ppl. a.* (UN-¹ 8 b.)
1535 STEWART *Cron. Scot.* (Rolls) II. 394 Tha thocht aneuche for to defend thair awin Into sic thrang, and keip thame vnouirthrawin. *a* **1586** SIDNEY *Arcadia* III. xxii, Yet shewed it most the perfection of the beautie, which could remaine unoverthrowne by such enimies. **1621** G. SANDYS *Ovid's Met.* I. (1626) 8 What such a force, vn-ouerthrowne, oppos'd, The higher-swelling Water quite deuoures. **1852** CLOUGH *Poems*, etc. (1869) I. 348 In the prostration to ancient tenets and habits the old character remains upright, unoverthrown and unsubdued.

† unover'trowable: see OVERTROWABLE *a.*

un'owed, *ppl. a.* [UN-¹ 8.] † Unowned.
1595 SHAKS. *John* IV. iii. 147 And England now is left To tug and scamble, and to part by th' teeth The vn-owed interest of proud swelling State.

un'own, *v.* [UN-² 3.] *trans.* To disown.
a **1657** R. LOVEDAY *Let.* (1663) 12 What comes it [to] to lease my self away?.. Tis to unown my self, tis to disclaime My will, my head, my hands, all that I am.

un'owned, *ppl. a.* [UN-¹ 8.]
1. Not possessed as property; destitute of an owner or possessor.
1611 COTGR., *Vuayves*,.. things which bee left, abandoned, escheated, or vnowned. **1635** J. HAYWARD tr. *Biondi's Banish'd Virg.* 57 The Law declareth things unowned to be his that first comes to the enjoying of them. **1681** O. HEYWOOD *Diaries*, etc. (1881) II. 229 They would cry it at the crosse with some other unowned goods. **1829** SOUTHEY *Sir T. More* I. 94 Like the dogs at Lisbon and Constantinople, unowned, unbroken to any useful purpose. **1884** *Pall Mall G.* 12 Jan. 5/1 Unowned wires, he admitted, must be dealt with.
transf. **1634** MILTON *Comus* 407 Lest som ill greeting touch attempt the person Of our unowned sister [= 350 our lost sister].
2. Unacknowledged; unadmitted.
1715 GAY *Epist. to Earl of Burlington* 40 Here unown'd infants find their daily food; For should the maiden mother nurse her son, 'Twould spoil her match. **1748** RICHARDSON *Clarissa* (1811) II. xliv. 321, I know not my own heart, if I

have any of that latent or unowned inclination. **1793** W. Roberts *Looker-on* No. 48 (1794) II. 205 An action unowned by the delicacy of its real author. **1865** Miss Yonge *Dove in Eagle's Nest* vii, The poor little unowned bride had more to undergo than her imagination had conceived. **1897** Pullen-Burry *Blotted Out* 65 [Her] unowned child..had blossomed into one of the most famous actresses of the day.

un'oxidated, *ppl. a.* (UN-[1] 8.)
1805 R. W. Dickson *Pract. Agric.* I. 446 A portion of oil, or of the basis of it in an unoxydated state being diffused through their composition.

un'oxidized, *ppl. a.* (UN-[1] 8, 5 b.)
Also, in recent use (1894) ***unoxidizable***.
1827 *Edin Rev.* XLV. 300 Partial productions of these pure unoxydized bases. **1857** Miller *Elem. Chem., Org.* 22 The amount of unoxidized sulphur in an organic compound.

un'oxygenated, *ppl. a.* (UN-[1] 8.)
1790 R. Kerr tr. *Lavoisier's Elem. Chem.* II. 187 We cannot procure them in their unoxygenated state. **1798** Abernethy in *Phil. Trans.* LXXXVIII. 108 Neither could I..so accustom the animal to the circulation of unoxygenated blood, as to lengthen the term of its existence. **1875** tr. *Schmidt's Desc. & Darwinism* (ed. 2) 20 The unoxygenated constituents of the blood. **1886** Huxley in *Life* (1900) II. 148 The sort of uphill exercise which routs out all the un-oxygenated crannies of my organism.

un'pacable, *a.* (UN-[1] 7 b.)
1544 Bale *Chron. Sir J. Oldcastle* 15 b, The vnpacable furye of Antichrist thus kyndled agaynst him.

un'paced, *ppl. a.* (UN-[1] 8.)
[**1775** Ash.] **1897** *Daily News* 17 Feb. 11/3 The principal item is a series tandem match, unpaced,..for £100.

un'pacifiable, *a.* (UN-[1] 7 b.)
1629 T. Adams *Serm.* Wks. 804 O the vnpacifiable madnesse, that this worlds musicke puts those into, who will dance after his Pipe. **1702** C. Mather *Magn. Chr.* IV. x. 217/1 He had an unpacifiable Dissatisfaction at himself.

unpa'cific, *a.* (UN-[1] 7.)
1774 T. Twining in *Recreat. & Stud.* (1882) 26 The ear left afloat..in the midst of all the flats, and shoals, and breakers..of this unpacific ocean! **1781** Warton *Hist. Kiddington* 71 Many such works of our disunited and unpacific ancestors were undoubtedly destroyed..in the early martial ages. **1837** Carlyle *Fr. Rev.* I. v. vi, The Curé ..marches unpacific, at the head of his militant Parish.

† **unpa'cificable,** *a. Obs.*[−1] (UN-[1] 7 b.)
1608 Topsell *Serpents* 136 The enemy within..sporteth her selfe in the consumption of those vitall parts, which wast and weare away by yeelding to her vnpacificable teeth.

un'pacified, *ppl. a.* (UN-[1] 8.)
1570 Levins *Manip.* 50 Vnpacifyed, *impacatus*. *c* **1611** Chapman *Iliad* XVIII. 299 Twelve youths..I'll sacrifice..to thee unpacified. *a* **1680** Charnock *Attrib. God* (1834) I. 283 The approach is to God as gracious, not to God as unpacified.
Hence **un'pacifiedly** *adv.*
1748 Richardson *Clarissa* (1811) V. xli. 373 She was going to speak with an aspect unpacifiedly angry.

un'pack, *v.* [UN-[2] 3, 5. Cf. Du. *ontpakken*.]
1. *trans.* To undo or open up (a pack, bale, etc.) and remove or release the contents.
1472-5 *Rolls of Parlt.* VI. 155/2 Then it be leeffull to the Collectours..to doo unpakke there tho Pakkes and Fardels. **1535** *Act 27 Hen. VIII*, c. 14 §1 Whiche packes so conveied ..to suche portes..to be shipped be never there unpacked. **1611** Cotgr., *Desempacquet*, to vnpacke, to vnloose a packe. **1739** J. Elton in Hanway *Trav.* (1762) I. I. v. 21 The custom-house officers are not to break open and unpack their bales. **1798** S. & Ht. Lee *Canterb. T.* II. 478 On the deck sat Lady Emily, unpacking a little basket of fruit. **1838** Dickens *O. Twist* xxiii, The beadle, stooping to unpack his bundle. **1873** Black *Pr. Thule* 34 Go away..and unpack your portmanteau.
fig. **1602** Shaks. *Ham.* II. ii. 614 This is most braue, That I..Must (like a Whore) vnpacke my heart with words. **1874** Ruskin *Hortus Inclusus* (1887) 15 The difficulty I had in unpacking my mind.
2. a. To take (something) out of a pack or packing.
1598 Hakluyt *Voy.* I. 210 That none of our said subiects shall vnlade..nor vnpacke..no kind of wares. **1669** Boyle *Certain Physiol. Ess.* (ed. 2) *Absol. Rest Bodies* 25 When..he had unpacked them [*sc.* a great parcel of glasses] and rang'd them. **1754** Ld. Hardwicke in Harris *Life* (1847) III. xii. 18 As company is to come soon,..your mother is very busy in unpacking her house [= furniture]. **1810** W. Selwyn *Law Nisi Prius* (ed. 2) II. 1189 Not having any directions from him respecting the goods, [defendant] caused them to be unpacked. **1825** Ld. G. Cavendish in *Biog. J. Gibson* (1911) 62 It has been unpacked, and placed on a temporary pedestal. **1894** A. Robertson *Nuggets* 38 He unpacked the gold and laid it..on the counter.
fig. **1596** Nashe *Saffron Walden* K 4 The strange vntraffiqu't phrases by him now vented and vnpackt. **1821** Lamb *Elia* I. *Imperfect Sympathies*, He brings his total wealth into company, and gravely unpacks it. **1841** H. Miller *O. R. Sandst.* vi. 107 The strata..have been unpacked and arranged by the uptilting agent. **1966** *Philosophy* XLI. 30 If we unpack what is meant by 'positive morality' we come down to the opinions of individual people. **1979** A. R. Peacocke *Creation & World of Sci.* i. 39 The theological enterprise has always involved much unpacking and elaborating of this image.
b. *transf.* To take (a person) out of a conveyance, dress, etc.
1690 Crowne *Eng. Frier* III, The elderly Ladies have been unpack'd a good while since. **1837** Dickens *Pickw.* xxii, A red-haired man..had unpacked himself from a cab at the same moment. **1898** *Westm. Gaz.* 21 May 3/2 My poor child, in what a state of..collapse must you have been when Myrtle unpacked you on your return!
c. *refl.* or *pass.* To get one's furniture, luggage, etc., unpacked.
1791 H. Walpole *Let. to Miss Berry* 27 Oct., I..thought it would be very uncomfortable to you, till you had unpacked yourselves, seen some few persons, adjusted your family, etc. **1812** Lady Granville *Lett.* (1894) I. 40 The Bessboroughs have been unpacked about a couple of hours.
3. To remove a pack or load from (a horse, carriage, etc.).
1570 Levins *Manip.* 5 To Unpacke, *esarcinare*. **1598** Florio, *Sbastare*, to vnpacke, to vnsaddle a cariers horse. **1835** W. Irving *Tour Prairies* 27 His first care was to unpack his horses, and put them in safe quarters. **1853** Douglas *Milit. Bridges* (ed. 3) 66 To unpack the carriage [carrying a pontoon].
4. *absol.* To perform the work of unpacking.
1837 W. Irving *Capt. Bonneville* II. 22 Two-thirds trappers,..and one-third camp-keepers; who cook, pack, and unpack. **1897** Mary Kingsley *W. Africa* 626 As her commander..asked me on board to lunch, I had to unpack again.
5. *Computers.* To convert (an item of stored data) *into* two or more separate items; to retrieve data from (a record). Cf. PACK *v.*[1] 3 g.
1954 *Computers & Automation* Dec. 22/2 *Unpack*, to separate packed items of information each into a separate machine word. **1959**, etc. [see PACK *v.* 3 g]. **1960** Gregory & Van Horn *Automatic Data-Processing Systems* iii. 104 The 13 instructions given above..are required to unpack each meter-reading card and set up the quantity for bill calculation. **1972** *Computer Jrnl.* XV. 199/1 A stream.. might be formed by one stream function which unpacks words into bytes.
Hence **un'packing** *vbl. sb.*
1472-5 *Rolls of Parlt.* VI. 155/2 Withoute unpakking or sight of such Clothes. **1797** *Monthly Mag.* III. 261/1, I was present at the unpacking of the machine. **1837** [Mrs. Maitland] *Lett. fr. Madras* (1843) 97 People never seem to be able to lay their private hands upon them till after they have finished all their unpacking. **1897** Mary Kingsley *W. Africa* 272 It was a bundle of bark cloth: I anxiously watched its unpacking.
attrib. **1829** in Willis & Clark *Cambridge* (1886) III. 103 Unpacking Rooms connected with the several Museums.

un'packed, *ppl. a.*[1] [UN-[1] 8. Cf. MDu. *ongepact*.]
1. Not made up in, or put into, a pack.
1495 *Acc. Ld. High Treas. Scot.* I. 220, xxv sekkis of vnpakkit woll. **1621** in Foster *Eng. Factories Ind.* (1906) I. 270 To imbale four or five fardells yett unpacked. *c* **1887** Miss M. Jones *Games Patience* 40 Any other unpacked card has a chance of being moved, but not so the King.
2. Not taken out of a pack or parcel.
a **1721** Prior *Ess. Opinion* ¶ 13 Loads of ill Pictures, and worse Books.., lye unpacked and unthought of when they come into the Country.

un'packed, *ppl. a.*[2] (UN-[1] 8 + PACKED *ppl. a.*[2])
1810 Bentham *Packing* (1821) 188 To persuade either a Jury, even though unpacked, or his fellow Judges.

un'packer, [f. UNPACK *v.*] One who unpacks.
1768 J. Wedgwood *Let.* 13 June (1965) 64 He writes a good Hand, and will be more useful in that Respect than as an unpacker. **1804** Mar. Edgeworth *Ennui* iii, By the awkwardness of the unpacker, the statue's thumb was broken. **1859** F. A. Griffiths *Artill. Man.* (ed. 8) 46 Polemen, peg-men, and unpackers of tents.

un'padlocked, *ppl. a.* (UN-[1] or UN-[2] 8.)
1681 *Penny Post* No. 5, That and the Press being unpadlockt, are two incomparable turns of the Liberty of the Subject! **1846** C. Dickens *Battle of Life* 60 One of the fire-proof boxes, unpadlocked and opened.

un'pagan, *a.* (UN-[1] 7.)
1614 Sylvester *Bethulia's Rescue* II. 452 The Lord Marshall..Transporteth speedy, neer Bethulia's side, Th' un-pagan Pagan.

un'paganize, *v.* (UN-[2] 6 c (*b*).)
1678 Cudworth *Intell. Syst.* I. iv. 191 *Contents*, The paganizing of that, which was intended for the unpaganizing of the world. **1801** Hel. M. Williams *Sk. Fr. Rep.* I. vi. 47 Christianity had long spread its doctrines throughout the Roman empire before the world was quite unpaganized.

un'paged, *ppl. a.* (UN-[1] 8.)
1874 Boase & Courtney *Bibl. Cornub.* I. 238/1 Postscript, 6 pages unpaged. **1898** *Sotheby's Sale Catal.* 6 Oct. 41 The rare unpaged leaf 'to the Christen reader'.

un'paid, *ppl. a.* [UN-[1] 8.]
1. Of persons: To whom payment has not been made; not receiving payment.
1375 Barbour *Bruce* I. 257 Quhethir he his lordis neid suld let, And pay fryst that he awcht,..Or leve onpayit his wyff. **1464** *Paston Lett.* Suppl. (1901) 83, I trow I xall be fayn to contente hem or ellys they xall be unpayyd. **1568** Grafton *Chron.* II. 313 A number of the souldyours.. whome king Peter promised to pay, came home agayne vnpayde. **1586** Sir A. Poulet in Ellis *Orig. Lett.* Ser. I. III. 10 Yf they shall say that they are unpayd of their wages. **1627** Drayton *Battle of Agincourt* xliii, The Church to pawne, would see her Challice layde, E'r shee would leaue one Pyoner vnpayde. *a* **1658** Lovelace *Poems* (1904) 125 Whilst thy unpay'd Musicians, Crickets, sing. **1728** Pope *Dunc.* II. 110 That suit, an unpay'd tailor snatch'd away! **1769** Burke *Obs. 'Pres. St. Nat.'* 8 If her armies are three years unpaid. **1837** McCulloch *Acc. Brit. Empire* II. 646 The risks arising from the frequent defaults of the unpaid overseers. **1891** *Daily News* 27 June 5/1 Unpaid children.. went to their work at six o'clock in the morning.
b. With *for*. (Cf. 3.)
1611 Shaks. *Cymb.* v. v. 307 Wilt thou vndoo the worth thou art vnpayd for By tasting of our wrath? **1618** J. Taylor (Water P.) *Penniless Pilgr.* Wks. (1630) 123 Master Taylor.. Vnask'd (vnpaid for) me both lodg'd and fed.
c. *the* (*Great*) *Unpaid*, the class of unpaid magistrates or justices.
1826 *Edin. Rev.* 441 We beg to be acquitted of all intention of affronting, or attacking the Great Unpaid. **1826** *Examiner* 727/2 The miserable canting spirit which actuates the 'Unpaid'.
2. Not handed over or given in payment; not discharged or cleared off by payment.
1387 Trevisa *Higden* (Rolls) IV. 117 Lisia..wente into Pers, ffor þe tribute was unpayde. **1424** *Paston Lett.* I. 16 The fees and the wages of the seid William..unpayed draweth a gret some to hys pouere degree. **1491** *Act 7 Hen. VII*, c. 20 §5 As often as it shall happen the seid annuall rent ..to be behynd and unpayd in part or in all. **1507** *Rec. St. Mary at Hill* 25 Yff it happ yᵉ said yerly ferme of v marke.. to be behynd..by a monithe vnpaid. **1547** in Feuillerat *Revels Edward VI* (1914) 26 The sum.., as by the bookes.. dothe apere more at large, is vnpayd. **1606** *Arraignm. & Execution Late Traitors* (Hindley II) 7 That his wife might have her jointure.., his sisters their legacies in his hand unpaid. **1661** Morgan *Sph. Gentry* IV. iii. 41 The party whose portion shall appear to be unpayed. **1764** Goldsm. *Hist. Eng. in Lett.* (1772) II. 20 Alexander..was indebted to him a large sum, which was still unpaid. **1848** Thackeray *Van. Fair* lii, A long arrear of unpaid wages. **1878** J. Davidson *Inverurie & Garioch* 349 The fines remaining unpaid.
fig. **1421** Hoccleve *Min. Poems* 169/817 His brothres reward had nat been vnpayed, Nad promesse of the Emperour him bownde To pardon. **1667** Milton *P.L.* v. 779 How we may best..Receive him coming to receive from us Knee-tribute yet unpaid. ? **1710** Congreve *To Sir G. Kneller*, Fame due to vast desert is kept in store, Unpay'd, till the deserver is no more. **1791** Cowper *Iliad* I. 112 The seer..spake, Nor vow nor hecatomb unpaid on us He charges.
b. Of debts or bills: Undischarged.
1483 *Act 1 Ric. III*, c. 2 Many worshipful Men..live in great Penury.., their Debts unpaid, and their Children unpreferred. **1492-3** *Rec. St. Mary at Hill* 194 Olde dettes that have be lefte vnpayde by the cherch wardenys. **1681** R. Knox *Hist. Ceylon* vii. 149 The Interest never runs up higher, tho the Debt lye seven years unpaid. **1754** in *Nairne Peerage Evidence* (1874) 52 A just true and lawful debt wholly resting unpaid. **1781** Cowper *Retirem.* 559 Anticipated rents, and bills unpaid. **1887** Gunter *Mr. Barnes* xiii. 96 She remembers she has unpaid bills.
c. Not rendered or discharged.
1611 Shaks. *Cymb.* III. v. 48 She pray'd me to excuse her keeping close, Whereto constrain'd.., She should that dutie leaue vnpaide to you Which dayly she was bound to proffer. **1717** Pope *Elegy Mem. Unfort. Lady* 48 What can atone.. Thy fate unpity'd, and thy rites unpaid? **1725** —— *Odyss.* xv. 213 With him all night the youthful strangers staid, Nor found the hospitable rites unpay'd.
3. Not paid *for*. Also without prep.
1465 *Paston Lett.* II. 233 [If] the blak hose be payid for, he wyll send the roset un-payd for. **1552** in Feuillerat *Revels Edw. VI* (1914) 124 The like charges of the said lorde.. beinge yet behinde and vnpaid for. **1611** Shaks. *Cymb.* III. iii. 24 Rustling in vnpayd-for Silke. **1653** W. Ramesey *Astrol. Restored* To Rdr. 11 The Drapers cloth on their back,..and all unpaid for. **1827** Pollok *Course T.* VIII. 433 A show unpaid for, paying to be seen! **1886** C. E. Pascoe *Lond. of To-day* xliii. (ed. 3) 379 Letters posted unpaid are charged double postage. **1895** Ld. Farrer in *Westm. Gaz.* 19 Feb. 2/1, I did not know before I joined the Council how good and how zealous unpaid work can be.
Hence **un'paidish** *a.* (from sense 1 c).
1829 E. Elliott *Village Patriarch* III. ix, Mark his unpaidish sneer, his lordly frown.

un'pain, *v.* (UN-[2] 3.)
1545 Raynald *Byrth Mankynde* 69 These pylles be of such efficacy and strength, yᵗ it alleuiateth and vnpayneth the byrth.

un'pained, *ppl. a.* (UN-[1] 8.)
c **1380** Wyclif *Sel. Wks.* III. 200 No defoulynge þerof [*sc.* marriage] may askape unpeyned. **1599** B. Jonson *Cynthia's Rev.* v. iii, But there's not one of these who are unpain'd, Or by themsevles unpunished. **1667** Milton *P.L.* VI. 455 Too unequal work we find Against unequal armes to fight in paine, Against unpaind, impassive. *a* **1758** Ramsay *To G. Drummond* xi, And here the Fair may walk unpain'd, Her flowing silks and shoes unstain'd. **1804** *Europ. Mag.* XLV. 61/1 Learning's rever'd abode he leaves With unpain'd soul. **1826** A. A. Watts *First Kiss* 87 A bliss too pure For evil spirits to behold unpained.

un'painful, *a.* [UN-[1] 7.]
† **1.** Not subject to pain. *Obs.*[−1]
? *c* **1425** *Lucidarie* (Fr. Schmitt 1909) 21 Aftir his owne kynde, he was unpayneful & undeedly.
2. Not causing or involving pain or discomfort.
1570 Levins *Manip.* 186 Vnpaynful, *immolestus*. **1628** Feltham *Resolves* II. lxxxii. 236 If we owe a Retribution for vnpainefull Courtesies. **1690** Locke *Hum. Und.* II. iv. §4 That being generally call'd..soft, which changes the Situation of its parts upon an easie and unpainful touch. **1713** *Guardian* No. 82, Those who make an honest man a visit..to make his following year unpainful. **1758** J. S. *Le Dran's Observ. Surg.* (1771) 95 The small Remainder of the Tumour was unpainful. **1823** J. Wilson *Marg. Lyndsay* ix. 67 That unpainful sympathy which is all the poor can afford or expect. **1851** Hawthorne *Twice-told T.* II. vi. 99 A sympathy with the young and gay; an unpainful interest in the business of others.
3. Marked or characterized by absence of pain.
1861 Mrs. Jenkin *Who breaks—pays* II. 261 The first unpainful feeling I have had for three quarters of a year.

un'paining, *ppl. a.* (UN-^{1} 10.)
1828 TENNYSON *Lover's T.* I. 609 Would I had lain Until ..the wild brier had driven Its knotted thorns thro' my unpaining brows.

un'paint, *v.* [UN-^{2} 4.]
1. *trans.* To free from paint.
1611 COTGR., *Defarder*, to vnpaint; to wash, take, or wype off, painting. **1844** *P. Parley's Ann.* V. 265 Nothing now remained but to unpaint the young urchin; and so Sally.. scrubbed till she was tired.
2. To paint out; to obliterate (something painted).
a **1717** PARNELL *Piety* 53 Unpaint the Love, that hov'ring over Beds, From glitt'ring Pinions guilty Pleasure sheds. **1755** JOHNSON *Dict.*, *To Dislimn*, to unpaint. **1866** VISCT. STRANGFORD *Select.* (1869) II. 320 An unobtrusive little coronet which my wife has had painted..upon the panels of her carriage, and which I defy all the powers on earth..to induce her to unpaint.

un'paintable, *a.* (UN-^{1} 7 b.)
1849 KINGSLEY *Misc.* (1859) II. 255 Farewell to unpaintable Lynmouth. **1893** *Guardian* 16 Aug. 1291 When he began to try to paint the unpaintable.
Hence **unpainta'bility, -ableness.**
1884 *Athenæum* 16 Aug. 218/1 The artists who complain of the 'unpaintableness' of current attire. **1888** *Pall Mall G.* 4 Oct. 5/2 The unpaintability of Mr. Gladstone.

un'painted, *ppl. a.* (UN-^{1} 8.)
1555 EDEN *Decades* (Arb.) 106 Rased or vnpaynted tables. **1604** S. HARRISON *Archs of Triumph* B j, I would not care if these vnpainted Pictures were more Costly to me, so that [etc.]. **1651** HOBBES *Leviath.* I. x. 45 An unpainted Buckler was a signe of..a common Souldier. **1762** GOLDSM. *Cit. W.* xcix, More ugly than an unpainted actress. **1771** R. CUMBERLAND *West Indian* Epil. 24 Unpainted cheeks with blush of health did glow. **1818** SHELLEY *Let. to Peacock* 8 Nov., Strange-looking unpainted window-shutters. **1855** DICKENS *Holly-Tree* i, The rooms..were all of unpainted wood.

un'paired, *ppl. a.*^{1} [UN-^{1} 8. Cf. Da. *uparret*, Sw. *oparad*, Du. *ongepaard*, G. *ungepaart*.] Not united or arranged in pairs; not forming one of a pair.
1648 HEXHAM II, *Onpaer*, Vn-even, or Vnpaired. **1748** RICHARDSON *Clarissa* IV. 50 All this vast difference in sentiments shews how unpair'd our minds are. **1812** CRABBE *Tales* iv. 5 Others, ill match'd, with minds unpair'd, repent. **1880** GÜNTHER *Fishes* 40 The Fins are divided into vertical or unpaired, and into horizontal or paired fins. **1883** MARTIN & MOALE *Vertebr. Dissect.* 133 A single unpaired air sac will be seen just beneath the anterior portion of the sternum.

†**un'paired**, *ppl. a.*^{2} [UN-^{1} 8.] Unimpaired, uninjured.
c **1400** *Destr. Troy* 13128 But thurgh wilys & wit he wan of his daunger. Vnpairit of his person priuely he stale.

†**un'paised**, *ppl. a. Obs.* [UN-^{1} 8 + PEISE *v.*] Not properly weighed or balanced; defective or excessive in weight.
1390 GOWER *Conf.* Prol. 64* He that hath his word unpeysed. **1561** NORTON & SACKV. *Gorboduc* I. i, Porrex the younger so vnpaised in state, Perhappes in courage will be raised also. **1581** STUDLEY tr. *Seneca, Herc. Œt.* I. 191 b, And coulde I brooke it, Toxeus, to see thy death with woe? That wert vnwaynde in yeares, and eake in pits [? *read* pith; L. *sanguine*] vnpaysde. **1602** MARSTON *Ant. & Mel.* II. iii. 1 Seize on reuenge, graspe the sterne bended front Of frowning vengeance, with vnpaized clutch.

un'palaced, *ppl. a.* (UN-^{2} 8.)
1859 J. S. MILL *Diss. & Disc.* I. 23 Let the State endowments be once withdrawn from the Church of England, her mitred and unpalaced prelates will indulge in no such delusion.

un'palatable, *a.* [UN-^{1} 7 b, 5 b.]
1. Not agreeable to the palate. Also in fig. context.
1682 DRYDEN *Medal* 148 The Man..Might laugh again, to see a Jury chaw The prickles of unpalatable Law. **1700** T. BROWN *Amusem.* viii. Wks. 1720 III. 76 Our Doctor.. cloys his Auditors with that unpalatable Ragoust. **1748** *Anson's Voy.* II. viii. 218 We found them [*sc.* pearl oysters] extremely tough and unpalatable. **1799** J. ROBERTSON *Agric. Perth* 206 The grass is coarse, unpalatable to cattle. **1846** SOYER *Cookery* 380 It would..cause the fillets to eat tough and altogether unpalatable. **1871** DARWIN *Desc. Man* II. xi. I. 416 It would be highly advantageous to a caterpillar to be ..recognised as unpalatable by all birds.
2. Unpleasant, distasteful, disagreeable.
1711 tr. *Werenfelsius' Disc. Logomachys* 201 These things, my Son, may at first seem, to your Age, unpalatable and hard. **1749** SMOLLETT *Regic.* IV. ii, Candid friendship that disdains to hide Unpalatable truth! **1829** SCOTT *Anne of G.* xxvii, The Duke's eye lowered gloomily on the deliverer of this unpalatable message. **1849** MACAULAY *Hist. Eng.* xx. IV. 467 The King commanded himself sufficiently to return thanks for this unpalatable counsel.
Hence **un'palatableness; ,unpalata'bility.**
1805 SAUNDERS *Min. Waters* 82 Perhaps the unpalatableness of this drink has caused it to be in worse credit than it deserves. **1934** WEBSTER, *Unpalatability.* **1974** *Nature* 25 Jan. 170/1 The potential unpalatability of a current policy designed to affect the demographic situation in the next century. **1981** *Birds* Summer 37/2 Inedible insects advertise their unpalatability by wearing warning colours—usually black and yellow or black and red.

un'pale, *v.* [UN-^{2} 4.] *trans.* To strip of pales or palings.
1779 H. WALPOLE *Let. to Cole* 3 Jan., I hope you have not been untiled or unpaled by the tempest on New-year's morning.

un'paled, *ppl. a.*^{1} [UN-^{1} 8.] Not furnished with a paling.
1607 in *Essex Rev.* XV. (1906) 45 The ch[urch]y[ar]d fence ys unpaled on the S. side. **1648** HEXHAM II, *Onbetuynt*, Vnhedged, Vnpaled, or Open.

un'paled, *ppl. a.*^{2} [UN-^{1} 8.] Not made pale.
1831 JAMES *Phil. Augustus* I. vi, The fire of his eye was unquenched, the rose of his cheek unpaled. **1885** 'C. E. CRADDOCK' *Proph. Gt. Smoky Mount.* vii, In a sunshine all unpaled, and against the upper regions of the air, splendidly blue.

unpali'sadoed, *ppl. a.* (UN-^{1} 8.)
1642 *Prince Rupert's Sp. to King* 4 Their graffes or ditches being dry and their vamures unpallisado'd. **1654** GAYTON *Pleas. Notes* III. iv. 91 His mouth was upon the West side like to be unpalisado'd for ever.

un'palled, *ppl. a.*^{1} [UN-^{1} 8.] Not palled or jaded.
a **1770** NUGENT in Dodsley *Coll. Poems* II. 187 By pain unbitter'd, and unpall'd by fear. **1809** *Edin. Rev.* XV. 111 Where the taste is unpalled by satiety of what is better. **1859** W. H. GREGORY *Egypt* II. 130 His appetite..is unpalled as much at the conclusion as at the commencement of the feast.

un'palled, *ppl. a.*^{2} *Cant.* [UN-^{2} 8 + PAL *sb.*^{1}] (See quot.)
1812 J. H. VAUX *Flash Dict.* s.v., A thief whose associates are all apprehended, or taken from him by other means, is said to be *unpalled.*

un'palliable, *a.* [UN-^{1} 7 b.] Incapable of being palliated.
1673 BP. S. PARKER *Reproof Reh. Transp.* 374 A manifest and unpalliable breach..of loyalty.

un'palliated, *ppl. a.* (UN-^{1} 8.)
[**1775** ASH.] **1798** SOUTHEY in Robberds *Mem. W. Taylor* (1843) I. 232 The only person who has ever..advised, and at times reproved, him, in unpalliated terms. **1827** SCOTT *Napoleon* xlii, There was never a more unpalliated case of.. arbitrary spoliation. **1860** PUSEY *Min. Proph.* 255 Jonah leaves his own character unexplained, its severity rebuked by God, unexcused and unpalliated.

un'palpable, *a.* Now *rare.* [UN-^{1} 7 b, 5 b.] Impalpable.
1538 ELYOT Addit., *Asomatos*, vnpalpable, or that can not be felt. **1576** G. BAKER tr. *Gesner's Jewell of Health* 109 b, The same bring to a fine powder in a brasse morter as in a maner unpalpable. **1584** R. SCOT *Discov. Witchcr.* IV. ii. (1886) 59 The opinion of them that hold a spirit to be unpalpable. **1611** COTGR., *Insensible*,..vnpalpable, vnfeelable. **1725** *Fam. Dict.* s.v. *Sallet*, An Ingredient never to be omited..provided it be not minutely beaten to an almost unpalpable Dust. **1876** MRS. WHITNEY *Sights & Ins.* xxvii, We sat in the baptism of the far, unpalpable spray.

un'palped, *a.* [UN-^{1} 9.] Not furnished with palps or feelers.
1884 SEDGWICK & HEATHCOTE tr. *Claus' Zool.* 470 The unpalped maxilla of the second pair [of mandibles].

un'palsied, *ppl. a.* (UN-^{1} 8.)
[**1775** ASH.] **1798** *Monthly Mag.* V. 367 'No God,' with lips unpalsied they declare. **1850** TENNYSON *In Mem.* cxxvii, The love that rose on stronger wings, Unpalsied when he met with Death.

un'pampered, *ppl. a.* (UN-^{1} 8.)
[**1775** ASH.] **1794** W. ROBERTS *Looker-on* No. 90 (1794) III. 448 Unpampered by servile compliance. **1844** DICKENS *Mart. Chuz.* xiv, Unspoiled, unpampered in her joys or griefs.

un'panel, *v.* [UN-^{2} 4.] *trans.* To unsaddle.
1620 SHELTON *Quix.* III. xi. 235 Good betide him that freed vs from the paines of vnpannelling the gray Asse;..yet if hee were here, I would not permit any other to vnpannell him. *a* **1739** JARVIS *Quix.* I. III. xi, If he were here, I would not consent to his being unpannelled.

un'panelled, *ppl. a.* (UN-^{1} 8.)
1883 BARING-GOULD *John Herring* xxxix, The unpanelled walls were plastered white.

un'panged, *ppl. a.* (UN-^{1} 8.)
1612 *Two Noble K.* I. i, But when could greefe Cull forth, as unpanged judgement can, fit'st time For best solicitation.

un'panniered, *ppl. a.* (UN-^{1} 8.)
1812 J. WILSON *Isle of Palms*, etc. 354 Th' unpannier'd ass slowly retires From the brown tents. **1869** BROWNING *Ring & Bk.* IX. 61 Even the poor ass, unpanniered and elate Stands.

un'panoplied, *ppl. a.* (UN-^{1} 8.)
1827 POLLOK *Course T.* VII. 422 Innumerous armies rose, unbannered all, Unpanoplied, unpraised.

un'panting, *ppl. a.* (UN-^{1} 10.)
1721 SOUTHERNE *Spartan Dame* III. ii, I sent this steel with tidings to his heart, Nor parted thence, till..I left the unpanting villain on the earth.

un'pantofle, *v.* (UN-^{2} 4.)
1643 in *Harl. Misc.* (Malh.) V. 335 They, whose part in a comedy allows them a robe and scepter; who.., as soon as they come to their exit, are un-pantoffled, and return to their own stature.

un'paper, *v.* [UN-^{2} 4.] *trans.* To remove paper from; *esp.* to strip of a paper covering.
1714 C. JOHNSON *Country Lasses* II. ii, The Holland curtains.., up with 'em—unpaper the screens, the sconces, and the andirons. **1769** J. SKEAT *Art Cookery* 23 The fat of venison..is apt to waste, so that it is always necessary to paper it;..just before you want to take it up, unpaper it. **1802** H. MARTIN *Helen of Glenross* I. 54 Dolly employed herself, unpapering and uncovering chairs and carpets. **1828** P. CUNNINGHAM *N.S. Wales* (ed. 3) II. 269 A coterie of these nymphs were unpapering their curls.

un'papered, *ppl. a.* (UN-^{1} 8.)
[**1775** ASH.] **1805** F. BURNEY *Let.* 29 May (1975) VI. 517 It is unfurnished, indeed, unpapered, & every way unfinished. **1851** N. HAWTHORNE in Bridge *Pers. Recollect.* (1893) 125 The boxes..are not all papered, but neither are they all unpapered. **1871** KINGSLEY *At Last* x, The walls were of cedar and other valuable woods, which good taste left still unpapered.

un'papering, *vbl. sb.* (UN-^{1} 13.)
1847 LE FANU *T. O'Brien* 326 Trimming of ruffles and unpapering of gold lace.

unpar, obs. form of UMPIRE.

un'paradise, *v.* [UN-^{2} 5, 6 b.]
1. *trans.* To turn out of, expel from, Paradise. Also *fig.*
1592 DANIEL *Compl. Rosamond* 456 Now did I finde my selfe vnparadis'd, From those pure fields. **1605** G. ELLIS *Lamentation Lost Sheep* G j b, With shame-sick Adam haue I hid my head, Vnparadiz'd, from my Angell-like state. *c* **1640** MILTON *Draft of P.L.* Poet. Wks. (Globe) 12 Adam Unparadized. **1839** F. BARHAM *Adamus Exul* 47 Widowed, desolate, And quite unparadised in heart. **1846** LOCKHART in *Ch. of Scot. Pulpit* II. 156 The old serpent, who deceived and unparadised our first parents. **1858** CASWALL *Poems* 170 Archangels guard the gates with flaming swords,..who at an earlier day Did man unparadise.
2. To deprive of the character of Paradise.
1647 FULLER *Wounded Consc.* 28 Thus a wounded conscience is able to unparadise Paradise it selfe. **1742** YOUNG *Nt. Th.* I. 187 That ghastly thought would drink up all your joy, And quite unparadise the realms of light. **1788** V. KNOX *Winter Even.* III. VII. vii. 45 This it was which unparadised an Eden. **1827** MONTGOMERY *Pelican Isl.* VI. 254 The serpent.., Whose guile unparadised the world. **1876** C. M. DAVIES *Unorth. Lond.* 370 Were man to enter Heaven as he now is, it would be unparadised for him at once.
Hence **un'paradised** *ppl. a.*
1872 O. W. HOLMES *Poet Breakf.-t.* i. 24 Nature is never wholly unkind. Economical as she was in my unparadised Eden,..still the damask roses sweetened the June breezes.

un'paradox, *v.* (UN-^{2} 3.)
1654 WHITLOCK *Zootomia* 322 The hardest Task is to perswade the erroneous obstinate..Woman-Hater, that.. any confirmations from History can un-paradox the worth ..of that Sex.

un'paragoned, *ppl. a.* (UN-^{1} 8.)
1611 CHAPMAN *Widowes T.* III. i, At hand, sir, with your unparagon'd sister: please you take your chair of honour, sir? **1611** SHAKS. *Cymb.* II. ii. 17 Rubies vnparagon'd. **1640** tr. *Verdere's Rom. of Rom.* III. xlix. 204 The unparragoned Knight of the Sun. **1824** MISS MITFORD *Village* Ser. I. 181 His little dog Viper, unparagoned of terriers. **1874** M. & FR. COLLINS *Vill. Comedy* xxii, Even Rough feels poetical as he sees the wondrous towers and spires unparagoned.

†**un'paragonized**, *ppl. a. Obs.*$^{-1}$ [UN-^{1} 8.] = prec.
1603 FLORIO *Montaigne* II. Ded., Give me leave (peerelesse, and in all good gifts vnparagonized Ladies).

†**un'paralable**, obs. var. UNPARALLELABLE *a.*
a **1639** W. WHATELEY *Prototypes* I. xi. (1640) 97 Here was an obedience incomparable and unparalable, no man ever did the like except our Lord Jesus Christ.

†**un'paralled**, obs. var. UNPARALLELED *ppl. a.*
1637 A. STAFFORD *Just Apol.* in *Fem. Glory* (1860) p. xlvi, They are unparall'd Scoldes. **1640** tr. *Verdere's Rom. of Rom.* III. vi. 20 The two little unparalled Worlds, that so graced her bosome.

un'parallel, *a.* [UN-^{1} 7, 5 b.]
1. Not parallel or correspondent.
1652 TH. PESTILL in Benlowes *Theoph.* C i, To That, Unparallel, This comes so neer, That 't is a Glimpse of Heav'n to leade Thee here. **1674** HICKMAN *Quinquart. Hist.* (ed. 2) 105 In this also the Parallel is unparallel. **1757** EDWARDS *Orig. Sin* II. ii. (1807) II. 237 How unlike and unparallel is this? **1826** LAMB *Elia* II. *Wedding*, Certainly there is a jealousy in unparallel subjects.
†**2.** = UNPARALLELED *ppl. a. Obs.*
1665 J. SPENCER *Prodigies* (ed. 2) 188 The black and terrible Monitors of that unparallel Destruction which ensued. **1666** J. SMITH *Old Age* 115 They had had so many ..experiences of his unparallel strength.
Hence **un'parallelness.**
1719 S. SEWALL *Diary* 4 Oct., I ride to Byfield Meeting-house; hear Mr. Payson's Son of the Unparallelness of Josiah.

un'parallelable, *a.* (UN-^{1} 7 b.)
1640 BP. HALL *Episc.* III. ix. 54 The unparallelable glory of this Church, and Nation. **1676** *Doctrine of Devils* 50 His transcendent, unimitable, unparallelable Miracles. **1703** J. SAVAGE *Lett. Antients* cxxi. 303 An Amour, which..I looked upon unparallelable. **1743** J. GLAS *Treat. Lord's Supper* ii. Wks. 1761 IV. 38 He expressed his unparallelable good-will to all his elect. **1813** SIR R. WILSON *Priv. Diary* (1861) I. 342 The artillery in unparalleled and unparallelable order. *a* **1843** SOUTHEY *Doctor* xxii. (1848) 537 Which cannot with propriety be distinguished by any other name than one derived from its unparalleled and unparallelable author.

un'paralleled, *ppl. a.* (UN-1 8, 5 b.)
In very common use from *c* 1610.
1594 DRAYTON *Leg. Matilda* xvi, The most iudiciall eyes Did giue the gole impartially to me; So did I stand vnparaleld and free. **1608** MACHIN *Dumbe Knt.* I. i, Dost thou not think, Shee is the mirrour of her beauteous sexe, Unparalleld, and uncompanioned? **1662** STILLINGFL. *Orig. Sacr.* III. i. §2 Those many unparalleld miracles, which were wrought among them. **1713** WARDER *True Amazons* (title-p.), Their..unparallelled Love to their Queen. **1770** *Junius Lett.* xli. (1788) 231 *note*, The..Judge..had the unparallelled impudence to tell [etc.]. **1814** SCOTT *Diary* 16 Aug. in *Lockhart*, Monuments..otherwise unparalleled in Britain. **1857** BUCKLE *Civiliz.* I. vii. 354 Progress..made in the face of these unparalleled disasters.
Hence **un'paralleledly** *adv.*, **-edness.**
1667 WATERHOUSE *Fire Lond.* 5 His intercurrent judgements of Fire between this first and that last president of unparalleledness. **1815** ANN SMITH *Diary* in *Life* (1851) 40 The freedom, sovereignty, and unparalleledness of his love. **1854** *Blackw. Mag.* LXXV. 448 It is unparalleledly impudent.

un'paralyzed, *ppl. a.* (UN-1 8.)
1846 WORCESTER (citing Goode). **1889** *Athenæum* 15 June 751/2 An unparalyzed system of misgovernment. **1893** W. R. GOWERS *Dis. Nerv. Syst.* (ed. 2) II. 399 The eyelids blink when the finger comes from the unparalysed side.

un'parboiled, *ppl. a.* (UN-1 8.)
1616 *Rich Cabinet* 56 An vnparboyld pastie of tainted venison.

un'parcelled, *ppl. a.* (UN-1 8.)
[**1775** ASH.] **1840** BROWNING *Sordello* VI. 219 But, portioned duly out, the Future vied Never with the unparcelled Present. **1844** KINGLAKE *Eothen* xii. 175 You find yourself..proving the mettle of your mare upon the broad and dreary downs, because you feel congenially with the yet unparcelled earth.

un'parched, *ppl. a.* (UN-1 8.)
1599 THYNNE *Animadv.* (1875) 49 Chaucer of purpose addethe that woorde 'Greene' to explane 'vnseriall', whiche signyfiethe vnsered, vnparched. **1648** HEXHAM II, *Onverdrooght*,..unparched.

un'parching, *ppl. a.* (UN-1 10.)
1818 MILMAN *Samor* XI. 237 Th' unconsuming fire Innoxious rang'd th' unparching edifice.

un'pardon, *v.* (UN-2 3.)
1685 BAXTER *Paraphr. N.T.* Matt. xviii. 34–35 *note*, How God is said..to demand the debt which he had forgiven, and to unpardon it again.

un'pardonable, *a.* (*adv.*) (UN-1 7 b, 5 b.)
1525 LD. BERNERS *Froiss.* II. cliii. 168 b/2 If they be [broken],..ye ryn in the churches sentence, and to be excommunycate on payne vnpardonable. **1561** T. NORTON *Calvin's Inst.* I. xiii. 36 b, An vnpardonable crime. **1647** CLARENDON *Hist. Reb.* I. §66 The Earl..thought the very suspecting him to be an injury unpardonable. **1676** GLANVILL *Seasonable Reflect.* 28 We may conclude safely from the Doctrine of the Apostle, that they are incurable and unpardonable. **1712** STEELE *Spect.* No. 312 ¶1 The most unpardonable Malefactor in the World. **1827** LYTTON *Pelham* iv, A most unpardonable fault. **1882** MISS BRADDON *Mt. Royal* I. ii. 51 There was nothing unpardonable in Miss Bridgeman's plainness.
b. As *adv.* Unpardonably.
1662 HICKERINGILL *Apol. Distressed Innoc.* Wks. 1716 I. 316 He is unpardonable credulous that will lend an Ear to your noise of the Gospel.

un'pardonableness. (UN-1 12; cf. prec.)
1646 HAMMOND *Tracts* 20 The unpardonablenesse of it is acknowledged. **1677** GILPIN *Demonol.* II. ix. 392 The note of unpardonableness, is indeed affixed to sins under several Denominations. *a* **1714** M. HENRY *Baptism* Wks. 1853 I. 496/2 A mistaken apprehension of the unpardonableness of sin committed after baptism. **1849** RUSKIN *Sev. Lamps* ii. §1. 28 It would be well if moralists less frequently confused the greatness of a sin with its unpardonableness. **1885** *Athenæum* 26 Dec. 852 The unpardonableness of the offence.

un'pardonably, *adv.* (UN-1 11, 5 b.)
1645 MILTON *Tetrach.* 12 Those mighty syllables..which take upon them to joyn heavn and hell together unpardnably till death pardon. **1811** MISS L. M. HAWKINS *C'tess & Gertr.* I. 111 We have both deviated most grievously and unpardonably from our duty. **1866** FREEMAN *Hist. Ess.* (1871) 9 English people—more unpardonably still—reject it.

un'pardoned, *ppl. a.* (UN-1 8.)
1565 ALLEN *Def. Purg.* xvii. 284 There was no sin so smaule vnpardoned, but [etc.]. **1651** BAXTER *Inf. Bapt.* 310 Are you sure so many thousands are all unpardoned? **1692** tr. *B. Jonson's Leges Conviv.* x, Like the old Lapithites, with the goblets to fight, Our own 'mongst offences un-pardon'd will rank. **1796** MRS. E. PARSONS *Myst. Warning* ii, [If] informed I was unpardoned, portionless and dependent. **1817** BYRON *Manfred* II. ii, He slew That which he loved,.. And died unpardon'd. **1858** FROUDE *Hist. Eng.* IV. 261 The unpardoned..affront which Henry had offered to the Spanish nation.

un'pardoning, *ppl. a.* (UN-1 10.)
1644 MILTON *Divorce* Introd. A4 b, His ungirt permissions, his venial and unvenial dispences, wherwith the Law of God pardoning and unpardoning hath bin shamefully branded. **1700** DRYDEN *Pal. & Arc.* II. 344 Curse on th' unpard'ning Prince, whom Tears can draw To no Remorse. **1725** POPE *Odyss.* xx. 351 Whom Pallas with unpard'ning fury fir'd. **1810** *Monthly Mag.* XXIX. 209 A rash, unruly, Un-pardoning soul. **1894** *Outing* XXIV. 13/2, 'I have been so hard, so unforgiving, so unpardoning,' she said.

un'pared, *ppl. a.* [UN-1 8.]
1. Of fruit: Not having the skin pared off.
c **1305** *Pilate* 232 in *E.E.P.* (1862) 117 Þe gayler him tok an appel; he seide hit was vnriȝt Vnpared an appel take, an heȝ man oþer a kniȝt. **14..** *Burlesques* ii. in *Rel. Ant.* I. 83 Adam, Adam, why ete thu the appull unpard? **1530** PALSGR. 652/2 Can you nat eate a peere onpared? **1658** EVELYN *Fr. Gard.* (1675) 190 The fruits being pared or unpared, according to ..your curiosity.
2. Of nails: Uncut, untrimmed.
1547 BOORDE *Introd. Knowl.* 117 Who shall let me, the deuyls nayles vnpared? **1598** DALLINGTON *Meth. Trav.* X iij, Wearing long vnpared nayles. **1635** QUARLES *Embl.* III. vi. 146 If the peevish Infant fights, and flies, With un-par'd weapons, at his mother's eyes. **1743** FRANCIS tr. *Hor., Epode* v. 60 Her unpar'd Thumbs Canidia gnaws.

†**un'paregal, -'peregal,** *a. Obs.* [UN-1 7.] Unequal.
c **1374** CHAUCER *Boeth.* III. pr. i. (1868) 63 So þat I trowe nat now þat I be vnparygal to the strokes of fortune. **1605** MARSTON *Dutch Courtezan* IV. i, Afore the Lord God, my knaverie growes unperegall; Tis time to take a nap.

†**un'parel,** *v. Obs.*-1 [UN-2 4.] *trans.* To divest of apparel.
1603 H. CROSSE *Vertues Commw.* N 1, Perhaps thou wilt say againe, I brought him not to beggery: did I lame him? did I vnparell him?

un'parented, *ppl. a.* [UN-1 8 and UN-2 8.]
1. Deprived of the status of a parent.
1650 B. *Discolliminium* 38 Our Politicall Parents..are now unparented or civilly dead.
2. Deprived or destitute of a parent or parents.
1668 WILKINS *Real Char.* II. xii. 295 *Orphan* is unparented. **1885** *American* X. 333 The unparented suggestion that each newcomer should add a stone to the growing pile. **1897** *Fortn. Rev.* 1 Feb. 225 A family of five children, three brothers and two sisters, unparented.

un-Pa'risianized, *ppl. a.* (UN-1 8.)
1858 MRS. GORE *Heckington* III. 160 The envy with which the still un-Parisianised Lady Frere surveyed the boudoir furniture.

un'parliament, *v.* (UN-2 6 b.)
1643 PRYNNE *Sov. Power Parl.* IV. 24 Such a grand difference is there now..between the Irish Rebels,..who may do what they please..; and the English (now un-Parliamented) Parliament. **1648** E. SYMMONS *Vind. Chas. I*, 382 They were once a true Parliament.., but now they swarm so much in evils..that they have plainly un-parliamented themselves.

unparlia'mentary, *a.* (UN-1 7.)
1626 JAS. I *Sp.* in *3rd Rep. Hist. MSS. Comm.* 68/1, I am come here to shew you your errors, and, as I may term them, unparliamentary proceedings in this Parliament. **1679** HOBBES *Behemoth* 89 All Unparliamentary raising of Mony upon the Subjects. **1701** SWIFT *Contests Nobles & Comm.* v, That unparliamentary abuse of setting individuals upon their shoulders who were hated by God and man. **1810** *Sporting Mag.* XXXV. 302 The Speaker stated..that..a member had used unparliamentary language. **1876** JEVONS *Logic Prim.* 18 A speech is unparliamentary when it does not agree with the rules of parliamentary debate.
Hence **unparlia'mentarily** *adv.*, **-ariness.**
1647 CLARENDON *Hist. Reb.* IV. §81 The Unparliamentariness of their Remonstrance. **1727** BOYER *Dict. Royal* II. s.v., Unparliamentarily. *a* **1797** H. WALPOLE *Mem. Geo. II* (1847) II. ii. 55 The use that had been made of the sacred name of the King, so often and so unparliamentarily.

un'parrel, *v. Naut.* (UN-2 4.)
1627 CAPT. SMITH *Seaman's Gram.* ix. 41 For more haste unparrell the mizen yard and lanch it and the saile ouer her Lee quarter. [**1694** MOTTEUX *Rabelais* v. x, We..for more haste unparrell'd the Misen yard, and lanch'd it and the Sail over her Lee-quarter.] **1706** PHILLIPS (ed. Kersey), To *Unparrel* a Yard, (in Sea-Language) is to take off the Frames call'd Parrels, that go round about the Masts.

†**un'parreled,** obs. var. UNPARALLELED *ppl. a.*
1639 W. H. *Zarain Aga* (title-p.), With one Unparreled, Cruell, Furious and Bloudy assault, made by the Turks. **1661** BOYLE *Physiol. Ess.* (1669) 284 Another Author quoted for writing an unparrel'd Story.

un'parriable, *a.* (UN-1 7 b.)
1813 SCOTT *Let.* in *Lockhart* (1839) IV. 91 A general reluctance to allow that any danger is near, until it is almost unparriable. **1826** *Blackw. Mag.* XIX. 393 How pretty had it been to dally for a few passes, and then, unparryable as the Chevalier St. George, to pierce through heart and back. **1836** in Russell *Mem. Moore* (1856) VIII. 275 A tone of irony.., which..is the most unparryable..weapon ever directed against the [Church's] vitals.

un'parroted, *ppl. a.* (UN-1 8.)
1817 GODWIN *Mandeville* I. 207 She expressed herself with the greatest ease; her sentiments were unparrotted and unstudied.

unpar'sonical, *a.* (UN-1 7.)
1858 MOTLEY *Corr.* (1889) I. 232 [Kingsley] seems a good fellow, and entirely unparsonical. **1889** 'F. ANSTEY' *Pariah* III. i, A manner which was un-parsonical, not to say secular.

†**un'part,** *v. Obs.*-1 [UN-2 9.] *trans.* To take apart.
1536 *MS. Rawl. D. 780* fol. 73 Not only vpon..framyng of one syde of the same brydge..butt also aswell in vnpartyng the frame ayen.

un'partable, *a.* (UN-1 7 b. Cf. IMPARTIBLE *a.*1)
c **1420** *Wycliffite Bible* Luke, Prol. i, Bi the entringe of the generacioun of vndepartable [*v.r.* unpartable] God. *c* **1555** HARPSFIELD *Divorce Hen. VIII* (Camden) 248 This only consent..is thought to uphold..this unparteable conversation and living together. **1587** GOLDING *De Mornay* xv. 272 That the Soule is a life by it selfe, a life all in one, vnpartable. **1611** COTGR., *Indivisible*,..inseperable, vnpartable.
Hence **un'partableness.**
1647 HEXHAM I, s.v. **1656** BLOUNT, *Individuality*, inseparableness, unpartableness.

unpar'taken, *ppl. a.* (UN-1 8 b.)
1807 ANNA SEWARD *Lett.* (1811) VI. 379 The single solitary Wight, who, in every one of these periodical olios, possesses his separate and un-partaken department.

unpar'taking, *ppl. a.* (UN-1 10.)
1606 DANIEL *Queen's Arcadia* IV. i, And now hath sorrow no worse plague I see, Then free and vnpartaking companie.

un'parted, *ppl. a.* (UN-1 8.)
1561 NORTON & SACKV. *Gorboduc* I. ii, When discent on one alone Makes single and vnparted reigne to light. **1587** GOLDING *De Mornay* xv. 280 The one vniuersall capable mind is and worketh whole and vnparted in euery man. **1613** CHAPMAN *Masque Inns Court* Plays 1873 III. 116 Twinns as of one age, so to one desire May both their bloods giue an vnparted fire. **1648** HEXHAM II, *Ongedeelt*, Vnparted, or Vnshared. **1718** PRIOR *Solomon* I. 188 The Object.. Becomes mixt Blackness, or unparted Light.

un'partial, *a.* [UN-1 7, 5 b.]
1. †**a.** Impartial, unbiassed, fair. *Obs.*
Very common from *c* 1590 to *c* 1660.
1579 W. WILKINSON *Confut. Fam. Love* B ij b, Then must the Judge sit vnparciall in judgement place. **1593** *Sidney's Arcadia* v. (1922) 201, I wayed the matter..with most unpartiall and farthest reach of reason. **1637** HEYWOOD *Royall King* 29 Rendring withall a full satisfactory reason to any unpartiall reader, why they are there. *a* **1662** SANDERSON in Walton *Life* (1796) 496 Upon the clear evidence of truth and reason, after a serious and unpartial examination of the grounds.
b. Free from inclination or fondness.
1844 THACKERAY *B. Lyndon* xv, The widow was not unpartial to me.
2. Unrestricted, ample. *rare*-1.
1787 BENTHAM *Def. Usury* xiii. 137 On the most unpartial and extensive signification.
Hence **un'partialness.**
a **1639** W. WHATELEY *Prototypes* II. xxxii. (1640) 127 O ignorant..creatures that we be, let us beg more wisdome and unpartialnesse to our selves at Gods hand. **1661** FELTHAM *Resolves* II. xxvii. 237 Even in the unpartialness of War.

†**unparti'ality.** *Obs.* (UN-1 12, 5 b.)
1579 W. WILKINSON *Confut. Fam. Love* B ij, In vniformenes of hart and vnpartialitye of minde. **1635** HEYWOOD *Hierarchy* IV. 232 Ovid speaking of the unpartialitie of the fatall Sisters.

†**un'partially,** *adv.* [UN-1 11, 5 b.] Impartially. (Common 1610–50.)
1576 W. RAWELY in Gascoigne *Steele Gl.* Wks. 1910 II. 139 This Glasse of Steele unpartially doth shewe Abuses all, to such as in it looke. **1599** SANDYS *Europæ Spec.* (1629) 248 The truth.., which I haue sincerely and unpartially endeavored to deliver. **1655** FULLER *Ch. Hist.* III. i. §3 About this time Doomes-day-book was made,..unpartially done with rigorous severity. *a* **1662** SANDERSON *Cases Consc.* ix. (1678) 172 Advisedly and unpartially to weigh the benefits.

†**un'partible,** *a. Obs.*-1 [UN-1 7, 5 b.]
= UNPARTABLE *a.*
c **1511** *1st Eng. Bk. Amer.* Introd. (Arb.) 32/1 We beleue in god the father, in god the sonne, and in god the holy gooste. The whyche be vnpartyble and one very god.

unpar'ticipant, *a.* (UN-1 7.)
1866 CARLYLE *Remin.* I. 282, I strictly unparticipant, sitting silently apart till it was done.

unpar'ticipate, *a.* [UN-1 7.] Not participant.
1824 J. H. WIFFEN tr. *Tasso's Jerusalem Delivered* II. xii. And what if some be unparticipate In this new crime?

unpar'ticipated, *ppl. a.* (UN-1 8.)
1678 CUDWORTH *Intell. Syst.* I. iv. 557 In all which several Ranks of Being they supposed One First Universal, and Un-participated,..and many Particular, or Participated Ones. **1781** COWPER *Friendship* 125 Some..are indeed a bog, that bears Your unparticipated cares Unmov'd and without quaking. *a* **1806** H. K. WHITE *Time* 563 Spirit, rear Thy flag on high!—Invincible, and throned In unparticipated might. **1821** BYRON *Cain* I. i, Creating worlds, to make eternity Less burthensome to His immense existence And unparticipated solitude!

unpar'ticipating, *ppl. a.* (UN-1 10.)
1795 COLERIDGE *Lett.* (1895) 148 An unparticipating propensity. **1817** —— *Biog. Lit.* xv. II. 16 It is throughout as if a superior spirit..were placing the whole before our view; himself meanwhile unparticipating in the passions. **1831** CARLYLE *Sart. Res.* I. iii, He was a man so still and altogether unparticipating, that to question him..was a thing of more than usual delicacy.

unpar'ticipative, *a.* (UN-1 7.)
1889 WHITTIER *Pr. Wks.* III. 222 Deep down under the squalid exterior, unparticipative in the..recklessness of the criminal, there is another self.

unpar'ticular, *a.* (UN-1 7.)
1828 L. HUNT *Byron & Contemp.* 93 Written by as unparticular a fellow as one should wish to see with a pair of scissors in his hand.

unpar'ticularized, *ppl. a.* (UN-1 8.)
[**1775** ASH.] **1823** BENTHAM *Not Paul* 67 Time as well as place being left thus unparticularized.

unpar'ticularizing, *ppl. a.* (UN-1 10.)
1835 WILLIS *Pencillings* I. xii. 90 The same lost unexamining, unparticularizing feeling which I cannot overcome in this place.

†**un'partied,** *ppl. a. Obs.*$^{-1}$ [UN-1 8.] Unassisted, unsupported.
1641 SIR E. DERING *Sp. on Relig.* 63 They..ought not to be bound up unheard, and unpartied.

†**un'partingly,** *adv. Obs.*$^{-1}$ [UN-1 11.] With close adherence.
1435 MISYN *Fire of Love* 44 þat, vanite spisyd.., to trewth vnpartyngly we draw.

unpar'took, *pa. pple.* (UN-1 8 b.)
1836 MRS. BROWNING *Rom. Margret* iv, That dream, by that ladye, Is certes unpartook.

un'party. (UN-1 12 b.)
1711 *Peace in Divinity* (title-p.), A Grave Author of Middle and Unparty Principles.

un'pass, *v.* (UN-2 3.)
1605 DANIEL *Queen's Arcadia* 694 *Clo.* Yes, sure, My promise is already past. *Tec.* And if it be, I trust you are so wise T'vnpasse the same againe for your owne good.

un'passable, *a.* [UN-1 7 b, 5 b.]
1. = IMPASSABLE *a.* Now *dial.*
Very common in 17th and 18th centuries.
1553 BRENDE *Q. Curtius* 132 In the daye time the countrey is wild and vnpassable, when they can nether finde any tracte nor waye to go in. **1579–80** NORTH *Plutarch* (1595) 314 The riuer..is vnpassable for any shallow it hath. **1649** F. ROBERTS *Clavis Bibl.* 500 Waters..very deep and unpassable. *a* **1698** TEMPLE *Ess. Heroick Virt.* Wks. 1720 I. 196 Vast and unpassable Mountains or Desarts. **1719** DE FOE *Crusoe* I. (Globe) 263 A Grove of Trees,..so thick, that it was unpassable. **1796** J. MOSER *Hermit of Caucasus* I. 192 The caverns were rendered slippery, and nearly unpassable. **1828–32** WEBSTER s.v., Unpassable roads. **1876–88** in Yks. and Somerset glossaries.
†**b.** As *adv.* Impassably. *Obs.*$^{-1}$
1632 LITHGOW *Trav.* IX. 390 The North side..beeing vnpassable steepe.
2. Incapable of being transcended or exceeded.
1570 DEE *Math. Pref.* 34 They can not prescribe.. certaine vnpassable boundes. **1656** JEANES *Fuln. Christ* 236 The Scotists..say farther, that the degree of Christ's grace was unpassable even by Gods absolute power. *a* **1683** OLDHAM *Wks.* (1686) 109 'Tis I..Who must new Worlds in Vice descry, And fix the pillars of unpassable iniquity.
3. Of money: Incapable of being passed or circulated.
1664 in *Aberdeen N. & Q.* (1910) III. 109/2 Ther was some unpassable money in the poors box. **1696** J. CARY *Ess. Coyn* 10 The Trade of England was apparently slackened since the Small Money was made unpassable. **1745** *De Foe's Eng. Tradesm.* (1841) I. xx. 188 A considerable quantity of false and unpassable money. **1828–32** WEBSTER s.v., Unpassable notes or coins.
Hence **un'passableness.**
1657 R. LIGON *Barbadoes* 75 The unpassableness of the wayes. **1674** EVELYN *Navig. & Comm.* 34 Grave Authors, who speak of the unpassableness of the Ocean. **1691** T. H[ALE] *Acc. New Invent.* 26 Its unpassableness, not to the Water, but to the Worm.

un'passageable, *a.* (UN-1 7 b.)
1592 R. D. *Hypnerotomachia* 94 The ruggednesse of the vnpassageable mountaine Caucasus.

un'passed, un'past, *ppl. a.* (UN-1 8, 5 d.)
1541 *Aberdeen Reg.* XVII. (Jam.), To returne hame on past to the tryst. **1597** MORLEY *Introd. Mus.* To Rdr., Like vnto a great Sea, which the further I entred into, the more I sawe before mee vnpast. **1647** COWLEY *Mistress* 115 Unpast Alps stop mee, but I'le cut through all, And march, the Muses Hanniball. [**1775** ASH, *Unpassed, Unpast.*] **1849** ROCK *Ch. of Fathers* III. x. 477 The strong unpassed wall between them and that defenceless town. **1884** *Knowledge* 4 July 6 Barriers as yet unpassed, and probably impassable.

†**un'passen,** *ppl. a. Obs.*$^{-1}$ [UN-1 8 b.] = prec.
1624 in Capt. Smith *Virginia* Pref. 4 Who loues to liue at home, yet looke abroad, And know both passen and unpassen road.

†**un'passible,** *a.*1 *Obs.* [UN-1 7.]
= UNPASSABLE.
1398 TREVISA *Barth. De P.R.* XV. iii. (1495) F iv/2 In many places in ye vttermeste endes [of Assyria] for dystemperate places ye londe in vnpassyble. [**1775** ASH.]

†**un'passible,** *a.*2 *Obs.* [UN-1 7, 5 b.]
= IMPASSIBLE *a.*
Freq. as an attribute of the Deity.
c **1450** *Mirour Saluacioun* (Roxb.) 140 The gude mens [bodies shall rise] fulle faire with out eend unpassible. **1533** tr. *Erasmus' Com. Crede* 23, I beleue in God the father almyghty vnuysyble and vnpassyble. **1587** GOLDING *De Mornay* iii. 35 First substances, vnchaungeable and vnpassible. **1623** LISLE *Anc. Mon.* (1638) 6 Christs body.. neuer dieth henceforth: but is eternal, and vnpassible.

un'passing, *ppl. a.* (UN-1 10, 5 d + PASSING *ppl. a.* 1, 3.)
1592 *Sc. Acts, Jas. VI* (1814) III. 531/1 The haill estaittis ..to remane in this toun vnpassing furth of the samyne. **1887** 'H. HALIBURTON' *Scotland's Sake* 219 An unpassing present of passionless repose. **1903** W. SHARP in *Life* (1910) 357 It deals in a new way with a subject of unpassing interest.

un'passionate, *a.* Now *rare.* [UN-1 7, 5 b.]
Common from *c* 1600 to *c* 1660.
1. Not influenced or swayed by passion or strong feeling; calm, self-possessed:
a. Of persons, disposition, etc.
1593 *Sidney's Arcadia* (1598) 439 That well appeased gesture, vnpassionate nature bestoweth vpon mankind. **1604** T. WRIGHT *Passions* II. i. 56 That which an vnpassionate mind detested, a passionate soule most effectually pursueth. **1673** CAVE *Prim. Chr.* II. i. 5 We are to be of a meek and unpassionate mind. **1747** CARTE *Hist. Eng.* I. 188 True wisdom..is ever cool and unpassionate when she takes a resolution. **1852** M. ARNOLD *Summer Night* 80 Ye Heavens, whose pure dark regions..though so great Are yet untroubled and unpassionate.
b. Of actions, feelings, etc.
a **1600** HOOKER *Eccl. Pol.* VI. v. §4 A calm, unpassionate, and just assignation of dreadful punishment. **1610** HEALEY *St. Aug. Citie of God* 532 Gods unpassionate and unaltering anger. **1683** E. HOOKER *Pref. Pordage's Mystic Div.* 48 A prettie and unpassionate replie, that a Steward once made to his angri Lord. **1702** C. MATHER *Magn. Chr.* II. ix. 29/1 He did with a very Unpassionate Aspect and Carriage then say, Friends, I thank you all.
†**2.** Unprejudiced, impartial. *Obs.*
1602 T. FITZHERBERT *Apol.* 6 But whether it be reason.. I leaue it to the iudgment of any indifferent & vnpassionate man. *a* **1648** DIGBY *Priv. Mem.* (1827) 243, I am sure you will say, who are yet an indifferent and unpassionate judge, that [etc.].

†**un'passionated,** *ppl. a. Obs.* [UN-1 8.] = prec.
1611 FLORIO, *Spassionato*, vnpassionated, sans passion. **1661** GLANVILL *Van. Dogm.* 100 A set of misconceits, which are..absurd to an unpassionated reason.

un'passionately, *adv.* (UN-1 11; cf. UNPASSIONATE *a.*)
1648 *Eikon Bas.* iv. 24 Make us unpassionately to see the light of Reason. **1661** COWLEY *Cromwell* Wks. 1906 II. 366 Truely and unpassionately reflecting upon the advantages of his person. **1707** *Reflex. upon Ridicule* (1717) I. 44 Those who unpassionately hear him, regard his Mystery as importunate Trifles.

un'passionateness. (UN-1 12.)
1611 COTGR., *Impassibilité*,..vnpassionatenesse. **1655** M. CASAUBON *Enthus.* iii. (1656) 159 Stoicks and Cynicks..who ..chose to beg, and to be trampled upon.., to make good their profession of un-passionatnesse. **1673** O. WALKER *Educ.* 205 If your election be..made..with indifferency, unpassionateness, and sincerity.

un'passioned, *ppl. a.* [UN-1 8.]
= UNPASSIONATE *a.*
a **1618** J. DAVIES (Heref.) *Witte's Pilgr.* Wks. (Grosart) II. 48/2 O you vnpassiond peacefull Harts That with me liue secure in meane estate. **1678** TEMPLE *Let.* Wks. 1720 II. 515 As unpassioned, and as uninteressed Concernment in the.. Service of my Master..as any Man can have. *a* **1764** MRS. CARTER in *Mem.* (1808) II. 103 With calm severity, unpassion'd Age Detects the specious fallacies of Youth.

un'passive, *a.* [UN-1 7.] †**a.** = IMPASSIVE *a.* 1. *Obs.* **b.** Active.
1602 WARNER *Alb. Eng.* XIII. lxxix. 326 Sufficeth vs to know he is..vnpassiue, vnmateriall, vncompounded, Infinite. **1768–74** TUCKER *Lt. Nat.* (1834) II. 568 The principal of those [habits] are faith, and hope, and charity,.. unpassive compliance, readiness to please, and easiness to be pleased.

unpast, variant of UNPASSED *ppl. a.*

un'paste, *v.* (UN-2 3.)
1598 FLORIO, *Spastare*, to vn-paste, to take away the paste or crust of any thing. **1668** R. STEELE *Husbandman's Calling* i. 9 Item, Spent each day..in dressing, painting,..and three hours more at Night in unpasting and undressing again.

un'pastor, *v.* (UN-2 6 b.)
1655 FULLER *Ch. Hist.* VIII. iii. §12 Preferring rather willingly to un-Pastor..themselves than to retain the place, without the power.

un'pastoral, *a.* (UN-1 7.)
1782 WARTON *Rowley Enq.* 95 This very unpathetic and unpastoral idea.., that 'the portcullis of the castle of his heart was fallen'. **1820** SCOTT *Monast.* xxviii, The swain cursed the nymph's bad humour with very unpastoral phrase and emphasis. **1865** RUSKIN *Sesame* 45 The most unpastoral [character] is, instead of feeding, to want to be fed.

un'pasturable, *a.* (UN-1 7 b.)
1796 W. H. MARSHALL *Planting* II. 38 Plantations of Alders should..be confined to swampy, low, unpasturable places.

un'pastured, *ppl. a.* [UN-1 8.]
1. Not led to pasture; unfed.
1548 ELYOT *Impastus*, vnfed, vnpastured, hungry. **1647** HEXHAM I, Vnpastured, *ongeweydt*. *a* **1800** COWPER *Death of Damon* 113 Go, go, my lambs, unpastur'd as ye are. **1821** SHELLEY *Adonais* xxvii, Why didst thou..Dare the unpastured dragon in his den?
2. Not employed for pasture.
1820 SHELLEY *Prometh. Unb.* III. ii. 49 It is the unpastured sea hungering for calm. **1872** BLACKIE *Lays Highl.* 3 Wandering..o'er the wide unpastured sea.

un'patched, *ppl. a.* (UN-1 8.)
[**1775** ASH.] **1824** MISS MITFORD *Village* Ser. I. I. 206 The ragged condition of those unpatched shoes. **1875** WHYTE MELVILLE *Katerfelto* xi, Excuse my freedom in an unpatched pair of breeches.

un'patented, *ppl. a.* (UN-1 8.)
1719 W. WOOD *Surv. Trade* 160 Any Land..that is unpatented, or not granted to some particular Person. **1809** MALKIN *Gil Blas* VIII. ix. ¶2 Invested with full powers to make the world his oyster, and leave nothing but the shell to his unpatented competitors. **1879** *Cassell's Techn. Educ.* IV. 33/1 Unpatented Inventions. **1903** *Westm. Gaz.* 27 Aug. 2/2 The various patented and unpatented medicines of the present day.

un'pathed, *ppl. a.* (UN-1 8.)
1611 SHAKS. *Wint. T.* IV. iv. 578 A wild dedication of your selues To vnpath'd Waters, vndream'd Shores. **1628** FELTHAM *Resolves* II. xxxvi. 111 The lonelinesse of vnpathed Desarts. **1671** MARTEN *Voy. Spitzbergen* in *Acc. Sev. Late Voy.* II. (1694) 30 She always keeps her strait way through these unpathed Waves. **1852** *Q. Rev.* Mar. 441 Three galleys..were sent across these unpathed waters. **1897** BARING-GOULD *Guavas* xiv, He..strode over the unpathed moor.

unpa'thetic, *a.* (UN-1 7.)
[**1775** ASH.] **1782** [see UNPASTORAL *a.*]. **1818** T. L. PEACOCK *Nightmare Abbey* iv, We are all..puppets of a blind and unpathetic necessity. **1903** *Times Lit. Supp.* 16 Jan. 16/1 The not unpathetic image of a big..ape.

un'pathwayed, *a.* (UN-1 9.)
1805 WORDSW. *Waggoner* VI. 24 While she roves..Along the smooth unpathwayed plain.

†**un'patience.** *Obs.* [UN-1 12, 5 b.] Lack of patience; impatience.
1380 *Lay Folks Catech.* (Lamb. MS.) 740 Be grucchyngge and vnpaciens and blasfemynge of god. *c* **1440** *Jacob's Well* 94 þe sexte fote depe of wose in wretthe is vnpacyence. *Ibid.*, Vnpacyens is full of malyce. **1483** CAXTON *Gold. Leg.* 361 b/2 Neuertheles was neuer sene in her signe of unpacyence but alwey swete wordes. **1549** COVERDALE, etc. *Erasm. Par. Gal.* i. 3 b, Lest any thynke that these my wordes are spoken either of hastynes or of vnpacience. **1643** J. STEER tr. *Exp. Chyrurg.* ix. 43 By reason of the Childs unpatience I could not make the Medicine stay.

†**un'patiency.** *Obs. rare.* [UN-1 12, 5 b.]
= prec.
1535 COVERDALE *Judith* viii. 24 They that..put them selues forth with vnpaciency and murmurynge agaynst God. **1558** KNOX *First Blast* (Arb.) 14, I might adduce histories, prouing..some for vnpaciencie to haue murthered them selues.

un'patient, *a.* Now *dial.* [UN-1 7, 5 b.] Impatient.
c **1380** WYCLIF *Sel. Wks.* II. 268 þes þat ben unpacient þat Goddis lawe riȝtid hem. **1387** TREVISA *Higden* (Rolls) II. 167 Ful vnpacient of pees,..and wlatful of sleuþe. *a* **1425** tr. *Arderne's Treat. Fistula*, etc. 22 If ȝe be vnobedient and vnpacient to my commandyngs. *c* **1485** *Digby Myst.* (1882) IV. 948 Nothinge ragid he, ne was vnpaciente. **1560** PILKINGTON *Expos. Aggeus* (1562) 37 The unpacient bearing of [God's scourge]..when it comes. *a* **1586** SIDNEY *Arcadia* I. xii, Though he were very unpatient of long deliberations. **1607** BEAUM. & FL. *Woman-Hater* III. i, *Gond.* Thou hadst better bin a devill. *Orian.* Why my unpatient Lord? **1651** *Fuller's Abel Rediv., Calvin* (1867) I. 321 The commissioners, unpatient of delay, assembled the people together. *a* **1704** T. BROWN *Ess. Women* Wks. 1711 IV. 157, I see..you are un-patient to object against me. **1861** GEO. ELIOT *Silas M.* xiv, The men are..so fiery and unpatient. **1886–96** in Lanc. and Durham glossaries.

†**un'patiently,** *adv. Obs.* [UN-1 11, 5 b.] Impatiently.
c **1425** *Orolog. Sapient.* i. in *Anglia* X. 335/23 þat þou take not vnpacientlye þat diuerse graciose visitacione. **1491** CAXTON *Vitas Patr.* (W. de W. 1495) I. cxi. 136/1 The sayd Sirryens..bare full unpacyently that they were brought in bondage. **1548** CRANMER *Catech.* 93 When such yong babes do not lye softly..they crie vnpatientlye. **1576** FLEMING *Panopl. Epist.* 186 It was manifest..that their minds were exceedingly molested, and tooke their repulse very unpatiently. **1610** HEALEY *St. Aug. Citie of God* XIX. iv. 759 Cato..would not haue done it but that he tooke Cæsar's victory so vnpatiently.

†**un'patientness.** *Obs.* [UN-1 12, 5 b.] Impatience.
1548 CRANMER *Catech.* 140 b, Their unpatientnes is encreaced by such aduersitie. **1587** FLEMING *Contn. Holinshed* III. 1391 Parries exclamation of outrage and vnpatientnesse.

unpatri'archal, *a.* (UN-1 7.)
1859 W. H. GREGORY *Egypt* I. 274 Jabbering and mumbling for a full hour in a most ungodlike, unpatriarchal manner.

un'patrimonied, *ppl. a.* (UN-1 8.)
1782 ELIZ. BLOWER *Geo. Bateman* I. 100 It is the misfortune of the unpatrimonied, that they can only shew their feelings in words.

un'patriot, *v.* (UN-2 6 b.)
1738 *Common Sense* II. 207, I fairly deliver him up to Freeman and Company to unpatriot and revile as much as they please.

unpatri'otic, *a.* (UN-1 7, 5 b.)
[**1775** ASH.] **1828** CARLYLE *Misc.* (1840) I. 362 The French wits of the period were as unpatriotic. **1853** LYTTON *My Novel* XII. xxv, A captain..undertook a long defence of army and navy, from the unpatriotic aspersions of the preceding speakers.

unpatri'otically, *adv.* (UN-1 11.)
1783 EARL MALMESBURY *Diaries & Corr.* II. 34 The clamour, which was very unpatriotically indeed attempted to be raised about it in Parliament. **1850** CARLYLE *Latter-d. Pamph.* i. 23 Of America it would ill beseem any Englishman ..to speak unpatriotically, if any of us even felt so. **1861** TROLLOPE *Tales All Countries* vii. 273 Unpatriotically acquiescent as to England's aristocratic propensities.

un'patriotism. (UN-^{1} 12, 5 b.)
1887 *Blackfriars Mag.* Jan. 225 In the desire..lay the germ of unpatriotism, a forgetting that they were Englishmen at all. [Freq. from *c* 1905.]

un'patroned, *ppl. a.* (UN-^{1} 8.)
1741 Warburton *Div. Legat.* II. Pref. p. xiv, This Disadvantage..gave his first Volume, unpatroned and unfriended as it was, so very kind a Reception.

un'patronized, *ppl. a.* (UN-^{1} 8.)
1620 J. Beale *Ded.* in *Hieron's Serm.*, etc. I. ¶2 The author of this present volume..left not only some members of it vnpatroniz'd, but the whole frame without a generall sustainer. **1661** Rawley *Resuscitatio* (ed. 2) Ded. a j, This unpatroniz'd Booke. **1751** Johnson *Rambler* No. 120 ⁋11 Unpatronized and unsupported, he cleared himself by the openness of innocence. **1814** Scott *Wav.* ii, The young officer..rose in the army with a rapidity far surpassing the usual pace of unpatronized professional merit. **1865** Mill *Repr. Govt.* vii. 158 Those who are desirous of voting for unpatronized persons of merit.

un'patterned, *ppl. a.* [UN-^{1} 8.]
1. Unexampled, unequalled. Now *arch.*
1621 Fletcher *Thierry & Theod.* III. i, To bring forth a second to your self, Was only worthy of my Virgin loss; And should I prize you less, unpattern'd Sir, Then being exemplify'd? **1641** Prynne *Dioc. Prel. Tyr.* I. 35 The unpatternd compliency both of the Judges, and Court of Star-Chamber. **1657** Bp. H. King *Poems* (1843) 48 What debt of service I do truly ow To your unpattern'd self. **1899** *Academy* 28 Oct. 479/2 Old Sam Butler, most singular and unpatterned of satirists.
2. Not decorated with a pattern.
1884 *Bazaar* 19 Dec. 658/1 The only rule seems to be that the fabric must be unpatterned.
3. Not formed or cast into a pattern.
1949 M. Mead *Male & Female* ix. 190 Man, the heir of tradition, provides for women and children. We have no indication that man..unpatterned by social learning, would do anything of the sort. **1960** T. McLean *Kings of Rugby* xi. 192 Too much unpatterned play. **1977** *Sci. Amer.* Jan. 117/1 Consider an analogous isomorphism exhibited by a sequence of unpatterned digits such as pi.

un'paunch, *v.* [UN-^{2} 4.] = PAUNCH *v.*^{1} 2.
1598 Florio, *Suiscerato*, vnbowelled, vnpanched. **1603** —— *Montaigne* I. xlviii. 159 To save themselves from the extreamitie of the cold, many advised to kil and vnpanch their horses, and enter into their panches. **1622** Mabbe tr. *Aleman's Guzman d'Alf.* I. 39 The old woman was vnpanching the belly of an old rotten sheepe.

un'pauperized, *ppl. a.* (UN-^{1} 8.)
1846 Worcester (citing *Q. Rev.*). **1896** W. D. Howells *Impressions & Experiences* 135 It could not have been said that she was wholly unpauperised before she took it [*sc.* money].

un'pausing, *ppl. a.* (UN-^{1} 10.)
1837 Lytton *Athens* II. 371 Restless and unpausing energy. **1857** Dufferin *Lett. High Lat.* (ed. 3) 334 Raging and bubbling up.., the unpausing wave sweeps on. **1898** G. Wyndham *Poems Shakespeare* 266 The pause in the first line ..is heavily pointed to prepare for the unpausing outburst of the last two.
Hence **un'pausingly** *adv.*
1891 *Athenæum* 4 July 36/2 The brisk and stirring kind [of story] that may be read unpausingly.

un'pave, *v.* [UN-^{2} 4.] *trans.* To lift or remove the paving of (a street, etc.).
1598 Florio, *Dimattonare*, to vnpaue, to vnbrick. **1623** tr. *Favine's Theat. Hon.* v. i. 44 During that yeare, the Primatiall Church..had the Altars vnpaued..and the Belles vn-hung. **1686** *Lond. Gaz.* No. 2147/2 They have unpaved the Streets. **1769** Falconer *Dict. Marine* (1780) s.v. *Waterspout*, This whirlwind['s]..general effects on houses were..forcing up the floors, and unpaving the rooms. **1827** Hood *Don't you smell fire?* iv, Here's a nice easy bit in the street, That M'Adam has lately unpaved! **1859** Sala *Tw. round Clock* (1861) 28, I might take one house and unroof it, one street and unpave it.

un'paved, *ppl. a.* (UN-^{1} 8.)
a **1533** Ld. Berners *Gold. Bk. M. Aurel.* (1546) P v, O Rome, I wepe not to see thy streetes vnpaued,..nor that the battylmentes fall downe. **1585** T. Washington tr. *Nicholay's Voy.* II. xviii. 51 b, A great and large place vnpaued. **1627** Hakewill *Apol.* II. vii. 123 The streetes of the citty lying then vnpaued. **1741** tr. *D'Argen's Chinese Lett.* xiii. 82 If most of its Streets were not crooked, narrow, rugged, and generally unpav'd. **1805** *Ann. Rev.* III. 18 In Philadelphia the privies are unpaved. **1833** M. Scott *Tom Cringle* xvi, We marched up through a hot, sandy, unpaved street. **1884** *Manch. Exam.* 14 Nov. 5/6 The roads were all unpaved earth roads.
fig. **1823** Byron *Juan* x. ii, The mode In which Sir Isaac Newton could disclose Through the then unpaved stars the turnpike road.
b. In allusive use: (cf. STONED *ppl. a.* 4).
1611 Shaks. *Cymb.* II. iii. 34 It is a voyce in her eares which Horse-haires, and Calues-guts, nor the voyce of vnpaued Eunuch to boot, can neuer amend.

unpa'vilioned, *a.* (UN-^{1} 9.)
[**1775** Ash.] **1819** Shelley *Prometh. Unb.* IV. 184 As the bare, green hill..Laughs with a thousand drops of sunny water To the unpavilioned sky. **1839** G. Darley *Nepenthe* I. 5 High on his unpavilioned throne The heaven's hot tyrant sat alone.

un'pawn, *v.* (UN-^{2} 3.)
1598 Florio, *Disimpegnare*, to vnpaune, to redeeme. **1636** Davenant *Wits* Wks. (1673) 169 We can't unpawn the Oaths We left at the Bar for the last Reckoning. **1680** *Lond. Gaz.* No. 1496/4 The Murderer..having unpawn'd and changed his Cloaths.

un'pawned, *ppl. a.* (UN-^{1} 8.)
1638 R. Baillie *Lett. & Jrnls.* (1841) I. 58 Would it not grieved them to see the subjects suffer by the relying upon unpauned trust? **1639** Massinger *Unnat. Combat* III. i, Tis well I have one [suit] Unpawnd in these dayes. **1728** Pope *Dunc.* I. 116 He roll'd his eyes that witness'd huge dismay, Where yet unpawn'd, much learned lumber lay. **1909** Stacpoole *Pools of Silence* ii, The cigarettes and the unpawned banjo.

†**un'pay,** *v.*^{1} *Obs.* [UN-^{1} 14, 5 d.]
1. *trans.* To displease.
1340 *Ayenb.* 50 Glotounye..is a vice þet þe dyeuel is moche myde ypayd, and moche onpayþ god.
2. To leave unpaid; not to pay.
1515 *Reg. Privy Seal Scotl.* I. 409/1 At every viage..he frelie and unpaying ony custumez may discharge and charge [etc.]. **1540** *Extr. Aberd. Reg.* (1844) I. 173 To..poind the personis for the rest of the taxt..of thame that hes vnpayit the samen. **1697** De la Pryme *Diary* 16 Oct., Mr. Elways did..grant unto his tennants..all their land to be tithe free, which they have unpay'd untill this time.

†**un'pay,** *v.*^{2} *Obs.*$^{-1}$ [UN-^{2} 3.] *trans.* To undo, make good.
1597 Shaks. *2 Hen. IV*, II. i. 133 Pay her the debt you owe her, and vnpay the villany you haue done her.

un'payable, *a.* [UN-^{1} 7 b, 5 b.]
1. Incapable of being paid: a. Of debts, etc.
1463 G. Ashby *Prisoner's Refl.* 44, I am put to vnpayable det. **1611** Cotgr., *Insolvable*, vnpayable, vnlikely to be payed. **1656** Earl Orrery *Parthen.* III. iv. 269, I finde my scores of gratitude are as unpayable to the Brother, as those of adoration are to the Sister. *a* **1716** South *Serm.* (1744) X. 295 The debt of a thousand talents due to him from her, yet by reason of this her great poverty..utterly unpayable. **1899** Mackail *W. Morris* ii. 27 The price is unpayable.
b. Of persons.
1856 Lever *Martins of Cro' M.* xxxi. 325 Our Club [would] become only an asylum for unpayable tailors. **1868** Carlyle in *Mrs. C.'s Lett.* (1883) I. 24 A poor creditor, unpayable, overheard Mrs. A. whispering, 'Let us keep' [etc.]
2. Incapable of paying; unremunerative.
1880 G. Sutherland *Tales Goldfields* 50 The goldfields were unpayable. **1896** in Morris *Austral-Eng.* (1898) 487 Unpayable Lines... Of these [railways] 33..do not pay working expenses.

un'paying, *ppl. a.* (UN-^{1} 10.)
1682 Dryden *Epil. to King & Queen* 26 We've none so great but their unpaying Masters. **1843** Syd. Smith *Amer. Debts* ii. ⁋3, I am astonished that the honest States of America do not draw a *cordon sanitaire* round their unpaying brethren. **1894** D. Campbell *Coleridge* vi. 121 Which he spent much of his time inditing in the form of letters to his unpaying correspondents!

un'payment. (UN-^{1} 12.)
a **1578** Lindesay (Pitscottie) *Chron. Scot.* (S.T.S.) I. 351, I know no cause quhairfoir, bot that he discordit witht his persone ffor wnpayment of his teindis.

un'peace. Now *arch.* [UN-^{1} 12, prob. after *unfrith.* (UN-^{1} 3). Cf. MDu. *onpays*, obs. Du. *onpaais*, Flem. *onpeys* (Kilian).] Absence of peace; dissension, strife.
a **1300** *Cursor M.* 414 He..sette þam in haly palais, þar neuer mai be of pride unpais. *Ibid.* 13306 To man þai wroght neuer vn-pes. *c* **1380** Wyclif *Sel. Wks.* I. 250 Men ben now redi to heeren of unpees, batailis, and strives. **1420–22** Lydg. *Thebes* III. 4260 Fell Ethyocles, Rote of vn-reste and causer of vnpes. *a* **1470** *Dives & Pauper* (W. de W. 1496) v. xvii. 219/1 He bad them absteyne them from all tokenes of unpacyence, of unpeas, and of crueltee.
1876 Morris *Sigurd* II. 89 Where unpeace and troubles and the griefs of the soul abide. **1906** Mary Cholmondeley *Prisoners* vi, There is an unpeace which passes understanding also.

un'peaceable, *a.* Now *rare.* [UN-^{1} 7 b. Cf. UNPEACIBLE *a.*]
1. Not disposed to peace; contentious, turbulent.
c **1520** M. Nisbet *Jas.* iii. 8 Naman may chastice the toung, for it is ane vnpeceable [*Wyclif* unpesible] euile. **1570** Drant *Serm.* E vj b, What warres..hath this foule and vnpeaceable woman brought to passe? **1608** Dod & Cleaver *Expos. Prov.* ix–x. 86 If our hearts..begin to grow turbulent and unpeaceable. **1682** *Sec. Plea Nonconf.* 66 The Arrians were Calumniators of the Orthodox, and so are the Papists, and unpeaceable Lutherans. **1860** Ruskin *Unto this Last* i. (1862) 25 An unpeaceable and often irrational person.
2. Characterized by want of peace or quiet.
a **1548** Hall *Chron., Hen. VI*, 101 The lord Scales and his company,..together in an vnpeaceable fury, set on their enemies. **1635** Brathwait *Arcad. Pr.* 55 We..live both in these factious and unpeaceable times. **1649** Milton *Eikon.* xviii. 165 Suttle and unpeaceable designes. **1702** Echard *Eccl. Hist.* III. vi. 408 His scandalous, irregular and unpeaceable Practices. **1770** Langhorne *Plutarch* V. 219 His unpeaceable and unsalutary conduct.
Hence **un'peaceableness.** (Common *c* 1655–*c* 1690.)
c **1475** *Cath. Angl.* 277/2 Vn Pesseabilnes, *impaciencia*,.. *inquietudo, proteruitas.* **1651** Baxter *Inf. Bapt.* 246, I would not have unpeaceableness and division to be encouraged. **1690** T. Burnet *Theory Earth* II. 193 The disorders of our passions,..and the unpeaceableness of the world.

un'peaceably, *adv.* (UN-^{1} 11; cf. prec.)
1651 Baxter *Inf. Bapt.* 121 The most able may not unpeaceably or intemperately contradict it. **1717** De Foe *Mem. Ch. Scot.* III. 16 It was alledged by the Persons that were thus taken up,..that they had not acted unpeaceably or undutifully to his Majesty in any Thing.

†**un'peaced,** *ppl. a.* *Obs.*$^{-1}$ [UN-^{2} 8.] Deprived of peace; disquieted.
c **1450** tr. *De Imitatione* III. xlvii. 117 If þou sette þy pes wiþ eny persone for þin owne felyng & lyvinge togidres, þou shalt be unstable & unpesed.

un'peaceful, *a.* (UN-^{1} 7.)
1611 Florio, *Inpacifico*, vnquiet, vnpeacefull. **1645** Milton *Tetrach.* 80 Man or wife who hates in wedloc, is perpetually unsociable, unpeacefull, or unduteous. **1647** Cowley *Mistr.*, *Wish* iii, Eas'd of unpeaceful thoughts. **1734** Thomson *Liberty* IV. 678 Immature, and red with glorious wounds, Unpeaceful death their choice. **1797** Lamb *'Alas! how am I changed'* 54 The not unpeaceful evening of a day Made black by morning storms. **1805** Wordsw. *Prelude* VI. 76 Lofty elms..Bestowed composure on a neighbourhood Un-peaceful in itself. **1831** Arnold *Let.* in Stanley *Life* (1858) I. 240 The violence of political quarrels seeming to be something shocking because it was so unpeaceful.

†**un'peacible,** *a.* In 4–5 **vnpesible, -peisyble, -peysible.** [UN-^{1} 7.] = UNPEACEABLE *a.*
1382 Wyclif *Jas.* iii. 8 The tunge..is an vnquyet, or vnpesible, yuel thing. **1388** —— *1 Thess.* v. 14 Britheren,.. repreue ȝe vnpesible men. **1398** Trevisa *Barth. De P.R.* XIII. xxvi. (Tollem. MS.), A criynge see and an unpesible is perilouse. *a* **1400** *New Test.* (Paues) App. i, Jas. iii. 8 Tunge no man may make tame, ful of vnpeisyble yuel. *c* **1430** *Life St. Katherine* (1884) 52 Lest he schold be accused..as wykked and vnpeysible. **1482** *Rolls of Parlt.* VI. 220/2 Many ..been of such evill disposition and unpesible, that the Maier..may not gyde..the people.
Hence †**un'peacibly** *adv.* *Obs.*$^{-1}$
a **1400** *Wycliffite Bible* 2 Thess. iii. 11 We han herd summe among ȝou for to wandre inquyet,..or inpesibli [*v.rr.* vnpesiblely, vnpesibly; L. *inquiete*].

un'peccable, *a.* [UN-^{1} 7 b, 5 b.] Impeccable.
1818 Bentham *Ch. Eng.* 333 Still, though never sinning, he was not yet unpeccable.

unpe'dantic, *a.* (UN-^{1} 7.)
1796 Burney *Mem. Metastasio* II. 316 This essay is sufficient to manifest..the solid, unpedantic cultivation of your happy talents. **1829** Lytton *Devereux* I. iv, He would speak of courts and kings in an easy and unpedantic strain. **1840** Mill *Dissert. & Disc.* (1859) II. 41 [The Americans'] cast of mind is altogether unpedantic and practical.

un'pedestal, *v.* (UN-^{2} 5.) Hence **un'pedestalled** *ppl. a.*
1821 *Tales Landlord, Witch of Glas Llyn* II. 38 Force me not to unpedestal you from the proud height to which my adoring fancy has raised you. **1839** Lady Lytton *Cheveley* (ed. 2) I. xii. 278 He did not think..there was any danger of George Sand's un-pedestaling the..Despinasses of the olden time. **1881** T. Hardy *Laodicean* II. iii, His well-curved youthful form looked like an unpedestaled Dionysus.

un'pedigreed, *ppl. a.* (UN-^{1} 8.)
1827 Pollok *Course T.* VIII. 90 Unscutcheoned all, Uncrowned, unplumed, unhelmed, unpedigreed. **1879** *Cassell's Techn. Educ.* IV. 246/2 The Yorkshire cow, or.. unpedigreed shorthorn.

un'peel, *v.* (UN-^{2} 9.)
1904 W. James *Let.* 16 June in R. B. Perry *Thought & Character W. James* (1935) II. 487 The original 'that' may vanish in the infinitely regressive superposition of human 'whats'—we can't today unpeel them wholly. *a* **1914** in *Penguin Bk. Austral. Ballads* (1964) 122 Then the sheila raced off squealin', And her clothes she was un-peelin'. **1969** *Washington Post* 14 Apr. A27/3 Aides believe that the Kennedy ploy..will ultimately unpeel Republican Senators from the anti-ABM forces.

un'peeled, *ppl. a.* (UN-^{2} 9.)
In Shaks. *L.L.L.* II. 88 the Quarto has *unpeeled* for *unpeopled* of the Folio.
1599 A. M. tr. *Gabelhouer's Bk. Physicke* 360/2 Take vnpeeled Barlye,..and Misleden of Abiete,..with his leaues. **1725** *Fam. Dict.* s.v. *Apricock-tree*, Those [apricots] that are over-ripe, whether peeled or unpeeled. **1750** G. Hughes *Barbados* 182 If this unripe fruit [of the Papaw] when unpeeled is boiled. **1814** Southey *Roderick* XVIII. 127 He.. held a natural cross Of rudest form, unpeel'd, even as it grew On the near oak that morn. **1887** Moloney *Forestry W. Africa* 361 Peeled Colocynth, and Mogador or Un-peeled Colocynth.

un'peerable, *a.* (UN-^{1} 7 b + PEER *v.*^{1})
1604 Webster *Malcontent* III. i, O unpeerable invention! rare!

un'peered, *ppl. a.* [UN-^{1} 8.] Unequalled, unrivalled.
1602 Marston *Antonio's Rev.* I. i, What a toplesse mount Of unpeer'd mischiefe have these hands cast up! **1636** Heywood *Challenge* I. i, Most unpeer'd Lady, that, not for ten Worlds. **1795** Macneill *Scotland's Scaith* v. xii, Roslin's banks, unpeered by ony, Save the muses' Hawthornden. **1855** Bailey *Mystic*, etc. 152 Where's the castle, that on yonder mountain piled Held the prince unpeered in honour?

un'peg, *v.* (UN-^{2} 4 b.) Also *fig.* Hence **un'pegging** *vbl. sb.*
1602 Shaks. *Ham.* III. iv. 193 Vnpegge the Basket on the houses top: Let the Birds flye. **1611** Cotgr., *Declaveter*, to vnbolt, vnpinne, vnpeg; loose from. **1863** W. C. Baldwin *Afr. Hunting* ii. 51 He at length charged against the side of the tent, unpegging two of the ropes. **1923** J. M. Keynes *Tract on Monetary Reform* 121 The present situation..did not begin until after the 'unpegging' of the leading exchanges in 1919. **1975** 'M. Yorke' *Small Hours* i. 14 A young woman came to unpeg them [*sc.* the clothes]. **1977** *Guardian Weekly* 7 Aug. 10/1 Unpegging sterling from the US dollar is a thoroughly sensible move. **1977** *Times* 29 Oct. 19/4 The Israel pound fell sharply as it was unpegged from

its official rate of 10 to the dollar. **1981** *Ibid.* 21 Jan. 11/4 They chat as they unpeg the washing.

un'pegged, *ppl. a.* (UN-¹ 8.)
1697 *View Penal Laws* 253 Neither shall any suffer his swine to run in any such Grounds or Woods unringed or unpegged.

unpeisyble, var. UNPEACIBLE *a. Obs.*

un'pen, *v.* [UN-² 5. Cf. OE. *onpennian*, and UNPEND *v.*] *trans.* To let out of, release from, a pen or enclosure.
a **1592** GREENE *Jas. IV*, IV. iii, The lamb is vnpent, the fox shal preuaile. **1766** BLACKSTONE *Comm.* II. 395 If one obstructs another's antient windows,.. fouls his water, or unpens or lets it out, &c. **1817** J. F. PENNIE *Royal Minstr.* II. 10 Young David from the fold His..playful lambs unpenn'd. **1820** CLARE *Poems* (ed. 3) 127 The shepherd.. Unpens and frees the captive sheep.
fig. **1818** KEATS *Endym.* III. 2 There are..who unpen Their baaing vanities, to browse away [etc.].

un'penal, *a.* (UN-¹ 7.)
1641 CLARENDON *Ess. Divine & Moral* Tracts (1727) 213 It [*sc.* the Law] may render me more potent to do hurt and injury, by making that damage and injury unpenal to me.

un'penanced, *ppl. a.* (UN-¹ 8.)
1624 MIDDLETON *Game at Chess* III. i, How dares your Pawn unpenanced.. Appear in this assembly?

un'pencilled, *ppl. a.* (UN-¹ 8.)
1628 FELTHAM *Resolves* II. xxiii. 76 There is no disposition, but hath a varnisht vizor, as well as an vnpencill'd face.

†**un'pend,** *v. Obs.*⁻¹ [UN-² 3.] = UNPEN *v.*
1565 GOLDING *Ovid's Met.* I. 4 b, Poure out your force,.. your headdes eche one vnpende, And from your open sprynges your streames with flowyng waters send.

†**un'penetrable,** *a. Obs.* [UN-¹ 7 b, 5 b.] Impenetrable.
c **1400** *Found. St. Bartholomew's* (1923) 17 As yt were with an vnpenytrable scochyn wardid and defendyd. **1581** J. BELL *Haddon's Answ. Osor.* 187 b, God accordyng to his unpenetrable counsell doth determine all thinges. **1630** J. TAYLOR (Water P.) *Pennilesse Pilgr.* Wks. I. 129/2 The Foundation and Walls are vnpenetrable, the Rampiers impregnable. **1652** G. HERBERT *Priest to the Temple* xxxiv. 152 To them an unpenetrable rock, an unaccessible desert.

un'penetrated, *ppl. a.* (UN-¹ 8.)
[**1775** ASH.] **1781** PENNANT *Hist. Quadrup.* I. 161 In some of those remote parts..unpenetrated yet by Europeans. **1831** CARLYLE *Sart. Res.* II. viii, An American Backwoodsman, who had to fell unpenetrated forests. **1868** MILMAN *St. Paul's* 160 The unpenetrated darkness of futurity.

un'penetrating, *ppl. a.* (UN-¹ 10.)
1748 RICHARDSON *Clarissa* (1768) I. 217 This, frequently, the unpenetrating world calls Humanity.

un'penitent, *a.* ? *Obs.* (UN-¹ 7, 5 b.)
1546 COVERDALE *Treatise on Lord's Supper* A v b, The vnpenitent herte of the persone whych receyueth it [*sc.* the sacrament]. **1562** PILKINGTON *Expos. Abdyas* 128 It [*sc.* absolution] is no more profitable thanne.. the communion is too an hypocrite or unpenitente sinner. **1651** HOBBES *Leviath.* III. xlii. 275 The Apostles had not the Power..to grant it [*sc.* Baptism] to the Un-penitent. **1801** SOUTHEY *Garci Ferrandez* II. iv, Fearless, unpenitent, unblest, Without a prayer they sunk to rest.

un'penned, *ppl. a.*¹ [UN-¹ 8.] Unwritten.
1587 TURBERV. *Trag. T.* A iv b, My booke.. I send,.. Though reason willes it rather left vnpend. **1594** R. WILSON *Coblers Proph.* II. i. 145 Loath was I that vnpend one iote of this should goe.

un'penned, *ppl. a.*² [f. UNPEN *v.*] Let out of a pen.
1596 W. SMITH *Chloris* viii, But I..My vnpend flocke vnto the mountaines led.

un'pennied, *a.* (UN-¹ 9.)
1822 LAMB *Elia* I. *Praise Chimney-Sweepers*, This is *saloop* —..the delight, and..the envy, of the unpennied sweep. **1848** CLOUGH *Amours de Voy.* I. 132 To introduce at assemblies To the unpennied cadets our cousins with excellent fortunes.

un'pensioned, *ppl. a.* (UN-¹ 8.)
1728 POPE *Dunciad* III. 330 Gay dies unpension'd with a hundred friends. **1732** —— *Hor. Sat.* II. i. 116 Could.. I not strip the gilding off a knave, Unplac'd, unpension'd..? **1771** *Ann. Reg., Chron.* 203/1, I come here unplaced, unpensioned, to give my vote voluntarily. **1817** BYRON *Mazeppa* iv, So sung his poets, all but one, Who, being unpension'd, made a satire. **1891** *Daily News* 15 July 3/1 Some of the unpensioned survivors of the Crimean and of the Indian Mutiny campaigns.

un'pensioning, *ppl. a.* (UN-¹ 10.)
1853 DICKENS *Bleak Ho.* xl, An ungrateful and unpensioning country.

un'pent, *ppl. a.* (UN-² 8.)
1820 SHELLEY *Prometh. Unb.* I. 688 We make there our liquid lair, Voyaging cloudlike and unpent Through the boundless element. **1861** LD. LYTTON & FANE *Tannhäuser* 52 Nor e'er Bade unpent passion wildly start Through the forced portals of thy heart. **1885–94** R. BRIDGES *Eros & Psyche* March xv, The hour When beauty, from its fleshy bud unpent, Flaunts like the corol of a summer flower.

un'people, *v.* [UN-² 4.]
1. *trans.* To divest or empty of people; to depopulate.
a **1533** LD. BERNERS *Gold. Bk. M. Aurel.* (1546) K vj b, Bycause thou hast vnpeopled the lanes and stretes of workemen and officers, and hast peopled it all about with infinite vacaboundes. **1594** KYD *Cornelia* IV. i. 106 [Caesar] hath vnpeopled most part of the earth. **1641** MILTON *Reform.* II. 60 They have unpeopl'd the Kingdome by expulsion of so many thousands. **1685** N. CROUCH *Eng. Emp. Amer.* i. 2 There is no such Torrid Zone where the heat is so noxious as to unpeople any part of the Earth. **1768** STERNE *Sent. Journ., Paris*, Thirty-five years..have unpeopled her dominions of the slaves of love. **1820** BYRON *Mar. Fal.* III. ii. 492 'Tis mine to sound the knell, and strike the blow, Which shall unpeople many palaces. **1865** W. G. PALGRAVE *Arabia* II. 328 Systematic ill government can do more to unpeople a land than..the Black Death.
transf. **1712** BLACKMORE *Creation* VII. 40 That costly banquets.. May crown thy table,.. Ransack the hills,.. The lake unpeople, and despoil the flood. **1781** *Westm. Mag.* IX. 263 Now, to unpeople ev'ry brook, The long-neglected mesh repairs.
b. *fig.* To divest or strip *of* something.
1823 CHALMERS *Serm.* I. iv. 114 When the business of devotion is thus unpeopled of all its externals.
2. To divest of the status of a people.
1653 O. SEDGWICK *Doubting Believer* 255 It is an unadvised folly in the suspension of Gods favour, to unsonne our selves, and unpeople our selves.

'unpeople, *sb.* [UN-¹ 12.] **a.** People excluded from 'the people' as understood politically. **b.** Unpersons.
1962 E. SNOW *Other Side of River* (1963) l. 380 There is less mystery in China today than in most Communist countries about what both people and 'unpeople' find unbearable. **1968** *Guardian* 28 Nov. 11/2 (*heading*) Czech unpeople down on the farm. **1970** *Guardian Weekly* 21 Mar. 6 People on foot on a hot road..walking from nowhere to nowhere... Tired people. Unpeople. **1975** P. LIVELY *Going Back* vii. 88 Who are those people the Greeks knew about —the ones who wander around the Styx? The unburied dead: grey, unpeople. I am one of them. **1975** LD. HAILSHAM *Door wherein I Went* vi. 28 Communists teach that there was no such person as Jesus at all... He is the unperson to end all unpeople.

un'peopled, *ppl. a.* [UN-¹ 8.] Not populated; uninhabited; without people.
In some contexts perhaps influenced by UNPEOPLE *v.*
a **1586** C'TESS PEMBROKE *Ps.* LXXVIII. xiv, He made them waste their weary yeares Roaming in vain in that unpeopled place. **1627** SPEED *England* xlv. §7 This Iland so small.. and so vnpeopled and vnprofitable. **1667** MILTON *P.L.* III. 497 The Paradise of Fools, to few unknown Long after, now unpeopl'd, and untrod. **1737** GLOVER *Leonidas* IV. 638 What suff'rings to compensate.. for unpeopled realms, And all this waste of nature? **1774** GOLDSM. *Nat. Hist.* VII. 131 The crocodile..found in unpeopled countries. **1816** WILSON *City of Plague* III. i. 122 He loves the silence Of an unpeopled reign. **1839** CARLYLE *Chartism* iv, Ireland will be burnt into a black unpeopled field of ashes. **1887** BOWEN *Æneid* VI. 269 The unpeopled realm of Death.

un'peppered, *ppl. a.* (UN-¹ 8.)
1648 HEXHAM II, *Ongepepert*, Vnpeppred, or without pepper. **1814** COLMAN *Vagaries Vind.* (1818) 203 Ye Novel-Readers!—such as relish most Plain Nature's feast, unpepper'd with a Ghost. **1846** LANDOR *Imag. Conv.* Wks. II. 16/1 A plate of unpeppered cucumbers.

unper'ceivable, *a.* [UN-¹ 7 b, 5 b.] Imperceptible.
a **1395** HYLTON *Scala Perf.* II. viii. (W. de W. 1494), Thorugh a pryue vnperceyuable worchyng of the holy ghost. *c* **1400** LOVE *Bonavent. Mirr.* (1908) 290 In a moment, that is in an vnperceyuable short tyme. **1603** FLORIO *Montaigne* II. xii. 284 Who knowes not how vnperceivable the neighbourhood betweene folly with the liveliest elevations of a free minde is. **1617** MORYSON *Itin.* III. 45 Their motion, being made in time vnperceiuable by vs. **1709** BERKELEY *Th. Vision* §72 The particles of the..vapours, which are themselves unperceivable. **1768–74** TUCKER *Lt. Nat.* (1834) I. 619 The chain of causes and effects..divides into so many unperceivable threads. **1801** *Monthly Mag.* XII. 422 One of those French reputations, which, when weighed in the European scale, is almost unperceivable. *a* **1882** T. H. GREEN *Proleg. Ethics* 347 That God is as unimaginable as he is unperceivable.
Hence **unper'ceivableness.**
1611 FLORIO, *Impercettibilita*, vnperceiuablenesse.

unper'ceivably, *adv.* [UN-¹ 11, 5 b: cf. prec.] Imperceptibly.
a **1395** HYLTON *Scala Perf.* II. viii. (W. de W. 1494), How it is wonderly & vnperceyuably chaunged..vnto the fayrnes of an angell. **1603** FLORIO *Montaigne* III. iv. 500, I vnperceauablie remooued those dolefull humours from hir. **1695** BP. ROCHESTER *Disc. Clergy* 39 With the Scriptures.. their Memories will unperceivably be filled. **1713** *Guardian* No. 56, [They] rolled their trains unperceivably beneath their habits.

unper'ceived, *ppl. a.* [UN-¹ 8.]
1. Without being perceived or noticed. Occas. const. *by* or *of.*
c **1350** *Will. Palerne* 1676 þat noþer clerk nor kniȝt.. Schal passe vnperceyued & pertiliche of-souȝt. *c* **1400** *Destr. Troy* 8657 Achilles grippit a gret speire,..Vnpersayuit of the prince prikit hym to. **1533** MORE *Apol.* iii. Wks. 848/1 They would..haue their false folies passe and repasse all vnperceiued. **1593** SHAKS. *Lucrece* 1010 The crow may.. unperceiv'd fly with the filth away. **1667** MILTON *P.L.* XI. 224 Hee alone..took his way, Not unperceav'd of Adam. **1725** POPE *Odyss.* XXII. 194 Behind the felon unperceiv'd they past. **1760–72** H. BROOKE *Fool of Qual.* (1809) III. 17 Unperceived of Harry, he displayed the bills to the company. **1834** *Tait's Mag.* I. 189/2 The intrenchment being cast up unperceived, in the middle of the night. **1875** JOWETT *Plato* (ed. 2) III. 67 Chance words..which fall unperceived on the reader's mind.
2. Not perceived; unobserved.
c **1500** *Three Kings' Sons* 84 Departid this yonge gentilman..so secretly that he was vnperceyued. **1581** MULCASTER *Positions* xxxiii. 120 Galene also maketh the litle vnperceiued, or for the smallnesse contemned, to be mother of all illes. **1665** BOYLE *Occas. Refl.* IV. ix, Moisture.. convey'd but by little and little.., and by unperceivd Passages, and yet.. able to impart Fertility. **1768** BOSWELL *Corsica* p. xii, Even the succession of Chiefs has been unperceived. **1790** COLERIDGE *Progr. Vice* 7 By unperceiv'd degrees she tempts to stray, Till far from Virtue's path she leads the feet away. **1842** IS. WILLIAMS *Baptistery* 43 Time marks not Death with unperceived tread Steal on behind. **1898** LUCY B. WALFORD *Archdeacon* II. ii, St. Andrews was unperceived, and drew back..disconcerted.
Hence **unper'ceivedly** *adv.*
1633 T. ADAMS *Exp. 2 Peter* ii. 18 That they may not too unperceivedly catch us, let me a little bare their hooke. **1663** BOYLE *Usef. Exp. Nat. Philos.* II. App. 352 Sometimes in filtration, some of the thinner parts of the oyl have unperceivedly passed through the paper. **1713** DERHAM *Physico-Theol.* III. iv. 78 Descending (though unperceivedly) gently down..to the Sea.

unper'ceiving, *ppl. a.* (UN-¹ 10.)
1723 WATERLAND *Sec. Vindic. Christ's Divinity* xxiii. 448 To make you at length sensible of Two Things, about which you have been hitherto very slow and unperceiving. **1803** *Monthly Mag.* XIV. 490 For an idea to exist in an unperceiving thing is a contradiction.

unper'ceivingness. (UN-¹ 12; or f. prec.)
1685 RENWICK *Serm.*, etc. (1776) 144 What unperceivingness of temper is this?

†**unper'ceptable,** *a.* [UN-¹ 7 b.] = next.
1683 MOXON *Mech. Exerc., Printing* xxiv. ¶ 19 The small un-level lying of every Sheet, though unperceptable in a small number of Sheets.

†**unper'ceptible,** *a. Obs.* [UN-¹ 7, 5 b.] Imperceptible; unperceivable.
1398 TREVISA *Barth. De P.R.* IX. ii. (Bodl. MS.), Noþing is more vncerteyne þanne tyme, noþing more vnperceptible. **1603** HOLLAND *Plutarch's Mor.* 1086 The diversitie of good things and evill is very small, and unperceptible by the sense. **1653** H. MORE *Antid. Ath.* II. i. §2 Matter.. unperceptible to any of our Senses. **1682** —— *Contn. Remark. Stor.* 10 A tugging..for his Sword by an invisible Hand. By which, I suppose, is meant an unperceptible hand.

unper'ceptive, *a.* (UN-¹ 7 b, 5 b.)
1688 H. MORE *Div. Dial.* II. v. 197 You seem to forget that the strokes of Nature levell not at particulars. For she is an unperceptive Principle. **1691** NORRIS *Pract. Disc.* 171 His Affections..are now become so unperceptive of any thing but the..relishes of the Animal Nature. **1768–74** TUCKER *Lt. Nat.* (1834) I. 298 Those who have asserted that..a perceptive being may be produced by a combination of unperceptive principles. **1882** *St. James' Gaz.* 30 March 3/2 He cut it out, good man, being unperceptive of the consequences.

un'perch, *v.* [UN-² 5.] *trans.* To dislodge from a perch. Also *fig.*
1579 LYLY *Euphues* (Arb.) 114 For honest recreation..vse hunting or haukeing, either rowse the Deere, or vnpearch the Phesant. **1646** CRASHAW *Steps to Temple* 27 Which when I lose, o may at once my Tongue Lose this same busie speaking art Vnpearcht, her vocall Arteries unstrung. *a* **1659** OSBORNE *Observ. Turks* Wks. (1673) 286 If he but offers to tune his note contrary to the true Dialect of State, he is straight unperched. **1716** M. DAVIES *Athen. Brit.* I. 320 Divines, who never fail to endeavour to unperche that good old Fox's well-meaning Book from its Post and Chain in our Churches. **1734** WATTS *Reliq. Juv.* 287 When..walking through a Grove,..we unperch'd a Squirrel and a Lark. **1846** LANDOR *Exam. Shaks.* Wks. II. 267/2 They never have unperched me from my calling.
Hence **un'perching** *vbl. sb.*
1589 WARNER *Alb. Eng.* Prose Add. 161 The vnpearching of other, should be fore-preachings to vs.

un'perched, *ppl. a.* (UN-¹ 8.)
1732 M. GREEN *The Grotto* 116 Moping like sick linnet.. Unperch'd, averse to fly or sing.

unperegal, var. UNPAREGAL *a. Obs.*

un'perfect, *a.* Now *rare.* [UN-¹ 7, 5 b.]
1. Of persons: Imperfect in respect of nature, conduct, or function.
a **1340** HAMPOLE *Ps.* cxxxviii. 15 Thou saghe mercifully my men, that ere vnperfyt. *c* **1380** WYCLIF *Sel. Wks.* II. 45 þei weren ȝit unperfit, and Petir, after þat Crist was risun.., synnede many weyes. **1402** *Jack Upland* in *Pol. Poems* (Rolls) II. 20 Certes..it seemeth that yee be unperfect. *c* **1449** PECOCK *Repr.* V. xiv. 560 Vnperfit men ben cumbrid in her freelnes..ouȝten chese ful ofte the..surer good to hem bifore the vnsurer good. **1549** COVERDALE, etc. *Erasm. Par. Heb.* 11 As the vnperfiter priesthood geueth place vnto the perfiter. **1594** CAREW *Huarte's Exam. Wits* xiv. 252 A man vnperfect and void of the gifts of nature. **1617** MORYSON *Itin.* II. 79 The wisest Counsels..are vncertaine, and the wisest men vnperfect. *a* **1628** F. GREVIL *Sidney* (1652) 12 What marvail can it be, if these Iacobs and Esaus strive..as well before as after they come out of such erring and unperfect wombes? **1766** A. NICOL *Poems* 14 O, Heavens! deliver me.. From one that's thriftless, nasty, unperfeit.
b. Inexpert, unskilled; not properly trained or practised; not thoroughly up in one's part.
c **1440** *Gesta Rom.* xliii. 170 (Harl. MS.), They wer.. vnperfite of the crafte, or vncunnynge in the mystery. *c* **1470** HENRY *Wallace* IV. 736 Rycht wnperfyt I am of Venus play. **1545** ASCHAM *Toxoph.* (Arb.) 20, I beyng an vnperfyte shoter. **1577–82** BRETON *Floorish upon Fancie* To Yng. Gentlemen, I was..in a place vnknowne..vnperfect to returne the waye I went. *c* **1600** SHAKS. *Sonn.* xxiii. 1 As an

vnperfect actor on the stage, Who with his feare is put besides his part.

2. Not brought to perfection or completeness; left unfinished, incomplete, or defective; not full in number, etc.: **a.** Of material things.

1382 WYCLIF *Ps.* cxxxviii. 16 Myn vnparfit thing seȝen thin eȝen. 1398 TREVISA *Barth. De P.R.* XVII. i. (Bodl. MS.), In some trene þe [humoure] is vnsufficiaunte and vnperfecte. *c* 1449 PECOCK *Repr.* II. ix. 193 The sympler and vnperfiter and lasse representing ymage. 1483 *Act 1 Ric. III*, c. 8 *Preamble*, Wollen clothes..unperfite and deceyvably made. 1535 COVERDALE *Wisd.* iv. 5 The vnparfecte braunches shalbe broken. *a* 1568 ASCHAM *Scholem.* (Arb.) 142 Plautus and Terence, with a litle rude vnperfit pamflet of the elder Cato. 1604 T. WRIGHT *Passions* Ep. Ded., The vncorrected copie..of three..was most vnperfit. 1626 BACON *Sylva* §546 Mushroomes..are likewise an unperfect Plant. 1683 MOXON *Mech. Exerc., Printing* 8 Some Trades are..sooner sold off, which renders the remainder of the un-sold Exercises unperfect. 1858 H. BUSHNELL *Nat. & Supernat.* xi. (1864) 342 The world..was made, including man, as a thing necessarily unperfect.

b. Of qualities, concepts, etc.

c 1380 WYCLIF *Wks.* (1880) 302 A fool..bryngiþ in a newe ordre þat is boþe heuy & vnperfiȝt. 1387 TREVISA *Higden* (Rolls) V. 53 He dede oon dede þat semede of unperfiȝt witte. *c* 1475 *Partenay* 5225 The pope assoiled hym ther benyngly, When [he] declared hade hys dedes vnperfight. 1535 COVERDALE *1 Cor.* xiii. 9 Our knowlege is vnparfecte, and our prophecienge is vnparfecte. 1551 T. WILSON *Logike* H iiij, An halfe argument, is an argument vnperfect. 1607 HIERON *Wks.* I. 150 Nurses..doe babble with them in their owne stammering and vnperfite language. 1614 RALEIGH *Hist. World* III. xii. 145 Taking vpon themselues the maintenance of the peace..which Agesilaus..had left vnperfect. 1656 SANDERSON *Serm.* (1689) 537 The sence hangeth unperfect unless we take in the former verse.

† **un'perfect**, *v.* *Obs.* [UN-^{2} 3.] *trans.* To render imperfect.

1548 GESTE *Pr. Masse* C vii, To renew the sayde sacryfyce is vtterlye to vnperfyt, & disable it quite. *a* 1586 SIDNEY *Arcadia* III. v, The dressing of her haire and apparell..left to a neglected chaunce, which yet coulde no more unperfect her perfections, than a Die..could loose his squarenesse.

un'perfected (now *unper'fected*), *ppl. a.* (UN-^{1} 8, 5 b.)

a 1513 FABYAN *Chron.* VII. 491 By reason of which..trewes the hostes were deseuered, and the ende of ye warre vnparfyted. *c* 1542 SURREY in *Tottel's Misc.* (Arb.) 29 A mark, the which (vnparfited, for time) Some may approche, but neuer none shall hit. 1625 K. LONG tr. *Barclay's Argenis* v. x. 363 The businesse yet stands well; the alliance unperfected; Argenis unmarried. 1657 W. RAND tr. *Gassendi's Life Peiresc* II. 192 He never willingly left anything unperfected. 1716–20 *Lett. fr. Mist's Jrnl.* (1722) I. 308 These..are but half Gentlemen,..debased, unperfected things. 1864 *Reader* No. 86. 219/2 An unperfected sketch. 1891 FARRAR *Darkn. & Dawn* xli, Shall any germ of good in man's soul perish unperfected?

† **unper'fection.** *Obs.* [UN-^{1} 12, 5 b.] Imperfection.

c 1380 WYCLIF *Sel. Wks.* III. 402 When unperfeccioun is putt upon God. 1388 —— *Ecclus.* xxxviii. 31 He schal ȝyue his herte in to the perfourmyng of werkes; and bi his wakyng he schal ourne vnperfeccioun. *c* 1535 NISBET *N.T.* (S.T.S.) III. 344 Christ..now dealis with us daylye, sufferyng our vnperfectiounn.

† **unper'fective**, *a.* (UN-^{1} 7, 5 b.)

1704 NORRIS *Ideal World* II. vi. 320 A pure and unmingled darkness, being..so very unperfective of our natures. *Ibid.* xii. 476 The knowledge of an unperfective object.

† **un'perfectly**, *adv.* *Obs.* [UN-^{1} 11, 5 b.] Imperfectly.

1398 TREVISA *Barth. De P.R.* VIII. xxix. (Bodl. MS.), Whanne it [*sc.* light] comeþ into fatte mater it is inperfitelich [1495 vnperfyghtly] ifonge & schedeþ hym þerinne vnperfitelich and semeþ derke withoute. *c* 1449 PECOCK *Repr.* v. xv. 564 It is no nede forto seie ther of eny thing vnperfitli and vnfully and therfore vnsauorili here. 1483 *Act 1 Rich. III*, c. 8 *Preamble*, Wollen Clothes..unperfitly made and deceyvably wrought. 1552 LATIMER *Serm. Lord's Prayer* vi. (1562) 47 b, We beleue vnperfectly, we loue vnperfectly, we suffer vnperfectly..; and so al thinges that we do, ar done imperfectly. 1561 DAUS tr. *Bullinger on Apoc.* 579 Besydes this, we se here vnperfitly. 1639 GENTILIS *Servita's Inquis.* (1655) 20 Yet was it not put to execution according to the Emperours mind, but onely unperfectly.

un'perfectness. Now *rare.* [UN-^{1} 12, 5 b.] Imperfection.

α. *a* 1325 *Prose Ps.* cxxxviii. 15 Þyn eȝen sen myn vnparfitnes. 1387 TREVISA *Higden* (Rolls) I. 5 Art, sciens and lawe al were i-falle,..but þe mercy of God had i-ordyned vs of lettres in remedie of vnparfiȝtnesse of mankynde. *c* 1449 PECOCK *Repr.* III. xi. 349 As he which ofte and miche synned, and as he which knewe his vnperfitnes. *a* 1568 ASCHAM *Scholem.* II. (Arb.) 144 Cicero him selfe doth complaine of this vnperfitnes, but more plainly Quintilian.

β. 1543 *Necessary Doctrine* e ii, These workes..for as moch as they be done in the faith of Christe,..theyr vnperfectnes is supplied. 1548 CRANMER *Catech.* 220 b, Althoughe he doth oftentimes ouercome sinne, yet this is a great vnperfectenes, y^t he dothe it not willingly. 1625 DONNE *Serm.* 669 If there had not been unbeliefe, weaknesse, unperfectnesse in that Faith. 1661 RUST *Origen's Opin.* 72 Seeing what..was likely to be the lot of some of them from the necessary unperfectness of their Natures. 1900 MARY KINGSLEY *Mem.* in G. H. Kingsley *Sp. & Trav.* vii. 193 In the very unperfectness of that specimen.

unper'flated, *ppl. a.* (UN-^{1} 8.)

1822–7 GOOD *Study Med.* (1829) II. 203 Confined and unperflated barracks.

un'perforate, *a.* [UN-^{1} 7.] = next.

1713 CHESELDEN *Anat.* (1722) 224 The Edges of this growing together, it continued unperforate.

un'perforated, *ppl. a.* (UN-^{1} 8, 5 b.)

1676 H. MORE *Remarks* 153 It will be hard then to find any evasion if the inward Vessel ascend not as it does when the bottom is unperforated. 1726 MONRO *Anat.* 113 The posterior unperforated Part of the Lamella. 1833 J. HOLLAND *Manuf. Metal* II. 196 An unperforated iron plate. 1884 BOWER & SCOTT *De Bary's Phaner.* 328 Very oblique, fibrously thickened (unperforated ?) end-surfaces.

unper'formable, *a.* (UN-^{1} 7 b, 5 b.)

1674 O. WALKER, etc. *Paraphr. Ep. St. Paul* (1675) 7 An unperformable supposition. 1818 BENTHAM *Ch. Eng.* 238 The unperformable obligation actually taken upon themselves by the Sponsors.

† **unper'formance.** *Obs.* [UN-^{1} 12.] Non-performance.

1608 HIERON *Defence* III. 138 Kneeling..is altogether accidentall and uncerteyne, and so, by consequence, liable to an unperformance.

unper'formed, *ppl. a.* (UN-^{1} 8.)

1442 *Rolls of Parlt.* V. 57/2 It may be founden..that parcell therof [*sc.* a will]..remayneth unperfourmede and not executed. 1483 *Ibid.* VI. 261/1 So that the said last Wille ..shall reste unperfourmed. 1573 DAUS tr. *Bullinger on Apoc.* 101 b, He shall most fully accomplish such thynges as we see as yet vnperformed. 1591 HARINGTON *Orl. Fur.* XXVI. xxxv. 208/2 Merlin,..by his passing wit, Set here (as yet) their vnperformed deeds. *c* 1611 CHAPMAN *Iliad* I. 59 If unperformed vows He blames in us. 1651 BAXTER *Inf. Bapt.* 308 That condition which is of necessity to the end, though some accidentals be unperformed. 1750 CHESTERF. *Let.* 8 Jan., They have done feats..unperformed by others. 1849 FITZGERALD *Lett.* (1889) I. 197 A large bill for service unperformed. 1870 BRYANT *Iliad* I. II. 41 Yet is the enterprise for which we came still unperformed.

unper'forming, *vbl. sb.* (UN-^{1} 13.)

1645 MILTON *Tetrach.* 31 No fals dealing, or unperforming should be thrust upon men without redress, if the covnant bee so divine.

unper'forming, *ppl. a.* (UN-^{1} 10.)

1670 DRYDEN *Conq. Granada* I. Epil., Yet, though he much has failed, he begs, to-day, You will excuse his unperforming play. 1706 WATTS *Horæ Lyricæ* II. 205 Ye vulgar charms of eyes and ears, Ye unperforming promisers! 1742 MELMOTH *Fitzosborne Lett.* (1749) 153 You..have placed in strong contraste their successful industry, with our unperforming ignorance. 1765 GOLDSM. *Ess.* ii. Wks. (Globe) 288/2 The public has been so often imposed upon by the unperforming promises of others. 1824 LAMB *Elia* II. *Capt. Jackson*, You..reeled under the potency of his unperforming Bacchanalian encouragements.

unperfumed, *ppl. a.* (UN-^{1} 8.)

1706 PHILLIPS (ed. Kersey), *Inodorous*, that is without Scent,..unperfumed. 1784 COWPER *Task* III. 732 Are not wholesome airs, though unperfum'd By roses,..To be preferr'd to smoke? 1860 FARRAR *Orig. Lang.* i. 1 Uttering things simple, and unperfumed.

un'perilous, *a.* (UN-^{1} 7.)

1621 in Kempe *Losely MSS.* (1836) 455 [A] not unpleasant waye, though not unperilous. 1628 FELTHAM *Resolves* II. xii. 33 The secure depths, in the most vnperillous Channell. 1805 WORDSW. *Prelude* v. 234 Where had we been..If in the season of unperilous choice..We had been followed! 1847 EMILY BRONTE *Wuthering Heights* xxxiii, Temperate mode of living, and unperilous occupations.

un'perishable, *a.* (UN-^{1} 7 b, 5 b.)

1548 UDALL *Erasm. Par. Luke* iii. 33 b, He that hath throughly conceiued the fyer of charitee & loue vnperishable. 1664 INGELO *Bentiv. & Ur.* II. vi. 366 The unperishable nature of the Soul. 1677 YARRANTON *Eng. Improv.* 23 The Moneys will be lent..upon unperishable Commodities. 1712 *Spect.* No. 537 ¶7 A contemplation on the unperishable part of his nature. 1793 SMEATON *Edystone L.* §93 The stone here..was..unperishable by the effects of weather. 1824 GODWIN *Hist. Commw.* I. 425 A king.. has an unperishable advantage over a popular assembly. 1858 BIRCH *Anc. Pottery* II. 396 The glyptic and graphic arts only exist in their later forms as exercised on unperishable materials.

Hence **un'perishableness.**

1648 JENKYN *Blind Guide* 48 This position..of a simple and absolute unperishablenesse. 1768–74 TUCKER *Lt. Nat.* (1834) II. 679 The spirituality and unperishableness of the soul.

un'perished, *ppl. a.* (UN-^{1} 8.)

c 1400 *Destr. Troy* 2460 He cast be course what shuld come after, Shuld neuer purpos vnperisshit be put to a yssu. *c* 1425 WYNTOUN *Cron.* v. xi. 3016 We ask..ȝour help at oure cete And we may als vnperist be. 1531 ELYOT *Gov.* III. vi, He presumed, that faythe beinge obserued unperisshed, shulde please all mighty god aboue all thinges. 1555 EDEN *Decades* (Arb.) 331 Any beastes whose skynnes they desyre to saue vnperysshed. 1624 CAPT. SMITH *Virginia* v. 198 The hull though..in the water, they found vnperished. 1652 T. FROYSELL *Gale Opportunity* 39 The sweet smelling spices of his lovely life..will imbalme him, and keep him unperisht in your thoughts many years. 1720 POPE *Iliad* XXIII. 402 Yon aged trunk.., Or hardy fir, unperish'd with the rains. 1857 RUSKIN *Pol. Econ. Art* 146 You can help some genius yet unperished.

un'perishing, *ppl. a.* (UN-^{1} 10.)

1561 T. NORTON *Calvin's Inst.* III. vi. 158 b, Ordeyned to heauenly incorruption and an vnperishing crowne. 1709 SHAFTESB. *Charac.* II. 371 Mighty Being!.. Unperishing in Grace, and of undecaying Youth! 1789 COWPER *Annus Memorabilis* 15 Deeds of unperishing renown. *c* 1800 COLERIDGE *On a Cataract* 1 Unperishing youth! Thou leapest from forth The cell of thy hidden nativity. 1852 BILLINGS *Baronial Antiq. Scot., Dunblane* II. 1 The Romans have left unperishing memorials of their far-reaching energy.

un'periwigged, *a.* (UN-^{1} 9.)

1779 R. GRAVES *Euphrosine* (1783) II. 110 Would'st thou enraptured nature's charm behold,..Un-painted and un-periwig'd survey?

un'perjured, *ppl. a.* (UN-^{1} 8.)

a 1700 DRYDEN (J.), Thou can'st not die unperjur'd, And leave an unaccomplish'd love behind. 1802–12 BENTHAM *Ration. Judic. Evid.* (1827) I. 382 They or he remain unperjured, all the others perjured. 1827 POLLOK *Course T.* v. 523 Days When, on the glittering dews of orient life, Shone sunshine hopes, unfailed, unperjured then.

un'permanency. (UN-^{1} 12, 5 b; cf. next.)

1864 R. F. BURTON *Mission to Gelele* II. 197 The unpermanency of the half-breed, and the frequency of sterile marriages amongst mulattos.

un'permanent, *a.* (UN-^{1} 7, 5 b.)

1630 J. TAYLOR (Water P.) *Wks.* II. 160/2 All the world may well be cal'd a Boat, Tost on the troublous waues of discontent, All subject vnto change vnpermanent. 1668 H. MORE *Div. Dial.* IV. xiii. 56 Because it was so short and unpermanent the Prophecy seems to take no express notice of it. 1748 RICHARDSON *Clarissa* III. 362 Who would not,.. to preserve so many essentials, give up so light, so unpermanent a pleasure? 1788 D. GILSON *Serm. Pract. Subj.* i. 9 The splendors he..pursued, have been found both unreal and unpermanent. 1804–9 BLAKE *Select. Milton, Los* 5 Not one moment Of Time is lost, nor one event of Space unpermanent.

un'permeable, *a.* (UN-^{1} 7 b, 5 b.)

[1775 ASH.] 1827 MONTGOMERY *Pelican Isl.* III. 159 Where unpermeable foliage made Midnight at noon.

unper'missible, *a.* (UN-^{1} 7, 5 b.)

[1775 ASH.] 1871 *Athenæum* 14 Jan. 57 The presence of man is held to be unpermissible.

unper'mitted, *ppl. a.* (UN-^{1} 8.)

1598 SYLVESTER *Du Bartas* II. i. *Eden* 306 Now Heav'ns eternall all-fore-seeing King..Thought good..That he [*sc.* man] should never taste fruits un-permitted. 1777 POTTER *Æschylus, Seven Chiefs* 180 Murd'rous is the rage that fires thee To deeds of death, to unpermitted blood. 1810 H. P. FORSTER *Ess. Princ. Sanskrit Gram.* Introd. p. xii, My friend,..I trust, will excuse this unpermitted mention of his name. 1851 CARLYLE *Sterling* I. xv, A rash, false, unwise and unpermitted step.

unper'mixed, *ppl. a.* (UN-^{1} 8.)

c 1545 G. WISHART *Conf. Faith* in *Misc. Wodrow Soc.* (1844) 14 Christ..hauynge two natures unpermyxte. 1577 tr. *Bullinger's Decades* 1097/2 Where I haue intreated of one person, and of bothe natures in Christ vnpermixed.

un'perpetrated, *ppl. a.* (UN-^{1} 8.)

1811 LAMB *Trag. Shaks.* Wks. 1908 I. 136 The painful anxiety about the act, the natural longing to prevent it while it yet seems unperpetrated.

unper'plex, *v.* (UN-^{2} 3.)

a 1631 DONNE *Poems, Extasie* 29 This Extasie doth unperplex (We said) and tell us what we love. 1665 J. SERGEANT *Sure Footing* 205, I believe you are in some wonderment..: I shall endeavour to unperplex you. *a* 1711 KEN *Edmund* Poet. Wks. 1721 II. 238 O Father! you can unperplex my Mind. 1819 KEATS *Lamia* I. 192 Not one hour old, yet of sciential brain To unperplex bliss from its neighbour pain.

unper'plexed, *ppl. a.* [UN-^{1} 8.]

1. Not puzzled or made uncertain.

1558 PHAER *Æneid.* VI. Qj b, Proud minds vnperplext Reioysing vile in sinne. *a* 1586 SIDNEY *Arcadia* III. iv, Desiring her (whose thoughts were unperplexed) to use for his sake..intercession. *a* 1711 KEN *Urania* Poet. Wks. 1721 IV. 452 With Judgment unperplex'd [she] Reviews the Text. 1728 YOUNG *Love Fame* v. 263 Bless'd with health, with business unperplex'd. 1824 CAMPBELL *Theodric* 192 Hers was the brow, in trials unperplexed, That cheered the sad. 1838 MRS. BROWNING *To M. R. Mitford* 10 Thou art unperplext,..To preach a sermon on so known a text!

2. Not involved or intricate.

1653 WALTON *Angler* i. 31 That good, plain, unperplext Catechism, that is printed with the old service book. *c* 1698 LOCKE *Cond. Und.* §39 Simple, unperplexed proposition belonging to the matter in hand. 1754 A. MURPHY *Gray's Inn Jrnl.* No. 104, My Arrangement has been grammatically just, unperplexed and clear. ? 1812 WORDSW. *Water fowl* 13 Progress intricate Yet unperplexed, as if one spirit swayed Their indefatigable flight. 1864 PUSEY *Lect. Daniel* 317 The unperplexed simple pleading.

un'persecuted, *ppl. a.* (UN-^{1} 8.)

1642 MILTON *Apol. Smect.* 11 Since I dare not wish to passe this life unpersecuted of slanderous tongues.

un'persecutive, *a.* (UN-^{1} 7.)

1664 H. MORE *Apology* 540 Whose errours..are.. themselves of a peaceable and unpersecutive Temper.

unperse'verance. (UN-^{1} 12.)

c 1449 PECOCK *Repr.* II. vii. 177 Vnstable vnconstaunce and variaunce and vnperseueraunce.

'unperson. [UN-^{1} 12: introduced by 'George Orwell'.] A person who, usu. for political misdemeanour, is deemed not to have existed and whose name is removed from all public records. In extended use, a person whose existence or achievement is officially denied or disregarded; a person of no political or social importance.

1949 'G. Orwell' *Nineteen Eighty-Four* ii. 159 Syme was not only dead, he was abolished, an *unperson*. **1954** *Economist* 18 Sept. 883/2 Beria is already an 'unperson', the record of his career 'unfacts'. **1961** *Guardian* 28 Apr. 8/5 The concentration camp was a factory for processing people into un-persons. **1962** *Listener* 15 Feb. 308/1 From the Soviet point of view they are 'unpersons', ignored or slandered in Soviet travesties of literary history. **1969** H. E. Salisbury *Siege of Leningrad* i. iii. 24 Berezhkov omits any mention of Dekanozov's name or of the Dekanozov-Weizsäcker meeting. Because of his execution in 1953 Dekanozov apparently has become an unperson. **1981** P. Dickinson *Seventh Raven* xi. 151 You've got absolutely nothing to do..in hospitals... Places like that tend to turn you into a kind of unperson. **1983** *Listener* 16 June 4/1 He omitted the then Foreign Secretary, Francis Pym, who seemed even then to have become an unperson.

Hence **un'person** *v.* to make into an unperson (usu. in *pa. pple.*); **un'personing** *vbl. sb.* Also *transf.*

1966 Page & Burg in *Soviet Stud.* XVIII. 96 (*title*) Unpersoned: the fall of Nikita Sergeyevitch Khrushchev. **1973** *Listener* 4 Jan. 8/2 On television... The addition of a face..turns the newsreader into a person, but the job then requires him to unperson himself. **1976** *Times Lit. Suppl.* 13 Feb. 156/3 The unpersoning process [in Czechoslovakia] had gathered momentum and many of the notables of 1968–69 were being rapidly transmogrified into the nobodies of the 1970s. **1977** *Listener* 16 June 790/2 One of them dead and the other efficiently unpersoned and confined to a political asylum. **1983** *Daily Tel.* 12 Mar. 14/2 In 1956, Bob..brought in Hamilton..as editorial director. .. But in the new edition it looks as if all the work was done by his successor, Harold Harris. 'It is no trivial matter to be "unpersonned",' says Hamilton.

un'personable, *a.* (UN-^{1} 7 b.)

1632 Holland *Cyrupædia* 46 A man for his body not unpersonable, and in regard of his minde, seeming no ignoble and base pesant.

un'personal, *a.* and *sb.* [UN-^{1} 7, 12, 5 b.]

†**a.** = IMPERSONAL *adj.*, *sb.* 1. **b.** Not personal.

1530 Palsgr. 83 Of verbes..some be parsonal, and some be unparsonals. *Ibid.* 614 This verbe..is ever used as an unparsonal. **1891** *Cent. Dict.*, *Unpersonal*, not personal; not intended to apply to the person addressed, as a remark.

unperso'nality. (UN-^{1} 12.)

1881 S. Lanier *English Novel* (1883) 91 As the third feature of the unpersonality revealed in this play, consider the fact that [etc.].

unper'sonified, *ppl. a.* (UN-^{1} 8.)

[**1775** Ash.] **1825** Coleridge *Aids Refl.* 82 An obscure impersonation of what the Atheist receives unpersonified under the name of Fate or Nature.

unper'spicuous, *a.* (UN-^{1} 7, 5 b.)

[**1775** Ash.] **1804** Ranken *Hist. France* iii. iv. III. 312 Their unclassical, often barbarous, and unperspicuous Latin. **1834** Southey in *Corr. w. C. Bowles* (1881) 294 Is not that evidence..of its exuberant fancy, its richness of diction, unperspicuous as it is.

unper'spirable, *a.* (UN-^{1} 7 b.)

a **1735** Arbuthnot (J.), Bile is the most unperspirable of animal fluids.

unper'spiring, *ppl. a.* (UN-^{1} 10.)

1881 T. Maclagan *Rheumatism* 5 In acute gout the skin is dry and unperspiring.

unper'suadable, *a.* [UN-^{1} 7 b, 5 b.]

†**1.** Not removable by persuasion. *Obs.*$^{-1}$

a **1586** Sidney *Arcadia* i. xv, Who (finding his sisters unperswadeable melancholy..) had for a time left her court.

2. Not susceptible to persuasion; obstinate.

1611 Florio, *Inpersuadibile*, vnperswadable. **1647** Trapp *Comm. Col.* iii. 6 Unperswadable, uncounsellable persons, that regard not good courses. **1668** Howe *Bless. Righteous* xii. 219 They..are utterly unperswadable towards God. **1748** Richardson *Clarissa* I. 48 A mind, till now, not thought either unpersuadable or ungenerous! **1817** T. L. Peacock *Melincourt* xxi, After a certain period of life..men in general become perfectly unpersuadable to all practical purposes. **1865** Carlyle *Fredk. Gt.* xviii. vii. V. 149 Deploring that sad mistake; but unpersuadable to stand, and try amendment of it.

absol. **1685** Baxter *Paraphr. N.T.* Matt. iii. 12 He will burn the unbelievers and unperswadable as chaff.

Hence **unper'suadableness.**

1615 Byfield *Expos. Colos.* iii. 6 They will not be persuaded by the..servants of God; and so they are children of unpersuadableness. **1685** Baxter *Paraphr. N.T.* Acts xxi. 14 His resolution and unperswadableness. **1748** Richardson *Clarissa* II. 57 Resentment and unpersuadableness are not natural to you. **1786** A. Gib *Sacr. Contempl.* 306 Children of disobedience, of unpersuadableness.

unper'suaded, *ppl. a.* (UN-^{1} 8.)

1534 More *Comf. agst. Trib.* iii. xix. Wks. 1242/1 If you had assented in woordes and in your mynde departed unperswaded. **1570** Dee *Math. Pref.* 10 Who can remaine.. vnpersuaded, to loue..the excellent Science of Arithmetike? **1709** Stanhope *Paraphr.* IV. 62 The present stupidity of this unpersuaded Man. **1777** Dodd *Let. to Johnson* 23 May in *Boswell*, Not a soul could be left unconvinced and unpersuaded. **1818** Shelley *Rosal. & Helen* 648 His very gestures touched to tears The unpersuaded tyrant, never So moved before. **1882** Farrar *Early Chr.* I. 540 Myriads of Jewish Christians remained secretly unpersuaded.

Hence **unper'suadedness.**

1617 Ainsworth *Annot. Ps.* lviii. 5 The serpent Python.. noteth..the unperswadednes which this Psalm showeth to be naturally in that beast.

†**unper'suasibleness, -'suasion.** *Obs.* (UN-^{1} 12.)

a **1684** Leighton *Com. 1 Pet.* ii. 7 The word here us'd for disobedience, signifies properly unpersuasion:..We are Children of disobedience, or unpersuasibleness.

unper'suasive, *a.* (UN-^{1} 7.)

1748 Richardson *Clarissa* (1811) V. 207, I traversed the room, and bit my unpersuasive lips..for vexation. **1783** Blair *Lect.* II. 122 That argumentative manner, bordering on the dry and unpersuasive, which is..the character of English Sermons. **1847** F. W. Newman *Hist. Hebrew Mon.* ix. 328 In his own town of Anathoth,..his [*sc.* Jeremiah's] extreme youth would make him unpersuasive to his neighbours. **1905** Holman-Hunt *Pre-Raphaelitism* II. 419 Actuality, without which all painting is characterless and unpersuasive.

Hence **unper'suasively** *adv.*

1855 Pusey *Doctr. Real Presence* 347 So not unpersuasively might it be said on this passage. **1865** Grosart *Lambs all Safe* 106, I have indeed written poorly and vnpersuasively.

†**unper'taining**, *ppl. a. Obs.*$^{-1}$ (UN-^{1} 10.)

c **1449** Pecock *Repr.* v. xiii. 552 Vsis and expendingis vnperteynyng to tho religiouns and to her persoones.

†**un'pertinent**, *a. Obs.* (UN-^{1} 7, 5 b.)

c **1380** Wyclif *Sel. Wks.* II. 388 In general crede ben conteyned many treuþis þat us nediþ not to dispute, but bileve hem as unpertinent. *c* **1400** *Apol. Loll.* 72 To warn men to fle in weddingis couetous lustis, and pride, and swilk oþer vices vnpertinent to þe mariage. *c* **1445** Pecock *Donet* 206 Maters vnpertinent to þe maters of þi preising and preiyng. **1579** Fulke *Heskins' Parl.* 439 This controuersie.. is vnpertinent to this cause. **1598** Florio, *Inpertinente*, vnpertinent, not fit, not belonging.

Hence †**un'pertinently** *adv. Obs.*$^{-1}$

c **1449** Pecock *Repr.* iv. iv. 441 Ellis this clausul..hadde be seid vnpertynently and vnhangingli fro the materis of the clausulis folewing.

unper'turbed, *ppl. a.* [UN-^{1} 8.] Not perturbed. (In *Physics*: cf. PERTURBED *ppl. a.* 2.)

1420–22 Lydg. *Thebes* ii. 1714 That he..Myght allone regnen in quiete;..Vnperturbed of Polymyte his brother. **1611** Cotgr., *Impassible*,..vnpassionate, vnperturbed. **1671** R. MacWard *True Non-conf.* 389 What in the ordinary and unperturbed condition of things would be accounted.. an usurpation. **1674** Boyle *Excell. Theol.* ii. iii. 150 The great plenty of unperturbed light that is reflected from snow. **1823** Scott *Quentin D.* xxvi, The King,.. unperturbed by the..violent gestures of the Duke. **1876** Geo. Eliot *Dan. Der.* vi, His own love seemed a guarantee of hers, since it was one with the unperturbed delight in her image. **1937** [see PERTURBED *ppl. a.* 2]. **1967** Margerison & East *Introd. Polymer Chem.* ii. 67 A 'poor' solvent, on the other hand, is one in which the polymer dimensions approach those of the unperturbed configuration. **1974** G. Reece tr. *Hund's Hist. Quantum Theory* xiv. 184 The function ψ^0 is a solution of the 'unperturbed' problem $H^{(0)}$.

Hence **unper'turbedness.**

1676 Hale *Contempl.* ii. (1677) 149 Nothing so much gratifies an ill Tongue, as when it finds an angry hearer: nor nothing so much disappoints and vexeth it as Calmness and Unperturbedness. **1867** Legge *Confucius* 265 A calm unperturbedness may be attained.

unpe'rused, *ppl. a.* (UN-^{1} 8.)

1553 in Strype *Eccl. Mem.* (1721) III. App. iii. 6 His letters, which..we have sent you here unperused by us. **1605** Bacon *Adv. Learn.* ii. xxiii. §6 He burned Sertorius papers unperused.

unper'vaded, *ppl. a.* (UN-^{1} 8.)

[**1775** Ash.] **1852** H. Rogers *Ecl. Faith* 388 That the Old Testament is unpervaded by any distinct traces of expectations of a future life.

unper'verse, *a.* (UN-^{1} 7.)

1868 Browning *Ring & Bk.* vii. 545 Either you have prayed him unperverse, Or I have talked him back into his wits.

unper'vert, *v.* (UN-^{2} 3.)

1655 Fuller *Ch. Hist.* x. iv. §64 His wife could never be unperverted again, but perished in her Judaism. **1768** Sterne *Sent. Journ., Paris*, I declare I had the credit all over Paris of unperverting Madame de V***.

unper'verted, *ppl. a.* (UN-^{1} 8.)

1653 W. Ramesey *Astrol. Restored* 203 So long as God upholdeth the order and course of Nature unperverted. **1674** Coke & Davis *England's Independency* (title-p.), Those who are yet unperverted to the Court or Church of Rome. **1782** J. Scott *Poet. Wks.* 4 Pleasing vestiges..Of unperverted Nature's golden reign. **1838** Keble *Serm.* ix. (1848) 238 What unperverted conscience can fail to see the offence? **1871** Fraser *Life of Berkeley* ix. 352 He was unperverted by controversial theology.

un'pestered, *ppl. a.* (UN-^{1} 8.)

1588 T. P. tr. *Orders Span. Fleet* in *Harl. Misc.* (1744) I. 114 That all soldiers have their room clean, and unpestered of chests, and other things. **1598** Barret *Theor. Warres* 103 It is a place of armes, and is to bee left free and vnpestered for onely the battell when it is to be set. **1824** Mactaggart *Gallovid. Encycl.* (1876) 233 Unpestered, sequestered, Deep hidden I remain.

unpe'titioned, *ppl. a.* (UN-^{1} 8.)

1675 Crowne *Calisto* iv, Thou hast pleas'd me so, My favors unpetition'd I'll bestow.

un'petrified, *ppl. a.* (UN-^{1} 8.)

1646 Sir T. Browne *Pseud. Ep.* ii. v. 91 All Corall is not hard, and in many concreted plants some parts remaine unpetrified. **1735** Thomson *Liberty* iii. 208 Their generous hearts, Unpetrify'd by Self, so naked lay..that [etc.].

un'petrify, *v.* (UN-^{2} 3.)

1815 *Hist. J. Decastro* iv. 22 This unpetrified the waiter, who seized a poker to drive her out of the house. **1838** Robertson *Let.* in Brooke *Life* (1865) I. 40 We all agreed that the distance of eighteen miles had a marvellous effect in unpetrifying us.

un'petticoated, *ppl. a.* (UN-^{1} 8.)

1846 *Browning Lett.* (1899) II. 321 Flush [the dog] hates all unpetticoated people. **1848** A. Herbert in Todd *Irish Nennius* Notes p. lvii, The unpetticoated government of their Milesian wives.

†**unpeysible:** see UNPEACIBLE *a. Obs.*

unphilan'thropic, *a.* (UN-^{1} 7.)

1831 Carlyle *Sart. Res.* ii. iv, I have heard affirmed..by not unphilanthropic persons, that [etc.].

unphi'losopher. (UN-^{1} 12.)

1829 Carlyle *Misc.* (1840) II. 219 The English Unphilosopher believes it without demonstration.

unphilo'sophic, *a.* (UN-^{1} 7.)

1776 *Phil. Trans.* LXXXV. 189 Those censures, which unphilosophic severity may throw on him. **1834** De Quincey *Autob. Sk.* Wks. 1853 I. 349 It would be unphilosophic to say, that [etc.].

unphilo'sophical, *a.* (UN-^{1} 7.)

1649 Milton *Eikon.* vi. 57 Straining her wise dictates to un-philosophicall purposes. **1656** Cowley *Davideis* i. Note x, One of the most unphilosophical opinions in all Aristotle. **1696** J. Edwards *Exist. & Provid. God* i. 31 This is unphilosophical, and therefore we may justly look upon the argument drawn from it as so too. **1771** *Encycl. Brit.* I. 652/1 The very supposition..must be unphilosophical, whimsical, and absurd. **1847** Helps *Friends in C.* i. i. 5 A man more fierce and unphilosophical in the pursuit of it I never saw. **1862** Goulburn *Educ. World* 30 Surely this statement is both unphilosophical and unscriptural.

absol. **1877** Laing *Bacon's Philos. Exam.* 15 The minds of the unphilosophical.

Hence **unphilo'sophicalness.**

1687 Norris *Coll. Misc.* (1699) 169 The unphilosophicalness of this their Hypothesis.

unphilo'sophically, *adv.* (UN-^{1} 11.)

1674 R. Godfrey *Inj. & Ab. Physic* 179, I should not easily have believed that any Physician had been..so unphilosophically bred, as to ascribe the cure of Diseases to the Devil. **1705** Clarke *Unch. Obligat. Nat. Relig.* (1716) 278 These latter indeed, explained themselves very weakly and unphilosophically. **1778** *Phil. Trans.* LXVIII. 814 An experiment thus loosely and unphilosophically made. **1830** Mackintosh *Eth. Philos.* Wks. 1846 I. 203 Believing unphilosophically, as well as dangerously, that there can be any measure..so useful [etc.]. **1854** James *Ticonderoga* III. 43 Sometimes..Woodchuck would talk, neither unphilosophically, nor unlearnedly,..upon a life to come.

unphi'losophize, *v.* (UN-^{2} 3.)

1713 Pope *Let. to Caryll* 14 Aug., Our passions, our interests, flow in upon us, and unphilosophise us into mere mortals.

unphi'losophized, *ppl. a.* (UN-^{1} 8.)

1828–32 Webster s.v., Unphilosophized revelation. **1900** F. H. Stoddard *Evol. Eng. Novel* 156 The honest, unbiassed, unphilosophized portrayal of life-conditions.

unphle'botomized, *ppl. a.* (UN-^{1} 8.)

[**1775** Ash.] **1791** [see UNPILLED *ppl. a.*^{2}].

unpho'netic, *a.* (UN-^{1} 7.)

1857 Ld. Campbell *Chief Justices* III. xlviii. 153 A word of two syllables without any unphonetic consonants. **1879** *Encycl. Brit.* IX. 634/2 French orthography is now quite as traditional and unphonetic as English. **1888** [see next].

Hence **unpho'neticness.**

1888 Sweet *Hist. Eng. Sounds* 68 Unphoneticness is mainly the result of the retention of originally phonetic spellings after they have become unphonetic through sound-change.

un'phrased, *ppl. a.* (UN-^{1} 8.)

1663 Sir G. Mackenzie *Religious Stoic* 145 He furnish'd only to the other Prophets the mater and subject unphrased. **1891** Meredith *One of our Conq.* xxxiii, That was the thought, unrevolved, unphrased, all but unconscious.

un'physical, *a.* (UN-^{1} 7.)

1593 Nashe *Christ's T.* V iij b, In another corner, enhabiteth a Phisition and a Coniuerer, who..can coniure vp an vnphisicall drabbe at all times. **1763** *Museum Rust.* I. 364 It will not contribute to the encrease..of the root, in the unphysical or over heavy manner in which I have seen it done. **1874** Tyndall *Fragm. Sci.* (1879) II. ix. 151 His notions of motion were entirely unphysical. **1885** *Century Mag.* XXIX. 953 Probably no unphysical argument addressed to genuine dynamiters would be likely to have any powerful effect.

So **un'physically** *adv.*

1782 Eliz. Blower *Geo. Bateman* I. 230, I cannot believe you would act so unphysically as to walk out clad so loosely.

un'physicked, *ppl. a.* (UN-^{1} 8.)

a **1596** *Sir T. More* iii. ii. 233 This is noe age for poets..; And, as great subiects of ther pen decay, Even so vnphisickt they doe melt away. **1641** Howell *Poem Royal* (1650) I 3, Free limbs, unphysic'd health, due appetite, Which no sauce else but Hunger may excite. **1691** Cotton in *Aubrey's Lett.*, etc. (1813) i. 20, I enjoy at present so firm and an unphysick'd health, that I hope to do somewhat before I die.

unphysio'logical, *a.* (UN-^{1} 7.)

[**1775** Ash.] **1859** Agassiz *Ess. Classification* 288 An entirely unphysiological principle. **1898** P. Manson *Trop. Diseases* xii. 202 Impaired by disease, or by trying unphysiological conditions.

Also **unphysio'logic** *a.* (chiefly *U.S.*); **unphysio'logically** *adv.*

1934 WEBSTER, *Unphysiologic.* **1948** *Endocrinology* XLIII. 118 The amount of food consumed..was unphysiologically large in most instances. **1969** *Obstetrics & Gynecol.* XXXIII. 419/1 It is unphysiologic for newlywed apareunia. **1970** *Nature* 17 Oct. 210/1 The significance of this effect *in vivo* may be limited, for it takes place *in vitro* only at unphysiologically high levels of glucose.

un'pick, *v.* Also 4–5 **-pike, -pyke.** [UN-^{2} 9.]

† **1.** *trans.* To pick (a lock); to undo (a door) in this way. Also *fig. Obs.*

1377 LANGL. *P. Pl.* B. XIII. 368 Atte laste I stale it, Or pryuiliche his purse shoke, vnpiked his lokkes. **1390** GOWER *Conf.* II. 347 Ek fulofte he goth a nyht..And with his craft the dore unpiketh. *c* **1412** HOCCLEVE *De Reg. Princ.* 1103 (MS. Reg. 17, D v 1), He dremethe theves come in, And on his coffres knokke,..And som of hem unpyke withe a sotelle gynne. **1433** LYDG. *St. Edmund* III. 1201 Another [thief] besy..To vnpyke lokys. *a* **1661** FULLER *Worthies, Kent* II. (1662) 76 Cunning his hands, who could unpick the Cabinets in the Popes Conclave.

2. To undo the sewing of (a garment, etc.); to take out (stitches). Also in fig. context.

[**1775** ASH.] **1808** JANE AUSTEN *Let.* 7 Oct. (1932) I. 217 Your gown shall be unpicked. **1809** MALKIN *Gil Blas* X. x. ¶14, I unpicked his pillow, where I found..fifty crowns. **1842** MRS. BROWNING *Grk. Chr. Poets* iii. Wks. (1904) 612 Was it not enough..that he was turned once, like her own cast imperial mantle,..but that he must be unpicked again by Eudocia..? **1856** MISS YONGE *Daisy Chain* I. vii, Ethel sat down..and began to assist in unpicking the merino.

absol. **1890** *N. & Q.* 5 July 12/2 While we boys 'unpicked', the bigger girls would sew the patchwork covers.

un'pickable, *a.* (UN-^{1} 7 b.)

1612 BEAUM. & FL. *Coxcomb* II. ii, Not a door open now, but double barr'd;..and their locks unpickable. **1862** *Catal. Internat. Exhib.* II. No. 5993, The so-called 'unpickable' locks. **1869** MRS. WHITNEY *We Girls* xii, She put her principles into her unpickable pocket.

un'picked, *ppl. a.* [UN-^{1} 8.]

1. Not picked out or selected; not freed from what is of inferior quality.

1587 PALFREYMAN *Baldwin's Mor. Philos.* To Rdr. (1600) B ij b, Some curious or scornfull person finding it vnpicked, emptie, barren of eloquence. **1641** MILTON *Prel. Episc.* 3 Whatsoever time, or the heedlesse hand of blind chance, hath drawne down..in her huge dragnet, whether Fish, or Sea-weed, Shells, or Shrubbs, unpickt, unchosen. **1765** *Museum Rust.* IV. 384 A small sample of each kind of seed, certified..to have been taken indifferently and unpicked out of the gross quantity gathered. **1830** M. DONOVAN *Dom. Econ.* I. 277 An inferior quality of wine will be afforded by unpicked clusters. **1887** in Moloney *Forestry W. Africa* 135 In a rough state unpicked, but simply roughly..sifted, it sells for £45 to £60 per ton.

2. Not gathered or culled.

1597 SHAKS. *2 Hen. IV*, II. iv. 397 Now comes in the sweetest Morsell of the night, and wee must hence, and leaue it vnpickt. **1612** PARKES *Curtain-Drawer* 4 Then Tobacco was an Indian, vnpickt and vnpiped, now made the common Iuy-bush of luxury.

3. Not unfastened or opened; not rifled or robbed. Also in fig. context.

1598 GREENE *Jas. IV*, I. ii, I cannot abide..a fat capon vncaru'd, a full purse vnpickt. *a* **1704** T. BROWN *Laconics* Wks. 1711 IV. 2 How is it possible..for a Woman to keep her Cabinet unpick'd, when every Rascal has got a Key to 't?

† **4.** Without incision. *Obs.*$^{-1}$

1605 J. MOSAN *Wirtzung's Gen. Pract. Phys.* 420 Bathing in sweet water is very profitable. So are also boxing cups set vnpickt vpon the sides, whereby to extract all windinesse.

un'picket, *v.* (UN-^{2} 3.)

1839 ALISON *Hist. Eur.* VII. lii. 191 Before..the horses in many places [could be] unpicketted, the British dragoons were upon them.

un'picketed, *ppl. a.* (UN-^{1} 8.)

1860 TRISTRAM *Gt. Sahara* xvi. 270 A large courtyard, where picketed horses, unpicketed mules,..jostled in hopeless confusion.

un'pickled, *ppl. a.* (UN-^{1} 8.)

1620 VENNER *Via Recta* vii. 132 The greene..Cucumbers preserued in a pickle..are much better then those that are eaten..vnpickled. **1757** W. THOMPSON *R.N. Advoc.* 9 Pickled, unpickled, and undrained Casks rolled away together.

unpic'torial, *a.* (UN-^{1} 7.)

1860 I. TAYLOR *Spir. Heb. Poetry* (1873) 80 Giving to the aerial aspect of Palestine that clear, sharp, and unpictorial visibility which is now its characteristic. **1884** *19th Cent.* May 813 The idea..was of the most unpictorial kind.

Hence **unpic'torially** *adv.*

a **1864** HAWTHORNE *Amer. Note-bks.* (1879) II. 168 He dresses very..unpictorially. **1887** HISSEY *Holiday on Road* 308 Outlined unpictorially sharp against the sky.

unpictura'bility, (UN-^{1} 12.)

1887 DUKE OF ARGYLL in *Mem.* (1906) II. 525 The multiplicity of motions..resulting, to my mind, in the same 'unpicturability'.

un'picturable, *a.* (UN-^{1} 7 b.)

1837–8 SIR W. HAMILTON *Lect.* (1859) I. xxxv. 312 Objects so different as the images of sense and the unpicturable notions of intelligence. **1888** J. MARTINEAU *Stud. Relig.* II. 337 By a mixture of the two, an insertion of unpicturable power between the successive picturable things.

un'pictured, *ppl. a.* (UN-^{1} 8.)

[**1775** ASH.] **1875** BROWNING *Aristoph. Apol.* 83 The hero of each painted monster—so Suggesting the unpictured perfect shape.

unpictu'resque, *a.* (UN-^{1} 7.)

1791 W. GILPIN *Forest Scenery* I. 54 The walnut is not an unpicturesque tree. **1821** CRAIG *Lect. Drawing*, etc. v. 301 It might be supposed that stone lying in regular layers, would be unpicturesque. **1870** LOWELL *Among my Bks.* Ser. I. (1873) 229 Looked at on the outside, New England history is dry and unpicturesque.

Hence **unpictu'resquely** *adv.*, **-ness.**

1840 POE *Domain Arnheim* Wks. 1864 I. 394 Our disorder may seem order—our unpicturesqueness picturesque. **1841** in H. H. Wilson *Trav. W. Moorcroft & G. Trebeck* I. I. i. 39 Bilaspur is not unpicturesquely situated. **1876** 'ANNIE THOMAS' *Blotted out* viii, My hair has been unpicturesquely out of order.

un'pieced, *ppl. a.* (UN-^{2} 8, 3.)

1483 CAXTON *Gold. Leg.* 231 b/2 His vestement..he ware ..so long that it was broken & unpeced.

un'pierceable, *a.* (UN-^{1} 7 b.)

1600 FAIRFAX *Tasso* XX. lxvi, Is he then vnpearceable.. That neither force nor foe he needes regard? **1611** COTGR., *Impenetrable*,..vnpierceable. **1801** SOUTHEY *Thalaba* II. viii, O'er the two remaining lives A cloud unpierceable had risen. **1849** MANGAN *Poems* (1903) 76 Conal's unpierceable shirt of mail.

un'pierced, *ppl. a.* (UN-^{1} 8.)

1593 B. BARNES *Poems* (Grosart) 95 Thine hart of Adamant, which none can wound: Thine eye of Adamant, vnperced found. **1607** CHAPMAN *Bussy d' Ambois* V. ii, Counsels (as your entrails) Should be unpierc'd and sound kept. **1633** P. FLETCHER *Purple Isl.* VI. xxix, Such is this famous Prince, such his unpierced beam. **1744** THOMSON *Autumn* 852 Where, unpierc'd by Frost, the Cavern sweats. **1759** *Phil. Trans.* LI. 377 The leaves on each side of the foil were pierced, while the foil itself remained unpierced. **1862** LYTTON *Str. Story* II. 192 My dark guess into the Shadowland unpierced by Philosophy. **1864** J. H. FOLEY in Willis & Clark *Cambridge* (1886) III. 223 An arch, unpierced,..making..a shallow recess.

un'piercing, *ppl. a.* (UN-^{1} 10.)

1768–74 TUCKER *Lt. Nat.* (1834) I. 512 Our unpiercing optics reaching a very little way into the chain of events around us.

un'piety. *Obs.*$^{-1}$ [UN-^{1} 12, 5 b.] Impiety.

1675 BAXTER *Cath. Theol.* II. 192 Some [children] the Parents apostatizing educate in Heresie or unpiety themselves.

un'pigmented, *ppl. a.* (UN-^{1} 8.)

1887 LUBBOCK in *Linn. Soc. Jrnl., Zool.* XX. 124 It is, however, easy to imagine that in unpigmented animals..the light might act directly on the nervous system. **1898** P. MANSON *Trop. Diseases* ii. 49 The earlier unpigmented phase [of the malaria parasite].

† **un'piked**, *ppl. a. Obs.* [UN-^{1} 8: see PICKED *ppl. a.* 2.] Untrimmed.

1542 UDALL *Erasm. Apoph.* 80 b, He brought theim foorth vnkembed, and vnpiked,..bare foote and bare-leggued.

un'pile, *v.* [UN-^{2} 3, 5.] *trans.* To demolish (a pile or heap); to remove from a pile. Also *absol.*

1611 COTGR., *Desamasser*, to vnheape, vnpile. **1792** *Comm. Jrnl.* XLVII. 363/1 The Expence of piling, unpiling, &c. &c. as is practised in His Majesty's Yards. **1847** *Infantry Man.* (1854) 27 *Unpile Arms.* At the word Unpile, the whole advance their right feet. **1871** MISS YONGE *Cameos* II. 281 The English began to unpile the fearful heaps of dead.

un'pilfered, *ppl. a.* (UN-^{1} 8.)

[**1775** ASH.] **1844** LOWELL *Prometheus* 298 That spirit which doth ever brood..on the unpilfered nest Of man's deep heart.

un'pillaged, *ppl. a.* (UN-^{1} 8.)

1753 GLOVER *Boadicia* I. i, Did not Prasutagus..On your insatiate emperor bestow Half of his rich possessions, vainly deeming, The rest might pass unpillag'd to his children?

un'pillared, *ppl. a.* [UN-^{1} 8 and UN-^{2} 8.] Not furnished with, deprived of, pillars.

1706 WATTS *Horæ Lyricæ* I. 77 Thou bulky globe,..That hangs unpillar'd in an empty space! **1728** POPE *Dunc.* III. 107 See, the Cirque falls, th' unpillar'd Temple nods.

† **un'pilled**, *ppl. a.*^{1} *Obs.* [UN-^{1} 8 + PILL *v.*^{1}]

1. Unpeeled.

1538 *Inv. W. Gebon of Sutterton, Linc.* (MS.), Hempe vnpillid and flaxe vnswyngled. **1562** PHAER *Æneid* C c iv, An vnshapen bunchy speare with barke unpilde. **1639** T. DE GRAY *Expert Farrier* 232 Beate the garlicke unpilled in a stone morter.

2. Not robbed or plundered.

1577 DEE *General & Rare Mem.* 4 Their Marchantlike Ships..may, in our Seas,..pas quietly vnpilled, vnspoyled, and vntaken by Pyrates. **1580** *Reg. Privy Council Scot.* III. 308 The remanent guidis..left unpilleit within the samin schip.

un'pilled, *ppl. a.*^{2} (UN-^{1} 8 + PILL *v.*^{2})

1791 HUDDESFORD *Salmag.* 140 No Doctor feed, no regimen advised, Unpill'd, unpoultic'd, unphlebotomiz'd!

un'pillowed, *ppl. a.* (UN-^{1} 8.)

1634 MILTON *Comus* 355 Perhaps..'gainst the rugged bark of som broad Elm [she] Leans her unpillow'd head. **1652** BENLOWES *Theoph.* XII. lxxii, We there, on grassy tufted tapestries..Leaning unpillow'd heads, view Nature's ants and bees. **1868** GEO. ELIOT *Span. Gipsy* 177 In carved dark-oaken chair, unpillowed, sleeps..a small man.

un'piloted, *ppl. a.* (UN-^{1} 8.)

[**1775** ASH.] **1794** COLERIDGE *Lett.* (1895) 122 Launching our frail and unpiloted bark on a rough sea of anxieties. **1820** SHELLEY *Witch Atl.* lxiii, We, the weak mariners of that wide lake,..Our course unpiloted and starless make O'er its wide surface. **1853** C. BRONTE *Villette* xxxv, You see me void of affection and religion,..unpiloted by principle or faith.

un'pin, *v.* [UN-^{2} 3, 4.]

1. *trans.* To withdraw the pin or bolt of (a door); to unbolt.

13.. *Coer de L.* 4212 On schal dwelle the clos withinne, The gate to unschette and unpynne, And stylly to unschette the lok. **1377** LANGL. *P. Pl.* B. XI. 108 Þe porter vnpynned þe ȝate. *Ibid.* XX. 328. *c* **1400** *Beryn* 484 'Away, dogg, with evil deth,' quod he, þat was within, And made hym al redy, the dorr to vnpyn. *a* **1547** SURREY *Æneid* II. 328 Sinon..Let fourth the Grekes enclosed in the womb, The closures eke of pine by stealth vnpind. **1596** DRAYTON *Legends* iv. 825 Peace, the good Porter, readie still at hand It doth un-pin. **1753** SMOLLETT *Ct. Fathom* xxix, The quaker..unpinned the other coach-door..and trundled himself into the mud. **1826** SCOTT *Woodst.* xiii, Joan unpinned the door, to demand who was without.

absol. **1377** LANGL. *P. Pl.* B. XVIII. 261 Prynces of þis place, vnpynneth & vnlouketh!

2. To remove pins or pegs from; to unfasten or detach in this way. Also *fig.*

1611 COTGR., *Declaveter*, to vnboult, vnpinne, vnpeg; loose from. **1633** G. HERBERT *Temple, Constancie* i, Whom neither force nor fawning can Unpinne, or wrench from giving all their due. **1673** R. HEAD *Canting Acad.* 76 Unpinning a wheel [he] took it off. *a* **1699** J. BEAUMONT *Psyche* XVI. xvii, Unclasp my Joints; unlace my nerves; and try My finest tenderest membranes to unpin. **1701** WARWICK *Mem. Reign Chas. I*, 6 They have in a great measure unpinned the firmness of the government. **1825** J. NICHOLSON *Operat. Mechanic* 500 When the upper part of the frame..is unpinned and removed.

transf. **1674** GREW *Anat. Plants* (1682) 228 [The atoms of] any fixed unodorable, or untastable Body..being not able to make any Smell or Taste, unless they were first dissolved; that is to say, unpin'd one from another.

3. To undo the dress of (a woman) by the removal of pins. Also *absol.*

1604 SHAKS. *Oth.* IV. iii. 35 *Æmilia.* Shall I go fetch your Night-gowne? *Desdemona.* No, vn-pin me here. *c* **1680** *Roxb. Ball.* (1891) VII. 459 Prithee begin; don't delay, but unpin. **1745** FIELDING *Tom Jones* XIII. iii, Mrs. Etoff, who had the honour to pin and unpin the Lady Bellaston. **1815** *Hist. J. Decastro* III. 331 Come and unpin me, O my dearest husband!

fig. **1641** MILTON *Animadv.* 9 The peremptory Analysis.. will be so hardy as once more to unpinne your spruce fastidious oratory, to rumple her laces [etc.].

4. a. To remove a pin or pins from (an article of dress, etc.); to detach by removing or releasing a pin or pins. Also in fig. context.

1605 ERONDELLE *Fr. Gard.* O 8 b, Go to, take of my cloathes vnpinne that, vntie this. **1630** I. CRAVEN *God's Tribunall* 33 A day..when all maskes shall be vnpinned, and all disguises taken off. **1662** GURNALL *Chr. in Arm.* III. xxx. 256 Unpinne this story, take off that gaudy pinrase, and nothing is left in the discourse. **1709** STEELE *Tatler* No. 36 ¶3 She..began to unpin her hood. **1740** RICHARDSON *Pamela* II. 21 He began to unpin my Handkerchief. **1769** LADY MARY COKE *Jrnl.* 8 Feb. (1892) III. 19 My Maids had pin'd up the train of my Sack to my back, and had forgot to unpin it. **1849** C. BRONTE *Shirley* xxv, Who gave you this little brooch? Let me unpin it and look at it. **1860** EMILY EDEN *Semi-attached Couple* vi, Sarah unpinned a gigantic bunch of camellias. **1887** FENN *Master of Cerem.* i, Unpinning a piece of paper that guarded the gay silks and wools.

b. *intr.* To become unpinned.

1716 LADY MONTAGU *Town Ecl., Tuesday* 74 Reaching the kettle made her gown unpin.

5. *trans. Chess.* To release (a piece that has been pinned). Hence **un'pinning** *vbl. sb.*

1878 S. LOYD *Chess Strategy* 145 The key unpins the Black Queen. **1906** A. C. WHITE *Tours de Force* p. xxxvii, The more general tasks can be grouped under several heads: checking, sacrificing, pinning and unpinning, [etc.]. **1967** V. NABOKOV *Speak, Memory* (rev. ed.) xiv. 289 Themes in chess..are such devices as forelaying, withdrawing, pinning, unpinning and so forth.

'unpin, *sb. Chess.* [f. the vb.] The action or fact of releasing a piece that has been pinned.

1922 HUME & WHITE *Good Compan. Two Mover* 187 There are six unpins, five of which are direct..while the sixth is an Interference Unpin. **1928** [see *half-pin* s.v. HALF II. i.].

un'pinched, *ppl. a.* (UN-^{1} 8.)

1648 HEXHAM, *Onvernepen*,..vnpinched. **1854** MRS. CARLYLE in Froude *Life in London* (1884) II. 164 Habits of *unpinched* housekeeping.

unpin'darical, *a.* (UN-^{1} 7.)

1729 YOUNG *Merchant* Pref., Nothing is so unpindarical as following Pindar on the foot.

un-pin-'downable, *a.* [UN-^{1} 7 b (*b*) + PIN *v.*^{1} 6 c.] That cannot be pinned down or defined.

1966 *Punch* 14 Feb. 249/2 Of all the great detectives he has the most un-pindownable character. **1973** *Guardian* 28 June 14/6 Harold Pinter is..our most tangible and un-pin-downable playwright.

† **un'pined**, *ppl. a. Obs.* [UN-^{1} 8.] Unpained; unpunished.

c **1200** *Trin. Coll. Hom.* 69 Þenche we ure giltes er þe dom cume,..þat god ne finde þanne on us no gilt unpined. *c* **1200** ORMIN 1367 Cristess Goddcunndnesse wass All cwicc & all unnpinedd. *c* **1290** *St. Edmund Conf.* 184 in *S. Eng. Leg.* I. 436 He nolde þat no lime un-pined scholde beo.

un'pinion, *v.* [UN-[2] 4.] *trans.* To deprive of pinions.
1593 NASHE *Christ's T.* G j, My wings her.. disobedience hath now cleane vnpinioned and broken. **1691** NORRIS *Pract. Disc.* 170 The Soul.. is not only broken and wounded in her Wings, but utterly unpinioned, she has dropt her Feathers.

un'pinioned, *ppl. a.*[1] [UN-[1] 8.] Not furnished with pinions.
1615 BRATHWAIT *Strappado* (1878) 26 Vnpiniond Muses (such as nere could flie) Further than vnplum'd birds now presse as high As Eagles.

un'pinioned, *ppl. a.*[2] [UN-[1] 8.]
1. Not having the pinions cut.
1622 F. MARKHAM *Bk. War* v. x. 199 His power must be .. vnrestrained, that flying with vnpinion'd wings it may seeme to be hid within the Skie of the greatest Actions.
2. Not bound or tied.
1775 ADAIR *Amer. Ind.* 394 When they were taking him unpinioned.. to the place of torture.

un'pinked, *ppl. a.* (UN-[1] 8.)
1596 SHAKS. *Tam. Shr.* IV. i. 136 Gabrels pumpes were all vnpinkt i' th heele.

un'pinned, *ppl. a.* [UN-[1] 8.]
a. Not fastened with a pin or pins.
1390 GOWER *Conf.* I. 293 He berth evere his mowth unpinned, So that his lippes ben unloke. **1568** *Depositions* XVI, 11 May (MS. Cant. Cath. Lib.), The said wif with her peticote vnpynned. **1655** tr. *Sorel's Com. Hist. Francion* VI. 18 Her waiting Gentlewoman had.. her Gorget unpinned. **1776** F. BURNEY *Diary* 6 Apr. (1889) II. 139 Two of her curls came quite unpinned, and fell lank, on one of her shoulders. **1821** M. EDGEWORTH *Let.* 27 Nov. (1971) 281 An end of her frill was unpinned.
b. Of a grenade: having had the pin (PIN *sb.*[1] 1 n) removed.
1974 P. DICKINSON *Poison Oracle* vi. 159 The Jap pilot who brought the plane down.. on to an inadequate runway with an assassin sitting beside him holding an unpinned grenade.

un'piped, *ppl. a.* [UN-[1] 8.] Not put into a pipe.
1612 [see UNPICKED *ppl. a.* 2].

un'pirated, *ppl. a.* (UN-[1] 8.)
1840 DE QUINCEY *Style* I. (1860) 194 We have lying before us.. the unpirated edition of Hartknoch.

un'pitched, *ppl. a.* [UN-[1] 8.] Not smeared or dirtied with pitch.
1634 SIR T. HERBERT *Trav.* 105 In this Riuer are some long, deepe prams, sowed together with hempe and cord (but vnpitcht or calkt). **1648** HEXHAM II, *Onbepeckt*, Vnpitcht, or Vndefiled with pitch.

†**un'piteous**, *a.* [UN-[1] 8, 5 b.]
†1. Impious, wicked. Also *absol. Obs.*
c **1374** CHAUCER *Boeth.* I. met. i. (1868) 4 But now.. myn vnpitouse [*Camb. MS.* vnpietous] lijf [L. *impia vita*] draweþ along vnagreable dwellynges in me. **1382** WYCLIF *Prov.* xxviii. 1 The vnpitouse [L. *impius*] fleeth, no man pursuende. *c* **1400** *Apol. Loll.* 61 ȝe schal not.. tak to hond to sey fals witnes for þe vnpitous.
2. Pitiless, unmerciful.
1390 GOWER *Conf.* III. 206 As the rages of the See Ben unpitous in the tempeste. *c* **1412** HOCCLEVE *De Reg. Princ.* 3371 It is ful hard To lakke mercy and ben vnpitous. **1447** BOKENHAM *Seyntys* (Roxb.) 15 Have mercy lord jhesu up on me And lese not my soule with unpetous men. *a* **1586** SIDNEY *Ps.* (1823) XL. vi, Lett them with shame be cloied,.. Who so unpittious be. **1612** T. JAMES *Corrupt. Script.* III. 8 Whilst the vnpitous man defouleth a rightfuller than himselfe. **1725** POPE *Odyss.* xx. 253 The tyrant, not the father of the skies! Unpiteous of the race thy will began. **1954** W. FAULKNER *Fable* 289 In our country, in our hard and unpiteous mountains, people used.. children as people in lands savage with dangerous animals used guns and bullets: to defend, preserve themselves.

un'piteously, *adv.* [UN-[1] 11.]
†1. Impiously, wickedly. *Obs.*
1382 WYCLIF *Prov.* xii. 2 Who forsothe trostith in his thoȝtis, vnpitously [L. *impie*] doth. —— *2 Pet.* ii. 6 Puttinge ensaumple of hem that weren to doynge yuel, or vnpitously.
2. Pitilessly; unmercifully.
1390 GOWER *Conf.* (1901) II. 470 He yit nevere unpitously Ayein the liges of his lond.. Thurgh crueltee vengaunce soghte. **1502** *Ord. Crysten Men* (W. de W. 1506) II. xvii. 130 Y^e darte y^t the deuyll casteth subtylly, & ryght unpytuously. **1513** BRADSHAW *St. Werburge* I. 3465 Whiche danes.. Punysshed vnpiteously all this region With a wofull plage of great crudelite. *a* **1856** SIR W. HAMILTON (Imp. Dict.), Oxford.. so unpiteously cramming her alumni with the shells alone.

†**un'piteousness.** *Obs.* [UN-[1] 12.]
1. Impiety, wickedness.
1382 WYCLIF *Lev.* xix. 7 If eny.. etith of it, he shal be cursid, and gilti of vnpitowsnes [L. *impietatis*]. —— *Ps.* v. 11 After the multitude of the vnpitousnessis [*v.r.* vnpiteuousnessis; L. *impietatum*] of hem, put hem awei.
2. Pitilessness; unmercifulness.
c **1380** WYCLIF *Sel. Wks.* III. 474 Leste Crist dampne ȝowe for traytouris and monquellers.. for ȝoure unpityuousnes. **1447** BOKENHAM *Seyntys* (Roxb.) 108 O unpetousnesse, o unryhtful Domys, and o pervers entent.
So †**unpiteousty**, impiety. *Obs.*[−1]
1382 WYCLIF *Ecclus.* xlvi. 23 He.. enhauncede his vois.. to don awey the vnpitouste [L. *impietatem*] of the folc.

un'pitiable, *a.* (UN-[1] 7 b.)
1646 BP. HALL *Devout Soul* xii. 42 The unpitiable, interminable, unmitigable tortures of those.. never-dying souls. **1748** RICHARDSON *Clarissa* (1811) VII. 34 Such as sad accident, or unpitiable presumption, threw in their way. **1844** in *Life A. Fonblanque* (1874) 259 An elderly gentleman with the military mania is as unpitiable a case as one of the same years in the measles. **1873** GEO. ELIOT in Cross *Life* (1885) III. 193, I.. am at that unpitiable stage of illness which is counterbalanced by extra petting.

un'pitiably, *adv.* (UN-[1] 11, 5 b.)
1821 SCOTT *Le Sage* Biogr. Mem. (1834) I. 419 Carambola is employed in reading to slumber the Member of the Council.., who unpitiably awakens at every instant when his reader stops.

un'pitied, *ppl. a.* (UN-[1] 8.)
a **1586** SIDNEY *Arcadia* II. xxix, With unpittyed teares idly protesting, he had rather die. **1601** *2nd Pt. Ret. fr. Parnass.* Prol. 85 To you we seeke to shew a schollers state, His scorned fortunes, his vnpittyed fate. **1693** G. STEPNEY in *Dryden's Juvenal* VIII. (1697) 197 Think what Rewards upon the Good attend, And how those fall unpitied who offend. **1735** BERKELEY *Querist* §335 Whether there be a more wretched, and.. a more unpitied case, than for men to make precedents for their own undoing? **1781** COWPER *Retirem.* 512 The unpitied victim of ill-judg'd expence. **1819** CRABBE *T. of Hall* XII. 305 While all beheld her just, unpitied pain, Grown in neglect! **1891** FARRAR *Darkn. & Dawn* xxxi, A herd of wretches clothed in rags, ill-fed, untended, unpitied.
So **un'pitiedly** *adv.*
1628 FELTHAM *Resolves* II. 296, I beg no more, then may keepe mee vncontemnedly, and vnpittiedly-honest.

un'pitiful, *a.* [UN-[1] 7.] Pitiless.
c **1449** PECOCK *Repr.* v. vi. 516 Vnpiteful questmongers and forsworen iurers. *c* **1510** BARCLAY *Mirr. Gd. Manners* (1570) D. vj, Unpitifull art thou and cruell tormentour Which thine owne proper minde thus drownest in errour. *a* **1563** BALE in Marbeck *Bk. of Notes* (1581) 753 The vnpitifull murderers are also the same bloudthirstie Prelates. **1651** tr. *De-las-Coveras' Don Fenise* 27 The unpitifull hardnesse of these rockes where I was abandoned. **1658–9** *Burton's Diary* (1828) III. 479 Where they have power, they are the unpitifullest people in the world.

un'pitifully, *adv.* [UN-[1] 11.] Pitilessly.
1598 SHAKS. *Merry W.* IV. ii. 215 He beate him most vnpittifully, me thought. **1709** MRS. MANLEY *Secret Mem.* (1720) III. 217 Never were Barbarian Pirates.. so unpittifully insulted.

un'pitifulness. [UN-[1] 12.] Absence of pity.
1526 *Pilgr. Perf.* (W. de W. 1531) 90 b, Periury, vnquyetnes, obduracion or vnpitefulnes. *a* **1586** SIDNEY *Arcadia* III. xviii, The unpitifulnes of his owne neere-threatning death. **1679** G. R. tr. *Boaystuau's Theat. World* II. 332 [The] unpitifulness of one violent Creature against another.

unpitous, -ness, -ty: see UNPITEOUS *a.*, etc.

†**un'pity.** *Obs.* [UN-[1] 12.]
1. Impiety, wickedness.
a **1340** HAMPOLE *Psalter* lxxii. 6 Hilde þai er in wickidnes & in þaire impite [*v.r.* vnpete]. *c* **1400** *Apol. Loll.* 62 Wam þu fynd wickid þu schall condempne of vnpite.
2. Lack of pity.
1447 BOKENHAM *Seyntys* (Roxb.) 72 O cruel tyraunth ful of unpyte. **1491** CAXTON *Vitas Patr.* (W. de W. 1495) I. cxlv. 155/2 Of leesynges, of couetise,.. of unpyte, of euyll mynde. **1653** H. WHISTLER *Upshot Inf. Baptisme* Pref., For preservation of.. freedom of holy Right herein, against Advances of Opposit unpitty.

un'pitying, *ppl. a.* (UN-[1] 10.)
1605 DRAYTON *Heroical Ep., Matilda to K. John* 12 As though thy hard vnpittying hand had sent me Some new deuised torture to torment me. **1646** CRASHAW *Carmen Deo Nostro, Weeper* xxvii, So sigh tormented sweets, oppress With proud unpittying fires. **1777** POTTER *Æschylus, Prom. Bd.* 10 Yet upbraid not My ruder and unpitying ruthlessness. **1796** MRS. M. ROBINSON *Angelina* I. 59 Instances.. where the purest sentiments have been contaminated.. by sordid and unpitying parents! **1846** MRS. A. MARSH *Father Darcy* II. i. 25 The proud, haughty, unpitying expression to be read there. **1870** 'L'ESTRANGE *Miss Mitford* I. vi. 173 All these evils fall with an unpitying hand on the devoted heads of their correspondents.

un'pityingly, *adv.* (UN-[1] 11.)
1741 RICHARDSON *Pamela* IV. 422 [She] listens eagerly to Stories told to the Disadvantage of Individuals of her own Sex: Will unpityingly propagate such Stories. **1817** LADY MORGAN *France* I. (1818) I. 9 The smallest infringement of the dreadful code was unpityingly punished. **1895** *Forum* (U.S.) Oct. 210 The effects.. would operate in a socialistic state even more rigidly, more unpityingly and more openly than they do now.

†**un'pizzled**, *a. Obs. rare.* (UN-[2] 5.)
1535 LYNDESAY *Satyre* 2765 Bot thay, lyke rams, rudlie in thair rage, Vnpysalt, rinnis amang the sillie ȝowis. **1552** —— *Monarche* 4707.

†**un'placable**, *a. Obs.* (UN-[1] 7 b, 5 b.)
1553 BALE *Vocacyon* 48 b, A perpetuall and vnplacable enemye. **1594** ? GREENE *Selimus* Prologue 10 You shall behold him character in blood The image of an unplacable King. *a* **1619** FOTHERBY *Atheom.* I. xiii. §3 (1622) 141 An vnplacable hatred. **1676** BP. N. FRENCH *Vnkinde Desertor* Pref., A hard-harted man, and our vnplacable enemy.

un'place, *v.* Now *rare.* [UN-[2] 5.] *trans.* To displace. Hence **un'placing** *vbl. sb.*
1554 in Gairdner *Hist. Eng. Ch. 16th c.* (1903) xvii. 349 The unplacing of so many godly laws set forth touching the true religion of Christ. **1597** BRETON *Arb. Amorous Deuices* Wks. (Grosart) I. 5/2 If God for goods shalbe vnplac'd. **1623** COCKERAM, *Dislocate*, to vnplace. **1876** R. A. ARNOLD in *Contemp. Rev.* June 31 No writhing.. can unplace them.

un'placed, *ppl. a.* [UN-[1] 8.]
1. Not assigned to, or set in, a definite place.
1512 *Northumbld. Househ. Bk.* (1770) 423 The Steward and Chaplaine must sit down in the Hall, and call unto them the Gentlemen if there be any unplaced above. **1591** SYLVESTER *Du Bartas* I. i. 529 Th' unplac'd Climates of that deep disorder. **1610** HOLLAND *Camden's Brit.* I. 77 Augustus gift unplaced lay, none would it undertake. **1849** G. R. GLIDDON *Otia Ægyptiaca* 39 My own List of Unplaced Kings.. who preceded the XVIIIth. Dynasty. **1861** HULME tr. *Moquin-Tandon* I. v. 34 Languages either unplaced or Indo-European (so called).
b. *Racing.* (See PLACE *v.* 5 d.)
1881 *Racing Analysis* I. 366 Aeronaut.. also ran unplaced at 135 and 196. **1883** *Sat. Rev.* 24 Nov. 665/2 Last year,.. Hackness started first favourite for the Liverpool Cup, and was unplaced.
2. Not appointed to a place or office.
1558 in Strype *Ann. Ref.* (1709) I. App. iv. 4 All such as governed.. and now remain unplaced and uncalled to Credit. **1575** GASCOIGNE *Glasse of Govt.* I. ii, It is not like that he should have returned from thence unplaced. **1732, 1771** [see UNPENSIONED]. **1823** J. WILSON *Marg. Lyndsay* xliii. 345 Young preachers, yet unplaced. **1849** MACAULAY *Hist. Eng.* ii. I. 241 The other fifteen were to be unplaced noble-men and gentlemen of ample fortune.

un'placid, *a.* (UN-[1] 7.)
1848 J. H. NEWMAN *Loss & Gain* III. vi. 335 His face had that worn, or, rather, unplacid appearance, which [etc.].

un'plagued, *ppl. a.* (UN-[1] 8.)
1550 CROWLEY *Last Trumpet* 50 Then thincke Gods iustyce could not leaue The[e] unplaged. **1560** BECON *New Catech.* Wks. 1564 I. 542 He shal not escape vnplaged, neither in this world nor in the world to come. **1592** SHAKS. *Rom. & Jul.* I. v. 19 Ladies that haue their toes Vnplagu'd with Cornes. **1833** DE QUINCEY *Rev. Greece* Wks. 1859 XI. 143 The inestimable advantage of being unplagued with a Turkish population.

un'plain, *a.* (UN-[1] 7.)
1390 GOWER *Conf.* I. 77 Who that is to trowthe unplein. **1500–20** DUNBAR *Poems* lxvi. 11 The figurit speiche, with faceis tua, The plesand toungis, with hartis unplane. *c* **1530** L. COX *Rhet.* (1899) 86 It was a great folye to put in tho wordes which made a playne mater to be vnplaine. **1538** ELYOT, *Salebrosus*, vnplayne, where a manne can not goo, excepte he do leape.
Hence **un'plainness.**
1619 SIR J. SEMPILL *Sacrilege Handled* 56 Paul then is wrong quarrelled for his vnplainenesse.

un'plain, *v.* (UN-[2] 3).
1611 FLORIO, *Dispianàre*, to vnplaine. **1638** N. WHITING *Albino & Bellama* 720 Though earldoms court her, her disdains Nonsuits their service, and her brow unplains.

†**un'plained**, *ppl. a.*[1] *Obs. rare.* [UN-[1] 8 + PLAIN *v.*] Unlamented.
1591 SPENSER *Daphn.* 79 That thou are bent To die alone, vnpitied, vnplained.

un'plained, *ppl. a.*[2] [UN-[1] 8; cf. PLAIN *a.*[1]] Not made plain.
1598 BARRET *Theor. Warres* IV. i. 98 They will breake and disaray,.. when they come to any straight or vnplained way.

un'plait, *v.* (UN-[2] 3.)
c **1374** CHAUCER *Boeth.* II. pr. viii. (1868) 61 It is a wondyr þat I desyre to telle, and forthi vnnethe may I vnpleyten [L. *explicare*] my sentense with wordes. *c* **1586** C'TESS PEMBROKE *Ps.* CIV. vii, Oile, whose juyce unplaites the folded brow. **1638** N. WHITING *Albino & B.* 76 Dull-aged Saturne .. his waightie head did bow, And with a smile unplaited every frowne. **1865** *Cornh. Mag.* Oct. 487 She unplaited her hair and threw it back.. over her shoulders. **1867** MISS BOWDEN *Fathers of Desert* 160 Paul unplaited all the fifteen ells, and then plaited them together again.
Hence **un'plaiting** *vbl. sb.*
1611 COTGR., *Desplissure*, an vnfoulding, vnplaiting. **1902** BARNES GRUNDY *Thames Camp* iv, This seemed a sensible idea, but why the unplaiting of her hair?

un'plaited, *ppl. a.* (UN-[1] 8.)
1659 W. CHAMBERLAYNE *Pharonnida* IV. I. 229 Where her richest ornament (Although with art unpleited) Nature in A lovely landscape wore. **1702** ADDISON *Dial. Medals* ii. (1726) 36 Rude from her forehead fell th' unplaited hair. **1877** DE COSSON *Cradle of Blue Nile* II. 73 Their hair, which they wear unplaited, is short and woolly.

un'plan, *v.* (UN-[2] 3.)
1819 BUSBY *Hist. Music* II. 490 The drama,.. first planned, and partly written, by.. Dr. Kenrick, and then.. un-planned, and re-written, by Rolt.

un'planed, *ppl. a.* (UN-[1] 8.)
[**1775** ASH.] **1810** CRABBE *Borough* xviii. 362 That floor, once oak, now pieced with fir unplaned. **1879** MISS BIRD *Rocky Mount.* 43 Two unplaned wooden shelves.

un'planished, *ppl. a.* (UN-[1] 8.)
1683 MOXON *Mech. Exerc., Printing* ii. ¶2 Brass well Planish't will be stiffer.. at half the thickness than unplanish't Brass will at the whole.

un'plank, *v.* (UN-[2] 4.)
1654 GAYTON *Pleas. Notes* III. xii. 74 Having no notice the place was unplankt and laid open. *c* **1660** J. GWYNNE *Milit. Mem.* (1822) 33 One man might.. cut down an arch of the bridge, or unplank it, and so make it inaccessible. **1834** J. S. MACAULAY *Field Fortif.* 246 While the repair of the third bay was in progress, the remaining bay was partly unplanked.

un'planked, *ppl. a.* (UN-[1] 8.)
1648 HEXHAM II, *Ongeberdert*, vnboarded, or vnplanckt. **1855** KINGSLEY *Westw. Ho!* xx, The upper-deck beams were left open and unplanked.

un'plant, *v.* (UN-[2] 3, 4. Cf. Du. *ontplanten.*)
1569 HAWKINS *3rd Voy.* (1878) 77 The vice Roy.. sent.. commandement to vnplant all things suspicious. **1575**

Veron's Dict. Lat.-Eng. (1584), *Explanto*, to vnplant, or pull vp. **1624** CAPT. SMITH *Virginia* IV. 163 Being enioyned by our Commission not to vnplant nor wrong the Saluages. *a* **1658** LOVELACE *Poems* (1904) 155 He.. Unplanted had this Plantane plant.

un'plantable, *a.* (UN-¹ 7 b.)
1683 *Pres. St. Jamaica* 2 It's imagined, if this Island were divided into eight parts,..[three parts are] Barren or unplantable. **1788** CLARKSON *Impol. Slave Tr.* 110 The rocky, unplantable parts.

un'planted, *ppl. a.* [UN-¹ 8. Cf. ON. *úplantaðr.*]
1. Not set in the ground; growing without having been planted. Also *fig.*
In first quot. rendering L. **implantatus*, a misreading of *implanatus* 'deceived'.
1382 WYCLIF *Ecclus.* xxxiv. 11 Who is vnplauntid, shal abound shreudenesse. **1600** SURFLET *Countrie Farme* 735 No more.. can the vine well.. endure after it is cut to be long kept vnplanted. **1639** WALLER *Battle Summer Isl.* I. 5 Figs there unplanted through the fields do grow. *a* **1750** A. HILL *Happy Man* 5 Unplanted groves rise round his shelter'd seat.
2. a. Of countries, etc.: Not occupied or colonized; not developed by cultivation.
1612 CAPT. SMITH *Proc. Virginia* 104 But God that would not it [*sc.* Virginia] should bee unplanted, sent Sir Thomas Gates.. to preserue us. **1660** F. BROOKE tr. *Le Blanc's Trav.* 354 The countrey remaining unplanted by any forrainers. **1719** DE FOE *Crusoe* II. (Globe) 436 To be lock'd up in an unplanted Island. **1807** J. BARLOW *Columb.* IV. 572 The future sires of our unplanted states.
b. Of ground: Not set with plants. Also *fig.*
? *a* **1800** PITT in *Nat. Rev.* (1892) XIX. 298, I.. left for thee my downy bed, Unplanted yet with thorns. **1805** *Monthly Mag.* XX. 110 [Land] unsown, unplanted, untilled.
3. Not put in position.
1615 G. SANDYS *Trav.* 38 At the East end.. lies a number of great Ordnance vnplanted.
4. *Sc.* Not provided with a minister.
a **1651** CALDERWOOD *Hist. Kirk* (1843) II. 186 It was ordeaned.. that Mr. George Hay.. preache in the unplanted kirks of Carrick.

un'plant-like, *a.* (UN-¹ 7 c.)
1837 *Edwards' Bot. Register* XXIII. pl. 1942 That there must be something of an animal nature infused into this most unplant-like production.

un'plaster, *v.* (UN-² 3.)
1598 FLORIO, *Sgommare*, to vngum, to vnplaister. **1671** TRENCHFIELD *Cap Gray Hairs* (1688) 38 As if you had undertaken the publick unplaistering of a painted Face.

un'plastered, *ppl. a.* (UN-¹ 8.)
1648 HEXHAM II, *Ongemortert*, Vnplaistered. **1669** WOODHEAD *St. Teresa* II. viii. 77 The Portall.. being ill floored, and the Walls unplaistered. **1804** SOUTHEY *Let. to Coleridge* 11 June, And so unplastered it [*sc.* a room] is likely to remain another winter. **1886** W. J. TUCKER *E. Europe* 411 Its dark-grey unplastered walls.

un'plastic, *a.* (UN-¹ 7, 5 b.)
1787 *Generous Attachment* IV. 231 Those [articles] which the subtle Mr. Archer.. endeavoured to hammer out of the unplastic disposition of the relentless Sir James. **1883** C. C. PERKINS *Italian Sculpture* III. i. 244 Statues of Apollo, Mercury, Minerva and Peace.. thoroughly unplastic in action and conception. **1894** *Illustr. Lond. News* 24 Mar. 364/3 The idea of harsh unplastic feeling.

un'plat, *v.* (UN-² 3.)
1591 PERCIVALL *Sp. Dict.*, *Destravar*, to vnplat, to vndoo. **1607** MARKHAM *Cavel.* VI. vi. 36 Then you shall vnplat both his maine and taile.

unpla'tonically, *adv.* (UN-¹ 11.)
1668 H. MORE *Div. Dial.* I. 288 That also, O Sophron, is very perversly and un-Platonically done of Cuphophron.

†**un'plausable**, *a. Obs.* [UN-¹ 7 b. Cf. next.] Unpraiseworthy.
1670 G. H. *Hist. Cardinals* III. III. 326 No body will rob himself.. of his hopes.. for an unplausable person.

un'plausible, *a.* (UN-¹ 7, 5 b.)
1575 FENTON *Gold. Epist.* (1582) 232 It shall not be.. the more vnplausible to the reader. **1604** BACON *Apol.* Wks. 1879 I. 436 This proceeding.. was a thing towards the people very unplausible. *a* **1677** BARROW *Serm.* Wks. 1687 III. xlv. 531 We never.. should.. embrace his institution, consisting of such unplausible Propositions, and precepts. **1757** HUME *Hist. Eng.* II. 198 He must have had some reasons, and perhaps not unplausible ones, for this affirmation. **1860** MILL *Lett.* (1910) I. 236 Nothing can be at first sight more entirely unplausible than his theory. **1891** F. W. NEWMAN *Early Hist. Cdl. Newman* 47 Your assumption is to me arbitrary and unplausible.

un'plausibly, *adv.* (UN-¹ 11, 5 b. Cf. prec.)
1733 W. CRAWFORD *Infidelity* (1836) 217 Some may allege, and not unplausibly, that [etc.]. **1795** BURKE *Regic. Peace* iv. Wks. IX. 56 Men would reason not unplausibly, that it would be better [etc.]. **1820** COLERIDGE *Lit. Rem.* (1839) IV. 138 Others, again, and not unplausibly, contend [etc.]. **1862** M. HOPKINS *Hawaii* 85 Cook's two ships.. appeared to them, not unplausibly, islands, the masts being trees.

†**un'plausive**, *a. Obs.* (UN-¹ 7.)
1606 SHAKS. *Tr. & Cr.* III. iii. 43 'Tis like heele question me, Why such vnplausiue eyes are bent? why turn'd on him?

un'playable, *a.* [UN-¹ 7 b.] Incapable of being played.
1833 LYTTON *Godolphin* xxxv, Having an unplayable hand and a bad partner. **1839** DARLEY *Introd. Beaum. & Fl.'s Wks.* p. xxvii, These.. form the real attraction of their 'plays,' altogether unplayable now. **1881** *Sat. Rev.* 2 July 14/1 The two slow bowlers seemed quite unplayable. **1884** *Lillywhite's Cricket Comp.* 39 The wicket was unplayable. **1902** CORNISH *Naturalist Thames* 33 After that, I must trust to the strength of the gut, for the fish would be unplayable.
Hence **un'playably** *adv.*
1955 *Times* 6 June 3/1 Before luncheon the occasional ball turned and lifted nastily, and the one that accounted for May did so almost unplayably. **1978** *Daily Tel.* 21 Feb. 13/6 Next the unplayably simple A flat, made to sound telling and enigmatic at the same time, a great success.

un'played, *ppl. a.* (UN-¹ 8.)
[**1775** ASH.] **1850** BOHN *Hand-bk. of Games* (1867) 161 The highest card unplayed of a suit. **1875** J. BISHOP *Otto's Violin* iv. 47 *note*, An unplayed violin does not improve.

un'pleadable, *a.* [UN-¹ 7 b, 5 b.]
†**1.** Improper for legal pleadings. *Obs.*⁻¹
1569 J. SANFORD tr. *Agrippa's Van. Artes* 85 b, The yeere diuided in XII monethes with the varieties of pleadable and unpleadable dayes.
2. Incapable of being pleaded or urged.
a **1716** SOUTH *Serm.* (1744) VII. 202 All ignorance, that is merely negative.., is utterly inconsistent with [this], and makes [it] absolutely unpleadable. **1869** BROWNING *Ring & Bk.* IX. 1443 A flight.. unpleadable in court!

un'pleaded, *ppl. a.* (UN-¹ 8.)
1682 OTWAY *Venice Preserved* IV. 55 Doom'd to die! condemn'd unheard! unpleaded!

un'pleasable, *a.* (UN-¹ 7 b.)
1561 T. NORTON *Calvin's Inst.* IV. xx. 170 Let parentes shew themselues so hard and vnpleasable to their children, ..that [etc.]. **1604** T. WRIGHT *Passions* I. viii. 31 To pleasure the unpleasable appetites, and lusts of the flesh. **1786** BURGOYNE *Heiress* II. ii, What a change have I made to please my unpleasable daughter! **1951** A. L. ROWSE *English Past* 24 The two sons were growing up not much to the liking of their virtuous, unpleasable mother.

un'pleasant, *a.* [UN-¹ 7.]
1. Not pleasant, displeasing: **a.** To the senses.
1538 ELYOT, *Rancidus*,.. vnsauery, or vnpleasaunt. **1551** TURNER *Herbal* I. 109 The colour is vnpleasanter and blacker. **1575** GASGOIGNE *Making of Verse* §5 Wordes of many syllables do cloye a verse and make it unpleasant. **1585** T. WASHINGTON tr. *Nicholay's Voy.* III. i. 69 b, An euill fauoured and vnpleasant harmonie. **1611** FLORIO, *Inameno*, vnpleasant to the view. **1667** DRYDEN *Dram. Poesy* Ess. (ed. Ker) I. 69 Does not the eye pass from an unpleasant object to a pleasant in a much shorter time than is required to this? **1725** DE FOE *Voy. round World* (1840) 253 In-numberable rills.. falling from the cliffs, making a barbarous and unpleasant sound. **1796** MME. D'ARBLAY *Camilla* IV. 223 The aspect of Mrs. Mittin.. was.. unpleasant to him. **1879** LUBBOCK *Sci. Lect.* ii. 32 Flies prefer unpleasant smells, such as those of decaying meat. **1892** *Photogr. Ann.* II. 103 A dilute solution.. changes the colour of the image to a not unpleasant brown.
Comb. **1869** TOZER *Highl. Turkey* II. 109 A most unpleasant-looking piece of water, marshy and full of reeds.
b. To the mind or feelings.
1535 COVERDALE *Ecclus.* xxii. 6 Euen so is the.. doctryne of wyszdome euer vnpleasaunt vnto fooles. *a* **1568** ASCHAM *Scholem.* II. (Arb.) 132 Preceptes in all Authors.. without applying vnto them the Imitation of examples, be.. barrayn, vnfruitfull and vnpleasant. **1596** SHAKS. *Merch. V.* III. ii. 254 The vnpleasant'st words That euer blotted paper. *a* **1679** HOBBES *Rhet.* I. xi. (1681) 28 Unpleasant are those things, which proceed from Necessity, as Cares, Study, Contentions. *c* **1721** MRQ. TULLIBARDINE in *10th Rep. Hist. MSS. Comm.* App. I. 126 Tho' your Majesty permitts me to wryte even on ane unpleasant subject. **1762** GOLDSM. *Nash* 200 That a man of pleasure leads the most unpleasant life in the world. **1839** THIRLWALL *Greece* III. xxvi. 419 To execute a commission which would require them to deliver many unpleasant truths. **1875** JOWETT *Plato* (ed. 2) I. 466 All of us.. had an unpleasant feeling at hearing them say this.
2. Unentertaining, unfacetious.
1712 *Spect.* No. 408 ¶4 It would be no unpleasant Notion, to consider the several Species of Brutes, into which we may imagine that Tyrants.. might be changed. **1768** *Junius Lett.* (1850) II. 220 In his assertions.. there is something really not unpleasant... It puts me in mind of the consulship which Caligula intended for his horse.
3. Unamiable.
1654 [see UNPLEASING *ppl. a.* b].
Hence **un'pleasantish** *a.*
1827 HOOD *Parthian Glance* 28, I can't but.. pronounce 'Heads or tails' with a child, an unpleasantish game. **1844** —— *Etching Moralised* 229 'Tis a rather unpleasantish job.

un'pleasantly, *adv.* (UN-¹ 11.)
1549 COVERDALE, etc. *Erasm. Par. Rom.* 34 Let him, that hath, gyue hym some thyng, not louryngly and vnpleasantly,.. but euen as one that rekeneth al he hath commen. **1551** BP. GARDINER *Explic., Christes Presence* 70 b, If fleshe did appeare, we should be vnpleasauntly disposed to the communion of it. **1677** GREW *Anat. Fruits* iv. §6 A White Corin, without taking off the Skin, sheweth not unpleasantly how the Seeds are fastned. **1718** DIGBY in Pope *Wks.* (1751) VIII. 34 We don't live unpleasantly in primitive simplicity and good humour. **1818** BYRON *Juan* I. ccxx, You've pass'd your youth not so unpleasantly. **1861** GEO. ELIOT *Silas M.* iv, The lane was becoming unpleasantly slippery.
Comb. **1804** WOLCOT (P. Pindar) *Gt. Cry* To Pitt, Machinery which has contracted a most unpleasantly-looking rust.

un'pleasantness. [UN-¹ 12.]
a. The quality of being unpleasant. (Also with *a* and pl.)
1548 ELYOT, *Iniucunditas*, vnpleasauntnesse. **1594** O. B. *Quest. Profit. Concern.* K 3 b, I stand in very little neede.. to haue these vnpleasantnesses renued or made lasting vnto me. **1596** BARROUGH *Meth. Physick* VIII. 461 So great inconuenience and vnpleasauntnesse of tast. **1603** HOLLAND *Plutarch's Mor.* 1156 The Mathematical rudiments which children be taught, at the beginning trouble them..; but this unpleasantnesse continueth not alwaies with them. **1635** J. SWAN *Spec. M.* vi. §2 (1643) 201 Sea-water.. by passing through divers windings.. of the earth, is deprived of all unpleasantnesse. *a* **1665** GOODWIN *Filled with the Spirit* (1670) 394 Which would occasion a great disparagement and unpleasantness in the World. **1808** L. MURRAY *Eng. Gram.* I. 455 Here there is some degree of harshness and unpleasantness [in the rhythm]. **1830** WORDSW. in C. Wordsw. *Mem.* (1851) II. 226 Another unpleasantness arose from the same cause. **1852** DICKENS *Bleak Ho.* xlv, I have made some advances out of pocket to accommodate these unpleasantnesses.
b. *the late unpleasantness* (U.S.), the American Civil War; also *transf.*
1868 D. R. LOCKE *Ekkoes from Kentucky* 23 (Th.), That cuss cum back here, doorin' the late onpleasantniss, kernel of a rigiment. **1872** *Harper's Mag.* Feb. 479/1 During our 'late unpleasantness' a convalescent hospital was established ..in Nashville. **1903** *N.Y. Times* 19 Sept. 3 The only soldier to be killed from Orange during the late unpleasantness with the Filipinos. **1930** S. HENRY *Conquering Great Amer. Plains* 33 When 'the late unpleasantness' terminated, the Texan drover lacked a satisfactory market. **1948** *Amer. Jrnl. Nursing* Dec. 770/2 Among the stamps of particular interest to nurses to come out of the 'late unpleasantness', are a Hungarian Red Cross series,.. and a German child welfare series. **1981** *Times* 25 Aug. 7/1 The British and the Germans ..were all of that older generation which well remembers the late unpleasantness between our two countries.

un'pleasantry. [UN-¹ 12.] Unpleasantness.
1830 'JON BEE' *Wks. S. Foote* IV. p. xli, It would have been well.. if this were all the unpleasantry to which he subjected himself. **1844** ALB. SMITH *Adv. Mr. Ledbury* xvi. Had he allowed himself to be depressed by every unpleasantry, he would have had a sad time of it. **1847** DE QUINCEY in *Tait's Mag.* XIV. 520 Without any 'unpleasantries' occurring. *Ibid.* Note, 'Unpleasantries'.. is a new word, launched a very few years back in some commercial towns. **1883** BURTON & CAMERON *Gold Coast* I. i. 16 A very low barometer, which suggested unpleasantries.

un'pleased, *ppl. a.* [UN-¹ 8.]
1. Not pleased; displeased. Now *rare.*
c **1450** tr. *De Imitatione* III. xxv. 96 As ofte tymes as I fele me unplesid & greved. **1520** CAXTON *Chron. Eng.* IV. 33/1 It was no meruayle all though the prynce was vnpleased. **1593** SHAKS. *Rich. II*, III. iii. 193 Me rather had, my Heart might feele your Loue, Then my vnpleas'd Eye see your Courtesie. **1613** CHAPMAN *Rev. Bussy d' Ambois* III. F 3 b, Hee that vnpleas'd to hold his place, will range. **1692** WASHINGTON tr. *Milton's Def. Pop.* ii. Wks. 1851 VIII. 65 God.. was extreamly unpleas'd with them for asking a King. **1733** HERVEY *Mem. Geo.* (1848) I. 198 A sort of unpleased smile. **1762** COWPER *Miss Macartney* 64 The phlegm of sullen elves, Who.. Extend no care beyond themselves, Unpleasing and unpleas'd. **1831** WORDSW. *Avon* 14 Never ..may the good Shrink from thy name, pure Rill, with unpleased ears. **1901** CLIVE HOLLAND *Mousmé* 204 Glances of frank admiration which Lou looked not unpleased to see.
†**2.** Unpaid. *Obs.*⁻¹
1604 MIDDLETON *Father Hubburd's T.* F 3, I am not worth ..three farthings: beside my Lodging vnpleasde.

un'pleasing, *ppl. a.* [UN-¹ 10, 5 b.] Not pleasing; displeasing, unpleasant:
a. To the senses.
c **1480** HENRYSON *Test. Cres.* 338, I mak Thy voice sa cleir, vnplesand, hoir, and hace. **1595** SHAKS. *John* III. i. 45 If thou ..wert grim, Vgly,.. Full of vnpleasing blots and sightlesse staines. **1617** WOODALL *Surg. Mate* (1639) 344 It hath an unpleasing taste. **1670** BAXTER *Cure Church-Div.* 169 Some of them will not take such unpleasing medicines. **1770** SIR J. REYNOLDS *Disc.* iii. (1778) 83 [Such] a figure.. may still have a certain union of the various parts, which may contribute to make them on the whole, not un-pleasing. **1797** DALLAWAY *Constantinople* v. 86 A man of rank, remarkably unpleasing in his countenance and figure. **1817** STEPHENS in Shaw *Gen. Zool.* X. II. 476 Each leap being accompanied by a note that is far from unpleasing. **1867** LADY HERBERT *Cradle L.* i. 15 Instruments which sounded unpleasing to English ears.
b. To the mind or feelings.
1533 BELLENDEN *Livy* IV. ii. (S.T.S.) II. 57 ʒe wald defend sic thingis vnder colour of ʒoure rigorus & vnplesand lawis. **1588** SHAKS. *L.L.L.* v. ii. 912 Cuckow, Cuckow: O word of feare, Vnpleasing to a married eare. **1605** *Gunpowder Plot* in *Harl. Misc.* (Malh.) III. 5, I thought it would not be unpleasing unto thee to join them together in the press. **1654** GATAKER *Disc. Apol.* 43 These Digressions.. will not be unpleasing to a Reader of no over-rigid and unpleasant Disposition. **1735** JOHNSON *Lobo's Abyssinia, Descr.* xv. 140 To put the unpleasing Remembrance of our past Labours out of our Minds. **1818** SCOTT *Br. Lamm.* ix, The first thing which recalled him to those unpleasing circumstances. **1885** *Manch. Exam.* 6 July 4/6 The appointment in itself must be unpleasing to the English Government.

un'pleasingly, *adv.* (UN-¹ 11.)
1597 MORLEY *Introd. Mus.* 82, I think it goeth but vn-pleasinglie to the eare. **1623** BINGHAM *Xenophon* 27 Young man you looke like a Philosopher, and speake not vnpleasingly. **1633** BP. HALL *Occas. Medit.* 319 This flowre is but unpleasingly fulsome for sent. **1852** MUNDY *Antipodes* III. viii. 251 The Van Diemonians, as they unpleasingly call themselves. **1862** CALVERLEY *Verses & Transl.* (ed. 2) 36 A happy child,.. Not unpleasingly apparelled In a tightish suit of blue.

un'pleasingness. (UN-¹ 12.)
1611 COTGR., *Mauplaisance*, vnpleasantnesse, vnpleasingnesse. **1652** HEYLYN *Cosmogr.* I. 123 The misery and un-pleasingness of his present condition. **1673** O. WALKER *Educ.* 228 A corrective to the harshness and unpleasingness of the other. **1727** BAILEY (vol. II) s.v. *Unpleasantness.*

†**un'pleasive**, *a. Obs.*[-1] (UN-[1] 7.)
1644 BP. HALL *Rem. Wks.* (1660) 108 Grief is never but an unpleasive passion; the rest have some life and contentment in them.

un'pleasurable, *a.* (UN-[1] 7 b.)
1768–74 TUCKER *Lt. Nat.* (1834) I. 373 Many of our waking hours pass irksome and insipid, unprofitable to others, and unpleasurable to ourselves. **1796** CHARLOTTE SMITH *Marchmont* IV. 183 Unpleasurable sensations. **1860** RUSKIN *Mod. Paint.* V. IX. xi. §22 Let no technical labour be wasted on things useless or unpleasurable. **1879** MRS. A. W. HUNT *Basildon* II. xvi. 288 The visit, though a melancholy one, would not be wholly unpleasurable to him!

un'pleasurably, *adv.* (UN-[1] 11.)
1826–7 DE QUINCEY *Lessing* Wks. 1859 XIII. 300 The comic interest..would at once disarm the inherent meanness in the subject, of all power to affect us unpleasurably.

un'pleasure. [UN-[1] 12.] **a.** Unpleasantness; (something that causes) displeasure.
1792 F. BURNEY *Jrnl.* Jan. (1972) I. 111, I told him, very truly, of the pleasure with which I had re-entered his Roof—but I [write] the *un*pleasures that followed! **1814** COLERIDGE *Lett.* (1895) 639, I don't like to use any words that might give you *un*pleasure. **1839** J. HODGSON in Raine *Mem.* (1858) II. 411 Walked about half a mile with great unpleasure.
b. *Psychoanal.* [tr. G. *unlust.*] The sense of inner pain, discomfort, or anxiety which results from the blocking of an instinctual impulse by the ego and is the opposite of the affect of pleasure.
1919 A. WOHLGEMUTH in *Brit. Jrnl. Psychol.* Monogr. Suppl. VI. I. 1 The affective elements are Pleasure-Unpleasure. **1925** I. A. RICHARDS *Princ. Lit. Crit.* xii. 95 Unpleasure being frustrated, chaotic, mal-successful activity. **1949** KOESTLER *Insight & Outlook* xv. 208 The nervous processes which determine the pleasure-unpleasure tone of emotional experience. **1974** *Nature* 11 Oct. 500/2 The monkeys' 'interest' overrode—so long as it lasted—their 'unpleasure'.

un'pleat, *v.* (UN-[2] 3.)
1614 J. DAVIES (Heref.) *Eclogue* 17 Droope not for that (man) but vnpleate thy browes. **1648** HEXHAM II, *Het haer ontvlechten*, to unpleat or untie ones Haire.

un'pleated, *ppl. a.* (UN-[1] 8.)
1612 W. PARKES *Curtaine-Dr.* (1876) 54 Let not the seruant with vnpleated browes and presented innocency abuse the trust committed to his charge. **1648** HEXHAM II, *Ongeployt*, Vnfoulded, or Vnpleated. **1889** *Daily News* 22 Oct. 6/1 These are necessarily in unpleated material, in order to give firmness to the whole.

un'pledged, *ppl. a.* (UN-[1] 8.)
1605 CHAPMAN *All Fools* v. ii. 68 *Val.* Ile be their pledge. *For.* Not yet Valerio; This hee must drinke unpledgd. **1630** J. TAYLOR (Water P.) *Thiefe* Wks. II. 123/1 If a Drunkard be vnpledgd a kan. **1741–2** GRAY *Agrippina* 21 They are aware Of th' unpledg'd bowl. **1823** S. ROGERS *Italy* 160 For deeds of violence..came the unpledged bowl, The stab of the stiletto. **1834** MOORE *Mem.* (1856) VII. 24 Sir Robert Peel ..is unpledged to any one for his next turn at the Charter House.

un'plenished, *ppl. a.* Chiefly *Sc.* (UN-[1] 8.)
1535 *Sc. Acts, Jas. V* (1814) II. 346/2 Ane grete part of þe Realme..hes bene þir mony ȝeris..vnplenissit. **1535** STEWART *Cron. Scot.* (Rolls) II. 532 Mony sted wnpleneist lyand waist. **1857** J. HAMILTON *Lessons fr. Gt. Biog.* 290 In a lonely unplenished room.

un'plet, *ppl. a. Sc.* [UN-[1] 8 b.] Unplaited.
c **1425** WYNTOUN *Cron.* II. i. 49 The tane half of hir haire vnplet.

†**un'pleyed**, *ppl. a. Sc. Obs.*[-1] [UN-[1] 8.] Not assailed at law.
1445 *Sc. Acts, Jas. II* (1814) II. 33/2 All & sindri landis.. as his fadir broukit þaim vndemandit and unpleyit of ony man befor ony Juge.

un'pliable, *a.* [UN-[1] 7 b, 5 b.]
1. Unyielding, obstinate, stubborn.
c **1400** *Wycliffite Bible* Heb. x. 23 We..holde the confessioun of oure hope vnbowynge [*v.r.* vnpliable; L. *indeclinabilem*]. **1603** HOLLAND *Plutarch's Mor.* 687 Their stiffenesse and unpliable disposition, the roughnesse also of their skinne, argueth their dry nature. **1627** I. BARGRAVE *Serm.* 4 Wee are all as oxen unpliable to the yoake. **1652** URQUHART *Jewel* 250 Such..sinners as should prove unpliable to the stamp of his wholesome admonitions. **1774** REID *Aristotle's Logic* iv. §3 It is somewhat unpliable to rules. **1885** S. COX *Expositions* I. 101 He saw a new heaven and a new earth,..free from all that renders it hostile or unpliable to the spirit of man.
2. Unbending, inelastic, stiff. Also *fig.*
1622 F. MARKHAM *Bk. War* I. x. 38 Buckram..is too stiffe and unplyable. **1747** COOKE in Hanway *Trav.* IV. lvi. (1762) I. 260 The paper was very hard and unpliable. **1759** *Phil. Trans.* LI. 290 [Wires] so unpliable and brittle, as to be rendered quite useless. **1773** JOHNSON 8 Oct. in Boswell *Tour Hebrides*, She had no notion of a joke,..had a mighty unpliable understanding. **1806** FORSYTH *Beauties Scotl.* IV. 31 The spruce..has unpliable branches. **1825** SCOTT *Betrothed* iii, A broad countenance, with heavy and unpliable features.
Hence **un'pliableness.**
1635 BRATHWAIT *Arcad. Pr.* 99, I feele very usually such a stiffnesse, or unpliablenesse in my selfe. *c* **1720** GIBSON *Diet Horses* i. (1731) 11 From an Unpliableness or Straitness of the Ligaments. **1754** HUME *Hist. England* I. 158 That the commons,..by their unpliableness and independance, were insensibly changing. **1787** BEST *Angling* (ed. 2) 9 The line by reason of their unpliableness must be much endangered.

un'pliancy. (UN-[1] 12; cf. next.)
1737 BRACKEN *Farriery Impr.* (1757) II. 106 The Stiffness and Unpliancy of our Limbs. **1831** CARLYLE *Misc. Ess., Schiller*, In all other provinces exhibiting a certain inaptitude, an elephantine unpliancy. **1842** PRICHARD *Nat. Hist. Man* 494 The aboriginal American is at once in the incapacity of infancy and unpliancy of old age.

un'pliant, *a.* [UN-[1] 7.]
1. Not bending readily or easily; stiff.
1624 WOTTON *Archit.* 89 The Chissell..being so hard an Instrument, and working vpon so vnpliant stuffe. **1720** WELTON *Suffer. Son of God* II. xvii. 465 Like Iron, which is ..unpliant, when it is not throughly softened by the Forge. **1735** SOMERVILLE *Chase* III. 120 His stiff unpliant Limbs Rooted in Earth, unmov'd..he stands. **1791** COWPER *Odyss.* XXI. 208 Thou wast not born to bend The unpliant bow, or to direct the shaft. **1825** GOOD *Study Med.* (ed. 2) IV. 330 We..render the dejected muscles torpid and unpliant. **1855** MILMAN *Lat. Chr.* XIV. x. VI. 610 The beautiful but too regular face, or the hard, but not entirely unpliant form.
2. Unyielding, obstinate, stubborn.
1659 EVELYN *Char. Eng.* 40 Ill Courtiers, unplyant, morose, and of vulgar address. **1674** *Govt. Tongue* 178 Men are..prone in all companies to arraign such an unpliant Person, as if he were an enemy to mankind. **1710** *Tatler* No. 214 ¶1 These are Persons of a stubborn, unpliant Morality. **1768–74** TUCKER *Lt. Nat.* (1834) II. 591 The love of rectitude becomes a preciseness and rigidity unpliant to the common occasions of life. **1821** JOANNA BAILLIE *Metr. Leg., Lady G.B.* li, The dull unpliant dame refused. **1822** GOOD *Study Med.* IV. 195 *Parodynia Implastica.* Unpliant Labour.
3. Not easily adapted or managed.
1717 ADDISON *Ovid's Met.* III. Notes, The short speeches ..which make the Latin very natural, cannot appear so well in our language, which is more stubborn and unpliant. **1751** JOHNSON *Rambler* No. 173 ¶12 By him who..enters late into the gay world with an unpliant attention and established habits.

un'pliantly, *adv.* (UN-[1] 11.)
[JOHNSON s.v. *Rigidly.*]

un'plight, *sb. Obs.* or *dial.* [UN-[1] 4 b.] Evil plight; danger, risk.
Cf. mod. Whitby dial. *unplight*, a state of disorder.
c **1330** *Assump. Virg.* (B.M. MS.) 194 ȝif I any þinge haue mys wrouȝt,..I it wole amende with my myȝt, That my soule haue no vnplyȝt.

†**un'plight, un'plite**, *v. Obs.* [UN-[2] 3: see PLIGHT *v.*[2]] *trans.* To unfold; *fig.* to evolve.
c **1374** CHAUCER *Boeth.* v. met. iv. (1868) 167 Yif þe þriuyng soule ne vnplitiþ no þing, þat is to sein ne doþ no þing by hys propre moeuynges. *c* **1430** *Pilgr. Lyf. Manhode* III. lvi. (1869) 164 The Scripture j vndide, and vnplytede it, and redde it. **1511** *Guylforde's Pilgr.* (Camden) 50 Ther was delyucrd to hym ye booke of Isaie ye prophete, and as he vnplight the booke he founde the place [etc.].

†**un'plitable**, *a. Obs.*[-1] (UN-[1] 7 b + *plite* PLIGHT *v.*[2]; intended to render L. *inexplicābilis.*)
c **1420** *Chaucer's Boeth.* I. pr. iv. (1876) 9 Whan..ther was estabelissed..greuos and vnplitable [*v.r.* inplitable] coempcion.

un'plotted, *ppl. a.* (UN-[1] 8.)
1598 J. DICKENSON *Greene in Conc.* (1878) 123 Leauing no deuice vnplotted, no deceipt vnpractised to make gratious her gracelesse selfe.

un'ploughed, *ppl. a.* [UN-[1] 8, 8 c. Cf. Du. *ongeploegd*, MLG. *ungeploget*, MSw. *oplögdher* (Sw. *oplöjd*), Da. *upløjet*, Norw. *upløgd.*]
1. Not turned up by the plough. Also with *up.*
1580 LUPTON *Sivqila* 25 What is it to sowe seede uppon the grasse or greene swarde, unplowed or undigged? **1613** W. BROWNE *Brit. Past.* I. ii. 328 Like to that smell, which oft our sense descries Within a field which long unplowed lyes. **1649** LOVELACE *The Scrutinie* iii, Like skilfull Minerallists that sound For Treasure in un-plow'd-up ground. **1765** A. DICKSON *Treat. Agric.* (ed. 2) 42 Allow two fields to lie unplowed;..they will produce very different plants. **1832** *Scoreby Farm Rep.* 4 in *Husb.* III. (L.U.K.), The ridge freshly turned up then covers the unploughed ground. **1891** MALDEN *Tillage* 106 To throw the split-furrows on to the unploughed land.
transf. **1839** HALLAM *Hist. Lit.* II. 287 The daring adventurer that violates their unploughed waters. **1859** MAURY *Phys. Geog.* ii. 38 This unploughed sea would be an oft-used thoroughfare. **1864** BRYANT *New & Old* 21 Brows unploughed by care.
2. Of books: Not trimmed with the plough.
1886 *W. George's Catal.* No. 129. 1 Cloth and boarded books are always edges unplowed (if so issued.)

un'ploughing, *vbl. sb.* (UN-[2] 8, 3.)
1740 TULL *Horse-hoeing Husb.* (1822) xiii. 166 The second is a sort of un-ploughing, for it turns the turf the same side uppermost as before it was ploughed at all.

un'plucked, *ppl. a.* (UN-[1] 8, 8 c. Cf. Du. *ongeplukt*, older Da. *uplukket*, Sw. *oplockad.*)
1568 SKEYNE *Pest* (1860) 8 The third part of the people.. war not left vnplukit away, be sic ane..manslayar. **1610** G. FLETCHER *Christ's Tri.* I. lviii, And you sweete flow'rs,.. Your selues vnpluckt would to his funerals hie. **1659** W. CHAMBERLAYNE *Pharonnida* I. iii. 75 His hands bereft His hoary head of all that time had left Unplucked before. **1819** CRABBE *T. of Hall* VIII. 860 The green cold moss above it grown, Unpluck'd of all but maiden hand. **1878** BROWNING *Poets Croisic* vii, Unplucked grace Of soul, ungathered beauty. **1889** CLARK RUSSELL *Marooned* vi. (1890) 27 The bird came to the table..somewhat prickly with unplucked quills. **1959** 'E. PETERS' *Death Mask* i. 8 Her brows were still high, shapely, and unplucked. **1974** *Times* 26 Oct. 8/8 Her chalk-white complexion, emerald, Kohl-rimmed eyes with unplucked eyebrows.

un'plug, *v.* [UN-[2] 4.] To remove a plug from; of an electrical appliance: opp. PLUG *v.* 1 e.
[**1775** ASH.] **1840** R. H. DANA *Bef. Mast* xxx, By unplugging the holes, we let the soap-suds off the decks. **1876** PREECE & SIVEWRIGHT *Telegraphy* 270 The whole of the resistance in each arm..should be unplugged. **1942** *Tee Emm* (Air Ministry) II. 141 Nothing is more annoying than to find..one glove [of an electrically-heated flying suit] unplugging itself every time you move your arm. **1969** A. GLYN *Dragon Variation* vi. 184 Mr. Jackson unplugged the television and turned out the lights.

un'plumb, *a.* (UN-[1] 7.)
1828 CARLYLE in Froude *Life* (1882) II. 27 She watches over her joiners..with an eye like any hawk's, from which nothing crooked, unplumb or otherwise irregular can hide itself.

un'plumb, *v.* [UN-[2] 4.] *trans.* To take out of lead coffins.
1796 BURKE *Let. to Noble Lord* Wks. VIII. 6 They unplumb the dead for bullets to assassinate the living. [**1845** FORD *Handbk. Spain* I. III. 389 Nor have the dead been unplumbed to furnish missiles of death against the living.]

un'plumbed, *ppl. a.* [UN-[1] 8.] Unsounded, unfathomed.
1623 W. C[RASHAW] *Fatal Vesper* B4b, The height whereof mans vnderstanding cannot aspire vnto, nor the vnplummeld [*sic*] depth thereof sinke vnto. *c* **1852** M. ARNOLD *Isolation* iv, The unplumb'd, salt, estranging sea. **1892** STEVENSON *Across the Plains* 216 Justice is not done to ..the unplumbed childishness of man's imagination.

un'plume, *v.* [UN-[2] 4. Cf. Du. *ontpluimen.*]
1. *trans.* To strip of plumes or feathers. Also in fig. context.
1587 GREENE *Carde of Fancie* (1593) I 3 b, He would vnplume thee of all his feathers, that like Æsops Crow thou mightest receiue the reward of thy rashnesse. **1608** L. MACHIN *Dumbe Knt.* I, Envies sword, Which like a rasor shall unplume thy crest. **1673** *Lady's Call.* I. i. §28 Should we have the like distinction observed, I fear many of our gaiest birds would be unplumed. **1744** H. BROOKE *Love & Van.* 95 She..Exalts the meek..; Of Pride unplumes the lofty crest. **1804** CHARLOTTE SMITH *Conversations*, etc. II. 202 The nest is robbed, and she a second time unplumes herself for the accommodation of her young. **1841** LADY F. HASTINGS *Poems* 212 When Time's allotted course is done, His wings unplumed, his hour-glass run.
2. *fig.* To deprive of distinction, prestige, etc.
1626 T. H[AWKINS] *Caussin's Holy Crt.* 82 Ladyes of court vnplume him, other women..filch from him. **1641** J. SHUTE *Sarah & Hagar* (1649) 55 God can soon unplume us, and take away that which swelleth us so. **1725** POPE *Odyss.* XIX. 104 Her lov'd Lord [may] unplume thy tow'ring pride. **1744** E. MOORE *Fables* xiv. 301 The partner of thy scorn'd embrace, Shall play the wanton in thy face, Each spark unplume thy little pride.
Hence **un'pluming** *vbl. sb.*
1592 NASHE *P. Pennilesse* E 2 b, We delight..in the vnpluming of pullerie, and quartering of Calues and Oxen.

un'plumed, *a.* [UN-[1] 8. Cf. Du. *ongepluimd.*] Not furnished with plumes or feathers.
[**1598** FLORIO, *Spennato*, vnfeathered vnplumed.] **1601** HOLLAND *Pliny* I. 338 They will..kill young pigeons whiles they be calow and unplumed. **1638** DAVENANT *Madagascar* 3 Their Arrowes were unplum'd, Their Bowes unstrung. **1777** POTTER *Æschylus, Agamemnon* 217 Like vulturs, which, their unplumed offspring lost, Whirl many a rapid flight. **1804** *Europ. Mag.* XLV. 413/2 Whether it was..plain or coloured, plumed or unplumed, covered or uncovered. **1871** H. KING *Ovid's Met.* VI. 946 Not with their birth Those pinions came;..young Calaïs And Zethes grew unplumed.
fig. **1818** MILMAN *Samor* VII. 267 Had it seem'd love, her very pride had quell'd The unplum'd phantasy.

unplummed, obs. var. UNPLUMBED *ppl. a.*

un'plundered, *ppl. a.* (UN-[1] 8. Cf. Du. *ongeplunderd*, Sw. *oplundrad.*)
1655 FULLER *Ch. Hist.* IX. v. §9, I count it a blessing that providence hath preserved such a treasure unplundred. **1855** SINGLETON *Virgil* II. 460 Then I..The pitiable corse, and arms Unplundered, to the sepulchre will bear. **1865** J. CAMERON *Malayan India* 263 To waste your time cutting the throat of a dead man while his house is yet unplundered.

un'plunge, *v.* (UN-[2] 3.)
a **1645** HEYWOOD *Fort. by Land & Sea* III. iii, Any meanes that can unplunge me from this gulf of trouble.

un'ply, *v.* [UN-[2] 3.] *trans.* To unfold, unfurl.
c **1330** *Arth. & Merl.* 5063 (Kölbing), Þese Sarrazins þo gun vnplie Her baners & after heiȝe. **13..** *K. Alis.* 3000 (Laud MS.), A clerk gan þe lettre vnplye. **1830** JAMES *De L'Orme* xxviii, A pistole for every fold he unplied in the rich white silk.

un'pocket, *v.* (UN-[2] 5.)
1611 FLORIO, *Sgaglioffare*,..to vnpouch or vnpocket. **1844** TUPPER *Heart* xi. 104 Mutual participation in profit and loss:..the bookseller pocketing the first, and the author un-pocketing the second. **1894** A. MORRISON *Mean Streets* 136 Sam unpocketed a greasy paper.
Hence **un'pocketed** *ppl. a.*
1797 MRS. M. ROBINSON *Walsingham* I. 102 A thousand times..did my eyes glance..at my unpocketed guinea.

unpo'etic, *a.* (UN-[1] 7. Cf. next.)
? **1619** CORBET *Death Q. Anne* Poems (1672) 126 Do not.. for an Epithite that fails, Bite off your Unpoetick Nails. **1786** MISS SEWARD in *Mrs. Delany's Life & Corr.* (1862) III. 395, I have seen nothing of him since he sunk into his very un-poetic union. **1812** J. WILSON *Isle of Palms*, etc. 371 Light Fauns, That the good owner's unpoetic soul Could

not..Imagine. **1863** 'OUIDA' *Held in Bondage* vi, There is something unpoetic, and coarse,..about blood and bruises.
Comb. **1865** G. MACDONALD *A. Forbes* xxxix, The most unpoetic-looking Mr. Cupples.

unpo'etical, *a.* (UN-^{1} 7. Cf. prec.)
a **1746** HOLDSWORTH *Remarks Virgil* (1768) 270 Ruæus's interpreting..is very unpoetical. **1776** MICKLE *Camoens' Lusiad* Introd. 149 A loose unpoetical paraphrase of the Lusiad. **1812** *Examiner* 4 May 284/1 The unpoetical lucubrations of Lord Coke. **1861** PALEY *Æschylus* (ed. 2) *Persians* 547 The superlative is here tame and unpoetical.

unpo'etically, *adv.* (UN-^{1} 11.)
1697 DRYDEN *Virgil* Notes 633 How unpoetically and baldly had this been translated: Thou shalt Marcellus be! **1756** J. WARTON *Ess. Pope* I. 7 How coldly and unpoetically Pope has copied the subsequent appeal to the nymphs. **1786** MRS. DELANY *Life & Corr.* (1862) II. 358 My poor muse has been asleep these thirty years, during which time I have been very unpoetically..employed!

un'poetized, *ppl. a.* (UN-^{1} 8.)
1831 SCOTT *Jrnl.* 26 Nov., I got home about midnight; but remain unpoetised and unspeeched.

un'pointed, *ppl. a.* (UN-^{1} 8.)
1533 *Extr. Aberd. Reg.* (1844) I. 149 Gif he thollis ony bestis to cum in the kyrkyerd frathinfurtht vnpundyt. **1539** *Reg. Privy Seal Scot.* II. 472/2 The said Johnne to be..unpoyndit and untrublit for ony actioun civile bigane.

un'pointed, *ppl. a.* [UN-^{1} 8.]
†**1.** Not furnished with tagged points or laces. *Obs.*
1574 HELLOWES tr. *Gueuara's Fam. Ep.* (1577) 254 His shirt ragged, his doublet lose and vnpoynted.
2. a. Not punctuated.
1593 MARLOWE *Edw. II*, v. iv, But read it thus, and thats an other sence:..Vnpointed as it is, thus shall it goe. **1641** PRYNNE *Antip.* 267 This ambiguous sentence unpointed, they take for a sufficient warrant, and most pittifully murthered the innocent King. **1655** FULLER *Ch. Hist.* III. 107 He returned unto them a Ridling Answere, altogether un-pointed.
b. Not provided with vowel-points or similar marks.
1640 SIR E. DERING *Carmelite* (1641) 30 Three words in Greek, whereof one was unpointed. **1659** BP. WALTON *Consid. Considered* 278 There is no such uncertainty in the Text unpointed, as is pretended by them. **1778** BP. LOWTH *Transl. Isaiah* Notes 236 It is upon a rasure in a third; and left unpointed at first, as suspected, in a fourth. **1845** *Proc. Philol. Soc.* II. 172 An *i*, written in certain cases, but more generally in unpointed texts only perceptible in the pronunciation. **1877** CAIRD *Philos. Kant* 203 Like the reader of unpointed Hebrew, who supplies for himself the vowels.
3. Not furnished with a point; lacking point or finish.
1632 B. JONSON *Magn. Lady* IV. iii, *Pro.* Which, ending here, would have shown dull, flat, and unpointed; without any shape or sharpness. **1681** DRYDEN *Abs. & Achit.* II. 502 But thou in Clumsy verse, unlickt, unpointed, Hast Shamefully defi'd the Lord's Anointed. **1887** BOWEN *Æneid* VI. 760 [He] leans on a lance unpointed and bright.
4. Not pointed *at*.
a **1555** J. PHILPOT *Apol.* (1559) A 5 b, That the simple people maye beware of their Pharisaical venome,..suffre them not to passe by you vnpointed at. **1642** HOWELL *For. Trav.* (Arb.) 13 Yet one's..personall conversation will still find out something new and unpointed at by any other.

un'pointing, *vbl. sb.* [UN-^{1} 13.] Omission of punctuation.
1612 T. JAMES *Corrupt. Script.* v. 10 The transposition..of words, or vnpointing of Books,..doe so farre alter the sense, and obscure the Author.

un'pointing, *ppl. a.* (UN-^{1} 10.)
1814 *Monthly Mag.* XXXVII. 240 She too stands mute, th' unpointing fingers fall.

un'poise, *v.* (UN-^{2} 3.)
1700 S. PARKER *Six Phil. Essays* 50 Instead of poizing, I look upon such a mass as rather fitted to unpoize and break the mystick Chains upon which the body of the earth hangs. **1800** COLERIDGE *Tri. Loyalty* 372 The violent pull..Unpois'd me and I fell. **1824** SYD. SMITH *Wks.* (1859) II. 185/2 The balance of Justice is unpoised.

un'poised, *ppl. a.* [UN-^{1} 8.] Unbalanced.
c **1600** W. FOWLER *Wks.* (S.T.S.) I. 260, Vnpoized hambers strikes vntimely howers. **1735** THOMSON *Liberty* II. 150 Oft on the brink Of ruin..Totter'd the rash Democracy; un-pois'd. **1827** HOOD *Mids. Fairies* lxi, Languid fish, unpois'd, grow sick and yearn. **1903** W. H. HUDSON *Rousseau* 7 The restless, flighty, unpoised Jean Jacques.

un'poison, *v.* (UN-^{2} 6 b.)
1598 FLORIO, *Suelenire*,..to vnpoison, to vnrankle. *c* **1620** in Farr *S. P. Jas.* (1848) 99 When sin befriends us, 'tis that we should dread The mighty one, that sin un-poisoned hath. **1644** G. PLATTES in *Hartlib's Legacy* (1655) 174 Their minds are so poysoned, that there is no other way to unpoyson them, but to win their belief. *c* **1685** SOUTH *Serm.* (1717) V. 43 Such a Course could not, but in a short time, have Unpoisoned their perverted Minds. **1868** BROWNING *Ring & Bk.* v. 1038, I was shaken wide awake, Doctored and drenched, somewhat unpoisoned so. **1896** in *Westm. Gaz.* 17 Sept. 5/1 His mind has been poisoned and 'un-poisoned', and he is now..open to receive information.

un'poisonable, *a.* (UN-^{1} 7 b.)
1628 FELTHAM *Resolves* II. lxxix. 226 It fell out to be part of Mithridates misery, that hee had made himselfe vnpoisonable.

un'poisoned, *ppl. a.* (UN-^{1} 8.)
[**1775** ASH.] **1821** LAMB *Elia* I. *Old Benchers I.T.*, So may the sparrows..unpoisoned hop about your walks! **1859** R. F. BURTON *Centr. Afr.* in *Jrnl. Geog. Soc.* XXIX. 197 Bows and arrows, the latter unpoisoned, but..cruelly barbed.

un'poisonous, *a.* (UN-^{1} 7.)
a **1843** *Encycl. Metrop.* (1845) VII. 306/2 The Unpoisonous,..the Fang-less Poisonous, and..the Fanged Poisonous Snakes.

un'polar, *a.* (UN-^{1} 7.)
1856 TYNDALL *Fragm. Sci.* (1879) I. 374 A simple unpolar force.

un'polarized, *ppl. a.* (UN-^{1} 8.)
1827–8 HERSCHEL in *Encycl. Metrop.* (1845) IV. 524 The unpolarized portion [of light] will continue to be half transmitted. **1856** SCOFFERN in *Orr's Circ. Sci., Pract. Chem.* 96 Whether the..rays be polarized or unpolarized. **1871** B. STEWART *Heat* (ed. 2) §179 If the vibrations have no reference to any particular plane, then the wave is unpolarized.

unpo'liced, *ppl. a.* (UN-^{1} 8.)
[**1775** ASH.] *a* **1797** H. WALPOLE *Mem. Geo. III* (1845) III. vii. 220 In a vast capital,—free, ungoverned, unpoliced, and indifferent to everything but its pleasures and factions!

un'policied, *ppl. a.* (UN-^{1} 8.)
1606 SHAKS. *Ant. & Cl.* v. ii. 311 Oh could'st thou speake, That I might heare thee call great Cæsar, Asse, vnpolicied. **1654** WHITLOCK *Zootomia* 448 The unpolicied Schollar. **1738** WARBURTON *Div. Legat.* I. 75 [Modern savages] being yet unpolicied, and in a State of Nature. **1947** AUDEN *Nones* (1952) 64 The unamerican survivor Hears angels drinking fruit-juice with their wives Or making money in an open Unpolicied air.

un'polish, *v.* (UN-^{2} 3.)
a **1697** AUBREY *Lives* (1898) I. 216 Denham was unpolished with the small pox: otherwise a fine complexion. **1748** RICHARDSON *Clarissa* (1768) V. 261 How anger unpolishes the most polite! **1823** MOORE *Mem.* (1853) IV. 69 His chimney pieces, by Bartollini, spoiled from over-polish; hopes to be able to un-polish them again.

un'polishable, *a.* (UN-^{1} 7 b.)
1687 J. REYNOLDS *Death's Vis.* Pref. (1713) 3 'Tis true such Matter is Restive, Refractory and Unpolishable Enough. *a* **1797** H. WALPOLE *Mem. Geo. II* (1822) I. 170 The duke's outside was unpolished, his inside unpolishable. **1836** LANDOR *Pericles & Asp.* Wks. 1846 II. 416 A coarse grained, unpolishable people. **1863** HAWTHORNE *Old Home* (1879) 344 The unpolishable ruggedness of the native character.

un'polished, *ppl. a.* [UN-^{1} 8, 5 b.]
1. Not made smooth or bright by polishing.
1382 WYCLIF *Deut.* xxvii. 6 An auter..of stonus vnfourmed and vnpolishid. *c* **1475** *Cath. Angl.* 293/1 (A.), Vn Pulysched..., *impolitus*. **1552** HULOET, Vnpollished, and not perfitly wrought, *raudus*. **1605** BACON *Adv. Learn.* II. xvii. §13 The better sort of Rules haue beene not vnfitly compared to glasses of steele vnpullished. **1662** J. BARGRAVE *Pope Alex. VII* (1867) 122 Another thin piece of jasper stone, unpollished. **1751** JOHNSON *Rambler* No. 166 ¶3 Fortitude, and probity,..are cast aside like unpolished gems. **1815** J. SMITH *Panorama Sci. & Art* I. 5 If the tool be unpolished. **1874** J. GEIKIE *Gt. Ice Age* vi. 73 Rough, unpolished angular fragments that have tumbled..from cliffs.
transf. **1635** SWAN *Spec. M.* iii. §2 (1643) 48 Both of them [*sc.* the heavens] remained as it were unpolished or unfinished untill the fourth day.
2. Inelegant or rude in respect of style, language, etc.; not carefully finished.
c **1489** SKELTON *Death Earl Northumbld.* 127 My wordes vnpullysht be, nakide and playne. **1575** LANEHAM *Let.* (1871) 15 The thing which heer I report in vnpolisht proez. **1585** DANIEL *Paulus Iouius* Pref., Wks. (Grosart) IV. 4 In like maner..haue I aduentured to place these my vnpolished labors on the Piller of your worthines. **1635** in *Verney Mem.* (1907) I. 99 Not daring to present any unpolished lines to such a judicious reader. **1673** *Phil. Trans.* VIII. 5178 Of which many pregnant Instances..are registred in these un-polish't Volumes. *a* **1704** T. BROWN *Satire Ancients* Wks. 1720 I. 26 To hear..Horace [called] an Author un-polished, languid, and without force. **1781** HARRIS *Philol. Enq.* III. xi. 468 At a time when the Languages of England and France were barbarous and unpolished. **1839** HALLAM *Hist. Lit.* I. v. §16 Budæus..is hard and unpolished. **1891** FARRAR *Darkn. & Dawn* xxii, It cannot be Chrysippus; the Greek is too modern, and too unpolished.
3. Left rude or imperfect.
1596 *Edward III*, I. i. 76 His lame vnpolisht shifts are come to light. **1647** CLARENDON *Contempl. Ps.* Tracts (1727) 527 To reduce our unpolished speculations and conceptions into a prompt and ready practice.
4. Not refined in manners or ways of living; marked or characterized by lack of culture.
1593 SHAKS. *2 Hen. VI*, III. ii. 271 The Commons, rude vnpolisht Hindes. **1647** CLARENDON *Hist. Reb.* I. §4 The spirit of Craft and Subtilty in some, and the Unpolished Integrity of others. **1672** DRYDEN *Def. Epilogue* ¶28 They were unlucky to have been bred in an unpolished age. **1703** J. SAVAGE *Lett. Antients* xxxvii. 99, I have had an unpolish'd Education..in Barbarous Nations. **1776** GIBBON *Decl. & F.* ix. (1788) I. 277 The unpolished wives of the barbarians. *c* **1815** JANE AUSTEN *Persuas.* ix, Their parents' inferior, retired, and unpolished way of living. **1853** LYNCH *Self-Improv.* v. 112 An unpolished man need not be an ill-mannered one.
Hence **un'polishedness**.
1647 CLARENDON *Hist. Reb.* VII. §279 That roughness and unpolishedness of his nature. **1652** J. WRIGHT tr. *Camus' Nat. Paradox* v. 90 Those hearts, which may bee said to bee of Iron for their rude unpolishedness.

unpo'lite, *a.* [UN-^{1} 8, 5 b.]
†**1.** Unpolished; unrefined. *Obs. rare.*
1646 G. DANIEL *Poems* Wks. (Grosart) I. 94 What but vnpolite fformes, and ffancies raw, Can such a time produce? **1726** WALDRON *Descr. Isle of Man* (1744) 93 However unpolite and savage..the Natives of Man may be. **1727** SWIFT *Further Acc. E. Curll* ¶1 A faithful, though unpolite historian of Grubstreet.
2. Lacking in politeness; impolite:
a. Of actions, conduct, etc.
1709 *Tatler* No. 140 ¶8 [He calls] my cousin Jenny Distaff, Madam Distaff; which..is very unpolite. **1753** RICHARDSON *Grandison* (1781) I. xxiii. 164 His unpolite behaviour to the dear creature. **1838** DICKENS *O. Twist* ix, As an apology to the company for his unpolite behaviour.
b. Of persons.
1712 *Spect.* No. 506 ¶4 The Spirit of Love..is very often..lost, by some little Accidents which the Careless and Unpolite never attend to. **1747** RICHARDSON *Clarissa* (1811) I. 205 An unpolite and disobliging brother. **1802–12** BENTHAM *Ration. Judic. Evid.* (1827) IV. 417 He will not be so unpolite..as to suffer this..suspicion to pass the bounds of his own lips. **1871** SMILES *Charac.* ix. 238 The unpolite impulsive man will..rather lose his friend than his joke.
†**3.** Unfashionable, inelegant. *Obs.*
1740 CIBBER *Apol.* I. 11 In these unpolite Amusements he has laugh'd like a Rake. **1741** WATTS *Improv. Mind* I. xvii, How ever they may be now fancied to sound unpolite or unfashionable. **1753** *Songs Costume* (Percy Soc.) 234 Next a coat of embroidery from foreigners come; 'Twou'd be quite unpolite to have one wrought at home.

unpo'litely, *adv.* (UN-^{1} 11, 5 b; cf. prec.)
1748 RICHARDSON *Clarissa* (1811) II. 72, I acted very unpolitely. **1857** DICKENS *Little Dorrit* II. xxiii, Arthur asked his pardon, if he had stared at him unpolitely.

unpo'liteness. [UN-^{1} 12, 5 b.]
†**1.** Lack of culture or refinement. *Obs.*
1702 ECHARD *Eccl. Hist.* 20 People of great Courage..and of no less Plainess and Unpoliteness. **1728** MORGAN *Algiers* I. iii. 49 A People so prone to Unpoliteness as were the natural Africans.
2. Want of politeness.
1707 *Refl. upon Ridicule* (1717) I. 28 Unpoliteness is a Vice that gives the World a Right to complain of us. **1748** RICHARDSON *Clarissa* (1811) III. 187, I have just carried unpoliteness far enough to make her afraid of me. **1858** CARLYLE in Froude *Life in London* (1844) II. 197 The shocking unpoliteness of breaking an express promise. **1880** *Athenæum* 5 June 725 Their own unpoliteness and ill temper.
†**3.** Inelegance. *Obs.*
1725 BLACKWALL *Sacr. Class.* (1727) I. 80 Sad outcries are made of the unpoliteness of the style.

un'politic, *a.* [UN-^{1} 7, 5 b.] Impolitic.
a **1548** HALL *Chron.*, *Hen. V*, 65 He imagined that all mischiefes..whiche chaunced in the common wealth should bee imputed and assigned to his vnpolitike doyng. **1591** G. FLETCHER *Russe Commw.* (Hakl. Soc.) 44 It might seeme..to be no bad nor unpollitique way for conteyning of so large a commonwealth. **1647** CLARENDON *Hist. Reb.* I. §150 The Circumstances and Proceedings..were very Unpolitick, and even Destructive to the Services intended. **1664** H. MORE *Myst. Iniq.* vi. 17 It had been the most unpolitick action..to offer them any strange God to worship. **1721** AMHERST *Terræ Fil.* No. 45 (1726) 240 In this odd, unpolitic manner, did I conduct myself. **1747** CARTE *Hist. Eng.* I. 268 The great slaughter..put their affairs into a condition, which rendered it very unpolitick to provoke new enemies. **1978** J. UPDIKE *Coup* (1979) i. 20 The unpolitic loyalty of the fearful.

unpo'litical, *a.* (UN-^{1} 7, 5 b.)
1643 CARYL *Sacr. Covt.* 22 Some have thought it unpoliticall to set a foote this Covenant. **1778** W. H. MARSHALL *Minutes Agric., Digest* 37 Feeding Farming-servants at their master's expence is unpolitical. **1792** A. YOUNG *Trav. France* 564 A proof that the measures of the National Assembly have been ill-judged, ill-advised, and unpolitical. **1894** *Thinker* VI. 63 This condition of things authorizes the political nations..to answer the call of the unpolitical populations for aid.
Hence **unpo'litically** *adv.*
1930 E. SITWELL *Alexander Pope* v. 63 The young and un-politically-minded Pope. **1962** *Times* 5 Dec. 17/6 It [*sc.* a film] is unpolitically concerned with people.

†**un'politicly**, *adv.* [UN-^{1} 11, 5 b.] Impoliticly.
1589 WARNER *Alb. Eng.* II. 160 A sport [*sc.* riding on horseback] lately vsed of our English youthes, but now..vnpollitickly..discontinued. *a* **1677** BARROW *Serm.* (1686) I. 407 We..deal as un-politickly, as the members of the body should act unnaturally, in subtracting mutual assistance. **1748** RICHARDSON *Clarissa* II. 64 Mr. Solmes..had told Her, that..I acted very unpoliticly.

†**un'politicness**. *Obs.* [UN-^{1} 12, 5 b.] Impoliticness.
1664 H. MORE *Apology* 532 It would lose the appellation of Veracity, and deserve the style of Unpolitickness.

un'pollarded, *ppl. a.* (UN-^{1} 8.)
1830 J. G. STRUTT *Sylva Brit.* 16 The Beggar's Oak is a fine sample of the real Park Oak, unpruned, unpollarded. **1891** E. R. PENNELL *Stream Pleas.* 124 The cut, with its unpollarded willows,..was like a bit of a French canal.

un'polled, *ppl. a.* [UN-^{1} 8.]
1. Uncut, unshorn.
1647 HEXHAM I, Vnpowled, *ongeschoren*. **1727** BAILEY (vol. II), *Unpolled*, the hair being uncut.
†**2.** Untold, uncounted. *Obs.*
1647 FANSHAW *Poems* 299 Though richer then unpoll'd Arabian wealth, and Indian Gold.
3. Not brought to, or recorded at, the poll; not having voted at an election.

1818 TODD, *Unpolled*, not registered as a voter. **1824** HOOK *Sayings & Doings* I. 134 There were upwards of a thousand freeholders unpolled. **1837** DICKENS *Pickw.* xiii, Fourteen unpolled electors. **1893** *Westm. Gaz.* 1 Jan. 6/1 There has always in this constituency been a wide margin of unpolled voters.

† **un'pollushed**, *ppl. a. Obs.*$^{-1}$ [Irreg. f. OF. *impollus, -ue*.] Unpolluted.
c **1489** CAXTON *Blanchardyn* v. 23 That by vyolent opressyon that traytour..shall enioye youre youghthe vnpolusshed.

unpo'llutable, *a.* (UN-^{1} 7.)
1711 G. HICKES *Two Treat. Chr. Priesth.* (1847) II. 77 After it is consecrated..it becomes..an unpollutable altar.

unpo'lluted, *ppl. a.* (UN-^{1} 8, 5 b.)
1602 SHAKS. *Ham.* v. i. 262 From her faire and vnpolluted flesh, May Violets spring. **1653** W. RAMESEY *Astrol. Restored* Ep. Ded. 2 Among the..graver sort of people in all Ages, this Science (being unpolluted and unsophisticated) hath been still had in most high esteem. **1732** BERKELEY *Alciphr.* III. §1 Honour is a noble unpolluted source of virtue. **1771** SMOLLETT *Humph. Cl.* (1815) 262 A man must tread with great circumspection to get safe housed with unpolluted shoes. **1812** J. WILSON *Isle of Palms* I. 21 A woman's unpolluted soul! **1865** DICKENS *Mut. Fr.* III. viii, The young river..unpolluted by the defilements that lie in wait for it on its course.

unpo'lluting, *ppl. a.* (UN-^{1} 10.)
1817 SHELLEY *Rev. Islam* IX. xviii, The shafts of falsehood unpolluting flew.

un'pollux, *v.* [UN-^{2} 6 b.] *fig.* To castrate.
1654 GAYTON *Pleas. Notes* III. vii, The story of the Castor [= beaver] un-polluxing himselfe is very well applyed.

un'pompous, *a.* (UN-^{1} 7.)
1656 W. DU GARD tr. *Comenius' Gate Lat. Unl.* 297 Jesus of Nazareth (rejected by the Jews for his un-pompous life). **1928** *Daily Express* 8 May 5 This is an unpompous age, and the tendency to poke fun at that ancient spectacle, grand opera,..does not decrease. **1946** D. WELCH *Jrnl.* 9 Apr. (1952) 197 He quickly dropped the 'sir' when he was sitting beside me... This I knew was a compliment in some way. I suppose I interpreted it as a tribute to an unpompous or young appearance. **1959** J. OSBORNE *World of Paul Slickey* I. iii. 29 We can safely say in a not unpompous way, blind Them with words! **1978** *Even. Stand* 29 Sept. 20/5 At yesterday's function Sir Peter read a neat, unpompous little speech.

un'pope, *v.* (UN-^{2} 6 b.)
1563 FOXE *A. & M.* 13 1 Benedictus vnderstanding them to be set against him..vnpoped him self. **1655** FULLER *Ch. Hist.* XI. v. §74 Rome will never so farr un-Pope it self, as to part with her pretended Supremacy. **1677** W. HUGHES *Man of Sin* II. xii. 212 They took the boldness to un-pope four of their Infallibilities. **1868** BROWNING *Ring & Bk.* x. 73 He is unpoped, and all he did I damn. **1880** —— *Pietro* 403 We're Pope—once Pope, you can't unpope us!

un'popular, *a.* [UN-^{1} 7, 5 b.] Not possessed of popular favour.
1647 CLARENDON *Hist. Reb.* I. §8 That Meeting being, upon very unpopular..reasons, immediately Dissolved. **1652** *Nicholas Papers* (Camden) 295 Those who put his Majesty on such unpopular and unpleasing things. **1731** CHESTERF. *Let.* 16 Jan. in *10th Rep. Hist. MSS. Comm.* App. I. 245 The disagreeable and unpopular situation we are at present in. **1855** MACAULAY *Hist. Eng.* xviii. IV. 163 James was unpopular because he was a Papist. **1863** H. COX *Instit.* III. iii. 628 An unpopular government.

unpopu'larity. [UN-^{1} 12; cf. prec.] The quality or fact of being unpopular.
1735 LD. LYTTELTON *Lett. Persian* (ed. 3) I. 214 You are afraid of the Unpopularity of the Sound. **1781** JOHNSON *L.P., Dryden* Wks. 1787 II. 412 The original impropriety, and the subsequent unpopularity of the subject. **1810** COLERIDGE *Friend* 355 The last War..had yet causes of unpopularity peculiar to itself. **1878** LECKY *Eng. in 18th C.* I. iii. 432 The Government was now too weak to bear the strain of additional unpopularity.

un'popularize, *v.* [UN-^{2} 6 c.] *trans.* To make unpopular.
1831 *Examiner* 185/1 The Citizen King is completely unpopularized. **1884** *Nonconf. & Indep.* 24 July 723/3 Spontaneous emigration..unpopularised a noble cause.

un'populate, *v.* [UN-^{2} 4.] *trans.* To depopulate.
1658 COKAINE *Trappolin* IV. ii, It is a frequent thing..To have the Plague..rage and even unpopulate places. **1880** *Cornh. Mag.* Dec. 673 The growth of manufactures..had been unpopulating the country to swell the towns.

un'populated, *ppl. a.* (UN-^{1} 8.)
1885 *Manch. Exam.* 4 Apr. 4/6 The march of the European invader into the unpopulated regions.

un'populous, *a.* (UN-^{1} 7.)
[**1775** ASH.] **1827** SCOTT *Chron. Canongate* iv, Some sequestered and unpopulous district. **1887** *Field* 24 Dec. 975/2 In so remote and unpopulous a part of the country.

un'populousness. (UN-^{1} 12: cf. prec.)
1599 SANDYS *Europæ Spec.* (1632) 208 The unpopulousnesse..makes that no one Country is defence for it selfe.

unporno'graphic, *a.* [UN-^{1} 7 a.] Not pornographic.
1938 *New Statesman & Nation* 23 July 156/2 This admirable and totally unpornographic novel. **1943** D. WELCH *Jrnl.* 20 Apr. (1952) 61 As Bernard Shaw said to me when we were all called to give evidence over the *Well of Loneliness* fuss, 'Here I am, asked to say something about this pathetic book, and I don't know what to do, because I know it's serious, unpornographic, but it's so bad as literature.' **1968** *Punch* 5 June 829/1 The story is not only quite unpornographic, it is also very funny.

un'porous, *a.* (UN-^{1} 7, 5 b.)
1822-7 GOOD *Study Med.* (1829) IV. 25 We behold the etherial fluids..transmitted..by substances still more solid and unporous. **1841** *Florist's Jrnl.* (1846) II. 121 Whenever we find the soil close and unporous.

† **un'portable**, *a. Obs.* [UN-^{1} 7 b, 5 b.]
1. Too burdensome or grievous to be borne; unbearable, intolerable.
1382 WYCLIF *Matt.* xxiii. 4 Greuouse chargis, and vnportable, or that mown nat be born. **1424** *Paston Lett.* I. 17 To here grete and unportable drede..in here spirites. *c* **1470** G. ASHBY *Active Policy* 172 Ther hath be in late daies ..To myche folk unportable punicion. **1526** *Pilgr. Perf.* (W. de W. 1531) 299 b, All the great & unportable paynes whiche it was thy blessed wyll to suffre. **1540** in Ellis *Orig. Lett.* Ser. III. III. 273 That I may be delyvered from the cure, and to me the unportable burden in governance of this House. **1611** SPEED *Hist. Gt. Brit.* IX. viii. 491 These important and vnportable matters did no whit moue him.
2. Extremely large.
1536-7 *Act Hen. VIII*, in Bolton *Stat. Irel.* (1621) 178 Whose Majestie..hath with the expence of an vnportable summe of his own treasure, defended vs.
3. Too heavy to carry.
a **1618** RALEIGH *Invent. Shipping* 9 Had their Cables of Iron chains held any great length, they had been unportable. **1728** E. SMITH *Compl. Housew.* Pref., [It] would fill an unportable volume. **1782** W. F. MARTYN *Geog. Mag.* II. 78 Which pieces are so large and unportable, that..a cart or wheel-barrow is necessary.

unpor'tentous, *a.* (UN-^{1} 7.)
1813 T. BUSBY *Lucretius* II. VI. 538 Clouds unportentous of the future storm.

un'portioned, *ppl. a.* (UN- 8.)
1744 YOUNG *Nt. Th.* VII. 1167 'Has virtue charms?'—I grant her heavenly fair; But if unportion'd; all will int'rest wed. **1747** FRANCIS tr. *Horace, Ep.* I. xvii. 69 My Sister lies unportion'd on my Hands. **1828-32** WEBSTER s.v., An unportioned daughter.

unport'manteaued, *ppl. a.* (UN-^{1} 9.)
1819 WHEWELL in Todhunter *Acc. Writ.* (1876) II. 33 We ..wended our way dolorous and discontented,.. untravelled and unportmanteaued.

un'portraited, *ppl. a.* (UN-^{1} 8.)
1611 GUILLIM *Heraldry* II. i. 39 Leigh reckoneth such vnportraicted bearing to bee good.

unpor'trayable, *a.* (UN-^{1} 7 b.)
1873 M. COLLINS *Squire Silchester* II. xi. 131 A mighty dusky unportrayable figure, stalking over the furrows.

† **un'portunate**, *a. Obs.* [UN-^{1} 7, 5 b.] Importunate.
a **1533** LD. BERNERS *Gold. Bk. M. Aurel.* (1536) p. iii, Amonge so many vnportunate wyndes and vnstable waters ther is great necessitee of good ores. **1603** HOLLAND *Plutarch's Mor.* 57 For they..are troublesome and unportunate hearers.

un'portuous, *a. rare*$^{-1}$. [UN-^{1} 7 + L. *portus* harbour. Cf. L. *importuōsus*.] Harbourless.
1797 BURKE *Regic. Peace* iii. ¶25 Had the West of Ireland been an unportuous coast, the French naval power would have been undone.

† **unpo'ssess**, *v. Obs. rare.* [UN-^{2} 3.] *trans.* To dispossess.
c **1449** PECOCK *Repr.* III. xvi. 380 Preestis..mowen iustli be vnpossessyd (that is to seie, mowen iustli be putt out of possessioun of the same godis). *a* **1542** WYATT in *Tottel's Misc.* (Arb.) 84 The holde that is geuen ouer, I vnpossest, so hangeth in balance Of warre.

unpo'ssessed, *ppl. a.* [UN-^{1} 8.]
1. Not possessed or owned; unoccupied.
1594 DANIEL *Compl. of Rosamond* ciii, Seeing how many seeke to vndermine The treasury that's vnpossest of any. **1603** KNOLLES *Hist. Turks* (1621) 105 The riuer was yet vnpossessed by the enemie. **1664** H. POWER *Exp. Philos.* 92 If you let in the outward ayr into the cavity unpossessed by the mercury. **1725** DE FOE *Voy. round World* (1840) 281 If he leaves the country unpossessed, he leaves it free for any other nation to come in. **1748** *Anson's Voy.* I. vi. 64 [Patagonia] is unpossessed by the Spaniards. **1833** WORDSW. *Itin. Poems, Iona* 12 A grace by thee unsought and unpossest.
† **2.** Not preoccupied; unprejudiced. *Obs.*
a **1586** SIDNEY *Arcadia* III. xv, When a while that instrument had made a brave proclamation to all unpossessed mindes of attention. **1665** J. SPENCER *Vulg. Proph.* 61 All the Heralds of Heaven had the badg of some divine Signs, whereby unpossest minds might easily distinguish them from Impostors. **1685** TEMPLE *Ess., Gardening* (1690) 11 The want of Demonstration or Satisfaction, to any thinking and unpossessed Man.
3. Not having possession *of* something.
1795 V. KNOX *Chr. Philos.* §22 *note*, The mind, unpossessed of virtue. **1840** GEN. P. THOMPSON *Exerc.* (1842) V. 69 A witness..absolutely unpossessed of all idea of obligation to speak the truth. **1899** F. T. BULLEN *Way Navy* 25 Many of them quite unpossessed of any knowledge of our most thrilling episode.
Hence **unpo'ssessedness**.
1819 COLERIDGE in *Lit. Rem.* (1836) II. 239 How truly Shakspearian is the opening of Macbeth's character given in the unpossessedness of Banquo's mind.

unpo'ssessing, *ppl. a.* (UN-^{1} 10, 5 d.)
1605 SHAKS. *Lear* II. i. 69 Thou vnpossessing Bastard, dost thou thinke [etc.]. **1757** MRS. GRIFFITH *Lett. Henry & Frances* (1767) II. 191 With a taste and relish for them all, yet unpossessing any of them.

unpossi'bility. (UN-^{1} 12, 5 b; cf. next.)
1621 AINSWORTH *Annot. Pentat., Exod.* xix. 8 The unpossibility of the Law, which is weake through the flesh. **1623** COCKERAM I I, Vnpossibilitie of beleefe, *Incredulitie*. *a* **1849** POE *King Pest* Wks. 1865 II. 372 It would be a matter of utter unpossibility. **1866** FLORENCE MARRYAT *For Ever & Ever* II. 194 Why, it would be an unpossibility, Sir.

un'possible, *a.* Now only *dial.* [UN-^{1} 7, 5 b.] Impossible. (Very common *c* 1400–1660.)
1362 LANGL. *P. Pl.* A. XI. 225 Poul prouiþ it is vnpossible riche men in heuene. *c* **1400** *Lanfranc's Cirurg.* 153 Þer is no þing vnpossible to stalworþe nature. **1453** in *Wars Eng. in France* (1864) II. 488 It is unpossible unto us so sone to purvey for the saide socours. **1471** FORTESCUE *Wks.* (1869) 535 The forsayd minor is now clerely proved unpossible. **1523** LD. BERNERS tr. *Froiss.* I. cxlv. 173 The frenchemen coude natte passe no way, without they wolde haue gone through the marshes, the whiche was vnpossyble. **1570** T. WILSON *Demosth. Orat., Life* 127 Vnpossible it is for anye one to deceyue him. **1610** FLETCHER *Faithful Shepherdess* II. i, Whose grief..to anothers eye May seem unpossible of remedy. **1697** BURGHOPE *Disc. Relig. Assemb.* 169 There's nothing requir'd of us..which is unpossible. **1773** GOLDSM. *Stoops to Conq.* II. i, By the laws, your worship, that's parfectly unpossible. **1825** BROCKETT *N.C. Words*, *Unpossible*, for impossible. The word is frequent with the vulgar in the North. **1844-** in Sc. and dialect use (*Eng. Dial. Dict.*). **1866** FLO. MARRYAT *For Ever & Ever* II. 194 That is an unpossible thing, Sir.
absol. **1581** MULCASTER *Positions* iv. 17 Nothing giuen to the vnpossible, where possibilitie must take place.
Hence † **un'possibleness**; † **un'possibly** *adv.*
1561 T. HOBY tr. *Castiglione's Courtyer* IV. Ss ii, The vnpossiblenes of yᵉ matter. **1658** OSBORNE *Adv. Son* Wks. (1673) 175 Therefore not unpossibly the cause why the Devil was so earnest..to make them commit if [*sc.* a sin]. **1659** —— *Misc. Ess. Paradoxes* 176, I confesse the Party may not unpossibly be very Rich.

un'posted, *ppl. a.* (UN-^{1} 8.)
[**1775** ASH.] **1860** W. H. RUSSELL *Diary India* I. 4 A few younger men, unposted, who expected to be attached to Queen's regiments.

unpost'ponable, *a.* (UN-^{1} 7 b.)
1854 J. WILSON *Let.* in *Mem.* (1859) 304 Whatever was not altogether imperative and un-postponable. **1890** GUNTER *Miss Nobody* xvii, Important and unpostponable business.

un'pot, *v.* (UN-^{2} 5.)
1754 JUSTICE *Scots Gard. Director* 127 As for the small Plants.., I do not choose to unpot them until Michaelmas.

un'potable, *a.* [UN-^{1} 7 b, 5 b.] Undrinkable.
1848 S. WELLS WILLIAMS *Mid. Kingd.* I. 14 The water.. is brackish and unpotable. **1902** *Act 2 Edw. VII*, c. 7 §8 The applicant..will..render the spirits unpotable..during use.

un'poulticed, *ppl. a.* (UN-^{1} 8.)
[**1775** ASH.] **1791** [see UNPILLED *ppl. a.*^{2}].

un'powdered, *ppl. a.* [UN-^{1} 8.]
1. Not sprinkled with salt.
c **1440** *Promp. Parv.* 366/2 On-powderyd, on-saltyd, *insalitus*. ? **1619** HIERON *Wks.* II. 484 As an vnpowdered masse of flesh..is enough to poyson with the stench. *Ibid.* 492 Those particulars..will, like so many vnpowdered morsels mixed in with others, make the whole lump to become vnsauory.
2. Not whitened with hair-powder.
1751 JOHNSON *Rambler* No. 109 ¶6 My hair unpowdered, and my hat uncocked. **1847** LYTTON *Lucretia* I. i, The dark hair which he wore unpowdered. **1898** R. S. HICHENS *Londoners* vii, Various footmen, powdered and unpowdered.
3. Not wearing face-powder; without face-powder.
1917 J. F. MACDONALD *Two Towns—One City* III. ii. 210 Flushed, and dishevelled, and unpowdered Fifine becomes. **1921** W. DE LA MARE *Mem. Midget* xli. 276 Her clear, unpowdered skin had the faint sheen of a rose. **1956** 'C. BLACKSTOCK' *Dewey Death* iii. 59 The fair hair was falling over her face; her skin was blotched and unpowdered. **1974** J. MANN *Sticking Place* v. 88 Look at her now, shabby, unpowdered.

un'power, *sb. Obs.* exc. *dial.* [UN-^{1} 12. Cf. NON-POWER.] Want of power; inability; weakness; helplessness.
c **1380** WYCLIF *Serm.* Sel. Wks. I. 371 Þis drede haþ no peyne, but unpower for to synne. **1402** *Jack Upland* in *Pol. Poems* (Rolls) II. 36 Then puttest thou on Christ.. unkunning, unpower, and evill will. *c* **1440** *Gesta Rom.* lii. 233 Þerfor do not aftir the worlde, ne abide not age, vnpower, or blyndnesse. *a* **1470** H. PARKER *Dives & Pauper* (W. de W. 1496) II. xiv. G iiij b, Yf it be soo that þᵗ othe be made..the man that he made it to can not..vnbynde hym from that othe..but nede or unpower excuse hym. **1847-** in south-western dial. glossaries.

† **un'power**, *v. Obs.* [UN-^{2} 4.] *trans.* To deprive of power.
1643 W. GREENHILL *Axe at Root* 8 Now the Lord did.. un-church them, un-power them, un-saint them. **1657** REEVE *God's Plea* 287 Why are they ministers, if they un-power, cassate their own function?

un'powerful, *a. rare.* (UN-^{1} 7.)
1611 FLORIO, *Impoderoso*, vnmightie, vnpowerfull. **1656** COWLEY *Davideis* I. 48 He..envy'd him a Kings unpowerful Hate. **1777** J. RICHARDSON *Dissert. East. Nations* 21 A distinct body of harmless and unpowerful people.
Hence **un'powerfulness**.
1625 DARCIE *Ann.* a 4 It lies meerely in their owne vn-powerfulnesse, that they do not ouerthrow his..Empire.

†**un'practic**, *a. Obs.* [UN-¹ 7.] Not practical.
1659 W. CHAMBERLAYNE *Pharonnida* IV. ii. 551 A speedy, though unpractic sympathy.

un'practicable, *a.* [UN-¹ 7 b, 5 b.] Impracticable. (Common 1650–1700.)
1647 CLARENDON *Hist. Reb.* III. § 176 Such Objections..as rendered it [*sc.* the proposition] Ridiculous and Unpracticable. **1673** *Remarques Humours Town* 52 They have made Love..unpracticable to the World. **1692** BENTLEY *Boyle Lect.* 16 Such unpracticable conditions as these. **1702** *Eng. Theophrast.* 135 Many things that seem'd unpracticable to their Thoughts.
Hence **un'practicableness**.
1667 OWEN *Indulg. & Tolerat. Consid.* 30 The unpracticableness of such an Indulgence. **1680** H. DODWELL *Two Lett.* (1691) 180 That unpracticableness wherewith they are changed. **1894** *N.W. Congregationalist* (U.S.) 5 Jan., There is a certain amount of unpracticableness about this.

un'practical, *a.* (UN-¹ 7, 5 b.)
1637 BP. REYNOLDS *Serm.* (1638) 26 To foment their jealousies and censures..by novell, speeious, and unpracticall Curiosities. **1668** HALE *Pref. to Rolle's Abridgm.* 5 Some of their Laws grew..obsolete, some unpracticall, some obscure. **1849** C. BRONTE *Shirley* vii, Caroline was feeling..what an unpractical life she led. **1890** R. 'BOLDREWOOD' *Col. Reformer* (1891) 152 An unpractical, unsuccessful enthusiast.
Hence **unpracti'cality**; **un'practically** *adv.*; **un'practicalness**.
1875 HOWELLS *Foregone Concl.* (1882) 313 That poor fellow with his whole stock of helplessness, dreamery and *unpracticality. **1880** *Athenæum* 18 Dec. 812/3 The delightful unpracticality of good Mrs. Brooke. **1881** *Trans. Obstet. Soc. Lond.* XXII. 5 Where we cannot foresee any immediate effect on practice, that is, so far as we can see, *unpractically. **1843** J. S. MILL *Let.* in *Wks.* (1963) XIII. 579 The chief fault seems to me that of entire *unpracticalness. **1880** VERNON LEE *Stud. Italy* II. iii. 49 To this charming unpracticalness..must be added the fact that [etc.].

†**un'practisable**, *a.* (UN-¹ 7 b, 5 b; cf. PRACTISABLE *a.*)
1594 in Halliwell *Lett. Sci. Subjects* (1841) 36 Converted to sundrie other uses..which have hetherto byn supposed to be unpractyzable. **1644** G. PLATTES in *Hartlib's Legacy* (1655) 295 It is neither unpossible, strange, nor unpracticeable.

un'practise, *v.* (UN-² 3.)
1727 *Art of Speaking in Publick* v. (ed. 2) 67 If you find it comes only from an ill Habit you have got,..you ought to take up a resolution of unpractising it.

un'practised, *ppl. a.* [UN-¹ 8.]
1. Not familiarized or skilled by practice; inexperienced, inexpert.
1551 ROBINSON tr. *More's Utopia* I. (1895) 49 Your newe made and vnpractysed soldiours. **1562** A. BROOKE *Romeus & Jul.* 1416 A wise mans wit vnpractised doth stand him in no steede. **1606** SHAKS. *Tr. & Cr.* I. i. 12 But I am..skillesse as vnpractis'd Infancie. **1672** MARVELL *Reh. Transp.* I. 207 To harden their unpractis'd modesty. **1748** *Anson's Voy.* III. viii. 380 Of so little consequence are the most destructive arms in untutored and unpractised hands. **1805** WORDSW. *Prelude* v. 589 In his youth..in that raw unpractised time. **1849** MACAULAY *Hist. Eng.* vi. II. 143 The most unpractised eye at once perceived that they were taller..than their successors. **1890** *Retrospect Med.* CII. 109 The unpractised operator is far less likely to do harm with the forceps than with version.
b. Const. *in*.
1665 BOYLE *Occas. Refl.* III. xx. 131 These are..altogether unpractis'd in that Civility. **1687** DRYDEN *Hind & P.* III. 614 The latter brood, who just began to fly, Sick-feathered and unpractis'd in the sky. **1759** HUME *Hist. England* I. 96 Albany..was totally..unpractised in their language. **1844** UPTON *Physioglyphics* Pref. p. ii, A person unpractised in authorship. **1900** *Longm. Mag.* Mar. 466 Supposing that I speak to anyone who is unpractised in the art.
2. Not practised; unemployed, untried.
1540 *Commemoration of Inestimable Graces of God* B ij, The old prouerbe..is not lefte vnpractised by the sayde Antichrist. *c* **1584** *An Abstract, Certaine Acts Parl.* (title-p.), Certaine Canons, Constitutions, and Synodals prouinciall.. for the most part heretofore vnknowen and vnpractized. **1611** BEAUM. & FL. *Maid's Trag.* II. i, I..must try Some yet unpractis'd way to grieve and die. **1686** *Col. Rec. Pennsylv.* I. 184 An unsafe and hetherto unpractised way in procedure. **1753** HANWAY *Trav.* XIV. x. (1762) II. 382 No barbarities were left unpractised. **1848** AKERMAN *Introd. Study Anc. & Mod. Coins* v. 90 This description of artifice seems to have been..unpractised among the Romans.
†**b.** Untraversed, unfamiliar. *Obs.*
1621 G. SANDYS *Ovid's Met.* I. (1626) 4 Ships..Then plow'd th' vnpractiz'd bosom of the Flood. **1778** BP. LOWTH *Transl. Isaiah* Notes 187 A journey..through desert and unpracticed countries.
Hence **un'practisedness**.
1628 EARLE *Microcosm.* (Arb.) 61 He ascribes all honestie to an vnpractis'dnesse in the World. **1672** FLAMSTEED in Rigaud *Corr. Sci. Men* (1841) II. 130 My unpractisedness in such observations at the first essays.

unprag'matical, *a.* (UN-¹ 7.)
1673 CAVE *Prim. Chr.* II. i. 6 Whoever would govern his life aright must be modest and unpragmatical.

un'praisable, *a.* [UN-¹ 7 b.]
1. That cannot be praised.
1483 *Cath. Angl.* 290/1 Vn Praysabylle, *illaudabilis.* **1892** A. LANG *Lett. Dead Authors* 178 Thou splendid warrior with the world at odds, Unpraised, unpraisable, beyond thy merit.
†**2.** Incapable of being appraised or valued; above valuation. *Obs.*
1526 *Pilgr. Perf.* (W. de W. 1531) 173 b, Thou shalt haue inestimable or vnpraysable rychesse. **1598** STOW *Surv.* 325 Vessels of gold, and siluer vnpraiseable, and many pretious stones.

un'praise, *v.* [UN-² 3.] *trans.* To dispraise.
c **1375** *Cursor M.* 27585 (Fairf.), We agh ilkman our-self vpraise & in our hert vs vnpraise [*Cott.* dispraise]. *a* **1500** *Praise of Women* in *Rel. Ant.* I. 275 To onpreyse womene, yt were a shame. **1728** YOUNG *Love Fame* VII. 45 Cannot thrice ten hundred years unpraise The boist'rous boy, and blast his guilty bays? **1729** SAVAGE *Wanderer* I. 345 Shou'd some nobler Bard their Worth unpraise, Deserting Morals, that adorn his Lays.

un'praised, *ppl. a.* (UN-¹ 8.)
1390 GOWER *Conf.* I. 229 If reson be wel peised, Ther mai no vertu ben unpreised. **1422** YONG tr. *Secreta Secret.* 130 Of the dyuersyte..of maneris wych ben praside and vn-prayside. **1570** LEVINS *Manip.* 50 Vnpraysed, *illaudatus.* **1590** SPENSER *F.Q.* II. x. 5 The land..was saluage wildernesse, Vnpeopled, vnmanurd, vnprou'd, vnpraysd. **1634** MILTON *Comus* 723 Th' all-giver would be unthank't, would be unprais'd. **1700** DRYDEN *Cymon & Iph.* 469 Unprais'd by me, tho' Heav'n sometime may bless An impious Act with undeserv'd Success. **1784** COWPER *Task* v. 539 There is yet a liberty,..by senators unprais'd. **1827** POLLOK *Course T.* VII. 422 Innumerous armies rose, unbannered all, Unpanoplied, unpraised. **1856** R. A. VAUGHAN *Mystics* IX. iii. II. 151 How many women..are far surpassing St. Theresa in their self-sacrifice and patience, unseen and unpraised of men. **1892** [see UNPRAISABLE 1].

un'praiseful, *a.* (UN-¹ 7.)
1868 LYNCH *Rivulet* CLII. ii, Not..with unpraiseful prayer We live below.

un'praiseworthy, *a.* (UN-¹ 7.)
1589 FLEMING *Virg. Georg.* IV. 59 Th' other king ill-fauoured is,..And vnpraiseworthy drags his large brode belly all along. **1876** LOWELL *Among my Bks.* Ser. II. 45 We do not mean to say that this minute exegesis is useless or unpraiseworthy.

un'pray, *v.* (UN-² 3.)
1611 COTGR., *Desprier*, to vnpray,..recall prayers. **1662** GURNALL *Chr. in Arm.* III. xiii. 102, I pray'd with so little faith, that I..unprayed my own prayer. **1676** HALE *Contempl.* I. 128 The freeness and purity of his obedience.. made him, as it were, un-pray what he had before prayed. **1842** FABER *Styrian Lake*, etc. 289 And he unprayed his curse, his passion sunk. **1862** CHR. G. ROSSETTI *Poems* (1904) 235/1 My sins unpray My prayer.

un'prayable, *a.* [UN-¹ 7 b.]
†**1.** Inexorable.
1382 WYCLIF *Lam.* iii. 42 Wee wickeli diden, and to wrathe terreden; therfore thou art vnpreiable [L. *inexorabilis*].
2. That cannot be uttered as a prayer. *rare.*
1941 T. S. ELIOT *Dry Salvages* ii. 9 The prayer of the bone on the beach, the unprayable Prayer at the calamitous annunciation.

un'prayed, *ppl. a.* [UN-¹ 8.]
1. Of persons: **a.** Not entreated or besought; unasked; uninvited. Also with *to*.
c **1374** CHAUCER *Troylus* IV. 513 Syn þat thow slest so fele ..Ayeins hir wil vnpreyed day and nyghte, Do me..this seruyse. *c* **1400** LOVE *Bonavent. Mirr.* (1908) 116 In that oure lord mekely vnpreide wente bodily to hele the sike seruaunt. *c* **1440** *Gesta Rom.* lxv. 290 (Add. MS.), The lyon, the Ape, and the Serpent, yelded hym mede, because he drew hem out of the pitte vnpraied. **1536** in *10th Rep. Hist. MSS. Comm.* App. V. 407 Whatsoever man..goeth in to anny such housse..unpraied or bidden. **1600** FAIRFAX *Tasso* XVI. xlv, To my sutors old what I denaid, That gaue I thee ..vnpraid. **1681** H. MORE in *Glanvill's Sadducismus* I. Postscr. 51 The holy Angels..which..reinforce the prayers of good and holy men..unprayed to themselves. **1849** M. ARNOLD *Fragm. of 'Antigone'* 5 Who, weighing that life well Fortune presents unpray'd, Declines her ministry.
†**b.** Not moved by prayer. *Obs.*⁻¹
1567 DRANT *Horace, Ep.* A iiij, If thou wouldest set Achilles oute,..Let him be swift, chafing, vnprayed, inflamde to vengaunce sone.
2. Not prayed *for*; without being prayed *for*.
1533 MORE *Apol.* xxviii. Wks. 894/1 Yf they leue nothing vnpraied for that mai perteine to the pacificacion of this diuision. **1703** DE FOE *More Reform.* 50 What Capital offence Could bar thee from the Priests Benevolence, That they..should..let thee live unbless'd, unprayed for Die.

un'preach, *v.* (UN-² 3.)
1692 BP. STRATFORD *Charge*, 5 *May* 22 Can they think, that he does in good earnest believe what he preaches, when he unpreaches the same again in his life? **1701** DE FOE *Trueborn Eng.* II. 256 The Clergy..Unpreach'd their Non-resisting Cant, and Pray'd To Heaven for Help. **1855** KINGSLEY *Westw. Ho!* xviii, To show the white feather in the hour of need, is to unpreach in one minute all that he had been preaching his life long.

un'preached, *ppl. a.* (UN-¹ 8.)
[**1775** ASH.] **1843** CARLYLE *Past & Pr.* III. xii, This unpreached, inarticulate,..forever-enduring Gospel.

un'preaching, *ppl. a.* [UN-¹ 10.]
1. Omitting or neglecting to preach; characterized by absence of preaching.
1549 LATIMER *6th Serm. bef. Edw. VI* (Arb.) 167 The deuill..hath set vppe a state of vnpreachynge prelacye in this Realme... He hath made vnpreachynge prelates. **1585** ABP. SANDYS *Serm.* iii. 60 Woe therefore to the idle and Idol pastor, to the dumme dogge, to the vnpreaching minister! **1630** J. TAYLOR (Water P.) *Sculler* Wks. III. 20/1 Who dares say that like a drone or moath, Like an vnpreaching Priest he liues by Sloath? **1660** PRYNNE *Unbish. Tim.* (ed. 2) 95 Idle, proud, ambicious, unpreaching Prelates. **1732** NEAL *Hist. Purit.* I. 372 There are severe expressions against the unpreaching clergy. **1828** J. T. RUTT *Burton's Diary* III. 203 Praising that Bishop at the expense of unpreaching prelates. **1850** MARSDEN *Early Purit.* iv. 124 Her successor on the throne..discouraged preaching... We became an un-preaching church.
†**2.** *spec.* Not undertaking the duty of preaching; merely reading the services of the Church. *Obs.*
1574 WHITGIFT *Def. Answ.* 482 Bycause a chylde may reade the booke, dothe it therefore mainteyne an vnpreaching ministerie? **1588** J. UDALL *Demonstr. Discipline* (Arb.) 38 If vnpreaching ministers cannot be made without the manifest breach of the commaundement of God. **1597** HOOKER *Eccl. Pol.* v. xxxii. § 3 That..we..maintaine an vnpreaching ministerie, is neither aduisedly nor truly spoken. **1642** FULLER *Holy & Prof. St.* v. xi. 402 Sacraments received from ignorant and unpreaching Ministers. **1710** H. BEDFORD *Vind. Ch. Eng.* 161 There were several unpreaching Ministers, whose..Business it was to read the publick Prayers.

unpre'carious, *a.* (UN-¹ 7.)
1712 BLACKMORE *Creation* II. 532 The Stars..grace the high expansion, bright By their own beams, and unprecarious light. **1745** YOUNG *Nt. Th.* VIII. 968 Bliss there is none, but unprecarious bliss. **1843** TIZARD *Brewing* 5 Even were brewing as simple and unprecarious as some are willing to imagine.

unpre'cautioned, *ppl. a.* (UN-¹ 8.)
1694 FRANCK *Northern Mem.* 128 Because unprecautioned how to distinguish the Elements,..she frequently encounters the boiling Water.

unpre'ceded, *ppl. a.* (UN-¹ 8.)
1846 WORCESTER (citing J. Johnson). **1884** *Law Times* 6 Sept. 320/2 Hostile acts unpreceded by declaration of war.

unprece'dental, *a.* [UN-¹ 7.] = next.
1768 CAPT. COOK in *Roy. Soc. Archives, Lett.* (1908) 18 This, I believe to be the reason for the unpresidental reception we met with here.

un'precedented, *ppl. a.* (UN-¹ 8.)
In frequent use from *c* 1760.
α. **1623** in Rushw. *Hist. Coll.* (1659) I. 101 To forbid the Judges against their Oathes..is a thing unpresidented in this Kingdom. **1650** WELDON *Crt. Jas. I*, 37 Which was a strange Judgement, and unpresidented. **1707** HEARNE *Collect.* II. 24 Yᵉ Delegates..declar'd the Drˢ sentence pronounc'd against him by himself, as Assessor, to be unjust and unpresidented.
β. **1716** ADDISON *Freeholder* No. 16 ¶ 5 Nor did the Legislature do any thing in this that was unprecedented. **1743** BULKELEY & CUMMINS *Voy. S. Seas* p. xiv, An audacious and unprecedented Action. **1837** HT. MARTINEAU *Soc. Amer.* II. 147 Some startling circumstance..which I was assured was unprecedented. **1874** GREEN *Short Hist.* viii. § 3. 487 A speech of unprecedented boldness.
Hence **un'precedentedly** *adv.*, **-ness**.
1678 MARVELL *Growth Popery* 46 There was but one Reason given herein for declining the granting Money, and that is the Unpresidentedness. **1826** T. TOOKE *Currency* 56 The late disastrous, and unprecedentedly numerous failures. **1884** *Manch. Exam.* 27 Nov. 5/4 The number of students attending was no doubt unprecedentedly great.

unprece'dential, *a.* [UN-¹ 7.] = prec.
a **1700** EVELYN *Diary* 19 July 1641, It was condemned as unprecedential, and not justifiable. **1846** WORCESTER (citing *Ec. Rev.*).

un'precedently, *adv.* (UN-¹ 11.)
1748 RICHARDSON *Clarissa* I. 242 The imaginary prerogative he was so unprecedently fond of asserting.

unpre'cipitable, *a.* (UN-¹ 7 b.)
1782 *Phil. Trans.* LXXIII. 76 Now this compound of calx of silver, and silver in its metallic form, may well be unprecipitable by iron.

unpre'cipitated, *ppl. a.* (UN-¹ 8.)
1663 BOYLE *Usef. Exp. Nat. Philos.* II. App. 314 The aqua fortis preserving none [of the silver] unprecipitated. **1698** COLLIER *Immor. Stage* i. 28 His Incidents are often surprising, and his Plots unprecipitated. **1850** L. HUNT *Autobiog.* viii. (1860) 150 The horse suddenly came to a stand,..and I was agreeably surprised to find myself.. unprecipitated over his head.

unpre'cise, *a.* (UN-¹ 7, 5 b.)
[**1775** ASH.] **1782** WARTON *Rowley Enq.* 47 Chatterton gave a vague unprecise explanation. **1820** *Monthly Rev.* XCI. 219 The antiquated and unprecise division of emotions into sublime and beautiful. **1858** CARLYLE *Fredk. Gt.* VIII. iv. II. 322 Here is the unprecise but indubitable fact.

unpre'cisely, *adv.* (UN-¹ 11; cf. prec.)
1869 ROSSETTI *Mem. Shelley* p. xcix, Lord Eldon either spoke loosely or was reported unprecisely.

unpre'cludible, *a.* (UN-¹ 7.)
1825 COLERIDGE *Lett., Conv.*, etc. (1836) II. 187 Demands on such quantity of time, as bodily pain and disqualification, with unprecludible interruption, have enabled me to make use of.

un'predicable, *a.* (UN-¹ 7 b, 5 b.)
1865 MASSON *Rec. Brit. Philos.* 392 Under the name of Faith..Hamilton affirmed..much which he declared to be utterly unpredicable in the name of Reason.

unpre'dict, *v.* (UN-² 7.)
1671 MILTON *P.R.* III. 395 Means I must use thou say'st, prediction else Will unpredict and fail me of the Throne.

unpre'dictable, *a.* (UN-¹ 7 b.)
In frequent use from *c* 1880.

1857 M. PATTISON *Ess.* (1889) II. 405 The constant tendency of discovery [is] to reduce to order classes of facts, once thought irregular and unpredictable. **1874** J. SULLY *Sensation & Intuition* 113 The many chances of some unpredictable accident.

Hence ˌ**unpredicta'bility**.

1920 S. ALEXANDER *Space, Time, & Deity* II. 324 Unpredictability is not limited to human determinism. **1955** *Bull. Atomic Sci.* Mar. 87/1 Their freedom imparts an unpredictability to historic events. **1977** J. L. HARPER *Population Biol. Plants* 769 Organisms in nature live in environments that contain rhythms and unpredictabilities, patterns and noise.

un'prefaced, *ppl. a.* (UN-¹ 8.)

[**1775** ASH.] **1801** BLOOMFIELD *Rural T.* (1802) 51 [He] straight began.. Th' unprefac'd History of his latter years. **1859** HOOKER in Darwin *Life & Lett.* (1887) II. 242 The three volumes, unprefaced by this, would have choked any Naturalist.

unpre'ferred, *ppl. a.* [UN-¹ 8.]

†**1.** Not advanced or promoted.

1483 *Act 1 Rich. III*, c. 2 §1 Mony worshipfull men.. were compelled.. to lyff in greate penurie.., their dettes unpaied and their childeryn unpreferred. **1564** HAWARD *Eutropius* x. 123 He.. would not see them vnpreferred to honoures. **1572** *Wills & Inv. N.C.* (Surtees, 1835) 370, I will yᵗ Alice my wyf &.. my doughters being vnmarried & vnpreferred shall haue their full portions of my goods. **1607** DEKKER *Northward-Hoe* IV. Wks. 1873 III. 45 A poore vnpreferd scholler. **1655** FULLER *Ch. Hist.* IX. vi. §36 Of which order fourteen only could be found.. which were unmarried, unpreferred to cures. **1697** COLLIER *Ess. Mor. Subj.* I. 25 There is no such way to make a Scholar, as to keep him under while he is young, or unpreferred.

2. Not regarded with preference.

1884 *Imperial Dict.* s.v.

†**un'pregnable**, *a.* [UN-¹ 7 b, 5 b.] Impregnable.

α. **1386** *Rolls of Parlt.* III. 225/1 The Mairaltee,.. were it never so unprenable. **1481** CAXTON *Godfrey* cxxxii. 196 A dongeon.. upon an hylle.., whiche the turkes helde so strongly that it is unprenable. **1560** DAUS *Sleidane's Comm.* 211 The Castell.. which for the situation was vnprennable.

β. **1545** ELYOT, *Inexpugnabilis*, vnpreignable. **1561** DAUS tr. *Bullinger on Apoc.* 536 Therefore was there neuer any thing.. so mightie or vnpregnable, whiche the inuincible power of God can not bring to naught. **1572** TWYNE *Dionysius' Surv. World* E iv b, Semiramis.. enuironed it wᵗ an vnpregnable wal. **1632** SHERWOOD s.v.

un'pregnant, *a.* (UN-¹ 7.)

1602 SHAKS. *Ham.* II. ii. 594 Yet I.. peake Like Iohn a-dreames, vnpregnant of my cause, And can say nothing. **1603** —— *Meas. for M.* IV. iv. 23 This deede vnshapes me quite, makes me vnpregnant And dull to all proceedings. **1868** *Lond. Rev.* 8 Aug. 166/2 His work has never been unpregnant in illustration of his mind. **1878** *N. Amer. Rev.* CXXVI. 48 No such interest can arise when the misfortune is unpregnant.

unpre'judged, *ppl. a.* (UN-¹ 8.)

[**1775** ASH.] **1888** *Times* 31 Aug. 3/1 The question of sovereignty remained unprejudged.

†**unpre'judicate**, *a. Obs.* [UN-¹ 7, 5 b.] Unprejudiced. (Common in 17th c.)

1609 *Hoby's Let. to T.H.* Printer to Rdr. 115 For the better satisfaction of the vnpreiudicate Reader. **1650** H. MORE *Observ.* in *Enthus. Tri.*, etc. (1656) 78 His humility and purity of mind and unprejudicate reason. **1679** J. GOODMAN *Penit. Pard.* I. i. 11 Discourses.. plain and intelligible to such unprejudicate minds.

Hence **unpre'judicately** *adv.*, **-ness**.

a **1662** SANDERSON *Cases Consc.* iii. (1678) 74 Doubts and difficulties meet to be.. unprejudicately weighed against those other probabilities. **1668** H. MORE *Div. Dial.* II. 416 All the difficulty is to get to that state of Unprejudicateness. **1683** E. HOOKER *Pref. Pordage's Mystic Div., Postscr.* 111 Shold you please to lai the.. Ear of conscientious unpræjudicateness as close to the voice of these Mysteries as I did.

†**unpre'judicated**, *ppl. a.* [UN-¹ 8.] = prec.

1633 PRYNNE *Histrio-m.* 2nd Ep. Ded., Imploring.. your unprejudicated affections too. **1644** JESSOP *Angel of Eph.* 63 Let the impartiall and unprejudicated Reader peruse his words. **1660** STILLINGFL. *Iren.* II. vi. §9 That evidence.. which will command assent from an unprejudicated mind.

†**unpre'judicating**, *ppl. a.* (UN-¹ 10.)

1602 CAREW *Cornwall* 69 Who (as I conceive) looked heerinto with an indifferent and unprejudicating eye.

un'prejudice. (UN-¹ 12, 5 b.)

c **1800** COLERIDGE in *Sotheby's Sale Catalogue* 20 Nov. (1899) 16 Religious Musings, which you will read with a Poets eye, with the same unprejudices. **1871** LOWELL *Study Wind.* 92 Carlyle.. has now been so long before the world that we may feel toward him something of the unprejudice of posterity.

un'prejudiced, *ppl. a.* [UN-¹ 8.]

1. Not affected prejudicially.

1613 HEYWOOD *2 Edward IV*, M 4 b, On whom I vow, Leauing King Lewis vnpreiudizde in peace, To spend the whole measure of my kindled rage.

2. Free from prejudice: **a.** Of persons, the mind, eye, etc.

1637–50 ROW *Hist. Kirk* (Wodrow Soc.) 437 Let the unprejudiced reader judge whither [etc.]. **1678** CUDWORTH *Intell. Syst.* 728 To the full Conviction of all Minds Unprejudiced, and Unprepossessed with false Principles. **1710** STEELE *Spect.* No. 4 ¶5, I have the high Satisfaction of beholding all Nature with an unprejudiced Eye. **1794** R. J. SULIVAN *View Nat.* II. 72 It is clear to unprejudiced reason, that experiments in philosophy should unremittingly be made. **1842** BORROW *Bible in Spain* xlix, Surely it is not the part of unprejudiced people to disparage that of which they are ignorant. **1885** J. PAYN *Talk of Town* II. 259 William Henry's affidavit will acquit you of all blame in this matter in the eyes of unprejudiced persons.

absol. **1739** GORDON (*title*), An Appeal to the Unprejudiced Concerning the present Discontents Occasioned by the late Convention with Spain. **1755** T. EDWARDS *New Transl. Psalms* 19 These few instances may be sufficient to convince the unprejudiced, that [etc.].

b. Of opinions, inquiries, etc.

a **1670** SOUTH *Serm.* (1715) IV. 291 Some such Principle of Reason.. universally granted by the unprejudiced Apprehensions of Mankind. **1709** ADDISON *Tatler* No. 101 ¶2 To consider Things in so unprejudiced a manner, that [etc.]. **1770** A. YOUNG *Six Months' Tour North* (1771) I. Pref. p. xiii, I was forced to make more than one honest farmer half drunk, before I could get sober, unprejudiced intelligence. **1809** *Med. Jrnl.* XXI. 307 An unprejudiced perusal of these cases. **1839** DE LA BECHE *Rep. Geol. Cornw.*, etc. iv. 101 Fair and unprejudiced discussion. **1856** OLMSTED *Slave States* 702 Reliable and unprejudiced information.

Hence **un'prejudicedly** *adv.*, **-ness**.

1674 BOYLE *Excell. Theol.* II. v. 230 By having the reasons it presents perspicuously proposed, and *unprejudicedly entertained. **1685** H. MORE *Paralip. Prophet.* li. 476 Whoever reads considerately and unprejudicedly the 23. Chapter,.. cannot but be fully assured. **1889** *Amer. Naturalist* Oct. 897 Let us consider this evidence as unprejudicedly.. as we can. **1672** H. MORE *Brief Reply* Pref. a ij, My impartialness and *unprejudicedness. **1704** CLARKE *Attrib.* (1706) 10 Hearing the Reason of the Case with Patience and Unprejudicedness.

unpreju'diciable, *a.* (UN-¹ 7 b.)

1673 O. WALKER *Educ.* 37 In denying all, or most of his desires, though the things be reasonable, or unprejudiciable.

unpreju'dicial, *a.* (UN-¹ 7.)

1641 *Vind. Smectymnuus* ix. 104 Not only un-prejudicial to the honour of Episcopacy, but behoveful to the Church. **1657** J. SERGEANT *Schism Dispach't* 156 A bare word, capable of a different (and so unprejudicial) signification.

unpreju'dicialness. (UN-¹ 12.)

1642 J. GOODWIN *Anti-Cavalierism* 10 The unprejudicialnesse or inoffensivenesse of it to Sauls kingly Throane and dignity.

un'prelate, *v.* (UN-² 6 b.)

a **1670** HACKET *Abp. Williams* II. (1693) 120 The Archbishop thought not himself absolute, till this man was unprelated.

unpre'latic, *a.* [UN-¹ 7.] = next.

1880 F. G. LEE *Ch. under Q. Eliz.* I. 215 In a fierce dispute.. the language uttered and written was both unprelatic and violent.

unpre'latical, *a.* (UN-¹ 7.)

1647 CLARENDON *Hist. Reb.* III. §198 The archbishop of York,.. by such Unprelatical, Ignominious Arguments, in plain terms advised him.. to pass that Act. *a* **1661** FULLER *Worthies, Leicester.* II. (1662) 129 Some highly commended the Zeal of the Bishop,.. whilest others condemned this in him, as an unprelatical act. **1857** TROLLOPE *Barchester T.* v, A new sofa had been introduced,.. most unprelatical and almost irreligious. **1858** BUSHNELL *Nat. & Supernat.* x. (1864) 329 Vindicator of.. a free unprelatical religion.

unpre'meditable, *a.* (UN-¹ 7 b.)

1768 STERNE *Sent. Journ., Fragment*, A capfull of wind.. comes against you.. with such unpremeditable puffs.

unpre'meditate, *ppl. a.* Now *arch.* [UN-¹ 8 b, 5 b.] = next.

1551 ROBINSON *More's Utopia* (1895) 2 As his talke cold not be fine and eloquent,.. but sodein and vnpremeditate. **1600** TATE in Gutch *Coll. Cur.* I. 7 Either unpremeditate, and in hot blood, or else upon.. grounded malice. **1651** *Life Father Sarpi* 174 His answers how unpremeditate soever. **1702** *Toleration* 10 There is something more excellent that men may hazard by unpremeditate Prayer. **1825** SOUTHEY *Tale Paraguay* III. xxxvi, The voice.. Is one which.. Utters all unpremeditate, at will, A modulated sequence.

unpre'meditated, *ppl. a.* (UN-¹ 8.)

1591 SHAKS. *1 Hen. VI*, I. ii. 88 Aske me what question thou canst possible, And I will answer vnpremeditated. **1619** A. NEWMAN *Pleas. Vis.* 2 His vnpremeditated words. **1699** BENTLEY *Phal.* 237 Both Comedies and Tragedies for some time were unpremeditated and extemporal. **1768–74** TUCKER *Lt. Nat.* (1834) II. 444 Those unpremeditated addresses to Heaven called ejaculations. **1814** SCOTT *Wav.* xxvi, The hint.. respecting Flora was not unpremeditated. **1878** STUBBS *Const. Hist.* xviii. III. 9 The scene in Westminster Hall.. was no unpremeditated pageant.

Hence **unpre'meditatedness**.

1802–12 BENTHAM *Ration. Judic. Evid.* (1827) I. 295 There is no such absolute incompatibility.. between recollectedness and unpremeditatedness. **1883** H. DRUMMOND *Nat. Law in Spir. W.* 280 The suddenness and unpremeditatedness of Prayer.

unpre'meditatedly, *adv.* (UN-¹ 11.)

1776 G. SEMPLE *Building in Water* 4 The cost did not exceed.. 100 guineas, as I had unpremeditatedly mentioned to Mr. Prior. **1826** DISRAELI *V. Grey* II. i, He could unpremeditatedly clothe his conceptions in language characteristic of the style of any particular author. **1884** *Contemp. Rev.* Feb. 250 There is not one of his writings which does not do for us.. as it were by the way and unpremeditatedly, what [etc.].

†**unpre'meditately**, *adv. Obs.* [UN-¹ 12; cf. UNPREMEDITATE *ppl. a.*] = prec.

1671 F. PHILIPS *Reg. Necess.* Ep. Ded., Answers not seldom suddainly and unpremeditately given. **1685** BOYLE *Of High Veneration* 1 Divines.. who.. talk of Him and his Attributes as freely and as unpremeditately, as.. of a Geometrical Figure. *a* **1721** in W. Ayre *Life Pope* (1745) I. 140, I, who always speak unpremeditately.

unpremedi'tation. (UN-¹ 12, 5 b.)

1807 *Ann. Rev.* V. 237 It has the vivacity of unpremeditation. **1884** W. BESANT *Dorothy Forster* xxxvi, Asking each other.. what means this naked plea of unpremeditation.

†**unpre'occupated**, *ppl. a.* (UN-¹ 8.)

1666 J. SERGEANT *Let. Thanks* 26 To all unprejudic't and unpreoccupated Understandings.

unpre'occupied, *ppl. a.* (UN-¹ 8.)

Frequent in recent use (1896–).

[**1775** ASH.] **1827** COLERIDGE *Lit. Rem.* (1839) IV. 408 Every reader whose imagination supplies an unpreoccupied, unrefracting medium to the Apostolic assertion. **1886** B. HARTE *Snowbound* 193 Lee, the only unpreoccupied.. spirit in the party.

†**un'preparate**, *ppl. a. Obs.*⁻¹ [UN-¹ 8 b.] Unprepared.

1576 TURBERV. *Venerie* 224 Let the scamony be unpreparate, the which you shall mingle amongst all those iuyces.

unprepa'ration. *rare.* [UN-¹ 12, 5 b.] Unpreparedness.

1627 BP. HALL *Holy Observ.* §77 Our cowardlinesse, our vnpreparation, is his aduantage. **1646** —— *Balm Gil.* 330 Thy unpreparation shall make him dreadfull. **1883** *Standard* 9 Jan. 2 The state of unpreparation may be imagined.

unpre'pare, *v. rare.* [UN-² 3 or UN-¹ 14.]

1. *trans.* To undo the preparation of.

1598 FLORIO, *Sparecchiare*, to vngarnish, to vnprepare, to vndecke.

2. To make unprepared; to unfit.

1645 MILTON *Tetrach.* 36 Nothing more unhallows a man, more unprepares him to the service of God in any duty. **1788** WESLEY *Wks.* (1872) VII. 154 No business.. can hinder any man.. unless it be such as unprepares him for heaven. **1852** LEVER *M. Tierney* iii, The gloom of the place.. equally unprepared me for what was to come.

unpre'pared, *ppl. a.* [UN-¹ 8.]

1. Of persons: Not in a state of preparation; not ready (for defence, reply, etc.).

1549 CHEKE *Hurt Sedit.* (1569) G ij b, Although ye thinke your selues able to match with a fewe vnprepared Gentlemen, and put them from their houses. **1555** EDEN *Decades* (Arb.) 79 Where so euer they fownde any of owre men vnprepared, they slewe them. ? **1606** DANIEL *Funeral Poem Earl Devon.* Wks. (1623) 11 He brauely came to disappoint his foe, And many times surpris'd him vnprepared. **1667** MILTON *P.L.* VIII. 197 What is more,.. renders us in things that most concerne Unpractis'd, unprepar'd, and still to seek. **1695** TRYON *Dreams* i. 3 Such discourses seem very.. extravagant to their unprepared Apprehensions. **1760** GOLDSM. *Cit. W.* iv, We were overtaken by a heavy shower of rain. I was unprepared; but they.. had large coats. **1818** BYRON *Ch. Har.* IV. cxxvii, Lest the truth should shine Too brightly on the unprepared mind. **1849** MACAULAY *Hist. Eng.* v. I. 662 Cornish was arrested.. and was brought altogether unprepared to the bar of the Old Bailey. **1889** GRETTON *Memory's Harkb.* 165 His Lordship requested one of the clergymen.. to preach the sermon. Naturally they one and all declined, as unprepared.

absol. *a* **1643** S. GODOLPHIN *Quatrains* ii. 11 The unprepar'd this grace do find, Ye cool and do refresh the mind.

b. Const. *for*, or *to* with inf.

1549 CHEKE *Hurt Sedit.* (1569) F ij, Exeter.. being.. vnfurnished, vnprepared, for so long a siege. **1678** *Proph. & Predict. Jas. Usher* (Hindley, III) 11 Look that you be not found unprepared for it. **1722** HAMILTON *Wallace* VIII. (1816) 135 Wallace.. Surpris'd the English, unprepar'd for fight. **1794** S. WILLIAMS *Hist. Vermont* 174 That they might not be wholly unprepared to begin their course. **1819** SCOTT *Leg. Montrose* xvii, Being taken by surprise, they were totally unprepared for resistance. **1865** DICKENS *Mut. Fr.* I. xv, I am rather unprepared to see you.

c. *spec.* Not prepared for death.

1594 SHAKS. *Rich. III*, III. ii. 65 'Tis a vile thing to dye,.. When men are vnprepar'd. *c* **1600** CHALKHILL *Thealma & Cl.* 1215 Death at no time finds goodness unprepared. **1611** BEAUM. & FL. *Maid's Trag.* V. i, Stir not; if thou dost, I'le take thee unprepar'd, thy fears upon thee, That make thy sins look double. **1665** BOYLE *Occas. Refl.* II. xi, Upon a Death Bed,.. that very Thought might justly prove Dismal to an unprepar'd Man. **1796** SOUTHEY *Joan of Arc* x. (1853) 124 Hurried the confessor To shrive them, lest with unprepared souls They to their death might go. **1846** MRS. A. MARSH *Father Darcy* II. xii. 215 The slaughter of hundreds.. of human beings totally unprepared.

transf. **1897** B. CAMM *Benedict. Mart. in Eng.* i. 31 Carried off by sudden and unprepared death before the priest could be summoned.

†**2.** Const. *of*. Not provided with. *Obs.*⁻¹

1732 J. LOUTHIAN *Form of Process* (1752) 45 If the Prisoner, through Ignorance, come unprepared of Lawyers.

3. Not made ready; left, introduced, taken, etc., without special preparation.

1595 SHAKS. *John* II. i. 560 This vnlook'd for vnprepared pompe. *a* **1751** BOLINGBROKE *Study Hist.* ii. (1752) I. 41 The events we are witnesses of.. appear to us very often original, unprepared, single, and un-relative. **1796** MME. D'ARBLAY *Camilla* V. 397 Her sight, thus unprepared,.. might be too affecting for his weak frame. **1838** G. F. GRAHAM *Mus. Comp.* 23/2 Monteverde began to introduce unprepared sevenths and ninths. **1858** GREENER *Gunnery* 376 An ordinary unprepared gun, taken from a number promiscuously. **1874** PUSEY *Lent. Serm.* 8 We take refuge in the thought, that these were not sudden unprepared apostasies.

unpre'paredly, *adv.* (UN-[1] 11; cf. prec.)
1606 Bp. Hall *Medit. & Vows* I. lvi. 63 If hee die suddainly, yet hee dies not vnpreparedly. **1684** J. Goodman *Old Relig.* II. vi. 319 It seems far the more pardonable to come, though somewhat unpreparedly, than not to come because of unpreparedness. **1780** S. J. Pratt *Emma Corbett* (ed. 4) I. 194 She hath an affecting trick of..shedding tears, which burst upon one so unpreparedly, that [etc.]. **1825** J. Neal *Bro. Jonathan* II. 134 We are like the young waterfowl,..launched upon their natural..element, unpreparedly. **1857** Gen. P. Thompson *Audi Alt.* I. xxxiv. 131 There is such a thing as going into danger with a full knowledge of where the danger lies, and there is doing it blindly and unpreparedly.

unpre'paredness. (UN-[1] 12.)
1627 in Foster *Eng. Factories India* (1909) III. 169 Any advantage possible to bee taken (by theire unpreparednes). **1640** Habington *Edw. IV*, 77 There could bee no excuse but in the unpreparednesse of his mind. **1684** [see prec.]. *a* **1716** Blackall *Wks.* (1723) I. 250 Our Unpreparedness for the Duty will not excuse the Omission of it. **1748** Richardson *Clarissa* VII. 416 They had, for..his unpreparedness for it [*sc.* his fate], but too much grounds for apprehension with regard to his future happiness. **1824** Bentham *Bk. Fallacies* Wks. 1843 II. 411/1 Supposing the unpreparedness real, the reasonable and practical inference is—say nothing. **1873** Spencer *Stud. Sociol.* ix. (1877) 213 The French..suffered catastrophes from this and other kinds of unpreparedness.

unpre'ponderating, *ppl. a.* (UN-[1] 10.)
1818 Ranken *Hist. France* v. i. V. 204 Henry..proposed to throw his weight into the unpreponderating scale.

unprepo'ssessed, *ppl. a.* (UN-[1] 8.)
1648 Boyle *Seraph. Love* (1659) 15 That with compos'd and unprepossessed thoughts you may judge of the Object, I propose to you. **1659** South *Serm.* (1679) 72 The Unprepossessed on the one hand, and the well disposed on the other. **1705** Stanhope *Paraph.* I. 39 The Miracle upon Lazarus..which put the unprepossessed Multitudes upon celebrating the Glories of this Mighty Prophet. **1768** Sterne *Sent. Journ.* (1775) I. 67 Being pretty much unprepossessed, there must have been grounds for what struck me the moment I cast my eyes over the parterre. **1818** Foster *Ess.* (1844) I. 468 A mind of..strong intelligence.., entirely unprepossessed with any theory or system.
Hence **unprepo'ssessedly** *adv.*
1748 Richardson *Clarissa* III. 211 Had she been left unprepossessedly to herself, she would have shewn favour to me.

unprepo'ssessing, *ppl. a.* (UN-[1] 10.)
1816 Tuckey *Narr. Exped. R. Zaire* iii. (1818) 108 The faces..were by no means unprepossessing. **1869** Tozer *Highl. Turkey* I. 154 The marsh used to bear the unprepossessing name of Borboros, or 'Mud'. **1889** W. S. Gilbert *Gondoliers* II. 39 It's extraordinary what unprepossessing people one can love if one gives one's mind to it.

unpre'posterous, *a.* (UN-[1] 7.)
a **1618** Sylvester *Elegiac Epistle* 79 That Hand alone,.. Un-partiall ever, Un-preposterous; How ever Other it may seem to us.

unpre'sageful, *a.* (UN-[1] 7.)
1882 Swinburne *Tristram of Lyonesse*, etc. 144 Unwittingly, with unpresageful eyes.

un'presbyterated, *ppl. a.* (UN-[1] 8.)
1650 Jeanes *Want of Ch. Govt.* (title-p.), Whether or no the Sacrament of the Lord's Supper may..be lawfully administered in an un-Presbyterated Church, that is, a Church destitute of Ruling Elders. **1656** G. Collier *Ans. 15 Quest.* 10 While this church is unpresbyterated.

un'prescient, *a.* (UN-[1] 7.)
1866 Lytton *Lost Tales Miletus, Secret Way* 15 Having heard all with not unprescient fears. **1874** Lewes *Probl. Life & Mind* I. 229 A blind impulse unprescient of means and end.

unpre'scribed, *ppl. a.* (UN-[1] 8.)
1642 Bp. Hall *Let. from Tower* 4, I have grated upon no mans conscience by the pressure..of the late Oath, or any unprescribed Ceremonie. **1690** C. Nesse *O. & N. Test.* I. 72 He left nothing unprescribed, that..mans foolish brain might find no room to foist anything into his service. **1768** R. Wood *Ess. Genius Homer* (1775) 170 A certain proportion of voluntary attention in one sex, and of unprescribed reserve in the other.

unpre'sentable, *a.* (UN-[1] 7 b.)
1828 *Q. Rev.* XXXVIII. 204 Another worse evil, the name of which, in his days, was not unpresentable, 'in prose or rhyme'. **1857** J. G. Wood *Objects Sea Shore* 55 A pair of snowy white trowsers were covered with the sable fluid, and rendered entirely unpresentable. **1876** T. Hardy *Ethelberta* xlviii, She still felt so distressed and unpresentable that she resolved not to allow Lord Mountclere to see her.
Hence **unpresenta'bility, -ableness.**
1862 Rossetti in *Fraser's Mag.* July 73 For years past it has..candidly admitted its own unpresentableness. **1882** 'Sarah Tytler' *Bride's Pass* ii, His unpresentability when fresh from some of his functions. **1886** Ruskin *Præterita* I. x. 330 My own shyness and unpresentableness were farther stiffened..by a patriotic and Protestant conceit.

unpre'sented, *ppl. a.* (UN-[1] 8.)
(*a*) **1523** in W. H. Turner *Select. Rec. Oxford* (1880) 42 All the trespassors..have byn permitted to passe unpresented. **1548** in Strype *Eccl. Mem.* (1721) II. App. Q. 57 We also.. advertise you, that for no Favour ye go about to excuse or leave unpresented, those that..have offended. **1620** Quarles *Div. Poems, Feast for Worms* IX. ix, No crime unsifted, no sinne unpresented, Can lurke unseene. **1732** J. Louthian *Form of Process* (1752) 185 You shall present no Person for Hatred, Malice, or Ill-will; nor leave any thing unpresented for Fear, Favour or Affection.
(*b*) **1657** Baynes in *Burton's Diary* (1828) II. 278 There are many things yet unpresented in the Petition. *c* **1732** in A. Thomson *T. Boston of Ettrick* (1895) 251 [He] was.. scrupulous of anything new or unpresented, until he was thoroughly satisfied of its necessity. **1895** Petrie *Egypt. Tales* Ser. I. Introd. 1 It is strange that..the oldest literature ..should yet have remained unpresented to English readers.
(*c*) **1864** G. A. Sala in *Daily Tel.* 25 Feb., I went back to New York unavoidably unpresented [to the President]. **1897** W. C. Hazlitt *4 Generations* II. 221 The Queen and the Court,..their almost affecting solicitude for the health even of the Unpresented.

unpre'servable, *a.* (UN-[1] 7 b.)
1841 E. Forbes in Geikie *Mem.* x. (1861) 277, I am.. drawing all the unpreservable animals..that fall in my way.

unpre'served, *ppl. a.* (UN-[1] 8.)
1648 Hexham II, *Onbehoeat*, Vnpreserved, or Vnsaved. [**1775** Ash.] **1859** Atkinson *Walks & Talks* 380 As good a day's fly-fishing as in almost any unpreserved stream in the kingdom.

un'pressed, *ppl. a.* [UN-[1] 8.]
1. a. Not pressed or squeezed; not subjected to pressure.
1552 *Acc. Ld. High Treas. Scot.* X. 123 Thre elnis, thre quarteris, unprest blak. **1606** Shaks. *Ant. & Cl.* III. xiii. 106 Haue I my pillow left vnprest in Rome,..to be abus'd By one that lookes on Feeders? **1615** G. Sandys *Trav.* 65 A beastly kind of vnpressed cheese. **1718** Prior *Solomon* I. 346 Unpress'd their Vintage, and untill'd their Ground. **1794** Mrs. Radcliffe *Myst. Udolpho* i, The forest-walk, where flowers unprest, Bow not their tall heads. **1812** Cary *Dante, Purg.* VI. 90 What boots it, that thy reins Justinian's hand Refitted, if thy saddle be unpressed? **1879** E. Arnold *Lt. Asia* IV. 90 On our bed there lay An unpressed pillow. **1932** W. Faulkner *Light in Aug.* xix. 419 A tall, loosejointed man with a constant cob pipe,..wearing always loose and unpressed dark gray clothes. **1968** J. Ironside *Fashion Alphabet* 96 Soft pleats with edges rounded and left unpressed. **1974** J. Flint *Cecil Rhodes* (1976) ii. 19 Rhodes was notable for the shabbiness of his unpressed suits. **1977** *Lancashire Life* Nov. 115/3 (*caption*) A dress with an intricately seamed bodice falling into unpressed pleats.
b. Not obtained by pressing.
1630 Quarles *Div. Poems* 309 Our tender Vine Should cheare thy palate with her unprest wine. **1708** J. Philips *Cyder* I. 414 Snails, that creep O'er the ripe Fruitage,..and unprest Cyder drink. **1802** Lamb *J. Woodvil* 111, Because your poet-born hath an internal wine,..unpressed in mortal wine-presses.
2. Not pressed into service; unconstrained.
1603 J. Davies *Microcosmos* Wks. (Grosart) I. 58/2 Our Kings might warre with Tenants of their owne, Who would vnprest haue yet bin prest for shame To follow their Liege-land-lords. **1871** H. King *Ovid's Met.* XIII. 43 The first to arms who sprang Unpressed, by no informer dragged to war.

†**un'prest**, *a. Obs.* [UN-[1] 7.] Not ready, willing, or well-disposed.
13.. *St. Erkenwolde* 285 Nas I a paynym vnpreste þat neuer thi plite knewe? **1568** T. Howell *Newe Sonets* (1879) 131 When Pen is vnprest, And witte wanteth conning thervnto adrest.

unpre'sumed, *ppl. a.* (UN-[1] 8.)
1741 Richardson *Pamela* I. p. xx, It adorn'd her with such un-presum'd Increase of Loveliness.

unpre'suming, *ppl. a.* (UN-[1] 10.)
1770 Akenside *Pleas. Imag.* IV. 16 An unpresuming guest. **1779** Moore *View of Soc. France*, etc. I. 28 Unpresuming in argument, and..as well bred as those who have no other pretension. **1793** V. Knox *Lett. to Yng. Nobleman* Wks. 1824 V. 91 To the entire exclusion of modest unpresuming men. **1830** W. L. Bowles *Ken* I. p. xviii, The descendant of the great though unpresuming Locke. **1866** Liddon *Bampton Lect.* i. (1875) 7 The most unpresuming of the titles of the Messiah.
Hence **unpre'sumingness.**
a **1859** De Quincey in H. A. Page *Life* (1877) II. xix. 199 Two sound qualities are at the root of these unpleasant phenomena—modesty or unpresumingness in the first place.

unpre'sumptuous, *a.* (UN-[1] 7.)
1704 Arwaker *Embassy Heaven* xi, Henceforth, I'll urge my unpresumptuous Prayer. **1784** Cowper *Task* v. 746 A propriety that none can feel, But who..Can lift to heaven an unpresumptuous eye. ?**1813** Lamb *Christ's Hospital* Wks. 1908 I. 182 The common mass of that unpresumptuous assemblage of boys. **1822** Wordsw. *Eccles. Sonn., Concl.* 3 The Word..with unpresumptuous faith explored.

unpre'sumptuously, *adv.* (UN-[1] 11.)
1846 Worcester (citing Thacher). **1850** W. Anderson *Regener.* 262 Such a state of mind..is sometimes..attained to unpresumptuously and legitimately.

unpre'tended, *ppl. a.* (UN-[1] 8.)
1611 Florio, *Impretenso*, vnpretended. **1649** Jer. Taylor *Gt. Exemp.* Disc. xx. §21 It is to be supposed he hath no great account to make for unpretended injuries.

unpre'tending, *ppl. a.* (UN-[1] 10.)
1697 Collier *Ess. Mor. Subj.* I. 101 Ought they not to be somewhat Frugal, and Unpretending in their Appearance? **1730** Pope *Let.* in Johnson *L.P.*, *Fenton*, Feeling himself honest, true, & unpretending to more than was his own. **1795–6** Wordsw. *Borderers* II. 933 The unpretending ground we mortals tread. **1827** Scott *Chron. Canongate* Introd., Mere dignity of mind and rectitude of principle, assisted by unpretending good sense and temper. **1859** J. Lang *Wand. India* 7 She..has brought up a large family in the most respectable and unpretending style. **1885** 'Mrs. Alexander' *At Bay* i, Charmed with the unpretending refinement of her surroundings. **1891** Farrar *Darkn. & Dawn* xliv, His house..was so unpretending as to excite the wonder of those who saw it.

unpre'tendingly, *adv.* [UN-[1] 11; cf. prec.]
1. Without pretence; genuinely.
1828 Moore in *Mem.* V. 264 It is impossible for a royal personage to be more naturally and unpretendingly unaffected.
2. Without pretension; unassumingly.
1855 Cdl. Wiseman *Fabiola* 359 Miriam would follow up, humbly and unpretendingly,..the instructions given by the holy Dionysius. **1859** W. Collins *Q. of Hearts* I. iv. 99 These narratives were written plainly and unpretendingly.

unpre'tendingness. [UN-[1] 12.] Absence of pretension; unassumingness.
1727 Boyer *Dict. Royal* II, Unpretendingness, *modestie*. **1768** *Woman of Honor* III. 254 There was in her..so sweet an unpretendingness..as astonished and captivated me. **1832** S. Austin tr. *Tour Germ. Prince* III. xi. 315 She is goodness, cordiality, and unpretendingness itself. **1863** Cowden Clarke *Shaks. Char.* xvii. 427 One of the most agreeable [scenes] in the whole play, by reason of its familiar domestic unpretendingness.

unpre'tentious, *a.* (UN-[1] 7.)
1859 E. FitzGerald in Shorter *Borrow & His Circle* (1913) 359 They are all perfectly quiet, sensible, and unpretentious girls. **1874** Micklethwaite *Mod. Par. Churches* 175 Unpretentious village towers. **1887** *Spectator* 26 Mar. 422/2 The story is quite simple and unpretentious.
Hence **unpre'tentiously** *adv.*, **-ness.**
1863 Geo. Eliot *Romola* ix, He wore that fortune..easily and unpretentiously. **1867** *Sat. Rev.* 17 Aug. 228/1 Its entire unpretentiousness of style..and unimaginative narrative.

un'prettiness. (UN-[1] 12; cf. next.)
1675 S. Sewall *Diary* 29 Apr., My Father..goes to live there, notwithstanding the littleness and unpretines of the house. **1753** Richardson *Grandison* (1781) III. vii. 49 She says, it is not pretty in a young Lady to sigh: But where is the un-prettiness of it?

un'pretty, *a.* (UN-[1] 7.)
1782 Mme. D'Arblay *Let.* 15 Oct., His English is blundering, but not unpretty. **1828** Miss Mitford *Village* Ser. III. 40 Too refined for the youths of her own station, and too unpretty to attract those above her. **1856** Susan Warner *Hills of Shatemuc* xxviii. 308 [She] shewed the white ivory between her not unpretty parted [lips].
Hence **un'prettily** *adv.*
1929 W. Faulkner *Sartoris* II. vi. 157 She mouthed her food unprettily. **1982** R. Barnard *Death & Princess* xiv. 141 The Princess Helena pouted unprettily.

unpre'vailing, *ppl. a.* [UN-[1] 10.]
1. Ineffective, unsuccessful.
1602 Shaks. *Ham.* I. ii. 107 *King.* We pray you throw to earth This vnpreuayling woe, and thinke of vs As of a Father. **1693** Locke *Educ.* §78 If she had left off sooner.. she had spoil'd the Child for ever, and, by her unprevailing Blows, only confirm'd her Refractoriness. **1716–20** *Lett. fr. Mist's Jrnl.* (1722) I. 292 Beauty draws but by a Hair, and that's but weak and unprevailing. *a* **1806** Horsley *Serm.* xxvii. (1816) II. 344 The bare unprevailing wish that we were what we necessarily understand we ought to be. **1813** Shelley *Q. Mab* VII. 248 The unprevailing malice of my Foe.
b. Quasi-*adv.* Ineffectively, vainly.
1632 Lithgow *Trav.* VII. 326 We were..assayled by the Cursares..; yet vnpreuailing, for we were well prouided with good Munition. **1817** Shelley *Rev. Islam* I. xiv, Wile baffled wile, and strength encountered strength, Thus long, but unprevailing.
2. Not prevalent or usual.
1859 Mill *Liberty* 97 It is only desired to restrain the employment of them against the prevailing opinion: against the unprevailing they may..be used without general disapproval.

un'prevalent, *a.* (UN-[1] 7.)
1690 Boyle *Christian Virtuoso* Pref. A 1, The formerly unprevalent Desires of those that would have it appear in Public. **1880** Ramsay in *Daily News* 26 Aug. 5/7 In 1855 the old idea was still not unprevalent.

†**unpre'varicate**, *a. Obs. rare.* [UN-[1] 7.] Not perverted.
1652 Charleton *Darkn. Atheism Dispelled* 27 To that unprevaricate judgment, that shall maturely perpend the contents.

unpre'varicating, *ppl. a.* (UN-[1] 10.)
1792 V. Knox *Serm.* viii. 186 The un-prevaricating dictates of a clear conscience.

unpre'ventable, *a.* (UN-[1] 7, 5 b.)
1616 *Rich Cabinet* 31 A cuckold is an vnpreuentable destiny. *a* **1670** Hacket *Abp. Williams* I. (1693) 21 Nineteen Parts of a great Incorporation should be Condemn'd, for the Frowardness, and that unpreventable by all the Power we had of the twentieth Part. **1787** Bentham *Def. Usury* iii. 29 There are so many unpreventable ways of letting it run out at the bung-hole. **1816** —— *Offic. Apt. Maximized, Extr. Const. Code* (1830) 55 Of this repugnance..the existence is unpreventable. **1895** *Voice* (N.Y.) 5 Sept. 1/2 One of those terrible, unforeseen, and apparently unpreventable accidents.
Hence **unpre'ventableness.**
1884 *Mind* July 342 The element of unpreventableness or inescapableness.

unpre'ventably, *adv.* (UN-[1] 11.)
a **1639** W. Whateley *Prototypes* I. xxi. (1640) 260 Though death should present itselfe to you naked,..and that in shew unpreventably. **1816** Bentham *Chrestom.* Wks. 1843 VIII. 82 Constantly and unpreventably it actually is so.

unpre'vented, *ppl. a.* (UN-[1] 8.)
1585 Greene *Planetomachia* H 4, Hee that seeketh to haue his purpose vnpreuented. **1602** Campion *Art Eng. Poesie* iv. 10 The more secure, the more the stroke we feele Of

vnpreuented harms. **1667** MILTON *P.L.* III. 231 Shall grace not find means, that.. Comes unprevented, unimplor'd, unsought? **1735** THOMSON *Liberty* III. 499 The meanly-patient death, That waits a tyrant's unprevented stroke.

unpre'ventible, *a.* (UN-^{1} 7.)
1676 *Doctrine of Devils* 120 This seems unpreventible where this Doctrine is entertained. **1885** DUCANE *Punishm. Crime* 124 The evils of the hulk system were.. unpreventible.

unpre'ventive, *a.* (UN-^{1} 7.)
1667 WATERHOUSE *Fire Lond.* 96 So dangerous a thing is that, which the consequence calls unpreventive wisdom.

un'priceable, *a.* [UN-^{1} 7.]
a. Inestimable.
a **1641** BP. MOUNTAGU *Acts & Mon.* (1642) 39 This unpriceable benefit conferred upon man.
b. That cannot be priced.
1951 P. LARKIN *XX Poems*, And to hear how the past is past and the future neuter Might knock my darling off her unpriceable pivot.

un'priced, *ppl. a.* [UN-^{1} 8.]
1. Beyond price; priceless.
1857 WHITTIER *Last Walk in Autumn* xvi, He, who to the lettered wealth Of ages adds the lore unpriced. **1858** NEALE *Bernard de M.* 27 Thine ageless walls are bonded With amethyst unpriced.
2. Not having the price affixed.
1888 *Athenæum* 15 Sept. 355/3 The books offered for sale are unpriced.

un'pricked, *ppl. a.* [UN-^{1} 8.]
1. Not marked with pricks or dots; †*spec.* (of a Hebrew text), unpointed.
1588 J. MELLIS *Briefe Instr.* F iij b, Diuers parcels more may remaine vnpricked in the Leager, which ought not to bee put in the Iournall. **1690** C. NESSE *O. & N. Test.* I. 426 The Septuagint, who in their unprick'd Bibles did read [etc.]. **1695** J. EDWARDS *Perfect. Script.* III. 493 These Interpreters in their unpricked Bibles mistook [the Hebrew text].
2. Not subjected to pricking; unpunctured.
1611 COTGR. s.v. *Plumer*, To pill, or vnhuske, a chestnut .. which .. few can doe easily, or with vnprickt fingers. **1882** J. PARKER *Apost. Life* I. 74 If your heart be left unpricked, .. the word has been in vain.
†3. Not turned sour. *Obs.*
c **1645** HOWELL *Lett.* (1650) I. 58, I have sent you a Runlet of it.. : and, if it com safe and unprick'd, I pray bestow som Bottles upon the Lady (you know).

un'prickled, *ppl. a.* (UN-^{1} 8.)
a **1711** KEN *Hymnotheo* Wks. 1721 III. 318 Sweet Rosebuds on unprickel'd Bushes blew. **1728** CHAMBERS *Cycl.* s.v. *Fish*, The Smooth, or un-prickled Hound-Fish.

un'prickly, *a.* (UN-^{1} 7.)
1660 *Catal. Plant. Cantab.* Index 23 Unprickly Sowthistle, *Sonchus lævis.* **1758** *Phil. Trans.* L. 513 Smooth or unprickly Sowthistle.

un'prided, *ppl. a.* (UN-^{2} 8, 6 b.)
1628 FELTHAM *Resolves* II. xxxiii. 104 Pittifull! that we should rather mischiefe our selves, then be content to be vnprided.

un'pried, *ppl. a.* (UN-^{1} 8 c.)
1757 *Hist. 2 Mod. Advent.* II. 191, I left no Corner unpryed into, to find out a Lady to my Taste.

un'priest, *v.* [UN-^{2} 6 b, 4. Cf. Du. *ontpriesteren.*]
1. *trans.* To deprive (a person) of the character or office of priest.
1550 BALE *Eng. Votaries* II. 63 b, If he were a secular prest, or one vnprested by them, he shuld clerely lose his benefyce. **1581** J. BELL *Haddon's Answ. Osor.* 285 One Stephen was made Pope, who.. doth first vnpriest, and after-wardes newpriest agayne all such as Const. before him had priested. **1641** R. BROOKE *Eng. Episc.* 74, I finde.. some others unpriested by Councells because ordained by Presbyters alone. **1691** GRASCOMBE *Reply Vind. Disc.* 11 To take away our Orders, and Unpriest and Unbishop us. **1713** CALAMY *Life Baxter* (ed. 2) xvii. 466 No Secular Power could Unbishop and Unpriest, or disable them. A Clergy-man's Authority (said they) is from God. **1839** J. ROGERS *Antipopopr.* xvii. §2. 340 Thousands of men may have.. brought disorder and nullity into the kirk, unpriesting the priesthood. **1868** BROWNING *Ring & Bk.* VI. 1870 Unpriest me, .. Remove me from the midst, no longer priest.
2. To deprive, or make free, of priests.
1844 MOZLEY *Ess.* (1878) II. 33 This ideal of a Church of course utterly unpriested it, and a priest, accordingly, Arnold could not tolerate.

un'priested, *ppl. a.* [UN-^{1} 8.] Not furnished with a priest.
1548 GESTE *Pr. Masse* E iij b, Paul spoke the selue same wordes vnto the vnprested Corinthians. **1596** BELL *Surv. Popery* III. x. 406 S. Paul.. did communicate the vnpriested Corinthians vnder both kinds. **1858** ALLINGHAM *50 Mod. Poems* (1865) 46 Though living unpriested and dying unshriven.

un'priestly, *a.* (UN-^{1} 7.)
1537 LATIMER *Serm. & Rem.* (Parker Soc.) 390 That un-priestly priest, whose damsel was brought to bed alate. **1546** BALE *Eng. Votaries* I. 66 Kynge Edgare.. rebuked the prestes.. for.. their vnprestlye aparellynges. **1611** SPEED *Hist. Gt. Brit.* IX. viii. 1 The two vnjust Intruders on the Crowne; .. the one by vnprincely forces, the other by vnpriestly fraud. **1790** PENNANT *London* 19 The people, enraged at his unpriestly conduct, would have torn him to pieces. **1837** J. H. NEWMAN *Proph. Office Ch.* 403 The Asmonæans, who, besides their unpriestly character, were many of them stained with crimes.

un'priestly, *adv.* (UN-^{1} 11.)
1554 BONNER *Articles* A iij, Whether they.. vse common games or playes, or behaue themselfes otherwyse vnpriestly and vnsemely.

un'prime, *a.* (UN-^{1} 7.)
1879 *Encycl. Brit.* IX. 839/1 Unprime fur seals part with their overhair very reluctantly.

un'primed, *ppl. a.* (UN-^{1} 8.)
[**1775** ASH.] **1862** THORNBURY *Turner* I. 265 Turner had the greatest horror of the picture being lined, having commenced it with sized colours on un-primed cloth. **1881** LE CONTE *Sight* 234 The position[s].. shown by the unprimed and the primed vinculum respectively.

un'primitive, *a.* (UN-^{1} 7, 5 b.)
1708 COLLIER *Eccl. Hist.* V. 481 [To] acquiesce under so unprimitive, and uncatholick a Practice. **1746** J. CHAPMAN *Popery* 2 The unscriptural, unprimitive Crudities of the Romish Principles. **1899** FILLEUL (*title*), A Sacerdotal Ministry in the Christian Church: Unscriptural, Unprimitive, and High Treason against Christ.

un'prince, *v.* (UN-^{2} 6 b.)
1602 CHETTLE *Hoffman* II. (1631) C 4, You were better vnknighted then vnprinced. *a* **1661** FULLER *Worthies, Warwick* III. (1662) 121 Queen Mary.. would not Unprince herself to Obey his Holiness.

un'princelike, *a.* and *adv.* (UN-^{1} 7 c, 11 b.)
1579 J. STUBBES *Gaping Gulf* F 4 b, This vnmanlike, vnprincelike, secrete, .. french kind of woeng [= wooing]. **1611** SPEED *Hist. Gt. Brit.* VII. xli. §2. 347 With shamelesse and vnprincelike lust, hee abused a Lady of great estate. **1639** FULLER *Holy War* I. xv. 23 Alexius.. most unprincelike brake his word.

un'princeliness. (UN-^{1} 12; cf next.)
1855 G. H. LEWES *Life & Wks. Goethe* I. IV. i. 310 The princely unprinceliness of selling to the Jews a diamond ring. **1860** FORSTER *Gr. Remonstr.* 97 Never was Kirk so rebellious, in flaming up.. against the sovereign's unprinceliness and ungodliness.

un'princely, *a.* (UN-^{1} 7.)
1536 Q. ANNE BOLEYN *Lett.* (1714) 38 Your unprincely and cruel usage of me. **1593** *Sidney's Arcadia* V. (1922) II. 201 Constant suffering, that your unprincely dealing hath purchased unto you. **1611** [see UNPRIESTLY *a.*]. **1613** SHERLEY *Trav. Persia* 29 As farre from.. vanity as from all vnprincely signes, or acts. **1649** MILTON *Eikon.* ix. 78 Not forgetting the unprincely usage, and.. the abolishing of Parlaments. **1748** RICHARDSON *Clarissa* (1811) II. 12 Nor would the unprincely wretch marry her till [etc.]. **1821** JOANNA BAILLIE *Metr. Leg.*, *Wallace* lxix, A base unprincely compact. **1881** TENNYSON *Cup* I. i, Some unprincely violence to a woman.

un'princely, *adv.* (UN-^{1} 11.)
a **1548** HALL *Chron. Hen. IV*, 7 b, He most tirannously and vnprincely said that [etc.]. **1611** SPEED *Hist. Gt. Brit.* IX. viii. 486/1 If Princes can bee thus vnprincely degenerous.

un'princess, *v.* (UN-^{2} 6 b.)
1663 R. STAPYLTON *Slighted Maid* II. 22, I have Unlorded my self and Unprincess'd thee, Granchild Fritilla.

un'principal, *a.* (UN-^{1} 7.)
1541 R. COPLAND *Guydon's Quest. Chirurg.* c ij, Howe many pryncypal membres be there, and howe many vnpryncypal?

un'principle, *v.* (UN-^{2} 6 b.)
1713 *Gentl. Instructed* II. 108 The Press has not only effeminated the Mind, but Unprincipl'd the Understanding. **1760–72** H. BROOKE *Fool of Qual.* (1809) I. 87 When I behold so many scoundrels.. I reflect, that they have been principled, or rather unprincipled, by such tutors as Mr. Vindex.

un'principled, *ppl. a.* [UN-^{1} 8.]
1. Not instructed or grounded *in* something.
1634 MILTON *Comus* 367, I do not think my sister so to seek, Or so unprincipl'd in vertues book. **1644** —— *Educ.* 3 Others betake them to State affairs, with souls so unprincipl'd in vertue, and true generous breeding, that [etc.].
2. Of persons, etc.: Not possessed of fixed, sound, or honourable principles of conduct.
1644 MILTON *Judgm. Bucer* 26 God.. will also give them .. to inform themselvs rightly in the midst of an unprincipl'd age. **1681** FLAVEL *Meth. Grace* v. 102 An unprincipled professor must be squeezed by some weight of affliction, ere he will yield one tear. **1771** GOLDSM. *Hist. Eng.* I. 353 Every office.. was bestowed on these unprincipled strangers. **1796** MME. D'ARBLAY *Camilla* V. 506 [It] opened to his unprincipled mind a scheme yet more flagitious. **1849** MACAULAY *Hist. Eng.* vi. II. 113 Several men not less unprincipled than Sunderland. **1878** E. JENKINS *Haverholme* 30 A couple of unprincipled rascals.
absol. **1834** *Tait's Mag.* May 222/2 These clamours of the wealthy, the timid, or the unprincipled.
3. Based upon, exhibiting, want of principle.
1782 V. KNOX *Ess.* cxx. (1819) II. 9 There are, indeed, many who are esteemed good sort of persons, but whose goodness is unprincipled. **1797** BURKE *Regic. Peace* ii. ¶22 Whilst the monarchies subsisted, this unprincipled cession was what the influence of the elder branch.. never dared to attempt on the younger. **1841** THACKERAY *Gt. Hoggarty Diam.* vii, I thought this rather cruel and unprincipled conduct. **1871** FREEMAN *Hist. Ess.* Ser. I. xi. 331 The ambition of Philip the Good was quite.. unprincipled.
Hence **un'principledness.**
a **1812** BUCKMINSTER *Serm.* (1827) 362 Their strange union.. of exquisite sensibility and practical unprincipledness. **1865** *Pall Mall G.* 12 Dec. 2 A settled unprincipledness has been eating its way into the public opinion of Europe.

un'print, *v.* (UN-^{2} 3.)
1842 S. R. MAITLAND *Notes* II. 81 Whatever he may say now, he cannot unprint his Vindication of Fox.

un'printable, *a.* and *sb.* [UN-^{1} 7 b, 12.]
1. *adj.* Not fit to be printed. (Common *c* 1893–.)
1871 *St. Paul's Mag.* Aug. 457 Articles that were utterly unprintable. **1898** *Punch* 9 July 10/1 What the groom says is unprintable!
2. *sb. pl.* Trousers; = UNMENTIONABLE *sb.*
1860 W. W. READE *Liberty Hall* I. iii. 32 Arrayed in black coat, tie, studs, waistcoat, unprintables.
Hence **un'printably** *adv.*
1934 WEBSTER, Unprintably. **1940** E. HEMINGWAY *For whom Bell Tolls* iii. 44 Go then unprintably to the campfire with thy obscene dynamite. **1965** D. FRANCIS *Odds Against* xi. 153 Jones-boy unprintably told Chico where he could find his coffee. **1977** *Gay News* 7–20 Apr. 23/2 It's infuriating trying to write about Anger because so much is unprintably scandalous.

un'printed, *ppl. a.* (UN-^{1} 8.)
1532 MORE *Confut. Tyndale* Wks. 627/2 When he cometh to my seconde boke, [he] goeth fro the first Chapiter to the third, as though the prynter had left the second vnprinted. **1551** RECORDE *Pathw. Knowl.* II. Pref., The other bookes, whiche now are lefte vnprinted. **1609** BOYS *Expos. Princ. Script.* 93 This may teach.. all superiours who prescribe lawes vnto other, to become first an vnprinted law them-selues. *a* **1683** OLDHAM *Wks.* (1686) 112 Wit should be open, .. Not lurk in sly unprinted privacy. **1729** T. INNES *Crit. Essay* (1879) 117 The most ancient now extant eve of the unprinted Irish historians. **1796** LAMB *Let. to Coleridge* in *Final Mem.* ii. 211 You have scarce enough unprinted to make a second volume with Lloyd. **1860** TYNDALL *Glac.* II. xiv. 299 The paper.. might have remained unprinted, had not another publication.. called it forth. **1884** A. R. PENNINGTON *Wiclif* viii. 247 He expresses himself still more strongly in his unprinted writings.

un'prison, *v.* [UN-^{2} 5.] *trans.* To free from prison.
1390 GOWER *Conf.* III. 202 Therbellis king of Bulgarie .. Justinian hath unprisoned. **1598** FLORIO, *Discarcerare*, to vnprison. **1633** HEYWOOD *Eng. Trav.* IV. H 3, Now is the Goale deliuerie; Through this backe gate Shift for your selues, I heere vnprison all. **1635** *To C'tess Huntington* Donne's Wks. 1912 I. 418 Fire rose, and each from other but unty'd, Themselves unprison'd were and purify'd. **1827** MONTGOMERY *Pelican Isl.* I. 119 Then the wind Unprisoned, blew its trumpet loud.

un'prisonable, *a.* (UN-^{1} 7 b.)
1878 M. & F. COLLINS *Vill. Comedy* I. xx. 269 The agile and unprisonable spirit of man.

un'prisoned, *ppl. a.*^{1} [UN-^{1} 8.] Not put in prison.
a **1844** CAMPBELL *Napoleon & Sailor* 10 They suffer'd him.. Unprison'd on the shore to roam.

un'prisoned, *ppl. a.*^{2} [UN-^{2} 8 or f. UNPRISON *v.*] Released from prison.
1840 DICKENS *Old C. Shop* lii, Perhaps not one of the unprisoned souls had been able [etc.].

†**unpri'vation.** *Obs.*$^{-1}$ [UN-^{1} 12.] Continuance (of existence).
a **1628** F. GREVIL *Cælica*, '*Down in the Depth*' iii, With glory scourging all the Sp'rits infernall, And vncreated hell with vnpriuation.

un'privileged, *ppl. a.* (UN-^{1} 8.)
1590 SWINBURNE *Testaments* 112 Such disposition.. maie be lawfullie and properlie said to be a testament, whether the same be.. priuiledged or vnpriuiledged. **1592** WARNER *Alb. Eng.* VII. xxxiv. 149 But of vnpriuiledged bloud yet had he store to spill. **1702** ROWE *Tamerl.* I. i. 100 The Boast and Master-piece of the great Maker, That wears in vain th' Impression of his Image Unpriviledged from thee. **1791** MACKINTOSH *Vind. Gallicæ* 255 They are a small body, united to the mass.., and returning to it, undistinguished and unprivileged, the majority of their children. **1818** HALLAM *Mid. Ages* (1819) I. 443 The arrangement.. had still left several kinds of artisans unincorporated, and consequently unprivileged. **1881** L. WALLACE *Ben-Hur* VI. ii, To dwell with none but lepers; to be utterly unprivileged.

un'prizable, *a.* [UN-^{1} 7 b.]
1. Not to be prized; of little worth.
1601 SHAKS. *Twel. N.* V. i. 58 A bawbling Vessell was he Captaine of, For shallow draught and bulke vnprizable.
†2. Beyond all price; inestimable. *Obs.*
1604 T. WRIGHT *Passions* V. iv. 246 Some gifts are.. so vn-prizable, that a man is never able perfitly to recompence them. **1616** BRETON *Good & Bad* Wks. (Grosart) 12/2 A Quiet Woman is.. a iewell vnprizeable and a ioy vnspeakable. **1634** W. TIRWHYT tr. *Balzac's Lett.* (vol. I) 258 She is rich, but my liberty is unprizeable.

un'prized, *ppl. a.* [UN-^{1} 8.]
†1. Unpriced; of which the price has not been fixed. *Obs.*
1445 *Extr. Aberdeen Reg.* (1844) I. 14 That thai sell na flesche vnprisit, .. vnder the payne of tynsal of the flesche.
2. Not prized or valued.
c **1600** DONNE *Elegy* iii. 6 Women are like the Arts, forc'd unto none, Open to all searchers, unpriz'd, if unknowne. **1615** G. WITHER *Fidelia* 707 Though my faith must now despised be, Vnpriz'd, vnualued at the lowest rate. **1648** HEXHAM II, *Ongelovet*, Vnprised, or Vnrated. **1821** WORDSW. *Italian Itinerant* 82 Seemingly a Thing despised; Even by the sun and air unprized.
†3. ? Priceless. *Obs.* (Probably = prec.)
1605 SHAKS. *Lear* I. i. 262 Not all the Dukes of watrish Burgundy Can buy this vnpriz'd precious Maid of me.

†**un'proachable**, *a.* *Obs.*$^{-1}$ [UN-^{1} 7b, 5b.] Unapproachable.
1544 BETHAM *Precepts War* I. cxvii. Fviij, The vnprocheable humanitie of Cesar.

†**un'probable**, *a.* *Obs.* [UN-^{1} 7b, 5b.]
a. Incapable of proof. **b.** Improbable, unlikely.
1532 MORE *Confut. Tyndale* Wks. 429/1 When Tyndall hath proued by thys vnprobable case, that women may consecrate the body of Christ. **1588** FRAUNCE *Lawiers Log.* Ded. ¶3 The unprobable assertion comprized in your last two Epithetes. **1602** T. FITZHERBERT *Apol.* 4 The one [point], no doubt in their owne opinions vncertayne, and in ours altogeather vnprobable, if not vnpossible. **1652** GAULE *Magastrom.* 108 Is not, then, the latter..supposition still more unprobable? **1684** BOYLE *Porousn. Anim. & Solid Bod.* vi. 104, I thought it not very unprobable that the great heat ..might cleave..some of the Crystalline Fragments.

†**un'probably**, *adv.* [UN-^{1} 11, 5b.]
1. Without good reason.
1613 PURCHAS *Pilgrimage* (1614) 62 The Iew not vnprobably thinketh that mixtures..were forbidden. **1721** STRYPE *Eccl. Mem.* I. I. 373 Being able to diminish, by the authority of wise and knowing men, things unjustly and unprobably crept in.
2. Without probability; improbably.
1606 *Choice, Chance*, etc. (1881) 53 Pardon me..if I speak vnprobably and Let me say what I think.

un'probated, *ppl. a.* (UN-^{1} 8.)
1570 LEVINS *Manip.* 50 Vnprobated, *improbatus*.

un'probed, *ppl. a.* (UN-^{1} 8.)
[1775 ASH.] **1827** POLLOK *Course T.* VI. 148 The frothy orator..leaving still the heart unprobed. **1866** C. J. VAUGHAN *Plain Words* xi. 211 He knows the misery..of having any unprobed, unexplored secrets between the heart and its God. **1879** BROWNING *Ivan Ivanovitch* 31 Each village death-begirt By wall and wall of pine—unprobed undreamed abyss.

unproble'matic, *a.* (UN-^{1} 7.)
1683 E. HOOKER *Pref. Pordage's Mystic Div.* 107 It beeing altogether unproblematic and without the less'st shadow of scrupl. **1944** C. G. MYRDAL et al. *Amer. Dilemma* II. 1032 The system of mores, conceived of as a homogeneous, unproblematic, fairly static, social entity. **1981** *Word 1980* XXXI. 196 Something that was not possible within the tonetic stress marks theory proves relatively unproblematic for the configurational model. **1984** *Listener* 19 Apr. 16/2 Nor is there any unproblematic external standard with which to compare competing paradigms.

unproble'matical, *a.* (UN-^{1} 7.)
1799 E. DU BOIS *Piece Family Biog.* I. 65 Which he [neglected]..for this plain and unproblematical reason.

un'processed, *ppl. a.* (UN-^{1} 8.)
1539 *Reg. Privy Seal Scot.* II. 472/2 The said Johnne to be ..unprocessit, unpoyndit, and untrublit for ony actioun civile bigane. **1959** *Times* 6 Mar. 11/7 The United States.. want the unprocessed raw materials. **1962** E. SNOW *Other Side of River* (1963) lxxix. 607 In Peking I had been assured that I would be permitted to take out unprocessed film. **1974** *Brit. Med. Jrnl.* 19 Jan. 109/2 Unprocessed bran is an ideal additive to the diet in such cases.

unpro'claimed, *ppl. a.* (UN-^{1} 8.)
1648 HEXHAM II, *Onverkondight*, vnproclamed. **1667** MILTON *P.L.* XI. 220 Against the Syrian King, who,.. Assassin-like had levied Warr, Warr unproclam'd. **1795–1802** WORDSW. *Excurs.* I. 94 Else surely this Man had not left His graces unrevealed and unproclaimed. **1844** DE QUINCEY *Greece under Rom.* Wks. 1858 VIII. 335 Armistices .., truces, or unproclaimed suspensions of war. **1878** B. TAYLOR *Deukalion* III. ii, The..Heir Who, unproclaimed, awaits his lordship.

un'procreant, *a.* (UN-^{1} 7.)
1870 LOWELL *Among my Bks.* Ser. I. (1873) 190 A knowledge..which comes of mere learning is sapless and unprocreant.

un'procreate(d, *ppl. a.* (UN-^{1} 8.)
1630 DRUMM. OF HAWTH. *Flowres of Sion, Hymne of Fairest Faire* 126 O most holie One, Vnprocreat'd [*ed.* 1711 unprocreate] Father, euer-procreat'd Sonne.

unpro'curable, *a.* (UN-^{1} 7b.)
1607 HIERON *Wks.* I. 351 The dignity of this estate..was vnprocurable, saue only by this infinit price. **1654** BOYLE in T. Birch *Life* B.'s Wks. 1772 I. p. liv, A barbarous country, where..chemical instruments were..unprocurable. **1864** CARLYLE *Fredk. Gt.* XVII. v. IV. 568 Draught-cattle seem absolutely unprocurable. **1875** JOWETT *Plato* (ed. 2) III. 29 Not of an Eleusinian pig, but of some unprocurable animal.

unpro'cured, *ppl. a.* (UN-^{1} 8.)
1534 MORE *Comf. agst. Trib.* II. Wks. 1177/2 [To] fall in the dyspleasure of God, or leaue Goddes pleasure vnprocured. *a* **1600** HOOKER *Serm. Pride* ⁋10, I bless thee ..for thy goodness,..not in regard of my merits,..but of thy mere unprocured benignity. **1655** JER. TAYLOR *Unum Necess.* vii. §3. 464 The meer ineffective, unprocured desirings or lustings after evil things.

unpro'curing, *vbl. sb.* (UN-^{1} 13.)
1622 MABBE tr. *Aleman's Guzman d' Alf.* I. 135 A man ought to venture his life, for the keeping of a friend,..for the vn-procuring of an enemie.

unpro'duceable, *a.* (UN-^{1} 7b.)
1802–12 BENTHAM *Ration. Judic. Evid.* (1827) II. 497 While the witnesses are alive and produceable,..when they are dead, or otherwise unproduceable. **1834** DE QUINCEY *Autob. Sk.* Wks. 1854 II. 313 Everybody agrees in our days to think this accomplishment..unproduceable, unless existing in an exquisite state of culture.

unpro'duceably, *adv.* (UN-^{1} 11.)
1865 MISS YONGE *Clever Woman* II. 206 To have an unproduceably eccentric melancholy bride.

unpro'duced, *ppl. a.* [UN-^{1} 8, 5b.]
1. Not brought into existence; uncreated.
1674 BOYLE *Ground's Corpusc. Philos.* 9 For their sakes that would have matter to be unproduced. **1712** BLACKMORE *Creation* p. iv, Those who believe an innate Idea of a Divine Being, unproduced by any Operation of the Mind. **1768–74** TUCKER *Lt. Nat.* (1834) I. 499 The rules of justice are apprehended immutable and unproduced, because you cannot draw them directly from any object before you.
2. Not extended or lengthened.
1768 *Phil. Trans.* LX. 250 A new equation, all whose roots shall fall upon the line OT unproduced. **1882** MINCHIN *Unipl. Kinemat.* 83 Supposing that the lines..intersect each other at a point, O, in their unproduced lengths.
Hence **unpro'ducedness**.
1862 F. HALL *Hindu Philos. Syst.* 37 Unproducedness thereby does not belong to them.

unpro'ductive, *a.* [UN-^{1} 7.]
1. Not productive: **a.** Const. *of*.
1756 BURKE *Subl. & B.* I. xix, The use of the passions.. cannot be..unproductive to ourselves of that noble..union of science and admiration. **1768–74** TUCKER *Lt. Nat.* (1834) II. 130 The enjoyment distilling from this source is sure and sincere,..and unproductive of future inconvenience. **1828** HAWTHORNE *Fanshawe* iii, A few months passed.. unproductive of events that [etc.]. **1839** CARLYLE *Chartism* x, Most paralytic, uninstructive: unproductive of any comfort to one!
b. Without const., or in attributive use.
1784 COWPER *Task* II. 124 The gloomy scenes Where beauty oft and letter'd worth consume Life in the unproductive shades of death. **1791** NEWTE *Tour Eng. & Scot.* 383 Shall..the poor..[be doomed] to unproductive labour, in order to gratify barbarian ignorance and pride? **1815** SCOTT *Guy M.* xv, Sampson picked up some other scholars..whose lessons were proportionally unproductive. **1849** COBDEN *Speeches* 4 Unproductive services like your fighting establishments..in a time of peace. **1870** BURTON *Hist. Scot.* lxxii. VII. 73 The king..does not see the use of their attempting to hold a meeting— in Scotland it would be dangerous, in England unproductive.
2. Not materially productive; not yielding crops, minerals, etc.
1766 *Parl. Deb.* (1813) XVI. 303/1 The harvest had failed, and was unproductive. **1796** WITHERING *Brit. Plants* (ed. 3) II. 389 A female plant..produced small unproductive seeds. **1855** *Orr's Circ. Sci., Inorg. Nat.* 222 Unproductive portions of the fields. **1877** RAYMOND *Statist. Mines & M.* 192 They are unproductive as yet in minerals.
Hence **unpro'ductively** *adv.*, **-ness**.
c **1815** JANE AUSTEN *Persuas.* xx, The anxious interval wore away *unproductively. **1813** SIR H. DAVY *Agric. Chem.* 177 Any particular ingredient which is the cause of their *unproductiveness. **1869** TOZER *Highl. Turkey* II. 343 The unhealthiness and unproductiveness of marshes.

unproduc'tivity. (UN-^{1} 12.)
1888 *19th Cent.* June 836 The unproductivity of the soil.

unpro'fanable, *a.* (UN-^{1} 7b.)
a **1641** BP. MOUNTAGU *Acts & Mon.* (1642) 178 Nor did the Romanes..hold any thing so sacred, sanctified and unprophanable, as Sibyll's Oracles. **1869** MRS. WHITNEY *We Girls* xii, The sanctity..would be as unprofanable as ever.

unpro'fane, *a.* (UN-^{1} 7.)
1576 FLEMING *Panopl. Epist.* 196 Passing..through Ægypt, there to conferre with the unprophane priestes, and learned Astronomers. **1646** MAYNE *Serm. Unity* 58 How seemingly holy,..how un-profane soever his Behaviour be.

unpro'faned, *ppl. a.* (UN-^{1} 8.)
1650 R. STAPYLTON *Strada's Low C. Wars* v. 125 The greatest wonder was..that..a few men..should before mid-night, when they began but in the evening, have nothing at all left entire or unprofaned. **1659** GAUDEN *Tears Ch.* III. iv. 274 They easily preserved the doctrine of Christian Religion uncorrupted, the Mysteries unprophaned. **1774** BEATTIE *Minstrel* II. xliv, May your influence unprofaned To god-like worth the generous bosom raise! **1818** BYRON *Ch. Har.* IV. lxvi, Surely that stream was unprofaned by slaughters. **1894** BLACKMORE *Perlycross* 435 Resting placidly, unprofaned, untouched.

unpro'fessed, *ppl. a.* (UN-^{1} 8.)
c **1430** *Paston Lett.* I. 30 The poure hous of Bromholm.., in wheche arn divers vertuous yongge men, monkes clad and unprofessyd. *a* **1450** in Myrc *Par. Pr.* (1902) 61 Alle þat leyne hand on preste or clerke..off religione professed or vnprofessud. **1808** SCOTT *Marm.* II. v, Sister Clare,..As yet a novice unprofess'd. **1809–14** WORDSW. *Excurs.* VII. 309 Whose mind could..beguile A solitude, unchosen, unprofessed.

unpro'fessing, *ppl. a.* (UN-^{1} 10.)
1748 RICHARDSON *Clarissa* (1811) V. 158 The unprofessing Mrs. Moore.

unpro'fessional, *a.* and *sb.* (UN-^{1} 7, 12.)
1806 *Med. Jrnl.* XV. 299 The solution unfortunately having become a very common medicine with unprofessional people. **1847** DE QUINCEY *Span. Mil. Nun* Wks. 1853 III. 59 No authority could overrule the concurrent testimony of all symptoms, and of all unprofessional opinions. **1895** *Westm. Gaz.* 31 July 8/1 As a wicket-keeper he has had no unprofessional superior. **1899** *Ibid.* 17 June 3/2 He had not intended any disrespect to the Court, or to do anything unprofessional.
sb. **1863** READE *Hard Cash* II. 244 The unexpected turn the evidence had taken..cleared Mr. Hardie with the unprofessionals.
Hence **unpro'fessionalism**.
1934 WEBSTER, *Unprofessionalism.* **1955** A. L. ROWSE *Expansion Elizabethan England* 382 The clue to English ill-success was, as usual, amateurishness, unprofessionalism, in the beginning. **1977** *Time* 28 Feb. 22/1 The Carter Administration was still marred in some areas by confusion and unprofessionalism; the staff work was sometimes shoddy and key memos poorly prepared.

unpro'fessionally, *adv.* (UN-^{1} 11.)
1840 WILLIS *Loiterings* III. 75 Your physician and dentist are distinguished persons, who meet you in Society, and call on you unprofessionally.

unpro'ficiency. [UN-^{1} 12, 5b.] †Lack of moral or spiritual progress.
1625 BP. HALL *Contempl.*, *O.T.* IV. iii. Wks. 870 As on the contrary, carelesnesse caries vs to a meere vnproficiency vnder the best meanes of God. **1665** BOYLE *Occas. Refl.* IV. ix. 59 'Tis no mean sign of Proficiency in Piety, to be apt to deplore ones unproficiency. **1691** NORRIS *Pract. Disc.* Pref. 4 The unproficiency of the World under such extraordinary Advantages.

unpro'ficient, *a.* and *sb.* (UN-^{1} 7, 12.)
a **1653** BINNING *Serm.* (1735) 464/2 This makes us such Unproficients in Mortification, so that scarce any Sin is killed.

un'profit, *sb.* (UN-^{1} 12. Cf. MDu. *onprofijt*, MLG. *unprofit*.)
1382 WYCLIF *Heb.* vii. 18 Forsoth reprouyng of the maundement bifore goynge is maad, for the vnsadnesse and vnprofyt of it. *a* **1420** *Wycliffite Bible* Eccl. i. 1 *marg.*, Kunnyng getun bi mannus weye is vnprofit and diseseful. *c* **1430** *Pilgr. Lyf Manhode* I. iii. (1869) 58 Who so hath on this garnement he dooth his profyt, with that that oothere doon here vnprofyt and here harm. **1483** *Cath. Angl.* 292/1 Vn Profett,..*incomoditas*. **1598** FLORIO, *Disutile*,..vn-profit. **1840** BROWNING *Sordello* V. 327 Through his youth's daybreak of unprofit, quite To his noon's labour.

†**un'profit**, *v.* *Obs.* (UN-^{2} 3.)
14.. *Latin-Ang. Voc.* (MS. Harl. 2257), *Incommodo*, vnproffite. **1541** R. COPLAND *Galyen's Terap.* 2 C iv, A clere and notable vntemperatnes,..which is the greatest cause.. that maye vnproffyte and anoye in the vlceres.

un'profitable, *a.* (UN-^{1} 7b, 5b.)
a **1325** *Prose Psalter* xiii. 4 Alle boweden, to-gider hij ben vnprofitable. **1390** GOWER *Conf.* I. 263 Envie..is..to mankinde unprofitable. *c* **1412** HOCCLEVE *De Reg. Princ.* 2268 Swiche an eschaunge [is] but vnprofitable. *c* **1435** *Chron. London* (Kingsford, 1905) 42 Demyng hym sylff..vtterly vnprofitable to the Rewle and good gouernaunces off the Rewme. **1526** TINDALE *Heb.* xiii. 17 That is an vnprofitable thynge for you. **1577** GOOGE tr. *Heresbach's Husb.* 139 So that the Master be not deceiued with an olde unproffitable flocke. **1630** CAPT. SMITH *Trav. & Adv.* xv. 27 Any beast unprofitable for service they kill. **1654** S. CLARKE *Eccl. Hist.* (ed. 2) I. 25 Such men as labor for shortlived honour are but like froth, which though it be uppermost, yet is unprofitablest. **1735** JOHNSON *Lobo's Abyssinia. Voy.* i. 7 To expose ourselves..to a Death almost certain and unprofitable. **1826** F. REYNOLDS *Life & Times* II. 377 This arduous, unprofitable, and ungracious office. **1878** LECKY *Eng. in 18th C.* II. vii. 302 Prizes offered..for reclaiming unprofitable bogs.
absol. **1838** *Penny Cycl.* XI. 345/2 To distinguish good from evil,..the profitable from the unprofitable.
†**b.** As *adv.* Unprofitably. *Obs.*$^{-1}$
c **1425** *Orolog. Sapient.* v. in *Anglia* X. 360/12 þat I hadde so vnprofitabil spendid þe tyme.

un'profitableness. (UN-^{1} 12, 5b; cf. prec.)
1526 TINDALE *Heb.* vii. 18 The commaundment..is disanulled, be cause of his weaknes and vnproffitablenes. **1641** PRYNNE *2nd Pt. Antip.* (title-p.), Touching the.. unprofitablenesse, and mischievousnesse of Lordly Prelates, both to King, State, Church. **1673** *Lady's Call.* II. ii. §54 Servants, whose unprofitableness usually increases together with their number. **1765** *Museum Rust.* IV. 269 The unprofitableness arising from their keeping men and horses for that work alone. **1837** HALLAM *Hist. Lit.* I. vi. §30 Their yellow leaves, their thousand folio pages, do not more repel us than the unprofitableness of their substance. **1875** MANNING *Mission H. Ghost* iv. 116 Learn, then,..your unprofitableness before Him.

un'profitably, *adv.* (UN-^{1} 11.)
1395 PURVEY *Remonstr.* (1851) 25 The comoun puple is.. vnprofitabli ocupied. *c* **1425** *Eng. Conq. Ireland* 142 Such that..al thynge vnprofytably wasteden, to harme of peesmen. **1508** FISHER *Wks.* (1876) 75 Euery worde spoken vnproufytably and in vayne. **1561** T. NORTON *Calvin's Inst.* IV. xx. 162b, This is not vnprofitablye appointed by the prouidence of God. **1611** B. JONSON *Catiline* I. i, I should not now vnprofitably spend my selfe in words. *a* **1677** BARROW *Serm.* Wks. 1687 I. xxxi. 451 To prevent this being necessarily and unprofitably deprived of our goods. **1737** GLOVER *Leonidas* IV. 237 Unprofitably wasting precious hours In vain discussion. **1819** SHELLEY *Cenci* II. ii. 140 Thus unprofitably I clasp the phantom of unfelt delights. **1856** DE QUINCEY *Confess.* Wks. I. 135 Impressing..a new movement upon dialogues that loitered painfully, or see-sawed unprofitably.

un'profited, *ppl. a.* (UN-^{1} 8, 8c.)
1601 SHAKS. *Twel. N.* I. iv. 22 Be clamorous, and leape all ciuill bounds, Rather then make vnprofited returne. **1796** COLERIDGE *Destiny of Nations* 381 Why, uninjured and unprofited, Should multitudes against their brethren rush? **1813** T. BUSBY *Lucretius* II. VI. Comm. p. xxii, Never to permit a circumstance of importance..to pass unprofited of, as a moral lesson. **1820** W. JAY *Prayers* 296 How un-profited have we been under the richest means of religious prosperity.

un'profiting, *vbl. sb.* (UN-^{1} 13.)
1867 H. BUSHNELL *Mor. Uses Dark Th.* (1869) 268 The key we start upon there is lower, by the whole unprofiting of a misspent life.

un'profiting, *ppl. a.* (UN-1 10.)
1616 B. JONSON *Epigr.* I. xc, The vnprofiting foole, Vn-worthy such a mistris. **1693** FLEETWOOD *Serm.* 18 Another sort of unprofiting Hearers, are represented..by the Seed that fell among the Thorns. **1880** *Victorian Rev.* I. 602 Finding themselves in a hopeless and unprofiting minority.

unpro'found, *a.* (UN-1 7.)
a **1859** DE QUINCEY *Posth. Wks.* (1891) I. 26 The joy of an infant, or joy-generation, without significance to an unprofound and common mind.

unpro'fuse, *a.* (UN-1 7.)
1727 THOMSON *To Mem. Newton* 68 O unprofuse magnificence divine!

unpro'gressive, *a.* (UN-1 7, 5 b.)
[**1775** ASH.] **1851** H. W. TORRENS *Jrnl. Asiat. Soc. Bengal* 40 Such a description of unprogressive civilization. **1869** TOZER *Highl. Turkey* I. 141 Their mode of life..left them..uninstructed and unprogressive. **1886** TENNYSON *Locksley Hall 60 Years After* 153 Cries of unprogressive dotage ere the dotard fall asleep!
Hence **unpro'gressively** *adv.*, **-ness.**
1800 COLERIDGE in C. K. Paul *Godwin* (1876) II. 13 Life is too melancholy a thing for men in general for the doctrine of unprogressiveness to remain popular. **1869** FARRAR *Fam. Speech* iv. (1870) 159 Tribes..in every stage of nomad unprogressiveness or squalid savagery. **1881** *Echo* 28 June 3/6 The Bulgarians of the Principality would be only too content to live quietly, stolidly, and unprogressively.

unpro'hibited, *ppl. a.* (UN-1 8.)
1641 MILTON *Animadv.* 51 Lest his conversation unprohibited, or unbranded, might breath a pestilentiall murrein into the other sheepe. **1679** C. NESSE *Antid. agst. Popery* 21 To abstain from unprohibited ceremonies as well as from unprohibited meats.

unpro'jected, *ppl. a.* (UN-1 8.)
1653 CROMWELL *Sp.* in *Harl. Misc.* (1810) VI. 63 Your call..is of God, and it hath been unprojected, unthought of by you and us. *a* **1715** SOUTH *Serm.* IV. 367 Heresies..have been often taken up at first by meer Accident, or upon some slight, trivial, unprojected Occasion. **1806** FOSTER *Ess.* (1844) I. 9 Some great, and as yet..unprojected, plan for the relief of their pressing physical wants.

unpro'jecting, *ppl. a.* (UN-1 10.)
1647 CLARENDON *Contempl. Ps.* Tracts (1727) 387 He is quiet and unprojecting, and even unconcerned to help himself. **1787** BENTHAM *Def. Usury* xiii. 179 Birmingham and Sheffield are pitched upon by you as examples, the one of a projecting town, the other of an unprojecting one.

unpro'lific, *a.* (UN-1 7, 5 b.)
a **1676** HALE *Prim. Orig. Man.* II. ix. (1677) 210 Inundation..drowns oftentimes many sorts of Insects, and renders their..Eggs unprolifick. **1724** GAY *Captives* Epil., [The dame] brings her unprolifick Spouse a Son. **1784** COWPER *Task* VI. 138 Th' icy touch Of unprolific winter. **1854** *Poultry Chron.* I. 62/2 Frequently a great part of the eggs are un-prolific. **1869** DUNKIN *Midn. Sky* 60 An unprolific part of Draco below Polaris.

un'promise, *v.* (UN-2 3.)
1598 FLORIO, *Spromettere*,..to vnpromise, to breake promise. **1605** CHAPMAN *All Fools* II. i. 70 Promises are no fetters; with that tongue Thy promise past, unpromise it againe. **1672** RAVENSCROFT *Cit. turned Gentl.* IV. i. 64 *Luc.* But you have promis'd I should be his Wife. *Jord.* If I promised you, I unpromise you.

un'promised, *ppl. a.* (UN-1 8.)
1596 SPENSER *F.Q.* V. v. 49 Say, and do all, that may thereto preuaile; Leaue nought vnpromist, that may him perswade. *a* **1689** MRS. BEHN *Fair Jilt* in *Novels* (1905) 102 He is unenjoyed, unpromised; and so am I.

un'promising, *ppl. a.* [UN-1 10.]
1. Not affording promise of excellence or success.
1663 J. SPENCER *Prodigies* 81 God often accomplisheth his biggest ends by means unpromiseing. **1721** *Lond. Gaz.* No. 5999/1 The Vintage Season,..though very backward and unpromising.., has..begun. **1786** tr. *Beckford's Vathek* 187 The Caliph, to whom these complaints were but unpromising auguries. **1827** SCOTT *Surg. Dau.* i, So you will often find.., under an unpromising and blunt exterior, professional skill and enthusiasm. **1871** FREEMAN *Norm. Conq.* IV. xix. 418 Hermann..began vigorously to build a church in the unpromising spot.
†2. Unprepossessing. *Obs.*
1632 MASSINGER & FIELD *Fatal Dowry* IV. i, *Liladam.* What d'ee take me for? *Pontalier.* A long thing with a most vnpromising face. **1669** CLARENDON *Ess.* Tracts (1727) 101 The beauty of the mind doth frequently reconcile..all men to the most unpromising countenances.
Hence **un'promisingness.**
1655 EARL ORRERY *Parthen.* I. II. 135, I doe now in some sort rejoyce at the unpromisingnesse of my Condition. **1727** BAILEY (vol. II), *Inauspiciousness*, unpromisingness.

un'promisingly, *adv.* (UN-1 11; cf. prec.)
1848 DICKENS *Dombey* xiii, Looking over his white cravat, as unpromisingly as Mr. Dombey himself could have looked.

unpro'motable, *a.* (UN-1 7 b.)
1836 CARLYLE *Corr. w. Emerson* (1883) I. 103, I suppose there is no more unpromotable, unappointable man now living in England than I.

unpro'moted, *ppl. a.* (UN-1 8.)
[**1775** ASH.] **1801** W. TAYLOR in Robberds *Mem.* (1843) I. 381 You must turn over the *Critical* to us unpromoted politicians.

un'prompted, *ppl. a.* (UN-1 8.)
1659 W. CHAMBERLAYNE *Pharon.* IV. iv. 32 To ask The way; for more his youth's unprompted fear Expects not there. *c* **1700** CONGREVE *To Cynthia* Wks. 1730 III. 291 And my tongue talks, unprompted by my heart. **1761** GLOVER *Medea* IV. i, Jason would have come Uncall'd, unprompted, but by love alone. **1810** CRABBE *Borough* x. 100 Then may you call in aid the moderate glass, But let it slowly and unprompted pass. **1860** TYNDALL *Glac.* I. 169 A respect for him, which this unprompted idea of his augmented.

un'promptly, *adv.* (UN-1 11.)
1837 CARLYLE *Fr. Rev.* II. II. vi, The Mutineer deputies vanish, not unpromptly.

un'promulgated, *ppl. a.* (UN-1 8.)
[**1775** ASH.] **1802-12** BENTHAM *Ration. Judic. Evid.* (1827) II. 474 Every law unpromulgated is, moreover, an Act of tyranny. **1836** J. GILBERT *Chr. Atonem.* ix. 387 The unpromulgated law of nature.

unpro'mulged, *ppl. a.* (UN-1 8.)
[**1775** ASH.] **1832** AUSTIN *Outl. Lect. Jurispr.* p. viii, Unwritten law, or unpromulged law, is law which flows immediately from some subordinate source.

un'prone, *a.* (UN-1 7.)
1611 *Coryat's Crudities* e i, Vlysses had a wife to lust vnprone. **1883** WRIGHT *Scientific Dogmatism* 9 The vain deceit which Philosophy was not unprone to keep company with.

unpro'nounce, *v.* (UN-2 3.)
1745 *Matrimony, pro & con.* 3 Could his loath'd Fair-One unpronounce 'I will', Not Worlds shou'd buy him to a Thing so ill.

unpro'nounceable, *a.* (UN-1 7 b.)
1831 SCOTT *Ct. Rob.* ii, Foreigners bearing unpronounceable names. **1863** MISS BRADDON *Aurora Floyd* xviii, Hock, the name of which was in fourteen unpronounceable syllables. **1889** DOYLE *Micah Clarke* xviii, A score of unpronounceable fights in the Styrian Alps.

unpro'nounced, *ppl. a.* [UN-1 8.]
1. Unuttered, unspoken.
[**1586** in *Bk. Univ. Kirk Scotl.* (1839) 298 We hold the said proces and sentence as unled, undecydit or pronuncit.] **1611** COTGR. s.v. *Cet*, Those [words] which begin..with *H* vnpronounced. **1628** MILTON *Vac. Exerc.* 4 Hail native Language, that..mad'st imperfect words with childish tripps, Half unpronounc't, slide through my infant-lipps. **1796** MME. D'ARBLAY *Camilla* V. 35 He wanted her to seize his meaning unpronounced.
2. Not prominent or distinct.
1863 DANA *Man. Geol.* 748 Although the grand systems in Zoology are unpronounced, there are still faint indications of them generally observable.

un'prop, *v.* (UN-2 4.)
1611 COTGR., *Destamper*, to vnprop; to take the tressles from. **1676** HOBBES *Iliad* II. 137 [They] strait unpropt their Ships. **1717** *Entertainer* No. 5. 29 Nor can they be assured their own Minions..may not more unprop the Throne, than guard it. **1897** P. WARUNG *Tales Old Régime* 114 "Ardy, jest unprop West!" Hardy obeyed, and lifted the cadaver to the centre of the chamber.

unpro'pense, *a.* [UN-1 7.] Unbiassed.
1640-1 LD. DIGBY *Parl. Sp.* 9 Feb. 17 To preserve an equall and un-propense judgment.

un'proper, *a.* Now *rare.* [UN-1 7, 5 b.]
†1. = IMPROPER *a.* 1. *Obs.*
c **1380** WYCLIF *Sel. Wks.* II. 269 We seen now bi a myror, in fer siȝt, and unpropre, but we shulen se after in blis þe firste trouþe face to face. **14..** *Voc.* in Wr.-Wülcker 589 *Improprium*, unpropre. **1594** BLUNDEVIL *Exerc.* I. xxii. (1597) 23 b, The vnproper [compound musical proportion] is, when to 3 numbers giuen, 2 other seuerall numbers are ioyned [etc.]. *a* **1619** FOTHERBY *Atheom.* I. i. §5 (1622) 8 So that Demonstrations are here vnproper and vnprofitable. **1661** CAMPION *Counterpoint* II. 122 The last close being to be made in the greater or sharp third, is unproper.
†b. *spec.* Of language. *Obs.*
c **1449** PECOCK *Repr.* I. v. 27 Bi vnpropre maner of speche and bi figure. *Ibid.*, In this present purpos of grounding and of the vnpropir speking vsid ther upon. **1550** VERON *Godly Saiyngs* B iv b, An abused and an vnpropre speache. *c* **1568** ASCHAM *Scholem.* II. (Arb.) 87 To traine his Scholler to a iudgement, in cutting out..ouer old and vnproper wordes. **1607** MARKHAM *Cavel.* II. xix. 203 Speaking of these loftie ayres, hee calles them Cariering horses; an epithiton most vnproper.
2. = IMPROPER *a.* 2. Now *dial.*
1581 MULCASTER *Positions* xxxix. 221 Ignorance..will cause them selues to be their owne Gnatoes, a most vnproper part, to be seene vpon a stage, when [etc.]. **1605** CAMDEN *Rem.* 14 It will not be vnproper I hope to this purpose if I note out of the epistles of..Busbequius. *a* **1659** OSBORNE *Piso & Vindex* Wks. (1673) 373 An endeavour no less indecent for men of Honour, than unproper for a Tyrant. **1678** MOXON *Mech. Exerc.* vi. 101 The use of which ..is unproper for me to meddle with in this Place. **1773** JOHNSON (ed. 4), *Unproper*,..unfit, not right. **1869-** in various dialect glossaries, etc.
3. = IMPROPER *a.* 3. *rare.*
1868 MRS. WHITNEY *P. Strong* ix, As foolish and happy and unproper as one pleases.
†4. = IMPROPER *a.* 4. *Obs.*
1604 SHAKS. *Oth.* IV. i. 69 Millions..nightly lye in those vnproper beds, Which they dare sweare peculiar.

†**un'properly,** *adv.* *Obs.* [UN-1 11, 5 b.] Improperly. (Freq. *c* 1560–*c* 1650.)
a. In respect of the use of words.
c **1340** HAMPOLE *Pr. Consc.* 8129 Ffor if endlesnes any end moght hald, þan war it endlesnes unproperly cald. **1398** TREVISA *Barth. De P.R.* v. xxxii. (Bodl. MS.), It is vnpropirliche seide þat oþer bestes haue backes. *a* **1425** tr. *Arderne's Treat. Fistula*, etc. 55 þai ar called emeroydez, bot neþerlez vnproperly. *a* **1470** H. PARKER *Dives & Pauper* (W. de W. 1496) I. xiii. 45/2 They take that Dulia full largely, and full unproprely. **1553** T. WILSON *Rhet.* 93 Long talke, and small matter, are spoken vnproperly, for we cannot measure either talke or matter by length or breadth. **1579** FULKE *Heskins' Parl.* 100 This worde sacrifice, is either taken properly, or vnproperly, and figuratiuely. **1636** M. WALBANCKE in *Ann. Dubrensia* (1877) 3 You to whom I may not unpropperly give the denomination of an Hero. **1678** MOXON *Mech. Exerc.* v. 95 They..say..'Lay a kerf in that piece of Stuff'; and sometimes, (but most unproperly,) 'Cut, or Slit that piece of Stuff'.
b. In other contexts.
1561 T. NORTON *Calvin's Inst.* II. 153 Those thinges yt were done in his nature of man, are vnproperly, & yet not without reason, geuen to hys Godhed. **1577** tr. *Bullinger's Decades* 463 Iustification is somtimes somewhat vn-properly attributed to workes. **1613** PURCHAS *Pilgrimage* I. viii. 41 A part of the hill Taurus (unproperly ascribed to Caucasus). **1683** MOXON *Mech. Exerc., Printing* ii. ¶2 They commonly, but unproperly, imploy Joyners to make them.

†**un'properness.** *Obs.* [UN-1 12, 5 b.] Lack of propriety or appropriateness.
1561 T. NORTON *Calvin's Inst.* IV. xix. 148 b, So that a godly sense be kept, although there be some vnpropernesse in the speaking. **1581** PETTIE tr. *Guazzo's Civ. Conv.* I. (1586) 23 b, You shall offende Boccace, rather with the vnpropernesse, then with the vnusualnesse of words. **1652** SPARKE *Prim. Devot.* 217 Their insufficiency..and unproperness for such imployment. **1692** TRYON *Gd. House-w.* i. (ed. 2) 8 The unproperness and contrariety of these Prescriptions to the end intended.

un'propertied, *ppl. a.* (UN-1 8.)
1793 ANNA SEWARD *Lett.* (1811) III. 217 The protecting influence of represented property, extending to the unpropertied. **1794** *Ibid.* 369 The ignorant and unpropertied mass of people. **1886** W. GRAHAM *Soc. Problem* 335 Since under it there is no safety for the unpropertied man. [Freq. in recent use.]

un'prophesiable, *a.* (UN-1 7 b.)
1883 LOWELL *Rich. III*, Latest Lit. Ess. (1891) 122 Like those pulses of pale flame with which the sky throbs at unprophesiable intervals.

unpro'phetic, *a.* (UN-1 7.)
1725 POPE *Odyss.* XXII. 13 Wretch that he was, of unprophetic soul! **1728** SAVAGE *Bastard* 47 Thus unprophetic, lately misinspir'd, I sung. **1821** SHELLEY *Ginevra* 124 Un-prophetic of the coming hours, The matin winds..awaken The earth. **1843** CARLYLE *Past & Pr.* II. viii, Alas, ye *un*-prophetic..! **1886** TENNYSON *Opening Indian & Col. Exh.* iii, Unprophetic rulers they.

unpro'phetical, *a.* (UN-1 7.)
1743 ELLIS *Knowl. Div. Things* 254 How unprophetical would it be, to say they should some time know what they already knew?

unpro'phetically, *adv.* (UN-1 11.)
1861 T. WRIGHT in *Pol. Poems* II. p. xxvii, Elmham warns the king (not unprophetically) of the..uncertain character of human life.

†**unpro'pice,** *a.* *Obs.*−1 [UN-1 7.] Unpropitious.
a **1529** SKELTON *Bk. 3 Fooles* Wks. 1843 I. 200 Shee is so debylyte, colde, vnpropyce, vnnaturall, and vndyscurrente.

unpro'pitiable, *a.* (UN-1 7 b.)
[**1775** ASH.] **1891** *Academy* 28 Mar. 296/1 That unpropitiable avenger who waits on secular misconduct.

unpro'pitious, *a.* (UN-1 7.)
1699 POMFRET *To Another Friend* 12 Beneath the pond'rous Weight Of angry Stars, and unpropitious Fate. **1702** ADDISON *Dial. Medals* ii. (1726) 65 Ye sue the unpropitious maid in vain. **1776** MICKLE *Camoen's Lusiad* Introd. 149 In the unpropitious age of a Cromwell. **1847** HELPS *Friends in C.* I. 39 The whole life appears to be shut up in the one unpropitious affection. **1875** JOWETT *Plato* (ed. 2) III. 425 Sleep and exercise are unpropitious to learning.
Hence **unpro'pitiousness.**
1844 W. H. SMYTH *Cycle Celestial Obj.* II. 6 Had this been done, every notion of stellar unpropitiousness and malevolence must have vanished.

unpro'pitiously, *adv.* (UN-1 11.)
1602 MARSTON *Ant. & Mel.* II, My legge is not altogether unpropitiously shap't. There's a word: unpropitiously? I thinke I shall speake unpropitiously as well as any courtier in Italy.

unpro'portion. [UN-1 12, 5 b.] Disproportion.
1844 KINGLAKE *Eothen* xvii. 265 You stare at the wide unproportion between this slender Company, and the boundless plains of sand.

†**unpro'portionable,** *a.* *Obs.* [UN-1 7 b, 5 b.] Disproportionate. Also const. *to*, or (rarely) *with*. (Common in 17th c.)
1586 T. B. *La Primaud. Fr. Acad.* I. 672 Too much increase and unproportionable growth..procureth the change and ruine of commonwealthes. **1613** PURCHAS *Pilgrimage* (1614) 39 The roofe is not to be thought vnproportionable. **1650** FULLER *Pisgah* v. xi. 163 To give a thing and take a thing is unproportionable with his [*sc.* God's] proceedings. **1697** C. LESLIE *Snake in Grass* (ed. 2) Advert., The Preface was an Eye-Sore, because of its Length, unproportionable to the Book. **1704** N. N. tr. *Boccalini's Advts. from Parnass.* III. 255 Some of her limbs swell to an unproportionable Bulk. **1766** *Compl. Farmer* s.v. *Surveying*, If you protract.., you will put your closes into unproportionable shapes.
Hence †**unpro'portionableness.** *Obs.*
1653 GAUDEN *Hierasp.* 74 This unproportionableness of the Creators dealing with man. **1659** —— *Tears Ch.* 586 The unproportionableness of any other Church-government than a right Episcopacy to the temper of England.

†**unpro'portionably**, *adv. Obs.* [UN-¹ 11; cf. prec.] Disproportionately.

1558–9 ABP. PARKER *Corr.* (Parker Soc.) 62 And now for the upholding of two or three years more of life, to heap unproportionably, I count it madness. **1594** R. ASHLEY tr. *Loys le Roy* 2 Being duely tempered for generation, and vnproportionably distempered for corruption. **1626** BACON *Sylva* §360 A Chameleon is a Creature about the Bignesse of an Ordinary Lizard: His Head vnproportionably bigge. **1641** J. JACKSON *True Evang. T.* III. 166 The Gospell too bids us 'not bee unequally yoaked,' but what is it to be unproportionably yoaked, if this bee not? **1790** *Phil. Trans.* LXXX. 355 Though nature..may permit a particular species of animal to become so unproportionably numerous. **1819** W. S. ROSE *Lett. fr. N. Italy* II. 172 There is, perhaps, no offence which is so unproportionably punished.

unpro'portional, *a.* (UN-¹ 7.)

1714 DERHAM *Prelim. Disc. to Astro-Theol.* (1726) p. xiii, Which are Motions [of the moon, etc.] so unproportional,.. that [they] are sufficient to subvert the whole Hypothesis.

unproportio'nality. (UN-¹ 12.)

1818 BENTHAM *Ch. Eng., Catech. Exam.* 273 Uncertainty, unproportionality, abstractiveness.., and degradingness.

unpro'portionally, *adv.* (UN-¹ 11.)

1820 HOGG *Tales & Sk.* (1836) II. 204 The next three volumes were..unproportionally thick.

unpro'portionate, *a.* Now *rare.* [UN-¹ 7, 5 b.] Disproportionate, unproportioned.

1581 MULCASTER *Positions* xxx. 109 The whole bodie..is anoyed with vnproportionate heat. **1601** DANIEL *Civ. Wars* VI. xxviii, No swelling member, vnproportionate, Growne out of forme. **1651** H. MORE *Second Lash* in *Enthus. Tri.*, etc. (1656) 184 Where is my Fancie distorted, unproportionate, unproper? **1679** J. GOODMAN *Penit. Pard.* III. v. 336 That the powers and objects are mis-matched and unproportionate to each other. **1897** *Advance* (Chicago) 21 Jan. 77 Unsound, unproportionate teachings.

So **unpro'portionately** *adv.*, **-ness.**

1495 *Trevisa's Barth. De P.R.* VII. xx. p iij b/2 A man is byrefte.. of his syght somtyme..for vnproporcyonat[n]es of the blacke of the eye to yᵉ spyryte of syghte. **1897** *Trans. Amer. Pediatric Soc.* IX. 22 The paralysis..progressing by degrees and sometimes unproportionately.

unpro'portioned, *ppl. a.* (UN-¹ 8, 5 b.)

c **1586** C'TESS PEMBROKE *Ps.* CXXXV. vii, What unproportion'd odds To thee, these idolls gold and silver beare? **1595** DANIEL *Civ. Wars* II. xix, Huge vnproportion'd mountaines. **1602** SHAKS. *Ham.* I. iii. 60 Giue thy thoughts no tongue, Nor any vnproportion'd thought his Act. **1650** BULWER *Anthropomet.* 186 Crook-back't men..are justly accounted unproportioned. **1712** ATTERBURY *Serm.* (1737) IV. 216 Such a mock worship,..how unproportioned it is to the Divine Nature. **1799** J. ROBERTSON *Agric. Perth* 231 A multitude of soldiers, unproportioned to the extent or fertility of Scotland. **1828** TENNYSON *Lover's Tale* I. 187 That porch, So unproportion'd to the dwelling-place.

unpro'posed, *ppl. a.* (UN-¹ 8.)

a **1700** DRYDEN (J.), The means are unpropos'd. **1884** *Imp. Dict.* IV. 513 The motion or candidate is as yet unproposed.

un'propped, *ppl. a.* (UN-¹ 8.)

1616 W. BROWNE *Brit. Past.* II. v. 342, I have beheld A widow vine stand, in a naked field,..Unpropt, unsuccoured, by stake or tree. **1675** OTWAY *Alcibiades* V. i, When success me to my wishes calls, I'll shake him off, and then unpropt he falls. **1700** DRYDEN *Meleager & Atalanta* 132 The Nerves no more sustain The Bulk; the Bulk unprop'd, falls headlong on the Plain. **1802–12** BENTHAM *Ration. Judic. Evid.* (1827) I. 396 The ceremony of an oath in its pure state, unpropped by that support. **1827** POLLOK *Course T.* II. 740 He..tried to stand Alone, unpropped, to be obliged to none.

unpro'scribable, *a.* (UN-¹ 7 b.)

1817 LADY MORGAN *France* III. (1818) I. 310 The unproscribable influence of fashion and beauty.

unpro'scribed, *ppl. a.* (UN-¹ 8.)

[**1775** ASH.] **1840** TYTLER *Hist. Scot.* (1864) III. 294 Not a baron who espoused the cause of the queen would have been left unproscribed.

un'prosecuted, *ppl. a.* (UN-¹ 8.)

1655 MOUFET & BENNET *Health's Improv.* xvi. 139 Tasting of every..part of mans body, not leaving the nails unprosecuted. **1665** BOYLE *Occas. Refl.* V. vi. 164 To make him leave his Endeavours unprosecuted. **1802–12** BENTHAM *Ration. Judic. Evid.* (1827) V. 97 The example is bad, when a man supposed to be guilty is seen to remain unprosecuted.

un'proselyte, *v.* (UN-² 3.)

1655 FULLER *Ch. Hist.* X. iv. §8. 63 It happily unproselyted some inclinable to his Opinions.

unpro'sodian, *a.* (UN-¹ 7.)

1836 MOORE *Mem.* (1856) VII. 160 Such an unprosodian school as Dublin College then was.

unpro'spected, *ppl. a.* (UN-¹ 8.)

1882 *U.S. Rep. Prec. Met.* 79 An unprospected part of the channel.

un'prosperable, *a.* (UN-¹ 7.)

1690 C. NESSE *O. & N. Test.* I. 298 Solitariness..is an unprofitable and unprosperable thing.

unpro'sperity. (UN-¹ 12, 5 b.)

a **1628** F. GREVIL *Sidney* (1652) 33 [He] left the success to his will, that governs the blinde prosperities and unprosperities of Chance. *Ibid.* 173 A perspective into vice, and the unprosperities of it. *a* **1843** SOUTHEY *Doctor* cxcvii. (1848) 525 The thriftless man..finds some satisfaction in imputing his un-prosperity to the Stars.

†**un'prosperly**, *adv. Obs.*⁻¹ [UN-¹ 11.] Unprosperously.

1608 P. GOLDING *Sleidane's Epit. Frossard* 62 The matter had falne out so vnprosperly before.

un'prosperous, *a.* (UN-¹ 7, 5 b.)

a **1578** LINDESAY (Pitscottie) *Chron. Scot.* (S.T.S.) I. 257 The king heirand of his wnprosperous iournay. ? **1586** HOOKER *Answ. Travers' Supplic.* §5 Which vnprosperous beginning of a thing..did..disgrace that order in their conceit. **1631** GOUGE *God's Arrows* III. §57. 289 No marvell therefore that the warre..was unprosperous. **1665** BOYLE *Occas. Refl.* VI. i, Endeavours, which..are oft-times so un-prosperous. **1776** ADAM SMITH *W.N.* I. x. II. (1869) I. 139 That unprosperous race of men, commonly called men of letters. **1861** M. ARNOLD *Pop. Educ. France* 185 Not that primary instruction is unprosperous in the Canton of Vaud. **1884** PEARSON in *Law Rep.* 26 *Chanc. Div.* 676 The tenant for life received nothing from the unprosperous year, 1881.

un'prosperously, *adv.* (UN-¹ 11; cf. prec.)

1630 *Camden's Hist. Eliz.* II. 117 Two famous Pilots.. sought as vnprosperously to discouer a neere way to East-India. **1650** JER. TAYLOR *Holy Living* ii. §6. 153 When a Prince fights justly, and yet unprosperously. **1663** BOYLE *Usef. Exp. Nat. Philos.* II. i. 10 It is possible to be safely made, though many..have but unprosperously attempted it. **1848** THACKERAY *Van. Fair* lvii, Her life, begun not unprosperously, had come down to..a long ignoble bondage. **1876** MISS YONGE *Womankind* xxxii, Love affairs come early and unprosperously.

un'prosperousness. (UN-¹ 12.)

a **1660** HAMMOND *Serm.* Wks. 1683 IV. 492 The unprosperousness of the arm of flesh. **1698** FRYER *Acc. E. India & P.* 88 The True Cause of the Unprosperousness of the Ancient Undertakers. **1741** RICHARDSON *Pamela* III. 117 After a Series of Unprosperousness in all they undertook.

un'prostitute, *ppl. a.* (UN-¹ 8 b; cf. next.)

1606 BIRNIE *Kirk-buriall* (1833) 28 Under these three conditions (to wit, of amplitude, ornacy, and vnprostitude [*sic*] chastity to any other vse). **1681** *Whole Duty Nations* 24 Retaining their Honour untouch'd,..and presenting to the Honour of Christianity a Supremacy unprostitute.

un'prostituted, *ppl. a.* (UN-¹ 8.)

1721 AMHERST *Terræ Fil.* No. 41 (1726) 213 Some future unprostituted, ungarbled history of a rebellion. **1753** *Gray's Inn Jrnl.* No. 29 (1756) I. 190 That unprostituted, dignified Independence, which will always do Honour to the Man. **1785** *Rolliad, Prob. Odes* xix. 96 With unprostituted pen,.. unmov'd by gain, I'll call thee..'most chaste of men'.

unpro'tected, *ppl. a.* (UN-¹ 8.)

a **1593** MARLOWE *Ovid's Elegies* II. ii. 12 Nor is her husband wise, what neede defence When vn-protected ther is no expence? **1597** HOOKER *Eccl. Pol.* V. i. §4 Such euils.. as men either destitute of grace diuine may commit, or vnprotected from aboue, indure. **1748** RICHARDSON *Clarissa* VII. 97 A defenceless unprotected woman. **1791** MRS. RADCLIFFE *Rom. Forest* iv, The idea of leaving his family unprotected. **1844** NOAD *Electricity* (ed. 2) 429 It is necessary to observe..that the lamps were unprotected. **1879** LUBBOCK *Sci. Lect.* ii. 41 It might be an advantage to a flower which was quite unprotected, to open early for the bees.

Hence **unpro'tectedly** *adv.*, **-ness.**

1823 *Blackw. Mag.* XIV. 461 Seeing their friends massacred unprotectedly all round them. **1824** MISS MITFORD *Village* Ser. I. 13 His unprotectedness, his utter defencelessness. **1895** MEREDITH *Amazing Marriage* xlvi, Lady Arpington's mention of Henrietta's unprotectedness.

un'protestant, *a.* (UN-¹ 7.)

1839 J. S. MILL in *Westm. Rev.* Apr. 504 The unprotestant and unchristian doctrines..which are extensively professed. **1841** WISEMAN *Remarks Lett. fr. Palmer* 53 How moderate, how un-Protestant, is the language of St. Epiphanius! **1881** W. R. SMITH *Old Test. in Jew. Ch.* i. 7 This point of view is, however, thoroughly unprotestant.

un'protestantize, *v.* (UN-² 6 c.)

1833 R. H. FROUDE *Rem.* (1838) I. 332, I wish you could get to know something of S. and W., and un--ise, un-Protestantise, un-Miltonise them. **1842** G. S. FABER *Prov. Lett.* (1844) II. 291 We must unprotestantise the National Church. **1895** *Bulwark* Sept. 98/1 Mr. Gladstone and Lord Salisbury..have vied with each other in unprotestantising the Church of England.

Hence **un'protestantizing** *vbl. sb.* and *ppl. a.*

1841 *British Critic* July 45 The unprotestantizing..of the national Church. **1847** H. MILLER *First Impr. Eng.* xiii. 244 The unprotestantizing leaven introduced into the mass of the English Establishment.

un'protestantlike, *a.* (UN-¹ 7 c.)

1641 MILTON *Animadv.* 35 Not caring otherwise to answer this un-Protestant-like Objection.

unpro'truded, *ppl. a.* (UN-¹ 8.)

[**1775** ASH.] **1777** PENNANT *Brit. Zool.* (ed. 4) IV. 9 Doctor Baster..counted 12,444 eggs under the tail, besides those that remained in the body unprotruded. **1812** *Examiner* 24 Aug. 541/2 You left scarcely one of his faults unprotruded on inspection.

unpro'trusive, *a.* (UN-¹ 7.)

1825 COLERIDGE *Aids Refl.* 148 *note*, The unprotrusive and unintellected Convolutes of the Brain.

un'proud, *a.* (UN-¹ 7.)

1570 LEVINS *Manip.* 217 Vnproude, *inglorius.* **1666** J. SERGEANT *Let. Thanks* 20 'Tis your weak and unproud conjecture. **1820** L. HUNT *Indicator* No. 16 (1822) I. 123 They spoke to me more familiarly than usual, and yet somehow or other, didn't seem so kind nor so *un*-proud. **1900** *Academy* 28 July 75 He is not unconscious nor unproud of this freedom.

un'provable, *a.* [UN-¹ 7 b.]

1. Incapable of being proved.

c **1425** WYNTOUN *Cron.* IX. xix. 2042 Eftyr þat he had beyn ..in exile Be fenȝheid fals suspicion, And all wnprowabil be resson. **1553** GRIMALDE *Cicero's Offices* II. (1556) 65 So we, dissenting from them, do saie again some thinges be prouable, some vnprouable. **1609** BP. HALL *Dissuas. Poperie* 35 A Religion, that depends wholly vpon nice and poore vncertainties, and vnproueable supposals. **1677** GILPIN *Demonol.* II. vii. 325 Though Satan's injections of Non-election be altogether unproveable. **1825** BENTHAM *Offic. Apt. Maximized, Indic.* (1830) 79 By an unpunishable and unprovable, though solemn act of insincerity. **1883** MYERS *Ess., Mod., Mazzini* (1885) 60 Unprovable speculations about the firmament.

†**2.** Incapable of succeeding. *Obs.*⁻¹

1653 BLITHE *Eng. Improver Impr.* xxiv. 156 Avoid the getting of Eaten, Bitten, Rough, and Brushy, all being un-proveable sets.

Hence **unprova'bility, -ableness.**

a **1881** BARRATT *Phys. Metempiric* (1883) 23 The unproveability of the hypothesis. **1883** *Contemp. Rev.* Nov. 697 There is always a great deal of vagueness, and..of unprovableness, in charges of immorality against a whole race.

†**un'prove**, *v. Obs.* [UN-² 3, 7. Cf. MDu. *ontproeven.*]

1. *trans.* To disprove; to deny or reject.

13.. *Gosp. Nicod.* 591 His folk vnproues him king, And kingdom claymes he. *c* **1440** *Promp. Parv.* 366/2 Onprevyn, or imprevyn,..*improbo.* *c* **1449** PECOCK *Repr.* I. xviii. 104 Thei schulen suffice forto vnproue this iiijᵉ opinioun here, as thei vnproven the ijᵉ opinioun there.

2. *intr.* To disapprove.

1528 GARDINER in Pocock *Rec. Reform.* (1870) I. 104 His holiness,..neither approving ne unproving, said, he had sent it to the cardinal.

Hence †**un'proving** *vbl. sb. Obs.*

c **1449** PECOCK *Repr.* IV. iii. 430 Thus miche is ynowȝ for vnprouyng of the seid skile.

un'proved, *ppl. a.* [UN-¹ 8.]

†**1.** Not put to proof or trial; untried. *Obs.*

c **1440** *Pallad. on Husb* I. 236 Preue eek thonpreued greyne afore eschaunge. *c* **1445** PECOCK *Donet* 7 Y wote weel þat.. scant ynouȝ oon leef schulde stonde vnprovid or colowrabily vnrebukid. **1550** BALDWIN *Mor. Philos.* K. iiij, Proue not thy frende wyth dammage, nor vse thou hym vnproued. **1561** B. GOOGE *Palingenius' Zodiac Life* I. A ij b, Willing to trede vnproued pathes that haue not yet ben gon. **1590** SPENSER *F.Q.* I. vii. 47 For to find a fresh vnproued knight.

2. Not demonstrated to be true or genuine.

1532 MORE *Confut. Tindale* Wks. 609/2 Both is his purpose on his part vnproued, & the contrarye to hym proued. **1533** FRITH *Answ. More* G 8, His mastership hathe lefte one thinge vnproued. **1628** DONNE *Serm.* (1640) 291 The proofe lies on their side; and it rests yet unproved. **1693** DRYDEN *Juvenal* VI. 313 Prov'd, or unprov'd, the Crime, the Villain dies. **1843** J. H. NEWMAN *Miracles* 63 A fact is not disproved, because the testimony is..insufficient, it is only unproved. **1866** GEO. ELIOT *F. Holt* xvii, The essence of bribery is that it should be legally proved; there is not such a thing..as unproved bribery. **1874** MAHAFFY *Social Life Greece* 335 However unproved or doubtful this ancient creed.

Hence **un'provedness.**

a **1400–50** *Alexander* 1019 For barnes in þar bignes it baldis þam mekill, Oft with vnprouednes in presse to pas out of lyfe.

un'proven, *ppl. a.* [UN-¹ 8 b.] = prec. 2.

1853 *Westm. Rev.* April 475 We do not expect the preacher to prove anything before unproven. **1875** JOWETT *Plato* (ed. 2) III. 149 Plato does not like to make an assertion which is unproven.

unpro'vide, *v.* (UN-² 3. Cf. DISPROVIDE *v.*)

1530 PALSGR. 768/2, I unprovyde, *Je despouruoys.* **1604** SHAKS. *Oth.* IV. i. 218 Ile not expostulate with her; least her body and beautie vnprouide my mind againe. **1793** A. MURPHY *Tacitus* I. 339 Increasing honours, he had no doubt, would unprovide his mind, and..produce the genuine features of his character.

unpro'vided, *ppl. a.* [UN-¹ 8, 5 b.]

1. Not furnished, supplied, or equipped (with something): **a.** Const. *of* (now *rare* or *Obs.*) or *with.*

1523 LD. BERNERS *Froiss.* I. cccxxi. 498 The countre was voyde, and vnprouyded of men of warre. **1579** SPENSER *Sheph. Cal.* May 114 The shepheards God so wel them guided, That of nought they were vnprouided. **1600** SURFLET *Countrie Farme* I. xvi. 105 The countrie farme being for the most part vnprouided of the benefits and easements of water. **1673** [R. LEIGH] *Transp. Reh.* 45 It being a thing wholly unlikely that the wise Astragon should be unprovided of such excellent authors. **1720** SWIFT *Fates of Clergymen* Wks. 1755 II. II. 22 Courts are seldom unprovided of persons under this character. **1735** BERKELEY in Fraser *Life* (1871) vii. 241 Those places where they are unprovided with churches. **1785** T. BALGUY *Disc.* 174 Men, whose understandings are..unprovided of the principles of knowledge. **1844** KINGLAKE *Eothen* viii, Assailants.. unprovided with regular means of attack. **1875** JOWETT *Plato* (ed. 2) III. 102 The actual drone is unprovided by nature with a sting.

b. Without const. Also *for* (a person, etc.).

(*a*) *a* **1586** SIDNEY *Arcadia* II. xii, And whose good haps do leave him unprovided, Condoling cause of friendship he will borrow. **1603** G. POWEL *Papist's Reas. for Toleration* 127 Whereby they haue left the Ministrie so marveilously vn-prouided and so beggerly. **1627** CAPT. SMITH *Seaman's Gram.* xii. 56 Neither should her Gunroome be vnprouided: not manned like a Merchant-man. **1760–72** H. BROOKE *Fool of Qual.* (1809) III. 78 Since you will go, you must not go unprovided. **1818** SCOTT *Br. Lamm.* xxv, We are totally and literally unprovided [*sc.* with provisions]. **1833** MACAULAY

Ess., War Succession in Spain ⁋12 The arsenals were deserted. The magazines were unprovided.
(*b*) **1530** PALSGR. 768/2 He shalbe hertely welcome, but I am yet unprovyded for him. **1603** BRETON *Mad World* Wks. (Grosart) II. 10/1 He..led me into his house, the doore open, as unfearefull of theeves, as vnprovided for strangers. **1725** DE FOE *Voy. round World* (1840) 333 As for going by water, that they were unprovided for.
c. Not provided for. (Cf. 4.)
1640 HABINGTON *Edw. IV*, 33 The inconvenience of raising a widow to his bed, who could bring nothing with her but her poverty, and an unprovided issue. **1892** CHILD *Ballads* IV. 391/2 The bower of an unprovided seamstress.
2. Not in a state of preparation or readiness; unprepared (to resist attack, make reply, etc.).
1525 LD. BERNERS *Froiss.* II. xxxiii. 41/2 So that whan oure enemyes come, let them nat fynde vs vnprouided. **1578** *Chr. Prayers* in *Priv. Prayers* (1851) 447 Take me not unawares and unprovided to thy judgment-seat. **1599** SHAKS. *Hen. V*, IV. i. 183 If they dye vnprouided. **1615** BRATHWAIT *Strappado*, etc. (1878) 334 Alas, faire queene, why should you thus assault the vnprouided fortresse of mine hart? **1647** COTTERELL *Davila's Hist. France* I. 43 The armed men..appearing on a sudden.., the King being found un-provided, and the Court disarmed. **1722** DE FOE *Plague* (1756) 140 The unprovided Condition that..the People were in at the first coming of the Calamity. **1805** SOUTHEY *Madoc in Azt.* II. 231 So saying, I left The astonish'd men, whose unprovided minds Fail'd them. **1819** SHELLEY *Cenci* III. i. 377 You are unprovided where to fly, How to excuse or to conceal.
3. Against which provision has not (or cannot) be made; unforeseen.
1514 BARCLAY *Cyt. & Uplondyshm.* (Percy Soc.) 9 Nought is more noysom..Than sodayne tempeste, and unprovyded colde. **1536** *Goodly Primer, Litany* Rivb, Sodeyn & vn-prouided dethe. **1627** C. MAGEOGHAGAN tr. *Ann. Clonmacnois* 75 The Emperor dyed of a sudaine and unprovided death. **1660** *Trial Regic.* 20 You must give your direct Answer, Guilty, or Not guilty. You cannot say, it is sudden, or unprovided. You spend time in vain. **1739** in *Cath. Rec. Soc. Publ.* VIII. 263 Her Death,..by the holy life she led, was not unprovided. **1817** F. LEWIS in *Parl. Debates* 1361 Very heavy expenses..under the head called 'unprovided services,' which ought to comprise nothing except what could not possibly be foreseen. **1841** ALISON *Hist. Eur.* IX. lxxii. 702 The unprovided expenditure of the year.
4. Not provided *for*. (Cf. 1 c.)
1575 GASCOIGNE *Glasse of Govt.* II. v, If ever I live to enherit Phylocalus, then Eccho shall not be unprovided for. **1647** CLARENDON *Hist. Reb.* I. §5 The necessary Subsistence of the household was provided for. **1676** TEMPLE *Let. to Sir J. Williamson* Wks. 1720 II. 413 They cannot, upon that Pretence, be pressed to Things..wholly unprovided for by the very Letter of the Treaty. **1794** S. WILLIAMS *Vermont* 239 Many officers..were then unprovided for. **1839** *John Bull* 15 Sept., The income upon which he and the unprovided for members of his family exist. **1897** *Outing* XXX. 376/2 Unprovided-for tasks are best decided by drawing lots.
5. Not furnished, supplied, or made ready.
1621 FLETCHER *Isl. Princess* I. ad fin., That's all That's un-provided,..The rest wee'l councel as we goe. **1726** LEONI *Alberti's Archit.* I. 21 b, You will have occasion for a great number of things.., and..if but one is unprovided, it may stop or spoil the whole Work.
Hence **unpro'videdly** *adv.*, **-ness.**
1567 *Reg. Privy Council Scot.* I. 522 He mycht *unprovidittie oppres..that innocent infant. **1652** URQUHART *Jewel* 112 Another young Lady..so unprovidedly was surprised. *a***1652** BROME *Covent Garden Weeded* II. ii, My unsetledneesse and *unprovidednesse..may well excuse us all. **1861** [MRS. A. J. PENNY] *Romance Dull Life* xl. 296 From the fear of unprovidedness during her stay in this great house.

un'providenced, *ppl. a.* (UN-¹ 8.)
*a***1661** FULLER *Worthies* I. (1662) 57 If those must be accounted unfortunate (which I in the true meaning of the word must interpret unprovidenced) who swim not in equal Plenty with others.

†**un'provident,** *a. Obs.* [UN-¹ 7, 5 b.] Improvident; incautious.
1572 BUCHANAN *Detection of Mary* (1727) 71 Ane Hous..prouydit for ane ȝoung Gentilman unprouydent be ȝouth. *c***1600** SHAKS. *Sonn.* x, Deny that thou bear'st loue to any, Who for thy selfe art so vnprouident. **1619** J. KING *Serm.*, etc. 39 Hath it made you proud,..and improvident, and un-provident against your enemies? **1658** J. WEBB *Cleopatra* VIII. II. 55 Must the unfortunate Alcamenes be ignorant, whence this unprovident ruine comes?

unprovi'dential, *a.* (UN-¹ 7, 5 b.)
1813 T. BUSBY *Lucretius* II. VI. Comm. p. x, Lucretius, reasoning from the unprovidential casualities of thunder, denies that it springs from the hand of Jupiter. **1837** LYTTON *Athens* I. 21 [He] reclaimed his barbarous subjects from a wandering and unprovidential life.

†**un'providently,** *adv. Obs.* (UN-¹ 11, 5 b.)
1611 FLORIO, *Improuidamente*, vnprouidently. **1805** FORSYTH *Beauties Scotl.* III. 354 Forests..unprovidently and wastefully destroyed.

un'proving, *ppl. a.* (UN-¹ 10.)
1640 BP. HALL *Episc.* III. §2 Since this one litigious, and unproving text is the onely place in the whole New Testament, that can beare any pretence for the lay-Presbytery. **1641** —— *Def. Humble Remonstr.* 118 Your unproving illustrations, and unregardable testimonies.

†**unpro'vised,** *ppl. a. Sc. Obs.* [UN-¹ 8, 5 b.] Unforeseen; unconsidered.
*c***1480** HENRYSON *Fables, Fox & Wolf* 162 This suddand deith and vnprouysit end Of this fals Tod. **1533** BELLENDEN *Livy* I. ii. (S.T.S.) I. 19 He wald nocht opin ane haisty and vnprovisit mater.

Hence †**unpro'visedly** *adv. Obs.*
1513 DOUGLAS *Æneid* VI. iii. 28 With his bois trump as he Went vnprowysitlie blawand by the se. **1567** *Sc. Acts, Jas. VI* (1814) III. 27/2 Proceding to ane pretendit mariage with him suddandlie, and vnprouisitlie thairefter.

unpro'vision. (UN-¹ 12, 5 b.)
*a***1638** MEDE *Wks.* (1672) 231 Whatsoever..among the Beasts of the field..is.., by un-provision, of all others the most wretched and miserable.

unpro'visioned, *ppl. a.* (UN-¹ 8.)
1796 COLERIDGE *Lett.* (1895) 189, I shall be again afloat on the wide sea, unpiloted and unprovisioned. **1827** POLLOK *Course T.* II. 242 Choosing, thus unshipped, Uncompassed, unprovisioned,..To swim a sea of breadth immeasurable.

unpro'vocative, *a.* (UN-¹ 7.)
Frequent in recent use.
1821 LAMB *Elia* I. *Grace before Meat*, At a poor man's table, or at the simple and unprovocative repast of children. **1893** *Scribner's Mag.* June 747/2 As he placidly walked along, unprovocative of even passing curiosity.

unpro'vokable, *a.* (UN-¹ 7 b.)
1803 BENTHAM *Mem. & Corr.* Wks. 1843 X. 403 Better..would it be if your..principals were as placable, or rather as unprovokable.

unpro'voke, *v.* (UN-² 3.)
1605 SHAKS. *Macb.* II. iii. 32 Lecherie, Sir, it prouokes, and vnprouokes: it prouokes the desire, but it takes away the performance.

unpro'voked, *ppl. a.* (UN-¹ 8.)
1585 ABP. SANDYS *Serm.* xv. 264 The voluntarie and vn-prouoked operation of the spirite. **1641** BP. HALL *Answ. Vind. Smectymnuus* To Rdr. A 3, When..the Smectymnuans,..unprovoked, unthought of,..flye in my face, as men wrongfully accused. **1712** STEELE *Spect.* No. 427 ⁋2 This Heroine had..out-done the whole Sisterhood of Gossips, in..unprovoked Malice. **1759** STERNE *Tr. Shandy* II. xii, These unprovoked strokes at my uncle Toby's [hobby-horse]. **1819** SCOTT *Ivanhoe* xli, To discover ..who have been my unprovoked enemies. **1849** C. BRONTE *Shirley* xxiii, In answer to unprovoked insult.
Hence **unpro'vokedly** *adv.*, **-ness.**
1663 BOYLE *Usef. Exp. Nat. Philos.* I. v. 95 Galen..some-where *unprovokedly and causelessly enough derides Moses. **1781** T. DAVIES *Mem. Garrick* (ed. 3) I. 23 He was rudely and unprovokedly attacked by a boisterous man. **1864** CARLYLE *Fredk. Gt.* XVI. xii. IV. 455 His conduct..has nothing of bad, at least of unprovokedly bad. **1856** FABER *Creator & Creature* II. i, God's..tenderness,..His extraordinary *unprovokedness.

unpro'voking, *ppl. a.* (UN-¹ 10.)
1710 FLEETWOOD *Serm.* 7 To..dash against the Stones the innocent and un-provoking Children. **1759** STERNE *Tr. Shandy* II. xii, But to hurt a brother..so unprovoking,—and so unresenting;—'tis base. **1821** COBBETT *Rur. Rides* (1885) I. 38 It is no very unprovoking reflection.

†**un'prudence.** [UN-¹ 12, 5 b.] Imprudence.
1382 WYCLIF *Prov.* xiv. 8 The vnprudence of foolis [is] erring. **1533** BELLENDEN *Livy* II. xvi. (S.T.S.) I. 193, I drede þat sum thing be done by vnprudence or folie of my pepill. **1652** GAULE *Magastrom.* 239 Whether you shall become poor by..luxuriousnesse, unprudence.

†**un'prudent,** *a. Obs.* [UN-¹ 7, 5 b.] Imprudent; unwise.
1382 WYCLIF *Mark* vii. 18 So and ȝe ben vnprudent, or vnwyse. **1395** PURVEY *Remonstr.* (1851) 119 In this vnprudent geuinge [of the Sacrament]. **1412–20** LYDG. *Chron Troy* I. 3650 For to provide þei ben graceles, Ful vnprudent and wilful rekeles. **1611** SPEED *Hist. Gt. Brit.* IX. xi. 555/2 Peirs,..to establish his interest in the vnprudent Prince,..filled the Court with buffons.

unpru'dential, *a.* (UN-¹ 7, 5 b.)
1650 MILTON *Eikon.* (ed. 2) xxviii. 224 [This] were the most unwise and unprudential act as to civil goverment. **1685** D. GRANVILLE *Lett.* (Surtees, No. 37) 198, I thought it not unprudentiall so to do. *a***1832** BENTHAM *Deontol.* (1834) II. 101 Of evil contingent on prudential or unprudential conduct.

†**un'prudently,** *adv. Obs.*⁻¹ (UN-¹ 11, 5 b; cf. UNPRUDENT.)
1412–20 LYDG. *Chron. Troy* II. 1474, I wondre gretly..What auenture..Vnprudently meveth now þi kyng Vn-to me to make swiche a sonde.

un'pruned, *ppl. a.*¹ [UN-¹ 8 + PRUNE *v.*¹] Not smoothed with the beak.
1820 KEATS *Eve St. Agnes* xxxvii, A dove..with sick unpruned wing.

un'pruned, *ppl. a.*² [UN-¹ 8 + PRUNE *v.*²] Not trimmed by cutting or lopping.
1593 SHAKS. *Rich. II*, III. iv. 45 Her Fruit-trees all vn-pruin'd, her Hedges ruin'd. **1621** BURTON *Anat. Mel.* III. iii. I. ii. 673 If they [*sc.* women] be not curbed in time, as an vnproyned tree. **1649** OGILBY tr. *Virg., Bucol.* ii. (1684) 12 On th' Elm my unprun'd Vines neglected are. **1743** FRANCIS tr. *Hor., Epodes* xvi. 52 Where..Vines unprun'd their blushing Clusters yield. **1801** SOUTHEY *Thalaba* XII. xviii, The unpruned taper flares a longer flame. **1863** HAWTHORNE *Our Old Home* II. 24 The hedges grow in unpruned luxuriance. **1882** *Garden* 21 Jan. 49/3 An idea prevails that birds are not so likely to spoil an unpruned tree.
b. In fig. uses.
1588 SHAKS. *L.L.L.* IV. ii. 18 After his..vnpolished, vneducated, vnpruned, vntrained..fashion. **1619** MIDDLETON *Love & Antiq.* B 3, A Common-wealth That is vndrest, vnpruin'd, wilde in her health. **1628** FELTHAM *Resolves* II. xxviii. 89 No man ha's preheminence, but wishes to preserue it in vnpruned state. **1814** *Monthly Rev.* LXXIV. 308 Addison lives, but not undecaying, nor unpruned. **1878** *Masque Poets* 181 They let their unpruned fancies roll Round some old theme like hop-vines round a pole.

un'prying, *ppl. a.* (UN-¹ 10.)
1771 MRS. GRIFFITH *Hist. Lady Barton* II. 269 He..should wait upon him at..a respectful and unprying distance. **1803** *Forest of Hohenelbe* II. 215 The unprying few that composed her humble circle.

unpsycho'logical, *a.* (UN-¹ 7.)
1885 *Athenæum* 8 Aug. 170/2 Hence the first main division into unpsychological and psychological ethical theories.

un'public, *a.* (UN-¹ 7.)
1643 W. GREENHILL *Axe at Root* A iv, Wee hope your spirits are all unselvished, that none are now unpublique. **1650** JER. TAYLOR *Holy Living* ii. §3. 90 Virgins must be retired and unpublick.

un'publishable, *a.* (UN-¹ 7 b.)
Also (quot. 1981) as *sb.*
1815 COLERIDGE *Lett.* (1895) 644 Making a MS. collection of all my poems—publishable and unpublishable. **1842** LYTTON *Zanoni* I. i, His unpublished—his unpublishable and imperishable opera of the 'Siren'. **1891** SMILES *J. Murray* I. 441 Irving says..that Moore showed him the Byron recollections, and that they were quite unpublishable. **1981** [see UNMENTIONABLE *a.* and *sb.* c].
Hence **un'publishably** *adv.*
1860 DE MORGAN in *Macm. Mag.* I. 223 Their ways of conducting themselves were unpublishably singular.

un'published, *ppl. a.* [UN-¹ 8.]
1. a. Not made generally known or accessible, esp. in print.
1607 MARKHAM *Cavel.* (title-p.), The discovery of the subtill trade..of horse-coursers:..Secrets before vnpublished. **1684** T. BURNET *Theory Earth* I. 261 The ancient glosses and catenæ upon Scripture..are many of them either lost or unpublisht. **1731** *Hist. Litteraria* III. 259 Authors..whose Writings still remain unpublished in the Libraries of Rome, Venice, and Paris. **1828** P. BUCHAN *(title)*, Ancient Ballads and Songs of the North of Scotland hitherto un-published. **1862** *Numism. Chron.* II. 104 Unpublished Greek Imperial Coins.
b. Of an author: having had no writings published.
1934 R. MACAULAY *Milton* 26 A severe judgment on a writer already so fruitful, though as yet unpublished. **1976** *Scotsman* 20 Nov. (Weekend Suppl.) 3/8 (Advt.), This second anthology of new poems..includes work by..other established poets as well as by very talented but previously unpublished poets.
2. Not divulged or disclosed.
1605 SHAKS. *Lear* IV. iv. 16 All blest Secrets, All you vn-publish'd Vertues of the earth Spring with my teares. *a***1850** BRYANT *The Past* 30 Labours of good to man, Unpublished charity, unbroken faith. **1886** MRS. HUNGERFORD *Mental Struggle* vii, 'Nobody can help me,' declares the as yet unpublished sinner.

un'pucker, *v.* (UN-² 3.)
[**1775** ASH.] **1831** CARLYLE *Sart. Res.* I. iii, Let but Teufelsdröckh open his mouth, Heuschrecke's also unpuckered itself into a free doorway. **1862** —— *Fredk. Gt.* XII. xi. III. 360 Belleisle..unpuckers his stern brow again.

un'puckered, *ppl. a.* (UN-¹ 8.)
[**1775** ASH.] *c***1830** *Encycl. Brit.* (ed. 7) III. 38/1 Ruminants, in which the cæcum is moderate in size and unpuckered. **1862** *Catal. Internat. Exhib., Brit.* II. No. 2747, A plain unpuckered surface.

un'puddled, *ppl. a.* (UN-¹ 8.)
*a***1618** SYLVESTER *Maidens Blush* 1437 When the Ægyptians could no more perceive Nile's over-floud, nor any mud to leave; But pure, unpuddled on the sand to slide. **1842** *Civil Eng. & Arch. Jrnl.* V. 128/1 The whole surface of the hill is to be left unpuddled.

un'puff, *v.* (UN-² 3.)
1591 SYLVESTER *Du Bartas* I. iv. 526 We might unpuff our Heart, and bend our Knee. **1598** FLORIO, *Disenfiare*, to vnswel, to vnpuffe, to alay, to asswage.

un'puffed, *ppl. a.* (UN-¹ 8.)
1608 SYLVESTER II. iv. IV. *Decay* 452 Pure in Religion, Wise in Counselling,..Un-puft in Sun-shine, un-appall'd in Storms.

†**un'puissant,** *a. Obs.*⁻¹ [UN-¹ 7, 5 b.]
= IMPUISSANT *a.*
?*c***1597** BACON *Let.* in *Resuscitatio* II. (1657) 91 A Letter, carrying so empty an offer of so unpuissant a service.

un'pulled, *ppl. a.* (UN-¹ 8, 8 c.)
*c***1440** *Pallad. on Husb.* XII. 230 Ek plauntis fair excuse To stonde vnpuld, that they be not to seke. *c***1450** *Two Cookery Bks.* 99 Cast x. or xij. oynons hole vnpullud, and lete hem seth togidre. *c***1536** BELLENDEN *Chron. Scot.* (1821) I. p. ix, The lillyis, and the violet, Unpullit, sone ar with the wind ouirset. **1551** CRANMER *Answ. Crafty & Sophist. Cavillation* To Rdr. A iij b, What auaileth it..so long as ii. chief rootes remayne vnpulled vp? **1608** H. CLAPHAM *Errour Left Hand* 72 Some doubts, which yet (as stumps) remaine behind vnpulled vp. **1641** EARL MONM. tr. *Biondi's Civil Wars* II. 95 If some few [houses] remained un-pulled down. **1694** DRYDEN *Love Triumph.* III. i, 'Tis indeed a Fruit; Seen and desir'd of all, while yet unpull'd. **1765** *Museum Rust.* V. 120 Ground as much over-run with sea-grims as any part else of the pasture which had been unpulled! **1895** *Westm. Gaz.* 15 June 3/2 The greatest of devils must be in that carriage [= a cable-tram], making it crawl along unpulled, unpushed.

un'pulleyed, *ppl. a.* (UN-¹ 8.)
1839 LANDOR *Andrea of Hungary* 16 But intellect.., unpullied and adrift, Burns its dull heart away in smouldering scorn.

un'pulped, *ppl. a.* (UN-[1] 8.)
1806 A. HUNTER *Culina* (ed. 3) 59 Some part of the vegetables may be left unpulped.

un'pulverize, *v.* (UN-[2] 6 c.)
1733 TULL *Horse-Hoeing Husb.* xxv. 417 Crushing has such a contrary Effect from squeezing, that if this Roller should be us'd when the Land is moist, it would be very pernicious, by unpulverizing it.

un'pulverized, *ppl. a.* (UN-[1] 8.)
[**1775** ASH.] **1839** *Mag. Dom. Econ.* IV. 214 A lump of unpulverised magnesia. **1883** *Daily News* 30 July 4/8 If he took French leave and went off..leaving..the Government undetected, the Opposition unpulverised.

un'pumpable, *a.* (UN-[1] 7 b.)
1831 DISRAELI *Young Duke* III. xiii, Arundel Dacre was proverbially unpumpable.

un'pumped, *ppl. a.* (UN-[1] 8, 8 c.)
1633 T. JAMES *Voy.* 98 The Ship to be left vnpumpt. **1669** BOYLE *Contin. New Exp.* xliv. 154 Air that yet remain'd unpump'd out. **1873** RUSKIN *Fors Clav.* xxxiii. 17 A real pump in a pump room,..instead of the unpumped Tweed.

un'punctated, *ppl. a.* (UN-[1] 8.)
1870 H. A. NICHOLSON *Man. Zool.* I. 247 *Spiriferidæ*... Shell punctated or unpunctated.

unpunc'tilious, *a.* (UN-[1] 7.)
1753 RICHARDSON *Grandison* (1781) III. xxiii. 237 Lovers, said she, are the weakest people in the world; and people of punctilio the most *un*-punctilious.

un'punctual, *a.* (UN-[1] 7.)
1740 POPE *Let. to Swift* Wks. 1751 IX. 333, I am a very unpunctual correspondent, tho' no unpunctual agent or friend. **1828** LYTTON *Pelham* II. xii, Very young men are seldom unpunctual at dinner. **1841** LADY LYTTELTON *Corr.* (1912) xii. 316 They are immensely unpunctual, and make the poor Queen wait for dinner. **1884** *Expositor* June 467, I am not unpunctual, as you know.

unpunctu'ality. (UN-[1] 12, 5 b; cf. prec.)
1814 JANE AUSTEN *Mansfield Park* II. iv. 84 Their remoteness and unpunctuality, or their exorbitant charges. **1828–32** WEBSTER. **1841** EMERSON *Ess.* Ser. I. vii. 230 The discomfort of unpunctuality..is of no nation. **1868** STANLEY *Westm. Abbey* ii. 71 He came to the Abbey with an ostentatious unpunctuality.

un'punctuated, *ppl. a.* (UN-[1] 8.)
1860 W. JAMES *Let.* 12 Aug. in R. B. Perry *Thought & Character W. James* (1935) I. 196 Alice must be locked up alone..to write a letter, unassisted, uncorrected and unpunctuated, to her loving brothers. **1866** MRS. STOWE *Lit. Foxes* 46 That little unpunctuated scrap of life's poetry. **1890** 'R. BOLDREWOOD' *Col. Reformer* (1891) 261 His usual slow, unpunctuated direction of speech.

un'punctuating, *ppl. a.* (UN-[1] 10.)
1866 DE MORGAN *Budget of Paradoxes* (1872) 139 Of this unpunctuating paradoxer I shall give an account in his own way.

un'puncturable, *a.* (UN-[1] 7 b.)
1891 *Daily News* 28 Nov. 6/1 An 'unpuncturable' tyre,..so constructed that the pressure of the air closes up holes. **1901** G. PASTON *Little Mem. 18th Cent.* 201 An equally unpuncturable power of self-delusion.

un'punishable, *a.* (UN-[1] 7 b.)
1531 *Dial. on Laws Eng.* II. 4 b, He is vnpunysshable of waste by the lawe. **1584** R. SCOT *Discov. Witchcr.* III. viii. (1886) 40 An impossible purpose is unpunishable. **1648** FAIRFAX, etc. *Remonstr.* 49 While your own proceedings admit themselves unpunishable. **1682** EVATS tr. *Grotius* (title-p.), In the Third [Book] is declared, What in War is Lawful, that is Unpunishable. *a* **1700** DRYDEN tr. *Ovid's Art of Love* 38 Th' unpunishable Pleasures of the Kind. *a* **1797** H. WALPOLE *Geo. II* (1847) I. ii. 334 It is the cause of sovereigns that their crimes should be unpunishable. **1802–12** BENTHAM *Ration. Judic. Evid.* (1827) I. 354 Mendacity..remains altogether unpunishable. **1837** CARLYLE *Fr. Rev.* I. v. i, Inertia alone is at once unpunishable and unconquerable.
Hence **un'punishably** *adv.*
1649 MILTON *Eikon.* xxviii. 230 It were yet absurd to think that the Anointment of God should..give them privilege, who punish others, to sin themselves unpunishably. **1829** BENTHAM *Justice & Cod. Petit.* 27 The now written, and above described unpunishably mendacious, pleadings.

un'punished, *ppl. a.* (UN-[1] 8.)
a **1340** HAMPOLE *Psalter* xxxiii. 16 He þat does ill, wen he not to be vnpunyst. **1387** TREVISA *Higden* (Rolls) VII. 185 Whos see after his deth none myȝte oppresse slepyng un-punsched. *c* **1440** *Alph. Tales* 276 So he had levur lefe þe blame vnpunysshid. **1484** CAXTON *Fables of Æsop* VI. xv. N viij b, Men ought not to leue hym vnpunysshed. **1512** *Helyas* in Thoms *Prose Rom.* (1828) III. 75 A good dede is never unrewarded nor an evyll unpunisshed. **1573** L. LLOYD *Marrow of Hist.* (1653) 136 They suffered theft to be un-punished. **1613** J. TAYLOR (Water P.) *Waterm. Suit* Wks. (1630) 174/1 Few or none escapes vnpunished if their faults be knowne. **1651** HOBBES *Leviath.* II. xxx. 183 Crimes ..which unpunished, seem Authorised. **1712** BLACKMORE *Creation* VII. 71 His sword unpunish'd criminals defy. **1766** GIBBON *Decl. & F.* vi. (1782) I. 163 The crime went not unpunished. **1827** POLLOK *Course T.* II. 553 An individual sovereignty, that none Created might, unpunished, bind or touch. **1875** JOWETT *Plato* (ed. 2) I. 319 The impious.. ought not to go unpunished.
Hence **un'punishedly** *adv.*
1561 T. NORTON *Calvin's Inst.* Pref. A iiij b, They doe so ..licentiously as vnpunishedly fome agaynst vs. **1611** FLORIO, *Impunitamente*, vnpunishedly.

un'punishing, *vbl. sb.* (UN-[1] 13.)
a **1340** HAMPOLE *Ps.* xciii. 11 þai hete til þaim selfe vnpunyssynge of syn. *a* **1662** HEYLIN *Laud* (1668) 354 The unpunishing of the first Tumult.

un'punishing, *ppl. a.* (UN-[1] 10.)
1644 MILTON *Divorce* II. iii. 41 Nay this is..to incarnat sin into the unpunishing and well pleas'd will of God.

un'punishingly, *adv.* [UN-[1] 11.] †With impunity.
1499 *Promp. Parv.* (Pynson), Onponysshingly, *impunite.*

†**un'punishment.** *Obs.*$^{-1}$ (UN-[1] 12.)
a **1555** PHILPOT *Exam. & Writ.* (Parker Soc.) 335 Yet eftsoons they be so hauwtiff with power, riches and unpunishment. **1648** HEXHAM II, *Ongestraftheydt* Vnpunishment, or Impunity.

un'purchas(e)able, *a.* (UN-[1] 7 b.)
1611 FLORIO, *Inacquisteuole*, vnpurchasable. **1792** W. ROBERTS *Looker-on* No. 18 (1794) I. 238 The unpurchasable beauties and chaste decorations of rural scenery. *a* **1834** COLERIDGE *Lit. Rem.* (1839) IV. 170 To others, they are not only not easy and cheap, but unpurchaseable and impossible too. **1880** MCCARTHY *Own Times* IV. 215 The country gentleman, whose own vote..was unpurchasable by any money bribe.

un'purchased, *ppl. a.* (UN-[1] 8.)
1545 *Test. Ebor.* (Surtees) VI. 236 Where as I covenante withe hym..to leave hym lande in yerlie value xls..and have unpurchased xxs value of it. ? **1608** *J. Reynard's Deliv.* in *Harl. Misc.* (1808) I. 187 Nor [is] any treasure of the earth ..left unpurchased. **1665** BOYLE *Occas. Refl.* IV. iii, As she is rich in Natures bounty, [she] appear'd..satisfy'd with the unpurchas'd Treasures she possesses. **1736** THOMSON *Liberty* v. 613 Justice, like the liberal light of Heaven, Unpurchas'd shines on all. **1781** COWPER *Hope* 343 But oh the strife,..and debate, The tidings of unpurchased heaven create! **1831** SCOTT *Ct. Rob.* xxviii, Let him keep unpurchased the crown, for which he has paid..a price which it is not worth. **1893** F. ADAMS *New Egypt* 75 The poor unpurchased and, so far, unpolluted free-lance.

†**un'pure**, *a. Obs.* [UN-[1] 7, 5 b. Cf. MDu. *onpuur*, MLG. *unpûr*, MSw. *opur.*]
1. Morally impure.
a **1375** *Lay Folks Mass Bk.* App. iv. 226 Of sunnes we beþ vnpure. **1393** LANGL. *P. Pl.* C. I. 116 (Ilchester MS.), For þay were prestes vnpure. *c* **1450** tr. *De Imitatione* III. xxxvi. 106 Hov vnpure all oure werkes are we weyle not. **1509** BARCLAY *Shyp of Folys* 258 b, Nought chaste thou techyst, but thynge vnpure and vyle. **1550** BALE *Eng. Votaries* II. F iij, Thus was the churche fylled wyth vnpure ministers. **1604** T. WRIGHT *Passions* v. 237, I hope such vnpure minds will amend their impure errours. **1624** DONNE *Devot.* 210 Of so vnpure constitutions, as that we can present no obiect but sin. **1742** in Wesley *Jrnl.* (1749) 41 Dost thou believe, thy heart must be thus unpure?
2. Not physically pure or clean.
a **1500** *Ratis Raving* I. 156 Quhilk is stinkand aire vnpure. **1548** *Act 2 & 3 Edw. VI*, c. 10 §1 Malte unpure and unseasonable. **1576** NEWTON *Lemnie's Complex.* 9 b, When the humours be not sufficiently..concocted and attenuate, vnpure Spirites proceede out of them. **1651** WITTIE *Primrose's Pop. Err.* IV. iii. 213 The mixture of pure, and unpure, that is to say, of different parts in..the same mixt body.
3. Not genuine or true.
1590 BURROUGH *Meth. Physick* 246 If one feuer do exceede the other, then it is called an vnpure hemitrice.
Hence †**un'purely** *adv.*, **-ness.** *Obs.*
1550 BALE *Eng. Votaries* II. A ij b They..teache the veryte of God *vnpurely. **1548** UDALL *Erasm. Par. Luke* ii. 20 b, For what point of *vnpurenes coulde suche a woman haue in bearyng childe, as..had conceiued by the onely power and vertue of God. **1573** T. CARTWRIGHT *Replye to Answ. Whitgift* 13 Christe..shall couer all oure vnpurenesse and not impute it vnto vs.

†**un'pured**, *ppl. a. Obs.* [UN-[1] 8.] Unpurified.
1398 TREVISA *Barth. De P.R.* XVII. i. (Bodl. MS.), þerin þe fedinge pured is itempred fro þe vnpured, as it is in þe guttes of a beeste. *c* **1400** MAUNDEV. (1919) 200 þei fynen the pured gold & casten awey the vnpured. **1579** LANGHAM *Gard. Health* 519 Put them in dishes with vnpured hony.

un'purgeable, *a.* (UN-[1] 7 b.)
1876 SWINBURNE *Erechtheus* 299 A stain of blood unpurgeable with tears.

un'purged, *ppl. a.* [UN-[1] 8.]
1. Not cleansed or freed from baser elements or admixture.
1555 EDEN *Decades* (Arb.) 268 Ginger Mechino..is sould vnclensed or vnpurged. **1601** SHAKS. *Jul. C.* II. i. 266 The Rhewmy, and vnpurged Ayre. *a* **1661** HOLYDAY *Persius* (1673) 306 This from th' unpurged earth made us desire To strain out veins of gold by purging fire. **1667** MILTON *P.L.* v. 419 Whence in her visage round those spots, unpurg'd Vapours not yet into her substance turn'd. **1788** V. KNOX *Winter Even.* II. IV. x. 61 Instruments sweeter than the unpurged ear ever heard. **1874** FARRAR *Christ* I. 118 Which to the dull unpurged ear was but inarticulate thunder.
2. Not freed or cleared from wrong-doing, accusation, etc.
1530 RASTELL *New Bk. Purgatory* III. viii. f 4 b, That the soule vnpurged maye do some meane & lowe seruyce to god in heuen. **1586** J. HOOKER *Hist. Irel.* in *Holinshed* II. 70/1 The prisoner deceased in the castell, and because he stood vnpurged, long he laie vnburied. **1642** MILTON *Apol. Smect.* 11 So long as I should suffer my honest estimation to lye unpurg'd from these insolent suspicions. **1653** JER. TAYLOR *Serm. for Year* I. xix. 250 Hell is wide open..to euery unpurged person. **1738** WESLEY *Ps.* VI. iii, Who dies unpurg'd for ever dies.
3. Not removed or cleared away.
a **1617** HIERON *Wks.* (1620) II. 415 That there is some secret euill in vs, which is vnpurged and vnreformed. **1682** FLAVEL *Fear* 39 The unpurged relicts of unbelief. **1835** T. MITCHELL *Acharn. of Aristoph.* 874 A man who had yet the unpurged pollution of a mother's blood upon him. **1884** *Chr. Commw.* 14 Feb. 415/2 The Church,..corrupted by the unpurged influences of the great Apostacy.

un'purified, *ppl. a.* (UN-[1] 8.)
1574 T. CARTWRIGHT *Full Declar.* a 2 b, That vnreuenged, and vnpurified shedinge off giltlesse bloud. **1617** MORYSON *Itin.* I. 10 Vnpurified siluer as it comes from the Mines. **1667** *Decay Chr. Piety* ii. 37 Our sinful Nation..is indeed now come out [of the furnace], but so unpurified, that [etc.]. *a* **1779** WARBURTON *Div. Leg.* VI. Notes, Wks. 1788 III. 576 This active Watchman of the Church militant will let nothing escape him,..nor leave any thing unpurified that has once passed through my hands. **1791** COWPER *Yardley Oak* 12 The conscience, yet Unpurified by an authentic act Of amnesty. **1832** G. R. PORTER *Porcelain & Gl.* 275 The presence of iron in the unpurified sea-sand and ashes of which it is composed.

un'purifying, *ppl. a.* (UN-[1] 10.)
1862 'SHIRLEY' (J. Skelton) *Nugæ Crit.* vii. 319 The discipline which teaches humility is not unpurifying.

un'purposed, *ppl. a.* (UN-[1] 8.)
1570 DEE *Math. Pref.* 15 Of second vnpurposed frute,.. arrising by Geometrie. **1606** SHAKS. *Ant. & Cl.* IV. xiv. 84 Do it at once, Or thy precedent Seruices are all But accidents vnpurpos'd. **1645** MILTON *Tetrach.* 32 The restorement of a freeborn man from an unpurpos'd, and unworthy bondage to a rightfull liberty. **1827** POLLOK *Course T.* v. 362 The lonely bard.., when forth he walked, Unpurposed. **1885** W. J. SENDALL *Calverley's Rem.* 53 The work which he has left behind him..is, as to much of it, unpurposed and fragmentary.

†**un'purposedly**, *adv. Obs.*$^{-1}$ [UN-[1] 11; cf. prec.] Not purposely.
a **1639** W. WHATELEY *Prototypes* I. xix. (1640) 185 Had they unpurposedly fallen to wanton embraces.

un'purpose-like, *a.* (UN-[1] 7 c.)
[**1825** JAM.] **1856** LEVER *Martins of Cro' M.* 22 The unpurpose-like vacuity, the intense vulgarity of his Oughterard friends.

un'purse, *v.* [UN-[2] 5, 4, 3.]
1. *trans.* To take (money) out of a purse; to disburse.
1390 GOWER *Conf.* II. 146 The time is ofte cursed, That evere was the gold unpursed, The which was leid upon the bok. **1570** LEVINS *Manip.* 191 To vnburse and vnpurse, *expendere, insumere.* **1580** HOLLYBAND *Treas. Fr. Tong*, *Grand d'esboursement d'argent*, a great vnpursing of mony. **1611** TOURNEUR *Ath. Trag.* v. i. (Stage direct.), Unpurses the gold.
2. To rob of one's purse.
1827 POLLOK *Course T.* VIII. 382 The uncivil robber, who unpursed The traveller on the highway.
3. To relax from a pursed state. Also *intr.*
1871 BROWNING *Pr. Hohenst.* 45 Now I permit your plump lips to unpurse. *c* **1880** R. BRIDGES in A. D. Coleridge *Eton in Forties* (1896) 174 Unpursed his mouth, empty his mighty chest, His run is o'er.

unpur'sued, *ppl. a.* (UN-[1] 8.)
1469 *Sc. Acts, Jas. III* (1814) II. 95/1 þe obligatione..sall prescrife & be of nain avail þe said fourtj ȝeris beand ronnyng & vnpersewit be þe law. **1531** *Reg. Privy Seal Scot.* II. 134/2 The saidis personis..to be..unaccusit, unfollowit, unpersewit,..for quhatsumever actioun or cryme. **1667** MILTON *P.L.* VI. 1 All night the dreadless Angel un-pursu'd Through Heav'ns wide Champain held his way. **1675** HOBBES *Odyssey* (1677) 189 To the ship we unpursued pass. **1782** J. SCOTT *Poet. Wks.* 235 Pale fear, who un-pursued still flies. **1810** SCOTT *Lady of L.* II. xxvi, This youth..Guided my steps not unpursued. **1861** CLARA F. BROMLEY *Woman's Wand. West. World* 168 They made a precipitate..retreat, but were unpursued.

unpur'veyed, *ppl. a.* [UN-[1] 8.]
†**1.** Of persons: Unprovided, unfurnished, unsupplied (with something): **a.** Const. *of.*
a **1300** *Cursor M.* 5444 'Now leue sun ioseph,' he said, 'O þe es [= am] i noght vnpuruaid'. *c* **1375** *Lay Folks Mass Bk.* 424 (Royal MS.), If þou of ane be vn-puruayde. **1471** *Paston Lett.* III. 4 It is soo that my brother is on purveyed off monye. *a* **1548** HALL *Chron., Edw. IV*, 197 You may thinke that kyng Edward was not..so vnpurueyed of counsail, to forsake thys beneficiall alliaunce. **1596** SPENSER *F.Q.* VII. vi. 14 All the heauenly crew Of happy wights, now vnpurvaide of light, Were much afraid.
†**b.** Without const. Also = not provided for.
1491 CAXTON *Vitas Patr.* (W. de W. 1495) I. cxlii. 153 b/1 That yf I wexed an almes gyuer, god sholde neuer leue me unpurueyed. *a* **1500** *Assemb. Ladies* 382 Than we began to dresse us in our gyse, That folk shuld see we were nat unpurvayd. **1509** BARCLAY *Shyp of Folys* 50 For one small faute..out is he cast bare and vnpuruayde. *c* **1530** *Court of Love* 561 And ye that ben unpurveyed, praye her eke Comfort you soon.
†**2.** Unprepared, not in readiness (to resist attack, etc.). *Obs.*
1387 TREVISA *Higden* (Rolls) VII. 111 In þe nyȝt.. Englische men..disperbled and chased þe enemyes unpurveied. *c* **1425** *Orolog. Sapient.* v. in *Anglia* X. 359/7 Take me not so vnpurueyed fro þis liȝte of life. *a* **1450** *Knt. de la Tour* (1906) 146 The .v. maidenes that were folys, that slepte and were vnpurueyed. *a* **1548** HALL *Chron., Hen. VIII*, 32 It was forsene that the kyng nor his people should be taken vnpuruyed. **1586** DAY *Eng. Secretorie* II. 114 It seemeth a matter incident to his accompt..that..he be not vnpurueyed in his owne person.
†**3.** Unforeseen; unexpected(ly). *Obs.*
c **1374** CHAUCER *Boeth.* II. pr. i. (1868) 30 Til þat she confounde wiþ vnsuffreable sorwe hem þat she haþ left in

despeir vnpurueyed [L. *inseperata*]. *c* **1425** WYNTOUN *Cron.* II. xvi. 1531 He slew of þaim a gret party As he come on vnpurvaid, Vnwarnyst wer þai. **1456** SIR G. HAY *Gov. Princes* Wks. (S.T.S.) II. 112 Rycht sa of ane unkynde ȝere ..men may better purvay na it war unknawin na unpurvayde of before. **1483** CAXTON *Gold. Leg.* 359 b/2 As they fled they..mette the holy body sodenly unpourueyed.

4. Of things: Not furnished beforehand.

a **1548** HALL *Chron., Edw. IV*, 243 He..left nothyng apperteignyng to the warre, vnpurueyed or vnlooked for.

un'pushed, *ppl. a.* (UN-[1] 8.)

[**1775** ASH.] **1895** [see UNPULLED].

unput, *ppl. a.* (UN-[1] 8, 8 c.)

Chiefly with advs. and preps.

c **1470** HENRY *Wallace* VI. 624 Dede corssys that lay wnputt in graiff. **1491** *Sc. Acts, Jas. IV* (1814) II. 225/1 The tennentis..sall remane vnput furth or removit. **1509** HAWES *Past. Pleas.* XXIX. (Percy Soc.) 143 Towarde Rome a great circuite aboute, There was no fyre that was un-put-out. **1565** in Hay Fleming *Reform. Scotl.* (1910) 611 Certane tymmer and glas unput in the memoriall. **1600** SURFLET *Countrie Farme* I. iii. 4 One tyle in the roofe..being left vnrepaired and vnput in againe, causeth others also to fall. **1665** SIR T. HERBERT *Trav.* (1677) 56 This holy Fire.. continued un-put out for many Generations. **1732** J. LOUTHIAN *Form of Process* 267 Which Act as yet remains unput to due Execution anent the forenamed Persons. **1843** MRS. BROWNING *Lett. R. H. Horne* (1877) I. 65 She has..a natural exaltation, perfectly unaffected and un-put-on. **1897** FLANDRAU *Harvard Episodes* 37 Bradley suddenly answered the unput questions by suggesting ways and means.

un'putrefied, *ppl. a.* (UN-[1] 8.)

1579 W. FULKE *Heskins' Parl.* 353 It was kept many yeres ..vnputrified. **1626** BACON *Sylva* §341 So wee see that Meat and Drinke will last longer, Vnputrified, or Unsowred, in Winter, than in Summer. **1663** BOYLE *Usef. Exp. Nat. Philos.* II. i. 25 An embrio..preserved unputrified for several years. **1735** ARBUTHNOT *Aliments* 180 No Animal unputrify'd, being burnt, yields any alkaline Salt. **1799** KIRWAN *Geol. Ess.* 60 The rhinoceros was found intire and unputrified. **1843** CARLYLE *Past & Pr.* III. x, All human things do require..to have some Soul in them,..were it only to keep the Body unputrefied.

un'putrid, *a.* (UN-[1] 7, 5 b.)

1657 B. W. tr. *Bauderon's Expert Phisic.* 72 An unputrid Synochus hath no small Analogy with an Ephemera.

unpytha'gorically, *adv.* (UN-[1] 11.)

a **1687** H. MORE *Conject. Cabbal.* (1713) 133 By all which terms is meant nothing else but Cybele or Vesta, but how Unpythagorically, any one may discern.

†**un'quaerable**, *a. Obs.*[−1] [UN-[1] 7 b + QUÆRE *v.*] Indubitable, certain.

1657 J. WATTS *Vind. Ch. Eng.* 58 An unquestionable and unquaerable Rule.

un'quaffed, *ppl. a.* (UN-[1] 8.)

[**1775** ASH.] **1812** BYRON '*If sometimes*' iii, If not the goblet pass unquaff'd, It is not drain'd to banish care.

un'quailed, *ppl. a.* (UN-[1] 8.)

1583 GOLDING *Calvin on Deut.* cxcix. 1237 Let vs..praye him to giue vs power to holde out vnquailed. **1613** W. BROWNE *Brit. Past.* I. iv, So Griefe..In longest journeys hath the strongest strength, And is at hand suppress, unquail'd at length. **1839** COLERIDGE *Constit. Ch. & State* (ed. 2) 145 The lion-hearted Luther with unquailed spirit.

un'quailing, *ppl. a.* (UN-[1] 10.)

1836 WHITTIER *Mem. T. Shipley* 49 The unquailing eye of innocence. **1853** ROCK *Ch. of Fathers* III. ix. 217 His heart was unquailing when he met his foemen. **1884** R. W. CHURCH *Bacon* i. 25 Elizabeth's..unquailing spirit at the time of the Spanish invasion.

Hence **un'quailingly** *adv.*

1845 [JANE ROBINSON] *Whitehall* lxviii, [He] fixed his eyes steadily and unquailingly upon him.

un'quaint, *a.* [UN-[1] 7.] † Uncunning, ignorant.

a **1340** HAMPOLE *Psalter* ciii. 26 Waytynges of þaim.. occupyes vn-quaynte men anence þaire saule. *Ibid.* cxl. 4 It is þe manere of vnquaynt men..to excuse þaim wiþ falshede.

†**un'quainted**, *ppl. a. Obs.*[−1] [UN-[1] 8.] Unfamiliar.

1587 W. FOWLER *Wks.* (S.T.S.) I. 26, I who was not muche acquent with such vnquented sight.

un'quakerish, *a.* (UN-[1] 7.)

1822 LAMB *Lett.* (1900) III. 80 It is a visiting, unquiet, unquakerish season.

un'quakerlike, *a.* (UN-[1] 7 c.)

1832 F. TROLLOPE *Domestic Manners of Americans* II. xxx. 154, I overheard many unquakerlike jokes. **1852** SAVAGE *R. Medlicott* I. iii, A fair..girl, with a most un-quakerlike expression of mirth in her eye.

un'quakerly, *a.* (UN-[1] 7.)

1846 B. BARTON *Select.* (1849) 41 The bell, with the somewhat unquakerly inscription of 'Mr. Barton's bell'.

un'quaking, *ppl. a.* (UN-[1] 10.)

1816 WILSON *City of Plague* II. iii. 99 That awful happiness That walks unquaking through the shades of death. **1881** RUSKIN *Bible Amiens* iv. §10 On the unquaking and fruitful earth.

un'qualifiable, *a.* (UN-[1] 7 b.)

With recent quots. cf. mod.F. *inqualifiable*.

a **1734** NORTH *Lives* (1742) 271 He would not put the Seals to any Commissions to Persons unqualifiable. **1871** *Union Rev.* 78 This unqualifiable proceeding. **1899** *Westm. Gaz.* 28 June 2/1 The march played over and over..with quite unqualifiable iteration.

unqualifi'cation. (UN-[1] 12.)

1657 W. MORICE *Coena quasi Κοινὴ* xvi. 261 Qualifications (I should think them rather unqualifications). **1708** HEARNE *Collect.* (O.H.S.) II. 106 He..express't his unqualification for yᵉ Place.

un'qualified, *ppl. a.* [UN-[1] 8.]

1. Not qualified or fitted; not having the necessary qualifications.

1556 LAUDER *Tractate* 364 Quhow God sall ȝow correct, Geue ȝe vnqualifeit hirds Elect. **1631** *Star Chamb. Cases* (Camden) 73 Allen, being a Vicar in Sudbury and beneficed and unqualifyed, accepted of another living. **1673** *S'too him Bayes* 22 The bishop would not have unqualify'd people read the scriptures. **1780** HARRIS *Philol. Enq.* I. iv. (1781) 27 As Translators are infinite, and many of them (to borrow a phrase from Sportsmen) unqualified Persons. **1836** JAS. GRANT *Random Recoll. Ho. Lords* ix. 192 He was always the unqualified denouncer of State prosecutions of the press. **1891** E. KINGLAKE *Australian at Home* 46 It is no use sueing a quack... Why did you employ him? You know he is unqualified.

b. Const. *for*, or *to* with inf.

1667 *Decay Chr. Piety* xix. 409 Till he have thus denudated himself..he is utterly unqualified for these Agones. **1689** S. JOHNSON *Remarks Sherlock's Bk.* 41 A Person may be unqualified by Law, to execute a Commission. **1736** BUTLER *Anal.* I. v. 113 Capable of naturally becoming qualified for States of life, for which they were once wholly unqualified. **1781** GIBBON *Decl. & F.* xviii. (1787) II. 109 Dominions which they were unqualified to govern. **1847** HARRIS *Life Ld. Hardwicke* I. 504 A minister..unqualified for his situation.

2. Not endowed with specific qualities.

1678 CUDWORTH *Intell. Syst.* 220 If he neither derived them from..unqualified Matter,..not yet from..an irrational and maleficent soul.

3. Not modified, limited, or restricted.

1796 MME. D'ARBLAY *Camilla* I. 76 [He] could scarce refrain from a smile at this unqualified opening. **1857** PRESCOTT *Philip II*, I. (1857) 145 His ardour did not precipitate him into any unqualified declaration of his passion. **1878** BOSW. SMITH *Carthage* 7 The unsparing and unqualified denunciations of Tyre and Sidon..in Joel and Amos.

un'qualifiedly, *adv.* [UN-[1] 11.] Without qualification.

1861 MILL *Repr. Govt.* iii. 57 On the question of strikes.. it is doubtful if there is so much as one among the leading members of either House, who is not firmly convinced that the reason of the matter is unqualifiedly on the side of the masters. **1862** R. H. PATTERSON *Ess. Hist. & Art* 107 M. Guizot..inculcates much too unqualifiedly the preservation of repose in statuary. **1873** MORLEY *Rousseau* II. 178 An exercise of sovereignty which might be atheistic, mahometan, or anything else unqualifiedly monstrous.

un'qualifiedness. (UN-[1] 12.)

1666 BOYLE *Hydrostatical Paradoxes* Pref. A 7 b, The unqualifiedness of most Readers, to examine Mathematical things. **1674** A. G. *Quest. Oath Allegiance* To Rdr. p. iii, My own unqualifiedness extreamly discourag'd me from doing it. **1720** S. PARKER *Biblioth. Bibl.* 65 The inadvertency and unqualifiedness of Copyers.

un'qualify, *v.* [UN-[2] 3.] *trans.* To make unqualified; to disqualify. (Common *c* 1675–1750.)

1655 SPURSTOWE *Wels of Salvation* 164 Earthly things defile the heart with..corrupt affections, which do unqualifie it for the reception of..precious promises. **1694** S. JOHNSON *Notes Past. Let. Bp. Burnet* I. 73 The Duke of York had unqualified himself for that High Office. **1709** ADDISON *Tatler* No. 103 ¶ 16 These particularities..in dress and behaviour..oftentimes..unqualify them from doing any Good in the World. **1794** MRS. A. M. BENNETT *Ellen* III. 72 His ill health..unqualified him to be a public [tutor]. **1836** T. ERSKINE *Baxter's Saint's R.* Pref. p. xxxiv, [To] unqualify the mind for present exertion. **1853** C. H. SPURGEON in *Daily News* 2 Feb. (1892) 6/1 If you think my years would unqualify me for your pulpit.

Hence **un'qualifying** *ppl. a.*

1737 *Common Sense* I. 30 The most unqualifying Circumstances for any Employment, where Bribery and Corruption can possibly enter.

un'qualifyingly, *adv.* (UN-[1] 11.)

1841 S. WARREN *Ten Thou.* v. i, Unqualifyingly submitting to every one of the requisitions.

un'qualitied, *ppl. a.* (UN-[2] 8.)

1606 SHAKS. *Ant. & Cl.* III. xi. 44 Madam, speake to him, Hee's vnqualited with very shame.

un'quality-like, *a.* (UN-[1] 7 c.)

1784 R. BAGE *Barham Downs* I. 100 An unaccountable unquality-like fit of the spleen.

un'quantified, *ppl. a.* (UN-[1] 8.)

1864 BOWEN *Logic* vi. 162 The same naked or unquantified Subject and Predicate. **1865** MILL *Exam. Hamilton* xxii. 443 Forms..in which unquantified conclusions can be drawn from unquantified premises.

un'quarrellable, *a.* (UN-[1] 7 b.)

1646 SIR T. BROWNE *Pseud. Ep.* VI. x. 323 There arising unto examination no such satisfactory and unquarrellable reasons. **1698** in Sir H. Dalrymple *Decisions* (1792) I It necessarily followed, that the sentence should be final, and unquarrellable.

un'quarrelled, *ppl. a.* (UN-[1] 8.)

1606 in De Foe *Hist. Ch. Scot.* II. Add. (1717) 224 By a just Sentence of a lawful Judge, standing unquarrelled and unreduc'd.

un'quarrelsome, *a.* (UN-[1] 7.)

1836 SIR H. TAYLOR *Statesman* xv. 101 A statesman should be..the most unquarrelsome of men.

un'quarried, *ppl. a.* (UN-[1] 8.)

1788 D. GILSON *Serm.* 19 The fragment of an useful Column, has more honour than the whole unquarried rock. **1901** *Daily News* 21 Feb. 6/3 It was the work of a poetic pioneer in the unquarried rocks of daily life.

un'quartered, *ppl. a.* (UN-[1] 8.)

[**1775** ASH.] **1887** BOWEN *Æneid* VI. 253 He..Flings on the flames whole bodies of bulls unquartered to blaze.

un'quashed, *ppl. a.* (UN-[1] 8.)

1647 N. BACON *Disc. Govt. Eng.* I. xlviii. 131 Preserving the particular sub-servient jurisdictions of the kingdome, intire and unquashed.

un'queen, *v.* [UN-[2] 6 b, 4.]

1. *trans.* To deprive of, depose from, the rank or position of queen.

1579 J. STUBBES *Gaping Gulf* D ij, Is it not more then probable..that the next prince..wyl drawe it [*sc.* England] also..under the law Salique, and so quite vnqueen the desolate sister? **1613** SHAKS. *Hen. VIII*, IV. ii. 171 Embalme me, Then lay me forth (although vnqueen'd) yet like A Queene. **1673** *Season. Disc. Maintain. Establ. Relig.* 9 Nor was she unqueen'd enough by all this. **1821** *To the King* 9 We must un-queen your wife, because she is immoral. **1833** H. COLERIDGE *Poems* I. 38 Old times unqueen thee, and old loves endear thee. **1873** *Athenæum* 22 Feb. 240/2 The divorce which was to unqueen Catherine of Arragon.

2. To remove the queen from (a hive).

1884 *Bee-keeping* 23 Unqueen your diseased stock, cutting out all queen-cells ten days after.

Hence **un'queened** *ppl. a.*

1820 SCOTT *Abbot* xxiii, Go thou..and render the usual service of the meal to this unqueened Queen. **1826** SOUTHEY *Vind. Eccl. Angl.* 388 The un-queened, un-sexed, un-Lutheranized, Christina.

un'queenlike, *a.* (UN-[1] 7 c.)

a **1683** OLDHAM *Wks.* 1686) 13 Unqueenlike pity marr'd her Royal Pow'r.

un'queenly, *a.* (UN-[1] 7.)

1865 SWINBURNE *Chastelard* IV. i. 164 Methinks I am growing unqueenly. **1884** *Truth* 13 Mar. 383/1 Her.. modest bearing and unqueenly ways.

un'quelled, *ppl. a.* (UN-[1] 8. Cf. MDu. *ongequelt*, ON. *úkvaldr*.)

? *a* **1400** *Morte Arth.* 3811 Qwhylles he es qwykke and in qwerte unquellyde with handis. **1605** SYLVESTER *Du Bartas* II. iii. *Law* 1307 Thou shalt dye quiet, thou shalt live unquell'd. **1654** FANSHAWE *Love for Love's Sake*, That so famous Queen For unquell'd valour. **1727** THOMSON *Summer* 509 Thy Meadows..rise unquell'd Against the Mower's Sythe. *a* **1800** COWPER *Iliad* (ed. 2) v. 121 Diomede unquell'd By that keen shaft, retreated. **1813** BYRON *Giaour* xxxii, A spirit yet unquell'd and high.

†**un'queme**, *a. Obs.* [OE. *uncwéme* (UN-[1] 7): cf. *uniqueme* UN-[1] 3), MSw. *oqväm*, MDa. *ukvem*.]

1. Displeasing.

c **1000** *Vercelli MS.* fol. 79 a, For þære [unsibbe] bið sio ure onsæᵹdnes Gode uncweme. *c* **1200** *Trin. Coll. Hom.* 9 Ure lif we leded richtliche toȝenes ure louerd.., ȝif we forbered al þat þat him is unqueme. *c* **1200** ORMIN 4629 All þatt follȝheþþ unnclænleȝȝc All iss Drihhtin unncweme.

2. Unfit, unsuitable; awkward.

a **1300** *Cursor M.* 12411 Þis tre..þat first vnquemest was to see Nu es it quem als it mai be. **1611** COTGR., *Maladroict*, vnwieldie, aukward, vnwheeme.

3. Uncomfortable, uneasy.

a **1300** *Cursor M.* 22597 Þe self angels sal quake vnqueme For dute of him þat all sal deme.

So †**un'quemable**, *a.*, **un'quemably** *adv.*, **un'quemefully** *adv.*, **un'quemely** [cf. MSw. *oqvämelika*] *adv.* Also **un'queme** *v.* [UN-[2] 3], to trouble, unsettle. *Obs.*

a **1300** *Cursor M.* 3566 Þe heued biginnes for to scak, His hend vnquemli for to quak. *Ibid.* 22551 Vnquemfulli þan sal þai quak, þat all þe erth it sal toscak. *c* **1400** *Destr. Troy* 2693 Þou qwene, þat vnqwemyt has on sum qwaint wise, The angur thee is, Ecuba, entrond on honde! *Ibid.* 13681 Þen fortune his fall felli aspies, Vnqwemys his qwate, & þe qwele turnys. *c* **1440** *Promp. Parv.* 366/2 On-qwemable, *inplacabilis*. *Ibid.*, On-qwemably, *inplacabiliter*.

un'quenchable, *a.* [UN-[1] 7 b, 5 b.] Incapable of being quenched; inextinguishable:

a. Of fire. (Also *fig.*)

1382 WYCLIF *Matt.* iii. 12 Chaffis he shal brenne with fyr unquenchable. *c* **1450** tr. *De Imitatione* III. lxiii. 147 Þei þat ..brennen in an unquenchable fire of charite. **1535** COVERDALE *Luke* iii. 17 He..shal burne the chaffe with vn-quencheable fyre. **1565** CALFHILL *Answ. Martiall's Treat. Cross* To Rdr. 2 To burne in hell wyth flames vnquenchable. **1627** HAKEWILL *Apol.* IV. xiv. §4. 462 That [fire] burneth eternally without feeding, and is vnquenchable. **1652** VAUGHAN *Mount of Olives* Wks. 1914 I. 169 Those furious and unquenchable burnings of hell (which the Scripture calls the lake of fire, &c.). **1741–2** GRAY *Agrippina* 128 The spark Unquenchable, that glows within their breasts. **1791** COWPER *Iliad* XVII. 107 Fierce as Vulcan's fire Unquenchable. **1811** LAMB *Genius of Hogarth* Wks. 1908 I. 106 Her unquenchable spark is not utterly out. **1825** MACAULAY *Ess., Milton* ¶ 50 Those mighty principles..have kindled an unquenchable fire in the hearts of the oppressed. **1870** BRYANT *Iliad* XVI. II. 119 The eager enemy hurled the blazing brands.., and wrapped the stern in flames Unquenchable.

b. Of thirst, hunger, or greed.

1567 JEWEL *Reply Harding* 735 The Pope..beinge diseased..with an vnquencheable thirst of monie. **1577** HOLINSHED *Hist. Scot.* I. 62/2 Hee was giuen to suche vnquenchable couetyse that nothing mighte suffice hym. *a* **1619** FOTHERBY *Atheom.* II. ii. §5. 204 Thus vnquenchable is the thirst of ambition. **1723** DE FOE *Col. Jack* (1840) 186 By these things he raised an unquenchable thirst in me.

1795 SOUTHEY *Maid of Orleans* II. 71 Often impatiently to quench their thirst Unquenchable, large draughts of molten gold They drink insatiate. **1857** ROBERTSON *Serm.* Ser. III. xix. 273 The more unquenchable his hunger for the high and the good, the sooner will he find that out. **1901** TROWBRIDGE *Lett. Mother to Eliz.* x. 51 Her thirst for information is apparently unquenchable.

c. In other contexts. (Common in recent use.)

a **1586** SIDNEY *Defence of Earl of Leicester* Wks. 1923 III. 65 An evident proof of an unquencheable malice. **1671** MILTON *Samson* 1422 The people on thir Holy-days Impetuous, insolent, unquenchable. **1805** WORDSW. *Prelude* I. 184 Firm devotion, zeal unquenchable. **1859** MILL *Liberty* iv. 164 Polygamy..seems to excite unquenchable animosity when practised by persons who speak English. **1883** *Harper's Mag.* Apr. 696/2 There is just the same unquenchable interest here.

Hence **un'quenchableness.**

1627 H. BURTON *Baiting Pope's Bull* 63 Wee pray God, that wee neuer come to feele the fierie vnquenchablenesse of it. **1629** in Hakewill *Apol.* (1630) Advts. Yy 4 b, Visiting him [*sc.* a bled man] I was amazed to see the vnquenchableness of this fire.

un'quenchably, *adv.* (UN-¹ 11.)

1652 GAULE *Magastrom.* 288 He..hath brought..his bookes to be burnt (by which himselfe might have burned un-quenchably). *a* **1711** KEN *Hymn.* Poet. Wks. 1721 II. 104 In pure Love Jesus on the Cross expir'd, That Sinners might unquenchably be fir'd. **1805** SCOTT *Last Minstrel* II. xvii, That lamp shall burn unquenchably, Until the eternal doom shall be. **1856** MRS. BROWNING *Aur. Leigh* III. 86 All true poets laugh unquenchably Like Shakespeare and the gods.

un'quenched, *ppl. a.* [UN-¹ 8.]

1. Unextinguished; unsuppressed:

a. Of fire or light. Also *fig.*

c **1200** ORMIN 10491 Inntill þatt fir þatt bærnenn shall A butenn ende unncwennkedd. ? *a* **1400** *MS. Cantab. Ff. ii. 38* fol. 26 (Halliw.) I lycken the worlde to fyre un-queynte. **1596** SPENSER *F.Q.* IV. v. 4 Vulcan..This pretious ornament ..wrought in Lemno with vnquenched fire. *a* **1626** BACON *Prayer* Wks. 1879 I. 340 My heart..hath been an unquenched coal upon thine altar. **1703** ROWE *Fair Penit.* II. D 4, If any Spark from Heav'n remain unquench'd Within her Breast. **1764** GOLDSM. *Trav.* 222 Their level life is but a smouldering fire, Unquench'd by want. **1812** BYRON *Ch. Har.* II. lxxv, Who but would deem their bosoms burn'd anew With thy unquenched beam, lost Liberty! **1836** *Lyra Apost.* (1849) 180 On high th' unquenched stars Blaze. **1882** FARRAR *Early Chr.* I. 286 Even amid the moral aberrations of heathenism it was granted to some..to keep that light unquenched.

b. Of feelings, qualities, etc.

1590 MARLOWE *2nd Pt. Tamburl.* V. iii, His teare-thyrsty and vnquenched hate. **1593** *Sidney's Arcadia* III. (1598) 367 Being depriued of her vnquenched desire. *a* **1625** FLETCHER *Woman's Prize* IV. iv, My unquench'd charity shall tell you thus much, (Though you deserve it well) you shall not beg. **1762** FALCONER *Shipwr.* III. 168 On the youthful mind th' impression cast Of ancient glory..; There all unquench'd by cruel fortune's ire, It glows. **1797** COLERIDGE *Osorio* V. 100 The Tyger, that with unquench'd cruelty, Still thirsts for blood. **1817** BYRON *Lament of Tasso* V, All unquench'd is still my better part. **1890** 'R. BOLDREWOOD' *Col. Reformer* (1891) 116 The ardour of his unquenched philanthropy.

†**2.** Of lime: Unslaked. *Obs.*

c **1500** *Melusine* 142 Barels full of vnquynched lyme. *c* **1550** H. LLOYD *Treas. Health* Uj b, Make an oyntment.. of Aloes and vnquenchyd lime wyth comon oyle. **1608** TOPSELL *Serpents* 43 Vnquenched Lyme, mixeth with Honnie and oyle. **1660** SHARROCK *Vegetables* 129, I.. sometimes have added unquenched lime into the infusions.

†**un'quert,** *sb. Obs.* [UN-¹ + QUERT, QUART *sb.*¹] Disquiet, annoyance, trouble, hurt.

a **1300** *Cursor M.* 1788 Þe leon suam beside þe hert, Til oþer did na beist vn-quert. *a* **1300** *E.E. Psalter* xxx. 15 To forgetelnes for vnquert Am I giuen. *a* **1400** *Minor Poems fr. Vernon MS.* I. 250/1121 Þis fals folk of Religioun..ben as riche in vnquerte As þeos oþure. *c* **1400** *Beryn* 2057 The man þat wrouȝt me this vnquert. *c* **1475** *Golagros & Gaw.* 675 Than thair hors vith thair hochis sic harmis couth hint, As crasit in vnquart quakand thai stand.

†**un'quert,** *a. Obs.* [UN-¹ + QUERT *a.*]

1. Disquieted, distressed.

a **1300** *E.E. Psalter* x. 2 Þair bowe..þai schot to make un-quert, In mirkenes rightwise of herte.

2. Unquiet, troublesome, wicked.

13.. in Herrig *Archiv Stud. Neu. Spr.* LXXXI. 310/95 Þis Pharesens weore vnquert, þey knewe not heor owne hert. *c* **1425** *Cast. Persev.* 3354 in *Macro Plays* 177 Þe Jeves þat were vnquert dressyd þee drynke. *c* **1470** HARDING *Chron.* CCX. ii, This wormes mete, this caryon full vnquerte, That some tyme thought in worlde it had no pere.

un'questionable, *a.* and *sb.* [UN-¹ 7 b, 12.]

1. Having an assured character or position; unexceptionable.

1603 DANIEL *Def. Rhime* G 3, The Generall Custome, and vse of Ryme..hauing beene so long..held vnquestionable. **1648** WILKINS *Math. Magic* I. xviii. 131 Attested by the experience of divers unquestionable witnesses. *a* **1687** PETTY *Pol. Arith.* i. (1690) 29 For what summ the Keepers of the Bank are unquestionable Security. **1796** MORSE *Amer. Geog.* II. 91 [It] would be incredible, were it not attested by the most unquestionable authors. **1828** LYTTON *Pelham* I. xvii, The rope was of the most unquestionable thickness. **1846** MRS. A. MARSH *Father Darcy* II. xiv. 237 His ability is great, his principles unquestionable.

2. Incapable of being doubted or disputed; indisputable, indubitable, certain.

1631 GOUGE *God's Arrows* III. §93. 353 The Crowne..by just and unquestionable title descended on her. **1695** J. EDWARDS *Perfect. Script.* 349 The learned professor.. renders it unquestionable that Moses..was the author. **1709** BERKELEY *Th. Vision* §150 The contrary being held an unquestionable truth. **1782** MARTYN *Geog. Mag.* I. 225 Authentic facts, and unquestionable evidence. **1850** HT. MARTINEAU *Hist. Peace* V. iii. (1877) III. 226 The evil was unquestionable. **1879** S. C. BARTLETT *Egypt to Pal.* xxi. 453 This is one of the unquestionable antiquities, the fountain of Elisha.

b. *sb.* An unquestionable fact or truth.

1661 GLANVILL *Van. Dogm.* 231 The love of God and our neighbour, those Evangelical unquestionables. **1898** *Westm. Gaz.* 1 Feb. 1/3 One of the unquestionables is, that the German Government cannot dare to challenge the hostility of Russia.

3. a. Not submitting to question; impatient.

1600 SHAKS. *A.Y.L.* III. ii. 393 *Orl.* What were his markes? *Ros.* A leane cheeke, which you haue not:..an vnquestionable spirit, which you haue not.

b. Not liable to question.

1649 MILTON *Tenure Kings* 19 What hath a native King to plead,..why he..should think to scape unquestionable, as a thing divine?

Hence **unquestiona'bility, -ableness.**

1727 BAILEY (vol. II), *Indisputableness,* unquestionableness. **1843** CARLYLE *Past & Pr.* II. vi, Our Religion is..a great heaven-high Unquestionability. **1873** HAMERTON *Intell. Life* III. viii. 112 The modern linguist can never fence him-self behind that stately unquestionableness which shields the Classical scholar.

un'questionably, *a.* [UN-¹ 11, 5 b.] Without or beyond question; indisputably, indubitably.

Chiefly in loose construction, qualifying the clause or sentence, as in (*a*).

(*a*) **1644** VICARS *God in Mount* 167 Such a Magistrate un-questionably is this present Lord Major. **1661** COWLEY *Cromwell* Wks. (1906) 365 It was bold unquestionably for a man..so outragiously to murder his Master. **1756** *Keysler's Trav.* I. 18 Europe is unquestionably not a little indebted to him. **1800** *Asiat. Ann. Reg., Char.* 7/2 Unquestionably a person of great prudence. **1884** F. TEMPLE *Relat. Relig. & Sci.* viii. 228 Newton's investigations were unquestionably pursued..in reliance on the truth of the uniformity of nature.

(*b*) **1655** FULLER *Ch. Hist.* XI. ii. §100 Wherein they conceived themselves to be before unquestionably estated. **1678** CUDWORTH *Intell. Syst.* 360 It might be made unquestionably evident. **1736** BUTLER *Anal.* I. vii, How unquestionably little..the pleasures and profits of it are at the best. **1740** CIBBER *Apol.* 318 Whose Repentance I have been unquestionably inform'd, appear'd [etc.]. **1846** HUXLEY in *Life* (1900) I. 28 It is an unquestionably dull day. **1894** ILLINGWORTH *Personality* iii. 60 Man finds the world outside him to be intensely, unquestionably real.

†**un'questionate,** *ppl. a. Obs.* [UN-¹ 8 b.] = next.

1423 JAS. I *Kingis Q.* cxxv, The maister portare, callit pacience,..frely let vs in, vnquestionate.

un'questioned, *ppl. a.* [UN-¹ 8.]

1. Of persons: Not subjected to questioning; uninterrogated.

1601 SHAKS. *All's Well* II. i. 211 More should I question thee..From whence thou cam'st, how tended on, but rest Vnquestion'd welcome. **1655** *Nicholas Papers* (Camden) II. 295 It lookes straingly that he passeth to and fro with that liberty he doth vnquestioned. **1742** RICHARDSON *Pamela* IV. 144, I could wish..that, even in Jest, my Mamma's Daughter might pass unquestioned. **1810** SCOTT *Lady of L.* I. xxix, That fellest foe might join the feast, And from his deadliest foeman's door Unquestioned turn. **1868** MORRIS *Earthly Par., Atl. Race* 45 Wherethrough, unquestioned of his race or name, He entered.

absol. **1898** B. GREGORY *Side Lights Confl. Meth.* 525 Permitting the great Questioner to be the great Unquestioned.

2. Not inquired into; unexamined.

1603 SHAKS. *Meas. for M.* I. i. 56 Our haste from hence is of so quicke condition, That it..leaues vnquestion'd Matters of needfull value.

3. Not called in question; undisputed.

c **1622** ROWLEY, etc. *Birth of Merlin* I. ii. 6 His safety being unquestion'd. **1653** W. RAMESEY *Astrol. Restored* 3 The case [is]..clear and unquestioned amongst rational men. **1712** ADDISON *Spect.* No. 469 ¶5 The stated and unquestioned Fee of his Office. **1781** COWPER *Expost.* 645 To praise him is to serve him, and fulfil..his unquestion'd will. **1809** CRABBE *Tales* IX. 62 He must be one with manners like her own, His life unquestion'd, his opinions known. **1885** *Manch. Exam.* 4 Feb. 4/7 She has put forward her largest claims, and..they pass unquestioned.

b. Quasi-*adv.* Without question.

1734 THOMSON *Liberty* IV. 862 On Aid, unquestion'd, liberal Aid was given.

Hence **un'questionedly** *adv.*

1644 DIGBY *Nat. Bodies* xxxiii. §5. 287 The memory, till then, keepeth quietly and vnquestionedly for the true obiect, what either the thought or chance..had patched up.

un'questioning, *ppl. a.* (UN-¹ 10.)

Both adj. and adv. (see next) are common from *c* 1860.

1828–32 WEBSTER (citing J. M. Mason). **1846** MRS. A. MARSH *Father Darcy* II. xxi. 356 Unquestioning obedience to the authority of his superiors. **1861** GEO. ELIOT *Silas M.* ii, The unquestioning activity of a spinning insect. **1875** E. WHITE *Life in Christ* IV. xxvii. 470 Schools which have.. accepted with unquestioning faith, the everlasting duration of the soul.

Hence **un'questioningly** *adv.*, **-ness.**

1857 SUSANNA WINKWORTH tr. *Life Tauler* 90 Inclined to follow..blindly and unquestioningly their spiritual masters. **1876** MRS. WHITNEY *Sights & Ins.* III. 98 His eyes were as steadfast as hers; but they had not her unquestioningness.

un'quibbled, *ppl. a.* (UN-¹ 8.)

1860 PRIOR *Anc. Danish Ball.* II. 266 He sware a clear unquibbled oath.

un'quick, *a. rare.* [UN-¹ 7. Cf. MDa. and Norw. *ukvik.*]

1. Lifeless, dead.

c **1449** PECOCK *Repr.* II. ix. 193 Ech lyuyng man is verier.. ymage of Crist..than is eny vnquyk stok or stoon. *Ibid.*, The making..of suche vnquyke gay ymagis.

2. Not lively or active.

c **1445** PECOCK *Donet* 208 Þat þou be not in eny of hem [*sc.* matters] to sluggy, vnquyke and heuy. *a* **1560** PHAER *Æneid* IX. (1562) Ee iij b, We wear our lyues in spending stele,..nor age vnquick enfebleth ought our mynds. **1925** D. H. LAWRENCE *Refl. Death Porcupine* 111 The novel..can't exist without being 'quick'. The ordinary unquick novel, even if it be a best seller, disappears into absolute nothingness.

un'quick, *v.* [UN-² + QUICK *v.*¹] *intr.* To lose vivacity.

1595 DANIEL *Civ. Wars* III. lxii, His sences droope, his steedy eye[s] vnquicke, And much he ayles.

un'quickened, *ppl. a.* (UN-¹ 8.)

1610 HEALEY *St. Aug. Citie of God* 489 Bodyes that haue a liuing soule (though as yet vnquickned by the spirit). **1639** BP. REYNOLDS *Lord's Supper* xvii, A bodily and un-quickned service. **1712** BLACKMORE *Creation* VI. 290 Which numerous, but unquicken'd progeny,..inwrapt within each other lie. **1755** H. WALPOLE *Lett.* (1846) III. 125 You may imagine our land-spirit will not be unquickened neither. **1868** BOYD *Less. Middle Age* 382 Shakspere..probably wrote, with pulse unquickened, the wildest bursts of Othello. **1876** MISS YONGE *Womankind* xi. 83 It is constant use of the powers that is needed, not only dead acquirement unquickened by exertion.

unqui'escent, *a.* (UN-¹ 7.)

1859 F. MAHONY *Rel. Father Prout* 385 The human breast ..Throbs thus unawed, Untamed and unquiescent.

un'quiet, *sb.* [UN-¹ 12, 5 b.] Absence or want of quiet; disquiet, disturbance.

1551 in Froude *Hist. Eng.* (1860) V. 328 Occasions of disorder and unquiet in the realm. **1592** KYD *Sp. Trag.* III. xv. 23 Nor dies Reuenge, although he sleepe awhile; For in vnquiet quietnes is faind. **1613** SHERLEY *Trav. Persia* 106 [It] did aggrauate both the griefe of my minde and unquiet of my bodie. **1668** PEPYS *Diary* 10 Jan., The unquiet which her ripping up of old faults will give me. **1746** ELIZA HEYWOOD *Female Spect.* No. 23 (1748) IV. 258 The cause of his own unquiet, and of that of one so dear to him. **1862** 'SHIRLEY' (J. Skelton) *Nugæ Crit.* i. 48 The unquiet and unrest of the day are gradually subdued as the evening descends. **1887** *Spectator* 1 Oct. 1300 The unquiet of the sea.

un'quiet, *a.* [UN-¹ 7, 5 b.]

1. Marked by unrest, disturbance, or disorder.

1523 [COVERDALE] *Old God & New* (1534) A j, In this so vnquiet & troblous estate of comen weales. *a* **1548** HALL *Chron., Hen. IV*, 32 b, The end of the vnquiet tyme of kyng Henry the fourth. **1634** SIR T. HERBERT *Trav.* 68 Their vnquiet Country,..lying twixt two great Kings, is a prey many times to the Turke or Persian. **1674** *Essex Papers* (Camden) I. 191, I have..writen at large.. concerning yᵉ unquiet motions which have of late bin in this Citty. **1743** *Johnson's Debates* (1787) II. 340 Measures which could produce no other effect than that of making their reign unquiet. **1796** MRS. M. ROBINSON *Angelina* III. 36 That I should not fear to sleep alone in the very apartments which were supposed to be unquiet. **1826** MISS MITFORD *Village* Ser. II. 126 Some relics of those picturesque but unquiet days. **1849** MACAULAY *Hist. Eng.* ii. I. 253 Temple himself, as was his wont in unquiet times, retired to his garden.

2. Not disposed to be quiet or inactive; restless, active, stirring (esp. so as to cause trouble).

1526 *Pilgr. Perf.* (W. de W. 1531) 2 b, This worlde..is and euer shall be vnquiet. **1560** DAUS tr. *Sleidane's Comm.* 442 Vnquiet and troublesome persons. *a* **1648** LD. HERBERT *Hen. VIII* (1683) 327 The more unquiet sort being..worn out and spent, the rest..came to a composition with the Emperor. **1697** WALSH *Dryden's Virg. Past.* Pref. ¶1 We.. can scarcely pass..a whole Day not ruffled by some unquiet Passion. **1701** SWIFT *Contests Nobles & Comm.* iv, Those hot, unquiet spirits, who disturb assemblies. **1719** —— *Abstr. Hist. Eng.* Wks. 1841 I. 545 Those perpetual troubles and vexations given to his kingdom by that unquiet people. **1849** MACAULAY *Hist. Eng.* vii. II. 253 The daring, unquiet, and vindictive seaman now sate in the councils. **1871** SMILES *Charac.* vii. 202 France has been the unquiet spirit among the nations of Europe.

b. In a state of physical unrest or commotion. Also in fig. context.

1535 COVERDALE *2 Esdras* xvi. 12 Yᵉ see aryseth up.., and the floudes of it are vnquyete. **1627** J. TAYLOR (Water P.) *Navy of Land Ships* Wks. (1630) 87/1 The tossing of the billow, and vnquiet surges of the sea. **1644** MILTON *Educ.* 2 To be tost and turmoild..in fadomles and unquiet deeps of controversie. **1707** MORTIMER *Husb.* 598 In case the Liquor [*sc.* cider in a cask] be unquiet. **1793** SMEATON *Edystone L.* §293 They found the sea so unquiet about the rocks, that [etc.]. **1853** KANE *Grinnell Exp.* xlix. (1856) 466 On every side..are the unquiet grinding floes. **1863** CONINGTON *Hor., Odes* IV. xii. 1 The gales of Thrace, that hush the unquiet Sea.

c. Not still or silent.

1655 STANLEY *Hist. Philos.* III. 45, I sent away the women lest they should be so unquiet.

3. Uneasy, perturbed, anxious: **a.** Of persons, the mind, look, etc.

1535 COVERDALE *Ps.* xli. 5 O my soule,..why art thou so vnquiete within me? **1582** N. LICHEFIELD tr. *Castanheda's Conq. E. Ind.* I. ix. 25 Being unquiet and greatly greeued at their falshood. *a* **1628** SIR J. BEAUMONT *Bosw. Field*, etc. (1629) 71 Whose counsels make men draw vnquiet breath. *c* **1698** LOCKE *Cond. Underst.* §6 (1754) 28 The mind.. hastens to some hypothesis to bottom it on; till then it is unquiet and unsettled. **1719** DE FOE *Crusoe* I. (Globe) 187, I slept unquiet. **1740** RICHARDSON *Pamela* II. 185 As the

Hours grew on . . my silly Heart was the unquieter. **1760–72** H. BROOKE *Fool of Qual.* II. 73 A countenance visibly unquiet and confused. **1831** JAMES *Phil. Augustus* I. viii, Walking up and down the hall, with an unquiet and somewhat irritated air. **1871** PALGRAVE *Lyr. Poems* 98 On the eve of the marriage morrow The bride is unquiet by night.

b. Of states or conditions.

1576 FLEMING *Panopl. Epist.* 199 The vnquiet estate of a tyrant. **1613** PURCHAS *Pilgrimage* (1614) 610 Guagida betwixt two stooles had vnquiet sitting, paying tribute [etc.]. **1665** BOYLE *Occas. Refl.* v. viii, The unquiet Pleasure that the sight of the Stars gives to this Child. **1679** *Establ. Test* 18 That insecurity . . makes . . their dayes unquiet. **1772** W. BUCHAN *Dom. Med.* 574 His sleep is unquiet with frightful dreams. **1802** WORDSW. *Excurs.* I. 873 Nine long years, She lingered in unquiet widowhood. **1844** LYTTON in *Life & Lett.* (1883) I. 115, I cried myself into an unquiet doze.

un'quiet, *v.* [UN-^{2} 3. Cf. INQUIET *v.*] *trans.* To disturb the quiet of; to disquiet.

Common *c* 1525–*c* 1625; also occurring in recent use.

1382 WYCLIF *Acts* xv. 19 For which thing I deme hem . . for to be not vnquyetid, or disesid. **1407** *Exam. Wm. of Thorpe* (MS. Rawl. C. 208) fol. 21, My conscience schulde euer be herwiþ ouer mesure vnquyetid. **1526** *Pilgr. Perf.* (W. de W. 1531) 15b, These irefull thoughtes . . neuer ceaseth to vnquiet and trouble the same. **1540** *Act 32 Hen. VIII*, c. 38 §1 The usurped power of the Bishop of Rome, hathe . . unquietid . . the subjectis of the same. **1576** LAMBARDE *Peramb. Kent* 322 They gaue him both othes and hostages to depart the Realme, and neuer after to vnquiet it. **1602** WARNER *Alb. Eng.* XII. lxxiii. 304 Thus erring Rome . . will our christian World vnqueate. **1648** GAGE *West Ind.* xii. 80 Who thought it safer sleeping in a whole skinne, then to be unquieted by fighting.

Hence **un'quieted** *ppl. a.*, **un'quieting** *vbl. sb.*

1538 in *Lett. Illustrious Ladies* (1846) III. 39, I was then half unquieted . . all day. *a* **1548** HALL *Chron., Hen. IV*, 20 To the great displeasure and long vnquieting of kyng Henry and his partakers. **1562** T. WILSON *Rhet.* (ed. 2) 72b, The gentleman . . departed with an vnquieted minde.

†**unquie'tation.** *Sc. Obs.* (UN-^{1} 12, 5b.)

1604 *Extr. Aberd. Reg.* (1848) II. 253 Na vtheris . . sall trubill this burgh, or mak ony vnquietatioun or perturbatioun in the same.

un'quietly, *adv.* [UN-^{1} 11, 5b.] Without being or keeping quiet; restlessly; *esp.* with disquiet or discomfort (of body or mind); uneasily.

c **1510** BARCLAY *Mirr. Gd. Manners* (1570) G iij, Least his giftes . . augment envy And cause him liue after much more vnquietly. **1565** COOPER *Thesaurus* s.v. *Inconstanter*, To be alway mouyng vnconstantly and vnquietly. **1592** CHETTLE *Kind-harts Dr.* (1841) 33 My quiet ghost (vn-quietly disturbed). **1605** SHAKS. *Lear* III. i. 2 *Kent.* Who's there besides foule weather? *Gen.* One minded like the weather, most vnquietly. **1640** BP. HALL *Chr. Moder.* I. xi. 109 When he was asked, what man lived most unquietly. **1671** SALMON *Syn. Med.* I. xxxviii. 86 They sleep little, and that unquietly. **1715** J. CHAPPELOW *Rt. way Rich* (1717) 79 The one bears the Trouble very unquietly. **1797** COLERIDGE *Christabel* I. 323 If she move unquietly [in sleep]. **1800** *Med. Jrnl.* III. 520 He slept very unquietly, and the pain . . extended up towards his shoulders. **1881** *Atlantic Monthly* XLIX. 51 Nell started, as from a dream, and then laughed slightly, but unquietly.

un'quietness. [UN-^{1} 12, 5b.]

1. A source of trouble or disquiet.

1514 BARCLAY *Egloges* II. (1570) Bib, When thou wouldest slepe . . , Then is their musike to thee vnquietnes. **1585** ABP. SANDYS *Serm.* 340 Some are troubled with one vnquietnes, and som with another. **1654** R. BAKER tr. *Balzac's Lett.* (vol. II) 13 If he have no other unquietness but what he is like to have from me.

2. An unquiet condition or state of things; a state of trouble or discord.

1523 [COVERDALE] *Old God & New* (1534) Aj, In this greate unquietnes of comen weales. **1560** DAUS tr. *Sleidane's Comm.* 216 The state of the prouince . . tendeth to greate vnquyetnes. **1603** in *Buccleuch MSS.* (Hist. MSS. Comm.) I. 48 Tumultuous behaviour . . whereby great unquietness did grow. **1674** *Essex Papers* (Camden) 262, I hope there will be nothing to disturbe yᵉ peace there, or bring any unquietnesse here. **1860** BP. S. WILBERFORCE *Addr. Cand. Ordination* 217 This evil of unquietness, religious strife, and discord.

3. The condition or fact of being restless or turbulent in conduct.

1526 *Pilgr. Perf.* (W. de W. 1531) 90b, Treason, fraude, . . periury, vnquyetnes, obduracion, . . with suche other. **1555** EDEN *Decades* (Arb.) 53 Isopes frogges to whom for theyr vnquietnesse Iupiter sent a hearon. **1647** N. BACON *Disc. Govt. Eng.* I. lvi. 160 The unquietnesse of some of the English brought the King to some thoughts of arbitrary rule. **1681** H. NEVILE *Plato Rediv.* 19 He cannot be denyed to be a great motive of the Peoples unquietness. **1724** WELTON *Chr. Faith & Pract.* 188 Men's unquietness and wavering in their principles. **1829** LYTTON *Disowned* 116 The unquietness and agitation of man's character.

b. Physical restlessness.

1670 EVELYN *Sylva* (ed. 2) 24 Stubbed Oak is the fittest Timber for the Case of a Sider-Mill . . as best enduring the unquietnesse of a ponderous Rolling-stone. **1856** MISS YONGE *Daisy Chain* I. i, An unquietness at the ends of her shoes, betraying the restlessness of the digits therein contained.

4. The condition of being disquieted or disturbed.

1548 ELYOT, *Inquies*, . . care, vnquietnesse, . . lacke of reste. **1553** BRENDE *Q. Curtius* VI. 110b, With a bashed countenaunce (wel declaring the vnquietnes of his minde). **1589** COOPER *Admon.* 243 To the great hindrance . . & vnquietnes of the church of God. **1638** R. BAKER tr. *Balzac's Lett.* III. 19 My unquietnesse would have continued still, if you had not taken the paines to calme it. **1649** T. FORD *Lusus Fort.* 93 Seeking rest in it's unquietnesse, but finding none. **1683** *Apol. Prot. France* vi. 93 Her great unquietness of Spirit. **1702** ECHARD *Eccl. Hist.* III. viii. 469 Being overprest with a Load of Grief and Guilt, he resolv'd to put an End to his Unquietness. *a* **1806** H. K. WHITE *Time* 628 Time . . Will waft him to repose . . Far from the unquietness of life. **1855** KINGSLEY *Misc.* (1859) I. 54 The Queen's continual unquietness will grow to contentment.

†**un'quietous**, *a. Obs.* [UN-^{1} 7.] Unquiet.

1553 BALE *Vocacyon* 37 The vnquietouse harte of the Captaine. **1641** *Cheke's Hurt Sedition* To Rdr. b, An unquietous kind of men.

un'quietude. (UN-^{1} 12, 5b.)

a **1639** WOTTON in *Reliq.* (1651) 318 That a rod or barre of iron . . will bewray a kind of unquietude and discontentment till it attain the former position.

un'quilleted, *ppl. a.* (UN-^{1} 8.)

1885 A. N. PALMER *Anc. Tenures in Marches N. Wales* 27 All the unquilleted fields that lie within the quilleted area.

un'quilt, *v.* (UN-^{2} 4.)

1611 FLORIO, *Discoltrare*, to vnquilt, to vnhill. **1634** MILTON *Comus* 614 Correction (Birch), He with his bare Wand can unquilt thy Joynts, And crumble every Sinew.

†**un'quit**, *ppl. a. Obs.* [UN-^{1} 8b, c.]

1. Unrequited; not repaid.

a **1300** *Cursor M.* 21431 Þe dai es gan, þe dett vn-quitte, þe bodi most beleue for it. *c* **1412** HOCCLEVE *De Reg. Princ.* 4177 Seruice vnquyt and murdre . . Bifore al-mightly god auxen vengeaunce. *c* **1450** *Cov. Myst.* (Shaks. Soc.) 308 That rebuke that he gaf me xal not be unqwyt. **1500–20** DUNBAR *Poems* xv. 41 Suppois the servand be lang vnquit, The lord sumtyme rewaird will it. *Ibid.* xlvii. 67 Vnquyt I do no thing. *a* **1542** WYATT in *Tottel's Misc.* (Arb.) 64 Thinke not alone vnder the sunne Vnquit to cause thy louers plaine.

2. Not quitted or left.

1603 B. JONSON *Sejanus* v. v, We must pray you hold your Guards Vnquit, when Morning comes.

†**un'quite**, *ppl. a. Obs. rare.* [UN-^{1} 8b, c.]

a. Unrequited. **b.** Unredeemed.

c **1450** *Mirk's Festial* 89 Þus þer schall no good dede be vnquyte. **1496** *Reg. Cupar Abbey* I. 251 That the saidis landis remayne with us and our successouris wnquite-owt be the lard of Burlie.

un'quitted, *ppl. a.* (UN-^{1} 8; cf. UNQUIT *ppl. a.* 2.)

1713 C'TESS WINCHELSEA *Misc. Poems* 243 Some rough Blast too far above conveighs, Or to unquitted Earth confines your weak Essays.

un'quivering, *ppl. a.* (UN-^{1} 10.)

a **1811** J. GRAHAME *Sabbath Walks* (1827) 81 The breast And wing unquivering of the wheeling lark. **1844** LD. HOUGHTON *Mem. Many Scenes* 195 He who . . with unquivering heart and hand can meet Ever distress. **1864** SALA in *Daily Tel.* 14 Dec., The same Indian . . , with unquivering lip and unfaltering eye.

un'quizzable, *a.* (UN-^{1} 7b.)

1829 MARRYAT *F. Mildmay* xv, Each was dressed out in . . most exact and unquizzable uniform.

†**unquod**, obs. variant of UNKED *a.*

a **1470** HARDING *Chron.* To Rdr., It wer an vnquod thyng, if we . . chaunge, that old menne haue write. **1548** UDALL *Erasm. Par. Luke* i. 22 He . . declared at large the cause of yᵗ his vnquod & straunge greting.

un'quotable, *a.* (UN-^{1} 7b.)

Hence, in recent use, *unquotability*.

a **1843** SOUTHEY *Doctor* ccxlii. (1848) 663 An epigram . . unquotable at length. **1862** J. H. BURTON *Bk. Hunter* 114 Words . . unquotable in this nineteenth century.

'unquote, *v.* [UN-^{2} 3.] *intr.* Used as a formula in dictation, etc.: terminate the quotation. See QUOTE *v.* 4c.

1935 E. E. CUMMINGS *Let.* Mar. (1969) 139 But he said that if I'd hold up publication of No Thanks for 15 days he'd kill unquote a page of Aiken. **1935**, etc. [see QUOTE *v.* 4c]. **1969** *New Yorker* 11 Oct. 48/2 Then Mr. Tanks announced the last downtown stop. He said, 'Madison Square Garden, Penn Station . . et cetera, et cetera, et cetera, unquote'.

un'quoted, *ppl. a.* [UN-^{1} 8.] That has not been quoted; not quoted (cf. QUOTE *v.* 7).

[**1775** ASH.] **1825** *Q. Rev.* XXXIII. 85 It is not easy to conceive that they could have existed as Scripture, unquoted, till the close of the fifth century. **1892** LE GALLIENNE *Retrosp. Rev.* (1896) I. 133 Not forgetting the unquoted 'Eve of St. Mark'. **1969** *Times* 2 May 31/6 Cranfields is an unquoted public company in flour milling and baking. **1977** JOHNS & GREENFIELD *Dymond's Capital Transfer Tax* iii. 54 (*heading*) Condition (4) Sale of unquoted shares or debentures.

unquoth, obs. or dial. var. UNCOUTH *a.*

1567 DRANT *Horace, Ep.* II. ii. Hiv, Thou must abandon vnquoth words. **1583** STUBBES *Anat. Abus.* II. H5b, These names . . are so vnquoth and strange to my eares, that [etc.]. **1615** W. HULL *Mirr. Maiestie* 113 An vnquoth sight and nouelty was . . seene in heauen. **1684** MERITON *Yorksh. Dial.* 64 An unquoth Dog hes monny barkers at. **1873** *Swaledale Gloss.* 27.

†**un'raced**, *ppl. a.*^{1} *Obs.* [UN-^{1} 8 + RACE *v.*^{4}] Not torn up.

c **1374** CHAUCER *Boeth.* IV. pr. i. (1868) 110 Yif þe þinges þat I haue concluded a litel here byforne ben kept hoole & vn-raced [*ed.* 1560 vnaraced; L. *inconvulsa*].

†**un'raced**, *ppl. a.*^{2} *Obs.* [UN-^{1} 8 + RACE *v.*^{3}] Unrazed.

c **1611** CHAPMAN *Iliad* XII. 5 Nor could the brode dike of the Greeks, nor that strong wall they made To guard their fleete, be long vnrac't.

un'raced, *ppl. a.*^{3} [UN-^{1} 8 + RACE *v.*^{1}] That has not taken part in a race.

1955 *Motor* 26 Jan. 57/1, 2-seater sports, one owner, pale green, unraced, £975. **1963** *Times* 21 May 3/6 Lord Derby's brown gelding, Robinson Crusoe, unraced as a two-year-old but winner of two races at Newmarket this season, gave a first rate display of stamina and gameness at Leicester yesterday. **1976** *Horse & Hound* 3 Dec. 9/4 Miles Away was bought by the combination at the Ballsbridge November Sales for 10,000 guineas, a record price in Ireland for an unraced gelding of his age.

un'racked, *ppl. a.*^{1} [UN-^{1} 8; cf. RACK *v.*^{5}] Not drawn from the lees.

1602 WARNER *Alb. Eng.* XIII. lxxvii. 319 Euen horror would from Tyrants, shame from harlots flow vnrack't. **1626** BACON *Sylva* §306 Pour the lees of the racked vessel into the unracked vessel.

un'racked, *ppl. a.*^{2} [UN-^{1} 8; cf. RACK *v.*^{3}]

1. Not exhausted by exactions.

1659 W. CHAMBERLAYNE *Pharon.* IV. ii. 440 Each in his own unracked inheritance Where born expired.

2. Not stretched or strained.

1887 BROWNING *Parleyings, C. Avison* ix, Because he . . spread out phrase unracked By modulations fit to make each hair Stiffen upon his wig.

un'racy, *a.* (UN-^{1} 7.)

1847 *Dublin Rev.* Sept. 228 The style . . is seldom chargeable with the defects of unracy or unidiomatic phraseology, commonly objected to Johnson's. *a* **1859** DE QUINCEY *Posth. Wks.* (1893) II. 151 Christianity in a soil so shallow and unracy as the Græco-Latin, could not [etc.].

un'railed, *ppl. a.* (UN-^{1} 8.)

[**1775** ASH.] **1842** *Rep. Comm. Children's Employment* 384 in *Parl. Papers* XVI. 1 Women and children employed to carry coal on their backs in unrailed roads. **1891** KIPLING & BALESTIER in *Century Mag.* Nov. 35/1 The unrailed bridge that crossed the irrigating-ditch. **1900** J. P. STRUTHERS in *Life* (1918) 267 He went down the little unrailed stair.

un'rainy, *a.* (UN-^{1} 7.)

1865 W. G. PALGRAVE *Arabia* I. 354 In this unrainy climate the roads are very seldom paved.

un'raised, *ppl. a.* [UN-^{1} 8.] Not raised, in various senses of the verb.

1523 LD. BERNERS *Froiss.* I. cccxxxviii. 529 So yᵗ by their neglygence the Siege shulde nat be vnreysed. **1599** SHAKS. *Hen. V*, Prol. 9 The flat vnraysed Spirits, that hath dar'd, On this vnworthy Scaffold, to bring forth So great an Obiect. **1694** DRYDEN *To Sir G. Kneller* 55 Flat Faces, . . Such as in Bantam's Embassy were seen, Unrais'd, unrounded. **1697** D. F. *Char. Dr. S. Annesley* 6 When Griefs come threatning on, or Comfort flows, He was undepress'd by these, unrais'd by those. **1809–14** WORDSW. *Excurs.* IV. 959 Go, demand Of mighty Nature, if 'twas ever meant That we should pry far off, yet be unraised. **1817** COLERIDGE *Biog. Lit.* II. 132 The poem . . is for the greater part written in language, as unraised and naked as any perhaps in the two volumes. **1873** HERSCHEL *Pop. Lect.* i. §7. 6 The raised portion still stands up above the unraised.

un'rake, *v.* [UN-^{2} 3 + RAKE *v.*^{1} 5.] *trans.* To uncover or expose by raking. Also *absol.*

?*a* **1400** *MS. Cantab. Ff.* i. 6, fol. 12 (Halliw.), Eke as charbokylle casteth ryght bemys, With rody lighte, as cole that is unrake. **1611** SPEED *Hist. Gt. Brit.* IX. xiii. 598 This againe vnraked the burning coales of enuie . . against the said Lord Duke. **1655** VAUGHAN *Silex Scint.* 60 When thou unrak'st thy fire, those sparks will bring New flames. *Ibid.*, When thy Nap's over, stir thy fire, unrake In that dead age. **1861** L. L. NOBLE *Icebergs* 91 At every dip of the oars it was like unraking the sparkling embers.

un'raked, *ppl. a.* (UN-^{1} 8. Cf. MDa. *uraget*, MSw. *orakadher*.)

1598 SHAKS. *Merry W.* v. v. 48 Where fires thou find'st vnrak'd, and hearths vnswept, There pinch [etc.]. **1659** MILTON *Hirelings* 128 [The] Lord of all things . . doubtles will command the people to make good his promises of maintenance more honorably unask'd, unrak'd for. **1683** J. REID *Scots Gard'ner* (1907) 38 Delve and mix [manure] together, to lye all winter un-raked. **1828–32** WEBSTER s.v., Land unraked. **1854** WHITTIER *Maud Muller* 64 Till the rain on the unraked clover fell.

un'rallied, *ppl. a.* (UN-^{1} 8.)

c **1644** W. CHAMBERLAYNE *Pharon.* II. iii. 255 Death . . in's march prevents The unition of unrallied regiments. **1662** HICKERINGILL *Apol. Distr. Innoc.* Wks. 1716 I. 273 Pompey blasphemously rav'd after his fatal and unrallied Pharsalian defeat. *a* **1835** HOGG *Dream Confirmed* in *C.L.* (1896) IV. 34/2 His ideas were as yet unrallied.

un'rancid, *a.* (UN-^{1} 7.)

1884 McLAREN *Spinning* 46 [In] the power of remaining fresh and unrancid . . olive [oil] is pre-eminent. **1888** J. ELLIS *New Christianity* x. 231 Unrancid oil.

un'ranged, *ppl. a.*^{1} (UN-^{1} 8; cf. RANGE *v.*^{1})

1633 FORD *'Tis Pity* I. i, Thou has mov'd a Majesty above, With thy unranged (almost) blasphemy. **1851** C. L. SMITH tr. *Tasso* IX. xxii, The Soldan rushes on, the foremost he, Upon the guards' unranged and startled pow'r.

†**un'ranged**, *ppl. a.*^{2} *Obs.* (UN-^{1} 8; cf. RANGE *v.*^{2})

1611 COTGR., *Pain de balle*, vnranged bread; or, a course bread wherein there is much chaffe. **1694** MOTTEUX *Urquhart's Rabelais* Pref. p. lxxx, That course, unraung'd Bread, or some of the great brown Houshold Loaf was good enough for such Shepherds.

un'rank, *v.* [UN-^{2} 3.] *trans.* To throw out of rank.

1611 COTGR., *Desarrengement*, an vnranking, disordering, disarraying. *Ibid.*, *Desfiler*, . . to vnranke, disorder; put off a file. **1640** tr. *Verdere's Rom. of Rom.* III. xli. 182 [They] charged the Christians through and through, till they scarce left a ranke [not] unranked.

un'ransacked, *ppl. a.* (UN-¹ 8. Cf. ON. *úrannsakaðr*, MSw. *oransakadher*.)

1529 MORE *Dyaloge* II. Wks. 187/1, I will for none hast leue any corner of the matter unransaked, as far as we can any doubte find therin. **1555** WATREMAN *Fardle Facions* II. viii. 178 Leauing no element vnransaked to get a gowbin for their glotenous gorge. **1603** KNOLLES *Hist. Turks* (1621) 651 His soldiers..left neither house nor corner thereof unransacked. **1785** COWPER *Let. to Newton* Wks. 1837 XV. 177, I shall not leave my books unransacked. **1845** [JANE ROBINSON] *Whitehall* xiv, Such carcasses as he imagined were yet unransacked. **1895** R. ELLIS in *Class. Rev.* Feb. 41/2 A still unransacked mine of quite new materials.

un'ransomed, *ppl. a.* (UN-¹ 8.)

1554 in *10th Rep. Hist. MSS. Comm.* App. V. 415 If the said silver platte be..unranesomid or redemid of the owners. **1599** SANDYS *Europæ Spec.* (1605) X 4 b, They are charitable among them selves, leaving no poore vnrelieved, no prisoner vnransomed. *a* **1625** FLETCHER *Hum. Lieut.* II. iv, 1 *Gent.* Do you grieve, we are come off? *Dem.* Unransom'd, was it? *2 Gent.* It was, Sir. **1669** EARL ORRERY *Parthen.* III. VI. 96 Giving me an unransomed Liberty. **1791** COWPER *Iliad* xxiv. 151 The Gods..say..that he still detains Amid his fleet..Unransom'd Hector. **1813** SCOTT *Rokeby* IV. vi, Safe and unransom'd [he] sent them home. **1877–9** RUSKIN *St. Mark's Rest* vii. §80 The Norman chief sent them home unransomed.

un'raptured, *ppl. a.* (UN-¹ 8.)

1742 YOUNG *Nt. Th.* IV. 261 Such contemplations.. should mount The mind still higher; nor ever glance on man, Unraptured, uninflamed. **1746** WARTON *Ode to Fancy* 114 Teach him to scorn with frigid art Feebly to touch th' unraptur'd heart. **1819** CAMPBELL *To Rainbow* 36 Nor ever shall the Muse's eye Unraptured greet thy beam.

un'rarefied, *ppl. a.* (UN-¹ 8.)

1660 BOYLE *New Exp. Phys. Mech.* xviii. 134 If that whole space had been full of unrarified Air.

un'rash, *a.* (UN-¹ 7.)

1669 CLARENDON *Ess.* Tracts (1727) 120 The temperate unrash and dispassionate man,..by being unmoved himself, discerns all advantages whilst he gives none.

un'ratable, *a.* (UN-¹ 7 b.)

1629 *Leather* 7 For common vse..vnratable value, and vnmatchable goodnesse. **1766** BURROW *Rep.* II. 1060 It would be most unreasonable that this Property which was always rateable before, should..be rendered unrateable. **1856** OLMSTED *Slave States* 560, I found that, more than any people I had ever seen, they were unrateable by dress, taste, forms, and expenditures.

un'rated, *ppl. a.* (UN-¹ 8.)

1648 HEXHAM II, *Ongelovet*, Vnprised, or Vnrated. **1703** *Act 2–3 Anne* c. 18 §15 The Values of any vnrated Goods imported. **1704** *Ibid.* c. 4 §8 Unrated Drugs..which are imported within the Days and Times last mentioned. **1772** *Ann. Reg., Chron.* 146/1 Duties due on certain unrated goods. **1896** *Daily News* 23 Apr. 5/5 The burdens upon rated and unrated property.

un'ratified, *ppl. a.* (UN-¹ 8.)

1611 SPEED *Hist. Gt. Brit.* IX. viii. 500 Some therefore haue imagined, that such Instruments might happily then be mentioned and drawne, and yet die vnratified, though the copies stand recorded. **1652** ROW *Let.* in *Hist. Kirk* (Wodrow Soc.) 538 Our Commissione of the Generall Assemblie..excommunicating most precious men transgressing unratified Acts. **1856** FROUDE *Hist. Eng.* II. 194 The parliament reviewed the Annates Act, which had been left unratified. **1887** *Pall Mall G.* 27 June 1/1 The Egyptian Convention is still unratified.

†**un'rationable,** *a. Obs.*⁻¹ [UN-¹ 7 b, 5 b.] Irrational.

a **1500** in *Ratis Raving*, etc. 6 Sic folkes suld erar be callyt bestes vnracionable, than man rasonable.

un'ravaged, *ppl. a.* (UN-¹ 8.)

[**1775** ASH.] **1796** BURKE *Let. to Noble Lord* Wks. VIII. 21 These obscene harpies..leave nothing unrent, unrifled, unravaged. **1888** *St. James's Gaz.* 11 Feb. 7/1 Few collections..can be more interesting, than underground and unravaged Cyprus.

un'ravel, *v.* [UN-² 3. Cf. Du. *ontrafelen*, †*ontravelen*.]

1. *trans.* To take out of a ravelled, tangled, or intertwined condition; to disentangle; also, to pull down, to undo (a woven fabric).

Freq. in fig. context: see quots. under (*a*).

(*a*) **1603** DEKKER *Wonderfull Yeare* Wks. (Grosart) I. 131 She..vnraueld the bottome of her frailetie at length. **1639** FULLER *Holy War* IV. i. 166 Frederick..unravelled the fair web of John Brens victory, even to the very hemme thereof. **1709** SWIFT *Tritical Ess.* Wks. 1755 II. I. 144 We shall be forced to..unravel in the night what we spun in the day. **1792** BURKE *Corr.* (1844) IV. 3 The web has been too long weaving to be unravelled in an instant. **1856** KINGSLEY in *N. Brit. Rev.* XXVI. 78 To unravel patiently the tangled web of good and evil. **1878** BROWNING *La Saisiaz* 81, I, link by link, unravelled any tangle of the chain.

(*b*) **1688** BOYLE *Final Causes Nat. Things* IV. 172 Those curious oval prisons in which they [*sc.* silkworms] enclose themselves, and which are unraveled into silk. **1727** [DORRINGTON] *Philip Quarll* (1816) 54 He was obliged to unravel the sail. **1768–74** TUCKER *Lt. Nat.* (1834) I. 352 As often happens in trying to unravel an entangled thread, while they loosen the knot in one place they draw it tighter in another. **1871** A. MEADOWS *Man. Midwifery* (ed. 2) 46 So intimate is the union in later months, that it is impossible to unravel the meshes. **1883** MARTIN & MOALE *Vertebr. Dissect.* 143 Unravel the small intestine, cutting it away from the mesentery.

transf. **1860** TYNDALL *Glac.* II. i. 227 By prisms we can unravel the white light into pure red, orange, yellow [etc.].

†**2.** *fig.* To reverse, undo, annul. *Obs.*

1644–7 CLEVELAND *Char. Lond. Diurn.* 2 It differs..as a black Witch doth from a white one, whose office is to unravell her inchantments. **1667** DRYDEN & DAVENANT *Tempest* IV. iv, All my designs Are ruin'd and unravell'd by this blow. **1673** *Lady's Call.* I. IV. §10, I wish they would.. unravel that injurious mirth by a penitential sadness. **1710** PALMER *Proverbs* 382 One season let slip, breaks the series of our conduct, unravels the order of life. **1762** H. WALPOLE *Vertue's Anecd. Paint.* (1765) I. 57 Though at last He wofully unravelled most of the pursuits of his early age. **1766** BLACKSTONE *Comm.* II. 248 After the land had descended to his issue, they would not unravel the matter again, and suffer his estate to be shaken.

3. To free from intricacy or obscurity; to make plain or obvious; to reveal or disclose.

1660 JER. TAYLOR *Ductor* I. iv. rule ii. §22 A religion that would..unravel all the intrigues of hearts. **1674** JEAKE *Arith.* (1696) 529 Simple Disjunct Proportions have at large ..been unravelled in the foregoing Part. **1709** STEELE *Tatler* No. 178 ¶1 With these..Passages..[he] was breaking his Brains Day and Night to..unravel their Sense. **1789** BELSHAM *Ess.* II. xxxii. 207 Without attempting to unravel all the intricacies of scholastic theology. **1827** LYTTON *Falkland* I. 23, I unravelled the intricacies which knit servility with arrogance. **1862** BURTON *Bk. Hunter* 377 To unravel the mystery of these primitive sculptures. **1884** A. R. PENNINGTON *Wiclif* vi. 188 Unravelling difficult questions of theology.

refl. **1791** PAINE *Rights of Man* 108 In a few days..the plot unravelled itself. **1863** STANLEY *Jew. Ch.* I. xiii. 295 As the story unravels itself.

4. *intr.* To come undone; to become unknit or disentangled. Freq. *fig.*

1650 T. VAUGHAN *Anthroposophia* 55 When the Harmony is broken.., the vitall Twist..Disbands and unravells. **1656** T. WATSON *One Thing Necessary* 53 Our life doth unravell apace. **1664** H. MORE *Myst. Iniq.* 566 As if to leave the Church of Rome were at last to unravel into a mere canting Paganism. **1744** YOUNG *Nt. Th.* VI. 158 In an eternity, what scenes shall strike!.. What webs of wonder shall unravel, there! **1768–74** TUCKER *Lt. Nat.* (1834) I. 489 My vehicle did not begin to unravel like a torn stocking. **1815** J. SMITH *Panorama Sci. & Art* II. 533 The stuff..increases in thickness.., and will not unravel when it is cut. **1820** SHELLEY *Prometh. Unb.* II. i. 23 As the burning threads Of woven cloud unravel in pale air.

Hence **un'ravelled** *ppl. a.*

1659 W. CHAMBERLAYNE *Pharon.* IV. v. 193 Whose serious souls are busied to compose Unravelled thoughts into a method. *a* **1720** J. HUGHES *Ode to Creator* ix, Proceed my muse! Time's wasting thread pursue, And see at last the unravel'd clue. **1762** FALCONER *Shipwr.* III. 41 'Tis mine the unravell'd prospect to display. **1814** BYRON *Lara* I. xvi, Vain thought! that hour of ne'er unravell'd gloom Came not again. **1859** SALA *Tw. round Clock* (1861) 168 The genuine Skye [terrier],..like an unravelled ball of worsted.

un'ravellable, *a.* (UN-¹ 7 b.)

1846 WORCESTER (citing *Phil. Mag.*). **1881** DUFFIELD *Don Quixote* I. p. xlvi, The putative Shelton renders an obvious printer's error.., and so makes unravellable nonsense of a phrase. **1885** H. O. FORBES *Wand. E. Archip.* 308 The unravellable matted wisp.

un'raveller. [f. prec.] One who unravels.

a **1704** T. BROWN *Wks.* (1715) III. 263 Mythologists are indeed..mighty Unravellers of the Fables of the old Ethnicks. **1764** P. HIFFERNAN *Earl of Warwick* I. i, Time.., th' unraveller of all The great events which actuate this world. **1814** MISS MITFORD in L'Estrange *Life* (1870) I. 189 An unraveller of state cyphers. **1889** *Athenæum* 20 Apr. 502/1 The 'improved' telephone is..dragged in to serve the purposes of fiction as an unraveller of crime.

un'ravelling, *vbl. sb.* [f. as prec.] The action of disentangling, etc.

1607 DEKKER *Knt.'s Conjur.* (1842) 32 When..the bottome of my patrimony came within 200 pound of vnraueling. **1668** DRYDEN *Dram. Poesy* Ess. (Ker.) I. 45 The Catastrophe, which..the French [call] *le denouement*, and we the discovery or unravelling of the plot. **1713** *Guardian* No. 36, Are not..all their pompous distinctions only so many unravellings of double meanings? **1742** WEST *Let.* in *Gray's Poems* (1775) 142 No unravelling of your web, dear Sir! only pursue it a little further. **1801** S. & HT. LEE *Canterb. T.* IV. 455 A mystery, the unravelling of which.. engaged all my attention. **1868** TYNDALL *Fragm. Sci.* (1871) 102 The mental exercise..involved in the unravelling of a language.

un'ravelling, *ppl. a.* [f. UNRAVEL *v.* 4.] Becoming unwound.

1827 MONTGOMERY *Pelican Island* III. 77 The unravelling clew not for a moment lost Hold of the silent hand that drew it out.

un'ravelment. [f. UNRAVEL *v.*] The process of unravelling.

1776 MICKLE *Camoens' Lusiad* Introd. 131 Collateral Episodes..assist..to facilitate and produce the Unravelment, or Catastrophe. **1779** HAMILTON *Wks.* (1886) VII. 586 The unravelment of the plot. **1835** *Court Mag.* VI. 244/1, I felt it as the unravelment of fate. **1880** BURTON *Reign Q. Anne* II. 319 His tedious work with the unravelment of all these difficulties.

un'ravished, *ppl. a.* (UN-¹ 8.)

(*a*) **1622** WITHER *Philarete* G iv, I would not permit an eare To attend vnrauisht heere.

(*b*) **1628** FELTHAM *Resolves* II. xxxvii. 114 Had not Dinah had so good a one [*sc.* face], she had come home vnrauished. **1717** POPE *Iliad* IX. 480 My beauteous captives thither I'll convey, And all the rest of my unravish'd prey. **1820** KEATS *Ode Grecian Urn* i, Thou still unravish'd bride of quietness!

un'ravishing, *ppl. a.* (UN-¹ 10.)

1781 WARTON *Hist. Eng. Poetry* III. 171 The more sober and unravishing ecstasies.

un'ray, *v.*¹ Now *dial.* [UN-² 4.] *trans.* and *refl.* To divest of clothes; to undress, strip.

1485 *Rutland Papers* (Camden) 16 The King shalbe vnraied and vnclothed by his Chamberlayn. **1510** *Bonavent. Mirr.* (Pynson) xiv. E iv b, Now take we here gode hede howe that high lorde of mageste unrayeth hym and doeth of his clothes. *c* **1550** CHEKE *Matt.* xxvii. 28 Vnraieng of him, [they] put on him a scarlet mantil. **1599** HAKLUYT *Voy.* II. II. 57 One of the Spaniards vnraied himselfe, and lept into the water. **1611** COTGR., *Desabiller*, to vncloath, vndresse, vnray. **1825–** in s.w. dialect glossaries.

absol. **1867** W. F. ROCK *Jim an' Nell* lxxix, Zum..chap 'll help thee to unray.

un'ray, *v.*² (UN-² 4; cf. RAY *sb.*¹)

1824 J. TELFER *Border Ball.* 133 The letters shone With such effulgence, that they half-unray'd Some minor names.

†**un'rayed,** *ppl. a.*¹ *Sc. Obs.* [UN-¹ 8.] = UNARRAYED *ppl. a.* 2.

c **1425** WYNTOUN *Cron.* III. ii. 322 (Cott.), Þai..set þar wachis for to se Qwhen wnrayid al was he.

un'rayed, *ppl. a.*² (UN-¹ + RAYED *ppl. a.*¹)

1830 TENNYSON *Arab. Nts.* 91 Dark-blue the deep sphere overhead, Distinct with vivid stars unrayed [1842 inlaid], Grew darker.

un'razed, *ppl. a.* (UN-¹ 8.)

1586 J. MUSH in J. Morris *Troub. Cath. Forefathers* III. (1877) 363 Not one Religious house standeth, not one altar unrased and undefiled. **1610** HOLLAND *Camden's Brit.* II. 101 They left scarce one village..unrased and unrifled. **1674–5** A. CAPEL in *Essex's Lett.* 3 Feb. (1770) 38 It will be a precedent very dangerous to the government here, that.. these very things [ordered to be erased] in after times shall appear unrazed.

un'razored, *ppl. a.* [UN-¹ 8.] Unshaven.

1634 MILTON *Comus* 290 As smooth as Hebe's their unrazor'd lips. **1774** *Westm. Mag.* II. 9 Apollo, the un-razored Macaroni God. **1845** LD. CAMPBELL *Chancellors* xlv. II. 153 By his flowing locks and unrazored lip [he] had captivated her affections. **1902** SNAITH *Wayfarers* xx, My unrazored chin passed without comment.

un'reachable, *a.* (UN-¹ 7 b.)

Freq. from *c* 1865. Also, in recent use, *un'reachableness*.

1593 *Sidney's Arcadia* v. (1622) 456 As their course neuer alters, so is there nothing done by the vnreachable ruler of them, but hath an euerlasting reason for it. **1802** SOUTHEY in Robberds Mem. (1843) I. 436, I would not remove to an unreachable distance from Herefordshire. **1846** RUSKIN *Mod. Paint.* II. III. I. v. §13 The apparent, though unreachable, nearness and promise of them.

Hence **un'reachably** *adv.*

1881 PALGRAVE *Vis. Eng.* 247 The..brimming jars In fiendish mock borne past their dungeon bars, Upheld unreachably high.

un'reached, *ppl. a.* (UN-¹ 8.)

c **1611** CHAPMAN *Iliad* XXI. 251 As he would try If all the Gods inhabiting the broad unreached sky Could daunt his spirit. **1679** DRYDEN & MULGRAVE *Ess. Sat.* 279 Now labour ..to climb That lofty hill, unreach'd by former time. **1713** C'TESS WINCHELSEA *Misc. Poems* 113 Between which two Extreams true Pleasure lies, O'er-run by Fools, unreach'd at by the Wise. **1818** BYRON *Ch. Har.* IV. cxxii, The unreach'd Paradise of our despair. **1878** WHITTIER *Seeking of Waterfall* 100 Evermore the end shall tell The unreached ideal guided well.

unre'acted, *ppl. a. Chem.* [UN-¹ 8.] Not having undergone reaction.

1950 *Jrnl. Amer. Chem. Soc.* LXXII. 10/1 If the recovered unreacted bismuth compound is considered, the yield..was 62·4%. **1977** A. HALLAM *Planet Earth* 33/3 After neutralizing or evaporating off any unreacted acid, the resulting rock solution is then sprayed into a hot flame.

unre'active, *a. Chem.* [UN-¹ 7 a.] Not reactive (REACTIVE *a.* 5 a).

1934 in WEBSTER. **1946** *Nature* 28 Sept. 437/1 In this substance..the Cl atoms are unreactive. **1965** PHILLIPS & WILLIAMS *Inorg. Chem.* I. x. 348 Molecules with very high dissociation energies such as C_2, N_2, and O_2 would be expected to be unreactive, while Li_2, Be_2, and F_2, with very low dissociation energies, would be reactive. **1978** *Jrnl. Physical Chem.* LXXXII. 2554/1 The zwitterion is relatively unreactive.

Hence **unreac'tivity.**

1946 *Nature* 14 Sept. 383/1 This chemical unreactivity of the fluorine atom of the FCH_2-group is shared by many of the compounds mentioned in this communication. **1978** *Jrnl. Physical Chem.* LXXXII. 2549 The unreactivity of glycine-like, α-amino acid zwitterions does not appear to be due to rate-limiting ring closure.

un'read, *v.* (UN-² 3.)

1533 MORE *Debell. Salem* Wks. 1025/1 Can I both gather vp al hys bookes & go hyde theim, & also make them that haue red them goe vnreade them agayne, or forget what they haue redde? **1797** *Monthly Rev.* XXIII. 511 Can his countrymen unread Freret, Boulanger, and Voltaire, or unlearn the sophisms which they have impressed?

un'read, *ppl. a.* [UN-¹ 8 b.]

1. Not read; unperused.

1456 SIR G. HAYE *Law Arms* (S.T.S.) 63 [He] held the letter in his hand unred. *a* **1553** UDALL *Roister D.* III. ii, Ye a woman? and your letter so long vnredde. **1596** SPENSER *F.Q.* IV. xii. 2 Then blame me not, if I haue err'd in count Of Gods, of Nymphs, of riuers yet vnred. **1693** *Dryden's Juvenal* VII. (1697) 173 His Muse had starv'd, had not a Piece unread, And by a Player bought, supply'd her Bread. **1728** POPE *Dunciad* III. 103 Her grey-hair'd Synods damning books unread. **1796** Mme. D'Arblay *Camilla* II. 389 She therefore determined that..she would..deliver the unread letter to Sir Hugh. **1838** Lytton *Leila* I. ii, An open manuscript..lay unread before the Moor. **1879** Froude *Cæsar* xxvii. 469 He burnt unread the correspondence of Pompey and Scipio.

2. Not instructed by reading. Also *absol.*

1606 Shaks. *Tr. & Cr.* I. iii. 24 The Wise and Foole, the Artist and vn-read,..seeme all affin'd, and kin. **1687** Dryden *Hind & P.* III. 409 And last, uncertain whose the narrower span, The clown unread, and half-read gentleman. *a* **1743** Savage *To John Powell* 47 To unread Squires, illiterately gay; Among the learn'd, as learned full as they. **1811** Byron *Hints fr. Hor.* 237 Unread,..Fool'd, pillag'd, dunn'd, he wastes his term away. **1865** *St. James's Mag.* Oct. 354 The Great Unread. **1884** *Graphic* 4 Oct. 358/1 The Khedive himself is far from unlearned and unread.

b. Const. *in* (a matter or subject).

1602 Warner *Alb. Eng.* IX. lii. 234 Such as be vnreade In that sweete Promise. **1790** Burke *Fr. Rev.* 185 Not being wholly unread in the authors. **1816** Coleridge *Lay Serm.* 314 A fact that none but the unread in history will deny. **1865** Meredith *R. Fleming* viii, Algernon was unread in the hearts of women.

un'readable, *a.* [un-¹ 7 b.]

1. Too dull or distasteful to read.

1802–12 Bentham *Ration. Judic. Evid.* Wks. 1843 VI. 441 Take up a history of an old French lawsuit, the evidence is absolutely unreadable. **1837** Hallam *Hist. Lit.* I. iv. §70 Making the entire work unreadable by the most patient..of mankind. **1867** Darwin in F. Darwin *Life & Lett.* (1887) III. 96 After the horrid, tedious, dull work of my present huge, and I fear unreadable, book.

2. Illegible through careless or indistinct writing.

1830 Miss Mitford *Village* Ser. IV. 182 Oh such letters! ..and in such a hand! so pretty and so unreadable! **1861** Wynter *Soc. Bees* 13 An immense number of letters..with directions perfectly unreadable to ordinary persons.

transf. **1839** Carlyle *Chartism* iii, The emblem of darkness, of unreadable confusion.

3. Inaccessible to any reader.

1852 C. B. Mansfield *Paraguay*, etc. (1856) 66 Whether I go down by steamer to Monte Video..or whether I go into the interior of San Paulo..is at present written in the Unreadable Book.

Hence **unreada'bility, un'readableness; un'readably** *adv.*

1780 F. Burney *Diary & Lett.* (1842) I. VII. 316 In the evening we had Mrs. Lambert, who brought us a tale, called 'Edwy and Edilda', by the sentimental Mr. W——, and unreadably soft, and tender, and senseless is it. **1838** J. S. Mill in *Westm. Rev.* Aug. 506 He could stop nowhere short of utter unreadableness. **1856** Vaughan *Mystics* II. VIII. vii. 74 Reason will not attempt to rescue him from condign sentence of unreadableness. **1870** Lowell *Among my Bks.* Ser. I. (1873) 338 Klopstock himself is..an immortality of unreadableness. *a* **1871** De Morgan *Budget Parad.* (1872) 123 It is a climax of unsaleability, unreadability, and inutility. *a* **1974** R. Crossman *Diaries* (1975) I. 564 She may be right that if you want to impress people you must make things unreadably long.

un'readily, *adv.* (un-¹ 11.)

1599 Hakluyt *Voy.* II. I. 117 Men being first inforced to write their actes..in barkes of trees, or otherwise perchance as vnreadily. **1755** Johnson, *Awkwardly*, clumsily; unreadily; inelegantly. **1804** Mitford *Inquiry* 75 Instruments like the harpsichord,..incapable or unreadily capable of variety in loudness. **1871** Proctor *Light Science* 138 It is astonishing how unreadily two sea-currents exchange their temperatures.

un'readiness. (un-¹ 12; cf. unready *a.*¹)

1526 *Pilgr. Perf.* (W. de W. 1531) 131 We shold expell all slouth & vnredynes in doynge our dutye to god. *a* **1548** Hall *Chron., Hen. VI*, 154 The Frenchemen hauing perfyte vnderstanding of the infirmitie and vnreadinesse..of Englande. **1611** Speed *Hist. Gt. Brit.* VII. xliv. §39. 366 Accusing him with sloath and vnreadinesse of Armes. **1665** Boyle *Occas. Refl.* To Sophronia, My Unreadiness to Publish these very long neglected Papers. *a* **1761** Law *Comf. Weary Pilgr.* (1809) 26 Every unreadiness to do good ..makes us schismaticks. **1861** Hughes *Tom Brown at Oxf.* ii, He couldn't realise the fact of his unreadiness in a boat. **1887** *Spectator* 5 Nov. 1494 Our unreadiness as to a sufficient supply of arms.

un'reading, *ppl. a.* (un-¹ 10.)

1829 *Edin. Rev.* L. 183 There is but one chance of making this unreading cast readers. **1852** H. Rogers *Ess.* (1874) I. vii. 348 The unreading 'philosophers who avoided books'. **1879** F. Harrison *Choice of Bks.* iv. (1886) 81 The idle and unreading world.

un'ready, *a.*¹ [un-¹ 7.]

1. Not in a state of readiness or preparation: a. Without const.

c **1340** Hampole *Pr. Consc.* 1990 If a man þat unredy es, Be tane with dede in his wykednes. **1382** Wyclif *2 Cor.* ix. 4 Lest when Macedonyes schulen come with me, and schulen fynde ȝou vnredy, we schamen [etc.]. *c* **1450** tr. *De Imitatione* I. xxiii. 31 Lyue so þat deþe finde þe neuer unredy. *c* **1560** *Jack Juggler* B ii b, And as you see for the most part our witts be best When wee be takyne most vnrediest. **1570** Foxe *A. & M.* (ed. 2) 69/2 Some other there were vnready and not so well prepared. **1603** J. Davies (Heref.) *Micro-cosmos* Wks. (Grosart) I. 56/2 Our force lies most dispersed at the Plow, Vnready, rude, and oft rebellious too. **1671** Clarendon *Hist. Reb.* IX. §30 Fairfax was..not in readiness to march; yet reported to be much more unready than he was. **1790** A. Wilson *Death* Poet. Wks. (1846) 64 And, if unready, we are caught by Death, He throws us howling to the gulph beneath. **1855** Macaulay *Hist. Eng.* xix. IV. 268 His enemies, while still unready, learned with dismay that he had taken the field in person.

absol. **1838** G. Johnston *Brit. Zoophytes* 102 Should the prey prove too tough, woe! to the unready!

b. Const. *to* with inf.

a **1300** *Cursor M.* 25478 Vnworthi am i..And al vnredi for to rise On domesdai be-for iustise. **1510–20** *Everyman* in Hazl. *Dodsley* I. 104 Full unready I am such reckoning to give. **1590** Spenser *F.Q.* I. v. 45 False Duessa..found the Faery knight Departed thence, albe his woundes wide Not throughly heald, vnreadie were to ride. **1615** W. Lawson *Country Housew. Gard.* (1626) 29 Want of strength may make them vnready to receiue sap. **1707** S. Sewall *Diary* 15 Dec., I express'd my self unready to vote for it. **1871** R. H. Hutton *Ess.* v. I. 125 If it be a righteous life and will..that stirs human nature thus deeply, and finds us..unready to adapt ourselves to it.

c. Const. *for*, †*of*, or *with*.

1617 Woodall *Surgeon's Mate* (1639) 191 He is an unworthy Chirurgion, which is at any time unready with such needfull instruments. **1702** Rowe *Tamerl.* I. i, Secure of Peace and for Defence unready. **1737** Whiston *Josephus, Antiq.* v. iii. §2 The Israelites grew so indolent, and unready of taking pains. *a* **1865** Keble *Lett.* (1870) 165 Very unready with any plan for meeting it. **1865** Ruskin *Arrows of Chace* (1880) II. 72, I am not usually unready for a controversy.

2. Not prepared or made ready.

c **1380** Wyclif *Sel. Wks.* II. 40 þerfore make þi tresoure in God, for..þis tresoure mai not perishe, to be unredi whanne þou hast nede. *a* **1500** *Ratis Raving* I. 1003 It is wnreddy payment That þow has fristit out or lent. **1542** Udall *Erasm. Apoph.* 187 It is an eivill man of warre that wil have his weapen unreadie when he should occupie it. *a* **1548** Hall *Chron., Edw. V*, 12 b, And so all thyng was vnredy, when this message came. **1632** Holland *Cyrupædia* 125 When he vieweth your forces, he will thinke his owne to be yet unready. **1721** Strype *Eccl. Mem.* II. xx. 405 The money was already when Cæsar had present need thereof.

†b. *Sc.* Not easy or plain. *Obs.*

1535 Stewart *Cron. Scot.* (Rolls) I. 440 Nocht ane..wist weill quhair away for till wend, The gait wes sa vnreddy and miskend.

3. Undressed; in deshabille. *Obs.* or *dial.*

In common use from *c* 1595 to 1640.

1591 Shaks. *1 Hen. VI*, II. i. 39 [*stage-dir.*] The French leape ore the walles in their shirts. Enter..Bastard, Alanson, Reignier, halfe ready, and halfe vnready. *Alan.* How now my Lords? what all vnreadie so? **1625** in Ellis *Orig. Lett.* Ser. I. III. 198 The Queene,..though she were unready,..hasted down a pair of stairs to meet him. **1678** *Yng. Man's Call.* 364 She desired to go..to dress her head, which by the violence of the wind was made all unready. **1823–** in Suffolk and Lincoln glossaries.

4. Not quick or prompt; hesitating, slow; †not responding readily to command.

1594 T. Bedingfield tr. *Machiavelli's Florentine Hist.* VI. (1595) 149 These newes grieued the Earle exceedingly, bicause he thought his army not fully paid, would be vnreadie. **1607–12** Bacon *Ess., Youth & Age* (Arb.) 260 Like an vnready horse that will neither stopp nor tourne. **1672** Sir T. Browne *Let. Friend* §22 To become more narrow-minded..and tenacious, unready to part with anything. **1708** Rowe *Royal Convert* I, There needs no more; For I would spare thee the unready tale. **1824** Miss Mitford *Village* Ser. I. 124 So alive and eloquent in conversation, that I feel more than ever puzzled and unready. **1855** Mrs. Gaskell *North & S.* vii, 'Mr. Thornton, I believe!' said Margaret, after a half-instant's pause, during which his unready words would not come. **1857** in Mrs. Gaskell *C. Bronte* (ed. 3) II. 138 She had become unready, nervous, excitable, and either incapable of speech, or talked vapidly.

Comb. **1670** Cotton *Espernon* II. 409 One of the most unwieldy, and unready footed Animals, that is to say, a Mule.

Hence †**un'ready** *v. trans.*, to undress. *Obs.*⁻¹

1593 *Sidney's Arcadia* III. (1598) 365 After his wife was departed to her fained repose, as long as hee remayned with his daughter, to giue his wife time of vnreadying her selfe.

un'ready, *a.*² [Later form of unredy *a.*, after prec. Cf. unrede b.] = redeless *a.* (but usually regarded as = prec. 1 or 4).

Only as an epithet of Ethelred II (died 1016): cf. Polydore Vergil *Angl. Hist.* (1534) VII. 124 'qui pigritia omnia faciebat'.

1580 Stow *Chron.* 134 Etheldrede, commonly called Unready. **1643** Baker *Chron.* (1653) 18 Ethelred,..by reason of his backwardnesse in Action, was commonly called the Unready. **1655** Fuller *Ch. Hist.* II. 136. **1867** Freeman *Norm Conq.* I. 286 A prince, who..has received no nobler historical surname than that of the Unready. *Ibid.* 327 The Unready King showed occasional glimpses of vigour.

un'real, *a.* (un-¹ 7.)

1605 Shaks. *Macb.* III. iv. 107 Hence horrible shadow, Vnreall mock'ry hence. **1645** Milton *Tetrach.* 60 Only for the fals keeping of a most unreal nullity, a mariage that hath no affinity with Gods intention. **1667** —— *P.L.* x. 471 Th' unreal, vast, unbounded deep Of horrible confusion. **1711** Steele *Spect.* No. 53 ¶3 You should..teach the Men not to be any longer dazzled by false Charms and unreal Beauty. **1746** Francis tr. *Horace, Epist.* II. i. 289 He gives a desperate Trial of his Art,..Who with unreal Terrours fills my Breast. **1810** Southey *Kehama* IV. iv, Musing so long he lay, that all things seem Unreal to his sense, even like a dream. **1842** Manning *Serm.* x. (1848) 139 Surrounding ourselves with an unreal world of hopes, and fears. **1871** Lowell *Study Windows* 153 Those who have most loudly advertised their passion for seclusion..have been mostly sentimentalists, unreal men.

spec. **1838** G. F. Graham *Mus. Comp.* 17/2 What are called passing notes, or unreal notes, and which are said not to form any real part of the melody or the harmony. **1883** A. Sidgwick *Fallacies* 42 The distinction between *Real* and what may be called *Unreal*. *Ibid.*, The name 'Unreal' as here applied to propositions, is somewhat wider than what is usually meant by 'verbal'.

un'realism. (un-¹ 12.)

1859 *Sat. Rev.* 29 Jan. 118/2 The ideal unrealism of statesmanship which invented Mr. Gladstone's mission. **1875** Lowell in *N. Amer. Rev.* CXX. 387 It is only a world of unrealism.

un'realist, *sb.* and *a.* [un-¹ 12, 7 a.]

A. *sb.* One who is not a realist. B. *adj.* Not realistic or realist.

1934 Webster, Unrealist, *n.* **1936** E. Gill *Let.* 10 Oct. (1947) 367 It is unrealist to write..saying 'art is a way of life ..that should govern all we do and make, not to say think'. **1938** A. L. Rowse in *Pol. Q.* Jan.–Mar. 24 The hopeless doctrinaires,..the chronic unrealists, who are the despair of the [Labour] Party. **1958** S. Spender *Engaged in Writing* 67 They, with their fairy stories,..are the unrealists. **1973** *Screen* Spring/Summer 40 Certain types of cinema (modern, realist, 'un-realist'. [etc.]). *Ibid.* 48 Films which are deliberately 'un-realist' (legends, fairy stories, films of the *phantastique* genre, etc.).

unrea'listic, *a.* (un-¹ 7.)

1865 Kingsley *Lett.* (1878) II. 215 The very unrealistic turn of mind which I have in common with this generation.

Hence **unrea'listically** *adv.*

1961 *Listener* 16 Nov. 797/2 Our critics often use their weapons unrealistically, and unhistorically. **1977** *Times Lit. Suppl.* 20 May 610/3 He kidded him for making American life unrealistically grim.

unre'ality. (un-¹ 12.)

1751 Warburton *Pope's Wks.* III. 42 They conclude in the most extravagant and senseless inferences; such as the unreality of matter; the reality of space. **1798** Lamb *Ros. Gray* xi, Past associations revived with the music—blended with a sense of unreality. **1850** Carlyle *Latter-d. Pamph.* vi. 8 Unreality is death, to Parliaments and to all things. **1880** E. White *Cert. Relig.* 45 They are seen in a glory mist which throws a certain unreality over their outlines.

b. With *an* and pl.

1817 Southey *Fragm. Th. on Son's Death* Wks. (1909) 741/1 They are not, though, Mere unrealities. **1843** Carlyle *Past & Pr.* IV. i, The unrealities, beaten into dust, flew gradually off. **1863** E. V. Neale *Anal. Th. & Nat.* 31 If time is not to become an unreality to us.

un'realizable, *a.* [un-¹ 7 b, 5 b.] Incapable of being realized, in various senses.

1840 Carlyle *Heroes* iv. (1841) 247 We may rejoice that he could not realise it; that it remained, after two centuries of effort, unrealisable. **1860** J. Young *Prov. Reason* 81 Power which is truly infir .e, must be for ever..unrealizable in its utmost extent. **1883** *St. James's Gaz.* 1 Dec. 7/2 The great financial establishments..are believed to be still overloaded with unrealizable stock.

un'realize, *v.* [un-² 3.] *trans.* To make unreal; to deprive of reality.

1804 Southey *Let.* in *Life* (1850) II. 259 The least breath stirring would have shaken the whole vision, and at once unrealised it. **1854** H. Miller *Sch. & Schm.* xv. 331 The painted canvass, and the..too palpable acting, served but to unrealize what I saw, and to remind me that I was merely in a theatre. **1875** Lowell *Spenser* Prose Wks. 1890 IV. 337 His fancy, habitually moving about in worlds not realized, unrealizes everything at a touch.

Hence **un'realizer; un'realizing** *ppl. a.*

1814 Southey *Roderick* x. 60 The flame..cast upon the leaves A floating, grey, unrealizing gleam. **1845** Mozley *Ess.* (1878) II. 127 How little do we feel the past! On flows Time, the great unrealiser. *a* **1859** De Quincey *Posth. Wks.* (1893) II. 204 This postulate of fiction..would have operated with an unrealizing effect upon all that followed.

un'realized, *ppl. a.* (un-¹ 8.)

[**1775** Ash.] **1803** *Man in Moon* (1804) 82 What real good are we to expect from this new scheme to which we so foolishly attach unrealized riches. **1852** H. Rogers *Ecl. Faith* 290 There is such a thing in the human mind as unrealised truth, both intellectual and spiritual. **1876** Mrs. Whitney *Sights & Ins.* xxx, Behind us a southwest wind was driving the mists, all unrealized by us, from off the mountain faces.

un'really, *adv.* (un-¹ 11.)

1855 Pusey *Doctr. Real Presence* Note E. 69 Some distinct case..in which proper terms..are, without any hint or notice, to be understood unreally.

un'realmed, *ppl. a.* (un-² 8, 4 + realm.)

1845 Bailey *Festus* (ed. 2) 386 That unrealmed tyrant drew his mortal dart And drave it through himself.

un'realness. (un-¹ 12; cf. unreal *a.*)

1834 Lytton *Pilgr. Rhine* v, The unrealness of literary fame.

un'reaped, *ppl. a.* (un-¹ 8.)

1577 Hellowes *Gueuara's Chron.* 143 Losse of their corne, both reapt and vnreapt. *a* **1625** Beaum. & Fl. *Cust. Country* IV. i, My first love here begun, rests here unreapt yet. **1670** Milton *Hist. Eng.* II. 39 In that place which only they had left unreap'd of all thir Harvest. **1737** Glover *Leonidas* IV. 370 There the corn Bent by its golden burthen sheds unreap'd Its plenteous seed. **1795** Southey *Joan of Arc* III. 7 The autumnal rains had beaten to the earth The unreap'd harvest. **1817** Kirby & Sp. *Entomol.* II. 480 Those moths..betake themselves to the yet unreaped fields. **1834** M. Scott *Cruise Midge* (1859) 289 Half of my beard has been left unreaped by that villanous razor of Brail's.

un'reason, *sb.* [un-¹ 12.]

†1. Unreasonable action or intention; injustice, impropriety. *Obs.*

a **1300** *Cursor M.* 3747 He has me don oft vn-resun And no[w] me reft mi benisun. **13..** *Metr. Hom.* (Vern. MS.) in *Archiv Neu. Spr.* LVII. 303 Wiþ muchel wrong and vn-resoun Dost þow me þis tresoun. *c* **1400** *Pilgr. Sowle* IV. ix. (Caxton) 62 It semeth me vnreson..that he that nought ne oweth shal payen for the dettour hym seluen. *c* **1500** *Priests of Peblis* 141 And that ȝe think vnressoun or wrang, Wee al and sundrie sings the samin sang. **1597** Skene *De Verb.*

Sign. s.v. *Tort*, Tort, et non reason, vn-reason, wrang, and vnlaw. **1609** [see UNLAW *sb.* 1].

†**2.** ***Abbot (of) Unreason***, a mock personage elected as the leading character in certain popular revellings formerly in Scottish use. *Obs.*

1496 *Acc. Ld. High Treas. Scot.* I. 270 To Gilbert Brade, ..for spilling of his hous in Striuiling be the Abbot of Vnresoun, x.li. **1555** *Sc. Acts Parlt., Mary* (1814) II. 500/1 It is..ordanit that in all tymes cumming na maner of persoun be chosin, Robert Hude nor Lytill Johne, Abbot of vnressoun, Quenis of Maij nor vtherwyse. *a* **1572** KNOX *Hist. Ref.* Wks. 1846 I. 40 The same Frear maid ane uther sermoun of the Abbote Unreassone, unto whome..he compared the prelattis of that age. [**1820** SCOTT *Abbot* xiv, and note.]

3. Absence of reason; indisposition or inability to act or think rationally or reasonably. (Common from *c* 1850.)

1827 CARLYLE *Misc.* (1840) I. 47 Other forms of Unreason have taken its place. **1847** HELPS *Friends in C.* I. vii. 115 Many a woman is brought up in unreason and self-will from these causes that he has given. **1861** M. ARNOLD *Pop. Educ. France* 174 A system which, to the loud blasts of unreason and intolerance, sends forth no certain counterblast. **1883** PATTISON *Mem.* (1885) 2 All my energy was directed..to free myself from the bondage of unreason.

b. That which is contrary to, or devoid of, reason.

1847 HELPS *Friends in C.* I. vii. 114 Women may talk the greatest unreason out of doors, and nobody kindly informs them that it is unreason. **1865** J. GROTE *Explor. Philos.* I. 210 That unreason or nonsense which it is the business of the higher part to convert into knowledge.

un'reason, *v.* [UN-[2] 4, 3.]

1. *trans.* (and *refl*). To deprive of reason.

a **1676** HALE *Prim. Orig. Man.* (1677) 343 We shall have such Solutions as must make us first unreason and unman our selves, before we can subscribe to them. **1755** SMOLLETT *Quix.* I. i. I. 2 The unreasonable usage..so unreasons my reason, that I have reason to complain of your beauty. **1829** T. HOOK *Bank to Barnes* 40 Were I to tease on, It would nearly unreason your reason.

2. To disprove, refute.

1661 R. L'ESTRANGE *State Divinity* 25 Their Reasons I have un-Reason'd already. *a* **1716** SOUTH *Serm.* (1744) XI. 257 However a man may for a while..seem to himself to unreason the equity of God's proceedings; yet [etc.].

un,reasona'bility. (UN-[1] 12; cf. next.)

14.. in *E.E.P.* (1862) 143 Arystotelle..sayethe that euery man nedethe To be ware of the vnresonabylite That comethe of the sensualite.

un'reasonable, *a.* (*adv.*) [UN-[1] 7 b.]

1. Not endowed with reason; irrational.

c **1340** HAMPOLE *Pr. Consc.* 599 He..fares als an unresonabel beste, þat his awen wille folowes. **1382** WYCLIF *2 Peter* ii. 12 Thes sotheli [ben] as vnresounable beestes. *c* **1400** *Destr. Troy* 4428 A Roid beste vnreasonable. *c* **1450** *Myrr. our Ladye* 287 But vnresonable creatures..prayse god, in that they do as god hathe..ordeyned them to do. **1509** BARCLAY *Shyp of Folys* 119 Other creatures that ar vnresonable Goeth on all foure. **1569** J. SANFORD tr. *Agrippa's Van. Artes* 69 b, All the Pagans..doo affirme.. that reasonable soules goo into unreasonable bodies. **1615** W. BEDWELL *Moham. Impost.* II. §9 We shall leade our life ..as beasts and vnreasonable creatures do. **1655** MOUFET & BENNET *Health's Improv.* 265 Nay, go to your Raven and Stag, those longest livers of all the unreasonable breathers. **1675** BROOKS *Gold. Key* 231 All the creatures, both reasonable and unreasonable, do in some sort set forth the praises of Christ. **1795** SOUTHEY *Soldier's Fun.* 35 Whilst his fellow-man..Must as the unreasonable beast drag on A life of labour. **1861** READE *Cloister & H.* lxxiii, There were buffaloes, lizards,..leopards; any unreasonable beast but the right one.

transf. **1592** SHAKS. *Rom. & Jul.* III. iii. 111 Thy wild acts denote The vnreasonable Furie of a beast.

2. Not acting in accordance with reason or good sense; not reasonable in conduct, demands, expectations, etc.

c **1375** *Cursor M.* 6614 (Fairf.), Quen þai þis sagh, qua soþ wil say, þa vnresonable folk þu3t na play. *c* **1400** *Comm. Luke* i. 22 (MS. Bodl. 143), þe puple of iewes semeþ lyk to doumb sacarie, whiche puple is so vnresonable þat it may not 3yue resoun of his dedis. **1483** CAXTON *G. de la Tour* e vi b, This newe kynge..was to them full hard and felon, & also to al his comyns he was vnresonable. **1496** *Act 12 Hen. VII*, c. vii, Divers unresonable and detestable persones..wilfully committe murdre. *a* **1548** HALL *Chron., Hen. VI*, 126 Least thei beyng nedy and innocente people, should be.. turmented with the vnreasonable men of warre. **1596** SHAKS. *Merch. V.* v. i. 203 What man is there so much vnreasonable, If you had pleas'd to haue defended it With any termes of Zeale. **1669** STURMY *Mariner's Mag.* I. i. 3 [This] will give the most reasonable men satisfaction; for the unreasonable, I care not a fig for them. *c* **1670** HOBBES *Dial. Com. Laws* (1681) 10 When the greatest part of Men are so unreasonable as they are. **1740** LD. HARRINGTON in *10th Rep. Hist. MSS. Comm.* App. I. 275, I hope therefore that I shall not be thought unreasonable in preferring this Petition to the King. **1829** SCOTT *Anne of G.* xxxiv, He was capricious, unreasonable, peremptory, and inconsistent. **1876** MOZLEY *Univ. Serm.* x. (ed. 2) 205 They are not so unreasonable as to expect that they can like persons without knowing them.

3. Not in accordance with reason; not based upon sound reason or good sense.

a **1340** HAMPOLE *Psalter* lxxvii. 76 Nurishynge of vnresonabill thoghtis. **1377** LANGL. *P. Pl.* B. VI. 153 For it is an vnresonable Religioun þat hath ri3te nou3te of certeyne. *c* **1450** *Cov. Myst.* (Shaks. Soc.) 221 O, holy prophete! graunt me mercy! Of my synnys unresonable. **1533** MORE *Debell. Salem* Wks. 983/1 To shew that the same spiritual law, which this man would proue vnreasonable, is not in dede proued vnreasonable. **1560** DAUS tr. *Sleidane's Comm.* 226 b, Neyther that he enforce them to any vnreasonable condicyon or vnworthye for them. **1660** *Trial Regic.* 54, I do hold the Prisoner's Plea vain, and unreasonable. **1688** BUNYAN *Jerus. Sinner Saved* (1886) 50 It would be the unreasonablest thing in the world to render hatred for love. **1711** ADDISON *Spect.* No. 164 ¶1 He contracted an unreasonable Aversion towards his Son. **1760** STERNE *Tr. Shandy* III. xxxi, I think it a very unreasonable demand. **1849** MACAULAY *Hist. Eng.* vi. II. 159 The panic was not unreasonable. **1885** 'MRS. ALEXANDER' *At Bay* iv, A vague, unreasonable anxiety about Elsie haunted him.

†**b.** Inequitable, unfair; unjustifiable. *Obs.*

? *a* **1400** *Morte Arth.* 3453, I rede thow rekkyne and reherse un-resonable dedis. **1525** LD. BERNERS *Froiss.* II. CXC. [clxxxvi.] 582 We haue to laye to his charge dyuers artycles vnresonable whiche requyre iudgement of punisyon. **1651** HOBBES *Leviath.* II. xxvi. 140 That..which thou thinkest unreasonable to be done by another to thy selfe.

4. Going beyond what is reasonable or equitable; excessive in amount or degree.

c **1380** WYCLIF *Wks.* (1880) 233 Lordis many tymes don wrongis to pore men by..vnresonable mercymentis & vnresonable taxis. *c* **1450** *Mirk's Festial* 101 Pharao.. oppressyth the pepull of Israell wyth bondage and wyth vnresynabull werkes. *c* **1460** FORTESCUE *Abs. & Lim. Mon.* xiv. (1885) 144 Yff this ordre be kept,..suytours..shall [not] be importunite or brocage optayne any vnresonable desires. **1542** BRINKLOW *Compl.* xxiv. (1874) 73 But the forkyd persecutors haue vnreasonable riches..in their handys. **1583** STUBBES *Anat. Abus.* II. C 8, Is not this too vnreasonable, to take a crowne..for writing six or seuen lines? **1617** MORYSON *Itin.* I. 220 No Christian may enter this place..except he will giue an vnreasonable reward. **1680** PRIDEAUX *Lett.* (Camden) 79 Y[e] unreasonable prices set upon Bibles. **1725** DE FOE *Voy. round World* (1840) 195 Almost any reasonable quantity might have been sold there; but the truth is, we had an unreasonable quantity. **1796** MME. D'ARBLAY *Camilla* III. 416 She could never again consent to interfere in his unreasonable requests. **1855** MACAULAY *Hist. Eng.* xix. IV. 373 He had to wait a most unreasonable time for a judgment. **1893** *Law Times* XCIV. 600/2 The [income] tax falls with..undue severity upon one class, and with unreasonable lightness upon others.

†**b.** As *adv.* Excessively, extremely. *Obs.*

1581 PETTIE *Guazzo's Civ. Conv.* II. (1586) 115 There are some, who coueting to be counted unreasonable honest, frowne [etc.]. **1583** STUBBES *Anat. Abus.* II. F 3, Thus..they make shooes vnreasonable deere.

un'reasonableness. [UN-[1] 12.]

1. The quality (in things or actions) of being unreasonable or at variance with reason.

1532 *Dial. on Laws Eng.* (ed. 2) II. xlviii. 122 It were a greate vnreasonablenes in the lawe if it shulde prohibit hym [etc.]. **1560** DAUS tr. *Sleidane's Comm.* 305 Considering the vnreasonablenes of the thing. **1645** VANE *Lost Sheepe* 24 The vnreasonablenesse of this assertion. **1691** RAY *Creation* I. (1692) 18 The folly and unreasonableness of this.. ungrounded Figment. **1748** *Anson's Voy.* III. ix. 388 The Commodore urging the unreasonableness of this procedure, from the inability of the forts to have done otherwise. **1778** MISS BURNEY *Evelina* xlvi, The folly and unreasonableness of this speech. **1830** GEN. P. THOMPSON *Exerc.* (1842) I. 248 There are depths of unreasonableness, which surpass all human folly. **1886** *Law Times Rep.* LIII. 660/1 The agreement is invalidated by the unreasonableness of the restriction.

†**b.** Unfairness, injustice. *Obs.*

a **1533** LD. BERNERS *Huon* xviii. 48 Ye..haue well herde the grete vnresonablenes that the kynge do too one of oure peres. *Ibid.*, The place wher as suche extorsyon and vnresonableness is vsed.

c. Immoderateness; excessiveness.

1665 SIR T. HERBERT *Trav.* (1677) 282 The Ambassadour ..acquainted his Master with the unreasonableness of the Turks demands. **1797** MRS. RADCLIFFE *Ital.* xxxi, The unreasonableness of her claims was forgotten.

2. The quality (in persons) of being unreasonable in action, demands, etc.

1542 UDALL *Erasm. Apoph.* 184 Here maye a manne doubte whether of these twoo thynges he ought rather to maruaill at, the kynges liberalitee in geuyng, orels the vnreasonablenes of the philosophier, in askyng. **1598** R. BERNARD tr. *Terence, Andria* v. i, You would (now at last) giue ouer to cumber me with your vnreasonablenesse. **1703** MRS. CENTLIVRE *Beau's Duel* v. i, Did ever man of your hairs ask such questions? I vow I blush at your unreasonableness. **1736** BUTLER *Anal.* I. vi. 156 This is vanity, conceit and unreasonableness. **1855** MACAULAY *Hist. Eng.* xv. III. 595 The difficulties by which the government was beset on all sides, the malignity of its enemies, the unreasonableness of its friends. **1879** L. STEPHEN *Hours in Library* Ser. III. 322 The grand unreasonableness of the average Englishman.

†**3.** Lack of reason; irrationality. *Obs.*

1598 FLORIO, *Irationalita*, vnreasonableness, brutishnes. **1647** H. MORE *Song of Soul* I. ii. 88 But what with judgement doth them both compare? Is't reason or unreasonableness, I pray.

un'reasonably, *a.* [UN-[1] 11.]

1. In a manner at variance with reason; without due observance of reason or good judgement.

c **1380** WYCLIF *Wks.* (1880) 12 3if þei coueiten vnresonabiliche þe housis..of here nei3eboris. *c* **1450** *Myrr. our Ladye* 109 By whyche..thow shuldest hate no creature vnreasonably. **1535** COVERDALE *2 Macc.* xiv. 23 Nicanor, whyle he abode at Ierusalem, ordred himself not vnreasonably. **1561** T. NORTON *Calvin's Inst.* I. 10 To passe ouer all the rest, which are much more vnreasonably foolish, Plato himself..vainly erreth in his round globe. **1641** R. BROOKE *Eng. Episc.* I. v. 27 Else Reason doth unreasonably determine me not to Marry. **1670** CLARENDON *Contempl. Ps.* Tracts (1727) 757 They only consider..how unreasonably men deal with them. **1729** LAW *Serious C.* x. 143 Do but suppose a man acting unreasonably. **1823** SCOTT *Quentin D.* xxiii, Said Quentin, not unreasonably offended at the turn thus given to his gallantry. **1881** BENHAM in *Macm. Mag.* XLV. 115/1 The Essay..was, not unreasonably, regarded as the most objectionable in tone.

2. To an unreasonable extent; excessively, immoderately.

a **1450** *Knt. de la Tour* (1906) 53 There be..other that be lykerous of moche mete and drinke, takyng unresonably therof. **1470–85** MALORY *Arthur* VII. i. 213, I am come hyder to praye you..to gyue me thre yeftes and they shalle not be vnresonably asked. **1512** *Act 4 Hen. VIII*, c. 6 §2 If..the same Collectours..unresonably delay or tary the said Marchauntes. **1568** GRAFTON *Chron.* II. 402 When they.. would ryde, they found horses vnreasonably deare. **1607** SHAKS. *Cor.* I. iii. 84 Fye, you confine your selfe most vnreasonably. **1697** WALSH *Life V.* ¶20 in Dryden *Virgil*, Venus grows..unreasonably confident. **1723** ATTERBURY *Serm.* (1726) I. ix. 314 To grant that to others, which we our selves perhaps..might be willing enough, unreasonably willing, to obtain from them. **1782** *Phil. Trans.* LXX. 352 Under all these disadvantages in the machine (if not unreasonably ill made) the rod *ef* will ascend to *d*. **1840** ALISON *Hist. Eur.* iii. VII. 109 A nation..unreasonably jealous of its military expenditure. **1884** *Law Rep.* 25 *Ch. Div.* 492 To discourage unreasonably early marriages.

†**un'reasonal**, *a. Obs.*[−1] (UN-[1] 7.)

1653 E. CHISENHALE *Cath. Hist.* 129 Therefore for the Doctor, to deny us to be a Church,..seems to me strange and unreasonall.

un'reasoned, *ppl. a.* [UN-[1] 8.]

1. Not gifted with reason; devoid of reason.

1582 STANYHURST *Æneid* IV. (Arb.) 115 Might not I my lief tyme..Spend lyk an vnreasoned wild beaste? **1805** EUGENIA DI ACTON *Nuns of Desert* II. 230 A wretch..so totally un-reasoned as to say [etc.].

2. Not evolved or developed by reasoning.

1790 BURKE *Fr. Rev.* 286 The citizens are interested from old prejudices and unreasoned habits. **1854** FERRIER *Inst. Metaph.* Introd. 3 An unreasoned philosophy, even though true, carries no guarantee of its truth. **1880** *Fraser's Mag.* May 658 Our unreasoned confidence that every vision of truth is in itself a glorious..vision.

un'reasoning, *vbl. sb.* (UN-[1] 13.)

a **1871** DE MORGAN *Budget Parad.* (1872) 317 He is..the ablest head at unreasoning,..of all who have tried in our day to attach their names to an error. **1889** 'MARK TWAIN' *Yankee at Crt. K. Arthur* xiii, It was the stubborn unreasoning of the time.

un'reasoning, *ppl. a.* (UN-[1] 10.)

(*a*) **1751** G. WEST *Education* lxii, The unreasoning vulgar willingly obey. **1800** COLERIDGE *Piccolom.* IV. vii, I cannot traffic in the trade of words With that unreasoning sex. **1865** PUSEY *Truth Eng. Ch.* 13 The authors..were mostly unsystematic, disjointed, unreasoning. **1883** *19th Cent.* May 773 That somewhat unreasoning personage who is called the British Public.

(*b*) **1812** L. HUNT in *Examiner* 11 May 289/2 The caprices of an unreasoning resentment. **1855** MILMAN *Lat. Chr.* XIV. i. VI. 357 An unthinking and unreasoning impulse of the inward being. **1878** E. WHITE *Life in Christ* (ed. 3) IV. xxvi. 437 There is no influence to which men yield so easily as to unreasoning fear.

Hence **un'reasoningly** *adv.*

1848 MRS. GASKELL *Mary Barton* xxxii, Job Legh pressed out of court, and Jem followed unreasoningly. **1885** *N. Amer. Rev.* March 194 Most fathers, schoolmen, and divines..have done so most unanimously and most unreasoningly.

un'reasty, *a.* (UN-[1] 7.)

1853 G. J. CAYLEY *Las Alforjas* II. 88 The first unreesty sample [of ham] we have met with since Seville.

un'reave, *v.* Now *dial.* [UN-[2] 3 + REAVE *v.*[3]] *trans.* To unravel.

1593 BILSON *Govt. Christ's Ch.* p. v, The warpe and webbe of the laie Presbyterie..hath so enfolded some mens wits, that they cannot vnreaue their cogitations from admiring their newe founde Consistories. **1594** SPENSER *Amoretti* xxiii, Penelope..Deuiz'd a Web..in which the worke that she all day did make, the same at night she did againe vnreaue. **1898** R. BLAKEBOROUGH *Wit*, etc. *N. Riding Yorks* 466 *Unreave*, to unwind.

†**un'reaved**, *ppl. a. Obs.*[−1] [UN-[1] 8 + dial. *reave* to strip (a roof or house).] Not stripped of its roof.

1646 BP. HALL *Balm of Gilead* i. §9 Couldst thou think that a Cottage, not too strongly built, and standing so bleak in the very mouth of the Windes, could..hold tight, and unreaved?

unre'bated, *ppl. a.* [UN-[1] 8.]

†**1.** Unblunted; undulled. *Obs.*

1579–80 NORTH *Plutarch* (1595) 241 He shewed the people the cruell fight of fensers at vnrebated swords. **1630** J. TAYLOR (Water P.) *Heauens Blessing* Wks. III. 118/2 Saint George (being armed at all points but especially) with an vnrebated courage. **1681** J. SCOTT *Chr. Life* iii. §1. 74 They are full of sharp and unrebated Desires. **1745** WESLEY *Wks.* (1872) VIII. 195 Those dogs of hell are let loose to prey upon your soul, with their whole unrebated strength.

2. Not subject to rebate or deduction.

1894 *Q. Rev.* Jan. 208 Thus the unrebated income-tax becomes..a special tax on labour.

un'rebel, *v.* (UN-[2] 6 b.)

1642 HOWELL *Twelve Treat.* (1661) 24 The Treatie began, which the Scot wold not conform himself to do, unless he were first unrebell'd and made Rectus in Curia.

unre'bellious, *a.* (UN-[1] 7.)

1570 LEVINS *Manip.* 226 Vnrebelliouse, *impertinax*. **1879** MORLEY *Burke* 205 A composed spirit.., an unrebellious temper.

unre'bukeable, *a.* (UN-^{1} 7 b.)
1530 TINDALE *Prol. Philippians* Wks. (1572) 52/1 He him selfe had liued in such false righteousnes, and holinesse Vnrebukeable. **1537** BIBLE *1 Tim.* vi. 14 That thou..be without spotte & vnrebukeable. *c* **1585** [R. BROWNE] *Answ. Cartwright* 80 There were those that..were vnrebukeable. **1619** W. SCLATER *Exp. 1 Thess.* 173 Plinie to Traian giues testimonie of Christians inoffensiue life; except in matter of their Superstition (as he calls it) they were vnrebukeable. **1650** S. CLARKE *Eccl. Hist.* 465 Justitiaries, and such as were unrebukeable in their lives. **1868** LYNCH *Rivulet* CLXI. iv, Not unrebukable am I, Not spotless Thy command have kept.
Hence **unre'bukeably** *adv.*
a **1639** HARSNET *Repent.* (1640) 182 Paul..lived before his Conversion as unrebukeably as any civill person doth.

unre'buked, *ppl. a.* (UN-^{1} 8.)
c **1445** PECOCK *Donet* 7 Scant ynouȝ oon leef schulde stonde vnprovid or colowrabily vnrebukid. **1547** BECON in *Certain Hom.* P iv b, He woulde rather suffer death..then to suffer whordom to be vnrebuked, euen in a King. **1697** C. LESLIE *Snake in Grass* (ed. 2) 107 Tho' they have let no suppos'd contempt of their own Books go unrebuked. **1857** SUSANNA WINKWORTH tr. *Life Tauler* xvi. 306 When one finds this evil inclination in a man,..and he remains unrebuked, all this is the world. **1870** MORRIS *Earthly Par.* II. III. 401 All unrebuked he let her soft eyes claim Kindness from his.

unre'buttable, *a.* (UN-^{1} 7 b, 5 b.)
1869 JAMES in *Law Rep.* 7 Equity 537 The strong and unrebuttable presumption.

unre'butted, *ppl. a.* [UN-^{1} 8.]
†**1.** Not repulsed or driven back. *Obs.*
c **1470** HENRY *Wallace* III. 131 Vnraboytyt [**1570** unrebutit] the Sothroun was in wer. **1513** DOUGLAS *Æneid* IX. xiii. 48 That onrebutit knycht Endlang the wallys put thame to the flycht.
2. Not disproved or refuted.
1884 *Law Times Rep.* L. 215/2 The evidence is clear and unrebutted that [etc.].

unre'callable, *a.* (UN-^{1} 7 b.)
1611 COTGR., *Irrevocable*, irreuocable, vnrecallable. **1628** FELTHAM *Resolves* II. lxxxix. 257 That which is done, is vnrecallable. **1798** SOUTHEY *Wife of Fergus* 39 The unrecallable vow That made me his. **1930** W. DE LA MARE *On the Edge* 293 Not that she had ever confessed this in so many raw unrecallable words.

unre'called, *ppl. a.* (UN-^{1} 8.)
1601 R. CHESTER *Love's Mart., K. Arthur* (1878) 43 Merlin..told him vnrecalled Time did stay [= await], To haste him from his pleasure thence away. *a* **1648** LD. HERBERT *Occas. Poems, To his Watch*, The doom of fate, whose unrecall'd decree You date, bring, execute. **1679** T. JENISON in R. Jenison *Popish Plot* 18 As long as your Oath stands unrecalled. **1742** YOUNG *Nt. Th.* II. 260 While she seems, nodding o'er her charge, to..give us up to licence, unrecall'd, Unmarkt. **1883** LD. MONCREIFF *Law Rep. 9 App. Cases* 317/2 While [the conveyance]..remained unrecalled it was absolute.

unre'calling, *ppl. a.* (UN-^{1} 10.)
1593 SHAKS. *Lucr.* 993 And euer let his vnrecalling crime Haue time to waile th' abusing of his time.

unre'canted, *ppl. a.* (UN-^{1} 8.)
[**1775** ASH.] **1826** *Q. Rev.* XXXIII. 356 After living in the unrecanted profession of The Confession of Faith.

unre'ceding, *ppl. a.* (UN-^{1} 10.)
1810 JANE PORTER *Scottish Chiefs* xxxviii, Why, then, this unreceding determination to invade us? **1881** *Scribner's Mag.* XXII. 810 A steady and unreceding advance.

unre'ceipted, *ppl. a.* (UN-^{1} 8.)
1881 *Cambridge Trifles* 3 Files of bills, receipted or unreceipted.

unre'ceivable, *a.* [UN-^{1} 7 b.]
1. Incapable of being received.
1611 COTGR., *Inadmissible*, vnadmittable, vnreceiuable, vnacceptable. **1802–12** BENTHAM *Ration. Judic. Evid.* (1827) V. 132 There is a receipt..whereby any man..may render his testimony unreceivable. **1877** M. ARNOLD *Last Ess. on Ch.* p. xxx, Those who had thrown it aside because what was presented to them under its name was so unreceivable.
†**2.** Unfit to receive one. *Obs.*$^{-1}$
1634 HERBERT *Trav.* 118 If that Kingdome haue a purgatory, so a conspiracie of..scalding sand, the burning Sun, and vnreceiueable Cottages, can make one.

unre'ceived, *ppl. a.* (UN-^{1} 8.)
1540 *Act 32 Hen. VIII*, c. 5 The residue of the said dett..remayning unlevied or unreceyvid by the said former execution. **1597** HOOKER *Eccl. Pol.* v. lvii. §5 Where the signes..of his grace are not either through contempt vnreceiued, or receiued with contempt. **1651** G. W. tr. *Cowel's Inst.* 66 It is much questioned whether Tenant for life..hath any right..to profits and fruits unreceived. **1725** BERKELEY *Lett.* Wks. 1871 IV. 112 Stock, and dividends unreceived make up the sum. **1748** RICHARDSON *Clarissa* (1811) V. xx. 235 Miss Howe's answer to my last unreceived. **1825** COLERIDGE *Aids Refl.* 196 The right though unreceived Owner of the House.

unre'ceiving, *ppl. a.* (UN-^{1} 10.)
1566 in *Three 15th Cent. Chron.* (Camden) 138 To quyat ye matter ye churche dores wer fayn to be closyd, and ye paryschyns to departe unreseyvynge for that day.

unre'ceptant, *a.* (UN-^{1} 7.)
1851 RUSKIN *Mod. Paint.* I. II. v. i. §5 To maintain themselves obstinately unreceptant of the good.

unre'ceptive, *a.* (UN-^{1} 7, 5 b.)
1778 HARTLEY *Pref. to Swedenborg's Heav. & Hell* p. xlviii, The self-hardened..render themselves unreceptive of mercy. **1865** M. PATTISON *Ess.* (1889) I. 349 To sharpen the attention of a defiant and unreceptive mind such as Wolf. **1877** 'H. A. PAGE' *De Quincy* II. xix. 147 That wholly unreceptive..mood which cannot even temporarily condescend to sympathy.

unrecep'tivity. (UN-^{1} 12, 5 b.)
1849 ALFORD *Gk. Test.* I. 524 Instances of unreceptivity of spiritual meaning.

unre'ciprocal, *a.* (UN-^{1} 7, 5 b.)
[**1775** ASH.] **1841** J. J. SYLVESTER in *Lond.*, etc. *Phil. Mag.* XVIII. 138 The unreciprocal implication of systems of equations.

unre'ciprocated, *ppl. a.* (UN-^{1} 8.)
1860 PATMORE *Faithful for Ever* 100 This poor, complaining wraith Of unreciprocated faith. **1887** RIDER HAGGARD *Jess* iv, Nor was the liking unreciprocated.

unre'cited, *ppl. a.* (UN-^{1} 8.)
1587 CHURCHYARD *Worth. Wales* (1876) 10 An act so noble..shall not passe my pen vnresited. **1662** BOYLE *Examen* vi. 72, I have left un-recited several..undesired Expressions. **1760–72** H. BROOKE *Fool of Qual.* (1809) III. 126 Did you..meet with any adventure..yet unrecited?

un'recked, *ppl. a.* (UN-^{1} 8.)
1808 SCOTT *Marm.* I. xvii, Unmark'd, at least unreck'd, the taunt. **1862** ELLICOT *Destiny of Creature* i. (1865) 5 These animals..die unrecked of and unheeded.

un'recking, *ppl. a.* (UN-^{1} 10.)
1868 GEO. ELIOT *Sp. Gipsy* 290 Unrecking of time-woven subtleties. **1873** MRS. WHITNEY *Other Girls* xxx, An utterance of hard unrecking distinctness.

un'reckingness. (UN-^{1} 12.)
1873 MRS. WHITNEY *Other Girls* xxx, The hard unreckingness was only the reflex of a tenderness quick, not dead.

un'reckon, *v.* (UN-^{2} 3.)
1561 EDEN *Art Navig.* II. vi, The dayes of the Moone beynge knowen, then unrekenyng or disrekenynge backwarde, we shall knowe the daye. **1598** FLORIO, *Discontare*, to vnreckon, to abate in reckoning.

un'reckonable, *a.* (UN-^{1} 7 b.)
1851 HAWTHORNE *Ho. Seven Gables* iv, An uncle..might..make her the ultimate heiress of his unreckonable riches. **1880** A. RALEIGH *Way to City* 267 It is even more so by unreckonable degrees.

un'reckoned, *ppl. a.* (UN-^{1} 8, 8 c. Cf. MDu. *ongerekent* (Du. *ongerekend*), MHG. *ungerechent* (G. *ungerechnet*), ON. *úreiknaðr*, Sw. *oräknad*, Da. *uregnet*.)
c **1340** HAMPOLE *Pr. Consc.* 2462 Na syn þan unrekend sal be. *c* **1450** *Cov. Myst.* (Shaks. Soc.) 166 Suche a carpynge is unknowe, Onrekenyd in my regne. **1464** *Mann. & Househ. Exp.* (Roxb.) 161 Afftyr the same rekenynge Keverstonys men..askyd more wiche was onrekenyd as thei seyd, vj. s. viij. d. **1551** BP. GARDINER *On Sacram.* 75 The foure substaunces, whiche this auctor..numbreth of Christ, might haue bene left vnrekened by tale. **1599** DANIEL *Musoph.* (1601) A iiij, Who doth touch the tenour of that vaine, Is held but vain; and his vnreckned pen The title but of Leuitie doth gaine. **1628** GAULE *Pract. The.* (1629) 100 These were his Names, Many and Great; yet is Jesvs (the Name aboue all names) vnreckoned. **1690** DRYDEN *Don Sebastian* III. i, Add that falshood To a long Bill that yet remains unreckon'd. **1875** LOWELL *Under Old Elm* 135 The casual gleanings of unreckoned years. **1879** BARING-GOULD *Germany* II. 283 The theory may be wrong,..the calculation put out by unreckoned elements.
b. With *for*.
1680 C. NESSE *Ch. Hist.* 452 God left not his cruelty long unreckon'd for. **1894** MRS. DYAN *Man's Keeping* (1899) 47 This unreckoned-for encounter..was a bitter pang.

unre'claimable, *a.* [UN-^{1} 7 b, 5 b.]
1. Incapable of being reclaimed or reformed; incorrigible: **a.** Of actions, qualities, etc.
1577 tr. *Bullinger's Decades* 438/1 The Iewes..for their vnreclaymeable affiaunce in the lawe are vtterly reiected. **1607** TOPSELL *Four-f. Beasts* 305 He..faleth into some furious and vnreclaimable euill qualities. **1652** SCLATER *Civ. Magistracy* (1653) 8, Men, who are full of savage and unreclaimable desires.
b. Of persons. Also const. *from*.
a **1656** BP. HALL *Serm. 2 Pet.* i. 10 Wks. 1863 V. 681 That dreadful place of torment, which is the unavoidable portion of careless and unreclaimable sinners. **1680** C. NESSE *Ch. Hist.* 195 He finds her unreclaimable from her idols. *a* **1716** BLACKALL *Wks.* (1723) I. 258 He is not unreconcileable to us until we become unreclaimable. **1717** FLEETWOOD *Burdett's Let.* 11 'Tis the Proceeding of the..tenderest Fathers..with their Sons, when so enormously ungracious, wicked, and unreclaimable.
absol. **1685** J. SCOTT *Chr. Life* II. iv. §1 To pour out the Vials of his Wrath upon the obstinate and unreclaimable.
†**2.** Untameable, uncontrollable. *Obs.*
1609 HOLLAND *Amm. Marcell.* 401 This kind of men so quicke and nimble, so untamed and unreclaimable. **1611** COTGR., *Bœuf bran*,..a kind of wild Oxe..vnreclaimable, and onely good for the shambles.
3. Not liable to be claimed back.
1777 POTTER *Æschylus, Supplicants* 107 That we might be permitted here to dwell Free, unreclaimable, inviolate.
Hence **unre'claimably** *adv.*
1645 BP. HALL *Peace Maker* vii. 57 Those..who doe pertinaciously, and unreclaimably maintaine Doctrines destructive to the foundation of Christian Religion. **1652** HEYLYN *Cosmogr.* III. 106 Unreclamably addicted to their antient Judaism.

unre'claimed, *ppl. a.* [UN-^{1} 8, 5 b.]
1. †**a.** Not summoned to return. *Obs.*$^{-1}$
c **1470** HARDING *Chron.* CXXII. ii, He then his lawe and peace alwaye proclaymed..And so held on to London vnreclaymed.
b. Not demanded back.
1748 EARL NUGENT *To Mankind* xviii, Wise nature mocks th' wrangling herd; For unreclaim'd, and untransfer'd, Her pow'rs and rights remain.
2. Not reclaimed from error or wrong-doing; not reduced to order or good ways; unreformed.
1602 SHAKS. *Ham.* II. i. 34 The flash and out-breake of a fiery minde, A sauagenes in vnreclaimed bloud of generall assault. **1611** SPEED *Theat. Gt. Brit.* IV. i. 138/1 Their manners vnreclaimed, and barbarisme.., doe witnesse no such ciuilitie sowen, to bee in that plot. **1757** W. WILKIE *Epigon.* IX. 281 Yet, unreclaim'd, from such atrocious deeds, To more and worse your desp'rate rage proceeds. **1827** POLLOK *Course T.* II. 483 In tormenting, pained; Unawed by wrath, by mercy unreclaimed. **1830** MACKINTOSH *Progr. Eth. Philos.* Wks. 1846 I. 256 They retain whatever was admirable in their unreclaimed state.
3. Untamed; unsubdued.
1618 LATHAM *Falconry* Contents, Of the Ostringer, and..Goshawke compared with other Fowles of the ayre, as they are vnreclaimed and wilde. **1631** CHAPMAN *Cæsar & Pompey* Plays 1873 III. 193 *Antony*: [of Cato]. Vnreclaimed man! **1693** DRYDEN *Ovid's Met.* XIII. *Acis* 81 Bullocks, unreclaim'd to bear the Yoke.
4. Uncultivated, wild.
1781 COWPER *Expost.* 468 This island, spot of unreclaim'd rude earth. **1832** *Planting* 23 (L.U.K.), [Such] unreclaimed lands..can seldom be prepared as above. **1856** OLMSTED *Slave States* 157 Land of this description..in its unreclaimed state.
Hence **unre'claimedness.**
1611 COTGR., *Sauvageté*, sauagenesse, wildnesse, unreclaimednesse. **1646** S. BOLTON *Arraignm. Err.* 28 Unreclaimednesse under any sin whatever will bring in errour.

unre'claiming, *ppl. a.* (UN-^{1} 10.)
1820 SHELLEY *Prometh. Unb.* III. iv. 187 Love Dragged to his altars..And slain amid men's unreclaiming tears.

unre'clining, *ppl. a.* (UN-^{1} 10.)
1777 POTTER *Æschylus, Prom. Bd.* 7 Therefore the joyless station of this rock Unsleeping, unreclining, shalt thou keep.

unrecog'nition. (UN-^{1} 12, 5 b.)
1869 MRS. WHITNEY *Hitherto* ix, Everybody who has a goading ambition has knowledge..of a cold exasperating unrecognition. **1875** HOWELLS *Foregone Concl.* (1882) 299 She kept her eyes upon him with a dreamy unrecognition.

un'recognizable, *a.* (UN-^{1} 7 b, 5 b.)
1817 COLERIDGE *Biog. Lit.* II. 83 When a number of successive lines can be rendered..unrecognizable as verse, ..by simply transcribing them as prose. **1847** LD. LINDSAY *Chr. Art* I. p. cxlii, He returned so disfigured.., that he was unrecognisable save by his voice.
Hence **unrecognizableness; -ably** *adv.*
1879 STEVENSON *Trav. Cevennes* 49 The mist had almost unrecognisably exaggerated their forms. **1883** H. DRUMMOND *Nat. Law in Spir. W.* 303 One of the most recognisable characteristics of life is its unrecognisableness.

un'recognized, *ppl. a.* (UN-^{1} 8.)
[**1775** ASH.] **1813** SHELLEY *Q. Mab.* VI. 189 Not a thought, ..Nor the events enchaining every will,..pass Unrecognized, or unforeseen by thee. **1861** [MRS. A. J. PENNY] *Romance Dull Life* xxxvii. 265 She felt she was still in unrecognised disgrace.

un'recognizing, *ppl. a.* (UN-^{1} 10.)
a **1814** *Witness* III. iii. in *New Brit. Theatre* I. 35 A kinsman proudly rich, Whose haughty and unrecognizing eye Had never glanc'd on him. **1858** SEARS *Athan.* II. x. 233 He walked to Emmaus with the two unrecognizing disciples. **1890** 'R. BOLDREWOOD' *Miner's Right* xxxviii, He gazed for one moment at me with strange, unrecognising air.
Hence **un'recognizingly** *adv.*
1891 COTES *2 Girls on Barge* 76 The Essingtons had passed us, unrecognisingly.

unreco'llected, *ppl. a.* (UN-^{1} 8.)
(*a*) **1733** WATTS *Philos. Ess.* (1734) 127 Our unrecollected and useless Dreams. **1802–12** BENTHAM *Ration. Judic. Evid* (1827) I. 276 Unrecollected, when occasion comes for recollecting it, it will be tantamount to silence.
(*b*) **1850** J. H. NEWMAN *Diffic. Anglic.* 235 Such a soul, so selfish, so unrecollected.

unreco'mmendable, *a.* (UN-^{1} 7 b.)
1830 MISS MITFORD *Village* Ser. IV. 237, I should have objected to it..as being utterly unrecommendable by one rational person to another.

unreco'mmended, *ppl. a.* (UN-^{1} 8.)
c **1550** CHEKE *Let.* in *Athenæum* 28 Aug. (1909) 237/2, I would rather that you would, unproved and unrecommended, do well. **1704** *Moderat. Displ.* v, A Notion undefin'd in Vertues Schools, Unrecommended by her sacred Rules. **1792** A. YOUNG *Trav. France* 190 Unknown and unrecommended at Nice, I expected nothing but what could be shot flying in any town.

un'recompensable, *a.* [UN-^{1} 7 b, 5 b.]
† Incapable of being remedied.
1526 *Pilgr. Perf.* (W. de W. 1531) 203 b, Surely this offence is..of man vnrecompensable. **1560** BECON *New Catech.* Wks. 1564 I. 304 Whiche miserye and wretchednesse was so greate and vnrecompensable, that from it..no creature..coulde delyuer me. **1587** FLEMING *Contn. Holinshed* III. 1329/1 The heinous and vnrecompensable defamation of the course of iustice.

un'recompensed, *ppl. a.* (UN-^{1} 8.)
1469 *Paston Lett.* II. 379 Yif ye any thyng doo..to the pleasir of my Lordes, it will neither be unremembrid ne unrecompensid. **1555** EDEN *Decades* (Arb.) 310 He shall returne..not vnrecompensed with iust rewards. **1581** A.

HALL *Iliad* I. 5 Thinkst thou it fit I leaue the maide, and emptie go my wayes Vnrecompenste. **1621** FLETCHER *Wild Goose Chace* IV. iii, Heaven will not see so true a love unrecompenc'd. *a* **1763** SHENSTONE *Ess.* Wks. 1777 II. 29 To retire at last unrecompensed..was beyond all power of resolution. **1822** LAMB *Elia* I. *Bachelor's Compl.*, The display of married happiness..is throughout pure, unrecompensed, unqualified insult. **1840–1** WORDSW. *Mem. Tour Italy* iii. 10 Yet not unrecompensed are they who learn [etc.].

† **unre'comptless**, *a.* [UN-^{1} 7, 15.] Incapable of being related or reckoned.

1593 LODGE *Misc. Pieces* (Hunter. Cl.) 14 Fvll fraught with vnrecomptles sweete Of your faire face that stole mine eie.

un'reconcilable, *a.* Now *rare.* (UN-^{1} 7b, 5b.)

1577 tr. *Bullinger's Decades* IV. ii. 574/1 That vnreconcileable and harde hart. **1618** *Fenton's Guicciard.* (ed. 3) 344 The Pope shewing signes of a person vnreconcileable against Alphonso. **1646** HAMMOND *Tracts* 25 Whether it be reconcileable or unreconcileable with a good conscience. **1685** BAXTER *Paraphr. N.T.* 2 Tim. iii. 3 Men that will not live in peace, but are unreconcileable. *a* **1716** [see UNRECLAIMABLE *a.* 1b]. **1896** *Advance* (Chicago) 2 Apr. 475/2 Teachings..absolutely unreconcilable with the teachings of the New Testament.

Hence **unreconcilableness; -ably** *adv.*

1650 *Vind. Hammond's Addr.* iii. §7 The *unreconcileablenesse of those two opinions (the one with the other). *c* **1620** BP. HALL *Contempl., O.T.* xv. vii, How much lesse shall the God of mercies bee *unreconcileably displeased with his owne. **1653** H. MORE *Antid. Ath.* I. ii. (1655) 6 The minde of man..will fully and unreconcileably disagree.

un'reconciled, *ppl. a.* (UN-^{1} 8, 5b.)

c **1450** *Myrr. our Ladye* 152 Wretched were that persone that..wolde be vnreconcyled and dysceuered from that holy vnyte. **1513** BRADSHAW *St. Werburge* I. 872 Dredynge sore the iustyce of god almyght For his fathers demerytes vnreconsyled On hym to fall. **1564** DORMAN *Proofe Cert. Art. Relig.* 33b, He..was forced to leaue the two places at a iarre vnreconciled. **1604** SHAKS. *Oth.* v. ii. 27 Any Crime Vnreconcil'd as yet to Heauen, and Grace. **1671** MRS. BEHN *Forc'd Marr.* I. ii, As those unreconciled to Heaven Would bear the pangs of death. **1711** G. HICKES *Two Treat. Chr. Priesth.* (1847) II. 48 The offering of unreconciled Christians. **1769** BURKE *Obs. 'Late St. Nat.'* 90 The unreconciled principles of the original discord of parties. **1817** SHELLEY *Rev. Islam* I. xxvii, He changed from starry shape..To a dire Snake, with man and beast unreconciled. **1873** SYMONDS *Grk. Poets* xii. 420 Yet the spirit and the flesh still remained in unreconciled antagonism.

† **unrecon'ciliable**, *a. Obs.* [UN-^{1} 7b, 5b.] Unreconcilable.

1589 T. WHITE *Serm. Paules Crosse* 47 Deuiding his [*sc.* Christ's] Bodie by vnreconciliable hatred among our selues. **1606** SHAKS. *Ant. & Cl.* v. i. 47 Let me lament..that our Starres Vnreconciliable, should diuide our equalnesse to this. **1628** tr. *Mathieu's Powerf. Favorite* 87 From this instant their mindes became vnreconciliable.

† **unreconciliate**, *ppl. a. Sc. Obs.*$^{-1}$ [UN-^{1} 8b.] Unreconciled.

1588 *Reg. Privy Council Scot.* IV. 283 Sa lang as the said deidlie feid..standis unreconsiliat.

unreco'nnoitred, *ppl. a.* (UN-^{1} 8.)

1899 *Westm. Gaz.* 13 Dec. 5/1 Country unreconnoitred is unknown in a military sense.

unrecon'structed, *ppl. a.* [UN-^{1} 8; cf. RECONSTRUCTION 1b.] *spec.* (orig. *U.S.*) Not reconciled to the outcome of the American Civil War; hence *gen.* not reconciled or converted to the current political orthodoxy; unreformed; die-hard.

1867 *Harper's Weekly* 9 Nov. 707/2 The Democratic candidates in Maryland are..of the 'unreconstructed' kind. **1869** *Nation* 25 March 221/2 Butler's Committee on Reconstruction reported in favor of extending..the time during which an 'unreconstructed' Southerner may retain his Government employment. **1877** LONGF. in *Life* (1891) III. 277 A letter from Mr. ——, of Washington, a fierce and 'unreconstructed' rebel. *a* **1936** KIPLING *Something of Myself* (1937) vii. 195 There came..with her married daughter the widow of a Confederate Cavalry leader; both of them were what you might call 'unreconstructed' rebels. **1944** *Univ. of Chicago Mag.* May 6 The young are in increasing numbers, not only in Oklahoma but in much of the vast inland region of our republic, moving to the cities, leaving the unreconstructed small towns to their elders and to decay. **1946** J. FLANNER in *New Yorker* 9 Mar. 80/1 Nuremberg defense counsel have just offered..an absolutely first-rate demonstration of the still unreconstructed prewar German mind. **1949** B. A. BOTKIN *Treas. S. Folklore* I. i. 4 As the type and symbol of the 'unreconstructed Southerner', Donald Davidson selects 'Cousin Roderick', an idealized Middle Georgia country gentleman, who combines the 'bearing of an English squire' with the 'frontier heartiness' of A. B. Longstreet's *Georgia Scenes*. What principally distinguishes Cousin Roderick from 'Brother Jonathan' (the Vermont 'unreconstructed Yankee' who resembles the Georgian in so many ways)..is the fact that he does not work with his own hands. **1962** A. SAMPSON *Anat. of Britain* xxx. 480 He and his board have reacted..to revelations about their monopoly, with the old-fashioned sang-froid of unreconstructed businessmen. **1968** *Economist* 6 Jan. 34/3 The trial had an even greater impact because of the blunt rebukes hurled at the defendants by Judge Harold Cox, once considered one of the more unreconstructed judges in the South. **1972** R. PLANT in Cox & Dyson *20th-Cent. Mind* II. iv. 91 The major opposition to Roosevelt's New Deal policies in fact came from these unreconstructed *laissez-faire* liberals who failed to realize that planning was necessary in order to make individual freedom a *real* possibility for the masses. **1973** [see RECONSTRUCTED *ppl. a.* b]. **1979** *Guardian* 2 Oct. 10/2 A further entrenchment of unreconstructed union power. **1981** 'A. CROSS' *Death in Faculty* i. 12 The place is pretty much unreconstructed..an ancient bathroom complete with mahogany bathtub.

unre'cordable, *a.* (UN-^{1} 7b, 5b.)

1874 M. COLLINS *Transmigr.* III. xviii. 271 That delicious unrecordable nonsense which some people fancy can only be talked once in a life-time.

unre'corded, *ppl. a.* (UN-^{1} 8.)

1585 ABP. SANDYS *Serm.* 287 Had Salomon neuer beene, or had his fall been vnrecorded. **1662** STILLINGFL. *Orig. Sacræ* II. i. §2 Supposing that God had left the matters of Divine revelation unrecorded at all. **1671** MILTON *P.R.* I. 16 Deeds..in secret done, And unrecorded left through many an Age. **1725** POPE *Odyss.* IV. 276 Antilochus, a name Not unrecorded in the rolls of fame. **1847** KEBLE *Serm.* Pref. p. lxviii, The more established theory of silent unrecorded Tradition. **1881** P. BROOKS *Candle of Lord* 133 A thousand unrecorded patriots helped to make Washington.

unre'cording, *ppl. a.* (UN-^{1} 10.)

1849 TENNYSON '*You might have won the Poet's name*' 7 A life that moves to gracious ends Thro' troops of unrecording friends.

† **unre'counselled**, *ppl. a. Sc. Obs.* [UN-^{1} 8.] Unreconciled.

1533 BELLENDEN *Livy* III. xix. (S.T.S.) II. 26 He declarit him Inemye and as ȝit vnreconsellit to þis man. **1565** *Reg. Privy Council Scot.* I. 407 The said unrecounsalit bluid and inymitie.

unre'counted, *ppl. a.* (UN-^{1} 8.)

1613 SHAKS. *Hen. VIII*, III. ii. 48 Marry this is yet but yong, and may be left To some eares vnrecounted.

unre'coverable, *a.* [UN-^{1} 7b, 5b.]

† **1.** That cannot be recovered; completely lost.

14.. *Brut* 319 ȝet thilk Northren wynd..lost good wiþoute nombre vnrecouerable. **1448** *Extr. Aberd. Reg.* (1844) I. 401 Al sumes..bath recouerable and unrecouerable. *a* **1500** *Chaucer's Dreme* 1753 This hasty farme had bene a feast, And now is unrecoverable. *a* **1586** SIDNEY *Arcadia* I. v, To lament the losse of such a jewell, so much the more, as that skilful men in that arte assured it was unrecoverable. **1617** MORYSON *Itin.* I. 278 The vnrecouerable losse of time. **1650** BAXTER *Saints' R.* III. ii. 281 Oh my unconceiveable unrecoverable loss!

2. From which no recovery is possible; past remedy or cure.

1561 DAUS tr. *Bullinger on Apoc.* 533 The most certaine, vnrecouerable, and most weightie destruction of Rome. **1584** R. SCOT *Discov. Witchcr.* XIII. xxxiv. (1886) 287 To make an unrecoverable wound in your bellie. **1608** MACHIN *Dumbe Knt.* III, I doe not think this ill Is yet so big as unrecoverable. **1644** VICARS *God in Mount* 1 An unrecoverable cursed estate of damnation. **1888** *Amer. Jrnl. Psychol.* Feb. 333 Loss of memory is so commonly associated with unrecoverable cases.

† **unre'coverably**, *adv. Obs.* [UN-^{1} 7b, 5b.] Irrecoverably.

c **1445** PECOCK *Donet* (1921) 160 ȝitt if þei be not vnrecouerabli [unre]dressable, þouȝ to so redresse happily longiþ sum labour. **1578** WALSHINGHAM in Nicolas *Life & T. Sir C. Hatton* (1847) 60 We shall estrange Scotland from us unrecoverably. **1628** T. SPENCER *Logick* 125 Thereby we finde, that this condition befalls them secretly, certainly, vnrecoverably. *a* **1652** BROME *Damoiselle* III. ii, [He is] most unrecoverably mad! **1690** BAXTER *Kingd. Christ* iv. (1691) 49 They are unrecoverably Extinct.

unre'covered, *ppl. a.*^{1} [UN-^{1} 8.]

1. From which no recovery is or has been made.

c **1611** CHAPMAN *Iliad* IX. 247 Consider these affairs in time,..And have the grace to turn from Greece fate's unrecover'd hour. **1612** DRAYTON *Poly-olb.* II. 74 Too late (alas) we find The softness of thy sword..To be the onely cause of vnrecouer'd spoile. **1630** J. TAYLOR (Water P.) *Siege Jerus.* Wks. 12 Then fell they to an vnrecouered wane.

2. Not recovered or regained.

a **1692** POLLEXFEN *Disc. Trade* (1697) 4 The other half Million..we may be sure they did not give us, or left unrecovered, but took it from us. **1855** M. ARNOLD *Balder Dead* III. 235 They bind us..To leave for ever Balder in the grave, An unrecover'd prisoner. **1897** *Daily News* 21 Jan. 6 A telegram..states that the body of Fowler is unrecovered.

3. Not having recovered (*from* something).

1737 PARNELL *Poems* 94 Lychenor following with a downward Blow, Reach'd in the Lake his unrecover'd Foe. **1860** FROUDE *Hist. Eng.* VI. 235 With a stomach unrecovered from the sea..he sate down..to a public English supper. **1880** EMMA MARSHALL *Troubl. Times* IV. 288 Being yet on my bed, unrecovered of that fore-mentioned illness.

† **unre'covered**, *ppl. a.*^{2} *Obs.* [UN-^{1} 8.] Not covered up, obvious.

1577 tr. *Bullinger's Decades* IV. i. 534/2 The vnfigured and vnrecouered promises..in the Psalmes.

un'recreating, *ppl. a.* (UN-^{1} 10.)

a **1861** T. WINTHROP *Life in Open Air* xii. (1863) 90 A feeble, restless, unrecreating slumber.

unre'cruitable, *a.* (UN-^{1} 7b. Cf. UNRECRUITIBLE *a.*)

[**1775** ASH.] **1884** *Imp. Dict.* IV. 514/2 Unrecruitable health, strength, &c.

unre'cruited, *ppl. a.* (UN-^{1} 8.)

1649 J. ARNWAY *Tablet* 33 To avoide the next storme which His unrecreuted Armie might not encounter. *a* **1661** FULLER *Worthies, Cheshire* I. (1662) 187 Had the Royalists pursued this Single Enemy, (as yet unrecruited with additional strength,) they had finally worsted him. **1712** BLACKMORE *Creation* V. 240 By unrecruited waste..His glorious stock long since had been consum'd. **1859** *Macm. Mag.* IV. 47 Lest the ranks of the ministry should be unrecruited by candidates from this first class of intelligence. **1891** E. KINGLAKE *Australians at Home* 107 The ranks of larrikins do not go unrecruited from among the sons of the more respectable poor.

† **unre'cruitible**, *a. Obs.* [UN-^{1} 7.] Incapable of getting recruits.

1644 MILTON *Educ.* 7 Their empty and unrecrutible [*ed.* 1738 unrecruitable] Colonells of twenty men in a company.

un'rectifiable, *a.* (UN-^{1} 7b.)

a **1678** STANLEY *Hist. Philos.* (1687) IX. 541/2 Such a person must be unlearned, and unrectifiable.

un'rectified, *ppl. a.* [UN-^{1} 8.]

1. Not corrected or amended.

1638 RIDER *Horace, Odes* III. xiv, You youths,..Forbeare all languages unrectifi'd. **1662** HIBBERT *Body Divinity* I. 306 Many things were left unrectified, which..they did not see. **1686** JEFFREYS in Howell *State Trials* (1811) XI. 591/2 That one mistake in point of law might not go unrectified. **1837** WORDSW. *Mem. Tour Italy* i. 329 Diligence uninspired, Unrectified, unguided..By godlike insight. **1895** W. H. HUDSON *Spencer's Philos.* 171 The unrectified egotistic emotions of the dweller in cave and wilderness.

2. Not purified or refined.

1663 BOYLE *Usef. Exp. Nat. Philos.* II. ii. 36 Unrectified spirit of man's blood. **1694** SALMON *Bate's Dispens.* 144/1 The Oil..stinks so abominably, that it is scarce possible to be used alone, especially unrectified. **1766** *Compl. Farmer* s.v. *Purging*, Unrectified oil of amber. **1840** HOOD *Kilmansegg, Misery* ix, Drops of unrectified spirit distill'd From the limbeck of Pride and Vanity.

unre'cumbent, *a.* (UN-^{1} 7.)

1784 COWPER *Task* V. 29 The cattle..seem half petrified to sleep In unrecumbent sadness.

† **unre'cuperable**, *a. Obs.*$^{-1}$ [UN-^{1} 7b, 5b.] = UNRECOVERABLE *a.* 2.

1430–40 LYDG. *Bochas* I. xxv. (1494) fij/1 For comfortles and vnrecuparable [**1558** unrecurable] Are thilke hepyd sorowes. *c* **1535** ELYOT *Let.* in *Gov.* (1883) p. cxvi, To my importable charges and unrecuperable decay of my lyving.

† **unre'curable**, *a. Obs.* [UN-^{1} 7b, 5b.] = UNRECOVERABLE *a.*

c **1450** *Cov. Myst.* (Shaks. Soc.) 313 Thus oure lawys dystroyd myth be, And to us alle unrecurabyl! **1465** *Paston Let.* II. 182 A newe mater a newe cost and many smale growe to a gret summe, and summe mater on-recurabyll. **1546** BALE *Eng. Votaries* I. 77b, An unrecurable dyshonoure it were unto yow. **1597** G. HARVEY *Trimming Nashe* Wks. (Grosart) III. 24 If this remedie helpe not, surely thou art vnrecurable.

† **unre'cured**, *ppl. a. Obs.* [UN-^{1} 8, 5b.] Not alleviated or remedied.

1430–40 LYDGATE *Bochas* I. x. (1494) djb/1 My sorowes let se If any sorowe or myscheef vnrecuryd May counturpeyce to that I haue enduryd.

† **unre'curing**, *ppl. a. Obs.*$^{-1}$ [UN-^{1} 10.] Not admitting of recovery.

1588 SHAKS. *Tit. A.* III. i. 90, I found her..Seeking to hide herselfe as doth the Deare That hath receiude some vnrecuring wound.

un'red, *a. rare*$^{-1}$. (UN-^{1} 7.)

a **1300** *Cursor M.* 24471 Þi face es wan as ros vnrede.

† **un'rede.** *Obs.* [OE. *unrǽd* (f. *un-* UN-^{1} 4a, b + *rǽd* REDE *sb.*^{1}), = OFris. *unrêd*, WFris. *on-*, *ûnrie(d)*, MDu. *onraet* (Du. *-raad*), OHG. (MHG.) *unrât* (G. *unrath*), ON. *úráð* (MSw. *oradh*, Sw. *oråd*, MDa. *urad*, Da. and Norw. *uraad*).] Lack of counsel or wisdom; evil counsel; folly.

c **893** K. ÆLFRED *Oros.* IV. xii. 210 Scipia..self sæde..þæt hit wære se mæsta unræd & se mæsta ȝedwola. *c* **1100** *O.E. Chron.* (MS. D) an. 1048, Ac hit þuhte unræd eallum folce. *c* **1205** LAY. 8011 Wale, wale, vnræd [*c* **1275** onread], mani cniht þu makest dæd. *c* **1250** *Gen. & Ex.* 1906, xii. ȝer or ysaac was dead Iacobes sunes deden un-red. *c* **1275** *Sinners Beware* 303 in *O.E. Misc.* 82 He gredeþ þanne heye, þe wrecches and þe vnsleye, þat luuede þe vnredes.

b. As the epithet given to King Ethelred II: see UNREADY *a.*^{2}

c **1210** *Leges Edw.* in Lambarde *Archaionomia* fol. 138b, Ældredus unrade,..Edmundus yrenside. ? *c* **1275** *Livere de Reis de Engletere* (Rolls) 96 Cesti Eilred aucone genz apelent Eilred Unred; e assez proprement.

unrede, variant of UNRIDE *a.*

unre'deemable, *a.* (UN-^{1} 7b, 5b.)

1584 *Reg. Privy Council Scot.* III. 672 Heretabill tennendreis unredimabill. **1593** *Sidney's Arcadia* III. (1598) 363 Zelmanes graue [shall] become her mariage bed,..before I will leaue a marke in my selfe of an vnredeemeable trespasse. **1611** COTGR., *Irrachetable*, vnredeemable; not to bee bought..at any price. **1813** L. HUNT in *Examiner* 11 Jan. 17/2 Men, who..would have left us, unredeemed and unredeemable, the habitual slaves of every species of despotism. **1856** RUSKIN *Mod. Paint.* III. IV. xv. §9 This absence of colour from rocks..was in their eyes an unredeemable defect.

unre'deemed, *ppl. a.* [UN-^{1} 8.]

† **1.** Unretrieved, unremedied. *Obs.*$^{-1}$

1526 *Pilgr. Perf.* (1531) 264b, That no circumstance sholde be lefte vnredemed that myght let thy saluacyon.

2. Not spiritually redeemed; unsaved.

1548 GESTE *Pr. Masse* I viijb, Ther shuld be made..prayer for the dead to..release them wyth al (as otherwyse vnredemed and payned). **1662** JER. TAYLOR *Three Serm.* (1663) 82 The state of a carnal, unredeemed, unregenerate person. **1760** LAW *Spir. Prayer* I. 76 Our redemption is this new birth; if this is not done,..we are still unredeemed. **1850** HAWTHORNE *Scarlet L.* xviii, Breathing the wild, free atmosphere of an unredeemed, unchristianized, lawless region.

absol. **1827** POLLOK *Course T.* VIII. 796 He stood With eye, of all the unredeemed, most sad.

3. Not recovered, ransomed, or released, by purchase or otherwise. (In quot. 1896 = IRREDEEMED.)

1554 [see UNRANSOMED]. **1572** N. ROSCARROCKE *Prelim. Verses* in Bossewell *Armorie*, Caparisons ther fixed hang,.. With armors fully furnished, and gauntlets vnredeemd. **1648** HEXHAM II, *Ongelost*, Vnredeemed, or Vnreleased. **1845** McCULLOCH *Taxation* I. i. 59 *note*, The land-tax redeemed amounts to 737,285*l.* a-year, and the unredeemed to 1,069,904*l.* a-year. **1856** KINGSLEY *Misc.* (1859) II. 3 [Lands] yet unredeemed from the wild beast and the wild hunter. **1896** *Daily News* 16 Oct. 5/3 The most elaborate [wreath] being sent by the other 'unredeemed' Italian city of Trieste.

b. *spec.* Not recovered from pawn.

1859 SALA *Tw. round Clock* (1861) 180 The articles sold.. are all pawnbrokers' pledges unredeemed. **1881** E. F. POYNTER *Among the Hills* II. 30 Teapot and candlesticks both had..been pledged and unredeemed.

4. Not remedied or relieved (*by* some good quality or feature); unmitigated; absolutely bad.

1805 W. ROSCOE *Leo X*, II. 22 A man so totally unredeemed by a single virtue. **1843** CARLYLE *Past & Pr.* III. xii, The unredeemed ugliness is that of a slothful People. **1862** 'SHIRLEY' (J. Skelton) *Nugæ Crit.* vi. 320 The villain of the piece, who is..an unredeemed and impossible blackguard. **1896** H. G. WELLS *Wheels of Chance* viii, He was not an unredeemed rough taking advantage of a mistake.

5. Not performed or realized.

1812 L. HUNT in *Examiner* 7 Dec. 770/2 Your promise has remained unredeemed. **1862** GOULBURN *Pers. Relig.* II. ix, The great gulf of unredeemed possibilities.

Hence **unre'deemedly** *adv.*

1885 *Athenæum* 28 Feb. 276/3 If she had..one touch of refinement,..instead of being unredeemedly vulgar.

†**un'redely**, *adv.* *Obs.*[−1] [UN-[1] 11; cf. next and OE. *unrǣdlíce*, ON. *úráðliga*.] Without restraint.

c **1200** *Trin. Coll. Hom.* 173 He bit here unbette sennes.. bigraden hem shameliche, and biten hem unradeliche.

†**un'redily**, *adv.* *Obs.* [UN-[1] 11, or f. UNREDY *a.* Cf. prec.] Without counsel or consideration; imprudently, unwisely, inadvisedly.

1398 TREVISA *Barth. De P.R.* XVII. lv. (Tollem. MS.), Auctoures meneþ þat yt is a ful violent herbe, and schall be take redily and warly; for he greueþ and soone sleþ, yf it is unredily [L. *indiscrete*] take to any person. *c* **1445** PECOCK *Donet* 142 Þerfore hem silf in þis maner þei biwamblen so rudely and so vnredily. *c* **1449** —— *Repr.* II. xx. 274 Al this vndirstonde not y of the Bible aloon, as summen ouer vnredili..vndirstonden.

†**unre'doubting**, *ppl. a.* *Obs.* [UN-[1] 10.] Not anticipative; unapprehensive.

1665 J. SERGEANT *Sure Footing* 49 That the Rule of Faith must be apt to justify unreflecting and unredoubting persons..is found most exactly in Tradition.

unre'dressable, *a.* (UN-[1] 7 b, 5 b.)

1607 S. COLLINS *Serm.* (1608) 81 If it had come any later, the euill had beene almost vnredressable. **1665** J. SERGEANT *Sure Footing* 41 That Principle which is the necessary Parent of such ruinous and unredressable disorders. **1716** M. DAVIES *Athen. Brit.* I. Pref. 55 He thereupon grew unredressable and irreconcilable with the whole order.

unre'dressed, *ppl. a.* (UN-[1] 8, 8 c.)

1563 *Reg. Privy Council Scot.* I. 244 All attemptatis committit upoun the subjectis of Scotland and unredressit for. **1590** SPENSER *F.Q.* IV. viii. 41 That vnto death had doen him vnredrest, Had not the noble Prince his readie stroke represt. **1617** CAMPION *Third Bk. of Ayres* xvii. 11 So may I dye vnredrest, Ere my long loue be possest. **1639** FULLER *Holy War* II. xxv. 76 Wearied with delayes, [he] returned back with his grievances unredressed. **1721** AMHERST *Terræ Fil.* No. 6 (1726) 30 The king's friends remain still unredress'd, and the king's honour unrepair'd to this day. **1806** *Ann. Rev.* IV. 886 An important public paper..which makes many allegations of grievance, still true, and still unredressed. **1877** MRS. OLIPHANT *Makers Flor.* ix. 230 Wickedness unwarned and wrong unredressed.

unre'duceable, *a.* (UN-[1] 7 b.)

1851 RUSKIN *Stones Ven.* I. p. x, I determined to separate the text and the unreduceable plates.

unre'duced, *ppl. a.* [UN-[1] 8.]

†**1.** *Sc.* Not annulled or repealed. *Obs.*

1572–3 *Reg. Privy Council Scot.* II. 185 The saidis first charter and confirmatioun following thairupoun standing unreducit. **1606** [see UNQUARRELLED]. *a* **1639** SPOTTISWOOD *Hist. Ch. Scot.* VI. (1655) 307 The sentence of forfeiture.. stood unreduced.

2. Unsubdued; not taken by force.

1689 *Apol. Fail. Walker's Acc.* 20 Whether some Men are not satisfy'd..Ireland be entirely lost,..and remain unreduc'd for some years, rather than Dissenters be employ'd in retrieving it. **1884** *Leeds Merc.* (Weekly Suppl.) 15 Nov. 6/2 Stirling Castle, the chief place of strength.., still remained unreduced.

3. *Med.* Not restored to a normal state.

1749 T. GATAKER *Le Dran's Operat. Surg.* 101 When an intestine is gangrened and remains unreduced. **1782** MONRO *Anat.* 39 The annihilation..of the head of a bone.., after an unreduced fracture. **1837** QUAIN *Elem. Anat.* (ed. 4) 57 Those cases of unreduced dislocations where the tendons slide over bones. **1857** T. WATSON *Lect. Physic* (ed. 4) I. 35 The dislocation remaining unreduced.

4. Not dissolved or comminuted.

1782 *Phil. Trans.* LXXIII. 63 Dr. Priestley having.. dissolved mercury in the nitrous acid,..constantly found a considerable proportion of it unreduced. **1815** J. SMITH *Panorama Sci. & Art* II. 609 Those [lands] which contain a large proportion of unreduced vegetable matter. **1880** J. DUNBAR *Pract. Papermaker* 24 The rags must..be..drawn out into fibre without having the smallest particle of rag unreduced to half-stuff.

5. Not brought down to simple terms; not applied *to* some use.

1798 HUTTON *Course Math.* I. 251 The rule may be applied at once to an unreduced equation. **1827** POLLOK *Course T.* VIII. 213 The bigot theologian, in minute Distinctions skilled, and doctrines unreduced To practice.

6. Unlessened, undiminished.

1830 BENTHAM *Offic. Apt. Maximized, Further Extr. Const. Code* 15 The emptional mode; according to which, mention is made of the greatest sum he will give for it, if unreduced. **1885** in *Longm. Mag.* Mar. (1900) 434 To enable them to maintain their existence, with unreduced vitality, against the severities of the climate.

7. *Phonetics.* Of a vowel sound or other phonetic element: not reduced (see REDUCED *ppl. a.* 6 b).

1953 K. JACKSON *Lang. & Hist. Early Brit.* 658 Unreduced forms are almost never found in Welsh. **1964** E. BLANCQUAERT in D. Abercrombie et al. *Daniel Jones* 300 English weakened syllables are pronounced unreduced.

unre'ducible, *a.* [UN-[1] 7, 5 b.] Irreducible.

1643 MILTON *Divorce* 44 By Laws commanding over the unreducible antipathies of nature. **1736** *Phil. Trans.* XXXIX. 333 This Rupture was..fixed and unreducible. **1768** *Woman of Honor* II. 159 Those have laughed at it in theory on judging it unreducible to practice. **1858** H. BUSHNELL *Nat. & Supernat.* xii. (1862) 276 There is nothing eccentric that..will not fall into the general aim of the plan..; no fantastic matter that is unreducible. **1861** SIR W. FAIRBAIRN *Iron* 14 An invention..to smelt otherwise useless and unreducible ores.

Hence **unre'ducibleness**.

1694 SOUTH *Serm.* (1698) III. 271 Their Strangeness and Unreducibleness to the common Methods and observations of Nature.

†**unre'duct**, *ppl. a.* *Obs.*[−1] [UN-[1] 8 b.] Unreduced.

1608 MIDDLETON *Fam. Love* III. i, Thought vnreduct to Art, Is but an Embrion in the truest sence.

†**un'redy**, *a.* *Obs.* [UN-[1] 7. Cf. UNREADY *a.*[2]] Not well advised; incautious, rash, foolish.

1387 TREVISA *Higden* (Rolls) II. 91 Eyþer manere summynge is as vnredy as oþer. **1393** LANGL. *P. Pl.* C. XIII. 216 An vnredy reue þi residue shal spene..in a myntewhile. *c* **1449** PECOCK *Repr.* Prol. 3 Ech such vngroundid and vnredy and ouer hasti..blamer.

unre'edified, *ppl. a.* (UN-[1] 8.)

1519 in *Somerset. & Dorset. N. & Q.* (1893) III. 244 Every half yere that the said scolehouse shall be unbuylded or unreedefyed. **1534** *Act 26 Hen. VIII*, c. 8 §1 By reason of whiche burninge .. many voide groundes .. [are] remayninge now at this daye unreedyfied. **1541** *Act 32 Hen. VIII*, c. 19 §1 Houses of habitation..whiche nowe are fallen downe decayed and at this tyme remayne unreedified.

un'reel, *v.* [UN-[2] 3.]

1. *trans.* To unwind from a reel or skein.

Chiefly *fig.* Quot. 1605 is echoed by several later writers, as in quot. 1652.

1567 GOLDING *Ovid's Met.* x. 122, I Beseech yee of Eurydicee vnreele the destinye. **1598** FLORIO, *Sgominare*,.. to vnreele yarne. **1605** SYLVESTER *Du Bartas* II. iii. III. *Law* 1377 Un-winde the bottom of old Times again, Of Ages past un-reel the snarled skain. **1606** J. RAYNOLDS *Dolarney's Prim.* (1880) 77 Ye fates vnreele my lou's sad destinie. **1652** BENLOWES *Theoph.* XII. lxxxvi, Unwinde Times ball again, Unreel through ages its snarl'd skain. **1889** *Engineer* 15 Nov. 413 A measured mile course was laid off by unreeling from an anchored stake buoy one mile of fine wire.

2. *intr.* To become unwound.

1886 *Tribune Bk. Sports* 163 (Cent.), The line will unreel faster than it is needed. **1899** *Westm. Gaz.* 13 Jan. 2/1 They shall mark the Empire's line unreel From Cairo to the Cape.

un'reelable, *a.* (UN-[1] 7 b.)

1611 COTGR., *Indevidable*, vnwindable, vnreelable. **1863** *All Year Round* 11 July 467/2 That the moth, in escaping from the cocoon,..cuts it, and renders it unreelable. **1887** *Encycl. Brit.* XXII. 62/2 Unreelable cocoons, *i.e.*, those which are pierced, torn, or cut.

un'reeve, *v.* [UN-[2] 3.] *trans.* To withdraw (a rope, etc.) from being reeved.

1600 in Hakluyt *Voy.* III. 847 Wee vnriued our sheates, tackes, halliers, and other ropes. *c* **1625** *Nomencl. Navalis* (Harl. MS.) s.v. *Reeve*, When wee would haue that Roape pulled out of the Block, &c. wee say vnreeue that Roape, or the Brases, Lifts, Sheats, &c. are vnreeued. **1692** *Capt. Smith's Seaman's Gram.* I. 81 To pull a Rope out of a Block is called unreeving the Rope. **1730** CAPT. W. WRIGLESWORTH *MS. Log-bk. of the 'Lyell'* 1 Aug., Yesterday afternoon unreeved the runing Rigging. **1745** P. THOMAS *Jrnl. Anson's Voy.* 148 We unreev'd [*sc.* the rope].. And reev'd a new one. **1804** *Naval Chron.* XII. 480 The chain-pumps were unrove, and leathered afresh. **1840** R. H. DANA *Bef. Mast* v, We..sent down the royal yards, and unrove the gear. **1883** *Man. Seamanship for Boys* 59 Jib or flying-jib stays can be unrove,..and then rove through the lacing.

refl. **1847** KIPPING *Sailmaking* 49 By the loosening of which they unreeve themselves.

b. *fig.* (See quots.)

1840 R. H. DANA *Bef. Mast* xxix, Cockroaches, fleas and other vermin..must have unrove their life-lines before the hatches were opened. **1867** SMYTH *Sailor's Word-bk.* 707 *Unrove his life-line*, departed this life.

Hence **un'reeved** *ppl. a.*[1], **un'reeving** *vbl. sb.*

1730 CAPT. W. WRIGLESWORTH *MS. Log-bk. of the 'Lyell'* 14 Aug., All our unreev'd Rigging is a shore. [**1775** ASH, *Unreeving*.] **1892** KIPLING *Life's Handicap* 182 The reeving and unreeving of the bed-tapes.

un'reeved, *ppl. a.*[2] (UN-[1] 8.)

1793 SMEATON *Edystone L.* Expl. Plate 18 The greater sheaves, before left unreeved.

†**unre'fellable**, *a.* (UN-[1] 7 b.)

1593 BILSON *Govt. Christ's Ch.* 258 Which to all..is an argument vnrefellable. **1622** F. MARKHAM *Bk. War* III. ix. 116 Doubtlesse I could hold..almost an unrefellable disputation therein.

unre'ferring, *ppl. a.* (UN-[1] 10.)

1655 FULLER *Ch. Hist.* III. ix. §5 He..began the innocent Order of the Garter, unreferring to any of his former atchievements. **1824** MISS L. M. HAWKINS *Mem.*, etc. I. 207 There is about them..so unreferring a recoil into themselves, that [etc.].

unre'fine, *v.* (UN-[2] 3.)

1792 W. ROBERTS *Looker-on* No. 27 (1794) I. 392 How I wish you could a little unrefine yourself. **1869** H. BUSHNELL *Wom. S.* v. 101 Where away goes the refinement of the polls, when the polls have unrefined the refiner?

unre'fined, *ppl. a.* [UN-[1] 8.]

1. Not refined in manners, feelings, or speech.

1595 W. CLERKE *Polimanteia*, etc. R iij, With Chausers praise, with Lydgate,..and such like, whose vnrefined tongues..wrote simplie and purelie as the times weare. **1704** SWIFT *T. Tub.* ix, The Vulgar dictates of unrefined Reason. **1756** BURKE *Vind. Nat. Soc.* Wks. I. 61 In these early and unrefined ages. **1807** G. CHALMERS *Caledonia* I. II. vi. 309 In this unrefined state, the Scoto-Irish long continued. **1861** WHYTE MELVILLE *Market Harb.* 60 A confirmed bachelor,..somewhat rough and unpolished and unrefined.

2. Not freed from gross or inferior matter.

c **1610** *Rates of Marchandizes* F 1 b, Camphire refined the pound. Camphire vnrefined. **1611** COTGR., *Borras Pierreux*, vnrefined Borax, as it comes out of the rocke, or mine. **1659** W. CHAMBERLAYNE *Pharon.* I. v. 65 Like gold yet unrefined. **1703** DAMPIER *Voy.* III. 55 Which makes it whiter and finer than our Muscovada, as we call our unrefin'd Sugar. **1791** NEWTE *Tour Eng. & Scot.* 108 Rocksalt in the raw and unrefined state. **1868** G. DUFF *Pol. Surv.* 190 Brazil sends us ..raw cotton and unrefined sugar. **1900** *Jrnl. Soc. Dyers* xvi. 10 Unrefined natural indigo.

Hence **unre'finedness**.

1607 WALKINGTON *Opt. Glass* 18 The vnrefinednesse of the spirits doe seeme to affect the soule.

unre'finement. (UN-[1] 12.)

1886 LINSKILL *Haven under Hill* i, Nor did [her speech].. strike you with any jarring sense of unrefinement.

unre'fining, *ppl. a.* (UN-[1] 10.)

1759 FRANKLIN *Ess.* Wks. 1840 III. 370 A plain, unrefining reader would think that..the issue could not but be happy.

unre'flected, *ppl. a.* [UN-[1] 8, 8 c.]

1. Not reflected *on* or *upon*; not thought over.

1670 CLARENDON *Contempl. Ps.* Tracts (1727) 372, I suffered those papers..to lie neglected and unreflected upon, during..my too great prosperity. **1720–1** *Lett. fr. Mist's Jrnl.* (1722) II. 71 That..their every Action..should pass uncensured and unreflected on. **1755** CHESTERF. in *World* No. 112. 66 All these unreflected and unexamined opinions of our cobler.

2. Not returned by reflection.

[**1775** ASH.] **1810** SCOTT *Lady of L.* v. x, The sun's last glance was glinted back,.. The next, all unreflected, shone On bracken green. **1869** TYNDALL in *Fortn. Rev.* 1 Feb. 245 In two directions we should have the solar light reflected; in two others unreflected.

unre'flecting, *ppl. a.* (UN-[1] 10.)

1665 J. SERGEANT *Sure Footing* 49 Unreflecting and unredoubting persons. **1704** J. TRAPP *Abra-Mulé* II. i. 498 Ill Success Renders a Sultan odious in the Eyes Of th' unreflecting Vulgar. **1769** *Junius Lett.* iii. (1788) 44, I place them to the account of an honest, unreflecting indignation. **1848** R. I. WILBERFORCE *Doctr. Incarnation* v. 128 The unreflecting simplicity of that early faith. **1891** MEREDITH *One of our Conq.* xxviii, She did not reflect;..she was unreflecting, feeling only a beyond and hidden.

absol. **1748** RICHARDSON *Clarissa* II. 281 The censures of the busy and the unreflecting.

Hence **unre'flectingly** *adv.*, **-ness.**

1696 J. SERGEANT *Method to Sci.* II. ii. 131 The Former comes by Experience Unreflectingly; the Later is attain'd by Study and Reflexion. **1816** COLERIDGE *Lay Serm.* (Bohn) 308 The habitual unreflectingness, which..may be susceptible of more or less palliation. **1854** A. G. HENDERSON tr. *Cousin's Philos. of Kant* p. lx, Thou wouldst not unreflectingly confer it upon the first comer. **1866** GEO. ELIOT *F. Holt* v, Quite unreflectingly, he drew forth a pair of spectacles.

unre'flective, *a.* (UN-[1] 7, 5 b.)

Also, in recent use, *unreflectively*.

1854 FARADAY *Exp. Res.* (1859) 466 The observant, but unreflective infant. **1874** SAYCE *Princ. Compar. Philol.* iii. 95 The unreflective fetichism of the savage.

unre'formable, *a.* [UN-[1] 7 b, 5 b.]

1. Incapable of being reformed or amended.

1583 GOLDING *Calvin on Deut.* cxvi. 711 They continued stubborne and vnreformable still. *a* **1600** HOOKER *Eccl. Pol.* VII. v. §8 The proud, tyrannical, and unreformable dealings of her bishops. **1624** BP. HALL *True Peace Makers* Wks.

(1625) 542 The vnreformable drunkard. **1648** OWEN *Righteous Zeal Encouraged* (1649) 14 To swim against the streame of an unreformable multitude. **1791** COWPER *Corresp.* (1824) II. 274 Endeavouring to reform the unreformable great. **1848** PHILLIMORE *Introd. Stud. Rom. Law* 319 If I may coin a word to express an evil it is so hard to describe, the unreformable Court of Chancery.

2. Incapable of being re-cast or altered.

1624 BEDELL *Lett.* i. 43 You had that same one onely immoueable and vnreformable rule of faith..recited in your hearing. **1649** *Bounds Publ. Obed.* 47 Unalterable and unreformable as a divine text. **1837** J. H. NEWMAN *Proph. Office Ch.* 267 This rule..is sole, unalterable, unreformable.

unrefor'mation. (UN-1 12.)

a **1656** BP. HALL *Wks.* (1863) V. 632 Yea, have not too many amongst us added to their unreformation an impudence in sinning?

unre'formed, *ppl. a.* [UN-1 8, 5 b.]

1. Of faults, etc.: Not amended or made good.

1528 CROMWELL in Merriman *Life & Lett.* (1902) I. 318, I trust that no defaulte..is lefte vnrefourmed. **1542** HEN. VIII *Declar.* A iv b, The kyng of Scottis dedes..could not..be passed ouer vnreformed. **1653** JER. TAYLOR *Serm. for Year* I. xii. 161 Every vicious habit, or unreformed sin. **1679** MOXON *Mech. Exerc.* viii. 145 Upon penalty..for every default Ten Shillings, and Ten Shillings every week it continues unreformed. **1694** S. BETHAL *Providences of God* 94 There being no such Traitors to the Strength of a Land ..as are unreformed Provocations.

2. Not reformed or made better; unimproved:

a. Of persons, the heart, etc.

1583 GOLDING *Calvin on Deut.* xxvii. 223 If wee..in the meane while leaue our heartes vnreformed. **1644** HAMMOND *Of Conscience* 44 Never to lye downe..unhumbled unreformed in any such sinne. **1671** MILTON *P.R.* III. 429 Who freed,..Unhumbl'd, unrepentant, unreform'd, Headlong would follow. **1717** DE FOE *Mem. Ch. Scot.* II. 27 The Church formally absolv'd him, and yet secretly believed him to be unreformed. **18..** MOORE (*title*), Musings of an Unreformed Peer. **1872** GEO. ELIOT *Middlem.* lxi, The unreformed provincial mind distrusted London.

b. Of practices, institutions, etc.

1614 *Act 12 Jas. I,* in Bolton *Stat. Irel.* (1621) 425 Your gracious disposition..towards the settling of this unreformed kingdom. **1792** BURKE *Let. to Dundas* Wks. 1812 V. 199 It is better to allow the evil, in order to correct it, than..to leave it under an illegal, and therefore an unreformed existence. **1840** ARNOLD in *Life* (1844) II. 189 If a system goes on long unreformed, it is not then reformed, but destroyed. **1849** MILL *Diss. & Disc.* (1859) II. 352 The majority of even the unreformed House of Commons. **1898** *Westm. Gaz.* 1 Mar. 2/1 Then I would rather that the Church should remain unreformed.

3. Not affected by the Reformation.

1788 BURKE *Sp. agst. W. Hastings* Wks. XIV. 20 [You] have seen in the unreformed countries of Europe churches filled with persons, who take sanctuary in them. **1892** MAYOR *Ep. James* p. xviii, The churches of Western Christendom, reformed and unreformed.

Hence **unre'formedness.**

1607 HIERON *Wks.* I. 248 Denouncing the heauy vengeance of God vpon vnreformednesse. **1655** S. ASHE *Funeral Serm. Gataker* 13 During the time of his impenitency and unreformednesse. **1677** I. MATHER *Preval. Prayer* (1864) 244 That which aggravateth our Unreformedness, is, that in the Time of our Trouble [etc.]. **1888** *Contemp. Rev.* Sept. 345 One who, in that day of its unreformedness, did not regard the constitution of the Royal Academy as absolutely perfect.

unre'fracted, *ppl. a.* (UN-1 8, 5 b.)

a **1676** HALE *Prim. Orig. Man.* (1677) 303 To distribute this Light..which unrefracted might have been too.. violent to the other parts of Nature. **1728** CHAMBERS *Cycl.* s.v. *Refraction,* The perpendicular Ray..will pass unrefracted to K. **1796** COLERIDGE *Destiny of Nations* 463 Whether thy Love with unrefracted ray Beam on the Prophet's purged eye. **1862** R. H. PATTERSON *Ess. Hist. & Art* 83 The purity and brilliance of unrefracted light.

unre'fracting, *ppl. a.* (UN-1 10.)

1827 COLERIDGE *Lit. Rem.* (1839) IV. 408 An unpreoccupied, unrefracting medium. **1863** J. C. MORISON *St. Bernard* III. v. 369 Looking through the pure unrefracting ether as we do at the stars.

unre'frainable, *a.* (UN-1 7 b.)

1828 E. IRVING *Last Days* 174 A wild, inconstant, unrefrained and unrefrainable disposition.

unre'frained, *ppl. a.* (UN-1 8.)

c **1550** ROLLAND *Crt. Venus* I. 825 With cruell mind thair vnrefrenit In this degre [he] Rehersit wordis iniurious. **1593** *Sidney's Arcadia* III. (1598) 354 Delay, the racke of vnrefrain'd desire. **1648** HEXHAM II, s.v. *Ontoomigh.* **1828** [see prec.].

unre'freshed, *ppl. a.* (UN-1 8.)

1736 ARBUTHNOT *Rules Diet* 384 Unrefresh'd by Sleep. **1769** FALCONER *Dict. Marine* (1780) s.v. *Water-spout,* A tract of land..unrefreshed by the wind. **1791** COWPER *Odyss.* IV. 955 Unrefresh'd with either food or wine. **1797** COLERIDGE *Remorse* I. ii, I am old and Heartless!.. Hectic and unrefreshed with rest. **1881** CHR. ROSSETTI *Later Life* 4 So unrefreshed by foregone weariness.

unre'freshful, *a.* (UN-1 7.)

1819 SCOTT *Leg. Montrose* xvi, The viands..were.. unrefreshful to my body. **1858** FARRAR *Eric* 361 Even his sleep seemed unrefreshful when the waking brought no change in his condition.

unre'freshing, *ppl. a.* (UN-1 10.)

1814 SCOTT *Wav.* xxxvii, His slumbers were broken and unrefreshing. **1870** MISS BRIDGMAN *R. Lynne* II. v. 115 He fell into a troubled and unrefreshing sleep.

unre'freshingly, *adv.* (UN-1 11; cf. prec.)

1889 *Scribner's Mag.* Aug. 164/2 It was unrefreshingly hot, and just about slack water scarcely ebbing at all.

un'reft, *ppl. a.* [UN-1 8 b.] Undespoiled.

1535 STEWART *Cron. Scot.* (Rolls) I. 291 His dochteris tua ..In tutorie to Cesar that he left, Into thair rycht for to kepe thame vnreft.

unre'fulgent, *a.* (UN-1 7.)

1879 STEVENSON *Edinburgh* 32 The unrefulgent sun going down.

unre'funding, *ppl. a.* (UN-1 10.)

[**1727** BOYER *Dict. Royal* II, Unrefunding, *qui ne rend jamais.*] **1744** YOUNG *Nt. Th.* VII. 831 When horror universal shall descend..On that enormous, unrefunding tomb, How just this verse!

unre'fusable, *a.* (UN-1 7 b, 5 b.)

1691 SEWEL, *Onontzeggelyk,* Vnrefusable, that which will take no denial. **1704** NORRIS *Ideal World* II. i. 37 Upon this fair and unrefusable supposition. **1843** CARLYLE *Past & Pr.* III. xii, The most unrefusable demand! **1865** MRS. WHITNEY *Gayworthys* xxvi, Skylie..said this with her most unrefusable expression.

Hence **unre'fusably** *adv.*

1710 NORRIS *Chr. Prud.* iii. 131 Happiness abstractly considered, which is necessarily and unrefusably lovely.

unre'fused, *ppl. a.* (UN-1 8.)

1548 in *Compl. Scotl.* (1872) 242 Because nothyng should be left..of your part vnrefused. **1648** HEXHAM II, s.v. *Ongeweygert.*

unre'fusing, *ppl. a.* (UN-1 10.)

a **1586** SIDNEY *Arcadia* III. x, Thinking..that beauty, carefully set forth, wold soone prove a signe of an unrefusing harborough. **1621** LADY M. WROTH *Urania* 374 What power had those instruments sweete speach, more sweete and vnrefusing conuersation ouer my heart? **1728** THOMSON *Spring* 38 There, unrefusing to the harness'd yoke They lend their Shoulder.

unrefutable, *a.* Now *rare.* (UN-1 7 b, 5 b.)

1594 NASHE *Christ's T.* (ed. 2) To Rdr., Henceforth..for an vnrefutable principle I will hold it. **1629** MASSINGER *Picture* IV. ii, As I must grant, It being vnrefutable in reason. **1859** HERSCHEL *Pop. Lect. Sci.* iii. §54 (1866) 140 That positive and unrefutable demonstration.

unre'futed, *ppl. a.* (UN-1 8.)

1589 GREENE *Menaphon* (Arb.) 38 In nature this is an vnrefuted principle, that [etc.]. **1846** LEWES *Hist. Philos.* IV. 85 So long must Berkeley remain unrefuted by any theory of perception. **1875** JOWETT *Plato* (ed. 2) III. 507 This argument of ours remains unrefuted.

unre'gainable, *a.* (UN-1 7 b.)

1649 J. H. *Motion to Parl. Adv. Learn.* 22 The time is unregainable. **1866** CARLYLE *Remin.* (1881) I. 281 The wild struggles..towards the unattainable, the unregainable.

un'regal, *a.* (UN-1 7.)

1611 SPEED *Hist. Gt. Brit.* IX. vi. 35 King Henry..seeing no issue of his long disquietnesse, and vnregall vsages. **1846** WORCESTER (citing *Ed. Rev.*). **1880** F. G. LEE *Ch. under Q. Eliz.* II. 240 With unregal meanness, she sent Lord Hunsdon..to 'draw him out' as regards religion. **1894** *Persian Pict.* 114 We stopped before an unregal gateway.

unre'gard, *sb.* (UN-1 12.)

a **1656** BP. HALL *Rem. Wks.* (1660) 256 When he saw a woman bowing her self forward too low in her devotion, [the cynic] could chide her for her unregard to those deities, which beheld her on all sides. **1876** *Gd. Words* 687 Worth yet shall..Outlive the death of unregard.

†**unre'gard,** *v. Obs.* [UN-2 3.] *trans.* To disregard.

1545 RAYNALD *Byrth Mankynde* Prol. C iv, Sholde men.. denye or vnregard the blessyd sacrament? **1600** ROWLANDS *Lett. Humours Blood* 4 Carelesse of wronges, and vn-regarding right. **1627** BP. HALL *Passion Serm.* 431 Not onely [hast thou]..smitten me, vn-regarded me, but, as it were, forgotten—yea, forsaken—me.

†**unre'gardable,** *a. Obs.* [UN-1 7 b.] Not deserving regard or consideration.

1614 RALEIGH *Hist. World* VIII. vi. 618 Neither is it vnregardable, that the Tyrants..were not all of them good men of warre. **1641** BP. HALL *Def. Humble Remonstr.* 118 Away then with those your unproving illustrations, and unregardable testimonies.

unre'gardant, *a.* (UN-1 7.)

1814 SOUTHEY *Roderick* x. 69 With fix'd eyes intent Yet unregardant of the countenance Whereon they dwelt.

unre'garded, *ppl. a.* (UN-1 8.)

1561 T. NORTON *Calvin's Inst.* I. Pref., Beyng in dede but one man alone, and vnregarded, but out of whoes mouthe came truthe. **1614** RALEIGH *Hist. World* III. (title-p.), When Israel was..an unregarded Nation. **1670** R. COKE *Disc. Trade* 62 A poor and unregarded Village. **1726** POPE *Odyss.* XVII. 612 Time steals away with unregarded wing. **1767** WILKES *Corr.* (1805) III. 100 That so many other publications.., full of the most deadly venom, should pass totally unregarded. **1813** BYRON *Corsair* II. v, Each bears a prize of unregarded charms. **1883** RUSKIN *Fors Clav.* xc. 172 In the dormitory..on an unregarded shutter..she cuts her notch.

b. Const. *by* or †*of.*

1571 GOLDING *Calvin on Ps.* xli. 18 We surmise him to be unregarded of God. **1612** W. PARKES *Curtaine-Dr.* (1876) 17 The lawes of nature,..vassayled, obliterate and vnregarded by him. **1728** R. MORRIS *Ess. Anc. Archit.* 13 Architecture is so unregarded by our modern Builders. **1805** WORDSW. *Prelude* XIII. 278 God..loveth us, When we are unregarded by the world. **1884** tr. *Lotze's Metaph.* 464 Many external stimuli, therefore, are unregarded by us.

Hence **unre'gardedly** *adv.*

1685 BOYLE *Salubr. Air* 12 Bodies..wont to be unregardedly compris'd under the confus'd name of Earths.

unre'gardful, *a.* (UN-1 7.)

1598 FLORIO, *Inconsiderato,* rash, vnregardfull, inconsiderate. **1812** J. HENRY *Camp. agst. Quebec* 183 Unregardful of the dogs, we awaited the management of the flight. **1853** RUSKIN *Stones Ven.* II. vi. 184 This is design unregardful of facts. **1879** FARRAR *St. Paul* I. 338 The sea which four times wrecked him with its unregardful storms.

unre'garding, *ppl. a.* (UN-1 10.)

c **1585** T. PROCTOR *Triumph of Truth* (1866) 5 Who vn-regarding of him self, forgets his Parents cares. **1593** *Sidney's Arcadia* III. (1922) II. 52 The debate betwixt Basilius shinnes and the unregarding fourmes. **1660** JER. TAYLOR *Ductor* III. v. rule 8 §29 Their not complying..is only then a sin when it is done with unregarding circumstances. **1720** POPE *Iliad* XX. 202 The lion,..viewing first his foes with scornful eyes,..Stalks careless on, with unregarding pride. **1732** J. WHALEY *Poems* 27 Unregarding of his useful Pains, The surly Carter wounds his [*sc.* a horse's] stretching Veins. **1851** KINGSLEY *Yeast* xvii, His employer..walked before him silent and unregarding.

unre'generacy. (UN-1 12, 5 b; cf. next.)

1622 W. WHATELY *Gods Husb.* II. 118 A man in his vtter vnregeneracy is dead in sinne. **1688** J. BUNYAN *Jerus. Sinner Saved* (1886) 49 Paul was the most outrageous of all the apostles, in the time of his unregeneracy. **1818** G. S. FABER *Horæ Mosaicæ* II. 293 He derives no benefit from the external sign, remaining still..in a state of unregeneracy. **1870** *Athenæum* 19 Nov. 652 Ned went to Astley's in the blackest state of unregeneracy.

unre'generate, *a.* and *sb.* (UN-1 7, 12, and 5 b.)

1612 T. TAYLOR *Comm. Titus* i. 12 What properties haue vnregenerate men, which are not more beseeming..beasts than men? **1651** BAXTER *Inf. Bapt.* 225 No man hath any sign given him..by which to judge of the unregenerate Elect. *a* **1740** WATERLAND *Inquiry Communion* Wks. 1823 IX. 483 In or by their natural, unregenerate state. **1795** COLERIDGE *Eolian Harp* 55 These shapings of the unregenerate mind. **1839** HALLAM *Hist. Lit.* III. ii. §31 The human virtues..of unregenerate men. **1876** CANON MOZLEY *Univ. Serm.* xiii. (1877) 237 Instances of what unregenerate human nature can attain to.

absol. **1655** JER. TAYLOR *Unum Necess.* vii. §2. 460 As in the unregenerate there might be some good.

fig. **1876** GEO. ELIOT *Dan. Der.* xxxvii, I was unregenerate then [in matters of art].

b. *sb.* An unregenerate person.

c **1625** BP. HALL *St. Paul's Combat* Wks. 1634 II. 441 Those carelesse unregenerates. **1627** —— *Salomon's Song Paraphr.* ii. 251 All the assemblies of aliens and unregenerates.

unre'generate, *v.* (UN-2 3.)

1861 LD. LYTTON & FANE *Tannhäuser* 9 Suffered for a space..To range the wide world, and assay their powers To unregenerate redeem'd mankind.

unre'generated, *ppl. a.* (UN-1 8.)

1579 W. WILKINSON *Confut. Fam. Love* B iij b, They are vnilluminated, vnregenerated. *a* **1791** V. KNOX *Serm.* (1792) iii. 49 Man in his corrupt and unregenerated state. **1826** SCOTT *Woodst.* xiv, I..have fought prizes when I was unregenerated.

Hence **unre'generatedness.**

1664 H. MORE *Myst. Iniq.* Pref. 5 In a state of Unregeneratedness, and utterly devoid of the Life of God.

unre'generating, *ppl. a.* (UN-1 10.)

1657 REEVE *God's Plea* 145 Were ever so many Pulpits despised? were there ever so many unregenerating sermons?

unregene'ration. (UN-1 12, 5 b.)

1625 PEMBLE *Justification* V. ii. 176 All men..which are in state of infidelity and vnregeneration. **1662** HIBBERT *Body Divinity* I. 119 Conforming us to the nature of the devil; pleading mans unregeneration. *a* **1812** H. MARTYN *20 Serm.* (1822) 224 The wickedness and unregeneration of his heart. **1870** MISS BRIDGMAN *R. Lynne* II. xiii. 270 Cheerfulness of disposition she considered a..sign of unregeneration.

un'regimented, *ppl. a.* (UN-1 8.)

1684 *List Military* Title-page, A general and compleat List Military..(Excepting the Un-Regimented Companies). *a* **1725** LD. WHITWORTH *Acc. Russia* (1758) 102 Unregimented Soldiers and free companies in the lesser garrisons of Ingria. **1850** CARLYLE *Latter-d. Pamphl.* i. 45 These outcast soldiers of his, unregimented roving banditti.

un'registered, *ppl. a.* [UN-1 8.]

1. Not entered in a register; unrecorded.

1604 E. G[RIMSTONE] *D'Acosta's Hist. Indies* IV. iv. 216 That which came for Merchants and private men being registred, and much that came vnregistred. **1606** SHAKS. *Ant. & Cl.* III. xiii. 119 Besides what hotter houres Vn-registred in vulgar Fame, you haue Luxuriously pickt out. **1679** C. NESSE *Antichrist* 235 By those few [witnesses] we may conjecture many more..lay hid unregistred. **1716** *Lond. Gaz.* No. 5467/1 The unregistered [part of the effects] is valued at half as much more. **1826** KIRBY & SP. *Entomol.* IV. 440 Its animal productions shall no longer remain unregistered and undescribed. **1871** *Leisure Hour* 9 Sept. 576/1 Unregistered letters and book packets.

2. Not made to register or correspond.

1816 SINGER *Hist. Cards* 133 It is printed upon vellum.., and the right margin is quite as irregular or unregistered as in the Dutch Speculum.

unre'gretful, *a.* (UN-1 7.)

1873 T. W. HIGGINSON *Oldport Days* vii. 196 [She] grew up into a well-behaved mediocrity, unregretful of the show-tent.

unre'gretfully, *adv.* (UN-1 11.)

1862 'SHIRLEY' (J. Skelton) *Nugæ Crit.* xi. 453, I remember, not unregretfully, the simple rustic procession.

unre'gretfulness. (UN-[1] 12.)
1876 L. TOLLEMACHE in *Fortn. Rev.* Jan. 117 To this unregretfulness..they owed much of [their] lighthearted joyousness.

unre'grettable, *a.* (UN-[1] 7 b.)
1768 *Woman of Honor* II. 120 A very unregrettable sacrifice of..an object of vanity.

unre'gretted, *ppl. a.* (UN-[1] 8.)
1676 ROW *Contin. Blair's Autobiog.* xii. (1848) 453 He died unregretted by good men. **1781** COWPER *Retirem.* 167 A few.., unregretted, are soon snatch'd away From scenes of sorrow. **1782** V. KNOX *Ess.* clxviii, Those [works] of the frothy declaimer are daily dropping unregretted into the gulph of oblivion. **1843** RUSKIN *Mod. Paint.* I. II. III. i. §3 All has passed unregretted as unseen. **1891** MEREDITH *One of our Conq.* xxv, Since she had taken a step..unregretted, if fatal.

unre'gretting, *ppl. a.* (UN-[1] 10.)
1800 P. L. COURTIER *Pleas. Solitude* III. 39 We,.. unregretting, other joys resign.

un'regular, *a.* Chiefly *dial.* (UN-[1] 7, 5 b.)
1609 DOULAND *Ornithoparcus' Microl.* 29 It hath his Finall regular place in *Dsolre*, or his vnregular in *alamire*. **1828–** in dialect glossaries, etc. **1884** 'MARK TWAIN' *Huck. Finn* xxviii, It's so kind of strange and unregular, I never see nothing like it.

un'regulated, *ppl. a.* (UN-[1] 8, 5 b.)
1721 AMHERST *Terræ Fil.* No. 1 (1726) 5 The universities, ..in their present unregulated state. **1791** BOSWELL *Johnson* an. 1744 ¶1 He undoubtedly had a warm and vigorous, though unregulated mind. **1808** SCOTT in *Lockhart* I. i. 35 These studies were totally unregulated. **1871** B. TAYLOR *Faust* (1875) I. Notes 282 An indolent unregulated habit of life.

unre'hearsable, *a.* (UN-[1] 7 b.)
1513 DOUGLAS *Æneis* XI. vi. 72 Of ws hail the remanis Bene punyst sore with onrehersabill panis.

unre'hearsed, *ppl. a.* [UN-[1] 8.]
1. Not related or mentioned; untold.
1472 *Cov. Leet Bk.* 378 All thees moo, whoos names be vndrewreton besyde many moo vnrehersyd. **1562** T. WILSON *Rhet.* (ed. 2) 76 b, The holie mother Church willeth me to leaue nothing vnrehearsed. **1613** SHERLEY *Trav. Persia* 92 A discourse proued true..by many examples which he would leaue unrehearsed. **1629** SIR W. MURE *True Crucifixe* 670 Exposd to paine, to horrors vnrehearsed. *a* **1800** COWPER *Odyss.* (ed. 2) XIV. 236, I could exhaust..the circling year Complete, my woes rehearsing, and at last Leave unrehearsed large portion of the toil. **1827** POLLOK *Course T.* x. 32 New scenes of bliss..unrehearsed by mortal tongue.
2. Not previously practised.
1845 E. HOLMES *Mozart* 289 The unrehearsed overture was then commenced. **1875** C. L. KENNEY *Mem. Balfe* 44 An alarm of fire through some unrehearsed effect in the incantation scene.

†un'reign, *v. Obs.*[−1] [UN-[1] 14.] *intr.* To fail to reign.
1434 MISYN *Mending Life* 122 As qwo say: syn in vs may vnrene [L. *non regnare*], bot it may not vnbe.

un'rein, *v.* (UN-[2] 4 b.)
1603 DANIEL *Paneg. Congrat.* lix, An imperiall lust, that being vnrain'd, Will hardly be resisted any where. **1694** ADDISON *Eng. Poets* Wks. 1721 I. 41 How negligently graceful he unreins His verse, and writes in loose familiar strains! **1702** DE FOE *Reform. Manners* I. 15 Tell us why he ..Unreins no Vengeance, lets no Thunders fly, When Villains prosper. **1707** TICKELL *Oxford* 273 Codrington and Steele, their verse unrein, And form an easy, unaffected strain. **1851** *Bentley's Misc.* Aug. 147 If a soldier's life..can atone for the sad consequences of unreining an ungovernable temper.

unre'ined, *ppl. a.* (UN-[1] 8.)
1609 DANIEL *Civ. Wars* VI. vi, Whil'st this wilde vnrained multitude..Ransacke the Cittie. **1628** FELTHAM *Resolves* II. viii. 18 When the Minde is madded with vn-reined passions. **1667** MILTON *P.L.* VII. 17 Least from this flying Steed unrein'd,..Dismounted, on th' Aleian Field I fall. **1751** J. BROWN *Shaftesb. Charac.* 312 The delirious flights of an unreined imagination. **1825** LONGF. *Burial of Minnisink* vii, Leading the war-horse of their chief..Uncurbed, unreined, and riderless. **1850** BLACKIE *Æschylus* II. 10 We cannot but condemn the spirit of unreined independence. **1851** C. L. SMITH tr. *Tasso* VI. xvii, Unreined By aught of fear, thy message here expound.

unre'jected, *ppl. a.* (UN-[1] 8.)
1757 DYER *Fleece* II. 81 There the tender eye May view.. the lame, employ'd, And unrejected age. **1778** CHATHAM in *Ann. Reg., Chron.* App. 247/2 His conversations..are..to my feeling too offensive to be continued, or unrejected.

unre'joiced, *ppl. a.* (UN-[1] 8.)
1814 BYRON *Lara* I. vii, Not unrejoiced to see him once again, Warm was his welcome. **1816** WORDSW. *Morning Gen. Thanksgiving* i, Thou, impartial Sun,..Not unrejoiced I see thee climb the sky.

unre'joicing, *ppl. a.* (UN-[1] 10.)
1726 THOMSON *Winter* (ed. 2) 267 In Russia's..Moors, Where Winter keeps his unrejoicing Court. **1745** WARTON *Pleas. Mel.* 230 Amid Siberia's unrejoicing wilds. *a* **1814** *Hortensia* II. iii. in *New Brit. Theatre* IV. 161 Within the castle walls, Let not one un-rejoicing soul be found. **1876** RUSKIN *Fors Clav.* lxxii. 388 The unrejoicing manner of travel adopted by the..modern tourist.

†un'reke, *v. Obs.* [UN-[2] 3 + REKE *v.*[3]] *trans.* To uncover, display.
1412–20 LYDG. *Chron. Troy* I. 2196 Whan þat Loue of manhod wolde speke, þe wode fire out of his brest to vnreke, ..Cometh Schame anoon, & outterly seith nay. *c* **1421** HOCCLEVE *Min. Poems* 117/197 Lo, frinde, nowe haue I myne entent vnreke of my longe tale.

†un'reken, *a. Obs.* [UN-[1] 7.] **a.** Unready, awkward. **b.** Uneasy; unpleasant; rough.
c **1250** *Gen. & Ex.* 2817 Louerd, ic am wanmol, vn-reken Of wurdes. *a* **1310** in Wright *Lyric P.* xxxvi. 100 Al unreken is my ro, Loverd Crist, whet shal y say? **13..** *Cursor M.* 24847 (Gött.), þaim bleu mani vnrekind [*Cott.* brem, *Edinb.* bremli] blast, þair mast raf.
Hence **†un'rekenly** *adv. Obs.*
a **1300** *Cursor M.* 15786 Wit maces and wit neues smert vn-rekenli on him [þai] ran.

unre'lapsing, *ppl. a.* (UN-[1] 10.)
1740 CHEYNE *Regimen* 27 To..establish in perpetual and unrelapsing Order and Purity, free and lapsed intelligent Beings.

unre'latable, *a.* (UN-[1] 7 b.)
1621 LADY M. WROTH *Urania* 276 The vn-relatable exquisitenesse of his youth. **1963** BRUNER & OLVER in J. S. Bruner *Beyond Information Given* (1974) xx. 361 The lists proceed from near to far items, from easily associated to almost unrelatable elements. **1968** *Listener* 1 Aug. 147/3 The relative pronoun hangs in the air, unrelatable to anything in particular.

unre'lated, *ppl. a.* [UN-[1] 8, 5 b.]
1. Not connected by blood; not akin.
a **1661** FULLER *Worthies, London* II. (1662) 207 But let others unrelated unto him write his Character. *a* **1677** BARROW *Serm.* (1686) III. 36 'Tis not the example..of a stranger, of one indifferent, or unrelated to us. **1706** DE FOE *Jure Div.* x. 219 Of foreign Breed, of unrelated Race,..A spurious Birth of intermingl'd Blood. *a* **1752** WARBURTON *Serm.* Wks. 1788 V. 79 They..despised the rest of the sons of Adam, who..were deemed to be naturally unrelated to them. **1875** MAINE *Hist. Inst.* iii. 65 The tribesmen of an alien and unrelated tribe. **1882** FARRAR *Early Chr.* II. 218 Seven emperors..for the most part entirely unrelated to one another.
2. Not standing in relationship or connexion.
1668 H. MORE *Div. Dial.* I. xxxv. 156 If they were so unrelated indeed in the..apprehension of them,..then I confess the Inference might be sound. **1701** NORRIS *Ideal World* I. ii. 92 For things to be only conditionally related.. is really to be unrelated to, and separated from one another. **1785** BURKE *Corr.* (1844) III. 42 Detached and unrelated offences. **1817** R. JAMESON *Cuvier's Ess. Theory Earth* (ed. 3) p. vii, Petrifactions are no longer viewed..as things isolated and unrelated to the rocks. **1860** TYNDALL *Glac.* I. i. 6 A theory..which..apparently referred a great number of unrelated phenomena to a common cause.
3. Not recounted or told.
1764 *Museum Rust.* IV. 32 Some peculiar circumstance in the soil,..or..some unrelated circumstance in the culture. **1796** MME. D'ARBLAY *Camilla* x. xiii, A reciprocal confidence that left nothing untold, not an action unrelated.
Hence **unre'latedness.**
1854 SYLVESTER *Coll. Math. Papers* (1908) II. 32 The number of singularities (including absolute unrelatedness and entire coincidence within the purview of the term).

unre'lating, *ppl. a.* (UN-[1] 10.)
1697 NORRIS *Treat. Sev. Subj.* (1698) 240, I would fain know, whether any of these Misconducts of Life be..more unrelating to our grand Concern [etc.].

unre'lational, *a.* (UN-[1] 7.)
1865 H. BUSHNELL *Vicar. Sacr.* III. v, A state unrelational with God. **1869** H. SPENCER *Princ. Psychol.* (1872) I. 181 The extremely unrelational states of different orders.

un'relative, *a.* (UN-[1] 7, 5 b.)
a **1751** BOLINGBROKE *Study Hist.* ii. (1752) I. 41 The events..appear to us very often..single, and un-relative, if I may use such an expression for want of a better in English. **1757** CHESTERF. *Lett.* (1774) II. 371 *A propos*, (an expression which is commonly used to introduce whatever is unrelative to it). **1776** BURNEY *Hist. Mus.* I. 62 If the mutations were too sudden and unrelative. **1819** BUSBY *Hist. Music* II. 122 The sudden and unrelative modulation from F to E♭.

un'relatively, *adv.* (UN-[1] 11, 5 b.)
a **1751** BOLINGBROKE *Study Hist.* ii. (1752) I. 46 They saw the measures they took singly, and unrelatively, or relatively alone to some immediate object.

unre'laxable, *a.* (UN-[1] 7 b.)
1860 RUSKIN *Mod. Paint.* V. 36 These pre-Raphaelite laws..are unrelaxed yet, and unrelaxable for ever.

unre'laxed, *ppl. a.* (UN-[1] 8.)
1508 *Reg. Privy Seal Scot.* I. 258/1 Throw the said Androis being..our souerane lordis rebell and at his horne unrelaxit thairfra. **1569** *Reg. Privy Council Scot.* I. 687 [He was] put to the horne,..quhairat he hes remanit lyke as he dois yit continewallie sensyne unrelaxt. **1589** *Ibid.* IV. 358. **1737** GLOVER *Leonidas* VIII. 611 The hosts Maintain in strong and unrelax'd array The conflict undecided. **1766** in Hansard *Parl. Debates* (1813) XVI. 286 To maintain, unrelaxed and unenervated, the fundamentals of the constitution. **1810** SOUTHEY *Kehama* II. xiii, At the length he raised His brow yet unrelax'd. **1825** SCOTT *Betrothed* ix, One wide-spread scene of..unrelaxed pursuit. **1862** LYTTON *Str. Story* II. 172 Unrelaxed, unmitigable indignation.

unre'laxing, *ppl. a.* (UN-[1] 10.)
1781 J. MOORE *View Soc. It.* xlvi. II. 4 A man of unrelaxing wisdom. **1796** BURKE *Letter to Noble Lord* Wks. VIII. 40 To support with unrelaxing vigilance every right, ..every franchise, in this my adopted..country. **1801** SOUTHEY *Thalaba* x. 233 His unrelaxing brow. **1822** KEBLE *Serm.* i. (1848) 5 The most blameless and unrelaxing diligence. **1890** 'R. BOLDREWOOD' *Col. Reformer* (1891) 75 The unrelaxing grip of the law.
Hence **unre'laxingly** *adv.*
[**1847** WEBSTER.] **1858** *Westm. Rev.* Oct. 310 He is unrelaxingly wedded to the conception of the Empire as it was.

unre'leased, *ppl. a.* (UN-[1] 8.)
c **1400** *Rom. Rose* 2729 In sorwe and thought..Ayee vnrelesed woo to make, Whether..they slepe or wake. **1619** in Foster *Eng. Factories India* (1906) I. 80 The fruicts..you may..perceave by your goods detencion these six months in customehouse, and yett unreleaced. **1679** OLDHAM *Sat. Jesuits* iii. (1681) 55 Souls in Purgatory unreleast. **1960** *Lang. & Speech* III. 109 (*heading*) On the perception of unreleased voiceless plosives in English. **1982** *Times* 13 Feb. 6/1 This successful, though unreleased, movie.

unre'lentable, *a.* [UN-[1] 7 b.] Incapable of relenting or giving way.
1611 COTGR., *Inflexible*,..vnrelentable, hard-hearted. **1716** M. DAVIES *Athen. Brit.* I. 113 The Popish Clergy.. render their respective Countries..Reformation-proof and Unrelentable to any redress.

unre'lentance. (UN-[1] 12.)
1637 JACKSON *Serm. Lk. xiii.* 5, 61 This unrelentance presupposeth some other fouler sin then rebellion.

unre'lented, *ppl. a.* [UN-[1] 8.] Unrelaxed.
1676 *Life Father Paul Sarpi* in *Brent's Counc. Trent* 90 This unrelented way of reading and writing..is a kind of intemperance. **1846** WORCESTER (citing Scott). **1876** *Whitby Gloss.* 206 *Ungeen*,..unthawed or unrelented.

unre'lenting, *ppl. a.* [UN-[1] 10, 5 b.]
1. Not softening or yielding; *esp.* not giving way to feelings of kindness or compassion.
(*a*) **1588** SHAKS. *Tit. A.* II. iii. 141 Be your hart to them, As vnrelenting flint to drops of raine. **1621** G. SANDYS *Ovid's Met.* v. (1626) 93 The blade from vnrelenting stone rebounds. **1749** SMOLLETT *Regicide* IV. ix, Him hath the unrelenting dagger torn From my parental arms. **1870** BRYANT *Iliad* v. I. 148 The unrelenting edge Cleft at its root the tongue.
(*b*) **1590** MARLOWE *2nd Pt. Tamburl.* v. iii, If the vnrelenting eares Of death and hell be shut against my praiers. **1593** SHAKS. *3 Hen. VI*, II. i. 58 The irefull Arme Of vn-relenting Clifford. **1634** COWLEY *Elegy R. Clerke* 27 Who hath such hard, such unrelenting Eyes, As would not weep when so much Vertue dyes? **1717** POPE *Iliad* XI. 178 These words..The youth address'd to unrelenting ears. **1774** *Monthly Misc.* June 309 Thy [*sc.* Death's] unrelenting hand..snatch'd Chaucer from our arms. **1813** BYRON *Br. Abydos* II. xxvii, Woe to thee, rash and unrelenting chief! **1844** H. H. WILSON *Brit. India* I. 257 To save him from falling alive into the power of his unrelenting foes. **1853** MISS YONGE *Heir of Redclyffe* xxxii, I don't think you can be very unrelenting when you see..how altered he is.
(*c*) **1608** *Yorksh. Trag.* x. 7 In the handes of vnrelenting lawes. **1647** STANLEY *Poems, Despair*, I will no more Vainly implore The unrelenting Destinies. **1697** DRYDEN *Æneis* VI. 763 These are the realms of unrelenting Fate. **1809–11** COMBE *Syntax* XV. 26 The car Of furious, unrelenting War Leaves the dire track of streaming gore. **1813** LAMB *Recoll. Christ's Hosp.* Wks. 1908 I. 186 The heavy unrelenting arm of this temporal power.
b. Not slackening or relaxing in respect of severity, harshness, or determination.
(*a*) **1609** DANIEL *Civ. Wars* IV. lxxxiii, [His] vnrelenting paines do neuer cease. **1656** COWLEY *Pindar. Odes* I. vi, Unrelenting torments prove The heavy Necessary effects of Voluntary Faults. **1743** FRANCIS tr. *Hor., Epodes* xvii. 44 You glow with unrelenting Fire, Till by the rapid Heat calcin'd, Vagrant I drive before the Wind. **1795** BURNS '*Now spring has clad*' 15 Love, wi' unrelenting beam, Has scorch'd my fountains dry. **1816** SHELLEY *Let.* in *Sothern's Catal.* No. 12 (1899) 51 Precipitous mountains, the abodes of unrelenting frost. **1844** H. H. WILSON *Brit. India* III. 377 The unrelenting pressure of the revenue system.
(*b*) **1614** JACKSON *Creed* III. xiii. §12 Vnrelenting perseuerance in traiterous plots. **1689** COTTON *Poems Sev. Occas.* 648 Bow-men of unrelenting Minds, Whose Shafts are Feathered with the Winds. **1715** ATTERB. *Serm.* (1734) I. 119 An Act..of deliberate and unrelenting Malice. **1788** GIBBON *Decl. & F.* xlii. IV. 245 The slaughter still raged with unrelenting fury. **1821** LAMB *Elia* I. *Old Benchers In. T.*, The long-resolved..puttings off of unrelenting bachelorhood. **1855** MACAULAY *Hist. Eng.* xiii. III. 316 With unwearied, unscrupulous and unrelenting ambition.
2. Not slackening or slowing down.
1817 SCOTT *Harold* v. x, With unrelenting pace, From grave to cradle [he] ran the evil race.
Hence **unre'lentingly** *adv.*, **unre'lentingness.**
1637 JACKSON *Serm. Lk. xiii.* 5, 61 It is one thing to be rebellious, another to bee *unrelentingly rebellious. **1777** POTTER *Æschylus, Furies* 409 Cloath'd in terrors we appear, Unrelentingly severe. **1812** L. HUNT in *Examiner* 4 May 275/1 [He] is..unrelentingly orthodox. **1869** TOZER *Highl. Turkey* II. 49 The Albanian soldiery..unrelentingly pursued their object. **1727** BAILEY (vol. II), *Impenitentness*, ..*unrelentingness. **1834** DE QUINCEY *Autob. Sk.* Wks. 1853 I. 359 Such in its unrelentingness was the persecution. **1861** GEO. ELIOT *Silas M.* viii, He had constantly suffered annoyance from witnessing his father's sudden fits of unrelentingness.

†unre'lentless, *a. Obs.* [UN-[1] 5 a.] Relentless.
1606 MARSTON *Parasit.* IV. G 4, Thinke how vnrelentles you were to her but supposed fault.

unre'lentor. [UN-[1] 12.] One who is relentless.
1818 KEATS *Endym.* IV. 600 He'll be shent, Pale unrelentor, When he shall hear the wedding lutes a playing.

†un'relevant, *a. Obs.*[−1] [UN-[1] 7, 5 b.] Irrelevant.
1650 in Davidson *Inverurie & Earld. Garioch* (1878) 313 The excuses always be[ing] found unrelevant.

unrelia'bility. (UN-[1] 12.)
1860 WORCESTER (citing *N.B. Rev.*). **1867** H. BUSHNELL *Moral Uses Dark Th.* (1869) 393 There must be surprises,

incalculable somersets, infinite unreliabilities, . . else [etc.]. **1883** *Harper's Mag.* Mar. 496/1 The unreliability of epitaphs . . is proverbial.

unre'liable, *a.* (UN-[1] 7 b.)
In common use from *c* 1860.
1840 DE QUINCEY in *Blackw. Mag.* XLVIII. 516 Alcibiades . . was too unsteady, and (according to Mr. Coleridge's coinage) 'unreliable'. **1859** MAURY *Phys. Geog.* xiv. 232 Wind and weather in this part . . are very unreliable and changeable. **1874** W. R. GREG *Rocks Ahead* 63 This calculation is . . not only unreliable, but purely deceptive.
Hence **unre'liableness**.
1862 F. HALL *Hindu Philos. Syst.* 86 They are involved in the suspicion of unreliableness. **1872** SPURGEON *Treas. Dav.* Ps. lxxiii. 4 The unreliableness of mere feelings shown.

unre'lievable, *a.* (UN-[1] 7 b, 5 b.)
a **1586** SIDNEY *Arcadia* I. x, My ruin being but by one unrelieveable. **1648** BOYLE *Seraph. Love* v. (1659) 39 No degree of Distress is unrelievable by his power. **1676** TEMPLE *Let.* Wks. 1720 II. 420 Finding the Swedes weak, divided, and unrelieveable by France. **1820** BENTHAM *Mem.* Wks. 1843 X. 517 Communicate not to a friend . . vexations of yours unrelievable by him. **1898** *Daily News* 29 July 2/6 No operative procedure should be suggested . . until the case had been . . found to be unrelievable by other means.
Hence **unre'lievableness**.
1654 'PALÆMON' *Friendship* 12 The unrelievablenesse of our bad condition.

unre'lieved, *ppl. a.* [UN-[1] 8.]
1. Not freed from some obligation.
1533 BELLENDEN *Livy* v. xii. (S.T.S.) II. 189 The senate . . wald nocht suffir him to be . . vnrelevit of þe vote be him made to apollo.
2. Not provided with relief; not aided or assisted.
1599 [see UNRANSOMED]. **1609** DRAYTON *Leg. T. Cromwell* 23 It better should him please, Farre out of sight to perish here vnknowne, Then vnrelieu'd bee pitied of his owne. **1656** COWLEY *Davideis* IV. 446 If unrelieved seven days by Israels aid, This bargain for ore-rated Life is made. **1694** F. BRAGGE *Disc. Parables* vii. 269 The thefts . . of such, whose unrelieved poverty forced to be thus wicked. **1719** J. ROBERTS *Spinster* 335 To leave the afflictions . . of their . . fellow-creatures neglected and unrelieved. **1757** W. WILKIE *Epigoniad* II. 49 Has . . unreliev'd the stranger left my door? **1857** RUSKIN *Pol. Econ. Art* 25 That none of their distresses should be unrelieved. **1885** C. E. PASCOE *Lond. of To-day* xxxii. 283 Many sufferers . . are altogether unrelieved for want of funds.
3. Not freed from depressing or monotonous character; not diversified or varied (*by* something).
1764 GIBBON *Misc. Wks.* (1814) IV. 397 Torments the more horrible in his . . solitary state, unrelieved by the hope of glory. **1828** *Q. Rev.* XXXVIII. 219 An unrelieved series of miseries and crimes. **1857** ROBERTSON *Serm.* Ser. III. vii. 112 Sacrifice alone, bare and unrelieved, is . . dead. **1882** FLOYER *Unexpl. Baluchistan* 248 An oval lake of rough boulders, quite flat, and unrelieved by tree or shrub.
Hence **unre'lievedly** *adv.*
1876 MEREDITH *Beauch. Career* xv, The poor are everlastingly, unrelievedly, in the abysses of the great sea. **1899** MACKAIL *Life Morris* II. 41 Modern glass, some of it unpainted, the rest . . unrelievedly hideous.

unre'ligioned, *ppl. a.* (UN-[2] 8.)
1674 PENN *Chr.-Quaker* I. xxv. 126 Thus is this Man Unravel'd, Unreligion'd, Unbottom'd as to his former State.

†**unreligi'osity**. *Obs.*[−1] [UN-[1] 12, 5 b.] Irreligiosity.
1382 WYCLIF *1 Esdras* i. 42 Of his vnclennesse and vnreligiosite [**1388** vnreligioustee; Vulg. *irreligiositas*], it is writen in the boc.

unre'ligious, *a.* [UN-[1] 7, 5 b.]
1. Irreligious.
1382 WYCLIF *1 Esdras* i. 24 Who so euere weren vnreligious ageȝn the Lord. *c* **1450** tr. *De Imitatione* I. xxiv. 34 þan shal . . euery vnreligious man sorowe. *c* **1500** *Melusine* xlii. 314 The monkes . . , whiche were of euyl, inordinate, & vnrelygious lyuyng. **1548** UDALL, etc. *Erasm. Par. John* xi. 74 Nothyng is more vnreligyouse than Jewish religion, whiche consisteth in visible thinges. **1577** FULKE *Answ. True Christian* 11 These vnreligious and vngodly opinions of God. **1606** DEKKER *Double PP* Wks. (Grosart) II. 163 Hee dare presse To th' Eaves of Bishops Pallaces: Where, harsh and vn-religious notes Hee singes against their Reuerend Coates. **1814** WORDSW. *Excurs.* IV. 607 If unreligious, let him be at once, Among ten thousand innocents, enrolled A pupil.
2. Non-religious: not connected with religion.
1855 MILMAN *Lat. Chr.* XIV. v. VI. 508 The popular poetry . . became profane, unreligious, at length in some parts irreligious. **1871** R. H. HUTTON *Ess.* I. 88 The difficulties involved in the conception of Creation being, however, totally unreligious. **1898** *Educat. Rev.* XV. 392 In the general movement . . , education has become quite unreligious.
Hence **unre'ligiously** *adv.*, **unre'ligiousness**.
c **1535** in Ellis *Orig. Lett.* Ser. III. II. 363 Whom, after myn opynyon, war better to be at large and dymyssed from ther bondage then so vnrelygiously to remayne ayenst ther conscyens. **1579** FULKE *Heskins' Parl.* 30 Although there be great rashnesse in some, and vnreligiousnesse in more. **1847** EMERSON *Poems, Blight* 38 We invade them impiously for gain; We devastate them unreligiously.

unre'linquishably, *adv.* (UN-[1] 11.)
1643 MILTON *Divorce* 28 To clogge a rational creature to his endles sorrow unrelinquishably.

unre'linquished, *ppl. a.* (UN-[1] 8.)
[**1775** ASH.] **1781** COWPER *Conversat.* 673 While at heart sin unrelinquish'd lies. **1806** FOSTER *Ess.* (1844) I. 16 Their . . unrepented and unrelinquished sins. **1881** MRS. OLIPHANT *H. Joscelyn* II. 304 That familiar unrelinquished name.

un'relishable, *a.* (UN-[1] 7 b, 5 b.)
1606 G. W[OODCOCKE] *Hist. Ivstine* Pref., A tun of Wine, which . . is made vn-rellishable by being mingled with some other compound. **1727** BAILEY (vol. II), *Disgustful*, unrelishable.

un'relished, *ppl. a.* (UN-[1] 8.)
1593 DRAYTON *Ecl.* ii. 10 My Rymes seeme harsh to thy vn-relish'd taste. **1863** MRS. WHITNEY *Faith Gartney's Girlh.* vii, Sleepless nights, . . and forgotten, or unrelished meals.

un'relishing, *ppl. a.* (UN-[1] 10.)
1611 FLORIO, *Insulso*, vnsauorie . . , vnrelishing, tastelesse. **1633** T. ADAMS *Exp. 2 Peter* i. 2 Idle, profane, and unrelishing compliments. **1676** GLANVILL *Seasonable Reflect.* 147 All things [in the other world] . . are uneasie and unrelishing at the best.

†**un'relishness**. *Obs.*[−1] [UN-[1] 12.] Lack of relish.
1615 A. NICCHOLES *Marr. & Wiving* vii. (1620) 19 The vnrealishnesse of that which is lawful, desire of that which is restrained.

unre'luctant, *a.* (UN-[1] 7, 5 b.)
1737 GLOVER *Leonidas* I. 233 Death, receive My unreluctant hand, and lead me on. **1774** *Trinket* 188 The consent is . . granted with an unreluctant frankness. **1820** SHELLEY *Ode Lib.* xi, The eager hours and unreluctant years. **1854** MILMAN *Lat. Chr.* III. iii. I. 316 An orthodox Empire would not repose in unreluctant submission under an Arian.

unre'luctantly, *adv.* (UN-[1] 11.)
1655 EARL ORRERY *Parthen.* II. III. 271 The Armenians have vnreluctantly submitted to that Government. **1768–74** TUCKER *Lt. Nat.* (1834) II. 289 It will sometimes carry them through self-denials unreluctantly upon proper occasions. **1799** HAN. MORE *Fem. Educ.* (ed. 4) I. p. xiv, Unreluctantly yielding themselves to be carried down the tide of popular practices. **1849** C. BRONTË *Shirley* xxix, She resigns herself to me unreluctantly. **1874** H. ROGERS *Orig. Bible* ii. 60 They unreluctantly received such as spontaneously sought their communion.

unre'maining, *ppl. a.* (UN-[1] 10.)
1817 SHELLEY *Rev. Islam* I. i, Like a brief dream of unremaining glory. **1818** —— *Rosal. & Helen* 997 My dream of unremaining gladness. **1936** A. E. HOUSMAN *More Poems* 63 Here the child comes to found His unremaining mound.

unre'markable, *a.* [UN-[1] 7 b, 5 b.]
1. Unworthy of remark or note.
1611 COTGR., *Irremarquable*, vnremarkable, . . no way to be noted. **1632** G. SANDYS *Ovid's Met.* XI. Notes 397 Nor is this vnremarkable, . . that the Kings-fisher being dead and hung vp by the Neb, turnes alwaies her belly to the wind. **1643** SIR T. BROWNE *Relig. Med.* 55 It is not unremarkable what Philo first observed, That [etc.].
†**b.** Incapable of being observed. *Obs.*[−1]
1644 DIGBY *Nat. Bodies* v. §2. 34 Our vnderstanding to make a compleate notion, must adde something else to this fleeting and vnremarkable superficies that may bring it vnto our acquaintance.
2. Not notable or striking.
1850 KINGSLEY *A. Locke* xxvii, As we may see by the histories of every remarkable, and many an unremarkable, man. **1853** G. J. CAYLEY *Las Alforjas* I. 155 We . . saw Arahal, an unremarkable white town, on a slight eminence. **1879** *St. George's Hosp. Rep.* IX. 520 An unremarkable sprinkling of other workers.

unre'marked, *ppl. a.* (UN-[1] 8, 8 c.)
[**1775** ASH.] **1793** *Minstrel* III. 159 The extreme attention of Edward to her daughter, was not unremarked by Jaqueline. **1830** HERSCHEL *Study Nat. Phil.* 348 It cannot be supposed, that all the indications of nature continually passed unremarked. **1871** FRASER *Life of Berkeley* x. 382 Some hitherto unremarked phases of the Berkleian conception.
(*b*) **1856** CRAIK *English of Shaks.* Pref., Not leaving any passage unremarked upon which seemed . . obscure.

†**unre'mediable**, *a.* *Obs.* Also 5 *Sc.* **vnremedable**, 6 **onremedabil**. [UN-[1] 7 b, 5 b.] Irremediable.
1382 WYCLIF *Tobit* x. 4 Thanne wepte his modir with vn-remediable teris. *c* **1480** HENRYSON *Want of Wyse Men* 63 (Bann. MS.), Sic sturtfull stering in to godis neis it stinkis; Bot he haif rew, all is vnremedable. **1549** *Compl. Scot.* 1 Ther cruel inuasions aperis to be onremedabil. *a* **1586** SIDNEY *Arcadia* II. x. (1912) 213 An unremediable mischiefe already committed. **1645** BP. HALL *Remedy Discontents* 125 The miseries of an unremediable disappointment. **1695** S. LOBB *Let. Dr. Bates* 21 An antecedent desert of hell, and a sinfulness so deserving (tho' not by an unremediable guilt).

un'remedied, *ppl. a.* (UN-[1] 8.)
Also in 16th c. *unre'medied*, Sc. *unre'medit*.
1563 *Reg. Privy Council Scot.* I. 250 Salang as this inobedience is unremedit. **1595** SPENSER *Clorinda* 8 The authors . . And workers of my vnremedied wo. **1644** MILTON *Divorce* (ed. 2) A 3 b, The unremedied lonelinesse of this remedy. **1768** BLACKSTONE *Comm.* III. 385 Should [these defects] . . continue unremedied and unsupplied. **1791** COWPER *Odyss.* II. 272 Waste will continue and disorder foul Unremedied. **1864** PUSEY *Lect. Daniel* 523 *note*, God is often said to 'awake' for His people, when He notices that which He had before left unremedied.

unre'member, *v.* [UN-[1] 14.] *trans.* To fail (or omit) to remember.
1484 in *Lett. Rich. III & Hen. VII* (Rolls) I. 78 Whiche [fidelity] we shalle not unremembre. **1616** W. HAIG in J. Russell *Haigs* vii. (1881) 159 Unremembering so kendspeckle a thing wherein they were put. **1983** *Spectator* 16 Apr. 22/2 We cannot unremember Auschwitz.

unre'memberable, *a.* (UN-[1] 7 b, 5 b.)
1803 *Ann. Rev.* I. 68 The topography of a country wherein every place has an unrememberable name. **1858** CARLYLE *Fredk. Gt.* II. iii. I. 89 The smallest flint-spark, in a world all black and unrememberable, will be welcome. **1887** SAINTSBURY *Hist. Elizab. Lit.* viii. 292 Vast heaps of things altogether unrememberable.

unre'membered, *ppl. a.* [UN-[1] 8.]
1. Not borne in mind; allowed to drop out of mind; forgot.
With early examples cf. UNREMEMBER *v.*
c **1400** *Found. St. Bartholomew's* xii. 17 Innumerable were schewid tokynnys of myracles, but . . they be almoyste vnremembred. **1422** YONG tr. *Secreta Secret.* 203 For als moche as good newe ensamples sholde not ben vnremembrid for lerynge of tho that arne to come. **1584** HUTTON *Let.* in Campbell *Chancellors* (1856) II. 273 Towards yourself leave not the causes of my presumptions unremembered. **1607** HIERON *Wks.* I. 260 This feare causeth them . . to be vnwilling to let any of it [*sc.* comfort of the Scriptures] fall to the ground vnremembred. **1641** MILTON *Reform.* II. 69 Nor must their sincere . . proceeding hitherto, be unremember'd. **1734** A. HILL *On Death Dennis* 9 The furious petulence, the jealous start, . . Veil'd in thy grave shall unremember'd lie. **1798** WORDSW. *Tintern Abbey* 31 Feelings too Of unremembered pleasure. **1816** SOUTHEY *Lay of Laureate* lxxvi, Where in elder time Earth's unremember'd conquerors held the sway. **1853** G. JOHNSTON *Nat. Hist. E. Borders* I. 29 A skirmish of unremembered date.
†**b.** (Left) unrecorded or unmentioned. *Obs.*
c **1477** CAXTON *Jason* 52 Hit is not to be vnremembrid that thenuie of . . Peleus grewe so terribly that he . . coude haue no reste. *a* **1513** FABYAN *Chron.* I. i, Whiche if any suche wonder had ben there wroughte, shuld nat haue ben vn-remembred [by] the wryters. **1570** FOXE *A. & M.* (ed. 2) 19/2 Which doubtles shoulde not haue bene vnremembred, if he had bene then in Rome. **1603** G. OWEN *Pembrokeshire* (1892) 219 For the better memorye of these . . members, not to suffer them vnremembered in this my Discripcion of their Country. *c* **1650** P. SMITH *Life Willet* in Fuller *Abel Red.* (1651) 565, I thought good . . to adde some remarkable things then unremembred or undiscovered.
†**2.** Of persons: Unmindful, forgetful. *Obs.*
1467 *Paston Lett.* II. 306 He thynkyth indoubted that William Worcetre shuld not be unremembred of this. *a* **1528** BP. R. FOX in Ellis *Orig. Lett.* Ser. II. II. 6, I am not un-remembred of my deutye towardes the Kyng. **1536** E. LEE *Ibid.* Ser. III. II. 326, I trust your Highnes is not unremembred, that [etc.].

unre'membering, *ppl. a.* (UN-[1] 10.)
1540 *Sc. Acts Parlt., Jas. V* (1814) II. 363/2 That he will nocht be vnremembrand and vngrate for þe gude . . seruice done to him. **1697** DRYDEN *Æneis* VI. 1020 That, unremembr'ing of its former Pain, The Soul may suffer mortal Flesh again. **1882** J. HAWTHORNE *Fort. Fool* I. xvii, It would become human like ourselves, and lose its thoughtless and unremembering happiness.

unre'membrance. (UN-[1] 12.)
c **1449** PECOCK *Repr.* IV. ix. 474 The vnknowing and the vnremembraunce of these thre . . notabilitees. **1725** WATTS *Logic* I. iv. §2 There are some Words which are negative in their original Language, but seem positive to an Englishman, . . as . . *Amnesty*, an Unremembrance or general Pardon.

unre'minded, *ppl. a.* (UN-[1] 8.)
[**1775** ASH.] **1881** M. C. HAY *Missing* II. 214, I never could allow him to be unreminded that [etc.].

†**unre'missible**, *a.* *Obs.* (UN-[1] 7, 5 b.)
1593 NASHE *Christ's T.* 30 There is the Tabernacle of the Lord, . . there if we shold drawe our blades, it were abhomination vnremissible. **1603** FLORIO *Montaigne* III. v. 511 It is a capitall crime, and vn-remissible offence.

unre'mitted, *ppl. a.* [UN-[1] 8.]
1. Not pardoned or cancelled.
1646 HAMMOND *Tracts* 27 Sin unretracted . . doth certainly stand upon the sinners score unremitted.
2. Not allowed to slacken or fall off; maintained at the same pitch or force; continuous.
Very common from *c* 1760.
1722–7 BOYER *Dict. Royal* II, Unremitted, (incessant), *continuel*. **1744** AKENSIDE *Pleas. Imag.* I. 430 Against the . . stubborn hill To urge bold Virtue's unremitted nerve. **1781** C. JOHNSTON *Hist. J. Juniper* I. 13 Her endeavours . . had been unremitted. **1820** SCOTT *Monast.* xi, Assiduity and unremitted attention. **1842** H. ROGERS *Introd. Burke's Wks.* I. 26 The fatigues of such years of unremitted toil.
3. Of persons: Unremitting.
1796 MORSE *Amer. Geog.* I. 329 Several men of abilities . . were unremitted in their endeavours. **1833** SIR W. HAMILTON *Discuss.* (1853) 588 The pastor . . ought to be . . unremitted in his superintendence of the masters.
Hence **unre'mittedly** *adv.*
1786 tr. *Beckford's Vathek* 22 His wives . . unremittedly supplied him with water. **1792** in J. Morse *Amer. Geog.* (1796) I. 510 Through which aperture the water unremittedly drops. **1889** *Engineer* 10 May 408 An advantage which Swansea has been striving for unremittedly, and will gain this autumn.

unre'mittent, *a.* (UN-[1] 7.)
1871 PALGRAVE *Lyr. Poems* 28 The lark scattering in the crystal morn His unremittent gush of silver rain. **1895** *Athenæum* 16 Feb. 224/2 An atmosphere of unremittent work.

unre'mittently, *adv.* (UN-[1] 11.)
1895 *Athenæum* 26 Oct. 576/3 Mr. Manns has laboured . . unremittently in the interests of native art.

unre'mitting, *ppl. a.* [UN-[1] 10.] Never relaxing or slackening; continuing with the same force; incessant: **a.** Of activity, etc.

1728 THOMSON *Spring* 700 Inspiring God! who boundless Spirit all, And unremitting Energy,.. agitates the Whole. **1768** BOSWELL *Corsica* ii. (ed. 2) 79 With unremitting constancy [he] endeavoured to restore the liberties of his country. **1819** BUSBY *Hist. Music* II. 256 We find in the music a continued and unremitting echo to the sense of the language. **1833** T. HOOK *Parson's Dau.* I. i, [They] lived in the most unremitting hostility towards each other. **1871** MACDUFF *Mem. Patmos* v. 56 Engaged in unremitting toil.

b. Of persons. Also quasi-*adv.*

1736 THOMSON *Liberty* IV. 711 Fleet on fleet Of barbarous pirates unremitting tore The miserable coast. **1796** MME. D'ARBLAY *Camilla* IV. 238 [She] was.. unremitting in boasting how well she had.. kept them in order. **1817** J. SCOTT *Paris Revisit.* (ed. 4) 359 He.. was unremitting in his exertions. **1876** BANCROFT *Hist. U.S.* I. xiii. 420 He was unremitting in argument and entreaty to prevent the taking of their lives.

Hence **unre'mittingness.**

1812 SHELLEY *Proposals* Pr. Wks. 1888 I. 283 Considering the unremittingness of its pressure. **1865** M. ARNOLD *Ess. in Crit.* vi. (1875) 243 The very intensity and unremittingness of its appeal.

unre'mittingly, *adv.* [UN-[1] 11.] Without remission; incessantly, continually.

1796 MME. D'ARBLAY *Camilla* IV. 184, I watched her unremittingly. **1824** DIBDIN *Libr. Comp.* 608 Having secretly and unremittingly formed his style. **1878** A. H. MARKHAM *Gt. Frozen Sea* i. 6 Officers and men were unremittingly engaged in the various duties.

unre'monstrant, *a.* (UN-[1] 7.)

1865 MEREDITH *R. Fleming* xxxix, As mute and unremonstrant as a fallen tree.

unre'monstrated, *ppl. a.* (UN-[1] 8 c.)

1818 BENTHAM *Ch. Eng. Catech. Exam.* 151 Such connivance should be left unremonstrated against. **1860** DICKENS *Lett.* (1880) III. 193 You are.. far too able a man to be left unremonstrated with by an admiring reader.

unre'morseful, *a.* (UN-[1] 7.)

c **1611** CHAPMAN *Iliad* IX. 597 O unremorseful man!.. thee a.. cruel spirit the Gods for plague have given. **1616** R. NICCOLS *Sir T. Overbury's Vis.* B I b, Vnremorsefull fate Did worke the falls of those two Princes dead. *Ibid.* C 2, Monsters.. vnremorsefull of my forepast woes. **1855** LYNCH *Rivulet* LXXVIII. v, By unremorseful joys, O, woo Our hearts to holy efforts still. **1876** STEDMAN *Victorian Poets* 316 Sebald and Ottima have murdered the latter's aged husband, and are unremorseful in their guilty love.

unre'morsefully, *adv.* (UN-[1] 11.)

1846 HAWTHORNE *Old Manse* II. 31 Thus making his own actual serpent.. the type of each man's.. unquiet conscience, and striking his sting so unremorsefully into the sorest spot.

†**unre'morseless,** *a.* *Obs.*[−1] [UN-[1] 5 a.] Remorseless.

1634 COWLEY *Elegy R. Clerke* 10 His mellifluous breath Could not at all charme unremorselesse Death.

unre'mote, *a.* (UN-[1] 7.)

1837 WHITTOCK *Bk. Trades* (1842) 239 (*Fruiterer*) The 'unremote' period when many of our most familiar garden products were introduced.

unre'movable, *a.* [UN-[1] 7 b, 5 b.]

†**1.** Incapable of being moved; immovable; steady, firm, constant. *Obs.*

a **1500** in *Ratis Raving*, etc. 11 The erde remanis euermare vnremouable. **1579** FULKE *Heskins' Parl.* 476 It still remaineth vnremouable, that a signe and the thing signified, be distinct things. *c* **1595** CAPT. WYATT *Dudley's Voy.* (Hakl. Soc.) 25 Caryinge soe great a majestie in his march with such unremovable resolucions in his proceedings. *a* **1642** BEDELL *Erasmus* in Fuller *Abel Rediv.* (1867) I. 91 He was of an unremoveable constancy. **1670** WALTON *Lives, Wotten* 72, I.. contracted with him an unremovable affection.

2. = IRREMOVABLE *a.* 1. Now *rare.*

a **1586** SIDNEY *Arcadia* I. v, He manifested himself an unremoveable suiter to her daughter. **1614** BP. HALL *Contempl., O.T.* VIII. v, Their neernesse of abode was an unremoveable barre of peace. *a* **1680** CORBET *Non-conf. Plea* (1683) 25 Unnecessary terms, that are unlawful to them by unremovable doubts of conscience. *a* **1740** WATERLAND *Sec. Def.* Wks. 1823 III. 70 This.. left the charge fixed and unremoveable upon the Pagans. **1752** CARTE *Hist. Eng.* III. 27 The lord Areskine, his constant and unremoveable guardian. **1802** *Sk. Paris* II. xlvii. 123 The pretended unremoveable rights.

Hence **unre'movableness.**

1611 COTGR., *Constance*,.. vnremoueablenesse. **1634** BP. HALL *Contempl., Resurrection* 276 They bragd of the surenesse of the place, and unremoveablenesse of that load.

unre'movably, *adv.* [UN-[1] 11, 5 b: cf. prec.] Irremovably.

1604 SIR T. CONINGSBY in *14th Rep. Hist. MSS. Comm.* App. II. 2 Yours unremovabelly, yf you remoufe him not. **1617** HIERON *Wks.* 1620 II. 236 That wee may bee so settled in a right way.., as that we may.. goe on sincerely, and vnremouably to the end. **1646** HAMMOND *Tracts* 102 So heavy an arreare of sinne lying unremovably upon every ones score.

unre'moved, *ppl. a.* [UN-[1] 8, 5 b.]

1. Not removed or done away with.

1455 *Rolls of Parlt.* V. 330/1 Whiche doubte.. unremoved, is not unlike to set.. division. **1674** R. GODFREY *Inj. & Ab. Physic* 4 So long as the spurious Ferment in both Stomach and Blood is unremoved. **1680** C. NESSE *Church Hist.* 363 This rubb and remora is still unremoved. **1812** CRABBE *Tales* III. 290 Gwyn something felt.. was wrong; He wish'd to know, for he believed the thing, If unremoved, would other evil bring. **1860** WESTCOTT *Introd. Study Gosp.* iii. 153 Their external disinclination for literature was unremoved.. by their special work. **1901** *N. Amer. Rev.* Feb. 236 The unremoved deteriorating influences.

b. Not removed or shifted in place.

a **1450** in *MS. Rawl. D.* 251 fol. 86, Let it ly iij dayes onremevyd. *c* **1490** *Paston Lett.* III. 338 Ye must send me wryghtyng.. hough longe.. [the plaster] shold abyd on hys kne unremevyd. **1563** HYLL *Art Garden.* (1574) 117 If they [*sc.* rape] growe to thicke, then remoue.. them,.. whereby the other vnremoued may growe the bigger in the roote. **1613** W. BROWNE *Brit. Past.* I. iv. 529 As yonder mill.. Yet by the head-strong torrent from his beame Is unremov'd. **1632** LITHGOW *Trav.* I. 31 [They] placed it in a high broad way, where it standeth vnremooued to this day. **1707** MORTIMER *Husb.* 472 Being sown very thin.. where they may stand unremoved in the Ground for two Years. **1784** *Phil. Trans.* LXXIV. 428 They continued unremoved in their several places. **1837** CARLYLE *Fr. Rev.* II. VI. viii, A hundred and eighty bodies of Swiss lie piled there; naked, unremoved till the second day. **1889** *21st Rep. Dep. Keeper Irel.* 16 Other testamentary Records, unremoved to this Department.

c. Fixed in place; firmly stationed.

1551 RECORDE *Pathw. Knowl.* I. xlii, Then sette I one foote of the compas vnremoued in B. **1591** HARINGTON *Orl. Fur.* IX. lxix, So great a sound, As seemed.. to remove the unremoved ground. **1667** MILTON *P.L.* IV. 987 Satan.. dilated stood, Like Teneriff or Atlas unremov'd. **1820** SHELLEY *Prometh. Unb.* IV. 380 Making shiver Thought's stagnant chaos, unremoved for ever. **1873** SYMONDS *Grk. Poets* x. 325 The mountain stands for ever unremoved.

†**2.** Firm, steadfast, constant. *Obs.*

1589 *Rare Tri. Love & Fort.* II. M 4, The unremoved love I beare my lady. **1606** G. WOODCOCK *Hist. Ivstine* xv. 64 With an vnremooued courage, neither arrogant in happinesse, nor altred in distresse. **1627** DRAYTON *Elegies, To Lady I. S.* 85 Your noble heart.. With vnremoued constancie is still The same it was. **1655** EARL ORRERY *Parthen.* II. VIII. 816 An unremoved resolve of sharing in his despair.

unre'munerated, *ppl. a.* (UN-[1] 8.)

(Freq. in 19th cent. use.)

[**1775** ASH.] **1895** J. WILLIAMS *Briefless Ballads* 51 We mourn in unremunerated pain Those brave old days. **1945** A. L. ROWSE *West-Country Stories* 3 His services were unremunerated.

unre'munerating, *ppl. a.* (UN-[1] 10.)

1855 [J. R. LEIFCHILD] *Cornwall* 247 If a mine.. just meets its working expenses at a low and unremunerating standard.

unre'munerative, *a.* (UN-[1] 7.)

Hence, in recent use, ***unremuneratively, -ness.***

1854 *Poultry Chron.* I. 26/2 Evidence that the raising of poultry was by no means the unremunerative folly idlers supposed it to be. **1869** TOZER *Highl. Turkey* II. 120 A girl is considered an expense and unremunerative.

†**unre'navigable,** *a.* *Obs.* (UN-[1] 7 b.)

1661 J. BOYS *Æneas* VI. 17 How gladly would they.. see blest light again? Fates thwart: an unrenavigable sound.. doth them surround.

†**un'rende(d,** obs. varr. UNRENT *ppl. a.*

c **1440** *Pallad. on Husb.* IV. 9 The trunkes sadde, in humor that abounde, Vnolde, vnrende. **1646** J. GREGORY *Notes & Obs.* 117 The suspension of these waters.. I no more marvaile at then that the thicke Clouds.. should hang in the Aire unrended under them.

un'renderable, *a.* (UN-[1] 7 b, 5 b.)

1860 RUSKIN *Mod. Paint.* V. VI. x. §8 The best beauty of flowers being wholly inimitable, and their sweetest service unrenderable by art. **1889** *Athenæum* 10 Aug. 187/3 A rendering of Sappho's unrenderable 'Ode to Aphrodite'.

un'rendered, *ppl. a.* (UN-[1] 8.)

[**1775** ASH.] **1851** MAYHEW *Lond. Labour* I. 199 Cakes, made of flour and 'unrendered' (unmelted) lard. **1865** GROSART *Palmer's Mem.* Introd. 15 The suggestive and invaluable treatise of M. Rémusat still lies unrendered.

unre'newable, *a.* (UN-[1] 7 b, 5 b.)

1548 GESTE *Pr. Masse* B ij, Christes body (whose creatyon is vnrenuable). **1977** *Church Times* 25 Feb. 7/2 Its chronic prodigality in the use of unrenewable fossil fuels.

unre'newed, *ppl. a.* (UN-[1] 8.)

1579 W. WILKINSON *Confut. Fam. Love* B iij b, They are.. vnrenewed, vngodded, vnsent. **1678** R. BARCLAY *Apol. Quakers* (1703) 363 Acting in their own natural and unrenewed Wills. **1683** J. CORBET *Free Actions* II. xvi. 24 Whatsoever an un-renewed person doth, hath necessarily.. a disconformity to Gods Law. **1764** J. WITHERSPOON *Pract. Treat. Regeneration* ii. §2 All unrenewed persons.. place their supreme happiness in something that is not God. **1828–32** WEBSTER s.v., The lease is unrenewed. **1865** GLADSTONE *Farewell Addr. Edinb. Univ.* 61 The spirit of the unrenewed world. *a* **1866** D. DUNCAN *Disc.* (1867) vii. 144 Prayer is not an exercise congenial to the unrenewed soul.

unre'nounceable, *a.* (UN-[1] 7 b.)

1851 [see next].

unre'nounced, *ppl. a.* (UN-[1] 8.)

[**1775** ASH.] **1851** MRS. BROWNING *Casa Guidi Wind.* II. 117 The people rose up in the dust.., and shouted.. 'Live the People,' who remained and must, The unrenounced and unrenounceable.

un'renovated, *ppl. a.* (UN-[1] 8.)

[**1775** ASH.] **1856** RUSKIN *Mod. Paint.* IV. v. xiv. §25 Age after age may only prolong the unrenovated ruin.

unre'nowned, *ppl. a.* Also 6 -nowmed. (UN-[1] 8. Cf. IRRENOWNED.)

1570 LEVINS *Manip.* 50 Vnrenowned, *incelebris.* **1594** MARLOWE & NASHE *Dido* IV. iii, The dreames.. that did beset my bed,.. Commaunds me leaue these vnrenowmed reames. **1827** POLLOK *Course T.* IX. 479 Nor unrenowned among the most renowned.. stood the bard. *a* **1851** MOIR *Sonn.* i, Nor unrenowned, as, with an ampler tide, Thou windest through the glens of Woodhouselee.

un'rent, *a.* (UN-[1] 7.)

1596 SPENSER *F.Q.* VI. vi. 40 Were not, that the Prince did him appeaze, He had not left one limbe of him vnrent. **1727** POPE, etc. *Art of Sinking* 102 Distended with the waters in 'em pent, The clouds hang deep in air, but hang unrent. **1796** BURKE *Let. Noble Lord* Wks. VIII. 21 These obscene harpies.. leave nothing unrent, unrifled. **1816** BYRON *Siege of Cor.* xxxiii, The hills that shake, although unrent. **1858** CARLYLE *Fredk. Gt.* V. v. I. 577 Daily had some loop fallen,.. but daily was he there to pick it up again, and keep the web unrent. **1879** R. T. SMITH *Basil Gt.* ix. 113 The garment without seam.. preserved unrent even by the soldiers.

un'rentable, *a.* UN-[1] 7 b.)

1826 GALT *Last of Lairds* v. 40 An untenanted and unrentable portion of the Laird's domain.

unre'paid, *ppl. a.* (UN-[1] 8.)

1655 EARL ORRERY *Parthen.* I. VIII. 456 To leave so liberall a guift vnrepay'd. **1697** CREECH in *Dryden's Juvenal* XIII. xvii. 334 Thy Loss continues, unrepaid by Pain. **1738** WESLEY *Hymn, To Thee, O Father of Mankind* iii, Nor shall their Love be unrepaid. **1750** JOHNSON *Rambler* No. 54 ¶10 We recollect.. a thousand favours unrepaid. **1826** SCOTT *Woodst.* xxviii, That my affection was not unrepaid. **1890** 'R. BOLDREWOOD' *Col. Reformer* (1891) 316 The very substantial aid in cash.. still unrepaid.

unre'pair. [UN-[1] 12, 5 b.] Lack of repair; disrepair, irrepair.

1843 THACKERAY *Irish Sk.-Bk.* II. xii. 225 A dismal state of unrepair. **1873** in *Daily News* 5 Mar. 2/4 He might send them to sea in a condition of unrepair, both as to equipment and hull. **1886** *American* XIII. 57 Everywhere the combined efforts of ill-construction and unrepair are visible.

unre'pairable, *a.* (UN-[1] 7 b, 5 b.)

1611 COTGR., *Irrecuperable*, vnrecouerable, vnrepairable. **1617** MORYSON *Itin.* II. 192 The losse of them would be for many yeeres vnrepairable. **1680** RUSHW. *Hist. Coll.* II. 301 These great Abuses are.. increased to the publick Nuissance, and likely to.. become unrepairable.

unre'paired, *ppl. a.*[1] [UN-[1] 8.] Not repaired.

1523 LD. BERNERS *Froiss.* I. ccccxxxiv. (1812) 762 Whan the frenche kynge went oute of that countrey it was vnrepayred,.. for all was brent and beaten downe. *c* **1550** W. CLOPTON in Halliwell *Shaks.* (1887) II. 171 Bentlye hath lefte the said manour place in great ruyne, and unrepayryd. **1617** CAMPION *3rd Bk. Ayres* ix. 11 Great sorrows vnrepayred Admit no meane in mourning. *a* **1637** B. JONSON *Underwoods, Execration Vulcan* 196 Paul's steeple.., though a divine Loss, remains yet as unrepair'd as mine. **1693** TATE *Dryden's Juvenal* xv. 5 Where, Thebes, thy Hundred Gates lie unrepair'd. **1721** [see UNREDRESSED]. **1805** SOUTHEY *Madoc* I. xii. 32 As the floods of spring had broken down Their barrier, so its breaches unrepair'd Were left. **1837** CARLYLE *Fr. Rev.* II. v. v, Robbers scour the Highways, which wear down unrepaired.

unre'paired, *ppl. a.*[2] [UN-[1] 8 c.] Not resorted *to.*

1615 T. ADAMS *Lycanthropy* 33 The Temples unrepaired and unrepaired to—neyther adorned nor frequented.

†**un'reparable,** *a.* *Obs.* (UN-[1] 7 b, 5 b.)

1611 SPEED *Hist. Gt. Brit.* IX. viii. §55. 503/1 His French affaires had sustained vnreparable impeachments. **1645** MILTON *Tetrach.* 90 We grant divorce.. not for lesse then many tedious and unreparable yeares of desertion.

unre'partable, *a.* (UN-[1] 7 b.)

1592 R. D. *Hypnerotomachia* 8 b, Compassed with fowlded haires of vnrepartable curiousnes.

unre'passable, *a.* (UN-[1] 7 b, 5 b.)

1600 J. PORY tr. *Leo's Africa* Introd. 35 A report, that the streights of Magellan were unrepassable. **1611** COTGR., *Irrepassable*, vnrepassable, ouer which no returne can be made. **1734** WATTS *Reliq. Juv.* 110 Narrow Limits indeed! and when once pass'd, they are unrepassable. **1794** H. BOYD *Ind. Observer* No. 49 ¶3 The eternal shore of the unrepassable river.

unre'payable, *a.* (UN-[1] 7 b.)

1881 SHAIRP *Aspects of Poetry* 312 A debt still unrepaid, perhaps now unrepayable.

unre'paying, *ppl. a.* (UN-[1] 10.)

1866 *Chamb. Jrnl.* Dec. 785 Another almost as unrepaying a branch of literary labour. **1868** R. L. POOLE in *Contemp. Rev.* Jan. 112 As we study the dry and unrepaying pages of the Ritual.

unre'pealable, *a.* (UN-[1] 7 b, 5 b.)

1601 DENT *Pathw. Heaven* 376 His decree is vnrepealeable. **1656** JEANES *Fuln. Christ* 180 An irreversible, and unrepealable promise of an omnipotent God. *a* **1711** KEN *Hymns Evang.* Poet. Wks. 1721 I. 151 Unrepealable and dreadful Doom. **1730** WATERLAND *Suppl. to Nat. Chr. Sacr.* iii. 21 That Love of God,.. which is unrepealable, abiding for ever. **1784** COWPER *Task* v. 610 Unrepealable enduring death. **1803** JANE PORTER *Thaddeus* xv, These words fell like an unrepealable sentence on the heart of Thaddeus. **1860** LOWELL *Election in Nov.* Prose Wks. 1890 V. 38 Truth is the unrepealable thing.

Hence **unrepeala'bility, -ableness.**

1651 W. DURHAM *Maran-atha* (1652) 24 The unrepealablenesse of this judgment, it can never be revers'd. **1820–30** COLERIDGE in *Lit. Rem.* (1838) III. 25 The unrepealability of their decisions.

unre'pealed, *ppl. a.* (UN-[1] 8.)

1479 in *Eng. Gilds* (1870) 417, I shall.. meyntene all laudable ordinauncez.. vnreuokid and vnrepelid. **1603** HOLLAND *Plutarch's Mor.* 1126 Say a man did abolish lawes, and yet withall leave behind unrepealed and uncondemned the doctrines and books of Parmenides. **1649** MILTON

Tenure Kings 13 Which Edict of his remaines yet unrepeald in the Code of Justinian. **1712** BLACKMORE *Creation* I. 626 Could they [*sc.* moist elements] dispense to lie below the land, With nature's law, and unrepeal'd command. **1771** *Junius Lett.* xlviii. (1788) 264 The resolutions..stand upon your Journals, uncontroverted and unrepealed. **1819** G. S. FABER *Dispensations* (1823) I. 180 That the original sentence continued wholly unaltered and unrepealed. **1891** FARRAR *Darkn. & Dawn* xlii, An unrepealed decree of the senate.

unre'peatable, *a.* [UN-[1] 7 b, 5 b.]
1. Too coarse to be re-uttered.
1843 MOZLEY *Ess.* (1878) I. 84 The most disgusting and unrepeatable indecencies went on. **1859** W. H. GREGORY *Egypt* II. 47 Droll but somewhat unrepeatable anecdotes. **1887** *Punch* 19 Mar. 136/2 An account of his most infamous exploits in unrepeatable language.
2. Incapable of being done or made again.
1880 LITTLEDALE *Plain Reas.* lxxv. 157 The..unrepeatable privilege and glory of being the first to unlock the doors of the kingdom. **1901** G. H. HOWISON *Limits of Evol.* 362 The absolutely singular and unrepeatable personality of each soul.

unre'peated, *ppl. a.* [UN-[1] 8.]
1. Not re-uttered or recounted.
a **1586** SIDNEY *Arcadia* II. xxix, To leave that unrepeated, which I finde my daughters have told you. **1649** MILTON *Eikon.* Pref. B ij, The further mention of his deeds..perhaps for the present age might have slept with him unrepeated. *a* **1839** PRAED *Poems* (1864) I. 236 Believe not that those uttered words In the far winds have fleeted..Uncherished, unrepeated.
2. Not renewed.
1786 *Francis the Philanthropist* II. 3 'If you are serious in your bets..I'll hold ye both, gentlemen.'..The bets were unrepeated. **1811** SCOTT *Don Roderick* II. xix, First shrill'd an unrepeated female shriek!

unre'pellable, *a.* (UN-[1] 7 b.)
1665 J. GADBURY *London's Deliv. Predicted* i. 3 Which.., by an (almost) uncontrolable and unrepellable siccity, dries up and destroys the Natural Powers.

unre'pelled, *ppl. a.* (UN-[1] 8.)
[**1775** ASH.] **1795** COLERIDGE *Plot Discov.* 27 Dreadful encroachments yet unrepelled. **1818** SHELLEY *Rosal. & Helen* 205 They sate With linked hands, for unrepelled Had Helen taken Rosalind's. **1850** BROWNING *Christmas Eve* xxi, I caught At the flying Robe, and unrepelled Was lapped again in its folds.

unre'pent, *v.* (UN-[2] 7.)
1833 CARLYLE *Ct. Cagliostro* Misc. Ess. 1872 V. 123 He..wanders necessitous hither and thither; repents, unrepents; knows not what to do.

unre'pentable, *a.* (UN-[1] 7 b, 5 b.)
1827 POLLOK *Course T.* x. 421 Unrepented deeds, Now unrepentable for evermore.

unre'pentance. (UN-[1] 12, 5 b.)
c **1410** *Wycliffite Bible* 1 John v. 7 *marg.*, Fynal unrepentaunce, bi which a man dieth in deedly synne. **1563** *Form Common Prayer* B iv, Thy pacyence beynge..ouercome at the laste, wyth oure obstynate vnrepentaunce. **1579** W. FULKE *Heskins' Parl.* 482 With vnreuerence and vnrepentance, they presume against..so high a mysterie. **1623** BP. HALL *Contempl.*, *O.T.* XIX. x, Hee might have averted it by his prayers: their unrepentance disabled him. **1661** COWLEY *Cromwell* Ess., etc. (1906) 372 Though the outward unrepentance of his death afford but small materials for the work of Charity. **1690** H. WHARTON *Serm.* (1700) 383 Man continuing in a state of unrepentance. **1860** BP. S. WILBERFORCE *Addr. Cand. Ordination* 45 To all..who do not, by actual unrepentance and unbelief, bar His gracious working. **1882** BESANT *All Sorts* II. 275 My brother is hardened in his unrepentance.

unre'pentant, *a.* (UN-[1] 7, 5 b.)
c **1380** WYCLIF *Sel. Wks.* III. 108 þurghe his wyckede and unrepentant herte. **1395** PURVEY *Remonstr.* (1851) 119 The curat shulde remove hem fro Goddis boord, if he parceyuith hem vnrepentaunt. *c* **1440** *Jacob's Well* 9 In þis cursyng, who-so deye vnrepentaunt, schal haue a dredeful ende! **1548** CRANMER *Catech.* 222 b, Unrepentaunte synners and vnbelevers. **1588** *Marprel. Epist.* (Arb.) 45 The soule of the vnrepentant papist. **1631** *High Commission Cases* (Camden) 213 The body of the unrepentant sinner. **1671** MILTON *P.R.* III. 429 Should I of these the liberty regard, Who,..unrepentant, unreform'd, Headlong would follow. **1813** SCOTT *Rokeby* III. xiv, Among the feasters waited near Sorrow, and unrepentant Fear. **1856** FROUDE *Hist. Eng.* I. 358 The two offenders were hopelessly unrepentant. **1869** MOZLEY *Univ. Serm.* ii. (1877) 34 False goodness is..an unrepentant type of evil.
absol. **1581** A. GOLDING *Test. 12 Patriarchs* 59 The Lorde, who either taketh away his benefites from the wicked,..or els reserueth them in the vnrepentant, to their endlesse punishment. **1617** J. BARBIER *Janua Ling.* 4 The sinnes of the vnrepentant.
Hence **unre'pentantly** *adv.*, **-ness**.
c **1440** *Promp. Parv.* 366/2 *On-repentawntly, *inpenitenter*. **1647** TRAPP *Comm. Matt.* xxvi. 75 Stephen Gardiner..both stinkingly and unrepentantly died. **1869** *Lyndesay's Wks.* 440 *marg.*, Princes that, unrepentantly, live amiss. **1561** DAUS tr. *Bullinger on Apoc.* (1573) 126 b, The *vnrepentauntnesse and lasciuiousnes of them. **1571** GOLDING *Calvin on Ps.* lxix. 29 This is the last curse..that foloweth the unrepentantnesse, of which he spake.

unre'pented, *ppl. a.* (UN-[1] 8, 5 c.)
[*a* **1500** in *Ratis Raving*, etc. 3 The synis that he has done, wnconfessyt of or rapentyt.] **1649** OGILBY tr. *Virgil's Æneis* VI. (1684) 255 Crimes at their last Hour unrepented were. **1659** GAUDEN *Slight Healers* (1660) 45 What peace can there be or true healing, while..the deepest wounds..are unpunished and unrepented? **1729** LAW *Serious C.* xxiii. 460 The guilt of unrepented sins. **1795** SOUTHEY *Joan of Arc* IX. 38 Sent before the Eternal Judge, With all their unrepented crimes upon them. **1806** [see UNRELINQUISHED]. **1830** G. S. FABER *Diffic. Romanism* (ed. 2) I. v. 168 An act of unrepented idolatry. **1867** H. MACMILLAN *Bible Teach.* xii. 243 Humbling discoveries..of secret, unsuspected, unrepented sins.
b. With *of* (†*on*, †*for*).
1597 HOOKER *Eccl. Pol.* v. lxxii. §13 Heapes of grieuous transgressions..vnrepented of. **1629** RUTHERFORD *Let. to Lady Kenmure* 15 Jan., Fear of God's anger for old, unrepented-of sins. **1645** E. CALAMY *Indictm. Eng.* 23 This sin alone unrepented on will shut a man out of heaven. **1646** FULLER *Wounded Consc.* xvi. (1647) 122 Some unrepented-for sinne. *a* **1716** BLACKALL *Wks.* (1723) I. 77 His known, allow'd, unrepented-of Breach of that one Law. **1824** MISS L. M. HAWKINS *Annaline* III. 209 Where sin unrepented of cannot enter. **1889** M. HOUSTON *Sylvanus Redivivus* 164 The burden of unrepented-of sins.

unre'penting, *ppl. a.* (UN-[1] 10.)
a **1586** SIDNEY *Arcadia* III. xiv, Wicked woman,..whose unrepenting harte can find no way to amend treason, but by treason. **1655** JER. TAYLOR *Unum Necess.* v. §3. 245 Unrepenting or habitual sinners. **1678** CUDWORTH *Intell. Syst.* 156 It goes on in one Constant, Unrepenting Tenor, from Generation to Generation. **1700** DRYDEN *Theod. & Hon.* 168 In unrepenting Sin she dy'd. **1730** A. PETRIE *Rules Good Deportm. Ch. Officers* 127 To their last Hour of unrepenting Death. **1790** GIBBON *Misc. Wks.* (1814) III. 396 The unrepenting tyrant had accomplished the measure of his sins. **1827** POLLOK *Course T.* VI. 496 The sword of Justice, red With..unrepenting wrath. **1839** HALLAM *Hist. Lit.* III. ii. §25 A Jesuit wrote a book to prove that unrepenting Protestants could not be saved.
Hence **unre'pentingly** *adv.*, **-ness**.
1615 HIERON *Wks.* I. 606 Such is the stablenesse of His counsell,..the vnrepentingnesse of His conferring sauing grace. **1789** CHARLOTTE SMITH *Ethelinde* (1814) V. 333 Though he now unrepentingly was gone where all his crimes were registered.

unre'pined, *ppl. a.* (UN-[1] 8, 8 c.)
1626 BP. HALL *Contempl.*, *O.T.* XXI. iii, To continue those [taxes] he found unrepined at.

unre'pining, *ppl. a.* (UN-[1] 10.)
1637 BP. HALL *Rem. Prophaneness* II. §11 (1662) 80 What unrepining subjection to the rod? **1654** *Nicholas Papers* (Camden) II. 118 That I may be able to keepe him in the present free and unrepyning humor. **1739** GLOVER *Hosier's Ghost* 65 Unrepining at thy glory, Thy successful arms we hail. **1815** SCOTT *Guy M.* xxix, She would sit up..to nurse me with the most unrepining patience. **1850** MRS. JAMESON *Leg. Monast. Ord.* 402 She endured all unrepining.
Hence **unre'piningly** *adv.*
1626 WOTTON *Let.* in *Rem.* (1651) 507 His indisputable will must be done, and unrepiningly received by his own Creatures. **1748** RICHARDSON *Clarissa* II. 237 [As] the will of Providence..leads, let me patiently and unrepiningly follow. **1876** BANCROFT *Hist. U.S.* I. ix. 277 He unrepiningly went to meet impoverishment..for the welfare of Massachusetts.

unre'placeable, *a.* (UN-[1] 7 b, 5 b.)
1801 SOUTHEY *Lett.* (1856) I. 153 Humphry Davy is an unreplaceable companion. **1856** RUSKIN *Mod. Paint.* IV. v. xx. §41 The head of the Lake of Geneva being..unreplaceable if destroyed. **1894** *Blackw. Mag.* Oct. 463 He was, like Napoleon, unreplaceable.

unre'placed, *ppl. a.* (UN-[1] 8.)
1883 LD. LYTTON *Life & Lett. Lytton* II. 36 There is a charm in sympathetic female companionship unapproached, and unreplaced, by any friendship.

unre'plenished, *ppl. a.* (UN-[1] 8.)
1562 BACON in D'Ewes *Jrnl.* (1682) 60/1 Few came to Service, and the Church so [was] unreplenished. **1614** GORGES *Lucan* VII. 280 The townes are vnreplenished. The champian vninhabited. **1660** BOYLE *New Exp. Phys. Mech.* xvii. 126 Some Air..kept the Mercury out of the unreplenish'd space. **1817** SHELLEY *Pr. Athan.* I. 59 Though his life..Was failing like an unreplenished stream. **1854** J. S. C. ABBOTT *Napoleon* (1855) I. 478 Gradually the unreplenished piles burnt out.

†**unre'pliable**, *a. Obs.* [UN-[1] 7 b, 5 b.] Unanswerable.
1653 R. BAILLIE *Dissuas. Vind.* (1655) 1 Arguments of no lesse than steel, and that unsheathed and shining, evident and unrepliable. **1663** GRIFFITH *Serm. Four Admirable Beasts* 23 His wise, unreprovable and unrepliable answers. **1716** M. DAVIES *Athen. Brit.* II. To Rdr. 41 The unreplyable A[rch]b[ishop] Tenison's Tract of Idolatry.

†**unre'pliably**, *adv. Obs.* (UN-[1] 11.)
1648 N. HOMES in J. Cotton *Congregat. Ch. Cleared* A 2, You will meet with..divers precious Saints..evidently and unrepliablely vindicated. **1715** M. DAVIES *Athen. Brit.* I. Pref. 34 Topicks..answer'd unrepliably innumerable times.

unre'plied, *ppl. a.* (UN-[1] 8, 8 c.)
1825 SCOTT *Talism.* vii, The Scottish barons..were not men to bear his scorn unobserved or unreplied to. **1856** LEVER *Martins of Cro' M.* xviii, Three [letters] of hers had been left unreplied to!

unre'plying, *ppl. a.* (UN-[1] 10.)
1791 COWPER *Iliad* v. 817 He spake; but Hector unreplying pass'd Impetuous. **1812** CARY *Dante, Parad.* I. 126 Oft-times, but ill accords the form To the design of art, through sluggishness Of unreplying matter. **1892** *Pall Mall G.* 16 Apr. 7/1 The voiceless lips of the unreplying dead.

unre'portable, *a.* (UN-[1] 7 b, 5 b.)
1611 SPEED *Hist. Gt. Brit.* IX. viii. §37 Which brought..his Kingdome to vn-reportable calamities. **1871** L. STEPHEN *Playgr. Europe* iii. 124 A volley of unreportable language from the Chamouni guides. **1883** *Harper's Mag.* Jan. 208/1 Stirring stories some of them, but as unreportable as the..metaphors in which they were portrayed.

unre'ported, *ppl. a.* (UN-[1] 8.)
1622 MALYNES *Anc. Law-Merch.* 284 This finesse of Siluer hid and vnreported in the bullion. **1808** MITFORD *Hist. Greece* III. 65 On some turn in the popular mind,..unreported by antient writers, they were imprisoned. **1850** THACKERAY *Pendennis* lxii, In consequence of that unreported conversation. **1884** *Marshall's Tennis Cuts* 21 Some unreported club or local handicap.

unre'posed, *ppl. a.* (UN-[1] 8.)
1827 POLLOK *Course T.* VII. 581 Great Ocean! strongest of creation's sons, unreposed, untired.

unre'poseful, *a.* (UN-[1] 7.)
1883 *Fortn. Rev.* July 118 The passions, and the foible of that unreposeful time.

unre'posing, *ppl. a.* (UN-[1] 10.)
1817 SHELLEY *Rev. Islam* II. i, The murmur of the unreposing brooks. **1862** MILMAN *Mem. Macaulay* 19 The ballad['s]..whole excellence is in..unreposing, unflagging, vigorous, stirring life.

unrepre'hended, *ppl. a.* (UN-[1] 8.)
a **1614** DONNE *Βιαθανατος* (1644) 195 Some of the Patriarches lived unreprehended in Polygamie. **1739** R. BULL tr. *Dedekindus' Grobianus* 40 Unreprehended there, supine, you lie.

unrepre'sentable, *a.* (UN-[1] 7 b, 5 b.)
1840 *Penny Cycl.* XVI. 20/2 Unrepresentable by any kind of musical instrument at present known. **1850** H. BUSHNELL *God in Christ* 156 The Unapproachable, and, as far as all measures of..conception are concerned, the Unrepresentable God.

unrepre'sentative, *a.* (UN-[1] 7.)
1832 A. W. FONBLANQUE *Eng. under 7 Administr.* (1837) II. 236 An unrepresentative House of Representation. **1884** *Pall Mall G.* 18 July 10/2 An irresponsible and unrepresentative House of Lords.
Hence **unrepre'sentativeness.**
1958 A. TOYNBEE *East to West* 221 This unrepresentativeness of the capital is one of its generic defects. **1980** BUTLER & PINTO-DUSCHINSKY in Z. Layton-Henry *Conservative Party Politics* viii. 198 Does Conservative unrepresentativeness harm the party in other ways?

unrepre'sented, *ppl. a.* [UN-[1] 8.]
1. Not represented by a member of a legislative body.
1681 *Jedburgh Town Council Records* 29 Sept. (MS.), That the Burgh may not be unrepresented by Magistrates, Councillors and others. *c* **1778** *Conquerors* 13 No subjects can be tax'd unrepresented. **1787** HAWKINS *Life Johnson* 502 The far greater number of the subjects of England..are unrepresented in parliament. **1849** MACAULAY *Hist. Eng.* i. I. 135 Very few unrepresented towns had yet grown into importance. **1884** *Manch. Exam.* 10 Sept. 5/3 The county..would [not] be indifferent to the claims of the unrepresented two millions.
2. Not represented by an instance, individual, etc.
1854 *Poultry Chron.* I. 350/2, 13 classes..were entirely unrepresented in the entries! **1885** *Mag. of Art* June 350 The exhibition at the Grosvenor Gallery, with Mr. Whistler at Suffolk Street, Mr. Burne Jones unrepresented,..is [etc.].
3. Not yet produced upon the stage.
1888 *Daily Telegr.* 13 Feb. (Encycl. Dict.), A single performance of hitherto unrepresented works.

†**unre'pressable**, *a. Obs.* [UN-[1] 7 b.] Irrepressible.
1607 MARKHAM *Cavel.* II. 95 Diuers horses..bee so vnrepressable in the violence of their furies, that [etc.].

unre'pressed, *ppl. a.* (UN-[1] 8.)
1583 GOLDING *Calvin on Deut.* xxxv. 211 His bearing with such blasphemie so as it hath full scope vnrepressed. **1803** EUGENIA DE ACTON *Ess.* I. 82 The fervour of a youthful mind,..if unrepressed by the precepts of..prudence. **1830** TENNYSON *Arab. Nts.* 74 Life, anguish, death, immortal love, Ceasing not, mingled, unrepress'd. **1861** TRENCH *Comm. Ep. Churches Asia* 50 Every disorder..which has remained unrepressed.

unre'pressible, *a.* [UN-[1] 7, 5 b.] Irrepressible.
1804 EUGENIA DE ACTON *Tale without Title* II. 158. **1846** WORCESTER (citing Dr. Barton).

unre'prievable, *a.* (UN-[1] 7 b.)
1593 NASHE *Christ's T.* 36 b, The best remedy of thyne vnreprlueable peruerse destiny was death. **1595** SHAKS. *John* v. vii. 48 There the poyson Is, as a fiend, confin'd to tyrannize, On vnrepreeuable condemned blood. *a* **1625** FLETCHER *Elder Brother* II. i, Thou unreprieveable Dunce! ..dost thou tell me I should?
Hence **unre'prievably** *adv.*
1594 NASHE *Unfort. Trav.* Ded., Vnrepriuebly perisheth that booke whatsoeuer to wast paper, which [etc.]. **1596** —— *Saffron Walden* F ij, His bedred stuffe..else would haue laine vnrepriuably spittled at the Chandlers.

unre'prieved, *ppl. a.* (UN-[1] 8.)
1667 MILTON *P.L.* II. 185 There to converse with everlasting groans, Unrespited, unpitied, unreprievd. **1735** SOMERVILLE *Chace* III. 213 But unrepriev'd he [*sc.* a captive fox] dies. **1820** SHELLEY *Prometh. Unb.* I. 423 The slow years Which thou must spend in torture, unreprieved.

unre'printed, *ppl. a.* (UN-[1] 8.)
[**1775** ASH.] **1872** W. MINTO *Eng. Lit.* I. i. 82 One of his unreprinted papers. **1885** *Athenæum* 5 Sept. 305/3 It was..intended to confine it to unreprinted pieces.

† **unre'proachable**, *a. Obs.* (UN-[1] 7b, 5b.)
1603 HOLLAND *Plutarch's Mor.* 244 The purenesse of our life and innocencie unreprochable. **1625** DONNE *Serm.* (1626) 40 These bills must be well testified, with vnreproachable witnesses. *a* **1711** KEN *Hymn.* Poet. Wks. 1721 II. 143 Whether God hears the Pray'rs of Saints or not, ..God unreproachable remains. **1737** WHISTON *Josephus, Hist.* I. ix. §4 An unreproachable witness. **1768** BLACKSTONE *Comm.* III. xxii. 347 Where the defendant bore a fair and unreproachable character.

unre'proached, *ppl. a.* (UN-[1] 8.)
1648 *Eikon Bas.* viii. 49 Sir John Hotham unreproached, unthreatned, uncursed by any language or secret imprecation of Mine. **1753** FOOTE *Englishm. in Paris* II, Full fifteen years, in wedlock's sacred bands, have I liv'd unreproach'd. *a* **1812** BUCKMINSTER *Serm.* (1827) 262 He passed through the world unreproached. He now sees, that his innocence..was unreproached, because unknown or despised.

unre'proachful, *a.* (UN-[1] 7.)
c **1720** GAY in *Pope's Wks., Addits.* (1776) I. 99 Friendly Congreve, unreproachful man! **1837** LYTTON *Athens* II. 574 An anxious, earnest unreproachful devotion of conjugal love. **1838** MRS. BROWNING *Seraphim* II. 362 With these forgiving hands upraising Their unreproachful wounds. **1869** LYTTON *Orval* 56 Nay, not till..all the love I render back With unreproachful tears.

unre'proachfully, *adv.* (UN-[1] 11.)
1671 CLARENDON *Hist. Reb.* x. §171 He could never have been rid of him again so unreproachfully, as by his changing his own countenance.

unre'proaching, *ppl. a.* (UN-[1] 10.)
1742 RICHARDSON *Pamela* xx. (1785) III. 103 Nay, [she would have] reproach'd you more, by her unreproaching obligingness. **1766** GOLDSM. *Vicar W.* xxii, That books were sweet unreproaching companions to the miserable. **1858** FARRAR *Eric* 15 An unreproaching conscience. **1876** GEO. ELIOT *Dan. Der.* lxiv, The unreproaching voice of birds.
Hence **unre'proachingly** *adv.*
1753 RICHARDSON *Grandison* (1781) V. xli. 257 How unreproachingly may we call each other by that sacred name!

unrepro'ducible, *a.* (UN-[1] 7, 5b.)
1880 GOLDW. SMITH *Cowper* vi. 92 It belongs to an unreproducible past. **1893** *Nation* (N.Y.) 18 May 371/1 Desperate efforts to reproduce the unreproducible. **1899** KIPLING *Stalky* 225 An unreproducible sniff..rounded the retort. [Freq. in recent use.]

unrepro'ductive, *a.* [UN-[1] 7.] Not reproductive.
1930 W. K. HANCOCK *Australia* viii. 161 Informed opinion was ready to welcome the report of the British Economic Mission (January 1929), which warned Australia that unreproductive developmental expenditure was imposing 'a heavy burden on the general community.' **1968** P. SCOTT *Day of Scorpion* (1973) II. ii. 330 Hers were the menstrual flows of a virgin, sour little seepages such as Barbie Batchelor had presumably sustained for a good thirty years of her unreproductive life.

unre'provable, *a.* Now *rare.* [UN-[1] 7b, 5b.] Irreprovable, irreproachable. (Common *c* 1550–1680.)
1382 WYCLIF *Tobit* x. 13 Monestende hir..to gouerne the hous, to ȝiue hirself vnreprefable. *c* **1385** CHAUCER *L.G.W.* 691 *Cleopatra*, Vnreprouable on to myn wyfhod ay, The same wolde I fele, lyf or deth. *a* **1548** HALL *Chron., Hen. VIII*, 227 In life and conuersacion vnreprouable. **1581** J. BELL *Haddon's Answ. Osor.* 76 b, Whose wordes and deedes we may accompt without exception unreproveable. **1615** G. SANDYS *Trav.* 135 She was..of life vnreproueable. **1635** PAGITT *Christianogr.* I. i. 4 Historiographers, and other unreproveable Authors. **1712** STEELE *Spect.* No. 302 ⁋14 Ye guardian Angels,..lead her gently hence innocent and unreprovable to a better Place. **1791** COWPER *Iliad* IX. 650 Thy wrath was unreproveable and just. **1851** RUSKIN *Stones Ven.* I. xxvii. §17 His work is absolutely unreproveable.
Hence **unre'provableness, -ably** *adv.*
1634 SANDERSON *Serm., Ad Mag.* iii. (1681) II. 286 See to it..that you walk orderly and unreproveably your selves. **1680** W. CLAGETT *Disc., Answ.* 24 The unreprovableness of the Spiritual man in assenting to the mysteries of the Gospel.

unre'proved, *ppl. a.* (UN-[1] 8.)
a **1400–50** *Alexander* 3092 For-þi ȝour werke ay be witt ȝe wirke vnreproued [*v.r.* vnreprefytt]. *c* **1400** *Found. St. Bartholomew's* (1923) 13 He..yn his techynge vnrepreuyd was fownde. **1420–2** LYDG. *Thebes* 4152 That we bygan we knyghtly han acheuyd Vpon our foon, with worship vnrepreuyd. **1578** WHETSTONE *Promos & Cass.* II. III. i, God graunt I scape this blacke day unreprev'd. **1590** SPENSER *F.Q.* II. vii. 16 The antique world..with glad thankes, and vnreproued truth, The gifts of soueraigne bountie did embrace. **1615** G. SANDYS *Trav.* 14 Yet haue the Christians their Churches, and vnreproued exercise of religion. **1667** MILTON *P.L.* IV. 493 With eyes Of conjugal attraction unreprov'd. **1703** DE FOE *More Reform.* 8 Let them expose thy Errors to the Town, Thou shalt go unreprov'd, 'till they repent. **1760–72** H. BROOKE *Fool of Qual.* (1809) III. 18 Man..riots at large and unreproved. **1820** SCOTT *Monast.* iv, The servants mingled,..unreproved and with freedom, in whatever conversation was going forward. **1861** LD. ACTON in Gasquet *Ld. A. & Circle* (1906) 165 Newman's view of the Council of Trent should not go unreproved.

unre'proving, *ppl. a.* (UN-[1] 10.)
1748 THOMSON *Cast. Indol.* I. xxviii, Here dwells kind ease, and unreproving joy. *a* **1850** MRS. BROWNING *Woman's Shortcomings* ii, She..Hears bold words, unreproving.

unre'publican, *a.* (UN-[1] 7.)
1878 *N. Amer. Rev.* CXXVI. 13 Erasmus's description of what he calls the unrepublican bird [*sc.* the eagle]. **1885** *Atlantic Monthly* April 450 The importation of uneducated, un-American, un-republican workmen.

† **unre'pugnable**, *a. Obs.* (UN-[1] 7b, 5b.)
c **1440** *Gesta Rom.* xxvii. 102 (Harl. MS.), Thow most sey iij. trewe poyntes, þat shul be vnrepugnable. **1611** SPEED *Hist. Gt. Brit.* VIII. ii. §11. 389/1 So mighty and almost vnrepugnable an enemie.

unre'pugnant, *a.* (UN-[1] 7.)
1594 HOOKER *Eccl. Pol.* III. ix. §1 When [Scripture gives] Positiue [laws], which way to make Lawes vnrepugnant vnto them. **1642** CHAS. I *Answ. to Bristol & Dorset* 3 Severall and farre different conceptions; yet none unrepugnant to reason. **1823** SCOTT *Quentin D.* xviii, The unrepugnant acquiescence of Hayraddin in their change of route.

unre'pulsable, *a.* (UN-[1] 7b.)
1814 JANE AUSTEN *Mansf. Park* xxxiv, Fanny..was trying ..to repulse Mr. Crawford, and avoid both his looks and inquiries; and he, unrepulsable, was persisting in both.

unre'pulsing, *ppl. a.* (UN-[1] 10.)
1748 RICHARDSON *Clarissa* (1811) IV. 254, I kissed her unrepulsing hand.

un'repulsive, *a.* (UN-[1] 7.)
1835 WILLIS *Pencillings* I. iii. 26 We sat down once more to clean cloths and unrepulsive food. **1946** D. WELCH *Jrnl.* 12 Jan. (1952) 185 The person who built this church was unclogged with 'book-learning' and so his church is unrepulsive and almost pretty and good.

un'reputable, *a.* (UN-[1] 7b, 5b.)
1698 COLLIER *Immor. Stage* vi. 240 The Athenians.. thought a Comedy so unreputable a Performance, that [etc.]. **1703** J. SAVAGE *Lett. Antients* cxiii. 277 It is.. unreputable to change ones Friends often. **1724** *Briton* No. 26 (1724) 115 Let Fools..of unreputable Praise be proud.

unre'puted, *ppl. a.* (UN-[1] 8.)
1596 *Edward III*, II. i. 436 An vnreputed mote, flying in the Sunne, Presents a greater substaunce then it is.

unre'quest, *v.* (UN-[2] 3.)
1552 HOOPER *Let.* Wks. (Parker Soc.) p. xx, When that I perceived my request for jurisdiction made before unto you, upon further deliberation I thought it good to unrequest that again.

unre'quested, *ppl. a.* (UN-[1] 8.)
1576 R. PETERSON *G. della Casa's Galateo* 60 To offer aduyse vnrequested. **1587** GOLDING *De Mornay* xxxiv. 634 How vnindifferent are these people, which will needes both beleeue and be beleeued of all men without witnesse and vnrequested [F. *sans enqueste*]. **1609** W. M. *Man in Moon* G 4 b, How hee would..proffer, vnrequested, many seruile ceremonies. **1641** EARL MONM. tr. *Biondi's Civil Warres* v. 93 Though unrequested on Henries behalfe, the soveraigntie of France was demanded on Charles. **1709** MRS. CENTLIVRE *Gamester* IV, Valere has..exposed my unrequested bounty. *a* **1768** SECKER *Serm.* (1771) V. vii. 136 Without this no Person would have..more Assistance in Distress from his Neighbour, than..unrequested Goodness [would] incline him to bestow.

unre'quired, *ppl. a.* [UN-[1] 8.]
1. Of persons: Not requested or asked; without being asked.
1412–20 LYDG. *Chron. Troy* I. 2405 But more frely, with herte ful entere, Liste vnrequered on my wo to rewe. **1514** BARCLAY *Cyt. & Uplondyshman* (Percy Soc.) 13 And unrequyred presentynge them, sayde she, O Lorde, these also my veray chyldren be! **1561** T. HOBY tr. *Castiglione's Courtyer* II. (1577) H vj b, They..that rashly before a greate man enter into talk vnrequired. **1594** T. BEDINGFIELD tr. *Machiavelli's Florentine Hist.* (1595) 172 Many times also vnrequired he did lend to those Gentlemen. **1634** BP. HALL *Contempl., N.T.* IV. xxxii. 266 So free, that he shall willingly undergoe it, when it is laid upon him; not so free as that he shall lay it upon himselfe, unrequired. **1748** RICHARDSON *Clarissa* (1811) III. 13 How artfully does he (unrequired) promise to observe the conditions?
2. Of things: Unasked for, unsought; not demanded or called for.
c **1510** BARCLAY *Mirr. Gd. Manners* (1570) G v, Desire thou none office nor cure... If it unrequired be geuen vnto thee,..do not the same despise. **1559** in Tytler *Hist. Scot.* (1864) III. 396 As I have found this your good mind unrequired,..I am bold to desire you..to continue in the same. **1687** BOYLE *Martyrd. Theodora* x. 179 A young Lady, in whose Sex, Courage is..an unrequired, if not an altogether improper, Vertue. **1818** SCOTT *Rob Roy* xxxix, His unrequired presence prevented me from speaking freely to Syddall.
3. Not requisite; unnecessary.
1847 C. BRONTE *J. Eyre* xxxv, He would make me sensible that it was a superfluity, unrequired by him. **1849** EASTWICK *Dry Leaves* 163 The caution was unrequired.

un'requisite, *a.* (UN-[1] 7, 5b.)
1594 HOOKER *Eccl. Pol.* III. xi. §16 Much may be requisite which the scripture teacheth not, and much which it hath taught, become vnrequisite. **1603** J. DAVIES (Heref.) *Microcosmos* Wks. (Grosart) I. 31/2 Too full Of fearefull thoughts, and cares vnrequisit. **1621** in Foster *Eng. Factories Ind.* I. (1906) 270 It is nott unrequizite that some Englishman accompany the goods. **1817** KEATINGE *Trav.* I. 278 Without allowing the meats to cool by unrequisite delay.

unre'quitable, *a.* (UN-[1] 7b, 5b.)
1584 W. WARNER *Syrinx* (1597) O j, Vnrequitable are the duties, wherein we are..indebted to our Mothers. **1617** DONNE *Serm.* Wks. 1839 VI. 3 There are persons which are unrequitable, though they be believed to loue. **1646** SIR T. BROWNE *Pseud. Ep.* v. xxi. 269 An unrequitable evil may ensue. **1683** KENNETT *Erasm. on Folly* 17 An unrequitable obligation.

unre'quital. (UN-[1] 12, 5b.)
1865 MRS. WHITNEY *Gayworthys* xxx, Old love sleeps, if it do not die. It has..its pains and its unrequital. **1867** *Spectator* 6 Apr. 386 Glorious in their unrequital.

unre'quited, *ppl. a.* (UN-[1] 8.)
a **1542** WYATT in *Tottel's Misc.* (Arb.) 53 Complaint for true loue vnrequited. **1622** J. HAGTHORPE in Farr *S.P. Jas. I* (1848) 347 If from a friend some trifle we receiue,..We think ourselues ungratefull if we leaue These vnrequited. **1634** BP. HALL *Contempl., N.T.* IV. iii, Who can ever say, Lord, this favour I did to the least of thine, unrequited? **1741–2** GRAY *Agrippina* 76 Benefits, too great To be repaid, Sit heavy on the soul, As unrequited wrongs. **1793** J. TWEDDELL *Rem.* (1815) 48 Productive..of unrequited blood-shed. **1814** WORDSW. *Excurs.* VI. 109 Being crazed in brain By unrequited love. **1857** J. H. NEWMAN *Serm. Var. Occas.* xii. 261 The times of patience,..of humble, unrequited service. **1893** [see UNREQUITER].
Hence **unre'quitedly** *adv.*, **unre'quitedness**.
1648 BOYLE *Seraph. Love* xiv. (1659) 94 So far from enabling us by them, to Requite his Love,..it encreases the Un-requitednesse of it. **1867** MISS BROUGHTON *Not wisely but too well* I. 108 Falling in love violently, and as it now appeared unrequitedly, with a man her superior in station.

unre'quitement. (UN-[1] 12.)
1890 TALMAGE *Manger to Throne* 425 In wrath at this unrequitement of the mercy..shown him.

unre'quiter. (UN-[1] 12.)
1893 A. KENEALY *Molly & Man-of-War* 94 The story of an unrequited love, and a sight of the photograph of the unrequiter.

unre'scinded, *ppl. a.* (UN-[1] 8.)
1716 in *Records of Stitchill* (S.H.S.) 173 So long as this Act stands unrescinded.

un'rescued, *ppl. a.* (UN-[1] 8.)
[**1775** ASH.] **1846** WORCESTER (citing *Ec. Rev.*).

† **unre'semblable**, *a.* (UN-[1] 7b.)
1678 CUDWORTH *Intell. Syst.* I. iv. 189 Thereby debasing both themselves and God, not glorifying Him according to His spiritual and unresembleable nature.

† **unre'semblant**, *a.* [UN-[1] 7.] Dissimilar.
1653 F. G. tr. *Scuderi's Artamenes* (1655) IV. VII. III. 191 One and the same Passion produced in them effects very unresemblant.

unre'sembling, *ppl. a.* (UN-[1] 10, 5d.)
1598 FLORIO, *Dissimile*,..vnlike, vnresembling. **1655** EARL ORRERY *Parthen.* I. VIII. 383 He had once seene some features not vnresembling his. **1683** DRYDEN *Ded. to Plutarch's Lives* 26 Malice will make a picture more unresembling than ignorance. **1702** S. PARKER tr. *Cicero's De Finibus* IV. 262 Some of your Unresembling Similitudes! **1799** LAMB *Let. to Southey* 2 March, Following, at unresembling distance, Sterne, and greater Cervantes.
Hence **unre'semblingly** *adv.*
1662 ORMONDE in Carte *Life* (1735) III. 23, I have the honour, how unworthily and how unresemblingly soever, to represent the Majesty of my Great Master. **1665** BOYLE *Occas. Refl.* I. i. 162 Not unresemblingly deals God with us.

unre'sented, *ppl. a.* (UN-[1] 8.)
1705 VANBRUGH *Mistake* III. i, You must not think so daring an affront to my family can go long unresented. **1711** ADDISON *Spect.* No. 99 ⁋7 One may tell another he.. Drinks, Blasphemes, and it may pass unresented. **1748** RICHARDSON *Clarissa* VII. 47 It is still a worse imputation, that she should pass over so mortal an injury unresented. **1811** MISS L. M. HAWKINS *C'tess & Gertr.* 239 He had suffered to pass, unnoticed and unresented, her former ill-humor. **1886** A. WEIR *Hist. Basis Mod. Europe* iii. 115 To suffer unresented the contemptuous demeanour of his unprofitable superiors.

unre'sentful, *a.* (UN-[1] 7.)
1773 MELMOTH tr. *Cato* (1777) I. 252 The same philosophers, who contended for this innoxious and unresentful character of the Deity. **1805** WORDSW. *Prelude* v. 414 A race of real children;..Not unresentful where self-justified. **1862** 'SHIRLEY' (J. Skelton) *Nugæ Crit.* x. 441 He bore the pang..with proud confidence and unresentful regret.
Hence **unre'sentfully** *adv.*, **-fulness**.
1862 LOWELL *Biglow P.* Ser. II. Poet. Wks. (1912) 320 Good-nature..becomes a positive crime when it leads us to look unresentfully on peculation. **1899** G. TYRRELL in Petre *Life* (1912) II. 16 Abounding in sympathy, unresentfulness, ..loyalty, fidelity.

unre'senting, *ppl. a.* (UN-[1] 10.)
1716 COLLIER tr. *Gregory of Nazianzus* 57 'Twas this [patience] which made..Stephen unresenting when ston'd 'to death'. **1759** STERNE *Tr. Shandy* II. xii, But to hurt a brother of such gentle manners,—..so unresenting;—'tis base. **1810** COLERIDGE *Friend* 358 To remain in nominal Peace and unresenting Passiveness with an insolent neighbour. **1861** GEO. ELIOT *Silas M.* iii, Godfrey..left the room, followed humbly by the unresenting Snuff.

unre'serve. [UN-[1] 12.] Absence of reserve; frankness.
1751 J. DUNCOMBE in *Richardson's Corr.* (1804) II. 273 He has rather more openness and unreserve than his brother. **1777** WRAXALL *Court of Berlin* (1799) I. 92, I was as much penetrated with her condescension and unreserve, as I was charmed by her..love of knowledge. **1826** DISRAELI *Viv. Grey* v. xi, 'May I really speak with freedom?'.. 'With the most perfect unreserve and confidence,' answered Vivian. **1862** LYTTON *Str. Story* I. 80 You have done well to confide in me with so generous an unreserve.

unre'served, *ppl. a.* [UN-[1] 8.]
1. Unrestricted, unlimited, absolute.
1539 HEN. VIII in *Wyatt's Wks.* (1816) II. 498 He will send to my Lady Regent..full and unreserved power..to..

conclude the same upon reasonable conditions. *a* **1729** ROGERS *19 Serm.* (1735) 311 An entire unreserved Obedience to his Commands. **1768–74** TUCKER *Lt. Nat.* (1834) II. 422 We may have an unreserved trust in His mercy. **1771** *Junius Lett.* lix. (1788) 321 A determination so entire and unreserved. **1818** SCOTT *Hrt. Midl.* xiv, A friend, ..whose attachment deserved her full and unreserved confidence. **1858** FROUDE *Hist. Eng.* III. 260 Her name is mentioned..with unreserved respect.

2. Free from reserve; frank, open.

1713 POPE *Lett.* (1735) I. 199 That we have lived many Years together in an unreserved Conversation. **1751** EARL ORRERY *Remarks Swift* ii. 15 Her manners were humane, polite, easy, and unreserved. **1827** R. PEEL *Let. To Croker* 3 Oct., In consequence of unreserved communications with you, you were in possession of my opinions. **1884** *American* VIII. 277 Mr. Bright was more unreserved in his language.

absol. **1756** COWPER *Wks.* (1837) XV. 278 The character of the open and unreserved, who thinks it a breach of friendship to conceal any thing from his intimates.

unre'servedly, *adv.* [UN-¹ 11.]

1. Without reservation or limitation; absolutely.

1651 BAXTER *Inf. Bapt.* 224 The entrance into Covenant, and acceptation of the terms of it (though not sincerely and unreservedly). **1687** BOYLE *Martyrd. Theodora* xi. 201, I should have been very much, if not unreservedly, guided by your wishes. **1768–74** TUCKER *Lt. Nat.* (1834) II. 399 We may trust unreservedly to the words..of the perfect wise man. **1823** SCOTT *Quentin D.* xxvi, My own person I have this morning placed unreservedly in your power. **1850** THACKERAY *Pendennis* ii, Everything was left unreservedly to her, except in case of a second marriage.

2. Without reserve; openly, frankly.

1718 ADDISON *Let. to Swift* 20 Mar., To tell you unreservedly, I have been unwilling [etc.]. **1747** RICHARDSON *Clarissa* (1811) I. 48 This I may the more unreservedly say to you. **1817** PONSONBY in *Parl. Deb.* 286/2 When the bill came before them, he should state his sentiments unreservedly. **1867** MRS. H. WOOD *Orville College* xxiii, Full of her griefs and grievances, she spoke out unreservedly.

unre'servedness. [UN-¹ 12.] The quality of being unreserved.

1648 BOYLE *Seraph. Love* (1659) 23 The tendernesse and unreserv'dnesse of his Love. **1713** POPE *Lett.* (1735) I. 203 I am conscious I write with more unreservedness than ever Man wrote, or perhaps talk'd to another. **1742** RICHARDSON *Pamela* IV. 226 An Unreservedness of Air and Behaviour, that I had not before seen so becoming. **1821** in Picton *L'pool Munic. Rec.* (1886) II. 391, I will do so with all unreservedness, but I hope with all due civility. **1844** STANLEY *Arnold* I. Pref. p. viii, The familiarity and unreservedness of epistolary intercourse. **1882** *Macm. Mag.* XLV. 304 The freedom..of his speech, its buoyancy and unreservedness.

† **un'resident**, *sb. Obs.*⁻¹ [UN-¹ 12.] = NON-RESIDENT *sb.* 2.

1683 *Col. Rec. Pennsylv.* I. 65 Publique houses to credit no Vnresident for above 20ˢ.

† **un'resident**, *a. Obs.*⁻¹ (UN-¹ 7.)

1574 *Reg. Privy Council Scot.* II. 352 Nor yit ar the unresident personnis admoneist.

unre'signed, *ppl. a.* (UN-¹ 8.)

a **1641** D. BAKER *Holy Practises* (1657) 11 Contrarie to the proprietarious or vnresigned will of our corrupt nature. **1893** F. ADAMS *New Egypt* 170 Petulant and unresigned with his own, but..submissive to dictation when it came.

† **unre'sistable**, *a. Obs.* [UN-¹ 7 b, 5 b.] Irresistible. (Common *c* 1590–1660.)

1581 SIDNEY *Apol. Poetrie* (Arb.) 67 Many of such writings, as come vnder the banner of vnresistable loue. **1610** B. JONSON *Alch.* III. iv, He will winne you By vnresistable lucke..Inough to buy a baronie. **1614** LITHGOW *Trav.* E I b, It pleased him..to send downe an vnresistable tempest. **1672** TEMPLE *Ess., Govt.* (1680) 88 The unresistable force and conquests of some Nations over others.

unre'sistably, *adv.* (UN-¹ 11, 5 b.)

a **1591** H. SMITH *Six Serm.* (1612) A 4 b, Till..Gods iust iudgements [came] as the whirle-winde suddenly, vnresistably.

† **unre'sistance.** *Obs.* (UN-¹ 12, 5 b.)

1644 HUNTON *Vind. Treat. Monarchy* iv. 27 Being authoritative, they authorize the Instrument, and give him an unresistance. *a* **1656** BP. HALL *Soliloquies* §66 How do they [*sc.* dumb creatures] bear our stripes with a trembling unresistance?

unre'sistant, *a.* (UN-¹ 7.)

1830 MANGAN *Poems* (1903) 283 The blast.., soon a tempest,..Will swoop down on its unresistant prey. **1884** *Cent. Mag.* XXIX. 7 He draws her, unresistant, to him.

unre'sisted, *ppl. a.* [UN-¹ 8, 5 b.]

1. Not resisted; not meeting with resistance; †irresistible.

1526 *Pilgr. Perf.* (W. de W. 1531) 66 b, Leest perauenture other herynge theyr infamy vnresysted, despyse theyr holy prechynge. *c* **1586** C'TESS PEMBROKE *Psalm* LXXI. ii, Show thy unresisted power, Working now thy wonted will. **1593** SHAKS. *Lucr.* 282 As corne ore-growne by weedes: so heedfull feare Is almost choakt by vnresisted lust. *a* **1614** DONNE *Βιαθανατος* (1644) 128 That for the spirituall good of another, a man should expose his own life, is an unresisted doctrine. **1651** BAXTER *Inf. Bapt.* Apol. 19 Our God..rather then Schism shall go unresisted, will [etc.]. **1705** ADDISON *The Campaign* 197 To Donavert, with unresisted force, The gay victorious army bends its course. **1789** MRS. PIOZZI *Journ. France* II. 370 Black heaths,..over which the unresisted wind sweeps. **1855** MACAULAY *Hist. Eng.* xviii. IV. 119 The white flag, which..had ranged the Channel unresisted. **1881** MEREDITH *Tragic Com.* i, An unresisted lady-killer is probably less aware that [etc.].

† **2.** Uninterrupted. *Obs.*⁻¹

1603 FLORIO *Montaigne* III. iii. 498 It hath three baye-windowes, of a farre-extending, ritch and vnresisted prospect.

Hence **unre'sistedly** *adv.*

1673 BOYLE *Ess. Effic. Effluviums* vi. 33 These pass unresistedly thorow the pores of all solid Bodies, and even Glass it self. **1845** E. WARBURTON *Crescent & Cross* I. 351 The influence of that discipline..was now sending them unresistedly to encounter..privation in the depths of Africa. **1889** WELCH *Text Bk. Naval Archit.* iii. 50 The purely hypothetical case of a vessel rolling unresistedly in still water.

unre'sistible, *a.* Now *rare.* [UN-¹ 7, 5 b.] Irresistible.

1608 *Great Frost* in *Arber's Garner* I. 90 The swift, violent, and unresistible land currents. *a* **1631** DONNE *80 Serm.* (1640) 358 Which reproofe is an uncontrollable sense, and an unresistible remorse. *Ibid.* 384. **1653** HOLCROFT tr. *Procopius, Vandal Wars* II. 38 To think the enemy unresistible because of his victory. **1760** STERNE *Tr. Shandy* III. xxxviii, A mighty and unresistible call within me. **1891** FARRAR *Darkn. & Dawn* lxvi, The Church..'by the unresistible might of weakness shook the world'.

Hence **unre'sistibleness, -ibly** *adv.*

1644 HUNTON *Vind. Treat. Monarchy* v. 45 He is like to goe alone in this wild untroden path of defending an unresistiblenesse on such supposals. **1685** BAXTER *Paraphr. N.T.* Jas. i. 13 God..tempteth no man to it (much less forceth them to it, or unresistibly..makes them sin).

unre'sisting, *ppl. a.* (UN-¹ 10.)

1625 K. LONG tr. *Barclay's Argenis* II. xi. 98 The River.. gently mingled itselfe with the unresisting Sea. **1653** JER. TAYLOR *Serm. for Year* I. xx. 270 The bondage of conquered, wounded, unresisting people. **1691** NORRIS *Pract. Disc.* 329 As a Stone..[falling] through an unresisting Medium. **1744** THOMSON *Spring* 440 To the Shore You gayly drag your unresisting Prize. **1786** tr. *Beckford's Vathek* 116 That unresisting languor, so frequently fatal to the female heart. **1855** MACAULAY *Hist. Eng.* xiii. III. 282 The Jacobites, silent and unresisting, became prisoners. **1874** J. GEIKIE *Gt. Ice Age* xxi. 270 The rocky crust of the earth must needs have been as unresisting as putty.

Hence **unre'sistingly** *adv.*, **-ness.**

1797 MRS. RADCLIFFE *Italian* vi, Ellena followed unresistingly up a path. **1844** KINGLAKE *Eothen* xxvi, They ..unresistingly left their property to the hands of the spoilers. **1883** *Knowledge* 20 July 34/2 Groaningly it may be, but still unresistingly. **1900** MRS. H. WARD *Eleanor* vi, Her attitude by its sad unresistingness appealed to Lucy.

† **un'resnably**, *adv. Obs.* [UN-¹ 11 + RENABLY *adv.*] Unreasonably.

1461 *Paston Lett.* (1904) IV. 16 An evyll rewlyd felawschep..ferd ryth fowle with the Undyr Scheryfe, and onresnably as I herd sey.

un'resolute, *a.* (UN-¹ 7, 5 b.)

1579 FENTON *Guicciard.* 36 Mens witts wandring, and their mindes vnresolute. **1581** E. CAMPION in *Confer.* III. (1584) O j, I am not vnresolute. **1600** HOLLAND *Livy* I. xiv. 11 Whilest the Cavallirie stood unresolute as it were, in a mammering whither to flie or fight. *a* **1628** F. GREVIL *Alaham* II. iv. Chorus ii, Those Scenes still tedious are, those Acts too long, Where thy unresolute Images be strong.

unre'solvable, *a.* (UN-¹ 7 b, 5 b.)

1611 FLORIO, *Irresolubile*, vnresolueable. **1624** WOTTON *Elem. Archit.* 18 The Triangle which hath the fewest sides and corners, is..vnresoluable into any other regular Forme then it selfe. **1694** SOUTH *Serm.* (1698) III. 306 Men of Parts .., after all their Study,..are forced to give them over as Things Unresolveable. **1744** YOUNG *Nt. Th.* VII. 606 Call; and with endless questions be distrest, All unresolveable, if earth is All. **1850** MᶜCOSH *Div. Govt.* (1852) 260 Others.. have distinctly recognised the importance of the will as an unresolvable and independent faculty. **1870** RUSKIN *Lect. Art* (1875) 181 Your telescope..reveals nebula beyond nebula, far and farther,..unresolvable. **1874** WILLSHIRE *Anc. Prints* ii. 12 Various examples which..link the time of surety to that of *unresolvable* doubt.

unre'solve, *sb.* (UN-¹ 12, 5 b.)

1679 MRS. BEHN *Feign'd Curtizan* III. i, Come, lay by all sullen unresolves! **1895** *Outing* XXVI. 345/1 Her heart was torn, her mind a chaos of unresolve.

unre'solve, *v.* (UN-² 3, 7.)

1675 HOWE *Living Temple* 109 That the same thing is not ..resolved and unresolved a thousand times in a day. **1707** *Reflex. upon Ridicule* 331 Adriastus resolves and unresolves in the same Moment. **1746** W. HORSLEY *Fool* (1748) I. 188 He..consider'd, resolv'd, and unresolv'd, all in the same Moment. **1805–6** CARY *Dante, Inf.* II. 39 As one who unresolves What he hath late resolved.

unre'solved, *ppl. a.* [UN-¹ 8, 5 b.]

1. Of questions, etc.: Undetermined, undecided, unsolved.

1577 HOLINSHED *Chron.* II. 445/2 For to confesse..myne ignorance, or rather vnresolued doubt herein, I can not satisfie my selfe with any thing that I haue red. **1621** *First Bk. Discipl.* 10 Because..Articles thereanent remaine yet unresolved, and referred to further conference. **1652** HEYLYN *Cosmogr.* I. 152 It is unresolved who this Samothes was. **1692** RAY *Disc.* III. ix. (1693) 348 So I leave this Question unresolved. **1754** EDWARDS *Freed. Will* II. iv. 48 [He] leaves all the Difficulty unresolved and the Question un-answered. **1856** FROUDE *Hist. Eng.* I. 101 Doubt on such a subject once mooted might not be left unresolved. **1856** *Orr's Circ. Sci., Pract. Chem.* 327 The reason of this is an unresolved enigma.

2. a. Uncertain or undetermined how to act; irresolute. Also *transf.* (quot. 1611).

1594 SHAKS. *Rich. III*, IV. iv. 436 To our Shores Throng many doubtfull hollow-hearted friends, Vnarm'd, and vnresolu'd to beat them backe. **1611** TOURNEUR *Ath. Trag.* II. i, With A kinde of unresolu'd unwilling pace. **1653** H. COGAN tr. *Pinto's Trav.* xvi. 52 Being unresolved what course to take. **1691** NORRIS *Pract. Disc.* 151 To be Doubtful and Unresolved in a business of such vast moment. **1725** DE FOE *Voy. round World* (1840) 67 A crew of unresolved divided rogues. **1777** ROBERTSON *Hist. Amer.* VI. (1778) II. 236 He..was still unresolved, when the violence of the viceroy..moved him to quit his residence. **1821** SCOTT *Pirate* xxxiv, Several were unresolved upon engaging in a.. conflict.

absol. *a* **1659** OSBORNE *Wks.* (1673) 675 Nor did the readiness of the Scots to arm portend less in the ears of the un-resolved, than a possibility of Conquest.

b. Uncertain in opinion; undecided.

1597 HOOKER *Eccl. Pol.* v. lxii. §18 S. Augustines doubtfulnes..should not be mentioned by them which presume to define peremptorily of that wherein he was content to professe himselfe vnresolued. **1649** F. ROBERTS *Clavis Bibl.* 259 Authors seem much unresolved herein. **1673** [R. LEIGH] *Transp. Reh.* 142 The way is so difficult and my guides unresolv'd. **1707** *Curios. in Husb. & Gard.* 235 Boyle..is very much unresolved, and knows not what to think of these..Vegetations. **1784** COWPER *Task* VI. 160 Unresolv'd Which hue she most approv'd. **1864** F. W. ROBINSON *Mattie, a Stray* III. 220 She [was] unresolved as to what was best and just—for others, as well as for herself!

† **c.** Const. *of. Obs.*

1655 FULLER *Ch. Hist.* II. vi. §32 Either displeased at the Collect read,..or unresolved of the Efficacy of the Gold pendent about the Patients Neck. **1697** DRYDEN *Æneis* IX. 1078 So Turnus..unresolved of flight, Moves tardy back.

† **3.** Not formed of set purpose. *Obs.*⁻¹

1649 JER. TAYLOR *Gt. Exemp.* II. viii. 68 If the backsliding be but the interruption of the first sanctity by a single act, or an unconfirmed, unresolved, unmalicious habite.

4. Not broken up or dissolved.

(*a*) *c* **1801** BUSBY *Dict. Music* s.v. *Canon*, There are various kinds of canons: as the..resolved, the unresolved, the finite, and the infinite canon. **1837** [MRS. MAITLAND] *Lett. fr. Madras* (1843) 56 Imagine a succession of unresolved discords, selected at random. **1869** OUSELEY *Counterp.* xvi. 127 The unprepared and unresolved sevenths..produced by its inversion.

(*b*) **1843** R. J. GRAVES *Syst. Clin. Med.* xxi. 252 The hepatisation [of the lung] remains unresolved. **1850** NICHOL *Archit. Heav.* 54 The cluster in Hercules..never appeared devoid of unresolved light about its central regions. **1898** *Allbutt's Syst. Med.* V. 894 Fibroid disease of the lung.. secondary to pleuritic effusion or unresolved pneumonia, &c.

Hence **unre'solvedly** *adv.*

1621 LADY M. WROTH *Urania* 182, I gaue my answers vn-resolued.

unre'solvedness. [f. prec.] Irresolution.

1628 LE GRYS tr. *Barclay's Argenis* 274 This vnresoluednesse of minde. **1642** H. MORE *Min. Poems* Wks. (Grosart) 174/1 Grave matrons will wax wanton and betray Their unresolv'dnesse in their wonted grace. **1694** KETTLEWELL *Comp. Penitent* 131 Remove from me perplexing doubts, and unresolvedness about my Duty. **1734** J. EDWARDS *Serm.* Wks. 1811 VII. 415 Many grow old, in an unresolvedness whether to embrace Christianity or not. **1888** *Pall Mall G.* 24 Feb., The apparent unresolvedness..of many of the English electors.

unre'solving, *ppl. a.* (UN-¹ 10.)

1697 CONGREVE *Mourn. Bride* I. vi, In long suspense she stands, Shifting the prize in unresolving hands. **1737** *Gentl. Mag.* VII. 120/1 Behold! sweet ruin! the unhappy scene, Now on my pen I unresolving lean.

unre'sounded, *ppl. a.* (UN-¹ 8.)

1755 YOUNG *Centaur* vi, Is it not also far too much for human gratitude to leave unproclaimed, unresounded, unadored?

unre'sounding, *ppl. a.* (UN-¹ 10.)

1841 MANGAN *Poems* (1903) 293 Forth flow the moments, ..And, as their unresounding stream Departs away [etc.]. **1854** FABER *Growth in Holiness* xiii. 223 The shore of that unresounding sea.

† **unre'spect**, *sb. Obs.* [UN-¹ 12.] Lack of respect; disrespect.

? **1615** SYLVESTER *Tobacco Battered* 822 Those, that on Earth will still..Offend their Friends, with a Most vn-Respect. *a* **1656** BP. HALL *Rem. Wks.* (1660) 251 A palpable unrespect to the blessed Angels of God.

unre'spect, *ppl. a.* [UN-¹ 8 b.] Unregarded.

1854 S. DOBELL *Balder* i. 4 As one Who in a temple passes unrespect Between the kneeling suppliant and the saint.

unre'spectable, *a.* (UN-¹ 7 b, 5 b.)

1765 LANGHORNE in *Collins' Wks.* 164 The small Marino, which however unrespectable with regard to power or extent of territory, has, at least [etc.]. **1789** J. WHITE *Earl Strongbow* II. 94 The unrespectable pride of being descended from some ancient..ruffian. **1802** MRS. J. WEST *Infidel Father* I. 41 With some pretty appellative..it did not look unrespectable at the bottom of a letter. **1850** KINGSLEY *A. Locke* xx. 151 Let those of the respectable press who are without sin, cast the first stone at the unrespectable. **1889** J. J. THOMAS *Froudacity* 187 The handful of malcontents whose unrespectable grievance he holds up to public sympathy.

unre'spected, *ppl. a.* [UN-¹ 8.]

† **1.** Unregarded, unnoticed. *Obs.*

a **1586** SIDNEY *Arcadia* III. xxviii, The last grone of his brother was the onely answere he could get to his unrespected eloquence. **1596** B. GRIFFIN *Fidessa* xxxvii, Whil'st I..doe sit in heauie plight, Wayling alone my unrespected loue. *a* **1628** F. GREVIL 5 *Years K. James* (1643) 42 There being none to look after him, it would passe unregarded, or unrespected. **1634** SIR T. HERBERT *Trav.*

149 Women..wrap themselues in a large receiuing sheet;.. they passe and repasse vnknowne and vnrespected.

2. Not held in respect or regard.

1595 Daniel *Civ. Wars* II. xx, Which wounds with griefe poore vnrespected zeale. 1610 Healey *St. Aug. Citie of God* XVI. i. 572 Through the second inundation of impietie.. Gods religion lay wholy vnrespected. 1647 Trapp *Comm. 1 John* iii. 1 Princes unknown are unrespected. 1735 Pope *Ep. Lady* 125 From loveless youth to unrespected age, No Passion gratify'd except her Rage. 1784 Cowper *Task* I. 747 Till sabbath rites Have dwindled into unrespected forms. 1829 Scott *Anne of G.* xxxiv, I am, as you say, an unrespected exile. 1865 W. G. Palgrave *Arabia* II. 66 A retreat..where he led a tranquil nor unrespected life.

†3. Not carefully considered. *Obs.*

1601 *Pasquil & Kath.* IV. 128 The man is such a man, That he is matchlesse! Oh, I shall prophane His name with vnrespected vtterance.

unre'spectful, *a.* [UN-1 7, 5 b.] Lacking in respect; disrespectful.

1611 Cotgr., *Inofficieux*, vnofficious,..vnrespectfull, vnkind. 1621 Bp. Mountagu *Diatribæ* 284 As vnrespectfull, vndutifull and sawcy a censure as the former. 1872 J. L. Sanford *Estimates Eng. Kings* 383 The unrespectful and invidious patronage of relatives.

unre'spectfully, *adv.* (UN-1 11; cf. prec.)

a 1648 Ld. Herbert *Hen. VIII* (1683) 99 He..behaved himself so un-respectfully to the Cardinal, that he was cast into Prison. 1709 Strype *Ann. Ref.* lii. 528 How odly and unrespectfully he was used by some of his Bristol ill-willers.

unre'specting, *ppl. a.* (UN-1 10, 5 b.)

1592 Daniel *Delia* xlix, Celestiall fires, and vnrespecting powers! That deigne not view the glory of your might. 1868 Milman *St. Paul's* 377 Their tombs were respected until the unrespecting fire.

unre'spective, *a.* [UN-1 7, 5 b.]

†1. Inattentive, heedless. *Obs.*

1594 Daniel *Cleopatra* III. i, When dissolute impiety possest Th' vnrespectiue mindes of such a people. 1594 Shaks. *Rich. III*, IV. ii. 29, I will conuerse with.. vnrespectiue Boyes: none are for me, That looke into me with considerate eyes. 1633 Bp. Hall *Hard Texts, O.T.* 239 A true hearted loving neighbour is better than an overlie and unrespective brother. [1822 Scott *Nigel* Introd. Ep., Bargaining for the objects of my curiosity with an unrespective shop-lad.]

2. Making no distinction; undiscriminating.

1606 Shaks. *Tr. & Cr.* II. ii. 71 Nor the remainder Viands We do not throw in vnrespectiue siue. 1648 Bp. Hall *Select Th.* xxxiv. 102 To cast the envy of their condemnation meerly upon the absolute will of an unrespective power. *a* 1656 Hales *Gold. Rem.* III. (1673) 53 These general and unrespective judgments of God, by famine, or sword, or the like. 1850 S. Dobell *Roman* i, She was not born To..bear Rude licence of the unrespective waves. 1866 J. B. Rose tr. *Virg. Ecl. & Georg.* 107 But onward, onward,..Doth unrespective Time..in silence move.

†3. Disrespectful, rude. *Obs.*

1611 Cotgr., *Irrespectueux*, vnrespectiue, inofficious, rude. *a* 1624 Bp. M. Smith *Serm.* (1632) 23 Nothing [is] more vncertain then the minds of the multitude..: humorous, clamorous, vnrespective. *a* 1643 J. Shute *Judgem. & Mercy* (1645) 197 So in David towards Saul;.. not one un-respective word comes from him.

†4. Not deserving of respect. *Obs.*−1

1626 Donne *Serm.* 825 Which to lesse reverend and unrespective Persons we should be lesse willing to do.

Hence **unre'spectively** *adv.*, **-ness**.

1611 Speed *Hist. Gt. Brit.* IX. xxiii. §112 This great victory made the English..carelesse,..and the Forts thereabout.. were *vnrespectiuelie regarded. 1633 Bp. Hall *Hard Texts, N.T.* 152 Were he so..I would haue forborne to speake unreverently and unrespectively to him. 1656 Trapp *Comm. Heb.* vii. 23 All our learning also is soon refuted with one black Theta, which..snappeth us unrespectively without distinction. 1611 Cotgr., *Inofficiosité*, vnofficiousnesse, *vnrespectiuenesse, or want of due respect. *a* 1628 F. Grevil *Sidney* vi. (1652) 75 Finding unrespectiveness in himself..not respected by this Princely Spirit.

†**unre'spectless**, *a.* *Obs.*−1 [UN-1 5 a.] Unrespective.

1614 Rowlands *Fooles Bolt* E 3 b, Can I regard this vnrespectlesse dealing, If one be longing sicke, is this call'd healing?

unrespirable, *a.* (UN-1 7 b, 5 b.)

1807 Aikin *Dict. Chem.* II. 94/2 Foul or unrespirable air. 1836 Brande *Chem.* 392 Ammonia is..acrid, and of course unrespirable. 1839 Ure *Dict. Arts* 991 The pit..is rendered unsafe..by the unrespirable gases.

un'respited, *ppl. a.* (UN-1 8.)

1593 Nashe *Christ's Teares* 30 The Marble flore of it they made slippery, with theyr vnrespited..blood-shed. 1667 Milton *P.L.* II. 187 There to converse with ever-lasting groans, Unrespited. 1708 J. Philips *Cyder* II. 618 Horror thus, And wild Uproar, and Desolation, reign'd Unrespited.

unre'sponding, *ppl. a.* (UN-1 10.)

1858 Lytton *What will He do?* I. xiv, He pressed Lionel's unresponding hand.

unre'sponsable, *a.* (UN-1 7 b, 5 b; cf. UNRESPONSIBLE *a.*)

a 1661 Fuller *Worthies, Essex* I. (1662) 346 Of whom when still alive, he justly..demanded reparations, though since his unresponsable memory can make us no satisfaction.

†**unre'sponsal**, *a.* *Obs. rare.* [UN-1 7, 5 b.]

1. = UNRESPONSIBLE 1.

1579 *Sc. Acts, Jas. VI* (1814) III. 145/2 In caiss the committar of þe wrang be vnresponsall, he sall for the first falt be put in þe stokkis. 1579 *Reg. Privy Council Scot.* III. 231 Williame Forbes,..a brokin and unresponsall man.

2. = UNRESPONSIBLE 2.

a 1670 Hacket *Abp. Williams* I. (1692) 106 A Tithe or a Crop of Hay or Corn, which are ready to be carried away by force, by unresponsal Men.

unre'sponsible, *a.* [UN-1 7, 5 b.]

†1. Lacking substance or standing. *Obs.*

1634 *Jedburgh Town Council Records* 28 Nov. (MS.), That no person..set any of their houses or buiths to unresponsible persons. 1710 *Ess. Hist. Last Ministry* 67 The losses sustain'd by employing Unresponsible Persons in the Collection of Taxes.

2. Irresponsible.

1653 [implied in *unresponsibleness*; see below]. 1786 Burke *Charges agst. W. Hastings* v. ix, Thereby..changing him from a minister of the Company..to a dependant upon an unresponsible power. 1797 Gillies *Aristotle's Ethics & Pol.* II. 59 *note*, A power unbalanced and unresponsible, and therefore..not made for man. 1802–12 Bentham *Ration. Judic. Evid.* (1827) II. 333 Because the judges are unexperienced, uninformed, numerous, unresponsible. 1852 Grote *Greece* II. lxxxi. X. 610 Vesting in Dionysius a single-handed power..above the laws—unlimited and unresponsible.

Hence ˌ**unresponsi'bility**, **unre'sponsibleness**.

1653 Gauden *Hierasp.* 439 That unresponsiblenesse to any other;..that independence or absolute liberty in their will. 1935 E. Hemingway *Green Hills of Africa* xii. 235, I.. settled, happily, with the darkness into the unresponsibility of victory; only emerging to direct M'Cola in where to cut.

unre'sponsive, *a.* [UN-1 7, 5 b.]

1. Unable to reply.

1668 Wilkins *Real Char.* 341 To render a man Vnresponsive, is to Confound, Poze, Puzzle, Non-plus.

2. Not responsive; irresponsive.

[1775 Ash.] 1816 Scott *Old Mort.* xxxviii, The hand.. turned cold within her grasp, and lay..unresponsive to her caresses. 1871 Macduff *Mem. Patmos* xviii. 242 All now dull, pulseless, unresponsive as the insensate stone. 1886 Hall Caine *Son of Hagar* I. iv, Hugh took the proffered hand with unresponsive coldness.

Hence **unre'sponsively** *adv.*, **-ness**.

1881 E. F. Poynter *Among the Hills* II. 114 She divined the blank unresponsiveness with which her questions would be met. 1898 'Merriman' *Roden's Corner* xxv. 266 Dorothy saw this in a glance, and her own face hardened unresponsively.

un'rest, *sb.* [UN-1 4, 12. Cf. WFris. *on-*, *ûnrêst*, MLG., MHG. *unreste*; MDu. *onraste* (Du. *onrast*), MLG., MHG. *unraste* (G. *unrast*); MDu. *onruste* (Du. *onrust*), MLG. *unruste* (LG. *unrust*, *unrüst*, *unrost*), and WANREST.] Absence of rest; disturbance, turmoil, trouble.

a 1340 Hampole *Psalter* lxxxiv. 8 þe vnrest of þis life. *Ibid.* cxviii. 165 Charite puttis away..vnrest of thoght. *c* 1374 Chaucer *Troylus* IV. 879 That cause is of þis sorwe and þis vnreste. 14.. *Rule Syon Monast.* liii. in *Collect. Topogr.* (1834) I. 31 In the dortour..none schal..make any noise of unreste, aboute makyng of ther beddes. *c* 1440 *Gesta Rom.* xlvii. 196 (Harl. MS.), Wher so euer..eny discorde or vnrest was regnynge. *a* 1513 Fabyan *Chron.* VII. 417 Which tourned hym to great dishonoure and his lordes to great vnrest. 1559 *Mirr. Mag.* (1563) V iv, Furth streamde the teares, recordes of his vnrest. 1638 W. Sclater *Serm. Experimentall* 50 A sweet soliloquie of David with his soul, checking it..for the disquiet, and unrest it passionately had plunged it self into. 1685 Dryden tr. *Lucretius* III. 273 If the foolish race of man..Cou'd find as well the cause of this unrest, And all this burden lodg'd within the breast. 1815 Byron *Parisina* v, And mutters she in her unrest A name. 1849 Robertson *Serm.* Ser. I. i. (1866) 10 The unrest and the agony that lie hid in the heart of man. 1873 Symonds *Grk. Poets* i. 18 To the anarchy and unrest of transition succeeds the demand for constitutional order.

b. In pl. Somewhat *rare*.

1477 Earl Rivers (Caxton) *Dictes* (1877) 17 Of thought cometh the wakyngis and vnrestis. 1513 Douglas *Æneid* XIII. ii. 74 Be all wais noysum and onrestis, And all that horribill was. *c* 1611 Chapman *Iliad* VIII. 405 Both Goddesses..contriving still afflicted Troy's unrests. 1628 Wither *Brit. Rememb.* VI. 1957 Nor, thereby, many other mens unrests Occasion they alone.

†**un'rest**, *v.* *Obs.* [UN-2 3.] *trans.* To disturb, trouble.

1382 Wyclif *1 Sam.* xxvi. 14 Who art thou that criest, and vnrestist the kyng? *c* 1430 *Life St. Kath.* (1884) 49 A Cyte.. whom noon aduersite troubleth..ne noon heuynesse vnresteth. *c* 1440 *Pallad. on Husb.* VI. 174 Good is hem to sle, For they the swarm vnrestith.

un'restable, *a.* (UN-1 7 b.)

1662 J. Chandler *Van Helmont's Oriat.* 74 This therefore is the unrestable appointment of the water, that by proceeding continually upwards and downwards, it [etc.].

un'rested, *ppl. a.*1 [UN-1 8.]

a. Not laid to rest. **b.** Not refreshed by rest.

a. 1607 Chapman *Bussy d'Ambois* V. iv. 154 My unrested soul. 1612 —— *Rev. Bussy d'Ambois* IV. v. 82 Th' unrested spirit of your slaughter'd brother.

b. [1775 Ash.] 1846 Worcester (citing Erving). 1940 N. Last *Diary* 22 Oct. in *Nella Last's War* (1983) iii. 81, I got up, tired and unrested, after a very broken night. 1981 D. Boggis *Time to Betray* xvii. 94 Nigel lay sleepily, unrested, worried.

un'rested, *ppl. a.*2 [UN-2 8, 5.] Thrown out of the rest.

1760–1 Smollett *Launcelot Greaves* xix, Sir Launcelot, perceiving his rival's spear unrested, had just time to throw up the point of his own.

un'restful, *a.* [UN-1 7. App. not in use between 16th and 19th century: cf. RESTFUL *a.*]

1. Restless, stirring, unquiet. (Freq. *c* 1875–.)

1382 Wyclif *Baruch* iv. 15 A folc vnsaciable, or vnrestful, and of an other tunge. *c* 1400 *Apol. Loll.* 104 þei are..vnschamful to axe,..vnrestful tul þei tak, vnkynd wan þei han tane. *a* 1420 *Wycliffite Bible* Prov. vii. 13 *marg.*, With wowing cheer; that is, vnresteful, and with out schame. *c* 1475 *Cath. Angl.* (A.) 305/1 Vn Restfulle, *inquietus*. 1533 More *Debell. Salem* Wks. 961/2 That good peacible folke.. should not for suche inquiete & vnrestfull wretches without some ruffle liue in peace long. 1553 *Primer in Lit. & Doc. Edw. VI* (1844) 474 We are..besieged of cruel and unrestful enemies. 1565 Abp. Parker *Corr.* (Parker Soc.) 237 The talk ..is much increased, and unrestful they be, and I alone they say am in fault. 1837 Carlyle *Fr. Rev.* II. v. ix, So wags.. this unrestful World, day after day. 1891 *Spectator* 7 Mar. 340/1 This unrestful and fussy energy.

†2. Disturbed, troubled. *Obs.*

a 1395 Hylton *Scala Perf.* II. xxvii. (W. de W. 1494), It bereth downe the thoughte: and makyth it vnrestfull. 1435 Misyn *Fire of Love* II. vi. 82 Lorde, þou art my takar, þat malicius prikkyngis of my fraward enmys me make not vnrestfull.

3. Marked by absence of rest or quiet.

14.. *Rule Syon Monast.* liii. in *Collect. Topogr.* (1834) I. 31 Suche as gretly rowte or make any unrestful noyse in ther sleppe..schal be purveyd a nother place, wher they may slepe withoute unrestyng of other. *c* 1445 Pecock *Donet* 94 þouȝ al þis lijf be..laboriose, vnrestful. 1542 Udall *Erasm. Apoph.* 242 The bedde of a persone beeyng in greate debte is an unrestefull thyng. 1548 Bodrugan *Epit. King's Title* (1873) 254 What properties procedeth of warre, but outragious costes,..consumyng anger, vnrestfull quietness. 1600 *Look About You* i. A 2, If drousie age keepe not thy stiffened ioyntes On thy vnrestfull bed. 1884 *Pall Mall G.* 9 Dec. 11/2 There is on every face a craving, unrestful expression.

Hence **un'restfully** *adv.*

1483 *Cath. Angl.* 305/1 Vn Restfully, *jnquiete, jnoportune*.

un'restfulness. (UN-1 12; cf. prec.)

1382 Wyclif *Luke* xi. 8 If he schal contynue knockynge, ..for his vnrestefulnesse he schal rise, and ȝyue to hym. *c* 1450 tr. *De Imitatione* III. xxxiii. 102 Of inordinate loue.. growiþ all vnrestfulnes of herte. 1491 Caxton *Vitas Patr.* (W. de W. 1495) II. 234 b/2 The holy fader..axed hym, yf.. he sholde praye god for hym; that he wolde releue hym from this unrestfulnesse. *c* 1557 Abp. Parker *Ps.* lv. 157, I would me flitche..to wildernes: More there to dwell, than here wyth such in such unrestfulnes. 1579 E. K. *Gloss. to Spenser's Sheph. Cal.* March (Emblem), Loue..vexeth the body..with vnrestfulnesse all night.

un'resting, *vbl. sb.* ? *Obs.* [f. UNREST *v.*, or UN-2 8.] The depriving of rest.

14.. [see UNRESTFUL *a.* 3]. 1615 T. Adams *Blacke Devill* 9 Well; gone he is out of this Man; and we must therein consider..1. His vnroosting. 2. His vnresting. [Hence in 1670 Eachard *Cont. Clergy* 68.]

un'resting, *ppl. a.* (UN-1 10.)

1582 Stanyhurst *Æneis* IV. (Arb.) 114 The poore vnresting Dido could catch no such happye Season too be quiet. 1604 A. Scoloker *Daiphantus* F 4 The wandring soule Seeking for rest in his vnresting spirit. *a* 1652 Brome *Eng. Moor* IV. iv, What is she? I am fear-struck Tis some unresting shadow. 1748 Thomson *Cast. Indol.* II. lxxxi, But ay the ruthless driver goads them on,..Ne ever find they rest from their unresting fone. 1812 Byron *Ch. Har.* I. lxxxiii, Life-abhorring gloom Wrote on his faded brow curst Cain's unresting doom. 1856 H. Dixon *Post & Paddock* x. 168 Those ballads, which they sing with such un-resting diligence. 1870 M. D. Conway *Earthw. Pilgr.* xxi. 256 This unresting life of the enquiring soul.

Hence **un'restingly** *adv.*; **un'restingness**.

1831 Carlyle *Sartor Res.* I. x, The silent Arachnes that weave unrestingly in our imagination. 1839 De Quincey *Roman Meals* Wks. (1854) III. 269 *note*, The German imagination has been most struck by the duration of the man's life,..the English, by the unrestingness.., his incapacity of repose.

un'restless, *a.* (UN-1 5 a.)

1513 Douglas *Æneid* IV. x. 13 The onrestles fey spreit.. Of this wnhappy Phenician Dido. 1894 in Heslop *Northumberland Gloss.* s.v.

†**un'restly**, *adv.* *Obs.*−1 [UN-1 11.] Not restfully.

1561 Hollybush *Hom. Apoth.* 6 b, If one slepeth vnrestly, let him eat lettice.

unre'stored, *ppl. a.* (UN-1 8.)

c 1445 Pecock *Donet* 87 His ordinaunce þat man..schulde be restorid into saluacioun, þouȝ aungel..was left vnrestorid. 1473 *Acta Auditorum* (1839) 25/2 To restore again the samyn [cattle] in sa fer as is vnrestorit. 1500–20 Dunbar *Poems* xxi. 64 O! quha sall weild the wrang possessioun,..Quhilk vnrestorit helpis no confessioun? *c* 1586 C'tess Pembroke *Ps.* CXL. iv, Flames shall fling them low, Ay unrestor'd to drown in deepest woe. 1606 Shaks. *Ant. & Cl.* III. vi. 27 Then does he say, he lent me Some shipping vnrestor'd. *a* 1649 Drumm. of Hawth. *Hist. Jas. V*, Wks. (1711) 81 Whose Father was banished for Treason ..and died un-restored. 1742 Young *Nt. Th.* II. 643 If unrestor'd by this, despair your cure. 1818 Byron *Ch. Har.* IV. xi, The Bucentaur lies rotting unrestored. 1860 Pusey *Min. Proph.* 596 The Jews He brought back, Edom He left unrestored. 1899 C. K. Paul *Memories* 129 The old unrestored choir of St. Paul's Cathedral.

unre'storing, *ppl. a.* (UN-1 10.)

1811 W. Taylor in Robberds *Mem.* (1843) II. 333 The corse, the spectre, the veiling pall, the unrestoring tomb. 1823 Lamb *Elia* II. *Old Margate Hoy*, Ships, and sumless treasures swallowed up in the unrestoring depths.

unre'strainable, *a.* (UN-^{1} 7 b, 5 b.)
1430–40 LYDG. *Bochas* III. xx. (1561) 86/1 Their colorike fumes, ye fury vnrestraynable. **1608** BP. J. KING *Serm.* 5 *Nov.* 34 In the timely execution of your Lawes, and.. coercion of their vnrestrainable audaciousnesse. **1609** HOLLAND *Amm. Marcell.* 187 Like as out of a drie wood the sparkes.., with an unrestrainable course, reach to the daunger of countrey townes. *a* **1711** KEN *Edmund* Poet. Wks. 1721 II. 111 Wonder not that a Virgin makes this Court, Of Love the unrestrainable Effort. **1815** ABERNETHY *Surg. Obs.* (ed. 2) 125 *note*, An unrestrainable hæmorrhagic tendency. **1863** MOUAT *Andaman Islanders* 227 An unrestrainable fit of laughter.
Hence **unre'strainably** *adv.*
1615 SANDYS *Trav.* 148 A Iew.. did poison his sonne, whom he knew to be vnrestrainably lasciuious. **1849** RUSKIN *Seven Lamps* i. §12. 23 There is occasionally a burst upwards and blossoming unrestrainably to the sky.

unre'strained, *ppl. a.* [UN-^{1} 8.]
1. Not kept in check or under control; allowed free course or vent.
a **1600** HOOKER *Remedie agst. Sorrow* (1612) 3 Naturall compassion.. caused them.. to poure forth vnrestrained teares. **1712** BERKELEY *Pass. Obed.* Wks. 1871 III. 131 So unrestrained [are] the passions of men. **1796** MME. D'ARBLAY *Camilla* V. 516 Her tears now flowed fast from unrestrained delight. **1828** LYTTON *Pelham* II. xxv, They all rose in a mirth sufficiently unrestrained to be any thing but patrician. **1879** M^{c}CARTHY *Own Times* II. xxiii. 172 He was attacked with all the bitterness of a.. very unrestrained animosity.
b. Not restricted or limited.
1622 [see UNPINIONED^2.] **1647** CLARENDON *Hist. Reb.* II. §41 There being.. an unrestrained Intercourse between the King's Camp and Edenborough. **1670** —— *Ess.* Tracts (1727) 184 The spacious fields of their unlimited and unrestrained contemplation. **1776** ADAM SMITH *W.N.* v. i. I. ii. (1904) II. 414 The emulation which an unrestrained competition never fails to excite. **1806** SURR *Winter in London* III. 219 The unrestrained intermixture of ranks.. is a remarkable trait of your national manners. **1856** KANE *Arct. Expl.* I. xxviii. 364 The men.. had frequent and unrestrained intercourse with them. **1899** *Allbutt's Syst. Med.* VII. 376 The 'unantagonised' or 'unrestrained' influence exerted by the cerebellum.
c. Not limited in application.
1827 JARMAN *Powell's Devises* II. 117 They admitted that the general words, if unrestrained, would carry the reversion.
2. Not subjected (or subject) to restraint in respect of action or conduct.
a **1586** SIDNEY *Arcadia* II. xxix, Zelmanes.. unrestrained parts, the minde & eie, had their free course to the delicate Philoclea. **1593** SHAKS. *Rich. II*, v. iii. 7 There.. he dayly doth frequent, With vnrestrained loose Companions. **1628** T. SPENCER *Logick* 34 The vnrestrained, and free choyse of the will. **1691** HARTCLIFFE *Virtues* 68 He that is guilty of the Excess, is said to be.. unrestrained and let loose to all Debauchery. **1751** EARL ORRERY *Remarks Swift* (1752) 67 With heads and hearts elated by affluence, and un-restrained by foresight or discretion. **1760–72** H. BROOKE *Fool of Qual.* (1809) III. 122 What will not power effect, when unrestrained by conscience? **1825** SCOTT *Betrothed* ii, The revellers were unrestrained by the stricter rules of good-breeding. **1864** TREVELYAN *Compet. Wallah* (1866) 349 The free and unrestrained life of an English lady. **1890** *Retrospect Med.* CII. 351 He walks about the room,.. and in many respects is unrestrained in his movements.
absol. **1770** GLOVER *Leonidas* (ed. 5) IV. 713 The un-restrain'd and free Will fly from danger.
b. In appositive use: Without restraint; unrestrainedly.
1596 *Edward III*, III. ii. 52 Slaughter and mischiefe walke within your streets, And, vnrestrained, make hauock as they passe. **1812** BYRON *Ch. Har.* I. lxxxix, While o'er the parent clime prowls Murder unrestrain'd. **1848** THACKERAY *Van. Fair* xxxv, The girls indulged unrestrained in their grief. **1867** E. F. BOWDEN *Fathers of Desert* 374 Vice stalks abroad unrestrained.
3. Free from restraint of manner; easy, natural.
1856 FROUDE *Hist. Eng.* I. ii. 159 His letters.. are simple, easy, and unrestrained. **1876** T. HARDY *Ethelberta* xliii, Whose manner.. had little in common with Sol's warm and unrestrained bearing.
Hence **unre'strainedness**.
[**1775** ASH.] **1889** *Pop. Sci. Monthly* July 296 No men on earth ever have had liberty in the sense of unrestrainedness of action.

unre'strainedly, *adv.* [UN-^{1} 11.] Without restraint.
1655 EARL ORRERY *Parthen.* II. III. 287 Shee shedd hirs [*sc.* tears] the more vnrestrain'dly. *Ibid.* II. VII. 653 Surena permitted Parthenissa unrestrainedly to visit him. **1852** THACKERAY *Esmond* I. ix, He.. yawned unrestrainedly. **1862** H. AÏDE *Carr of Carrlyon* II. 57 She and her child wept unrestrainedly. **1876** MISS YONGE *Womankind* v. 32 She will see enough of them unrestrainedly to understand their dispositions.

unre'straint. (UN-^{1} 12.)
1804 *Ann. Rev.* II. 235 The spirit of antijacobinism was as yet so strongly bent on the restoration of royal un-restraint. **1867** MILL *Subj. Women* (1869) 66 His conduct.. in the unrestraint of home. **1885** *Encycl. Brit.* XVIII. 146/1 A simple and fine and light stroke,.. and unrestraint in the flow of writing.

unre'stricted, *ppl. a.* (UN-^{1} 8.)
1766 SMOLLETT *Trav.* xvii, His military power and unrestricted authority. **1785** H. WALPOLE *Mod. Gardening* Wks. 1798 II. 537 They extended their branches unrestricted. **1807** WORDSW. *White Doe* IV. 60 Happy as others of her kind, That.. Range unrestricted as the wind. **1854** RÖHNER *Mus. Composition* III. 197 Unrestricted Canon is founded upon a melodic subject which [etc.]. **1884** *Contemp. Rev.* Oct. 525 The unrestricted intermeddling of the State.
Hence **unre'strictedly** *adv.*; **-'strictedness**.
1844 W. H. MAXWELL *Wand. Highl.* I. 195 To him, every discovery.. is unrestrictedly unfolded. **1846** G. S. FABER *Lett. Tractar. Secess.* 42 The unrestrictedness of his own liberty and power. **1861** WHYTE MELVILLE *Good for Nothing* I. 293 A process.. that the weaker sex seldom leave unrestrictedly to their servants.

unre'strictive, *a.* (UN-^{1} 7, 5 b.)
1817 H. T. COLEBROOKE *Algebra*, etc. 329 The foregoing rule.. is unrestrictive. **1863** COWDEN CLARKE *Shaks. Char.* xx. 504 Temperament, un-restrictive teaching, and a desire to amend.

un'resty, *a. Obs.* exc. *Sc. dial.* [UN-^{1} 4, 7. Cf. WFris. *on-*, *ûnrestich*, MDu. *onrustich* (Du. *onrustig*), MLG. *unrust-*, *unrostich*.] Unquiet; full of unrest.
a **1340** HAMPOLE *Psalter* cxl. 10 Kepe me fra lettyngis of vnristy men. *c* **1374** CHAUCER *Troylus* v. 1355, I dar not pleyne more, But humbely.. Yow wryte ich myne vnresty sorwes sore. *c* **1412** HOCCLEVE *De Reg. Princ.* 116 Boote fonde I non In myn vnresty bed lenger to lye. ? *a* **1500** *Lydgate's Ballad* in Thynne *Chaucer* (1530) 374/2 Unto vnresty bothe rest and remedye Fruteful to al tho that in her assye. **1606** S. GARDINER *Bk. Angling* 137 Worldly cares maketh a man very vnrestie with himself.

unre'sultive, *a.* (UN-^{1} 7.)
1833 MRS. BROWNING *Prometh. Bound* 451, I discern An empty wish,—and unresultive work.

unre'tained, *ppl. a.* (UN-^{1} 8.)
[**1775** ASH.] **1822** COLERIDGE *Lett.* (1895) 720 The taste for unconnected, and for that reason unretained single thoughts.

unre'taliated, *ppl. a.* (UN-^{1} 8.)
1683 TRYON *Way to Health* 630 Men.. turn the natural use of things into Wantonness, which cannot pass unretaliated. **1805** FOSTER *Ess.* (1806) I. 62 The overawed timidity and unretaliated injuries of the unfortunate beings within his power. **1831** SCOTT *Cast. Dang.* xix, Obliged to submit to national insults, unretaliated and un-revenged.

unre'tarded, *ppl. a.* (UN-^{1} 8.)
1615 T. ADAMS *Lycanthropy* 7 What Paul speakes of his unretarded execution of Christs message. **1636** B. JONSON *Discov.* Wks. (Rtldg.) 747/1 Which they will utter unretarded without any shamefastness. **1793** V. KNOX *Let. to Yng. Nobleman* Wks. 1824 V. 109 Then go on in your virtuous progress, unretarded by those.. who laugh at your virtuous solicitude. **1820** E. KEAN in *9th Rep. Hist. MSS. Comm.* App. 488/2 Friends such as will come uninvited, [and] go unretarded.

un'retched, *ppl. a. rare*$^{-1}$. [UN-^{1} 8 c.] Not stretched *out*.
1674 N. FAIRFAX *Bulk & Selv.* 33 When our Author tells us.. of a *now* longer than Ages, and a being unretcht out.

unre'tentive, *a.* (UN-^{1} 7, 5 b.)
1748 CHESTERF. *Lett.* (1774) I. 336 Discovering to them such an unretentive weakness as must convince them that you will tell it to twenty others. **1782** BAKER *Biog. Dramatica* I. 238/2 So unretentive was his memory. **1825** COLERIDGE *Aids Refl.* 363 You are not so unretentive a Scholar as to have forgotten the *pateris et auro* of your Virgil. **1851** [J. B. HUME] *Poems Early Years* 165 What further may have chanc'd my sleepy brain, In unretentive dulness, noted not.

un'retinued, *ppl. a.* (UN-^{1} 8.)
1855 SINGLETON *Virgil* I. 378 To be left Forlorn unto herself she seemeth, aye, Un-retinued.

unre'tired, *ppl. a.* (UN-^{1} 8.)
1648 HEXHAM II, *Ongeweken*, Vnretyred, or Vnretreated. **1766** W. GORDON *Gen. Counting-ho.* 36 Bills unretired at the dates they are payable.

unre'torted, *ppl. a.* (UN-^{1} 8.)
1618 *Barnevelt's Apol.* Ded. A 4 Else I shrewdly feare, lest many.. fall away to that side, where we are assaulted with vnretorted weapons.

unre'touched, *ppl. a.* (UN-^{1} 8.)
1880 SWINBURNE *Stud. Shakes.* 218 Possibly we have a survival of some lines' length, not unretouched by Fletcher.

unre'tractable, *a.* (UN-^{1} 7 b.)
1627 JACKSON *Creed* VI. x. §1 That God.. did set the course of nature a-going with an irresistible and unretractable swinge. **1900** OMOND *Romantic Triumph* 276 An unretractable gift to France.

unre'tracted, *ppl. a.* (UN-^{1} 8.)
1646 HAMMOND *Tracts* 27 Any such act of sin unretracted by repentance. **1697** COLLIER *Ess. Mor. Subj.* II. 66 Malevolence shewn.. in a single Outrage unretracted. **1739** *Wks. Learned* I. 73 Content to leave the Calumnies of Fatalism and Spinozism unretracted. **1834** MACKINTOSH *Revolution of 1688* ix. 257 To consider the silence of the King as a virtual assent to their unretracted condition. **1855** MILMAN *Lat. Chr.* XIV. iv. VI. 502 The monkish Latin satire maintained its unretracted protest against the Church.

unre'treating, *ppl. a.* (UN-^{1} 10.)
1791 COWPER *Iliad* v. 590 The powers of Troy.. the Grecians dense Expected, unretreating, void of fear. **1858** J. ROBERTSON *Poems* 78 As light is mixed in the unretreating air.

† **unre'trievable**, *a. Obs.* (UN-^{1} 7 b, 5 b.)
1705 STANHOPE *Paraphr.* I. 241 The unretrievable Misery of those who will not suffer themselves to be rescued from Destruction.

unre'trievingly, *adv.* (UN-^{1} 11.)
1844 MRS. BROWNING *Cry of Children* 145 They.. Are worn as if with age, yet unretrievingly The harvest of its memories cannot reap.

un'retrograde, *a.* (UN-^{1} 7.)
1817 MALTHUS *Popul.* (ed. 5) II. 231 A regular and unretrograde increase.

un'retted, *ppl. a.* (UN-^{1} 8.)
1839 URE *Dict. Arts* 490 Unretted flax. **1856** *Farmer's Mag.* Nov. 379 Either green or unretted straw.

unre'turnable, *a.* [UN- 7 b, 5 b.]
† **1.** Admitting of no return. *Obs.*
Chiefly as a rendering of L. *irremeabilis*.
1513 DOUGLAS *Æneid* VI. i. 60 The naimcouth hous, that Laborinthus hait, Full of wrinkillit vnreturnable dissait. *Ibid.* vii. 4 The fludis bank.., Quhais passage is vnreturnable went. **1611** COTGR., *Irremeable*, vnreturnable, or, from which one cannot goe backe. **1648** HEXHAM II, *Onwederkeerlick*, vnreturnable [Kil. *irremeabilis*].
2. Incapable of being returned.
1740 RICHARDSON *Pamela* (1741) II. 343, I am even oppress'd with unreturnable Obligations. **1788** MRS. HUGHES *Henry & Isabella* III. 151 The unexpected, and as he esteemed it, unreturnable proof of friendship he had given him. **1795** *Jemima* II. 195 Having such unreturnable benefits to thank him for. **1884** *Marshall's Tennis Cuts* 114 He can.. place it in the opposite corner at such a pace that the stroke is practically unreturnable.
Hence **unre'turnably** *adv.*
1513 DOUGLAS *Æneid* v. x. 81 Laborynthus.. a thousand slychtis wrocht, For to dissave all wncouth tharin brocht, To wavir and er thar wnreturnably. **1788** MRS. HUGHES *Henry & Isabella* II. 72 Where there is a certain equality.. of advantages, so as to leave neither parties unreturnably obliged to the other.

unre'turned, *ppl. a.* [UN-^{1} 8.]
1. Not having returned or come back.
1589 *Reg. Privy Council Scot.* IV. 428 The Chancellair.. being yit unreturned oute of Lauder. **1600** FAIRFAX *Tasso* xv. xxvi, They whom storme hath forced that way sence, Are drowned all, or vnreturn'd from thence. **1802** *Noble Wanderers* I. 131 Selisme was still unreturned:—.. my suspicions gained strength. **1885** W. WATSON *Sonn., Soudanese* 13 Thousands that weep their warriors unreturn'd.
2. That is not reciprocated or responded to.
a **1643** S. GODOLPHIN *Constancy* i, Love unreturn'd, howe'er the flame Seem great and pure, may [etc.]. **1710** ADDISON *Tatler* No. 250 ¶10 Supercilious Looks, unreturned Smiles. **1766** GOLDSM. *Hermit* xvii, Dost thou.. grieve for friendship unreturned? **1820** SCOTT *Monast.* xx, I.. will brook no insult unreturned. **1896** *McClure's Mag.* VI. 492 The proud and unreturned gaze of the dead who have died in their glory.

unre'turning, *ppl. a.* (UN-^{1} 10.)
a **1628** F. GREVIL *Sidney* (1652) 159 Yet these unreturning steps seemed well worth the observing. **1816** BYRON *Ch. Har.* III. xxvii, And Ardennes.. Grieving.. Over the unreturning brave. **1856** WHITTIER *Panorama* 507 Ghosts of unreturning sails. **1897** *Outing* XXIX. 440/2 We grew weary of waiting for the unreturning hounds.

unre'turningly, *adv.* (UN-^{1} 11; cf. prec.)
1818 SHELLEY *Rosal. & Helen* 668 Like a vile weed Which the sea casts unreturningly. **1845–6** TRENCH *Huls. Lect.* Ser. II. ii. 175 That sepulchre, to which it had seen its sons.. unreturningly descend.

unre'vealable, *a.* (UN-^{1} 7 b, 5 b.)
1611 COTGR., *Irreveland*, vnreuealable, not to be reuealed. ? **1826** COLERIDGE *Ne Plus Ultra* 11 The Dragon foul and fell —The un-revealable, And hidden one. **1846** G. MOORE *Power of Soul* (ed. 2) 9 These proposers of an unrevealable divinity.

unre'vealed, *ppl. a.* (UN-^{1} 8, 5 b.)
1529 MORE *Dyaloge* I. Wks. 167/2 If there were any thing.. that in the church sometyme was doubted and reputed for vnreueled and vnknowen. **1543–4** *Act 35 Hen. VIII*, c. 5 §1 Untrue accusacions.. kept secret unreveled. **1592** KYD *Sp. Trag.* III. ii. 9 If this incomparable murder.. Shall vnreueald and vnreuenged passe. **1651** HOBBES *Leviath.* III. xl. 250 The effect.. of the unrevealed will, and of the power of God. **1697** DRYDEN *Æneis* VI. 374 Ye realms, yet unreveal'd to human sight. **1732** BERKELEY *Alciphr.* v. §27 Religion of any kind, either revealed or unrevealed. **1798** LAMB *R. Gray* iv, The secret, unrevealed, hung upon his conscience. **1850** TENNYSON *In Mem.* xxxi, The rest remaineth unreveal'd; He told it not. **1875** MANNING *Mission H. Ghost* i. 9 God in His unrevealed mercies will [etc.].

unre'vealing, *ppl. a.* (UN-^{1} 10, 5 d.)
1628 FELTHAM *Resolves* II. xxiv. 79 The Physician that hath a Soueraigne Receit, and dyeth vnreuealing it, robbes the world of many blessings. **1835** LYTTON *Rienzi* II. iii, The greater barons.. preserved a strict and unrevealing silence. **1899** G. MATHESON *Stud. Portr. Christ* xv. 182 We have all our unrevealing moments—our moments when the spring of life seems dry.

unre'venged, *ppl. a.* (UN-^{1} 8.)
1533 BELLENDEN *Livy* IV. xv. (S.T.S.) II. 105 Than tempaneus.. drew þame all togidder.., nocht vnrevengit of his Inemyis. **1553** EDEN *Treat. New Ind.* (Arb.) 39 Hauinge thus sustayned so greuous iniuries vnreuenged. **1621** BRATHWAIT *Nat. Embassie* (1877) 27 Her husbands death,.. effected, but not vnreuenged. **1669** SHADWELL *Royal Shepherdess* II, *Neander.* O Madam! your eyes will revenge your quarrels. *Evadne.* Or they must be unreveng'd, for you. **1726** POPE *Odyss.* XVI. 277 With such a foe th' unequal fight to try, Were by false courage unreveng'd to die. **1796** *Monthly Mag.* II. 449 Ampanani never bled unrevenged. **1821** SHELLEY *Hellas* 1021 Keep holy This jubilee of unrevenged blood!

unre'vengeful, *a.* (UN-[1] 7.)
1660 *Nicholas Papers* (Camden) IV. 220 The Kinge of Englands..unreuengefull disposition. *a* **1670** HACKET *Abp. Williams* I. (1693) 191 He was un-revengeful,..and no longer displeased with those he overcame.

unre'vengefulness. (UN-[1] 12.)
a **1586** SIDNEY *Arcadia* II. ix, A Tyrant also, not thorow.. unrevengefulnes,..but..of a wanton crueltie.

unre'venging, *ppl. a.* (UN-[1] 10.)
a **1593** MARLOWE & NASHE *Dido* IV. i, Curse that vnreuenging Ioue, Whose flintie darts slept in Typhous den. **1711** POPE *Lett.* (1735) I. 169 The unrevenging Spirit of primitive Christianity.

unre'vengingly, *adv.* (UN-[1] 11.)
1650 B. *Discolliminium* 15 A King..that..Reign'd justly, peaceably, and un-revengingly after.

un'revenue, *v.* (UN-[2] 4.)
1673 BP. S. PARKER *Reproof Reh. Transp.* 142 They had unrevenued the Clergy.

un'revenued, *ppl. a.* (UN-[1] 8.)
1641 MILTON *Reform.* I. 22 He that will mould a modern Bishop into a primitive, must yeeld him to be..undiocest, unrevenu'd, unlorded.

un'reverence, *sb.* [UN-[1] 12, 5 b.]
†**1.** Lack of reverence; irreverence. *Obs.*
1388 WYCLIF *Ecclus.* xxv. 29 The ire and vnreuerence of a womman is grete schenschipe. **1422** YONG tr. *Secreta Secret.* 135 Wreth engendryth vnreuerence, Vnreuerence engendryth enemyte. **1491** CAXTON *Vitas Patr.* (W. de W. 1495) V. xiv. 343 b/2 Defaultes commysed in the unreuerence of god. **1526** *Pilgr. Perf.* (W. de W. 1531) 237 That is the moost vnreuerence that may be done to god. **1597** BEARD *Theatre God's Judgem.* (1612) 317 The disobedience, vn-reuerence, & contempt of children towards their parents. **1649** W. SCLATER *Comm. Malachy* (1650) 27 Unreverence more displeaseth, than outward observance can please. **1684** BAXTER *Answ. Theol. Dial.* 16 Praying with the Hatt on, is..a sign of unreverence.
2. Used as the negative of REVERENCE *sb.* 6.
1823 W. H. LYTTLETON in *Corr. Lady Lyttleton* (1912) 248 The sooner I see your Un-Reverence a-shooting the better I shall be pleased.

un'reverence, *v.* [UN-[2] 3.] *trans.* To treat irreverently.
1553 BALE *Vocacyon* 11 This write I, not in vnreuerencinge the sacrament, but [etc.]. **1642** FULLER *Holy & Prof. St.* III. xxiv. 222 S. Paul thought their materiall Church..abused and unreverenced, by their lay meetings of Love-feasts therein.

un'reverenced, *ppl. a.* (UN-[1] 8.)
a **1470** H. PARKER *Dives & Pauper* (1496) 35/2 Oftentyme that crosse that the preest holdeth..is full unreuerenced. **1603** KNOLLES *Hist. Turks* (1621) 101 The sepulchre of our blessed Sauiour..not vnreuerenced by the Turkes themselues. **1881** H. JAMES *Portr. Lady* lii, She saw..the dry, staring fact that she had been a dull un-reverenced tool.

†**un'reverency.** (UN-[1] 12.)
c **1680** *Roxb. Ball.* (1874) II. 195, I must not come in place where their friends merry be, Lest I should my son disgrace with my unreverency.

un'reverend, *a.* [UN-[1] 7, 5 b.]
†**1.** Irreverent. *Obs.* (Common *c* 1580–1660.)
1562 in Strype *Ann. Ref.* xxviii. (1709) 295 All unreverend speaking of God's holy predestination. **1584** R. DUDLEY *Lett.* 161 Inveying against their souerain with..vnreuerend tearmes, and insolent controlmentes. **1591** SHAKS. *Two Gent.* II. vi. 14 Fie, fie, vnreuerend tongue, to call her bad. **1613** DEKKER *Four Birdes Noah's Arke* Wks. (Grosart) V. 20 Cleanse my heart..from all foule, loose and vnreuerend languages. **1659** W. CHAMBERLAYNE *Pharon.* IV. i. 257 That it might unreverend gazers tell It once was sacred. **1820** LAMB *Elia* I. *Oxford in Vac.*, They rather hold such curiosities to be impertinent—unreverend.
2. Unworthy of reverence.
[**1828–32** WEBSTER.] **1874** J. THOMSON *City Dreadf. Nt.* XVIII. iv, Long grey unreverend locks befouled with mire. **1876** GEO. ELIOT *Dan. Der.* lxii, The presence of this unreverend father..affected Mirah with..shame and grief.
Hence †**un'reverendly** *adv.*, irreverently. *Obs.*
1603 KNOLLES *Hist. Turks* (1621) 352 Thou hast vnreuerendly spoken. **1663** BOYLE *Usef. Exp Nat. Philos.* II. iv. 118 He..was wont..(unreverendly enough) to compare our Physitians to Bishops. **1673** *S'too him Bayes* 24 Whose person you shall not find me speak so unreverendly of.

un'reverent, *a.* Now *rare.* [UN-[1] 7, 5 b.]
1. Irreverent: **a.** Of actions, conduct, etc.
In frequent use from *c* 1550 to *c* 1640.
1388 WYCLIF *Ecclus.* xxiii. 17 Thi mouth be not customable to vnreuerent speche. **1532** MORE *Confut. Tindale* Wks. 622/1 Such euyl fashion of vnreuerent railing vpon great personages. **1583** BABINGTON *Commandm.* (1590) 220 If we be parentes, and greeued with vnreuerent regarde in our children of vs. **1608** WILLET *Hexapla Exod.* 62 The Corinthians were chastised..for vnreuerent receiuing of the Lords supper. *a* **1661** FULLER *Worthies, Yorks.* III. (1662) 206 Greatly guilty in his ill language, which to any Author was uncivil, to a Bishop unreverent. **1858** H. BUSHNELL *Nat. & Supernat.* x. (1864) 313 That unreverent feeble laxity, that lets the errors be as good as the truths.
b. Of persons.
1526 *Pilgr. Perf.* (W. de W. 1531) 85 b, Se thou be not vnreuerent or stately of behauour to thy company. **1552** in *Vicary's Anat.* (1888) App. xvi. 313 A swearer, or an vnreuerent vser of his mouth. **1612** T. TAYLOR *Comm. Titus* ii. 12 They durst not shewe themselues..so vnreuerent and retchles in hearing, as most men doe. **1675** BAXTER *Cath. Theol.* I. I. 9 We must be very fearful and not unreverent and rash, in ascribing such a..lusus of notions to God.
transf. *c* **1590** *Sir T. More* II. iv. 134 Your vnreuerent knees, Make them your feet to kneele to be forgyuen! **1593** SHAKS. *Rich. II*, II. i. 123 Wert thou not Brother to great Edwards sonne, This tongue..Should run thy head from thy vnreuerent shoulders.
†**2.** = UNREVEREND *a.* 2. *Obs.*[-1]
1576 LAMBARDE *Peramb. Kent* 256 Erasmus opinion and iudgment touching such vnreuerent Reliques. **1659** W. CHAMBERLAYNE *Pharon.* III. iv. 356 Their rage Neglected youth slights like unreverent age.
Hence †**un'reverentness**, irreverence. *Obs.*
1579 NORTHBROOKE *Dicing* 32 [They] that do vse and handle vpon scaffolds Gods diuine mysteries with such vnreuerentnes. **1636** HENSHAW *Horæ Succ.* 294 That unreverentnesse..which they durst not use to this or that Mr Gentleman, they use to God.

†**un'reverently,** *adv.* *Obs.* [UN-[1] 11, 5 b.] Irreverently; without reverence. (Common *c* 1510–1660.)
c **1386** CHAUCER *Pars. T.* ¶582 Whan they treten vnreuerently the sacrement of the Auter. **1421** HOCCLEVE *Jereslaus' Wife* 218 He answerde and spak vnreuerently. *c* **1449** PECOCK *Repr.* V. xv. 563 The ix[e] principal gouernaunce for which summe of the lay peple vnwijsly and vnreuerentli blamen the clergie. **1543** GRAFTON *Contn. Harding* 460 His corps was brought vnreuerently from the toure..vnto Poules. **1576** FLEMING *Panopl. Epist.* 80 That is supposed a loose kinde of writing, to talke of any man vnreuerently. **1638** BP. MOUNTAGU *Art. Enq. Visit.* A 4 b, Hath any of your parish unreverently used your Minister? *a* **1677** MANTON *Serm. Ps. cxix*, cxxxi. Wks. 1725 I. 605/1 Will not God be as severe to me, if I behave my self unreverently?

unre'versable, *a.* (UN-[1] 7 b, 5 b.)
1802–12 BENTHAM *Ration. Judic. Evid.* (1827) I. 141 The decision remaining unreversed, and, but for legislative authority, unreversable.

unre'versed, *ppl. a.* (UN-[1] 8.)
1591 SHAKS. *Two Gent.* III. i. 223 The doome (Which vnreuerst stands in effectuall force). **1648** PRYNNE *Plea for the Lords* 63 His sentence..remaines..unreversed. **1657** *Decree Excheq., Hatfield Chase* 7 While the said Decree stands in force, and unreversed. **1802–12** [see prec.]. **1855** MACAULAY *Hist. Eng.* xiii. III. 271 A legal sentence, passed in due form, and still unreversed. **1878** ABNEY *Treat. Photogr.* xxxiv. 278 It is possible to obtain an unreversed impression of the thermal spectrum.

†**unre'vessed, -'vested,** *pa. pple.* *Obs.* (UN-[2] 4, 8.)
c **1450** *Chron. London* (Kingsford, 1905) 131 Whan the bysshope hadde don the masse and whas unrevessed. **1483** CAXTON *G. de la Tour* c vij b, When he had songen and was vnreuested it was not knowen where he bicam.

unre'viewed, *ppl. a.* (UN-[1] 8.)
[**1775** ASH.] **1819** BUSBY *Hist. Music* II. 255 There are particular..reasons why his Te Deum should not pass unreviewed. **1837** CARLYLE *Fr. Rev.* I. VI. iii, After long unreviewed centuries.

unre'viled, *ppl. a.* (UN-[1] 8.)
1470 HARDYNG *Chron.* Pref. p. x, As lyon fell he putte hym forth in prese, The werre maynteynde and kepte hym vnrevylde.

unre'vised, *ppl. a.* (UN-[1] 8.)
[**1775** ASH.] **1845** *Syd. Smith's Wks.* (1859) II. 333/1 The following unrevised fragment. **1847** STANLEY *Arnold* Suppl. 22 The unblotted, unrevised manuscript. **1897** GOLDW. SMITH *Guesses Riddle Exist.* 83 Readers of the Bible who continue to use the unrevised version.

unre'vivable, *a.* (UN-[1] 7 b.)
1802–12 BENTHAM *Ration. Judic. Evid.* (1827) V. 171 When I say unrevivable, I mean by common law.

unre'vived, *ppl. a.* (UN-[1] 8.)
1631 WEEVER *Anc. Funeral Mon.* 417 Old, moth-eaten, vnreuiued penall Lawes. **1680** H. MORE *Apocal. Apoc.* xi. 106 That..they may not seem to prophesie and be dead at the same time, nor lye too long unburied or unrevived. **1877** CONDER *Basis Faith* ii. 75 Those memories of the past, unrevived for years.

†**un'revocable,** *a.* *Obs.* (UN-[1] 7 b, 5 b.)
1535 STEWART *Cron. Scot.* (Rolls) II. 581 Vnreuocabill, withoutin fraude or gyle, At thair plesour sic peax for to compyle. **1589** GREENE *Menaphon* (Arb.) 43 The heauens.. sent vnreuocable Fates to depriue me of her life. **1608** L. MACHIN *Dumbe Knight* III, My vow..is like fate still unrevocable. **1616** B. PARSONS *Mag. Charter* 2 By an unrevocable patent.

un'revocably, *adv.* (UN-[1] 11.)
1472 in Ramsay *Bamff Charters* (1915) 29 Assignit hym unrevocably to the said annualerent of sex markis.

unre'voked, *ppl. a.* [UN-[1] 8.]
1. Not revoked, recalled, or annulled.
1479 [see UNREPEALED]. **1570** LEVINS *Manip.* 50 Vnreuoked, *irreuocabilis.* **1667** MILTON *P.L.* v. 602 Hear all ye Angels,..Hear my Decree, which unrevok't shall stand. **1740** CIBBER *Apol.* (1756) I. 310 This unrevoked order of silence. **1790** COWPER *Mother's Pict.* 112 Time, unrevok'd, has run His wonted course. **1835** *Court Mag.* VI. 35/1 The morrow arrived, and the Sultan's command remained unrevoked. **1858** LD. ST. LEONARDS *Handy-bk. Prop. Law* xx. 157 The general gift in your will to your child..will belong to him if you leave it unrevoked.
†**2.** Not called back. *Obs.*[-1]
1654 GAYTON *Pleas. Notes* II. vi. 59 As she unrevoked ran Shee thought each tree to be a man.

unrevo'lutionized, *ppl. a.* (UN-[1] 8.)
1804 LARWOOD *No Gun Boats* 39 The old Lillies of unrevolutionized France.

unre'volved, *ppl. a.* (UN-[1] 8.)
[**1775** ASH.] **1891** MEREDITH *One of our Conq.* xxxiii, That was the thought, unrevolved, unphrased, all but unconscious, in Nesta.

unre'volving, *ppl. a.* (UN-[1] 10.)
1843 CARLYLE *Past & Pr.* III. xi, Of an idle unrevolving man the kindest Destiny..can bake and knead nothing other than a botch.

unre'wardable, *a.* (UN-[1] 7 b.)
c **1445** PECOCK *Donet* 94 Not wip-stonding synne is.. vncleene, vnrewardable, punyschable.

unre'warded, *ppl. a.* [UN-[1] 8.]
1. Not rewarded; unrequited.
c **1412** HOCCLEVE *De Reg. Princ.* 2890 No goode dede vnrewardid is, or quytte. *c* **1440** *Alph. Tales* lxxxi. 64 God will hafe no gude dede vnrewardid. **1512** *Helyas* in Thoms *Prose Rom.* (1828) III. 75 A good dede is never unrewarded ne an evyll unpunysshed. **1576** ABP. SANDYS *Serm.* (1585) 171 Their seruice was vnrewarded, because it was vncontinued. **1628** R. H. *J. Owen's Epigr.* I. 7 Verses giuen for a New-yeeres gift, vnrewarded. **1656** SIR E. NICHOLAS in *N. Papers* (Camden) III. 270 None can..imagine that so glorious an act can possibly be unrewarded. **1712** BLACKMORE *Creation* VII. 74 While Heaven's adorers..Their unrewarded innocence maintain. **1779** *Mirror* No. 35, My obsequious services in the drawing-room passed unrewarded. **1821** BYRON *Sardanap.* III. i. 357 Slain! unrewarded!..that's hard, poor slave. **1863** MOUAT *Andaman Islanders* 153 Our persevering search, and our repeated use of the line, were unrewarded with the success we desired.
2. Unpunished.
1621 J. TAYLOR (Water P.) *Unnat. Father* Wks. (1630) 140/1 God did neuer suffer Murder to goe vnrewarded. **1907** *Verney Mem.* II. 128 Wickedness does not go for ever unrewarded.

unre'wardedly, *adv.* (UN-[1] 11.)
1888 *Scribner's Mag.* Dec. 757/1 He had transfused two months of her life with such a delicate sweetness, so unrewardedly.

unre'warding, *vbl. sb.* (UN-[1] 13.)
a **1586** SIDNEY *Arcadia* III. xiv, It was the unrewarding, & not the evil employing her service, which grieved her.

unre'warding, *ppl. a.* (UN-[1] 10.)
1653 JER. TAYLOR *Serm. for Year* I. xix. 255 He findes it an unrewarding interest, to walk seven dayes..only to see a place from whence he must come back in an hour. **1854** LEVER *Dodd Family Abroad* lxx. 592 [It] is a very unrewarding process. **1882** MYERS *Renewal of Youth* 120 [To] come bootless back from the unrewarding quest.

unrhe'torical, *a.* (UN-[1] 7, 5 b.)
[**1775** ASH.] **1822** DE QUINCEY *Confess.* 78 The literal and unrhetorical use of the word *myriad.* **1859** G. WILSON *Mem. E. Forbes* ii. 68 The style..is strikingly unrhetorical. **1875** E. WHITE *Life in Christ* IV. xxiv. 405 Certain unrhetorical explicit statements of doctrine.

un'rhymed, *ppl. a.* (UN-[1] 8; cf. UNRIMED.)
1828 CARLYLE *Misc.* (1857) I. 219 The grand unrhymed Romance of his earthly existence. **1848** LONGF. *Secret of Sea* iv, With a soft, monotonous cadence, Flow its unrhymed lyric lines.

un'rhythmic, *a.* (UN-[1] 7.)
1884 *Athenæum* 2 Aug. 142/2 No unrhythmic verse was ever yet remembered beyond the generation that produced it.

un'rhythmical, *a.* (UN-[1] 7.)
Also, in recent use (1904), ***unrhythmically***.
1777 RICHARDSON *Persian & Arab. Dict.* 1935 Discordant, unrhythmical, wretchedly composed verse or prose. **1840** DE QUINCEY *Style* Wks. 1859 XI. 167 Excess of awkwardness, or of inelegance, or of unrhythmical cadence. **1871** *Edin. Rev.* Apr. 432 His lines are never unrhythmical.

un'ribbed, *ppl. a.* (UN-[1] 8.)
[**1775** ASH.] **1834** K. H. DIGBY *Mores Cath.* v. viii. 288 See, then to what a distance your unribbed bark is driven. **1851** RUSKIN *Stones Ven.* I. xxix. §3 When the vaulting is unribbed, as in plain waggon vaults.

un'rich, *a.* (UN-[1] 7.)
1875 MORRIS *Æneid* XII. 519 By fruitful fishy Lerna's flood was once his life and gain, And unrich house.

†**un'rid,** *ppl. a.*[1] [UN-[1] 8 b.] Unridden.
1640 H. MILL *Night's Search* I. 194 Give me a jade unrid, that's plump and fat.

un'rid, *ppl. a.*[2] *Sc.* and *dial.* [UN-[1] 8 b. Cf. ON. *úrudd-r* (Norw. *urudd, urydd,* Sw. *orödd,* Da. *uryddet*) uncleared.] Not put in order.
1637 RUTHERFORD *Lett.* (1664) 132 So marches lie still unrid & counts uncleared betwixt us. **1824** [CARR] *Craven Dialect* 5 Awr house is vara unrid and grimy. **1856** CARLYLE *Lett.* (1904) II. 179 [More of] my Book..lies in heaps ahead of me, in the unrid state.

un'ridden, *ppl. a.* (UN-[1] 8 b.)
(*a*) **1574** *Richmond. Wills* (Surtees) 248 Horses at Burghe. Ridden horsses and mares, xv... Stages and fillies unreden, xij. **1607** MARKHAM *Cavel.* IV. 5 Foales, vnridden horses, or horses that are of any..sobrietie in iourneying. **1831** JAMES *Phil. Augustus* III. v, Horses..which have stood there unridden for months. **1857** DUFFERIN *Lett. High Lat.* (ed. 2) 83 Having caught, saddled and bridled the three unridden ponies.
(*b*) **1615** *Extr. Aberd. Reg.* (1848) II. 323 Leaving the saidis merches unridden.

un'riddle, *sb.* *rare*[-1]. [UN-[2]; cf. next.] A solution of a riddle.
1756 *Connoisseur* No. 107 ¶7 Reading over the Riddles, and Unriddles, the Questions, and the Answers.

un'riddle, *v.* [UN-^{2} 3. Cf. G. *enträtseln.*] *trans.* To solve, explain (a mystery, etc.). (Cf. RIDDLE *v.*^{1} 2.)

a **1586** SIDNEY *Arcadia* III. vii, But nowe Amphialus helped to unriddle his doubts; for he [etc.]. **1634** PEACHAM *Compl. Gent.* xii. 111, I will give you..examples of these, with which..you may easily unriddle the rest. **1648** PRYNNE *Plea for Lords* 63 Let him..unriddle and assoyle..his owne Dilemma. **1714** ADDISON *Spect.* No. 567 ¶7 If any sagacious Person can fairly unriddle it, I will print his Explanation. **1785** REID *Intell. Powers* IV. ii. 371 Take this description altogether, and it would require an Œdipus to unriddle it. **1820** KEATS *Hyperion* II. 150 No, no-where can [I] unriddle ..why ye..Should cower beneath..untremendous might. **1858** MERIVALE *Rom. Emp.* liii. VI. 218 To unriddle some of the perplexing questions. **1885** MISS BRADDON *Wyllard's Weird* I. 194 If we can unriddle the railway mystery, all may yet come right.

refl. **1653** R. C[ODRINGTON] *Lloyd's Marrow of Hist.* 1 This at first may seem a paradox; but upon a deliberate consideration it will easily unriddle itself.

absol. *a* **1642** SUCKLING *Goblins* I. i, Pray, unriddle. **1710** PARNELL *Hermit* 207 Confess th' Almighty just, And where you can't unriddle, learn to trust. **1768** H. WALPOLE *Myst. Mother* IV. vi, Unriddle, priest. My soul is too impatient To wait [etc.].

Hence **un'riddling** *vbl. sb.*

a **1680** BUTLER *Char. Religion* Wks. (1908) 306 They..are wonderfull acute at unriddling of Mysteries. **1821** BYRON *Juan* III. xxviii, The cause being past his guessing or unriddling.

un'riddleable, *a.* (UN-^{1} 7 b.)

1647 EVELYN *Let.* in *Diary*, etc. (1852) III. 6 Things were never more unriddleable than at this instant of time. *a* **1675** LIGHTFOOT *Serm.* Wks. 1684 II. 1246 These difficulties..in Scripture..are not unriddleable riddles, and tyring-irons never to be untied, but [etc.].

un'riddled, *ppl. a.* [UN-^{1} 8.] Unsolved.

1823 BYRON *Juan* XI. iii, This unriddled wonder, The World.

un'riddler. [f. UNRIDDLE *v.*] One who, or that which, solves or explains.

1657 TRAPP *Comm. Job* xxxvi. 22 A Teacher of perplexed things, an unriddler of Riddles. **1663** BOYLE *Usef. Exp. Nat. Philos.* I. iii. 64 If our posterity be not much happier unriddlers then..we have been. **1824** SCOTT *St. Ronan's* iii, He was also a deviser of charades and an unriddler of riddles. **1871** EARLE *Philol. Eng. Tongue* 365 That frequent unriddler of philological problems, the Hebrew language.

†**un'ride**, *a.* *Obs.* Also 3 vnrude, 5 -ruyde; 4–5 vn-, 6 unryde, 4 oun-, 5 onride, vnrid; 4 vnrede. [OE. *unȝerýde* (ME. *unirude* UN-^{1} 3) rough, violent, f. *ȝerýde* (once), ? smooth, pleasant; of obscure origin. Cf. UNRUDE *a.*^{1}]

1. Severe; causing much suffering.

c **1200** ORMIN 4779 All þiss wass utenn wiþþ unnhal þurrh swiþe unnride unnhæle. *Ibid.* 4784 Her wass unnseoll þe unnride inoh Till an mann forr to dreȝhenn. *c* **1300** *Havelok* 1981 He haues a wunde in the side, With a gleyue, ful unride,..And he haues on þoru his þe, þe vnrideste þat men may se. *c* **1380** *Sir Ferumb.* 747 Wel neȝ ys guttes þat swerd him ran, & made hym a wounde ounride. *a* **1400** *St. Alexius* (Laud 108) 542 Al þat folk þat stod be-syde þat say þe sorwe so vnruyde, þey wepe ful tendreliche. *c* **1460** *Towneley Myst.* III. 40 Man..was put out, in that tyde, In wo & wandreth for to be, in paynes full vnrid To knawe.

2. Of large size; of great size and strength; so large as to be cumbersome or unwieldy.

c **1220** *Bestiary* 646 Ðanne cumeð ðis elp unride. *a* **1240** *Sawles Warde* in *O.E. Hom.* I. 249 Euch an [*sc.* devil] bereð ..an unrude raketehe gled-read of fure. *c* **1300** *Havelok* 1795 þe barre..was unride, and gret ynow. *c* **1380** *Sir Ferumb.* 3691 þe dent of þat sper oun-ryde. *a* **1400** *Sir Per.* 1160 To morne..salle we togedir playe With wapyns unryde. ? *a* **1600** *Merline* 1501 (Percy Folio), His tayle was great...his bodye was unryde with-all.

b. Large in number; numerous.

c **1300** *Havelok* 2947 [All] it sawe..Hwou he it bar with mikel pride For his barnage þat was vnride. *c* **1330** *King of Tars* 142 The soudan gederet an ost unryde.

c. Large in extent. *rare*$^{-1}$.

13.. *Metr. Hom.* (MS. Ashm. 42) fol. 136, An vnridde spase es now Makid betwix vs and ȝow þat none of vs maie come ȝou nere Ne none of ȝou maie come here.

3. Rough; violent.

a **1300** *Cursor M.* 24845 þe wind ras gains þam vnride. **1338** R. BRUNNE *Chron.* (1810) 174 þe noyse was vnride, it lasted alle day. *c* **1350** *Ipomedon* 6492 Is knyght non, That darre fyght wyth hym alonne, So is the fende vnryde. *a* **1400–50** *Alexander* 739 Reviles he þis oþire renke with vnrid [*v.r.* vnrode] speche. *c* **1470** *Golagros & Gaw.* 630 [He] raught to the renk ane rout wes vnryde.

un'rid(e)able, *a.* (UN-^{1} 7 b.)

Common in recent use. Hence *unrid(e)a'bility.*

1881 *Daily News* 5 Jan. 6/5 Over a fine open country, till the land became almost unrideable. **1883** C. HOWARD *Roads Eng. & Wales* (ed. 3) 94 Steep unrideable ascents and descents.

un'rideably, *adv.* (UN-^{1} 11. Cf. prec.)

1851 KINGSLEY *Yeast* i, Lancelot had bought him..for half his value, as unrideably vicious, when he had killed a groom.

†**un'ridely**, *adv.* *Obs.* Forms: (see quots.). [OE. *unȝerýdelíce* (rare), f. *unȝerýde*: see UNRIDE *a.*] Violently, roughly, harshly.

c **1200** ORMIN 15567 *note*, And oferrwarrp þær i þe flor Unnriddliȝ þeȝȝre bordess. *a* **1225** *Juliana* 54 [Juliana] reat him mitte raketehe unrudeliche swiðe. *a* **1300** *Cursor M.* 24391 It raght mi hert al thoru þe rote, Vnrideli on me rane. **13..** *Gaw. & Gr. Knt.* 1432 þer as þe rogh rocher vn-rydely was fallen. *a* **1400–50** *Alexander* 566 þen rekils it vnruydly & raynes doune stanys. *Ibid.* 638 If any of his feris Raged with him vnridly. *c* **1400** *Song Roland* 990 He rent hym vnredly euyn to the sadill.

un'ridge, *v.* (UN-^{2} 4.)

1647 TRAPP *Comm. Rev.* i. 16 The word..slits open, and as it were, unridgeth the conscience.

unri'diculous, *a.* (UN-^{1} 7.)

1646 SIR T. BROWNE *Pseud. Ep.* VII. xvi. 372 If an indifferent and unridiculous object could draw his habituall austerenesse unto a smile.

un'rife, *a.* (UN-^{1} 7.)

1599 T. M[OUFET] *Silkwormes* 4 His brother Linus first began The Flaxmans craft (a secret then vnrife).

un'rifled, *ppl. a.*^{1} (UN-^{1} 8 + RIFLE *v.*^{1})

1603 KNOLLES *Hist. Turks* (1621) 83 Nothing..left vnpolluted and defaced, no place vnsought, no corner vnrifled. **1653** JER. TAYLOR *Serm. for Year* I. xix. 246 The estate..remains unrifled, and descends upon the heir. **1743** FRANCIS tr. *Hor., Odes* III. xxiv. 1 Though of th' unrifled Gold possest Of gorgeous Ind. **1835** *Court Mag.* VI. 205 Sing Birds!..Give thanks in song for your unrifled nest! **1864** I. TAYLOR *Words & Places* 171 The hope of capturing the rich and unrifled prize.

fig. **1637** HEYWOOD *Royall Kings* Prol., No History We have left unrifled.

un'rifled, *ppl. a.*^{2} (UN-^{1} 8 + RIFLE *v.*^{3})

1860 *All Year Round* No. 73. 546 The shot of the ordinary unrifled service gun is round.

un'rig, *v.* [UN-^{2} 4.]

1. *trans.* To divest (a ship) of its rigging (both standing and running).

1579–80 NORTH *Plutarch* (1595) 541 He vnrigged and bestowed his ships in docks. **1615** *Britain's Buss* in Arber *Garner* III. 632 That the other two weeks be also spent..in unrigging and laying up the Buss. **1667** *Lond. Gaz.* No. 169/4 They were constrained to Unrigg her, and to take down her Topmast. **1720** DE FOE *Capt. Singleton* xiv. (1840) 240 We unrigged our top-masts. **1768** *Ann. Reg., Chron.* 106/1 Some sailors began to unrig the ships. **1806** A. DUNCAN *Nelson* 124 A broadside..nearly unrigged the Foudroyant. **1820** SCORESBY *Acc. Arct. Reg.* II. 451 It would be necessary first to discharge the cargo, and to unrig the ship.

b. *absol.* To remove or take down rigging.

a **1647** PETT in *Archaeologia* (1796) XII. 227 Friday the 16th, we unrigged, and shot the bridge. **1799** NELSON in Nicolas *Disp.* (1845) III. 238 Malta then was half-starving, and the Ships had unrigged. **1897** tr. *Nansen's Farthest North* II. vii. 327 We..rigged up mast and sail. But..we were soon obliged to unrig, and take to paddling.

c. In pres. pple. = Being unrigged.

1673 *Lond. Gaz.* No. 773/4 The other, mounted with 24 Guns, is now unrigging. **1810** *Naval Chron.* XXIII. 121 A small frigate unrigging.

d. *trans.* (See quot.)

1769 FALCONER *Dict. Marine* (1780), *Dégarnir le cabestan*, to unrig the Capstern, by taking off the voyol, and unshipping the bars.

2. *transf.* To strip of clothes; to undress.

1591 LYLY *Endym.* III. iii, Vnrigge mee. Hey ho! **1693** *Dryden's Juvenal* xiv. (1697) 367 The Shrine was..lin'd with a strong Guard of Souldiers, who had an Eye to their God..lest he should be stoln, or unrigg'd. **1723** *Pres. St. Russia* I. 162 The French Gentlewoman,..whom they had almost unrigged, withal telling the Men that they had stript first. **1793** WOLCOT (P. Pindar) *Ep. to the Pope* 132 Out with her ear-rings and the Dame unrig. **1820** SCOTT *Monast.* xvi, He secured my spare doublet..—I was enforced to beat a retreat before I was altogether unrigged. **1880–** in Shropshire and Yks. use (*Eng. Dial. Dict.*).

absol. **1693** CONGREVE *Old Bach.* v. i, *Bell.* I wou'd unrig. *Setter.* I attend you, Sir. **1865** MRS. WHITNEY *Gayworthys* v, Gabriel..fibbed again when he said he didn't feel much like rigging up for a party;' which had been true but for the last five minutes since he unrigged.

b. To unharness.

1690 *Lond. Gaz.* No. 2552/3 The Sailors went ashore and unrigged his Horse. **1881** DUFFIELD *Don Quixote* II. 575 The express command of his master that..Rozinante should not be unrigged.

un'rigged, *ppl. a.* [f. prec., or UN-^{1} 8.]

a. Divested of rigging. **b.** Not furnished with rigging.

a **1593** MARLOWE *Edw. II*, II. ii, While in the harbor ride thy ships vnrigd. —— *Dido* III. i, Yet..are my ships vnrigd, My Sailes all rent. **1623** in Foster *Eng. Factories Ind.* II. (1908) 215 The carricke..nowe lyeth alltogeather unrigged. **1695** *Lond. Gaz.* No. 3088/3 The Ships that lay hard by unrigg'd. **1748** *Anson's Voy.* III. iv. 330 Our shrowds were loose, and our top-masts unrigged. **1799** *Hull Advertiser* 30 Mar. 1/4 She being totally unrigged, struck. **1830** *Encycl. Brit.* (ed. 7) II. 633/2 An unrigged boat. **1834** MARRYAT *P. Simple* II. 281 Our guns became..hot from quick firing... By this time we were almost..unrigged.

un'right, *sb.* *Obs.* exc. *arch.* [OE. *unriht* (f. *un-* UN-^{1} 12 + *riht* RIGHT *sb.*^{1}), = OFris. *on-*, *unriucht* (WFris. *on-*, *ûnjucht*, NFris. *ünrocht*), MDu. (Du.) *onrecht*, OS. *unreht* (MLG., LG. *unrecht*, LG. *-regt*), OHG. (MHG.) *unreht* (G. *unrecht*), Norw. *urett*, (M)Da. *uret*, (M)Sw. *orätt.*]

1. Wrong, wrong-doing, iniquity.

Beowulf 1264 Siþðan goldsele Grendel warode, unriht æfnde. *a* **1122** *O.E. Chron.* (Laud MS.) an. 1100, He on middewardan his unrihte buten behreowsunge..ȝewat. *c* **1205** LAY. 6553 Vnriht him wes leof, and rihtwisnesse him wes lað. *c* **1330** R. BRUNNE *Chron. Wace* (Rolls) 11513 Com, & amende þyn vnright, þat þou so slowe ffrolle oure knyght. *c* **1380** WYCLIF *Sel. Wks.* II. 91 þis is a trewe man, and unriȝt is not in him. *c* **1449** PECOCK *Repr.* v. iii. 498 The oon [god] is maker of riȝt and of good thingis, and the other is maker of vnriȝt and of badde thingis. *a* **1547** SURREY in *Early XVI Cent. Lyrics* xlv. 46 Prowd people that drede no fall, clothed with falshed and vnright. **1578** PROCTOR *Gorgeous Gallery Inventions* B ij, Well mayst thou wayle thy want of troth; & rue thy great vnright. **1610** H. BROUGHTON *Job* xxvii. 4 My lippes shall not speak the vnright. [**1876** FREEMAN *Norm. Conq.* V. xxiv. 394 It was because they still spake of right that right in the end outlived unright.]

b. In the phr. *to do* (or *work*) *unright.*

c **888** K. ÆLFRED *Boeth.* xxxviii. §3 Forþamðe ðu ær cwæde ðæt he unriht dyde þæt he lete unwitnod ða yflan. *c* **1000** ÆLFRIC *Deut.* xxxi. 29 þonne ȝe unriht wirceað beforan drihtene. *a* **1300** *Cursor M.* 24158 Ye Iuus,..Vn-reufulli yee wirc vnright. **13..** *Ibid.* 5084 (Gött.), I am a-knau i did vnriht. *c* **1412** HOCCLEVE *De Reg. Princ.* 5040 [God] may done non vnright. **1535** COVERDALE *Zeph.* iii. 5 But the iust Lorde that doth no vnright, was amonge them. *a* **1547** SURREY in *Early XVI Cent. Lyrics* xlv. 16 All such as wourke vn-right. **1607** J. DAVIES *Summa Totalis* G 2, With neither Will, nor Pow'r to do vnright.

2. Unfairness, injustice (done or suffered).

c **888** K. ÆLFRED *Boeth.* xxxix. §9 Hwylc unriht mæȝ beon mare þonne ȝeþafiȝe [etc.]. *c* **1020** *Ags. Laws* (Thorpe) I. 388 We nellað ȝeþafian þæt unriht. *c* **1175** *Lamb. Hom.* 115 He scal wissian mid wisdome his folke and unriht aleggen. **1297** R. GLOUC. (Rolls) 8625 More vnriȝt þan he dede ne miȝte nomon ise. *c* **1325** *Spec. Gy Warw.* 613 To suffre wrong and vnriht For þe loue of god almiht. *c* **1400** *Beryn* 557 That were grete vnryȝte, To aventur oppon a man þat with hym did nat fiȝte. **1456** *Cov. Leet Bk.* 290 Boldly to fight, Yf any man of curage wold bid you vnright. **1530** TINDALE *Pract. Prelates* A v b, There was neuer creature that sofred so greate vnright so pacyentlye..as he. **1581** A. HALL *Iliad* IX. 162 Suffice it him he hath me wrongde, and that his own vnright Doth hel him like a man forlorne.

b. In phr. *to do one unright*, or variations of this.

c **1200** *Vices & Virtues* 113 Nis him idon non unriht. *c* **1250** *Gen. & Ex.* 1276 Ðor ben he boðen feren pliȝt, ðat here neiðer sal don oðer un-riȝt. **13..** *K. Alis.* 7491 (Laud MS.), And amendyng I bidde þee to Of vnriȝth þat is me do. **1340** *Ayenb.* 221 Hi ssolle loki hare bodi þe on to þe oþre.. treweliche wyþ-oute do onriȝt þe on to þe oþren. *c* **1402** LYDG. *Compl. Bl. Knt.* 334 Notwithstonding his man-hood ..Love unto him did ful greet unright. **1532** TINDALE *Expos. Matt.* (1550) F vij b, Be patient..., what soeuer vnright be done the. **1599** DANIEL *Lett. Octauia to M. Antonius* xxii, Is it, that loue doth take no true delight In what it hath,..Which drawes you on to doe vs this vnright?

3. *with* (also *on*) *unright*, wrongfully, unjustly.

Beowulf 2739 Ic..ne sohte searoniðas, ne me swor fela aða on unriht. ? *a* **900** K. ÆLFRED *Laws* §1 Ne wilna þu þines nehstan ierfes mid unryhte. *c* **1205** LAY. 7374 þu ahtest me to ȝulden ȝauel of þine londe, And þu hit halst on unriht. **1297** R. GLOUC. (Rolls) 4040 He nom it verst mid vnriȝt, & broȝte þat lond in wo. **13..** *E.E. Allit. P.* B. 1142 He loses hit ille, As hit were rafte wyth vnryȝt & robbed wyth þewes. *a* **1425** *Cursor M.* 19012 (Trin.), þat ihesus..ȝe dude on rode wiþ vnriȝt. **1563** FOXE *A. & M.* 564/1 To discerne in what wise ther iudgement passed, whether with right or vnright.

4. An instance of wrong or wrong-doing; a wrong or unjust act.

c **888** K. ÆLFRED *Boeth.* xvi. §4 Betwuh þyllecum un-rihtum wæs him [*sc.* Nero]..underþeod eall þes middanȝeard. *a* **1122** *O.E. Chron.* (Laud MS.) an. 1086, Maniȝe oðre unriht hi dydan, þe sindon earfeþe to areccenne. *c* **1200** *Vices & Virtues* 79 Ða ðat he hadde mid maniȝe unrihtes biȝeten. *a* **1300** *Cursor M.* 11812 þis herods ..vn-rightes biginnes to ripe! *c* **1380** *Sir Ferumb.* 1031 þe Sarasyns..schullaþ abigge þys ounriȝt. *c* **1400** tr. *Secreta Secret., Gov. Lordsh.* 59 Draw to þe þe good wylles of þy subgitz, and putte away þaire vnryghtys and wronges. ? *a* **1500** *Chester Pl.* III. 142, 40 dayes and 40 nightes Rayne shall fall for ther vnrightes. **1528** LYNDESAY *Dreme* 262 Partycipant thay wer of thare vnrychtis.

un'right, *a.* [OE. *unriht* (f. *un-* UN-^{1} 7 + *riht* RIGHT *a.*), = OFris. *on-*, *unriucht* (WFris. *on-*, *ûnrjucht*, NFris. *ünrocht*), MDu. and obs. Du. *onrecht*, OS. *unreht* (MLG. and LG. *unrecht*, LG. *-regt*), OHG. (MHG.) *unreht* (G. *unrecht*), ON. *úréttr* (Norw. *urett*, Da. *uret*, MSw. *orätter*, Sw. *orätt*).]

1. Not right, just, or equitable; improper, unfair, wrong. Now *Sc.* or *arch.* (common in 16th c.).

c **888** K. ÆLFRED *Boeth.* xxxviii. §3 Ic..wundrie forhwy swa rihtwis dema æniȝe unrihte ȝife wille forȝifan. *c* **1000** *Ags. Ps.* (Thorpe) cxviii. 104 Ic me betst oncneow, þæt ic unrihte weȝas ealle of-eode. *c* **1200** *Vices & Virtues* 121 Unriht domesmann. **1297** R. GLOUC. (Rolls) 8726 He let grede þoru al þe lond þe vnriȝte lawes vndo. *c* **1375** *Cursor M.* 26711 (Fairf.) He salle..on domisday haue wreyers harde, þat is to say..þe werlde, þe deuil, his didis vnriȝt. *c* **1449** PECOCK *Repr.* III. xix. 415 Open it is..thilk deede or gouernaunce in him silf is vnriȝt and wrong. **1532** MORE *Confut. Tindale* Wks. 545/2 [To] walke in the commaundementes of life, & do nothing that is vnright. **1603** J. DAVIES (Heref.) *Microcosmos* 157 These senseless spunges of Improbity Are full of pleasure, but it is vnright. **1627** BP. HALL *Dauids Ps. Metaphr.* i, The man vnright, As chaffe.., With euery blast Is cast on hie. **1856** W. H. GILLESPIE *Truth Evang. Hist.* vii. 129 Such un-right and self-inconsistent depravation. **1880** G. MACDONALD *Diary Old Soul* 16 Feb., If I should slow diverge..Into some thought, feeling, or dream unright.

absol. **1610** H. BROUGHTON *Job* xxix. 17, I brake the tuskes of the vnright.

†**2.** Incorrect; inexact. *Obs. rare.*

1562 TURNER *Herbal* II. 32 Amatus gyueth an vnryght duche name vnto Sion when he calleth it bauchbungen. **1591** WOTTON in *Reliq.* (1685) 641, I..alleg'd further, that the Copy was unright. **1605** VERSTEGAN *Dec. Intell.* i. 17 So many haue aleaged so many vnright and vnlykely causes thereof.

†**un'right**, *adv. Obs.* [OE. *unrihte* (f. *un-* UN-[1] 11 b + *rihte* RIGHT *adv.*), = MDu. *onrechte* (Du. *onrecht*), OS. and OHG. *unrehto* (MHG. *unrehte*, G. *unrecht*), Da. *uret*, Sw. *orätt.*] Improperly; not in the right way; wrongly.

Beowulf 3059 þa wæs ȝesyne þæt se sið ne ðah þam ðe unrihte inne ȝehydde wræte under wealle. *a* **1000** *Ags. Ps.* (Thorpe) cxviii. 78 Beon þa oferhydeȝan ealle ȝescende, þe me unrihte ahwær gretan. *c* **1374** CHAUCER *Troylus* v. 661 Hym thought..þat þe sonne wente his course vnright. *a* **1400** *Northern Passion* 1624 þai lukyd tyll hys fete full bryght; Sone þai sayd þai lay vnryght [*v.r.* noghte aryghte]. *c* **1480** HENRYSON *Test. Cres.* 205 As King Royall he raid vpon his Chair, The quhilk Phaeton gydit sum tyme vnricht. **1513** DOUGLAS *Æneid* XIII. Prol. 138 Gyf thou hes afore tyme gayn onrycht, Followand sa lang Virgill, a gentile clerk. ? **1555** COVERDALE tr. *Bk. Death* vii. 24 Therefore wryteth gregory not vnright whan he saith [etc.]. **1603** J. DAVIES (Heref.) *Microcosmos* 167 See how blinde a Guide Is lothsome Lust, that leades men so vnright.

†**un'right**, *v.*[1] *Obs. rare.* [f. UNRIGHT *sb.* or *a.* Cf. MDu. *onrechten*, MHG. *unrechten*, to do injustice, treat unjustly.] *trans.* To wrong, injure.

1390 GOWER *Conf.* I. 176, I wolde swiche tales sprede.. That I scholde al his love unrihte. *Ibid.* II. 355 That he thurgh eny sleihte myhte Hire lusti maidenhod unrihte. **1647** in Rushworth *Hist. Coll.* IV. (1701) I. 555 Rather than they will be unrighted in the matter of their Honesty and Integrity,..they will lose all.

†**un'right**, *v.*[2] [UN-[2] 4. Cf. OFris. *on(t)riuhta*, MDu. *ontrechten* (Du. *-richten*), MLG. *entrihten*, OHG. *intrihtan* (MHG. *entrechten*, G. *-richten*).] *trans.* To deprive of rights.

c **1449** PECOCK *Repr.* III. xvi. 386 This man mai not iustli be vnriȝtid and vnpossessid, that is to seie, be putt out of riȝt and out of possessioun of the seid..good.

un'righted, *ppl. a.* [UN-[1] 8.] Not righted.

[**1775** ASH.] **1883** F. M. PEARD *Contrad.* II. 269 If the wrong were unrighted,..then—what would become of her?

un'righteous, *a.* Forms: (see RIGHTEOUS *a.*). [OE. *unrihtwís* (UN-[1] 7 + RIGHTEOUS). Cf. ON. *úréttvís* (MDa. *uretvis*, Sw. *orättvis*).]

1. Not righteous or upright; unjust, wicked: **a.** Of persons.

c **888** ÆLFRED *Boeth.* xxxvii. §1 Geher nu an spell be ..þam unrihtwisum cyningum. *c* **1000** *Ags. Gosp.* Luke xvi. 10 Se þe ys on lytlum unrihtwis, se ys eac on maran unrihtwis. *c* **1175** *Lamb. Hom.* 115 þe nihȝeðe unþeau is þet þe king beo unrihtwis. *c* **1200** *Trin. Coll. Hom.* 19 Alle þe unrihtwise men..hersumieð þe deuel. *c* **1380** WYCLIF *Sel. Wks.* III. 19 Alle unriȝtwise men þat serven to him [*sc.* the devil] as hise trewe knyȝtis. **14..** *Tundale's Vis.* 274 þou art not lele iustise, þou art fals and unryghtwyse. **1474** CAXTON *Chesse* 28 Cambyses..had an vnrightwis juge. **1526** TINDALE *Heb.* vi. 10 God is not vnrighteous that he shulde forget youre worke. **1572** R. T. *Discourse* 48 The Sadduces ..were most vnrightuous. **1651** HOBBES *Leviathan* III. xlii. 306 There being nothing in mens Manners that makes them righteous, or unrighteous. **1712** M. HENRY *Expos., Isaiah* lv. 7 Here's a Call..to the Wicked, and the Unrighteous Man. ? **1791** BENTHAM *Draught Code* Wks. 1843 IV. 316 An unrighteous judge, or rather a judge who would otherwise be unrighteous. **1871** JOWETT *Plato* I. 158 Many men are utterly unrighteous, unholy, intemperate.

absol. *c* **825** *Vesp. Psalter* v. 6 Ne ðorhwuniað ða unrehtwisan biforan eȝum ðinum. *c* **1200** *Vices & Virtues* 83 Ic wile tache ðo unrihtwisen ðine weiȝes. *a* **1400** *New Test.* (Paues) App., 1 Pet. iii. 18 For onys Crist was for oure synnes deed, þe riȝtwyse for the vnriȝtwise. **1623** R. CARPENTER *Conscionable Christian* 14 What then shall the vnrighteous be able to say..for themselues? **1712** M. HENRY *Expos., Isaiah* lv. 7 The Unrighteous that live in the neglect of plain Duties. **1835** *Wilson's Tales Borders* I. 58/1 The innocent have been left to perish amang the unrighteous.

b. Of actions, etc.

971 *Blickl. Hom.* 33 Se awyrȝda gast is heafod ealra unrihtwisra dæda. *c* **1250** *Gen. & Ex.* 2014 His wif wurð wilde, and nam in ðoȝt vn-riȝt-wis luue. *a* **1300** *Cursor M.* 29507 O thrijn wijs Mai cursing be tald onrightwijs. *c* **1400** *Destr. Troy* 3539 The rape vnrightwis of his Riche qwene. **1481** CAXTON *Reynard* xlii. (Percy Soc.) 160 Somme helpe them forth in theyr vnryghtwys dedes. **1535** COVERDALE *2 Macc.* iv. 35 The vnrightuous death of so godly a man. **1590** SPENSER *F.Q.* II. x. 60 Octauius here lept into his roome, And it vsurped by vnrighteous doome. **1667** MILTON *P.L.* III. 292 Thir own both righteous and unrighteous deeds. **1725** POPE *Odyss.* IX. 630 Angry Neptune heard th' unrighteous prayer. **1846** MRS. A. MARSH *Father Darcy* II. xxi. 365 Those who have dared to prostitute holy things to unrighteous purposes. **1863** 'OUIDA' *Held in Bondage* i. I. 17 He was..full of most unrighteous oaths.

†**c.** Incorrect, false. *Obs.*[−1]

1507 *Extr. Aberd. Reg.* (1844) I. 437 That the mettis and mesouris be assait,..and quhar thai be fundin unrichtuus be distroit.

2. Not rightly due or deserved.

1855 SINGLETON *Virgil* II. 100 Anchises' offspring..from his soul Compassionated their unrighteous lot.

Hence **un'righteous** *v.*, to make unrighteous.

1593 NASHE *Christ's T.* K ij b, Thou that ere this hast disparradiz'd our first Parent Adam, and vnrightuouzd the very Angels.

un'righteously, *adv.* [OE. *unrihtwíslíce* (UN-[1] 11 + RIGHTEOUSLY *adv.*). Cf. ON. *úréttvísliga* (MDa. *uretvislige*, MSw. *orätvislika*).] In an unrighteous manner; unjustly, wrongfully.

c **897** K. ÆLFRED *Gregory's Past. C.* liv. 425 Ic cwæð to ðæm unryhtwisum, ne do ȝe unryhtwislice. *a* **1200** in Kemble *Cod. Dipl.* IV. 24 Butan he toforan ðam deaðe ..ȝebete ðæt he unrihtwislice forȝette. *a* **1300** *Cursor M.* 18274 Qui gaf þou rede þis ilk iesu to crucifi, Wit-vten skil, vn-rightwisli? **1382** WYCLIF *Wisdom* xii. 13 For not vnriȝtwisly thou demest dom. *c* **1425** AUDELAY *XI Pains Hell* 333 What chamful end þay haue þat leuyn here vnryȝtwysly. **1509** BARCLAY *Shyp of Folys* (1570) 29 Remember Richarde..In Englande reigning vnrightwisely a while. **1559** *Mirr. Mag.* 43 Was never prince that other dyd oppresse Un-righteously, but died in distresse. **1611** BEAUM. & FL. *Philaster* II. i, Who unrighteously Holds wealth or state from others, shall be curst. **1687** DRYDEN *Hind & P.* III. 1077 Their Foes a deadly Shibboleth devise: By which unrighteously it was decreed [etc.]. *a* **1768** SECKER *Serm.* (1770) V. 422 Whether they do not..persecute most unrighteously..both Christian Faith, and natural piety. **1807** FOSTER *Ess.* (1844) I. 21 They have sometimes been most unrighteously accused. **1847** PRESCOTT *Peru* III. vii. I. 428 The distribution of spoil so unrighteously acquired.

un'righteousness. [f. UNRIGHTEOUS *a.*] The quality of being unrighteous; an instance of this, an unrighteous action.

c **825** *Vesp. Psalter* v. 7 Ðu fedest..alle ða ðe wircað unrehtwisnisse. *c* **1055** *Byrhtferth's Handboc* in *Anglia* VIII. 332 Iniquitas on lyden on englisc ys ȝecweden unrihtwisnys. *c* **1200** *Vices & Virtues* 37 Ðurh his unrihtwisnesse he bringþ his saule in to helle pine. *a* **1300** *E.E. Psalter* xxxvi. 7 In man..Unrightwisnes þat es doand. *c* **1380** WYCLIF *Wks.* (1880) 240 A grete vnriȝtwisnesse regneþ among lordis whanne þei wolen not distroie pride. **1422** YONG tr. *Secreta Secret.* 132 Vnryghtuossnes disherityth kynges and Pryncis. **1535** COVERDALE *2 Esdras* vii. 35 The righteousnesses shall watch, and the vnrighteousnesses shall beare no rule. **1590** BABINGTON *Expos. Commandm.* 70, I am not worthie to beholde the height of Heauen, for the multitude of my vnrighteousnesse. **1611** BIBLE *Rom.* i. 18 The wrath of God is reueiled from heauen against all..vnrighteousnesse of men. *a* **1677** BARROW *Serm.* Wks. (1686) II. v. 80 The inherent unrighteousness consequent upon Adam's sin. ? *a* **1758** WITHERSPOON *Ess.* Sel. Wks. 1804 I. 36 He is a God ..with whom unrighteousness can have no communion. **1833** S. HOOLE *Discourses* xv. 200 The unrighteousness of living to himself alone. **1871** JOWETT *Plato* II. 330 If only he can..be pure from evil or unrighteousness.

un'rightful, *a.* Now *rare.* [UN-[1] 7.] Unrighteous, unjust, wrong.

a **1325** *Prose Psalter* c. 3 Y ne sett nouȝt to-fore myn eȝen þyng vnryȝtful. **1393** LANGL. *P. Pl.* C. XI. 215 A rybaud þei engendrede and a gome vnryghtful. *c* **1440** *Jacob's Well* 285 An Heremyte ȝaf hym to ydell & vnryȝtefull thouȝtys,..for hym thouȝte þat god was vnryȝtfull. **1482** *Monk of Evesham* (Arb.) 85 The onrightful scheding of mennys blode. **1545** BALE *Myst. Iniq.* 15 Pylate the vnryghtfull iudge. *a* **1586** SIDNEY *Astr. & Stella* Sonn. v. x, A rightfull prince by unrightfull deeds a tyrant groweth. **1606** G. W[OODCOCKE] *Hist. Ivstine* XXII. 84 Obiecting vnto them sometime their vnrightfull entrapping of Hanno. **1664** MORE *Myst. Iniq.* iv. 11 Malicious or inconsiderate spirits, that..pass unrightfull censures upon what is at least allowable.

1880 MCCARTHY *Own Times* IV. 336 The unrightful things that were sometimes done.

un'rightfully, *adv.* Now *rare.* [UN-[1] 11.] Without right; unjustifiably, unfairly, wrongly.

a **1325** *Prose Psalter* cv. 6 We han wroȝt vnryȝtfullich. *c* **1374** CHAUCER *Boeth.* I. met. v. (1868) 23 Anoienge folk treden..vnryȝtfully in þe nekkes of holy men. **1433** *Rolls of Parlt.* IV. 455/1 Whan they been often tymes unrightfully empeched. **1470–85** MALORY *Arthur* VIII. ii. 276 That is vnryghtfully asked, said kyng Melyodas. **1513** BRADSHAW *St. Werburge* I. 336 A kynge..In batayle slayne vnryghtfully, now a martyr gloryous. *c* **1557** ABP. PARKER *Ps.* xxxvi. 99 The wordes of hys mouth be unrightfully wayed.

1793 JEFFERSON *Writ.* (1859) IV. 61 Between restraining it ourselves, and permitting her enemies to restrain it unrightfully, is no difference. **1866** HOWELLS *Venet. Life* iv. 53 A great humbug and unrightfully in the guide-books.

un'rightfulness. Now *rare.* [f. UNRIGHTFUL *a.*] The quality of being unrightful.

a **1250** *Owl & Night.* 1742 Ic nolde þat vnrihtfulnesse Me at þen ende ouercome. *a* **1325** *Prose Psalter* vii. 15 Lo, þe sinner doþ vnryȝt-fulnesse. **1382** WYCLIF *John* vii. 18 This is sothfast, and vnriȝtfulnesse is not in him. ? *c* **1450** in Roy *Rede me*, etc. (Arb.) 183 The wrathe of god is shewyd..vpon cruelnes and vnryghtfulnes of these men. *a* **1470** H. PARKER *Dives & Pauper* (W. de W. 1496) II. xvii. 128/1 Periury is cause..of all unrightfulnesse.

1821 JEFFERSON *Autobiog.* Writ. 1892 I. 62 The unrightfulness and inefficacy of the punishment of crimes by death.

†**un'rightly**, *a. Obs.*[−1] [UN-[1] 7. Cf. next and OE. *unrihtlic.*] Wrong, erroneous.

1422 YONG tr. *Secreta Secret.* 161 Verite caste doune, whan any vnryghtly thynge is preferrid to trouthe.

un'rightly, *adv.* Now *rare.* [OE. *unrihtlíce* (UN-[1] 11 + RIGHTLY *adv.*), = MDu. *onrechtelike* (obs. Du. *-lijk*), MLG. *unrechtelíken*, OHG. *unrehtlîhho* (MHG. *unrehtlîche*, etc.), ON. *úréttliga* (MDa. and Da. *urettelig*, MSw. *orätlika*).] Not rightfully; unfairly, wrongly.

a **900** *O.E. Martyrol.* 18 May 84 Fram þæm mannum..þa he ær unrihtlice ofsloh on þyssum life. *c* **1000** *Rule St. Benet* (1888) 104 Unrihtlice he ne ȝedihte [nan þing]. *c* **1425** *Eng. Conq. Ireland* 128 To setten yn har londes, Thay that wyth streynth & vnryghtly weren out i-dryue. **1544** BALE *Chron. Sir J. Oldcastell* 55 b, Not all vnryghtlye ded sayenct Augustyn speake yt. **1583** tr. *Maison Neuve's Gerileon* I. 29 b, Thereby to burden you with the fault, wherein not vnrightly you are culpable. **1643** PRYNNE *Sov. Power Parl.* III. 108 If any inferiour Officers..unrightly governe the people, they may lawfully be resisted by them. **1878** *Prodigal Son* IV. in Simpson *Sch. Shaks.* 110 We are such honest folk that we covet nothing unrightly.

†**un'rightness.** *Obs.* [UN-[1] 12.] Unfairness.

c **1445** PECOCK *Donet* 134 þei ben..forbodis of oure vniustness, of oure vnriȝtnes anentis oure neiȝboris.

†**un'righty**, *a. Obs.*[−1] [UN-[1] 7 + RIGHT *a.* Cf. Du. *onrechtich* (Du. *-ig*), MLG. *unrichtich*, OHG. *unrihtig* (G. *unrichtig*), etc.] Devoid of right condition.

c **1315** SHOREHAM I. 1075 þou wreþest god almyȝty, To holy cherche on-bouxam þart, Makest þy selue on-ryȝty.

un'rimed, *ppl. a.* [UN-[1] 8 a.] = UNRHYMED *ppl. a.*

1774 [W. MITFORD] *Ess. Harmony Lang.* 142 Rimed verse ..is far inferior to unrimed. **1886** SKEAT *Wars Alex.* p. xx, Any other unrimed alliterative poem.

un'rimple, *v.* (UN-[2] 4. Cf. Du. *ontrimpelen.*)

1800 *Monthly Mag.* X. 318 Fresh blossoms of diction [would] unrimple their roseate petals.

un'rimpled, *ppl. a.* (UN-[1] 8.)

[**1775** ASH.] *a* **1839** GALT *Demon Destiny* III. (1840) 21 The placid waters..Were all unrimpled by the gentle air.

un'rind, *v.* Also 6 vnrine. [UN-[2] 4. Cf. G. *entrinden.*] *trans.* To strip of rind or bark. Hence **un'rinded** *ppl. a.*[1]

1382 WYCLIF *Gen.* xxx. 37 Jacob takynge green popil ȝerdis..a parti vnryendide hem. **1598** FLORIO, *Sbucciare*,.. to pare..or vnbarke or vnrinde trees. **1611** COTGR., *Escorcée*,..the pilled, or vnrinded part of a Plant. **1648** HEXHAM II, *Ontschoeyen*, to Pill or Vnrinde a tree.

b. *fig.* To undress.

1872 T. HARDY *Under Greenw. Tree* IV. ii, I've been forced to go upstairs and unrind myself.

†**un'rinded**, *ppl. a.*[2] *Sc. Obs.* [UN-[1] 8 + RIND *v.*[2]] Unrendered; not melted down.

1581 *Burgh Rec. Edinb.* (1882) IV. 217 The talloun bocht be him als weill ryndet and vnryndet. **1702** in W. R. Mackintosh *Glimpses of Kirkwall* (1887) 42 That none of the flesshers exact any more than twentie pennies Scots for the merk of unrynded tallow.

un'ringed, *ppl. a.* [UN-[1] 8. Cf. MDu. *ongeringet*, older Da. *uringet.*] Of swine: Not furnished with a nose-ring. (Cf. UNRUNG *ppl. a.*[2])

1510 *Burgh Rec. Prestwick* (Maitl. Club) 42 For þe wrangwis worttyne of þar swyne, & wnryngyt. **1576** GASCOIGNE *Steele Gl.* (Arb.) 70 Like rude vnringed swine. **1624** in H. Maclean *Watermillock Reg.* (1908) 157 Sub poena for every swine so unringed iiij[d]. **1664** BUTLER *Hud.* II. II. 310 Is't fit [it] should..Be forc'd t' impeach a broken hedge, And Pigs unring'd. **1733** in Climenson *Hist. Shiplake* (1894) 307 No person..shall suffer his hogs to go unringed.

un'rinsed, *ppl. a.* (UN-[1] 8.)

1661 FELTHAM *Resolves* (ed. 8) II. i. 174 Loose and unrins'd expressions are the..spurcitious exhalations of a corrupted mind. **1847** LANDOR *Hellenics, Thrasymedes & E.* 6 Ye shall not..taste From unrinsed barrel the diluted wine. **1860** FLOR. NIGHTINGALE *Nursing* i. 14, I have actually seen ..the utensils..put back, unrinsed, under the bed.

un'rioted, *ppl. a.* (UN-[1] 8.)

1627 MAY *Lucan* IX. 235 A chast vnriotted house, and neuer stain'd With her Lords fortune.

un'rip, *v.* [UN-[2] 9 + RIP *v.*[2]]

1. *trans.* To strip (a house or roof) of tiles, slates, etc. (Cf. RIP *v.*[2] 2 c.) Now *dial.*

a **1513** FABYAN *Chron.* VII. 414 [They] vnryppyd the howse in dyuers places that the rayne..myght entre. **1543** in Parker *Dom. Archit.* (1859) III. 61 Serching, vnryppyng, new tylyng and poyntyng ouer the west syde of the Quenes pallet chambre. **1887** PARISH & SHAW *Kentish Gloss.* 129 To unrip the roof of a stable or outbuilding, is to take off the tiles, slates, &c.

2. a. To lay open, slit up, or detach, by ripping.

Stigmatized in 1708 as 'a barbarous, improper word' (*British Apollo* No. 75, 2/1; cf. quot. 1880). In 19th c. somewhat rare in literary use; but freq. in dialect.

1534 [see b]. **1594** SHAKS. *Rich. III.* I. iv. 212 [Thou] Did'st breake that Vow, and with thy treacherous blade, Vnrip'st the Bowels of thy Sou'raignes Sonne. **1601** B. JONSON *Poetaster* III. iv, You should ha' seene me vnrip their noses now, and haue sent 'hem to the next barbers, to stitching. **1661** WALTON *Angler* I. v. (ed. 3) 122 We heard as high a contention amongst the beggers, Whether it was easiest to rip a cloak, or to unrip a cloak? **1700** SWIFT *Poems, Mrs. Harris' Petition* 11 My smock was unript, And, instead of putting it [= a purse] into my pocket, down it slipt. **1743** FIELDING *J. Wild* IV. ix, He unript the lining of his waistcoat and pulled forth several jewels. **1837** MARRYAT *Dog Fiend* xi, They..proceeded to unrip them [*sc.* bags]. **1863** MISS BRADDON *Aurora Floyd* xxi, He took his clasp-knife..[and] carefully unripped a part of one of the seams in the waistcoat. **1880** *Plain Hints Needlework* 106 To say un-rip, as is often heard, is at least manifestly wrong, to describe the act of tearing open.

b. In fig. contexts.

1534 R. WHITINTON *Cicero* I. G vij, Amytes and loue that lesse delyte vs..wyse men iudge rather to become vs by lytell and by lytell to vnrippe them than sodaynly to cutte them awaye. **1586** HOOKER *Disc. Justification* §5, I cannot stand now to vnrip this building, and to sift it piece by piece. **1611** BEAUM. & FL. *Philaster* I. i, Though thy breath doth strike me dead..I have unript my breast. *a* **1652** A. WILSON *Inconstant Ladie* IV. iii, Thy lookes are full of honestie; I dare Vnrip my breast to thee. **1697** COLLIER *Ess. Mor. Subj.* II. 67 As Cato well observes, though in the Phrase of a Taylor, Friendship ought not to be Vnrip'd, but Vnstitch'd.

refl. **1614** J. COOKE *Greene's Tu Quoque* E 1, Had'st thou not vnrip't thy selfe to me, I should neuer haue knowne thee.

†**c.** To break (a seal); to open (a sealed document). *Obs.*

1583 GREENE *Mamillia* 26 b, His daughter..receiuing the Letter, could scarcely stay to vnrip the seale, while she came in her closet. **1633** FORD *'Tis Pity* v. i. 2, *Friar.* Looke there, 'tis writt to thee. (Gives the letter.) *Gio.* From whom? *Friar.* Vnrip the seales and see. **1634** HEYWOOD *Maidenh. well lost* I. 47 b, His seal'd Commission He had vnript.

†**3.** *fig.* **a.** To rip up, bring to light or notice, expose to view. *Obs.*

1577 SIR W. DRURY in Grosart *Spenser's Wks.* I. 66, I would not seem to unrip old matters. **1591** *Troub. Raigne K. John* i. 88 Before I once open my mouth to vnrippe the shameful slaunder of my parents. **1615** BRATHWAIT *Strappado* 211 For many Errors and fowle crimes I knowe.. Which I'le in part vnrip, and so make cleare. **1633** FORD *'Tis Pity* III. F 3 b, You haue vnript a soule, so foule and guilty, ..I maruaile how The earth hath borne you vp.

b. To unfold, disclose, reveal, make known. Now *rare.*

1579–80 NORTH *Plutarch* (1595) 832 When he beganne to vnrip his whole intents and practises..he..offended the Senate. **1598** MARSTON *Pygmal., Sat.* ii. 143 Delphick Apollo, ayde me to vnrip These intricate deepe Oracles of wit. **1615** BRATHWAIT *Strappado*, etc. (1878) 253 Her blush, her smile, her biting of her lip, did all the secrets of her hart vnrippe. **1755** SMOLLETT *Quix.* II. 296 You may unrip, and unload, all that lies upon your sorrowful heart. **1928** BARRIE *Peter Pan* II, in *Plays* 42 Unrip your plan, Captain.

†**c.** To undo, annul. *Obs.*

1622 BACON *Hen. VII*, 176 Hee could not now with his Honour so vnrippe, and (in a sort) put a Lye vpon all that hee had said and done before.

Hence **un'ripped** *ppl. a.*; **un'ripping** *vbl. sb.*

1641 MILTON *Animadv.* 8 Such an unripping, such an Anatomie of the shiest, and tenderest particular truths. **1707** MORTIMER *Husb.* 144 Let down the Bag by unripping of the Hoop. **1850** THACKERAY *Pendennis* xi, Milly..took an unripped satin garment off the only vacant seat.

un'ripe, *a.* [OE. *unripe* (f. *un-* UN-¹ 7 + *ripe* RIPE *a.*), = WFris. *on-*, *ûnryp*, NFris. *ünrip(þ*, MDu. (Du.) *onrijp*, OHG. *unrîfi* (MHG. *unrîf*, G. *unreif*).]

†**1.** Of death: Untimely, premature. *Obs.*

c **1000** ÆLFRIC *Gloss.* in Wr.-Wülcker 149 *Immatura* [*mors*], unripe deað. **1548** UDALL *Erasmus Par. Luke* vii. 69 b, The unripe death of the young strieplyng. *a* **1586** SIDNEY *Arcadia* II. vi, Dorilaus, whose unripe death doth yet..draw teares from vertuous eyes. **1633** P. FLETCHER (*title*), Elisa, or An Elegie upon the Unripe Decease of Sr Antonie Irby.

2. Immature; not arrived at full development.

a **1340** HAMPOLE *Psalter* cxviii. 147, I ran in barnhede, þat is vnrype til perfeccioun. **1548** UDALL *Erasm. Par. Luke* 141 b, That same stemme of the Judaicall figtree brought foorth..vnsauourie, & vnripe people. **1620** *Southampton Court Leet Rec.* (1907) III. 582 The teaching of a Stranger ..vnripe of yeres. *a* **1639** WALLER *Battle Summer-Isl.* I. 59 So in this northern tract our hoarser throats Utter unripe and ill-constrained notes. **1659** W. CHAMBERLAYNE *Pharon.* II. iii. 612 Yet Justice slumbers I' the prosecution of his unripe fate. **1700** DRYDEN *Sigism. & Guisc.* 254 Resolv'd his unripe Vengeance to defer, The Royal Spy..Sought not the Garden. **1704** J. TRAPP *Abra-Mulé* I. i. 33 Thy tender Innocence, and unripe Beauty. **1819** SHELLEY *Peter Bell 3rd* Prol. 15 The First Peter—he who was Like the shadow in the glass Of the second, yet unripe. **1847** EMERSON *Each & All* 38 Beauty is unripe childhood's cheat. **1891** *Spectator* 28 Feb., To try unripe and ill-conceived schemes for improving their condition.

b. Of years or age.

1568 GRAFTON *Chron.* II. 120 The election beyng vnfree, and the yeres vnripe, eche of them almost of necessitie must hate the other. **1596** SPENSER *F.Q.* VI. ii. 9, I whose vnryper yeares are yet vnfit For thing of weight. **1633** P. FLETCHER *Purple Isl.* Ep. Ded., These raw Essayes of my very unripe yeares. **1659** W. CHAMBERLAYNE *Pharon.* IV. v. 235 The old Experienced courtiers kneel; by which..those of unriper age [etc.]. **1800** WORDSW. *Brothers* 297 The boy..of unripe years, a stripling only. **1814** CARY *Dante, Parad.* XVII. 77 His unripe age Yet holds him from observance.

3. Of fruit, etc.: Not matured by growth.

a **1250** *Owl & Night.* 320 Mi stefne is bold..& þin is iliche one pype Of one smale weode vnripe. **1382** WYCLIF *Rev.* vi. 13 As a fijge tree sendith his vnripe fyges. **1535** COVERDALE *Wisd.* x. 7 The vnripe and vntymely frutes that growe vpon the trees. **1555** EDEN *Decades* (Arb.) 67 While they be soure and vnripe, they are white. **1614** R. TAILOR *Hog hath lost Pearl* II, Unripe fruit will ask more shaking before they fall than those that are. **1732** ARBUTHNOT *Rules of Diet* in *Aliments*, etc. I. 247 Unripe, they are sour, and rather astringent. **1798** COLERIDGE *Fears in Solitude* 9 Fresh and delicate As vernal corn-field, or the unripe flax. **1849** CLARIDGE *Cold Water Cure* 112 To eat plentifully of common unripe plums. **1882** *Garden* 4 Feb. 72/3 Unripe wood is liable to get injured by frosts.

transf. *a* **1425** tr. *Arderne's Treat. Fistula*, etc. 93 Rude [roset] is made of vnripe oile and of rosez. **1693** SIR T. BLOUNT *Nat. Hist.* 250 Erastus affirms..that..there hath been Unripe and Unconcocted Silver found in Mines. **1751** WARBURTON *Pope's Wks.* IV. 128 *note*, The image is taken from half-formed unripe lightning, which streams along the sky. **1799** KIRWAN *Geol. Ess.* 279 No. 10. Red and yellow, unripe pouzzolana. *Ibid.*, Unripe black pumice. **1884** J. PHIN *Dict. Apiculture* 73 Unripe Honey.—Honey from which the water has not been sufficiently evaporated.

un'riped, *ppl. a.* [UN-¹ 8.] Unripened.

1423 JAS. I *Kingis Q.* xiv, Thou ȝouth, of nature Indegest, Vnrypit fruyte with windis variable.

un'ripely, *adv.* (UN-¹ 11.)

1597 MIDDLETON *Wisd. Solomon* ii. 3 Unripely withering in a flowery prime. **1755** JOHNSON, *Crudely*,..unripely; without due preparation.

un'ripened, *ppl. a.* (UN-¹ 8.)

1588 KYD *Househ. Philos.* Wks. (1901) 244 Mellons..that ..taste like Goords and Cowgomers which also hang vpon the earth vnripened. **1589** [? LYLY] *Pappe w. Hatchet* D iij b, Vnripened youthes, whose wisedomes are yet in the blade. **1611** SPEED *Hist. Gt. Brit.* IX. xii. §63. 682/2 They would not haue found that euer this Iland brought forth a Prince of such excellency at so vnripened yeares. **1675** HAN. WOOLLEY *Gentlew. Comp.* 181 Take of unripened Galls one dram. **1720** POPE *Iliad* XXIII. 671 The errors of unripen'd age. **1768–74** TUCKER *Lt. Nat.* (1834) II. 228 To..wade through the mud of indolence, with the slender staff of unripened reason. **1831** SCOTT *Ct. Rob.* ix, The vehemence of their own appetite for raw fruits and unripened wines. **1895** *Cent. Mag.* Aug. 542/2 All the unripened nymphs that played at hide-and-seek among the maples.

un'ripeness. (UN-¹ 12.)

a **1340** HAMPOLE *Psalter* cxviii. 147, I bifore come in vn-rypnes and i cried. **1548** ELYOT, *Immaturitas*, vnrypenesse, to muche haste in dooyng a thynge before the tyme. **1593** *Sidney's Arcadia* v. (1922) II. 199 The unripenesse of theyr age. **1625** BACON *Ess., Delays* (Arb.) 525 The Ripenesse, or Vnripenesse of the Occasion (as we said) must euer be well weighed. **1678** MARVELL *Growth Popery* 42 In this state of uncertainty and unripeness, the House Adjourned. **1783** *Phil. Trans.* LXXIII. 244 The unripeness of the barley. **1844** PRICE in Stanley *Arnold* I. iv. 196 The unripeness of England for a free and unfettered discussion. **1886** C. SCOTT *Sheep-farming* 46 Let the same conditions or unripeness be present in any kind of roots, and their effects will be much the same.

un'ripening, *ppl. a.* (UN-¹ 10.)

1864 SWINBURNE *Atalanta* 531 Death Crushes with sterile feet the unripening ear.

unripped, -ripping: see UNRIP *v.*

un'rippled, *ppl. a.* (UN-¹ 8.)

[**1775** ASH.] **1816** BYRON *Siege Cor.* xix, The sea..was unrippled as glass may be. **1882** FARRAR *Early Chr.* I. 248 The unity so secured is but the stagnancy of the unrippled water. **1883** *Congregationalist* Nov. 902 The secret of our unrippled intercourse is that we have always acted on the principle of non-intrusion.

un'ripplingly, *adv.* (UN-¹ 11.)

a **1861** T. WINTHROP *Life in Open Air* viii. (1863) 63 Its current, unripplingly smooth,..bore on our bark.

un'risen, *ppl. a.* (UN-¹ 8 b.)

[**1775** ASH.] *a* **1806** H. K. WHITE *To Morning* ii, The lark ..soars till the unrisen sun Gleams on her speckled breast. **1879** MISS BIRD *Lady's Life in Rocky Mount.* 139 The moon, as yet unrisen here.

un'ritual, *a.* (UN-¹ 7.)

1791 ANNA SEWARD *Lett.* (1811) III. 80 The quiet dispassionate simplicity of unritual devotion.

unritua'listic, *a.* (UN-¹ 7.)

1876 ALEXANDER *Bampton Lect.* (1877) 6 A religion, tolerant, unritualistic, and unsectarian.

un'rivalable, *a.* (UN-¹ 7 b.)

1834 SOUTHEY *Doctor* I. 34 The present unique, unrivalled, and unrivalable production.

un'rivalled, *ppl. a.* (UN-¹ 8.)

1591 SHAKS. *Two Gent.* v. iv. 144, I heere..Plead a new state in thy vn-riual'd merit, To which I thus subscribe. **1667** MILTON *P.L.* III. 68 Uninterrupted joy, unrivald love In blissful solitude. **1693** DRYDEN *Juvenal* x. 492 But your Endymion,..Unrivall'd, shall a Beauteous Dame enjoy. **1708** J. PHILIPS *Cyder* II. 7 Thou view'st..what Unrival'd Authors by their Presence made For ever venerable. **1771** *Junius' Lett.* lxvii. (1772) II. 305 *note*, In the memoirs of private treachery they stand first and unrivalled. **1849** MACAULAY *Hist. Eng.* iv. I. 445 Unrivalled powers of argument and eloquence. **1877** MRS. OLIPHANT *Makers Flor.* xv. 369 [He] had shown himself unrivalled and above all competitors.

†**un'rive,** *v. Obs.* [UN-² 9 + RIVE *v.*¹] *trans.* To tear apart; to open up.

1592 WYRLEY *Armorie, Capitall de Buz* 109 Such one as.. troubles makes him faster for to twind Fast gaged band of loue, and scorns to liue More rather then the same he will vnriue. **1652** BENLOWES *Theoph.* VI. xciv, Thus, they..Into each others knowledge dive; And, by consent, thoughts, else inscrutable, unrive.

unrive, obs. var. of UNREEVE *v.*

un'riven, *ppl. a.* (UN-¹ 8 b. Cf. MSw. *orivin*, Sw. *orifen.*)

c **1400** *Sege Jerus.* 607 ȝit wer þe Romayns as rest, as þey fram Rome come, Ronnen ouer [*v.r.* vnrevyn] eche a renk, & noȝt a ryng brosten. **1817** MOORE *Lalla R., Veiled Prophet* III. 219 The last sole stubborn fragment, left unriv'n, Of the proud host that late stood fronting Heav'n. **1845** HIRST *Com. Mammoth*, etc. 25 Mocking, as he rushed on unriven, The innocuous bolts of mighty heaven.

un'rivet, *v.* [UN-² 3.]

1. *trans.* To undo, unfasten, or detach, by the removal of rivets.

1591 HARINGTON *Orl. Fur.* XLV. lxxii, No more the damsels force did now preuayle To pierce a plate, or to vn-riuet nayle. **1627** DRAYTON *Agincourt* 46 Their Curates are vnriuetted with blowes. **1631** *Celestina* XVIII. 181 Who hewes, and unriviteth the finest maile but it [*sc.* the sword]? **1755** T. H. CROKER *Orl. Fur.* XXXI. xxi, While from their shields immense the sides they tear, Armour unrivetted, and mail unbound. **1758** GOLDSM. *Mem. Protestant* (1895) II. 83 At nine o'Clock..our Chains were again unrivetted. **1863** CONINGTON *Hor., Odes* III. v. 18 Should aught but death the prisoner's chain Unrivet. **1885** *Law Rep.* 15 *Q.B.D.* 360 The belts..could be removed from the shafting altogether by being unrivetted or unlaced.

2. *fig.* To undo, loosen, relax, detach, etc.

1620–51 I. JONES *Stone-Heng* (1725) 13 He..sought to be ..revenged on the British Nobility, who had wholly un-rivetted his Designs. **1665** BRATHWAIT *Comment Two Tales* (1901) 78 Some..unriveted the very Secrets of their own Brests, and told him what they most desired. **1706** BAYNARD in Floyer *Hot & Cold Bath.* II. 199 Nothing is harder than to unrivet a wrong Notion. **1803** SCOTT *Let.* in *Lockhart* (1837) I. xi. 378 We sincerely hope Mrs. Ellis and you will unrivet yourselves from your forest. **1853** MISS E. S. SHEPPARD *Ch. Auchester* III. 158 Before I had spoken or even unriveted my gaze.

Hence **un'rivetting** *vbl. sb.*

1611 COTGR., *Desrivement*, an vnriuetting. *a* **1662** HEYLYN *Laud* (1668) 370 By which he screwed himself so far into his Majesties good opinion, that whosoever undertook the unrivetting of him, made him faster in it. **1885** W. MORRIS in Mackail *Life* (1899) II. 134 Only the complete unriveting of the chain will really free us.

†**unro.** *Obs.* (See also UNRUFE.) [UN-¹ 4, 12. Cf. ON. *úró* (Norw., MDa., and Da. *uro*, MSw. and Sw. *oro*), NFris. (Sylt) *unruu*, MLG. *unro(u)we*, MHG. *unruowe*, *unruo* (G. *unruhe*).] Unrest, disquiet.

a **1300** *Cursor M.* 7438 Ai quen he [*sc.* Saul] was trauaild mast Thoru a wreche vn-roful gast, And he [*sc.* David] bigan to gleu or sing, Of his vn-ro he tok lething. *Ibid.* 28250 In kyrk i wroght oft syth vn-ro Quen goddis seruis was to do. **13..** *Metr. Hom.* in *Archiv Stud. neu. Spr.* LVII. 250/2 Wiþ pyne and vnreste and vn-Ro. *a* **1400** *Sir Perc.* 362 Thou wirkeste thiselfe mekille unroo.

Hence †**un'roful** *a.* (See prec., quot. *a* 1300.)

†**un'roast,** obs. variant of next.

1665 PEPYS *Diary* 21 Dec., A good chine of beef..; but, being all frost-bitten, was most of it unroast.

un'roasted, *ppl. a.* (UN-¹ 8.)

1377 LANGL. *P. Pl.* B. v. 612 Tho Adam and Eue eten apples vnrosted. **1600** HAKLUYT *Voy.* III. 511 The worst in the ship thought scorne..of sodden lambe, which they disdained to eate vnrosted. **1622** FLETCHER *Sea-Voy.* III. i, Why should we consume thus, and starve,..And she live there that bred all our miseries, Unrosted, or unsod? **1751** J. HILL *Hist. Plants* 281 A decoction of the raw or unroasted seeds is a powerful diuretic. **1839** URE *Dict. Arts* 693, 19 hundred weight of limestone are employed; constituting nearly 1 of limestone for 3 of unroasted ore. **1882** *U.S. Rep. Prec. Met.* 600 Two parcels of pyrites of 20 tons each—one roasted, the other unroasted.

un'robbed, *ppl. a.* (UN-¹ 8.)

1393 LANGL. *P. Pl.* C. XIV. 1 He may walke vnrobbed Among pilours in pees yf pacience hym folwe. *c* **1450** *Mirk's Festial* 39 A man myght goo wher he wold vnrobbet, wyth his good yn hys hond. *c* **1530** LD. BERNERS *Arth. Lyt. Bryt.* (1814) 318 They leue no house vnrobbed. **1599** HAKLUYT *Voy.* II. I. 238 Although you haue set so many eyes to looke there for your benefit, that you escape vnrobbed of the slaues. **1660** EVELYN *The Late News* 2 Those ready Jewels of honour (the only Treasure he is, or can be unrob'd of). **1794** H. WALPOLE in Miss Berry *Jrnls.*, etc. (1865) I. 436 At night I went to Lady Onslow's,..and came back unrobbed. **1891** *Pall Mall G.* 24 Dec. 2/3 An amateur bushranger..'stuck up' a coach, which, however, got away unrobbed.

un'robe, *v.* [UN-² 4.] To divest of a robe or robes: **a.** *trans.* or *refl.* Also const. *of.*

1598 FLORIO, *Spogliare*,..to disaray, to vnrobe. **1687** in *Magd. Coll. & Jas. II* (O.H.S.) 25 Several went into the outward Chapel to unrobe themselves. **1711** G. HICKES *Two Treat. Chr. Priesth.* (1847) II. 290 He robed and unrobed himself in his throne. **1797** COLERIDGE *Christabel* I. xxvi, But now unrobe yourself; for I Must pray, ere yet in bed I lie. **1838** ELIZA COOK *Love's First Dream* iii, It fades..; Leaving the spirit, unrobed of light, In darkness and tears behind. **1850** R. G. CUMMING *Hunter's Life S. Afr.* xii. I. 263, I considered myself..fortunate in having secured so noble a specimen of the lion,..and I at once set men to work to unrobe him. **1874** SPURGEON *Treas. Dav.* lxxxii. 7 How quickly death unrobes the great!

b. *absol.* (for *refl.*).

1743 YOUNG *Nt. Th.* IV. 44 When, on their exit, souls are bid unrobe,..And drop this mask of flesh behind the scene. **1766** ENTICK *London* IV. 117 There is no vestry room for the minister to robe and unrobe. **1837** MCCULLOCH *Acc. Brit. Empire* II. 240 The Lords also adjourn..to unrobe. **1855** MACAULAY *Hist. Eng.* xv. III. 574 The King..unrobed, took his seat,..and listened..to the debate.

Hence **un'robing** *ppl. a.*

1810 MONTGOMERY *West Indies*, etc. 157 Still the unrobing spirit cast Diviner glories to the last.

un'robed, *ppl. a.* (UN-¹ 8.)

[**1775** ASH.] **1861** H. MACMILLAN *Footnotes fr. Page Nat.* 189 Unrobed prophets that see no sad visions themselves. **1899** *Westm. Gaz.* 8 May 5/1 The two Archbishops entered unrobed.

unro'bust, *a.* (UN-¹ 7.)

[**1775** ASH.] **1891** HANNAH LYNCH *G. Meredith* 36 Deeming our taste questionable and unrobust.

un'rocked, *ppl. a.* (UN-¹ 8.)

With the Sc. quots. in (*a*) cf. ROCKED *ppl. a.* 1, quot. *a* 1500, and ROCK *v.*¹ 1, quot. 1796.

(*a*) *c* **1480** HENRYSON *Fables, Fox, Wolf & Husb.* 116 Schir, be the Rude, vnroikkit now ȝe raif. **1530** LYNDESAY *Test. Papyngo* 969 Thow rauis vnrockit,..So to reproue ryches or properttie. *a* **1583** POLWART *Flyting w. Montgomerie* 802 (Tullib. MS.), Proud slaif, ȝe raif vnrokkit.

(*b*) **1648** HEXHAM II, *Ongewieght*, vnrocked. [**1775** ASH.] **1892** *Daily News* 4 Feb. 5/8 The absolute stillness of her tall masts, unrocked by any motion of the sea.

un'roll, *v.* [UN-^{2} 3, 5, 7. Cf. Du. *ont-*, Ger. *entrollen.*]

1. *trans.* To open out from a rolled-up state; to uncoil.

1412–20 LYDG. *Chron. Troy* III. 171 Ful kny3tly þei han take her weye..with baneris..displaied, And her penouns vnrollid euerychon. **1523** LD. BERNERS *Froiss.* I. ccxli. 145/1 [He] rested on the felde, and caused his banerr to be vnrolled. **1611** COTGR., *Desrouler*, to vnroule, vnfould, lay open. *a* **1700** EVELYN *Diary* 15 Jan. 1645, On which lay the 5 Bookes of Moses, and the Commandments a little unrowled. **1769** MRS. RAFFALD *Eng. Housekpr.* (1778) 89 Then unroll the cloth, and roll it tight again. **1786** ABERCROMBIE *Gard. Assist.* 267 Turf..when to be laid, unrolled, joining..close edge to edge. **1828** DUPPA *Trav. Italy*, etc. 98 In this Museum [at Naples] is carried on the operation of unrolling the ancient papyri. **1873** J. RICHARDS *Wood-working Factories* 122 By unrolling the blade on the floor, it can be tested as to straightness.

refl. **1815** SCOTT *Guy M.* xxxviii, Rolling up..the long lash of his horsewhip, and then by a jerk causing it to unroll itself into the middle of the floor. **1855** KINGSLEY *Westw. Ho!* xvii, Till not..an armadillo [dare] unroll himself.

b. In fig. contexts.

1678 DRYDEN *All for Love* v. i, Time has unrowl'd her Glories to the last, And now clos'd up the Volume. **1750** GRAY *Elegy* 50 But Knowledge to their eyes her ample page ..did ne'er unroll. **1757** —— *Bard* 106 But oh! what solemn scenes on Snowdon's height Descending slow their glitt'ring skirts unroll? **1818** BYRON *Ch. Har* IV. clvii, Until thy mind..unroll In mighty graduations, part by part, The glory. **1866** LE FANU *All in Dark* xiii, One could see..that she was reading to herself the romance that was unrolled within her pretty girlish head. **1876–89** R. BRIDGES *Growth of Love* xlvii, The busy mind Will in one woeful moment more upwind Than lifelong years unroll of bitter or black.

c. To extend, spread out; to disperse.

1813 SCOTT *Trierm.* III. xii, And still..Were..bastions dimly seen, And Gothic battlements between Their gloomy length unroll'd. **1817** SHELLEY *Rev. Islam* I. xxxviii, Wisdom had unrolled The clouds which hide the gulf of mortal woe. **1831** SCOTT *Cast. Dang.* iii, The mist had settled upon the hills, and unrolled itself upon brook, glade, and tarn.

d. *fig.* To develop or expand fully.

1854 EMERSON *Lett. & Soc. Aims, Eloquence*, Jenny Lind ..complained of concert-rooms and town-halls, that they did not give her room enough to unroll her voice. *a* **1871** GROTE *Eth. Fragm.* iv. (1876) 92 That all these elements are really present, is shewn most incontestably when the sentiment comes to be deliberately unrolled.

2. *intr.* To become unrolled. Also *fig.*

1588 SHAKS. *Tit. A.* II. iii. 35 Euen as an Adder when she doth vnrowle To do some fatall execution. ? **1797** BLAKE *Four Zoas* IX. 20 The Books of Urizen unroll with dreadful noise! **1807** J. BARLOW *Columb.* II. 132 The venturous soul Bids greater powers and bolder thoughts unrol. **1816** J. WILSON *Misc. Poems* 194 As the clouds of the morning unroll. **1827** FARADAY *Chem. Manip.* xx. 532 To fold..this projecting part down, in such a manner as to..prevent the slip from unrolling.

†**3.** *trans.* To remove from a roll or list. *Obs.*$^{-1}$

1611 SHAKS. *Wint. T.* IV. iii. 130 If I make not this Cheat bring out another,..let me be vnrold, and my name put in the booke of Vertue.

Hence **un'rolled** *ppl. a.*^{1}; **un'roller; un'rolling** *vbl. sb.* and *ppl. a.*^{1}

1805 LUCCOCK *Nat. Wool* 113 When we find a line of sand strewed along the *unrolled fleece. **1890** *Retrospect Med.* CII. 27 Passing the unrolled end [of the bandage] over the shoulder and down the back. **1843** *For. Q. Rev.* II. 364 A pale-faced *unroller of dusty records. **1648** HEXHAM II, *Een Ontrollinge*, an *Vnroling, or an Vnfolding. **1856** STANLEY *Sinai & Pal.* i. 3 There is..no unrolling of a great drama, no beginning, middle and end of a moral progress. **1870** BURTON *Hist. Scot.* lxi. VI. 93 The unrolling of secrets. **1699** C. HOPKINS *Crt. Prosp., Peace* iii, *Unrowling Waves steal softly to the Shore. *a* **1850** BRYANT *To a Cloud* 9, I would I were with thee..To rest on thy unrolling skirts.

un'rolled, *ppl. a.*^{2} [UN-^{1} 8. Cf. G. *ungerollt.*] Not rolled; not subjected to rolling.

1573 TUSSER *Husb.* (1878) 100 See when ye rowle it, the weather be drie, or else it were better vnrowled to lie. **1600** [see STONE *sb.* 16 c] **1640** HOWELL *Dodona's Gr.* 114 Hee.. left no stone unrolld to bring this mighty worke to passe. **1839** DE LA BECHE *Rep. Geol. Cornwall*, etc. viii. 241 The prevalence of unrolled chalk flints above the green sand. **1851** *Quart. Jrnl. Geol. Soc.* VII. 359 The local and unrolled character of such surface-accumulations.

un'rolling, *ppl. a.*^{2} (UN-^{1} 10.)

1647 CLARENDON *Contempl. Ps.* Tracts (1727) 503 With downcast looks, and unrowling or fixt eyes.

un'rollment. *rare*$^{-1}$. [UNROLL *v.*] The action of unrolling.

1878 G. D. BOARDMAN *Creative Week* 124 You cannot unroll what was not inrolled... And yet these Gentlemen.. confound *Unrollment* with transmutation.

un-'Roman, *a.* (UN-^{1} 7.)

1682 *Whitelocke's Mem.* Pref., A more degenerate un-Roman generation. **1848** DENNIS *Cities & Cem. Etruria* iv. I. 97 Its mode of construction is decidedly un-Roman. **1864** PUSEY *Lect. Daniel* v. 284 The un-Roman retreat of Cestius Gallus.

un'romanized. *ppl. a.* (UN-^{1} 8 a (*c*).)

1771 WHITAKER *Hist. Manchester* I. 312 Before the third century the fruit appears to have..stocked the.. unromanized regions of Shetland with large plantations of the trees. **1847** WEBSTER, *Unromanized*,..not subjected to the principles or usages of the Roman Catholic Church. **1855** MILMAN *Lat. Chr.* XIV. vii. VI. 530 The kindred language enabled them to communicate..with the un-Romanised races. **1861** CRAIK *Hist. Lit.* I. 36 Evidence of the comparatively un-romanized condition of the Early English church.

unro'mantic, *a.* (UN-^{1} 7.)

1731 SWIFT *Let. to Gay & Duchess of Queensberry* 28 Aug., I own it is a base, unromantick spirit in me. **1824** MISS L. M. HAWKINS *Annaline* I. 41 If I were a young man, I should not like such an unromantic proceeding. **1850** THACKERAY *Pendennis* lxxi, This unromantic conclusion to a rather sentimental scene.

unro'mantical, *a.* (UN-^{1} 7.)

1850 THACKERAY *Pendennis* xlvii, Mr. Pen was blushing whilst he made this reply to his unromantical friend.

unro'mantically, *adv.* (UN-^{1} 11.)

1846 WORCESTER (citing Allen). **1884** W. BLACK in *Athenæum* 11 Oct. 463/1 Her unromantically long spinsterhood.

unro'manticized, *ppl. a.* (UN-^{1} 8 a (*c*).)

1855 MILMAN *Lat. Chr.* XIV. vi. VI. 525 Toulouse owns only her own unidealised, unromanticised Counts.

un'roof, *v.* (UN-^{2} 4.)

1598 FLORIO, *Disculminare*,..to vnroofe, or vntile a house. **1607** SHAKS. *Cor.* I. i. 222 Sdeath, The rabble should haue first vnroof't the City Ere so preuayl'd with me. **1779** HERVEY *Nav. Hist.* II. 457 Three hundred houses were unroofed by it. **1844** KINGLAKE *Eothen* viii, They actually unroofed a great part of the building. **1868** FREEMAN *Norm. Conq.* viii. II. 288 Houses were unroofed, and the timbers were thrown into the fosse.

transf. **1804** COLLINS *Scripscrap* 59 Time had unroof'd all the thatch from his pate. **1862** JAS. GRANT *Capt. of Guard* xii, Servers, pages, and pantrymen..unroofed the huge pasties of pigeons and venison.

Hence **un'roofed** *ppl. a.*^{1}, stripped of the roof, made roofless; **un'roofing** *vbl. sb.*

a **1550** LELAND *Itin.* (1768) II. 68 At the which tyme al the Chirch..lay to wast, and was *onrofid. **1779** *Phil. Trans.* LXX. 68 The sight of this town, unroofed, half buried under black scoriæ and ashes. **1814** SCOTT *Wav.* lxiii, Unroofed cottages, trees felled for palisades, and bridges destroyed. **1876** BRYANT *Flood of Years* 79 Temples stand Unroofed, forsaken by the worshippers. **1831** JAMES *Phil. Augustus* I. xv, The *unroofing of the hovels.

un'roofed, *ppl. a.*^{2} [UN-^{1} 8.] Not furnished with a roof; not roofed in.

[**1775** ASH.] **1805** EUGENIA DE ACTON *Nuns of Desert* II. 203 Miss Blenheim..had repaired to the un-roofed temple. **1851** RUSKIN *Stones Ven.* I. xiv. §18 Walls surrounding un-roofed courts.

transf. *a* **1854** H. REED *Lect. Eng. Lit.* ii. (1855) 83 The rude places of the open and unroofed world.

un'roost, *v.* [UN-^{2} 5 and 7.]

1. *trans.* To dislodge from a roost or perch. Also *fig.*, to dislodge or force out of a place, to drive out or away.

1598 FLORIO, *Disnidare*, to vnroost, to vn-nest. **1611** SHAKS. *Wint. T.* II. iii. 74 Thou dotard, thou art woman-tyr'd: vnroosted By thy dame Partlet heere. **1647** TRAPP *Comm. Rev.* xiv. 20 The Pope being driven from Rome, shall flie and sit, till Christ shall unroost him. **1682** BUNYAN *Holy War* 236 He also saw..how he was unroosted and made to quit the Castle. **1780** JOHNSON *Let. to Mrs. Thrale* 12 June, Though I am sorry that you should be so outrageously unroosted, I think that Bath has had you long enough. **1834** M. SCOTT *Cruise Miage* II. 12 Shoving the blade to the drowning man, with some danger of being unroosted myself in the attempt.

2. *intr.* To leave a roost; *fig.* to rise from bed.

1614 J. COOKE *Greene's Tu Quoque* L 3, [It is] time to goe to Church, and not a man vnroosted. **1821** CLARE *Vill. Minstr.* II. 24 The crows, unroosting as he comes in sight.

Hence **un'roosted** *ppl. a.*; **un'roosting** *vbl. sb.*

1615 [see UNRESTING *vbl. sb.*]. **1691** DRYDEN *K. Arthur* IV. i, The pass is free; The unroosted fiends have quitted this abode.

un'root, *v.* [UN-^{2} 4 b and 7.]

1. *trans.* To tear, pluck, or dig up by the roots. Also in fig. context and *transf.*

1570 LEVINS *Manip.* 178 To vnroote, *eradicare.* **1593** G. HARVEY *New Letter* B 3, Riotous Vanitie was wont to roote so deeply, that it could hardly be vnrooted. **1601** SHAKS. *All's Well* v. i. 6 Be bold you do so grow in my requitall, As nothing can vnroote you. **1635** SHIRLEY *Coronat.* IV, His love was firm to you, and cannot be Unrooted with one storme. **1687** DRYDEN *Song St. Cecilia's Day* vii, Trees unrooted left their Place. **1740** PITT *Æneid* VI. 9 To feed the fires, [some] unroot the standing woods. **1774** GOLDSM. *Nat. Hist.* I. 133 There are sometimes whole plains unrooted from the main lands, by floods and tempests. **1852** TH. ROSS tr. *Humboldt's Trav.* I. iii. 130 The causes that unroot these weeds at depths where..the sea is but slightly agitated.

b. *fig.* To eradicate, clear away, remove or detach altogether. Also **un'rooting** *vbl. sb.*

c **1449** PECOCK *Repr.* I. ii. 8 Forto meete a3ens the firste bifore spoken opinioun, and forto vnroote and updrawe it. *Ibid.*, This vnrooting of the first opinioun. **1574** HELLOWES *Gueuara's Fam. Ep.* (1577) 181 Vices be so euill to be vnrooted where they once take place. **1603** G. OWEN *Pembrokeshire* iii. (1892) 36 The Conqueror..purposed to haue vnrooted the Saxon or Englishe tongue out of England. *Ibid.* iv. 38 He gaue diuerse of them theire ancient landes to hold of him, and did not vtterlye vnroote them. **1738** WARBURTON *Div. Legat.* I. 277 They unrooted and destroyed all that good to Society. **1856** DICKENS *Lett.* (1880) I. 419 My present idea, if nothing should arise to unroot me sooner, is to stay here until the middle of May.

2. *intr.* To lose root-hold; to withdraw the root from the soil.

a **1616** BEAUM. & FL. *Bonduca* III. i, Make their strengths totter, and their topless fortunes Unroot and reel to ruine. *c* **1800** W. BLAKE *Four Zoas, Last Judgem.* 39 The trees unroot; The rocks groan horrible and run about.

un'rooted, *ppl. a.*^{1} [UN-^{1} 8 c + ROOT *v.*^{1} 7.] Not rooted *out.*

1550 BALE *Image both Churches* xiv. II. Nj, Nothinge shalbe vnrooted out that the heauenly father hath not planted. **1567** *Satir. Poems Reform.* vi. 108 Leif nathing that belangis to the Paip Unrutit out as it had neuer bene. **1649** MILTON *Eikon.* xvii. 155 So long as they remain'd in any of his three Kingdoms unrooted out. **1661** ARNWAY *Tablet* (ed. 3) 154 Can you imagine..The rooters up of Religion and Monarchy can be unrooted out; seeing the Loppers of the branches brak their neckes? **1859** SALA *Twice round Clock* 384 Gambling dens in Leicesterian slums, yet unrooted out by lynx-eyed policemen.

un'rooted, *ppl. a.*^{2} [UN-^{1} 8.] Not furnished with roots.

1648 HEXHAM II, *Ongewortelt*, Vnrooted. **1650** BAXTER *Saints' R.* IV. 588 What makes..the green blade of unrooted faith, to wither before the heat of persecution? **1849** *Sk. Nat. Hist., Mammalia* IV. 172 The molar teeth..are cylindrical, unrooted. **1893** *Barrows' Parl. Relig.* II. 1542 Hinduism is not the idolatry and unrooted polytheism of savages.

un'rope, *v.* [UN-^{2} 4 b.] *trans.* To detach by undoing a rope. Also *absol.* for *refl.* in *Mountaineering.*

1883 *Philadelphia Times* 30 July (Cent.), The horse was unroped from the wagon and turned loose. **1883** *Pall Mall G.* 1 Sept. 4/1 They unroped themselves, and sent three of their four guides to see what was the matter. **1902** G. BELL *Let.* 3 Aug. (1927) I. vii. 146 About 6 we got to where we could unrope—having been 48 hours on the rope. **1957** J. MASTERS *Far, Far the Mountain Peak* 67 She began to unrope, and a moment later the second *cordée* had joined them.

un'roped, *ppl. a.* (UN-^{1} 8.)

1881 BLACKMORE *Christowell* ii, An avalanche of pots from the unroped crate fell..upon him.

un'rosined, *ppl. a.* (UN-^{1} 8.)

1714 E. WARD *Field-Spy* 9 Where dejected Scrapers us'd to..Thrash their smooth Cats-guts with unrozen'd Bows.

un'rotted, *ppl. a.* (UN-^{1} 8.)

c **1440** *Pallad. on Husb.* x. 201 And thenne vnroted wol the grape abide. **1844** H. STEPHENS *Bk. Farm* II. 488 The unrotted stubble..may form obstacles under..the plough. **1876** ROCK *Text. Fabr.* i. 2 The few unrotted shreds still cleaving to its bones.

un'rotten, *a.* (UN-^{1} 7.)

1574 R. SCOT *Hop Garden* 33 Rather vse no dung than vnrotten dunge about the dressing of your Hoppes. **1683** J. REID *Scots Gard'ner* II. ii, Let not the root of any tree stand on..unrotten-manure. **1742** YOUNG *Nt. Th.* II. 564 Since friends grow not thick on ev'ry bough, Nor ev'ry friend unrotten at the core. **1763** MILLS *Pract. Husb.* II. 20 The yet un-rotten straw might be apt to clog the shares of the drill.

un'rouged, *ppl. a.* (UN-^{1} 8.)

1837 CARLYLE *Fr. Rev.* III. II. vii, Further aloft reigns Mère Duchesse with her unrouged Amazons. **1887** RUSKIN *Præterita* II. 39 Unveneered, unrouged, and well finished things.

un'rough, *a.* [UN-^{1} 7; cf. OE. *unrúh.*] Not rough; *spec.* not rough-chinned; unbearded.

c **1440** *Pallad. on Husb.* VII. 186 And thus the kinges [of bees] may be fonde:..in colour shynyng pure, And smothe, vnrough. **1605** SHAKS. *Macb.* v. ii. 10 There is Seywards Sonne, And many vnruffe youths, that euen now Protest their first of Manhood.

un'roughened, *ppl. a.* (UN-^{1} 8.)

[**1775** ASH.] **1865** CARLYLE *Fredk. Gt.* XIX. vii. V. 572 Cavalry, unroughened, make sad sliding.

un'round, *a.* (UN-^{1} 7. Cf. WFris. *on-, ûnroun*, Du. *onrond.*)

1588 LUCAR tr. *Tartaglia's Colloq. Shooting* App. 24 To make round pellettes of unround yron pellettes by two waves. **1676** NEWTON in Rigaud *Corr. Sci. Men* (1841) II. 383 This [image]..will be..not much unround, unless the angles be very unequal. **1877** E. SANG (*title*), The Toothing of Unround Discs, which are intended to Roll upon each other.

un'round, *v.* (UN-^{2} 6 a.)

Now *spec.* in phonetics: cf. ROUND *v.* 1 c. Also **un'rounding** vbl. sb.

1611 COTGR., *Desrondir*, to vnround, vnbow, vncompasse. **1648** HEXHAM II, *Ontronden*, to vnround, or take away the roundnesse of any thing. **1874** H. SWEET in *Trans. Philol. Soc.* 471 Rounded front vowels are often unrounded. *Ibid.* 475 Rounding of back [vowels]; unrounding of front. **1877** —— *Handbk. Phonetics* 25 This vowel..is best obtained by unrounding (u).

un'rounded, *ppl. a.* (UN-^{1} 8.)

1519 HORMAN *Vulg.* 112 b, Rounded heare becometh men: and vnrounded women. *a* **1631** DONNE *Elegies* xi. 33 Unfil'd pistolets..Which, negligently left unrounded, looke Like many angled figures, in the booke Of some great Conjurer. **1694** DRYDEN *To Sir G. Kneller* 55 Flat Faces, such as wou'd disgrace a Skreen,..Unrais'd, unrounded. **1815** J. SMITH *Panorama Sci. & Art* I. 388 Three teeth rounded from point to point;..three full teeth, unrounded. **1852** LYELL *Man. Elem. Geol.* vii. (ed. 4) 82 Similar unrounded nodules of flint. **1877** SWEET *Handbk. Phonetics* 17 The narrow back unrounded vowels.

†**un'rounged,** *ppl. a.* *Sc. Obs.* [UN-^{1} 8 + ROUNGE *v.*^{3}] Unclipped.

15.. *Aberd. Reg.* (Jam.), The baileyeis chargit him to take the Inglis grot vnrovngit for thre sous in pament.

un'rousable, *a.* (UN-¹ 7 b.)
1894 MRS. DYAN *Man's Keeping* xvi, Urquhart submitted to all [this]..with unrousable apathy.

un'roused, *ppl. a.* (UN-¹ 8.)
[**1775** ASH.] **1802** COLERIDGE *Dejection* 4 This night, so tranquil now, will not go hence Unrous'd by winds. **1834** *Tait's Mag.* I. 540/2 In that visionary world, Unroused by Pleasure's fierce extreme. **1882** FLOYER *Unexpl. Baluchistan* 214 Totally unroused reasoning powers.

un'routed, *ppl. a.* (UN-¹ 8.)
1622 FLETCHER *Prophetess* IV. v, Of all the Persian Forces, one strong Squadron..Stands firm, and yet unrouted. **1888** *Leisure Hour* Sept. 594/1 The ladies..did not leave him with so much as an unrouted doubt on this point.

unrove, var. of UNRUFE *Sc. Obs.*

un'row, *v.* (UN-¹ 14, or UN-² 3.)
1897 F. T. BULLEN *Cruise 'Cachalot'* xiv, My gloomy cogitations were abruptly terminated by the order to 'unrow'—we were alongside.

†**un'rowed,** *ppl. a. Obs.* [UN-¹ 8 + ROW *v.*⁷] Not having the nap raised.
1487 *Act 3 Hen. VII*, c. xi. §1 The seid Clothes..arne..conveyed out of this realme, unroweed and unshorne. **1535**, **1541**, **1643** [see UNBARBED 1].

un'royal, *a.* [UN-¹ 7.]
1. Unbefitting or inappropriate to a king or queen.
a **1586** SIDNEY *Arcadia* II. ix, He..sent them with unroyall reproches to Musidorus. *a* **1680** CHARNOCK *Attrib. God* (1834) I. 71 A Roman king, who counted it the most unroyal thing to be religious. **1780** W. BECKFORD *Italy* (1834) I. 62, I scolded in an unroyal style. **1842** FR. A. KEMBLE *Rec. Later Life* (1882) II. 239 The unroyal indignity of being waited upon after her guests. **1880** F. G. LEE *Ch. under Q. Eliz.* II. 155 With unroyal discourtesy and unwomanly harshness.
b. Not associated with royal authority.
1867 BAGEHOT *Eng. Constitution* 99 The unroyal species of cabinet government.
2. Not of royal rank or birth.
a **1618** J. DAVIES *Witte's Pilgr.* Wks. (Grosart) II. 35/2 Then, Rimes how ere vnroiall run you on, You may, in time, perhaps come neer that Crowne. **1814** MOORE *Mem.* (1852) II. 21 A certain *un*-royal person in Derbyshire. **1861** TROLLOPE *Framley P.* III. 230 That none of the blood royal shall raise to royal honours those of the subjects who are by birth un-royal.
Hence **un'royally** *adv.* Also **un'royalist.**
1777 POTTER *Æschylus, Choephoræ* 345 My royal father, who unroyally Wast murder'd! **1788** MME. D'ARBLAY *Diary* 11 Feb., He is so privileged a favourite with all the Royal Family, that he utters all his flights to them almost as easily as to unroyalists. **1829** MOORE *Mem.* (1854) VI. 38 Not quite liking to refuse him, as being always so unroyally good-humoured and good-natured.

un'rubbed, *ppl. a.* (UN-¹ 8.)
c **1380** WYCLIF *Sel. Wks.* III. 231 As a horce unrubbed, þat haves a sore back, wynses when..rubbed on his rugge. **1648** HEXHAM II, *Onbestreken*, Vnrubbed, or Vnsmeared. **1847** GEO. ELIOT in Cross *Life* (1885) I. 161 You are a bright golden sovereign to me, with edges all unrubbed. **1877** MEREDITH *Lett.* (1912) I. 282, I am consequently dull, unrubbed, no reflector.

un'rubbish, *v.* (UN-² 4.)
1645 MILTON *Colast.* 26 This under-work of scowring and unrubbishing the low and sordid ignorance of such a presumptuous lozel.

un'rubrical, *a.* (UN-¹ 7.)
1843 LD. COLERIDGE in *Life & Lett.* (1904) I. 115 Commencing the service..with..a hymn is unrubrical, uncatholick.

un'ruddered, *ppl. a.* (UN-¹ 8 or UN-² 8.) **-ing,** *vbl. sb.* (UN-² 8.)
1804 LARWOOD *No Gun Boats* 12 Better to give all than suffer their Gun Boats to remain in even an unruddered, unmasted, unordonanced existence. *Ibid.* 15 The inutility of dismasting, unruddering, or scuttling.

†**un'rude,** *a.*¹ *Obs.* [var. of UNRIDE *a.*, but prob. associated with RUDE *a.*]
1. Violent, rough, dreadful.
c **1400** *Laud Troy Bk.* 17162 Ther were ȝit..of sqwyers gret multitude, And ȝaff thanne strokes wel vnrude. **1513** DOUGLAS *Æneid* VI. ii. 114 The laithlie flude Cochitus, with his drery bosum vnrude. *Ibid.* v. 3 Hellis flude of Acheron; With holl bisme, and hiduus swelth wnrude. **1825** JAMIESON s.v., This term is still used in Ayrs[hire], and expl. 'Base, vile, diabolical; detestable;' as, 'unrude bleeries,' abominable falsehoods.
2. Rude, unmannerly, uncouth.
1561–2 W. FULLWOOD in *Ballads*, etc. (Percy Soc.) 57 For you may see he is in deed An unrude simple man. **1599** B. JONSON *Ev. Man out of Hum.* IV. i, The good Gentleman vouchsaft to make him his companion,..and now see how the vnrude Rascall back-bites him! **1616** —— *Masque of Christmas* 116 They have need o' mending: unrude people they are, your Courtiers. *a* **1630** J. TAYLOR (Water P.) *Wit & Mirth* cii, Truly, said the fellow [*sc.* a countryman], I am no schollar, I am altogether vnrude, and very ingrum.
Hence †**un'rudeness,** rudeness. *Obs.*⁻¹
1561–2 W. FULLWOOD in *Ballads*, etc. (Percy Soc.) 57 A Supplication to Eldertonne for Leache's Unlewdnes, Desiring him to pardone his manifest unrudenes.

un'rude, *a.*² [UN-¹ 7.] Not rude; mannerly.
1648 HERRICK *Hesper., Panegerick to Pemberton* 31 Manners knowes distance, and a man unrude Wo'd soon recoile, and not intrude His Stomach to a second Meale.

†**un'ruefully,** *adv. Obs.* [UN-¹ 11.] Unmercifully, pitilessly.
a **1300** *Cursor M.* 24023 Vn-reufulli þai can him raipe. *Ibid.* 24158 Vn-reufulli [*Edin.* vnrewfullik] yee wirc vnright.

†**unrufe** (also unrove), Sc. var. UNRO *Obs.*
c **1470** *Gol. & Gaw.* 499 May nane do thame na deir... Yit sal I mak thame vnrufe. *c* **1550** *Clariodus* (Maitl. Cl.) 44 3it glaidlie for his saik I sould ȝow love, That this regioun hes brocht from sik unrove. *c* **1550** ROLLAND *Crt. Venus* II. 446 Quhy sufferis thow ane creature mortall, For none defalt to incur sic vnrufe?

un'ruffable, *a.* (UN-¹ 7 b.)
1837 DICKENS *Pickw.* xxxiii, Sam..obeyed all his master's behests with..unruffable composure.

un'ruffed, *a.* (UN-¹ 9.)
1872 COUES *N. Amer. Birds* 133 Bill moderate, unruffed, but with a little tuft of feathers at the base of the rictus.

un'ruffle, *v.* [UN-² 7 and 3.]
1. *intr.* To become smooth or tranquil.
1697 DRYDEN *Æneis* I. 212 Where e're he guides His finny Coursers,..The Waves unruffle, and the Sea subsides. **1871** [see UNRUFFLING *ppl. a.*²].
2. *trans.* To restore from a ruffled state.
1827 LAMB *Wife's Trial* Wks. 1908 II. 805 A witch..can by a backward charm Unruffle the foul storm she has just been raising. **1833** LADY GRANVILLE *Lett.* (1894) II. 148 This does not seem to unruffle Dolly's plumes.

un'ruffled, *ppl. a.* [UN-¹ 8.]
1. a. Not affected by any violent feeling; not agitated or disturbed; calm, unmoved.
1659 W. CHAMBERLAYNE *Pharonnida* Ded., I have, with an unruffled confidence, given these papers a capacity of being publicly viewed. **1712** ADDISON *Spect.* No. 381 ¶4 His Temper is even and unruffled. **1751** SMOLLETT *Per. Pic.* xcv, 'Why shouldn't I lend a hand?'..(answered the unruffled Pipes). **1754** *Connoisseur* No. 4 ¶9 Whose conversation flows with one even tenor, undisturb'd by sentiment, and unruffled by passion. **1829** LYTTON *Devereux* II. ii, The most unruffled composure. **1874** GREEN *Short Hist.* vii. §3. 369 Her mind was unruffled by the spiritual problems which were vexing the minds around her.
b. Not excited by drinking.
1709 STEELE *Tatler* No. 27 ¶2 When he is himself, and unruffled with Intemperance. **1748** *Anson's Voy.* III. vii. 363 Perceiving that after they had dispatched four or five bottles.., the Mandarine still continued unruffled.
2. Not physically ruffled or made rough:
a. Of water, etc. Also in fig. context.
1713 ADDISON *Cato* I. iv, Calm and unruffled as a summer-sea. **1757** W. WILKIE *Epigon.* v. 135 A lake..Whose surface smooth, unruffled by the breeze, The hills inverted shows. **1814** WORDSW. *Excurs.* II. 365 Days unruffled by the gale Of public news or private. **1824** MISS L. M. HAWKINS *Annaline* II. 229 Crags mantled in unruffled snow. **1883** TYNDALL in *Knowledge* 3 Aug. 73/2 Between the ferry and this bridge, the river Niagara flows unruffled.
b. Of feathers, leaves, the forehead, etc.
1816 WILSON *City of Plague* II. iv. 106 Like an angel With hair unruffled in its radiance. **1821** SCOTT *Kenilw.* v, Now for..an open and unruffled brow! **1854** *Poultry Chron.* I. 328/2 A pen of birds..unruffled in their plumage. *a* **1878** SIR G. SCOTT *Lect. Archit.* (1879) I. 320 Here the Byzantinesque foliage is nearly all of the plain unruffled form.
3. Not furnished with ruffles.
c **1825** LD. COCKBURN *Mem.* i. (1856) 13 A shirt fastened at the neck by a black ribbon, and except on dress days unruffled.
Hence **un'ruffledness.**
1858 HAWTHORNE *Fr. & It. Note-bks.* (1881) II. 177 His propriety, his cleanliness and unruffledness. **1880** RUSKIN *Hortus Inclusus* (1887) 77 The perfect cleanliness and unruffledness of white cap [in Chartres] is always a marvel.

un'ruffling, *ppl. a.*¹ [UN-¹ 10.] Not ruffling; not becoming ruffled.
1762 FALCONER *Shipwr.* II. 307 Th' involving clue, Swell'd by the wind, aloft unruffling flew. **1797** SOUTHEY *Donica* 19 The powerless storm unruffling swept Across the calm dead lake.

un'ruffling, *ppl. a.*² [f. UNRUFFLE *v.*] Becoming unruffled.
1871 TENNYSON *Last Tourn.* 368 As, when a gust hath blown, Unruffling waters re-collect the shape Of one that in them sees himself.

un'ruinable, *a.* (UN-¹ 7 b.)
a **1693** *Urquhart's Rabelais* III. viii. (1708) I. 353 Nature, having a fervent desire..to eternize, and continue them..unruinable. **1706** WATTS *Horæ Lyricæ* II. 163 The spirit..flies upward, an undoubted guest Of the third heaven, th' unruinable sky. *a* **1740** —— *Remnants of Time* ix. Wks. 1753 IV. 612 May the unruinable world be but my portion.

†**un'ruinated,** *ppl. a. Obs.* [UN-¹ 8.] = next.
1566–7 *Reg. Privy Council Scot.* I. 498 Of the haill ludgeing walles..thair is na thing left unruinated and doung in drosse. **1610** BP. HALL *Apol. Brownists* §30. 74 These you will proue vnruinated Towers of that Babell. **1658** BROMHALL *Treat. Specters* II. 175 They should leave nothing unruinated and not pull'd down.

un'ruined, *ppl. a.* (UN-¹ 8.)
1610 J. HEALEY *St. Aug. Citie of God* 4 So long the City should continue unruined. *a* **1649** DRUMM. OF HAWTH. *Hist. Jas. III*, Wks. (1711) 58 He sent to all such of his Friends, whom his Disasters had left unruined, to take Arms for the King. **1820** BENTHAM *Liberty of Press* Wks. 1843 II. 283/1 Under whom it has hitherto been my good hap to live unhanged,..unbanished and unruined. **1853** RUSKIN *Stones Ven.* II. vii. §46. 268 He can still see the strong sweep of the unruined traceries drawn on the deep serenity of the starry sky.

un'rulable, *a.* (UN-¹ 7 b.)
1680 H. DODWELL *Two Lett.* (1691) 68 Preventing the occasion or increase of passion, which will be also so much easier if it be taken before it grow unrulable. **1716** M. DAVIES *Athen. Brit.* II. 289 Rendring a Country-property..unattainable as well as unrulable even by an Hereditary Pretender. **1881** in J. Hatton *New Ceylon* vii. 185 People..found to be unruleable by other nations.

un'rulableness. *rare*⁻¹. (UN-¹ 12. Cf. prec.)
c **1445** PECOCK *Donet* 94 þouȝ al þis lijf be foule..for wijldenes and vnreuleablenes, in tyme of ȝongþe.

un'rule. [UN-¹ 12.] Absence of rule or government.
1422 YONG tr. *Secreta Secret.* 136 Whyle he regnyd in this vnrule.., into the land of Irlande he arryuete. *c* **1425** WYNTOUN *Cron.* v. xii. 3724 (Wemyss MS.), Forthy it nedis þat ressoune Thyne vnreullis habandoun.
1818 SCOTT *Rob Roy* xxii, Now let's hear..how, in the name of unrule, they got here at this time o' night. **1861** *Sat. Rev.* II. 670 A very few years more of republican unrule.

un'ruled, *ppl. a.* [UN-¹ 8.]
1. Not ruled or governed; ungoverned, disorderly.
c **1375** *Sc. Leg. Saints* xxx. (*Theodera*) 107 Certis, vnreulyt ware my wil gyf for þe my-self I suld spil. *a* **1395** HYLTON *Scala Perf.* III. i. (W. de W. 1494), For charyte vnruled tourneth somtyme in to vyce. *c* **1425** WYNTOUN *Cron.* v. xiii. 4717 (Cott. MS.), Our Lady..repruffit hym fast Off his wnrewllit wilfulnes. *a* **1513** FABYAN *Chron.* VII. 530 Theyse vnrulyd Company gatheryd vnto them great multytude of the commons. **1538** STARKEY *England* II. ii. 180 Man ys then myserabul..when reson ys ouer-run and vnrulyd affectys gouerne and reyne in hys ordur of lyfe. **1596** SPENSER *St. Irel.* Wks. (Globe) 617/1 The realme was left, like a shipp in a storme,..unruled, and undirected of any. **1615** CHAPMAN *Odyss.* IV. 925 But their unrul'd acts show their minds' estate. **1655** GENTILIS *Servita's Inquis.* xxxi. 136 Because the desire of gain is so unruled, that..it doth induce men to commit things against honesty. **1813** HOGG *Queen's Wake* Concl. xvii, To end this strife, unruled and vain, Let all the three be called again. **1897** *Westm. Gaz.* 29 Mar. 3/1 The same strong and unruled passions.
†**2.** Not decided or decreed. *Obs.*⁻¹
1456 *Paston Lett.* I. 387 The atteynte abidith unreuled til the next terme.
†**3.** Irregular. *Obs.*⁻¹
1551 RECORDE *Pathw. Knowl.* I. Defin., They haue no syde equall to an other.., neither keepe they any rate in their corners, and therefore are they counted vnruled formes.
4. Not having ruled lines.
1888 E. M. GALLAUDET *Life T. M. Gallaudet* 23 It is written on unruled paper.
Hence **un'ruledly** *adv. rare.*
1580 HOLLYBAND *Treas. Fr. Tong, Desreigléement*, vnruledly. **1587** [see UNRULILY *adv.* 2, quot. 1561].

un'ruleful, *a. Sc.* and *dial.* (UN-¹ 7.)
1438 *Sc. Acts, Jas. II* (1814) II. 32/2 Quhare þar is ony rebellys or vnrewlful men within ony castellys or fortalicis resett or haldyn. **1678** in Wodrow *Hist. Suff. Ch. Scot.* (1722) I. App. 191 Spilling the Country by unreasonable and unruleful men. **1898** in *Eng. Dial. Dict.* s.v.

†**un'rulely,** obs. variant of UNRULY *a.*
a **1581** in Marbeck *Bk. of Notes* 540 If our passions be so vnrulely,..then doth impatiencie ouer master vs. **1653** HOLCROFT *Procopius, Goth. Wars* IV. 153 He took order..to be rid of his unrulely Lombards, who were infinitely disorderly.

†**un'rulily,** *adv. Obs.* [f. UNRULY *a.*]
1. Immoderately.
c **1445** PECOCK *Donet* 98 Liȝtnessis,..whanne þei ben vnmesurably and vnreulili aȝens doom of resoun. *c* **1456** —— *Bk. Faith* (1909) 109 Manye of the lay peple whiche..attenden over unreulili to the Bible.
2. In an unruly or disorderly manner.
1549 CHEKE *Hurt Sedit.* (1569) D ij, Ye..vnrulilye haue ruled, where ye listed to commaund. **1561** T. NORTON *Calvin's Inst.* II. ii. 11 b, Wylde horses whyche..dooe range vnrulyly [**1587** vnruledly] and wythout measure. **1571** GOLDING *Calvin on Ps.* lvi. 8 The ungodly have unrulily roysted without let. **1610** C. NESSE *O. & N. Test.* I. 312 Evil concupiscence..groweth unrulily headstrong.

†**un'ruliment.** *Obs.*⁻¹ [-MENT.] = next.
1596 SPENSER *F.Q.* IV. ix. 23 They breaking forth with rude vnruliment, From all foure parts of heauen doe rage full sore.

un'ruliness. [f. next.] The quality of being unruly. (Of persons, animals, etc.)
1547 *Act 1 Edw. VI*, c. 12 §1 The Insolency and Unruliness of Men. **1577** B. GOOGE *Heresbach's Husb.* III. 150 You must keepe the Boare from them; for with his vnrulinesse, he maketh them to cast. **1577** tr. *Bullinger's Decades* 301/1 Therein doth patience make proofe of it self, ..that it neuer breaketh forthe to immoderate vnrulynesse. **1638** RAWLEY tr. *Bacon's Life & Death* 210 For the Quieting of the vnrulinesse of the spirits. **1684** J. S. *Profit & Pleas. United* 14 For the better preservation of your Cattle, both from sickness and hurt, which may happen through their unruliness. **1695** J. EDWARDS *Perfect. Script.* 440 Excellent caveats..touching..unruliness of the tongue. **1704** *Dict. Rust.* s.v. *Mare*, His own unruliness being so great, the Cure [of the colt] may be very difficult. **1768–74** TUCKER *Lt. Nat.* (1834) II. 356 We ascribe the..unruliness of inordinate desires..to the fatal effects of original sin. **1805** WORDSW. *Prelude* VI. 392 Some vapoured in the unruliness of joy. **1858** FROUDE *Hist. Eng.* IV. xix. 110 The governments affected to regret the unruliness of their subjects.

un'ruly, *a.* (and *sb.*) Forms: 5-6 vnruely, 6-7 vnrulye, -lie, 6- unruly; 5 onreuli, vnrewely, 6 vnrewly. [UN-[1] 7 + RULY *a.*[2]]

1. Not amenable to rule or discipline; ungovernable; disorderly, turbulent:

a. Of persons.

1400 R. DE GREY in Ellis *Orig. Lett.* Ser. II. I. 4 Hitt woll be an unruely Cuntrie within short tyme. **1422** YONG tr. *Secreta Secret.* 160 When they were full woxen, prowte, onreuli, fiers, and presumpteous. *a* **1533** LD. BERNERS *Gold. Bk. M. Aurel.* (1559) U ij, Sith the worlde is so chaungeable, and the people so vnruly. **1592** GREENE *Disput.* 20 Ouer kind fathers make vnruly daughters. **1665** BOYLE *Occas. Refl., Disc.* §iv. i. 53 That he should of all others prove the most unruly, who alone has been endowed with Reason to rule himself withall. *a* **1715** BURNET *Own Time* I. iv. (1897) I. 108 The dispersing of that little unruly army. **1781** COWPER *Tiroc.* 262, I blame not those who..O'erwatch the num'rous and unruly clan. **1855** MACAULAY *Hist. Eng.* xvi. III. 685 William had found it no easy matter to decide what course should be taken with that capricious and unruly body. **1896** W. K. LEASK *H. Miller* 29 He seems rather to have become an unruly lad.

sb. and *absol.* **1611** SPEED *Hist. Gt. Brit.* IX. xxii. §31. 807/1 These vnrulies presently chose him for their ringleader. **1684** BUNYAN *Pilgr.* II. (1900) 265 All things must be managed here to..the warning of the Unruly. **1782** PRIESTLEY *Inst. Relig.* (ed. 2) I. p. xli, We cannot possibly warn all the unruly.

transf. **1667** DRYDEN *Ind. Emperor* IV. iv, Th' unruly Sword will no distinction make. **1888** BARRIE *When a Man's Single* xii, She softly pushed the invalid's unruly hair off his brow.

b. Of animals. Also in fig. context.

1565 COOPER *Thesaurus* s.v. *Bos*, Restie or vnrulie oxen. **1577** GOOGE *Heresbach's Husb.* 141 b, To keepe the weaker [sheep]..from the strong and vnruly. *Ibid.* 145 The horned, by reason of theyr weapons, are hurtful, and vnruely. **1627** J. TAYLOR (Water P.) *Navy of Land Ships* Wks. (1630) 91/1 A ship is an vnruly beast. **1682** SHEFFIELD (Dk. Buckhm.) *Ess. Poetry* 8 The Muses most unruly Horse. **1768-74** [see UNSHAKEN 2]. *a* **1821** V. KNOX *Serm.* Wks. 1824 VI. 196 Like the spirited and unruly steed.

c. Of the heart, tongue, passions, etc.

1526 TYNDALE *Jas.* iii. 8 The tonge can no man tame. Yt is an vnruely evyll full off deedly poyson. **1598** BARRET *Theor. Warres* I. ii. 11 A generous minde, not subiect vnto passions and vnrulie fits. **1612** T. TAYLOR *Comm. Titus* i. 6 An vnruly heart will breake out one time or other. *a* **1674** CLARENDON *Surv. Leviath.* (1676) 239 When his unruly invention suggests to him an addition to the Text. **1712** POPE *Spect.* No. 408 ¶7 Young Men whose Passions are not a little unruly. **1729** BUTLER *Serm.* Wks. 1874 II. 40 To imagine he keeps that unruly faculty [*sc.* the tongue] in due subjection. **1800** COLQUHOUN *Comm. Thames* viii. 262 It is impracticable to control their unruly passions. **1846** KEBLE *Lyra Innoc.* (ed. 3) 293 Nor time nor tune are there, Yet sounds the unruly joy.

d. Characterized by disorder or disquiet.

1439 *Cases bef. King's Council* (Selden) 105 Wawton.. seid..it is the unruliest session that I haue euer sey in Bedford. **1582** STANYHURST *Æneis* I. (Arb.) 21 These vnrulye reuels..thee sea king Neptun awaked. **1805** WORDSW. *Prelude* I. 136 The Poet, gentle creature as he is, Hath, like the Lover, his unruly times.

†**2.** Of things: Unmanageable. *Obs.*

1577 GOOGE *Heresbach's Husb.* III. 158 When they sitte, with theyr vnruly spurres they breake theyr egges. **1598** FLORIO *Dict.* To Rdr. 9 A more vnruly..vessell then the biggest hulke on Thames. **1633** HERBERT *Temple, Ch. Porch* xli, Wit's an unruly engine, wildly striking Sometimes a friend, sometimes the engineer. **1681** R. KNOX *Hist. Ceylon* 9 These Ploughs..if heavier..would sink and be unruly in the mud.

†**3.** Violent; incurable. *Obs.*

1596 SPENSER *F.Q.* VI. vi. 5 Their wounds..had festred priuily, And ranckling inward with vnruly stounds, The inner parts now gan to putrify. **1606** G. WOODCOCKE *Lives Emperors* in *Hist. Ivstine* K k 6 Dying of an vnruly disease.

4. Stormy, tempestuous; impetuous.

1593 SHAKS. *Lucrece* 869 Unruly blasts wait on the tender spring; Unwholesome weeds take root. **1605** —— *Macb.* II. iii. 59 The Night ha's been vnruly; Where we lay, our Chimneys were blowne downe. **1647** CLARENDON *Hist. Reb.* v. §449 The standard itself was blown down..by a very strong and unruly wind. **1697** DRYDEN *Virg. Georg.* III. 396 He makes his way o'er Mountains, and contemns Unruly Torrents, and unfoorded Streams.

un'ruminated, *ppl. a.* (UN-[1] 8.)

1735 BOLINGBROKE *Study Hist.* (1752) I. 4 Those who.. store their minds with crude un-ruminated facts and sentences.

un'rummaged, *ppl. a.* (UN-[1] 8.)

†**a.** **1591** RALEIGH *Last Fight Reuenge* cij, The ships growne foule, vnroomaged, and scarcely able to beare anie saile for want of balast.

b. **1775** ASH s.v., Unrummaged. **1910** *Athenæum* 29 Jan. 117/3 No relevant archives have remained unrummaged.

un'rumple, *v.* (UN-[2] 3.)

1694 ADDISON *Virg. Georg.* IV. Wks. 1721 I. 22 Daffadils, that late from earth's slow womb Unrumple their swoln buds. **1728** GARDINER tr. *Rapin Of Gardens* (ed. 3) 36 Wide o'er the Garden now she sheds Perfumes, Unrumples her swol'n Buds, and gayly blooms.

un'rumpled, *ppl. a.* (UN-[1] 8.)

1641 W. CARTWRIGHT *Siege* II. ii, We cannot keep a pleat unrumpled..for them. **1692** WOOD *Life* (O.H.S.) IV. 25, I shall put it into the hands of Dr Levet that he might convey it to you..unrumpled. **1776** MRS. DELANY *Life & Corr.* Ser. II. (1862) II. 218, I leave the rest of her unpacking to your delicate fingers. I hope to hear she arrives unrumpled —feathers and all. **1821** SCOTT *Kenilw.* iv, You must..wear ..your falling band unrumpled and well starched. **1865** MRS. WHITNEY *Gayworthys* xxiii, Her bright hair was put back over her ears, not quite unrumpled.

un'run, *ppl. a.* [UN-[1] 8 b.] Not past or completed.

1474 *Acta Dom. Audit.* (1839) 37/1 þe tak of þe said landis ..for sa mony termes now to cum as was vnrunnyn of þe xix ȝeris. **1591** *Knaresb. Wills* (Surtees) I. 176 The reste of the yeares I have to come unron.

un'rung, *ppl. a.*[1] [UN-[1] 8 b + RING *v.*[2]] Not sounded by ringing.

1422-61 in *Cal. Proc. in Chanc. Q. Eliz.* (1827) I. Introd. 20 It wer better bell unrogne at þe sauntes tyme þan þe messe unsogne. **1742** BLAIR *Grave* 53 The Great Bell has toll'd, unrung, untouch'd.

un'rung, *ppl. a.*[2] [UN-[1] 8 b + RING *v.*[1]] = UNRINGED *ppl. a.*

1548 *Fen Laws* in Thompson *Hist. Boston* (1856) 643 No swine were to be put in the fens unrung. **1654** in Picton *L'pool Munic. Rec.* (1883) I. 191 Swyne that shalbee found unrung. **1707** MORTIMER *Husb.* 530 He let his Hogs go into his Orchard unrung. **1727** E. LAURENCE *Duty of Steward* 125 Paying Ten shillings for each Hog suffer'd to be unrung or unyoked. **1885** W. RYE *Hist. Norfolk* 114 Men were often prosecuted for..keeping unrung pigs, or savage dogs.

un'runkled, *ppl. a. Sc.* (UN-[1] 8.)

1721 RAMSAY *Keitha* 43 Her..brow, smooth as th' unrunkled deep.

un'ruptured, *ppl. a.* (UN-[1] 8.)

[**1775** ASH.] **1862** A. MEADOWS *Man. Midwifery* VI. i. 211 Even if the membranes are unruptured, we shall generally be able to feel a small coil. **1875** BROWNING *Aristoph. Apol.* 118 Odusseus..Holding as surely on to Herakles, Who touched Zeus, link and link, the unruptured chain!

un'rusted, *ppl. a.* (UN-[1] 8.)

a **1653** BINNING *Serm.* (1845) 257 Take heed to walk suitably and preserve your seal of adoption unblotted, unrusted. **1797** COLERIDGE *Osorio* IV. iii, The point Is bright, unrusted with the villain's blood! **1851** MRS. BROWNING *Casa Guidi Wind* I. 1086 Bring thoughts and words, Unrusted by a tear of yesterday's. **1868** *Lond. Rev.* 19 Dec. 670/2 The book..has the quality of gold, and will keep unrusted for an age.

un'rustling, *ppl. a.* (UN-[1] 10).

1749 COLLINS *Superst. Highlands* vi, For watchful, lurking, 'mid the unrustling reed, At those mirk hours the wily monster lies.

un'ruth. Now *arch.* (UN-[1] 12.)

c **1440** *Jacob's Well* 294 To haue..vnrewthe of hem þat arn in peyne. **1888** W. MORRIS *Dream of J. Ball* iv. 32 All this hast thou lost for..a little winking of the eyes amidst murder and wrong and unruth. **1899** W. S. BLUNT *Satan Absolved* 18 Thy Will found counterpart Only in Man's un-Will, Thy Truth in his un-Truth,..Ruth in his un-Ruth.

un'ruthfully, *adv.* [UN-[1] 11.] = UNRUEFULLY *adv.*

c **1375** *Cursor M.* 24023 (Fairf.), Vnreuþfulli þai con him raipe. *Ibid.* 24158 Vn-reuþfulli ȝe wirk vn-riȝt.

uns, obs. Sc. form of OUNCE *sb.*[1]

unsa'bbatical, *a.* (UN-[1] 7.)

1882 'EDNA LYALL' *Donovan* x, A most unsabbatical.. shooting-jacket. **1896** *Daily News* 6 April 2/3 For an altogether unsabbatical outburst of levity.

un'sabred, *ppl. a.* (UN-[1] 8.)

1820 BENTHAM *Liberty of Press* Wks. 1843 II. 283/1 Under whom it has..been my good hap to live unhanged, unsabred, unimprisoned.

unsacer'dotal, *a.* (UN-[1] 7.)

1844 J. S. MILL in *Edin. Rev.* LXXIX. 33 The Papacy could..indulge within certain limits their [*sc.* the Franciscans'] most unsacerdotal preference of grace to the law. **1847** MAURICE *Relig. World* I. iii. 71 Such an utterly unsacerdotal people as the Mahometans. **1860** *All Year Round* No. 44. 412 Popes who have scandalised mankind by their unsacerdotal vices.

unsacer'dotally, *adv.* (UN-[1] 11.)

1834 H. O'BRIEN *Round Towers Irel.* 502 They then very unsacerdotally make a serpent bite him.

un'sack, *v.* [UN-[2] 5.] *trans.* To take out of a sack. Also *fig.*

14.. *Voc.* in Wr.-Wülcker 581 *Exsacco*, to vnsacke. **1598** FLORIO, *Dissaccare*, to vnsacke, to emptie out of a sacke. **1846** LANDOR *Imag. Conv.* Wks. II. 81/2 The state is founded on follies, the Church on sins. Come then, unsack them.

un'sackable, *a.* [UN-[1] 7 b.] Not sackable.

1980 *Daily Tel.* 14 Feb. 14/8 It is a fair description of the real world of unsackable functionaries whom not God nor Sir Derek Rayner nor TNT will remove. **1984** *Listener* 12 July 17/2 The system introduced in the 1940s..made the men who handled the catches in the registered fishing ports unsackable.

un'sacked, *ppl. a.* [UN-[1] 8.] Not plundered.

1590 MARLOWE *2nd Pt. Tamburlane* IV. iii. 59 This same Boy..must..Rifle the kingdomes I shall leaue vnsackt. **1595** DANIEL *Civ. Wars* v. lxxxvi, From yonder turrets yet vnsackt, Your valiant fellows stand your worth to see. **1791** COWPER *Iliad* XII. 14 The city yet Of royal Priam was unsack'd. *c* **1813** SOUTHEY *At Santarem* 4 Loth to leave Rich Lisbon yet unsack'd, he kept his ground.

un'sacrament, *v.* (UN-[2] 6 b.)

1642 T. FULLER *Holy & Prof. St.* v. xi. 402 Whereas the profanenesse of a bad man administring it, doth unsacrament baptisme itself.

unsacra'mentally, *adv.* (UN-[1] 11.)

1840 G. S. FABER *Christ's Disc. Capernaum* 62 Under the phraseology of Eating the Flesh and Drinking the Blood of Christ, the same vital doctrine..is successively propounded .., first unsacramentally, next sacramentally.

†**un'sacred**, *ppl. a.*[1] *Obs.* [UN-[1] 8.] Unconsecrated.

1382 WYCLIF in Knighton *Chron.* (Rolls) II. 161 þe Sacrament of the Autere white and ronde and like tyl oure brede or ost unsacrede. **1387** TREVISA *Higden* (Rolls) VII. 263 Thomas wolde ȝit nouȝt assent, but..wente his wey unsacred. *c* **1440** *Alph. Tales* 112 þai cownceld þe preste to feche ane hoste þat was vnsacred & giff hym.

un'sacred, *ppl. a.*[2] [UN-[2] 8.] Deprived of sacred character.

1652 HOWELL *Giraffi's Rev. Naples* II. 35 A Jesuite was also beheaded, but he was unsacred and degraded first of his function.

un'sacred, *a.* [UN-[1] 7 and 5 b.] Not sacred; profane.

1608 SYLVESTER *Du Bartas* II. iv. III. *Schisme* 188 Th' unsacred Altar sudden slent in twain. *a* **1641** BP. MOUNTAGU *Acts & Mon.* (1642) 204 No person, uncleane, common, unsacred, must approach unto Gods altar. *c* **1712** W. KING *Case Consc.* Wks. 1776 III. 249 If from a place unsacred you should take A sacred thing,..Or an unsacred thing from sacred place. **1755** LAVINGTON *Moravians Compared* 113 The Valentinians' unsacred Sacraments, and profane Initiations. **1872** SWINBURNE *Under Microscope* 28 The unsacred secrets of no Eleusinian initiation.

un'sacredly, *adv.* (UN-[1] 11.)

1852 S. R. MAITLAND *8 Ess.* 37 No doubt Orpheus sung *Ho perso il caro ben*, and the chorus followed him..naturally, and *un*sacredly, and operatically.

unsacri'ficeable, *a.* (UN-[1] 7 b, 5 b.)

1580 W. FULKE *Stapleton Confut.* II. iv. 82 That great and vnsacrificable sacrifice (as I may call it). **1618** AINSWORTH *Annot. Lev.* vii. 18 The Greek translateth it sundry wayes, a thing polluted, unsacrificeable, and profane. [**1650** TRAPP *Comm. Lev.* vii. 18 Kept beyond the time; and so uneatable, unsacrificeable.]

un'sacrificed, *ppl. a.* (UN-[1] 8.)

[**1775** ASH.] **1849** ROCK *Ch. of Fathers* I. ii. I. 91 The bread which is unsacrificed is then changed into what is sacrificed. **1855** PUSEY *Doctr. Real Presence* 483 In Thy Temple, where thou art sacrificed unsacrificed.

†**un'sad**, *a. Obs.* [UN-[1] 7. Cf. OE. *unsæd* unsated (= obs. Du. *onzat*).]

1. Not firm or steadfast; unreliable.

1382 WYCLIF *Rom.* xv. 1 The feblenesse of syke men, or vnsadde in feith. *c* **1386** CHAUCER *Clerk's T.* 995 O stormy peple vnsad and euere vntrewe. *c* **1412** HOCCLEVE *De Reg. Princ.* 705 O lord! þis world vnstabyl is, & vnsad. **1455** *Rolls of Parlt.* V. 341/2 Blynded with unsad trust and promysse of mariage. **1495** *Cov. Leet Bk.* 564 þe vnsadde demeasnyng & dealyng þat he hath be of in tymes past.

2. Not firm, hard, or solid.

1398 TREVISA *Barth. De P.R.* VI. v. (Tollem. MS.), The childes flesche, þat is newe bore, is tendir, nesche, quauy and unsad. *c* **1440** *Promp. Parv.* 491/2 Thoke, as onsadde fysche, *humorosus*.

3. Free from sadness.

a **1450** *Le Morte Arth.* 1508 Off sorow were they neuyr vnsad, Myght they neyther drynke ne ete.

Hence †**un'sadness**. *Obs.*

1382 WYCLIF *Heb.* vii. 18 Reprouyng of the maundement bifore goynge is maad, for the vnsadnesse and vnprofyt of it. **1398** TREVISA *Barth. De P.R.* XVII. cl. (Bodl. MS.), þere it is iseide þat..it happiþ & comeþ of vnfastenes & vnsadnes of þe tre.

un'sad, *v.* (UN-[2] 6 a.)

1640 QUARLES *Sighes* xvii, We'l change our Scene, & we'l unsad our Stile; We'l teach your sighes to sing.

un'sadden, *v.* (UN-[2] 6 a.)

1654 WHITLOCK *Zootomia* 483 It unsaddens the melancholy, quickens the dull, awaketh the drowsie. **1748** RICHARDSON *Clarissa* (1811) IV. 355 The unsaddened heart ..will not now, I hope, give the sable turn to every address of the man she dislikes not. *Ibid.* V. 224 [He] began to untwist and unsadden his features.

un'saddened, *ppl. a.* (UN-[1] 8.)

? *c* **1840** MRS. BROWNING *Paraphr. Homer, Hector & A.* 2 The nurse..Bore on her bosom the unsaddened child.

un'saddle, *v.* [UN-[2] 4, 5. Cf. older Du. and Flem. *ontsadelen* (Du. *ontzadelen*), OHG. *intsatalôn* (MHG. *entsatelen*, G. *entsatteln*).]

1. *trans.* To remove the saddle from (a horse, etc.). Also *absol.*

1382 WYCLIF *Gen.* xxiv. 32 He ladde hym into the hows of herbergrye and unsadelynge dischargide the camelis. *c* **1440** *Promp. Parv.* 367/1 Onsadelyn hors,..*desterno*. **1560** BIBLE (Geneva) *Gen.* xxiv. 32 He vnsadeled the camels and broght lytter & prouander. **1609** ARMIN *Ital. Taylor* B 3 b, When you shall see The bargaine full assignd, Vnsaddle me, and leaue me sold. **1716** B. CHURCH *Hist. Philip's War* (1865) I. 43 The Horses that he and his company came on standing at the door (for they had not been unsaddled). **1798** *Hull Advertiser* 8 Sept. 1/4 After a march of ninety miles, without unsaddling our horses. **1837** W. IRVING *Capt. Bonneville* II. 263 Their horses, too, were unsaddled, and turned loose to graze. **1890** 'R. BOLDREWOOD' *Col. Reformer* (1891) 185 His attendants proceeded to unsaddle the whole troop.

2. To dislodge from a saddle. Also *fig.*

a **1470** H. PARKER *Dives & Pauper* (Pynson, 1493) x. v, Therfore..kepe you wele in the sadyl of pacience, & let no angre,..no tribulacion, no seknesse unsadle you of pacience. **1564** BULLEYN *Dial. agst. Pest.* 42 b, Helpe me, my horse starteth, and had like to haue..vnsadled me. **1623** DONNE *Serm.* 176 A froward and peremptory Refuter unsaddles me at first. *a* **1700** EVELYN *Diary* 22 March 1649, Another..whose ambition..is resolved to neglect no tentative..that may unsaddle the General, and fairly hold him the stirrup. **1821** HUISH *Life Geo. III*, I. 10/1 Magnus ..engaged Otho personally, and unsaddled him. **1860** ADLER *Prov. Poet.* xviii. 404, I expect to unsaddle many a knight on the fair centre of the bridge.

3. To free from spectacles.

1753 SMOLLETT *Ct. Fathom* xl, The prince unsaddled his nose, and..our hero was introduced in form.

Hence **un'saddling** *vbl. sb.* Also *attrib.*

[**1775** ASH.] **1855** KINGSLEY *Westw. Ho!* ii, Sir Richard Grenvile's house is like a very tavern, with eating and drinking, and unsaddling. **1892** *Star* 15 June 4/2 The small unsaddling paddock. **1951** *People* 3 June 7/5 Horses shied; off scampered the rabbit to the unsaddling enclosure. **1972** D. FRANCIS *Smokescreen* iv. 51 We walked down from the stands and over towards the unsaddling enclosures.

un'saddled, *ppl. a.* [UN-[1] 8. Cf. OE. *unsadelod*, *ungesadelod*, MDu. *ongesadelt* (Du. *ongezadeld*), G. *ungesattelt*; NFris. *unsadeld*, Da. *usadlet*, Sw. *osadlad*.] Not saddled. Also *transf.* (cf. prec. 3).

1623 FLETCHER & ROWLEY *Maid in Mill* iv. ii, If thy spectacles be not easie, Keep thy nose unsadl'd, and ope thine ears. **1817** *Blackw. Mag.* I. 57/1 There were at her wedding fifty saddled asses, and unsaddled asses without number. **1892** *Daily News* 28 Sept. 3/5 Each mounted soldier leading an unsaddled charger.

unsadness: see UNSAD *a.*

un'safe, *a.* [UN-[1] 7.]

1. Not enjoying safety; exposed to danger or risk.

1605 SHAKS. *Macb.* III. ii. 32 Vnsafe the while, that wee must laue Our Honors in these flattering streames. *a* **1618** RALEIGH *Rem.* (1664) 151 People that were..un-safe, or unsure for their lives. **1676** HALE *Contempl.* I. 277 Which makes the man's estate unquiet and unsafe, because he hath many competitors. **1892** TENNYSON *Foresters* IV. i, I have let them know Their lives unsafe in..our woods.

2. a. Of actions, etc.: Involving, or not free from, danger or risk.

1597 HOOKER *Eccl. Pol.* v. xlii. §2 Yet others should be taught how unsafe it was to continue his friends. **1604** SHAKS. *Oth.* v. i. 43 Let's think't vnsafe To come into the cry. **1611** —— *Wint. T.* II. ii. 30 These dangerous, unsafe Lunes i' th' King. **1662** J. DAVIES tr. *Olearius' Voy. Ambass.* 84 This great number of slaves make it unsafe to walk the streets..unarm'd. **1722** WODROW *Corr.* (1843) II. 665 Our Assembly..declared the unsafe tendency of several propositions advanced by them. **1798** S. & HT. LEE *Canterb. T.* II. 168 [He] thought its appearance so unsafe, that..he chose to mount a horse. **1836** THIRLWALL *Greece* xxii. III. 259 A small number whom it appeared unsafe to trust. **1864** E. A. PARKES *Pract. Hygiene* 427 Rain water may be unsafe, if the tanks are not clean.

b. Of ways or places: Dangerous from natural or other causes.

1621 in Foster *Eng. Factories Ind.* (1906) I. 274 The tyme of winter had made the wayes unsafe. **1650** in *Verney Memoirs* (1907) I. 464 The wayes are everywhere unsafe for travell. **1686** HORNECK *Crucif. Jesus* xxii. 661 Where the roads are unsafe, there men carry swords. **1748** *Anson's Voy.* III. ii. 315 Full of sharp-pointed coral rocks, which..renders it a very unsafe place to lie at. **1781** COWPER *Heroism* 33 Oh, bliss precarious, and unsafe retreats! **1830** WORDSW. *Russian Fugitive* II. ii, And midway in the unsafe morass, A single Island rose Of firm dry ground. **1891** FARRAR *Darkn. & Dawn* xx, While Nero..made the streets..unsafe with riot and assault.

c. ***unsafe period***, the part of the menstrual cycle during which conception is most likely.

1961 G. GREENE *Burnt-Out Case* III. i. 82 He sometimes allowed her to be alone during her monthly or unsafe periods. **1969** *Times* 20 Nov. 3/3 The Roman Catholic Church has revised its ideas about the..'unsafe period' and now makes it four days around the mid-point of the female cycle.

3. Not to be trusted to; unreliable.

1601 SHAKS. *Twel. N.* III. iv. 88 No obstacle, no incredulous or vnsafe circumstance,..can come betweene me, and the full prospect of my hopes. **1615** G. SANDYS *Trav.* 92 A number of wracks..did miserably testifie the unsafe protection of that harbour. **1660** JER. TAYLOR *Ductor* II. iii. rule 14 §2 The topick of traditions..was..false in many things, and therefore unsafe in all questions. **1815** J. SMITH *Panorama Sci. & Art* II. 635 Land..on which it is deemed unsafe to sow grain, on account of the worm. **1863** *Smith's Dict. Bible* II. s.v. *Phut*, Such mere similarity of sound is a most unsafe guide. **1894** A. ROBERTSON *Nuggets* 34 We say 'As unsafe as a bank', after what has occurred in Melbourne.

un'safely, *adv.* [UN-[1] 11.] In an unsafe manner; without safety or surety.

1621 G. SANDYS *Ovid's Met.* x. (1626) 209 Valour vnsafelie copes with valiant foes. **1692** DRYDEN *Eleonora* 368 Take it,..before my rage Unsafely just, break loose on this bad Age. **1774** BEATTIE *Minstr.* II. xl, Even there, if left without a guide, The young adventurer unsafely plays. **1870** PROCTOR *Other Worlds* ii. 45 It may not unsafely be asserted, that..those elements..exist in..every single star.

un'safeness. [UN-[1] 12.] The quality of being unsafe.

1673 *S'too him Bayes* 89 As for the unsafeness of it, if uncontroulable libertie prove safe, all's well. **1678** CUDWORTH *Intell. Syst.* I. v. 794 Unevenness and Unsafeness of..[Plotinus's] Temper. **1884** *Law Times* 22 Nov. 64/1 The unsafeness and impropriety of the manner of removal.

un'safety. [UN-[1] 12, 5b.] Absence or want of safety.

1596 BACON *Max. Com. Law* Ep. Ded. (1630) A 4, The great hollownesse and vnsafety in assurances of lands. **1614** —— *Charge touching Duels* 9 It may cause suddaine stormes in Court, to the disturbance of his Majestie, and vnsaftie of his person. *a* **1684** LEIGHTON *Com. 1 Pet.* iii. 15 Perceiving the unsafety and vanity of these..external things. **1844** J. WATSON in Churton *Mem.* (1861) II. 222 The unsafety of determining authorships by internal evidence. **1872** HOWELLS *Wedding Journ.* ix, The unsafety of all bridges of that design.

un'sage, *a.* (UN-[1] 7.)

1584 HUDSON *Du Bartas' Judith* v. 305 And, with their wicked hands, and words vnsage, They did our sacred messengers outrage.

un'sagely, *adv.* (UN-[1] 11.)

1801 MOORE *Morality* 71 The plain good man..Pursues his course, unsagely blest, His tutor whispering in his breast.

un'said, *ppl. a.* [OE. *unsǽd* (UN-[1] 8b), = NFris. *unsad*, MDu. *ongeseit*, Du. *ongezegd*, MLG. *ungesegget*, *-gesecht*, MHG. *ungesaget*, *-geseit* (G. *ungesagt*), ON. *úsagðr* (Sw. *osagd*, (M)Da. *usagt*, Norw. *usagd*).] Not said or uttered.

c **1000** ÆLFRIC *Hom.* II. 466 Eac þæs dæȝes godspel is swiðe earfoðe læwedum mannum to understandenne..; i we hit lætað unsæd. *c* **1375** *Sc. Leg. Saints* xxx. (*Theodera*) 234 Theodera þane cane hyr pray þat scho wald tel hyr..& lef vnsad til hyr richt nocht. *c* **1425** *Cast. Persev.* 693 in *Macro Plays* 98 þer-fore I am mad massenger..þorwe all þe world ..vnsayd sawys for to seye. *c* **1440** *Alph. Tales* 324, I hafe lefte þe laste colett vnsaid. *c* **1450** *Merlin* x. 143 Merlyn.. tolde hym alle these thynges, that nought be lefte vn-seide. **1532** MORE *Confut. Tindale* Wks. 345/2 He held..that al diuine seruice may be left vnsaied without ani sinne. **1593** *Sidney's Arcadia* v. (1922) II. 192 Leaving nothing unsaide which a filthy minde can imagine. **1609** DONNE *Elegie Mrs. Boulstred* 1 Death I recant, and say, unsaid by mee What ere hath slip'd, that might diminish thee. **1699** BENTLEY *Phal.* 46 This was..a thing unsaid before. **1730** SWIFT *Poems, Traulus* II. 20 He..Talks whate'er comes in his head; Wishes it were all unsaid. **1805** SCOTT *Last Minstrel* v. xxvii, Half his tale he left unsaid. **1848** THACKERAY *Van. Fair* lxvi, You leave me under the weight of an accusation which, after all, is unsaid. **1889** WALPOLE *Life Ld. J. Russell* II. 266 Forced, therefore, to leave unsaid the words..necessary for his own defence.

un'sailable, *a.* (UN-[1] 7b.)

1570 LEVINS *Manip.* 4/15 Vnsaylable, *innauigabilis.* **1587** GOLDING *De Mornay* vii. 102 Ye shall make the Sea for the most part vnsayleable. **1627** MAY *Lucan* v. H 8b, Cæsar.. findes The sea vnsaileable for dangerous windes.

un'sailed, *ppl. a.* (UN-[1] 8, 8c.)

a **1572** KNOX *Hist. Ref.* Wks. 1846 I. 293 To bring this head to pass,..the Quein Regent left no point of the compas unsailled. **1807** J. BARLOW *Columb.* I. 457 There spreads, belike, that other unsail'd main I sought so long. **1866** SWINBURNE *Poems & Ball., Lament.* 86 Lo, what hath he seen or known Of..the wave Unbeholden, unsailed-on? **1870** MORRIS *Earthly Par.* II. III. 272 'Twixt inaccessible cliffs and unsailed sea.

un'sailorlike, *a.* (UN-[1] 7c.)

1841 THACKERAY *Yellowplush Papers* Wks. 1898 III. 375 Nothing can be more unsailorlike than his namby-pamby starlit descriptions. **1865** J. CAMERON *Malayan India* 41 The unsightly and unsailorlike aspect of the craft.

un'sailorly, *a.* (UN-[1] 7.)

1883 STEVENSON *Treas. Isl.* II. ix, I think his conduct unsailorly.

un'sained, *ppl. a.* Now *arch.* [UN-[1] 8. Cf. OE. *ungeseġnod*, MDu. *ongesegent* (Du. *ongezegend*), MLG. *ungesegnet*, MHG. *ungesëgenet*, *-ent* (G. *ungesegnet*).] Unblessed; *esp.* not formally blessed or protected by a blessing.

a **1275** *Ancr. R.* 312 [A] wardein, þet wit & wereð us euer wið þe unseiene [*Cotton MS.* unseinede] gostes. **1513** *Acc. Ld. High Treas. Scot.* IV. 417 To Thomas Drummond, alias Thom Unsanit,..vij li. **1691** R. KIRK *Secret Commw.* i. (1815) 10 Those who are unseened or unsanctified (called Fey). **1881** W. GREGOR *Folk-Lore N.-E. Scotl.* xi. 62 To carry off unsained and unchurched mothers.

un'saint, *v.* [UN-[2] 6b.] *trans.* To deprive of saintly character or status.

1572 R. T. *Discourse* 29 Thomas Becket, whom King Henry dyd vnsainte, and disgrade. **1594** *Zepheria* xiv, No neuer shall that face..Emblemisht be, defaced or unsaynted, Till death shall blot it. **1612** T. JAMES *Corrupt. Scripture* IV. 51 The Master of the sacred Palace hath vnsainted him. **1655** GURNALL *Chr. in Arm.* I. 114 Satan's scope in accusing the Christian,..is to unsaint him, and perswade him he is but an hypocrite. **1701** HOWE *Some Consid. Pref. Enquiry* 29 Power..to saint themselves, and unsaint all other men, at their own pleasure. **1766** ENTICK *London* IV. 123 That saint's bones being..burnt, and unsainted, by the powers in being. **1834** SOUTHEY *Doctor* liv. (1848) 122 Most assuredly they ought to be unsainted! **1870** *Temple-Bar Mag.* XXIX. 186 Young women..mutter in tender tremulous voices, which..might unsaint an anchorite.

Hence **un'sainted** *ppl. a.*[1]

1851 MORIER *Adv. Hajji Baba* II. vi. 172, I marvelled how of a sudden I had become such an unsainted lion.

un'sainted, *ppl. a.*[2] [UN-[1] 8.] Unsanctified; not canonized.

a **1642** SUCKLING *Acc. Relig.* Ep., Wks. (1648) 100 The Fathers of the Church..had slept now un-Sainted in their Graves,..benighted with Oblivion. **1647** WHARTON *Bellum Hybern.* 1 As Iohn Booker prognosticated in his un-sainted state-lying-Kalender. **1768** [W. DONALDSON] *Life Sir B. Sapskull* I. vii. 90 St. Austin,..Chrysostom, and many other sainted and unsainted fathers. **1862** E. ARNOLD *Hymn of Priestess of Diana* iii, O ear, that hears no word..unfit! O breast, which thought unsainted never felt! **1895** *Outing* April 6/1 Shame! shame! upon those unsainted ones!

un'saint-like, *a.* (UN-[1] 7c.)

1681 J. SCOTT *Chr. Life* iii. 225 Our wicked and unsaint-like Lives. **1891** *Pall Mall G.* 19 March 3/3 The saint's [*i.e.* John Wesley] very unsaint-like love affairs.

un'saintly, *a.* (UN-[1] 7.)

Also, in recent use (1887–), *unsaintliness*.

1659 GAUDEN *Tears Ch.* II. xix. 209 What (I pray) can be more unsaintly, than to..delight and glory..in most unjust and uncharitable actions? **1809** FOSTER *Ess.* (1844) I. 272 There is something unsaintly spread over the character. **1837** GEN. P. THOMPSON *Exerc.* (1842) IV. 301 Bring up the most unsaintly cases you can find. **1899** B. HARRADEN *Fowler* I. ix, A most unsaintly-looking pair of shoes.

†**un'saked**, *a. Obs.* [UN-[1] 9 + SAKED *a.*] Innocent.

a **1300** *Cursor M.* 572 Alle virtus has saul i-wis, þat vte o sin vnsaked is. *Ibid.* 17336, I am vn-saked of his blod.

un'salaried, *ppl. a.* (UN-[1] 8.)

1836 DISRAELI *Runnymede Lett.* (1885) 185 Happy England, whose fortunes are supervised by such an unsalaried steward! **1866** *Ch. Times* 1 Sept. 277/3 The cost ..has been borne..chiefly by its founder, the unsalaried secretary. **1898** *Dict. Nat. Biog.* LVI. 247/1 A comfortable though unsalaried post as tutor.

un'saleable, *a.* and *sb.* (UN-[1] 7b, 12.)

1565 COOPER *Thesaurus* s.v. *Merx*, Vnsalehable ware. **1644** MILTON *Areop.* (Arb.) 60 Sermons..vented in such numbers,..as have now wellnigh made all other books unsalable. **1692** RAY *On Creation* (ed. 2) Advt., By publishing a Second Edition of a Book, with large Additions, to render the former worthless and unsalable. **1762** STERNE *Tr. Shandy* VI. xxxiii, An unsaleable piece of cambrick. **1798** *Hull Advertiser* 23 June 4/4 Middling and ordinary qualities are quite unsaleable. **1817** COLERIDGE *Biogr. Lit.* I. 178 The unsaleable nature of my writings. **1860** RUSKIN *Unto this Last* (1862) 112 A horse is useless, and therefore unsaleable, if no one can ride.

sb. **1811** BYRON *Hints from Hor.* 657 'Scott's thirty thousand copies sold,' which must sadly discomfit poor Southey's unsaleables. **1843** E. FITZGERALD *Lett.* (1889) I. 116 A desperate collection of pictures..: among them old unsaleables by Maclise.

Hence **unsalea'bility**; **-ableness.**

1872 DE MORGAN *Budget of Paradoxes* 123 A climax of *unsaleability, unreadability, and inutility. **1775** ASH, *Unsaleableness. **1903** *Saturday Rev.* 10 Jan. 43/1 The unsaleableness of landscape.

un'salt, *a.* (UN-[1] 7. Cf. OE. *unsealt*, Du. *onzout*, ON. *úsaltr*, Icel. *ósaltur*, older Sw. *osalt*.)

1435 MISYN *Fire of Love* 89 þis warld..has also salt vnsalt, sauyr vnsauyrd. **1598** FLORIO, *Fresco*, fresh, new, vnsalt. **1935** E. BOWEN *House in Paris* II. ix. 143 Here the sea air was washed unsalt by the rain.

un'salt, *v.* (UN-[2] 6 and 7. Cf. Du. *ontzouten*, G. *entsalzen*.)

1547 *Bk. of Marchantes* c ij, Of suche wares their store houses are ful, and these be called, store hous masses, or salted masses. That god..ryght soone vnsalte and water it. **1611** COTGR., *Dessaler*, to vnsalt; make fresh; become fresh.

un'saltatory, *a.* (UN-[1] 7.)

1846 FORD *Gatherings from Spain* xxiii. 334 Our immelodious labourers and unsaltatory operatives.

un'salted, *ppl. a.* (UN-[1] 8. Cf. NFris. *unsalted*, (M)Sw. *osaltad*, (M)Da. *usaltet*.)

c **1440** *Promp. Parv.* 366/2 On-powderyd, on-saltyd, *insalitus.* **1541** R. COPLAND *Guydon's Quest. Chirurg.* Q i, A maturatife made with butter wel wasshed and vnsalted. **1579** LANGHAM *Gard. Health* 473 Pease.., whether they be gray or white vnsalted. **1600** SURFLET *Countrie Farme* v. xvi. 682 Sprinkled with neats blood mingled with oile oliue vnsalted. **1725** *Fam. Dict.* s.v. *Poupelin*, Good melted and unsalted Butter. **1731** ARBUTHNOT *Aliments* (1735) 187 The Cure of this Distemper lies in a Diet of fresh unsalted things. **1820** SCORESBY *Acc. Arctic Reg.* I. 342 Unsalted mutton and beef. **1860** O. W. HOLMES *Elsie V.* vii, Villages lying along the unsalted streams.

b. *fig.* (See quots.)

1602 MARSTON *Antonio's Rev.* IV. ii, Your unsalted fresh foole is your onely man. **1619** HIERON *Wks.* II. 489 It is impossible for a man of an vnsalted heart, so to counterfait the language of Canaan. **1649** MILTON *Eikon.* xiv. 139 Compiler of that unsalted and Simonical praier annex'd. **1879** ATCHERLEY *Trip Boërland* 208 'Unsalted' horses, *i.e.* those which have not passed through the ordeal [of the disease].

unsa'lubrious, *a.* (UN-[1] 7, 5b.)

1781 J. MOORE *View Soc. It.* II. 97 Descending from that town..we traversed an unsalubrious plain to Sermonetta. **1951** M. MCLUHAN *Mech. Bride* (1967) 118/2 Nobody can do much about changing the noisy and unsalubrious character of the big cities in which most of us live and work. **1971** *Daily Tel.* 13 Dec. 7/8 There have been demonstrations in several [French] jails recently against unsalubrious conditions.

unsa'lubrity. (UN-[1] 7, 5b.)

1694 FALLE *Jersey* ii. 78 The Unsalubrity of any Country arising chiefly from a low Ground, and a stagnating Air and Water.

un'salutary, *a.* (UN-[1] 7 and 5b.)

1770 LANGHORNE *Plutarch* V. 219 His unpeaceable and unsalutary conduct. **1778** *Eng. Gazetteer* (ed. 2) s.v. *Norfolk*, The air..is aguish, and otherwise unsalutary. **1840** FORSTER *Treat. Pop. Progr. Eng. Hist.* p. xlviii, It is fearful, but not unsalutary, to cast a parting glance at it. **1846** LANDOR *Imag. Conv.* Wks. I. 544/2 It is just..to shake a salutary fear into..stupid despots, when they shake an unsalutary one into thousands.

unsa'luted, *ppl. a.* (UN-¹ 8.)

1542 BECON *Pathw. Prayer* xxxvi. O vii, He that leaueth̄e God vnsaluted with his prayers at these thre tymes. *a* **1586** SIDNEY *Arcadia* III. ii, My sleepes were inquired after, and my wakings never unsaluted. **1607** SHAKS. *Cor.* V. iii. 50 You Gods, I pray, And the most noble Mother of the world Leaue vnsaluted. **1694** tr. *Milton's Lett. State* 260 We have given him in Command, not to pass by your Lordships Unsaluted in our Name. **1795** [see next]. **1805** WORDSW. *Prelude* IV. 47 The rooms, the court, the garden were not left Long unsaluted. **1821** SCOTT *Pirate* xxiii, He suffered them to go away unsaluted.

unsa'luting, *ppl. a.* (UN-¹ 10.)

1795 COLERIDGE *Lett.* (1895) 144, I met you in Redcliff, and, unsaluted and unsaluting, passed by the man to whom [etc.].

un'salvable, *a.* (UN-¹ 7 b and 5 b.)

1624 T. SCOTT *Vox Pop.* II. 14 He found the rootes of eithers discontent so deepe, and the sore so vnsalueable, that hee gaue it ouer. **1638** CHILLINGW. *Relig. Prot.* I. v. §60 The words by you cited, and charged with unsalvable contradiction. **1659** FULLER *App. Inj. Innoc.* II. 102 Else we were all..in an unsaluable condition. **1895** SALMOND *Chr. Doctr. Immort.* VI. iv. 668 Neither to make the heathen unconditionally unsalvable, nor to represent salvation as possible apart from Christ.

Hence **unsalva'bility, -ableness.**

1684 H. MORE *Answer* xiv. 105 Touching the Idolatrousness of the Church of Rome, and the Unsalvableness of those in her Communion. **1891** *Wesleyan Method. Mag.* June 465/1 The unsalvability of any heathen.

un'salvatory, *a.* (UN-¹ 7.)

1850 CARLYLE *Latter-d. Pamph.* iii. 6 Dalai-Lama pills, manufactured let not refined lips hint how, and quite *un*salvatory to mankind.

un'salved, *ppl. a.* (UN-¹ 8. Cf. MHG. *ungesalbet*, G. *ungesalbt*, Du. *ongezalfd.*)

a **1240** *Ureisun* in *O.E. Hom.* I. 202 Hwoa þerf beon unsalued þet haueð se mihti salue. **1641** MILTON *Prel. Episc.* 23 Nor caring how slightly they put off the verdit of holy Text unsalv'd. **1837** YOUATT *Sheep* xvii. 549 The *laid* wool ..was..lower in price than the white or unsalved wool.

†**un'same**, *v. Obs.* [UN-² 6 + SAME *a.*] *trans.* To alter, change.

1632 QUARLES *Div. Fancies* II. xxxiii, What secret mischiefe can Vn-same thy peace? 'Twas not the selfe same Man.

†**un'samen**, *adv. Obs.* [UN-¹ 11 b.] Not in union or harmony.

a **1400–50** *Alexander* 605 With grete glesenand eȝen grymly he lokis, þat were..sett vn-samen of serelypy hewys.

un'sampled, *ppl. a.* [UN-¹ 8.]

†**1.** Unexampled. *Obs.*

a **1638** MEDE *Wks.* (1672) 220 The unsampled irregularity of our whole nature. **1675** ALSOP *Anti-sozzo* 312 The Burning of Rome and his unsampled Butcheries.

2. Untried; not experienced.

1890 *Pall Mall G.* 28 Aug. 1/2 It is the unknown and the unsampled that bewilders us.

unsanctifi'cation. (UN-¹ 12, UN-² 8.)

a **1684** LEIGHTON *Comm. 1 Pet.* i. 2 (1693) 28 From present unsanctification, a Man cannot inferre that he is not Elected. **1804** *Europ. Mag.* XLV. 96/2 Whether this tavern had, from the time of its unsanctification, been always kept by Quakers, cannot now be ascertained.

un'sanctified, *ppl. a.* (UN-¹ 8.)

1570 *Homilies* II. *Agst. Rebellion* III. (1859) 570 Rebels.. leave the Sabbath day of the Lord unsanctified. **1602** SHAKS. *Ham.* V. i. 252 She should in ground vnsanctified haue lodg'd. **1650** BULWER *Anthropomet.* 199 In the Indies, among barbarous and unsanctified Nations. **1747** DODDRIDGE *Col. Gardiner* 28 A Heart as yet quite unsanctified. **1796** MME. D'ARBLAY *Camilla* V. 430 My own prayers may be too unsanctified to be heard. **1827** POLLOK *Course T.* x. 306 The others..stand unsanctified, unpardoned, sad. **1855** MILMAN *Lat. Chr.* XIV. viii. VI. 578 To the Ecclesiastic belonged the chancel, not to be entered by unsanctified feet.

Hence **un'sanctifiedly** *adv.*, **-ness.**

1634 LD. WARRISTON *Diary* (S.H.S.) 226, I most confesse ..the unsanctifiednes of my affections. **1650** HUBBERT *Pill Formality* 183 Thou livest..unholily, and unsanctifiedly.

un'sanctify, *v.* (UN-² 6 c.)

1594 *Zepheria* xxv, Let not disdayne thy soule vnsanctifie. **1633** PRYNNE *Histrio-m.* 648 If therefore Stage-playes unsanctifie or pollute the one,..needes must they defile the other too. **1693** SHADWELL *Volunteers* IV, *Lettice.* You may see the most unhallow'd sight. *Hackwell.* Will it not unsanctifiy my eyes? **1831** WORDSW. *Yarrow Revisited* 91 Nor deem that localised Romance..Unsanctifies our tears. **1862** BURTON *Bk. Hunter* IV. 323 To imagine any process by which they could be unsanctified.

Hence **un'sanctifying** *ppl. a.*

a **1859** MACAULAY *Hist. Eng.* xxiv. (1861) V. 193 The sanctity of their profession has an unsanctifying influence on them.

unsancti'monious, *a.* (UN-¹ 7.)

a **1797** H. WALPOLE *Geo. II* (1847) III. vi. 158 A woman of so unsanctimonious a character.

un'sanction, *v.* (UN-² 4.)

1854 PATMORE *Angel in Ho., Betrothal* 160 Love blabb'd of is a great decline; A careless word unsanctions sense.

un'sanctioned, *ppl. a.* (UN-¹ 8.)

1784 COWPER *Task* II. 524 Their [*sc.* sages'] rules of life Defective and unsanctioned. **1833** J. H. NEWMAN *Arians* I. iii. 64 From a fear of using unsanctioned language on a sacred subject. **1866** C. J. VAUGHAN *Plain Words* vi. 92 'Society'..is a thing not unnoticed, not unsanctioned by Him who made us.

un'sanctity. (UN-¹ 12.)

a **1639** W. WHATELEY *Prototypes* II. xxvi. (1640) 81 Those rules..doe discover rather the unsanctity of love in other respects, than the excesse. **1838** S. BELLAMY *Betrayal* 85 From whose Unsanctity incense doth ev'n recoil.

†**un'sanctuary.** (UN-¹ 12.)

? **1615** SYLVESTER *Tobacco Battered* 709 In som Play-house, or some Ordinary, Or in som piece of som Vn-sanctuary.

un'sandalled, *ppl. a.* (UN-¹ 8.)

1772 MASON *Eng. Garden* I. 16 Many a glade..where if Art E'er dar'd to tread, 'twas with unsandal'd foot. **1820** SHELLEY *Prometh. Unb.* III. i. 15 As ice wounds unsandalled feet. **1887** BOWEN *Æneid* IV. 518 One foot all unsandalled, her robe ungirdled, she stands.

un'sanded, *ppl. a.* (UN-¹ 8.)

1843 *Farmer's Mag.* Jan. 29/2 The unsanded spot is visible to this day.., being almost bare of grass.

un'sane, *a.* [UN-¹ 7, 5 b.]

†**1.** Unsound, unhealthy. *Obs.*

c **1690** tr. *Plutarch's Mor.* (1718) IV. 177 A Man begotten by an unsane Body, does not therefore deserve Punishment.

2. Lacking sanity. *rare.*

1867 H. BUSHNELL *Moral Uses Dark Th.* 267 It results.. not that we are insane, but short of perfect sanity, practically unsane.

un'sanguine, *a.* (UN-¹ 7.)

1728 YOUNG *Ocean* lxxi, Prophetic schemes, And golden dreams, May I, unsanguin, cast away! **1862** [ELIZ. JOHNSTON] *Gifts & Graces* xxiv. 238 To one of her unsanguine disposition such cheerfulness was very admirable. **1883** LYTTON *Life & Lett. Ld. L.* II. 25 The unsanguine nature of his disposition.

Hence **un'sanguineness.**

1841 LADY LYTTELTON in *Corr.* (1912) 309 This, however, is..only my usual unsanguineness.

un'sanitary, *a.* (UN-¹ 7 and 5 b.)

1871 GEO. ELIOT *Middlemarch* xxiii, In any grim street of that unsanitary period. **1883** *Century Mag.* XXVI. 77 Unsanitary dwellings.

un'sanitated, *ppl. a.* (UN-¹ 8.)

1888 *Daily Tel.* 5 Mar. (Encycl. Dict.), Unsanitated workrooms, or..sweating dens.

unsa'ponifiable, *a.* (UN-¹ 7 b.)

1885 W. L. CARPENTER *Soap & Candles* 91 Estimation of Unsaponifiable Oils in Fats.

unsa'ponified, *ppl. a.* (UN-¹ 8.)

1839 URE *Dict. Arts* 729 The unsaponified fat of the coccus insect.

†**un'sapory**, *a. Obs.* [UN-¹ 7 and 5 b + SAPOR.] Unsavoury.

1638 SIR T. HERBERT *Trav.* (ed. 2) 13 A meale..unsapory and offensive. *Ibid.* 241 The cheese is..of an unsaporie taste.

un'sapped, *ppl. a.* (UN-¹ 8.)

1768 STERNE *Sent. Journ., Act of Charity*, Two upright vestal sisters, unsapp'd by caresses. **1896** *Amer. Ann. Deaf* Feb. 106 Sound and vigorous in body, unsapped in vitality.

un'sappy, *a.* (UN-¹ 7. Cf. OE. *unsæpiȝ.*)

a **1722** LISLE *Husb.* (1757) 248 A small, thin, unsappy leaf.

unsarra'd, dial. var. UNSERVED *ppl. a.*

un'sashed, *ppl. a.* (UN-¹ 8.)

[**1775** ASH.] **1841** DICKENS *Barn. Rudge* xli, A gleam of sun shining through the unsashed window.

un'satable, *a.* [UN-¹ 7 b.] Insatiable.

1850 BROWNING *Easter Day* xxvi, His saints..knew He would not disallow Their spirit's hunger,..Unsated,—not unsatable.

un'sated, *ppl. a.* (UN-¹ 8.)

1693 DRYDEN *Juvenal* VI. 185 Tir'd with the Toyl, unsated with the Sin. **1744** YOUNG *Nt. Th.* VI. 69 Long life might lapse, age unperceiv'd come on; And find the soul unsated with her theme. **1798** FERRIAR *Illustr. Sterne*, etc. i. 6 His imagination..unsated by a long acquaintance with literary folly. **1834** LYTTON *Pompeii* III. x, Now contracting, now lengthening, its folds, in pain and unsated anger. **1879** FARRAR *St. Paul* I. 177 To the High Priest therefore he went, unsated by all his previous cruelties.

Hence **un'satedness.**

1845 BAILEY *Festus* (ed. 2) 258 Contrasting the pure joys of earlier years With the unsatedness of current sin.

un'satiable, *a.* Now *rare.* [UN-¹ 7 b and 5 b.] Of persons, desires, etc.: Insatiable. (Common *c* 1540–*c* 1675.)

(*a*) **1382** WYCLIF *Baruch* iv. 15 He brouȝte vpon hem..a folc vnsaciable. *c* **1440** *Alph. Tales* 523 With mony we sall fyll þine vnsaciable harte. **1500–20** DUNBAR *Poems* xvii. 38 Sum wald tak all this warldis breid,..Throw hairt vnsatiable. *a* **1540** BARNES *Wks.* (1573) 342/1 Beecause you bee..vnsaciable belly Gods. **1631** GOUGE *God's Arrows* III. §70. 311 To them that are unsatiable in sin. **1684** BURNET tr. *More's Utopia* 21 When any unsatiable Wretch..resolves to inclose many thousand Acres of Ground.

(*b*) *c* **1440** J. SHIRLEY *Dethe K. James* 28 All mene saye that the unsacionable [*sic*] covetise was the..cause of the Kynges dethe. *a* **1513** FABYAN *Chron.* VII. ccxxiv. 251 The vnsaceable couetous [*sic*] of Ranulph. **1535** COVERDALE *Judith* Contents ii, The vnsaciable desyre that Nabuchodonosor had to raigne. **1579** W. WILKINSON *Confut. Fam. Love* To Rdr. p. iv b, Vnsatiable greadines. **1643** SIR T. BROWNE *Relig. Med.* I. §47 That essence, whose infinite goodnesse is able to terminate the desires of it selfe, and the unsatiable wishes of ours. **1692** N. MATHER *Pref. Owen's Disc. Holy Sp.* (1693) A 3 b, An unsatiable Desire to do Service to Christ. **1810** *Monthly Mag.* XXIX. 321 His hate [is] unsatiable, where he mistrusts.

(*c*) **1528** ROY *Rede me* (Arb.) 102 They are the divels fornace, Oven infernall vnsaciable. **1691** tr. *Emilianne's Frauds Rom. Monks* (ed. 3) 375 An unsatiable Gulf which swallows all, and gives up nothing again.

un'satiableness. Now *rare.* [UN-¹ 12 and 5 b.] Insatiability.

1539 ELYOT *Cast. Helthe* (1541) 28 To content the unsaciablenes of wanton appetites. **1547** RECORDE *Judic. Ur.* 1 Unsaciablenes is never satisfied. **1656** EARL MONM. tr. *Boccalini's Advts. fr. Parnass.* 437 To satisfie the ravenous and dog-like unsatiableness of such a company of starvelings. *a* **1699** J. BEAUMONT *Psyche* XVI. ccxxx, O pardon my Unsatiableness, Since Thou thy self alone art cause of it. **1823** BENTHAM *Not Paul* 282 The unsatiableness of Paul's ambition.

†**un'satiably**, *adv. Obs.* UN-¹ 11 and 5 b.)

1540–1 ELYOT *Image Gov.* 154 b, They vnsaciably fedde therewith theym selues. **1583** GOLDING *Calvin on Deut.* xlix. 291 To haue crammed and glutted themselues after that fashion vnsatiably. **1615** J. STEPHENS *Satyr. Ess.* II. ii. 236 The steame of a roasted ioynt attracts his nostrils vnsatiably. *a* **1665** J. GOODWIN *Filled w. the Spirit* xix. (1670) 540 By following Lusts and Pleasures unsatiably.

un'satiate, *a.* (UN-¹ 7 and 5 b.)

Frequent *c* 1540–1650; now *rare.*

1528 ROY *Rede me* (Arb.) 78 The dayly cravynge..Of the vnsaciate fryer beggers. **1594** SHAKS. *Rich. III*, III. v. 87 (Q.), When that my mother went with child Of that vnsatiate Edward. **1614** RALEIGH *Hist. World* III. 51 The unsatiate desire of man to obtaine more and more thereof. **1681** DRYDEN *Abs. & Achit.* I. 987 But save me most from my Petitioners, Unsatiate as the barren Womb or Grave. **1876** MORRIS *Sigurd* III. 183 Their eyes are all unsatiate of gazing on his face.

un'satiated, *ppl. a.* (UN-¹ 8 and 5 b.)

1701 NORRIS *Ideal World* I. viii. 436 To behold the bright Sun of truth with an unwearied, as well as unsatiated eye. **1745** H. WALPOLE *Lett.* (1846) II. 90 The Prince of Wales has had unsatiated curiosity about him. **1812** J. HENRY *Camp. agst. Quebec* 48 Though we gorged the stomach, the appetite was unsatiated. **1880** NICHOL *Life Byron* 143 The feeling of affronted or unsatiated pride.

absol. **1890** SARAH J. DUNCAN *Soc. Depart.* 364 [We] looked at them with all the pleasure of the uncritical and the unsatiated.

un'satiating, *ppl. a.* (UN-¹ 10.)

1768 TUCKER *Lt. Nat.* (1834) II. 312 He might have excited sensations..permanent, unfading, and unsatiating. **1786** tr. *Beckford's Vathek* 3 The Eternal or unsatiating Banquet.

un'sating, *ppl. a.* (UN-¹ 10.)

1818 KEATS *Endym.* I. 816 So delicious is the unsating food. **1863** GILCHRIST *Life Blake* I. 73 There is something unsating about them, a perfume as of a growing violet.

un'satire, *v.* (UN-² 6 b.)

1638 N. WHITING *Albino & Bellama* To Ld. Lovelace 16 Some worthy peer, Whose very name unsatire can a jeer.

unsa'tirical, *a.* (UN-¹ 7.)

1592 G. HARVEY *Four Lett.* iii. 44 Those vnsatyricall Satyres, which M. Spencer long since embraced with an ouerloouing Sonnet.

unsatis'faction. [UN-¹ 12 and 5 b.]

1. Absence of satisfaction.

1643 DIGBY *Observ. Relig. Med.* (1644) 36 Nor have [I] any unsatisfaction in believing there are Spirits. **1675** T. PLUME *Life Hacket* in Hacket *Cent. Serm.* p. xliii, He thought the permission of conventicles did shew great irresolution and unsatisfaction in the truth. **1865** MRS. WHITNEY *Gayworthys* xxx, An earnestness that searched through all things even to unsatisfaction and scepticism. **1880** CARPENTER in *Mod. Review* I. 49 The unsatisfaction (if I may revive an obsolete word) of resting in any inherent 'potency' of Matter as the *ultima ratio* of the existing Kosmos.

†**2.** Unsatisfactoriness. *Obs.*

1645 BP. HALL *Remedy Discontents* 94 The mean valuation of all these earthly things, for their transitorinesse, unsatisfaction, danger. **1668** R. STEELE *Husbandman's Calling* vi. §5 Thence he learns the unsatisfaction of the creature and that God and Heaven are the only rest of the soul.

unsatis'factorily, *adv.* (UN-¹ 11 and 5 b.)

1657 F. ROBERTS in Spurgeon *Treas. Dav.* III. 239 Augustine also expounds the words much to the same effect, but altogether as unsatisfactorily. **1685** BAXTER *Paraphr. N.T.* A 3, Many..are too large and costly for this use: some ..are unsatisfactorily brief. *c* **1714** POPE *Let.* Wks. 1751 VII. 138 To shew you how very unsatisfactorily you write,.. you've never told me how you do. **1794** R. J. SULIVAN *View Nat.* IV. 11 Materialism, as I have repeatedly said, and I hope not unsatisfactorily proved, is [etc.]. **1838** JAMES *Louis XIV*, III. 50 Completing that which had been thus imperfectly and unsatisfactorily begun. **1884** *Law Rep. 12 Q.B.D.* 583 The scope and effect of an Act so unsatisfactorily framed.

unsatis'factoriness. (UN-¹ 12.)

1643 PRYNNE *Sov. Power Parl.* I. (ed. 2) Pref. A 2 The insufficiency and unsatisfactorinesse of all late Printed Pleas. **1679** J. GOODMAN *Penit. Pard.* I. iv. 113 The emptiness and unsatisfactoriness of all the Incomes of sin.

1807 G. CHALMERS *Caledonia* I. II. vi. 275 The unsatisfactoriness of the one, and the silence of the other, lead us to suppose [etc.]. 1876 LOWELL *Among my Bks.* Ser. II. I. 6 The unsatisfactoriness of science leads Faust to seek repose in worldly pleasure.

unsatis'factory, *a.* (UN-¹ 7.)
1637–50 ROW *Hist. Kirk* (Wodrow Soc.) 65 This ansuer wes judged..unsatisfactorie. 1652 BENLOWES *Theoph.* Pref., All external splendours being unsatisfactory. 1714 R. FIDDES *Pract. Disc.* II. 212 The very enjoyments of life..are ..in themselves unsatisfactory. 1777 J. RICHARDSON *Dissert. East. Nations* 9 [It] opens a wide field for unsatisfactory enquiry. 1818 COBBETT *Pol. Reg.* XXXIII. 692 To assert without stating particulars, would be unsatisfactory. 1843 BETHUNE *Sc. Fireside Stor.* 88 As his visit proved unsatisfactory, he determined to make his stay short. 1890 *Retrospect Med.* CII. 17 The treatment of this dangerous complication is most unsatisfactory.

un'satisfiable, *a.* [UN-¹ 7b.]
1. Incapable of being satisfied.
1539 TAVERNER *Gard. Wysd.* II. 26 Onles thou haddest bene an euell man & with money unsatisfyable. 1593 G. HARVEY *Pierce's Super.* To Friends, Aduisedly weigh..the impossible satisfaction of vnsatisfiable expectation. 1648 GAGE *West Ind.* 76 An unsatisfiable minde and greedy covetousnesse. 1680 C. NESSE *Church Hist.* 60 Their envy and ambition are restless and unsatisfiable. 1802 PALEY *Nat. Theol.* xxvi. Wks. (1834) 545/1 Well-directed tastes and desires, compared with the dominion of..unsatisfied, and unsatisfiable passions. 1896 DK. ARGYLL *Philos. Belief* 544 The unsatisfied, and apparently unsatisfiable, desires of men.
†**2.** For which no satisfaction can be made. *Obs.*
1593 G. HARVEY *New. Let.* B 3 b, The more notorious the offence, and the more vnsatisfiable the Iniurie was. 1648 SYMMONS *Vind. Chas. I*, 166 Until we have quite destroyed him, whom we hate,..for those unsatisfiable wrongs, which ourselves have done him.
Hence **un'satisfiableness**, **-ably** *adv.*
1647 TRAPP *Comm. 1 John* ii. 17 There is a curse of *unsatisfiablenesse lies upon the creature. 1664 INGELO *Bentiv. & Ur.* VI. 350 [Appetites which] do gall the Soul by a ravenous unsatisfiableness. 1652 N. CULVERWEL *Lt. Nature* II. 70 The Hart pants *unsatisfiably after the water-brooks.

un'satisfied, *ppl. a.* [UN-¹ 8 and 5b.]
1. Not satisfied in respect of something desired; not having obtained all that, or as much as, is wished for: **a.** Predicatively, also const. *with*, †*of*.
c 1430 LYDG. *Min. Poems* (Percy Soc.) 31 Thou tolde me, frende,..That thou kneuhest one..Unsatisfied a day in tymes twelfe. a 1586 SIDNEY *Arcadia* III. xviii. (1912) 457 So the more they strake, the more unsatisfied they were with striking. 1592 SHAKS. *Rom. & Jul.* II. ii. 125 *Rom.* O wilt thou leaue me so vnsatisfied? *Iuli.* What satisfaction can'st thou haue to night? 1597 HOOKER *Eccl. Pol.* v. lx. §7 That the Church..should repell them and see them dye vnsatisfied of these their Ghostly Desires. 1613 SHAKS. *Hen. VIII*, IV. ii. 55 Though he were vnsatisfied in getting,..yet in bestowing..He was most Princely. 1685 DRYDEN *Lucretius* III. 155 Unsatisfy'd with all that Nature brings; Loathing the present, liking absent things. 1758–63 GIBBON *Misc. Wks.* (1814) III. 41 His ambition was yet unsatisfied. 1808 MITFORD *Hist. Greece* IV. 457 They were unsatisfied with the composition of the appointed embassy. 1866 GEO. ELIOT *F. Holt* i, To feel a woman's hunger of the heart for ever unsatisfied. 1897 MARY KINGSLEY *W. Africa* 52 A warning to others of the dangers of being unsatisfied.
b. Attributively.
1611 SHAKS. *Cymb.* I. vi. 49 The Cloyed will: That satiate yet vnsatisfi'd desire. 1665 MANLEY *Grotius' Low C. Wars* 279 Casting their unsatisfied eyes upon his countenance, they gratefully reverenced that tender Age. a 1704 T. BROWN *Sat. agst. Woman* Wks. 1730 I. 57 Raging with unsatisfy'd desire. 1757 FOOTE *Author* I, You know the unsatisfied mind of man, no sooner is one object possessed, but another starts up. 1849 GROTE *Greece* II. l. VI. 355 Bitter and as yet unsatisfied hatred against Platæa. 1871 MORLEY *Carlyle* in *Crit. Misc.* Ser. I. (1878) 168 The deep unrest of unsatisfied souls.
2. Not satisfied in respect of information or knowledge; doubtful, dubious.
1575 CHURCHYARD *Chippes* 38 b, At whoes elloquence the heerars rather stoede astoned than vnsatysfyed in any poynt or parssell. 1602 SHAKS. *Ham.* v. ii. 351 Report me and my causes right To the vnsatisfied. 1646 SIR T. BROWNE *Pseud. Ep.* 187 In submission to future information, we are unsatisfied unto great dubitation. 1655 FULLER *Ch. Hist.* IX. ii. §25 Others were unsatisfied in the Authenticalness of the instrument, who never did..see the original. 1736 BUTLER *Anal.* II. viii. 384 It will yet leave the mind in a very unsatisfied state.
†**b.** Not certain *of* something. *Obs.*
1665 MANLEY *Grotius' Low C. Wars* 593 They mistrusted their Borders, and were unsatisfied of their more inward Garrisons.
3. Not satisfied with some circumstance, result, etc.; dissatisfied, displeased.
Common in latter half of the 17th cent.; now *rare*.
a 1648 LD. HERBERT *Hen. VIII* (1683) 526 Both Princes remained unsatisfied of the others actions. 1652 J. WRIGHT tr. *Camus' Nat. Paradox* x. 253 Miestas [was] very unsatisfied with his Son's deportments. 1669 TEMPLE *Let. to Trevor* Wks. 1720 II. 202 He seemed a good deal unsatisfied that the Spanish Ambassador had received the Advice from England. 1731 *Gentl. Mag.* I. 436 Fortune.. declar'd that whoever was unsatisfied with their Lot should complain to her. 1795 V. KNOX *Chr. Phil.* vi. I. 57 When he is observed, he is ashamed; and when he has done, he is unsatisfied. 1883 *American* VI. 250 Mr. Freeman is.. unsatisfied with the review.
†**b.** Not satisfied by being paid. *Obs.*
1654 WHITLOCK *Zootomia* 130 The short, and long is now no sight so unpleasant as their unsatisfied Doctor. 1796 MME. D'ARBLAY *Camilla* IX. viii. V. 174 If they [*sc.* gamesters] were left unsatisfied, the credit of the young man would fall a sacrifice of their ill treatment.
4. Not settled by payment, etc.
1588 SHAKS. *L.L.L.* II. i. 139 If then your father will restore But that one halfe which is vnsatisfied, We will giue vp our right in Aquitaine. 1632 in *10th Rep. Hist. MSS. Comm.* App. V. 483 Howe the same debt was paid..and what is yet behinde and unsatisfied. 1682 SCARLETT *Exchanges* 114 Upon pain of forfeiture of twenty five Guilders, and the Bill to be accounted unsatisfied. 1763 *Act 4 Geo. III*, c. i. 29 The Monies so remaining unsatisfied, or not discharged. 1879 F. HITCHMAN *Publ. Life Beaconsfield* I. 182 He was deeply in debt, and had a number of unsatisfied judgments out against him.
Hence **un'satisfiedly** *adv.*
1661 BOYLE *Style of Script.* 172 Some of them,..after having Unsatisfiedly Travell'd thorough all sorts of Human Volumes, have Rested..only in these Divine Ones.

un'satisfiedness. [UN-¹ 12.] The condition of being unsatisfied. (Freq. in 17th cent.)
1646 LD. DIGBY in Carte *Ormonde* (1735) III. 476 Rather out of an unsatisfiedness of his safety..than [etc.]. 1653 GAUDEN *Hierasp.* 74 Whence that unsatisfiedness, which carries the soul of man..to this height of coveting after a blessed eternity. 1741 RICHARDSON *Pamela* II. 387, I may.. rejoice in that happy State, where is..no Unsatisfiedness. 1860 PUSEY *Min. Proph.* 13 The soul..seeks to distract herself from her unrest and unsatisfiedness. 1886 LINSKILL *Haven under Hill* xxii, He had seen her loneliness, her soul's dimness and unsatisfiedness.

†**un'satisfy**, *v. Obs.* (UN-² 3.)
1652 SHIRLEY *Doubtful Heir* Ded., I have presumed thus rather to let you know I can still honour you than unsatisfy myself by neglecting the first opportunity of presenting my service.

un'satisfying, *ppl. a.* (UN-¹ 10.)
1656 JEANES *Fuln. Christ* 234 Not resting therefore in this unsatisfying answere, we will in the next place shew [etc.]. 1665 BOYLE *Occas. Refl.* IV. xiii, Parting with unsatisfying Trifles. 1760–2 GOLDSM. *Cit. W.* xxxvii, In this also.. enthusiastic confidence or unsatisfying doubts terminate all our inquiries. 1813 SHELLEY *Q. Mab* IV. 248 Days of unsatisfying listlessness. 1837 LYTTON *Athens* I. 469 With this unsatisfying reply the messenger returned. 1879 MᶜCARTHY *Own Times* xxviii. II. 351 The political results of the war were to many minds equally unsatisfying.
Hence **un'satisfyingness**.
1650 TRAPP *Comm. Gen.* xxv. 29 The curse of unsatisfyingness that lies upon them [*sc.* carnal pleasures]. 1883 H. DRUMMOND *Nat. Law in Spir. W.* 363 Its vagueness to the mere intellect,..its satisfying unsatisfyingness, its vast atmosphere.

un'satisfyingly, *adv.* (UN-¹ 11.)
1653 JER. TAYLOR *Serm. for Year* iii. 41 They speak variously, and uncertainly, and unsatisfyingly.

un'saturable, *a.* (UN-¹ 7b and 5b.)
1535 STEWART *Cron. Scot.* (Rolls) II. 426 Sleipand in sleuth,..Vnsaturabill als of gulositie. 1816–30 BENTHAM *Offic. Apt. Maximized, Extr. Const. Code* 16 The perpetual saturation of appetites essentially unsaturable.

un'saturate. *Chem.* [UN-¹ 12.] Any unsaturated compound, esp. an unsaturated fat or fatty acid. Cf. *polyunsaturate* sb. s.v. POLYUNSATURATED *a.*
1934 *World Petroleum* Apr. 123/2 Whereas straight run fuel contained less than two percent unsaturates, cracked gasoline contained from 10 to 40 percent unsaturated compounds. 1959 LOGAN & MAGGIOLO in E. S. Pattison *Industr. Fatty Acids* v. 41 These unsaturates can be cleaved to produce monobasic and dibasic acids and their derivatives. 1974 *Radiation Res.* LIX. 109 When these substances undergo moderately rapid reaction the surface temperature of the unsaturate is considerably higher than 77°K.

un'saturated, *ppl. a.* (UN-¹ 8; cf. SATURATED *ppl. a.* 3b.)
1758 REID tr. *Macquer's Chym.* I. 395 That portion of the Acid which remains unsaturated will dissolve the Mercury. 1791 *Phil. Trans.* LXXXI. 219 Any surplus of..air would only have remained unsaturated. 1832 *Nat. Philos., Electr.* ii. §53 (L.U.K.), Its unsaturated matter would have exerted an attractive force on the fluid. 1866 *Notices Proc. R. Inst. Gt. Brit.* IV. 417 The two nitrogen arms which are left exposed sufficiently indicate that two attraction units remain unsaturated. 1872 *Phil. Mag.* XLIII. 259 A radical ..is a portion of a molecule, a group of atoms, the affinities of which do not wholly saturate one another, the radical being uni-, bi-, tri-, quadri-, &c. valent, according as 1, 2, 3, 4,..affinities are left unsaturated. 1879 ROOD *Chromatics* xviii. 307 He must mainly use the pale unsaturated colours of nature. 1916 *Jrnl. Amer. Chem. Soc.* XXXVIII. 778 It has been generally assumed that what is known as a bivalent element must be tied by two bonds to another element or elements, or remain with an 'unsaturated valence'. 1951 I. L. FINAR *Org. Chem.* iv. 67 The acetylenes are unsaturated hydrocarbons that contain one triple bond. 1982 J. E. FERNANDEZ *Org. Chem.* v. 89 The alkenes are unsaturated: that is they contain fewer hydrogen atoms than the alkanes.

unsatu'ration. *Chem.* [UN-¹ 12.] The condition of a compound, esp. an organic one, of having one or more multiple bonds in its molecule. Cf. SATURATION 3a.
1885 REMSEN *Org. Chem.* 209 The condition of unsaturation is met with among carbon compounds in several forms. 1932 I. D. GARARD *Introd. Org. Chem.* v. 59 The cause, or explanation, of the unsaturation is not the same in all instances. 1964 N. G. CLARK *Mod. Org. Chem.* vii. 115 Chemical reagents attack the site of unsaturation but this occurs less readily than in the case of the related olefins. 1975 *Sci. Amer.* Mar. 78/3 The greater the unsaturation in a fat or a wax, that is, the greater the number of double bonds, the more likely it is that the substance will be liquid at low temperatures.

unsau, variant of ONSAW *Obs.*

†**un'saught**, *sb. Obs.* [Late OE. *unseht* (f. *un-* UN-¹ 12 + *seht* SAUGHT *sb.*), **unsaht*, = ON. and Icel. *úsátt*, *ósátt*, *úsǽtt*, MSw. *osät*, MDa. *usæt*.] Discord, dissension; hostile speech.
a 1122 *O.E. Chron.* (Laud MS.) an. 1052, Hi macodon mæst þet unseht betweonan Godwine eorle & þam cynge. c 1205 LAY. 11456 Wuileð Romleode cumen to þissere þeode,..& maken vnsæhte. a 1300 *Cursor M.* 28198 Wit flitt, wit brixil,..Myn euen-cristen haue i hurt, And oft vn-saght o him i said. 1710 RUDDIMAN *Gloss.* s.v. *Saucht*, *To live in unsaucht*, i.e. trouble. 1808 JAMIESON.

†**un'saught**, *a. Obs.* [Late OE. *unseht* (f. *un-* UN-¹ 7 + *seht* SAUGHT *a.*), **unsaht* = ON. and Icel. *úsáttr*, MSw. *osatt*, *osätt*, MDa. *usaat* in sense 1.]
1. At variance or enmity; hostile.
c 1100 *O.E. Chron.* (MS. D.) an. 1067, Eadric cild & þa Bryttas wurdon unsehte. c 1205 LAY. 3930 Þas breþren weren swa wode..þat al heo weren vn-sahte. 1303 R. BRUNNE *Handl. Synne* 482 With holy chyrche þey ben vnsaght. c 1350 *Lybeaus Disc.* 1421 For þey were unsauȝte [*v.r.* vnsyȝt] And eiþer oþres fo. 13.. *St. Erkenwald* 8 In Hongyst dawes þat þe Saxones vnsaȝt had ene sende hyder. ? a 1400 *Morte Arth.* 1306 That here are semblede in sale, vn-sawghte mott ȝe worthe! c 1475 *Golagros & Gaw.* 456 Than thai schupe for to assege segis vnsaught.
2. Dissatisfied, displeased.
? a 1300 *Salomon & Sat.* (1848) 275 Hit is mony gedelyng when me him ȝeueþ a lutel þyng, waxen wol vnsaþt. a 1310 in Wright *Lyric P.* xii. 42 Ant swore somme unsaht, That hem wes werk by-taht, longe er hit were lyht. 1390 GOWER *Conf.* III. 153 Of thilke folk that were unsauhte Toward here king for his pilage. c 1400 *Destr. Troy* 5057 Yf we be cause of þi kene yre, And þou vnsaght of þi sight sothely of vs two.
3. Not at ease; embarrassed; troubled, distressed.
a 1375 *Joseph Arim.* 64 Þe kyng..wolde haue red of his folk,.. & þei forsaken hit han, & he vnsauht sittes. a 1400 *Sir Perc.* 2152 Thenne was scho unsaughte. Scho gret and cried in hir mone. a 1450 *Le Morte Arth.* 3189 The kynge gan lowde crye and calle, As marred man of wytte vnsaught. 1513 DOUGLAS *Æneid* XII. v. 201 This Chorineus als so fast Ruschit on his fa, thus fyrefangit and onsaucht.
Hence †**un'saughtly** *adv.*; †**un'saughtness**.
a 1000 in *Vercelli MS.* fol. 80 b, Þurh þæt þonne ariseð unsehtnesse betweoh twam cyningum & twam ȝebroðrum. c 1200 ORMIN 7187 Alle þa þatt lufenn toþþ & woh & unnsahhtnesse. ? a 1400 *Morte Arth.* 1501 Vnsaughtely he saide hyme þese sittande wordez. *Ibid.* 1847 Vnsaughtyly þey sette thane appone oure sere knyghttez.

un'saveable, *a.* (UN-¹ 7b.)
1647 TRAPP *Marrow Gd. Authors* in *Comm. Ep.* 613 One that is unsaveable, or one that is undone by himself. 1874 M. ARNOLD in *Contemp. Rev.* Oct. 816 All the devices to save those unsaveable things, the Bible-miracles.

un'saved, *ppl. a.* (UN-¹ 8.)
1648 HEXHAM II, *Onbehoedt*, vnpreserved, or vnsaved. [1775 ASH.] 1818 BENTHAM *Ch. Eng., Catech. Exam.* 437 Why are these [souls] to be left unsaved..? 1838 S. BELLAMY *The Betrayal* 168 And there did answer these, unseen, but loud,..th' unsaved Of earth. 1866 B. NORTH *Ourselves* 36 A man..when he says he does not know the Lord..confesses that he is unsaved.

un'saving, *ppl. a.* (UN-¹ 10.)
1628 FELTHAM *Resolves* II. lxiii. 179 If hee takes policie, that is both endlesse and vncertaine:..What to day is good, is to morrow vnsaving. 1714 POPE *Lett.* (1737) VI. 46, I would no more make a judgment of an author's genius from a damning critick, than I would of a man's religion from an unsaving zealot.

†**un'savour**, *v.* [UN-¹ 14.] *intr.* To have no savour or agreeableness.
a 1547 SURREY *Poems, Eccl.* iv. 58 In boost of owtwarde works he taketh no delight, Nor wast of wourds; suche sacryfice unsauereth in his sight.

un'savoured, *ppl. a.* (UN-¹ 8.)
1435 [see UNSALT *a.*]. 1562 J. HEYWOOD *Prov. & Epigr.* (1867) 139 As yl is this othing: Ill sauerd sumthing, as vnsauerd nothyng. 1580 HOLLYBAND *Treas. Fr. Tong* s.v. *Goguelu*, A nice one, an vnsauoured one, a proud foole. 1897 *Allbutt's Syst. Med.* II. 880 Of what possible service are.. blows unfelt, salts and feathers unsavoured?
Hence **un'savouredly** *adv.*
1603 FLORIO *Montaigne* I. xxv. 84 He that meanes to speake vnsavouredly.

†**un'savourest**, obs. superl. of UNSAVOURY *a.*
1599 SANDYS *Europæ Spec.* (1605) Y 1 b, All which [*sc.* idols] are the vnsavorest dregs to the Iew in the world.

un'savourily, *adv.* [UN-¹ 11.]
†**1. a.** So as to savour ill. **b.** Without savour; insipidly. *Obs.*
14.. *Langland's P. Pl.* C. XVI. 49 (MS. Laud 656), Here sauce was oversoured & vnsauerilich ygrounde. c 1440 *Promp. Parv.* 367/1 Onsaveryly, *insipide*. c 1449 PECOCK *Repr.* v. xv. 564 It is no nede forto seie ther of eny thing vnperfitli..and therfore vnsauorili here.
2. In an unpleasant or disagreeable manner.
1611 COTGR., *Mausadement*, harshly, vnsauorily. 1641 MILTON *Animadv.* 60 So often and so unsavourily has it been repeated, that the Reader may well cry, Downe with it. 1647 TRAPP *Marrow Gd. Authors* in *Comm. Ep.* 646 Yea

many times most unseasonably and unsavourily.. they fell into those absurd disputes. **1899** *Westm. Gaz.* 21 Mar. 2/1 Tenanted by myriads of penguins, which nest unsavourily on the steep slopes.

un'savouriness. [UN-¹ 12.]

†**1.** Want of savouriness; insipidity. *Obs.*

1398 *Trevisa's Barth. De P.R.* XIX. lii. (1495) kk iiij, The nynthe sauour hyght werysshenesse & vnsauerynesse. **1548** ELYOT, *Insulsitas*,.. foolysshenesse, vnsauourynesse, lacke of grace. **1721** BAILEY, *Insipidity*, Unsavouriness, Flatness.

2. The quality of being unsavoury or disagreeable.

1557 in Hakluyt *Voy.* (1598) I. 296 Any anoyance, stinke, or other vnsauorinesse.. in the shippe. **1571** GOLDING *Calvin on Ps.* xxxiii. 7 It is an unsaverines not worthy the disproving. **1617** WOODALL *Surg. Mate* (1639) 356 If any person, for the unsavourinesse of a medicine, will refuse helpe [etc.]. **1646** SIR T. BROWNE *Pseud. Ep.* IV. x. 202 If we concede a nationall unsavourinesse in any people, yet shall we finde the Iewes lesse subject hereto then any. **1664** T. GOUGE *Chr. Directions* xx. 173 The unsavouriness of thy words and speeches. **1727** A. HAMILTON *New Acc. E. Ind.* I. iii. 44 The Sea affords Variety of Fish, but not savoury. I believe their unsavouriness proceeds from the extreme Saltness of the Sea-water. **1765** STERNE *Tr. Shandy* VII. xxxii, In the little peevish contentions of nature betwixt hunger and unsavouriness. **1864** R. KERR *Gentlem. House* 291 Flies.. follow their noses, and their presence.. is but an index of unsavouriness. **1884** *Manch. Exam.* 23 Sept. 5/2 Mudbanks.. in their unsightliness and unsavouriness when exposed.

†**un'savourly,** *adv. Obs.* [UN-¹ 11.] = UNSAVOURILY *adv.*

1377 LANGL. *P. Pl.* B. XIII. 43 Her sauce was ouer soure & vnsauourely grounde. *a* **1395** HYLTON *Scala Perf.* II. xxxii. (W. de W. 1494), This seeth the soule.. not.. nakydly and vnsauourly as dooth a clerke that seeth hym by his clergye onely. **1540–54** CROKE *13 Ps.* (Percy Soc.) 20 My fode doeth taste vnsavourly. **1592** GREENE *Groat's W. Wit* (1617) 8 Our fathers Precepts.. were most vnsauerly to one of your yeeres applyed. **1660** HICKERINGILL *Jamaica* 38 Without it other things seem to want their taste, or relish out unsavourly.

†**un'savourness,** obs. var. UNSAVOURINESS.

1422 YONG tr. *Secreta Secret.* 98 Saltnesse, & vnctuosite, Egrenesse & vnsauournesse.

un'savoury, *a.* [UN-¹ 7.]

†**1.** Having no savour; not attractive to the taste; tasteless, insipid. *Obs.*

a **1225** *Ancr. R.* 262 Loke nu hwo grucche.. of mistrum, oðer leane mel of unsauure metes, of poure pitaunce? **1377** LANGL. *P. Pl.* B. xv. 425 Fresshe flesshe other fisshe whan it salt failleth, It is vnsauory. *c* **1400** LOVE *Bonavent. Mirr.* (1908) 108 Til thoruȝ his mercy.. the vnsauery water and colde of aduersitie.. be torned in to wyne and conforte. **1477** NORTON *Ord. Alch.* v. in Ashm. (1652) 74 Also is Weerish tast called Unsavoury. **1576** NEWTON *Lemnie's Complex.* I. 87 Choler is bitter:.. Phlegme, vnsavery as water. **1601** BP. W. BARLOW *Defence* 89 The white of an egge, without salt, is flash, and vnsavery, sayth Job. **1610** BP. CARLETON *Jurisd.* 261 The Pope would hereby prooue vnsauery salt good for nothing but to be troden vnderfoot of men. **1652** GAULE *Magastrom.* 284 Crying out.., tread me under feet, as unsavory salt. **1784** COWPER *Task* I. 125 Hard fare! but such as boyish appetite Disdains not; nor the palate, undeprav'd By culinary arts, unsav'ry deems.

transf. **13..** *E.E. Allit. P.* B. 822 Þis vn-sauere hyne Louez no salt in her sauce. **1548** UDALL *Erasm. Par. Luke* xix. 141 b, That same stemme of the Judaicall figtree brought foorth.. vnsauourie, & vnripe people. **1585** GREENE *Planetomachia* F 4 b, Phlegme.. doulce, vnsauory & natural.

b. *fig.*

c **1449** PECOCK *Repr.* I. xvi. 89 If such maner of arguyng.. schulde be sett in sermonyng, the sermon schulde be ful vnsauory. *c* **1450** tr. *De Imitatione* II. viii. 48 Hov dry & hov harde þou art wiþoute ihesu! hov unsauory, hov veyne, if þou coueite eny þinge wiþoute ihesu! **1534** MORE *Treat. Passion* Wks. 1291/1 The context of the story shuld.. seme very farre vnsauery, by reason of the often interposicion of the iniciall letters. **1540** MORYSINE *Vives' Introd. Wysd.* G ij, Bodely workes be unsavery, excepte they have sauce from the hart. **1603** HOLLAND *Plutarch's Mor.* 1188 Some.. will say.. that the oracles.. be none of his [*sc.* Apollo's], because they are but rudely made and unsavery. **1634** MILTON *Comus* 742 The good thereof Consists in mutual and partak'n bliss, Unsavoury in th' injoyment of it self.

†**c.** *Bot.* (See quots.) *Obs.*

1548 TURNER *Names Herbes* (E.D.S.) 77 Symphytum petreum..; this herbe.. may be called in english vnsauery Margerum. **1597** GERARDE *Herbal* II. 948 *Abrotanum Inodorum*, Vnsauorie Sothernwood,.. growes flat vpon the grounde with broade leaues. **1660** *Catal. Plant. Cantab. Index* 6 Unsavoury field Cranes-bill, *cicutæ folio inodorum.* **1728** BRADLEY *Dict. Bot.*, *Thymum Inodorum*, Unsavory Thyme.

2. a. Unpleasant or disagreeable to the taste.

c **1380** WYCLIF *Serm.* Sel. Wks. II. 46 For scheep ben goode for to ete, and getis fleish is unsavery. *c* **1400** *Pilgr. Sowle* (Caxton, 1483) IV. ii. 58 These fowle buskes and wylde myght nought fructyfyen no.. lusty fruyte, but bytter and vnsauoury. **1555** EDEN *Decades* (Arb.) 222 The flesshe of this beaste is fylthy and vnsauery. **1577** B. GOOGE *Heresbach's Husb.* II. 86 b, The geathered Olyue, if it lye to long in heapes, putrifieth by reason of heate, and makes vnsauery oyle. **1617** WOODALL *Surg. Mate* (1639) 356 An approoved good Medicine, and not much unsavovry to bee taken. **1667** MILTON *P.L.* v. 401 Unsavourie food perhaps To spiritual Natures. **1812** J. HENRY *Camp. agst. Quebec* 97 Towards March they become unsavoury, but in no way tainted. **1856** KANE *Arct. Expl.* II. iii. 42 As unsavory a dose of flax-seed and quinine as was ever honored by the name of beer.

b. Disagreeable or offensive to the sense of smell, or to refined feelings.

1539 ELYOT *Cast. Helthe* 55 These excrementes be none other, but matter superfluouse and vnsauery. **1582** STANYHURST *Æneis* III. (Arb.) 78 Thee victals.. They do leaue haulf mangled with sent vnsauerye bepoudred. **1591** UNTON *Corr.* (Roxb.) 199 In his sicknes none could endure to be with him, he was so unsavorie. *a* **1656** BP. HALL *Rem. Wks.* (1660) 108 Those.. which scent an unsavory breath turne their heads aside. **1684** *Contempl. St. Man* II. vi. (1699) 196 Unsavoury Smells, so proper unto Prisons. **1725** POPE *Odyss.* IV. 598 Unsavoury stench of oil. **1784** COWPER *Task* IV. 196 The smoke of lamps, The pent-up breath of an unsav'ry throng. **1825** WATERTON *Wand. S. Amer.* II. 103 An unsavoury little beast, called bug.

fig. **1547** J. HARRISON *Exhort. Scottes* 213, I will stirre that vnsauery sinke of treson and trecherie.

Prov. **1546** J. HEYWOOD *Prov.* (1867) 30 Great bost and small roste, Maketh vnsauery mouthes.

3. Unpleasant, disagreeable, distasteful.

c **1380** WYCLIF *Wks.* (1880) 177 þei sclaundren goddis lawe.. & maken it vnsawory to worldly men. *c* **1386** CHAUCER *Pars. T.* ¶ 510 Thurgh which bitternesse euery good dede of his neighebor semeth to hym bitter and vnsauory. *c* **1440** *Gesta Rom.* xxiii. 80 This is an vnsavery question; this rebavde we saw never before. *c* **1456** PECOCK *Bk. of Faith* (1909) 116 Oold custom.. wole make that these bokis at first schulen be unsavery. **1573** TUSSER *Husb.* (1878) 17 To keepe no more but needfullie, and count excesse vnsauerie. **1591** SAVILE *Tacitus, Hist.* III. xxvi. 130 All that tended to safety was vnsauory. **1637** GILLESPIE *Eng. Pop. Cerem.* IV. viii. 37 This.. will be very unsavory language, to many Arminianized Conformitans. **1657** SPARROW *Bk. Com. Prayer* 256 Suppose some Preachers should be so careful, as not to vent any thing unsavoury. **1845** JAMES *Arrah Neil* v, You came hither upon an unsavory errand.

†**b.** Ill-natured. *Obs.*⁻¹

1568 T. HOWELL *Arb. Amitie* (1879) 45 Then pleasant speech suppresse, and faine a sowre unsauerie looke.

4. Objectionable on moral grounds; having an unpleasant or disagreeable character or association.

a. Of persons.

1401 *Pol. Poems* (Rolls) II. 52 For Sathanas by ȝour sawes is sent into soulis, that ben ful unsavery. *c* **1450** tr. *De Imitatione* I. xxiv. 33 O þou most wrecchid and unsauory synner, what shalt þou answere god? **1552** HULOET, Vnsauery queane, *blittea meretrix.* **1605** CAMDEN *Rem.* 219 That they be the salt of the earth, and if the salt once appall, the world must needes waxe vnsauerie. **1849** JAMES *Woodman* vi, They are very unsavoury fellows.

b. Of things, language, etc.

1536 ELYOT in Croft *E.'s Gov.* (1883) I. p. cxxvi, Unsavery gloses and commentes. **1550** BALE *Eng. Votaries* II. iii, Professinge the vnsauery vse of Sarum. **1586** W. WEBBE *Eng. Poetrie* (Arb.) 54 The motion of some vnsauery loue, such as in the sixt Eglogue he seemeth to deale withall. **1615** DAY *Festivals* Ep. Ded., The Unsavorie Pamphlets.. that have passed the Presse as well as Sermons. **1657** TRAPP *Comm. Ezra* vi. 11 Those.. who turne it into a.. pest-house of noysome lusts by their unsavoury speeches. **1723** WODROW *Corr.* (1843) III. 26, I heard some account of his unsavoury carriage when a student.., and that he was stopped in his licentiatory trials for some immorality. **1882** *Athenæum* 23 Dec. 842/3 A number of grim anecdotes and unsavoury details. **1894** SIR E. SULLIVAN *Woman* 44 There are many unsavoury laws in our code.

un'sawed, *ppl. a.* [UN-¹ 8.] Not saw-edged. Also = next (Ash, 1775).

1786 ABERCROMBIE *Gard. Assist.*, *Arr.* 42 Mock privet,.. Oval unsawed leaved. **1799** *View Agric. Lincoln.* 128 An unsawed sharp reaping hook.

un'sawn, *ppl. a.* (UN-¹ 8 b.)

1572 *Wills & Inv. N.C.* (Surtees) I. 349 Wood tymber for buylding, bords sawen and vnsawen. **1678** MOXON *Mech. Exerc.* v. 95 When he draws back his Saw, the Work-man bears it lightly off the unsawn Stuff. **1865** CAMERON *Malayan India* 31 Huge rafts of unsawn newly-cut timber.

un-'Saxon, *a.* (UN-¹ 7.)

1848 LYTTON *Harold* IV. iii, A lover of things un-Saxon. **1877** TENNYSON *Harold* II. ii, When that un-Saxon blast.. drave and crack'd His boat on Ponthieu beach. **1885** SWEET *O.E. Texts* 177 Both texts show several un-Saxon forms.

un'say, *v.* [UN-² 3, 7. Cf. OE. *ontsecgan* (once), to renounce, abjure, OHG. *antsagên*, MHG. (G.) *entsagen*, MDu. (Du.) *ontzeggen*.]

†**1.** *trans.* To deny. *Obs.*

c **1460** *Oseney Reg.* 167 Fore þᵉ saide Richard.. may not vnsay but þat þᵉ saide Hugh of Tywe yafe.. the foresaide tenement.

2. To withdraw, retract, or revoke (something said or written).

1483 *Vulgaria abs Terentio* 29 J say & vnsay itt. **1557** N.T. (Genev.) *Acts* xi. 18 *note*, That they were not ashamed to vnsay that wherof they had vniustely blamed Peter. **1571** GOLDING *Calvin on Ps.* lxxiii. 1 They openly unsaid that which they had sayd afore. **1613** T. MILLES tr. *Mexia's Treas. Anc. & Mod. T.* II. 964/2 So shall you be sure, neuer to vnsay your owne words. **1687** *Reflect. on Hind & Panther* 21 He has Face enough to say or unsay any thing. **1741** RICHARDSON *Pamela* III. 322 The less you said against her, the less you'd have to unsay. **1819** SHELLEY *Cenci* IV. i. 137 For thine own sake unsay those dreadful words. **1884** W. C. SMITH *Kildrostan* 53 Yet you can speak thus calmly of unsaying All we have said.

transf. **1745** AKENSIDE *Odes Sev. Subjects, On Love* x, Even now, While thus I preach the Stoic strain, Unless I shun Olympia's view, An hour unsays it all again.

b. *intr.* (Freq. in 17th cent.)

1575–85 ABP. SANDYS *Serm.* vii. 111 That it is good Christendome to lie, sweare, and forsweare, to say and vnsay to any. **1646** EVANCE *Noble Order* 3 How can God be said to Say and unsay? **1692** WASHINGTON tr. *Milton's Def. Pop.* ii. 43 Who would trust him.. that in things of so great concern says and unsays without any consideration? **1878** SPURGEON *Treas. Dav.* Ps. cxvi. 11 It is so much easier to say than to unsay.

Hence **un'saying** *vbl. sb.*; **un'sayer.**

1583 GOLDING *Calvin on Deut.* clxxxix. 1177 Hee is no vnsaier as mortall men bee. **1647** HEXHAM I. s.v., An Vnsaying of that which one hath spoken or written. **1669** STILLINGFL. *Serm.* x. (1673) 190 As though the unsaying what we had done.. were abundant compensation.. for the affronts. **1710** STEELE *Tatler* No. 178 ¶ 2 A most happy art in saying and unsaying. **1856** R. A. VAUGHAN *Mystics* XIII. i. II. 301 Such saying and unsaying is not convenient merely,.. but in the highest degree artistic.

†**un'sayed,** *ppl. a. Sc. Obs.* [UN-¹ 8 + SAY *v.*²] Untried.

a **1598** FERGUSON *Scot. Prov.* (1667) 7 All things are good unseyed.

un'scabbard, *v.* (UN-² 5.)

1611 FLORIO, *Sfoderare*, to vn-sheathe, to vn-scabbard. **1813** SCOTT *Rokeby* II. xxi, A warlike form.. steps 'twixt Wilfrid and his foe; Nor then unscabbarded his brand. **1848** STEINMETZ *Hist. Jesuits* I. 130 The fiend of religious persecution unscabbarded the sword.

un'scabbarded, *ppl. a.* (UN-¹ 8, or f. prec.)

1562 in Strype *Stow's Surv.* (1720) II. 307/1 No Man shall go in the Streets.. with Bow bent,.. nor with Sword unscabber'd. **1804** LARWOOD *No Gun Boats* 37 The unscabbarded sword of the bombastic Invader.

un'scalable, *a.* (UN-¹ 7 b and 5 b.)

1579–80 NORTH *Plutarch* (1595) 1083 After he had measured the height of the wall, he reported that the place was not vnscalable. **1611** SHAKS. *Cymb.* III. i. 20 Your Isle, which stands As Neptunes Parke, ribb'd, and pal'd in With Oakes vnskaleable. **1652** HEYLYN *Cosmogr.* III. 222 High and unscalable walls. **1751** R. PALTOCK *P. Wilkins* I. 91, I saw no Entrance into the Island,.. nor any thing but the same unscalable Rock. **1818** KEATS *Endym.* III. 23 There are throned seats unscalable But by a patient wing. **1850** LYNCH *Theoph. Trinal* xi. 211 The frowning unscalable rocks of worldly custom.

un'scalded, *ppl. a.* (UN-¹ 8.)

1615 J. STEPHENS *Satyr. Ess.* (ed. 2) vi. 189 That mountebank preparing oyle which kept his hands vnscalded.

un'scale, *v.*¹ [UN-² 4, 4 b + SCALE *sb.*²]

1. *trans.* To clean (fish, etc.) from scales.

a **1510** STANBRIDGE *Vulgaria* (W. de W.) A vj b, *Desquamo*, [I] vnscale fysshe. **1598** FLORIO, *Scagliare*, to skale or vnskale fish. **1655** MOUFET & BENNET *Health's Improv.* 168 [Shrimps] are unscaled, to vent the windiness which is in them, being sodden with their scales. **1719** *Glossogr. Angl. Nova*, Disquamation, is an unscaling a Fish, or the like.

2. *fig.* To free (the eyes or sight) from scales.

1635 QUARLES *Embl.* III. Prol. 44 Grones fresht with vowes, and vowes made salt with teares, Vnscale his eyes. **1644** MILTON *Areop.* (Arb.) 72 Methinks I see her as an Eagle.. purging and unscaling her long abused sight at the fountain it self of heav'nly radiance. **1827** POLLOK *Course T.* I. 3 Thou who of old The prophet's eye unscaled. **1867** H. MACMILLAN *Bible Teach.* xiii. 265 The Spirit unscales our eyes, and unveils Christ before us.

un'scale, *v.*² [UN-² 7 + SCALE *v.*³] *intr.* To climb down again.

c **1470** HARDING *Chron.* CCXVIII. i, They shot their gonnes, and with their ladders scaled, But nought auailed, thei were so wel of bet, When they our hoste sawe anone they vnscaled.

un'scaled, *a.* [UN-¹ 9 + SCALE *sb.*²] Not furnished with scales; smooth-skinned.

1562 BULLEIN *Bulwarke, Bk. Simples* 78 b, Vnscaled Fyshes, as Eeles, Tenches. **1647** HEXHAM I, Vnscaled, *ongeschubt.*

un'scaled, *ppl. a.*¹ [UN-¹ 8 + SCALE *v.*²] Not having the scales removed.

1585 HOLINSHED *Chron.* II. *Hist. Scot.* 128/2 Now had the king appointed for euerie one of their chambers one man apparelled in garments pretilie deuised and made of fish skins vnskaled [L. *haud desquammatis*].

un'scaled, *ppl. a.*² [UN-¹ 8 or UN-² 8 + SCALE *sb.*²] Not darkened by scales; free or freed from scales.

1827 POLLOK *Course T.* VII. 527 Messengers Of peace,.. whose eye, unscaled, Saw up the path of immortality. **1844** IS. WILLIAMS *Baptistery* xxiv. 251 We learn to look with your unscaled eyes On all things here we prize.

un'scaled, *ppl. a.*³ [UN-¹ 8 + SCALE *v.*³] Unascended.

1812 J. WILSON *Isle of Palms*, etc. 373 The cliffs, In unscaled majesty, must frown no more. **1860** TYNDALL *Glac.* I. ii. 21 The Weisshorn, then.. unscaled. **1886** *Pall Mall G.* 6 Aug. 5/2 Vast glaciers and unscaled snowfields.

un'scalped, *ppl. a.* (UN-¹ 8.)

1726 C. LYMAN in S. Penhallow *Hist. Wars New-England* 22 We found seven dead upon the spot: Six of whom we scalpt, and left the other unscalpt. [**1775** ASH.] **1814** SOUTHEY *Lett.* (1856) II. 388 Philip had waylaid and murdered a party of these Indians, and left them unscalped. **1884** NOURSE *Early Rec. Lancaster, Mass.* 229 Women and children, scalped or unscalped, were paid for at half price.

un'scaly, *a.* (UN-¹ 7.)

1715 GAY *Trivia* II. 416 The joynted lobster and unscaly soale.

un'scandalize, *v.* (UN-² 6 c.)

1781 CHARL. BURNEY in *Early Diary F. Burney* (1889) II. 294, I said a great deal to her to *un*scandalize her, but I don't know whether I did at last.

un'scandalized, *ppl. a.* (UN-[1] 8.)
1618 T. GAINSFORDE *Hist. P. Warbeck* 78 [He] may sit downe with a safe conscience, but not vnscandalized or maligned of some of his owne rancke.

un'scandalous, *a.* (UN-[1] 7.)
1614 R. HARRIS *Samuel's Funerall* (1618) To Rdr., He much respected..euery learned and vnscandalous Preacher. *a* **1628** F. GREVIL *Sidney* (1652) 3 This representing of.. actions of men unfeigned and unscandalous Images.

un'scannable, *a.* (UN-[1] 7 b.)
1815 W. TAYLOR in Robberds *Mem.* (1843) II. 458 The lines..are unscannable. **1856** BADHAM in *Cambr. Ess.* 291 Hopeless nonsense and unscannable verse. **1876** M. COLLINS *Fr. Midn. to Midn.* II. ii. 223 Analytic unscannable blank verse.

un'scanned, *ppl. a.* (UN-[1] 8.)
1577 HOLINSHED *Chron.* II. *Descr. Irel.* 5, I woulde haue beene easily perswaded..to rest as a lukewarme Neuter in omitting the one and the other vnskande. **1595** DANIEL *Civ. Wars* I. xciii, What he had in hand Left it [*sc.* the vision] to his diuerted thoughts vnskand. **1607** SHAKS. *Cor.* III. i. 313 This Tiger-footed-rage, when it shall find The harme of vnskan'd swiftnesse. **1652** BENLOWES *Theoph.* VII. lxxxvi, O Light unscann'd! Of wisdom every glance Beams only from Thy countenance. **1813** SHELLEY *Q. Mab* III. 15 Turn thee, surpassing Spirit! Much yet remains unscanned. **1842** J. B. FRASER *Allee Memroo* II. 283 Furtive sidelong glances.. which left nothing unobserved or unscanned. **1872** CALVERLEY *Fly Leaves, Motherhood* 92 Where the sunbeams fall Unscanned upon the broken wall.

un'scanted, *ppl. a.* (UN-[1] 8.)
1599 DANIEL *Musoph.* 846 Maiestie..with her full face,.. with all her raies, Vnscanted of her parts, vnshadowed In any darkened poynt.

†un'scapable, *a. Obs.* [UN-[1] 7 b.] Unescapable.
1382 WYCLIF *Wisd.* xvii. 16 Vnscapable, or that myȝt not be fled, nede he suffrede. *c* **1449** PECOCK *Repr.* v. vi. 514 The synne is as it were vnscapeable and vnavoidable of him. *c* **1455** —— *Folewer* 95 þis vnscapable peruertid doom. **1554** KNOX *Faythf. Admon.* G 5 To instructe vs that lyuelye fayth ..is able to carye vs thorowe such parelles as be unscapable to nature.

Hence **†un'scapably** *adv. Obs.*
c **1449** PECOCK *Repr.* III. v. 308 If eny man be in contrarie wise vndisposid vnscapabili. *Ibid.* v. vi. 516. *c* **1455** —— *Folewer* 95 þe doom of resoun is derkid ful oft..vnscapabli bi passions of þe louȝer wittis.

un'scared, *ppl. a.* (UN-[1] 8.)
1742 R. BLAIR *Grave* 247 The high-fed worm..Riots unscared. **1784** COWPER *Task* iv. 561 Then sleep was.. unscar'd By drunken howlings. **1842** J. WILSON *Chr. North* I. 46 Birds..sung their best, unscared on hedge, bush, and tree. **1878** B. TAYLOR *Deukalion* IV. iv. 159 These simple lives may own contentment now unscared.

un'scarfed, *ppl. a.* (UN-[1] 8; cf. SCARF *v.*[1])
1634 SIR T. HAWKINS tr. *Caussin's Holy Court* III. 58 The great God..was vnscarfed in the crib..in such sort, that you need lift vp but simple clothes to know him.

un'scarified, *ppl. a.* (UN-[1] 8.)
[**1775** ASH.] *a* **1834** COLERIDGE *Lit. Rem.* (1836) II. 239 An unsullied, unscarified mirror!

un'scarred, *ppl. a.* (UN-[1] 8.)
1594 SHAKS. *Rich. III*, IV. iv. 209 So she may liue vnscarr'd of bleeding slaughter. **1598** B. JONSON *Ev. Man in Hum.* I. iv, Is't like, that factious beauty will preserue The soueraigne state of chastitie vnscard? **1607** SHAKS. *Timon* IV. iii. 161 The vnscarr'd Braggerts of the Warre. **1817** BYRON *Mazeppa* xvii, Flanks unscarr'd by spur or rod. **1866** MISS MULOCK *Noble Life* xiv, A battle from which no woman ever comes out unwounded or unscarred. **1884** *Harper's Mag.* Mar. 524/2 Solid and defiant as it looks, the sea has not left it unscarred.

un'scathed, *ppl. a.* (UN-[1] 8. Cf. ON. and Icel. *ú-, óskaðaðr*, MSw. *oskadhad*, Sw. *oskadad.*)
Before 19th cent. *Sc.* and somewhat rare.
c **1375** *Sc. Leg. Saints* vii. (*James min.*) 608 þat I and þai.. In gud fath sal vnschait be. **1425** *Sc. Acts Parlt., Jas. I* (1814) II. 11/2 Quhil it be knawin..at þe cuntre be vnscaithit of þaim. **1461** *Extr. Aberd. Reg.* (1844) I. 22 That man..sal..kepe the toun vnscathit..of all dettis and chargis acht be hym. **1567-8** *Reg. Privy Council Scot.* I. 613 To be unharmit, unskaythit, or unmolestit be ony of the liegis. **1787** BURNS *Tam Samson's Elegie* xvii, Unskaith'd by Death's gleg gullie, Tam Samson's livin! **1827** LYTTON *Falkland* 25, I passed through the ordeal unshrinking, yet not unscathed. *a* **1862** BUCKLE *Misc. Wks.* (1872) I. 103 That intellect which had conducted them unscathed through such..dangers. **1882** A. W. WARD *Dickens* i. 9 Whatever his experiences of this kind may have been, he passed unscathed through them.

†un'scathely, *a. Obs.*[-1] [UN-[1] 7. Cf. ON. *úskaðligr* (MSw. *oskadheliker*).] Harmless.
13.. *St. Erkenwald* 278 þe skilfulle & þe vnskathely skelton ay to me.

un'scathing, *pres. pple.* [UN-[1] 5 d.] Unharming.
1437 *Dunfermline Reg.* (Bann. Cl.) 285 þai sel kepe þe wateris lauchfully vnskathand vthir.

un'scattered, *ppl. a.* (UN-[1] 8.)
1531 ELYOT *Gov.* I. ii, Whiche..was wonderfully pacified, and the armie unscatered, by the maiestie of Agamemnon. **1814** WORDSW. *Excurs.* IV. 453 The cawing rooks, and seamews from afar, Hovering..By the rough wind unscattered. **1941** in M. Gowing *Britain & Atomic Energy 1939-45* (1964) 400 The 'elastically' scattered neutrons are deviated only through small angles by the collisions and to a final approximation may be treated as unscattered. **1966** D. G. BRANDON *Mod. Techniques Metallogr.* 48 The thickness of film that will reduce the unscattered transmitted intensity to $1/e$ of its original value is given by $t = 20V/\rho$.

†un'scauberked, *ppl. a. Obs.*[-1] [UN-[1] 8.] Unscabbarded.
c **1430** *Pilgr. Lyf Manhode* I. cxxv. (1869) 66 That oother ..hadde his swerd vnshethed and vnscauberked.

un'scavengered, *ppl. a.* (UN-[1] 8.)
1846 DICKENS *Pict. Italy* Lyons, etc., The undrained, unscavengered qualities of a foreign town.

un'scent, *v.* (UN-[2] 4.)
1632 QUARLES *Div. Fancies* IV. xxxi, Weeds that fall Into thy Garden,..Whose loathsom smel unscent thy sweeter Flow'rs.

un'scented, *ppl. a.* (UN-[1] 8.)
[**1775** ASH.] **1784** COWPER *Task* I. 416 Who..Renounce the odours of the open field For the unscented fictions of the loom. **1884** *Girl's Own Paper* 26 Jan. 271/3 Employ a mild, unscented soap at night. **1914** [see SAPELE]. **1979** C. MCCARRY *Better Angels* I. x. 92 Philindros was odourless; he ..used an unscented soap.

un'sceptical, *a.* (UN-[1] 7.)
1851 MRS. BROWNING *Casa Guidi Wind.* II. 92 Forgive, that I forgot the mind which runs Through absolute races, too unsceptical!

un'sceptre, *v.* (UN-[2] 4. Cf. Du. *ontsc(h)epteren*, G. *entsceptern, -zeptern.*)
1594 *Zepheria* xxxviii, Needes must I wish..That thou vnsceptred be of natures royaltie. **1628** QUARLES *Argalus & P.* I. Wks. (Grosart) III. 247/1 If he had, with his victorious hand, Unsceptred halfe the Princes in the land. **1642** T. CASE *God's Rising* (1644) 8 The Enemies of Gods truth and people would..not unscepter him only, but un-essence him. **1897** F. THOMPSON *New Poems* 110 Unsceptre thee of state and place!

un'sceptred, *ppl. a.* [UN-[1] 8 and UN-[2] 8.] Having no sceptre; deprived of a sceptre.
1752 YOUNG *Brothers* I. i, How say'st, unsceptred boaster! This to me! **1798** *Anti-Jacobin* No. 24, So..the unscepter'd Lear Heav'd the loud sigh. **1820** KEATS *Hyperion* I. 19 Upon the sodden ground His old right hand lay..dead, Unsceptred. **1854** J. D. BURNS *Vis. Proph.* 20 The idols fall unsceptred from their thrones.

un'scheduled, *ppl. a.* (UN-[1] 8.)
1889 *Daily News* 24 July 3/1 Consumers [of electric light] in the unscheduled districts.

un'scholar, *sb.* (UN-[1] 12.)
1545 ASCHAM *Toxoph.* (Arb.) 38, I tell you plainlye, scholer or vnscholer,..I wolde thinke it were my dutie..to set forwarde that thing.

un'scholar, *v.* (UN-[2] 6 b.)
1823 CHALMERS *Serm.* I. 351 You cannot unscholar demagogues down to the level of an untaught multitude.

un'scholarlike, *a.* (UN-[1] 7 c.)
1616 CHAMPNEY *Voc. Bps.* 70 Hence likewise is solved that vnscholerlike question. **1716** M. DAVIES *Athen. Brit.* III. 24 Dissenting Sermons,..full of such Unscholar-like Vulgarities. **1760** STERNE *Tr. Shandy* III. xxxvi, 'Tis just as discreditable and unscholar-like a question, Sir. **1834** *Gentl. Mag.* CIV. I. 10 The Duke of Bedford he represented as coarse and unscholarlike. **1881** *Athenæum* 30 July 140/2 The execution of the work can only be described as essentially unscholarlike.

un'scholarly, *a.* (UN-[1] 7.)
1784 SIR W. JONES *Gods of Greece* Wks. 1799 I. 269 The confusion of analogy in the names of the planets is inelegant, unscholarly, and unphilosophical. **1879** MISS YONGE *Cameos* IV. xviii. 206 The unscholarly way in which the debate had been conducted. **1884** *Athenæum* 16 Feb. 215/3 Strype..states that the custom of ordaining unscholarly candidates speedily passed away.

unscho'lastic, *a.* (UN-[1] 7.)
1690 LOCKE *Hum. Und.* III. x. 242 It was to the unscholastick Statesman, that the Governments of the World owed their..Liberties. **1701** NORRIS *Ideal World* II. xii. 441 Which way of speaking is also not altogether unscholastick. **1826** J. GILCHRIST *Lect.* 63 The understanding of every commonsense, unscholastic inquirer. **1843** BETHUNE *Sc. Fireside Stor.* 120 This piece of ethical philosophy..is perhaps new to the schoolmen, though by no means new to their unscholastic brethren.

un'school, *v.* (UN-[2] 3.)
1820 MILMAN *Fall Jerusalem* 10 We must unschool our royal pupil, And cast him back to the common herd of men. **1862** LOWELL *Biglow P.* Ser. II. ii. ℙ3 [I] have heard those talk of England, who..could not unschool their lips from calling her the Mother-Country. **1862** LYTTON *Str. Story* II. 159 If I unschool myself to believe that in what I have just experienced there is no mental illusion.

un'schooled, *ppl. a.* and *a.* [UN-[1] 8, 9.]
1. Uneducated, untaught.
1594 HOOKER *Eccl. Pol.* IV. xiv. §2 They were..poore, simple, vnschooled altogether and vnlettered men. **1615** SYLVESTER *Job Triumphant* Proem 54 Mine un-schooled and unskilfull Muse. **1762** FALCONER *Shipwr.* I. 184 In art unschool'd, each veteran rule he prized. **1865** GROTE *Plato* I. vi. 222 He especially warns Dionysius against talking about these matters to unschooled men. **1873** BLACKIE *Lett. to Wife* (1909) 222 The vulgar unschooled mind.
b. *spec.* Not educated at school; not made to attend school. Also *absol.*
1841 EMERSON *Ess., History* ad fin., The Indian, the child, and unschooled farmer's boy. **1847** *Eng. Rev.* No. II. 18 There were only 21,609 children unschooled. **1898** *Daily News* 14 Oct. 4/7 It is the unschooled that make the gaolbirds.
2. Untrained, undisciplined.
1589 NASHE *Anat. Absurditie* Ep., From such entercourse of excuse, let my vnschooled indignities conuert them selues to your courtesie. **1602** SHAKS. *Ham.* I. ii. 97 It shewes..a Minde impatient, An Vnderstanding simple, and vnschool'd. **1811** MISS L. M. HAWKINS *C'tess & Gertr.* I. 69 Any power, that her..experience might give her over the errors of so unschooled a husband. **1838** PRESCOTT *Ferd. & Is.* x. II. 8 A panic-struck mob, unschooled by discipline or experience. **1871** MISS BRADDON *Lovels of Arden* iii. 41 A generous and somewhat lofty nature, perhaps, but unschooled and unchastened as yet.
b. Not affected or made artificial by education; natural, spontaneous.
1815 MOORE *Epil. to Lady Dacre's Ina* 43 When lovely Woman, all unschool'd and wild, Blush'd without art. **1873** M. ARNOLD *Lit. & Dogma* iii. 100 The artless, unschooled perception of a child. **1883** R. BRIDGES *Prometheus* 648 The unschooled promptings of his best desire.
3. Not provided with a school.
1872 M. COLLINS *Princess Clarice* II. ii. 28 A dingy village, undrained and unschooled.

un'science. (UN-[1] 12 and 5 b.)
c **1374** CHAUCER *Boeth.* v. pr. iii. (1868) 156 It nys nat oonly vnscience, but it is deceiuable oppinioun..fer fro þe soþe of science. **1603** FLORIO *Montaigne* III. xii. 629 Purposely I treate of nothing, but of nothing; nor of any one science, but of vnscience. **1878** PUSEY (*title*), Un-science, not Science, Adverse to Faith. A Sermon preached before the University of Oxford. **1896** *Trans. Victoria Inst.* XXVIII. 200 This Method..has been influential both in the science and the unscience of all time.

un'scienced, *a.* (UN-[1] 9.)
1891 *Harper's Mag.* July 316/1 What a work like Mr. James's..does for the unscienced reader is [etc.].

unscien'tific, *a.* (UN-[1] 7.) Also *absol.*
[**1775** ASH.] **1813** F. S. N. DOUGLAS *Ess. Greeks* ii. 85 The admiration, with which the beautiful Caryatides..inspire the most unscientific. **1827** FARADAY *Chem. Manip.* vii. 204 This distinction is known to be very unscientific, but it is convenient in operations. **1877** *N. & Q.* 22 Dec. 498/1 In this matter of Latin pronunciation old fogies like myself are ..on the side..of the unscientific.

unscien'tifically, *adv.* (UN-[1] 11.)
[**1775** ASH.] **1794** HUTTON *Philos. Light*, etc. 107 A principle perhaps no less unscientifically conceived;..that of reflected heat. **1858** GREENER *Gunnery* 278 Unscientifically formed projectiles. **1886** *Contemp. Rev.* Jan. 11 To talk then, in..[nature's] name, of the rights of conscience,..is to talk unscientifically.

un'scintillating, *ppl. a.* (UN-[1] 10.)
1807 J. BARLOW *Columb.* v. 676 Prometheus like, to snatch a beam of day And homeward bear the unscintillating ray.

un'scissored, *ppl. a.* (UN-[1] 8.)
1608 SHAKS. *Per.* III. iii. 29 (Q.[1]), Till she be married, madam,..Vnsistered [*read* Vnsissered]..shall this hair of mine remain. *c* **1631** T. CAREW *Elegy Death Donne* 5 The uncisor'd Churchman. *a* **1639** —— *Poems, To my Friend G. N.* 64 Nor, on a Marble Tun, his face besmear'd With grapes, is curl'd uncizard Bacchus rear'd.

un'scoffed, *ppl. a.* (UN-[1] 8.)
1622 WITHER *Philarete* B 4 b, What hopes haue I to passe vnscoft I pray..?

un'scolded, *ppl. a.* (UN-[1] 8.)
[**1775** ASH.] **1855** E. FORBES *Lit. Papers* vi. 176 We like this book too well to permit us to pass over a fault unscolded.

†un'scomfited, *ppl. a. Obs.* [UN-[1] 8.] Unconquered.
c **1400** *Found. St. Bartholomew's* 23 The vertu in her conceyuyd of vnskunfitid feith. *Ibid.* 34 The coronacioun of the most vnskunfitid kynge of Englonde, Henry the secunde.

un'sconced, *ppl. a.* (UN-[1] 8 + SCONCE *sb.*[4] or *v.*[2])
1735 SAVAGE *Progr. Divine* 17 Him, quite unsconc'd, the butt'ry book shall own.

un'scorched, *ppl. a.* (UN-[1] 8.)
1601 SHAKS. *Jul. C.* I. iii. 18 His Hand, Not sensible of fire, remain'd vnscorch'd. **1612** WARNER *Alb. Eng.* XI. lxvii. 285 Thogh thou could'st buzze about the flame, & keepe vnskorcht thy wings. **1651** STANLEY *Poems, Love Deposed* iv, We..unscorch'd may Like atoms play, And wanton in the sunshine of your eyes. **1816** SCOTT *Antiq.* xviii, The moss and wild flowers were unscorched. **1843** PRESCOTT *Mexico* II. iv. I. 247 From all these fiery trials..he came out unscorched. **1856** FROUDE *Hist. Eng.* ix. II. 345 If he threw them [*sc.* toads] into the fire, they hopped back to him unscorched.

un'score, *v.* (UN-[2] 3. Cf. SCORE *v.* 6.)
1621 BP. MOUNTAGU *Diatribæ* 184 Goe and unskore your margine with those many quotations,..ranged wel-nigh from the top to the bottome of that page.

un'scored, *ppl. a.* (UN-[1] 8.)
1596 NASHE *Saffron Walden* T ij b, He hath..not left anie ..Almain scribe..vncompared or vnscoard. **1818** BUSBY *Gram. Mus.* 491 He..should ascertain his powers of invention, in unscored Composition. **1894** *Westm. Gaz.* 7 Mar. 2/1 He will leave no point unscored in favour of the people.

un'scorned, *ppl. a.* (UN-[1] 8.)
a **1425** tr. *Arderne's Treat. Fistula*, etc. 4 He that skorneþ other men shal not go away vnskorned. **1622** WITHER *Philarete* M 4, I..yet, vnscorned, serue a gentle Nymph. **1721** YOUNG *Revenge* I. i, Africk I quell'd, in hope by that to purchase Your leave to sigh unscorn'd. **1828** WORDSW. *Power of Sound* 51 Unscorned [be] the peasant's whistling breath.

un'scornful, *a.* (UN-[1] 7.)
1858 TENNYSON in Ld. Tennyson *Memoir* (1897) I. 427 He is such a good fellow, so unscornful and genial.

un'scornfully, *adv.* (UN-[1] 11.)
1844 tr. *Mem. Babylonian Princess* II. 307 Hanging his majestic head, and unscornfully pacing to and fro in his narrow cage.

un'scornfulness. (UN-[1] 12.)
1840 L. HUNT *Leg. Florence* II. i, Your look, madam, is wondrous logical;..and cramm'd with scorn, from pure unscornfulness.

un'scotch, *v.* (UN-[2] 3.)
1839 F. A. GRIFFITHS *Artill. Man.* 191 Unsling gun and carriage. Limber up. Hold on. Unscotch the wheels.

un'scotted, *ppl. a. local.* [UN-[1] 8 + SCOT *sb.*[2] 3.] Not subject to a 'scot' or tax.
1865 *Level of Hatfield Chase* (Notice of Annual Meeting) 18 Oct., The Owners of Unscotted Lands affected by 'The Level of Hatfield Chase Act, 1862.'

un'scottified, *ppl. a.* (UN-[2] 8.)
1773 JOHNSON 1 May in *Boswell*, You are the most unscottified of your countrymen. **1858** E. B. RAMSAY *Remin.* (ed. 2) v. 39 Numerous examples..might be taken from the works of Robert Burns..which lose their charm altogether when *unscottified*.

un-'Scottish, *a.* (UN-[1] 7.)
1825 *Monthly Rev.* CVI. 14 The Un-Scotish name of Griffiths.

un'scoured, *ppl. a.* (UN-[1] 8. Cf. Sw. *oskurad.*)
c **1460** *Stans Puer ad Mensam* 58 in *Babees Bk.* 30 Brynge no knyves vnskoured to the table. **1567** DRANT *Horace, Ep.* iii. cvj, Thy witte is not of meanest sorte; it doth not lye vnskowrde. **1592-3** *Act 35 Eliz.* c. 10 §1 Beinge rawe unscowred..as yt cometh from the Weavers Beame. **1603** SHAKS. *Meas. for M.* I. iii. 171 Like vn-scowr'd Armor. **1630** J. TAYLOR (Water P.) *Jacke-a-Lent* Wks. I. 115 Making the band of vnscowred Halberdiers retire. **1702** *Guide for Constables* 141 He that scours not his ditches..shall forfeit 12 pence for every rod so left unscoured. **1830** CARLYLE *Misc.* (1840) II. 345 Her kettles hung unscoured on the wall. **1894** *Outing* XXIV. 229/1 A handful of unscoured worms.

un'scourged, *ppl. a.* (UN-[1] 8.)
c **1412** HOCCLEVE *De Reg. Princ.* 1257 They þat swymmen in richesse..Vnscourgid ay of any aduersitee. **1648** HEXHAM II, *Ongegeesselt*, Vnwhipped, or Vnscourged. **1825** CAMPBELL *Hallowed Ground* 5 Man..Erect and free, Unscourged by superstition's rod.

un'scramble, *v.* [UN-[2] 3.] **1.** *trans.* To reverse the process of scrambling (eggs). Also in *fig.* contexts.
This would appear to be the earlier sense though pre-1926 printed evidence has not been found.
1926 R. H. TAWNEY *Relig. & Rise of Capitalism* ii. 88 But the discovery of the sage who observed that it is not possible to unscramble eggs had already been made. **1928** C. SANDBURG *Good Morning, America* 18 Can you unscramble eggs?.. J. Pierpont Morgan's query as to court decrees dissolving an inevitable industrial combination. **1969** *P.E.N.* IX. 46 She quoted, as an example, 'Mr. Enoch Powell called last night for the denationalisation of all State-owned industries and explained exactly how to unscramble the eggs.' **1980** J. WAINWRIGHT *Tainted Man* 131 You demanded retribution..*your* law..unscrambles all eggs.
2. To put into or restore to order; to disentangle; to make sense of (something) confused; to extricate from (or *from*) a state of confusion or muddle; to separate into constituent parts; to 'dismantle' (an organization or system); *spec.* to restore (a signal) by applying the reverse of the process previously used to scramble it; to render intelligible in this way.
1923 WODEHOUSE *Inimitable Jeeves* x. 104, I collapsed on to the settee and rather lost interest in things for the moment. When I had unscrambled myself I found that Jeeves and the child had retired. **1927** [see SCRAMBLE *v.* 3c]. **1952** *Times* 17 Nov. 6/1 The Government propose to 'unscramble' nationalized road haulage service. **1955** [see SCRAMBLE *v.* 3c]. **1956** *Archivum Linguisticum* VIII. 153 Since Trubetzkoy's untimely death the task of unscrambling them [*sc.* phonology and phonemics] has been pursued with wearisome halts. **1956** AUDEN & KALLMAN *Magic Flute* (1957) 116 So english, remodel Our lines as you please, Unscramble the drama and jumble the keys. **1958** *Times* 19 Aug. 9/2 Very broadly the intention seems to be to 'unscramble' from the French legislature those territories which wish to become federated. **1959** *Daily Tel.* 6 Mar. 14/3 By putting money in a box attached to a set the viewer automatically 'unscrambles' the transmission. **1963** *Ibid.* 10 Jan. 1/8 The process of 'unscrambling' Northern Rhodesia ..will take very much longer. **1973** 'I. DRUMMOND' *Jaws of Watchdog* ii. 31 The message was unscrambled by a radio on a fast, low-profile motor-yacht. **1974** *Listener* 9 May 597/1 When the Conservatives returned to office in 1951 they didn't unscramble the National Health Service. **1978** R. LUDLUM *Holcroft Covenant* xxxvi. 420 You should bring him instead a potion to unscramble his doddering brains. **1981** *Sunday Express* (Colour Suppl.) 12 July 33/4 Only those who pay the extra rental are provided with a device to unscramble the film signals. **1983** *Listener* 18 Aug. 8/1 It was often more fruitful than trying to unscramble what he was actually saying.
Hence **un'scrambled** *ppl. a.*; **un'scrambling** *vbl. sb.*
1955 J. G. DAVIS *Dict. Dairying* (ed. 2) 993 (*caption*) Unscrambling machine. **1958** *Listener* 25 Sept. 463/2 The unscrambling attachments to the receiving sets. **1959** *Times Lit. Suppl.* 16 Jan. 30/3 To be brought up short on page 78 by a sentence scrambled by the printer almost beyond unscrambling. **1959** *Daily Tel.* 6 Mar. 14/3 In another method, the 'unscrambling' is done by dialling, as on a telephone. **1959** *Times* 11 June 5/7 The transparency of the texture and the clean, fresh sounds of unscrambled timbres. **1964** L. DEIGHTON *Funeral in Berlin* xxx. 156 There was a din of unscrambled noise before Charlotte Street switched the scrambler into the circuit.

un'scrambler. [f. prec. + -ER[1].] A device for unscrambling scrambled messages or signals.
1968 A. B. CARLSON *Communication Systems* v. 218 The system shown..is a simplified speech scrambler... Show that an identical system will suffice as an unscrambler. **1976** 'A. HALL' *Kobra Manifesto* vi. 80 We began reading the signals as they came off the integral unscrambler. **1979** *Maclean's Mag.* 26 Mar. 59/1 Methods range from such simple expedients as wrapping antennas with aluminum foil to black-market sales of 'unscramblers' that decode signals.

un'scraped, *ppl. a.* (UN-[1] 8. Cf. ON. *úskrapaðr*, (M)Sw. *oskrapad*, MDa. *uskrabet.*)
1725 RAMSAY *Gentle Sheph.* IV. i, With vile, unscrapit tongue. **1881** *Cheq. Career* 323 They threw it [*sc.* a dead iguana] on the coals, unscraped and uncleaned. **1887** MOLONEY *Forestry W. Africa* 427 The coated or unscraped sort is similarly prepared, excepting that the rhizomes are unscraped; this is sometimes called Black Ginger.

†**un'scrapen,** *ppl. a. Obs.*[−1] [UN-[1] 8 b.] = prec.
1599 GARNET *Let. to Parsons* May (Stonyhurst MSS.), I was willing to let it go naturally, that you may rather mend it, if it be necessary, or deliver it unscrapen.

un'scratched, *ppl. a.* (UN-[1] 8.)
1595 SHAKS. *John* II. i. 225 To saue vnscratch'd your Citties threatned cheekes. *a* **1667** JER. TAYLOR *Lib. Proph.* (1817) 394 They are his image undefiled, unscratched, unbroken by any act or consent of their own. **1853** DICKENS *Bleak Ho.* lxiii, You must make up your mind to remain *unscratched* [*sc.* out of a will].

un'scrawled, *ppl. a.* (UN-[1] 8.)
1612 BRINSLEY *Lud. Lit.* 39 That the schollars keep their copies and books fair, vnblotted and vnscrauled.

un'screen, *v.* (UN-[2] 5.)
1628 WITHER *Brit. Remembr.* v. N xi b, Secrets to unskreene, That cannot by our mortall eyes be seene. **1635** QUARLES *Embl.* III. vii. 28 Unskreen those Heav'nly lamps, or tell me why Thou shad'st thy face. **1654** GAYTON *Pleas. Notes* IV. viii. 223 But he bustling still to unscreen her fully, she then shreekt out.

un'screened, (*ppl.*) *a.* [UN-[1] 8, 9.]
1. Not protected or covered with a screen.
1648 BOYLE *Seraph. Love* xxvi. (1659) 167 Their being expos'd (unskreen'd) to the Sun's refulgent beams. **1783** R. GRAVES *Euphrosyne* II. 113 Yet in those eyes we see..(More bright un-screen'd) the pow'r..To make new conquests. **1801** *Monthly Mag.* XII. 224 If I sit unscreened, with my back to the fire. **1859** GEO. ELIOT *A. Bede* liv, The little, grey, desolate-looking hamlet, unscreened by sheltering trees. **1891** *Nature* 20 Aug., Similar actions on cometary matter, unscreened as it is by an absorptive atmosphere.
2. a. Not passed through a screen; unsifted.
1851 LAXTON *Builder's Price Bk.* 132 Gravel unscreened, 5s. od. Per cubic yard. **1888** *Encycl. Dict.* s.v., Unscreened coal. **1900** *Daily News* 21 May 2/1 Unscreened town's refuse.
b. Not investigated or checked for security: see SCREEN *v.* 4c.
1970 R. CLAPPERTON *Victims Unknown* xi. 101, I have been severely criticised..for authorising the employment on intelligence work of an unscreened individual. **1979** H. KISSINGER *White House Years* xix. 748 The beady eye of Secret Service agents Ready and McLeod, who were not about to leave me to the mercy of unscreened foreigners.

un'screw, *v.* [UN-[2] 3 and 7. Cf. WFris. *ont-*, *ûntskroeve*, *-je*, Du. *ontschroeven.*]
1. *trans.* To slacken or detach by turning a screw (either separate or forming part of the thing turned).
1651 DAVENANT *Gondibert* I. VI. xiii, His Hilts round Pommel he did then unskrew. **1669** STURMY *Mariner's Mag.* V. i. 2 You may unscrew the perpendicular from the sight. **1683** MOXON *Mech. Exerc., Printing* xxii. ¶4 He must unskrew the Skrew of his Composing-stick. **1722** DE FOE *Plague* (1754) 71 They found Ways to unscrew the Locks. **1739** LABELYE *Piers Westm. Bridge* 24 They were secured by proper Iron-work; which being unskrew'd, would permit the Sides..to part asunder. **1815** J. SMITH *Panorama Sci. & Art* II. 24 Shut the stop-cock, and unscrew the syringe. **1848** DICKENS *Dombey* xlix, He..unscrewed his hook, screwed his fork into its place, and did the honours of the table. **1900** HASLUCK *Model Engin. Handybk.* 118 This rod ..can be lengthened..by unscrewing one of the joints.
b. To remove the stopper from (a flask) by unscrewing.
1653 URQUHART *Rabelais* I. xxiv. 114 He unscrewed his borracho (which was a great Dutch leathern bottle).
c. *intr.* To undergo, or admit of, being unscrewed.
1822 T. MITCHELL *Aristoph.* II. 225 Like the tones of a lyre, When the pins and pegs are unscrewing. **1874** H. H. COLE *Catal. Ind. Art S. Kens. Mus.* 166 Amulet Case... It unscrews at one end. **1888** RUTLEY *Rock-Forming Min.* 21 Fitted on a separate stand the foot of which unscrews.
2. *fig.* (In various applications.)
1605 B. JONSON *Volpone* v. vii, To the Court..will I; and if't be possible, Vn-screw my Aduocate, vpon new hopes. ?*a* **1616** FLETCHER, etc. *Q. Corinth.* III, I should curse my fortune..to be made the ginne To unscrew a Mothers love unto her Son. **1627** N. BURLEY in Capt. Smith *Seaman's Gram.* a ij, What long trauels..Haue made thee know, thou ..do'st vnscrew To those that want like knowledge. **1664** H. MORE *Myst. Iniq.* 295 The Thirteenth Chapter would not fail to unscrue the meaning with the considerate and intelligent. **1761** CHURCHILL *Rosciad* 468 Courtiers will, like reasonable creatures, Suspend vain Fashion, and unscrew their features.

un'screwed, *ppl. a.* [UN-[1] 8.] Not furnished with a screw.
1887 D. A. LOW *Machine Draw.* 18 If the countersunk head be lengthened so as to take up the whole of the unscrewed part of the bolt.

un'scribbled, *ppl. a.* (UN-[1] 8.)
1628 EARLE *Microcosm., Child* (Arb.) 21 His Soule is yet a white paper vnscribled with obseruations of the world.

†**un'scried,** *ppl. a. Obs.*[−1] [UN-[1] 8.] Undescried.
1560 ROLLAND *Seven Sages* 86 Thay..Wan to the Gold.. and vnscryit come away.

†**un'scrip,** *v.* (UN-[2] 4.)
c **1430** *Pilgr. Lyf Manhode* II. xii. (1869) 79 A cherl..wole bineme hem her burdouns and vnscrippe hem of here scrippes.

un'scriptural, *a.* (UN-[1] 7.)
1653 GAUDEN *Hierasp.* 14 How unscriptural..do they seem to many..Christians? **1683** E. HOOKER *Pref. Pordage's Mystic Div.* 71 Unwritten Traditions, inhumane inventions, unscriptural institutions. **1719** WATERLAND *Eight Serm. Div. Christ* iii. 103 That is as manifestly unscriptural, false, and groundless, as either Socinian or Arian. **1782** PRIESTLEY *Corrupt. Chr.* II. VII. 104 Wickliffe..saw nothing unscriptural in extreme unction. **1825** COLERIDGE *Aids Reflect.* 311 The View or Scheme..I believe to be altogether unscriptural. **1849** MACAULAY *Hist. Eng.* vi. II. 112 Prelacy was abhorred..both as an unscriptural and as a foreign institution.
Hence **un'scripturally** *adv.*, **-alness.**
1677 W. HUGHES *Man of Sin* III. ii. 27 Besides the unscripturalness of such visits. **1824** D. RUSSELL *Covenants* (1843) 182 Some have spoken very..unscripturally of the good works and holy tempers of believers. **1868** MIALL *Congregationalism in Yorks.* 15 Cartwright had openly proclaimed..the unscripturalness of the Anglican hierarchy.

unscriptu'rality. (UN-[1] 12.)
1733 *Revolution Politicks* vi. 18 The Unscripturality and Irregularity of the Doctrine. **1827** G. S. FABER *Sacr. Calend. Prophecy* (1844) II. 19 The flagrant unscripturalities of that notoriously apostatising period.

un'scripture, *sb.* [UN-[1] 12 b.] *attrib.* Unscriptural.
1697 G. KEITH *2nd Narr. Proc. Turner's Hall* 9 They that find..Fault with unscripture Language.

un'scripture, *v.* (UN-[2] 4.)
1690 STILLINGFL. *Charge* 11 Sept. 6 They who go about to Unbishop Timothy and Titus, may as well Unscripture the Epistles, that were written to them.

†**un'scripturely,** *a. Obs.*[−1] [UN-[1] 7.] Unscriptural.
1549 LATIMER *2nd Serm. bef. Edw. VI*, To Rdr. (Arb.) 48 This maintenance of so many vnscripterlye opinions.

un'scrubbed, *ppl. a.* (UN-[1] 8.)
[**1775** ASH.] *c* **1900-** in periodical use.

un'scruple, *v.* (UN-[2] 4.)
1647 M. HUDSON *Div. Right Govt.* II. ii. 75 To unscruple all vocabular doubts and difficulties, let us but look into the fourteenth Ch. of Gen.

un'scrupled, *a.* [UN-[1] 9.] Unscrupulous.
1813 SCOTT *Rokeby* VI. vii, In their favour oft we see Unscrupled, useful men like thee.

un'scrupled, *ppl. a.* (UN-[1] 8; cf. SCRUPLE *v.* 4.)
1665 BOYLE *Occas. Refl.* VI. iii. 195 Either the same [practice], or little better, may be found unscrupled at among our selves.

unscrupu'losity. (UN-[1] 12; cf. next.)
1847 HARRIS *Life Ld. Hardwicke* III. 270 The unscrupulosity with which he ever gratified his passion. **1879** GEO. ELIOT *Theo. Such* xi. 191 The dirty work of unscrupulosity.

un'scrupulous, *a.* (UN-[1] 7.)
1803 GODWIN *Chaucer* xli. II. 265 A person..boundless in ambition, and unscrupulous in his choice of means for gratifying it. **1829** SCOTT *Anne of G.* xix, The priest took instant and unscrupulous possession of his seat of honour. **1875** JOWETT *Plato* II. 222 The worse he is the more unscrupulous he will be.
Hence **un'scrupulously** *adv.*, **-ness.**
1808 MITFORD *Hist. Greece* IV. 356 Their unscrupulousness in using the arbitrary powers of democratical government. **1833** J. H. NEWMAN *Arians* iv. §ii. 315 This mere handful of divines unscrupulously pressing forward into the highest ecclesiastical stations. **1879** FARRAR *St. Paul* xxxviii. II. 248 The unscrupulousness of a worldly ecclesiasticism. **1884** CHURCH *Bacon* iii. 61 Lawyers..who unscrupulously pushed their way to preferment.

†**un'scrutable,** *a. Obs.* (UN-[1] 7 b, 5 b.)
1562 COOPER *Answ. Priv. Masse* 96 b, Is it not merueilous, ..and to oure iudgement vnscrutable, that [etc.]? [**1775** ASH.]

un'scrutableness. (UN-[1] 12; cf. prec.)
1657 J. SERGEANT *Schism Dispatch't* 449 The profound unscrutableness of those mysteries.

un'scrutinized, *ppl. a.* (UN-[1] 8.)
1728 MORGAN *Hist. Algiers* I. v. 167 Their Consciences he leaves wholly unscrutinized. **1795** BENTHAM *Protest agst.*

Law Taxes 52 His unscrutinized notion of its supposed tendency to check litigation. **1802–12** —— *Ration. Judic. Evid.* (1827) I. 478 Scrutinized or unscrutinized, evidence may speak. **1852** J. H. NEWMAN *Scope Univ. Educ.* 60 Every received but unscrutinized assertion.

un'scrutinizing, *ppl. a.* (UN-^{1} 10.)
1802–12 BENTHAM *Ration. Judic. Evid.* (1827) I. 123 Unreflecting and unscrutinizing caprice. **1872** MORLEY *Voltaire* i. 9 Unscrutinising acquiescence in half-thoughts and faint guesses.

un'scrutinizingly, *adv.* (UN-^{1} 11; cf. prec.)
1891 HAN. LYNCH *G. Meredith* 136 He adores her unscrutinizingly.

un'sculptured, *ppl. a.* (UN-^{1} 8.)
[**1775** ASH.] **1816** SHELLEY *Mont Blanc* 27 The aethereal waterfall, whose veil Robes some unsculptured image. **1891** *Cent. Dict., Unsculptured,*..in *zoology,* smooth; without elevated or impressed marks on the surface.

un'scummed, *ppl. a.* (UN-^{1} 8. Cf. Sw. *oskummad.*)
c **1440** *Pallad. on Husb.* VIII. 128 A sester of vnscomed hony. **1562** *Apol. Priv. Masse* (1850) 40 If the servant would leave the pot unscummed.

un'scure, *v. s. dial.* [UN-^{2} 3. Cf. Isle of Wight *skure* to secure.] *trans.* To untie, undo.
1749 MRS. ROBERT GOADBY *Carew* v. 51 They were now all employed in unscuring the Children from his Back. [Cf. *Ibid.* 49 It was quickly resolved to tie two to his Back.]

un'scutcheoned, *ppl. a.* (UN-^{1} 8.)
1827 POLLOK *Course T.* VIII. 89 No King, no subject was; unscutcheoned all, Uncrowned, unplumed.

un'scythed, *ppl. a.* (UN-^{1} 8.)
a **1818** in Scott *Hrt. Midl.* i, Skiddaw hears afar The rattling of the unscythed car.

un'seal, *v.* [UN-^{2} 3, 4. Cf. MDu. *ontsegelen,* (Du. *-zegelen*), OHG. *intsigilan* (MHG. *entsigelen,* G. *-siegeln*).]
1. *trans.* To remove a seal from, to break the seal of (a letter, etc.).
c **1425** *Seven Sag.* (P.) 1054 His emys bokes he vnselde. *c* **1425** AUDELAY *XI Pains Hell* 179 Þe angel..lad him to þe blak pit þo, With vij. selys was selid treuly... Anon he vnselid þe pit þore. **1596** SHAKS. *Merch. V.* v. i. 275, I haue better newes in store for you Then you expect: vnseale this letter soone. **1666** in *10th Rep. Hist. MSS. Comm.* App. V. 23 He..resolved to unseale the bags. **1693** DRYDEN *Persius* VI. 37 Nor yet [will I] unseal the Dregs of Wine that stink Of Cask. **1746** FRANCIS tr. *Horace, Epist.* I. vii. 12 The long Lawyer's Plea unseals our Wills. **1791** COWPER *Odyss.* III. 495 Charging high the cup With wine of richest sort, which she..First broach'd, unsealing the delicious juice. **1818** COLERIDGE in *Encycl. Metrop.* (1845) I. Introd. 33 Henceforward the book is unsealed for him; the depth is opened. **1851** LONGF. *Gold. Leg.* I. *Court-yard,* Then was the family tomb unsealed. **1884** *Cassell's Fam. Mag.* Mar. 203/1 The oven is then unsealed, and the coke withdrawn.
fig. **1830** MRS. HEMANS *Songs Affec., Spirit's Return* i, This long-shut heart for thee shall be unseal'd.
2. *fig.* **a.** To free from some constraining influence; to allow free action to.
1589 GREENE *Menaphon* (Arb.) 59 She ought to shut vp her dores, and solemnize continuall night, till her husband, her sunne, making a happie return, vnsealeth her silence. **1652** BENLOWES *Theoph.* I. lxxxviii, Renew my heart, direct my tongue, unseal My hand. **1826** MRS. HEMANS *Forest Sanctuary* II. xxx, When stars..are shining, How their soft glance unseals each thought of thee! **1847** EMERSON *Compensation* ii, And why when mirth unseals all tongues Should mine alone be dumb?
b. To free from the condition (or necessity) of remaining closed. (Cf. SEAL *v.*^{1} 6 b.)
With reference to the eyes (*b*) probably in part replacing UNSEEL *v.*
(*a*) *a* **1586** SIDNEY *Arcadia* I. ii, I pray you (said Musidorus, then first unsealing his long silent lips) what countries be these? **1621** QUARLES *Div. Poems, Esther* iii, Memucan..Vnseal'd his serious lips, and thus bespake. **1815** SCOTT *Guy M.* xli, Speaking as if his utmost efforts were unable to unseal his lips beyond the width of a quarter of an inch. **1852** MERIVALE *Rom. Emp.* (ed. 2) iii. I. 129 Cicero's mouth was unsealed. **1884** *Manch. Exam.* 24 Nov. 5/2 Gladstone..is therefore extremely anxious that his lips should..be unsealed.
(*b*) *a* **1652** BENLOWES *Theoph.* XI. xxx, Still to have toting waits unseal thine eyes. **1700** DRYDEN *Ovid's Met., Ceyx & Alcyone* 303 The God disturb'd with this new Glare of Light.., unseal'd his Sight. **1725** POPE *Odyss.* XV. 8 In sleep profound the Son of Nestor lies; Not thine, Ulysses! Care unseal'd his eyes. **1855** SINGLETON *Virgil* I. 364 Others 'neath rueful Tartarus he sends; Grants slumbers, and withdraws [them], and the eyes At death unseals. **1863** COWDEN CLARKE *Shaks. Char.* xiii. 333 The discovery of that patron's baseness..acts like a talisman to unseal his eyes.
3. To disclose, reveal.
1640 FLETCHER, etc. *Coronation* II. i, If this preserve thee not, I must unseal Another mistery. **1871** B. TAYLOR *Faust* (1875) II. II. iii. 147 He the future hath unsealed.
Hence **un'sealer; un'sealing** *vbl. sb.*
1683 JANE LEAD *Revelation* (title-p.), An Essay towards the Unsealing, Opening and Discovering The Seven Seals. **1844** LOWELL *Leg. Brittany* II. xxii, Remembering when he stood Not fallen yet, the unsealer of her heart. **1895** W. WATSON *Hymn to Sea* i, While, with throes, with raptures, with loosing of bonds, with unsealings,—Youth..wakes like a wondering rose.

un'sealable, *a.* [UN-^{1} 7 b.] Incapable of being sealed.
1831 E. IRVING *Expos. Rev.* I. 91 The apocalypse is..an unsealed and unsealable book.

un'sealed, *ppl. a.*^{1} [UN-^{1} 8. Cf. MDu. *ongesegelt,* Du. *ongezegeld,* G. *ungesiegelt.*]
1. Not stamped or marked with a seal.
1377 LANGL. *P. Pl.* B. XIV. 292 Wynneth he nauȝt with weghtes fals ne with vnseled mesures. **1492** *Extr. Aberd. Reg.* (1844) I. 419 Conuikit..for the wrangwiss haldin of a wrang pek of less mesour, and unselit. **1550** *Southampton Court Leet Rec.* (1905) I. 9 We present that [they]..sell beere and wyne by vnlawful and vnsealled measures contrary to the statute. **1629** *Leather* 15 The Market is full of excellent Leather;..all this in the Morning lyes vnsealed. **1660** in J. Davidson *Inverurie,* etc. (1878) 361 Giv onie person have ane unseilit stoup they sall braik the same.
fig. **1680** C. NESSE *Church Hist.* 447 They could never kill the souls of any of Gods sealed ones, as they did of the unsealed.
2. Not having a seal imposed or attached; not closed by means of a seal.
c **1430** *Pilgr. Lyf Manhode* I. xxxvi. (1869) 22 He þat holt his swerd naked, and þe keyes vnbownde, naked and vnseeled. **1523** LD. BERNERS *Froiss.* I. ccccxxv. 301/2 So he toke the letters vnsealed, and retourne in to Englande agayne. **1646** *Bury Wills* (Camden) 192 All my bookes, papers, and parchments vnsealed. **1665** BOYLE *Exp. & Obs. Conc. Cold* Pref. c 6, Judging it fit to make further Trial, with an unseal'd Weather-glass. **1726** BERKELEY in Fraser *Life* Wks. 1871 IV. 140 In case it be a bond in form, or..a promissory note unsealed. **1793** T. TWINING in *Recreat. & Stud.* (1882) 184 Sending the parcel unsealed that you might have read..the MS. **1848** W. H. KELLY tr. *L. Blanc's Hist. Ten Y.* II. 89 This letter..was..delivered, unsealed, to M. de Montalivet.
fig. *a* **1649** CRASHAW *Carmen Deo Nostro, Hymn St. Thomas* 54 When this dry soul those eyes shall see, And drink the unseal'd sourse of thee. **1820** SHELLEY *Prometh. Unb.* IV. 115 The murmurings Of the unsealed springs. **1831** [see prec.].
transf. **1868** *Rep. U.S. Commissioner Agric.* (1869) 278 Moisture, emanating in part from unsealed honey,.. becomes condensed in the hive from external cold.
3. *fig.* Not formally confirmed or ratified.
1601 SHAKS. *All's Well* IV. ii. 30 Therefore your oathes Are words and poore conditions, but vnseal'd. **1665** J. SPENCER *Vulg. Proph.* 87 That very many of these Modern Prophecies have been very punctually accomplish'd, though unseal'd by any divine Sign attending the delivery of them. **1831** JAMES *Phil. Augustus* II. iii, My fate is yet an unsealed one.

un'sealed, *ppl. a.*^{2} [UN-^{1} 8 + SEEL *v.*^{2} Cf. UNSEAL *v.* 2 b (*b*).] Not closed.
1800 COLERIDGE *Piccolom.* I. xi, The unsealed eye Of Jupiter's glad children born in lustre.

un'seam, *v.* [UN-^{2} 4.] *trans.* To undo the seam or seams of (a garment, etc.). Also *fig.*, to rip up.
1592 GREENE *Groat's W. Wit* (1617) 28 In a thread-bare cloake,..his hose vnseamed. **1605** SHAKS. *Macb.* I. ii. 22 Till he vnseam'd him from the Naue to th' Chops, And fix'd his Head vpon our Battlements. **1608** BEAUM. & FL. *Four Plays in One* I. iii, Nor a vein runs here From head to foot, but Sophocles would unseame, and..shoot his scornfull blood Into their eyes. **1631** in *Verney Mem.* (1907) I. 131 Our barke..had her bottome strucken out and was unseamed. **1812** BYRON *Ch. Har.* I. lxxvii, One gallant steed is stretch'd a mangled corse; Another, hideous sight! unseam'd appears. **1824** in *Spirit Pub. Jrnls.* (1825) 194 Giving Mr. Trotter a thump on the eye, and unseaming his shirt from top to bottom! **1848** T. AIRD *Chr. Bride* I. xiii, The monster's.. tusks backward glance To gather fury for his onset dread, To unseam her lovely limb.

un'seamanlike, *a.* (UN-^{1} 7 c.)
1726 SHELVOCKE *Voy. round World* 7 His unseamanlike behaviour in the late storm. **1865** *Sat. Rev.* 2 Sept. 301/2 The idea of a French Sailor as a weedy, unseamanlike kind of 'loafer'.

un'seamed, *ppl. a.* [UN-^{1} 8. Cf. Du. *ongezoomd,* MLG. and MHG. *ungesûmet,* G. *ungesäumt,* Sw. *osömmad.*] Having no seam.
1592 SYLVESTER *Tri. Faith* II. xlix, The Schismatiks.. renting Christ's unseamed coat in twain. **1635** F. WHITE *Sabbath* 310 The unseamed coat of Christ.

un'searchable, *a.* and *sb.* [UN-^{1} 7 b, 12, and 5 b.]
1. That cannot be searched into, so as to be ascertained or exactly estimated; inscrutable.
1382 WYCLIF *Rom.* xi. 33 Hou incomprehensyble ben his domes, and his weyis vnserchable. *c* **1400** *Found. St. Bartholomew's* 43 God, that makith grete and vnsercheable thyngis with-owte numbre. **1549** LATIMER *3rd Serm. bef. Edw. VI* (Arb.) 100 Mans hart is vnserchable. **1584** B. R. tr. *Herodotus* II. 77 They fell..to discourse..of Nilus, the head whereof was vnsearchable, and not to be knowne. **1622** PEACHAM *Compl. Gent.* viii. 69 To consider how Nature.., by an vnsearchable and stupendious worke, sheweth vs [etc.]. **1667** MILTON *P.L.* VIII. 10 To relate Things else by me unsearchable, now heard With wonder. **1703** ROWE *Ulysses* IV. i, 'Tis all the mighty working of the gods, Unsearchable and dark to human Eyes. **1759** JOHNSON *Rasselas* xi, The unsearchable will of the Supreme Being. **1809–14** WORDSW. *Excurs.* III. 112 Lost in unsearchable eternity. **1835** THIRLWALL *Greece* I. vi. 193 As his might is irresistible, so is his wisdom unsearchable. **1876** R. BRIDGES *Sonn.* viii, The unsearchable and secret aims Of nature.
b. *sb.* An unsearchable thing.
1725 WATTS *Logick* I. vi. §1 It is a vast Hindrance..if we spend too much of our Time and Pains among Infinites and Unsearchables. **1741** —— *Improv. Mind* I. xviii, To busy yourselves..amongst unsearchables.
2. That cannot be sought for.
1878 B. TAYLOR *Pr. Deukalion* III. v. 128 A something lost, Because vnsought, perchance unsearchable, Assails my sight.
Hence **un'searchableness, -ably** *adv.*
1611 FLORIO, *Inscrutabilità,* *vnsearchableness. *a* **1653** BINNING *Serm.* (1845) 38 God's unsearchableness, God's unchangeableness. **1683** BURNET tr. *More's Utopia* 197 Unless, according to the unsearchableness of his Mind, he is pleased with a variety of Religions. **1856** RUSKIN *Mod. Painters* IV. v. v. §21 In an Italian twilight..there is still unsearchableness, but an unsearchableness without cloud or concealment. **1873** SYMONDS *Grk. Poets* ix. 290 The unsearchableness of God's dealings. **1706** STEVENS *Span. Dict.* I, *Inscrutablemente,* inscrutably, *unsearchably. **1746** HERVEY *Refl. Flower Garden* 21 The various Expedients which Providence, unsearchably wise, uses. **1847** DE QUINCEY *Sp. Mil. Nun* Wks. 1862 III. 98 A female..who.. perished by a fate so unsearchably mysterious.

un'searched, *ppl. a.* [UN-^{1} 8, 8 c.]
1. Not searched; unexamined, uninvestigated:
a. In predicative use, after *leave, go, pass,* etc.
1526 *Pilgr. Perf.* (W. de W. 1531) 131 b, It shall leaue no corner of our soules..vnserched. *a* **1548** HALL *Chron., Edw. V,* 7 Watchyng, that no person..should passe vnserched. **1621** FLETCHER *Thierry & Theod.* v. i, Since you have your tricks..we will not leave a wrinkle of you unsearcht. **1691** T. H[ALE] *Acc. New Invent.* 12 Suffering a Ship..to lye..in Harbour unsearched. **1765** WILKES *Corr.* (1805) II. 138 The two trunks..were suffered to go out of Rome unsearched. **1832** G. DOWNES *Lett. Cont. Countries* I. 399 The custom-house officers..letting all ours [*sc.* luggage] pass unsearched. **1865** DICKENS *Mut. Fr.* III. vi, The chimney was not left unsearched.
b. In attributive use.
1568 *Jacob & Esau* I. iii. Bj, Whatsoeuer mysterie the Lorde therein ment, Must be referred to his vnserched iudgement. **1615** CHAPMAN *Odyss.* XXIV. 640 Pallas spake To Ioue..And askt of him, what his vnsearched mind Held vndiscouer'd. *a* **1649** CRASHAW *Carmen Deo Nostro, To C'tess Denbigh* 36 The self-shutt cabinet of an unsearcht soul. **1753** *Chambers' Cycl.* Suppl. s.v. *Fossile Shells,* Other yet unknown or unsearched seas and shores. **1821** BYRON *Heaven & Earth* iii. 912 The ocean..grasps each drowning hill, Nor leaves an unsearch'd cave. **1879** FARRAR *St. Paul* xxxi. II. 24 That unsearched borderland which lies between the natural and the supernatural.
2. Not searched *for.*
1730 A. GORDON *Maffei's Amphith.* p. x, All which..have been unsearch'd for, and unknown.

un'searching, *ppl. a.* (UN-^{1} 10.)
1599 DANIEL *Musoph.* (1602) C iij b, Then would they only labour to extend Their now vnsearching spirits beyond these bounds Of others powres, wherein they must be pend. **1828–32** WEBSTER (citing J. Q. Adams).

un'seared, *ppl. a.* [UN-^{1} 8.]
1. Not made sear; unwithered.
1599 THYNNE *Animadv.* (1875) 48 That is, (as some do expounde this worde vnseriall,) vnsered, vnsinged, vnwithered. **1829** J. L. KNAPP *Jrnl. Nat.* 102 Preserving.. a portion of its foliage unseared by frosts. *a* **1847** ELIZA COOK *Like the Evergreen* iii, It remaineth unseared in the deluge of light.
fig. **1827** POLLOK *Course T.* III. 153 The stripling youth of plump, unseared hope. **1863** W. LANCASTER *Præterita* 37 We'll keep a merry heart up still, Unsered, fresh, young, and callow.
2. Not made hard or callous.
1860 TRENCH *Serm. Westm. Abbey* vi. 59 Many things which he would have shrunk back from at first, while his conscience was yet unseared.

†**un'season,** *sb. Obs.*$^{-1}$ [UN-^{1} 12.] *in unseason,* out of season.
a **1400–50** *Alexander* 4439 ȝoure sowping in vnseson, ȝoure surfete of drinkis.

un'season, *v.* [UN-^{2} 4.] *trans.* To deprive of seasoning or relish. In quots. *fig.*
1590 SPENSER *F.Q., To Sir W. Raleigh,* Why doe I send this rusticke Madrigale, That may thy tunefull eare vnseason quite? ? *a* **1600** *Nobody & Someb.* in Simpson *Sch. Shaks.* (1878) I. 310 The remembrance that I was a king, Unseasons the content of povertie. **1728** THEOBALD *Double Falshood* I. ii, What Fortune soever my Going shall encounter, cannot be good Fortune; What I part withal unseasons any other Goodness.

un'seasonable, *a.* [UN-^{1} 7 b.]
1. Not suited to, not in accordance with, the time or occasion; untimely, inopportune.
c **1448** *Ten Commandments of Love* in *Stow's Chaucer* (1561) 342 b, Take measure in langage,..For mesure.. Thynges vnseasonable setteth in season. **1591** *Acts Privy Council* (1900) XXI. 123 The unordinate and unseasonable taking of the same [spawn] by the common fishers. **1607–12** BACON *Ess., Dispatch* (Arb.) 248/1 To chuse tyme is to save tyme, and an vnseasonable mocion is but beating the ayre. **1667** MILTON *P.L.* VIII. 201 Whence haply mention may arise Of somthing not unseasonable to ask. **1718** *Freethinker* No. 7. 42 A Notion prevails..that Marriage in Lent, is at least unseasonable. **1752** JOHNSON *Rambler* No. 207 ⁋9 Unseasonable importunity of discontent. **1817** JAS. MILL *Brit. India* II. v. v. 522 The English fleet,..dispersed by the weather, incurred considerable danger of a very unseasonable rencounter. **1839** W. C. TAYLOR *Anc. Hist.* xvii. §2 (ed. 2) 501 This rash conspiracy induced Galba to sully the commencement of his reign by unseasonable severities. **1844** H. H. WILSON *Brit. India* II. 497 The omission to inspect the accounts was unseasonable and injudicious.
transf. **1722** STEELE *Consc. Lovers* III. i, The familiar, learned, unseasonable Puppy!
b. Of time: Not suitable for the action specified or implied.
Freq. (with *hour*) implying an unusual time of the night.
1595 SHAKS. *John* IV. ii. 20 This acte..Being vrged at a time vnseasonable. **1621** in Foster *Eng. Factories Ind.* I. (1906) 261 The said ship..at last at unseasonable time made tryall to com for Petapolie. **1674** *Jackson's Recant.* B 1, To let them out at unseasonable hours, and stay up for them, till it

be early. **1715** De Foe *Fam. Instruct.* I. iii. (1841) I. 62 Who knows but God may bless instruction, though begun at an unseasonable time. **1759** Franklin *Ess.* Wks. 1840 III. 218 Neither did they conceive the time to be unseasonable for an application to the crown. **1800** Mrs. Hervey *Mourtray Fam.* II. 176 If I presume to intrude upon you at an unseasonable hour. **1838** Lytton *Leila* I. vi, The alarm it might occasion..if he endeavoured at so unseasonable an hour, to force an entrance.

c. As *adv.* Unseasonably; out of season.
a **1634** Chapman *Bussy d'Ambois* III. (1641) 42 How most unseasonable thou playest the Cucko, In this thy fall of friendship. **1680** R. L'Estrange tr. *Erasmus' Colloquies* 174 This came very Unseasonable; Or if there had been any Errour, it might have been dissembled.

2. Of fish, etc.: Not in season.
c **1450** *Cal. Letter-bks. London, D.* (1902) IV. 198 Ye shalle not suffre no fysshe corrupt ne unsesynable to be solde. **1477** [see victual *sb.* 1 γ]. **1488–9** *Act 4 Hen. VII*, c. 21 Aswell grete fisshes unsesonable as the seid frie. **1533–4** *Act 25 Hen. VIII*, c. 7 Kyllyng of salmons when they be unsesonable and not holsome for manns body. **1563** in *Liturg. Serv. Q. Eliz.* (1847) 488 The same poor which either lack food, or else that which they have is unseasonable and cause of sickness. **1653** Walton *Angler* vi. 133 The old Salmon..grow sick in fresh waters, and by degrees unseasonable. **1677** *Quarter Sess. Rec.* (N. Riding Rec. Soc.) VII. 6 A Startforth yeoman for catching ten unseasonable fish called scurfes. **1842** *Act 5–6 Vict.* c. 106 §74 If any Person shall..have in his Possession any..unclean or unseasonable Salmon or Trout.

†**b.** Not properly matured; unseasoned. *Obs.*$^{-1}$
1515 *Nottingham Rec.* III. 344 We present Ser John Bagula for makyng on seysnabulle tyle. **1548** *Act 2 & 3 Edw. VI*, c. 10 §1 Sondrie persons..made myche Malte unpure and unseasonable.

3. Of weather: Not appropriate to the season of the year; *esp.* stormy, tempestuous. Also of days, seasons, etc., marked by such weather.
a **1513** Fabyan *Chron.* VII. 433 Great scarcete of corne and frute..by meane of vnsesonable wederynge. **1593** Shaks. *Rich. II*, III. ii. 106 An vnseasonable stormie day. **1602** in Moryson *Itin.* (1617) II. 261 Their Haruest was so vnseasonable, and their Corne was so destroied by the weather, as numbers of subiects will vndoubtedly die of famine. **1610** Holland *Camden's Brit.* 466 By reason of vnseasonable weather the corne..was choked and blasted in the eare. **1645** Boate *Ireland's Nat. Hist.* xxi. (1652) 166 The ripeness of the fruits..is greatly retarded by the abundance of unseasonable rain. **1696** Ray in *Lett. Lit. Men* (Camden) 203 Heer hath been a very unseasonable Summer, for the most part very cold and wet. **1707** Mortimer *Husb.* 212 A cold, dry, unseasonable Spring. **1820** Shelley *Prometh. Unb.* II. iv. 52 The unseasonable seasons drove With alternating shafts of frost and fire, Their ..pale tribes to mountain caves. **1854** *Poultry Chron.* I. 578/1 Notwithstanding the cold, dark, unseasonable day. **1879** S. C. Bartlett *Egypt to Pal.* xx. 442 Plucking lilies of the field from beneath the unseasonable snow.

un'seasonableness. [f. prec.] The quality or fact of being unseasonable: **a.** Of weather.
1523 Fitzherb. *Husb.* §14 The vnseasonablenes of the wether. **1577** B. Googe *Heresbach's Husb.* I. 2 b, Yf either the vnseasonablenesse of the weather, or sicknesse cause me to keepe my bed. **1600** Surflet *Country Farme* v. x. 674 The Oxen..better indure the vnseasonablenes of times, and..draw a deeper draught. **1695** Luttrell *Brief Rel.* (1857) III. 515 The lords justices, considering the unseasonablenesse of the weather, have..prohibited the exportation of corn. **1796** *Phil. Trans.* LXXXVI. 280 During last January, nothing was more common than to hear expressions of the unseasonableness of the weather. **1853** C. M. Yonge *Heir of Redclyffe* II. i. 2 Mrs. Ashford put the matter off for the present by the unseasonableness of the weather. **1971** *Daily Tel.* 3 July 9/1 Summer..is the season when unseasonableness becomes most glaring and least sufferable.

b. Of time.
1548 Udall *Erasm. Par. Luke* iv. 49 b, He neuer did so muche as laie for his excuse the importunitee or vnseasonablenesse of tyme. **1628** in Rushw. *Hist. Coll.* (1659) I. 582 Our next Argument is drawn..from the unseasonableness of the time. **1656** Earl Monm. tr. *Boccalini's Pol. Touchstone* (1674) 273 About one a clock at night, forty Carts..were seen to enter the Royal Palace..: and because of the unseasonableness of the time..inquiry was made [etc.]. **1694** *Phil. Trans.* XVIII. 45 They were generally taken notice of,..because of the unseasonableness of the time for Grashoppers. *a* **1748** Watts *Disc. Educ. Childr.* ix. (1795) 177 The unseasonableness of the midnight hour [for dancing].

c. Of actions, etc.
1610 Healey *Theophrastus* (1616) 49 Vnseasonnablenesse is a troublesome..assaulting of those with whom we haue to doe. **1693** *Mem. Ct. Teckely* III. 28 The unseasonableness of the ill Policy of the Turks. **1741** Richardson *Pamela* IV. 387 Forgive, dearest Sir, the Unseasonableness of your very impertinent..Pamela. **1799** Han. More *Fem. Educ.* (ed. 4) I. 14 A sneer, not at the truth of religion,..but at its gravity, its unseasonableness. **1815** Jane Austen *Emma* I, The suddenness and..the unseasonableness with which the affair burst out. **1884** *Manch. Exam.* 1 July 3/1 The unseasonableness of the proposed discussion.

un'seasonably, *adv.* [un-^{1} 11.] In an unseasonable manner; at an unfitting time; out of season.
1588 Lambarde *Eiren.* IV. xix. 603 It wil fall out unseasonablie. **1589** Warner *Alb. Eng.* Prose Add. 164 Whilest he vnseasonably amongst blowes, deliuered vnregarded perswasions of Peace. **1610** Healey *Theophrastus* (1616) 12 A Pratler or Babler..vnseasonably setting vpon any stranger. **1687** Wood *Life* (O.H.S.) III. 233 That night there should have been an illumination in the quadrangle, but by the folly of the proctor it was unseasonably done the night before. **1719** De Foe *Crusoe* II. (Globe) 332, I unhappily and unseasonably disturb'd him. **1780** *Mirror* No. 72, The thoughts of futurity..may surely sometimes, not unseasonably, press upon our imagination. **1819** Shelley *Cenci* IV. iv. 2 Lady, my duty to his Holiness Be my excuse that thus unseasonably I break upon your rest. **1868** *Rep. U.S. Commissioner Agric.* (1869) 21 Unseasonably cool and..wet weather set in, followed by early frosts.

un'seasoned, *ppl. a.* [un-^{1} 8.]
1. Not made palatable by seasoning.
1582 Stanyhurst *Æneis* IV. (Arb.) 108 Caucasus haggish Bred the, with a tigers soure milck vnseasoned. **1601** *Song of Mary* D j b, If it may be, let this vnseasoned cup Of sorrow passe. **1611** Florio, *Incondite uiuande*, vnseasoned meates.

b. Not appreciative of dainties.
1598 Marston *Sco. Villanie* 169 For whose vnseasoned palate I wrote the first Satyre, in some places too obscure.

2. Not matured by growth or time. Also in fig. context.
1601 B. Jonson *Poetaster* v. iii, We haue no vacant eare, now, to receiue The vnseason'd fruits of his officious tongue. **1641** Best *Farm. Bks.* (Surtees) 32 The best stricles..are made of froughy, unseasoned oake. **1683** Moxon *Mech. Exerc., Printing* iii, If they be made of unseason'd Stuff,..as the Stuff dries it shrinks. **1832** *Planting* 74 (L.U.K.), Comparative trials of seasoned and unseasoned wood in the same building. **1833** Loudon *Encycl. Archit.* §243 Unseasoned timber, or other materials.

b. Not habituated by time or experience.
1601 Shaks. *All's Well* I. i. 80 'Tis an vnseason'd Courtier, good my Lord, Aduise him. **1608** Day *Law Trickes* III. ii, These words..Are but like Ignes Fatui, to delude Greene and vnseason'd wits. **1614** Latham *Falconry* I. ix. 33 These hawkes being vnseasoned in their bodies. **1638** Shirley *Mart. Soldier* I. ii, Your unseason'd valour Had thrice ingag'd our fortunes and our men Beyond recovery. **1730** *2nd Contin. Baker's Chron.* 531/2 The unseason'd Orkney Men immediately yielded themselves. **1770** Pittman *European Settlem. Mississ.* p. viii, The twenty-first regiment ..being..unseasoned to such a climate, suffered almost as much. **1840** E. E. Napier *Scenes & Sports For. Lands* II. App. 243 The exposure of his unseasoned person alternately to night damps and the burning rays of the sun. **1857** Dickens *Dorrit* I. xxxii, The depressed unseasoned prisoner.

†**3.** Unseasonable. *Obs.*
1589 Cooper *Admon.* 21 Their virulent and unseasoned speeches. **1597** Shaks. *2 Hen. IV*, III. i. 105 These vnseason'd howres perforce must adde Vnto your Sicknesse. **1598** —— *Merry W.* II. ii. 174 The which hath something embolded me to this vnseason'd intrusion. **1615** Brathwait *Strappado*, etc. (1878) 282 Each..tun'd their odes with that vnseasoned time. **1796** Mme. D'Arblay *Camilla* I. 202 Camilla looked hastily away, and her whole set, abashed by so unseasoned an inquiry, cast down their eyes.

†**4.** Rendered unhealthy. *Obs.*$^{-1}$
1638 Sir T. Herbert *Trav.* (ed. 2) 213 A great and lovely Citie,..over-topt by no hill, unseasoned by no marishes.

un'seasoning, *ppl. a.* (un-^{1} 10.)
a **1617** Hieron *Wks.* (1619) II. 474 This miserie of hauing none among them but an vnseasoning and vnsufficient minister.

un'seat, *v.* [un-^{2} 5.]
1. *trans.* To dislodge from a seat (*esp.* on horseback).
1596 Spenser *F.Q.* IV. x. 10 Whom boldly I encountred.. And by good fortune shortly him vnseated. **1784** Cowper *Task* VI. 553 His horse..Rush'd to the cliff, and..stood. At once the shock unseated him. **1835** W. Irving *Tour Prairies* 177 Beatte was nearly unseated from his saddle. **1845** J. Coulter *Adv. in Pacific* xvi. 247 The boat plunged down.. with so violent a shock, that nearly all were unseated. **1895** Scully *Kafir Stories* 170 My horse..wheeled sharply to the right, completely unseating me.
transf. **1609** Holland *Amm. Marcell.* 84 But Constantine ..displaced and unseated this huge masse. **1839** Marryat *Phant. Ship* ii, The probing of the wound would half unseat my reason. **1891** *Cent. Dict.* s.v., To unseat a boiler; to unseat a valve.

2. To dislodge from some place or position; to deprive of rank or office.
1611 Speed *Hist. Gt. Brit.* Summary, In Germany by intrusion they vnseated the Sueuians. **1661** J. Davies *Civ. Warres* 371 [They] resolved next morning to unseat the Parliament once more. **1826** Hood *Recipe for Civiliz.* 89 Whereas a cook would soon unseat him [*sc.* Apis], And make his own churchwardens eat him. **1870** Emerson *Soc. & Solit.* iv. 67 A greater power of carrying the thing loftily, and with perfect assurance,..might..unseat any sovereign, and abrogate any constitution in Europe and America. **1878** Taylor *Deukalion* III. vi. 135 The Gods of races I unseat, as Time or Tyranny of old Unseated them.

b. *spec.* To deprive of, or depose from, a seat in Parliament or other representative body.
1834 *Tait's Mag.* I. 541/1 Had one third of the exceptions held good, it was clear the Governor must be unseated. **1882** Sergt. Ballantine *Exper.* xxx. 294 The first case..was speedily disposed of by unseating the member.

un'seated, *ppl. a.* [un-^{1} 8.]
†**1.** *U.S.* Of land: Unsettled, unoccupied. *Obs.*
1662 *Laws of Virginia* lxxii. 43 [It] must in a short time leave the greatest part of the Countrey, unseated and unpeopled. **1689** *Col. Rec. Pennsylv.* I. 318 Where land is unseated. **1724** *Acts Assembly Pennsylv.* (1762) I. 102 Exempting..all unsettled Tracts or Parcels of Land, That is to say, such Tracts of Land as..are unseated. **1800** *Farmer's Reg.* 29 March (Thornton), The owners of unseated lands in Westmoreland. **1877** Burroughs *Taxation* 208.

2. Not seated; not provided with a seat.
[**1775** Ash.] **1883** D. C. Murray *Hearts* ix, She was still unseated, and he approached her.

unseaulich: see unsewly *a.*

un'seaworthiness. (un-^{1} 12. Cf. next.)
1824 *Cowen's Rep.* (N.Y. State Supreme Crt.) 106 Every vessel has a point of time at which it..arrives at a situation of unseaworthiness. **1832** McCulloch *Dict. Commerce* 648 Unseaworthiness may be caused in various ways, such as want of repair, want of stores [etc.]. **1875** *Economist* 27 Feb. 246/1 Ought not the underwriters to have been able to plead 'unseaworthiness'?

un'seaworthy, *a.* (un-^{1} 7.)
1820 Tomlins *Law Dict.* (ed. 3) I. s.v. *Insurance*, A ship ..sailed on her voyage in an unseaworthy state. **1857** Dickens *Dorrit* II. xxvi, Drowning men clinging to unseaworthy spars. **1896** 'H. S. Merriman' *Sowers* xxxiv, A sailor never believes that his own ship is unseaworthy.

†**un'second,** *v. Obs.*$^{-1}$ (un-^{1} 14.)
1616 J. Lane *Contn. Sqr.'s T.* x. 59 Wear't not as good to have betraid oure lord, as to vnsecond him, as twice wee did?

un'seconded, *ppl. a.* [un-^{1} 8.]
1. Not backed up or supported.
1597 Shaks. *2 Hen. IV*, II. iii. 34 O Miracle of Men! Him did you leaue (Second to none) vn-seconded by you. **1608** [Tofte] *Ariosto's Sat.* III. (1611) 33 So that in rank of fauour, I alone Stood still vnseconded of any one. **1691** T. H[ale] *Acc. New Invent.* 9 Nor lay this long unseconded by concurrent Advices from Portsmouth. **1734** Thomson *Liberty* I. 166 Unseconded by art, the spinning race..idly toil. **1778** Hamilton *Wks.* (1886) VII. 558 He attempted, single and unseconded, to possess himself of one of the enemy's field-pieces. **1809–14** Wordsw. *Excurs.* VI. 221 He ..Urged unremittingly the stubborn work, Unseconded, uncountenanced. **1884** *Law Times* 8 Nov. 27/2 [A] result.. obtained by his own unseconded efforts.

b. *spec.* (See second *v.*^{1} 3.)
1816 *Monthly Mag.* XLI. 144 Applause revives. All cry, To France, To France! And Westmoreland unseconded remained. **1865** *Reader* 27 May 594/3 His proposal was unseconded, and fell to the ground.

†**2.** Unparalleled, unique. *Obs.*$^{-1}$
1646 Sir T. Browne *Pseud. Ep.* III. vii. 120 Even as in the body of man from putred humours..there have succeeded strange and unseconded shapes of wormes.

un'secrecy. *rare*$^{-1}$ (un-^{1} 12.)
159. H. Walpole in *Cath. Rec. Soc. Publ.* V. 225 By some mens unsecrecy, which I will not name, my iourney is much known.

un'secret, *a.* (un-^{1} 7.)
a **1586** Sidney *Arcadia* III. xviii, Which hopes, Hate (as unsecrete as Love) could not conceale. **1606** Shaks. *Tr. & Cr.* III. ii. 133 Who shall be true to vs When we are so vnsecret to our selues? **1614** Raleigh *Hist. World* IV. iv. §8. 251 Hee was driuen by necessitie to trust many, of whom he stumbled vpon some, that were vnsecret. **1655** Earl of Norwich in *Nicholas P.* (Camden) II. 259 For what I heare of my being thought vnsecret (a hard censure after fifty yeares seruice in your Royall Family).

un'secret, *v.* [un-^{2} 4.] *trans.* To disclose.
1607–12 Bacon *Ess., Counsel* (Arb.) 318 But lett Princes beware that the vnsecreting of theire affaires come not from themselves. **1654** Whitlock *Zootomia* 447 Things nere done hee'l sweare; All he unsecrets: such black Sheep beware. **1659** Fuller *App. Inj. Innoc.* III. 17 They say, It is ..another thing, to look on Gods Secrets, in some sort unsecreted. **1666** Bp. S. Parker *Free & Impart. Censure* 65 The Intrinsick Essence of any one Being is no more explain'd & unsecreted after all their Labour, then it was afore.

unse'creted, *ppl. a.* (un-^{1} 8.)
1750 G. Hughes *Barbados* 246 The more gross returns back unsecreted to the radical Vessels.

un'secretness. (un-^{1} 12.)
1526 *Pilgr. Perf.* (W. de W. 1531) 110 Vnkyndnesse, Vntrustynesse or vnsecretnesse, Discorde or contencyon.

unsec'tarian, *a.* and *sb.* (un-^{1} 7 and 12.)
adj. **1847** Webster (citing Buckham). **1854** *Edin. Rev.* Oct. 413 Their devotion to the one God and his Prophet [is] unsectarian in its character. **1887** Ruskin *Præterita* II. 195 A standard of the purest unsectarian Christianity.
sb. **1888** *Pall Mall G.* 20 Nov. 4/1 In Sheffield the victory was with the Unsectarians, in Manchester it was with the Sectarians.

unsec'tarianism. (un-^{1} 12; cf. prec.)
1866 *Spectator* 1 Dec. 1325 Making such a fuss about unsectarianism in religion.

unsec'tarianize, *v.* (un-^{2} 6 c (*b*).)
1832 J. S. Mill *Let.* 17 Sept. in *Wks.* (1963) XII. 118 The editor & his writers..are but Unitarians & liberals, unsectarianized. **1836** —— *Diss. & Disc.* (1859) I. 200 The very first step..should be to unsectarianize them [*sc.* the Universities] wholly.

un'secular, *a.* (un-^{1} 7.)
1846 Worcester (citing *Ec. Rev.*). **1849** A. Baker in J. Aiton *Domest. Econ.* (1857) 33* All will agree..that they [*sc.* buildings] should have..a humble unsecular air. **1859** Dickens, etc. *Haunted House* vi, We were every Sunday advertising the establishment in an unsecular way.

un'secularize, *v.* (un-^{2} 6 c (*b*).)
1816 A. Knox *Rem.* (1844) I. 66 The humbled and unsecularized priesthood of the English Church. **1842** Pusey *Crisis Eng. Ch.* 127 Our Church has been in part un-Catholicized by those who helped..to unsecularize her. **1897** W. C. Hazlitt *Ourselves* 60 The clergy..more or less unsecularise them [*sc.* women].

†**unse'cure,** *a. Obs.* (un-^{1} 7 and 5 b.)
1636 [Denham] *Destr. Troy* (1656) 2 Now but an unsecure and open Bay. **1685** Ld. Perth in *Lond. Gaz.* No. 2031/7 They render us unquiet and unsecure at home. **1700** Blackmore *Job* 67 He in his prosperous state is unsecure.

1726 LEONI *Alberti's Archit.* II. 100/1 It may be unsecure against sudden incursions of enemies. **1729** T. INNES *Crit. Ess.* (1879) 184 Looking on their religion as unsecure as long as the queen's authority was acknowledged.

b. Const. *of*, or *to* with inf.

? *a* **1685** ROSCOMMON *Virgil's Sixth Ecl.* Poems (1749) 77 None who under that protection came Was ever ill receiv'd, or unsecure of fame. **1693** FLEETWOOD *Serm.* 13 Depending ..on Accidents in Nature, which are varying every Day, uncertain, unsecure to be relied upon.

unse'cured, *ppl. a.* (UN-[1] 8.)

1780 BURKE *Œcon. Reform* Wks. 1906 II. 319 A supply of unsecured money..wholly at the discretion of ministers. **1821** SCOTT *Kenilw.* xli, He left, therefore, the Countess's door unsecured on the outside. **1866** *Sat. Rev.* 22 Sept. 361/1 All corn, therefore, unsecured, cut or uncut, is considerably discoloured. **1882** DE WINDT *Equator* 86 Their jet-black hair was unsecured and allowed to fall in profusion down their backs.

† **unse'curity.** *Obs.*[−1] (UN-[1] 12 and 5 b.)

1591 CONINGSBY *Jrnl. Siege Rouen* in *Camden Misc.* I. 64 Lytle provision commeth to our markett, what for the unsecurytie of the passage for pore men.

unse'date, *a.* (UN-[1] 7.)

1823 HONE *Anc. Mysteries* 262 Their obsolete costume and hobbling walk are sport for the unsedate.

un'sedentary, *a.* (UN-[1] 7.)

1814 WORDSW. *Excurs.* VII. 193 Meanwhile the unsedentary Master's hand Was busier with his task. **1915** W. B. YEATS *Tribute to Thomas Davis* (1947) 15 A gallant unsedentary man.

unse'duce, *v.* (UN-[2] 3.)

1664 N. INGELO *Bentiv. & Ur.* Index, *Misoplanus*, one that hates Cheaters, takes pains to discover their Frauds and to unseduce the deceiv'd.

unse'duced, *ppl. a.* (UN-[1] 8 and 5 c.)

1565 [see UN-[1] 5 c]. **1611** SHAKS. *Cymb.* I. iv. 173 If shee remaine vnseduc'd..you shall answer me with your Sword. **1667** MILTON *P.L.* v. 896 Unshak'n, unseduc'd, unterrifi'd His Loyaltie he kept. **1721** SOUTHERNE *Spartan Dame* II. i, Among so many false one man yet true, Unshaken, unseduced. **1751** SMOLLETT *Per. Pic.* lxxxi, He remained unshaken, unseduced, preserving his attachment for me. **1830** MACKINTOSH *Progr. Eth. Philos.* (1862) 200 Having been unseduced by the temptations either of scepticism, or of useless idealism. **1866** FELTON *Anc. & Mod. Gr.* I. xi. 195 Still unseduced, unstained by vice.

unse'ducible, *a.* (UN-[1] 7.)

1869 *Lyndesay's Wks.* 436 *marg.*, A judge, come from afar, unwavering, unseducible.

un'see, *v. rare.* [UN-[1] 14 and UN-[2] 3.] *trans.* To avoid seeing; to leave, or make, unseen.

a **1395** HYLTON *Scala Perf.* II. xl. (W. de W. 1494), Whan he sheweth him the soule may not vnsee hym, for he is lyghte. **1865** J. GROTE *Explor. Philos.* I. 243 We cannot unsee the prospect before us. **1871** KINGSLEY *At Last* xvii, At last we had seen it; and we could not unsee it.

un'seeable, *a.* [UN-[1] 7 b.] Invisible.

a **1400** in *Hampole's Wks.* (1895) I. 124 Our blyssed vnseable god may be perseyued alanle be inly vnderstandyng. *Ibid.* 165 It is..nerhand vnpossibull to a fleshle saule..for to ryse in knawyng of vnseabull þ[i]nges. ? **1531** TINDALE *Exp. 1st Ep. John* Wks. (1572) 427/2 Of the very Sacrament it selfe we know no other thyng then that we come thether to see an vnseable miracle. **1548** GESTE *Pr. Masse* C ii, That the substance of ye bred, whiche is vnseable, shuld be worshipped. **1719** DE FOE *Vis. Angelic World* 44 To see things unseeable, as St. Paul heard things unutterable. **1880** *Boston Jrnl. Chem.* Dec. 134/2 It is assumed that spirit is unseeable.

Hence † **un'seeably** *adv. Obs.*

a **1395** HYLTON *Scala Perf.* II. xi. (MS. Bodl. 592), Þee fforȝifnesse of synne is doon goostli and vnseabli þoruȝ grace of þe hooligoost. *Ibid.* II. xxx, He was vnseabli felid in þe myȝtes of her soulis.

un'seeded, *a.* [UN-[1] 9.] Not having or bearing seed.

1884- *Imp. Dict.*, etc.

un'seeded, *ppl. a.* [UN-[1] 8.] Unsown.

[**1775** ASH.] **1791** COWPER *Odyss.* IX. 140 The unseeded and unfurrow'd soil..food for blatant goats supplies. **1828-32** WEBSTER, *Unseeded*,..not sown. (Local.) *N. England.*

un'seeing, *vbl. sb.* (UN-[1] 13.)

1860 RUSKIN *Mod. Paint.* V. VIII. i. §14. 164 False seeing is unseeing,—on the negative side of blindness.

un'seeing, *ppl. a.* [UN-[1] 10, 5 d. Cf. OE. *unȝeséonde* not yet seeing, MHG. *unsëhende* (G. *unsehend*) in sense 2.]

† **1.** Unseen, invisible. *Obs.*

a **1300** *Cursor M.* 25010 Wit þis word 'heuen' þou vnderstand Al gastli thing and vnseand.

2. Not seeing; lacking sight.

Freq. in recent use, esp. with *eyes*.

1591 SHAKS. *Two Gent.* IV. iv. 209 Else by Ioue, I vow, I should haue scratch'd out your vnseeing eyes. *c* **1600** —— *Sonn.* xliii, How would thy shadowes forme, forme happy show,..When to vn-seeing eyes thy shade shines so? **1795** SOUTHEY *Joan of Arc* IV. 66 With a full eye, that of the circling throng And of the visible world unseeing, seem'd Fix'd upon objects seen by none beside. **1819** *Monthly Mag.* XLVIII. 33 As one who, sever'd from the maid he loves, Rolls an unseeing eye on all beside. *a* **1830** LD. COCKBURN *Mem.* (1856) 17 But the garden!..unseen and unseeing, it was a world of its own. **1873** MISS BRADDON *Lucius Davoren* I. 57 He looked at his friend's face with blank unseeing eyes. **1888** D. C. MURRAY *Weaker Vessel* ii, After an apparently unseeing glance at one of its pages.

3. With object: Without seeing.

1632 LITHGOW *Trav.* x. 445, I haue gone eighteene leagues,..vnseeing house or Village. **1798** SOUTHEY *Joan of Arc* (ed. 2) I. I. 124, I sat in silence,..unheeding and unseeing all Around me.

Hence **un'seeingly** *adv.*

1893 MARIE CORELLI *Barabbas* xxxiii, Barabbas went out, wandering almost unseeingly in the open street.

un'seeking, *ppl. a.* (UN-[1] 5 d, 10.)

1583 *Reg. Privy Council Scot.* III. 586 Quhairintill his Hienes hes occupeit himself..unseiking the hurt and ruyne of quhatsumevir his subjectis. **1799** COLERIDGE *Lett.* (1895) 272 He might as well have been in England as at Goslar, in the situation which he chose and with his unseeking manners. **1878** MRS. STOWE *Poganuc P.* xxiii. 207 Love faithful, devoted, unseeking of self, and asking only to bless.

† **un'seel,** *v. Obs.* [UN-[2] 3.]

1. *trans.* To unsew (the eyes of a hawk, etc.); *fig.*, to open, unclose.

1530 PALSGR. 766/2, I unceyle a haukes eyes, or other byrdes, I cut the stytches that closed his eyes togyther. *a* **1587** Q. ELIZ. in Puttenham *Eng. Poesie* III. xx. (Arb.) 255 Then dazeld eyes with pride, which great ambition blinds, Shalbe vnseeld by worthy wights. **1612** J. DAVIES (Heref.) *Muse's Sacr.* Wks. (Grosart) II. 37/1 Vnseele mine Eyes, that long thy Light to see. **1652** BENLOWES *Theoph.* XI. xxx, Still to have toting waits unseel thine eyes In bed, at board.

2. To unsew or uncover the eyes of (a hawk, etc.). Also *fig.*

1530 PALSGR. 766/2 Unceyle your pigyon and..he wyll go from your hauke. **1575** TURBERV. *Falconrie* 91 Watche hir all that nighte that you unseale hir. **1612** WARNER *Alb. Eng.* XIII. lxxvi. 315 This Athiest and that Epicure grant thou whom they offend That I vnceele, and of my Verse thy Glory be the end. **1618** LATHAM *Falconry* xxvii. 124 Let them haue the rest [*sc.* doves] giuen vnseild with some few feathers drawne from them. **1686** BLOME *Gentl. Recr.* II. 36 In the Evening by Candle-light unseal her, giving her something to tyre upon. **1728** CHAMBERS *Cycl.* s.v. *Falcon*, Give her a bit or two upon the Lure, and unseel her.

† **unseeled,** obs. var. UNCEILED *ppl. a.*

1594 NASHE *Unfort. Trav.* I iij, Whiles I, thorough a crannie of my vpper chamber vnseeled, had beheld all this sad spectacle.

† **un'seeliness.** *Obs.* [UN-[1] 12. Cf. OE. *unȝesǣliȝnes.*] Unhappiness.

a **1300** *E.E. Psalter* xiii. 7 Forbreking and vnselines ai [are] In waies of þaim. *c* **1374** CHAUCER *Boeth.* IV. pr. v. (1868) 131 Þus see I wel..what blisfulnesse or ellys what vnselinesse is establissed in þe desertys of goode men and of shrewes.

† **un'seely,** *a. Obs.* [OE. *unsǣliȝ* (*un-* UN-[1] 7 + *sǣliȝ* SEELY *a.*), = WFris. *on-*, *ûnsillich*, NFris. *unsaleg*, MDu. *onsâlich* (Du. *onzalig*), MLG. *unsalich*, OHG. *unsâlig* (MHG. *unsâlich*, *unsælic*, *-ec*, G. *unselig*).]

1. Of persons: **a.** Unfortunate, unhappy, miserable, wretched; deserving pity.

a **900** *Juliana* 450 Ic þec halsiȝe..þæt þu miltsiȝe me..þæt [ic] unsæliȝ eall ne forweorþe. *a* **1023** WULFSTAN *Hom.* (1883) 52 Deofol..ȝedeð swa þurh þæt, þæt unsæliȝ man wisdomes ne ȝymeð. *c* **1200** ORMIN 4812 Unnseliȝ mann Amm icc onn eorþe wurrþenn. *c* **1275** *xi Pains Hell* 7 in *O.E. Misc.* 147 Vnsely gost hwat dostu here? *c* **1374** CHAUCER *Boeth.* IV. pr. iv. (1868) 124 ȝit mot it nedes be þat shrewes ben more wrecches and vnsely. **1388** WYCLIF *Rom.* vii. 24 Y am an vnceli man; who schal delyuer me fro the bodi of this synne? **14..** *Seven Points Wisd.* iii. (MS. Douce 114) fol. 108 Loo I vnselye..sowht abowte to gete me a wyfe. **1513** DOUGLAS *Æneid* I. xi. 36 The fey wnsely Dido, For the mischeif to cum predestinate, Mycht not refrene. *Ibid.* V. viii. 86 Vnsilly wycht! quhow did thi mynd invaid Sic gret wodnes? *a* **1555** PHILPOT tr. *Curio* Exam. & Writ. (Parker Soc.) 418 Barbarous words by the which unto unsely [L. *incautis*] and foolish folk they avaunt themselves to be marvelled at.

b. Bringing misfortune on oneself or others; unlucky; evil-doing, wicked.

a **900** *Andreas* 561 Þæt..Iudea cynn wið Godes bearne ahof hearmcwide, hæleð unsæliȝe. *a* **1200** *St. Marher.* 16 Sathanas the unseli, the..of parais lihte so lahe. *c* **1205** LAY. 2531 Bi hire he hæfde twein sunen ah beine heo weoren unseli. *a* **1300** *Cursor M.* 1223 Vnseli caym..God and man þan was..hated. **1340-70** *Alex. & Dind.* 987 We ben of-set wiþ no sinne for vnsely godus. *c* **1400** LOVE *Bonavent. Mirr.* (1908) 225 How paciently..he resceyuede that false feyned clippynge and traitoures cusse of that vnsely disciple. **1412-20** LYDG. *Chron. Troy* II. 4233 Vnhappy woman, causere of oure peyne, Hard & vnsely.

c. Of animals: Mischievous, harmful.

13.. *Gaw. & Gr. Knt.* 1562 Þe lorde..Swez his vncely swyn, þat swyngez bi þe bonkkez, & bote þe best of his brachez þe bakkez in sunder. **1804** R. COUPER *Poetry* II. 84 My bacon ham..Th' unseely tyke has ta'en.

2. Of things, conditions, etc.: Causing or involving, accompanied by, misfortune or unhappiness.

a **900** *Genesis* 637 Sum hire æt heortan læȝ æppel unsælȝa. **13..** *Metr. Hom.* (MS. Ashm. 42) fol. 148 b, To þat ilk vnceli lande þare he bees bonden fote and hand Full hard wiþ þe deuils band. **13..** *Cursor M.* 15842 (Gött.), 'Ha men,' he said, 'quat ȝe er of ane vnseli toght'. *c* **1374** CHAUCER *Boeth.* II. pr. iv. (1868) 39 Þe most vnsely kynde of contrarious fortune. **1412-20** LYDG. *Chron. Troy* II. 3249 A! Priam kyng! vncely is þi chance! *a* **1450** *Northern Passion* (D.) 2024 We han pleyd vnseli plawis. **1513** DOUGLAS *Æneid* IV. Prol. 230 Lo! with quhat thocht, quhat bitternes and pane Luif vnseilly breidis in euery wycht! *a* **1828** *Young Allan* i. in *Buchan's Ball.* (1875) II. 11 There fell a-rousing them amang, On an unseely time.

† **un'seem,** *a. Obs.*[−1] [UN-[1] 7 + SEEM *a.*]

= UNSEEMLY *a.* 1.

c **1425** in *Anglia* VIII. 139/11 Vnmesurabil laghter or vnsem and vnmanerly berynge of body.

un'seeming, *pres. pple.* [UN-[1] 13.] Not seeming or appearing.

1588 SHAKS. *L.L.L.* II. i. 156 You..wrong the reputation of your name, In so vnseeming to confesse receyt Of that which hath so faithfully beene paid.

un'seeming, *ppl. a.* [UN-[1] 10, 5 d.]

† **1. a.** Unbecoming, unseemly; = UNBESEEMING *a.* 2. *Obs.*

a **1340** HAMPOLE *Psalter* lxxii. 15 Lo þis misemand [*v.r.* vnsemand] þing folous. **1382** WYCLIF *Prov.* xxvi. 7 So vnsemende thing is in the mouth of foolis a parable. **1535** STEWART *Cron. Scot.* (Rolls) III. 146 But quhois counsall nother prince nor king Ma gif consent to sic wnsemand thing. **1549** COVERDALE, etc. *Erasm. Par. Rom.* 33 Cutte out of thy mynde superfluous and vnsemyng desyres. **1662** BAXTER *Saints' R.* III. xi. 473 Unsavoury, harsh, and unseeming [*ed.* 1650 unseemly] language.

b. In predicative use, sometimes with dependent clause. *Obs.*

c **1400** *Destr. Troy* 3891 He spake neuer dispituosly,..Ne sagh, þat was vnsemond, slipped hym fro. *c* **1400** *Laud Troy Bk.* 10029 Hit is foly and vnsemyng A man to leue on fals dremyng. *c* **1460** G. ASHBY *Dicta Philos.* 967 On erthe ther is no thing so vnsemyng As a kynge to be in predacion. **1549** COVERDALE, etc. *Erasm. Par. Rom.* 27 Vnseamyng is it for loue of suche a meane, to dispise the ende. **1550** BALE *Eng. Votaries* II. 29 Remembrynge..that nothynge was more vnsemynge, than an olde dottynge fole..so to rage.

c. Const. *for* or *to*. *Obs.*

1382 WYCLIF *Prov.* xxvi. 1 What maner snoȝ in somer,.. so vnsemende is to the fool glorie. *c* **1400** *Destr. Troy* 1846 Þat hynd..þat ye kepe in youre company..As subiecte vnto syn, vnsemyng for you. **1536** BELLENDEN *Cron. Scot.* (1821) I. 64 With thir, and siclike inhumane cruelteis, unsemand to ane prince. **1592** WYRLEY *Armorie* 20 As these things are vnseeming for him to weare.

d. With direct object. *Obs.*

1592 GOLDING *De Mornay* (ed. 2) i. 12 He is tempted of his lustes, a thing altogether vnseeming the Godhead. **1620** MASON *Newfoundland* 5 Fishing is a beastly trade and unseeming a Gentleman. **1648** GAGE *West Ind.* 44 The beds only were unseeming this great state, very poor. **1701** *Stanley's Hist. Philos.* (ed. 3) 100, I think it most unseeming a Philosopher to sell his advice.

2. Unapparent. *rare.*

1923 D. H. LAWRENCE *Birds, Beasts & Flowers* 174 The elephants ponderously, with unseeming swiftness, galloped uphill in the night.

Hence † **un'seemingness.** *Obs.*

1540 WYATT in Flügel *Neuengl. Lesebuch* I. 348 Here I allegid the vnsemingnes to gyve credence to his word.

un'seemingly, *adv. rare.* [UN-[1] 11; cf. prec.] Unbecomingly.

1619 A. NEWMAN *Pleas. Vis.* (1840) 13 Euen some of.. tender age Vnseemingly can vaunt how they will..carouse. **1656** *Eirenikon* 28 Love..Unseemingly doth not itself behave. **1897** *Westm. Gaz.* 23 Dec. 2/3 That ophthalmia is unseemingly rife still is proved by [etc.].

† **un'seemlily,** *adv. Obs.* [UN-[1] 11.]

= UNSEEMLY *adv.*

1483 *Cath. Angl.* 329/2 Vn Semelily, *jndecenter*, *jnconuenienter*. *a* **1661** HOLYDAY *Juvenal* (1673) 177 Such [gifts] as thou..dost unseemlily receive at the same times.

un'seemliness. [f. next, or UN-[1] 12.]

1. The quality of being unseemly in respect of action, conduct, etc.

c **1380** WYCLIF *Sel. Wks.* III. 43 Unsemelynes schulde not be in Cristes Chirche. **1549** UDALL, etc. *Erasm. Par. 2 Thess.* iii. 11 b, Getting their liuyng with their owne handes, rather than to be greuouse vnto other with shamles crauinges & vnsemelines. **1577** tr. *Bullinger's Decades* 510/2 What vnseemelinesse soeuer is committed against God and his Church. **1678** WANLEY *Wond. Lit. World* V. i. §82. 466/2 The Emperour did expostulate the unseemliness of the deed with him. **1829** LYTTON *Devereux* I. xiii, I saw the unseemliness of fighting with my preceptor, and a priest. **1871** JOWETT *Plato* IV. 170 His virtue being such, that he never..fell into any great unseemliness.

2. The quality of being unseemly in appearance; uncomeliness.

1597 A. M. tr. *Guillemeau's Fr. Chirurg.* 23/1 The cleavinge in the lippes is such an vnseemlines and deformitye. **1603** G. OWEN *Pembrokeshire* (1892) 44 Parchinge of the sunne, and starveinge with cold is a cheefe cause of the vnseemelynes of the comon people of the countrey. **1846** LANDOR *Imag. Conv.* Wks. I. 195 *Johnson.* It makes an unseemly appearance in the type. *Tooke.* The unseemliness is not equal to the absurdity.

un'seemly, *a.* (and *sb.*) [UN-[1] 7. Cf. ON. *úsǿmilig-r* (Icel. *ósæmilegur*, Da. *usømmelig*, Norw. *usømeleg*, etc.).]

1. Unbecoming, unfitting; indecent.

a **1310** in Wright *Lyric P.* viii. 31 Ofte in song y have hem set, that is unsemly ther hit syt. **1338** R. BRUNNE *Chron.* (1810) 171 Þei did a foule trespas, it was vnsemely þing. *a* **1400-50** *Alexander* 99 For soth it is vnsemely slike sawis of a prynce. *c* **1440** *Promp. Parv.* 367/1 On-semely, *indecens*, *inconveniens*. **1542** HEN. VIII *Declar. Scots* A iv, With that vnsemely dissimulation, we were not a lytell moued. **1597** HOOKER *Eccl. Pol.* v. xlviii. §4 Things in themselues vnholie or vnseemely we may not aske. **1645** USSHER *Body Div.* 218 That no unseemely behaviour proceed from us. **1692** E. WALKER tr. *Epictetus' Mor.* l, Nor would they anything unseemly say. **1738** WATERLAND *Chr. Sacr. Expl.* Appendix i. 6 An unseemly Reflection upon..The Sacrifices of God. **1791** COWPER *Odyss.* XVII. 243 A squalid beggar..in unseemly garb attir'd. **1824** DIBDIN *Libr. Comp.* 616 Shall..

all editions be passed over in a sort of unseemly silence? **1855** MACAULAY *Hist. Eng.* xvii. IV. 39 The news..threw him into a passion..which hurried him into many foolish and unseemly actions. **1871** FREEMAN *Norm. Conq.* xviii. IV. 155 To offer to William..an insult as unseemly as it was senseless.

absol. **1880** *Sat. Rev.* 7 Aug. 162/2 Partaking not a little of the unwise as well as of the unseemly.

b. Const. *for* (†*of, to*) and with inf.

a **1300** *Body & Soul* in *Map's Poems* (Camden) 335 Thouȝ art unsemly for to se, uncomli for to cussen suwete. *c* **1375** *Sc. Leg. Saints* xxi. (*Clement*) 659 Sayand, vnsemly ware to se cristine man begare to be. *c* **1445** PECOCK *Donet* 139 Ful vnseemely and vntreuli it is to seie þat [etc.]. **1551** RECORDE *Pathw. to Knowl.* I. Def., It shall not be vnsemely to call all suche shapes, formes and figures [etc.]. **1581** MULCASTER *Positions* ii. 5 It is a thing not vnseemely for me to deale in. **1583** STUBBES *Anat. Abus.* I. P vij, How vnhonest soeuer, or vnseemly of christian eares his argument be. *a* **1598** ROLLOCK *1 Thess.* (1606) 183 Any thing, that is vnsetting, or vnseemlie to this Christian calling. **1667** MILTON *P.L.* x. 155 Unseemly to beare rule, which was thy part.., had'st thou known thy self aright. **1843** LYTTON *Last Bar.* VIII. vii, Unseemly it may be for one of your quality..to quit this place with me.

c. *sb.* An unseemly thing.

1654 WHITLOCK *Zootomia* Pref. A 7 The Candid Interpreter of modest Endeavours, not Exacter of Impossibles, or unseemlies.

2. Uncomely, unhandsome.

c **1340** HAMPOLE *Pr. Consc.* 5023 Þair bodys sal alle unsemely be, And foul, and ugly, opon to se. **1390** GOWER *Conf.* I. 96 Which of alle kinde Of wommen is thunsemlieste. **1393** LANGL. *P. Pl.* C. II. 55 The dupe dale and durke vnsemely to se to. *c* **1400** *Pilgr. Sowle* (Caxton) IV. xxxviii. (1859) 63 He found..an old vnsemely one. I ne can nought calle hyr lady. *a* **1513** FABYAN *Chron.* VI. cxciv. 198 The Erle..prayed his wyfe..yt she wold..make her selfe as fowle and as vnsemely as she coude. **1581** PETTIE *Guazzo's Civ. Conv.* II. (1586) 114 A man of unseemlie personage. **1683** MOXON *Mech. Exerc.*, *Printing* xvii. ¶2 Their Faces stand closer or wider assunder, which is unseemly, when the Letter comes to be Printed. **1684** J. S. *Profit & Pleas. United* 138 If you buy your Bees, Observe they be..Smooth and Shining; Rejecting the Rough and unsemly Ones. **1838** *Civil Eng. & Arch. Jrnl.* I. 394/2 Making the vessel frightfully crank and most unseemly to look at. **1843** JAMES *Forest Days* ii, In other respects he was not an unseemly man. **1870** DICKENS *E. Drood* i, He lies, dressed, across a large unseemly bed.

un'seemly, *adv.* [UN-[1] 11. Cf. ON. *úsœmiliga* (Icel. *ósæm-*).] In an unseemly or unbecoming manner.

c **1375** *Cursor M.* 24504 (Fairf.), On him mi heued I shoke & saide, vn-semeli, leue sone, artow graide! ?*a* **1400** *Morte Arth.* 1044 The syghte had he rechide, How vn-semly that sott satt sowpande hym one. *c* **1449** PECOCK *Repr.* II. x. 207 Ellis it wolde folewe that ther yn thei diden vnaccordingli and vnsemeli. **1591** DRAYTON *Harmonie of Ch.*, *Song of Annah* 8 Nor yet vnseemly speak such things, so proud and arrogant. **1610** HOLLAND *Camden's Brit.* 297 English women..rode very unseemely astride, like as men doe. *a* **1641** BP. MOUNTAGU *Acts & Mon.* (1642) 293 In which action hee..demeaned himself..unseemly for a King. **1725** POPE *Odyss.* I. 292 Yon' jovial Troop..Unseemly flown with insolence and wine. **1871** B. TAYLOR *Faust* (1875) I. xii. 143 Ah, thought I, in my conduct has he read it,—Something immodest or unseemly free?

un'seen, *ppl. a.* and *sb.* [UN-[1] 8 b, 12. Cf. OE. *unȝesewen*, MDu. *ongesien* (Du. *ongezien*), OHG. *ungesëhan* (MHG. *ungesëhen*, G. *-gesehen*), NFris. *unseen*; ON. and Icel. *úsénn, ósénn*.]

1. Not seen; not apprehended by sight; unperceived, invisible.

a. *a* **1225** *Leg. Kath.* 1784 For he halt in his hond..alle ischepene þing, sehene & unsehene. *a* **1225** *Ancr. R.* 312 Þet wit & wereð us euer wið þe unseiene [*v.r.* unsehene] gostes. *c* **1375** *Cursor M.* 566 (Fairf.), Saule..has vnderstandynge clene of þinge sayde and vnseyne. **1390** GOWER *Conf.* II. 247 If a man wol ben unsein, Withinne his hond hold clos the Ston, And he mai invisible gon. *c* **1440** *Jacob's Well* 263 No counseyl may be hyd in þe vnseyn & vnknowyn.

β. *a* **1300** *Cursor M.* 566 Saul..has als vnderstanding clene O thing it seis and of vnsene. **1387–8** T. USK *Test Love* I. Prol. (Skeat) l. 57 Wherthrough..arn the unsene privitees of god made to us sightful and knowing. *c* **1470** HENRY *Wallace* x. 626 Off the out watch thus chapyt thai wnseyn. **1500–20** DUNBAR *Poems* lxxxv. 39 Haile, schene, vnseyne with carnale eyne! **1590** SPENSER *F.Q.* II. i. 1 Himselfe he frees by secret meanes vnseene. **1644** DIGBY *Nat. Bodies* xix. §8 When by meanes of an vnseene haire, they [*sc.* jugglers] draw light bodies to them. **1681** COTTON *Wond. Peak* 59 When a..Ship..Suddenly strikes upon some unseen Rock. **1750** GRAY *Elegy* 55 Full many a flower is born to blush unseen. **1798** S. & HT. LEE *Canterb. T.* II. 27 [He] saw her there, and was not himself unseen. **1855** TENNYSON *Maud* I. IV. v, Do we move ourselves, or are moved by an unseen hand..? **1867** H. MACMILLAN *Bible Teach.* Pref. p. xii, The work of the world is carried on by the unseen force of steam.

absol. **1829** CARLYLE *Misc.* (1840) II. 226 The veil and mysterious Garment of the Unseen. **1841** MYERS *Cath. Th.* III. xxxiv. 125 Concerning the Unseen..no device..can preclude the possibility of Doubt.

b. Const. *of* (= by). Also *absol.*

a **1586** SIDNEY *De Mornay* Wks. 1923 III. 305 Looke up to that same only King..Who,..unseene of any mortall wight, Beholdeth all things. **1623** BP. HALL *Contempl.*, *O.T.* XVIII. iv, What an idleness it is for foolish hypocrites to hope they can dance in a net, unseen of heaven! *c* **1800** R. CUMBERLAND *John De Lancaster* (1809) II. 161 Davis..had entered the room, unseen of young Owen. **1802** J. BAILLIE *1st Pt. Ethwald* IV. iii, Through the dank and through the dry, Through th' unseen of mortal eye.

2. Not seen previously or hitherto; *esp.* †unfamiliar, strange, unknown.

a **1200** *St. Marher.* 10 Þa seh ha hwer set an unsehen unwiht,..blaccre þen euer eni blamon. *a* **1300** *Cursor M.* 5946 Þe frosse deid all vp be-dene, Þe hepes o þam war gret vnsene Þat men gadird on þe grund. *Ibid.* 9091 Þat scrift was soruful and vn-sene,..þat salamon yod vnder. *a* **1400–50** *Alexander* 2536 Be þis ser Philip son..of feȝtand folk Had semblid ane vnsene sowme. **1435** MISYN *Fire of Love* 69 Bot in treuth in me is cunne an vnsein Ioy. **1549** COVERDALE, etc. *Erasm. Par. Rom.* 25 If it be an vnsene and a hiddeous presumpcion, that the clay should with the potter pratle. **1592** R. D. *Hypnerotomachia* 55 A Diamond..of a huge and unseene bignes. **1604** E. G[RIMSTONE] *D'Acosta's Hist. Indies* VII. xxiii. 565 A bird as bigge as a Crane,.. but of a strange and vnseene form. **1667** MILTON *P.L.* XII. 361 A Starr Unseen before in Heav'n. **1725** BERKELEY *Proposal*, etc. Wks. 1871 III. 230 Unseen countries and after ages may feel the effects of his bounty.

b. Of passages for translation: Not previously read. Hence as *sb.*, an unprepared passage.

1879 C. S. JERRAM *Anglice Reddenda* Pref., An exercise book in 'unseen', that is, unprepared translations. **1882** *Athenæum* 30 Dec. 897/2 A proposal..to substitute 'unseens' for 'set books' in..examinations. **1892** J. EDGAR (*title*), Latin Unseens. *Ibid.* 23 A specimen unseen from Livy. **1897** E. S. SMITH (*title*), Greek Unseens in Prose and Verse.

†**3.** Unskilled, inexperienced. *Obs.*

1606 HOLLAND *Sueton.* 254 Neither was he unseene in Musick. **1653** W. RAMESEY *Astrol. Restored* 279 Somewhat difficult to those who are as yet altogether unseen therein. **1682** T. FLATMAN *Heraclitus Ridens* No. 63 (1713) II. 142 For any Man now to wonder at it, would but shew him very much unseen in the English History.

†**un'seenly**, *adv.* *Obs.*[−1] [UN-[1] 11; cf. *unseȝenlike* s.v. UN-[1] 3.] Invisibly.

1398 TREVISA *Barth. De P.R.* VIII. xxviii. (Bodl. MS.), Þe vertu of liȝt worcheþ vnseynlich [L. *invisibiliter*] feling and meuynge in beestes.

un'segmented, *ppl. a.* (UN-[1] 8.)

1848 *Proc. Berw. Nat. Club* II. 297 Body ovate, ventricose,..even and unsegmented. **1875** HUXLEY & MARTIN *Elem. Biol.* 206 Its posterior unsegmented part.. nearly as long as the segmented part.

un'seizable, *a.* (UN-[1] 7 b.)

1862 R. H. PATTERSON *Ess. Hist. & Art* 44 Beauty,.. beaming forth like an essence, felt but unseizable, in the wide sunny landscape. **1885** MEREDITH *Diana* xiii, She swam above them in a cocoon of her spinning, sylphidine, unseizable.

†**un'seize**, *v.* *Obs.* [UN-[2] 3.]

1. *trans.* To detach from something held or that holds; *spec.* in hawking.

1575 TURBERV. *Faulconrie* 95 When she hath fedde, take it from hir and vnseaze hir. **1622** MABBE tr. *Aleman's Guzman d' Alf.* I. To Vulgar, Who is hee that can be so happy as to ..unseaze himselfe from thy griping talons? **1635** QUARLES *Embl.* I. xii. 1 Be thy lips skrew'd so fast To th' earth's full breast? For shame, for shame unseise thee. *Ibid.* 3 Unseise thy lips. **1728** CHAMBERS *Cycl.* s.v. *Falcon*, To which if she come well..and hastly seize it, let her cast two or three bits thereon. That done, unseize, take her off the Lure.

2. To let go, take one's hands off.

1663 TUKE *Adv. 5 Hours* I. 8 He, at the stroke, unseas'd me, and gave back.

un'seized, *ppl. a.* (UN-[1] 8.)

a **1400–50** *Alexander* 5334, I sall surely þe saue vnsesid of þe berbrens. **1681** DRYDEN *Abs. & Achit.* I. 258 If unseiz'd, she glides away like wind; And leaves repenting Folly far behind. *a* **1700** EVELYN *Diary* 6 Sept. 1666, Watching at all places contiguous to unseised houses. **1818** KEATS *Endym.* II. 464 He was..content to see An unseiz'd heaven dying at his feet. **1895** *Nat. Counc. Congregat. Ch.* (U.S.) 177 The unseized opportunities of this..mission field.

†**unsel**, *a.* and *sb.* *Sc.* and *north.* *Obs.* Also 6 vnsall, -sale, -sell, 7 ouncel. [var. of UNSELE *a.*]

1. *adj.* Unlucky, wretched; wicked.

c **1375** *Sc. Leg. Saints* xv. 40 Gais furth, I send ȝou, I ȝou tel, as lammys amang wolfis vnsel. **1500–20** DUNBAR *Poems* xiv. 79 Off Sathanis senȝie syne sic ane vnsall menȝie..was nevir hard nor sene. *a* **1583** MONTGOMERIE *Flyting* 87 (Tullib. MS.), Arpit angrie Ettercoip, and auld vnsell aip. *a* **1614** J. MELVILL *Diary* (Wodrow Soc.) 49, I haiff dreamed an unsell dream.

b. As *adv.* Wickedly, vilely.

a **1583** POLWART *Flyting w. Montgomerie* 622 (Tullib. MS.), He was ane fals schismatik, notorlie namit; Baith hurdome, & homeceid, vnsell he vsit.

2. *sb.* A vile or worthless person; a wretch.

kittie unsel (*Sc.*): see KITTY[1] 1.

155. LYNDESAY *Play* 2038 (Bann. MS.), Quhat sayis thow, cairle, art thow Gud Counsale? Swyth, pass the hence, vnhappy vnsale. *a* **1583** MONTGOMERIE *Flyting* 282 There ane elf on ane ape ane vnsell begat. **1677** NICOLSON in *Trans. Royal Soc. Lit.* IX. 321 Unsell, wretched fellow. **1691** RAY *N. Co. Words* (ed. 2) 150 *Unsel*, Nomen..opprobriosum. **1825** JAMIESON s.v., In Dumfries-shire, *Scoury unsell* is a contemptuous designation applied to a child, by one who is in bad humour. **1894** *Northumb. Gloss.* 757.

b. The Evil One. *rare.*

c **1669** GARBUTT *One Come from Dead* (1675) 27 He is right the Devils Child, the Ouncels Elfe. *Ibid.* 26.

†**un'selde**, *adv.* *Obs.* [OE. *unseldan* (*un-* UN-[1] 11 b + *seldan*: see SELD *adv.*), = Du. *onzelden*, G. *unselten*, ON. *úsjaldan*.] = next.

Only in phr. with *oft*: cf. ON. *oft úsjaldan*.

a **950** *Laws Edw. & Guthrum* Prol. in Thorpe *Ags. Laws* I. 166 Þa witan eac..oft & unseldan þæt seolfe ȝeniwodon. *c* **967** *Canons of Edgar* ibid. II. 278 Mislice men agyltað oft & unseldon þurh deofles scyfe. *c* **1320** *Sir Tristr.* 2313 Oft and vnselde Of triamour tok he pray.

un'seldom, *adv.* [UN-[1] 11 b. Cf. prec.] *not unseldom* (misused for), not rarely, not infrequently.

Du. *niet onzelden* is similarly used.

1658 W. BURTON *Itin. Anton.* 204 It is a thing not unseldome seen. **1686** PARR *Life of Usher* 83 Gaming..too often administred to Passion,..and not unseldom to Duelling. *a* **1836** MRS. SHERWOOD *Nun* ii, They not unseldom spent the afternoon under the cedar-trees. **1860** TRENCH *Deficiencies Eng. Dict.* 64 Johnson..quotes, not altogether unseldom.., Hacket's Life of Archbp. Williams. **1882** *Athenæum* 23 Sept. 401/2 A style which was generally diffuse, and not unseldom obscure.

†**un'sele**, *sb.* *Obs.* Forms: 1 unsæl, 2–3 un-, vnsel, 4–5 vnsell, -sele; 4 vncel(e, 5 vnceyll(e. [OE. *unsǽl* (*un-* UN-[1] 12 + *sǽl* SELE *sb.*) = ON. and Icel. *úsæla, ósæla* unhappiness.]

1. Unhappiness, misery; misfortune, ill luck.

a **1023** WULFSTAN *Hom.* (1883) 236 Þa deoflu..wæron on miclum unsælum, and þa englas wæron on swiðe micelre blisse. *c* **1205** LAY. 30541 Unsel him wes on mode. *a* **1250** *Owl & Night.* 1263 Ich wolde þer hi wel vnderstonde scholde þat sum vnsel heom is ihende. *c* **1275** *xi Pains Hell* 90 in *O.E. Misc.* 149 Snaken..dreyeþ heom in-to a wel þer heo þolyeþ al vn-sel. **1338** R. BRUNNE *Chron.* (1810) 278 Þe Scottis I telle for sottis, & wrecchis vnwar, Unsele dyntis to dele þam drouh to Dunbar. **13..** *Guy Warw.* (A.) 1267 Of an vnsele y may ȝou telle, & ȝe wil a stounde duelle. *a* **1400** *Hymns Virgin* (1867) 106 Þat þou..help to sauen hem from vncele, So þat heore soules beo not schent. *c* **1400** *Laud Troy Bk.* 5985 Ector thanne with mochel vnsele Graunted his askyng. *c* **1460** *Towneley Myst.* xii. 3 Here is mekyll vnceyll, and long has it last.

b. Unseemly matter. *rare*[−1].

a **1400** *Minor Poems fr. Vernon MS.* 503/377 Bi heore onswere þei wuste ful wel þat þei hedde spoken muchel vncel.

2. An improper time.

c **1200** *Trin. Coll. Hom.* 13 Ȝef man haueð to done mid his rihte spuse on unsele oðer an untime þan man faste sal.

†**un'sele**, *a.* *Obs.* [OE. *unsǽle* (UN-[1] 7), = ON. and Icel. *ú-, ósæll* (Sw. *osäll*, Da. *ussel*), unhappy, wretched, Goth. *unsēls* evil, wicked. Cf. SELE *sb.*] **a.** Unlucky, bad. **b.** Unfortunate, wretched.

c **1050** *Voc.* in Wr.-Wülcker 421 *Inprobus*, unsæle, ȝemah. *a* **1200** *Moral Ode* 199 Nere namon elles ded ne sec ne nan unsele. *c* **1275** LAY. 23868 Þe king was onseale þat he euere þoht wiþ Arthur to fihte. *c* **1300** *Prov. Hendyng* in *Rel. Ant.* I. 113 Holde ich no mon for vnsele Oþer whyle þah he fele Sum þyng þat him smerte. **13..** *Cursor M.* 6149 (Gött.), Þaim he did þair asking haue, For to reue þat folk vn-sele.

Hence †**un'sel(e)ly** *adv.* *Obs.*[−1]

c **1275** LAY. 7022 Suþþen was his sone king, þat onselliche lifuede.

unse'lect, *a.* (UN-[1] 7.)

1826 MISS MITFORD *Village* Ser. II. 256 A prodigious bundle of autographs, particularly unselect. **1867** P. FITZGERALD 75 *Brooke St.* II. xiii, Select, even in their unselect way. **1882** *Athenæum* 2 Sept. 299/1 The modern Jew as he lives and moves among the unselect.

unse'lecting, *ppl. a.* (UN-[1] 10.)

[**1828–32** WEBSTER.] **1895** *Daily News* 11 June 4/7 Realists try to look at life with the unselecting eyes of the camera.

un'self, *sb.* (UN-[1] 12.)

1822 COLERIDGE *Lett., Convers.*, etc. II. 116 There was neither self nor unself in the flash..of pleasurable sensation. **1893** J. PULSFORD *Loyalty to Christ* II. 367 Let us examine ..whether His spirit of unself, or the spirit of self and of the world, be the more in us.

un'self, *v.* (UN-[2] 6 b, 8.) Also **un'selfed** *ppl. a.*, **un'selfing** *vbl. sb.*

1654 WHITLOCK *Zootomia* 265 Canst thou afford lying, Dissembling,..and servile unselfing thy free born Minde, or Body? **1668** H. MORE *Div. Dial.* II. 28 God himself, who is that pure, free, and perfectly-unselfed Love. **1765** J. BROWN *Chr. Jrnl.* 286 O to be unearthed, unselfed, that I may be like him! **1806** SURR *Winter in Lond.* III. 121, I cannot unself or unsex myself sufficiently to write in the narrative form; it must be I—I—I, and all about me—me —me. **1856** FABER *Creator & Creature* (1886) 55 Holiness is an unselfing of ourselves. **1868** BROWNING *Ring & Bk.* VII. 707 The grotesque intrigue To make me and my friend unself ourselves. **1890** J. PULSFORD *Loyalty to Christ* I. 39 His unutterable sympathy..and His utterly unselfed character.

unself'changing *ppl. a.*, **-de'licious** *a.*, †**-'interessed** *ppl. a.*, **-'knowing** *ppl. a.*, **-like** *a.*, **-ness**, **-re'flecting**, **-'valuing** *ppl. adjs.*, **-'willedness**. (UN-[1] 7, 7 b, 8, 10, 12; cf. SELF 1 e, 1 f.)

1591 SYLVESTER *Du Bartas* I. ii. 212 The World's owne Matter is the waxen Lump, which, *un-self-changing, takes all kind of stamp. *Ibid.* iii. 1057 Such were not yerst Cincinnatus, Fabricius, Serranus, Curius, who *vn-self-delicious,..With ploughs triumphant plough'd the Roman lands. **1664** H. MORE *Exp. 7 Epist.* viii. 134 Thou art a lover of unity, *un-self-interessed, a foe to no body. **1685** —— *Paralip. Prophet.* l. 465 That full, free, and absolute unself-interessed Good. **1649** MILTON *Eikon.* ix. 78 He twitts them with his Acts of grace; proud, and *unself-knowing words in the mouth of any King. **1598** SYLVESTER *Du Bartas* II. ii. IV. *Columnes* 195 All Solids else (cast in the Aire) reflect *Un-self-like-forms: but in a Globe each tract seems still the same. **1886** G. MACDONALD *What's Mine's Mine* xx, He would have attracted attention anywhere, if only from his look of quiet *unselfness. **1668** H. MORE *Div. Dial.* II. 69 Like an *un-self-reflecting and an *un-self-valuing childe. **1684** —— *Answer* 242 The Wheels and living Creatures being..acted by the spirit, does not signifie an Earthly state in them, but..an *Unselfwilledness.

unself'conscious, *a.* (UN-[1] 7.)
1866 G. MACDONALD *Ann. Q. Neighb.* xxviii, Instances of quiet unselfconscious faith. **1884** RUSKIN *Fors Clav.* xcvi. 286 One who has in some signal..unself-conscious way done her duty. **1899** S. BROOKE *Eng. Lit.* 146 This poem.. belongs to the joyous, unself-conscious time.
So **unself'consciousness**.
1838 J. STERLING *Ess.*, etc. (1848) I. 199 One other great form of poetry..in which self-consciousness projects itself into external figures, and appears as unself-consciousness. **1894** LUCY H. M. SOULSBY *Home Rule* 32 It may be urged that theatricals teach unself-consciousness, but this form of unself-consciousness is worth very little.

unselfconsciously, *adv.* (UN-[1] 11.)
1903- [Listed in *N.E.D.* (1926) as 'in recent use'.] **1921** H. CRANE *Let.* 26 Nov. (1952) 72, I..carry these encumbrances ..deftly and un-selfconsciously. **1958** P. WINCH *Idea of Social Sci.* IV. iv. 102 Science..applies its criteria unselfconsciously. **1977** P. STREVENS *New Orientations Teaching of Eng.* ii. 17 Young children (say, age 6–13)..tend to learn easily and unselfconsciously.

un'selfish, *a.* (UN-[1] 7. Cf. Da. *uselvisk*, Sw. *osjälfvisk*.)
1698 J. NORRIS *Pract. Disc.* IV. 289 That Noble and Generous, disinteressed and unselvish Kind of Love. **1714** H. GROVE *Spectator* No. 588 ¶2 Notwithstanding which, the Inclination is nevertheless unselfish. **1834** T. KEBLE in *Tracts for Times* No. 43. 14 St. Paul, that most heroic, and (if there were such a word,) that most *unselfish* of men. **1851** LONGF. *Gold. Leg.* Epil. 10 Rise up..And scatter with unselfish hands Thy freshness on the barren sands. **1880** McCARTHY *Own Times* xl. III. 224 One of the most unselfish men that ever lived.
Hence **un'selfishly** *adv.*, **un'selfishness**.
1812 COLERIDGE *Lit. Rem.* (1836) I. 351 The unselfishness of self-love in the hopes and fears of religion. **1850** LYNCH *Theoph. Trinal* v. 77 A most womanly unselfishness. **1862** SHIRLEY (J. Skelton) *Nugæ Crit.* v. 218 A cause, whose success demanded perfect union and unselfishness. *Ibid.* x. 435 Steady, sagacious, moderate, never unselfishly imprudent. **1863** 'OUIDA' *Held in Bondage* I. 185 None will ever love you more unselfishly than I.

un'selfished, *ppl. a.* [UN-[2] 8.] Deprived of selfish qualities; rendered unselfish.
1643 W. GREENHILL *Axe at Root* A iv, The Axe is at the root of our Tree, wee hope your spirits are all unselvished, that none are now unpublique.

†**un'selfly**, *adv.* (UN-[1] 11.)
1605 SYLVESTER *Du Bartas* II. iii. III. *Law* 253 All Beings Be not (or else un-selfly be) But, from my Being, all their Being gather.

un'sellable, *a.* [UN-[1] 7 b.] Lacking a buyer; that no one wants to buy.
1975 *Daily Tel.* 22 Oct. 16 The Wardle farm was derelict and regarded as unsellable before the family..bought it two years ago. **1981** *Times Lit. Suppl.* 18 Sept. 1061/1 New ways of getting the johns to spend their money on previously unsellable old tat.

un'selling, *ppl. a.* (UN-[1] 10; cf. SELLING *ppl. a.* 1.)
a **1704** T. BROWN *Dial. Dead* Wks. 1711 IV. 98 As a Bookseller hates an unselling Author. **1720** *Humourist* 124 As you may see in certain unselling Dialogues of the Art of Poetry.

†**un'selth**. *Obs.* [OE. *unsǽlþ* (*un-* UN-[1] 12; also *unȝesǽlþ*, see UN-[1] 3), = OHG. *unsâlida*, *unsâlda*, *unsâltha* (MHG. *unsælde*, MLG. *unsâlde*, etc.).] Unhappiness, infelicity, misery.
c **888** K. ÆLFRED *Boeth.* x, þæt is seo mæste unsælð on þys and weardan life. *c* **1000** *Ags. Ps.* (Thorpe) xiii. 7 Hie wilniað ealle mæȝne oþera manna unsælþa. *a* **1200** *Moral Ode* 374 Nis þer sorewe ne sor, ne neure nan vn-sealþe. *c* **1250** *Gen. & Ex.* 3026 Ðo wex vn-selðe on hem wel hard. *c* **1315** SHOREHAM I. 823 Na more ne greueþ hyt ihesus..þaȝ eny best deuoured hyt, Oþer eny oþer onselþe. *c* **1425** *Eng. Conq. Ireland* 50 Euery selth hath wnselth at þe end.

unsembly, obs. var. UNSEEMLY *a.*

†**un'seminared**, *ppl. a.* *Obs.*[−1] [UN-[2] 8.] Deprived of virility.
1606 SHAKS. *Ant. & Cl.* I. v. 11 Tis well for thee, That being vnseminar'd, thy freer thoughts May not flye forth of Egypt.

†**un'sene**, *a.* *Obs. rare.* [UN-[1] 7 + SENE *a.* Cf. OE. *unȝeséne* and ON. *úsýnn*.] Invisible; not obvious.
c **1200** *Trin. Coll. Hom.* 47 On ure helendes lichame wiðuten sene, þe holie saule wiðinne unsene. *c* **1250** *Gen. & Ex.* 2878 Ic..swanc and michel sorwe dreȝ; ȝet ist vnsene hu ic it bi-teȝ?

†**un'sensably**, *adv.* [UN-[1] 11.] = UNSENSIBLY *adv.* 1.
a **1395** HYLTON *Scala Perf.* II. xxiv. (MS. Bodl. 592), Not in bodili liknesse but vnsensabli bi preuie hid presence of his goostli myȝt.

†**un'sensate**, *a.* *Obs.*[−1] [UN-[1] 7, 5 b.] Insensate.
1561 EDEN *Arte Nauig.* Pref., Yf they be lyuely members and not wythered or otherwyse vnsensate by reason of dead fleshe.

unsen'sational, *a.* (UN-[1] 7.)
Also, in recent use, *unsensationalism*, *-ally* adv.
1854 GEO. ELIOT tr. *Feuerbach's Essence Christianity* xxii. 213 God sees..all objects of sense in an unsensational manner. **1865** *Pall Mall G.* 8 Aug. 11 The name of a French novel, quiet and unsensational. **1881** 'RITA' *My Lady Coquette* xxii, Altogether life is very drowsy and unsensational.

un'sense, *v.* [UN-[2] 6 b.] *trans.* To deprive of sense; *esp.* to render insensible.
1611 FLORIO, *Disensato*, sencelesse, vnsensed, out of reason. **1793** *Minstrel* I. 185, I was a little unsensed by my sudden souse into the stream. *a* **1809** T. PAINE *Farmer's Dog* Poems (1834) 163 And get such mischief by the hit As should unsense him of his wit. **1851** BORROW *Lavengro* I. 331 One blow given with the proper play of his athletic arm, will unsense a giant. **1895** *Educat. Rev.* Sept. 158 The mind has been unsensed or dematerialized.

un'sensed, *ppl. a.* (UN-[1] 8.)
1667 JER. TAYLOR *Dissuas. Popery* II. I. §2. 75 They tell you the Scripture is but a dead letter, Unsensed Characters, words without sense, or unsensed. **1675** R. FLEMING *Short Acc. Doctr. Rom. Ch.* 6 They have no..authentick record to prove their Religion, but what is a Mass of dead unsensed Characters. **1734** WATERLAND *Imp. Doct. Holy Trinity* i. 18 We do not mean unsensed Characters, or empty Sounds. **1876** MRS. WHITNEY *Sights & Ins.* vi, They were like apparitions shining out of the unsensed. **1897** F. THOMPSON *New Poems* 22 The incredible excess of unsensed sweet, And mystic wall of strange felicity.

†**unsensi'bility**. (UN-[1] 12, 5 b. Cf. next.)
1551 ROBINSON tr. *More's Utopia* II. (1895) 204 For to be wythowte greyffe, not hauinge health, that they call vnsensybylyte and not pleasure. *a* **1650** MAY *Satyr. Puppy* (1657) 13 A passionate Man is..nor Man nor Beast: for he wants the sence of the one, and in some kinde the vnsensibilitie of the other.

un'sensible, *a.* *Obs.* exc. *dial.* or as *nonce-wd.* [UN-[1] 7, 5 b.]
1. = INSENSIBLE *a.* 1.
c **1380** WYCLIF *Serm.* Sel. Wks. II. 55 It was bigynnyng of tyme unsensible to mannis witt. *Ibid.* 148 þei trowen to sensible wordis, and oþer signes þat men maken, but unsensible wordis of Goddis Sone..þei trowen litil or nouȝt. *c* **1400** *Apol. Loll.* 100 To a-wowe is, a resonable creature to obey him to his souereyn, to kep sum hard þing þat is sensible, or vns[ens]ible. **1534** MORE *Treat. Passion* Wks. 1335/2 Vnder anye of the twoo outwarde sensible Sacramentes..the whole inwarde vnsensyble Sacramente.. is..fullye conteyned. **1581** E. CAMPION in *Confer.* III. (1584) Q j b, That you say vnsensible, it is true, if you meane the spirituall grace, which is not subiect to sense. **1587** GOLDING *De Mornay* xv. 285 To extend reason from.. things sensible to things vnsensible,..from bodily to spirituall. **1656** M. CASAUBON *Enthus.* To Rdr., Neither do I think so meanly of any truth, that can be reduced to any reality, whether sensible or unsensible.
b. = INSENSIBLE *a.* 1 b.
1545 RAYNALD *Byrth Mankynde* Y vj, The blud the whiche daylye and hourely, by vnsensyble swettinge euaporatith. *a* **1586** SIDNEY *Arcadia* I. xiii, It being set upon such an unsensible rising of the ground, as you are come to a pretty height before almost you perceive that you ascend. **1614** BREREWOOD *Lang. & Relig.* 12 For which reason, the corruption of speech growing upon them, by little and little, the change hath been unsensible. **1633** PRYNNE *Histrio-m.* 957 No man becomes extreamely vitious on a sudden, but by unsensible gradations.
c. Imperceptible by reason of minuteness.
1551 RECORDE *Pathw. Knowl.* I. Def., A Poynt..is named of Geometricians that small and vnsensible shape, whiche hath in it no partes. **1571** DIGGES *Pantom.* I. xv. E ij, The angle..groweth so acute, and vnsensible, that great errour ensueth the least mistakyng. **1602** FULBECKE *Pandectes* 9 The present time is so small and unsensible, that it is almost of no continuance.
2. = INSENSIBLE *a.* 2.
1555 EDEN *Decades* (Arb.) 53 If the greefes of them bee to thee vnsensible by reason of thy..longe sickenes.
3. = INSENSIBLE *a.* 3 a.
c **1532** TINDALE *Answ. More* Wks. (1572) 279/1 [Christ] dyed not to purchase such honour vnto vnsensible thinges, that [etc.]. *c* **1555** HARPSFIELD *Divorce Hen. VIII* (Camden) 252 Unless he be as unsensible as a man that will put and hold his finger in the hot fire and say the fire burneth not. **1583** MELBANCKE *Philotimus* S ij, The two vnsensible pictures. **1611** COTGR., *Cal*, a thicke, and vnsensible skin, or brawnie hardnesse of skin. **1627** *Lisander & Cal.* I. 11 The secret places of Calista's affection, which were not marble, nor of any unsensible matter. **1677** W. HUBBARD *Narrative* Postscr. 10 The unsensible and hardhearted Monster answered, he liked it very well.
b. = INSENSIBLE *a.* 3 b, 3 c.
1568 TURNER *Herbal* III. 50 Rasis in his Simples writeth that the Methel maketh num or vnsensible. *a* **1616** BEAUM. & FL. *Wit without M.* II. iv, Your Land has lain long bedrid, and unsensible. **1632** J. HAYWARD tr. *Biondi's Eromena* 191 Her often swounding kept her alive by making her become unsensible of the sharpenesse of the paine which shee felt. **1669** WORLIDGE *Syst. Agric.* 160 When the doors are shut.. they [*sc.* bees] are dark, and unsensible of so small a heat. **1891** in G. L. Gower *Surrey Words* (1893) 44, I was unsensible for loss of blood.
4. = INSENSIBLE *a.* 4 a.
(*a*) **1610** HEYWOOD *Gold. Age* IV. i, Vnsensible of loue, or amorous pitty. **1621** G. SANDYS *Ovid's Met.* VIII. (1626) 167 They the time beguile with speech: Vnsensible of stay. **1692** SOUTH *Serm.* (1697) I. 498, I mean not, that he is unsensible of the good it self, but that..he is wholly unsensible..of the Benignity of him that does it. *a* **1804** in Miss Betham *Biog. Dict. Celebrated Women* 452 She thought herself..too unsensible of our Lord's love to her.
(*b*) **1663** GERBIER *Counsel* a ij, It would doubtlesse make me pass for uncensible, how your Majesty..inherited that same clemency. **1664** INGELO *Bentiv. & Ur.* v. 39 One not altogether unsensible that he hath over-charg'd his Vocation with burthensome Cares. **1719** W. WOOD *Surv. Trade* 24, I am not unsensible, how very disadvantagious it is for us [etc.]. **1735** J. PRICE *Stone-Br. Thames* 16, I am not unsensible that it may be suggested [etc.].
b. = INSENSIBLE *a.* 4 b.
1619 J. KING *Serm.* 2, I thinke there is none so unsensible that is not moved hereat. **1650** O. SEDGWICK *Christ the Life* 26 Dull and unsensible men; of such did one long since complain, That [etc.]. **1676** ETHEREDGE *Man of Mode* II. i, *Town.* Methinks you speak very feelingly, Brother. *Old Bell.* I am but Five and Fifty, Sister, you know, an Age not altogether unsensible! *a* **1699** J. KIRKTON *Hist. Ch. Scot.* (1817) 65 Many a sober man was tempted to exceed, lest he should be condemned as unnatural, disloyal, unsensible.
5. = INSENSIBLE *a.* 5.
1560 PILKINGTON *Expos. Aggeus* Dd ij, Lyke vnreasonable beastes and vnsensyble. **1565** STAPLETON *Fortr. Faith* 136* What is now more reuiled of vnsensible protestants then the shauen crowne of reuerent priesthood? *a* **1586** SIDNEY *Arcadia* I. iv, He found some of his aunswers..not unsensible. **1814** [MARY BRUNTON] *Discipline* xxii. 26 The poor lad was not so unsensible, but he knew to do his bidding. **1861** GEO. ELIOT *Silas M.* xiv, When the drink's out of 'em, they aren't unsensible.
6. Not showing good or sound sense.
a **1586** SIDNEY *Arcadia* III. xix, For nothing can be more unsensible, then to thinke what one doth, & to forget the end why it is done. **1858** BAGEHOT *Lit. Stud.* (1879) II. 154 The strongest *unsensible* feeling in Scott was perhaps his Jacobitism.

†**un'sensibleness**. *Obs.* [UN-[1] 12 and 5 b. Cf. prec.] Insensibility.
a **1568** COVERDALE *Bk. Death* xxxvii. (1579) 171 That is a very blockish vnsensiblenesse of wilde madde barbarous people. **1571** GOLDING *Calvin on Ps.* xxviii. 5 Through stubbornnesse [they] harden themselues vntoo vnsensiblenesse. **1603** FLORIO *Montaigne* II. xii, I commend not that vnsensiblenesse, which is neither possible nor to be desired. **1676** I. MATHER *K. Philip's War* (1862) 94 Our great unsensibleness of the Displeasure of the Lord, in suffering these abominations to be perpetuated. **1730** BAILEY (fol.), *Indolency*, unsensibleness of Pain or Grief.

†**un'sensibly**, *adv.* *Obs.* [UN-[1] 11, 5 b.]
1. = INSENSIBLY *adv.* 1.
1627 ABP. ABBOT in Rushw. *Hist. Coll.* (1659) I. 444 So being unsensibly hatched, it came flying into the World. **1679** C. NESSE *Antichrist* 213 It stole into the world..unsensibly, and at unawares.
b. Unknowingly, unconsciously.
1658 J. JONES *Ovid's Ibis* 127 Though unsensibly she shed bitter tears for her transgression.
2. = INSENSIBLY *adv.* 2.
1565 JEWEL *Reply Harding* 217 That after so many wordes ..ye shoulde be founde so nakedly, and so vnsensibly to deceiue the people. **1596** SPENSER *State Irel.* Wks. (Globe) 622/2 The later [statute]..is soe unsensibly contryved that it scarce carryeth any reason in it.

†**un'sensical**, *a.* *Obs.*[−1] [UN-[1] 7.] Nonsensical.
1692 S. JOHNSON *Argument* 18 His Unsensical Apothegm, 'No Bishop, no King'.

un'sensitive, *ppl. a.* (UN-[1] 7 and 5 b.)
Also, in recent use (1895–), *unsensitiveness*.
1610 HEALEY *St. Aug. Citie of God* 283 One [soul] liuing in all bodies vnsensitiue, onely hauing life. **1816** *Monthly Mag.* XLI. 209 But figures never affect the feelings; numerical calculations go on in an unsensitive part of the mind. **1838** MILL *Diss. & Disc.* (1859) I. 323 In a world which, for any but the unsensitive, is not a place of contentment. **1881** P. BROOKS *Candle of Lord* 273 Some knowledge which the life in its best health was too hard and unsensitive to take.

un'sensitized, *ppl. a.* (UN-[1] 8 a (*c*).)
1889 *Anthony's Photogr. Bull.* II. 53 An unsensitized piece ..will soon cause discoloration on any sensitized paper placed against it.

†**un'sensive**, *a.* *Obs.*[−1] [UN-[1] 7.] Not perceptible by the senses.
1616 J. LANE *Contn. Sqr.'s T.* x. 284 Feare bears it knowne, thoughe (ofte) no man knoes how, Yea ofte b' vnsensive meanes (as clerkes avowe).

un'sensual, *a.* (UN-[1] 7.)
1850 LYNCH *Theoph. Trinal* v. 76 Wisdom hath a pure unsensual love. **1866** *Sat. Rev.* 3 Mar. 255/2 It is true, that ..Plato dwells prominently on the anti-sensual, or at least on the unsensual, side of love.

un'sensualize, *v.* (UN-[2] 6 c.)
1792 W. ROBERTS *Looker-on* No. 29 (1794) I. 410 Love is so unsensualized and sublimed above passion, that it has forgotten its old retreats. **1796** COLERIDGE *Destiny of Nations* 80 For Fancy is the power That first unsensualises the dark mind, Giving it new delights. *a* **1849** H. COLERIDGE *Ess.* (1851) II. 147 Certain divines who thought to unsensualize mankind by making the body as disgusting as possible. **1889** *Spectator* 7 Sept., An almost Pharisaic observance of the rites and ceremonies which unsensualised them.

un'sensuous, *a.* (UN-[1] 7.)
1850 MRS. BROWNING *Sonn., H. S. Boyd* 12 Till Sensuous and Unsensuous seemed one thing, Viewed from one level. **1856** R. A. VAUGHAN *Mystics* I. 270 The higher calm of unsensuous, imageless contemplation.

un'sent, *ppl. a.* Also 8 *Sc.* unsenn. [UN-[1] 8 b and 8 c. Cf. ON. *úsent* (Da. *usendt*).]
1. Not sent for, unsummoned. (Cf. b.)
c **1530** *Crt. of Love* 174 Of your free will ye should have come unsent. **1717** RAMSAY *Elegy Lucky Wood* ii, Death, wha came unsenn To Lucky Wood.
b. With *for* expressed.
1501 *Plumpton Corr.* (Camden) 157 If I wold come up unsent for. **1598** DALLINGTON *Meth. Trav.* X 3 b, They take one of a suddaine, comming vnlooked for and vnsent for. *a* **1641** BP. MOUNTAGU *Acts & Mon.* (1642) 298 Herod, unsent for, went to visit him. **1673** WYCHERLEY *Gentl. Dancing-Master* v, We Fiddlers, Sir, often come unsent for. **1717** DE FOE *Mem. Ch. Scot.* II. 36 But Mr. Andrew Melvin

..went unsent for. **1753** Richardson *Grandison* (1781) IV. xiv. 104 That no third person, unsent for, can be welcome.

2. Not sent or dispatched.

In recent use esp. of letters or telegrams.

c **1550** Crowley *Inform. & Petit.* iv b, The same Spirite.. wytnesseth wyth my conscience that I renne not vnsent. *c* **1586** Sidney *Arcadia* I. vi, He armed himselfe, and those few of his servants he had left unsent. **1608** Dod & Cleaver *Expos. Prov. xi–xii.* 122 That we goe not unsent. **1647** Jer. Taylor *Lib. Proph.* vi. 124 More able men may be unsent then sent. **1841** *Fraser's Mag.* Jan. 111/2 Ye came na here unsent, and ye maun perform your errand. **1855** Kingsley *Westw. Ho!* xxvii, Her strange affection for the English was not unsent by Heaven.

b. With advs. or preps.

1549 Paget in Froude *Hist. Eng.* (1860) V. 182 Send for all the council that be remaining unsent abroad. **1606** Bp. Hall *Heaven upon Earth* xiii. Wks. (1625) 83 Thy heauenly Physician,..vnsent to, sends thee..a soueraigne remedie. **1656** in Picton *L'pool Munic. Rec.* (1883) I. 176 Whylst they stay at home unsent away.

un'sentenced, *ppl. a.* (un-^{1} 8.)

1526 *Customs of Pale* in *Archæol.* (1893) LIII. 373 The king's iudicate officers..shall..suffer no accion to departe unsentenced before them. **1612** *Two Noble K.* v. i. 163, I could doombe neither; that which perish'd should Goe too't unsentenc'd. **1661** Heylin *Hist. Ref.* Q. Mary (1670) 6 The King..privately marryeth her within few days after his return, the divorce being yet unsentenced betwixt him and the Queen. **1822** Beddoes *Brides' Trag.* iv. ii, Some vengeance will fall on us in the night If he remain unsentenced. **1862** Shirley (J. Skelton) *Nugæ Crit.* 140 To leave them rather unsentenced and in hope to the mercy.. which alone can fully extenuate..their guilt. **1896** *Harper's Mag.* April 672/2 The secular judge..forgot his duty, and Joan went to her death unsentenced.

unsen'tentious, *a.*

[**1775** Ash.] **1846** Worcester (citing *Qu. Rev.*).

un'sentient, *ppl. a.* (un-^{1} 7 and 5 b.)

1768–74 Tucker *Lt. Nat.* (1834) I. 315 We may admit a sentient composed of unsentient parts. *Ibid.* 583 An eternal First Cause, whether intelligent or unsentient. **1835** J. Young *Lect. Intell. Philos.* xlviii. 485 There could be no sensation in an unsentient being. **1864** Bowen *Logic* xiii. 422 Only in the sentient mind, and not in the unsentient matter of the body.

unsenti'mental, *a.* (un-^{1} 7.)

1752 H. Walpole *Let.* 23 June (1974) XXXVII. 340 He ..was even so unsentimental as to talk, of desiring to make her happy. **1810** Scott in *Lockhart* (1839) III. 228 The despair..gave me a most unsentimental horror for sentimental letters. **1853** C. Bronte *Villette* xxi, Never man had a more unsentimental mother than mine. **1898** Haddon *Stud. Man* xiv. 409 An unsentimental survival of this pretty custom.

Hence **unsentimen'tality; -'mentalize** *v.*; **-'mentally** *adv.*

1824 Hook *Sayings & Doings* III. 168 Gaieties.. calculated..to enliven and unsentimentalize the mind. *Ibid.* Ser. ii. I. 28 The impropriety and unsentimentality of her behaviour. *Ibid.* xiv. III. 300 She was..most unsentimentally employed in swallowing a very hearty supper. **1837** Lewis *Lett.* (1870) 84 For the sake of.. unsentimentalizing the cause of the Catholic clergy. **1847** L. Hunt *Men, Women, & B.* II. ii. 25 The unsentimentalizing effects of the gallantry of the court of Charles II.

un'sentinelled, *ppl. a.* (un-^{1} 8.)

1817 *Edin. Rev.* XXVIII. 87 The old castle..was ungarrisoned and unsentinelled. **1859** *All Year Round* No. 36. 219 A huge gateway, not unsentinelled.

†**un'separable,** *a. Obs.* (un-^{1} 7 b and 5 b.)

1398 Trevisa *Barth. de P.R.* xvi. v. (Bodl. MS.), þe onynge is vnseperable so þat þei mowe not afterward be parted atwynne. **1532** More *Confut. Tindale* Wks. 495/1 Was himself..companion to saynt Poule, & that so continuall and so vnseparable, yt..he neuer departed from him? **1561** T. Hoby tr. *Castiglione's Courtyer* iv. Xxiij b, This is the beawtye vnseperable from the high bountye. **1587** Golding *De Mornay* v. 67 Fire..hath in it both heate and brightnesse vnseparable. **1645** Milton *Divorce* (ed. 3) i. i. 7 The first institution will be objected to have ordain'd marriage unseperable. **1697** Jeremy Collier *Ess. Mor. Subj.* i. 5 Self-love..is an unseparable Passion of humane nature. **1737** *Gentl. Mag.* VII. 14/2 Placed between two Words joyned together in unseparable Concord.

Hence **un'separableness.**

1587 Fenner *Def. Ministers* 116 Hee maketh the case of both alike in regarde of the propertie and vnseparablenes of the bande.

†**un'separably,** *adv. Obs.* (un-^{1} 11 and 5 b.)

1532 More *Confut. Tindale* Wks. 514/2 And with them the godhead vnseperably ioyned. **1586** W. Webbe *Eng. Poetrie* (Arb.) 80 Thys verse is alwayes vnseperably adioyned vnto the Hexameter. **1622** Callis *Stat. Sewers* (1647) 14 A pretty difference, where the act to be done is unseparably tied to ones person, and where not. **1698** S. Clarke *Script. Justif.* iv. 18 That Pardon is unseparably join'd with Justification.

†**un'separate,** *ppl. a. Obs.* (un-^{1} 8 b, 5 b; cf. next.) Hence †**un'separateness.** *Obs.*$^{-1}$

1553 *Short Catech.* in *Liturgies*, etc. (Parker Soc.) 513 True faith and works *unseparate. **1563** Foxe *A. & M.* 540 As heat followeth euer with the fire vnseparate there from. **1591** Jas. I *Lepanto, Chorus Angel.* 11 Our onlie one vnseparate, And yet in persons three. **1668** H. More *Div. Dial.* I. 121 Then Rest and Unseparateness of parts are all one,..and *Unseparateness and Union all one.

un'separated, *ppl. a.* (un-^{1} 8.)

1545 Coverdale *Def. Certain Chr. Man* E iiij b, Therfore will we discerne these thre thinges,..but so that they remayne vnseparated. **1577** tr. *Bullinger's Decades* iii. vi. 373/1 He being one and the same Christ vnseperated. **1620** Quarles *Medit.* i, Three speciall Attributes of God.., all Vnseparated From Gods pure Essence. *a* **1671** Ld. Fairfax *Mem.* (1699) 99 The two Houses of Parliament.., so great an Authority which was then unseparated from the Royal interest. **1725** Pope *Odyss.* x. 585 To whom Persephone, entire and whole, Gave to retain th' unseparated soul. **1860** Farrar *Orig. Lang.* ii. 44 The field and the snow were unseparated. **1893** Tuckey *Amphioxus* 104 The unseparated mesoblast fold.

†**un'separately,** *adv. Obs. rare.* [un-^{1} 11, 5 b.] Inseparably.

1580 Hollyband *Treas. Fr. Tong, Indissolublement*, vnseparately. **1593** Nashe *Christ's T.* A ij, She thought the Lord vnseparately tyde to his Temple.

un'septate, *a. Bot.* (un-^{1} 7.)

1900 Jackson *Gloss. Bot. Terms* 283 *Unseptate*,..applied to a plant which has not partitioning divisions.

un'septated, *a. Bot.* (un-^{1} 8 a(*b*).)

1899 J. R. Green *Soluble Ferments* xx. 325 A fungus which developes a much-branched unseptated mycelium.

un'sepulchre, *v.* (un-^{2} 5.)

1856 in *Oxford Ess.* 217 As his ploughshare unsepulchred the 'empty helmets and the mighty bones' of the buried foemen.

un'sepulchred, *ppl. a.* (un-^{1} 8.)

c **1611** Chapman *Iliad* xxii. 306 Dead, vndeplor'd, Vnsepulcherd; he lies at fleete. **1624** Quarles *Sion's Elegies* ii. 21 Unsepulchred my murthred people lye. **1795** Southey *Joan of Arc* ix. 42 For hills of human slain, unsepulchred, Steam pestilence. **1816** Byron *Ch. Har.* iii. lxiii, The Stygian coast Unsepulchred they roam'd, and shriek'd each wandering ghost. **1862** Grattan *Beaten Paths* I. 142 To discover the unsepulchred, uncoffined, and uncereclothed tailor, standing stiff against the chapel wall.

un'sepultured, *ppl. a.* (un-^{1} 8.)

[**1847** Webster.] **1862** R. H. Patterson *Ess. Hist. & Art* 269 Some unsepultured one, who had departed to join the troop of shivering ghosts. **1897** Gomme *C. Macfarlane's Camp of Refuge* Introd. p. lxv, The cause that so many men were slaughtered and lay unsepultured.

†**unse'quester,** *v. Obs.* (un-^{2} 3.)

1664 Kath. Philips *Poems* 146 By a flame from thy blest Genius lent..Unsequester our Fancies, and create A Worth that may upon thy Glories wait.

unse'questered, *ppl. a.* (un-^{1} 8.)

1654 Whitlock *Zootomia* 149 Which if impartially compared,..our Librarys might be repreived, and our Colledges unsequestred. **1655** Fuller *Ch. Hist.* xi. iii. §6 His unsequestred Spirit so supported him, that [etc.].

unse'rene, *a.* (un-^{1} 7.)

1664 Ingelo *Bentiv. & Ur.* v. 124 How unserene are all the Joyes..upon Earth! **1829** Lamb in *The Gem* 26 The sad orbs..blinded through unserene drops for her dead lord.

un'serious, *a.* (un-^{1} 7.)

1655 Earl Orrery *Parthen.* ii. v. 493 To speake any thing unserious. **1673** Flavel *Saint Indeed* 199 Frothy, vain and unserious persons. **1755** Wesley *Wks.* (1872) II. 326 Any one who behaved in a light or unserious manner. **1860** Hawthorne *Fr. & It. Note-bks.* (1871) II. 357 A plaything, a trifle, an unserious affair.

Hence **un'seriousness.**

1680 H. Dodwell *Two Lett.* (1691) To Rdr. §9 The lives and unseriousness of some of our conformable Clergy. **1973** I. Robinson *Survival of English* ii. 62, I am not discussing in this book the gross popular examples of breakdown or coarsening..nor shall I more than mention the increasing unseriousness of the denominational press. **1978** *Detroit Free Press* 5 Mar. B 9/1 Aliette works so hard she brooks no unseriousness.

un'serrated, *ppl. a.* (un-^{1} 8.)

1840 *Cuvier's Anim. Kingd.* 79 The edge of the long inferior incisors is unserrated.

un'served, *ppl. a.* [un-^{1} 8.]

1. Not served or furnished with something; not attended to.

c **1350** *Leg. Rood* (1871) 85 Sen sekenes es sent to þe þir men sall noght vnserued be, þai sall haue nayles or þai ga. **1433** *Rolls of Parlt.* IV. 439/1 Yf I shuld paye hem, youre Household, Chambre and Warderope..shuld be unservid and unpaide. **1542** Udall *Erasm. Apoph.* 302 Onely Phocion was remainyng unserved by reason that the poison had been all consumed by the others. *a* **1585** Montgomerie *Cherry & Slae* 1083 Who came uncald, unserv'd shuld sit. *a* **1600** Deloney *Jack of Newberie* iv, Well, looke there be not one hog vnserued. **1624** *Essex his Ghost* 16 His people I hope will turne your golden..Coates into Coates of Male,.. rather then your Soueraigne..shall bee vnserued. **1786** R. Heathcote *Sylva* (1788) 256 His boy therefore sent away unserved a customer. **1804** R. Anderson *Cumbld. Ball.* 79 The witch weyfe begg'd in our back seyde, But went unsarra'd away. **1832** Ht. Martineau *Each & All* iii. 33 Conscience awakes..to the cry of unserved humanity. **1899** *Daily News* 3 Nov. 7/6 Several of their unserved guns were shelled vigorously.

b. *spec.* Not attended to by a priest or incumbent. (See serve *v.* 14.)

The app. early instance in Wyclif's *De Ecclesia* is prob. an error for 'unlerned', the reading of MS. Bodl. 788.

1562 in Strype *Ann. Ref.* (1709) I. xxxi. 312 So that the people be not unserved or defrauded of a reasonable minister. **1587** Holinshed *Chron.* (ed. 2) III. 1142/1 Where through died manie..priests, so that a great number of parishes were vnserued. **1643** Baker *Chron., Q. Mary* 106 This yeer..was great mortality, and specially of Priests, so as many Churches were unserved. **1765** Blackstone *Comm.* I. 466 It permits an infant to present a clerk..rather than.. suffer the church to be unserved till he comes of age.

2. Not worshipped, regarded, or observed.

1387 Trevisa *Higden* (Rolls) II. 85 þese feyned goddes.. beeþ i-serued in Chestre... þan is Pluto not vnserued, god of helle. **1390** Gower *Conf.* I. 355 The cherche is brent, the priest is slain,..The lawe is lore and god unserved. *c* **1450** *Mirk's Festial* 267 Mony seyntys-dayes we leuen yn þe ȝere vnseruet; for þay ben so many þat we may not serue hom all. **1532** More *Confut. Tindale* Wks. 495/2 Nor saint Paule.. meaneth not yet they shall leaue the sacramentes vnserued which God hath taught.

3. *Law.* **a.** Of writs, summonses, etc.: Not served upon a person.

1465 *Paston Lett.* II. 201 The shyrf sayd playnly that he ..derst not serve it [*sc.* a writ],..and so it ys yet unservyd. **1476** *Acta Auditorum* (1839) 49/2 þe persons of þe inqueste allegeit before þe lordis þat þe said breve wes vnseruit. **1908** *Daily Chron.* 10 Jan. 3/5 The constabulary were withdrawn, and the processes remained unserved.

†**b.** *Sc.* Not returned as heir. *Obs.*

1490 *Acta Dom. Conc.* (1839) 125/2 Patrik and William.. sall nocht fortify þe partij þat beis one seruit be that inquest.

4. Not served up.

1871 Ruskin *Fors Clav.* iii, The waiter then and there packed his knapsack and departed,..leaving my dinner unserved.

5. With *for*: For which service has not been done.

1555 *Inv. Ch. Goods* (Surtees) 157, xij li bequeithed..to the finding of a prieste there for iij yeares.., whereof remayned unserved for at the tyme.., xiijs. iiijd.

†**un'serviable,** *a. Obs.*$^{-1}$ [un-^{1} 7 b.] Unserviceable.

1544 Betham *Precepts War* i. xcii. E vj b, They [*sc.* gunners] be vnseruyable, and can do no good.

†**un'service.** *Obs.* (un-^{1} 4 b, 12.)

1611 Florio, *Disseruitu*, vnseruice, disseruice. **1624** Massinger *Parl. Love* i. v, Where you tax us for unservice, lady, I never knew a soldier yet that could Arrive into your favour.

un'serviceable, *a.* [un-^{1} 7 b and 5 b.]

1. Of things: Not capable of being employed for their proper purpose.

1535 *Wardr. Kath. Arragon* 33 in *Camden Misc.* III, The thurde [chair] is broken and unservesable. **1590** Spenser *F.Q.* i. xi. 25 The beast..his late wounded wing vnseruiceable found. **1600** in *St. Papers, Dom.* (1869) 437 The others [= signets] having become unserviceable from long use. **1663** Boyle *Usef. Exp. Nat. Philos.* ii. App. 328 Besides a not despicable quantity of terrestrial and unserviceable matter. **1690** Locke *Hum. Und.* iii. iii. §17 The supposition..is so..unserviceable to any part of our knowledge. **1713** Berkeley *Guard.* No. 35, His intellectuals, I observed, were grown unserviceable by too little use. **1737** tr. *Le Comte's Mem. & Remarks China* Pref., They might not be unserviceable to those who might..take up such a design. **1801** *Farmer's Mag.* Aug. 339 The horse I hire.. may be in any degree serviceable or unserviceable. **1830** H. N. Coleridge *Grk. Poets* 1 A perusal of these Introductions may not be unserviceable to many well educated readers. **1857** Dickens *Dorrit* i. xxxii, What with her flapping cap, and..her unserviceable eye.

b. *spec.* Of ships, guns, etc.

1610 Holland *Camden's Brit.* 35 The ships..so shaken with the tempest, that they became altogether unserviceable. **1618** in *Essex Rev.* (1908) XVII. 102 The moderne use doth altogether exclude the caliver as unservicable. **1707** *Lond. Gaz.* No. 4362/2, 10 Ships were destroyed.., and several others rendred wholly unserviceable. **1748** *Anson's Voy.* ii. iv. 165 Three four pounders, which were altogether unserviceable. **1811** *Regul. & Orders Army* 91 The disposal of Unserviceable Arms. **1865** Cameron *Malayan India* 246 It is not that the forts are ungarrisoned,..but that they are unserviceable. **1876** Voyle & Stevenson *Milit. Dict.* 446/2 *Unserviceable*, the term is applied..to all stores which are no longer of use, being either obsolete or worn out.

2. Of persons: Unable to be of service; not rendering service or help; useless.

1598 Hakluyt *Voy.* I. 240 You haue too much liuing, and are vnseruiceable to your prince, lesse will serue you. **1614** W. B. *Philosophers Banquet* (ed. 2) 121 One that would be vnseruiceable to him, and vnprofitable to the Commonwealth. **1655** *Nicholas Papers* (Camden) II. 217, I did long since tell you that poore man would be made onseruiceable to you. **1856** Kane *Arct. Expl.* II. i. 13 Our sick are about the same;..McGary and Riley unserviceable. **1865** Dickens *Mut. Fr.* iii. ii, I am an unserviceable friend of hers.

b. *spec.* Not capable of rendering military (or naval) service.

1596 Spenser *State Irel.* Wks. (Globe) 653/2 The rebells ..will turne away all theyr rascall people, whom they thinke unserviceable. **1601** Shaks. *All's Well* iv. iii. 152 Fiue or sixe thousand, but very weake and vnseruiceable: the troopes are all scattered. **1681** Luttrell *Brief Rel.* (1857) I. 151 Poor soldiers rendred unserviceable by age, wounds, &c. **1786** Burke *Art. agst. W. Hastings* Wks. 1842 II. 191 The country troops..would be ill-disciplined and unserviceable, if not worse. **1834** Marryat *P. Simple* I. 124 Some of them were retained, but most of them sent on shore as unserviceable. **1881** Jowett *Thucyd.* I. 146 The Plataeans had already conveyed to Athens their wives,..with the rest of their unserviceable population.

transf. **1867** Smyth *Sailor's Word-bk.* 707 *Unserviceable ticket*; this is made out in the same manner, and requires the same notations, as a sick-ticket.

3. Marked by disinclination to be of service.

1614 Raleigh *Hist. World* v. vi. 657 Such men of note.. as had any way discouered an vnseruiceable disposition towards the Romans.

4. Prejudicial, disadvantageous.

1698 Norris *Pract. Disc.* IV. 386 To reform his Temper, which I'm afraid is more unserviceable to Religion than any Hypothesis of mine can be.

Hence **unservicea'bility.**

1884 *Cyclists' Tour. Cl. Gaz.* Nov. 335/1 The unserviceability of the new substitute.

un'serviceableness. (UN-[1] 12; cf. prec.)
1611 COTGR., *Inutilité,*..vnseruiceablenesse. 1640 SANDERSON *Serm.* (1681) II. 173 The unserviceableness of any thing to edification. 1683 PEPYS *Diary at Tangier* in *Life, etc.* (1841) I. 452 The unserviceableness of the Mole by reason of those winds. *a* 1832 BENTHAM *Draught of Code* Wks. 1843 IV. 399 How many bad and unserviceable ones have, by this very unserviceableness, become popular! 1864 MISS YONGE *Trial* II. 20 The unserviceableness of his maimed arm.

un'serviceably, *adv.* (UN-[1] 11.)
1611 COTGR., *Inutilement,*..vnseruiceably. 1661 BEVERIDGE *Priv. Th.* (1709) 156 What is the reason, I have hitherto liv'd so unserviceably to God? 1695 WOODWARD *Nat. Hist. Earth* I. 48 It..does not enlarge the Dimensions of the Globe, or..lye idly and unserviceably there.

un'servicelike, *a.* (UN-[1] 7 c.)
1614 ANDREWES *Serm. on Easter Day* 39 They see how vnseruicelike our seruice is.

un'servile, *a.* (UN-[1] 7.)
1701 COLLIER *M. Aurel.* IV. xlix. 61 Does the present Accident hinder your being Honest..and Unservile? 1773 MRS. GRANT *Lett. fr. Mount.* (1807) I. ii. 19 We are charmed with..unservile courtesy in the lower class. 1847 CARLYLE in Froude *Life in Lond.* (1884) I. 409 Reporters to the daily papers, whose industry is the humblest of all real or unservile kinds in literature. 1866 ELIZA METEYARD *Wedgwood* II. 273 Wedgwood's exquisite yet unservile copies of antique art.

un'set, *v.* [UN-[2] 3, 7. Cf. OE. *unsettan* (once), to take down.]
1. *trans.* To put out of place or position; to undo the setting of.
1602 MARSTON *Ant. & Mel.* III. Wks. 1856 I. 37 O, you spoyle my ruffe, unset my haire. 1611 COTGR., *Desplanter,*.. to vnplant, vnset, remoue. 1761 GRAY *Lett.* (1900) II. 204 The man was sent for: he unset it; it was a paste not worth 40 shillings. 1775 MRS. DELANY in *Life & Corr.* Ser. II. (1862) II. 105 There is some hazard in unsetting enamel for fear of chipping the edges. 1836 MARRYAT *Midsh. Easy* xxxii, How could he put the young men to fresh tortures by removing splints and unsetting limbs? 1884 *Law Times* 1 Nov. 8/1 On the morning in question Dawson had unset the gun.
2. *intr.* To get out of place or position.
1703 THORESBY *Let. to Ray, Spelk,* a wooden splinter tied on, to keep a broken bone from bending or unsetting again.

un'set, *ppl. a.* [UN-[1] 8 b, 8 c. Cf. Du. *ongezet* in sense 1.]
†**1.** Of time or place: Not previously appointed or arranged. *Obs.*
Chiefly in phr. *at unset steven*: see STEVEN *sb.*[2] 2.
c 1386 [see STEVEN *sb.*[2] 2]. 1430–40 LYDG. *Bochas* II. xxi. (1494) h iiij/1 At the vnset houre their falsnesse he wyll quyte. 1476 *Paston Lett.* III. 162 The Duke toke grete corage to goo..to conquer them, butt the[y] berded hym att an onsett place. 1543–*a* 1600 [see STEVEN *sb.*[2] 2]. *a* 1600 MONTGOMERIE *Misc. Poems* v. 47 For man may meit at unset stevin, Thoght montanis nevir meitis.
†**b.** Of events: Not predetermined; unfixed, uncertain. *Obs.*
1550 BALDWIN *Mor. Philos.* P vi, But yf that the chaunce of thynges be vnset, It is folly to feare that we knowe we maye let. 1559 *Mirr. Mag., O. Glendour* xxvii, Of thinges to cum the haps be so vnset That none but fooles may warrant of them make.
†**2.** Not seated at table. *Obs.*[-1]
c 1475 *Rauf Coilȝear* 148 'Gang begin the buird,' said the Coilȝear. 'That war vnsemand, forsuith, and thy self vnset.'
3. Not assigned or allocated (*to* one); unlet.
1480 *Acta Dom. Conc.* (1839) 70/2 Land..haldin of our souuerain lorde and fre vnset for termes or for male. 1523 *Lincoln Wills* (L. Rec. Soc.) V. 120, I will that..all myne inward stuf that was myne owne unset to my wyf remayne to..my daughters. 1580–1 *Reg. Privy Council Scot.* III. 358 To warrand the same unsett, sauld, assignit, or disponit to utheris. 1736 in Picton *L'pool Munic. Rec.* (1886) II. 165 There are some few back seats yet unsett. 1825–9 MRS. SHERWOOD *Lady of Manor* I. viii. 334 During the absence of Lord T——, the family-mansion had remained untenanted, the houses of servants and dependents unset.
4. With advs. Not set *down, forth, out, up,* etc.
c 1445 PECOCK *Donet* 138 þese ij..forbodis of avoutrye.., whi ben not þei stillid and vnsett forþ expressely? 1530 PALSGR. Introd. p. v, I have..assayde..that there shulde fewe wordes..worde for worde be unsetforthe. 1547 *Act 1 Edw. VI,* c. 6 §1 The same poore persons..be now unoccupied and unset aworke. 1594 HOOKER *Eccl. Pol.* III. xi. §8 They vrge that God left nothing in his word vndescribed,..nothing vnset-downe. 1629 HOBBES *Thucyd.* 75 The Athenians..recriminated the Megareans, for hauing tilled holy ground, and vnset-out with bounds. 1639 *Knaresb. Wills* (Surtees) II. 168 One new stand bed unsett upp.
5. †**a.** *unset leek,* a (young) leek not transplanted. *Obs.*
1530 PALSGR. 249/2 Onsetleke, *porret.* 1563 HYLL *Art Garden.* (1593) 128 If you desire only to haue vnset Leekes. 1601 HOLLAND *Pliny* II. 424 Ashes for to be drunke with the juice of unset leeks in cold water. 1611 COTGR., *Porrette,* Maidens Leeke, bladed Leeke, vnset Leeke.
b. Not planted.
1573 TUSSER *Husb.* (1878) 75 Set..yoong bay and his berie. Or set their stone, vnset leaue out none. 1577 HARRISON *England* III. viii. (1878) II. 57 Notwithstanding that they haue remained there vnset by the space of fortie dais and more: yet some [saffron heads]..haue brought foorth two or three floures a peece. 1597 GERARDE *Herbal* I. i. 2 Common Medow grasse groweth of it selfe, vnset or vnsowen, euery where. 1653 BLITHE *Eng. Improver Impr.* 169 Shouldst thou be occasioned..to keep thy sets longer unset, be thou sure thou get their Roots into the ground.
c. Not furnished with plants.
c 1600 SHAKS. *Sonn.* xvi, Many maiden gardens yet vnset, With vertuous wish would beare your liuing flowers.
6. Not placed in a setting; unmounted.
1561 T. HOBY tr. *Castiglione's Courtyer* II. R i b, A iewell that vnsett seemeth faire. *c* 1592 BACON *Conf. Pleasure* (1870) 15 If these rich peeces be so faire vnsett, what are they sett? 1684 *Lond. Gaz.* No. 1906/4 An Emerald unset,..having a narrow Bizel. 1702 *Ibid.* No. 3811/4 Lost.., a large Diamond-drop,..unset. 1884 *West. Daily Press* 20 June 7/5 Necklets of unset amethysts,..and other stones. 1891 *Science-Gossip* XXVII. 36/1 Lack of uniformity in unset specimens.
7. Not composed or arranged.
1631 BRATHWAIT *Whimzies, Traveller* 93 Not an irregular haire about him, nor an unset looke to attend him, nor an uncomposed cringe to accoutre him. 1821 LAMB *Elia* I. *Ears,* Those unconnected, unset sounds are nothing to the measured malice of music.
8. Not surgically set.
a 1661 FULLER *Worthies, General* I. (1662) 61 An unset bone is better then a bone..ill set.
9. Of the sun: Not gone beneath the horizon.
1860 W. W. READE *Liberty Hall* I. ix. 158 Though very pretty she was only a moon with the sun unset, for [etc.].

†**un'sete,** *a. Obs.* Also **unseete.** [UN-[1] 7. Cf. SETE *a.* and UNSETY *a.*]
1. Unbecoming, improper; bad.
a 1310 in Wright *Lyric P.* viii. 31 For-thi on molde y waxe mot, that y sawes have seid un-sete. *Ibid.* xv. 49 Gabbes, les, ant luthere lore, sunnes bueth un-sete. *c* 1325 *Body & Soul* in *Map's Poems* (Camden) 342 A! thou foule flesch, unseete, Ful of falsnesse.
2. Unpleasant; painful.
a 1310 in Wright *Lyric P.* iv. 23 That i telle a povre play, that furst is feir ant seththe un-sete. *c* 1320 *Sir Tristr.* 1238 His bon brast vnder skinne, His sorwe was vnsete.
3. Unwholesome. (Cf. UNSETY *a.*)
13.. in *Archiv Stud. neu. Spr.* LXXXI. 319 þe watures bitter and vnseete were ymad boþe gode and swete. 1387 TREVISA *Higden* IV. 11 His frendes trowede þat unsete mete þþat he hadde i-ete at soper was cause of his siknesse.
4. Of persons: Ill-disposed; dissatisfied or discontented.
a 1310 in Wright *Lyric P.* xii. 43 This mon that Matheu ȝef A peny that wes so bref; this frely folk unsete, ȝet he ȝyrnden more.

unsett, var. of UMSET *v. Obs.*

un'setting, *ppl. a.* [UN-[1] 10.]
†**1.** Unbecoming, unfitting. *Obs.*
1567 DRANT *Horace, Ep.* B ij, I will tell them..what doth becom, and what unsetting is. *a* 1598 ROLLOCK *1 Thess.* (1606) 183 Any thing that is vnsetting, or vnseemlie to this Christian calling.
2. Not going beneath the horizon.
1607 *Merry Devil Edmonton* III. ii. 101 Thou bright vnsetting star..! 1819 CRABBE *T. of Hall* xix. 543 Some spoke of wonders they before had seen, When on their travels..: How they beheld for months th' unsetting sun. 1844 LOWELL *Prometheus* 230, I Shall be a power and a memory,..a light Unsetting as the pole-star. 1869 MCLAREN *Serm.* Ser. II. viii. 132 The full light of the unsetting Sun.
fig. 1838 MRS. BROWNING *An Island* xxvii, The undim Unsetting Godlight.

un'settle, *v.* [UN-[2] 3 and 7.]
1. *trans.* To undo from a fixed position; to unfix, unfasten, loosen.
1598 FLORIO, *Discasciare,*..to make loose the teeth, to dismount artillerie, to vnsettle anything. [1755 JOHNSON, *To Unsettle,* v.a., to move from a place.] 1818 KEATS *Endymion* IV. 414 He..strives in vain to unsettle and wield A Jovian thunderbolt.
2. To force out of a settled condition; to deprive of fixity or quiet:
a. a state of things, institutions, etc.
1651 HOBBES *Leviath.* II. xxvii. 154 Such as..take upon them..to unsettle the Lawes with their publique discourse. 1679 ALSOP *Melius Inq.* I. i. 91 To set Religion upon its proper Basis, and unsettle it from the feeble foundations upon which former Ages had erected it! *a* 1700 EVELYN *Diary* 21 April, 1695, Never were so many private Bills pass'd for unsettling estates. 1704 ATTERBURY *On 1 Tim.* ii. 7 Those Mighty Events, that fix, or unsettle the Peace of the World. 1803 WORDSW. '*England! the time is come*' 4 Old things have been unsettled. 1849 MACAULAY *Hist. Eng.* i. I. 71 This theory, though intended to strengthen the foundations of government, altogether unsettles them. 1884 *Leeds Merc.* 15 Nov. 6/4 Such a struggle..must unsettle all the institutions of the country.
b. beliefs, thoughts, the mind, etc.
1644 MILTON *Divorce* (ed. 2) I. viii. 19 They should but seek..to unsettle our constancie with timorous and softning suggestions. 1662 STILLINGFL. *Orig. Sacr.* III. i. §2 When men bent their wits to unsettle the Beleef of such things as tended to Religion. 1671 in *Verney Mem.* (1907) II. 354 My thoughts are unsettled. 1759 SARAH FIELDING *C'tess of Dellwyn* II. 261 His Father had unsettled his Resolution. 1794 MRS. RADCLIFFE *Myst. Udolpho* xlvii, The long struggle which Agnes suffered..at length unsettled her reason. 1816 SCOTT *Bl. Dwarf* xviii, The shock was even sufficient to unsettle his wits. 1839 DICKENS *Nickleby* iv, None of those ill-judged comings home twice a year that unsettle children's minds so. 1885 *Spectator* 25 July 971/2 That his mind had been unsettled by his peril.
c. persons (in respect of beliefs, etc.).
1833 COLERIDGE *Table Talk* (1884) 225 What is the spirit which seems to move and unsettle every other man..at this time? 1851 HELPS *Comp. Solit.* xii. 236 Provided they do not, as they would say, unsettle their neighbours. 1880 R. G. WHITE *Every-Day Eng.* 140 A phonetic printing of those two words would unsettle all these people.
3. *intr.* To become unsettled.
1605 SHAKS. *Lear* III. iv. 167 His wits begin t' vnsettle. 1624 SANDERSON *Serm.* I. 102 The house cannot but unsettle apace, and without speedy repairs fall to the ground. 1643 MILTON *Divorce* 8 Their wild affections unsetling at will have been as so many divorces to teach them experience. *a* 1859 DE QUINCEY *Posth. Wks.* (1891) I. 14 He gazes, and slowly under the blazing scenery of his brain the scenery of his eye unsettles.
4. *trans.* To clear of settlers.
1895 *Advance* (Chicago) 11 Apr. 991/1 Probably no [other] section of our country has ever been un-settled so rapidly.
Hence **un'settling** *vbl. sb.* and *ppl. a.*
Also, in recent use (1901), *unsettler.*
1665 BOYLE *Occas. Refl.* I. vii, Troublesome and unsettling Employments. 1775 ASH, *Disconcerting,* p.a.,.. unsettling, discomposing. 1828 MISS MITFORD *Village* Ser. III. 70 The unsettling, and the journey, and the settling again,..fairly killed her. 1866 *Cornh. Mag.* XIII. 437 Christianity..must have raised among the believers in the Law very unsettling questions much akin to these. 1894 H. GARDENER *Unoff. Patriot* 10 The unsettling times which brought Methodism..into the ranks of established things.

un'settleable, *a.* (UN-[1] 7 b.)
1864 CARLYLE *Fredk. Gt.* XVI. iii. IV. 276 All details being, in the interim, either got settled, or got flung into corners as unsettleable.

un'settled, *ppl. a.* [UN-[1] 8, or f. UNSETTLE *v.*]
1. Not peaceful, tranquil, or orderly; disturbed; not (yet) quietly or firmly established.
1591 SYLVESTER *Du Bartas* I. ii. 424 Of winged Clouds the wide inconstant House, Th' unsettled Kingdome of swift Æolus. 1659 *Nicholas Papers* (Camden) IV. 265 The new and unsettled Government in England. 1697 DRYDEN *Æneis* I. 791 My cruel fate, And doubts attending an unsettled state, Force me to guard my coast from foreign foes. 1759 STERNE *Tr. Shandy* I. xi, But the two extremes are more common, and in a greater degree in this unsettled island. 1800 MRS. HERVEY *Mourtray Fam.* I. 41 The hurry and unsettled state which..had attended their first arrival in the country. 1826 SCOTT *Woodst.* v, The times were dangerous and unsettled. 1876 BANCROFT *Hist. U.S.* I. vi. 171 A report of a committee concerning the unsettled government of Virginia.
b. Of weather, etc.: Changeable, variable.
1707 MORTIMER *Husb.* 587 If unsettled or moist Weather happen at the time of its working. 1773 COOK *Voy.* (1777) I. 59 The wind continued unsettled. 1803 MARY CHARLTON *Wife & Mistress* IV. 114 His health, which was yet very unsettled. 1879 FROUDE *Cæsar* xvi. 255 The weather was too unsettled for his fleet..to join him.
Comb. 1788 J. WHITE *Jrnl. Voy. N.S. Wales* (1790) 105 Strong breezes, with unsettled-looking weather.
c. That has not yet settled down; still in a state of flux or motion.
1691 J. HARRINGTON *Introd.* in *Wood's Ath. Oxon.* II. a i b, The Graces of Measure and numbers..are not to be expected in a rude and unsettled Language. 1845 J. PHILLIPS *Geol.* in *Encycl. Metrop.* VI. 552/1 [Remains of plants] might be long suspended in the unsettled water, and be transported along with the finer matter. 1894 MRS. DYAN *Man's Keeping* (1899) 100 The dust flying in unsettled clouds about him.
2. Not settled in a particular place or position.
1594 HOOKER *Eccl. Pol.* II. vi. §3 To set himselfe in an house of cedar trees, and to behold the arke of the Lord's couenant vnsetled. 1729 T. INNES *Crit. Ess.* (1879) 284 The Francs..appear in history as a people unsettled, roving up and down. 1761 CHURCHILL *Rosciad* 988 Next follows Sheridan—a doubtful name, As yet unsettled in the rank of Fame. 1782 MARTYN *Geog. Mag.* I. iii. I. 205 A considerable encampment of these unsettled Arabs. 1807 J. BARLOW *Columb.* II. 212 These tribes have forester'd the fruitful zone, Their seats unsettled, and their name unknown. 1863 BOYD *Graver Th. Country Parson* vii. 106 They were a race of hunters; unsettled, cruel and deceitful. 1896 *Harper's Mag.* XXIII. 26/1, I am a single woman, unsettled as yet.
b. *Path.* Not confined to a definite part or spot.
1793 ABERNETHY *Surg. Ess.* 18 He was..teized with unsettled rheumatic pains. 1819 LADY MORGAN *Autobiog.* (1859) 267 A severe illness, arising..from unsettled gout.
3. Not settled or staid in character; of a restless or turbulent disposition.
1594 *Selimus* 823 Resolue to venture it, Fortune doth fauour euery bold assay, And t'were a trick of an vnsetled wit Because [etc.]. 1595 SHAKS. *John* II. i. 66 All th' vnsetled humors of the Land, Rash, inconsiderate, fiery voluntaries. 1607 *Puritan* I. iv. 31 Many desprate, vnsetled souldiours. 1675 HAN. WOOLLEY *Gentlewom. Comp.* 38 These unstaid dimensions argue unsetled dispositions. 1803 *Censor* 1 July 84, I am sorry you seem so unsettled; I now..advise you to settle in service. 1837 HT. MARTINEAU *Soc. Amer.* II. 63 Young people, who might be 'unsettled'; that is, not sufficiently subservient. *Ibid.* III. 136 Too many of them are unsettled, reckless, slovenly.
b. Marked by absence of regularity, uniformity, staidness, or tranquillity.
c 1714 POPE *Lett.* (1735) I. 150 What is commonly called an unsettled Life (and what you with too much unjust Severity call a Vagabond Life). 1787 BURNS *Let. to Jas. Smith* 11 June, Should I stay, in an unsettled state, at home, I would only dissipate my little fortune. 1824 MISS L. M. HAWKINS *Annaline* I. 307 High compassion called forth at her unsettled and forlorn condition. 1825 LAMB *Mr. Liston* Wks. 1908 I. 315 The orthography varying, according to the unsettled usage of the times. 1830 *Forrester* II. 270, I have already told you..of the unsettled life I led, after the loss of my mother.
c. Unsteady; unquiet.
1794 MRS. RADCLIFFE *Myst. Udolpho* xxviii, She..then viewed the face with a long unsettled gaze. 1810 SOUTHEY

Kehama xv. xii, How often did she .. from unsettled slumber start, and hear The Winds that moan above!

4. Undetermined, unresolved.

1593 MARLOWE *Lucan* I. 264 Now light had quite dissolu'd the mysty night, And Cæsars mind vnsetled musing stood. **1600** HAKLUYT *Voy.* III. 667 The Spaniard is not so simple, vnsetled & vncertaine in his determinations, as .. to make our papers his Bulwarks. **1618** GAINSFORD *Hist. P. Warbeck* ¶27 Such humility .. won the hearts of many as yet unsettled unto him. **1671** MILTON *P.R.* IV. 326 Uncertain and unsettl'd [he] still remains, Deep verst in books and shallow in himself. *a* **1768** SECKER *Serm.* (1770) IV. 2 What the prophet Elijah said to the Israelites belongs equally to all of this unsettled Character: How long halt ye between two Opinions? **1823** MRS. HEMANS *Siege of Valencia* v, Ere yet th' unsettled heart hath closed its long Impatient conflicts. **1897** MARY KINGSLEY *W. Africa* 360 The chiefs came in an unsettled state of mind, and showed at first much opposition to the conclusion of a treaty.

5. Of the mind: Unbalanced, disturbed.

1611 SHAKS. *Temp.* v. i. 59 A solemne Ayre, and the best comforter To an vnsetled fancie. **1693** *Dryden's Juvenal* xiv. (1697) 353 It shews a manifest unsetled Brain. **1751** JOHNSON *Rambler* No. 141 ¶2 A combination of circumstances acting when his imagination was unoccupied, and his judgment unsettled. **1779** *Mirror* No. 17, Such violent procedure might have effects too dreadful upon a brain which .. is already much unsettled. **1807** CRABBE *Par. Reg.* III. 180 Accounts perplex'd, .. My mind unsettled, and my will unmade. **1825** SCOTT *Betrothed* xxvii, Is his brain unsettled, .. or is there some dreadful mystery in these broken words?

b. Of persons: Mentally affected.

1611 SHAKS. *Wint. T.* I. ii. 325 Do'st thinke I am so muddy, so vnsetled, To appoint my selfe in this vexation? **1768** STERNE *Sent. Journ., Maria,* She said, she was unsettl'd much at that time. **1823** S. ROGERS *Italy, Foscari* 121 Unnerved, and now unsettled in his mind. **1879** *Cassell's Techn. Educ.* IV. 107/1 A failure so annoyed him, that he became unsettled, .. and at length died by his own hand.

6. a. Not assigned by will.

1671 SHADWELL *Humourists* III, Your Estate, by being unsettled, may come to be divided among the Lawyers, after I have killed you. **1800** MRS. HERVEY *Mourtray Fam.* II. 232 You shall not .. command a sixpence of my fortune, which I shall keep unsettled, as a check upon you.

b. Undischarged, unpaid.

1811 *Regul. & Orders Army* 214 The Nature of the Claims of any Man which remain unsettled. **1816** 'QUIZ' *Grand Master* II. 53 Here parcels of unsettl'd bills.

c. Not determined or fixed; not freed from doubt or uncertainty; undecided.

1844 J. S. MILL (*title*), Essays on Some Unsettled Questions of Political Economy. **1857** RUSKIN *Pol. Econ. Art* ii. §65, I haven't made up my mind about the number yet, and there are several other points in the system yet unsettled. **1884** *Imp. Dict.* s.v., An unsettled dispute.

7. Not occupied by settlers.

1724 [see UNSEATED *ppl. a.* 1]. **1788** *Encycl. Brit.* (ed. 3) I. 617/2 This immense extent of unappropriated western territory, or vacant unsettled land. **1859** CORNWALLIS *Panorama New World* I. 154 Those occupying runs in the then 'unsettled' districts. **1869** FROUDE *Short Stud., Educ.* (1871) 328 A new and unsettled country.

Hence **un'settledly** *adv.*

1599 JAS. I *Basilikon Doron* (1603) 115 Neither looking sillely, like a stupide pedant, nor unsetledly. **1651** CULPEPPER *Astrol. Judgem. Dis.* Ep. A 3 b, That so you may .. not float unsetledly upon the waves of Errour. **1685** *Case of Doubting Conscience* 4 The Ballance no longer hangs in *aequilibrio*, or moves unsetledly this way or that. **1725** N. BAILEY *Erasm. Colloq.* (1878) I. 72 Whenever any one that is your Superior speaks to you, .. look neither .. saucily, malapertly, nor unsettledly. **1824** SCOTT *Redgauntlet* ch. vii, If I thought you were unfortunate in former undertakings, .. which might cause you to live unsettledly.

un'settledness. [f. prec.] The quality or condition of being unsettled.

1619 LD. HERBERT *Corr.* in *Life* (1886) 346 And for their unsettledness, it is such as .. they know not whom to trust. **1682** FLAVELL *Fear* 81 The unsetledness and distraction of our own thoughts. **1748** HARTLEY *Observ. Man* I. iv. §6. 495 Sceptical Unsettledness and fool-hardy Impiety. **1799** J. ROBERTSON *Agric. Perth* 427 The present unsettledness in the value of grain. **1832** *Examiner* 436/1 A sense of unsettledness pervades everything. **1873** MORLEY *Rousseau* II. 209 If the former is not acquired .., a man grows up with a drifting unsettledness of will.

un'settlement. [f. UNSETTLE *v.*, or UN-^{1} 12.]

1. The act or process of unsettling.

1648 FAIRFAX, etc., *Remonstr.* 8 To entertain motions tending to the unsettlement of what you had resolved. **1691** T. H[ALE] *Acc. New Invent.* p. iv, Whoever attempts the settlement of any Question, which would be the unsettlement of any mens Interest [etc.]. **1844** LD. BROUGHAM *A. Lunel* III. xiv. 106 The universal unsettlement of all received ideas, and ancient opinions. **1862** TROLLOPE *N. Amer.* I. 221 Delay in travelling .. causes the unsettlement of a settled purpose.

2. Unsettled state or condition.

1650 BAXTER *Saints' R.* IV. i. §4 They have .. lived in much trouble and unsettlement, and have just overcome them. **1655** *Nicholas Papers* (Camden) II. 281 The yet great vnsetlement in England. **1681** *Treat. E. India Trade* 10 Our Neighbours are not now at leasure .. to make their Advantage of our Unsettlement, during the Transition from one Stock to another. **1867** H. W. WILBERFORCE in *Ess. Relig. & Lit.* II. 342 A general spirit of unsettlement and presumption. **1875** E. WHITE *Life in Christ* xxviii. v. 492 A not uncommon feeling is that .. 'the faith' is of such a quality that reasoning upon it .. is likely to lead to unsettlement.

un'settling, *vbl. sb.* and *ppl. a.*: see UNSETTLE *v.*

† **un'sety,** *a. Obs.*$^{-0}$ = UNSETE *a.* 3.

c **1440** *Promp. Parv.* 367/1 On-sety, *idem quod* on-holsum, *supra.* [*Ibid.* 365/2 On-holsum, *insalubris.*]

† **un'seven,** *v. Obs.*$^{-1}$ [UN-^{2} 6 a.] *trans.* To reduce from seven in number.

1655 FULLER *Ch. Hist.* XI. 137 He much decryed the necessity thereof, (though not so far as to un-seven the Sacraments of the Church of Rome).

† **un'sever,** *v. Obs.*$^{-1}$ (UN-^{2} 7.)

1609 HEYWOOD *Brit. Troy.* v. cx, Both his lips unsever, His head bends backe, legs stride.

un'severable, *a.* (UN-^{1} 7 b, 5 b.)

1579 TOMSON *Calvin's Serm. Tim.* 234/2 Hee sheweth the thinges which are alwayes ioyned with faith, and are as it were vnseuerable. **1644** DIGBY *Nat. Soul* xi. §5. 438 They .. yet were vnseuerable from one an other, as being compartes of the same substance.

un'severably, *adv.* (UN-^{1} 11, 5 b.)

c **1425** in *Anglia* VIII. 153 Wheþere for þee, þat as vnseuerably was ioyned to god [etc.]. **1548** GESTE *Pr. Masse* C iij b, Only soch a presence of christes body in the bread wherwyth they both shuld be vnseuerably personed. **1561** T. NORTON *Calvin's Inst.* II. 81 By whose knittyng together they might perfectly and vnseuerably cleaue vnto God.

unse'vere, *a.* (UN-^{1} 7.)

1646 CODRINGTON *Life or Death Essex* 11 If any unseverer houres of leisure offered themselves in his study. **1651** JER. TAYLOR *Serm. for Year* II. xxii. 284 Angry against servants for .. easing their labours with a lesse prudent and unsevere refreshment.

un'severed, *ppl. a.* (UN-^{1} 8.)

1453 *Rolls of Parlt.* V. 231/2 The said .. Archers shall be .. kept hole, undepartid, undevided and unsevered. **1513** DOUGLAS *Æneis* IX. viii. 133 Sa lang as thai sammyn vnsyverit war. **1607** SHAKS. *Cor.* III. ii. 42, I haue heard you say, Honor and Policy, like vnseuer'd Friends, I' th' Warre do grow together. **1657** H. KING *Departure* 28 'Tis only the Triumphant Church where we Shall in unsever'd neighbourhood agree. **1712** BLACKMORE *Creation* I. 645 The unsever'd parts the greatest pressure bear. *a* **1800** COWPER *Odyss.* (ed. 2) XIV. 530 He .. honouring Ulysses most, On Him the long unsever'd chine bestow'd. **1849** M. ARNOLD *Strayed Reveller, Sonnet* 5 One lesson .. Of Toil unsever'd from Tranquillity. **1885** *Manch. Exam.* 2 Feb. 6/2 How long this tie would remain unsevered .. is open to doubt.

Hence **un'severedly** *adv. rare*$^{-1}$.

1661 BOYLE *Style of Script.* 209 The .. Scripture was so Unsever'dly his Study.

unsew, *v.* [UN-^{2} 3.]

1. *trans.* To undo the sewing of (a garment, etc.); to remove the stitches from.

1362 LANGL. *P. Pl.* A. v. 48 Heo wolde vn-souwen hire smok and setten þer an here. **1382** WYCLIF *Lev.* xiii. 45 He shal haue his clothis vnsewyd [L. *dissuta*], the heed nakid, the mouth couered with the cloothe. **1491** CAXTON *Vitas Patr.* (W. de W. 1495) I. xxxix. 54/1 He commaunded hym to doo thynges agaynst reason, as .. to unsowe his gowne, and after to sowe it agayne. **1552** HULOET, Vnsow, .. *resuo.* **1611** COTGR., *Descoudre,* to vnsowe, vndoe stitches. **1712** tr. *De Marolles' Mem.* 104 A pair of Old-Shooes unsew'd on both Sides. **1728** CHAMBERS *Cycl.* s.v. *Marroquin,* The Skins .. are taken out, drain'd on a Rack, unsewed, the Sumac taken out [etc.]. **1809** MALKIN *Gil Blas* x. x. ¶14, I often observed the old man at work upon his pillow, unsewing and sewing it up again. **1848** THACKERAY *Van. Fair* xxxiv, When she unsewed herself, and let out of her dress all those .. valuables which she had secreted in the wadding.

fig. **1340** *Ayenb.* 184 Salomon þus zayþ: 'þer no guod red ne ys, þet uolk to-ualþ and is al onzauwed. **1620** SHELTON *Quix.* II. lx. 411 Sancho was amazed, and purposed not to vnsow his lips, as long as he was in that company. **1661** FELTHAM *Resolves* II. xliii. 268 Even in those [friendships] that have been ill contracted, Cato's advice is good, They are rather to be unsewed then cut. **1853** READE *Chr. Johnstone* 181 Time was to be given him to unsew a connection which he could not cut asunder.

2. To unwrap, uncover, set free, by the removal of stitches.

1390 GOWER *Conf.* III. 315 Thei founde A bodi ded, which was bewounde In cloth of gold .. Unsowed was the bodi sone. **1692** O. WALKER *Grk. & Rom. Hist.* 270 Bacchus being born in Arabia, or rather unsowed from the Thigh of his Mother Semele. **1740** RICHARDSON *Pamela* (1824) I. 113 So I took off my undercoat, and .. unsewed them [*sc.* papers] from it.

Hence **un'sewer; un'sewing** *vbl. sb.*

1611 COTGR. s.vv. *Descouseur, Descousure.*

un'sewed, *ppl. a.* (UN-^{1} 8, 8 c.)

Also with advs., as *together, up.*

a **1225** *Ancr. R.* 344 Cloðes unseouwed bireined oðer unwaschen. *c* **1325** *Pilate* 169 in *E.E.P.* (1862) 115 Oure louerdes curtel he dude on .. þat vnsued was of þred. **1535** COVERDALE *John* xix. 23 The cote .. was vnsowed from aboue, wrought thorow and thorow. **1550** BALE *Image Both Ch.* II. Pref. A iiij b, An heape of barbarous tearmes and vnsowed togither sentences. **1596** SPENSER *F.Q.* VI. iv. 14 But the bare ground .. Must be their bed, their pillow was vnsowed. **1603** J. DAVIES (Heref.) *Extasie* Wks. (Grosart) I. 90/2 On either side from her Armes to her Wast, It was vnsow'd, and made with Buttons fast. **1765** STERNE *Tr. Shandy* VIII. i, If slits in petticoats are unsewed up.

un'sewered, *ppl. a.* (UN-^{1} 8.)

1844 R. H. HORNE *New Spirit of Age* I. 113 The unsewered, undrained, and uncleansed localities. **1864** R. A. ARNOLD *Cotton Fam.* 440 The unsewered towns of the south. **1885** *Atlantic Monthly* Apr. 467/1 Roadways, ungraded, unsewered, and unpaved.

† **un'sewly,** *a. Obs.* Also 3 unseaulich. [UN-^{1} 7, with obscure second element.] Uncomely.

a **1225** *Ancr. R.* 10 Ich am blac & tauh hwit, heo seið, unseaulich wiðuten, & shene wiðinnen. *c* **1450** *Mirk's Festial* 81 In lykenes of a ȝong chyld wyth long herus, and hory, and vnsewly [*Douce MS.* vnsemely].

un'sewn, *ppl. a.* [UN-^{1} 8 b.] = UNSEWED *ppl. a.*

1648 HEXHAM II, *Ongenaeyt,* Vnsowne, or not Sowne on. **1869** *Athenæum* 25 Sept. 396 Why, we ask, do they [German publishers] send out books unsewn?

un'sex, *v.* [UN-^{2} 6 b.] *trans.* To deprive or divest of sex, or of the typical qualities of one or other (*esp.* the female) sex. Also *fig.*

1605 SHAKS. *Macb.* I. v. 42 Come you Spirits, That tend on mortall thoughts, vnsex me here. **1793** MURPHY *Tacitus* I. 73 If a woman can thus unsex herself at the head of the eagles. **1844** MRS. BROWNING *To G. Sand* 13 Beat purer, heart, .. Till God unsex thee on the heavenly shore. **1852** SMEDLEY *L. Arundel* xxxviii. 289 A foreign education, than which we know not a better receipt for unsexing the minds of the daughters of Albion. **1955** AUDEN *Shield of Achilles* i. 27 A day that meekly takes The potter's cuff, a gravel that as concrete Will unsex any space which it encloses.

Hence **un'sexing** *vbl. sb.* and *ppl. a.*

[**1775** ASH.] **1812** *Examiner* 11 May 302/2 Her unsexing ambition. **1851** *Illustr. Lond. News* 27 Sept. 395/2 In reply to the objection of unsexing.

un'sexed, *ppl. a.* (UN-^{1} 8, or f. UNSEX *v.*)

1797 MATHIAS *Purs. Lit.* IV. Adv. p. ii, Our unsexed female writers now instruct or confuse us and themselves in the labyrinth of politics. **1827** SCOTT *Surg. Dau.* xi, I doubt the propriety of your being under the charge of this unsexed woman. **1860** O. W. HOLMES *Elsie V.* xvi, To think that a woman is never to be a woman again, whatever she may come to as an unsexed angel. **1876** T. HARDY *Ethelberta* viii, To have an unsexed judgment is as precious as to be an unsexed being is deplorable.

un'sexual, *a.* (UN-^{1} 7.)

Also, in recent use (1905), **unsexually.**

1819 SHELLEY *Peter Bell 3rd* VI. xix, Turned to a formal puritan, A solemn and unsexual man. **1834** DE QUINCEY *Autob. Sk.* Wks. 1853 I. 353 An air of something unsexual, mannish, and .. ludicrous. **1875** WHITNEY *Life Lang.* x. 207 The world of untraceably sexual or of unsexual objects.

un'shackle, *v.* [UN-^{2} 4 b. Cf. Du. *ontschakelen.*]

1. *trans.* To free from a shackle or fetter. Also *fig.*

1611 COTGR., *Destraver,* to vnshackle, vngyue. **1650** GENTILIS *Considerations* 129 But to doe it [*sc.* overcome his enemy] when he is shackled and bound, without unshackling or unbinding is very much. **1699** SOUTH *Serm.* (1715) IV. 518 Unshackle his Nature, and turn his Desires loose, and then you shall see what he will choose. **1827** POLLOK *Course T.* VII. 464 The patriot bands that .. unshackled nations. **1828–32** WEBSTER s.v., To unshackle the hands.

b. To untie, detach.

1694 ECHARD *Plautus* 195 Only t'unshackle your rope, that hangs at your heels.

2. *Naut.* To remove a shackle from (a chain, etc.).

1840 R. H. DANA *Bef. Mast* vii, We hove in upon our chain, and after stoppering and unshackling it again and again, .. we at length tipped our anchor. **1899** F. V. KIRBY *Sport E.C. Africa* ix. 97 Unshackling the anchor, I put the shackle in my pocket.

un'shackled, *ppl. a.* [UN-^{1} 8.]

1. Not shackled or fettered. Also *transf.*

[**1775** ASH.] **1816** BYRON *Parisina* xvii, These hands are chain'd, but let me die At least with an unshackled eye. **1821** SCOTT *Pirate* xli, Cleveland and Bunce .. were permitted to walk unshackled.

2. Not restricted or impeded *by* something.

1776 BURNEY *Hist. Mus.* I. p. xiii, Freedom of thought, unshackled by the trammels of authority. **1782** MISS BURNEY *Cecilia* III. ii, Surrounded as you are by the opulent and the splendid, unshackled by dependance. **1853** HUXLEY in *Life & Lett.* (1900) I. 115 To be unshackled by anything that may prevent you taking the highest places. **1884** *Law Times* 17 May 42/2 The discretion of the court was unshackled by any obligation of hearing evidence.

b. Unrestricted, unimpeded, unhampered, free.

1796 MME. D'ARBLAY *Camilla* III. 21, I can desire no one to abstain from pursuing the dictates of their own sense of honour. I leave you, therefore, unshackled. **1820** BYRON *Mar. Fal.* III. ii. 534 Ages of prosperity and freedom To this unshackled city. **1850** GROTE *Greece* II. lxvii. VIII. 450 The full and unshackled force of comedy.

un'shade, *v.* (UN-^{2} 4 b.)

1611 COTGR., *Desumbrer,* to vnshade, or depriue of shadow. **1625** QUARLES *Sion's Sonn.* ii. 1 Vnshade thy Face, cast backe those golden Locks. **1633** P. FLETCHER *Purple Isl.* XII. li, Ah now unshade thy face, uncloud thy sight.

un'shaded, *ppl. a.* [UN-^{1} 8.]

1. a. Not darkened or obscured by shade; not covered by a shade or blind.

a **1668** DAVENANT *To Queen* Wks. (1673) 218 Faire as unshaded Light; or as the Day In its first birth. **1792** WORDSW. *Descr. Sk.* 101 There, all unshaded, blazing forests throw Rich golden verdure on the lake below. **1843** *Florist's Jrnl.* (1846) IV. 78 A small uncovered and unshaded bed of prepared earth. **1880** MISS BIRD *Japan* II. 187 Buildings .. with .. unshaded windows.

b. Not provided with shade; fully exposed to light (or heat).

1802 H. MARTIN *Helen of Glenross* III. 166 No nankeen monkey figures then frisked round a muslin-dressed dabbish, unshaded mamma. **1837** HT. MARTINEAU *Soc.*

Amer. II. 49 We passed an unshaded meadow, where the grass had caught fire.

2. 'Not having shades in coloring' (Webster, 1828); not modified or toned down.

1823 MRS. HEMANS *Vespers Palermo* II. i, A very boy, on whose unshaded cheek The spring-time glow is lingering. **1893** W. H. HUDSON *Patagonia* 138 Nothing here surprised me more than the song of the British wren—a current of sharp high unshaded notes.

3. Not marked with shading lines.

1868 LYELL *Princ. Geol.* (ed. 10) II. 348 The annexed map, all the lands which are shaded belonging to the Australian and those which are unshaded to the Indian region. **1880** C. R. MARKHAM *Peruv. Bark* 325 The identical plant figured in Plate X...(the unshaded branch with capsules).

un'shadow, *v.* [UN-² 4 b.] *trans.* To free from shadow; *fig.* to disclose, reveal.

In quot. 1599 = SHADOW *v.* 7; perh. an error.

1550 THOMAS *Ital. Dict., Sgombrare*, to vnshadowe or leaue voide. **1595** R. BARNFIELD *Cynthia* To Rdrs. (Arb.) 44, I will vnshaddow my conceit: being nothing else, but an imitation of Virgill. **1599** R. LINCHE *Anc. Fiction* I iv, This picture of Honor..was oftentimes set forth with two wings on the shoulders thereof, intending & vnshadowing thereby, that honour and glorie doe as it were lend wings vnto men of vertue and merit. **1818** BYRON *Let. to Moore* 2 June, The dawn gleams over the Grand Canal, and unshadows the Rialto. **1821** SOUTHEY *Vis. Judgem.* i. 51 To thy mortal sight shall the Grave unshadow its secrets. **1895** A. MACHEN *Three Impostors* 93, I, too, burned with the lust of the chase, not pausing to consider that I knew not what we were to unshadow. **1926** D. H. LAWRENCE *David* xv. 121 Is my heart fireless..? Kindler! it shall not be so! My heart shall shine to Thee, yea, unshadow itself. **1953** A. CLARKE *Moment Next to Nothing* II. 41 All that men think of would be immaterial Could they but watch these women shadowing, Unshadowing themselves.

un'shadowable, *a.* (UN-¹ 7 b.)

1640 BP. REYNOLDS *Passions* xxxiii. 402 There are indeed some Attributes of God..absolutely inimitable, and unshadowable by any excellency in mans soule. **1885** TENNYSON *Anc. Sage* 238 The gain of such large life as match'd with ours Were Sun to spark—unshadowable in words.

un'shadowed, *ppl. a.* [UN-¹ 8.] Not covered or darkened by shadow.

1593 B. BARNES *Poems* (Grosart) 10 Whose shadow trembling on her louely face He left vnshadow'd. **1599** DANIEL *Musophilus* 846 Maiestie..Shining with all her beames, with all her raies,..vnshadowed In any darkened point. **1682** WHELER *Journ. Greece* III. 268 Nothing but a Rock..unshadowed by Trees. **1823** MRS. HEMANS *Vespers Palermo* III. i, The skies themselves..Unshadow'd by a cloud. **1855** [MISS COBBE] *Ess. Intuitive Morals* 111 The true splendour of the Sun..in a heaven of unshadowed light. **1870** MORRIS *Earthly Par.* III. IV. 53 In the unshadowed noontide light.

fig. **1649** QUARLES *Virgin Widow* v. i, Thou before whose open eye All unshadow'd secrets lye. **1661** GLANVILL *Van. Dogm.* 238 He alone sees all things with an unshadowed comprehensive Vision, who eminently is All. **1828** LD. GRENVILLE *Sinking Fund* 85 The bare and unshadowed outline of the view..of these interesting topics. **1891** FARRAR *Darkn. & Dawn* xxxv, A beauty as yet unshadowed by evil secrets and base desires.

un'shafted, *a.* (UN-¹ 9.)

1883 R. BRIDGES *Prometheus* 798 The white unshafted darts of day.

un'shakeable, *a.* (UN-¹ 7 b.)

1611 COTGR., *Inescroulable*, vnshakeable. **1621** S. WARD *Happiness of Practice* 16 The wise, that build on the Rocke of Doing, vnshakeable. *a* **1715** SOUTH *Serm.* IV. viii. 328 A Bottom so firm and sure for Christianity to rest upon, that it cannot be placed upon a surer and more unshakable. **1866** HARE *Guesses* 106 There is still one rock indeed, stout and bold and unshakable as can be desired. **1890** *Times* 6 Feb. 5/1 He is Stambouloff's brother-in-law, and consequently unshakeable in his post.

b. Of belief, conviction, etc.

a **1677** BARROW *Serm.* Wks. 1687 I. 471 To express..his unshakeable Faith in God..under so fierce a trial. **1711** in *10th Rep. Hist. MSS. Comm.* App. V. 188 This fundation of unshakeable patience. **1805** SOUTHEY *Madoc* II. xxvii. 377 With..unshakeable resolve My soul maintains its purpose. **1891** FARRAR *Darkn. & Dawn* xviii, To these good Christians that doctrine was an unshakeable conviction.

Hence ˌ**unshak(e)a'bility**; **un'shakeably** *adv.*

1864 HAWTHORNE *S. Felton* (1872) 167 Desire nothing too fervently, not even life; yet keep thy hold upon it.. unshakably. **1907** W. JAMES in *Philos. Rev.* Jan. 9 The result claimed [from yoga, etc.]..is strength of character, personal power, unshakability of soul. **1952** GERTH & MARTINDALE tr. *Weber's Ancient Judaism* xv. 387 The complete unshakability of its communities by the foreign environment from which they segregated themselves.

† **un'shaked**, obs. variant of next.

a **1586** SIDNEY *Arcadia* III. xii, The horses with smooth running, their staves with unshaked motion, obediently performed their cholericke commandements. **1593** *Sidney's Arcadia* IV. (1922) II. 107 An unshaked magnanimity. **1601** SHAKS. *Jul. C.* III. i. 70, I do know but One That vnassayleable holds on his Ranke, Vnshak'd of Motion. **1611** —— *Cymb.* II. i. 68 Keepe vnshak'd That Temple thy faire mind. **1642** H. MORE *Song of Soul* II. iii. IV. xiv, Wherein we stedfast stand, unshak'd, unmov'd.

un'shaken, *ppl. a.* [UN-¹ 8 b and 8 c.]

1. Not shaken or agitated.

c **1460** [see UN-¹ 5 c]. **1602** SHAKS. *Ham.* III. ii. 201 Which now like Fruite vnripe stickes on the Tree, But fall vnshaken, when they mellow bee. **1712** BLACKMORE *Creation* I. 343 These strong, unshaken mounds, resist the shocks Of tides. **1762** FALCONER *Shipwr.* II. 314 [The canvas] lies at length unshaken by the wind. **1798** W. L. BOWLES *Poems, St. Michael's Mt.* 75 Firm as stands the rock's unshaken base.

2. Not moved from a firm position or state; unweakened; steadfast, steady.

1548 UDALL, etc. *Erasm. Par. John* i. 12 Able to stand stable and vnshaken against al temptacions of the deiuill. **1613** SHAKS. *Hen. VIII*, III. ii. 199 My Duty..Should the approach of this wilde Riuer breake, And stand vnshaken yours. **1659** W. CHAMBERLAYNE *Pharon.* I. iii. 384 With such unshaken confidence as we Pray on the expanded wings of faith. **1711** STEELE *Spect.* No. 75 ⁋7 A firm and unshaken Expectation of another Life. **1768–74** TUCKER *Lt. Nat.* (1834) II. 361 He will never get an unshaken seat in the saddle, who never rides an unruly horse. **1823** SCOTT *Quentin D.* xxii, The Bishop cast a melancholy but unshaken look upon the grisly satellite. **1848** MRS. JAMESON *Sacr. & Leg. Art* II. 188 Her unshaken constancy. **1883** A. ROBERTS *O.T. Revis.* ii. 29 The tradition..remains unshaken.

3. Not shivered or cracked. *rare.*

1573 TUSSER *Husb.* (1878) 42 Now sawe out thy timber.. to haue it vnshaken, and ready to sale. **1828** *Craven Gloss. Unshacken*, not cracked.

4. Not shaken out; unscattered.

1765 *Museum Rust.* IV. 134, I found a considerable quantity of the nameless grass, the seed unshaken.

Hence **un'shakenly** *adv.*

1882 MISS C. F. WOOLSON *Anne* 384 Feeling drearily, unshakenly sure.

† **un'shakened**, *ppl. a. Obs.*⁻¹ (UN-¹ 8.)

1659 FULLER *App. Inj. Innoc.* I. 49* My words stand an un-shakened truth.

un-Shake'spearian, *a.* (UN-¹ 7.)

a **1834** COLERIDGE *Lit. Rem.* (1836) II. 115 One of the most un-Shakespearian speeches in all the genuine works of our poet. **1875** DOWDEN *Shakspere* 55 Even if it were a work of Shakspere, we should still call it un-Shaksperian.

un'shaking, *ppl. a.* (UN-¹ 10.)

1818 MILMAN *Samor* VII. 956 A soft step approach'd Light as the wren along the unshaking spray.

un'shakingly, *adv.* (UN-¹ 11.)

1846 WORCESTER (citing *Qu. Rev.*).

† **un'shale**, *v. Obs.* [UN-² 5.]

1. *trans.* **a.** *fig.* To disclose, reveal, expound.

c **1576** THYNNE *Animadv.*, etc. (1875) 108 To vnshale this dowte, and laye abrode this clowdye hidden speache. **1606** MARSTON *Parasit.* IV. G 2, I wil not vnshale the rest before it be ripe. **1611** in Coryat *Crudities* 12 *marg.*, Those courteous Dames called cortesans (as M. Thomas himselfe hath elegantly vnshaled the word vnto vs). *a* **1652** BROME *Novella* II. i, *Nic.* I could unshale a plot. *Pi.* Ny noble Nicolo out with't I say.

b. To strip.

1604 MARSTON *Malcontent* I. iii. B 2 b, *Pietro.* Speake: vnshale him quick. *Mal.* With most tumbler-like nimblenes.

2. To unhusk.

1611 COTGR., *Goussepiller*,..to vnshale, or take pulse out of the swads. **1681** R. KNOX *Hist. Ceylon* 11 They unshale their Rice from its outward husk by beating it in a mortar.

un'shaled, *ppl. a.* [UN-¹ 8.] Not taken out of the pod or husk.

a **1661** HOLYDAY *Juvenal* (1673) 43 With whose vineger And unshal'd bean d'ye swell? **1733** TULL *Horse-Hoeing Husb.* xiii. 159 Beans..so large as to fill the Bushel almost as full when shal'd as unshal'd.

un'shamed, *ppl. a.* [UN-¹ 8. Cf. MHG. *ungeschamt, -schemt*, MDa. *uskæmmet.*]

a. Not put to shame. **b.** Unashamed.

1382 WYCLIF *2 Tim.* ii. 15 To ȝyue thi self prouable, or able, werk man to God, vnschamyd, or worthi not for to be schamed. **1450** *Rolls of Parlt.* V. 176/2 If it ever shall like our Lord, that I dey otherwise than in my bedde, my blode unshamed. *a* **1470** HARDING *Chron.* CXX. xiv, Thus by witte she kept her selfe vnshamed. **1562** LEGH *Armory* (1597) 62 To keepe his cote armour vnshamed in tryall. **1700** DRYDEN *Pal. & Arc.* III. 741 Unsham'd, though foil'd, he does the best he can. **1725** C. PITT *Vida's Art of Poetry* ii. 76 Th' immortal Virgil..Shines out unsham'd, and tow'rs above the rest. **1838** MRS. BROWNING *Seraphim* I. 289 Are ye unshamed that ye cannot dim Your alien brightness to be liker Him? **1897** H. N. HOWARD *Footsteps Proserpine* 97 Afraid to die, This other love thou wouldst unshamed deny?

un'shamefaced, *a.* (UN-¹ 9 b.)

1533 FRITH *Mirror* A vii b, They..with vnshamefaced beggynge, polle them so nye, that in a maner they leue nothinge behinde. **1545** JOYE *Exp. Dan.* 145 The vnshamefaced arrogant boldenes and serpentine fraudes of anticryste. **1603** HOLLAND *Plut. Mor.* 23 This so bolde and unshamefaced queane. **1647** LILLY *Christian Astrology* cviii. 540 Cruel men,..bloody minded, unshameface't, sumtuous.

Hence **un'shamefacedness.**

1596 LADY BACON *Let.* in Birch *Mem.* (1754) II. 218 Both unchast and impudent, with as it were an incorrigible unshamefacedness. **1611** COTGR., *Impudence*, impudence,.. vnshamefac'dness. **1632** HOLLAND *Cyrupædia* 4 It seemeth, that unthankefulnesse is accompanied especially with unshamefacedness.

† **un'shamefast**, *a. Obs.* [UN-¹ 7.] Immodest:

a. Of persons, the mind, heart, etc.

a **1100** *Voc.* in Wr.-Wülcker 337 *Impudens*, unsceamfæst. *c* **1380** WYCLIF *Sel. Wks.* III. 469 Suche a bischop is raþer an unschamefast dogge þen a bischop. **1382** —— *Dan.* viii. 23 There shal ryse a kyng vnshamfast in face. *a* **1470** TIPTOFT *Orat. G. Flamineus* (Caxton, 1481) f iv/2 Peradventure thou hast be prodigal unto wantone & unshamefast creatures. **1535** COVERDALE *Ecclus.* xxiii. 6 An vnshamefast and obstinate mynde. **1592** GREENE *Disput.*, etc. 26 Take heede of her that hath an vnshamefast eye. **1608** WILLET *Hexapla Exod.* 128 An hard heart..vnshamefast in euill things.

b. Of conduct, actions, etc.

c **1400** *Found. St. Bartholomew's* (1923) 49 He was nat forȝeitfull of the vnshamefaste boldnes wher that euer the mayde he sawh aloyne. **1407** *Exam. Wm. of Thorpe* Prol. (MS. Rawl. C 208), þoruȝ her olde & her newe vnschamefast synnes. **1436** *Rolls of Parlt.* IV. 501/2 Ye grete dredeles and unshamefast Perjurie, that orriblely contynueth. *a* **1533** LD. BERNERS *Gold. Bk. M. Aurel.* (1546) N n j b, Thy shame is so shamefull, and thy malyce so unshamefast, that I can not answere the. **1586** FERNE *Blaz. Gentrie* 63 This law..would peradventure call some backe from vnshamefast lasciuiousnes.

† **un'shamefastly**, *adv. Obs.* [UN-¹ 11. Cf. prec.] Immodestly.

1382 WYCLIF *Pref. Ep. St. Jerome* i, More wilnyng other mennus thingis shamfastli to lernen, than his owne vnshamefastli to prece forth. *c* **1440** *Promp. Parv.* 367/1 Onschamefastly, *inpudenter.* **1561** T. HOBY tr. *Castiglione's Courtyer* Zz 2 Not to loue promotions so,..nor vnshamefastlye to begg any office. **1580** T. LUPTON *Sivqila* 63, I am sure a greate sorte woulde not..so vnshamefastly, and so commonly vse that filthy vice. **1632** SHERWOOD, Unshamefastly, *eshontément.*

† **un'shamefastness.** *Obs.* (UN-¹ 12.)

Common *c* 1540–1590.

? *a* **1400** *Wycliffite Bible* Job xv. 27 (MS. Bodl. 277), Outward fatnesse, that is vnschamefastnesse, hangith doun of his sidis. *a* **1470** TIPTOFT *Orat. G. Flamineus* (Caxton, 1481) f iv b/1 Supposest thou with thy..vnshamefastnes to get that worshipful fame which they gate? **1520** *Calisto & Melib.* A iij b, Theyre enbawmyng & theyre vnshamfastnes. **1549** CHALONER *Erasm. on Folly* R j b, Whiche their sayd iugglyng they conueigh yet by so happie an vnshamefastnesse, as..Ciuilians haue cause..to enuie. **1608** WILLET *Hexapla Exod.* 403 Contrarie hereunto are immodestie and vnshamefastnes. **1653** W. RAMESEY *Astrol. Restored* 73 This is the face of boldness,..unshamefastness, resoluteness and confidence.

† **un'shameful**, *a.* [UN-¹ 7.] Shameless.

c **1400** *Apol. Loll.* 104 þei are..vnschamful to axe, bolde to denay. *c* **1430** *Life St. Kath.* (1884) 45 O thou most vnschameful dogge! **1561** T. HOBY tr. *Castiglione's Courtyer* IV. Qq iii b, [It] maketh them desperate for yᵉ wronges & vnshameful dealing that they receiue. **1566** PAINTER *Pal. Pleas.* I. 192 b, Reforme thy unshamefull and disordinate appetites. **1648** HEXHAM II, [*Onschamel*], Vnshamefull, Impudent, or Brazen fact.

† **un'shamefully**, *adv. Obs.* [UN-¹ 11.] Shamelessly.

c **1375** *Sc. Leg. Saints* xxxii. (*Justin*) 387 The feynde.. becuth vnschamefully to diffule hyre thru lychery. *c* **1400** *Found. St. Bartholomew's* 48 It is no prudent mannys dede ..suche a conseyuyd desire yn herte so vnshamfully to vttyr. *c* **1430** *Wycliffite Bible* (1850) I. 61/2 To prece forth his owne [studies] vnshamefully. **1561** T. HOBY tr. *Castiglione's Courtyer* Yy iv, Not to praise himself vnshamefully and out of reason. **1648** HEXHAM II, *Onbeschaemdelick*, vnshamefully, or impudently. *a* **1660** *Contemp. Hist. Irel.* (Ir. Archæol. Soc.) II. 26, I will..prove you to be a lyer, in what you unshamfully formerly asserted.

† **un'shamefulness.** *Obs.* [UN-¹ 12.] Shamelessness.

c **950** *Lindisf. Gosp.* Mark vii. 21 From innueard.. ofcymeð unrehtwisnise, esuicnis, unsceomfulnise. **1357** *Lay Folks Catech.* 468 Of this syn [*sc.* pride] comes..Despite, and ypocrisie, and unshamefulnesse. *c* **1440** *Jacob's Well* 77 þe seuenthe cornere of wose in pride is vnschamfulnes. **1534** BARNES *Suppl. Hen. VIII*, E 2, But oh lorde God, what an vnshamefulnes is this? thus to delude with wordes all the hole worlde? **1648** HEXHAM II, *Onbeschaemtheyt*, Vnshamefulnesse.

† **un'shameless(ness.** *Obs.* (UN-¹ 5 a.)

1555 H. PENDILTON in Bonner *Homilies* 41* The vnshameles breakynge of the deade mennes testamentes. **1565** COOPER *Thesaurus*, *Impudentia*, impudencie; vnshamelesnesse.

† **un'shamely**, *adv. Obs.*⁻¹ [UN-¹ 11. Cf. OE. *unsceamlīce.*] Shamelessly.

c **1375** *Sc. Leg. Saints* xv. (*Barnabas*) 162 Ethnykis, þat oysit sa nakit one-schamely to ga.

† **un'shamous**, *a. Obs.*⁻¹ [UN-¹ 7.] Shameless.

a **1500** in *Asloan MS.* fol. 274 Of thare syn sum schrewis are vnschamous.

un'shape, *v.* [UN-² 3, 4. Cf. MHG. *entschepfen.*] *trans.* To deform; to destroy. Also *fig.*

a **1400** *New Test.* (Paues) App. 219 Vnschapynge þer body wiþ newe manere of degyse. **1603** SHAKS. *Meas. for M.* IV. iv. 23 This deede vnshapes me quite. **1857** DE QUINCEY *Whiggism* Wks. VI. 77 The sandy columns of the Great Desert, which the caprices of the wind build up and scatter, shape and unshape, within..a minute.

unshape, obs. var. UNSHAPEN *a.*

un'shapeable, *a.* [UN-¹ 7 b.] Having no definite shape; shapeless.

Also *unshapable* (Worcester, 1846, citing Good).

1630 *R. Johnson's Kingd. & Commw.* 115 The unshapeable and rough Mountaine Grampius. **1846** LOUISA S. COSTELLO *Tour Venice* 369 Like the back of some huge antediluvian monster, unshapeable and mysterious.

un'shaped, *ppl. a.* [UN-¹ 8. Cf. ON. *úskapaðr*, Sw. *oskapad*, Da. *uskabt.*] Not reduced or moulded into shape; imperfectly formed; left rude or rough. Freq. *fig.*

1572 BOSSEWELL *Armorie* 11 A sleue, vnshaped, and vnsowed. **1602** SHAKS. *Ham.* IV. v. 8 Her speech is nothing, Yet the vnshaped vse of it doth moue The hearers to

Collection. *c* **1680** P. AYRES *Embl. Love* (1906) 355 See how the bear industriously does frame, And bring in time to form, her unshaped young. **1730** BAILEY (fol.), *Mola Carnea* ..is a spungy unshaped Substance, without Bones or Bowels. **1798** WORDSW. *P. Bell* 296 All the unshaped half-human thoughts Which solitary Nature feeds. **1841** BROWNING *Pippa Passes* II. Poems (1905) 179/1 Shall to produce form out of unshaped stuff Be Art? **1860** HAWTHORNE *Marb. Faun* ii, He spoke..with the Tuscan rusticity of accent, and an unshaped sort of utterance.

Hence **un'shapedness**.

1587 GOLDING *De Mornay* x. 166 A certeine vnshapednesse; which is the cause of all mishapennesse.

† **un'shapeful**, *a. Obs.*⁻¹ (UN-¹ 7.)

1598 CHAPMAN *Hero & Leander* III. 298 Her right hand leand on her hart-bowing knee, Wrapt in vnshapefull foulds.

† **un'shapefulness**. *Obs.*⁻¹ [UN-¹ 12.] Shapelessness.

1535 *Trevisa's Barth. De P.R.* XIII. xxii. 181/1 It was called Abyssus, for vnshapfulnesse: for it was dystynguyed with no fourme nor shape.

† **un'shapeless**, *a. Obs.*⁻¹ (UN-¹ 5 a.)

1640 J. GOWER *Ovid's Festiv.* I. 4 A rude unshapelesse load.

un'shapeliness. (UN-¹ 12; cf. next.)

1741 RICHARDSON *Pamela* I. p. xxvi, What, in the Name of Unshapeliness, cou'd he find to complain of, in a beautiful Girl of Sixteen. *a* **1834** COLERIDGE *Constit. Ch. & State* (1839) 118 *note*, Gold or silver ingots,..their unshapeliness and want of the mint impression. **1871** ALABASTER *Wheel of Law* 252 Its unshapeliness has not prevented Buddhists from claiming it as made by the foot of Buddha.

un'shapely, *a.* (UN-¹ 7. Cf. ON. *úskapligr* (Sw. *oskaplig*, Norw. *uskapleg*) misshapen, etc.)

c **1200** *Trin. Coll. Hom.* 163 Ðe meshakele [is] of medeme fustane,..ðe corporeals sole, and unschapliche. **13..** *Guy Warw.* (A.) 7160 His bodi..is michel,..Fram þe nouel vpward vnschepliche. ? *a* **1400** *Morte Arth.* 1099 Schouelle-fotede was that schalke..With schankez unschaply. *c* **1485** *Digby Myst.* (1882) III. 1158 On-shaply þou art to see! **1589** PUTTENHAM *Eng. Poesie* (Arb.) 89 Our auncient rymers.. many times made their meetres..of such vnshapely wordes as would allow no conuenient Cesure. **1615** CROOKE *Body of Man* 113 It is an vnshapely body, very loose, all glandulous. **1645** BOATE *Ireland's Nat. Hist.* (1652) 64 Things like Boats, but very unshapely, being nothing but square peeces of timber made hollow. **1752** HUME *Ess. on Original Contract* II. xii. (1777) I. 471 The people being commonly very rude builders,..it is natural to imagine, that their workmanship must be a little unshapely. **1802** PLAYFAIR *Illustr. Hutton. Th.* 114 An immense mass of solid rock, naked and unshapely. **1874** J. FISKE *Cosmic Philos.* I. ii. I. 26 An apparently-solid edifice, which fell into unshapely ruin at the first rude blast of criticism.

un'shapen, *a.* [UN-¹ 8 b. Cf. OE. *unsceapen*, *ungesceapen*, MDu. *ongescapen* (Du. *-schapen*), MLG. *ungeschapen*, OHG. *-scaffan* (MHG. and G. *-schaffen*).] = UNSHAPED *ppl. a.*

13.. *Cursor M.* 367 (Gött.), þe mater of foure elementis, þat ȝeit was þan of forme vnschapin. *c* **1350** *Athanasian Creed* in *MS. Bodl. 425* fol. 69 b, Vnshapen fadir unshapen son is, Vnshapen heli gost in blis. **1387** TREVISA *Higden* (Rolls) II. 163 Al þe longage of þe Norþhumbres..is.. scharp, slitting, and frotynge and vnschape [L. *incondita*]. *a* **1560** PHAER *Æneid* IX. (1562) Ff i b, An vnshapen bunchy speare..Sir Pandare whirling threw. **1594** SHAKS. *Rich. III*, I. ii. 251 (Q 1), Will she yet debase her eyes..On me that halt, and am vnshapen thus. **1646** SIR T. BROWNE *Pseud. Ep.* III. vi. 116 A Bear brings forth her young informous and unshapen. **1695** J. EDWARDS *Perfect. Script.* 322 This unshapen mass without form and void. **1728** R. MORRIS *Ess. Anc. Archit.* 42 Columns were originally made of unshapen Trees. **1747** CARTE *Hist. Eng.* I. 44 A rough unshapen stone, of an enormous size. *a* **1814** *Mermaid* I. ii. in *New Brit. Theatre* II. 478 They ran to mock her hump'd unshapen form. **1872** MORLEY *Voltaire* 9 Pale unshapen embryos of social sympathy.

Hence **un'shapeness**.

1398 TREVISA *Barth. De P.R.* XIII. xxii. (Tollem. MS.), It was clepid *abbissus* for unschapnesse,..for it was distinged with no forme noþer schappe. **1648** HEXHAM II, *Ongeschapenheydt*, Vncreatednesse, or Vnshapennesse.

un'shared, *ppl. a.* [UN-¹ 8.] Not shared with, or by, another or others.

c **1616** W. BASSE *Shakespeare* Poet. Wks. (1893) 116 Thy unmolested peace, vnshared Caue, Possesse as Lord, not Tenant, of thy Graue. **1667** MILTON *P.L.* IX. 880 For bliss, as thou hast part, to me is bliss, Tedious, unshar'd with thee. *a* **1774** W. WHITEHEAD *Enthusiast* xii, Each bliss unshar'd is unenjoy'd. **1809–14** WORDSW. *Excurs.* IX. 587 Merely from a wish To impart a joy, imperfect while unshared. **1886** GURNEY, etc. *Phantasms of Living* I. 458 Both sensory and non-sensory hallucinations are idiosyncratic and unshared.

Hence **un'sharedness**.

1896 G. MATHESON *Lady Ecclesia* vii. 57 It was not the fault of my new faith, but of its unsharedness.

un'sharp, *a.* (UN-¹ 7. Cf. OE. *unscearp*, Du. *onscherp*).

1611 FLORIO, *Inaspro*, vnsowre, sweet, vnsharpe. **1889** *Anthony's Photogr. Bull.* II. 204 People often call unsharp, fuzzy pictures 'artistic'.

Hence **un'sharpness**.

1961 in WEBSTER. **1967** E. CHAMBERS *Photolitho-Offset* xi. 161 Normal action of the diffusing stop, when all the small apertures are clear, results in a moderate degree of unsharpness. **1977** J. HEDGECOE *Photographer's Handbk.* 314/2 Overall unsharpness can be caused by gross misfocus.

un'sharpened, *ppl. a.* (UN-¹ 8.)

1620 E. BLOUNT *Horæ Subs.* 385 The place where our thoughts cannot be perturbed, nor our sences vnsharpened. **1813** SCOTT *Rokeby* I. v, Though no human ear, Unsharpen'd by revenge and fear, Could e'er distinguish horse's clank.

unshathiness, -shathy: see UN-¹ 3.

un'shattered, *ppl. a.* (UN-¹ 8.)

1634 BP. HALL *Serm.* Wks. II. 427 Where brasse meets with clay, how can that brittle stuffe escape unshattered? **1657** THORNLEY tr. *Longus' Daphnis & Chloe* 191 How intire and unshatter'd their horns. **1809** COLERIDGE *Friend* 123 Their own good health and unshattered nerves. **1870** WILBERFORCE *Heroes Hebrew Hist.* 175 His casting down.. left their rising spirit unshattered.

un'shaveable, *a.* (UN-¹ 7 b.)

1809 *Q. Rev.* I. 214 A *harrie*, or [one] of any other unshaveable cast.

un'shaved, *ppl. a.* (UN-¹ 8; cf. next.)

1648 HEXHAM II, *Onbeschoren*, Vnshorne, or Vnshaved. **1862** *Lond. Rev.* 30 Aug. 192 The sturdy philosophy of the unshaved Warrington. **1900** G. SWIFT *Somerley* 66, I found Dobson unshaved and in the tattered remnants of a dress-suit.

un'shaven, *ppl. a.* [UN-¹ 8 b. Cf. prec. and MDu. *ongescaven*.]

1. Not shaved.

1382 WYCLIF *2 Sam.* xix. 24 The feet vnwasshen, and the beerd vnshauen. *c* **1450** *Mirk's Festial* 125 þis man..abode half schauen and half vnschauen tyll þe Monday aftyr. **1532** MORE *Confut. Tindale* Wks. 430/2 Though beefore those ceremonyes vsed, priestes myghte consecrate vnshauen & vnannoynted,..yet nowe can there none dooe so, syth there is no priest made vnshauen and vnannoynted. **1646** SIR T. BROWNE *Pseud. Ep.* v. 269 The indiciduous and unshaven locks of Apollo. **1759** STERNE *Tr. Shandy* II. iv, My uncle began..to dismiss his barber unshaven. **1838** DICKENS *O. Twist* xxi, The unwashed, unshaven, squalid, and dirty figures. **1863** MISS BRADDON *Aurora Floyd* xxii, His unshaven chin, dark with the blue bristles of his budding beard. **1870** BLACK *Kilmeny* iii, He went about in a frightfully unshaven and ragged condition.

2. Not smoothed or planed.

a **1547** SURREY *Æneid* IV. 527 Their oares..from wood they bring, And mastes vnshaue, for hast to take their flight.

Hence **un'shavenness**.

1667 WATERHOUSE *Fire Lond.* 62 What avails Sampson's strength, if God give a key to the secret of it which resides in its unshavenness.

un'shawl, *v.* (UN-² 7 and 4.)

1817 LADY MORGAN *France* II. (1818) I. 238 While I was unshawling, I caught the first stanzas of the following song. **1828** MISS MITFORD *Village* Ser. III. 62 [She] sate down on her dear sofa, and was forthwith unclogged, unshawled and unbonneted. **1849** C. BRONTË *Shirley* vii, And now Caroline had..to help them to unshawl.

un'sheaf, *v.* (UN-¹ 3.)

a **1722** LISLE *Husb.* (1757) 182 [He] unsheafed some of his wheat to dry it.

† **un'sheaf**, obs. var. UNSHEATHE *v.*

1658 tr. *Bergerac's Satyr. Char.* xvi. 67 I'le not unsheafe, to drive your enemy by death far from you.

un'sheared, *ppl. a.* [UN-¹ 8.] = UNSHORN.

1707 MORTIMER *Husb.* 481 The part [of the rose-tree] unsheared will spend that Strength and Sap. **1788** tr. *Chenier's St. Morocco*, etc. I. 283 Their household furniture consists in a mat, two sheep-skins, unsheard, to sit upon [etc.]. **1826** HOOD *Stag-eyed Lady* 27 A trail Of bristly hair —that, honour'd and unshear'd, Grew downward.

un'sheathe, *v.* [UN-² 4, 5.]

1. *trans.* To dislodge.

c **1374** CHAUCER *Troylus* IV. 776 Than shal no mete or drynk come in my mouthe, Til I my soule out of my breste vnsheþe. **1593** SHAKS. *Lucr.* 1724 She sheated in her harmless breast A harmful knife, that thence her soul unsheathed.

2. To draw (a weapon) out of the sheath or scabbard. ***to unsheathe the sword***, to begin hostilities or slaughter. (Cf. SHEATHE *v.* 2.)

a **1542** WYATT *Ps.* xxxvii. 41 They have unsheathed eke their bloudye brands. *a* **1547** SURREY *Æneis* IV. 774 Aeneas ..his glistering sword unshethes,..[and] the cabels cut in twaine. **1600** *1st Pt. Sir J. Oldcastle* v. x. 78 Wherefore were your sharpe edgde kniues vnsheathde? **1649** MILTON *Eikon.* ix. 78 Never was King less in danger of any violence from his Subjects, till he unsheath'd his Sword against them. **1683** WALLER *Invasion of Turks* 60 Unsheathing the destructive sword. **1807** J. BARLOW *Columb.* VI. 686 Are these..the swords Thy hand unsheath'd and gave the savage hordes? **1884** A. R. PENNINGTON *Wiclif* v. 176 The sword of the persecutor would be unsheathed against him.

fig. and *transf.* **1692** A. PITCAIRNE *Babell* 287 He did his trustie tongue unsheath... It was a blade that he could trust. **1774** GOLDSM. *Nat. Hist.* VII. 335 Nature has furnished her [*sc.* the grasshopper] with an instrument at her tail,..which she can sheathe and unsheathe at pleasure. **1810** SOUTHEY *Kehama* XVI. xiv, The Beast.., His mouth half-open, and his teeth unsheath'd. **1855** KINGSLEY *Westw. Ho!* xxvii, A tame leopard, whose claws might be unsheathed..at any moment.

3. To take out of, strip of, a sheath or covering. Also *fig.* and *refl.*

1638 N. WHITING *Albino & Bellama* 2275 At time of rest her body she unsheathed, And housed within the linen walls her limbs. **1664** H. POWER *Exp. Philos.* I. 30 If you unsheath her body, and take off her spotted short crustaceous wings. **1875** SEARS *Serm. & Songs* 6 When our spiritual senses are first unsheathed. **1893** J. PULSFORD *Loyalty to Christ* II. 225 Sing for joy;..and others will be moved to unsheathe themselves of their wintry earthliness.

4. *intr.* 'To come out from a sheath' (*Cent. Dict.*).

Hence **un'sheathing** *vbl. sb.*

1611 COTGR., *Desgaine*, an vnsheathing..of a weapon. **1823** LAMB *Elia* II. *Old Margate Hoy*, Whistling to the sheathing and unsheathing of their cutlasses. **1871** MACDUFF *Mem. Patmos* 152 The unsheathings of that terrible sword.

un'sheathed, *ppl. a.* [f. prec. or UN-¹ 8.]

1. Of a weapon: Drawn from the sheath; not covered by a sheath.

c **1430** *Pilgr. Lyf Manhode* I. xxxv. (1869) 22 It is bettere the swerd be shethed than vnshethed. *a* **1593** MARLOWE *Ovid's Eleg.* II. ii. 64 My hands an vnsheath'd shyning weapon haue not. **1611** COTGR. s.v. *Blanc*, A naked or vnsheathed..sword. **1638** SUCKLING *Aglaura* III. i, Blesse me, what means this unsheath'd minister of death [= a sword]? **1700** DRYDEN *Pal. & Arc.* II. 253 He..with his Sword unsheath'd..Commands both Combatants to cease their Strife. **1814** SCOTT *Lord of Isles* II. xxiii, Do dirks unsheathed suit bridal cheer? **1842** BORROW *Bible in Spain* x, He held his unsheathed knife in his hand.

fig. **1830** MRS. HEMANS *Songs Affec.*, *Spirit's Return*, Yet something,..as that unsheathed spirit-glance I met, Made my soul faint.

2. Not protected by a sheath or sheathing; uncovered, exposed.

1691 T. H[ALE] *Acc. New Invent.* 9 Any unsheathed or Wood-sheathed Ships. *Ibid.* 24 Not only in sheathed Ships ..but unsheathed too. **1790** BEATSON *Nav. & Mil. Mem.* I. 126 An unsheathed fire ship..was left to act as an advice-boat. **1884** BOWER & SCOTT *De Bary's Phaner.* 393 The delicate unsheathed parts of the vascular bundles.

un'shed, *ppl. a.* [UN-¹ 8 b.]

1. Not shed or poured out.

c **1450** *Mirk's Festial* 242 Forto haue savytte gyltles blode vnsched on boþe parties. **1667** MILTON *P.L.* XII. 176 To blood unshed the Rivers must be turnd. **1768–74** TUCKER *Lt. Nat.* (1834) II. 483 He..can make the same mass of blood exist at once unshed in the wafer, and shed in the cup. **1816** BYRON *Dream* v, An unquiet drooping of the eye, As if its lid were charged with unshed tears. **1880** MISS BRADDON *Just as I am* v, Dulcie's eyelids were heavy with unshed tears.

2. Unparted.

1596 SPENSER *F.Q.* IV. vii. 40 His faire lockes..He let to grow..Vncomb'd, uncurl'd, and carelesly vnshed.

† **un'sheen**, *a. Obs.*⁻¹ (UN-¹ 7.)

a **1400** *Sir Degrev.* 1656 Some lorkus undur tres In slowes unshene.

un'sheet, *v.* (UN-² 4.)

a **1814** *Sorceress* III. i. in *New Brit. Theatre* III. 20, I saw Th' accursed robbers..With hideous burglary unsheet a corpse. **1888** JACOBI *Printers' Vocab.*, *Unsheet*, to withdraw the interleaving sheets between printed work which have been placed there to prevent set-off.

un'sheeted, *a.* (UN-¹ 9.)

[**1775** ASH.] **1816** J. WILSON *City of Plague* I. iv. 52 Down the drunken wretch doth lie Unsheeted in the cemetery. *Ibid.* 53 The bodies Of the unsheeted dead.

un'shell, *v.* [UN-² 5. Cf. Du. *ontschillen*, *-schellen*.] *trans.* To extract from, to strip of, the shell. (Chiefly *fig.*)

1599 NASHE *Lenten Stuffe* D iij, Of him and none but him, ..that euer Yarmouth vnshelled or ingendred. **1611** COTGR., *Challer*,..to shale, or vnshell, Nuts, &c. **1642** FULLER *Holy & Prof. St.* II. x. 90 Our Perkins brought the schools into the Pulpit, and unshelling their controversies out of their hard school-terms, made thereof..wholsome meat for his people. **1652** BENLOWES *Theoph.* VI. xvii, Thou, Love,..did'st unshell My Spirit (fledg'd with Grace) from that disorder'd cell. **1761** MURPHY *Citizen* II, Sir! Turn out pray, turn out —you won't—Then I'll unshell you. **1819** SCOTT *Leg. Montrose* v, By this time he was unshelled, and stood before the fire. **1892** *Sat. Rev.* 17 Dec. 719/1 You have got but to unhusk and unshell it, and there it is.

Hence **un'shelled** *ppl. a.*¹; **un'shelling** *vbl. sb.*

a **1668** LASSELS *Voy. Italy* (1698) II. 277 Whose ingenious book gives light to many books by the unshelling of a world of ancient customs. **1799** SHERIDAN *Pizarro* IV. i, O'er her unshelled brood the murmuring ring-dove sits not more gently.

un'shelled, *ppl. a.*² [UN-¹ 8. Cf. NFris. *unskelled*, MDu. *ongescelt* (Du. *ongescheld*), MHG. *ungeschelt* (G. *ungeschält*).] Not taken out of the shell. Also (of husks), unremoved.

1594 NASHE *Terrors of Night* G iij b, Their naturall vnshelled shining mother pearle proportions might be more imprintingly apprehended. **1647** WITHER (*title*), Amygdala Britannica, Almonds for Parrets. A Dish of Stone-Fruit, partly shel'd and partly unshel'd. **1769** *Phil. Trans.* LIX. 382 Ten gallons of the pease, with the husks unshelled. **1802** *Naval Chron.* VIII. 28 Sweet almonds, unshelled.

un'shelterable, *a.* (UN-¹ 7 b.)

1841 LYTTON *Nt. & Morn.* II. x, As if to protect him even from the wrath of the unshelterable flame.

un'sheltered, *ppl. a.* (UN-¹ 8.)

1599 DANIEL *Musoph.* Wks. (1602) C i b, For this it practises to dissipate Th' vnsheltred troupes. **1665** BOYLE *Occas. Refl.* IV. xx, Shunning all beaten Paths, and unshelter'd Grounds. **1667** *Decay Chr. Piety* vi. 143 [To] leave him unsheltred to that scorching wrath of God. **1726** LEONI *Alberti's Archit.* I. 28 An open place, unshelter'd either by Woods or Hills. **1760–72** H. BROOKE *Fool of Qual.* (1809) II. 133, I did not dare to leave my child alone and unsheltered. **1815** KIRBY & SP. *Entomol.* IV. I. 85 We should soon be..unsheltered, except by caves. **1855** [J. R. LEIFCHILD] *Cornwall* 64 A bleak and unsheltered country.

un'sheltering, *ppl. a.* (UN-¹ 10.)

1614 R. TAILOR *Hog hath lost Pearl* I. i, Whilst dear Carracus Wanders..through th' unshelt'ring field, Seeking me. **1766** GOLDSM. *Vicar* xxiii, My son, observe this bed of straw, and unsheltering roof. **1892** *Pall Mall G.* 2 Dec. 2/2 Mr. Mitchell still roams the unsheltering streets.

un'shelve, *v.* (UN-² 5.)
a **1819** *Edin. Rev.* (Seager), To unshelve books. **1876** *Nature* 13 Jan. 206/2 He is not likely to unshelve works of travel of a past generation.

†**un'shend**, obs. var. UNSHENT.
c **1440** *Pallad. on Husb.* XII. 610 Al yeer Thy duc attende, . . or laste Vnshende.

†**un'shending**, *ppl. a. Obs.*⁻¹ [UN-¹ 10.] Not harming or injuring.
c **1450** *Mirour Saluacioun* (Roxb.) 162 So was crist borne of the thy maydenhode vnsheendyng.

un'shent, *ppl. a.* Now *arch.* [UN-¹ 8b. Cf. OE. *unscended*, MDu. *ongescendet*, *-scent*, *-scant* (obs. Du. *ongeschent*, Du. *ongeschend*), OHG. *ungeschendet* (MHG. *ungescant*), etc.] Uninjured, unharmed, unspoiled, etc.
1303 R. BRUNNE *Handl. Synne* 2733 Vndyrstand . . þat . . wrong Iugement Shul neuer more be vnshent. *a* **1400** *Minor Poems fr. Vernon MS.* 680/6 þer nis no mon fer ne nere þat may him-seluen saue vn-schent, But he þat casteþ . . To kepe wel Cristes Comaundement. *a* **1400–50** *Alexander* 2143 If at ȝe shap ȝow to shount vnschent of oure handis. *c* **1460** *Towneley Myst.* xv. 3 If thou wyll saue thy self vnshent. **1597** BP. HALL *Sat.* IV. i, Ho! all ye Females that would liue vnshent. **1628** WITHER *Brit. Rememb.* I. 975 In hope their number keep them shall unshent. **1653** J. TAYLOR (Water P.) *Cert. Trav. Uncert. Journ.* 20 Time never was, nor n'ere I thinke shall be, That Truth (unshent) might speake, in all things free. **1817** KEATS *Sleep & Poetry* 379 The patient weeds, that now unshent by foam Feel all about their undulating home. **1868** BROWNING *Ring & Bk.* III. 1409 Let the priest retire, unshent, unshamed, Unpunished. **1898** T. HARDY *Wessex Poems* 62 Like one of those the Furnace held unshent.

un'shepherded, *ppl. a.* (UN-¹ 8.)
1850 BLACKIE *Æschylus* I. 194 Depart, ye sheep unshepherded. **1880** *Blackw. Mag.* Mar. 283 A strange flock, evidently unshepherded.

un'sheriff, *v.* (UN-² 6b.)
a **1661** FULLER *Worthies, Kent* II. (1662) 95 But he was soon un-Sheriffed by the Kings death, and another of more true Integrity substituted in his room.

un'shewed, *ppl. a.* [UN-¹ 8.] Unshown.
c **1386** CHAUCER *Par. T.* ¶999 Right so fareth synne þat longe tyme is in a man vnshewed. **1559** W. BERCHER *Nobil. Women* Pref. (Roxb.) 90 That no parte shoulde be vnshewed vnto me, a gentleman . . wolde nedes have me with hym in to the contreye.

un'shewing, *ppl. a.* [UN-¹ 10.] †Secret.
1598 R. MARKHAM in *Harington's Nugæ Ant.* (1804) I. 242 When a man hath so manie shewing friendes, and so manie unshewing enemies.

un'shielded, *ppl. a.* (UN-¹ 8.)
1700 DRYDEN *Ovid's Met.* XII. 135 Th' inviolable Body stood sincere; Though Cygnus . . scornful offer'd his unshielded Side. *c* **1790** A. WILSON *Poems, Tears of Britain*, Soon will the tempest . . This unshielded bosom most fatally wound. **1817** SCOTT *Harold* III. viii, Unshielded, mail-less, on he goes Singly against a host of foes. **1883** *Hardwick's Photogr. Chem.* 290 Exposing a small slip of the sensitive paper, unshielded, to the sun's rays.

un'shiftable, *a.* [UN-¹ 7b.]
†**1.** Incapable of helping oneself. *Obs.*
1622 S. WARD *Life of Faith in Death* 118 These fooles . . neuer thinke of the euill day, and when away they see they must goe, how vnshyftable are they! **1633** T. ADAMS *Exp. 2 Peter* ii. 9 How unshiftable otherwise shall we be in that houre, how unable to answer at the day of Iudgement!
2. Incapable of being shifted; immovable.
1890 W. J. GORDON *Foundry* 36 Secured so as to be unshiftable in a sea-way.

un'shifted, *ppl. a.* (UN-¹ 8.)
1643 GREAVES *Morbus Epidemicus* 9 Filth, and nastinesse in Diet, . . unshifted apparrell, &c. **1674** N. FAIRFAX *Bulk & Selv.* 182 It never shall be, or at least never was it body unshifted. **1863** HAWTHORNE *Our Old Home* (1879) 268 Wearing the unbrushed coat, unshifted linen, and unwashed faces of yesterday.

un'shiftiness. (UN-¹ 12.)
1870 *Sat. Rev.* 23 April 538/2 A molluscous man, too, suddenly ejected from his long-accustomed groove, . . presents just as wretched a picture of helplessness and unshiftiness.

un'shifting, *ppl. a.* (UN-¹ 10.)
1811 WORDSW. *To Beaumont* 18 An unshifting weather-cock. **1817** CHALMERS in *Edin. Rev.* Mar. 15 A small and unshifting population.

un'shifty, *a.* (UN-¹ 7. Cf. UNSHIFTINESS.)
1570 LEVINS *Manip.* 111 Vnshifty, *improuidus.*

un'shimmering, *ppl. a.* (UN-¹ 10.)
1868 GEO. ELIOT *Span. Gipsy* 50 All thought-teaching form Utters itself in firm unshimmering hues.

un'shingled, *ppl. a.* (UN-¹ 8.)
1611 in *Essex Rev.* XV. 47 The church is unleaded and unshingled. *c* **1805** A. WILSON *Foresters*, The owner, indolent and poor, His house unshingled and without a door.

un'shining, *ppl. a.* (UN-¹ 10.)
1682 CREECH *Lucretius* v. 158 Else the Sun hath secret stores of Heat, Dark and unshining stores, but vastly great. **1867** E. F. BURR *Ecce Cœlum* iii. 63 [The earth] seemed . . so different from them [*sc.* the heavenly bodies], so unshining.

un'ship, *v.* [UN-² 5, 4, 7. Cf. Du. *ontschepen*, G. *entschiffen.*]
1. *trans.* To take out of, remove or discharge from, a ship; to put on shore (or into a boat, etc.) from a vessel.
a **1450** *Contn. Brut* 542 He . . saylet toward Normaundy, and londit at Hogges, . . and vnshippit his pepill. **1497** *Naval Acc. Hen. VII* (1896) 324 Ladders for to Shep men and vnship men with. **1523** LD. BERNERS *Froiss.* I. ccxviii. 113b/2 The kynge of Ciper . . arriued at Douer, . . and refreshed hym tyll all his cariage was vnshipped. **1568** GRAFTON *Chron.* II. 210 They vnshipped their horse and harneys, not knowing in what part of England they were. **1624** CAPT. SMITH *Virginia* v. 174 They vnshipped all their goods . . into their Boats. **1641** W. HAKEWIL *Libertie of Subject* 102 Impositions are not paid upon the buying and selling of Merchandize, but when they are to ship or unship. **1719** DE FOE *Crusoe* II. (Globe) 426 In the Voyage . . he had had the Misfortune to be five Times shipp'd and unshipp'd. **1726** SWIFT *Gulliver* II. i, We unshipped our goods. **1837** HT. MARTINEAU *Soc. Amer.* II. 6 All hands were busy in unshipping the cargo, to lighten the vessel. **1885** *Act 48–49 Vic.* c. 41 §17 Any harbour . . at which vessels can . . ship or unship goods or passengers.
refl. *a* **1604** HANMER *Chron. Irel.* (1809) 253 They forthwith landed, and unshipped themselves.
b. To deprive of, dismiss from, a ship.
1829 MARRYAT *F. Mildmay* xxi, I should have unshipped him next cruise.
2. *Naut.* To detach or remove (esp. a mast, rudder, or oar) from a fixed place or position.
1598 HAKLUYT *Voy.* I. 235 We were not able to beare in, but by violence were constrained to take the sea agayne, our Pinnesse being vnshipt. **1769** FALCONER *Dict. Marine* (1776), *Dégarnir le cabestan*, to unrig the capstern, by taking off the voyol, and unshipping the bars. **1773** COOK *S. Voy.* (1777) II. ii. I. 205 He . . dived under the boat, and . . unshipped the rudder. **1806** PIKE *Sources Mississ.* (1810) 102 Obliged to unship our mast to prevent its rolling overboard. **1865** DICKENS *Mut. Fr.* I. i, The speaker at the same time unshipping his scull on that side. **1874** BEDFORD *Sailor's Pocket Bk.* viii. 241 So that . . the apparatus . . may . . be . . unshipped and re-shipped again at pleasure.
fig. **1816** *Sporting Mag.* XLVII. 277 Crocken . . beat a Knightsbridge wheelwright . . by unshipping his jaw in the fourth round.
b. In general use.
1793 SMEATON *Edystone L.* §140 Unshipping the tackle belonging to the lantern. **1832** *Lincoln Herald* 13 Jan. 2 John Page saw Clarke unship the flag on the top of the governor's house. **1839** F. A. GRIFFITHS *Artill. Man.* 87 No 1 unships the handspike. **1882** SALA *Amer. Revis.* (1885) 384 Tell the porter not to unship the little one-legged flap table . . fixed to the wall of the car.
3. *intr.* **a.** To admit of being detached or removed.
1834 MARRYAT *P. Simple* II. 30 Six large pieces of iron, . . with a gimblet at one end of each, and a square at the other, which fitted to a handle which unshipped. **1844** STEPHENS *Bk. Farm* III. 1169 The top-sides . . are fitted to ship and unship as occasion may require. **1862** *Catal. Internat. Exhib., Brit.* II. No. 2256, The upper ladders unship by means of shifting levers.
b. To become detached.
1867 SMYTH *Sailor's Word-bk.* 161 *Capstan-bar Pins*, pins inserted through their ends to prevent their unshipping. **1883** *Pall Mall G.* 13 Mar. 10/2 The boat's rudder unshipped and caused the boat to capsize.
4. To undergo unloading from a vessel.
1860 DICKENS *Christmas Stories, Message fr. Sea* i, Such other cargo as was . . unshipping at the pier.
5. *trans.* **a.** Of a horse: To unseat, throw (the rider).
1831 SCOTT *Let.* in *Westm. Gaz.* 14 June (1904) 12/2 My forester walks by his [*sc.* the pony's] head for fear a start or sudden stumble should unship me altogether. **1853** R. S. SURTEES *Sponge's Sp. Tour* lxvii, One [horse] has still his muzzle on, lest he should unship his rider and eat him.
b. To unbalance, upset.
1827 CHALMERS in Hanna *Life* (1851) III. 163, I really fear lest his [*sc.* Irving's] prophecies may unship him altogether.
Hence **un'shipped** *ppl. a.*, **un'shipping** *vbl. sb.*
1868 MORRIS *Earthly Par.* (1870) II. III. 389 A ring of Icelanders, who sat Upon the bales of *unshipped goods. **1497** *Naval Acc. Hen. VII* (1896) 327 Ladders for shippyng & *vnshippyng of men. **1709** *Act 8 Anne* c. 7 §17 The Persons . . to whose Hands the same shall knowingly come, after the unshipping thereof. **1803** *Act 43 Geo. III*, c. 132 §28 To prevent the fraudulently unshipping or re-landing of Goods.

un'shiplike, *a.* (UN-¹ 7c.)
1842 DICKENS *Amer. Notes* (1868) 46 A sullen, cumbrous, ungraceful, unshiplike leviathan. **1859** —— *Lett.* (1880) II. 101, I thought her [*sc.* the Great Eastern] the ugliest and most unshiplike thing these eyes ever beheld.

un'shipment. (f. UNSHIP *v.*)
1846 WORCESTER (citing *Penny Mag.*). **1879** MISS BRADDON *Vixen* III. 273 Mr. Vawdrey . . came round to assist in the unshipment of Violet's belongings.

un'shipped, *a.* [UN-¹ 9.] Not provided with a ship.
1720 DE FOE *Capt. Singleton* v. (1840) 82 We were . . all upon a level, as to our travelling, being unshipped. **1725** —— *Voy. round World* (1840) 200 We should be like a company of freebooters loose and unshipped. **1827** POLLOK *Course T.* II. 241 Choosing, thus unshipped, Uncompassed, unprovisioned, . . To swim a sea of breadth immeasurable.

un'shipshape, *a.* (UN-¹ 7.)
1883 *Harper's Mag.* Jan. 198/2 Never was seen so unshipshape and disreputable a locomotive as that on duty here.

un'shipwrecked, *ppl. a.* (UN-¹ 8.)
c **1637** H. KING *The Sovereign* 14 That golden constellation . . guides the seaman . . Safe and unshipwrack'd through the troubled streams.

un'shirted, *a. U.S. slang.* [UN-¹ 9.] In phr. ***unshirted hell***, serious trouble; 'a bad time'.
1932 *Sun* (Baltimore) 6 Jan. 10/3 When he proposed certain policies on prohibition . . he was given what is known in rural districts hereabouts as 'unshirted hell'. **1954** F. P. KEYES *Royal Box* v. 67 She and his playboy son are going to fall for each other and then there will be unshirted hell. **1979** H. KISSINGER *White House Years* xxi. 897 I've been catching unshirted hell every half-hour from the President who says we're not tough enough.

un'shivered, *ppl. a.* (UN-¹ 8.)
1597 BP. HALL *Sat.* V. iii, Theirs, like anuilles, bore the hammers head, Our glasse can neuer touch vnshiuered. ? **1827** MRS. HEMANS *Last Constantine* x, So may thy helmet tower Unshiver'd through the storm.

un'shivering, *ppl. a.* (UN-¹ 10.)
1818 MILMAN *Samor* VIII. 555 On Went Samor with unshivering naked foot.

un'shocked, *ppl. a.* (UN-¹ 8.)
1712 TICKELL in *Spect.* No. 532, Thy spotless Thoughts unshock'd the Priest may hear. **1774** FOOTE *Cozeners* II, You must have the heart of a tiger, to stand unshocked at such a horrible scene. **1816** BYRON *Prisoner of Chillon* vi, The very rock hath rock'd, And I have felt it shake, unshock'd. **1891** H. HERMAN *His Angel* 57 Though her seasoned ear . . remained unshocked by an occasional outburst.

un'shod, *ppl. a.* [UN-¹ 8b, or f. UNSHOE *v.* Cf. UNSHOED *ppl. a.* and Sw. *oskodd.*]
1. Of persons, or the feet: Having a shoe or shoes not put on, or taken off; not wearing shoes, barefooted.
c **897** K. ÆLFRED *Gregory's Past. C.* v. 45 Ðonne bið us suiðe fracoðlice oðer fot unscod. *c* **1000** ÆLFRIC *Deut.* xxv. 10 Nemne hine ælc man on Israhela folce unsceoda. *a* **1300** *Cursor M.* 15099 Tuelue or ma o men vnscod þan has he wit him broght. **1382** WYCLIF *Isaiah* xx. 3 As wente . . Isaie nakid and vnshod. *Ibid.* 4. **1596** SPENSER *F.Q.* II. xi. 23 There follow'd fast at hand two wicked Hags, . . Their feet vnshod, their bodies wrapt in rags. **1627** DRAYTON *Battle of Agincourt* 26 Vnshod, and without stockings are the best. **1693** tr. *Emilianne's Hist. Monast. Ord.* 156 The Order of the Unshod Carmelites. **1728** POPE *Dunc.* III. 114 Men bearded, bald, . . shod, unshod. **1781** COWPER *Ep. Prot. Lady* 16 With unshod feet they yet securely tread. **1849** C. BRONTE *Shirley* xxxiii, He left his shoes on the mat; mounted the stairs unshod. **1870** ROSSETTI *Burden Nineveh* ix, Any god Before whose feet men knelt unshod.
absol. **1382** WYCLIF *Deut.* xxv. 10 The hows of the vnshod. **1847** F. PRANDI tr. *Cantu's Ref. Europe* I. 212 The Order of the Unshod.
transf. **1535** COVERDALE *Deut.* xxv. 10 And his name shalbe called in Israel, the vnshodd house.
2. Of horses: Having cast a shoe or shoes; not furnished with shoes.
1523 LD. BERNERS *Froiss.* I. xviii. 9/2 Most part of their horses [were] hurt on their back, nor they had nat wherwith to shoo them, that were vnshodde. **1530** PALSGR. 768/2 Your horse is unshod of bothe his hynder fete. **1610** HOLLAND *Camden's Brit.* 529 They use their Horses unshod. **1680** *Lond. Gaz.* No. 1569/4 One dark bay Nag, . . lately rowelled, and trots all, and unshod. **1839** DARWIN *Voy. Nat.* x. 225 [It] would soon disable an unshod horse from taking part in the chase.
3. Not protected by an iron rim, toe-piece, etc.
1497 *Naval Acc. Hen. VII* (1896) 87 A pair wheles vnshodd. **1557** in Raine *Richmond. Wills* (1853) 101 One yron bound wayne and ij. unshode cowpes. **1601** in Moryson *Itin.* II. (1617) 204 Ten Culuerings . . mounted vpon vnshod wheeles. **1660** *Act 12 Chas. II*, c. 4 *Rates*, Shovells, unshod, the dozen, iijs. iiijd. **1869** A. HUME *Brit. Antiq.* 27 The unshod wooden wheels of timber carriages.

un'shodden, *ppl. a.* (UN-¹ 8b.)
1836 F. MAHONY *Rel. Father Prout* 176 It is far from my purpose . . to tread on such solemn ground save with . . feet duly unshodden. **1838** LYTTON *Calderon* iv, To place our unshodden feet upon the necks of kings.

un'shoe, *v.* [UN-² 4. Cf. OE. *an-*, *on-*, *unscóȝian*, MDu. *ontscoeyen*, *-scoen* (Du. *-schoeien*), MLG. *entschoien*, OHG. *in(t)scuohôn* (MHG. *entschuohen*, G. *-schuhen*).] *trans.* To remove a shoe or shoes from; to strip or deprive of shoes.
1481 CAXTON *Reynard* xix. (Arb.) 45 Whan Isegrym was vnshoed, Tho muste . . his wyf lye doun in the grasse [etc.]. **1530** PALSGR. 768/2, I unshoo a horse, *je deferre.* **1591** SYLVESTER *Du Bartas* I. iii. 767 O Moon-wort! tell us where thou hid'st the Smith, Hammer, and Pincers, thou unshoo'st them with? **1628** tr. *Mathieu's Powerfull Fav.* 1 They are unshod of their high shooes that eleuated them aboue others. **1653** CULPEPPER *Eng. Phys. Enlarged* (1656) 163 Moon-wort is an herb which they say wil . . unshoo such Horses as tread upon it. **1677** GILPIN *Demonol.* I. xiii. 102 They were told . . that this did unshoo their Foot, and afflicted them with Thirst and Want. **1827** HONE *Every-day Bk.* II. 197 They were to unshoe themselves. **1868** HOLME LEE *B. Godfrey* xliii, Joan unshod her feet.
transf. **1852** BURN *Naval & Mil. Techn. Dict.* II. 302/1 To Unshoe a wheel, *ôter la bande, les bandes de roue.*
b. ***unshoe-the-horse***, the plant moonwort. ? *Obs.*
1635 SWAN *Spec. M.* vi. §4 (1644) 251 The Italians call it Vnshoe-the-horse; because if they tread upon it, they lose their shoes. **1653** CULPEPPER *Eng. Phys. Enlarged* (1656) 163 Country people that I know, cal it Unshoo the Horse. **1878** DICKINSON *Cumbld. Gloss.* 85 *Unshoe the horse*, I have heard the *Botrychium Lunaria* plant so called.
Hence **un'shoeing** *vbl. sb.*

1580 HOLLYBAND *Treas. Fr. Tong, Dechaussement*, an vnshoing. **1653** URQUHART *Rabelais* I. xxii. 95 Gargantua.. played..at [the game] the unshoing of the Asse.

un'shoed, *ppl. a.* [UN-¹ 8, or f. UNSHOE *v.* Cf. MDu. *ongescoeit, -scoet* (Du. *-schoied*, †*-schoed*), MLG. *ungeschoiet*, MHG. *-schuohet* (G. *-schuht*), ON. *úskúaðr* (Da. *uskoet*).] = UNSHOD *ppl. a.* Also *transf.*

1388 WYCLIF *Isaiah* xx. 3 As my seruaunt Ysaie ȝede nakid and vnshood. *c* **1440** *Pallad. on Husb.* I. 860 A menstruate vngird womman, vnshood, Vntressed. **1479** *Cely Papers* (Camden) 19 To bye for me a carthe at Caleys..unschude the wyllys [= wheels]. **1530** TINDALE *Deut.* xxv. 10 His name shalbe called in Israel, the vnshoed housse. *a* **1564** BECON *Wks.* Pref. ciij b, The shooe, that is moulde with thee, is the shooe of him that is vnshood. **1865** H. H. DIXON *Field & Fern, South* 34 There are ponies, too,..fat and unshoed.

un'shook, obs. or arch. var. UNSHAKEN *ppl. a.*

1633 FORD *Broken H.* v. ii, Stretch out Thine arm with vigour, and unshook virtue. *a* **1644** QUARLES *Sol. Recant.* IX. ii. 42 They gain the Port..With Ribs unshook. **1736** THOMSON *Liberty* IV. 430 On the groaning mast With unshook knee to know their giddy way. **1893** KIPLING *Many Inventions* p. ix, May I look with heart unshook On blow brought home or missed.

un'shop, *v.* [UN-² 5.] (See quot.)

1839 F. LIEBER *Pol. Ethics* II. iv. §38. 349 High rewards were paid for discovering any disobedience, or even for 'unshopping,' that is, throwing out of employment, highly skillful hands.

un'shored, *a.* [UN-¹ 9.] Shoreless.

1881 MASSON *De Quincey* 63 Unshored astronomical abysses.

un'shorn, *ppl. a.* [UN-¹ 8 b. Cf. OE. *unscoren*, MDu. *ongescoren* (Du. *-schoren*), OHG. *ungescoran* (MHG. *ungeschorn*, G. *-schoren*), ON. *úskorinn* (Sw. *oskuren*, Da. *uskaaren*).]

1. Not shorn, cut, or cropped: **a.** Of cloth.

1464 *Rolls of Parlt.* V. 564/2 [No person shall buy] eny Wolles than unshorn, or take promesse of bargayn of eny Wolles than unshoren. **1486** *Bk. St. Albans* b v, A dagon or pece of Rough blanket vnshoron. **1535-** [see UNBARBED 1]. **1597** SHAKS. *Lover's Compl.* 94 His phenix downe began but to appeare Like vnshorne veluet. **1675** HOBBES *Odyssey* (1677) 232 He wore a purple vest, Unshorn, and lin'd. **1700** DRYDEN *Flower & Leaf* 266 White Velvet, but unshorn, for Cloaks they wore. **1716** GAY *Trivia* I. 47 True Witney broad-cloth, with its shag unshorn.

b. Of persons or animals, hair, etc.

c **1449** PECOCK *Repr.* I. xx. 118 The heer of wommennys heed vnschorn. **1565** COOPER *Thesaurus* s.v. *Intonsus*, Sheepe vnshorne. **1577** B. GOOGE *Heresbach's Husb.* 138 Bye not your Sheepe but washed and vnshorne. **1596** W. SMITH *Chloris* xlviii, Those curled locks which thou wast wont to twist, Vnkempt, vnshorne, and out of order beene. **1628** MILTON *Vac. Exerc.* 37 Listening to what unshorn Apollo sings. **1693** DRYDEN tr. *Ovid's Met.* I. 766 As the Locks of Phœbus are unshorn. **1820** KEATS *Eve St. Agnes* viii, All amort, Save to St. Agnes and her lambs unshorn. **1848** THACKERAY *Van. Fair* xxxix, The caresses of the old gentleman, unshorn and perfumed with tobacco.

c. Of corn, fields, etc.

1573 TUSSER *Husb.* (1878) 105 Some mowe vp their hedlonds and plots among corne, and driuen to leaue nothing, vnmowne, or vnshorne. **1601** CAMPION *Wks.* (1909) 21 A Meadow yet vnshorne. **1631** QUARLES *Samson* Wks. (Grosart) II. 155/2 His rip'ned Corne; Whereof, some part..stood unshorne. **1697** DRYDEN *Virg. Past.* v. 98 The mountain-tops unshorn, the rocks, rejoice. **1757** AKENSIDE *Pleas. Imag.* I. 316 The pathless woods unshorn That wave o'er huge Olympus. **1810** SCOTT *Lady of L.* I. xxvi, Of mountain fir, with bark unshorn. *a* **1850** BRYANT *Prairies* 2 These are..The unshorn fields, boundless and beautiful. **1873** SYMONDS *Grk. Poets* vii. 222 This garland..Of wilding flowers plucked from an unshorn meadow.

2. *fig.* Not reduced or diminished; not deprived *of* something.

1818 BYRON *Ch. Har.* IV. lxxii, An Iris sits..and..bears serene Its brilliant hues with all their beams unshorn. **1818** KEATS *'There is a charm'* 12 One who was great through mortal days, and died of fame unshorn. **1821-2** SHELLEY *Chas. I*, II. 142 To his God Alone he must deliver up his trust, Unshorn of its permitted attributes.

un'shortened, *ppl. a.* (UN-¹ 8.)

1744 YOUNG *Nt. Th.* VI. 542 Unshortened by progression infinite! Futurity for ever future! **1805** *Ann. Rev.* III. 244 Every tax should..leave unshortened to speculation his casting-net, and to industry his oar. **1855** *Poultry Chron.* III. 496/1 The buds..may be left unshortened until the end of September. **1878** RUSKIN *Notes* 77 His full, final, unshortened strength is in these [drawings].

un'shot, *ppl. a.* [UN-¹ 8 b.]

1. a. Not fired or let off.

1544 *Exped. Scotl.* in *Fragm. Sc. Hist.* (1798) 14 The Scottes fledde from theyr ordinaunces, leuyng them vnshot. **1686** WALLER *Night Piece* 32 He..With Cupid's pointed Arrows plays; They, with a touch, they are so keen, Wound us unshot, and She unseen. **1899** J. MILNE *Romance of Pro-Consul* vi. 52 For his own gun, he snatched an unshot one which the man was struggling to release from its cover.

b. Not struck by a shot; not shot *at*.

[**1755** JOHNSON.] **1897** *Outing* XXIX. 368/1 The deer left suddenly and unshot. *Ibid.*, We found them easily,..and as before they whirled away unshot at to the cover.

2. Of grain: Not come into ear; not sprouted.

1854 H. MILLER *Sch. & Schm.* xxv. 527 Fields..waving with the yet unshot corn. **1893** *Times* 8 June 12/4 Barley and oats had been lying in the soil for a long time unshot.

3. Not shot out or deposited.

1882 *Pall Mall G.* 7 Oct. 1 France is full of the unshot, unburned rubbish of her last financial orgie.

un'shot, *v.* (UN-² 5.)

1805 JAMES *Milit. Dict.* (ed. 2), *To unshot a gun*, to take the ball out of a piece of ordnance.

un'shotted, *ppl. a.* [UN-¹ 9.] Not loaded with shot.

1802 *Naval Chron.* VII. 18 The Phœnix fired a gun.. unshotted. **1856** FROUDE *Hist. Eng.* vii. II. 229 Mere idle sounds, like the bellow of unshotted cannon.

un'shoulder, *v.* [UN-² 4.]

1. *trans.* (See quot.) *rare*⁻⁰.

1598 FLORIO, *Spallare*, to vnshoulder, to put ones shoulders out of ioint.

2. To remove from the shoulder.

1625 MARKHAM *Souldiers Accid.* 11 The two Rankes next it must vnshoulder their Musquets. **1650** R. ELTON *Military Art* (1659) 192 Unshoulder your Musket and poyse. **1859** R. F. BURTON in *Jrnl. Geog. Soc.* XXIX. 414 At a short distance they halt, unshoulder their burdens. **1882** ELWES tr. *Fr. Benguella to Yacca* I. xii. 346 The goods all unshouldered and dispersed.

un'shouldered, *a.* (UN-¹ 9.)

1790 SPEECHLY *Culture Vine* 6 The berries of this species ..compose long unshouldered bunches.

un'shout, *v.* (UN-² 3.)

1607 SHAKS. *Cor.* v. v. 4 Vnshoot the noise that banish'd Martius; Repeale him, with the welcome of his Mother.

un'shovel, *v.* [UN-² 4 b.] *trans.* To uncover by removing a shovel-hat.

1836 T. HOOK *G. Gurney* III. 228 'Sir,' said my clerical friend, unshovelling his head, 'I am extremely glad to see you'.

un'shovelled, *ppl. a.* (UN-¹ 8.)

[**1775** ASH.] **1828** *Craven Gloss.*, *Unshooled*, not shovelled, uncleansed. **1855** WHITMAN *Song of Myself* xxii, Sea of the brine of life and of unshovell'd, yet always-ready graves.

un'showered, *ppl. a.* [UN-¹ 8.] Not moistened by showers.

1629 MILTON *Hymn Nativ.* xxiv, Nor is Osiris seen.. Trampling the unshowr'd Grasse with lowings loud. **1873** SYMONDS *Grk. Poets* vii. 196 Bringing Oedipus to die among the unshowered meadows of those Dread Ladies.

un'shown, *ppl. a.* (UN-¹ 8 b.)

1606 SHAKS. *Ant. & Cl.* III. vi. 52 You..haue preuented The ostentation of our loue; which left vnshewne, Is often left vnlou'd. **1614** SYLVESTER *Bethulia's Rescue* IV. 45 Though, as unknown, to pass unshown shee ween, Her Odors made her smelt, her Jewels seen. **1648** HEXHAM II, *Ongetoont*, Vnshowne, or Vndemonstrated. **1832** L. HUNT *Gentle Armour* ii. 16 The stranger, with his face unshewn, Rides in. **1865** M. ARNOLD *Ess. Crit.* 286 Marcus Aurelius saw it [Christianity] with its future yet unshown.

un'showy, *a.* (UN-¹ 7.)

1838 LYTTON *Alice* III. vi, There was another, equally hard-favoured and unshowy,..and that virtue was Justice.

un'shrine, *v.* [UN-² 5.] *trans.* To remove from, cast out of, a shrine. Also *fig.*

1599 *Life Sir T. More* in Wordsw. *Eccl. Biog.* (1853) II. 181 We have of late unshrined him [*sc.* Thomas of Canterbury]. **1609** HOLLAND *Amm. Marcell.* 230 The image of Apollo Chomeus being displaced, unshrined, and brought to Rome. **1652** BENLOWES *Theoph.* VII. xvii, Could'st thou.., from each golden cell, unshrine Those beams. **1807** J. BARLOW *Columb.* IX. 612 Descartes.. Unshrines old errors and propounds his own. **1827** CARLYLE *Germ. Rom.* I. 5 Musäus grasped his satirical hammer; and with lusty strokes, defaced and unshrined the false divinity.

un'shrined, *ppl. a.* [UN-¹ 8.] Not enshrined; unburied.

1297 R. GLOUC. (Rolls) 10661 Sein tomas body..adde ileye an erþe vnssrined vifti ȝer. **1614** GORGES *Lucan* VI. 242 If that she..doe finde A carkasse on the ground vn-shrinde. **1846** WORCESTER (citing Southey).

un'shrinement. (f. UNSHRINE *v.*)

1891 *Athenæum* 21 March 382/3 Of the disposal of St. Thomas's skeleton at the unshrinement there are two stories.

un'shrinkable, *a.* (UN-¹ 7 b.)

1885 *Army & Navy Co-op. Soc. Price List* July 1300 Flannels..Unshrinkable so-called. **1897** *Voice* (N.Y.) 1 Apr. 3/4 The Methodist vote is one of the unshrinkable assets of that party.

Hence **ˌunshrinka'bility**.

1934 in WEBSTER. **1946** *Nature* 5 Oct. 476/2 A high degree of unshrinkability is obtained with 10 per cent of polymer within the fibres. **1963** A. J. HALL *Textile Sci.* v. 249 This treatment is continued until almost complete unshrinkability is obtained.

un'shrinking, *ppl. a.* [UN-¹ 10.] Not shrinking or drawing back; unyielding, firm.

1605 SHAKS. *Macb.* v. viii. 42 The which no sooner had his Prowesse confirm'd In the vnshrinking station where he fought, But like a man he dy'de. **1706** WATTS *Horæ Lyr.* II. (1743) 169 He that unshrinking and without a Groan, Bears the first Wound. **1799** SHERIDAN *Pizarro* IV. ii, Thy unshrinking ears may at last be feasted with the music of my cries. **1845** M. PATTISON *Ess.* (1889) I. 15 A union of prudence, tact, firmness, and unshrinking principle. **1878** B. TAYLOR *Deukalion* I. iv. 34 The firm-set lips, And level glance of thine unshrinking eyes.

Hence **un'shrinkingly** *adv.*

1826 MRS. HEMANS *Forest Sanctuary* I. xlv, There was one, with whom..Thou might'st perchance, unshrinkingly have died. **1857** SUSANNA WINKWORTH tr. *Life Tauler* 135 They..unshrinkingly declared their adherence to all that they had hitherto taught.

un'shrived, variant of next.

[**1775** ASH.] **1812** J. WILSON *Isle of Palms*, etc. 258 Had unshrieved guilt for one moment been there, His heart had turn'd to stone! **1819** SHELLEY *Cenci* IV. i. 89 As she shall die unshrived and unforgiven. **1820** SCOTT *Monast.* xxiii.

un'shriven, *ppl. a.* (UN-¹ 8 b.)

a **1225** *Ancr. R.* 314 Me telleð..of on oðer mon þet..deide unschriuen þerof. *a* **1300** *Cursor M.* 23122 Vn-scriuen war þai at þair end, Bot deied in dedli sin. *c* **1395** *Plowman's Tale* III. vii, Though all her paryshe dye vnshriue. *c* **1440** *Jacob's Well* 181 For on dedly synne vnschreuyn, þou schalt be dampnyd. *c* **1450** *Mirk's Festial* 100 He may do..mony venyall synnys vnshryuen. **1813** HOGG *Queen's Wake* 287 Sires, in dread of sins unshriven. **1850** S. DOBELL *Roman* i. 9 Thoughts, which..would have gone..down to hell, unblest, unshriven. **1858** [see UNPRIESTED].

un'shroud, *v.*¹ [UN-² 5, 3.]

1. *trans.* To strip of a shroud; *fig.* to uncover, lay bare, expose. Also **un'shrouding** *vbl. sb.*

1594 SOUTHWELL *M. Magd. Funeral Teares* 27 b, Yea, would he haue bin so venturous, as to haue stayed the vnshrowding of the corse? **1633** P. FLETCHER *Purple Isl.* XII. xxv, At length the piercing Sunne his team unshrouds, And with his arrows th' idle fogge doth chase. **1653** A. WILSON *Inconstant Ladie* V. iii, Vnshroud thyselfe thou night-rauen. *a* **1773** FERGUSSON *Poems* (1879) 177 Turn, fair Amanda! cheer your swain, Unshroud him from his veil of woe. **1791** E. DARWIN *Bot. Gard.* II. 133 Now the broad Sun his golden orb unshrouds. **1821** SCOTT *Kenilw.* viii, Unshrouding the dark lantern, which had hitherto only emitted an indistinct glimmer. **1824** CAMPBELL *Dream* 26 Methought I beheld two hands a space Slow unshroud a spectre's face.

2. To open out.

1846 *New Monthly Mag.* Dec. 488 Without.. unshrouding the folds of my mantle, I stalked towards the sofa.

un'shroud, *v.*² [UN-² 4.] *trans.* To strip (a vessel) of shrouds or ropes.

1584 HUDSON *Judith* II. (1608) 36 The quiet see..growes .., And lastly beates the banks, and ships vnshrouds.

un'shrouded, *ppl. a.* [UN-¹ 8.] Not wrapped in, or covered with, a shroud. Also *fig.*

1410 HEALEY *St. Aug. Citie of God* 384 So be thy face unshrouded And thy pure hornes unclouded! **1742** BLAIR *Grave* 152 There's not a Dungeon-Slave, that's bury'd In the High-way, unshrouded and uncoffin'd, But..sleeps as sound as He. **1799** SHERIDAN *Pizarro* III. ii, He will..open ..his unshrouded eyes, and bless me with his last look. **1823** PRAED *Troubadour* I. 516 They walked upon the earth, Unshrouded, in a ghastly mirth. **1855** SINGLETON *Virgil* II. 266 Had Cytherea not a token deigned From the unshrouded Sky.

un'shrubbed, *a.* (UN-¹ 9.)

1610 SHAKS. *Temp.* IV. i. 81 Who..with each end of thy blew bowe do'st crowne My boskie acres, and my vnshrubd downe.

un'shrunken, *ppl. a.* (UN-¹ 8 b.)

1862 LYTTON *Str. Story* II. 39 With enough of vigour for years to come..in the unshrunken muscle of his limbs. **1897** *Allbutt's Syst. Med.* IV. 475 When the skin is cut into..it remains unshrunken.

un'shuffled, *ppl. a.* (UN-¹ 8.)

[**1775** ASH.] **1901** *Munsey's Mag.* XXIV. 871/2 Playing with unshuffled cards.

un'shunnable, *a.* (UN-¹ 7 b.)

1604 SHAKS. *Oth.* III. iii. 275 'Tis destiny vnshunnable, like death. **1839** F. BARHAM tr. *Grotius' Adamus Exul* v. 47 Deadly rage, And the black hurricane of thick despair Urge on the unshunnable doom. **1890** FURNESS *Variorum Shaks.* VIII. Pref. p. vii, It makes no difference whether the unshunnable outcry is in French, or German, or English.

un'shunned, *ppl. a.* (UN-¹ 8.)

1603 SHAKS. *Meas. for M.* III. ii. 63 An vnshun'd consequence, it must be so. **1648** HEXHAM II, *Ongemijdt*, Vnshunned, or Vn-avoided.

un'shunning, *ppl. a.* [UN-¹ 10.] † Unavoidable.

1593 Q. ELIZ. *Boeth.* V. pr. i. 50 Order it self that goes on with an vnshonning [L. *inevitabili*] turne.

un'shunted, *ppl. a.* (UN-¹ 8.)

1873 F. JENKIN *Electr. & Magn.* xvi. §3 The sensibility.. of the unshunted galvanometer.

un'shut, *v.* [UN-² 3, 7. Cf. OE. *unscyttan.*]

1. *trans.* To open or unlock (a door, etc.); †to undo (a lock). Now *rare*.

13.. *Coer de L.* 4212 On schal dwelle the clos withinne, The gate to unschette and unpynne, And stylly to unschette the lok. *c* **1315** SHOREHAM I. 2228 Nou, lord, þat coudest maky open þet no man coude ounschette. **1370-80** *Visions of St. Paul* 198 in *O.E. Misc.* 228 He opened þe Mouþ of þat put, Hit stonk foule woȝon hit was vn-schut. *c* **1412** HOCCLEVE *De Reg. Princ.* 679 My purs I wole vnschete. **1470-85** MALORY *Arthur* XI. iii. 574 Anone as he had vnshet the wyndowe. *c* **1475** *Mankind* 52 in *Macro Plays* 3 On-schett yowur lokke, & take an halpenye. **1530** PALSGR. 768/2, I unshote, I open, *je defferme. Ibid.*, Unshote the doore. [Cf. 285/2 Unshittyng, *deffermure.*] **1611** COTGR., *Deffermer*, to open; to vnshut, or vndoe a thing shut. **1873** BROWNING *Red Cott. Nt.-cap* 274 Compare such paragon With any scarabæus of the brood That..keeps wing in wingcase;.. the couple yonder..never bade unshut from sheath the gauze.

absol. *c* **1430** LYDG. *Min. Poems* 52 Off Abyssi this Aungel bar the keyes, Callid *Clauis Dauid* to shettyn and vnshette.

fig. *c* **1412** HOCCLEVE *De Reg. Princ.* 1573 Thre causes ben, whiche I þe wole vnschette And open a-non, whi þou schalt with hire dele. **1513** DOUGLAS *Æneid* XII. Prol. 121 Gymp gerraflouris thar royn levys vnschet. **1589** FLEMING *Virg. Georg.* II. 24, I enter..on things of old and ancient praise,.. being bold t'vnshut or open holie springs.

b. *intr.* To become open.

1390 GOWER *Conf.* II. 102 Ther is no dore, which mai charke, Wherof an yhe scholde unschette. *a* **1400** *Stockholm Med. MS.* II. 390 in *Anglia* XVIII. 317 Ley hem on neuer so strong a lok, It schal onschetyn & onstrok. **1649** G. DANIEL *Trinarch., Hen. V*, cxxix, Wee..need not feare an Asse's Load Of Solar Earth, can force the Gates vnshutt.

2. *dial.* To unharness (a horse).

1817 in Burne *Folk-Lore* (1883) 611 His team's unshut, his whip's laid up. **1841** HARTSHORNE *Salop. Ant.* Gloss., *Unshut*, to unlink, or ungear horses. **1879** *Shropshire Word-bk.* 310.

un'shut, *ppl. a.* [f. prec. or UN-^{1} 8 b.]

1. Opened, unclosed; not closed or shut.

c **1384** CHAUCER *H. Fame* III. 1953 And be day..Been al the dores opened wide And be nyght echon vnshet. **1426** LYDG. *De Guil. Pilgr.* 23403 The gate..Of the castel stood vnshet. **1491** CAXTON *Vitas Patr.* (W. de W. 1495) II. 259/2 An hous the whiche byfore outwarde is moche ornate..but behynde all unshytte &..ruynous. ? **1606** ROWLANDS *Terrible Battell* (Hunterian Cl.) 36 From eare to eare thou hast a mouth vnshut. **1691** E. TAYLOR *Behmen's Theos. Philos.* 331 Whereby we ascend into his Arms, the unshut Light-World. **1849** M. ARNOLD *Forsaken Merman* 44 Where great whales come sailing by, Sail and sail, with unshut eye. *a* **1851** MOIR *Poems, Tombless Man* iii, And, in the midst,.. An unshut gateway.

2. Not shut *up*.

1610 BP. HALL *Apol. agst. Brownists* lv. 134 The plague.. of sinne vnshut vp and vncouered.

un'shutter, *v.* (UN-^{2} 4.)

1861 HUGHES *Tom Brown at Oxf.* xvii, He unshuttered the little lattice window of the room on the ground-floor. [Also in recent use (1901-).]

un'shuttered, *ppl. a.* (UN-^{1} 8.)

1845 JAMES *Arrah Neil* II. iii. 39 From an open door, or unshuttered window, the lights..served also for the benefit of the passenger. **1883** 'OUIDA' *Wanda* I. 58 She seated herself here by the unshuttered casement.

un'shy, *a.* (UN-^{1} 7.)

1748 RICHARDSON *Clarissa* II. 45 It would be doing Mr. Solmes a spight, to wish him such a shy, un-shy girl. **1841** LADY LYTTELTON *Let.* 29 July, I was thinking how totally unshy I was!

un'shyly, *adv.* (UN-^{1} 11.)

1814 LADY LYTTELTON *Let.* 12 Sept., Pretty [German school-]girls of all ages answering very unshyly.

unsib, *sb.*: see UN-^{1} 3 (s.v. *unisibbe*).

†**un'sib**, *a.* *Obs.* [UN-^{1} 7. Cf. OE. *ungesib*, OHG. *unsibbi*, *-sippi* (MHG. *unsippe*), Goth. *unsibjis*.] Not related, not of kin. In quots. *absol.*

c **1200** ORMIN 2474 And ȝhot [= she it] forrhall wiþþ alle menn Wiþþ sibbe & wiþþ unnsibbe. **1303** R. BRUNNE *Handl. Synne* 1198 To holy land, ȝyf þou haue hyt hette; Syb, ne vnsyb, may hyt lette.

un'sick, *a.* (UN-^{1} 7. Cf. older Du. *onziek*, ON. *úsjúkr*, MSw. *osiuker*, MDa. *usjug*.)

a **1500** *Chaucer's Dreme* 1205 And I..Up rose..Hole and vnsicke, right wele at ease. *c* **1540** COPLAND *Hye Way to Spyttel Ho.* 198 Bedrid folke, and suche as can not crave,.. But not every unseke stoborne knave. **1594** DANIEL *Cleopatra* K 4 b, What comforts vnsicke Eloquence can sound, And yet all fayles vs in the poynt of trying.

un'sicker, *a.* *Obs.* exc. *Sc.* [UN-^{1} 7. Cf. NFris. *unseker*, MDu. *onseker* (Du. *onzeker*), MLG. *unseker*, OHG. *unsichûre* (MHG. and G. *unsicher*), MDa. *usekker*, Da. *usikker*, Sw. *osäker*.] Uncertain; unsafe; insecure.

a **1225** *Ancr. R.* 144 Deað þet we beoð siker of & unsiker hwonne. *c* **1325** *Metr. Hom.* 83 Gode ensaumpil may thai lere, Unsikir of thaim self to be. *c* **1330** R. BRUNNE *Chron. Wace* (Rolls) 9636 Bot þer hap was al vnsyker; For synne of Octa..Dide al his felawes & hym be lorn. **1387** TREVISA *Higden* (Rolls) VIII. 327 Þe buldyng uppon.. unsikergrounde bygynneþ to slyde. *c* **1412** HOCCLEVE *De Reg. Princ.* 41 Thus vnsikir of my smal lyfloode. **1470–85** MALORY *Arthur* XVII. xxiii. 724 Galahad prayed yow to remembre of this vnsyker world. **1533** BELLENDEN *Livy* IV. v. (S.T.S.) II. 66 He had levir returne to rome with sikkir victorie þan vnsikkir pece of wolchis. *a* **1578** LINDESAY (Pitscottie) *Chron. Scot.* (S.T.S.) I. 33 It was vnsickir to comit his lyfe and honoure in the binding wp of bandis witht the Earle of Douglas. **1796** BURNS *To Colonel de Peyster* iii, Dame Life,..Oh! flickering, feeble, and unsicker I've found her still. **1819** W. TENNANT *Papistry Storm'd* (1827) 5 Thou ..flaff't thy wings, and in a crack Flew frae th' unsicker stance!

Hence **un'sickerness**, uncertainty. Also **un'sickerly**, unsafely, insecurely.

c **1340** HAMPOLE *Pr. Consc.* 9049 Alle þe sykernes þat had Ennoc and Ely..War noght bot als unsykernes. **1387** TREVISA *Higden* (Rolls) III. 287 Þou schalt have.. unsikernes..of þy children ende. ? *a* **1400** *Morte Arth.* 966 Thow saynned the vnsekyrly to seke to these mountez. *c* **1440** *Jacob's Well* 221 A-forn me I se vnsykernes to wythstonde feendys þat temptyn me. *a* **1568** in *Bannatyne MS.* (Hunterian Cl.) 201/55 With wrechitnes wofull away thow wendis; The deid certane, the hour vnsickirnes.

un'sickled, *ppl. a.* (UN-^{1} 8.)

1820 SHELLEY *Let. Mar. Gisborne* 278 The surface of the unsickled corn Trembles not in the slumbering air.

un'siege, *v.* (UN-^{2} 4 b.)

1592 SYLVESTER *Tri. Faith* III. xi, Hee..Whom Heav'nly arms, from Assur did unsiege; The most religious, matchlesse Ezechias. **1594** *Zepheria* xxv, Let not disdayne thy soule vnsanctifie,..Vnsieging where it seekes to fortifie With deadly frownes the canons of the brow.

un'sifted, *ppl. a.* [UN-^{1} 8. Cf. Du. *ongezift*.]

1. Not passed through a sieve; unstrained.

1589 COGAN *Haven Health* (ed. 2) iv. 25 When meale wholly vnsifted..is made into Bread. **1628** MAY *Virg. Georg.* I. 5 The ground one yeare at rest; forget not than.. to hearten it againe..with unsifted ashes. **1784** COWPER *Task* VI. 108 Swallowing..The total grist unsifted, husks and all. **1870** TYNDALL *Fragm. Sci.* (1871) 138 Pure unsifted solar light is white.

2. Unexamined, unscrutinized.

1620 QUARLES *Div. Poems, Feast for Worms* IX. ix, No crime unsifted, no sinne unpresented, Can lurke unseene. **1826** SOUTHEY *Lett.* (1856) IV. 38 There must be abundant matter of unsifted information in our public collections. **1858** GLADSTONE *Homer* I. 219 A poet who, as to facts, was at the mercy of unsifted information. **1882** PUSEY *Paroch. & Cathedr. Serm.* i. 3 The unsifted, unexamined conscience of a sinner.

3. Untried, inexperienced.

1602 SHAKS. *Ham.* I. iii. 102 You speake like a greene Girle, Vnsifted in such perillous Circumstance.

un'sighed, *ppl. a.* (UN-^{1} 8, 8 c.)

1814 WORDSW. *Laodamia* 100 The past unsighed for, and the future sure. **1898** R. W. SETON WATSON *Scotland for Ever* 38 Queen Elizabeth..sank, unsighed for, to a gilded grave.

un'sighing, *ppl. a.* (UN-^{1} 10.)

a **1743** LD. HERVEY *Epist.* i. 65 The change I cou'd unsighing see. **1822** BYRON *Juan* VIII. lxvii, The solitudes Of this unsighing people of the woods. **1838** MRS. BROWNING *Vanities* v, Those ye love are not unsighing.

un'sight, *sb.* [UN-^{1} 12.] Lack of sight or seeing.

c **1412** HOCCLEVE *De Reg. Princ.* 5002 The ymages.. Maken folke þenke on god..Whan þe ymages þei be-holden & seen; Were oft vnsyte [*v.r.* vnsight] of hem causith restreyntes Of þoughtes gode. **1898** HARDY *Wessex Poems* 163 In vain do I urge my unsight To conceive my lost prize.

un'sight, *v.* [UN-^{2} 6 b.]

1. *trans.* To deprive of sight. *rare.*

1615 CHAPMAN *Odyss.* IX. 595 Their full bags so sore, With being vnemptied; but their shepheard more, With being vnsighted. **1638** N. WHITING *Il Insonio Insonnadado* 468 His armed brow fell down; and lighting right His antlers did the marching god unsight.

2. In *pa. ppl.* Of a coursing dog: Deprived of a sight of the hare.

1825 *Sporting Mag.* XVI. 268/2 If one or both dogs be unsighted, owing to the hare running through bushes or a live hedge,..the course shall be deemed to end there. **1876** *Coursing Calendar* 124 Miss Alice on a strong inside led Handicraft, who threw her head up as though unsighted.

3. *trans.* Of a participant in a game: to deprive (another player or an official) of a clear view. Freq. in *pa. pple.*

1923 *Daily Mail* 15 Jan. 11 The referee..was unsighted and so, apparently, was the linesman to whom he appealed. **1928** *Daily Express* 8 June 17/2 Gibbons..would have been caught by slip if the wicketkeeper had not unsighted that fieldsman. **1951** *Sport* 30 Mar.–5 Apr. 10/2, I felt sorry for Hendon's goalkeeper, Reg Ivey, who was unsighted both times and had hitherto played a very sound game! **1972** *Times* 3 Mar. 7/2 Mr Kelly was travelling some two to three lengths behind Mr Smith and inevitably that unsighted him for a reasonable distance in front of Mr Smith. **1976** *Alyn & Deeside Observer* 10 Dec. 3/2 It was afterwards revealed that the umpire had been unsighted and had not seen the ball hit by a Chester player in the circle.

4. To make unseen. *nonce.*

1914 HARDY *Satires of Circumstance* 17 Nor God nor Daemon can undo the done, Unsight the seen.

†**un'sight**, *ppl. a.*^{1} *Obs.* [? var. of UNSIGHTED *ppl. a.* 1.] Only in phr. ***unsight, unseen***, without inspection or examination.

? **1622** MIDDLETON & ROWLEY *Old Law* III. i, Take that at hazard, sir...Unsight, unseen, I take 3. to one. **1632** BROME *North. Lasse* II. i, I would I had his Neece unsight and unseen I faith for her monies sake. **1710** PALMER *Proverbs* 352 A generous mind..gives unsight and unseen, and trusts the Divine Goodness for the return. **1764** CHESTERF. *Lett.* (1774) II. 479 He tells you true as to Comtesse Cosel's diamonds, which certainly nobody will buy here unsight unseen, as they call it. **1790** COWPER *Private Corr.* (1824) II. 217 My very best compliments attend Mrs. Hill, whom I love, unsight unseen, as they say. **1810** *Splendid Follies* I. 167 So you don't dance with me?.. Bernard, I find, is to enjoy that felicity, unsight unseen.

un'sight, *ppl. a.*^{2} [UN-^{1} 8 b.] Unsighed for.

a **1618** SYLVESTER *Elegiac Epistle* 8 What Sea..Could.. drown a Sidney's Name..so quickly,..So vn-bewayled, so vn-sigh't, vnsung?

un'sightable, *a.* (UN-^{1} 7 b.)

a **1420** *Wycliffite Bible* 1 Tim. i. 17 To the kyng of worldis, vndeedly and invisible [*MS. Magd. Coll. Cambr.* vnsiȝtable]. **1893** LEVESON-GOWER *Surrey Words* 44 Trees ..very unsightable from anywhere.

un'sighted, *ppl. a.* [UN-^{1} 8.]

1. Unexamined; unperceived, unseen.

1584 *Reg. Privy Council Scot.* III. 687 To subscrive.. letters presentit be thame,..unsichtit first and fund ressounable be the officiaris of his estait. *a* **1642** SUCKLING *'When, Dearest'* i, Beauties that from worth arise, Are like the grace of Dieties, Still present with us, though unsighted. **1898** MEREDITH *Poems, Day Dau. Hades* ix, Sights that made the unsighted appear.

2. Not furnished with a sight.

1891 *Cent. Dict.* s.v., An unsighted gun.

†**un'sightful**, *a.*, **-fully**, *adv.* *Obs.*$^{-1}$ [UN-^{1} 7, 11.] Invisible; invisibly.

c **1375** *Sc. Leg. Saints* l. (*Catharine*) 369 A god.. wnsichtfull and sichtfull bedene. *Ibid.* xxxvi. (*John Baptist*) 331 Þat quha hofine is..resawis þan þe haly gaste vnsichtfully.

†**un'sightily**, *adv.* *Obs.*$^{-0}$ [UN-^{1} 11.] Invisibly.

c **1440** *Promp. Parv.* 367/1 On-syghtyly, *invisibiliter*.

un'sightliness. (UN-^{1} 12; cf. next.)

1611 FLORIO, *Sparutezza*,..vnhandsomnesse, ill-fauorednesse, vnsightlinesse. **1647** TRAPP *Comm. Matt.* xiii. 54 The unsightlinesse of his person. **1648** MILTON *Observ. Peace Ormond* Wks. 1851 IV. 559 The unsightliness of such a Ceremony. **1676** WISEMAN *Surgery* I. xiv. 66 If the unsightliness and pain be in the Legs. **1845** FORD *Handbk. Spain* 122 Time has healed the wounds of our ecclesiastical ruins, but in Spain they remain in all the unsightliness of recent onslaught. **1874** MICKLETHWAITE *Mod. Par. Churches* 35 The argument from their unsightliness is of no value.

un'sightly, *a.* [UN-^{1} 7. Cf. MDu. *onsicht(e)lijc*, *-lic* (Du. †*onzichtelijk*), invisible, ugly, MLG. *unsichtlik*, MHG. *unsihtlîh*, *-lîch* invisible.] Unpleasing to the eye; unhandsome, ugly.

In first quot. perhaps = 'unable to see'.

a **1425** *Cursor M.* 6706 (Trin.), Who so smiteþ out his þralles eȝe And makeþ him vnsiȝtiliȝe [*Gött.* vnsihti for to sie; *Cott.* vn-mighti for-to seie]. **1548** UDALL *Erasm. Par. Luke* xviii. 139 Beeyng a slouenly felowe and vnsightly in his geare. **1594** T. B. *La Primaud. Fr. Acad.* II. 59 The face woulde bee euill fauoured and vnsightly, if it were hairy. **1634** MILTON *Comus* 629 A small unsightly root, But of divine effect. **1673** [R. LEIGH] *Transp. Reh.* 82 They.. betray their breeding by..an unsightly bow. **1757** W. WILKIE *Epigon.* VI. 162 Now the place Unsightly shrubs o'erspread. **1784** COWPER *Task* II. 588 There..it compresses hard The..most unsightly bones. **1855** PRESCOTT *Philip II*, I. iii. I. 34 The unsightly trophies of the heads and limbs of numerous victims. **1892** STEVENSON *Across the Plains* vi, You can never have dwelt in a country more unsightly than that part of Caithness.

b. Applied to immaterial things.

1605 SHAKS. *Lear* II. iv. 159 Good Sir, no more: these are vnsightly tricks. **1644** MILTON *Areop.* (Arb.) 76 Truth,.. whose first appearance to our eyes..is more unsightly and unplausible than many errors. **1787** COWPER *Poet's N. Year's Gift* 8 To wish thee fairer is no need,..or more freed From temper-flaws unsightly. **1810** WORDSW. *Ess. Epitaphs* ¶6 The unsightly manner in which our monuments are crowded together.

†**un'sightly**, *adv.* *Obs.*$^{-1}$ [UN-^{1} 11.] In an unsightly manner.

1726 LEONI *Alberti's Archit.* I. 5/1 No Building..can be placed more unsightly or inconveniently, than in a Valley.

†**un'sighty**, *a.* *Obs.* [UN-^{1} 7. Cf. MDu. *onsichtich* (obs. Du. *onzichtig*), MLG. *unsichtich*, MHG. *unsihtic*, *-ec* (older G. *unsichtig*) invisible.] **a.** Unsightly. **b.** Invisible.

13.. *Cursor M.* 6706 (Gött.), Qua-so smytes vte his thrales eye, And mas him vnsihti for to sie. *c* **1440** *Promp. Parv.* 367/1 On-syghty, *invisibilis*.

un'signable, *a.* (UN-^{1} 7 b.)

1802 CANNING *Let.* in *Diaries Ld. Malmesbury* (1844) IV. 96, I commit the paper to your discretion. If signable people should fall in your way, or if unsignable,..use it.

un'signalized, *ppl. a.* (UN-^{1} 8 a (*c*).)

[**1775** ASH.] **1810** COLERIDGE *Friend* 314 A newly-invested Knight appearing with his blank unsignalized Shield.

un'signalled, *ppl. a.* (UN-^{1} 8.)

1868 GEO. ELIOT *Sp. Gipsy* 81 In haste He rushed unsignalled through the corridor. **1874** BLACKIE *Self-Cult.* 40 An unsignalled railway train.

un'signatured, *ppl. a.* (UN-^{1} 8.)

1807 BRYDGES *Censura Lit.* III. 342 Such notes..as appear unsignatured at the bottom of the page. **1877** BLACKIE *Wise Men* 338 Blind inorganic hinderment, mere man Unsignatured, uncharactered.

un'signed, *ppl. a.* (UN-^{1} 8.)

1598 CHAPMAN *Hero & Leander* III. 148 She..Tolde him how poore was substance without rites, Like bils vnsignd. **1694** *Lond. Gaz.* No. 3017/4 All such Adventurers that took out any Tickets..(either signed or unsigned). **1740** *Col. Rec. Pennsylv.* IV. 417 Bills..unsign'd by either [the Governor or the Secretary]. **1753** *Scots Mag.* Jan. 47/2 Three unsigned letters were..put into the post-office. **1812** COMBE *Syntax, Picturesque* xxv, On the wing there upwards sprung A flight of Dockets, who were join'd By dire Certificates unsign'd. **1885** 'MRS. ALEXANDER' *At Bay* viii, These lines were unsigned, and might be meant for any one, as there was no address.

un'signed, *a.* *Math.* [UN-^{1} 9.] Of a number: without a plus or minus sign, or a bit representing this.

1953 *Electronic Engin.* Jan. 6/1 One advantage possessed by the complement notation for signed numbers is that the processes of addition and subtraction can be carried out by exactly the same methods on signed and unsigned numbers. **1970** O. DOPPING *Computers & Data Processing* xvii. 273 The 'compare' instruction can hardly be used for numerical information except when it is certain that all the keys are unsigned, that all keys have a plus sign, or that all keys have a minus sign. **1979** *Sci. Amer.* June 18/2 The problem asks whether for different values of *n* it is possible to pair each number in one subset with a number in the other so that the 2*n* sums and absolute, or unsigned, differences of the numbers in each pair are all distinct.

un'signeted, *ppl. a.* (UN-[1] 8.)
1585 *Reg. Privy Council Scot.* IV. 15 Be vertew of the saidis letters purchest be him unsignetit.

†**unsig'nificancy.** *Obs.* [UN-[1] 12, 5 b. Cf. next.] Insignificance.
1659 HEYLIN *Animadv.* in Fuller *App. Inj. Innoc.* (1840) 501 But we shall see..that the activity of the next Convocation will make amends for the silence and unsignificancy of this. **1685** in *15th Rep. Hist. MSS. Comm.* App. VIII. 133 The unsignificancie of the militia.

†**unsig'nificant**, *a.* *Obs.* [UN-[1] 7 and 5 b. Cf. UNSIGNIFYING.] Not significant, unmeaning; insignificant. (Freq. *c* 1635–*c* 1665.)
1603 HOLLAND *Plutarch's Mor.* 643 Yet will they.. participate with them in a kinde of voice, not altogether inarticulate and unsignificant. **1630** *R. Johnson's Kingd. & Commw.* 82 The Duke..is but a voice unsignificant; for the Senate carrieth the sword. **1673** R. ALLESTREE *Ladies Calling* I. 123 She..is like..to give but an unsignificant attendance at it.
Hence †**unsig'nificantly** *adv.* *Obs.*
1644 MILTON *Areop.* (Arb.) 74 The Temple of Janus.. might now not unsignificantly be set open. *a* **1662** HEYLIN *Laud* (1668) 5 Which words had been impertinently, and unsignificantly used.

unsig'nificative, *a.* (UN-[1] 7, 5 b.)
1664 H. MORE *Myst. Iniq.* 227 They are not unsignificative of that Wisdom that is said to be more quick and moving then any motion.

un'signified, *ppl. a.* (UN-[1] 8.)
[**1775** ASH.] **1809** BUCKMINSTER in *Biogr. Mem.* (1831) 17 As to the..most important charge in the review, that of unsignified alterations.

un'signifying, *ppl. a.* (UN-[1] 10.)
1665 J. SERGEANT *Sure Footing* Ep. Ded., They carry the war out of the bounds of Science..and transfer it to a kind of Spatium Imaginarium of Fancy and unsignifying sounds. *a* **1680** GLANVILL in *Disc.*, etc. (1681) 407 Such a Faith as this is that which St. James writes so earnestly against, as dead, and unsignifying (of it self alone) to the purpose of Justification. **1727** DE FOE *Syst. Magic* I. iii. (1840) 65 Muttering over them some unsignifying significations. **1884** *Encycl. Brit.* XVII. 86/1 A tune is named generally after some place, as 'York',..or by some other unsignifying word.

†**unsile**, *v.* *Sc.* [UN-[2] 3 + SILE *v.*[3]] = UNSEEL *v.*
1628 SIR W. MURE *Spirit. Hymn* 229 He doth vnsyle the eyes alone Of soules sincere. **1629** —— *True Crucifixe* 32 The Serpent offring..to vnsile his sight.

un'silenceable, *a.* (UN-[1] 7 b.)
1678 *Lively Oracles* iii. §70. 279 How sadly will conscience then revenge all its stifled admonitions by an unsilenceable clamor. **1875** M. ARNOLD *God & Bible* iii. 131 The great, standing, unsilenceable, unshaken witness. **1884** *Harper's Mag.* Mar. 524/2 The winds moaned with unsilenceable grief.

un'silenced, *ppl. a.* (UN-[1] 8; cf. SILENCED *ppl. a.* b.)
1615 CHAPMAN *Odyss.* Ep. Ded. xlvi, Singing their praises in unsilenced story. **1828** MISS MITFORD *Village* Ser. III. 294 One, however, of his adversaries..still remained unsilenced. **1865** MRS. WHITNEY *Gayworthys* xix, This unsilenced haunting 'If' of fruitless regret. **1923** *Autocar* 7 Dec. 1151/2 Unsilenced engines. **1971** *Daily Tel.* (Colour Suppl.) 12 Nov. 21/4 A motor-bike of approximately six litres, unsilenced. **1981** M. KENYON *Zigzag* xxv. 171 Kelly's new unsilenced gun was shaping up..effectively.

un'silent, *a.* [UN-[1] 7.] ? Causing a noise, notorious.
1597 Q. ELIZ. in Nichols *Progr.* (1805) III. B 7, More at this time we will not write of this unsilent subjecte.

unsi'licified, *ppl. a.* (UN-[1] 8.)
1877 HUXLEY *Anat. Inv. Anim.* iii. 117 Silicious spicula, the majority of which..contain a fine central canal filled with an unsilicified substance.

unsilly, variant of UNSEELY *a.* *Obs.*

un'silvered, *ppl. a.* (UN-[1] 8.)
1772 *Phil. Trans.* LXII. 100 The back-horizon-glass was silvered,..the upper part being left unsilvered. *a* **1853** PEREIRA *Polarized Light* (1854) 113 This combination of Fresnel's rhomb and an unsilvered glass. **1895** *Outing* XXVI. 397/1 The mirror..has a small unsilvered spot in the centre.

un'similar, *a.* (UN-[1] 7.)
Rarely used without preceding negative.
1768 TUCKER *Lt. of Nat.* (1834) I. 274 It is not unsimilar to a declaration of St. Paul's. **1804** EUGENIA DE ACTON *Tale without Title* II. 161 This speech, which..was seriously made upon an occasion not unsimilar, raised a laugh. **1863** MRS. OLIPHANT *Salem Chapel* ii, They..[were] much of an age, and not unsimilar in worldly means.

un'simple, *a.* (UN-[1] 7. Cf. MDu. *onsimpel.*)
1541 COPLAND *Galyen's Terap.* A ij b, For to a symple dysease a symple healynge is due, and to a composed dysease a healynge vnsymple. *a* **1750** A. HILL *Wks.* (1753) II. 274 Every thing is..unsimple, that has foreign and unnatural annexions. **1797** LAMB *Let. to Coleridge* 13 Feb., I wonder you do not perceave..something unsimple and artificial in the expression, 'voiced a sad tale'. **1862** H. AÏDÉ *Carr of Carrl.* II. 230 The very unsimple manners of the English lady (they could hardly be called affected, they were so much a part of herself).

unsim'plicity. (UN-[1] 12.)
1855 KINGSLEY *Westw. Ho!* iv, In his simple unsimplicity, and cunning foolishness.

un'simplify, *v.* [UN-[2] 3.] *trans.* To make less simple; to state in a more complex form.
1858 F. W. FABER *Foot of Cross* iv. 219 Why should she.. unsimplify her worship, by disuniting in thought what God had united. **1960** R. A. KNOX *Occas. Sermons* xx. 94 We try to simplify modern politics, by making them all black and white, all heroes and villains; and in doing that we only unsimplify ourselves. **1975** *Sci. Amer.* Oct. 100/1 (Advt.), To understand, then, why there is a controversy, it is necessary to unsimplify the issue.

un'simulated, *ppl. a.* (UN-[1] 8.)
1840 DE QUINCEY *Style* Wks. 1858 XI. 171 Ebullitions of absolute unsimulated feeling. **1894** A. K. H. BOYD *St. Andrews* 126 To which the driver replied, with unsimulated heartiness.

un'sin, *v.* [UN-[2] 4 b, 6 b.]
1. *trans.* To annul (a sin) by subsequent action.
1628 FELTHAM *Resolves* II. lxxxix. 257 When a sinne is past, griefe may lessen it, but not vnsinne it. **1670** CLARENDON *Contempl. Ps.* Tracts (1727) 593 They who.. observe the other injunction of the prophet..have unsinned their former sins. **1705** J. DUNTON *Life & Errors* 405, I can't Un-Sin the Errours of my past Life. **1868** BROWNING *Ring & Bk.* IV. 285 The proper process of unsinning sin Is to begin well-doing somehow else.
2. To free (a person) from being a sinner.
c **1629** DONNE *Serm.* (1640) 645 *Expeccabis*; and if in our language, that were a word in use, it might be translated, 'Thou shalt un-sin me', that is, look upon me as a man that had never sinned.
3. To maintain or prove to be no sin; to divest of the character of a sin.
1682 SOUTHERNE *Loyal Brother* v. i, Gifted Rogues, That ..zealously, upon a fit of Conscience, Sin or Unsin Rebellion to the Croud. *a* **1715** SOUTH *Serm.* IV. 123 He who defends it [*sc.* a sin], utterly denies its Guilt, and (as I may so speak) absolutely unsins it.

unsin'cere, *a.* [UN-[1] 7 and 5 b.]
1. = INSINCERE *a.* 1: **a.** Of actions, etc.
1577 tr. *Bullinger's Decades* 566/1 The consideration of the vnsincere feare of God. **1646** HAMMOND *Death-bed Repent.* 62 Sure there is such a thing as unsincere resolution. **1683** TEMPLE *Mem.* Wks. 1720 I. 410 To act an unsincere Part either in Friendship or in Love. **1718** *Freethinker* No. 83, An affected, unsincere Humility towards God.
b. Of persons. Also *absol.*
1617 HIERON *Wks.* 1620 II. 155 Judas [was] an apostle, yet what careth God for him, being vnsincere? **1664** H. MORE *Myst. Iniq.* xxii. 85, I cannot pronounce any thing in the behalf of the unsincere, but that Hell it self is their portion. **1700** CONGREVE *Way of World* I. C 1 b, What, I warrant he's unsincere, or 'tis some such Trifle. *c* **1742** SHENSTONE *Song*, *'On ev'ry tree'* v, My friends..Might well demand one tender tear; For when was Damon unsincere?
†**2.** = INSINCERE *a.* 2. *Obs.*
1664 BOYLE *Exper. touching Colours* 197 The Light of a Candle..made unsincere, and..Ting'd with a Yellow Colour. **1666** DRYDEN *Ann. Mirab.* ccix, But ah! how unsincere are all our Joys! **1725** POPE *Odyssey* IV. 1060 O why, Penelope, this causeless fear, To render sleep's soft blessings unsincere?
Hence **unsin'cereness.**
1683 TEMPLE *Mem.* Wks. 1720 I. 435 When the Dutch should grow more impatient of the Slowness or Unsincereness of their Allies Proceedings in the General Treaty.

unsin'cerely, *adv.* (UN-[1] 11, 5 b.)
c **1555** HARPSFIELD *Divorce Hen. VIII* (Camden) 65 The adversaries, that..have so unfaithfully and unsincerely demeaned themselves. **1684** *Pennsylv. Arch.* I. 91 As unsincerely all along as I have been dealt with.

†**unsin'cerity.** *Obs.* [UN-[1] 12 and 5 b.]
1. Impurity; admixture. Cf. INSINCERITY 1.
1668 BOYLE *Physiol. Ess.* 108 A Spirit of Sea-Salt may without any unsincerity be so prepar'd, as to dissolve the body of crude Gold.
2. Lack of sincerity; = INSINCERITY 2.
1646 HAMMOND *Tracts* 42 An argument of the unsincerity of that contrition. **1692** NORRIS *Two Treat. Div. Light* I. 67 See the Inconsistency and Unsincerity of this Writer! **1707** *Reflex. upon Ridicule* (1717) II. 189 All this opens a prospect to the Bottom of their Hearts, and manifests their Unsincerity.

un'sinew, *v.* [UN-[2] 6 b and 4.]
1. *trans.* To weaken the sinews of; to render weak or feeble; to enervate.
1598 FLORIO, *Sneruare*, to vnsinew, to weaken ones bodie. **1639** FULLER *Holy War* v. xv. 255 It is not so much the climate, as bad and unwholesome diet,..which unsineweth those Northern nations when they come into the South. **1645** WITHER *Vox Pacif.* 119 This imprudencie will..Your bones unsinnew, and your joynts untie. **1693** DRYDEN *Persius* VI. 89 Now Toys and Trifles from their Athens come, And Dates and Pepper have unsinnew'd Rome. **1845** *Blackw. Mag.* LVII. 781 Death unsinews the hand that held her against the world.
b. *fig.* To weaken, enfeeble.
1599 DANIEL *Musoph.* Wks. (1602) B iii j b, This skill.. Vnsinewes all your powres, vnmans you quite. **1609** G. BENSON *Serm. 7 May* 57 The want of this knowledge vnsinewes the powers of a man. **1697** DRYDEN *Æneis* Ded. ¶84 The affected purity of the French has unsinnewed their heroic verse. **1744** AKENSIDE *Epistle to Curio* 160 What spells unsinew'd thy determin'd soul? **1866** LYTTON *Lost Tales Miletus*, *Secret Way* 16 The hold Of a strong phantasy, which, night and day,..unsinews life.
2. (See quot.)
1753 *Chambers' Cycl.* Suppl. s.v. *Sinew*, To unsinew a horse,..is to cut the two tendons on the side of the head, about five inches under the eyes.

un'sinewed, *ppl. a.* [f. prec. or UN-[1] 8.] Not furnished with sinews; not sinewy or strong; weakened in sinews, enfeebled.
1541 R. COPLAND *Guydon's Form.* S iij, The seconde intencyon is accomplysshed by hote yron in vnsynewed places..and by corosyues, in meane places. **1615** DANIEL *Hymen's Tri.* II. i, Those vnsinewed amorous heardsmen. **1678** DRYDEN *All for Love* I. i, Can any Roman see and know him now,..Unbent, unsinew'd, made a woman's toy? **1863** W. LANCASTER *Præterita* 116 Old brand, art shamed with my unsinew'd gripe? **1872** R. W. BUCHANAN *St. Abe* II. v, As each Saint sank unsinew'd, In his arm-chair he continued: 'Goodman Jones' [etc.].
b. *fig.* (Cf. prec. 1 b.)
1602 SHAKS. *Ham.* IV. vii. 10 O for two speciall Reasons, Which may to you (perhaps) seeme much vnsinnowed, And yet to me they are strong. **1643** *Lanc. Tracts Civil War* (Chetham Soc.) 169 From him I must expect an unsinewed and faithles agreement. **1683** DRYDEN (& SOAME) tr. *Boileau's Art Poetry* III. 189 Without these Ornaments before our Eyes, Th' unsinew'd Poem languishes. **1746** FRANCIS tr. *Horace*, *Sat.* II. i. 3 My Lines are weak, unsinew'd, others say.

un'sinewy, *a.* (UN-[1] 7 and 5 b.)
1622 J. HAYWARD *David's Tears* To Rdr. A 8 Some other form-lesse vnsinewie writings. **1641** EARL MONM. tr. *Biondi's Civil Wars* Ep. Ded., I doe not praise the soft unsinnowy goodnesse of Henry the sixth. *a* **1658** CLEVELAND *Poems*, *Agst. Ale* iv, May Bards that drink thee, write a small, Unsubstanc'd Line pedantical, Unsinewy, ænigmatical.

un'sinful, *a.* (UN-[1] 7.)
1598 FLORIO, *Impeccabile*, that cannot sin,..vnsinfull. **1681** BAXTER *Answ. Dodwell* iii. 22 They may command any unsinful thing, and excommunicate him that doth not obey. **1767** COWPER *Lett.* (1863) 94 They who are his servants here, shall pay him an unsinful obedience for ever. **1893** A. WHYTE *Bunyan Char.* Ser. I. i. 6 Our Lord made His own unselfish and unsinful will to bow to silence and to praise before the holy will of His Father.
Hence **un'sinfulness.**
1598 FLORIO, *Impeccabilita*, vnsinfulnes, puritie. **1681** BAXTER *Answ. Dodwell* iii. 22 One that knoweth the unsinfulness of all things in the world that are such.

un'sinfully, *adv.* (UN-[1] 11. Cf. prec.)
c **1400** *Apol. Loll.* 15 No creature mai do iustli,..perfitly, vnsinfully,..ani þing, not but if God wirk þat þing bi him. **1627** SANDERSON *Serm.* I. 265 He did it unwittingly, and therefore..unsinfully, as to that species of sin. **1862** T. A. TROLLOPE *Marietta* I. ii. 30 No usance could be unsinfully received.

un'sing, *v.* (UN-[2] 3.)
1701 DE FOE *True born Eng.* II. 242 They soon their New Deliverer Despise;..Unsing their Thanks, and pull their Trophies down. **1876** H. GARDNER *Sunflowers*, *Rose Garden* 21 A thought once thought is never unthought, Or a melody sung unsung!

un'singable, *a.* (UN-[1] 7 b.)
1882 *Athenæum* 4 Feb. 153/2 The lyrics throughout the volume are as unlike songs—as 'unsingable' and unlyrical —as ever.

un'singed, *ppl. a.* [UN-[1] 8. Cf. Du. *ongezengd.*] Not singed; untouched by fire.
1599 [see UNSEARED]. **1646** SIR T. BROWNE *Pseud. Ep.* VII. x. 358 He was cast into a Cauldron of burning oyle, and came out againe unsinged. **1697** DRYDEN *Æneis* XI. 1158 By thee protected, with our naked soles, Through flames unsinged we march. **1737** EARL ORRERY *Let. to Swift* 15 Mar., Let the thunder burst where it will, so that you are safe, and unsinged. **1755** DODDRIDGE *'Let Jacob'* iv, Then let the fires their rage display,..Unburnt, unsinged, He leads them through. **1834** T. MOORE in Walpole *Life Ld. J. Russell* (1889) I. 203 You at least come safe and unsinged out of the furnace. *a* **1850** BRYANT *Medit. Rhode Isl. Coal* 54 That men might to thy inner caves retire, And there, unsinged, abide the day of fire.

un'singled, *ppl. a.* (UN-[1] 8.)
1697 DRYDEN *Æneis* IV. 221 The Stags, a trembling Train In Herds unsingl'd, scour the dusty Plain.

un'singleness. (UN-[1] 12.)
a **1658** DURHAM *Comm. Rev.* (1660) 189 Sinfull defects, and unsinglenesse and want of zeal.

unsinka'bility. (UN-[1] 12. Cf. next.)
1865 *Times* 11 Mar. 8/6 He, too, puts speed first of all.., and armour-plating or 'unsinkability' nowhere. **1891** *Naut. Mag.* Mar. 236 The unsinkability of cargo-carrying vessels.

un'sinkable, *a.* (UN-[1] 7 b.)
Also, in recent use (1912), ***unsinkableness.***
1655 MRQ. WORCESTER *Cent. Inv.* Index p. ij, An unsinkable Ship. **1861** *Times* 10 July, Unsinkable Iron Ships. **1883** *Fisheries Exhib. Catal.* 62 Unsinkable Suits for Fishermen.

un'sinking, *ppl. a.* (UN-[1] 10.)
Also, in recent use (1920), ***unsinkingly.***
1705 ADDISON *Italy* 191 All the dewy Strand Lyes cover'd with a smooth, unsinking Sand. **1816** J. WILSON *City of Plague* I. iii. 38 Let me walk the waves of this wild world Through faith unsinking. **1821** BYRON *Cain* III. i. 529 Oh! thou..whose unsinking Blood darkens earth and heaven! **1823** MRS. HEMANS *Siege Valencia* ii. 429 Enough of woe.. For man to bear, unsinking.

un'sinnable, *a.* (UN-[1] 7 b.)
1570 FOXE *A. & M.* (ed. 2) 2059/2 By that power or authority he is not become vnsinneable. **1612** R. SHELDON *Serm. St. Martin's* 57 It was impeccable, vnsinneable, and not capable of any the lest spot of sinne.

un'sinning, *vbl. sb.* (See UNSIN *v.* 2.)

c **1629** DONNE *Serm.* (1640) 645 It is only this expeccation, this unsinning, this taking away of sins formerly committed, that restores me. **1681** J. SCOTT *Chr. Life* I. iv. 471 Till by an actual unsinning and Revocation of the Facts, we have totally cross'd and discharged them.

un'sinning, *ppl. a.* (UN-¹ 10.)

c **1375** *Sc. Leg Saints* xvi. (*Magdalene*) 34 Mare Ioy is With angelis.. Of a synful, pennance dowand, þane nyne & nynte vnsynnand. **1642** MILTON *Apol. Smect.* 23 To expell quite the unsinning predominance of his anger. *a* **1680** CHARNOCK *Attrib. God* (1834) II. 652 Above the unsinning angels, and perfectly renewed spirits in glory. **1705** STANHOPE *Paraphr.* II. 392 That First Covenant.. promised Immortality to unsinning Obedience. **1760–72** H. BROOKE *Fool of Qual.* (1809) III. 31 In compassion to Adam, and.. to his yet unsinning progeny. **1837** LYTTON *Athens* II. 567 Great Jove! a grateful spectacle—if thus May it be said unsinning. **1872** BUSHNELL *Serm. Living Subjects* 419 He chooses this most passive, most unsinning, unoffending creature.

un'siphon, *v.* [UN-² 5, 7.] *trans.* To deprive of the function of a siphon. Hence **un'siphoned** *ppl. a.*

1878 J. A. RUSSELL *Sanitary Houses* 19 Traps may be unsiphoned by a body of water coming down the soil pipe, ..making suction behind it. **1884** E. F. WILLOUGHBY *Hygiene* v. 194 This simple.. preventative of unsyphoning is ..little appreciated. **1894** *Times* 20 Feb. 3/6 The unsyphoned traps.. of the waterclosets.

un'sister, *v.* (UN-² 6 b.)

1875 TENNYSON *Q. Mary* I. i, There will be plenty to sunder and unsister them again.

un'sistered, *ppl. a.* (UN-¹ 8.)

1738 G. LILLO *Marina* II. i, I vow'd.. That all unsister'd shou'd this heir of mine Remain till she were marry'd. **1860** O. W. HOLMES *Prof. Breakf.-t.* x, A lonely and unsistered creature.

un'sisterliness. (UN-¹ 12.)

1748 RICHARDSON *Clarissa* I. 296 Don't let me be surprized at your seeming unsisterliness. **1879** STEVENSON *Edinburgh* iv. 16 Never did four walls look down upon an uglier spectacle than these sisters rivalling in unsisterliness.

un'sisterly, *a.* (UN-¹ 7. Cf. Du. *onzusterlijk*, Sw. *osysterlig*.)

1747 RICHARDSON *Clarissa* (1811) I. 96 Your Bell's unsisterly behaviour. *c* **1815** JANE AUSTEN *Persuas.* vi, Mary was not so repulsive and unsisterly as Elizabeth. **1860** W. S. HAYWARD *Beautiful Demon* 103 You wrong me, Regina. It is cruel, it is unsisterly of you.

† **un'sisting,** *ppl. a.* (Of doubtful meaning.)

1603 SHAKS. *Meas. for M.* IV. ii. 92 That spirit's possest with hast, That wounds th' vnsisting [*Fol. 4* insisting] Posterne with these strokes.

un'sitten, *ppl. a.* (UN-¹ 8 b. Cf. SIT *v.* 31 b.)

1611 A. STANDISH *Commons Compl.* 20 If they finde any [wild ducks'] egges therein that be vnsitten.

† **un'sitting,** *ppl. a. Obs.* [UN-¹ 10.] Unbecoming, unfitting. (Common *c* 1390–1550.)

Freq. in later eds. misread or misprinted as *unfitting*: cf. the note to UNFITTING.

c **1390** CHAUCER *Troylus* II. 307 Were it þyng þat me þoughte vnsittynge To yow nold I no suche tales brynge. **1390** GOWER *Conf.* III. 143 It were an unsittende thing. *c* **1412** HOCCLEVE *De Reg. Princ.* 2361 þat vn-to hygh degre, Vnsittynge is to swere in any wise. **1456** T. BECKINGTON *Corr.* (Rolls) II. 144 The unsittyng, unleful, and unlawful quarell. **1533** MORE *Apol.* xii. Wks. 872/1 The priestes agaynste laye people.. haue vsed.. to speake vnsyttyng woordes. **1567** TURBERV. *Epit.*, etc. 91 Vlysses wiues renowne Unsitting is for hir whose loue endureth but a stowne. **1585** HOLINSHED *Descr. Scotl.* Ded., It is much vnsitting for him that professeth Diuinitie, to applie his time any otherwise.

Hence † **un'sittingly** *adv. Obs.*

c **1412** HOCCLEVE *De Reg. Princ.* 2349 As he þat custumably Clappith and ianglith.. Moot othir while speke vnsittyngly. *Ibid.* 3639 Fresche apparaile and herte leccherous Unsittynly ben in a Prince ioynt. **1476** *Paston Lett.* III. 153 It was nott thowght.. that I dalt onkyndly or onsyttyngly, but that I was moor onresonably dalte with.

un'sizeable, *a.* [UN-¹ 7 b.]

† **1.** Unequal in size; not of the proper or exact size. *Obs.*

1653 BLITHE *Eng. Improver Impr.* 197 Make your Horses and Oxen as equall as you can possibly; if they be unsizeable, your highest draw up your lowest, and your lowest draw down the highest. **1678** MOXON *Mech. Exerc.* v. 78 [Do not let] the edge of your Hatchet cut too deep into the stuff, lest you.. spoil your stuff by making it unsizeable. **1704** *Lond. Gaz.* No. 3888/3 The 35 Tun of unsizeable and crackt Brass Ordance. **1716** B. CHURCH *Hist. Philip's War* (1867) II. 26 Bullets.. so unsizeable that some of them were forc'd to make slugs while they were ingag'd.

2. Of excessive size; too large or bulky. *Obs.*

1698 FRYER *Acc. E. India & P.* 9 An unsizeable Sword to their Backs. *Ibid.* 162, I was made at by an unsizable Snake. **1710** *Tatler* No. 241 ¶ 3, I am not without hopes, that by this method I shall bring some unsizable friends of mine into shape and breadth. **1736** T. PRINCE *Chron. Hist. New Eng.* I. 250 If I now proceed to the End of this Second Section, ..it will make the First Volume too unsizeable.

fig. **1755** PITT in *Anecd.* (1810) I. xii. 202 This unsizable project, impracticable and desperate as it is,.. will.. bring bankruptcy upon Great Britain. **1759** FRANKLIN *Ess.* Wks. 1840 III. 529 And who or what are these proprietaries? In the province, unsizable subjects and unsufficient lords.

3. Not grown to a proper size; immature.

1746 R. GRIFFITHS *Ess. Conservacy Thames* 52 [They] annually destroy infinite Numbers of unsizeable Smelts. **1759** *Act 33 Geo. II*, c. 27 §13 Any Spawn, Fry, or Brood of Fish, or any unsizeable Fish, or any Fish out of Season. **1833** J. CORNISH in *Rep. Sel. Comm. Brit. Channel Fisheries* 148 Millions of young and unsizeable fish. **1887** *Field* 24 Dec. 953/2 The keepers are.. instructed to.. prosecute the possessors of unsizeable pike.

Hence **un'sizeableness.**

1746 *Lond. Mag.* 324 Diversity of Weapons.., Unsizeableness of the Men, and Want of.. Discipline in their Officers.

un'sized, *ppl. a.*¹ [UN-¹ 8 + SIZE *v.*¹]

† **1.** = UNASSIZED. *Obs.*⁻¹

1613 *Southampton Court Leet Rec.* (1907) III. 469 Having made view of vnsissed bread in the markett [and] findinge.. howshold Loaves of no assize.

2. Not made of an exact size or fit; not formed or sorted into sizes.

1700 CONGREVE *Way of World* IV. I. 3, I must have been let out and piec'd in the sides like an unsiz'd Camlet. **1857** *Local Act 20 & 21 Vict.* c. 141 Sched. (C), Slates.. Unsized Rag, Half Rag, Queen or sized Rag. **1877** RAYMOND *Statist. Mines & Mining* 426 Several tests made in concentrating unsized ore.

un'sized, *ppl. a.*² [UN-¹ 8 + SIZE *v.*²] Not treated with size.

1794 KIRWAN *Elem. Min.* (ed. 2) I. 461 Filtres formed of unsized paper. **1827** FARADAY *Chem. Manip.* ix. 235 The thinner varieties of unsized paper, or white blotting-paper. **1888** JACOBI *Printers' Vocab.*, *Unsized paper*, paper made entirely without size, and consequently very absorbent and adapted for plate printing.

un'skated, *ppl. a. rare.* [UN-¹ 8.] Not skated on.

1936 DYLAN THOMAS *Twenty-Five Poems* 19 December's pools.. Lie this fifth month unskated.

un'sketchable, *a.* (UN-¹ 7 b.)

1851 CURTIS *Nile Notes* 213 Sundry veiled spectres were sketching the unsketchable.

un'skilful, *a.* [UN-¹ 7.]

† **1.** Unreasonable. *Obs.*

c **1370** *Lay Folks' Catech.* (L.) 1342 Glotony.. is an vnskylful lykyng or loue in tast or tastynge of mete or drynke. **1377** LANGL. *P. Pl.* B. XIII. 277 Of vnboxome speche,.. of scoffyng and of vnskilful berynge. *c* **1400** *Pilgr. Sowle* (Caxton) I. xxx. (1859) 34 They shold serue theyr creatour.. with resonable werkes doyng, and vnskylful werkes forbering. *c* **1491** *Chast. Goddes Chyld.* (Caxton) 25 Her rest was full short by cause it was unskilfull and also unlefull.

† **b.** Undiscerning; unwise, foolish. *Obs. rare.*

c **1374** CHAUCER *Troylus* I. 790, I may not endure þat þow dwelle In so vnskilful [*v.r.* onskylful] an opynyoun. *c* **1449** PECOCK *Repr.* III. xix. 413 But that this seiyng is vnskilful may be schewid thus. **1568** GRAFTON *Chron.* II. 30 Robert Losaunge that.. by the gift of a thousand pound to the King, was made Bishop of Thetforde, repented him after, and bewayled that vnskilfull deede.

† **2. a.** Ignorant of propriety. *Obs.*⁻¹

c **1475** *Rauf Coilȝear* 159 Schir, thow art vnskilfull,.. Thow byrd to haue nurtour aneuch, and thow hes nane.

† **b.** Ignorant *of* something. Also with inf. or dependent clause. *Obs.*

a **1547** SURREY *Æneis* II. 493 Striken with dred, vnskilfull of the place. **1573** TUSSER *Husb.* (1878) 106 Ill huswife vnskilful to make hir owne chees. **1600** HOLLAND *Livy* XXII. xxxi. 451 They fell unadvisedly into an ambush, and being unskilfull of the countrie,.. they were soon enclosed among many. **1667** MILTON *P.L.* XI. 32 Unskilful with what words to pray, let mee Interpret for him.

3. Lacking in skill; inexpert.

1565 GOLDING *Cæsar* 32 The whyche pollicie, though it hadde taken place agaynst sauage and vnskylfull people, yet was not Ariouistus so folysh to loke that it should preuaile against oure army too. **1573** TUSSER *Husb.* (1878) 15 The father an vnthrift, what hope to the sonne? The ruler vnskilfull, how quickly vndonne? **1617** MORYSON *Itin.* II. 49 At his first entering the gouernment, when he was yet vnskilfull in the affaires of that State. **1639** in *Verney Mem.* (1907) I. 183 Ther was never soe Rawe, soe unskilfull and soe unwilling an Army brought to fight. **1709** BERKELEY *Th. Vision* §12 Those unskilful in optics. **1765** *Museum Rust.* IV. 460 This operation is nice, and may prove dangerous in unskilful hands. **1840** THACKERAY *Shabby-genteel Story* vi, He was not unskilful at this kind of exercise. **1867** M. E. G. DUFF in *N. Brit. Rev.* XLVII. 484 The attempts of the foreign evangelizers may often be unskilful enough.

absol. **1565** COOPER *Thesaurus*, *Imperitum vulgus*, the ignorant, rude, or vnskilfull. *c* **1580** [see VOID *v.* 11]. **1612** B. JONSON *Alch.* To Rdr., It is onely the disease of the vnskilfull to thinke rude things greater then polish'd. **1726** LEONI *Alberti's Archit.* III. 12 b, It hardly happens.. that what delights the Judges, shou'd at the same time strike the Unskilful. **1762** FALCONER *Shipwr.* II. 251 The gallant boatswain.. Prompt to direct the unskilful still appears.

transf. **1687** P. AYRES *To Dryden* 15 Could my unskilful pen augment his fame.

b. Displaying lack of skill; clumsy.

a **1586** SIDNEY *Arcadia* I. ix, No more.. then.. the diligent Pilot in a daungerous tempest doth attend the unskilful words of a passinger. **1614** LATHAM *Falconry* II. vii. 94 Such Hawkes haue beene euelly ordered, and continued in vncleane and vnskilfull keeping. **1651** HOBBES *Leviath.* III. xxxii. 195 When it seemeth so, the fault is either in our unskilfull Interpretation, or erroneous Ratiocination. **1737** GLOVER *Leonidas* III. 250 Assyria's sons Their brazen helms display, th' unskilful work Of rude Barbarians. **1798** LAMB *R. Gray* xiii, His wounds by unskilful treatment had been brought to a dangerous crisis. **1831** JAMES *Phil. Augustus* I. vii, De Coucy.. took the instrument, over the strings of which he threw his hand, in a bold but not unskilful manner.

un'skilfully, *adv.* [UN-¹ 11.]

† **1.** Unreasonably; without good reason; to an unreasonable extent. *Obs.*

1338 R. BRUNNE *Chron.* (1810) 152 þe kyng.. said he was redy, þe testament to fulfille of kyng William, & þat his men fulle ille vnskilfully nam. **1387** TREVISA *Higden* (Rolls) IV. 433 Ȝif it is good to lyve, it is sacrelegy to forsake it unskilfulliche. *c* **1400** LOVE *Bonavent. Mirr.* (1908) 147 We haue ensaumple that we schulle not lette to do gode werkes for occasioun of sclaundre vnskilfully taken of othere. *a* **1470** H. PARKER *Dives & Pauper* (W. de W. 1496) IV. xxv. 192/2 We sholde loue all men.. with drede to offende them unskylfully.

† **2.** Without discernment; foolishly; ignorantly.

1340–70 *Alex. & Dind.* 871 For almus-dede do ȝe non as ȝe demen alle, But skarsete & skaþe vn-skilfully fonden. **1390** GOWER *Conf.* III. 251 Tarquinus made unskilfully A werre.. Ayein a toun with walles stronge. *c* **1460** G. ASHBY *Dicta Philos.* 1211 He wol.. euery thinge determen wilfully, Ayenste Reason, & eke vnskilfully. **1565** COOPER *Thesaurus* s.v. *Inscienter*, Thei sayde he did vnskilfully. **1603** SHAKS. *Meas. for M.* III. ii. 156 Therefore you speake vnskilfully: or, if your knowledge bee more, it is much darkned in your malice.

3. In an unskilful manner; inexpertly.

1565 COOPER *Thesaurus*, *Imperite*, vnexpertly, vnskilfully, vnlearnedly. **1664** H. MORE *Myst. Iniq.* 496 Upon which Grotius doth freely and not unskilfully comment after this manner. **1685** BOYLE *Enq. Notion Nat.* vii. 266 To clear all those unskilfully framed axioms and phrases, I found to be so intricate.. a task [etc.]. **1735** JOHNSON *Lobo's Abyssinia*, *Voy.* v. 29 One [of the muskets] being unskilfully charged too high, flew out of the Soldier's Hand. **1768–74** TUCKER *Lt. of Nat.* (1834) II. 381 That it is highly blasphemous.. to imagine that God should have contrived His order of second causes so unskilfully. **1848** MISS MITFORD in L'Estrange *Life* (1870) III. xii. 213 The story is very unskilfully told, with an entire want of dramatic power. **1885** *Law Times Rep.* LIII. 325/2 The defendant.. negligently and unskilfully navigated.. the said vessel.

un'skilfulness. [UN-¹ 12.] The quality of being unskilful; inexpertness, †ignorance.

c **1410** *Lanterne Liȝt* 115 God forbediþ þe vnleful takyng of oþir mennes goodis & so.. refreyneþ þe vnskilfulnes of mannes dede. **1544** BETHAM *Precepts* I. ccii, Theyr vnskylfulnesse is the great destruction of the whole hoste, when they knowe not howe for to kepe theyr arraye. **1576** FLEMING *Panopl. Epist.* ¶iiij, In consideration of the gatherers vnskilfulnesse. **1613** PURCHAS *Pilgrimage* (1614) 399 They double their numbers at foure, as we doe at ten, through vnskilfulnesse in numbring. **1691** HARTCLIFFE *Virtues* 231 Hence we are obliged not to impose upon any Man's ignorance or unskilfulness. **1748** *Anson's Voyage* II. x. 242 The indolence and unskilfulness of the Spanish sailors. **1776** GIBBON *Decl. & F.* vi. (1782) I. 193 The siege ..was protracted to the tenth year.. by the unskilfulness of the besiegers. **1828** LYTTON *Pelham* III. xi, Tyrrell, who believed he should readily recruit himself by my unskilfulness in the game, fell easily into the snare. **1869** DK. ARGYLE *Primeval Man* III. 100 This.. may be due to the unskilfulness of early art.

un'skill. [UN-¹ 12 and 4 b. Cf. ON. and Icel. *úskil*, *óskil* (Norw. dial. *uskil*, etc., MSw. *oskiäl*, etc., Sw. *oskäl*, MDa. *uskæl*, Da. *uskel*, in sense 1 or 1 b).]

† **1.** Improper or foolish conduct; folly; wrongdoing; wrong. *Obs.*

c **1175** *Lamb. Hom.* 65 Lauerd forȝef us ure unskile, and alswa we alle oðre wile. *c* **1275** *XI Pains Hell* 58 in *O.E. Misc.* 148 [He] þat.. nolde leten his fleysses wil, Ac folewede al þat wes vnskil. *c* **1300** *Cursor M.* 201 How Iuus wit þer gret vnschill Wend his vprisyng to dill. **1303** R. BRUNNE *Handl. Synne* 8798 Ȝyf þou dedyst euer þat vnlawe,.. þou hast synned yn moche vnskyl. *c* **1420** *Sir Amadace* (Camden) lxvii, I wille do the no vnskille, Thou schalt dele hit atte thi wille, The godus that here now is. *a* **1500** *Ratis Raving* I. 1033 Bot always serf hyme elyk,.. Bot gif he do the al wnskill.

† **b.** Want of reason; unreasonableness. *Obs.*

c **1380** WYCLIF *Sel. Wks.* II. 415 If we taken hede to þingis þat touchen þis staat, we moun fynde fulli unskil in ech of hem. *a* **1500** *Ratis Raving* I. 1269 It louis weill to leif be wyll, And callis resone oft vnskill.

† **2.** *with unskill*: **a.** Wrongly, wrongfully, improperly. (Also with *at*.) *Obs.*

c **1200** ORMIN 427 Swa we don itt wiþþ unnskill þatt itt maȝȝ anngrenn oþre. *c* **1250** *Gen. & Ex.* 3506 Ne slo ðu noȝt wið hond ne wil, Ne rend, ne beat noȝt wið vn-skil. *c* **1330** R. BRUNNE *Chron. Wace* (Rolls) 12643 Ȝif y ha lore hit at vnskyle, Y schal hit wynne eft when God wyle. *c* **1330** *King of Tars* 712 So long i wis hit is agon, I have ilived in prison of ston, With wrong and muchel unskille.

† **b.** Unreasonably, excessively. (Also with *till*, *to*.) *Obs.*

c **1220** *Bestiary* 433 He bit us don ure bukes wille, eten and drinken wið unskil. *a* **1300** *Cursor M.* 26991 Hop es god at hald wit houe, Bot til [*Fairf.* to] vnskil noght worth a gloue. **13..** *Guy Warw.* 514 After þe hete me comeþ a chele, þat me greueþ wiþ vn-skele.

3. Lack of skill; inexpertness; †ignorance (*of* something). Now *arch.*

1565 MARTIAL in Harding *Answ. to M. Ivelle's Challenge* A 3 b, Where the faultes of the printers be infinite for the vnskill of the language. **1576** LAMBARDE *Peramb. Kent* 293 I ..doe preferre plaine vnskill and ignorance, before vaine lying and presumptuous arrogance. **1598** SYLVESTER *Du Bartas* II. i. I. *Eden* 276 That even light Pirrhon's wavering fantasies Reave him the skill his un-skill to agnize. **1611** FLORIO, *Inarte*, vnartnesse, ignorance, vnskill. **1905** J. BRIERLEY *Eternal Relig.* 100 Hence more and more the idea will prevail that ignorance, unskill in things,.. is in itself a kind of lower morality.

un'skilled, *ppl. a.* [UN-¹ 8.]

1. Not skilled or expert *in* something; ignorant *of*; untrained or unable *to*.

1581 T. HOWELL *Deuises* H iv, Thus harte to faine vnskilde, in being whole is broke. 1612 DRAYTON *Poly-olb.* iv. 174 In fing'ring some unskill'd, but only us'd to sing Unto the other's harp. 1693 DRYDEN *Persius* III. 63 Down goes the Wretch at once, unskill'd to swim. 1717 POPE *Iliad* IX. 568 Thy youth as then in sage debates unskill'd. 1725 —— *Odyss.* IV. 1021 Thus he [spoke], unskill'd of what the Fates provide! 1791 COWPER *Iliad* v. 77 Unskill'd to spell aright The oracles predictive of the woe. 1823 MRS. HEMANS *Vespers of Palermo* III. v, If in this unskill'd, you stand alone Amidst our court of pleasure. 1863 H. COX *Instit.* I. viii. 123 The members of the committee are usually unskilled in the rules of evidence.

b. Without const.

1693 PRIOR *To C'tess of Exeter* 3 Unskill'd and young, yet something still I writ, Of Ca'ndish Beauty join'd to Cecil's Wit. *a* 1749 A. HILL *Epilogue* 20 The world's wide stage.. Sees some act nobly, others play unskill'd. 1818 SHELLEY *Rosal. & Helen* 1066 An unskilled hand..had the marble warmed With that pathetic life. 1856 KANE *Arct. Expl.* II. 94 Butter..melted from salt beef;..the unskilled might call it tallow. 1871 JOWETT *Plato* I. 154 None of us unskilled individuals can..become physicians.

c. *spec.* Not skilled in some handicraft; devoid of technical training.

1851 MAYHEW *London Labour* II. 323/1 With unskilled labourers it is otherwise. 1856 FROUDE *Hist. Eng.* I. 4 Any able-bodied unskilled labourer earns as soon as he has arrived at man's estate.

2. Not involving or requiring skill; displaying lack of skill.

1833 HT. MARTINEAU *Tale of Tyne* i. 8 All works of tillage have been mixed up together under the name of unskilled labour. 1849 G. TICKNOR *Span. Lit.* I. 109 If their unskilled verses were preserved at all. 1869 FROUDE *Short Stud.* (1871) 337 Take the lowest and most unskilled labour of all, that of the peasant in the field.

†**un'skilly**, *adv.* [UN-¹ 11.] Unskilfully.

1648 HEXHAM II, *Hoetelen*, to doe a thing unskilly,..to Bungle. 1658 tr. *Ussher's Ann.* 142 Which Artemon the Engineer, Ephorus the Historian doth unskilly confound with Artemon Periphresus.

†**un'skilwise**, *a. Obs.* [UN-¹ 7.]

1. Irrational; not endowed with reason.

c 1340 HAMPOLE *Pr. Consc.* 166 Þat man þat..lyves als an unscylwys best, Þat nother has skil, witt, ne mynde. ? *a* 1375 *Relig. Pieces fr. Thornton MS.* 63 For þou..gafe hym lordechipe and powere Abowen all oþer vnskillwise creatures sere.

2. Unreasonable, excessive.

a 1340 HAMPOLE *Psalter* lxxxv. 10, I..ioy in þe wiþouten vnscilwis sikirnes. *a* 1350 *St. Barthol.* 367 in Horstm. *Altengl. Leg.* (1881) 123 Þai gaf him many unskilwis scorn. 1357 *Lay Folks Catech.* (T.) 493 Glotony..is ane unskilwise likyng, or loue, In taste, or in takyng of mete and of drynk.

So †**un'skilwisely** *adv. Obs.*

a 1300 *Cursor M.* 19149 Es it..resun þat we Calanged for ur gode dede be? Vn-skilwisli þan can yee blam. *a* 1340 HAMPOLE *Psalter* xxxv. 7 Men, þat lifis rightwisly, and..ill men, þat lifis vnscilwisly.

un'skimmed, *ppl. a.* (UN-¹ 8.)

1634 T. JOHNSON *Parey's Chirurg. Wks.* xxiv. vi. 891 A certaine thinne skinne..like unto that..over vnscimmed milke. 1687 MONTAGUE & PRIOR *Hind & P. Transv.* 12 He ..could not on a sudden Knead up with unskim'd Milk this Reas'ning Pudding. *a* 1722 LISLE *Husb.* (1757) 275 They wean them with unskimmed cow's-milk. 1858 FLINT *Milch Cows* 309 Sweet milk cheese is made of the unskimmed milk. 1894 *Westm. Gaz.* 20 April 8/1 The milk..is very often skimmed, and the skimmed milk mixed with unskimmed.

un'skin, *v.* [UN-² 4.] *trans.* To divest of skin; to flay. Also *fig.*

1598 FLORIO, *Discotennare*, to flea, to vnskin. *a* 1652 BROME *New Acad.* IV. ii, I'le..not only unmask, but unskin her face too. 1655 MOUFET & BENNET *Health's Improv.* xxx. 278 Flaying and unskinning themselves as it were of reasons robe. 1935 T. S. ELIOT *Murder in Cathedral* i. 20 And our hearts are torn from us, our brains unskinned like the layers of an onion.

un'skinned, *ppl. a.*¹ [UN-² 8, or f. prec.] Stripped of the skin.

1607 MARKHAM *Cavel.* VII. 63 Then casting that powder vpon any vnskinde part, it will presently bring on the skinne againe. 1790 J. WILLIAMS *Shrove Tues.* 24 Deal out contumely with dread.., Nor make that ulcerous that's scarce unskinn'd.

un'skinned, *ppl. a.*² [UN-¹ 8.] Not having the skin taken off.

[1775 ASH.] 1882 J. F. S. GORDON *Prov. Moray* I. 36 Unskinned peas boiled into a soup were also a favourite dish. 1899 *Daily News* 7 June 8/3 They threw the unskinned animal on the embers.

un'skirmished, *ppl. a.* (UN-² 8 c.)

1627 DRAYTON *Agincourt* 24 And more then this, his Iourneyes to fore-slowe He scarce one day vnskirmish'd with doth goe.

un'skirted, *ppl. a.* (UN-¹ 8.)

[1775 ASH.] 1886 *Col. & Ind. Exhib., Catal. Exhibits N.S. Wales* (ed. 2) 93 Wool,..Six unskirted fleeces off prize ewes.

un'slack, *a.* (UN-¹ 7. Cf. OE. *unsleac, unslæc.*)

1622 WITHER *Philarete* O 7 b, Thy ioynts are yet nimble, thy sinnewes vnslacke.

un'slacked, *ppl. a.* [UN-¹ 8.]

1. Unslackened, unrelaxed.

1593 NASHE *Christ's T.* 24 b, God is mooued and mollified ..with often, and vnslacked intercessions. 1848 AIRD *Herod. & Azala* I. i, Still their [*sc.* lions'] fronts were racked With lust of blood, their forms were still unslacked.

2. Of lime: (see SLACKED *ppl. a.* 2).

1656 EARL MONM. tr. *Boccalini's Advts. fr. Parnass.* I. xxi. (1674) 22 Tyrannies are laid with..the unslackt Lime of.. injustice. 1703 MOXON *Mech. Exerc.* 286 Unslackt or Quick Lime. 1760 BROWN *Compl. Farmer* II. 17 Unslacked lime beat to powder. 1808 *Phil. Trans.* XCVIII. 346 They.. were in the highly caustic or unslacked state. *c* 1860 H. STUART *Seaman's Catech.* 63 Neither should unslacked lime ..be allowed below.

3. Of thirst, etc.: Not slacked.

1798 COLERIDGE *Anc. Mar.* III. iv, With throat unslack'd [1805 unslaked], with black lips bak'd Ne could we laugh, ne wail.

un'slackened, *ppl. a.* (UN-¹ 8.)

1770 GLOVER *Leonidas* (ed. 5) VI. 418 They well may keep the field, Who with unslaken'd [1772 unslacken'd] nerves endur'd that day. 1844 MRS. BROWNING *Sonn., Patience* 7 Ocean girds Unslackened the dry land. 1870 *Daily News* 23 Apr., He drove down a narrow road..followed by the waggon and horses with unslackened speed. 1890 'R. BOLDREWOOD' *Miner's Right* xlii, Still the quartz-crushing machine..went thundering on..unchecked, unslackened.

un'slackening, *ppl. a.* (UN-¹ 10.)

1768–74 TUCKER *Lt. Nat.* (1834) I. 628 To turn his steps into the way that..unslackening prudence would have led. 1793 W. ROBERTS *Looker-on* No. 85 (1794) III. 371 After an unslackening course of..fasting, mortification, and watchfulness. 1836 KEBLE in *Lyra Apost.* (1849) 18 Faster each hour, on Time's unslackening gale, The dreaming world drives on. 1848 MILL *Pol. Econ.* I. xi. § 1 There is no obstacle to an increase of production..of unslackening rapidity.

un'slain, *ppl. a.* [UN-¹ 8 b. Cf. ON. and Icel. *úsleginn* in sense 2, MSw. *oslaghin* in sense 1, Sw. *oslagen* in sense 3.]

1. Not put to death; not killed.

c 1250 *Gen. & Ex.* 1332 Ðo wurð abraham friȝti faȝen, for ysaac bi-leaf un-slaȝen. 13.. *Gaw. & Gr. Knt.* 1858 Myȝ[t] he haf slypped to be vn-slayn, þe sleȝt were noble. *c* 1400 *Laud Troy Bk.* 18250 Prest, ne clerk,..Leffte the Gregais non vn-sclayn. 1470–85 MALORY *Arthur* x. lix. 515, I shalle be with yow by that day yf I be vnslayne or vnmaymed. *a* 1533 LD. BERNERS *Gold. Bk. M. Aurel.* ii. (1535) 101 b, They leaue no cattayle vnslayne, no gardeyne vnrobbed. 1555 PHAËR *Æneid* III. (1558) F iiij, Saue of Troy this last remayne, The leauinges of Achilles wyld and Grekes abiectes onslayne. 1633 T. STAFFORD *Pac. Hib.* I. ix. (1821) 117 The rest which were unslaine, returned into the Castle. *a* 1661 HOLYDAY *Juvenal* (1673) 187 To Ceres's son-in-law few kings descend Unslain. 1715 TICKELL *Iliad* I. 112 Nor does the god complain Of vows withheld or hecatombs unslain.

fig. *c* 1412 HOCCLEVE *De Reg. Princ.* 1972 O deth!..his hy vertu astertith Vnslayn fro þe. 1674 R. GODFREY *Inj. & Ab. Physic* 8 Spurious Mercurial [remedies], and ill-made Antimonial ones, that..have the Mercury unslain. 1779 COWPER *Olney Hymns* lvii, One sin, unslain, within my breast, Would make that heav'n as dark as hell.

†2. Uncut, unmown. *Obs.*

c 1440 *Pallad. on Husb.* I. 239 Lupyne and ficchis slayn.. are as dongyng, londis boote. And let hem drie vnslayn, and vp they drinke The londis iuce.

†**unslake**, obs. var. UNSLAKED *ppl. a.*

1660 SHARROCK *Vegetables* 19 Unto the ashes of every hill [*sc.* heap] you must put a peck of unslake Lime.

un'slak(e)able, *a.* (UN-¹ 7 b.)

1820 C. R. MATURIN *Melmoth* xxviii. IV. 262 An unslakeable appetite for the restored splendours of her former state. 1872 C. KING *Mountain. Sierra Nev.* i. 21 In a few miles, the unslakable desert has drunk it dry.

un'slaked, *ppl. a.* [UN-¹ 8.]

1. Of lime: Unslacked.

1598 FLORIO, *Calce vergine*, vnslaked lyme. 1651 FRENCH *Distill.* I. 4 Take unslaked Lime, and Linseed Oil, mix them well together. 1669 STURMY *Mariner's Mag.* v. xii. 67 Plaster..four parts, of Unslak'd Lime one part. 1816 SCOTT *Old Mort.* xxi, Would ye build a wall with unslaked mortar? 1837 J. T. SMITH *Vicat's Mortars* 79 Those hydraulic mixtures, which are used unslaked, and ground previous to mixture. 1889 *Science-Gossip* XXV. 151/1 The leaves are.. chewed with a little unslaked lime.

2. Unrelaxed.

a 1625 FLETCHER *Chances* II. ii, A likely man, a man Made up like Hercules, unslak'd with service.

3. Of thirst, etc. (See SLAKE *v.*¹ 10.)

1692 DRYDEN *Don Sebastian* III. i, Her desires new rouz'd, And yet unslak'd, will kindle in her fancy. 1805 [see UNSLACKED 3]. 1818 BYRON *Ch. Har.* IV. cxxiv, We gasp away..; unfound the boon, unslaked the thirst. 1874 FARRAR *Christ* 36 Stung by remorse, yet still unslaked with murder.

un'slandered, *ppl. a.* (UN-¹ 8.)

1621 SANDERSON *Serm.* I. 24 If seldom truth scape unslandered, marvel not: the reasons are evident. 1648 HEXHAM II, *Ongelastert*, Vnslaundered, or Vncalumniated.

un'slate, *v.* (UN-² 4.) Also *fig.*

1598 FLORIO, *Scoppare*, to vntile, to vnslate. 1637 SALTONSTALL *Eusebius' Constantine* 70 Some of the Chappels by his command were unslated. 1648 HERRICK *Hesper.*, *To the Detracter*, A fellon take it, or some Whit-flaw come For to unslate, or to untile that thumb! 1795 COLERIDGE *Lines at Shurton Bars* 39 Where stands one solitary pile Unslated by the blast. 1872 BRIERLEY *Cotters of Mossburn* xxiii, He's gone clean off his head. Unslated.

un'slaughtered, *ppl. a.* (UN-¹ 8.)

1719 YOUNG *Par. Job* 230 Hov'ring o'er Th' unslaughter'd host, [the eagle] enjoys the promis'd gore. *a* 1800 COWPER *Odyss.* (ed. 2) XI. 463 The woful end Of other Greecians,..Who 'scap'd, indeed, unslaughter'd from the field of Ilium. 1827 SOUTHEY *Hist. Penins. War* II. 553 The few mules and horses which remained unslaughtered. 1870 *Eng. Gilds* 354 *margin*, Having..goats, sheep, or swine, and selling them unslaughtered.

un'slave, *v.* (UN-² 4 b. Cf. Du. *ontslaven.*)

a 1618 SYLVESTER *Maiden's Blush* 1641 I'll give you all the golden good I have,..your Brother to un-slave. 1633 P. FLETCHER *Poet. Misc.*, *A vow* 25 Thou freest Servant, from this yoke unslave me. 1719 D'URFEY *Pills* VI. 210 Suppose a Man does all he can, To unslave himself from a scolding Wife. 1729 SWIFT *Let.* 31 Oct., L—— C——, who doth his duty of a good governor in unslaving this kingdom as much as he can.

†**unslaw(e**, obs. varr. UNSLAIN *ppl. a.*

a 1400 in *Eng. Gilds* (1870) 354 Þulke, þat..byggeth get, shep, swyn, & a-ȝen selleþ vn-shlawe [*sic*]. *c* 1430 *Syr Gener.* (Roxb.) 8159 Thei that gate in, and wer vnslaw, The gates thei shet.

†**un'sleakable**, *a. Obs.*⁻¹ [UN-¹ 7 b.] Unquenchable.

c 1400 *Apol. Loll.* 75, I schal brenne þe chaffe wiþ fire vnslekable.

†**un'sleaked**, *ppl. a. Obs.* [UN-¹ 8.] = next.

1525 *Grete Herbal* cxix. (1529) Hj, Lyme, whan it is vnsleked. 1594 PLAT *Jewell-ho.* 55 Fill a sheepes gut with smal vnsleakt limestones. 1615 G. SANDYS *Trav.* 69 A composition of Rusma..and vnsleakt lime.

un'slecked, *ppl. a.* [UN-¹ 8. Cf. MSw. *osläkt*, Sw. *osläckt.*] = UNSLACKED *ppl. a.* 2.

Frequent *c* 1570–*c* 1600.

c 1386 CHAUCER *Can. Yeom. Prol. & T.* 806 Vnslekked lym, Chalk, and gleyre of an ey. 1563 T. GALE *Antidot.* II. 53 Take vnslecked Lime, and quench it in water. 1607 TOPSELL *Four-f. Beasts* 365 Take..so much vnslect lime as will make that hony thicke like paast.

un'sleek, *a.* (UN-¹ 7.)

1859 TENNYSON *Elaine* 811 Then she that saw him lying unsleek, unshorn,..Utter'd a little tender dolorous cry.

un'sleep, *v.* (UN-² 3.)

1555 *Inst. Gentleman* *iii b, Slepe once passed cannot be vnslept againe.

†**un'sleepiness.** *Obs.* [UN-¹ 12.] Sleeplessness.

1540 R. JONAS *Byrth Mankynde* 70 b, Agaynste vnslepynesse, that is, when the chylde..wanteth his due and naturall reste.

†**un'sleeping**, *vbl. sb. Obs.* [UN-¹ 13.] Lack of sleep.

a 1425 tr. *Arderne's Treat. Fistula*, etc. 56 Brennyng with greuous prikkyng, and smertyng, and vnslepyng. *Ibid.* 72 If þat þe thenasmon last long, it bringeþ to..vnslepyng and feblenes of vertu.

un'sleeping, *ppl. a.* (UN-¹ 10.)

1667 MILTON *P.L.* v. 644 The unsleeping eyes of God. 1744 THOMSON *Autumn* 415 She sits Conceal'd, with folded Ears; unsleeping Eyes. 1777 POTTER *Æschylus, Prom. Bd.* 7 The joyless station of this rock Unsleeping, unreclining, shalt thou keep. 1805 SOUTHEY *Madoc in Wales* III. 195 The unsleeping eye Of justice. 1863 LD. LYTTON *Ring Amasis* II. 293 Dear heart! Again you have passed a whole night long unsleeping.

fig. *a* 1613 OVERBURY *A Wife*, etc. (1614) H 2, Policie is the vnsleeping night of reason. 1796 COLERIDGE *Destiny of Nations* 106 Whose unheard name..Unsleeping Silence guards. 1802–12 BENTHAM *Ration. Judic. Evid.* (1827) I. 428 Unerring and unsleeping steadiness. 1841 ELPHINSTONE *Hist. Ind.* II. 520 The unsleeping suspicions of Aurangzib were stirred up.

Hence **un'sleepingly** *adv.*

1877 *Daily News* 16 Jan. 4/5 Our pressure must be friendly, but very firm and unsleepingly watchful.

un'sleeve, *v.* (UN-² 4 b, 5.)

1598 FLORIO, *Dimanicare*, to vnhandle, to vnhaft, to vnsleeue. *Ibid.*, *Smanicare*, to unsleaue. *a* 1814 *Gonzanga* IV. vii. in *New Brit. Theatre* III. 143 Unsleave thy arm, that I may kiss a mark, stamped there indelible by nature's finger.

un'slept, *ppl. a.* [UN-¹ 8 b, c.]

1. Not having slept.

a 1500 *Chaucer's Dreme* 1836 An aged knight..With visage..pale, as man longe unslept. 1500–20 DUNBAR *Poems* lxxviii. 9 The sentence lay full evill till find, Vnsleipit in my heid behind. 1876 J. GRANT *One of the '600'* i. 10 My poor mother, pale, anxious, and unslept,..stole softly into my room. 1894 FROUDE *Life & Lett. Erasmus* 230, I hurry on board unsupped and unslept.

2. Not slept *in*; not slept *off*.

1821 BYRON *Sardanap.* I. ii, Is this moment A fitting one for the resumption of Thy yet unslept-off revels? 1864 MISS YONGE *Trial* I. 289 She had..found..never before, Mr. Ward's bed unslept in. 1880 MRS. PARR *Adam & Eve* xxxv. 476 The untasted food, the unslept-in bed.

†**un'slickt**, var. UNSLEAKED or UNSLECKED *ppl. adjs.*

1573 *Arte of Limning* C iv, Vnslickt lyme. Poulder of white bones. 1605 TIMME *Quersit.* III. 180 Take unslickt lime: let it lye in spring water.

un'sliding, *ppl. a.* (UN-¹ 10.)

1806 O. GREGORY *Treat. Mechanics* I. 101 Let E be the unsliding body, which acts in the direction EK.

un'sling, *v.* [UN-² 3, 4 b.] *trans.* To detach from a sling; to free from being slung or suspended.

(*a*) 1630 CAPT. J. SMITH *True Trav.* xx. 40 Many of them were got to the top to unsling the maine saile. 1783 in *Naval*

Chron. (1802) VIII. 364 [We] unslung our lower yards. **1815** BURNEY Falconer's Marine Dict. 603/2 To unsling is to take off the slings from boats, butts, buoys, yards, etc. **1839** F. A. GRIFFITHS Artill. Man. 187, [No.] 7..slings, and unslings the gun, and lashes it to the pry pole.

(b) **1688** HOLME Armoury III. xix. (Roxb.) 153/1 Vnsling your musket. **1798** Naval Chron. XXV. 200 An Arab.. unslung his carbine. **1818** SCOTT Rob Roy xxx, He.. commanded his soldiers to unsling their firelocks. **1838** JAMES Robber iii, Lord Harold unslung his sword, and gave it to one of the servants. **1865** VISCT. MILTON & W. B. CHEADLE N.-W. Passage by Land vii. 101 He unslings his pack, and sets to work to construct a..wooden trap.

un'slip, *v.* [UN-^{2} 3, 4 b.]

1. *trans.* To let slip, set free.

1611 FLORIO, Sguinzagliare, to vncouple, to vnslip, to let goe as Spaniels. **1801** SURR Splendid Misery III. 215 'Tis not the sudden impulse of a fleeting passion that has unslipped from caution's trammel a rebellious tongue. **1846** WHITTIER To Southern Statesman 6 When thy eager hand With game afoot, unslipped the hungry pack To hunt down Freedom in her chosen land.

2. To slip back.

1892 ZANGWILL Bow Mystery 125 [He] went downstairs, [and] unslipped the bolt of the big lock.

un'slipping, *ppl. a.* (UN-^{1} 10.)

1606 SHAKS. Ant. & Cl. II. ii. 129 To hold you in perpetuall amitie, To make you Brothers, and to knit your hearts With an vn-slipping knot. **1822** AINSLIE Land of Burns 71 The unslipping bauns o' matrimony.

†**un'slissed**, *ppl. a. Obs.* [UN-^{1} 8, after obs. Du. *ongeslist.*] Unslacked.

1597 A. M. tr. Guillemeau's Fr. Chirurg. 26 b/2 Like vnslissed lime. **1599** [see SLISS *v.*].

un'slit, *ppl. a.* (UN-^{1} 8 b.)

1679 MOXON Mech. Exerc. ix. 164 Bauk, a peece of Fir unslit, from four to ten Inches square.

un'slockenable, *a. Sc.* [UN-^{1} 7 b.] Unquenchable.

c **1520** M. NISBET Luke iii. 17 The caffis he sal birne with fire vn-sloknabile. **1856** H. S. RIDDELL Matt. iii. 12 He will burn up the caff wi' unslockenable fire.

un'slockened, *ppl. a. north.* and *Sc.* [UN-^{1} 8.] Unextinguished.

1434 MISYN Mending Life 126 O mery lufe, stronge, rauischand, byrnand,..vnslokynd, þat all my saull brynge to þi seruis. **1435** —— Fire of Love 97 þis lufe to fyre vnslokynd I lykyn. **1596** DALRYMPLE tr. Leslie's Hist. Scot. (S.T.S.). II. 164 Not willing to leiue ane spunk vnsloknet, [he] receiuet in fauour the Erle of Angus. **1896** CROCKETT Grey Man xxxiii, There burned a still and unslockened fire in her eye.

un'sloken, *ppl. a. rare*$^{-1}$. [Cf. prec.] = UNSLAKED *ppl. a.* 3.

1871 SWINBURNE Songs bef. Sunrise, Tenebræ 23 A slow song beaten and broken, As it were from the dust and the dead, As of spirits athirst unsloken.

un'slot, *v. north.* and *Sc.* [UN-^{2} 3.] *trans.* To unfasten (a door).

1819 W. TENNANT Papistry Storm'd (1827) 46 Thus said, Don Andrew..Unslot his yett, and out gaed whiddin'. **1855** [ROBINSON] Whitby Gloss. s.v., To Unslot or Unsteck, to unlatch, to open.

un'slothful, *a.* (UN-^{1} 7.)

1648 HEXHAM II, Ontraegh, vnslothfull, vigilent. **1887** E. JOHNSON Antiq. Mater. 251 Your unslothful love unto the glory of God.

un'slothfulness. (UN-^{1} 12.)

1700 RAY Persuas. Holy Life Add., Unslothfulness in Labour, if I may make such a Word, is the means to preserve health.

†**un'slow**, *a. Obs.* [OE. *unsláw* (UN-^{1} 7).] Not slow; active, quick, swift.

In Beowulf 2564 the emendation *unslaw* has been suggested for the MS. reading *unglaw*.

c **1000** ÆLFRIC Saints' Lives xxv. 375 Hi slogon þa togædere unslawe mid wæpnum. *a* **1023** WULFSTAN Hom. x. (1883) 72 Se ðe wære full slaw, weorðe se unslaw to cyrican. **1382** WYCLIF Prov. vi. 11 If forsothe thou shul be, shal come as a welle thi rip. *c* **1400** Destr. Troy 908 The dragon..gird him agayne with a grym noyse: Mony slecynges vnslogh throughe hys slote yode. **1483** Cath. Angl. 343/2 Vn Slawe, *vbi* wyghte.

un'sluice, *v.* [UN-^{1} 4 b, 5.]

1. *trans.* To let out as from a sluice; to allow to flow.

1611 FLORIO, Schiuso,..vnshut, vnlockt, vnsclused. **1648** HERRICK Hesper., Sailing fr. Julia, Forbeare (In my short absence) to unsluce a teare. *a* **1711** KEN Hymns Evang. Poet. Wks. 1721 I. 237 Unsluce his Blood, till now undrein'd. **1787** Generous Attachment I. 167 Enough to unsluice the water from any female eye. **1826** J. MONTGOMERY Chron. Angels Wks. 1841 IV. 309 Angels, with healing virtue in their wings,..unsluice earth's bosom-springs.

2. To furnish with an outlet.

1652 BENLOWES Theoph. III. xcv, Here did she seal her lips, unsluice her eyes To flowing rhet'ric. **1700** DRYDEN Ovid's Met., Mel. & Atalanta 365 Now lofty Calidon in Ruines lies; All Ages, all Degrees unsluice their Eyes. **1721** YOUNG Revenge II. ad fin., I must unsluice my overburthen'd heart And let it flow.

un'slumbering, *ppl. a.* (UN-^{1} 10.)

1718 G. SEWELL Proclam. Cupid 17 High God,..Who pierces Nature with unslumb'ring Eyes. **1787** Generous Attachment IV. 184 So many hours..devoted to unslumbering nights. **1841** JAMES Brigand xxix, There will be an unslumbering eye upon you which you cannot escape. **1862** TYNDALL Mountaineer. xii. 95 We wound along the meadows, by the slumbering houses, and the unslumbering river. **1887** BOWEN Æneid IV. 199 A hundred altars, on each an unslumbering fire.

absol. **1831** CARLYLE Sart. Res. I. viii, But Him, the Unslumbering,..we see not.

un'slumbrous, *a.* (UN-^{1} 7.)

1818 KEATS Endym. I. 912 How dark the dreadful leisure Of weary days, made deeper exquisite, By a fore-knowledge of unslumbrous night!

†**un'sly**, *a.* (*adv.*) *Obs.* [UN-^{1} 7, 11 b. Cf. ON. *úslœg-r* not sly or cunning.]

1. Of persons: Unskilful, unwise, foolish, careless.

c **1275** Sinners Beware 302 in O.E. Misc. 82 He gredeþ þanne heye, þe wrecches and þe vnsleye, þat luuede þe vnredes. *a* **1300** Cursor M. 21631 Mani o trouth es sua vn-slei, þai tru noght bot þat þai se wit ei. *c* **1340** HAMPOLE Pr. Consc. 1938 þarfor me thynk he es unsleghe þat mas hym noght here redy to deghe. **1382** WYCLIF Prov. xxiii. 28 She waiteth in the weie, as a thef; and whom vnsleiȝ [**1388** vnwar] she seeth, she shal slen. *c* **1425** Cast. Persev. 2781 In all hys werkis he is vnslye; mekyl of hys lyf he hath myspent. *c* **1450** Mirk's Festial 6 Vnsley old man, goo heþen! for I se apon þe mony meruayles.

2. Unskilfully made or done; awkward.

a **1300** Cursor M. 1684 þou lok þi werk be noght vnslei. **13..** Northern Passion 1356 (Camb. MS. Gg. I. 1), Als þei droth [= drew] þe tre on heie, þe werk waxed so vnsleie. *a* **1585** POLWART Flyting w. Montgomerie 159 To answere thee In sermon short I am content; And sayes thy similitudes vnslie Are na wayes verie pertinent.

b. As *adv.* Unskilfully, awkwardly.

a **1400** Northern Passion 144/217 (Camb. MS. Gg. 5. 31), þe tre..was wroght so vnsclegh þat it was schortir þan þe make Be four fute.

†**un'slyly**, *adv. Obs.*$^{-1}$ [UN-^{1} 11. Cf. prec.] Unskilfully, clumsily.

? *a* **1400** Morte Arth. 979 He slewe hir un-slely, and slitt hir to þe navylle.

un'smart, *a.* (UN-^{1} 7.)

c **1480** HENRYSON Fables, Prol. 23 Ane Bow that is ay bent Worthis vnsmart and dullis on the string. *a* **1817** JANE AUSTEN Watsons (1879) 330 The convenient though very un-smart family equipage. **1861** G. F. BERKELEY Eng. Sportsman i. 13 To tell an American..that you guess 'he's pitching it in considerable smart', and departing from un-smart fact, is no insult whatever.

Hence **un'smartness**.

1802 MISS BERRY Jrnl. (1865) II. 147 A general unsmartness of appearance pervaded them all.

un'smeared, *ppl. a.* (UN-^{1} 8.)

1648 HEXHAM II, Onbestreken, vnrubbed, or vnsmeared. **1805** FORSYTH Beauties Scotl. II. 179 Some farmers keep a few sheep perfectly unsmeared for domestic uses. **1825** R. WILSON Hist. Hawick xxvi. 267 Wool..of the white or unsmeared sorts.

un'smelled, un'smelt, *ppl. a.* (UN-^{1} 8, 8 b.)

[**1775** ASH.] **1812** Monthly Mag. XXXIV. 15 Odors may exhale unsmelt. **1856** G. WILSON Gateways Knowl. 83 Unsmelled or odourless incense.

un'smelling, *ppl. a.* (UN-^{1} 10.)

c **1440** Pallad. on Husb. IX. 71 The marl hath veynys [of water] thynne, vnsmellyng best [L. *nec optimi saporis*]. **1674** N. FAIRFAX Bulk & Selv. 47 All tastless, nothing relishing; all unsmelling, nothing scented.

un'smelted, *ppl. a.* (UN-^{1} 8.)

1824 MACTAGGART Gallovid. Encycl. (1876) 470 While earth Unsmelted will around her axle fly. **1887** Daily News 11 July 3/6 Black or unsmelted tin.

unsmethe: see UN-^{1} 3.

un'smiled, *ppl. a.* (UN-^{1} 8 a, c.)

1841 LADY F. HASTINGS Poems 26 They pass'd me ever —all unsmiled on—by. **1860** S. DOBELL in Macm. Mag. Aug. 328 In that pure face where woe grown bright Seems rapture chastened to the mild And equal light of smiles unsmiled. **1867** JEAN INGELOW Story of Doom v. 161 Pale she was As lily yet unsmiled on by the sun.

un'smiling, *ppl. a.* (UN-^{1} 10.)

1826 MISS MITFORD Village Ser. II. II. 129 Her fixed, settled, unsmiling silence hung over the banquet like a cloud. **1847** C. BRONTË J. Eyre xxxi, An unsmiling..gaze it was. **1873** DIXON Two Queens XIX. v. 26 Charles, with meek, unsmiling face, knelt in his chapel.

Hence **un'smilingly** *adv.*, **un'smilingness**.

1873 MISS BROUGHTON Nancy II. 65 The utter unsmilingness of his expression. **1879** HOWELL L. Aroostook xxvi, 'Is it something disagreeable?' asked Stainford lightly. 'It's right,' assured Lydia, unsmilingly.

un'smirched, *ppl. a.* (UN-^{1} 8.)

1602 SHAKS. Ham. IV. v. 119 The chaste vnsmirched brow Of my true Mother. **1784** COWPER Task III. 73 Matrons.. of character unsmirch'd, And chaste themselves. **1813** Examiner 1 Feb. 73/2 He courts the applause of unsmirched artificers. **1884** Fortn. Rev. Mar. 321 [His] innocence is unsmirched by any electioneering experience.

un'smirking, *ppl. a.* (UN-^{1} 10.)

1750 CHESTERF. Lett. 18 Jan., An open, chearful, but unsmirking countenance.

un'smitten, *ppl. a.* (UN-^{1} 8 b.)

13.. E.E. Allit. P. B. 732 Nay for fyfty..I schal for-gyue alle þe gylt..& let hem smolt al unsmyten smoþely atonez. *c* **1425** in Anglia VIII. 177 She myghte byholde þe compas of þe material sunne wiþ þe sighte of hir eyen vnsmyten ageyn. *c* **1430** Wycliffite Bible Gen. xxxii. 8 (MS. Bodl. 277), þe ooþir cumpanye whiche is left vnsmyten schal be saued. **1435** MISYN Fire of Love 34 With mynde vnsmytyn to heuyns þe self itt raises & stirris to lufe. **1648** HEXHAM II, Ongesmeten, vnsmitten, or vnstricken. **1743** YOUNG Nt. Th. IV. 158 Too long I set at nought the swarm Of friendly warnings, which around me flew; And smil'd, unsmitten. **1805** WORDSW. Prelude VI. 50 Four years and thirty..Have I been now a sojourner on earth, By sorrow not unsmitten. **1868** MILMAN St. Paul's 41 The godless John alone remained unsmitten, untouched.

un'smokable, *a.* (UN-^{1} 7 b.)

1892 Nation (N.Y.) 15 Sept. 201/3 Cigars..to the cultivated taste unsmokable.

un'smoked, *ppl. a.* [UN-^{1} 8.]

1. Not exposed to smoke.

1648 HEXHAM II, Onberoockt, Vnsmoaked. **1828–32** WEBSTER, Unsmoked,..not dried in smoke. **1890** Spectator 31 May, Men and women who consciously exult in the fresh air, the unsmoked sky. **1894** Daily News 1 Mar. 5/3 Unsmoked bacon of a particular cut.

2. Not consumed by smoking.

1731 SWIFT Cassinus & P. 24 His ancient pipe in sable dy'd, And half unsmok'd, lay by his side. **1827** DE QUINCEY Last Days of Kant Wks. 1854 III. 121 He smoked a pipe of tobacco..so rapidly, that a pile of reliques partially a-glow remained unsmoked. **1894** H. NISBET Bush Girl's Rom. 20 Turning abruptly..and flinging away his unsmoked cigar.

un'smokified, *ppl. a.* (UN-^{1} 8.)

a **1693** Urquhart's Rabelais III. xxxvii. 311 Having ravined his..Loaf, whereof no Morsel had been unsmoakified.

un'smoking, *ppl. a.* (UN-^{1} 10.)

1559 MORWYNG Evonym. 298 Tiles made of red earth.. must be..set on fire with unsmoking coles.

un'smoky, *a.* (UN-^{1} 7.)

1675 HAN. WOOLLEY Gentlew. Comp. 122 Then broil it.. over a temperate and unsmoaky fire.

un'smooth, *a.* [UN-^{1} 7. Cf. OE. *unsmóðe* (usually *unsméðe*).] Not smooth; rough.

1597 A. M. tr. Guillemeau's Fr. Chirurg. 9/2 A suture is vnsmothe and rugged. **1621** FLETCHER Thierry & Theod. III. i, Can there be any way unsmooth, has end So fair? **1638** MAYNE Lucian (1664) 356 May my limbes be for ever rough, and my chinne unsmooth. **1667** MILTON P.L. IV. 631 Those dropping Gumms, That lie bestrowne unsightly and unsmooth, Ask riddance. **1786** BURNS Lament v, Alas! Life's path may be unsmooth! **1856** MRS. BROWNING Aur. Leigh VI. 165 A peasant's brow, Unsmooth, ignoble, save to me and God.

b. Of sounds, speech, etc.

1610 G. FLETCHER Christ's Vict. xliii, How may weake mortall ever hope to file His unsmooth tongue, and his de-prostrate stile? **1642** FULLER Holy & Prof. St. II. viii. 79 Yet his own Poems are harsh, and unsmooth. **1812** COLERIDGE in Lit. Rem. (1836) I. 366 Its unsmooth mixture of the vocal and the organic..of language. **1846** MANGAN Poems (1903) 41 The things I sing of in verse unsmooth.

c. Of manners or conduct.

1648 HERRICK Hesper., Hymn to Graces, Give me.. Sweetnesse to allay my sowre And unsmooth behaviour. **1782** V. KNOX Ess. clxv. II. 328 A-propose, pray do you reconcile your unsmooth address to those rules of decorum?

Hence **un'smoothness**.

1597 A. M. tr. Guillemeau's Fr. Chirurg. 9/2 We perceave noe vnsmoothnes; than [= but] all even and smothe.

un'smooth, *v.* [UN-^{2} 6 a.] *trans.* To deprive of smoothness; to ruffle.

1621 G. SANDYS Ovid's Met. IX. (1626) 181 Yet Iupiters last words Vnsmooth her forehead with obseru'd distaste. **1654** W. MONTAGU Dev. Ess. II. viii. 155 Her forehead not unsmooth'd by any wrinkle. **1805** Miniature No. 33 (1806) II. 166 Wine..which causes..the reverend churchman to unsmooth his episcopal sanctity. **1849** M. ARNOLD New Sirens 123 Storms unsmooth'd your folded valleys.

un'smoothed, *ppl. a.* [UN-^{1} 8.] **a.** Not made smooth; left rough, uneven, etc. **b.** Of data, etc. (cf. SMOOTH *v.* 1 e). **c.** Of a voltage: with any ripple left in.

1614 WITHER Sat. to King 30 Let it not therefore now be deemed strange, My vnsmooth'd lines their rudenesse do not change. **1648** HEXHAM II, Ongevlackt, vnplained, or vnsmoothed. **1841** LYTTON Nt. & Morn. I. i, The clothes.. were thrown carelessly about, unsmoothed, and unbrushed. **1866** G. STEPHENS Runic Mon. I. 225 A tolerably even slab, ..unsmoothed except by the hand of nature. **1945** 16th Census: Population: Diff. Fertility: Women by Children under 5 (U.S. Bureau of Census) 2/2 An indication of the effect of inaccuracy in reported ages of women on the fertility statistics is given by a comparison of the unsmoothed figures with the smoothed figures. **1957** Practical Wireless XXXIII. 557/1 The frequency of the mains input is 50 c.p.s. and the output 'unsmoothed' H.T. has a 100 c.p.s. ripple. **1981** Jrnl. Geophysical Res. LXXXVI. 8002/1 The relative velocities are computed from the unsmoothed data.

un'smote, *ppl. a.* [UN-^{1} 8 b.] Unsmitten.

1815 L. HUNT Feast Poets 147 Ye shall try..how well ye can bear What Dryden has witness'd, unsmote with despair. **1815** BYRON Destr. Sennacherib vi, The might of the Gentile, unsmote by the sword.

un'smotherable, *a.* (UN-^{1} 7 b.)

c **1624** DONNE Serm. Wks. 1839 V. 304 That unsmotherable, that unquenchable spirit of adoption. **1766** J. ADAMS Diary 13 Jan., The unsmotherable pride of his own heart. **1837** DICKENS Pickw. xxviii, To the unsmotherable delight of all the porters.

un'smothered, *ppl. a.* (UN-^{1} 8.)

[**1775** ASH.] **1840** MANGAN Poems (1903) 136 The startled soul, upbounding from the mire Of earthliness,.. Unsmothered by the lethargy of years. **1891** SIR W. M.

CONWAY *Guide E. Pennine Alps* p. viii, I made way willingly ..and, as was intended, overheard the unsmothered remark.

un'smutched, *ppl. a.* (UN-[1] 8.)
[1775 ASH.] **1809** MALKIN *Gil Blas* II. iv. ¶12 Purer than unsmutched snow. **1879** TOURGEE *Fool's Err.* viii. 37 [The estate] came into his hands a new toy, unsmutched by any suspicion that [etc.].

un'smutty, *a.* (UN-[1] 7.)
1698 COLLIER *Immor. Stage* i. 54 The Expression of his Theodore was altogether unsmutty. **1764** *Museum Rust.* II. 225 If smutty seed be worse than unsmutty.

un'snaffled, *ppl. a.* (UN-[1] 8 a.)
[1775 ASH.] **1846** LANDOR *Exam. Shaks.* Wks. II. 280/2 There is not one of them that doth not sweat at some secret sin committed, or some inclination toward it unsnaffled.

un'snaky, *a.* (UN-[1] 7.)
1851 DE QUINCEY *Pope* Wks. 1858 IX. 26 [He] might, with advantage, have amputated this unsnaky chapter on snakes.

un'snap, *v.* [UN-[2] 3 and 7.]
1. *trans.* To reverse or undo the action of snapping; to release or detach by undoing a snap or catch.
1862 DICKENS *Somebody's Luggage* ii, As if nothing should ever tempt her to unsnap that snap [of the fingers]. **1901** *Munsey's Mag.* XXV. 736/2 The colt..was led in, the tie strap was unsnapped from his halter, and he was allowed [etc.]. **1904** A. L. ARTUS *Mere English* 62 At dusk of the day we unsnapped our teeth, And spewed him out.
2. *intr.* To give way with a snap.
1866 MEREDITH *Vittoria* vii, After he had drawn the seal ..over the lamp, the green wax bubbled and unsnapped.

un'snapped, *ppl. a.* (UN-[1] 8.)
[1775 ASH.] **1864** SKEAT *Uhland's Poems* 282 Round his limbs..Clings, unsnapped, the fetters' might. **1891** C. DAWSON *Avonmore* 162 Each harp has yet an unsnapped string That waits the touch of God.

un'snare, *v.* (UN-[2] 4 b.)
1550 THOMAS *Ital. Dict.*, *Dislacciare*, to vnsnare. **1611** COTGR., *Desreté*, vnsnared,..deliuered out of a net. [In modern dicts.]

un'snarl, *v.* [UN-[2] 3 and 7.] *trans.* To disentangle.
1555 WATREMAN *Fardle Facions* I. i. 27 Some fel into errours whereout they could neuer unsnarle themselues. **1633** P. FLETCHER *Purple Isl.* I. lvii, For ever had this Isle in that foul ditch..strai'd,..Had not the King..Unsnarl'd that chain. *a* **1699** T. BEAUMONT *Psyche* III. cxc, How Shall I unsnarle my Promise, and contrive That..the Saint may live! **1879** P. BROOKES *Influence of Jesus* iv. 160 Material fact and impalpable vision shoot through each other and cannot be unsnarled. **1893** KATE D. WIGGIN *Cathedr. Courtship* 53 It is Salemina who always unsnarls the weekly bill.
intr. **1844** 'J. SLICK' *High Life N.Y.* II. xxviii. 167 All on 'em seemed kinder tangled up and trying to unsnarl all over the floor. **1876** MRS. WHITNEY *Sights & Ins.* xxiii, Things do cool down. And snarls unsnarl just by putting quietly away.
Hence **un'snarling** *vbl. sb.*
1640 FULLER *Joseph's Coat* 189 Ones Excellency may consist in the unsnarling of a knowne controversie.

un'sneaped, *ppl. a.* [UN-[1] 8.] Unchecked.
1647 H. MORE *Song of Soul* III. ii. 2 When centrall life its outgone energie Doth spreaden forth, unsneep'd by foe-man keen.

un'sneck, *v.* orig. *north.* and *Sc.* [UN-[2] 3.] *trans.* and *intr.* To unlatch.
1785 W. HUTTON *Bran New Wark* (E.D.S.) 199 The girl unsneck'd the raddle heck. **1806** JAMIESON *Pop. Ball.* II. 339 She drew the bar, unsneck'd the door. **1825-** in northern dial. glossaries, etc. **1932** L. G. GIBBON *Sunset Song* i. 77 She unsnecked the door of the kirkyard wall, passing through to the Manse. **1948** A. JOBSON *This Suffolk* iii. 50 A little wicket gate..snecks and unsnecks, to let one in or out. **1967** 'G. NORTH' *Sergeant Cluff & Day of Reckoning* xv. 139 Mole..unsnecked the door of the bedroom.

un'snecked, *ppl. a. north.* and *Sc.* [UN-[1] 8.] Unlatched; off the latch.
1796 R. GALL *Tint Quey* 67 [To] gang an' leave the door unsnecket. **1824** CARR *Craven Gloss., Unsnecked*, unlatched.

un'sned, *ppl. a. Sc.* [UN-[1] 8 b.] Uncut.
1513 DOUGLAS *Æneid* IX. xi. 44 Onsned branchis wavand heyr and thayr. **1887** *Suppl. Jamieson* 180 In the West of S. some thirty years ago a common street cry was, 'Birk besoms; heather besoms; sned an' onsned!'

un'snib, *v.* [UN-[2] 3.] *trans.* To unfasten (a catch); to unlatch.
1904 GLEGG & DUNCAN *Law Reparation Scotl.* (ed. 2) ii. 39 When he unsnibs the window to clean it. **1966** J. MCCLENAGHAN *Moving Target* xiv. 148 He unsnibbed the chain which held the dogs together, and..they slipped away. **1980** R. HILL *Spy's Wife* xxiii. 178 She snibbed her bedroom door, but after a few seconds in bed got up and unsnibbed it.

un'snubbable, *a.* (UN-[1] 7 b.)
Also, in recent use (1898), ***unsnubbableness.***
1847 BP. W. HOW in *Mem.* (1898) 31 It is a most unsnubbable cat. **1898** C'TESS VON ARNIM *Eliz. & Germ. Gard.* 93 You can't snub that sort of people; they're unsnubbable.

un'snuffed, *ppl. a.* (UN-[1] 8.)
[1775 ASH.] **1825** LD. COCKBURN *Mem.* ii. (1856) 124 The smoky unsnuffed candles in greasy tin candlesticks. **1837** CARLYLE *Fr. Rev.* I. v. v, This latter, as nocturnal Vice-President,..sits sleepless, with lights unsnuffed. **1879** W. COLLINS *Rogue's Life* xiii, With one long unsnuffed candle lighting us smokily.

un'soaked, *ppl. a.* (UN-[1] 8.)
1570 LEVINS *Manip.* 50 Vnsoked, *insopitus.* [1775 ASH.]

un'soaped, *ppl. a.* (UN-[1] 8.)
[1775 ASH.] **1837** DICKENS *Pickw.* xxiv, The unsoaped of Ipswich brought up the rear. **1859** GEO. ELIOT *A. Bede* ii, Bessy belonged unquestionably to that unsoaped, lazy class of feminine characters.

un'sober, *a.* [UN-[1] 7. Cf. MDu. *onsober.*]
†**1.** Uncontrolled, immoderate. *Obs.*
c **1400** *Destr. Troy* 3800 Dyamede..was..Vnsober with seruaundes,..Dredfull in dole for dissait þat he vsit. *Ibid.* 12507 The sea was vnsober, sondrit the nauy. **1535** JOYE *Apol. Tindale* (title-p.), To..defende himself ageinst so many sclaunderouse lyes fayned vpon him in Tindals vncharitable and vnsober Pystle. **1589** FLEMING *Virg. Georg.* II. 35 Ne hath he seene (hard) yron lawes nor pleadinges at the bar Vnsober, mad, and quarellous. **1648** HERRICK *Hesper.*, *To J. Wingfield*, For ordaining, that thy words not swell To any one unsober syllable. *a* **1680** BUTLER *Char.*, *Mel. Man*, He..takes Pleasure in nothing but his own un-sober Sadness.
2. Unregulated in conduct; not staid or grave.
1542 UDALL *Erasm. Apoph.* 134 A young strepleyng must remedylesse from excessive and unsober revellyng come home lesse honest. **1550** BALE *Eng. Votaries* II. 88 Her eyes, her talke, her pase, all were vnsober, wylde, and wanton. **1637** R. CLERKE *Serm.* 485, I censure it [*sc.* drinking of healths] not simply, but for some unsober Ceremonies, that become not Christians. **1682** *Gov. Pennsyl.* 10 All that..are not convicted of Ill Fame, or unsober and dishonest Conversation. **1730** A. PETRIE *Rules Good Deportm. Ch.-Officers* 121 [Deacons] must not be Drunkards, nor Unsober, nor Covetous. **1812** W. TENNANT *Anster F.* II. xlii, Th' unsober spirit of the fiddle. **1829** LANDOR *Imag. Conv.* II. 309 She is verily an unsober jade, who in her gravest humour will lead thee into quarrels, and in her gayest will pick thy pocket.
3. Affected by, addicted to, drinking.
1611 FLORIO *Insobrio*, vnsober, drunken. **1846** LANDOR *Imag. Conv.* Wks. II. 193/1 We must do all we have to do, while the nation is feasting and unsober. **1852** MUNDY *Antipodes* I. 164 The loss or destruction of these fragile liabilities in the hands of rough, careless, and unsober characters.
Hence **un'soberness.**
1548 ELYOT, *Immodestia*, malapertnesse,..vnsobrenesse. **1681** KETTLEWELL *Chr. Obed.* v. ii. 605 Several instances of unsoberness, when there is no scandal to our Brethren joined with them.

un'sober, *v.* [UN-[2] 6 a.] *trans.* To make unstaid.
1856 FABER *Creator & Creature* III. i. (1858) 334 While we grow in merits we are getting hugely into debt to the greatness..of God's mercies, and this at times unsobers us.

un'soberly, *adv.* [UN-[1] 11.] Without sobriety or restraint; immoderately.
c **1400** *Destr. Troy* 2506 Lest it tyde after, þat ye be drepit with dole,..Your sones vnsoberly slayne in the place. *Ibid.* 12494 Sodonly the softe winde vnsoberly blew. **1547** *Homilies* I. *Contention* I. S ij b, So vnsoberly to reason and dispute, that..they fal to chiding and contencion. **1551** CRANMER *Answ. Cavillation* 8 Which counsell if you had.. folowed, you wolde not haue doone so vnsobrely in manny thynges, as you haue doone.

unso'briety. (UN-[1] 12 and 5 b.)
1669 R. FLEMING *Fulfill. Script.* (1726) 155, I think without any challenge of unsobriety such a remark very suitable.

unsocia'bility. (UN-[1] 12, 5 b. Cf. next.)
1758 WARBURTON *Div. Legat.* Pref., Wks. 1788 II. 326 A Principle which subverted the whole system of their religion, namely, the unsociability of the Christian faith. *a* **1797** BURKE *Regic. Peace* i. Wks. 1802 IV. 445 The systematick unsociability of this new-invented species of republick. **1837** LYTTON *E. Maltrav.* I. v, He..had his fits of unsociability. **1885** C. E. PASCOE *London of To-day* xiii. 125 The Richmond Club members invited guests to their dinner-table, and thus escaped the charge of unsociability.

un'sociable, *a.* [UN-[1] 7 b and 5 b.]
1. Not sociable or companionable; not readily or pleasantly associating with others.
1600 HOLLAND *Livy* 292 The Tyburts..had in times past joined armes with the Frenchmen, a savage and unsociable nation. **1646** H. LAWRENCE *Comm. Angells* 188 Men were so form'd for Communion, as no doctrine can be avowed for good, which renders them unsociable. **1703** *Rules Civility* 274 [Baseness] rather makes them to be accounted base, vindictive, savage, and unsociable. **1841** DICKENS *Barn. Rudge* i, He looked unsociable enough. **1871** JOWETT *Plato* II. 319 Whether a man is righteous and gentle, or rude and unsociable. **1899** W. T. GREENE *Cage-Birds* 32 At other times..he is unsociable with his kind.
b. Of disposition, conduct, etc.
1630 J. TAYLOR (Water P.) *Water-Cormorant* Wks. III. 1 His best seruice is harsh and vnsociable. **1688** SAVILE *Lady's New-Years Gift* 13 The Sullen are apt to place a great part of their Religion in Dejected and Ill-humour'd Looks, putting on an unsociable Face. **1710** *Tatler* No. 149 ¶5 A severe, distant, and unsociable temper. **1802** MAR. EDGEWORTH *Moral T.*, *Forester* vii, Surprised at his unsociable silence. **1861** PALEY *Æschylus* (ed. 2) *Agam.* 314/2 You would..reproach them for their unsociable behaviour.
2. Not readily or naturally going together; incompatible, incongruous.
1611 SPEED *Hist. Gt. Brit.* 779/1 This Ecclesiasticke text is handled elsewhere, and seemeth vnsociable to our begunne Subiect. **1697** COLLIER *Ess. Mor. Subj.* I. 26 If Sense and Learning are such unsociable imperious things. **1779** JOHNSON *L.P.*, *Cowley* ad fin., A boundless verse, a headlong verse,..seem to comprise very incongruous and unsociable ideas. **1827** POLLOK *Course T.* v. 558 Combining things Unseemly, things unsociable in nature, In most absurd communion.
b. Incapable of, averse to, uniting.
1676 BOYLE in *Phil. Trans.* II. 785 The Vial..contain'd two unsociable Liquors. **1678** NEWTON *Let.* Boyle's Wks. 1772 I. p. cxiv, There is a certain secret principle in nature, by which liquors are sociable to some things, and unsociable to others.
3. Devoid of, interfering with, social intercourse.
1638 SIR T. HERBERT *Trav.* (ed. 2) 164 An old rotten weather-beaten Inn..placed in part of an unsociable desart. **1642** HOWELL *For. Trav.* (Arb.) 45 Many Colonies..which lye squandered up and down in disadvantagious unsociable distances. **1861** LD. LYTTON & FANE *Tannhäuser* 105 As one ..Sunder'd by savage seas unsociable From kin and country.
Hence **un'sociableness; un'sociably** *adv.*
1611 FLORIO, *Insociabilita*, *vnsociablenesse. **1644** PRYNNE *Ch. Govt.* xii. 7 An extraordinary strangnes, unsociablenesse, and coldnesse of brotherly affection. **1871** SMILES *Charac.* ix. 258 The comparative unsociableness of the Englishman. **1665** BRATHWAIT *Comm. Two Tales* 2 None should be so *unsociably retired, as to ingross his Conceits to himself. **1787** J. WHITE *Voy. N.S. Wales* (1790) 58 The pavement..is so very unsociably narrow, that two persons cannot walk with convenience together. **1977** *Gramophone* June 117/2 Such indiscretions apart, and the inevitable rash of black sheep playing music at unsociably high volumes..the show had much to offer the keen visitor. **1981** A. FRASER *Splash of Red* xiii. 145 She had once been prepared to toil unsociably for the whole of August.

un'social, *a.* [UN-[1] 7 and 5 b.] Not social; not inclined for, adapted to, or fond of society:
a. Of persons (or animals).
1731 A. HILL *Adv. Poets* Ep. p. vii, Even Tartary, uncultivated, and unsocial, as she is, has given the World a Tamerlane. **1758** L. TEMPLE *Sketches* (ed. 2) 67 To be perpetually wise, is forbidding, unsocial, and something that does not become human Nature. **1817** KIRBY & SP. *Entomol.* xvi. II. 12 Neither of these motives can operate in causing unsocial insects to congregate. **1889** GRETTON *Memory's Harkb.* 298 My unsocial neighbour startled me.. by gravely propounding that he [*sc.* Scott] was not a Christian.
transf. **1781** COWPER *Charity* 126 To give the pole the produce of the sun, And knit th' unsocial climates into one.
b. Of habits, conditions, etc.
unsocial hours, socially inconvenient working hours.
1734 A. HILL *On Death of Dennis* 1 Adieu! unsocial excellence! at last Thy foes are vanquish'd. **1744** HARRIS *Three Treat.* (1765) 152 A solitary, unsocial State, can never supply tolerably the common Necessaries of Life. **1791** BOSWELL *Johnson* 25 June 1763, The mode of dining..at such houses in London, is..particularly unsocial. **1826** LAMB *Elia* II. *Pop. Fallacies* xv, What savage unsocial nights must our ancestors have spent..! **1884** *Century Mag.* XXVIII. 620 The unsocial effect of the drinking habit.
1973 *Times* 4 Dec. 1/1 A proposed unsocial hours payment in recognition of the odd times of the day and night that a [train] driver has to report for duty. **1976** *Evening Post* (Nottingham) 17 Dec. 15/7 (Advt.), Waiter-waitress required for Lenton Hall of Residence... Good holidays and unsocial hours payment for week-end work. **1982** *Economist* 13 Nov. 50/1 If the government is to avoid the annual pay squabble with the nurses the new review body should first establish realistic pay scales..taking into account the unsocial hours. **1984** *Brit. Med. Jrnl.* 21 July 145/2 The unsocial hours during which most emergency operating is done has meant that much of it has been unsupervised.
c. Of disposition, temper, etc.
1739 GLOVER *London* 212 Benignant peace With hospitality begin to sooth Unsocial rapine, and the thirst of blood. **1775** SHERIDAN *Rivals* v. i, Perhaps the recollection of a deed my conscience cannot justify may haunt me in such gloomy and unsocial fits, that [etc.]. **1816** *Remarks Eng. Mann.* 3 Our unsocial turn he ascribes to 'that independence Britons prize too high'. **1837** HALLAM *Hist. Lit.* I. ii. §15 The man himself was of too unsocial and forbidding a temper to conciliate them. **1885** *Manch. Exam.* 12 Feb. 4/7 The unsocial selfishness which excluded the toiling populations from their national health-giving scenes.
Hence **un'socialism,** (*a*) the quality of being unsocial; (*b*) an absence of socialism (*rare*).
1849 HANNA *Mem. Chalmers* II. 422 Behind all his assumed unsocialism there lay a true warm heart. **1889** G. B. SHAW *Fabian Ess. Socialism* 4 The gambling spirit urges man to..secure some acres of her [*sc.* Stepmother Earth]... This is Private Property or Unsocialism.

un'socialist, *sb.* and *a.* [UN-[1] 12, 7.]
A. *sb.* One who is not a socialist. **B.** *adj.* Not socialist.
1892 G. B. SHAW *Fabian Soc.* 6 Socialist statesmanship must..consist largely of taking advantage of the party dissensions between the Unsocialists. **1893** —— *Impossibilities of Anarchism* 4 It was bad enough to have to contend with the conservative forces of the modern unsocialist State. **1935** N. MITCHISON *We have been Warned* IV. 423 She'd been afraid..in strange, unsocialist towns. **1967** *Spectator* 28 July 103/3 To an unsocialist, socialism is as unmoral as it is fatuous. Suez revealed the extent to which the Conservative party has given up the idea of an unsocialist morality. **1979** *Guardian* 9 Oct. 4/8 You can't.. let this community be destroyed. It's un-Christian, let alone unsocialist.

unsoci'ality. (UN-[1] 12. Cf. UNSOCIAL *a.*)
1852 LEVER *M. Tiernay* xlv, All his habits were temperate, even to the extent of unsociality. **1873** MORLEY *Rousseau* I. 278 The bitter, irritable, and suspicious form which this unsociality now first assumed.

un'socially, *adv.* (UN-[1] 11.)
1656 J. SERJEANT in *Blount's Gloss.* A 8, Nay homebred heads unsocially did strive T'estrange themselves.

† **un'sociated**, *ppl. a.* (UN-1 8.)
1706 WATTS *Horæ Lyr.* II. 230 O happy pair! Envy'd by yet unsociated souls Who seek their faithful twins!

un'socket, *v.* (UN-2 5.)
a **1711** KEN *Hymns Evang.* Poet. Wks. 1721 I. 161 It racks his Joints, unsockets all his Bones. *a* **1745** SWIFT *Right of Prec.* Wks. 1841 II. 75/1 Not to oblige him [*sc.* an old parson] uncover in the cold, and unsocket his head with both hands. **1881** TENNYSON *Cup* II. ii. 159 Great Goddess, whose storm-voice Unsockets the strong oak.

un'sod, *ppl. a.* [UN-1 8 b.] = next.
a **1250** *Owl & Night.* 1007 Hi eteþ fys & fleys vnsode, Suych wolues hit hadde tobroude. **1562** WHITEHORNE *Ord. Souldiours* xxxiv. 43 Addinge to the sayde mixture that is vnsod..haulfe a parte of baye salte. **1577** B. GOOGE *Heresbach's Husb.* I. 31 b, A bushell of sodden meate, made of three quarters wet and vnsodde. **1622** FLETCHER *Sea-Voy.* III. i, Why should we consume thus,..And the live there that bred all our miseries, Unrosted, or unsod? *a* **1634** CHAPMAN *Alphonsus* III. i. 142 A schinken of good raw bacon, And that's a common meat with us, unsod.

un'sodden, *ppl. a.* [OE. *unsoden* (UN-1 8 b), = MDu. *ongesoden* (Du. *-zoden*), OHG. *unca-*, *unkisotan* (MHG. *ungesoten*, G. *ungesotten*), MSw. *osudhin*, MDa. *usaaden*, Da. *usoden* in sense 1.]
1. Unboiled, uncooked.
c **1000** *Sax. Leechd.* II. 38 Sceapes hohscancan unsodenne tobrec, ȝedo þæt mearh on þa eaȝan. **1511** FABYAN *Will* in *Chron.* (1815) p. v, If my said monethes mynde fall in Lent, or upon a fysshe day, than I will that the said .xxiiij. peces of fleshe be altered unto saltfyche or stokfyshe, unwatered and unsodeyn. **1571** GOLDING *Calvin on Ps.* lviii. 10 Like unsodden flesh, and such as hathe scarce yit felt the first warmth of the fyre. **1608** WILLET *Hexapla Exod.* 247 The manna..was raw and vnsodden.
2. Not sodden or soaked. Also *fig.*
1818 SHELLEY *Eugan. Hills* 295 The plains that silent lie Underneath; the leaves unsodden. **1859** MEREDITH *R. Feverel* xxii, A non-dancing, stout-dining congregation, in the midst of which a gay young guardsman..would not have obtruded his unsodden spirit.

† **un'soft**, *a. Obs.* [UN-1 7. Cf. MDu. *onsoft*, *-saft*(*e*, etc. *sacht*(*e*, etc. (Du. *onzacht*), MLG. *unsacht*, OHG. (MHG.) *unsamft* (G. *unsanft*).] Not soft; hard, severe.
c **1275** *Serving Christ* 25 in *O.E. Misc.* 91 Þer is þe sunfulle vnsofte to beon. *c* **1386** CHAUCER *Merch. T.* 1824 He kisseth hire ful ofte With thilke brustles of his berd vnsofte. **1390** GOWER *Conf.* I. 283 Mi wofull herte is so tobete, That all my wittes ben unsofte And I am wroth. **1430–40** LYDG. *Bochas* v. vii. (1494) r j b/2 And Affricans felt full vnsoft Whan she to theym list be contrarye. *c* **1470** HENRY *Wallace* x. 332 Quham euir he hyt, thair sawchnyng was wnsoft. **1513** DOUGLAS *Æneid* II. ii. 96 The north wynd onsoft Held thaim abak.

† **un'soft**, *adv. Obs.* [OE. *unsófte* (f. *un-* UN-1 11 b + *sófte* SOFT *adv.*), = WFris. *on-*, *ûnseaft*, *-sêft*, *-sacht*, MDu. *onsacht*(*e*, *-socht*(*e*, etc. (Du. *onzacht*), MLG. *unsachte*, OHG. *unsamfto* (MHG. *unsanfte*, G. *unsanft*).] Not softly; severely.
a **900** *Guthlac* 858 (Gr.), Hu he monȝe..ȝehælde..þe hine unsofte adle ȝebundne..ȝesohtun. *c* **1000** *Sax. Leechd.* II. 260 Hwær mon unsofte ȝetilað on forewearde þa adle. ? *a* **1400** LYDG. *Chorle & Birde* (Roxb.) 10 And who desireth to clymbe hygh a lofte Be sodeyn turne falleth ofte unsofte. **1430–40** —— *Bochas* VI. (1494) t ii b/1 Another honde griped full vnsofte Which cast another in greate aduersite. **1509** HAWES *Past. Pleas.* XXXII. (Percy Soc.) 159 In holly bushes they did hange aloft, Theyr hedes downeward for to fall unsofte. **1579** SPENSER *Sheph. Cal.* July 12 This reede is ryfe, that oftentime Great clymbers fall vnsoft.

un'softened, *ppl. a.* (UN-1 8.)
1645 HAMMOND *Death-bed Repent.* 29 When the hard heart is unsoftned, unhumbled. **1715** ATTERBURY *Serm.* (1734) III. 121 Impatient of Delay, and unsoftned by all these Applications. **1789** T. TWINING *Aristotle's Treat. Poetry* 352 The unsoftened and unflattered character of Achilles. **1802** *Noble Wanderers* II. 143 The multitude of his sins were unsoftened by a single charity. **1855** [J. R. LEIFCHILD] *Cornwall* 76 The same primitive rock..is still durable and unsoftened. **1857** N. HAWTHORNE *Eng. Note-Bks.* (1870) II. 291 Scenery..with very hard outlines, which are unsoftened..by any foliage.

un'softening, *ppl. a.* (UN-1 10.)
1857 DICKENS *Dorrit* II. xxx, She.., with an unsoftening face, looked at the worked letters within. **1873** PATER *Stud. Hist. Renaiss.* 74 This last passion would be the most unsoftening..of all.

† **un'soilable**, *a. Obs.* [UN-1 7 b + SOIL *v.*2 4.] Unanswerable, irrefutable.
c **1449** PECOCK *Repr.* II. v. 162 An other vnsoilable proof for this..principal conclusioun is sett bifore.

† **un'soilably**, *adv. Obs.* [UN-1 11; cf. prec.] Indisputably.
c **1445** PECOCK *Donet* 141 As it is bifore sufficientli and vnsoilably provid.

† **un'soiled**, *ppl. a.*1 *Obs.*−1 [UN-1 8 + SOIL *v.*2 3.] Unsolved, unanswered.
1533 MORE *Answ. Poysoned Bk.* Wks. 1061/2 That question Christ left vnsoyled.

† **un'soiled**, *ppl. a.*2 *Obs.* [UN-1 8 + SOIL *sb.*3 8 or *v.*3] Not covered or treated with manure.
1616 MARKHAM *Cheap Husb.* (ed. 2) 46 You shall remoue her into the best grasse you haue, which is fresh and unsoiled.

un'soiled, *ppl. a.*3 [UN-1 8.] Not soiled or dirtied. Also in fig. context.
c **1592** MARLOWE *Jew of Malta* II. 419 *Lod.* This is thy Diamond, tell me, shall I haue it? *Bar.* Win it, and weare it, it is yet vnsoyl'd. **1649** LOVELACE *Poems* 131 Which.. Lookes..Like Gold in Canvas, or with dirt Unsoyled Ermins close begirt. **1686** DRYDEN *To Mem. Mrs. Anne Killigrew* iv, Her Arethusian Stream remains unsoil'd..and undefil'd. **1784** COWPER *Task* IV. 212 Time, as he passes us, has a dove's wing, Unsoil'd and swift. **1818** SCOTT *Hrt. Midl.* iii, A white handkerchief was thrust into the muzzle of the piece, and returned unsoiled or blackened. **1867** MORRIS *Jason* II. 71 With unsoiled feet scarce touching the wet way.
fig. **1603** SHAKS. *Meas. for M.* II. iv. 155 My vnsoild name, th' austeerenesse of my life,..Will..your accusation ouerweigh. **1699** LD. TARBUT in *Pepys' Diary*, etc. (1870) 691 That common opinion that young infants (unsoiled with many objects) do see apparitions which are not seen by those of older years. **1704** D'URFEY *Abrad. & Panthea* i. 9 Yet shall her honour be unsoil'd and clear. **1815** CHALMERS *Let.* in Hanna *Life* (1850) II. 29 An unsoiled gracefulness and brilliancy of character. **1848** JAMES *Sir T. Broughton* I. 159 Her spirit [was] unsoiled by the world.

un'soiling, *vbl. sb.* (UN-2 4.)
1895 *Funk's Stand. Dict.*, *Unsoiling*, the act or process of removing soil, as for working a bed of brick-clay.

un'solaced, *ppl. a.* (UN-1 8.)
[**1775** ASH.] **1796** COLERIDGE *Ode to Departing Year* v, By the Earth's unsolaced groaning, Seize thy terrors, Arm of might! **1862** [ELIZ. JOHNSTON] *Gifts & Graces* XXII. 215 Unsolaced by ministering hands of loved ones.

un'sold, *ppl. a.* [UN-1 8 b. Cf. MSw. *osalder*, Sw. *osåld*.] Not disposed of by sale.
1362 LANGL. *P. Pl.* A. v. 122 Bote nedde þe grace of gyle i-gon a-mong my ware, Hit hedde ben vn-sold þis seuen ȝer. **1388** WYCLIF *Acts* v. 4 Whethir it vnseld was not thin; and whanne it was seld, it was in thi power? **1489** *Paston Lett.* III. 354 If Bayard be onsolde, I pray yow late hym be made fatte. *a* **1513** FABYAN *Chron.* (1811) 594 All suche marchaundyse, beyng than vnsolde, to be forfayted vnto the kyng. **1583** MELBANCKE *Philotimus* R iv b, Pertinax..did rather leaue his wood vnsould, then abate one blancke of his price. **1620** in Foster *Eng. Factories Ind.* I. (1906) 207 The last yers corrall is unsould. **1683** MOXON *Mech. Exerc.*, *Printing* 8 Some Trades are..sooner sold off, which renders the remainder of the un-sold Exercises unperfect. **1725** DE FOE *Voy. round World* (1840) 246, I always reserved a small quantity of all goods unsold. **1809** PINKNEY *Trav. France* 57 When the property of the emigrants is unsold. **1878** JEVONS *Prim. Pol. Econ.* 100 She begins to fear that she may have to carry her butter back unsold.

un'solder, *v.* [UN-2 3. Cf. Flem. *ontsouderen* (Kilian).] *trans.* To undo the soldering of. Also *fig.*, to dissolve.
1538 ELYOT, *Replumbo*, to vnsowlder. **1611** COTGR., *Dessoulder*, to vnsolder, loose, dissolue. **1633** T. ADAMS *Exp. 2 Peter* ii. 5 Who feares..that his marrying a wife should unsoulder his conjunction with Christ? **1813** *Examiner* 12 Apr. 237/2 The leaden coffin being unsoldered, a body appeared. **1842** TENNYSON *Morte d'Arth.* 14 The sequel of to-day unsolders all The goodliest fellowship of famous knights Whereof this world holds record. **1889** *Anthony's Photogr. Bull.* II. 171 The weak point of the lamp..is the danger of unsoldering its parts by this down rush of the flame.

un'soldered, *ppl. a.* [UN-1 8.] Not fixed or closed with solder. Also *fig.*
1641 J. TAYLOR (Water P.) *Reply* (title p.), A Rusty, Rayling,..Lying Libell,..lately written by an impudent unsoder'd Ironmonger. **1876** PREECE & SIVEWRIGHT *Telegraphy* 303 The soldering iron, and fire-pot,..are more or less cumbersome, and lead to unsoldered joints remaining in the wire. **1891** CLARK RUSSELL *Curatica* 104 If he is a plumber, he will not leave your pipes unsoldered.

un'soldier, *v.* [UN-2 6 b and 4.] *trans.* To divest of the character of a soldier or soldiers.
1611 FLORIO, *Dissoldato*, vnsoldiered. **1776** S. J. PRATT *Pupil of Pleas.* II. 53 A tender woman will..unsoldier the boldest of us. **1780** —— *Emma Corbett* (ed. 4) II. 67 Death sometimes comes at the bottom of the account to unsoldier a man. **1791** MACKINTOSH *Vind. Gallicæ* 286 Two grand operations conduct to it—arming the people, and unsoldiering the army.

un'soldiered, *ppl. a.* [f. prec. or UN-1 8.] Free from, not attended by, soldiers. Also as *adv.*, in an unsoldierly manner.
1609 HEYWOOD *Brit. Troy* XV. xi, The people yssue free, Th' unsouldierd fields and deserts plaine to see. **1618** FLETCHER *Loyal Subj.* I. i, This young Prince..drew 'em up ..so poorly, So raggedly and loosely, so unsouldier'd, The good Duke blush'd. **1834** DISRAELI *Rev. Epick* 35 Behold With eager homage..This mystical Omnipotence who breathes Unsoldiered edicts to a martial world.

un'soldierlike, *a.* (UN-1 7 c.)
1590 SIR J. SMYTH *Disc. Weapons* Ded. 3 Their infinite vnsoldiorlike proceedings and disorders. **1600** DYMMOK *Ireland* (1843) 41 That advantage which was geven them by this unsoldior lyke encampinge. **1652** J. WRIGHT tr. *Camus' Nat. Paradox* III. 50 The unsoldier-like countenance of Iphigenes. **1721** DE FOE *Mem. Cavalier* (1840) 291 This was the most unsoldier-like action. **1777** ROBERTSON *Hist. Amer.* II. 80 From their unsoldier-like impatience..their general permitted them to retire. **1810** SYD. SMITH *Wks.* (1859) I. 193/1 Those allowances have been abused in the meanest.. and most unsoldier-like manner. **1861** G. MUSGRAVE *By-Roads* 300 An abnormal and most unsoldierlike condition of things, which involved all the elements of weakness, incompetency, and defeat.

un'soldierly, *a.* (UN-1 7.)
1598 BARRET *Theor. Warres* II. i. 29 [An] vnsoldiarly trick of a training captaine. **1644** PRYNNE & WALKER *Fiennes' Trial* 33 The most absurd, irrational, if not unsoldierly distinction, that ever was heard of in the world. **1693** RYMER *Short View of Tragedy* 134 The General..should..have turn'd his Eyes away from so unsouldierly an Execution. **1721** DE FOE *Mem. Cavalier* (1840) 299 Avoiding..the putting any unsoldierly extremities upon us. **1863** KINGLAKE *Crimea* II. 356 This movement..was scarcely wrong or unsoldierly. **1895** *Eclectic Mag.* Mar. 294 The unsoldierly appearance of a dandified subaltern.

† **un'soldiery**, *a. Obs.* [UN-1 7.] = prec.
1598 BARRET *Theor. Warres* II. i. 22 That the souldiers take not example from him of vnsoldiarie negligence. **1648** (*title*), An Elegie on the Most Barbarous, Vnparallel'd, Vnsouldiery Murder, committed at Colchester upon..Sir Charles Lucas and Sir George Lisle.

un'sole, *v.* (UN-2 4. Cf. Du. *ontzolen*.)
1598 FLORIO, *Dissolare*,..to part as the shoe from the sole, to vnsole. **1611** COTGR., *Dissemeler*, to vnsole, or pull the soles off a shoe. **1805** J. BOARDMAN *Dict. Veterinary Art* s.v. *Sole*, A horse that has been unsoled..will recover in a month's time.

un'solemn, *a.* [UN-1 7.]
† **1.** Uncelebrated. *Obs.*
c **1374** CHAUCER *Boeth.* I. pr. iii. (1868) 11 Of wyche folk þe renoun is neyþer ouer oolde ne vnsolempne [L. *incelebris*].
2. Not solemn; lacking in formal gravity.
c **1555** HARPSFIELD *Divorce Hen. VIII* (Camden) 124 The power..of that kind of vowe is stronger than in..a single unsolempe vow. **1660** JER. TAYLOR *Ductor* I. ii. rule 8 §30 Conscience can oblige a Judge to an unsolemn absolution. **1825** R. P. WARD *Tremaine* II. 106 The not unsolemn rhythm of the regular trot of the horses. **1885** *Law Rep. 14 Q.B.D.* 702 A thing..which by the rules of the House is disorderly and unsolemn.
b. *Law.* Of a will: Informal.
1590 SWINBURNE *Testaments* 18 Vnsolemne testamentes are so tearmed, whereas the solemnities of the Ciuil law.. are omitted. *a* **1661** HOLYDAY *Juvenal* (1673) 50 Our lawiers therefore now call those ancient ones 'solemn testaments', as the latter sort unsolemn. **1726** AYLIFFE *Parergon* 527 Such a perfect Will may either be a solemn or unsolemn will. **1774** S. HALLIFAX *Rom. Law* 34 The Privilege of Unsolemn Testaments granted to Soldiers. **1844** H. TENNANT *Notary's Man.* ii. 32 The word 'Codicillus' or Codicil..denotes any unsolemn last will, in which no heir is named.
Hence **un'solemnly** *adv.*
1821 J. HODGSON in J. Raine *Mem.* (1857) I. 367 He read the prayers very unsolemnly.

un'solemnized, *ppl. a.* (UN-1 8.)
1603 TAMWORTH in E. Lodge *Illustr.* (1791) III. 229 He is enfermed by deathenesse [*sic*]; and that made him unsolempnized at the coronacion.

unso'licitated, *ppl. a.* (UN-1 8.)
1807 COGAN in *Treat. on Passions*, etc. (1813) II. 470 The thoughts which suggest themselves to the mind, not only unsolicitated, but completely unexpected.

unso'licited, *ppl. a.* [UN-1 8.]
1. Of persons: Not approached with solicitation; unasked.
1588 SHAKS. *Tit. A.* IV. iii. 60 Of my word, I haue written to effect, Ther's not a God left vnsollicited. **1613** —— *Hen. VIII*, II. iv. 219, I then..got your leaue To make this present Summons vnsolicited. **1680** C. NESSE *Church Hist.* 365 The devil..steps in..though unsolicited by those conspirators. **1756** CONNOISSEUR No. 116 ¶2 The graduate in medicine, finding himself unsolicited for prescription or advice. **1813** COLERIDGE *Lett.* (1895) 604 A number of unsolicited, unknown yet predetermined plauditors in the theatre. **1851** HUXLEY in *Life & Lett.* (1900) I. 90 He had previously been civil enough to sign my certificate.., unsolicited. **1883** MEREDITH *Melampus* x, Not unsolicited, ..the pendulous flower of the plants of sloth..answered question and squeeze.
b. *spec.* Not asked in marriage.
1750 JOHNSON *Rambler* No. 73 ¶2 My aunts, being.. neither young nor beautiful,..were suffered to live unsolicited.
2. Not asked for; given or done voluntarily.
1689 SAVILE *Let. to Dissenter* 30/2 Thanks must be voluntary, not only unconstrained, but unsolicited. **1782** MISS BURNEY *Cecilia* II. v, [He called] to bring her..fresh and unsolicited intelligence. **1818** SCOTT *Br. Lamm.* xxv, I am obliged to your lordship for your unsolicited intercession. **1847** HARRIS *Ld. Hardwick* III. 107 This appointment was entirely the unsolicited act of His Majesty.
3. Not affected or influenced.
1857 MILLER *Elem. Chem.*, *Org.* 184 If thus, whilst unsolicited by any extraneous chemical forces, its molecular arrangement is so readily altered.
Hence **unso'licitedly** *adv.*
1815 W. H. IRELAND *Scribbleomania* 285 He..refused the first ecclesiastic dignities, which were unsolicitedly pressed upon him.

unso'licitous, *a.* (UN-1 7.)
(*a*) **1668** CLARENDON *Vind.* Tracts (1727) 66 Which refusal, and many others, shew how unsollicitous I have always been in the way of getting. **1768–74** TUCKER *Lt. Nat.* (1834) II. 453, I could easily conceal this slip of memory,.. but I choose to let it stand, agreeably with the character of the Searches, unsolicitous to hide their defects. **1778** SIR J. REYNOLDS *Disc.* (1779) 21 That natural energy of men engaged in real action, unsolicitous of grace. **1817** BENTHAM *Parl. Reform* Introd. 110, I have not been unsolicitous in my endeavours to collect it. **1884** *19th Cent.* Feb. 198 Yet St. Matthew is admitted..to be unsolicitous as to order of time. **1891** MISS DOWIE *Girl in Karp.* 259 With the fortune that attends the unsolicitous.

(*b*) **1758** JOHNSON *Idler* No. 9 ¶3 How many unsolicitous hours should I bask away, warmed in bed.., could I.. tumble from thence in a moment.

Hence **unso'licitousness**.

a **1683** OWEN *Gospel Grounds* Wks. 1851 V. 449 An unsolicitousness about present affairs and future events.

un'solid, *a.* [UN-^{1} 7, 5 b. Cf. G. *unsolid*.]

1. Not materially solid.

1611 COTGR., *Insolide*, vnsolide, vnsound. **1615** CHAPMAN *Odyss.* XI. 60, I.. would not suffer any one to dip Within our offring, his vnsolide lip, Before Tiresias. **1646** MAYNE *Serm. Unity* 38 A thin, unsolid, brittle, painted blast of wind. **1690** LOCKE *Hum. Und.* II. iv. §5 The continuity of unsolid, inseparable, and immoveable Parts. **1733** WATTS *Philos. Ess.* v. i. (1734) 116 'Tis not solid Extension, for that is Body or Matter... 'Tis not empty or unsolid Extension, for that is pure Space. **1768–74** TUCKER *Lt. Nat.* (1834) I. 298 Nor is it conceivable that any assortment of unsolid..parts should form a solid.. body. **1829** J. PHILLIPS *Geol. Yorks.* 73 These unsolid materials fall and waste away into slopes. **1896** *Daily News* 22 Jan. 5 German manufacturers are advised..to forsake the making of unsolid or ugly furniture.

fig. **1845** MILL *Diss. & Disc.* (1859) II. 256 The breaking up of the great unsolid structure which Charlemagne had raised.

2. *fig.* Having no substance or sound basis.

1593 in *Maitl. Club Misc.* (1840) I. 58 The presbiterie debarris Connald Strutheris for his vnsolid speichis..fra the communioune at this present seasoun. **1639** W. SCLATER *Worthy Commun.* 37 Its cleare, that this Consubstantiation of the Lutherans is unsolid. **1642** MILTON *Apol. Smect.* 45 Unsolid and corrupted judgements both in doctrine and life. **1730** THOMSON *Winter* 753 Whither now are fled..those unsolid hopes Of happiness? **1792** G. WAKEFIELD *Mem.* (1804) I. 115 The generality of them [*sc.* criticisms] are triviall or unsolid. **1854** H. MILLER *Sch. & Schm.* 204 To separate the solid from the unsolid thinking contained in my abstract. **1873** M. ARNOLD *Lit. & Dogma* p. xxiv, To what is unsolid in the New Testament he applies a negative criticism ably enough.

3. Lacking solid worth or merit.

1731 A. HILL *Advice to Poets* 193 But ah! far short the unsolid tinklers rise, Nor soar, but flutter, in the muse's skies.

Hence **un'solidly** *adv.*; **un'solidness**.

1611 COTGR., *Insolidement*, vnsoundly, vnsolidely. *a* **1684** LEIGHTON *Comm. 1 Peter* ii. (1693) 261 Consider this as our happiness, and the unsolidness of other comforts, and priviledges. **1755** JOHNSON, *Loosely*,..unsolidly; meanly; without dignity.

unso'lidity. (UN-^{1} 12, 5 b; cf. prec.)

1736 BAILEY (fol.) Addit., *Unsolidity*, unsolidness, unsoundness. **1802–12** BENTHAM *Ration. Judic. Evid.* (1827) V. 22 Wearing on the face of it a proof of its own injustice, a proof of the unsolidity of the ground. **1889** *Atlantic* May 655/2 The pen that has indulged itself to an extent disproportionate..to the apparent unsolidity of its topic.

un'solomonize, *v.* (UN-^{2} 6 c.)

1755 J. SHEBBEARE *Lydia* (1769) I. 60 We should then.. squeeze him to a confession of the truth, or unsolomonise him by superior wisdom.

†**unsolu'bility.** *Obs.*$^{-1}$ (UN-^{1} 12, 5 b.)

1789 J. KEIR *Dict. Chem.* 29/2 The absolute unsolubility of bismuth.

†**un'soluble**, *a. Obs.* [UN-^{1} 7, 5 b.] Insoluble; *fig.* unanswerable, irrefutable.

1559 AYLMER *Harborowe* K 3 b, I do not vrge this, as an vnsoluble reason. **1587** GOLDING *De Mornay* x. 170 Let us conclude..by vnsoluble reasons..that God..did in deede create the World of nothing. **1756** F. HOME *Exper. Bleaching* 279 By the..influence of the air, it [*sc.* lime] becomes an unsoluble earth.

unsolute, app. an error for *unsolide* UNSOLID *a.*

1611 SPEED *Th. Gt. Britain* I. xxxiii. 63/1 The Aire vpon the East and South part is both thicke and foggie, by reason of the Fennes and vnsolute grounds.

un'solvable, *a.* [UN-^{1} 7 b and 5 b.]

†**1.** Insolvent. *Obs.*$^{-1}$

1656 COWLEY *Misc.* Pref. ¶5, I have the real excuse of the honestest sort of Bankrupts, which is, to have been made Unsolvable..by some notorious accidents and publike disasters.

2. Insoluble.

[**1775** ASH.] **1821** J. Q. ADAMS *Report Weights & Meas.* 79 The problem, hitherto unsolvable to man, of squaring the circle. **1865** *Reader* 4 Feb. 130/1 He alone has produced paintings, before which we stand..as though they were unsolvable enigmas. **1894** S. FISKE *Holiday Stories* (1900) 155 Who had assumed the name..and hidden the receipt in our butler's pantry were unsolvable mysteries.

absol. **1894** H. GARDENER *Unoff. Patriot* 6 Human longing to solve the unsolvable.

Hence **un'solvableness**, ˌ**unsolva'bility**.

1884 *Nonconf. & Indep.* 10 Jan. 30/1 The question is depressing to the spirits in its very unsolvableness. **1947** *Jrnl. Symbolic Logic* XII. 7 They become decision problems of recursively enumerable sets of positive integers of the same degree of unsolvability as the complete set *K*. **1979** *Sci. Amer.* May 131/1 One approach for circumventing unsolvability is to limit the kinds of statements given to the computer.

†**un'solve**, *v. Obs.* [UN-^{2} 9.] *trans.* To solve.

1631 QUARLES *Samsòn* xii. 16 Perchance, my Fancy would have bin so kinde, T' unsolve the doubts of my perplexed minde. **1639** G. DANIEL *Ecclus.* Induct. 75 Ah! deare, I faint: can only this vnsolve The sentences which wisedome doth involve?

un'solved, *ppl. a.* (UN-^{1} 8.)

1665 SIR R. HOWARD *Four New Plays* Pref. A 4, If this were let pass, the Argument is yet unsolv'd in it self. **1697** DRYDEN *Æneis* Ded. ¶70 As Virgil propounds a riddle, which he leaves unsolved. **1741** WATTS *Improv. Mind* I. i. (1786) 17 Those knots and perplexities which have hitherto been unsolved. **1827** POLLOK *Course T.* v. 62 Vain question this,..and worthy to be left Unsolved. **1886** F. M. CRAWFORD *Tale Lonely Parish* v, He nevertheless represented in the minds of all an unsolved enigma.

†**un'solvible**, *a. Obs.* [UN-^{1} 7.] = UNSOLVABLE *a.* 2.

1664 H. MORE *Exp. 7 Epist.* x. 164 If unsolvible otherwise, there is still the more assurance of undeniable Demonstration.

†**un'some**, *a. Obs.* [UN-^{1} 7. Cf. *unisome* (UN-^{1} 3).] At variance; hostile.

c **1205** LAY. 3931 Al heo weren vn-sahte & a heo weren vn-some. **13..** *R. Gloucester's Chron.* (Rolls) App. G. 134 Hit bifel þat time..For defaute of weyes muche folc was vnsome.

un'son, *v.* [UN-^{2} 6 b.] *trans.* To deprive of the character or status of a son.

1652 BP. HALL *Rem. Wks.* (1660) 144 He may so sin as to be frowned on,..not so as to be unsonned, or dis-herited. **1653** O. SEDGWICK *Doubting Believer* 255 It is an unadvised folly in the suspension of Gods favour, to unsonne our selves, and unpeople our selves. **1752** YOUNG *Brothers* III. i, Thy heart, how dead to ev'ry call of nature! Unson'd! unbrother'd! nay, unhumaniz'd! **1882** G. MACDONALD *Weighed & Wanting* III. 165 The father came back.. determined..that his son, having unsonned himself, should no more be treated as a son.

un'sonlike, *a.* and *adv.* (UN-^{1} 7 c, 11 b.)

1657 OWEN *Communion*, etc. III. v. 300 A Spirit of bondage..casting them into an unsonlike frame of Spirit. **1687** R. L'ESTRANGE *Answ. Diss.* 41 Not among the Persecutors of the Dissenters; which he (most Un-son-like) Reflects upon in this Clause. **1690** C. NESSE *O. & N. Test.* I. 314 Their irreverent and unson-like repartee. **1879** CHR. G. ROSSETTI *Seek & Find* 315 An vnsonlike, unsympathetic, grudging spirit.

un'sonorous (formerly *unso'norous*), *a.* (UN-^{1} 7, 5 b.)

1720–1 *Lett. Mist's Jrnl.* (1722) I. 62 Words harsh, and altogether unsonorous, and..incongruous in meaning. **1821** *Monthly Mag.* LI. 12 The harsh and unsonorous letters j and s.

un'sonsy, *a. Sc.* and *north.* [UN-^{1} 7.]

1. Luckless, unlucky, ill-omened, uncanny.

1560 ROLLAND *Seven Sages* 47 The Mairch [= marrow] heirof I sall declair, The quhilk pertenis to ȝour vnsonsie Air. *Ibid.* 82 That may serve weill sic ane vnsonsie Sanct. **1683** G. M[ERITON] *Yorks. Dial.* (1684) 71 You are unsawncy, I think by my life. **1728** RAMSAY *Anacreontic on Love* 32 He leugh, and with unsonsy jest, Cry'd,..Did not my arrow flie right smart? **1771** FOOTE *Maid of B.* II, My father was so unsaunzy as to gang out with Charley in the forty-five. **1814** SCOTT *Wav.* lxvii, At these unsonsy hours the glen has a bad name. **1897** W. BEATTY *Secretar* xiv. 105 As unsonsy a place as I could have chanced on.

2. Unhandsome, plain.

1894 CROCKETT *Raiders* xxi, I'm nane so unsonsy yet, though I be auld eneuch to be the laddie's mither.

†**un'soot**, *a. Obs.* [UN-^{1} 7.] = UNSWEET *a.*

1420–2 LYDG. *Thebes* I. 574 Al be that some founde ful vnsoote Rather a pley of werre than of pees. **1430–40** —— *Bochas* I. iv. 1628 This flood..Causid also scarsete off vetaile, That many a man felte ful vnsoote. **1579** SPENSER *Sheph. Cal.* Dec. 118 And I..Sike follies nowe haue gathered as too ripe, And cast hem out, as rotten and vnsoote.

un'soothed, *ppl. a.* (UN-^{1} 8.)

1648 HEXHAM II, *Ongevleyt*, Vnflattered, or Vnsoothed. **1814** BYRON *Lara* II. viii, Cheerful was his gate; For there the wretched ne'er unsoothed withdrew. **1853** RUSKIN *Stones Ven.* II. iii. §10 The irritated pride of the antagonists remained unsoothed by the love-feast of St. Stephen's day.

un'soothfast, *a.* [UN-^{1} 7. Cf. OE. *unsóþfæst*.] Not truthful or true.

a **1300** *Cursor M.* 26874 Þof his scrift vnsothfast be, It sal him serue o thinges thre. **1570** LEVINS *Manip.* 36 Vnsoothfast, *infidelis*.

unso'phistical, *a.* [UN-^{1} 7.]

†**1.** Unsophisticated. *Obs.*$^{-1}$

1741 *Compl. Fam.-Piece* I. i. 58 Take red and unsophistical Oil of Petre.

2. Not sophistical.

[**1775** ASH.] **1836** LANDOR *Peric. & Asp.* xcv, Certainly these words are very unsophistical. **1886** J. PULSFORD *Infold. & Unfold. Div. Genius* 13 With childlike unsophistical affections, let us love 'the Maker of Heaven and earth'.

Hence **unso'phistically** *adv.*

1794 R. J. SULIVAN *View Nat.* II. 309 If..men would allow themselves the free exercise of their reason..when unsophistically established. **1890** W. JAMES *Princ. Psychol.* I. xiii. 500 A formulation of the facts which offers itself so naturally and unsophistically.

unso'phisticate, *ppl. a.* (UN-^{1} 8 b. Cf. next.)

1607 MARKHAM *Cavel.* VI. Ded., Yet when I shall be tride, I hope I shall proue vnsophisticat. **1659** T. PECKE *Parnassi Puerp.* 172 Few English men dare purchase an Estate; Unless your Wisdom's unsophisticate The Title vouch. **1688** NORRIS *Lett.* 165 The unsophisticate and genuine relish of the Soul. **1760** WESLEY *Prim. Physick* Pref. ¶3 Medicines..good in their Kind; pure, genuine, unsophisticate. **1781** COWPER *Conversat.* 451 Nature, unsophisticate by man, Starts not aside from her Creator's plan. **1867** LOWELL *Fitz Adam's Story* 605 Men unsophisticate, rude-nerved as bears.

unso'phisticated, *ppl. a.* [UN-^{1} 8.]

1. Unmixed, unadulterated.

1630 J. TAYLOR (Water P.) *Begger* Wks. I. 98/1 Vnsophisticated drinke, That neuer makes men stagger. **1664** BOYLE *Exp. touching Colours* 141 Take Blew, but Unsophisticated, Vitriol. **1706** E. WARD *Wooden World Diss.* (1708) 17 He never wants for two Sorts of Liquors, the Good and the Bad;..and that to be sure unsophisticated with the other. **1861** in *Daily Chron.* 12 Sept., An infusion made from the unsophisticated [tea-] leaves. **1894** *Cosmopolitan* XVII. 128 Pure air and a sky unsophisticated with the lights and smokes of civilization.

2. Not tampered with, altered, or falsified; uncorrupted, genuine.

1664 H. MORE *Myst. Iniq.* 438 They shall use the Sword of the Spirit,..which is unsophisticated Reason and Scripture. **1690** D. GRANVILLE *Lett.* (Surtees) 234 This low ebb of pure unsophisticated devotion. **1790** BURKE *Fr. Rev.* 128 We preserve the whole of our feelings still native and entire, unsophisticated by pedantry and infidelity. **1843** [MRS. MAITLAND] *Lett. fr. Madras* p. v, To give the correspondence in its genuine unsophisticated state. **1897** MARY KINGSLEY *W. Africa* 380 It was difficult to tell.. which was the bottom of the canoe and which was the unsophisticated log.

3. Not sophisticated in habits, manners, or mind; natural, ingenuous, inexperienced.

1665 BOYLE *Occas. Refl.* IV. iii. 16 If some Ladies..were bound to change Dresses with this unsophisticated and unadorn'd Maid. **1668** H. MORE *Div. Dial.* II. 362 They shall be..untainted and unsophisticated by the unwholesome Converse of men. **1814** JANE AUSTEN *Mansf. Park* xxiv, Her young, unsophisticated mind. **1854** THACKERAY *Newcomes* II. 118 What an unsophisticated little country creature you are! **1873** TRISTRAM *Moab* xiii. 234 Trotter..drew out the unsophisticated fish as fast as he could bait his hook.

Hence **unso'phisticatedness**.

1858 ABP. BENSON in *Life* (1899) I. 139 Some..footmen.. took away my umbrella, but amazed my unsophisticatedness in making me keep my hat on my head. **1866** ALGER *Solit. Nat. & Man* IV. 336 To appreciate natural unsophisticatedness more highly, and conventionality more lowly.

unsophisti'cation. (UN-^{1} 12.)

1825 T. HOOK *Sayings* Ser. II. II. 356 Affecting delight.. at their unsophistication and curiosity. **1846** MRS. GORE *Eng. Char.* (1852) 29 The unsophistication which exposes the less wary classes..to be quacked to death by plausible doctors. **1887** T. HARDY *Woodlanders* III. 99 A proposal due rather to his unsophistication than to his prudence.

†**un'sopited**, *ppl. a. Sc. Obs.* [UN-^{1} 8.] Not put to rest.

1734 KEITH *Hist. Ch. & St. Scot.* 186 To beget and maintain Friendship..after so late and as yet unsopited Jars.

un'sordid, *a.* (UN-^{1} 7, 5 b.)

1857 SMILES *Stephenson* xxxiv. 464 Though a thrifty and frugal man, [he] was essentially unsordid.

un'sore, *a.* (UN-^{1} 7. Cf. OE. *unsár*, ON. *úsárr*, MSw. *osar*, MDa. *usaar*.)

1500–20 DUNBAR *Poems* lxxxiii. 23 Thane had my dyt beine all in duill,..Quhair now I sing with heart onsair.

un'sorrowed, *ppl. a.* (UN-^{1} 8.)

1597 HOOKER *Eccl. Pol.* v. lxxii. §13 What heapes of grieuous transgressions haue we committed,..and yet cleane passe them ouer vnsorrowed for, and vnrepented of. **1619** FLETCHER *M. Thomas* II. iv, *Val.* What shall I do? *Cel.* Dye like a fool unsorrow'd, A bankrupt fool, that flings away his Treasure.

un'sortable, *a.* (UN-^{1} 7 b.)

1716 M. DAVIES *Athen. Brit.* II. 289 An Arian, Papist and Jacobit, dealing in their respective unsortable patch-work, make up to themselves unseizable Chymera's.

un'sorted, *ppl. a.* [UN-^{1} 8.]

1. Not arranged or put in order.

1533 MORE *Apol.* xlvii. Wks. 921/2 Good Tomme Truthe ..bringeth neuer a wytnesse with hym, and all hys euydence vnsorted. **1741** WATTS *Improv. Mind* xx. (1786) 408 Their ideas..will lie in the brain unsorted, and thrown together without order. **1861** WYNTER *Soc. Bees* 22 The last letters ..are, of course, vnsorted, and have to go through that process as the train proceeds. **1895** *Educat. Rev.* Nov. 352 A new science has been developed out of what were unsorted and uninterpreted fragments.

†**2.** Unfitted, unsuitable. *Obs.*$^{-1}$

1596 SHAKS. *1 Hen. IV*, II. iii. 13 The purpose you undertake is dangerous, the Friends you haue named vncertaine, the Time it selfe vnsorted.

un'sought, *ppl. a.* [UN-^{1} 8 b, c. Cf. MDu. *ongesocht* (Du. *ongezocht*), MHG. *ungesuochet* (G. *ungesucht*), Da. *usøgt*, Sw. *osökt*.]

1. Not searched out or sought after; not sought or asked for.

a **1225** *Ancr. R.* 324 A wummon þet haueð forloren hire nelde..secheð hine anonriht,..and God forloren uor sunne schal liggen unsouht fulle seoue dawes. **1374** CHAUCER *Troylus* I. 809 Vnknowe vnkyst and lost þat is vn-sought. *a* **1395** HYLTON *Scala Perf.* II. xiv. (W. de W. 1494), Vnresonably he werkith þat leuith the souereyn gode.. vnsought and vnloued. *a* **1470** GREGORY *Chron.* in *Hist. Coll. Cit. Lond.* (Camden) 192 They lefte noo thynge unsoffethe, and they serchyd all that nyght. *a* **1548** HALL *Chron., Hen. VI*, 103 A thyng discended from heauen, of theim vnsought, vnimagined and not deuised. **1576** GASCOIGNE *Kenelworth Castle* Wks. 1910 II. 92 Nothing shall rest unsought, That may bring pleasure to your mind. **1634** MILTON *Comus* 732 The Sea o'refraught would swell, and th' unsought diamonds Would so emblaze the forhead of the Deep,..that [etc.]. **1688** T. FLATMAN *Lines to Abp. Sancroft* 1 When I Your unsought Glories view'd,..some great thing to Write I meant. *c* **1708** FENTON *First Fit of Gout* 19 Whence comes this unsought honour unto me?

1751 WARBURTON *Pope's Wks.* IX. 247 To the issue of that unasked and unsought compliment these words allude. **1837** LOCKHART *Scott* IV. i. 13 This novel seems to me to possess ..a kind of simple unsought charm. **1856** KANE *Arct. Expl.* II. iii. 44 How often relief has come at the moment of extremity, in forms strangely unsought.

b. Not obtained by search or effort. Freq. in loose const.: Without being sought for; without search.

c **1350** *Ipomadon* 6519 Nowe I se vnsoughte, My travayle hedyr is all in vayne! *c* **1368** CHAUCER *Compl. Pite* 104 What maner thinge may encrese my wo That haue I redy vnsoghte euyr where. *c* **1400** *Ywaine & Gaw.* 798 Bot the knight thar fand thai noght; Than was thar mekil sorow unsoght. *c* **1460** *Towneley Myst.* III. 97 In erth I se right noght Bot syn that is vnsoght. ? *a* **1500** *Chester Pl.* (Shaks. Soc.) 206 Endles paine muste I have unsoughte To my rewarde. **1596** SPENSER *F.Q.* VI. iv. 28 Oftimes..sorrowes of the mynd Find remedie vnsought, which seeking cannot fynd. **1601** SHAKS. *Twel. N.* III. i. 168 Loue sought, is good: but giuen vnsought, is better. **1671** MILTON *P.R.* II. 59 Thus they out of their plaints new hope resume To find whom at the first they found unsought. **1725** RAMSAY *Gentl. Sheph.* III. ii, That's kind unsought. **1784** COWPER *Task* III. 288 What pearl is it..which the poor..Seek and obtain, and often find unsought? **1817** SCOTT *Harold* Introd. 55 Oft at such season, too, will rhymes unsought Arrange themselves in some romantic lay. **1855** *Poultry Chron.* III. 338/2 The greatest gain will often, unsought and unwished, attend the first-class.

c. With advs., esp. *for*.

1611 FLORIO, *Inesplorato*, unsought out. **1622** WITHER *Philarete* M 3 b, Those sad Straines..Which you composd, when greatest discontent Vnsought-for helpe to your Inuention lent. **1650** CROMWELL *Let.* 12 Sept. (Carlyle), Which we earnestly desire may not be laid aside unsought after. **1727** [DORRINGTON] *P. Quarll* (1816) 26, I had him.. by mere accident, unexpected, and unsought for. **1816** WILSON *City of Plague* III. ii. 137 Unsought-for bliss Coming..from all the points of heaven. **1863** H. COX *Instit.* I. x. 249 This arrangement..at least was unsought for by him.

2. † **a.** Unassailed. *Obs. rare.*

a **1300** *Cursor M.* 2440 He luued hir wil mare þan are, For wirscipp þat sco did him win, And sco vnsoght saccles o sin. *c* **1400** *Sowdone Bab.* 2081 Ye bene biseged in this toure... Charles wole not leve you vnsought.

b. Unasked; without being requested.

a **1500** *Chaucer's Dreme* in *C's Wks.* (1598) 359/1 So verily, ech thing vnsought, He said as he had knowne my thought. **1613** HIERON *Bridegroome* 18 Christ leadeth his Church with benefits, and that vnsought to. *a* **1704** T. BROWN *Sat. Quack* Wks. 1720 I. 71 Death, tho' unsought, waits on thy murd'ring Quill. **1873** SYMONDS *Grk. Poets* xi. 392 Then on my lyre, unasked, unsought, there flew A grasshopper. **1878** B. TAYLOR *Deukalion* I. vi. 49 Ere ye approach me, I shine unsought.

3. Unexamined, unexplored.

c **1375** *Cursor M.* 26637 (Fairf.), Hit faris of shrift as dos of wound þat lange vnsoȝt is to þe grounde. **1400** tr. *Secreta Secret., Gov. Lordsh.* 48, I haue noght left vnsoght no stede no temple whare Philosophers vsyd to wryte. **1426** LYDG. *De Guil. Pilgr.* 4450 And ther ys no corner vnsouht, But that I go to euery place. **1590** SHAKS. *Com. Err.* I. i. 136 Loth to leaue vnsought Or that, or any place that harbours men. **1600** FAIRFAX *Tasso* XV. xxvii, So that this mighty sea is yet unsought, Where thousand isles and kingdoms lie unknown. **1625** QUARLES *Sion's Sonn.* xv. 6 Thus..no place I left unsought, No eare vnask'd.

4. Not resorted to; untried.

1582 STANYHURST *Æneis* IV. (Arb.) 109 No meane vnattempted, ne vnsoght..leauing. **1626** CHAS. I in *Buccleuch MSS.* (Hist. MSS. Comm.) I. 264 We..have left no means unsought that might truly enable us to these great works. **1708** ROWE *Royal Convert* III. i, Is there a Remedy in human Wisdom, My Mind has left unsought, to help this Evil?

un'soul, *v.* [UN-[2] 6 b and 4. Cf. Du. *ontzielen*, G. *entseelen*.]

1. *trans.* To deprive of spirit or courage.

a **1634** CHAPMAN *Rev. for Honour* I. i. 204 For shame, sir! .. Your sad appearance, should they thus behold you, Would half unsoul your army. **1641** SHIRLEY *Cardinal* II. i, Such Another were enough to unsoul an Army; Ignobly talk of patience till they drink And reel to death?

2. To deprive of soul; to make soulless. Also const. *of*.

1652 BENLOWES *Theoph.* I. xxi, Such are their ranting catches, to unsoul And out-law man. **1654** COKAINE *Dianea* IV. 336 But Cruelty..spoiles, unbowels, unsoules the world. *a* **1743** OZELL tr. *Brantome's Sp. Rhodom.* (1744) 123 Heaps of Bodies they had un-soul'd and deprived of vital air. **1805** WORDSW. *Prelude* XII. 83 Even so could I unsoul As readily by syllogistic words Those mysteries of being. **1858** J. CULROSS *Lazarus Revived* 46 There is a way of making truth plain and comprehensible by unsouling it of all that is.. most precious in it.

3. To deprive of the essential qualities of a soul.

1653 H. MORE *Antid. Ath.* Wks. (1712) 13 You may as soon unsoul the Soul. *a* **1680** CHARNOCK *Attrib. God* (1834) I. 88 [When] we seem to deny the being of God,..we seem also to unsoul our souls.

un'souled, *ppl. a.* [f. prec. or UN-[1] 8. Cf. G. *entseelt*; also MHG. *ungesêlt* (obs. G. *ungeseelt*), G. *unbeseelt*.] **a.** Deprived of soul. **b.** Not endowed with soul.

1596 SPENSER *F.Q.* VII. vii. 46 Death..[is not] ought to see, but like a shade to weene, Vnbodied, vnsoul'd, vnheard, vnseene. **1620** SHELTON *Quix.* I. IV. v. 336, I know not what vnsouled folke they be, and so without conscience. **1633** FORD *Love's Sacr.* I. ii, Thus, bodies walke vnsold. **1722** HAMILTON *Wallace* v. (1816) 67 The chief retires,..While twenty foes unsoul'd, adorn the fatal scene. *a* **1750** A. HILL *Ronald & Dorna* v, Trembling, I wait, unsoul'd, till you inspire. **1800** COLERIDGE *Piccolom.* I. iv. 127 The painful toil ..Left me a heart unsoul'd and solitary. **1840** MANGAN *Poems* (1903) 136 To be The world's applauded and degraded martyr, Unsouled, enthralled. **1885-94** R. BRIDGES *Eros & Psyche* Mar. xii, Her fair Hellenic empire.. For which she had..left her wanton images unsoul'd In Babylon and Zidon.

un'soulish, *a.* (UN-[1] 7.)

1890 J. PULSFORD *Loyalty to Christ* I. 226 He felt for the moment that he was living a miserably thin, formal, unsoulish life.

† **un'sound**, *sb. Obs.* [UN-[1] 12. Cf. MHG. *ungesunt* (obs. G. *ungesund*) in sense 1.]

1. Physical unsoundness; malady or sickness; a wound or sore.

c **1205** LAY. 29315 þe king him gon crepen an heonden and a futen, swulc he mid unsunde al uorwunded weore. *a* **1300** *Marina* 207 in Horstm. *Altengl. Leg.* (1878) 173 þer heo lay mid vnsounde Fourteniht faste ybounde. *c* **1315** SHOREHAM I. 82 Water wasscheþ þe felthe a-wey, þer me wesscheþ by liste þe on-sounde.

2. Harm, distress, annoyance.

13.. *E.E. Allit. P.* C. 58 Did not Ionas in Iude such Iape sum-whyle, To sette hym to sewrte, vnsounde he hym feches? *Ibid.* 527 He þat is to rakel to renden his cloþez, Mot efte sitte with more vn-sounde to sewe hem togeder. *c* **1470** *Golagros & Gaw.* 590 Was neuer sa vnsound set to my hert.

un'sound, *a.* [UN-[1] 7. Cf. NFris. *ünsün* (*-sünj*), MLG. *unsund* (hence Sw. *osund*, Da. *usund*); also MDu. *ongesont* (Du. *ongezond*), MLG. *ungesund*, MHG. *ungesunt* (G. *ungesund*).]

1. Of persons, etc.: Not physically sound; unhealthy, diseased; †suffering from wounds or injuries.

c **1320** *Sir Tristr.* 1175 Men wounded him and band Vnsounde. *Ibid.* 3342. *c* **1330** *King of Tars* 522 Summe heore scolles icleved, With serwe thei weore unsounde. *c* **1400** *Destr. Troy* 1255 þai hurlet hym fro horse fete, & of hond toke, Set hym in his sadill þof he vnsound were. *a* **1450** *Le Morte Arth.* 2165 Oute of the felde was he drayne, For he was seke and sore vn-sounde. *c* **1470** HENRY *Wallace* VIII. 787 The wery ost..Wysche woundis with wyn, off thaim that was wnsound. **1513** DOUGLAS *Æneid* IV. i. 1 The Queyn, with havy thochtis onsound, In euery vane nurisis the greyn wound. **1601** B. JONSON *Poetaster* III. v, Enuy..Shall find me solid, and her teeth vnsound. **1667** *Decay Chr. Piety* viii. 211 And like an unsound limb, the healing of one Sore is the breaking out of another. **1722** DE FOE *Plague* (1896) 57 It brought abundance of unsound people to the markets. **1787** 'G. GAMBADO' *Acad. Horsemen* (1809) 47 It seems as if one might work a lame horse thus, and keep his unsound leg quiet. **1824** BYRON *Def. Transf.* I. i. 564 Merrily! merrily! never unsound, Shall our bonny black horses skim over the ground! **1879** HARLAN *Eyesight* vi. 80 An eye with a high degree of short-sight is almost always an unsound one.

b. *transf.* Of wounds, ailments, etc.

c **1400** *Destr. Troy* 495 Medea the mylde..Wox pale for pyne..With a Sykyng vnsounde, þat sonet to hir hert. **1596** SPENSER *F.Q.* VI. iv. 16 But that same Ladies hurts no herbe he found Which could redresse, for it was inwardly vnsound. **1613** HEYWOOD *Brazen Age* H 2 b, I did neglect the smart: At length it rankled and it grew vnsound. **1813** J. THOMSON *Lect. Inflam.* 425 The unsound appearances of the granulations show to what a stand the animal powers are put on such occasions.

† **c.** Quasi-*adv.*, in the phrase *to sigh unsound*.

? *a* **1400** *Morte Arth.* 3290 Ofte he syghede vn-sownde, and said theis wordes. *a* **1440** *Sir Degrev.* 316 The eorl hovede and beheld..How they fayre in the feld, And syght unsound. *c* **1470** *Gol. & Gaw.* 638 For pure sorow of that sight thai sighit vnsound.

d. Of substances, plants, fruits, etc.: Not in sound or good condition.

1617 MORYSON *Itin.* III. 273 Officers..who oversee the shambles, that no vnsound meate be sold. **1707** MORTIMER *Husb.* 167 Some Lands will make unsound Cheese, notwithstanding all the Care the good Housewife can take. **1815** A. T. THOMSON *Lond. Disp.* 402 In some places the grapes are..picked from the stalks, and freed from all the unsound ones with great care. **1855** *Poultry Chron.* III. 546/1 Shake the earth from the roots, cut off any unsound parts.

2. Morally corrupt or vitiated; wicked, evil.

13.. *E.E. Allit. P.* B. 575 þe venym & þe vylanye & þe vycios fylþe, þat by-sulpez mannez saule in vnsounde hert. ? *a* **1400** *Morte Arth.* 3942 [He] ses theme alle in a soppe.. With the Sarazenes vn-sownde enserclede a-bowte. **1597** HOOKER *Eccl. Pol.* v. iv. §1 That wherein vnsounder times haue done amisse, the better ages ensuing must rectifie, as they may. **1601** WEEVER *Mirr. Mart.* A 7 b, Seeking how she might the more inhaunce me, Though lewd my hauiour was, vnsound my carriage. **1811** LAMB *Hogarth* Wks. 1908 I. 107 That he..took a pleasure in exposing the unsound and rotten parts of human nature. *a* **1862** BUCKLE *Civiliz.* (1869) III. iii. 130 If the people are unsound,..the nation perishes.

b. Not sincere or true.

1714 GAY *Sheph. Week* IV. 104 Boobyclod soon drops upon the ground, A certain token that his love's unsound.

3. Unwholesome, unhealthy.

1598 FLORIO, *Insanare*,..to make vnsound, or vnholsome. **1660** F. BROOKE tr. *Le Blanc's Trav.* 385 The Mine of Porto ..is..of little benefit for want of workmen, by reason of the unsound ayre. **1707** MORTIMER *Husb.* 179 In unsound Pasture they reckon it the best for Lambs to run with the Ewes. *c* **1830** *Glouc. Farm Rep.* 18 (L.U.K.), In summer they depasture on the unsound grass land.

4. Not mentally sound or normal; not sane.

a **1547** SURREY *Æneis* II. 308 But we goe on, vnsound of memorie. *Ibid.* IV. 11 When all unsound, her sister of like minde Thus spake she to. **1642** tr. *Perkins' Prof. Bk.* iv. 131 If a man of unsound memory..exchange the same land with a stranger. **1693** *Humours Town* 32 A debilitated Body, and unsound Mind. **1746** FRANCIS tr. *Hor., Sat.* II. iii. 400 His Master sure..Must have confess'd the Slave unsound of Brain. **1818** CRUISE *Digest* (ed. 2) V. 538 Finding that Nicholas Hume..was not an idiot or person of unsound mind. **1898** *Daily News* 9 Nov. 4/5 The jury found..that he was occasionally unsound in mind.

5. Not soundly based in reasoning or fact.

1595 SPENSER *Epithal.* 237 Modesty, That suffers not one looke to glaunce awry, Which may let in a little thought vnsownd. **1631** GOUGE *God's Arrows* 210 The ground of the objection is unsound. **1641** MILTON *Ch. Govt.* ii. 6 Therfore it is unsound to say that God [etc.]. **1746** DUNKIN tr. *Horace, Epist.* I. ii. 22 When doating Monarchs urge Unsound Resolves, their Subjects feel the Scourge. **1818** BYRON *Ch. Har.* IV. vii, Waking Reason deems Such over-weening phantasies unsound. **1849** MACAULAY *Hist. Eng.* x. II. 614 Their old theory, sound or unsound, was at least complete and coherent. **1873** M. ARNOLD *Lit. & Dogma* vi. 180 When they air their unsound criticism in public.

b. Of persons in respect of opinion or belief.

1597 HOOKER *Eccl. Pol.* v. lii. §4 So Eutyches, of sound beliefe.., became vnsound by denying the difference. *a* **1658** DURHAM *Comm. Rev.* (1660) 187 If an unsound hypocriticall man may be sent Minister of Christ? **1680** C. NESSE *Church-Hist.* 196 God tenderly covers Asa's frailty,.. which he would not do for unsound Jehu. **1891** LD. ACTON in *Westm. Gaz.* 10 Oct. (1906) 2/3 St. John, I have even heard, was unsound about Old Testament dates and authorships.

6. Lacking in solidity or firmness.

1590 SPENSER *F.Q.* II. xi. 20 Of such subtile substance and vnsound, That like a ghost he seem'd, whose graue-clothes were vnbound. **1760** BEATTIE *The Hares* 170 Some new phenomenon..Which..From its proud summit to the ground Proves the whole edifice unsound. **1800** SOUTHEY *St. Gualberto* viii, The pile was ruinous, the base unsound. **1844** *Act 7 & 8 Vict.* c. 84 §46 If an unsound Party Wall.. be pulled down and rebuilt. **1856** KANE *Arct. Expl.* I. 126 The ice is too unsound for us to attempt to ride with a large team.

7. Of sleep: Broken or disturbed.

1584 C. ROBINSON, etc. *Handf. Pleas. Delights* (Arb.) 44 My sleepe vnsound hath dreadfull dreams.

un'sound, *adv.* [UN-[1] 11 b.] Not soundly.

1595 DANIEL *Civil Wars* III. lxii, The now sad king..still muses, sleepes vnsound.

† **un'sound**, *v. Obs.* [UN-[2] 6 b.] **a.** *trans.* To tear or rend. **b.** To make unsound.

c **1450** *Mirour Saluacioun* (Roxb.) 97 Jacob sonnes thaire brothere cote with thaire handis vnsoundid. **1560** W. BALDWIN *Funeralles K. Edw. Sixt* A iv b, When thou hast his ..person found, I will thou shalt his helthy body vnsound.

† **un'soundable**, *a.*[1] *Obs.*[−1] [UN-[1] 7 b.] Not sounding well; improper.

c **1440** *Alph. Tales* 408 It wer ane vnsondabyll thyng to do, if it sulde be he lefte & I taryd with þe.

un'soundable, *a.*[2] [UN-[1] 7 b, 5 b.] Incapable of being sounded; unfathomable.

1627 JACKSON *Creed* VI. v. §1 Some Schoole-braines have beene so puzled in passing this unsoundable gulfe, as to suspect [etc.]. **1660** F. BROOKE tr. *Le Blanc's Trav.* 216 The so famous Nile..sallying, as some say, out of an unsoundable lake. *a* **1684** LEIGHTON *Comm. 1 Pet.* ii. (1693) 295 The thoughts of God are..deep, and unsoundable by us. **1843** CARLYLE *Past & Pr.* III. xi, There shall be a depth of Silence in thee..; a Silence unsoundable. **1884** *Graphic* 4 Oct. 358/2 His eyes will be large, black, with long lashes and unsoundable. **1897** BARING-GOULD *Guavas* vii, One track.. betwixt unsoundable bogs.

† **un'sounded**, *ppl. a.*[1] *Obs.*[−1] [UN-[1] 8: cf. SOUND *v.*[3]] Not healed.

1420-2 LYDG. *Thebes* II. 2438 Wherto shuld I write..of the sorowe that Polymytes Mad in hym-silf to sen hym so forwounded, His greuous hurtes, his sooryS, ek vnsounded.

un'sounded, *ppl. a.*[2] Also 6 unsounde. [UN-[1] 8.] Not sounded, uttered, or pronounced; not made to sound.

1530 PALSGR. Introd. 16 No vowell is left unsounded..in a frenche worde. *c* **1532** DU WES *Introd. Fr.* in *Palsgr.* 899 If the next worde..be a consonant, than shall the said *s* remayne unsounde. **1807** J. BARLOW *Columb.* v. 766 Every honest Muse with horror flings The name unsounded from her sacred strings. **1865** *Trans. Philol. Soc.* 15 The unsounded syllable of the third person plural of the French verb. **1884** H. R. HAWEIS *Musical Life* 119, I keep my Strad. in a cabinet behind glass. There he rests unsounded and unstrung.

un'sounded, *ppl. a.*[3] [UN-[1] 8.]

1. Not sounded or plummeted; unfathomed.

1591 SHAKS. *Two Gent.* III. ii. 81 Orpheus Lute,..Whose golden touch could..Make Tygers tame, and huge Leuiathans Forsake vnsounded deepes, to dance on Sands. **1616** W. BROWNE *Brit. Past.* II. i. 130 The tyde..whereon his carre should sweepe, Deckt with the riches of th' unsounded deepe. **1651** T. STANLEY *Poems, Venus Vigils* 77 Piercing through the unsounded sea. **1861** L. L. NOBLE *Icebergs* 243 Where with the surf around its shoulders..it stood far up from the unsounded valleys of ocean.

b. *fig.* or in fig. contexts.

1593 SHAKS. *2 Hen. VI*, III. i. 57 Glouster is a man Vnsounded yet, and full of deepe deceit. **1607** CHAPMAN *Bussy D'Ambois* III. F 1, O the vnsounded Sea of womens bloods, That when tis calmest, is most dangerous. **1634** JACKSON *Creed* VII. xix. §6, I would request every ingenuous sober reader..not adventure to saile in a narrow..and unsounded sea only with the help of a generall carde. *a* **1750** A. HILL *The Muse to the Writer* xxxiii, This is a subject, that, outstretching thought, Through depths unsounded, wit's long plummet draws. **1826** MRS. HEMANS *Forest Sanctuary* lxxi, Th' unsounded gulfs of human woe! **1876** SWINBURNE *Erechtheus* 939 Mine unknown children of unsounded years. **1878** EMERSON in *N. Amer. Rev.* CXXVI. 409 To good men, as we call good men, this doctrine of Trust is an unsounded secret.

2. Unprobed, unexamined.

c **1620** ROBINSON *Mary Magd.* 534 Vaine woman!..shall thy heart vnsounded, still remaine vnsound?

un'soundly, *adv.* [UN-¹ 11.]

† **1.** So as to do hurt or harm; injuriously. *Obs.*

13.. *E.E. Allit. P.* B. 201 Ne neuer so sodenly soȝt [God] vn-soundely to weng, As for fylþe of þe flesch þat foles han vsed. **13..** *Gaw. & Gr. Knt.* 1438 Þenne þay beten on þe buskez, & bede hym vp ryse, & he vnsoundyly out soȝt seggez ouer-þwert.

2. In an unsound or unsolid manner.

1594 HOOKER *Eccl. Pol.* Pref. viii. §1 All such partes of the word of God..no lesse unsoundly taught and interpreted by all authorized English pastors, then by antichrists factors themselues. **1611** COTGR., *Insolidement*, vnsoundly, vnsolidely,..feebly. **1668** H. MORE *Div. Dial.* II. v. 195 If it were notable to bear such small Fillips, it would be a sign that things hung very crazily and unsoundly together. **1828–32** WEBSTER s.v., He sleeps unsoundly. **1851** MANSEL *Proleg. Log.* i. 2 That it is possible to transgress those [mental] laws, or to think unsoundly.

un'soundness. [UN-¹ 12.]

1. The quality of being physically or materially unsound. Also *fig.*

1599 SANDYS *Europæ Spec.* (1605) V 2 b, The bond of common feare, is the strongest indeed of all other,..and the daunger once past falles in sunder of his owne vnsoundnesse. **1614** LATHAM *Falconry* II. i. 79 When through our disorder..we haue wrought their [*sc.* hawks'] vnsoundnes, we forget to looke backe. **1763** MILLS *Pract. Husb.* III. 449 If these [livers] were livid or corrupted, they offered others, as the unsoundness of the first might be owing to some casual distemper. **1820** STARKIE *Rep. Cases N.P.* II. 81 If a horse be affected by any malady which renders him less serviceable for a permanency, I have no doubt that it is an unsoundness. **1860** TYNDALL *Glac.* II. xix. 333 The unsoundness of ice at and near its melting point. **1880** *Encycl. Brit.* XII. 189/2 A pimple on the body where the saddle would cover it is an unsoundness in a hunter while it lasts. *Ibid.*, A temporary cough is also an unsoundness.

b. Unwholesomeness.

1660 F. BROOKE tr. *Le Blanc's Trav.* 370 A Colony.. displanted for the unsoundnesse of the ayre.

2. The quality of being unsound in belief, opinion, principles, etc.

1597 HOOKER *Eccl. Pol.* v. lxii. §6 By reason of vnsoundnes in the highest articles of Christian faith. **1641** MILTON *Animadv.* 20 They need not carry such an unworthy suspicion over the Preachers of Gods word, as to tutor their unsoundnesse with the Abcie of a Liturgy. **1680** S. MATHER *Iren.* 3 Fundamental unsoundness and Corruption of Judgment. **1769** J. GILL *Body Pract. Divinity* II. ii. 302 They..agree to differ..and not charge one another with unsoundness and heterodoxy. **1794** G. ADAMS *Nat. & Exp. Philos.* II. xvii. 259 It was not uncommon formerly to suspect every one who professed to pursue the light of nature, of unsoundness of principles. **1841** [MRS. MOZLEY] *Lost Brooch* II. 71 Every sermon of his betrays his unsoundness. **1877** *Smith & Wace's Dict. Chr. Biog.* I. 11/2 The breach was widened by mutual accusations of unsoundness in the faith.

b. Of doctrine, principles, etc.

1586 HOOKER *Answ. Travers* §6 Any thing that shalbe spoken concerning the vnsoundnes of my Doctrine. **1607** *Stat.* in *Hist. Wakefield Gram. Sch.* (1892) 61 The unsoundnes of his or theire religion. **1712** ADDISON *Spect.* No. 507 ¶6 The Unsoundness of this Principle..is.. universally acknowledged. **1844** H. H. WILSON *Brit. India* I. 551 The unsoundness of the conclusion..might inspire a reasonable distrust of the correctness of the persuasions. **1881** WESTCOTT & HORT *Grk. Test.* Introd. §93 The presumed unsoundness of the text.

3. The quality of being mentally unsound.

1825 MACAULAY *Ess., Milton* ¶14 Perhaps no person can be a poet..without a certain unsoundness of mind. **1856** J. W. H. WILLIAMS (*title*), On Unsoundness of Mind, in its medical and legal considerations. **1884** *Law Rep.* 27 *Ch. Div.* 119 The soundness or unsoundness of mind of the alleged lunatic.

† **un'soundy,** *a. Obs.*⁻¹ Irreg. var. UNSOUND *a.*

a **1529** SKELTON *E. Rummyng* 35 Her eyen gowndy Are full vnsoundy, For they are blered.

unsouped, obs. variant of UNSUPPED.

un'sour, *a.* (UN-¹ 7. Cf. OE. *unsúr*, ON. *úsúrr*.)

1611 FLORIO, *Inaspro*, vnsowre, sweet. **17..** RAMSAY *To D. M'Ewen* ii, Health, T' enjoy ilk hour a saul unsow'r.

un'soured, *ppl. a.* (UN-¹ 8. Cf. NFris. *unsürred*, MSw. *osyrdh* (Sw. *osyrad*), older Da. *usuret* (Da. *usyret*); Du. *ongezuurd*, MHG. *ungesiuret* (G. *ungesäuert*) chiefly of bread, = unleavened.)

1626 BACON *Sylva* §341 Wee see that Meat and Drinke will last longer, Vnputrified, or Vnsowred, in Winter, than in Summer. **1685** DRYDEN *Horace* I. ix. 26 Secure those golden early joyes, That Youth unsowr'd with sorrow bears. *c* **1791** BURNS *To Mr. Maxwell* i, Health, ay unsour'd by care or grief. **1853** C. BRONTE in Mrs. Gaskell *Life* (1858) 471 A serene spirit and an unsoured disposition!

un'sowed, *ppl. a.* [UN-¹ 8. Cf. MDu. *ongesaeit* (Du. *ongezaaid*), G. *ungesäet*, Da. *usaaet*, Sw. *osådd*.] = next.

1648 HEXHAM II, *Onbezaeyt landt*, an vnsowed land, or a Fallowe field. **1791** COWPER *Odyss.* IX. 125 Earth unsow'd, untill'd, brings forth for them All fruits, wheat, barley, and the vinous grape.

un'sown, *ppl. a.* Also 4 unsowe, -sawe. [UN-¹ 8 b. Cf. OE. *unsáwen* (of land), ON. *úsáinn*, and prec.]

1. Of seed: Not sown; left without being sown. Also of vegetation: Growing without having been sown.

c **1374** CHAUCER *Former Age* 10 Corn vp-sprong vnsowe of mannes hond. ? **15..** in Thynne *Animadv.*, etc. (1875) 88 Wher the seyd of god is vnsawn. **1539–40** *N.C. Wills* (Surtees) 169 All my corne sowen and unsowen. **1573** TUSSER *Husb.* (1878) 85 Sowe lintels ye may, and peason gray. Keepe white vnsowne, till more be knowne. **1626** BACON *Sylva* §546 Mushromes..come vp so hastily; As in a Night; And yet they are Vnsowne. **1693** DRYDEN *Ovid's Met.* I. 138 The Flow'rs un-sown, in Fields and Meadows reign'd. **1883** R. W. DIXON *Mano* I. iv. 10 The crops remained unsown this year.

2. Of land: Not supplied with seed.

c **1400** *Gamelyn* 83 He þought on his landes þat lay vnsawe. *a* **1513** FABYAN *Chron.* IV. lxxv. 53 The grounde was vntylled and vnsowen, Wherof ensued great scarsytie. **1539** *Act 31 Hen. VIII*, c. 5 Duryng all suche time as the same landes shalbe and remayne vnsowen. **1600** SURFLET *Countrie Farme* I. xxiv. 147 The trampling which they keepe about trees, medowes, and vnsowne places. **1626** BACON *Sylva* §482 If the Ground lie fallow, and vnsowne. **1725** POPE *Odyssey* IX. 143 Nor knows the soil to feed the fleecy care,..But uninhabited, untill'd, unsown It lies. **1730** LYTTELTON *Epist. to Pope* 28 Unhappy Italy!..Her cities [are] desert and her fields unsown. **1842** TENNYSON *Dora* 71 Dora.. went her way Across the wheat, and sat upon a mound That was unsown.

un'span, *v. rare.* (UN-² 3 + SPAN *v.*² Cf. OE. *un-, onspannan*, Du. *ontspannen*.)

1648 HEXHAM II, *Ontspannen*,..to Vnspan, or to Vnyoake. *Ibid.*, *Een Ontspanninge*,..an Vnbending, or an Vnspanning. **1659** W. CHAMBERLAYNE *Pharon.* III. v. 92 The grave sad man, Whose counsel could conspiracies unspan When ready to give fire. **1914** T. A. BAGGS *Back from Front* xxiv. 120 They unspanned in a neighbouring field and invited me to supper.

un'spaned, *ppl. a. Sc.* [UN-¹ 8.] Unweaned.

1500–20 DUNBAR *Poems* lxxv. 36 My clype, my vnspaynit gyane With moderis milk ȝit in ȝour mychane.

† **un'spang,** *v. Obs.* [UN-² 4 b.] *trans.* To detach (horses) from a cart.

1580 HOLLYBAND *Treas. Fr. Tong*, *Desteler les chevaux*, to lose horses, or vnspang them from the carte. **1611** COTGR. s.v. *Desteler*.

un'spangled, *ppl. a.* (UN-¹ 8.)

1628 QUARLES *Argalus & P.* I. Wks. (Grosart) III. 251/1 Whenas the universall shade Of the unspangled heaven.. had made An utter darknesse.

un'spar, *v.* [UN-² 3. Cf. Du. *ontsperren*, OHG. *intsperran, -en* (MHG. *ent-, ensperren*).] *trans.* To unbar (a door, etc.); to open.

c **1200** ORMIN 12158 Cristess þohht wass sperrd swa wel ..þatt naness kinness sinnfull lusst Ne mihhte itt næfre unnsperrenn. *a* **1225** *Ancr. R.* 70 Heo schal habben leaue to openen [*MS. B.* unsperren] hire þurl enes oðer twies. **1393** LANGL. *P. Pl.* C. XXI. 89 The blood sprang doun by þe sper, and vnsperrede þe knyghtes eyen. *Ibid.* 272 A spirit..bit vnsperre þe ȝates. *a* **1542** WYATT in *Tottel's Misc.* (Arb.) 225 Lyke as the birde within the cage enclosed, The dore vnsparred, her foe the hawke without. **1599** T. M[OUFET] *Silkwormes* 12 How feately then vnsparred she the doore. **1611** COTGR., *Desverouiller vn huis*, to..vnsparre a doore. **1808** SCOTT *Marm.* I. iv, Forty yeomen..The lofty palisade unsparr'd And let the drawbridge fall.

un'sparable, *a.* (UN-¹ 7 b.)

c **1449** PECOCK *Repr.* V. vii. 519 Sithen it is profitable..and vnsparable that such a meyr and such a bischop shulden be in tyme comyng.

un'spared, *ppl. a.* [UN-¹ 8. Cf. MDu. *ongespaert* (Du. *ongespaard*), MLG. *ungesparet*, MHG. (and G.) *ungespart*; ON. *úsparðr* (Sw. *ospard*, Da. *usparet*, dial. *uspard*).]

1. Not spared or reserved. †Also in loose const., without sparing, unsparingly.

13.. *St. Erkenwolde* 335 in Horstm. *Altengl. Leg.* (1881) 273 With vnsparid murthe. **1535** STEWART *Cron. Scot.* (Rolls) I. 504 Euerilk man, baith ill and gude vnspaird, As he had wrocht, sall get ane just rewaird. **1667** MILTON *P.L.* x. 606 Thou therefore..whatever thing The Sithe of Time mowes down, devour unspar'd. **1881** RUSKIN *Love's Meinie* iii. §87 Unspared labour, and attentive skill.

† **2.** Indispensable. *Obs.*⁻¹

1614 T. ADAMS *Physicke fr. Heaven* Wks. (1629) 291 No Physitian then cures of himselfe; no more then the hand feedes the mouth;..though the Physitian and the hand be vnspared instruments to their seuerall purposes.

† **un'sparely,** *adv. Obs.* [UN-¹ 11. Cf. ON. *úsparliga* (MSw. *osparlika*).] Unsparingly.

a **1225** *Juliana* 59 Heo as þe deouel spurede ham to donne, dude hit unsparliche. **13..** *Gaw. & Gr. Knt.* 979 Chefly þay asken Spycez, þat vn-sparely men speded hom to bryng. ? *a* **1400** *Morte Arth.* 235 Thane spyces vn-sparyly þay spendyde there-aftyre. *Ibid.* 3160 Thus they..Spendis vnsparely, þat sparede was lange.

un'sparing, *ppl. a.* [UN-¹ 10.]

1. Showing no forbearance or mercy.

a **1586** SIDNEY *Arcadia* III. vii, The pittilesse launce ..(angry with being broken)..full of unsparing splinters, lighted upon that face. **1599** DANIEL *Musoph.* 323 No, no, vnsparing Time will prowdly send A warrant unto Wrath. **1649** MILTON *Eikon.* Pref. C, The unsparing Sword of Justice. **1770** GLOVER *Leonidas* (ed. 5) VI. 166 Unsparing Mars Heap'd carnage round thee. **1781** COWPER *Lett.* 2 Apr., Men of a rough and unsparing address. **1818** MITFORD *Hist. Greece* V. 155 Unsparing of himself, he seems however to have been strongly disposed to be considerate of others. **1844** KINGLAKE *Eothen* viii, Cool, decisive in manner, unsparing of enemies. **1869** TOZER *Highl. Turkey* II. 244 His unsparing, merciless character,..never diverted from its fell purpose.

2. Not niggardly; liberal, lavish.

1667 MILTON *P.L.* v. 344 Fruit of all kindes..She gathers, ..and on the board Heaps with unsparing hand. **1736** THOMSON *Liberty* v. 584 Unsparing love Their endless treasure, and their deeds their praise. **1781** COWPER *Expost.* 677 Gratitude and temp'rance in our use Of what he gives, unsparing and profuse. **1819** SHELLEY *Cyclops* 167 See, here are sheep,..Here are unsparing cheeses of pressed milk. **1856** *N. Brit. Rev.* XXVI. 23 The four or five ideas..are.. turned over and over again with so unsparing a profuseness, that [etc.].

Hence **un'sparingness.**

1818 MITFORD *Hist. Greece* V. 426 His extraordinary.. successes, but especially his profuse unsparingness of himself,..had [etc.].

un'sparingly, *adv.* (UN-¹ 11. Cf. prec.)

a **1500** *Bernardus de cura rei fam.* (1870) 2 Þe man þat spendis Vnsparandly mar þan his rent extendis. *a* **1631** DONNE *Lament. Jeremy* II. ii, The Lord unsparingly hath swallowed All Jacobs dwellings. **1805** SOUTHEY in Robberds *Mem. W. Taylor* (1843) II. 85, I am squeezing out the whey, and shall cut out unsparingly. **1849** MACAULAY *Hist. Eng.* I. I. 98 On the chief ministers..the vengeance of the nation was unsparingly wreaked.

un'sparkling, *ppl. a.* (UN-¹ 8.)

[**1775** ASH.] **1816** WILSON *Misc. Poems* 293 Unsparkling eyes where smiles appear More mournful far than many a tear. **1895** W. M. ROSSETTI *D. G. Rossetti* I. 171 Tall, finely formed, with..greenish-blue unsparkling eyes.

† **un'sparpled,** *ppl. a. Sc.* [UN-¹ 8.] Undivided.

1508 *Reg. Privy Seal Scotl.* I. 253/1 For keping of his heretage..unsparpalit and unanalyt in favouris of his sone.

un'spatial, *a.* (UN-¹ 7.)

1865 J. GROTE *Moral Ideals* (1876) 370 Concurrently.. there is going on thought in our spiritual, unspatial, being. **1884** tr. *Lotze's Metaph.* 185 Every real Thing..would have to be itself infinitely divisible into unspatial multiplicities.

un'spawned, *ppl. a.* (UN-¹ 8.)

[**1775** ASH.] **1814** *Monthly Mag.* XXXVII. 335 She instant resolv'd such a gala to give, As thro' ages unspawn'd should continue to live. **1847** STODDART *Angler's Comp.* 214 The female parr..retaining..the unspawned ova. **1884** *St. James' Gaz.* 11 Jan. 4 The death of..many unspawned fish.

un'speak, *v.* (UN-² 3.)

1605 SHAKS. *Macb.* IV. iii. 123 Euen now I put my selfe to thy Direction, and Vnspeake mine owne detraction. **1615** G. WITHER *Fidelia* 1222, I will vnspeake againe what is mis-spoken.

unspeaka'bility. (UN-¹ 12. Cf. next.)

1845 CARLYLE *Cromwell* (1871) II. 93 No modern reader can conceive the..unspeakability of this fact.

un'speakable, *a.*, *sb.*, and *adv.* [UN-¹ 7 b and 5 b.]

1. Incapable of being expressed in words; inexpressible, indescribable, ineffable.

a **1400** *Hampole's Wks.* (1895) I. 199 Þe vnspekeabill & þe vnmesurabill charite, bothe of þe ffadire and of þe sone. *a* **1425** tr. *Arderne's Treat. Fistula*, etc. 37 It may neuer be cured..but if it plese god..for to help wiþ his vnspekeable vertu. *c* **1445** PECOCK *Donet* 84 A þing..fer aboue alle creaturis speche vnspekable. **1534** MORE *Treat. Passion* Wks. 1346/1 It is chaunged by an vnspeakeable woorking, although it seme bread to vs that be weake. *a* **1586** SIDNEY *Arcadia* I. i, The flocke of unspeakeable vertues laid up..in that best builded folde. **1615** W. LAWSON *Country Housew. Gard.* (1626) 6 It is vnspeakable, what fatnesse is brought to low grounds by Inundations of waters. **1675** TRAHERNE *Chr. Ethics* 204 Those bodies are superadded, certainly for unspeakable and most glorious ends. **1754** *Connoisseur* No. 6 ¶4, I had the unspeakable mortification to see my favours sometimes not inserted. **1841** W. SPALDING *Italy & It. Isl.* II. 57 The laws and the system of society conspired together to work unspeakable evils. **1871** MORLEY *Carlyle* in *Crit. Misc.* Ser. I. 216 He had the unspeakable advantage of being ..respectable.

absol. **1831** CARLYLE *Sart. Res.* II. ix, In what words..[can we] speak even afar-off of the unspeakable?

b. *spec.* Indescribably or inexpressibly bad or objectionable.

Freq. of 'the Turk', after quot. 1876. Also *absol.*

1831 CARLYLE in *Westm. Rev.* July 6 How they sailed.. into Paynim land; fought with that unspeakable Turk, King Machabol. **1843** —— *Past & Pr.* I. iii, How ye came among us, in your cruel armed blindness, ye unspeakable County Yeomanry! **1876** —— *Let.* in *Mem.* (1881) II. 311 The unspeakable Turk should be immediately struck out of the question, and the country left to honest European guidance. **1896** *Advance* (Chicago) 30 Jan. 153/1 We were..even more guilty than the Unspeakable himself. **1902** CROSLAND (*title*), The Unspeakable Scot.

c. *sb.* An ineffable being.

1843 CARLYLE *Past & Pr.* III. xv, Through all thy.. melancholy Business and Cant, there does shine the presence of a Primeval Unspeakable.

2. Incapable of being spoken or uttered; that may not be spoken.

1568 H. B. tr. *P. Martyr, Ep. Rom.* 224 They are called vnspeakeable sighes, for that we speake not expressedlye what the spirite asketh. **1611** BIBLE *2 Cor.* xii. 4 He..heard vnspeakeable wordes, which it is not lawfull for a man to vtter. **1770** GLOVER *Leonidas* (ed. 5) x. 574 Leonidas, whose looks Declar'd unspeakable applause.

3. *U.S.* Unwilling or unable to speak.

1888 *Advance* (Chicago) 29 Nov., The distinguished but unspeakable witness. **1890** Lowell *Lett.* (1894) II. 465 My dog..looks up at me as who should say, 'You are become unspeakable as one of us, poor old fellow!'

4. *adv.* Unspeakably, indescribably.

1635 Pagitt *Christianogr.* 34 Beyond the Land of Cathaie, which they prayse to be civill, and unspeakable rich. **1657** Baxter *Call to Unconverted* (1660) 59 How certainly and unspeakable happy you may be if you will.

Hence **un'speakableness.**

a **1586** Sidney *Arcadia* I. xi, The unspeakablenes of his griefe. **1657** J. Smith *Myst. Rhet.* 54 That we may rather conceive the unspeakablenesse then the untruth of the relation. **1691** Bunyan (*title*), The Greatness of the Soul, and unspeakableness of the loss thereof. **1963** B. Friedan *Feminine Mystique* viii. 182 After the loneliness of war and the unspeakableness of the bomb,..women as well as men sought the comforting reality of home and children.

un'speakably, *adv.* [f. prec.] Unutterably, indescribably.

1526 *Pilgr. Perf.* (W. de W. 1531) 154 The clere syght of fayth..gyueth more ioye vnspekably to the contemplatyue seruauntes of god, than [etc.]. **1597** Hooker *Eccl. Pol.* v. liv. §8 God hath in Christ vnspeakablie glorified the nobler..part of our nature. **1647** H. More *Song of Soul* Notes 358 Some inhabit God himself, who is unspeakably infinite. **1681** Flavel *Meth. Grace* x. 224 It is unspeakably delightful. **1705** *Phil. Trans.* XXV. 1910 A Confluence..of unspeakably small Salt Particles. **1754** Edwards *Freed. Will* iv. v. 226 Man is..unspeakably different from a meer Machine. **1842** Dickens *Amer. Notes* (1850) 150/1 The effect is said to be unspeakably absurd. **1871** Le Fanu *Rose & Key* II. 298 It was unspeakably provoking.

un'speaking, *vbl. sb.* (un-¹ 13.)

1860 Ruskin *Mod. Paint.* V. 164 False speaking [is] unspeaking,—on the negative side of silence.

un'speaking, *ppl. a.* [un-¹ 10. Cf. OE. *unsprecende*, OFris. *unsprekand*, MDu. *onsprekende* (obs. Du. *onsprekend*), OHG. *unsprĕchente* (MHG. *unsprĕchende*) in sense 2 (chiefly of children).]

†1. Unspeakable, ineffable. *Obs.*⁻¹

1340 *Ayenb.* 266 Ich yze*ȝ* þe ilke onspekynde an[d] ontodelinde mageste of þe holy trinyte.

2. Not speaking; unable to speak. Also *fig.*

1382 Wyclif *Job* xxxviii. 9 With clothis of vnspekende childhed. —— *Ps.* viii. 3 Of the mouth of vnspekende childer..thou performedist preising. **1611** Shaks. *Cymb.* v. v. 178 His description Prou'd vs vnspeaking sottes. **1796** Eliza Hamilton *Lett. Hindoo Rajah* (1811) II. 81 All was placid uniformity, and unspeaking regularity of feature. **1811** Shelley *Mother & Son* iii, The proofs of an unspeaking sorrow dwelt Within her ghastly hollowness of eye. **1935** E. Bowen *House in Paris* II. iv. 129 Karen herself had more than once been the victim of that unspeaking smile.

†un'spear, *v.*¹ *Obs.* [un-² 4 + spear *v.*¹] *trans.* To unbar; to open.

c **1250** *Gen. & Ex.* 25 Quhu lucifer..held hem sperd in helles male til god..unsperd al ðe fendes sped. **1377** Langl. *P. Pl.* B. xviii. 259, I here..How a spirit speketh to helle & bit vnspere þe ȝatis. *c* **1400** *Laud Troy Bk.* 1039 When it was with-inne ther lippes, Faste to-gedur hit hem grippes, That thei myȝt not her mouth vn-spere. *c* **1430** Lydg. *Min. Poems* (Percy Soc.) 54 Late at eve thou wolt unspere the gate. *c* **1450** Capgrave *Life St. Aug.* 20 Poncian vnsperd þe bok and say wel þat it was a bok longing to cristen feith.

unspear, *v.*² [un-² 4 b + spear *v.*³] *trans.* To free from being transfixed.

1859 Geo. Eliot *Adam Bede* xxxii, Mrs. Poyser,..unspearing her knitting, began to knit again with her usual rapidity.

un'specialized, *ppl. a.* (un-¹ 8.)

1874 E. D. Cope *Orig. Fittest* xviii. (1887) 398 The Doctrine of the Unspecialized. **1886** G. Allen *Maimie's Sake* xv, A vague flood of unspecialized emotion. **1902** S. & B. Webb *Hist. Trade Unionism* (ed. 5) Introd. p. x, The general mass of unskilled and unspecialised labour.

un'specie. (un-¹ 12 b.)

1711 *Lond. Gaz.* No. 4822/4, 13 unspecie Exchequer Bills, of 100 *l.* each. *Ibid.* No. 4825.

unspe'cific, *a.* (un-¹ 7.)

1807 W. Coxe *Hist. House of Austria* II. 713 It is no wonder so unspecific a declaration..should not be followed by any important consequence. **1822–7** Good *Study Med.* (1829) III. 417 An incidental and unspecific irritation of the prepuce. **1884** *Solicitors' Jrnl.* 8 Nov. 26/2 A contract for the sale of unspecific goods.

†unspe'cificate, *a.* and *sb.* *Obs.* [un-¹ 7, 12.]

1. *adj.* (See quot.)

1674 *Phil. Trans.* IX. 70 This Aerial Salt,..whilst in the Air, is altogether un-specificate, I mean, freed from all Union with..any Seminal principle.

2. *spec.* Unsexed. Also as *sb.*

1734 *Prompter* 19 Nov. 2/1 It is a Prodigy to see an Actor, General, Plastick, and unspecificate. *Ibid.* 4 Dec. 2/1 One of these Vocal Unspecificates.

†unspe'cificated, *ppl. a.* *Obs.* [un-¹ 8.] = prec. 1.

1651 French *Distill.* v. 162 Whether this *primum ens salium* be so unspecificated.., or no, it matters not much. **1675** E. W[ilson] *Spadacrene Dunelm.* 65 There are unspecificated acids in the humours of our Body.

un'specified, *ppl. a.* (un-¹ 8.)

1624 Heywood *Gunaik.* ix. 427, I desire to leave nothing unspecified, or not remembered in this worke. *a* **1661** Fuller *Worthies, London* II. (1662) 204 The laxity of so populous a place leaving them as unspecified as it found them. **1883** *Specif. Alnwick & Cornhill Railway* 14 Facilitating the construction of any unspecified works.

un'specked, *ppl. a.* (un-¹ 8.)

[**1775** Ash.] **1781** Cowper *Truth* 281 A demeanour holy and unspecked. **1868** Geo. Eliot *Sp. Gipsy* 234 Gazing from his narrow shoal of sand On the unspecked round of blue and blue.

un'speckled, *ppl. a.* (un-¹ 8.)

1570 Levins *Manip.* 50 Vnspeckled, *immaculatus.* [**1775** Ash.] **1887** Morris *Odyss.* x. 525 A sheep of black unspeckled, of all thy flock most fair.

†un'spectable, *a.* *Obs.* [un-¹ 7 b, 5 b.] Incapable of being regarded.

1502 Atkynson tr. *De Imitatione* III. iii. (1893) 197 The vnspectable & inestymable Ioy in heuen. **1526** *Pilgr. Perf.* (W. de W. 1531) 16 We be not worthy to come to that vnspectable glory.

un'spectacled, (*ppl.*) *a.* (un-¹ 8, 9.)

1791 Huddesford *Salmag.* 140 Why did your will the Pylian chief decree Three centuries unspectacled to see. **1824** Scott *St. Ronan's* xiv, Many a nose, spectacled and unspectacled, was popped out of the adjoining windows. **1893** *Atlantic Monthly* Feb. 146/2 She pored over them with unspectacled eyes.

un'speculating, *ppl. a.* (un-¹ 10.)

1828 Pusey *Hist. Enq.* I. 109 A recurrence to practical and unspeculating Christianity.

un'speculative, *a.* (un-¹ 7.)

1659 *Gentl. Calling* 40 Their whole time..to be taken up in other unspeculative Exercises. **1674** *Govt. Tongue* 160 Some unspeculative men may not have the skill to examine their assertions. **1874** J. Donaldson *Apost. Fathers* 51 This unspeculative character of the apostolic teaching. **1891** T. Hardy *Tess* xii, She obeyed the signal to wait for him with unspeculative repose.

un'sped, *ppl. a.* [un-¹ 8 b.] **a.** Not having succeeded in an errand or effort. **b.** Not accomplished or discharged; not brought to a successful result or issue.

a **1300** *Cursor M.* 17596 For-þi þaa Iuus war full medd, þair sandes come again vn-spedd. **1390** Gower *Conf.* III. 293 So was he come ayein unsped. *c* **1450** *Myrr. our Ladye* 82 That prayer..is neuer lefte vnspedde. *a* **1533** Ld. Berners *Gold. Bk. M. Aurel.* xxxviii. (1536) 67 b, Nor for all the affaires of his house, he wolde not leaue one of thempire vnsped. *a* **1568** in *Bannatyne MS.* (Hunter. Cl.) 617/8 Onsped speche bettir vnspokin be. **1624** Quarles *Job* xiii. xxiv, To Athens, gown'd, he goes, and..Returnes unsped. **1717** Garth *Ovid's Met.* xiv. (1732) 477 Thus Diomedes Venulus withdraws; Unsped the Service of the common Cause. **1895** R. Bridges *Ode to Music* iv. iii, When the winds fatigued..Have left the drooping banks unsped.

un'speechful, *a.* (un-¹ 7.)

1853 Faber *All for Jesus* (1854) 365 Lighting up their land of pain and unspeechful expectation.

†un'speed. *Obs.* [OE. *unspéd* (un-¹ 12), = WFris. *on-*, *ûnspoed*, MDu. *onspoet* (Du. *onspoed*), OS. *unspôd* (MLG. *unspôt*), OHG. *unspuot*, *-spuet*, chiefly in sense 2. Cf. wanspeed.]

1. Poverty. (OE. only.)

c **950** *Lindisf. Gosp.* Mark xii. 44 Ðios..of unspoed hire alle ðe hæfde sende. *c* **1000** *Ags. Ps.* (Spelman) lxxxvii. 9 Eaȝan mine sarȝodon for unspeda [L. *inopia*].

2. Lack of good speed or success; misfortune, detriment, harm.

a **1300** *Cursor M.* 10468 If þou mai na barns brede, Quam wites þou þin aune vnspede? *Ibid.* 15420 Bot to þaim þat þe cheping did, it fel to mikel vnspede. **14..** *Northern Passion* (MS. I.) 1214 Ȝet þei maden at vnspede in his riht hand to halde a rede. *c* **1440** *Lay Folks Mass Bk.* (MS. C.) 88 To þe priest herken þan Hys office.., And answere þere-to.., Or on a boke þy-selfe it rede, I wate þerfore nane unspede.

3. Unprofitable labour.

a **1300** *Cursor M.* 4230 Bot al his quainning for to rede Or for to spek, it war vn-spede.

†un'speedful, *a.* *Obs.* [un-¹ 7.] Unprofitable; of no avail.

a **1340** Hampole *Psalter* cxxviii. 4 When þei..seme vnspedful in all þat þei did here. *c* **1374** Chaucer *Boeth.* v. pr. vi. (1868) 178 Prayeres, þat ne mowen nat ben vnspedful..whan þei ben ryȝtful. *c* **1440** *Jacob's Well* 184 Ȝif þis handyl be wrong, it is vnspedefull to werke wyth. **1482** *Monk of Evesham* (Arb.) 29 Thy contynual prayer..may not be onspedeful before the presens and goodnes of god. **1570** Levins *Manip.* 186 Vnspeedful, *inexpeditus.*

un'speedy, *a.* [OE. *unspédiȝ* (un-¹ 7), = MDu. *onspoedich* (Du. *-spoedig*), OHG. *unspuotîg*. Cf. wanspeedy *a.*]

†1. Poor, indigent. (OE. only.) *Obs.*

c **893** K. Ælfred *Oros.* I. i. §23 þa ricostan men drincað myran meolc, & þa unspediȝan & þa þeowan drincað medo. *c* **1000** Ælfric *Hom.* I. 578 He ȝeendebyrde þone unspediȝan fiscere ætforan ðam rican casere.

†b. Of land: Barren, unproductive. *Obs.*⁻¹

a **1000** *Genesis* 962 Ðesæton þa æfter synne sorȝfulre land, eard & eðyl unspediȝran.

†2. Unprofitable; unsuccessful.

a **1300** *E.E. Psalter* lxxxviii. 34 Ne wemme mi witeworde, and þat forthga Of mi lippes, vnspedy noght make þa. *a* **1340** Hampole *Psalter* xvi. 14 Make þaim vnspedy and kast þaim down. *c* **1449** Pecock *Repr.* I. xvi. 89 The werk ther of schulde be the vnsaueryer and the vnspedier.

3. Slow, sluggish. *rare.*

1615 G. Sandys *Trav.* 117 The water..passing along with a mute and vnspeedy current.

un'speered, *ppl. a.* Latterly *Sc.* [un-¹ 8.] Unasked; without inquiry. Also with *at.*

13.. *Gaw. & Gr. Knt.* 918 Wich spede is in speche, vnspurd may we lerne. *a* **1568** in *Bannatyne MS.* (Hunter. Club) 641/44 Than suld I..cum to yow, I ken the gait onsperd. **1599** Jas. I Βασιλ. Δωρον Ep. Ded., It will not come vncalled, neither speake vnspeered at.

un'spell, *v.* [un-² 3.]

1. *trans.* To undo or dissolve (a spell).

1611 Cotgr., *Descharmer*, to vncharme, vnspell, frustrate a charme. **1671** Tuke *Adv. 5 Hours* v. (ed. 3) 94 *Her.* Sure w'are enchanted, and all we see's illusion. *Cam.* Allow me, Henrique, to unspel these Charms.

2. To free from a spell.

1635 Quarles *Embl.* iv. xv, Ah, if my voyce could, Orpheus-like, unspell My poore Eurydice, my soul, from hell. **1681** Dryden (Tate) *Abs. & Achit.* II. 117 Such Practices as These, too gross to lye Long unobserv'd,..The more judicious Israelites Unspell'd, Though still the Charm the giddy Rabble held. **1777** Johnson *Let. to Mrs. Thrale* 6 Oct., I am glad Master unspelled you, and run you all on rocks. **1890** *Handbk. Folklore* (ed. Gomme) 132 A prince is transformed into a loathsome beast;..he is unspelled and they marry.

†3. To decipher, read. *Obs.*⁻¹

1665 Sergeant in Digby *Nat. Bodies* *4 Even that great Soule, which fathomes th' Universe, Unspells the Heaven's broad volume.

4. (See quot.)

1846 *Printing Apparatus for Amateurs* 34 In the process of distributing [the type] the word is unspelt, beginning with the first letter of the word.

Hence **un'spelling** *vbl. sb.* Also *attrib.*

1897 A. Nutt in K. Meyer *Voy. Bran* II. 16 Manawyddan obtains..the unspelling of the land. **1902** —— *Leg. Holy Grail* 52 The unspelling theme. *Ibid.* 53 In Crestien..it is subordinated to the unspelling quest.

un'spellable, *a.* (un-¹ 7 b.)

1852 Mundy *Antipodes* II. 97 Unspellable intonations..supply the place of the letters. **1872** 'Mark Twain' *Roughing it* xxiv, A Spanish saddle,..furnished with the ungainly sole-leather covering with the unspellable name.

un'spelled, *ppl. a.* [un-¹ 8.] Not put under a spell.

1684 Tate *Medea to Jason* 12 No doubt but he.., with the fierce Bulls, unspell'd had fought. **1806** M. A. Shee *Rhymes Art* 27 While yet unspell'd, unplighted you remain, Pause, ere you join the art-enamour'd train.

un'spelt, *ppl. a.* (un-¹ 8 b.)

1892 Meredith *Sage Enamoured* i, Her eyes were the sweet world desired of souls, With something of a wavering line unspelt.

†unspen, *v.* *Obs.*⁻¹ [un-² 3 + spen *v.*] *trans.* To release.

a **1225** *Ancr. R.* 158 Seint Johan baptiste..ine his iborenesse unspende [*v.r.* unspennede] his feder tunge into prophecie.

un'spendable, *a.* (un-¹ 7 b.)

1876 Mrs. Whitney *Sights & Ins.* III. xiv. 263 Every day a large piece of unspendable delight in the anticipation,..to last us [etc.].

†un'spended, obs. var. unspent *ppl. a.*

c **1440** *York Myst.* xxv. 450 Haue [= half] my gud I have vnspendid Poure folke to geue it till. **1533** Bellenden *Livy* III. xxv. (S.T.S.) II. 48 He was fer rvn in ȝeris, and few dayis vnspendit of his live. **1564** *Wills & Inv. N.C.* (Surtees, 1835) I. 225 So mutch hay vnspended as is valud to ijs.

un'spent, *ppl. a.* [un-¹ 8 b.]

1. Not expended; not employed or used.

1466 *Mann. & Househ. Exp.* (Roxb.) 326 He ad of myn onspente in is and, vj.s. viij.d. **1483** in *Somerset Med. Wills* (1901) 239 As moch as that shal..remayne unspent of the seid xij torches. **1550** Crowley *Last Trump* 269 If ought remayne vnspent Upon thyne owne necessity. **1632** Lithgow *Trav.* vii. 313 The French men had only left unspent..three-score and nine Chickens of Gold. **1674** Hobbes *Odyssey* (ed. 2) 9 We had Wine enough as yet unspent. **1745** in Picton *L'pool Munic. Rec.* (1886) II. 110 A proportionable part of what remains unspent. **1895** *Westm. Gaz.* 24 May 5/2 The revolver..contained one spent and five unspent cartridges. **1899** *Parlt. Debates* LXVII. 554/2 What [he]..pressed was the use of the unspent balance for that purpose.

2. Unexhausted; not used up.

c **1611** Chapman *Iliad* xiv. 344 For fervour of his unspent strength. **1663** Dryden *Ep. to Charleton* 36 Whose Fame..Flies like the nimble journeys of the Light; And is, like that, unspent too in its flight. **1732** Pope *Ess. Man* I. 274 All are but parts of one stupendous whole,..That..extends thro' all extent, Spreads undivided, operates unspent. **1770** Glover *Leonidas* (ed. 5) xii. 355 He impell'd His spear. The point with violence unspent..reach'd the Persian's throat. **1799** Cowper *Castaway* 39 So long he, with unspent pow'r, His destiny repell'd. **1857** Emerson *Poems*, '*Give all to Love*' ii, High and more high It dives into noon, With wing unspent.

un'sphere, *v.* [un-² 5.] *trans.* To remove (a star, etc.) from its sphere. Also in fig. context.

1611 Shaks. *Wint. T.* I. ii. 48 Though you would seek t'vnsphere the Stars with Oaths. **1643** Howell *Parab. reflect. Times* 5 Touching the malignant Planets..I put them over to you, that..they may be unspher'd or extinguished. **1796** C. Anstey *Pleaders' Guide* (1803) 124 Th' adventrous Engineer Who swore he would the Earth unsphere,..Give him but where to set his foot. **1820** Milman *Fall Jerus.* 117 If ye have seen the moon unsphered, And the stars fall. **1857** P. Freeman *Princ. Div.*

Serv. II. 57 Thus too did it supply..a new centre or centres for the gravitation of its mighty forces..in lieu of that which had been, so to speak, unsphered.
fig. **1632** MILTON *Penseroso* 88 Where I may..unsphear The spirit of Plato. **1806** H. K. WHITE *Fragments* vi, Mine ear Longs for some air of peace,..That may the spirit from its cell unsphere. **1882** J. BROWN *Horæ Subs.* 3rd Ser. 4 Many have been the attempts to unsphere the spirit of a joke and make it tell its secret.
Hence **un'sphered** *ppl. a.*
1598 CHAPMAN *Hero & Leander* III. 186 Thou..That..with the wings Of thy vnsphered flame visitst the springs Of spirits immortall. **1833** H. COLERIDGE *Poems* I. 41 Like a spectre of an age departed, Or unsphered Angel woefully astray—She glides along. **1849** M. ARNOLD *New Sirens* 251 The sunk eyes, the wailing tone, Of unspher'd, discrowned creatures.

un'spiable, *a.* (UN-^{1} 7 b.)
1615 SYLVESTER *Job Triumph.* I. 367 Him would I seek..Whose works are great,..Unspiable, Unspeakable by Man.

un'spiced, *ppl. a.* (UN-^{1} 8.)
1655 MOUFET & BENNET *Health's Improv.* vi. 48 A great difference..betwixt fri'd meats and bak't meats, spiced and unspiced, salt and fresh. **1899** *Westm. Gaz.* 11 Aug. 8/1 There are English firms which export the genuine unspiced article in tins.

un'spied, *ppl. a.* (UN-^{1} 8.)
14.. *Chaucer's Troylus* IV. 1457 (Harl. MS.), It is ful hard to halten vnspied Bifor a crepul. *a* **1542** WYATT '*Take heed by time*' v, To love unspied is but a hap; Therefore, take heed! **1561** NORTON & SACKV. *Gorboduc* I. ii. 317 Traiterous corrupters of their pliant youthe Shall have unspied a muche more free accesse. **1624** QUARLES *Sion's Elegies* I. xxii, Thinke you to flourish euer? and (vnspide) To shoot the flowers of your fruitlesse pride. **1667** MILTON *P.L.* IV. 529 I must walk round This Garden, and no corner leave unspi'd. *a* **1740** TICKELL *Misc., Fatal Curiosity* 5, I..went prepared to pry,..Resolv'd to find some fault before unspy'd. **1798** in A. D. Coleridge *Eton in Fourties* (1896) 14 When waving fresh each woolly wing, That..serv'd..to hold unknown, unspied, A loaf or pudding in.

un'spike, *v.* [UN-^{2} 3, 4 b.]
1. *trans.* To extract a spike from (a cannon).
1680 *Exact Jrnl. Siege Tangier* 6 The Moors took our Guns.., and unspik'd them, & clear'd them. **1842** R. BURN *Naval & Mil. Dict.* (1852) 118/2 *Désenclouer*, to unspike a piece of ordnance. *c* **1860** H. STUART *Seaman's Catech.* 14 Suppose your gun is spiked.., how will you unspike it?
2. To release by the removal of a spike.
1846 *Edin. Rev.* Oct. 504 In this case the iron bar [*sc.* rail], worn thin and unspiked, gets detached from the plank.

un'spiked, *ppl. a.* (UN-^{1} 8; cf. SPIKED $a.^2$ 3 a, b.)
[**1775** ASH.] **1902** *Daily Chron.* 16 July 8/6 Six [rail-] chairs..had been left unspiked. **1904** *Westm. Gaz.* 8 Sept. 7/1 They..[captured 97] cannon, mostly unspiked. **1969** *Lithos* II. 138 Unspiked measurements of Sr^{87}/Sr^{86} and Sr^{88}/Sr^{86} were made for all other samples. **1980** *Nature* 31 Jan. 438/2 Completely separate sets of equipment were used for spiked and unspiked sample solutions, thus eliminating the possibility of cross-contamination.

un'spillable, *a.* (UN-^{1} 7 b.)
1885 *Chamb. Jrnl.* 560 Our readers will be acquainted with the unspillable ink-bottle.

un'spilled, -'spilt, *ppl. a.* (UN-^{1} 8, 8 b. Cf. MDa. and Da. *uspildt*.)
1573 TUSSER *Husb.* (1878) 35 Then haue of thine owne, without lending vnspilt, what followeth needfull, here learne if thou wilt. **1641** in Rushw. *Hist. Coll.* (1692) I. 217 The very Blood that runs unspilt in our Veins. **1643** DENHAM *Cooper's H* (1668) 7 That bloud, which thou and thy great Grandsire shed,..Had been unspilt. **1837** DICKENS *Pickw.* v, The first care of the two unspilt friends was to extricate their unfortunate companions from their bed of quickset. **1877** BROWNING *La Saisiaz* 369 Only grant my soul may carry high through death her cup unspilled.

un'spin, *v.* (UN-^{2} 3. Cf. Du. *ontspinnen*.)
a **1585** in Holinshed *Chron.* II. 416/1 Oh cruel fates! the which so soone, his vitall thred vnsponne. **1638** MAYNE *Lucian* (1664) 304 Is't not in your power to change, and unspinne their decrees? **1638** N. WHITING *Albino & Bellama* 1176 My teeming fancy strives..to..make those garden-minutes see the sun Entombed in darkness, and the earth unspun Ere they expire. *a* **1703** J. POMFRET *Last Epiphany* vi, Whilst backward all the Threads shall haste to be unspun. **1845** MOZLEY *Ess.* (1878) II. 102 The web was respun, that it might be unspun again.

un'spirit, *v.* [UN-^{2} 4.] *trans.* To deprive of spirit.
1607 B. JONSON *Volpone* III. v, I am unmask'd, unspirited, undone. **1647** TRAPP *Marrow Gd. Authors* in *Comm. Ep.* 604 We may not neglect the body,..maserate and unspirit our selves overmuch. **1687** NORRIS *Coll. Misc.* (1699) 367 Nor did I ever think that it could be in the Power of any Temporal loss, so much to discompose and unspirit my Soul.

un'spirited, *ppl. a.* [UN-^{1} 8.] Destitute of spirit; spiritless.
1621 FLETCHER *Thierry & Theod.* II. i, A poor, cold, unspirited, unmanner'd..fool. **1649** ARNWAY *Tablet* 74 Leave no stone unmoov'd, to cousen an unspirited (and so apt to be unchristen'd) Nation into the way..of the Alcoran. **1751** SMOLLETT *Per. Pick.* lxxxv, The new productions of the stage,..generally unspirited and insipid.
Hence **un'spiritedness**.
1669 OWEN *Exp. Ps.* cxxx, 15 Vnspiritedness and disability unto Duty, in doing or suffering.

un'spiritual, *a.* (UN-^{1} 7.)
1643 MILTON *Divorce* 3, I see it the hope of good men, that those irregular and unspirituall Courts have spun their utmost date in this Land. **1679** PULLER *Moder. Ch. Eng.* 494 These Divisions (the Character of a Carnal and Unspiritual Temper)..dishonour the Protestant Cause. **1818** BYRON *Ch. Har.* IV. cxxv, Circumstance, that unspiritual god and miscreator. **1872** LIDDON *Elem. Relig.* v. 175 Prayer ceases to be itself, by degenerating..into a mechanical and unspiritual routine.
Hence **un'spiritually** *adv.*; **-ness**.
1642 D. ROGERS *Naaman* 476 Through that unspiritualnesse of our heart. **1669** OWEN *Expos. Ps. cxxx*, 352 The more spiritual any man is, the more he sees of his unspiritualness in his spiritual Duties. **1863** H. ALLON *Mem. J. Sherman* Coll. Life i. 53 Unspiritualness had generated scepticism. **1871** TYLOR *Prim. Cult.* II. 325 Those..may say..that I have written..unspiritually of spiritual things.

unspiritu'ality. (UN-^{1} 12, or f. prec.)
1842 SARA COLERIDGE in Coleridge *Aids Refl.* App. C. (1843) II. 384 Calvin..missed this truth..neither from natural inability, nor from unspirituality, nor from a tendency to rationalism, but [etc.]. **1863** GROSART *Small Sins* 27 Despondent..through..coldness, deadness, unrealness, unspirituality.

un'spiritualize, *v.* [UN-^{2} 6 c.] *trans.* To divest of spiritual qualities.
a **1716** SOUTH *Serm.* (1727) VI. 243 Enjoyments..such as ..will by Degrees certainly indispose, and unspiritualize the Mind. **1846** HAWTHORNE *Old Manse* II. 115 Those evil habits..which unspiritualize man's nature. **1851** RUSKIN *Mod. Paint.* II. III. II. v. §17, I recollect no single instance of a naked angel that does not look..unspiritualized. **1881** H. DRUMMOND *Ideal Life* (1897) 133 God would never unspiritualise three-fourths of man's active life by work, if work were work, and nothing more.

un'spiritualized, *ppl. a.* [UN-^{1} 8.] Not made spiritual.
1816 COLERIDGE *Lay Serm.* (1839) 291 The idolism of the unspiritualized understanding. **1878** T. SINCLAIR *Mount* v. 100 The unspiritualised 'man of land,' when left to his instincts, is sufficiently marked in history the slave-maker of his fellows.

un'spit, *v.* [UN-^{2} 4 b.] *trans.* To remove from a spit.
1574 T. NEWTON *Health Mag.* I iij b, Rosted fleshe is then best to be vnspitted and taken from the broche. **1611** COTGR., *Desembrocher*, to vnspit; pull off the broach. **1648** HEXHAM, *Ontspeten*, to Vnspit, or to Vnbroach a peece of meate. **1798** in *Spirit Public Jrnls.* (1799) II. 290 The pigs and geese were all unspitted. **1820** T. MITCHELL *Aristoph.* I. 116 The science which he displays in boiling, roasting, spitting, and unspitting.

un'spleened, *ppl. a.* (UN-^{1} 8.)
1633 FORD *'Tis Pity* I. ii, Yet the villanie of words..may be such, As would make any vnspleen'd Doue, Chollerick.

†**un'spleeted**, *ppl. a.* (UN-^{1} 8. Cf. SPLEET $v.^1$)
1609 C. BUTLER *Fem. Mon.* F 8 Lay the vnspleeted hiue along hard by.

un'splendid, *a.* (UN-^{1} 7.)
1809 SYD. SMITH *Serm.* II. 307 In the tumult of life the man, who can please for the passing hour, is..greater than him who has difficult, and unsplendid virtues.

un'splint, *v.* (UN-^{2} 4 b.)
1615 MARKHAM *Country Contentm.* I. i. 24 Let it so rest nine daies at least, before you vnsplint it.

un'split, *ppl. a.* (UN-^{1} 8 b. Cf. Du. *ongesplit*, MSw. *osplitad*, older Da. *usplit*.)
1656 EARL MONM. tr. *Boccalini's Advts fr. Parnass.* 262 To repair those his Gallies, which were yet unsplit. **1802–12** BENTHAM *Ration. Judic. Evid.* (1827) II. 194 The man is split into two persons..: or, he remaining unsplit, an ideal person is fabricated to speak of the real one. **1875** BENNETT & DYER tr. *Sachs' Bot.* 72 The originally unsplit fragments of cell-wall.

†**un'spoil**, $v.^1$ *Obs.* [UN-^{2} 9.] *trans.* To despoil.
a **1400** *Sir Perc.* 742 Now es Percyvelle lyghte To unspoyle the rede knyghte.

un'spoil, $v.^2$ [UN-^{2} 3.] *trans.* To restore from being spoiled.
1778 MISS BURNEY *Evelina* xxxiv, And what good will that do now?—that won't unspoil all my clothes. **1834** MAR. EDGEWORTH *Helen* xliii, 'I am quite spoiled, I believe,' said Helen; 'you must unspoil me'.

un'spoilable, *a.* (UN-^{1} 7 b.)
1836 E. HOWARD *R. Reefer* lv, He contrived..to spoil our almost unspoilable meals. **1888** MARZIALS *Life V. Hugo* 204 One trusts that Master Georges and Miss Jeanne were unspoilable.
Hence **un'spoilableness**.
1873 C. M. YONGE *Pillars of House* I. XI. 232 Geraldine thought it was a great proof of his unspoilableness. **1881** *Daily News* 1 Oct. (Encycl. Dict.), A prevalent style of furniture and decoration should have this character of what may be called unspoilableness.

un'spoiled, *ppl. a.* [UN-^{1} 8.]
1. Not despoiled or plundered; not taken as plunder.
c **1500** *Melusine* xxxvi. 256 None passed by the said Fortresse vnspoyled. **1513** *Life Hen. V* (1911) 34 All Churches..shoulde be kepte inviolat, vnspoyled and vnharmed. **1577** DEE *General & Rare Mem.* 4 Their Marchantlike Ships..may..pas quietly vnpilled, vnspoyled, and vntaken by Pyrates. **1603** KNOLLES *Hist. Turks* (1621) 268 The Bassa..began..with fire and sword to wast that part of the countrey which yet remained vnspoiled. **1697** DRYDEN *Æneis* XI. 890 Unspoil'd shall be her Arms, and unprofan'd Her holy Limbs with any Human Hand. **1802** J. BAILLIE *2nd Pt. Ethwald* I. ii, A land of peace! Where yellow fields unspoil'd..smile gladly. **1870** BRYANT *Iliad* v. I. 177 He left the corpse of Periphas unspoiled where he had fallen.
2. Not spoiled or deteriorated.
1732 POPE *Ep. Bathurst* 226 O teach us, Bathurst! yet unspoil'd by wealth! That secret rare. **1746** COLLINS *Ode to Pity* iv, He sung the female heart, With youth's soft notes unspoil'd by art. **1821** V. KNOX *Grammar Schools* 117 An unspoiled boy,..possessing talent and sensibility. **1860** H. MARRYAT *Resid. Jutland* I. xiv. 209 The Castle of Rosenborg ..is a fine specimen of the period, and is unspoiled by modern improvements. **1888** CHILD *Ballads* III. 1/1 This precious specimen..of the unspoiled traditional ballad.

un'spoilt, *ppl. a.* [UN-^{1} 8 b.] = prec. 2.
1796 MME. D'ARBLAY *Camilla* III. 180 An original feeling, unspoilt by the apathy of satiety. *Ibid.* IV. 353 Having brought with her whatever was unspoilt of her Tunbridge apparel. **1884** *World* 20 Aug. 20/1 An unspoilt English girl. **1925** C. CONNOLLY *Let.* 8 Apr. in *Romantic Friendship* (1975) 68, I hope to see some good unspoilt villages. **1939** *Country Life* 11 Feb. p. v (Advt.), 3 miles south of Dorking in beautiful unspoilt country, with lovely views. **1968** T. WOLFE *Electric Kool-Aid Acid Test* v. 59 Kesey wasn't primarily an outdoorsman. He wasn't that crazy about unspoilt Nature.

un'spoke, arch. variant of next.
1605 SHAKS. *Lear* I. i. 239 A tardinesse in nature, Which often leaues the history vnspoke That it intends to do.

un'spoken, *ppl. a.* [UN-^{1} 8 b, 8 c, 5 d. Cf. (M)Du. *ongesproken*, MLG. *ungesproken*, MHG. *ungesprochen*.]
1. Not spoken *of*. †Also with *to*.
1375 BARBOUR *Bruce* xv. 268 Till king Robert will we gang, That we haf left vnspokyn of lang. *c* **1530** L. COX *Rheth.* (1899) 62, I can nat let passe his diuine wysdome vnspoken of. **1588** KYD *Househ. Philos.* Wks. (1901) 284 Albeit somethings vnspoken of might be reuiued and produced. **1607** S. COLLINS *Serm.* (1608) 35, I am faine to passe by some things of moment, vnspoken-to here. **1634** SIR T. HERBERT *Trav.* 147 The [Persian] women as vnseene may passe vnspoken of.
2. Not spoken, unsaid, unuttered; not expressed in speech.
c **1449** PECOCK *Repr.* III. xiv. 373 The oon premisse is expressid.., and the other premysse is stille vnspokun for schortnes. **1461** *Paston Lett.* II. 76 Desyreng the said schref if ony thyng of the Kyngs comaunded were be hynd unspoken by hym self that [etc.]. **1548** W. PATTEN *Exped. Scotl.* L v, Causes..that..ar better vnspoken then vttred. **1577** GRANGE *Golden Aphrod.* K iij, No doubte but I.I. wished his wordes vnspoken. **1611** SHAKS. *Cymb.* v. v. 139 Thou'lt torture me to leave vnspoken, that Which to be spoke, wou'd torture thee. **1640** QUARLES *Enchyrid.* III. xxxii, A word unspoken is like the Sword in thy Scabberd, thine. **1773** GOLDSM. *1st Epil. to 'Stoops to Conq.'*, And that our friendship may remain unbroken, What if we leave the Epilogue unspoken? **1818** COLERIDGE in *Encycl. Metrop.* I. Introd. 13 The unspoken alphabet of nature. **1862** SHIRLEY (J. Skelton) *Nugæ Crit.* v. 210 Rigorous edicts..which punished the unspoken thought as well as the visible act.
3. Not spoken *to*; unaddressed.
1616 HIERON *Wks.* II. 23, I shall also teach that which shall be for the best behoofe of euery one in this assembly, that so none may goe away vnspoken to. **1721** KELLY *Scot. Prov.* 249 When People out of Bashfulness leave..a Person unspoken to. **1855** TROLLOPE *Warden* vi, She had sat the whole evening through.., not speaking, and unspoken to.
4. *Sc.* Without having spoken. $rare^{-1}$.
1597 in *Spalding Cl. Misc.* (1841) I. 91 Jonet Wischert.. commandit..Katherine Ewyn to ryss airlie befoir the sone, on betechit hir self to God, and on spokin.
b. (See quot.)
1825 JAMIESON, *Unspoken water*, water..brought..to the house of a sick person, without the bearer's speaking either in going or returning.

un'spongy, *a.* (UN-^{1} 7.)
a **1774** GOLDSM. *Surv. Exp. Philos.* (1776) I. 366 When an unspongy or solid body sinks in a vessel of water.

unspon'taneous, *a.* (UN-^{1} 7.)
1791 COWPER *Odyssey* xx. 419 Wide they stretch'd Their jaws with unspontaneous laughter loud. **1885** *Wesleyan Method. Mag.* Dec. 955/2 Cases of unspontaneous Scripture-study. **1896** *Westm. Gaz.* 15 Dec. 2/1 His acting ..is so mechanical,..so painfully unspontaneous.

unspon'taneously, *adv.* (UN-^{1} 11.)
1640 REYNOLDS *Treat. Passions* xlii. 545 Whereby the Will of man is..inforced or unspontaneously determined to the producing of such Effects.

un'spool, *v.* [UN-^{2} 3.] *trans.* To unwind (thread, tape, etc.) from a spool; *spec.* in *Cinematogr.*, to project (a film); also *intr.* of the thread, etc., or the film shown. Also *fig.*
1940 *Amer. Speech* XV. 205/1 *Unspool*, to project a film. **1961** S. PLATH in *London Mag.* Aug. 8 The heath grass glitters and the spindling rivulets Unspool and spend themselves. **1962** A. NISBETT *Technique Sound Studio* 271 *Spill*,..to unspool a quantity of tape by accident. **1973** *Listener* 22 Feb. 254/2 The new play..unspools inside Christopher's head. **1980** *Times* 10 Oct. 14/1 A noisy adventure film..opened (or unspooled as local jargon has it) in Delhi.

un'sported, *ppl. a.* [UN-^{1} 8 + SPORT *v.* 11 b.] Open.
1871 'M. LEGRAND' *Cambr. Freshm.* xi. 200 Come on, Golightly, your door is unsported.

un'sportful, *a.* (UN-^{1} 7.)
1837 CARLYLE *Fr. Rev.* II. IV. iv, 'A Republic!' said the Seagreen, with one of his dry, husky, *unsportful* laughs, 'what is that?'

un'sporting, *ppl. a.* (UN-¹ 10.)
1859 W. H. GREGORY *Egypt* II. 388 Then we beat the bed of the river, but in a most unsporting manner. 1894 *19th Cent.* July 130 A most pernicious and unsporting custom.
Hence **un'sportingly** *adv.*, **un'sportingness.**
1932 R. CAMPBELL *Taurine Provence* 17 The 'unsportingness' of hunting an animal in an enclosure. *a* 1974 R. CROSSMAN *Diaries* (1976) II. 222, I was now in the dock for unsportingly challenging the rules when I'd lost a round in the parliamentary game. 1978 R. V. JONES *Most Secret War* xxv. 217 The Joint Intelligence Committee decided, very unsportingly, I thought, to hold back Colvin's account while they invited Ewen Montague..to write an officially approved account.

un'sportsmanlike, *a.*, *adv.* (UN-¹ 7 c, 11 b.)
1754 *Connoisseur* No. 31 ¶12 It is unsportsman-like to admit dunghill cocks into the Pit. 1789 WOLCOT (P. Pindar) *Subj. for Painters* Wks. 1816 II. 34 On which he..cry'd, 'See, ho!' Then jump'd (unsportsman like) upon his hare. 1803 in *Spirit Pub. Jrnls.* VII. 298 We stayed till it was dark, that we might not be seen returning in such an unsportsmanlike manner. 1845 FORD *Handbk. Spain* 107 They use nets, spears, night lines, and every unsportsmanlike abomination. 1873 G. C. DAVIES *Mount. & Mere* ii. 8 It was all very well once in a way, but too unsportsmanlike to be repeated often.

un'sportsmanly, *a.* and *adv.* (UN-¹ 7, 11.)
1778 [W. H. MARSHALL] *Minutes Agric.* 9 Sept. 1776, To behave in this churlish, unsportsmanly manner! *Ibid.*, I will not suffer any man to trample unsportsmanly upon me with impunity.

un'spot, *v.* (UN-² 4.)
1598 FLORIO, *Dimacchiare*, to vnspot, to take away spots. *a* 1711 KEN *Hymnotheo* Poet. Wks. 1721 III. 115 It seem'd an easier labour at first Sight, T' unspot Leopards, or wash Ethiops white.

un'spottable, *a.* (UN-¹ 7 b.)
a 1711 KEN *Christophil* Poet. Wks. 1721 II. 516 Robes unspottable and bright.

un'spotted, *ppl. a.* [UN-¹ 8.]
1. Not marked with spots; free from any spot or stain.
1382 WYCLIF *1 Pet.* i. 19 Bi the precious blood of the lomb vndefoulid and vnspottid. 1446 LYDG. *Nightingale Poems* i. 185 The lombe vnspotted, the grounde of Innocence. ? 1567 STOWE in *Three 15th C. Chron.* (Camden) 143 About that tyme [1567] were many congregations of the Anabaptysts in London, who cawlyd themselvs Puritans or Unspottyd Lambs of the Lord. 1626 BOSWORTH *Arcadius & Sepha* II. 219 The tables did unspotted carpets hold Of Tyrian dyes. 1643 (*title*), The Parliaments Unspotted-Bitch: in answer to Prince Roberts Dog. 1709 ADDISON *Tatler* No. 97 ¶2 Her beauty was natural and easy, her Person clean and unspotted. 1743 FRANCIS tr. *Hor., Odes* II. v. 24 Like the Moon's unspotted Light, O'er the Waves. 1804 SHAW *Gen. Zool.* V. 73 Unspotted Salmon, *Salmo Immaculatus*... Salmon with unspotted body. 1835 J. DUNCAN *Beetles* (Nat. Libr.) 220 The head, thorax, and scutellum are velvet black, and unspotted. 1870 HOOKER *Stud. Flora* 353 Leaves lanceolate acute unspotted.
2. Not morally stained; unblemished, pure:
a. Of persons, the mind, etc.
c 1400 *Found. St. Bartholomew's* (1923) 48 She..myghtly troid them vndir foit, vnspottid euermore abidyng. *c* 1450 *Myrr. our Ladye* 140 Sonne of the clene and vnspotted vyrgyn. 1526 TINDALE *Jas.* i. 27 To kepe hym silfe vnspotted from the worlde. 1576 GASCOIGNE *Kenelw. Castle* Wks. 1910 II. 108 The stately tower of your unspotted myndes. 1629 PRYNNE *Anti-Armin.* 84 Being thus rescued from the power of sinne, may they keepe themselues vnspotted from it. 1709 ADDISON *Tatler* No. 75 ¶4 My Sister Jenny..is as unspotted a Spinster as any in Great Britain. 1743 FRANCIS tr. *Hor., Odes* I. xxiv. 9 Modesty, unspotted Maid, And Truth in artless Guise array'd. 1812 CRABBE *Tales* vi. 346 A heart unspotted, and a life unblamed. 1863 CONINGTON *Horace, Odes* I. x. 17 Thou lay'st unspotted souls to rest.
b. Of character, qualities, etc.
1455 *Rolls of Parlt.* V. 280/2 Alwey kepyng oure trouthe to his said Highnesse unspotted and unbrused. *a* 1568 ASCHAM *Scholem.* II. (Arb.) 87 The vnspotted proprietie of the Latin tong,..whan it was..at the hiest pitch of all perfitenesse. 1579 SPENSER *Two Commend. Lett.* i. ad fin., The.. inuiolable Memorie of our vnspotted friendshippe. 1638 M. GRIFFITH in Hearne *Collect.* (O.H.S.) I. 160 Christendome cannot shew in one person..a more Angelical Life, unspotted of yᵉ Worlde & the Flesh. 1665 BUNYAN *Holy Citie* 73 The twelve Apostles, in their own pure, primitive, and unspotted Doctrine. 1712 STEELE *Spect.* No. 276 ¶2, I am a Woman of an unspotted Reputation. 1772 PRIESTLEY *Inst. Relig.* (1782) II. 132 A being of unspotted purity. 1841 BROWNING *Pippa Passes* II. 136 Never to overtake the rest of me, All that, unspotted, reaches up to you.
Hence **un'spottedly** *adv.*; **un'spottedness.**
1598 FLORIO, *Puramente*, purely, cleanlie, *vnspottedlie. 1602 F. HERING *Anat.* 6 He may religiously, vnspottedly, and charily, preserue the precious health and life of man. 1598 FLORIO, *Purità*, puritie, clenlines, neatenes, *vnspottednes. 1624 DONNE *Devotions*, etc. (ed. 2) 303 Doeth the Son dwell bodily in this flesh, that thou shouldst looke for an unspottednesse here? 1682 INGELO *Bentiv. & Ur.* (ed. 4) IV. 156 The unspottedness of our Virgin-life. 1706 tr. *Liger's Compl. Florist* 273 A violation of the candor and unspottedness of her Manners. 1828 T. BROWN *Serm.* 86 Valens spared Paulinus out of respect to the unspottedness of his life.

un'spoused, *ppl. a.* (UN-¹ 8.)
1587 FLEMING *Contn. Holinshed* III. 1299 Unspoused Pallas present is, O Phebus bright retire.

un'spouselike, *a.* (UN-¹ 7 c.)
1611 SPEED *Hist. Gt. Brit.* VIII. vi. 401/2 All which vnprincelie and vn-Spouslike vsage..was, because shee onely should not liue in comfort.

†**un'sprayed,** *ppl. a.*¹ *Obs.* [UN-¹ 8 + SPRAY *sb.*¹] Not furnished with sprays or branches.
1486 *Bk. St. Albans, Her.* a j b, Adam the begynnyng of man kynde was as a stokke vnsprayde and vnfloreshed.

un'sprayed, *ppl. a.*² [UN-¹ 8 + SPRAY *v.*⁴] Not sprayed with a chemical.
1894 *Times* 19 Nov. 4/4 Neither Puritan nor The Bruce yielded any diseased tubers on the unsprayed portions of the crop.

un'spread, *ppl. a.* Also 7 **unspreaden.** [UN-¹ 8 b.] Not spread (out).
1589 FLEMING *Virg. Georg.* III. 44 Lodging all night long he lies..Vpon a couch vnmade (vnspread). 1642 H. MORE *Song of Soul* II. iii. 21 Remember that some things unspreaden be, How shall it find them out? 1644 G. PLATTES in *Hartlib's Legacy* (1655) 188 Where dung hath..layen unspread for a moneth or six weeks. 1776 C. KEITH *Farmer's Ha'* lxi, The dishes set on unspread table. 1827 POLLOK *Course T.* VI. 633 Bounding immensity, unspread, unbound! 1838 MRS. BROWNING *Young Queen* 1 The shroud is yet unspread. 1844 —— *Confessions* iii, Unquickened, unspread My fire dropt down.

un'spread, *v.* (UN-² 3.)
1661 K. W. *Conf. Charac.* (1860) 69 He's so used to spread cloaths, that he's ne're well but when he's unspreading of aprons.

†**un'sprighty,** *a.* *Obs.*⁻¹ [UN-¹ 7.] Not sprightly or lively.
1607 MARKHAM *Cavel.* VIII. 14 Anie of these constant and vnsprity carriages are signes of dulnes.

un'spring, *v.* [UN-² 7, 4 b. Cf. OE. *onspringan*, OS. *antspringan*, Du. *ontspringen*, OHG. *intspringan* (MHG., G. *entspringen*).]
†1. *intr.* To burst open. *Obs.*⁻¹
13.. *K. Alis.* (W.) 2902 Mury hit is in sonne-risyng! The rose openith and unspryng [*Laud MS.* wile vpspringe].
2. *trans.* To release or detach by pressing a spring.
1802 JAMES *Milit. Dict.*, *To unspring*, a word of command formerly used in the exercise of cavalry. *Ibid.*, Unspring your carbine. 1833 *Reg. Instr. Cavalry* I. 96 'Unspring' by disengaging the swivel from the carbine. 1859 F. A. GRIFFITHS *Artill. Man.* (ed. 8) 48 Unspring arms.

un'springing, *ppl. a.* (UN-¹ 10.)
1821 MILMAN *Judicum Regale* 140 The red havoc of unspringing fire.

un'springy, *a.* (UN-¹ 7.)
1672 *Phil. Trans.* VII. 5167 An Un-springy Fluid (which presseth but as a Weight not as a Spring). 1936 *Scrutiny* IV. 398 The new verse moves line by line, the characteristic single line having..an evenly distributed weight—a settled, quite unspringy balance.

un'sprinkled, *ppl. a.* [UN-¹ 8.] Not sprinkled with water, etc.; *spec.* not baptized by sprinkling.
1648 HEXHAM II, *Ongewatert*, vnwatered, or vnsprinckled. 1735 SAVAGE *Progr. Divine* Wks. 1775 II. 112 Let babes of poverty convulsive lie; No bottle waits, tho' babes unsprinkl'd die. 1802–12 BENTHAM *Ration. Judic. Evid.* (1827) II. 659 If the child remains unsprinkled,..no registration is to take place. 1843 TIZARD *Brewing* 62 Unsprinkled malt.

un'sprung, *ppl. a.*¹ [UN-¹ 8 b.] Not having sprung up or sprouted.
1600 FAIRFAX *Tasso* I. xlix, His hopes Vnsprong, his cares were fit to mowe. 1684 J. S. *Profit & Pleas. United* 106 To prevent the Crows or daws falling on the Corne unsprung.

un'sprung, *ppl. a.*² [UN-¹ 8 b + SPRUNG *ppl. a.*²] Not provided with a spring or springs. Of a (dance-)floor: not constructed so as to be resilient.
1928 C. F. S. GAMBLE *Story N. Sea Air Station* i. 32 The floats of seaplanes were practically unsprung. 1939 M. ALLINGHAM *Mr Campion & Others* I. viii. 171 A small unsprung dance-floor. 1973 R. PERRY *Ticket to Ride* xii. 162 Both bunks boasted a mattress of sorts, thin and unsprung.

†**un'spulyied,** *ppl. a.* *Sc. Obs.* [UN-¹ 8.] = UNSPOILED *ppl. a.* 1.
1513 DOUGLAS *Æneid* XI. xi. 134 My self..the reuthfull corps..sall cary away, Onspulȝeit of hir armour or array. 1559 *Extr. Aberd. Reg.* (1844) I. 316 The sklayttis, tymmir, and stanis..that are in place onspoulȝet. *a* 1578 LINDESAY (Pitscottie) *Chron. Scot.* (S.T.S.) II. 285 That nane mycht travell onspuilȝeit on bayth the sydes. *a* 1670 SPALDING *Troub. Chas. I* (1850) I. 157 To saif..his houssis on spolȝeit, and his freindis and seruandis on plunderit.

un'spun, *ppl. a.* (UN-¹ 8 b. Cf. OHG. *ungispunnan* (MHG. *ungespunnen*, G. *-sponnen*), ON. *úspunninn* (older Da. *uspunden*, Sw. *ospunnen*).)
1545 *Rates of Custom* a vi, Cotton vnsponne..xxvi.s. viii.d. 1565 COOPER *Thesaurus*, *Linum infectum*, flaxe vnspunne. 1571 *Wills & Inv. N.C.* (Surtees, 1835) 352, I haiue in the howse spunn and vnsponne vj ston of lynt. 1586 in Kyd *Wks.* (1901) 340 Her thred still holds, thine perisht though vnspun. 1827 FARADAY *Chem. Manip.* ii. 49 A filament of unspun silk.

unspurd, obs. var. UNSPEERED *ppl. a.*

†**un'spurn,** *v.* *Obs.*⁻¹ [UN-² 9.] *trans.* To force open.
a 1300 *K. Horn* 1074 (Camb. MS.), Horn gan to þe ȝate turne, And þat wiket vnspurne [*v.r.* op spurne].

un'spurred, (*ppl.*) *a.* [UN-¹ 8, 9.]
1. Not urged on by a spur. Also *fig.*
a 1635 CORBET *Iter Bor.* Poems (1647) 12 His Mare went truer then his Chronicle; And..unspurr'd, unbeaten, Brought us sixe miles. 1865 MEREDITH *R. Fleming* xviii, The replenished glass enabled Stephen to add the picturesque bits of the affray, unspurred by a surrounding eagerness of his listeners. 1886 *Pall Mall G.* 31 July 2/2 Not altogether unspurred by hints from home.
2. Not furnished with a spur.
1852 C. W. HOSKYNS *Talpa* xvi. 133 Grazing Mr. Greening's unspurred foot with the point of the leader's stretcher.

un'squandered, *ppl. a.* (UN-¹ 8.)
[1775 ASH.] 1799 J. ROBERTSON *Agric. Perth* 416 The public have a right to any effects he left unsquandered away. 1812 CRABBE *Tales* xx. 175 His pension, with what sums remain Due or unsquander'd.

†**unsquare,** obs. f. ANSWER *v.*
c 1420 *Avow. Arth.* xix, The tother vnsquarut him withskille.

un'square, *v.* [UN-² 3, 6 b, 7.]
a. *trans.* To divest of squareness; to undo the squaring of. b. *intr.* To lose squareness of form or structure.
1611 FLORIO, *Disquatrare*, to vnsquare. 1790 *Trans. Soc. Arts* VIII. 168 [The loom] is not liable to unsquare; and yet ..may be more easily removed than the old loom. 1872 DE MORGAN *Budget of Paradoxes* 470 Montucla charges Cluvier with unsquaring the parabola, which Archimedes had squared as tight as a glove.

un'squared, *ppl. a.* [UN-¹ 8.] Not made square; not reduced to a square form or section.
1549 COVERDALE, etc. *Erasm. Par. 1 Cor.* viii. 23 b, An idole..hathe no more Godhead in it, than an other vnsquared piece of tymber. 1598 GRENEWEY *Tacitus, Germanie* ii. (1622) 262 They..vse to all buildings vnsquared and vnwrought timber. 1633 T. ADAMS *Exp. 2 Peter* ii. 5 An unsquared stone..must not be put into the building of Christ. 1664 EVELYN *Sylva* xxix. 90 Such Trees as one would leave round, and unsquar'd. 1798 HUTTON *Course Math.* II. 95 To find the Solidity of Round or Unsquared Timber. 1883 STEVENSON *Treas. Isl.* IV. xix, The log-house was made of unsquared trunks of pine.
fig. 1592 KYD *Sp. Trag.* III. xi. 23 The more he growes in stature.., The more vnsquard, vnbeuelled he appeares. 1606 SHAKS. *Tr. & Cr.* I. iii. 159 With tearmes vnsquar'd, Which from the tongue of roaring Typhon dropt, Would seeme Hyperboles. 1607 MARSTON *What you will* Induct., Were I to passe Through publick verdit, I should feare my forme, Least ought I offerd were unsquard or warp'd.

un'squeamish, *a.* (UN-¹ 7.)
1893 *Athenæum* 4 Feb. 157/3 This pushing, unsqueamish age.
Hence **un'squeamishly** *adv.*; **un'squeamishness.**
1922 F. L. LUCAS *Seneca & Elizabethan Tragedy* iv. 97 With Tudor unsqueamishness the audience then proceeded to watch Tereus dining off his son's flesh. 1959 *Times* 24 Jan. 7/7 The Calvinism that Burns satirized..was unsqueamishly aware of man's carnal nature. 1970 *Daily Tel.* 6 Feb. 17 The nurses are..tireless. All the virtues of the Victorian heroine are there, with unsqueamishness added for good measure. 1976 *National Observer* (U.S.) 27 Mar. 19/2 Vidal's fiction is true to the spirit of 1876, an age that was unsqueamishly exploitive and loved the grand scale.

un'squeezed, *ppl. a.* (UN-¹ 8.)
1683 MOXON *Mech. Exerc.*, *Printing* xi. ¶1 The natural Spring that all these Joynts have, when they are unsqueez'd. 1736 THOMSON *Liberty* v. 198 Rich, as unsqueez'd favourite, to them, Is he who can his Virtue boast alone! 1757 GARRICK *Lilliput* Prol. 8 Gently you'll ride, as in a Fairy Dream, Your Hoops unsqueez'd. 1824 MACTAGGART *Gallovid. Encycl.* (1876) 29 The primrose..and the crawtae grow unsqueez'd and unlooked at.

un'squire, *v.* (UN-² 6 b.)
1721 SWIFT *Let. to King at Arms* Wks. 1841 II. 70/2 If this should be the test of squirehood, it will go hard with a great number of my fraternity,..who must all be unsquired because a greyhound will not be allowed to keep us company.

†**un'squissed,** *ppl. a.* *Obs.*⁻⁰ [UN-¹ 8.] Unsqueezed.
1648 HEXHAM II, *Ongepijnden honigh*, Vnpressed, or Vnsquissed hony.

unsta'bility. Now *rare.* (UN-¹ 12, 5 b.)
a 1470 *Dives & Pauper* (W. de W. 1496) VI. x. 247/2 Eue synned more by freelte and unstabylyte..than by shrewednes. 1572 *Wills & Inv. N.C.* (Surtees, 1835) 386 Perceivynge..the vnstabilitie and soden changes of the worlde,..and the vncertentye of deathe. 1603 KNOLLES *Hist. Turks* (1621) 50 The head was forthwith strucke off from this miserable carkasse (the mirrour of honours vnstabilitie). 1646 P. BULKELEY *Gospel Covt.* v. 363 When you see uncertainty and unstability of all things. 1886 *Science* 5 Nov. 401/2 The unstability of such an association is..beginning to be understood.

un'stable, *a.* [UN-¹ 7, 5 b. Cf. obs. Du. *onstabel*, MHG. *unstabel.*]
1. a. Not remaining steadily in the same place; apt to move or be moved about.
a 1225 *Ancr. R.* 122 Ne scheaweð heo þet heo is dust, & vnstable þinc, þet mid a lutel wind of a word is anon to blowen. *a* 1340 HAMPOLE *Ps.* x. 1 If i doe i sall be like a sparou, þat is, vnstabile and lyght. 1388 WYCLIF *Gen.* iv. 14 Y schal be vnstable of dwellyng and fleynge aboute in erthe. 1483 *Cath. Angl.* 357/2 Vn Stabylle, *argus, vagus.* 1597 R. TOFTE, etc. *Laura* I. xviii, If Sea no other thing doth shew to bee Than most vnstable waters moouing oft. 1634 SIR T. HERBERT *Trav.* 91 Sands..in great drifts..so light and vnstable, that the high wayes are neuer certaine. 1653 W.

RAMESEY *Astrol. Restored* 179 Aries,..though it be a sign fiery, yet is it moveable and unstable.

b. Not steady in position; readily swaying or shaking; liable to swing or fall.

1390 GOWER *Conf.* I. 200 Now herke how thilke unstable whel, Which evere torneth, wente aboute. **1393** LANGL. *P. Pl.* C. XI. 37 Stonde he neuere so styfliche þorgh sterynge of the bote, He bendeþ and boweþ, þe body is vnstable. *c* **1480** HENRYSON *Fables, Cock & Fox* 199 Thy strenth is nocht, thy stule standis vnstabill. *a* **1542** WYATT in *Tottel's Misc.* (Arb.) 38 So foloweth me remembrance of that face: That with my teary eyn, swolne, and vnstable, My desteny to beholde her doth me lead. **1567** *Gude & Godlie B.* (S.T.S.) 106 As quheill vnstabill and caffe befoir the wind. **1600** FAIRFAX *Tasso* XIX. xiii, When the still windes stirre not th' vnstable maine. **1736** THOMSON *Liberty* IV. 302 On each hand Amazing seen amid unstable waves, The splendid palace shines. **1760** GOLDSM. *Cit. W.* ii, A strange people.. who have founded an empire on this unstable element [*sc.* the ocean]. **1857** BUCKLE *Civilis.* vii. 347 The sailor is naturally more superstitious than the soldier, because he has to deal with a more unstable element. **1873** MAXWELL *Electr. & Magn.* I. 141 The body therefore is unstable even when constrained to move parallel to itself, *à fortiori* it is unstable when altogether free.

c. Of movement: Unsteady; irregular.

1549 *Compl. Scot.* vi. 54 It makkis ane onstabil reuolution in thre hundretht xlviij dais. **1819** SCOTT *Ivanhoe* xlii, Down he came, with an unstable step and a strong flavour of wine.

d. *Mech.* Of equilibrium (q.v.).

1839 G. BIRD *Nat. Philos.* 31 The body will be in a state of unstable equilibrium. **1860** *All Year Round* No. 69. 450 An acrobat balances a ladder on his shoulder; on the ladder, perhaps will mount a child... The whole are in unstable equilibrium.

2. Not stable in purpose; vacillating, fickle, changeable.

c **1290** *S. Eng. Leg.* I. 319/685 Wraþþe he berth luytel ȝwyle:..Glad and bliþe, and onstable of þat he hath to done. **1297** R. GLOUC. 10507 He made of þe olde lawes is chartre atte laste,..& aselede is vaste inou, Ac suþþe as vnstable man wiþ sede & wiþ drou. *c* **1305** *Pilate* 183 in *E.E.P.* (1862) 116 Alle þat ihurde þis cas Wondrede moche of þemperour, þat he vnstable was. *c* **1380** WYCLIF *Sel. Wks.* II. 10 Þis Emperour..was unstable as watir. *c* **1400** *Destr. Troy* 8057 Hit is a propertie apreuit..To all wemen..To be vnstable & not stidfast. *c* **1450** tr. *De Imitatione* III. l. 121 Euery man is a lyer, sike, unstable, and slydyng. *c* **1485** *Digby Myst.* (1882) III. 588 Woman, why art þou so onstabyll?.. why art þou a-ȝens god so veryabyll? **1509–10** *Act 1 Hen. VIII*, c. 11 Many lyght and unstable Persons. *a* **1548** HALL *Chron., Hen. V*, 38 The Cambers, otherwise called the vnstable Welshemen. **1607** SHAKS. *Cor.* III. i. 148 It must omit Reall Necessities, and giue way the while To vnstable Slightnesse. **1653** MILTON *Ps.* v. 25 In his faltring mouth unstable No word is firm. **1661** SOUTH *Serm.* (1715) III. 192 Such Pretenders may beguile Factious and Unstable Minds. **1791** WOLCOT (P. Pindar) *Lousiad* III. ix, [A deed] Which Cain perform'd, in godliness unstable. **1855** MACAULAY *Hist. Eng.* xv. III. 613 His nature, lamentably unstable, was not ignoble. **1891** FARRAR *Darkn. & Dawn* xxv, Onesimus was too unstable to withstand the combined temptations by which he was surrounded.

absol. **1582** N. T. (Rhem.) *2 Pet.* iii. 16 Certaine things hard to be vnderstoode, which the vnlearned and vnstable depraue. **1630** H. LYNDE (*title*), Via Devia: The By-Way: Mis-leading the weake and vnstable into dangerous paths of Error. **1650** BAXTER *Saints' R.* III. xi. §18. 497 Drawing off the unstable from the doctrine and way of life.

3. a. Not fixed in character or condition; exposed to vicissitude or chance; apt to change or alter; variable.

c **1340** HAMPOLE *Pr. Consc.* 1420 Þe worlde is swa unstable, Alle þat men sese þar-in es chaungeable. *c* **1375** *Lay Folks Mass-Bk.* (MS. B.) 390 þo weders grete & vnstable, Lord make gode. **1387** TREVISA *Higden* (Rolls) I. 139 Hap was vnstable and vnstedefast; ones wiþ þat oon side, and eft wiþ þat oþer. *c* **1412** HOCCLEVE *De Reg. Princ.* 705 O lord! þis world vnstabyl is. *c* **1450** tr. *De Imitatione* III. lxiv. 149, I finde all vnferme & vnstable, what euere I beholde oute of þe. **1513** DOUGLAS *Æneid* XI. viii. 118 The variant chance Of our onstabill lyfe. *a* **1542** WYATT in *Tottel's Misc.* (Arb.) 35 Vnstable dreame,..Be stedfast ones, or els at least be true. *a* **1642** KYNASTON *Leoline & Sydanis* 141 O wretched state unstable Of mortal men! **1657** in *Verney Mem.* (1907) 560 These giddy and unstable times. **1768** BOSWELL *Corsica* ii. 73 The Genoese..were..in an unstable, and perilous condition. **1796** MME. D'ARBLAY *Camilla* III. 75 We must allow to our unstable virtues all the encouragement that can prop them. *Ibid.* V. 540 The perpetual vicissitudes of our unstable condition. **1829** HOOD *Eugene Aram* 46 Or is it some historic page Of kings and crowns unstable? **1863** H. COX *Instit.* III. iii. 628 That all oligarchies and democracies are unstable. **1884** CHURCH *Bacon* ix. 223 English seemed to him too homely to express the hopes of the world, too unstable to be trusted with them.

b. *spec.* in *Chem.*

1849 D. CAMPBELL *Inorg. Chem.* 216 Its [*sc.* suboxide of copper] salts are very unstable. **1857** MILLER *Elem. Chem., Org.* 59 Grape sugar forms definite but unstable combinations with the alkaline bases. **1890** *Retrospect Med.* CII. 2 The chloral hydrate is, comparatively, an unstable compound.

c. *Physics.* (Cf. STABLE *a.* 3 d.)

1904 F. SODDY *Radio-Activity* viii. 123 Our knowledge of unstable atoms is necessarily limited. *Ibid.* 124 Radio-activity..has thus introduced us to a whole series of new unstable elements. **1924** O. LODGE *Atoms & Rays* ii. 33 The possibility of building up still more complex, and probably still more unstable, elements..remains a subject for future discovery. **1981** C. E. SWARTZ *Phenomenal Physics* xxxiii. 715 Most elements exist naturally as a mixture of several isotopes... The diagram shows all of the stable isotopes, and many of the unstable ones.

4. Not firm or solid; insecure.

1565 JEWEL *Repl. Harding* (title-p.), The Weake and vnstable Groundes of the Romaine Religion. **1613** PURCHAS *Pilgrimage* (1614) 597 The Earth was couered with sand, which yeelded an vnstable footing.

un'stable, *v.* [UN-² 5.] † *trans.* To free *of.*

1612 T. ADAMS *Gallant's Burden* 32 If our harts be vnstabled of these beastiall lusts.

un'stabled, *ppl. a.*¹ [UN-¹ 8.] Not established or made stable.

1622 *Babington's Wks.* 9 Complaints of wauering weakenesse and vnstabled [*ed.* **1596** vnstayned (*read* vnstayed)] mutability..brought against vs. **1681** RYCAUT tr. *Gracian's Critick* 120 A tottering Cottage, founded on an unstabled Sand.

un'stabled, *ppl. a.*² [UN-¹ 8.] Not put into a stable.

1853 C. BRONTE *Villette* xxxix, Behold the branchless tree, the unstabled Rosinante!

un'stableness. [f. UNSTABLE *a.*] The condition of being unstable; instability: **a.** Of persons, the mind, etc.

c **1380** WYCLIF *Sel. Wks.* II. 58 Medling of freris cloþis telliþ unstablenesse [in virtue] of þes ordris. **1387** TREVISA *Higden* II. 175 Þe vnstabilnesse of þouȝtes schal be bytokened by many manere dyuersite of cloþinge. *c* **1425** *Eng. Conq. Irel.* 136 Thegh thay, throgh kynd falsnesse & vnstablenesse that yn ham ys, lytyl tel of othes. **1539** ELYOT *Cast. Helthe* 75 Unstablenesse of wytte and slipper remembraunce. **1590** GREENWOOD *Answ. Gifford* 13 Your vnstablenes in denying and affirming with one breath. **1646** P. BULKELEY *Gospel Covt.* v. 368 By reason of our unstablenesse of spirit, we are apt to make many a breach. **1676** HALE *Contempl.* II. 49 Unstableness, Vanity, Love of Pleasures, Easiness to be corrupted in Youth. **1815** W. H. IRELAND *Scribbleomania* 124 His natural unstableness debars him from adopting any fixed mode of action.

b. Of conditions, life, etc.

c **1340** HAMPOLE *Pr. Consc.* 353 Þe unstabelnes of þis werld. *c* **1374** CHAUCER *Boeth.* II. pr. iv. (1868) 43 Þe vnstablenesse of fortune. *c* **1430** LYDG. *Compl. Bl. Knt.* 457 Thy stormy wilful variaunce I-meynt with chaunge and gret vnstablenesse. *c* **1440** *Gesta Rom.* lxxxix. 411 A woman.. that sawe..the synnes, and the vnstablenesse, that was in the worlde. *a* **1589** PALFREYMAN *Baldwin's Mor. Philos.* (1600) 52 O world thou hast so many countenaunces in thy vanitie, that thou leadest all wandering in vnstablenesse. **1601** SIR W. CORNWALLIS *Ess.* II. xxxvi, The frailty and vnstablenes of wealth. **1670** in Somers *Tracts* I. 27 To shew unto those insolent Commanders of the Army, the Unstableness of their Condition. **1807** G. CHALMERS *Caledonia* I. III. vii. 421 A weaker prince would have lost his crown, considering its unstableness.

un'stably, *adv.* [UN-¹ 11. Cf. prec.] In an unstable manner; unsteadily.

a **1380** *Eufrosyne* 390 in Horstm. *Altengl. Leg.* (1878) 178 I stunte, I stonde, vnstabli I stalke. **14..** *Wyclif's De Ecclesia* (1851) p. xiii, But her þenken trewe men þat þe fend failiþ her, & goiþ vnstably [*v.r.* unstable] bi two weies. *c* **1440** *Promp. Parv.* 367/2 Onstabylly, *instabiliter.* **1502** ATKYNSON tr. *De Imitatione* III. xix. 212 He standeth casually and vnstably that castith nat all his busynes in the. **1611** COTGR., *Instablement*, vnstably, vnsteadily. **1654** ELLISTONE & SPARROW tr. *Boehme's Myst. Magnum* lxxvi. 579 As Adam suddenly and unstably therein, departed from his Glory. **1830** PUSEY *Hist. Enq.* II. 109 Others, who are unstably 'halting between the two opinions'. **1879** THOMSON & TAIT *Nat. Phil.* I. I. §351 A particle placed on the inner circle.. would move perpetually in that circle, but unstably.

un'stack, *v.* [UN-² 3.] *trans.* To remove, take down, from being stacked or piled up.

1859 R. F. BURTON *Centr. Afr.* in *Jrnl. Geog. Soc.* XXIX. 414 The porters..unstack the loads propped against the trees. **1863** W. THORNBURY *True as Steel* III. 39 The enemy ..already were beating the alarm, unstacking their weapons, and gathering outside their tents. **1888** *Pall Mall G.* 18 Feb. 6/2 In unstacking some timber..the men came across a newly-made sparrow's nest.

un'stacked, *ppl. a.* (UN-¹ 8.)

[**1775** ASH.] **1846** WORC. (citing More). **1884** *Spectator* 4 Oct. 1326/1 She has left some wood unstacked at home.

un'stagnant, *a.* (UN-¹ 7.)

1822–7 GOOD *Study Med.* (1829) III. 45 A pure and unstagnant air.

un'stagy, *a.* (UN-¹ 7.)

1882 *Macm. Mag.* XLVI. 332/2 A room altogether natural and unstagey. [Freq. in recent use.]

un'staid, *a.* Also 6–7 **unstaied, -stayed,** etc. [UN-¹ 7.]

1. Of persons: Not staid or regulated in deportment or conduct.

c **1550** CHEKE *Matt.* xxiii. 25 Thei be called in greek ἀκρατεῖς,..which we mai cal rightli vnstaid. **1621** BURTON *Anat. Mel.* III. ii. II. iii. 567 When they are so new fangled, so vnstaide, so prodigious in their attires. **1636** HEYWOOD *Love's Mistr.* v. L 4, Now Psiche, you must see your sisters judg'd, Vnstaid Petrea, and unkind Astioche.

transf. **1591** SHAKS. *Two Gent.* II. vii. 60 How will the world repute me For vndertaking so vnstaid a iourney?

†**b.** Of a hawk: Not properly trained. *Obs.*⁻¹

1614 LATHAM *Falconry* I. v. 21 With the first of these three orders, I haue reclaimed an outragious vnstaied hawke.

2. Of the mind, etc.: Not subjected to restraint or control; unrestrained, unregulated.

(*a*) **1579** E. K. *Ded. to Spenser's Sheph. Cal.* §5 His vnstayed yougth had long wandred in the common Labyrinth of Loue. **1593** SHAKS. *Rich. II*, II. i. 2 Will the King come, that I may breath my last In wholsome counsell to his vnstaid youth? **1603** KNOLLES *Hist. Turks* (1621) 158 All those vaine delights which vnstaied youth most desireth.

(*b*) **1587** HOLINSHED *Chron.* III. 488/1 To lash out whatsoeuer his vnstaied mind affoorded. **1605** ROWLANDS *Hell's Broke Loose* (Hunterian Club) 23 The easier to beguile The simple sort, which haue vnstayed mindes. *a* **1678** H. SCOUGAL *Disc. Imp. Subj.* (1735) 136 Our blood is hot, and our spirits unstayed and giddy. **1685** BAXTER *Paraphr. N.T.* 1 Tim. iii. 11 Women..in danger..of unstayed Levity. **1812** CARY *Dante, Purg.* x. 112 O poor and wretched ones! That..lean your trust Upon unstaid perverseness. **1832** L. HUNT *Sir R. Esher* i. 38 Unripe and unstaid thoughts, the vanities of youth. **1840** LOWELL *The Moon* 5 My soul was like the sea,..Moaning in vague immensity,..Unrestful and unstaid.

(*c*) **1592** LYLY *Gallathea* III. i, I feele my thoughts vnknit, mine eyes vnstaied. **1638** BRATHWAIT *Spirit. Spicery*, etc. 398 Those poore objects wherewith my unstayed eyes were fed.

(*d*) **1590** SPENSER *Muiopot.* 161 To the gay gardins his vnstaid desire Him wholly caried, to refresh his sprights. **1612** DRAYTON *Poly-olb.* xi. 348 Ethelbald..by the wise reproofe of godly Bishops brought From those vnstay'd delights by which his youth was caught.

3. Not settled or stable in opinion or resolve; not clearly determined or decided.

1561 T. NORTON *Calvin's Inst.* I. 5 That vnstayed and wandring opinion of the maiestie of God. **1603** HARSNET *Pop. Impost.* 121 If they had brought the old renowmed Reliques from Rome, some unstayed body would haue made question whether they had been Saints bones indeed. **1613** BP. HALL *Serm.* v. 93 A private man unsettled in opinion, is ..troublesome and useless: but a public person unstayed is dangerous. **1631** WEEVER *Anc. Funeral Mon.* 515 King Henry,..vnstayed in religious resolutions, did cut them off vpon false suggestions. *a* **1750** A. HILL *Muse to Writer* viii, While roving thus, uncenter'd and unstaid, I lik'd by turns, and did by turns refuse.

4. Liable to change or alter; uncertain.

1586 DAY *Eng. Secretary* I. (1595) 116 Is there anie thing on earth so assured, that by vnstaied incertaintie is not continuallie guided? **1628** FELTHAM *Resolves* II. xlvi. 135 Change is the great Lord of the World; Time is his Agent, that brings in all things to suffer his vnstaid Dominion. **1642** H. MORE *Song of Soul* III. iii. 15 They frisque about in circulings unstay'd.

Hence **un'staidly** *adv.*

1556 GRIMALDE *Cicero's Offices* III. 123 Nothing.. vniustly, nothing wantonly, nothing vnstayedly is meete to be done. **1571** GOLDING *Calvin on Ps.* xxxvii. 9 If we were not shifted hither and thither unstayedly. **1611** COTGR., *Incontinemment*,..disorderedly, vnstayedly, immoderately.

un'staidness. [f. prec.]

1. Absence of staidness in conduct or opinion.

c **1550** CHEKE *Matt.* xxiii. 25 For ie clense yᵉ outward part of yᵉ cup..but yᵉ insijd is ful of robri and vnstaidnes. **1583** GOLDING *Calvin on Deut.* xxxviii. 227 That we must not defile our selues with any vnchastitie or vnstayednesse. **1650** HOLYDAY *Persius' Sat.* v. 41 Nothing hinders thee..But Luxurie. That doth seduce thy weake Unstayednesse. **1675** BARCLAY *Apol. Quakers* xi. §8. 358 The unstayedness of their Minds. **1828** E. IRVING *Last Days* 326 The former [trait] expressing haste, precipitancy, and unstayedness.

†**2.** Physical unsteadiness. *Obs.*

a **1586** SIDNEY *Arcadia* I. ix, With a kind of shaking unstayednes over all his body. **1607** MARKHAM *Cavel.* VII. 59 When..the orifice by the vnstaidnes of the Farriers hand, is made too great.

un'stain, *v.* [UN-² 3.] *trans.* To free from stain or stains.

1639 N. WHITING *Albino & Bellama*, etc. H 10, What other errours thou findest, let thy pen amend, excusing the presse, and un-staining the Authour. **1639** FULLER *Holy War* II. ix. 55 They sought to unstain their credits by going again. **1687** J. REYNOLDS *Death's Vis.* vii, How Blooming Trees..Unstain Dy'd Cloaths, and call their Atoms forth.

un'stainable, *a.* (UN-¹ 7 b.)

1584 LODGE *Hist. Forbonius & Prisc.* (Shaks. Soc.) 96 Alas, unfortunate Ægyptian! whose faithful affections are so immutable, as thy naturall colour is unstainable. **1864** CARLYLE *Fredk. Gt.* XVII. i. IV. 502 The unstainable fidelity of Weingarten Senior. **1878** GROSART *H. More's Poems* Mem. Introd. p. xxii/1 A pure white life unstained and unstainable as the light.

un'stained, *ppl. a.* [UN-¹ 8.]

1. Not stained or (dis)coloured; spotless, clean, pure.

1555 in Feuillerat *Revels Q. Mary* (1914) 182 The same white cloth of sylver vnstayned. **1597** SHAKS. *2 Hen. IV*, v. ii. 114 Th' vnstained Sword that you haue vs'd to beare. **1629** MILTON *Hymn Nativ.* iv, The hooked Chariot stood Unstain'd with hostile blood. **1736** THOMSON *Liberty* v. 556 Languedocian skies, That, unstain'd ether all, diffusive smile. **1807** CRABBE *Par. Reg.* I. 24 By sighs unruffled or unstain'd by tears. **1860** TYNDALL *Glac.* I. xiv. 97 The unstained blue of heaven. **1899** *Allbutt's Syst. Med.* VIII. 903 An unstained or faintly stained zone..across the bacillus. **1918** *Heal & Son Catal.: Cottage Furnit.* 3 This furniture is left quite plain, unstained and unpolished. **1936** 'N. BLAKE' *Thou Shell of Death* ii. 27 A cream-washed bedroom, furnished..with unstained oak.

2. Not morally stained or sullied; unblemished, untarnished.

1573 DAUS tr. *Bullinger on Apoc.* (ed. 2) 84 The Byshops began to defile the Lordes supper and other vnstained doctrines of fayth. *a* **1586** SIDNEY *Arcadia* II. x, Any sparkes of unstained duety lefte in them towardes me. **1624** QUARLES *Job* xv. 19 Preserue he then, vnstained in his brest, A milke-white Conscience. **1689** D. GRANVILLE *Lett.* (Surtees) 81 The consideration whereof hath..kept me untainted and unstained. **1744** THOMSON *Spring* 761 The towering Seat.. of his Empire; which, in Peace, Unstain'd he holds. **1746** FRANCIS tr. *Horace, Epist.* II. ii. 196 A Person, who maintain'd A due Decorum, and a Life unstain'd. **1813** SHELLEY *Q. Mab* VII. 236 No year of my eventful being Has passed unstained by crime and misery. **1863** MRS. H. WOOD *Verner's Pride* xviii, He was proud of his independence, his unstained name.

Hence **un'stainedness.**

1685 H. MORE *Paralip. Prophet.* 327 Sacerdotal,.. because of the unstainedness of their condition as to

Externals. **1727** BAILEY (vol. II), *Pureness,..* Unspottedness, Unstainedness.

un'staled, *ppl. a.* (UN-¹ 8.)
1883 LD. R. GOWER *Reminisc.* I. i. 5 A source of intense pleasure, ever fresh and unstaled.

un'stalked, *a.* (UN-¹ 9.)
1875 HUXLEY & MARTIN *Elem. Biol.* 93 Free swimming unstalked bells. **1884** ELLACOMBE *Plant-Lore Shaks.* 115 Female blossoms.. completely sessile or unstalked.

un'stalled, *ppl. a.* (UN-¹ 8.)
[**1775** ASH.] **1829** LYTTON *Devereux* IV. i, My horse stood unstalled at the gate.

un'stamped, *ppl. a.* [UN-¹ 8. Cf. MDa. *ustampet.*]
1. Not crushed by stamping.
1594 PLAT *Jewell-ho.* II. 46 Malaghie reasons.. either stampt or unstampt. **1595** R. SOUTHWELL *Mæoniæ, Christ's Bloody Sweat* 3 Sweete oliue, grape of blisse,.. vnstampt, vntoucht of presse. **1648** HEXHAM II, *Ongestooten Peper,* Vnstamped Pepper.
2. Not marked by stamping; not stamped with a device or official mark: **a.** Of metals.
1622 *Strange Accid.* in *Harl. Misc.* (1808) I. 26/2 Silver of three sorts, all unstamped. *a* **1643** GODOLPHIN *Sonn. fr. Harl. MS.* 25 Like unstamped gold I weigh each grate. **1767** *Curiosities of London* 71 Putting in the unstamped piece with his forefinger and thumb. **1801** *Farmer's Mag.* 196 A bit of unstamped bullion. **1853** TRENCH *Proverbs* 15 The same advantage.. which.. has the recognised coin of the realm over the rude unstamped ore.
b. Of paper or publications.
1809 R. LANGFORD *Introd. Trade* 13 Country Bankers can .. issue bills of exchange on unstamped paper. **1855** *Instructions to Postmasters* June, Unstamped Publications.. can be forwarded.. under the regulations of the Book Post. **1861** *Sat. Rev.* 23 Nov. 532 So all the benefits of a free press, unstamped, unexcised, may be altogether thrown away.
3. Not having a stamp affixed.
1892 'H. S. MERRIMAN' *Slave of Lamp* xxi, Posting an unstamped letter addressed to England.

Unstan ('ʌnstən). The name of the site of a chambered tomb on Mainland, Orkney, used *attrib.* to denote a type of early neolithic pottery originally found on that site.
1932 *Proc. Prehistoric Soc.* VII. 64 The hatched and shaded Triangle motif occurs on the Unstan bowls. **1954** S. PIGGOTT *Neolithic Cultures* viii. 248 The bulk of the pottery .. can best be classed as Unstan ware from the thirty or so vessels found in that tomb. **1978** *Times* 27 May 3/3 One post-hole also yielded shreds of 'Unstan' pottery, characteristic of the early Neolithic period of the Orkney Islands.

un'stanchable, *a.* [UN-¹ 7 b.]
1. Incapable of being stopped or ended.
c **1374** CHAUCER *Boeth.* II. pr. vii. (1868) 58 By þe regard of eternite, þat is vnstaunccheable [L. *inexhausta*] and infinit. **1430-40** LYDG. *Bochas* VIII. xvii. (1558) 12 With heed enclyned no word he spake again, Fyll in wepinge, with subbyng vnstaunchable. **1571** GOLDING *Calvin on Ps.* xxiii. 6 Gods goodnesse is unstaunchable. **1670** SWAN *Spec. M.* 440 The wounds of the Hæmorrhois procure unstanchable bleeding. **1837** CARLYLE *Necklace, Misc. Ess.* (1840) V. 104 He burst into unstanchable blubbering of tears. **1880** SWINBURNE *Stud. Shaks.* (ed. 2) i. 51 That perpetual source of debate unstanchable and inexhaustible dispute.
2. Unquenchable, insatiable.
1426 LYDG. *De Guil. Pilgr.* 13053 Evere ther glotons appetyt Ys so ful off ffals delyt, So gredy and so vnstaunchable. *c* **1430** *Pilgr. Lyf Manhode* III. xiv. (1869) 142 Vnstaunchable is my wille;.. my affeccioun may haue no fulfillinge. **1440** J. SHIRLEY *Dethe K. James* (1818) 25 Consideryng his unstaunchable covetise. **1590** *Serpent of Deris.* A iij b/2 His greedy unstancheable thirste of covetousnes. **1625** JACKSON *Creed* V. xxxii. §3. 307 The flames of.. ill-kindled loue.. hath caused his stonie heart to boyle over with vnstaunchable bloudie malice.

un'stanched, *ppl. a.* [UN-¹ 8.]
1. a. Not satisfied; unsated.
c **1374** CHAUCER *Boeth.* II. pr. vi. (1868) 54 Rycchesse may nat restreyne auarice vnstaunched. **1591** LYLY *Endym.* II. ii, I will.. teare the flesh with my teeth, so mortall is my hate, and so eger my unstaunched stomacke. **1596** SHAKS. *3 Hen. VI,* II. vi. 83 Stifle the Villaine, whose vnstanched thirst Yorke, and yong Rutland could not satisfie. **1613** HEYWOOD *Silver Age* III. i, His maw Vnstaunch't, He still the thicke Nemean groues doth stray.
b. Unrestrained; not stopped.
1621 *N. Riding Rec.* (1894) 34 Being unstaunchte they [*sc.* deer] raunge over all the adjacent fieldes. **1826** SCOTT *Woodst.* xiv, I conjure thee by the unstanch'd wound. **1850** BLACKIE *Æschylus* II. 263 Fresh and unstaunched woes.
2. Not made staunch or water-tight.
1607 J. CARPENTER *Plaine Mans Plough* 220 Slugging on the waves of this ocean with an unstancht ship. **1760-72** H. BROOKE *Fool of Qual.* (1809) II. 126 The elements.. came pouring from unstanched roofs.
fig. **1610** SHAKS. *Temp.* I. i. 51 Though the Ship were.. as leaky as an vnstanched wench.

†**un'stanged,** *ppl. a. Obs.*⁻¹ [UN-¹ 8.] Not stung.
13.. *Metr. Hom.* (MS. Ashm. 42) fol. 126 b, Nedders vnstangid sall þai bere; Poysonouse drink sall þaim noȝt dere.

un'starch, *v.* [UN-² 4.] *trans.* To free from stiffness.
1600 B. JONSON *Cynthia's Rev.* III. ii, [He] dares not smile Beyond a point, for fear t'unstarch his look. **1641** J. TRAPP *Theol. Theol.* iv. 174 [Paul] unstarcht the Oratours speech (as one phrases it) afore Felix. **1683** KENNETT *Erasm. on Folly* 32 He cannot unstarch his gravity.
Hence **un'starching** *vbl. sb.*
1647 TRAPP *Comm. 1 Cor.* i. 17 Witness his [*i.e.* Paul's] artificiall unstarching of the Oratours speech, *Act.* 26.

un'starched, *ppl. a.* [UN-¹ 8.] Not starched; *fig.* free from stiffness.
[**1775** ASH.] **1827** *Archæologia* XXI. 254 An unstarched or unplaited pocket. **1861** T. A. TROLLOPE *La Beata* I. vi. 124 The unstarched ease of her own undisguised character. **1894** MRS. DYAN *Man's Keeping* II. 137 You look.. as limp as an unstarched collar.

un'starred, *ppl. a.* [UN-¹ 8.] Not marked with a star or asterisk; not decorated with a star; *spec.* of a Parliamentary question: denoting that a written reply is required. Also *fig.*
[**1775** ASH.] *a* **1849** J. C. MANGAN *Poems* (1859) 65 Perfect bliss, unstarred with woe. **1854** S. DOBELL *Balder* iii. 12 The keeper of the palace-gate.., although he come In fashion as a commoner, unstarred, Lets the prince pass. **1890** HESSELS *Latin-A.S. Glossary* p. xli, I trust that.. no A.S. words [are] left unstarred. **1902** *Hansard Commons* 18 June 958 To ask the First Lord of the Treasury if arrangements can be made by which the answer to an unstarred Question shall be communicated to the Member asking the Question within an hour after the sitting of the House on the day.. the Question is asked. **1919** LD. CURZON in *Hansard Lords* 11 Mar. 633 His alternative, I think, was this—that one is to assume that a Question in future, starred or unstarred, is a Question only. **1978** T. WILLIS *Buckingham Palace Connection* i. 10 Prayers had been said, and the business of the afternoon began, as usual, with a series of four Unstarred Questions.

un'started, *ppl. a.* [UN-¹ 8.]
1. Unstartled.
1659 W. CHAMBERLAYNE *Pharonnida* I. IV. 215 Sound sleeps, unstarted innocence, Softn'd their Beds.
2. Not started or begun.
[**1775** ASH.] **1898** *Daily News* 14 Nov. 5/1 Three blocks are now approaching completion,.. and only two remain unstarted.

un'starting, *ppl. a.* (UN-¹ 10.)
1748 RICHARDSON *Clarissa* (1811) VI. 118 Unbroken, unstarting slumbers.

un'startled, *ppl. a.* (UN-¹ 8.)
1659 W. CHAMBERLAYNE *Pharonnida* I. I. 96 Desp'rate men, Unstartled with those dangers. *Ibid.* III. v. 474 Unstartl'd at The Rivers depth. **1796** COLERIDGE *Destiny of Nations* 346 The plough-man.. Turned up fresh sculls unstartled. **1823** MRS. HEMANS *Siege of Valencia* i, Train'd to hear The trumpet's blast unstartled. **1833** M. SCOTT *Tom Cringle* xix, [The snake], the only unstartled thing in the neighbourhood, continued steadily.. on its course.

un'startling, *ppl. a.* (UN-¹ 10.)
1729 SAVAGE *Wanderer* II. 230 Calm thoughts the deed revolve, And now, unstartling, fix the dire resolve. **1891** J. C. ATKINSON *Moorland Par.* 38, I have been accustomed to regard the sheep as a quiet unimpressive sort of creature, with unstartling habits.

un'state, *v.* [UN-² 6 b.]
1. *trans.* To deprive of state, rank, or estate.
c **1586** C'TESS PEMBROKE *Ps.* LXXXIX. xiv, Takes he his weapon? thou the edge rebatest... Would march with kingly pomp? thou him unstatest. **1605** SHAKS. *Lear* I. ii. 108, I would vnstate my selfe, to be in a due resolution. **1611** SPEED *Hist. Gt. Brit.* IX. viii. 490/2 [They] proceeded to vnstate him of that goodliest portion of France. **1624** F. WHITE *Repl. Fisher* 572 The Romane Pope hath a direct power to depose and vnstate them [*sc.* kings]. **1879** J. TODHUNTER *Alcestis* 30 Alack! the best of us May Zeus unstate.
2. To deprive of the character of a state.
1647 WARD *Simp. Cobler* 22 States are unstated, Rulers growne Over-rulers.. Churches decayed.

un'stated, *ppl. a.* [UN-¹ 8.] Not stated or declared.
[**1775** ASH.] **1864** PUSEY *Lect. Daniel* i. 14 Daniel.. left unstated the grounds of his non-participation in their steadfastness. **1900** *Westm. Gaz.* 19 June 9/3 The assertions he makes, and especially the points he leaves unstated.

un'stately, *a.* (UN-¹ 7.)
1860 RUSKIN *Mod. Painters* V. 296 Within certain black and unstately iron railings.

un'statesmanlike, *a.* (UN-¹ 7 c.)
1796 LD. SHEFFIELD in *Ld. Auckland's Corr.* (1862) III. 357 The miserable unstatesmanlike mode of taxation which has prevailed. **1837** LYTTON *Athens* I. 456 A daring, but no unstatesmanlike stroke of policy. **1880** MCCARTHY *Own Times* IV. 397 Mr. Gladstone's sudden resolve was openly condemned as petulant and unstatesmanlike.
Hence **un'statesmanlikely** *adv.*
1846 MRS. GORE *Eng. Char.* I. 326 There are moments.. when the strongest ministerial mind becomes unstatesmanlikely enfeebled.

unstathelfast, *a.*: see UN-¹ 3.

un'station, *v.* (UN-² 3.)
1840 BROWNING *Sordello* v. 603 The men and women stationed hitherto Will I unstation.

un'stationary, *a.* (UN-¹ 7.)
1832 WHEWELL in *Life* (1881) 149, I shall be very unstationary (if there be such a word) for the next three weeks.

un'stationed, *a.* (UN-¹ 9.)
1760 C. JOHNSTON *Chrysal* I. 23 Though I could give their ships information how to avoid our squadrons, yet they fell into the hands of unstationed privateers.

unsta'tistic, *a.* (UN-¹ 7.)
1839 CARLYLE *Chartism* iv. (1858) 21 So much can observation altogether unstatistic.. ascertain for itself.

unsta'tistical, *a.* (UN-¹ 7.)
1868 VISCT. STRANGFORD *Select.* (1869) II. 304 That unstatistical city [Constantinople].

un'statutable, *a.* [UN-¹ 7 b.] Not in accordance with, contrary to, a statute or statutes.
1634 LAUD *Wks.* (1857) VI. 388 That they use not long, undecent hair,.. nor any other like unstatutable novelty. **1691** *Case of Exeter Coll.* 22 These severe and unstatutable proceedings. **1723** SWIFT *Argts. agst. Power Bps.* Wks. 1841 II. 218/2 In the present bishop of Meath's case that plea did not avail, although the lease were notoriously unstatutable. **1794** BURKE *Corr.* IV. 237 A deputation to remonstrate against an unstatutable arrangement proposed for the succession to the provostship. **1851** J. B. MOZLEY *Lett.* 208 The President has summarily squashed the whole scheme, on the ground of being unstatutable.
Hence **un'statutably** *adv.*
1688 in *Magd. Coll. & Jas. II* (O.H.S.) 224 The one being unstatutably admitted. **1721** N. AMHERST *Terræ Fil.* No. 27 (1726) 147 That he governs his college arbitrarily, unjustly, and unstatutably. **1876** *Encycl. Brit.* V. 228/2 The establishment of 'vicars', or, as they are now more usually but unstatutably called, 'minor canons'.

un'staunch, *a.* Also unstanch. [UN-¹ 7.] Not sound, firm, watertight, etc.
1606 WARNER *Alb. Eng.* XVI. ci. 400 Who can lesse than smile that sees vnstanch and riueld faces, To shelter coylie vnderneath Fannes. *a* **1674** MILTON *Hist. Mosc.* v. Wks. 1851 VIII. 505 The Ships being unstaunch,.. sunk by the way. **1896** E. A. KING *Ital. Highways* 223 Not one [column] has proved unstanch through.. the storms of these long.. centuries.

unstaunchable, -ed: see UNSTANCHABLE, etc.

un'staved, *ppl. a.* [UN-¹ 8.] Not furnished with staves.
1481-90 *Howard Househ. Bks.* (Roxb.) 333 My Lord paied to J. Gravele uppon vj. bylles staved, and v. unstaved, iij. s. iiij. d.

un'stayable, *a.* (UN-¹ 7 b.)
1633 T. ADAMS *Exp. 2 Peter* ii. 2 There is.. in these a desperate and unstayable precipitation. **1940** G. GREENE *Power & Glory* II. i. 113 It had been set up in a minute clearing by a small farmer the forest must have driven out, .. an unstayable natural force which he couldn't defeat with his machete. **1980** D. K. CAMERON *Willie Gavin* xviii. 177 He had risen on the unstayable tide of his master's success.

un'stayed, *ppl. a.*¹ [UN-¹ 8 + STAY *v.*¹] Not stayed or stopped; unhindered, unimpeded.
1600 FAIRFAX *Tasso* XX. xciii. 382 A thunderbolt he was.. that.. of his comming swift, and flight vnstaid, Eternall signes in hardest rockes hath wrought. **1638** JUNIUS *Paint. Ancients* 314 His vast and unstayed understanding. **1820** PRAED *Poems* (1864) II. 40 Unchecked, unstayed, he hurries on. **1851** MRS. BROWNING *Casa Guidi Wind.* I. 730 To strike electric influence through a race, Unstayed by city-wall and barbican.

un'stayed, *ppl. a.*² [UN-¹ 8 + STAY *v.*²] Unsupported, †unstable.
1594 T. B. *La Primaud. Fr. Acad.* II. 184 For one kinde thereof [*sc.* consent] is firme and stedfast, and another weake and vnstayed. **1596** SPENSER *F.Q.* VI. i. 20 He.. layd On hideous strokes.. That oft he made him stagger as vnstayd. *a* **1649** DRUMM. OF HAWTH. *Poems* Wks. (1711) 55 Some young Phaeton, Whose skilless and unstayed Hand May prove the Ruin of the Land. **1881** CHR. ROSSETTI *Pageant,* etc., *Late Life* iii, Bear Thou in mind.. our feebleness unstayed Except Thou stay us.

un'stayed, *ppl. a.*³ [UN-¹ 8 + STAY *sb.*² 3.] Not furnished with, or confined by, stays.
1820 PRAED *Bachelor* 97 My waist, unvexed, unstayed, By fetters of the tailor's trade. **1894** *Idler* Sept. 140 In hygienic clothing, A waist and heels deep-loathing, Thy unstayed figure freely flounders.

unstayed, obs. var. UNSTAID *a.*

un'stayedness. [f. UNSTAYED *ppl. a.*²] Lack of support.
1874 PUSEY *Lent. Sermons* 326 He clad Himself with our fear, that He might array our unstayedness with the solidity of His virtue.

un'staying, *ppl. a.* [UN-¹ 10.] Not stopping or pausing.
1616 W. BROWNE *Brit. Past.* II. iv. ad fin., I feare,.. Ere I have ended my sad history, Unstaying Time may bring on his last houre. **1682** OTWAY *Venice Preserved* IV. i, If I not revenge, With.. unstaying fury, Thy sufferings. **1845** E. JONES *Studies* (1879) 186 Laughing maids, unstaying,.. O'er the lights shall dart. **1883** B. SMITH *Life Ld. Lawrence* II. 449 His unstaying and pitiless advance across the wilds of Central Asia.

un'steadfast, *a.* [UN-¹ 8 and 5 b. Cf. ON. *ústaðfast-r* (older Da. *ustadfæst*).]
1. Of persons, the mind, etc.: Not steadfast in conduct or opinion; inconstant, fickle.
a **1200** *Moral Ode* 241 in *O.E. Hom.* I. 175 þo boð þa þe weren her a þanke unstedefeste. *c* **1200** *Trin. Coll. Hom.* 61 We turnen ofte to him and fro him, for we beð unstedefaste. *a* **1300** *Cursor M.* 6516 þi folk.. has don a suik; Sin þat þou com fra þam last, þou sal þam find ful vn-stedfast. **1340-70**

Alex. & Dind. 944 Huo wolde wene þat a weih woxen on elde Were wist for vnstedefast of word or of dede? *c* **1450** *Mankind* 207 in *Macro Plays* 8, I am onstedfast in lywynge; my name ys 'Mankynde'. **1502** ATKYNSON tr. *De Imitatione* III. xxii. 214, I am ryghte feble and vnstedfaste. **1568** GRAFTON *Chron.* II. 193 This king was..vnstedfast of maners and disposed to lightnesse. **1601** CAMPION *Bk. Ayres* xiv. 4 My heart..is dismaid by thee, Who art so cruell and vnsteadfast growne. **1647** H. MORE *Song of Soul*, etc. 319 When my weakened soul Unstedfast, into this Outworld doth reel. *a* **1850** ROSSETTI *Dante & Circle* I. (1874) 123 He answers Dante, confessing his unsteadfast heart. **1850–1** LONGF. *Gold. Leg.* ii. *Village Church*, Pardon in me The oscillation of a mind Unsteadfast.

absol. **1825** COLERIDGE *Aids Refl.* 379 In the perfect foreknowledge that they would confirm the disbelieving, alienate the unsteadfast.

2. Not remaining in the same state; liable to change or alteration: **a.** Of the world, life, etc.

c **1200** *Moral Ode* 320 in *O.E. Hom.* II. 229 We wilneð after wereldes wele þe longe ne mai ilaste, And legeð mast al ure swinc on þing unstedefaste. **1456** SIR G. HAYE *Law Arms* (S.T.S.) 33 Be caus of this divisioun, all the warld is in a wylde thocht, unstedefast. **1475** *Bk. Noblesse* (Roxb.) 3 Thoroughe sodein and variable chaunces of unstedfast fortune. *a* **1500** in *Ratis Raving*, etc. 22 Leid thi lyf with thaim that the louis for the day of the vnstedfast lyf. **1574** HYLL *Conject. Weather* i, Then shall follow an unstedfast Winter. **1591** SPENSER *Daphn.* 518 For all mens states alike vnstedfast be. **1600** TOURNEUR *Transf. Metam.* iv, Subiect unto th' unstedfast moone's controle.

b. Of persons, qualities, etc.

1483 CAXTON *Gold. Leg.* 388 b/2 Whome ought I better to chese of thyse two, or the kyng puyssaunt pardurable..or one seek unstedfast. **1513** MORE *Rich. III* (1883) 6 With large giftes he get hym unstedfaste frendeshippe. **1535** COVERDALE *Prov.* v. 6 She regardeth not the path of life, so vnstedfast are hir wayes, that thou canst not knowe them. **1600** HOLLAND *Livy* 671 The assured loialtie of the captaines..was but vaine, fickle, and unsteadfast.

3. Not firmly established or fixed; readily moving or changing place; not firm or steady.

13.. *Propr. Sanct.* 158 in *Archiv Stud. neu. Spr.* LXXXI. 93 He made Nettes to beo cast In to þe se vnstudefast. **1398** TREVISA *Barth. De P.R.* XII. xxxii. (Bodl. MS.), þe pecock haþ an vnstedefaste and an yuel schape heede. **1563** *Mirr. Mag., Induct.* xxxiii, Her iyes vnstedfast rolling here and there. **1596** SHAKS. *1 Hen. IV*, I. iii. 193 As full of perill.. As to o're-walke a Current, roaring loud, On the vnstedfast footing of a Speare. **1657** AUSTEN *Fruit Trees* II. 28 The farther off the Branches are from the Roote, the more loose, and unsteadfast they are. **1793** WORDSW. *Descr. Sk.* 252 Bare steeps, where Desolation stalks, afraid, Unsteadfast, by a blasted yew upstay'd. **1864** DORA GREENHILL *Lyra Myst., Soul Garden.* xii, These Lilies..That quiver with unsteadfast light.

fig. **1817** JAS. MILL *Brit. India* II. v. vii. 621 The unsteadfast basis on which the power of the leaders at Poonah was placed.

Hence **un'steadfastly** *adv.*

1559 GUEST *Let. to Cecil* in Strype *Ann. Ref.* (1709) I. App. xiv. 38, I have neither ungodly allowed anything against the Scripture, neither unstedfastly done anything contrary to my writing. **1611** COTGR., *Inconstamment*,.. vnstedfastly, mutably, waueringly.

un'steadfastness. [f. prec.] The quality of being unsteadfast: **a.** Of persons or conduct.

a **1300** *Cursor M.* 27793 O suernes cums..vnstedfastnes, o will wandring. **1384** CHAUCER *L.G.W.* Prol. 526 A ful gret neglygence Was it to the to write onstedefast-nesse Of women. *c* **1440** *Promp. Parv.* 367/2 Onstedefastnesse, *instabilitas.* *a* **1500** *Chaucer's Dream* 200 Wherefore I doubt ..Her variance and vnsteadfastnes. *a* **1548** HALL *Chron., Hen. VIII*, 144 b, Then was rehersed to the Frenchemen their doublenes [and] their vnstedfastnes. **1649** BP. REYNOLDS *Hosea* ii. 91 The falsenesse and unstedfastnesse of our Hearts. **1694** KETTLEWELL *Comp. Persecuted* 58 Let not any other Persons unsteadfastness in thy ways..cause me to waver. *a* **1850** ROSSETTI *Dante & Circle* I. (1874) 99 Many times I cursed the unsteadfastness of my eyes. **1860** PUSEY *Min. Proph.* 90 God, in answer, promises to heal.. their fickleness and unsteadfastness.

b. Of life, fortune, etc.

1508 *Dunbar's Poems* (S.T.S.) 321/19 Sen in this warld thare is no sekernes,..I tak my leve at all vnstedfastnes. **1561** BECON *Sick Man's Salve* (1572) 5 O the vnstedfastnesse of mans life! **1585** T. WASHINGTON tr. *Nicholay's Voy.* IV. xxix. 150 b, By chaunge of time and vnstedfastnesse of fortune this so flourishing a citie is brought to..ruine.

un'steadied, *ppl. a.* (UN-[1] 8.)

1809–14 WORDSW. *Excurs.* VII. 115 A Priest he was by function; but..By books unsteadied, by his pastoral care Too little checked. **1865** *Sat. Rev.* 19 Aug. 240/1 It is not the drunkenness of the unsteadied hand, the rolling gait, and stammering tongue.

un'steadily, *adv.* [UN-[1] 11. Cf. UNSTEADY *a.*] In an unsteady manner.

1556 J. HEYWOOD *Spider & Flie* Bb iij b, To se these flies now: so vnstedily stagger, So late so redie. **1690** LOCKE *Hum. Und.* III. x. §31 He that uses his Words loosly and unsteadily, will either be not minded, or not understood. *c* **1700** CONGREVE *Ovid's Art of Love* Wks. 1773 III. 276 This way and that unsteadily they rove, And, never fix'd, are fugitives in Love. **1738** BOLINGBROKE *Idea Patriot King* (1749) 71 Considering how unsteadily and unsystematically even the best of men are apt often to proceed. **1817** COLERIDGE *Lay Serm.*, '*Blessed are ye*' 37 The cup of sorrow overflows by being held unsteadily. **1847** DE QUINCEY *Sp. Mil. Nun* Wks. 1853 III. 60 As idle as the flapping sail that fills unsteadily with the breeze upon a stranded ship. **1897** MRS. E. L. VOYNICH *Gadfly* I. vii, The man approached unsteadily along the water side.

un'steadiness. [f. next.] The quality of being unsteady.

1611 COTGR., *Volubilité*,..vnsteadinesse, or an inconstant mouing. **1646** H. LAWRENCE *Comm. Angels* 120 The cause of loosenes, and laxenesse, and unsteddines in our course. **1698** FRYER *Acc. E. India & P.* 2 The unsteadiness of the Weather. **1722** WOLLASTON *Relig. Nat.* v. (1724) 85 If things are now and then mis-shaped, this infers no unsteadiness or mistake in nature. **1796** MME. D'ARBLAY *Camilla* v. 7 The unsteadiness of the boat. **1808** MITFORD *Hist. Greece* III. 88 The gross evils inherent in the Athenian constitution; its irremediable unsteadiness, its gross tyranny. **1869** TANNER *Clin. Med.* (ed. 2) 289 The insidious form begins by numbness,..unsteadiness on the legs,..till the loss of power is complete. **1875** *Economist* 16 Jan. 68/1 The unsteadiness of the [stock-]markets.

un'steady, *a.* [UN-[1] 7. Cf. OFris. *un-*, *onstedich*, MLG. *unstedich*, MHG. *unstætec* (G. *unstätig*); MDu. *onstadich*, LG. *unstadig*; etc.]

1. Not steady in position; not firm or secure; not held or kept steady.

1598 FLORIO, *Insollare*, to make loose or vnsteadie. **1601** HOLLAND *Pliny* II. 440 Some there bee, who..advise their patients to wash their unsteedie teeth with the said infusion. **1622** MABBE tr. *Aleman's Guzman d' Alf.* I. 258 Walking to and fro on the vnsteddy legges of Dis-rest. **1703** DE FOE *Hymn to the Pillory* viii, The Statesmen..Who guide us with unsteady hand. **1743** R. BLAIR *Grave* 205 The busto moulders, and the deep-cut marble, Unsteady to the steel, gives up its charge. **1800** COLERIDGE *Christabel* II. 590 Christabel in dizzy trance Stumbling on the unsteady ground. **1815** SCOTT *Guy M.* li, He glanced at some passages of the letters with an unsteady eye and an agitated mind. **1867** MORRIS *Jason* VI. 238 On their quest [they]..began to plough The unsteady plain.

transf. **1885** 'MRS. ALEXANDER' *At Bay* v, Her voice was unsteady, and Glynn noticed that she was trembling.

2. Not steady or constant in respect of conduct or purpose; fluctuating, fickle, wavering.

1598 DALLINGTON *Meth. Trav.* X 2 b, Men of light and vnsteadie braines, haue commonly sudden and sharpe conceites. **16..** MIDDLETON, etc. *Old Law* v. i, Our unsteady fancies Would question whether we yet lived or no. **1647** CLARENDON *Hist. Reb.* I. §49 So fluctuating and unsteady a testimony is the Applause of Popular Councils. **1677** YARRANTON *Eng. Improv.* a 3 b, I could not imagine which way what I lay down in my Book..should in this unsteady Age ever come to be put into Practice. **1712** BERKELEY *Pass. Obed.* Wks. 1871 III. 121 The violent humours and unsteady opposite wills of a multitude of savages. *a* **1770** JORTIN *Serm.* (1774) III. 16 The tyranny of evil habits, and the easy descent from an unsteddy virtue to those habits. **1819** KEATS *Otho* I. i, You have intrigued with these unsteady times To admiration. **1849** FROUDE *Nemesis of Faith* 136 Unsteady minds began to grow uneasy. **1871** B. TAYLOR *Faust* II. I. v. 6 Let naught howe'er it sound make thee unsteady.

absol. **1828** MOIR *Mansie Wauch* Prelim., The unsteady may take a hint concerning what it is possible for one of..a stout heart to go through with. **1872** [see UNSTEADY *v.*].

3. Marked or characterized by absence of steadiness or regularity; not regular, even, or uniform.

1690 LOCKE *Hum. Und.* II. xiv. §22 If the Motion of the Sun were as unequal as that of a Ship driven by unsteady Winds. **1759** STERNE *Tr. Shandy* II. ii, The unsteady uses of words, which have perplexed the clearest and most exalted understandings. **1798** SOUTHEY *Henry the Hermit* 58 The lamp that stream'd a long unsteady light. ?**1821** BRYANT *Winter Piece* 4 When the unsteady pulse Beat with strange flutterings. **1862** A. MEADOWS *Man. Midwifery* 186 Unsteady gait; when the woman walks the chest is held back. **1884** *Truth* 13 Mar. 372 The badness of the road is aggravated by unsteady driving, and a defective type of rolling stock.

un'steady, *v.* [UN-[2] 6 a.] *trans.* To deprive of steadiness; to render unsteady.

1532 W. WALTER *Guystarde & S.* A ij, The wretched lyfe of osyosyte..Unstedyeth the wyt. **1646** H. LAWRENCE *Comm. Angels* 122 How doth hee unsteddy our steps, and intimidate us, by putting scruples in our wayes. **1748** RICHARDSON *Clarissa* VII. xliv. 176 Unless the shock..(by unsteadying my hand) shall divert my aim from his head. **1812** *Examiner* 24 Aug. 540/1 Shot, shells, grape,..could not unsteady the step..of the..infantry. **1872** H. BUSHNELL *Serm. Living Subj.* 245 Waiting always on the unsteady, unsteadies even the sense of principle. **1883** STEVENSON *Treas. Isl.* ii, I was quite unsteadied by all that had fallen out.

Hence **un'steadying** *ppl. a.*

1865 MASSON *Rec. Brit. Philos.* 174 A point whence the appearance of an unusual amount of unsteadying thought may be dated.

un'steek, *v.* Now *dial.* [UN-[2] 3.] *trans.* To undo, unfasten, open. Also *fig.*

c **1250** *Hymn* in *Trin. Coll. Hom.* App. 258 He mai binde & to breke... He mai luke & unsteke michte of al þinge. *c* **1250** *Gen. & Ex.* 2828 Aaron..can wel speken; ðu salt him meten and vnsteken Him bodeword min. *a* **1300** in Horstmann *Altengl. Leg.* (1875) 26 He gethþ þe Dore to vnsteke. **1390** GOWER *Conf.* II. 128 Thus whanne he hath his cofre loken, It schal noght after ben unstoken. *c* **1400** *Laud Troy Bk.* 8239 Many a coffre was vnstoken, To drawe out robes that were y-loken. **1855**, **1868** in Yks. glossaries (*unsteck*).

b. In *pa. pple.* not clearly distinguishable from 'not closed, left open' (UN-[1] 8). Cf. UNSTOKEN.

13.. *Sir Beues* (A.) 1663 þe chaumber dore a fond vnsteke. *c* **1350** *Lybeaus Disc.* 1450 At a posterne unsteke Lybeaus gan out-breke. *c* **1470** HENRY *Wallace* IX. 1655 Gat nane, bot ane, with lyff out off that sted, For that the ȝet so lang wnstekit was.

un'steel, *v.* (UN-[2] 6 b.)

1748 RICHARDSON *Clarissa* V. 215 Why then should this enervating pity unsteel my foolish heart? **1851** C. L. SMITH tr. *Tasso* III. xxv, Her strokes on one descend Already trembling, suppliant and unsteeled.

un'steeled, *ppl. a.* (UN-[1] 8.)

1744 W. WHITEHEAD *Atys & Adrastus* 409 Why was I singl'd to perform the Part, Unsteel'd my Soul, unpetrified my Heart? **1760–72** H. BROOKE *Fool of Qual.* (1809) III. 75 My conscience was yet unsteeled. **1899** R. BRIDGES *Pater Filio* 2 Sense with keenest edge unused, Yet unsteel'd by scathing fire.

un'steep, *v.* (UN-[2] 3 + STEEP *v.*[1])

1598 FLORIO, *Dimollare*, to vnsteepe. **1633** P. FLETCHER *Purple Isl.* VI. xvii, Anon the rattling hail On earth poures down his shot..; His powder spent, the Sunne puts off his vail, And fair his flaming beauties now unsteeps.

un'steeped, *ppl. a.* (UN-[1] 8.)

1626 BACON *Sylva* §402 Next the wheat simple of itself, unsteeped and unwatered. *Ibid.*, There was also other wheat sown unsteeped. **1766** *Compl. Farmer* s.v. *Seed*, The ground had been prepared exactly in the same manner for the steeped and the un-steeped grain. **1853** *Nicholson's Operat. Mechanic* (ed. 4) 407 For the purpose of discharging the colour out of the unsteeped flax or hemp.

un'steered, *ppl. a.* (UN-[1] 8. Cf. MSw. *ostyrad*, Sw. *ostyrd*.)

1729 SAVAGE *Wanderer* III. (1761) 49 Like a frail Bark thy weaken'd Mind is tost, Unsteer'd, unbalanc'd, 'till its Wealth is lost. **1886** *Pall Mall G.* 23 Feb. 4/2 The unsteered, storm-driven voyage of the crazy craft.

un'stemmed, *ppl. a.*[1] [UN-[1] 8 + STEM *v.*[2] Cf. MDu. *ongestemt*.] Not stemmed or stopped.

1732 BERKELEY *Serm. to S.P.G.* 25 This unstemmed Torrent of Profaneness.

un'stemmed, *ppl. a.*[2] [UN-[1] 8 + STEM *v.*[4] 3 a.] Not having the stalk and midrib removed.

1883 J. R. DODGE *Manuf. Tobacco* iii. 24 The law established the rate at 5 cents per pound for unstemmed smoking, with 2 cents for stemmed. **1894** *Times* 16 Aug. 6/5 (U.S. tariff), Wrapped tobacco, unstemmed.

un'stenched, *a.* (UN-[1] 9.)

1822 COBBETT *Rur. Rides* (1885) I. 103 It is one of those pretty, clean, unstenched, unconfined places that [etc.].

†**un'stented**, *ppl. a.* *Sc. Obs.* [UN-[1] 8 + STENT *v.*[2]] Not assessed.

1605 *Extr. Aberd. Reg.* (1848) II. 272 To disburding thame of the taxatioun of fyue hundreth pundis,..quhilk sowme of fywe hundreth pundis lyis yit vnstentit.

un'step, *v.* (UN-[2] 5, 7 + STEP *v.* 11, 7.)

1853 READE *Christie Johnstone* xiii. 202 Flucker.. unstepped his mast in two fathom water. **1883** *Man. Seamanship for Boys* 243 If there is anything wrong at the mast-head,..unstep the mast and rectify it. **1883** *Pall Mall G.* 9 May 2/1 The novelty consists in the mast being made to unstep in rough weather.

un'stercorated, *ppl. a.* (UN-[1] 8.)

1821 SCOTT *Pirate* iv, A man's mind always grovelling in mould, stercorated or unstercorated.

†**un'stern**, *a.* *Obs.* Also 4 **vnsterne**, **-sterin**, **-sturen**. [App. an alteration of *austern* AUSTERE *a.*, by association with STERN *a.*] Severe, stern.

a **1300** *Cursor M.* 464 Bot he was merred of hys mint, Fulson he fand vnsterne stint. *Ibid.* 3461 þair strut it was vn-stern stith. *Ibid.* 24540 (Edinb.).

†**un'sternly**, *adv.* *Obs.* Also 4 **vnsturne-**, **vnsturen-**, **vnsterly**. [f. prec. + -LY.[2]] Severely, sternly; grimly.

a **1300** *Cursor M.* 7450 O bodi gret, o granis lang, Vnsternli [*Gött.* vnsterly] semed he be strang. *Ibid.* 16031 þai stert þam forth vnsterli [*Gött.* vnsternli], Wit a ful bald bere.

un'stick, *v.* [UN-[2] 3.] **1.** To cause to become unstuck.

1706 STEVENS, *Desempegar*,..to unstick, unglew. **1748** RICHARDSON *Clarissa* VII. 125 The other [foot] riveted to its native earth, bemired..beyond the possibility of unsticking itself.

2. *Aeronaut. intr.* (occas. *refl.*). To take off (*from* the surface of the ground, water, etc.).

1912 *Aero* May 134/1 It attains a high speed when running awash and 'unsticks' (*decoller*) very easily. **1913** *Flight* 19 Apr. 432/1 A head wind helps them materially to 'unstick' themselves from the water. **1913** *Captain* Sept. 1074/2 It is necessary to design the floats with the greatest care, so that they may 'unstick', or leave the water easily. **1926** *Chambers's Jrnl.* Sept. 581/2 It needs almost as long a run as the ordinary aeroplane to 'unstick'. **1964** G. LYALL *Most Dangerous Game* xix. 152 When she unstuck from the water ..we went away low. **1977** J. GARDNER *Werewolf Trace* i. 15 The British Airways Trident unstuck from the cold stressed-concrete.

Hence **un'sticking** *vbl. sb.*

1926 'N. SHUTE' *Marazan* vi. 206, I took the whole length of the aerodrome to get off. It was some time since I had flown a Thirty-four, and unsticking was never her strong point at the best of times.

'unstick, *sb. Aeronaut.* [f. the vb.] The moment of take-off. Also *attrib.*

1935 C. G. BURGE *Encycl. Aviation* 606 *Unstick*, the moment during the take-off when an aerodyne definitely leaves either the ground (or a solid platform) or water. **1936** *Jrnl. R. Aeronaut. Soc.* XL. 519 Stalling to the extent of losing two-thirds of the static thrust, while it increases the 'unstick' time due to reduced acceleration, has only a small effect on the length of the take-off run. **1966** D. Francis *Flying Finish* xii. 154 Inside the windowless lavatory compartment it was impossible to tell the exact moment of unstick, but the subsequent climb held me close anyway against the wall, as I faced the tail. **1969** K. Munson *Pioneer Aircraft 1903–14* 154/2 The 1904 multiplane had an 'unstick' speed of some 31 m.p.h. and was tested at Streatham, but apparently made no flights of significant length.

un'stiffen, *v.* (UN-[2] 6.)
1611 Florio, *Distirizzare*, to vnstiffen, to vnbenum. **1855** Mrs. Gaskell *North & S.* xxvi, Then her rigid face unstiffened from its gray frostbound expression. **1894** A. Robertson *Nuggets*, etc. 20 The prospect of a fee unstiffened his rheumatic joints.

un'stiffened, *ppl. a.* (UN-[1] 8.)
1648 Hexham II, *Ongestijft*, Vnstifned, or Loose. **1889** Swinburne *Study B. Jonson* 96 The poem..would be worthy of very high praise if the texture..were unstiffened and undisfigured by..awkward inversions. **1893** *Daily News* 17 Apr. 6/3 Some..have determined to abide by the unstiffened dresses of last year.

un'stiffening, *vbl. sb.* (UN-[1] 13.)
1832 Coleridge *Lett.* (1895) 761 A sort of unstiffening of my long dormant joints and muscles.

un'stifled, *ppl. a.* (UN-[1] 8.)
1742 Young *Nt. Th.* II. 121 Art, brainless art! our furious charioteer (For nature's voice unstifled would recal) Drives headlong. **1842** Browning *Christina* iv, Just this or that poor impulse Which for once had play unstifled, Seems the sole work of a life-time. **1863** *Pilgr. over Prairies* I. 156 A profusion of nut-brown hair..fell unstifled by cap, untortured by steel or curl paper.

un'stigmatized, *ppl. a.* (UN-[1] 8 a (*c*).)
[**1775** Ash.] **1778** [W. H. Marshall] *Minutes Agric., Digest* 6 Should this Impostor be suffered to stroll abroad unstigmatized. **1806–7** J. Beresford *Miseries Hum. Life* VII. lxxi, Who..manage their inuendos so adroitly, that you are obliged to let them pass unstigmatized. **1814** Wordsw. *Excurs.* VII. 798 Nor left unstigmatized those fatal fields On which the sons of mighty Germany Were taught a base submission.

un'still, *a.* (UN-[1] 7. Cf. OE. *unstille*, OHG. *unstilli*, MLG. *unstil*, obs. Du. *onstil*.)
[**1648** Hexham II, *Onstil*, Vnstill, or Disquiet.] **1743** C. Wesley in *Jrnl.* (1805) I. 247 Some very unstill sisters, who always..tried who could cry loudest. **1823** E. Moor *Suffolk Words* 184 A maid undressing an unstill child. **1903** Kipling in *Windsor Mag.* Sept. 363/1 She never kept still. She kept very unstill.
Hence **un'stillness**. (In quots. after OE. *unstillnes*, *-nys*.)
1846 Thorpe tr. *Ælfric's Hom.* II. 375 He..tries these five senses, who through curiosity and unstillness wastes them uselessly. **1875** *Anderida* I. vii. 121 When some..attendants discovered the unstillness to Osgood's companions.

un'stilled, *ppl. a.* (UN-[1] 8. Cf. Sw. *ostillad*.)
1648 Hexham II, *Ongestilt*, Vnstilled, or Vn-appeased. **1817** Coleridge *Biog. Lit.* ix. I. 140 Unstilled yearning, and an original ebulliency of spirit. **1874** Pusey *Lent. Serm.* 43 To hear the cries of their unstilled hunger.

un'stimulated, *ppl. a.* (UN-[1] 8.)
[**1775** Ash.] *a* **1800** Cowper *Iliad* (ed. 2) XXIII. 469 He..wept to see..his own Unstimulated coursers thrown behind. **1825** Scott *Talism.* xxii, The future..glittered with such hues, as..his unstimulated imagination had not been able to produce. **1882** Vines tr. *Sachs' Bot.* 893 The elasticity of the stimulated and of the unstimulated filament is the same.

un'stimulating, *ppl. a.* (UN-[1] 10.)
[**1828–32** Webster.] **1844** J. Epps *Dom. Homœop.* 147 Plain, nutritious, unstimulating food. **1899** Fr. H. Burnett *De Willoughby Claim* xiii, A lifetime of narrow, unstimulating years.

un'sting, *v.* [UN-[2] 4.] *trans.* To deprive of a sting.
1612 J. Davies (Heref.) *Muse's Sacr.* Wks. (Grosart) II. 79/1 God unstings such angry Waspes and Bees. **1656** Trapp *Comm. 1 Cor.* xv. 56 Christ having unstinged death, and as it were disarmed it. **1692** South *Serm.* (1697) II. 564 He has disarmed his Afflictions, unstung his Miseries. **1827** Pollok *Course T.* II. 341 For temporal death, although unstinged, remained. **1850** R. Simpson *Mem. Worth* vi. 83 [Death] was unstinged when it encountered him.
Hence **un'stinged** *ppl. a.* (Cf. UNSTUNG[2].)
1782 J. Brown *Nat. & Rev. Relig.* III. ii, An unstinged and sweetened death.

un'stinted, *ppl. a.* (UN-[1] 8: see STINT *v.*)
1480 *Cov. Leet Bk.* 438 Þe seid Maire & Recordor maynteyn the..Frankleyns of þe Forreins..contynually to go vnstynted, and the Comons of the Cite be stynted, no man to passe his rate. **1599** Sandys *Europæ Spec.* (1632) 41 To all such..as should oppose against his Soveraigntie and unstinted power. **1622** Callis *Stat. Sewers* (1647) 24 A general Law unstinted and unbounded. *a* **1711** Ken *Hymn Festiv.* Poet. Wks. 1721 I. 410 Saints..crop unstinted Shares In the twelve pleasant Fruits it bears. **1740** Somerville *Hobbinolia* III. 29 With unstinted Joy His Heart o'erflows. **1811** Scott *Don Roderick* I. ix, Lands, where the near Sun Gives with unstinted boon ethereal flame. **1877** 'H. A. Page' *De Quincey* II. xvi. 20 His unstinted, if not reckless liberality.
Hence **un'stintedly** *adv.*
1849 Rock *Ch. of Fathers* I. i. 8 Both these prelates borrowed unstintedly from the book of St. Osmund. **1883** *Standard* 13 April 6/4 General Angus..condemns the management unstintedly.

un'stinting, *ppl. a.* [UN-[1] 10.]
†**1.** Unceasing. *Obs.*$^{-1}$
c **1380** Wyclif *Sel. Wks.* III. 52 Alle angels.., and alle powers in þis world,..crien bi vois and unstyntinge to þee.
2. Ungrudging, lavish.
1845 Herschel *Ess.* (1857) 644 The spirit in which the demands of science have been met..has been..munificent and unstinting. **1883** W. E. Norris *No New Thing* xi, With so unstinting a hand had he ministered to the necessities of the poor.
Hence **un'stintingly** *adv.*
1857 Ruskin *Pol. Econ. Art* 200 All of these should be completely and unstintingly given. **1885** Agnes Clerke *Pop. Hist. Astron.* 147 He poured his earnings unstintingly into his crucibles.

un'stirrable, *a.* (UN-[1] 7 b.)
a **1340** Hampole *Psalter*, etc. (1884) 506 Made be þai vnstirabil as a stane til þat þi folke pass.

un'stirred, *ppl. a.* (UN-[1] 8.)
α. **13..** *E.E. Allit. P.* B. 706 At a stylle stollen steuen, vnstered wyth syȝt, Luf lowe hem bytwene lasched so hote. *c* **1375** *Sc. Leg. Saints* xliv. (*Lucy*) 255 Vnsterit scho stud stil as a crag. **1513** Douglas *Æneid* VII. xi. 53 Vnsterit lang tyme and vnmovit, Itale Now birnis into fury bellicale. **1535** Stewart *Cron. Scot.* (Rolls) III. 61 Neuir ane ox wes ȝokkit into bow, Bot lay full still into thair stall wnsteird.
β. *a* **1340** Hampole *Psalter* xxv. 12 Mi fote..departid not fro þi ryȝtwysnes bot stod vnstird ogeyne alle sclaunders. **1470–1** *Rolls of Parlt.* VI. 233/1 Uncompelled, unstirred or undesired soo to doo. **1551** Recorde *Pathw. Knowl.* I. xiv, Set the one foote of the same compasse vnsturred, in the eande of the other line. **1589** Fleming *Virg. Georg.* II. 28 Vnstird it doth remaine, And conquereth..by lasting many yeares. **1624** Gataker *Transubst.* 55 The selfe same body..sitting there still unstirred and untouched. **1628** Feltham *Resolves* 221 Like the Wind..It disperses Exhalations from the muddy Earth, which would, vnstirr'd, infect it. **1699** Bentley *Phal.* 506 It was immortal Vellum..that could last for ten Ages, though untouch'd and unstirr'd. **1830** Mrs. Hemans *Lady of Provence* 11 Many a Chatillon.., Unstirr'd by the ringing trumpet's breath, His shroud of armour wore. **1843** Ruskin *Mod. Paint.* I. II. v. iii. §27 Glassy pools, upon which the drinking cattle cast an unstirred image. **1882** 'Ouida' *Maremma* I. 192 The ilex leaves..drooping above their heads, unstirred by any breeze.

un'stirring, *ppl. a.* (UN-[1] 5 d, 10.)
1. Not causing to stir or give way. *rare*$^{-1}$.
c **1375** *Sc. Leg. Saints* vii. (*Jas. minor*) 785 Al vnsterynge þe stekyne Of þe presone & þe selynge.
2. Not stirring or moving; inactive.
a **1684** Leighton *Comm. 1 Peter* iv. (1849) II. 323 A slothful, unstirring life, will make a sickly, unhealthy life. **1818** Milman *Samor* III. 210 The dead unstirring ocean bears them on. *a* **1851** Moir *Night-Hawk* i, The midnight moon Looks sombred o'er the forest depths, that sleep Unstirring.

un'stitch, *v.* [UN-[2] 3.] *trans.* To remove stitches from; to detach or separate in this way.
1538 Elyot, *Resuo*,..to vnstytche. **1639** T. de Gray *Expert Farrier* 331 Stop both your horse eares;..stitch them up, and..[later] unstitch them. **1648** Hexham II, *Ontnaeyt*, vnsowne, or vnstitcht. **1688** R. L'Estrange *Tully's Offices* 79 As Wise men say of..Ill Grounded Friendships; 'tis better to unstich than to tear them all to pieces on a suddain. *a* **1774** Goldsm. tr. *Scarron's Com. Romance* (1775) II. 25 When he scuffled with anybody,..he ever tore or unstitched the cloaths of his adversary. **1860** *Ure's Dict. Arts* (ed. 5) I. 547 After washing, the pieces [of calico] are unstitched, and put in the hydro-extractor.

un'stitched, *ppl. a.* [UN-[1] 8.] Not stitched; unsewed.
1599 A. M. tr. *Gabelhouer's Bk. Physicke* 304/1 Nether doth the sinewe water so greate harme in an vnstitched wounde as it doth in a stitched. **1856** Geo. Eliot *Ess.* (1884) 86 To the typical German..it is indifferent..whether or not his book have every other leaf unstitched.

†**un'stithe**, *a.* *Obs.*$^{-1}$ [UN-[1] 7.] Not strong; feeble, weak.
c **1400** *Destr. Troy* 117 Till it fell hym by fortune, faintyng of elde, Unstithe for to stire, or stighttill the Realme.

un'stock, *v.* [UN-[2] 5 and 4.]
1. *trans.* **a.** To remove (a ship) from the stocks.
a **1547** Surrey *Æneis* IV. 524 Where the Troyans fast Fell to their worke, from the shore to unstock High rigged ships.
b. To dismount (a gun).
1598 Florio, *Scalcagnare*,..to vnstock, or dismount any kinde of great ordinance or artillerie.
c. To remove the stock from (a gun, etc.).
1706 Phillips (ed. Kersey), *To Unstock a Gun*, is to take off its Stock. **1726** Shelvocke *Voy. round World* 70 After we had got well to sea, we unstock'd our anchors and brought them aft. **1849** W. S. Mayo *Kaloolah* viii, Unstocking my rifle-barrel.
2. To deprive of stock.
1647 Digges *Unlawf. Taking Armes* 169 The husbandmans store being consumed, the pastures unstocked,..we shall be devoured by famine. **1667** Waterhouse *Fire Lond.* 169 Turned out of their callings, and unstocked by the loss of that ruffle.
3. To empty of occupants.
1655 G. S. in Hartlib *Ref. Commonw. Bees* 28, I am confident, had I continued my digestions any considerable time, I had soon unstock[ed] nigh a dozen of Hives. **1865** W. G. Palgrave *Arabia* II. 328 The conflict of the Roses did not unstock the England of a few years later.

un'stocked, *ppl. a.* [UN-[1] 8.]
1. Not furnished with a stock.
1388 in Nicolas *Hist. Royal Navy* (1847) II. 475 La hulk ..ove lapparaill..v. ankres dont un de eux est unstokked. **1497** *Naval Acc. Hen. VII* (1896) 290 Serpentynes.. stokked cxvj, vnstokked xxv. **1513** N. West in Ellis *Orig. Lett.* Ser. I. I. 70 A greate piece of ordenaunce of iij. yerds longe and mor, unstocked. **1599** Hakluyt *Voy.* II. II. 107 We had nowe but two ankers left vs, which were vnstocked and in hold. **1681** *Cal. Treas. Bks., 1681–5*, 4 The value of 200 barrels of guns or muskets unstocked. **1805** W. Hunter in *Naval Chron.* XIII. 8 Our anchors being unstocked, as is the custom in Indiamen,..we found great difficulty in.. steadying them, in order to get the anchors in the stocks.
2. Not provided with a stock of goods.
1633 D. R[ogers] *Treatise Sacr.* i. 161 A poore unstockt man is easily perceived in his wares, the small store and choice therof.
3. Not stocked with animals, etc.
1697 Walsh *Life V.* ¶7 in Dryden *Virgil*, Wars had laid Italy almost waste; the Ground was Uncultivated and Unstock'd. **1750** T. Carte *Hist. Eng.* II. 719 The lands lay uncultivated and the farms unstocked, by reason of.. continual depredations. *a* **1787** G. White *Selborne* vii, This chase remains un-stocked to this day. **1794** R. J. Sulivan *View Nat.* I. 24 One bold and inartificial whole, unstocked with animation.
4. (See STOCK *sb.*[1] 44.)
1825 T. Hook *Sayings* Ser. II. II. 94 While sleepy lacqueys, their hose ungartered, and themselves unstocked, are crawling down the second staircase to breakfast.

un'stockinged, *ppl. a.* (UN-[1] 8.)
[**1775** Ash.] **1812** W. Tennant *Anster F.* II. xxvii, Her roguish boys with bare unstocking'd feet. **1845** Talfourd *Vac. Rambles* I. 232 They were clad in brown serge, unstockinged.

†**un'stoic**, *v.* *Obs.*$^{-1}$ (UN-[2] 6 b.)
1735 Swift *Let.* in Maggs *Cat.* No. 445 (1923) 238, I long apprehended you would have the power to corrupt me. I shall therefore unstoick myself to attend you.

un'stoken, *ppl. a.* *Obs.* or *dial.* [Cf. UNSTEEK *v.* b.] Opened; not closed or shut.
1421 Hoccleve *Min. Poems* 151/333 On a nyght..Left was the Erles Chambre dore vnstoken. **1828** Carr *Craven Gloss.*, *Unstoken*, unshut.

un'stolen, *ppl. a.* (UN-[1] 8 b. Cf. MDu. *ongestolen*.)
1533 J. Heywood *Johan & Tib* (Brandl) 246 Yet it may lye safe ynough vnstolen. **1837** Carlyle *Misc. Ess.* (1840) V. 19 The world would let us keep it unstolen for Fourteen whole years.

un'stone, *v.* [UN-[2] 3 and 4.]
1. *trans.* To convert from a stony state.
1594 Carew *Tasso* (1881) 49 But let his hand that hardest harts gently Doth pierce, them both vnstone and mollifie. *Ibid.* 92 This fained sorrow drew from many a freake True teares, and harts vnstoand most hardened.
2. To castrate.
1611 Cotgr., *Escouiller*, to geld, lib, vnstone, cut away the stones of. *a* **1693** *Urquhart's Rabelais* III. xxxi. 255 He had unstoned Friar Caulderiel.

†**un'stonied**, *ppl. a.* *Obs.*$^{-1}$ [UN-[1] 8.] Unastonished.
c **1475** *Golagros & Gaw.* 642 Thair wes na staluart vnstonait, so sterne wes the stound!

un'stoniness. (UN-[1] 12. Cf. next.)
1661 J. Childrey *Brit. Baconica* 49 The unstoniness of the Country.

un'stony, *a.* (UN-[1] 7.)
1611 Florio, *Insassoso*, vnstonie, without stones. **1675** Evelyn *Terra* (1676) 132 The dust of unstony high-wayes, where the drift of Cattel, and much passage is.

un'stooping, *ppl. a.* (UN-[1] 10.)
1593 Shaks. *Rich. II*, I. i. 121 The vn-stooping firmenesse of my vpright soule. **1816** Byron *Ch. Har.* III. xlvii, As stands a lofty mind, Worn, but unstooping to the baser crowd. **1818** Milman *Samor* II. 272 The crash Of branches rent by his unstooping helm. **1869** Ruskin *Q. of Air* (1874) 17 She wears the crested and unstooping helmet.

un'stop, *v.* [UN-[2] 3 and 7. Cf. (M)Du. *ontstoppen*.]
1. *trans.* To free from being stopped up or closed.
(*a*) **1398** Trevisa *Barth. De P.R.* XVII. xiii. (Bodl. MS.), Comyn merche vnstoppeþ and openeþ þe splene and brekeþ þe stone. *c* **1489** Caxton *Sonnes of Aymon* xii. 306 He.. vnbounde hym and vnstopped his eyen. *c* **1561** Veron *Free-will* 57 b, Except the Lorde did..unstop their eares, and cleare the eyes of theyr myndes. **1584** Cogan *Haven Health* ix. 31 It maketh..the bellie laxatiue,..and vnstoppeth the veines. **1611** Bible *Isaiah* xxxv. 5 Then..the eares of the deafe shalbe vnstopped. **1637** N. Whiting *Albino & Bellama* 1963 Who will not..Galen try, To weaken humours, and unstop the pores? **1700** Motteux *Quix.* (1733) II. 186 The first thing we did was to unty the Hands of Zoraida's Father, and to unstop his Mouth. **1809** Malkin *Gil Blas* VII. vii. ¶9 My heart was softened, and my ears were unstopped. **1871** Spurgeon *Treas. Dav.* Ps. li. 15 He..fears to speak till the Lord unstops his shame-silenced mouth.
(*b*) **1530** Palsgr. 768/2 Unstoppe nat the bottell tyll we shall drinke on it. **1584** B. R. tr. *Herodotus* II. 102 Priuily vnstopping one or two of hys bottles, the wyne flowed out. **1604** E. G[rimstone] *D'Acosta's Hist. Indies* IV. xii. 241 When the melting is finished, they vnstoppe the pottes and draw forth the mettall. **1645–50** Boate *Ireland's Nat. Hist.* xvii. §7 (1652) 138 The Iron it self descendeth to the lowest part of the furnace, called the Hearth; the which being filled, ..they unstop the Hearth, and open the mouth thereof. **1660** Boyle *New Exp. Phys. Mech.* I. 21 To unstop the Valve to let out any Air. **1742** *Lond. & Country Brew.* I. (ed. 4) 73 In the Spring you must unstop your Vent-hole, and thereby see whether your Drink doth ferment or not. **1758** Reid tr. *Macquer's Chym.* I. 265 Unstop all the registers of the

reverberatory. **1823** J. Badcock *Dom. Amusem.* 45 If the bottle be stopped, the colour will presently disappear; but when it is unstopped, the colour soon returns again. **1854** *Hull Improv. Act* 32 [To] make, rebuild, clear out, unstop, or in anywise alter any sewer. **1866** Furnivall *Bk. Quinte Essence* 4 *marg.*, After many days unstop your distiller.

transf. **1664** Boyle *Exper. Colours* 35 Such White Fumes I have seen afforded by unstopping a Liquor.

b. *intr.* To become opened.

c **1440** *Ipomydon* 1261 Ipomydon was sore travailed... Hys arme vnstoppid; þe blode gan falle.

2. To pull or draw out (an organ-stop).

1855 Browning *Master Hugues* 139 Say the word, straight I unstop the Full-Organ, Blare out the mode Palestrina.

3. (See stop *v.* 28.)

1840 R. H. Dana *Bef. Mast* xxv, They were heave-ho-ing, stopping and unstopping, pawling, catting, and fishing for three hours.

Hence **un'stopping** *vbl. sb.*

1611 Cotgr., *Desbouchement*, an vnstopping. **1660** Boyle *New Exp. Phys. Mech.* xxxvii. 314 Upon the unstopping of the Glass. **1676** More *Remarks* 83 Upon the unstopping of the lower end, all the water.. will run down.

un'stoppable, *a.* (un-^{1} 7b.)

1836 T. Hook *G. Gurney* v, 'And,' said I, 'you carried home your spoils'. 'Not I,' exclaimed my unstoppable companion. **1895** W. Platt *Women* 15 A cattle-train—a blind, rolling, unstoppable force.

Hence **,unstoppa'bility; un'stoppably** *adv.*

1961 Webster, Unstoppably. **1966** D. F. Jones *Colossus* i. 13 There is no way of walking back. The whole point is the Project's unstoppability. **1975** K. P. Barr in Barr & Line *Ess. Information & Libraries* iii. 40 He had..the entire programme in his head from the start and moved firmly and unstoppably towards its completion. **1980** R. Adams *Girl in Swing* xii. 125 He was generous to the point of embarrassment, having..a kind of baffling unstoppability when it came to paying restaurant bills. **1984** *Times* 11 Aug. 19/8 An audience of adults and children chattered unstoppably.

un'stopped, *ppl. a.* [un-^{1} 8. Cf. Sw. *ostoppad* in sense 2.]

1. Not stopped up or closed.

1398 Trevisa *Barth. De P.R.* vii. x. (Bodl. MS.), þe weies of þe brayne be vnstopped of þat humoure. *c* **1440** *Jacob's Well* 216 ȝif ȝoure pyt in his entrees be stylle opyn & vnstoppyd. **1513** Sir E. Howard in Ellis *Orig. Lett.* Ser. iii. I. 149 He hath bored an C agore hoolis in her and left unstopte, that the water cam in. **1599** T. M[oufet] *Silkwormes* 58 If also carelesnesse haue left a rift, or chincke vnstopped in thine aged wall. *a* **1608** Dee *Relat. Spir.* i. (1659) 419 The hole which was not greater then the thickness of a brick unstopped. **1683** Boyle in *Phil. Trans.* XVII. 636, I have kept the Bottle of prepar'd Water..in the same unstopt Vessel. **1758** *Ann. Reg., Chron.* 96/2 Suffocated..by the steam of 40 buts of unstopped beer. **1825** J. Nicholson *Operat. Mechanic* 719 Gilding the unstopped parts with the proper amalgam. **1887** *Field* 24 Dec. 952/2 Our fox ran within short distance of main earths in a wholly unstopped country.

†**2.** Unstuffed. *Obs.*$^{-1}$

1434 *E.E. Wills* (1882) 102, iij quisshonus of the same colour vn-stopped.

3. Not stopped or hindered.

1621 G. Sandys *Ovid's Met.* iii. (1626) 60 So haue I seene an unstopt torrent glide With quiet waters. *Ibid.* xv. 319 He might, vnstopt, haue entred without feare: But I withstood. **1796** *Ann. Reg.* 168 Let the frequent wain, unstopp'd by rains, Clear the dry hayfield of its dusky piles! **1803** *Edwin* I. x. 152 That Edwin is no more, the voice of rumour, unstopped by opposition, has long declared. **1816** J. Scott *Paris Revisit.* (ed. 3) 20 We passed on with our trunks unopened and unstopped.

4. *Phonetics.* (See stopped *ppl. a.* 7.)

1874 H. Sweet in *Trans. Philol. Soc.* 471 Relaxation: a) stopped consonants to unstopped:..b) unstopped to diphthongal vowel. **1877** —— *Handbk. Phonetics* 78, 79.

5. *spec.* Of verse-lines: Not ending with a stop.

1874 Furnivall in *Trans. New Shaks. Soc.* I. 73 Shakspere's often use of the unstopt line.

un'stopper, *v.* (un-^{2} 3, 4.)

1839 F. A. Griffiths *Artill. Man.* 185 [He] runs the carriage up and back, assists to hold on the fall, stoppers and unstoppers it. **1860** *Family Economist* 7 Jan. 15/1 Unstoppering.—This operation is..likely to be required.., for the stoppers of decanters, smelling-bottles, &c... frequently become fixed. **1879** *Man. Artill. Exerc.* 473 Stopper and shift the fall. Unstopper.

un'stoppered, *ppl. a.* (un-^{1} 8.)

1861 Wynter *Soc. Bees* 455 An unstoppered bottle of ipecachuana.

un'stopple, *v.* (un-^{2} 3, 4.)

1611 Cotgr., *Destoupé*, vnstopped, vnstoppelled. *a* **1693** *Urquhart's Rabelais* iii. Prol. 6 There did he..unbung it,.. unstopple it [F. *destouppoit*].

un'store, *v.* [un-^{2} 4 and 5.]

1. *trans.* To deprive of stock.

1618 Breton *Court. & Countryman* A 4 b, Your state is weakened and your Land wasted, your woods vntimberd, your Pastures vnstored.

2. To take out of store.

1883 *Daily News* 18 Sept. 3/3 Until the furniture and other articles..stored hastily..have been unstored and examined.

un'stored, *ppl. a.* [un-^{1} 8.]

1. Not supplied with a store or stores; unfurnished. Const. *of, with.*

1603 Knolles *Hist. Turks* (1621) 1209 The fields at length lay now untilled, the pastures unstored. **1636** Pagitt *Christianogr.* (ed. 2) iii. 92 Neither was our Countrey unstored of reliques. **1807** J. Barlow *Columb.* ix. 92 And mark thy native orb!.. Tho' still unstored with light her silver horn. **1854** Lever *Dodd Family Abroad* lxxiii. 611 My ungifted and unstored intellect.

2. Not stored up; unhoarded.

a **1770** Akenside *Inscriptions*, '*Ye powers unseen*' 27 Nor shall a passion move Across my bosom unobserv'd, unstor'd By faithful memory.

un'storied, *ppl. a.* (un-^{1} 8.)

[**1775** Ash.] **1880** *Contemp. Rev.* Mar. 425 He laid his 'Prentice-hand upon the fair Unstoried smoothness of the column. **1890** 'R. Boldrewood' *Col. Reformer* (1891) 224 Farewell they of the unstoried herd!

un'stormed, *ppl. a.* (un-^{1} 8.)

1695 Addison *To Somers* Wks. 1721 I. 7 To you the Hero of my verse reveals His great Designs,..determining the doom Of Towns Unstorm'd, and Battels yet to come.

un'stormy, *a.* (un-^{1} 7.)

1823 Byron *Age of Bronze* ii, A calm, unstormy wave, Which over-sweeps the world.

un'stout, *a.* (un-^{1} 7.)

1545 Ascham *Toxoph.* i. (Arb.) 75 Make moche of those shaftes of youres, for they knowe neyther stoute nor vnstoute. **1746** D. Graham *Writings* (1883) I. 107 Long to resist they seem'd unstout.

un'stoved, *ppl. a.* (un-^{1} 8.)

[**1775** Ash.] **1863** *Act 26 Vict.* c. 22 Refined Sugar unstoved, pounded, crushed, or broken.

un'stow, *v.* [un-^{2} 3.] *trans.* To take out of stowage; to clear (a hold, etc.) of the articles stowed in it.

1726 Shelvocke *Voy. round World* 75 Half the hold must have been unstow'd to get at them. **1745** P. Thomas *Jrnl. Anson's Voy.* 106 We..unstow'd the Anchor, to be in Readiness. **1800** Colquhoun *Comm. Thames* ii. 59 The Lumpers unstowed the casks in the hold. **1856** Kane *Arct. Expl.* I. x. 105 We have to unstow the hold, and deposit its contents in the store-house. **1891** *Labour Commission* Gloss., *Unstowing* or *Breaking out*, the act of conveying the goods packed in a ship from the place occupied whilst travelling to the square immediately under the hatchway.

fig. **1748** Smollett *Rod. Rand.* xli, When they found my hold unstowed, they went all hands to shooling and begging.

un'stowed, *ppl. a.* [un-^{1} 8.] Not stowed.

[**1775** Ash.] **1884** *Imp. Dict.* IV. 519/3 Unstowed cargo or cables.

un'straight, *a.* (un-^{1} 7.)

1650 J. Nicoll *Diary* (Bann. Cl.) 39 The unstraght Royall airmy, or these quha foght for the King. **1671** [R. MacWard] *True Non-conf.* 122 The Church-policie..only holdeth out indirect, unstraight and ambiguous rules, applicable to any forme. **1860** H. Marryat *Resid. Jutland* I. 8 On the opposite side..rise the tall unstraight church spires.

un'straightened, *ppl. a. rare*$^{-0}$. (un-^{1} 8.)

[**1775** Ash.] **1846** Worcester (citing Taylor).

unstraight'forward, *a.* (un-^{1} 7.)

1887 A. C. Yate *Eng. & Russia* 443 Blame attaches solely to the Liberal Government then in power, for its tortuous and unstraightforward policy.

un'straightness. (un-^{1} 12.)

a **1693** *Urquhart's Rabelais* iii. xliv. 363 The unstreightness is so irregular, or the Corruption so evident.

un'strain, *v.* [un-^{2} 3.] *trans.* To free from strain; to relax. Chiefly *fig.*

1616 B. Jonson *Masques, Love freed fr. Ignorance*, 'Lesse they could the knot vn-straine Of a riddle, which she put. **1650** Fuller *Pisgah* ii. xi. 236 Since which time the Levites had unstrained their credit by their exemplary zeale against the Idolaters. **1843** E. Jones *Sens. & Event* 120 Omnipotent sleep shall thy life unstrain. **1883** R. Haldane *Workshop Receipts* Ser. ii. 125/1 To clean morocco leather, strain well over a board;..when done, unstrain the leather, and dry.

†**un'strainable,** *a. Sc. Obs.* [un-^{1} 7b + strain *v.*^{2}] Not distrainable.

1609 Skene *Reg. Maj.* Table 62 The Lord of ane vnstrenzeabill tenement, may saise the samine in his awin hands, for the arrierages, and byrunne fermes.

un'strained, *ppl. a.* [un-^{1} 8, 8c.]

1. Not subjected to straining or stretching; free from strain. Also *fig.*

13.. *E.E. Allit. P.* A. 248 Pensyf, payred, I am forpayned, & þou in a lyf of lykyng lyȝte In paradys erde, of stryf vnstrayned. **1612** Drayton *Poly-olb.* ix. 418 Taking a milk-white Bull, vnstrained with the yoke. **1690** Child *Disc. Trade* viii. 132 The Dutch..would buy our unstrained Cloth, and carry it into Holland, and there strain it. **1882** Minchin *Unipl. Kinemat.* 126 The ratio of the strained to the unstrained area. **1894** *Westm. Gaz.* 1 June 1/1 Their loyalty to the Cabinet would be unstrained by the work and worry of an Autumn Session.

transf. **1659** W. Chamberlayne *Pharonnida* v. ii. 158 That usurped diadem; which he..beheld without His unstrained reach.

b. With *for*: Not strained after.

1748 Richardson *Clarissa* (1811) VI. 177 The blush.. was a deep-dyed crimson, unstrained for.

2. Not forced or produced by effort.

1580 Stanyhurst *Æneis*, etc. (Arb.) 152 Heere percase carpers wyl twight his iollitye youthful. Strong reason vnstrayned that weake obiection aunswers. **1627** Hakewill *Apology Power & Providence of God* i. ii. 13 Which [Greek word] by an easie and vnstrained derivation, implies the breath of God. *a* **1639** T. Carew *Poems* (1651) 130 The true brood of Actors, that alone keep naturall unstrain'd Action in her throne. **1776** Mickle *Camoens' Lusiad* Introd. 140 The most natural unstrained harmony, is the just characteristic of the style of Camoens. **1802** Lamb *G. F. Cook* Wks. 1908 I. 47 This quality of unstrained mirth..is a prime feature in his character. **1871** Mrs. Whitney *Real Folks* xii, The pure, clear spaces where such things seemed to be fit and unstrained. **1898** *Contemp. Rev.* Aug. 188 Honours, like the gentle rain from heaven, fell upon him unstrained.

3. Not passed through a strainer; not cleared or purified by straining.

1828–32 Webster s.v., Unstrained oil. **1853** Royle *Mat. Med.* (ed. 2) 477 Press out the juice, and evaporate it, unstrained, to a proper consistence.

un'straitened, *ppl. a.* (un-^{1} 8.)

1665 Glanvill *Scepsis Sci.* (ed. 2) i. 2 All those enoblements that were suitable to the measures of an unstraightned Goodness. [**1755** Johnson, *Unstraitened*, not contracted.] **1855** Singleton *Virgil* II. 473 On their fainty shoulders bear they off Their bows unstraitened.

un'strange, *a.* (un-^{1} 7.)

c **1391** Chaucer *Astrol.* ii. §17 To knowe the verrey degree of any maner sterre straunge or vnstraunge after his longitude.

un'strangulable, *a.* (un-^{1} 7b.)

1824 Lamb *Lett.* (1886) II. 190 Are we unstrangulable, I ask you?

un'strap, *v.* (un-^{2} 4b.)

1828 Spearman *Brit. Gunner* (ed. 2) 178, [No.] 2 unstraps the rammer-head,..and [no.] 4 unstraps the sponge. **1836** Dickens *Sk. Boz, Gt. Winglebury Duel*, Up started the ostlers,..unstrapping, and unchaining, and unbuckling. **1862** *Cornhill Mag.* V. 34, I had a large cape folded up with my *valise*; so unstrapping this [etc.].

Hence **un'strapping** *vbl. sb.*

1851 *Household Words* IV. 299/2 She..busies herself with the unstrapping of my knapsack.

unstra'tegic, *a.* (un-^{1} 7.)

1831 Carlyle *Sart. Res.* iii. iii, The most undiplomatic and unstrategic of these [men].

un'stratified, *ppl. a.* (un-^{1} 8.)

[**1775** Ash.] **1802** Playfair *Illustr. Hutton. Th.* 57 The unstratified minerals exist..in veins intersecting the stratified. **1873** Dawson *Earth & Man* xi. 269 Boulder clay ..is usually destitute of any lamination or subordinate stratification; whence it is often called Unstratified Drift.

un'streaked, *ppl. a.* (un-^{1} 8.)

[**1775** Ash.] **1861** Whyte Melville *Good for Nothing* I. 101 Her black hair was as yet unstreaked with a line of grey. **1871** Geo. Eliot *Middlem.* xxxvi, Mrs. Viney's openness and simplicity were quite unstreaked with suspicion.

un'stream, *v. Educ.* [un-^{2} 3 + stream *v.* 14: cf. *unstreamed* s.v. un-^{1} 8a(*a*).] *trans.* In a school, to end the practice of streaming different abilities; to fail to stream in this way. Also *absol.*

1961 *Listener* 12 Oct. 565/3 Primary headmasters who have unstreamed their schools report that they have been able to raise the standard of work of the school as a whole. **1969** *Guardian* 29 Sept. 12/2 As a head, when a majority of the staff wanted it, he unstreamed a school. **1971** *Daily Tel.* (Colour Suppl.) 2 Apr. 18 (*caption*) You can't unstream—as the Swedes have done—and still hang on to classroom discipline.

Hence **un'streaming** *vbl. sb.*

1964 *Listener* 3 Dec. 904/1 Teachers..oppose unstreaming because they think it would threaten the interests of the 'A' stream. **1972** *Guardian* 9 June 9/5 Unstreaming, or teaching children in mixed ability groups.

†**un'strenge,** *v. Obs. rare.* [un-^{2} 6a, 7 + *strenge* strength *v.*] **a.** *trans.* To unstrengthen. **b.** *intr.* To lose strength.

a **1225** *Leg. Kath.* 1269 Is nu se storliche unstrenget ower strengðe..swa þet [etc.]? *a* **1225** *Juliana* 44 Heo unstrengeð þerwið ant we strengeð on ham.

†**un'strength,** *sb. Obs.* [un-^{1} 12.] Lack of strength; weakness, feebleness.

c **1200** Ormin 16915 Þatt follc þatt..nohht ne darr ȝet stiȝhenn upp To follȝhenn heȝhe mahhtess..Forr hiss flæshess unnstrenncþe. *a* **1225** *Ancr. R.* 232 We iknowen ure owune feblesce & ure owune muchele unstrencðe. *a* **1250** *Owl & Night.* 751 Hwy atwitestu me myne vnstrengþe? **1382** Wyclif *2 Macc.* iii. 24 Alle that weren hardye for to obeye to hym..weren togidre turnyd in to vnbyndynge, or vnstrengthe, and inward dreed.

†**un'strength,** *v. Obs.* [un-^{2} 6b.] *trans.* To weaken, enfeeble.

a **1225** *Ancr. R.* 138 Þis fette kelf haueð þe ueondes strencðe to unstrencðen, & forte makien buwen touward sunne. *Ibid.* 274 Heo unstrencðeð þe unwiht [*v.r.* unwicht] & deð him suluen o fluhte anonrihte.

un'strengthen, *v.* [un-^{2} 6.] *trans.* To deprive of strength; to weaken.

1598 Florio, *Sgagliardare*,..to enfeeble, to vnstrengthen. **1604** Marston *Malcontent* ii. iii. D j, If griefe that..Beduls the eye, vnstrengthens all the blood, Chance to remooue me to another world. **1890** Talmage *From Manger to Throne* 244 Enervated by his long fasting, and doubly unstrengthened by a sudden relaxation.

Hence **un'strengthening** *vbl. sb.*

1623 Sir J. Eliot in J. Forster *Life* (1864) I. 166 Reason affected not the cries..of the people, nor policy the unstrengthening of the state.

un'strengthened, *ppl. a.* (un-^{1} 8.)

1597 Hooker *Eccl. Pol.* v. viii. §4 Surely the Church..is neither of capacity..so weak, nor so unstrengthened, I know, with authority from above. **1806–20** Wordsw. *Resting-place* 3 If we advance unstrengthened by repose.

1836 *Going to Service* xviii. 233 The thin places left unstrengthened, and broken loops untaken up.

'unstress, *sb. Phonetics.* [UN-^{1} 12.] Absence of stress; the pronunciation of a syllable, etc., without stress.

1945 E. K. CHAMBERS *Eng. Lit. at Close of Middle Ages* i. 61 In this play aureate language . . is exaggerated, almost to the point of burlesque, and is accompanied by anapaestic unstress, but not alliteration. **1953** C. E. BAZELL *Linguistic Form* iii. 30 In the case of phonemic oppositions, the most striking case of a contradiction between the criteria of freedom of distribution and frequency would be the opposition of stress and unstress. **1970** B. M. H. STRANG *Hist. Eng.* vi. 341 Hesitation between the spellings *u* and *o* in unstress does not indicate a sound midway between the two phonemes.

un'stressed, *ppl. a.* (UN-^{1} 8.)

1883 H. SWEET in *Trans. Philol. Soc.* 212 Not only in most unstrest syllabls of polysyllabic words, but also in the unstrest monosyllabic words. **1927** W. DEEPING *Kitty* ix. 118 There seemed to be comfort for him in those fields... So peaceful and unstressed. **1946** P. BOTTOME *Lifeline* ii. 17 The peasants . . unstressed, simple people.

un'stressedness. (UN-^{1} 12. Cf. prec.)

1894 F. J. CURTIS *Rimes Clariodus* 48 In its unstressedness it was not long *ē*.

un'stretch, *v.* [UN-^{2} 3, 7.] *trans.* and *intr.* To relax, slacken.

1611 COTGR., *Destendre*, to vnbend, slacken, vnstretch. **1825** J. NICHOLSON *Operat. Mechanic* 752 The mechanism by which the strings of a violin are stretched or unstretched. **1888** *Philos. Mag.* Feb. 109 An annealed iron wire which is being heated when . . it is stretched by a slight weight . . suddenly unstretches.

Hence **un'stretching** *vbl. sb.*

1611 COTGR., *Destenture*, an vnbending, vnstretching, slackening. **1844** *Civil Eng. & Arch. Jrnl.* VII. 365 The consequent stretching and unstretching [of the rope].

un'stretched, *ppl. a.* (UN-^{1} 8, 8 c.)

1648 HEXHAM II, *Ongereckt*, Vnstretched, . . or Vnextended. **1678** CUDWORTH *Intell. Syst.* 781 A Substance whose Duration is Vnextended or Vnstretched out in Time.

un'strewed, *ppl. a.* (UN-^{1} 8.)

[**1775** ASH.] **1791** COWPER *Iliad* VIII. 569 On the river's brink . . space he found unstrew'd With carcases. *Ibid.* x. 235 A vacant space . . Unstrew'd with bodies of the slain.

un'striated, *ppl. a.* (UN-^{1} 8.)

1877 HUXLEY *Anat. Inv. Anim.* viii. 480 Bundles of muscular fibres, usually unstriated. **1895** *Naturalist* 339 Numerous small unstriated pebbles.

un'stricken, *ppl. a.* (UN-^{1} 8 b.)

1548 ELYOT, *Impercussus*, vnstryken. [Also in Baret, Florio, and Hexham.] **1848** T. AIRD *Nebuchadnezzar* I. ii, He . . lies through night unstricken by the winds. **1863** KINGLAKE *Crimea* (ed. 4) II. vi. 137 Those who remained unstricken [by cholera].

un'stridden, *ppl. a.* (UN-^{1} 8 b.)

1570 LEVINS *Manip.* 61 Vnstriden horse, *incons[c]ensus*.

un'stride, *v.* (UN-^{2} 3.)

1635 QUARLES *Embl.* III. ii. 21 If the fool unstride His prauncing Stallion, thou mayst up and ride.

unstridu'losity. (UN-^{1} 12.)

1871 BROWNING *Pr. Hohenst.* 1363 Dumb menace in that mouth, Malice in that unstridulosity!

un'strike, *v.* [UN-^{2} 9.] (See quot. 1678.)

1614 LATHAM *Falconry* I. iii. 10 Then vnstrike her hood, and lure her . . with a bitte or two of meate. [**1678** PHILLIPS (ed. 4), *To Unstrike the hood*, in Faulconry, to draw the strings that it may be in a readiness to pull off.] **1852** R. F. BURTON *Falconry Valley Indus* iii. 26 After slipping the knot that held the jesses to the leash, I gently 'unstruck' my Shikrah's hood, [and] pulled it off.

un'striking, *vbl. sb.* (UN-^{2} 3, 8.)

1567 *S.P. Dom. Eliz.* XLIV. 17 (P.R.O.), The vnstrikinge shavinge Blackinge newe nailinge bucklinge and letheringe of . . decaied Corselettes . . sore cankared and Rustie.

un'striking, *ppl. a.* (UN-^{1} 10.)

1768–74 TUCKER *Lt. Nat.* (1834) II. 36 The mental eye . . will see it obscure, unstriking, and no better than common objects. **1880** 'MARK TWAIN' *Tramp Abroad* II. 223 A monotonous variety of unstriking dishes.

un'string, *v.* [UN-^{2} 4 and 4 b.]

1. a. *trans.* To relax or remove the string(s) of (a lyre, bow, etc.).

(*a*) **1611** FLORIO, *Discordare*, . . to vnstring, to vntune. **1621** BURTON *Anat. Mel.* I. ii. iii. xv, A musitian will string and vnstring his lute. **1725** POPE *Odyssey* VIII. 107 His golden lyre Demodocus unstrung. *a* **1774** W. WHITEHEAD *Enthusiast* xv, Enthusiast, go, unstring thy lyre; In vain thou sing'st. **1869** SPURGEON *Treas. Dav.* Ps. xxi. 1 Our weakness unstrings our harps, but his strength tunes them anew.

(*b*) **1707** E. SMITH *Phædra & Hippolitus* II. 24 His idle Horn on fragrant Mirtles hung, His Arrows scatter'd, and his Bow unstrung. **1833** J. RENNIE *Alph. Angling* 52 Let us suppose that a bow . . be bent and unstrung in the water. **1856** 'STONEHENGE' *Brit. Rural Sports* 507/1 To Unstring the Bow. [Directions follow.]

b. To undo the strings of (a purse). Also *absol.*

1681 *Swearing Master* 1 Come Wil, unstring, and pay your Groat. **1685** *Roxb. Ball.* (1888) IV. 285 Now unstring your purse, and be kind to the poor. **1771** COLMAN *Prose Sev. Occas.* (1787) III. 188 To swathe and dress it [he] first unstrings his purse. **1861** GEO. ELIOT *Silas M.* ix, My father wasn't quite so ready to unstring as some other fathers I know of. **1884** *Manch. Exam.* 11 June 5/1 They would have to unstring the national purse, and find the money.

2. a. To detach from a string. Also *fig.*

1697 DRYDEN *Virg. Past.* VI. 29 For want of better Bands His Garland they unstring, and bind his Hands. **1763** GIBBON *Misc. Wks.* (1814) V. 387 Unstringing the beads from the rosary of antiquity. **1850** R. G. CUMMING *Hunter's Life S. Africa* xvi. I. 367 Having unstrung the dice, . . they rattle them between their hands, and drop them on the ground.

b. To detach from union; to separate, sever.

1674 N. FAIRFAX *Bulk & Selv.* 46 So do but unstring my soul and body, . . the thing is gone.

3. a. To render lax or weak; to disorder (the nerves, etc.).

1700 DRYDEN *Ovid's Met.* XII. 748 Light was the Wound; but in the Sinew hung The Point: and his disabled Wing unstrung. **1768–74** TUCKER *Lt. Nat.* (1834) II. 273 Terror and trepidation would unstring our nerves. *Ibid.* 498 So far as to unstring the very sinews of government. **1800** S. & HT. LEE *Canterb. T.* IV. 51 The very apprehension . . might unstring her nerves. **1817** SHELLEY *Rev. Islam* XI. xx, That voice unstrung his sinews, and he threw His dagger on the ground. **1845** M. PATTISON *Ess.* (1889) I. 26 His conscience must have been unstrung by the . . engagement he had made.

b. To unnerve, upset (a person).

1897 MISS F. F. MONTRÉSOR *At Cross Roads* ii, I could not live with so much sympathy, it would unstring me.

c. *intr.* Of the nerves: to be released from tension, to become lax.

1906 HARDY *Dynasts* II. VI. v. 308 My nerves unstring, my friends, my flesh grows weak. **1972** D. BLOODWORTH *Any Number can Play* xv. 130 He systematically slackened his body and mind . . feeling the knots twitch loose, the nerves unstring.

Hence **un'stringing** *vbl. sb.* and *ppl. a.*

1824 LADY GRANVILLE *Lett.* (1894) I. 256 The fatigue and worry . . have been very unstringing. **1833** HT. MARTINEAU *Cinnamon & Pearls* ii. 28 It gave more time for the unstringing of his nerves.

un'stringed, *ppl. a.* [UN-^{1} 8.] Not furnished with a string or strings; not arranged on a string. Also *transf.*, not accompanied by music.

1593 SHAKS. *Rich. II*, I. iii. 162 An vnstringed Vyall, or a Harpe. **1599** NASHE *Lenten Stuffe* D iij b, Or thou wilt commend thy muse to sempiternity, and haue images . . erected to her after the vnstringed silent interment and obsequies. **1655** SPURSTOWE *Wels Salvation* 73 Like loose and unstringed pearles.

un'strip, *v.* Now *dial.* and *rare.* [UN-^{2} 9.] *trans.* To strip.

1596 WARNER *Alb. Eng.* XII. lxxvii. 313 The Oste and Ostlers . . Came in, where he, almost vnstript, but wholly skar'de, did stand. **1637** R. ASHLEY tr. *Malvezzi's David Persecuted* 250 Any, to whom he may unstrip himselfe, and discover the secrets of his heart. **1654** GAYTON *Pleas. Notes* IV. xxiv. 281 The Villaine . . charg'd Leandra to unstrip her. **1691** T. H[ALE] *Acc. New Invent.* 27 The . . continuance of these Ships . . in their sheathing, without their being in all that time unstripp'd, for the necessary searching of their bottoms. **1764** GOLDSM. *Hist. Eng. in Lett.* (1772) II. 182 Pretended patriotism unstripped of its mask. **1823** E. MOOR *Suffolk Words* 460. **1905** in *Eng. Dial. Dict.*

un'striped, *ppl. a.* (UN-^{1} 8.)

a **1841** *Encycl. Metrop.* (1845) VII. 493 The unstriped variety of muscular fibre. **1859** *Todd's Cycl. Anat.* V. 262/1 In man and mammalia the tracheal muscles belong to the unstriped variety. **1882** *Garden* 28 Jan. 69/2 The unstriped form produces seed readily in cultivation.

un'stripped, *ppl. a.* [UN-^{1} 8.] Not stripped; not removed by stripping.

1676 HOBBES *Iliad* 158 Upon the field unstript they left these two. **1822** J. H. ALLAN *Bridal of Caolchairn* 278 An unsafe footway formed of the trunk of trees . . unstripped of their bark, and destitute of either plank or rail. **1822** COBBETT *Rur. Rides* (1830) 19 Here are farmers unable to pay men for working for them... There lie the hop-poles unstripped. **1888** *Field* 7 Jan. 27/1 Those growers whose crop [of tobacco] is still unstripped from stalks.

un'striving, *ppl. a.* (UN-^{1} 10.)

1868 W. R. GREG *Lit. & Soc. Judgm.* 62 Unambitious and unstriving, . . he finds that everything conspires to teach him the same lesson.

un'strong, *a. Obs.* or *dial.* [OE. *unstrang*, f. *un-* UN-^{1} 7 + *strang* STRONG *a.*] Not strong; feeble, weak. Also *absol.*

a **900** *O.E. Martyrol.* 13 Aug. 146 His þrowung wæs þe lengre . . þy þe hyra handa wæron unstrange hine to acwellanne. *c* **960** *Rule St. Benedict* (1885) lxiv. 121 þæt þa strangan furðor wilnien, and þa unstrangan . . heora þeowdom ne forfleon. *c* **1200** ORMIN 7911 Maȝȝdenn child iss all unnstrang Affterr wifmanne kinde. *a* **1250** *Owl & Night.* 561 þu art lutel and vnstrong. **13..** *R. Gloucester's Chron.* (Rolls) App. G. 49 Her was hunger & hete; wo was þe vnstronge. **1382** WYCLIF *1 Cor.* xi. 30 Therfore among ȝou manye syke, and vnstronge, or feble. **1398** TREVISA *Barth. De P.R.* xviii. xiii. (Bodl. MS.), Breste plates and oþer armure bi þe whiche vnstronge places of mannes bodie beþ warded. *c* **1440** *Pallad. on Husb.* I. 1110 The chaumburs in the bathis may be wrought . . other weyis fele . . al though they be vnstrenger [*v.r.* unstronger]. **1868** ATKINSON *Cleveland Gloss.* 551 He's varrey unstrong, puir chap.

un'struck, *ppl. a.* (UN-^{1} 8 b, 8 c.)

1615 J. TAYLOR (Water P.) *Faire & fowle Weather* B 3, As a measure fild with Oates or Rye Vnstrooke and heap'd, doth lye confusedly. **1705** J. PHILLIPS *Blenheim* 40 Over dank, and dry, They journey . . unstruck with Horror at the sight Of Alpine Ridges bleak. **1728** YOUNG *Ocean* lv, Who can gaze On restless seas, Unstruck with life's more restless state? **1790** BEATSON *Nav. & Mil. Mem.* I. 251 General Hawley . . sent orders to set fire to the tents, which were still unstruck in the camp. **1838** J. HILDYARD in *Life & Lett. S. Butler* (1896) II. 311 Could I bring my unstruck-off sheets with me, and insert the few remarks . . in them? **1897** *Westm. Gaz.* 29 July 7/2 She had seen 'unstruck' matches lying on the shop floor.

un'strucken, *ppl. a.* (UN-^{1} 8 b.)

c **1620** FLETCHER *False One* II. i, If this inhumane stroak be yet unstrucken.

un'struggling, *ppl. a.* (UN-^{1} 10.)

1822 MILMAN *Martyr of Antioch* 65 Bounteous God! That . . leaves you . . To feed unstruggling the fierce beast of rapine . . ! **1868** GEO. ELIOT *Sp. Gipsy* 241, I should . . rest for ever from the thought of bliss, And wear my weight of life's great chain unstruggling.

un'strung, *ppl. a.* [f. UNSTRING *v.*, or UN-^{1} 8 b.]

1. Having the string(s) relaxed or removed:

a. Of a harp, etc.

1598 FLORIO, *Scordato*, . . put out of tune, vnstrung. **1633** [? F. DAVISON] *Ps. 137* iii, Our mute harpes, untun'd, unstrung, Up wee hung On greene willowes. **1694** PRIOR *Hymn to Sun* viii, 'Till Nature's Musick lyes unstrung. **1738** WESLEY *Ps.* CXXXVII. ii, Our Harps . . We cast aside, untun'd, unstrung. **1820** BYRON *Juan* v. xxxvi. (MS.), As silent as an unstrung drum. **1821** SHELLEY *Adonais* xxxvi, The song, Whose master's hand is cold, whose silver lyre unstrung. **1871** MACDUFF *Mem. Patmos* 333 The unstrung tuneless harp.

transf. **1613** CAMPION *Descr. Lords Maske* Wks. (1909) 99 The good old Sage is silenc't, her free tongue That made such melodie, is now vnstrung. **1646** CRASHAW *Steps Temple, Ps. 137* 21 O may at once my tongue Lose this same busie speaking art, Unpearch't, her vocall Arteries unstrung. **1784** COWPER *Task* II. 728 His voice, unstrung, Grew tremulous, and mov'd derision more Than rev'rence.

b. Of a bow. Also = not strung.

1744 W. WHITEHEAD *Atys & Adrastus* 259 Behind him hung His rat'ling Quiver, and his Bow unstrung. **1797** *Encycl. Brit.* (ed. 3) II. 209/2 Now the long-bow (when unstrung) may be most conveniently covered. **1831** JAMES *Phil. Augustus* I. iv, His features . . had expanded like an unstrung bow. **1856** FITZGERALD *Salámán* (1879) 69 Salámán Call'd for an unstrung Bow—himself the cord Fitted unhelpt.

2. Weakened, relaxed; unnerved.

1692 DRYDEN *Don Sebastian* v. iii, These Sinews are not yet so much unstrung, To fail me. **1746** HERVEY *Medit. Among Tombs* 57 The Nervous Arm is unstrung; the brawny Sinews are relaxed. **1794** R. J. SULIVAN *View Nat.* II. 49 In the Sirocco wind at Naples, . . the whole system is unstrung, and the nerves seem to lose . . their tension. **1847** C. BRONTË *J. Eyre* xxix, It gave new tone to my unstrung nerves. **1866** LE FANU *All in Dark* v, Their entertainer remained behind unstrung and melancholic.

un'stubbling, *vbl. sb.* (UN-^{2} 9.)

1778 [W. H. MARSHALL] *Minutes Agric., Digest* 85 General reflections on Unstubbling.

un'stuccoed, *ppl. a.* (UN-^{1} 8.)

1882 *Cent. Mag.* XXIII. 645 The houses are built in long low lines of gray, unstuccoed adobe.

un'stuck, *ppl. a.* [UN-^{1} 8 b.] **a.** *to come unstuck*, to come to grief: see COME *v.* 25 d. **b.** *to get, come*, etc., *unstuck* (Aeronaut.), to get into the air, to take off: cf. UNSTICK *v.* 2.

1913 A. E. BERRIMAN *Aviation* xvi. 157 It is not easy to acquire a proper flight-speed while trying to rise from the water, and it is only with considerable difficulty that pilots are able to get some machines 'unstuck'. **1920** *Flight* 17 June 639/2 The machine had a very low landing-speed, got 'unstuck' after a very short run, and was very easy to fly. **1934** *Ibid.* 8 Feb. 121/2 No one seeing her for the first time would have expected her to come unstuck so quickly as she did. **1958** 'N. SHUTE' *Rainbow & Rose* viii. 295 We came unstuck at the fourth flare. **1979** *Truck & Bus Transportation* Apr. 16/3 With the motors running at high pitch, the end of the asphalt loomed up very quickly and with a deft flick of the wrist by the 'skipper' the aircraft became 'unstuck' just in time.

un'studied, *ppl. a.* [UN-^{1} 8.]

1. Not meditated on; neglected as a subject of study or thought.

c **1380** WYCLIF *Wks.* (1880) 192 þus bi þis nouelrie of song is goddis lawe vnstudied & not kepte. ? **1608** *Reynard's Deliv. fr. Turks* in *Harl. Misc.* (1744) I. 183 There is . . no language, be it never so barbarous, or hard to learn, left unstudied. **1614** in Overbury *A Wife*, etc. A 4 b, For that word, 'A goodly woman,' Prints it selfe in such a letter That it leaues vnstudied no man.

2. Not having studied; unversed (*in* something).

1642 MILTON *Apol. Smect.* 15, I . . was not unstudied in those authors which are most commended. **1650** BAXTER *Saints' R.* I. vii. 104 Men voyd of Learning, and strength of parts, unstudied and untaught. **1685** E. BOHUN *Life Jewell* in *Apol.* 30 That Learned Prelate . . was not so unstudied in the nature of Councils, as [etc.]. **1817** COLERIDGE *Lay Serm.* 77 The strict, but unstudied and uninquiring, Religionists of every denomination. **1846** HAWTHORNE *Mosses* 85 The young stranger . . was not unstudied in the great poem of his country.

†**b.** Not spent in or devoted to study. *Obs.*$^{-1}$

1645 MILTON *Tetrach.* Int. A 3 b, To cloak the defects of their unstudied yeers.

3. Not elaborated by study or care; not laboured or artificial.

1657 H. KING *Poems* 122 They bring Course and unstudy'd stuffs for offering. **1674** HICKMAN *Quinquart. Hist.* (ed. 2) Ep. A 3 Had I thought so unstudied a scrible meet to be exposed to publick view. **1697** DRYDEN *Virg. Georg.* Ded., A clearness of Notion, express'd in ready and unstudied Words. **1730** THOMSON *Winter* 468 With sense refin'd, . . Unstudy'd wit, and humour ever gay. **1798** S. &

Ht. Lee *Canterb. T.* II. 57 This scheme was not quite so unstudied as it appeared. **1817** W. Godwin *Mandeville* I. 207 She expressed herself with the greatest ease, her sentiments were unparrotted and unstudied. **1856** *N. Brit. Rev.* XXVI. 233 He had a homely,—apparently unstudied mode of expression. **1884** Church *Bacon* ix. 220 Easy and unstudied as his writing seems.

un'studious, *a.* (un-[1] 7.) Also *absol.*
1663 Boyle *Usef. Exp. Nat. Philos.* I. 9 To live ignorant or unstudious of the laws and constitutions of that great Commonwealth. **1841** Myers *Cath. Th.* III. §17. 64 The boundary line between them is really more indistinct than the unstudious would suppose. **1859** Helps *Friends in C.* Ser. II. I. 228 Besides, how encrusted their names are with the curses of unstudious boys.

unstuff, *v.* [un-[2] 3, 4.]
1. *trans.* To empty (*of* people).
c **1450** *Merlin* xx. 358 Moo [men] he myght haue hadde yef he wolde, but he seide he wolde not lete the reame be vnstuffed of peple.
2. To free from being stuffed.
1611 Cotgr., *Desestouffer*, to emptie, euacuate, vnstuffe. **1675** Han. Woolley *Gentlew. Comp.* 163 Saffron is a great Cordial, and unstuffs the pipes of the Lungs. **1852** *Meanderings of Mem.* I. 56 The brain [it] will scavage and the breast unstuff.

un'stuffed, *ppl. a.* [un-[1] 8.] Not stuffed; †unfurnished.
1480 *Wardr. Acc. Edw. IV*, (1830) 131 Pilowe beres off fustian unstuffed, iiij. **1573** *Arte of Limning* A iij, A litle borde..couered with a calues skin raysed or vnderstuffed with wolle or floxe or else vnstuffed. **1592** Shaks. *Rom. & Jul.* II. iii. 37 Where vnbrused youth with vnstuft braine Doth couch his lims, there golden sleepe doth raigne. **1647** H. More *Song of Soul* II. To Rdr., If any space be left out unstuffd with Atoms.

un'stumbled, *ppl. a.* (un-[1] 8.)
1399 Langl. *Rich. Redeles* II. 82 Ho so had kunnynge and conscience bothe, To stonde vnstombled and stronge in his wittis.

un'stung, *ppl. a.*[1] [un-[1] 8 b.] Not stung.
1615 Goddard *Neaste of Waspes* F iij, Why howe nowe Waspes, are you returnd agen? I knowe vnstung remaines a worlde of men And therefore once more out. **1807** Crabbe *Birth of Flattery* 147 Such was the fiend, and so secure of prey, That only Misery pass'd unstung away. **1816** Kirby & Sp. *Entomol.* xx. II. 203 Some of them flew after me; I escaped however unstung. **1864** 'Annie Thomas' *D. Donne* III. 135 He knew too that the Bishop knew it also, and was unstung by the knowledge.

un'stung, *ppl. a.*[2] [f. unsting *v.*] Having the sting removed; deprived of the sting.
1671 Janeway (*title*), Death Unstung; A Sermon [on Rev. xiv. 13] at the funeral of T. Mowsley. **1687** Renwick *Serm.*, etc. (1776) 333 To the believing soul death is unstung.

un'stunned, *ppl. a.* (un-[1] 8.)
[**1775** Ash.] **1797** Coleridge *Osorio* III. i. 11 What ear unstun'd..might bear up against The rushing of your congregated wings?

†**un'sturted,** *ppl. a. Sc.* [un-[1] 8.] Undisturbed.
1535 Stewart *Cron. Scot.* (Rolls) III. 265 To the thrid day the parteis baith did ly Into thair tentis wnsturtit richt still.

un'sty, *v.* (un-[2] 5.)
1614 Markham *Cheap Husb.* I. i. 90 The orderliest feeding of Swine is..in the Morning earely when you vnstie them [etc.].

un'stylish, *a.* (un-[1] 7.)
1863 Mrs. Whitney *F. Gartney's Girlh.* vi, Her respectable but somewhat unstylish figure and dress.

unsub'duable, *a.* (un-[1] 7 b and 5 b.)
1611 Cotgr., *Invincible*,..vnsubduable, vnconquerable. **1622** W. Whately *God's Husb.* II. 108 The most mischievous,..and but by his strength vnsubduable corruptions of their nature. **1810** Southey *Kehama* xviii. v, Her Father's eye..spake..Stern patience unsubduable by pain. **1840** Carlyle *Heroes* iv. (1858) 291 Unsubduable granite, piercing far and wide into the Heavens! **1878** P. Bayne *Purit. Rev.* xi. 499 An unsubduable capacity to make the best of things.

unsub'dued, *ppl. a.* (un-[1] 8.)
1590 Spenser *F.Q.* III. iii. 38 T'afflict the other Saxons vnsubdewd. *a* **1628** F. Grevil *Sidney* (1652) 99 The yet unsubdued Princes of Germany. *c* **1630** Sanderson *Serm.* II. 312 There may lurk in our hearts some secret noysome lust undiscovered, and so unsubdued. **1712** Blackmore *Creation* IV. 9 If dread of death still unsubdued remains. **1794** S. Williams *Vermont* 170 His passions unsubdued, undisciplined. **1831** James *Phil. Augustus* II. iv, The still unsubdued terror of the bishop. **1863** Conington *Horace, Odes* IV. xiv. 8 They know thee now, thy strength in war, Those unsubdued Vindelici.
absol. **1835** Milman *Nala & Damayanti* 32 In his wicked thought the dastard—her yet powerless to subdue, On the unsubdued stood gazing.
Hence **unsub'duedness.**
a **1665** Goodwin *Filled w. the Spirit* vi. (1670) 141 Weakness in Faith,..unsubduedness of the Flesh. *a* **1732** T. Boston *Crook in Lot* (1805) 165 Unsubduedness of spirit. **1839** Pusey in Liddon *Life* (1893) II. 142 Vanity, unsubduedness, self in some form, has been the source of all heresy. **1878** Abp. Benson *Let.* in *Life* (1901) 176 It is, I am afraid, interior unsubduedness.

un'subject, *a.* (un-[1] 7.)
1382 Wyclif *Heb.* ii. 8 In that thing that he sugetide alle thingis to him, he lefte no thing vnsuget [*v.r.* vnsugetted] to him. **1583** Golding *Calvin on Deut.* xlviii. 281 Not any of vs ..can excuse himselfe to bee vnsubiect to such naughtinesse. **1597** Hooker *Eccl. Pol.* v. lxx. §4. 294 Aboue the highest mooueable sphere there is nothing which feeleth alteration,..but all things immutable, vnsubiect to passion. **1652** Benlowes *Theoph.* v. lxiii. 75 'Tis but a Creature, though its Essence be To change unsubject. **1672** Penn *Spir. Truth Vind.* 36 Perhaps he hath followed an Erronious Judgment, or Unsubject Affection. **1754** Miss Boothby in *Life Johnson* (1805) 75 Thus is whirled about this little machine [= Miss Boothby], which..contains a mind unsubject to rotation. **1788** D. Gilson *Serm. Pract. Subj.* xiii. 368 Were the residence of man unsubject to mutation. **1842** Tennyson *Will Waterproof* 86 My head, Which bears a season'd brain about, Unsubject to confusion. **1881** Cleland *Evol., Express. & Sens.* p. x, No doubt spirit seems a vague and intangible entity because unsubject to those methods.

unsubject, *v.* (un-[2] 6 b.)
1647 Digges *Unlawf. Taking Arms* 114 Women cannot unmarry, nor the people unsubject themselves.

unsub'jectable, *a.* (un-[1] 7 b.)
1829 Bentham *Corr.* Wks. 1843 XI. 29 Statements unsubjected and unsubjectable to the test of cross-examination.

unsub'jected, *ppl. a.* (un-[1] 8.)
138. [see unsubject *a.*]. **1513** Douglas *Æneid* VII. vii. 67 All cuntre wnsubiekyt wnder our wand. **1693** *Mem. Ct. Teckely* III. 83 There remain'd nothing but Mongats unsubjected to the Emperor. **1697** C. Leslie *Snake in Grass* (ed. 2) 252 This shews them..the utter Inconsistency of that Principle (to use their own Word) of an *Un-subjected* Light within, to all Rule, Order, or Good Government. **1758** Akenside *Ode to Gentlemen Eng.* x, Shall war's heroic arts no more engage The unbought hand, the unsubjected mind? **1800** Coleridge *Piccolom.* I. xii, A new army Unsubjected to my control. **1823** Scott *Quentin D.* i, Wild beasts..who, if unsubjected by his arts, would..have torn him [*sc.* the keeper] to pieces. **1829** Southey *Sir T. More* I. 269 The unsubjected natives..recovered the greater part of their country.
Hence **unsub'jectedness.**
1682 Penn *Salut. Faithf. Friends* 5 Such as these,.. by a loose Conversation, or Highmindedness and Unsubjectedness cause grief.

unsub'jection. (un-[1] 12 and 5 b.)
a **1653** Binning *Sinner's Sanct.* xx. Wks. (1735) 271 His Unsubjection and unsubmissive Disposition towards the good Pleasure of the Lord. **1658** Manton *Exp. Jude* iv. 227 Which argueth much unsubjection of heart to Christ.

un'subjectlike, *a.* and *adv.* (un-[1] 7 c, 11 b.)
1590 *Acts Privy Counc.* (1899) XIX. 406 Lady Broome lyveth soe disorderly and unsubjectlyke. **1606** Bp. J. King *Serm.* Sept. 21 A forrest of the most..vnchristian, vnsubject-like practises, that ever were heard of.

un'subjugate, *v.* (un-[2] 3.)
1834 Sir H. Taylor *Artevelde* II. v. ii, Those powers by this nocturnal inroad wild Surprised.., vainly I essayed To rally and unsubjugate.

un'subjugated, *ppl. a.* (un-[1] 8.)
[**1775** Ash.] **1837** Lytton *Athens* I. 416 Babylon alone remained unsubjugated by the Mede.

unsu'blimable, *a.* (un-[1] 7 b.)
1753 *Chambers' Cycl.* Suppl. s.v. *Sublimable*, Those things, which render unsublimable bodies sublimable. **1803** *Phil. Trans.* XCIII. 26 The apparent sublimation of the common flowers of zinc at the instant of their production, though totally unsublimable afterwards.

unsu'blimed, *ppl. a.* (un-[1] 8.)
1694 Salmon *Bate's Dispens.* 416/2 Some prepare it.. with the crude Sulphur and unsublimed Salt. *Ibid.* 610/1 The unsublimed Sal-Armoniack. **1771** *Phil. Trans.* LXI. 125 Any solution or combination of tin, unsublimed or undistilled. **1814** Scott *Wav.* xxiii, A simple and unsublimed taste now, like my own, would perfer a jet d'eau at Versailles to this cascade.

unsub'merged, *ppl. a.* (un-[1] 8.)
1883 *Century Mag.* XXVII. 188 Only a thin scattered fringe of bluffs was unsubmerged.

unsub'mersible, *a.* (un-[1] 7, 5 b.)
1891 W. K. Brooks *Oyster* 58 Two beautiful unsubmersible claires [= oyster-tanks].

unsub'mission. (un-[1] 12.)
1845 Jane Robinson *Whitehall* II. 252 After this evidence of unsubmission, he was detained..a close prisoner. **1865** Pusey *Eirenicon* 15 A spiritual disease, which is part of man's unsubmission to his God.

unsub'missive, *a.* (un-[1] 7 and 5 b.)
a **1653** [see unsubjection]. *a* **1716** South *Serm.* (1744) X. v. 154 A stubborn unsubmissive frame of spirit in men. **1849** Eastwick *Dry Leaves* 55 [He] would hardly brook a band of unsubmissive strangers so near his own throne. **1868** Lynch *Rivulet* cxxv. ii, The lord of quarrel..And unsubmissive will.
Hence **unsub'missiveness.**
Also *unsubmissively* adv. (Webster, 1847).
1868 Pusey *Serm. Pharisaism* 7 Heresy, unbelief, misbelief, unsubmissiveness,..spring from pride.

unsub'mitting, *ppl. a.* (un-[1] 10.)
1730 Thomson *Autumn* 840 A generous race Of unsubmitting spirit. **1783** W. F. Martyn *Geog. Mag.* II. 366 Those unsubmitting heroes. *a* **1796** Burns *'All devil as I am'* 8 The honest man.., Whose unsubmitting heart was all his crime. *a* **1835** Mrs. Hemans *Abencerrage* III. viii, Heroic spirits, unsubmitting yet. *Ibid.* xviii, A sterner tone of unsubmitting thought.

†**unsu'bordinate,** *a. Obs.* (un-[1] 7 and 5 b.)
1641 Milton *Reform.* II. 66 A certaine unquestionable Patriarchat, independent and unsubordinate to the Crowne. **1678** Cudworth *Intell. Syst.* f 2 b, An Absolute, Independent, and Un-subordinate Co-equality. **1709** Shaftesb. *Charac.* (1711) II. 335 Perpetual Strifes..shew either no Controul, or several uncontroul'd and unsubordinate Powers in Nature.

unsu'bordinated, *ppl. a.* (un-[1] 8.)
1658 Bp. Reynolds *Lord's Supper* xii. Wks. 600 There was no Schism in the Body, no part unsubordinated, or unjoynted from the rest.

†**unsu'bordinately,** *adv. Obs.* (un-[1] 11, 5 b. Cf. unsubordinate *a.*)
1634 Bp. Reynolds *Shieldes of Earth* (1636) 19 This belongeth only unto Princes (and that independently, and unsubordinately to any higher power or person, save God).

†**unsubordi'nation.** *Obs.* (un-[1] 12, 5 b.)
1656 Jeanes *Mixt. Schol. Div.* 43 This is a sufficient argument, that in the manner of the soules being there is an unsubordination unto all second causes.

unsu'borned, *ppl. a.* (un-[1] 8.)
1656 Osborne *Observ. Turks* 3 Such marks of Worship.. as he was pleased to impresse upon their yet unsuborned imaginations. **1689** Hickeringill *Ceremony-Monger* Concl. ii, The Legislative Power (unsuborn'd by Priest-craft). **1754** Hume *Hist. Eng.* I. 467 The very pulpits were bedewed with unsuborned tears. **1797** Burke *Regic. Peace* iii. 30 Such a tone..is the true, unsuborned, unsophisticated language of genuine natural feeling.

†**un-sub-presbytery.** *Obs.* (un-[1] 12.)
1659 Gauden *Tears Ch.* 449 Factions, confusions are the genuine fruites of an un-sub-Presbytery.

unsub'scribed, *ppl. a.* (un-[1] 8, 8 c.)
1571 Bp. Lesley in Bercher *Nobility Women* (Roxb.) 26 Those Letters..were unsubscribid. **1639** Fuller *Holy War* III. viii. 122 A concealed Christian,..with letters unsubscribed with any name, gave them..intelligence. **1682** Scarlett *Exchanges* 358 Bills unsubscribed are like Bonds without Seals, and are not obligatory at all. **1754** Richardson *Grandison* V. 326 A call for supper makes me leave my paper unsubscribed. **1791** Cowper *Let. to W. Bagot* 21 Sept., He had sold..a hundred of the unsubscribed-for copies.

unsub'scribing, *ppl. a.* (un-[1] 10.)
1790 Cowper *Let. to J. Hill* 17 Sept., The sum subscribed ..will defray the expense of printing; which is as much as, in these unsubscribing days, I had any reason to promise myself. **1837** *Westm. Rev.* July 73 As far as the unsubscribing public were concerned. **1851** H. D. Wolff *Madrilenia* 50 Three rows of benches, where the bourgeoisie and unsubscribing portion of the aristocracy can take places.

unsub'servient, *a.* (un-[1] 8.)
1656 Bramhall *Replic.* ii. 84 These observations..are so innocent, so indifferent, and so unsubserviant to either party, that I hoped they might pass without any censure.

unsub'sided, *ppl. a.* (un-[1] 8.)
1804 Eugenia de Acton *Tale without Title* III. 192 Their joy was mixed with a still unsubsided surprise. **1815** Scott *Guy M.* xxxix, The froth of the last draught of twopenny yet unsubsided on his upper lip.

un'subsidized, *ppl. a.* (un-[1] 8.)
1756 *World* No. 204 ⁋2 Certain unsubsidized pamphleteers. **1807** Syd. Smith *Lett. Catholics* iv, The winds, those ancient and unsubsidised allies of England. **1875** *N. Amer. Rev.* CXX. 125 The criticism and denunciation of the unsubsidized press.

unsub'sistence. (un-[1] 12, 5 b.)
1642 D. Rogers *Naaman* 180 From the old yrkesomenesse, vanity, bondage and unsubsistence.

un'substanced, *ppl. a.* (un-[1] 8.)
a **1658** [see unsinewy]. **1838** S. Bellamy *Betrayal* 162 A vasty world of form Unsubstanc'd.

unsub'stantial, *a.* [un-[1] 7 and 5 b.]
1. Having no real basis or foundation in fact.
c **1455** Pecock *Folewer* 114 þe dyuersite..was not but in wordis oonli and in fame of þe peple wiþout þe trouþ, which ful oft is founde ful vntrewe, vnsubstancial and perilose. **1715** Rowe *Lady Jane Gray* IV. 48 The vain Dream Of Empire, and a Crown,..With all those unsubstantial empty Forms. **1776** Gibbon *Decl. & F.* xiii. I. 399 These deep but unsubstantial meditations. **1810** Southey *Kehama* VII. xi, Nor build on unsubstantial hope thy trust. **1833–4** J. Phillips *Geol.* in *Encycl. Metrop.* (1845) VI. 688/2 Every new, fanciful, and unsubstantial theory. **1883** Sir H. Cotton in *Law Rep. 11 Q.B. Div.* 532 If the counter-claim is frivolous and unsubstantial.
2. Having no bodily or material substance.
1592 Shaks. *Rom. & Jul.* v. iii. 103 Shall I beleeue that vnsubstantiall death is amorous? **1605** —— *Lear* IV. i. 7 Welcome then, Thou vnsubstantiall ayre that I embrace. **1671** Milton *P.R.* IV. 399 Darkness..brought in lowring night Her shadowy off-spring, unsubstantial both. **1742** Young *Nt. Th.* IX. 118 What lengths of far-fam'd ages..roll along In unsubstantial images of air! **1794** G. Adams *Nat. & Exp. Philos.* III. xxix. 198 Time and space, which in themselves are unsubstantial, inanimate, and destitute of intelligence. **1827** Pollok *Course T.* III. 412 Of all the phantoms,..Most unsubstantial, unessential shade, Was earthly Fame. **1871** L. Stephen *Playgr. Eur.* ii. 82 Hill and plain, apparently unsubstantial as a mountain mist. **1885** R. Bridges *Eros & Psyche* I. vi, To man's purer unsubstantial part The brightness of her presence was addressed.
b. Lacking in substance or solidity. Also *Comb.*
1617 Hieron *Wks.* II. xxvi. 363 If you shall pill it [*sc.* a rush], what is vnder it but a kind of spongious, vnsubstantiall substance? **1773** *Cook's Voy.* III. xi. III. 690 They taste not unlike a green cocoa-nut, and, like them, probably they yield a nutriment that is watry and unsubstantial. **1825** J. Neal *Bro. Jonathan* II. 195 Wasted

away, in her unsubstantial proportions. **1842** DICKENS *Amer. Notes* (1850) 18/1 The suburbs are..even more unsubstantial-looking than the city. **1848** MILL *Pol. Econ.* I. xi. §3. 203 We can scarcely conceive more unsubstantial or temporary fabrics.

Hence **unsub'stantialness**.

1860 PUSEY *Min. Proph.* 465 The unsubstantialness of it all, the unsubstantiality of his lies.

unsubstanti'ality. [f. prec.] The quality of being unsubstantial; insubstantiality.

1838 A. CLISSOLD *Pract. Nature* 182 If we allow this doctrine of unsubstantiality to prevail. **1847** C. BRONTË *J. Eyre* xxiv, Something of unsubstantiality and uncertainty had beset my hopes. **1860** [see prec.]. **1883** *Fortn. Rev.* Apr. 565, I have no consciousness of what happened, after this feeling of unsubstantiality came upon me.

unsub'stantialize, *v.* (UN-[2] 6 c.)

1809–14 WORDSW. *Excurs.* IX. 66 While the gross and visible frame of things..seems All unsubstantialized. **1894** S. BROOKE *Tennyson* v. 148 The sudden unsubstantialising of the outward world..was Wordsworth's frequent feeling.

unsub'stantially, *adv.* (UN-[1] 11.)

1529 *Act. 21 Hen. VIII*, c. 16 §1 Wares whiche they untruely, subtely, unsubstauncially, and dysceytfully have made. [**1847** WEBSTER.] **1890** W. H. DAWSON *Unearned Increment* vii. 84 It matters not to the speculator how unsubstantially his houses are built. **1972** P. D. JAMES *Unsuitable Job* iii. 96 The sitting-room was elegantly but unsubstantially furnished.

unsub'stantiate, *a.* (UN-[1] 7, 5 b.)

1890 *Cath. News* 3 May 4/3 A second glance..is enough to expose the unsubstantiate fraud.

unsub'stantiate, *v.* [UN-[1] 6.] *trans.* To divest of substance; to render unsubstantial.

1799 COLERIDGE *Lett.* (1895) 284 Death!—that..so unsubstantiates the living things that one has grasped. **1819** CHALMERS *Congregat. Serm.* (1836) I. 345 You unsubstantiate all the solemnity of his proclaimed sayings. **1881** FRASER *Berkeley* 91 The premises that unsubstantiate matter, they would argue, unsubstantiate everything.

unsub'stantiated, *ppl. a.* (UN-[1] 8.)

[**1775** ASH.] **1837** HT. MARTINEAU *Soc. Amer.* II. 139 An unsubstantiated rumour of his having been seen conversing with slaves. **1856** FROUDE *Hist. Eng.* II. 46 Wolsey..set aside these unsubstantiated rumours.

unsubstanti'ation. (UN-[1] 12.)

1881 FRASER *Berkeley* 201 [Berkeley] would probably have been satisfied with this acknowledgment, as a sufficient unsubstantiation of matter.

un'subtle, *a.* (UN-[1] 7.)

a **1500** *Ratis Raving* I. 877 For sen [? *read* few] vnsubtill that are fals Eschapis vnhyngyt be the hals. **1942** A. L. ROWSE *Cornish Childhood* ii. 29 My father..was a man of simple texture, upright, hard-working..but he was uneducated, unintrospective, unsubtle. **1978** R. NIXON *Mem.* 526 The Soviets moved troops to the Chinese border in an unsubtle attempt to tie up Chinese forces and prevent them from going to the aid of Pakistan.

Hence **un'subtly** *adv.*

1934 in WEBSTER. **1959** *Times* 24 Oct. 9/1 French vowels fall unsubtly from her lips. **1976** *Daily Tel.* 8 July 16 Anyone who goes around announcing, or unsubtly implying, that he is so terribly tough, aggressive and exciting is unlikely to be any of those things.

unsub'verted, *ppl. a.* (UN-[1] 8.)

[**1775** ASH.] **1809–14** WORDSW. *Excurs.* III. 149 Pyramid Of Egypt, unsubverted, undissolved. **1835** KIRBY *Hab. & Inst. Anim.* I. v. 186 The reefs of coral that were left unsubverted. **1872** BRIERLEY *Cotters of Mossburn* xxiv. 245 Invested with much of the feeling and understanding of unsubverted human nature.

unsuc'ceedable, *a.* (UN-[1] 7 b.)

1646 SIR T. BROWNE *Pseud. Ep.* I. ii. 6 Whereof had he remained assured, he had continued silent, nor would his discretion attempt so unsucceedable a temptation.

unsu'cceeded, *ppl. a.* (UN-[1] 8.)

1667 MILTON *P.L.* v. 821 To binde with Laws the free, And equal over equals to let Reigne, One over all with unsucceeded power. **1831** T. HOPE *Ess. Origin Man* III. 229 To many a man the storms of the day remain unsucceeded by a serene sunset.

unsuc'ceeding, *ppl. a.* (UN-[1] 10.)

1639 FULLER *Holy War* IV. xxix. 220 None will willingly father unsucceeding villany. **1661** BOYLE *Certain Physiol. Ess.* (1669) 75 The Second Essay Of Un-succeeding Experiments.

unsuc'cess. [UN-[1] 12 and 5 b.] Lack of success, failure; an instance of this.

a **1586** SIDNEY *Arcadia* II. viii, He deemed his unsuccesse [**1590** unsuccessings] proceeded of their unwillingnes to have him prosper. **1655** *Nicholas Papers* (Camden) II. 292 The late busines, whose vnsuccess, as hee thought, wolde prooue of aduantage to Cromwell. **1710** STRYPE *Life & Acts of E. Grindal* vii. 70 These Unsuccesses were justly looked upon to proceed from the punishing Hand of Heaven. **1797** J. PINKERTON *Hist. Scotland* I. 86 Fortune preserved his government from any signal unsuccess. **1837** MISS MITFORD *Country Stories* (1850) 129 Chilled by so much unsuccess, the ardour of my pursuit began to abate. **1883** SWINBURNE *Misc.* (1886) 128 The definitions he gives us of his object and the tests which these offer of his success and unsuccess.

unsuc'cessful, *a.* [UN-[1] 7 and 5 b.] Not attended by, not meeting or attaining, success.

a. Of actions, endeavours, etc.

1617 MORYSON *Itin.* II. 48 Griefe of vnsuccessefull loue. **1651** BAXTER *Infant Baptism* 161 They are cited by Conradus Bergius in his most excellent Pacificatory (though hitherto much unsuccessfull) Treatise. **1685** DRYDEN *Sylvæ* Pref. ¶6 These..deserve the pains I have taken with them, which I hope have not been unsuccessful, or unworthy of my author. **1744** BERKELEY *Siris* §6 Which trials I never knew unsuccessful. **1809** COLERIDGE *Friend* 37 An unsuccessful attempt to deceive him. **1837** LOCKHART *Scott* II. xii. 407 Mr. Southey's application was unsuccessful. **1863** W. C. BALDWIN *Afr. Hunting* vii. 300, I have shot nothing; two hard unsuccessful days.

b. Of persons.

1659 W. CHAMBERLAYNE *Pharon.* II. i. 309 The unsuccessful rebel thus secured By speedy flight. **1714** ADDISON *Spect.* No. 592 ¶1 Which, as I am informed, are the Plays of many unsuccessful Poets artificially cut and shreaded for that Use. **1790** BEATSON *Nav. & Mil. Mem.* I. 100 To be unsuccessful or unfortunate, is generally to be criminal in the opinion of mankind. **1828** LYTTON *Pelham* II. x, My unsuccessful opponent..preferred a petition against me, for what he called undue means. **1890** 'R. BOLDREWOOD' *Col. Reformer* (1891) 152 If a man doesn't make money..he is regarded only as an unpractical, unsuccessful enthusiast.

absol. **1750** JOHNSON *Rambler* No. 87 ¶9 The unsuccessful vent their discontent upon those that excel them. **1898** 'H. S. MERRIMAN' *Roden's Corner* iv, So many sail to those distant havens of the unsuccessful.

unsuc'cessfully, *adv.* [UN-[1] 11. Cf. prec.] Without success.

1649 J. H. *Motion to Parl. Adv. Learn.* 35 Propensions.. which if disobeyed succeeded untowardly and unsuccessfully. **1664** DRYDEN *Rival Ladies* Ep. Ded. ¶2 Fortune.., with which wisdom does often unsuccessfully struggle in the world. *a* **1674** MILTON *Free Commw.* Wks. 1851 V. 425 Nor was the heroic Cause unsuccessfully defended to all Christendom, against the Tongue of a famous and thought invincible Adversary. *a* **1721** SHEFFIELD (Dk. Buckhm.) *Wks.* (1753) II. 177 Several letters shew his punctual performance of it, tho' unsuccessfully. **1819** SCOTT *Ivanhoe* xxv, Has your suit, then, been unsuccessfully paid to the Saxon heiress? **1873** PROCTOR *Expanse Heav.* 287 Our short-lived race..has.. not unsuccessfully carried out the daring scheme [etc.].

unsuc'cessfulness. (UN-[1] 12 and 5 b.)

c **1630** SANDERSON *Serm.* (1681) 307 The weakness, frailty, and unsuccessfulness of mens devices. **1687** BOYLE *Martyrd. Theodora* ix. 171 The unsuccessfulness he had hitherto met with in his attempt. **1742** *Johnson's Debates* (1787) II. 107 The unsuccessfulness of their endeavours. **1761** STERNE *Tr. Shandy* IV. vi, When recollecting the unsuccessfulness of his first effort in that attitude. **1837** CARLYLE *Fr. Rev.* III. IV. vi, Custine was..found guilty..of one thing, unsuccessfulness.

†**unsuc'cessible,** *a. Obs.*$^{-1}$ [UN-[1] 7.] Not admitting of succession.

1579 FULKE *Refut. Rastel* 736 So great blasphemie, as none can lightly be greater,..because it taketh away the eternall and vnsuccessible priesthood of Christ.

†**unsuc'cessing,** *vbl. sb.* (See UNSUCCESS, quot. *a* 1586.)

unsuc'cessive, *a.* [UN-[1] 7 and 5 b.]

†**1.** Unsuccessful. *Obs.*$^{-1}$

1617 WOODALL *Surg. Mate* Pref. (1639) B 6 b, To keepe a Iournall in writing..as well of the unsuccessive applications, as of the successive.

2. Not exhibiting succession.

1646 SIR T. BROWNE *Pseud. Ep.* 345 Although we be measured by the Zone of time,..yet can we not thus.. summe up the unsuccessive and stable duration of God. *a* **1676** HALE *Prim. Orig. Man.* I. iii. 90 Such parts of the visible Universe as are incorruptible, unalterable, and unsuccessive. **1737** A. BAXTER *Enq. Nat. Human Soul* 375 If this necessary Being hath no change or succession in his nature, his existence must of course be unsuccessive. **1811** A. McLEAN *Comm. Heb.* Wks. 1847 II. 281 He hath an unsuccessive priesthood, which passeth not from him to any other.

Hence **unsuc'cessively** *adv.*, †unsuccessfully.

1707 *Lond. Gaz.* No. 4333/4 The Union with Scotland,.. so often..unsuccessively attempted,..is the Joy..of all Your..Subjects.

unsuc'cessiveness. (UN-[1] 12. Cf. prec.)

1737 A. BAXTER *Enq. Nature Human Soul* 375 On the other hand, it is, I think, scarce intelligible, to apply this successiveness or unsuccessiveness (so to speak) to time itself, or to eternity, abstractedly taken.

un'succourable, *a.* (UN-[1] 7 b.)

1593 *Sidney's Arcadia* (1598) IV. 414 That in the ende some one or other might hap to do an vnsuccourable mischiefe. **1599** SANDYS *Europæ Spec.* (1605) Z 4 An vnexplicable & vnsuccorable calamitie. **1611** FLORIO, *Insoccoreuole*, vnsuccourable.

un'succoured, *ppl. a.* (UN-[1] 8.)

1422 YONG tr. *Secreta Secret.* 183 He shal be vnsocowrid whan he moste nede hath. **1596** SPENSER *F.Q.* IV. viii. 51 Him wretched thrall vnto his dongeon [he] brought, Where he remaines, of all vnsuccour'd and vnsought. **1616** W. BROWNE *Brit. Past.* II. v. 342, I have beheld A widow vine stand..Unpropt, unsuccoured, by stake or tree. **1660** *Gentl. Calling* v. 78 The many unsuccour'd extremities of the Poor. **1807** J. BARLOW *Columb.* VII. 225 He..Hems on all sides the long unsuccour'd place. **1864** *Realm* 17 Feb. 5 Is Germany to leave her kindred unsuccoured, because they cannot be counted by millions?

unsu'ccumbing, *ppl. a.* (UN-[1] 10.)

a **1833** MRS. BROWNING *Tempest* ad fin., High-seeming Death, I..have hope..of showing to thy face An unsuccumbing spirit.

un'sucked, *ppl. a.* (UN-[1] 8.)

a **1652** BROME *City Wit* IV. i, Were't not a sin to let such a foole passe unsuckt? **1667** MILTON *P.L.* IX. 583 The Teats Of Ewe or Goat dropping with Milk at Eevn, Unsuckt of Lamb or Kid.

un'sued, *ppl. a.* (UN-[1] 8, 8 c.)

1594 W. WEST *2nd Pt. Symboleographie, Chancerie* § 139 It can not be intended, that..he would have left the elder bond and debt, being of a greater summe, unsued for. **1616** T. ADAMS *Soules Sicknesse* 27 Gilianus..rewarded deserts vnsued to. **1629** MASSINGER *Picture* I. i, I will not leave a saint unsued to For your protection. **1842** WORDSW. *Poems* p. x, Such is the grace Which, though unsued for, fails not to descend With heavenly inspiration.

†**unsuffera'bility.** [UN-[1] 12.] Incapacity of suffering.

c **1425** *St. Mary of Oignies* I. v. 38 in *Anglia* VIII. 137 She lafte þe manhede of Criste, and helde vp hir mynde to þe godhede & mageste, þat she myghte fynde comforte in his vnsufferabilite.

un'sufferable, *a.* and *adv.* Now *rare* or *Obs.* [UN-[1] 7 b, 11 b, 5 b.]

1. Incapable of being suffered with patience or equanimity; not to be tolerated or endured; going beyond all natural limits: **a.** Of injuries, wrongs, etc.

a **1325** *MS. Rawl. B.* 520 fol. 31 b, We undoinde so muche unsufferable luere of oure poeple..stabblissez ant ordeinez [etc.]. *c* **1440** *Promp. Parv.* 367/2 On-sufferabyl, or ontollerable, *intollerabilis, insufferabilis.* *c* **1449** PECOCK *Repr.* III. xvii. 395 Ellis vnsufferable myscheuys of hasty domes wolde ofte falle. **1533** BELLENDEN *Livy* I. xviii. (S.T.S.) I. 100 Þe haterent and vnsufferabil tyrannye of kingis. **1597** HOOKER *Eccl. Pol.* v. xxx. §3 We know no reason wherefore any man should yet imagine it an vnsufferable euill. **1621** in Foster *Eng. Factories Ind.* (1906) I. 301 To call them to accompt..for these unsufferable wrongs. **1660** JER. TAYLOR *Ductor* I. ii. rule 8 §30 The injustice may be frequent and unsufferable. **1725** POPE *Odyssey* II. 69 Unsufferable wrong Cries to the Gods, and vengeance sleeps too long. **1763** LD. HALIFAX in *10th Rep. Hist. MSS. Comm.* App. I. 361 The Outrages..are most abominable and unsufferable.

b. Of actions, conduct, qualities, etc.

1548 GESTE *Pr. Masse* D ij, What an vnsufferable mockedge is this..of God. **1582–3** *Reg. Privy Council Scot.* III. 541 A power strange and unsufferabill to be in the persoun of ony inferior subject. **1608** MACHIN *Dumb Knt.* v. i 3, Thine adulterat..lust, Shamefull and grosse and most vnsufferable. **1651** BIGGS *New Disp.* ¶250 Unsufferable fallacies..are couched under these four. **1711** STEELE *Spect.* No. 38 ¶10 The unsufferable Affectation you are guilty of in all you say and do. **1720** SWIFT *Let. to Yng. Clergyman* Wks. 1755 II. II. 12 The common unsufferable cant of taking all occasions to disparage the heathen philosophers. *a* **1774** GOLDSM. tr. *Scarron's Com. Romance* (1775) I. 27 Upon these vast accomplishments, he had built an unsufferable degree of pride.

c. Of persons. Also *absol.*

1382 WYCLIF *2 Macc.* viii. 5 Machabeus..was maad vnsuffreable to heithen men; forsothe the wrath of the Lord is conuertid in to mercye. *c* **1450** HOLLAND *Houlate* 926 Thir birdis ilkane Besocht Natur to cess that vnsufferable. *c* **1470** HENRY *Wallace* I. 267 Unsouerable are thir pepille of Ingland. **1586** T. B. *La Primaud. Fr. Acad.* I. 112 The more that an ignorant man is lift up unto some excellencie of dignitie.., the more unsufferable he is. **1619** A. NEWMAN *Pleas. Vis.* (1840) 49 All know (vnsufferable Man) they [*sc.* women] are..beyond compare. **1678** MRS. BEHN *Sir P. Fancy* I. i, The pertest unsufferable fool he ever saw.

2. Too distressing, severe, or painful to be borne; going beyond the limits of physical endurance: **a.** Of outward things.

a **1340** HAMPOLE *Psalter* cxlvii. 6 As wha say, vnsufferabil ware þat kald, if he lesid it noght. **1382** WYCLIF *Num.* xi. 10 Thanne Moyses herde the puple wepynge bi meynees,.. and to Moyses it was seen a thing vnsuffrable [L. *intoleranda*]. **1395** PURVEY *Remonstr.* (1851) 22 Thei wolen putten to a man confessid to hem, greuouse chargis and vnsuffrable. **1544** BETHAM *Precepts War* I. cxxiii. G ij b, They were ashamed, that they dydde not abyde suche lyke labours, yea and moche more vnsufferable. **1562** TURNER *Baths* 8 An unsufferable raynye, windye, or colde weather. **1613** PURCHAS *Pilgrimage* (1614) 720 The high ridges..are vnsufferable for cold. **1658** T. WALL *Charact. Enemies Ch.* 53 [To] lie under the..dreadful apprehensions, or unsufferable strokes of divine wrath. **1729** SAVAGE *Wanderer* II. 50 Like noon-tide summer-suns the rays appear, Unsuff'rable, magnificent and near! **1742** *Lond. & Country Brew.* III. (1743) 202 An unsufferable, ill palated oily Juice, that will spoil all the Liquor. **1869** SPURGEON *Treas. David* Ps. xviii. 6 The king heard it in his palace of light unsufferable.

b. Of pain, grief, fear, etc.

c **1374** CHAUCER *Boeth.* III. pr. vii. 79 Grete sekenesse and ..grete sorwes vnsuffrable. **1388** WYCLIF *Judith* xiv. 17 Vnsuffrable drede and tremblyng felde doun on hem. *a* **1425** tr. *Arderne's Treat. Fistula*, etc. 40 Þe pacient felep as it war vnsufferable ychyng. *c* **1425** *St. Christina* xvi. in *Anglia* VIII. 125 She was stired of god vnto an vnsufferabil priste. *c* **1445** PECOCK *Donet* 71 For eesing of his vnsuffrable fleischli freelte. *a* **1589** PALFREYMAN *Baldwin's Mor. Philos.* (1600) 140 b, Conscience..worketh..vnsufferable torments,..to the condempnation of the vngodly. **1595** CLERKE *Polimanteia* S j b, To my vnsufferable and vnpitied griefe. **1639** S. DU VERGER tr. *Camus' Admir. Events* 301 A torture unsufferable unto this young gentlewoman. **1700** BLACKMORE *Job* 138 My fullness gives unsufferable pain. **1722** DE FOE *Hist. Plague* (1754) 261 The unsufferable Torment of the Swellings.

†**3.** Incapable of self-restraint. *Obs.*$^{-1}$

1387 TREVISA *Higden* (Rolls) V. 61 Þis was a swiþe evel man,..and he was unsuffrable of leccherie [L. *libidinis impatientissimus*].

†**4.** Not involving suffering. *Obs.*$^{-1}$

1548 GESTE *Pr. Masse* C vj, They greuously erre, who hold opinion yt our faultes ar pardoned through theyr vnsufferable & vnbloudy sacrificing of christes bodi.

†**5.** Incompatible. *Obs.*⁻¹

a **1586** SIDNEY *Arcadia* III. x, Eternity, and Chaunce are things unsufferable together.

†**6.** As *adv.* = UNSUFFERABLY *adv.* 1. *Obs.*

c **1420** *Prose Life Alex.* 76 Than commanded Alexander þat þay schuld make many fyres. For it began for to be vnsufferable calde. **1683** MOXON *Mech. Exerc., Printing* xi. ¶23 Sometimes the Inck proves so unsufferable Pale, that [etc.].

Hence **un'sufferableness**.

1611 FLORIO, *Inpatibilita*, vnsufferablenesse. **1677** HORNECK *Gt. Law Consid.* iv. 175 His passions..represent to his mind..the unsufferableness of the disgrace. **1679** KID in Hickes *Spirit of Popery* (1680) 2 There is something in a Christians condition, that can never put him without the reach of unsufferableness.

un'sufferably, *adv.* [UN-¹ 11 and 5 b.]

1. Intolerably; unendurably.

c **1440** *Promp. Parv.* 367/2 On-sufferably.., *intollerabiliter*. **1644** PRYNNE & WALKER *Fiennes's Trial* App. 20 Captain Bagnall..was baffled unsufferably by the Defendant..before the Councell. **1661** PEPYS *Diary* 31 May, [His mother] being so unsufferably foolish and simple. **1702** ECHARD *Eccl. Hist.* I. vi. 138 Finding his Soul unsufferably oppress'd. **1727** DE FOE *Hist. Appar.* iv. (1840) 28 Saturn and Jupiter are uncomfortably dark, unsufferably cold.

†**2.** Without suffering. *Obs.*⁻¹

1548 GESTE *Pr. Masse* C vj b, We ar already redemed..by ye ones offering of christ neuer to be reuyued eyther sufferablye or vnsufferably, bloudely or vnbloudely.

†**un'sufferance.** *Obs.* [UN-¹ 12.]

1. Impatience.

a **1400** *Spec. Vitæ* (MS. Bodl. 2685) fol. 79 Þe syns of þe hert bene þese:..vnconable gladnes, Vnsuffrance & werldly drerines.

2. Impassiveness.

1611 FLORIO, *Inpassibilita*, vnsufferance. **1625** GILL *Sacr. Philos.* IV. 32 That Stoicall vnsufferance of His mind, which Clemens Alex[andrinus]..thought not to bee subject either to joy or sorrow.

un'suffered, *ppl. a.* [UN-¹ 8.]

1. Not suffered; unendured.

1549 COVERDALE, etc. *Erasm. Par. 2 Cor.* 52 b, For your welth I leaue nothyng vndone and vnsuffered. [**1775** ASH.]

†**2.** Unsufferable. *Obs.*

c **1611** CHAPMAN *Iliad* III. 6 Eschuing the vnsufferd stormes, shot from the winters starre. *Ibid.* VIII. 198 O Father Ioue, hath euer yet thy most unsuffred hand Afflicted, with such spoile of soules, the king of any land? *Ibid.* XI. 530, XIX. 357.

†**un'suffering,** *vbl. sb.* *Obs.*⁻¹ [UN-¹ 13.] Impossibility of enduring.

1382 WYCLIF *2 Macc.* ix. 10 No man mizte beere hym, for vnsuffryng [L. *intolerantiam*] of stynke.

un'suffering, *ppl. a.* [UN-¹ 10, 5 d.]

1. Not permitting or enduring. *rare.*

1568 *Reg. Privy Council Scot.* I. 626 Unsufferand the said Johnne..to be supportit..be the said hous. **1570** LEVINS *Manip.* 137 Vnsuffering, *impatiens*.

2. Not undergoing suffering.

1717 ATTERBURY *Serm.* (1737) III. 153 Can a man so treated..be said to be in an unsuffering state? **1736** THOMSON *Hymn Seasons* 75 For the Great Shepherd reigns; And His unsuffering kingdom yet will come. **1838** H. BLUNT *Sev. Ch. Asia* 24 To an extent, to which the fairest mansion of the unsuffering Christian is utterly a stranger.

unsu'fficed, *ppl. a.* (UN-¹ 8.)

1586 L. LLOID *Pilgr. Princes* 13 Yet vnsufficed here with hee slue the Queenes owne sonne. *a* **1644** QUARLES *Sol. Recant.* vi. 3 Who multiply their loynes and years, yet have Souls unsuffic'd with good. *c* **1850** NEALE *Hymns East. Ch.* (1866) 103 Hell fire fierce and unsufficed.

†**unsu'fficience.** *Obs.* (UN-¹ 12, 5 b.)

1445 in *Wars Eng. in France* (1861) I. 467 Letters.. deliverede for paiement into the Staple, and for unsufficience..refusede. *c* **1455** PECOCK *Folewer* 123 Vnsufficience of kunnyng longyng to eny effect.

†**unsu'fficienced,** *ppl. a.* (UN-² 4, 8.) *Obs.*

a **1661** FULLER *Life Smith* (1675) b 2, Allowing dispensation to such who were unsufficienced by weaknesse.

†**unsu'fficiency.** *Obs.* (UN-¹ 12 and 5 b.)

1580 HOLLYBAND *Treas. Fr. Tong*, *Incompetence*, not meete or fitte for, vnsufficiencie. **1594** HOOKER *Eccl. Pol.* II. viii. §3 The vnsufficiencie of the light of Nature. **1597** *Ibid.* v. lxxxi. §14 There are Ciuill as well as Ecclesiasticall Vnsufficiencies, Non-residences, and Pluralities. **1625** T. GODWIN *Moses & Aaron* IV. i. 172 The Arabians perceiuing the vnsufficiency of their knowne gods, dedicated their altars, *Ignoto Deo*. **1661** K. W. *Conf. Charac.*, [*Empirick*] (1860) 65 The weakness and unsufficiency of other doctors.

†**unsu'fficient,** *a.* *Obs.* [UN-¹ 7 and 5 b.]

1. = INSUFFICIENT *a.* 1.

1395 PURVEY *Remonstr.* (1851) 82 It is not declarid..that the clerk was vnsufficient, neither vnable. *c* **1445** PECOCK *Donet* 145 And þanne, wherto schulde þe sufficient be lefte, and þe vnsufficient be taken,..in a purpos so necessarye? *c* **1450** *Myrr. our Ladye* 137 We oughte to knowe oure selfe vnsuffycyente & therfore pray for helpe. *a* **1513** FABYAN *Chron.* VI. cxlix. 136 Consyderynge the vnablenesse of Hilderich the kynge, that he was vnsufficient to rule so great a charge. **1535** COVERDALE *Bible* Prol. ¶7 As for the commendacyon of Gods holy scripture..I am farre vnsufficient therto. *a* **1617** HIERON *Wks.* (1619) II. 474 This miserie of hauing none among them but an vnseasoning and vnsufficient minister. **1646** SIR T. BROWNE *Pseud. Ep.* I. iii. 9 Being unprovided, or unsufficient for higher speculations.

2. = INSUFFICIENT *a.* 2.

1398 TREVISA *Barth. De P.R.* XVII. i. (Bodl. MS.) fol. 185 b, Also in some trene þe [humoure] is vnsufficiaunte and vnperfecte. **1482** *Monk of Evesham* (Arb.) 109 Wat sum euer may be seyde of hyt by mannys mowthe, ful lytyl hyt ys, and onsufficient to expresse the ioy of myne herte. **1551** ROBINSON tr. *More's Utopia* I. (1895) 96 He perceiued the same stocke of money to be to litel, and vnsufficient. **1597** HOOKER *Eccl. Pol.* v. lx. §7 When vnder vnsufficient pretences wee defraude them of such ordinarie outward helpes as wee should exhibit. **1625** GILL *Sacr. Philos.* Pref., You say that reason is an unsufficient meane, and unable to bring us to the knowledge of those things. **1656** JEANES *Mixt. Schol. Div.* 5 Our Saviour's discourse sheweth, that these were weak and unsufficient grounds.

Hence †**unsu'fficiently** *adv.*; **-ness**. *Obs.*

1398 TREVISA *Barth. De P.R.* VII. xxxi. (Bodl. MS.), Whanne þe lunges beþ igreued with..bocches..he seruеþ þe hert *vnsufficientlich of aier. *c* **1440** *Alph. Tales* 143 One of þe cardynals when he hard þis, began to gruche agayne þe pope, & said he demyd vnsufficientlie. *c* **1455** PECOCK *Folewer* 204 Ellis y wolde graunte þat y vnsufficientli nombrid þe poyntis of goddis lawe in þe..tablis. *a* **1600** HOOKER *Eccl. Pol.* VI. vi. §13 Absolving of unsufficiently disposed penitents. **1685** PETTY *Will* p. v, The admeasurement of the lands..was most unsufficiently and absurdly managed. **1533** *Reg. Mag. Sig. Scot.* 286/2 Sua that oure soverane lord and his liegis be nocht begylit tharewith anent the *unsufficientnes of the samyn.

†**un'suffisance.** *Obs.* [UN-¹ 12, 5 b.]

= INSUFFISANCE.

c **1400** *Pilgr. Sowle* (Caxton) I. xviii. 19 Yf I personelly shold not be herde..for myn vnsuffysaunce.

†**un'suffisant,** *sb.* *Obs.* [Cf. next.] Insufficiency.

1387 TREVISA *Higden* (Rolls) VII. 381 It is seide þat kyng William..wolde haue depreved hym for unsufficiant [*v.r.* unsuffysant; L. *insufficientiam*] of lettrure. **1425** *Rolls of Parlt.* IV. 267 Ye grete unabilte and unsuffisante, that the same Wauter felte in hymself.

†**un'suffisant,** *a.* *Obs.* [UN-¹ 7, 5 b.]

= INSUFFISANT *a.*

c **1400** *26 Pol. Poems* 136 Though I be, lorde, vnsuffisaunte, Any helpe to gete of the, Yet..*Parce michi, domine!* **1423** *Rolls of Parlt.* IV. 255 Thoo werkes of Brouderie there founden unsuffisant. *c* **1440** *Pallad. on Husb.* I. 196 Olyuys grete out of that lond wol reke With drasty, wattry fruyt..Unsuffisaunt the costis forto acquyte.

un'suffocate, *v.* (UN-² 3.)

1818 BYRON *Juan* I. cxxx, Like the apparatus Of the Humane Society's beginning, By which men are unsuffocated gratis.

un'suffocative, *a.* (UN-¹ 7.)

1822 GOOD *Study Med.* I. 536 When this difficulty [of breathing] is moderate and unsuffocative.

un'sugared, *ppl. a.* (UN-¹ 8.)

1592 NASHE *Four Lett. Confut.* E iij, Your vnsugred pilles ..would not haue beene so harsh in the swallowing. **1626** BACON *Sylva* §883 Trie it with Sugar put into Water, formerly Sugred; And into other Water Vnsugred. **1871** *Daily News* 11 Feb., They may hereafter have an unsugared pill to swallow.

unsu'ggestive, *a.* (UN-¹ 7).

1797 LAMB *Let. to Coleridge* 10 Jan., My eyes are heavy and sleepy, and my brain unsuggestive. **1866** MARK LEMON *F. Lyle* II. 198 A single cup and saucer,..a diminutive teapot!—so unsuggestive of the pleasant gossip with which 'taking tea' is generally associated. **1900** *Daily News* 23 Feb. 5/1 The design was unsuggestive of date.

Hence **unsu'ggestiveness.**

1858 *Househ. Words* XIX. 181/2 An expression of countenance which..was a combination of aggression and pronounced patience, with a dogged unsuggestiveness.

†**un'suing,** *vbl. sb.* *Obs.*⁻¹ [UN-¹ 13.] Lack of agreement.

c **1425** *Saints' Lives* in *Anglia* VIII. 195/35 Vnsuynge of englyshe, as vmwhile soþeren, oþere-while norþen.

†**un'suit,** *a.* *Obs.*⁻¹ [UN-¹ 7.] Unfitting.

1704 J. BLAIR in W. S. Perry *Hist. Coll. Amer. Col. Ch.* (1870) I. 135 Aspersed with the most unsuitest imputations as if I had been raising sedition or rebellion.

un'suit, *v.* [UN-¹ 14.]

1. *trans.* To be at variance with.

1635 QUARLES *Embl.* IV. xv. 241 The sprightly Twang of the melodious Lute Agrees not with my voice; and both unsuit My untun'd fortunes.

2. To render unsuitable.

1869 *Pall Mall G.* 8 July 3/2 The health of the former cripple unsuiting her for convent life. **1902** *Daily Chron.* 8 Dec. 8/5 Their training..completely unsuits them for the proper performance of the duties.

unsuita'bility. (UN-¹ 12, 5 b. Cf. next.)

1814 MRS. J. WEST *Alicia de Lacy* III. 220 The unsuitability of her white glittering dress for such a purpose. **1866** DICKENS *Lett.* (1880) II. 249 A limited reference to its unsuitability to these pages [of *All the Year Round*]. **1880** A. R. WALLACE *Isl. Life* 102 Anomalies of distribution other than such as may be connected with unsuitability of climate.

un'suitable, *a.* (UN-¹ 7 b and 5 b.)

1597 HOOKER *Eccl. Pol.* v. xxxviii. §3 Wanton, or light or vnsuteable harmonie, such as only pleaseth the eare. **1601** SHAKS. *All's Well* I. i. 170 Virginitie like an olde Courtier, weares her cap out of fashion, richly suted, but vnsuteable. **1665** BOYLE *Occas. Refl.* I. iii, I make him but very unsuitable Returns for the Blessings..I have receiv'd. **1671** MILTON *P.R.* III. 132 Hard recompence, unsutable return For so much good, so much beneficence. **1831** JAMES *Phil. Augustus* II. iv, At so unsuitable an hour. **1869** TOZER *Highl. Turkey* II. 346 The expression..would hardly appear unsuitable. **1890** 'R. BOLDREWOOD' *Col. Reformer* (1891) 216 He thought..him not wholly unsuitable as a companion.

b. Const. *to* or *for*.

a **1586** SIDNEY *Arcadia* III. xxiii, An unkinde answere,.. but not unsutable to the rest of your behaviour. **1601** SHAKS. *Twel. N.* II. v. 222 Hee will smile vpon her, which will now be so vnsuteable to her disposition,..that [etc.]. **1651** HOBBES *Leviath.* III. xlii. 293 Their ordinary maintenance was not unsuitable to their employment. **1768–74** TUCKER *Lt. Nat.* (1834) II. 547 If our devotion be over-strained it becomes unsuitable for practice. **1780** *Mirror* No. 94, A train of thinking..neither unpleasing nor unsuitable to the character of a rational being. *a* **1834** COLERIDGE *Lit. Rem.* (1838) III. 382 Never did so wise a man adopt means so unsuitable to his end. **1879** HARLAN *Eyesight* ix. 131 Ground-glass globes are condemned..as unsuitable for school purposes.

un'suitableness. (UN-¹ 12.)

a **1586** SIDNEY *Arcadia* III. vii, The unsutablenes of a weake broken voice to high brave wordes. **1644** MILTON *Areop.* (Arb.) 73 To suppresse opinions for the newnes, or the unsutablenes to a customary acceptance. *a* **1697** SOUTH *Serm.* (1715) II. 167 The real Unsuitableness, that every thing sinful, or dishonest, bears to the Nature of Man. **1754** EDWARDS *Freed. Will* IV. viii. 239 The Unsuitableness of such a Necessity to the Liberty..of the divine Being. **1845** LD. CAMPBELL *Chancellors* lxxxiii. (1857) IV. 135 From the unsuitableness of his manner and style he is not.. entertaining. **1886** *Law Times* LXXXII. 173/2 Those who allege my unsuitableness for the high position I now hold.

un'suitably, *adv.* (UN-¹ 11.)

1624 GATAKER *Transubst.* 198 Their religion indeed being ..patched together out of olde condemned heresies and unsutably composed. *a* **1715** SOUTH *Serm.* IV. 110 That natural..Sensibility of Mind, which renders them apprehensive of any Thing done unsuitably to their Nature. **1774** WARTON *Hist. Eng. Poetry* I. 396 The modern monuments unsuitably placed in Westminster-abbey. **1859** *Habits of Gd. Society* iii. 143 He has never attempted to dress ..unsuitably to his station. **1898** *Westm. Gaz.* 27 Aug. 2/1 When a girl marries unsuitably.

un'suited, *ppl. a.* [UN-¹ 8, 8 d.]

†**1.** Not sued *for*. *Obs. rare*⁻¹.

1599 *Extr. Aberd. Reg.* (1848) II. 189 Sindrie our subjectis ..sustening gryt loss..in thair persones and gudes, be the piracie of Ingland, quhilkis..hes lyin ouer vnsuted for.

2. Not suited or adapted; unfitted, unfit.

1598 *Sidney's Astr. & Stella* li, My heart..is euen irkt that so sweet Comedie, By such vnsuted speech should hindred be. **1657** AUSTEN *Fruit Trees* II. 74 Therefore are his waies often so unsuted to the apprehensions of men. **1677** GILPIN *Demonol.* III. ix. 55 A work..such as had neither bee unsuited to the power of Christ, nor unlawful in it self. **1819** SCOTT *Ivanhoe* xliv, Like a garment unsuited to the climate in which I seek to dwell. **1847** SMEATON *Builder's Man.* 142 It is unsuited for the purpose to which it is applied. **1861** BUCKLE *Civiliz.* II. i. 136 The municipal privileges..being unsuited to the habits of the people.

b. Not accommodated or supplied.

1796 BURKE *Let. Noble Lord* Wks. VIII. 59 So that no constitution-fancier may go unsuited from his shop.

un'suiting, *ppl. a.* (UN-¹ 10.)

1596 HARINGTON *Metam. Ajax* I 2 b, Yet I will end with this good counsell, not vnsuting to the text I haue thus long talked of. **1604** SHAKS. *Oth.* IV. i. 78 (Q. 1), A passion most vnsuting such a man. **1639** FULLER *Holy War* v. xix. 261 The armie will be very heterogeneous, patched up of different people unsuiting in their manners. **1685** DRYDEN *Lucretius* III. 161 Leave those joys, unsuiting to thy age, To a fresh Comer. **1852** M. ARNOLD *Human Life* 16 Winds from our side the unsuiting consort rive.

un'sullen, *a.* (UN-¹ 7.)

1605 MARSTON *Dutch Courtezan* II. i, What harty gratefulnes, Unsulleine silence, unaffected modesty.

un'sulliable, *a.* (UN-¹ 7 b.)

1766 J. MACGOWAN *Death* (1814) 560 Blessed afflictions, which..have fitted me for those usulliable mansions of uninterrupted felicity! **1881** *Contemp. Rev.* Apr. 568 One block of long white light unsullyable Glows in deep azure.

un'sullied, *ppl. a.* (UN-¹ 8.)

1588 SHAKS. *L.L.L.* v. ii. 352 By my maiden honor, yet as pure As the vnsullied Lilly. **1621** G. SANDYS *Ovid's Met.* III. (1626) 56 The linked Deities their Graces fix! Where Roses with vnsullied Lillyes mix! **1717** LADY M. W. MONTAGU *Let. to C'tess of Mar* 18 April, That lovely bloom of complexion, unsullied by art. **1755** J. G. COOPER *Tomb Shaks.* 26 Here Fancy sat, (her dewy fingers cold Decking with flow'rets fresh th' unsullied sod). **1828** LYTTON *Pelham* I. xiv, Gloves of most unsullied doeskin. **1863** M. J. BERKELEY *Brit. Mosses* i. 3 Stems..of a clear unsullied green.

b. In fig. use.

1659 W. CHAMBERLAYNE *Pharon.* Ded., My more youthful labours..passed the public view unsullied by the cloudy aspect of the most critic spectator. **1665** MANLEY *Grotius' Low C. Wars* 113 His Mind, that never was greedy after Wealth, and, in that respect, unsullied and upright. **1743** FRANCIS tr. *Hor., Odes* IV. v. 29 Nobly conscious of unsullied Fame. **1774** W. WHITEHEAD *Plays & Poems* II. 171 The pure unsullied thoughts, and sallies of our souls. **1849** MACAULAY *Hist. Eng.* II. 247 In the midst of a corrupt court he had kept his personal integrity unsullied. **1879** FARRAR *St. Paul* I. 256 The unsullied sanctity of Jehovah's Temple.

Hence **un'sulliedness.**

1863 MRS. WHITNEY *F. Gartney's Girlh.* xx, Her sweet look and fair unsulliedness of attire. **1865** W. H. GILLESPIE *Arg. Being & Attrib. God* IV. ii. (1871) 142 Holiness is moral stainlessness, spotlessness, unsulliedness.

un'sulphurated, *ppl. a.* (UN-1 8a(*b*).)
1825 J. NICHOLSON *Operat. Mechanic* 768 About as much [gold] as was reserved unsulphurated from the mass.

unsul'phureous, *a.* (UN-1 7.)
1781 *Encycl. Brit.* (ed. 2) VII. 4932/1 To separate Mercury out of an unsulphureous Ore by Distillation.

un'sulphurized, *ppl. a.* (UN-1 8a(*c*).)
1846 *Mechanic's Mag.* 4 July 2/2 Gutta percha either sulphurised or unsulphurised.

un'sultry, *a.* (UN-1 7.)
1826 J. WILSON *Noctes Ambr.* (1855) I. 170 On a chosen day of cloudless sunshine, yet unsultry air.

un'summable, *a.* (UN-1 7b.)
1667 WATERHOUSE *Fire Lond.* 112 A Mart of Trade and a Mine of Wealth, [of] which the inexhaustion of this last twenty-six years by Sums unsummable,..would be incredible.

un'summed, *ppl. a.* [UN-1 8.]
1. Not summed up; uncounted.
a **1400–50** *Alexander* 1991 For as þis sede þat I send vnsoumed [*v.r.* vnsowmyd] is euer, So ben we.. vnnowmyrd. **1579** *Richmond. Wills* (Surtees) XXVI. 286 Some of these gold and mony above writen. By those unsomed iij c. *ijli. vjs. viijd.* **1649** G. DANIEL *Trinarch., Hen. IV*, cclxiv, The wise Man has an vnsumm'd Librarye; Himselfe and Man, and Bookes, are all his Bookes. **1772** MASON *Eng. Garden* I. 18 Egregious madness; yet pursu'd With pains unwearied, with expense unsumm'd. **1791** COWPER *Iliad* II. 568 So the Grecians swarm'd An unsumm'd multitude o'er all the plain. **1857** H. MILLER *Test. Rocks* vi. 239 Armed with the experience in evil of unsummed ages. **1869** MᶜLAREN *Serm.* Ser. II. xi. 194 After unsummed eternities of advance.
†**2.** (See quot. and cf. SUMMED 1.) *Obs. rare.*
1615 LATHAM *Falconry* ¶3b, Vnsumm'd is when a Hawkes feathers are not come forth, or els not com'd home to their full length.

un'summered, *a.* (UN-1 9.)
1879 TENNYSON *Pref. Poem to Brother's Sonn.* III. Poems (1894) 574/1 And, now to these unsummer'd skies The summer bird is still.

un'summerlike, -ly, *adjs.* (UN-1 7, 7c.)
1869 *Chamb. Jrnl.* Oct. 655/1 The unsummerly summer of eighteen sixty-nine. **1880** *Cassell's Mag.* 440 Another unsummer-like fashion. **1883** MISS BROUGHTON *Belinda* IV. ii, A chill and unsummerlike night.

un'summoned, *ppl. a.* (UN-1 8.)
1474 *Acta Audit.* (1839) 35/2 Henry..protestit þat þe decrete..suld turne him to na preiudice becauss he was vnsummond. **1480** *Acta Dom. Conc.* (1839) 55/2 The lordis ..ordanis him to hafe lettres to summond his prufis þat Is vnsummond gife he ony has. **1633** P. FLETCHER *Purple Isl.* v. xli, The lazie sense still sleeps, unsummon'd with his drum. **1673** DRYDEN *Marr. à la Mode* IV. v, Like an unsummon'd guest. **1763** MALLET *Elvira* III. iii, She [is].. unsummon'd too To this high task. *a* **1800** COWPER *Odyss.* (ed. 2) XXII. 551 Then bid Penelope with her attendants down, Nor leave unsummon'd one of all the train. **1839** MRS. JAMESON *Visits & Sk.* II. 74 Those whom the rules of etiquette allowed to approach unsummoned and pay their respects. **1860** FORSTER *Gr. Remonstr.* 31 An unsummoned tenant..could not take his place in the Council.

un'summoning, *vbl. sb.* (UN-2 3, 8.)
1632 in Nichols *Hist. Leics.* (1804) IV. 386 Paid apparitor for summoning and unsummoning.

un'sumptuary, *a.* (UN-1 7.)
1720–1 *Lett. fr. Mist's Jrnl.* (1722) I. 83 Should rigid unsumptuary Laws pass the House [etc.].

un'sundered, *ppl. a.* [UN-1 8. Cf. MDu. *ongesondert*, MLG., MHG. *ungesundert* (G. *ungesondert*).] Not parted or separated.
1594 NASHE *Unfort. Trav.* H ij b, Those siluer pipes,..by many edged vnsundred writhings.., strayed from bough to bough. **1609** HEYWOOD *Brit. Troy* v. xxiv, The stout Centaures came... They seemed at first halfe horse halfe man unsundred. [Also in Minsheu, Sherwood, and Hexham, s.v.]

†**un'sunderly**, *adv. Obs.* [UN-1 11.] Inseparably.
c **1440** *Gesta Rom.* xliv. 174 Late vs in this wordle be so vnsundirlye couplid to the holye trenitee, that [etc.].

un'sung, *ppl. a.* [UN-1 8b. Cf. MHG. and G. *ungesungen*, Sw. *osjungen*.]
1. Not sung; not uttered by singing.
1422–61 in *Cal. Proc. in Chanc. Q. Eliz.* (1827) I. Introd. 20 It wer better bell unrogne at þe sauntes tyme þan þe messe unsogne. **1539** *Abst. Protocols Town Clerks Glasgow* (1897) IV. 118 Geif it faillies to be left on-sung thre nychtis togidder. **1613** W. BROWNE *Brit. Past.* I. i. 8 Drawne by time ..To sing those layes as yet unsung of any. **1843** CARLYLE *Past & Pr.* III. v, Thy Epic, unsung in words, is written in huge characters on the face of this Planet. **1860** FABER *Bethlehem* 100 Numberless unlanguaged and unsung Magnificats. **1889** STEVENSON *South Seas* III. vi. (1900) 265 [They] gave up the unsung remainder of their ballet.
2. Not celebrated in or by song.
1667 MILTON *P.L.* VII. 253 Thus was the first Day..: Nor past uncelebrated, nor unsung By the Celestial Quires. **1697** DRYDEN *Æneis* VII. 1014 Nor Œbalus, shalt thou be left unsung. **1701** ADDISON *Let. from Italy* 14 Here..not a mountain rears its head unsung. **1743** YOUNG *Nt. Th.* IV. 533 Why doubt we, then, the glorious truth to sing, Tho' yet unsung, as deem'd, perhaps, too bold? **1805** [see UNHONOURED]. **1828** CARLYLE *Misc.* (1840) I. 343 A thousand battle-fields remain unsung. **1875** F. I. SCUDAMORE *Day-Dreams* 10 It is one of the unsung beauties of the earth.

un'sunk, *ppl. a.* (UN-1 8b.)
a **1300** *Cursor M.* 2847 Es noþer leued, ne tre, ne gress, Ne nathing of þat land vn-sonken [*v.rr.* vn-sunkyn, vnsunke]. *c* **1586** C'TESS PEMBROKE *Ps.* LXIX. vi, Keepe me safe unsunck, unmyred. **1611** SPEED *Hist. Gt. Brit.* IX. xii. §56 Not halfe of their Shippes escaped vntaken or vnsuncke. *a* **1687** H. MORE *Conject. Cabbal.* (1713) 77 The Angels and the Souls of Men unsunk into generation. [*Ibid.* All Souls as they descend εἰς γένεσιν.] *c* **1740** A. HILL *To Author of 'Pamela'* 28 What..Though taste like thine each void of time can fill, Unsunk by spleen. **1824** BYRON *Juan* XVI. xcix, The Sinking Fund's unfathomable sea..leaves The debt unsunk, yet sinks all it receives. **1837** CARLYLE *Fr. Rev.* I. II. iv, Nimble old man, who..in the worst confusion will emerge, cork-like, unsunk.

un'sunned, *ppl. a.* [UN-1 8.]
1. Not penetrated or reached by sunlight; not exposed or accessible to the sun.
1607 TOURNEUR *Rev. Trag.* III. F 1, [I] did wish his impudent grace To meete her here in this vn-sunned-lodge. **1634** MILTON *Comus* 398 The unsun'd heaps Of Misers treasure. **1652** BENLOWES *Theoph.* X. lxxvi, Why start'st? Unlock thy unsunn'd hoard. **1759** MASON *Caractacus* 22 The unsunn'd silver of the mine. **1797** COLERIDGE *Limetree Bower* 14 That branchless ash, Unsunn'd and damp. **1806** R. MANT *Poems, Country Gent.* I. 32 Where..horror shaggs the unsunn'd precipice. **1860** FLOR. NIGHTINGALE *Nursing* ix. 49 The unsunned sides of narrow streets. **1885** JEAN INGELOW *Sleep of Sigismund* xxxviii, With name unsaid and fame unsunned He walks that was King Sigismund.
b. *fig.* Not made patent or public.
1809–14 WORDSW. *Excurs.* VII. 281 With his cheerful throng Of open projects, and his inward hoard Of unsunned griefs. **1821** J. HODGSON in J. Raine *Mem.* (1857) I. 347 He has promised to communicate to our Society some very curious and unsunned letters of Lord Dacre's. **1862** *Athenæum* 30 Aug. 278 The unsunned historical treasures in the possession of the London Corporation.
2. Not touched or affected by the light or heat of the sun. Also *fig.*
1611 SHAKS. *Cymb.* II. v. 13, I thought her As Chaste, as vn-Sunn'd Snow. **1795** SOUTHEY *Vis. Maid of Orleans* I. 311 As white as unsunn'd snow, Or as the spotless lily of the vale. **1820** *Ellen Fitzarthur* 54 Crystal drops of unsunned dew. **1843** F. E. PAGET *Warden of Berkingholt* 119 The unsunned purity..of the Master of Berkingholt Union.
b. Not coloured or tanned by the sun.
1821 CRAIG *Lect. Drawing*, etc. vi. 344 The dark, yet clear, complexion of the Italians, which would ill suit on unsunned English faces. **1835** WILLIS *Pencillings* II. xlix. 80 They venture to drop their jealous veils and ramble about in their unsunned beauty. **1882** *Century Mag.* XXV. 103 A lady ..[with] pure, unsunned complexion.
fig. **1830** TENNYSON *Confess. Sensit. Mind* 140 In my morn of youth, The unsunn'd freshness of my strength.
3. Not lighted up by the sun. Also *fig.*
1840 LADY C. BURY *Hist. of Flirt* xvi, Her still countenance unsunned by a smile. *a* **1864** HAWTHORNE *Amer. Note-Bks.* (1879) I. 36 All the near landscape lay unsunned. **1874** FARRAR *Christ* II. lix. 350 The unsunned outer darkness of miserable self-condemnation.

un'sunny, *a.* (UN-1 7.)
1859 TENNYSON *Pelleas & Ettarre* 176 We marvel at thee much, O damsel, wearing this unsunny face To him who won thee glory. **1860** FABER *Bethlehem* ii. (1865) 87 The warm air of the noon has heated the unsunny forest.

†**un-'sun-seen**, *ppl. a.* (UN-1 8d.)
1654 BLOUNT *Acad. Eloq.* 48 An un-Sun-seen cave.

†**un-'sunshine**, *v.* (UN-2 6b.)
1659 FULLER *App. Inj. Innoc.* III. 31 Military preparations ..must needs give our Nation great troubles, and (for the time) un-Sunshine England.

†**un'superable**, *a. Obs.* (UN-1 7b and 5b.)
1526 *Pilgr. Perf.* (W. de W. 1531) 241 The vnsuperable loue & goodnes of god. **1617** MINSHEU s.v. (hence in Sherwood). **1644** DIGBY *Nat. Bodies* i. §4. 3 It..is the occasion of exceeding great errours, and entangleth one in vnsuperable difficulties. **1777** POTTER *Æschylus, Agamemnon* 293 To wear The form of friendship, and with circling wiles Inclose him in th' unsuperable net.

unsu'perfluous, *a.* (UN-1 7.)
1571 GOLDING *Calvin on Ps.* lxii. 11 How unsuperfluous this warning is, wee learne by daylye experience. **1634** MILTON *Comus* 773 Natures full blessings would be well dispenc't In unsuperfluous eeven proportion. **1832** L. HUNT *Poems* 197 Swans..which..glide With unsuperfluous lift of their proud wings. **1842** J. WILSON *Chr. North* (1857) I. 145 Not scanty but unsuperfluous fare is theirs.

unsuper'scribed, *ppl. a.* (UN-1 8.)
a **1711** KEN *Sion* Poet. Wks. 1721 IV. 390 A silken Cord around his Neck was hung, At which unsuperscrib'd a Letter hung. **1748** RICHARDSON *Clarissa* I. 163 [A] letter.. from my mother, unsealed, and unsuperscribed also.

unsuper'seded, *ppl. a.* (UN-1 8.)
[**1775** ASH.] **1857** TOULMIN SMITH *Parish* 133 The anomalies that have hence arisen leave the action of the Parish unsuperseded. **1890** 'R. BOLDREWOOD' *Col. Reformer* (1891) 162 That much-abused but as yet unsuperseded garb.

unsuper'stitious, *a.* (UN-1 7.)
1652 SPARKE *Prim. Devot.* (1660) 469 This kinde of Sortilegium was usual with Antiquity, such an undeceitful, and unsuperstitious Lottery. **1863** *Blackw. Mag.* Sept. 291 If we consult history in an unprejudiced, unsuperstitious spirit.

unsuper'vised, *ppl. a.* (UN-1 8.)
1899 *Educat. Rev.* Dec. 470 He is, unsupervised, irresponsible. [Common in recent use.]

un'supped, *ppl. a.* [UN-1 8.] Without having supped; supperless.
1382 WYCLIF *Dan.* vi. 18 The kyng..slepte vnsoupid [L. *incœnatus*], and metis be not brouȝt to byfore hym. **1483** *Cath. Angl.* 350/1 Vn Sowped, *jncenatus.* **1508** KENNEDIE *Flyting w. Dunbar* 382 Sic reule gerris the..sitt vnsoupit off beȝond the sey. *c* **1563** *Jack Jugler* in *Four Old Plays* (1848) 43, I wolde gladly byne vnsupped, soo you had your fyll. **1609** BIBLE (Douay) *Dan.* vi. 18 The king went to his house, and slept unsupped. **1894** [see UNSLEPT 1].

unsu'pplanted, *ppl. a.* (UN-1 8.)
1708 J. PHILIPS *Cyder* II. 384 Gladsome they quaff, ..[and] well bedew'd repair Each to his Home with unsupplanted Feet.

un'supple, *a.* (UN-1 7.)
1621 G. SANDYS *Ovid's Met.* II. (1626) 43 Againe shee struggl'd to haue stood on end: But, those vnsupple sinewes would not bend.

un'suppled, *ppl. a.* (UN-1 8.)
1761 EARL PEMBROKE *Milit. Equitation* (1762) 8 A raw, unsuppled, and unprepared lad, who is put at once upon a rough horse.

unsu'ppliable, *a.* (UN-1 7b.)
1638 CHILLINGW. *Relig. Prot.* I. ii. §67. 77 The unsuppliable defect of any necessary Antecedent. **1793** HOLCROFT tr. *Lavater's Physiog.* vi. 42 Are they not equally indispensable, equally unsuppliable? **1802–12** BENTHAM *Ration. Judic. Evid.* (1827) III. 413 Why admit it, under the danger of incorrigible incorrectness and unsupplyable incompleteness?

un'supplicated, *ppl. a.* (UN-1 8.)
1634 BP. HALL *Contempl.*, *N.T.* IV. xii, Saul himself would ..offer a burnt-offering to the Lord, rather than the Philistines should fight with him unsupplicated.

unsu'pplied, *ppl. a.* [UN-1 8, 8c.]
1. Not supplied or provided with something.
1599 Q. ELIZ. in Moryson *Itin.* (1617) II. 56 Therefore we command you, not onely to raise no more [men], when these shall be decaied, but to keepe them vnsupplied [*sc.* with money] that are already. **1618** HALES *Let. fr. Synod of Dort* Gold. Rem. (1673) 23 When the Church was unsupplied, either by the death, or absence, or sickness of their Pastor. **1709** STRYPE *Ann. Ref.* vii. 106 Forced to keep them [*sc.* divines] in the Church, lest otherwise it should be wholly unsupplied. **1712** STEELE *Spect.* No. 294 ⁋1 Every Man who ..is unmindful of the unsupplied Distress of other Men. **1784** COWPER *Task* v. 31 The cattle..wait Their wonted fodder; not like hung'ring man, Fretful if unsupply'd.
b. Const. *with* (also †*by*, *of*).
1616 HIERON *Wks.* II. 37 They..shall not be left vnsupplyed of earthly things. **1652** DAVENANT *Verses to Author* in Benlowes *Theoph.*, Her Pow'r,..which unsupply'd By what wise Art would carefully provide, Is but love's lightning. **1740** JOHNSON *Blake* Wks. 1787 IV. 360 The town was..unsupplied with almost every thing necessary for supporting a siege. **1844** STOCQUELER *Handbk. Brit. India* 254 Its principal defect, as a place besieged, would consist in its being..unsupplied with drinkable water.
2. Not met or satisfied; not made up or replaced.
1616 BRETON *Good & Bad* 2 A Worthy King:..his bosome must not be searched, his will not disobeyed, his wants not unsupplied, nor his place vnregarded. **1700** DRYDEN *Sigism. & Guiscard.* 38 But, prodigal in ev'ry other Grant, Her Sire left unsupply'd her only Want. **1768** BLACKSTONE *Comm.* III. 385 These defects,..should they, after all, continue unremedied and unsupplied, still [etc.]. **1788** V. KNOX *Winter Even.* lii. (1790) I. 453 Nor is the loss of a Goldsmith's..sentimental strain unsupplied by a Cowper.
3. Not provided or furnished.
1808 G. EDWARDS *Pract. Plan* iv. 59 In fine, nothing need be left unsupplied in any respect.

unsu'pportable, *a.* [UN-1 7b and 5b.]
1. a. Too objectionable or annoying to be endured with equanimity or patience.
1586 SIDNEY *Let. to Walsingham* 14 Aug., We are now four monethes behynd [with pay], a thing unsupportable in this place. **1654** *Nicholas Papers* (Camden) II. 91 Indeed D. Gloucesters carriage to all persons is unsupportable. **1679** SOUTH *Serm.* (1697) I. 130 A disgrace put upon a man in company is unsupportable. **1710** ADDISON *Tatler* No. 221 ⁋4 A passionate Woman..is one of the most unsupportable Creatures in the World. **1792** BURKE *Let. to Langrishe* Wks. 1842 I. 558 The unsupportable mortification of asking his neighbours..for their votes.
b. Too oppressive or distressing to be endured; unendurable, intolerable.
1602 SIR R. WILBRAHAM *Jrnl.* (1902) 50 Tyme and treasure, the wast wherof is unsupportable. **1644** MILTON *Divorce* (ed. 2) A3b, As well may he..redeem himself from unsupportable disturbance, to honest peace. **1750** G. HUGHES *Barbados* 17 This hardship is not so unsupportable to them. **1788** CLARA REEVE *Exiles* II. 215 This thought was unsupportable; it led to despair. **1801** CHARLOTTE SMITH *Lett. Solit. Wand.* II. 243 The most unsupportable of all her distresses. **1832** BREWSTER *Nat. Magic* xii. 309 A heat.. unsupportable by the spectators. **1885** FARGUS *Slings & Arrows* 140 Had he by word or gesture shown that the constant presence of the man who had done his best to kill him was unsupportable.
2. That cannot be supported by physical strength.
1688 HOLME *Armoury* III. 312/2 Goalers..when they meet with sturdy and unruly Prisoners, to Lock and Chain them to some strong Post, or unsupportable Block.
3. Not admitting of support or defence; indefensible.
1710 SIR J. ST. LEGER *Managers Pro & Con.* 21 To support that unsupportable Sense of the Homilies, the

Doctor produces the concurrent Opinions of many Learned Fathers. **1777** *Burke's Corr.* (1844) II. 191 The unsupportable claim of this country to the right of taxing America without reserve. **1904** A. H. Sayce *Monument Facts & Higher Critical Fancies* (ed. 2) i. 18 The unsupported and unsupportable assumptions of the modern scholar. **1984** *Times* 6 June 5/3 The present overregulated system of air transport was quite unsupportable.

Hence **unsu'pportableness**; **-ably** *adv.*

1664 H. More *Myst. Iniq.* Pref. 4 To be affected, nay deeply and unsupportably afflicted. **1672** Wilkins *Nat. Relig.* ii. vii. 386 'Tis the unsupportableness of this, that many times doth cause men..to chuse..death rather than life. *a* **1697** South *Serm.* (1715) II. 177 His Conscience.. assures him, that he shall be infinitely, unsupportably miserable, if he does it.

unsu'pported, *ppl. a.* [un-[1] 8.]

1. Not supported by aid or assent; not backed up or corroborated.

1420–2 Lydg. *Siege Thebes* iii. 2985 Farwel wisdam..For lakke only of supportacioun. For vnsupported..Amphiorax sighen gan ful sore. **1609** Daniel *Civ. Wars* iii. lxxix, He.. will not avouch thy fact, But let the weight of thine owne infamie Fall on thee, vnsupported, and vnbackt. **1646** Sir T. Browne *Pseud. Ep.* Pref., To despaire the favourable looke of learning upon our single and unsupported endeavours. **1753** *Stewart's Trial* 270 Deposing to a long romantic story, in which he is altogether unsupported. **1798** S. & Ht. Lee *Canterb. T.* II. 393 An idle..unsupported assertion. **1812** Wellington in Gurw. *Desp.* (1837) IX. 349 Leaving behind them unprotected and unsupported the guns of Captain M'Donald's troop. **1854** Greenwood *Haps & Mishaps* 54 Yet thus far have I taken not one lonely and unsupported step.

b. Const. *by*.

1694 Atterbury *Serm.* (1726) I. iii. 103 How utterly unsupported either by the Secular Arm, or Secular Wisdom! **1752** Johnson *Rambler* No. 194 ¶ 12 What can be expected from reason unsupported by fashion, splendour, or authority? **1831** T. Hope *Ess. Orig. Man* II. 235 This doctrine is..too unsupported by anything we see, to have had many adherents. **1897** Mary Kingsley *W. Africa* 618 This statement is utterly unsupported by facts.

†**c.** Not bold or confident. *Obs.*

1697 Collier *Ess. Mor. Subj.* i. 210 Whereas a diffident and unsupported Behaviour in a Clergyman, is often suppos'd to proceed from ignoble Qualities.

2. Not physically supported or sustained.

1635 Person *Varieties* i. 33 The false-Prophet Mahomet, his Chest of Iron,..doth hang miraculously unsupported of any thing. **1681** Stair *Instit.* ii. xxvi. 97 Whether Convalescence can be proven otherways, then by going unsupported to Kirk and Mercat, I have seen no decision. **1707** Mortimer *Husb.* 106 [Peas] run upon the ground unsupported with sticks. **1813** Scott *Rokeby* ii. xiv, Now, like the wild-goat, must he dare An unsupported leap in air. **1862** Ansted *Channel Isl.* ii. xi. 288 The falling in of the unsupported roof.

fig. **1667** Milton *P.L.* ix. 432 Her self, though fairest unsupported Flour, From her best prop so farr, and storm so nigh. **1776** Gibbon *Decl. & F.* I. 328 On the slightest touch, the unsupported fabric of their pride and power fell to the ground.

Hence **unsu'pportedly** *adv.*; **-ness**.

1825 *Q. Rev.* XXXII. 286 Mr. Bowles tells us (as insidiously, and as unsupportedly as usual) Pope was much more explicit. **1890** J. H. Stirling *Philos. & Theol.* xvi. 307 Contingency in the sense of unsupportedness, the powerlessness of things in themselves.

unsu'pporting, *ppl. a.* (un-[1] 10.)

1595 Daniel *Civ. Wars* v. cv, For loosing war abroad, at home lost peace; Being with our vnsupporting selues close pent. **1653** Taylor *Serm. for Year* i. xiii. 165 People whose arme is all flesh, whose foot is all leather, and an unsupporting skin.

unsu'pposable, *a.* (un-[1] 7 b and 5 b.)

1650 Fuller *Pisgah* 373 Such sacriledge being unsupposable in that age. **1701** Beverley *Apoc. Quest.* 44 It is utterly Unsupposeable, That All the little Turns of History..should have Place in it. **1814** Scott *Wav.* lvii, Were such an unsupposable case to happen.

unsu'pposed, *ppl. a.* [un-[1] 8.]

†**1.** As *adv.* Unexpectedly. *Obs.*[−1]

c **1425** *St. Christina* xxiv. in *Anglia* VIII. 128/34 Sodeynly and vnsupposid alle hir body was taken of spirite, & turnyd in to a whirlynge about.

2. Not supposed or imagined.

[**1775** Ash.] **1821** Coleridge *Lett., Convers.*, etc. II. 38 If that judgment were given avowedly, on the mere unbelieved possibility, on an unsupposed supposition of the worst.

unsu'ppressable, *a.* (un-[1] 7 b.)

1781 Moore *View Soc. & Mann. Italy* I. 220 How many of our acquaintance..have we seen doing painful penance at the Hay-market; and, in the midst of unsuppressable yawnings, calling out, Charming! exquisite! bravissimo, etc.

unsu'ppressed, *ppl. a.* (un-[1] 8.)

1621 G. Sandys *Ovid's Met.* x. (1626) 212 Their feet, unwet, the sea might well haue borne: Or vnsuppressed stalks of standing corne. **1649** Milton *Eikon.* xxvi. 208 Driv'n away by unsuppressed Tumults. *a* **1691** Bp. Barlow *Rem.* (1693) 277 The unsuppressed Abby Lands are a fourth of the whole. **1809–14** Wordsw. *Excurs.* v. 118 Simple manners, feelings unsuppresst And undisguised. **1855** Milman *Lat. Chr.* xiv. vii. VI. 557 The secret influence of these teachers, unsuppressed by years of persecution. **1881** Miss Braddon *Asphodel* II. 145 That suppressed gout.. was only another name for unsuppressed ill-temper.

unsu'ppressible, *a.* (un-[1] 7, 5 b.)

1669 Earl Orrery *Parthen.* iii. vi. 184 If some unsuppressible groan force it selfe from me.

un'suppurative, *a.* (un-[1] 7.)

1822 Good *Study Med.* II. 271 A multitude of tumours or tubercles of different degrees of inflammation, some suppurative, some unsuppurative.

unsur'charge, *v.* (un-[2] 3.)

1642 Fuller *Holy & Prof. St.* ii. xxii. 144 Our Herald knows also to cure the surfet of Coats, and unsurcharge them, and how to wash out stained colours.

unsure (ʌn'ʃʊə(r), ʌn'ʃɔə(r)), *a.* [un-[1] 7.]

1. Not safe against attack or mishap; liable to danger or risk; exposed to hazard or peril; insecure.

a **1400–50** *Alexander* 2136 Bot, for þe cite was vnsure, þe seggis within Miȝt noȝt þe braidis a-bide of bernes enarmed. *c* **1520** in *Yorks. Archæol. Jrnl.* (1892) XII. 208 Who that puttith his trust in them I call hym most unsure. *a* **1542** Wyatt *Poems* (1913) I. 350 There is a rok..of suche nature, That drawithe the yron from the woode, And leveth the ship unsure. **1586** J. Hooker *Hist. Irel.* in *Holinshed* II. 73/2 In Wales..he found his defense so weake, and vnsure, that [etc.]. **1600** Holland *Livy* ix. 345 [They] had seene by experience..how unsure a cittie they inhabited and not unpregnable. **1649** G. Daniel *Trinarch., Hen. IV*, cclii, Hee knew his Claime, and how vnsure he sate Midst many enimies.

b. Not affording or conducive to safety; lacking in security; unsafe, liable to yield or give way.

1426 Lydg. *De Guil. Pilgr.* 13355 Placys that be most peryllous,..Most dredful and most vnsure, Ther I logge, off nature. *c* **1530** More *Answ. Frith* Wks. 842/2 If ye will.. deale surely for youre self, ye should rather leaue your vnsure waye whiche ye belieue, and come..to beleue as we doe. *a* **1547** Surrey *Æneid* ii. 31 Now but a bay, and rode vnsure for ship. **1588** *Reg. Privy Council Scot.* IV. 299 Throw the multitude of deidlie feidis and unsure passage. **1609** Holland *Amm. Marcell.* 201 Neither is it possible..to set firme footing upon the ground, so unsure it is and slipperie. *a* **1661** Holyday *Juvenal* (1673) 232 The ship.. made but of unsure or dangerous planks. **1727** P. Walker *Biogr. Presbyt.* (1827) I. 225 A very loose unsure Foundation. **1774** Burke *Sp. Amer. Tax.* Wks. II. 420 It was indeed a very curious show, but utterly unsafe to touch, and unsure to stand on. **1830** Cunningham *Brit. Paint.* II. 200 It seems they make unsure work at that church. **1866** G. Macdonald *Ann. Q. Neighb.* vi, Down the oak staircase ..[I] came very deliberately, feeling the unsure contact of sole and wax.

2. Marked or characterized by uncertainty or unsteadfastness; dependent on chance or accident; liable to fail; uncertain, precarious.

c **1412** Hoccleve *De Reg. Princ.* 16 Bysily in my mynde I gan revolue The welthe onsure of everye creature. *c* **1430** Lydg. *Min. Poems* (Percy Soc.) 197 The world unsuyr, fortune transmutable. *c* **1449** Pecock *Repr.* v. xiv. 560 Vnperfit men..ouȝten chese ful ofte the sikerer and surer good to hem bifore the vnsurer good. **1509** Barclay *Shyp Folys* 17 b, He that is symple, and on the grounde doth lye, ..Is surer by moche than he that lyeth on hye: Nowe vp, nowe downe vnsure as a Balaunce. **1559** *Mirr. Mag.* Bj, Ryches and promocion be vaine thynges and vnsure. **1584** C. Robinson, etc. *Handf. Pleas. Delights* D 3 b, Svch bitter fruit thy loue doth yeelde,..such hope vnsure. **1614** T. Adams *White Devil* 37 Their dwelling, like Cains, [is] very vnsure. **1629** Maxwell tr. *Herodian* 108 Holding it a sufficient guerdon of an vnsure Soueraignty. **1641** Baker *Chron., Edw. VI*, 82 King Edward supposing his state to be most safe when indeed it was most unsure. **1711** Pope *Temple Fame* 508 Unsure the tenure, but how vast the fine! **1755** J. Duncombe in *Connoisseur* No. 50. 296 Whose houses are as unsure a possession, as if they were built with cards. **1848** T. Aird *Chr. Bride* ii. xvi, Old dragon Erc must we secure;..our scheme were else unsure. **1873** M. Arnold *Lit. & Dogma* 138 The moral is, what an unsure stay, then, must miracles be!

3. a. Of persons, etc.: Not to be trusted or relied upon; unreliable, untrustworthy.

c **1445** Pecock *Donet* 208 þou schalt considre..how brotyl, vnsure a wrecche þou art. *a* **1470** Harding *Chron.* Ded. v, That people..Hath..been so vntowarde, So vnstedfast, inconstaunte, and vnsure, That [etc.]. *Ibid.* xxxix. viii, [Catellus] Tenne yere reigned,..And dyed so vnder his vnsure deité. *a* **1589** Palfreyman *Baldwin's Mor. Philos.* (1600) 70 Hee is..deceiptfull, of his promise vnsure. **1610** Healey *St. Aug. Citie of God* (1620) 409 The senses are weake, dull and vnsure teachers. **1635** Heywood *Hierarchy* vi. 331 Than th' Heart of man..There's nothing more inconstant and vnsure. **1653** Holcroft *Procopius, Goth. Wars* iv. 145 If we prove unsure to them, we shall not be trusty to you. **1790** Burke *Fr. Rev.* 94 They are always bad citizens, and perfectly unsure connexions. **1807** Coleridge *Lett.* (1895) 513 Which *sures* are such very unsure folks that [etc.]. **1867** Swinburne *Songs bef. Sunrise* (1871) 58 Though she slay them, yet shall they trust in her, For unsure there is nought nor unjust in her. **1888** Stevenson *Black Arrow* 21 Keep an eye on Sir Daniel; he is unsure.

†**b.** Weak, feeble. *Obs. rare*[−1].

1432–50 tr. *Higden* (Rolls) VI. 51 Grawntynge to theyme a lytelle wyne..thro the whiche the unsure flesche [L. *caro infirma*] scholde be noryschede.

4. Subject to doubt or uncertainty; not fixed, sure, or certain; doubtful.

c **1445** Pecock *Donet* 107 If in dyuynite were no strenger groundis..dyuynite were a symple and an vnsure faculte. **1534** More *Treat. Passion* Wks. 1279/2 Sure sory looking, for the vnsure time of deathe. *a* **1586** Sidney *Arcadia* i. iv, A thing no more unpleasant, then unsure, for the preserving of vertue. **1595** Daniel *Civ. Wars* ii. iv, That, in the smoake of innouations strange Builde huge vncertaine plots of vnsure pride. **1612** R. Carpenter *Soule's Sent.* 90 The speedy approach of death, sure in the end, vnsure in the time. **1646** Sir T. Browne *Pseud. Ep.* ii. vi. 100 It will be unsure to rely on any preservative. **1691** *Weesils* ii. 10 Conquest unsure made you refuse before. **1849** Cupples *Green Hand* xiv, In the unsure dusky sight I had of it, certainly, it [*sc.* a landmark] wore somewhat of that look.

5. Of persons, etc.: Lacking certainty, assurance, or confidence; not sure, assured, or certainly knowing; uncertain. Const. *of*, *for*, *to*, or with clause.

c **1400** *Destr. Troy* 11540 And now is nedfull for noye..All my gold for to geue,..Kepid in hurd, holdyn full long;.. And I vnsure of my-self, my sorow is the more. **1412–20** Lydg. *Chron. Troy* iv. 2144 She wolde for no þing be vnsure Of puruyaunce, nor with-oute stoor. *a* **1461** *Pol. Poems* (Rolls) II. 241 Ful unsewyr atte the laste may he be To sette hys herte in swyche abundaunce. *a* **1500** *Chaucer's Dreme* 1732 Wild beastes..ran as of their lives unsure. **1534** More *Comf. agst. Trib.* i. vi. (1573) 14 b, So blind is our mortalitie .., so vnsure also what maner mind we wil haue to morow. **1564** Feckenham *Let. to Cecil* in Strype *Ann. Ref.* xlv. (1709) 460 Being always after unsure, how, or by what means, he might be..knit thereunto again. **1579** Fenton *Guicciard.* i. 15 He is..of nothing more vnsure then to find remedy in his perils. **1595** Daniel *Civ. Wars* ii. xlvii, And here my sou'raigne to make longer stay T' attend for what you are vnsure will fall May slippe th' occasion and incense their will. *a* **1618** Raleigh *Observ.* (1651) 56 Numbers of people that were..thrust out of their habitations, or unsafe, or unsure for their lives. **1628** Bp. Hall *Old Relig.* 147 That God euer heares vs, wee are as sure, as wee are vnsure to be heard of Saints. **1679** in Wodrow *Hist. Suff. Ch. Scott.* (1722) II. App. xviii. 18 Not finding it fit to unhinge himself of the one Party, while he was yet unsure of the other. *a* **1850** Rossetti *Dante & Circle* (1874) 49 Thus, being all unsure which path to take. **1855** Sir J. Paget in *Mem. & Lett.* (1901) 209, I am unsure whether I can ever again have time. **1884** A. Vambéry *Life & Advent.* vii. (1889) 71 Unsure of my discovery, I did not address him.

b. Without const.

a **1500** *Chaucer's Dreme* 894 Thus was I in a joyous dout, Sure and unsurest of that rout. *a* **1536** Tindale in Marbeck *Bk. of Notes* (1581) 366 For then shall the conscience be vnsure, doubting [etc.]. *a* **1555** Latimer *Let.* in Foxe *A. & M.* (1563) 1327/1 If they saye they bee vnsure, when shall you bee sure that hathe so doubtefull teachers and vnsure? **1624** Heywood *Gunaik.* iv. 193 A man within himselfe unsure. **1896** Mrs. Caffyn *Quaker Grandmother* 155 His mother looked as meek and unsure as a grocer's widow.

6. Marked or characterized by lack of sureness, assurance, or certainty.

1633 P. Fletcher *Purple Isl.* viii. xiii, With him went Doubt, stagg'ring with steps unsure, That every way, and neither way enclin'd. **1829** Cunningham *Brit. Paint.* I. 207 His touch was unsure and he painted somewhat coarsely. **1867** M. Arnold *New Poems* 132 Light ignorance, and hurrying, unsure thoughts. **1883** R. W. Dixon *Mano* ii. i. 66 Never would he..His friend forsake, or make his faith unsure.

un'sured, *ppl. a.* (un-[1] 8.)

1595 Shaks. *John* ii. i. 471 For by this knot, thou shalt so surely tye Thy now vnsur'd assurance to the Crowne, That [etc.].

un'surely, *adv. rare.* [un-[1] 11.] Uncertainly; insecurely.

1595 Daniel *Civ. Wars* ii. cxix, The vanity of greatness he had tride, And how vnsurely standes the foote of pride. **1645** Hammond *View Infallib.* 38 Scripture when surely sensed..is a different medium from the same Scripture sensed unsurely.

un'sureness. [un-[1] 12.]

1. Uncertainty; insecurity.

1430–40 Lydg. *Bochas* i. i. (1494) A vi b/1 Where they stode first in sykernesse Of ioye..Oute of their rest they fyll in vnsurenesse In sorowe and sighynge. *c* **1440** *Eng. Conq. Ireland* 51 And euery Surnesse hath vnsurnes at the ende. **1530** Palsgr. 285/2 Unsurenesse, *deseurete*. **1565** Cooper *Thesaurus* s.v. *Infirmitas*, What vnsurenes doe you see in the mariage hetherto? **1573** *Satir. Poems Reform.* I. 275 The greit frailtie and vnsureness of all strenthis eirthly. **1611** Speed *Hist. Gt. Brit.* vi. xxii. 226 The state of man..doth shew..with what vnsurenesse the seat of maiesty is possest. **1863** Holme Lee *A. Warleigh* III. 133 Her hints to Rachel ..touching the unsureness of the future.

†**2.** Unsteadiness, fickleness. *Obs.*[−1]

a **1470** Tiptoft *Tulle on Friendsh.* (Caxton, 1481) C ij, There ben two thynges, which prove in many men lightnesse and unsurenesse.

†**un'surety.** *Obs.* [un-[1] 12.] Insecurity, uncertainty.

c **1460** Fortescue *Abs. & Lim. Mon.* v. (1885) 119 What dishonour is this, and abatynge of the glorie of a kynge. But yet it is most to his vnsuyrte. **1483** *Act 1 Rich. III*, c. 1 § 1 By privey and unknowen feoffementes greate unsuertie..and grevous vexacions daily growen among the King's Subgiettis. **1534** More *Comf. agst. Trib.* iii. Wks. 1219/1 Of the vnsuretye of landes and possessions. **1563** *Mirr. Mag.* (ed. 2) S j, To shewe thereby the vnsuerty in this life, Marke wel my fal. **1609** J. Davies (Heref.) *Humours Heaven* i. lxxiii, Where's vnsuretie, feare must needs be there. **1625** R. Horn *Shield of Righteous* 86 Earthly Princes are subiect to.. great vnsuretie of life and estate.

un'surfeiting, *ppl. a.* (un-[1] 10.)

1653 Gauden *Hierasp.* 70 To follow him with all obediential love;..unsatiably satisfied with his unsurfetting-sweetness. **1772** Jas. Usher *Clio* (ed. 3) 140 The engaging image..of easy unsurfeiting joys.

un'surgical, *a.* (un-[1] 7.)

1807 S. Cooper *First Lines Surg.* 201 To increase these evils by rough handling of the part is..unsurgical. **1884** C. B. Kelsey *Dis. Rectum & A.* xi. 297 The operation is rough, uncertain, and unsurgical. **1897** *Allbutt's Syst. Med.* II. 1057 The harpoon designed..for this purpose produces an unsurgical wound.

un'surging, *ppl. a.* (un-[1] 10.)

1619 Drayton *Poems, Matilda* 344 As a Ship, that in a quiet Calme Flotes vp and downe on the vnsurging Seas.

unsur'mised, *ppl. a.* (UN-^{1} 8.)
[1775 ASH.] **1818** KEATS *Isabella* xliii, She had devised.. How her short absence might be unsurmised. **1885** *Encycl. Brit.* XVIII. 681/2 Michelangelo..was opening men's eyes ..to possibilities of achievement as yet unsurmised.

unsur'mountable, *a.* [UN-^{1} 7 b and 5 b.]
1. Incapable of being surpassed or exceeded. *rare.*
1611 COTGR., *Insurmontable*, vnsurmountable, vnexceedable. **1745** YOUNG *Nt. Th.* VIII. 328 That unsurmountable extreme of guilt!
2. Incapable of being surmounted or overcome; insurmountable: **a.** Of difficulties, etc. (Common in 18th c.)
1701 *Lond. Gaz.* No. 3713/1 We passed the Mountains.. Which were thought unsurmountable. **1757** FOOTE *Author* I. Wks. 1799 I. 141 The obscurity..of your birth, will prove an unsurmountable bar. **1788** *Trifler* No. 11. 134 The Prolixity of six and thirty Stanzas in a Pastoral Tale, proves an unsurmountable Exception. **1911** RIKER *Henry Fox* II. 126 The obstacle was not unsurmountable.
b. Of feelings.
c **1740** MRS DELANY *Life & Corr.* (1861) I. 29 The courtship..was awkward to Gromio (who saw too well my unsurmountable dislike). **1771** GOLDSM. *Hist. Eng.* II. 85 An unsurmountable aversion to the English government. **1791** BURKE *Let. to Memb. Nat. Assemb.* 50 If disgust, if unsurmountable nausea, drive them away from such spectacles,.. I cannot blame them.
3. Inextinguishable, unquenchable.
1725 *Fam. Dict.* s.v. *Fever*, It causes a violent Heat and unsurmountable Thirst.
Hence **unsur'mountableness.**
1894 *Thinker* VI. 76 Superstitious faith in nature's unsurmountableness.

unsur'mounted, *ppl. a.* (UN-^{1} 8.)
[1775 ASH.] **1787** T. MONRO, etc. *Olla Podrida* No. 25 ¶ 1 Difficulties unsurmounted in biography.

unsur'passable, *a.* (UN-^{1} 7 b and 5 b.)
1611 COTGR., *Insurmontable*,..vnsurpassable, vnvanquishable. **1799** W. TAYLOR in Robberds *Mem.* (1843) I. 243 The descriptive parts of this idyll are capital—are unsurpassable. **1837** CARLYLE *Fr. Rev.* I. III. iii, For freshness of style,..that opening Harangue of his was unsurpassable. **1876** *Contemp. Rev.* June 36 A sea-board.. capable of producing..fruits, in quantities unsurpassable.
Hence **unsur'passably** *adv.*
1859 RUSKIN *Two Paths* App. I. 254 Entirely, admirably, unsurpassably right, under the conditions. **1872** *Carlyle's Schiller* Wks. 1899 XXV. 226 Dannecker..has unsurpassably cut this head in marble for us.

unsur'passed, *ppl. a.* (UN-^{1} 8.)
[1775 ASH.] **1818** BYRON *Ch. Har.* IV. xxxix, Oh, victor unsurpass'd in modern song! **1840** THACKERAY *Barber Cox* Nov., A speech..unsurpassed for eloquence. **1882** *Nature* XXV. 429 On such a topic he is entitled to speak with at least an unsurpassed authority.

unsur'prised, *ppl. a.* (UN-^{1} 8.)
1591 FLORIO *2nd Fruites* 77 A pawn that could passe the pikes of seuen places vnsurprised. **1593** MARLOWE *Edw. II*, II. v, Though deuorsed from king Edwards eyes, Yet liueth Pierce of Gaueston vnsurprizd. **1629** H. BURTON *Truth's Triumph* 250 They may be certain of keeping their weak fort of vncertainty vnsurprised. **1655** FULLER *Wounded Consc.*, etc. (1867) 314 Nor was there any Herb or Flower in the whole Garden left unsurprised with fear. **1841** EMERSON *Eng. Traits* xiv. *Literature*, The unique fact in literary history, the unsurprised reception of Shakespeare. **1876** T. HARDY *Ethelberta* xxxv, She..gave him an unsurprised gesture of recognition. **1882** CHR. ROSSETTI *Resurgam* Poems (1904) 412 Strenuous thro' day and unsurprised by night He runs a race with Time and wins the race.

unsur'prising, *ppl. a.* (UN-^{1} 10.)
1671 WOODHEAD *St. Teresa* I. Pref. 34 Purity from committing any, foreknown, and unsurprising, venial sin. **1688** in Ellis *Orig. Lett.* Ser. I. III. 351 It was no unsurprising spectacle. **1740** CIBBER *Apol.* 69 Without this ..the Performance will come out..somewhere defectively, unsurprizing to the Hearer. **1927** *New Republic* 12 Oct. 219/1 The unsurprising result is a sermon of the first class, and a novel of the third. **1975** *Listener* 18 Dec. 819/1 Adaptations of Dickens's works..are meant to make you feel good. This is unsurprising, as..it could be argued that this is exactly how Dickens intends you to feel.
Hence **unsur'prisingly** *adv.*
1961 in WEBSTER. **1972** *Bankers Mag.* (Boston, Mass.) Winter 73/1 Unsurprisingly, no agency has ever approved any proposal that would reduce its own supervisory role. **1979** *Field* 28 Nov. 1417/2 The passage concluded unsurprisingly.

unsu'rrendered, *ppl. a.* (UN-^{1} 8.)
[1775 ASH.] *a* **1800** COWPER *Iliad* (ed. 2) VII. 376 Helen is mine, an unsurrender'd prize For ever. **1827** JARMAN *Powell's Devises* II. 123 None of this reasoning is now applicable to a devise of unsurrendered copyholds. **1848** J. MARTINEAU in *Life* (1902) I. 185 Military parties were told off to..search every house for the unsurrendered arms. *a* **1850** J. C. CALHOUN *Wks.* (1863) I. 147 It must..remain unsurrendered and unimpaired in the people of the several States.

unsu'rrendering, *ppl. a.* (UN-^{1} 10.)
1840 CARLYLE *Heroes* iii. ¶ 13 The face of one wholly in protest, and life-long unsurrendering battle, against the world.

unsu'rrounded, *ppl. a.* (UN-^{1} 8.)
[1775 ASH.] **1813** T. BUSBY *Lucretius* I. I. Comm. p. xxix, We cannot imagine an unsurrounded convex. **1859** CORNWALLIS *Panorama New World* I. 242 There she lay,.. unsurrounded by the comforts that were most needful. **1863** TYNDALL *Heat* ix. 283 The lamp is naked, unsurrounded by its camera.

unsur'veyable, *a.* (UN-^{1} 7 b.)
1833 CARLYLE *Misc.* (1840) IV. 256 Every Man..reaches downwards and upwards unsurveyable, fading into the regions of Immensity and of Eternity. **1847** HARE *Guesses* (ed. 3) 383 The field of operation is so vast and unsurveyable.

unsur'veyed, *ppl. a.* (UN-^{1} 8.)
1546 in *Vict. Co. Hist., Warwick.* II. (1908) 303/1 Divers Chantries unsurveyed and no rentalls thereof delyvered. **1758** JOHNSON *Idler* No. 3 ¶ 3 My predecessors..had the whole field of life before them, untrodden and unsurveyed. **1843** *Penny Cycl.* XXV. 241/2 In 1833..more than three-fifths of the island [was] unappropriated and unsurveyed. **1879** MISS BIRD *Lady's Life in Rocky Mount.* 120 Such as it is, Estes Park is mine. It is unsurveyed, 'no man's land'.

unsuscepti'bility. (UN-^{1} 12, 5 b. Cf. next.)
[1775 ASH.] **1805** *Monthly Mag.* XX. 231 Proofs of the permanency of the state of Unsusceptibility of the Small Pox. **1850** ROBERTSON *Serm.* Ser. III. ix. (1857) 133 That which ought to be men's shame becomes their boast—unsusceptibility of any fresh emotion.

unsu'sceptible, *a.* [UN-^{1} 7 and 5 b.]
†**1.** Unable to receive and retain. *Obs.*$^{-1}$
1692 DRYDEN *Cleomenes* IV. 43 Some Men are made of such a leaky Mould, That their fill'd Vessels can no fortune hold:..Of that unsusceptible Make am I.
2. Not susceptible *of* some operation, influence, etc.; = INSUSCEPTIBLE *a.* a.
(*a*) **1731** SWIFT *Strephon & Chloe* 86 While she a Goddess dy'd in Grain Was unsusceptible of Stain. **1799** KIRWAN *Geol. Ess.* 5 What then should render these facts and the circumstances attending them unsusceptible of testimony? **1816** BENTHAM *Chrestom.* 99 Although not perhaps completely susceptible, it is however not altogether unsusceptible, of a remedy. **1868** M. PATTISON *Academ. Org.* iv. 69 Statements..entirely unsusceptible of proof. **1890** *Retrospect Med.* CII. 237 Cases where the sugar..is unsusceptible of entire removal from the system by dietetic treatment alone.
(*b*) **1751** JOHNSON *Rambler* No. 153 ¶ 16 An old friend, who professed himself unsusceptible of any impressions from prosperity or misfortune. **1784** *Cook's 3rd Voy.* IV. ii. II. 310 They are certainly not wholly unsusceptible of the tender passions. **1814** SOUTHEY *Let. to J. King* 27 Feb., My skin..may very possibly be unsusceptible of this particular irritation. **1849** MACAULAY *Hist. Eng.* ix. II. 519 His serene intellect, singularly unsusceptible of enthusiasm, and singularly averse to extremes.
b. Const. *to.* = INSUSCEPTIBLE *a.* b.
1872 SANFORD *Estimates Eng. Kings* 400 They rendered him comparatively unsusceptible to the feelings of resentment and implacability.
3. Not readily liable to impressions; = INSUSCEPTIBLE *a.* c.
1779 *Mirror* No. 14, Men unfeeling and unsusceptible, commonly beat the beaten track with activity and resolution. **1860** FROUDE *Hist. Eng.* VI. 92 She was unsusceptible; she had no experience in love. **1893** F. F. MOORE *I Forbid Banns* xxvii, Surely the ivory—that most unsusceptible of materials—was warm from her hand.

unsu'sceptive, *a.* (UN-^{1} 7 and 5 b.)
1825 GOOD *Study Med.* (ed. 2) II. 373 The habit, or idiosyncracy of most anatomists fortunately renders them altogether unsusceptive of its impression.

†**unsu'spect,** (*ppl.*) *a. Obs.* Chiefly *Sc.* [UN-^{1} 7, 8 b, and 5 b.] Not subject to suspicion.
c **1380** WYCLIF *Sel. Wks.* II. 107 þe dedis þat Crist dide, ben unsuspect evydence þat Crist is boþe God and man. **1388** —— *Ecclus.* xxv. 9, I magnefiede nyne thingis vnsuspect of the herte. **1409** in *Exch. Rolls Scotl.* IV. p. ccxi, Askand thaim to be submitted to thaim and to their counselis unsuspect apon sic complaintis. *c* **1480** HENRYSON *Fables, Wolf & Lamb* 74, I oblis me rycht heir, That I sall byde ane vnsuspect Assyis. **1512** *Reg. Privy Seal Scotl.* I. 369/2 Befor the lordis of counsale or utheris unsuspect jugis. **1583** *Leg. Bp. St. Androis* 139 Grit oethes he sweirs,..And bad thame hald him vnsuspect. **1606** SYLVESTER *Du Bartas* II. iv. I. *Tropheis* 1055 David's foule defect Was yet un-seen, uncensur'd, un-suspect. **1665** GLANVILL *Def. Van. Dogm.* 83 Though his writings were never so unsuspect and certain in the main. **1678** SIR G. MACKENZIE *Crim. Laws Scot.* I. xxvi. §6 (1699) 134 Proved by most unsuspect Witnesses.

unsu'spectable, *a.* (UN-^{1} 7 b.)
1660 H. MORE *Myst. Godl.* VII. x. 323 That vigorous passion and elevation of spirit, and yet all so unsuspectable of any humane artifice. **1748** RICHARDSON *Clarissa* III. 108 Shall the man be guilty, yet expect the woman to be guiltless, and even unsuspectable?

unsu'spectably, *adv.* (UN-^{1} 11. Cf. prec.)
1748 RICHARDSON *Clarissa* III. 30 Grief so unsuspectably sincere.

unsu'spected, *ppl. a.* [UN-^{1} 8 and 5 b.]
1. Without being suspected.
c **1530** MORE *Answ. Frith* Wks. 833/1 Our english heretikes..might there imprynt theyr heresies amonge other matters, & so sende them hither vnsuspected. **1660** *Nicholas Papers* (Camden) IV. 251 To haue occasion therby to act unsuspected something..contrary vnto his professions. **1725** DE FOE *Voy. round World* (1840) 97 The governor putting so much confidence in us, that we might go on shore in the very fort unsuspected. **1798** S. & HT. LEE *Canterb. T.* II. 123 [He was] enabled, unsuspected, to trace ..the emotions of the heart he best loved. **1813** COLERIDGE *Remorse* II. i. 57 But I had traced her, stolen unnotic'd on them, And unsuspected..heard the whole.
2. Not regarded with suspicion; not considered to be suspicious or doubtful.
a **1586** SIDNEY *Arcadia* I. xiv, Hoping that (going for a woman) my lookes would passe, either unmarked, or unsuspected. **1594** SHAKS. *Rich. III*, III. v. 23 That ignoble Traytor, The dangerous and vnsuspected Hastings. **1603** KNOLLES *Hist. Turks* (1621) 147 For his too profuse bountie he could not be vnsuspected of his brother. **1670** CLARENDON *Hist. Reb.* XII. §129 Those principal heads of the Clans who..were of known, or unsuspected Affection to the King. **1747** J. LIND *Lett. Navy* (1757) I. 16 The courage of our common seamen is hitherto generally unsuspected. **1760** *Ann. Reg., Hist.* 39/2 They will find, both in his fortune and his virtue, abundant matter for just and unsuspected panegyric. **1827** SCOTT *Chron. Canongate* vi, Well judging that he would observe more wholesome caution if he conceived his character unsuspected, than if he were detected. **1855** MACAULAY *Hist. Eng.* xviii. IV. 234 Russell, as far as can now be discovered, was still unsuspected.
absol. **1800** *Asiat. Ann. Reg., Proc. E. Ind. Ho.* 115 It was not justice to confound the unsuspected with the suspected.
b. Const. *to* with inf., or *of*.
1647 CLARENDON *Hist. Reb.* I. §202 Those Infusions proceeded from those unsuspected to have any inclinations to Change. **1800** *Asiat. Ann. Reg., Proc. E. Ind. Ho.* 137/2 The director..was quite unsuspected of being concerned in the sale of it.
3. Not suspected to exist, or to bear a certain character; not thought of.
1620 J. TAYLOR (Water P.) *Jack a Lent* B 3 b, Some againe ..doe scout into..diuers secret vnsuspected places. **1654** FULLER *Two Serm.* 23 Many a close, secret and unsuspected Christian. **1693** CONGREVE in *Dryden's Juvenal* XI. (1697) 284 This Day..thou shalt perceive Whether, my self I keep those Rules I give, Or else, an unsuspected Glutton live. **1759** STERNE *Tr. Shandy* II. xvii, An unsuspected fissure in thy master's pocket. **1784** COWPER *Task* VI. 545 A storm was near, An unsuspected storm. **1810** SCOTT *Lady of L.* I. xxv, The mountain-maiden show'd A clambering unsuspected road. **1874** J. GEIKIE *Gt. Ice Age* iii. 26 It..opens up new channels of discovery which otherwise might have remained unsuspected and unknown.
Hence **unsu'spectedness.**
1655 FULLER *Ch. Hist.* X. ii. §27 They hoped..(by the strangenesse of the act, and unsuspectednesse of the actors) to amuze all men. **1802-12** BENTHAM *Ration. Judic. Evid.* (1827) II. 433 The popularity, the unsuspectedness, is not purchased, but at the expense of appropriate experience.

unsu'spectedly, *adv.* [UN-^{1} 11.]
1. Without being suspected.
1645 W. JENKYN *Stil-Destroyer* 44 Poyson is..given.. under the notion of good food.., and so it is taken unsuspectedly. **1663** BOYLE *Usef. Exp. Nat. Philos.* II. 267 The subtle murtherers do as unsuspectedly as fatally, execute their malice or revenge. **1695** D. TURNER *Apol. Chyrurg.* 24 That he the more unsuspectedly may carry on his Cheats. **1720** MRS. MANLEY *Power of Love* 156 Caton understood no Geography but what had been taught her.. in the Country of Love, whence Fauxgarde might unsuspectedly betray her to his wish. **1808** HAN. MORE *Cœlebs* xiii. I. 172 Till he has unsuspectedly landed his opponent in the pure ethics of the gospel.
b. Beyond suspicion; evidently.
1748 RICHARDSON *Clarissa* (1811) III. 2 Grief so unsuspectedly sincere, for an escape so critical.
2. Unsuspectingly.
1826 P. POUNDEN *France & Italy* 177 The Jews.. unsuspectedly bear in their hands the prophetic records.

unsu'spectful, *a.* [UN-^{1} 7.] Unsuspicious.
1781 GIBBON *Decl. & F.* xxxiii. (1787) III. 334 The credulous and unsuspectful count had armed the province.

unsu'spectfulness. (UN-^{1} 12. Cf. prec.)
1852 LEVER *M. Tiernay* xlii, 'What a glorious gift is unsuspectfulness,' said he, feelingly.

unsu'spectible, *a.* (UN-^{1} 7.)
1802-12 BENTHAM *Ration. Judic. Evid.* (1827) II. 105 Of all conceivable sources the most trustworthy and unsuspectible.

unsu'specting, *ppl. a.* [UN-^{1} 10, 5 d.] Not suspecting; not harbouring any suspicion.
1595 DANIEL *Civil Wars* IV. lxxiii, He such deepe aduise applide..To circumuent an vnsuspecting wight, Before he could discerne of their despight. **1703** ROWE *Fair Penit.* II. ii. 594 My unsuspecting, valiant, honest Friend. **1703** —— *Ulysses* I. i, Temper..open as the Day and unsuspecting. **1776** GIBBON *Decl. & F.* xii. I. 339 They..indulged their appetite for revenge and plunder, by frequent descents on the unsuspecting shores of Asia, Greece, and Africa. **1864** PUSEY *Lect. Daniel* iii. 160 [His] simple unsuspecting trust.. in the Romans. **1891** FARRAR *Darkn. & Dawn* xxxiii, He.. ventured to make her an unsuspecting agent in his little plot.
b. Const. *of*, or with direct object.
1654 R. CODRINGTON tr. *Iustine* XIII. 221 The Traytors.. unsuspecting their advance..were assaulted themselves. **1725** POPE *Odyssey* IX. 522 He felt their fleeces..and let them safely go, All unsuspecting of their freight below. **1758** GOLDSM. *Mem. Protestant* (1895) II. 108, I had the Pleasure of seeing them, unsuspecting my Design, and greedily catching at the seeming Victory. **1838** FOSTER *Ess.* (1844) I. 565 To take this step..unsuspecting of the advantage that would be taken of a needy youth. **1885** FARGUS *Slings & Arrows* 114 The moment when, utterly unsuspecting of our contiguity, Eustace Grant would find himself confronted by me.
Hence **unsu'spectingness.**
1883 H. JAMES *Portraits of Places* xii. 253 Her quiet-eyed unsuspectingness only makes her the more a part of his delicate entertainment.

unsu'spectingly, *adv.* [UN-^{1} 11.] Without suspicion.
1656 JER. TAYLOR *Deus Justif.* Pref. 3 It became almost a shame to examine what the world believed so unsuspectingly. **1787** A. HILDITCH *Rosa* II. 44 He waited patiently and unsuspectingly her return. **1798** *Lit. Mem. Living Authors* II. 162 Those talents which he had unsuspectingly cultivated in the groves of the academy. **1818** LADY MORGAN *Autobiog.* (1859) 94 One of those

charming *causeries* with the general, to which he unsuspectingly lent himself. **1883** D. C. MURRAY *Hearts* viii, For a moment she felt as a swimmer feels when he floats unsuspectingly into a sudden, powerful eddy.

unsu'spended, *ppl. a.* (UN-[1] 8.)
1701 NORRIS *Ideal World* I. ii. 111 If an ideal proposition be an actual unsuspended truth. **1792** WORDSW. *Descr. Sk.* 39 While unsuspended wheels the village dance. **1891** T. HARDY *Tess* xxxvi, His thought had been unsuspended; he was becoming ill with thinking.

unsu'spicion. [UN-[1] 12.] Lack of suspicion or suspiciousness.
1792 W. ROBERTS *Looker-on* No. 10 (1794) I. 134 In such a case..the vanquished has nothing to shame him, unless truth and unsuspicion can do it. *a* **1849** H. COLERIDGE *Ess.* (1851) I. 315 A calm unsuspicion, a grave taking of the matter for granted. **1876** 'ANNIE THOMAS' *Blotted out* xxv, I fear that Sydney, in his unsuspicion, will be readily won.

unsu'spicious, *a.* (UN-[1] 7).
1595 DANIEL *Civil Wars* IV. xxxv, But vnsuspicious magnanimitie Shames such effects of feare, and force to show. **1671** MILTON *Samson* 1635 His guide..unsuspitious led him. **1727** THOMSON *Britannia* 110 Like brothers live, in amity combin'd, And unsuspicious faith. **1777** ROBERTSON *Hist. Amer.* III. I. 211 The unsuspicious confidence of a man conscious of no crime. **1825** SCOTT *Talism.* xx, The unsuspicious object of the dark treachery. **1871** B. TAYLOR *Faust* (1872) II. III. 165 This place all unsuspicious I forsook For Cytheræa's fane.
b. Const. *of* or with clause.
1589 WARNER *Alb. Eng.* 158 Her Sister,..simply unsuspitious of the sequell, prouided..a pyle of dry Faggots. **1796** MME. D'ARBLAY *Camilla* III. 279 Unsuspicious of his remarks..[she] was gay. *Ibid.* V. 7 Edgar [was] not wholly unsuspicious such an accident might happen. **1825** SCOTT *Betrothed* iii, He was not unsuspicious, though altogether fearless, of the result.
Hence **unsu'spiciously** *adv.*; **unsu'spiciousness.**
a **1812** BUCKMINSTER *Serm.* (1827) 94 Epistles ..*unsuspiciously authentic. **1854** THACKERAY *Newcomes* i, Little lambkin was lying unsuspiciously at the side of the wolf. **1809** MAR. EDGEWORTH *Manœuvring* iv, A fluent panegyric upon the hereditary *unsuspiciousness of his temper. *a* **1834** COLERIDGE *Lit. Rem.* (1836) II. 267 Her absolute unsuspiciousness, and holy entireness of love.

unsu'stainable, *a.* (UN-[1] 7 b.)
a **1677** BARROW *Serm.* Wks. 1687 I. 255 A weapon..whose impression is altogether inevitable and unsustainable. **1716** M. DAVIES *Athen. Brit.* III. 61 [To] revive an unsustainable Cause, so often sunk, and so often irretrievably baffled. **1740** *Phil. Trans.* XLI. 414 This Notion is certainly as unsustainable as the First. **1857** TOULMIN SMITH *Parish* 297 It was unanimously held that these pleas were unsustainable. **1885** SIR J. BACON in *Law Times' Rep.* LII. 210/2 The application is wholly unsustainable.

unsu'stained, *ppl. a.* [UN-[1] 8.]
1. Not materially sustained or supported.
1630 DRUMM. OF HAWTH. *Flowers Sion, Hymn Passion* 9 Seeing..How vnsustain'd the Earth still steadfast stands. **1667** MILTON *P.L.* IX. 430 Each Flour..whose head..Hung drooping unsustained. **1725** POPE *Odyssey* XII. 517 All unsustain'd between the wave and sky, Beneath my feet the whirling billows fly.
2. Not supported by assistance, etc.
1697 DRYDEN *Æneis* XI. 1238 The Volscians quit the Field; And, unsustain'd, the Chiefs of Turnus yield. **1719** YOUNG *Par. Job* 236 Hale are their young, from human frailties freed; Walk unsustain'd, and unassisted feed. **1809–14** WORDSW. *Excurs.* VI. 767 With a sigh She spake, yet, I believe, not unsustained By faith in glory [etc.]. **1856** KANE *Arct. Expl.* II. xii. 129 A penalty is denounced against ..the accuser for his unsustained prosecution. **1876** BANCROFT *Hist. U.S.* I. i. 17 Unsustained by Cartier, Roberval accomplished no more than a verification of previous discoveries.
3. Not maintained at a uniform level of excellence; flagging in interest.
1817 COLERIDGE *Biog. Lit.* xiv. II. 9 An unsustained composition from which the reader collects rapidly the general result unattracted by the component parts.

unsu'staining, *ppl. a.* (UN-[1] 10.)
1818 SHELLEY *Julian* 538 One unsustaining reed. **1820** —— *Sensit. Pl.* 78 The light winds which from unsustaining wings Shed the music of many murmurings. **1880** MISS BIRD *Japan* II. 267 Rice and eggs were..unsustaining food.

† **unswac,** *a.*: see SWAC *a.*

un'swaddle, *v.* [UN-[2] 4.] *trans.* To free from, take out of, swaddling bands or clothes.
1580 NORTH *Plutarch* (1595) 382 His wife did vnswadell the young boy to wash and shift him. **1633** B. JONSON *Tale Tub* I. iv, Puppy ha' scarce unswadled my legges yet. **1662** GREENHALGH in Ellis *Orig. Lett.* Ser. II. IV. 16 When they had brought it to the altar, four or five were busied in uncovering and unswaddling the roll. **1853** G. J. CAYLEY *Las Alforjas* I. 184 Standing at the foot of the mattress, we fell back like tragic heroes, so as not to unswaddle our feet in lying down.
fig. **1600** NASHE *Summer's Last Will* Prol., Their censures we wey not, whose sences are not yet vnswadled. **1631** FULLER *David's Punishm.* vii, As when a tender rose begins to blow, Yet scarce unswaddled is.

un'swallowed, *ppl. a.* (UN-[1] 8, 8 c.)
13.. *E.E. Allit. P.* B. 1253 Alle þat swypped vnswolȝed of þe sworde kene, Þay wer..broþely broȝt to babyloyn. **1663** WATERHOUSE *Fortescutus Illustr.* 398 Thinking his unswallowed-down carcase happiness..enough for him. **1760** H. BROOKE *Fool of Qual.* (1809) I. 70 The guests..sat some time with open mouth, and unswallowed victuals. **1837** CARLYLE *Fr. Rev.* II. III. iv, A man may moderate its paroxysms,..and keep himself unswallowed on the top of it [*sc.* a 'whirlpool of Babylonish confusions']. **1859** TENNYSON *Geraint & Enid* 1479 The brawny spearman let his cheek Bulge with the unswallow'd piece, and turning, stared.

un'swan, *v.* (UN-[2] 6 b.)
1864 BROWNING *Worst of it* 6 Not you, the pride Of the day, my swan, that a first fleck's fall On her wonder of white, must unswan, undo!

un'swan-like, *a.* (UN-[1] 7 c.)
1837 DICKENS *Pickw.* xxx, Mr. Winkle..was being assisted over the ice by Mr. Weller, in a very singular and un-swan-like manner.

unswar(e, obs. ff. ANSWER *sb.* and *v.*

un'swathable, *a.* (UN-[1] 7 b.)
1846 LANDOR *Imag. Conv.* Wks. I. 78/1 There not being bone nor muscle nor blood enough.., he collapses into unswathable flabbiness.

un'swathe, *v.* [UN-[2] 4.] *trans.* To free from swathings; to unswaddle.
a **1400** *Octovian* 302 Her chylderen sche douȝte þer to baþe; Sche sat adoun hem to vnswade. **1598** FLORIO, *Sfasciare*, to vnswathe, to vnbind. **1604** DRAYTON *Moses Map Miracle* 13 This most sweete princesse..Soone on her knee vnswathes it as her owne. **1711** ADDISON *Spect.* No. 90 ¶7 About Nine a Clock..an old Woman came to unswathe me. **1788** MRS. HUGHES *Henry & Isabella* I. 115 Sir George ..insisted upon the nurse's immediately unpinning and unswathing him. *a* **1822** SHELLEY *Fragm. Unf. Drama* 207 Spring indeed Came to unswathe her infants. **1837** P. KEITH *Bot. Lex.* s.v. *Bulb*, An Egyptian mummy that was lately unswathed in this country. **1896** *Allbutt's Syst. Med.* I. 419 At the end of every three hours the child is unswathed.
fig. **1593** NASHE *Christ's T.* I j b, I will vnswathe thy breast with my sharpe knyfe. **1827** COLERIDGE *Lit. Rem.* (1839) IV. 319 Spinoza himself describes his own philosophy as in substance the same with that of..the Cabalists—only unswathed from the Biblical dress. **1833** TENNYSON in Ld. Tennyson *Mem.* (1897) I. 115 The clouds unswathe them from the height. **1873** H. ROGERS *Orig. Bible* i. 42 How came any of them to unswathe themselves from all these lifelong notions.

un'swayable, *a.* (UN-[1] 7 b.)
1607 SHAKS. *Cor.* v. vi. 26 To this end, He bow'd his Nature, neuer knowne before, But to be rough, vnswayable, and free. *a* **1945** E. R. EDDISON *Mezentian Gate* (1958) i. 5 He was..hard-necked and unswayable in policy. **1979** *United States 1980/81* (Penguin Travel Guides) 84 Bostonians..have the Irish tradition of impassioned and unswayable conviction.

un'swayed, *ppl. a.* [UN-[1] 8.]
1. Unwielded; uncontrolled.
1594 SHAKS. *Rich. III*, IV. iv. 470 Is the Chayre emptie? is the Sword vnsway'd? Is the King dead? *c* **1600** —— *Sonn.* cxli, Nor my fiue sences can Disuade one foolish heart from seruing thee, Who leaues vnswai'd the likenesse of a man, Thy proud hearts slaue..to be.
2. Uninfluenced, unaffected.
1615 SANDYS *Trav.* III. 154, I will declare what I haue obserued, vnswayed with either of their vices. **1652** BENLOWES *Theoph.* II. li, Make haste Lest you into despair be cast: The Judge unsway'd. **1718** J. HUGHES *Patriot* 14 Where's the patriot, by these virtues known, Unsway'd by others' passions, or his own? **1808** WELLINGTON in Gurw. *Desp.* (1835) IV. 249 It was my opinion (unswayed, I trust, by any unworthy motives) that [etc.]. **1847** HARRIS *Life Ld. Hardwicke* II. 327 Perseverance in the strict line of honesty and duty, unswayed by any considerations of this nature.
3. Unmoved, unstirred.
1851 HAWTHORNE *Snow Image*, etc. (1883) 200 The drops of rain that came down in monotonous succession, unswayed by a breath of wind.
Hence **un'swayedness.**
a **1656** HALES *Gold. Rem.* I. (1673) 246 That constancy and unswayedness in our lives and actions.

un'swear, *v.* [UN-[2] 3, 7. Cf. OFris. *unswera, und-, untswera*, MDu. *ontsweren* (Du. *ontzweren*), MLG. *entsweren*, MHG. *untswern.*] *trans.* To retract (something sworn or asserted).
1595 SHAKS. *John* III. i. 245 [To] Vn-sweare faith sworne. **1596** *Edward III*, II. i. 326 Thinkst that thou canst unsweare thy oth againe? *c* **1640** J. SMYTH *Lives Berkeleys* (1883) I. 94 The kinge repents and purposeth to undoe and vnsweare what to his Barons hee had done. **1690** DRYDEN *Amphitryon* IV. i, Think what thou wert, and who cou'd swear too much? Think what thou art, and that unswears it all. **1706** DE FOE *Jure Div.* IV. 79 Their vow'd Allegiance early they withheld, ..And unswore all Allegiance to his Line. **1829** LANDOR *Imag. Conv.* II. 447 What you propose to swear to-morrow you will unswear the day after. **1874** SWINBURNE *Bothwell* II. xvii, He..shall oversay the word he said In your own ear, or else unswear it.
absol. **1591** SPENSER *M. Hubberd* 1058 Who would not oft sweare, And oft vnsweare, a Diademe to beare? **1681** HICKFRINGILL *Sin Man-catching* Wks. 1716 I. 175 False Witnesses, whose Tongues can swear and unswear. *a* **1734** NORTH *Lives* (1826) I. 88 Her adversary defamed her for swearing and unswearing. **1872** TENNYSON *Last Tourn.* 637 Unsay it, unswear!
Hence **un'swearing** *vbl. sb.*
[**1775** ASH.] **1822** SHELLEY *Chas. I*, II. 321 Thou wilt preside Over a knot of censurers, To the unswearing of thy best resolves.

un'sweat, *v.* (UN-[2] 3.)
1644 MILTON *Educ.* 7 The interim of unsweating themselves..may..be taken up in recreating and composing their travail'd spirits.

un'sweated, *ppl. a.* (UN-[1] 8.)
1774 W. MASON *Heroic Postcript to Chambers* 12 Each glittering orb the sacred features bore Of George..Unfil'd, unsweated, all of sterling weight. **1891** *Daily News* 5 Oct. 2/3 Matches, the produce of unsweated match makers.

un'sweating, *ppl. a.* (UN-[1] 10.)
1693 DRYDEN *Juvenal* III. 178 In Frost and Snow, if you complain of Heat, They rub th' unsweating Brow, and swear they sweat.

un'sweepable, *a.* (UN-[1] 7 b.)
1866 RUSKIN *Crown Wild Olive* (1873) 4 The little piece of dead ground within..was thus left, unsweepable by any ordinary methods.

un'sweer, *a. Sc. rare.* [UN-[1] 7.] Not lazy or unwilling; not heavy or sad.
a **1500** *Ratis Raving* I. 1012 Be lel,..Honest, wnswere, & answer fare. *Ibid.* 1264 This eild is thowles and wnswere, And ȝarnis play, and al blycht chere.

un'sweet, *a.* [OE. *unswéte* (UN-[1] 7), = WFris. *on-, ûnswiet*, OS. *unswôti*, MLG. *unsote*, MDu. *onsoete* (Du. *onzoet*), OHG. *unsuozi* (MHG. *unsüeze*, G. *unsüss*). Cf. UNSOOT *a.*]
1. Unpleasant, disagreeable, distasteful.
c **890** WÆRFERTH tr. *Gregory's Dial.* IV. xxxvii. 318 þæt.. of þære ea wære reocende se mist..unswetes stences. *c* **1000** *Saxon Leechd.* II. 48/14 þonne ne biþ he to unswete to ȝestincanne. *c* **1320** *Sir Tristr.* 968 Tristrem, y telle it þe, A þing, is me vnswete. *c* **1384** CHAUCER *H. Fame* I. 72 A floode of helle vnswete. **1412–20** LYDG. *Chron. Troy* II. 895 Þe meschef of her vnhappy fyne, And how Fortune was to hem vnswete—Al þis was tolde..of þe poete. *Ibid.* III. 3928, I hope..so mortally to greue þe Grekis alle,..þat þei & þou shul fele ful vnswete. **1509** FISHER *Wks.* I. 279 Worldly pleasures were to hym vnswete. **1590** SPENSER *F.Q.* II. vii. 14 The troublous stormes, that tosse The priuate state, and make the life vnsweet. **1603** J. DAVIES (Heref.) *Microcosmos* Wks. (Grosart) I. 34 Wakfull thoughts..That make their sleepes vnsweet, and yet as short. **1633** T. ADAMS *Exp. 2 Peter* ii. 8 Yet how unsweet were our sacrifice, the bran and dregs of our dotage. **1848** L. HUNT *Jar Honey* i. 7 Provided the result..be not un-sweet to the reader. **1876** MEREDITH *Beauch. Career* III. i. 2 Certain terms in the letters.., unsweet to ladies, began to trouble his mind.
b. Of a person. *rare.*
? *a* **1600** in *Percy Folio* (1867) I. 114 Alle the contraye had wonder greatt Fro whens she com, that foule vnswete; They sawe neuer of so fowlle a thyng.
2. Not sweet or pleasant to the taste.
c **1440** *Pallad. on Husb.* IX. 72 Slak sonde [yields water] lymous and lene, vnswete & depe. **1530** PALSGR. 328/2 Unswete, *mal sauouré.* **1547** *Homilies* I. *Falling fr. God* II. ¶3 We..bring forth wild grapes, that is to say, sour works, unsweet, unsavoury, and unfruitful. *a* **1643** J. SHUTE *Judgem. & Mercy* (1645) 201 God will poure him out of his mouth as a man doth that that is unsavory and unsweet that troubles his tongue. **1661** LOVELL *Hist. Anim. & Min.* 202 But the flesh is soft, unsweet, ferine, mucous.
3. Not smelling sweetly.
1605 BRETON *Olde Man's Lesson* Wks. (Grosart) II. 17/1 Which is the sweetest Beast in the world? A Ciuit Cat. And which is the moste vnsweet? A dogge when he hath eaten carrion. **1607** TOPSELL *Four-f. Beasts* 110 Tame Conies which are kept in a close and vnsweet ayre. **1825** *Q. Rev.* XXXI. 381 Edinburgh has been (to use a gentle term) unsweet in former times. **1860** THACKERAY in *Cornh. Mag.* II. 635 The canals not unsweet, and busy and picturesque with old-world life. **1879** *Pall Mall Budget* 17 Oct. 12 That damp, chill, and unsweet little cluster of rooms.
fig. **1811** LAMB *Hogarth* Wks. 1908 I. 107 That his imagination was naturally unsweet, and that he delighted in raking into every species of moral filth.
4. Unpleasant to the ear.
1579 G. HARVEY *Commend. Let.* in *Spenser's Wks.* (1912) 641/1 The sweetest Farewell..that so vnsweete a Tong, and so sowre a paire of Lippes can affoorde. *a* **1586** SIDNEY *Astr. & Stella* lxxxiv, My Muse, to some eares not vnsweet, Tempers her words [etc.]. **1589** FLEMING *Virg. Georg.* To Rdr., How vnsweete a sound so euer they seeme to make in the eare. *a* **1616** B. JONSON *Epigr., On Famous Voy.* Wks. 817 When the noise doth beate Vpon your eares, of discords so vn-sweet. **1875** CLODD *Childh. Relig.* i. 2 If you wish to open..your ears to the sounds that give forth no unsweet notes. **1894** MRS. H. WARD *Marcella* I. 312 A little laugh, which..was not unsweet.
5. Not sweetly attractive.
1866 MISS MULOCK *Noble Life* xiv, Nor was her face unsweet now; but it bore tokens of what she had gone through.
Hence **un'sweetly** *adv.*; **un'sweetness.**
1596 BARROUGH *Meth. Physick* (ed. 3) 425 Which deceit.. you may easilie find out by the vnsweetnes of smelling. **1842** MRS. BROWNING *Grk. Chr. Poets* i. ¶1 The voice..sang not unsweetly, if more faintly than before.

un'sweeten, *v.* (UN-[2] 6 a.)
1611 FLORIO, *Disadolcire*, to vnsweeten. *a* **1634** CHAPMAN & SHIRLEY *Chabot* v. iii. 14 Were all my joys essential, and so mighty As the affected world believes I taste, This object were enough to unsweeten all.

un'sweetened, *ppl. a.* (*sb.*) [UN-[1] 8.] Not sweetened.
[**1775** ASH.] **1817** PEACOCK *Melincourt* I. 53 Sir Telegraph poured some cream into his unsweetened tea. **1844** MRS. BROWNING *Dead Rose* ii, The breeze..,—If breathing now, —unsweetened would forgo thee. **1880** *Act 43 & 44 Vict.* c. 24 §123 Unsweetened foreign spirits.
b. *ellipt.* as *sb.*, unsweetened gin. ? *Obs.*
1886 GREEN & HALL *Jack in Box* (Brit. Libr. MS. LCP 53369 Q) f. 37, And if to hint sir, I might be so bold. *Jack.* Unsweetened with a little water cold. **1890** BARRÈRE & LELAND *Dict. Slang* II. 390/1 Those who are partial to the *unsweetened* or 'Old Tom'.—*Bird o' Freedom.* **1910** WODEHOUSE *Psmith in City* xii. 100 The messengers were.. endeavouring to restore their nerve with about sixpenn'orth of the beverage known as 'unsweetened'.

un'swell, *v.* [UN-^{2} 7.] *intr.* To recover from a swollen state.
c **1374** CHAUCER *Troylus* IV. 1146 Ebben gan þe welle Of here teris, and þe herte vnswelle. *Ibid.* V. 214 But þo bygan a lytel his herte vnswelle, Thorugh teris, which þat gonnen vp to welle. **1530** PALSGR. 328/2 Unswolne, *desgourdy*. **1580** HOLLYBAND *Treas. Fr. Tong*, *Se desenfler*, to vnswel, to asswage. **1658** A. FOX *Würtz' Surg.* II. xxviii. 195 When the Fracture is opened the Member unswels, if the matter runs out. **1663** BOYLE *Usef. Exp. Nat. Philos.* II. v. xi. 229 Her whole hand, which was before tumid, unswelled again. **1753** N. TORRIANO *Gangr. Sore Throat* 26 On Friday Morning.. the Throat appeared unswelled, and there was a greater Freedom in swallowing. **1778** EARL PEMBROKE *Milit. Equitation* (ed. 3) 117, I have seen by repeated experiments legs swell, and unswell, by leaving litter, or taking it away.

un'swept, *ppl. a.* [UN-^{1} 8 b.]
a. That has not been swept.
1597 MIDDLETON *Wisd. Solomon* xii. 3 A house-room long unswept will gather dust. **1607** SHAKS. *Cor.* II. iii. 126 The Dust on antique Time would lye vnswept. **1678** R. L'ESTRANGE *Seneca's Morals, Of Anger* vii. II. 73 A spot upon a Dish.., or an unswept Hearth. **1683** DRYDEN *Life Plutarch* in *P.'s Lives* (1700) I. 24 To these he added a curious collection.., that he might leave nothing unswept behind him. **1760** STERNE *Tr. Shandy* III. xix, His head [was] like a smoke-jack;—the funnel unswept, and the ideas whirling round and round about in it. **1821** LAMB *Wks.* (1908) I. 511 The intolerable crash of the unswept cinder, betwixt your foot and the marble. **1852** JAMES *Pequinillo* II. 63, I have left nothing unswept for want of a broom.
transf. **1851** CARLYLE in Froude *Life* (1884) II. 84 The town had a dirty unswept look still.
b. Of the wing of an aircraft: not swept-back (see SWEPT *ppl. a.* 3), not having sweepback or sweep-forward (see SWEEP- 3).
1946 *Jrnl. Brit. Interplanetary Soc.* VI. 95 The application of sweep-back to wing shapes implies a swept V-shaped wing, in which the centre section is effectively unswept. **1977** *R.A.F. News* 11–24 May 6 (Advt.), Wingspan: 63 ft. unswept.

unswere, obs. f. ANSWER *v.*

un'swerved, *ppl. a.* (UN-^{1} 8, 8 c.)
1849 M. ARNOLD *Fragm. of 'Antigone'* i, Justice not infring'd, Makes his own welfare his unswerv'd-from law. **1869** LOWELL *Under the Willows* 295 Simple souls Unswerved by culture from their native bent.

un'swerving, *ppl. a.* [UN-^{1} 10.] Not turning aside; steady, constant.
1694 KETTLEWELL *Comp. Penitent* 136 Keep up clear knowledge and unswerving righteousness in my Soul. **1797** COLERIDGE *Osorio* V. i. 9 She moved steadily on Unswerving from the path of her resolve. **1810** *Monthly Mag.* XXIX. 211 That unswerving loyalty To thee. **1858** *Househ. Words* XIX. 165/1 The same unswerving face at the wheel. **1878** BOSW. SMITH *Carthage* 317 But Fortune.. was unswerving in her devotion to the son.

un'swervingly, *adv.* (UN-^{1} 11. Cf. prec.)
1805 in A. Duncan *Nelson* (1806) 339 The unswervingly patriotic Nelson. **1834** L. RITCHIE *Wand. by Seine* 65 The Seine.. flows calmly and unswervingly on. **1896** TOUT *Edw. I*, iv. 81 Henry Lacy.. remained unswervingly faithful to Edward.

un'swilled, *ppl. a.* (UN-^{1} 8.)
1645 MILTON *Colast.* 25 His farewell.. is to be a concluding taste to his jabberment in law, the flashiest and the fustiest that ever corrupted in such an unswill'd hogshead.

un'swing, *v.* (UN-^{2} 3.)
1835 JAMES *Gipsy* ii, The pot was unswung from the cross-bars that sustained it. **1856** J. STRANG *Glasgow & Clubs* 395 To unswing a golden fleece was a common trick.

un'swingled, *ppl. a.* (UN-^{1} 8.)
1538 *Inv. W. Gebon of Sutterton, Linc.* (MS.), Hempe vnpillid and flaxe vnswynglid.

un'swollen, *ppl. a.* (UN-^{1} 8 b.)
1648 HEXHAM II, *Ongeswollen*, vnswollen, or vnpuffed. **1812** COLMAN *Br. Grins, Reckoning w. Time* x, My lank purse unswoln by fees.

†**un'swore**, *ppl. a.* [UN-^{1} 8 b.] ? = next.
a **1400** *Gloss* in *Rel. Ant.* I. 7 *Jusjurandum*, a othe unswore.

un'sworn, *ppl. a.* [UN-^{1} 8 b. Cf. MHG. *ungesworn*, MSw. *os(v)orin*, Sw. *osvuren*, MDa. *us(v)oren*, not having sworn.]
1. Of persons: Not subjected to, or bound by, an oath.
1529 MORE *Dialoge* Wks. 133/2 For none of them can tel what was said to an other, & yet they be vnsworne also. **1533** —— *Debell. Salem* Wks. 973/1 Yet are there many that dare secretely detecte,.. and wyll not vncalled and vnsworen, tel no tale at all. **1581** LAMBARDE *Eiren.* I. x. (1588) 58 Albeit that it be the first Oath that I find to have bene ministred to Iustices of the Peace, yet I thinke they were neither unsworne before, nor at any time after. **1602** SEGAR *Hon. Mil. & Civ.* I. v. 7 That no Citizen unsworne, should remaine out of Italie more then three yeares. **1678** DRYDEN *All for Love* V. i, Is there one God unsworn to my Destruction? **1701** PRIDEAUX *Direct. Ch.-wardens* 11 Whatever they do.., while unsworn, is all to their own wrong. **1710** J. CHAMBERLAYNE *St. Gt. Brit.* I. II. xv. 128 There are in this Court Three Officers unsworn. **1852** *Fraser's Mag.* March 246/1 He may consequently be supposed, to use the language of the law, 'to stand unindifferent as he stands unsworn'. **1884** CHURCH *Bacon* iii. 75 An unsworn and unpaid member of the Learned Counsel.
2. Not confirmed by, or sworn as, an oath.
a **1623** SWINBURNE *Spousals* (1686) 11 Of Spousals, some be sworn and some unsworn; that is to say, some Spousals be confirmed by an Oath and some contracted without an Oath. *a* **1800** COWPER *Odyssey* (ed. 2) x. 419 When, therefore, nought of all her solemn oath Unsworn remain'd, I climb'd her stately bed. **1843** *Act 6–7 Vict.* c. 22 (title), The Admission, in certain Cases, of unsworn Testimony in Civil and Criminal Proceedings. **1887** *Pall Mall G.* 9 July 9/2 Granting summonses.. on unsworn information.

unsyght, -syker, var. UNSAUGHT *a.*, UNSICKER.

unsy'llabic, *a.* (UN-^{1} 7.)
1864 JEAN INGELOW *Poems* 69 What work so high as mine, .. Nature's.. unsyllabic voices to combine. **1932** W. L. GRAFF *Language & Languages* 56 The sound that possesses the highest degree of sonority in a syllable is called syllabic or sonant, the others are unsyllabic or con-sonant. **1964** H. KURATH in D. Abercrombie et al. *Daniel Jones* 146 There is no difference in the system of consonants, except that unsyllabic /ə/.. appears only in dialects that lack postvocalic /r/. **1970** *Publ. Amer. Dial. Soc. 1968* L. 6 The unsyllabic phone [ə].. will here be treated as the semi-vowel /ə/.

un'syllabled, *ppl. a.* [UN-^{1} 8.] Not formed into, not expressed in, syllables.
1594 SOUTHWELL *M. Magd. Funeral Teares* 69 b, The heart pressing out the vnsillabled breath at once. **1594** *Zepheria* xl, If she shall attend what fortunes sequeld The *naufrage* of my poore afflicted barke, Then tell, but tell in words unsillabled. **1832** MOTHERWELL *Jeanie Morrison* ix, When freely gushed all feelings forth, Unsyllabled—unsung. **1843** CARLYLE *Past & Pr.* II. xvii, With gaspings, gesturings, with unsyllabled cries. **1873** MRS. WHITNEY *Other Girls* xxxiii, She was.. trying to put something clearly into syllables that said itself, unsyllabled, to her.

unsyllo'gistical, *a.* (UN-^{1} 7.)
1638 CHILLINGW. *Relig. Prot.* vi. §14. 334 To the first proposition of this unsyllogisticall syllogisme, I answer [etc.].

unsym'bolic, *a.* (UN-^{1} 7.)
1871 EARLE *Phil. Eng. Tongue* 211 Infantine speech is unsymbolic. **1878** H. G. GUINNESS *End of Age* 130 The Apocalypse.. translated into unsymbolic language.

unsym'bolicalness. (UN-^{1} 12. Cf. prec.)
1681 H. MORE *Exp. Dan.* v. 149 Which Writing.. is called Scripture, and for its plainness and unsymbolicalness, as I may so speak,.. the Scripture of Truth.

un'symbolized, *ppl. a.* (UN-^{1} 8 a *c.*)
[**1775** ASH.] **1881** H. SWEET in *Trans. Philol. Soc.* 196 Bell's providing a sign.. for the very rare (ɫv), while leaving the frequently occurring (sj), (ʃj), (ʃv), (jv), unsymbolized.

unsy'mmetrical, *a.* (UN-^{1} 7.)
1755 JOHNSON, *Disproportionate*, unsymmetrical. **1816** R. JAMESON *Char. Min.* (ed. 2) 207 A Crystal is said to be.. Unsymmetrical, when two ranges of facets situated one above another, on each extremity, exhibit a want of symmetry. **1830** LINDLEY *Nat. Syst. Bot.* 141 An imbricated calyx with.. unsymmetrical flowers, definite pendulous ovules. **1893** TUCKY *Amphioxus* 119 This is an unsymmetrical movement of the mesoblastic somites.
Hence **unsy'mmetrically** *adv.*
1755 JOHNSON, *Disproportionately*, unsuitably, unsymmetrically. **1839–47** *Todd's Cycl. Anat.* III. 603/1 These ganglia are disposed unsymmetrically throughout the body. **1879** SPENCER *Data of Ethics* i. §1. 4 The unsymmetrically-pierced disk of an eccentric.

un'symmetrized, *ppl. a.* (UN-^{1} 8 a *c.*)
1825 LAMB *Last Ess. Elia, Wedding*, Visitors huddled up in corners; chairs unsymmetrised; candles disposed by chance.

un'symmetry. (UN-^{1} 12.)
1867 SPENCER *Principles of Biol.* II. 129 Each member of a plant will display.. unsymmetry or asymmetry where there is partial or entire departure from a balance of surrounding actions. **1867** J. M. WILSON in Farrar *Ess. Lib. Educ.* 274 The pelargonium, and its more visible unsymmetry.

unsympa'thetic, *a.* (UN-^{1} 7; cf. SYMPATHETIC *a.* 2 b.)
1823 BYRON *Island* IV. xiii, But calm and careless heaved the wave below, Eternal with unsympathetic flow. **1857** MRS. GASKELL *C. Brontë* II. 327 The critical, unsympathetic public. **1867** H. MACMILLAN *Bible Teach.* ii. 36 We are not left in the power of blind unsympathetic nature. **1937** L. MACNEICE in *Ess. & Stud.* XXII. 145, I have recently been to an exhibition of nineteenth-century French painting and was surprised to find it so unsympathetic. **1946** *Ann. Reg. 1945* 438 Dreiser was a most unsympathetic personality, yet during the 1920's he was regarded as probably the most impressive figure in American literature since Walt Whitman. **1968** B. FOSTER *Changing Eng. Lang.* ii. 75 *Sympathetic* and *unsympathetic* have latterly taken on an extra meaning in imitation of French idiom (or possibly also Spanish), where *sympathique* means 'likable'. **1981** *Daily Tel.* 12 Feb. 16/6 An insidious invasion, unfamiliar, unsympathetic, alien.
Hence **unsympa'thetically** *adv.*
1861 DICKENS *Gt. Expect.* vii, The ridgy effect of a wedding-ring, passing unsympathetically over the human countenance.

unsympathiza'bility. (UN-^{1} 12.)
1818 COLERIDGE in *Lit. Rem.* (1836) I. 144 A craving for sympathy in exact proportion to the oddity and unsympathizability of what he proposes.

un'sympathized, *ppl. a.* (UN-^{1} 8 a *c*, 8 c.)
1818 MRS. SHELLEY *Frankenst.* xv, Finding myself unsympathized with, [I] wished to tear up the trees.

un'sympathizing, *ppl. a.* (UN-^{1} 10.)
1735–6 SAVAGE *Volunteer Laureat* iv. 7, I, jocund Spring, unsympathizing, see. **1768–74** TUCKER *Lt. Nat.* (1834) II. 628 When they come out into the world they.. become partial, overbearing, and unsympathizing. **1828** LYTTON *Pelham* II. xix, The same stern, cold, unsympathising reserve, which made him.. an object of universal conversation and dislike. **1882** FARRAR *Early Chr.* I. 89 Jews .. by whom the name and work of the Apostle of the Gentiles were regarded.. with unsympathising coldness.
Hence **un'sympathizingly** *adv.*
1856 R. A. VAUGHAN *Mystics* I. ii. I. 16 Unless, indeed, the enquiry were conducted unsympathizingly.

un'sympathy. (UN-^{1} 12.)
1856 BP. WILBERFORCE in *Life* (1881) II. 305 How true the unsympathy as well as the sympathy of nature. **1871** PALGRAVE *Lyrical Poems* 19 The mountains in their gray unsympathy.. Mock'd her.

unsyn'tactical, *a.* (UN-^{1} 7), **-ally**, *adv.* (UN-^{1} 11.)
1865 FARRAR *Chap. Lang.* 93 The fact.. shows that their unsyntactical character is merely an accident of language. **1879** —— *St. Paul* II. 258 This general exhortation is then carried into details, unsystematically indeed, and even unsyntactically, but [etc.].

unsyste'matic, *a.* (UN-^{1} 7.)
1770 BURKE *Pres. Discont.* 71 His single, unsupported, desultory, unsystematic endeavours. **1780** —— *Œcon. Reform.* Wks. III. 285 A blind unsystematick observance of every trifle. **1836** J. GILBERT *Chr. Atonem.* ii. 45 The Bible ..is, in general, an unsystematic, miscellaneous communication. **1862** 'SHIRLEY' (J. Skelton) *Nugæ Crit.* x. 430 We miss the spontaneous and unsystematic music.. of the true ballad. **1875** B. W. RICHARDSON *Dis. Mod. Life* 11 The naming of these groups.. has been unsystematic and fanciful.

unsyste'matical, *a.* (UN-^{1} 7.)
1780 BURKE *Œcon. Reform.* Wks. III. 235 Thus, between the resistance of power, and the unsystematical process of popularity, the undertaker and the undertaking are both exposed. **1791** PAINE *Rights of Man* 58 A wild unsystematical display of paradoxical rhapsodies. *a* **1812** BUCKMINSTER *Serm.* (1827) 208 The occasional, and unsystematical addresses of your ministers.

unsyste'matically, *adv.* (UN-^{1} 11. Cf. prec. and UNSYSTEMATIC *a.*)
1738 [see UNSTEADILY]. **1865** *Trans. Philol. Soc.* 15 One is systematically and the other unsystematically wrong. **1879** [see UNSYNTACTICALLY *adv.*].

un'systematizable, *a.* (UN-^{1} 7 b.)
1799 SOUTHEY in *Sir H. Davy's Rem.* (1858) 42 The unconnected and unsystematizable fables of Hindoo absurdity. **1858** H. BUSHNELL *Nat. & Supernat.* ii. (1864) 41 Some desultory, unsystematizable action.

un'systematized, *ppl. a.* (UN-^{1} 8.)
1832 F. BURNEY *Mem. Dr. Burney* III. 323 His internal resources were too diffuse and unsystematized. [**1847** WEBSTER.] **1849** *Edin. Rev.* April 290 Fragments of uncertain, inaccurate, ill-remembered, unsystematised information. **1863** *Austin's Jurispr.* III. 277 The bulk and uncognoscibility of unsystematized law. **1870** *Athenæum* 17 Sept. 359/3 The last stage of what we may term unsystematized volunteer aid in a campaign.

unt: see UNCT *v. Obs.* (to anoint).

†**un'tache**, *v. Obs.* [UN-^{2} 9 + TACHE *v.*^{2} 1.] *trans.* To carve (a beaver or curlew).
14.. in *Porkington MS. 10* fol. 188 A Bytter vntachyd. **1486** *Bk. St. Albans* F vij b, A Bevure untachid. **1508** *Bk. of Kerving* (W. de W.) A j b, Vntache that curlewe. [Hence in later lists.]

un'tack, *v.*^{1} [UN-^{2} 3 + TACK *v.*^{1}]
1. *trans.* To take apart, break up.
1641 MILTON *Reform.* II. 54 The little adoe, which me thinks I find in untacking these pleasant Sophismes. *a* **1715** BURNET *Own Time* VII. (1734) II. 401 If they [*sc.* the Lords] should untack the Bill, and separate one from the other. [Cf. TACK *v.*^{1} 5.]
b. To detach (*from* something); to set free.
1667 MARVELL *Instr. Dutch Wars* Poems (1870) 153 Ruyter forthwith a squadron doth untack. *a* **1677** BARROW *Serm.* (1683) II. 49 It alone can untack our minds and affections from this world. **1741** RICHARDSON *Pamela* II. 21 Besides, I must all undress me in a manner to untack [the papers].
2. To detach by the withdrawal of tacks. Also *absol.*
1693 EVELYN *De la Quint. Compl. Gard.* II. 41 We must never begin to Prune an Espalier.. until it be quite untack'd. **1707** MORTIMER *Husb.* 138 When the Blanket.. is full, they untack it and carry it away, and empty it. **1718** J. LAURENCE *Fruit-Gard. Kalendar* 43 To Exercise his Knife.. in correcting the great Disorders of his.. Peach-trees; first untacking them from the Wall.

un'tack, *v.*^{2} [UN-^{2} 4 + TACK *sb.*^{7} b, *v.*^{5}] *trans.* To remove the saddle and bridle from (a horse). Also *absol.*
1962 W. FAULKNER *Reivers* viii. 185 We went back to the barn and untacked and Lycurgus brought a bucket and a rag and Lycurgus washed him down.. before stabling and feeding him. **1977** F. PARRISH *Fire in Barley* iv. 40 Would you like me to untack her?.. Take off the saddle and bridle?

un'tackle, *v.* (UN-^{2} 4, 4 b. Cf. Du. *onttakelen*.]
1. *trans.* To strip (a vessel) of tackle. Hence *untackled* ppl. a.
1552 HULOET, Vntakle a shyppe, *exarmare nauem*. **1598** GRENEWEY *Tacitus, Ann.* II. v. 40 At length the sea growing lower, and the wind more fauourable, the lame and

vntackled shippes..returned. **1626** Laud *Fast Serm.* 15 That no Tempest may vntackle them,..or hewe down their Masts. **1656** Davenant *Siege of Rhodes* i, I'le to our Gallies haste, Untackle ev'ry Mast.

2. To unharness (a horse).

1573 Tusser *Husb.* (1878) 62 But vse to vntackle them once in a day. **1885** *Even. News* 25 July 2/6, I then untackled the horse from the car.

3. To free from tackling or fastenings.

1905 'Q' (Quiller Couch) *Shining Ferry* iv, Groping for the rod, [she] drew the float ashore and untackled it.

un'tactful, *a.* (un-[1] 7.)

1860 E. Eden *Semi-attached Couple* xx. I. 181 When her vanity was in a state of mortification, she became unusually untactful. **1900** *Daily News* 20 Oct. 3/1 The untactful conduct of a few of his friends.

un'tagged, *ppl. a.* [un-[1] 8.] Not furnished with a tag or tags.

1557 North *Gueuara's Diall Pr.* iv. viii. (1568) 129 The courtier..that is content to tye his hose with vntagged poynts. *a* **1625** Fletcher *Woman's Prize* iv. iii, And your Money..if I forfeit, Make me a Jack o' Lent, and break my shins For untag'd Points and Compters. **1705** E. Ward *Hud. Rediv.* ii. 27 Or else those Points we shew our Art in Must often go untag'd. **1714** *Welsh Monster* 26 Tag'd or untag'd, his biting Satyrs..Were spun..exquisitly fine.

un'tailed, *ppl. a.*[1] [un-[1] 8 and un-[2] 8.] **a.** Not furnished with a tail. **b.** Deprived of a tail.

1611 Florio, *Discodato*, vntailed, curtailed. **1648** Hexham ii, *Ongestaert*, Vntailed, or a Horses taile cutt off as our English horses are. **1807** in *Spirit Pub. Jrnls.* XI. 79 He acknowledged that the os coccygis in untailed animals was indeed no tail. **1836** Fonblanque *Eng. under 7 Administr.* (1837) III. 285 The old story of the untail'd fox's quarrel with tails.

†**un'tailed**, *ppl. a.*[2] *Obs. rare.* Also *Sc.* **wntaillȝied.** [un-[1] 8.] Unentailed.

1461 *Paston Lett.* II. 80 Bothe the forseyd manerys were ontayled. *a* **1578** Lindesay (Pitscottie) *Chron. Scot.* (S.T.S.) I. 47 The landis that was wntaillȝied.

un'tailorly, *a.* (un-[1] 7.)

1775 S. J. Pratt *Liberal Opin.* (1783) III. 82 That you may be permitted to go by so genteel and untaylorly a conveyance to the place of execution.

un'taint, *v.* (un-[2] 6 b.)

1855 Bailey *Mystic*, etc. 80 That heart-soothing herb..Held to untaint from sin the savage soul.

†**un'taint**, *ppl. a.* [un-[1] 8 b.] Untainted.

1638 W. Lisle *Heliodorus* ix. 159 Let him passe Along with them, to keepe vntaint the Lasse.

un'taintable, *a.* (un-[1] 7 b.)

a **1610** Healey *Epictetus, Life* (1616) A 5, His life was spotlesse and vntaintable. *a* **1670** Hacket *Cent. Serm.* (1675) 238 His integrity was untaintable. **1895** *Cent. Mag.* July 339 One like himself should praise him! Soul of grace, untaintable white brightness!

un'tainted, *ppl. a.* [un-[1] 8.]

†**1.** Not attainted. *Obs.*[-1]

1594 Shaks. *Rich. III*, iii. vi. 9 And yet within these fiue houres Hastings liu'd, Vntainted, vnexamin'd, free, at libertie.

b. Not dishonoured. *rare*[-1].

1627 Drayton *Agincourt* ccxlvi, Now Excester with his vntaynted Reare Came on, which long had labour'd to come in.

2. Not affected by any physical taint.

c **1600** Shaks. *Sonn.* xix, Him in thy course vntainted doe allow, For beauties patterne to succeding men. **1651** Vaughan *Benefit by Enemies* Wks. 1914 I. 99 Vultures..flock to them, but passe by the sound and untainted bodies. **1725** Bolingbroke *Let. to Swift* 24 July, But the attainder is kept..prudently in force, lest..his bad leaven should sour that sweet, untainted mass. **1760–72** H. Brooke *Fool of Qual.* (1809) IV. 127 Her..flesh remained..pure and untainted. **1810** Southey *Kehama* x. iv, The stream..delights to lie..at rest Beneath the untainted sky. **1861** Ld. Lytton & Fane *Tannhaüser* 8 Till came the crack of that tremendous Doom..and on the lurid world Let in effulgence of untainted light.

3. Of qualities, etc.: Unsullied, unblemished, perfectly pure.

1590 Greene *Never too late* (1600) 41 Isabel, whose beauty is deuine,..whose constancy vntainted. **1625** B. Jonson *Staple of N.* ii. iv, A Gentleman..Of an vntainted credit. **1673** Temple *Obs. United Prov.* Wks. 1720 I. 53 A Man of..deep Understanding, with untainted Integrity. **1750** Collins *Superstit. Highlands* i, Let us wish him..joy untainted, with his destined bride. **1786** Mme. D'Arblay *Diary* 28 Nov., There was an evidence of her untainted worth in her very countenance. **1809–14** Wordsw. *Excurs.* viii. 241 Where is..The character of peace,..And honest dealing, and untainted speech? **1831** Scott *Ct. Rob.* x, The knight passed on, not unmoved with wonder, though untainted by fear. **1879** R. K. Douglas *Confucianism* iv. 93 No virtue can remain untainted without learning.

4. Of persons, etc.: Free from moral taint.

c **1590** *Sir T. More* iv. v. 103 Liuing thus vntainted, you are well. **1593** Shaks. *2 Hen. VI*, iii. ii. 232 What stronger Brest-plate then a heart vntainted? **1651** W. Durham *Maran-atha* (1652) 24 The Judge of Israel..is..untainted in point of Judicature. **1689** D. Granville *Lett.* (Surtees) 81 The consideration whereof hath..kept me untainted and unstained. **1709** Addison *Tatler* No. 75 ¶9 From such an untainted Couple, we can hope to have our Family rise to its ancient Splendour of Face. **1763** Churchill *Poems* I. 86, I her snares defy, And look on riches with untainted eye. **1814** Byron *Lara* i. xxiii, He will not that untainted line belie. **1815** Scott *Guy M.* xvi, Persons..untainted perhaps in morals, and fair in character. **1890** J. Pulsford *Loyalty to Christ* I. 170 Very few ever come forth untainted, from scenes and circumstances of temptation.

b. Const. *by*, *with*, or †*of*.

1612 T. Taylor *Comm. Titus* i. 6 The goodnes of God in keeping them altogether..vnreprooueable, that is vntainted of greiuous crimes. **1649** *Alcoran* p. iv, To keep thy selfe untainted of their follies. **1710** Addison *Spect.* No. 9 ¶3 This Sir-name of King, which..declared the Owners of it to be altogether untainted with Republican..Principles. **1757** Foote *Author* ii. (1777) 10/2 If George remains as untainted by affluence, as he has been untempted by distress. **1802** G. Canning *Poet. Wks.* (1827) 36 A statesman..By power uncorrupted, untainted by gold. **1850** Kingsley *A. Locke* ii, He alone was untainted with the sin around him.

Hence **un'taintedly** *adv.*, **un'taintedness.**

1611 Cotgr., *Pudiquement*, chastly, purely, vntaintedly, modestly. **1640** Bp. Hall *Rem. Wks.* (1660) 37 The light hath a quality..Of purity and untaintednesse in respect of any mixture of corruption. **1686** tr. *Chardin's Trav. Persia* 30 A Person untaintedly faithful to the Grand Vizier. **1817** Chalmers *Astron. Disc.* iv. 139 The untaintedness of his glory.

un'tainting, *ppl. a.* (un-[1] 10.)

1813 Shelley *Q. Mab* iv. 132 The untainting light of day.

un'tak(e)able, *a.* (un-[1] 7 b.)

1652 Earl Monm. tr. *Bentivoglio's Hist. Relat.* 11 A place which is thought almost untakable. **1882** Paxton Hood *Cromwell* iii. 65 Nutt..was an untakable man, and he had several pirate ships.

un'taken, *ppl. a.*[1] Also 4 **untak(e**, 5–6 *Sc.* **untane**, 5 **wntayne**, etc. [un-[1] 8 b, c, and 5 c. Cf. ON. *útekinn*, MSw. *otakin.*]

1. Not taken by force; not made prisoner; uncaptured.

c **1350** *Will. Palerne* 1280 Riȝt fewe went a-wey vnwoundet or take. *c* **1400** *Song of Roland* 89 He left vntak the toun, and to his tent ridis. *c* **1470** Henry *Wallace* v. 853 Lest he in strenth wntayne, This haill kynryk he wyll wyn. **1523** Ld. Berners *Froiss.* I. xciii. 115 Sir Robert Dartoyes was sore hurte, and scapedde hardely vntaken. **1577** Dee *General & Rare Mem.* 4 Their Marchantlike Ships..may..pas quietly vnpilled, vnspoyled, and vntaken by Pyrates. **1610** Holland *Camden's Brit.* 499 Albeit the foulers doe..catch great store of young water-foule, yet..abundance..remaineth untaken. **1697** Dryden *Æneis* x. 1173 Untouch'd thy Arms, untaken be thy Sword. **1722** De Foe *Col. Jack* (1840) 188 The most prosperous untaken thief. **1768–74** Tucker *Lt. Nat.* (1834) II. 562 A wise general will..leave no little stronghold untaken behind him. **1847** Mrs. A. Kerr tr. *Ranke's Hist. Servia* 317 Whilst that [fort] remained untaken. **1870** Morris *Earthly Par.* III. iv. 108 That he..scarce had trod Untaken on its floor.

2. Not taken, in other senses of the verb. Also const. *from.*

1456 Sir G. Haye *Law Arms* (S.T.S.) 204 He levis it [*sc.* the consecrated wafer] untane for despising of the sacrament. **1474** *Cov. Leet Bk.* 410 In case the oportunite of this tyme shuld nowe..be vntaken or sett a-part. **1543–4** *Act 35 Hen. VIII*, c. 6 §3 The Jurie is like to remayne untaken for defaulte of Jurors. **1586** T. B. *La Primaud. Fr. Acad.* i. 159 It is expedient sometime to leave untaken that which a man may lawfully take. **1600** Surflet *Countrie Farme* ii. lxv. 412 The honie..which is left vntaken from them. **1613** Sherley *Trav. Persia* 4, I left no paines untaken to accelerat it [*sc.* a journey]. **1735** Bolingbroke *Study Hist.* i. (1752) 7 That they might leave no liberty untaken. **1880** 'Ouida' *Moths* xvii, Resolute to leave no pains untaken.

b. With advs., as *away*, *down*, *off*, *up.*

1483 *Acta Audit.* in *Acta Dom. Conc.* II. Introd. 120 The malis and fermes..to be untakin up be ony party. **1526** Tindale *2 Cor.* iii. 14 Vntill this daye remayneth the same coverynge vntaken awaye. **1539–40** Coverdale in Money *Parish Goods Berks.* (1879) p. vi, All the beams..remain still untaken down. **1562** Turner *Herbal* ii. 33 If they [*sc.* lentils] be sodden with theyr shilles vntaken of. **1610** J. Dove *Advt. Seminaries* 3 That veile..untill this time hath continued untaken away. **1683** J. Reid *Scots Gard'ner* (1907) 77 Bark..untaken off at the upper end. **1701** *Col. Rec. Pennsylv.* II. 43 All other lands that are mine untaken up. **1822** A. Cunningham *Tradit. T.* (1887) 136 My supper shall be the untaken-down spirit. **1836** [see unstrengthened].

c. With other constructions.

1583 A. Melvill in *J. Melvill's Autob. & Diary* (Wodrow Soc.) 155 Na obstinat Papist..hes it sufferit lang to converse amangs us, untean ordour withe. **1647** Clarendon *Hist. Reb.* iii. §105 The King and Queen sate untaken notice of. **1904** E. Nesbit *Phœnix & Carpet* vii. 127 The four children found themselves at Waterloo Station quite untaken-care-of.

un'taken, *ppl. a.*[2] (un-[2] 3, 8.)

1893 Baring-Gould *Cheap Jack Zita* II. 150 Whether taken and confiscated I cannot say... But I have paid ten pounds to have it untaken and set at liberty.

un'taking, *vbl. sb.* (un-[2] 3, 8.)

1656 O. Sedgwick *Humble Sinner Resolved* vi. §5. 47 If I take a servant, I take him so, that..I can put him off againe; but if I take a wife, there can be no untaking on my part.

un'taking, *ppl. a.* [un-[1] 10, 5 d.] **a.** *Sc.* Without taking. **b.** Not receptive; not attractive.

1587 *Reg. Privy Council Scot.* IV. 168 Giff the Quene of England culd not persave hir awin securitie untaking his Majesteis moderis lyff. **1683** Moxon *Mech. Exerc., Printing* 377 When the Balls do not Take, the Un-taking part of the Balls that touches the Form will be left White. **1885** O. Crawfurd *Woman's Reput.* i, She has a harsh voice or an untaking manner.

untalelich: see un-[1] 3.

un'talented, *ppl. a.* (un-[1] 8.)

1753 Richardson *Grandison* (1754) VI. i. 6 This is the sort of stuff you must be satisfied with from a poor untalented girl. **1815** *Zeluca* III. 141 The means the untalented have of filling up their time. **1831** Carlyle *Sart. Res.* ii. viii, Your numerous talented men, and your innumerable untalented men. **1981** *London Rev. Bks.* 19 Nov.–2 Dec. 16 Wittgenstein..was impatient with untalented or lazy pupils.

un'talkative, *a.* (un-[1] 7.)

1739 J. Spence in *Academy* 20 Feb. (1875) 191/3 He's..untalkative, tolerably read and a great dealer in Relicks. **1866** *Standard* 29 June 5/3 Government is extremely untalkative, while the..telegraph communication with..Germany is almost completely interrupted.

un'talked, *ppl. a.* (un-[1] 8 c.)

1592 Shaks. *Rom. & Jul.* iii. ii. 7 That run-awayes eyes may wincke, and Romeo Leape to these armes, vntalkt of and vnseene. **1669** Dryden *Tyrannic Love* iii. i, Th' unknown, untalk'd of man is only blest. **1807** E. Weeton *Let.* 3 Dec. (1969) I. 53 She has for a long time been untalked of. **1926** G. Bell *Let.* 25 Jan. (1927) II. xxvi. 745 We seem to have left such a lot of things untalked about.

un'tall, *a.* (un-[1] 7. Cf. tall *a.* 1 c.)

c **1395** *Plowman's Tale* i. iii, The other side ben poore and pale,..And seeme caitives sore a-cale..; Who toteth on hem, they ben untall.

un'tame, *a.* [un-[1] 7. Cf. Du. *ontam*, OHG. (MHG.) *unzam* (G. *unzahm*), MDa. *utam*, (M)Sw. *otam.*] Not tame or gentle; wild.

1382 Wyclif *Ecclus.* xxx. 8 The vntame hors shal scapen hard. **1390** Gower *Conf.* I. 287 Whanne al his resoun was untame. **14..** *Voc.* in Wr.-Wülcker 589 *Indomitus*, vntame, wylde. **1555** Eden *Decades* (Arb.) 376 If the vntame brayne of Wyndam had..gyuen eare to the counsayle. **1584** R. Scot *Discov. Witchcr.* xii. xv. 204 How untame by nature these vipers..are. **1609** Bp. Hall *David's Ps. Metaphr.* viii, Thou hast..stretcht his raigne Vnto the heards, and beasts vntame. **1655** W. Hammond *Death* 54 The whole world obeys Creation's law; only untame man strays.

Hence **un'tameness.**

1727 Bailey (vol. II), *Ungentleness*, Untameness, Rudeness. **1871** Kingsley *At Last* xvii, In curious contrast to the natural tameness of the Kinkajou was the natural untameness of a beautiful little Night-Monkey.

un'tame, *v.* (un-[2] 3.)

1646 Shirley *Upon Death of C. Dalby* Wks. 1833 VI. 449 Nor did his courage know to make a pause, When honour call'd so loud, and such a cause As would untame a hermit.

un'tam(e)able, *a.* (un-[1] 7 b.)

(*a*) **1576** Fleming tr. *Caius' Dogs* D 2, Be the bull neuer so monsterous,..neuer so vntameable. **1577** Hellowes *Gueuara's Chron.* 58 The Parthians were a people so vntameable to be subdued, that [etc.]. **1607** Topsell *Four-f. Beasts* 112 The Indian little Pig-Cony..is..more tractable in hand; howbeit vntamable. **1692** Dryden *Don Sebastian* i. i, Still untameable! In what a ruine has thy head-strong Pride..plung'd thy People. **1764** Harmer *Observ.* viii. §11. 326 The Arabs have been always looked upon as an untameable people. **1774** Goldsm. *Nat. Hist.* III. 343 This animal..[is] more savage and untameable than any other quadrupede. **1818** Milman *Samor* vii. 172, I know thee now, majestic Rebel! thee The untraceable, untameable! **1833** J. Rennie *Alph. Angling* 25 The pike is held to be a more wild, untameable fish than the carp. **1870** N. F. Hele *Aldeburgh* vii. 77 They [*sc.* short-horned owls] are very untameable. **1890** *Spectator* 11 Jan., Cruel and untameable though they [*sc.* the Masai] seem.

fig. **1836** F. Mahony *Rel. Father Prout* 274 A genuine poet..enjoys the mental chase in proportion to the wild and untameable nature of the game.

(*b*) **1567** R. Mulcaster *Fortescue's De Laud. Leg.* 92 The lustes of the fleash are wanton, & almoste vntamable. **1571** Golding *Calvin on Ps.* ix. 21 He subdeweth their untamable wilfulnesse by force. *a* **1677** Barrow *Serm.* Wks. 1687 I. 33 His own unsatiable desires,..and untameable passions, will disquiet him. **1742** Young *Nt. Th.* v. 262 A Pomp untameable of Weed prevails. **1768–74** Tucker *Lt. Nat.* (1834) II. 380 This vigour and untamable violence of the sensitive faculties. **1818** Shelley *Let.* Pr. Wks. 1888 II. 224 The untameable profusion and loveliness of nature. **1860** Hawthorne *Marb. Faun* xviii, It was a delight to behold this untamable water.

Hence **un'tam(e)ably** *adv.*

1807 *Trans. Linn. Soc.* (1808) IX. 177 In a state of confinement, they appear to be untameably savage.

un'tam(e)ableness. (un-[1] 12, or f. prec.)

1662 T. Brooks *Crown & Glory of Christianity* 404 The Greeks call it an Adamant from its untameableness. **1790** Bewick *Hist. Quadrup.* 144 The Rhinoceros..possesses all the properties ascribed to that animal,—rage, untameableness,..and immense strength. **1837** Carlyle *Misc., Diamond Necklace* xiv, Her grand quality is rather to be reckoned negative: the 'untameableness' as of a fly. **1865** M. Arnold *Ess. Crit.* 179 By his intensity, by his untamableness,..[Heine] is Hebrew.

un'tamed, *ppl. a.* [un-[1] 8. Cf. ON. *útamdr*, Sw. *otamd*, Norw. *utamd*: also OHG. *ungizamot*, MHG. *ungezamt*, and untemed *ppl. a.*] Not tamed (in various senses); wild; unsubdued.

(*a*) *a* **1340** Hampole *Psalter* xxiv. 11 He leris..sothfastnes thurgh þe whilke he is vntamed. **1382** Wyclif *Jer.* xxxi. 18 Y am lerned as a ȝungling vntamed. **1495** Glanvil *Barth. De P.R.* xviii. lxviii. 831 Suche asses be grete..and vntamyd. **1535** Coverdale *Ecclus.* xxx. 8 An vntamed horse wylbe harde. **1596** Spenser *F.Q.* v. i. 2 Bacchus, that with furious might All th' East, before vntam'd, did ouerronne. **1623** Bingham *Xenophon* p. ii, Of vntamed beasts, the most were wilde Asses. **1659** Chamberlayne *Pharon.* iv. iii. 248 Base Amarus,..more beastly rude Than untamed Indians. **1718** Prior *Solomon* i. 199 Untam'd and fierce the Tiger still remains. **1762** Falconer *Shipwr.* ii. 518 Like some strong watch-tower nodding o'er the deep,..Untamed he stood. **1817** Moore *Lalla R., Veiled Prophet* iii. 226 He..there, untam'd, the approaching conq'ror waits. **1868** *Rep. U.S.*

Commissioner Agric. (1869) 254 A door for the inroads of untamed swine.

(*b*) **1585** ABP. SANDYS *Serm.* xii. 205 Which thing rightly ..weied, would bridle these vntamed affections of ours. **1600** *1st Pt. Sir J. Oldcastle* v. viii. 8 There dwell vntamed thoughts that hardly stoupe To such abasement. **1653** W. RAMESEY *Astrol. Restored* To Rdr. 11 His wilde untamed accustomary life. **1746** FRANCIS tr. *Horace, Art of Poetry* 177 With untam'd Fury let Medea glow. **1781** GIBBON *Decl. & F.* xxvii. (1787) III. 38 Their native fierceness was yet untamed. **1840** DICKENS *Old C. Shop* xlv, Monsters, whose like they almost seemed to be in their wildness and their untamed air. **1859** F. MAHONY *Rel. Father Prout* 385 The human breast..Throbs thus unawed, Untamed and unquiescent.

(*c*) **1600** SURFLET *Countrie Farme* III. xlix. 539 The perries which are pressed out of wilde peares, and all such as are vnhusbanded, vntamed. **1623** J. TAYLOR (Water P.) *Discov. by Sea* A8b, The windes and seas continued still their course,..vntam'd [seemed] their force. **1743** FRANCIS tr. *Hor., Odes* IV. xiv. 23 The Winds arise And work the Seas untam'd. *c* **1790** COLERIDGE *Death Chatterton* 159 Where Susquehannah pours his untamed stream. **1818** MILMAN *Samor* VIII. 130 The strong freedom of thy untam'd locks. **1841** CARLYLE *Heroes* i. (1904) 33 The untamed Forests and dark brute Powers of Nature. **1865** F. PARKMAN *Pioneers of France in New World* (1876) p. x, An untamed continent; vast wastes of forest verdure.

Hence **un'tamedly** *adv.*, **un'tamedness**.

1592 LYLY *Gallathea* II. v, Curse..the vntamednes of thy affections. **1612** AINSWORTH *Annot. Ps.* xl. 2 The untamednesse of the tongue. **1653** BLITHE *Eng. Improver Impr.* xxviii. 196 If the horse be kindly used, and taken of his untamednesse by degrees,..he is made a horse for ever. **1706** STEVENS *Span. Dict.* I, *Seneramente*,..wildly, untam'dly, outrageously. **1727** BAILEY (vol. II), *Wildness*, Untamedness, Furiousness.

†un'tameful, *a. Obs.*⁻¹ [UN-¹ 7.] Untameable.

1607 TOPSELL *Four-f. Beasts* 745 Their Epithites..are most cleare demonstrations of their disposition; as sowre,.. vnhonest, vntameful, harmeful.

un'tampered, *ppl. a.* (UN-¹ 8, 8c.)

1682 *Lenten Prol.* 52 If it dare speak th' untamper'd Nations sence. **1827** POLLOK *Course T.* VIII. 25 The true untampered witness of the heart. **1856** AYTOUN *Bothwell* II. xviii, The juice Of the untampered vine. **1858** FROUDE *Hist. Eng.* IV. 290 The Bible, as edited by Cranmer, was left untampered with.

un'tangible, *a.* (UN-¹ 7, 5b.)

[**1775** ASH.] **1816–30** BENTHAM *Offic. Apt. Maximized, Extr. Const. Code* 6 The special good will,..tangible or untangible, naturally flowing from these sentiments. **1818** T. L. PEACOCK *Nightmare Abbey* xii, No, sir, genuine untangible ghosts.

un'tangle, *v.* [UN-² 3 and 7.]

1. *trans.* To free from a tangled state.

1550 THOMAS *Ital. Dict.*, *Disbrigare*, to vntangle any thyng encombred, tangled, or carefull. **1573** TUSSER *Husb.* (1878) 135 See then..ech pole ye out get. Which being vntangled aboue in the tops, Go carrie to such as are plucking of hops. **1592** SHAKS. *Rom. & Jul.* I. iv. 91 This is that very Mab that..bakes the Elf-locks in foule sluttish haires, which once vntangled, much misfortune bodes. *c* **1696** PRIOR *Love Disarmed* 35 Untangle but this cruel Chain, And freely let Me fly again. **1871** B. TAYLOR *Faust* (1875) II. 31 Useless webs she long untangled, Dragging them to air and light.

intr. *a* **1668** LASSELS *Voy. Italy* (1670) II. 415 Sometimes meeting too thick in the arches of the wooden bridge,..they ..are stopt for an hour together without being able to untangle.

b. In fig. uses. Also *refl.*

1601 SHAKS. *Twel. N.* II. ii. 41 O time, thou must vntangle this, not I. *a* **1625** FLETCHER *Fair Maid Inn* II. i, My care now Must be to untangle this division, That our most equal flames may be united. **1677** WYCHERLEY *Pl. Dealer* v. iii, He's the best in England at untangling a flourish, Madam. **1702** VANBRUGH *False Friend* III. iii, If Leonora's innocent, she may untangle all. **1883** D. C. MURRAY *Hearts* xx, The letter went unwritten. She would leave it to events to untangle themselves. **1894** *Advance* (Chicago) 19 Apr., They must untangle their own fate.

2. To set free, to release, from entanglement.

1576 TURBERV. *Venerie* 36 Vntangle him out of the net or stall and let him go. **1588** DEE in Ellis *Lett. Eminent Lit. Men* (Camden) 46 [We will] endeuour our selues..diligently to ryd and vntangle our selues from hence. **1648** FANSHAWE *Il Pastor Fido* 89 Come, fumbler, let me see; I can my self untangle without thee. **1652** J. WRIGHT tr. *Camus' Nat. Paradox* v. 900 Like..Fowlers, who glad to see the innocent Creatures fall into their Gins, instead of untangling them doe ingage them further in their Snares. **1898** HOWELLS *Open-eyed Conspir.* 173 The young..have not had our experience in getting untangled, and think they are never going to get out alive.

un'tangled, *ppl. a.* [UN-¹ 8.] Free from entanglement.

1539 TAVERNER *Erasm. Prov.* (1545) 27 Meanyng that it is excedyng harde for such as flowe in worldly goodes to haue a mynde vntangled with the same. **1598** FLORIO, *Sciolto*, loose, free,..vnsnared,..vntide, vntangled.

un'tanned, *ppl. a.* [UN-¹ 8. Cf. Du. *ongetand.*] Not subjected to tanning.

1535 *Act 27 Hen. VIII*, c. 14 §5 Any manner of Lether tanned or untanned. **1555** EDEN *Decades* (Arb.) 361 Sackes made of raw or vntande hydes. **1639** T. DE GRAY *Expert Farrier* 320 Take the shreds of white leather untanned. **1683** MOXON *Mech. Exerc.*, *Printing* 386 Sheep Skins untan'd, used for Ball Leathers. **1709** LITTLEBURY *Herodotus* II. 194 A small Buckler compos'd of untann'd Hides. **1821** CAMPBELL *Song of Hybrias* 2 A right good shield of hides untanned. **1844** H. STEPHENS *Bk. Farm* II. 400 Untanned sheep-skin is employed to sew on the capes of the collars. **1883** BURTON & CAMERON *Gold Coast* I. 137 Long leather gaiters..and untanned shoes.

un'tap, *v.* (UN-² 9, 7.)

1622 MABBE tr. *Aleman's Guzman d'Alf.* II. 229 If I should suffer her still to vntap my vessel, she would suck me dry at last. **1689** N. LEE *Princ. Cleve* II. iii, Does not your Politician,..after all his Plotting, Drudging and Sweating at Lying, retire to some little Punk and untap at Night?

un'tapered, *ppl. a.* (UN-¹ 8.)

[**1775** ASH.] **1851** RUSKIN *Stones Ven.* I. viii. §9 The Egyptian shaft is often untapered, like the Northern.

un'tapestried, *ppl. a.* (UN-¹ 8.)

1849 JAMES *Woodman* ii, The fourth side of the room was untapestried. **1851** SIR F. PALGRAVE *Norm. & Eng.* I. 206 It was an untapestried Hall; the bowing walls freshly built with untempered mortar.

†un'tapis, *v. Obs.* [UN-² 7 + TAPIS *v.*¹] *intr.* To come out of cover or hiding.

1602 *2nd Pt. Return Parnass.* II. v. 830 At the vnkennelling, vntapezing, or earthing of the Fox. **1634** MASSINGER *Very Woman* III. v, Now I'll untappice. (Comes forward with the bottle.)

un'tapped, *ppl. a.* (UN-¹ 8. Cf. Da. *utappet.*)

In frequent use (esp. fig.) from *c* 1890.

[**1775** ASH.] **1779** WARNER in Jesse *Selwyn* (1844) IV. 254 An untapped barrel of ale. **1863** BATES *Nat. Amazons* I. 143 Untapped [india-rubber] trees still growing in the wilds. **1889** C. EDWARDES *Sardinia* 164 What a fund of mirth..lay untapped within him!

un'tarnishable, *a.* (UN-¹ 7b.)

1887 in A. Adburgham *Shops & Shopping* (1964) vii. 77 A thread of untarnishable gold or silver interwoven with the worsted. **1888** *Microcosm* (N.Y.) Dec. 1 The same.. untarnishable metal [*sc.* aluminium] wrought into every variety of cooking utensils.

un'tarnished, *ppl. a.* (UN-¹ 8.)

1732 GREEN *Grotto* 185 Come, nymph,..With charms untarnish'd, innocence Display, and Eden shall commence. **1798** S. & HT. LEE *Canterb. T.* II. 386 The yet untarnished bridal vestments she..saw packed. **1818** MILMAN *Samor* VII. 386 Yon flag..shook Untarnish'd in the sun its blazon broad. **1859** TENNYSON *Enid* 501 If I fall her name will yet remain Untarnish'd. **1876** E. JENKINS *Blot on Queen's Head* 14 Its glorious and wondrous colours remained fresh and untarnished.

†un'tarpage. *Obs.*⁻¹ [UN-² 5. Cf. UNTAPIS *v.*] An instance of unharbouring an animal.

c **1700** *Fox-chace* 88 in *Roxb. Ballads* (1871) I. 363 Then to Skipland Wood he goes,..An untarpage there we had, Which made our Huntsmen full glad.

un'tarred, *ppl. a.* [UN-¹ 8. Cf. Sw. *otjärad*, Du. *ongeteerd.*] Not smeared, etc., with tar.

1579 W. WILKINSON *Confut. Fam. Love* 24 Least that M. Rogers should scape vntarred with their opprobrious Eloquence. *c* **1610** *Rates of Marchandizes* E3b, Cordage Tard or vntard the hundred waight. **1769** FALCONER *Dict. Marine* (1780), *Cordage blanc*, White, or untarred cordage. *a* **1844** CAMPBELL *Napoleon & Brit. Sailor* 35 A wherry.. Untarr'd, uncompass'd, and unkeel'd. **1875** KNIGHT *Dict. Mech.* 2773/2 An untarred cord or rope.

un'tarried, *ppl. a.* (UN-¹ 8.)

1438 in *Wars Eng. in France* (1864) II. 438 We have disposed oure cousin..to passe in al haste, for whoos passage untaried we pray you that ye doo to hym your devoir.

un'tartarized, *ppl. a.* (UN-¹ 8a*c.*)

1737 BAILEY (vol. II) Add., *Untartarized* (in Chymistry) not mixed with tartar.

un'tasked, *ppl. a.* (UN-¹ 8.)

[**1775** ASH.] **1802** WORDSW. *Excurs.* I. 384 To pass the remnant of his days, untasked With needless services. **1850** DICKENS *D. Copperfield* iv, Miss Murdstone never could endure to see me untasked.

un'taste, *v.* (UN-² 4.)

1609 DANIEL *Civ. Wars* VIII. lxxxiii, Whil'st he himself, deceiu'd, suffers with them: And could not..Vntaste them of this violent disgust.

un'tasteable, *a.* (UN-¹ 7b, 5b.)

1656 BLOUNT, *Ingustable*,..untasteable. **1674** GREW *Disc. Mixture* iii. §16 In any fixed unodorable, or untastable Body.

un'tasted, *ppl. a.* (UN-¹ 8.)

1538 ELYOT, *Illibatus*, vntouched, vntasted. **1593** *Extr. Aberd. Reg.* (1848) II. 89 The aill being untaistit nor yit price maid thairupoun. **1665** BOYLE *Occas. Refl.* IV. v, [He] pour'd it untasted on the Ground. **1725** POPE *Odyss.* XXII. 100 Th' untasted viands, and the jovial bowl. **1802** MAR. EDGEWORTH *Moral T.* II. 11 With a yet untasted pinch of Snuff between her fingers. **1823** SCOTT *Quentin D.* vii, The old Lord..placed the untasted wine-cup before him. **1849** MACAULAY *Hist. Eng.* vi. II. 71 The dishes were removed untasted from the table.

b. In fig. uses.

1606 SHAKS. *Tr. & Cr.* II. iii. 130 All his vertues,..like faire Fruit in an vnholesome dish, Are like to rot vntasted. **1692** DRYDEN *Don Sebastian* II. i, A new Scene of yet untasted Joys. **1742** R. BLAIR *Grave* 76, Bursts of sorrow gush from either eye, Fast falling down her now untasted cheek. **1818** [S. WESTON] *La Scava*, etc. 44 A garbled essay of his abilities, for the most part misunderstood and untasted. *a* **1865** MRS. GASKELL *Wives & Dau.* (1866) I. 67 The squire withdrew into his study to read the untasted newspapers.

un'tasteful, *a.* (UN-¹ 7.)

1618 WITHER *Juvenilia, Abuses Stript* II. i, He marres the bounty of his loving feast By his ill chusing some untastefull guest. **1884** A. VAMBÉRY *Life & Adv.* vii. 60 My patient and untasteful occupation.

un'tastefully, *adv.* (UN-¹ 11.)

1828–32 WEBSTER (citing *Br. Rev.*). **1863** *Pilgr. over Prairies* II. 157 A tunic..profusely and untastefully ornamented with red beads.

un'tasting, *ppl. a.* (UN-¹ 10.)

1707 E. SMITH *Phædra & H.* III. 31 Cydonian Oyl, Whose balmy Juice glides o'er th' untasting Tongue.

un'tasty, *a.* (UN-¹ 7.)

1566 DRANT *Horace, Sat.* III. Gjb, If one..drincke nothing but vinaiger, untastie and unfyne. *a* **1733** LD. BINNING *Lady's Complaint* v. in Maidment *Ball.* (1844) 62 But camblet's an untasty thing.

un'tattered, *ppl. a.* (UN-¹ 8.)

[**1775** ASH.] **1856** N. HAWTHORNE *Eng. Note-bks.* (1879) I. 363 Banners..so untattered, that I think they must be modern.

unta'ttooed, *ppl. a.* (UN-¹ 8.)

1884 G. TURNER *Samoa* vii. 89 Variegated..with neat regular stripes of the untattooed skin.

un'taught, *ppl. a.* [UN-¹ 8b.]

1. Not enlightened or trained by teaching; uninstructed, ignorant.

c **1340** HAMPOLE *Pr. Consc.* 5873 Maysters [shall give account] of þair disciples..þat þai lete be unthewed, and untaght ga. **1382** WYCLIF *Ecclus.* viii. 5 Comune thou not to a man vntauȝt. *c* **1460** *Play Sacram.* 558 [636] Syr, thu art ontawght to come in thus henly [*sic*]. **1567** DRANT *Horace, Ep.* I. i. Gvj, The greater companye, in vertue few, and base, Vntaught blockheads, braineles. **1596** SHAKS. *1 Hen. IV*, I. iii. 43 He call'd them vntaught Knaues, Vnmannerly. **1602** *2nd Pt. Return Parnass.* v. i. 1986 With vntaught hand, and with vntuned hart. **1649** DAVENANT *Love & Hon.* III. ii. 3 Fit only to perswade the easinesse Of untaught babes. **1709** STEELE *Tatler* No. 167 ¶1 The rude and untaught Multitude. **1784** COWPER *Task* II. 359 He teaches those to read, whom schools dismiss'd, And colleges, untaught. **1847** C. BRONTE *J. Eyre* xxxii, Wholly untaught, with faculties quite torpid, they seemed to me hopelessly dull. **1882** BESANT *All Sorts* xxviii, The crude theories of untaught, if generous, youth.

absol. **1382** WYCLIF *1 Chron.* xxv. 8 Thei leyden lottis by their whilis euenly,..the tauȝt and vntauȝt to gyder. **1728** CHAMBERS *Cycl.* s.v. *Substantive*, The Taught have the Advantage of the Untaught. *a* **1832** CRABBE *Posth. Tales* II. 169 He knew not how For the untaught and ill-taught to allow.

Prov. *c* **1530** in *Songs, Carols*, etc. (E.E.T.S.) 129 Better it is to be wnborne than wntawght. **1557** F. S[EAGER] *School Virtue* Ciij, The common prouerbe remember ye oughte, 'Better vnfedde then vn-taughte'.

b. Const. with inf., *in*, or objective complement.

1581 HOWELL *Devises* Mij, Like a childe agayne, vntaught the sleightes of dayntie mindes. *a* **1593** MARLOWE *Hero & Leander* I. 392 Her mind pure, and her toong vntaught to glose. **1642** H. MORE *Song of Soul* II. III. iii. 42 Untought In subtilties they shew themselves in jangling stout. **1683** DRYDEN *Ovid's Ep.*, *Helen to Paris* 139 My hand is yet untaught to write to Men. **1762** SIR W. JONES *Arcadia* Poems, etc. (1772) 135 Daphne, yet untaught in am'rous lore, Felt..pains unknown before. **1784** COWPER *Tiroc.* 379 Untaught The knowledge of the world, and dull of thought! **1794** WORDSW. *Guilt & Sorrow* xxxiii, We gazed with terror on their gloomy sleep, Untaught that soon such anguish must ensue. **1827** KEBLE *Chr. Y.*, *Convers. St. Paul* vi, His strain'd eye..Still gazing, though untaught to bear Th' insufferable light.

c. Of animals, etc.

1697 DRYDEN *Æneis* VI. 348 Four sable bullocks, in the yoke untaught. **1725** POPE *Odyss.* VII. 153 The balmy spirit of the western gale Eternal breathes on fruits untaught to fail. **1743** FRANCIS tr. *Hor.*, *Epodes* xvi. 57 Where Goats untaught forsake the flowery Vale. **1817** BYRON *Mazeppa* ix, A noble steed,..Wild as the wild deer, and untaught. **1863** CONINGTON *Horace, Odes* III. iii. 14 For this..tigers drew Thy glorious car, untaught to slave In harness.

2. Not imparted or acquired by teaching; hence, natural, spontaneous.

c **1445** PECOCK *Donet* 6 Bettir it is..þan forto leve alle suche þingis vnwritun and vntauȝt. *c* **1449** —— *Repr.* I. xx. 127 This other maner of..witnessing bi Holi Scripture, which is left here vnseid and vntauȝt. **1533** MORE *Answ. Supper of Lord* I. xvii. Wks. 1064/1 Leauing that vntaught til yᵉ time of his maundy supper. *a* **1586** SIDNEY *Arcadia* III. xxiv, Delivering from his hart two or three (untaught) sighes. **1611** SHAKS. *Cymb.* IV. ii. 178 'Tis wonder That an inuisible instinct should frame them To Royalty vnlearn'd, Honor vntaught. **1656** COWLEY *Davideis* I. 821 Flocks of Birds..Teaching their Maker in their untaught lays. **1712** STEELE *Spect.* No. 276 ¶3, I have a natural Voice, and a pretty untaught Step in Dancing. **1742** GRAY *Spring* 7 The untaught harmony of spring. **1836** CDL. WISEMAN *Lect. Cath. Ch.* (1847) 3 Many doctrines untaught by Him. **1865** TYLOR *Early Hist. Man.* ii. 19 The untaught signs made by born deaf-mutes.

Hence **un'taughtness**.

1840 S. CLARK in *Mem. Jrnls. & Lett.* (1878) 131, I have to suffer from my untaughtness.

un'tawed, *ppl. a.* (UN-¹ 8 + TAW *v.*¹ 2.)

1545 *Rates of Customs* biv, Graye vntawed the timber, iiis. iiiid. *Ibid.* bvii, Lettuis vntawed the timber, iis. vid. **1617** *Bk. Rates Marchandise* G2, Furres:..Budge, blacke vntawed. **1642** *Ibid.* D2b, Letwis..Vntawed. **1662** *Stat. Irel.* (1786) II. 406 Furs:..Calabar, untawed the timber, containing forty skins, 6s. 8d.

un'tax, *v.* [UN-² 4b.] *trans.* To exempt from a tax; to remove a tax from.

c **1831** E. ELLIOTT *Corn-Law-Rhymes* (1833) 102 Who will untax our bread? **1834** HT. MARTINEAU *Moral* III. 119 To untax the prime necessary of life.

un'taxable, *a.* [UN-[1] 7 b and 5 b.]

†**1.** That cannot be taxed or charged with wrong-doing. Also const. *of. Obs.*

a **1610** HEALEY *Cebes* (1616) 137 Behold there a faire and florishing matrone, enthroned in state,..yet vntaxable of profuseness. **1624** BP. MOUNTAGU *Gagg* 130 It is not said, that They kept the commandements of God... But they walked in them.. untaxable, unblameable. *a* **1688** W. CLAGETT *17 Serm.* (1699) 289 His untaxable justice in bringing upon them that punishment.

2. Not liable to taxation.

1648 HEXHAM II, *Onschatbaer*, Vntaxable, or Free and Franck. **1818** BENTHAM *Ch. Eng.* p. x, The Lower House was indeed untaxable. But the Upper House..taxed themselves.

un'taxed, *ppl. a.* [UN-[1] 8. Cf. G. *untaxirt*, older Da. *utaxeret* in sense 2.]

†**1.** Unassailed; unchallenged. *Obs.*

c **1460** *Oseney Reg.* 17 Ordeynyng þat all maner possessions..sure to yow..vntaxid abyde. **1605** BACON *Adv. Learn.* I. vii. §7 In common speech (which leaves no virtue untaxed) he was called..a divider of cummin seed. **1645** G. DANIEL *Poems* Wks. (Grosart) II. 101 May not I,.. To my best Child, Vtter a Truth vntax'd? *a* **1691** BOYLE *Hist. Air* (1692) 76 A mistake that must not pass untaxed amongst learned men.

2. Not required to pay taxes.

1464–5 in *Acta Parlt. Scot.* (1875) XII. 31/2 Any personis ..within þe boundis of thare office vntaxt. **1746** WARTON *Progr. Discontent* 119, I..din'd untax'd, untroubled, under The portrait of our pious founder. **1776** ADAM SMITH *W.N.* v. ii. (1904) II. 513 Those who exercise the untaxed employments. **1826** LAMB *Wks.* (1908) I. 389 The Beadle.. looks like a whole parish, full, important—but untaxed. **1835** LYTTON *Rienzi* IX. iv, To live unbutchered by the Barons, and untaxed by their governors.

un'taxing, *ppl. a.* (UN-[1] 5 d.)

1851 LYTTON *Not so bad* 134 A College; Where teacher and student alike the subscriber, Untaxing the Patron,.. The State,..Or the briber.

unte: see UNCT *v. Obs.* (to anoint).

un'teach, *v.* [UN-[2] 3.]

1. *trans.* To cause (a person) to forget or discard previous knowledge. Occas. const. *to* with inf.

1532 TINDALE *Expos. Matt. v–vii*, 36 b, Thou hast vntaught hir to feare God. **1650** BAXTER *Saints' R.* III. 535 We have a double task; first to unteach them, and then to teach them better. **1802–12** BENTHAM *Ration. Judic. Evid.* (1827) I. 8 The peasant wants only to be taught, the lawyer to be untaught. **1833** *Q. Rev.* XLIX. 72 Much of their time was employed in *un*teaching them to read. **1845** KEBLE in A. Mozley *Lett. Newman* (1891) II. 473 You have taught me so, and I scarce think you can unteach me. **1870** EMERSON *Soc. & Solit.* vii. 135 Every new step in improving the engine restricts one more art of the engineer,—unteaches him.

b. With double object. (Also in passive.)

1620 SIR T. MATTHEW tr. *St. Augustine's Confessions* III. xii. 121 To teach me that which was good, and to vnteach me that which was otherwise. **1661** BOYLE *Style of Script.* 148 The Complaint was ordinary, That the Reading of the Bible untaught them the Purity of the Roman Language. **1732** BERKELEY *Alciphr.* v. §24 Gentlemen are untaught by the world what they have been taught at the college. **1743** FRANCIS tr. *Hor., Odes* II. ii. 19 But Virtue can the Croud unteach Their false, mistaken Forms of Speech. **1814** BYRON *Lara* I. iv, His faults..Might be untaught him by his varied lot.

2. *absol.* To undo previous knowledge or teaching.

1531 ELYOT *Gov.* I. xv, It is difficulte to put out of the mynde that whiche is ones settilled,..and verily moche more to unteache than to teache. **1573** TUSSER *Husb.* (1878) 63 To teach and vnteach in a schoole is vnmeete. *a* **1589** PALFREYMAN *Baldwin's Mor. Philos.* (1600) 74 The.. burthen beeing..verily much more to vnteach then to teach. **1839** BAILEY *Festus* 317 Once—teach and unteach—nay, to use more arts Than would outdo the Devil of his throne.

3. To remove from the mind (something known or taught) by different teaching.

1562 TURNER *Herbal* II. 57, I will be content..to vntech my error, whiche I haue taught before. **1633** T. ADAMS *Exp. 2 Peter* ii. 12 That the holy Ghost should sit in the Chaire, to crosse and unteach their principles. **1643** SIR T. BROWNE *Relig. Med.* II. §8 Wee doe but learne to day, what our better advanced judgements will unteach to morrow. **1709** O. DYKES *Eng. Prov.* (ed. 2) 92 Over-grown Habits may be untaught by diligent Care. **1801** *Monthly Mag.* XII. 590 Must not the Anti-gallicans seek fresh sophists to unteach all their lessons of the last decennium? **1857** ELLIS & BLACKBURN *Rep. Cases Q. Bench* VII. 190 Reasons.. instilled into her in the process of unteaching those prayers.

Hence **un'teaching** *vbl. sb.*

1876 W. CORY *Lett. & Jrnls.* (1897) 414 The inevitable *un*teaching of young men, the purging from delusion.

un'teachable, *a.* [UN-[1] 7 b.]

1. Incapable of being instructed.

c **1475** *Cath. Angl.* 378/2 (A.), Vn Techeabylle, *indocibilis*. **1580** HOLLYBAND, *Indocile*, vntractable, vnteachable. **1594** T. B. *La Primaud. Fr. Acad.* II. 188 The ignorant person that knoweth not himselfe..is as vnteachable a beast as can be. **1645** MILTON *Tetrach.* 42 Our Saviour at no time exprest any great desire to teach the obstinate and unteachable Pharises. **1707** *Reflex. upon Ridicule* 387 They are more unteachable, more heady, more interested. **1797** COLERIDGE *Osorio* IV. iv. 182 And so the babe grew up..A pretty boy, but most unteachable. **1871** MEREDITH *H. Richmond* xlvii, I chafed at his unteachable spirit.

absol. and as *sb.* **1819** SHELLEY *Cyclops* 492 Let us with some comic spell Teach the yet unteachable. **1850** CARLYLE *Latter-day Pamph.* ii. 14 If I had schoolmasters,..do you imagine I would set them on teaching a set of unteachables..?

2. Incapable of being imparted by teaching.

a **1667** PETTY in Sprat *Hist. R. Soc.* 306 This being infinite and almost unteachable by words. **1813** SCOTT *Rokeby* I. xxvi, His was minstrel's skill, he caught The art unteachable, untaught. **1860** EMERSON *Cond. Life* v. (1861) 116 We are continually surprised with graces..not only unteachable, but undescribable. **1867** LEWES *Hist. Philos.* (ed. 3) I. 215 Opinions..which in other dialogues Socrates is made to exhibit as untaught, perhaps unteachable.

Hence **un'teachableness.**

1607 HIERON *Wks.* I. 462 Doe not ignorant persons continue in blindnes and vnteachablenes? **1702** PENN *Fruits Solit.* II. §243 The worst part of this Vanity is its Unteachableness. **1850** L. HUNT *Autobiog.* II. 79 When kings themselves tried hard to make honest men republicans by their apparent unteachableness.

un'teaching, *ppl. a.* (UN-[1] 10.)

1587 FENNER *Def. Ministers* 137 The Senate of teaching and vnteaching Elders. **1610** BP. HALL *Apol. Brownists* xxvii. 70 What Congregation of Christendome..affoorded you the necessary patterne of an vnteaching Pastor, or an vnfeeding Teacher? **1642** MILTON *Apol. Smect.* 56 The Prelats..after their preferment most usually change the teaching labour of the word, into the unteaching ease of Lordship over consciences, and purses.

un'team, *v.* [UN-[2] 4 b.] *trans.* To unyoke.

1548 ELYOT, *Interiungo*, to vnteeme the horses, that they maie reste. **1592** WARNER *Alb. Eng.* VIII. xlii. 158 Our Cattell vnto stronger draughts we..would vnteame. **1667** JER. TAYLOR *Gt. Exemp.* (ed. 4) II. 310 Since Justice and Authority laid by the Rods and Axes as soon as the Sun unteamed his chariot. **1675** COTTON *Scoffer Scoft* 81 Let the Hours unteam thy Horses.

absol. **1662** J. DAVIES tr. *Olearius' Voy. Ambass.* 413 The Muscovian Ambassador having cudgell'd one of the Waggoners, all the rest would unteam and return homewards.

un'tearable, *a.* (UN-[1] 7 b.)

1648 HEXHAM II, *Onverscheurlick*, Vntearable. **1859** F. FRANCIS *Newton Dogvane* iv, The pudding appeared,..an indigestible mass, composed of untearable steak. **1900** POLLOK & THOM *Sports Burma* 252 Shooting-suits..of some strong untearable material.

un'teased, *ppl. a.* (UN-[1] 8.)

[**1775** ASH.] **1843** E. JONES *Sens. & Event* 71 These multitudinous varying boughs, Unteased with leaves slept still.

un'teaseled, *ppl. a.* (UN-[1] 8.)

[**1775** ASH.] **1877** C. GEIKIE *Christ* II. 38 A piece of raw unteazled cloth.

un'technical, *a.* (UN-[1] 7.)

1845 *Encycl. Metrop.* II. 751/1 These authorities are of two kinds, untechnical and technical. **1860** GEO. ELIOT *Mill on Fl.* III. vii, Tom's untechnical mind. **1882** FARRAR *Early Chr.* I. 149 The word occurs but once in his letter, and that in its purely general and untechnical signification.

un'technically, *adv.* (UN-[1] 11. Cf. prec.)

1818 CRUISE *Digest* (ed. 2) IV. 381 The intention of the parties, however untechnically expressed.

un'tedded, *ppl. a.* (UN-[1] 8 + TED *v.*[1])

c **1380** WYCLIF *Sel. Wks.* II. 301 þes lumpis failen here, as mowen gras þat were unteddid.

un'teem, *v.* [UN-[2] 3 + TEEM *v.*[1]] *trans.* To unburden, discharge.

1635 [GLAPTHORNE] *Lady Mother* III. i, Lest the full clouds..unteeme their big wombd laps And raise a sudden deluge. **1683** in J. Russell *Haigs* (1881) 314 It seems to me that Europe is unteaming herself to plant these Western parts of the world.

un'teemed, *ppl. a. dial.* [UN-[1] 8 + TEEM *v.*[2]] Unemptied.

1641 H. BEST *Farm. Bks.* (Surtees) 53 Wee sette (att night) the..two last waines to the mowe brest, and leave them unteamed till the morninge.

un'teinded, *ppl. a. Sc.* [UN-[1] 8.] Untithed.

1527 *Burgh Rec. Prestwick* (Maitl. Club) 52 For the wrangus takin in of peis ontendyt. **1663** *Min. Baron Court of Stitchill* (S.H.S.) 25 For hydeing and conceiling of his cornes in the yaird unteynded.

†**un'teinted**, *ppl. a. Obs.* [UN-[1] 8. Cf. F. *teinté.*] Untinted, uncoloured.

1745 *Phil. Trans.* XLIII. 525 [He] produced several Samples of the Apples; an unteinted Russetting; a Russetting changed in Complexion.

†**un'teld**, *v. Obs.*[—1] [UN-[2] 4 + TELD *sb.* b.] *trans.* To clear of tents or awnings.

a **1400** *Morte Arth.* 737 Qwen all was schyppede that scholde, they schounte no lengere, Bot vntelde [*MS.* ventelde] them tyte.

†**un'tell**, *v. Obs.* (UN-[2] 3.)

? **1603** HEYWOOD *Woman killed w. Kindness* (1617) G 2, That time could turne vp his swift sandy glasse, To vntell the dayes, and to redeeme these houres.

un'tellable, *a.* [UN-[1] 7 b, 5 b.] Unspeakable, unutterable; indescribable.

In earlier use somewhat rare. Freq. from *c* 1880. The absence of evidence from 16th to 19th c. is remarkable.

1382 WYCLIF *Ecclus.* xxxvi. 16 Fulfil Syon with thin vntellable vertues, and thi puple with thi glorie. *c* **1410** *Lantern Li3t* 136 Feer intollerable, drede vntellable. *c* **1425** *St. Eliz. of Spalbeck* in *Anglia* VIII. 113 With sobbynges & weymentynges vntelabil. *c* **1440** *Promp. Parv.* 367/2 Ontelleable, *inenarrabilis*. **1513** DOUGLAS *Æneid* I. xii. 6 Thi desyir, lady, is Renewing of ontellable sorow. **1552** ABP. HAMILTON *Catech.* (1884) 16 The glore of the saule quhilk is untelabil. **1830** MRS. OPIE in Brightwell *Mem.* (1854) 246 It fills me with untellable wonder and admiration of him. **1865** TRENCH *Gustavus Adolphus* ii. 76 Which, though not absolutely untellable, had yet better remain untold. **1886** RUSKIN *Præterita* I. 422 The joy of approved love, and the untellable, incalculable motive of its sympathy.

Hence **un'tellably** *adv.*

c **1425** *St. Eliz. of Spalbeck* in *Anglia* VIII. 109/21 Whanne þese and oþere lyke are doon often and vntellably. **1513** DOUGLAS *Æneid* VIII. ix. 38 The fader than..full tenderly Apone him hingis, wepand ontellably. **1889** *Missionary Herald* Feb. 50 [The character of the people] is terribly bad,..untellably bloodthirsty, cruel, and lascivious.

un'telling, *ppl. a. north.*, *Sc.* and *U.S. dial.* [UN-[1] 10.]

1. Innumerable, countless.

a **1300** *Cursor M.* 2107 Inde, and pers, and arabi,..And mani oþer vntelland contre. *Ibid.* 6441 Þis ilk folk was vntelland, þat moyses had vnder hand. **1816** G. MUIR *Clydesdale Minstrelsy* 7 The royal banner that has splendid flown Its annual course for ages past untellin'. **1825** JAMIESON, *Untelling*, adj.,..denoting what cannot be counted. Roxb. **1834** *Chambers's Edin. Jrnl.* 28 June 170/1 It being untelling the number of lodgers who used to elope without coming to a settlement. **1925** E. C. SMITH *Mang Howes* 1 The road was thrang wui droves o nout—aa keinds, untellin. **1951** H. GILES *Harbin's Ridge* iii. 18 It's untelling the times me and Faleecy John have walked the snake-back of that barnyard fence.

2. = UNTELLABLE *a.*

1823 HOGG *Shepherd's Cal.* i, It was untelling what land that man possessed. **1885** [J. TOD] *More Bits fr. Blinkbonny* i, It was untellin' what Tibbie did for poor Mrs. Gemmell. **1941** *Sat. Even. Post* 10 May 36/2 A man's notions are untelling.

†**un'temed**, *ppl. a. Obs.* [OE. *untemed* (UN-[1] 8), = MLG. *untem(m)et*, MDa. *utæm(me)t*, Da. *utæmmet*. Cf. OE. *unȝetemed*, MDu. *ongetemmet*, *-temt* (Du. *ongetemd*), MLG. *ungetemet*, G. *ungezähmt*.] Untamed.

a **1000** *Gloss.* in Wr.-Wülcker 226 *Edomitus* [sic], untemed, wilde. *a* **1100** *Cambridge Ps.* xxxii. 17 Leas *vel* untemed hors. **1388** WYCLIF *Ecclus.* xxx. 8 An hors vntemyd ..schal ascape hard. **1398** TREVISA *Barth. De P.R.* XVIII. lxxvii. (Bodl. MS.), Onager is a wilde asse..and suche asses been grete..& vntemed. *c* **1420** *Prose Life Alex.* 8 A prynce of Macedoyne broghte þe kyng a horse vn-temed, a grete and a faire.

un'temper, *v.* (UN-[2] 3.)

1685 COTTON tr. *Montaigne* I. 233 Examples have demonstrated to us that..the study of sciences does more soften and untemper the courages of men than any way fortifie and incite them. **1758** REID tr. *Macquer's Chem.* I. 65 By the same operation Steel may be untempered.

†**un'temperable**, *a.* (UN-[1] 7 b, 5 b.)

= INTEMPERABLE *a.*

1571 tr. *Buchanan's Detect. Mary* (1572) H iij, A woman.. in..corrupt affectiounis vnbridelit, vntemperable by her estayt, raging by hyr power.

†**un'temperance.** *Obs.* (UN-[1] 12 and 5 b.)

1541 R. COPLAND *Galyen's Terap.* 2 A. iv, The fyrste maner [of ulcers] haboundeth by the vntemperaunce of the flesshe subiecte. **1587** FLEMING *Contn. Holinshed* III. 1268 The successors may be taught by their predecessors,.. sobrietie by their vntemperance. **1614** GORGES *Lucan* IV. 124 The hazards that ensue,..From the vncertaine motions grew, When then the aires vntemperance drew.

†**un'temperant**, *a.*: see UNTEMPERATE *a.* 2 (quot. 1388).

†**un'temperate**, *a. Obs.* [UN-[1] 7, 5 b.]

1. a. Of weather, etc.: = INTEMPERATE *a.* 1.

1525 LD. BERNERS *Froiss.* II. cxxiv. 353 In Castyle there is no thynge but harde rockes and Mountaynes,..and an vntemperate ayre. *a* **1548** HALL *Chron., Hen. VI*, 137 Of these vntemperate stormes rose suche a scacety, that wheat was sold at iii.s. iiii.d. the busshell. **1614** *Archdeaconry of Essex* (MS.) *Minutes* fol. 101 [The weather] was wett and vntemperate.

b. Distempered, disordered. *rare*[—1].

1539 ELYOT *Cast. Helthe* (1541) 17 b, [To] the bodyes untemperate, suche meates or drynkes are to be gyven, which be in power contrary to the distemperance.

2. = INTEMPERATE *a.* 2.

1388 WYCLIF *Ecclus.* xxxi. 23 Colre..and gnawyng to an vndiscreet either vntemperat [*C.C. Coll. Camb. MS.* vntemperaunt] man. **1561** T. NORTON *Calvin's Inst.* I. xiii. 43 b, [They] that do delite in an vntemperate desyre of speculacion. **1589** COOPER *Admon.* 2 A lamentable state of time it is, wherin such vntemperat boldenes is permitted. **1607** MARKHAM *Cavel.* II. 101 If the Ryder haue an vntemperate hand, which euer pulleth..vpon the horses mouth. *a* **1633** CARY *Edw. II* (1680) 16 The King, by his untemperate and undiscreet actions, had lost the hearts of his People.

3. = INTEMPERATE *a.* 3.

a **1589** PALFREYMAN *Baldwin's Mor. Philos.* (1600) 116 Youth vntemperate, and full of carnall affections, quickly turneth the bodye into age. **1592** NASHE *P. Penilesse* G ij b, Vntemperate venerie, and that hatefull sinne of selfe-loue. **1613** SHERLEY *Trav. Persia* 55 Hee that can restraine himselfe from being transported by vntemperate appetites. **1625** SHIRLEY *Love Tricks* II. ii, I would not leaue Rufaldo for a world Of rash, vntemperate youth.

Hence †**un'temperately** *adv. Obs.*

1398 TREVISA *Barth. De P.R.* XVII. clxxxviii. (Bodl. MS.), Wyne drinkinge vntemperatlych is to man kinde..venym. **1548** UDALL, etc. *Erasm. Par. John* ii. 14 b, When their geastes..haue their mouthes out of taste, & powre in drinke vntemperately. **1560** DAUS tr. *Sleidane's Comm.* 237 b, They hearde also howe vntemperately the Freers that were collocutours handled the matter. **1602** SEGAR *Hon., Mil. & Civ.* IV. i. 209 He that immoderately and vntemperately pampereth his own body.

†**un'temperateness.** *Obs.* [UN-[1] 12, 5 b.]
1. Distempered physical condition.
1398 TREVISA *Barth. De P.R.* XVII. ii. (Bodl. MS.), þe temporat place bringeþ oute of vntemporatenes and makeþ it gode to ete. **1541** R. COPLAND *Galyen's Terap.* C iv, Some dysease of the lyuer, or the weykenes of the party greued, the which is none other thynge but a clere and notable vntemperatnes. **1580** BLUNDEVILLE *Horsemanship* IV. 36 b, To learne at the Physicians handes, which.. as touching the weakenesse of the Liuer, proceeding of the vntemperatenesse thereof, will bid you to heale euerie such vntemperatenesse by his contrarie. **1597** A. M. *Guillemeau's Fr. Chirurg.* 35 b/1 The glowinge Cautery..amendeth the vntemperatnes of that parte. **1621** BURTON *Anat. Mel.* I. ii. v. iii, An innate burning vntemperatnesse, turning blood and choler into melancholy.
2. = INTEMPERATENESS 1.
1577 tr. *Bullinger's Decades* 238/2 A dwelling place coueniently situated against the vntemperatenesse of the ayre. **1594** R. ASHLEY tr. *Loys le Roy* 26 The vntemperatenes of Winter, and Sommer. *a* **1656** USSHER *Ann.* (1658) 723 The work..being hindred by no untemperatenesse of the weather. **1665** MANLEY *Grotius' Low C. Wars* 405 Many of his men,..by the untemperateness of the Air,..dyed. **1758** J. S. *Le Dran's Observ. Surg.* (1771) Dict., *Intemperies*, an Unseasonableness, Untemperateness.
3. = INTEMPERATENESS 2.
1578 TIMME *Calvin on Gen.* 213 By reason of vntemperatnesse they doe degenerate from their nature. **1599** MINSHEU *Span. Gram.* To Students, Vntemperatenes, Vnshamefastnes, Vnfaithfulnes, and Vnthankefulnes. **1637** SALTONSTALL *Eusebius' Constantine* 137 Untemperatenesse of life, covetousnesse, murder.

†**un'temperature.** *Obs.*[−1] [UN-[1] 12, 5 b.] Distempered state.
a **1604** HANMER *Chron. Irel.* (1809) 396 [After the] Earthquake..there followed..a continuall untemperature of the ayre, with a filthy skurfe.

un'tempered, *ppl. a.* [UN-[1] 8. Cf. MDu. *ongetempert*, Du. *ongetemperd*, MHG. *ungetempert*.]
1. Unregulated; not moderated or controlled.
1377 LANGL. *P. Pl.* B. IX. 102 Wolde neuere þe faithful fader his fithel were vntempred. *a* **1547** SURREY *Eccl.* v. 52 What lyef leede testeye men that consume their dayes In inwarde freets, untempred hates. **1561** NORTON & SACKV. *Gorboduc* III. i, Your eldest sonne, misledd By traitours framde of young vntempered wittes Assembleth force against your yonger sonne. **1631** A. WILSON *Swisser* III. ii, I wilbee your Stickler, You too untemper'd Vermin! **1808** WM. MITFORD *Hist. Greece* I. 584 Every untempered government must be jealous. *Ibid.* III. 72 The spirit of party will pervade a state with..untempered and..lasting violence.
b. Unmodified, unqualified. Freq. const. *by*.
1768–74 TUCKER *Lt. Nat.* (1834) II. 603 The utmost rigour of legal justice untempered by equity. **1794** S. WILLIAMS *Vermont* 203 The spirit of monarchy, untempered by representation. **1847** H. ROGERS *Ess.* (1860) I. 240 His eyes ache with that too untempered brilliance. **1868** FREEMAN *Norm. Conq.* x. II. 481 Rigid justice, untempered by mercy.
2. Of lime or mortar: Not properly mixed and prepared. Also in fig. context.
c **1440** *Pallad. on Husb.* III. 395 Vntempred lime yf with the graffes be Putte in the plages. **1535** COVERDALE *Ezek.* xiii. 11 Y[e] wall, that ye haue dawbed with vntempered morter. **1637** GILLESPIE *Eng. Pop Cerem.* III. i. 7 He laboureth to plaister over his Superstition with the vntempered morter of this quidditative distinction. **1661** COWLEY *Cromwell* Wks. 1906 II. 362 That none of these untempered Mortars can hold out against the next blast of Wind. **1755** YOUNG *Centaur* v. 311 This castle was built out of the various ruins of many demolish'd forts of infidelity,.. and cemented with untemper'd mortar. **1826** SOUTHEY *Vind. Eccl. Angl.* 44, I have not been labouring in the quarries for thirty years, that I should build with untempered mortar. **1896** A. D. COLERIDGE *Eton in Forties* 8 His gloves..[being] bedaubed..with untempered mortar.
transf. **1781** COWPER *Hope* 627 To storm the citadels they build in air, And smite th' untemper'd wall, 'tis death to spare.
b. Not properly digested or concocted.
1822 GOOD *Study Med.* II. 757 The untempered fluid contained in the tubercles. *Ibid.* IV. 695 A defective secretion of the rete mucosum, which..seems to be.. untempered or imperfectly elaborated.
c. Unhardened.
1820 GOOD *Syst. Nosology* 427 Bones untempered in their substance, and incapable of affording their proper support. **1825** J. NICHOLSON *Operat. Mechanic* 322 A screw of untempered steel. **1839** NOAD *Electricity* 239 A disc of untempered steel.

un'tempering, *ppl. a.* (UN-[1] 10.)
1599 SHAKS. *Hen. V*, v. ii. 241 My blood begins to flatter me, that thou doo'st [love me], notwithstanding the poore and vntempering effect of my Visage.

un'tempested, *a.* (UN-[1] 9.)
1846 WORCESTER (citing Millman). **1890** 'R. BOLDREWOOD' *Col. Reformer* (1891) 244 The serene untempested heavens of the isles of the blest.

untem'pestuous, *a.* (UN-[1] 7, 5 c.)
1864 SWINBURNE *Atalanta* 400 Like kindled lights in untempestuous heaven.

un'templed, *a.* (UN-[1] 9.)
1850 S. DOBELL *Roman* v. 61 A bare Untempled spot, unblest, unconsecrate. **1855** BAILEY *Mystic* 16 He, the untempled God, above man's thought.

un'temporary, *a.* (UN-[1] 7.)
1784 R. BAGE *Barham Downs* I. 235 Oh, for the actual, undisturbed, untemporary enjoyment of two such friends!

un'temptable, *a.* (UN-[1] 7 b.)
1819 *Monthly Mag.* XLVIII. 306 With this second marriage, the untemptable Adam is extremely delighted. **1837** SIR F. PALGRAVE *Merch. & Friar* iv. 243 They wish to earn the character of the most untemptable and rigid justice.

un'tempted, *ppl. a.* [UN-[1] 8.]
1. Not tempted; unassailed by temptation.
1607 BEAUM. & FL. *Woman-Hater* IV. i, Can you imagine A Maid, whose beauty could not suffer her To live thus long untempted? **1652** BP. HALL *Invis. World* III. xii, Those objects of dread, and horror,..not so confined to their hell, as to leave us untempted. **1716** GAY *Trivia* II. 287 Careful observers,..Untempted,..contemn the jugler's feats, Pass by the Meuse, nor try the thimble's cheats. **1757** [see UNTAINTED *ppl. a.* 4 b]. **1809–14** WORDSW. *Excurs.* VIII. 259 Those..yet untempted to forsake The simple occupations of their sires. **1865** GROSART *Mem. H. Palmer* 44 The issue of profound meditation,..not untempted of doubt. **1890** 'R. BOLDREWOOD' *Col. Reformer* (1891) 366 An unworn, untempted nature.
b. Not due to or resulting from temptation or enticement.
1744 AKENSIDE *Ep. Curio* 67 Yet must you one untempted vileness own. **1753** FIELDING *Eliz. Canning* Wks. 1903 XI. 39 A pitch of wanton and untempted inhumanity, beyond all possibility of belief. **1871** RUSKIN *Fors Clav.* vii. 23 There is no physical crime..so without parallel in its untempted guilt, as the making of war machinery.
2. Unattempted, untried. *rare*[−1].
1744 AKENSIDE *Pleas. Imag.* i. 573 Let the breath of thy extended praise Inspire my kindling bosom to the height Of this untempted theme.

†**un'tempter.** *Obs. rare.* (UN-[1] 12.)
1382 WYCLIF *Jas.* i. 13 Sotheli God is vntempter [L. *intentator*] of yuel thingis, forsothe he temptith no man.

un'temptible, *a.*, **-ibly,** *adv.* (UN-[1] 7, 11.)
1828 E. IRVING *Serm.* I. p. lxvii, Infallibility and holiness untemptible..in that which hereto-fore had been human, fallible and temptible flesh. **1858** BUSHNELL *New Life* xiii, Absolute purity is untemptible, as in God. *Ibid.*, God..is untemptible. *Ibid.*, He can make us untemptibly pure.

un'tempting, *ppl. a.* (UN-[1] 10.)
1824 LYTTON in *Life & Lett.* (1883) I. 294 The poor animal..bent his head languidly over the untempting food. **1859** F. E. PAGET *Curate Cumberworth* 353 A schoolboy repugnance to go back to my smoky lodgings, and Mrs. Ferrall's untempting fare.
Hence **un'temptingly** *adv.*
[**1847** WEBSTER.] *a* **1856** H. MILLER *Rambles Geologist* (1858) 357 The day was still unfavorable, and the [geological] sections seemed untemptingly indifferent.

un'temptingness. (UN-[1] 12. Cf. prec.)
1646 HAMMOND *Sinnes* 12 The naturall intrinsecall untemptingnesse of that sinne.

un'temsed, *ppl. a.* [UN-[1] 8.] Unsifted.
1641 BEST *Farm. Bks.* (Surtees) 105 Wee have received a pecke and a halfe more of tempsed meale from the one, than wee have had of the other, of untempsed meale.

untena'bility. (UN-[1] 12, 5 c. Cf. next.)
1644 PRYNNE & WALKER *Fiennes' Trial* 76 The weaknesse and untenability of it was no ground of its surrender. **1841** HERSCHEL *Ess.* (1857) 188 The complete untenability of a simple aqueous doctrine. **1884** *Law Times* 1 Nov. 7/1 The untenability of the modern American contention.

un'tenable, *a.* [UN-[1] 7 b and 5 b.]
1. Incapable of being held against attack.
1647 CLARENDON *Hist. Reb.* VIII. §60 Having lain so long with such a strength before so vile and untenable a place, without reducing it. *a* **1671** LD. FAIRFAX *Mem.* (1699) 9 In a council of war the Town was judged untenable. **1769** ROBERTSON *Chas. V*, IV. Wks. 1813 V. 418 That ill-provided and untenable fort. **1796** *Campaigns 1793–4*, I. I. ix. 91 The post..was abandoned as untenable. **1844** H. H. WILSON *Brit. India* II. 54 Measures were taken to render the position of the besiegers untenable. **1879** *Cassell's Techn. Educ.* I. 287 The fire of the Prussian artillery rendered the interior of the works..untenable.
b. *fig.* (Cf. sense 2.)
1692 DRYDEN *Juvenal* (1697) p. lii, Casaubon..thinks it time to abandon a Post that was untenable. He acknowledges that Persius is obscure in some places. **1765** STERNE *Tr. Shandy* VIII. xxxiv, If there was any one post more untenable than the rest, he would be sure to throw himself into it. **1807** *Med. Jrnl.* XVII. 534 An impartial retrospect..will..convince Mr. Dawson, that he has occupied untenable ground. **1880** M[c]CARTHY *Own Times* lxiii. IV. 429 He withdrew from what he felt to be an untenable position.
c. Incapable of being occupied or retained.
1699 BOYER *Dict. Royal* s.v., His new Lodgings were made in a Moment as untenable as the others. **1721** AMHERST *Terræ Fil.* No. 40 (1726) 211 Not content with.. college-offices, they have lately found out a method of augmenting them with good livings, which, according to statutes and prescription, are untenable together. **1860** *Merc. Marine Mag.* VII. 291 A ship could lay there in safety when Table bay would be untenable. **1883** STEVENSON *Silverado Sq.* 5 The site has proved untenable.
2. Incapable of being maintained or supported.
1650 FULLER *Pisgah* II. xiii. 268 A Tenet unteinable with truth. **1664** H. MORE *Apol.* 507, I am..far from rejecting or condemning the Opinion of the Schools from being altogether untenable. **1724** WATERLAND *Farther Vindic. Christ's Divin.* Introd., Their main Scheme appearing so gross, and so untenable, that they..are..ashamed to own it. **1835** THIRLWALL *Greece* iii. I. 78 A not untenable hypothesis. **1886** *Law Rep. 31 Chanc. Div.* 365 The claim is of the most untenable description.
Hence **un'tenableness.**
1833 G. S. FABER *Recapit. Apostasy* 40 The untenableness of the various names..crudely propounded by the wantonness of expositorial licence. **1846** LEWES *Hist. Philos.* IV. 95 The untenableness of the theory of innate ideas.

un'tenant, *v.* [UN-[2] 4, 5.]
1. *trans.* To dislodge from a dwelling.
1614 T. ADAMS *Devils Banquet* 104 Hee gets possession of their affections, whence all the power of man cannot vntenant him.
2. To deprive of a tenant or tenants.
1640 SHIRLEY *St. Patrick for Irel.* I. i, You know I can Untenant hell, dispeople the wide air. **1796** COLERIDGE *Destiny of Nations* 35 All Those blind Omniscients, those Almighty Slaves Untenanting creation of its God. **1799** *Monthly Rev.* XXVIII. 528 It is only wonderful that the official cadastres should not wholly have untenanted the soil. **1832** R. CHAMBERS *Eminent Scotsmen* I. 46 The Reformation untenanted its walls. **1846** M'GEE *Irish Writers* 30 Dempster..began to untenant every niche in the national temple of Ireland. **1861** LD. LYTTON & FANE *Tannhäuser* 67, I, whose heart of all that lived in it He hath untenanted.
3. To depart from, to quit.
1795 COLERIDGE *Lines at Shurton Bars* iv, Untenanting its beauteous clay My Sara's soul has wing'd its way.

un'tenantable, *a.* (UN-[1] 7 b.)
a **1661** FULLER *Worthies, Essex* I. (1662) 347 Winchester Castle was..ordered to be made Untenable; but the over-officious malice of such who executed the Order (wilfully mistaking the word) made it Untenantable. **1772** *Ann. Reg., Chron.* 141/1, 400 houses..destroyed, or rendered untenantable. **1774** *Phil. Trans.* LXV. 274 They may so abound with fleas as to become untenantable. **1833** WHEWELL *Astron.* vii. 64 The apparently frozen and untenantable regions in the neighbourhood of the pole. **1862** GALTON *Vac. Tour.* 208 Beds untenantable, charges unconscionable, is the state of things now as then.

un'tenanted, *ppl. a.* [UN-[1] 8.] Not occupied by a tenant or tenants.
1673 TEMPLE *Ess. Irel.* Wks. 1720 I. 117 The Country seems to be full stock'd, no Ground that I hear of being untenanted. **1677** YARRANTON *Eng. Improv.* 16 There needed not one House to stand empty and untenanted. **1741** RICHARDSON *Pamela* II. 203 A pretty little Farm and House, untenanted. **1808** SCOTT *Marm.* II. Introd., All silent now—for now are still Thy bowers, untenanted Bowhill. **1887** *Spectator* 22 Oct. 1413 There are not now so many untenanted spaces on the globe suitable for human habitation.
fig. **1830** CARLYLE *Misc.* (1872) III. 53 In that hour thou wilt look back on thy untenanted life.

un'tended, *ppl. a.* [UN-[1] 8.]
1598 FLORIO, *Incustodito*, not kept, not looked vnto, vntended. **1732** LYTTELTON *Progr. Love* i. 17 His flock.. untended lay, To ev'ry savage a defenceless prey. **1736** THOMSON *Liberty* v. 10 Let Asia's woods, Untended, yield the vegetable fleece. **1794** WORDSW. *Guilt & Sorrow* lxiii, Nor shall she perish there, untended and alone! **1807** J. BARLOW *Columb.* VI. 160 He comes..untended by his usual train. **1854** H. MILLER *Sch. & Schm.* xi, The hedges [were] gapped by the almost untended cattle. **1861** *Peaks, Passes & Glac.* Ser. II. I. 163 The same fitful glare from the pine-log fire, as the untended embers crumble together!

un'tender, *a.* [UN-[1] 7.]
1. Not tender in dealing with others; ungentle, unkind. Also const. *of*.
1605 SHAKS. *Lear* I. i. 108 So young, and so vntender? **1611** —— *Cymb.* III. iv. 12 Why tender'st thou that Paper to me, with A looke vntender? *c* **1678** J. B. in *Spirit of Popery* (1680) 75 Is it reasonable..to be thus tender of a few men, and untender of the grand Concerns of..our Master? ?*c* **1710** CONGREVE *Lament. Helen over Hector* 9 In all which time..Not one untender Word or look of Scorn, Which I too often have from others born. **1774** BEATTIE *Minstrel* II. xxxi, Let untender thoughts afar be driven. **1825** LAMB *Elia* II. *Wedding*, Is there not something untender..in the hurry which a beloved child is sometimes in to tear herself from the paternal stock. **1898** G. W. E. RUSSELL *Collect. & Recoll.* ii. 14 In those untender days he was considered too delicate to remain at a Public School.
†**2.** Not having a tender conscience; lacking in religious susceptibility. Also *transf. Obs.*
a **1658** DURHAM *Comm. Rev.* (1660) 187 We will find, that many who have been untender, have had hand at this work. **1680** in *Proc. Soc. Antiq. Scot.* XLV. 235 This wofull dreadfull defection in these two emenent men is to be lamented... Among them Mr. Castairs elder is the most unsound and untender. **1730** T. BOSTON *Mem.* (1899) 37 He, being both a weak and untender man, was unacceptable to the parish. *Ibid.* 136 The untender carriage of some ministers in Nithsdale. **1765** J. BROWN *Chr. Jrnl.* 262 Untender professors loudly bawl against the sins of others. *a* **1812** MACLEAN *Disc.* Wks. 1848 VI. 195 By an untender walk guilt has accumulated upon the conscience.
3. Not immature.
1879 BAIN *Educ. as Science* xii. 416 The effect produced on tender years will be submerged in the un-tender years that follow.
Hence **un'tenderness.**
a **1658** DURHAM *Comm. Rev.* (1660) 181 There was much ..unwatchfulness and untenderness in both these respects before God. **1680** in *Proc. Soc. Antiq. Scot.* XLV. 248 An untenderness and sinfull love of life. **1724** E. ERSKINE *Serm.* Wks. (1791) 122 If through untenderness ye provoke him to withdraw. **1883** *Century Mag.* 55 This education..he had never got.—Hence his untenderness.

un'tendered, *ppl. a.* [UN-[1] 8.] Not offered.
1607 MIDDLETON *Michaelmas Term* III. iv. 45 Is not the day past, the money untendered? **1611** SHAKS. *Cymb.* III. i. 10 Cassibulan..granted Rome a Tribute, Yeerely three thousand pounds; which (by thee) lately Is left vntender'd.

un'tenderly, *adv.* (UN-[1] 11.)
? *a* **1400** *Morte Arth.* 1144 Vn-tenderly fro þe toppe þai tiltine to-gederz. *c* **1425** WYNTOUN *Cron.* VII. ii. 128 (Cott. MS.), He sende þaim in to Normondy, þar tretyt þai war wntendyrly. **1651** WARRISTON *Diary* (S.H.S.) II. 143, I heard of Suynton's..leaving of all family exercises..and walking untenderly on the Lords Day. *a* **1658** DURHAM *Comm. Rev.* (1660) 188 A Minister..prone to foster their securitie, or rifle their wounds untenderly. **1780** S. J. PRATT *Emma Corbett* (ed. 4) III. 154, I have too much contributed to her happiness for her to treat me untenderly. **1856** MRS. BROWNING *Aur. Leigh* II. 823 If I spoke untenderly This morning,..pardon it. **1868** BROWNING *Ring & Bk.* VI. 196 The snow-white soul that angels fear to take Untenderly.

un'tenible, *a.* [UN-[1] 7.] Untenable.
1783 HAILES *Antiq. Chr. Ch.* 135 A conclusion most illogical and untenible.

† **un'tennanted**, *ppl. a. Obs.*[−1] [UN-[1] 8.] Not furnished with a tenon.
1678 MOXON *Mech. Exerc.* v. 84 Make also a Tennant on each un-Tennanted end of the Stiles.

un'tense, *v.* [UN-[2] 3, 7.] *trans.* and *intr.* To render or become less tense or rigid; to relax.
1970 N. FLEMING *Czech Point* i. 7, I hooked my ski-sticks on to the T-bar and with some difficulty untensed my leg muscles. **1970** E. TIDYMAN *Shaft* (1971) i. 10 Anderozzi untensed: Shaft wasn't going to run. **1976** A. J. RUSSELL *Pour Hemlock* vii. 72 She untensed and started walking again. **1978** *Times Lit. Suppl.* 1 Dec. 1406/4 The triplets helped Tomlinson to un-tense his diction.

un'tent, *v.* (UN-[2] 4, 4 b.)
1606 SHAKS. *Tr. & Cr.* II. iii. 178 Why, will he not vpon our faire request, Vntent his person, and share the ayre with vs? **1611** FLORIO, *Stendare*, to remooue the tents of a camp, to vntent.

unten'taculated, *ppl. a.* (UN-[1] 8.)
a **1830** MCCULLOCH *Attributes* (1843) III. 394 The untentaculated Medusæ.

un'tented, *ppl. a.*[1] [UN-[1] 8 + TENT *v.*[4]] Unprobed, undressed.
1605 SHAKS. *Lear* I. iv. 322 Th' vntented woundings of a Father's curse Pierce euerie sense about thee. **1822** MILMAN *Martyr of Antioch* 65 With open and untented wounds. **1828** SCOTT *Aunt Margaret's Mirror* ad fin., The wounds of an untented conscience.

† **un'tented**, *ppl. a.*[2] *Obs.* [UN-[1] 8 + TENT *v.*[2]] Not tempted.
1725 in Peterkin *Ork. & Zetl.* (1822) I. 223 The straight pathes of virtue and untented honesty.

un'tented, *ppl. a.*[3] *Sc.* or *arch.* [UN-[1] 8 + TENT *v.*[1]] Unheeded, unregarded.
1791 J. LEARMONT *Poems* 61 The least untentit, lowse spoke word, Gars them draw the duellin' sword. *c* **1800** R. GILL *Elegy Pudding Lizzie* xiii, While busy time still jogged on, Unmark'd, untented. **1867** MORRIS *Jason* x. 300 Great herds of deer and neat,..Seeming all wild.., For quite untented here and there they ran.

un'tented, *ppl. a.*[4] [UN-[1] 8 + TENTED *ppl. a.*] Not furnished with a tent or tents.
1891 *Cent. Dict.* s.v., An untented army;..an untented field.

un'tenty, *a. Sc.* [UN-[1] 7.] Careless, heedless.
1819 SCOTT *Leg. Montrose* x, What is to become of me, if Gustavus..should be lamed among their untenty hands! **1893** STEVENSON *Catriona* vii, I would never be so untenty as to commit myself.

‖**untergang** ('ʊntərgaŋ). [Ger., = decline, downfall.] An irreversible decline, esp. leading to the destruction of culture or civilization.
1938 L. MACNEICE *I crossed Minch* ix. 133 The Untergang, the collapse of civilisation. **1962** *Listener* 12 July 51/2 There were times when Zarathustra—and, I believe, Nietzsche himself—longed for the *Untergang*, the going down, the descent, among the many, for the many, into death. **1965** *New Statesman* 30 July 166/1 The rooms and houses seemed on a depressingly small scale for a civilisation which it had always pleased me to think of as suffering the disease of gigantism which afflicts societies in full *untergang*.

† **un'termed**, *ppl. a.* [UN-[1] 8.] Unbounded, unlimited.
c **1586** C'TESS PEMBROKE *Ps.* CV. ii, He eternally that treaty mindeth, Which him to us untearmed ages bindeth. **1633** FORD *Love's Sacr.* III. iii, Thy reward..Shall be our speciall thanks, and loue vn-term'd.

‖**untermensch** ('ʊntərmɛnʃ). Pl. **-menschen**. [Ger.] Esp. with reference to the Nazi régime (1933–45): a racially inferior person, a sub-human person. Cf. ÜBERMENSCH.
1964 *Punch* 13 May 723/1 A Negro American..is a benighted *Untermensch*. **1966** *Sat. Rev.* (U.S.) 26 Mar. 34 To the Germans, Lithuanians were *Untermenschen*, a second-class people to be exploited and, when politically expedient, enslaved. **1974** A. GODDARD *Vienna Pursuit* II. 60 The Jews were shown to be people beyond the pale—*untermenschen* who had murdered Christ. **1981** R. BARNARD *Sheer Torture* xii. 132 Maria-Luisa had been shouting insults... Comes from the gutter. Scum. *Untermensch*.

† **un'terminable**, *a. Obs.* (UN-[1] 7 b, 5 b.)
a **1677** MANTON *Serm. Ps. cxix.* (1725) 436/2 Eternal Duration implies an immutable and unterminable abode in Being.

un'terminably, *adv.* (UN-[1] 11, 5 b.)
1631 R. SKENE in A. Craig *Pilgr. & Hermit* 3 For the singular and ever bound duetie, wherevnto..I ever acknowledge my selfe to be vnterminably tied, to loue, serue, and honour, You and Yours.

un'terminated, *ppl. a.* (UN-[1] 8.)
[**1775** ASH.] **1853** KANE *Grinnell Exp.* xxvii. (1856) 225 The broad, unterminated expanse of ice. **1891** E. T. DIXON *Found. Geom.* 33 Any unterminated straight line.

un'terminating, *ppl. a.* (UN-[1] 10.)
1821 SCOTT *Biogr. Mem.* (1834) I. 368 The unterminating succession of misfortunes.

‖**unteroffizier** ('ʊntərɔfi'tsiːr). *Mil.* [Ger.] A German non-commissioned officer.
1917 T. E. LAWRENCE *Let.* 10 July (1938) 228 We entered Akaba..with 600 prisoners, about 20 officers, and a German unteroffizier. **1942** *Order of Battle of German Army* (U.S. War Dept. General Staff) 33 *Hauptgefreiter*, no equivalent grade... *Unteroffizier*, Corporal. **1980** R. BUTLER *Blood-Red Sun at Noon* (1981) I. i. 22 *Unteroffizier* Neumann was..shot down.

un'terraced, *ppl. a.* (UN-[1] 8.)
[**1775** ASH.] **1879** STEVENSON *Trav. Cevennes* 166 The ground, where it was unterraced, was usually too steep.

† **un'terred**, *ppl. a. Obs.*[−1] [UN-[1] 8.] Uninterred.
1633 MARMION *Fine Companion* I. i, Those That lye unterr'd, wanting their funerall rites.

unte'rrestrial, *a.* (UN-[1] 7.)
1746 YOUNG *Nt. Th.* IX. 1752 The natives of this world sublime, Of this so foreign, un-terrestrial sphere. **1813** SHELLEY *Q. Mab* VII. 175 No pain assailed His unterrestrial sense.

un'terrifiable, *a.* (UN-[1] 7 b.)
1875 HELPS *Soc. Press.* xxiii. 352 There remain no unterrifiable witnesses but children.

unte'rrific, *a.* (UN-[1] 7.)
1788 H. DOWNMAN *Infancy* VI. 637 The stream Of lightning,..safe convey'd, In unterrific silence, to the ground. **1831** CARLYLE *Sart. Res.* II. iii, Not unterrific was the aspect; but we looked on it like brave youths. **1887** RUSKIN *Præterita* II. 393 A majestic, but unterrific fortalice of cliff.

un'terrified, *ppl. a.* (UN-[1] 8.)
Also *U.S.* 'derisively applied to the Democratic party': **1832–63** in Thornton *Amer. Gloss.* s.v.
1609 DANIEL *Civ. Wars* VI. lxxviii, Yet standes he stiffe, vndash't, vnterrifi'd. **1670** FLATMAN *Death of Albemarle* v, Ever unterrified his valour stood Like some tall rock amidst a sea of blood. **1753** SMOLLETT *Ct. Fathom* xli, The chevalier, unterrified by this dreadful salutation, desired he would accompany him to a more convenient place. **1764** *Ann. Reg., Chron.* 87/1 The robin..comes in..unterrified by the number of persons. **1821** SHELLEY *Adonais* iv, He went, unterrified, Into the gulf of death. **1856** OLMSTED *Slave States* 178 The attempt to suppress discussion has given every advantage to the unterrified partisans on both sides.

un'terrifying, *ppl. a.* (UN-[1] 10.)
1691 NORRIS *Pract. Disc.* 149 What a mild and unterrifying thing is Death to such a Man as this! **1821** LAMB *Elia* I. *Chapter on Ears*, The genuine unterrifying aspects of my pleasant-countenanced host and hostess. **1877** SWINBURNE *C. Brontë* 79 Lips already whitened..by the present shadow of unterrifying death.

† **un'testate**, *a.* [UN-[1] 7, 5 b.] Intestate.
c **1440** *Jacob's Well* 20 þe godys of here tenauntys þat dyen vntestate. **1559** *Richmond. Wills* (Surtees) 138 Not willinge to dye untestate,..I provide..this my last will. **1591** SAVILE *Tacitus, Hist.* II. 89 If they dyed vntestate the ordinary course of the law..was obserued. **1600** ROWLANDS *Lett. Humours Blood* iv. 65 It was his fathers lucke of late to die Untestate. **1617** MINSHEU. (Hence in Hexham.)

un'tested, *ppl. a.* [UN-[1] 8.]
† **1.** Intestate. *Obs.* (Cf. prec.)
1570 FOXE *A. & M.* (ed. 2) I. 409/1 The courte [of Rome]..aspired how to vsurpe the goods of them that die vntested. **1586** SPENSER *Will* Wks. 1882 I. p. xvii, Suche as dye untestyd. **1608** in *T. Pont's Acc. Cunningham* (Maitl. Cl.) 183 Johne Blair..deceist vntestit in the moneth of Januar, 1604 zeiris.
2. Not tested or proved.
[**1775** ASH.] **1828–32** WEBSTER (citing *Adams' Lect.*). **1881** FITCH *Lect. Teach.* 179 To leave him unquestioned and untested. **1884** CHURCH *Bacon* viii. 197 His whole doctrine of 'Forms'..is an example of loose and slovenly use of unexamined and untested ideas.

un'testicled, *ppl. a.* (UN-[2] 8, 4.)
1668 WILKINS *Real Char.* 291 So *Ox* is untesticled or gelt Bull.

† **un'tetche**. *Obs.*[−1] [UN-[1] 4 b + *tetche* TACHE *sb.*[1]] Wrongful act; fault.
c **1350** *Will. Palerne* 509 His maners were so menskful, a-mende hem mi3t none, & seþþe forsoþe til þis time non vntetche he ne wrou3t.

un'tether, *v.* (UN-[2] 4 b.)
[**1775** ASH.] **1888** W. G. BLACK *Heligoland* 9 The herd-girl who comes to untether the patient sheep.

un'tethered, *ppl. a.* (UN-[1] 8.)
[**1775** ASH.] **1826** W. A. MILES *D. Barrow* 5 [These evidences, etc.] give a free untethered flight to the imagination. **1907** *Daily Chron.* 6 June 5/5 Old untethered horses and donkeys..browsing on the slopes.

un'tewed, *ppl. a.* [UN-[1] 8 + TEW *v.*[1]] Untrimmed.
1591 LYLY *Endym.* II. ii, That..cruell enemie that beareth rough and vntewed lockes vpon his bodie.

un'thack, *v.* [UN-[2] 4.] = UNTHATCH *v.*
c **1400** *Pepysian Gospel Harmony* 22 Hij cloumben on þat hous and vnþakkeden it.

† **unthank**, *sb. Obs.* [OE. *unþanc* masc. (f. UN-[1] 12 + *þanc* THANK *sb.*), = OFris. *unthonk* (WFris. *ontank*, NFris. *untoonk*), MDu. *ondanc* (Du. *ondank*), MLG. *undank*, OHG. *undanch*, *unthank* (MHG. *undanc*, G. *undank*) ingratitude, displeasure, etc.; ON. *úþökk* fem., a reproach, censure, etc. (MSw. *othak*, Sw. *otack*, MDa. and Da. *utak* ingratitude, etc.).]
I. 1. Absence of gratitude or good-will; unfavourable thought or feeling; ill-will, disfavour; displeasure expressed in actions or words.
c **893** K. ÆLFRED *Oros.* IV. x. § 11 þa wæs Hannibale æfter hiera hæðeniscum ȝewunan þæt and wyrde swiþe lað, & him unþanc sæde þæs and wyrdes. *a* **1000** *Sal. & Sat* 98 Ðonne hiene on unðanc..R. ieorrenga ȝeseceð. *c* **1205** LAY. 22370 Mid Arðure he win dronc; þat him wes mucheles unðonc. **13..** *E.E. Allit. P.* C. 55 þenne þrat moste I þole, & vnþonk to mede. *c* **1380** WYCLIF *Sel. Wks.* I. 256 And in travaile aboute þese goodis..stondiþ al þe mede in þis liif, and al unþank of peyne of helle. *c* **1386** CHAUCER *Reeve's T.* 161 Vnthank come on his hand that boond hym so. **1435** MISYN *Fire of Love* 92 Frenschyp..has also a grete likynge with it knytt in qwhilk it adyls no meyde ne vnþanke. **1483** *Cath. Angl.* 381/2 Vn Thanke, *demericio*. **1557** *Tottel's Misc.* (Arb.) 203 Vnthanke to our desert be geuen, Which merite not a heauens gift to kepe.
b. In the phrase *to have unthank*.
c **1325** in Wright *Pol. Songs* (Camden) 327 But unthank have the bishop that lat hit so go. **13..** *E.E. Allit. P.* B. 183 For þeft, & for þrepyng, vnþonk may mon haue. *c* **1380** *Sir Ferumb.* 3061 'Wel depardieux,' quaþ þis barouns, 'ounþank habbe þat spare'.
2. An act or circumstance causing displeasure or annoyance; an offence or injury.
c **897** K. ÆLFRED *Gregory's Past. C.* xlix. 379 And ða forðyðe he forwandode ðæt he swa ne dyde, ða aȝeaf he hit [*sc.* ðæt feoh] to unðances. *c* **1000** *Apollonius of Tyre* 26 Cweðe ȝe þæt ic..eow dide æfre æniȝne unþanc? *c* **1050** *O.E. Chron.* (MS. C) an. 1049, Eac fela oðra unþanca þe he him dyde. *c* **1205** LAY. 11769 þe eorl Caredoc..3et hit mai ilimpe; hit is þe an vnðonke. *a* **1225** *Ancr. R.* 202 Uor lure of eie worldliche þinge, oðer of freond, oðer uor eni unðonc. **13..** *Guy of Warw.* 5311 His brond..brac vnto his hond. 'Allas,' quaþ Gij, 'þis vnþang! Were no may y me nou3t lang'.
II. In uses denoting disinclination, reluctance, or involuntariness.
3. In genitive, used adverbially, = Unwillingly; compulsorily; against a person's wish or will; without one's consent; also, involuntarily.
The genitive is similarly used in OFris., MDu., OHG., etc.
c **960** *Laws Edgar* in Thorpe *Laws* I. 264 Niman [hi] unþances þone teoðan dæl to þam mynstre. ? **1066** *O.E. Chron.* (MS. C) an. 1066, Tostiȝ..nam of þam butse karlon sume mid him, sume þances, sume unþances. *c* **1175** *Lamb. Hom.* 17 Gif þu agultest wið þine efen-nexta unðonkes, bet hit þin þonkes hu se þu miht wið him. *a* **1300** *Cursor M.* 27192 [It] sceus quat nede Was man at drau him to þis dede, ..Quar vnthankes [*Fairf.* queþer vnþankis] or wit will, And quatkin strengh him draf þer-till.
b. More freq. with poss. adj. (or sb. in poss. case).
c **893** K. ÆLFRED *Oros.* II. ii. § 1 Hi swaþeah heora unðances mid swicdome hie beȝeaton. *c* **1100** *O.E. Chron.* (MS. D) an. 905, þa ȝerad Æþelwold æðeling..þone ham æt Winburnan & æt Tweoxnam þæs cynges unþances. *c* **1200** ORMIN 7194 Miccle bettre iss to þe mann..To don all hiss unnþannkess god þan ifell hise þannkess. *c* **1205** LAY. 4502 Brennes..hauede heo biwedded, & ihaued heo to bedde, al hire vnðonkes. *a* **1240** *Sawles Warde* in *O.E. Hom.* I. 247 Strengðe stont nest hire, þat 3ef ei wule in, warschipes vn þonkes, warni strengðe fore, þat is hire suster, ant heo hit ut warpe. *c* **1330** R. BRUNNE *Chron. Wace* (Rolls) 14172 Wyþ hym to fighte leuere he wylde þan, his vnþankes, to þem 3elde. **13..** *Coer de L.* 2208 Natheles many he cleaved, And their unthanks ther bylived. *c* **1450** *St. Cuthbert* (Surtees) 201 þis virgyne þus hir vnthankes fyled perceyued þat sho was with chiled. *a* **1470** HARDING *Chron.* L. iv, Kyng Edward with long shankes Brought it awaye again, the Scottes vnthankes. *Ibid.* LXVIII. ii, Vpon the north sea bankes, He faught with theim in battaill their vnthankes.
c. Without inflection in absolute use.
a **1225** *Juliana* 36 He schal unþonc in his teð cuðen þe þat tu wilnest. [Cf. TOOTH *sb.* 5.] *c* **1230** *Hali Meid.* 47 þurh þis weorre, he 3arkeð þe, unþonc hise [*v.r.* in his] teð, þe blisse ..of cristes icorene. *c* **1330** R. BRUNNE *Chron. Wace* (Rolls) 6093 Walwes þey tok, al his vnthank, & leddym to Atyngal. **1338** —— *Chron.* (1810) 241 þe Walsch com þam ageyn, did our men alle arere, þat turnyng þer vnthank, as heuy was þe charge, Vnder þam alle sank.
4. *at one's unthanks*, against one's will.
a **1400–50** *Alexander* 4698 Forþi enhabete 3e in angwysch at 3oure vnthankis. *c* **1420** *Anturs of Arth.* 424 (Thr.), Or he weldene my landes, at myne vn-thankes. By alle þe welthe of this werlde, he salle þame neuer welde.

un'thank, *v.* [UN-[2] 3.] *trans.* To unsay or recall one's thanks to.
1640 SHIRLEY *Love's Cruelty* III. iii, *Duke*. We are not pleasd, she should depart. *Seb.* Then I'le vn-thanke your Goodnesse.

un'thanked, *ppl. a.* (UN-[1] 8.)
1562 LEGH *Armory* Pref., Suche they are, as be gone from the world, of whome I am sure to be vnthanked. **1634** MILTON *Comus* 723 If all the world Should in a pet of temperance feed on Pulse,..Th' all-giver would be unthank't, would be unprais'd. **1666** DRYDEN *Ann. Mirab.*

cxcii, Their batter'd Admiral too soon withdrew, Unthank'd by ours for his unfinish'd Fight. **1700** —— *Pal. & Arc.* I. 388 Unwelcom Freedom and unthank'd Reprieve. **1814** COLERIDGE *Lett.* (1895) 630 Unthanked, and left worse than defenceless, by the friends of the Government. **1897** H. N. HOWARD *Foot-steps Proserpine* 95 Though unthanked he fall Midway.., His soul shall mount to Heav'n.

un'thankful, *a.* [UN-[1] 7. Cf. OE. *unþancful*, OHG. *undancfol.*]

1. Not earning thanks or gratitude; unacceptable, unappreciated, thankless; disagreeable.

c **1400** *Apol. Loll.* 45 What þing þat þu werkyst is vnþankful to þe Holi Goost. **1533** BELLENDEN *Livy* I. x. (S.T.S.). I. 56 Baith þe pepil[s]..beheld þis vnthankful sicht. *Ibid.* I. 60. **1598** SYLVESTER *Du Bartas* II. i. III. *Furies* 626 Those that (broken with unthankfull toyl) Seek others' Health. **1623** J. TAYLOR (Water P.) *Discov. by Sea* B7, Which make themselues sicke with drinking such vnthankfull healths. **1759** GOLDSM. *Bee* No. 8 ¶14 It is, therefore, one of the most unthankful offices in the world. **1815** COLERIDGE *Lett.* (1895) 642 To be a prophet is..an unthankful office. **1855** *Poultry Chron.* III. 363 It must be an unthankful task for judges to award prizes to inferior birds.

†**b.** Inadequate, insufficient. *Obs.*[-1]

1491 *Reg. Aberdon.* (Maitl. Cl.) I. 328 Gyf it beis fundin onthankful payment be þe said Jhone to þe said vicar.

2. Not rendering thanks; not feeling or exhibiting gratitude.

1499 *Contempl. Sinners* Prol. A v b, Vnthankfull mannes myndes. **1526** TINDALE *2 Tim.* iii. 2 Men shalbe.. vnthankfull, vnholy, churlisshe. **1565** COOPER *Thesaurus*, *Animus ingratus*, an vnthankfull harte. **1602** *2nd Pt. Return fr. Parnass.* III. ii. 1199 An vnthankefull Viper that will sting the man that reuiued him. **1647** N. BACON *Disc. Govt. Eng.* I. lvii. 168 These concurring with unnaturall troubles from most unthankfull sonnes. **1702** *Eng. Theophrastus* 91 He that in silence suppresses a favour received is an unthankful Fellow. **1722** DE FOE *Relig. Courtsh.* I. ii. (1840) 77, I do not think you will ever be unthankful. **1768** ROSS *Helenore* 60 I'm seeking after twa unthankfu' men. **1805** WORDSW. *Prelude* VII. 543 Could a youth..Sit, see, and hear, unthankful, uninspired?

absol. **1535** COVERDALE *Luke* vi. 35 The Hyest..is kynde, euen to the vnthankfull. **1893** J. PULSFORD *Loyalty to Christ* II. 367 The Good Shepherd giveth Himself to the unthankful and the evil.

transf. **1614** B. JONSON *Barth. Fair* III. i, The husbandman ought not, for one unthankful year, to forsake the plough. **1615** BRATHWAIT *Strappado*, etc. (1878) 326 But time vnthankfull time, too soone forgot the Gem she had. **1665** BOYLE *Occas. Refl.* v. vii, The Thorns and Thistles that are the unthankful Earths wonted productions.

b. Const. *for* or †*of* (a thing), *to* (a person).

c **1500** KENNEDIE *Passion of Christ* 373 As seik vnthankfull to þe medicinar. **1542** BRINKLOW *Compl.* iii. 16, I pray God, that we be not vnthanckful for that delyuerance. **1580** J. HAY in *Cath. Tract.* (S.T.S.) 33 That I swild nocht appear to be onthankfwll of the said benefeit. **1610** DONNE *Pseudo-martyr* 289 When Otho..became vnthankfull to the Pope. **1711** STEELE *Spect.* No. 82 ¶5 Your Ingratitude..shall not make me unthankful for the Good you have done me. **1729** LAW *Serious C.* xi. 171 Quarrelsome with others, and unthankful to God. **1855** SINGLETON *Virgil* II. 394 He looks back, Unconscious of events, and for escape Unthankful.

3. Characterized by ingratitude.

1614 BP. HALL *Contempl.*, *O.T.* v. vi. 107 If yee had said, Choose vs another gouernour, it had been a wicked and vnthankfull motion. **1643** *Secrets Discovered* (title-p.), Their perfidious, deceitful, and unthankful proceedings against the welfare of this Kingdom. **1665** BOYLE *Occas. Refl.*, etc. (1848) 54 It were..unthankful towards the Father of Lights, not to make use of the great Light we receive..by the Moon. **1721** KELLY *Scot. Prov.* 188 When they whom we have supported make unhandsome, and unthankful Returns.

un'thankfully, *adv.* [UN-[1] 11.] Ungratefully.

a **1470** HARDING *Chron.* CXXXIII. i, He awnswered hym full vnthankefully. **1531** ELYOT *Gov.* III. ii, The riches that he hym selfe gaue hym, whiche the other unthankefully dothe attribute to his owne fortune. **1577** tr. *Bullinger's Decades* 285/2 Such as do vnthankfully abuse the benefites..of their good God. *c* **1620** MORYSON *Itin.* IV. v. iii. (1903) 475 This all experienced strangers doe confesse, but they vnthanckfully misconceaue the cause. **1697** *Verdicts conc. Virgil & Homer* v. 21 If these shipwrackt Banditti came sneakingly to Carthage, they go from it as unthankfully. **1814** WORDSW. *Excursion* IV. 479 You judge unthankfully; distempered nerves Infect the thoughts. **1848** DICKENS *Dombey* xlvii, A stubborn disposition..unthankfully indulged in.

un'thankfulness. [UN-[1] 12.] Ingratitude.

Very frequent from *c* 1550 to *c* 1650.

c **1500** in *Asloan MS.* (S.T.S.) II. 220 Vnthankfulness of man thrillit his [*sc.* Christ's] hart. **1553** T. WILSON *Rhet.* 102 b, Suche should suffer death as felons, whiche were found faultie with vnthankfulnesse. **1617** MORYSON *Itin.* II. 89 Without great vnthankefulnesse..he could not have beene questioned upon this weake ground. *a* **1665** J. GOODWIN *Filled w. the Spirit* ii. (1670) 28 The Spirits with-drawing of himself from men..proportionably to mens unthankfulnes, neglect, and opposition to him. **1728** YOUNG *Love Fame* v. 173 When surfeit or unthankfulness destroys..our solid joys. **1803** MALTHUS *Popul.* IV. ix. 563 If the proposed relief be given, it is of course received with unthankfulness. **1850** LYNCH *Theoph. Trinal* viii. 145 For pride will in thy doings lurk, And in thine heart unthankfulness.

un'thanking, *ppl. a.* [UN-[1] 10.] Not giving thanks (for something); ungrateful.

1902 KIPLING *Five Nations* (1903) 138 Arid, aloof, incurious, unthinking, unthanking, gelt. **1932** CHESTERTON *Chaucer* i. 36 We may sometimes be unthinking about it; unthinking and especially unthanking.

un'thatch, *v.* [UN-[2] 4. Cf. OE. *unþeccan* and UNTHACK *v.*] *trans.* To strip of thatch.

1699–1700 *Laws Nevis* xxx. §4 (1740) 25 That the Constables..may the better know what Houses to unthatch. **1771** *Ann. Reg.*, *Chron.* 104/1 Many peasants were under the necessity of unthatching their houses to maintain their cattle. **1894** *Daily News* 23 May 6/5 They think the landlords are wrong to unthatch a tenant's house.

un'thatched, *ppl. a.* [UN-[1] 8.] Not covered with thatch.

1570 LEVINS *Manip.* 50 Vnthatched, *intectus.* **1629** [see UNTRELLISED]. **1633** HALL *Occas. Medit.* 279 An old unthached Cottage. **1664** INGELO *Bentiv. & Ur.* v. 33 Streight Cottages, unthatch'd above, full of Smoak and Rain within. *a* **1860** ALB. SMITH *Med. Student* (1861) 58 An unthatched cottage on a common. **1897** *Daily News* 1 Oct. 2/6 The storm was accompanied by drenching rain, and..a large number of unthatched corn stacks were completely saturated.

un'thaw, *v.* Now *dial.* [UN-[2] 9 and 7.] *trans.* and *intr.* To thaw. Also *fig.*

1598 FLORIO, *Disquagliato*, melted, vnthawed, liquified. **1633** T. JAMES *Voy.* 77 In the woods, wee found the Snow partly wasted away... The ponds were almost vnthawd: but the sea..[was] all firme frozen. **1699** T. BROWN *Gent. Holland* Wks. 1711 IV. 316 The Men..are cold to such a degree, that neither Love nor Wine can unthaw them. **1764** J. G. COOPER *Power Harmony* I, The flood of life, Loos'd at its source.., Flows like some frozen silver stream unthaw'd, At a warm Zephyr of the genial Spring. **1847–** in southern dial. glossaries. **1895** *Times* 23 Jan. 9/3 Harcourt..would not or could not unthaw.

un'thawed, *ppl. a.* [UN-[1] 8.] Not thawed; remaining frozen.

1611 FLORIO, *Indileguato*, vnthawed, vnuanished. **1657** H. KING '*Tell me, you stars*' 10 Or give her my flame to melt that snow Which yet unthaw'd does on her bosom grow. **1665–6** *Phil. Trans.* I. 260 Solid Ice, that continued a considerable while unthaw'd. **1734** POPE *Hor. Sat.* II. ii. 14 Your wine lock'd up, your Butler stroll'd abroad, Or fish deny'd (the river yet unthaw'd). **1774** *Phil. Trans.* LXV. 122 Whilst that [snow]..continues so many hours unthawed. **1825** HOOK *Sayings & Doings* II. 283 His maiden aunt, whose heart had remained unthawed for upwards of sixty winters. **1856** MRS. BROWNING *Aur. Leigh* VII. 243 [She bore] A babe upon her breast,..Unseasonable outcast on such snow Unthawed to this time.

unthe'atric, *a.* (UN-[1] 7.)

1858 LYTTON *What will He do* I. ix, The cobbler yielded to the impulse of an untheatric man.

unthe'atrical, *a.* (UN-[1] 7.)

1745 AYRE *Mem. Pope* I. 92 His Opera called Rosamond ..did not succeed on the Stage, being wholly un-theatrical. **1898** *Westm. Gaz.* 12 Dec. 2/1 The piece..is remarkably untheatrical in style.

†**un'thee**, *v. Obs.* [UN-[1] 14 + THEE *v.*[1]] *intr.* To fail to thrive; to be unsuccessful.

c **1470** ASHBY *Active Policy* 330 Who that is withoute.. pite,..he shall vnthe. —— *Dicta Philos.* 784 So shal he thriue or vnthe.

unthe'matic, *a.* (UN-[1] 7.)

1888 KENNEDY *Revised Lat. Primer* 94 Personal Endings in Unthematic and Thematic Verbs.

†**un'thende**, *a. Obs.* [ME. *unthēnde*, f. *un-* UN-[1] 10 + *thēnde*, pres. pple. of THEE *v.*[1]]

1. Not in good condition; bad or poor in quality or kind.

1377 LANGL. *P. Pl.* B. v. 177, I ete there vnthende fisshe and fieble ale drynke. *a* **1400** *Partonope* 6660 He was so megere and so vnthende,..So hugely wasted a-wey is he. **1447** BOKENHAM *Seyntys* (Roxb.) 27 My penne also..ful ny is waxyn unthende. *a* **1470** H. PARKER *Dives & Pauper* (W. de W. 1496) I. iv. 35/2 Oftentyme that crosse that the preest holdeth in his honde is full unreuerenced & unthende.

b. Unwholesome.

c **1425** *Cast. Persev.* 2262 in *Macro Plays* 145 þi metis & drynkys arn vnthende, whanne þei are out of mesure take.

2. Unthriving; unprosperous.

c **1400** *Pety Job* 654 in *26 Pol. Poems* 142 The worldes wyles ryght nat me payes, For they ben false and full vnthende. *c* **1412** HOCCLEVE *De Reg. Princ.* 2464 Rightwisnesse..out of this ile Purposeth fully for to fare & wende, So is our reule vnthrifty & vnthende. *c* **1425** *Cast. Persev.* 510 in *Macro Plays* 92 Who-so wyl alwey foly fle, In þis werld schal ben vnthende.

b. Weak, feeble.

c **1425** *Cast. Persev.* 287 in *Macro Plays* 85 Nakyd I am, as ȝe may se. a! Lord God in trinite! Whow Mankende is vnthende! *c* **1440** *Promp. Parv.* 367/2 On-thende, *invalidus.*

Hence †**un'thendely** *adv. Obs.*

c **1440** *Promp. Parv.* 367/2 On-thendly, *invalide.*

untheo'logical, *a.* (UN-[1] 7.)

1641 MILTON *Animadv.* 16 This untheologicall Remonstrant. *a* **1656** BP. HALL *Let.* in *Rem. Wks.* (1660) 300 To argue from Scripture negatively in things of this nature is somewhat untheological. **1865** *Reader* 14 Oct. 420/2 The untheological or secularist philologist. **1893** LIDDON, etc. *Life Pusey* I. 365 The dull untheological temper of the time.

untheo'retic, *a.* (UN-[1] 7).

1809 COLERIDGE *Friend* 87 Did those, who opposed the theories of Innovators, conduct their untheoretic Opposition..to a happier Result? **1863** GEO. ELIOT *Romola* III. vi, The untheoretic virtues of her godfather.

untheo'retical, *a.* (UN-[1] 7.)

1797 *Monthly Mag.* III. 227 The bass..is no where untheoretical.

un'theorizing, *ppl. a.* (UN-[1] 10.)

1820 LAMB *Elia* I. *Two Races of Men*, I would put it to the most untheorizing reader..whether [etc.]. **1856** RUSKIN *Mod. Paint.* IV. v. App. ii, I..set myself..to see the Alps in a simple, thoughtless, and untheorizing manner.

†**un'thew.** *Obs.* [OE. *unþéaw*: see UN-[1] 4 b and THEW *sb.*[1]] A bad habit or custom; a vice.

c **897** K. ÆLFRED *Gregory's Past. C.* 23 Feorðe [ðara dæla] is hu he his agene unðeawas ongietan wille. *c* **1175** *Lamb. Hom.* 107 Twelf unþeawes beoð on þissere weorlde to hermen alle monnen. *a* **1200** *Moral Ode* 346 þat buð ða þe heom sculdeð ȝeorne wid elche un-ðeawe. *a* **1250** *Owl & Night.* 194 He is of worde swyþe gleu, And him is loþ eurich vnþeu. **1303** R. BRUNNE *Handl. Synne* 4850 A chylde þat wyþ vnþewys wexyþ wylde, þat wyl boþe myssey and do. **13..** *E.E. Allit. P.* B. 190 Man may mysse þe myrþe, þat much is to prayse, For such vnþewez as þise & þole much payne. *a* **1400** *Relig. Pieces fr. Thornton MS.* 54 þe conscience, þat chases owte alle vnthewes, and calles in alle gud vertus.

†**un'thewed**, *ppl. a. Obs.* [UN-[1] 8.]

1. Ill-mannered; unruly, wanton.

c **1200** ORMIN 2186 Forr son se maȝȝdenn wurrþeþþ bald, Ȝho wurþeþþ sone unnþæwedd. *Ibid.* 6371. *c* **1250** *Ten Abuses* 9 in *O.E. Misc.* 185 Child un-þeaud [*v.r.* vnþewed]. *c* **1325** *Metr. Hom.* 112 That ilke childe Was sa unthewed and sa wilde, That alle the schathe that he moht do, He did. *c* **1340** HAMPOLE *Pr. Consc.* 5873 Maysters of þair disciples alswa, þat þai lete be unthewed, and untaght ga, And chastid þam noght. **1390** GOWER *Conf.* I. 144 Thus is schewed What is to ben of Pride unthewed.

2. Unrefined, coarse.

c **1250** *Gen. & Ex.* 2555 Summe he deden in vn-ðewed swinc,..Muc and fen ut of burȝes beren.

†**un'thewful**, *a. Obs.* [UN-[1] 7.] Unmannerly; unseemly.

c **1050** *Voc.* in Wr.-Wülcker 425 *Indisciplinatorum*, unþeawfulra. *a* **1200** ORMIN 2191 Full wel birrþ ure maȝȝdenn ben Forrshamedd, ȝiff mann brinngeþ Biforenn hire unnþæwfull word. *c* **1320** in Wright *Pol. Songs* (Camden) 159 Suche chaffare y chepe at the chapitre, That maketh moni thryve-mon un-theufol to be.

un'thick, *a.* (UN-[1] 7. Cf. ON. *úþykkr.*)

1587 W. FOWLER *Wks.* (S.T.S.) I. 65/196 The passage owt and going furthe wes high and rair vnthik.

un'thickened, *ppl. a.* (UN-[1] 8.)

[**1775** ASH.] **1870** ROLLESTON *Anim. Life* 119 The thickened glandular three-fourths of these segments are separated off from the ventrally placed and unthickened fourth. **1884** BOWER & SCOTT *De Bary's Phaner.* 160 The unthickened portion of the membrane.

un'thievish, *a.* (UN-[1] 7.)

1858 GEN. P. THOMPSON *Audi Alt.* II. lxxxi. 39 The unthievish portion of mankind.

un'thimble, *v. Cant.* [UN-[2] 4.] *trans.* (See quot.)

1812 J. H. VAUX *Flash Dict.* s.v., To *unthimble* a man, is to rob, or otherwise deprive him of his watch.

un'think, *v.* [UN-[2] 3.] *trans.* To remove from thought; to annul or reverse by a mental effort. Also *absol.*

c **1600** CHALKHILL *Thealma & Cl.* 537 Still the king burns, and still his working brain Plots and displots, thinks and unthinks again. **1613** SHAKS. *Hen. VIII*, II. iv. 104, I do beseech You (gracious Madam) to vnthinke your speaking, And to say so no more. **1640** C. HARVEY *Confusion* i, One while I think, and then I am in pain To think how to unthink that thought again. **1675** J. HOWE *Living Temple* I. iii. 109 That the same thing is not thought and unthought, resolved and unresolved a thousand times in a day. **1709** O. DYKES *Eng. Prov. & Refl.* (ed. 2) 6 There's no unthinking a Misfortune, after it has befallen us for want of Precaution or Foresight. **1811** *Henry & Isabella* I. 6 They knew not how to think, and unthink so often that this world is, and is not a good place. **1818** COBBETT *Pol. Reg.* XXXIII. 527 To imagine that gags..will induce the people to unthink their present thoughts and unfeel their present feelings! **1849** *D'Israeli's Cur. Lit.* II. 428 Bayle stands among those masters of the human intellect who taught us to think, and also to unthink! **1894** ILLINGWORTH *Personality* iv. 91 There is no question of the inevitableness of this conclusion; we cannot avoid it, we cannot unthink it.

'unthink, *sb.* [UN-[1] 12.] Passive acceptance; failure to use logical reasoning.

1958 *Spectator* 14 Nov. 641/2 Mr. Wechsler..got on his feet rampaging against 'latrine prose' and the tedious doctrine of 'un-think'. **1961** *Guardian* 9 June 11/6 The undiscriminating unthink of the new middle class. **1974** P. GORE-BOOTH *With Great Truth & Respect* 421 And let us not talk of a 'Lost Empire'; that is a piece of 'unthink' which implies that, if only we had been cleverer, Australia would still have been governed from London.

unthinka'bility. (UN-[1] 12. Cf. next.)

1865 MILL *Exam. Hamilton* 134 An endeavour to think what cannot be thought..is the test by which we ascertain its unthinkability. **1897** F. H. BALFOUR *Unthinkables* 11 This involves unthinkabilities just as unthinkable as either of the other two.

un'thinkable, *a.* and *sb.* [UN-[1] 7 b.]

1. Too great, numerous, etc., to be conceived or apprehended by thought; unimaginable.

c **1430** *Life St. Kath.* (1884) 48 þey sawe al þe prison ful of vnthencable and vnspecable swetnesse of sauour. *a* **1450** *Myrr. our Ladye* 183 Wherfore the nombre of crownes is to be beleued vnthyncable. **1526** *Pilgr. Perf.* (W. de W. 1531) 28 b, He hath gyuen..treasour spirituall whiche be in valour vnthynkable. **1623** LISLE *Ælfric on O. & N. Test.* p. xxiv, The losse whereof is vnspeakeable, vnthinkable, vnsufferable misery. **1674** N. Fairfax *Bulk & Selv.* 193 The unthinkable care and forecast in all its evennesses and entwinings. **1879** M. Pattison *Milton* 112 The bathos is unthinkable. **1897** *Westm. Gaz.* 6 July 2/1 You wander..in cool glades of unthinkable beauty.

2. Incapable of being framed or grasped by thought; incogitable.

c **1445** Pecock *Donet* 84 A þing fer aboue alle creaturis þouȝt vnþenkable. *c* **1530** tr. *Erasmus' Serm. Ch. Jesus* (1901) 7 Jesus, whiche by an vnspeakable, nay, with an vnthynkable reason, is borne God of God. **1830** W. Taylor *Hist. Surv. Germ. Poetry* I. 453 Separate from her To live is quite unthinkable—is death. **1884** H. Spencer in *Contemp. Rev.* July 33 From whatever point of view we consider it, Bentham's proposition proves to be unthinkable.

absol. and *sb.* **1871** Jowett *Plato* III. 134 The negative of measure or limit; the unthinkable, the unknowable; of which nothing can be affirmed. **1897** F. H. Balfour (*title*), Unthinkables.

Hence **un'thinkably** *adv.*

1526 *Pilgr. Perf.* (W. de W. 1531) 244 b, The paynes yᵗ he suffred..excedeth vnthynkably all the paynes that ony creature myght suffre. **1895** *Young England* XVI. 30/1 Our hearths are warmed by the stored-up sunshine of unthinkably distant ages.

un'thinker. (un-¹ 12.)

1837 Carlyle *Fr. Rev.* I. iv. i, Thinkers and unthinkers.. are spontaneously at their post.

un'thinking, *ppl. a.* [un-¹ 10.]

1. Not exercising the faculty of thought; thoughtless; unreflecting, undiscriminating.

1676 Glanvill *Ess. Philos. & Relig.* i. 29 The shallow, unthinking Vulgar, are sure of all things. **1683** D. A. *Art Converse* 14 Women are generally an unthinking sort of Creatures. **1748** Smollett *R. Random* vii, I was no longer a pert unthinking coxcomb. **1780** *Mirror* No. 72, The effect of scenes like that I have described, on minds neither frigid nor unthinking. **1849** Macaulay *Hist. Eng.* iii. I. 393 Even the unthinking King showed some signs of concern. **1868** Morris *Earthly Par.* I. i. 311 Then swelled his vain unthinking heart with pride.

absol. **1697** C. Leslie *Snake in Grass* (ed. 2) p. ii, Atheism takes none But the Un-thinking and Debauch'd. **1769** Robertson *Chas. V*, ii. Wks. 1813 V. 238 Even the most unthinking were shocked. **1873** Proctor *Expanse Heav.* 298 That steadfastness which, to the unthinking, would have had no significance.

2. Characterized by absence of thought.

1688 R. Pepys *Let.* in *S. Pepys' Life* (1841) II. 127 The unthinking conduct of a violent passion. **1693** T. Creech in *Dryden's Juvenal* xiii. (1697) 324 All laugh to find Unthinking Plainness so o'er-spread thy Mind. **1709** Addison *Tatler* No. 75 ¶8 You see a deep Attention and a certain unthinking Sharpness in every Countenance. **1796** Mme. D'Arblay *Camilla* I. 25 Even in the unthinking period of earliest youth. **1832** Lytton *Eugene A.* i. xi, When I see the unthinking and lavish idolatry you manifest. **1873** Black *Pr. Thule* xiv, She walked on, in a blind and unthinking fashion.

3. Not possessing the faculty of thought.

a **1688** Cudworth *Immut. Mor.* (1731) 299 If all Being.. may..arise out of the dark Womb of unthinking Matter. **1710** Berkeley *Princ. Hum. Knowl.* §10 They who assert that figure, motion,..do exist without the mind in unthinking substances. **1794** R. J. Sulivan *View Nat.* IV. 8, I can never conceive, that a capacity of thinking can be the effect of the combination and motion of unthinking elements.

un'thinkingly, *adv.* [un-¹ 11.] Without thought; unreflectingly.

1717 Mrs. Centlivre *Cruel Gift* iv, Cardono's Love unthinkingly obey'd me. **1768–74** Tucker *Lt. Nat.* (1834) II. 27 Yet are we still liable unthinkingly to fall into little artifices for working upon the divine affections. **1829** Arnold in Stanley *Life* (1844) I. 235 The part which you object to, was not put in unthinkingly. **1884** J. Gilmour *Mongols* 222 These phrases are often uttered unthinkingly.

un'thinkingness. (un-¹ 12.)

a **1695** Ld. Halifax *Char. Chas. II* (1750) 4 In this kind of Indifference or Unthinkingness,..I will suppose he might pass some considerable part of his Youth. **1744** *Lond. Mag.* 27 Men begin to be convinced that Indolence and Unthinkingness, are the greatest Blessings upon Earth. **1796** Mme. D'Arblay *Camilla* I. 229 [He will] never go astray again, in wicked unthinkingness of this great mercy. **1857** Bagehot *Biog. Stud.* 53 The unfeeling unthinkingness of our Home administration. *a* **1866** J. Grote *Exam. Utilit. Phil.* xviii. (1870) 297 To make a state of unthinkingness desirable for the human mind.

un'thinned, *ppl. a.* (un-¹ 8.)

1648 Hexham, *Ongedunt*, Vnthinned. **1816** Byron *Siege Cor.* xxix, Fast they fill The ranks unthinn'd, though slaughter'd still. **1848** Aird *Frank Sylvan* ii, With ear Patient attend his [*sc.* the gardener's] manifold complaints Of birds unthinned.

†**un'thirlable,** *a. north. Obs.* (un-¹ 7 b.)

1483 *Cath. Angl.* 383 Vn Thyrleabylle, *jnpenetrabilis.*

†**un'thirled,** *ppl. a.*¹ *north. Obs.* [un-¹ 8.] Unpierced, unopened.

1435 Misyn *Fire of Love* 74 To qwhome herefore so sal be opynd þe wyndow vnþirlyd of all.

†**un'thirled,** *ppl. a.*² *Sc. Obs.* [un-¹ 8.] Unsubjugated.

1533 Bellenden *Livy* iii. xxv. (S.T.S.) II. 48 Sa lang as Coriolos stude fre and vnthirlit to romanis. **1536** — *Cron. Scot.* (1821) I. 148 We, as maist vailyeant pupil,..hes kepit us evir unthirllit to Romane dominioun.

un'thirsty, *a.* (un-¹ 7.)

[**1775** Ash.] **1882** J. Parker *Apost. Life* I. 74 To the unthirsty man the Bible spring is without attraction.

†**un'tholeful,** *a. Obs.*⁻¹ [un-¹ 7.] Intolerable.

a **1425** tr. *Arderne's Treat. Fistula*, etc. 39 Som hauyng a ful gret brennyng..and vntholeful smertyng.

†**un'tholemood,** *a.* and *sb. Obs.* [un-¹ 7, 12. Cf. next and ON. *úþolinmóðr* a., *-mǿði* sb.]

1. *adj.* Impatient.

c **1200** *Vices & Virtues* 13 Ac ȝif..godd me wolde swingen mid ani swinge,..ic was ðar aȝean unþolemod.

2. *sb.* Impatience.

a **1400** *Spec. Vitæ* (MS. Bodl. 1885) 139 b, Vnboxsomnesse and vntholemode, Grucchyng also and drerynesse.

†**un'tholemoodness.** *Obs.* [OE. *unþolemódness* (un-¹ 12). Cf. prec.] Impatience.

c **1000** *Confess. Peccat.* (Toller), þurh unðolemodnesse. *c* **1200** *Vices & Virtues* 13 *Inpaciencia* hatte an oðer senne, þat is, unþolemodnesse. *a* **1340** Hampole *Psalter* i. 1 Whaim ..na tribulacioun bryngs in till gruchynge or vntholemodnes. *a* **1400** *Spec. Vitæ* (MS. Bodl. 1885) fol. 140 Vntholmodnesse wrong wol lere A man þat wil noȝt bledly here [etc.]. *a* **1400** in *Hampole's Wks.* (1896) II. 289 Vntholemodnes oure soueraines to. *a* **1500** in *Ratis Raving*, etc. 4 The þrid temptacioune is in-paciens or vntholemudnes.

†**un'tholing,** *ppl. a. Obs.* [un-¹ 10. Cf. ON. *úþolandi*, MSw. *otholande*, in sense 1.]

1. Intolerable.

a **1300** *Cursor M.* 25892 þe paine of hell, How hard it es, and vntholand. *a* **1300** *E.E. Psalter* cxxiii. 4 (E.), þurgh hap hade ouerfaren owr saule water vnþoland [*v.r.* vntholandlik]. **1340** *Ayenb.* 265 þer me geþ uram chele in to greate hete of uere, and buoþe onþolyinde.

2. Impatient.

a **1300** *Cursor M.* 28208 Ic ha ben wrath and vn-tholand Quen i was bunden in godds band.

un'thong, *v.* (un-² 3, 4 b.)

1829 Landor *Imag. Conv.* II. 308, I would..unthong the drenching-horn from my stable-door. **1843** E. Jones *Sens. & Event* 4 His muscles glisteningly unthonged As burst each ringing peal [of laughter].

un'thorned, *a.* (un-¹ 9.)

1803 Moore *Ep. to Miss Moore* 6 When every night my weary head Sunk on its own unthorned bed.

un'thorny, *a.* (un-¹ 7.)

1646 Sir T. Browne *Pseud. Ep.* i. v. 18 It were some extenuation of the curse, if..there still remained a Paradise or unthorny place of knowledge.

un'thorough, *a.* (un-¹ 7.)

1868 W. R. Greg *Lit. & Soc. Judgm.* 277 Some singular inconsistencies, which..showed how imperfect and unthorough was his political philosophy. **1891** Atkinson *Moorland Par.* 142 Knowing..how utterly unscientific and unthorough all such investigations then were.

un'thoroughfaresome, *a.*, **-ness**, *sb.*

= unthroughfareness, -some.

1868 Trench *Engl. Past & Pres.* 74.

un'thought, *sb.* (un-¹ 12.)

1866 Mrs. Whitney *L. Goldthwaite* xii, Something different in thought and purpose from the apparent unthought about her. **1892** P. W. Clayden *Eng. under Coalition* xv. 315 To show to which side the charge of credulity, of rashness and of unthought belonged.

un'thought, *ppl. a.* [un-¹ 8 b, 8 c. Cf. MHG. *ungedaht* (G. *ungedacht*), Du. *ongedacht.*]

1. a. Not thought of, unexpected.

a **1548** Hall *Chron., Hen. VI*, 110 b, While kyng Charles did politiquely consider..what a sodain and vnthought chaunce of a smal thyng, might do in a battaill. **1653** J. Taylor (Water P.) *Cert. Trav. Uncert. Journ.* 16 Undeserv'd, unlook'd for, and unthought From them my purse and person both were fraught. **1738** G. Lillo *Marina* ii. i, The hot salt tears this unthought loss drew from me. **1745** Young *Nt. Th.* viii. 114 As they spin our hours On Fortune's wheel, where accident unthought Oft, in a moment, snaps life's strongest thread. **1903** Kipling 5 *Nations, Wage-Slaves* 61 They that have wrought the end unthought Be neither saint nor sage.

b. With *on, of, out.* (Cf. think *v.*² 5 c, 7 b, 15.)

1538 Elyot, *Inopinatus*, vnthought on or vnloked for. *a* **1586** Sidney *Arcadia* i. iv, It may be, his pen with more leasure doth polish the rudenesse of an unthought-on songe. **1596** Shaks. *1 Hen. IV*, iii. ii. 141 The day..That..This gallant Hotspur..And your vnthought-of Harry chance to meet. **1621** Lady M. Wroth *Urania* 451 One night he came vnlook'd for to our house, but not vnthought on by me. **1666** Boyle *Orig. Forms & Qual.* 418 By a way unthought on (that I know of) by any Body. **1676** Hale *Contempl.* i. 52 A little..accident..may put a period to all those pleasures.. in an unthought of moment. **1713** Berkeley *Hylas & Phil.* iii. Wks. 1871 I. 356 What security can I have..that no unthought-of objection or difficulty will occur hereafter? **1748** Richardson *Clarissa* (1811) III. xxxvi. 216 Consequences, unthought of by you or me. **1860** Froude *Hist. Eng.* V. 490 A return to communion with the See of Rome was unthought of. **1890** 'R. Boldrewood' *Col. Reformer* (1891) 449 This distant, long-dry, unthought-of reservoir. **1919** M. K. Bradby *Psycho-Anal. & its Place in Life* x. 12 An unthought-out attitude is shown and resulting unhappiness. **1933** W. E. Orchard *From Faith to Faith* vi. 80 It may..reveal to those who cling to a merely traditional and un-thought-out orthodoxy what it is that often inspires such liberalism. **1978** R. Ludlum *Holcroft Covenant* xiv. 163 There were canvases with bold dashes of color and heavy, un-thought-out lines.

†**2.** (With complement or *ellipt.*) Not regarded in a certain (specified or implied) way. *unthought long*, without feeling time long. *Obs.*

1595 Spenser *Epithal.* 378 Thou likewise didst loue, though now vnthought. *a* **1637** B. Jonson *Underwoods, Eupheme* ix. 44 As spirits had stolne her spirit in a kisse,.. And left her lovely body unthought dead! *a* **1806** in R. Jamieson *Pop. Ballads* I. 94 He harpit to the king, To haud him unthought lang.

3. Unimagined; not devised in thought.

1639 Cokaine *Masque* Dram. Wks. (1874) 10 Forsake the woods, fond Satyr, and but try The unthought difference 'twixt them and us! **1672** Marvell *Reh. Transp.* ii. (1674) 46, I wish it unsaid as it was unthought. **1743** Young *Nt. Th.* v. 147 Each salutation may slide in a sin Unthought before. **1815** Milman *Fazio* 67 Is't to be mad..To speak with..continuous flow, Yet know not how the unthought words start from me? **1850** Thackeray *Pendennis* lxxii, If you knew..how I lie awake and think of those hard sentences,..and wish them unspoken, unthought!

†**4.** Unheeded, disregarded. *Obs.*

1640 Yorke *Union Hon.* 185 [He] returned from his unthought banishment, [and] tooke King Richard prisoner.

†**5.** Unpremeditated. *Obs.*

1648 *Pol. Ballads* (1860) I. 74 With speech unthought, quick revelation,..See a new Teacher of the Town.

un'thoughted, *ppl. a.* [un-¹ 8.] Not contemplated; not formed in thought.

1598 Rowlands *Betraying of Christ* (Hunterian Cl.) 9 What furies guided this misguided swarme? To bend their force against vnthoughted harme. **1860** O. W. Holmes *Elsie V.* xiv, There are states of mind..which remain not only unworded, but unthoughted, if such a word may be coined for our special need.

un'thoughtful, *a.* [un-¹ 7.]

1. Not taking thought, unmindful or regardless, *of* something.

1456 Sir G. Haye *Govt. Princes* Wks. (S.T.S.) II. 141 Wyne..makis man to be unthochtfull of his honour. **1702** C. Mather *Magn. Chr.* iv. x. 220/2 He was not unthoughtful of the Time when publick Ones [*sc.* sermons] might be expected from him. **1728** R. Morris *Ess. Anc. Archit.* 106 How unthoughtful of the Affair in hand? **1887** R. F. Burton *Arab. Nts.* (abr. ed.) III. 71 We have foes who are not unthoughtful of us.

2. Unthinking, thoughtless.

a **1533** Ld. Berners *Gold. Bk. M. Aurel.* xxxvii. (1536) 67 They as vnthoughtfull,..leaue the iust trauayle, and take vniust idelnes. *a* **1667** Cowley *Ess. in Verse & Prose, Solitude* iv, Here let me, careless and unthoughtful lying, Hear the soft winds above me flying. **1698** Norris *Pract. Disc.* IV. 62 People..that have..a lazy, unthoughtful, list-less, yawning way of talking of Religion. **1715** Jane Barker *Exilius* i. 72 The vulgar Part of the Africans are extremely unthoughtful and unpolished. *a* **1834** Coleridge *Lit. Rem.* (1836) II. 10 Without which poetry becomes..evaporated into a hazy, unthoughtful, day-dreaming. **1895** C. Scott *Apple Orchards* 131 The reckless, unthoughtful, but ill-directed youth of to-day.

Hence **un'thoughtfully** *adv.*; **un'thoughtfulness.**

1661 J. Fell *Hammond* 205 During the current of that Tyranny,..he kept a constant equable serenity and unthoughtfulness in outward accidents. **1701** Norris *Ideal World* i. vi. 322 Never was any question..more ignorantly and unthoughtfully moved. **1709** Mrs. Manley *Secret Mem.* (1736) IV. 185 Should he begin by this unthoughtfulness of enterprize, it would render him.. formidable. **1884** E. W. Benson in *Life* (1899) II. 29 A ceaseless reproach to the unthoughtfulness of this busy existence.

un'thrall, *v.* [un-² 4 b.] *trans.* To emancipate, set free.

c **1586** C'tess Pembroke *Ps.* cxviii. v, God answere gave me when I called, And me inlarging, me unthralled. **1650** H. B. *To Vaughan* in Vaughan *Anima Magica*, But who from envies sordid mire Is washt,..a light shall see, (Unthral'd from errors Sophistry). **1652** Howell *Giraffi's Rev. Naples* ii. 28 Thou chopst his neck, who thy head did unthral.

un'thralled, *ppl. a.* (un-¹ 8.)

[**1775** Ash.] **1865** W. G. Palgrave *Arabia* I. 136 A sort of chivalresque knight-errants and representatives of unthralled freedom.

un'thrashed, -'threshed, *ppl. a.* [un-¹ 8. Cf. Sw. *otröskad.*]

1. Of corn, etc.: Not thrashed.

α. **1561** *Wills & Inv. N.C.* (Surtees, 1835) 193, xx threives of wheat unthresshed. **1573** Tusser *Husb.* (1878) 56 Such wheat..vnthreshed till March in the sheafe let it lie. **1660** in *Sadler St. Papers* (1809) III. 360 Barley, threshed and unthreshed. **1766** *Compl. Farmer* s.v. *Harvest*, Wheat keeps better when stacked in the ear unthreshed. **1798** *Hull Advertiser* 24 Mar. 2/3 Insurance upon..outhouses, and upon unthreshed stock therein. **1885** *Athenæum* 5 Sept. 298/1 A wooden stage on which unthreshed corn is placed. **1891** T. Hardy *Tess* xlviii, The unthreshed sheaves remaining untouched.

β. **1702** *Guide for Constables* 136 Carts carrying..corn unthrashed. **1799** J. Robertson *Agric. Perth* 323 Others throw hay or unthrashed corn in handfuls upon the snow to feed them. **1844** H. Stephens *Bk. Farm* II. 286 The unthrashed corn..is delivered into the machine.

fig. **1853** Ruskin *Stones Ven.* III. ii. §27 It is to be remembered, that knowledge in this form may be kept..in such unthreshed disorder that it is of no use.

2. Unbeaten, unflogged.

1892 *Daily News* 5 Oct. 3/1 A couple of youths..tore the lower part of it, but they ran off unthrashed.

†**un'thrashen,** *ppl. a. Obs. Sc.* and *north.* [un-¹ 8 b. Cf. MHG. (G.) *ungedroschen.*] = prec. 1.

1482 *Acta Auditorum* (1839) 109/1, xij thrafe vnthreschin corne. **1537** *Stanlowe Cell Inv.* (P.R.O.), vj thrayf of vnthrashen Barlycorne. **1578** *Reg. Privy Council Scot.* II. 680 The said unthreschin corne. **1601** in *T. Pont's Acc. Cunningham* (Maitl. Cl.) 180 Ane mow of vnthressin beir.

1629 *Orkney Witch Trial* in *County Folk-Lore* III. (1903) 77 Ye said ye may give me ane lock.. out of the cassie under the unthreachin corne.

un'thread, *v.* (UN-² 3.)
Chiefly in figurative uses.
1595 SHAKS. *John* v. iv. 11 Vnthred the rude eye of Rebellion, And welcome home againe discarded faith. **1634** MILTON *Comus* 616 He with his bare wand can unthred thy joynts, And crumble all thy sinews. **1699** BOYER *Royal Dict.* I, *Desenfiler*, to unthread a Needle. **1801** LAMB *Lett.* (1900) II. 40 Who can disentangle and unthread the rich texture of Nature and Poetry,.. without spoiling both lace and coat? **1818** KEATS *Isabella* xxxvii, The while it did unthread the horrid woof Of the late darken'd time. **1847** DE QUINCEY *Sp. Mil. Nun* Wks. 1854 III. 43 Under Kate's guidance.. they soon unthreaded the labyrinth of rocks. **1865** MISS BRADDON *Doctor's Wife* x. 93 Threading and unthreading her needle very often.

un'threaded, *ppl. a.* (UN-¹ 8.)
[**1775** ASH.] **1895** K. GRAHAME *Golden Age* 109 A signal for retreat.. into unthreaded copses.

un'threatened, *ppl. a.* (UN-¹ 8.)
1647 CLARENDON *Hist. Reb.* II. §86 The Arch Bishop.. lodged.. in Whitehall; which place was likewise not unthreatned in their seditious meetings. **1648** [see UNREPROACHED]. **1813** WORDSW. '*Stay, bold Adventurer*' 25 All around Had darkness fallen.. unthreatened, unproclaimed. **1818** COLEBROOKE *Import Colonial Corn* 108 Yet are his productions not unthreatened.. by dangerous rivalship of less skilful.. artists.

un'thrid(den, *ppl. adjs.* [UN-¹ 8 b + THREAD *v.* 4.] Unthreaded.
1843 E. JONES *Sensation & Event* 125 He stands again before the unthridden gloom. **1866** MRS. WHITNEY *Gayworthys* iv, Piny forests, untouched, unthrid.

un'thrift, *sb.* (and *a.*). [UN-¹ 4 a, 12. Cf. WANTHRIFT.]
†**1.** A malpractice; a defect or fault in conduct.
1303 R. BRUNNE *Handl. Synne* 12339 þer ys an vnþryfte þat doþ moche skaþe yn shryfte. *c* **1430** *Pilgr. Lyf Manhode* II. cxxii. (1869) 121 þis mantelle.. was maad for to.. mantelle with my defautes, and consele myne vnthriftes.
2. Want of thrift or economy; neglect of thriving or doing well; †dissolute conduct, loose behaviour, impropriety.
13.. *E.E. Allit. P.* B. 516 Hit is sothe, þat alle mannez wyttez To vn-þryfte arn alle þrawen with þoȝt of her herttez. *c* **1374** CHAUCER *Troylus* IV. 431 To don his wo to falle, He rought nought what vnthrift þat he seyde. *c* **1400** *Pilgr. Sowle* (Caxton, 1483) III. viii. 55 These ben the children of tristesse,.. ful of ydelnes and al maner vnthrifte. *a* **1475** G. ASHBY *Dicta Philos.* 469 That the myddyl of your liffe be not spent In ydelnesse, ne in vnthrifte myswent. **1483** *Cath. Angl.* 385/2 Wn Thryfte, *deuigencia*.
1721 KELLY *Sc. Proverbs* 250 Many one blames their Wife, for their own unthrift. **1830** CARLYLE *Misc.* (1840) II. 320 The Hof public openly finding her guilty of Unthrift. **1860** *All Year Round* No. 53. 62 No idleness was allowed in her house; no unthrift, no useless dawdlings. **1887** *American* XIV. 23 Both fell an easy prey to every adverse circumstance which poverty and unthrift can offer.
3. An unthrifty (†unthriving), shiftless, or dissolute person; a spendthrift, prodigal.
Freq. *c* 1520–1690. Occas. *to play the unthrift*.
c **1330** R. BRUNNE *Chron. Wace* (Rolls) 7231 Go we now, & sle þat vnþrift. *c* **1375** *Sc. Leg. Saints* xl. (*Ninian*) 661 þai.. tretyt weile þat vnthrifte, til eld had it brocht fra schrifte. **1491** CAXTON *Vitas Patr.* (W. de W. 1495) I. cxl. 152 b/2 At theyr metynge togyder this Unthryft gaaf hym a buffeth. **1509** BARCLAY *Shyp of Folys* 142 b, A folysshe man rurall If he a churle, a fole and vnthrift be, The more he loketh to come to hye degree. **1556** *Chron. Grey Friars* (Camden) 73 Vacobondes that wold not labor, but play the unthryftes. *a* **1602** W. PERKINS *Cases Consc.* (1619) 74 The young vnthrift in the Gospell, called the Prodigall child. **1639** FULLER *Holy War* 124 If he played the unthrift with this golden occasion. **1693** DRYDEN *Persius* iv. 237 Shall I.. My Friends disgrace, And be the first lewd Unthrift of my Race? **1765** BLACKSTONE *Comm.* I. 295 When a man on an inquest of idiocy hath been returned an unthrift and not an idiot, no farther proceedings have been had. **1821** SCOTT *Kenilw.* xxxi, The Earl of Oxford, a young unthrift, whom Foster had more than once accommodated with loans. **1862** SIR H. CAIRNS in *Times* 2 Jan., The Roman law made no distinction between unthrifts and idiots.
fig. **1571** E. WOLLAY *Pl. Pathway* 14 Wee know what thanckes wee owe to God for all his giftes; Yet contrary we showe to him ourselves unthriftes. **1654** GATAKER *Disc. Apol.* 18 As we count him a bad Husband, that foloweth game on the Market-day, so may we as wel count him a spiritual unthrift, that spends the Sabbath in that sort.
†**b.** One who is prodigal *of* something. *Obs.*
1640 QUARLES *Enchyrid.* I. xciii, Fury.. being an unthrift of its owne strength. *a* **1659** in *Bann. Club Misc.* (1827) 324, I do confess thou 'rt sweet, yet find Thee such an unthrift of thy sweets. **1666** SPURSTOW *Spir. Chym.* lix. 175 The most of men are such unthrifts of time.
4. *attrib.* or as *adj.* Prodigal, spendthrift.
a **1562** G. CAVENDISH *Wolsey* (1893) 45 Thow hast allwayes byn a prowd, presumpcious, disdaynfull, and a very onthryft waster. **1592** NASHE *P. Penilesse* A ij b, Sir Rowland Russet-coat.. hath much adoo.. to keepe his vnthrift elbowes in reparations. **1596** SHAKS. *Merch. V.* v. i. 16 In such a night Did Iessica steale from the wealthy Iewe, And with an Vnthrift Loue did runne from Venice. **1650** VAUGHAN *Silex Scint.*, *Regeneration* vi, The unthrift Sunne shot vitall gold A thousand peeces. **1865** A. CARY *Ballads*, etc. 66 When I met a man, unthrift and lorn. **1869** LOWELL *Cathedral* 142 This unthrift housekeeping that will not brook A dish warmed-over at the feast of life.
Hence **un'thrift-like** *a.* or *adv.*
1603 HEYWOOD *Wom. Killed w. Kindn.* (1617) D 4 b, Now Nichlas you want money; And vnthrift-like would eate into your wages.

†**un'thriftfully,** *adv. Obs.* (UN-¹ 11.)
1549 CHEKE *Hurt Sedit.* (1569) G i b, That such plentie of vittayle, as was aboundauntly in euery quarter,.. is nowe all wastfully and vnthriftfully spent.

†**un'thriftihead.** *Obs.* [UN-¹ 12.] Thriftlessness.
1590 SPENSER *F.Q.* II. xii. 18 The quicksand of Vnthriftyhed. *Ibid.* III. xii. 25 Emongst them was sterne Strife,.. Vnquiet Care, and fond Vnthriftihead.

un'thriftily, *adv.* [UN-¹ 11.] In an unthrifty manner; prodigally; †dissolutely.
13.. *E.E. Allit. P.* B. 267 þay.. controeued agayn kynde contrare werkez, & vsed hem vn-þryftyly vchon on oþer. *c* **1386** CHAUCER *Can. Yeom. Prol. & T.* 893 If a man wole aske hem pryuely, Why they been clothed so vnthriftily. **1493** *Festivall* 53/2 Truly to laboure & not to slombre & slepe slewffully & vnthryftely. **1509** BARCLAY *Shyp of Folys* b ij b, Some thynkinge them self moch wyse & commendable Thoughe al theyr dayes they lyue vnthryftely. **1571** GOLDING *Calvin on Ps.* xxxvi. 8 The ungodly ronne ryot unthriftely in their oune wickednes. **1605** WILLET *Hexapla Gen.* 436 All such as spend their time vnthriftily. **1697** COLLIER *Ess. Mor. Subj.* II. Pref., Our Attainments cannot be over-large; and yet we manage a narrow Fortune, very Vnthriftily. **1909** FIRTH *Last Years Protectorate* I. 8 The government had not managed the treasury unthriftily.

un'thriftiness. [UN-¹ 12.]
1. The quality of being unthrifty; thriftlessness, prodigality, wastefulness; †dissoluteness.
c **1430** *How the Good Wyf* 154 in *Babees Bk.* (1868) 43 Pride, reste, & ydilnes, makiþ on-þriftines. *a* **1475** G. ASHBY *Dicta Philos.* 116 Wele manered people bene of goode lif,.. Euel named bene often in striff, And men fle theim for thair vnthriftynesse. **1509** BARCLAY *Shyp of Folys* 141 b, Sawynge in hym sede of moche vnthryftynes And than to spoyle hym; and leue hym pore and bare. *a* **1548** HALL *Chron.*, *Hen. VIII*, 149 b, Some fell to drinkyng,.. and stealyng of Dere in Parkes, and other unthriftines. **1609** DEKKER *Gull's Horn-bk.* 35 You are to cherish the vnthriftinesse of such yong tame pigions, if you be a right gentleman. **1642** FULLER *Holy & Prof. St.* I. xiv. 46 Neither wasting his paternall estate by his unthriftinesse, nor marring it by parcelling his ancient mannours.. among his younger children. **1688** R. HOLME *Armoury* III. 266/2 Unthriftiness, Slothfulness, Carelessness, and Rashness in Business. **1710, 1802–74** in Sc. glossaries (defining *Wanthrift*).
2. Lack of thriving in growth.
1707 MORTIMER *Husb.* 394 When any of its Roots happen to perish,.. the unthriftiness of its Branches will quickly discover it. *Ibid.* 418 The grubbing up of Woods and Trees may be needful upon the account of their Unthriftiness. **1950** *N.Z. Jrnl. Agric.* Apr. 327/1 At the first sign of unthriftiness calves should be drenched with phenothiazine. **1955** W. W. DENLINGER *Complete Boston* 83 Much of the unthriftiness and langor that are charged to worms are caused by other diseases. **1973** *Country Life* 7 June 1660/1 If the calves are under stress.. unthriftiness or mortality will follow.

un'thrifty, *a.* [UN-¹ 7. Cf. WANTHRIFTY *a.*]
1. Producing or bringing about no advantage, profit, or gain; tending to, resulting in, or marked by thriftlessness, waste, or extravagance; unprofitable, wasteful; harmful.
c **1374** CHAUCER *Troylus* IV. 1530, I-wys my dere herte trewe We may wel stele a-way as ye deuyse And fynde swyche vnthryfty weyes newe. *c* **1412** HOCCLEVE *De Reg. Princ.* 2464 Rightwisnesse.. out of this ile Purposeth fully for to fare & wende, So is our reule vnthrifty & vnthende. *c* **1470** ASHBY *Active Policy* 681, I mene nat for vnthrifty Cowardise, wheche is in al Realmes abhominable. **1513** DOUGLAS *Æneid* IX. x. 25 Quhat onthrifty God in sic foly Hes ȝou bywavyt heyr till Italy? **1529** *Supplic. to King* (E.E.T.S.) 40 Common players at all vnthryftye games. **1579** NORTHBROOKE *Dicing* 60 b, Venerous people haue all their whole pleasance, Their vice to nourishe by this vnthriftie daunce. **1590** SPENSER *F.Q.* I. iv. 35 Full many mischiefes follow cruell Wrath;.. Vnmanly murder, and vnthrifty scath. **1627** SIR R. COTTON in Rushw. *Hist. Coll.* (1659) I. 471 The spending of much Munition, Victuals and Money,.. is counted an unthrifty error. **1647** CLARENDON *Hist. Reb.* I. §147 The Subject might be taught how unthrifty a thing it was, by too strict a detaining of what was His, to put the King as strictly to enquire what was his Own. **1652** BENLOWES *Theoph.* III. lxvii, Unthrifty death has spread where thriving peace did range. **1697** DRYDEN *Virg. Georg.* I. 226 Tough Thistles.. kill'd the Corn, And an unthrifty Crop of Weeds was born. **1776** ADAM SMITH *W.N.* v. ii. II. 473 They are all more or less unthrifty taxes that increase the revenue of the sovereign.. at the expence of the capital of the people. **1809** MALKIN *Gil Blas* IX. vi. ¶3 The commerce of the eyes being so unthrifty, I had recourse to different agents. **1819** SCOTT *Leg. Montrose* ii, Having by unthrifty courses reduced a fair patrimony to a nonentity. **1869** FREEMAN *Norm. Conq.* III. xii. 101 The rebuilding.. had been possibly interrupted during the unthrifty reign of Malger.
†**b.** Of language: Unprofitable, idle. *Obs.*
c **1440** *Alph. Tales* 215 Oft sithes, with þer vnthrifti language, hym at had rewle of þaim þai provoked.. to be angrie. **1467** *Mann. & Househ. Exp.* (Roxb.) 172, I wolde avysse ȝowe to sese.. of ȝower onthreffety langwage.
2. Not thriving or flourishing; lacking vigour or promise in growth. (Cf. THRIFTLESS *a.* 1.)
c **1440** *Promp. Parv.* 367/2 Onthryfty, *idem quod* onthende [*Ibid.*, Onthende, *invalidus*]. **1484** CAXTON *Fables of Æsop* III. iii, Thynke now, how thow arte lene and vnthryfty. **1486** *Bk. St. Albans* b vij b, Euell meetis to make her vnthrefti. **1674** N. FAIRFAX *Bulk & Selv.* Ep. Ded., Such an underly Shrub in Knowledge, and unthrifty Sucker in Philosophy as I am. **1709** *Phil. Trans.* XXVI. 450 The Cow was very unthrifty, for which they gave her Cow Physick. **1796** C. MARSHALL *Gardening* xii. (1813) 145 Consider the soil about an unthrifty tree. **1831** YOUATT *Horse* viii. 122 The horse will lose flesh;.. his coat will be unthrifty, and readily come off. **1846** LANDOR *Imag. Conv.* Wks. II. 224/1 That.. we should think it expedient to plant unthrifty thorns over bitter wells of blood.
transf. **1812** *Examiner* 11 May 292/1 Poor, ill-cultivated.. soils, the early appearance of which was unthrifty, show.. very thin.
b. Characterized by absence of well-being; indicative of unprosperousness.
c **1400** *Three Kings Cologne* 24 þer was nothyng left bote.. a litel cave vndir erþe and a litil vnthrifti hows tofore þe cave. *c* **1425** *MS. Sloane 73* fol. 201 Whanne þi bagge chaungiþ clene out of þe rede colour.. in to a manere of an vnþryfty wan colour. *a* **1450** *Knt. de la Tour* 9 Atte the yongest doughtres hous it was turned up-so-doun, and alle unthrifti. *c* **1529** LATIMER in Foxe *A. & M.* (1563) 1298/2 Whiche vnthriftye state that wee be borne vnto, is come vnto vs for oure owne desertes.
3. Loose or lax in respect of conduct, morals, or virtue; unchaste, wanton, profligate.
1388 *Pol. Poems* (Rolls) I. 272 Goddes dere halydayys ar noght, non observantur honeste; For onthryfty pley ys worght. *a* **1450** *Knt. de la Tour* 30 The good women.. that hathe not take the state of the unthrifti women that bene euelle women of her body. *c* **1485** *Digby Myst.* (1882) II. 558 Non shall in heuyn posses that be so vnthryfty. **1523** LD. BERNERS *Froiss.* I. ccclxxxvi. 660 Suche rybaudes and vnthriftye people, as desyred nothynge but yuell and noyse. **1530** in W. H. Turner *Select. Rec. Oxford* (1880) 80 Certen onthryfty persons brekyng of the Kyngs pesse. *a* **1571** JEWEL *On Thess.* (1583) 219 Withdrawe thy selfe from the companie, of such vnthriftie, and light, and suspected persons.
transf. *c* **1400** *Pilgr. Sowle* (Caxton, 1483) II. lvii. 55 Thou madest me to lede a ful vnthryfty lyf. **1476** *Stonor Papers* (Camden) II. 7 Comaunde me to the Cloke [= clock], and pray hym to amend his unthryffte maners: ffor he strykes euer in vndew tyme. **1535–6** *Act 27 Hen. VIII*, c. 28 ¶1 Reformacion of suche unthrifty carnall and abhomynable lyvyng.
4. Not thrifty, economical, or frugal; careless or improvident of one's means or substance; wasteful, extravagant, prodigal. (Cf. THRIFTLESS *a.* 3.)
1532 HERVET *Xenophon's Househ.* 59 The grounde doth best examyne, which be good, and whiche be vnthryfty husbandes. **1551** ROBINSON tr. *More's Utopia* II. (Arb.) 87 The vnthrifty heire suffereth ye houses that his father buylded.. to fall in decay. **1596** BACON *Max. & Use Com. Law* II. (1635) 49 Or to be in hazard of undoing his house by unthrifty posterity. **1639** J. TAYLOR (Water P.) *Part this Summers Trav.* 18 Such an unthrifty Rascall as thou will never be worth such a halter, it cost me two pence. **1662** HIBBERT *Body Divinity* I. 197 The wormes shall have his carkass, and unthrifty heires his estate. **1684** J. GOODMAN *Old Relig.* 336 A querulous, uneasy, lean, hungry and unthrifty sort of people. **1780** S. J. PRATT *Emma Corbett* (ed. 4) II. 108, I am one of those whom the world calls an unthrifty fellow. **1849** HAWTHORNE *Twice-told T.* 213 Next comes a sledge, laden with wood for some unthrifty house-keeper. **1904** *Verney Mem.* II. 215 Before the wine arrives, this unthrifty host discovers that he does not require it.
fig. *c* **1600** SHAKS. *Sonn.* iv, Vnthrifty louelinesse why dost thou spend, Vpon thy selfe thy beauties legacy? **1659** O. WALKER *Oratory* 109 This ingrafting.. parenthesis, if it argues a good wit, it shews a weak and unthrifty Orator. **1682** MRS. BEHN *False Count* II. i, Should we be unthrifty in our loves, And for one moment's joy give all away? **1703** ROWE *Fair Penit.* II. i, Oh wherefore did I play th' unthrifty Fool, And wasting all on others, leave myself Without one thought of Joy to give me comfort?
absol. **1876** BANCROFT *Hist. U.S.* II. xlii. 567 To insure an estate even to the sons of the unthrifty.
b. Prodigal or lavish *of* something; unsparing.
1620 DONNE *Serm.* (1640) 418 God is content to be told, that he is unthrifty, and prodigall of his servants lives. **1670** COTTON *Espernon* II. vi. 289 He was not altogether so unthrifty of his own Interest. **1713** BLACKMORE *Creation* v. 243 Of light unthrifty, and profuse of day, The ruin'd globe has spent his latest ray.

un'thrilled, *ppl. a.* (UN-¹ 8.)
[**1775** ASH.] *a* **1861** MRS. BROWNING *Ragged Schools London* xxii, Calm, unthrilled in Our heart's pulses.

†**un'thrive,** *v. Obs.* [UN-² 7.]
1. *intr.* To fail to thrive; to be unprosperous.
c **1380** WYCLIF *Sel. Wks.* II. 411 In Cristis tyme and long aftir proof þe Chirche,.. but siþ it haþ unþrivun. **1390** GOWER *Conf.* II. 211 For that a man scholde al unthryve Ther oghte no wisman coveite. **1426** LYDG. *De Guil. Pilgr.* 23767 God wil,.. to chastice hem, his hond with-drawe, suffre her goodes to vnthryve. **1465** *Paston Lett.* II. 237 Upon trust of Calles promise, we may soon onthryve. **1477** NORTON *Ord. Alch.* Proem, in Ashm. (1652) 7 Whereby they were pore and made to unthrife. **1618** LITHGOW *Pilgrim's Farew.* E 1, If hee vnthrives, hee hates anothers weele. *a* **1706** EVELYN *Sylva* II. viii. (1776) 419 Shade and dripping.. are certainly causes of their [*sc.* trees'] unthriving till removed.
2. *trans.* To make unprosperous.
a **1550** *Image Hypoc.* II. 345 in Skelton *Wks.* (1843) II. 427/1 His expectatyves Many a man vnthrives.

un'thriven, *ppl. a.* Now *Sc.* (UN-¹ 8 b. Cf. WANTHRIVEN.)
1680 W. ALLEN *Peace & Unity* 136 Such as were but Babes still, and unthriven in the Life and Spirit of Christianity. **1825** JAMIESON, *Crile*,.. a child or beast that is unthriven. **1875** W. ALEXANDER *Ain Folk* 187 Willikie had assumed an unthriven look.

un'thriving, *ppl. a.* [UN-¹ 10.]
†**1.** Not doing well; lacking merit or excellence; unworthy. *Obs.*
c **1325** *Metr. Hom.* 130 Als did unthriuand [*v.r.* unthrewand] Giezye, That wex unhale thoru his gilrye. **13..** *Gaw. & Gr. Knt.* 1499 Good is your speche, Bot þrete

is vn-þryuande in þede þer I lende. *c* **1400** *Destr. Troy* 4893 And we..Answarth hym..with angur & skorne, With thretyng vnthriuand. *c* **1460** *Wisdom* 784 in *Macro Plays* 784 Here was a meny on-thryvande.

2. Not growing vigorously or thriving; not prospering or flourishing.

1600 SURFLET *Countrie Farme* III. xlvi. 517 After you haue thus cut it you may take the vnthriuing grafts [etc.]. **1628** QUARLES *Argalus & P.* III. Wks. (Grosart) III. 276/2 My quill would wast Th' unthriving stock of my bespoken time. **1673** *Lady's Call.* II. ii. §49 They will often find temtation enough here to discard their honesty, as the most unthriving trade. **1793** *Residence in France* (1797) I. 121 An unthriving tree of liberty, which seems to wither under the baneful influence of the *bonnet rouge*. **1848** AIRD *Mother's Blessing* II. ii, Filling up With stakes the gaps of the unthriving hedges. **1875** W. ALEXANDER *Ain Folk* 59 The poor wan bairnie.. looked even more shrivelled and unthriving than before.

3. Bringing no gain or profit; unprosperous.

1617 BP. HALL *Quo Vadis?* §5 Whiles in the meane season, their vnthriuing intermission is assailed with a thousand suggestions. **1624** HEYWOOD *Gunaik.* IX. 442 Hee was compelled..to prostitute his owne bodye to unnaturall lusts, for bruitish and unthriving gaine. *a* **1656** in *Raleigh's Remains* 110 It is now more than a seasonable time to alter the course of so unthriving a husbandry. *a* **1722** LISLE *Husb.* (1757) 107 The vetches continued in an unthriving way till the first of February. **1723** MRS. HOWARD in *Lett. C'tess Suffolk* (1824) I. 111 Sincerity is so very unthriving, that I can never give consent that you should practise it.

Hence **un'thrivingly** *adv.*, **un'thrivingness.**

13.. *E.E. Allit. P.* B. 135 A þral þryȝt in þe þrong vnþryuandely cloþed. **1387** TREVISA *Higden* (Rolls) IV. 397 Þe childe was i-bore to fore his tyme, and þerfore it was so unþryvyngeliche and so evel i-schape. **1704** *Dict. Rust.* s.v. *Enclosures*, The unthrivingness of Trees.

un'throne, *v.* [UN-² 4. Cf. Du. *onttronen*, G. *entthronen*.] *trans.* To dethrone.

1611 COTGR., *Desthroner*, to disthronize, or vnthrone. **1637** EARL MONM. tr. *Malvezzi's Romulus & Tarquin* 9 Amulius is not content to have unthron'd his brother. **1658** W. CHAMBERLAYNE *Loves Vict.* I. 13 Do not..Unthrone thy soul with this unmanly passion. **1665** DRYDEN *Indian Queen* V. i, Think, what pride, unthroned, must undergo. **1721** SOUTHERNE *Spartan Dame* III. i, She means to bring her Father in again, And to unthrone her Husband. **1838** TUPPER *Proverb. Philos.* 167 The shock that splitteth the globe, shall not unthrone thy self-possession. **1883** WHITELAW *Sophocles, Oedipus King* 386 Creon..Seeks to unthrone me, springing unawares.

Hence **un'throning** *vbl. sb.* (also *attrib.*).

1653 W. RAMESEY *Astrol. Restored* 324 An un-throning of some King. **1661** J. DAVIES *Civil Warres* 216 They resolved to send him four (as one called them) un-throning bills.

un'thronged, *ppl. a.* (UN-¹ 8.)

1648 HEXHAM II, *Ongedrongen sitten*, to Sitt unpressed or unthronged. [**1775** ASH. **1847** WEBSTER.]

†**un'throughfareness.** [UN-¹ 12.] Impenetrability.

1674 N. FAIRFAX *Bulk & Selv.* 112 The soul not agreeing with body, so much as in that one belonger of unthroughfareness.

†**un'throughfaresome,** *a.* [UN-¹ 7.] Impenetrable.

1674 N. FAIRFAX *Bulk & Selv.* 138 Body being a stour unweildsom thing, or at least a boaky unthroughfaresom thing.

un'thrown, *ppl. a.* (UN-¹ 8 b, 8 c; cf. THROW *v.* 32 d.)

a **1547** SURREY *Æneis* II. 605 No stone vnthrown, nor yet no dart vncast. **1642** T. WILSON *Jerichoes Down-fall* (1643) 86 Wherefore downe must the house, leave not one stone upon another unthrowne downe. **1651–7** T. BARKER *Art of Angling* (1820) 6 If any of the Line falleth into the water before the Flie, it is better unthrown then thrown. *a* **1716** SOUTH *Serm.* (1842) III. 522 As long as the old ferment remains unthrown out, a man cannot be safe. **1959** G. GREENE *Complaisant Lover* I. i. 4 *Victor* (*quite unthrown*). Take him any way. **1977** C. WOOD *James Bond, Spy who loved Me* xiv. 128 Bond tried to appear unthrown.

un'thrust, *ppl. a.* (UN-¹ 8 b.)

[**1775** ASH.] **1842** MRS. BROWNING *Grk. Chr. Poets* iv. Wks. (1904) 623 Objurgation vain To soulless nature, powerless to contain One ill unthrust upon it!

un'thumbed, *ppl. a.* (UN-¹ 8.)

[**1775** ASH.] **1797** COLERIDGE *Lett.* (1895) 7 His various works, uncut, unthumbed, have been preserved free from all pollution. **1846** MRS. GORE *Eng. Char.* (1852) 99 In his time, newspapers..were unthumbed in the pantry.

un'thwarted, *ppl. a.* (UN-¹ 8.)

[**1775** ASH.] **1805** WORDSW. *Prelude* IX. 523, I with him believed..that we should see the earth Unthwarted in her wish. **1853** WHITTIER *Trust* 18 Resting..upon His will Who moves to His great ends unthwarted by the ill. **1872** RUSKIN *Fors Clav.* xvi. 12 Such as the unthwarted sun in his season brings.

†**unthwyuond,** *pres. pple. Obs.* (Origin and meaning obscure; the alliteration requires *tw.*)

c **1400** *Destr. Troy* 6360 The xij [= twelfth] vnthwyuond, þat twyet not in fight, Was..mightful Henex. *Ibid.* 6378 With xxij [= two and twenty] vnthwyuond twyet to filde.

un'ticketed, *ppl. a.* (UN-¹ 8.)

[**1775** ASH.] **1865** TYLOR *Early Hist. Man.* viii. 203 An unticketed collection. **1899** *Westm. Gaz.* 20 Apr. 7/1 The unticketed crowd..was..perfect in its quiet behaviour.

un'tickled, *ppl. a.* (UN-¹ 8.)

1736 CHESTERFIELD *Fogg's Jrnl.* No. 377 ¶5 There is not an ear in the whole country untickled.

un'tidily, *adv.* (UN-¹ 11.)

c **1440** *Promp. Parv.* 367/2 On-tydely. **1530** PALSGR. 472/2, I bungyll, or do a thyng untydyly, or lyke an yvell workeman. [**1775** ASH.] **1825** JAMIESON s.v., She was very untidily dressed. **1847** C. BRONTE *J. Eyre* viii, Untidily folded articles pinned to her shoulder. **1885** *Manch. Exam.* 12 Jan. 6/3 The table over which the remains of a fish dinner were untidily scattered.

un'tidy, *a.* [ME. *untīdi* (UN-¹ 7), = WFris. *on-*, *ûntidich*, MDu. *ontidich* (Du. *ontijdig*), MLG. *untidich*, OHG. *unzitich* (MHG. *unzitec*, *-zitic*, G. *unzeitig*), MSw. *otidig*, (M)Da., Norw. *utidig* untimely, unseasonable, unfavourable, etc.]

†**1.** Untimely, unseasonable; unsuitable, unseemly.

a **1225** *Leg. Kath.* 2400 Aflei from ham al uuel, Weorre & weane baðe, & untidi wederes! **1377** LANGL. *P. Pl.* B. xx. 118 With his vntydy tales he tened ful ofte Conscience and his compaignye. **1393** *Ibid.* C. x. 262 The tarre is vntydy þat to þyne sheep by-longeþ. *c* **1440** *Promp. Parv.* 367/2 On-tydy, *intemptatus* (P. *intemperatus*). **1661** J. ARNWAY *Tablet* 91 Hitherto ye are come by an untidy Parliament, wherein.. many..made grievous..shiprack of the Faith.

2. Of poor, mean, or uncared-for appearance; not kept in good order; not neat or orderly.

For the break in the evidence (as in the *adv.* above), cf. the history of TIDY *a.* (esp. sense 4).

c **1350** *Will. Palerne* 1455 Sche schal..haue mo solempne cites and semliche casteles, þan ȝe treuly han smale tounes or vntydi houses. *a* **1529** SKELTON *E. Rummyng* 151 Theyr lockes about theyr face, Theyr tresses vntrust,..Full vntydy tegges, Lyke rotten egges. **1545** BALE *Image Both Ch.* I. ix. (1550) Ki, Bishoppes, preestes, monkes,..were poore, abiecte, and vntydye. **1570** FOXE *A. & M.* (ed. 2) I. 116 Therfore this vntydie ground of ours, bringeth forth so many weedes.

[**1775** ASH.] **1824** CARR *Craven Gloss.* 119 *Unheppen*,.. indecent, untidy. *a* **1825** FORBY *Voc. E. Anglia*, *Untidy*, unclean; sluttish. **1855** *Poultry Chron.* II. 541 The untidy one [*sc.* bee-keeper] permits cobwebs to occupy the corners of the bee-shed. **1884** F. M. CRAWFORD *Rom. Singer* I. 4 There can be nothing so untidy about a house as children and chickens.

Hence **un'tidiness.**

[**1775** ASH.] **1845** E. B. BARRETT *Lett. Browning* (1899) I. 115, I rather like blots than otherwise—being a sort of patron-saint of all manner of untidyness. **1875** W. S. HAYWARD *Love agst. World* 13, I must be in a dreadful state of untidyness.

un'tidy, *v.* [UN-² 3, or f. UNTIDY *a.*] *trans.* To make untidy.

1891 R. DOWLING *Isle of Surrey* 112 He was busy tidying, or rather untidying, his room all one day. **1893** BARING-GOULD *Cheap Jack Zita* I. 192 The wildness of her appearance thus untidied by the wind.

un'tie, *v.* [OE. *untīgan* (UN-² 3, 7).]

1. *trans.* To release, set free, detach, by undoing a cord or similar fastening.

c **1000** *Ags. Gosp.* Matt. xxi. 2 Þonne sona finde ȝyt ane assene ȝetiȝȝede..: untiȝeað hiȝ, and lædað to me. *Ibid.* Mark xi. 5 Hwæt do ȝyt þone folan untiȝende? **13..** *K. Alis.* 784 (Laud MS.), He it [*sc.* Bucephalus] vntyed & lete gon. **1388** WYCLIF *Mark* xi. 5 Thei..founden a colt tied bifor the ȝate,..and thei vntieden hym. **1530** PALSGR. 768/2, I untey, ..*je deslie*. Untey my hosen. **1581** A. HALL *Iliad* VIII. 147 His goodly steedes the Marine god..vnties. *c* **1586** C'TESS PEMBROKE *Ps.* XCI. ii, From snare..He shall thee sure unty. **1639** T. DE GRAY *Expert Farrier* 236 Untye him, and give him meat. **1659** HAMMOND *On Ps.* lx. 6 As when the master reaches out his shooe to his meanest servant, to be untyed and taken off by him. **1719** DE FOE *Crusoe* II. (Globe) 494 They said,..if they untied her [*sc.* a cow], they should see which Way she went. **1725** POPE *Odyss.* IX. 208, I climbed my vessel's lofty side; My train obeyed me, and the ship unty'd. **1794** WORDSW. *Guilt & Sorrow* lxiv, They..busily ..untie Her garments. **1847** EMERSON *Daemonic Love* 148 Therefore comes an hour from Jove Which his ruthless will defies, And the dogs of Fate unties.

absol. **1638** JUNIUS *Paint. Ancients* 193 The unlearned.. use to think it a matter of greater strength..to teare asunder, than to unty.

b. To free from a confining or encircling cord, bond, etc.

c **1450** *Cov. Myst.* (1922) 224 Goo forthe,..and lazare ȝe vntey, And all his bondys losyth hem asundyr. *a* **1533** LD. BERNERS *Huon* ci. 333 Huon came to yᵉ fote of yᵉ ladder, where as he founde Gerames as then not vntyed. **1596** SHAKS. *Tam. Shr.* II. i. 21, I prethee sister Kate, vntie my hands. **1683** MOXON *Mech. Exerc.*, *Printing* xxii. ¶7 He unties all the Pages of that Quarter. **1747** MRS. GLASSE *Cookery* ii. 38 Untye your Cucumbers, but take care the Meat don't come out. **1781** COWPER *Charity* 471 With slow deliberation he unties His glitt'ring purse. **1819** SHELLEY *Peter Bell 3rd* VI. vii, All these Reviews the Devil made Up in a parcel.. Peter..Untied them—read them. **1891** FARRAR *Darkn. & Dawn* lv, The executioner has untied your hands.

c. In various fig. uses.

13.. *Cast. Love* (H.) 1603 Hevyn and erthe shull byn aleyde, And the foure elementes shull be unteyede. **1390** GOWER *Conf.* III. 21 If thou be forto wyte In eny point.. Wherof thi wittes ben unteid. **1565** COOPER, *Linguam resoluere*,..to vntie his tongue. **1586** DAY *Eng. Secretary* I. (1625) 87 Before this time the like breach..was neuer seene betweene vs: but what (mischiefe) shal I now terme it..that ..hath in this vilde sort, giuen meanes to vntie vs. **1605** SHAKS. *Macb.* IV. i. 52 Though you vntye the Windes, and let them fight Against the Churches. *a* **1654** SELDEN *Table-T.* (Arb.) 66, I cannot bind my self, for I may untye my self again. **1655** EARL ORRERY *Parthen.* I. VI. 131, I will vntye my Soule from that Cley which invirons it. *a* **1845** WORDSW. *Eccl. Sonn.*, *Crusaders* 10 When Heaven unties Her inmost, ..tenderest harmonies. **1847** DISRAELI *Tancred* IV. iv, We shall be at Hebron before they untie their eyelids.

2. To undo, unfasten (a cord, knot, etc.); also *transf.* to relax (a hold).

1590 SPENSER *F.Q.* I. xi. 42 He forst him to vnty One of his grasping feete. **1602** *2nd Pt. Return Parnass.* III. iv. 1378 If he will not vnty the purse stringes of his liberality. **1639** J. TAYLOR *Summers Trav.* (Hindley, III) 17 You might have untied it [*sc.* a halter], that it might have serv'd another time. *a* **1718** PRIOR *Love Disarmed* 39 The Chain I'll in Return unty; And freely Thou again shalt fly. **1791** COWPER *Odyssey* VIII. 339 A snare Of bands indissoluble, by no art To be untied. **1858** TROLLOPE *Dr. Thorne* iii, The old squire of Greshamsbury, whose shoe ribbons Dr. Fillgrave would not have objected to untie. **1885** 'MRS. ALEXANDER' *Valerie's Fate* i, She untied and removed her veil.

fig. **1581** G. ELLIOT in Arber *Garner* VIII. 208 Even then (by God's great goodness..) all their..devilish devices and practises were so broken and untied in me that [etc.].

b. *fig.* To solve or clear away (a difficulty). Freq. with *knot* in fig. sense (cf. KNOT *sb.*¹ 10).

(*a*) *a* **1586** SIDNEY *Arcadia* II. xiii, The love of him commaundid him to preserve his life: which knot might well be cut, but untied it could not be. **1601** SHAKS. *Twel. N.* II. ii. 42 O time, thou must vntangle this, not I; It is too hard a knot for me t'vnty. **1643** R. BAKER *Chron.*, *Stephen* 65 A Gordian knot, which no Writer helpes me to unty. **1732** BERKELEY *Alciphr.* VI. §32 He will endeavour to untie knots as well as tie them. **1746** FRANCIS tr. *Hor.*, *Sat.* II. v. 56, I know the Doubles of the mazy Laws, Unty their Knots, and plead with vast Applause. **1761** STERNE *Tr. Shandy* IV. vii, That is cutting the knot, said my father, instead of untying it. **1818** COBBETT *Pol. Reg.* XXXIII. 714 We cannot cut the knot: we must, therefore, take time to untie it. **1889** S. WALPOLE *Life Ld. J. Russell* II. 374 The new King tried to cut instead of untying the Gordian knot.

(*b*) **1611** SHAKS. *Cymb.* V. iv. 149 'Tis still a Dreame..Or senselesse speaking, or a speaking such As sense cannot vntye. **1649** DAVENANT *Love & Hon.* IV. iv. 80 We must to Delphos sure t'untie these doubts..with an oracle. **1654** JER. TAYLOR *Real Pres.* 65 The whole party wanders in eternal intricacies, and inextricable riddles; which.. themselves cannot untie.

c. *fig.* To dissolve (a bond, esp. of union).

(*a*) **1634** B. JONSON *Love's Welcome* Wks. (1641) 282 A true-love Knot will hardly be unti'd. **1651** HOBBES *Leviath.* IV. xlvii. 385 First, the Power of the Popes was dissolved... And so was untyed the first knot. **1671** R. MACWARD *True Non-conf.* 166 Unless the error be of greater importance,.. it ought not to unty the bond of the unity of the Catholick Church. **1784** COWPER *Task* II. 685 Profusion..unties the knot Of union. **1805** SCOTT *Last Minstrel* VI. ii, Land of my sires! what mortal hand Can e'er untie the filial band, That knits me to thy rugged strand! **1895** *Daily News* 15 Nov. 7/3 If a husband got tired of his wife,..the State winked at a collusive suit by which the knot was untied.

(*b*) **1606** SHAKS. *Tr. & Cr.* II. iii. 111 The amitie that wisedome knits, not folly may easily vntie. **1610** —— *Temp.* V. i. 253 Come hither Spirit, Set Caliban and his companions free: Vntye the Spell. *a* **1683** SIDNEY *Disc. Govt.* iii. §15 (1698) 316 But if these obligations were untied, we may easily guess [etc.].

3. *intr.* To become loosened or untied.

1590 *Tarlton's Newes Purgat.* 30 He threwe his armes about him with such violence, that his wide sleeue vntyed. **1651** JER. TAYLOR *Serm. for Year* II. v. 59 Then their resolution unties like the cords of vanity or the gossamere against the violence of the Northen winde. *Ibid.* II. xxiii. 290 Their promises are but fair language,..and disband and unty like the air that beat upon their teeth, when [etc.].

Hence **un'tied** *ppl. a.*¹

1565 COOPER s.v. *Recinctus*, *Zona recincta*, a girdle vntied. **1619** FLETCHER *Knt. Malta* V. i, I am..a vessel crack'd, A Zone unti'd. **1891** T. HARDY *Tess* xlvii, She..had to supply the man with untied sheaves.

un'tied, *ppl. a.*² [UN-¹ 8.]

1. Not tied, in various senses.

c **1374** CHAUCER *Troylus* II. 752, I am myn owene woman wel at ese,..Right yong and stond vntyd in lusty lese. **1390** GOWER *Conf.* I. 307 Suche adaies be now fele..That lete here tunges gon unteid. *Ibid.* II. 117 Mi sorwe is everemore unteid, And secheth overal my veines. **1398** TREVISA *Barth. De P.R.* V. xxiii. (Bodl. MS.), þat partie of þe tunge þat is nyȝe þe pipe of þe lunges is vntied. **1509** HAWES *Past. Pleas.* XVIII. (Percy Soc.) 86 Myne owne I am, what that I lyste to do I stand untyed. *a* **1529** SKELTON *Agst. Venemous Tongues* 4, I care muche the lesse what euer they say, For tunges vntayde be rennyng astray. **1617** DANIEL *Coll. Hist. Eng.* 114 There were Excesses to many committed in a time so vntied as this was. **1651** HOBBES *Leviath.* II. xviii. 89 The untyed hands of that Man..that hath the Soveraignty. **1725** POPE *Odyss.* IX. 158 A port there is, inclos'd on either side, Where ships may rest, un-anchored, and unty'd. *c* **1730** RAMSAY *Bonny Tweedside* iv, Unty'd to a man..We never can thrive. **1888** *Stamford Mercury* 27 Apr., An untied beerhouse, cottages and land.

2. Wrongly used for 'unloosed'.

1608 SHAKS. *Per.* IV. ii. 160 If fires be hot, knives sharp, or waters deep, Untied I still my virgin knot will keep.

†**un'tiffed,** *ppl. a.* [UN-¹ 8: see TIFF *v.*¹] Unadorned.

a **1225** *Ancr. R.* 420 To Godes eien heo is lufsumere, þet is, uor þe luue of him, untiffed wiðuten.

†**un'tight,** *sb. Obs.*⁻¹ [UN-¹ 12 + TIGHT *sb.*¹ Cf. Du. *ontucht*, OHG., MHG. *unzuht* (G. *unzucht*).] An immoral act or practice.

a **1300** *Body & Soul* in *Map's Poems* (Camden) 336 Ȝwanne thouȝ me tauȝtist on untiȝth, an me gan ther offe mone. [*Ibid.* 341 (Vernon MS.), Whon I dude an untiht.]

un'tight, *a.* (UN-¹ 7.)

1622 F. MARKHAM *Bk. War* I. vi. 21 However crazie or untight my pore Vessell may be, it must stil put forth into the Sea. **1622** MALYNES *Anc. Law-Merch.* 142 If the ouer-loope of the Ship be vntyth, or the Pumpe be faultie. **1815** W. FINLAYSON *Scot. Rhymes* 27 Like some poor bodie, in his mind untight. **1823** P. NICHOLSON *Pract. Build.* 336 When lime has been long kept in..untight casks.

un'tighten, *v.* (UN-^{2} 3.)

[1775 ASH.] 1836 BROWNING *Porphyria's Lover* 46, I untightened next the tress About her neck.

until (ʌn'tɪl), *prep.* and *conj.* Forms: α. 3 *Orm.* **unntill,** 4–7 **vn-,** 4–9 **untill** (7 **untell**), 4, 6 **vn-,** 5–6 **untyll** (5 **unetyll**); 4–5 **vn-,** 5 (9 *arch.*) **untille,** 5 **un-, vntylle** (**yn-**); 4–7 **vntil,** 5–6 **vntyl,** 4– **until.** β. 4 (9 *dial.*) **ontil,** *Sc.* 5 **ontyll, onetil,** 5–6 **ontill.** [ME. (originally northern) *untill*, f. ON. *und* (retained only in *unz*, *undz* = *und es*), = Goth. *und* (and *untē*), OS. *und* (usually *unt*), OFris. *und* (*ont*), up to, as far as + *till* TILL *prep.* and *conj.*]

A. *prep.*

In poetry occasionally put after the sb. (or pron.).

I. Local (and derived senses), dative, etc. Latterly *Sc.* and *north.*

1. To, unto (denoting motion to and reaching a person or place); = TILL *prep.* 1.

c 1200 ORMIN 1399 Forr whatt teȝȝ fellenn sone dun Off heoffne unntill helle. a 1300 *Cursor M.* 5123 Þan he went vntil his in. c 1330 R. BRUNNE *Chron. Wace* (Rolls) 13086 Wiþ hym vntil wode þey fled. c 1380 *Sir Ferumb.* 2311 Þe Amerel vn-til a wyndow ran. a 1450 *Le Morte Arth.* 3858 Streyght vnto hys bed he yode, And clepyd the bysshope hym vntylle. 1478 *Eng. Misc.* (Surtees Soc. 85) 37 Unto all theis untill whome this presentes shal com. 1526 TINDALE *Matt.* iv. 3 Then came vntyll hym the tempter. 1561 *Godly Q. Hester* (1873) 12 Then shall I brynge her the kynge untyll. 1590 SPENSER *F.Q.* I. xi. 4 He rousd himselfe full blith, and hastned them vntill. ? a 1800 *Jock o' the Side* xiii. in Scott *Min.*, When they cam the gate until. 1824 J. TELFER *Border Ball.* 43 It dirlit upthrow the twinklinge holes, The second lifte untille.

b. Up to (a point or limit); as far as; so as to reach; = TILL *prep.* 1 b.

c 1330 R. BRUNNE *Chron. Wace* (Rolls) 10554 Fro þe Weste or Est vntil Moungow He was told of non honour. 1338 —— *Chron.* (1810) 42 Þe folk vntille Humber to Suane gan þei loute. c 1440 *York Myst.* xxxvii. 52, I prechid in Neptalym, þat lande, And Zabulon even vn-till ende. 1535 COVERDALE *Judg.* xx. 1 Then wente the children of Israel out and gathered a congregacion,..from Dan vntill Bersaba. 1552 *Bk. Com. Prayer, Communion*, Upon the holy dayes.. shalbe sayde al that is appoynted.., vntyl the ende of the Homelie. 1599 HAKLUYT *Voy.* II. I. 211 Staires of yron ascending vp vntill the midst of the pillers. 1616 J. LANE *Contn. Sqr.'s T.* XI. 311 A woman..Which att her necke, vntill her dugges dependinge, Wore the ritch rubie. a 1765 *Ld. Thomas & Fair A.* xxviii. in Child *Ball.*, Lord Thomas ..strake the dagger untill his heart.

c. In contact with; against.

c 1440 *Pallad. on Husb.* III. 1138 Sarmentes..Vntil a reed for turnyng bounden fast. 1785 R. FORBES *Ulysses* 38 He shook the blade, an'..Set the heft to the ground, The nib until his breast. a 1803 *Cruel Mother* iii. in Child *Ball.* I. 221/1 She's set her back untill an oak. *Ibid.* iv.

2. To, towards; unto; = TILL *prep.* 2.

a 1300 *Cursor M.* 23286 Þai..Ne wald noght here bot þair delices, þat drogh þam vntil oþer vices. 1303 R. BRUNNE *Handl. Synne* 6484 Þogh now we ȝaue alle þy gode vntyl pore mannes fode. 1338 —— *Chron.* (1810) 237 Ȝit auanced he þat file vntille a faire þing. c 1440 *Pallad. on Husb.* I. 448 Mynge hit yurne Tyl euery part vntyl on body turne. c 1535 FISHER *Wks.* II. (E.E.T.S.) 429 Howe terribly shall he lay this vntyll our charge, whan we shal be called vntyll a rekenynge for this matter! 1566 STERNHOLD & H. *Ps.* cxxxix. 6 It is so hye that I the same Can not attayne vntill. 1587 M. GROVE *Pelops & Hipp.* (1878) 77 Perchance ye gods haue you preseru'd vntil some better end. c 1675 in *Shirburn Ball.* (1907) 171 Good or euill, which his minde was bent vntill. c 1800 in Chambers *Pop. Poems Scotl.* (1862) 64 Ge—en—tlemen o' the Jury, Ye'll answer until a' your names. 1814 SCOTT *Wav.* x, The Laird..had devoted his leisure *untill* tillage and agriculture.

†**b.** *like until*, like; resembling. *Obs. rare.*

c 1375 *Leg. Rood* (1871) 123 It was like untill a heuyn. c 1400 MAUNDEV. (Roxb.) vii. 26 Þe fruyt..es lyke vntill hostez.

3. Indicating the person towards whom an action, feeling, statement, etc., is directed. Freq. after verbs of telling, teaching, calling, doing, giving, making, listening, etc. = TILL *prep.* 3.

a 1300 *Cursor M.* 1069 Vntil his broþer nith he bare. 1357 *Lay Folks' Catech.* (T.) 56 Seuen dedis of merci until oure euen-cristen. 1377 LANGL. *P. Pl.* B. Prol. 227 Tauerners vn-til hem tolde þe same. c 1400 *Rule St. Benet* (Verse) 378 Al þat scho sal tech oþer vntill. 1417 *York Memo. Bk.* (Surtees) I. 183 He that es noght obeiant untill sercheours and till his crafte. c 1450 LOVELICH *Grail* lvi. 77 What is that the vntylle? 1470–85 MALORY *Arthur* XVIII. xv. 752 She cryed on loude vntyl hym. a 1500 *Coventry Corpus Chr. Pl.* 966 The furst byddyng, Wyche Moses dyd rede vs vntill. 1521 FISHER *Serm. agst. Luther* iv. D v, He shal be a comforter vntyl vs. 1565 J. HALL *Crt. Virtue* 31 The rounde earth he hath forth lente The sonnes of mortall men vntyll. 1567 *Gude & Godlie B.* (S.T.S.) 82 Than ȝe present ane peirles sing, Of lyfe serene, the warld vntill. a 1780 *Archie o' Cawfield* xxxv. in Child *Ball.*, The lieutenant Until a bonny lad said..'Who is the man..?' *Ibid.* xxxvi.

†**4.** Up to (a given number); amounting or extending to. *Obs. rare.*

c 1400 MAUNDEV. (Roxb.) xxii. 102 Diuerse bestez, as marmusetes, apes and oþer many vntil iii^m or iiii^m. 1539 BIBLE (Great) *Matt.* xviii. 22 Lorde howe oft shall I forgeue my brother..: Tyll seuen tymes? Iesus sayeth vnto him: I saye not vnto the vntill seuen tymes: but seuenty times seuen tymes. 1582 N. T. (Rhem.) *Luke* ii. 37 And she was a widow vntil eightie and foure yeres.

II. With reference to time.

5. Onward till (a time specified or indicated); up to the time of (an action, occurrence, etc.); = TILL *prep.* 5.

a 1300 *Cursor M.* 1424 Stil ai stod þai wandes thre Fra adam tim until noe. c 1340 HAMPOLE *Pr. Consc.* 555 Þe wilk reches fra þe bygynnyng Of mans lyfe un-til þe endyng. a 1352 MINOT *Poems* (ed. Hall) iii. 39 All þat land vntill þis day Fars þe better for þat iornay. c 1420 *Anturs of Arth.* (T.) 702 Þay made hyme..a knyghte of þe tabylle rownde, Vn-tille his lyues ende. a 1466 *Paston. Lett.* Suppl. (1901) 105, I pray zow that hyt may be repytyd un tyll the tyme that I speke with zow. 1539 BIBLE (Great) *Luke* xvi. 16 The lawe and the Prophetes raygned vntyll Iohn. 1554 in Feuillerat *Revels Q. Mary* (1914) 154 From the laste daye of Maye.. vntill the vj^t daye of June. 1592 *Arden of Feversham* III. vi. 36, I doo but slip it vntil better time. 1652 J. WRIGHT tr. *Camus' Nat. Paradox* x. 229 Intreating him to stay there untill further intelligence from him. a 1682 SIR T. BROWNE *Tracts* (1683) 138 With little action with foreign Nations untill the union of the Heptarchy under Egbert. 1721 MORTIMER *Husb.* (ed. 2) II. 133 [To] hang them up until the end of February. 1754 in *Nairne Peerage Evid.* (1874) 55 Taking upon himself the stile or title of lord Nairn..until pay[men]t. 1853 THACKERAY *Eng. Hum.* i. 10 He waits and waits until nightfall. 1889 *Science-Gossip* XXV. 255/2 Brooks's comet..may be visible..until the end of the year.

b. With (usu. after) a negative, = TILL *prep.* 5 b.

1543 *Star Chamber Cases* (Selden) II. 267 Straungers.. will not vtter their wares..vntill the Faire. 1590 SHAKS. *Mids. N.* II. ii. 117 Things growing are not ripe vntill their season. 1628 tr. *Mathieu's Powerfull Favorite* 103 Tiberius ceased not vntill such time as the Senate did content him. 1671 tr. *Frejus' Voy. Mauritania* 21 Although this be a countrey where, untill this very day, we see no man so venterous as to hazard himself, but by Hostages. 1764 H. WALPOLE *Otranto* v, Until this hour I never set eyes on this damsel. 1872 J. L. SANFORD *Estimates Eng. Kings, Chas. I*, 333 He did not become a person of real importance..until the death of his elder brother. 1893 W. O. MORRIS *Napoleon* (1894) 158 Nelson had not left Europe until the second week of May.

c. Followed by an adv. (or advb. phrase) of time. = TILL *prep.* 5 c.

1338 R. BRUNNE *Chron.* (1810) 58 Godwyn..fro London went away, He stode vntille no more, defaute he mad þat day. 1538 ELYOT, *Etiamnum*, vntyll than. 1539 BIBLE (Great) *Num.* xiv. 19 As thou hast forgeuen this people from Egipte euen vntyll now. 1582 N.T. (Rhem.) *Matt.* xi. 12 From the dayes of Iohn the Baptist vntil novv. a 1631 DONNE *Paradoxes* (1652) 81 A vertue which,..untill then, is kept with a modest chastity. 1648 HEXHAM II, *Tot wanneer?* Untill when? 1721 in *Cath. Rec. Soc. Publ.* VIII. 301 From the end of Compline untill after Prime the next day. 1764 H. WALPOLE *Otranto* v, It was not until after frequent discourses with Isabella..that he was persuaded. 1826 *Art Brewing* (ed. 2) 126 [It] has, until lately, been a question among chemists. 1838 *Encycl. Metrop.* (1845) XXV. 175/2 The results..cannot be appreciated until after the lapse of years. 1849 ROCK *Ch. of Fathers* I. v. 385 Until late in the thirteenth century. 1873 F. HALL *Mod. Eng.* p. xv, Until four years ago.

6. Before (a specified time).

1887 LADY BRASSEY *Last Voy.* 201 Having quite abandoned all hope of our appearing until the morning.

B. *conj.* (See TILL *conj.*)

Not common during 18th c.; in freq. use from c 1820.

a. Up to the time that; till the point or degree when; = TILL *conj.* 1. Also with *that*.

c 1300 *Harrowing of Hell* (Auch.) 29 [They were in woe] Vntil Crist loked þaim vnto. 1338 R. BRUNNE *Chron.* (1810) 56 Þei..duelled þer for drede, Untille þe kyng turned, & his wrath ouer ȝede. c 1440 *Pallad. on Husb.* I. 619 The cok..his briddis hateth Vntil the crest uppon theire hedis growe. 1526 TINDALE *Luke* xxiv. 49 Tary ye in..Jerusalem vntill ye be endewed with power. 1556 LAUDER *Tractate* 481 The Maledictione of the pure Sall on ȝow and ȝour seid Indure, Vntyll that ȝe be rutit oute. 1580 in *10th Rep. Hist. MSS. Comm.* App. IV. 426 [The jury] shall contynue together.. untill they be fullie agreed upon their verdicte. 1602 *Ld. Cromwell* IV. v. 39 Now get you in, vntill I call for you. 1684 BUNYAN *Pilgr.* II. (1900) 228 He..did them all abuse; Until that I..arose. 1729 T. INNES *Crit. Essay* (1879) 267 In the meantime, until exact copies be published,..variations and alterations..may be shown [etc.]. 1764 H. WALPOLE *Otranto* v, Manfred..pushed on the feast until it waxed late. 1802 *Lochmaben Harper* xvi. in Scott *Min.*, The fiend dought they do but listen him to, Until that the day began to daw. 1870 M. ARNOLD *St. Paul & Prot.* 9 Man is altogether passive in this call, until the Holy Spirit enables him to answer it.

ellipt. 1596 SHAKS. *Merch. V.* III. ii. 149 As doubtfull whether what I see be true, Vntill confirm'd, sign'd, ratified by you. 1855 *Poultry Chron.* III. 296/2 After this, until feathered, they should be fed on rich food.

b. With negative (expressed or implied) in the principal clause, = TILL *conj.* 1 b. Also with *that*.

a 1300 *E.E. Psalter* xciii. 15 For lauerd sal noght his folke schouue awai,..Vntil þat rightwisenes Be turned in dome. c 1340 HAMPOLE *Pr. Consc.* 3213 Na man may..Out of þat hard payn þam wyn, Until þe fire haf wasted þair bandes of syn. *Ibid.* 3271 Til þat sight þai may never wyn, Until þai be clensed þar of al syn. c 1477 *Stoner Papers* (Camden) II. 29 Fore we may nat go yn-tylle ȝe comme. 1535 COVERDALE *Job* xiv. 12 But when man slepeth, he ryseth not agayne, vntill the heauen perish. 1590 SHAKS. *Com. Err.* v. i. 115, I will fall prostrate at his feete, And neuer rise vntill my teares..Haue won his grace to come in person hither. 1662 DRYDEN *To Ld. Chancellor* 32 In open Prospect nothing bounds our Eye Until the Earth seems join'd unto the Sky. 1692 E. WALKER tr. *Epictetus' Mor., On Enchiridion*, That Truth they could not find Until the Morning-Star..form'd the Gospel Day. 1766 SMOLLETT *Trav.* iv, It will not freeze at all, until it has deposited all its salt. 1798 WORDSW. *Peter Bell* Prol. 4 Through the clouds I'll never float Until I have a little Boat. 1868 MORRIS *Earthly Par.* I. 187 No man living should see this Until that thou..Hast given it to the seneschal. 1893 *Spectator* 22 July 101 The answer..will probably not be published until these pages are in our readers' hands.

ellipt. 1895 C. J. CORNISH *Wild England of to-day* 248 Often they will..not move until almost trodden on.

c. In similar sense without a negative: Before the time that; before. Cf. TILL *conj.* 1 c.

1601 J. WEEVER *Mirr. Martyrs* A 3 b, One tale is good vntill another's told. 1621 ELSING *Debates Ho. Lords* (Camden) 51 He refused to yield..untell the fees..were payed him. c 1645 HOWELL *Lett.* (1655) II. 70 'Tis held a great part of incivility for maidens to drink wine untill they are married. 1841 J. R. HOPE-SCOTT in R. Ornsby *Mem.* (1884) I. 305 There will probably be an interval of six months, at least, until they can meet. 1852 ROCK *Ch. of Fathers* III. 76 The unfitness of man's soul to go to heaven until cleansed from every smallest speck of sin.

d. = TILL *conj.* 1 d.

1609 HOLLAND *Amm. Marcell.* 417 Mallobantes..was much troubled, thinking it long untill he might advance his standerd against the enemie. 1611 R. FENTON *Treat. Usury* 97 The time is not long, vntill thou must trust him with a far greater matter. 1804 LADY HUNTER in *Jrnl. Sir M. Hunter* (1894) 202 We had not sat long until one roll of the ship brought such a sea on deck as [etc.].

e. So long or so far that; = TILL *conj.* 1 e.

c 1440 *Pallad. on Husb.* III. 1143 In water first this opium relent, Of sape vntil hit ha similitude. 1535 COVERDALE *Jer.* xliv. 27 All the men of Iuda..shal perish with the swearde, ..vntill they be vtterly destroyed. 1567 JEWEL *Def. Apol.* VI. vii. 625 They eate, vntil they be faine to per-breake. 1598 *Epulario* K iij, Heat it vntill the Cheese curd. 1652 CULPEPPER *Eng. Physic.* 5 If the decoction stand..for two or three days untill the yellow colour be changed black. 1748 *Anson's Voy.* I. viii. 82 We were obliged to bear away until they had made all fast. 1764 H. WALPOLE *Otranto* v, A silly wench, who has heard stories of apparitions until she believes them. 1836 THIRLWALL *Greece* III. 247 The flames were spread by the wind, until almost the whole island was left bare. 1901 *Scribner's Mag.* XXIX. 511/2 It was comparatively easy to repeat the drawing until the whole design was acccurately copied.

ellipt. 1827 FARADAY *Chem. Manip.* xviii. 476 A mixture made by rubbing down very poor cheese with water.., until of the consistency of cream.

†**f.** ***so long (...) until***, = TILL *conj.* 1 f. *Obs.*

1470–85 MALORY *Arthur* VII. xxxi. 263 So this syr Gareth rode soo longe in that forest vntyl the nyghte came. 1565 COOPER *Thesaurus* s.v. *Eatenus*, Thou shouldest so longe beare vntill he had..neglected those lawes. 1595 in *Cath. Rec. Soc. Publ.* V. 346 The Universitie of Oxford, where he continwed so longe untill he was thought fitt for the degree of Bacheler of Artes. 1597 BEARD *Theatre God's Judgem.* (1612) 129 Eating grasse like oxen, even so long untill his haire was growne stiffe. 1651 WITTIE tr. *Primrose's Pop. Err.* 226 Wee must persist so long in the use of remedies, untill ..we perceive [etc.].

g. ***unless and until***: see UNLESS *prep. phr.* 2 c.

until(l, erron. varr. (now dial.) of INTIL *prep.*

a 1300 *Cursor M.* 2501 Þai fled and fell vntill a sogh. c 1375 *Ibid.* 2692 (Fairf.), Our lorde went vp vn-til [*Cott.* in-til] his blis. 1858 in *N.W. Linc. Gloss.* (1877) 264 Chuck some more stoäns until her [*sc.* a cart].

un'tile, *v.* [UN-^{2} 4.] *trans.* To strip (a roof, etc.) of tiles. (Common c 1590–1760.)

c 1400 *Destr. Troy* 9114 The taburnacle titly vntild was aboue. 1468–9 *Paston Lett.* Suppl. (1901) 123 Ye shall have doubyll cost for to untylle your howsys ayen. 1536 *MS. Rawl. D. 780* fol. 94 b, Rypyng and vntyllyng the Rouffes. 1589 *Whip for Ape* A iij, Cathedrall Churches he would faine vntile. 1604 T. WRIGHT *Passions* v. §3. 182 Pull down this rafter, cut that beame, vntile the house. 1633 HEYWOOD *Eng. Trav.* I. ii, Rough tempests rise, Vntile the roofe, which ..Left vnrepaired, the stormy showres beat in. 1690 LUTTRELL *Brief Rel.* (1857) II. 5 [The wind] untiled the tops of most houses more or lesse. 1713 *Lond. Gaz.* No. 5103/2 The Houses have been..Untiled..by the Wind. 1774 G. WHITE *Selborne* lxi, I untiled the eaves of a house where many pairs build.

fig. 1648 HERRICK *Hesper.*, *To the Detractor* 4 A fellon take it, or some Whit-flaw come For to unslate, or to untile that thumb! 1699 T. BROWN *Sev. New Coll.* 60 What, is your House until'd already, and is it come to a Rupture between you?

un'tiled, *ppl. a.* [UN-^{1} 8.] Not covered with tiles.

1377 LANGL. *P. Pl.* B. XIV. 252 Had þei no þyng but of pore men her houses were vntyled! 1600 BRETON *Pasquil's Passe* Wks. (Grosart) I. 8/1 From dwelling in a house that is vntilde..good Lord deliuer me. 1649 J. H. *Motion to Parl. Adv. Learn.* 20 Our houses were..untiled and obvious to.. injuries of the weather. a 1721 PRIOR *Down-Hall* xxxvii, A low ruin'd white Shed..Untyl'd and unglaz'd.

un'till, *v.* (UN-^{2} 3.)

1733 TULL *Horse-Hoeing Husb.* vi. 52 It rather Untills the Land, and Anticipates the subsiding of the Ground.

un'tillable, *a.* (UN-^{1} 7 b.)

1714 *Welsh Monster* 26 In a wild Corner of the World,.. Worthless, untillable, and barren. 1791 COWPER *Iliad* I. 398 On the shore..Of the untillable and barren deep. 1812 BRACKENRIDGE *Views Louisiana* (1814) 27 An extensive region of open plains and meadows, interspersed with bare untillable hills. 1889 *Times* 20 Apr. 5/1 A considerable portion of the district being untillable.

un'tilled, *ppl. a.* (UN-^{1} 8.)

1297 R. GLOUC. (Rolls) 7667 Muche lond þer is As al wast & vntuled [*v.rr.* vntyled, -teled]. 1377 LANGL. *P. Pl.* B. XV. 451 Heth and vntiled erthe. 1382 WYCLIF *Ezek.* xxxvi. 36, I the Lord haue..plantid vntilied [1388 vntilid] thingus. 1445 in *Anglia* XXVIII. 277 Londys which were vntilied. 1469 *Paston Lett.* Suppl. (1901) 128 Thei byd them lete there land lye on tilled. 1538 STARKEY *England* 12 The erth ..els schold haue leyne..rude and vntyllyd. 1598 SYLVESTER *Du Bartas* II. i. *Eden* 598 There lives the Sea-Oak in a little shell; There growes untill'd the ruddy Cochenel. 1638 JUNIUS *Paint. Ancients* 245 An unbroken or untilled ground. ? 1674 TRAHERNE *Poems Felicity* (1910) 86 A Globe of Gold must Barren be, Untill'd & Useless. 1766 *Compl. Farmer* s.v. *Hoeing*, The tilled earth receives an advantage from these dews, which the untilled does not. **1819** SHELLEY *England* 7 A people starved and stabbed in the untilled field. **1874** STUBBS *Const. Hist.* I. ii. 19 The wide forests and untilled plains are common property.

fig. **1592** R. D. *Hypnerotomachia* 95 Fearing to offend hir ..with my rude and vntilled toong. **1651** JER. TAYLOR *Holy Dying* ii. §4 His beastly nature, and desart and untilled manners. **1803** WORDSW. *Poems Nat. Indep.* I. xx. 6 Men unto whom..minds not stinted or untilled are given.

†**un'tilthed,** *ppl. a. Obs. rare.* [UN-¹ 8.] = prec.

1495 GLANVIL. *Barth. De P.R.* XIV. xlviii. F i b/2 That londe þat is tilthyd hyghte Ager and þat londe that is vntylthyd [*Bodl. MS.* vntilied] highte Rus.

†**un'tilward,** *prep. Obs.*⁻¹ [f. UNTIL *prep.* + -WARD. Cf. TILWARD.] Toward.

a **1300** *Cursor M.* 15739 Iesus went him forþerward.. Vntilward a littel yard O cedron ouer þe strand.

un'timbered, *ppl. a.*¹ [UN-¹ 8.]

1. Not furnished with timbers; frail.

1606 SHAKS. *Tr. & Cr.* I. iii. 43 Where's then the sawcy Boate, Whose weake vntimber'd sides but euen now Coriual'd Greatnesse? **1814** SIR R. WILSON *Priv. Diary* (1861) II. 371 The vessel of state is yet too weak and untimbered to buffet the waves.

2. Unprovided with timber; not wooded.

1808 PIKE *SourcesIssiss.* II. App. (1810) 8 The vast tract of untimbered country..between the..Missouri, Mississippi, and the western Ocean. **1828–32** WEBSTER s.v., Untimbered land.

un'timbered, *ppl. a.*² [UN-² 4, 8.] Stripped of timber; deforested.

1618 BRETON *Court. & Countryman* A 4 b, Your state is weakened and your Land wasted, your Woods vntimberd, your Pastures vnstored.

†**un'time,** *sb. Obs.* [OE. *untíma* (UN-¹ 12, 4 b), = ON. and Icel. *útími, ótími* (MSw., Norw. dial. *otime*).]

1. *in* (earlier *on*) *untime*, at an unsuitable, improper, or wrong time. Also in pl.

Cf. ON. *í útíma*, MSw. *i otima, i otimom*, in same sense.

c **897** K. ÆLFRED *Gregory's Past. C.* xxi. 153 Swa se læce, ðonne he on untiman lacnað wunde, hio wyrmseð & rotað. *c* **1000** ÆLFRIC *Saints' Lives* xii. 76 Ælc þæra manna þe yt oððe drincð on untiman on þam halȝan lenctene. *c* **1200** *Trin. Coll. Hom.* 207 He habbe ofte agilt on golliche dedes, on untime oðer on unluuede stede. *a* **1225** *Ancr. R.* 344 Of vres misseide wiðuten ȝeme of heorte oðer in untime. **1303** R. BRUNNE *Handl. Synne* 2962 3yf þou þys foly haunte..Yn vntyme,..For soþe þou synnest þer dedly. *c* **1386** CHAUCER *Pars. P.* ¶1051 A man shal nat ete in vntyme, ne sitte the lenger at his table to ete for he fasteth. *c* **1440** *Jacob's Well* 105 To pleyin at þe tablys,..& at swyche oþere vayn pleyis, in vntyme & out of mesure. **1486** *Bk. St. Albans, Hawking* c vii b, A lombe that was borne in vntime. *a* **1500** in *Ratis Raving*, etc. 18 Oft fore thocht of his riches he walkis in wntymis.

b. *untimes* (gen. sing.), untimely, untimeous.

a **1300** *Cursor M.* 27799 O suernes cums..Vntimes spech or to be still. *c* **1470** HENRY *Wallace* IX. 1630 This hour.. thow mycht haiff beyn away; Wntymys thow art, for it is scantly day.

2. a. A bad time, inclement season. (OE. only.)

a **1023** WULFSTAN *Hom.* 297 Ic asende ofer eower land ælcne untiman, þæt bið eȝeslice great haȝol..and unasecgendlice þunras. *c* **1130** *O.E. Chron.* an. 1124, Ðes ilces ȝeares wæron fæla untime on Englelande, on corne & on ealle westme.

b. An unsuitable time for action.

14.. *Northern Passion* (MS. I) 601 Thys is vn tyme of þe nyghte, In thys tharkenesse to preue ȝoure myghte.

†**un'time,** *a. Obs.* [OE. *untíme* (UN- 4 b).] Untimely; ill-timed.

c **1000** ÆLFRIC *Saints' Lives* xii. 74 Se dysiȝa dranc butan bletsunge..He his feorh forlet and ȝebohte swa ðone untiman drenc. *c* **1200** *Trin. Coll. Hom.* 13 Continencia: ..Ðat feorðe is, þat man þe spuse haueð, his golliche deden wið-teo, swo hit be untime. **1338** R. BRUNNE *Chron.* (1810) 227 Whan he com to lond Tiþing com him vntime, Sir Lowys dede he fond. **1414** *26 Polit. Poems* 56 Slouþe vn-tyme eft mon swete When it is hot, and gloweþ as glede.

†**un'timeable,** *a. Obs.*⁻⁰ [UN-¹ 7 b.] Untimely.

1570 LEVINS *Manip.* 4 Vntymeable, *intempestiuus.*

un'timed, *ppl. a.* (UN-¹ 8.)

[**1775** ASH, *Untimed*, not timed, not regulated as to time.] **1888** MEREDITH *Poems* (1898) II. 168 With thee, O fount of the Untimed! to lead.

†**un'timeless,** *a. Obs.* [UN-¹ 5 a.] Untimely.

1602 CHETTLE *Hoffman* v. (1631) I 2, In memory of his vntimelesse fall.

un'timeliness. [f. next.] The quality of being untimely.

1580 HOLLYBAND *Treas. Fr. Tong, Importunité*, vntimelinesse. **1656** JER. TAYLOR *Let. to Bp. Rochester* 87 The solemnities..and untimeliness of temporal death. **1670** G. H. *Hist. Cardinals* II. II. 169 Had not the untimeliness of his death prevented it. **1846** TRENCH *Mirac.* xxxi. 438 Putting out of sight the untimeliness of even seeking fruit, and of that pretence of fruit. **1850** L. HUNT *Autobiog.* II. xi. 54 The latter calamity, by a most unfortunate climax of untimeliness, took place a little before his enemy's reverses.

un'timely, *a.* [UN-¹ 7. Cf. MDa. *utimelig* of weather, etc.]

1. Coming before the proper or natural time; premature: **a.** Of fruit. Also, not fully or properly ripened; immature.

1535 COVERDALE *Isaiah* xxviii. 4 It shal happen vnto him, as to an vntymely frute before the haruest come. **1561** DAUS tr. *Bullinger on Apoc.* 209 That yᵉ vntimely figges fal downe in great plentie. **1568** BIBLE (Bishops') *Rev.* vi. 13 Euen as a figge tree casteth her vntimely figges. **1644** MILTON *Educ.* 2 These are not matters to be wrung from poor striplings, like..the plucking of untimely fruit. **1825** A. L. BARBAULD '*Praise to God*' vi, Should the fig-tree's blasted shoot Drop her green untimely fruit.

b. Of birth(s).

1538 ELYOT, *Abortus*, an vntymely byrthe. **1634** T. JOHNSON tr. *Parey's Chirurg. Wks.* XXIV. XXX. 921 The causes of abortion or untimely birth, whereof the child is called an abortive, are many. **1710** BERKELEY *Princ. Hum. Knowl.* §151 Monsters, untimely births, fruits blasted in the blossom. **1755** JOHNSON, *Abortment*, an untimely birth.

c. Of death, fate, etc.

1548 ELYOT, *Praematura mors*, vntymely death. **1596** DRAYTON *Leg. Matilda* 648 Some say, the King repentant for this Deed,..Offered His Teares on my vntimely Graue. **1599** B. JONSON *Cynthia's Rev.* I. i, Th' untimely fate of that too beauteous boy. **1651** HOBBES *Leviath.* II. xxix. 167 The bodies of children, gotten by diseased parents, are subject.. to untimely death. **1709** ADDISON *Tatler* No. 154 ¶5 Souls of Infants..snatched away by untimely Ends. **1776** GIBBON *Decl. & F.* xii. I. 322 A life of pleasure or virtue,..of indolence or glory, alike led to an untimely grave. **1819** SCOTT *Ivanhoe* xlii, Their guide pointed with solemn air to the untimely bier of Athelstane. **1847** PRESCOTT *Peru* I. 452 Heaven..bringing them all to an untimely and miserable end.

d. In other contexts.

1565 COOPER *Thesaurus* s.v. *Praecox*, Vntimely laughter & that happeneth very soone, as before the childe is fortie dayes olde. *c* **1586** C'TESS PEMBROKE *Ps.* LVIII. iv, O let their brood..of springing thornes Be by untimely rooting over-throwne. **1634** SIR T. HERBERT *Trav.* 157 Few of them attending patiently the death of their Predecessours, but by impious meanes labour their vntimely establishment. **1746** BERKELEY *Sec. Let. Tar-water* §9 Unhappy drinkers.. bringing on the untimely symptoms of old age.

e. Perishing before due time. *rare*⁻¹.

1605 SYLVESTER *Du Bartas* II. iii. *Law* 667 Som, thrill'd with..shafts, through hundred holes Shall ghastly gasp-out our untimely soules.

2. Unseasonable (in respect of the time of year).

a. Of frost, blight, etc.

1576 GASCOIGNE *Steele Gl.* 455 So those imps..Are.. nipt, with such untimely frosts. **1591** SPENSER *Daphn.* 238 O that so faire a flower so soone should fade, And through vntimely tempest fall away. **1730** THOMSON *Spring* 115 If brush'd from Russian wilds a cutting gale Rise not, and.. breathe Untimely frost. **1751** W. WHITEHEAD *Hymn to Nymph* 46 Life's latter fruits..at last fall off Shook by no boist'rous, or untimely blasts. **1797** GODWIN *Enquirer* I. v. 35 [It] may..suffer an untimely blight. **1847** LONGF. *Ev.* I. ii. 98 The harvests in England By untimely rains or untimelier heat have been blighted. **1853** C. BRONTE *Villette* xxxii, I have read of those who sowed in tears, and whose harvest..perished by untimely blight.

b. In other contexts.

1593 DRAYTON *Shepherd's Garl.* iv. 33 O dismall day,..O stormy winter,..O most vntimely and eclipsed morrow. **1627** ABP. ABBOT in Rushw. *Hist. Coll.* (1659) I. 448 It is an unseasonable time to brew now, and as untimely to cut Wood. **1712** *Spect.* No. 404 ¶3 By the Assistance of Art and an hot Bed, we may possibly extort an unwilling Plant, or an untimely Sallad. **1879** STEVENSON *Trav. Cevennes* 40 They were cutting aftermath,..which gave the neighbourhood.. an untimely smell of hay.

3. Unseasonable, ill-timed, inopportune.

1581 J. FIELDE (*title*), A Caveat for Parsons Hovvlet, concerning his vntimely flighte, and scriching in the cleare day lighte of the Gospell. **1590** SPENSER *F.Q.* II. x. 68 So vntimely breach The Prince him selfe halfe seemeth to offend. **1607–12** BACON *Ess., Of Empire* (Arb.) 298 The vnequall and vntimely interchaunge of pressing power. **1617** WOODALL *Surg. Mate* (1639) 3 Many dangers attending the unskilfull or untimely use thereof. **1665** BOYLE *Occas. Refl.*, etc. (1848) 68 Men's overeager and untimely pursuits of several desirable things. **1756** C. LUCAS *Ess. Waters* III. 240 [It is] wise and just in general; but often..untimely; that is, too late. **1796** MME. D'ARBLAY *Camilla* II. 370 [She] felt so much hurt by this untimely sight, that..she bent her eyes another way. **1830** PRAED *Poems* (1865) I. 234 All untimely question Ruffles the temper. **1867** FREEMAN *Norm. Conq.* I. v. 328 The cause of all this untimely activity.

b. Of hours: Unusually late (or early).

1827 SCOTT *Highl. Widow* v. ad fin., There are many who are still unwilling, at untimely hours, to pass the oak-tree.

un'timely, *adv.* [UN-¹ 11. Cf. MSw. *otimelika* in sense 1.]

1. At an unsuitable or improper time; unseasonably, inopportunely.

Not in common use before the end of the 16th cent.

c **1200** *Trin. Coll. Hom.* 11 Swilche oðre [sins]..alse ben oueretes and untimeliche eten alehuse. **1382** WYCLIF *Ps.* civ. 28 He sente dercnessis, and made derc; and vntymely he fullfilde not [L. *non exacerbavit*] his woordis.

1596 SPENSER *F.Q.* v. v. 29 Now is the time, that I vntimely must Thereof make tryall, in my greatest need. **1596** *Edward III*, III. i. 184 Thus my tale is donne: We haue vntimly lost, and they haue woone. **1618** ROWLANDS *Night Raven* (1620) D 2 b, I behold abuses..By such as doe vntimely haunt the street. **1667** KATH. PHILIPS *Poems* 111 He only dies untimely who dies late. **1702** ROWE *Tamerl.* III. ii, If I not press untimely on his leisure, You would [etc.]. **1743** W. WHITEHEAD *Ann Boleyn to Hen. VIII*, 74, I fell untimely, and lament my Fall. **1828** SCOTT *F.M. Perth* xxii, To avenge the deed expelling Thee untimely from thy dwelling. **1882–3** *Schaff's Encycl. Relig. Knowl.* II. 851/2 The moment for this controversy was very untimely chosen by the Pope.

2. Before the proper or natural time; prematurely.

a **1586** SIDNEY *Arcadia* III. x, O sweet youth,..how untimely subject it is to devotion? **1611** GUILLIM *Heraldry* II. iv. 46, I haue inserted the same (although vntimely) in this place, which otherwise I would haue reserued to some other. **1660** *Trial Regic.* 36 When that Blessed King was untimely taken away. **1721** POPE *Ep. to Earl Oxford* 2 'Till Death untimely stopp'd his tuneful tongue. **1766** *Museum Rust.* VI. 74 Trees..untimely taken off, before they arrive at any valuable maturity. **1833** HT. MARTINEAU *Loom & Lugger* I. ii. 17 Legs bowed from having been made untimely to bear the weight of the swollen body. **1857** PUSEY *Real Presence* i. 64 Melanchthon..prolonged the conference, only lest he should seem to break it off untimely.

un'timeous, *a.* Chiefly *Sc.* Forms: 5 wn-, 6–7 vn-, untymous, 6 untimus, 7–8 untimous; 6 untymeus, 7 -tymeous, 9 -timeous. [Alteration of earlier *untimes, untymys* (see UNTIME *sb.* 1 b), by assimilation to adjs. in -(E)OUS. For this change of ending cf. UNDEEMOUS *a.*]

1. Unseasonable; = UNTIMELY *a.* 2, 3.

a **1500** *Ratis Raving* 95 Tak not delyt in morne slepinge, Wntymous eting na drynkynge. *a* **1584** MONTGOMERIE *Cherrie & Slae* 397 Vntymous spurring spillis the steid. **1586** *Reg. Privy Council Scot.* IV. 74 The inoportune and untymous sutes of divers personis. **1640** R. BAILLIE *Canterb. Self-convict.* Pref., We could not but leave..to you..the legacie of an untimous repentance. **1670** RAY *Prov.* 280 Of untymous persons:..He is as welcome as snaw in harvest. **1823** SCOTT *Quentin D.* xvi, It required all the authority.. which Quentin could exert over him, to restrain his irreverent and untimeous jocularity. **1883** *Contemp. Rev.* Oct. 612 You do not find yourself oppressed by untimeous volunteered franknesses.

b. Of times (esp. of the night).

1728 RAMSAY *Monk & Miller's Wife* 60 Wha's that gi'es fowk a fright At sic untimous time of night? **1836** M. SCOTT *Cruise Midge* I. 349 Wha makes such an indecent uproar.. at such an untimeous season? **1837** BARHAM *Ingol. Leg.* Ser. I. *Grey Dolphin*, To inquire who sought admittance at that untimeous hour. **1894** CROCKETT *Raiders* iii, It was this which had raised me at such untimeous hours.

2. Premature; = UNTIMELY *a.* 1.

1536 BELLENDEN *Cron. Scot.* (1821) II. 408 He..was prevenit be untimus deith. **1603** JAS. I. Βασιλ. δῶρον To Rdr. A 8 b, So as this their great concurrence in curiositie..hath inforced the vn-timous divulgating of this booke. **1634** CANNE *Necess. Separ.* 88 If his death was vntimous, it was rather for his secret intentions crossing his fathers courses. **1646** R. BAILLIE *Anabaptism* (1647) 66 The change..ere long..brought upon him an untimous and cruell death. **1828** MOIR *Mansie Wauch* xiii, I believe he came to some untimeous end.

un'timeously, *adv.* Chiefly *Sc.* [UN-¹ 11, or f. prec.] = UNTIMELY *adv.*

1513 DOUGLAS *Æneid* VI. vii. 11 Ȝoung babbeis..From the sweit lyf twynnit vntymusly. **1533** BELLENDEN *Livy* II. xv. (S.T.S.) I. 188 The romanis..had bene vntymuslie invadit be þe wolchis. *a* **1578** LINDESAY (Pitscottie) *Chron. Scot.* (S.T.S.) I. 56 Scho pairtit wntymouslie witht ane deid bairne. **1640** BAILLIE *Lett.* (1841) I. 262 The cold[ness] of the good old Generall..did shortlie cast water on this spunk, beginning most untymouslie to reek. *a* **1670** SPALDING *Troub. Chas. I* (1851) II. 273 This commvnion wes thocht to be vntymouslie givin heir. **1821** SCOTT *Kenilw.* xv, It must be some perilous cause puts her Grace in motion thus untimeously. **1851** BORROW *Lavengro* lxxi, My husband..came to his death untimeously. **1894** HALL CAINE *Manxman* I. x, Dreaming that the poor lad has come to his end untimeously.

†**un'timing,** *ppl. a. Obs.*⁻¹ [UN-¹ 10.] Careless, regardless.

c **1350** *Commem. Dead* 20 in Horstm. *Altengl. Leg.* (1881) 146 If þe preste, þat schryues þe, Vn-timand or so rekles be Þat he gif þe noght penance right [etc.].

un'timorous, *a.* (UN-¹ 7.)

a **1548** HALL *Chron., Edw. IV*, 196 b, A man of suche haute corage,..and vntimerous audacite,..as fewe or none was sene in hys tyme. *Ibid., Rich. III*, 56 b, Let us..set on our enemies like vntimerous Tigers.

un'tinct, *ppl. a.* [UN-¹ 8 b.] Untinged.

1642 H. MORE *Song of Soul* II. 68 A reall infinite matter, distinct And yet proceeding from the Deitie, Although with different form as then untinct.

un'tinctured, *ppl. a.* [UN-¹ 8.]

1. *fig.* Untinged, uncoloured, unaffected. Const. *by* or *with*.

1760–2 GOLDSM. *Cit. W.* lxvi, Simple gratitude, untinctured with love. **1769** E. BANCROFT *Guiana* 329 They are not untinctured with vanity. **1774** GOLDSM. *Nat. Hist.* II. 397 [Zebras] caught sufficiently young, so as to be untinctured by their original state of wildness. **1801** *Lusignan* I. 113 A degree of awe..not untinctured with [fear]. **1866** *Q. Rev.* Apr. 327 Oracles of the common law, but untinctured by scholarship. **1874** H. ROGERS *Orig. Bible* i. 43 Virtue..untinctured with..austerity.

2. In literal use; *spec.* in *Her.*

1880 WARREN *Book-plates* ii. 10 The arms are..at that period untinctured.

un'tine, *v. Obs.* exc. *dial.* Forms: 1 untynan, 2 untinen, 3 untunen (ontune), 5 vntynde, 9 *dial.* untine. [OE. *untýnan* (var. of *an-, ontýnan*), f. *un-* UN-² 3 + *týnan* TINE *v.*¹, = OHG. *antzûnen, inzûnen* (G. *entzäunen*).]

1. *trans.* To open.

c **950** *Lindisf. Gosp.* Matt. ii. 11 [Hia] untyndon striona hiora. *Ibid.* ix. 30 Untynde weron ego hiora. *c* **1000** ÆLFRIC *Gen.* xli. 56 Iosep untynde ealle þa bernu. *c* **1200** *Trin. Coll. Hom.* 115 Openeð ȝiure gaten, and ech gate untineð ȝiu seluen to-ȝenes þe king of blisse. *c* **1205** LAY. 9781 Amarȝen þa hit dæi wes duren heo vntunden. *Ibid.* 18949 Nis nan cniht..þe..þe ȝeten mihten un-tunen [*v.r.* ontune]. **1888**

DONALDSON *Takin' th' New Year in* 8 (E.D.D.), Hoo told me hoo'd untined th' door.

2. To separate, sever.

c **1495** *Epitaffe*, etc. in *Skelton's Wks.* (1843) II. 392 Howe durst thou [*sc.* Death] his flessh and spyryte vntynde?

† **un'ting**, *v. Obs.* [UN-² 4 b. Cf. TINGER² and s.w. dial. *ting* to bind, fasten together.] *trans.* To loosen (a cart-body) so as to prepare it for tipping. So † **un'tinger**. *Obs. rare.*

1587 FLEMING *Contn. Holinshed* III. 1544/2 There attended..eight men called vntingers, to loose and vndoo the tackle of euerie court immediatlie before the vnloding or sheluing thereof [at Dover harbour]. *Ibid.* 1545/1 When the first court came nigh to the place where he should vnlode, one vntinged it, and the driuer proceeded with his court.. into the ouze or water.

un'tinged (-'tɪndʒd), *ppl. a.* (UN-¹ 8.)

1664 BOYLE *Exp. Hist. Colours* III. 191 In a Darken'd Room..where it may appear what Beams [of light] are Unting'd. **1732** SWIFT *Let. to Gay* 10 July, Pope has the same defect..: neither is my lord Bolingbroke untinged with it. **1744** W. WHITEHEAD *Atys & Adrastus* 283 The foaming Boar['s]..horny Sides repel Unting'd the plumy Shaft, and blunted Steel. ? *a* **1813** LAMB *Christ's Hosp.* Wks. 1908 I. 180 This religious character in him is not always untinged with superstition. **1817** COLERIDGE *Lay Serm.* p. xxiii, Not a ray of light could enter, untinged by the medium through which it passed. **1882** FLOYER *Unexpl. Baluchistan* 61 Copper gives green, and the untinged limestone snowy white.

un'tinned, *ppl. a.* (UN-¹ 8.)

[**1775** ASH.] **1825** J. NICHOLSON *Operat. Mechanic* 400 A little sea-water is..put into..an untinned copper kettle. **1859** F. S. COOPER *Ironmongers' Catal.* 88 Saucepans.. Tinned,..Untinned. **1898** *Daily News* 6 Sept. 4/6 Frequent detections of unsound food, tinned and untinned.

un'tint, *ppl. a. Sc.* [UN-¹ 8 b.] Not lost.

1513 DOUGLAS *Æneid* I. x. 43 The auld Troiane geir..fra the storme of see is left ontynt.

un'tinted, *ppl. a.* (UN-¹ 8.)

1849 C. BRONTË *Shirley* xxix, There she is, a lily of the valley, untinted, needing no tint. **1866** R. M. FERGUSON *Electr.* 29 The space included between those two lines..is left untinted.

un'tipped, *ppl. a.*¹ [UN-¹ 8 + TIPPED *ppl. a.*¹]

1. Not furnished with a tip.

1679 *Lond. Gaz.* No. 1373/4 A Case of seven Tip Razors, ..with eight other Razors, &c. some Tipt, some Untipt. **1775** ASH, *Untipped*,..*Untipt.*

2. *spec.* Of a cigarette: without a filter tip. Also *absol.*

1968 *Times* 15 Nov. 8/8 More men than women smoke heavily, inhale deeply and prefer untipped cigarettes. **1969** J. ELLIOT *Duel* I. iii. 67 'Smoke?'.. We both took untipped and she lit them. **1973** H. GILBERT *Hotels with Empty Rooms* xiii. 111 The smoke from a hundred untipped Gitanes lay low in the air.

un'tipped, *ppl. a.*² [UN-¹ 8 + TIP *v.*⁴] Not presented with a gratuity.

1860 W. W. READE *Liberty Hall* I. xi. 203 The untipped ostler scowling from the yard.

untira'bility. (UN-¹ 12. Cf. next.)

1855 *Household Words* X. 31/2 Hence..a rapidity of hæmatosis, which explains the untirability of the wings of birds.

un'tirable, *a.* Also **untireable.** (UN-¹ 7 b.)

1607 TOPSELL *Four-f. Beasts* 31 They are..of hardest hoofe, a leane body, but of a generous and vntierable stomack. **1607** SHAKS. *Timon* I. i. 11 A most incomparable man, breath'd as it were, To an vntyreable and continuate goodnesse. **1836** T. ALLSOP *Lett. & Recol. Coleridge* II. 226 The sympathy and untireable kindness of my revered friend. **1846** MRS. GORE *Eng. Char.* (1852) 38 The Chaperon has, constitutionally, an untirable voracity. **1875** M. COLLINS *Sweet & Twenty* II. xix, It might have gone on for ever, if everyone had been as untireable as Charlie Hawker.

† **un'tire**, *v.*¹ *Obs.* [UN-² 4.] *trans.* To undress. Also *refl.* and *fig.*

1597 BEARD *Theatre God's Judgements* 342 Who being suspected, was in the presence of many vntired, and found to be a man. **1613** PURCHAS *Pilgrimage* (1614) 536 Then doe they vntire themselues, and..eate the cheere in the Platters. **1651** *Life Diazius* in Fuller *Abel Rediv.* 143 Diazius in his youthfull dayes had cloath'd His heart with Popery... When he was inspir'd By Heaven, he searcht for truth, and soon untyr'd Himselfe.

un'tire, *v.*² [UN-² 3.] *trans.* To free from being tired; to rest.

In quot. 1845 after Sp. *descansar* (as in quot. 1853).

1677 *Phil. Trans.* XII. 919 A way of untiring a Soldier after a long march, *viz.* by making a Decoction of Mugwort, and washing the feet therewith. **1845** FORD *Handbk. Spain* I. 162 Let [him] remember..to invite his friend to walk in and untire himself. **1853** G. J. CAYLEY *Las Alforjas* I. 170 He..pressed us to bait our horses and *descansar* (untire) ourselves at his farm.

un'tired, *ppl. a.* [UN-¹ 8.] Not tired or exhausted; unwearied.

1594 SHAKS. *Rich. III*, IV. ii. 44 Hath he so long held out with me, vntyr'd, And stops he now for breath? **1616** W. BROWNE *Brit. Past.* II. i. 10 The great effects of vntirde industry. *a* **1660** *Contemp. Hist. Irel.* (Ir. Archæol. Soc.) II. 21 Greate is the preparation, by thundering proclamations and untyred poastes to and fro. **1753** HANWAY *Trav.* III. xxxviii. (1762) I. 175 With..untired attention he applied himself to business. **1799** WORDSW. *Influence Nat. Obj.* 32 Exulting like an untired horse That cares not for his home. **1839** T. MITCHELL *Frogs of Aristoph.* 651 *note*, The canary, with its untired throat and labyrinth of sounds. **1889** A. LANG *Lett. Lit.* iii. (ed. 2) 37 The poor have..in him an untired advocate and friend.

b. Const. *by*, *with*, and †*of*.

1600 FAIRFAX *Tasso* I. lii, Vntear'd in fight, vntir'd with hurt or wound. **1624** HEYWOOD *Gunaik.* v. 226 Most patient of labour, untyred with travell. **1698** ATTERBURY *Serm.* (1734) IV. 235 When the Mind is fresh and vigorous, untired with the Business of the Day. **1802** H. MARTIN *Helen of Glenross* III. 139, I am still untired of sight or visits. **1813** BYRON *Corsair* I. xii, Unmoved by absence,..And yet ..untired by time. **1839** ARNOLD in Stanley *Life* (1844) II. 175, I was so perfectly untired by my past work.

Hence **un'tiredly** *adv.*

1855 FABER *Growth in Holiness* xxvi. 481 Fervour..thus immediately and untiredly..works at present duties.

un'tiring, *ppl. a.* (UN-¹ 10.)

Common from *c* 1850.

1822 B. W. PROCTER *Girl of Provence* xxiv, The untiring seasons bring, for aye, To night rich slumber, and fresh life to day. **1859** JEPHSON *Brittany* xix. 312 The passengers were chiefly English, those untiring travellers. **1871** WHYTE MELVILLE *Sarchedon* I. 20 Yet a few more furlongs of those smooth untiring strides.

Hence **un'tiringly** *adv.*

[**1847** WEBSTER.] **1860** RUSKIN *Unto this Last* iv. §82 No scene is continually and untiringly loved, but one rich by joyful human labour.

un-'Titaned, *a.* [UN-¹ 9.] Sunless.

1635 QUARLES *Embl.* II. i. 3 Thy Torch will burn more clear In night's un-Titan'd Hemisphere.

untithea'bility. (UN-¹ 12. Cf. next.)

1885 A. N. PALMER *Anc. Tenures Marches N. Wales* 28 The untitheability of the common fields of Erbistock.

un'titheable, *a.* (UN-¹ 7 b.)

1775 *Ann. Reg., Chron.* 133/2 This gentleman..filed a bill for..the tythe of lands before held untytheable. **1885** A. N. PALMER *Anc. Tenures Marches N. Wales* 28 The existing untitheable tract of arable and hay land.

un'tithed, *ppl. a.* [UN-¹ 8. Cf. OE. *untéoðod*, and UNTEINDED *ppl. a.*]

1. On which no tithe is levied.

1621 BP. MOUNTAGU *Diatribæ* 540, I will complaine vpon thee vnto the Prytanes, because thou detainest..to thine owne vse, the consecrated inwards..that belong vnto the gods, vntithed. **1801** HELEN M. WILLIAMS *Sk. Fr. Rep.* I. vi. 57 The lavish produce of the earth unfeudalized, and untythed. **1845** MᶜCULLOCH *Taxation* II. iv. 176 It then encourages cultivation as much on the untithed as it discourages it on the tithed lands. **1871** LONGF. *Div. Trag.* II. i. 35 In thy court-yard grows the untithed rue.

2. Not receiving tithes.

1827 POLLOK *Course T.* VIII. 81 Not from him Could be distinguished then the priest untithed.

un'title, *v.* (UN-² 4.)

1824 HOOK *Sayings* II. 48 His Lordship untitled himself with the greatest safety.

un'titled, *ppl. a.*¹ [UN-¹ 8.]

1. Having no title or right (to rule).

1605 SHAKS. *Macb.* IV. iii. 104 O Nation miserable! With an vntitled Tyrant, bloody Sceptred.

2. Unnamed, undesignated.

1612 W. PARKES *Curtaine-Dr.* (1876) 11 When these things were thus vnknowne, and vntitled, a good and happy world was I then.

3. Not distinguished by a title.

1798 S. & HT. LEE *Canterb. T.* II. 425 There, untitled and unknown, may we fix our home. **1825** J. NEAL *Bro. Jonathan* I. 71 What have we to do with the blazonry of an old people any more than..he, the untitled Adam? **1856** EMERSON *Eng. Traits, Aristocr.*, An untitled nobility possess all the power without the inconveniences that belong to rank. **1870** BURTON *Hist. Scot.* lvi. V. 400 They have precedence over the untitled clergy.

absol. **1859** *Habits of Gd. Society* 26 My Lady A——..can scarcely appreciate the wide diffusion of wit and intellegence among the untitled.

un'titled, *ppl. a.*² [UN-² 8. Cf. UNTITLE *v.*] Deprived of the title of.

1596 SPENSER *F.Q.* v. ix. 42 But false Duessa, now vntitled Queene, Was brought to her sad doome.

un'tittering, *ppl. a.* (UN-¹ 10.)

1749 in A. Dobson *Fielding* (1883) 137 Girls of an untittering Disposition.

untittle'tattling, *ppl. a.* (UN-¹ 10.)

1779 H. WALPOLE in Tovey *Gray's Lett.* (1900) II. 92 There is not so untittle-tattling a village as Twickenham in the island.

† **un'tituled**, *ppl. a. Obs.*⁻¹ [UN-¹ 8.] = UNTITLED *ppl. a.*¹ 2.

1610 HEALEY *St. Aug. Citie of God* XVII. xiv. 640 Hee made all the 150, entitling them sometimes with other names,.. and leauing some others vntituled at all.

unto ('ʌntʊ), *prep.* and *conj.* Forms: α. 4– unto (5 untoo), 4–7 vnto (5 *north.* vntew), 5, 6 *Sc.* wnto. β. 5–6, 7 *Sc.*, 9 *dial.* onto (5 onne-to, *Sc.* one-to). [f. on the analogy of UNTIL *prep.*, by substitution of TO *prep.* in place of the northern equivalent *til* TILL *prep.* Cf. the independent OS. *untô.*]

Since the end of the 17th c. less frequent, and employed chiefly in poetry, or in formal, dignified, or archaic style, or after Biblical use. Very rare in standard writers of the 18th c., and hence noted by Johnson as 'now obsolete'.

A. *prep.* (Ordinarily governing a sb. or pron.) In poetry often placed after the sb. or pronoun.

I. Indicating spatial or local relationship.

1. Expressing or denoting motion directed towards and reaching (a place, point, or goal); = TO *prep.* 1.

a **1300** *Cursor M.* 17547 Helias..Was taken up als vnto heuen. *c* **1300** *Havelok* 2399 Cum nu swiþe un-to him. **1338** R. BRUNNE *Chron.* (1810) 104 Vnto þe se side chaced þei Sir Lowys. **1387** TREVISA *Higden* (Rolls) II. 123 And the seete of Welles was chaungede vn to Bathe. *c* **1420** *Anturs of Arth.* (T.) 111 Vn-to þat grysely gaste Sir Gaweayne es gane. *c* **1440** *Alph. Tales* 215 He tuke bread & keste vnto it [*sc.* a swine]. *c* **1475** *Rauf Coilȝear* 5 Thay past vnto Paris. **1526** *Pilgr. Perf.* (W. de W. 1531) 4 Theyr iourney out of Egypte vnto the countre of Jerusalem. *a* **1548** HALL *Chron., Hen. VIII*, 85 He called unto him a seruaunt of the kynges. **1587** HOLINSHED *Chron.* (ed. 2) III. 1187/1 The campe remooued from Linton brigs vnto salt Preston. **1590** SHAKS. *Mids. N.* III. ii. 310, I told him of your stealth vnto this wood. **1633** G. HERBERT *Temple, The Bag* iv, He did repair unto an inne. **1654** H. DUNSTER in Quincy *Hist. Harvard Univ.* (1840) I. 19 The place unto which I go, is unknown to me. **17..** *Jock o' the Side* xiii. in Caw *Poet. Museum*, When they cam the gates unto. **1768** ROSS *Helenore* 83 We came unto a gentle place. **1801** WORDSW. *Prioress' T.* 52 A little scholar..Who day by day unto this school hath gone. **1866** EMERSON *Daemonic & Celest. Love* 48 So shall the lights ye pour amain Go..Through from the empyrean walls Unto the same again. **1887** MORRIS *Odyssey* I. 90 Then speed we..Hermes the Flitter, to go Unto the isle Ogygia.

b. In various fig. uses. (Cf. TO *prep.* 1 b.)

c **1440** *Alph. Tales* 218 With þatt sho come agayn vnto hur selfe, & thankid God. *Ibid.* 448 When he come vnto his spyrittis agayn. **1526** TINDALE *Heb.* vii. 19 By which hope we drawe nye vnto god. **1535** COVERDALE *Psalm* xxiii. 4 Which lifteth not vp his mynde vnto vanite. **1538** STARKEY *England* 21 Though..I dowtyd no thyng of thys mater, that you so ernystely moue me vnto. **1568** GRAFTON *Chron.* II. 263 They put all their goodes vnto the Englishmens pleasures. **1600** HOLLAND *Livy* 1123 In this last speech he came neere unto the LL. of the Senat, and touched them to the quick. **1606** G. WOODCOCK *Hist. Ivstine* v. 27 It was secretly come vnto their eare, that [etc.]. **1639** LD. DIGBY *Lett. conc. Relig.* (1651) iv. 87 It is a farre more evident impossibility, then what you drive unto. **1683** *Pennsylv. Archives* I. 60, I cannot but believe yᵗ you will take my great Wrong..unto your serious consideration. **1801** WORDSW. *Troilus* 63 In that very place My Lady first me took unto her grace. **1838** MRS. BROWNING *The Sleep* i, Of all the thoughts of God that are Borne inward unto souls afar.

c. With ellipsis of verb of motion. (Cf. TO *prep.* 1 c.)

a **1593** MARLOWE & NASHE *Dido* II. i, Let vs vnto our ships,..why stay we here? **1596** SHAKS. *Tam. Shr.* II. i. 316, I will vnto Venice To buy apparell. **1768** ROSS '*To the Begging*' iv, I'll then unto the cobler, An' cause him sole my shoon.

2. In the direction of; directed towards; = TO *prep.* 2.

a **1300** *Cursor M.* 10479 Sco lift hir hend vn-to þe lift, And þus to prai sco gaf a scift. **1338** R. BRUNNE *Chron.* (1810) 217 Unto þe kinges partie Edward turned tite. **1390** GOWER *Conf.* I. 8 Unto him which the heved is The membres buxom scholden bowe. *Ibid.* 45 Whanne I..caste up many a pitous lok Unto the hevene. **1535** COVERDALE *Gen.* xiv. 22, I lift vp my honde vnto the Lorde. *Ibid.* xlix. 8 Thy fathers children shall stoupe vnto the. ? *a* **1600** '*Gentle heardsman*' i. in *Percy Folio* (1868) III. 526 Vnto the towne of Walsingham which is the right and ready way? **1611** [see LIFT *v.* 5]. **1796** BURNS '*When Januar' wind*' iii, I bow'd fu'low unto this maid. **1858** WHITTIER *Cable Hymn* i, Lean down unto the white-lipped sea The voice of God to hear!

fig. **1535** COVERDALE *Prov.* ii. 18 Hir house is enclyned vnto death, and hir pathes vnto hell. —— *Dan.* ix. 3, I turned me vnto God..for to praye. **1826** SCOTT *Woodst.* i, There is no light in England that shall come nigh unto it.

b. At. (Esp. after *look*, †*smell*. Cf. TO *prep.* 2 b.)

a **1300**- [see LOOK *v.* 23]. *a* **1400** *New Test.* (Paues) Acts iii. 4 Peter wiþ Ioon bihelde vnto hym. *c* **1430** *Pol., Rel. & L. Poems* (1903) 180 A semeli man to ben a king, A graciouse face to loken vnto. **1535** COVERDALE *Bel. & Dr.* 18 The kinge loked vnto yᵉ altare. **1579** TOMSON *Calvin's Serm. Tim.* 222/2 Ministers..must marke why this office is given them; ..it is not because a few should be sene vnto [= looked up to]. **1594** HOOKER *Eccl. Pol.* II. v. §7 God made flowers sweet and beautiful, that being seen and smelt unto they might so delight. **1670** J. SMITH *Eng. Improv. Reviv'd* 213 The Root smelled vnto is good for the same purpose. **1848** AIRD *Chr. Bride* II. vii, Majestic men who looked unto the skies.

c. In (a specified course or direction, *lit.* or *fig.*). Cf. TO *prep.* 2 c, e.

a **1300** *Cursor M.* 2117 Þis land lies mast vnto þe south. *Ibid.* 2120 Þe thrid part..lies mast vnto þe west. *c* **1386** CHAUCER *Miller's T.* 386 [To break] an hole an heigh vp on the gable Vnto the gardynward. *c* **1400** *Melayne* 135 He sawe a bryghtenes of a beme Vp vn-to heuenwarde glyde. **1549** COVERDALE, etc. *Erasm. Par. Rom.* Prol. + v, Such a newe herte and lusty corage vnto the lawe warde, canste thou neuer come by.

† d. Indicating a means of access. (OE. *tó* and *intó.*) *Obs.*⁻¹

1535 COVERDALE *2 Kings* iv. 5 She wente, and shut the dore vnto her with hir sonnes.

3. Indicating the limit or dimension of a movement, extension, or continuance in space: As far as; even to; not short of; = TO *prep.* 3.

Occas. correlative to *from* (the remoter of two limits).

a **1300** *Cursor M.* 24346 Quen we na hele moght se on him, Fra hefd vnto þe fote. *a* **1325** *Prose Psalter* cvi. 3 Fram þe rysyng of þe sunne vnto þe goynge adoune. *c* **1330** R. BRUNNE *Chron. Wace* (Rolls) 181 Mayster Wace..rymed [his romance]..vnto þe Cadwaladres. *c* **1400** *Destr. Troy* 95 All the ferlies þat fell vnto the ferre ende. *c* **1470** *Gol. & Gaw.* 1313 All thi braid landis, Or all the renttis fra thyne vnto Ronsiwall. *c* **1500** *Melusine* xxxvii. 297 He..sawe melusyne within the bathe vnto her nauell. **1535** COVERDALE *Exod.* xxxviii. 4 A brasen gredyron of net worke rounde aboute, from vnder vp vnto the myddest of the altare.

1548–9 (Mar.) *Bk. Com. Prayer, Communion of Sick*, With the firste parte of the exhortacion and all other thynges unto the Psalme. **1597** Lyly *Wom. in Moon* I. i, The rundle of this Massiue earth, From vtmost face vnto the Centers point. **1768** Ross *Helenore* 31 Ye see her rigs run just unto our ain. *a* **1774** Goldsm. *Hist. Greece* I. 223 A strong haven, with walls reaching unto the city. **1801** Wordsw. *Un-to Loverd. T.* 198 My throat is cut unto the bone. **1812** Cary *Dante, Parad.* xxii. 149 This petty area..from the havens stretched unto the hills.

b. In figurative uses.

1508 Dunbar *Ballad Ld. Stewart* 5 Onto the sterris vpheyt is thyne honour. **1535** Coverdale *Ps.* xxxv. 5 Thy mercy (O Lorde) reacheth vnto the heauen. **1591** Drayton *Harmonie of Church, Song Jonah* 2 My voice I did extend Unto the Lord. **1609** Bp. Hall *David's Psalms Metaphr.* viii, Thou hast..stretcht his raigne Vnto the heards, and beasts vntame.

4. Upon (and in contact with); on, against; = to *prep.* 5a.

a **1300** *E.E. Psalter* cxvii. 26 Settes miri daie in thickenesse, Vnto horn þat of weued esse. *c* **1386** Chaucer *Wife's T.* 973 She leyde hir mouth vn-to the water doun. *c* **1440** *Alph. Tales* 368 Þe ymage..fell down vnto þe hard erth. **1480** *Cov. Leet Bk.* 447 The pepull..carryen their Donge,..& leyen hit vnto the walles & yate. **1535** Coverdale *Exod.* xxii. 8 He hath not put his hande vnto his neghbours good. **1550** T. Lever *Serm.* (Arb.) 135 Beware therefore that ye staye not your selfe vnto a bryttell staffe. **1559** Q. Eliz. in Strype *Ann. Ref.* (1709) I. ii. App. x. 440 We have but a weake staff to leane unto. **1602** Marston *Antonio's Rev.* iv. iii, Thou bur, that only sticks Unto the nappe of greatnesse. **1607, 1624** [see lean *v.* 2, 2c]. **1768** Ross *Helenore* 21 She..lean'd her head unto the kindly tree. **1836** R. Allan *Evening Hours* 98 The hope thus to press thee Unto my fond bosom.

fig. c **1386**, *c* **1400** [see stand v. 76f, g].

b. In contiguity or proximity to; in front of; by, close beside. Cf. to *prep.* 5b.

1590 Shaks. *Com. Err.* i. ii. 91 Wilt thou flout me thus vnto my face? **1606** —— *Ant. & Cl.* iv. xiv. 29 What thou would'st do Is done vnto thy hand. **1677** W. Hughes *Man of Sin* iii. iii. 79 Which..plainly gives them the lye unto their Teeths.

5. Expressing relative location (esp. with *nigh* or *near*).

1526 Tindale *Mark* v. 21 Iesus..was nye vnto the see. **1558** *Child. Marr.* 145 Nether in his house.., nether within iiij myle compas vnto the same Citie. **1600** J. Pory tr. *Leo's Africa* iii. 171 Neere vnto the said plaine are diuers woods. *Ibid.* v. 262 The citie of Tunis..hath no mountaines nigh vnto it. **1768** Ross *Helenore* 89 They began to speer Gin they were unto Flaviana near.

fig. **1526** Tindale *Heb.* vi. 8 But that grounde..is reproved, and is nye vnto cursynge. **1539** Bible (Great) *Lev.* xxv. 49 Any that is nye of kynne vnto hym. **1548** Udall, etc. *Erasm. Par. Matt.* xii. 75 b, He is moste nere and moste dere vnto me. **1785** Burns *Letter to J. Goudie*, Auld Orthodoxy [is]..Nigh unto death. **1870** Morris *Earthly Par.* III. 390 Death had need be near Unto such men.

II. Indicating a temporal relationship.

6. Until (a final limit in time); till as late as; = to *prep.* 6 and 6c.

a **1300** *Cursor M.* 24739 All mi liue vn-to min end, In hir loueword þof i moght spend. *a* **1325** *Prose Psalter* lxxxix. 15 Lord, be þou turned vnto nov. *Ibid.* cxii. 2 Be þe name of our Lord blisced, nou of þis & vnto heuen. **1382** Wyclif *Ps.* cxii. 2 Be the name of the Lord blissid; fro this now and vnto the world. *c* **1386** Chaucer *Man of Law's T.* 765 Kepeth this child..vn to myn hoom comynge. *c* **1440** *Alph. Tales* 439 Þer devotelie he servid our Ladie vnto his lyfis ende. **1480** *Cov. Leet Bk.* 436 Certain Common pastures belongyng to the seid Cite vnto nowe. **1484** Caxton *Fables of Alfonce* ix, The wulf..hyd hym self nyghe them vnto the nyght. **1523** Ld. Berners *Froiss.* I. lxvii. 89 The bysshoppe..toke hym as his lorde, vnto suche season as somme other shulde come. **1539** Bible (Great) *Rom.* v. 13 For euen vnto the lawe was synne in the worlde. **1582** N. T. (Rhem.) *Luke* xvi. 16 The law and the prophets, vnto Iohn. **1613** *Acts Privy Council* 4 Yow shall..keepe the same unto suche tyme as.. publicacion shall [be] moved thereof. **1691** in E. Walker *Epictetus* (1692) A 1 b, All good and perfect Gifts..Which Mortals have from th' Womb unto the Tomb. **1801** Wordsw. *Troilus* 56 She..there so graciously did me behold, That hers unto the death my heart I hold. **1896** 'Ian Maclaren' *K. Carnegie* 356 Doctor Manley..praises Kate unto this day.

7. After a negative, = until *prep.* 5b.

c **1400** *Brut* 322 The clergye..wolde not graunte hit vnto Ester next comyng. **1450–80** tr. *Secreta Secret.* lviii. 34 Shewe not thi thought vnto tyme thou performe thi wille. **1485** Caxton *Paris & V.* (1868) 11 Never I shal have playsyr ne Ioye unto the tyme that I knowe. **1515** in Leadam *Star Chamber Cases* (Selden) II. 88 He neuer vnto this last yere knew eny man occupye a nothur mans Craft without Interrupcion. **1559** W. Cunningham *Cosmogr. Glasse* 105 Before the sonne be vnder th' Earth, which is not vnto .6. of the clocke.

III. Expressing the relation of aim, design, destination, result, consequent status or condition.

8. In order to begin, perform, accomplish, or obtain. Cf. to *prep.* 8b.

a **1300** *E.E. Psalter* ciii. 24 Oute sal man ga vnto his werke. **1303** R. Brunne *Handl. Synne* 9098 Vn-to þe karolle asswyþe he ȝede. *c* **1400** *Destr. Troy* 10734 The sun in his sercle set vnto rest. *c* **1440** *Alph. Tales* 424 In þe mornyng he went vnto his prayers. **1470–85** Malory *Arthur* vii. xxvi. 271 Many bold knyghtes wente vnto mete. **1587** Turberv. *Trag. T.* (1837) 134 The Lady, somewhat hungrie, fell unto the Cates. **1596** R. L[inche] *Diella*, etc. D 7, They all sat downe vnto a soone-made feast. **1768** Ross *Helenore* 68 Unto their supper they right yaply fa'.

b. With a view to; for the purpose of; for. Cf. to *prep.* 8.

c **1440** *Pallad. on Husb.* iii. 1166 This wyne al medicine is take vnto. **1486** *Naval Acc. Hen. VII* (1896) 10 Diuers cabilles of hym bought vnto the Kyngs use. **1487** in Nichols *Illustr. Manners & Exp.* (1797) 83 For hokes and hengles unto the skolehouse dore,..and for nailes to the same dore, $4\frac{1}{2}$*d.* **1539** Cranmer *Let.* in *Misc. Writ.* (Parker Soc.) 396, I pray you that the same may be delivered unto the said Whitchurche unto printing. **1549** Thomas *Hist. Italye* (1561) 74 b, Vpon a very smal warnyng they [*sc.* galleys] may be furnyshed out vnto the sea. **1582** N. T. (Rhem.) *Mark* i. 4 Preaching the baptisme of penance vnto remission of sinnes. **1592** Warner *Alb. Eng.* viii. xlii. 158 Our Cattell vnto stronger draughts we..would vnteame.

9. Indicating a condition, state, or situation, conferred or imposed upon a person. Cf. to *prep.* 9.

a **1300** *E.E. Psalter* xviii. 16 Mi helper ai he isse, And mi bier vn-to blisse. *c* **1400** *Destr. Troy* 1418 Wemyn & wale children vnto wo put. *a* **1425** tr. *Arderne's Treat. Fistula* 34 Vnto a loueable ende wiþ goddes help aboute half a ȝere I cured hym. *c* **1440** *York Myst.* xxxvii. 319 Vnto my dome I schall þame drawe, And juge þame worse þanne any Jewe. *c* **1529** Latimer in Foxe *A. & M.* (1563) 1298/2 Which vn-thriftye state that wee be borne vnto. **1548** in Starkey *England* (1878) p. xciii, If vnto Office they after bee electe. **1591** Drayton *Prayer of Mardocheus* iv, To destroy and bring us unto nought. **1603** Knolles *Hist. Turks* (1621) 1119 Some [traitors] they roasted, and some they put vnto the Tenalia. **1648** Wilkins *Math. Magic* i. xi. 75 That slavery, which those..Nations were subjected unto. **1710** Blackwell *Schema Sacrum* v. 103 The Decree of Divine Reprobation..necessarily inferred Man's Fall, Sin and Damnation violenting him (as it were) unto the same. **1807** Wordsw. '*Nuns fret not*' 8 The prison, unto which we doom Ourselves.

10. Indicating result, effect, or consequence: So as to result in, bring about, cause, or produce; = to *prep.* 10.

a **1300** *Cursor M.* 24746 Þof mans wijt be neuer sa strait, Sco mai well bring it vnto nait. **1430–40** Lydg. *Bochas* ii. 2812 Senacherib..Leffte his siege & took hym onto flyht. *c* **1440** *Alph. Tales* 440 He was ferd at þai or þer fadurs shulde desyre hym to be maryd or to fall vnto syn. **1526** Tindale *1 Cor.* xv. 34, I speake this vnto youre rebuke. **1591** Drayton *Harmonie of Church* x, They..by their sin provoke Him unto ire. **1601** Breton *Longing Blessed Heart* xxii, Th' Artificer..bringes his hand vnto his heads deuise, Longes till he see, what it will come vnto. **1660** *Nicholas Papers* (Camden) IV. 250 The unexpected..admitting to audience and afterwards vnto treatie of the Portugal ambassador.

11. Indicating a resultant condition, status, or capacity: In or into the character, nature, or quality of; = to *prep.* 11, 11b.

13.. *E.E. Allit. P.* A. 772 Quat-kyn þyng may be þat lambe, Þat þe wolde wedde vnto hys vyf? **1390** Gower *Conf.* I. 114 This lord a worthi ladi hadde Unto his wif. *c* **1400** *Rule St. Benet* (Verse) 1374 If þat þe priores wor dede, þo same..Wold ches me vnto priores. **1470–85** Malory *Arthur* i. vii. 43 We wille haue Arthur vnto our kyng. **1556** *Chron. Gr. Friars* (Camden) 28 The gray freeres chaungyd their habbetts from London rossette unto whytt gray. **1590** Shaks. *Mids. N.* i. i. 207 (Q.), Hee hath turnd a heauen vnto a hell! **1599** Drayton *Idea* xlvi, I meruaile not thou feelst not my delight..Whose stomack vnto gaule hath turn'd thy foode. **1609** Bible (Douay) *2 Kings* xxi. 14 And they shal be unto waste, and unto spoile to al their adversaries. **1749** C. Wesley *Hymns* I. 57 Turn unto Flesh my Heart of Stone.

12. Indicating the object of desire, right, or claim. Cf. to *prep.* 12, 12b.

1338 R. Brunne *Chron.* (1810) 57 He þat had gode right vnto þe regalte. **1530** Palsgr. 538/1 By what meanes is he entyteled unto these landes. **1535** Coverdale *Ps.* cxviii. 20 The very feruent desyre that I haue allwaye vnto thy iudgmentes. **1593** Nashe *Christ's T.* 29 b, There is no better clayme vnto wealth. **1738** in *Nairne Peerage Evid.* (1874) 42 Such personal estate as he..shall become..intitled unto.

IV. Followed by an expression denoting or indicating a limit in extent, number, amount, or degree.

13. a. Up to as many, as much, or as often as. Cf. to *prep.* 13.

a **1300** *Cursor M.* 12648 Ai to iesu was cummen neir Vn-to þe eild of thritte yeir. *a* **1325** *Prose Psalter* lii. 4 Þer nys non þat doþ god, þer nys non vn-to on. *c* **1400** *Brut* 295 Shippez & barges were take, vnto þe noumbre of .CC. & xxx. *c* **1500** *Melusine* xxiii. 156 There nys thing..that I shuld reffuse you vnto myn owne deth. **1526** Tindale *Mark* vi. 23, I will geve it the, even vnto the one halfe of my kyngdom. **1530** in Leadam *Star Chamber Cases* (Selden) II. 46 It was.. unknowne what the charges..would drawe vnto. **1596** Shaks. *1 Hen. IV*, iv. i. 129 What may the Kings whole Battaile reach vnto? *Vernon.* To thirty thousand. **1610** Healey *St. Aug. Citie of God* xix. i. 752 Thus doth the number arise vnto twelve. **1663** Bp. Patrick *Parab. Pilgr.* xiv, There cannot be so much interruption given to them, as the scratch of a pin among us amounts unto. **1812** Cary *Dante, Parad.* xxiii. 57 Not..Unto the thousandth parcel of the truth, My song might shadow forth that saintly smile. **1895** Petrie *Egypt. Tales* Ser. i. 70 He came again unto him, even unto six times. **1896** 'Ian Maclaren' *K. Carnegie* 328 There is nothing unto life itself I would not give for your good.

b. Down to (an ultimate grade, point, or number).

a **1325** *Prose Psalter* cxxxiv. 8 Þe which..smote þe first borne of Egipt fram man vnto beste. **1515** *St. Papers Hen. VIII*, II. 11 The King..dyd conquyre all the lande, unto lytyll. **1535** Coverdale *Exod.* xxii. 4 Yf yᵉ theft be founde by him alyue (from the oxe vnto the Asse or shepe). **1592** Shaks. *Rom. & Jul.* i. iii. 11 Faith I can tell her age vnto an houre. *a* **1623** Fletcher *Love's Cure* v. iii, No Town in Spain, from our Metropolis Unto the rudest hovel. **1646** Sir T. Browne *Pseud. Ep.* 274 The whole world perished unto eight persons before the floud.

c. So as to be equivalent or equal to. Cf. to *prep.* 14.

1568 Grafton *Chron.* II. 308 Three Millions of Scutes of Gold,..the which do come unto sterlyng money, fyve hundreth thousand pound. **1660** Willsford *Scales Commerce* i. 108 How much comes 10d. a day unto by the year?

14. To such an extent or degree, so far, as to cause; so much as to bring about or result in; = to *prep.* 14b.

1382 Wyclif *2 Kings* xx. 1 In tho dayes sijknede Ezechias vnto [1388 til to] the deeth. *a* **1425** tr. *Arderne's Treat. Fistula*, etc. 73 Be þai brissed and boiled in watre vnto mene þikkenez. *c* **1425** *St. Christina* xvi. in *Anglia* VIII. 125 She was stired of god vnto an vnsufferabil þriste. *c* **1440** *Alph. Tales* 154 Þe Emperour tuke it vnto so grete wrath, þat he garte smyte of his head. *Ibid.* 408 He fell into a dispayre, vnto so mekull þat he myght not liff with-owten venyall syn. **1542–5** Brinklow *Lament.* 3 To persecute vnto dethe all and euery godly person. **1571** Golding *Calvin on Ps.* xxxviii. 5 Through stubbornnesse [they] harden themselues vntoo vn-sensiblenesse. **1611** Cotgr., *Esgoüer*,..to eat vnto sacietie. **1640** Bp. Reynolds *Passions* xv. 141 Those vanities what hee seeth doe provoke others unto loathing. **1652** Sclater *Civ. Magistracy* (1653) Ep. Ded., His Singular Contentation accompanyed with Temperance unto Admiration. **1812** Cary *Dante, Purg.* xxiv. 22 That face beyond him, pierced Unto a leaner fineness than the church. **1896** 'Ian Maclaren' *K. Carnegie* 153 [The] fields, now yellow unto harvest, shone in the moonlight.

V. Expressing addition or accumulation, attachment, appurtenance, or possession.

15. a. Denoting attachment, union, adherence, or kinship to a person. Cf. to *prep.* 16.

1338 R. Brunne *Chron.* (1810) 65 Felawes vnto þefes, to robbours of ilk cuntre. *Ibid.* 90 With scrite vnto William Sir Dunkan him bond. **1423** Jas. I *Kingis Q.* cxxxiii, Lat wisedom ay vnto thy will be Iunyt. *c* **1440** *Alph. Tales* 219 [She] wold not be wed vnto a wurthi man þat wold hafe had hur. **1470–85** Malory *Arthur* x. liii. 501 A ful noble Knyghte nyghe kynne vnto sire Launcelot. **1535** Coverdale *Gen.* ii. 24 For this cause shal a man..cleue vnto his wife. **1544** in Leadam *Star Chamber Cases* (Selden) II. 279 Factoures vnto one Jacob vanganspole merchaunt of Andwerpe. **1591** Drayton *Harmonie of Church, Song Sol.* vii. 25, I am unto my Love a faithful friendly fere. **1601** *Important Consid. Priests* 21 Some of his own subiects were ..drawne, rather to adhere vnto them then to himselfe. **1649** Lovelace *Lucasta, Paradox* iv, The God that constant keepes Unto his Dieties. **1658** *Ibid.*, *Sanazar* 190, I was ally'd dear Uncle unto thee In blood, but thou alas not unto me.

b. Denoting fastening, securing, or junction to something.

1470–85 Malory *Arthur* viii. xxxiv. 326 He loked vpon bothe his handes that were fast bounden vnto two knyghtes. **1535** Coverdale *Gen.* xlix. 11 He shall bynde his foale vnto the vyne. **1585** T. Washington tr. *Nicholay's Voy.* ii. 47 Two sides are washed by the sea, and the thyrd ioyneth vnto the firme land. **1646** Sir T. Browne *Pseud. Ep.* 239 The use of the Navell is to continue the infant unto the Mother. **1662** Dryden *To Ld. Chancellor* 32 Nothing bounds our Eye Until the Earth seems join'd unto the Sky. *a* **1881** Rossetti *House of Life* i, Still some golden hair Unto his shoulder clinging, since the last Embrace.

16. Denoting appurtenance or possession. Freq. after verbs, as *appertain*, *behove*, *belong*, *long*, *pertain*, q.v. Cf. to *prep.* 17, 17b.

1390 Gower *Conf.* I. 6 The vice Which longeth unto this office. **1445** in *Anglia* XXVIII. 273 He þat knowith the fadirlaw vnto themperours sone. *a* **1450** *Knt. de la Tour* cxvii. 159 Suche an instrument as longithe vnto a mynstralle. **1513** Bradshaw *St. Werburge* i. 452 Elflede.. Doughter vnto Oswy. **1568** Grafton *Chron.* I. 144 He was Cosyn germaine unto him on the fathers syde. **1594** Drayton *Sonn.* viii, Vnto the World, to Learning, and to Heauen, Three nines there are, to euerie one a nine. **1634** Bp. Reynolds *Shieldes of Earth* (1636) 19 This belongeth only unto Princes. **1682** Sir T. Browne *Chr. Mor.* iii. §8 So may'st thou be..a Father unto thy contemporaries. **1768** Ross *Helenore* 60 Ye maun, I ween, unto the kards belang. **1845** Bailey *Festus* (ed. 2) 194 From this highest orb, the crown of space And footstool unto Heaven.

17. By way of increase to; in addition to; with, besides; = to *prep.* 15.

1526 Tindale *Acts* ii. 41 The same daye there were added vnto them aboute a thre thousande soules. **1535** Coverdale *Ecclus.* xviii. 6 There maye nothinge be taken from them, nothinge maye be put vnto them. **1595** Shaks. *John* iv. iii. 46 This is the very top, The heighth, the Crest: or Crest vnto the Crest Of murthers Armes. **1600** —— *A.Y.L.* i. ii. 250, I should haue giuen him teares vnto entreaties. **1642** Denham *Sophy* ii. i. 18 Wisedome he ha's, and to his wisedome courage: Temper to that, and unto all, successe. **1660** Sharrock *Vegetables* 19 Unto the ashes of every hill [*sc.* heap] you must put a peck of unslake lime. **1896** 'Ian Maclaren' *K. Carnegie* 329 You have many friends, and may God add unto them good men and faithful.

VI. Expressing comparison or correspondence, relation to a standard, etc.

18. After words denoting correspondence, agreement, comparison, proportion, etc. = to *prep.* 21.

See also like *a.* 1, resemble *v.*¹ 2, 6, resembling 1b.

c **1325** *Metr. Hom.* 37 For mani man mai bisend be Unto the rede, als thinc me. *c* **1386** Chaucer *Prol.* 243 Vn to swich a worthy man as he Acorded nat..To haue with sike lazars Aqueyntance. **1423** Jas. I *Kingis Q.* clv, The pantere, like vnto the smaragdyne. *c* **1460** *Towneley Myst.* iii. 506 Like vnto the turtill. **1553** Eden *Treat. New Ind.* (Arb.) 5 Which ..he thought to be muche inferiour vnto his. **1591** Drayton *Harmonie of Church, Song Sol.* ii. 6 No more the sons unto my Love may ought compared be. **1611** Cotgr. s.v. *Deschargé*, [A colour] neere vnto a light blew, or of a light blew; light. **1634** T. Johnson *Parey's Chirurg.* Wks. xxiv. vi. 891 A certaine thinne skinne..like unto that..over vnscimmed milke. **1644** Digby *Two Treat.* ii. (1645) 67 When a thing is identifyed unto the soule [etc.]. **1809–14** Wordsw. *Excurs.* ix. 56 A throne that may be likened unto his. **1875** Jowett *Plato* (ed. 2) III. 30 The second principle is like unto it.

19. With regard to; in respect of; as to, concerning; = TO *prep.* 22.

c **1400** *Cursor M.* 25119 (Cott. Galba), Seuin askinges er þarin to rede.. both vnto lifing here a space, and whare oure sawl more mister hase. **1502** *Ord. Crysten Men* (W. de W. 1506) I. iii. C iii, And this is vnto the sygnyfycacyon of the salte. **1520** *Chron. Calais* (Camden) 92 And as unto ladies ther were.. the duches of Norfolk, with her iij doughters. **1591** *Wills & Inv. N.C.* (Surtees, 1860) 199 For engrossing his will, twice vnto paipar, after vnto parchment *1l xs.* **1611** BIBLE *Rom.* vi. 11 Likewise reckon yee also your selues to be dead indeed vnto sinne. **1641** J. JACKSON *True Evang. T.* I. 3 A Commentator unto the Text askes the question. **1669** N. MORTON *New Eng. Memorial* (1910) 46 They also brought a full intelligence in reference unto the particulars. **1729** LAW *Serious C.* x. 147 We are to live wholly unto God. **1778** Ross *Helenore* 22, I ken nought unto his dispraise. **1885–94** R. BRIDGES *Eros & Psyche* Jan. xxi, Shut thy soft ear unto his clamour thin.

20. In comparison or as compared with; in relation to; = TO *prep.* 18.

c **1400** *Rom. Rose* 5600 [He] never shal make his richesse Asseth unto his gredinesse. *a* **1500** in *Ratis Raving*, etc. 4 Al his seknes [is] lytill, in comparesone one-to the luf at god schawyt till ws. **1539** BIBLE (Great) *Matt.* vi. 34 Sufficient vnto the daye, is the trauayle therof. *a* **1566** R. EDWARDS *Damon & Pithias* (1571) Hij b, But now I see there is no garde vnto a faithfull friend. **1682** SIR T. BROWNE *Chr. Mor.* III. §8 So may'st thou be coetaneous unto thy elders. **1768** Ross *Helenore* 93 But a' their cushel-mushel was but jest, Unto the coal that brunt in Lindy's breast. **1842** TENNYSON *Locksley Hall* 152 All thy passions, match'd with mine, Are as moonlight unto sunlight. —— *Talk. Oak* 107 As cowslip unto oxlip is, So seems she to the boy. **1854–5** LONGF. *Hiawatha's Wooing* I As unto the bow the cord is, So unto the man is woman.

21. In accordance, agreement, or correspondence with; according to; after; = TO *prep.* 20.

c **1420** *Contn. Brut* 340 So oure Kyng.. graunted hem trewes certyn yeres vnto her axyng. **1430–40** LYDG. *Bochas* I. 492 Whan he us made onto his liknesse, He putte vn bothe into Paradis. **1515** *Festivall* (W. de W.) 117 We praye you of a place to bury his body unto his worshypp. **1596** SPENSER *State Irel.* Wks. (Globe) 613/2 Lawes ought to be fashioned unto the manners.. of the people to whom they are ment. ? *a* **1600** in *Percy Folio* (1867) I. 63 Shooes of gold the porter had on, And all his other rayment was vnto the same. **1602** SHAKS. *Ham.* I. iii. 23 Therefore must his choyce be circumscrib'd Vnto the voyce and yeelding of that Body, Whereof he is the Head. **1710** BLACKWELL *Schema Sacrum* viii. 151 Disposing of Angels.. suitably unto the Tenor of their own Actings. **1803–6** WORDSW. *Ode Intim. Immort.* 96 And this hath now his heart, And unto this he frames his song. **1842** TENNYSON *Ld. of Burleigh* 80 A trouble.. perplex'd her.. With the burthen of an honour Unto which she was not born. **1870** MORRIS *Earthly Par.* III. 418 Meanwhile to Kiarton,.. Unto all seeming, life went merrily.

b. As far as; to the extent of. Cf. TO *prep.* 20 b.

1502 *Ord. Crysten Men* (W. de W. 1506) II. ix. I viii, To socour our neyghbour in kepynge hym vnto our power in place and in tyme that he.. falle not. **1642** tr. *Perkins' Prof. Bk.* III. §205. 92 Unto divers respects a man shall take by a liverie of seisin which he made in his owne right.

VII. Expressing relations in which the idea of course or direction tends to blend with the dative use.

22. After words denoting attention, care, trust, etc.; = TO *prep.* 24.

Freq. after verbs, as *apply, attend, betake, hearken, intend, listen, look*: see these words.

a **1300** *Cursor M.* 255 To laud and Inglis man i spell.. Sumquat vnto þat thing to tent. *c* **1386** CHAUCER *Sqr.'s T.* 67 Vn to my firste I wole haue my recours. *c* **1440** *Alph. Tales* 446 He fell vnto his prayers. **1455** *Paston Lett.* I. 326 Not to plese to geve trust or confidence unto the sinistrez.. rapportes of our sayd ennemyes. *c* **1477** CAXTON *Jason* 20 My herte Iugeth that ye shall haue grete Regard vnto my good wil. **1535** COVERDALE *Ps.* xvi. 1 Herken vnto my prayer. **1585** T. WASHINGTON tr. *Nicholay's Voy.* I. xviii. 21 The castle.. hath been so ill looked vnto.. it is againe fallen into the hands of the Barbaries. **1613** JACKSON *Creed* I. §iv. i. 219 Whose beleefe vnto diuine Oracles hath beene confirmed. **1642** *Remonstr. Ch. Irel.* 5 He wanted powder, having no more.. than his Bandeleers to trust unto. **1656** EARL MONM. tr. *Boccalini's Advts. fr. Parnass.* I. xlvii. 95 Flocks.. grow lean.. through the meer carelesness of him that looks unto them. **1710** BLACKWELL *Schema Sacrum* v. 104 It was.. Man alone, voluntarily hearkening unto Satan. **1812** CARY *Dante, Parad.* v. 119 Say on; and trust As unto gods.

23. Against, in respect of opposition or hostility. Cf. TO *prep.* 25 b.

a **1300** *E.E. Psalter* liii. 5 Torne iuels vnto mi faas. *a* **1400** *New Test.* (Paues) Acts iv. 1 As þei stoden.. þer kome fallande vnto hem prestes.. ande Saduceys. **1412–20** LYDG. *Chron. Troy* IV. 2452 Archilogus A mortal cours ran vn-to Brumvs. **1439** *Rolls of Parlt.* V. 17/2 Phelip.. hath contynuelly.. made werre unto the seide John. *a* **1450** *Knt. de la Tour* 120 So it befell he had do a forfeit vnto the kinge Dauid. **1585** T. WASHINGTON tr. *Nicholay's Voy.* I. xvii. 19 b, [They] dyd daily make warre vnto his highnesse. **1591** SHAKS. *1 Hen. VI*, IV. i. 73 Then gather strength, and march vnto him straight.

24. Indicating the person addressed, etc.; = TO *prep.* 26. Usu. after verbs, as *cry, say, speak, tell*.

a **1300** *E.E. Psalter* xxvi. 6 (E.), I sall synge and salm sai Un-to-Loverd. *Ibid.* xc. 15 He cried vnto me witerli. **1338** R. BRUNNE *Chron.* (1810) 99 Lowys wrote his letter vnto þe kyng Henry. **1390** GOWER *Conf.* I. 282 To speak a goodli word unto me. *c* **1440** *Alph. Tales* 122 þis suster said vnto hur brother. *c* **1450** CAPGRAVE *Life St. Aug.* 5 The book of Seynt Augustin.. on-to his sistir, a widow. **1477** *Stonor Papers* (Camden) II. 28, I spake vnto my lady.., and she wold scarsely oppyn hir mouthe vnto me. **1511** in W. H. Turner *Select. Rec. Oxford* (1880) 2 The mayer answered aȝen onto the forsayd John. **1535** COVERDALE *Deut.* xxxii. 46 Yᵉ wordes, which I testifye vnto you this daye. **1569** *Southampton Crt. Leet Rec.* (1905) I. 56 Be yt comaunded vnto all those.. that they make chimnes. **1610** J. HEALEY *St. Aug. Citie of God* XVII. v. 628 These words of the Prophet vnto Heli. **1643** CARYL *Expos. Job* I. 635 Would you know what the visiting of God is? It is praying unto him. **1710** BLACKWELL *Schema Sacrum* vi. 112 Some special One of their Number intimateth the great News unto the Shepherds. **1768** Ross *Helenore* 101 The squire well saw't, an' unto Lindy says [etc.]. **1844** WHITTIER *Texas* 32 Let the North unto the South Speak the word befitting both. **1896** 'IAN MACLAREN' *K. Carnegie* 328 John,.. is this all you have in your heart to say unto me?

b. To or for the worship of; in honour, adoration, or salutation of; = TO *prep.* 26 b.

a **1300** *E.E. Psalter* lxv. 15 Offrand meryhed, gode þat be, Sal I offre unto þe. *a* **1400** *New Test.* (Paues) Acts xxi. 25 Demande þat þei abstene hem fro þinge þat es sacrified vnto idoles. **1430–40** LYDG. *Bochas* VIII. 552 Egipceins dide.. Ther sacrefises & rihtes.. Vnto Isis. *c* **1440** *Pallad. on Husb.* I. 1178 Laude, ymne,.. & songe vnto The flour of Iesse spronge in Bethleem. **1526** TINDALE *Acts* xvii. 23, I founde an aultre wher in was written: vnto the vnknowen god. **1598** LODGE *Looking-Gl. Lond. & Eng.* H 2 b, Villaines, why skinck you not vnto this fellow? **1599** SHAKS. *Much Ado* v. iii. 22 Now vnto thy bones good night. **1615** W. BEDWELL *Arab. Trudg.* L 1, *Aba' lkibla*, was an idoll.. which.. the Arabians did.. offer sacrifice vnto. **1842** MACAULAY *L. Regillus* ii, Unto the Great Twin Brethren We keep this solemn feast. **1882** BIBLE (R.V.) *Exod.* xxxii. 8 They have made them a molten calf,.. and have sacrificed unto it.

25. Expressing or denoting response, responsive action, or reaction. = TO *prep.* 27, 27 b.

Freq. with *assent, consent, obey*, etc. (q.v.).

c **1440** *Alph. Tales* 448 He wolde not consent vnto hur to ly by hur. **1502** *Ord. Crysten Men* (W. de W. 1506) I. ii. 12 Whan Adam & eue.. dysobeyed unto God. **1518** in Leadam *Star Chamber Cases* (Selden) II. 148 The said bille is vncerteyn and insufficient to be aunswerd vnto. **1576** GASCOIGNE *Steel Glas* (Arb.) 59 To yeld good smacke vnto their daintie tongues. **1597** HOOKER *Eccl. Pol.* v. lxii. §13 Nature as much as is possible inclineth vnto validities and preseruations. **1612** DRAYTON *Poly-olb.* iv. 175 Some.. only us'd to sing Unto the other's harp. **1710** BLACKWELL *Schema Sacrum* vii. 140 To say Amen, unto Isaiahs Description of our Lord. **1768** Ross *Helenore* 88 Afore mishap had forc'd him to comply Unto a match. **1881** N. T. (Revised) *Luke* xiv. 6 They could not answer again unto these things.

VIII. Supplying the place of, assuming or taking over the functions of, the dative.

26. Denoting the recipient of a gift or the like, or the person affected by an event, etc. = TO *prep.* 29.

a **1300** *E.E. Psalter* ciii. 22 Lyoun whelpes.. seke fra god mete vnto þa. *c* **1380** *Antecrist* in Todd *3 Treat. Wyclif* 134 þei putten grete penaunce unto men, þere Cristis charge is liȝt. **1426** in *Surtees Misc.* (1890) 10 þe charge.. þat is put vnto me. *c* **1440** *Alphabet of Tales* 207 He putt þaim [*sc.* his goods] vnto þe bisshopp. *c* **1470** HENRY *Wallace* I. 447 Syluir and gold he gert on to him geyff. **1532** HERVET *Xenoph. Househ.* 32 b, As for suche thynges,.. we deliuered them vnto a woman. **1581** in *Lanc. & Cheshire Wills* (1893) 3 I geue and bequeath vnto Richard.. tenne shepe. **1610** HOLLAND *Camden's Brit.* I. 726 Deliuering vnto him a verge of gold. **1678** BUNYAN *Pilgr.* I. 168 This could not but be a great grief unto him. **1695** in *Jrnl. Friends' Hist. Soc.* Oct. (1915) 173 She hath borne unto mee three sonnes. *c* **1708** FENTON *First Fit of Gout* 19 Whence comes this unsought honour unto me? **1768** Ross *Helenore* 88 Nory.. a glack of bread an' cheese.. unto Lindy gees. **1814** CARY *Dante, Inf.* xxiii. 5 He told What fate unto the mouse and frog befel. **1829** in *Nairne Peerage Evid.* (1874) 76 We are graciously pleased to give and allow unto Caroline baroness Nairn an annuity. *a* **1865** EMERSON *Woodnotes* II. 342 Unto every race and age He emptieth the beverage.

b. Indicating the recipient of an impression, the holder of an opinion or the like; used esp. after verbs, as *appear, seem, †think*, etc. Cf. TO *prep.* 29 b.

a **1470** HARDING *Chron.* (MS. Lansd.) Pref. vi, If it lyke vn to ȝour owne avyse.. To Comforte now.. ȝour pore subgite. **1526** TINDALE *Luke* xxiv. 11 Their wordes semed vnto them fayned thinges. **1599** SHAKS. *Much Ado* III. v. 55, I am now in great haste, as may appeare vnto you. **1611** SPEED *Hist. Gt. Brit.* IX. xviii. §29 It was thought vnto the Protector, and vnto the whole Councell, that [etc.]. *a* **1613** BACON *Case Post-nati Scot.* Wks. 1826 V. 116 For it seemeth admirable unto me, to consider [etc.]. **1710** BLACKWELL *Schema Sacrum* viii. 147 One Attribute seemeth more Dear unto him than another.

27. For the advantage, benefit, convenience, use, or disposal of; for. Cf. TO *prep.* 30.

a **1300** *E.E. Psalter* lxx. 8 In þe ai alle mi singinge. Made am i als fortakeninge Vnto mani. *a* **1400** *New Test.* (Paues) Acts ii. 41 Ande þat day weren wonnen vnto God ande turned abowte þreo þowsande. **1539** BIBLE (Great) *Gen.* iii. 21 Unto the same Adam also and to his wife dyd the Lorde God make lethren garmentes. **1591** DRAYTON *Harmonie of Church, Song Sol.* v. 15 Then opened I the door unto my Love at last. **1613** HEYWOOD *Silver Age* I. i. B 3, Expose thy selfe Vnto that monstrous beast of Cicily, Cal'd the Chimera. **1664** BUTLER *Hud.* II. i. 616 By which Astrologers .. can tell What strange Events they do foreshow Unto her Under-world below. *a* **1678** H. SCOUGAL *Disc. Imp. Subj.* (1735) 179 A happiness we can never secure unto our selves. **1702** C. MATHER *Magn. Chr.* III. 178 An opportunity.. to Vindicate another great Man, unto the Churches of our Lord Jesus Christ. *a* **1714** in Ledwich *Antiq. Sarisb.* 6 Therein you may find many an excellent Lore That unto your Wives you may teach. *a* **1784** *Hobie Noble* i. in Child *Ball.*, For in it there was baith meat and drink, And corn unto our geldings gay. **1816** WORDSW. *Ode, 1814*, 51 Those palms and amaranthine wreaths Unto their martyred Countrymen decreed. **1891** *Cornh. Mag.* Dec. 664 He took unto himself a village maid, and settled in Lyndhurst.

b. Indicating the person or thing towards which an action, feeling, etc., is directed; = TO *prep.* 30 b.

Freq. with *beholden, †holden* (HOLD *v.* 10 b), *recommend*, etc.

a **1300** *E.E. Psalter* xviii. 13 And fra outen.. Forbere vnto þi hine ai. **13..** *Cursor M.* 1069 (Gött.), Vnto his broþer ire he bare. *a* **1400** *New Test.* (Paues) Acts xxvi. 27 Ande þo kenge Agrippa trowes vnto þo prophetes. *c* **1440** *Alph. Tales* 103 He askid hym whi he wuld not ryse vnto hym. *c* **1465** *Stonor Papers* (Camden) I. 70 Y weir be-hold unto yow. **1508** KENNEDIE *Flyting w. Dunbar* 482 Lat newir this synfull sot Do schame.. vnto your nacion! **1555** in *Rep. Hist. MSS. Comm.* Var. Coll. IV. (1907) 283 The leke paines.. shall ronne and be unto all those free Burgesses. **1587** in *Cath. Rec. Soc. Publ.* V. 137 Goolde.. referred me over unto Mr. Baylye to be payed upon youre head. **1623** in *Eng. Hist. Rev.* July (1919) 408 Delivered to St. Raby.. as a present.. without any fees or charge unto him. **1654–66** EARL ORRERY *Parthen.* (1676) 378 More from a desire of being alone, than from any aversion she seem'd to have unto it. **1710** BLACKWELL *Schema Sacrum* vii. 130 Our Lord.. having all their Iniquities.. imputed unto him. **1763** C. SMART *Song to David* lxxiv, Sweeter [is].. The glory of thy gratitude, Respired unto the Lord. **1796** MME. D'ARBLAY *Camilla* IV. 169 The Lord be good unto me! **1803** C. K. SHARPE *Lett.* (1888) I. 165 If Jane hath done this fault, woe be unto her! **1887** E. JOHNSON *Antiq. Mater.* 251 Your unslothful love unto the glory of God.

28. Denoting the relation of an adj. (or derived sb. or adv.) to a sb. indicating a person or thing to which its application is directed or restricted. = TO *prep.* 33.

Used in construction with many adjs.; cf. TO *prep.* 33, and see MERCIFUL *a.*, OPEN *a.* 15, SUBJECT *a.*, TRUE *a.* 1 c, UNKINDFULLY *a.*, UNTOLERABLE *a.*, etc.

1300 GOWER *Conf.* II. 285 Hast thou be scars or large of yifte Unto thi love? *c* **1407** LYDG. *Reson & Sens.* 948 The which.. wern.. vn-to manne ryght vayllable. *c* **1450** *Crt. Of Love* 14, I can-not write Unto the princes.. No termes digne unto her excellence. **1485** *Digby Myst.* III. 8, I am soveren of al soverens subjugal On-to myn empere. **1526** TINDALE *Acts* xxvi. 19, I was not disobedient vnto the hevenly vysion. **1593** in J. Morris *Troub. Cath. Forefathers* Ser. III. (1877) 124 Yet their life-labour is.. costly unto us. **1639** S. DU VERGER tr. *Camus' Admir. Events* 301 A torture unsufferable unto this young gentlewoman. **1669** OWEN *Exp. Ps. cxxx*, 15 Vnspiritedness and disability unto Duty, in doing or suffering. *a* **1687** PETTY *Pol. Arith.* (1690) 72 It will be dangerous unto England, that Ireland should be in the Hands of any other Nation. **1795–6** WORDSW. *Borderers* 2168, I (so filled With horror is this world) am unto thee The thing most precious that it now contains. **1801** —— *Troilus & Cresida* 83 So cruel do not be Unto the blood of Troy,.. As Juno was unto the Theban blood.

b. After *known, unknown, †uncouth, †unwist, †unwitting*, etc.; = TO *prep.* 33 b.

In later use (esp. in or after Biblical usage) with *known*.

a **1400** *New Test.* (Paues) Acts xix. 17 þis was made knowne vnto alle þe Iewes. **1423** JAS. I *Kingis Q.* lxiii, Quhen sall ȝour merci rew vpon ȝour man, Quhois seruice is ȝit vncouth vnto ȝow? **14..** HOCCLEVE *Minor P.* 231/418 How [we] thidir come, vn-to vs vnwist. *c* **1440** *Generydes* 3396 Vppe they rose,.. And chaungyd horses onto them bothe vnknowyng. **1514** BARCLAY *Cyt. & Uplondyshman* (Percy Soc.) 32 Seth God wyll be unknowen unto us. **1556** *Chron. Grey Friars* (Camden) 17 The othe that he made un to the kynge of Ynglonde unwyttynge unto the pope. **1605** SHAKS. *Lear* I. iv. 224 By making this well knowne vnto you. **1795–6** WORDSW. *Borderers* 628 If compassion.. Be known unto you. **1843** —— *G. Darling* 7 One.. Known unto few but prized as far as known.

IX. † **29.** = *to* with the infinitive. *Obs.*

c **1352** MINOT *Poems* (ed. Hall) v. 25 King Edward vnto sail was ful sune dight. *a* **1400** *Northern Passion* 461 (Camb. MS. Gg 5. 31), þare come downe a aungell.. Vnto comforthe ihesu well still. ? **1481** *Cely Papers* (Camden) 203 Any thing that I cane do unto ples ye.

B. *conj.* † **a.** = UNTIL *conj.* a. Also (*a*) with *that*.

(*a*) *a* **1300** *E.E. Psalter* xciii. 15 (H.), For Laverd sal noght his folke schonne awai, Ne his heritage for-lete never a dai; Unto þat rihtnes be turned in dome with quert. *a* **1425** tr. *Arderne's Treat. Fistula*, etc. 61 þe pacient ow to abide still in þe watre, vnto þat þe blode.. chaunge into fairer colour. *c* **1475** *Partenay* 4132 In thys place abide vnto that ye see Ho bering hym best and ho better haue. **1556** *Chron. Gr. Friars* (Camden) 19 A gret multytude.. there abode seven dayes contynually unto that the kynge.. came.. toward Grenewich.

(*b*) **1303** R. BRUNNE *Handl. Synne* 9055 þys songe sunge þey yn þe chercheȝerd.. Vn-to þe matynes were alle done. *c* **1381** CHAUCER *Parl. Foules* 647 Almyghty queen vnto this ȝer be gon I axe respit. **1411** *E.E. Wills* (1882) 20 Also y wille .. þat lucie my wyf haue gouernauns þer-of.. vn-to þe forseyd william be of age xviij. ȝhere. *c* **1489** CAXTON *Sonnes of Aymon* ix. 223 They wente to bed, & slepte vnto the daye appered. **1526** *Pilgr. Perf.* (W. de W. 1531) 2 b, It is & euer shall be vnquiet, vnto I come to the. **1549** *Wills & Inv. N.C.* (Surtees, 1860) 132, I give vnto my wife my house vnto my boy be of xxiiij yeirs of age. **1572** MASCALL *Plant. & Graff.* (1592) 52 The which may also keepe vnto the new come againe.

† **b.** = UNTIL *conj.* b. Also with *that*. *Obs.*

1303 R. BRUNNE *Handl. Synne* 5994 Here synne shal noþer be forȝyuen ne slakyn Vn-to þey ȝelde þat þey haue takyn. *c* **1400** *Northern Passion* (H.) 958 þe men þan letted for no thing Vnto þai come to herod. *c* **1425** in *Anglia* VIII. 139/46 She.. hadde no reste in spirite, vnto she hadde made a-seth. *c* **1457** *Stonor Papers* (Camden) I. 53, I can.. not gefe hym no comfort onto that I have wurd fro yowr maistership. **1502** *Ord. Crysten Men* (W. de W. 1506) I. ii, None were baptysed vnto that yᵗ he were suffycyentlye cathecysed. **1535** BP. TUNSTALL in Strype *Eccl. Mem.* (1721) I. App. lix. 147 The commissioners.. occupied the said auditors so long, that unto they were dispatched we could not have them [etc.]. **1573** J. TYRIE *Refutation* Pref. 6 Wnto he proue that he defendes that same caus,.. he will neuer caus me to beleue nor graunt that [etc.].

† **c.** So that at length; = UNTIL *conj.* e. *Obs.*

a **1395** HYLTON *Scala Perf.* I. xci. (W. de W. 1494), My dere chyldern whyche I bere..vnto cryste be ayenshapen in you. *c* **1400** tr. *Secreta Secret., Gov. Lordsh.* 84 Alle þes þinges shal be vpon þe fyr all a nyght and a day, vnto all þayre stryngh be out passyd. *c* **1425** tr. *Arderne's Treat. Fistula*, etc. 73 Boile it agayne vnto it be ane vntement haldyng fast ynoȝ. **1502** ATKYNSON tr. *De Imitatione* III. xii. (1893) 207 This sensuall appetite is to be subdued..vnto it haue lerned to be content with fewe thynges. **1541** R. COPLAND *Guydon's Quest. Chirurg.* Q j b, Apply vpon it a maturatife..vnto the scar be fallen.

†**d.** = UNTIL *conj.* d. *Obs.*

1490 *Plumpton Corr.* (Camden) 100, I thinke long unto I here word from you.

un'toasted, *ppl. a.* (UN-¹ 8.)

1769 MRS. RAFFALD *Eng. Housekpr.* (1778) 361 Lay untoasted sippets round the inside of the dish. **1865** DICKENS *Mut. Fr.* I. vii, Mr. Venus dives, and produces another muffin, yet untoasted.

un'tochered, *ppl. a.* Chiefly *Sc.* (UN-¹ 8.)

1823 BYRON *Juan* XI. xlix. *note*, The '*untochered*' but 'pretty virginities'..of the *then* day. **1850** A. MCGILVRAY *Poems* 65 His sons..marry poor Untochered lasses. **1866** FREEMAN *Hist. Ess.* i. (1871) 12 Whom his father had left unmarried and untochered.

†**unto-come,** *v. Obs.*⁻¹ [f. UNTO + COME *v.* Cf. TO-COME *v.*] *intr.* To arrive, come to a place.

c **1440** *Alph. Tales* 102 On a tyme Petur & Clemett vnto-come þer þis Matidiana begid hur meatt.

†**untofore,** *prep. Obs.*⁻¹ [f. UNTO, after TOFORE *prep.*] = TOFORE *prep.* I c.

c **1430** LYDG. *Min. Poems* (Percy Soc.) 86 Theyr labour.. They..remembred by writyng ful notable, Unto-fore God a thyng ful commendable.

un'toggle, *v.* (UN-² 4 c.)

1859 F. A. GRIFFITHS *Artill. Man.* (ed. 8) 213, [Nos.] 5 and 6..shift side-tackles, untoggle breeching, and span it when the gun is in. **1883** *Man. Seamanship for Boys* 129 The first reef-beckets must be untoggled when taking in the third reef.

un'toiled, *ppl. a.* [UN-¹ 8, 8 c.]

†**1.** Untilled, uncultivated. *Obs.*

1578 LYTE *Dodoens* I. ii. 4 The common wormwood groweth naturally in..dry, rude, and untoyled places. **1601** HOLLAND *Pliny* II. 224 It commeth up..in untoiled and neglected places, and namely, common high waies. *a* **1633** G. HERBERT tr. *Cornarus on Temp.* (1634) 40 The reducing of many rude and untoiled places..to cultivation. **1683** J. REID *Scots Gard'ner* (1907) 80 Trenching doth well prepare ..untoil'd ground.

2. Not subjected to, or overcome by, toil.

1598 SYLVESTER *Du Bartas* II. ii. *Babylon* 262 Un-toyld, un-tutor'd, sucking tender food, We learn'd a language all men understood. **1649** G. DANIEL *Trinarch., Hen. V*, ccli, A Iollitie Sprung from vntoyled Limbes. **1744** ELIZA HEYWOOD *Female Spect.* No. 9 (1748) II. 143 He who preserves it [*sc.* hope]..is untoiled with disappointment, and never loses the prospect of his wish.

3. Not toiled *for*; got without toil.

1651 H. VAUGHAN *Olor Iscanus, To best Couple* 20 Like the dayes Warmth may all your Comforts be, Untoil'd for, and Serene as he.

un'toileted, *ppl. a.* (UN-¹ 8.)

1819 MOORE *Mem.* (1853) II. 325 Obliged to fly from bed and home, unshaved, untoileted.

un'toiling, *pr. pple.* and *ppl. a.* (UN-¹ 10.)

1748 THOMSON *Cast. Indol.* I. xix. It is of vanities most vain, To toil for what you here untoiling may obtain. **1821** BYRON *Cain* II. ii, It is not with the earth..I feel at war, but that I may not profit By what it bears of beautiful, untoiling. **1839** CARLYLE *Chartism* vii, The Toiling Classes of mankind declare..to the Untoiling, that they will be governed.

un'told, *ppl. a.* [OE. *unteald* (UN-¹ 8 b), = MDu. *ongetellet, -telt* (Du. *ongeteld*), MLG. *ungetelt* (LG. *-tald*), MHG. *ungezalt, -zelt* (G. *ungezahlt, -zählt*), ON. *útalið̃r, útaldr*, (M)Da. *utalt.*]

†**1. a.** Not counted or reckoned; not counted out or paid. *Obs.*

c **1000** *Sax. Leechd.*, etc. III. 264 Be ðam dæȝe spræc se wisa Augustinus,..ȝyf he byð forlæten unteald, þær rihte awent eall ðæs ȝeares ymbryn þwyres. *c* **1386** CHAUCER *Miller's T.* 594 Certes were it gold Or in a poke nobles all vntold, Thou sholdest have. *a* **1400** *Octouian* 821 He tok the floryns all vntold. **14..** *Tundale's Vis.* 64 He went..To a mon to ascon his pay For thre horsis that he had sold For the whych the pennys wer untold. *c* **1600** SHAKS. *Sonn.* cxxxvi, Among a number one is reckon'd none. Then in the number let me passe vntold.

†**b.** Not enumerated or reckoned up; unspecified. *Obs.*

a **1300** *Cursor M.* 18549 þaa Iuus sau þis ilk man do signes sere—þe blind to se, þe dumb at here,..And oþer takens fele vn-teld. *c* **1340** HAMPOLE *Pr. Consc.* 7447 Wha couth þan telle..Alle þe syns..And leve nane untald, gret ne smale, þe whilk a man has here fallen in. *c* **1425** *Cursor M.* 23139 (Trin.), In pride & triccherу..And in vntolde synnes fele. *a* **1450** *Le Morte Arth.* 3239 Forthe went they..To syr mordred and hys lordis,..And an C knyghtis all vn-tolde. **1607** TOURNEUR *Rev. Trag.* II. i, Fair trees..Are cut to maintain head-tires—much untold—All thrives but chastity, she lies a cold.

2. Uncounted, unreckoned, because of amount or numbers; immense, vast.

untold gold (= any amount of gold), prob. originally in sense 1 a (= not carefully or exactly counted).

a **1400–50** *Alexander* 2677 þare fand he tresour vntald. *c* **1440** *Gesta Rom.* viii. 22 þe kyngdom of hevene, in þe which is tresour vntold. **1672** W. WALKER *Parœm.* 24 You may trust him in the dark; with untold gold. **1754** *Connoisseur* No. 18 ¶ 3 He..boasts that you may safely trust him with untold gold. **1782** COWPER *Alex. Selkirk* 25 Religion! what treasure untold Resides in that heavenly word! **1849** GROTE *Greece* II. liv. VI. 605 The untold number of these barbarians was reported as overwhelming. **1853** J. H. NEWMAN *Hist. Sk.* (1873) I. I. ii. 83 All the untold riches of his treasury.

b. With plural sbs.: In large numbers; numberless, countless.

? *a* **1500** *Peblis to the Play* 46 The bagpyp blew, and thai out threw out of the townis vntald. **1659** W. CHAMBERLAYNE *Pharon.* I. III. 4 A fruitful pasture..Where in untold droves did feed His bellowing herds. **1819** SHELLEY *Mask of Anarchy* lxxii, Ye who suffer woes untold. **1868** HELPS *Realmah* viii. I. 280 Untold ages have passed since the day when [etc.]. **1874** GEIKIE *Gt. Ice Age* xxvii. 376 The genial climate..lasted for untold centuries.

c. With abstract sbs. Unmeasured, unlimited.

In early ME. *unitald fultum* occurs (*Cott. Hom.* 233).

1781 COWPER *Table-t.* 330 Incomparable gem! thy worth untold. **1825** J. NEAL *Bro. Jonathan* I. 60 His mouth was agitated..with untold sorrow. **1868** MORRIS *Earthly Par.* I. 147 He seemed to see the ancient sage Shrivelled yet more with untold age. **1875** T. W. HIGGINSON *Hist. U.S.* xxi. 212 It had also cost the Americans untold suffering.

3. Not related or recounted.

c **1386** CHAUCER *Pars. T.* ¶ 1010 Lat no blotte be bihynde, lat no synne been vntoold as fer as thow hast remembraunce. *c* **1400** *Destr. Troy* 563 The truthe of the tale [is] vntold to your ere. *a* **1450** *Knt. de la Tour* (1868) 12 Whanne a man is shreue, he shulde leue no thinge vntolde. **1533** MORE *Debell. Salem* Wks. 1009/1, I haue..proued afore that he must mene so: or elles must haue left his tale vntold. **1565** STAPLETON tr. *Staphylus' Apol.* 175 b, Rather then to suffer a..heresy vncomptrolled, or the truthe vntolde. **1623** MIDDLETON & ROWLEY *Sp. Gipsy* I. v, The cause..shall be to all the world untold. *a* **1645** MILTON *Arcades* 41 Where ye may more neer behold What shallow-searching Fame hath left untold. **1700** DRYDEN *Pref. to Fables* ¶ 13 Such tales shall be left untold by me. **1796** MME. D'ARBLAY *Camilla* x. xiii, A reciprocal confidence that left nothing untold, not an action unrelated. **1827** MRS. HEMANS *Last Constantine* xxv, In their mien..Things by the brave untold may fearfully be read! **1875** J. P. HOPPS *Princ. Relig.* xvii. 53 Until a thought or a disclosure is comprehended, it is as though it were untold—it is not revealed.

4. Not informed (of a fact).

1590 SPENSER *F.Q.* I. iii. 38 For the old man well knew he, though vntold, In..magicke to haue wondrous might.

†**un'tolerable,** *a. Obs.* (UN-¹ 7 b and 5 b.)

1382 WYCLIF *Judith* xiv. 17 Vntolerable drede and trembling fel vp on hem. **1422** YONGE tr. *Secreta Secret.* 182 He was..a crowel Tyraunt ontollerabill. *c* **1440** *Alph. Tales* 147 The bitter payn of hell..is vntollerable vnto me. **1535** COVERDALE *Bible* Ded., The vntollerable iniuries..done vnto God. **1597** MORLEY *Introd. Mus.* 154 Which is a thing vntolerable except [etc.]. **1612** T. TAYLOR *Comm. Titus* iii. 1 Those in authority, who may..returne our frowardnes with vntolerable displeasure.

un'tolled, *ppl. a.* (UN-¹ 8 + TOLL *v.*³)

1592 GREENE *Conny Catch.* II. 5 That no man may buy a horse vntould, nor the toule be taken without lawful witnesses. [See TOLL *v.*³ 3.] **1775** ASH, *Untolled*, not tolled; not diminished by the toll.

un'tomb, *v.* [UN-² 5.] *trans.* To disentomb. Also *fig.*

1594 *Zepheria* i, All in the humble accent of my Muse,.. My grieues I here vntoombe. Sweete, them peruse. **1614** GORGES *Lucan* VI. 243 The babe within the mothers wombe With gashing wound she will vntombe. **1646** SIR T. BROWNE *Pseud. Ep.* VII. xviii. 382 The wonderfull corps of Antæus untombed a thousand years after his death by Sertorius. **1712** T. STAVELEY *Hist. Churches* 271 Being advised once to untomb the bones of an enemy. **1840** THACKERAY *Paris Sk.-bk.* (ed. 2) II. 229 The fair Rachel has been trying to revive this *genre* and to untomb Racine.

un'tombed, *ppl. a.* [UN-¹ 8.] Not provided with, or placed in, a tomb. Also *transf.*

1560 J. HEYWOOD *Thyestes* D i, That whiche the worste was wont to be, were heere a wisshed thyng, That them theyr father sawe vntombde [L. *insepultos*]. **1582** STANYHURST *Æneis* I. (Arb.) 29 But loa, the proper image of corps vntumbed apeered In dreame too Dido. **1818** MILMAN *Samor* IV. 510 The burial on cold battle field, unhymn'd, Unmourn'd, untomb'd. *Ibid.* XII. 234 Th' untomb'd slumbers of far battle vales. **1835** TALFOURD *Ion* IV. i, Spirits that have left..their plague-tormented flesh To rot untomb'd.

un'tone, *v.* [UN-² 6 b.] *trans.* To deprive of tone. Hence **un'toned** *ppl. a.*¹

1803 C. W. ETHELSTON *Suicide* 9 Is there a hope that o'er this unton'd frame Awakened Health her wonted glow shall spread? **1847** H. BUSHNELL *Chr. Nurt.* II. ii. (1861) 266 Nothing..untones more completely the divine affinities of the childish nature.

un'toned, *ppl. a.*² (UN-¹ 8 + TONED *ppl. a.*)

1807 J. BARLOW *Columb.* IX. 104 But frail at first his frame, with nerves ill strung, Unform'd his footsteps, long untoned his tongue. **1896** A. H. KEANE *Ethnol.* xii. 326 A distinctly polysyllabic group of untoned languages. **1897** *Daily News* 12 Jan. 6/5 Its dominant black and blue, its almost strident red, its untoned white.

un'tongue, *v.* [UN-² 4. Cf. older Du. *onttongen.*] *trans.* To deprive of (the use of) the tongue; to render speechless.

1598 FLORIO, *Dislinguare*, to vntoong. *c* **1600** CHALKHILL *Thealma & Cl.* 3136 Speak he could not,..they had him quite untongued. **1628** FELTHAM *Resolves* II. lix. 170 It hath vntongued some on the sudden; and from some hath snatcht their naturall abilities. **1655** FULLER *Ch. Hist.* XI. 218 Such ..condemn him in keeping such a Diary about him in so dangerous days. Especially he ought to untongue it from talking to his prejudice.

un'tongued, *ppl. a.* [UN-¹ 8.] Destitute of a tongue; tongueless.

a **1600** M. COSOWARTH *Ps. xxx.* in Farr *S.P. Eliz.* (1845) II. 407 The mute and the untounged dust. **1623** MIDDLETON & ROWLEY *Sp. Gipsy* I. iii, If every orator of folly plead In silence, like this untongu'd piece of violence. **1648** HEXHAM II, *Ontongigh*,..Vntongued, or without a tongue. **1891** C. DAWSON *Avonmore* 28 Untongued voices whispered..comfort to the troubled breast.

un'tongue-tied, *ppl. a.* (UN-¹ 8 d.)

1640 BROME *Sparagus Gard.* II. iv, Ide give another hundred Peeces now..that I might be untongue ty'd, And triumph o're my adversary.

un'tonsed, *ppl. a.* [UN-¹ 8.] Unlopped.

1819 J. HODSON in J. Raine *Mem.* (1857) I. 231 The abundance of untonsed trees..give a richness..to all the suburban villages.

un'tonsured, *ppl. a.* (UN-¹ 8.)

1855 MILMAN *Lat. Chr.* VI. 359 Schools of medicine.. freely admitted untonsured..students. **1863** GEO. ELIOT *Romola* III. xxiii, There came the train of untonsured secular priests.

un'tooled, *ppl. a.* (UN-¹ 8.)

1862 BURTON *Bk. Hunter* 381 Whatever sort of work.. went on around these untooled fragments of the living rock.

un'toomly, *adv.* [UN-¹ 11.] Hastily; hurriedly.

c **1400** *Destr. Troy* 1822 Antenor vntomly turnet his way Withoutyn lowtyng.

un'tooth, *v.* (UN-² 4. Cf. Du. *onttanden*, G. *entzahnen.*)

1791 COWPER *Odyssey* xviii. 37 As men untooth a pig pilf'ring the corn. **1820** *Blackw. Mag.* VII. 678 We called to untooth them your friend the gay dentist.

un'toothed, (*ppl.*) *a.* [UN-¹ 9, UN-² 8. Cf. G. *ungezähnt.*] Not having, deprived of, teeth.

1513 MORE *Rich. III* (1883) 6 Hee came into the worlde with the feete forwarde,..and (as the fame runneth) also not vntothed. **1550** THOMAS *Ital. Dict.*, *Isdentato*, vntoothed, or without teethe. **1603** S. HARSNET *Pop. Impost.* 136 An olde weather-beaten Croane,..hollow eyed, vntoothed. **1611** FLORIO, *Disdentato*, vntoothed, toothlesse.

un'toothsome, *a.* [UN-¹ 7.]

1. *fig.* Unpalatable, disagreeable.

1548 UDALL *Erasm. Par. Luke* Pref. vi, Suche thynges as these, so ferre contrarie to all mennes..thynkyng, and thynges so vntouthsome for menne to be fond on. **1583** BABINGTON *Commandm.* (1590) 354 Vntoothsome is that trueth euer, that treadeth downe my liking. **1632** SHIRLEY *Hyde Park* II. iv, You shall not ask me..How old I am—a question most untoothsome. *a* **1680** CHARNOCK *Attrib. God* (1834) II. 89 Their doctrine was..untoothsome to the world.

2. Unpleasant or unattractive to the taste.

1576 R. PETERSON *G. della Casa's Galateo* 99 The selly sickman, to whom al cates neuer so..sweete, seeme vntoothsome. **1601** HOLLAND *Pliny* I. 407 Their grapes..be very harsh and in tast untoothsome. **1630** J. TAYLOR (Water P.) *Wks.* I. 60/1 The drugs, the drenches, and vntoothsome drinks. **1655** MOUFET & BENNET *Health's Improv.* 245 Nay .., is it not unwholesom, heavy and untoothsom without Salt?

Comb. **1900** *Morning Post* 3 March 5/7 A sparse, dried, untoothsome-looking herbage, which man and beast accepted as fodder.

Hence **un'toothsomeness.**

1623 BP. HALL *Contempl., O.T.* XIX. x, The asse was (besides the untoothsomnesse) an impure creature.

un'top, *v.* [UN-² 4. Cf. TOP *v.*¹] *trans.* To deprive of a top. Also *fig.*

1598 FLORIO, *Disculminare*, to vntop, to vnroofe, or vntile a house. **1630** J. TAYLOR (Water P.) *Bk. Martyrs* Wks. III. 141/1 So our Eliza stoutly did begin Untopping and beheading Romish sin. [**1775** ASH.]

un'topped, *ppl. a.* [UN-¹ 8.] Not deprived of the top.

1864 R. L. DE COIN *Cotton & Tobacco* 273 You will leave [tobacco] plants untopped enough to produce all the seeds you may want.

untor'mented, *ppl. a.* (UN-¹ 8.)

c **1374** CHAUCER *Troylus* I. 1004 Troylus..wex of his wo as who seyth vntormentid But hotter weex his loue. **1648** [see UNTORTURED]. **1744** YOUNG *Nt. Th.* VII. 774 Was it then.. Too much for chaos to permit my mass A longer stay with essences unwrought, Unfashion'd, untormented into man? **1868** MORRIS *Earthly Par.* I. I. 393 If thou couldst forget, And live unholpen, lonely, loveless yet, But untormented. **1869** RUSKIN *Q. of Air* iii. §145 With perfect, untormented serenity of ease.

un'torn, *ppl. a.* [UN-¹ 8 b.]

1. Not torn or lacerated.

c **1547** GARDINER in Foxe *A. & M.* (1563) 751 We shoulde not..mangle them or cut them, but suffer them to stand vntorne. **1599** T. M[OUFET] *Silkwormes* 18 They..Leaue yet no leaues vntorne that may be seene. **1621** G. SANDYS *Ovid's Met.* I. (1626) 3 The yet-free Earth..(Vntorne with ploughs). **1649** F. ROBERTS *Clavis Bibl.* 513 Preserving them un-torn in the Lyons Den. **1791** COWPER *Iliad* XXIV. 26 Apollo, with compassion touch'd Ev'n of the lifeless Hector, ..preserved him, although dragg'd, untorn. **1855** BROWNING *Saul* v, Our sheep..are white and untorn by the bushes. **1890** *Retrospect Med.* CII. 249 The..tissue is usually torn through in front,..but remains untorn behind.

2. Not taken away by force.

c **1691** SOUTH *Serm.* (1717) V. 443 As long as that small remainder of Land, belonging to the Church, shall continue yet untorn from her.

un'torrefied *ppl. a.* (UN-[1] 8.)
1829 TOGNO & DURAND *Mat. Med.* 190 The untorrefied coffee seems to possess very energetic tonic properties.

un'torture, *v.* (UN-[2] 4 b.)
1650 FULLER *Pisgah* 58 To rectify his mistake, and to untorture him from the apprehension of his son's supposed death.

un'tortured, *ppl. a.* (UN-[1] 8.)
1648 HEXHAM II, *Ongepijnt*, Vnpained,..Vntortered, or Vntormented. **1813** SCOTT *Rokeby* VI. xiii, Thy racks could give thee but to know The proofs, which I, untortured, show.

†**unto'smitten**, *ppl. a. Obs.* (UN-[1] 8 b.)
1382 WYCLIF *Rom.* Prol., The Tessalonycensis..kepten the feith of treuthe, vntosmyten.

un'tossed, *ppl. a.* (UN-[1] 8.)
1611 FLORIO, *Inagitato*, vnmooued, vntossed. **1819** BYRON *Juan* II. clxxxi, The sands untumbled, the blue waves untost.

un'tottering, *ppl. a.* (UN-[1] 10.)
1637 C. DOW *Answ. to H. Burton* 203 The onely way to have constant and untottering comfort. **1671** CLARENDON *Dial.* Tracts (1727) 324 That they may keep the ship steady and untottering in that troublesome and unruly sea.

ˌuntoucha'bility. [f. UNTOUCHABLE *a.*: see -ILITY.] The quality or state of being untouchable; the condition or status of an untouchable; the social practice of having a class or caste of untouchables. Also *transf.*
1919 F. B. FISHER *India's Silent Revolution* v. 110 The depressed classes are now holding Untouchability Conferences at frequent intervals. **1928** *Speeches Maharaja of Baroda* 244 The question of untouchability was particularly Hindu. **1929** *Nineteenth Cent.* Dec. 763 His own system..tends to perpetuate such cruel social abuses as untouchability and child marriage. **1952** A. R. RADCLIFFE-BROWN *Structure & Function in Primitive Society* vii. 138 An extreme sanctity or untouchability attached to a chief born of a brother and sister who were themselves children of a brother and sister. **1958** *Times* 9 Sept. 9/6 The origin of untouchability in Japan is not clear. **1978** L. HEREN *Growing up on The Times* ii. 44 Untouchability, surely the greatest injustice in the history of mankind. **1979** J. WAINWRIGHT *Tension* xvii. 59 She has a perpetual air of untouchability about her. **1982** *Times* 24 June 3 Among the first generation [of Asians], untouchability is practised..in Britain... The Hindus of Southall have a separate temple for their untouchables.

un'touchable, *a.* and *sb.* [UN-[1] 7 b.]
A. *adj.* **1. a.** Incapable of being touched; immaterial.
1567 JEWELL *Def. Apol.* 239 Theophylacte saithe, The Body of Christe is Eaten; but the Godheade is not Eaten: bicause it is vntoucheable, and vncomprehensible vnto our senses. **1611** COTGR., *Immateriel*,..impalpable, vntouchable.
absol. **1833** S. AUSTIN *Char. Goethe* I. 185 Differentializing the Unchangeable and Untouchable.
b. Beyond the reach of touch.
1622 G. G. *Creat. Praysing God* 33 The vntouchable height of his [*sc.* God's] glory. **1886** J. PARKER *Apost. Life* II. 169 With the heavens above it, hell below it, an untouchable horizon round about it. **1890** HALL CAINE *Bondman* III. i, Seas beneath of an untouchable depth.
c. *fig.* Unapproachable, unrivalled.
1867 E. YATES *Forlorn Hope* xv, A worthy woman, untouchable in Mangnall, devoted to the backboard. **1884** —— *Recoll.* I. 189 In his day untouchable as a romantic actor.
2. a. Exempt from touch; that one may not touch.
1607 S. COLLINS *Serm.* (1608) 46 Euery mans conscience is as free and as vntouchable as anothers before God, one price was paid for all. **1647** TRAPP *Comm. Jas.* iii. 7 Sons of Belial, untamable, untractable, untouchable. **1661** FELTHAM *Resolves* II. lxvi. 327 Were not their Persons Sacred, that is, by the Laws of God and Man, untouchable as to prejudice. **1737** *Gentl. Mag.* VII. 35/1 Her Majesty's Foot hitch'd in the Stirrup, and the Horse dragg'd her along.., but the untouchable Foot retain'd the grave Spaniards from intermedling in so delicate an Affair. **1879** J. HINGSTON *Austral. Abroad* ix. 101 The graves..are held as sacred and untouchable by the present owners.
b. *spec.* That cannot legally be interfered with or made use of.
1734 SWIFT in Mrs. Delany *Life & Corr.* (1861) I. 524, I hope the young lady has an untouchable settlement. **1815** *Zeluca* I. 263 Your own untouchable property. **1874** W. R. GREG *Rocks Ahead* 45 Declaring this peasant's farm inalienable,..untouchable for any debt.
3. a. Too bad, unpleasant, defiling, etc., to touch. *spec.* of Hindus: see sense B; also *transf.* from this sense.
1873 MRS. WHITNEY *Other Girls* x, Fried potatoes, or whatever else was economical and untouchable. **1909** *Indian Spectator* 23 Oct. 843/2 Persons in mourning are.. considered to be defiled and untouchable for some days. **1910** *Times* 29 July 5/6 In non-essentials Brahmanism soon found it expedient to relax the rigour of caste obligations, as for instance to..travel even in their own country in railways ..without incurring the pollution of bodily contact with the 'untouchable' castes. **1943** G. MUFF *Let.* in *Times* 8 July 5/5 There was a gulf between the public school and the elementary school—a caste system; when all the while we knew the child of the worker was neither 'untouchable' nor belonged to a depressed class. **1963** T. & P. MORRIS *Pentonville* ii. 27 The work of the general work cleaners is of 'untouchable' status and is frequently given to the Maltese and 'blacks' for this reason. **1979** A. BRINK *Dry White Season* III. vii. 237 He is untouchable, protected by the entire bulwark of his formidable system.
B. *sb.* A Hindu of a hereditary low caste, contact with whom was regarded as defiling members of higher castes. Also *transf.* and *fig.* Cf. HARIJAN.
Use of the term, and the social restrictions which accompany it, were declared illegal in the constitution adopted by the Constituent Assembly of India in 1949 and of Pakistan in 1953.
1909 *Indian Spectator* 23 Oct. 843/2 Our untouchables were not clean. **1911** *Times* 2 Feb. 5/5 When it is remembered in what manner the lower classes are treated in daily life it may appear strange that the higher castes should be so..alarmed at the prospect of the untouchables ceasing to be regarded as Hindus. **1920** *Asiatic Review* XVI. 172 The term 'untouchable', as a name for the 'depressed classes', or 'outcastes', is a revival of the most ancient designation of these people. **1926** in *N.E.D.* s.v. *untouchable* adj. **1928** *Daily Express* 22 May 10/2 Those in Whitehall may go on thinking there is something extremely meritorious in treating Russia as a diplomatic untouchable. **1931**, etc. [see HARIJAN]. **1960**, **1969** [see ETA, ETA[3]]. **1975** *Guardian* 27 Jan. 5 Five hundred Untouchables—low caste Indians—marched on Downing Street yesterday. **1978** N. J. CRISP *London Deal* vi. 104 'Well, I've become a non-copper.' 'You mean you've been suspended?'.. 'A modern untouchable.' **1981** G. PRIESTLAND *Priestland's Progress* vi. 93 The Indian untouchable who becomes a Christian often has to pay a heavy price for his liberation.
Hence **un'touchableness**, the state or condition of being untouchable.
1909 *Times of India* (Mail ed.) 23 Oct. 19/3 The Hon. Mr. Ghokale..thought if only the untouchableness went, it would be a comparatively easy matter to help these classes. **1916** *Indian Review* Feb., in M. K. Gandhi *Coll. Works* (1964) XIII. 232 This miserable, wretched, enslaving spirit of 'untouchableness'. **1970** *Daily Tel.* 7 Feb. 9/6 It [*sc.* Verdi's 'Macbeth']..had to overcome our strong proprietorial feelings about the untouchableness of Shakespeare.

un'touched, *ppl. a.* [UN-[1] 8.]
I. 1. a. Not touched with the hand (finger, foot, etc.): not handled or treated by hand, etc.
1382 WYCLIF *2 Kings* xxiii. 18 The citeȝeens..vntouchid laften the boonys of hym. *c* **1440** *Pallad. on Husb.* VI. 4 Now euery grayne almeest hath floures swete; Vntouched now the tilman let hem growe. **1502** ATKYNSON tr. *De Imitatione* I. xiii. (1893) 162 A bell untouchyd is not perfytely knowen whether it be hole..or dyscrased. *a* **1586** SIDNEY *Arcadia* III xvi, I pray you..to let my maides take my body untouched by you. **1673** [R. LEIGH] *Transp. Reh.* 43 Romances are thumb'd more than.. Gondibert is Dogs-ear'd, while the Rabbies are untoucht. **1697** DRYDEN *Æneis* x. 1173 Untouched thy arms, untaken be thy sword. **1725** POPE *Odyssey* II 396 Untouch'd and sacred may these vessels stand Till great Ulysses views his native land. **1801** SCOTT *Glenfinlas* xxxviii, Untouch'd, the harp began to ring. **1816** J. WILSON *City of Plague* I. ii. 26 Buy poison, and 'twill lie for years untouch'd Beneath thy pillow. **1877** HUXLEY *Physiogr.* p. viii, The manuscript remained untouched until last year.
b. Not touched by another body, etc.; †*spec.* (quot. 1730), unmagnetized.
a **1595** SOUTHWELL *Mæoniæ, Christ's Bloody Sweat* 3 Fat soile, full spring, sweete oliue, grape of blisse, Vntil'd, vndrawne, vnstampt, vntoucht of presse. **1730** *Phil. Trans.* XXXVI. 295 Of Touched Iron or Steel (or of Untouched, so long as it remains in a Posture which gives it Polarity). **1736** THOMSON *Liberty* IV. 416 Even yet untouch'd by daring keel, be theirs The vast Pacific.
c. Not approached, crossed, or traversed.
1628 MAY *Virg. Georg.* III. 75 Let us follow the Woods, and Lands Vntouch'd. **1729** T. INNES *Crit. Essay* I. 28 The northern wall..was of no use at all to keep off the enemies, who leaving it untouch'd, passed easily over the narrow Friths. **1882** H. S. HOLLAND *Logic & Life* 50 We are carried forward to explore new regions of our souls as yet untouched and untrodden.
2. a. Not affected physically, esp. in an injurious manner; not damaged, harmed, or meddled with; unhurt, uninjured; intact. Const. *by*, †*of*.
c **1400** *Found. St. Bartholomew's* 62 Of an howse vntouchid yn myddyl of the fyer. *c* **1440** *Jacob's Well* 183 His suster..be þe vertu of schryfte, was vntowchyd of þe fyir. **1526** *Pilgr. Perf.* (W. de W. 1531) 136 b, Whiche came out safe & vntouched of ye fyre. **1571** GOLDING *Calvin on Ps.* xvi. 10 No one [of the faithful] becommeth partaker of incorruptible lyfe, untowched of rotting. **1603** KNOLLES *Hist. Turks* (1621) 101 The Sultan..polluted the sepulchre of our blessed Sauiour,..of all nations vntouched & reuerenced. **1666** BOYLE *Orig. Forms & Qual.* 112 The Rudiments of the Chick..is nourish'd..onely by the White of the Egg... In effect you may see the Chick furnish'd not onely with all the necessary, but divers other parts,..whilst the Yolk seems yet as it were untouch'd. **1690** DRYDEN *Don Sebastian* V. ii, Untouch'd, and Seal'd, as when intrusted with me, Such I restore it [*sc.* a paper]. **1736** THOMSON *Liberty* II. 246 Then stood untouch'd the solid base Of Liberty, the Liberty of Mind. **1749** JOHNSON *Van. Hum. Wishes* 35 Untouch'd his Cottage, and his Slumbers sound, Tho' Confiscation's Vulturs clang around. **1820** SHELLEY *Hope, Fear, & Doubt* 9 Nor did I hope to pass Untouched by suffering, through the rugged glen. **1856** KANE *Arct. Expl.* I. 317 We landed at the point where we left our life-boat a year ago, and to our great joy found it untouched! **1890** OMAN *Hist. Greece* 303 The plague had left the rest of Greece almost untouched.
†**b.** Not having had sexual connexions; immaculate, chaste, undefiled. *Obs.*
c **1400** *Found. St. Bartholomew's* 49 She skapid vntowchid. *c* **1450** *Myrr. our Ladye* 171 O vntouwched mother of the kynge of peace. *Ibid.* 296 Yet that maydes wombe is alway vntowched. **1577** tr. *Bullinger's Decades* 62/2 The vntouched Virgine Marie. **1621** LADY M. WROTH *Urania* 343 Shee loues the Prince of Iambolly much better then the King;..yet on my conscience shee is vntouched, and iust to her Husband. *a* **1649** DRUMM. OF HAWTH. *Hist. Jas. II*, Wks. (1711) 31 The earl..sought..to have her in marriage, alledging her untouched of his brother. **1683** DRYDEN tr. *Ovid, Helen to Paris* 30 Rude force might some unwilling Kisses gain, But that was all he ever could obtain... Untouch'd the Youth restor'd me to my friends.
c. Not used at all, left intact; *esp.* not partaken of, untasted.
1538 ELYOT, *Illibatus*, vntouched, vntasted. **1577** B. GOOGE *Heresbach's Husb.* 36 Lupines,..for the bitternesse thereof whyle it is greene, they [*sc.* cattle] leaue vntouched. *a* **1589** MASCALL *Govt. Cattle* (1596) 69 Cattell..leaue many tufts of grasse here and there vntouched. **1610** HOLLAND *Camden's Brit.* I. 303 Choosing rather..to send away whole dishes vntouched, than other commers vnbidden to call for more viands. **1666** EARL ORRERY *St. Lett.* (1742) 184 The 10,000 *l.* stock..I humbly beg your grace will keep.. untouched to answer a dead lift with. **1679** PEPYS *Mem. Royal Navy* (1906) 5 A further Reserve [of Supplies] remain'd untoucht in Magazine. **1725** POPE *Odyssey* x. 447 Untouch'd before thee stand the cates divine. **1798** J. NAISMITH *Agric. Clydesdale* 93 The pastures are allowed to grow untouched, from..May to..August. *a* **1828** *Arab. Nts.* (1853) 328 A great quantity of provisions left untouched. **1839** THACKERAY *Fatal Boots* Dec., That famous rum-punch..which she and my sisters left untouched. **1863** MISS BRADDON *Aurora Floyd* ii, He had sent his dinner away untouched.
3. Not worked upon or at; not touched or treated by way of improvement, alteration, operation, etc.
1726 LEONI *Alberti's Archit.* I. 39/1, I am..for preserving the old Structures untoucht. **1736** T. PRINCE *N. Eng. Chronol.* II. II. 231 The General Frame of Diocesan Episcopacy had no doubt remain'd untouched. **1815** J. SMITH *Panorama Sci. & Art* II. 778 In engraving upon copper, every part which is to be white must be left untouched. **1833–4** *Encycl. Metrop.* (1845) VI. 706/1 The mighty forests of America, untouched by human industry. **1862** *Catal. Internat. Exhib., Brit.* II. No. 3168, Untouched and coloured photographs. **1884** THOMPSON *Tumours of Bladder* 41 [He] found a large tumour, which, after consultation, was left untouched.
II. 4. Not dealt with in discourse, etc.; not treated, written about, or spoken of; unmentioned. Also with *upon*.
c **1380** WYCLIF *Sel. Wks.* III. 362 þus no þing untouchid in þis lawe shulde be dun or axid to do. **1382** —— *Joshua* viii. 35 No thing..that Moyses comaundide, he left vntowchyd; but alle thingis he openyde [**1388** declaride] before al the multitude. **1532** MORE *Confut. Tindale* Wks. 609/2 Wherein whoso consider what I haue aunswered hym, shal..perceiue that it had been better for him to haue lefte that matter vntouched. **1594** SHAKS. *Rich. III*, III. vii. 19, I..left nothing..Vntoucht, or sleightly handled in discourse. **1667** BOYLE *Orig. Forms & Qual.* (ed. 2) 293 The nature of our present discourse forbids me to leave it altogether untouch'd. **1697** [C. LESLIE] *Snake in Grass* (ed. 2) 307 In his Answer..he passes this Section of their Diabolical Possessions, wholly untouch'd. **1793** WORDSW. *Descrip. Sketches* Ded. ¶4, I might have inscribed to you a description of some of the features... But the Alpine steeps of the Conway..remain yet untouched. **1841** SPALDING *Italy & It. Isl.* I. 150 The earliest progress of Grecian art.. must here be left untouched. **1866** G. STEPHENS *Runic Mon.* I. p. vi, The comparatively few hitherto almost untoucht and unredd older or Old-Northern Runic pieces. **1900** *Handbk. Austral. Assoc., Melbourne* 74 The aquatic worms are an untouched group.
(*b*) **1746** ELIZA HEYWOOD *Female Spect.* No. 24 (1748) IV. 319 They will needs have us take up the pen again, and promise to furnish us with a variety of topics yet untouched upon. **1856** CARLYLE *Lett. Emerson* (1883) II. 258, I must end, in mid-course; so much still untouched upon.
5. a. Not affected, modified, or influenced, esp. in a prejudicial or adverse manner.
a **1586** SIDNEY *Def. Earl Leicester* Wks. 1923 III. 67 If awncient undouted and untouched nobility bee worthi to match with the most noble hows that can bee. **1593** *Sidney's Arcadia* V. (1622) 475 How can any lawes..be obserued, if the law-giuers, and law-rulers bee not held in an vntouched admiration? **1696** PRIOR *Presented to King* 32 Be William's Life untouch'd, as is his Fame. **1699** BENTLEY *Phal.* 232 In the third Verse..Mr. Stanley corrected it.., as appears by his Translation, utile; the other word he leaves untouch'd. **1732** BERKELEY *Alciphr.* I. §9, I will shew you..That whatever was sound and good we leave untouched, and encourage it to grow in the Mind of Man. **1761** STERNE *Tr. Shandy* IV. xxix, In the case cited,..where *patriae* is put for *patris*, *filia* for *filii*, and so on—as it is a fault only in the declension, and the roots of the words continue untouched. *a* **1763** W. KING *Anecd.* (1818) 163 Clodia..was descended from an old Patrician family... Her behaviour was modest, and her reputation untouched. **1894** H. DRUMMOND *Ascent Man* 182 [In North Queensland you] will find the child of Nature still untouched, and neither by intercourse nor imitation removed by one degree from the lowest savage state.
b. Not affected or prejudiced in mind or feeling; not biassed or moved by excitement or emotion; unmoved, undisturbed, calm.
1616 T. ADAMS *Div. Herball* 89 Some Sage, honest policie; ..such as may stand with an vntouched conscience. **1697** VANBRUGH *Æsop* I. i, Is it possible any thing that I am Father of, can be untouch'd with so much Merit? **1709** STEELE & SWIFT *Tatler* No. 71 ¶4 If a Man could be untouched at so warm an Accusation. **1748** RICHARDSON *Clarissa* VII. i. 3 The roughest and most untouched creature that ever enter'd a sick man's chamber. **1768–74** TUCKER *Lt. Nat.* (1834) II. 678 Every one proceeding by a softness and milkiness of temper, untouched by injuries, unmoved at offences. **1805** WORDSW. *Prelude* V. 182 Think not that I could pass along untouched By these remembrances. **1838** LYTTON *Alice* I. x, Her heart is as yet untouched;—if she can love you, may you deserve her affection. **1876** MISS BRADDON *J. Haggard's*

Dau. II. 60 The young people were..untouched by the blighting influence of this aggrieved spinster.

6. Not equalled in respect of excellence or high character; unexampled, unparalleled.

1736 THOMSON *Liberty* II. 194 Greece in their view, and glory yet untouch'd, Their steady column..held its way Triumphant. **1878** GROSART *H. More's Poems* p. xxxiii, I have been struck with the untouched perfection of all that arrests you in reading.

7. Not entered upon; not begun.

1876 *Coursing Cal.* 21 The day finished at dusk, with only twenty-seven trials, leaving the all-aged stake untouched.

Hence **un'touchedness.**

1889 KIPLING *From Sea to Sea* (1899) I. xviii. 145 The utter untouchedness of the town was one-half the charm.

un'touching, *ppl. a.* [UN-¹ 5 d, 10.]

1. Not touching (something).

1602 W. BASSE *Three Past. Elegies* i. (1893) 46 My flocks ..saw their maisters eie Perus'd in things vntutching their estate. **1632** LITHGOW *Trav.* VII. 327 Their flight will bee the length of a Cables Rope, vntouching Water. **1846** MANGAN *Poems* (1903) 6 Untouching the earth I then sped forth To Inver-lough.

b. Not having contact.

a **1811** J. GRAHAME *Poems* (1827) 88 Like that untouching cincture which enzones The globe of Saturn.

2. Having no effect upon the feelings; unaffecting.

1745 ELIZA HEYWOOD *Female Spect.* No. 10. II. 204 All the Protestations they made..were..unfelt by themselves, and equally untouching to those they were address'd.

un'touchingly, *adv.* (UN-¹ 11. Cf. prec. 2.)

1861 MISS YONGE *Young Stepmother* iii. 26 Albinia had been strongly interested by the touching facts, so untouchingly narrated.

untoward (ʌntəˈwɔːd, ʌnˈtəʊəd), *a.* [UN-¹ 7.]

†**1.** Not having or showing inclination, disposition, or readiness *to* or *for* something; disinclined.

1526 *Pilgr. Perf.* (W. de W. 1531) 42 b, Syth of our selfe we be insufficient & all vntowarde to all goostly thynges. **1575** VAUTROLLIER *Luther on Ep. Gal.* 252 If Satan did not vexe vs inwardly with spirituall tentations,..we should become vtterly careles, negligent, and vntoward to all good workes. **1594** CAREW *Huarte's Exam. Wits* i. (1596) 5 Those who are vntoward for one science, are very apt to another. **1628** WITHER *Brit. Rememb.* Pref. 713 Yea, so untoward was I to conforme My Will,..That [etc.]. **1665** MANLEY *Grotius' Low C. Wars* 73 The Captains were yet not skilled in managing their Men, and the Men were untoward to be commanded.

†**b.** Showing lack of proficiency or aptitude; inept, slow. *Obs. rare.*

1557 NORTH *Gueuara's Diall Pr.* Prol. A ij, Greate travayle taketh a scole maister in teaching an untowarde scholler. **1592** NASHE *Four Lett. Confut.* F 4 Lamentable, that an indifferent vntoward ciuill Lawyer..should be no more set by but..thrust aside.

2. Of persons (or animals), their disposition, etc.: Difficult to manage, restrain, or control; intractable, unruly, perverse.

In frequent use from *c* 1580 to *c* 1700.

1526 TINDALE *Acts* ii. 40 Save youre selves from this vntowarde generacion. **1548** UDALL, etc. *Erasm. Par. Luke* i. 16 b, If the same commyng of yᵉ Lorde shoulde fynde the hertes of men slouthfully sluggyng, & vtterly vntowarde. **1587** *Norton's Calvin's Inst.* III. xxiv. 326 b, The vnchangeable decree of God concerning the destruction of the wicked is the ground of their vntoward disposition. **1624** GATAKER *Good Wife* 3 It is no small vexation for a man to find vntoward and vnfaithful cariage toward him in those.. that feed at his boord. *a* **1654** —— *Antid. Errour* (1670) 54 The verie prohibitions..of the Law..ar to mans untoward spirit, but as water to qick lime. **1656** EARL MONM. tr. *Boccalini's Pol. Touchstone* (1674) 257 The very untoward Spanish Mules, who are so..given to lay about them with their heels. **1714** GAY *Sheph. Week* v. 53 Th' untoward creatures to the stye I drove. **1771** MACKENZIE *Man Feel.* vii, The young man was so untoward in his disposition. **1789** BELSHAM *Ess.* I. iii. 55 This..answer..mollified the untoward and uncourtly disposition of the House. **1814** JANE AUSTEN *Mansf. Park* ii, A most untoward gravity of deportment. **1817** BYRON *Mazeppa* viii, The devil!—I'm loth to do him wrong, It might be some untoward saint. **1865** M. ARNOLD *Ess. Crit.* ix. (1875) 379 The untoward generation of metaphysical Article-makers.

transf. **1809** W. IRVING *Knickerb.* I. i, The untoward planet pertinaciously continued her course, notwithstanding that she had..a whole university of learned professors opposed to her conduct.

b. Of things: Difficult to manipulate, work, deal with, or perform; stubborn, stiff.

1566 DRANT *Sat.* I. x. E vj, Why maye not we inquyre.. if the matter to vntoward, hath made his style to harde. **1601** B. JONSON *Poetaster* I. i, Nay looke, what a rascally vntoward thing this poetrie is. **1620** SANDERSON *Serm.* (1632) 101 God ..out of mankinde, as out of an vntoward lumpe of clay,.. maketh vp vessels for the vse of his Sanctuary. **1664** BUTLER *Hud.* II. II. 293 A Vow Which afterward he found untoward, And stubborn to be kept. **1693** CONGREVE *Old Bach.* III. viii, Pish! This is the untowardest lock [of hair]. **1799** J. ROBERTSON *Agric. Perth* 278 A piece of untoward ground.. cannot be improved with equal success in any other way. **1831** CARLYLE in Froude *Life* (1882) II. 203 A noisy, untoward lodging-house. **1833–5** J. H. NEWMAN *Hist. Sk.* Ser. III. (1873) 49 Basil had to deal on all hands with most untoward materials. **1875** TAIT & STEWART *Unseen Universe* ii. (1878) 81 There is a periodicity even in such untoward phenomena.

†**c.** Awkward, clumsy; ungainly, ungraceful.

1590 SPENSER *F.Q.* I. viii. 31 But very vncouth sight was to behold, How he did fashion his vntoward pace. **1592** LYLY *Gallathea* II. i, I neither like my gate, nor my garments; the one vntoward, the other vnfit. **1628** FORD *Lover's Mel.* v. i, I am..so poor and feeble, That my untoward joints can scarcely creep Unto the grave. **1632** LITHGOW *Trav.* x. 433 Their..Ploughes..are only fastned with Straw..to their bare Rumps, marching..three or foure in a Ranke, and as many men hanging by the ends of that vntoward Labour. **1658** A. FOX *Würtz' Surg.* II. xviii. 125, I will write now of Knees that are much pained..and grow untoward and unshaped. **1762** H. WALPOLE *Vertue's Anecd. Paint.* (1765) III. 65 His drawing even of the neck and shoulders..[was] incorrect and untoward. *a* **1791** SIR J. REYNOLDS in Boswell *Johnson* an. 1739, Accompanying his thoughts with certain untoward actions [*ante* 'improperly called convulsions'].

3. Characterized or attended by misfortune, calamity, vexation, or annoyance; unlucky, unfortunate, ill-starred: **a.** Of conditions, times, etc.

1570 T. WILSON tr. *Demosth. Orat.* vii. 95 Thorowe the Lacedemonians vntowarde lucke. **1603** HOLLAND *Plutarch's Mor.* 238 The diseases, the debts, the hard usage of men to their owne wives, and the untoward life betweene them. **1782** WOLCOT (P. Pindar) *Lyric Odes* vii, The courtly Abington's untoward Star Wanted her reputation much to mar. **1805–6** WORDSW. *Char. Happy Warrior* 68 Who, with a toward or untoward lot,..Plays, in the many games of life, that one [etc.]. **1868** ROGERS *Pol. Econ.* ii. (1876) 103 A man ..should have a..reserve from which he can draw when the times are untoward. **1878** STUBBS *Const. Hist.* III. xviii. 88 No untoward omen..threw a shadow over the second epoch of the war. **1898** 'H. S. MERRIMAN' *Roden's Corner* xxx, Percy..looked back later to this as one of his most untoward hours.

b. Of occurrences, enterprises, etc.

Esp. with *accident, circumstance, event,* and in very frequent use from *c* 1800.

1632 LITHGOW *Trav.* x. 482 When Charles the fift returned from that vntoward voyage of Algier. **1638** SIR T. HERBERT *Trav.* (ed. 2) 92 The report of this vntoward massacre is soone knowne. **1647** CLARENDON *Hist. Reb.* III. § 1 An untoward, and in truth an unheard of accident, which brake many of the King's measures. **1760** STERNE *Tr. Shandy* III. xxiv, The foulmouth'd trumpet of Fame carried it from ear to ear, with this untoward circumstance along with it. **1798** W. HUTTON *Autobiog.* 115 An untoward trade is a dreadful sink for money. **1814** JANE AUSTEN *Mansf. Park* i, She could hardly have made a more untoward choice. **1833** HT. MARTINEAU *Berkeley* I. ii, There were no untoward delays. **1893** LIDDON *Life Pusey* I. viii. 176 He felt anxious as to the untoward influence..of these books.

absol. **1887** RUSKIN *Præterita* II. 120 Every soul of us has to do its fight with the Untoward, and for itself discover the Unseen.

4. Unfavourable or adverse to progress; unpropitious, unprosperous.

1621 in Foster *Eng. Factories Ind.* (1906) I. 283 The wayes soe untoward that in the best season..they are unpassable for carts. **1662** J. DAVIES tr. *Olearius' Voy. Ambass.* 391 Bridges, raised very high,..so untoward to pass over, that they put a man into a fright. **1725** *Portland Papers* (Hist. MSS. Comm.) VI. 120 We came down by a very steep, untoward descent. **1731** CAPT. W. WRIGLESWORTH *MS. Log-bk. of the 'Lyell'* 4 Mar., Wee have had a very untoward ugly Sea all these 24 Hours. **1791** SMEATON *Edystone L.* 145 The weather being untoward, the short sea..occasioned.. a motion of the yawls. **1833** HT. MARTINEAU *Three Ages* II. 35 The present had been an untoward season, as regarded the nation's prosperity. **1849** GROTE *Hist. Greece* II. xliv. V. 381 An untoward storm drove the vessel to the island. **1886** C. SCOTT *Sheep-farming* 83 In untoward seasons..the lambs often do not exceed 100 per cent. of the ewes.

5. a. At variance with good conduct or propriety; indecorous, unseemly, improper; foolish.

1628–9 DIGBY *Voy. Medit.* (Camden) 57 Because idlenesse should not fixe their mindes vpon any vntoward fansies. **1658** T. WHITE in Spurgeon *Treas. Dav.* Ps. lxxiii. 17 They came to a very wicked man's house, where they had very untoward entertainment. **1695** WOODWARD *Nat. Hist. Earth* III. (1723) 179 Some Men there are who have made a very untoward Use of this. **1709** STRYPE *Ann. Ref.* I. i. 44 The popish priests..took frequent occasion..to speak very untoward words against the Queen. **1802** WORDSW. *Resolution & Indep.* 53 When I with these untoward thoughts had striven.

†**b.** Marked by lack of reason or fitness. *Obs.*

1682 H. MORE *Annot. Glanvill's Lux O.* 95 If you paraphrase (*me*) thus, My Hypostasis consisting of my Humane and Divine Nature, it will be as untoward sence. **1701** NORRIS *Ideal World* I. v. 225 It seems..untoward, to inquire whether a thing be,..before we know what it is we inquire about. **1733** BERKELEY *Th. Vision Vind.* § 6 Such is the ill effect of untoward defences and explanations of our faith.

†**6.** Of taste: Disagreeable; unpleasant. *Obs.*⁻¹

1662 J. DAVIES tr. *Mandelslo's Trav.* 245 It had so untoward a taste, that the Sea-men would not take it for their..drink.

†**un'toward,** *prep. Obs.* [f. UNTO *prep.* + -WARD. Cf. UNTILWARD.] Toward; in the direction of.

1390 GOWER *Conf.* II. 20 Whanne I am mi ladi fro And thenke untoward hire drawe. *Ibid.* 215 Nevere for no worldes good Min herte untoward hire stod. *Ibid.* III. 127.

un'towardliness. (UN-¹ 12. Cf. next.)

1598 BARCKLEY *Felic. Man* v. 427 The fathers felicitie is deminished by the childrens vntowardlinesse. **1603** FLORIO *Montaigne* I. xxv. 86 Who..could..winke at..my vntowardlinesse, and such other faults that were in mee. **1707** *Pennsylv. Hist. Soc. Mem.* X. 235 The more privileges the more presumption and untowardliness.

un'towardly, *a.* Now *rare.* [UN-¹ 7.]

1. Unbecoming, improper.

1483 *Cov. Leet Bk.* 511 Not beyng content with such answer [he] desired a copy of þat Evidence,..&..other vntowardly wordes there vttered. **1598** GRENEWEY *Tacitus, Ann.* I. ii. 3 Little doubt but Augustus, complaining of the yong mans vntowardly behauior, caused his exile to be confirmed. **1693** LOCKE *Educ.* 70 [Children] frequently learn from unbred or debauched Servants..untowardly Tricks and Vices.

b. Froward, perverse, ill-disposed.

1561 T. HOBY tr. *Castiglione's Courtyer* IV. Z z iii, Not to be haughtie, enuious,..contentious nor vntowardlye. **1598** BARCKLEY *Felic. Man* v. 427 If they [*sc.* children] prooue vntowardly and giuen to lewdnesse, what greater griefe can happen to a man? *a* **1678** H. SCOUGAL *Disc. Imp. Subj.* (1735) 193 Sad and heavy looks, morose and untowardly deportment. **1712** STEELE *Spect.* No. 442 ¶ 3 The Serene or Cloudy, Jovial or Melancholy, Untowardly or Easy [Temper]. **1791** WASHINGTON *Let.* Writ. 1892 XII. 85 If you are disobliging, self-willed, and untowardly, it is hardly to be expected that they will engage themselves in unpleasant disputes with you. **1887** *S. Cheshire Gloss.* 320 Ay, he's..an unto'artly yowth, is Joe.

2. Awkward, clumsy.

1611 COTGR., *Faire le pied de veau,* to make an vntowardlie, or clownish leg; or, to vse a foolish lifting vp of the leg in dauncing, &c. *a* **1642** SIR W. MONSON *Naval Tracts* II. (1704) 270/1 They went the most untowardly way I ever saw. **1668** ETHEREDGE *She wou'd if she cou'd* III. ii, Well, thou hast seduc'd me; But I shall look so untowardly.

3. Ill-suiting; adverse; unfavourable.

1756 C. LUCAS *Ess. Waters* II. 257, I have observed at Spa ..one most untowardly effect. **1856** CARLYLE *Let.* 22 Feb. (Encycl. Dict.), Travelling is at all times very untowardly to me. **1864** —— *Fredk. Gt.* xv. iii. IV. 32 The Expedition does not improve in promise;..the march one of the most untowardly.

untowardly (ʌntəˈwɔːdlɪ, -ˈtəʊəd-), *adv.* [UN-¹ 11.]

1. Unskilfully, awkwardly, clumsily, badly.

1550 BALE *Apol.* 146 b, That rawe and ragged clause whych ye haue vntowardly torne out of hys xxi. homely. **1561** T. NORTON *Calvin's Inst.* III. 159 No man shal go so vntowardly, but he shal euery day get some ground, though it be but litle. **1576** R. PETERSON *G. della Casa's Galateo* 105 Their cloathes doe sit vppon them so vntowardly. **1642** FULLER *Holy & Prof. St.* IV. ix. 281 Generally the most dexterous in spirituall matters are left-handed in temporall businesse, and go but untowardly about them. **1667** DRYDEN *Sir Martin Mar-all* v. i, He played well, and yet methinks he held his lute not untowardly. **1697** DAMPIER *Voy.* I. 190 They rig their Ships but untowardly,..and are as meanly furnished with Warlike Provisions. **1762** STERNE *Tr. Shandy* VI. xxxiii, A large uneven thread..running along the whole length of the web, and so untowardly, you cannot so much as cut out..a fillet. **1764** HARMER *Observ.* ix. 23 There is no scripture from whence he attempts to deduce it, as he doth the time of the latter rain, though very untowardly.

b. Unsuitably (for use).

1686 PLOT *Staffordsh.* 352 If there be any such land that lyes so untowardly.

2. Unluckily; unpropitiously; with likelihood or suggestion of misfortune or mishap.

1568 GRAFTON *Chron.* II. 262 As he lept out of his ship,.. he fell so vntowardly, that the blood brast out of his nose. **1571** GOLDING *Calvin on Ps.* ii. 8 Least this Prophecie should bee spoken in vayne, yea and untowardly concerning the largenesse of dominion. **1599** SHAKS. *Much Ado* III. ii. 134 O day vntowardly turned! **1603** HOLLAND *Plutarch's Mor.* 108 Which as many as use, worke their own.. destruction, dauncing..a daunce untowardly about a pits brinke. **1699** BENTLEY *Phal.* Introd. 2 Mr. B. here seems to enter upon his work a little untowardly and ominously.

b. Unsuccessfully; unfortunately.

1649 J. H. *Motion to Parl. Adv. Learn.* 35 There were some propensions and aversions,..which if disobeyed succeeded untowardly and unsuccessefully. **1679** *Hist. Jetzer* 26 The Prior swore things went very untowardly against them. *a* **1722** LISLE *Husb.* (1752) 180 Such barley.. will come away very untowardly in the malting. **1815** JANE AUSTEN *Emma* xxxvi, If things are going untowardly one month, they are sure to mend the next. **1889** GRETTON *Memory's Harkb.* 269 On his death-bed he..sent urgently for the clergyman, who untowardly happened to be from home.

3. Rudely, roughly; frowardly.

1682 BUNYAN *Holy War* 223, I charge you, therefore,.. that you carry it not ruggedly, or untowardly to my Captains, or their men. **1693** SOUTHERNE *Maid's Last Prayer* II. ii, Give me thy Hand dear Bully; Faith, I'm sorry you provok'd me to use you so untowardly. **1868–9** BROWNING *Ring & Bk.* IX. 259 Let the heifer bear the yoke! ..What if..all untowardly she pursue her way With groan and grunt?

untowardness (ʌntəˈwɔːdnɪs, -ˈtəʊəd-). [UN-¹ 12.]

1. Disinclination to be accommodating or pleasant; perversity, obstinacy.

1481 *Cov. Leet Bk.* 500 We fynde them therunto in no wyse towardly disposed,..which their vntowardnesse sᵉwneth not to oure pleasure. **1538–9** HENRY VIII in *Wyatt's Wks.* (1816) II. 501 Continuing our good mind and affection to join with him (his said untowardness and coldness in that behalf notwithstanding.) **1569** in Bolton *Stat. Irel.* (1621) 339 Which is occasioned by the sluggardy, idlenesse and vntowardnes of the Marchants. **1607** HIERON *Wks.* I. 129 Gods first work in them is..to remooue their naturall vntowardnesse, and to make their hearts more.. pliable vnto good. **1658** *Whole Duty Man* 120 Complain not of the hardness of the duty, but of the untowardness of thy own heart. **1723** *Pres. St. Russia* I. 16 The Untowardness of these People made me astonished. **1765** MRS. MACAULEY *Hist. Eng.* II. 232 Finding him not at so entire leisure to discipline their untowardness as in time of peace. **1873** HAMERTON *Intell. Life* II. ii. 54 Our untowardness was a hopeful sign.

b. Const. *to* (esp. with inf.).

c **1547** LATIMER in Foxe *A. & M.* (1563) 1352/1 So should I haue bene without this inwarde sorrow of my harte, to see suche vntowardnes of you bothe to godlines. **1557** EARL WESTMORLD. in Lodge *Illustr. Brit. Hist.* (1791) I. 287, I ame sory to see suche an untowardnes to serve in the Bushopriche men as ys now. **1579** J. STUBBES *Gaping Gulf* E j b, If ther be . . a generall vntowardnes to desirc that statc of lyfe.

†**2.** Lack of good progress or promise, *esp.* in respect of physical condition. *Obs.*

1538 AUDLEY in *St. Papers Henry VIII*, I. 588 Besechyng you to travayle therin [*sc.* the suit] and to advertise me . . of the towardnes or ontowardnes therof. **1555** WATREMAN *Fardle Facions* II. viii. 184 Yf thei spie vntowardnes in the infante, deformitie, or lacke of lymmes, [they] commaunde it to be slayne. **1601** HOLLAND *Pliny* I. 359 Even in trees as well as in other living creatures, there is a certaine infelicitie, which may be well tearmed, A dwarfish untowardnesse.

†**3.** Lack of aptitude; awkwardness. *Obs.*

1598 FLORIO, *Inettudine*, vnaptnesse, vntowardnesse, grossenes. **1604** T. WRIGHT *Passions* v. iii. 176 Some . . eloquent [men], . . for lack of action or rather vntowardnesse, . . were accounted infants. **1622** F. MARKHAM *Bk. War* v. ii. 168 There will be such disparity and untowardnesse in his actions, that all his labour will be to little or no purpose.

4. Unpropitiousness; adverseness.

1778 [W. H. MARSHALL] *Minutes Agric., Observ.* 101 The untowardness of circumstances prevented any Experiment . . from being made. **1803–5** WORDSW. *Rob Roy's Grave* 62 Through untowardness of fate . . He came an age too late. **1847** HELPS *Friends in C.* I. iii. 44 The untowardness of things present, the miseries of the past. **1871** MORLEY *Vauvenargues* in *Crit. Misc.* 7 His nature had such . . quality that the perpetual untowardness of circumstances left no evil print upon him.

†**un'towards**, *a. Obs.* [Cf. TOWARDS *prep.* and *adv.*] = UNTOWARD *a.* 1 and 2.

1525 in Ellis *Orig. Lett.* Ser. III. I. 360 Ther is no wise man but wool thinke . . that it apperith, seing they be thus vntowards, that they be lincked together, for commonlye they aggreid in oon aunswer. **1548** UDALL, etc. *Erasm. Par. John* 40 The lustes of thie worlde maketh many one vntowardes to bee taughte.

†**un'towe(n**, *ppl. a. Obs.* Forms: (see quots.). [OE. *unȝetoȝen* (UN-¹ 8 b), = OHG. *ungizogan*, *unkazogan*, etc. (MHG. and G. *ungezogen*, obs. G. *unzogen*), MLG. *un(ge)togen* uneducated, undisciplined, ill-bred, etc., MSw. *otughin* improper, disreputable, etc. Cf. WANTON *a.*] Untaught, untrained; unmannered, wanton.

c **1000** ÆLFRIC *Hom.* I. 576 Fisceras and unȝetoȝene menn ȝeceas Drihten him to leorning-cnihtum. *c* **1225** *Ancr. R.* 102 Eni totilde ancre . . þet bekeð euer utward ase untowe brid ine cage. *Ibid.* 372 So tendre of þe bodie þet hit iwurðe untowen. *a* **1240** *Sawles Warde* in *O.E. Hom.* I. 245 For alle hit beoð untohene ant rechelese hinen. *Ibid.* 267 To . . leaden him . . nawt efter wil, þe untohe lefdi, . . ah efter þat wit wule, þat is husebonde. *a* **1310** in Wright *Lyric P.* viii. 32 Thah told beon tales untoun in toun. **13..** *Metr. Hom.* in *Archiv Stud. neu. Spr.* LVII. 252/1 Þis ilke childe was so vntoun and so wylde. *c* **1425** in *Anglia* VIII. 145 Wiþ hir vntoune & lacches songes [she] kyndeliþ þe fyre of lecchery.

Hence †**un'towe(n)ly** *adv.*, wantonly; **un'towe(n)ship**, wantonness. *Obs.*

a **1225** *Ancr. R.* 170 Schomeleas is þe mon oðer þeo wummon þet deð eni untoweschipe, oðer seið, biuoren ancren. *a* **1230** *Hali Meid.* 22 3ef 3e þenne hondlið ow in ei stude untuliche [*v.r.* untoheliche]. *a* **1240** *Sawles Warde* in *O.E. Hom.* I. 247 Nis hare nan þe ne þearf ofte untoheliche ant gulteð ilome. *c* **1450** *Cursor M.* 10135 (Laud MS.), I rede of hem ye here That may you help in your mystere And leve your vntounship a-while.

un'town, *v.* (UN-² 6 b.)

1783 WOLCOT (P. Pindar) *Odes R.A.'s* VI. i, Find me in Sodom out . . Ten gentlemen, the place shan't be un*town'd.*

un'trace, *v.* [UN-² 4 b.] *trans.* To free (horses) from the traces.

1604 MIDDLETON *Father Hubburd's T.* B 1, The fiery Horses of the Sun Were from their golden-flaming Car vntrac'de. **1819** W. S. ROSE *Lett. N. Italy* I. 87 We again put to the horses, necessarily untraced during the preceding operation.

un'traceable, *a.* (UN-¹ 7 b.)

1661 BOYLE *Style of Script.* 20 Who can alone . . fathom the depths of Satan, and track him through all his windings and (otherwise untraceable) Labyrinths. *a* **1684** LEIGHTON *Comm. 1 Pet.* i. (1693) 199 If the wayes of Gods universall providence be untraceable. **1758** *Monthly Rev.* 507 A proper and salutary quantity of this untraceable fluid. **1782–3** W. F. MARTYN *Geog. Mag.* I. 335 The untraceable way by which Divine Wisdom issues from the infinite ocean of God. **1807** *Med. Jrnl.* XVII. 293 The . . hooping-cough . . was untraceable to any apparent source. **1883** J. PARKER *Apost. Life* II. 167 Physical circumstances . . operate in a subtle and often untraceable manner upon our . . spiritual constitution. *absol.* **1818** MILMAN *Samor* VII. 172, I know thee now, majestic Rebel! thee The untraceable, untameable!

Hence **un'traceableness**; **un'traceably** *adv.*

1856 RUSKIN *Mod. Paint.* III. IV. xvii. §4 This comparative Dimness and Untraceableness of the thoughts which are the sources of our admiration. **1875** WHITNEY *Life Lang.* x. 207 The world of untraceably sexual or of unsexual objects.

un'traced, *ppl. a.* (UN-¹ 8.)

1641 G. SANDYS *Paraphr. Song Sol.* III. i, No Angle my unwearyed Feet Vntraced left. **1643** DENHAM *Cooper's H.* 11 Through untrac'd ways, and airy paths I flye. **1713** C'TESS WINCHELSEA *Misc. Poems* 63 More wakeful Trundle . . Follows the scent untrac'd by nobler Hounds. **1809–14** WORDSW. *Excurs.* VI. 662 There are . . good reasons why we should not leave Wholly untraced a more forbidding way. **1826** MILMAN *Anne Boleyn* 51 That vast body That shall bespread the world, uncheck'd, untrac'd—Like God's own presence. **1900** *Daily News* 20 Sept. 5/3 It is needless for me to say that a number of these [removals] remain untraced.

un'tracked, (*ppl.*) *a.* Also 6–7 untract. [UN-¹ 8 and 9. The spelling *untract* is due to TRACT *sb.*² 8–11 and *v.*² 4–5. Cf. UNTRACTED.]

1. Through which no way has been found or made; not furnished with a track or path.

α. **1603** KNOLLES *Hist. Turks* (1621) 309 The rest . . hauing on horsebacke all alone by vncouth and vntract waies, trauailed three dayes without meat. **1684** OTWAY *Atheist* III. 32 Drawn by wing'd Horses through the untract Air. **1706** ROWE *Ulysses* III. 40 So the Eagle . . beholds his hardy youthful Offspring Forsake the Nest, to try his tender Pinions, In the wide untract Air.

β. **1612** BP. HALL *Contempl.* IV. 353 That they might not erre in that sandy and vntracked wildernesse. **1659** T. PECKE *Parnassi Puerp.* 172 The untrack'd path to Bliss. **1750** CARTE *Hist. Eng.* II. 391 After a long day's march through untracked ways. **1812** A. PLUMTRE *Lichtenstein's S. Africa* I. 350 The road was untracked and fatiguing. **1830** *New Monthly Mag.* Hist. Reg., Jan. 8/1 Regions yet untracked by any Europeans. **1894** *Outing* XXIII. 347/2 A long, dark object lying . . on the untracked snow beneath the trees.

2. Not tracked or traced; not followed up.

1680 OTWAY *Orphan* III. 504 At midnight thus the us'rer steals untract [**1735** untrack'd] To make a visit to his hoarded gold. **1872** RUSKIN *Fors Clav.* xiv. 12 Just persons . . untracked by the hounds of war. **1890** 'R. BOLDREWOOD' *Miner's Right* (1899) 146/2 A reflection of the deed still untracked and unavenged.

untracta'bility. (UN-¹ 12. Cf. next.)

1791 BURKE *Th. French Aff.* Wks. VII. 58 His untractability to these leaders . . alone prevented that part of the arrangement.

un'tractable, *a.* Now *rare.* [UN-¹ 7 b, 5 b.]

1. = INTRACTABLE *a.* 1. (Common *c* 1550–1800.)

1538 ELYOT, *Insanus*, madde, peuyshe, . . vntractable. **1548** UDALL, etc. *Erasm. Par. Matt.* xviii. 75 Yf he be so vntractable that he wyll not be moued neyther wyth shame, nor wyth feare of iudgemente. **1586** T. B. *La Primaud. Fr. Acad.* I. 320 His horses . . are become resty, furious, and untractable. *a* **1619** FOTHERBY *Atheom.* I. xii. §4 (1622) 130 Pharaoh . . was as stiffe, and as vntractable, as a rocke. **1670** COTTON *Espernon* II. VIII. 409 Birds . . of those kinds which with us are the most wild, and untractable. **1714** R. FIDDES *Pract. Disc.* II. 300 Persons of a base and untractable temper. **1777** ROBERTSON *Hist. Amer.* v. II. 78 The untractable arrogance of Narvaez. **1818** [see UNTAMEABLE *a.*]. **1824** MISS L. M. HAWKINS *Annaline* III. 32 His followers . . [were] more furious and untractable from the dreadful excesses they had committed.

2. = INTRACTABLE *a.* 2.

1601 HOLLAND *Pliny* II. 118 Other hearbs, hideous to the eye, and untractable in hand. *c* **1630** RISDON *Surv. Devon* (1810) 5 Hills are untractable to tillage. **1667** MILTON *P.L.* x. 476 But I Toild out my uncouth passage, forc't to ride Th' untractable Abysse. **1743** W. EMERSON *Fluxions* 85 If you have an untractable Fluxion that will answer to none of the Forms. **1823** SCOTT *Quentin D.* xxiv, He . . wrung bitterly the hands, which his mail-gloves rendered untractable. **1837** WHEWELL *Hist. Ind. Sci.* II. 177 There was room, among these hitherto untractable irregularities, for the additional results of the theory.

Hence **un'tractableness.**

1599 SANDYS *Europæ Spec.* (1605) T 3, The vntractablenesse of Papacy to it. *a* **1600** HOOKER *Serm. on Pride* I. §9 Disobedience of children, stubbornes of servants, vntractablenesse in them, who . . should . . bee also subiect. **1690** LOCKE *Hum. Und.* IV. xx. §5 In the Dulness or Untractableness of those Faculties for want of Use. **1752** H. WALPOLE *Lett.* (1846) II. 432 Will they ever expect a peaceable prelate, if untractableness is thus punished? **1817** JAS. MILL *Brit. India* II. IV. ii. 70 The untractableness of his own disposition.

untrac'tarian, *a.* (UN-¹ 7.)

1846 CAROLINE FOX *Jrnls.* (1882) II. 64 His untractarian and unsectarian convictions, and his broad charity.

†**un'tracted**, *ppl. a. Obs. rare.* [UN-¹ 8.] = UNTRACKED *ppl. a.* 1.

1610 HEALEY *St. Aug. Citie of God* XVIII. i. 654 My way lying through deserts, and vntracted woods. **1649** OGILBY tr. *Virgil, Georgics* III. 42 Meane while let us seek Groves . . and search untracted woods. **1680** *Tides* (MS. Bodl. Add. A. 202) 14 By what tædious, crooked, and untracted Journeys through that world of variety itt passes.

†**un'tractible**, *a. Obs.* [UN-¹ 7.] = UNTRACTABLE *a.* 1.

1670 G. H. tr. *Hist. Cardinals* III. i. 226 Who were 18 in number, all obstinate and untractible.

†**un'tractibleness.** *Obs.* (UN-¹ 12. Cf. prec.)

1676 HUBBARD *Happiness of a People* 23 When that Generation . . manifested such untractibleness and impatience.

un'traded, (*ppl.*) *a.* [UN-¹ 8 and 9.]

†**1. a.** Unskilled, inexperienced, unfamiliar. *Obs.*

1542 UDALL *Erasm. Apoph.* 172 No manne beeyng untraded in philosophie is an apte . . persone to bee a kyng. **1548** —— *Erasm. Par. Luke* i. 7 A people not vtterly vntraded or vnentred in his discipline. **1570** LEVINS *Manip.* 50 Vntraded, *insolens.*

†**b.** Not customary; unhackneyed. *Obs.*

1606 SHAKS. *Tr. & Cr.* IV. v. 178 By Mars his gauntlet thanks, Mocke not, that I affect th' untraded Oath.

†**2.** Not frequented, *spec.* for trade. *Obs.*

1600 HAKLUYT *Voy.* III. 682 Our English that to steale the first blessing of an vntraded place, will perhaps secretly hasten thither. **1603** H. CROSSE *Vertues Commw.* (1878) 44 Two waies are proposed, . . the first is combersome, intricate, vntraded, ouergrowne.

un'tradesmanlike, *a.* (UN-¹ 7 c.)

1863 *Sat. Rev.* XV. 175/1 If any manufacturer did more than this, he would certainly be behaving in a very untradesmanlike manner.

un'trading, *ppl. a.* (UN-¹ 10.)

1691 LOCKE *Lower. Interest* (1696) 60 Men . . leave Estates to their Children in Land, as . . not so liable to Casualties as Money, in untrading or unskilful Hands. **1828–32** WEBSTER s.v., An untrading country or city.

un'trafficked, *ppl. a.* (UN-¹ 8.)

1596 NASHE *Saffron-Walden* K iv, When I record (as I doo often) strange vntraffiqu't phrases, by him new vented and vnpackt, as of *incendarie* for fire.

un'tragic(al, *adjs.* (UN-¹ 7.)

1837 CARLYLE *Fr. Rev.* I. v. vi, The nodus of a drama, not untragical, crowding towards solution. *Ibid.* II. v. xii, Emblems not a few . . of the tragic and the untragic sort.

un'trainable, *a.* (UN-¹ 7 b.)

1864 ELIZ. MURRAY *E. Norman* I. 276 She was as untrained as a young savage, and apparently untrainable.

un'trained, *ppl. a.* [UN-¹ 8.]

1. Not trained by instruction or experience.

1548 UDALL *Erasm. Par. Luke* xxiv. 180 b, Yet these shadowes of thynges visible wer geuen for a tyme to the grosse and vntrained people. **1591** SHAKS. *1 Hen. VI*, I. ii. 73, I am by birth a Shepheards Daughter. My wit vntrayn'd in any kind of Art. **1633** G. HERBERT *Temple, Content* ii, Gad not abroad at ev'ry quest and call Of an untrained hope or passion. **1642** MILTON *Apol. Smect.* 55, I cannot say that I am utterly untrain'd in those rules. **1805** WORDSW. *Prelude* x. 197 Men who, to business of the world untrained, Lived in the shade. **1823** SCOTT *Quentin D.* xv, The low size, and wild, shaggy, untrained state of the animal. **1834** NEWMAN *Par. Serm.* (1837) I. xxii. 325 Nothing is done effectually through untrained human nature. **1864** [see prec.].

2. *spec.* Not trained in military exercises.

1591 SMITH *Instr. Military* (1595) Ep. Ded. 8 That the people of kingdomes . . should bee disarmed, vntrayned, and vnexercised, for feare of reuoltes. **1608** tr. *J. de Gheyn's Exercise of Arms* 1 b, To instruct the vntrained souldiers. **1667** MILTON *P.L.* XII. 222 For life To noble and ignoble is more sweet Untraind in Armes. **1726** POPE *Odyssey* XIX. 212 Untrained to martial toil I lived inglorious in my native isle. **1770** GLOVER *Leonidas* (ed. 5) VII. 510 The unabating fortitude of Greece Maintains her line, th' untrain'd Barbarians charge In savage fury.

3. Not trained in figure.

1871 *Figure Training* 17 The untrained form of the dairy-maid.

Hence, in recent use, **untrainedness.**

†**un'traist**, *a. Sc. Obs.* [UN-¹ 7.] Unreliable. Also †**un'traisted** *ppl. a.*, unexpected, unlooked for; †**un'traistful** *a.*, unbelieving; †**un'traisty** *a.*, untrustworthy.

1456 SIR G. HAYE *Law Arms* (S.T.S.) 170 Peple . . flowand and *untraist in all thair dedis. **1530** LYNDESAY *Test. Papyngo* 367 Sen ilke court bene vntraist and transitorie, Cheangyng als oft as woddercok in wynd. **1533** BELLENDEN *Livy* III. ix. (S.T.S.) II. 304 Na thing mycht happin less [*sic*] *vntrastit nor less belevit þan þe samyn. *c* **1375** *Sc. Leg. Saints* viii. (*Philip*) 93 *Vntrastefull folk of þat land fore gret invy tuk hym & band. **1567** *Gude & Godlie B.* (S.T.S.) 214 Traist the *vntraistie quha that will.

un'traitored, *ppl. a.* (UN-¹ 8.)

1840 CLOUGH *Dipsychus* II. viii. 23 Yet I could deem it better too to starve And die untraitored.

un'trammelled, *ppl. a.* (UN-¹ 8.)

In common use from *c* 1850.

[**1775** ASH.] **1795** R. ANDERSON *Life Johnson* 201 He . . has adopted all the good sense of Aristotle, untrammelled by his forms. **1867** LEWES *Hist. Philos.* (ed. 3) I. 1 Through the history of thought, how difficult it has been to keep the scientific attitude untrammelled. **1888** OMAN *Hist. Greece* xvi. (1901) 161 No previous constitution . . had given the . . citizens such untrammelled power to sway the state.

un'trampled, *ppl. a.* (UN-¹ 8.)

1648 HEXHAM II, *Ongetreden*, Vntrodden, or Vntrampled. **1817** MOORE *Lalla R., Fire-Worshippers* 320 To die upon that Mount of Flame— . . Before her last untrampled Shrine! **1861** GLADSTONE *Iliad* I. 329 They reluctant paced the margin of the free untrampled main. **1900** S. PHILLIPS *Paolo & Fr.* I. 4 Still have we foes untrampled, wavering friends.

un'tranquil, *a.* (UN-¹ 7.)

1817 KEATS *Sleep & Poetry* 263 Nought more untranquil than the grassy slopes Between two hills. **1850** J. H. NEWMAN *Diffic. Anglic.* 76 Fanatical doctrine and untranquil devotion. **1869** TYNDALL *Notes Lect. Light* §188 A tranquil pellucid portion . . and a turbid or untranquil portion.

un'tranquillize, *v.* (UN-¹ 6 c.)

1874 M. COLLINS *Transmigr.* II. viii. 153 Why should mere physical ideas trouble and untranquillize the brain?

un'tranquillized, *ppl. a.* (UN-¹ 8 a c.)

1846 WORCESTER (citing Goode). **1857** DE QUINCEY *Whiggism* Wks. VI. 145 Unwilling to leave us with . . the agitations of sympathy in the reader as yet untranquillised.

untran'sacted, *ppl. a.* (UN-¹ 8.)

c **1825** HOGG *Tales & Sk.* (1837) V. 146 Business that . . must remain untransacted.

untran'scended, *ppl. a.* (UN-¹ 8.)

1846 MANGAN *Poems* (1903) 39, I also found . . Fasting as Christ hath recommended, And noble councillors untranscended. **1852** BAILEY *Festus* (ed. 5) 171 A spirit.. Who..sojourns In untranscended light.

untranscen'dental, *a.* (UN-^{1} 7.)
1865 MRS. WHITNEY *Gayworthys* xxi, I think Wealthy felt it so, in her untranscendental way.

untran'scribable, *a.* (UN-^{1} 7 b.)
1874 in *Folklore* (1919) XXX. 149 An untranscribable baboon song. **1883** *Harper's Mag.* July 177 1 Students and amateurs..labouring with untranscribable details.

un'transferable, *a.* (UN-^{1} 7 b and 5 b.)
1649 HOWELL *Pre-em. Parlt.* 6 Though the Soverainty remaine still entire, and untransferable in the person of the Prince. **1794** COLERIDGE *Lett.* (1895) 71 The Demetrius is dry, and utterly untransferable to modern use. **1858** J. MARTINEAU *Stud. Christianity* 80 The personal character and untransferable nature of Sin. **1881** P. BROOKS *Candle of Lord* 326 The habits are rigid, uniform and untransferable.

untrans'ferrable, *a.* (UN-^{1} 7 b.)
1826 C. ANDERSON *Gen. Dom. Constitution* 378 That department of parental training, which is at once unpurchaseable and untransferrable.

untrans'ferred, *ppl. a.* (UN-^{1} 8.)
1748 EARL NUGENT *To Mankind* xviii, For unreclaim'd, and untransfer'd, Her pow'rs and rights remain.

untrans'formable, *a.* (UN-^{1} 7 b, 5 b.)
1570 DEE *Math. Pref.* 2 The generall Formes..are constant, vnchaungeable, vntransformable. **1851** SYLVESTER *Coll. Math. Papers* (1904) I. 230 All the distinct systems of ..conjugate forms that have been, and will be given, are mutually untransformable.

untrans'formed, *ppl. a.* (UN-^{1} 8.)
[**1775** ASH.] **1890** *Retrospect Med.* CII. 218 It..leaves masses of starchy food untransformed in the stomach. [Freq. from *c* 1900.]

untrans'gressed, *ppl. a.* (UN-^{1} 8.)
1621 QUARLES *Div. Poems, Esther* iii, Let him proclayme (which vntransgressed be) His royall Edict. *a* **1866** J. GROTE *Exam. Utilit. Phil.* i. (1870) 23 A general and untransgressed rule.

†**un'transible**, *a. Obs.*$^{-1}$ [ad. L. *intransibilis*: see UN-^{1} 7, 5 b.] That cannot be crossed.
1644 DIGBY *Nat. Soul* x. §7. 428 There is..no vntransible gappe, or Chaos to seuer them.

un'transitory, *a.* (UN-^{1} 7.)
1632 QUARLES *Div. Fancies* III. xlv, That Time untransitory. **1644** —— *Sheph. Orac.* v, Whose Kingdome's endlesse and untransitory.

untranslata'bility. (UN-^{1} 12. Cf. next.)
1860 G. P. MARSH *Lect. Eng. Lang.* xxvii. 611 Of this untranslatability of single words..German offers us many examples.

untrans'latable, *a.* (UN-^{1} 7 b, 5 b.)
Very common from the beginning of the 19th c.
1655 FULLER *Ch. Hist.* v. v. §36 Some few [words] untranslatable, without losse of life or lustre. **1694** *Gracian's Courtier's Oracle* A 3 b, The French Author..counts him unintelligible, and by consequence untranslatable. **1742** GRAY *Lett.* II. 28 Pray put me the following lines into the tongue of our modern Dramatics:..To me they appear untranslatable. **1811** COLERIDGE *Table-t.* (1835) II. 353 The excellence of verse, he said, was to be untranslatable into any other words. **1880** T. HODGKIN *Italy & Inv.* I. ii. I. 193 The untranslateable grandeur of Claudian's epithet.
Hence **untrans'latableness**; **-'latably** *adv.*
1817 COLERIDGE *Biogr. Lit.* II. 160 The infallible test of a blameless style; namely, its untranslatableness in words of the same language without injury to the meaning. **1855** SMEDLEY *Occult Sciences* 250 Concerning dreams—*ut de accentibus somni*—as he untranslatably styles them. **1889** *Athenæum* 16 Nov. 671/1 The ugly proceedings untranslatably known as *brique*.

untrans'lated, *ppl. a.* [UN-^{1} 8.]
1. Not turned into another language.
1530 PALSGR. 34 [Those writers] have left none auctours written in the latyn tonge untranslated. **1540** MORYSINE *Vives' Introd. Wysd.* A 5, No one boke untranslated..hath halfe soo many holsome documentes as this hathe. **1651** HOBBES *Leviath.* III. xxxviii. 244 Which ought not to have been left untranslated..in the Latine. **1768** TUCKER *Lt. Nat.* II. III. xxx. 458 The term translated Everlasting, ought to be preserved untranslated, as a kind of technical term. *a* **1778** PEGGE *Anonym.* (1809) 472 We have in English now, several untranslated French words. **1852** LEWIS *Meth. Obs. & Reason. in Pol.* I. 105 Others may resort to periphrasis, or may use the original word untranslated. **1883** A. ROBERTS *O.T. Revis.* iv. 83 'Bethel' is rendered..'the house of God', but should have been left untranslated.
2. Not transferred to another sphere.
1746 YOUNG *Nt. Th.* IX. 1753 This world sublime,.. Where mortal, untranslated, never stray'd. **1878** B. HARTE *Man on Beach* 58 Of course, he will be there to see his untranslated Goddess.

untransmigrated, *ppl. a.* (UN-^{1} 8.)
1821 SCOTT *Kenilw.* xxii, Thus, Alasco will leave your pewter artillery untransmigrated.

untrans'missible, *a.* (UN-^{1} 7, 5 b.)
1590 SWINBURNE *Testaments* 173 Because the testator maie if he will, make that transmissible, which otherwise is vntransmissible. **1882–3** *Schaff's Encycl. Relig. Knowl.* I. 472 The apostolic office was..unique and untransmissible.

untrans'mitted, *ppl. a.* (UN-^{1} 8.)
[**1775** ASH.] **1802–12** BENTHAM *Ration. Judic. Evid.* (1827) III. 447 The nature of original untransmitted evidence. **1820** SHELLEY *Prometh. Unb.* III. iii. 171 Those Who bear the untransmitted torch of hope Into the grave.

untrans'mutable, *a.* (UN-^{1} 7 b, 5 b.)
1611 FLORIO, *Intrasmutabile*, vntransmutable. **1682** H. MORE *Annot. Glanvill's Lux O.* 52 Spirits specifically different, are untransmutable one into another. *a* **1776** HUME *Ess.* (1777) II. 351 Each character..appears to me, in practice, pretty durable and untransmutable.

untran'smuted, *ppl. a.* (UN-^{1} 8.)
1666 BOYLE *Orig. Formes & Qual.* 409 The untransmuted Rain water. **1805** WORDSW. *Prelude* VI. 464 The untransmuted shapes of many worlds.

†**untransparable**, *a. Obs.*$^{-1}$ [UN-^{1} 7 b.] = next.
a **1618** RALEIGH *Rem.* (1644) 210 The unjust Magistrate that fancieth to himself a solid and untransparable body of Gold, every ordinary wit can vitrifie, and make transparent.

untrans'parent, *a.* [UN-^{1} 7 and 5 b.] Not transparent; opaque.
1591 SYLVESTER *Du Bartas* I. i. 290 Suppose an Earth.. without Hill or Plaine, A Heav'n un-hanged, un-turning, un-transparent. **1675** EVELYN *Terra* (1676) 33 An impalpable whitish Sand, untransparent. **1754** *Phil. Trans.* XLVIII. 659 The matter appeared of a dark blackish colour, untransparent. **1862** TYNDALL *Mountaineer.* v. 38 The water [resolves itself] to transparent vapour, and the vapour to untransparent cloud. **1888** O. CRAWFURD *Sylvia Arden* 361 So dark and untransparent was the flood water.

untrans'passable, *a.* (UN-^{1} 7 b.)
1594 DANIEL *Cleopatra* N 8, Are these the bounds y' haue giuen Th' vntranspassable barres, That limit pride so short..?

untrans'planted, *ppl. a.* (UN-^{1} 8.)
[**1775** ASH.] **1832** *Planting* 3 (L.U.K.), Equal, if not superior to untransplanted seedlings.

untran'sportable, *a.* (UN-^{1} 7 b.)
1611 FLORIO, *Intransporteuole*, vntransportable. **1838** EMERSON *Addr., Lit. Ethics*, Truth is..so untransportable and unbarrelable a commodity.

untran'sported, *ppl. a.* [UN-^{1} 8.]
1. Not conveyed or carried.
1549 *Acc. Ld. High Treas. Scot.* IX. 357 Chargeing him to keip Schir Robert Bowis, Inglisman, untransporttit hame in his awin cuntre.
2. Not carried away by feeling.
1641 EARL MONM. tr. *Biondi's Civil Wars* II. 72 Hee received all these injuries not onely untransported, but with a setled judgement. **1701** COLLIER *M. Aurel.* p. xxiii, He.. was Religious without Affectation, untransported and free from Eagerness upon all occasion. **1768–74** TUCKER *Lt. Nat.* (1834) II. 586 To preserve an even steady temper,.. untransported by allurements.

untrans'posed, *ppl. a.* (UN-^{1} 8.)
1751 JOHNSON *Rambler* No. 86 ¶10 To preserve the series of sounds untransposed in a long composition, is..very difficult. **1810** BENTHAM *Offic. Apt. Maximized, Def. Econ.* (1830) 21 The thread of his argument is delivered unbroken, and the parts of it untransposed.

untransub'stantiated, *ppl. a.* (UN-^{1} 8.)
1672 H. MORE *Brief Reply* 325 The said Individual matter untransubstantiated and remaining Bread still. **1830** G. S. FABER *Diffic. Romanism* (ed. 2) 143 The unconsecrated, and therefore (in latin phrase) the untransubstantiated, bread and wine. **1854** MILMAN *Lat. Chr.* III. vii. I. 467 The Redeemer's spiritual presence, yet undefined and untransubstantiated.

†**untran'sumed**, *ppl. a. Obs.*$^{-1}$ (UN-^{1} 8. Cf. TRANSUME *v.* 1.)
1526 *Sc. Acts, Jas. V* (1814) II. 313 þ^t he sall bring þe writingis laitlie maid be our souerane lorde..vntransumyt auctentily.

un'trapped, *ppl. a.* (UN-^{1} 8.)
1648 HEXHAM II, *Onbeklicht*,..Vnsurprised, or Vntrapt. *Ibid.*, *Onbetrapt*, Vntrapped, or Vnsnared. [**1775** ASH.]

un'trapped, *a.* [UN-^{1} 9.] Of a sink or drain: Not fitted with a trap.
1860 FLOR. NIGHTINGALE *Nursing* 15 An untrapped sink may..spread fever..among the inmates of a palace. **1877** TEALE *Dangers to Health* 7 A rain water tank, which had an untrapped overflow into the drain. **1884** *19th Cent.* May 847 Untrapped drains.

un'travellable, *a.* (UN-^{1} 7 b.)
1652 HEYLYN *Cosmogr.* III. 113 Full of untravellable Desarts. **1846** *Chr. Watchman* Sept., Fearful precipices and rocky passes..abound in this almost untravellable district.

un'travelled, *ppl. a.* [UN-^{1} 8.]
1. That has not travelled.
1585 T. WASHINGTON tr. *Nicholay's Voy.* Ep. Ded., They are among men vntrauelled as Hesperus among the smaller starres. **1611** BEAUM. & FL. *Philaster* I. i, If they should, I say, they were never abroad:..it writes them directly untravel'd. **1667** SPRAT *Hist. R. Soc.* 73 Untravell'd Gentle-men,..and Generals, that had scarce ever before seen a Battel. **1712** ADDISON *Spect.* No. 407 ¶1 That an untravelled Englishman cannot relish all the Beauties of Italian Pictures. **1812** SCOTT *Let.* in *Lockhart* (1837) III. 19 Sophia and Walter hold their heads very high among their untravelled companions. *a* **1862** BUCKLE *Misc. Wks.* (1872) I. 524 We rarely find an untravelled man who is not full of prejudice.
transf. and *fig.* **1606** *Sir G. Goosecappe* I. ii. B i, *Fo.* Why this is the vntrauaild rudnes of our grose Englesh ladies now. **1764** GOLDSM. *Traveller* 8 Where'er I roam,..My heart untravell'd fondly turns to thee. **1805** *Ann. Rev.* III. 199 The author is apparently untravelled in continental literature. **1861** GEO. ELIOT *Silas M.* i, To their untravelled thought a state of wandering was a conception as dim as the winter life of the swallows.

2. Not travelled over or through.
1661 FELTHAM *Resolves* II. xlix. 281 He..that is illiterate, and unactively lives hamletted in some untravaill'd village. *a* **1720** J. HUGHES *Ode to Creator* 35 Beyond the untravell'd limits of the sky. **1762** FALCONER *Shipwr.* 335 Pilots, tutor'd to divine Th' untravell'd course by geometric line. **1809–14** WORDSW. *Excurs.* VI. 455 To the deep shade of those untravelled Wilds. **1864** R. S. HAWKER *Quest Sangraal* 41 Neither landmarks, nor fences, bounded..the bold, free, and untravelled Cornish domain.
fig. **1646** SIR T. BROWNE *Pseud. Ep.* To Rdr. A 5, Wee.. are oft-times faine to wander in America and untravelled parts of truth. **1672** LLOYD *F.S. on Bp. Wilkins* 27 He shewed it in whatsoever Argument he undertook; sometimes beating out new untravel'd ways, sometimes repairing those that had been beaten already.

un'traversable, *a.* (UN-^{1} 7 b, 5 b.)
1856 RUSKIN *Mod. Paint.* III. 200 The endless undulation of the untraversable hills. **1890** *Spectator* 3 May, The Southern desert..is practically untraversable and uninhabitable.

un'traversed, *ppl. a.* (UN-^{1} 8.)
[**1775** ASH.] **1807** J. BARLOW *Columb.* I. 57, I..Tamed all the dangers of untraversed waves. *Ibid.* IX. 37 To thee is given To..inquire of heaven, To mark untraversed ages. **1843** RUSKIN *Mod. Paint.* I. II. IV. iv. §6 Few, if any, of the rocks of nature are untraversed by delicate and slender fissures. **1876** A. S. MURRAY *Mythol.* iii. 37 A personification of the untraversed regions of the sea.

un'tread, *v.* [UN-^{2} 3.] *trans.* To retrace.
1592 SHAKS. *Ven. & Ad.* 908 She treads the path that she untreads again. **1596** —— *Merch. V.* II. vi. 10. **1615** G. SANDYS *Trav.* 169 Vntreading a good part of the fore-said alley, we entered the Ile. *a* **1659** OSBORNE *Ess.* iii. 36 Who onely knew the Way to untread the Maze, in which Man had lost Himself. **1710** NORRIS *Chr. Prud.* viii. 398 He has made abundance of false steps..which..he would willingly untread. **1837** DE QUINCEY *Revolt of Tartars* Wks. 1854 IV. 153 The question was formally debated..whether, even at this point, they should untread their steps.

un'treadable, *a.* (UN-^{1} 7 b.)
1857 LIVINGSTONE *Trav.* xxiii. 461 Impassable forests and untreadable bogs.

un'treasure, *v.* [UN-^{1} 4, 3.] *trans.* To rob, or empty, of a treasure. Also const. *of.*
1600 SHAKS. *A.Y.L.* II. ii. 7 In the morning early, They found the bed vntreasur'd of their Mistris. **1819** MOORE *Mem.* (1853) III. 64 Niches untreasured of their busts, and rooms depopulated of their statues. *a* **1859** J. MITFORD (Webster), The quaintness with which he untreasured, as by rote, the stores of his memory.

un'treatable, *a.* [UN-^{1} 7 b, 5 b.]
†**1.** Intractable; incapable of being treated or dealt with; unmanageable. *Obs.*
c **1374** CHAUCER *Boeth.* II. pr. viii. (1868) 61 For-as-mochel as thow shalt nat wenen..þat I bere vntretable batayle ayenis fortune. **1430–40** LYDG. *Bochas* I. xv. 5638 For Narcisus was nat merciable Toward Echcho,..But in his port was founden ontretable. *c* **1450** BURGH *Secrees* 2196 Yif he be wood and vntretable, He may..thy Reem destroye. **1509** BARCLAY *Shyp of Folys* 68 If that deth vntretable Arrest the with his mace. **1571** GOLDING *Calvin on Ps.* ii. 9 The greater part avanceth itselfe against him with untreatable feercenesse. **1604–5** in *Trans. Roy. Hist. Soc.* Ser. IV. IV. 137 Parishioners doe fynde mutch faulte with his untreatable reading in the tyme of public prayer. **1675** G. R. tr. *Le Grand's Man without Passion* 137 Anger that wild and untreatable Passion. *a* **1745** SWIFT *Serm.* Wks. 1765 XVI. 31 [It] caused many of them..to be..supercilious and untreatable.
2. Not admitting of medical treatment.
1865 *Q. Rev.* July 33 Untreatable by any known remedy, this malady would seem now to have nearly worn itself out.
Hence **un'treatableness**.
1693 C. MATHER *Wonders Invisible World* Def. A 2, The unaccountable Frowardness, Asperity, Untreatableness, and Inconsistency of many persons.

un'treated, *ppl. a.* (UN-^{1} 8 and 8 c.)
c **1456** PECOCK *Bk. of Faith* (1909) 120 The articlis which ben spokun in the Represser, and left there untretid. **1665** BOYLE *Occas. Refl.* a6 b, Themes..untreated of by others. **1666** —— *Orig. Forms & Qual.* B 2 b, He has left most of the other Qualities Untreated of. **1883** *Pall Mall G.* 10 Nov. 4/1 The untreated sewage of London. **1890** *Retrospect Med.* CII. 292 The risk of leaving untreated a clot [etc.].

†**un'tree**, *v.* (UN-^{2} 4.)
1611 FLORIO, *Disarborare*, to vntree, to cut downe trees. **1624** *Trag. Nero* III. (1633) D 4, The shores And hollow caves of forrests now untreed.

un'trellised, *ppl. a.* (UN-^{1} 8.)
1629 GAULE *Holy Madn.* 340 He keepes an open House: but..it is the Roofe vnthatcht, or Windowes vntrellessed; for the Doore is neuer vnbolted.

un'trembling, *ppl. a.* (UN-^{1} 10.)
1570 LEVINS *Manip.* 137 Vntrembling, *intrepidus*. **1708** J. PHILIPS *Cyder* I. 109 Nor untrembling can'st thou see, How from a scraggy rock..hardy men..Cut samphire. **1742** BLAIR *Grave* 386 Then might the Debauchee Untrembling mouth the Heav'ns. **1846** KEBLE *Lyra Innoc.* 179 Not to the quick untrembling gaze..Loves He to say, Go higher. **1881** A. AUSTIN in *Macm. Mag.* XLIII. 403 The roll of that untrembling diapason that makes all things tremble.
Hence **un'tremblingly** *adv.*
a **1832** BENTHAM *Deontol.* (1832) II. 12 Stand up untremblingly, then, and avow that [etc.].

untre'mendous, *a.* (UN-^{1} 7.)
1820 KEATS *Hyperion* II. 155 Why ye, Divinities,..Should cower beneath what, in comparison, Is untremendous might.

un'tremulous, *a.* (UN-^{1} 7.)
1826 MRS. HEMANS *Forest Sanctuary* I. lxx, I heard a sweet..strain Piercing the flames, untremulous and clear. **1832** MISS MITFORD *Village* V. 348 Thy cheek unflush'd; Thy lip untremulous. **1853** C. BRONTE *Villette* xxi, Here was the seal..deftly dropped by untremulous fingers.

un'trenched, *ppl. a.* [UN-^{1} 8 and 8 c.] **a.** Not entrenched. **b.** Not trenched by digging. **c.** Not encroached *upon*.
[**1775** ASH.] **1807** J. BARLOW *Columb.* v. 759 Untrench'd before the town, they dare oppose Their fielded cohorts to the forted foes. **1849** JOHNSTON *Exp. Agric.* 101 Whether oats are after lea trenched or untrenched, or after turnips. **1887** BROWNING *Parleyings, G. de Lairesse* xi, Yonder space extends Untrenched upon by any vagrant tree.

†**un'trend,** *v. Obs.*$^{-1}$ [UN-^{2} 3.] *trans.* To unroll.
a **1272** *Luue Ron* 195 in *O.E. Misc.* 99 þis rym..ich þe sende open and wiþ-vte sel; Bidde ic þat þu hit vntrende.

un'trended, † **-trend,** *ppl. a.* (UN-^{1} 8: see TREND *v.* 2 b.)
c **1395** *Plowman's Tale* II. 594 He culleth the sheep as doth the cook; Of hem they taken the woll untrend. **1805** LUCCOCK *Nat. Wool* 301 That the quality of the untrended wool is not so good as the other.

un'trespassed, *ppl. a.* (UN-^{1} 8.)
1854 S. DOBELL *Balder* iii. 14 The untrespassed rest Of immemorial pastures.

un'trespassing, *ppl. a.* (UN-^{1} 10.)
1642 MILTON *Apol. Smect.* 22 Others were sent..as it were at large, in the midst of an untrespassing honesty.

un'tress, *v.* (UN-^{2} 4 b.)
1587 A. DAY *Daphnis & Chloe* (1890) 18 Chloe..vntressed quickly her golden wirie lockes.

un'tressed, *ppl. a.* [UN-^{1} 8.] Not arranged in tresses; loose, dishevelled.
c **1381** CHAUCER *Parl. Foules* 268 Her gylt heares with a gold threde Ybounde were, vntressyd [*Camb. Univ. MS.* vntrussede] as she lay. *c* **1386** —— *Knt.'s T.* 1431 Hir brighte heer was kempd vntressed [*MSS. Camb. & Lansd.* vntrussed] al. **1412–20** LYDG. *Chron. Troy* III. 4124 Vntressid hir her abrod gan sprede, Like to gold wyr, for-rent & al to-torn. *c* **1440** *Pallad. on Husb.* I. 861 A..womman, vnshood, Vntressed, al aboute to goon is good. **1582** STANYHURST *Aeneis* I. (Arb.) 33 Troy dames..with locks vntressed al hanging. **1621** G. SANDYS *Ovid's Met.* VII. (1626) 131 Her haire Vntrest, her garments loose. *a* **1849** H. COLERIDGE *Poems* (1851) II. 387 She..with her untress'd hair Still wiped the feet.

†**un'trest.** [UN-^{1} 12.] Mistrust.
c **1400** *Lanfranc's Cirurg.* 17 Greet drede, ouþir vttereste [*read* vntreste; *v.r.* vntryst] of heelþe of his wounde. *c* **1450** *Mirour Saluacioun* (Roxb.) 132 Be vntrest and incredulitee he dos some grete disese.

un'triable, *a.* (UN-^{1} 7 b.)
1612 S. STURTEVANT *Metallica* 78 An vntryable inuention is a new proiect or discouery, whose worth and goodnesse requireth no tryals.

†**un'trial,** *a. Obs.* [Of obscure origin.] ***gentleman untrial***: (see quot. 1486).
1486 *Bk. St. Albans, Heraldry* B iij b, Ther be ij dyuerse Gentylmen made of gromys that be nott gentilmen of cote-armure nother of blode. Oon is calde in armys a gentylman vntriall, that is to say made vp emong religyous men as priorys, Abbottis, or Byschoppis. **1562** LEGH *Armorie* 27 b, The eight is called a gentleman vntrial, and such is he, as being brought vp in an Abbey, or with a bishop [etc.]. **1600** W. WATSON *Decacordon* (1602) 257 This vntriall gentleman was one of that nobleman father Parsons spies. *Ibid.* 270 Our Frankelings, Gentlemen vntriall, or substantiall Yeomen.

un'tributary, *a.* (UN-^{1} 7.)
[**1775** ASH.] **1796** COLERIDGE *Watchman* 27 April, The probable Loss and Gain of unprotected and untributary Independence.

†**un'trick,** *a. Obs.*$^{-0}$ (UN-^{1} 7. Cf. TRICK *a.*^{1} and *adv.* 2.)
1570 LEVINS *Manip.* 121 Vntricke, *inconcinnus*.

un'tried, *ppl. a.* [UN-^{1} 8.]
1. Not tried, proved, or tested.
1526 *Pilgr. Perf.* (W. de W. 1531) 132 That no worde passe out vntryed & nothynge entre vnexamyned. *a* **1586** SIDNEY *Arcadia* I. iii, Her skin like burnisht gold, her hands like silver ure untryde. **1591** SPENSER *F.Q.* I. iii. 34 Loth was that other..To taste th' vntryed dint of deadly steele. **1647** COWLEY *Mistr., Encrease* iii, So the new-made, and untride Spheres above, Took their first turn from th' hand of Jove. **1697** DRYDEN *Virg. Georg.* IV. 781 Four fair Heifars yet in Yoke untry'd. **1739** LABELYE *Piers Westm. Bridge* 28 Not to leave one single square Foot in the whole Surface of the Foundation untried. **1783** CRABBE *Village* II. 146 When smit with Glory's charms, The untried youth first quits a father's arms. **1833** HT. MARTINEAU *Cinnamon & Pearls* v. 95 Can anything equal the presumption of human decisions on untried matters! **1871** DIXON *Tower* III. i. 1 A man of untried power.
absol. **1839** CARLYLE *Chartism* ix, The New, Untried ascertains how it will fit itself into the arrangements of the Old. **1887** MEREDITH *Ballads & P.* 112 She marched toward the gloomy gate Of earth's Untried.
2. Not tried by a judge.
a **1618** SYLVESTER *Job* IV. 12 Against Job began his wrath to flame,..And..his Foe-friends, for so strict Condemning Job, untry'd and unconvict. **1784** COWPER *Task* v. 398 Condemn'd untried, Cruelly spar'd, and hopeless of escape! **1824** S. SMITH *Wks.* (1859) II. 32 Cruel Treatment of Untried Prisoners. **1842** DICKENS *Amer. Notes* v, The best Jail for untried offenders in the world.

un'trifling, *a.* (UN-^{1} 10.)
a **1743** SAVAGE *Epitaph Young Lady* 7 Modest knowledge, fair untrifling youth.

un'trig, *a. Sc.* [UN-^{1} 7.] Not neat or trim.
1821 GALT *Ann. Parish* xvii. 160 His wife kept an untrig house. **1850** MCGILVRAY *Poems* 197 She is so big, and so untrig.

un'trilled, *ppl. a.* (UN-^{1} 8.)
1866 *Jrnl. Amer. Oriental Soc.* VIII. 342 The production of this untrilled *r* may be carried as far back in the mouth as we choose. **1869** ELLIS *E.E. Pron.* II. 603/1 The peculiar English untrilled *r*. **1874** SWEET in *Trans. Philol. Soc.* 471 Untrilled consonants.

un'trilling, *vbl. sb.* (UN-^{2} 3, 8.)
1874 SWEET in *Trans. Philol. Soc.* 471 Untrilling [is] a common phenomenon in..English, in which the trilled *r* is quite lost.

un'trim, *a.* (UN-^{1} 7.)
1570 LEVINS *Manip.* 131 Vntrym, *inconcinnus*. **1898** N. MUNRO *J. Splendid* xv, His hair was untrim.

un'trim, *v.* [UN-^{2} 3.]
1. *trans.* To deprive of trimness or elegance; to strip of ornament.
c **1600** SHAKS. *Sonn.* xviii, Euery faire from faire some-time declines, By chance, or natures changing course vntrim'd. **1611** J. DAVIES (Heref.) *Sco. Folly* cxcvii, Their hairlesse scalpes..Barely affirme they were vntrimm'd by trulls. **1832** HOOD *Ode to J. Hume* 40 Don't trim though, but untrim their [*sc.* soldiers'] jackets.
2. To unbalance.
1884 HARROP *Bolingbroke* i. 21 The success of the French King's intrigues at Madrid had threatened..to untrim the balance of power.

un'trimmable, *a.* (UN-^{1} 7 b.)
1863 HAWTHORNE *Our Old Home* (1879) 361 Shovelling the untrimmed and untrimmable ideas out of his mind.

un'trimmed, *ppl. a.* [UN-^{1} 8.]
1. Not put in good order or condition; not carefully or neatly arranged or attired.
In quot. 1595 the word has been variously explained, and may be formed on UNTRIM *v.*
1532 HERVET *Xenophon's Househ.* 18 b, The horse beareth hym..that wyll se the grounde be nat let alone vntylled and vntrymmed. **1540** HYRDE tr. *Vives' Instr. Chr. Wom.* (1541) I ii, A mayde nat pyked, and fayre, and wanton..: but sad, pale, and vntrimmed. **1592** R. W[ILMOT] *Tancred & Gism.* v. ii, So let thy tresses..Vntrimmed hang about thy bared necke. **1595** SHAKS. *John* III. i. 209 The deuill tempts thee heere, In likenesse of a new vntrimmed Bride. **1648** J. QUARLES *Fons Lachrym.* 71 Man's like a house..; If we survay The inward rooms, there we may find enough Of untrim'd natures slattish houshold-stuff. **1813** SCOTT *Rokeby* I. xxxii, Yon untrimm'd lamp, whose yellow gleam Is mingling with the cold moonbeam. **1817** BYRON *Beppo* xlvi. *note*, Without the sex, our sonnets Would seem unfinish'd, like their untrimm'd bonnets.
2. Not made trim by cutting, pruning, or otherwise reducing to shape.
1625 K. LONG tr. *Barclay's Argenis* v. xi. 367 The pleasing young Groves..with their deepe silence and untrimmed simplicity. **1633** FORD *Love's Sacrifice* v. i, A crooked leg, a scambling foot,..or such an untrimm'd beard As yours. **1687** *Lond. Gaz.* No. 2307/4 The said Nag is..rough Coated and untrim'd. **1808** SCOTT *Marm.* III. Introd., Prune the vine, But..leave untrimm'd the eglantine. **1848** AKERMAN *Introd. Study Coins* iv. 56 A grim bearded untrimmed head. **1892** OLDFIELD *Man. Typog.* v, A demy 8vo. page measures, untrimmed, about $8\frac{3}{4}'' \times 5\frac{1}{2}''$.
fig. **1849** M. ARNOLD *New Sirens* 138 Germs, your untrimm'd passion overgrew. **1863** [see UNTRIMMABLE *a.*].
3. Not properly balanced.
a **1732** GAY *Fables* (1738) II. v. 44 The boat untrimm'd admits the tide.
Hence **un'trimmedness.**
1883 H. JAMES *Portr. Places* viii. 167 [The old castle's] quiet rustiness and untrimmedness only help it to be familiar.

un'tripe, *v.* (UN-^{2} 4.)
1611 COTGR., *Estripé*, vntriped, vnbowelled, with his..bowels about his heeles. **1653** URQUHART *Rabelais* I. xliii. 190 The broile and defeat, wherein Tripet was untriped [F. *estripé*]. **1808** E. S. BARRETT *Missled General* 69 We must either embowel them, or they will untripe us.

†**untrist,** *sb. Obs.* [UN-^{1} 12 + TRIST *sb.*^{1}] Distrust. Also †**un'trist** *a.* [UN-^{1} 7 + TRIST *a.*^{1}], unfaithful; unbelieving.

†**un'tristed** *ppl. a.* [UN-^{1} 8 + TRIST *v.*] Unhoped for.

†**un'tristy** *a.* [UN-^{1} 7.] Faithless; unreliable.
1390 GOWER *Conf.* II. 151 Jelousie of his *untrist Makth that full many an harm arist. *c* **1400** *Comm. Luke* i. 19 (MS. Bodl. 143), In beyng doumb he suffriþ þe peyne of vntrist disseruyd. *c* **1374** CHAUCER *Troylus* III. 839 Whi hastow mad Troylus to me *vntriste? *c* **1460** *Towneley Myst.* xxvii. 210 Me thynk you all vntrist to trow,..All that the prophetys told to you before, it is no trane. **1387** TREVISA *Higden* (Rolls) VII. 115 A Goddes man seide..þat þere was to comen and *untristed [L. *insperatum*] a lordschipe fro Fraunce. *Ibid.* III. 265 þe firste tweie artes beeþ untrusty [*Cotton MS.* *vntrysti.] *c* **1400** *Destr. Troy* 11973 þan happit hom to mete The traytor with tene, vntristy Eneas. *c* **1460** *Promp. Parv.* (Winch. MS.), On-trysty, *idem quod* thende.

un'trite, *a.* (UN-^{1} 7.)
1781 T. TWINING in *Recreat. & Stud.* (1882) 110 There is very little pleasing or untrite in his melody or harmony.

un'triumphable, *a.* (UN-^{1} 7 b.)
1663 BUTLER *Hud.* I. ii. 502 This blood..Which now y' are bent to throw away In vain, untriumphable fray. **1768** *Woman of Honor* I. 161.

untri'umphant, *a.* (UN-^{1} 7.)
1659 GAUDEN *Serm.*, etc. (1660) 72 A civil intestine War, where victory itself is sad and untriumphant. **1858** CARLYLE *Fredk. Gt.* IX. xi. II. 536 The French Ambassador..did much intriguing,..first in a signally triumphant way, and then in a signally untriumphant.

un'triumphed, *ppl. a.* (UN-^{1} 8.)
1627 MAY *Lucan* VIII. O 6, I..Suffer'd you only, when I conquer'd all, To goe vntriumph'd.

un'trod, *ppl. a.* [UN-^{1} 8 b, 8 c. Cf. older Da. *utraadd*, Sw. *otrådd*.] = next.
1593 MARLOWE *Lucan* I. 567 Clashing of armes was heard in vntrod woods. **1601** SHAKS. *Jul. C.* III. i. 136 Mark Antony..will follow..Thorough the hazards of this vntrod State, With all true Faith. **1633** FORD *Broken H.* III. v, That remedy Must be a winding-sheet,..And some vntrod-on corner in the earth. **1667** MILTON *P.L.* III. 497 The Paradise of Fools,..now unpeopl'd, and untrod. **1737** GLOVER *Leonidas* II. 151 The secret paths, Which..through the forests wind, Untrod by human feet. **1771** *Hunter's Georgian Ess.* II. 10 Sheep..are never found in countries untrod by man. **1864** J. BROWN *Minchmoor* 6 We..looked down its grassy and untrod avenue to the pallid, forlorn mansion. **1879** BROWNING *Halbert & Hob* 49 Untrod Leave this last step we reach.

un'trodden, *ppl. a.* [UN-^{1} 8 b.] Not trodden or stepped on; untraversed. Also in fig. context.
a **1300** *E.E. Psalter* xvii. 31 Mi God un-filed [L. *inpolluta*; *E., H.* un-troden] es his wai.
1535 COVERDALE *Ps.* cvi[i]. 4 They wente astraye..in an vntroden waye. **1593** *Sidney's Arcadia* IV. (1922) II. 119 Vagabonding in those untroden places. **1606** MARSTON *Parasitaster* IV. G 4, Vntrodden snow is not so spotless. **1656** COWLEY *Davideis* I. 28 Guid my bold steps..In these untrodden paths to Sacred Fame. **1735** BERKELEY *Querist* §418 So many roads untrodden, fields untilled, houses desolate. **1760–2** GOLDSM. *Cit. W.* lxxxvii, Those untrodden forests..which formerly covered the face of the country. **1826** MRS. HEMANS *Forest Sanctuary* I. xiii, The red grapes untrodden strew'd the ground. **1849** GROTE *Greece* II. xxxviii. V. 57 A wild, woody, and untrodden country.
Hence **un'troddenness.**
1644 DIGBY *Nat. Bodies* xxiii. § 1. 203 The ruggednesse, and vntrodenesse of the pathes we haue walked in. **1681** R. FLEMING *Fulfilling Script.* II. Pref. (1726) 249 The untroddenness of this path, the weight..of the truths, with some study..to believe what I wrote.

un'trolled, *ppl. a.* (UN-^{1} 8 + TROLL *v.* 2.)
1693 S. HARVEY *Juvenal* ix. 12 Hard Fate! untroll'd is now the Charming Dye.

un'trophied, *a.* (UN-^{1} 9.)
1756 W. WHITEHEAD *Elegy* iv. 61 O why, Britannia, why untrophied pass The patriot deeds thy godlike Sons display? *a* **1861** T. WINTHROP *Life in Open Air* x. (1863) 81, I entered skulkingly, as a gameless hunter may, and hid my untrophied head beneath a mound of ancient hay.

†**un'troth.** *Obs.* [UN-^{1} 12. Cf. TROTH *sb.*, UNTRUTH, and WANTROTH.]
1. Unfaithfulness, treachery; = UNTRUTH 1. (Common *c* 1385–*c* 1450.)
c **1374** CHAUCER *Troylus* v. 1448 He þought ay wel he hadde his lady lorn, And þat Ioues..Hym shewed hadde in sleep þe signyfyaunce Of hire vntroþe. *c* **1384** —— *H. Fame* I. 384 But weleaway the harme the routhe That hath betyd for suche vntrouthe. *c* **1425** *Eng. Conq. Irel.* 8 Bot Robert..for no t[h]ynge wold do thynge wher-of he myght be þer-after i-wyted of wntrowth. **1483** CAXTON *G. de la Tour* E viii b, He slewe his broder Amon that suche desloyalte and untrouth had done to his Suster. **1523** LD. BERNERS *Froiss.* I. ccxxxi. 313 The kyng..pituously complayned hym of ye untrouthe of his men, shewyng howe they had all forsaken him. *a* **1548** HALL *Chron., Hen. VI*, 154 b, The capitaines perceyuing their vntrought & trayterous demeanour, retrayted themselves into the Castell or Palaice, where..they sore molested and vexed the vntrew citizens. **1606** G. W[OODCOCKE] *Hist. Ivstine* XI. 45 Which deed..might rather be imputed to the oresight of light credit, then to any vntroth or infidelity.
b. Wickedness, mischief. *rare.*
1470–85 MALORY *Arthur* XVII. viii. 702 Thenne dyd they grete vntrouthe; they slewe clerkes and preestes. **1484** CAXTON *Fables of Æsop* I. iv, The euylle hongry peple..by theyr grete vntrouthe and malyce robben..the poure folke.
2. Unbelief; = UNTRUTH 2.
c **1380** WYCLIF *Sel. Wks.* II. 204 þe fadir..seide, Sire, Y bileve; helpe myn untrouþe. *a* **1395** HYLTON *Scala Perf.* II. vi. (Bodl. MS.), þei schulden streiȝt flee to heuene,..hadde þei do neuer so myche synne bifore in time of her vntrouþe. *c* **1400** *Apol. Loll.* 28 Crist..miȝt not do ani vertu þer, for þe vntrouþ.
3. Falsehood; = UNTRUTH 3.
c **1386** CHAUCER *Man of Law's T.* 687 This false knyght was slayn for his vntrouthe. *c* **1449** PECOCK *Repr.* II. xv. 234 Thei worschipiden God bi ydolatrie, and therfore by vntrouthe. *a* **1592** GREENE *Alphonsus* II. ii, If you find my words to be vntroth, Then let me die to recompence the wrong.
b. = UNTRUTH 3 b.
1581 T. HOWELL *Deuises* I ij, A false vntroth to me the same doth seeme. **1598** R. BERNARD tr. *Terence, Phormio* II. ii, If then I had spoken an vntroath. **1623** FLETCHER & ROWLEY *Maid in Mill* IV. i, There will be a yard of dissimulation At least (City measure) and cut upon an untroth or two.
†**4.** A company (of summoners). *Obs.*$^{-0}$
1486 *Bk. St. Albans* f vi b, An vntrouth of sompneris.

† **un'trothful**, *a. Obs.*⁻¹ [UN-¹ 7.] Unbelieving.
a **1400** *New Test.* (Paues) Acts xiv. 2 Þo Iewes þat wore vntrowþeful stired persecucyone.

un'trouble, *v.* (UN-² 4 b.)
a **1684** LEIGHTON *Comm. 1 Pet.* v. (1849) II. 468 Art thou troubled with fears, enemies, and snares? untrouble thyself of that, for He is with thee.

un'troubled, *ppl. a.* [UN-¹ 8.]
1. Not subjected to trouble or disquiet.
1484 *Acta Auditorum* (1839) *146/2 Þe said venerable fader..salbe vntrublit for þat some. **1531** *Reg. Privy Seal Scot.* II. 134/2 The saidis personis..to be..unmolestit, and untrublit, for quhatsumever actioun or cryme. **1590** SPENSER *F.Q.* I. i. 33 Vntroubled night they say giues counsell best. *Ibid.* II. vii. 15 With how small allowaunce Vntroubled Nature doth her selfe suffise. *a* **1625** FLETCHER *Love's Pilgrimage* IV. ii, Make your spirit an untroubled way To pass to what it ought. **1648** BOYLE *Seraphick Love* (1659) 14 A sight, whose glory made them look on fading Beauties, with..untroubled eyes. **1671** MILTON *P.R.* IV. 401 Our Saviour meek and with untroubl'd mind..betook him to his rest. **1743** FRANCIS tr. *Hor., Odes* II. x. 17 He who enjoys th' untroubled Breast, Of Virtue's awful Lore possest. **1816** WILSON *Misc. Poems* 268 Thou with that untroubled voice. **1846** MRS. A. MARSH *Father Darcy* II. ii. 62 The priest preserved all the usual untroubled gravity and dignity of his demeanour. **1890** 'R. BOLDREWOOD' *Col. Reformer* (1891) 246 Untroubled by care or consuming anxiety.
2. Not rendered turbid. Also *fig.*
c **1614** SIR W. MURE *Dido & Æneas* II. 776 Whose vertew's streame vntrubled still runnes pure. **1662** CHARLETON *Myst. Vintners* (1675) 191 The equal distribution of the Spirits of the liquor, which always rendreth bodies clear and untroubled. **1810** SOUTHEY *Kehama* x. iv, The stream..there delights to lie, Untroubled and at rest Beneath the untainted sky. **182.** MRS. HEMANS *Evening Prayer* iv, Fresh within your breasts th' untroubled springs Of hope make melody.
Hence **un'troubledness**.
a **1660** HAMMOND *Wks.* (1683) IV. 479 He hath..robb'd ..the Sceptick of his indifference and untroubledness.

un'troublesome, *a.* (UN-¹ 7.)
1757 MRS. GRIFFITH *Lett. Henry & Frances* (1767) IV. 208 My Companion is a chearful, civil, untroublesome Person. **1848** MILL *Pol. Econ.* v. vii. §3. II. 436 The progress of industry is gradually affording other modes of investment almost as safe and untroublesome. **1894** *Blackw. Mag.* Mar. 393 Things which make cricket easy and untroublesome.
Hence **un'troublesomeness**.
1874 MICKLETHWAITE *Mod. Par. Churches* xxiv. 185 Above all, its [*sc.* gas's] exceeding untroublesomeness.

† **un'trow**, *v. Obs.* [UN-¹ 14.]
1. *intr.* To lack faith.
c **1200** *Trin. Coll. Hom.* 197 On alle þese limpes ne untrowede neure Iob to-ȝenes ure drihten.
2. *trans.* To have no belief in; to disbelieve.
c **1380** WYCLIF *Sel. Wks.* II. 400 But who shulde untrowe Petris sentence? **1387** TREVISA *Higden* (Rolls) I. 17 Wondres beþ not al to be vntrowed [L. *discredenda*]. *a* **1395** HYLTON *Scala Perf.* II. xxxii. (Bodl. MS.), He seeþ it so sooþfastli þoruȝ grace þat he may not vntrowe it.

† **un'trowable**, *a. Obs.* [UN-¹ 7 b.] Unbelievable, incredible.
1382 WYCLIF *Judg.* xx. 5 My wijf traueylynge with vntrowable woodnes of lust. —— *Esther* ii. 15 She was ful semeli, and with vntrouable fairnesse. *c* **1475** *Cath. Angl.* 394/1 (A.), Vn Trowabylle, *incredibilis, incredulus.* **1533** BELLENDEN *Livy* IV. xiv. (S.T.S.) II. 99 Þe samyn is na les difficill..þan vntrowabil. **1552** LYNDESAY *Monarche* 2760 Nynus..rasit vp one gret arme.., Quhose nummer bene.. vntrowabyll.

un'trowed, *ppl. a. Obs.* exc. *arch.* [UN-¹ 8.] Unbelieved, uncredited.
1432 *Rolls of Parlt.* IV. 405/2 For..unreasonable excesse of suche lyes, or sum other untrowed meschevyng. **1434** MISYN *Mending Life* 126 More tollerabyll it wer to þe a vntrowyd greife to suffyr þen ons syn deedly. *a* **1583** MONTGOMERIE *Flyting* 372 (Tullib. MS.), Vntrowit be thy tounge, ȝit tratling all tymes. *a* **1657** SIR W. MURE *Sonn., Vile Priest* 11 Quhose..tounge vntrou'd Hath oft intrappit many a wanton wench.

† **un'trowful**, *a. Obs.* [UN-¹ 7.] Unbelieving.
c **1375** *Sc. Leg. Saints* v. (*John*) 360 Sancte Iohne tuk of þan his kirtill, and to þe vntreufull gawe it till. *Ibid.* xiii. (*Mark*) 35. *c* **1380** WYCLIF *Sel. Wks.* II. 204 O kynrede untroweful, how longe shal I be wiþ ȝou!

† **un'trowing**, *ppl. a. Obs.* [UN-¹ 10.] Faithless.
c **1320** *Sir Tristr.* 1731 Her wening was al wouȝ Vntroweand til hem to.

† **untrowness**: see UNTRUENESS.

un'truced, *a.* (UN-¹ 9.)
c **1613** MIDDLETON *No Wit like Woman's* III. i, All those four Maintain a natural opposition And untruc'd war the one against the other.

un'truckling, *ppl. a.* (UN-¹ 10.)
1850 MRS. BROWNING *Prometh. Bound* 89 But revile not me For the firm will and the untruckling hate.

un'true, *a.* and *adv.* [OE. *untréowe*, *unȝetréow(e*, etc. (UN-¹ 7, 11 b), = NFris. *untraw*, WFris. *on-*, *ûntrou*, MDu. *on(ge)trouwe* (Du. *ongetrouw*, usu. *ontrouw*), MLG. *un(ge)truwe*, OHG. *un(gi)triuwi*, *-gitrûwi*, *-getreowe* (MHG. *un(ge)triuwe*, G. *un(ge)treu*), ON. *útryggr* (MSw. *otrygger*, (M)Da. *utryg*), Goth. *untriggws*.]
A. *adj.* 1. Of persons, etc.: Unfaithful, faithless.
c **1040** *Laws Cnut* in *Liebermann* I. 330 Ȝyf hwylc man sy swa untrywe ðam hundrede. *c* **1290** *St. Edmund* 100 in *S. Eng. Leg.* I. 434 Ich wot wel, ȝuyt men miȝhten finde.. Summan..untreowore to is wiue. *c* **1300** *K. Horn* 645 Þe kyng rod on hontynge,..ant Fykenyld bi is syde, þat fals wes ant vntrewe. *a* **1340** HAMPOLE *Psalter* xxx. 9 To..haf ill susspeccioun of a trew frend, or goed of an vntrew. **1390** GOWER *Conf.* I. 21 The world as of his propre kynde Was evere untrewe. **14..** HOCCLEVE *Of Pride* (MS. Laud Misc. 735) fol. 69, Fy vp on tonges vntrew, They displeasaunce in lordis courtes brew. **1446** LYDG. *Two Nightingale Poems* ii. 17 To take vengeaunce On false lovers whiche that bien vntriewe. *c* **1489** CAXTON *Sonnes of Aymon* xii. 285 Yᵉ gretest traytour & the vntruest kyng of the worlde. *a* **1547** SURREY in *Tottel's Misc.* (Arb.) 219 For my vaunt I dare well say my blood is not vntrue. *a* **1548** [see UNTROTH 1]. **1611** SHAKS. *Cymb.* I. v. 86 When to my good Lord I proue vntrue, Ile choake my selfe. **1700** DRYDEN *Flower & Leaf* 564 The Men inglorious Knights, the Ladies all untrue. **1738** WESLEY *Ps.* v. iii, The Hearts unkind and Hearts untrue Are both abhor'd by Thee. **1802** LEYDEN *Mermaid* vi, Know that thy favourite fair is dead, Or Proves to thee and love untrue. **1818** WORDSW. *'Not seldom'* 6 The smoothest seas will sometimes prove, To the confiding Bark, untrue. **1879** FROUDE *Cæsar* xx. 341 He had refused to believe that Labienus could be untrue to him.
absol. *a* **1400** *Pauline Ep.* (Powell) Titus i. 15 To þe fuylyd ..and to þe vntrewe no thyng is clene. **1866** MORRIS *Ayenb.* 270 *margin*, The untrue, the evil, thieves, &c., are dark.
2. Contrary to fact; false; erroneous.
13.. *E.E. Allit. P.* A. 897 Neuer lesyng ne tale vn-trwe, Ne towched her tonge for no dysstresse. *c* **1370** *Hymns Virg.* (1867) 108 And ȝif þei talke of tales vn-trewe, þou torn hem out of þat entent. *c* **1400** *Cursor M.* 28012 (Cott. Galba), Ȝe traist ouer mekill in thing vntrew. **1446** LYDG. *Two Nightingale Poems* ii. 80 Feynt and vntriew thyne exposicioun. **1531** *Pilgr. Perf.* (W. de W.) 187 b, Sooner shall heuen and erth be dissolued, than one..lettre of yᵉ lawe of god shold be vnfulfylled or founde vntrue. **1577** B. GOOGE *Heresbach's Husb.* I. 43 Others thinke it an assured remedie..; but Columella thinkes it vntrue. **1612** SIR J. DIGBYE *Let.* in *10th Rep. Hist. MSS. Comm.* App. I. 609 But for myne owne parte, I holde this like the reste, to bee alltogeather untrue. **1644** MILTON *Areop.* 38 When God shakes a Kingdome..'tis not untrue that many..false teachers are then busiest in seducing. **1765** *Museum Rust.* IV. 400, I do not apprehend that it any ways tends to prove my assertion untrue. **1802–12** BENTHAM *Ration. Judic. Evid.* (1827) III. 360 The motives by which a man may be urged to give credit to untrue facts. **1875** JOWETT *Plato* (ed. 2) IV. 156 There is nothing true which is not from some point of view untrue.
absol. **1807** WORDSW. *White Doe* 836 Less would not..be due To us, who war against the Untrue. **1882** *N. & Q.* 6th Ser. VI. 429/2 Belief in the untrue. **1891** *Science-Gossip* XXVII. 1/1 It has all the fascination of the untrue for the popular taste.
3. Dishonest; unfair, unjust; wrong.
1393 LANGL. *P. Pl.* C. I. 98 And boxes ben broght forþ.. To vnder-take þe tol of vntrewe sacrifice. **1399** —— *Rich. Redeles* I. 11 By drede, or be dyntis or domes vntrewe. **1444** *Rolls of Parlt.* V. 105/2 Be cause it was of untrue makyng, and untru stuff, no man sette therby. **1495** *Act 11 Hen. VII*, c. 24 §1 Every untrue verdite herafter geven. **1542–3** *Act 34–35 Hen. VIII*, c. 20 Untrue and fained recoveries to be had against them. *Ibid.*, To thentent by fraude, covyne, and untrue meanes..to bynde and defeate theyre heyres. **1596** DALRYMPLE tr. *Leslie's Hist. Scot.* (S.T.S.) I. 199 To..craue the succour..of God and man against the Romane vntrue tyrannie. **1622** in Foster *Eng. Factories Ind.* (1908) II. 44 Wee shall fynde it deficulte to..cleare their demaunds, which what they are or howe untrewe wee are not justly posest. **1865** PUSEY *Truth Eng. Ch.* 5 Nothing..so dispels untrue prejudice as personal intercourse.
4. Not straight or direct; inexact; not agreeing with a standard.
c **1220** *Bestiary* 77 in *O.E. Misc.* 3 Ðer he wurdeþ heil & sund,..Ne were his bec untrewe. *Ibid.* 111 His muð is ȝet untrewe. **1503–4** *Act 19 Hen. VI*, c. 6 §1 Deceivable and untrewe Beames and Scales. *a* **1513** FABYAN *Chron.* ccxxvi. (1516) 147 b/1 This Henry chastysed the olde vntrewe mesure, and made a yerde of the length of his owne Arme. **1780** COWPER *Progr. Error* 571 None sends his arrow to the mark in view, Whose hand is feeble, or his aim untrue. **1844** H. STEPHENS *Bk. Farm* III. 891 Thereby producing wool of unequal size, and therefore untrue. **1867** A. BARRY *Sir C. Barry* ii. 57 The perspective gives an untrue figure.
b. Improper, imperfect.
1541 R. COPLAND *Guydon's Quest. Chirurg.* C i, There is ii. maners of consolydacyon, one is trewe,..and yᵉ other is vntrue consolydacyon. **1884** tr. *Lotze's Metaph.* i. 23 One of the oldest thoughts in Philosophy is that of the opposition between true being and untrue being.
B. *adv.* = UNTRULY *adv.*
a **1310** in Wright *Lyric P.* xlii. 114 Whose loveth untrewe, his herte is selde seete. *c* **1386** CHAUCER *Prol.* 735 Or ellis he moot telle his tale vntrewe Or feyne thyng or fynde wordes newe. *c* **1600** SHAKS. *Sonn.* lxxii, Least your true loue may seeme falce in this, That you for loue speake well of me vntrue. **1622** J. TAYLOR (Water P.) *Merry-Fery-Wherry Voy.* Wks. (1630) 13/1 Some fooles would say I flatter'd, spake vntrue.

† **un'trueful**, *a. Obs. rare.* [UN-¹ 7.] Untruthful, false.
c **1380** WYCLIF *Serm.* Sel. Wks. I. 137 Wole þou not be untrewful but trewe in bileve. **1491** CAXTON *Vitas Patr.* (W. de W. 1495) I. lxxviii. 120/1 Orygenes by his false doctryne hadd gyuen many untruefull techynges contrary to the holy scrypture.

un'trueness. [UN-¹ 12. Cf. OE. *unȝetréowness*.]
a. Unfaithfulness. b. Absence of trueness or truth; falsity, inexactness.
a **1200** *Moral Ode* 265 (Lamb. MS.), Þa þe untrownesse [*v.r.* untrewnesse] duden þon þe ho sculden bon holde. **1727** BAILEY (vol. II), *Falsness*, falshood, untrueness. **1862** F. HALL *Hindu Philos. Syst.* 161 This untrueness does not belong to the universe,..for the causes of that universe..are free from all defect. **1886** HUXLEY in *Fortn. Rev.* Dec. 789 If there be gradations in untrueness.

un'truism. [f. UNTRUE *a.*, after TRUISM.]
1. An untruth.
1845 *Q. Rev.* LXXV. 115 This continual repetition of amiable untruisms. **1857** TROLLOPE *Barchester T.* vi, No one but a preaching clergyman can revel in platitudes, truisms, and untruisms; and yet receive..the same respectful demeanour.
2. That which is untrue.
1868 VISCT. STRANGFORD *Select.* (1869) I. 188 This tiresome literary trick of making an appeal..to the genius of Untruism.

un'truly, *adv.* [OE. *untréowlice* (UN-¹ 11), = MDu. *ontrouwelike* (obs. Du. *ontrouwelijk*), MHG. *untriuwelîche*, ON. *útrúliga* (MSw. *otrolika*, older Da. *utrolig*).]
† 1. Unfaithfully, dishonestly; guilefully, treacherously. *Obs.*
c **893** K. ÆLFRED *Oros.* IV. v. §5 Agothocles ȝedyde untreowlice wið hiene. **1303** R. BRUNNE *Handl. Synne* 1834 She..here wedlak Ful falsly an on-truly brak. **1340** *Ayenb.* 44 Huanne me heþ riȝtuolle wyȝtes and riȝtuolle mesures and zelleþ ontreweliche. *c* **1400** *Destr. Troy* 12074 Achilles ..with treson in þe temple vntruly was slayn. **1444** *Rolls of Parlt.* V. 107/2 The Slayes and Yern therto belangyng, untruly were..wrought. **1495** *Act 11 Hen. VII*, c. 24 §1 Jurrours untruly gevyng ther verdite. **1532–3** *Act 24 Hen. VIII*, c. 1 §1 Great multitude of Hydes..is vntruely insufficiently and deceyvably tanned. *a* **1548** HALL *Chron., Hen. V*, 78 b, Ye..ought to haue kept your faith and promise, whiche you haue vntruly and vnhonestly broken.
2. Incorrectly, falsely.
c **1380** WYCLIF *Wks.* (1880) 430 For þanne..goddis lawe shulde be vntreweliere knowun boþe bi clerkis & bi comyns. *c* **1394** *P. Pl. Crede* 312 Þere we lengeden full longe..For-to all þis freren folke weren founded in townes, And tauȝten vntrulie. **1425** *Paston Lett.* I. 19 Johne Wortes, that.. affermith hym untrewely to be my cousyn. *c* **1449** PECOCK *Repr.* Prol. 4 Whiche summe of the comoun peple vnwijsly and vntreuli iugen and condempnen to be yuele. ? *a* **1533** FRITH *Another Bk. agst. Rastell* C viij b, Now are we come to the fourth erroure where Rastel vntrulye reporteth on me [etc.]. **1579** FULKE *Heskins' Parl.* 438 He would get credite to that which is vntruely ascribed to Saint Iames. **1625** DONNE *Serm.* (1640) 26 It is..dangerously said,..that it is not absurd to say..that God does sometimes speake untruly. **1839** HALLAM *Hist. Lit.* II. cvi. §8 It was said foolishly..of Shakspeare, and we may be sure untruly, that he never blotted a line. **1864** PUSEY *Lect. Daniel* 122 They allege, even untruly, that he copied the prayer of Nehemiah.
3. Inexactly; not in a true course.
1844 MARDON *Billiards* 107, I cannot recollect a single instance of the balls having run untruly.

† **untrum**, *v.*: see UN-¹ 14.

† **un'trum**, *a. Obs.* Also 4 ontrom. [OE., f. *un-* UN-¹ 7 + *trum* strong.] a. Weak, ailing, ill.
c **825** *Vesp. Ps.* civ. 37 [God] utalaedde hie in seolfre & golde & ne wes in cyn heara untrum. *c* **900** tr. *Baeda's Hist.* IV. xxiv. 346 Wæs þær in neaweste untrumra monna hus. **971** *Blickl. Hom.* 217 Þa wearð he untrum on feforadle. *a* **1200** *St. Marher.* 22 Þa..tuhen alle to hire bodi þe untrume weren, and hefden hare heale.
b. Diffident, hesitating.
c **1315** SHOREHAM *Poems* I. 595 Þanne auȝte we wel aryȝt to be To fange hym on-tromme.

† **un'trumness.** *Obs.* [OE., f. prec. Cf. UN-¹ 12.] Weakness, infirmity; ill-health.
c **897** K. ÆLFRED *Gregory's Past. C.* liv. 423 Forðæm wæs sanctus Paulus ȝecostod mid his modes untrumnesse. *c* **1000** *Ags. Gosp.* Matt. viii. 17 He onfeng ure untrumnessa. *a* **1122** *O.E. Chron.* (Laud MS.) an. 1043, Be þes cynges ȝelæfan.. for his mycelre untrumnysse. *c* **1200** ORMIN 5379 Forr to takenn hæle att himm Off iwhillc unntrummnesse. *Ibid.* 18329 Icc amm i me sellfenn wac & full off unntrummnesse.

un'trumpeted, *ppl. a.* (UN-¹ 8.)
[**1775** ASH.] **1861** READE *Cloister & Hearth* i, The strange history of a pair, who lived untrumpeted, and died unsung. **1864** E. SARGENT *Peculiar* III. 298 The important and hazardous though untrumpeted labours of a scout.

un'trunked, *ppl. a.* (UN-² 5, 8.)
1582 STANYHURST *Æneid* II. (Arb.) 63 At leingth with rounsefal, from stock vntruncked, yt harssheth.

un'truss, *v.* [UN-² 4 b.]
1. *trans.* To free from a pack or burden. *rare.*
1390 GOWER *Conf.* II. 294 With this worde his Asse anon He let untrusse. *c* **1430** *Pilgr. Lyf Manhode* II. xlvii. (1869) 94 Whan vntrussed thus j was, j was rauished in to the ayr an hygh. *c* **1530** LD. BERNERS *Arth. Lyt. Bryt.* (1814) 484 There he saw the goodly yong squyers vntrussing of their somers & cariages. **1598** FLORIO, *Sfardellare*,..to vntrusse, or disburthen.
2. To unfasten or undo (a pack, etc.); to remove or free from some fastening.
c **1400** *Pilgr. Sowle* (Caxton, 1483) II. xlv. 51 He vntrussed my fardel, and soone was I taught that sooth was that he seyde. **1570** GOOGE *Pop. Kingd.* IV. 56 The Pedler doth his packe vntrusse, the Host his pots doth fill. **1600** in Swayne *Sarum Churchw. Acc.* (1896) 148 Laborer to untrusse the bels, 6d. **1777** SHERIDAN *Trip Scarb.* v. ii, Now..that I am untrussed [= set free], give me leave to thank thee for the very extraordinary reception I have met with.
b. *fig.* To put off, discard.

1608 CHAPMAN *Byron's Consp.* III. iii, Be free, all worthy spirits, And stretch yourselves for greatness.., Untruss your slaveries.

3. To undo, unfasten (a 'point' of a garment). In later use chiefly allusively (see quot. 1721). *Obs.* exc. *Hist.*

1577 HOLINSHED *Hist. Eng.* I. 8/2 He was slain..by one of his own soldiers, as he was about to vntrusse his pointes. **1614** SYLVESTER *Bethulia's Rescue* II. 78 For..while hee plyes T' untrusse his Points, [he] them (fumbling) faster tyes. **1622** MABBE tr. *Aleman's Guzman d'Alf.* II. 356 One of the Souldiers was going to vntrusse a point. **1721** BAILEY, *To untruss a Point*, i.e. to unbutton one's Breeches in order to ease his Body. **1727** SOMERVILLE *Fables, Welshman & Fly*, A noisy fly..perch'd upon his worship's crown;..his skin he tore, And stuff'd himself with human gore. At last, in manners to excel, Untruss'd a point, some authors tell. **1739** [see POINT *sb.*[1] B. 5]. **1796** *Grose's Dict. Vulgar T.* s.v. **1837** BARHAM *Ingol. Leg.* I. *Grey Dolphin*, The Clerk of Chatham was untrussing his points preparatory to seeking his truckle-bed.

b. In fig. contexts.

1591 LYLY *Endym.* III. iii, Loue..kept such a tumbling in his bodie, that he was glad to vntrusse the poynts of his hart. **1622** DEKKER *Virg. Martir* II. i, Vntrusse the Cod-peece point of our reward. **1891** MEREDITH *One of our Conq.* xiii, Lawyers can be brought to untruss a point over a cup of claret.

c. *absol.* To unfasten one's points; to undo one's dress (*spec.* one's lower garments).

1592 NASHE *P. Penilesse* D iv b, Off with thy gowne and vntrusse, for I meane to lash thee mightily. **1604** E. GRIMSTONE *Siege Ostend* 67 Making a shewe as if hee went to vntrusse. **1648** HERRICK *Hesper.*, *Upon Pagget*, Untrusse, his Master bade him; and that word Made him take up his shirt. *a* **1683** OLDHAM *Rem.* (1684) 123, I must beg my Reader's Distance: as if I were going to Untruss. **1705** HICKERINGILL *Priest-cr.* II. vi. 57 To do which Business, they untrussed, and stript themselves. **1837** BARHAM *Ingol. Leg.* I. *Leech* (1905) 84 Now strip thee, Master Marsh, and that quickly: untruss, I say!

transf. **1649** W. M. *Wandering Jew* 19 His breeches if hee takes wide strides, will untrusse of themselves.

4. To undo or unfasten the garments of (a person); to assist in undressing. Also *refl.*

a **1625** FLETCHER *Elder Brother* IV. iv, Well done, give me my night-cap. So. Quick, quick, untruss me. **1786** tr. *Beckford's Vathek* 99 [He] had untrussed himself to eat with greater advantage. **1809** MALKIN *Gil Blas* X. ix. ¶11 They also undressed Beatrice and Scipio, who..gravely allowed themselves to be untrussed. **1861** READE *Cloister & H.* lv, Soon he bade me untruss him, for he felt sadly.

†**5.** *fig.* **a.** To expose, disclose, reveal. *Obs.*

1600 ROWLANDS *Lett. Humours Blood* iv. 63 Who nominates his Bread and Cheese a name, (That doth vntrusse the nature of the same). **1601** B. JONSON *Poetaster* v. iii, Our Muse is in mind for th' vntrussing a poet. **1651** CLEVELAND *Poems* 20 Yet here's not all, I cannot half untruss &c. it's so abominous.

†**b.** To take apart, dissect, disintegrate. *Obs.*

a **1618** J. DAVIES (Heref.) *Witte's Pilgr.* Wks. (Grosart) II. 37/1 Then, to vntrusse him..Whose Muse hath power to vntrusse what not? Was a vaine cast. **1645** MILTON *Colast.* 16 But hee goes on to untruss my Arguments, imagining them his Maisters points. **1651** CLEVELAND *Poems* 20 Scatter th' accumulative King; untruss That five-fold fiend.

un'trussed, *ppl. a.* [UN-[1] 8, or f. prec.]

†**1.** Unburdened. *Obs.*[−1]

a **1225** *Ancr. R.* 350 þeo men þet..goð untrussed lihte ase pilegrimes touward heouene.

†**2.** Untressed; loose. *Obs.*

c **1400** [see UNTRESSED *ppl. a.*]. **1494** *Lydgate's Bochas* VI. Prol. 32 Hir here vntrussyd [*MSS.* vntressid, -ed] harde sharpe and horryble. *a* **1529** SKELTON *E. Rummyng* 147 Theyr lockes about theyr face, Theyr tresses vntrust. **1587** TURBERV. *Trag. T.* (1837) 30 Untrust her haire hoong rounde about her head. **1600** FAIRFAX *Tasso* XVIII. xxvii. 320 The Dryads..Whose armes, halfe naked; lockes vntrussed bee.

3. Having the garments unfastened or undone.

1544 PHAER *Regim. Lyfe* (1553) I iiij, Ye ought.. to lette your backe be vntrussed in the sommer. **1596** LODGE *Wits Misery* (Hunter. Cl.) IV. 69 His common course is to go alwaies vntrust, except when his shirt is a washing. **1607**, **1647** [see UNGARTERED 1]. **1652** BENLOWES *Theoph.* XI. iv, All his clothes so loosely spread, He's so untrust, as if it were not long to bed. **1822** SCOTT *Nigel* v, Three or four pages in the royal livery, but untrussed, unbuttoned. **1829** *Q. Rev.* XXXIX. 106 The poor boy who..has stood untrussed and trembling before him.

†**b.** Of points: Unfastened. *Obs.*

1589 GREENE *Span. Masquerado* Wks. (Grosart) V. 244 His cappe pulde ouer his eies, and his pointes vntrust. **1616** R. C. *Times' Whistle* v. 2135 Old Monsier Grey-beard with your poynts vntrust.

4. Not trussed for cooking.

1846 SOYER *Cookery* 217 Have four spring chickens untrussed.

un'trusser. [f. UNTRUSS *v.* 5.] †A severe critic.

1599 B. JONSON *Ev. Man out of Hum.* II. i. E iij b, Welcome gentlemen: and how doest thou, thou Grand Scourge, or Second Vntrusse [*sic*] of the time? **1601** —— *Poetaster* v. iii, Ambitiously affecting the title of the vntrussers, or whippers of the age. *Ibid.* To Rdr. 141 *Pol.* Will you not answere then the libells? *Avt.* No. *Pol.* Nor the vntrussers?

un'trussing, *vbl. sb.* [f. UNTRUSS *v.*] The action of the vb., chiefly in fig. senses.

1597 *Return fr. Parnass.* II. i. 762 One that will give his scholler leave to prove as verie a dunce as his father and nere commaunde the untrussinge of his points. **1601** B. JONSON *Poetaster* IV. vii, Come, wee'll goe see how forward our iourney-man is toward the vntrussing of him. **1602** DEKKER (*title*), Satiro-Mastix, or, the Untrussing of the Humorous Poet. **1603** SHAKS. *Meas. for M.* III. ii. 190 Marrie this Claudio is condemned for vntrussing.

un'trust, *sb.* [UN-[1] 12. Cf. WANTRUST.]

1. Unbelief, distrust. Now *rare.*

a **1225** *Ancr. R.* 332 þeos two unðeawes, untrust and ouer-trust, beoð þes deofles tristren. **1382** WYCLIF *Rom.* iv. 20 In the byheeste of God he doutide not with vntrust. **1390** GOWER *Conf.* II. 147 This fievere of Jelousie Somdel.. groweth of sotie, Of love, and somdiel of untrust. **1421–2** HOCCLEVE *Dialog* 336 Frendshipes lawe nat worth wer a myte, If þat vntrust vn-to it wer annexid; Vntrust hath many a wight ful sore vexid. *c* **1450** *Cov. Myst.* (Shaks. Soc.) 153 Alas!.. For my grett dowth and fals beleve,.. My fals vn-trost hath wrought myscheve! **1581** HOWELL *Devises* M j, Condemde thou art for thine vntruste. **1890** J. PULSFORD *Loyalty to Christ* I. 152 We should linger over the words 'Our Father', till nothing of doubt, or untrust, remains.

†**2.** Untrustworthiness. *Obs.*

1430–40 LYDG. *Bochas* Prologue 429 To shewe thun-trust off al worldli thyng. **1563** *Mirr. Mag.* X ii, Of my death let ..princes wete The worldes vntrust, that they there-by be taught. **1579** HAKE *Newes out of Powles* (1872) H iij, Suche is the vntruste that is in man, moe men can speake plausibly in time of good happe,..then [etc.].

†**un'trust**, *v.* *Obs.*[−1] [UN-[1] 14.] *intr.* To have no confidence; to be in despair.

a **1225** *Ancr. R.* 332 Dred wiðuten hope makeð mon untrusten, and hope wiðute dred makeð ouertrusten.

un'trustable, *a.* (UN-[1] 7 b.)

1863 KINGSLEY *Water-Bab.* iii. 118 Dennis will look up at you with his..good-natured untrustable Irish grey eye.

un'trusted, *ppl. a.* (UN-[1] 8.)

1552 HULOET, Vntrusted, *perfidus.* *a* **1586** SIDNEY *Arcadia* III. xix, I could wish my faith untried, and my counsell untrusted. *c* **1710** CONGREVE *Of Pleasing* 13 The untrusted wretch to secresy pretends, Whispering his nothing round to all as friends. *a* **1750** A. HILL *Picture of Love* 41 Curb your untrusted hearts while yet they're free. **1796** MME. D'ARBLAY *Camilla* IV. 389 Even her beloved sister..is untrusted.

un'trustful, *a.* (UN-[1] 7.)

1569 PRESTON *Cambyses* C j b, Untrustfull traitor and corrupt Judge, how likest thou this complaint? **1829** SCOTT *Anne of G.* xxviii, The untried and untrustful services of those, whom we have only known as..malignant neighbours.

†**un'trustiness.** *Obs.* [f. UNTRUSTY *a.*] Unfaithfulness. (Common *c* 1545–1625.)

1526 *Pilgr. Perf.* (W. de W. 1531) 110 These be yͤ vices, ..Sleyghtnesse or deceyte,..Vntrustynesse or Vnsecretnesse. *a* **1548** HALL *Chron.*, *Edw. IV*, 232 Such is the end of vntrustynes & promisbrekyng. **1614** R. HARRIS *Samuels Funerall* (1618) 16 Ah our idlenesse and vntrustines! and all. **1685** BAXTER *Paraphr. N.T.* Rom. iii. 4 All [shall] be silenced that dare accuse him of untrustiness or lying.

†**un'trusting**, *vbl. sb.* (UN-[1] 13.)

c **1440** *Jacob's Well* 294 þe synnes of þe herte arn þise:.. vntrustynge, wrong wenyng, foly loue [etc.].

un'trusting, *ppl. a.* (UN-[1] 10.)

1861 [H. S. CUNNINGHAM] *Wheat & Tares* 364 She had been suspicious, untrusting, ungenerous.

†**un'trustly**, *adv.* *Obs.*[−0] [UN-[1] 11.] Unfaithfully, unreliably.

c **1440** *Promp. Parv.* 368/1 On-trostly (*P.* ontruly, or ontrustly, *infideliter*, *insecure*).

un'trustworthiness. (UN-[1] 12. Cf. next.)

1808 BENTHAM *Sc. Reform* 91 The mass of evidence,..the comparative untrustworthiness of which is thus recognised. **1867** FREEMAN *Norm. Conq.* I. ii. 10 To show the untrustworthiness of the traditional account.

un'trustworthy, *a.* (UN-[1] 7.)

1846 WORCESTER (citing *Ec. Rev.*). **1853** RUSKIN *Stones Ven.* III. ii. §20 Knowledge is not only very often unnecessary, but it is often untrustworthy. **1878** BOSW. SMITH *Carthage* 314 The Gauls, untrustworthy as ever—except when led by Hannibal—were drawn up on a hill to the left.

un'trusty, *a.* [UN-[1] 7.]

1. Untrustworthy, not to be trusted (to), unreliable: **a.** Of things.

1387 TREVISA *Higden* (Rolls) III. 265 þe firste tweie artes beeþ untrusty [*L. erroneæ*]. **1430–40** LYDG. *Bochas* I. 3026 So variable she [*sc.* Fortune] is in hir delites, Hir wheel vntrusti & frowardli meuyng. **1593** T. LODGE *Phillis* H 3 b, Tongue vntrustie, subtil sighted, Wanton will, with change delighted. **1609** HOLLAND *Amm. Marcell.* 67 The residue.. abandoning the Islands as an untrustie place of defence. **1639** FULLER *Holy War* II. xvii. 67 Relying on their own strength, which never is more untrusty then when most trusted. **1677** GILPIN *Demonol.* 58 Others..make them the Effects of our untrusty and deceitful Senses. **1842** MANNING *Serm.* xvii. (1848) 253 It is a dubious and untrusty faith,.. which is reconcileable with an ambitious life. **1870** MORRIS *Earthly Par.* III. IV. 8 To bid them come aboard, and take such rest As they might have of the untrusty sea.

b. Of persons.

1430–40 LYDG. *Bochas* VIII. xxv. 3000 His cosyn Modred, vntrusti & vnstable. *c* **1440** *Promp. Parv.* 148/1 False, and vntrosty, *perfidus.* *a* **1513** FABYAN *Chron.* (1516) 20 b/1 Edricus was..vntrusty and false of thought and promyse. **1542** UDALL *Erasm. Apoph.* 294 To mistruste an untrustie persone, is a poincte of wysedome. **1597** J. PAYNE *Royal Exch.* 14 The vntrustie that borrow moche, and repay.. little. **1642** D. ROGERS *Naaman* 435 Faithfull in the cheefe treasure, and yet untrusty in the smaller. **1691** E. TAYLOR *Behmen's Theos. Philos.* 421 In Adam all Men became untrusty. **1846** W. CROSS *Disruption* xxix, The untrusty domineering laun'-steward. **1876** MORRIS *Sigurd* IV. 327 She dwells with a folk untrusty and a king that knows not ruth.

†**2.** Unfaithful *to* another. *Obs.*

1553 GRIMALDE *Cicero's Offices* III. (1556) 142 How manye mo, thinke ye, were vntrue, and vntrusty to that king. **1575** GASCOIGNE *Glasse of Govt.* I. v, I was never yet untrusty to any of you both. **1612** T. TAYLOR *Comm. Titus* ii. 10 A strong theefe is he, that is vntrusty to him that trusteth him.

un'truth. [OE. *untréowþ*, *untríewþ* (UN-[1] 12). Cf. ON. *útrygð*, also UNTROTH, WANTRUTH.]

1. Unfaithfulness; lack of fidelity, loyalty, or honesty. Now *arch.* and *rare.*

c **893** K. ÆLFRED *Oros.* III. xi. §5 He..him wende from Antigones hamfærelte micelra untreowða. *Ibid.* IV. v. §5. *a* **1122** *O.E. Chron.* (Laud MS.) an. 1086, þa Dænescan.. wurdon awende to þære meste untriwðe. **1340** *Ayenb.* 17 þe uerste boȝ of prede þet is ontreuþe. **1400** tr. *Secreta Secret.*, *Gov. Lordsh.* 62 Hold trewly þy fayth hyght, ffor euer moor to all vntreuthe folwys euyl ende. *c* **1489** CAXTON *Sonnes of Aymon* xvi. 387 Be my suretees, I praye you,..Ye knowe that I dyde never vntrewth. **1559** *Mirr. Mag.* C ij, I through flattery abused his wanton youth, And his fonde trust augmented my vntruth. **1593** SHAKS. *Rich. II*, II. ii. 101, I would to heauen (So my vntruth had not prouok'd him to it) The King had cut off my head.

1859 TENNYSON *Elaine* 126 He never spake word of reproach to me, He never had a glimpse of mine untruth. —— *Guinevere* 537 Too wholly true to dream untruth in thee.

†**2.** Unbelief; lack of faith. *Obs.*

c **1380** WYCLIF *Serm.* Sel. Wks. I. 45 He shal reprove þe worlde of þe synne of untreuþe. *Ibid.* II. 20 Crist woundride of his kyn, for þe untreuþe þat þei hadden.

3. Falsehood, falsity.

1439 *Cases bef. King's Council* (Selden) 105 To sey the playn trouth and nouȝt to melle it with eny ontrouth. **1482** in *Surtees Misc.* (1890) 40 To put down all falssett and untrewit. **1559** BP. SCOT in Strype *Ann. Ref.* (1709) I. App. x. 32 Bringinge..others from the truthe unto untruthe. **1577–82** BRETON *Toyes Idle Head* Wks. (Grosart) I. 27/2 Such youthes there are..As with vntrueth their Ladies fancies feede. **1587** GOLDING *De Mornay* Pref., But yet cannot any vntruth preuayle..against truth... For vntruth is contrary to nature. **1632** LITHGOW *Trav.* I. 2 This stinging censure of absurd vntrueth. **1748** RICHARDSON *Clarissa* III. 299 For his boldness in hoping to make me..testify to his great untruth. **1843** CARLYLE *Past & Pr.* III. i, A poor braggart; fast hastening to be a falsity and speaker of the Untruth. **1873** SPENCER *Stud. Sociol.* xi. (1877) 265 Everyone discovers the untruth of this assumption.

b. A falsehood; a false or incorrect statement.

c **1449** PECOCK *Repr.* III. xvii. 396 It is open that tho ij opinions, conclusiouns, and holdingis..ben errouris and vntreuthis. **1565** JEWEL *Reply Harding* 554 Therefore M. Harding concludeth this mater with twoo vntruethes bothe togeather. **1585** in *Cath. Rec. Soc. Publ.* V. 109 He saythe it is a great untruthe and cannot be prooved. **1634** SIR T. HERBERT *Trav.* 2 All Trauellers are subject to imputations of vntruths. **1651** HOBBES *Leviath.* I. viii. 36 So singular a truth (as they think it, though it be many times an untruth they light on). *a* **1716** BLACKALL *Wks.* (1723) I. 23 A very strange Paradox, or rather a most palpable Untruth. **1756** *Gentl. Mag.* XXVI. 144 The author of three letters..is taken into custody for the virulent abuse, and notorious untruths they contain. **1819** SCOTT *Leg. Montrose* ii, I would be loath to reply to you with an untruth. **1863** P. BARRY *Dockyard Econ.* 215 He..asserts either an impudent or an ignorant untruth.

Comb. **1799** SOUTHEY *Devil's Walk* liii, He is an untruth-telling whoreson.

4. Inexactness.

1869 RANKINE *Machine & Hand-tools* Pl. H 9, The washers have sufficient play..to allow them to accommodate themselves to any untruth..on the surface of the nut.

Hence **un'truther**, one who utters untruths.

1889 JEROME *Three Men in Boat* vii, 'You are an untruther,' I replied, getting roused.

un'truthful, *a.* [UN-[1] 7. Cf. UNTROTHFUL.]

†**1.** Unbelieving, infidel. *Obs.*

c **1375** *Sc. Leg. Saints* xxvii. (*Machor*) 846 Dewenik can to cetnes pas, to folk þat þan wntreuthfull was. **1456** SIR G. HAYE *Law Arms* (S.T.S.) 108 The traytouris untreuthfull sais that the grete Cane is lord of all the warld.

2. Not truthful; untrue.

[**1847** WEBSTER.] **1854** PATMORE *Angel in Ho.* I. viii. 5 The candid skies At our untruthful strangeness laugh'd. **1871** JOWETT *Plato* II. 20 As men become better such theories appear more and more untruthful to them.

Hence **un'truthfully** *adv.*, **un'truthfulness.**

[**1847** WEBSTER, *Untruthfully.] **1879** *Temple Bar Mag.* Sept. 45, 'I am sorry', says Tremaine, untruthfully. **1830** CARLYLE *Misc. Ess.* (1872) III. 53 But it always is our duty ..not to avoid unweddedness by *untruthfulness. **1863** MANSEL *Lett., Lect.*, etc. (1873) 239 The glaring untruthfulness and incongruity of the story.

un'tuck, *v.* [UN-[2] 3.] *trans.* To undo or free from being tucked up.

1611 COTGR., *Destrousser*, to vntrusse, vntucke. **1765** STERNE *Tr. Shandy* VIII. ix, When Bridget untucked the feet of the bed. **1857** J. G. WOOD *Com. Obj. Seashore* 67 In due time it untucks itself, and tosses away the indigestible portions of its food. **1882** *Blackw. Mag.* July 15/1 With a dignified gesture he untucked his legs from under him.

un'tucked, *ppl. a.* [UN-[1] 8 + TUCK *v.*[1]] **a.** Of cloth: Not stretched or tentered. **b.** Not tucked up; loose.

1467 *Rolls of Parlt.* V. 621 To bie rawe Clothes, untoked and unfulled. **1592–3** *Act 35 Eliz.* c. 10 §1 Eyche Kersey.. beinge rawe, unscowred, untucked, and unwett. **1597** SHAKS. *Lover's Compl.* 31 Her haire nor loose nor ti'd in formall plat,..For some vntuck'd, descended her sheu'd hat. **1797** *Monthly Mag.* III. 536 Another, ungirded, or untucked, called *Orthostades*, or streight robes.

un'tuckered, *a.* (UN-^{1} 9.)
1713 ADDISON *Guardian* No. 109 ¶5 One of those Untuckered Ladies whom you are so sharp upon on Monday was sennight. *Ibid.* No. 140 ¶1 The attacks he has made on the untuckered stays and short petticoat.

un'tufted, *ppl. a.* (UN-^{1} 8, 9.)
1872 COUES *N. Amer. Birds* 206 Very small; head untufted.

un'tumbled, *ppl. a.* (UN-^{1} 8.)
1675 WYCHERLEY *Country Wife* v. 91 Women of quality, like the richest Stuffs, lie untumbled and unask'd for. **1781** *Gentl. Mag.* LI. 616 The ocean [was] left in an easy untumbled bed. **1819** BYRON *Juan* II. clxxxi, The sands untumbled, the blue waves untost.

untu'multuated, *ppl. a.* (UN-^{1} 8.)
1659 GAUDEN *Tears Ch.* 107 They were left to their free votes and untumultuated suffrages.

untu'multuous, *a.* (UN-^{1} 7.)
1741 LADY HARTFORD *Lett.* (1805) III. 193 Necessitated to see nothing but what offers itself to me in the most easy and untumultuous manner. **1786** *Francis the Philanthropist* I. 23 Tasting the untumultuous enjoyments of rational society. ? **1818** KEATS *Ep. to Reynolds* 91 An untumultuous fringe of silver foam. **1897** F. THOMPSON *New Poems* 16 In skies that no man sees to move Lurk untumultuous vortices of power.

un'tunable, *a.* [UN-^{1} 7b.]
1. Not tuneful; unmelodious, inharmonious, harsh-sounding.
1545 ELYOT, *Absonus voce*, he that hath an vntunable voyce. **1569** SANFORD *Agrippa* 185b, The vnpleasaunte and vntunable roringe of Asses. **1595** SPENSER *Col. Clout* 374 Or be the shepheards which do serue her laesie,.. Or be their pipes vntunable and craesie. **1655** tr. *Sorel's Com. Hist. Francion* IV. 11 The most untunable musick in the world. **1688** in Wood *Life* (O.H.S.) III. 274 A boy..with a cat under his coat..made her make..an untunable noise. **1748** MELMOTH *Fitzosborne Lett.* lix. (1749) II. 100 [It] might probably give musick to those lines in Horace, which now seem so untuneable. **1796** BURNEY *Mem. Metastasio* III. 307 Constructed in measures wholly untuneable. **1841** D'ISRAELI *Amen. Lit.* I. 100 The Normans could not endure the Saxons' untunable consonants. **1887** W. G. PALGRAVE *Ulysses* 34 The four church bells..have been ringing a very hospitable, though untuneable, peal.
b. *fig.* or in fig. context.
1591 SHAKS. *Two Gent.* III. i. 208 In dumbe silence will I bury mine [*sc.* news], For they are harsh, vn-tuneable, and bad. **1599** SANDYS *Europæ Spec.* (1605) B2b, I will not heere warble long vpon this vntuneable harsh string. **1610** P. HOLLAND *Camden's Brit.* I. 8 It is wholly patched up of untuneable discords and jarring absurdities. **1645** [see UNATONABLE 1]. **1661** J. STEPHENS *Procurations* 129 That which..in him..seemeth..untunable and out of square and friendly compasse.
2. Incapable of being tuned.
1801 BUSBY *Dict. Mus.* s.v.
3. Not appreciative of music.
1851 KEBLE *Occas. Papers & Rev.* (1877) 251 The colours are spread before the blind; the music falls on untunable ears.
Hence **un'tunableness.**
1611 COTGR., *Desaccord*, a jarre, discord, untuneablenesse. **1659** H. MORE *Immort. Soul* III. ix. 420 The tenderer Ear cannot but feel..some harshness and untunableness or other, in the best consorts of Musical Instruments and Voices. **1691** NORRIS *Pract. Disc.* 217 As the untunableness of one or two Instruments discommends the whole Musical Consort. **1756** J. WARTON *Ess. on Pope* I. ii. 65 The harshness and untuneableness of modern languages. **1832** *Westm. Rev.* Oct. 357 An age which finds beauties in untuneableness, and believes exact intonation would be an evil and a loss.

un'tunably, *adv.* [UN-^{1} 11.] Unmelodiously, inharmoniously.
1504 in *Archiv Stud. neu. Spr.* CXX. 423 A harpe gewythe sownd as yt ys set: The harper may wreste vntvnably. **1564** J. RASTELL *Confut. Jewell's Serm.* 111b, This would sound ..vntuneablie. **1610** HOLLAND *Camden's Brit.* I. 131 A Poet ..sung not untunably in this maner. **1653** H. COGAN tr. *Pinto's Trav.* lxxiii. 301 They fell to playing on divers instruments.., though very barbarously and untunably.

†**un'tune,** *sb. Obs.*$^{-1}$ [UN-^{1} 12.] The state of being out of sorts.
1603 FLORIO *Montaigne* III. xiii. 646 Men..much troubled and vexed with their bellies untune and disorder.

un'tune, *v.* [UN-^{2} 4.]
1. *trans.* To put out of tune; to render inharmonious. Freq. in fig. context.
1598 FLORIO, *Distonare*, to vntune. **1602** *2nd Pt. Return Parnass.* v. i. 1996 The cold of wo hath quite vntun'd my voyce. **1643** HERLE *Answ. Ferne* 15 There would be a discontinuity in the whole, enough to..untune the Organ of the Creation. **1711** ADDISON *Spect.* No. 135 ¶9 We have drawn two Words into one, which has likewise very much untuned our Language. **1743** in *Mem. Eliz. Carter* (1808) II. 55 When..The last dread thunders..Untune the concord of the spheres. **1807** J. BARLOW *Columb.* VIII. 45 The drum's rude clang, the war wolf's hideous howl,.. Untuned the harp for all but misery's pains. **1856** C. READE *Never too late* III. 106 The quail['s]..Crake!—crake!—crake! untuning the night. **1876** SWINBURNE *Erechtheus* 1741 Never tear Shall stain for shame nor groan untune the song.
refl. *a* **1661** HOLYDAY *Juvenal* (1673) To Rdr., Certainly I believe he [*sc.* Horace] injuriously untun'd himself in his fall from the ode to the satyre.
b. *fig.* To disorder; to discompose; to render unapt or averse *to* (something).
1638 N. WHITING *Albino & Bellama* 343 Madam, what passion does untune your mind? *a* **1657** R. LOVEDAY *Lett.* (1659) 199 The continuance of my trouble..does often untune and discompose my soul. **1697** DRYDEN *Virg. Past.* IX. 71 Cares and Time Change all things, and untune my Soul to Rhyme. **1753** HOGARTH *Anal. Beauty* xiv. 119 Do we not see in most collections that much time disunites, untunes, blackens, and by degrees destroys even the best preserved pictures. **1798** BLOOMFIELD *Farmer's Boy, Autumn* 228 Disappointed hope untunes the Soul. **1822** SCOTT *Halidon Hill* II. ii, *Gordon.* If music touch thee—*Swinton.* It did, before disasters had untuned me. **1860** EMERSON *Cond. Life* vii. 232 Despair is no muse, and untunes the active powers.
2. *intr.* To go out of tune. *rare*$^{-0}$.
1598 FLORIO, *Discordare*, to disagree, to vntune, to contend, to iarre.
†3. *absol.* ? To relax, unbend. *Obs.*
1609 *Everie Wom. in her Humor* A2b, Come thou hast bene a sinner: vnloade, discharge, vntune, confesse, is venus dominatrix? art not in loue?

un'tuned, *ppl. a.* [UN-^{1} 8, or f. UNTUNE *v.*]
1. a. Not tuned; not made tuneful or melodious; also, rendered untuneful.
1592 DANIEL *Delia* xxi, Vexing with vntun'd moane her dainty eares. **1594** SHAKS. *Rich. II*, I. iii. 134 Rouz'd vp with boystrous vntun'd drummes. **1612** CHAPMAN *Rev. Bussy d'Ambois* I. i, The cities' bells Jangling together in untun'd confusion. **1630** DRAYTON *David & Goliah* 294 The harmony of the vntuned'st string Torments the spirit which so torments the King. **1702** POPE *Sappho* 229 Untun'd my lute, and silent is my lyre. **1733** *Satirist* 9 For Sat'rists write in so untun'd a Strain, Thy claim no Title to th' harmonious Train. **1773** J. HERRIES *Elem. Speech* 53 A string in an instrument broken or untuned.
transf. **1590** SHAKS. *Com. Err.* v. i. 310 That heere my onely sonne Knowes not my feeble key of vntun'd cares. *c* **1626** BOSWORTH *To Fairest Lady* 5 O that it might have been While she had liv'd, and had my verses seen, Before sad cries deaf'd my untuned ears. **1684** EARL ROSCOM. *Ess. Transl. Verse* 337, I lose my Patience, when, with Sawcy Pride, By untun'd Ears I hear His Numbers try'd.
b. Not furnished with a tune.
1853 READE *Chr. Johnstone* 69 The Newhaven men..are agreed that this song lifts them through more work than untuned fishermen can manage.
2. *fig.* Not brought into, put out of, a state of harmony or concord; disordered.
1602 *2nd Pt. Ret. fr. Parnass.* v. i. 1986 With vntaught hand, and with vntuned hart. **1648** J. BEAUMONT *Psyche* XVII. v, At the first,..when in th' untuned Deep Each Thing was wroth and snarled with his brother. **1687** *Death's Vision* v, The Intellective, Vital Flame..Is Thoughtless struck, and Dies By the Untun'd Contexture of the Un-thinking Frame! **1794** GODWIN *Caleb Williams* 65 Mr. Tyrrel would have gone also; his mind was untuned. **1805** WORDSW. *Prelude* IV. 145 For cold and raw the air was, and untuned. **1834** MACAULAY *Ess. Pitt* ¶27 When his mind was untuned.
3. Of an electronic device: not tuned to any one frequency; able to deal with signals of a wide range of frequencies. Also *transf.*
1905 *Electrician* Mar. 822/1 A forest would have great influence in impeding if not in staying altogether the transmission of signals over its surface, more especially in an untuned system. **1962** SIMPSON & RICHARDS *Physical Princ. Junction Transistors* vii. 136 Small-signal operation in the region beyond cutoff is usually confined to two types of amplifier: 1. The tuned band-pass type... 2. The untuned wide-band or video amplifier. **1978** G. SIMS *Rex Mundi* vii. 47 The disorganisation..extended even to the absence of.. canned *bouzouki* music. Instead there was the untuned blare of a radio station.

un'tuneful, *a.* (UN-^{1} 7.)
1709 *Brit. Apollo* No. 9. 3/2 My Voice is so Hoarse and Untuneful. **1760** STERNE *Tr. Shandy* IV. *Slawkenb. T.*, Harsh and untuneful are the notes of love, Unless my Julia strikes the key. **1803** *Monthly Mag.* XVI. 25 He had a voice rough and untuneful. **1830** TENNYSON *The Owl* II. 6 Her voice untuneful grown, Wears all day a fainter tone. **1890** *Pall Mall G.* 24 June 2/3 Liszt's ambitious but untuneful.. Symphony.
Hence **un'tunefully** *adv.*, **un'tunefulness.**
1881 *Athenæum* 25 June 840/2 So does he demonstrate Byron's innate untunefulness. **1884** *Manch. Exam.* 19 Feb. 5/2 A cold which causes a man to sing untunefully.

un'turbaned, *a.* (UN-^{1} 9.)
1801 SOUTHEY *Thalaba* II. xxvii, Unturban'd and unsandal'd there, Abdaldar stood before the Flame. **1887** W. G. PALGRAVE *Ulysses* 14 Visited by turbaned and unturbaned pilgrims.

un'turbid, *a.* (UN-^{1} 7.)
1820 SCOTT *Monast.* ii, The little brook..danced carelessly on from stream to pool, light and unturbid.

un'turf, *v.* (UN-^{2} 4.)
1890 *Nature* 27 Nov. 80/1 A wild hill-top..had been unturfed, the turves and gorse being piled in heaps.

un'turn, *v.* (UN-^{2} 3, 7.)
1816 KEATS *Sonn. when L. Hunt left Prison*, Think you he naught but prison walls did see, Till, so unwilling, thou unturn'dst the key? **1825** J. NICHOLSON *Operat. Mechanic* 320 Then, unturning the finger-screw,..I released the screw from the wheel. *Ibid.* 322 Screws..which are prevented from unturning by tightening the finger-nuts.

un'turnable, *a.* (UN-^{1} 7b.)
1847 TENNYSON *Princ.* II. 186 That iron will, That axelike edge unturnable. **1891** H. HERMAN *His Angel* 14 Honesty, sterling and unturnable, was emblazoned there.

un'turned, *ppl. a.* [UN-^{1} 8.]
1. Not turned over, round, away, etc.
c **1550** [see STONE *sb.* 16c]. **1575** *Gamm. Gurton* I. iv. 12 So see in all the heaps of dust thou leave no stone vnturned. **1665** R. OLIVER in Earl Orrery *St. Lett.* (1742) 120, I will leave no stone unturned, till I find out the root, from whence those wicked branches grow. **1670** [see STONE *sb.* 16c]. **1760** LAW *Spir. Prayer* II. 79 Whilst man stood in his first perfection, unturned from God. **1814** *Monthly Mag.* XXXVIII. 438 Oft I took, and oft return'd This key, and left the lock unturn'd. **1822** BYRON *Vis. Judgem.* lxvii, Behold a candidate with unturn'd coat! **1904** E. RICKERT *Reaper* 303 He wanted to see how much ground was unturned.
2. Not shaped by turning.
1816 J. SMITH *Panorama Sci. & Art* I. 61 The part thus left unturned may be cut off either in the lathe or afterwards. **1875** *Carpentry & Join.* 88 The head..of the bed..may be made of unturned posts.

un'turning, *ppl. a.* [UN-^{1} 10.]
1. Not turning round; not revolving.
1591 [see UNTRANSPARENT *a.*].
2. Not turning back or aside; continuing in a straight course; undeviating.
1593 Q. ELIZ. *Boeth.* IV. pr. vi. 93 Yf the euerlasting purenes of Godes mynde doth prescribe an vnturning order of causes. *c* **1611** CHAPMAN *Iliad* XV. 254 The clamorous fray Calls out a lion,..and his abhorred view Turns headlong in unturning flight (though vent'rous) all the crew. **1862** T. A. TROLLOPE *Marietta* iv, The long unturning path.

un'tusked, *a.* (UN-^{1} 9.)
1859 *All Year Round* No. 32. 129 The untusked elephants of Ceylon have 'tushes'.

un'tutelar, *a.* (UN-^{1} 7.)
1667 WATERHOUSE *Fire Lond.* 2 Men may see the dreadful effects of providence, untutelar to their acquisitions.

un'tutored, *ppl. a.* [UN-^{1} 8.]
1. Uneducated, untaught; simple, unsophisticated; †rude, boorish: a. Of persons.
1593 SHAKS. *3 Hen. VI*, v. v. 32 Vntutor'd Lad, thou art too malapert. **1598** SYLVESTER *Du Bartas* II. ii. *Babylon* 262 Un-toyld, un-tutord,..We learn'd a language all men understood. **1618** FLETCHER *Loyal Subj.* IV. iii, We are two simple maids, untutor'd here Sir. **1663** J. SPENCER *Prodigies* 15 Those Secretaries of Nature..fell under the hatred of the untutor'd rabble. **1725** POPE *Odyss.* I. 491 What God to your untutor'd youth affords This headlong torrent of amazing words? **1780** BENTHAM *Princ. Legisl.* xviii. §17 *note*, It is not for this that the untutored many could have originally submitted themselves to the dominion of the few. **1809–14** WORDSW. *Excurs.* v. 840 The untutored bird may..so construct..her nest..That the thorns wound her not. **1858** MERIVALE *Rom. Emp.* lii. VI. 66 [These] women..were exceptions to the mass of the untutored matrons of Rome. **1878** H. S. PALMER *Sinai* iv. 75 The superstitious and untutored inhabitants of the Desert.
b. Of the mind, intellect, etc.
1597 *Pilgr. to Parnassus* I. 9 Urge mee to advise youre younge untutord thoughts. **1619** A. NEWMAN *Pleas. Vis.* (1840) 7 Vaine will vntam'd, vntutored, Left Reasons rule. **1693** PRIOR *To Dr. Sherlock* 29 Thy even Thoughts with so much Plainness flow; Their Sense untutor'd Infancy may know. **1732** POPE *Ess. Man* I. 99 The poor Indian! whose untutor'd mind Sees God in clouds, or hears him in the wind. **1784** COWPER *Task* II. 570 A relaxation of religion's hold Upon the roving and untutor'd heart Soon follows. **1837** DISRAELI *Venetia* III. vii, Her unsophisticated and untutored spirit. **1867** PEARSON *Hist. Eng.* I. 15 Their wants were still undeveloped, their taste untutored.
c. Of instruments (esp. pen or pencil).
1611 RICH *Honest. Age* (Percy Soc.) 7, I come not to implore a Lawrell Crowne, Wherewith to decke my rude untutred quill. **1623** J. TAYLOR (Water P.) *Discov. by Sea* C2b, What my vntutor'd Pen cannot sufficiently commend, I am forced with silence to ouerpasse. **1706** E. WARD *Wooden World Diss.* (1708) A6b, This rough Draught of my untutor'd Pencil. **1748** *Anson's Voy.* III. viii. 380 Of so little consequence are the most destructive arms in untutored and unpractised hands. **1865** F. PARKMAN *Champlain* iv. (1875) 240 A scene oddly portrayed by the untutored pencil of Champlain.
d. Of places or conditions.
1751 W. WHITEHEAD *Hymn to Nymph* 312 Ev'n then, the scene We now behold to such perfection wrought, Charm'd with untutor'd wildness. **1760** W. SMITH *Disc. Public Occas.* (1762) 119 The Propagation of Christ's religion through the untutored parts of the earth. **1796** MME. D'ARBLAY *Camilla* V. 204 The children of untutored nature. **1809** WORDSW. *Poems Nat. Indep. & Liberty* II. xiii, Is it among rude, untutored Dales..only, that the heart is true? **1887** *Cornh. Mag.* Jan. 39 A camping-out expedition in the untutored woodlands.
2. Not produced or formed as the result of education or training; not improved by instruction.
1593 SHAKS. *Lucr.* Ded., The worth of my vntutord Lines. **1644** MILTON *Educ.* 2 Besides the ill habit which they get of wretched barbarizing..with their untutor'd Anglicisms. **1744** AKENSIDE *Pleas. Imag.* I. 422 The gracious Power Who first awakened my untutored song. **1768** BOSWELL *Corsica* iii. (ed. 2) 196 Those heroes whose untutored patriotism had shone with such lustre. **1788** GIBBON *Decl. & F.* xliv. IV. 334 The laws of marriage,..the authority of parents,..are ascribed to the untutored wisdom of Romulus. **1810** CRABBE *Borough* i. 122 We prune our hedges, prime our slender trees, And nothing looks untutor'd and at ease. **1859** JEPHSON *Brittany* v. 61 The rough untutored vocal expression of worship offered by a whole congregation. **1873** SYMONDS *Grk. Poets* viii. 251 The peculiar glories of Aristophanes style are its untutored beauties.
3. Not subject to a tutor or tutors.
1641 MILTON *Reform.* II. 72 Where under a free, and untutor'd Monarch, the..most prudent men..have in their power the supreame..determination of highest Affaires.

†**un'twight,** *pa. pple. Obs.* [UN-^{1} 8b. Phaer also uses *twight* for 'touched'.] Untouched: intact.
1558 PHAER *Æneid* I. Bj, For her to him her father gaue a virgyn yet ontwight. *Ibid.* II. Civb, Whiles yet hys kingdom stood ontwight.

†**un'twind**, *v. Obs. rare.* [UN-^{2} 3.] = next. Hence **un'twinding** *vbl. sb.*
c **1460** *Promp. Parv.* (Winch.) 323 On-wyyndyn or ontwyndyn, *destorqueo.* a **1542** WYATT *Penit. Ps.* xxxvii. 104 All wicked folk reversed shall untwind. **1592** WYRLEY *Armorie* 34 Their linked chaines do binde Bigge ships so fast, they cannot soone vntwinde. **1597** SHAKS. *2 Hen. IV*, II. iv. 213 Why then let..gaping Wounds vntwin'd the Sisters three. **1608** MACHIN *Dumb Knt.* II. D 2 b, Euen with ease, and gentle tangled knots, Thou shalt vntwind thy clew of miseries. **1642** R. CARPENTER *Experience* III. v. 47 The untwinding of my heart from all idle affection to these low base things of earth.

un'twine, *v.* [UN-^{2} 3. Cf. WFris. *ont-, un-twine*, Du. *onttwijnen*.]

1. *trans.* To untwist; to undo by untwisting or disentangling. Freq. in fig. context.
c **1407** LYDG. *Reson & Sens.* 1252 To shewen..How the threde shal be vntwyned Of hir lyf. **1447** BOKENHAM *Seyntys* (Roxb.) 43 Or than deth the threed untwyne Of oure fatal web. **1551** T. WILSON *Logike* B ij b, Knitting together true Argumentes, and vntwining all knotty Subtiltees. **1577** HOLINSHED *Chron.* I. *Hist. Irel.* 14/1 This knotte (saith our Authour) might be vntwyned with more facilitie thus. **1601** CAMPION *Bk. of Ayres* II. ix. 6 The sprites..Affect for pastime to vn-twine her tressed haire. a **1656** HALES *Gold. Rem.* III. (1673) 24 Idleness, Fulness, and Lust, they are a three-fold cord, twisted by the devil, and hardly untwined and severed by any man. a **1687** WALLER *Thyrsis, Galatea* 41 Since the Sisters did so soon untwine So fair a thread, I'll strive to piece the line. **1793** BURNS *'O Poortith cauld'* i, O why should Fate sic pleasure have, Life's dearest bands untwining? **1813** SCOTT *Rokeby* III. xxii, On his sad brow nor mirth nor wine Could e'er one wrinkled knot untwine. **1847** J. MARTINEAU *Chr. Life* 347 Philosophy..endeavours to untwine the finished web of thought.

b. *fig.* To dissolve, undo, destroy.
13.. *E.E. Allit. P.* B. 757 'What for twenty,' quoth þe tolke, 'vntwynez þou hem þenne?' a **1470** HARDING *Chron.* LXXIII. v, With hoost full great of Britons..On Douglas water the Saxons he did vntwine. **1523** SKELTON *Garl. Laurel* 1445 This goodly flowre with stormis was vntwyned. a **1529** —— *P. Sparowe* 282 O cat.., The fynde was in thy mynde Whan thou my byrde untwynde. **1560** DAUS tr. *Sleidane's Comm.* 274 b, So did also the frendshyp..not a litle greue you and full ofte haue assayed that the same might be vntwyned. **1594** CAREW *Huarte's Exam. Wits* 322 At the instant when he beginneth to be shaped, he likewise beginneth to be vn-twined. **1625** QUARLES *Sion's Sonn.* ix. 1 The world cannot vntwine The joyfull vnion of His heart, and Mine. **1718** POPE *Iliad* XVI. 950 There ends thy glory! there the fates untwine The last, black remnant of so bright a line.

2. To detach, remove, release, extract, by untwisting. Also *fig.*
a **1568** ASCHAM *Scholem.* I. (Arb.) 75 Whom all the Siren songes of Italie could neuer vntwyne from the maste of Gods word. **1582** STANYHURST *Æneis* IV. (Arb.) 108 When death hath vntwined my soule from carcas his holding. **1600** FAIRFAX *Tasso* XX. cxxx, His strong arme..She would haue thrust away, loos'd, and vntwin'd. **1611** SHAKS. *Cymb.* IV. ii. 59 Let the stinking-Elder (Greefe) vntwine His perishing roote with the encreasing Vine. **1799** SHERIDAN *Pizarro* I. i, He sued to..untwine the sword from my determined grasp. **1841** BROWNING *Pippa* Introd. 199 Untwine me from the mass Of deeds which make up life. **1846** LANDOR *Imag. Conv.* Wks. II. 46/2 Some privy councillor..come to untwine and wheedle your secrets out of you.

3. *intr.* To become untwisted or undone.
1592 *Arden of Feversham* IV. iv. 80 What, so familiare?.. Vntwyne those armes. *Ales.* I, with a sugred kisse let them vntwine. **1644** MILTON *Divorce* (ed. 2) vi. 14 For strait..his silk'n breades untwine, and slip their knots. **1871** B. TAYLOR *Faust* II. III. 266 Soon shall, I fear me, The sweet bond untwine!

Hence **un'twining** *vbl. sb.*
1577 HOLINSHED *Chron.* I. *Hist. Irel.* 1 b, And that our Irishe hystorie..yeeldeth al these commodities, I trust the indifferent reader, vpon the vntwyning thereof, will not denie. **1626** BACON *Sylva* §494 Which is caused by the untwining of the Beard by the Moisture. **1664** POWER *Exp. Philos.* III. 177 Our thread by often untwining broke it self.

un'twineable, *a.* (UN-^{1} 7 b.)
1609 J. MELTON *Sixefold Politician* v. 73 That damnable and vntwineable traine and owsell of perdition. **1617** J. MOORE *Mappe Mans Mort.* III. viii. 234 The most strong and vntwineable cable.

un'twined, *ppl. a.* (UN-^{1} 8, or f. UNTWINE *v.*)
1649 LOVELACE *Lucasta, A Forsaken Lady* v, Must we.. Be dragg'd on still By the weake Cordage of your untwin'd will?

un'twinkling, *ppl. a.* (UN-^{1} 10.)
1880 AGNES GIBERNE *Sun, Moon, & Stars* 175 A brilliant untwinkling star-like form.

†**un'twinned**, *ppl. a.*^{1} *Obs.*$^{-1}$ [UN-^{1} 8.] Unparted, undivided.
c **1450** *Mirour Saluacioun* (Roxb.) 1 Ye blyssed Trinitee In o substaunce vntwynned.

un'twinned, *ppl. a.*^{2} [UN-^{1} 8.] *Cryst.* Not furnished with a twin.
1879 RUTLEY *Stud. Rocks* x. 97 Untwinned crystals [of albite] are rare. **1888** —— *Rock-forming Min.* 277.

un'twirl, *v.* (UN-^{2} 3.)
a **1703** WALLIS in Greenwood *Eng. Gram.* (1711) 283 Untwirling the twine that intwisteth between.

un'twist, *sb.* [UN-^{2} 3, 8.] A reversive twist.
1889 *Telegr. Jrnl.* 26 April 467/2 Each coil of the cable.. as it comes out receives a twist in the opposite direction, or 'untwist'.

un'twist, *v.* [UN-^{2} 3 and 7.]

1. *trans.* To restore from a twisted state; to untwine. Also in fig. context.
1538 ELYOT, *Retexo*, to vntwyste. **1587** GREENE *Penelope's Web* Wks. (Grosart) V. 151 A shift to make her work endlesse, by vntwisting as much in the night as she woue in the day. c **1590** L. BRYSKETT *Mourning Muse* 148 Which made them eftsoones feare the daies of Pirrha shold..their fatall threds vntwist. **1626** JACKSON *Creed* VIII. x. §1 The Sonne of God..began to untwist that triple cord, wherewith our first parents..were bound by Satan. **1632** MILTON *L'Allegro* 143 Untwisting all the chains that ty The hidden soul of harmony. **1700** DRYDEN *Ovid, Pythagorean Philos.* 381 Restless they soon untwist the Web they spun. **1731** SWIFT *Nymph going to Bed* 19 She..Untwists a wire, and from her gums A set of teeth completely comes. **1760** R. BROWN *Compl. Farmer* II. 68 Hempen ropes cut small and un-twisted, are beneficial [as manure] for lands. **1823** J. BADCOCK *Dom. Amusem.* 54 Hop plants, growing round a pole..; if you untwist any, and confine them in the contrary direction, they die. a **1834** COLERIDGE *Friend* (1837) III. 213 Cutting the knot which it cannot untwist. **1860** GEO. ELIOT *Mill on Fl.* III. vi, Bob had drawn out..[and began] to untwist his canvas bag.
transf. **1834** COLERIDGE *Table-t.* (1835) II. 295 A serpent ..makes a fulcrum of its own body, and seems for ever twisting and untwisting its own strength.

b. *fig.* and in fig. context. To dissolve, break up, decompose.
1611 SPEED *Hist. Gt. Brit.* VIII. vii. §39. 408 The English supposing the Normans to have fled,..began in eager pursuit carelesly to vntwist and display their ranckes. **1640** SIR J. WRAY *Speech* in Rushworth *Hist. Coll.* (1692) I. 40 The Divisions of Great Britain have half untwisted our Long Union. a **1644** QUARLES *Hieroglyphikes* i. 21 Whose errour-chacing beams..untwist The clouds of ignorance. **1653** JER. TAYLOR *Serm. Year* I. xiii. 168 The faith of very many men, seems a duty so weak.., is so often untwisted by violence, or ravel'd and intangled in weak discourses. **1727** THOMSON *To Mem. Newton* 98 Ev'n light itself..Shone undiscover'd, till his brighter mind Untwisted all the shining robe of day. **1751** WARBURTON *Pope's Wks.* I. 105 *note*, The prismatic glass..untwisting, by its obliquities, those threads of light. **1896** A. AUSTIN *England's Darling* I. i, The outlandish dogs..Untwisting what he bound, and to their will Enserfing all.

†**2.** To disentangle by explanation or exposition; to expound, make plain. *Obs.*
1577 tr. *Bullinger's Decades* 5/2 This is the brief summe of the holy fathers tradition, whiche it is best to vntwist more largely. **1606** SYLVESTER *Du Bartas* II. iv. *Magnif.* 1314 Hee ..at pleasure frees Such doubts, as..might have taskt, t' untwist, The Brachman, Druide, and Gymnosophist. a **1625** FLETCHER *Woman Pleas'd* v. i, Tis a Witch sure, And by her means he came to untwist this Riddle. **1660** JER. TAYLOR *Worthy Commun.* Introd. 8 The Holy Communion ..is too much untwisted and nicely handled by the writings of the Doctors. **1773** TOPLADY in Boswell *Johnson* 7 May, You have untwisted this difficult subject with great dexterity.

3. To loosen, detach, or set free, by untwining. Also *fig.*
1637 S. MARMION *Cupid & Psyche* I. iii. 394 He took her wrist, And wrung it hard, and did her hands untwist. **1638** SIR T. HERBERT *Trav.* (ed. 2) 167 A raging storme.. separated us; insomuch as we had hardly recovered our companies, had not the..jingling of the Cammells bells revoked, yea untwisted us out of these Caspian or Zagrian straits. a **1652** J. SMITH *Sel. Disc.* iv. 86 Our souls,.. untwisting themselves from all corporeal complications. **1692** DRYDEN *Don Sebastian* III. i, *Alm.* How can we better dye than close embrac'd, Sucking each others Souls while we expire?.. *Emp.* No I'll untwist you: I have occasion for your stay on Earth.

4. *intr.* To pass out of a twisted condition; to become untwined.
1589 PUTTENHAM *Eng. Poesie* III. xviii. 156, I will well that ye wist, The thred is spon, that neuer shall vntwist. a **1703** WALLIS in Greenwood *Eng. Gram.* (1711) 282 If one of the twines of the twist do untwist, The twine that untwisteth, untwisteth the twist. **1728** CHAMBERS *Cycl.* s.v. *Hygrometer*, The Cord or Gut twisting and untwisting..will indicate the Change of Moisture. **1786** BONNYCASTLE *Astronomy* xi. 184 As the thread untwists, the globe..will turn round its axis. **1825** J. NICHOLSON *Operat. Mechanic* 435 Either of the two palls *x* and *y* may..prevent the strands from untwisting. **1897** GRANT ALLEN *Type-writer Girl* i, There..you shall see spring buds untwisting.
fig. **1653** JER. TAYLOR *Serm. for Year* I. ii. 22 His purposes untwist as easily as the rude conjuncture of uncombining cables. **1670** EACHARD *Cont. Clergy* 67 Sometimes the words naturally fall asunder;..sometimes they untwist.

Hence **un'twist** *ppl. a.*, = UNTWISTED *ppl. a.*^{2}
1607 MARSTON *What you will* II. i, My spirit is untwist; My heart is raveld out in discontents. **1647** N. WARD *Simple Cobler* 30 When States dishelv'd [= dishevelled] are, and lawes untwist, Wise men keep their tongues. **1651** JER. TAYLOR *Serm. for Year* II. xv. 190 By little and little our strongest resolutions be untwist, and crack in sunder.

un'twistable, *a.* (UN-^{1} 7 b.)
1816 *Monthly Mag.* XLII. 521 The origin of the profoundest impressions, and the most untwistable associations. **1879** THOMSON & TAIT *Nat. Phil.* I. I. §109 A perfectly flexible, untwistable cord.

un'twisted, *ppl. a.*^{1} [UN-^{1} 8.] Not twisted or twined.
1575 TURBERV. *Faulconrie* 97 Threade it with untwisted threade. **1825** J. NEAL *Bro. Jonathan* III. 323 Have you forgotten..how you broke away from us like the Philistine from the untwisted flax? **1865** TYLOR *Early Hist. Man.* vii. 188 The warp consists of strands of un-twisted fibre. **1866** R. M. FERGUSON *Electr.* 21 A magnetic bar, suspended by.. a few untwisted filaments of cocoon silk.

un'twisted, *ppl. a.*^{2} [f. UNTWIST *v.*] Taken out of a twisted state.
1611 FLORIO, *Sfilaccio*, okame of vntwisted ropes. **1629** FORD *Lover's Melancholy* IV. 59 If the Fates Haue spun my thred and my spent clue of life Be now vntwisted. ? **1738** WARBURTON *Div. Legat.* II. App. (R.), The solar light is not less real in the rainbow where it's rays become thus untwisted. **1848** BUCKLEY *Iliad* 26 The ropes have become untwisted.
fig. a **1700** B. E. *Dict. Cant. Crew, Untwisted*, Undone, Ruin'd. **1756** *Monitor* No. 35. I. 329 Mrs. Bull..cries out, ..Lord, Doctor! we are all untwisted, all undone. **1785** GROSE *Dict. Vulgar T.* s.v.

un'twisting, *vbl. sb.* [f. UNTWIST *v.*] The action or result of taking out of twist; also *pl.*, untwisted fibres or threads.
1591 PERCIVALL, *Deshiladura*, vntwisting. **1611** FLORIO, *Sfiaccij*, vntwistings, rauelings, lint for Chirurgions. **1651** BAXTER *Inf. Bapt.* 92 There should be no difficulty in the untwisting of all this which Mr. T. hath so ravelled. **1728** CHAMBERS *Cycl.* s.v. *Hygrometer*, This alternate Twisting and Untwisting in a Cord. **1875** R. F. MARTIN tr. *Havrez' Winding Mach.* 27 Without any untwisting of the eight strands.

un'twitted, *ppl. a.* (UN-^{1} 8.)
1651 H. VAUGHAN *Of the Benefit by our Enemies* ad. fin., Neither must wee leave them untwitted with that [saying] of Solon.

†**un'twitten**, *ppl. a. Obs.*$^{-1}$ (Meaning obscure.)
1613 R. C. *Times' Whistle* (1871) 132 When every gull may see his booke's vntwitten, And Epigrams as bad as e're were written.

†**unty3tel**, *adv. Obs.*$^{-1}$ (Obscure; perh. an error for *unsty3tel*: see STIGHTLE *v.*)
13.. *Gaw. & Gr. Knt.* 1114 þay dronken & daylyeden, & dalten vnty3tel.

un'tying, *vbl. sb.* [f. UNTIE *v.*] The action of the vb.
1597 A. M. tr. *Guillemeau's Fr. Chirurg.* 45 b/2 Concerninge the vntyinge [of a bandage]. a **1637** B. JONSON *Horace's Art Poetrie* 274 Nor must the fable..have a god come in; except a knot Worth his untying happen there. **1644** HUNTON *Vind. Treat. Monarchy* vii. 55 The non observance of it by the King did not amount to an untying of the bond of subjection in the people. **1668** DRYDEN *Ess.* (ed. Ker) I. 86 For the contrivance of the plot, 'tis..withal easy; for the..untying of it, 'tis so admirable, that [etc.]. a **1844** CAMPBELL *Song, 'How delicious'* i, When two mutual hearts are sighing For the knot there's no untying. **1891** T. HARDY *Tess* xlvii, Tess..was one of those who best combined strength with quickness in untying.

un'typable, *a. Med.* and *Biol.* [UN-^{1} 7 b.] That cannot be assigned to a specific type.
1950 *Britannica Bk. of Year* 682/2 Untypable. **1961** *Lancet* 22 July 173/2 Both strains [of Staphylococci] were untypable. **1977** *Ibid.* 14 May 1047/1 The isolate derived from the mincer was of serotype 1, and that from the butter beans was untypable.

un'typical, *a.* (UN-^{1} 7.)
1848 MOZLEY *Ess.* (1878) I. 345 It is not untypical of Luther's temper. **1884** *Harper's Mag.* Apr. 771/2 An instance, not untypical of London.

†**un'ulcerate**, *ppl. a. Obs.* (UN-^{1} 8 b.)
1590 BARROUGH *Meth. Physick* v. xxvi. (1596) 356 Of an vnulcerate cancre, there often proceedeth an vlcerate tumor. **1634** *Lowe's Chirurg.* (ed. 3) IV. xvi. 115 The unulcerate [cancer], is called the hidden Cancer.

un'ulcerated, *ppl. a.* (UN-^{1} 8.)
[**1775** ASH.] **1879** *St. George's Hosp. Rep.* IX. 431 The ileum presented several as yet unulcerated swellings.

un'ullaged, *ppl. a.* (UN-^{1} 8.)
1646 in Picton *L'pool Munic. Rec.* (1883) I. 180, 65 tunnes of un-ulleged Wynes.

un-'ultra, *a.* (UN-^{1} 7.)
1817 LADY GRANVILLE *Lett.* (1894) I. 97 He says these un-ultra men have neither the *petit maître* or grand polished manner of *vieille cour* Frenchmen.

‖**unum necessarium** ('uːnəm nɛsɪ'sɛərɪəm). [mod.L., ad. Vulgate *unum est necessarium* one thing is necessary (Luke x. 42).] The one, or the only, necessary thing; the essential element.
1931 H. H. HENSON *Let.* 21 Oct. (1950) 63 So long as episcopacy is looked upon as the *unum necessarium* of a Christian Church, I am sure that no reunion with the presbyterian and congregational churches is possible. **1937** *Times Lit. Suppl.* 15 May 379/1 Mr. Wilkins has the *unum necessarium* of a storyteller in this kind. **1938** W. S. CHURCHILL *Marlborough* IV. xxxi. 522 His exclusion was, he said, the *unum necessarium*.

ununder'standable, *a.* (UN-^{1} 7 b.)
a **1631** DONNE *Serm.* i. (1634) 8 Let him have known..ununderstandable things, unrevealed decrees of God. a **1843** SOUTHEY *Common-pl. Bk.* Ser. II. (1849) 251 The vile and ununderstandable Machabeo he ranks with Homer and Virgil! **1872** BRIERLEY *Cotters of Mossburn* xxiv. 252 There is something very 'ununderstandable' going on between Luke Brundrett and Miss Louisa Gerrard. **1891** H. HERMAN *His Angel* 46 He stammered a few ununderstandable words.

ununder'standing, *ppl. a.* (UN-^{1} 10, 5 b.)
1611 FLORIO, *Inintelligente*, vnunderstanding. a **1658** LOVELACE *Lucasta, Peinture*, Let's walk hand in hand, And smile at this un-understanding land. **1862** MRS. N. CROSLAND *Mrs. Blake* II. 219, I know that the most crystalline phrases..have been dragged through the mud of common un-'understanding' usage. **1891** H. HERMAN *His*

Angel 77 The thoughtless ununderstanding girl was gone, and a blushing..woman stood there in her stead.

ununder'stood, *ppl. a.* (UN-^{1} 8 b.)
1639 FULLER *Holy War* IV. v. 174 With us they consent in ..the overplus of Merits, Services ununderstood, Indulgences. **1655** —— *Ch. Hist.* IX. i. §50 English being.. in the most Parishes of Wales utterly un-understood. **1860** PUSEY *Min. Proph.* 537 The deep saying, ununderstood even by Joseph and Mary. **1880** BARING-GOULD *Mehalah* vii, Some such vague sea of ununderstood, unestimated elements.

un'unified, *ppl. a.* (UN-^{1} 8.)
1862 H. SPENCER *First Princ.* §37 Knowledge of the lowest kind is ununified.

ununiform (ʌn'ju:nɪfɔ:m), *a.* (UN-^{1} 7.)
1659 ALLESTREE *Gentl. Calling* v. §25. 85 Nor will they be so Ununiform, as not to have their Drink bear a full proportion with their Meat. **1697** COLLIER *Ess. Mor. Subj.* I. 101 How patched and ununiform does it..make the Figure of some Families? **1749** HURD *Hor. Ars Poet.* 54 Let the manners be uniform, or, if ununiform, yet consistently so, or uniformly ununiform. **1842** GWILT *Archit.* Gloss. s.v. *Casting*, The ununiform texture of the material.

un'uniformed, *a.* (UN-^{1} 9.)
1867 MOTLEY *Corr.* (1887) II. 263, I, of course, was ununiformed, having left my official finery at Vienna. **1898** D. C. MURRAY *Tales* 140 Uniformed and ununiformed men were chaffing each other.

ununi'formity. (UN-^{1} 12.)
1749 HURD *Hor. Ars Poet.* 54 Here is a manifest ununiformity. **1803** *Monthly Mag.* XV. 3 We now reserve only enough of the diphthongal spelling to add to the un-uniformity of our very anomalous language.

un'uniformly, *adv.* (UN-^{1} 11.)
1656 [? J. SERGEANT] tr. *T. White's Peripat. Inst.* 171 It must alwayes be mov'd ununiformly. **1891** C. CHAPMAN *Preorganic Evol.* 166 Any one familiar with the action of physical laws in masses of matter *un*uniformly composed and related *un*symmetrically to 'forces external to it'.

un'uniformness. (UN-^{1} 12. Cf. UNUNIFORM *a.*)
1716 S. CLARKE *Several Lett.* 41 The different Attributes of which One Uniform Being are not a Variety of Parts, or an un-Uniformness (if I may so speak) of the Necessity by which it exists; but [etc.].

unu'nitable, *a.* (UN-^{1} 7 b.)
1678 CUDWORTH *Intell. Syst.* 564 Minds or Intellects.. who also are absolutely Ununitable to any Bodies. **1881** P. BROOKS *Candle of Lord* 183 To us they seem to stand opposite, over against each other, ununited, ununitable.

unu'nitableness. (UN-^{1} 12.)
1664 H. MORE *Myst. Iniq.* 336 The Ununitableness of the Kings of the Age into one Head.

†**unu'nite**, *v. Obs.* [UN-^{1} 14.] *trans.* To abstain from uniting.
1596 R. L[INCHE] *Diella*, etc. F 1 b, You ruthlesse Fates.., Why ioy you so in vnuniting vs?

ununited (ʌnju:'naɪtɪd), *ppl. a.* (UN-^{1} 8.)
1587 GOLDING *De Mornay* ii. 19 In vnvnited diuersitie wee finde waste. **1626** SIR D. DIGGES *Sp.* in Rushw. *Hist. Coll.* (1659) I. 302 Scotland..ununited, Ireland not setled in peace. **1678** CUDWORTH *Intell. Syst.* 795 In the World to come, they should..continue Pure Souls, Ununited to any Body. **1736** BUTLER *Anal.* I. iii. 59 Ten Men united, might be able to accomplish, what ten thousand..wholly ununited, could not. **1738** WARBURTON *Div. Legat.* I. 251 Unsupported by, and ununited with the State. **1852** M. ARNOLD *Tristr. & Iseult* II. 89 But, since living we were ununited, Go not far..from my grave. **1872** ERICHSEN *Surg.* (ed. 6) I. 301 Ununited Fractures and False Joints.

ununi'versitied, *ppl. a.* (UN-^{2} 4 and 8.)
1655 FULLER *Hist. Cambr.* 14 On the Kings letters Patents Northampton was un-universitied, the Scholars therein returning to the place from whence they came.

unup'braided, *ppl. a.* (UN-^{1} 8.)
1682 MRS. BEHN *City-Heiress* II. ii, Knowest thou not he has abus'd my fame, And does he think to pass thus unupbraided? **1683** —— *Ovid's Ep. Oenone to Paris* 239 Then unupbraided with my wrongs thou'dst been. **1746** YOUNG *Nt. Th.* IX. 695 Nor stands thy wrath depriv'd of its reproof, Or un-upbraided by this radiant choir. **1864** SWINBURNE *Atalanta* 1668 Each unupbraided, each without rebuke Convicted.

unup'braiding, *ppl. a.* (UN-^{1} 10.)
1780 *Mirror* No. 109, The quiet and unupbraiding sorrows of Louisa. **1816** L. RICHMOND *Let.* in Grimshawe *Mem.* (1828) 362 Your affectionate unupbraiding, and liberal conduct. **1831** W. SEWELL *Clergym. Recreat.* (1835) 89 Friends whom we lov'd in anguish hide Their unupbraiding look.

unup'braidingly, *adv.* (UN-^{1} 11.)
a **1711** KEN *Hymns Evang.* Poet. Wks. 1721 I. 96 A Conscience unupbraidingly sincere.

unup'held, *ppl. a.* (UN-^{1} 8 b.)
1827 POLLOK *Course T.* VI. 630 God of truth!.. Thyself unmade, un-governed, unupheld! **1850** NICHOL *Archit. Heav.* 241 Shall aught that it contains be unupheld by the same preserving law?

unup'lifted, *ppl. a.* (UN-^{1} 8.)
1802 WORDSW. *Excurs.* II. 575 Resting on its lid In silent grief their un-uplifted heads. **1833** —— *'Most sweet it is'* 1 With unuplifted eyes To pace the ground. **1891** J. L. ALLEN *Sister Dolorosa* x, She passed him with unuplifted eyes.

un'upright, *a.* (UN-^{1} 7.)
1585 *Reg. Privy Council Scot.* III. 758 Throw sik craftie and unupricht dealing. [**1775** ASH.]

un'uprightness. (UN-^{1} 12.)
a **1680** T. GOODWIN *Work Holy Ghost* III. v, That sense of his sin and own Un-uprightness.

unur'bane, *a.* (UN-^{1} 7.)
1759 STERNE *Tr. Shandy* II. ii, So, Sir Critic, I could have replied; but I scorn it. 'Tis language unurbane.

†**un'ured**, *a. Obs.*$^{-1}$ [UN-^{1} 9 + *ure* EURE *sb.*] Unfortunate, unhappy.
c **1510** *Songs* (MS. Royal, App. 58) in *Anglia* XII. 266 But kepe hyt styll yn remembrance With my vnvrid desteny.

†**un'ured**, *ppl. a. Obs.* [UN-^{1} 8 + URE *v.*] Unaccustomed, unused.
1567 DRANT *Hor., Sat.* I. x, A Greek poeme I dreamed to indite, (A Romaine I disioynde by sea, vnured so to write). **1610** *Histrio-m.* II. 241 This toung's unur'd to carpe or contrary.

un'urged, *ppl. a.* [UN-^{1} 8.]
1. Not urged or incited to some course of action.
1590 SHAKS. *Com. Err.* II. ii. 115 The time was once, when thou vn-vrg'd wouldst vow, That neuer words were musicke to thine eare. **1628** FELTHAM *Resolves* I. xxxv. 33 If hee reueales ought vn vrged, my aduice is..free. **1648** HERRICK *Hesper., Twelfe Night* iii, Let not a man then be seen here, Who unurg'd will not drinke. **1838** FR. A. KEMBLE *Rec. Later Life* I. 187 [The] teeming soil produced, unurged, the means of life. **1868** GEO. ELIOT *Sp. Gipsy* 243 You..are brave, unurged by aught Save the sweet overflow of your good will.
2. Not thrust or pressed upon one.
1594 KYD *Cornelia* IV. i. 160 Shall we then..Submit vs to vnurged slauerie? **1595** SHAKS. *John* v. ii. 10 Albeit we sweare..an vn-urg'd Faith, To your proceedings. *a* **1614** DONNE *Βιαθανατος* (1644) 37 Augustine, Anselm, and Hierome, betray themselves by unurged confessions. *a* **1689** MRS. BEHN *Fair Jilt* (1887) 33 She leaves nothing unurged that might debauch and invite him. **1728** ELIZA HEYWOOD tr. *Mme. de Gomez's Belle A.* (1732) II. 128 Being one day alone with his Son, he..left unurg'd those Arguments which he had prepar'd in his Mind.

un'urn, *v.* (UN-^{2} 5.)
1837 A. TENNENT *Vis. Glencoe* 48 Foul human relics grisly shown,..From the dark grave unurn'd.

un'urned, *ppl. a.* (UN-^{1} 8.)
1830 MANGAN *Poems* (1903) 284 What time my unurned Ashes lie trodden in the churchyard dell. **1834** LD. HOUGHTON *Mem. Tour in Greece* 95 Let him not be deeply mourned, As dead in-glorious, or cast out unurned.

un'usable, *a.* (UN-^{1} 7 b.)
1825 SYD. SMITH *Wks.* (1850) 418 All seems doubly dear in proportion as it is antiquated, worthless, and unusable. **1884** *Eng. Illustr. Mag.* May 494 [The cave] is now inaccessible and unusable.

†**un'usage.** *Obs.*$^{-1}$ (UN-^{1} 12.)
c **1374** CHAUCER *Boeth.* II. pr. vii. (1868) 57 What for difficulte of weyes and..what for defaute of vn-usage [and] entercomunynge of marchaundise [L. *commercii insolentia*].

un'use. (UN-^{1} 12.)
1611 FLORIO, *Indisusanza*, vnuse, disuse. **1835** *Wilson's Tales Borders* I. 289 Allowing..the heel o' a kebbuck to gaun to unuse [= waste]. **1861** DUTTON COOK *P. Foster's Dau.* III. 126 He spoke with that heavy breathing and unuse of the nose peculiar to Jews.

unused (ʌn'ju:zd), *ppl. a.* [UN-^{1} 8.]
1. Unaccustomed (esp. *to* something, or with inf.) (now freq. with pronunc. ʌn'ju:st before *to*).
1297 R. GLOUC. (Rolls) 4367 Vor þer ȝe abbeþ nou vif ȝer of batayle vn-vsed be. *c* **1449** PECOCK *Repr.* IV. iii. 431 Suche persoones as ben vnkunnyng and vnvsid in vertues. **1538** ELYOT, *Inceduus*, vnvsed to be cutte. *a* **1586** SIDNEY *Arcadia* III. xxvi, So that, unused to a way of courtesie,..he hastily went away. **1604** SHAKS. *Oth.* v. ii. 349 One, whose subdu'd Eyes, Albeit vn-vsed to the melting moode, Drops teares. **1697** DRYDEN *Æneis* x. 815 Æneas couch'd his Spear, Unus'd to Threats, and more unus'd to Fear. **1741-2** GRAY *Agrippina* 17 A thousand haughty hearts, unus'd to shake When a boy frowns. **1796** MME. D'ARBLAY *Camilla* V. 436 [She was] unused to transact any sort of business for herself. **1827** FARADAY *Chem. Manip.* ix. 235 The student who is unused to the examination of papers. **1868** MORRIS *Earthly Par.* I. I. 411 Her gaoler's torches filled with light The dreary place, blinding her unused eyes. **1870** *Ibid.* III. IV. 362 He..felt the golden circle of the crown..upon his unused head.
transf. **1617** CAMPION *Third Bk. of Ayres* xxviii. 8 Hils [would prove] too high for my unused pace.
2. Not made use of; unemployed.
1398 TREVISA *Barth De P.R.* VI. xxix. (Bodl. MS.), Yren ..rosteþ if it is to longe vnne vsed. *c* **1480** HENRYSON *Fables, Fox, Wolf & H.* ii, The oxin wes vnwsit, ȝoung and licht. **1546** *Sc. Acts, Mary* (1814) II. 472 þe said remissioune blank & obligatioune.. one vsit. **1590** SPENSER *F.Q.* I. viii. 30 A bounch of keyes.., The which vnused rust did ouergrow. **1604** SHAKS. *Ham.* IV. iv. 39 (Q. 2), Sure, he.. gaue vs not That capabilitie..To fust in vs vnvsd. **1819** SHELLEY *Cenci* v. iii. 125 Some dull old thing, Some outworn and unused monotony. **1860** FORSTER *Gr. Remonstr.* 37 A maxim not unused by even Norman kings. **1887** *Spectator* 22 Oct. 1415 One of the churches..is unused, being considered dangerous.
3. Not in use; unusual; unwonted. Now *arch.*
1513 DOUGLAS *Æneid* VI. i. 33 By a quent vnvsit [L. *insuetum*] way to knaw, Towart the frosty poil artik he flaw. **1568** GRAFTON *Chron.* II. 390 Inuentyng flatteryng wordes and vnused termes. **1570** T. NORTON tr. *Nowel's Catech.* 32 b, Neither is it vnused among men,..to be suretie..for an other. **1637** G. DANIEL *Genius of Isle* 417 My frozen witts, ..Enlivened by a Splendor far more great, Have vnus'd Raptures. **1671** R. MACWARD *True Non-conf.* 127 Yet I wish you had..forborn the hard and unused expression of an Inward Crown. **1835** BROWNING *Paracelsus* I. 767 In unused conjuncture, When sickness breaks the body. **1867** MORRIS *Jason* VI. 497 Strange dainty things they ate, Of unused savour.
Hence **un'usedness.**
1593 *Sidney's Arcadia* (1598) v. 466 Comparing the vn-usednesse of this act with the vnripenesse of their age. **1865** MRS. WHITNEY *Gayworthys* i. (1879) 10 That air of unusedness which a black silk dress..may keep.

unuseful (ʌn'ju:sfʊl), *a.* [UN-^{1} 7.]
a. Unprofitable, useless. (Very common in 17th c.)
In 18th and 19th-c. use chiefly with negatives.
1598 DALLINGTON *Meth. Trav.* Vj, Bowling, carding, dicing, and other vnlawful and vnvseful games. **1624** HEYWOOD *Gunaik.* v. 219 Gold and silver they despise,.. esteeming it rather an unusefull burden than a profitable merchandize. **1675** GREW *Nature of Mixture* 6 Which Definition..is both Vnintelligible, and Vnuseful. **1726** LEONI *Alberti's Archit.* I. 57 b, A new, and not unuseful Invention. **1788** PRIESTLEY *Lect. Hist.* I. iii. 32 It is no unuseful sentiment that we collect from reading [etc.]. **1817-8** COBBETT *Resid. U.S.* (1822) 216 This may be no unuseful hint for the English Boroughmongers. **1827** J. MONTGOMERY *Pelican Isl.* II. 160 Still-life was theirs, well pleasing to themselves, Nor yet unuseful. **1977** *Western Morning News* 1 Sept. 8/1 A correspondent in Derriford, Plymouth, says he finds it is the unnecessary or 'unuseful' noises which annoy him most. **1982** *N. & Q.* Aug. 357/2 The transference of the term to English literature is unuseful. **1984** *Ibid.* June 259/1 The concatenation of Rolle, Langland and Wycliffe is decidedly unuseful.
b. Const. *to*; also *for*, *towards*.
1625 K. LONG tr. *Barclay's Argenis* II. xx. 133 The streamers unusefull to the sailes, and onely hanging for bravery. **1653** H. MORE *Antid. Ath.* II. x. §3 Birds that will flutter with their wings when..as yet [they are] utterly unuseful for flying. **1733** W. CRAWFORD *Infidelity* xvi, The Law of Nature..became unuseful to the End it was made for. **1756** BURKE *Subl. & B.* IV. i, Something not unuseful towards a distinct knowledge of our passions. **1793** *Residence in France* (1797) II. 10 My ideas..may not be unuseful to..my countrymen.

un'usefully, *adv.* [UN-^{1} 11. Cf. prec.] Uselessly, unprofitably.
1626 LD. CONWAY in Rushw. *Hist. Coll.* (1659) I. 231 Whereas divers jealousies have been raised in the House, that the Moneys have been expended unusefully. *a* **1680** GLANVILL *Sadducismus* (1681) I. 180 Such as will not unusefully nor unseasonably conclude this First Part. **1747** *Phil. Trans.* XLIV. 588, I thought it might not unusefully be joined with Alum. **1799** E. DU BOIS *Piece Family Biog.* I. 111 He is not unusefully occupied. **1885** *Manch. Exam.* 12 Jan. 5/1 Prudent men..might discharge such functions not unusefully.

un'usefulness. [UN-^{1} 12.] Uselessness.
1694 R. BURTHOGGE *Reason* ix. 268 His notion of a Person, the unusefulness of it to the salving of the Holy Trinity shewed. *c* **1850** JAS. SKINNER in *Life* (1883) 120 The notion of ——'s usefulness to the Church and of ——'s so-called unusefulness is a purely human..notion. **1886** *N. Amer. Rev.* Sept. 304 Frivolous unusefulness, or passion for diversion and excitement.

un'ushered, *ppl. a.* (UN-^{1} 8 c.)
1659 W. CHAMBERLAYNE *Pharon.* Introd. A 5 Wonder not, that I appear un-usher'd in with a Train of Encomiums. **1865** W. G. PALGRAVE *Arabia* II. 28 Death unushered in by any direct morbid change.

†**un'using**, *vbl. sb. Obs.* (UN-^{1} 13.)
c **1550** CHEKE *Matt.* xxv. 26 Neglecting and vnusing of his commandementes. **1598** FLORIO, *Disusanza*, disuse, an vnusing.

†**un'using**, *ppl. a. Obs.*$^{-1}$ [UN-^{1} 10.] Not usually resorting.
1605 DANIEL *Philotas* 267 My brother..I left behinde, lest the conspirators Seeing him here vnusing to this place, ..might shift away.

un'usual, *a.* [UN-^{1} 7 and 5 b.] Not usual; uncommon; exceptional.
In common use from *c* 1630.
1582 STANYHURST *Æneis* II. (Arb.) 60 Priamus..On rusty shoulders sloa clapt his vnusual armoure. **1596** SHAKS. *Tam. Shr.* III. ii. 98 Some Commet, or vnusuall prodigie. **1628** WITHER *Brit. Rememb.* 284 God will..Put some unusuall Plague in execution. **1682** LISTER *Godartius Of Insects* 28 This is a Rare and unusuall Catterpillar. **1724** SWIFT *Drapier's Lett.* iv, A new governor, coming at an unusual time, must portend some unusual business. **1773** *Life N. Frowde* 56, I returned to my Book.., in a Situation quite unusual to what I had ever before experienced. **1821** SCOTT *Kenilw.* xli, Varney received his profligate servant with a rebuke of unusual bitterness. **1877** HUXLEY *Physiogr.* 196 A cloud of unusual size and shape was seen hanging over the mountain.
Hence **unusu'ality.**
1799 W. TAYLOR in Robberds *Mem.* (1843) I. 259 They have..an unusuality which startles. **1807** SOUTHEY *Let. to J. May* 27 Jan., From its unusuality it would have a better chance of being read. *a* **1849** POE *Marginalia* lvi, It is to be said of Sallust..that his obscurity, his unusuality of expression,..bore the impress of his genius.

un'usually, *adv.* [UN-^{1} 11.] In an unusual manner; to an unusual extent; uncommonly, exceptionally.
1615 CROOKE *Body of Man* 263 If her monthly courses do stop vnvsually. **1620** T. GRANGER *Div. Logike* 246 More obscurely, and vnusually when the negatiue particle is set before the coniunction discretiue. **1796** MME. D'ARBLAY

Camilla I. 355 Camilla, unusually thoughtful, walked alone into the garden. **1818** Scott *Hrt. Midl.* x, She was unusually cross and fretful. **1871** Le Fanu *Rose & Key* II. 123 Very unusually for him, he was first to speak.

un'usualness. [un-^{1} 12.] The quality of being unusual or exceptional.

1579 W. Wilkinson *Confut. Fam. Love* To Rdr., The vnusualnesse of their Methode. **1626** C. Potter tr. *Sarpi's Hist. Quarrels* 399 Beleeuing it an indignity (besides the vnusualnesse of the matter) which would diminish his Reputation. **1668** Wilkins *Real Char.* 9 Varying the way of pronunciation, according to the unusualness and difficulty of several sounds to several Countries. **1718** *Entertainer* No. 43. 306 Some Persons..wondered at the Unusualness of his Running in that Place. *a* **1754** Carte *Hist. Eng.* (1755) IV. 402 The unusualness of the thing served to countenance the unreasonable outcries. **1836** M. Scott *Cruise Midge* I. 120 Totally unconscious of the unusualness of her costume. **1876** Geo. Eliot *Dan. Der.* iv, The answer may seem to be ..in..a certain unusualness about her, a decision of will.

†**un'usuring,** *ppl. a.* (un-^{1} 10.)

1622 Middleton *Hon. & Virt.* in Bullen *O. Pl.* VII. 361 All the wealth Which thou with an unusuring hand hath got.

†**un'utile,** *a. Obs.* Also *Sc.* 5 **wnwtyle,** 6 **onutil.** [un-^{1} 5 b.] Useless; = inutile *a.*

c **1425** Wyntoun *Cron.* ii. viii. 700 (Cott. MS.), þai þat duelt in to þat ile Wnhonest was and wnwtyle. **1541** R. Copland *Galyen's Terap.* B iv, But after y^t the present dysease is all togyther knowen, than the cause prymytyfe is totally vnutyle. **1549** *Compl. Scot.* 28 The file..is vorne ande cassin auaye as ane thing onutil to serue to do ony gude verk.

un'utilized, *ppl. a.* (un-^{1} 8, 5 b.)

1868 W. R. Greg *Lit. & Soc. Judgm.* 466 It is too probable that the negro race..is doomed..to pass away neglected and unutilized.

unuttera'bility. (un-^{1} 12. Cf. next.)

1837 Carlyle *Fr. Rev.* ii. i. iii, They come; with hot unutterabilities in their heart.

un'utterable, *a.* and *sb.* [un-^{1} 7 b, 5 b.]

A. *adj.* 1. a. Transcending utterance; inexpressible, ineffable; = unspeakable *a.* 1.

a **1586** Sidney *De Mornay* (1587) 33 The vnvtterable cause which Plato teacheth vs vnder two names. **1621** Fletcher *Thierry & Theod.* ii. i, He is, Sir, The most unutterable coward that e'er nature Blest with hard shoulders. **1652** Benlowes *Theoph.* v. lxxviii, That most unutterable blaze Of Heav'n's all-luminating rays. **1746** Hervey *Refl. Flower Garden* 115 One transient Glimpse of those unutterable Beatitudes would captivate our souls. **1771** Beattie *Minstrel* i. xliv, Hags, that suckle an infernal brood, And ply in caves th' unutterable trade. **1806** J. Beresford *Miseries Human Life* iv. xxxii, A barrow of cat's meat, the un-utterable contents of which employ your eyes and nose. **1831** James *Phil. Augustus* I. vi, The unutterable multitude of weathercocks, with which every pinnacle of the castle was adorned. **1873** Proctor *Expanse Heav.* 304 By unutterable pace the light swept to them.

absol. **1896** *Edin. Rev.* Oct. 302 The vision of the utterable passes into the vision of the unutterable.

b. Of sorrow, anger, or other emotion.

1658 T. Wall *Charact. Enemies Ch.* 9 The carnal delights which he has promised you will turn to unutterable dolours of soul. **1697** Congreve *Mourn. Bride* iv. vii, What means these Tears, but Grief unutterable? **1707** E. Smith *Phædra & Hipp.* iv. 50 How it wounds my Soul! To think of your unutterable Sorrows! **1766** Goldsm. *Vicar* xxix, Our bliss shall be unutterable. **1832** Coleridge *Lett.* (1895) 762 Yours, with unutterable and unuttered love and regard. **1880** 'Ouida' *Moths* II. vi. 185 She turned her face with unutterable scorn..on it.

c. In the phr. *unutterable things*.

a **1711** Ken *Psyche* Poet. Wks. 1721 IV. 299 Bless'd Paul ..was..heav'nly things unutterable taught. [Cf. 2 Cor. xii. 4.] **1727** Thomson *Summer* 848 They..talked the flowing Heart, Or sigh'd and look'd unutterable Things! **1791** W. Maxwell in Boswell *Johnson* (1831) I. 381 Jacob Behmen, whom Law alleged..to have seen *unutterable things*. **1818** Byron *Juan* i. xc, Juan wander'd by the glassy brooks, Thinking unutterable things. **1873** Black *Pr. Thule* ii, Sheila..rarely speaks, but looks unutterable things with her soft..eyes.

2. a. That may not be uttered or spoken.

1656 Cowley *Davideis* iv. 260 Witness th' unutterable Name, there's nought Of private ends into this question brought. **1708** Watts *Horæ Lyricæ* (1727) 161 My Tongue ..with a noble Aim Attempts th' unutterable Name, But faints. **1883** Whitelaw *Sophocles, Ajax* 773 Dread words, unutterable, back he flung.

b. Incapable of being uttered; unpronounceable.

1849 *Jrnl. Amer. Oriental Soc.* I. 423 The endless, and to a European, unutterable jargons of the other class. **1852** *Jrnl. Ethnol. Soc.* (1854) III. 271 The peculiarly harsh, deep-toned guttural, unknown and unutterable to the European. **1867** Whitney *Lang.* iii. 95 Sounds..in the alphabet of one tongue which are unutterable by the speakers of another.

B. *sb.* 1. An unutterable thing.

1788 J. Newton in W. Roberts *H. More* (1835) II. 126 The Apostle Paul..was rapt into the third heavens, saw invisibles, and heard unutterables. **1797** Mrs. A. M. Bennett *Beggar Girl* II. 51 Rosa did not faint or betray any of the unutterables some of our young readers may expect.

2. *pl.* Trousers. (Cf. unmentionable *sb.*)

1843 Mrs. Romer *Rhone, Darro*, etc. I. 322 His..short unutterables, garnished down the seams with silver buttons. **1860** *Slang Dict.* 242.

Hence **un'utterableness.**

1681 H. More *Exp. Dan.* iii. 75 The ineffableness and unutterableness of the admirable union..of the Humane nature with the Divine. **1890** J. Pulsford *Loyalty to Christ* I. 162 With what unutterableness of meaning, we breathe the prayer!

un'utterably, *adv.* [f. prec.] Inexpressibly, indescribably; unspeakably.

1746 Hervey *Refl. Flower Garden* 111 At that awful, that unutterably important Juncture. **1801** Coleridge *Lett.* (1895) 352, I need not observe..how unutterably silly and contemptible these opinions would be. **1866** Mrs. Whitney *Leslie Goldthwaite* xi, I'll..thank you unutterably, if you'll only let me have my way in this. **1885** 'Mrs. Alexander' *At Bay* viii, The sweet eyes were unutterably sad.

un'uttered, *ppl. a.* [un-^{1} 8.]

1. Not given out in trade. *rare*.

1463 *Cases bef. King's Council* (Selden) 111 Fer which cause the seid wolles ben yet as by youre seid suppliaunt unuttred. **1618** Gainsford *Glory Eng.* i. ix. 77 That the countrey commodities might be vnuttered.

2. Not uttered or expressed.

1651 J. Reading *Guide Holy City* 347 Hee cannot know the unuttered secrets of the heart. **1696** Tate & Brady *Ps.* cxxxix. 4 Thou know'st..My yet un-utter'd Words intent. *a* **1771** Gray *Dante* 5 Anguish, that unutter'd wrings My inmost Heart. **1798** Southey *St. Patrick's Purgatory* xxvi, How should he pass that molten flood?.. A Fiend, as in a dream, 'Thus!' answer'd the unutter'd thought. **1844** A. B. Welby *Poems* (1867) 72 As..meeting glances tell The unuttered tale of love. **1883** J. Parker *Tyne Ch.* 277 Self-control..begins upon the subtle and un-uttered thought.

absol. **1843** Carlyle *Past & Pr.* iii. v, The cloudy-browed ..Practicality..has in him what transcends all logic-utterance: a Congruity with the Unuttered.

unu'xorial, *a.* (un-^{1} 7.)

1877 Blackmore *Cripps* xxi, Unconjugal, perhaps, is what I mean; unuxorial, or what it may be.

un'vaccinated, *ppl. a.* (un-^{1} 8.)

1871 *Daily News* 28 Jan., We need..somebody to look after unvaccinated children. **1883** Lyon Playfair in *Scotsman* 25 June 7/7 In this way nearly half..of the unvaccinated die.

un'vacillating, *ppl. a.* (un-^{1} 10.)

1821 Scott *Kenilw.* xvii, Like one..whose only safety consists in moving onwards, by firm and unvacillating steps. **1825** Beddoes *Let.* in *Poems* (1851) 166 In the unvacillating soar of song.

†**un'vadable,** *a. Obs.*$^{-0}$ (un-^{1} 7 b. See vade *v.*)

1611 Cotgr., *Immarcessible*, incorruptible, vnuadeable, vnwitherable.

unvail, obs. f. unveil *v.*

†**un'vailable,** *a. Obs.* Also 5 *Sc.* **wnwalable,** 6 **vnuaylable,** etc. [un-^{1} 7 b.] Of no avail; unavailing; useless.

a **1500** in *Ratis Raving*, etc. 24 Al that is bot vanite and lycht, transitoure blythnes, wnwalable. **1502** Atkynson tr. *De Imitatione* iii. l. (1893) 236 Mannes helpe is but vayne & vnuaylable in such nedis. **1612** T. Taylor *Comm. Titus* iii. 5 Without which..it would be vnuailable to regeneration. **1679** C. Nesse *Antichrist* 228 Julian the 2d. who threw Peters keys into Tyber as unvaileable.

un'vain, *a.* (un-^{1} 7.)

1863 Cowden Clarke *Shaks. Char.* xvi. 396 Her habit of speech is perceptibly un-vain. **1897** *Harper's Mag.* Apr. 748 A tyrant may be unvain.

unvale'tudinary, *a.* (un-^{1} 7, 5 b.)

1650 Bulwer *Anthropomet.* i. 11 This ought not to be accounted among the non-natural or unvaletudinary figures.

†**un'valid,** *a. Obs.* (un-^{1} 7, 5 b.)

1658 W. Burton *Itin. Anton.* 172 Where I found not sufficient proof for what I met with,..I rejected it as unvalid. *a* **1660** *Contemp. Hist. Irel.* (Ir. Archæol. Soc.) I. 133 Why did you..embrace such a groundlesse and unvalid a peace?

un'valuable, *a.* [un-^{1} 7 b, 5 b.]

†1. Of inestimable value; = invaluable *a.* 1. *Obs.* (Common in 17th c.)

1569 T. Norton *Warning agst. Papists* A ij, Thinke vpon the..miseries that we all shalbe like to susteine by losse of her vnualuable presence. **1591** Horsey *Trav.* (Hakl. Soc.) 160 The riches..caried owt of these citties..was unvaluable. *a* **1616** Beaum. & Fl. *Lit. Fr. Lawyer* iii. i, That Jewel, Because it had no flaw, you held unvaluable. **1691** W. Nicholls *Answ. Naked Gospel* 21 When he hath sent his only begotten Son..to purchase our Redemption by such an unvaluable price. **1691** Ray *Creation* ii. (1692) 4 The use of our Hand, that unvaluable Instrument. **1712** *Lond. Gaz.* No. 5037/6 The Blessings of Peace are unvaluable.

†b. Incalculable; = invaluable *a.* 1 b. *Obs.*

1638 Rous *Heav. Acad.* 132 It is an unvaluable losse, that men doe so much divide the outward Teacher from the inward. *a* **1661** Fuller *Worthies, Yorks.* iii. (1662) 225 Debasing the Forraign estimation of our Cloth to the unvaluable damage of our Nation. *a* **1683** Oldham *Rem.* Wks. (1686) 6 Her Dowry..Which..we never gain But with unvaluable Cost.

2. Of no value, worthless; = invaluable *a.* 2. Now *rare*.

1615 T. Adams *England's Sickness* 57 If nature..deny health, how vnualuable are their riches. *a* **1674** Clarendon *Surv. Leviath.* (1676) 55 To render those precious words unvaluable and of no signification. **1728** R. Morris *Ess. Anc. Archit.* 89 The unvaluable Deformities of Singleness and Novelty. **1766** *Museum Rust.* VI. 15, I think the burnet so unvaluable, as to design to root it out of my ground. **1860** Ruskin *Unto this Last* (1862) 118 In proportion as it leads away from life it is unvaluable or malignant.

Hence **un'valuableness.**

1665 Dk. Ormonde in Earl Orrery *St. Lett.* (1742) 133 The cry was so great, upon the unvaluableness of the clothes given to the soldiery, that [etc.].

†**un'value,** *v. Obs.*$^{-1}$ [un-^{2} 6 b.] *trans.* To deprive of value.

1550 Bale *Eng. Votaries* ii. 33 Peruersely alleging Malachyes prophecye, as though [it]..in hys mouthe myght vnualue or dysable their masses.

un'valued, *ppl. a.* [un-^{1} 8, 5 b.]

1. Not estimated or fixed in value; extremely great or valuable. Now *rare*.

1586 Marlowe *1st Pt. Tamburl.* i. ii, Whatsoeuer you esteeme of this successe, and losse vnvalued, Both may inuest you Empresse of the East. **1594** Spenser *Amoretti* lxxvii, There in a siluer dish did ly twoo golden apples of vnualewd price. **1607** Middleton *Fam. Lov.* i. ii, Art or nature never yet could set A valued price to her unvalued worth. **1638** Aleyn *Hen. VII*, 73 He..drew him clad In furniture of an unvalued worth. **1662** H. Hibbert *Body of Divinity* II. 30 The saving benefits of his unvalued passion. **1713** Johnson *Guard.* No. 4 ¶3, I have been so happy in my searches..that I have found unvalued repositories of learning. **1736** Thomson *Liberty* v. 503 The kind Art, that, of unvalu'd price, The fam'd and only picture, easy, gives. **1820** Shelley *Arethusa* 60 Through the weltering floods, Over heaps of unvalued stones [= jewels].

b. Not subjected to formal valuation.

1807 *Ann. Rev.* V. 176 If real property, instead of passing entire and unvalued to the heir at law, were put up to the highest bidder.

2. Not regarded as of value.

1602 Shaks. *Ham.* i. iii. 19 Hee may not, as vnuallued persons doe, Carue for himselfe. **1615** G. Wither *Fidelia* 707 Though my faith must now despised be, Vnpriz'd, vnualued at the lowest rate. **1670** Clarendon *Contempl. Ps.* Tracts (1727) 740 The inestimable, tho' unvalued benefit of health, we seldom thank God for. **1823** Mrs. Hemans *Siege Valencia* viii, I have cast Thy life's fair honour, in my wild despair, As an unvalued gem upon the waves. **1852** Mrs. Stowe *Uncle Tom's C.* xxxv, A hard-tempered sire, on whom that gentle woman had wasted a world of unvalued love. **1870** Lowell *Among my Bks.* Ser. i. (1873) 203 Recalling and confirming our own unvalued sensations and perceptions.

un'vamped, *ppl. a.* (un-^{1} 8.)

1638 Ford *Lady's Trial* i. i, The newest news, unvampt. [**1775** Ash.] **1880** *E. Cornwall Gloss.* 105 *Unvamped*, not added to or embellished.

un'vanquishable, *a.* Also 4 **unuenkus-,** 5 *Sc.* **unvencusable.** [un-^{1} 7 b.] Incapable of being vanquished or overcome.

1382 Wyclif *Wisd.* v. 20 He shal take the sheeld vnuenkusable. **1456** Sir G. Haye *Bk. Knychthede* vii. (S.T.S.) 56 Man has..stark curage unvencusable. **1561** T. N[orton] tr. *Calvin's Inst.* iii. xxi. 239 The vpholdyng stay of sounde affiance..to make vs vnuanquishable among so many dangers. **1613** Jackson *Creed* i. xv. §3 Ouid faines Nisus his vnuanquishable fortune, to haue been seated in one haire. **1657** Earl Monm. tr. *Paruta's Pol. Disc.* 162 He waged War with people..who were till then thought unvanquishable. **1728** Eliza Heywood tr. *Mme. de Gomez's Belle A.* (1732) II. 76 Able to make some little Incroachments on that Liberty which seem'd unvanquishable. **1813** Shelley *Q. Mab* iii. 120 Toil and unvanquishable penury. **1865** Dickens *Mut. Fr.* i. ii, He is only stunned by the unvanquishable difficulty of his existence.

un'vanquished, *ppl. a.* Also 4 **vnuenkushid,** 5 **vnuenquiste,** 6 *Sc.* **unvencust, wnwencust,** etc. [un-^{1} 8.] Not vanquished or overcome; unsubdued.

1382 Wyclif *Ecclus.* xviii. 1 God alone..dwelleth vnuenkushid king withoute ende. ? *a* **1400** *Morte Arth.* 2049 The vassalage of Viterbe to daye schalle be reuengede! Vnuenquiste for þis place voyde schalle I neuer! *c* **1510** More *Picus* Wks. 23 Enforce thy self..to stande, Unvainquished against the deuils might. **1548** Udall, etc. *Erasm. Par. John* xvi. 97 b, Ye shalbe through my spirite strong and vnuanquished. **1614** Gorges *Lucan* vi. 221 Deare mates we yet vnuanquisht stand. **1697** Dryden *Æneis* v. 290 Unvanquish'd Scylla now alone remains. **1770** Glover *Leonidas* (ed. 5) ii. 49 The gods conceal, how long our strength May stand unvanquish'd. **1820** Shelley *Prometh. Unb.* i. 315 'Tis but some passing spasm, The Titan is unvanquished still. **1883** J. Parker *Apost. Life* II. 279 Such an unvanquished devil mocks the impotent exorcist.

un'vantaged, *ppl. a.* (un-^{1} 8.)

1791 Cowper *Iliad* xi. 868 Yet, even thus, unvantag'd and on foot, Superiour honours I that day acquir'd To theirs who rode.

un'variable, *a.* Now *rare.* (un-^{1} 7 b and 5 b.)

c **1425** *St. Mary of Oignies* ii. vii. in *Anglia* VIII. 169/40 þe most soueryan sympyl and vnvaryabil megures. *c* **1440** *Pallad. on Husb.* i. 354 Grauellis dolue in iij naturis vary: In red, & hoor, & blak vnvariable. *a* **1586** Spenser *De Mornay* (1587) i. 5 Wee must imagine..of all these so constant diuersities, one (vnuariable) alwaies like it selfe. **1624** Wotton *Elem. Archit.* 8 A steadie and vnuariable light. **1697** Collier *Ess. Mor. Subj.* ii. 189 It becomes the Greatness of the Deity, to work by the most comprehensive, unvariable Methods. **1738** Warburton *Div. Legat.* II. 213 In the fullest and most unvariable Manner. **1759** Johnson *Rasselas* xlviii, She..would gladly be fixed in some unvariable state. **1896** W. M. Thomson *Leaders of Chr. & Anti-Chr. Th.* 7 To impose a fixed and unvariable creed is to build prison walls round the soul.

Hence **un'variableness; un'variably** *adv.*

1611 Florio, *Inuariabilitá*, vnuariablenesse. **1644** Featly *Roma Ruens* 7 The immutability of our faith, or unvariablenesse of the doctrine..of the church. **1734**

KAMES *Decis. Crt. Sess.* (1799) 13 The real right..continues unvariably the same till the last farthing be recovered.

un'variant, *a.* [UN-^{1} 7, 5 b.] Unchanging.
1582 STANYHURST *Æneis* IV. (Arb.) 111 His mynd vnuariant [L. *immota*] doth stand, tears vaynelye doe gutter.

un'varied, *ppl. a.* (UN-^{1} 8 and 5 b.)
1570 LEVINS *Manip.* 51 Vnuaried, *inuariatus*. **1690** LOCKE *Hum. Und.* II. xiv. §13. 87 Whether he can keep one unvaried single Idea in his Mind without any other. **1748** *Anson's Voy.* III. iii. 328 The equable and unvaried character which he had hitherto preserved. **1791** NEWTE *Tour Eng. & Scot.* 2 The unvaried and uninteresting voids of life. **1840** THIRLWALL *Greece* lvii. VII. 241 He seasoned the plain unvaried meal by his cheerful..conversation. **1879** G. ALLEN *Colour Sense* iv. 38 The unvaried panorama of green over-head and brown beneath.
Hence **un'variedly** *adv.*
1780 M. MADAN *Thelyphthora* II. 242 The word..which we have as uniformly and unvariedly translated *adultery*.

un'variegated, *ppl. a.* (UN-^{1} 8.)
a **1763** SHENSTONE *Ess. Men* Wks. 1768 II. 130 Large, unvariegated, simple objects have the best pretensions to sublimity. **1846** WORCESTER (citing *Edin. Rev.*).

un'varnished, *ppl. a.* [UN-^{1} 8.]
1. *fig.* Of statements, etc.: Not embellished or rendered specious; plain, direct.
1604 SHAKS. *Oth.* I. iii. 90, I will a round vn-varnish'd Tale deliuer, Of my whole course of Loue. **1780** BURKE *Sp. at Bristol* Wks. III. 367 This is a true, unvarnished, undisguised state of the affair. **1790** WOLCOT (P. Pindar) *Adv. Future Laureat* II. i, Were I monarch of this mighty isle! By verse unvarnish'd should my merits smile. **1806** SURR *Winter in Lond.* II. 238 State to this company, without exaggeration, and without palliation, your own unvarnished story! **1883** MISS M. BETHAM-EDWARDS *Disarmed* xxxi, Valerian..had set out with the intention of adhering to the unvarnished truth, but finally ended in romancing.
b. Of persons, etc.: Unsophisticated, unpolished; plain and simple.
1827 POLLOK *Course T.* VIII. 107 A congregation..Of unappendaged and unvarnished men; Of plain, unceremonious human beings. **1831** [MARY BERRY] *Soc. Life Eng. & France* 192 Strong appeals to all the unvarnished feelings of human nature. **1864** MRS. H. WOOD *Verner's Pride* xli, Lady Verner liked Lord Garle..ten times better than she liked unvarnished Jan.
2. Not covered with, or as with, varnish.
1758 REID tr. *Macquer's Chym.* I. 372 Into an unvarnished earthen dish put the quantity of Tin you intend to calcine. **1784** COWPER *Task* VI. 174 The deep dark green of whose unvarnish'd leaf, illumines more The bright profusion of her scatter'd stars. **1875** SIR T. SEATON *Fret-Cutting* 33 The mortification of ultimately finding some place left unvarnished or unfinished.
Hence **un'varnishedly** *adv.*
1824 HOGG *Tales & Sk.* V. 68, I had kept by the naked truth too unvarnishedly.

un'varying, *ppl. a.* (UN-^{1} 10.)
1690 LOCKE *Hum. Und.* II. xiv. §18 We cannot keep by us any standing unvarying measure of Duration. **1757** AKENSIDE *Pleas. Imag.* III. 418 With contempt I gazed On that tame garb, and those unvarying paths. *a* **1763** SHENSTONE *Elegies* iii. 52 The generous rustics mourn'd the friendly swain, But Pow'r and Wealth's unvarying cheek was dry! **1803** MATHIAS *Purs. Lit.* (ed. 12) 320 *note*, At the general..Boarding houses, the expences of which are liberal, unvarying, and regulated. **1825** SOUTHEY *Tale of Paraguay* IV. xxx, All was verdant there throughout the unvarying year. **1897** MARY KINGSLEY *W. Africa* 96 Apparently endless walls of mangrove, unvarying in colour, unvarying in form, unvarying in height.
Hence **un'varyingly** *adv.*; **un'varyingness**.
1814 SHELLEY *Ess. & Lett.* (1887) 151 Mediocrity alone seems unvaryingly to escape rebuke. **1851** SPENCER *Soc. Stat.* 40 An unvaryingness which renders the eclipse of a hundred years hence predicable to a moment! **1861** GEO. ELIOT *Silas M.* xvii, His..more wavering nature, too averse to facing difficulty to be unvaryingly simple and truthful.

un'vascular, *a.* (UN-^{1} 7.)
1846 OWEN *Comp. Anat. Invert.* 224 In the Diodon the dental plates consist wholly of hard or unvascular dentine.

un'vaulted, *ppl. a.* (UN-^{1} 8.)
1589 IVE *Fortific.* 25 As for the passage from one flanke vnto another, that may bee left vnuaulted. **1777** T. WARTON *Ode Vale-Royal Abbey* 51 Beneath yon tower's unvaulted gate, Forlorn she sits.

un'vaulting, *ppl. a.* (UN-^{1} 10.)
1797 MATHIAS *Purs. Lit.* IV. 338 Yet with unvaulting sober wishes blest, Ambition fled with envy from my breast.

un'veil, *v.* [UN-^{2} 4 and 4 b.]
1. *trans.* To free (the eyes, etc.) from a veil so as to give clearer sight. Also in fig. context.
1599 *Warn. Faire Wom.* II. 872 Now she unvailes their sight, and lets them see The horror of their foule immanity. **1650** HUBBERT *Pill Formality* 109 Hereby the understanding is unvailed. **1678** BUTLER *Hud.* III. II. 1085 Truth no more unvail'd your Eyes, Than Maggots are convinc'd to Flies.
2. To disclose, display, allow to appear, by removing a veil or covering.
1657 THORNLEY tr. *Longus' Daphnis & Chloe* 43 Daphnis ..could not be merry, because he had seen..her beauty which before was not unvailed. **1692** DRYDEN *Don Sebastian* I. i, Unveil the Woman; I wou'd view the Face That warm'd our Mufti's Zeal. **1754** GRAY *Progr. Poesy* 86 What time.. To him the mighty Mother did unveil Her awful face. **1797** MRS. RADCLIFFE *Italian* xxvii, I claim the privilege.. awarded me, and bid you unveil your countenance. **1817** SHELLEY *Rev. Islam* I. xx, She unveiled her bosom. **1820** —— *Witch Atlas* Ded. vi, If you unveil my Witch, no priest nor primate Can shrive you of that sin. *fig.* **1667** MILTON *P.L.* IV. 608 Till the Moon Rising in clouded Majestie, at length Apparent Queen unvaild her peerless light. **1725** POPE *Odyssey* VI. 36 When the gay morn unveils her smiling ray. **1747** HERVEY *Contempl. Night* (1748) II. 81 She unveils her peerless Light, and becomes 'the Beauty of Heaven'.
b. *absol.* and *refl.* Also *fig.*
1770 GLOVER *Leonidas* (ed. 5) x. 170 She unveils, Then with a voice, a countenance compos'd, Go, Medon [etc.]. **1819** SCOTT *Ivanhoe* xxxvii, The Grand Master commanded Rebecca to unveil herself. **1862** J. H. NEWMAN *Two Worlds* i, Unveil, O Lord, and on us shine In glory and in grace.
c. *spec.* To remove the covering from (a statue, etc.) so as to display it for the first time in public.
1865 *Punch* 23 Sept. 17 Paulina (Britannia) unveils the Statue. **1884** *American* VII. 218 The statue..was unveiled recently at Utrecht.
3. *fig.* To uncover, disclose, display, reveal.
1606 SHAKS. *Tr. & Cr.* III. iii. 200 The prouidence.. Keepes place with thought; and almost like the gods, Doe thoughts vnuaile in their dumbe cradles. **1638** CHILLINGW. *Relig. Prot.* I. Ded. §3 The lustre of this blessed Doctrine I have here endeavoured to uncloud and unveile. **1700** DRYDEN tr. *Ovid, Pythagorean Philos.* 212 For I will..Dark Oracles unveil, and open all the Skies. **1796** KIRWAN *Elem. Min.* (ed. 2) I. p. ix, Hitherto its treasures have been unveiled only to my eyes. **1860** PUSEY *Min. Proph.* 421 Man veils foul deeds under fair words; God, in His word, unveils the foulness. **1885** MRS. ALEXANDER *At Bay* viii, What secrets would that meeting unveil?
b. To display to the sight; to make visible.
1656 COWLEY *Davideis* IV. 804 When the new Ebb of Night Did the moist world unvail to humane sight. **1740** DYER *Ruins Rome* 36 While the vine-mantled brows The pendent goats unveil. **1791** MRS. RADCLIFFE *Rom. Forest* ii, Un-veiling the whole face of Nature. **1821** SHELLEY *Hellas* 624 The splendour of the moon, When as the wandering clouds unveiled or hid Her boundless light. **1872** JENKINSON *Guide Eng. Lakes* (1879) 115 The summit is gained, and an exquisite prospect is unveiled.
4. *intr.* To become free from a veil or covering.
1655 H. VAUGHAN *Silex Scint.* I. 73 When first thy Eies unveil, give thy Soul leave To do the like. **1849** LONGF. *Lighthouse* vii, Eager faces, as the light unveils, Gaze at the tower.
Hence **un'veiler**; **un'veiling** *vbl. sb.* and *ppl. a.*
1674 BOYLE *Excell. Theol.* I. i. 44 Much better encomiasts of the Divine mysteries..than *unvailers. **1611** FLORIO, *Disuelamento*, an *vnualing. **1768–74** TUCKER *Lt. Nat.* (1834) II. 421 Lest they should esteem the very unveiling of mystery indiscreet. **1854** GOSSE (*title*), The Aquarium; an Unveiling of the Wonders of the Deep Sea. **1885** *Harper's Mag.* March 644/2 The unveiling of Fielding's bust at Taunton. **1802** J. BAILLIE *1st Pt. Ethwald* I. ii, Th' *unveiling moon Which calls the advent'rer forth.

un'veiled, *ppl. a.* [UN-^{1} 8, or f. UNVEIL *v.*] Not covered with, free or freed from, a veil.
1606 N. B[AXTER] *Sydney's Ourania* E 3 b, Leauing faire Tellus with vnuailed face, Drie and vnmantled. **1659** W. CHAMBERLAYNE *Pharon.* II. ii. 236 The unveiled face of War Looks big with horror. *Ibid.* III. v. 336 He dares Affront unveiled report. **1717** LADY M. W. MONTAGU *Let. to Pope* 1 April, Their wives and daughters..go unveiled. **1801** SOUTHEY *Thalaba* VI. xxviii, Unveil'd women bade the advancing youth Come merry-make with them! **1825** SCOTT *Talism.* vi, Richard's unveiled contempt for his brother sovereigns. **1890** J. PULSFORD *Loyalty to Christ* I. 213 His higher and unveiled teaching belongs only to His disciples.
Hence **un'veiledly** *adv.*; **un'veiledness**.
1661 BOYLE *Physiol. Ess.* (1669) 37 Not yet knowing.. what use you will make of what has been unveiledly communicated to you. **1902** R. C. MOBERLY *Christ our Life* xxi. 178 This unveiledness of face; this reflecting, as a mirror, of the being of God.

un'veined, (*ppl.*) *a.* (UN-^{1} 8, 9.)
1826 MISS MITFORD *Village* II. 173 The flowers unveined and colourless. **1869** RUSKIN *Q. of Air* §82 Under gray sky, unveined by vermilion or by gold.

un'velvetly, *adv.* (UN-^{1} 11.)
1663 WATERHOUSE *Fortescutus Illustr.* 424, The hard hand of power unvelvetly lined.

un'vendable, *a.* (UN-^{1} 7 b.)
1753 HANWAY *Trav.* III. xlvii. (1762) I. 217 They were utterly unvendable. **1893** *Daily News* 15 June 5/2 These.. precious but entirely unvendable books.

un'vendible, *a.* (UN-^{1} 7, 5 b. Cf. prec.)
1642 *Compl. Ho. Commons* 7 That unvendible commodity of Ship-mony. **1747** W. HORSLEY *Fool* (1748) II. 274 It is best to lay them [*sc.* taxes] on Things unvendible. **1841** D'ISRAELI *Amen. Lit.* III. 95 Nearly a third of Pope's original subscription edition..[was] left unvendible. **1859** MASSON *Brit. Novelists* 81 To..carry off that otherwise unvendible work.
Hence **un'vendibleness**.
1618 in Foster *Eng. Factories Ind.* (1906) I. 42 The unvendiblenesse of the rest [of the goods].

unve'neered, *ppl. a.* (UN-^{1} 8.)
[**1775** ASH.] **1887** RUSKIN *Præterita* II. 39, I had my father's love..of unveneered, unrouged, and well finished things.

un'venerable, *a.* (UN-^{1} 7 b.)
1611 SHAKS. *Wint. T.* II. iii. 77 For euer Vnvenerable be thy hands, if thou Tak'st vp the Princesse. **1616** CHAMPNEY *Voc. Bps.* 224 A Bishop howsoeuer vnuenerable he be,..so long as he is a Bishop,..suffereth not the losse of his Pastorall vocation. **1836** J. H. NEWMAN in *Lyra Apost.* 127 O aged blind Unvenerable! **1867** SWINBURNE *Ess. & Stud.* (1875) 148 So excellent and noble a thing that even error cannot make it unvenerable.

un'venged, *ppl. a. Obs.* exc. *arch.* (UN-^{1} 8.)
1382 WYCLIF *Job* xxiv. 12 The liues of woundid men.. God suffreth not vnuengid [L. *inultum*] to gon awey. *a* **1470** H. PARKER *Dives & Pauper* (W. de W. 1496) VI. xiii. 253/1 The..pryde of araye that is now used in this londe..wyll not be unuenged. **1855** SINGLETON *Virgil* I. 159 Moaning.. for the loves Which he, unvenged, hath lost.

un'venial, *a.* (UN-^{1} 7.)
1589 NASHE *Almond for Parrat* B ij b, He wil be-pistle thee so peuishly, with allegations of vnuenidall [*sic*] sinnes. **1644** MILTON *Divorce* (ed. 2) Pref. A 4 b, His venial and unvenial dispences.

un'venom, *v.* [UN-^{2} 4.] *trans.* To deprive of venom.
1611 FLORIO, *Disuiperato*, vnuipered, vnuenomed. **1675** ALLESTREE *Art Contentm.* xi. 206 He may..unvenem all those calamities which are to others the gall of Asps. **1906** F. THOMPSON in *Dublin Rev.* Apr. 381 You did, with thrift of holy gain, Unvenoming the sting of pain, Hive its sharp heather-honey.

un'venomed, *ppl. a.* [UN-^{1} 8.] Without being envenomed.
1597 BP. HALL *Sat.* Postscr., If thou maist spit vpon a toade unvenomed, why maist thou not speak of a vice without danger?

un'venomous, *a.* (UN-^{1} 7.)
1659 GAUDEN *Tears Ch.* 297 Their errour is not solitary, nor the sting of their schisme either soft, or blunt, or unvenomous. **1774** GOLDSM. *Nat. Hist.* VII. 100 The toad ..is an harmless, defenceless creature, torpid and unvenemous.

un'ventable, *a.* (UN-^{1} 7 b + VENT *v.*^{2})
1633 T. ADAMS *Exp. 2 Peter* ii. 4 But O..the unventable sorrow of the goates on his left!

un'vented, (*ppl.*) *a.* [UN-^{1} 8, 9.] Not provided with a vent or outlet; not allowed to issue.
c **1618** FLETCHER *Mad Lover* II. i, Things like our selves, as sensual, vain, unvented Bubbles, and breaths of air. **1624** QUARLES *Job Militant* xvi. 26 I'me full, and I must speake, Or, like vnuented vessels, I must breake. **1630–40** —— *Funeral Elegies* xviii, The false teare, that's forc'd, or slides by Art,..Or dares (unvented) come to composition. **1866** GEO. ELIOT *F. Holt* xi, The company..perhaps felt the more, as they seated themselves with an expectation unvented by utterance.

un'ventilated, *ppl. a.* [UN-^{1} 8.]
1. Not purified (as) by, not provided with means of, ventilation.
1712 BLACKMORE *Creation* II. 706 For, should the air unventilated stand, The idle deep, corrupted, would contain Blue deaths. **1743** S. HALES *Ventilators* 144 Ventilated and unventilated Hops. **1849** in Huxley *Life & Lett.* (1900) I. 50 The lower and main decks are utterly unventilated. **1877** TEALE *Dangers to Health* 14 Unventilated water closets.
2. Not ventilated or discussed.
1872 LATHAM. Also in recent use (1916).

un'ventured, *ppl. a.* (UN-^{1} 8 and 8 c.)
1605 SYLVESTER *Du Bartas* II. iii. *Vocation* 631 Our way to vertue lyes so..plain, With pain-lesse Honour and unvent'red Gain. ? **1608** *Reynard's Deliv. fr. Turks* in *Harl. Misc.* (1744) I. 183 There is no Coast..left unsought,..no People, never so wild, left unventured upon. **1854** S. DOBELL *Balder* xxiii. 117 Nor less above yon midway crag the calm Unventured summit.

un'venturous, *a.* (UN-^{1} 7.)
1865 LOWELL *Ode Harvard Commem.* 14 The common grave Of the unventurous throng.

un'venued, *ppl. a.* [UN-^{1} 8. Cf. VENUE 2.] †Not hit or wounded in fencing.
1581 PETTIE tr. *Guazzo's Civ. Conv.* III. (1586) 135 b, They ly so open that they are soone venued..: and if they do chaunce to scape vnuenued or vnhurt, yet they leaue the world in doubt of their honestie.

unve'racious, *a.* (UN-^{1} 7 and 5 b.)
Hence, in recent use (1922), *unveraciously*.
1845 MRS. CARLYLE *Lett.* (1883) I. 301 A quick tact for detecting everything unveracious. **1894** JEAFFRESON *Bk. Recoll.* II. xvii. 33 The unveracious man left the drawing-room, which he never again entered.

unve'racity. (UN-^{1} 12 and 5 b.)
1839 CARLYLE *Chartism* v, What is injustice? Another name for disorder, for unveracity, unreality. **1843** —— *Past & Pr.* III. i, Such super-incumbent weight of Unveracities. **1870** RUSKIN *Lect. Art* (1875) 96 They will never permit themselves in uselessness or in unveracity.

un'verdant, *a.* (UN-^{1} 7.)
1646 G. DANIEL *Poems* Wks. (Grosart) I. 120 The Earth vnverdant may goe seeke Her Flowers in Winter. ? *c* **1710** CONGREVE *Ovid's Art of Love* III. Wks. 1730 III. 308 Ungraceful 'tis to see..A Leaf-less Tree, or an unverdant Mead. **1859** W. H. GREGORY *Egypt* I. 20 The parched, baked, and unverdant clay that had replaced the greensward of Western city parks.

un'verifiable, *a.* (UN-^{1} 7 b.)
1861 MAINE *Anc. Law* v. 114 A non-historic, unverifiable, condition of the race. **1876** SPENCER *Princ. Sociol.* Pref., Many facts from other sources had to be sought out and incorporated; and..I left them in an unverifiable state.

un'verified, *ppl. a.* (UN-^{1} 8.)
[**1775** ASH.] **1816** J. GILCHRIST *Philos. Etym.* p. iii, There is not one of them which he has been obliged to abandon.. as contradicted or unverified by experimental evidence. **1867** SPENCER *First Princ.* (ed. 2) II. iii. 159 The looking-glass..proves how deceptive is sight when unverified by

touch. **1887** *Spectator* 24 Sept. 1273 The array of loose statements and unverified conjectures.

un'veritable, *a.* (UN-¹ 7 b.)
1589 PUTTENHAM *Eng. Poesie* I. xii. (Arb.) 42 They could not..vse in their lauds any maner of grosse adulation of vnueritable report. **1646** SIR T. BROWNE *Pseud. Ep.* VII. x. 359 All these [beliefs] proceeded upon unveritable grounds.

un'verity. (UN-¹ 12.)
1572 FORREST *Theophilus* in *Anglia* VII. 81 To tell fable of unveryte. **1574** *Life 70th Abp. Canterb.* Pref. E 3 b, Lest.. the sowishe papiste..gredily swallow uppe this litle vomited gobbett of written vnverities.

un'versed, *ppl. a.*¹ [UN-¹ 8.] Inexperienced.
1675 *Camden's Hist. Eliz.* III. 328 A young man raw and unversed in military matters. **1712** BLACKMORE *Creation* I. 437 The bright Natives of th' unlabour'd Field, Unverst in Spinning, and in Looms unskill'd. **1779** J. MOORE *View Soc. Fr.* (1789) I. iv. 27 A stranger..unversed in their language. **1808** MITFORD *Hist. Greece* IV. 232 A collegue..unversed in military command. **1885** R. BUCHANAN *Annan Water* xxiv, He was unversed in the ways and the by-ways of the great city.

un'versed, *ppl. a.*² [UN-¹ 8.] Not versified; not expressed in verse.
1648 HEXHAM II, *Ongerijmt*, Vnversed, or without Rhime. **1891** *Cent. Dict.* s.v., Thoughts unversed.

un'versified, *ppl. a.* (UN-¹ 8.)
[**1775** ASH.] **1846** WORCESTER (citing Scott).

†**un'verty,** *a. Sc. Obs.*⁻¹ [UN-¹ 7.] Imprudent.
1456 SIR G. HAYE *Law Arms* (S.T.S.) 236 Nocht that ony ambassadouris war sa unverty, na sa folily avisit.

un'vessel, *v.* (UN-² 5.)
1633 FORD *Love's Sacr.* V. iv. L 2 b, So; I grow sweetly empty; all the pipes Of life vn-vessel life. **1656** TRAPP *Comm.* (ed. 2) *Acts* xv. 24 The word signifies unvesselling them, unpacking them,..scattering them.

un'vest, *v.* [UN-² 4.]
1. *trans.* To divest, strip.
1609 BIBLE (Douay) *Lev.* vi. 11 He..shal be unvested of his former vestments. **1610** GUILLIM *Heraldry* III. vii. 106 This being mortified and vnuested of the verdour which sometimes it had.
2. *refl.* and *absol.* To divest (oneself) of ecclesiastical vestments.
1740 CHALLONER *Gard. Soul* (1801) 87 The priest returns ..to the sacristy and unvests himself. *c* **1771** in E. H. Burton *Life Challoner* (1909) I. ix. 140 The Bishop having unvested, remained kneeling. **1853** DALE tr. *Baldeschi's Ceremonial* 15 They assist the sacred Ministers to unvest.

un'vestal, *a.* (UN-¹ 7.)
1757 MRS. GRIFFITH *Lett. Henry & Frances* (1767) IV. 4 Our Vestal..has lately..had a Flame lighted up in her Breast, but of a most unvestal Kind.

unve'xatious, *a.* (UN-¹ 7.)
1802–12 BENTHAM *Ration. Judic. Evid.* (1827) II. 373 The collection of..evidence in a mode thus comparatively undilatory, unexpensive, unvexatious.

un'vexed, *ppl. a.* (UN-¹ 8.)
1456 SIR G. HAY *Gov. Princes* Wks. (S.T.S.) II. 125 The mannis persone restis..in the nycht, and the membris and the wit ar bathe unvexit. **1485** *Acta Dom. Conc.* (1839) *94/1 To be..Joisit be him vnvext be þaim bot as law will. **1508** *Reg. Privy Seal Scotl.* I. 234/2 To..defend [them]..unvexit and undistroublit. **1595** SHAKS. *John* II. i. 253 With a blessed and vn-vext retyre,..We will beare home that lustie blood againe. **1611** DONNE *Anat. World* 363 In whom all white, and red, and blew (Beauties ingredients) voluntary grew, As in an unvext Paradise. **1697** DRYDEN *Virg. Georg.* II. 659 Unvex'd with Quarrels, undisturb'd with Noise. **1791** HUDDESFORD *Salmag.* 105 Unvex'd by the cares that ambition and state has. **1809** MALKIN *Gil Blas* VIII. ii. ¶9 Which put forth shoots like a plantation in a fat and unvexed soil. **1864** TENNYSON *En. Arden* 526 Unvext She slipt across the summer of the world. **1869** LOWELL *Ode to Happiness* 71 These in unvexed dependence lie, Each 'neath his strip of household sky.

un'vicar, *v.* (UN-² 6 b.)
c **1561** UNDERHILL *Autobiog.* (Camden Soc.) 157 Yff I hadde your auctoryte I wolde be so bolde to unvycker hym.

†**un'viciate,** *ppl. a. Sc. Obs.*⁻¹ (UN-¹ 8 b.)
1593 *Sc. Acts, Jas. VI* (1816) IV. 25/2 Sa mony of the rentis & fruittis thairof as ar presentlie frie and vnviciat.

un'vicious, *a.* (UN-¹ 7.)
1456 SIR G. HAY *Gov. Princes* Wks. (S.T.S.) II. 136 Gude quhete brede and gude lycht flesche and gude unvicious wynis.

†**un'vict,** *a.*, **un'victed,** *ppl. a. Obs.* [UN-¹ 7, 8, 5 b.] = INVICT *a.*
1560 PHAER *Æneid* IX. (1562) E e ij, Depe mourning maks them slack, vnuicted strengthes begin to pal. *Ibid.* x. Gg ij, That shield which..the fyry-puissant god vnuict, gaue thee with golden grates.

†**un'victable,** *a. Obs.*⁻¹ [UN-¹ 7.] Invincible.
1533 BELLENDEN *Livy* II. xxi. (S.T.S.) I. 217 The fabis [= Fabii]..belewit þir vnvictaible [*v.r.* invincibill; L. *invicta*] armoure and wappinnys mycht nother be winccust nor ȝit resistit.

unvic'torious, *a.* (UN-¹ 7.)
1611 FLORIO, *Inuittorioso*, vnuictorious. **1853** CARLYLE in Froude *Life* (1884) II. 135, I am a most unvictorious man surely. **1892** RIDER HAGGARD *Nada* xxi, Never before for many years had a Zulu impi returned unvictorious.

un'victualled, *ppl. a.* (UN-¹ 8.)
1484 *Cov. Leet Bk.* 519 Wherthorough..straungers resortyng to þe seid Cite..were vnvittailled. **1549** CHEKE *Hurt Sedit.* (1569) F ij, Exeter..being in the middest of Rebelles, vnuittailed, vnfurnished, vnprepared, for so long a siege. **1598** SYLVESTER *Du Bartas* II. ii. *Babylon* 351 Jayes, that in their wyerie gail Can ask for victuals, and unvictual'd rail. **1648** HEXHAM II, *Ongespijst*, Vnvictualled.

un'viewed, *ppl. a.* (UN-¹ 8.)
1570 LEVINS *Manip.* 51 Vnuewed, *inæstimatus*. **1608** SYLVESTER *Du Bartas* II. iv. *Schism* 971 Another cals on Heav'n's un-viewed Lights. **1641** PEACHAM *Worth of a Penny* 27 Our Ladies..will..shiver in the hardest frost, rather than they will suffer their bare necks and breasts to passe your eyes unviewed. **1712** BLACKMORE *Creation* VI. 475 From thee, Democritus, it lay conceal'd,..'Twas by the Coan's piercing eye unview'd. **1810** CRABBE *Borough* i. 164 But who to thee (A wonder yet unview'd) shall paint the sea?

un'vigilant, *a.* (UN-¹ 7, 5 b.)
1611 FLORIO, *Inuigilante*, vnuigilant, vnwatchful. **1648** HEXHAM II, *Onwacker*, Vnwakened, or Vnvigilent. **1891** ATKINSON *Moorland Par.* 324 A wild wary bird..so dazed.. by hunger and cold as to become dulled, muffled, unvigilant.

un'vigorously, *adv.* (UN-¹ 11.)
1641 MILTON *Ch. Govt.* I. v. 25 Many other courses he tries,..but so unvigorously, that I do not feare his winning of many to his cause.

†**un'vinceable,** *a. Obs.*⁻¹ [UN-¹ 7 b.] = next.
a **1567** *Dunbar's Lament for Makaris* 25 (Bann. MS.), That strang, vnvynsable tirrand.

†**un'vincible,** *a. Obs.* (UN-¹ 7 and 5 b.)
1554 *Dial. on Laws Eng.* I. xvi. 28 b, Though ignorance vnuincible of a statute excuse the party against God. *a* **1557** MRS. M. BASSET tr. *More's Treat. Passion* M.'s Wks. 1392/2 To sende hym..a myghtye stronge vnuyncible armie of Aungels from heauen. **1594** CAREW *Huarte's Exam. Wits* xiii. 205 Imagination..deuiseth the engins..wherby vnuincible fortresses are won. *a* **1612** H. BROUGHTON *Wks.* (1662) III. 713 The assertion..is by an unvincible consequent denied by the Geneveans. **1658** J. WEBB *Cleopatra* VIII. III. 69 Fanc[y]ing her Troops unvincible had this great person fought at their head.
Hence †**un'vincibleness;** †**un'vincibly** *adv.*
1581 FULKE in *Confer.* III. (1584) U iiij b, Though the communion vnder both kindes bee proued vnuincibly by that testimonie. **1611** FLORIO, *Inuincibilita*, vnuincibleness.

un'vindicated, *ppl. a.* (UN-¹ 8.)
1654 GAYTON *Pleas. Notes* III. v. 97 Whom those Inchanters, Moors, and Witches..had coffin'd up unvindicated untill this present houre. **1879** CHR. ROSSETTI *Seek & F.* 220 His [*sc.* Christ's] royalty, scoffed at by malice, remained unvindicated.

unvin'dictive, *a.* (UN-¹ 7.)
[**1775** ASH.] **1857** J. W. DONALDSON *Chr. Orthod.* 333 With an unvindictive selection of epithets. **1883** CROFT *Elyot's Governour* II. 650/2 Anecdote of [Emperor Augustus], illustrating his unvindictive nature.

un'vintaged, *ppl. a.* (UN-¹ 8.)
1869 BLACKMORE *Lorna D.* xxxiii, That eternal morning, when crag and chasm shall be no more, neither hill and valley, nor great unvintaged ocean.

†**un'violable,** *a. Obs.* (UN-¹ 7 b, 5 b.)
1565 COOPER *Thesaurus*, *Inuiolabilis*,..vnuiolable. **1583** GOLDING *Calvin on Deut.* iii. 14 This order..ought to be vnuiolable. **1596** SIR H. KNYVETT *Def. Realme* Ded. (1906) 9 The fountaine of unviolable faith. **1624** CAPT. SMITH *Virginia* IV. 144 Such a firme peace, as most men there thought sure and vnuiolable. **1656** EARL MONM. tr. *Boccalini's Advts. fr. Parnass.* II. lxi. (1674) 213 Religion, Faith, and unviolable Friendship. **1718** ROWE tr. *Lucan* 255 Who views the Gorgons with intrepid Eyes, And your unviolable Flood defies?
Hence †**un'violably** *adv. Obs.*
1534 tr. *Lyndwode's Const. Provinc.* 3 b, We charge & commaunde the constitucions..to be vnuiolably obserued & kept. **1647** HEXHAM I, Vnviolablely, *onverderffelicken*.

†**un'violate,** *ppl. a. Obs.* [UN-¹ 8 b, 5 b. Cf. next.] = INVIOLATE *a.*
a **1548** HALL *Chron., Hen. V*, 39 To thentent that this league and amitee should be kept unviolate. **1570** T. NORTON tr. *Nowel's Catech.* 11 Any other matter of great importance, wherein we are..to mainteine vnuiolate the honor of God. *a* **1589** PALFREYMAN *Baldwin's Mor. Philos.* (1600) 127 b, Common lawes..ought to bee..kept vnuiolate. **1681** *Whole Duty Nations* 24 The retaining their Honour untouch'd, unviolate by any creature.

un'violated, *ppl. a.* (UN-¹ 8, 5 b.)
1555 EDEN *Decades* (Arb.) 342 The nation..dooth not longe keepe the condicions of peace vnuiolated. **1590** SHAKS. *Com. Err.* III. i. 88 Th' vnuiolated honor of your wife. **1639** FULLER *Holy War* II. vi. 51 His tombe is unviolated at this day. **1671** MILTON *Samson* 1144 The pledge of my unviolated vow. **1727** THOMSON *Britannia* 134 Unviolated, him the virgin sings. **1786** BURKE *Art. agst. W. Hastings* Wks. 1842 II. 215 A treaty of peace.., unviolated on his part. **1861** WYNTER *Soc. Bees* 20 The letter..reaches the person to whom it is directed, apparently unviolated. **1891** MEREDITH *One of our Conq.* xxv, Not until we are driven back upon an unviolated Nature, do we call to the intellect to think radically.

un'violenced, *ppl. a.* (UN-¹ 8.)
a **1711** KEN *Hymns Evang.* Poet. Wks. 1721 I. 146 He ever lives unviolenc'd by ill, Who to his God devoted, has no will. —— *Hymnarium* Ibid. II. 142 How God..Governs unviolenc'd Contingency.

un'virgin, *v.* (UN-² 6 b.)
1638 N. WHITING *Albino & Bellama* 2593 It seems some roister bold Them to unvirgin cunningly did lurk.

un'virginal, *a.* (UN-¹ 7.)
1546 BALE *Eng. Votaries* I. 29 b, If their unvirginall vowes had not bene, lytle should the worlde haue neded thys lecherous learnynge.

un'virgined, *ppl. a.* (UN-² 6 b, 8.)
1602 WARNER *Alb. Eng.* x. lix. 258 Her now vn-virgin'd Eyes did shame to view the common Light. **1638** MAYNE *Lucian* (1664) 167 The other tooke his bride, led her into his chamber, and a while after brought her forth unvirgin'd.

un'virginlike, *a.* (UN-¹ 7 c.)
1671 H. M. tr. *Erasm. Colloq.* 361, I am much afraid, lest some unvirginlike thing was committed that night.

un'virile, *a.* (UN-¹ 7, 5 b.)
1884 H. S. WILSON *Stud. Hist.*, etc. 122 James..was unstable, pedantic, undignified, and unvirile.

†**un'virtuate,** *v. Obs.*⁻¹ [UN-² 6 c.] *trans.* To render ineffective.
1611 SPEED *Hist. Gt. Brit.* IX. xxiv. §125 Neither continuance of time, nor subtilty of ayre could checke or vn-vertuate the strength [of the poison].

un'virtue. (UN-¹ 12.)
1869 W. M. ROSSETTI in *Q. Eliz. Academy*, etc. II. 108 Every Un-virtue has Both her service and her council. **1869** RUSKIN *Q. of Air* §141 Evil by outlawry and unvirtue.

un'virtuous, *a.* (UN-¹ 7.)
1432 *Paston Lett.* I. 32 The whiche lak or defaulte mighte be caused by ungodely or unvertuous men. *c* **1456** PECOCK *Bk. of Faith* (1909) 149 Forto so bileeve withoute evydence is unresonable, and therfore unvertuose. *a* **1548** HALL *Chron., Hen. IV*, 19 He beyng netteled with these vncurteous ye vnuertuous prickes..serched out the authours. **1586** FERNE *Blaz. Gentrie* 16 The coate-armours, and nobilities of the vaine and vnvertuous Gentlemen. **1645** MILTON *Tetrach.* 54 An opinion both ungodly, unpolitic, unvertuous, and void of all honesty and civil sense. **1741** RICHARDSON *Pamela* III. 44 It must be a very unvirtuous Man, that can form any other Ideas..than those of..Pity for you. **1867** *Month* VI. 17 An unvirtuous Priest..ruins many souls in these days. **1886** A. WEIR *Hist. Basis Mod. Europe* ii. 37 He was [deeply] involved in the unvirtuous statecraft of his time.
Hence **un'virtuously** *adv.*; **un'virtuousness.**
a **1500** *Bernardus de cura rei fam.* (E.E.T.S.) 10/245 Wyrk thow oder wnwerteusly or vele. **1520** *Caxton's Chron. Eng.* IV. 32 b/2 Many tymes he regned vnuertuously that is a kynge borne. **1682** N. INGELO *Bentiv. & Ur.* IV. (ed. 4) 115 Love less, and you will love better and longer. You love Arete unvertuously. **1843** CARLYLE *Past. & Pr.* III. ii, It was the terror..of doing unworthily, doing unvirtuously, which was their word for un*manf*ully. **1865** W. H. GILLESPIE *Argt. Being & Attrib.* III. iii. §6 The same sort of thing holds with regard to..unvirtuousness.

†**un'vised,** *ppl. a. Obs.* [UN-¹ 8.]
a. Unintended. **b.** Unadvised.
a **1300** *Cursor M.* 28569 Drunkennes if it vnvisd be. **1609** R. G. *Good speed to Virginia* C 4 b, They holde it an vnuised course to set the same attempt on foote againe.
Hence †**un'visedly** *adv.*, imprudently. *Obs.*
c **1470** HENRY *Wallace* XI. 231 A lord off court.. Wnwisytly sperd, with outyn prouisioun; 'Wallace, dar ye go fecht on our lioun?'

†**un'visible,** *a. Obs.* (UN-¹ 7 and 5 b.)
1388 WYCLIF *Tobit* xii. 19 Y vse vnuysible meete. *c* **1402** LYDG. *Compl. Bl. Knt.* 623 When Vulcanus..with a cheyne vnvisible yow bounde. **1483** CAXTON *Cato* c j b, The whyche hath myght..vpon alle thynges vysyble and vnuysyble. **1558** BP. WATSON *Sev. Sacram.* vii. 36 Christ geueth vnto vs his vnuisible graces, in sensible sacramentes. **1593** *Pass. Morrice* F ij b, I would I..went not so vnuisible. [Also Hexham and Ash s.v.]
Hence †**un'visibleness;** †**un'visibly** *adv.*
c **1380** WYCLIF *Sel. Wks.* III. 522 It is nedeful þat it be understonden *unvesibily. **1647** HEXHAM I, Vnvisible, or unvisibly. **1721** STRYPE *Eccl. Mem.* III. 279 You..adore the same flesh in substance, altho' unvisibly [*orig.* invisible] in the sacrament, which we al shal se in the latter day visible. **1611** FLORIO, *Inuisibilita*, *vnuisiblenesse.

un'visionary, *a.* (UN-¹ 7.)
1794 R. J. SULIVAN *View Nat.* II. 167 Whatever turns the mind intensely upon unvisionary contemplation. **1870** RUSKIN *Lect. Art* (1875) 48 A measured..observance of the quite unvisionary facts of the surrounding world.

un'visitable, *a.* [UN-¹ 7 b.]
1. a. Unable to visit. **b.** Unfit to be visited.
1638 WOTTON in *Reliq.* (1672) 570 The B. of Lincoln being in an unvisitable case himself. **1832** MISS MITFORD *Village* V. 38 A series of bachelor lords, whose female companions have been thoroughly unvisitable.
2. Not suitable for visiting.
1749 FIELDING *Tom Jones* XIII. iii, The next morning..she huddled on her clothes, and at a very unfashionable, unseasonable, unvisitable hour, went to Lady Bellaston.

un'visited, *ppl. a.* [UN-¹ 8.] Not visited, in various senses.
(*a*) **1549** LATIMER *Ploughers* (Arb.) 31 He goeth on visitacion daylye. He leaueth no place of hys cure vnuisited. **1600** HAKLUYT *Voy.* III. 171 There remayned some farre remote Countries vnvisited by them. **1693** S. HERVEY *Juvenal* ix. 13 The Play-House and the Parks unvisited must lie. **1799** WORDSW. *Nutting* 17, I came to one dear nook Unvisited. **1853** KANE *Grinnell Exp.* xxiv. (1856) 197 Another opportunity of seeing the unvisited shores of Wellington Sound.
(*b*) *a* **1586** SIDNEY *Arcadia* III. xxvi, Giving order to his brother to keepe the prisoners safe, and unvisited. **1588**

SHAKS. *L.L.L.* v. ii. 358 You haue liued in desolation heere, Vnseene, vnuisited. **1612** in *Buccleuch MSS.* (Hist. MSS. Comm.) I. 126, I resolved to leave him unvisited until I should receive answer. **1734** MRS. DELANY *Life & Corr.* (1861) I. v. 447 She must live unvisited by me till I know where to find her. **1831** CARLYLE *Sart. Res.* II. v, Thus was the young man..not unvisited by hosts of true Sky-born. **1868** PUSEY *Lent. Serm.* viii. (1883) 165 While His members are..sick and by us unvisited.

(*c*) **1667** MILTON *P.L.* II. 398 In some milde Zone [we may] Dwell not unvisited of Heav'ns fair Light. **1760–72** H. BROOKE *Fool of Qual.* (1809) II. 158 Abandoned by God, and unvisited by his gracious motions in the heart. *c* **1815** JANE AUSTEN *Persuas.* viii, The utter impossibility..that he could be unvisited by remembrance. **1831** CARLYLE in Froude *Life* (1882) II. 189 The day [being] unvisited by any adventure except a little message from Mrs. Austin. **1870** BRYANT *Iliad* IX. I. 281 So have I Had many a night unvisited by sleep.

un'visor, *v.* [UN-^{2} 4. Cf. UNVIZARD *v.*] *trans.* To strip of a visor; to unmask.

1572 BUCHANAN *Detect. Mary* (1727) 28 This..Strangeris Hap was to spill the Play, and unvisor all the Disguising. **1602** WARNER *Alb. Eng.* x. lviii. 255 The Barricados Feast, when Guise vn-vizard was. **1630** J. TAYLOR (Water P.) *Vertue of Tayle* Wks. II. 126 Whilst I vnmaske, vnvisor, or vnveile The vertues of a Taylor and a Tayle.

un'visored, *ppl. a.* [UN-^{1} 8.] Not wearing a visor; not masked.

1827 POLLOK *Course T.* VIII. 24 On their grim features, now The plain unvisored index of the soul,..No smile of hope..was seen. **1881** *Daily News* 8 Apr. 5/3 Un-visored foes in open fray he'll meet.

un'vital, *a.* (UN-^{1} 7.)

1661 RUST *Origen's Opin.* 79 The matter she [*sc.* the soul] is then muchsurrounded with being all of that unvital temper. **1837** WHEWELL *Hist. Induct. Sci.* III. 129 Lavoisier showed that the atmospheric air..[contains] an *unvital* air, which he thence called *azot*. **1854** E. G. HOLLAND *Mem. J. Badger* x. 171 Some dry and unvital difference in theological belief. **1865** M. ARNOLD *Ess. Crit.* i. 23 A sphere..perfectly unvital, a sphere in which spiritual progression is impossible.

Hence **un'vitalness**.

1661 RUST *Origen's Opin.* 69 Purged from all material unvitalness or mortality.

un'vitalized, *ppl. a.* (UN-^{1} 8.)

1874 LEWES *Probl. Life & Mind* I. 116 The inorganic, unvitalised material becoming there transformed into organisable, vitalised material.

un'vitiated, *ppl. a.* (UN-^{1} 8.)

1632 B. JONSON *Magn. Lady* IV. viii, Render then Your Neice a Virgin and unvitiated, And make all plaine and perfect (as it was). **1779** FORREST *Voy. N. Guinea* 297 The poor Papua people..follow nature unvitiated, and sing most melodiously. **1797** B. S. BARTON *New Views* p. xv, The traditions of a people cannot be preserved long in a pure, unvitiated stream. **1838** LYTTON *Alice* II. i, Her unvitiated and guileless taste had a logic of its own. **1864** DISRAELI in *Daily Tel.* 22 Sept., To breathe and enjoy pure and unvitiated air.

unvitresci'bility, (UN-^{1} 12), **unvi'trescible**, *a.* (UN-^{1} 7.)

1782 WEDGWOOD in *Phil. Trans.* LXXII. 309 A clay sufficiently apyrous or unvitrescible. **1786** —— *Ibid.* LXXVI. 401, I..found it to answer my wishes completely ..in..increasing its unvitrescibility.

unvitri'fiable, *a.* (UN-^{1} 7 b, 5 b.)

1758 REID tr. *Macquer's Chem.* I. 7 A species of Earth absolutely unvitrifiable in its nature. **1778** PRYCE *Min. Cornub.* 253 The micose clay..is known to be absolutely unvitrifiable. **1879** *Cassell's Techn. Educ.* II. 338/2 The alkali ..facilitates the vitrification of the earthy particles, which separately are unvitrifiable.

un'vitrified, *ppl. a.* (UN-^{1} 8.)

[**1775** ASH.] **1779** *Encycl. Brit.* (ed. 2) IV. 2674/1 Another sort of glass,..[having] some unvitrified particles in its substance. **1839** URE *Dict. Arts* 1160 The superficial film of colours will remain unvitrified. **1888** *Encycl. Brit.* XXIV. 264/1 The vitrified walls are supported by masses of unvitrified stone.

un'vitriolized, *ppl. a.* (UN-^{1} 8.)

1757 tr. *J. F. Henckel's Pyritologia* 298 That sort..yet remaining unvitriolized as the other [*sc.* white pyrites].

un'vizard, *v.* [UN-^{2} 4.] *trans.* = UNVISOR *v.* Also *absol.* for *refl.*

1620 E. BLOUNT *Horæ Subs.* 490 Whereas they that are more cunning in their trade, are hardly visible, if not vnvizarded, which is my now endeuour to doe. **1642** *Remonstr. Ch. Ireland* 6 But others more fully unvizard themselves, professing, That they would have a King of their owne. **1655** EARL ORRERY *Parthen.* II. v. 469 Merinzor..began lately so much to unvizard his designes, that [etc.]. **1911** H. G. WELLS *New Machiavelli* IV. i. 388 People who unvizard to talk more easily at a masked ball.

Hence **un'vizarding** *vbl. sb.*

a **1628** F. GREVIL *Life Sidney* (1652) 113 The unvizarding of this masked triplicity.

un'vizarded, *ppl. a.* [UN-^{1} 8.] = UNVISORED *ppl. a.*

1612 N. FIELD *Woman a Weathercock* v. ii. Stage direct., Enter Scudmore unvizarded.

un'vocable, *a.* [UN-^{1} 7.] Incapable of utterance.

1826 GALT *Last of Lairds* xiii. 118 The same genial power ..prompteth unvocable as well as intelligent nature to.. rejoice in the spring.

un'vocal, *a.* (UN-^{1} 7.)

1773 J. HERRIES *Elem. Sp.* 58 The simple elements of speech [include] some vocal, some unvocal, some open, some shut. **1858** CARLYLE *Fredk. Gt.* IV. ii. I. 393 He is a man to keep the world's tongue wagging,..though himself of very unvocal nature. **1885** *Athenæum* 17 Jan. 94/3 The composer indulges in unvocal intervals and harsh progressions.

un'vocalized, *ppl. a.* (UN-^{1} 8.)

1855 C. R. LEPSIUS *Stand. Alphabet* 39, *h* belongs, therefore, to the unvocalised strong fricatives. **1878** BRISTOWE *Th. & Pract. Med.* 477 The result is that unvocalised air escapes through the chink.

un'voice, *v.* [UN-^{2} 4.] *trans.* To deprive of voice; *spec.* in *Phonetics*, to utter with 'breath' in place of 'voice'.

1637 N. WHITING *Albino & B.* 402 As though an Incubus ..Enclaspt their bosomes, and un-voyc'd their tongues. *Ibid.* 702. **1879** SWEET *Coll. Papers* (1913) 456 In Russian, as in French, a high final vowel is often unvoiced after a breath stop. **1888** —— *Eng. Sounds* 19 Liquids and nasals are not often unvoiced.

Hence **un'voicing** *vbl. sb.*

1887 SKEAT *Eng. Etym.* Ser. I. 392 Unvoicing of voiced consonants. **1888** SWEET *Eng. Sounds* 198 This unvoicing of weak stops.

un'voiced, (*ppl.*) *a.* (UN-^{1} 8, 9. Cf. VOICE *v.* 5, 7 b.)

1859 EMERSON *Art & Criticism* Wks. 1903 XII. 298 A book holding so many memorable and heroic facts,..things unvoiced before. **1874** HOLLAND *Mistr. Manse* i. 10 That word, ineffable to man,..Remains unvoiced since time began. **1881** W. E. DICKSON *Pract. Organ-building* ix. 119 A wooden pipe, similarly put together but unvoiced.

un'voiceful, *a.* (UN-^{1} 7.)

1872 HOWELLS *Wedd. Journ.* ix, The unvoiceful stir of the new week had begun again.

un'voidable, *a.* [UN-^{1} 7 b + VOID *v.* 3.] Irreversible.

1725 BAILEY *Erasm. Colloq.* (1877) 173 He will from on high pronounce that unvoidable sentence.

†**un'voided**, *ppl. a. Obs.* [UN-^{1} 8.] = UNAVOIDED *ppl. a.* 2 a.

1612 R. DABORNE *Chr. turn'd Turke* 228 How idle then were he Should striue to crosse vnuoided desteny?

un'volatile, *a.* (UN-^{1} 7, 5 b.)

1823 LADY GRANVILLE *Lett.* (1894) I. 228 A straight Dutch road, broad and unvolatile as the natives.

un'volatilize, *v.* (UN-^{2} 6 c.)

1875 BROWNING *Aristoph. Apol.* 201 Who would imprison, unvolatilize A violet's perfume.

un'volatilized, *ppl. a.* (UN-^{1} 8.)

1807 AIKIN *Dict. Chem. & Min.* I. 37/2 The ashes being the fixed or unvolatilized part of the plant.

†**un'volatized**, *ppl. a. Obs.* (UN-^{1} 8.)

1669 W. SIMPSON *Hydrol. Chym.* 347 Deprav'd matter.. un-volatiz'd by the ferment.

un'voluntary, *a.* ? *Obs.* (UN-^{1} 7, 5 b.)

1570 LEVINS *Manip.* 107 Vnvoluntarie, *inuitus*. **1632** tr. *Bruel's Praxis Med.* 66 An vnuoluntary motion in the part which vsually did moue of its owne accord. *a* **1676** HALE *Prim. Orig. Man.* I. i. (1677) 30 They are not acts that are imperate by the Will, but they are in a manner natural and unvoluntary. **1706** E. WARD *Wooden World Diss.* (1708) 21 'Tis unvoluntary, to be sure, if he spill of the one or the other. **1725** *Fam. Dict.*, *Diabetes*,..an unvoluntary Discharge of Urine. **1834** *Tait's Mag.* I. 10/1 The unvoluntary listener to his grey-haired father's earnest prayers.

unvo'luptuous, *a.* (UN-^{1} 7.)

1871 GEO. ELIOT *Middlem.* xxiii, He had written stanzas as pastoral and unvoluptuous as his flute-playing.

un'vote, *v.* [UN-^{2} 3 and 7.]

1. To reverse or annul by revoting.

trans. **1647** in *7th Rep. Hist. MSS. Comm.* App. 456/2 They were forced to unvote what they had passed the day before. **1708** *Deplorable State of New Eng.* 35 The Business was so managed..that altho'..one Day it was Voted, That the Fort should be Attack'd, it was by'nd by, Unvoted again. *intr.* **1647** R. KENTISH *Serm. to Comm.* (1648) 12 They.. will vote and un-vote, as the times turn. **1653** *Pol. Ballads* (1860) I. 108 They voted, unvoted, as fancy did guide.

2. *trans.* To deprive by a vote. Const. *of*.

1658 J. HARRINGTON *Prerog. Pop. Govt.* I. vii. 35 If they unchirotonized or unvoted God of the Kingdome.

Hence **un'voting** *vbl. sb.*

1642 HOWELL *Twelve Treat.* (1661) 40 A Bill for the unvoting, and utter exclusion of the Spirituall Lords from the Parliament. **1643** PRYNNE *Sov. Power Parl.* IV. 24 His Majesties..unvoting of their Votes in Parliament.

un'voting, *ppl. a.* (UN-^{1} 10.)

1839 CARLYLE *Chartism* ix, Shall we blame the unvoting disappointed millions..?

un'vouched, *ppl. a.* [UN-^{1} 8, 8 c.] Not guaranteed by evidence; not vouched *for*.

1775 L. SHAW *Hist. Moray* 134 This wholly unvouched account. **1783** HAILES *Antiq. Chr. Ch.* iii. 56 This hypothesis, fanciful at the best and unvouched. **1858** FROUDE *Hist. Eng.* IV. 496 [A legend] unvouched for, unalluded to by any contemporary authority. **1878** J. DAVIDSON *Inverurie* vii. 244 A picture..which, if unvouched, would now surpass belief.

unvouch'safed, *ppl. a.* (UN-^{1} 8.)

1661 BOYLE *Style of Script.* 246 God has Veyl'd in an Obscure..Stone an Attractivenesse (Unvouchsaf'd to Diamonds and Ruby's). ? **1810** WORDSW. *Maternal Grief* 19 Beams of that celestial light To all the Little-ones on sinful earth Not unvouchsafed.

un'vowed, *ppl. a.* [UN-^{1} 8.] Not bound by a vow; not rendered on account of a vow.

1570 LEVINS *Manip.* 51 Vnuowed, *inuotiuus*. *a* **1600** HOOKER *Eccl. Pol.* VII. xxiii. §4 They had the free and unvowed oblations of men. **1615** G. SANDYS *Trav.* 229 If vnuowed to another Order,..he vowes in this order. **1856** MRS. BROWNING *Aur. Leigh* VI. 57 Some equal poise of sex, some unvowed love Inviolate. **1878** *Masque Poets* 151 She sat apart In widowed saintliness, an unvowed nun.

un'vowelled, (*ppl.*) *a.* (UN-^{1} 8, 9. Cf. VOWEL *v.* 3.)

1624 SKINNER in *Ussher's Lett.* (1686) 357, I note..That Moses left unvowelled Copies to the Tribes, save one which had both Accents and Vowels to the custody of the Priests. **1894** W. WRIGHT in *Bibl. Soc. Rec.* (N.Y.) Aug., A set of plates of the unvowelled Bible.

un'voyageable, *a.* (UN-^{1} 7 b.)

1667 MILTON *P.L.* X. 366 This unvoyageable Gulf obscure. **1809–14** WORDSW. *Excurs.* V. 342 Here standing, with the un-voyageable sky..Stretched overhead. **1853** RUSKIN *Stones Ven.* II. 10 The lifeless, impassable, unvoyageable plain.

un'voyaged, *ppl. a.* (UN-^{1} 8.)

1816 J. WILSON *City of Plague* III. iii, A kingdom Lying unknown amid unvoyaged seas. **1856** RUSKIN *Mod. Paint.* III. IV. xiv. §8 The flowing flame of some calm unvoyaged river.

un'vulcanized, *ppl. a.* (UN-^{1} 8.)

1884 KNIGHT *Dict. Mech.* Suppl. 916/2 A material..made of unvulcanized rubber and other substances.

un'vulgar, *a.* [UN-^{1} 7 and 5 b.]

†**1.** Uncommon, unusual; above the common, refined, rare. *Obs.*

1598 SYLVESTER *Du Bartas* II. i. 40 O! furnish me with an un-vulgar stile. **1615** J. STEPHENS *Satyr. Ess.* I. xv. 192 In his behauiour hee would seeme French, Italian, Spanish, or any thing, so he may seeme vnvulgar. **1654** GAYTON *Pleas. Notes* IV. v. 199 There were no living..with us, unlesse something new and unvulgar be in our houses. **1713** BERKELEY *Hylas & Phil.* Pref., When they have taken a circuit through so many refined and unvulgar notions. **1736** WELSTED *Wks.* (1787) 427 Philosophers..too unvulgar to relish any Divinity that is not Pagan.

2. Free from vulgarity.

1819 L. HUNT *Indicator* No. 3 (1822) I. 19 The whole story is..unvulgar and..sweetly serious. **1839** J. H. FRERE *Aristoph. Knights* p. iv, That admirable and most unvulgar exhibition of vulgar life, the Pickwick Papers.

un'vulgarize, *v.* (UN-^{2} 6 c.)

1811 LAMB *Hogarth* Wks. 1908 I. 95 The quantity of thought..would alone unvulgarize every subject which he might choose. **1881** *Mag. Art* IV. 290/2 It might..have.. made the entire aspect of English home-life delightful, unvulgarising a domestic nation.

un'vulgarized, *ppl. a.* (UN-^{1} 8.)

1858 *Nat. Rev.* Oct. 352 The grace and depth of unvulgarised emotions.

un'vulgarly, *adv.* [UN-^{1} 11.] †Uncommonly, remarkably.

1602 MARSTON *Antonio's Rev.* III. iv, I haue taken a murre, which makes my nose run most patheticallie, and vnvulgarlie.

†**un'vulnerable**, *a. Obs.* (UN-^{1} 7 b, 5 b.)

1607 SHAKS. *Cor.* v. iii. 72 The God of Souldiers.. informe Thy thoughts with Noblenesse, that thou mayst proue To shame vnvulnerable. **1666** *Third Advice to Painter* 20 Leave then (said he) th' unvulnerable Keele.

†**un'vulnered**, *ppl. a. Obs.*$^{-1}$ [UN-^{1} 8, 5 b. Cf. VULNERATE *v.*] Unwounded.

1613 HEYWOOD *Silver Age* III. i, This Lyons case shall on our shoulders hang, Wee'l arme our body with th' vnvulner'd skin.

un'wadded, *ppl. a.* (UN-^{1} 8.)

[**1775** ASH.] **1835** DICKENS *Sk. Boz, Scenes* xi, Can our friend in the military uniform ever..descend to the comparatively un-wadded costume of every-day life?

un'wafered, *ppl. a.* (UN-^{1} 8.)

1844 STOCQUELER *Handbk. Brit. India* 218 Scraps of paper ..un-wafered or unsealed.

†**un'wafted**, *ppl. a. Sc.* [UN-^{1} 8.] = UNWEFT *ppl. a.*

1662 *Stirling Burgh Rec.* I. 239 Ilk weaver is to leave the bounds of a large inch at the end of each pair [of plaids] unwafted.

un'waged, *ppl. a.* [UN-^{1} 8.] **a.** Not recompensed with wages; unpaid. **b.** Not receiving a wage, out of work. Also *absol.*

1538 LATIMER *Serm. & Rem.* (Parker Soc.) 397 His highness should..remember them with some piece of some broken abbey..; for, as I hear, the vicars and other ministers sing and say unwaged. *c* **1550** *Dice Play* (Percy Soc.) 11 With less relief of victuals than had the worst unwaged adventurer here. **1563** *Mirr. Mag.* M iij, Now all stormy gales Of..rancor vtterly are swaged, And we our owne to lyve or dye vnwaged. **1971** DALLA COSTA & JAMES in *Power of Women* (1975) 33 (*heading*) The productivity of wage slavery based on unwaged slavery. **1981** *Evening Mail* (Birmingham) 30 Apr. 22/2 (Advt.), Women's Theatre

Group presents their new play on Nuclear Power, Breaking Through, at Small Heath Community School... £1·50 waged, £1 unwaged. **1982** *Libr. Assoc. Rec.* (Vacancies Suppl.) 30 Nov. p. cxlviii, The cost will be £2 per line for waged persons or £1 per line for those who are unwaged. **1982** *Guardian* 24 Feb. 10/4 They're supposed to do unwaged work for their whole lives.

un'wagged, *ppl. a.* (UN-[1] 8.)
1788 HURDIS *Village Curate* (1797) 94 The silent pointer.. Now motionless.. stands, one foot lift up, His nostril wide-distended, and his tail Unwag'd.

un'wailed, *ppl. a.* (UN-[1] 8.)
1802 J. BAILLIE *2nd Pt. Ethwald* v. ii, Where dying warriors groan unheard, and things Horrid to nature are as though they were not, Unwail'd, unheeded.

†**un'waindandly,** *adv. Sc. Obs.* [UN-[1] 10, 11.] Unsparingly.
c **1425** WYNTOUN *Cron.* VI. xv. 1526 Quhen þat he.. spilt gret blude vnwayndandly [*v.r.* vnwanandly].

un'wainscot(t)ed, *ppl. a.* (UN-[1] 9.)
1709 *Phil. Trans.* XXVI. 481 The Top or Cieling of an Un-wainscotted Church.

un'waited, *ppl. a.* (UN-[1] 8 c.)
1592 TIMME *Ten Eng. Lepers* E 4 b, Pride.. disdaineth to go alone, unwaited upon. *c* **1618** FLETCHER *Mad Lover* II. i, To wander up and down unwaited on.. Is for a Sowter's Soul, not an old Souldiers. **1648** HEXHAM II, *Onverbeydt*, Un-attended, Un-expected, or Vnwaited for.

un'waked, *ppl. a.* (UN-[1] 8.)
1390 GOWER *Conf.* III. 258 Sche unwaked Abedde lay, but what sche mette God wot. *a* **1720** J. HUGHES *Barn-elms* 4 Smooth was the Thames, his waters sleeping lay, Unwak'd by winds. **1824** PRAED *Troubadour* III. 192 You might think the instrument Unwaked by any touch replied To all its master said or sighed.

un'wakened, *ppl. a.* (UN-[1] 8.)
1621 G. SANDYS *Ovid's Met.* XII. (1626) 245 Vnwakened with the tumult of this fray, Dissolu'd in death-like sleepe, Aphidus lay. **1667** MILTON *P.L.* v. 9 So much the more His wonder was to find unwak'n'd Eve With Tresses discompos'd. **1835** CAMPBELL *Dead Eagle* 14 Whilst yet the unwakened world was dark below.

un'wakening, *ppl. a.* (UN-[1] 10.)
1818 MILMAN *Samor* XI. 882 Some knelt before their cold deaf Gods, some scoff'd.. Their stony and unwakening thunders. **1821** BYRON *Sardanap.* IV. i, The realm Of thy stern, silent, and unwakening twin [*sc.* Death].

un'waking, *ppl. a.* (UN-[1] 10.)
1818 MILMAN *Samor* IV. 23 Within the grave She slept unwaking.

un'walkable, *a.* [UN-[1] 7 b.] **a.** Unfit for walking in. **b.** Unable to walk. **c.** Unfit for walking on.
1813 MME. D'ARBLAY *Diary* (1846) VII. 7 How teased I am.. by this eternal unwalkable weather! **1831** HOWITT *Seasons* 273 Even the unwalkable infant sits propt with sheaves. **1976** *N.Y. Times Mag.* 12 Sept. 85/2 The top step is 2 feet high and unwalkable. **1981** *New Scientist* 16 July 141 A nasty mixture of coal slurry and raw sewage makes the sand unwalkable. **1982** *London Rev. Bks.* IV. xxiv. 8/3 These proud owners of this awful model house, tripping around on an artistic but farcically unwalkable pattern of paving-stones.., conduct themselves with a sober sense of import and duty.

un'walked, *ppl. a.*[1] [UN-[1] 8.] Unfulled.
1488 *Acta Dom. Concil.* (1839) 95/2 A wob of tanny claith, ..deliuerit.. to þe said Robert in vnwawkit claith. **1570** *Wills & Inv. N.C.* (Surtees) 348, xiiij yards of vnwaukid caresey and xvj yards of playne whit vnwaukid. **1583** *Durham Wills & Invent.* (Surtees) 78 In unwalked cloth, xiij yeirds of white cearsey [etc.]. **1601** in *T. Pont's Acc. Cunningham* (Maitl. Cl.) 179 Fyve pair of vnwalkit blankettis.

un'walked, *ppl. a.*[2] [UN-[1] 8.] **a.** Not made to walk. **b.** Not traversed by walking.
1607 TOPSELL *Four-f. Beasts* 400 Let him rest vnwalked, for feare of loosening his hooues. **1648** HEXHAM II, *Onbewandelt*, Vnwalked, not Haunted, or Vnfrequented.

un'walking, *ppl. a.* (UN-[1] 10.)
1789 H. WALPOLE *Let. to Conway* 5 Sept., I am so unwalking, that prospects are more agreeable to me when.. I look at them through a window.

un'wall, *v.* [UN-[2] 4. Cf. Du. *ontwallen.*] *trans.* To deprive of, to free from, a wall or walls; to demolish (a wall).
1598 FLORIO, *Smurare*, to vnwall, to raze.. any walles. **1641** TRAPPE *Theol. Theol.* i. 26 *margin*, Christ shall unwall (or cast down the wals) of all the children of Seth. **1663** DAVENANT *Siege Rhodes* Wks. (1672) 8 It were more honour, Sultan, to assail A publick Strength.. Then to unwall this private Tenement. **1686** J. S[ERGEANT] *Hist. Monast. Convent.* 176 The Masons unwalled and unclosed the Conclave.

un'walled, (*ppl.*) *a.* [UN-[1] 8 and 9.] Not furnished with, or defended by, a wall.
c **1440** *Jacob's Well* 114 Slowthe makyth þe as a cyte vnwallyd. **1542** ELYOT s.v. *Arabia*, The townes ar vnwalled, bycause the people doo alwaye lyue in peace. **1577** HARRISON *England* II. xiii. (1877) I. 255 The citie.. laie then vn-walled. **1589** BIGGES *Sum. Drake's W. Ind. Voy.* 31 There was onely so much of this straight vnwalled, as might serue for the issuing of the horsemen. **1638** SIR T. HERBERT *Trav.* (ed. 2) 336 China has no fewer than.. 2000 wall'd Townes; 4000 unwalled. **1690** C. NESSE *O. & N. Test.* I. 14 The soul now dwells in an unwalled, unfortifyed city. **1760–2** GOLDSM. *Cit. W.* cxxii, An unwalled town, called Islington. **1807** J. BARLOW *Columb.* x. 540 Cities unwalled stand sparkling to the sun. **1860** O. W. HOLMES *Elsie V.* xviii, The round unwalled horizon of the open sea.

un'wallet, *v.* (UN-[2] 5.)
a **1739** JARVIS *Quix.* II. IV. xiv, The lacquey laughed, unsheathed his calabash, and un-walleted his cheese.

†**un'wallowable,** *a.* (see UNWELEWABLE *a.*).

un'wallowed, *ppl. a. Sc.* [UN-[1] 8.] Unfaded.
c **1425** WYNTOUN *Cron.* IV. Prol. 7 A garland.. Grene suld lestand be lang quhile, Vnwallowit [*v.r.* wn-walewit] throu ony interwall Off tyme, bot ay in vertu haill.

un'wandered, *ppl. a.* [UN-[1] 8. Cf. MDu. *ongewandert*, G. *ungewandert*; older Da. *uvandret*, Sw. *ovandrad.*] **a.** Untraversed. **b.** Of persons: Untravelled.
1654 E. JOHNSON *Wonder-wkg. Provid.* 35 Pilots, missing ofttimes of their skill on those unwandered Coasts. **1799** W. TAYLOR in Robberds *Mem.* (1843) I. 279 In Wales I am unwandered, and should like to go some summer's day. **1868** BROWNING *Ring & Bk.* I. 751 My soul.. in its pilgrimage O'er old unwandered waste ways of the world.

un'wandering, *ppl. a.* (UN-[1] 10.)
a **1568** COVERDALE *Fruitful Less. Passion* (1593) To Rdr., Thus the penitent findeth the waie, the reformer the vndoubted vnwandring truth. **1740** CIBBER *Apol.* v. 92 The Disproportion of his lower Features,.. with an unwandering Eye hanging over them. **1791** COWPER *Iliad* XIII. 48 He.. bound their feet With golden tethers.., that unwand'ring they might wait Their Lord's return. *a* **1864** HAWTHORNE *Amer. Note-bks.* (1879) II. 158 He was a pattern of diligence and unwandering thought. **1867** M. ARNOLD *Epil. to Lessing's Laocoon* 190 Only a few the life-stream's shore With safe unwandering feet explore.

un'waning, *ppl. a.* (UN-[1] 10.)
1807 COLERIDGE *To Wordsworth* 41 Hope sprang forth like a full-born Deity,.. With light unwaning on her eyes. **1855** BROWNING *Cleon* 130 That years and days.. Follow each other with unwaning powers. *a* **1865** TENNYSON *Mystic* 15 Always there stood before him.. Dim shadows but unwaning presences.

un'wanted, *ppl. a.* (UN-[1] 8.) Also *absol.* as *sb.*
1697 CONGREVE *Mourn. Bride* III. viii, [A] return so unwish'd, unwanted too, it seems. **1731** A. HILL *Advice to Virgins* 10 Yet modest excellence will oft descend To thank unwanted caution in a friend. **1808** MITFORD *Hist. Greece* IV. 476 Yet exhortation.. seems not to have been unwanted. **1864** 'ANNIE THOMAS' *D. Donne* I. vii. 167 Finding some one located at Donne Place who would prevent his occupying the distressing position of third and unwanted one. **1886** MANNING in *Contemp. Rev.* May 693 The duty society owes to the lives of unwanted children. **1932** *New Statesman* 10 Sept. 284/2 We don't take no notice although she did 'ave a little Unwanted. **1949** *Here & Now* (N.Z.) Oct. 18/1 The new freedom has to be weighed against the risk of rearing a generation of unwanteds, filled with.. hostility. **1976** *Daily Record* (Glasgow) 4 Dec. 31/5 The problem is not peculiar to Saints... Bigger teams heave out unwanteds, their feet not touching the ground.

un'wanton, *a.* (UN-[1] 7.)
1606 MARSTON *Parasit.* III. E 3, In heauy sadnes & vnwanton phrase there lies all the braine worke. **1894** E. F. BENSON *Dodo* 248 A woman's anger is always much more unwanton that that of a man.

†**un'wappered,** *ppl. a. Obs.*[−1] [UN-[1] 8 + WAPPERED, fatigued.] Unexhausted.
1612 *Two Noble K.* v. iv, We come towards the gods Yong, and unwapper'd, not halting under Crymes Many and stale.

†**un'ward,** *ppl. a. Obs.*[−1] [UN-[1] 8 b + *ward*, ad. ON. *varðr*, p.p. of *verja* to defend.] Unprotected.
c **1250** *Gen. & Ex.* 480 Lamech droȝe is arwe ner... Caim unwarde it under-feng,.. and starf wið-ðan.

un'warded, *ppl. a.* [UN-[1] 8.] Unguarded; undefended.
1382 WYCLIF *Gen.* xlii. 12 The vnwardid thingis [L. *immunita*] of this loond. **1553** T. LEVER *Serm.* (Arb.) 58 Take heede, that the vncleane spirite of ignoraunce.. fynde no place vnwarded, where he may creepe in agayne. **1553** BRENDE *Q. Curtius* 55 There was one Tiriotes, which.. escaped by a gate that was vnwarded. **1674** JACKSON *Recant.* E 3 b, The High-way-man may do what he list, and meet with more Booties than if the Road lay unwarded. **1858** *Household Words* XIX. 64/1, I pass through the strong gates, now unwarded from the Infidel.

unwardly, obs. var. UNWARELY *adv.*

un'ware, *a.*, *sb.*, and *adv.* Now only *arch.* [OE. *unwær* (UN-[1] 7, 12, 11 b), = ON. *úvarr* (MSw. *ovar*). Cf. UNWARES.]
1. a. Unwary, incautious; not on one's guard.
c **897** K. ÆLFRED *Gregory's Past. C.* xv. 89 Oft eac ða unwaran lareowas for eȝe ne durron cleopian. **971** *Blickl. Hom.* 61 Þa scinlæcan þa þe galdor-cræftas.. begangaþ, & mid þæm unwære men beswicaþ. *c* **1000** ÆLFRIC *Hom.* II. 538 Ȝif ðu unwær bist, þu bist ðe swiðor ȝeswenct. *c* **1200** *Vices & Virtues* 45 Ðe unware mann ðe ðis ȝeherð, ðingþ ðat he seið him god rad. *c* **1205** LAY. 7810 Nu þohte Julius Cezar (ah þer he wes to vnwar), he þohte swa forð teon æfter þere Temese. *a* **1225** *Ancr. R.* 274 Hwonne þeo sunnen þet weren ȝare ibet kumeð eft.. & sleað þeo unwarre soule. *c* **1307** LANGTOFT *Chron.* (Rolls) II. 252 For Scottes Tell i for sottes, And wrecches unwar; Unsele Dintes to dele Tham drohu to Dumbar. **1388** WYCLIF *Prov.* xxiii. 28 Sche schal sle hem, whiche sche schal se vnwar. *c* **1450** tr. *De Imitatione* III. xliv. 115 If he miȝt bringe hedily þe unware man into þe gnare of deceite. *Ibid.* I. 121 Fro suche fables & unwar men, lorde, defende me, þat I falle not into her hondes. **1509** BARCLAY *Shyp of Folys* 37 Suche ar vnware and gyuen to neglygence, ..Makynge no prouysyon for the tyme to come. **1557** *Tottel's Misc.* (Arb.) 230 Now vaunt thee loue which.. wounded hast a wight vnwise, vnweaponed and vnware. **1624** H. MASON *Art of Lying* ii. 35 Unware men are ouer-reached and caught.
b. Of actions: Done incautiously.
a **1395** HYLTON *Scala Perf.* II. xviii. (Bodl. MS.) fol. 110 An vnware stiringe of himsilf schulde caste him doun aȝen worse þan he was bifore. **1398** TREVISA *Barth. De P.R.* v. xxiv. (Bodl. MS.), þe þrote is ofte igreued.. by vnwise and vnwar taking of mete and of drinke.
2. a. Unaware, ignorant. Const. *of*, *that.*
c **1374** CHAUCER *Troylus* I. 304 Lo he.. was ful vnwar þat loue hadde his dwellynge with-inne þe subtile stremes of here eyen. *c* **1400** *Destr. Troy* 1183 Vnwar of þe weghes þat by the walles lay,.. He busket to þe banke with a bolde chere. **1421–2** HOCCLEVE *Complaint* 375 He that it owght agayne it to hym toke, Me of his haste vnware. **1523** LD. BERNERS *Froiss.* I. cvii. 128 We shall entre whyle they be at supper, and vnware of vs. **1563** *Mirr. Mag.* A a iij, O hedeles trust, vnware of harme to cum. **1590** SPENSER *F.Q.* II. iv. 17 So me weake wretch,.. vnware of such mishap, She brought to mischiefe.
ellipt. *c* **1611** CHAPMAN *Iliad* XVI. 109 Ajax seeing.. that he shook a headless spear, a little while unware. **1866** HARDY *Wessex Poems* (1898) 10, I lived unware, uncaring all that lay locked in that Universe taciturn and drear.
b. Quasi-*adv.* Without knowing it; in ignorance, innocently.
c **1386** CHAUCER *Pars. T.* 885 Of this brekynge comth eek ofte tyme that folk vnwar wedden or synnen with hire owene kynrede. **1390** GOWER *Conf.* II. 2 Thus bringeth he many a meschief inne Unwar, til that he be meschieved. *c* **1450** *Merlin* xxvi. 493 He put vp his goode swerde for doute leste he slough eny man vn-war. **1532** MORE *Confut. Tindale* Wks. 598/1 After that he.. therby made him giue sentence vnware against himselfe. **1533** —— *Apol.* 191 b, He playn reproueth his owne processe, & excuseth the clergye hym selfe vnware. *c* **1614** SIR W. MURE *Dido & Æneas* I. 963 Her self, vnwar, thus doth her self betray, And feels the force of this small archer's bowe. **1671** MILTON *P.R.* I. 225 The erring Soul Not wilfully mis-doing, but unware Misled.
3. Unexpected, unforeseen.
c **1374** CHAUCER *Boeth.* v. met. i. (1868) 151 It haþ hys propre causes of whiche causes þe cours vnforseyn and vnwar semiþ to han maked happe. *c* **1386** —— *Man of Law's T.* 427 Vp on thy glade day haue in thy mynde The vnwar wo or harm þat comth bihynde. *c* **1407** LYDG. *Reson & Sens.* 6181 They turne nat as doth a phane With vnwar wynde. **1430–40** —— *Bochas* VIII. 2192 Hih clymbyng vp haþ ofte an vnwar fall. **1509** HAWES *Past. Pleas.* xxxv. (Percy Soc.) 180 At a tyme unware my dette shal be dewe. *a* **1548** HALL *Chron., Edw. IV*, 218 b, Least.. the common people hereafter.. might.. excite an unware rebellion.
4. Unknown (*to* one).
1390 GOWER *Conf.* III. 44 Who dar do thing which love ne dar? To love is every lawe unwar. **1529** MORE *Dyaloge* II. Wks. 190/2 If there came amonge them vnware to you some spies. *a* **1536** WYATT *Wks.* (1913) I. 130 If I had suffred this to you unware, myn were the fawte, & you nothing to blame.
5. As *sb.* **a.** In phr. *on*, *in*, or *at unware*, unawares, unexpectedly.
c **1070** *O.E. Chron.* (MS. C) an. 1066, þa com Harold cyning.. into Tinan on unwaran. *c* **1100** *Ibid.* (MS. D) an. 1043, Man ȝerædde þan cynge þæt he rad.. to Wincestre on un-wær. **14..** *R. Gloucester's Chron.* 1966 (MS. Digby 205), This prince al in vnware toward hem þan drouȝ. **1561** NORTON & SACKV. *Gorboduc* II. ii, Shall I geue leasure by my fonde delayes To Ferrex to oppresse me at vnware?
b. Unwariness, carelessness.
1475 *Bk. Noblesse* (Roxb.) 27 By unware of theire purveiaunce [they] met withe the said Haniballe at certen streightes and narow places.
6. *adv.* **a.** Without warning; unexpectedly.
c **1100** *O.E. Chron.* (MS. D) an. 1050, Hi comon unwær on heom on ealne merȝen. *Ibid.* an. 1067. *c* **1386** CHAUCER *Frankl. T.* 1356 On thee Fortune I pleyne That vnwar wrapped hast me in thy cheyne. **1387** TREVISA *Higden* (Rolls) V. 219 He was bysette.. in a harde battaille þat fil uppon hym unwar [L. *inopino*] in þe Ester day. **1426** LYDG. *De Guil. Pilgr.* 13548 They sawh on komen ffaste by, Vnwar, with a gret company. **1454** *Paston Lett.* I. 282 William.. and Robert come uppon hem onwarre, and theruppon chasid hem. *c* **1510** MORE *Picus* Wks. 26 Death stealeth on full slily and unware. **1591** SPENSER *Virg. Gnat* Ded. 5 If that any Oedipus vnware Shall chaunce.. To reade the secrete of this riddle rare. **1613** W. BROWNE *Brit. Past.* I. iv. 498 Seeking the place of Charitie's resort, Unware I hapned on a Princes Court. **1616** J. LANE *Contn. Sqr.'s T.* VIII. 180 In each quarter, they prepare, to charge the campes sodainlie and vnware. **1875** MORRIS *Æneid* VI. 104 No face of any care, O maiden, can arise on me in any wise unware.
b. Unwarily, incautiously.
1545 TAVERNER *Erasm. Prov.* 55 Whiche stones so sone as a man vnware take vp, forthwith he receiueth a wound of the scorpion.

†**un'warely,** *adv. Obs.* [OE. *unwærlice* (UN-[1] 11), = ON. *úvarliga* (MSw. *ovarlika, -ligha*, MDa. *uvarlige*).]
1. Incautiously; without taking heed.
c **893** K. ÆLFRED *Oros.* IV. x. §9 Him com onȝen Hanno se cyning unwærlice, & þær ofslaȝen wearð. **971** *Blickl. Hom.* 57 Swa we þonne þa gastlican lare unwærlice ne sceolan anforlætan. *c* **1100** *O.E. Chron.* (MS. D) an. 1068, Æfter þisum coman Haroldes sunas.. into Taw-muðan, & þær unwærlice up-eodon. *a* **1300** *Cursor M.* 8894 Bot vn-warli sco sett hir don Apon þis ilk tre wit chance. **1398** TREVISA *Barth. De P.R.* XII. xiii. (Bodl. MS.), Vnwarliche he falleþ into a candel oþur into fuyre and.. brenneþ hym selfe. *a* **1425** tr. *Arderne's Treat. Fistula*, etc. 8 Discouer neuer the leche vnwarly the counsellez of his pacientez. *c* **1480** HENRYSON *Fables, Cock & Fox* 81 (Bann. MS.), Wn-warlye winkand, [the cock] walkit vp and doun, And syne to chant and craw he maid him boun. **1560** DAUS tr. *Sleidane's Comm.* 428 The soldiours of the garrison chaunced than to be some what vnwarely without the gates. **1592** LYLY *Gallathea* I. iii. 20, I shall.. vnwarelie blabbe out something by blushing at euery thing.

2. Without warning; unexpectedly.
c **1200** *Trin. Coll. Hom.* 191 A wiche wise he hem wile bisette þanne þe hem unwarliche his dintes gieð. *c* **1374** CHAUCER *Boeth.* I. met. i. (1868) 4 For elde is comen vnwarly vpon me. **1390** GOWER *Conf.* III. 252 So mai we knowe bothe tuo Unwarli what oure wyves do. **1412–20** LYDG. *Chron. Troy* IV. 2232 But vp-on hym, vnwarly, or he wende, Cam myȝty Troylus. **1447** BOKENHAM *Seyntys* (Roxb.) 22 Unwarly, er he wyst what it ment Wyth thy wycchecraft hys lyf was shent. **1514** PACE in Ellis *Orig. Lett.* Ser. III. I. 176 Thys post departide so hastyly and so unwarly that [etc.]. *a* **1542** WYATT in *Tottel's Misc.* (Arb.) 65 Vnwarely so was neuer no man caught..as I of late. **1596** SPENSER *F.Q.* IV. iii. 8 Yet one [stroke]..Through Cambels shoulder..vnwarely went.

un'wareness. Now *arch.* [UN-[1] 12. Cf. OE. *unwærness.*] Unwariness, incautiousness.
1388 WYCLIF *Prov.* xiv. 8 The vnwarnesse of foolis errith. *c* **1400** *Destr. Troy* 445 Þis vnwarnes of wit wrixlis hys mynd. **1436** *Pol. Poems* (Rolls) II. 190 Be ware of Walys, Criste Jhesu mutt us kepe, That it make not [us]..to wepe,..if it go his waye By unwarenesse. **1509** BARCLAY *Shyp of Folys* (1570) 25 But when he had obteyned great honours,..Then his vnwarenes caused him to wayle. **1544** BETHAM *Precepts War* II. xliv. Lj, The defaulte can not be escaped ne holpen, and al through thyne vnwarenesse. **1899** T. HARDY *Wessex Poems* 97 [She'll think] That my words were not unwareness, but deceit of her.

un'wares, *adv., sb.,* and *a.* Now *arch.* [Late OE. *unwæres, unwares,* f. *unwær* UNWARE *a.*]
A. *adv.* **1.** Without warning; unexpectedly, suddenly.
a **1122** *O.E. Chron.* (Laud MS.) an. 1004, Forþam þe hi unwares comon, & he fyrst næfde þæt he his fyrde ȝegadrian mihte. *Ibid.* an. 1093, Hine þa Rodbeard..unwæres besyrede & ofsloh. *c* **1400** *Found. St. Bartholomew's* 44 Here gladnes was turnyd yn-to waylyng;..vnwarys brake vp an violent tempest. **1512** *Helyas* in Thoms *Prose Rom.* (1828) III. 72 Makaire came wening to smite him al unwars. **1556** ROBINSON tr. *More's Utopia* To Rdr. (Arb.) 20 Yet haue I in this by chaunce, that on my side vnwares hath fallen, so..behaued myself, that [etc.]. **1615** CHAPMAN *Odyss.* IV. 112 One, murderously, Unwares, unseen, bereft my brother's life. **1642** H. MORE *Song of Soul* III. ii. xxvi, Unwares they find a sly still silver light. *c* **1745** A. SKIRVING *Tranent Muir* v, Menteith the great, where Hersell sate, Un'wares did ding her ower, man. **1805–6** CARY *Dante, Inf.* I. 52 When all unwares is gone, he inwardly Mourns, with heart-griping anguish. **1887** MORRIS *Odyssey* XII. 288 If all unwares upon us a blast of the wind should come.

†**b.** *his unwares,* without his knowledge; unforeseen by him. *Obs.*
1468 *Paston Lett.* II. 328 He hathe promysyd that there schall come non; and if ther do his unwarys, yowr answer may be thys.

†**c.** Const. *of,* or *to* (a person). *Obs.*
c **1510** in *Mem. Hen. VII* (Rolls) 286 So came he to the King's secret chamber door unwares of the King. **1532** TINDALE *Expos. Matt.* v. 20 Least anie vncleane thyng hadde touched theim unwaeres to all menne. **1625** BACON *Ps. xc.* ii, As a watch by night, that course doth keepe, And goes and comes vnwares to them that sleepe.

2. Unknowingly; without knowledge or intention; unintentionally.
13.. *Cursor M.* 2018 (Gött.), Bitid a day he was for-swonken, And vnwaris of win was dronken. **1526** TINDALE *Heb.* xiii. 2 Thereby have dyvers receaved angels into their houses vnwares. **1553** T. WILSON *Rhet.* 54 He did it not willyngly, but vnwares, and by chaunce. **1593** SHAKS. *3 Hen. VI,* II. v. 62 It is my Fathers face, Whom in this Conflict, I (vn-wares) haue kill'd. **1610** HOLLAND *Camden's Brit.* I. 260 Tirrell him seeing not Unwares him slew with dint of arrow shot. **1642** H. MORE *Song of Soul* II. I. ii. 35 But to return, Lest what we aim'd at we unwares omit.

B. *sb.* †**1.** *in unwares,* = A. 2. *Obs.*
a **1300** *Cursor M.* 2018 Bitid a day he was for suonken, And in vnwars o wyn was drunken.

†**2.** *at unwares,* = A. 1. *Obs.*
In common use *c* 1575–1610.
a **1547** SURREY *Æneis* IV. 90 Like to the..Hinde..which chasing with his dartes Aloofe, the shepheard smiteth at unwares, And leaves unwist in her the thirling head. **1576** LAMBARDE *Peramb. Kent* 208 The Danes..came freshly vpon the English Mariners at vnwares. **1581** STYWARD *Mart. Discipl.* I. 28 Hauing aduauntage of such as lie in scowte, who waite their time to assaile them at vnwares. **1606** G. W[OODCOCKE] *Hist. Ivstine* VI. 32 The Thebanes..began a new plot of cunning purposing..to set vpon them at vnwares. **1632** HOLLAND *Cyrupædia* 31 They that are skilfull to circumvent their enimies, can..put them first in a good conceit of themselves, and then surprize them at unwares.

C. *adj.* †**1.** Unwary, incautious. *Obs.*
1548 UDALL, etc. *Erasm. Par. Matt.* vii. 33 b, To the intent he maye poyson with hys heresye, them that be vnwares and negligent. **1565** STAPLETON tr. *Bede's Hist. Ch. Eng.* 27 Thinking to steale vppon them and so easely obtaine the victory ouer them, as vnwares and vnarmed.

†**2.** Unexpected, unlooked-for. *Obs.*
1548 UDALL, etc. *Erasm. Par. Matt.* xxvi. 26 b, As a thing vnwares & not looked for. *a* **1586** SIDNEY *Arcadia* III. x, The most..comfortable ayre, which an unwares sigh might bestow upon them.

†**un'waried,** *ppl. a. Sc. Obs.* [UN-[1] 8.] Not cursed.
1513 DOUGLAS *Æneid* II. xi. 108 So was I quyte miscareit, That noder god nor man I left wnwareit [*v.r.* unwaryit].

un'warily, *adv.* [UN-[1] 11. Cf. UNWARY *a.*]
†**1.** = UNWARELY *adv.* 2. *Obs.*
1568 GRAFTON *Chron.* II. 94 King Richard..drue him toward Aubeuyle.., and fell vpon the Frenchmen vnwarily. **1593** SHAKS. *John* v. vii. 63 The best part of my powre..Were in the Washes all vnwarily, Deuoured by the vn-expected flood.

2. Incautiously, imprudently; inadvertently.
1580 HOLLYBAND *Treas. Fr. Tong* s.v. *Bric,* When a word vnwarilie spoken, is taken for a confession. **1594** SPENSER *Amoretti* xvi, One day as I vnwarily did gaze On those fayre eyes. **1634** SIR T. HERBERT *Trav.* 213 One speckled fish the Seamen fed vpon vnwarily. **1670** CLARENDON *Contempl. Ps.* Tracts (1727) 382 Being unwarily ensnared by the vanities and levities of the world. **1712** ADDISON *Spect.* No. 435 ¶5 Any little Extravagance into which they are sometimes unwarily fallen. **1758** JOHNSON *Idler* No. 12 ¶1 We all either voluntarily or unwarily at least once an hour confess the truth. **1822** W. IRVING *Braceb. Hall* xvi, She had unwarily approached too near the bank. **1891** *Law Times* XCI. 32/1 Pointing out the pitfalls into which they unwarily fall.

un'wariness. [UN-[1] 12.] The quality of being unwary.
1544 BETHAM *Precepts War* I. xxiii. Cij, Leste by hys vnwarynesse, some mischaunce & damage do ensue. **1593** *Sidney's Arcadia* III. (1922) II. 58 Thisbes punishment for my rashe unwarinesse. **1649** J. TAYLOR *Great Exemplar* II. 123 He who is angry with a servants vnwariness. **1693** LOCKE *Educ.* 166 The inconsiderate heats and unwariness of Youth. **1711** ADDISON *Spect.* No. 256 ¶3 The same Temper of Mind..betrays us into such Slips and Un-warinesses as are not incident to Men of a contrary Disposition. **1870** MORRIS *Earthly Par.* III. 95 Thorgerd..would watch some gesture or some word to catch From his unwariness.

†**unwarl,** metathetic var. UNWRALL *v. Obs.*
1387 TREVISA *Higden* (Rolls) I. 9 As laborintus..haþ many..wyndynges and wrynkelynges þat wil nouȝt be vnwarled.

un'warlike, *a.* (UN-[1] 7 c.)
1590 SPENSER *F.Q.* III. xi. 44 With womanish teares, and with vnwarlike smarts, Priuily moystening his horrid cheek. **1597** BEARD *Theatre God's Judgem.* I. vii. 21 Ioshua and his poore people (though vnwarlike and vnacquainted with such actions). *c* **1654** WALLER *Panegyric to Ld. Protector* 78 He safely might old troops to battle lead, Against th' unwarlike Persian. **1697** DRYDEN *Virg. Georg.* II. 239 Cæsar, whose victorious Arms Avert unwarlike Indians from his Rome. **1739** GLOVER *London* 473 Thy sons..vainly deem'd that wealth Could..protect Unwarlike freedom. **1841** ELPHINSTONE *Hist. Ind.* I. 525 The inhabitants of the cultivated country were not unwarlike. **1878** STUBBS *Const. Hist.* III. xviii. 73 The only three unwarlike kings who had reigned since the Conquest.
Hence **un'warlikeness.**
1864 PUSEY *Lect. Daniel* v. 269 [Babylon's] deliberated unwarlikeness stands in strange contrast to its subsequent energy in rebelling.

un'warm, *a.* (UN-[1] 7.)
1694 *Lond. Gaz.* No. 2946/4 He has a Click in his walk when unwarm with one of his hinder Legs. **1824** COLERIDGE *Lett., Convers.,* etc. II. 170 Induced by the very fine but unwarm day.

un'warm, *v.* [UN-[2] 6 a.] *intr.* To grow cold.
1826 HOOD *Irish Schoolm.* xi, With horrid chill, each little heart unwarms.

un'warmed, *ppl. a.* (UN-[1] 8.)
a **1625** FLETCHER *Hum. Lieut.* IV. iii, What ever may compel..A Heart un-warm'd to melt in Loves desires. **1648** HEXHAM II. s.vv. *Ongewermt, Onverwermt.* **1716** POPE *Basset-Table* 76 But of what marble must that breast be form'd, To gaze on Basset, and remain unwarm'd? **1850** BRYANT *Journ. Life* 6 Broken gleams of brightness, here and there, Glance through, and leave unwarmed the death-like air. **1866** WHITTIER *Snow-Bound* 31 Unwarmed by any sunset light The gray day darkened into night. **1894** PARRY *Stud. Gt. Composers, Schubert* 230 The boys suffered..from living and working in unwarmed rooms.

un'warming, *ppl. a.* (UN-[1] 10.)
1736 A. HILL *Zara* I. i. 9 Monarchs, Like the Sun, Shine but in vain, unwarming, if unseen. **1794** BURNS *Lament* 6 With woe I nightly vigils keep, Beneath thy wan unwarming beam. **1800** CAMPBELL *Beech Tree's Petition* 4 Though bush or floweret never grow My dark unwarming shade below. *a* **1834** COLERIDGE *Lit. Rem.* (1836) I. 277 The pale unwarming light of hope. **1866** WHITTIER *Snow-Bound* 152 For such a world and such a night Most fitting that un-warming light.

un'warn, *v.* (UN-[2] 3.)
1612 in *10th Rep. Hist. MSS. Comm.* App. I. 574 The state being advertised of his purpose, thei have sent order to the Retorri of Padoa to unwarne that assembly. **1613** H. SAVILE in J. Hunter *Deanery of Doncaster* (1828) II. 137, I must unwarne you in halfe a sheete of paper..y[t] you loose not y[r] labour to come to me accordinge to my last entreatie.

un'warned, *ppl. a.*[1] and *adv.* [OE. *unwarnod* (UN-[1] 8). Cf. MDu. *ongewa(e)rnet,* OHG. *ungiwarnôt* (MHG. *ungewarnet,* G. *ungewarnt*), Sw. *ovarnad.*]
1. Not warned or forewarned.
c **1000** *Law Northumb. Priests* in Thorpe *Laws* II. 294 Ȝif preost oðerne unwarnode læte þæs, þe he wite, þæt him hearmian wille, ȝebete þæt. **1297** R. GLOUC. (Rolls) 1176 He let also arere Vpe þe water stronge hous, þat hii vnwarned nere. **1338** R. BRUNNE *Chron.* (1810) 13 Scho purueid þat poyson.. Brittrik hir lord..Unwarned drank þerof a drauht. **1382** WYCLIF *2 Macc.* viii. 6 And he aboue cummynge to castels and cytees, vnwarnyd [L. *improvisas*], brente hem. **1422** YONG tr. *Secreta Secret.* 175 Hit was not y-holde proesse ne chyualry to assayle a man vnwarnyd. **1456** *Cov. Leet Bk.* 295 Because no persones shuld be greued be these ordenaunces vnwarned, we ordeyn þat þes ordenaunces be radde to euery of þe seid officers. **1693** LOCKE *Educ.* (1699) 152 As un-experienced young Men are apt to do, if they are unwarn'd. **1715** RAMSAY *Great Eclipse* 23 When this strange darkness overshades the plains, 'Twill give an odd surprise t' unwarned swains. **1791** COWPER *Odyssey* I. 48 So now Ægisthus..him at his return Hath foully slain, though not unwarn'd by us, That he would surely perish. **1806** J. FOSTER *Ess.* (ed. 2) I. 39 Human beings, entering on life, with..unwarned carelessness of heart. **1823** MRS. HEMANS *Vespers Palermo* III. iv, He must not die unwarn'd. **1877** MRS. OLIPHANT *Makers Flor.* ix. 230 Wickedness unwarned and wrong unredressed were rampant.

b. Const. *of.*
c **1400** *Song of Roland* 314 [They] may..haue vs euyn as they lest, And we vn-warnyd þer-of in this tid. *c* **1425** WYNTOUN *Cron.* III. ii. 330 Vnwarnyt of thare spyise,..[he] went to bed. *c* **1470** HENRY *Wallace* VIII. 182 Wallace off Beik wnwarnyt than was he. **1513** DOUGLAS *Æneid* XII. x. 8 The Latynis.., Quhilk of hys cumming tho onwarnyt weyr.

†**2.** *adv.* Without warning or announcement.
c **1250** *Gen. & Ex.* 2682 Bi a lond weiȝe he wente riȝt, And broȝte vn-warnede on hem fiȝt. *c* **1325** *Song of Yesterday* 170 in *E.E.P.* (1862) 137 Sum men seiþ þat deþ is a þef, And al vnwarned wol on hym stele. **1407** *Exam. W. de Thorpe* (MS. Rawl. C 208) fol. 6 b, Þei ben sodeynli & vn-warned brouȝt forþ to ben apposid of aduersaries. *c* **1450** *Mirk's Festial* 39 Þe kyng hymselfe wold mony a tyme vnwarned come to þe mete.

3. Unannounced. Also with *-for.*
a **1400** *Minor Poems fr. Vernon MS.* 231/379 Kep vs..from temptaciun of þe fende, Of sodeyn deþ vnwarned to telle, And also from þe pyne of helle. **1641** BP. HALL *Serm.* Wks. 1837 V. 455 One..makes sudden embargoes, and un-warned inroads into the adjoining country. **1882** PIAZZI SMITH in *Nature* XXVI. 552 An interval quite long enough to allow of an unwarned-for cyclone having meanwhile entered the country.
Hence **un'warnedly** *adv.*
15.. *Exam. W. de Thorpe* in Foxe *A. & M.* (1563) 145/2 They be sodeinly and vnwarnedly brought forth to be apposed of their aduersaries.

†**un'warned,** *ppl. a.*[2] [UN-[1] 8 + WARN *v.*[3]] Not guarded or protected.
a **1240** *Sawles Warde* in *O.E. Hom.* I. 255 For nis his strengðe noht wurð bute hwer se he ifindeð eðeliche ant wake unwarnede of treowe bileaue.

un'warning, *vbl. sb.* [UN-[1] 13.] Absence of warning; †*of unwarning,* without premeditation.
13.. *Metr. Hom.* (MS. Ashm. 42) fol. 146 b, If wrethe come of vnwarnynge Late it haue in þe no dwellinge.

un'warning, *ppl. a.* [UN-[1] 10.] †Unguardedly.
1609 SKENE *Reg. Maj.* 115 Gif any man rydes vpon ane headstrong horse, and vnwarning runnes in ane water.

†**un'warnished,** *ppl. a. Obs.* [UN-[1] 8.]
a. Unprepared; unfurnished. **b.** Unwarned.
c **1425** WYNTOUN *Cron.* II. xvi. 1532 Vnwarnyst wer þai and vnarrayit. *c* **1430** *Pilgr. Lyf Manhode* II. cxxxii. (1869) 127 Iudas also was not vnwarnished of hem [*sc.* tools] whan he slowh the kyng jhesu. *Ibid.* IV. lix. 204 My fader, þat was put on þe cros, was not vnwar[ni]shed [F. *desgarny*] of swich a brest al were it nouht neede to shewe it. *c* **1475** *Cath. Angl.* 403/1 (A.), Vnwernyschit, *ex inspirato, ex inprouiso.* **1513** DOUGLAS *Æneid* XI. i. 46 Gif ye vnwarnist beis callit to the fycht. **1535** STEWART *Cron. Scot.* (Rolls) I. 221 Wn-warneist als tha war of ony wicht.
Hence †**un'warnishedly** *adv. Obs.*
1513 DOUGLAS *Æneid* VII. ix. 64 The landwart folkis..flokkis furth richt fast wnvarnystly. *Ibid.* IX. vi. 87.

un'warp, *v.* [UN-[2] 3.] *trans.* **a.** To uncoil, straighten out. **b.** To restore from being warped or prejudiced.
[In the transl. of *Maison Neuve's Gerileon* (1583) I. 64 b, app. a misprint for *vnwrap,* rhyming with *hap.*]
a **1659** OSBORNE *Essex's Death* Wks. 239 This had not been said, but..to unwarp their judgements..that may be drawn aside, by the goodness of Sir Henry Woottons parts. **1670** EVELYN *Sylva* (ed. 2) xxv. 122 When the bark is off, they unwarp it before the fire. **1733** HERVEY *Mem. Geo. II.* (1848) I. 257 The Queen herself was enough prejudiced too on this side, till Sir Robert Walpole unwarped her from it. **1802** LEYDEN *Mermaid* xii, Unwarp, unwind his oozy coils.

un'warped, *ppl. a.* [UN-[1] 8.] Not warped (*lit.* and *fig.*).
1744 THOMSON *Spring* 925 Honest Zeal unwarp'd by Party-Rage. **1759** ROBERTSON *Hist. Scotl.* III. Wks. 1813 I. 208 A heart unwarped by political interest. **1836** *Johnsoniana* 205 Totally devoid of all deceit,..and unwarped by any vice. **1855** KINGSLEY *Glaucus* 53 Long lines of tall elms,..their boughs unwarped by any blast.

un'warping, *ppl. a.* (UN-[1] 8.)
1828–32 WEBSTER (citing Dwight). **1902** *How to make Things* 26/2 So as to produce an unwarping flap.

un'warrant. (UN-[1] 12.)
1876 MRS. WHITNEY *Sights & Ins.* II. xi. 100 It would only be to reveal to me by the unwarrant, how strangely sweet the warrant might be.

unwarranta'bility. (UN-[1] 12.)
1836 G. S. FABER *Prim. Doctr. Election.* I. v. 57 The..delusive unwarrantability..of preferring any such prayer.

un'warrantable, *a.* (UN-[1] 7 b.)
1612 SELDEN *Illustr. Drayton's Poly-olb.* iv. 215 An un-warrantable report goes, that it was for his martial delivery of the King's daughter from the Dragon. **1642** FULLER *Holy & Prof. St.* III. xix. 203 If God bolts the doores..against him, he is not..to make his escape by unwarrantable courses. **1757** SMOLLETT *Reprisal* I. vii, An unwarrantable insult. **1783** BURKE *Rep. Aff. India* Wks. XI. 16 An unwarrantable extension or application of the municipal Law of England. **1847** H. ROGERS *Ess.* (1874) I. v. 218 Alterations of a most unwarrantable description. **1874** H. R. REYNOLDS *John Bapt.* ii. 83 It is an unwarrantable conjecture that the human intelligence is the highest form of mind.

b. *spec.* Of deer: (see quot. 1798).

1798 HEY *Lect. Div.* iv. 337 A Keeper in a King's Forest told me, certain Venison was unwarrantable; that is, could not be sent in return to the Warrants issued by the Officers of the Crown. **1888** *Daily News* 29 Oct. 6/8 Two young unwarrantable deer were shot at a previous hunt.

Hence **un'warrantableness**.

1633 T. ADAMS *Exp. 2 Peter* ii. 6 The unwarrantablenesse of their designes. *a* **1653** BINNING *Usef. Case Consc.* (1693) 7 The Conscience and Conviction of the Unwarrantableness of it for the want of Authority. **1713** E. CALAMY *Life Baxter* (ed. 2) xviii. 486 To prove the unwarrantableness of a Nations defending their Rights and Liberties. **1880** MUIRHEAD *Gaius* II. §104 *note*, Studemund's revision has also shown the unwarrantableness of the *endo mandatela*.

un'warrantably, *adv.* (UN-¹ 11.)

1634 CANNE *Necess. Separ.* 70 They found it.. unwarrantably to be used for the edifying of the body of Christ. **1682** C. IRVINE *Hist. Scott. Nomencl.* Ded. *vj, You, ..when they threw away their own Lives unwarrantably, bemoaned their madness. **1734** *Col. Rec. Pennsylv.* III. 561 Unwarrantably confined in a loathsome Goal. **1808** COLERIDGE *Lett.* (1895) 527 You have been, perhaps rather unwarrantably, severe on my morals. **1830** MACKINTOSH *Eth. Philos.* Wks. 1846 I. 198 Humility..has of late been unwarrantably used to signify that painful consciousness of inferiority which is the first stage of envy. **1890** *Spectator* 30 Aug. 262/1 His name is unwarrantably dragged into a controversy with which he has nothing to do.

un'warranted, *ppl. a.* (UN-¹ 8.)

Also, in recent use (1891-), *unwarrantedly* adv.

1577 tr. *Bullinger's Decades* 416 It doth sharpely rebuke.. him, for his unwarranted rashenesse. **1587** *Norton's Calvin's Inst.* IV. 490 *margin*, Extreame annointing [is] a forcelesse and vnwarranted ceremonie. **1633** HART *Diet of Diseased* Introd. 8 Ignorant and unwarranted Physitians. **1651** HOBBES *Leviathan* II. xxii. 116 The Assembly cannot Represent any man in things unwarranted by their Letters. **1748** MELMOTH *Fitzosborne Lett.* xlix. (1749) II. 36 Every eminent writer, without indulging any unwarranted licences, has a language which he derives from himself. **1817** JAS. MILL *Brit. India* II. IV. v. 216 The Directors.. condemned..the rapacious and unwarranted proceedings of their servants. **1862** LYTTON *Str. Story* II. 50, I should be utterly unwarranted in supposing that..they were insane.

†**un'warrayed**, *ppl. a.* [UN-¹ 8 + WARRAY *v.*] = next.

1411-12 HOCCLEVE *De Reg. Princ.* 2211 Castelx, by feith, dreden non assailynge, By feith, þe Citees standen vnwerreyed.

un'warred, *ppl. a.* [UN-¹ 8 + WAR *v.*¹] Unassailed, unattacked.

1390 GOWER *Conf.* I. 357 And so thei deden overal,..So that thei leften nothing stonde Unwerred, bot onliche Archade.

un'warren, *v.* (UN-² 6 b.)

a **1500** in Arnolde *Chron.* (1811) 19 That alle the wareyn of Stanes..be vnwareyned and vnforested for euermore.

un'wary, *a.* [UN-¹ 7.]

1. Not wary; unguarded, incautious: **a.** Of persons (or animals).

In Langland's *Piers Pl.* A. IV. 24 two manuscripts have 'vnwary', but the correct reading is doubtful.

1579 SPENSER *Sheph. Cal.* Dec. 10 O soueraigne Pan.., Which..Doest saue from mischiefe the vnwary sheepe. **1596** —— *F.Q.* VI. x. 3 T'entrap vnwary fooles in their eternall bales. **1598** FLORIO, *Disauedere*,..to be vnwarie, not to regard. **1624** GATAKER *Wife in Deed* 63 There is no woman almost so vnwise or vnwarie, that will buy an earthen pitcher,..but she will view it well first. **1651** HOBBES *Leviathan.* III. xxxvii. 234 The private actions of an ignorant, unwary man. *a* **1715** BURNET *Own Time* (1766) I. 263 These were his true principles tho' he had disguised them in order to catch un-wary readers. **1759** ROBERTSON *Hist. Scot.* VII. Wks. 1813 I. 513 No wonder pretexts so plausible should impose on the unwary queen. **1820** SCORESBY *Acc. Arctic Reg.* II. 178 The fish were numerous and unwary. **1896** W. K. LEASK *H. Miller* iv. 99 The unwary disputant emerged in a highly battered condition.

absol. **1637** EARL MONM. tr. *Malvezzi's Romulus & T.* 177 Tarquin is not to be ranked amongst the unwary. **1707** ATTERBURY *Serm.* (1726) II. 174 Its Emissaries are..very busy in Corners, to seduce the Unwary. **1848** MRS. JAMESON *Sacr. & Leg. Art* I. 70 With..flexile claws..stretched out to seize and entangle the unwary.

b. Of actions, conduct, the mind, etc.

1610 G. FLETCHER *Christ's Vict.* I. lxxxiv, With that the mightie thunder dropt away From Gods unwarie arme. **1643** SIR T. BROWNE *Relig. Med.* I. §1 Those principles my Parents instilled into my unwary understanding. **1697** DRYDEN *Virg. Georg.* II. 415 Sparkling fire, from hinds' unwary hands. **1703** ROWE *Ulysses* I. i, 'Tis rash, and savours of unwary Youth. **1747** HERVEY *Contempl. Night* (1748) II. 12 How often has an unwary glance, kindled a Fever of irregular Desire in our Hearts? **1803** GOUV. MORRIS in Sparks *Life & Writ.* (1832) III. 180 It is a most unwary step. **1867** LADY HERBERT *Cradle L.* v. 151 An unwary emptying of their..leather water-bottles before half the day was over.

†**2.** Unexpected. *Obs.*⁻¹

1590 SPENSER *F.Q.* I. xii. 25 All in the open hall amazed stood, At suddeinnesse of that vnwarie sight.

un'washable, *a.* and *sb.* (UN-¹ 7 b, 12.)

1839 MRS. KIRKLAND *New Home* xxxiv. 231 Those [ladies] who had unwarily sported silks and other unwashables, looked acid and uncomfortable.

un'washed, *ppl. a.* [UN-¹ 8, 8 c.]

1. Not washed; not cleaned by washing.

?*a* **1390** *Form of Cury* in Warner *Antiq. Culin.* (1791) 21 Take Hares,..and seeþ hem with þe blode unwaisshed in broth. *a* **1400** *Northern Passion* 346 Wasche fote and hand we pray þe, þat nokyn thyng vn wessched be. *c* **1440** *Promp. Parv.* 368/1 On-waschyd, *illotus.* **1543** TRAHERON *Vigo's Chirurg.* II. IV. ii. 66 It is good to laye vppon the place vnwashed woulle. **1605** R. F. *Dedekind's Sch. Slovenrie* (1904) 30 Then with your unwasht knife to cut your meate can breede no hurt. **1675** HAN. WOOLLEY *Gentlew. Comp.* 179 Take Mallows and Mercury unwasht. **1751** AKENSIDE *Ode to T. Edwards* vi, The sophist..With unwashed hands and lips profane. **1815** SCOTT *Guy M.* xliv, She proceeded with unwashed hands to arrange the stipulated bed-linen. **1890** *Anthony's Photogr. Bull.* III. 232 The emulsion is an unwashed one.

fig. **1607** B. JONSON *Volpone* Ep. ¶2, I..haue loathed the vse of such foule, and vn-wash'd Baudr'y. **1611** —— *Catiline* II. i, A slanderous, beastly, vnwash'd tongue. **1849** LEVER *Con Cregan* xv, Wickedness in its most unwashed state.

2. a. *spec.* Of persons: Not having washed; not usually washed or in a clean state.

1595 SHAKS. *John* IV. ii. 201 Another leane, vnwash'd Artificer, Cuts off his tale, and talkes of Arthurs death. *a* **1727** *Ballad on Quadrille* viii, The King of late..made, of many a Squire and Lord, An unwash'd Knight of Bath. **1781** COWPER *Table-t.* 152 Clubs..To which th' unwash'd artificer repairs. **1822** SCOTT *Nigel* Introd. Ep., All the unwashed artificers connected with literature. **1865** KINGSLEY *Herew.* xviii, Why should not beggars go unwashed? **1868** [T. WRIGHT] *Great Unwashed* Pref., Others who..are by the unwashed workers looked upon as swells.

b. *absol.* Those who are not usually in a clean state; the 'lower orders'. Freq. with *great.*

(*a*) **1830** LYTTON *Paul Clifford* I. p. xix, He is certainly a man who bathes and 'lives cleanly', (two especial charges preferred against him by Messrs. the Great Unwashed). **1833** HOOK *Parson's Dau.* II. 119 The 'fat and greasy', and the 'great unwashed,' bowed and smiled their best. **1850** THACKERAY *Pendennis* xxx, Gentlemen, there can be but little doubt that your ancestors were the Great Unwashed. **1868** [T. WRIGHT] *The Great Unwashed* Pref., Whenever.. I speak of working men, or the working classes, it is in the 'great-unwashed' sense.

(*b*) **1840** *Tipperary Constitution* 21 Aug. 2/3 The learned gentleman then briefly addressed the few *unwashed*, who were attracted to the scene. **1853** in Thornton *Amer. Gloss.* 920 A great portion of the unwashed, as well as the 'unterrified' left the hall. **1859** F. MAHONY *Rel. Father Prout* 417 The 'waters of instruction' are to be plentifully supplied to the unwashed.

3. Not washed *off* or *out.*

1628 MAY *Virg. Georg.* III. 94 Sweat unwash'd off [will] stick Vpon their new-shorne skins. **1842** MRS. BROWNING *Grk. Chr. Poets* ii. ¶ 6 His happy Athenian associations gave a colour, unwashed out by tears, to his mind and works.

Hence **un'washedness**.

1890 W. BOOTH *In Darkest England* II. ii. 106 You can have a thorough wash-up at last, after all these days of unwashedness. **1893** *Harper's Mag.* Jan. 186/2 Various perfumes of un-washedness and misery.

un'washen, *ppl. a.* Now *arch.* [OE. *unwæscen* (UN-¹ 8 b). Cf. (M)Du. *ongewasschen*, MLG., MHG., and G. *ungewaschen*, OHG. *ungiwasgan.*] = UNWASHED *ppl. a.* Also *fig.*

c **1000** *Sax. Leechd.* II. 108 Nim sigelhweorfan þa smalan unwæscene. *c* **1200** *Trin. Coll. Hom.* 57 On swinke, on unwasshen weden, on smerte swinginge. *a* **1225** *Ancr. R.* 82 Ful speche is as of lecherie, & of oðre fulðen þet unweaschene muðes spekeð oðer hwule. **13..** *E.E. Allit. P.* B. 34 For-þy hyȝ not to heuen in haterez to-torne, Ne in þe harlotez hod & handez vnwaschen. **1388** WYCLIF *Mark* vii. 2 Whanne thei hadden seen summe of hise disciplis ete breed with vn-waisschen hoondis. **1421-2** HOCCLEVE *Min. Poems* 116/182 Vnwasshen gold shall wasshe a-way that vice. *c* **1430** LYDG. *Min. Poems* (Percy Soc.) 256 Loth to ryse,..With unwassh handys reedy to dyneer. *c* **1450** *M.E. Med. Bk.* (Heinrich) 124 Take vnwasshe loombes wolle. **1526** TINDALE *Matt.* xv. 20 To eate with vnwesshen hondes defyleth nott a man. **1608** BP. HALL *Pharisaism & Christ* (1609) 642 The Pharise [finds fault] with vnwashen hands. **1648** J. BEAUMONT *Psyche* XVI. lxxvi, Prophane unwashen feet farr hence must be, This holy ground belongs to Sanctity. **1832** GEN. P. THOMPSON *Exerc.* (1842) II. 42 Whoever has brains so unwashen as to give up the guidance of himself..to any man. **1856** HAWTHORNE *Eng. Note-bks.* (1870) II. 44 The town..has a very sordid, grimy, shabby, unswept, unwashen aspect. **1870** MORRIS *Earthly Par.* II. III. 435 So from the lower end they came, ill clad, Houseless, unwashen, yet with faces glad.

un'wassailing, *ppl. a.* (UN-¹ 10.)

1826 LAMB *Lett.* (1886) II. 238 Old Christmas is a coming, to the confusion of Puritans,..Quakers, and that unwassailing crew.

un'wastable, *a.* (UN-¹ 7 b.)

1575 LANEHAM *Let.* (1871) 44 [Jupiter] seemz too be..in store of municion, vnwastabl. **1623** LISLE *Ælfric on O. & N. Test.* Pref. b 2 b, That vnwastable light,..which they had of old time shining, rather than burning in their sepulchers.

un'wasted, *ppl. a.* [UN-¹ 8.]

1. Not wasted or consumed.

1340-70 *Alex. & Dind.* 236 Hit scholde nouht lesen his liht..While þe weke & þe waxe vn-wasted lasteþ. *c* **1400** *Found. St. Bartholomew's* 61 What myghte falle to them.. that hastid with a desire to that place of vnwastid pite. **1561** T. NORTON *Calvin's Inst.* IV. xvii. 121 b, The fleshe of Christ is like a riche and vnwasted fountaine. **1625** DONNE *Serm.* 26 Whose meale and oyle God preserved unwasted. **1659** W. CHAMBERLAYNE *Pharon.* I. i. 178 So they preserve his name —A yet unwasted pyramid of fame. **1713** BLACKMORE *Creation* I. 671 Why have those rocks so long unwasted stood? **1826** MILMAN *Anne Boleyn* 35 Unwasted by the pains of earth, Thou didst bring forth the fair immortal birth. **1846** KEBLE *Lyra Innoc.* 73 Through the dim chinks of this decaying earth Gleams, ever and anon, th' unwasted fire.

2. Not laid waste; undevastated.

1570 FOXE *A. & M.* (ed. 2) I. 362 b/1 The kyng might haue had his land vnwasted, and his treasure vnconsumed. **1785** BURKE *Sp. Nabob of Arcot's Debts* Wks. IV. 276 Several of the petty princes of the most southerly of the unwasted provinces. **1836** THIRLWALL *Greece* II. xvi. 331 Tempted by the prospect of saving their still unwasted fields and dwellings.

3. Not impaired by waste.

1758 J. DALRYMPLE *Ess. Feudal Property* (ed. 2) 59 The lord came into the practice of giving a whole year's rent for the king's right of waste, and got the lands safe and unwasted to himself.

un'wasteful, *a.* (UN-¹ 7.)

1570 LEVINS *Manip.* 186 Vn-waystful, *frugalis.*

un'wastefully, *adv.* (UN-¹ 11.)

1618 BACON *Ord. Chancery* (1642) 15, 15 lines in every sheet thereof written orderly and unwastfully.

un'wasting, *ppl. a.* (UN-¹ 10.)

1387-8 T. USK *Test. Love* III. iii. (Skeat) l. 127 Wete, I doe brenne; unwasting, I langour and fade. **1722** POPE *Two Chorus's to 'Brutus'* ii. 41 Purest love's unwasting treasure. **1818** MILMAN *Samor* III. 222 Sleets From their unwasting granary barb their darts. **1846** KEBLE *Lyra Innoc.* 143 The Living Fount Of pure unwasting fire. **1868** LYNCH *Rivulet* CXXVIII. iv, 'Seek treasure of unwasting worth,' He said.

un'watched, *ppl. a.* (UN-¹ 8.)

c **1425** WYNTOUN *Cron.* IV. v. 499 All vnwachit sodanely Thai fell on sleip. **1548** UDALL *Erasm. Par. Luke* iv. 41 b, Of all these dooeth our enemie leaue not one thyng vn-watched, whereby he maie drawe vs to damnacion. **1593** DONNE *Sat.* ii. 98 But when he sells or changes land, he impaires His writings, and (unwatch'd) leaves out *ses heires.* **1602** SHAKS. *Ham.* III. i. 197 Madnesse in great Ones, must not vnwatch'd go. **1795** COLERIDGE *Silver Thimble* 49 And I from unwatch'd needle's erring point Had surely suffer'd on each finger-joint Those wounds. **1812** CRABBE *Tales* xi. 458 Rarely from town, nor then unwatch'd, he goes. **1850** TENNYSON *In Mem.* ci, Unwatch'd, the garden bough shall sway. **1870** BRYANT *Iliad* I. I. 30 Thou ever dost suspect me, Nor can I act unwatched.

un'watchful, *a.* (UN-¹ 7.)

1611 FLORIO, *Inuigilante*, vnuigilant, vnwatchfull. **1651** JER. TAYLOR *Serm. for Year* II. xx. 256 They are..incurious in their walking, unwatchfull in their circumstances. **1720** A. PETRIE *Rules Good Deportm.* (1877) 118 It is not discreet nor just in Ministers..to be unwatchfull over their Flock. *a* **1740** WATTS *Ess. Var. Subj.* (1795) 271 Every christian, even the weak and the unwatchful. *c* **1750** J. NELSON *Jrnl.* (1836) 40 You are more light and unwatchful than you used to be. **1805** WORDSW. *Prelude* II. 300, I..difference Perceived in things, where, to the unwatchful eye, No difference is. **1869** LOWELL *Cathedral* 213 Its once grim bulwarks, tamed to lovers' walks, Look down unwatchful on the sliding Eure.

Hence **un'watchfully** *adv.*, **-fulness**.

1611 FLORIO, *Inuigilanza*, vnwatchfulnesse. *a* **1658** DURHAM *Comm. Rev.* (1660) 181 There was much.. unwatchfulnesse and untendernesse in both these respects before God. **1682** W. ROGERS *Seventh Pt. Chr. Quaker* 78 No wonder if the High as well as the Low come to a Loss through their unwatchfulness. **1787** in *Jrnl. Friends Hist. Soc.* XIX. 92 Through unwatchfulness and the depravity of my heart. **1860** TRENCH *Serm. Westm. Abb.* xxxi. 354 Whether thou wilt be still watchful over thyself, when there is so much to persuade to unwatchfulness. **1867** RUSKIN *Time & Tide* (1872) 75 In summing the observation of past life not un-watchfully spent.

†**un'water**, *sb.* *Obs.*⁻⁰ (UN-¹ 12 b. Cf. UNWATERED *ppl. a.* 1 b.)

1611 COTGR., *Camelot plenier*, vnwater Chamlet.

un'water, *v.* [UN-² 4.] *trans.* To drain of water, to carry off water from; *spec.* in *Mining* (see b).

The word occurs as a mistranslation in: *a* **1300** *E.E. Psalter* lxxvii. 23 (E., H.), He smot þe stane, and watres outran, And scaldand unwatred [L. *inundaverunt*] þai ilkan.

a. 1642 C. VERMUYDEN *Disc. Fennes* 5 By these Out-falls the said Rivers and Lands unwater themselves. **1872** W. F. BUTLER *Gt. Lone Land* iv. (1875) 60 The St. Croix [river] unwatering the great tract of pine land. **1880** HAUGHTON *Phys. Geogr.* x. 192 The rivers of China unwater the whole eastern slope of the table-land.

b. 1769 SMEATON in Glynn *Treat. Power Water* (1853) 99 The first complete engine..at work..for draining or unwatering a lead mine. **1778** PRYCE *Min. Cornub.* 146 Many more valuable Lodes have been discovered, than those they were driving to unwater. **1865** J. T. F. TURNER *Slate Quarries* 22 The pits are unwatered by one engine pump. **1883** *Encycl. Brit.* XVI. 458/1 Siphons have been used for unwatering workings in special cases.

Hence **un'watering** *vbl. sb.*

1778 PRYCE *Min. Cornub.* 152 The innumerable Adits.. are of some importance to the unwatering of the Mines. **1909** R. H. RICHARDS *Text-bk. Ore Dressing* xv. 452 Unwatering devices are used to diminish the water carried by sand, or the sand carried by water. **1935** *Economist* 21 Dec. 1283/2 Their consulting engineer on the spot estimated that the unwatering of the old mine should commence about the beginning of February. **1976** *Northern Miner* (Toronto) 19 Aug. 13/3 Stage 1 included.. unwatering, sampling and surface and underground drilling.

un'watered, *ppl. a.* [UN-¹ 8. Cf. older Flem. *onghewaetert* (Kilian), Du. *ongewatert*, G. *ungewässert.*]

1. Not sprinkled, moistened, or artificially supplied with water.

c **1440** *Pallad. on Husb.* x. 111 Tyl hit be hard, vnwattred must hit [*sc.* land] be, Lest al the werk corrupte humydite. **1648** HEXHAM II, *Ongewatert*, Vnwatered, or Vnsprinckled. **1731** POPE *Ep. Burlington* 125 Un-watered see the drooping sea-horse mourn. **1899** *Daily News* 12 June 7/5 To facilitate cavalry charges the main thoroughfares remained unwatered.

b. Of dress materials: (see WATER *v.* 9).

1535 in *Archaeol.* IX. 248 A long gowne of unwatered chamblette. **1583** *Rates Custome ho.* B ij, Chamlets watered and vnwatred. **1648** HEXHAM II, *Ongewatert Kamelot*, Vnwatered Chamlot. **1706** *Lond. Gaz.* No. 4189/4 Coarse unwatered Camblets. **1750** LADY JANE COKE *Lett.* (1899) 61 I have given half-a guinea for an unwatered tabby.

†**2.** Not soaked or steeped in water. *Obs.*

1511 FABYAN *Will* in *Chron.* (1811) p. v, Than I will that the said .xxiiij. peces of fleshe be altered unto saltfyche or stokfyshe, unwatered and unsodeyn. **1570** LEVINS *Manip.* 51 Vnwatred, *immaceratus.* **1648** HEXHAM II, *Ongeweyckt*, Not laid in water, or Vnwatered, as Harberdine, &c.

3. Not mixed with water; undiluted.

1562 TURNER *Herbal* II. 35 b, Entre into a bath, and drynke vnwatered wyne after. **1576** GASCOIGNE *Steele Gl.* 582 Augustus Cæsar..seldome dranke his wine unwatered. **1648** HEXHAM II, *Ongewaterden wijn*, Vnwatered wine, or Vn-mixed with water. **1870** EMERSON *Soc. & Solit.*, *Farming*, The farmer has a great health;..his milk at least, is un-watered. **1887** BOWEN *Æneid* v. 78 Twain huge flagons of wine unwatered.

b. *Finance.* (See WATERED *ppl. a.* 4 c.)

1893 *Westm. Gaz.* 29 June 6/1 The 25 per cent. represents 1,250 per cent. on the original unwatered capital, or over £687,000 on a real capital of £55,000.

4. Of land, a district, etc.: Not provided with a natural supply of water; waterless. Also in fig. context.

1600 SURFLET *Countrie Farm* VI. vii. 740 In hot, drie, and vnwatered places. **1794** A. YOUNG *Trav.* (ed. 2) II. 152 The country (that I saw) is poor and unwatered, in the Milanese. **1794** VANCOUVER *Agric. Cambridge* 55 The grass..is chiefly inferior to that.·.which grows..upon unwatered ground. **1828** J. MONTGOMERY *Tombs Fathers* Wks. 1841 IV. 178 Kedron's unwater'd brook is dumb. **1860** PUSEY *Min. Proph.* 14 The soul of the sinner is..unfruitful;..for it is..unwatered by the Fountain of living waters. **1890** 'R. BOLDREWOOD' *Col. Reformer* (1891) 100 The unwatered region away from the river.

un'watery, *a.* [OE. *unwæteriȝ* (UN-^{1} 7).] Not supplied with or containing water.

c **1000** *Ags. Gosp.* Luke xi. 24 He gæð þurh unwæterie stowa, reste secende. *a* **1300** *E.E. Psalter* cvi. 4 Thei erreden in wildernesse, in vnwatri place. **1382** WYCLIF *Ps.* lxxvii. 40 In to wrathe thei to-striden hym in vnwatri place.

1739 C. WESLEY *Hymns* 222 Divinely led the Favourites pass Th' Unwatry Deep, and emptied Sea. **1872** BROWNING *Fifine* cii, How..The solid surface-shield was outcome..Of simple dew at work to save itself amid The unwatery force around. **1877** BLACKIE *Wise Men* 67 Age to youth May sooner pass than from unwatery crust Be birth of water.

un'wavering, *ppl. a.* (UN-^{1} 10.)

1570 LEVINS *Manip.* 137 Vnwauering, *immotus.* **1667** H. MORE *Disc. Faith* (1713) 579 Forasmuch as Faith..is nothing but an unwavering assent to some Doctrine [etc.]. **1721** STRYPE *Eccl. Mem.* II. II. i. 253 To shew how unwavering she continued in her formerly declared purpose. **1739** C. & J. WESLEY *Hymns* 12 With Steps unwav'ring, undismay'd Give me in all thy Paths to tread. **1801** COLERIDGE *Triumph Loyalty* I. 330 All objects there will teach me Unwavering Love. **1856** FROUDE *Hist. Eng.* (1858) I. 409 An unwavering pursuit of a single policy. **1884** A. R. PENNINGTON *Wiclif* III. 120 He was as unwavering in his tone as in his reply to the 'motley doctor'.

Hence **un'waveringly** *adv.*

1830 COLERIDGE *Constit. Ch. & State* I The mark, to which my convictions and wishes have..unwaveringly pointed. **1872** TENNYSON *Gareth & Lynette* 139 When the Queen..Found her son's will unwaveringly one, She answer'd craftily.

un'waving, *ppl. a.* (UN-^{1} 10.)

1706 J. WEAVER *Orchesography* 28 Examples of waving and unwaving Positions, where the Feet turn and return both on the same side. **1818** MILMAN *Samor* VII. 650 The yellow crown Of the unwaving forest. **1835** LYTTON *Rienzi* x. viii, Not a breeze stirred the dark cypress and unwaving pine.

†**un'wax**, *v.*^{1} *Obs.* [UN-^{2} 7.] *intr.* To grow or become less; to decrease. Also *fig.*

13.. *Coer de L.* 2844 Thus began our folk unwexe, And dyede for hungyr and for woo. *c* **1400** *Pepysian Gosp. Harmony* (1922) 14 For it bihoued nedes þat Jesus wex & þat he vnwex. **14..** in Maskell *Mon. Rit.* (1847) III. 353 Of a man it is seid, the more he wexith the more he unwexith.

un'wax, *v.*^{2} [UN-^{2} 4.] *trans.* To deprive of wax; to remove the wax from.

1817 KIRBY & SP. *Entomol.* II. 148 On the seventh day the part covering the head and trunk of the young female [bee], if I may so speak, is almost entirely unwaxed.

un'waxed, *ppl. a.* [UN-^{1} 8 + WAX *v.*^{2}] Not treated with wax.

c **1410** *Master of Game* (MS. Digby 182) xxi, Oþer meane hornes vnwexed beth goode ynogh for hem [*sc.* wood-men]. [**1775** ASH.] **1832** G. R. PORTER *Porcelain & Gl.* xv. 313 The unwaxed under-side of the glass. **1886** *Pall Mall G.* 6 April 1/1 Two rather steep.., uncarpeted, and unwaxed, staircases.

†**un'way**. *Obs.* [UN-^{1} 4 b. Cf. MDu. *onwech* (Du. *onweg*), MLG. *unwech*, MHG. *unwec* (G. *unweg*), MDa. *uvej.*] A place without ways.

a **1340** HAMPOLE *Ps.* cvi. 40 He made þaim to erre in vnway [L. *in invio*] & noght in way.

†**un'wayed**, *a.* *Obs.* [UN-^{1} 9. Cf. MDu. *ongheweget*, MDa. *uvejet.*]

1. Not provided with ways or roads.

In both passages rendering L. (*terra*) *invia*.

1382 WYCLIF *Ezek.* xv. 8 Whanne Y shal..ȝyue the loond vnwaied and desolat. —— *Hos.* ii. 3 Y shal putte hir as a wildrenesse, and ordeyne hir as a lond vnweyed.

2. Of horses: Not accustomed to ways or roads; hence, restive, intractable.

1607 MARKHAM *Cavel.* IV. 15 If the horse be yong and vn-wayed. *c* **1640** [? SHIRLEY] *Capt. Underwit* II. ii, She kicks and flings out like a Colt unwayed. *a* **1642** SUCKLING *Let.* Wks. (1648) 82 As Colts that are unway'd, and will not go at all.

un'weakened, *ppl. a.* (UN-^{1} 8.)

1648 HEXHAM II, *Ongekrenckt*, vnweakned, or vn-enfeebled. **1662** BOYLE *Def. Doct. Air* 74 The unweakned pressure of the outward Air. **1828** CARLYLE *Misc.* (1840) I. 201 His heart, though torn, is yet unweakened. **1856** RUSKIN *Mod. Paint.* IV. v. xix. §22 The unweakened and active intellects of Van Eyck and Albert Durer. **1871** KENNEDY *Publ. Sch. Lat. Gram.* (1874) 35 Numerous words keep their root-vowel *a* unweakened in the second member of their compounds.

un'weal. [UN-^{1} 12.] Unhappiness; distress.

a **1300** *Cursor M.* 5714 To-quils was of israel þe folk ledd wit mikel vn-wel [*v.r.* vn-wele]. *a* **1850** ROSSETTI *Dante & Circle* I. (1874) 39 Since thou alone hast made my heart to feel This sadness and unweal.

†**un'wealful**, *a.* *Obs.* [UN-^{1} 7.] Unhappy; causing misfortune or unhappiness.

1412-20 LYDG. *Chron. Troy* II. 4234 Vnwelful woman, disturber of oure pes, þou haste vs brouȝt in meschef & in were. *Ibid.* 8112 To Grekis pleinly þis ryvaille So mortal was & so infortunat, So vnwelful and disconsolat.

†**un'wealfulness**. *Obs.* [UN-^{1} 12. Cf. prec.] = next.

a **1555** J. PHILPOT tr. *Curio's Def. Christ's Ch.* (1842) 387, I perceive thou art more happier than all these, Calistus; but it shameth me nothing to be accounted among them, and to be partaker of this unwellefulness with them.

†**un'wealsomeness**. *Obs.*$^{-1}$ [UN-^{1} 12.] Unhappiness.

1382 WYCLIF *Ps.* xiii. 3 To-brosing and vn-welsumnesse [L. *infelicitas*] in the weies of hem, and the weie of þes thei knewen not.

†**un'wealth**. *Obs. rare.* [UN-^{1} 12.] Lack of prosperity.

a **1300** *Cursor M.* 28697 þou do him vnder-stand alsua Hu lang þat adam was in wa, And þai þat of his body sprang, Hu þair vnwelth þam lasted lang. *c* **1412** HOCCLEVE *De Reg. Princ.* (Roxb.) 32 To live..ever after in sorwe & unwelthe.

un'wealthiness. (UN-^{1} 12. Cf. next.)

1886 *Pall Mall G.* 23 Oct. 14/1, I have continued in the same state of un-wealthiness as formerly.

un'wealthy, *a.* (UN-^{1} 7.)

c **1412** HOCCLEVE *De Reg. Princ.* 1287 He sparith hem that vnwelthy heer ben. **1582** STANYHURST *Æneis* II. (Arb.) 46 My father vnwelthy mee sent..hither. **1809-14** WORDSW. *Excurs.* v. 132 An unwealthy mountain Benefice. **1876** MORRIS *Æneid* VIII. 105 The senate poor of that unwealthy folk Cast incense there. **1895** P. WHITE *King's Diary* iii, An unwealthy Tory peer and his pompous belongings.

†**un'wealy**, *a.* *Obs.*$^{-1}$ [UN-^{1} 7.] Poor; unwealthy.

a **1300** *E.E. Psalter* lxxviii. 8 (E.), For þat un-weli [*v.r.* poure; L. *pauperes*] for to se Swiþe mikel made are we.

un'weaned, *ppl. a.* Also 6 -waynde, -wain'd. [UN-^{1} 8.] Not weaned; †immature.

1581 STUDLEY tr. *Seneca, Herc. Œt.* I. 191 b, Coulde I brooke it Toxeus, to see thy death with woe? That wert vnwaynde in yeares, and eake in pits vnpaysde. **1596** FITZ-GEFFREY *Sir F. Drake* (1881) 30 Blinde with affection, ignorant of truthe, Vnwain'd from self-love, never at a staye. **1607** CHAPMAN *Bussy d' Ambois* IV. i. 17 Or still-unwean'd sweet Moon-calues with white faces. **1799** SHERIDAN *Pizarro* I. i. 13 In peace as gentle as the unweaned lamb. **1807** COGAN *Treatise on Passions* (1813) II. 310 An unweaned affection for peculiarities which have no other claim upon us. **1844** H. STEPHENS *Bk. Farm* III. 1123 The lambs remain unweaned, until they wean themselves. **1871** WHYTE-MELVILLE *Sarchedon* I. 3 Like sucking fawn and unweaned child.

un'weapon, *v.* [UN-^{2} 4. Cf. MDu. *ontwapenen*, *-wapen* (Du. *-wapenen*), MHG. *entwâpenen*, *-wâpen*, *-wâfen* (G. *-waffnen*).] *trans.* To deprive of a weapon or weapons.

a **1586** SIDNEY *Arcadia* III. xxviii, Hee was no more amazed with his being vnweaponed, then with the suddainnesse thereof. **1611** FLORIO, *Disarmare*, to disarme, to vn-weapon. *a* **1646** J. GREGORY *Posthuma, Assyrian Mon.* (1650) 248 One night a Plague of Mice came upon him, and unweaponed his souldiers, by devouring their Harness-ties of Leather. **1662** HIBBERT *Body Divinity* II. 106 He beats down our enemies before us, unweaponing them.

un'weaponed, *ppl. a.* [UN-^{1} 8. Cf. OE. *unȝewǣpnod*, MDu. *ongewapent* (Du. *-wapend*), MHG. *ungewâfent*, *-wâpent* (G. *ungewaffnet*, *-wappnet*).] Not equipped with or bearing a weapon or weapons; unarmed.

c **1200** *Trin. Coll. Hom.* 191 Ðus flited þe fiend wið alle men;..and þo ben alle unwepnede þe ne hauen mid hwan hie hem werien. *c* **1205** LAY. 5654 þeo cnihtes weoren vnwepned, þa þe wæne heo wes ȝeueðe. *c* **1425** *Eng. Conq. Irel.* 22 So as we bene..well y-wepned,..ne dout no man þat such vnwepned rascayll any power haw ows to wyth-stond. **1513-14** *Act 5 Hen. VIII*, c. 6, Wheras they [*sc.* surgeons]..have ben entreatid as Herawdes of Armes aswell in batelles and feldes as other places ther for to stond unharnesed and unwapenned. **1553** BALE *Vocacyon* 28 b, The cruell murtherers..cowardly slewe them all vnarmed & vn-weaponed. *c* **1618** RALEIGH *Disc. War* (1850) 2 Instruments of much advantage against unweaponed men. **1642** VICARS *God in Mount* 66 Being all unweaponed, and coming onely in a fair and unoffensive manner. **1823** *Monthly Mag.* LV. 409 He hastes his armour off to throw, And stands un-weapon'd. **1874** SPURGEON *Treas. Dav.* IV. 371 Not by the aid of others, but by his own unweaponed hand his marvellous conquests have been achieved.

fig. **1549** COVERDALE, etc. *Erasm. Par. 2 Cor.* 57 b, As lowe and weake as ye thinke vs, yet are we not vnweaponed, nor without strength to suppresse the aduersaries of the gospel. **1594** MARLOWE & NASHE *Dido* I. ii, Our hands are not prepar'd to lawles spoyle..: Such force is farre from our vnweaponed thoughts. **1624** MASSINGER *Bondman* IV. iv, Hee's more a slaue, then Fortune Or Miserie can make me, that insults Vpon vnweapon'd Innocence. *a* **1628** F. GREVIL *Cælica* xx, Since unweaponed care makes men forlorne, Let me first make your Dogge an Vnicorne. **1859** G. WILSON *Mem. E. Forbes* iv. (1861) 131 An accuracy [with the stethoscope]..such as the experience of forty years had often failed to bring to the unweaponed physician.

un'wearable, *a.* (UN-^{1} 7 b.)

[**1775** ASH.] **1846** WORCESTER (citing Grant). **1906** *Daily Chron.* 22 June 4/2 The merry crowd..laughs for the fifteenth time at an unwearable joke.

unweari'bility. (UN-^{1} 12. Cf. next.)

1853 HAWTHORNE *Eng. Note-bks.* (1883) I. 464 In instance of Charles Dickens's unweariability.

un'weariable, *a.* [UN-^{1} 7 b.] Incapable of being or becoming wearied or tired; indefatigable, unremitting.

App. disused in the 18th cent., and reintroduced in the 19th, when it came into common use.

a. Of persons or things.

1561 T. NORTON *Calvin's Inst.* I. 47 An enemie that is..in diligence and celeritie vnweriable. **1594** HOOKER *Eccl. Pol.* I. iv. §1 Desire to resemble him in goodnes maketh them vnweariable. **1608** BP. HALL *Char. Virtues & V.* II. (1614) 259 If the others eare were as vnweariable as his tongue. **1626** —— *Contempl.*, *O.T.* XXI. vi, He is vnweariable with our requests. **1694** in R. H. Story *W. Carstares* (1874) 234 A great fervency in expression, and unweariable lungs, are mistaken by the poor ignorant for zeal and piety.

[**1775** ASH.] **1810** SOUTHEY *Kehama* XVI. xix, That unweariable foe, With will relentless follows still. **1854** THOREAU *Walden* (1863) 253 So long-winded was he and so unweariable. **1899** MACKAIL *W. Morris* II. 217 Through all that period, his sister was his..unweariable nurse.

b. Of qualities, conditions, or actions.

1571 GOLDING *Calvin on Ps.* xxv. 5 He hung uppon God with unweeriable constancie. **1594** HOOKER *Eccl. Pol.* Pref. 17 An vnweariable desire of receyuing instruction. **1627** J. CARTER *Plain Expos.* 5 It requireth vnweariable labour and paines all our life long. **1651** GATAKER in Fuller *Abel Rediv.* (1867) I. 242 An insatiable ardour and unweariable endeavour of continual..hearing or reading.

1813 SHELLEY *Q. Mab* VII. 198 Resolved to wage unweariable war With my almighty Tyrant. *a* **1842** ARNOLD *Hist. Rome* (1845) III. 141 The Numidians..chased them with unweariable speed. **1880** MISS BIRD *Japan* II. 260 Their unweariable good nature.

Hence **un'weariableness**.

1647 TRAPP *Comm. Acts* vi. 5 Famous for their unweariableness in God's work. **1652** W. BROUGH *Sacr. Princ.* 64 Why such unweariablnesse to have my will?

un'weariably, *adv.* [UN-^{1} 11. Cf. prec.] Without wearying; indefatigably.

1612 T. TAYLOR *Comm. Titus* i. 8 Hereby thou art like God, he sparseth abroad, he vnweariably giveth good, to good and bad. **1643** E. SYMMONS *Loyal Subjects Belief* 65 Those graces and gifts..which in his service you have..most faithfully and unweariably expended. **1856** HAWTHORNE *Eng. Note-bks.* (1870) II. 40 A variety of mountain outlines that I could have studied unweariably. **1879** H. W. WARREN *Recr. Astron.* xii. 258 Rendered apparent, static, and unweariably operative.

un'wearied, *ppl. a.* [UN-^{1} 8. Cf. OE. *unȝewērigod.*] Of persons, things, etc.: Not wearied, tired, or tired out; also, never becoming weary; indefatigable.

a **1240** *Sawles Warde* in *O.E. Hom.* I. 261 þe oðre..iblescede gastes þe beoð a biuore godd..ant singeð a un-werȝed. *a* **1400-50** *Alexander* 3622 þe pepill..ware petusly woundid Of Olifauntis..; All at vnweried a-way wynnes in þe stoundis Durst neuir his face to his faes eft on fold bide. *a* **1548** HALL *Chron.*, *Hen. VI*, 141 b, The vnweried chieftain & manly warrior. **1596** SHAKS. *Merch. V.* III. ii. 296 The best condition'd and vnwearied spirit In doing curtesies. **1632** LITHGOW *Trav.* I. 27 They intreated me to come vp in the Caroch, but I..would not, replying..my body [was] vnwearied. *a* **1684** LEIGHTON *Comm. 1 Pet.* ii. (1693) 472 The Soul that is most active, and unwearied in Sin. **1707** *Curios. in Husb. & Gard.* 313 We might spend whole Years unwearied in the Examination of them. **1791** COWPER *Iliad* XVIII. 293 The sun, Unwearied minister of light. **1816** WILSON *City of Plague* II. ii. 79 The fairy..On plumes unwearied..floateth still. **1818** MILMAN *Samor* VIII. 95 If yet this heart unwearied may bear on. **1871** JOWETT *Plato* II. 10 The unwearied and disinterested seeker after truth.

b. Of qualities, actions, conditions, etc.: Marked by absence of abatement; unremitting.

1561 T. NORTON *Calvin's Inst.* I. 8 b, He..cesseth not to shewe hys vnweried bountifulnesse vpon miserable sinners. **1594** HOOKER *Eccl. Pol.* I. iii. §2 [The sun] as a Giant doth runne his vnwearied course. **1625** GODWIN *Moses & Aaron* (1641) A 2 b, An unwearied assiduity in perusing those sacred Oracles. **1678** VAUGHAN *Thalia Rediv.* 64 The Wisdom of the Bee, And her unwearied Industry. **1704** J. TRAPP *Abra-Mulé* II. i. 367 Had not my Care, My vigilant, unweary'd Diligence Still balk'd..the Visier's Conduct. **1782** MISS BURNEY *Cecilia* II. iii, The ludicrous mixture of groups kept her attention unwearied. **1820** SCOTT *Monast.* vi, The active and unwearied exercise of his sharp and piercing intellect. **1861** TRENCH *Comm. Ep. Churches Asia* 69 The unwearied activity of Christ in his Church. **1876**

BANCROFT *Hist. U.S.* II. xxx. 259 Bond..languidly thanked him for his faithful and unwearied exertions.

un'weariedly, *adv.* (f. prec., or UN-¹ 11.)
1653 BAXTER *Chr. Concord* 99 Shall it be said that Separatists will..lay out all their pains unweariedly to divide the Church..? **1673** HICKERINGILL *Greg. F. Greyb.* 149 The importunities of those..unweariedly troublesome spirits. *a* **1715** BURNET *Own Time* (1766) I. 253 He was.. unweariedly active to very little purpose. **1750** CHESTERF. *Lett.* (1774) II. 50 Absolute perfection is..unattainable, but ..a man of parts may be unweariedly aiming at..it. **1818** BENTHAM *Ch. Eng.* Introd. 54 The epithet so hardily and unweariedly bestowed upon it. **1860** FROUDE *Hist. Eng.* VI. 395 He worked unweariedly in the service of the public. **1893** J. PULSFORD *Loyalty to Christ* II. 135 Unweariedly intent on bringing Her earth-born children into Her glorious House.

un'weariedness. (f. as prec., or UN-¹ 12.)
1617 HIERON *Wks.* II. 101 Yet for largenesse,..for vnweariednesse, the louing kindnesse of the Lord doth farre exceed it. **1642** S. ASHE *Best Refuge* 35 Their frequency and unweariednesse in Prayer. **1702** E. CALAMY *Life & Times Baxter* i. 8 He prosecuted all his Studies with Unweariedness and Delight. **1837** CARLYLE *Misc. Ess.* (1840) V. 123 Working therein long years, with a filial unweariedness. **1884** FAIRBAIRN *Catholicism* (1899) 42 Unweariedness in well-doing.

un'wearily, *adv.* [f. UNWEARY *a.*, or UN-¹ 11.] Unweariedly.
1434 MISYN *Mending Life* 111 If þa forsake seculer occupacions & erandis, & rise vnwerily to þinke & pray. **1435** —— *Fire of Love* 82 Vnwerily it byrnys þo þingis to fulfil þat it seys & knawes plesynge to god.

un'weariness. (UN-¹ 12.)
1611 FLORIO, *Infaticabilita*, vnwearinesse. **1906** *Daily Chron.* 8 May 5/5 A young white kid, symbolical of unweariness.

un'wearisomeness. (UN-¹ 12.)
1649 EARL MONM. tr. *Senault's Use Passions* (1671) 312 The Labourer..endeavoreth to overcome the sterility of the soil by the unwearisomeness of his labour.

un'weary, *a.* [OE. *unwériȝ* (UN-¹ 7).] Not weary (*of*); free from weariness; unwearied.
c **893** K. ÆLFRED *Oros.* v. xi. §4 þæt mon þæt fæsten bræce, & on fuhte dæȝes & nihtes, simle an legie æfter oþerre un-weriȝ. *c* **1000** *Sax. Leechd.* I. 76 Drince þonne on niht nistiȝ, þreo full fulle; þonne bið he sona unweriȝ. *a* **1340** HAMPOLE *Psalter* xvii. 37 þou has gifen me vnwery brennynge to wirke þe goed and put away slawnes. *c* **1374** CHAUCER *Troylus* I. 410 If harme agree me wher-to pleyne I þanne? I not ne whi vnweri þat I feynte. *c* **1425** *Orolog. Sapient.* ii. 20 in *Anglia* X. 339 In to whomme angeles desyrene to loke and beholde with vnwerye felicite. *c* **1475** *Cath. Angl.* 414/2 (A.), Vn Wery, *jndefessus.* **1606** SYLVESTER *Du Bartas* II. iv. *Magnificence* 168 With unweary limb, Wade thorough Foords, and over Chanels swim. **1659** EEDES *Christ's Exalt.* Ep. Ded., He set himself to the serious study of the Hebrew tongue when he was 40 years old, and such was his unweary industry, that [etc.]. **1818** MILMAN *Samor* IX. 183 If thine eternal thunderbolts are yet Unweary of their function dire. **1844** MRS. BROWNING *Patience taught* 8 Ocean girds Unslackened the dry land, savannah-swards Unweary sweep. **1859** *Habits of Gd. Society* vii. 248 You must not obtrude your unweary mirth at a visit of condolence.

†**un'weary**, *v.* [UN-² 4 b.] *trans.* (and *refl.*). To restore from weariness; to refresh or rest.
Chiefly in translations of Fr. (*se*) *delasser*.
1530 PALSGR. 769/1, I unwerye,..*je delasse.* **1580** HOLLYBAND *Treas. Fr. Tong, Se delasser*, to vnweary himselfe. **1650** EARL MONM. tr. *Senault's Man bec. Guilty* 175 Are not Allegories impertinent? when to un-weary men's minds, they abuse them. **1652** LOVEDAY tr. *Calprenede's Cassandra* I. 43 Having taken a house in the Towne, we there unwearied ourselves for some dayes. **1687** ETHEREDGE *Let.* Wks. (1888) p. xxv, Not being able to prevail with him to stay a day and unweary himself.
absol. *a* **1698** TEMPLE *Health & Long Life* Wks. 1720 I. 281 Bathing..unwearies and refreshes more than any thing, after too great Labour and Exercise.
b. *refl.* To relieve or ease (oneself) *of* something.
1633 EARL MANCH. *Al Mondo* (1636) 161 A good man.. by this surplus of paine, unwearies himselfe of paine.

un'wearying, *ppl. a.* [UN-¹ 10.]
1. That does not grow or become weary; unremitting, untiring.
1600 J. MELVILL *Autob. & Diary* (Wodrow Soc.) 463 An unweireing and constant occupatioun in doctrine, prayer, and praise. **1762** FALCONER *Shipwr.* I. 22 She o'er the spacious flood..Unwearying wafted her commercial store. **1824** MISS L. M. HAWKINS *Annaline* III. 1 Her unwearying attendant..sought for it. **1843** CARLYLE *Past & Pr.* IV. vii, The Heavens, unwearying in their bounty, do send other souls into this world. **1856** KANE *Arct. Expl.* I. xiv. 158 [The dogs] walk in straight and curved lines with anxious and unwearying perseverance.
2. Not causing or producing weariness.
1799 W. TAYLOR in Robberds *Mem.* (1843) I. 297 The unwearied and unwearying eloquence of Mackintosh. **1858** HAWTHORNE *Fr. & It. Note-bks.* (1872) I. 11 Stately edifices prolonging themselves in unwearying magnificence and beauty. **1886** *Athenæum* 24 April 548/3 Success presently waited..upon the unwearying charms of her person and conversation.

un'wearyingly, *adv.* (UN-¹ 11, or f. prec.)
1835 BECKFORD *Recoll.* 86 Scientific researches unwearyingly pursued in calm and studious retirement. **1866** MEREDITH *Vittoria* xxix, The lamp burned unwearyingly. **1889** *Sat. Rev.* 23 March 349/1 The Carlyles themselves were unwearyingly kind to her.

†**un'weather.** *Obs.* [OE. *unweder* (UN-¹ 4 b), = OFris. *unweder* (NFris. *unwedder*), (M)Du. *onweder*, LG. *unweder* (*-wêr*, *-wär*), MHG. *unweter* (G. *unwetter*), ON. *úveðr* (MSw. *ovädher*, Sw. *oväder*, (M)Da. *uvejr*, Norw. dial. *uveer*, etc.).] Bad, rough, or stormy weather.
c **950** *Lindisf. Gosp.* Luke viii. 24 He..ȝeðreade þæt wind & hroeðnise *vel* unweoder ðæs wætres. *c* **1000** *Rule of Chrodegang* vi, Sylle man..ælcum breðer fif punda ȝewihte wines, ȝif þa unwedru his ne forwyrnað. *c* **1250** *Gen. & Ex.* 3058 Moyses ȝede vt, helde up is hond, And al ðis vnweder ðor atwond. [**1658** PHILLIPS, *Unweather*, (Sax.) a storm or tempest. Hence in Bailey (1721).]

un'weathered, *ppl. a.* [UN-¹ 8.] Of rocks, etc.: Not exposed to, unaffected by, the action of the weather or atmosphere.
[**1775** ASH.] **1843** PORTLOCK *Geol.* 527 The more compact variety [of rock], where unweathered, is distinctly porphyritic. **1860** TYNDALL *Glac.* II. xx. 338 In no case was he able to discover these fissures in the sound unweathered ice. **1884** *Leisure Hour* Aug. 493/2 Extensive quarries from which fresh, unweathered material could be procured.

un'weave, *v.* [UN-² 3, 7. Cf. (M)Du. *ontweven*, OHG. *antwepan* (MHG. and G. *entweben*).]
1. *trans.* To take out of a woven, intertwined, or entangled state or condition; esp. to unravel or undo (a woven fabric).
Freq. in fig. context, and in allusion to the story of Penelope (*Odyssey* II. 96-105).
1542 UDALL *Erasm. Apoph.* 63 b, Then used she this policie, to unweave in the night as much werke, as she had made up in the daye before. **1565** COOPER, *Texta soluere*, to vnweaue that one hath wrought. **1592** SHAKS. *Ven. & Ad.* 991 Now she [*sc.* love] unweaves the web that she has wrought; Adonis lives. *a* **1637** B. JONSON *Celebration of Charis* ix. 50 Nor do wrongs, nor wrongs receive, Nor tie knots, nor knots un-weave. **1640** G. SANDYS *Chr. Pass.* I. 81 That I should thus unweave the web of Fate. **1859** TENNYSON *Enid* 1114 She..pluck'd the grass,..And into many a listless annulet, Now over, now beneath her marriage ring, Wove and unwove it. **1875** JOWETT *Plato* (ed. 2) I. 461 Weaving instead of un-weaving her Penelope's web.
absol. **1631** BRATHWAIT *Eng. Gentlew.* 49 Chuse rather with Penelope to weaue and vnweaue, than to giue Idlenesse the least leaue.
fig. *a* **1625** FLETCHER *Love's Cure* v. iii, Custom..You did unweave, and had the power to charm A new creation in me. **1634** HEYWOOD *Witches of Lanc.* IV. G 4 b, Vnweave my age O time, to my first thread. **1820** KEATS *Lamia* II. 237 Philosophy will clip an Angel's wings,..Empty the haunted air, and gnomed mine—Unweave a rainbow. **1849** DE QUINCEY *Eng. Mail Coach* Wks. 1862 IV. 349 Light unwove the mazes of darkness.
b. To untwine (the fingers).
1863 BARING-GOULD *Iceland* 271 Several of the men came up, and endeavoured to unweave the fingers [from the sword]. **1897** —— *Guavas* xviii, She plaited the fingers together and unwove them, to again re-plait them.
†**2.** To make clear by exposition; to expose, disclose. Also *absol.* *Obs.*
1642 H. MORE *Song of Soul* II. ii. III. xxv, They're mixt, soild and contaminate, But truth doth clear, unweave, and simplifie. **1647** R. STAPYLTON *Juvenal* 48 Dædalus, who flying viewed the whole world (if we believe the poets), or that (if we unweave their fables) made discoveries of the world by sea with his winged sailes.
3. *intr.* To become disentangled. In quot. *fig.*
1798 SOTHEBY tr. *Wieland's Oberon* IV. lviii, How wonderfully strange my fate unweaves!
Hence **un'weaving** *vbl. sb.*
1706 STEVENS *Sp. Dict.*, *Desteximiento*, unweaving. **1847** HELPS *Friends in C.* I. vi. 89 The sleep-inducing weavings and unweavings of political combination. **1893** J. PULSFORD *Loyalty to Christ* II. 112 What unweavings and siftings and cleansings we shall have to undergo!

un'web, *v.* [UN-² 3.] *trans.* To unweave. (In quot. *fig.*)
1882 P. HOOD *Cromwell* iii. 98 Eliot was engaged in unwebbing the abominations and the intricacies of the Court.

un'webbed, *ppl. a.* (UN-¹ 8.)
1768 PENNANT *Brit. Zool.* II. 492 The feathers..long, slender and unwebbed. **1768** —— in *Phil. Trans.* LVIII. 92 The shafts [of the feathers are] broad and very thin; the vanes unwebbed. **1804** BEWICK *Brit. Birds* II. 179 Its feathers appear all unwebbed, and look like silky hair. **1872** COUES *N. Amer. Birds* 219 Toes all of the same length, unwebbed at base.

un'wed, *ppl. a.* [UN-¹ 8 b.] = next.
In quot. 1562 perhaps f. UN-² 8.
1513 DOUGLAS *Æneid* VI. v. 27 Small childrin, and ȝoung damicellis vnwed. **1562** J. HEYWOOD *Prov. & Epigr.* (1867) 191, We wold wed the sooner.., showyng plaine, That I should the sooner be vnwed againe. **1590** SHAKS. *Com. Err.* II. i. 26 This seruitude makes you to keepe vnwed. **1790** MRS. WHEELER *Westmoreland Dial.* (1821) 47 Be a gud lass, ..en keep the oel unwed en tac can. **1816** BYRON *Ch. Har.* III. lv, Though unwed, That love was pure. **1835** MILMAN *Nala & Damayanti*, etc. 91 Unwed wert thou in virgin bloom. **1873** SYMONDS *Grk. Poets* xi. 353 Timas, whom unwed Persephone locked in her darksome bed. **1967** E. S. GARDNER *Case of Queenly Contestant* (1973) viii. 103, I would keep on working as long as I was able. Then I would go to a home for unwed mothers and have my child. **1981** R. MCCLURE *Coram's Children* x. 124 In 1764 forty-nine children were reclaimed by their parents, often unwed mothers.

un'wedded, *ppl. a.* [UN-¹ 8.]
1. Of persons: Not wedded; unmarried. Also *absol.*
a **1230** *Hali Meid.* 13 (Titus MS.), þa ilke sari wrecches, þat i þat ilke fule wurðinge, unweddede, walewio. **1303** R. BRUNNE *Handl. Synne* 7352 þe fyrst [manner of lechery] ys fornycacyoun, Whan two vnweddyd haue mysdon. **1377** LANGL. *P. Pl.* B. xx. 111 Al manere men wedded & vnwedded. *c* **1430** *Syr Gener.* (Roxb.) 8699 Haue ye noo drede That my ladie vnwedded is? **1484** CAXTON *Fables of Æsop* VI. xvi, To them [*sc.* the aged] is better to be vnwedded than to be euer in trouble with an euyl wyf. **1577** tr. *Bullinger's Decades* 231/2 If a woman play the harlotte with an vnwedded man. *c* **1590** MARLOWE *Faustus* i, So shall the subiects of euery element Be alwaies seruiceable to vs three; ..Sometimes like women, or vnwedded maides. **1718** ROWE tr. *Lucan* IX. 1134 Unwedded Pallas lent a Sister's aid [to Perseus]. **1791** COWPER *Odyssey* XI. 44 Brides, youths unwedded, seniors.., And girls. **1825** SCOTT *Betrothed* xix, A richly-dowered maiden, unwedded, and unlikely to wed. **1877** E. R. CONDER *Basis Faith* v. 225 A large proportion of the..most vigorous in body and mind die unwedded or childless.
transf. *c* **1792** COWPER *Death of Damon* 89 My rambling vines, unwedded to the trees, Bear shrivell'd grapes. **1811** LAMB *Elia* I. *Bachelor's Complaint*, Cerasia..sent away a dish of Morellas..to her husband,..and recommended a plate of less extraordinary gooseberries to my unwedded palate. **1837** LYTTON *Athens* I. 377 Pisistratus conducted himself towards the fair Cæsyra with a chastity.. unwelcome to her affection... The unwedded wife communicated the mortifying secret to her mother.
2. Free from, unattended by, marriage.
1804 *Europ. Mag.* XLV. 192/2 'Twixt wedded and unwedded loving Great is the difference, they say. **1822** MILMAN *Martyr of Antioch* 101 The saintly quiet of the unwedded state. **1882** FARRAR *Early Chr.* II. 114 Expressions which..convey no such exaltation of the unwedded life.
Hence **un'weddedness**.
1830 CARLYLE *Misc.* (1840) II. 368 It is not always our duty to marry; but it is always our duty to abide by right;.. not to avoid unweddedness by untruthfulness.

un'wedge, *v.* [UN-² 3.] *trans.* (and *refl.*). To free from a wedged condition. Also *fig.*
1611 FLORIO, *Discugnare*, to vnwedge. **1622** MABBE tr. *Aleman's Guzman d'Alf.* II. 88 He fell off from me by degrees, by a little and a little vnwedging himselfe from mee. **1680** *Exact Jrnl. Siege Tangier* 12 Nine guns..which he had Unspiked and Unwedged.

un'wedgeable, *a.* [UN-¹ 7 b.] Incapable of being split by wedges; uncleavable.
In mod. use only in echoes of the Shaks. passage, with a tendency towards the wider meaning 'very hard, stubborn, or difficult to deal with': freq. used by Carlyle.
1603 SHAKS. *Meas. for M.* II. ii. 116 Mercifull heauen, Thou rather with thy sharpe and sulpherous bolt Splits the vn-wedgable and gnarled Oke, Then the soft Mertill. [**1802–12** BENTHAM *Ration. Judic. Evid.* (1827) V. 521 Men, like oaks, are..'gnarled and unwedgeable;' facts, like deals, are fissile.] **1837** CARLYLE *Misc.* (1840) V. 135 He, being unwedgeable, has remained in antiquarian cabinets. **1880** *Spectator* 5 June 722 Propositions which lie buried in these gnarled and unwedgeable periods.

†**un'wedset**, *ppl. a.* *Obs.* [UN-¹ 8 b. Cf. WADSET *v.*] Not put in pledge.
1480 *Acta Dom. Conc.* (1839) 70/2 Land..fre vnset for termes or for male and vnwedset.

un'weeded, *ppl. a.* [UN-¹ 8. Cf. Du. *ongewied.*]
1. Of ground: Not cleared of weeds. Also *fig.*
In later use freq. in fig. context in echoes of quot. 1602.
1602 SHAKS. *Ham.* I. ii. 135 Oh fie, fie, 'tis an vnweeded Garden That growes to Seed; Things rank, and grosse in Nature Possesse it meerely. **1624** USSHER *Serm.* 48 The field is the same, but weeded now, unweeded then. **1796** MORSE *Amer. Geog.* I. 654 The human mind, like an unweeded garden, has been suffered to shoot up in wild disorder. **1817** COLERIDGE *Lay Serm.* 19 The evils of a rank and un-weeded Press. **1824** J. TELFER *Border Ball.* 32 The wood it was dern, unweeded, and wild. **1842** *New Monthly Mag.* I. 400 All the rashness, insolence, and brutality of an un-weeded and newly-raised constabulary.
2. Not cleared away or rooted up as weeds. In quots. *fig.*
1626 JACKSON *Creed* VIII. v. §1 All men by nature (that is from the unweeded relikes of our first parents' pride) are prone to over-value themselves. **1645** HAMMOND *Death-bed Repent.* 29 The..hospitable soyle, contrary both to the thorny and stony ground, the one when the cares of the world are unweeded, unmortifyed, the other when [etc.].

unweel, Sc. var. of UNWELL *a.*

un'weened, *ppl. a.* Now *arch.* [UN-¹ 8. Cf. OE. *unge-*, *unwéned.*] Not thought of or imagined; unexpected.
c **1374** CHAUCER *Boeth.* IV. pr. vi. (1868) 139 What so euer þou mayst seen þat is don in þis world vnhoped or vnwened. **1813** HOGG *Queen's Wake* 85 The night unweened had passed away, And dawning ushered in the day. **1894** F. S. ELLIS *Reynard the Fox* 194 When one weens no thing at all, The thing unweened will straight befal.

†**un'weeningly**, *adv.* *Sc.* *Obs.* [UN-¹ 11.] Unexpectedly.
c **1375** *Sc. Leg. Saints* vi. (*Thomas*) 463 Quhen men venis beste þat þai sal lyfe in lykine.., þan cumys ded vnwenandly.

un'weeping, *ppl. a.* (UN-¹ 10.)
1598 DRAYTON *Heroical Ep.* Poems (1605) 55 b, We hold no obijts, no sad exequies Vpon the death-daies of vnweeping eies. **1783** JUSTAMOND tr. *Raynal's Hist. Indies* II. 321 Behold if thou can'st, with an unweeping eye the man who enriches us condemned to perish with misery.

†**un'weeting**, *vbl. sb. Obs.*$^{-1}$ [UN-^{1} 12.] Ignorance.

14.. *Wycliffite Bible* Acts iii. 17 (New Coll. MS. 67), Now, breþeren, I woot þat bi þe vnwetinge [L. *per ignorantiam*] ȝe diden.

un'weeting, *ppl. a.* Now *arch.* [UN-^{1} 10, 5 d. Cf. MDu. *onwetende* (Du. *onwetend*), MLG. *unwetende*, Sw. *ovetande*, and UNWITTING *ppl. a.*]

1. = UNWITTING *ppl. a.* 1.

1303 R. BRUNNE *Handl. Synne* 11253 ȝyf þou vnwetyng hyt haue, hyt helpeþ þe nat so moche to saue As ȝyf þou asked hyt by name. **1387–8** T. USK *Test. Love* III. vii. (Skeat) l. 66 Who that..coveyteth thing unknowe, unweting he shal be quyted. **1590** SPENSER *F.Q.* I. x. 66 She..in an heaped furrow did thee hyde, Where thee a Ploughman all vnweeting fond. **1634** MILTON *Comus* 539 To inveigle and invite th' unwary sense Of them that pass unweeting by the way. **1667** —— *P.L.* x. 335 Hee..saw his guileful act By Eve, though all unweeting, seconded Upon her Husband. *a* **1718** PARNELL *Fairy Tale* 62 'Twas grief..Which made my steps unweeting rove Amid the nightly dew. **1768** C. SHAW *Monody* vi, In vain—Perverse, still on th' unweeting head 'Tis thine thy vengeful darts to shed. **1803** W. S. ROSE *Amadis* 82 All who to his bow'rs unweeting came. **1855** SINGLETON *Virgil* I. 42 When Through the unweeting mountains here and there Rove living creatures. **1878** T. HARDY *Ret. Native* II. iv, This unweeting manner of performance is the true ring by which..a fossilized survival may be known from a spurious reproduction.

b. Const. *of.* = UNWITTING *ppl. a.* 1 b.

1591 SPENSER *Teares Muses* 491 Then wandreth he in error and in doubt, Vnweeting of the danger hee is in. *a* **1592** T. WATSON *Tears of Fancy* xlix, His hounds vnweeting of his sodaine change, Did hale and pull him downe. **1717** E. FENTON *Homer's Odyssey* 91 Me, O King, The Minister of adverse Fate malign'd, Unweeting of Mishap. **1735** SOMERVILLE *Chase* III. 280 Joyous he scents The rich Repast, un-weeting of the Death That lurks within. **1793** COLERIDGE *The Rose* 13 When unweeting of the guile Awoke the prisoner sweet. **1812** CARY *Dante, Purg.* III. 91 They stopp'd:..the same did all Who follow'd, though unweeting of the cause. **1870** BRYANT *Iliad* XVIII. II. 225 Two shepherds walked with them,..all unweeting of the evil nigh.

c. With objective clause. = UNWITTING *ppl. a.* 1 c.

1590 SPENSER *F.Q.* III. x. 22 He..stood aloofe, vnweeting what to doe. **1621** QUARLES *Div. Poems, Esther* Introd., A few from many they extracted forth,..Vnweeting where the most reward belongs. **1805–6** CARY *Dante, Inf.* XXX. 139, I..all the while Excused me, though unweeting that I did. **1814** WORDSW. *Lines written in copy of Excurs.* 9 He conned the new-born Lay..; Unweeting that to him the joy was given. **1864** BRYANT *Cloud on Way* 39 Haply, leaning o'er the pilgrim, all unweeting thou art near, Thou mayst whisper words..of comfort in his ear.

†**2.** In absolute constructions. *Obs.* = UNWITTING *ppl. a.* 2.

c **1386** CHAUCER *Can. Yeom. T.* 767 (Camb. MS.), He slyly tok it out, this cursede heyne, Vnwetynge this prest of this false craft. *c* **1400** *Destr. Troy* 8594 Ector..Went out wightly, vnwetyng his fader. *c* **1400** LOVE *Bonavent. Mirr.* (1908) 74 After that his parens weren gone homwarde, he dwelled stille there in Jerusalem, hem vnwetynge. *c* **1470** HARDING *Chron.* XVIII. vi, He helde Estrylde as his loue and leman, Therof his wife vnwetyng. *c* **1483** *Chron. London* (1827) 123 Oweyn..hadde iij or iiij^{or} chyldren be here, unwetyng the comoun peple tyl that sche were ded.

ellipt. **1398** TREVISA *Barth. De P.R.* XVII. xii. (Bodl. MS.), Wormod..exciteþ þe smel after slepe ȝif it is ileide vnweting vnder þe heed.

3. = UNWITTING *ppl. a.* 3.

(*a*) **1387–8** T. USK *Test. Love* I. vii. (Skeat) l. 110 Some of hem token money for thy chambre,..unwetinge of the renter. *a* **1400** *Partonope* 8931 In-to a chambre..Vnwetyng of any wight they hym lede. **1454** *Paston Lett.* I. 287 God wote my wif delyvered all, myn unwetyng. *c* **1483** *Chron. London* (1827) 131 The fals contryved evidents that weren sealed be old tyme with the comoun seall, unwetynge of them.

(*b*) **1579** FENTON *Guicciard.* III. 168 From whence,..vnweeting to the Duke,..he went to Coma. **1590** SPENSER *F.Q.* III. iii. 57 She resolu'd, vnweeting to her Sire, Aduent'rous knighthood on her selfe to don.

†**4.** Ignorant, uninformed, unlearned. *Obs.*

1483 CAXTON *Gold. Leg.* 86/2 She said..he shold abyde wythout and not come in as he that were not worthy but unwetyng. **1706** J. PHILIPS *Cerealia* 70 Have I so long..my lore Communicated to th' unweeting hind?

5. = UNWITTING *ppl. a.* 4. *rare*$^{-1}$.

1793 BURNS '*The last time*' ii, The unweeting groan, the bursting sigh, Betray the guilty lover.

un'weetingly, *adv.* Now *arch.* [UN-^{1} 11. Cf. prec. and UNWITTINGLY *adv.*] Unknowingly; unconsciously; †without it being known.

a **1400–50** *Alexander* 134 Furþe..withouten fole he passis his way, Vn-wetandly to any wee. **14..** *Chaucer's Pardoner's T.* 24 (Corpus MS.), Lord vnkyndely lay by his doughtres tuo vnwetyngly, So drunke he was. *a* **1542** WYATT '*And if*' Wks. 1913 I. 176 To frame all wel, I ame content That it were done unwetingly. **1596** SPENSER *F.Q.* v. viii. 15, I..found them faring so, As by the way vnweetingly I strayd. **1671** MILTON *Samson* 1680 They only set on sport and play Unweetingly importun'd Thir own destruction to come speedy upon them. **1792** D. LLOYD *Voy. Life* 30 Prone to the lap of lewd Licentiousness The high-flown rabble throngs unweetingly. **1802** J. BAILLIE *1st Pt. Ethwald* IV. iv, Woggarwolfe..once before unweetingly has served us. *a* **1849** H. COLERIDGE *Ess.* (1851) II. 157 Shakspeare..assumes the utmost pomp of diction on these occasions, complying, unweetingly, with Aristotle's precepts.

un'weft, *ppl. a.* [UN-^{1} 8 b. Cf. Sw. *oväfd.*] Unwoven.

1865 MRS. WHITNEY *Gayworthys* xliii, Every filament unweft shall be gathered from..its entanglement.

un'weighed, *ppl. a.* [UN-^{1} 8. Cf. Da. *uveiet*, Sw. *ovägd.*]

1. Not weighed.

1481–90 *Howard Househ. Bks.* (Roxb.) 348, lix. bales of Gene wode unweyed. **1535** COVERDALE *1 Kings* vii. 47 Salomon let all the apparell be vnweyed [**1539** vnwayed, **1611** vnweighed] because the metall was so moch. **1555** *Inv. Ch. Goods* (Surtees) 153, xlv sowes of leade unwaied. **1697** WALSH *Life Virgil* ¶ 7 in *Dryden's Virgil*, Massy Plate, unweigh'd to a great value.

transf. **1852** BAILEY *Festus* (ed. 5) 171 Such we hold Thy sanctity of nature, and unweighed Largess of light.

2. Not deliberately considered; not pondered before utterance or expression; hasty, inconsiderate.

a **1586** SIDNEY *Arcadia* II. xxii, Disgraced with wandring eyes, and vnwaied speeches. **1598** SHAKS. *Merry W.* II. i. 23 What an vnwaied Behauiour hath this Flemish drunkard pickt..out of my conuersation! **1697** COLLIER *Ess. Mor. Subj.* I. 111 If an Emperour throws out an unweigh'd Sentence, must we be governed by it? **1725** POPE *Odyss.* I. 84 Daughter! what words have pass'd thy lips unweigh'd? **1828–32** WEBSTER s.v., To leave arguments or testimony unweighed. **1850** J. F. COOPER *Ways of Hour* II. 241 Much unmerited misery is..entailed by such unweighed assertions and opinions.

†**un'weighing**, *ppl. a. Obs.*$^{-1}$ [UN-^{1} 10. Cf. prec. 2.] Thoughtless; inconsiderate.

1603 SHAKS. *Meas. for M.* III. ii. 147 A very superficiall, ignorant, vnweighing fellow.

un'weighted, *ppl. a.* (UN-^{1} 8; cf. WEIGHTED *ppl. a.* 2 c.)

1883 ANNIE THOMAS *Mod. Housewife* 23 My heart was unweighted, my brow unclouded, by a single household perplexity. **1898** *Daily News* 9 April 6/3 Put to the test of touch, the silks proclaim themselves to be pure and unweighted. **1927** BOWLEY & STAMP *National Income 1924* 23 The unweighted average is obtained by adding up the percentages and dividing by the number of them. **1966** *Rep. Comm. Inquiry Univ. Oxf.* II. 260 (*heading*) Student/staff ratios (unweighted) for certain universities. **1977** *Econ. & Social Rev.* (Dublin) VIII. 146 In cases where an unweighted regression applied to all twenty-six Irish counties would yield inefficient estimates, re-estimating the equation with Dublin omitted is in practice equivalent to applying a full correction for heteroscedasticity.

un'weighty, *a.* (UN-^{1} 7. Cf. G. *unwichtig*, Da. *uvigtig.*)

1621 LADY M. WROTH *Urania* 458 Speaking of a friuolous and vnwaighty businesse God knowes. *a* **1674** CLARENDON *Surv. Leviath.* (1676) 29 The instances and arguments given by him are very unweighty.

†**un'weirded**, *ppl. a. Sc. Obs.*$^{-1}$ [UN-^{1} 4 b, 9.] Subject to adverse fate; ill-fated.

c **1590** MONTGOMERIE *Sonnets* xlviii. 12 Thou art vnweirdit, I a woful wrech.

un'welcome, *sb.* [UN-^{1} 12.]

1. Unwelcomeness.

1603 FLORIO *Montaigne* III. iii. 495 Gentlye to beare..the importunitie of yeares, the vnwellcome of wrinckles, and such like minde-troubling accidents. **1654** WHITLOCK *Zootomia* 33 Since I must quarter the forces of two Garrisons, it will be prudence to dissemble the unwelcome of the one, and silently to welcome the other.

2. Lack of welcome; a cold reception. *rare.*

1912 D. H. LAWRENCE *Trespasser* i. 2 A stranger..was assured of his unwelcome.

un'welcome, *a.* [UN-^{1} 7. Cf. med.Du. *onwillecome* (Du. *onwelkom*), G. *unwillkommen*, Da. *uvel-*, Sw. *ovälkommen.*] Not welcome or acceptable; unpleasing.

Rare before *c* 1590. In freq. use from *c* 1665.

c **1325** in *Pol. Songs* (Camden) 330 His meyne is unwelcome, comen hii erliche or late. **13..** *E.E. Allit. P.* B. 49 If vn-welcum he were to a worþlych prynce. *a* **1586** SIDNEY *Arcadia* III. xvi, Unwelcome curtesie is a degree of injury. **1591** SHAKS. *Two Gent.* II. iv. 81, I thinke 'tis no vn-welcome newes to you. **1624** FLETCHER *Wife for Moneth* II. i, Death is unwelcome never, Unless it be to tortur'd minds..That make their own Hells. **1661** BOYLE *Style of Script.*, To Rdr. A 7 b, There can as little be an unwelcomer as an unjuster Complement plac'd upon me, than [etc.]. **1670** R. MONTAGU in *Buccleuch MSS.* (Hist. MSS. Comm.) I. 469 Your Lordship's letter..was much unwelcomer to me than any I yet received from you. **1728** ELIZA HEYWOOD tr. *Mme. de Gomez's Belle A.* (1732) II. 174 The Importunities of his unwelcome Tenderness. **1751** JOHNSON *Rambler* No. 153 ¶ 1 He that has an unwelcome message to deliver. **1817** SCOTT *Harold* III. vii, He whose daring lay Hath dared unwelcome truths to say. **1840** BARHAM *Ingol. Leg.* I. *H. Harris* (1905) 126 The unwelcome news of his grandson's dangerous state. **1869** TOZER *Highl. Turkey* II. 171 A name of ridicule..unwelcome to their ears.

un'welcome, *v.* [UN-^{1} 14.] *trans.* To receive uncordially.

1890 *Atlantic* April 550/2 [The] half-concealed ridicule with which the poor old fellow's sallies are liable to be welcomed—or unwelcomed.

un'welcomed, *ppl. a.* (UN-^{1} 8.)

1548 W. PATTEN *Exped. Scotl.* F 1 b, Yf they had kept pointment..they shoulde neyther haue bene vnwelcumed nor vnlooked for. **1590** SPENSER *F.Q.* III. vii. 8 At last..She askt..what vnwonted path Had guided her, vnwelcomed, vnsought? **1614** LITHGOW *Trav.* P 1 b, The vnwelcomed Arabs inuironed, and inuaded vs with a storme of arrowes. **1651** VAUGHAN *Olor Iscanus, Boet.* I. met. i. 20 Life adds unwelcom'd length unto my dayes. **1768** HOOLE *Cyrus* III. 36 Doom'd again to banishment, Unseen, unwelcom'd, [he] swells this heart with anguish. **1836** KEBLE *Lyra Apost.* 182 How count we then lost eve and morn, The bell unwelcom'd, prayer unsaid. **1893** *Harper's Mag.* Dec. 26 The Great Love comes to you at last Unwelcomed.

un'welcomely, *adv.* (UN-^{1} 11.)

1642 ROGERS *Naaman* 87 How doth Naaman take it? Surely very ill, and unwelcomly. **1718** TAVERNER *Artful Wife* v. i. 60 The Thought of him intrudes unwelcomely. **1792** CHARLOTTE SMITH *Desmond* III. 23 The task of chiding you..falls on me most unwelcomely. **1833** SIR F. B. HEAD *Bubbles fr. Brunnen* 121 A calculation which very unwelcomely kept forcing itself into my mind. **1882** C. C. HOPLEY *Snakes* xxvii. 495 A 'water moccasin'..had been seen..unwelcomely close to a southern residence.

un'welcomeness. (UN-^{1} 12.)

1682 BOYLE *Let.* Wks. 1772 VI. 43 But, together with that unwelcome news, you send me what does much alleviate the unwelcomeness of it. **1727** BAILEY (vol. II). **1876** GEO. ELIOT *Dan. Der.* vii, Her words..had the unwelcomeness which all unfavourable fortune telling has.

un'welcoming, *sb.* (UN-^{1} 13.)

1838 MRS. SMYTHIES *Fitzherbert* II. ii. 34 What has sent the young, the brave,..among the cold, the unwelcoming of frigid regions?

unwelde, etc.: see UNWIELD, etc.

un'welded, *ppl. a.* (UN-^{1} 8.)

[**1775** ASH.] **1846** WORCESTER (citing Turner). **1885** C. G. W. COOKE *Workshop Receipts* Ser. IV. 12/1, (1) unwelded, (2) welded, (rolled) goods.

†**un'welewable**, *a. Obs. rare.* [f. UN-^{1} 7 b. Cf. WALLOW *v.*^{2} and UNWALLOWED *ppl. a.*] That will not fade; unfadable.

1382 WYCLIF *1 Pet.* i. 4 In to heritage vncoruptible, and vndefoulid, and vnwelewable [L. *immarcescibilem*], that shal not fade. *Ibid.* v. 4 The vnwelewable crowne of glory.

un'well, *a.* Also 5 *north.* vnwele; *Sc.* 7 **unweal**, 9 **un-, onweel.** [UN-^{1} 7. Cf. NFris. (Sylt) *unwel*, WFlem. *onwel*, G. *unwohl.*] **a.** Not well or in good health; somewhat ill; indisposed.

Before 1780 almost always north. E., Sc., Anglo-Irish, or U.S. Not in Johnson (edd. 1–4). In very frequent use from *c* 1785. 'Crabbe..told us that Lord Chesterfield was the first person who introduced the word 'unwell' into common use, and..it was forthwith admitted into the vocabulary of fashion' (**1825** C. WORDSW. in Overton & W. *Life* (1888) 36).

c **1450** *St. Cuthbert* (Surtees) 3649 A man was seke and vnwele. **1653** URQUHART *Rabelais* I. vi. 30 Gargamelle began to be a little unwell in her lower parts. **1666** MRS. CARSTAIRES in *J. Carstaire's Lett.* (1846) 161 My sister still contanues unwell. The doctour thinks she is in great hazard. *a* **1700** EVELYN *Diary* 10 Oct. 1659, I..tooke lodgings..for all the winter, my son being very unwell. **1737** BERKELEY *Let.* Wks. 1871 IV. 248 My three children have been ill...George is still unwell. **1750** C. GIST *Jrnls.* (1893) 34, I was unwell and stayed in this Town to recover myself. **1755** CHESTERF. *Let.* 8 Oct., I am what you call in Ireland, and a very good expression I think it is, *unwell.* **1757** MRS. GRIFFITH *Lett. Henry & Frances* (1767) I. 218, I hope that it is only your spleen, which makes you fancy yourself unwell. **1768** CHESTERF. *Let.* 17 Oct., I am, neither well nor ill, but *unwell.* **1788** ANNA SEWARD *Lett.* (1811) II. 117, I have been so unwell with a violent cough. **1826** SCOTT *Jrnl.* (1890) I. 231, I am well-nigh choked with the sulphurous heat of the weather—or I am unwell. **1856** J. RICHARDSON *Recoll.* I. 61 Morris..suddenly retired as if taken unwell! **1882** TENNYSON *Promise of May* III. i, Mr. Steer still continues too unwell to attend to you.

b. *euphem.* Having menstrual discharges.

1844 DUNGLISON *Med. Dict.* (ed. 4) s.v. **1934** J. RHYS *Voyage in Dark* I. vi. 78 When I was unwell for the first time it was she who explained to me, so that it seemed quite all right. **1964** E. BOWEN *Little Girls* II. iii. 96 Miss Kinmate, herself *unwell* today, had not the slightest intention of going in.

Hence **un'wellness.**

1653 DOROTHY OSBORNE *Lett.* (1888) 140 You..never send me any of the new phrases of the town... Pray what is meant by *wellness* and *unwellness?* **1755** CHESTERF. *Let.* 8 Oct., This *unwellness* affects the mind as well as the body, and gives them both a disagreeable inertness. **1865** W. M. PUNSHON in Macdonald *Life* (1887) 250 This chronic 'unwellness' is difficult to understand. **1876** DARWIN in *Life* (1887) I. 69 Owing to frequently recurring unwellness, and to one long and serious illness.

un'wemmed, *ppl. a.* [OE. *unwemmed* (UN-^{1} 8). Cf. OE. *ungewemmed*, OHG. *ungawemmit.*]

1. Spotless, pure, immaculate. Now *arch.*

a. Of persons. Also const. *in*, *of.*

c **950** *Rituale Dunelm.* (Surtees) 104 Ðerh ðone vnwoemmedo drihten..crist. *a* **1175** *Cott. Hom.* 237 Ure halende wes accenned of þam unwemmede mede sante Marie. *c* **1200** ORMIN 2877 Jesu Cristess hird Iss clene, & all unnwemmedd Inn hire trowwþe towarrd Godd. *c* **1225** *Ancr. R.* 10 To ancren..þe witeð ou from þe worlde, ouer alle oðre religiuse, clene & unwemmed. *a* **1300** *E.E. Psalter* xviii. 14 Þan vnwemmed be I sal, And I sal be clensed clene Of gilte. **1382** WYCLIF *Col.* i. 22 For to haue ȝou hooly, and vnwemmid, and with oute reprof bifore hym. *c* **1400** *Prymer* in Maskell *Mon. Rit.* (1847) II. 40 Thou toke sum tyme the shap of oure bodi, in childynge of the unwemmed vyrgyn. *c* **1500** *Lancelot* 2097 This flour wnwemmyt of hir wirginitee. **1513** DOUGLAS *Æneid* x. Prol. 106 Thou tuke mankynd of ane onwemmyt mayd. **1570** LEVINS *Manip.* 51 Vnwembed, *immaculatus.* *a* **1643** CARTWRIGHT *Ordinary* II. ii, *Moth* [an^{e} antiquary]. 'Tis hard to find a Damosel unwenned [*sic*], They being all Coltish and full of Ragery.

absol. *a* **1300** *E.E. Psalter* xxxvi. 19 Lauerd daies of vn-wemmid knawes he. *a* **1325** *Prose Psalter* xxxvi. 19 Our Lord knew þe dedes of þe vnwemmed. **1382** Wyclif *Song Sol.* v. 2 Opene thou to me,..my culuer, myn vnwemed.

b. Of the body, etc.

c **1000** Ælfric *Saints' Lives* xxiii. B. 437 Þu wære symle fæmne oncnawen, and þinne lichaman hæbbende clæne and unwemmed. *c* **1200** Ormin 2816 Allmahhtiȝ Drihhtin..þatt nu liþ..I þin unnwemmedd wambe. *c* **1375** *Sc. Leg. Saints* iii. (*Andrew*) 442 [The] firste man, þat wes mad of vnwemmyterd. **1382** Wyclif *Heb.* xiii. 4 Honorable wedding in alle thingis, and bed vnwembid [*v.r.* vnwemyd bed].

c. Of qualities, etc.

c **1000** *Lambeth Psalter* c. 2 And ic anȝyte weȝe on unwemmed. *a* **1300** *E.E. Psalter* xviii. 8 Lagh of lauerd vnwemmed esse, Tornand saules in to blisse. *c* **1366** Chaucer *A.B.C.* 91 Signe of þin vnwemmed maidenhede. *c* **1375** *Sc. Leg. Saints* xxxvi. (*John Baptist*) 466 Þe firste is of virginite, þat ay vnuemmyt kepit he. *c* **1449** Pecock *Repr.* v. i. 477 A clene and an vnwemmed religioun. *c* **1872** J. Addis *Eliz. Echoes* (1879) 68 A love unwemmed, guiltless of attaint.

†**2.** Not hurt, injured, or scarred. *Obs.*

c **1200** Ormin 14735 All swa summ Ysaac attbrasst Unnwundedd & unnwemmedd. *a* **1300** *Cursor M.* 21046 Bot noþer him harmd, hefd ne fott. For als he was o lust vn-lame Als was vnwemmed his licam. **1375** Barbour *Bruce* xx. 376 He had gret ferly That sic a knycht..Micht in the face vnwemmyt be.

3. Not physically spotted or stained. Now *dial.*

a **1300** *Cursor M.* 19504 Godd him geit, þat euer es god, Vn-wemmed his hend in sacles blod. **1876** *Whitby Gloss.* 208/1 *Unwemm'd*, without wrinkle or stain; unblemished.

†**4.** Unblemished; flawless. *Obs. rare.*

c **1475** *Partenay* 6569 And so haue I done after my simplesse, Preseruing, I trust, mater and sentence Vnwemmed, vnhurt. **1501** Douglas *Pal. Hon.* II. xxx, Vnwemmit wit deliuerit of all dangeir.

Hence **un'wemmedness.** *rare.*

c **1200** Ormin 2388 Þatt ȝho mihhte A libbenn i clene maȝȝþhad, & inn unnwemmeddnesse. *Ibid.* 2875, 8220, 10098.

un'wept, *ppl. a.* [UN-[1] 8 b.]

1. Not wept or mourned for; unlamented.

1594 Shaks. *Rich. III*, II. ii. 65 Our fatherlesse distresse was left vnmoan'd, Your widdow-dolour, likewise be vnwept. **1633** P. Fletcher *Purple Isl.* I. xx, Had not that great Hart..piti'd thy wofull plight; There hadst thou lien unwept, unburied. **1637** Milton *Lycidas* 13 He must not flote upon his watry bear Unwept. **1725** Pope *Odyss.* v. 402 A shameful fate now hides my hapless head, Unwept, unnoted, and for ever dead! **1766** Goldsm. *Vicar* xxi, If you fall, though distant, exposed, and unwept by those that love you. **1805** Scott *Last Minstrel* VI. i, The wretch..shall go down To the vile dust,..Unwept, unhonour'd, and unsung. **1848** Buckley *Iliad* 413 Patroclus lies at the ships, an unwept, unburied corse.

2. Of tears: Unshed. *rare*[−1].

1816 Byron *Parisina* xx, Those tears..in its depth endure, Unseen, unwept, but uncongeal'd.

un'wered, *ppl. a. rare.* [UN-[1] 8. Cf. OE. *unwered.*] Unwatched, unguarded.

a **1400** *Pistill of Susan* 124 Þe wif werp of hir wedes vn-werde.

†**un'werked,** *ppl. a. Obs.*[−1] [f. UN-[1] 8 + ON. *verka* (MSw. *värka*, Sw., Norw. *verka*, Da. *virke*) to work, fashion.] Unworked, unwrought.

c **1430** *Chev. Assigne* 175 'Nowe lefte ther ony ouer vn-werkethe..?' And he recheth her forth haluendele a cheyne.

unwerred, -werreyed: see UNWARRED, UNWARRAYED *ppl. adjs.*

un'wet, *a.* [UN-[1] 7.] Not wet or moistened.

1433 *Rolls of Parlt.* IV. 451 Clothes..holdyng xiiii yerdes in lenght, and yeerde brodeunwette; or elles xii yerdes wette. *c* **1440** *Pallad. on Husb.* XII. 463 Cedur vnwet wol dure. **1585** Jas. VI *Ess. Poesie* (Arb.) 27, I no wais can, vnwet my cheekes, beholde My sisters made..macquerels olde. **1594** Kyd *Cornelia* II. 234 When sand within a Whirl-poole lyes vnwet. **1621** G. Sandys *Ovid's Met.* x. (1626) 212 Their feet, vnwet, the sea might well haue borne. **1683** Moxon *Mech. Exerc., Printing* xxiv. ¶9 The un-wet upper part of.. the Quire. *c* **1746** Collins *Ode Liberty* 69 He pass'd with unwet feet thro' all our land. **1789** E. Darwin *Bot. Gard.* I. 157 [To] bathe unwet their oily forms, and dwell With feet repulsive on the dimpling well. **1815** Kirby & Sp. *Entomol.* xiii. (1816) I. 425 Their bodies being kept unwet by a coating of air. **1840** N. Hawthorne *Biogr. Sk.* (1879) 178 It was like Gideon's fleece, unwet with dew. **1891** Atkinson *Last of Giant-killers* 234 Emerging from it unwet as well as unharmed.

b. Of the eye: Not suffused with tears; tearless.

1601–3 Daniel *Certaine Epistles* 58 He lookes thereon As from the shore of peace with vnwet eie. **1700** Dryden *Sigism. & Guisc.* 673, I meant to meet My Fate with..Eyes unwet. *a* **1743** Ld. Hervey *Epist.* i. 82 Thy breast unruffled, and unwet thy eye. **1823** S. Rogers *Italy, Brides Venice* 135 Eyes not unwet..with grateful tears. **1845** Jerrold *St. Giles* v. (1851) 43 The woman, lifting her apron to her unwet eye.

un'wetted, *ppl. a.* (UN-[1] 8.)

1664 Boyle *Exp. touching Colours* 56 The Unwetted Parts of the same Bodies. **1815** Kirby & Sp. *Entomol.* i. (1816) I. 16 By means of which she [*sc.* a spider] resides unwetted in the bosom of the water. **1892** Ld. Lytton *King Poppy* Prol. 281 The flash of her unwetted sandal.

†**unweved,** *pa. pple. Obs.*[−1] [? UN-[2] 9.] Struck off.

c **1330** *King of Tars* 199 (MS. Vernon), Mony an helm þer was vn-weued, And mony a Bacinet to-cleued.

unwex, variant of UNWAX *v.*[1] *Obs.*

un'wheel, *v.* (UN-[2] 4.)

1632 G. Hughes *Saints Losse*, Ded., Your charet is unwheeled, and your horsemen throwne. **1889** Talmage *Serm.* 28 Apr., God is not dead. The chariots are unwheeled.

unwheeme, var. UNQUEME *a. Obs.*

un'whet, *v.* (UN-[2] 3.)

1599 T. M[oufet] *Silkwormes* 55 Satiety their stomacks will vnwhet. **1885** R. Bridges *Nero* I. III. v, Come,..be seated. Let not the horrid sight Unwhet your appetites.

un'whetted, *ppl. a.* (UN-[1] 8.)

a **1644** Quarles *Sol. Recant.* x. 10 If th' unwhetted edge be blunt, the arm Must give more strength. **1648** Hexham II, *Een ongewet mes*, an Vnwhetted knife.

un'whig, *v.* [UN-[2] 6 b + WHIG *sb.*] *trans.* To divest of the character or opinions of a Whig.

1825 Moore *Sheridan* II. 38 Pitt..turned to the person who sat next him, and said, 'I'll *un-Whig* the gentleman for the rest of his life!' **1832** *Q. Rev.* XLVII. 80 Moore did not, indeed, return unwhigged, but he has dealt with American manners not less hardly than Mrs. Trollope. **1892** *Pall Mall G.* 4 May 2 Unwhigging the Duke of Devonshire.

un'whigged, *ppl. a.* [UN-[1] 8 + WHIG *v.*[3]] Not turned sour.

1756 Home *Bleaching* 79 A piece of cloth..was laid in butter milk unwhigged.

un'whiglike, *a.* (UN-[1] 7 c.)

1808 Syd. Smith in Lady Holland *Mem.* (1855) II. 48 He behaved in an unwhiglike manner.

un'whining, *ppl. a.* (UN-[1] 10.)

a **1750** A. Hill *Poems* Wks. 1753 IV. 119 Bid tears, unwhining, find their source within.

un'whip, *v.* [UN-[2] 3.] *trans.* To cast loose smartly.

1683 Moxon *Mech. Exerc., Printing* xxii. ¶7 Before the Cords are unwhipt from the Pages.

un'whipped, un'whipt, *ppl. a.* [UN-[1] 8, 8 b, c.]

1. Not punished (as) by whipping; not flogged or beaten.

1605 Shaks. *Lear* III. ii. 53 Tremble thou Wretch, Thou hast within thee vndivulged Crimes Vnwhipt of Iustice. **1732** Lady M. W. Montagu & Ld. Hervey *Verses to Pope* 69 If..Unwhipt, unblanketed, unkick'd, unslain, That wretched little carcase you retain. **1737** Pope *Hor. Epist.* II. ii. 18 Once..I caught him in a lie, And then, unwhipp'd, he had the grace to cry. **1863** Holland *Lett. Joneses* xiii. 197 The unwhipped coward rubs his hands over his clever boorishness and brutality. **1889** H. M. Stanley in *Daily News* 4 Dec. 5/2 Numerous peoples..who were as yet unwhipped out of their native arrogance.

transf. **1899** *Westm. Gaz.* 27 June 10/1 Time for fishing in unwhipped waters.

2. (See WHIP *v.* 17.)

1867 Smyth *Sailor's Word-book* 291 Feazings, the fagging out or unravelling of an unwhipped rope.

3. Not directed by the interests of a political party; not subject to a party whip.

1959 *Manch. Guardian* 11 Aug. 6/4 The argument for the independent 'unwhipped' councillor. **1971** Hindell & Simms *Abortion Law Reformed* xi. 233 It might..turn out that members would cast their ballots to some extent along party lines, even though unwhipped. **1979** *Guardian* 6 July 26/2 The plan is for an unwhipped vote on a motion covering the principle of the return of the death penalty.

un'whirled, *ppl. a.* (UN-[1] 8.)

1760 Sterne *Tr. Shandy* IV. xxxi, [To] make an example of him, as the first Shandy unwhirled about Europe in a post-chaise.

un'whiskered, *a.* (UN-[1] 9.)

1812 Byron *Waltz* xi. *note*, Buonaparte is un-whiskered, the Regent whiskered. **1828** Hook *Sayings & Doings* I. 105 His neckcloth..was tied lightly round his neck, and his plump unwhiskered cheeks festooned over its upper edge.

un'whisperable, *a.* and *sb.* [UN-[1] 7 b.]

a. *adj.* Unmentionable even in a whisper.

1853 Mrs. Gore *Dean's Daughter* II. 193 Turbid waters ..worthy only of the four rivers of an unwhisperable region.

b. *sb.* Trousers. *slang.*

1837 *Knickerbocker Mag.* March 288 How could he..see about procuring himself a new pair of unwhisperables from his host, when [etc.]. **1863** G. A. Sala *Captain Dangerous* I. Pref. p. vi, Unprotected females didn't venture in 'unwhisperables' into the depths of Norwegian forests.

un'whispered, *ppl. a.* (UN-[1] 8.)

1821 T. W. Hill *Select. Papers* (1860) 26 An unwhispered *s*. *Ibid.* 27 The symbols for the unwhispered letters. **1835** Lytton *Rienzi* IV. ii, How many unwhispered and solemn rites hast thou witnessed by thy native Nile!

un'whited, *ppl. a.* (UN-[1] 8.)

1621 in Kempe *Losely MSS.* (1836) 458 Mercheants for linin, dyaper, damaske, and of all kynds, but all unwhyted. **1648** Hexham II, *Ongewit*, Vnwhited, or Vnbleached.

un'whitened, *ppl. a.* (UN-[1] 8.)

[**1775** Ash.] **1833** Loudon *Encycl. Archit.* §62 The unwhitened mud and rough stone cottages of England.

un'whitewashed, *ppl. a.* (UN-[1] 8.)

1797 J. C. Davie *Let.* July in *Lett. from Paraguay* (1805) 118, I would have had the whole house..left unwhitewashed. **1846** Worcester (citing Philips). **1866** Augusta Wilson *St. Elmo* i, A rude unwhitewashed paling. **1893** J. W. Barry *Stud. Corsica* 196 An uninhabited cottage with..unwhitewashed walls. **1909** M. B. Saunders *Litany Lane* III. xx. 188 It is to be feared that in her suppressed excitement she betrayed the unwhitewashed Hilda.

†**un'whittle,** *v. Obs.*[−1] [UN-[2] 4 + WHITTLE *sb.*[2]] *trans.* To remove a 'whittle' or shawl from.

1654 Gayton *Pleas. Notes* II. i. 34 The Lady lik'd his pregnant fancy, and presently unwhitled, and swathed them [*sc.* babes] to her Paramor.

†**un'whole,** *a. Obs.* Forms: α. 1–4 **unhal** (3 *Orm.* **unnhal**), 3–4 **unhale.** β. 3, 5 **unhole** (3 **onhole**), **unhol**, 4 **unholl**, 5 **unhool.** [OE. *unhál* (*un-* UN-[1] 7 + *hál* WHOLE *a.*), = OHG. *unheil*, *unhail*, Goth. *unhails* unsound, ON. *úheill* insincere, Norw. dial. *uheil* unhealthy, decayed.]

1. Not in good health; unsound, unhealthy; diseased, infirm, sick.

α. *c* **888** K. Ælfred *Boeth.* xi. §1 Sume habbað bearn ȝenoȝe, ac þa beoþ hwilum unhale oððe yfele & unweorþe. *c* **1000** Ælfric in *O.E. Hom.* I. 296 Unȝemetȝod fæsten, & to mycel forhæfdnyss on æte & on wæte deð þone man unhalne. *c* **1200** Ormin 4778 Hiss bodiȝ toc To rotenn bufenn eorþe All samenn... All þiss wass utenn wiþþ unnhal þurrh swiþe unnride unnhæle. *Ibid.* 9393 Ȝiff þatt tin eȝhe iss all unnhal. *c* **1205** Lay. 17187 Þa men þe beoð un-hal, heo fareð to þan stane. *c* **1325** *Metr. Hom.* 35, I gif the blind.. thair siht,..I mac unhale men al hale.

β. *a* **1225** *Ancr. R.* 112 Lo þus þe hole half & te cwike dole drowen þet vuele blod ut frommard þe unhole. *c* **1275** *Sinners Beware* 308 in *O.E. Misc.* 82 He seyþ þenne, Myne Poure vn-hole hyne To eure dure come. **1379** *Glouc. Cath. MS.* 19 No. I. I. iv. fol. 12 Ellys the body is vnholl & ther after schewith him the vryn. *c* **1425** *Cursor M.* 5137 (Trin.), Her fadir lay vnhol in bedde.

b. Spiritually or morally unsound.

c **1000** Ælfric *Hom.* II. 470 Se ðe wenð þæt he hal sy, se is unhal. *c* **1275** *Moral Ode* 114 in *O.E. Misc.* 62 Nis no witnesse al so muchel so monnes owe heorte. For so seyþ þat vnhol is him seolue hwat him smeorteþ. *c* **1325** *Metr. Hom.* 129 Man quaim sinne mad unhale.

c. Of unsound mind. *rare*[−1].

13.. *E.E. Allit. P.* B. 1681 His hert heldet vnhole, he hoped non oþer Bot a best þat he be, a bol oþer an oxe.

d. Unsincere. *rare*[−1].

a **1352** Minot in *Pol. Poems* (Rolls) I. 74 In hert he was unhale, He come thare moste for mede.

2. Of food, etc.: Unwholesome. *rare*[−1].

a **1225** *Ancr. R.* 370 Ne nomen heo neuer ȝeme hwat was hol, hwat was unhol te eten ne to drincken.

3. Imperfect; defective; incomplete. *rare*[−1].

a **1300** *Cursor M.* 23563 For-þi þat godd has ai wroght al, Of his werkes es noght vnhale [*Trin.* vnhool].

un'wholesome, *a.* and *sb.* [UN-[1] 7. Cf. older Flem. *onheylsaem* (Kilian), MHG. (G.) *unheilsam*, ON. *úheilsamr* (MSw. *ohelsamber*).]

A. *adj.* **1. a.** Not beneficial, salutary, or conducive to morals, etc.; detrimental or prejudicial to health of mind.

c **1200** Ormin 7177 And tatt iss eȝȝþerr himm & hemm Unnhalsumm to þe sawle. **1554** T. Sampson *Let. to Trew Professors* A vi b, Where haue ye your ground in the scripture for this your vnholsome housell. **1657** Hobbes *Absurd Geom.* 16 You..can not expect to publish any unholesome doctrine without some Antidotes from me. **1888** H. M. Stanley in *Standard* (1889) 6 Apr., All unwholesome and evil conjectures. **1889** *Times* 8 Apr. 9/1 A mischievous demagogue who has acquired an unwholesome popularity by discreditable methods. **1900** L. B. Walford *One of Ourselves* xiv, They are keen on doing anything they shouldn't, anything improper and unwholesome.

b. Not promoting or conducive to, harmful or prejudicial to, well-being, good condition, soundness, etc.; hurtful, noxious.

a **1400–50** *Alexander* 4387 Þe kind of þire customs we kepe euire-mare, þe quilk, I hope, ser, þe to hald vnhalesom it ware. **1628** May *Virg. Georg.* I. 6 Nor is't unwholesome to subdue the Land By often exercise. **1664** Butler *Hud.* II. i. 794 I'd be loath..To free your heels by any course, That might b' unwholesome to your Spurs. **1787** Winter *Syst. Husb.* 84 When waters remain..on the ground which.. produce rank unwholesome weeds. **1812** Byron *Ch. Har.* I. liii, And must they fall..To swell one bloated Chief's unwholesome reign? **1828** Scott *F.M. Perth* xiii, Perhaps farther stay were unwholesome for my safety.

2. Not favourable to or promoting good health; not salubrious, wholesome, or healthful; injurious to health: **a.** Of food, etc.

1297 R. Glouc. (Rolls) 9115 He willede of an lampreye to ete, Ac is leches him vorbode vor it was vnholsom mete. *c* **1380** Wyclif *Wks.* (1880) 475 Þe mynging of þes þingis is vnholsum to man to take. *c* **1440** *Pallad. on Husb.* II. 187 The water that gooth thorgh the leden penne Is rust corrupt, vnholsum. *c* **1455** Pecock *Folewer* 22 To men is ȝouun þe witt of smellyng, bi which þei schulen knowe sumwhat afer what bodies ben vnholsom to be take vnto her nurischyng. **1482** Caxton *Polycron.* III. xxxi. 152 b, That vnholsomme mete that he hadde eten at soper. **1528** Paynell *Salerne's Regim.* E ij b, Salte meate..is vnholsome for sicke folkes. **1577** Googe *Heresbach's Husb.* 146 A grosse vnholsome kinde of milke. **1622** Peacham *Compl. Gent.* xv. 193 Hauing your..reputation abased, while you sit taking your vnwholesome healthes. **1665** Manley *Grotius' Low C. Wars* 473 Their flesh they found to be unwholsom for food. **1726** Leoni *Alberti's Archit.* I. 65 Its water is unwholsom to drink. **1774** Pennant *Tour Scotl. in 1772*, 305 Fever.. originating from unwholesome food. **1855** Macaulay *Hist. Eng.* xii. III. 233 Leprosies, such as strange and unwholesome diet engenders. **1876** Bancroft *Hist. U.S.* III. viii. 122 Sick at heart, and enfeebled by unwholesome diet.

transf. **1855** *Orr's Circ. Sci., Inorg. Nat.* 202 The water cannot be in any other than an unwholesome state, and unfit for general use.

b. Of places, conditions, etc.
c 1455 PECOCK *Folewer* 22 þe witt of smellyng, bi which þei schulen knowe.. what bodies ben vnholsom if with hem þei maken her nyȝ dwellyng. a 1533 BERNERS *Gold. Bk. M. Aurel.* (1546) Q j b, For meate corrupteth in an vnholsome potte. 1579 STEVENS in Hakluyt *Voyages* (1589) 160 Raine so vnholesome, that if the water stand a little while, all is full of wormes. 1613 PURCHAS *Pilgrimage* 486 Alexandria is very vnholesome, as the graue of that Alexandria we before mentioned. 1653 in *Verney Mem.* (1904) I. 551 Unwholesome smells.. and most noysome stinks. 1718 BERKELEY *Jrnl. Tour Italy* Wks. 1871 IV. 592 A small river seemed to render it marshy and unwholesome. 1779 *Mirror* No. 41 ¶5 The vicinity of.. the lake.. she was sure must be extremely unwholesome. 1847 G. HARRIS *Life Ld. Hardwicke* I. 207 The walls were not dry, but very damp and unwholesome. 1859 DICKENS *T. Two Cities* I. ii, As the waves of an unwholesome sea might do. 1867 SMYTH *Sailor's Word-bk.* 707 *Unwholesome ship*,.. a sugar ship diverted from her former trade, and not properly cleansed.

c. Of climate, air, etc.
1555 EDEN *Decades* (Arb.) 87 The great heate and vnholsome ayer. 1592 BRETON *Pilgr. Paradise* Wks. (Grosart) I. 14/1 Shee bit her taile, with such vnholsome breath, As.. stung her selfe to death. 1653 W. RAMESEY *Astrol. Restored* 267 It shews.. unwholsom infectious Mists. c 1690 in *10th Rep. Hist. MSS. Comm.* App. I. 139 The air is most unwholesome, and agrees very ill with him. 1726 LEONI *Alberti's Archit.* I. 64 Any very deep Valley reaking with unwholsome Steams. 1796 MORSE *Amer. Geog.* I. 750 The atmosphere is very hot, moist and unwholesome. 1825 SCOTT *Talism.* vi, The alternations of the unwholesome climate. 1859 LANDOR *Hellenics* 26 Why should we stand beneath This hollow tree's unwholesome breath?

3. a. Of persons: Not sound in respect of morals, character, etc.; morally tainted or corrupted.
c 1374 CHAUCER *Troylus* IV. 330 O olde, vnholsom and mysbyleued man. 1602 SHAKS. *Ham.* IV. v. 82 The people muddied, Thicke and vnwholsome in their thoughts and whispers.

b. Not sound in health; diseased, infirm, sick.
1656 OSBORN *Adv. Son* I. 33 Fly, with Joseph, the Embraces of great Ladyes; lest you.. see your leggs rot in the stocks of the Physitian: they being often unwholsome. 1732 ARBUTHNOT *Rules of Diet* (1736) 415 Children born healthy, often contract the Disease from an unwholsom Nurse. 1848 THACKERAY *Van. Fair* lxi, An unwholesome little Miss of seven years of age.
transf. 1847 C. BRONTË *J. Eyre* i, Large and stout,.. with a dingy and unwholesome skin. 1889 MRS. OLIPHANT *Poor Gentleman* xliv, Those white, unwholesome, greasy hands.
Comb. 1858 *Household Words* XVIII. 519/2 A middling-sized man, with a sharp, unwholesome-looking face.

†**c.** *Naut.* (See quot.) *Obs.*
1627 CAPT. SMITH *Seaman's Gram.* xi. 52 If she draw little water and be long, she may try and ride well, but neuer hull well, which is called an vnwholsome ship. [1867 SMYTH *Sailor's Word-bk.* 707.]

†**4.** *Sc.* Ugly; repulsive. *Obs.*⁻¹
c 1480 HENRYSON *Fables, Paddock & Mouse* 64 Thocht I vnhailsum be to luke vpon.

5. Impaired; defective. *rare*⁻¹.
1604 SHAKS. *Oth.* IV. i. 124 Prythee beare Some Charitie to my wit, do not thinke it So vnwholesome.

B. *sb.* An unwholesome thing.
1858 *Brit. Q. Rev.* LVI. 358 We find him [Lilly].. leaving.. Neve and Wodehouse to provide, as usual, tables of the wholesomes and unwholesomes.

Hence **un'wholesomely** *adv.*
c 1455 PECOCK *Folewer* 51 It is science to knowe.. what metis.. wole nurische vs vnholsomli. 1563 FOXE *A. & M.* 1712/2 Madam, you were best to come out of the raine. For you sit vnwholesomlye. 1628 WITHER *Brit. Rememb.* VIII. 199 Thy Children oft unwholsomly are fed. 1860 FLOR. NIGHTINGALE *Nursing* 10 The air.. unwholesomely close and foul. 1875 HELPS *Soc. Press.* xiii. 174 The eyes of an unwholesomely curious world.

un'wholesomeness. [f. prec. + -NESS.]
1. Unsound or impaired health; unhealthiness.
c 1449 PECOCK *Repr.* I. xiii. 68 Thanne thou etist hony aloon... And this feding schal turn into thin vnhoolsumnes.

2. Unhealthy character (of locality, climate, air, etc.); insalubrity, unhealthfulness.
a 1513 FABYAN *Chron.* VII. 377 By reason of yᵉ vnholsomnes of the countre. 1598 HAKLUYT *Voy.* I. 396 The vnwholesomnesse of the aire, and corruption of the waters in the hote time of the yeere. 1623 in Foster *Eng. Factories Ind.* (1908) II. 181 The unholsomnes of this clymeatt. 1626 BACON *Sylva* §777 The Wholesomenesse or Vnwholesomenesse, as well of Seasons, as of the Seats of Dwellings. 1697 WALSH *Life Virgil* ¶2 in Dryden's *Virgil*, The Unwholsomness of his Native Air. 1726 LEONI *Alberti's Archit.* I. 65/1 The damps.. will come to you with double.. unwholsomness. 1758 in Dodsley *Fug. Pieces* (1761) II. 84 The Unwholesomeness of the Rust and Verdegrease Suffusions. a 1843 SOUTHEY *Common-pl. Bk.* Ser. II. (1849) 245/2 In the unwholesomeness of this shade the tree.. could not possibly flourish. 1879 *Cassell's Techn. Educ.* IV. 42/1 The unwholesomeness of sewage.

3. The state or quality of being unwholesome as, or unfit for, food, etc.
1548 *Act 2 & 3 Edw. VI*, c. 10 §1 The unholsomenes of the drincke.. made thereof. 1587 GOLDING *De Mornay* xiv. 249 Iudging.. of the wholsomnes or vnwholsomnes of foode by the taste thereof. 1633 T. ADAMS *Exp. 2 Peter* ii. 20 The unwholesomenesse of his dyet. 1651 STANLEY *Poems* 37 Th' unwholsomnesse of fruit. 1863 *N. & Q.* 3rd Ser. IV. 249 The Scottish objection to eels as an article of food is mainly due to their supposed unwholesomeness.

4. Lack of moral wholesomeness; viciousness.
1881 *Sat. Rev.* 15 Jan. 88/2 Happily its unwholesomeness is often lessened by the folly of the language into which the author falls. 1897 *Advance* (Chicago) 25 Mar. 389/1 The absence of [disapprobation of sinners].. is a sure sign of unwholesomeness and decay.

†**un'wide,** *a. Obs.* [UN-¹ 7. Cf. OE. *unwid*, ON. *úviðr*.] Narrow, confined.
a 1300 *Cursor M.* 8667 At ans bath.. we.. vr barns bar. In wanes war we stad vn-wide.

†**un'wield,** *sb. Obs. rare.* In 4 **unwelde, vnweilde.** [UN-¹ 12.] Feebleness, weakness, impotence.
13.. *E.E. Psalter* lxx. 9 (V.), Ne for-werpe me in un-welde, In time when I am of elde. c 1375 *Cursor M.* 3563 (Gött.), And haue man ben neure so bald, Quen þat he bicomis alde, Til vnweild [he] bigines to falle.

†**un'wield,** *a. Obs.* [UN-¹ 7.]
1. Feeble, weak, impotent; = UNWIELDY *a.* 1. Freq. from c 1400 to c 1450.
c 1220 *Bestiary* 57 Siðen hise limes arn unwelde. c 1250 *Gen. & Ex.* 347 Vn-welde woren and in win Here owen limes. ? a 1366 CHAUCER *Rom. Rose* 359 Al woxen was her body vnwelde, And drie,.. for elde. c 1386 —— *Reeve's Prol.* 32 Oure olde lemes mowe wel been vnweelde. 14.. *Sir Beues* (L.) 34 He.. Wexed febull and vn-welde. c 1480 *Bk. of Brome* (1886) 106 Hys body gane vax on-wylld.
absol. a 1300 *Cursor M.* 10539 Sal naman negh þat vnweild.

2. Difficult or cumbrous to manipulate or handle; unwieldy. *rare.*
1390 GOWER *Conf.* I. 312 The reyni Storm fell doun algates And al here takel made unwelde. a 1440 *Sir Eglam.* 309 A clobb of yron.. That was mekylle and fulle unwelde.

Hence †**un'wieldness.** *Obs.*⁻¹
1437-8 *Rolls of Parlt.* V. 439 In cas that anny of the seide Lordes.. fall to suche unweldenesse or impotence.

un'wieldable, *a. rare*⁻¹. [UN-¹ 7 b.] Unwieldy.
1500-20 DUNBAR *Poems* xxvi. 98 Full mony a waistless wallydrag, With wamis vnweildable.

†**un'wielded,** *ppl. a. Obs.*⁻¹ [UN-² 6, 8.] Made feeble.
a 1300 *Cursor M.* 23642 þai [*sc.* the wicked] sal vnweldid be wit bale.

un'wieldily, *adv.* [f. UNWIELDY *a.* + -LY².] In an unwieldy or awkward manner; cumbrously.
c 1610 CHAPMAN *Iliad* To Rdr. A 5, Their long words Shewe in short verse, as in a narrow place, Two opposites should meet, with two-hand swords; Vnweildily, without or use or grace. 1611 COTGR., *Inhabilement*,.. weakely; vnweldily, vneasily. 1697 DRYDEN *Virg. Georg.* IV. 623 His finny Flocks about their Shepherd play... Unweildily they wallow first in Ooze, Then in the shady Covert seek Repose. 1830 *Fraser's Mag.* I. 24 It slides amain, unwieldily, Into the universal sea. 1848 T. AIRD *Summer Day, Noon* 39 The cottar's cow.. comes Cantering unwieldily. 1862 SMILES *Engineers* III. 101 Locomotives.. dragging themselves unwieldily along at.. five or six miles an hour.

un'wieldiness. [f. UNWIELDY *a.*]
1. The quality of being incontrollable or unrestrainable; indocility.
1571 GOLDING *Calvin on Ps.* iii. 5 Such as either blame fortune, or.. with vnruly rage power out the vnweeldinesse of their sorow. a 1680 CHARNOCK *Attrib. God* (1682) 173 The more unwieldiness there is in our Spirits, the more carnal our affections are in worship, the more evidence there is of the strength of that revolted state.

†**2.** The state or condition of being weak or feeble; weakness, infirmity. *Obs.*
1575 FENTON *Gold. Epist.* (1582) 263 This age of vnweldiness beginnes at fiftie yeares. 1610 HEALEY *St. Aug. Citie of God* XIX. iv. 757 Strength, beauty, vigour and actiuity, are all subuerted by.. sicknesse, faintnesse, and vnweeldinesse. 1698 FRYER *Acc. E. India & P.* 306 The South Wind.. brings Listlessness and an Unweildiness over the whole Body. 1737 SWIFT *Let. to J. Temple* Feb., She is quite sunk with years and unwieldiness, as well as a very scanty support.
transf. 1651 H. MORE *Enthus. Tri.* (1662) 4 The enormous strength of Imagination (which is yet the Soul's weaknesse or unwieldinesse).

3. Awkwardness or clumsiness in respect of bulk, build, or movement; *esp.* awkward corpulence; clumsy size or vastness.
1577 B. GOOGE *Heresbach's Husb.* IV. 163 b, Columella would haue you keepe for euery gander, three geese, thinking by reason of their vnweldynesse, this number to suffise. 1612 T. TAYLOR *Comm. Titus* iii. 1 Who is he that carrieth flesh about with him, that findeth not the heauinesse and vnweldines of it vnto any thing that is good? 1665 GLANVILL *Scepsis Sci.* xi. 62 The supposed unwieldiness of its massie bulk. 1709 ADDISON *Tatler* No. 116 ¶5 The Weight and Unweildiness of the Garment. 1712 —— *Spect.* No. 464 ¶5 Poverty.. preserving them from Gouts, Dropsies, Unwieldiness, and Intemperance. 1794 G. ADAMS *Nat. & Exp. Philos.* III. 271 If we should suppose animals vastly large,.. a heaviness and unwieldiness would arise which [etc.] 1809 *Med. Jrnl.* XXI. 115 An unwieldiness in motion and hurried respiration when walking. 1850 KINGSLEY *A. Locke* xxxvi, At last, after days of painful crawling, I dragged my unwieldiness to the tree foot. 1879 *Cassell's Techn. Educ.* II. 165/2 In the ordinary descriptions of field-carriages the weight and unwieldiness of the trail alone would be a serious objection to such a method of draught.
fig. a 1631 DONNE *Love's Diet* 1 To what a combersome unwieldinesse And burdenous corpulence my love had growne. 1673 ALLESTREE *Lady's Call* II. iii. §12. 219 Greatness is now grown to such an unweildiness, that it cannot stoop tho to the most Christian Offices.
transf. a 1677 BARROW *Serm.* (1678) 3 Whatever evil.. backwardness, inhability, unwieldiness and confusion of thought beget, Wisdom prevents. 1774 [W. MITFORD] *Ess. Harmony Lang.* 132 This line has also been admired for its expressive unwieldiness. Its form is.. by no means peculiarly suited to give the idea of unwieldiness. 1866 DICKENS *Mugby Junct.* ii, With that absurd sense of unwieldiness of mind and body weighing him down. 1875 HELPS *Soc. Press.* iii. 48 The largeness, the unwieldiness, and the temporary nature of habitation in these great centres of population.

4. The condition or character of being difficult to guide, direct, or control by reason of extent or size. Also *fig.*
1599 SANDYS *Europæ Spec.* (1605) V 1, Since that is great properly which is great in the actions, which one as often impeacheth by vnwildinesse in the bigge, as by weakenesse in the little. 1600 HAKLUYT *Voy.* III. 79 Considering the swift course and way of the ships, and the vnwieldinesse of them to stay and turne as a man would wish. 1610 HOLLAND *Camden's Brit.* I. 696 The disordered vnwealdinesse of their owne armie. 1764 BURN *Poor Laws* 226 The objections against county workhouses.. seem to require peculiar attention. There is something of unwieldiness in the prospect. 1809 MALKIN *Gil Blas* IX. i. ¶7 Noted for the unwieldiness of their ambition. a 1873 LYTTON *Pausanias* I. v, Armies too large rot by their own unwieldiness into decay. 1898 'MERRIMAN' *Roden's Corner* ii, The unwieldiness of the empire.

un'wieldly, *a.* [In early use f. UNWIELD *sb.* + -LY¹; later a variant of UNWIELDY *a.*
Many quots. for *unwieldly* in reprints from 1681 onwards have, on verification in first edd. or the MSS., proved to be misprints of UNWIELDY *a.*, as in quots. 1681–1730. The prevalence of the misprint may be the chief source of the form.]

†**1.** Impotent; weak; = UNWIELDY *a.* 1. *Obs.*
a 1300 *Cursor M.* 23642 (Edinb.), þir sal haf weldnes of wale, þa sal unweldli be wit bale.

2. = UNWIELDY *a.* 2–4. Also *transf.*
a 1513 FABYAN *Chron.* VII. (1516) 153/2 He was vnweldly by reason of ouer ladynge of Flesshe, and myght not well trauayll. *Ibid.* 161 b/2 [They] made them a Mamet of a Fatte and vnwyldely as.
[1681 *Sanderson's Serm.* 95 As Saul's armour did [sit] upon Davids [back]; unweildly, and sagging about his shoulders. 1730 BAILEY, *Inhabile*,.. unmeet, unfit, unwieldly, not nimble.]
1763 CHURCHILL *Ghost* I. 261 Horrid, unweildly, without Form,.. in the rear, That Post of Honour, should appear Pomposo. 1858 FABER *Foot of Cross* ii. 93 The interlacings and unfoldings of an unwieldly thunder-cloud. 1881 *Athenæum* 19 March 393/3 Unwieldly though the German language is in conversation and for every-day purposes. 1888 MURIE in Kingsley *Riverside Nat. Hist.* IV. 404 Such a great, unwieldly, horned bird as the rhinoceros hornbill.

un'wieldly, *adv. rare.* [Cf. prec.] In an unwieldy manner.
1793 WORDSW. *Evening Walk* 231 Thence issuing oft, unwieldly as ye stalk, Ye crush.. your flow'ry walk.

†**un'wieldsome,** *a. Obs.* [UN-¹ 7.]
1. Of age: Impotent; = UNWIELDY *a.* 1 c. *rare*⁻¹.
1567 GOLDING *Ovid's Met.* VII. 85 From dull vnweildsome age to youth he backward drew.

2. Unwieldy.
1579-80 NORTH *Plutarch* (1595) 748 Alexander.. perceiuing that his armie was very heauy and vnwildsom to remoue, for the.. spoiles they had with them. 1601 SIR W. CORNWALLIS *Disc. Seneca* (1631) 38 Like prisoners.. debarred exercise, fat, and unwieldsome. 1674 N. FAIRFAX *Bulk & Selv.* 138 Body being a stour unweildsom thing,.. it cannot stir without asking another bodies leave to crowd by.

unwieldy (ʌnˈwiːldɪ), *a.* Forms: 5–7 **unweldy**, 6 **-ye**, 6–7 **-ie**; 5–7 **unweeldy**, 5 **-weeldi**, 6 **-ie**; 6–7 **unwealdy**, **-ie**; 6–8 (9) **unweildy** (6 **-weyldy**, *Sc.* **wnveildy**), 6–7 **-ie**; 6– **unwieldy**, 7 **-ie**; 6–7 **unwildy**, 6 **-wildie**, *Sc.* **-wyldy**. (Also 5–7 **vn-**, 5–6 **on-**.) [UN-¹ 7, 5 b + WIELDY *a.* Cf. the early UNWIELD *a.* and UNWIELDLY *a.*]

†**1.** Of persons, the body, etc.: Lacking strength; weak, impotent; feeble, infirm. Also const. with preps., as *for*, *of*, *to* (with inf.). *Obs.*
c 1386 CHAUCER *Manciple's Prol.* 55 So vnweldy was this sory palled goost. 1421-2 HOCCLEVE *Dialog* 248 My lymes sumdell now vnweldy be. 1442 in *Proc. King's Counc. Irel.* (Rolls) App. 274 The said Erlle.. is aged, vnweldy and vnlustie. 1513 DOUGLAS *Æneid* VIII. v. 71 Furth held the king vnweildy in auld ȝeris. 1584 R. SCOT *Discov. Witchcr.* I. vi. (1886) 10 A toothless, old, impotent, and unweldie woman. 1606 G. WOODCOCKE *Hist. Ivstine* XXXIV. 111 Altogither giuen to sloath, and growne so vnweeldy through dayly ryot. 1621 T. GRANGER *Expos. Eccles.* xii. 321 So doe olde men, because they are vnweaIdie, and vnable to auoide dangers. 1659 W. CHAMBERLAYNE *Pharon.* I. iii. 72 At that stroke his Limbs Slack their unwieldy Nerves.
absol. 1550 CROWLEY *Way to Wealth* 685 To releue the vnweldy that be not able to labour for theire fode.
(*b*) 1570 FOXE *A. & M.* (ed. 2) I. 80/1 Narcissus.. was vnwieldy for his age to gouerne that function alone. 1588 T. HUGHES *Misfort. Arthur* I. ii. 13 Any wight vnwildie of herselfe. 1592 NASHE *P. Penilesse* E 2 b, To corrupt the braine, and make it vnapt and vnweldie for anything. 1642 FULLER *Holy & Prof. St.* II. xix. 128 The weilding of his sword hath not made him unweildie to do any other work.

†**b.** Of age, etc.: Characterized or attended by infirmity, weakness, or impotence. *Obs.*
1430-40 LYDG. *Bochas* I. 2127 In his vnweeldi age He was compellid to holden his passage Out off Thebes. c 1450 —— *Secrees* 645 Yif inpotence of his vnweldy age, In his desirs put hym nat abak. 1502 *Will of Wilbey* (Somerset Ho.), Oppressed with gret unweldy age. a 1592 GREENE *Jas. IV*, III. iii, Mine age vnweldie and vnmeete for toyle. 1659 W. CHAMBERLAYNE *Pharon.* II. iii. 167 Although unwieldy age allow Not strength to sell my life at such a rate Honour aimes at. 1685 DRYDEN tr. *Horace, Odes* I. ix. 28 E're with'ring time the taste destroyes, With sickness and unwieldy years!

2. Of persons or animals: Moving ungracefully or with difficulty, by reason of corpulence or ponderousness; lacking litheness or flexibility; awkward, clumsy.

1530 PALSGR. 328/2 Unweldye, boystouse, *lourt.* **1538** STARKEY *England* 79 In a dropcy the body ys vnweldy, vnlusty, and slo. **1563** B. GOOGE *Eglogs*, etc. (Arb.) 69 A bluddy Butcher byg and blunt, a vyle vnweldy knaue,..at hym..let dryue. **1602** *2nd Pt. Return Parnass.* III. ii. 1257 Then the old vnweldy Camels gin to dance. **1650** R. STAPYLTON *Strada's Low-C. Wars* x. 11 Others that wore Armes which made them unweldier, not so nimble to avoid a hurt. **1677** PLOT *Oxfordsh.* 134 The motion of so unwildy Creatures as Elephants. **1741** J. WILFORD *Mem.* App. 41 From the unwieldiest Beast of Land or Deep. **1779** *Mirror* No. 8, I have seen the unwieldy burgess changed into a slender gentleman. **1823** SCOTT *Quentin D.* xxix, He was, though now somewhat unwieldy, a powerful, athletic man. **1867** E. F. BOWDEN tr. *Fathers of Desert* 149 An unwieldy Bactrian camel had gone mad.

transf. **1553** T. WILSON *Rhet.* 2b, Nothyng is more nedefull, then..to cherishe these our lompishe and vnweldie natures. **1606** CHAPMAN *Gent. Usher* III. ii. 174 She shall have an unweldie and dull soule If she be nothing moov'd with my poore tongue. **1635** A. STAFFORD *Panegyricke* in *Female Glory* e 7, The toylesome burthen of unweldy clay.

b. Characterized by clumsy massiveness, awkward shape, or ponderousness.

1582 STANYHURST *Æneis* III. (Arb.) 83 When that..strayts shal be opned neere craggy vnwieldye Pelorus. **1596** SPENSER *F.Q.* VI. viii. 28 Th' other Knight, Whom with his weight vnweldy downe he held. **1610** HOLLAND *Camden's Brit.* I. 39 As a ship of exceeding great bulke..endangered through the own unweldy hugenesse. **1671** MILTON *Samson* 54 But what is strength without a double share Of wisdom, vast, unwieldy, burdensom. **1720** POPE *Iliad* XVII. 834 As when two mules..Drag some vast beam, or mast's unwieldy length. **1753** HOGARTH *Anal. Beauty* vi. 30 Elephants and whales please us with their unwieldy greatness. **1793** T. BEDDOES *Observ.* 101 Two cases of unwieldy corpulence. **1828** LYTTON *Pelham* II. xxi, His person..was of no unwieldy obesity. **1856** KANE *Arct. Expl.* I. xx. 260 Of such unwieldy bulk as not unfrequently to be mistaken for the walrus. **1892** *Photogr. Ann.* 374 On account of its unwieldy dimensions.

c. Expressed, manifested, or exhibited in a clumsy, awkward, or ungraceful manner; awkwardly performed.

a **1635** CORBET *Poems* (1807) 107 What a sting Of lust do their unwildy daunces bring? **1648** J. BEAUMONT *Psyche* VII. xxxii, O'rpowr'd with most unweildy thanks and praise. **1728** THOMSON *Spring* 776 The broad Monsters..flounce, and tumble in unwieldy Joy. **1748** *Anson's Voy.* II. i. 124 Their motion being the most unweildy that can be conceived. **1789** COWPER *On Queen's Visit to London* 20 [Water] Up-spouted by a whale in air, T'express unwieldy joy. **1824** MISS FERRIER *Inher.* lxxviii, The manners of Lady C..made her feel her own as something unwieldy and overgrown. **1850** L. HUNT *Autobiog.* xvii. (1860) 268 Two grampuses..interested us extremely by their unwieldy gambols.

3. a. Of weapons: Difficult to handle or wield. Also *transf.*

a **1547** SURREY *Æneid* II. (1557) C ii b, The aged man.. Forceless..cast his weake unweldy dart. **1595** *Locrine* III. iv. 44 This great vnwildie club. **1646** H. LAWRENCE *Comm. Angells* 173 The weapon would be too heavy, to unweildy for us to use. **1700** S. L. tr. *Fryke's Voy. E. Ind.* 160 With my unwildy weapon..I struck him into the left side. **1719** DE FOE *Crusoe* II. (Globe) 368 These Swords were strange great unweildy Things. **1745** P. THOMAS *Jrnl. Anson's Voy.* 289 Pole-axes like ours, but somewhat more rough and unweildy.

b. Difficult to control, guide, move, manipulate, etc., by virtue of size, shape, or weight; clumsily massive, awkwardly large; unmanageable.

1552 ELYOT s.v. *Inhabilis*, A ship that by reason of the biggenesse is vnwildie. **1644** MILTON *Areop.* (Arb.) 71 Untill hee see our small divided maniples cutting through at every angle of his ill united and unweildy brigade. **1663** COWLEY *The Complaint* v, The dull work of thy un-weildy Plough. **1679** MOXON *Mech. Exerc.* ix. 161 These Doors are commonly un-weildy to lift off and on. **1774** J. BRYANT *Mythol.* II. 408 Ships, which were unwieldy, and of great burden. **1814** LD. J. RUSSELL in S. Walpole *Life* (1889) I. 75 His legs being quite swollen and unwieldy. **1865** KINGSLEY *Herew.* xxi, A pole..which he dragged after him, like an unwieldy tail. **1879** S. C. BARTLETT *Egypt to Pal.* xix. 406 Division-walls,..composed of large and un-wieldy stones.

c. *fig.*, *transf.*, and in fig. context.

1538 STARKEY *England* iii. 79 We haue ouer-many [priests], wych..make our polytyke body vnweldy and heuy. **1589** *Almond for Parrat* B iij, His..burlibond adiunctes, that so pester his former edition with their vnweldie phrase, as no true syllogisme can haue elbowe roome. **1612** DRAYTON *Poly-olb.* ix. 139 [To] make us Britains beare Th' vnwieldy Norman yoke. **1632** LITHGOW *Trav.* IV. 144 This vnwealdy body [of the Ottoman dominion in Persia] hauing two heads, began to decline. **1665** BOYLE *Occas. Refl.* IV. xix. 125 Though an unwieldy Affluence may afford some empty Pleasure to the Imagination. *a* **1704** T. BROWN *Praise Poverty* Wks. 1720 I. 113 Raising their own Fortunes to an unweildy Bulk. **1744** AKENSIDE *Pleas. Imag.* III. 117 Hints deep-omened with unwieldy schemes, And dark portents of state. **1777** BURKE *Let. to Sheriffs of Bristol* Wks. III. 187 The unwieldy haughtiness of a great ruling nation. **1796** MORSE *Amer. Geog.* I. p. vi, The second fault of Guthrie's Grammar..is its unweildy and disproportionate account of Great Britain. **1807** J. BARLOW *Columb.* VI. 331 Athenian youths, the unwieldy war to meet, Couch the stiff lance. **1826–7** H. NEELE *Lit. Rem.* (1829) 49 The 'Iliad' [of Chapman] is written in the cumbrous and unwieldy old English measure of fourteen syllables.

absol. **1702** STEELE *Funeral* III. 44 That strong Masculine thing..pretends to all the Tenderness in the World! and would Fain put the Unwieldy upon us for the Soft, the Languid!

4. Indisposed to submit to guidance or command; restive, recalcitrant, indocile. Also const. *to.*

1513 DOUGLAS *Æneid* XIII. vi. 34 [He] went..the onweldy common pepill ilkane To caus adres eftir thar facultie. **1549** COVERDALE, etc. *Erasm. Par. Titus* 28 That nacion beyng rebellious and vnweyldy to be ordered. **1584** LODGE *Alarum* E iv, What praise deserueth he that will proffer..the raine to an unwildie colt? **1611** SPEED *Hist. Gt. Brit.* IX. xvi. §30. 659/2 The Flemings grew vnweildie to his commandements. **1730** T. BOSTON *Mem.* vi. (1899) 67 In the forenoon I thought my heart was very unweildy.

fig. and *transf.* *c* **1611** CHAPMAN *Iliad* XIV. 13 As when with vnwieldie waues, the great Sea forefeeles winds, That both waies murmure. **1641** MILTON *Reform.* I. 13 Exact Reformation is not perfited at the first push, and those unweildy Times of Edward 6. may hold some Plea by this excuse. *a* **1699** J. BEAUMONT *Psyche* x. ccclxxxvii, He knows the heat of this unweildy Passion, And will allow it brave Immoderation.

†5. Inexpert or awkward (*in* doing something); incapable, unpractical. *Obs.*

1666 J. DAVIES *Hist. Caribby Isles* 201 They are..so fearful and unwieldy in the handling of Armes, that they are easily reduc'd under subjection. **1709** STEELE *Tatler* No. 27 ¶2 A Rake..is a poor unwieldy Wretch, that commits Faults out of the Redundance of his good Qualities.

un'wifed, *a.* [UN-^{1} 9. Cf. UNWIVED *ppl. a.*] Not made a wife.

1834 LYTTON *Pilgr. Rhine* xix, The unwifed mother that ..casts her babe upon the river.

un'wifelike, *a.* (UN-^{1} 7 c.)

1853 MISS YONGE *Heir of Redclyffe* xxxi, I can't be so unwife-like after all; for..nothing makes me feel so small and foolish as that humility of his!

un'wifely, *a.* (UN-^{1} 7.)

1864 'ANNIE THOMAS' *D. Donne* III. 183 His wife's illness came from a most unwifely frame of mind. (Also in recent use.)

un'wig, *v.* [UN-^{2} 4.] *trans.* To divest of a wig.

1819 *Metropolis* II. 125 A button..entangling with her peruque, unmasked, or rather *unwigged* the Virgin of the Sun. **1897** *Westm. Gaz.* 6 Aug. 8/2 A tradition as to Baron Martin having unwigged himself..at Durham.

un'wigged, *ppl. a.* [UN-^{1} 8.] Not covered with a wig.

1845 LD. COCKBURN *Circuit Journeys* (1888) 269 [Lord] Moncrieff..went..and heard his friend..preach. He was unwigged, but perfectly well known in that congregation. **1895** J. C. SNAITH *Mistr. D. Marvin* v, His unshaved chin, his unwigged head.

†un'wight, *sb. Obs.* [UN-^{1} 4 b. Cf. ON. *úvættr* evil spirit.] An evil being or spirit; a fiend or monster; *spec.* the devil.

a **1200** *St. Marher.* 3 Ne þole þu neauer þe unwiht þat he weorri mi wit. *c* **1205** LAY. 15734 Nat ic..wha hine biȝate inne weorlde riche, no whaðer hit weore unwiht. *a* **1225** *Ancr. R.* 238 Hwo se..uihteð..aȝan þe unwiht of helle. *Ibid.* 300 þe sunfule is þe unwihtes lond. *a* **1250** *Owl & Night.* 33 Vnwyht, heo seyde, awey þu fleo. *Ibid.* 218 Hwi dostu þat vnwihtes doþ? þu singest anyht & nouht aday. *c* **1230** *Hali Meid.* 41 þu forhores te wið þe unwiht of helle. *c* **1275** *Sinners Beware* 4 in *O.E. Misc.* 72 þeos holy gostes myhte.. wisse vs and theche To wyten vs wyþ þan vnwihte, þat ..þencheþ vs to bipeche.

b. Used as *adj.* (but the Cotton MS. has *unwrþ* 'unworth', rhyming with *noȝt wrþ*).

a **1250** *Owl & Night.* (Jesus MS.) 339 þu..makest þi song so vnwiht þat me ne telleþ of þe nowiht.

†un'wight, *a. Obs.*$^{-0}$ (UN-^{1} 7.)

1570 LEVINS *Manip.* 120 Vnwight, *inualidus.*

un'wild, *a.* [UN-^{1} 7. Cf. MDu. *onwilt.*] Not wild; tame.

a **1400** *Religious Pieces fr. Thornton MS.* 89 Thou was witty and wyse, thi werkes vn-wylde. **1608** TOPSELL *Serpents* 88 Both these sorts [of wasps], both wilde and vnwilde.

†un'wild, *v. Obs.*$^{-1}$ [UN-^{2} 6 a.] *trans.* To tame.

1598 SYLVESTER *Du Bartas* II. i. *Handy-crafts* 277 Abel desirous still at hand to keep His Milk and Cheese, vnwildes [F. *dessauvage*] the gentle Sheep To make a flock.

un'wilful, *a.* [UN-^{1} 7.]

1. Involuntary; unintentional; undesigned.

1398 TREVISA *Barth. De P.R.* VII. xviii. (Bodl. MS.), Un-wilful rennyng of teeres falleþ in þe yȝen somtyme of outeward causes. *c* **1430** *Life St. Kath.* (1884) 38 þe vnwylfulle confession of fendes ys not to be sette lyght by. *c* **1450** *Myrr. our Ladye* 51 He that leuyth oughte by vnwylfull neglygence..synneth not deadly. **1577** tr. *Bullinger's Decades* 511/1 Of sinnes some are wilfull and some vnwilfull, or in-forced. **1603** H. CHETTLE *Eng. Mourn. Garment* D 2, How euer wilfull or vnwilfull the acte was, done it was. *a* **1711** KEN *Hymnotheo* Poet. Wks. 1721 III. 128 Few Years will wash away unwilful Taints. **1751** RICHARDSON *Clarissa* (ed. 4) I. 7 To make excuses..for the perhaps not unwilful slights of those whose approbation we wish to engage.

2. Not wilful, obstinate, or perverse. *rare.*

1570 LEVINS *Manip.* 186 Vnwilfull, *illicentiosus, continens.* **1863** COWDEN CLARKE *Shaks. Char.* vii. 184 As if, at his years, Lear..could become unwilful, and even pliable.

un'wilfully, *adv. rare.* [UN-^{1} 11. Cf. prec.]

1. Unintentionally; involuntarily; undesignedly.

1382 WYCLIF *Prol. Bible* iii. 5 Citees of refuyt..for hem that shedden blood vnwilfully, not of purpos. **1627** SANDERSON *Serm.* I. 265 He did it unwittingly, and therefore unwilfully.

†2. Against one's wish or will. *Obs.*$^{-1}$

1435 MISYN *Fire of Love* 52 Qwho wilfully god despisyd in dedely syn in casting down, vnwilfully after þis lyfe, god demand, sal be dampnyd.

†un'will, *sb.*^{1} *Obs.* [OE. *unwilla* (UN-^{1} 4 b, 12), = MLG. *unwille*, MDu. *onwille* (Du. *onwil*), OS. **unwillo* (gen. *unwilles*), OHG. *unwillo* (MHG., G. *unwille*), ON. and Icel. *úvili* (Da. *uvilje*, Sw. *ovilja*), displeasure, reluctance.]

1. Used adverbially, in genitive (usually with possessive pron.): Against one's will; unwillingly.

The normal OE. genitive *unwillan* is replaced by *unwilles* on the analogy of *willes* (see WILL *sb.*^{1} 10) and other adverbial genitives. For the adverbial use, cf. OS. *unwilles*, MLG. *unwillens*, older Flem. *onwillens*, MDu. *mijns onwillen.*

c **893** K. ÆLFRED *Oros.* VI. xxxviii, Siþþan sæton þa Gotan þær on lande, sume be þæs caseres willan, sume his unwillan. *c* **1000** in Thorpe *Laws* II. 182 ðif he hit dide unwilles. *c* **1000** ÆLFRIC *Saints' Lives* ix. 87 þeah þu mine hand ahebbe to ðinum hæþenȝilde, And swa þurh me ȝeoffriȝe mines unwilles. *a* **1225** *Juliana* 6 (Roy. MS.), Affrican ..ȝettede him his dohter, & wes sone ihondsald al hire unwilles. *c* **1375** *Sc. Leg. Saints* vii. (*James*) 373 þe men als þare wnwillis Suld to þe prince be brocht thrillis.

b. *at* (or *again*) *one's unwilles*, = prec. *rare*$^{-1}$.

Cf. ON. *at uvilja einhvers* against one's will.

c **1400** *Anturs of Arth.* 424 (Ireland MS.), ȝette schalle thou wring thi hondus,..Or any we schild hom weld, atte my unnewilles [*Douce MS.* agayne myne vmwylles].

2. Something displeasing or undesired; that which is against a person's will or wish; (one's) dislike or aversion.

c **1000** in *Sal. & Saturn* (1848) 262 Nafu ðu to yfel ellen. ðeah ðe sum unwilla on becume. *a* **1023** WULFSTAN *Hom*, 12 He dryhð deofles wyllan and godes unwillan. *a* **1200** *St. Marher.* 13 Ich mot nede, ant neoðeles min unwil hit is to don al þat ti wil is. *c* **1200** *Trin. Coll. Hom.* 123 Here [he] wuneð on wanrede and poleð his unwille. *a* **1225** *Juliana* (Bodl. MS.) 7 Ha wes him sone ihondsald þah hit hire unwil were. *a* **1250** *Owl & Night.* 422 þu farest so doþ þe ille, Euerich blisse him is vnwille. *a* **1300** *Cursor M.* 25261 Lauerd gif vs to Grace in erth þi wil to do, For to forber all þin vnwil.

un'will, *sb.*^{2} [UN-^{1} 12 + WILL *sb.* Cf. prec.]

1. The fact or condition of being displeased or offended; displeasure.

1872 WHITLEY STOKES *Goidelica* 182 Great folly, since thou hast proposed (?) to go to death, to be under the unwill of Mary's Son. **1895** K. MEYER *Voy. Bran* i. 14 Woe to him that shall be under His unwill.

2. Lack of will or purpose.

1899 W. S. BLUNT *Satan Absolved* 18 Thy Will found counterpart Only in Man's un-Will, Thy Truth in his un-Truth.

un'will, *v.* [UN-^{2} 3.]

1. a. *trans.* To will or resolve the reverse of (something one has willed); = UNRESOLVE *v.*

1650 HOWELL *Giraffi's Rev. Naples* I. 120 He would will and unwill a thing at the same instant. **1678** R. L'ESTRANGE *Seneca's Morals* III. 50 It is the Business of my Age to Unwill one day, that which I Will'd Another. **1849** J. A. CARLYLE tr. *Dante's Inf.* 16 One who unwills what he willed. **1870** J. H. NEWMAN *Gram. Assent* I. iv. 69 That which willed it, can unwill it. **1871** BROWNING *Pr. Hohenst.* 1472 What if the event demonstrate her unwise, If she unwill the thing she willed before?

b. With reference to WILL *sb.*^{1} (= testament).

1660 R. COKE *Power & Subj.* 23 Therefore if a Man make twenty Wills, yet when he will, he may unwill them all. **1854** WARTER *Last of Old Squires* xviii. 195 [He saw] that there was a democratic Desire abroad to *unwill* what good Men in former Days had *willed.*

c. To revoke or reverse (one's will or purpose).

1871 BROWNING *Balaust.* 163 Wouldst thou..Unwill thy will to reign a righteous king?

2. To divest of volition; to deprive (a person) of will-power.

1844 MRS. BROWNING *Duchesss May* III. vi, Now, your will is all unwilled—now, your pulses are all stilled. **1891** MEREDITH *One of our Conq.* I. xii. 232 The precedent of submission is a charm upon the faint-hearted through love: it unwinds, unwills them.

unwille, *a.*: see UN-^{1} 3.

un'willed, *ppl. a.* [UN-^{1} 8 + WILL *v.*^{1}]

1. Not willed or intended; not decided by the will; involuntary; unintentional; undesigned.

a **1540** BARNES *Wks.* (1573) 309/1 For our Lord can easely beare and suffer an vnwilled ignoraunce. **1598** FLORIO, *Inuoluto*, vnwilled, neuer consenting. *a* **1711** KEN *Hymnarium* Poet Wks. 1721 II. 133 We..are judg'd by Law innate, And God for unwill'd Failings will abate. ? **172.** A. HILL *Verses for Mr. Savage* 25 Some secret fate for guilt unwill'd..Plung'd me thus deep in sorrow's searching flood. **1791** E. DARWIN *Bot. Garden* II. 93 She speaks..With words unwill'd, and wisdom not her own. **1803** JANE PORTER *Thaddeus* vi, This unfortunate event..was completely un-willed on my part. **1854** S. DOBELL *Balder* xxiv. 168 At first ..[it] Did stir thee with no more than an unwilled Attention. **1857** G. MACDONALD *Poems* (1867) 68 My heart with unwilled love grew warm.

2. Undesired. *rare*$^{-0}$.

1648 HEXHAM II, *Ongewilt*, Vnwilled, or not liked off.

3. Left without being willed or purposed.

1863 LD. LYTTON *Ring Amasis* II. 291 Fool, to forget that Will can only be annihilated by Will; that good unwilled is evil willed.

un'willing, *ppl. a.* [OE. *unwillende* (UN-[1] 10), = ON. and Icel. *ú-, óviljandi.* Cf. MLG. *unwillendes.* Re-formed in 16th cent.]

†**1.** Of persons: Not intending, purposing, or desiring (to do a particular thing). *Obs.*

c **897** K. ÆLFRED *Gregory's Past C.* xxxiii. 214 Ðæt hie [*sc.* the impatient] ne hliepen unwillende on ðæt scorene clif unðeawa. *c* **1330** R. BRUNNE *Chron. Wace* (Rolls) 862 Wyþ þat schote his ffader he slow; Al unwylland þat draught he drow.

2. Of persons, etc.: Not inclined, willing, or ready; averse, reluctant, loath. Also in fig. context.

In quot. 1606 the comparative is used with adverbial force, = more unwillingly.

c **1000** in *Ags. Hom.* (Assmann) 180 Min drihten hit wat, þæt ic hit unwillende do, þæt ic æfre þas dæda ʒefremme. **1538** ELYOT, *Inuitus*,.. vnwyllynge, or agaynste a mannes wylle. **1586** MARLOWE *1st Pt. Tamburl.* II. i, Marching.. with vnwilling souldiers faintly arm'd. **1593** SHAKS. *Rich. II*, I. iii. 245 You gaue leaue to my vnwilling tong, Against my will, to do my selfe this wrong. **1606** G. WOODCOCKE *Hist. Ivstine* IX. 40 To which request Phillip vrged he should of reason so much the vnwillinger condiscend. **1644** MILTON *Areop.* (Arb.) 32 The tardiest, and the unwillingest of them that praise yee. **1746** FRANCIS tr. *Horace, Epist.* I. viii. 9 With unwilling Ear The Voice of Comfort, or of Health I hear. **1761** GRAY *Descent of Odin* 49 Unwilling I my lips unclose. **1817** SHELLEY *Rev. Islam* XI. xiv, On each unwilling heart Unusual awe did fall. **1849** JAMES *Woodman* vii, Evidently intended to bring up unwilling eels out of their native mud. **1870** BRYANT *Iliad* IV. I. 106, I fully yield me to thy wish Though with unwilling mind. **1897** NICHOLSON *Golspie* 22 This unwilling workman's curse lay on the family for ever.

absol. *a* **1586** SIDNEY *Arcadia* II. xxvii, Thus armed, thus governed, forcing the unwilling,..they came headlong towarde this lodge. *a* **1658** LOVELACE *Poems* (1904) 193 Fates lead the willing, but unwilling draw. **1765** BLACKSTONE *Comm.* I. 44 Counsel acts only upon the willing, law upon the unwilling also.

b. Const. *to* with inf., or with clause.

In very frequent use from *c* 1630, usu. with *to* and inf.

1533 SIR T. MORE *Debell. Salem* Wks. 1030/2, I..shewe my selfe vnwilling that the priestes should doe it neither. **1548** ELYOT s.v. *Respuo*, To be vnwillyng to here hym speake. *a* **1586** SIDNEY *Arcadia* II. ix, And so went they away from verie unwilling people to leave them. **1618** SELDEN *Hist. Tithes* III. vi. 1114 Every man..would have been the unwillinger to have specially endowed the church. **1664** in *Verney Memoirs* (1907) II. 212, I am unwilling you should be soe much alone. **1725** DE FOE *Voy. round World* (1840) 115, I was unwilling to run any more risks. **1765** *Museum Rust.* IV. 287 We should be very unwilling to offend him. **1821** SCOTT *Kenilw.* vi, I own I were unwilling he should learn what nowise concerns him. **1878** BROWNING *La Saisiaz* 28 Then my fellow takes the tale up, not unwilling to aver..'I knew him best of all'.

c. *transf.* of things.

1592 SHAKS. *Ven. & Ad.* 1051 Her eyes,..being open'd, threw unwilling light Upon the wide wound..in his soft flank. **1593** —— *Lucr.* 309 As each unwilling portal yields him way. **1692** DRYDEN *Don Sebastian* III. i, Why shou'd you pluck the green distasteful Fruit From the unwilling Bough. **1697** —— *Virg. Georg.* I. 144 For he, with frequent exercise, commands The unwilling soil, and tames the stubborn lands. **1704** TRAPP *Abra-Mulé* II. i. 416 A stiff unwilling Bow. **1748** GRAY *Alliance* 43 There industry and gain their vigils keep, Command the Winds, and tame th' unwilling Deep. **1848** MRS. GASKELL *M. Barton* iv, She.. lighted the unwilling fire, borrowing a pair of bellows to make it burn the faster. **1896** *Idler* March 291/2, I..pushed open the unwilling baize-covered door.

†**3.** Undesirous *of* something. *Obs. rare.*

a **1575** tr. *Pol. Verg. Eng. Hist.* (Camden, No. 29) 54 Neyther partie was unwilling of peace. **1590** PEELE *Polyhemnia* Wks. 1829 II. 210 On lusty horse That, angry with delay,.. Would snort,..Unwilling of his master's tarriance.

†**4.** *unwilling to* (*unto*), contrary to the will or desire of (a person). *Obs. rare.*

1555 EDEN *Decades* (Arb.) 334 They shall not touche any thynge of yowres vnwyllyng vnto yow. **1654** GAYTON *Pleas. Notes* IV. 171 Your hair (unwilling to your self) discovers you.

†**5.** Involuntary; unintentional; unwilled. *Obs.*

1535 *Trevisa's Barth. De P.R.* VII. lv. 105 b/2 Somtyme comyth vnwyllynge pyssynge, and that euyll hyghte.. Diabethica passio. **1587** GOLDING *De Mornay* 519 This high preest shalbe the..speech of God, cleere from sinne aswel willing as vnwilling. **1596** SHAKS. *Tam. Shr.* IV. i. 159 Patience I pray you, 'twas a fault vnwilling. **1687** DRYDEN *Hind & P.* III. 842 Good fortune may present some happier time, With means to cancel my unwilling crime.

6. Performed or manifested, expressed or avowed, reluctantly or unwillingly.

1613 in *Sidney's Arcadia* (1629) 343 Then went hee towards Pyrocles..and acquainted him with his vnwilling absenting himselfe. **1659** W. CHAMBERLAYNE *Pharon.* IV. v. 403 That soft delays..to an unwilling stay His fierce pursuers would ere long betray. **1665** BP. PATRICK *Parab. Pilgr.* viii. 29 It can [not] be acceptable to God to see men crouch in this fashion to him, and..afford him their unwilling prostrations. **1741** W. WHITEHEAD *Danger Writing Verse* 235 Must the Muse th' unwilling task pursue? **1764** GOLDSM. *Trav.* 352 Fictitious bonds, the bonds of wealth and law, Still gather strength, and force unwilling awe. **1822** MILMAN *Belshazzar* 93 Oh! bear a brief unwilling banishment From thine own home, my heart. **1855** MACAULAY *Hist. Eng.* xv. III. 529 That sagacity and energy which had..extorted the unwilling admiration of his enemies.

un'willingly, *adv.* [f. prec. + -LY[2].]

1. Contrary to one's will; against one's wish or desire; reluctantly.

In frequent use from *c* 1550.

a **1533** FRITH *Disput. Purgat.* Wks. (1572) 19/2 If thou do it for feare or vnwillyngly. *a* **1568** ASCHAM *Scholem.* I. (Arb.) 43 What soeuer the mynde doth learne vnwillinglie with feare. **1647** CLARENDON *Hist. Reb.* I. (1702) I. 5 The late abuse having..driven his Majesty unwillingly out of that course. **1667** LILLY *Hist. Life & Times* (1715) 88 A new Parliament was called, whereunto I was unwillingly invited by two Messengers. *a* **1715** BURNET *Own Time* (1897) I. ii. 42 They very unwillingly hearkened to that proposition. **1797** S. & HT. LEE *Canterb. T.* (1799) I. 141 Not unwillingly, [he] resigned his place to some ladies. **1818** SCOTT *Br. Lamm.* ix, His was a mind unwillingly roused from contemplative inactivity. **1848** DICKENS *Dombey* ii, [He] departed by no means unwillingly. **1883** MISS BROUGHTON *Belinda* III. ix, She has withdrawn her unwillingly-captured hand.

transf. *a* **1713** in Lady M. W. Montagu *Lett.* (1887) I. 83 In this cold climate where the sun appears Unwillingly.

b. In loose construction.

a **1586** SIDNEY *Apol. Poetrie* (Arb.) 51 Though a man should graunt their first assumption, it should followe (me thinkes) very unwillingly, that good is not good, because better is better. **1665** J. WEBB *Stone-Heng* (1725) 140 The Design of which..follows, the narrowness of the Plate unwillingly depriving you of two of the Entrances at the Trench. **1671** MILTON *Samson* 14 This day a solemn Feast the people hold,..unwillingly this rest Thir Superstition yields me.

†**2.** Involuntarily; unintentionally. *Obs.*

1594 SHAKS. *Rich. III*, II. i. 55 If I vnwillingly, or in my rage, Haue ought committed that is hardly borne. **1644** NYE *Gunnery* (1670) 2 A Monk did unwillingly let fall a spark of fire upon Brimstone and Saltpeter. **1660** COKE *Power & Subj.* 152 If a man slea another not lurking.., or unwillingly, or of necessity.

un'willingness. [f. as prec. + -NESS.] The state or condition of being unwilling, reluctant, or loath; reluctance; disinclination.

1593 SHAKS. *Rich. II*, I. iii. 149 Norfolke: for thee remaines a heauier dombe, Which I with some vnwillingnesse pronounce. *c* **1600** CHALKHILL *Thealma & Cl.* 51 How fain she would have..made Her grief, though with unwillingness, to set Open the floodgates of her speech. **1615** E. S. *Britain's Buss* E 2 b, The difficulties that Vnwillingnes hath obiected. **1694** F. BRAGGE *Disc. Parables* VII. 248 Unwillingness in doing anything, as if 'twere.. forced from one, rather than proceeded from a free inclination. **1720** WODROW *Corr.* (1843) II. 532 Which made me apprehend his unwillingness was not so great as was talked of. **1796** MME. D'ARBLAY *Camilla* V. 52 [He] had ..been forced into the party, though with added unwillingness. **1825** LAMB *Elia* II. *Wedding*, To this unwillingness..may be traced the difference of opinion on this point. **1883** F. M. PEARD *Contrad.* I. 34 Leigh went towards it with some unwillingness.

b. Const. *to*, or with *that* and clause.

In very frequent use with *to* from *c* 1650.

(*a*) **1594** SOUTHWELL *M. Magd. Funeral Teares* 6 The vnwillingnesse that his image should die with her. *a* **1665** J. GOODWIN *Filled w. the Spirit* (1670) 313 [These] do not argue any the least degree of unwillingness in God that men should be saved. **1665** BOYLE *Occas. Refl.* IV. xii. 80 My Unwillingness that one Theme should detain us any longer. **1884** *Leeds Merc.* 24 Oct. 4/4 His profound unwillingness that the question..should be mooted.

(*b*) **1605** LD. MOUNTAGUE in *Facsimiles Nat. MSS.* IV. 10 The unwillingnesse I sawe in her to my goeing downe. **1631** GOUGE *God's Arrows* I. §11. 16 Gods unwillingnesse to plague the righteous with the unrighteous. **1712** STEELE *Spect.* No. 427 ¶1 The Unwillingness to receive good Tidings. **1855** MACAULAY *Hist. Eng.* xxii. IV. 785 An unwillingness to run any great risk. **1882** BESANT *All Sorts* xxxiv. (1898) 236 Unwillingness to admit new things..and reluctance to unlearn old things.

†**un'willy,** *a. Obs.* [UN-[1] 7. Cf. OHG. (G.) *unwillig* (MHG. *unwillic*), (M)Du. *onwillig*, ON. *úviljugr* (Da. *uvillig*, Sw. *ovillig*).]

1. Unwilling (*to* do something); averse.

c **1200** *Trin. Coll. Hom.* 93 Sinne hem is loð to leten, and unwilliche to bete. **1395** PURVEY *Remonstr.* (1851) 139 A man vnmyghti othir vnwilli to gouerne it duli. *c* **1440** *Promp. Parv.* 314 Lothe, or vnwylly, *involuntarius, inspontaneus.* *c* **1475** *Cath. Angl.* 418/2 (A.), Vn Wylly, *coactus, jnuitus.*

2. Involuntary. *rare*[−1].

1398 TREVISA *Barth. De P.R.* VII. lv. (1495) 269 Somtime comyth vnwylly pyssynge. [Cf. UNWILLING *ppl. a.* 5.]

un'wily, *a.* [UN-[1] 7.] Not wily, artful, or cunning; †simple, silly.

a **1300** *Cursor M.* 738 He ches a littel best þe quilk es noght vnwiliest. *c* **1475** *Cath. Angl.* 418/1 (A.), Vn Wyly; *vbi* fonde. **1594** W. PERCY in Arber *Garner* (1895) VI. 149 Unwily man! why couldst not keep thee there? **1603** FLORIO *Montaigne* I. xxiv. 63 The plaine husbandman, or the vnwily shoomaker. **1612** W. PARKES *Curtaine-Dr.* (1876) 12 The skins or cases that the vnwily serpents of our age haue cast. **1846** WORCESTER (citing *Eclectic Rev.*).

†**un'wimple,** *v. Obs.* [UN-[2] 4. Cf. MDu. *ontwimpelen.*] *trans.* To remove the wimple from.

c **1430** *Syr Gener.* (Roxb.) 9953 She vnwimpled hir..And wipt hir face. **1470–85** MALORY *Arthur* X. xxxix. 476 Thenne she vnwympeled her vysage.

†**un'win,** *sb. Obs.* [UN-[1] 12. Cf. OS. *unwunni*, OHG. *unwunna* (MHG. *unwunne, unwünne*).] Grief, sorrow, distress.

c **1175** *Lamb. Hom.* 71 Kep us..from iwilch heued sunne, þet he ne bringe us in to unwune. *a* **1200** *Moral Ode* 208 Adam and his of-sprung..Wes fele undret wintre an helle pine and an unwunne. *c* **1275** *Sayings of Bede* 160 in Horstm. *Alteng. Leg.* (1881) 507 Hy shulen to þere ounwinne. *a* **1300** in *E.E.P.* (1862) 21 Sinne me hauiþ in care ibroȝt, broȝt in mochil vn-winne. *c* **1310** in Wright *Lyric P.* xv. 47 Un-wunne haveth myn wonges wet. *a* **1400** *Northern Passion* 1242 Of me þai hafe gret syn At gaffe me vppe to þis vnvyn. *c* **1480** *Bk. of Brome* (1886) 96 As they hadyn hym ferder inne Ther he sawe woll mykyll on-wyn. ? *a* **1500** *Chester Pl.* XXIV. 471 Lord, on this I can not myn,.. Thee in mischeif or any vnwyn To shew thee such a will.

†**un'win,** *a. Obs.*[−1] [App. f. after prec.] Grievous.

c **1320** *Sir Tristr.* 1235 Þe leuedi of heiȝe kenne, His woundes schewe..he lete, To wite his wo vnwinne.

un'wincing, *ppl. a.* (UN-[1] 10.)

1802 WOLCOT (P. Pindar) *Pitt & Statue, Thief* 21 As soon as Justice had perform'd her part Upon the Rogue's unwincing hide. **1813** *Examiner* 1 Feb. 73/2 A haughty unwincing firmness against every attack.

unwind (ʌn'waɪnd), *v.*[1] [UN-[2] 3. Cf. OE. (rare) *unwindan, onwindan*, = (M)Du. *ontwinden*, OS. *antwindan*, OHG. *intwindan* (MHG. and G. *ent-*), to untwist, disentangle.]

1. a. *trans.* To wind off, move back, or detach (a wrapping, covering, bandage, etc.); to undo the folds or convolutions of (thread, tape, or the like); to untwine, untwist.

c **1325** *Lai le Freine* 189 Therto he yede and it [*sc.* a furred skin] vnwond, And the..child therin he fond. *c* **1440** *Promp. Parv.* 368 On-wyndyn, or on-twynyn.., *detorqueo.* **1597** A. M. tr. *Guillemeau's Fr. Chirurg.* 43 b/2 To wind, and agayne vnwinde the same [bandages]. **1599** SHAKS. *Hen. V*, I. ii. 101 Gracious Lord, Stand for your owne, vnwind your bloody Flagge. **1605** BACON *Adv. Learn.* II. xviii. §8 Skaynes or Bottomes of thread.. bee vnwinded at large, when they come to be vsed. **1713** BLACKMORE *Creation* VI. 294 Engendering heats these one by one unbind, Stretch their small tubes, and hamper'd nerves unwind. **1759** in *Phil. Trans.* LI. 55 The pod [= cocoon] could not be easily unwinded. **1817** SHELLEY *Rev. Islam* V. lvii, She did unwind Her veil. **1818** KEATS *Endym.* II. 851 The fair visitant at last unwound Her gentle limbs, and left the youth asleep. **1839** DICKENS *Nickleby* xxix, 'Pooh! pooh!' said Mr. Folair, unwinding his comforter.

refl. **1740** R. BROOKES *Art Angling* 10 As soon as the Pike takes the Bait,..the Line unwinds itself off the Trimmer. **1831** SCOTT *Ct. Rob.* xvi, A skein of fine silk..unwinding itself as it descended.

b. *fig.* and in fig. context.

1387–8 T. USK *Test. Love* III. ix. (Skeat) l. 77 In this boke be many privy thinges wimpled and folde; unneth shul leude men the plites unwinde. **1482** CAXTON *Polychron.* 5 b, My wytte is full lytil to vnwynde the wrappynges of so wonderful werkes. *a* **1586** SIDNEY *Arcadia* II. xx, That it should have neded a stronger vertue then his, to have unwound so deeply an entred vice. **1591** SHAKS. *Two Gent.* III. ii. 51 As you vnwinde her loue from him; Least it should rauell. *a* **1613** OVERBURY *Remedy of Love* 8, I mean not to blot out what I have taught, Nor to unwinde the web that I have wrought. *c* **1620** Z. BOYD *Zion's Flowers* (1855) Introd. 13 Thou me unwind that knotty snarled clue. **1669** GLANVILL *Catholic Charity* 52 He..hath many prejudices ..; and these are not to be torn off all at once, but softly, and by degrees to be unwound. **1820** SHELLEY *Witch Atl.* lxx, And she unwound the woven imagery Of second childhood's swaddling bands. **1858** O. W. HOLMES *Aut. Breakf.-t.* viii, Unwinding the endless tapestry of time. **1908** S. E. WHITE *Riverman* xlvi, There's an awful lot of red-tape to unwind, as there always is in such cases.

refl. **1659** W. CHAMBERLAYNE *Pharon.* III. iii. 315 Here his harsh thoughts unwound Themselves in pleasure.

absol. **1638** SIR T. HERBERT *Trav.* (ed. 2) 1 If my new thoughts have added to your bottom, I know you will unwinde gently for feare of ravelling.

c. To cause to uncoil; to free from a coiled state.

1634 SIR T. HERBERT *Trav.* 53 These Wormes they vnwinde with a Pinne and come out daintily. **1638** N. WHITING *Albino & Bellama* Author to Bk. 48 Nor beg those niggards' eyes, who grudge to see A watch unwinded in perusing thee. **1810** *Encycl. Brit.* (ed. 4) XX. 532/1 It is indeed difficult to determine the exact extent of the spiral vessels.., for it is by unwinding them alone that they can be known. **1834–6** *Encycl. Metrop.* (1845) VIII. 641/2 At this instant the spring..is now unwound again.

fig. *a* **1613** OVERBURY *Characters, Melancholy Man*, His imagination..keeps his mind in a continuall motion, as the poise the clocke: he winds up his thoughts often, and as often unwinds them.

d. *fig.* To relieve from tension or anxiety, to cause to relax. *colloq.*

1958 B. MALAMUD in *Partisan Rev.* Spring 180 He managed to unwind himself and relax. **1975** 'W. HAGGARD' *Scorpion Tail* ix. 131 They sat down..the almost neat whisky unwound her.

2. a. To roll, twist, or turn back the wrapping, bandaging, or covering of (a body, etc.); to unwrap. Also, to untwine thread from (a bobbin); to free (a person) *from* bonds, etc.

1596 SPENSER *F.Q.* VI. viii. 27 Then, turning backe vnto that captiue thrall, Who all this while stood..bound,..He from those bands weend him to haue vnwound. **1597** A. M. tr. *Guillemeau's Fr. Chirurg.* 20 b/2 He then vnwyndeth his needle, and openeth the lippes of the wounde. **1608** SYLVESTER *Du Bartas* II. iii. *Vocation* 203 Can I thus (alas!) Rudely vnwinde me from the kinde embrace Of their deer arms. **1882** CAULFEILD & SAWARD *Dict. Needlework* 507/2 To unwind a bobbin so that the thread hanging from it is to be longer. **1902** *Munsey's Mag.* XXVI. 585/1 In he [*sc.* a doctor] came,..and unwound and wound me again.

fig. and in fig. context. **1609** B. JONSON *Sil. Wom.* II. iv, I would roule my selfe for this day, in troth, they should not vnwinde mee. **1697** CONGREVE *Mourn. Bride* II. ix, The conqueror is mine! In chains unseen I hold him by the heart, And can unwind or strain him as I please.

†**b.** *refl.* To free, disengage, or extricate (oneself) from an entanglement, difficulty, etc. *Obs.*

Chiefly employed in figurative contexts.

1561 T. NORTON *Calvin's Inst.* II. 100 Out of these snares we shall easily vnwinde our selues, if we well consider [etc.]. **1597** HOOKER *Eccl. Pol.* v. iv. §2 To vnwinde themselues where the snares of glosing speech doe lye to intangle them. **1601** [? MARSTON] *Pasquil & Kath.* (1878) II. 370 Vnwinde thy selfe from out the Labyrinth Of gaping wonder. **1656** W. MONTAGUE *Accompl. Wom.* 63 Without the thrid that she gave, how could he [*sc.* Theseus] ever have unwinded himself out of those Mazes? **1691** NORRIS *Pract. Disc.* 41 The Pythagoreans taught their disciples..that they must unwind themselves even from their very Bodies, if they would be good Philosophers. **1692** DRYDEN *Don Sebastian* v. i, You could unwind your self from all these dangers. **1701** NORRIS *Ideal World* I. vi. 412 To unwind ourselves from this intanglement.

3. *intr.* To undergo uncoiling or unwinding; to become free from a convoluted state. Also *fig.* and *transf.*

1656 T. WATSON *One Thing Necess.* 19 He is like a watch, when he hath been wound up towards heaven, he doth quickly unwinde to earth, and sinne again. **1681** J. SCOTT *Chr. Life* I. iv. 385 Our holy Fervours will be very apt to cool, our good Purposes to slacken and unwind. **1707** MORTIMER *Husb.* 223 Put the Bottoms into clean scalding Water, and..then will they easily unwind. **1818** BYRON *Ch. Har.* IV. cxxiii, Who loves, raves—'t is youth's frenzy—but the cure Is bitterer still, as charm by charm unwinds Which robed our idols. **1834–6** *Encycl. Metrop.* (1845) VIII. 635/1 As the spring unwinds and acts with less power. **1839** BAILEY *Festus* 334 Would I might die outright! And slip the coil without waiting it unwind. **1860** O. W. HOLMES *Elsie V.* x, She danced with a kind of passionate fierceness,..her round arms wreathing and unwinding.

b. *fig.* To obtain relief from tension or anxiety; to relax. *colloq.*

1938 D. BAKER *Young Man with Horn* IV. vii. 276 He was tired... If he'd ever unwound and relaxed, it would have been all over, he couldn't have lifted a finger. **1958** *Radio Times* 3 Oct. 34/1 (Advt.), After interviews Edana finds she can 'unwind' with 'Aspro' and a cup of tea. **1982** M. RUSSELL *Rainblast* iii. 14 He loved the solitude.. Helped him unwind.

4. *trans.* To open up, to trace or retrace to an issue, outlet, or end. Also in fig. context.

1716 GAY *Trivia* II. 86 Still the wandring passes forc'd his stay, Till Ariadne's clue unwinds the way. **1744** YOUNG *Nt. Th.* VI. 162 How shall the blessed day of our discharge Unwind, at once, the labyrinths of fate. **1760** STERNE *Tr. Shandy* IV. *Slawkenb. Tale*, The fifth act..terminates in unwinding the labyrinth and bringing the hero.. to a state of rest. **1864** BRYANT *Little People of Snow* 213 A cloud of twittering swallows..turn and wheel again, Unwinding their swift track.

fig. **1821** BRYANT *Ages* viii, He whose eye Unwinds the eternal dances of the sky.

Hence **un'winding** *vbl. sb.*

Also, in recent use (1915), *unwinder.*

1648 HEXHAM II, *Een ontdraeyinge*,..an Vnwinding. **1708** WATTS *Horæ Lyricæ* (1727) 161 The dull unwinding of Life's tedious Thread. **1760–72** H. BROOKE *Fool of Qual.* (1809) II. 13 The solution of all knots, and unwinding of all intricacies. **1825** J. NICHOLSON *Operat. Mechanic* 515 The balance, having now all the velocity it would acquire from the unwinding the spring. **1866** MRS. RITCHIE *Village on Cliff* xiv, The whole thing seemed running through her head like the unwinding of a skein. **1895** *Model Steam Engine* 23 The unwinding of a reel of cotton. **1933** H. G. WELLS *Bulpington of Blup* ix. 398 He began..to play with himself that tedious parlour game known as 'unwinding'. **1977** A. MORICE *Scared to Death* xiv. 94 There is something anti-climactic about going straight home..when the curtain comes down and it is quite pleasant to indulge in some gentle unwinding.

attrib. **1889** SLEEMAN *Torpedoes* (ed. 2) 235 The torpedo is launched, and the engine started which is to work the unwinding reels or drums. **1971** D. CLARK *Sick to Death* ii. 23 The unwinding part of the day when most people like to take their ease.

unwind (ʌn'waɪnd), *v.*² [UN-² 4 + WIND *sb.*] *trans.* To deprive (a person) of wind or breath.

1788 *Lond. Mag.* 264 Here, as well as at the pit of the stomach you may unwind him.

un'winding, *ppl. a.* [UN-¹ 10.] Straight; not deviating.

1886 J. PARKER *Apost. Life* III. 67 Stopping-places where we may sit down awhile, and then soon be up again to pursue life's unwinding and immeasurable road.

un'window, *v.* (UN-² 3.)

1710 C. SHADWELL *Fair Quaker Deal* III. 38 Shall we ravish all the Women we meet with, and un-window the Houses?

un'windowed, *a.* (UN-¹ 9.)

[**1775** ASH.] **1820** MATURIN *Melmoth* IV. 52 The low, narrow, and unwindowed rooms. **1897** in W. H. Tomkins *Selborne* (1905) 9 The simple, white-washed, unwindowed gable-side.

†**un'windowed**, obs. north. var. UNWINNOWED.

1578 *Knaresb. Wills* (Surtees) I. 135 Hard corne threshed and unwindowed. **1592** *Wills & Inv. N.C.* (Surtees, 1860) 209, x score bus[h]ells of rye, unwindowed, 20l. Wheat, unwindowed, 4l. 6s. 8d.

un'windy, *a.* (UN-¹ 7.)

1580 in *Liturg. Serv. Q. Eliz.* (1847) 571 The weather being fair, temperate and unwindy. **1848** DICKENS *Haunted Man* iii, His shady corner, where the wind was used to spin with such un-windy constancy.

†**un'wine.** *Obs.* [OE. *unwine* (UN-¹ 4 b), = ON. and Icel. *ú-*, *óvinr* (Norw. *uvin*, MSw. *ovin*, Sw. *ovän*, (M)Da. *uven*).] An enemy or foe.

1050 *Will* in Thorpe *Charters* 584 Ȝif ic onȝen ne cume, þat þu it nefre ne let weldon mine unwinan after me. *c* **1100** *O.E. Chron.* (MS. D) an. 1075, þæt he mihte..his unwinan unþancas don. *c* **1175** *Lamb. Hom.* 53 þos men þe þus to-draȝed heore euencristene bi-hinden..beoð cristes unwines. *c* **1200** ORMIN 19838 þatt time þatt Herode wass Unnwine wiþþ Filippe. *a* **1225** *Leg. Kath.* 1221 Eð were ure lauerd.. to awarpen his unwine.

b. *spec.* The Evil One. (So MSw. *ovin.*)

a **1225** *Ancr. R.* 178 þet te Holi Gost ledde ure Louerd into onliche stude..for to beon itempted of þe unwine, of helle. *a* **1225** *Juliana* 35 Were me swa wið þen vnwine;..þet þu beo..iheiet eaure in eorðe. *a* **1240** *Ureison* in *O.E. Hom.* I. 197 Ne þole þu þene unwine þet he me arine.

un'winged, *a.* [UN-¹ 9.] Lacking wings; wingless.

1601 HOLLAND *Pliny* II. 39 The unwinged Locusts called Tryxalides. **1658** ROWLAND tr. *Moufet's Theat. Ins.* 976 Of these then come the unwinged Glow-worms. *a* **1711** KEN *Psyche* Poet. Wks. 1721 IV. 216 Our unwing'd Arms shall round each other lie. **1753** *Chambers' Cycl.* Suppl. s.v. *Vine-grub*, Both the winged and the unwinged Vine-grubs. **1848** MRS. JAMESON *Sacr. & Leg. Art* I. 37 Two un-winged colossal-looking angel heads.

fig. **1659** W. CHAMBERLAYNE *Pharon.* III. v. 157 He..ends His journey, ere a thought unwinged with love Could lead him forth of 's court. **1818** MILMAN *Samor* VI. 274 For what thought Unwing'd by inbreath'd Godhead e'er might dream Of glory [etc.].

un'winged, *ppl. a.* [UN-² 8.] Deprived of wings.

1613 W. BROWNE *Brit. Past.* I. iii, And so did she.. Conjecture Time unwing'd, he came so slow. **1681** RYCAUT tr. *Gracian's Critick* 73 On the other Side was falling the unwinged Icarus..into the Water.

†**un'wink**, *v. Obs.*⁻¹ [UN-² 3.] *intr.* Of the eye: To open.

c **1440** *Pallad. on Husb.* IV. 25 Whan that their eyen gynneth forto unwynke [L. *aperire*].

un'winking, *ppl. a.* [UN-¹ 10.]

In very frequent use *c* 1855–*c* 1900.

1. Marked by absence of winking; characterized by watchfulness or vigilance.

1782 V. KNOX *Ess.* xvii. ¶9 That unwinking vigilance which a delicate..father will judge necessary in the care of daughters. **1833** MRS. BROWNING *Tempest* 88 The open eyes Of that dead man,..With their unwinking, unexpressive stare. **1857** DICKENS *Dorrit* II. xxviii, The attitude..was now expressive of unwinking watchfulness. **1876** GEO. ELIOT *Dan. Der.* xxv, No fish could have maintained a more unwinking silence. **1896** A. MORRISON *Child Jago* 326 His eyes were red with strained, unwinking attention.

transf. a **1873** B. HARTE in *Fiddletown*, etc. (1873) 127 The sands had a dreadful unwinking glare.

2. Not winking; never closing the eyes.

1811 LAMB *Edax on Appetite* Wks. 1908 I. 153 The broad, unwinking eye of the world. **1863** COWDEN CLARKE *Shaks. Char.* viii. 201 She watches her prey, lynx-eyed, unwinking upon him. **1880** L. WALLACE *Ben-Hur* 227 Such answer as might be looked for from the unwinking sphinx.

transf. **1875** MISS BIRD *Sandwich Isl.* 5 A white, unwinking, scintillating sun.

Hence **un'winkingly** *adv.* (Freq. from *c* 1890.)

1849 C. BRONTE *Shirley* x, A formidable eye..looked as steadily, as unwinkingly, at you as if it were a steel ball soldered in her head. **1891** J. H. PEARCE *Esther Pentreath* III. viii, She found Aichel..unwinkingly there on the watch.

†**un'winly**, *adv. Obs.* [UN-¹ 11. Cf. WINLY *adv.*] Unpleasantly; sadly, sorrowfully.

13.. *Coer de L.* 6744 Wher be these hethene pawtener, That have the cyte..i-take? Unwynnely I schal yow wake. *a* **1400** *Sir Degrev.* 823 Sche doys me unwynly to wak, With wongus ful wete. ?*a* **1400** *Morte Arth.* 955 Thane this wafulle wyfe un-wynly hym gretez. *c* **1460** *Towneley Myst.* xx. 189 Here is oone of his men that thus vnwynly gars vs wake.

un'winnable, *a.* [UN-¹ 7 b.] Not winnable; *esp.* of fortresses: Impregnable.

1536 BELLENDEN tr. *Boece, Descr. Alb.* ix. (1541) B vi b, This crag is callit the Bas; vnwynnabill be ingyne of man. **1551** ASCHAM *Let.* Wks. 1865 I. II. 256 Many castles stand on the tops of these rocks unwinnable. **1596** DALRYMPLE tr. *Leslie's Hist. Scot.* (S.T.S.) II. 289 The place quhilk naturalie was wnwinnable,..was gyuen ouer on condiciounis. **1621** LADY M. WROTH *Urania* 345 The Castle is impregnable, and she vnwinable, and thus his [= the prisoner's] misfortune fell. *a* **1670** SPALDING *Troub. Chas. I* (1850) I. 291 The assaillantis fynding the place..vnwynnable without gryte skaith. **1972** D. HALBERSTAM *Best & Brightest* 495 The war was unwinnable, or at least it was for a civilized government. **1975** F. BRESLER *You & Law* 148 What would make the case absolutely unwinnable would be if the tenant was also coloured. **1980** *Daily Mail* 24 Dec. 15/5 The fifth year of his unwinnable Vietnam-style war.

transf. **1588** A. KING tr. *Canisius' Catech.* 23 Giwe me.. a valkryffe harte,..a stoute and vnwinnable, that na tribulation may mak veirie.

un'winning, *ppl. a. rare.* [UN-¹ 10.]

†**a.** Unconciliatory. *Obs.* **b.** Unattractive.

1655 FULLER *Ch. Hist.* II. ii. §7 Pride being an unwinning Quality, rendering the Proud party scorned by his Betters. **1890** 'L. FALCONER' *Mlle. Ixe* ii, Her affection for this sickly, spoilt, and most unwinning child.

un'winnowed, *ppl. a.* (UN-¹ 8. Cf. UNWINDOWED.)

1552 HULOET, Vnwinewed wheate, *acerosum frumentum.* **1624** USSHER *Serm.* 48 The graine [is] the same, but winnowed now, unwinnowed then. **1635** QUARLES *Embl.* II. vii. 1 The world's a heap, whose yet unwinnowed grain Is lodg'd with chaff. [**1775** ASH.] **1844** H. STEPHENS *Bk. Farm* II. 273 The unwinnowed heap is becoming less. **1860** SWINBURNE *Queen-Mother* II. i, We are the chaff, The gross un-winnowed husks of your fanned wheat. **1884** *Cent. Mag.* Jan. 443/1 The unwinnowed sweepings of English haymows.

un'winter, *v.* [UN-² 6 b, 5.]

1. *intr.* and *trans.* To lose, or divest of, the qualities of winter.

1611 FLORIO (citing Dante), *Suernare*, to wax Sommer,.. to vnwinter. **1892** C. E. NORTON *Dante's Par.* xxvii. 179 Ere January be all un-wintered [It. *sverni*] by that hundredth part which is down there neglected. **1944** L. MUMFORD *Condition of Man* iv. 108 Spring was coming to Western Europe: the darkness and cold were almost over. But it did not unwinter suddenly.

†**2.** *trans.* To drive out of winter quarters. *Obs.*

1642 *Let. Student Oxf.* 1 Whatsoever forces shall take up armes to unwinter his Majesty from Oxford.

un'wintry, *a.* (UN-¹ 7.)

1852 M. ARNOLD *Tristr. & Iseult* I. 63 His closed eye doth sweep O'er some fair unwintry sea, Not this fierce Atlantic deep.

un'wiped, *ppl. a.* (UN-¹ 8, 8 c.)

?**1602** in *Donne's Poems* (1912) I. 404 The mind..is like a Table-book, Which, th'old unwipt, new writing never took. **1605** R. F. *Dedekind's Sch. Slovenrie* (1904) 36 Your unwipte knife. **1648** BOYLE *Seraph. Love* (1659) 100 A Fatherly Impatience of seeing a Spot unwip'd off in the Face he loves. **1716** SWIFT *Acc. E. Curll* Wks. 1841 I. 834/2 Recollecting that his own [breech] was unwiped, he abated of his fury. **1797** COLERIDGE *Osorio* IV. 223 His rosy face besoil'd with un-wiped tears. **1852** JAMES *Pequinillo* III. 132 The unwiped noses of the horse-chestnuts. **1855** BROWNING *Fra Lippo Lippi* 36 The slave that holds..his weapon..yet unwiped.

un'wire, *v.* (UN-² 4.)

1822 SCOTT *Peveril* xxvii, I will..unwire this fresh flask, to begin a brimmer. **1851** W. COLTON *Ship & Shore* v. 88, I must unwire that cage and liberate the captive.

un'wisdom. [OE. *unwísdóm* (UN-¹ 12), = OHG. *unwîstuom*, *-tuam*, *-tôm.*]

1. Lack or absence of wisdom; ignorance, folly, stupidity.

In very frequent use till *c* 1390, and (as a new formation) from *c* 1843, when its currency was due to, or stimulated by, Carlyle. There is lack of evidence from 1612 to 1832.

c **825** *Vesp. Psalter* xxi. 3 God min ic cleopiu..on naeht & nales to unwisdome me. *c* **897** K. ÆLFRED *Gregory's Past C.* xlix. 375 Ða ðe unmedome bioð to ðære lare oððe for ȝioȝuðe oððe for unwisdome. *c* **1205** LAY. 3383 We habbet idon unwisdom þat we mine fader habbet vnderfon mid þirtti cnihten. *a* **1225** *Ancr. R.* 278 Bihold i..þine soule, oðer two [things]—sunne & ignorance, þet is, unwisdom & unwitenesse. *a* **1300** *E.E. Psalter* xxxvii. 5 Stanke and roten mine erres er ma, Fra face of mine vnwisdome swa. **1382** WYCLIF *Prov.* xv. 14 The mouth of foolis is fed with vnwisdam. *c* **1449** PECOCK *Repr.* II. iii. 150 Schamed of her folie and of her vnwisdom and pride. *a* **1470** H. PARKER *Dives & Pauper* (Pynson, 1493) VI. x. s vi/1 Woman lowede hir and knowlegide hir vnwisedom and hir foly. **1509** FISHER *Funeral Serm. C'tess Richmond* Wks. (1876) 301 All we..may saye by lamentable complaynt of our vnwysdome vnto him, Ah domine si fuisses hic. **1535** STEWART *Cron. Scot.* (Rolls) II. 117 For and ȝe do, ȝe ar abill to tak Throw sic wnwisdome..greit skayth. **1612** T. JAMES *Corrupt. Scripture* III. 13 Forsooth vnwisedome is,..which is plenteous in euill.

1832 *Westm. Rev.* Apr. 321 The unwisdom of persecuting the Saint-Simonians. **1839** CARLYLE *Chartism* iv. (1840) 27 The Earth..bountifully sends food and increase; if man's un-wisdom did not intervene and forbid. **1873** SPENCER *Stud. Sociol.* 170 The unwisdom of officialism is daily illustrated.

2. With *a*, etc.: **a.** An instance of folly or ignorance; an unwise act.

1303 R. BRUNNE *Handl. Synne* 5046 A grete vnwysdom for soþe hyt ys. **1850** CARLYLE *Latter-d. Pamph.* vii. 42 Is.. the fruit of an unwisdom doubtful? **1855** KINGSLEY *Misc.* (1859) I. 8 A learned statement of facts in answer to some unwisdom of a Quarterly reviewer. **1869** F. W. NEWMAN *Misc.* 98 It has been pronounced an unwisdom in any one to write in a dramatic form, unless [etc.].

b. An unwise Power or Being. *nonce-use.*

1839 CARLYLE *Chartism* v. (1858) 27 A world understood always to be made and governed by a Providence and Wisdom, not by an Unwisdom.

unwise (ʌn'waɪz), *a.* [OE. *unwís* (UN-¹ 7), = NFris. *unwis*, *-wiss*, (M)Du. *onwijs*, OS. (MLG.) *unwîs*, OHG. *unwîs*, *unwîsi* (MHG. *unwîse*, G. *unweise*), ON. *úviss* (MSw. and Sw. *ovis*, Da. and Norw. *uvis*), Goth. *unweis.*]

1. Lacking or deficient in (practical) wisdom, discretion, or prudence; indiscreet, imprudent, foolish. Also const. *in.*

c **825** *Vesp. Psalter* xci. 7 Wer unwis ne oncnaweð & dysiȝ ne onȝiteð ða. **971** *Blickl. Hom.* 89 Ic wæs..unwisum netenum ȝelic ȝeworden. *c* **1175** *Lamb. Hom.* 111 þet is mildheortnesse þet þe wisa mon mid steore þene unwisan irihleche. *c* **1200** ORMIN 16954 Forr unnwis mann iss blunnt. *a* **1225** *Ancr. R.* 74 Hwose euer wule mei gon in & leden uorð hore asse: þet is, hore unwise soule. *c* **1290** *S. Eng. Leg.* I. 469/250 Heo was puyrliche vnwys in sawe and in spelle. *c* **1315** SHOREHAM III. 312 Ich wot hy beþ Vnwyser þane þe wode. *c* **1325** *Metr. Hom.* 110 Thar mai we graithe ensampel take, Unwise felawschip to forsake, And hald us imang wise men. *c* **1380** WYCLIF *Wks.* (1880) 411 þis telliþ an opyn blasfemye, þat crist was vnwiss in þis. **1415** HOCCLEVE *To Sir J. Oldcastle* 77 Thow art vnwys thogh thow thee wys pretende. *c* **1455** PECOCK *Folewer* 38 [They] holden him þerfore in þat neuer þe vnwiser þan creaturis whiche knowen þe same trouþis. **1526** *Pilgr. Perf.* (W. de W. 1531) 86 Saye not as many an unwyse persone sayth. **1573** *New Custom* I. i, Yea, doth! then the more vnwise man you. **1645** MILTON *Tetrach.* 42 When as he should bee not unwiser then the Serpent. **1660** —— *Way estab. Free Commw.* 6 A nation.. unwise in thir counsels. *c* **1700** *Short Acc. Scotland* 56 The younger and unwiser of the Bishops. **1746** FRANCIS tr. *Horace, Epist.* I. v. 22 The grave Disgrace of being thought unwise. **1827** CARLYLE *Misc.* (1840) I. 47 A class of unwise men. **1871** BROWNING *Pr. Hohenst.* 1472 What if the event demonstrate her unwise?

transf. **1390** GOWER *Conf.* I. 339 Thus seith the wilde unwise tonge Of hem. **1533** GAU *Richt Vay* 32 Thair onwisz hartis war blyndit. **1831** CARLYLE *Sart. Res.* I. i, That unwise science, which..'By geometric scale Doth take the size of pots of ale'.

b. *absol.* as sing. or pl.

c **825** *Vesp. Psalter* xiii. 1 Cweð se unwisa in his heortan, nis god. *a* **1300** *Floriz & Bl.* 1016 Ac Floris cleppen hire bigon, And he him also unwise [F. *si fait que fol*]. *c* **1315** SHOREHAM I. 355 Þat fleisch wiþ sleuþe and glotonie ..[acombreþ] þoun-wyse. **1362** LANGL. *P. Pl.* A. IX. 84 3e wyse, soffreþ þe vn-wyse wiþ ow for to libbe. **1484** CAXTON *Fables of Æsop* I. xvii, The vnwyse displeseth there, where as he supposeth to please. *a* **1542** WYATT in *Tottel's Misc.* (Arb.) 86 For the vnwise Had not ysene such a beast before. **1647** N. WARD *Simp. Cobler* 25 He that instructs a foole, may act th' unwise. **1725** POPE *Odyss.* VIII. 559 Th' unwise prevail,.. And by the god's decree proud Ilion falls. **1806** H. K. WHITE *Let.* 25 June, The religion of Jesus Christ is.. wisdom to the unwise. **1871** JOWETT *Plato* I. 367 The opinions of the unwise are evil.

2. Not marked, distinguished, or prompted by (practical) wisdom; characterized by lack of sound judgement; injudicious.

1390 GOWER *Conf.* I. 166 It is an unwys vengance. **1393** LANGL. *P. Pl.* C. I. 49 Pylgrimis & palmers.. Wenten forth in hure way with meny vn-wyse tales. *a* **1425** tr. *Arderne's Treat. Fistula*, etc. 44 If þe fynger.. haue be long vnheled of vnwise cure. **1513** Q. KATH. in Ellis *Orig. Lett.* Ser. III. I. 153 With my servants unwise demeanur I am noo thing wel contente. **1590** BARROUGH *Meth. Physick* I. xxiv. (1596) 40 There goeth before this euill [*sc.* epilepsy] an vnwise state of the bodie and mind. **1594** SHAKS. *Rich. III*, IV. i. 52 Be not ta'ne tardie by vnwise delay. **1678** BUTLER *Hud.* III. iii. 518 This Gambol thou advisest, Is of all others, the unwisest. **1798** S. & HT. LEE *Canterb. T.* II. 4 Lady Lettingham exacted one compliance, even her brother thought not unwise. *a* **1800** COWPER *Odyss.* (ed. 2) xv. 12 It were a deed unwise, To sojourn longer here. **1809** COLERIDGE *Friend* 158 The conduct.. was equally unwise in private life and to individuals. **1846** MRS. A. MARSH *Father Darcy* II. iv. 85 These revolting and most unwise persecutions. **1855** MACAULAY *Hist. Eng.* xx. IV. 522 It would be unwise to bring the prisoners to trial.

†**3.** Out of one's senses; mad. *Obs.*⁻¹

Cf. Flem. *on-wijs* 'demens' (Kilian) and OE. *on unwís* 'in a mad manner'. Similarly Sc. *no wise* = mad.

a **1400** *Morte Arth.* 3817 Schountes he no lengare; Bot alls vnwyse wodewyse he wente at the gayneste. **1481** CAXTON *Reynard* xxviii. (Arb.) 68, I lepe here and there, as an vnwyse [Du. *onvroet*] man.

un'wisely, *adv.* [OE. *unwíslíce* (UN-¹ 11), = MDu. *onwiselike*, *-lijc* (Du. *onwijslijk*), MLG. *unwîslike*, OHG. *unwîslîho* (MHG. *-wîslîche*, G. *-weislich*), MSw. *ovislika*, Norw. *uvislege*, Da. *-lig.*] In an unwise, injudicious, or foolish manner; imprudently, foolishly.

c **897** K. ÆLFRED *Gregory's Past. C.* xv. 93 Ðæt is ðæt he hie ȝedweleð & unwislice ȝeiecð ða idelnesse. *c* **1000** *Sax. Leechd.* II. 232 Ðif hio bið unwislice to lange forlæten. *a* **1225** *Ancr. R.* 338 Þauh no mon hit nute, oðer wolde þet ei hit wuste, oðer ȝemeleasliche do hit, oðer to unwisliche, to muchel, oðer to lutel. **1362** LANGL. *P. Pl.* A. XI. 270 Þanne wrouȝte I vnwisly, wiþ alle þe wyt þat I lere. *c* **1375** *Cursor M.* 27047 (Fairf.), Þe þrid letting makis mani mad quen þai vn-wiseli ar drad after rising to falle againe. *c* **1440** *Jacob's Well* 286 Þe hermyte thouȝte þat þis was vnwysely don. *c* **1455** PECOCK *Folewer* 60 Holdyng him silf to seie trewli and wiseli, whanne he seieþ vntrewli and vnwiseli. *a* **1513** FABYAN *Chron.* VII. 309 Kynge Rycharde, walkyng vnwysely about the castell to espye the feblenes therof. *a* **1586** SIDNEY *Arcadia* II. xx, Some unwisely liberall, that more delight to give presentes, then pay debtes. **1605** CHAPMAN *All Fools* III. i. 471 Since you have usd the matter so unwisely. **1647** CLARENDON *Hist. Reb.* II. (1702) I. 112 Every man unwisely thought him whom he found an Enemy to his Enemies, a Friend to all his other affections. **1744** THOMSON *Spring* 136 The skilful Farmer.. Nor.. The little trooping Birds unwisely scares. **1774** BURKE *Sp. Amer. Tax.* 47 If intemperately, unwisely, fatally, you sophisticate and poison the very source of government. **1805** WORDSW. *Ode to Duty* iii, They.. who, not unwisely bold, Live in the spirit of this creed. **1860** FROUDE *Hist. Eng.* V. 389 The same story of authority unwisely caught at and unwisely used. **1899** B. HARRADEN *Fowler* III. i, An unwisely-worded disparagement.

†**unwiseman.** *Obs.* [f. UNWISE *a.*] A fool or simpleton.

1400 tr. *Secreta Secret., Gov. Lordsh.* 65 Gyf no fayth to þe sawys of vnwysmen. *a* **1470** TIPTOFT *Orat. G. Flamineus* (Caxton, 1481) 4/2 And thou unwyseman to thy grete shame when thou remembrest thyne owne.. simplenesse then [etc.]. *c* **1520** M. NISBET *2 Pet.* iii. 17 Be nocht desauet be errour of vnwisemen.

un'wiseness. [UN-¹ 12. Cf. OE. *unwísness* ignorance.] Lack or absence of practical wisdom; foolishness, folly, imprudence.

a **1340** HAMPOLE *Psalter* lxviii. 7 God þou wate myn vn-wisnes. **1807** *Monthly Mag.* XXIV. 331 An unwiseness, which would not be expected from his sagacity. **1859** T. S. HENDERSON *Life E. Henderson* iv. 200 The wiseness or un-wiseness of the means he might employ. **1887** ANNE ELLIOTE *Old Man's Favour* I. II. ii. 208 The worthy merchant admitted the unwiseness of that cheque.

un'wish, *v.* [UN-² 3.]

1. *trans.* To retract, cancel, or abrogate (a wish, choice, etc.).

1594 SOUTHWELL *Mary Magd. Funeral Tears* 48 b, If that wish had taken effect, I would now vnwish it again. *a* **1639** W. WHATELEY *Prototypes* II. xxiv. (1640) 12 Had not Job cause to unwish his former wishes. **1651** N. BACON *Disc. Govt. Eng.* II. xxxiv. 267 Who.. lived to disdesire and unwish their former choise by late repentance. **1853** MISS YONGE *Heir of Redclyffe* i, 'Never was a more absurd wish,' said Charles..; 'unwish it forthwith'. **1864** MISS SMEDLEY *Linnet's Trial* II. IV. i. 222, I hope you won't un-wish your wish as soon as it is gratified.

absol. **1881** MISS YONGE *Lads & Lasses Langley* ii. 110 Frank was left to wish and unwish.

2. To make an end of by wishing; to wish away or annihilated. Also *refl.*

1599 SHAKS. *Hen. V*, IV. iii. 76 Now thou hast vnwisht fiue thousand men: Which likes me better, then to wish vs one. **1658** SIR T. BROWNE *Hydriot.* v. 71 The most tedious being is that which can unwish it self, content to be nothing, or never to have been. **1697** COLLIER *Ess. Mor. Subj.* II. 179 Were I sure never to be pleased, my next Business should be to unwish my self, and pray for Annihilation.

b. To wish or desire (a circumstance or thing) not to be.

1628 QUARLES *Argalus & P.* II. 71 Performe, performe what now it is too late, T' unwish againe, too soone to violate. **1646** SIR T. BROWNE *Pseud. Ep.* I. x. 38 To desire there were no God, were plainly to unwish their owne being. **1709** O. DYKES *Eng. Prov. & Refl.* (ed. 2) 170 Crack'd Maiden-heads cannot be set together again, like broken China,.. by unwishing the Misfortune. **1821** BYRON *Sardan.* IV. i. 275 Do not poison all My peace left, by unwishing that thou wert A father. **1876** MISS BROUGHTON *Joan* I. xxviii, What we wish to-day, often we unwish to-morrow.

c. *refl.* To seek to remove (oneself) from a particular class or category by wishing; to wish not to be something.

1615 HALL *Contempl.*, *O.T.* IX. vii, How many shall unwish themselves Christians, when God's revenges have found them out! **1633** T. ADAMS *Exp. 2 Peter* ii. 10 At that dreadfull day how many shall unwish themselves Christians?

Hence **un'wishing** *vbl. sb.*

1699 R. L'ESTRANGE *Fables* II. lxxii. 69 This Levity, of Wishing, and Unwishing, is.. the Great Bus'ness and Mistake of Humane Life.

un'wished, *ppl. a.* [UN-¹ 8, 8 c.]

1. a. Not wished, desired, or asked for; undesired.

1583 BABINGTON *Commandm.* To Gentl. of Glam., What proofe this latter hath, and what vnwished matter to furnish out a larger complaint, I spare to speake. **1621** QUARLES *Div. Poems, Esther* i, In lavish Cups.. Came wine unwisht. **1626** W. BOSWORTH *Arcadus & Sepha* II. 790 Those griefs.. never ceas'd to move A desp'rate end, for that unwisht mischance Still gnawing on my soul. **1725** POPE *Odyss.* IV. 113 Heaping unwish'd wealth, I distant roam. **1730** THOMSON *Winter* 53 Nor is the night unwish'd; while vital heat,.. and joy, the dubious day forsake. **1757** AKENSIDE *Pleas. Imag.* II. 401 Not poison, nor sharp fire,.. Were at that season an unwished exchange. **1855** *Poultry Chron.* III. 338/2 The greatest gain will often, unsought and unwished, attend the first-class.

b. Unwanted, unwelcome, unpleasing.

a **1586** SIDNEY *Arcadia* I. xiv, Her unwished presence gave my tale a conclusion, before it had a beginning. **1590** SHAKS. *Mids. N.* I. i. 81 His Lordship, whose vnwished yoake, My soule consents not to giue soueraignty. **1697** CONGREVE *Mourn. Bride* III. viii, You seem much surprised At.. [a] return so.. unexpected!.. And so unwish'd, un-wanted too, it seems.

2. *unwished-for*, = prec.

1617 MINSHEU s.v., Un-wished for. **1632** LITHGOW *Trav.* II. 71 Humide vapours.. accompany the unwished-for-bed of my repose. **1708** J. PHILIPS *Cyder* II. 155 When.. unwish't for Rain Descended. **1807** E. S. BARRETT *Rising Sun* III. 169 Why.. do you thus force your unasked—your unwished-for counsels upon me? **1918** *Glasgow Herald* 21 July 4/2 An echo—modified.. by reinforcements of sound at one point or an unwished for diminuendo at another. **1959** 'O. MILLS' *Stairway to Murder* v. 49 Her collection of unwished-for guests.

un'wishful, *a.* (UN-¹ 7.)

[**1775** ASH.] **1876** *Whitby Gloss.*, *Unwishful*, reluctant; undesirous. **1894** MRS. GAMLIN *G. Romney* 166 Her attire was the most simple, so unwishful was she to attract admiring eyes.

un'wishing, *ppl. a.* (UN-¹ 10.)

1743 FRANCIS tr. *Hor., Odes* III. xvi. 31, I.. to th' unwishing Few with Joy A bless'd and bold Deserter fly. **1772** JAS. USHER *Clio* (ed. 3) 131 Without it [*sc.* content] we can never enjoy undisturbed unwishing tranquillity. **1951** S. SPENDER *World within World* iii. 120 When he even no longer feels desire, he can in an idle, abstract and unwishing kind of way prove to himself.. that the hidden life of forbidden wishes exists.

un'wist, *ppl. a.* *Obs.* or *arch.* [UN-¹ 8 b.]

†**1.** Unknown to one; without it being known.

c **1374** CHAUCER *Troylus* II. 1294 Hire entent.. Was for to loue hym vnwist, if she myghte. **1382** WYCLIF *Gen.* xxxv. 22 Ruben ȝede, and slepte with Bala, the secundarye wijf of his fader, that to hym was not vnwist. **1420–22** LYDG. *Thebes* I. 494 And vttrely remembre, ȝif the lyst, Thy byrth and blood ar bothe two vnwist. *c* **1500** *Lancelot* 219 How he fra that stede In sacret wyss wnwyst away was tak. *a* **1547** SURREY *Æneis* IV. 397 Unfaithfull wight! to cover such a fault Coldest thou hope unwist to leve my land? **1590** SPENSER *F.Q.* III. ii. 26 Of hurt vnwist most daunger doth redound. *Ibid.* ix. 21 Then of them all she plainly was espyde To be a woman wight, vnwist to bee, The fairest woman wight, that euer eye did see.

†**b.** Const. *by*, *of*; *to*, *unto* (or with dat.). *Obs.*

In (*a*) freq. in the 16th c. in the archaic phrase 'unwist of any wight'.

(*a*) *c* **1385** CHAUCER *L.G.W.* 1653 *Hypsipyle*, But on-wist of hire fadyr is she gon To Tessaly. *c* **1500** *Lancelot* 1139 Prevaly, unwist of any wicht. **1587** TURBERV. *Trag. T.* (1837) 153 Unwist of any wight, The murther was unseene. **1590** SPENSER *F.Q.* V. i. 9 It was kept in store In Ioues eternall house, vnwist of wight. **1848** BAILEY *Festus* (ed. 3) 200 There is a secret sign whereby the soul Feels certainty of safety.., public to the universe,.. And yet unwist of by a single world.

(*b*) *c* **1412–20** LYDG. *Chron. Troy* I. 3585 Þat sche with hym schal in-to Grece wende.., Vnwist hir fader & euery other wyȝt. **1420–2** —— *Thebes* III. 4081 To hym the tyme vn-knowen and vnwist. **1476** *Paston Lett.* III. 153, I did it nott onwyst to hyr cowncell. *c* **1500** *Lancelot* 658 For to your folk this mater is wnwist. **1596** SPENSER *F.Q.* IV. iv. 27 The shield and armes.. Which Triamond had worne,.. to his friend vnwist.

†**2.** Lacking knowledge (*of* something); unknowing; not knowing how. *Obs.*

c **1374** CHAUCER *Troylus* I. 1400 Now quod Pandare er owres twyes twelue, He shal be ese vnwyst of it hym selue. *a* **1547** SURREY *Æneis* IV. 91 The shepheard smiteth at [the hind] unwares, And leaves unwist in her the thirling head. **1596** SPENSER *F.Q.* V. i. 22 When he wak't.., He found him selfe, vnwist, so ill bestad, That lim he could not wag.

3. *arch.* Not known or recognized; strange.

1757 W. THOMPSON *Poems, Nativity* xvi, Three Seers unwist the Captain-glory led, Of awful Semblance. **1836** MRS. BROWNING *Poet's Vow* II. xxi, Still between the sound and me, White creatures like a mist Did interfloat confusedly, —Mysterious shapes unwist!

un'wistful, *a.* (UN-¹ 7.)

[**1775** ASH.] **1861** LD. LYTTON & FANE *Tannhaüser* 8 So reap'd she honour of unwistful men, Roman, or Greek. **1865** MRS. WHITNEY *Gayworthys* v, What is this space, this circumstance,.. that can.. keep them so unwistful of each other?

†**un'wit**, *sb.* *Obs.* [UN-¹ 12 + WIT *sb.* Cf. ON. *úvit* (MSw. *ovit*, Norw. *uvit*), Goth. *unwiti*; also WANWIT, and OE. *unȝewit* stupidity.]

1. Lack of wit or practical knowledge; ignorance; stupidity, folly.

c **1200** ORMIN 6003 3iff he nohht ne follȝheþþ witt, Acc unnwitt all wiþþ wille Inn all þatt iss onnȝæn Drihhtin. *a* **1225** *Juliana* 22 Hwi destu us ba so wa, þurh þi muchele unwit? *a* **1300** *Cursor M.* 13936 Yee wat quat i am, and mi kin, O yur vn-witt quine wald yee blin? **1340** *Ayenb.* 82 3ef wyt of þe wordle ne is bot folye ase zayþ þe wrytinge, and childhede, and onwyt. *c* **1380** WYCLIF *Serm.* Sel. Wks. II. 374 God mai not faile on his side for noun-power or unwitt. *c* **1400** *Pilgr. Sowle* v. xiv. (MS. Bodl. 770) 99/1 It is verey vnwytte to any erthly creature.. to trowen [etc.]. **1468** *Chron. Eng.* in Hearne *R. Glouc.* (1724) 482/1 His hondes.. shewethe sumwhat vnwyt and necclygence, for he vtterliche leueth the kepyng of hem.

2. An imprudent or foolish act.

c **1200** ORMIN 8045 Þatt ifell gast maȝȝ oferr þa þatt follȝhenn barrness þæwess Inn illc unnwitt, inn illc unnitt. *a* **1300** *Cursor M.* 13657 Þou caitif for-lorn In sin was.. born, Queþer þou wenis vs nu here O þine vn-wittes for to lere.

Hence †**un'withead**, folly. *Obs.*

1340 *Ayenb.* 19 Zuych folie is wel y-cleped onwythede.

†**un'wit**, *v.*¹ *Obs. rare.* [UN-¹ 14.] *intr.* To know not; to be ignorant *of* something.

c **1374** CHAUCER *Boeth.* v. pr. vi. (1868) 175 Whan þat god knoweþ any þinge to be, he ne vnwoot nat [L. *non nesciat*] þat þilke þinge wanteþ necessite to be. **1382** WYCLIF *2 Cor.* i. 8 We wolen not ȝou for to vnwite of oure tribulacioun.

†**un'wit**, *v.*² *Obs.* [UN-² 4.] *trans.* To deprive of wit or wits.

1604 SHAKS. *Oth.* II. iii. 182 And then.. (As if some Planet had vnwitted men) Swords out.. In opposition bloody.

un'witch, *v.* Now *arch.* [UN-² 3.] *trans.* To free from witchcraft; to uncharm; = UNBEWITCH *v.* Also *refl.*

1580 HOLLYBAND *Treas. Fr. Tong*, *Desensorceler*, to vn-witch. **1584** R. SCOT *Discov. Witchcr.* III. x. 44 Iesus Christ shall unwitch us. **1601** HOLLAND *Pliny* II. 296 Even the very serpents as they may bee burst by enchauntment, so they can unwitch themselves. **1625** PURCHAS *Pilgrims* II. 1268 Like a.. Deuill witching and unwitching the superstitious vulgar. *c* **1640** DEKKER, etc. *Witch Edmonton* II. i, I would have thee so good as to unwitch me. **1764** FOOTE *Mayor of G.* II. Wks. 1799 I. 184, I am unwitch'd, and that you shall know to your cost. **1775** G. A. BELLAMY *Apology* VI. 95 They stopped the play,.. ordering all the singers to unwitch themselves. **1884** BLACK *Jud. Shakespeare* xxiv, Come man, unwitch thee! Collect thy senses.

absol. *a* **1656** ROLLE *Abridgment* (1668) I. 45 She is a white Witch, and can witch and unwitch.

†**unwite**, var. ME. *unweote* (UN-¹ 3).

unwith'drawing, *ppl. a.* (UN-¹ 10.)

1634 MILTON *Comus* 711 Wherefore did Nature powre her bounties forth, With such a full and unwithdrawing hand? **1757** MRS. GRIFFITH *Lett. Henry & Frances* (1767) II. 122 Else where-fore, with an unwithdrawing hand, did he create them?

unwith'drawn, *ppl. a.* (UN-¹ 8 b.)

[**1775** ASH.] **1829** SIR W. HAMILTON *Discuss.* (1853) 22 The veil of Isis is thus still unwithdrawn. **1836** JAMES GIBSON in *Lectures on Popery* x. 12/2 A thousand years of ecclesiastical decisions and unwithdrawn claims. **1866** SIR F. LOCKWOOD in *Daily News* 23 Nov. 7/1 The disgraceful charge made against her husband was still unwithdrawn.

un'witherable, *a.* (UN-¹ 7 b.)

1611 COTGR., *Immarcessible*,.. vnuadeable, vn-witherable. **1917** SAINTSBURY *Hist. Fr. Novel* I. 382 This reed, which waves.. with unwitherable greenness.

un'withered, *ppl. a.* (UN-[1] 8.)
1599 THYNNE *Animadv.* (1875) 48 She..dothe signyfye the oke to be grene and vnseriall, that is..vnwithered, of freshe coolor. **1616** SURFL. & MARKH. *Countrey Farme* 500 Whilest they are in grasse or vnwithered cockes. **1634** HABINGTON *Castara* I. (Arb.) 27 The roses in her cheekes unwithered. **1659** W. CHAMBERLAYNE *Pharon.* I. ii. 211 Whilst youth doth unwithered last. **1745** COLLINS *Epist. to Sir T. Hanmer* 4 She sees her myrtles bloom, Green and unwither'd o'er his honour'd tomb. **1818** MILMAN *Samor* VII. 563 Ye see Mine arm unwither'd, my unbroken sword. **1894** *Outing* XXIV. 307 The poplar branches on top still had unwithered leaves.
fig. **1640** FLETCHER, etc. *Coronation* v. i, The yet unwither'd blush That speaks the innocence of mine [*sc.* soul]. **1826** *Literary Souvenir* 349 A nameless charm, By age unwithered. **1842** J. WILSON *Chr. North* I. 248 There is in their unwithered hearts, warm love enough for all [etc.]. **1875** M. G. PEARSE *D. Quorm* p. ix, She has an unwithered faith in the Sword of the Spirit.

un'withering, *ppl. a.* (UN-[1] 10.)
1743 R. BLAIR *Grave* 696 We wish to be where sweets unwithering bloom. **1784** COWPER *Task* III. 570 The spiry myrtle with unwith'ring leaf. **1801** SOUTHEY *Thalaba* V. v, Cypress groves Every where scatter'd in unwithering green. **1839** MOORE *Alciphron* iii. 193 The same unwithering face. **1881** LOWELL *To J. G. Palfrey* 3 As 't were a wreath Unwithering in the adverse popular breath.

unwith'held, *ppl. a.* (UN-[1] 8 b.)
1727 THOMSON *To Mem. Newton* 146 Ye..Who saw him ..All unwithheld, indulging to his friends The vast unborrow'd treasures of his mind.

unwith'holden, *ppl. a. arch.* (UN-[1] 8 b.)
a **1834** COLERIDGE *Lit. Rem.* (1838) III. 192 It is not asserted, that..man unwithholden would not be a Yahoo, morally inferior to the swallow.

unwith'holding, *ppl. a. rare*[−1]. (UN-[1] 10.)
1810 COLERIDGE in *Lit. Rem.* (1838) III. 243 The literary chit-chat and unwithholding frankness of a rich genius.

†**unwith'sayable,** *a. Obs.*[−1] [UN-[1] 7 b.] = UNGAINSAYABLE *a.*
c **1450** *Mirour Saluacioun* (Roxb.) 129 Be the vnwithsayable prayere of marie oure mediatrice.

unwith'stood, *ppl. a.* [UN-[1] 8 b.] Not withstood or hindered; unopposed; also, not successfully opposed.
1595 DANIEL *Civ. Wars* II. vii, And stately Thames, inricht with many a flood,..Glides on with pompe of waters vnwithstood. **1708** J. PHILIPS *Cyder* I. 591 Cressy Plains, And Agincourt, deep-ting'd with Blood, confess What the Silures Vigour unwithstood Cou'd do in rigid Fight. **1757** W. WILKIE *Epigon.* I. 18 When the barb'rous tyrant, unwithstood, His hot revenge shall quench in Grecian blood. **1819** SHELLEY *Masque A.* xxxvi, As if their own indignant Earth..Had turned every drop of blood By which her face had been bedewed To an accent unwithstood. **1848** AIRD *Nebuchad.* v. ii, A band..bore the centre of the Persians back... Deep was pushed that column unwithstood.

†**un'witness.** *Obs.*[−1] [f. UNWIT *sb.*] = UNWITTING *vbl. sb.* 2.
1527 ANDREW *Brunswyke's Distyll. Waters* lxviii. L iv b/1 Water [of motherwort] is good agaynste vnwytnes [*other ed.* melancoly], and madnes of the hede.

un'witnessed, *ppl. a.* (UN-[1] 8.)
1407 *Exam. Wm. of Thorpe* (MS. Rawl. C. 208) fol. 33 b, For truþe whanne it is sowen may not ben vnwitnessid. **1592** SHAKS. *Ven. & Ad.* 1023 Trifles, unwitnessed with eye or ear. **1594** HOOKER *Eccl. Pol.* Pref. iii. §12 Lest their zeale to the cause should any way be unwitnessed. **1615** CHAPMAN *Odyss.* x. 711 Circe..as she came Vanisht againe, vnwitnest by our eyes. **1652** BENLOWES *Theoph.* XIII. xxvi, Th' unwitnest witnes of his love. *a* **1750** A. HILL *Wks.* (1753) II. 66 The unwitnessed reflections of solitude. *a* **1800** COWPER *Odyss.* (ed. 2) x. 583 My friends, who with complaints, By thee unwitness'd, wear my heart away. **1812** CRABBE *Tales* xii. 253, I..share unwitness'd pomp, unenvied power. **1890** 'R. BOLDREWOOD' *Col. Reformer* xiii, The mighty ocean was as yet a wonder unwitnessed by the bold Australian.

un'witted, *a. rare*[−1]. [UN-[1] 9.] Witless.
1828 *Lights & Shades* II. 133 Being at the same time unprincipled, unmannered, uncredited, unwitted, undunned.

†**un'witted,** *ppl. a. Obs.*[−1] [UN-[1] 8.] Unknown.
1582 STANYHURST *Æneis* I. (Arb.) 34 For to shak hands freendly fear bars, now gladnes on haleth. But the case vnwytted theym lets.

†**un'witten,** *ppl. a. Obs.* [UN-[1] 8 b.] = prec.
1456 SIR G. HAY *Gov. Princes* (S.T.S.) II. 112 Men wald purvay thame that thai suld pas with lesse cost and scathe, and save mony mennis lyfis, na it war unwittyn.

†**un'witter,** *a. Obs.* [UN-[1] 7. Cf. ON. *úvitr* (MSw. *oviter*).] Unknowing, foolish.
c **1205** LAY. 16023 þu ært unwis & vnwiter a ræde.

†**un'witterness.** *Obs.* [UN-[1] 12. Cf. prec.] Uncertainty.
a **1300** *Cursor M.* 26646 þerof haue we resuns fiue þat man agh hastili him scriue, þe first o ded vnwiternes, þat man wat neuer quen it es.

un'wittily, *adv.* [f. UNWITTY *a.*, or UN-[1] 11.]
†**1.** In an ignorant, unwise, or foolish manner; unwisely. *Obs.*
1362 LANGL. *P. Pl.* A. III. 101 Unwittily, ywys, wrouht hastou ofte. **1375** BARBOUR *Bruce* VI. 523 (Edin. MS.), To thaim, and nothyr ellys quhar Had [he] ey, and wrocht unwittily. ? *a* **1400** *Morte Arth.* 3802 þofe we hafe vnwittyly wastede oure selfene. **1548** ELYOT, *Inargute*, vnwittily, without subtilitee. **1560** DAUS tr. *Sleidane's Comm.* 135 Where they condempne the baptisme.., it is vnwittely [L. *inscienter*] done of them.
2. In a manner displaying lack of wit or facetious humour.
1661 COWLEY *Cromwell* Wks. 1906 II. 371 This Man was wanton and merry (unwittily and ungracefully merry) with our Sufferings. **1884** *Imp. Dict.* IV. 524/2.

†**un'witting,** *vbl. sb. Obs.* [UN-[1] 13.]
1. Lack of knowledge; ignorance.
1382 WYCLIF *Acts* iii. 17, I woot that by vnwittinge [L. *ignorantiam*] ȝe diden, as and ȝoure princes. **1620** T. GRANGER *Div. Logike* 34 The involuntarie vnwitting causeth, or effecteth a thing being ignorant thereof.
2. Unsoundness of mind; insanity.
1527 ANDREW *Brunswyke's Distyll. Waters* xvi. B. ij, [Borage-] water..is good agaynst madnes or vnwytyng [G. *unsvnnigkeit*] and melancolye.

un'witting, *ppl. a.* [OE. *unwitende* (UN-[1] 10, 5 d), = OS. *unwitandi*, OHG. *unwizzanti, -enti*, etc., MHG. *unwizzende* (G. *unwissend*), ON. *úvitandi* (Norw. *uvitande*, MSw. *ovitande*, Sw. *ovetande*, Da. *uvidende*), Goth. *unwitands*. Cf. UNWEETING *ppl. a.*]
Rare after *c* 1600, until revived (perhaps after UNWEETING *ppl. a.*) *c* 1800.
1. Having no knowledge or cognizance of a particular fact, thing, etc.; not knowing, unaware, unconscious; hence, unheeding, regardless. Sometimes quasi-*adv.* (= UNWITTINGLY *adv.*).
pred. *c* **893** K. ÆLFRED *Oros.* v. xiv. (1883) 248 He eac moniȝ tacen self ȝedyde..þeh he hie unwitende dyde. *Ibid.* v. xv. 250 He oft unwitende sloȝ mid his heafde on þone waȝ. *c* **1375** *Cursor M.* 19100 (Fairf.), [I] vnderstande þat ȝe him slogh vn-witande. **1382** WYCLIF *Joshua* xx. 3 Whoso euer a lijf hath smytun vnwitynge. *c* **1400** *Pilgr. Sowle* I. xiii. (Caxton, 1483) 7 He was weschen vnwiting, and nought willyng hym self..that he ne myght..discerne to chesen good ne euyl. *a* **1450** *Mirk's Festial* 30 Scho..toke Seynt Steuen's bonys ynstude of hyr maystyrs, vnwyttyng. **1513** DOUGLAS *Æneid* III. ix. 53 My falloschip vnwitting forȝet me heir. *c* **1580** SIDNEY *Ps.* xxxv. vii, Then abiects, while I was unwitting quite, Against me swarme. **1613** FLETCHER, etc. *Hon. Man's Fort.* II. i, I crave your Lordships pardon, your sudden apprehension on my steps made me to frame an answer unwitting and unworthy your respect.
1801 SOUTHEY *Thalaba* VIII. ii, His lean fingers play'd, Unwitting, with the grass that grew beside. **1852** KINGSLEY *Andromeda* 50 No word, once spoken, returneth, Even if uttered unwitting. **1868** MORRIS *Earthly Par.* I. I. 407 From her lips unwitting came a moan.
attrib. **1582** STANYHURST *Æneis* II. (Arb.) 53 Thee crack rack crashing the vnwitting pastor amazeth. **1833** H. COLERIDGE *North. Worthies* 5 The danger of which he had been the unwitting cause. **1884** *Chr. Commonwealth* 21 Feb. 439/2 Popular practice..imposes that ceremony [*sc.* baptism] on an unwitting babe.
b. Const. *of.*
1412–20 LYDG. *Chron. Troy* IV. 4863 þou knewe nouȝt of þat offence, But fully were vnwytinge of þe dede. **1609** HOLLAND *Amm. Marcell.* A j, Both of them.., unwitting of so much themselves, giving place to Christ. **1612** FIELD *Woman a Weathercock* II. i. D 1, This strange shape He altogether is vnwitting of.
1876 BLACK *Madcap Violet* xxv, Drummond, all unwitting of any change. **1887** BOWEN *Æneid* III. 569 On the Cyclops coast, of the course unwitting, we run.
c. With direct object or objective clause.
(*a*) *c* **1400** *Sc. Trojan War* II. 712 It plesed to Pryame þe kyng, As wnwittand þar purposyng. **1869** 'OUIDA' *Tricotrin* xix, 'But?' asked the child,..unwitting the frightful truth that lay in the words.
(*b*) **1810** SCOTT *Lady of L.* III. xx, Children that, unwitting why, Lent the gay shout their shrilly cry. **1814** —— *Lord of Isles* v. xv, Unwitting from what source it came. **1866** SALA *Barbary* 229 Quite unwitting that he is to be made king over Israel.
†**2.** In absolute constructions. (Also with *of.*)
a **1300** *Cursor M.* 12525 Iesus still him efter stal, Ioseph and mari vnwittand. *c* **1380** WYCLIF *Wks.* (1880) 56 Petir..wolde haue lettid cristis deþ.., him wnwyttyngge. *c* **1386** CHAUCER *Can. Yeom. T.* 767 (Ellesm. MS.), He slyly tooke it out.., Vnwityng this preest of his false craft. *c* **1400** *Brut* 325 þe Englissh men..drenchyng al þe men þat were þerin, vnwytyng hem þat þey weren of þat cuntre. *c* **1455** PECOCK *Folewer* 134 Whilis y kepe þe contraries of þo deedis so priueli to me, hem it vnwityng. **1456** SIR G. HAYE *Law Arms* (S.T.S.) 227 Unwittand his ost, he passis fra his company in the woddis. **1500–20** DUNBAR *Poems* ix. 138, I schryve me of all cursit cumpany, All tymes both witting and vnwitting me. **1586** HOOKER *Hist. Irel.* in *Holinshed* II. 130/1 Others of Mounster, who before (and vnwitting the Butlers) had [etc.]. **1598** STOW *Survey* 323 The Lord Gray of Ruthen,.. vnwitting the Sergeantes and against their willes (as they said), was first placed. **1622** MABBE tr. *Aleman's Guzman d'Alf.* II. (1623) 189 Which things,..the Captaine unwitting thereof, I clapt up closely within my trunks.
†**3.** Without the knowledge of (also with possessive adjs.), unbeknown *to*, a person. *Obs.*
(*a*) *a* **1300** *Cursor M.* 3874 Bisid Iya al night he lai, His vnwitand, til it was dai. *c* **1375** *Sc. Leg. Saints* xxix. (*Placidas*) 534 Nere-by, his vnwittand, his sonnis twa ware duelland. **1454** *Paston Lett.* I. 287 My wif delyvered all, myn unwetyng. **1470** *Ibid.* II. 412 He sente to my Lady.., my onwetyng, or wythout eny preyer of me. **1513** DOUGLAS *Æneid* IV. vi. 51 With dissimulance wenyt thow, wnfaithfull wycht, Thow mycht.., myne vnwitting, steill furth of my land?
(*b*) **1340** *Ayenb.* 37 [To] nyme..oþre manne þinges wyþ wrong and onwytinde and wyþ-oute wylle of þe lhorde. *c* **1386** CHAUCER *Frankl. T.* 228 Vnwityng of this Dorigen at al This lusty Squier..Hadde loued hire. **1535** STEWART *Cron. Scot.* (Rolls) I. 531 That samin nycht..[Donald] Come on the king..With greit power wnwitanad of this king. *Ibid.* III. 23 Tha dressit thame till go Towart his oist .., Onwittand than of ony Scottis wicht.
(*c*) **1386** *Rolls of Parlt.* III. 226/1 Alle suche wronges hav ben unwytyng to us. **1531** ELYOT *Gov.* III. vi, A gentilman, ..unwyttynge to any persone, dyd cut of his owne eares. **1556** *Chron. Grey Friars* (Camden) 17 The othe that he made un to the kynge of Ynglonde unwyttynge unto the pope. **1630** R. N[ORTON] tr. *Camden's Hist. Eliz.* I. 135 The two Earles.., vnwitting to the rest, presently withdrew themselues. **1633** B. JONSON *Tale Tub* IV. i, Ile marry her to you, Vnwitting to this Turfe.
4. Performed unwittingly; unintentional; unpremeditated.
1818 BENTHAM *Ch. Eng.* Introd. 248 Authors of the unwitting and unwilling transgression. **1856** MISS MULOCK *J. Halifax* xxxvii, The unwitting indication of some crotchets of mine. **1871** FREEMAN *Norm. Conq.* xviii. IV. 268 Whether this sacrilege was designed or unwitting, it was speedily avenged.
b. Unconscious.
1840 LOWELL *Irene* 21 Her large charity (An all unwitting, childlike gift in her).
5. *Path.* (See quot.)
1822–7 GOOD *Study Med.* (1829) I. 159 *Pica..Insulsa*, Un-witting pica. [So called] from want of correct taste or discrimination.

un'wittingly, *adv.* [f. prec. + -LY[2], or UN-[1] 11.] Not wittingly, knowingly, or intentionally; unconsciously, inadvertently; ignorantly.
In very frequent use *c* 1380–*c* 1630, and from *c* 1815. For the break in the history, cf. prec.
1375 BARBOUR *Bruce* XVI. 248 The gude king said..it wes in his awn foly, For he raid sa vnvittandly, So fer befor. **1388** WYCLIF *Joshua* xx. 3 Whoeuer sleeth vnwyttyngli a man. *c* **1400** *Cursor M.* 29392 (Cott. Galba), Of him þat dose a light trispase To prest or clerk vnwitandly. **1483** CAXTON *Gold. Leg.* 211/1 The prynce that bete y[e]..did it unwittyngly. **1526** *Pilgr. Perf.* (W. de W. 1531) 163 b, Yf a persone..omyt..agaynst theyr wyll vnwytyngly ony worde or wordes of theyr duty. **1581** HANMER *Jesuites Banner* H 4 b, Yet was it done of ignoraunce, and vnwittingly. **1626** JACKSON *Creed* VIII. xxi. §3 This acknowledgment was first madde (though unwittingly) by the multitude. **1654** BRAMHALL *Just Vind.* ii. 27 Who..if he hold any errours unwittingly and unwillingly, doth implicitely [etc.].
1794 COLERIDGE *Lett.* (1895) 112, I unwittingly (for I did not know it at the time) borrowed a thought from you. **1808** SCOTT *Marm.* v. xviii, Unwittingly, King James had given, As guard.., The man most dreaded under Heaven By these defenceless maids. **1833** HT. MARTINEAU *Tale of Tyne* ii. 24 He unwittingly spoiled their little arrangements. **1883** WHITELAW *Sophocles, Trachin.* 727 When men have stumbled all unwittingly Anger has pity.

un'wittingness. [f. UNWITTING *ppl. a.*]
†**1.** Lack of knowledge; ignorance. *Obs. rare.*
a **1300** *E.E. Psalter* xxiv. 7 Giltes of mine youthe in thoghte And mine un-witandnesses [L. *ignorantiæ*] min noght. **1611** FLORIO, *Inscibilita*, ignorance, vnwittingnesse. **1668** J. WILSON tr. *Erasmus' Praise of Folly* (1913) 176 Nor does he cover their crime with any other excuse than that of unwittingnesse—because, saith he, 'they know not what they do'.
2. Absence of realization; unconsciousness.
1873 MRS. WHITNEY *Other Girls* xviii, 'Why don't we preach it ourselves,' said Desire, with inimitable unwittingness. **1876** MEREDITH *Beauch. Career* II. iii. 44 A lovely melting image of her stole over him; all the warmer for her unwittingness in producing it.

un'witty, *a.* [OE. *unwittiȝ* (UN-[1] 7), *unȝewittiȝ*, = OHG. *unwizzîg, -îk* (MHG. *unwitzic*), MSw. *ovitugher*, Norw. *uvitug*, Da. *uvittig*. Cf. WANWITTY *a.*]
1. Lacking or deficient in wit, intelligence, or knowledge; ignorant, unwise, witless. Now *rare.*
c **1000** ÆLFRIC in Assmann *Ags. Hom.* 29 Ðe weras, ȝe wif, and ða unwittiȝan cild. *c* **1205** LAY. 786 þat nan ne beo so wilde, nan swa unwitti þat word talie. **13..** *E.E. Allit. P.* C. 511 Wymmen vnwytte þat wale ne couþe þat on hande fro þat oþer. **1382** WYCLIF *Ecclus.* xvi. 20 In alle these thingus mys felende, or vnwittie, is the herte. *c* **1450** LOVELICH *Grail* xliii. 410 Wel mown they for folis itold be, and vnwitty & madde. *c* **1490** CAXTON *Rule St. Benet* 120 A token of an vnwytty mynde. **1541** R. COPLAND *Guydon's Quest. Chirurg.* B ij, A Cyrurgyen..oughte nat to be a foole, vnwytty, nor of rude vnderstandynge. **1584** HUDSON *Du Bartas' Judith* IV. (1608) 60 [Lot's] wife, that was vnwittie, Cast back her eye. **1617** BP. HALL *Quo Vadis* §10, I know not wherein Lewis the Eleuenth shewed himselfe vnwitty, but [etc.]. **1670** MILTON *Hist. Eng.* v. 239 One of her waiting Maids; a Maid ..not unhansom nor unwitty; who [etc.]. **1859** TENNYSON *Merlin & V.* 344 These unwitty wandering wits of mine.
absol. *c* **1000** ÆLFRIC *Hom.* II. 532 Wel deð se ðe unwittiȝum styrð mid swinglum. ȝif [etc.]. *c* **1400** *Apol. Loll.* 25 Wiþ him al þe world schal fiȝt aȝen þe vnwitti.
†**b.** Unexperienced *in* something. *Obs. rare.*
1594 DANIEL *Cleopatra* 167 Inur'd to warres, in womens wiles vnwitty,..thou fell'st to loue in earnest.
†**2.** Of actions, etc.; Characterized by lack or absence of knowledge; senseless, foolish. *Obs.*
c **1200** *St. Marher.* 6 Stute nu and stew þine unwitti wordes. **1435** MISYN *Fire of Love* 54 Qwhilst þou herys of þe wisyst man vnwittiest dede. **1471** RIPLEY *Comp. Alch.* v. xliii. in Ashm. (1652) 158 Therfore ther Warkes provyth unwytty. *a* **1548** HALL *Chron., Hen. V*, 77, I maruell at his vnwitty doyng and rashe enterprise. **1550** *Acts Privy Counc.* III. 73 Those unwitty and superstitiouse vowes. **1587** M. GROVE *Pelops & Hipp.* (1878) 130 Of vnwittie spending.
3. Not witty or facetious.
1637 HEYLIN *Antid. Lincoln.* I. 1 It was an old, but not unwitty application of the Lo: Keeper Lincolns,..that [etc.]. *a* **1763** SHENSTONE *Levities, Simile* 23 He..Pours forth unwitty jokes, and swears, And bawls. **1849** FROUDE *Nemesis of Fate* ix. 60 He was acute, not unwitty, and with

a *savoir faire* about him. **1871** W. ALEXANDER *Johnny Gibb* xviii, A mannie says to me, '..Paul hed naething adee wi' sic plantin';..'t wusna that oonwutty o' the carlie.

un'wive, *v.* [UN-² 3.] *trans.* To deprive (a person) of a wife. Also *refl.*

1611 FLORIO, *Dismogliare*, to unwiue. **1633** FORD *Broken H.* II. ii, Had this sincerity beene reall once, My Orgilus had not beene now vn-wiu'd. **1759** SARAH FIELDING *C'tess of Dellwyn* II. 147 He was at once unwived, unhoused, and undone. **1824** MEDWIN *Convers. Byron* I. 95, I began by being jilted, and ended by being unwived. **1851** W. B. MACCABE *Bertha* III. 376, I can do more strange things than unwive myself and wive you.

un'wived, *ppl. a.* [UN-¹ 8. Cf. MDu. *onghewijft* wifeless, MHG. *ungewîbet* maiden; and UNWIFED *a.*] Not having a wife or wives; wifeless.

1570 LEVINS *Manip.* 51 Vnwyued, *inuxoratus, cœlebs.* **1611** FLORIO, *Smogliato*, without a wife, unwiued. **1612** SELDON *Illustr. Drayton's Poly-olb.* viii. 357 A competent number of Virgins might be sent ouer to furnish his vnwiu'd Batchelers. [**1775** ASH.] **1827** HOOD *Widow* 63 He look'd so lone, and so unwiv'd, That soon the Widow Cross contriv'd To fall in love. **1866** LYTTON *Lost Tales Miletus* 32 Of his stalwart chiefs [he selected]..all the bravest yet un-wived. **1873** E. H. CLARKE *Sex in Educ.* 63 The old story of unwived Rome and the Sabines.

†**un'wiving,** *ppl. a. Obs.* [UN-¹ 10.] **a.** Of or pertaining to celibacy. **b.** Celibate.

1550 BALE *Apol.* Ep. Ded. p. iiii, *Vouere* in that place pertayneth no more to their vnwiuing state, than [etc.]. *Ibid.* 81 b, Wher is now..the vnwyuyng vowe of prestes. **1550** —— *Eng. Votaries* II. 33 b, The ordre of prodygyouse buggerers, otherwyse called vnwyuynge masmongers.

†**un'wlap,** *v. Obs.*⁻¹ [UN-¹ 3.] *trans.* To free or release from a covering.

1388 WYCLIF *Jer.* li. 25 Y schal vnwlappe [L. *evolvam*] thee fro stoonys.

un'woeful, *a.* [UN-¹ 7.] †Free from pain.

1570 LEVINS *Manip.* 186 Vnwoful, *indolens.*

un'woman, *v.* [UN-² 6 b.]

1. *trans.* To deprive of the qualities or traits of a woman; to remove from the category of women. Occas. *refl.* Also const. *of.*

1611 FLORIO, *Disdonnare*, to vnwoman. **1614** T. ADAMS *Divells Banket* 5 A degenerate woman, unwomaned..of both modestie and chastitie. **1621** G. SANDYS *Ovid's Met.* II. (1626) 37 Shee, whose wicked deeds Vnwoman'd her. **1631** BRATHWAIT *Eng. Gentlew.* 123 One weary of her sexe, forbore not to vnwoman her selfe, by assuming not onely a virile habit, but a virago's heart. **1744** ELIZA HEYWOOD *Female Spect.* No. 5 (1748) I. 263 There is nothing..so shocking to the..modesty of our sex,..that we may not..degenerate into, if we proceed to unwoman ourselves. **1839** MRS. BROWNING *Romaunt Page* xxv, My love..shall requite No woman, whether dark or bright, Unwomaned if she be. **1863** MRS. OLIPHANT *Salem Chapel* xxi, Not all her personal wretchedness could unwoman the minister's mother so much as to make her forgive..Phœbe's presumption.

2. To unsex (a woman). *rare*⁻¹.

1827 *Lancet* 20 Oct. 71 Taking away the ovaries altogether ..would unwoman her.

un'womanize, *v.* [UN-² 6 c.] *refl.* To render unwomanly.

1744 ELIZA HEYWOOD *Female Spect.* No. 6 (1748) I. 273 When a woman unwomanizes herself, renounces the softness of her nature.

un'womanlike, *a.* (UN-¹ 7 c.)

1635 R. JOHNSON *Hist. Tom a Lincolne* (1828) 108 All these her unwomanlike demeanours. **1786** *Ann. Reg.* II. 29/1 She then cursed and swore in the most unwoman like manner.

un'womanliness. (UN-¹ 12.)

1854 H. JAMES *Let.* in R. B. Perry *Thought & Character W. James* (1935) I. 135 The machinery by which it works is lying, theft, fraud and every species of unmanliness and unwomanliness. **1882** *Society* 4 Nov. 12/2 The heroine..seems to glory in her unwomanliness.

un'womanly, *a.* [UN-¹ 7.]

1. Not befitting or characteristic of a woman; inappropriate to womanly character.

App. disused or rare in the 17th and 18th c.; cf. next.

1529 MORE *Dyaloge* II. Wks. 198/2 The women folowing the crosse wyth many an vnwomanly songe. **1589** COOPER *Admon.* 39 The vilenesse of her tongue, and other vnwomanly behauiour. **1592** DANIEL *Compl. Rosamond* lxxxiii, Offring me most vnwomanly disgrace. **1608** W. CRASHAW *Newes fr. Italy* xxi. 54 This monstrous vnkindnes and unwomanly answer pierced his heart.

1821 SCOTT *Kenilw.* xli, She appealed to Foster..not to permit her to be treated with unwomanly violence. **1843** HOOD *Song of Shirt* i, A woman..in unwomanly rags. **1865** 'ANNIE THOMAS' *Theo Leigh* xl, A decrepid old woman..with hard, bony, unwomanly shoulders, displayed in a hard, bold, unwomanly manner. **1896** 'H. S. MERRIMAN' *Sowers* xix, It was..the face of a womanly woman engaged in un-womanly work.

2. Lacking the qualities or traits of a woman.

1866 G. MACDONALD *Ann. Q. Neighb.* vi, The most hurtful of all beings,..an unwomanly woman. **1886** *Chr. Herald* (N.Y.) IX. 223 The woman of Samaria was hard, impure, and unwomanly.

un'womanly, *adv.* [UN-¹ 11.] In a manner unbecoming a woman.

App. not used in 18th and early 19th c.; cf. prec.

c **1400** *Pilgr. Sowle* IV. xxxviii. (MS. Bodl. 770) 79 b/2 Þis same..helde a parlement ful vnwommanlie befor þe kynges presence. **1565** CALFHILL *Answ. Martiall* 78 b, She most vnwomanly scratched out the eyes of..hir owne sonne. **1684** BUNYAN *Pilgr.* II. 13 For your poor Children's sakes, do not so unwomanly cast away yourself.

1883 D. C. MURRAY *Hearts* x, An evil story, though..not ..a sad one, and all through most unwomanly womanly. **1891** KIPLING *Light that Failed* xiii, To justify herself, she began, unwomanly, to weigh the evidence.

un'womb, *v.* (UN-¹ 5.)

1594 *Zepheria* ix, Like daintie Midwife Flora to vnwoombe Sweet babes of Tellus and Hiperion. **1674** *Jackson's Recant.* A 2, As if both the Globes..had been unwomb'd from the formless Chaos.

un'won, *ppl. a.* [UN-¹ 8 b. Cf. (M)Du. *ongewonnen*, MHG. *ungewunnen*, unconquered.]

1. Not won, in various senses. Also const. *by.*

1593 Q. ELIZ. *Boeth.* I. pr. i. 5 A woman did apeare..of fresche coulor and unwon strengh [L. *inexhausti vigoris*]. *Ibid.* met. iv. 4 Who so quiet in setled life..His chire vn-wonne [L. *invictum vultum*] preserues. **1818** MILMAN *Samor* VI. 33 Caswallon..Drives onward, he nought deeming won, while aught Remains unwon. **1855** M. ARNOLD *Haworth Churchyard* 117 She..leaves Half her laurels unwon, Dying too soon. **1874** PUSEY *Lent. Serm.* 14 The soul yet unwon by His grace. **1892** BP. WESTCOTT in *Daily News* 16 March 5/7 The coal remains there to this day unwon.

2. *spec.* Of women: Not successfully wooed.

1601 DANIEL *Cleopatra* I. Wks. F v b, I must die free, And die my selfe vncaptiu'd and vnwonne. **1837** W. MAGINN *Shakesp. Papers* (1859) 287 The anticipation of the lost dinner and unwon lady. **1850** MRS. BROWNING *Sonn. fr. Portuguese* xiii, Seeing that I stand unwon, however wooed.

†**un'wonder,** *v. Obs. rare.* [UN-² 6 b.] *trans.* To divest of the qualities of a wonder.

1655 FULLER *Ch. Hist.* II. vi. §17 Others easily unwonder the same [continency] by imputing it partly to his Impotence. *a* **1661** —— *Worthies* I. (1662) 197 But know Reader, that this Wonder is now Unwonder'd.

un'wondering, *ppl. a.* (UN-¹ 10.)

1788 WOLCOT (P. Pindar) *Peter's Prophecy* Wks. 1816 I. 455 Wiser now, th' un-wond'ring world..Gives all poor Herschel's glory to his glass. **1818** MILMAN *Samor* IX. 144 Soft and weak, (Pursued the unwondering Stranger)..There is a strength, that is not of the arm.

†**un'wone,** *v. Obs.*⁻¹ [UN-² 3. Cf. MHG. *entwonen*, G. *-wöhnen.*] *trans.* = UNWONT *v.* a.

1340 *Ayenb.* 32 And zuo he him onwoneþ þe dyeuel wel uor to done.

†**un'wone,** *a. Obs.*⁻¹ [UN-¹ 7. Cf. NFris. *unwenn*, OE. *unȝewuna*, MDu. *onghewone* (Du. *ongewoon*), OHG. *unga-*, *ungewon* (MHG. *ungewon*) unaccustomed.] Unwonted; unusual.

a **1300** *Cursor M.* 10139 It es vncuth and vnwon [*v.r.* vn-wone] þe fader to be-cum þe sun.

†**un'woned,** *ppl. a. Obs.*⁻¹ [UN-¹ 8.] = UNWONTED *ppl. a.* I.

c **1455** PECOCK *Folewer* 89 Þis mater is sumwhat straunge and vnwonyd to be talkid.

un'wont, *ppl. a.* Now *rare* or *Obs.* [UN-¹ 8 b. Cf. G. *ungewohnt, -wöhnt.*]

1. Unusual; uncustomary; = UNWONTED *ppl. a.* I.

c **1400** *Found. St. Bartholomew's* 46 The man awakid was afrayed of this vnwount vision and..lost his wytte. *c* **1475** *Cath. Angl.* 423/2 (A.), To be vn Wonte, *dessuere, dessuescere.* *c* **1520** BARCLAY *Jugurth* (1557) 40 b, The vnwonte and sodayne feare of this treason. **1533–4** *Acts 25 Hen. VIII*, c. 21 §3 Yf it be thought..that dispensacions..in any suche cause unwonte shall passe. **1556** OLDE *Antichrist* 52 b, A fearfull and an unwont blasing starre appeared. *a* **1568** COVERDALE *Bk. Death* III. xii. (1579) 300 If one die an vn-wonte death. **1611** COTGR., *Insolite*, strange, vnused, vnaccustomed, vnwont. **1664** BUTLER *Hud.* II. iii. 1185 He..with Activity unwont, Essay'd the lofty Beast to mount. **1816** *Monthly Mag.* XLI. 527 E'en in the chapel watch unwont is kept. **1827** POLLOK *Course T.* I. 114 But what concern hangs on thy countenance, Unwont within this place?

b. *poet.* Of persons: Strange *in* manner. *rare*⁻¹.

a **1843** BAMFORD *Wild Rider* IV, Poems (1864) 76 The knight, from that day, Was altered in look, and unwont in his way.

2. Not wont, used, or accustomed *to* do something. Cf. UNWONTED *ppl. a.* 2 (*a*).

1552 R. MORYSINE in Tytler *England* (1839) II. 136 He hath a face unwont to disclose any hid affection of his heart. **1596** SPENSER *F.Q.* VI. xi. 40 Groomes..Vnwont with heards to watch, or pasture sheepe. **1810** SCOTT *Lady of L.* II. vii, Though [thou art] all unwont to bid in vain. **1823** MRS. HEMANS *Siege Valencia* 171 A stem Unwont to bend or break. **1829** SCOTT *Anne of G.* xiii, I am unwont to press my favours.

Hence **un'wontness.** *rare.*

1552 HULOET, Vnwontenes, *insolentia, dissuetudo.* **1570** T. WILSON tr. *Demosth. Orat.* iv. 35 Beholde what an insolencie and vnwoontnesse the man is growne vnto.

†**un'wont,** *v. Obs. rare.* [UN-² 3. Cf. UNWONE *v.*] **a.** *trans.* = DISACCUSTOM *v.* 2. **b.** To disappoint.

1580 HOLLYBAND *Treas. Fr. Tong, Se Desaccoustumer*, to vnwoont. **1629** GAULE *Pract. & The.* 107 If (at any time) his Power and Will shall surprize mine vnwariness, or vn-wont mine expectation.

un'wonted, *ppl. a.* [UN-¹ 8. Cf. UNWONT.]

1. Not wonted, usual, or habitual; not commonly heard, seen, practised, etc.; infrequent.

In very frequent use from *c* 1810.

1553 BRENDE *Q. Curtius* 177 b, They put the Macedones in terrour, troublyng with their vnwonted crye. **1579** E. K. *Ded. to Spenser's Sheph. Cal.* §1 Old and vnwonted words. **1580** T. WILSON *Rhet.* (ed. 2) 197 His maister marueilyng..at suche an vnwonted [1553 vnwonte] kindnesse. **1611** B. JONSON *Catiline* I. i, A strange vn-wonted horror doth inuade me. **1668** GLANVILL *Sadducismus* 6 Epocha's made of those unwonted events. **1713** ROWE *Jane Shore* I. ii, Man..Shall pity thee, and with unwonted Goodness, Forget thy Failings. **1743** FRANCIS tr. *Hor., Epodes* v. 88 Soon the Wretch my Wrath shall prove, By Spells unwonted taught to love. **1764** H. WALPOLE *Otranto* ii, It is not seemly for me to hold farther converse with a man at this unwonted hour. **1808** SCOTT *Marm.* III. xxi, His own menials..Beheld..the grisly Sire, In his unwonted wild attire. **1847** C. BRONTE *J. Eyre* vii, Difficulties in habituating myself to new rules and un-wonted tasks. **1863** STANLEY *Jew. Ch.* xix. 428 The constant expectation of some new Prophet appearing in the most secluded or unwonted situation. **1876** FREEMAN *Norm. Conq.* (ed. 2) IV. 291 Those who survived kept up life on strange and unwonted food.

b. Not wont to appear; rarely seen.

1784 COWPER *Task* VI. 301 Spring..calls the unwonted villager abroad With all her little ones. **1825** SCOTT *Talism.* xviii, It seemed as if a tear (unwonted guest) were gathering in his dry and glazened eye.

2. Not made familiar by practice; unused or unaccustomed to something. Used (*a*) predicatively with *to*, or ellipt., and (*b*) attrib.

(*a*) *a* **1586** SIDNEY *Arcadia* II. xi, Philoclea..tenderly moved her feete, unwonted to feele the naked ground. **1628** MAY *Virg. Georg.* III. 99 The Fishes..Float dead..to the shore: Sea-calves unwonted to fresh rivers fly. **1828–32** WEBSTER s.v., A child unwonted to strangers. **1870** BRYANT *Iliad* II. I. 51 Boys unwonted to the tasks of war.

(*b*) **1791** COWPER *Iliad* I. 735 So He; then Juno,..smiling still, from his unwonted hand Received the goblet. **1822** MILMAN *Martyr Antioch* 108 Are not these chambers thine, That with their splendour load my unwonted eyes?

3. Going beyond ordinary limits. *rare*⁻¹.

1642 MILTON *Apol. Smect.* 11 If I shall be large, or un-wonted in justifying my selfe to those who know me not.

Hence **un'wontedness.**

1594 SOUTHWELL *M. Magd. Funeral Teares* 8 b, Let..the vnwontednesse of the miracle plead her pardon. *a* **1652** BROME *Mad Couple* II. i, I confesse it is (by reason of my unwontednesse to it) some difficulty for me. **1698** FRYER *Acc. E. India & P.* 251 We encountred two horrid Shapes both for Grandeur and Unwontedness. **1861** GEO. ELIOT *Silas M.* iv, A too bewildering dreamy sense of unwontedness in his position. **1895** *Daily News* 7 Nov. 5/3 A girdle of rubies which may have given a faint shock of unwontedness to the experience of even a Vanderbilt bride.

un'wontedly, *adv.* [f. prec., or UN-¹ 11.] In a strange, unwonted, or unusual manner; unusually; uncommonly.

1638 R. BAKER tr. *Balzac's Lett.* (vol. II) 140 It must be a very extraordinary vertue that transported him so unwontedly. **1648** HEXHAM II, *Ongewoonlick*, Vnwontedly, or Vn-usually. **1815** SCOTT *Antiq.* xviii, Both his brothers slept unwontedly deep and heavily. **1833** *New Monthly Mag.* XXXVIII. 433 Specimens..are not unwontedly seen invading the snowy surface. **1851** HELPS *Comp. Solit.* vi. 85 The unwontedly sunny pane in December. **1867** 'OUIDA' *C. Castlemaine's Gage* 16 Her heart stirred strangely and unwontedly.

†**un'wontly,** *adv. Obs.*⁻¹ [UN-¹ 11.] Contrary to custom.

1540 R. JONAS *Birth of Mankynde* 15 b, If..she haue had dayly and vnwontly her flowres.

un'wooded, *ppl. a.* [UN-¹ 8.] Destitute of wood or trees; treeless.

1628 MAY *Virg. Georg.* IV. 125 Shepheards collect These flowers..On plaine unwooded Valleyes. **1784** *Cook's Voy.* I. 30 That lifeless brown which prevails in countries..that are unwooded. **1816** SOUTHEY *Poet's Pilgr.* I. iii. 83 The un-wooded open land. **1860** O. W. HOLMES *Elsie V.* x, A dark, deep dell, unwooded, save for a few..native larches. **1870** MORRIS *Earthly Par.* III. IV. 326 The rugged mountain's bare unwooded feet.

†**un'woody,** *a. Obs.*⁻¹ (UN-¹ 7.)

1635 SWAN *Spec. M.* vi. §4 The tender and unwoodie branches of shrubs and trees.

un'wooed, *ppl. a.* (UN-¹ 8.)

1570 LEVINS *Manip.* 51 Vnwowed, *impetitus.* *c* **1600** SHAKS. *Sonn.* liv, They liue vnwoo'd and vnrespected fade. **1806** SURR *Winter in Lond.* III. 30 A maiden of the..kindest nature flattered me by an unwooed affection. **1830** TENNYSON *Arabian Nts.* 80 The solemn palms were ranged Above, unwoo'd of summer wind. **1882** MISS BRADDON *Mt. Royal* I. iii. 96 She would have blushed..for her folly in having loved unwooed.

†**un'woolled,** *a. Obs.* [UN-¹ 9.] Lacking wool; shorn.

1538 *Aberdeen Reg.* (MS.) XVI. (Jam.), Small wn-wollit skynnis, sic as hoyg schorlingis. **1648** HEXHAM II, *Ongewolt*, vnwolled, or bare of wool.

†**un'woollen,** *a. Obs.* [UN-¹ 7.]

1570 LEVINS *Manip.* 62 Vnwollen, *non laneus.*

†**un'word,** *v. Obs. rare.* [UN-² 4.] *trans.* To deprive of words; to make speechless.

a **1625** FLETCHER *Nice Valour* II. i, You should have found my thanks paid in a smile If I had fell unworded. **1654** GAYTON *Pleas. Notes* IV. ix. 230 Uncardinall'd, Unlorded,

Outed of all his hopes, but not Unworded; He..Curses Knight-Errants.

un'wordable, *a.* [UN-[1] 7 b.] Incapable of being expressed in words; unutterable.

c **1660** in *Memoirs of Whiston* (1749) 561 There is but one God the Father,..glorious and unwordable in all his Attributes. *Ibid.* 565 God['s]..Purity and unwordable Holiness. **1877** S. COX *Salv. Mundi* ix. 198 St. Paul..heard what he calls 'unwordable words'. **1882** [LEES & CLUTTERBUCK] *Three in Norway* xxxvi. 337 An unwordable calm, an in-describable tranquillity.

un'worded, *ppl. a.* [UN-[1] 8.]

1. Not expressed in words.

1860 MRS. C. CLIVE *Why Paul Ferroll killed his Wife* iii, With all this unworded she accosted him. **1860** [see UNTHOUGHTED]. **1865** MRS. WHITNEY *Gayworthys* xxi, The unworded intercourse between this husband and wife. **1898** MEREDITH *Poems* II. 132 This lone-laid wife was moved to feel Unworded things and old To her pained heart appeal.

2. Lacking words; silent. *rare*[−1].

1886 R. W. GILDER *Lyrics* 116 So, still unworded, save in memory mute, Rest thou, sweet hour of viol and of lute.

unwordily, -wordy, Sc. varr. UNWORTHILY, UNWORTHY.

un'wordy, *a. rare.* [UN-[1] 7.] Not diffuse or verbose; concise.

[**1775** ASH.] **1840** DE QUINCEY *Style* Wks. 1859 XI. 280 The culture of an unwordy diction.

un'work, *sb.* (UN-[1] 12.)

1854 WHITTIER *Yankee Gipsies* Prose Wks. I. 343 The comfortable philosophy..is the real life of this city of unwork.

un'work, *v. rare.* [UN-[2] 3, 5. Cf. OE. *unwyrcan* to undo; also OHG. *intwurchen, -wirken*, MHG. *entwürken, -wirken* to destroy.]

†**1.** *trans.* To undo or detach (*from* something).

a **1548** HALL *Chron. Hen. IV*, 8 But his workyng vnwrought king Richard from his croune.

†**2.** To spoil, mar, or destroy. *Obs.*[−1]

1587 GOLDING *De Mornay* xvii. 308 The punishments bewray..that wee chastise in vs, not that which God hath made or wrought in vs, but that which wee our selues haue vndone or vnwrought.

3. To release from an intertwined condition.

1634 C. BUTLER *Fem. Mon.* (ed. 2) 92 If they light in..a ded hedg, your best way is, softly to unwoork the hedg til you coom to them.

4. To undo by contrary action.

1726- [see UNWROUGHT *pa. pple.*]. **1909** W. OGILVIE *Whaup o' the Rede* VII. vii, Thy lady mother..Unwrought the wrong of Wat Harden's hate With her love.

unworka'bility. (UN-[1] 12.)

1881 *Nature* XXIV. 371 The then existing laws..were in a state of..confusion and unworkability. **1886** *Times* 7 April 9/1 The unworkability of his plan.

un'workable, *a.* [UN-[1] 7 b.]

1. a. Not workable; not capable of being worked, put into operation or practice, etc.

Freq. from *c* 1880.

1839 URE *Dict. Arts* 984 The mine is rendered unworkable until..fresh air is introduced. **1861** MILL *Repr. Govt.* vii. 152 Some profess to think the plan unworkable. **1869** A. MACDONALD *Love, Law & Theol.* vi. 102 Lord Aberdeen's Act is quite unworkable. **1887** W. S. S. TYRWHITT *New Chum in Bush* v. 84 To prevent his run being rendered unworkable by having the best parts of it taken from him.

b. Of ships: Unmanageable.

1853 KANE *Grinnell Exp.* xxiii. (1856) 186 She had split her rudder-post so as to make her unworkable. **1885** *Athenæum* 5 Dec. 726/3 The soldiers were untrained..and the ships unworkable.

c. Impossible to manage, direct, control, etc., on account of size, numbers, or lack of coherence.

1862 'SHIRLEY' (J. Skelton) *Nugæ Crit.* ix. 426 An undisciplined and unworkable rabble. **1874** MORLEY *Compromise* 83 The participation of large numbers of people ..immediately becomes unworkable. **1895** E. OWEN *Wks. G. Edwards* p. xiii, The large and unworkable parish of Wrexham. **1896** BADEN-POWELL *Matabele Campaign* v, We have broken up the original..Force as an unworkable and rather overpaid organization.

2. Of materials: Incapable of being worked upon or wrought into shape.

1854 H. MILLER *Sch. & Schm.* iii. 57 The white stone.. is a beautiful though unworkable rock. **1867** W. W. SMYTH *Coal & Coal-mining* 47 Of the measures..the upper half contains only a few unworkable beds. **1879** *Cassell's Techn. Educ.* II. 163/2 Alpaca wool..laid aside..as useless, unworkable material.

fig. **1856** R. A. VAUGHAN *Mystics* IX. i. II. 134 Mystics imperfectly subservient—unworkable raw material, and as such flung into the fire.

Hence **un'workableness**; **un'workably** *adv.*

1877 MORLEY *Crit. Misc.* Ser. II. 60 The absolute unworkableness of the new constitution. **1879** *Contemp. Rev.* Oct. 290 The unworkableness of the various systems proposed. **1927** C. HOLLIS *Amer. Heresy* 164 A plan, unworkably complicated. **1972** W. A. PANTIN *Oxford Life* iii. 25 As late as 1850 some people thought that a Congregation which might amount to over 100 would be unworkably large.

un'worked, *ppl. a.* [UN-[1] 8. Cf. OHG. *ungaworaht, ungewurchet* (MHG. *ungeworht*, G. *-wirkt*), MLG. *ungewercht*; also UNWROUGHT and UNWERKED *ppl. adjs.*]

1. Not wrought into shape; not worked upon.

1730 BAILEY (fol.), *Unwrought* (of *un* and *weorcian*, Sax.), unworked. **1862** J. NEWTON in *Trans. Hist. Soc. Lancs. & Chesh.* (N.S.) II. 103 Flint implements..obtained by a few adroit cleavages from the unworked boulders amidst which they lie. **1865** LUBBOCK *Preh. Times* viii. 265 One single unworked flint.

2. Not worked in or operated upon. Chiefly *fig.*

1817 LADY MORGAN *France* (1818) II. 190 Drawing from the unworked mine of fancy and imagination. **1858** GLENNY *Gard. Every-day Bk.* 83/1 This applies to all kinds of unworked subjects. **1874** RAYMOND *Statist. Mines & Mining* 365 Harris Gulch..contains much unworked ground. **1884** *Longm. Mag.* Mar. 486 The ingenuity of inventors..would not allow so fine a field for invention to remain long unworked.

b. = UNWROUGHT *ppl. a.* 3 b.

1883 GRESLEY *Gloss. Coal-m.* 268 *Unwrought* or *Unworked*, coal or other mineral which has not been mined or worked away.

un'worker. *rare.* [UN-[1] 12.] = NON-WORKER.

1843 CARLYLE *Past & Pr.* I. ii, Workers, Master Workers, Un-workers, all men, come to a pause.

un'working, *ppl. a.* (UN-[1] 10.)

1696 LOCKE *Lower. Interest* (ed. 2) 43 Lazy and Unworking Shopkeepers in this being worse than Gamesters. **1724** *Briton* No. 24. 105 Petty includes People of all Professions and Offices..in his unworking Tenth of the Nation. **1830** BOWLES *Life Bp. Ken* I. 201 Obese Bishops, oscitant Deans, and 'unworking' Clergy! **1843** CARLYLE *Past & Pr.* III. ix, The partridge-nets of an Unworking Dilletantism. **1848** MILL *Pol. Econ.* V. x. §3. II. 495 A practice essentially bad, that of converting the working classes into unworking classes.

un'workmanlike, *a.* [UN-[1] 7 c.] Unlike a workman; unworthy of a good workman; badly executed or finished.

1647 HEXHAM I, Vnworkemanlike, *niet gelijk een werckmeester.* **1730** BAILEY (fol.), *Inartificial*, artless, unworkmanlike. **1756** C. SMART tr. *Horace, Sat.* II. iii. II. 131 What was carved in an unworkman-like manner. **1820** *Edin. Rev.* XXXIII. 354 He tacks them together in such a clumsy and unworkmanlike style. **1873** HAMERTON *Intell. Life* X. i. 338 The unworkmanlike haste with which it was put together. **1895** *Mod. Stm. Eng.* 64 An unfinished, unworkmanlike appearance is imparted to the whole machine.

un'workmanlike, *adv.* (UN-[1] 11 b.)

1727 BAILEY (vol. II), *Inartificially*, artlesly, unworkmanlike.

un'workmanly, *a.* [UN-[1] 7.] Unworkmanlike.

1542 BALE *Myst Iniq. P. Pantolabus* (1545) 86 b, For lyke an vnworkemanlye dawber he hath done yt with vntempred claye. **1706** PHILLIPS (ed. Kersey), *Inartificial*, being without Art, Artless, Unworkmanly. **1894** *Season* X. 36/1 The quality of the serge is not fine enough to look 'unworkmanly'. *Ibid.* 58/2 Designed for unworkmanly people.

un'workmanly, *adv.* ? *Obs.* [UN-[1] 11.] In a manner uncharacteristic of a good workman.

1555 WATREMAN *Fardle Facions* Pref. 7 Clad..with rawe felle and hide, full vnworkemanly patched together. **1555** EDEN *Decades* (Arb.) 94 A golden cheyne vnwoorkmanly wrought.

un'world, *v.* [UN-[1] 6 b.]

1. *trans.* To deprive of the qualities of a world; to undo as a world. Also *refl.*

1647 N. WARD *Simple Cobler* 20 Take away the least *vericulum* out of the world, and it unworlds all, potentially. **1674** N. FAIRFAX *Bulk & Selv.* 155 The worlds driving up to any thing of Gods being, would as much ungod him, and over and above unworld it self. **1875** BROWNING *Aristoph. Apol.* 106 Such world has, of two courses, one to choose: Unworld itself,—or else [etc.]. *Ibid.* 116 'Unworld the world,' frowns he, my opposite. I cry 'Life!'

2. To deprive of a share in worldly activities.

1868 H. BUSHNELL *Serm. Living Subj.* 404 Why is he [*sc.* a soldier] allowed no more to have any world..? Is he thus unworlded to take the mettle out of him?

un'worldliness. [f. next, or UN-[1] 12.] Unworldly character.

1803 D. WORDSWORTH *Jrnl.* 28 Aug. (1941) I. 286 That visionariness which results from a communion with the unworldliness of nature. **1824** CAMPBELL *Theodric* 217 A wildly sweet unworldliness of thought. **1852** ROBERTSON *Serm.* III. xviii. (1857) 266 Unworldliness is this—..to have the world, and not to let the world have us; to be the world's masters, and not the world's slaves. **1874** MAHAFFY *Soc. Life Greece* v. 161 The gentleness and the unworldliness of the man who loved..the world so keenly.

un'worldly, *a.* [UN-[1] 7.]

1. Of a type transcending or exceeding what is usually found or experienced in the world.

1707 G. HICKES *Two Treat. Chr. Priesth.* (1711) II. 5 That pre-eminent unworldly Power..which the Spiritual Governours..have over their Spiritual Subjects. **1817** COLERIDGE *Lay Serm.* 73 The impressive example of their un-worldly feelings. **1848** AIRD *Chr. Bride* I. xxiv, Sequestered they in love's unworldly dream. **1863** COWDEN CLARKE *Shaks. Char.* xi. 291 They are in another world, and they revel in unworldly thoughts and unworldly associations.

Comb. **1805** WORDSW. *Prelude* IV. 290 A wild, unworldly-minded youth.

b. Of persons: Actuated by other than worldly or sordid motives; spiritually-minded.

1825 T. HOOK *Sayings* Ser. II. III. 180, I know you are guileless, Ma'am, and unworldly. **1844** KINGLAKE *Eothen* xx, This unworldly Sphynx has watched and watched like a Providence. **1855** MILMAN *Lat. Chr.* VII. vi. III. 225 The pious but not unworldly merchants of Venice.

2. Not belonging to this world; celestial.

1765 STERNE *Tr. Shandy* VII. vi, That all powerful fire which..lights the spirits through unworldly tracts!

un'wormeaten, *ppl. a.* (UN-[1] 8 b.)

1653 W. RAMESEY *Astrol. Restored* 12 Wood which we desired to keep..un-worm-eaten.

un'wormed, *a.* [UN-[1] 9.] Not worm-eaten.

1895 *Athenæum* 9 Feb. 178/1 The ordinary reader may see a perfect unwormed copy at the British Museum.

†**un'wormed**, *ppl. a. Obs. rare.* [UN-[1] 8.] Of a dog: Not having the lytta or 'worm' removed from the tongue.

1618 FLETCHER *Women Pleased* IV. iii, She is mad with Love, As mad as ever unworm'd dog was, Signior. **1817** *Gentl. Mag.* July 40/2 Inflicting a penalty on those who neglected it, and the destruction of the dog unwormed.

†**un'wormwooded**, *a.* [UN-[1] 9 b.] Not bitter or caustic.

1628 FELTHAM *Resolves* II. xx. 66 Vn-wormwooded Iests I like well; but they are fitter for the Tauerne, then the Maiestie of a Temple.

un'worn, *ppl. a.* [UN-[1] 8 b, c.]

1. Not impaired, decayed, or wasted by use, weather, etc.

a **1586** SIDNEY *Ps.* VIII. viii, What things els of waters traceth The unworn pathes, his rule embraceth. **1602** J. DAVIES (Heref.) *Mirum in Modum* Wks. (Grosart) I. 29/2 For in Not-beeings bottome, being fast, Ought would to worse then nought, vnworen wast. **1616** *Extr. Aberd. Reg.* (1848) II. 342 Stanes..[that] abyde baith wind and wather, vnworne or consumeit. *a* **1677** BARROW *Serm.* Wks. 1686 II. 98 This great Machine.., unimpaired in its beauty, unworn in its parts. **1757** YOUNG *Paraphr. Job* Wks. I. 215 Will the tall Reem..Submit his unworn shoulder to the yoke. **1771** *Phil. Trans.* LXI. 466 Any two of them, that appeared to be perfect and unworn. **1813** BYRON *Giaour* 1059 There read of Cain the curse and crime, In characters unworn by time. **1818** SHELLEY *Julian* 540 The colours of his mind seemed yet unworn. **1877** MRS. OLIPHANT *Makers Flor.* iv. 102 The beautiful countenance yet unworn with anything worse than the sweet sorrows of a visionary love. **1883** 'OUIDA' *Wanda* I. 41 Those cool, vast, unworn mountain solitudes.

b. Not worn or thrown *off*.

1748 RICHARDSON *Clarissa* VII. lxxviii. 258 The unworn-off effects of the midnight revel.

c. Not exhausted or worn out.

1882 PUSEY *Paroch. & Cathedr. Serm.* vi. 80 A dull heavy temper He will transform into patient unworn endurance for love of Jesus.

2. Free from deterioration or weakening; unimpaired, fresh.

1757 BURKE *Sublime & Beautiful* Introd. ad. fin., In the morning of our days, when the senses are unworn and tender. **1831** CARLYLE *Sartor Res.* II. iii, The unworn Spirit is strong. **1846** C. BRONTË in Mrs. Gaskell *Life* (1857) II. 5 While their minds are mostly unemployed, their sensations are all unworn. **1855** BROWNING *In Three Days* i, See how I come, unchanged, unworn!

absol. **1851** HELPS *Comp. Solit.* xi. 214 The knowledge to be gained [by travel]..is for the young and the unworn.

3. Of dress, etc.: Not hitherto worn; not actually worn.

1798 S. & HT. LEE *Canterb. T.* II. 226 One who appeared to him to be adorned with the unworn jewels of the Marchioness. **1819** WORDSW. *Misc. Sonn.* I. xxi, [She] Put on fresh raiment—till that hour unworn. **1861** WHYTE MELVILLE *Good for Nothing* I. 140 And yet..the white dress ..might have been consigned unworn to its place in the wardrobe. **1894** *Daily News* 7 April 5/3 [In this] painting of Mr. Gladstone..the pince-nez would have been better unworn.

un'worried, *ppl. a.* (UN-[1] 8.)

[**1775** ASH.] **1818** KEATS *Endym.* I. 75 Not one fleecy lamb ..but pass'd unworried By angry wolf. **1899** SIR E. RUSSELL *That reminds me* 197 All..have lady typewriters constantly at work. They look cool and unworried, and receive a caller [etc.].

†**un'worship**, *sb.*[1] *Obs.* [OE. *unweorþscipe* (UN-[1] 12).]

1. Absence of honour, respect, or reverence; dishonour; disgrace.

In frequent use from *c* 1400 to *c* 1450.

c **888** K. ÆLFRED *Boeth.* xxvii. §2 Hwæþer þu nu mæʒe onʒitan hu micelne unweorðscipe se anwald brengð þam unmedeman ʒif he hine underfehð? *c* **1200** *Vices & Virtues* 53 For ðare unwurscipe ðe me nimð hit al swa unwurðliche swa me nimð ðat bread (of ðæ borde). **13..** *Guy Warw.* (A.) 1857 Unworþschip it wer to me, ȝif y schuld iusti wiþ þe. *a* **1395** HYLTON *Scala Perf.* II. ii. (Bodl. MS.), þe trespas and þe vnworschip was endeles greet. *c* **1430** *Pilgr. Lyf Manhode* II. xvii. (1869) 81 Wurshipe,..what seyst thou? the unwurshipe is thine. *c* **1440** *Jacob's Well* 165 ȝif þou sodaynly..brekyst out woordys of vnworschype to god. *a* **1470** H. PARKER *Dives & Pauper* (W. de W. 1496) IV. i. 160/2 Thus for scornyng & vnworshyp that the sone dyde to the fader began fyrste boundage.

2. An act or instance of disgrace or dishonour; a slight. *rare.*

c **1200** *Vices & Virtues* 97 After maniȝe unwurðscipes ðe he for me hier þolede. **1387-8** T. USK *Test. Love* I. v. (Skeat) l. 24 Why, than,..suffre ye such wrong..? Me semeth, to you it is a greet unworship.

un'worship, *sb.*² *rare*⁻¹. [UN-¹ 12 + WORSHIP *sb.*] Lack or absence of divine worship.

1860 PUSEY *Min. Proph.* 75 All half-belief is unbelief; all half-repentance unrepentance, all half-worship is unworship.

†**un'worship**, *v. Obs.* [UN-² 3.] *trans.* To deprive of honour or dignity; to treat with indignity, disrespect, or irreverence. Also *refl.*

c **1380** WYCLIF *Wks.* (1880) 462 Men seyen þat þe pope wole biclippe worldly worchip, & not trewe men for goddis sake, lest he vnworchipe hym silf. **1387–8** T. USK *Test. Love* II. vi. (Skeat) l. 125 Yet is he worthy, for shrewdnesse, to be unworshipped. *a* **1425** tr. *Arderne's Treat. Fistula*, etc. 75 þerfor it schal noȝt vnworschip [*overlined* ne schame] a lech for to spede profitably with fewer þings and liȝter. *c* **1450** *Mirk's Festial* I. 87 þe lest synne þat a man doth, hyt vnworshypyth God. *a* **1470** H. PARKER *Dives & Pauper* (W. de W. 1496) II. i. 110/2 Graunte vs grace no thynge to do.. wherby thy name sholde be vnworshyped or ashamed in vs.

Hence †**un'worshipping** *vbl. sb. Obs.*

1382 WYCLIF *Ecclus* i. 38 Lest parauenture thou falle, and bringe to thi soule vnwrsheping [L. *inhonorationem*]. *c* **1400** LOVE *Bonavent. Mirr.* (1908) 154 The cause was for the gostly fire of his zele,.. for the vnworschippynge of his fader. *c* **1450** *Myrr. our Ladye* 208 The vnworshypynge and offense of god.

un'worshipful, *a.* [UN-¹ 7.]

1. Unworthy or devoid of esteem or honour.

c **1374** CHAUCER *Boeth.* III. met. iv. (1868) 75 Nero..ȝaf somtyme to þe dredeful senatours þe vnworshipful setes of dignites. *c* **1471** FORTESCUE *Wks.* (1869) 456 Indygence in them is not only unworschipfull, but yt may do the most harme. *a* **1664** FRANK *Serm.* (1672) 206 That poor contemptible condition, and unworshipful pickle they found Him in. **1851** CARLYLE *Sterling* I. v, Its high dignitaries..; its worships and worships unworshipful:.. a mad world, my masters.

2. Characterized by lack of divine worship.

1862 FABER *Hymn*, '*The Unbelieving World*' i, The wide-spreading world, How lovely..it seems, How full of realities, pure and divine, Yet how bent on unworshipful dreams! **1893** W. A. BARTLETT in *Advance* (Chicago) 21 Dec., So long as the churches are willing to worship in an unworshipful way by proxy.

†**un'worshiply**, *adv.* [UN-¹ 11.] Irreverently.

1303 R. BRUNNE *Handl. Synne* 981 Ne þou shalt swere vnwurschyply [F. *folement*], By oure lorde.

un'worshipped, *ppl. a.* [UN-¹ 8.] Not worshipped or adored; not held in reverence or esteem.

a **1395** HYLTON *Scala Perf.* II. xiv. (Bodl. MS.), Vnresonabli he werkiþ þat loueþ not þe souereyn good,..þat is god vnsouȝt and vnloued, vnknowen and vnworschipid. *c* **1430** *Life St. Kath.* (1884) 42 Whom þou byddest be wyth oute worshep hit schal be suffisant to hem to abyde in her owne houses vnworscheped. *a* **1513** FABYAN *Chron.* VII. (1811) 452 The holye seruyce of God [has been] lefte, and holye churche vnworshypped and vnhonouryd. **1587** GOLDING *De Mornay* 595 Had it not bene a cryme to haue left them vnworshipped for Gods? **1667** MILTON *P.L.* v. 667 He resolv'd..to..leave Unworshipt, unobey'd, the Throne supream. **1796** B. S. BARTON *Mem. Fasc. Faculty Rattlesnake* 17 The former [Being]..was merely acknowledged and named, but unworshipped and neglected. **1837** CARLYLE *Fr. Rev.* I. I. i, Thus..had this grand-nephew of the great Richelieu to glide about; unworshipped by the world. **1850** S. DOBELL *The Roman* viii, Oft the unworshipp'd angel passeth While we..adore his footsteps in the sand.

un'worshipping, *ppl. a.* (UN-¹ 10.)

1828 WEBSTER (citing J. M. Matthews), *Unworshiping*, a., not worshiping; habitually neglecting the worship of God. **1906** BP. MOULE in *Off. Rep. Church Congress* 411 In this day of unchastened, uncontrite, unworshipping thought upon religion.

un'worth, *sb.* [UN-¹ 12. Cf. Du. *onwaarde*, G. *unwerth*, Da. *uværd* worthlessness; also WANWORTH *sb.*]

†**1.** Lack of merit or desert. *Obs. rare.*

1340 *Ayenb.* 35 þe þridde manere of gavelinge is ine ham þet habbeþ onworþ to lene of hire hand. *Ibid.* 270 Dyad he [*sc.* Christ] is, þou hest hueruore: and to sterue þou hest onworþ?

2. Lack or absence of worth; unworthiness.

1835 CARLYLE in Froude *Life* (1884) I. 41 Do you reckon ..that style (mere dictionary style) has much to do with the worth or unworth of a book? **1872** RUSKIN *Fors Clav.* xiv. 9 Nature and Heaven command you..to discern worth from unworth in everything. **1896** A. AUSTIN *England's Darling* III. i, Why hath the King Laid this great meed on my unworth?

†**un'worth**, *a.*¹ *Obs.* [OE. *unweorþ*, *unwurþ*, etc. (UN-¹ 7), = OHG. *unwërd* (MHG. *unwërt*, G. *unwerth*), MLG. *unwert*, MDu. *onwert*, *onwerd*, etc. (Du. *onwaard*), ON. *úverðr*. Cf. WANWORTH *a.*]

1. = UNWORTHY *a.* 1–3: **a.** Of persons.

c **893** K. ÆLFRED *Oros.* IV. vii. §4 Æt þæm feorðan cirre hie sendon Hannan heora þone unweorðestan þeȝn, & he hit abæd. *c* **1000** *Rule of Chrodegang* 70 Preost þe bið cypa & of þam arist of wædlan to rican men, & of unwurðum men to wurðfullum. *c* **1200** *Vices & Virtues* 5 Sume oðre forlæteþ ðe world..and sone hem seluen healdeð for hali, and unwurð healdeþ of oðre. *c* **1205** LAY. 3464 He biðe vn-worð & lah þe mon þe litul ah. *c* **1230** *Hali Meid.* 33 Ȝif þu iwurðest him unwurð, & he ase unwurð þe. *c* **1275** *Prov. Ælfred* 316 (Trin. Coll. MS.), Swo is moni gadeling godelike on horse, wlanc on weiȝe, and unwurþ on wike. **1340** *Ayenb.* 132 þeruore þe uerþe stape is of þise uirtue: wylni to by y-knawe, and y-healde uor uyl and onworþ. *c* **1425** in *Minor Poems fr. Vernon MS.* 641/143 For þou vnworthe resawes me [= Christ], þu belewys noȝt þat I suld be he. **1603** M. M. *Ane Godlie Dreame* xviii, O wretch vnworth, my dayes are vainlie spent.

b. Of things.

c **960** ÆTHELWOLD *Bened. Rule* (Schröer) 138 þæt heora heortan furþum mid wacum mettum and unweorþum ne syn ofersymede. *c* **1205** LAY. 24656 And elche untuhtle Heo talden vnwurðe. *a* **1250** *Owl & Night.* 770 Vuel strengþe is lutel wrþ Ac wisdom ne wrþ neuer vnwrþ. *c* **1320** *Cast. Love* 1112 Woldestou þi finger ȝeue..So vnworth and so vyl chaffare to bugge? **1340** *Ayenb.* 215 Ase þe werm is uoul, and lite, þing onworth.

c. With dative, or with preps. (esp. *to*).

c **888** K. ÆLFRED *Boeth.* xxviii, Hu ne wes he þeah ælcum witum lað & unweorð? *c* **1000** ÆLFRIC *Saints' Lives* xvi. 367 Se idela ȝylp us beo æfre unwurð. *c* **1175** *Lamb. Hom.* 49 His beoden beoð aweriede and unwurðe gode. *c* **1200** *Trin. Coll. Hom.* 89 þe alre unwurþeste wig one to riden. *a* **1225** *Leg. Kath.* 1531 Stille þine wordes, for ha beoð me unwurð. *a* **1225** *Ancr. R.* 50 þe blake cloð bitockneð þæt ȝe beoð blake & unwurðe toward þe worlde wiðuten. *c* **1300** *Beket* 653 Unworth ich am of holi churche wardeyn forto beo. **1340** *Ayenb.* 49 þis zenne is zuo onworþ to gode, þet he dede rine uer bernınde..ope þe cite of sodome.

2. Undeserved; = UNWORTHY *a.* 4a. *rare*⁻¹.

a **1240** *Lofsong* in *O.E. Hom.* I. 207 Bi þe herde hurtes and þe unwurðe wowes ðet he..willeliche þolede.

Hence †**un'worthhead**, contempt. *Obs.*

1340 *Ayenb.* 17 þe uerste boȝ of prede is ontreuþe, þe oþer onworþhede, þe þridde ouerweninge. *Ibid.* 29 þe uerþe [sin] is onworþhede of penonce.

un'worth, *a.*² [UN-¹ 7 + WORTH *a.*] Not worthy of (something); = UNWORTHY *a.* 6. Const. with (*a*) sbs., esp. *while*, or (*b*) vbl. sbs.

(*a*) **1587** TURBERV. *Trag. T.* (1837) 5 Wherein if ought unworth the presse thou finde Unsavorie,.. Impute it to the troubles of my minde. **1664** J. WILSON *Projectors* III, Perhaps is may not be unworth your while. **1736** BAILEY *Housh. Dict.* s.v. *Goats*, Which if true or not would not be unworth the while of the curious in anatomy to enquire. **1848** LOWELL *Fable for Critics* 458 You may..deem it not unworth your while to review it. **1903** T. HARDY *Dynasts* I. v. vi, Some poor dolt unworth captivity.

(*b*) **1592** G. HARVEY *Four Lett.* iii. 25 Baggage stuffe, vnworth the aunswering, or reading. **1645** MILTON *Tetrach.* 6 Many things might be noted..not ordinary, nor unworth the noting. **1691** J. WILSON *Belphegor* v. iii, He'll tell ye the Story..not unworth your hearing.

†**un'worth**, *v. Obs.* [OE. *unweorðian* (f. *unweorþ* UNWORTH *a.*¹), = MDu. *onwerden*, MLG. *unwerden*, ON. *úvirða*, to slight, etc.; cf. also G. *entwerthen* to deprive of value.]

1. *trans.* To treat (a person or thing) disparagingly or with disdain; to slight, despise.

c **950** *Lindisf. Gosp.* John viii. 49 Ic diuul ne hafo.., ah ic uorðiȝe faeder min & ȝie un-uorðade mec. *c* **1000** ÆLFRIC in Assmann *Ags. Hom.* 93 Seo cwen..ne unwurðode na þe ænne mid þan, ac ealle þine ealdormenn and eac þine þeȝnas. *c* **1200** *Trin. Coll. Hom.* 181 For we..swo..unwurðeð ure drihten, wurðeð þe deuel. *c* **1200** ORMIN 18285 Hefiȝlike he shameþþ þe & shendeþþ & unnwurrþeþþ. **1340** *Ayenb.* 8 Huo þet onworþeþ his uader and his moder. *Ibid.* 84 Uirtue makeþ wynne heuene, and onworþi þe wordle.

2. To dishonour (something).

c **1200** *Trin. Coll. Hom.* 213 He sholde..noht shenden godes shafte,..ne swo unwurðin godes handiwerc.

un'worthily, *adv.* [f. UNWORTHY *a.*, or UN-¹ 11. Cf. MDu. *onwerdichlike* (Du. *onwaardiglijk*), MLG. *unwerdichliken*, MHG. *unwirdec-*, *unwërdeclîche* (G. *unwürdiglich*); also ON. *uvirðiliga*, *-uliga* scornfully.]

1. Without being worthy, fit, or qualified; without having sufficient merit or ability; unmeritedly.

c **1290** *Beket* 654 in *S. Eng. Leg.* I. 125 Luytel wuyrth ich am of holi churche wardein for-to beo, And al-so vnwurthþe-liche þar-to i-nome. **1303** R. BRUNNE *Handl. Synne* 3037 Vnwrþyly art þou made gentyl ȝyf þou yn wurdys and dedys be yl. *a* **1340** HAMPOLE *Psalter* lxx. 1 As þai sall be [shamed] þat here vnworthily resayfes fals honurs. *c* **1410** *Lanterne of Liȝt* 60 Whanne þei resceyue þe sacramentis, þei gon to hem vnworþili. **1526** TINDALE *1 Cor.* xi. 27 Whosoevere shall..drynke off the cuppe vnworthely. *a* **1586** SIDNEY *Arcadia* I. xiii, My name is Basilius, unworthily Lord of this country. **1670** MILTON *Hist. Eng.* III. Wks. 1851 V. 96 So hee..enjoy'd unworthily the rewards of lerning and fidelity. **1849** ROCK *Ch. of Fathers* I. 269 Acknowledging that whatsoever they had, was bestowed unworthily upon each one of them by God.

2. In a manner falling short of one's worth, excellence, or merit; without contributory fault or demerit; undeservedly.

Not always clearly distinguishable from sense 3.

a **1340** HAMPOLE *Psalter* lxxiii. 23 Rise god,..damyn þat þou ert vnworthily handelde of ill prestis. **1509** BARCLAY *Shyp of Folys* 25 But he and all his were murdred for theyr hyre. And nat vnworthely. **1598** YONG *Diana* 59, I bewailed my great mishap, knowing that he, whom most of al I loued, had so vnworthily forgotten me. **1607** E. GRIMSTONE tr. *Goulart's Mem. Hist.* 327 Marryed to an honest Gentlewoman, whom he entreated most unworthily. **1634** SIR T. HERBERT *Trav.* 83 [Nicanor] beginnes with Antiochus, sonne of Alexander, whom vnworthily he slue. **1712** STEELE *Spect.* No. 497 ¶4 Can any thing shew your Holiness how unworthily you treat Mankind? **1784** T. TWINING in *Recreat. & Stud.* (1882) 129 The Dean and Chapter..lay all the blame on him for suffering Johnson to be so unworthily interred. **1829** SIR W. NAPIER *Penins. War* II. 263 This arrangement was adopted after a struggle in the cabinet..; nevertheless, sir John Cradock was used unworthily.

b. Without sufficient appreciation; in an undervaluing or disparaging manner; derogatorily.

1599 HAKLUYT *Voy.* II. II. 135 Either thinking too worthily of the Spaniards valure,..or too vnworthily of them that vndertooke this iourney against him. **1651** HOBBES *Leviath.* II. xxxi. 190 That those Philosophers, who sayd the World, or the Soule of the World was God, spake unworthily of him. **1725** BROOME *Pope's Odyss.* Notes VII. II. 150 If then we look upon the Odyssey as all fiction, we consider it unworthily. *a* **1768** SECKER *Serm.* (1771) V. 416 Imagining that God can enjoin religious Cruelties,..is thinking..unworthily and absurdly of him.

3. In an unworthy, unbecoming, or improper manner; unbecomingly, unfitly, improperly.

1377 LANGL. *P. Pl.* B. xv. 238 And þat conscience and cryst hath yknitte faste, þei vndon it vnworthily, þo doctours of lawe. **1390** GOWER *Conf.* III. 169 Whan thou to such on as schal deie The worschipe of thi god aweie Hast yoven so unworthely. *c* **1449** PECOCK *Repr.* IV. i. 416 Summe.. vniustli and vnworthili blamen and vndirnymen the clergie. **1456** SIR G. HAYE *Govt. Princes* (S.T.S.) 82 A prince..for ..lusty delytis destroyand his awin gudis unworthily. **1535** COVERDALE *2 Macc.* v. 16 Them toke he in his hondes vnworthely, & defyled them. **1663** BP. PATRICK *Parab. Pilgr.* xxx, Thou blushest not..to think and do most unworthily, being altogether insensible of thy own Nature. *a* **1677** BARROW *Serm.* Wks. 1686 III. 63 In being discontented we behave our selves very unbeseemingly and unworthily. **1847** TENNYSON *Princ.* v. 177 One loves the soldier, one The silken priest of peace, one this, one that, And some unworthily. **1875** WHITNEY *Life Lang.* viii. 136 The name of Georgium Sidus, with which..it was unworthily sought to flatter a monarch.

†**4.** With indignation or resentment. *Obs. rare.*

In quots. tr. L. *indigne* (*ferens*).

1382 WYCLIF *2 Macc.* vii. 39 The kyng kyndlid with wrath,..berynge vnworthily hym self scornyd. —— *Mark* xiv. 4 Ther weren summe beringe vnworthily, or heuyli, with ynne hem silf.

un'worthiness. [f. as prec., or UN-¹ 12.]

1. The character or quality of being unworthy; lack of worth, absence of merit. †Occas. with *to*.

a **1340** HAMPOLE *Psalter* ci. 18 þat knawis þaire frelte & vnworthynes. *c* **1400** LOVE *Bonavent. Mirr.* (1908) 119 With grete drede of hir vnworthinesse that hir teres schulde touche oure lordes feete. **1447** BOKENHAM *Seyntys* (Roxb.) 2 The unwurthynesse Bothe of hys persone and eek hys name. **1485** *Rolls of Parlt.* VI. 274/1 The aforesaid Actes of Atteindre or Forfeiture, disableing, unworthi[n]esse, and unableing. **1526** *Pilgr. Perf.* (W. de W. 1531) 169b, The vylenesse, vnkyndnesse, & vnworthynesse of man to that loue. **1582** BENTLEY *Mon. Matrones* III. 278 Not remembering, good Lord, mine vnworthinesse..nor frailtie of my passed yeeres. **1631** GOUGE *God's Arrows* III. §22. 223 Mans unworthinesse and unfitnesse to appeare in Gods sight. **1675** DRYDEN *Aurengz.* IV. i. 1784 You will be kind to my Unworthiness. **1712** STEELE *Spect.* No. 448 ¶1 For Men ..do not keep up a lively Abhorrence of the least Unworthiness. **1771** *Junius Lett.* xlvi. (1772) II. 173 The people..would probably over-look his immediate unworthiness. **1855** MACAULAY *Hist. Eng.* xvii. IV. 60 It would be absurd to reject, on account of his unworthiness, the inestimable services which it was in his power to render. **1884** A. R. PENNINGTON *Wiclif* viii. 255 The unworthiness of the ministers hinders not the effect of the Sacrament.

b. With *an* (and pl.), *that*, *this*.

1533 BELLENDEN *Livy* II. vi. (S.T.S.) I. 149 Traisting to revenge this vnwourthynes be sum..hardy Interprise. **1653** JER. TAYLOR *Serm. for Year* I. xxiii. 304 If it [*sc.* jesting] mingles with any sin, it puts on the nature of that new unworthinesse. **1856** F. W. FABER *Creator & Creature* III. i, The very unworthinesses and short-comings of the creature. **1880** 'OUIDA' *Moths* II. 85, I think such a marriage a great unworthiness, a great disgrace.

c. With poss. pron., as a fictitious title.

1853 KINGSLEY *Hypatia* I. 239 Pambo asked his name... 'My unworthiness is called Peter the Reader.'

†**2.** Inappropriate or improper action. *Obs.*⁻¹

1608 in *Buccleuch MSS.* (Hist. MSS. Comm.) I. 76 It was unworthiness in your Majesty's officers to find him for a Ward.

†**un'worthly**, *a. Obs.* [OE. *unweorþlic* (UN-¹ 7).] Of little consequence or worth; base, mean.

c **1230** *Hali Meid.* 33 Ȝif þu art unwurðlich & wraðeliche ilatet. **13..** *E.E. Allit. P.* B. 305 With her vn-worþelych werk me wlatez with-inne. **1340** *Ayenb.* 132 Huanne þe man þoleþ in þolemodnesse þet he by uoulliche y-draȝe, and ase persone onworþlych.

†**un'worthly**, *adv. Obs.* [OE. *unweorþlice* (UN-¹ 11), = MDu. *onwerdelike* (Du. *onwaardelijk*), MLG. *unwerde-*, *unwertliken*, OHG. *unwerdlîhho* (MHG. *unwertlîche*).]

= UNWORTHILY *adv.* 1–3.

c **1200** *Trin. Coll. Hom.* 99 Ech þe understandeð þat holi husel unwurðliche. *c* **1200** [see UNWORSHIP *sb.* 1]. *a* **1225** *Ancr. R.* 130 Vor heo witeð unwurðliche ancre nome, & al þet heo euer wurcheð. **13..** R. BRUNNE *Handl. Synne* 981 Ne þou shalt swere vnwurschyply [*Dulwich MS.* vn-wurply; F. *folement*], By oure lorde. *a* **1400–50** *Alexander* (D.) 869 Vnworthly þou wroght..When þou was bowne with a brande my body to shende.

†**un'worthness.** *Obs.* [OE. *unweorþnes* (UN-¹ 12) in sense 1, = OHG. *unwerdnissa*.]

1. Contempt, scorn.

1340 *Ayenb.* 9 Wreþe oþer onworþnesse þet geþ liȝtliche.. uor to harmi oþren. *Ibid.* 19 Zuo is onworþnesse [*glossed* despit] þet is wel grat zenne.

2. Worthlessness.

1587 R. HOVENDEN in *Collect.* (O.H.S.) I. 212 Neyther.. ded [he] procure..rather the unworthenes of the lease then the..benefitt of the Colledge.

unworthy (ʌn'wɜːðɪ), *a.*, *adv.*, *sb.* [UN-[1] 7. Cf. MDu. *onwerdich* (Du. *onwaardig*), OS. *unwerdig*, MLG. *unwerdich*, OHG. *unwirdîg* (MHG. *unwirdic*, *-ec*, G. *unwürdig*), ON. *úverðugr* (Norw. *uverdug*, Sw. *ovärdig*, Da. *uværdig*), also UNWORTH and WANWORDY *adjs.*]

A. *adj.* **I. 1.** Of things: Deficient in worth; having little or no value; worthless.

In later use chiefly ellipt. from 3 b.

a **1240** *Wohunge* in *O.E. Hom.* I. 281 Ne was neauer unwurði þing chepet swa deore. **1375** BARBOUR *Bruce* IV. 196 Ane hamelat neir thair-by, A litill toune and vnworthy. **1398** TREVISA *Barth. De P.R.* XVII. cxv. (Bodl. MS.), Barlich.. haþ þe fouleste strawe of alle corne & vnworthieste stobles. *c* **1440** *Gesta Rom.* xiii. 43 Loo! what I haue suffred for the, where as I put non vnworthier thing for the then my owne body. *c* **1445** PECOCK *Donet* 33 Whanne a man.. beriþ in his hond sum pore vnworþi sticke. *c* **1532** DU WES *Introd. Fr.* in *Palsgr.* 896 Myn accustomed poore and unworthy servyce. **1599** SHAKS. *Hen. V*, I. ii. 228 France being ours, wee'l bend it to our Awe.. Or lay these bones in an vnworthy Vrne. **1618** J. TAYLOR (Water P.) *Penniless Pilgr.* D 2, My poore vnable and vnworthy pen. **1634** BP. HALL *Contempl.*, *N.T.* IV. vi, Our weak and unworthy prayers. **1697** DRYDEN *Virg. Georg.* II. 517 Whose leaves.. become the unworthy browse Of buffaloes. **1819** SHELLEY *Cenci* III. i. 129 These limbs, the unworthy temple of Thy spirit. **1854** *Poultry Chron.* II. 78/1 To withhold.. prizes in any of the classes in which the specimens are deemed unworthy.

b. Not reputable; hurtful or injurious to reputation; discreditable.

1693 DRYDEN *Exam. Poet.* Ded. ¶ 1 A kind of contempt for those who have risen by unworthy ways. **1735** THOMSON *Liberty* III. 376 Unworthy joys! that wasteful leave behind.. No secret ray to glad the conscious soul. **1795–6** WORDSW. *Borderers* I. 255, I suspect unworthy tales Have reached his ear. **1813** SHELLEY *Q. Mab* v. 163 Blunting the keenness of his spiritual sense With narrow schemings and unworthy cares. **1882** BESANT *All Sorts* xxvi, She repressed her indignation at this unworthy suggestion.

2. Of persons: Not worthy; lacking worth or merit; undeserving; hence, despicable, contemptible.

α. *a* **1240** *Wohunge* in *O.E. Hom.* I. 279 Schomeliche spateling of unwurði ribauz. *a* **1300** *Cursor M.* 23882 Amang þaa hirdes am i an, Sa wreche vnworthi wat i nan. *c* **1375** *Ibid.* 20015 (Fairf.), Al if I be vn-worþi man. *c* **1400** MAUNDEV. (Roxb.) iii. 10 He pryues þaim þat him think vnworthy. **1456** SIR G. HAYE *Law Arms* (S.T.S.) 302 Quhen princis prayis for unworthy personis, God is offendit. **1535** COVERDALE *Ecclus.* xxix. 32 Yet shall he be taken as vnworthy, & heare many bytter rough wordes. **1596** SHAKS. *Merch. V.* II. i. 37 So may I.. Misse that which one vnworthier may attaine. **1617** WOODALL *Surg. Mate* Pref., Wks. (1639) B 3, Unworthy impostors under the names of Surgeons. **1686** W. DE BRITAINE *Hum. Prud.* xi. 49 External Fortunes may befal the un-worthyest Persons. **1737** E. LEWIS *Let. to Swift* 30 June, [A] family.. brought to ruin by that unworthy man lord Kinnoul. **1823** SCOTT *Quentin D.* xv, Campo-basso, the un-worthy favourite of Duke Charles, with.. his base, treacherous spirit. **1835** JAMES *Gipsy* iii, An unworthy blackguard of that name. **1846** MRS. A. MARSH *Father Darcy* II. viii. 136 The authority confided to me—unworthy—by the church.

absol. *c* **1400** tr. *Secreta Secret.*, *Gov. Lordsh.* 52 He þat geuys þe giftys.. to vnworthy and to hem þat has non nede. **1555** EDEN *Decades* (Arb.) 59 Fortune.. sumtymes fauoureth the vnworthyest. **1602** [see SPURN *sb.*[1] 4]. *a* **1658** LOVELACE *Poems* (1659) 30 'Tis the same wrong th' unworthy to inthrone. **1864** FOX tr. *K. Ælfred's Boeth.* (1895) 97 Canst thou now understand how great dishonour power brings on the un-worthy when he receives it?

β. *c* **1475** *Cath. Angl.* 424/1 (A.), Vn Wordy, *jndignus, jgnobilis*. **1796** R. GALL *Tint Quey* (1819) 29 This is a bonny speech.. To come frae your unwordy head. *c* **1820** HOGG *Tales & Sk.* (1837) II. 147 Ah! the unwordy rascal!

b. Conventionally or devotionally used as an expression of humility.

c **1532** DU WES *Introd. Fr.* in *Palsgr.* 1036 Written by your unworthy servant. **1660** ALLESTREE *Gentl. Calling* 171 O most.. bountiful Lord, who.. hast in an extraordinary measure abounded to me thy unworthiest Servant. *a* **1700** in *Cath. Rec. Soc. Publ.* IX. 334 S[tr] Agnes of the Jnfant Jesus. Prioueresse unworthy. **1754** *Ibid.* VIII. 249 S[iste]r Agnes Howard Abbess unw[orth]y.

3. With const. Not of sufficient merit, excellence, or worth. **a.** With *to* (Sc. †*till*) and inf. (Chiefly of persons.)

a **1300** *Cursor M.* 14927 Crist and his moder do me to spede! þat vn-worthi es for to rede. *a* **1310** in Wright *Spec. Lyric P.* 73 Jesu, thah ich be unworthi To love the. *c* **1400** *Destr. Troy* II. 629, I wot me vnworthy þis wirdis to fall. *c* **1449** PECOCK *Repr.* IV. iii. 428 Thanne bi lijk argument.. ech gouernaunce and ech thing.. weren vnleeful and vnworthi to be had and vsid. *c* **1450** *St. Cuthbert* (Surtees) 2709, I am vnworthy.. Slike hy degre to come toward. **1526** *Pilgr. Perf.* (W. de W. 1531) 84 b, Proclamynge themselfe synners & vnworthy to lyue. **1563** A. NOWELL in *Lett. Lit. Men* (Camden) 21 [To] iudge whether it [= his MS. Catechism] were not unwoorthie.. to be maide publike. **1651** HOBBES *Leviath.* II. xxvii. 159 He.. is.. thought unworthy to have any charge, or preferment in Warre. **1667** MILTON *P.L.* XII. 91 Since hee [*sc.* man] permits Within himself unworthie Powers to reign Over free Reason. **1671** —— *P.R.* IV. 346 The rest [are].. unworthy to compare With Sion's songs. **1715** POPE *Iliad* II. 862 His troops in forty ships Podarces led,.. Nor he unworthy to command the host. **1789** COWPER *Queen's Visit* 67 The cumb'rous throng, Not else unworthy to be fear'd. **1827** POLLOK *Course T.* I. 121 Unworthy is your servant To stand in presence of the King. **1865** KINGSLEY *Herew.* xl, His soul, unworthy to be delivered from evil.

b. With *of*, †*to*, †*for* (something specifed), or clause.

1382 WYCLIF *Tobit* iii. 19 Or I was vnwrthi to hem, or thei parauenture to me weren not wrthi. —— *Acts* xiii. 46 ȝe.. han demed vs vnworthi of [**1388** to] euere lasting lyf. *c* **1386** CHAUCER *Clerk's T.* 359 Lord, vndigne and vnworthy Am I, to thilke honour. **1565** COOPER *Thesaurus*, *Amicitia indigni*, vnworthy of friendship. **1589** HAKLUYT *Voy.* To Rdr. ¶ 9, I accompt him vnworthy of future fauours. **1608** SHAKS. *Per.* II. v. 40, I am unworthy for her schoolmaster. **1615** SIR W. MURE *Misc. Poems* xiv. 14 Quhich endit ye dayes of this sensuall slaue, Wnwordy the earth sould ȝeild him a graue. **1674** *Jackson's Recant.* A 4, I thought my self unworthy of a forreign Plantation. **1784** COWPER *Task* III. 731 Neglected Nature pines, Abandon'd, as unworthy of our love. **1823** MRS. HEMANS *Siege Valencia* ii. 157 The noble daughter of Pelayo's line Hath nought to ask, unworthy of the name Which is a nation's heritage. **1849** MACAULAY *Hist. Eng.* ii. I. 250 Nor did he appear to the public unworthy of his high fortunes.

c. Of superior worth or merit. (Const. *to*.)

1746 FRANCIS tr. *Hor.*, *Sat.* II. ii. 139 Why lives in deep Distress A Man unworthy to be poor?

4. a. Of treatment, etc.: Not deserved, warranted, or justified; unmerited.

Chiefly of treatment, fortune, etc., below the deserts or merit of the person or persons concerned.

1382 WYCLIF *2 Macc.* xiv. 42 Cheesynge for to dye nobly, rather than.. aȝeinis his birthis for to be ledd with vnworthi wrongis. *a* **1425** tr. *Arderne's Treat. Fistula* etc. 30 It seemeþ.. vnworþi for to vse wele þingis y-giffe þat kan noȝt gette hym mo þingis. **1533** BELLENDEN *Livy* IV. viii, With mony vthir nocht vnwourthy lovingis. **1560** DAUS tr. *Sleidane's Comm.* 402 b, This vnworthie and lamentable fortune of the Norinbergians. **1596** SPENSER *F.Q.* VI. iv. 34 He inly touched was With tender ruth for her vnworthy griefe. **1603** KNOLLES *Hist. Turks* (1621) 146 [They] ceased not.. vntill they had wrought his vnworthie destruction. **1648** T. BEAUMONT *Psyche* VII. cxviii, The holy Travellers through Cold.. And northern Blasts, took their unworthy way. **1700** DRYDEN *Theodore & Hon.* 127 Mov'd with unworthy Usage of the Maid. **1854** TRENCH *Synonyms N.T.* 194 Absolutely unworthy suffering there is none. **1879** FROUDE *Cæsar* xxii. 368 The unworthy treatment of their great enemy.

†**b.** Dishonouring, low, mean. Const. *to*. *Obs.*

1694 J. COLLIER *Misc. Ess.* I. i. 33 How unworthy and unchristian it is to play upon the Indigence.. of another.

5. That has not requisite worth or merit; inferior to or below what is merited or deserved; base.

1533 BELLENDEN *Livy* II. xiv. (S.T.S.) I. 184 Thinkand richt vnworthy þat þare hail sollicitude.. was direkkit to na vthir fyne. **1598** YONG *Diana* 130 This villany did the traitor Alfeus work,.. for the contempt, which she had of his vnworthy affection. **1606** SHAKS. *Ant. & Cl.* III. xiii. 84 Your Cæsars Father oft.. Bestow'd his lips on that vnworthy place, As it rain'd kisses. **1662** STILLINGFL. *Orig. Sacræ* III. iii. §4 Far be such unworthy thoughts from our apprehensions of a Deity. **1760** *Impostors Detected* IV. iii. II. 190, I represented to him how unworthy the profession.. was to one of his character. **1820** LAMB *True Story* Wks. 1908 I. 256 A little festival.. (though it must bear an unworthier name).. in honour of her guest's recovery.

b. Beneath or below, unbecoming or unbefitting, the character, repute, or dignity *of* a person, etc.; not worthy or deserving *of* notice, etc.

1697 DRYDEN *Æneis* XII. 1156 A wound unworthy of our state to feel. **1700** —— *Pref. Fables* ¶ 14 Some people [think].. these tales.. unworthy of my pains. **1733** POPE *Let. to Swift* 2 April, I will take care to suppress things unworthy of him. **1780** *Mirror* No. 73, Some of them are new, and not unworthy of notice. **1869** TOZER *Highl. Turkey* I. 303 A series of domestic tragedies.. hardly unworthy of the palace of Atreus at Mycenæ.

II. With ellipse of *of*. **6.** Not deserving, meriting, or worthy of. **a.** Of persons. †Also *absol.*

1382 WYCLIF *Job* xxx. 2 Thei weren trowid vnwrthi that lif [L. *vita ipsa indigni*]. —— *Ecclus.* xxv. 11 Blisful.. [is he] that seruede not to the vnwrthi hymself [L. *indignis se*]. **1535** *Lett. Suppress. Monast.* (Camden) 103 The poore house which I under God.. (though unworthye suche a cure) have hadde mynistration and rule of. *a* **1589** PALFREYMAN *Baldwin's Mor. Philos.* (1600) 64 b, Hee is.. much vnworthy honour, that seeketh his owne wealth and oppresseth other. **1600** SHAKS. *Much Ado* II. iii. 216 (Q.), How much he is vnworthy so good a lady. **1634** SIR T. HERBERT *Trav.* 219 Iorwerth.. was thought vnworthy the Crowne and dignitie. **1718** POPE *Iliad* IX. 88 Curs'd is the man,.. Unworthy property, unworthy light,.. who delights in war. **1794** MRS. RADCLIFFE *Myst. Udolpho* li, She again beheld.. Valancourt unworthy the esteem and tenderness she had once bestowed upon him. **1836** DICKENS *Sk. Boz*, *New Year*, Until he proves himself unworthy the confidence we repose in him. **1874** DASENT *Half a Life* III. 78 This only shows you are quite unworthy such luck.

b. Of things, etc.

1634 SIR T. HERBERT *Trav.* 207 A place not vnworthy the remembrance. **1661** EARL ORRERY *St. Lett.* (1742) 18 It may not be unworthy your grace's observation, that [etc.]. **1697** DRYDEN *Virg. Georg.* III. 6 All other themes.. Are worn with use, unworthy me to write. **1718** PRIOR *Poems* Postscr., A Panegyric, not unworthy the Pen of some future Pliny. **1765** *Museum Rust.* IV. 334 Agriculture.. is.. not unworthy even the patriot's care. **1809** SYD. SMITH *Serm.* II. 335 Many men.. imagine, that this department of medicine is unworthy the name of science. **1832** R. & J. LANDER *Exped. Niger* I. i. 26 Nothing seemed unworthy his acceptance, from fine scarlet cloth to a child's farthing whistle. **1882** *Daily News* 19 Aug. 4/7 Nor is it unworthy notice that [etc.].

7. Not befitting or suiting (a person, etc.); derogatory to the dignity, standing, or character of; below the level of.

1646 H. LAWRENCE *Comm. Angells* 99 Other sins have their aggravations; but this is.. the most unworthy a man. **1682** *B. Whitelocke's Mem.* Pref., His posthumous work contains.. many things most false, and unworthy so great a name. **1720** POPE *Iliad* XX. 244 Unmanly pride, Unworthy the high race from which we came. **1761** HUME *Hist. Eng.* III. lii. 128 Rigours.. unworthy men of their profession. **1798** S. & HT. LEE *Canterb. T.*, *Yng. Lady's T.* II. 394 For her father to expatiate on such baubles, was unworthy both his experience and sex. **1810** SOUTHEY *Kehama* VII. v, The wings of Eagle or of Cherubim Had seem'd unworthy him. **1852** J. H. NEWMAN *Idea of a University* (1873) 53 It would.. have been unworthy a genius.. so analytical as Aristotle's, to have laid it down that [etc.]. **1885** 'MRS. ALEXANDER' *At Bay* i, A silly after-glow of boyish folly, unworthy his experience and maturity.

B. *adv.* Unworthily: in a manner unworthy *of* (something). Also *ellipt.* (cf. 6–7).

1661 EARL ORRERY *St. Lett.* (1742) 19 This would engage him to walk not unworthy such an honour. **1708** *Caldwell Papers* (Maitl. Club) I. 217 Our sins in walking unworthy of y[e] great mercy God hath blest us with. **1740** RICHARDSON *Pamela* (1741) II. 377, I hope I shall not behave unworthy of the good Instructions. **1760–72** H. BROOKE *Fool of Qual.* (1792) V. 43 Letting him know how unworthy he should have acted by his daughter, had he imposed.. upon her. **1804** EUGENIA DE ACTON *Tale without Title* III. 7 Let us not act unworthy of beings who have a hope in futurity.

C. *sb.* An unworthy person.

Used only in expressed or implied contrast to WORTHY *sb.*

1616 BRETON *Good & Badde* (title-p.), Descriptions of the Worthies, and Vnworthies of this Age. Where The Best may see their Graces, and the Worst discerne their Basenesse. *a* **1661** FULLER *Worthies* I. (1662) 73 The Worthies of England being your Subject, you have mingled many Unworthies among them. **1886** *Encycl. Brit.* XX. 614/2 John Wilmot.. was one of the unworthies of the reign.. of Charles II. **1893** E. PEACOCK in *N. & Q.* 22 July 72 Bothwell, Knox,.. and other worthies and unworthies of the troubled Marian period.

†**un'worthy**, *v.* *Obs. rare.* [UN-[2] 6 a, or f. prec. Cf. UNWORTH *v.*, MHG. *unwirdigen*, and G. *entwürdigen*.]

1. *trans.* To dishonour; to do discredit to.

c **1230** *Hali Meid.* 35 þis is sunne, & ec uncunnelicheð þe, & unwurðeð [*v.r.* unwurdgeð] þi bodi. **1628** FELTHAM *Resolves* II. liii. 156 b, To feed that dispersiue humour, all wayes shall be trodden, though they never so much vnworthy the man.

2. To asperse or vilify. Hence **un'worthying** *ppl. a.*

1654 WHITLOCK *Zootomia* 459 They know not how to raise their slender Merits, but by levelling others that excell them in any thing, with their unworthying Tongues.

un'wound (ʌn'waʊnd), *ppl. a.*[1] [UN-[1] 8 b. Cf. MDu. *onghewonden*, MHG. and older G. *ungewunden*.] Not wound (up).

1648 HEXHAM II, *Ongewonden*, Vnwound, or Vnwrapped. **1719** J. HUGHES *Morning Apparition* 4 Dumb o'er my pillow hung my watch unwound. **1824** MISS MITFORD *Village* Ser. I. 222 As the hand of an unwound clock stands at one hour of the day. **1897** BRAM STOKER *Dracula* iv, My watch was still unwound.

un'wound, *ppl. a.*[2] [UN-[2] 8, or f. UNWIND *v.*[1]] Released from a coiled or twisted state; untwisted.

1707 MORTIMER *Husb.* 305 Which Thatching most tie on with Withs, but old pitched Ropes unwound, is much cheaper. **1818** MILMAN *Samor* VIII. 34 The soul, unwound its coarse material chains, Basks in its own divinity.

un'woundable, *a.* [UN-[1] 7 b.] Incapable of being wounded.

1611 COTGR., *Imblessable*, vnhurtable, vnwoundable. **1698** S. CLARKE *Script. Just.* Introd. B 2, In these lie all my strength.. and.. I hope to be unwoundable. **1731** BAILEY (ed. 2). **1875** TENNYSON *Q. Mary* v. v, Callous with a constant stripe, Unwoundable.

Hence **un'woundableness.** *rare*[−0].

1660 BLOUNT (ed. 2), *Invulnerability*, unwoundableness.

un'wounded, *ppl. a.* [OE. *unwundod* (UN-[1] 8), = MDu. *onghewondet* (Du. *ongewond*). Cf. G. *unverwundet*.] Not wounded; unhurt.

a **1000** *Genesis* 183 Ne þær ænig com blod of benne, ac him breᵹo engla of lice ateah liodende ban, wer unwundod. *c* **1200** ORMIN 14735 All swa summ Ysaac attbrast Unnwunndedd & unnwemmedd. *c* **1350** *Will. Palerne* 1280 Riȝt fewe went a-wey vn-woundet or take. *c* **1400** *Destr. Troy* 10696 Aiax.. vnwoundit, i-wis, out of wothe paste. *c* **1450** *St. Cuthbert* (Surtees) 7098 Cuthbert men vnwounded eschapid. **1502** ATKYNSON tr. *De Imitatione* III. xl. (1893) 229 If thou vse nat on euery hande thy shylde of pacyence, thou shalt nat be longe vnwounded. **1614** TOMKIS *Albumazar* I. vii, With these walk as unwounded as Achilles, Dipp'd by his mother Thetis. **1651** DAVENANT *Gondibert* II. III. xl, Vex'd that the Empire which your wound did gaine, Was by a young unwounded Army fought! **1700** DRYDEN *Ovid's Met.* XIII. 434 Hector from the Field unwounded went. **1777** POTTER *Æschylus*, *Choephoræ* 376 [The] envenom'd viper, That poisons with a touch th' unwounded body. **1831** SCOTT *Ct. Rob.* xvi, He covered his eyes with the unwounded hand. **1863** W. C. BALDWIN *Afr. Hunting* vi. 185 An un-wounded cow giraffe.

fig. and *transf.* **1579** E. K. *Gloss. to Spenser's Sheph. Cal.* Oct. 41 Woundlesse armour, vnwounded in warre, doe rust through long peace. **1622** FLETCHER *Span. Cur.* I. i, We may hear praises when they are deserv'd, Our modesty unwounded. **1624** MASSINGER *Parl. Love* V. i, Provided my fair name Had been unwounded. **1735** POPE *Ep. Lady* 260 She, who can.. hear Sighs for a daughter with unwounded ear. **1816** SOUTHEY *Poet's Pilgr.* II. iii. 169 Unwounded here Judæa's balm distill'd Its precious juice. **1818** MILMAN *Samor* IV. 406 The beardless Troilus, Unwounded by soft Cresseide's arrowy eyes.

absol. **1768–74** TUCKER *Lt. Nat.* (1834) I. 517. I expect.. that the healed will accompany me as undisturbedly as the unwounded along our future progress.

un'woven, *ppl. a.* (UN-[1] 8 b.)

1429 *Rolls of Parlt.* IV. 360/2 þe yerne þat leveth un-woven. **1467** *Act 7 Edw. IV*, c. 3 To him or them that espieth or maketh Proof of any such unwoven Yarn. **1566** *Wills &*

Inv. N.C. (Surtees, 1835) 260, xv yerds of lining clothe with garne for harden clothe vnwoven. **1648** HEXHAM II, *Ongeweven*, Vnwoven. **1902** *Westm. Gaz.* 1 Oct. 2/3 Death .. shakes th' unwoven thread Thridding the shuttle, and the story's told.

†**un'wracked**, *ppl. a. Obs.* [UN-¹ 8.] Not wrecked.

1627 DRAYTON *Elegies, Lady Aston's Depart. Spain* 41 Let them for her sake, Who to thy safeguard doth her selfe betake, Escape vndrown'd, vnwrackt [**1748** unwreck'd].

†**un'wrall**, *v. Obs.*⁻¹ [UN-² 3 + WRALL *v.* Cf. UNWARL *v.*] *trans.* To unwind, unroll.

1387 TREVISA *Higden* (Rolls) I. 9 My witt is ful luyte to unwralle þe wrappyinges of so wonder werkes.

un'wrap, *v.* [UN-² 3, 4, 7.]

1. *trans.* To remove the wrapping from; to uncover by removing a wrapping or the like. Also *refl.*

Before *c* 1820 somewhat rare; cf. sense 2.

c **1386** CHAUCER *Man of Law's Prol.* 5 So soore artow ywoundid That verray nede vnwrappeth al thy wounde hid. **1530** PALSGR. 769/1 Unwrappe this same and looke what is in it. **1580** HOLLYBAND *Treas. Fr. Tong, Dessiller*, to vnwrappe his eies, to restore the sight. *a* **1618** SYLVESTER *Pibrac's Titrastica* lxxxiii, Her spightfull Cords shee can so closely knit, That though at last wee happen to un-wrap us; The print thereof still in our Fames will sit. **1825** J. NEAL *Bro. Jonathan* II. 119 The man-slayer was unwrapping the bundle. **1859** GEO. ELIOT *A. Bede* xxii, He had wrapped the box up in a great many covers, that he might see Hetty unwrapping it with growing curiosity.

fig. **1889** R. BRIDGES *Sonn.* xxix, The sun's first rays, That lift the dark west and unwrap the night.

†**b.** *fig.* To unfold, reveal, disclose, explain. *Obs. rare.*

c **1374** CHAUCER *Boeth.* IV. pr. vi. (1868) 133 þou hast ȝeuen .. me to vnwrappen þe hidde causes of þinges. **1593** *Sidney's Arcadia* III. (1629) 366, I will disclose my greatest secret... I will, I say, unwrap my hidden estate. **1600** FAIRFAX *Tasso* XVII. lxxxvii, That so I could the Catalogue vn-wrap Of thy great nephewes, yet vnborne.

c. To deliver *out of*, release *from*, free *of*, some envelopment; to liberate or set free. Also *fig.*

1561 T. NORTON *Calvin's Inst.* I. 12 Like a maze, out of which we can not vnwrapp our selues, vnlesse [etc.]. **1568** EARL OF SUSSEX in E. Lodge *Illustr. Brit. Hist.* (1791) II. 6 And, lastly, to foresee that these Scotts on bothe sydes packe not together, so as to unwrappe .. ther mystres owte of all present slaunders, purge her openly [etc.]. **1620** SHELTON *2nd Pt. Don Quix.* xlviii. 321 Vnwrapping him from the Sheet and the Quilt, they pinched him. *c* **1825** BEDDOES *Poems, Torrismond* I. iv, Unwrap me of my years, and hunt me .. Into my mother's womb! there unbeget me!

2. To open, unwind, or unroll (what is wrapped or wound); †to unfurl (a sail). Also *fig.*

Rare before 19th cent.; cf. sense 1.

1387 TREVISA *Higden* (MS. Cott. Tib.) fol. 3, þis matyre .. haþ meny .. wyndyngs and wrynkklyngs þat wol noȝt be vnwrappid. *Ibid.*, My wyt ys ful lytel to vnwrappe þe gret hardnes of so wondre werks. **1582** STANYHURST *Æneid* III. (Arb.) 76 Our sayls vnwrapped vphoysing, .. thee rough seas deepelye we furrowe. **1807** J. BARLOW *Columb.* III. 821 Where the savage leader lay .. [he] directs his eager way, Unwraps the tyger's hide, and strives .. To close the wound. **1860** RUSKIN *Unto this Last* ii. (1896) 60 Rags unwrapped from the breasts of goodly soldiers dead. **1894** A. ROBERTSON *Nuggets*, etc. 27 He unwrapped his blankets, [and] spread them on the bed.

b. (See quot.)

1859 T. LUND *Elem. Geom. & Mensuration* III. 316 We may call attention to two cases of curved surfaces, where the surface can be unwrapped, so as to form a plane surface.

3. *intr.* To undergo unwrapping or unwinding.

1833 WHEWELL *Astron.* 218 A stone at the end of a string, when the string is whirled round, and is allowed to wrap round the hand, or to unwrap from it. *c* **1888** YEATS *Poems* (1912) 261 Joy .. stirs the young kid's budding horn, And makes the infant ferns unwrap.

un'wrapped, *ppl. a.* [UN-¹ 8.] Not wrapped (up).

1570 LEVINS *Manip.* 51 Vnwrapped, *infasciatus.* **1648** HEXHAM II, *Ongewonden*, Vnwound, or Vnwrapped. **1921** *Daily Colonist* (Victoria) 20 Mar. 8/1 Why buy soap in packages when you can buy it cheaper 'unwrapped'? **1968** D. E. ALLEN *British Tastes* iii. 77 Bread, being brought to the door and made more by small local bakers, tends to be unwrapped (and, of course, unsliced) more frequently than elsewhere. **1978** A. NEAVE *Nuremberg* vii. 78 He handed over to Andrus and myself odd little packets of food and three bars of unwrapped chocolate for analysis.

†**un'wrast**, *a.* (and *sb.*). *Obs.* Forms: 1–3 **unwræst** (3 **-wærste**), **-wreast**, 1, 3–5 **-wrest**, 3–4 **-wreste** (3 *Orm.* **-wresste**); 2–3, 5 **unwraste**, 4–5, *Sc.* 6 **-wrast**. Also 3–4 **on-** (4 **oun-**), 4–5, *Sc.* 6 **vn-**. [OE. *unwræst*, *unwrést* (UN-¹ 7).]

1. Of a poor, worthless, or vile quality or condition; sorry, miserable; of little account: **a.** Of persons.

c **893** K. ÆLFRED *Oros.* III. i. §5 Hi Læcedemonie .. to þon ȝedydon þæt hi hi selfe leton æȝþer ȝe for heane ȝe for unwræste. *c* **1200** *Trin. Coll. Hom.* 29 Vnwreste þu best ȝef þu wreche ne secst hwanne þu time siest. *c* **1205** LAY. 26450 Cuðeð eower kinge, [Bruttus beoþ bolde] ac heo beoð unwræste italde. *a* **1225** *Leg. Kath.* 1260 Hwet nu, unwreste men & wacre þen eni wake! *c* **1350** *Lybeaus Disc.* 2118 The menstrales .. Hadde ryche yftes wythalle, And they that weryn unwrest.

b. Of things.

a **1122** *O.E. Chron.* (Laud MS.) an. 1052, And ȝewendon heom on an to Ealdulfes næse, & wearð him þær on anon unwræste scipe. *c* **1200** *Trin. Coll. Hom.* 29 Ful mai þe þinke, þat forcuðer haueð faire weden and þu unwreste. *c* **1205** LAY. 16307 þenne þat hæfd is unwræst þe hælp is þæ wurse. *c* **1300** *Havelock* 2821 Him to binden faste Vp-on an asse swiþe un-wraste.

2. a. Of persons: Addicted to evil, wickedness, or vice; wicked.

a **1225** *Ancr. R.* 124 þenc hu þe gode holi mon .. blescede þe unwreste hond þet hefde ihermed him. *a* **1240** *Wohunge* in *O.E. Hom.* I. 283 And tu .. was unwreste folk of world to hoker lahter. **13..** *K. Alis.* (W.) 878 What dostow here, unwrast gome? .. He! fyle ateynte horesone! To misdo was ay thy wone. *c* **1380** *Sir Ferumb.* 2905 þys schrewede Sarsyns þat wern ounwraste. *c* **1535** M. NISBET *N.T. in Scots* (S.T.S.) III. 349 He .. schawis how menn augtht to behaue thaim towart sick as be vnwrast.

absol. and as *sb.* *a* **1225** *Ancr. R.* 68 Me ileueð þet vuel sone, & te unwreste bliðeliche lieð on þe gode. *c* **1320** *Castle of Love* 335 Heo him made a-gulte, þulke vn-wreste, And biswikide him. *c* **1330** *Arth. & Merl.* 6964 (Kölbing), It were ille, ȝif eueriche vnwrest hadde his wille.

b. Of actions, etc.: Characterized by wickedness or evil; iniquitous.

a **1122** *O.E. Chron.* (Laud MS.) an. 1131, ðif þær wære hure an unwreste wrenc. *a* **1175** *Cott. Hom.* 235 Ac si laȝe sone adiliȝde þurh unwreaste leahtrum. *a* **1250** *Owl & N.* 178 Suche wordes beoþ vnwreste. *c* **1275** LAY. 7033 For þisse onwreste [laȝe] al men him hatede. *c* **1315** SHOREHAM I. 1581 þanne aȝte .. wyues nauȝt aȝens men Non onwrestnesse werche, Ac þolye, And nauȝt onwrest op-sechen hy. **13..** *Seuyn Sages* (W.) 1917 For mine thre unwrast dede. *c* **1400** *St. Alexius* (Laud 622) 738 Sergeauntz .. despised hym fast. þe wasshyng of her vessel þai cast on hym euerydel, þat was swiþe vnwrast. *c* **1425** *Cursor M.* 9475 (Trin.), þis foule synne was so vnwrast.

3. Untrustworthy, unreliable. Const. *of. rare*⁻¹.

1393 LANGL. *P. Pl.* C. XXI. 313 He were [= would be] vnwrast of hus worde, þat witnesse is of trewþe.

Hence †**un'wrastness**; also †**un'wrastship**, wickedness. *Obs.*

a **1225** *Ancr. R.* 304 Min owune unwrestschipe hit dude. *c* **1315** [see prec. 2 b]. *c* **1320** *Castle of Love* 1143 For vre vnwrestschupe here þe coroune of þornes on his hed he beere.

†**un'wraste**, *adv. Obs.* [UN-¹ 11 b.] = next.

c **1205** LAY. 19414 Bruttes .. lætten swiðe hokerliche of Lote .. and duden swiðe vnwraste alle his haste. *Ibid.* 2546, 19290, 28415. *a* **1225** *Ancr. R.* 268 Heo beoð to woke, & to unwreste iheorted þet .. herdeliche ne uihteð.

†**un'wrastly**, *adv. Obs.* [OE. *unwræstlice*, f. *unwræst* UNWRAST *a.*]

1. In a weak or feeble manner; weakly, poorly.

c **1050** *Byrhtferth's Handboc* in *Anglia* VIII. 334 þys hiw ealde uðwitan ȝesettan aȝen þam þingum þe zenodotus se eficisca esne unwræstilice ȝesette. *a* **1225** *Ancr. R.* 294 ȝif þu, þuruh þine ȝemeleaste, werest te erest wocliche [*Trin. MS.* unwreastliche].

2. Basely, wickedly.

c **1320** *Cast. Love* 1468 Sikerliche vnwrestlyche he deeþ þat such Fader ne loueþ with al his þouȝt.

un'wrathful, *a.* (UN-¹ 7.)

1542 UDALL *Erasm. Apoph.* Table, Vnwrathfull speakyng. **1548** —— *Erasm. Par. Luke* iii. 49 The merciable & vnwrathefull maker of the law euangelicall. **1775** ASH.

un'wrathfully, *adv.* (UN-¹ 11.)

1542 UDALL *Erasm. Apoph.* 61 *marg.*, Unwrathfully spoken. *Ibid.* 285 Yᵉ noumbre of thynges unwrathefully & prudentely dooen.

unwray, variant of UNWRY *v. Obs.*

un'wreaked, *ppl. a.* [UN-¹ 8.] Not revenged or requited; unavenged.

1590 SPENSER *F.Q.* III. xi. 9 How suffrest thou such shamefull cruelty, So long vnwreaked of thine enimy? **1605** *Play of Stucley* in Simpson *Sch. Shaks.* (1878) 208 Who'll let his kinsmans blood unwreaked rest? **1613** CHAPMAN *Rev. Bussy D'Ambois* IV. G 3 b, So wilde, so mad, Shee cannot liue, and this vnwreakt sustaine. **1855** SINGLETON *Virgil* II. 398 Not over me, unwreaked, Nor long, shalt thou .. exult, In conquest. **1884** *Macm. Mag.* Nov. 20/1 Unless the accused has an enemy .. with an unwreaked grudge against him. **1887** MEREDITH *Ballads & P.* 98 Hoarse for slaughter yet unwreaked.

†**un'wreaken**, *ppl. a. Obs.*⁻¹ [UN-¹ 8 b. Cf. OE. *unwrecen.*] = prec.

1592 R. WILMOT *Tancred & Gism.* v. ii. H 1, Shall I then vnwreaken downe descend? Shall I not worke some iust reuenge on him?

un'wreathe, *v.*¹ [UN-² 3. Cf. UNWRITHE *v.*] *trans.* To free from a wreathed or entwined condition; to disentwine, untwist. Also *refl.*

1591 PERCIVALL *Sp. Dict.*, *Destorcer*, to vnwreath, *detorquere.* **1660** BOYLE *New Exp. Phys. Mech.* Digress. 379 The Beards of wilde Oats .. continually wreath and unwreath themselves according to the even, light variations of the temperature of the ambient Air. **1731** BAILEY (vol. II), *Unwrithen*, unwreathed, untwisted, straitened. **1810** SOUTHEY *Kehama* XVI. xix, The Beast .. Unwreathes his rings and strives to fly. **1822** SHELLEY tr. *Calderon's Mag. Prodig.* III. 75 Leafy Vine, unwreath thy bower.

un'wreathe, *v.*² [UN-² 4.] *trans.* To divest of a wreath or wreaths.

(In quot. *absol.*)

1852 GROTE *Greece* II. lxx. IX. 137 Probably the operations of wreathing and unwreathing must here have been performed by the soldiers symbolically.

un'wreathed, *a. rare*⁻⁰. [UN-¹ 9.] Wreathless.

1731 BAILEY (vol. II), *Unwreathed*, .. without a wreath.

un'wrecked, *ppl. a.* (UN-¹ 8.)

1748 [see UNWRACKED]. **1775** ASH. **1896** R. BRIDGES *Fair Brass* ii, An effigy of brass .. Lieth in the sombre aisle Of this old church unwreckt.

†**un'wree**, *v. Obs.*⁻¹ [UN-² 3 + WREE *v.*] *trans.* To free (a person) from accusation; to clear.

a **1225** *Ancr. R.* 308 ȝif þu wreiest þe wel her, God wule unwreien [L. *excusat*] þe þer.

†**un'wrench**, *sb. Obs.* [OE. *unwrenc* (UN-¹ 4 b, 12).] An evil or base trick, artifice, or turn; a vice or sin.

c **897** K. ÆLFRED *Gregory's Past. C.* xxxiii. 215 Ða ȝeðyld .. for ðæm unwrence ðære unȝeðylde .. he forlet. *a* **1023** WULFSTAN *Hom.* 54 Mid ðam unwrencan bið Antecrist eal afylled. *c* **1200** *Trin. Coll. Hom.* 79 ȝif þe unfele man .. mid felefolde wiȝeles teð him to unwrenches. *a* **1225** *Ancr. R.* 268 Vor þet is his unwrench .. þet holi men mest dredeð. *c* **1250** *Owl & N.* 169 Ne speddestu noȝt mid þine unwrenche, For ich am war.

un'wrench, *v.* [UN-² 9.] *trans.* To open or detach by wrenching.

1818 MILMAN *Genius* 27 While Rape unwrench'd her wither'd grasp That clung unto the tomb. **1832** J. MONTGOMERY *Cholera Mount* Wks. 1841 IV. 170 The blue pest, whose gripe no art can shun, No force unwrench.

un'wrenched, *ppl. a.* [UN-¹ 8.] Not subjected to wrenching.

[**1775** ASH, *Unranched, Unwrenched.*] **1784** COWPER *Task* IV. 446 Nor will he leave Unwrench'd the door, however well secur'd. **1800** COLERIDGE *Piccolom.* v. vi. 72 To him Nothing on earth remains unwrenched and firm, Who has no faith.

unwrest, variant of UNWRAST *a. Obs.*

†**un'wrest**, *v. Obs.* Also 5 *pa. t.* and *pa. pple.* **vnwrast**(e; 7 **vnrest**. [UN-² 9.] *trans.* To undo, detach, or dislocate, by wresting or wrenching.

c **1450** LOVELICH *Merlin* 13942 The ȝate closed aȝen also faste as hit ne hadde neuere ben vnwraste. **1470–85** MALORY *Arthur* VIII. xxxiv. 326 Bothe his handes .. were fast bounden vnto knyghtes; .. sodenly he pulled them bothe to hym, and vnwrast his handes. **1509** BARCLAY *Shyp of Folys* 25 Haddest thou leuer se Thy sonnes necke vnwrested wyth a rope, Than [etc.]. **1598** FLORIO, *Distorcere*, .. to wriggle, to wrest, to vnwrest. **1613** DANIEL *Coll. Hist. Eng.* II. 139 Their occasions made them somewhat to vnrest [**1617** unwrest] the Soueraigntie from that height whereunto hee had strayned it.

un'wrested, *ppl. a.* [UN-¹ 8.] Not wrested or strained.

1653 *Nissena* 116 Whose wisdom hath always been equal to their unwrested and immaculate Justice. **1712** J. MORTON *Nat. Hist. Northampton.* 7 'Tis .. a natural and unwrested observation, that the rivers [etc.]. **1771** WHITAKER *Hist. Manch.* I. 265 The plain unwrested import of the word.

Hence **un'wrestedly** *adv.*, without forcing.

1615 G. SANDYS *Trav.* 91 Vnto this lamentable subuersion .. may that prophesie of Sibyls be vnwrestedly applied.

un'wresting, *ppl. a.* (UN-¹ 10.)

1595 DANIEL *Civ. Wars* I. xcix, Let vnwresting charity beleeue That then thy oth with thy intent agreed.

†**un'wried**, *ppl. a. Obs.*⁻¹ [UN-¹ 8.] Not twisted or wrested.

1558 PHAER *Æneid* VI. P iij b, Whan thou duely hast it [*sc.* a bough] spied Lay thou theron thy hand, for willingly with eas, onwried, Itself it shall releas.

un'wrinkle, *v.* [UN-² 3.]

1. *trans.* To free (the brow, etc.) from wrinkles; to smooth (a wrinkled surface).

1611 COTGR., *Desplisser*, to .. vnwrinkle, vncrumple. *Ibid.* s.v. *Desfroncer*, To cleere, vncloud, or vnwrinckle his visage. **1725** RAMSAY *Gentl. Sheph.* v. iii, See how much joy unwrinkles every brow. **1784** J. POTTER *Virtuous Villagers* II. 185 By unwrinkling the brow of care, [it has] given place to calm contentment. **1822** SCOTT *Nigel* Introd. Epist., To unwrinkle a brow bent with the furrows of daily toil. **1880** MEREDITH *Tragic Com.* x. 181 He unwrinkled the letter carefully for it to be legible.

2. *intr.* To become free from wrinkles.

1827 *Perils & Captivity* (Constable's Misc.) 85 Foreheads, lowering and sulky, began to unwrinkle.

un'wrinkled, *ppl. a.* [UN-¹ 8.] Free from wrinkles; smooth.

In freq. use from *c* 1820, esp. with 'brow' or 'forehead'.

1576 NEWTON *Lemnie's Complex.* I. vi. 36 b, The forhead smoth, cheerefull and vnwrynckled. **1592** *Sir T. More* III. i. 172 Mercie, whose maiestick browe Should be vnwrinckled. **1643** DAVENANT *Unfort. Lovers* III. D 4 b, Thy brow Is quite unwrinckled. *a* **1649** CRASHAW *Glorious Epiphany* 28 The world's one, round, Æternall year, Whose full and allunwrinkled face Nor sinks nor swells with time or place. **1783** MASON *Du Fresnoy's Art Paint.* 283 So the liberal vest In large, distinct, unwrinkled folds should fly. **1784** COWPER *Task* IV. 4 The wintry flood, in which the moon Sees her unwrinkled face reflected bright. **1801** COLERIDGE *Fragm., The Moon* 5 Trees, herbage, snake-like stream, un-wrinkled Lake. **1864** BRYANT *Sella* 510 Still she kept her fair Unwrinkled features. **1881** *Longmans' Notes on Bks.* 31 Aug. 83/2 The unwrinkled portrait which Cromwell feared that Lely might draw of himself. **1885** [W. H. WHITE] *Mark Rutherford's Deliverance* vii, Her dress was unwrinkled.

fig. **1582** BENTLEY *Mon. Matrones* 74 To leane to .. God, and his smooth and vnwrinkled Church. **1648** CRASHAW *Delights Muses, Musicks Duell* 39 A Nightingale .. Trayles her plaine Ditty in one long-spun note, .. A cleare unwrinckled song. **1822** COLERIDGE *Lett., Conv.*, etc. II. 79,

I am, with unwrinkled confidence,.. Your affectionate friend.

†un'writ, *ppl. a.* [UN-¹ 8 b.] = UNWRITTEN.

1485 *Waterford Arch.* in *10th Rep. Hist. MSS. Comm.* App. V. 320 The.. usages and privieleges.. that bene writte and unwritt. **1612** CHAPMAN *Rev. Bussy d'Ambois* II. i. 119 God's unwrit edicts. **1656** in *Verney Mem.* (1907) II. 51 [A letter] that had been better unwritt.

un'write, *v.* [UN-² 3.] *trans.* To cancel or abrogate the writing of (something); to annul or rescind (a writing).

1586 J. HOOKER *Hist. Irel.* in *Holinshed* II. 104/2 What he wrote he meant not to vnwrite. **1593** B. BARNES *Poems* (Grosart) 6 Since mercylesse she made that chartyre,.. Sign'd with those hands which neuer can vnwrite it. **1641** MILTON *Animadv.* 65 Yee write them in your closets, and unwrite them in your Courts. **1820** KEATS in Rossetti *Life* (1887) 96 My poor poem, which I would willingly take the trouble to unwrite, if possible. **1861** *Court Life at Naples* II. 269 It is easier to unsay than to unwrite cross words. **1888** GLADSTONE in *Daily News* 6 Nov. 6/3 You cannot un-write or rewrite the law of time.

un'writeable, *a.* (UN-¹ 7 b.)

1780 T. TWINING *Recreat. & Stud.* (1882) 76 In gracing, he does the most beautiful, most unassignable, most unwritten and unwriteable things I ever heard. **1801** SOUTHEY *Let. to G. C. Bedford* 19 Aug., These are unwriteable things—the gossip, and the playfulness. **1873** EARLE *Philol. Eng. Tongue* (ed. 2) 110 The first [vowel] we call by an unwriteable name.

†un'writhe, *v. Obs.*⁻⁰ [UN-² 3. Cf. OE. *un-, onwrīþan.*] *trans.* = UNWREATHE *v.*¹

1611 COTGR., *Destortiller*, to vnwrith, vnwind, open, vnwrap. **1731** BAILEY (vol. II), *Unwrithen*, unwreathed, untwisted, straitened.

un'writing, *ppl. a.* (UN-¹ 10.)

1663 COWLEY *Ode upon Verses of Ld. Broghills* i, I wrote, and wrote, but still I wrote in vain,.. A rich, unwriting Hand, carry'd the Prize away. **1728** POPE *Dunc., M. Scriblerus*, A deluge of Authors covered the land: Whereby.. the peace of the honest unwriting subject was daily molested. **1828–32** WEBSTER s.v., An unwriting citizen.

un'written, *ppl. a.* Also 4 unwrite. [UN-¹ 8 b. Cf. OE. *unwriten* (*unge-, uná-*), ON. *úritinn.*]

1. Not committed to writing; left unrecorded.

1362 LANGL. *P. Pl.* A. XI. 255 (MS. Univ. Coll. Oxford), Myn name [was] entred In ye legende of lyf.. Or elles vnwrite [B. vnwriten, C. vnwryten] for wiled. *c* **1440** *Jacob's Well* 115 þat none of here talys schulde be vnwretyn. *c* **1445** PECOCK *Donet* 6 Bettir it is.. þan forto leve alle suche þingis vnwritun and vntauȝt. **1533** TINDALE *Supper of Lord* B v, More muste gyve vs leaue to beleue his vn-wrytten vanityes (verities I shoulde saye) at leasure. **1577** tr. *Bullinger's Decades* 774/1 An vnwritten tradition of the Apostles. **1635** J. TAYLOR (Water P.) *Very Old Man* C 3, They.. might from Sire to Son Have been unwritten Chronicles, and by Tradition shew Times mutabillity. **1650** BAXTER *Saints' R.* II. iv. §3. 200 It was a former Record.. delivered to us, and not onely an unwritten Testimony. **1792** S. ROGERS *Pleas. Mem.* II. (1801) 59 High o'er the hearth his forest-trophies hung;.. Each vast antler.. unwritten records bore, Of gallant feats. **1851** HAWTHORNE *Snow Image, Old News* (1879) 153 Diseases unwritten in medical books. **1878** H. SWEET in *Trans. Philol. Soc.* 404 The characteristic features of a hitherto unwritten dialect.

absol. **1880** MEREDITH *Tragic Com.* (1881) 114, I have seen, have seen ahead, seen where all is dark, read the unwritten.

b. Of laws, etc.: Not formulated in written codes or documents; not reduced to writing; oral.

1456 SIR G. HAYE *Law Arms* (S.T.S.) 128 Be all lawis wryttin and unwrittin. **1596** SPENSER *State Irel.* ¶ 12 The Brehoone lawe.. is a certayne rule of right unwritten, but delivered by tradition from one to another. **1641** MILTON *Ch. Govt.* I. iii. 11 Those unwritten lawes and Ideas which nature hath ingraven in us. *c* **1670** HOBBES *Dial. Com. Laws* (1681) 3 Equity is a certain perfect Reason that interpreteth and amendeth the Law written, it self being unwritten, and consisting in nothing else but right Reason. **1765** BLACKSTONE *Comm.* Introd. I. 63 The municipal law of England.. may.. be divided into two kinds:.. the unwritten, or common law; and.. the written, or statute law. **1856** EMERSON *Eng. Traits, Universities* Wks. (Bohn) II. 93 That an unwritten code of honour deals.. an even-handed justice. **1888** T. W. REID *Life W. E. Forster* (ed. 2) II. vii. 294 The unwritten law of the Land League.

c. Not written *of* or about.

1761 in *Hull Museum Publ.* (No. 102) 13 Which, having been hitherto concealed and unwritten of, is.. worthy of a general knowledge.

2. Not written upon. Also with *on.*

1542 in T. A. Beck *Ann. Furnes* (1844) App. 87 [He] sealyd therwyth vij. blanckes in perchement then beyng blanckes and unwryttene. **1555** EDEN *Decades* (Arb.) 57 A white paper vnwritten, vpon the which yow may.. wryte what yow lyste. **1583** GOLDING *Calvin on Deut.* lxix. 423 This disposednes is as a white vnwritten paper. **1664** SOUTH *Serm.* (1715) II. 46 Like unwritten paper,.. it.. is white.. and fair for an after-Inscription. *a* **1700** EVELYN *Diary* 27 Oct. 1664, He then.. ask'd me if I had any paper about me unwritten and a crayon. **1760–2** GOLDSM. *Cit. W.* xlvi, When the large unwritten page presents its snowy spotless bosom to the writer's hand. **1833** T. HOOK *Parson's Dau.* I. xi, So that no possible spot or corner of her letters should escape unwritten on. **1873** B. HARTE *Fiddletown* 26 The unwritten side of one of these squares.

un'wroken, *ppl. a.* [UN-¹ 8 b. Cf. MDu. *onghewroken* (Du. *ongewroken*), OHG. *ungirohhan, unkirochan* (MHG. and G. *ungerochen*), and UNWREAKEN.] = UNWREAKED *ppl. a.*

a **1300** *Cursor M.* 13067 Ouer mikel has þou spoken, And þat sal noght be al vn-wroken. *c* **1400** *Destr. Troy* 4195 þat any lord of our londe shuld lacche soche a skorne Vnwrokyn with wondis. **1513** DOUGLAS *Æneid* II. x. 197 This day wnwrokin we sall neuir al be slane. *Ibid.* IV. xii. 30, XI. xiv. 19. **1600** FAIRFAX *Tasso* VIII. lxvi. 155 Yet all this season were we willing blinde, Offended, vnreueng'd, wrong'd, but vnwroken.

un'wronged, *ppl. a.* (UN-¹ 8.)

1598 FLORIO, *Inoffeso*, vnoffended, vntoucht, vnwrongd. **1628** GAULE *Pract. The.* (1629) 352 There lies he now, though by some (perhaps) vnremembred, yet by others not vn-wronged. **1789** E. DARWIN *Bot. Gard.* II. 15 Unwrong'd,.. They guard, the Kings of Needwood's wide domains, Their sister-wives. **1841** MRS. BROWNING *Q. Annelida, Complaint* iii, Now is he false—alas, alas!—although Unwronged! **1870** BRYANT *Iliad* I. I. 22 Unwronged and with no cause for tears.

un'wrongful, *a.* (UN-¹ 7.)

1876 MORRIS *Sigurd* II. 123 Till over a world unwrongful new-born shall Baldur ride.

†un'wronging, *vbl. sb. Obs.*⁻¹ [UN-¹ 13.] Non-committal of a wrong.

c **1449** PECOCK *Repr.* III. xvi. 382 Experience schewith.. how manye.. wrongis schulden be.. menteyned for riȝtis and vnwrongingis.

unwrought (ʌnˈrɔːt), *ppl. a.* [UN-¹ 8 b, c. Cf. OE. *unȝeworht*, MLG. *ungewrocht*, MDu. *onghewrocht, -wracht*, Du. *ongewrocht.*]

1. Not made, done, formed, performed, etc.; left in an unfinished or incomplete state; uncompleted, unperformed.

c **1375** *Sc. Leg. Saints* x. (*Matthew*) 143 Sa þare warke lewit vnwrocht, Fore vndire-stand vthire þai na mocht. *c* **1450** *Myrr. our Ladye* 268 She lefte no verteu vnwroughte in the worlde. *c* **1611** CHAPMAN *Iliad* II. 117 The work that should have wreaked our wrong.. lies unwrought. **1819** SHELLEY *Peter Bell 3rd* VII. xx, Love's work was left unwrought—no brood.. took wing.

2. Not formed or fashioned by being worked on; *esp.* of materials (as fabrics, stone, or metals): Still in a crude, raw, rude, or natural state; not worked into a finished condition; undressed; = RAW *a.* 2 a, ROUGH *a.* 16.

In very frequent use from *c* 1600, esp. with *stone, iron.*

c **1400** *Pilgr. Sowle* (Caxton, 1483) V. xiv. 107 God hymself is nature vnformed and vnwrought. **1455** *Rolls of Parlt.* V. 325/1 Never any thing of Silke.. in eny wise wrought, but in rawe Silk allone unwrought. **1463–4** *Act 19 Hen. VII*, c. 21 All other maner of Sylkes,.. rawe or unwrought. **1503** [see RAW *a.* 2 a]. **1545** *Rates of Custom* b i b, Enkyll the pounde vnwrought, iiii d. **1548** COVERDALE, etc. *Erasm. Par. 1 Cor.* viii. 23 b, An other vnsquared piece of tymber, or an vnwrought stone. **1571** GOLDING *Calvin on Ps.* lxxiv. 5 The unwrought and rough timber-logs. **1601** [see ROUGH *a.* 16]. **1616** W. BROWNE *Brit. Past.* II. iv. 587 Brests softer farre than tufts of unwrought silke. **1673** TEMPLE *Obs. United Prov.* Wks. 1720 I. 66 We then carry'd out our Wools unwrought. **1719** W. WOOD *Surv. Trade* 85 Every Country which.. returns us unwrought Materials to be manufactured here. **1773** HAWKESWORTH *Cook's Voy.* I. v. II. 57 We saw also some pieces of glass and flint among them unwrought. **1799** *Hull Advertiser* 11 May 1/1 A large quantity of unwrought Alum-Rock. **1827** G. HIGGINS *Celtic Druids* 212 Very large unwrought stones. **1841** ELPHINSTONE *Hist. India* I. 371 The cocoa-nut tree and the bamboo furnish all the materials for construction unwrought. **1896** *Daily News* 11 Feb. 2/4 Unwrought steel and cast and wrought iron.

fig. **1641** MILTON *Ch. Govt.* II. Concl. 62 Men.. whose unchast'ned and unwrought minds [were] never yet.. subdu'd under the true lore of religion. **1886** MᶜNEILL *Sir Tristrem* p. xx, After having lain unwrought into any new forms for a couple of centuries, the story [etc.].

b. Not developed or worked *out.*

1877 MISS YONGE *Cameos* III. x. 84 He must choose.. whether to continue the art that should diffuse knowledge for good or evil, or leave it unwrought out.

3. a. Of a mine, etc.: Not worked. Also in fig. context.

1669 EARL SANDWICH tr. *Barba's Art of Metals* I. (1674) 7 [The mine] lay unwrought for four or five years. **1670** PETTUS *Fodinæ Reg.* 86 Where he findeth a Meer unwrought, he shall score on the Spindle one score. **1796** MORSE *Amer. Geog.* II. 209 This island abounds with iron, lead, and copper mines, though unwrought. **1839** DE LA BECHE *Rep. Geol. Cornwall*, etc. xv. 617 In 1778, also, these iron-lodes still remained unwrought. **1863** N. HAWTHORNE *Our Old Home* II. 15 Treasures of wit and wisdom.. still in the unwrought mines of human thought.

b. Of coal: Not hewn out, excavated, or won.

1789 J. WILLIAMS *Min. Kingd.* I. 8 The whole coal wall, that is the unwrought coal. **1883** [see UNWORKED 2 b].

c. Of land: Not tilled, laboured, or cultivated.

1600 FAIRFAX *Tasso* I. lxiv, Or proue at least.. Their harts were fertill land, although vnwrought. **1876–** in north. dialect and Sc. use.

4. Not employed in, not subjected or inured to, labour. *rare.*

1550 W. LANE in Froude *Hist. Eng.* (1860) V. 285 Out of the decay of tillage springeth the scarcity of corn and the people unwrought. **1628** MAY *Virg. Georg.* II. 55 Then make strong hedges to keep cattell out, Young beasts especially, and yet unwrought.

un'wrought, *pa. pple.* [f. UNWORK *v.*] Put back or restored to a former condition; undone.

1726 POPE *Odyssey* XIX. 177 The woof unwrought the Suitor-train surprize. **1850** MRS. BROWNING *Sonn. fr. Portuguese* xiv, These things.. may Be changed, or change for thee,—and love, so wrought, May be unwrought so.

un'wrung, *ppl. a.* [UN-¹ 8 b.] Not pinched or galled.

1604 SHAKS. *Ham.* III. ii. 253 (Q. 2), Your Maiestie, and wee that haue free soules, it touches vs not, let the gauled Iade winch, our withers are vnwrong. [Hence freq. in later echoes of the phrase, or occas. (in recent use) of the word.]

†un'wry, *v. Obs.* [OE. *onwréon, unwréon* (UN-² 3). Cf. OHG. *intrîhan, inrîhan* 'revelare'.]

1. *trans.* To reveal or expose to sight by the removal of a covering; to uncover, lay bare.

α. *c* **825** *Vesp. Psalter* xvii. 16 Onwriȝen werun steaðelas ymbhwyrftes eorðan. *c* **1000** *Ags. Ps.* (Thorpe) cxviii. 18 Onwreoh þu mine eaȝan. *c* **1290** *Beket* 2278 in *S. Eng. Leg.* I. 172 þe Cardinales nolden nouȝt is bodi al on-wreo [*c* **1300** unwreo]. **1340** *Ayenb.* 58 Hi onwriþ þane pot, and þe uleȝen vlyeþ þerin.

β. *c* **975** *Rushw. Gosp.* Mark ii. 4 He.. unwreoȝon þæt hus.. þær he wæs. *c* **1000** ÆLFRIC *Hom.* II. 334 Ða licmen his neb þærrihte unwruȝon. *a* **1225** *Ancr. R.* 328 þo he schulde unwrien his wunden. **13..** *K. Alis.* 336 (Laud MS.), His aristable he gan vnwriȝene [*v.r.* vnwreone]. *c* **1374** CHAUCER *Troylus* I. 858 To hym byhoueth first vnwre [*v.rr.* onwrye, vnwry] his wounde. *c* **1430** *Lanfranc's Cirurg.* 85 Unwrey al þe bon, in kuttynge awey al þe flesch. *c* **1440** *Jacob's Well* 197 He ros out of his graue,.. & vnwryed þe munkys in here beddys.

b. *refl.* To uncover (oneself); to make naked.

a **1225** *Ancr. R.* 56 Bersabee.. unwreih hire ine Dauies sihðe. *Ibid.* 58 þurh þet heo unwrien ham ine monne eih sihðe.

2. *fig.* To reveal, disclose, make known (some hidden thing or fact, sin, etc.); to communicate or divulge (a matter).

a c **825** *Vesp. Psalter* xxxvi. 5 Onwrih dryhtne weȝ ðinne. *c* **1000** *Ags. Gosp.* Luke xvii. 30 Æfter þysum þingum bið on þam dæȝe þe mannes sunu onwriȝen bið. **1340** *Ayenb.* 88 Uor hyer ne zyþ non onwryȝe þe uayrhede of god, bote ase hit by ine ane ssewere. *Ibid.* 174 þe zike ssel onwri his ziknesse.

β. *c* **950** *Lindisf. Gosp.* Matt. x. 26 Nowiht forðon [bið] ȝedeȝled þæt ne se unwriȝen. *c* **1055** *Byrhtferth's Handboc* in *Anglia* VIII. 334 Griphia.. byð ȝesett þær þa deopan þing beoð unwroȝene. *a* **1200** *Moral Ode* 160 in *O.E. Hom.* I. 169 Al scal þer bon þanne unwron, þet men wruȝen her. *a* **1225** *Leg. Kath.* 1769 þer me unwreah me þe wei, þet leadeð to liue. **1297** R. GLOUC. (Rolls) 10457 God wot wuch is herte was, vor he nolde him noȝt vnwre. þe erchebissop him asoilede. *c* **1330** *Amis & Amil.* 783 When þe douke com in to þat won, þe steward oȝain him gan gon, Her conseyl for to vnwrain. *c* **1380** *Sir Ferumb.* 1849 Y wil her, as y can, my message to þe ounwrye. *c* **1407** LYDG. *Reson & Sens.* 18 Or [= ere] I do specifye Myn entent for to vnwrie, Or ferther in this boke procede.

Hence **†unwrye(n)** *ppl. a. Obs.*

a **1225** *Ancr. R.* 58 3if eni unwrie put were, & beste feolle þer inne, he hit schulde ȝelden þet þene put unwreih. **1340** *Ayenb.* 88 Hyer ne zyþ non onwryȝe þe uayrhede of god. *Ibid.* 112, 244.

†uny, *v. Obs.* Also 5 vnye. [ad. OF. *uni-er* (1371 in Godef.), or *uni-r* (12th–13th c.; F., Sp., and Pg. *unir*, It. *unire*), a. L. *ūnīre* to UNITE. Cf. UNE *v.*] *trans.* To form, combine, or join into one; to make one; to unite.

Freq. from *c* 1435 to 1535; in later use chiefly *Sc.* The chief types of construction are illustrated by the different groups of quotations.

(*a*) **1433** *Rolls of Parlt.* IV. 441/2 Pretendyng yat all his Auncestres.. have had ye Estate, Honour and Dignite, as annexed, unied and appurtenaunt to ye seid Castell, Honour and Lordship. **1483** CAXTON *Gold. Leg.* 435/2 How our lord wold unye or joyne our humanyte to his dyuynytee by grete loue. **1502** *Ord. Crysten Men* (W. de W. 1506) I. iv. D ij b, By the baptem the soule.. is incorporat and vnyed with holy chirche. *c* **1510** MORE *Picus* Wks. 13/1 That prayer.. not onelye presenteth the mind to the father: but also vnieth it with hym by vnspeakeable wayes. **1550** J. COKE *Eng. & Fr. Heralds* § 128 Whiche realme.. [he] conquered, uniynge it to the Crowne of Espayne.

(*b*) *c* **1450** *Myrr. our Ladye* 294 The prayer of a multytude that is vnyed togyther in charyte. *a* **1513** FABYAN *Chron.* VI. cxciii. 196 He made Dunstanne.. bisshop of Worceter, and vnyed and knyt into one the prouynce & lordshyppes of Englande. **1523** LD. BERNERS *Froiss.* I. ccclxxxi. 640 That there be no villayns nor gentylmen, but that we may be all vnyed toguyder. **1541** COPLAND *Galyen's Terap.* A j, Howe Phylosophy and eloquence are.. vnyed togyther by offyce and actyon.

(*c*) *c* **1460** FORTESCUE *Abs. & Lim. Mon.* ii. (1885) 112 Euery comunalte vnyed of mony parties must nedis haue an hed. **1482–3** in *Eng. Gilds* (1870) 310 That they.. a Gilde or Fraternyte.. of the men of the seid Crafte and other, myght make, vnye, founde,.. and stablissh. **1509** *Sc. Acts, Jas. IV* (1814) II. 267/1 It sall be lefull till his grace to diuide schirefdomez & create, vny, & annex þe sammyne. **1512** *Helyas* in Thoms *Prose Rom.* (1828) III. 135 In the which time.. should be unyed and congregeed the princes of christendom for to passe over the sea.

(*d*) **1562** WINȜET *Wks.* (S.T.S.) II. 41 In Christe Iesus is na commixtioun,.. bot bayth the twa naturis vniit in ane persoun. **1596** DALRYMPLE tr. *Leslie's Hist. Scot.* I. 84 At last.. the Britanis of Cambrie.. war vniit in ane people vndir ane law.

refl. *c* **1440** *Gesta Rom.* xli. 26 The Sone of god vnyede hym to mankynde to þe dethe. **1494** *Cov. Leet Bk.* 558 That they.. applye them-self to Joyn & vnye themself or to be contributory to other Craft. **1562** WINȜET *Wks.* (S.T.S.) II. 43 The Sone of God.. be vniing Him self to man.. wes maid man.

Hence **†unying** *vbl. sb. Obs.*

1517 *Love's Bonavent. Mirr.* xv. (W. de W.) I iv b, Puttynge a-way occasyon.. that myght drawe yᵉ.. soule.. fro the vnyenge & knyttyng to her spouse Jhesu chryst.

† **un'yark**, *v. Obs. rare.* [UN-² 3 + YARK *v.* b.] *trans.* To undo or open (a gate).
a **1400–50** *Alexander* 2147 Þai vnȝarked him þe ȝatis & ȝald him þe keys. *Ibid.* 3209 Þan ȝode þai furthe & vnȝarkid þe ȝatis of þe cite.

un'yeaned, *ppl. a.* [UN-¹ 8.] **a.** Unborn. **b.** Not having given birth. Also *fig.*
[**1775** ASH.] **1868** GEO. ELIOT *Sp. Gipsy* 148 Trust That men call blind; but..is blind Only as unyeaned reason is. **1884** MISS M. LINSKILL *Betw. Heather & North. Sea* vi, The loss of the ewes, and the unyeaned lambs. **1894** C. VICKERMAN *Woollen Spinning* 46 Sheep..much prized in unyeaned state.

unyelde, var. UNNEALED *ppl. a. Obs.*

unyement, obs. f. OINTMENT.

unyeown, obs. Sc. f. ONION.

† **un'yerded**, *ppl. a. Sc. Obs.* [UN-¹ 8 + *ȝerded*: see YIRD *v.*] Not buried.
1596 DALRYMPLE tr. *Leslie's Hist. Scot.* I. 121 Lat him end his lyf vpon ane fork, and [be] kastne by vnȝerdet.

un'yielded, *ppl. a.* [UN-¹ 8.] Not yielded or surrendered.
1640 BP. HALL *Chr. Moder.* II. xi. 101 Here were no tricks of inferences,..no violent deduction of unyeelded sequels. **1700** DRYDEN *Pal. & Arc.* III. 651 O'erpower'd, at length, they force him to the Ground, Unyielded as he was.

† **un'yielden**, *ppl. a. Obs.*⁻¹ [UN-¹ 8 b.] = prec.
1553 BRENDE *Q. Curtius* VIII. 154 b, Alexander lefte his fotemenne to subdue suche as were yet vnyelden.

un'yielding, *vbl. sb.* (UN-¹ 13.)
1848 DICKENS *Dombey* xl, Looking upon him with neither yielding nor unyielding, liking nor hatred.

un'yielding, *ppl. a.* [UN-¹ 10.]
1. Of substances (or their structure): Not yielding to force or pressure; unpliant, unbending; stiff, hard. Also const. *to.*
1658 ROWLAND tr. *Moufet's Theat. Ins.* 926 In physicks we see those things that are most stiffe and unyeelding, to be resisted and beaten off with the most soft things. **1736** THOMSON *Liberty* v. 87 How shall this thy mighty Kingdom stand? On what unyielding base? **1744** ARMSTRONG *Art Preserv. Health* II. 537 Hard unyielding unelastic bone. **1768–74** TUCKER *Lt. Nat.* (1834) II. 405 A soil unyielding to pressure. **1805** SOUTHEY *Madoc* II. x. 105 On the unyielding skin the temper'd blade Bent. **1854** OWEN in *Orr's Circ. Sci., Org. Nat.* I. 228 A firm and unyielding support to the large head. **1889** MRS. E. KENNARD *Landing a Prize* vii, An unyielding ledge of wood.
2. Of persons, etc.: Not yielding, surrendering, submitting, or giving way; firm, obdurate, obstinate. Also const. *to.*
1592 SHAKS. *Ven. & Ad.* 423 Remoue your siege from my unyeelding hart. **1724** A. HILL *Prol. to Sir T. Overbury* 15 He swims, unyielding, against Fortune's Stream. **1736** THOMSON *Liberty* IV. 982 His unyielding Son these doctrines drank, With all a Bigot's rage. **1777** POTTER *Æschylus, Seven Chiefs* 191 Ah! what frentic rage possest Each unyielding, ruthless breast! **182.** BRYANT *Hymn to Death* 146 When the earth Received thee, tears were in unyielding eyes And on hard cheeks. **1839** HALLAM *Hist. Lit.* iv. vii. §19 The unyielding claw of a cold-blooded animal. **1890** 'R. BOLDREWOOD' *Col. Reformer* (1891) 333 Of all people in the wide world,..his cousin was..the most unyielding to argument.
transf. **1806** BYRON *Childish Recollections* 6 Unyielding pangs assail the drooping mind. **1850** SCORESBY *Cheever's Whalem. Adv.* i. [An] instance..of what commerce can do against unyielding laws of Nature. **1909** *Daily Chron.* 28 Sept. 5/4 The storm-driven snows had buried and bound the dogs in unyielding frost.
3. Characterized by firmness or obstinacy.
1677 GILPIN *Demonol.* II. ii. 189 A kind of unnatural fury, which hurries Men with violence into an unyielding stifness. **1736** THOMSON *Liberty* v. 370 A zeal unyielding in their country's cause. **1779** *Mirror* No. 8, I..observed an obstinate unyielding silence. *a* **1812** BUCKMINSTER *Serm.* (1827) 60 Unyielding virtue is admired by the corrupt, disinterested goodness by the selfish. **1848** BUCKLEY *Iliad* 227 The Greeks were routed, and an unyielding tumult ensued. **1882** BESANT *All Sorts* xxi, She..sat bolt upright, the picture of unyielding determination.
Hence **un'yieldingly** *adv.*
[**1847** WEBSTER.] **1884** PEMBER *Earth's Earliest Ages* i. 14 They hold..opinions of their own, and are unyieldingly tenacious of them. **1889** STANLEY in *Daily News* 25 Nov. 5/8 There is a virtue..even in striving unyieldingly.

un'yieldingness. (UN-¹ 12, or f. prec.)
1613 DANIEL *Coll. Hist. Eng.* III. 160 Vpon..the vnyeeldingnesse of King Malcolm,..nothing was effected. **1617** HIERON *Wks.* II. 369 That phrase of a stony heart, a fit terme to note out the stiffenesse and sturdinesse, and vnyeeldingnesse thereof. *a* **1843** *Encycl. Metrop.* (1845) VII. 263/2 An un-yieldingness being imparted to the mass. **1850** L. HUNT *Autobiog.* II. xi. 53 His generalship..came to nothing before the unyieldingness of English, and the advent of Prussian soldiers.

un'yoke, *v.* [OE. *unȝeocian* (UN-² 4 b). Cf. older Du. *ontjocken*, Du. *ontjukken*, MHG. and G. *entjochen.*]
1. *trans.* To loose (a draught-animal, etc.) from the yoke; to free from harness.
c **1000** ÆLFRIC *Gram.* xlvii. (Z.) 277 *Disiungo*, ic ungeociȝe oððe totwæme. **1398** TREVISA *Barth. De P.R.* XVIII. xiv. (Bodl. MS.), Þan þei vnȝoke hem and bringe hem to þe stalle. **1565** COOPER *Thesaurus, Bouem disiunctum curare*, an oxe vnyoked. **1597** SHAKS. *2 Hen. IV*, IV. ii. 103 Our Army is dispers'd: Like youthfull Steeres, vnyoak'd, they tooke their course East, West, North, South. **1613** HEYWOOD *Brazen Age* II. D 3, My swannes I haue vnyoakt. **1628** MAY *Virg. Georg.* III. 98 The weeping Plowman tother Oxe alone Vnyokes. **1681** D'URFEY *Progr. Honesty* i, The Beasts unyok'd from Teams, Ran lowing to the distant Mead. **1708** J. PHILIPS *Cyder* II. 38 Soon as the Hind, fatigu'd, Unyokes his Team. **1720** POPE *Iliad* XXIII. 596 The chief himself unyokes the panting steeds. **1843** BETHUNE *Sc. Fireside Stor.* 148 While the coachman was preparing to unyoke his cattle. **1870** BRYANT *Iliad* VIII. I. 262 Unyoke the steeds..And set their food before them.
refl. **1832** HT. MARTINEAU *Ella of Gar.* ii. 18 The girls of the family unyoked themselves from the harrow which they were drawing over the..sandy soil.
† **b.** (See YOKE *sb.* 2, *v.* 3.) *Obs.*
1573 [see sense 4 a]. *a* **1589** MASCALL *Govt. Cattle* (1596) 274 Some..vse to ring them [*sc.* hogs] at Michaelmas..; they doe vnyoake them soone after Michaelmas.
c. To disconnect (the plough) from a draught-animal. Also in fig. context.
1821 SCOTT *Pirate* v, It's a finished field with me—I must unyoke the pleugh, and lie down to wait for the deadthraw.
2. *fig.* To liberate, release, deliver from oppression, etc. Also *refl.*
1387 TREVISA *Higden* (Rolls) V. 367 Þo was..Italy unȝoked and delyvered of þe ȝokke of Constantynnoble. **1593** B. BARNES *Poems* (Grosart) 3 So whiles shee sleightly gloas'd, with her new pray, Mine hartes eye..Vnyoak't himselfe, & closely scap't away. **1638** N. WHITING *Albino & Bellama* 5 When British Isles..From sad oppression had unyok'd their necks. **1641** MILTON *Ch. Govt.* II. 61 The property of Truth is,..to unyoke and set free the minds and spirits of a Nation. **1687** MIÉGE *Gt. Fr. Dict.* II. s.v., To unyoke himself out of Bondage, or Slavery. [Hence in Phillips (1706).]
absol. (for *refl.*). **1606** WARNER *Alb. Eng.* xv. xcviii. 388 Too aduantagiously from out our Rubrick they vnyoke, And Canons old and new by them are, too securely, broke.
3. To disconnect, unlink, disjoin. Also *fig.*
1595 SHAKS. *John* III. i. 241 And shall these hands,..So newly ioin'd in loue,..Vnyoke this seysure, and this kinde regreete? **1812** H. & J. SMITH *Rej. Addr., Arch. Atoms* 154 The milkman..With sudden sink unyokes the clinking pail. **1862** TROLLOPE *N. America* I. 109 At the rapids the large rafts are, as it were, unyoked, and divided into small portions.
4. a. *absol.* To remove the yoke from an animal.
1573 TUSSER *Husb.* (1878) 32 Let hogs be roong, both old and yoong. No mast vpon oke, no longer vnyoke. **1601** HOLLAND *Pliny* I. 593 When thou [*sc.* the husbandman] doest unyoke and give over thy daies worke. **1612** DRAYTON *Poly-olb.* I. 533 Here I'll unyoke awhile, and turn my steeds to meat. **1794** JAS. DONALDSON *View Agric. Carse of Gowrie* 24 The ploughmen..are in the stable by five o'clock, and unyoking about ten, are employed in cutting grass.
fig. **1610** FLETCHER *Faithf. Sheph.* I. i, Ever be thy honour spoke, From that place the morn is broke, To that place Day doth unyoke. **1667** JER. TAYLOR *Gt. Exemp.* (ed. 4) II. 310 It is..but reason such an anger should unyoke, and goe to bed with the Sun.
b. *fig.* To cease from labour, etc.; to give over work.
1594 NASHE *Terrors of Night* C iij b, To nothing more aptly can I compare the working of our braines after we haue vnyoakt and gone to bed. **1602** SHAKS. *Ham.* v. i. 59 Who builds stronger then a Mason, a Shipwright, or a Carpenter? *Clown.* I, tell me that, and vnyoake. **1889** SKRINE *Mem. Thring* 225, I am hastening to unyoke. But I must not do so till I account for something still left unsaid.
Hence **un'yoking** *vbl. sb.*
1667 MIÉGE II. s.v., An unyoaking, or Unyoking. **1835** THIRLWALL *Greece* I. 221 The unyoking of the oxen.

un'yoked, *ppl. a.*¹ [UN-¹ 8.] Not provided with or subjected to a yoke; not wearing a yoke. Also *fig.*
1573 TUSSER *Husb.* (1878) 93 Now hunt with dog, vnyoked hog. **1596** SHAKS. *1 Hen. IV*, I. ii. 220, I know you all, and will a-while vphold The vnyoak'd humor of your idlenesse. *c* **1611** CHAPMAN *Iliad* VI. 321 That..we may Twelue vn-yok't Oxen of a yeare, in this thy Temple slaye. **1697** DRYDEN *Æneis* VI. 58 Sev'n Bullocks, yet unyok'd, for Phœbus chuse.

un'yoked, *ppl. a.*² [UN-² 4 b, 8, or f. UNYOKE *v.*] Set free from the yoke. Also *fig.*
1700 A. PHILIPS *Pastorals* II. ad. fin., With songs the jovial hinds return from plough; And unyok'd heifers, loitering homeward, lowe. **1751** W. WHITEHEAD *Hymn to Nymph of Bristol Spring* 146 The panting Swain..at evening led His unyok'd heifers to the common stream. **1888** A. H. SMITH *Cat. Gems Brit. Mus.* 191 Rustic with yoke of oxen,..the oxen unyoked from cart and lying down before it.

un'yolden, *ppl. a. Obs.* [UN-¹ 8 b.]
1. Not yielded or surrendered; †unpaid.
a **1325** *MS. Rawl. B.* 520 fol. 29 b, Þe duwe seruices of þulke feos..beth with-drawen ant vn-ȝolde. *c* **1386** CHAUCER *Knt.'s T.* 1784 By the force of twenty is he take Vnyolden, and ydrawe vnto the stake. **1418–20** *Siege of Rouen* in *Archaeol.* XXI. 55 Whyle that Synt Katerynes was unȝolde. *c* **1425** WYNTOUN *Cron.* VIII. xi. 1720 Þaim thocht mare honeste Vnȝoldin to sla Þame in melle. **15..** *Christ's Kirk* 177 in *Maitland Folio MS.* 154 For hir saik he wes vnȝoldin Sewin myle quhen he wes chaist. **1575** GASCOIGNE *Weedes, Fruit of Fetters* viii, Whyles the hope of mine unyolden harte..did labor for reliefe.
2. Unrequited; unavenged. *rare*⁻¹.
c **1400** *Destr. Troy* 2216 If we, þat are worthy,..Take harme, other hethyng, or hurtys vnȝoldyn, Of any erdyng in erthe.

un'youthful, *a.* (UN-¹ 7.)
1859 J. PAYN *Foster Brothers* xv. 256 His heavy and somewhat unyouthful brows. **1881** M. C. HAY *Missing* II. 80 Her staid, unyouthful guardian.

un'youthfully, *adv.* (UN-¹ 11.)
1891 H. LYNCH *G. Meredith* 80 Dahlia's lover is legal, sharp, and unyouthfully serious.

un'zealous, *a.* (UN-¹ 7.)
1643 PRYNNE *Sov. Power Parl.* App. 217 What then will be our portion, if we be unzealous, negligent, perfidious to it? **1649** MILTON *Eikon.* ix. 84 Those men whose superstition Zealous or unzealous would [etc.]. **1801** *Monthly Rev.* XII. 589 An unzealous tardiness of preparation.
Hence **un'zealously** *adv.*, **-ness.**
1615 HIERON *Wks.* I. 603 Our vnzealousnes, and..our Laodician lukwarmnesse. **1647** TRAPP *Comm. Matt.* v. 45 Is not..our ancient fervour and forwardness [turned] into a general lukewarmness and unzealousness? **1871** *Leisure Hour* 284/2 Some [dancing dervishes],..of the 'earth earthy', shuffled unzealously along.

un'zip, *v.* [UN-² 3, 7: cf. next.] **1.** *trans.* To unfasten the zip of; to unfasten (a zip). Also *transf.* and *fig.*
1939 L. MACNEICE *Autumn Jrnl.* iii. 18, I shall..make the world my sofa, Unzip the women and insult the meek. **1951** G. FRANKAU *Oliver Trenton* xvi. 138 Sancha..unzipped her skirt. **1959** *Encounter* Aug. 75/2 When his lips are sealed, not even a loving wife can unzip them. **1972** R. QUILTY *Tenth Session* I. 140 Shirley..emerged with a brace of glistening Carlsbergs... She tossed one over and perched again to unzip her can. **1976** 'D. FLETCHER' *Don't whistle 'Macbeth'* 156 Unzip me, please? **1979** R. JAFFE *Class Reunion* I. xi. 105 She reached for the zipper of her skirt and unzipped it.
2. *intr.* To unfasten by means of a zip. Also *fig.*
1971 *Daily Tel.* 11 Oct. 11 (Advt.), A double bed that simply unzips into two singles when preferred. **1979** D. ATTENBOROUGH *Life on Earth* i. 19 DNA..is shaped like two intertwined helices. During cell division, these unzip, splitting the molecule.

un'zipped, *ppl. a.* [UN-¹ 8; partly also f. prec.] With the zip unfastened; not zipped up. Also *fig.*
1951 N. BLAKISTON *Canon James* 69 He could not turn his eyes away from its nakedness, its shameless unzipped modernity. **1971** 'M. UNDERWOOD' *Trout in Milk* ix. 105 A pair of unzipped trousers. **1978** J. GARDNER *Dancing Dodo* xxvii. 218 The men wore protective silver coveralls, unzipped and with the hoods down. **1980** J. MCCLURE *Blood of Englishman* v. 46 He lay unzipped from pubic arch to jaw bone.

un'zipper, *v.* [UN-² 3: cf. next.] *trans.* = UNZIP *v.* 1.
1961 in WEBSTER. **1977** J. CHEEVER *Falconer* 202 He unzippered the sack.

un'zippered, *ppl. a.* [UN-¹ 8; partly also f. prec.] = UNZIPPED *ppl. a.*
1953 *Manch. Guardian Weekly* 20 Aug. 7/1 He had on linen slacks, a polo shirt, and an unzippered linen coat. **1960** M. K. JOSEPH *I'll soldier no More* 291 Reaching inside his unzippered windcheater.

un'zoned, (*ppl.*) *a.* [UN-¹ 8, 9.]
† **1.** (See quot.) *Obs.*⁻¹
1662 STANLEY *Hist. Chaldaick Philos.* viii. 24 The unzoned Gods are Sarapis and Bacchus;..they are called unzoned, for that they use their power freely..in the Zones, and are enthroned above the conspicuous Deities.
2. Not girt with a zone, belt, or girdle; uncinctured.
1718 PRIOR *Solomon* II. 167 Full, tho' unzon'd, her Bosom rose. **1799** CORRY *Sat. London* (1803) 58 The Circassian slave, the unzoned waist, the pendent workbag. **1804** ANNA SEWARD *Lett.* (1811) VI. 142 Other bands of lovers..of sultry regions are shewn fanning the unzoned beauty. **1854** S. DOBELL *Balder* iii. 11 One all unzoned in her deep haunts ..Hastes not to hide her breast.

uo, uoaman, uolc, uoluel, uor-, uot, southern ME. varr. FOE, FOEMAN, FOLK, FULFIL *v.*, FOR-, FOOT *sb.*

‖ **uomo universale** ('womo univer'sale). Pl. uomini universali. [It., = universal man.] A man who excels in the major fields of learning and action. Cf. *Renaissance man* s.v. RENAISSANCE 1 d.
1963 *Times* 28 May 10/7 The newspaper poses the question who is to replace this *uomo universale*, with his good and bad traits. **1979** *Guardian* 16 May 12/6 Time was when the prestigitating [*sic*] Uomo Universale was considered a pillar of any civilised society. **1983** *Punch* 4 May 28/2 Some others, by comparison, are positive *uomini universali.*

-uous (juːəs), a compound suffix, repr. L. *-uōs-us* (*-a, -um*), OF. or AF. *-uous, -uos* (F. *-ueux*), occurring in a number of adoptions from L. (or F.), as *fructuous, halituous, impetuous, †monstruous, †portentuous, sumptuous, tempestuous, virtuous*; and hence by analogy employed with the sense 'of the nature of, consisting of' in a few E. formations on L. stems, as *ambiguous* (1528–), *strenuous* (1599–), †*subsiduous* (1490), *torrentuous* (1840–).
By assimilation, OE. *rihtwis* ('righteous') became *rightuous* in the 15–16th c.

uox, southern ME. variant of FOX *sb.*

up (ʌp), *sb.* [From UP *adv.*¹ and ² or *a.*]
1. a. One who or that which is up, in various senses. *rare.*

1536 *Rem. Sedition* i b, Say, farewell welth, where lust is lyked, and lawe refused, where uppe is sette downe, and downe sette uppe. **1759** STERNE *Tr. Shandy* I. xi, With us, you see, the case is quite different:—we are all ups and downs in this matter;—you are a great genius;—or..a great dunce. **1890** *Punch* 22 Feb. 85 It's the up-and-down bizness of life, mate, as makes it such fun—for the ups. **1895** M. CORELLI *Sorrows Satan* iv, It implies..that one must choose an up or a down,—genius is the Up, money is the Down.

b. A rise or elevation in the ground. Also in fig. context. (Cf. UP AND DOWN *sb.* 1 a.)

1637 RUTHERFORD *Lett.* (1664) 32 But Oh the windings, the turnings, the up's & the down's, that he hath led me through. **1755** WALPOLE *Let. to Bentley* 18 Sept., The bad choice of the situation in such a country; it is all *ups* that should be *downs*.

2. †**a.** The action of arising from bed. *nonce-use.*

1602 MARSTON *Ant. & Mel.* III. E 3, Here ile sleepe till that the sceane of vp Is past at Court.

b. A rise in life; a spell of prosperity; a success. Usu. pl., and contrasted with *down(s)*. (Cf. UP AND DOWN *sb.* 2 a.)

1844 DICKENS *Mart. Chuz.* xvi, And as fraudulent transactions have their downs as well as ups; the major was occasionally under a cloud. **1857** LOCKER *Lond. Life* 20 Life is chequer'd, a patchwork of smiles and of frowns; We valued its ups, let us muse on its downs. **1890** DOYLE *Sign of Four* xii, I've had ups in my life, and I've had downs.

c. A rise in price or value.

1897 *Westm. Gaz.* 19 June 6/3 But there were downs as well as ups, and we find the embryo South-Western..with its £50 shares at 43.

d. A state of mental stimulation or excitement. Cf. HIGH *sb.* 1 h. *U.S. colloq.*

1966 ROTE & WINTER *Lang. Pro Football* III. 144/1 *Up*,..state of being emotionally prepared for a game. **1979** *N.Y. Times* 1 Apr. 9/2 Young women want to be with it. The shapes in your ad are all sleek and slim and they come in colors you can get an up from.

e. Phr. *in two ups*: see TWO *sb.* 2 g.

3. An 'up' train or coach.

1849 F. B. HEAD *Stokers & Pokers* ix. 82 Her daughter.. listens for the rumbling of 'the $3\frac{1}{4}$ A.M. goods up'. **1884** *Graphic* 15 Nov. 503/2 To spend pleasant quarters of an hour in waiting for the 'ups' and 'downs'.

4. Colloq. phr. *on the up-and-up.*

a. Honest(ly), straightforward(ly), 'on the level'. orig. and chiefly *U.S.*

1863 *Humboldt Reg.* (Unionville, Nevada) 4 July 2/1 Now that would be business, on the dead up-and-up. **1929** D. HAMMETT *Red Harvest* vii. 71 He phoned the old man's residence to find out if the check was on the up-and-up. **1932** WODEHOUSE *Hot Water* i. 20, I kept telling her the whole thing had been strictly on the up-and-up, but she wouldn't listen. **1952** M. ALLINGHAM *Tiger in Smoke* iii. 65 They've *got* to be on the up-and-up, see? **1974** P. DE VRIES *Glory of Hummingbird* xiii. 200 Thus I ended..on the up-and-up. I had restored some honesty to..a thoroughly shady enterprise.

b. Steadily rising, improving, or increasing; prospering, successful.

1930 *Sun* (Baltimore) 18 Aug. 6/1 From now on, we are led to believe, law and order will be on the up and up, as the current phrase is. **1937** G. HEYER *They found him Dead* xiii. 265 He certainly wasn't on the up-and-up when I knew him. He was picking up a living doing odd jobs for any firm that would use him. **1959** *Encounter* Oct. 25/2 Private travel is on the up and up. **1971** *Farmer & Stockbreeder* 23 Feb. 10 (*heading*) Drainage work on the up and up. Drainage work completed in England and Wales during the coming year is likely to reach an all-time high.

5. In Winchester College Football, a forward.

1869 *Wykehamist* Oct. 6/1 J. W. Barry, a good and persevering 'up'. **1900** R. T. WARNER *Winchester* ix. 142 It begins with a 'hot' or scrimmage, in which all the 'ups' take part. **1975** *Oxf. Compan. Sports & Games* 397/2 In the 15-a-side—XV—game, a team is composed of eight 'ups', four 'hotwatchers', and three 'behinds' or 'kicks'.

6. *U.S. slang.* A prospective customer.

1942 BERREY & VAN DEN BARK *Amer. Thes. Slang* §542/21 *Forward, front, up*, a prospective customer in a store. **1949** *N.Y. Times* 1 May 62 The hottest salesman who ever turned a looker into an up. **1977** *Drive* Sept.–Oct. 112/1 You go to buy a car, offering your Old Faithful in part-exchange... In New York, you would be the up. 'I'm sitting at my desk. The guy comes through the door, so I gotta get up. See?'

7. = UPPER *sb.*[2] Freq. in *pl. slang.*

1969 R. JAFFE *Fame Game* xi. 164 Bonnie had taken a pill, one of the little cache of Ups Bonnie got from the queens in the gay bars. **1972** M. PEREIRA *Singing Millionaire* iii. 31 'Meth', he said,..'not meths. Methedrine. Speed. Up. Chrystal. Crank.' **1978** P. G. WINSLOW *Coppergold* 172 'She did take pills, ups, if you get me.' Capricorn understood her to mean amphetamines.

up (ʌp), *a.* [f. UP *adv.*[1] and [2]. Cf. UPSIDE.

In senses 2 and 4 sometimes hyphened; cf. UP- *prefix* 2 a and 2 b.]

1. a. Dwelling up-country. **b.** Situated on high ground. *rare.*

13.. *K. Alis.* 7053 (Laud MS.), þise Sereses als I fynde, þe vppest folk ben of al ynde. *c* **1710** CELIA FIENNES *Diary* (1888) 128 To persons born in up and dry Countryes.

2. a. Of trains or coaches: Going or running up; up-going. (See UP *adv.*[1] 6 d.)

1784 J. PALMER *Papers Reform Posts* (1797) App. IV. 40 All the Letters..are sent by the up Coach at night. **1815** *Ann. Reg., Chron.* 57 The up coach, by the way of Cashel, was attacked. **1841** COL. HAWKER *Diary* (1893) II. 216 For an up train to bring it back. **1844** ALB. SMITH *Adv. Mr. Ledbury* I. ii. I. 12 The up-mail-trains of the railway. **1868** M. COLLINS *Sweet Anne Page* II. 160 They caught an up-stage, which landed them in Piccadilly at six. **1890** 'R. BOLDREWOOD' *Col. Reformer* (1891) 131 The up coach leaving and the down one just coming in.

b. Belonging to, connected with, up-going trains, coaches, etc.

1840 *Osborne's London & Birm. Railw. Guide* 67 The rails ..constituting the road used by trains coming up to town and hence..called the up side. **1852** *Mechanic's Mag.* 6 Nov. 369 [He] observed the scarp next the up-line give way. **1885** *Law Times' Rep.* LII. 622/2 The booking-office at Risca is on the up platform. **1895** *Law Times* C. 133/2 A cottage near the up side of the railway line.

3. a. Of fermented liquors: Effervescing, effervescent.

1815 *Sporting Mag.* XLV. 251 Beer's nothing if not up. **1815, 1828** [see b]. **1840** *Dom. Brewing* 46 The beer is soon what is commonly called *up*. **1910** H. G. WELLS *Hist. Mr Polly* iv. 107 Mr. Johnson, at large: '*Ain't* the beer up! It's the 'eated room.' **1934** S. BECKETT *More Pricks than Kicks* 12 Their bottled stout was particularly excellent and well up.

b. *transf.* Sparkling, excited; cheerful, vivacious.

1815 J. SCOTT *Visit Paris* (ed. 2) 21 Their faces all sparkling and *up*, as we say of soda water. **1828** *Examiner* 806/1 As vain and flippant as a butterfly, and as 'up' as sparkling champagne. **1893** *Sat. Rev.* 7 Jan. 23/2 Mr. Gilfillan was too hurried, too perfervid, 'too much up', if we may borrow an expression from the effervescence of a harmless beverage.

4. a. Directed, inclining or sloping, upwards; ascending.

1869 [see UP-BEAT *sb.* 1]. **1876** STAINER & BARRETT *Dict. Mus.* 61/2 Alternate bowing will lead to the recurrence of an up-bow on every alternate down-beat. **1901** *Feilden's Mag.* IV. 412/1 If there be long lengths of them horizontal, or with slight up gradient. **1905** ELINOR GLYN *Viciss. Evangeline* 138 He said..that..that up look under the eyelashes was the affair of the devil!

b. Of a lift, escalator, etc.: ascending, moving upwards, carrying persons to a higher floor. Also applied to the button which operates or summons this.

1948 G. V. GALWEY *Lift & Drop* v. 124 Lord Swale..was usually the sole first occupant of the 'up' lift. **1967** 'M. CARREL' *Dark Edge of Violence* v. 42 The man then slammed the gate and punched the 'Up' button. **1976** J. WAINWRIGHT *Bastard* i. 16 He fell down the escalator. The 'up' escalator.

5. In a state of emotional or nervous stimulation, either naturally or as a result of taking drugs; excited, elated; at a peak of performance. Cf. HIGH *a.* 16 c. *colloq.*

1942 [see SNOW *v.* 7]. **1964** H. SELBY *Last Exit to Brooklyn* 49 Waiting for the time to fly, as it does when you're up on bennie. **1972** *Times* 31 May 7/6 She is playing lovely tennis. In the language of the game, she is really 'up' for this one. **1975** W. SAFIRE *Before Fall* I. v. 55 He's too 'up' to sleep —can you sit around with him until he runs out of gas? **1981** *Gossip* (Holiday Special) 10/2 He was very up about his job (in the CBS studio mailroom) and people in general.

6. *Particle Physics.* Applied to a quark carrying a flavour with a charge of $+2/3$; symbol u (U 4 a). [See note s.v. S 15. The name first appeared in print later than the symbol u.]

1975 *Sci. Amer.* Oct. 41/3 Gell-Mann designated the three quarks u, d and s, for the arbitrary labels 'up', 'down' and 'sideways'. **1977** *McGraw-Hill Yearbk. Sci. & Technol.* 208/1 The common baryons, the proton and the neutron, are composed of only up (u) and down (d) quarks (proton = uud, neutron = udd). **1978** *Nature* 2 Feb. 406/3 The best known meson is the pion (π) which is a combination of an up and a down quark. **1982** *Sci. Amer.* Nov. 134/1 Charm, like up, down and strange, is a quark flavor.

up, *v.* [f. UP *adv.*[1] Cf. OE. *uppian* (once), to mount up, rise. With senses 3 and 4 cf. the uses placed under UP *adv.*[1] 30.]

I. *trans.* **1. a.** To drive up and catch (swans, etc.) so as to provide with the mark of ownership. Cf. UPPING *vbl. sb.*[2] 1. ? *Obs.*

1560–1 in W. H. Turner *Select. Rec. Oxford* (1880) 285 For uppyng the ground byrde in porte meade. **1584–5** *Order for Swans*, The Swan-heard..shall vp no Swan nor make any sale of them, without the Maister of the Swannes..be present. **1602–3** in Willis & Clark *Cambridge* (1886) III. 595 Item yᵉ swanherd for vpping swans, ijˢ.

†**b.** To carry out, perform (the practice of 'upping').

1593 [see UPPING *vbl. sb.*[2] 1].

†**2.** To make up, form, or compose *of* something.

a **1658** CLEVELAND *London Lady* 102 An Animal together blow'd and made, And up'd of all the shreds of every Trade.

3. To raise up (a weapon, etc.), esp. to or upon the shoulder. Cf. sense 8 b.

1885 RIDER HAGGARD *K. Solomon's Mines* iv, Good.. upped gun, and let drive at..a young cow. **1887** G. R. SIMS *Mary Jane's Mem.* 104 She ups her stick and begins to belabour him across the shoulders.

4. *Naut.* **a.** (See sense 8 c.) **b.** To heave or haul up.

1890 CLARK RUSSELL *Marriage at Sea* vii, There's no English port for her unless she ups hellum and tries back'ards again. **1904** KIPLING *Traffics & Discov.* 133 After us've upped trawl, us'll be glad of a tow.

5. a. *Cards.* To raise (a bid, stake, etc.). Cf. RAISE *v.*[1] 34 a. Also *transf.* Chiefly *U.S.*

1915 *Munsey's Mag.* Apr. 488/1 I'd 'a' upped it till the hot place froze over! *Ibid.* 489/1 I'll up that! the old man was saying. **1942** BERREY & VAN DEN BARK *Amer. Thes. Slang* §746/3 *Raise*, go (it) one (*or* more) better, hike, press, up. **1984** *Listener* 3 May 16/1 Some competitors see it as his way of upping the ante.

b. To increase or raise (prices, production, mechanical power, etc.). *colloq.* (orig. *U.S.*).

1934 *Amer. Speech* IX. 76/1 In Birmingham on September 17, Dr. Sterling J. Foster..warned his hearers that 'if a certain fatal mistake is made, taxes will be upped on every house in the city'. **1943** *Sun* (Baltimore) 1 Dec. 9/3 (*heading*) Shot of water ups engine power. **1953** W. BURROUGHS *Junkie* xi. 116 You can only buy P.G. so often, or the druggist gets wise. Then he packs in, or ups the price. **1957** WODEHOUSE *Over Seventy* viii. 94 These negotiations are better left to one's agent. I have instructed mine to arrange for a flat payment of ten guineas, to be upped, of course, if they want to know what I had for dinner at that amusing château in the wine country. **1969** *Daily Tel.* 16 Apr. 23/2 This 28 per cent. increase now ups the annual bill of the trade from £36 million to about £47 million. *a* **1974** R. CROSSMAN *Diaries* (1975) I. 108 I'd talked this over with the Dame before lunch and cautiously suggested that we should make our target 135,000 houses... Harold immediately upped me to 150,000. **1978** G. A. SHEEHAN *Running & Being* x. 135 Athletes upped their practice time fivefold.

c. To promote in rank. *colloq.*

1945 H. BROWN *Artie Greengroin* 182 Someday that mess sergeant is going to fill the Spam full of arsenic and knock off the whole company for a laugh. The day he does that they'll probably up him to tech. **1970** G. F. NEWMAN *Sir, You Bastard* iii. 111 Both the detectives' names and ranks were correct; neither was upped to DCS. *a* **1974** R. CROSSMAN *Diaries* (1975) I. 609 Harold Wilson breezed up and said 'Meet your new Lord President.'..They were astonished that Harold had upped me into the stratosphere.

d. To improve, to 'boost'. *colloq.*

1968 *Globe & Mail* (Toronto) 17 Feb. 28 You can up your morale all so easily. **1976** *Daily Express* 29 June 5/4, I did make a perfunctory attempt to up my image by purchasing chic glasses.

II. *intr.* **6. a.** To rise to one's feet; to get up from a sitting or recumbent posture; to arise; to rise from bed. Also in fig. context.

1643 QUARLES *Embl.* II. xiv. 2 The true-bred Gamester ups a fresh, and then, Falls to 't agen. **1647** BP. CORBET *Poems* (1807) 226 Nor can these figures in thy rest endeere, As not to up when chanticleere Speaks the last watch. **1825** JENNINGS *Observ. Dial. W. Eng.* 109 Jerry Nutty..upp'd avaur tha lork. **1913** M. ROBERTS *Salt of Sea* vi. 177 The bloke nods and ups on 'is feet. **1915** C. H. SORLEY *Lett.* (1919) 255 Suddenly the division ups and marches to Aldershot.

b. *colloq.* and *dial.* To start up, come forward, begin abruptly or boldly, to say or do something. Usu. followed by *and*. Cf. UP *adv.*[1] 33.

(*a*) **1831** LOVER *Leg.* 82 The bishop ups and he tells him that he must mend his manners. **1865** DICKENS *Mut. Fr.* IV. xiii, Then we both of us ups and says, that minute, 'Prove so!' **1867–** in general dialect use (*Eng. Dial. Dict.*). **1879** R. BROWNING *Ned Bratts* 125 She ups with such a face, Heart sunk inside me: 'Well, pad on my prate-apace!'

(*b*) **1883** STEVENSON *Treas. Isl.* xxix, And you have the Davy Jones's insolence to up and stand for cap'n over me! **1884** 'MARK TWAIN' *Huck. Finn* xxv, All of a sudden the doctor ups and turns on them. He says: [etc.]. **1898** 'H. S. MERRIMAN' *Roden's Corner* xxvii, A gesture that served..to ..invite the Frenchman to up and smite him. **1935** E. E. CUMMINGS *Let.* 31 Jan. (1969) 135 And he ups and hands Am [*Eimi*] such a boost as would knock Karl Marx's whiskers out of Benjamin G. Woozeythought's cabinet d'aisance. **1958** 'A. GILBERT' *Death against Clock* 81 So you upped and fled. **1961** O. NASH *Coll. Verse* 33 One of these days not too remote I'll probably up and cut your throat. **1973** *Black World* Jan. 62/1 It did no good. I upped and died. **1979** J. RATHBONE *Joseph* I. i. 20 As soon as we could we upped and fled.

7. To move upwards; to rise or ascend. Also with *it*.

1737 OZELL *Rabelais* II. 103 A Chimney-sweeper *ups* and *downs* it in a Chimney, with his long Broom. *c* **1810** COLERIDGE *Lit. Rem.* (1838) III. 328 He flounders backward and forward, now upping and now downing. **1825** LADY GRANVILLE *Lett.* (1894) I. 360 What an odd thing life is, and how it ups and downs.

8. *to up with*: **a.** To come out with (a story, etc.). *rare*⁻¹. Cf. OUT *v.* 4 b.

1715 M. DAVIES *Athen. Brit.* I. 31 Sir Thomas up's with a Story of the Curs baiting of the Butcher's Dog.

b. *colloq.* To raise (the arm, etc.); to elevate; to lift or pick up.

1760 H. BROOKE *Fool of Qual.* (1809) I. 63 She ups with her brawny arm. **1825** T. HOOK *Sayings* Ser. II. II. 356 Mrs. South..'upped with the turbot and popped it into the dish'. **1851** H. NEWLAND *The Erne* 37 Had he upped with his pilgrim-staff, and broken the man's heretical head. **1887** G. R. SIMS *Mary Jane's Mem.* 30 He ups with the spade in a minute.

c. *Naut.* To place (the helm or tiller) so as to carry the rudder to leeward.

1860 W. H. RUSSELL *Diary India* I. 95 And there..stand the four Chinese helmsmen,..upping with the helm and downing with it.

up (ʌp), *adv.*[1] Forms: 1– **up**, 4–7 **vp**, 5–6 *Sc.* **wp**; 1–7 **upp**, 4–6 **vpp**; 3–5 **uppe**, 3–7 **vppe** (5 **wppe**, 6 **huppe**); 3–5, 9 *dial.* **op**, 4 **ope**, 5 **oppe**, **hoppe**, **hope**; 5, 6 *Sc.* **vpe**, **wpe**, 6 **upe**. [OE. *upp*, *up*, = OFris. *up*, *op* (WFris. *op*, NFris. *ap*), OLFr. **up* (MDu. *up*, *op*, Du. *op*), OS. *up* (MLG., LG. *up*), ON. *upp* (Norw. *upp*; MSw. *up*, *op*, Sw. *upp*, Da. *op*), related to OHG. *ûf* (MHG. *uf*, *ouf*, G. *auf*) and Goth. *iup*.

There does not appear to be sufficient evidence for the assumption that the normal OE. form was *ūp*, and that *ŭpp*, *ŭp* are due to the influence of *uppe* UP *adv.*[2] and *uppan* UP *prep.*[1], unless it is assumed that the same change has taken place in all the related languages except High German.]

I. Denoting actual movement or direction in (or in relation to) space.

1. a. To or towards a point or place higher than another and lying directly (or almost directly) above it; so as to raise or bring, come or tend, to or towards a highter position in space.

Freq. denoting the elevating or rising of only part of the thing spoken of.

c **888** K. ÆLFRED *Boeth.* xxxiv. § 11 Hwæðer þu nu onȝite forhwy þæt fyr fundiȝe up & sio eorðe ofdune? *a* **1000** *Riddles* lv. [liv.] 4 Hyse..hof his aȝen hræȝl hondum up. *c* **1000** *Sax. Leechd.* III. 252 Æfter heora ȝerepe ȝæð seo ea up..& ofer flett eall þæt egiptisce land. *a* **1122** *O.E. Chron.* (Laud MS.) an. 1099, Ðises ȝeares..asprang up..sæ-flod. *a* **1225** *Ancr. R.* 280 He iseih hu ueole þe grimme wrastlare of helle breid up on his hupe. *c* **1280** *Vox & Wolf* 75 Wen me shulde þat on op winde, þat oþer wolde adoun winde. **13..** *Gaw. & Gr. Knt.* 1192 Ho..stel to his bedde, Kest vp þe cortyn [etc.]. **1340–70** *Alex. & Dind.* 483 Whan þe watur wiþ þe wind þe wawus vp casteþ. *a* **1400** *Pistill of Susan* 229 To the ȝate ȝaply þei ȝeoden..And he lift vp þe lach and leop ouer þe lake. *c* **1420** *Anturs of Arth.* 408 He wayned vp his viser fro his ventalle. **1423** JAS. I *King's Q.* clxv, Quhere sum were slungin..vnto the ground, Full sudaynly sche hath [them] vp ythrungin. *c* **1450** *Mirk's Festial* 2 Þe see schall aryse vp yn hyr styd, soo þat þe watyr schall be hear then ayny hyll. **1535** *MS. Rawl.* 777 fol. 86, A smale Rope for the plommers to pull vppe there Irons vnto the leades. **1548** ELYOT, *Scintillatio*,..a sparkelyng vp of fire. **1570** DEE *Math. Pref.* 35 Catchyng hold of their Shyps, and hoysing them vp aboue the water. **1598** SHAKS. *Merry W.* IV. ii. 57 Ile creepe vp into the chimney. **1610** B. JONSON *Alch.* II. iii, Shee'll mount you vp, like quick-siluer, Ouer the helme. **1622** J. TAYLOR (Water P.) *Farew. to Tower-bottles* A 3 b, Thus like Times Football was I often tost In Dock out Nettle, vp downe. **1640** tr. *Verdere's Rom. of Rom.* III. xxx. 129 The Knight of the Eagles presently lift up his Bever. **1667** MILTON *P.L.* III. 574 Thither his course he bends..; but up or downe,..[it is] hard to tell. **1706** MOTTEUX *Vanbrugh's Mistake* Epil., Nor.., With Glass drawn up, Drive about Covent-Garden. **1766** G. WILLIAMS *Let.* in *G. Selwyn* (1843) II. 42 After he has pulled up his stockings. **1772** HUTTON *Bridges* 99 A large ram of iron..being lift up to the top of them. **1805** *Naval Chron.* XIV. 154 The hatches had bursted up. **1827** FARADAY *Chem. Manip.* iii. (1842) 77 The air..will immediately pass up by the hair or wire.

transf. **1843** *Penny Cycl.* XXVI. 419/1 Voices..capable of extending their compass by running up into a falsetto. **1890** *Good Words* Aug. 520/2 The barometer..is going up at a tremendous rate.

b. Towards or above the level of the shoulders or head.

Beowulf 2575 Hond up abræd ðeata dryhten, gryrefahne sloh. *a* **900** *O.E. Martyrol.* 18 April 58 þonne he hof his hond upp to hiofonum, þonne hofon þa deor heora fotas upp. *c* **1000** ÆLFRIC *Exod.* viii. 17 Aaron ahefde up hys hand. *c* **1250** *Gen. & Ex.* 3057 Moyses..helde up is hond. *a* **1300** *Cursor M.* 4767 Oft he liftud vp his hend To godd, þat he helpe þam wald send. **1387** TREVISA *Higden* (Rolls) VIII. 11 He..haf up his handes and seide, 'I praye [etc.]'. **1455** E. CLARE in *Paston Lett.* I. 315 Than he hild up his hands and thankid God. **1590** LODGE *Euphues Gold. Leg.* (1887) 21 Casting up his hand he felt hair on his face. **1639** E. SPENSER in *Lismore Papers* Ser. II. (1888) IV. 75 He heaved vp his sticke with an intent..to haue strooken me. **1719** DE FOE *Crusoe* I. (Globe) 256, I saw one of the Villains lift up his Arm with a great Cutlash..to strike one of the poor Men. **1853** *Public School Matches* 14 The wicket-keeper puts up his hands. **1887** MRS. PERKS *From Heather Hills* I. vi. 114 Eliza's hands went up in horror.

c. So as to raise into a more erect (or level) as well as elevated position.

c **897** K. ÆLFRED *Gregory's Past C.* liv. 425 Ne hebbe ȝe to up eowre hornas. Ðonne ahebbað ða synfullan swiðe up hira hornas [etc.]. **971** *Blickl. Hom.* 187 'Rære up þin heafod.'..þa ahof Paulus up his heafod. *a* **1300**– [see LIFT *v.* 5 c]. **1390** GOWER *Conf.* I. 219 With that he pulleth up his hed, And made riht a glad visage. **1535** COVERDALE *Job.* x. 15 Yf I be rightuous, yet darre I not lift vp my heade. —— *Ezek.* viii. 17 Purposly to cast vp their noses vpon me. **1570** *Satir. Poems Reform.* I. 90 Than did sum Lords lyft vp yair hornis on hie. **1607** MARKHAM *Cavel.* II. 208 The horse..dare neyther tosse vp his heade, nor ducke it downe. **1678, 1756** [see TOSS *v.* 11]. **1875** WHYTE-MELVILLE *Riding Recoll.* (1878) 48 Up go their heads to avoid the pain.

d. So as to raise a thing from the place in which it is lying, placed, or fixed.

For the specific sense 'into a vehicle (boat, etc.)', see TAKE *v.* 90 b *e*, PICK *v.* 21 e.

c **900** *Baeda's Hist.* III. xv. (1890) 200 þa scipmen þa oncras upp teon, & in þone sæ syndon. *c* **1000** ÆLFRIC *Gen.* vii. 17 Ða wæteru..ahefdon up ðone arc. —— *Saints' Lives* viii. 212 Hine ȝelæhte an hors..mid toðum and hefde him upp. *c* **1052** *O.E. Chron.* (MS. C), Hiȝ brudon up ða sona heora ancran. *a* **1300**– [see TAKE *v.* 90 a]. **1382** WYCLIF *2 Esdr.* ii. 1, I heuede vp the win, and ȝaf to the king. **1387** TREVISA *Higden* (Rolls) VII. 349 A whirlewynd..lefte up sixe rafters of þe cherche. *c* **1430** *Two Cookery Bks.* 5 Þan take hem vp of þe water after þe fyrst boylyng. **1458** in Parker *Dom. Archit.* III. 41 Som oute of her sadels flette to the grounde... Her kyn..caught hem uppe with care. *a* **1533** LD. BERNERS *Huon* lxi. 213 They weyed vp theyr ancres & lyft vp theyr saylles. **1535** COVERDALE *2 Esdr.* ii. 1, I toke vp the wyne, and gaue it vnto ye kynge. **1602**– [see DIP *v.* 5]. **1662**– [see GET *v.* 80 j]. **1694** *Lond. Gaz.* No. 3023/1 As soon as they could get up their Anchors they sailed away. *a* **1704**– [see PICK *v.* 21 b]. **1725** T. LEWIS *Antiq. Hebr. Rep.* III. 270 When she had lift it [*sc.* a shoe] up. **187.** B. HARTE *High Water Mark* Wks. (1873) 70 She dipped up the water to cool her parched throat.

e. So as to invert the relative position of things or surfaces; so as to have a particular surface facing upwards.

a **1300** in *E.E.P.* (1862) 21 Turne him uppe, turne him down,..ouer al þou findist him blodi oþer wan. *c* **1340** HAMPOLE *Pr. Consc.* 673 What es man in shap bot a tre Turned up þat es doun. *Ibid.* 1602 Þus es þis world turned up þat es doune. *c* **1375** *Sc. Leg. Saints* xxii. (*Lawrence*) 489 Þe rostit syd turne vpe & ete. **1611**– [see TURN *v.* 81 c, g, h, i]. **1853** DE QUINCEY *Autobiog. Sk.* Wks. I. 189 'We tossed up,' to settle the question... 'Heads' came up. **1863** 'CAVENDISH' *Whist* (ed. 5) 37 In trumps, if king or queen is turned up.

2. a. Towards a point overhead, or away from the surface of the earth; into the air.

Beowulf 1373 þonon yðȝeblond up astiȝeð won to wolcnum. *c* **888** K. ÆLFRED *Boeth.* vii. § 3 þonne ic up ȝefere ..swa se earn ðonne he up ȝewit bufan ða wolcnu. **971** *Blickl. Hom.* 143 þa apostolas tuȝon hie up & hie ȝesetton on ..neorxna wange. *c* **1000** ÆLFRIC *Saints' Lives* xxvii. 100 Æfter ðysum wordum ȝewende se engel up. *c* **1220** *Bestiary* 64 Ðer-ouer he fleȝeð, and up he teð, til ðat he ðe heuene seð. **1382** WYCLIF *Acts* i. 9 He was lift vp, and a cloud receyuede hym. **1526** *Pilgr. Perf.* (1531) 166 As a ball, which yf it be tossed and cast vp streyght, it falleth down [etc.]. **1535** COVERDALE *Job* xxxix. 27 Doth the Aegle mounte vp..at thy commaundement? **1591** RALEIGH *Last Fight Reuenge* B 4 b, Doubting least S. Richard would haue blowne them vp and himselfe. **1599**– [see BLOW *v.* 24]. **1647** N. BACON *Disc. Govt. Eng.* I. lvii. 167 Like a vapour mounted up by the Clergy. **1833** J. HOLLAND *Manuf. Metal* II. vii. 189 The fresh coals ..will throw up,..as usual, a body of thick smoke. **1853** *Public School Matches* 16 An appeal to the umpire, and up goes the ball.

b. With defining adv. or prep. phrase.

c **900** tr. *Baeda's Hist.* III. xvi. (1890) 202 þa he þa se biscop ȝeseah..þone rec up ofer þære burȝe wallas ahefenne. **971** *Blickl. Hom.* 123 Þes Hælend þe nu up on þysne heofon.. astaȝ. *c* **1000** in *Wulfstan's Hom.* (1883) 100 He stah up to ðam stepele and of ðam stepele hof upp on lyfte. *c* **1200** ORMIN Ded. 234 Þurrh þatt he [*sc.* Christ] stah forr ure god Upp inntill heffness blisse. **1297** R. GLOUC. (Rolls) 168 [To] bloue hom here & þere vp in þe luft anhei. *c* **1340** HAMPOLE *Pr. Consc.* 5027 Alle þat er gude..sal..up in-to þe ayre be ravyste. *c* **1375** *Sc. Leg. Saints* i. (*Peter*) 559 A day he sat þame till, vp in hewine quhen he suld fle. **1482** *Monk of Evesham* (Arb.) 107 Now sche was lyfte vppe an hye. **1539** BIBLE *2 Sam.* xviii. 9 He was lifte vp betwene heuen & erthe. **1593** SHAKS. *Ven. & Ad.* 853 Here the gentle larke..mounts vp on hie. **1617** MORYSON *Itin.* I. 206 Vines growing up high upon the Elmes. **1680** C. NESSE *Ch. Hist.* 284 Him..whom he hop'd to help up upon the lofty gallows. *a* **1721** SHEFFIELD (Dk. Buckhm.) *Wks.* (1753) I. 12 The sigh..Up tow'rds the heavens like a bright meteor soar'd. **1824** JAS. TELFER *Border Ball.* 42 They sprang upthrough the welkin high. **1904** SPENCER & GILLEN *Northern Tribes Australia* xv. 487 Then he took him away up into the sky.

c. To some height above the ground or other surface; from or off the ground; *spec.* to a seat on horseback; to or towards the mast-head.

c **897** K. ÆLFRED *Gregory's Past. C.* 173 Ðonne hi hebbað ..ða earce up. *c* **1200** ORMIN 16705 All swa se Moysæs Hof upp þe neddre i wesste. *c* **1205** LAY. 30607 Heo wunden up seiles to coppe. *c* **1290** *S. Eng. Leg.* I. 41/232 Lupe þou up bi-hynde me. *Ibid.* 134/961 He..a-rerde op is baner. **1377** LANGL. *P. Pl.* B. XVIII. 52 Poysoun on a pole þei put vp to his lippes. **1382** WYCLIF *John* iii. 14 As Moyses reride vp a serpent in desert. *c* **1400** *Destr. Troy* 10858 And pull vp a port, let hom passe furthe. *c* **1440** *Generydes* 2262 Generydes leppe vppe vppon his stede. **1450** *Bk. Hawkyng* in *Rel. Ant.* I. 297 Lete the spanyell flusch up the covey. *c* **1450** *Coventry Myst.* (1922) 301 And he xal make hym to..gon up on a leddere. **1508** DUNBAR *Gold. Targe* 236 And swyth vp saile vnto the top thai stent. **1582** STANYHURST *Æneis* III. (Arb.) 87 Foorth we take oure passadge, oure sayles ful winged vp hoysting. **1606** SHAKS. *Ant. & Cl.* v. ii. 56 Shall they hoyst me vp, And shew me to the showting Varlotarie Of censuring Rome? **1629**– [see PUT *v.* 56 b]. **1697** DAMPIER *Voy.* 416 Having fine handsome weather, we got up our Yards again. **1738** *Voy. up Thames* 31 Having put up a Sail in one of the small Wherries. **1821** SCOTT *Pirate* xl, Up goes the Jolly Hodge, the old black flag.

d. So as to be suspended aloft or on high; into a hanging position.

c **1000** ÆLFRIC *Joshua* x. 26 Iosue hi ofsloh ða & siððan up aheng on fif wacum boȝum. *a* **1200** *Vices & Virtues* 49 He ðe weiȝþ upp mid his fingre heuene and ierðe. **1297**– [see HANG *v.* 29 a, b, c]. *c* **1375** *Sc. Leg. Saints* xxxiii. (*George*) 780 Þane gert he men but mare hang hyre hey vpe be þe hare. **1430–40** LYDG. *Bochas* VIII. 1890 How he hymsilfe heng up bi the hals. **1536**– [see TRUSS *v.* 7]. **1711** ADDISON *Spect.* No. 47 ¶ 3 The Dutch..hang up in several of their Streets what they call the Sign of the Gaper.

3. a. From beneath the horizon to the line of vision.

c **888** K. ÆLFRED *Boeth.* xxxix. § 13 Þonne hate we hine morȝensteorra, forþam he cymð eastan up. *c* **937** *Brunanburh* 13 Siððan sunne up..glad ofer grundas. *a* **1000** *Narrat. Angl. Conscr.* (1861) 30 Mid þy ða ærest se mona up eode. *c* **1386** CHAUCER *Sqr.'s T.* 365 Er þat the sonne gan vp glyde. *c* **1400** *Destr. Troy* 755 Whan þe day vp droghe & the dym voidet. *Ibid.* 8455 When the sun vp set with his softe beames. **1508** DUNBAR *Gold. Targe* 4 Wp sprang the goldyn candill matutyne. —— *Tua Mariit Wemen* 512 Quhill that the day did vp daw. **1556–1632** [see FETCH *v.* 21 h]. **1655** H. VAUGHAN *Silex Scint.* I. 73 Yet, never sleep the Sun up; Prayer shou'd Dawn with the day. **1698** [see TURN *v.* 81 q]. **1744** THOMSON *Winter* 878 The welcome Sun, just verging up at first, By small Degrees extends the swelling Curve.

fig. **1807** J. BARLOW *Columb.* I. 204 The sun's blue ray Topt unknown cliffs and call'd them up to day.

b. From below the level of the earth, water, etc., to the surface. With (*a*) intransitive and (*b*) transitive verbs, and freq. with the addition of a prepositional phrase (*of the earth*, etc.).

With *grow*, etc., in reference to plants, passing into sense 4. For further examples with trans. verbs, see DELVE *v.*[4], DIG *v.* 14, GRUB *v.* 3, TURN *v.* 81 r, WEIGH *v.* 6 b.

(*a*) *Beowulf* 1619 Sona wæs [he] on sunde,..wæter up þurh-deaf. *c* **888** K. ÆLFRED *Boeth.* xxxiv. § 6 Þæt wæter.. cymð þonne up æt þæm æwelme. *c* **893** —— *Oros.* I. i. § 9 Seo ea..up aspryngð neh þæm clife. *c* **975** *Rushw. Gosp.* Matt. xiii. 5 Hræþe cuomun [hie] upp forþon þe hie næfdon heanisse eorðe. *c* **1000** ÆLFRIC *Gen.* ii. 5 Ælcne telȝor on eorðan, ær ðan ðe he up asprunge.., & eall gærs..ær ðan ðe hi up asprytton. *c* **1220** *Bestiary* 579 Ðe sipes [= ships] sinken..., ne cumen he nummor up. **1297** R. GLOUC. (Rolls) 165 þe wind þere..Vp of þe erþe ofte comþ. *a* **1300**– [see SPRING *v.*[1] 8 c]. **1303** R. BRUNNE *Handl. Synne* 9767 Vpp of hys graue a fyre vpp smote. **13..** *E.E. Allit. P.* A. 35 So semly a sede moȝt fayly not, Þat springande spycez vp ne sponne. **1530** PALSGR. 692/1 It is a plesaunt syght to se the water ryse up..out of a spring. **1535** COVERDALE *Job* xiv. 2 He commeth vp, and falleth awaye like a floure. **1667** MILTON *P.L.* VII. 456 Living Creatures..out of the ground up rose. **1835** MARRYAT *J. Faithful* i, My father burst up from the cabin. **1844** DICKENS in *Story of his Life* (1870) 156, I am here—just come up from underground. **1866** SHUCKARD *Brit. Bees* 223 A thick and prodigious quantity of the common mustard plant shot up.

(*b*) *c* **900** *Baeda's Hist.* III. vii. (1890) 168 Hædde biscop heht his lichoman up adon. *a* **1000** *Narrat. Angl. Conscr.* (1861) 35 Hy..delfaþ gold up of eorþan. *c* **1000** ÆLFRIC *Gen.* xxxvii. 28 Hi tuȝon hine up of þam pytte. *c* **1000** —— *Saints' Lives* xxi. 136 Eadgar cyning..wolde þæt se halȝa wer wurde up ȝedon. *a* **1122** *O.E. Chron.* (Laud MS.) an. 963, He nam up Sancta Kyneburh & S. Kynesuið. *c* **1375** *Sc. Leg. Saints* xxxvi. (*Baptist*) 561 Sarazenis syne vpe can ta.. his banis. **1387** TREVISA *Higden* (Rolls) VII. 77 Hircanus took up þre þowsand talentes of kyng David his grave. *c* **1440** *Promp. Parv.* 118 Delvyn vp owte of the erthe, *effodio*. **1494** *Acc. Ld. High Treas. Scot.* I. 251 Sertane wrychtis..takand wpe the auld schype, that was sunkyne..in the watter. **1548** HALL *Chron.*, *Richard III*, 27 b, Some saye that kynge Richard caused the priest to take them vp,..and to put them in a coffyne. **1563** FULKE *Meteors* (1571) 66 b, When they plowe the grounde [they] turne vp syluer, among the clottes. **1588** SHAKS. *Tit. A.* v. i. 135 Oft haue I dig'd vp dead men from their graues. **1632** MILTON *Penseroso* 109 That thy power Might..call up him that left half told The story of Cambuscan bold. **1660** SHARROCK *Vegetables* 100 This he onely did by casting up their nests. **1748** *Anson's Voy.* II. viii. 219 The taking up oysters from great depths..by Negro slaves. **1821** SCOTT *Pirate* xxxvi, Go down below, my girls, ..and send up the rare old man. **1851** MRS. BROWNING *Casa Guidi Wind.* II. 325 Ye called up ghosts, believing they were slack To follow [etc.].

c. So as to detach from being fixed in the soil or other surface.

See also GRUB *v.* 3, PLUCK *v.* 8 b, PULL *v.* 35 b, ROOT *v.*[1] 6.

a **1100** in Napier *O.E. Glosses* I. 2903 *Euulsum*, *i. abscisum*, ut alocene, up aliþode. *c* **1200** ORMIN 9285 Illc an treo.. Shall bi þe grund beon hæwenn upp. **1297** R. GLOUC. (Rolls) 10264 Ech tre were vp mored þat it ne spronge namore þere. **1362** LANGL. *P. Pl.* A. VII. 104 Summe, to plese perkyn, pykeden vp þe weodes. *a* **1400–50** *Alexander* 409 þis diuinour..ȝede..herbis to seche, Reft þam vp be þe rotis. *c* **1440** *Pallad. on Husb.* VIII. 14 Er the Canyculer, the hounde, ascende Haue vp the fern and seggis to be brende. *c* **1550** CHEKE *Matt.* xiii. 29 Leest in weeding ye darnel, ye pluck vp also ye corn. **1573** TUSSER *Husb.* (1878) 37 A pike for to pike them [*sc.* vetches] vp handsom to drie. **1699** DAMPIER *Voy.* II. III. vi. 67 By tearing up the Trees by the Roots. *a* **1701** MAUNDRELL *Journ. Jerus.* (1707) 144 In gathering their Corn,..they pluck'd it up by handfuls from the roots. **1738** *Voy. up Thames* 79 The Humour..of grubbing up every Tree in the Neighbourhood. **1841** *Jrnl. R. Agric. Soc.* II. II. 229 The turnips were taken up and carted.

d. From the stomach into, or out at, the mouth; out of the sea on to the shore, etc.

c **1000** *Sax. Leechd.* I. 74 Wiþ þon ðe men blod upp wealle þurh his muð. *c* **1315** SHOREHAM *Poems* I. 778 He soffreþ wel to be kest op, And ȝet to be honoured. **13..** *E.E. Allit. P.* C. 340 Þe whal wendez at his wylle & a warþe fyndez, & þer he brakez vp þe buyrne. **1377** LANGL. *P. Pl.* B. v. 379, I glotoun girt it [*sc.* food] vp, er I hadde gone a myle. **1484**– [see CAST *v.* 83 b, c]. **1541** ELYOT *Image Gov.* 23 He immediately wolde vomit vp colar. **1570** GOOGE *Popish Kingd.* IV. 53 And miserably they reele, till as their stomacke vp they lay. **1599, 1622** [see FETCH *v.* 21 b]. **1610, 1648** [see BELCH *v.* 4 b]. **1693**– [see VOMIT *v.* 2 b]. **1733**– [see THROW *v.* 48 b]. **1863** ROBSON *Bards of Tyne* 433 Whey, she had bowk't the sma' beer up.

fig. *c* **1205** LAY. 3532 Þa alles vppe abræc, hit wes god þet heo spæc. *a* **1225** *Ancr. R.* 426 Hwon his blowinge ne geineð nout, þeonne bringeð he up some luðer word. **1633** T. ADAMS *Exp. 2 Peter* ii. 22. 1094 Sinne, like *Stibium*, will tarry with no body: up it must.

4. a. So as to extend or rise to a higher point or level, esp. above the surface of the ground. With (*a*) intransitive and (*b*) transitive verbs.

For the use with *run*, etc., in reference to plants, cf. sense 3 b. With *build*, *make* (see MAKE *v.* 96 a, b), etc., restoration is freq. implied (cf. sense 20 b).

(*a*) *a* **900** *O.E. Martyrol.* 21 Dec. 222 On þam wæron þa wealdleðer swa upȝetiȝed, swa swa hiȝ urnon to heofenum up. *c* **1000**– [see sense 26 a]. **1387** TREVISA *Higden* (Rolls) VI. 305 A piler of liȝt þat stood up from his body into hevene. **1390** GOWER *Conf.* I. 173 As the Netle which up renneth The..Roses brenneth. **1530** TINDALE *Exod.* ix. 32 The barly was shott vp [1611 in the eare] & the flaxe was boulled. **1582** STANYHURST *Æneis* IV. (Arb.) 107 If ye be delighted, too see new Carthage vp hoouering. **1610** HOLLAND *Camden's Brit.* I. 288 There riseth up an high mount. **1611** BIBLE *Exod.* ix. 32 The wheat and the rye..were not growen vp. **1699** EVELYN *Kal. Hort.* (ed. 9) 97 If Plants run up to Seed over-hastily. **1726** SWIFT *Gulliver* III. iii, One..plate of adamant, shooting up to the height of about two hundred yards. **1731**– [see RUN *v.* 81 a]. **1840** [see GROW *v.* 13 b]. **1858** LYTTON *What will He do?* I. iv, At the rear of the palace soars up the old Abbey. **1878** SMILES *R. Dick* i. 3 It shoots up into a tall rocky point.

(*b*) **971** *Blickl. Hom.* 127 Þonne is þær..ȝeworht..up oþ mannes breost heah. *c* **1200** ORMIN 9204 Nu sket shall illc an dale beon All heghedd upp & filledd. *c* **1205** LAY. 8716 Þa þet work [*sc.* a castle] wes up iset, heom wes alles þa bet. **1297** R. GLOUC. (Rolls) 3023 Þe king..let rere up chirchen. **1338** R. BRUNNE *Chron.* (1810) 88 Whan he was at London, a haule he did vp wright. **1382** WYCLIF *2 Esdr.* ii. 17 Bilde we vp the wallis of Jerusalem. *Ibid.* iii. 1 Thei bilden vp the ȝatis of the floc. **1390** GOWER *Conf.* I. 53 To him that Thebes ferst on hyh Up sette. *c* **1400** *Destr. Troy* 1535 Priam..byld vp a bygge towne of þe bare vrthe. *c* **1440** *Pallad. on Husb.* I. 435 When that is drie, vp walle hit euery side In lyke maner. **1479** *Nottingham Rec.* II. 390 That the seid howse be fensyd, reryd and made upp. **1509** HAWES *Past. Pleas.* xxxv. (Percy Soc.) 182 He stretched hym up and lyft his axe a lofte. **1596** DALRYMPLE tr. *Leslie's Hist. Scot.*

(S.T.S.) I. 173 Quhen he had bigit the wal wpe agane. **1687-** [see RUN *v.* 81 j]. **1730** THOMSON *Autumn* 137 On either hand ..groves of masts Shot up their spires. **1788** J. MAY *Jrnl. & Lett.* (1873) 86 To-day finished laying up the house, and put on the roof. **1812** L. HUNT in *Examiner* 12 Oct. 642/2 The carpenters that knock up our hustings. **1873** H. SPENCER *Stud. Sociol.* xi. 287 Here are lighthouses we have put up to prevent shipwrecks.

b. With indication of a point of measurement.

c **1400** *Destr. Troy* 1548 The walle..of marbill was most fro þe myddes vp. **1473-4** *Acc. Ld. High Treas. Scot.* I. 30 Brade clath for ij goonis and ij kirtillis..for the lyning of thaim fra the waist vpe. **1877** RUSKIN *St. Mark's Rest* Suppl. i. 5 All the rest mere flat wall, wainscoted two-thirds up, eight feet or so.

c. So as to form a heap or pile, or become more prominent. (Also in fig. expressions.)

See also CAST *v.* 83 e, EARTH *v.* 3, MAKE *v.* 96 b, PUFF *v.* 4, 5, RIDGE *v.* 2, RISE *v.* 10 c, SWELL *v.* 2, THROW *v.*[1] 48 d.

c **1310** *Prov. Hendyng* 142 (MS. Harl. 2253), Bynd þine tonge wiþ bonene wal; Let hit don synke, þer hit up swal. **1523** FITZHERB. *Husb.* §13 In the begynnynge of Marche, rydge it vppe agayne. **1535** COVERDALE *Job* xvi. 4 Then shulde I heape vp wordes agaynst you. —— *Zech.* ix. 3 Tyrus shal..heape vp syluer as the sonde. **1576** FLEMING *Panopl. Epist.* 372 Ignoraunce doth..pile them vp one vpon another. **1586** A. DAY *Eng. Secretorie* I. (1595) 140 You must needs heap vp no other but extremities vppon her. **1611** BIBLE *Eccl.* ii. 26 To the sinner hee giueth..to gather and to heape vp. **1664** EVELYN *Sylva* (1679) 10 Your plants beginning now to peep, should be earthed up. **1718** BP. HUTCHINSON *Witchcraft* i. 8 They can huff up their Bellies, that they may seem much swell'd. **1751** JORTIN *Serm.* (1771) II. 37 Some heap up riches. **1776** SEMPLE *Building in Water* 109 To rise or bank up the Bed of the River. **1825** JAMIESON, *Hot*,..a small heap of any kind carelessly put up. **1837** P. KEITH *Bot. Lex.* 37 The vessels become convoluted and swell up into a bunch. **1839** URE *Dict. Arts* 751 The sediment called smitham is taken out, and piled up in heaps.

5. a. So as to raise or rise from a horizontal, relaxed, or drooping posture to an upright or nearly upright position.

a **900** *Genesis* 1675 [Hie] to heofnum up hlædræ rærdon. *a* **1240** *Wohunge* in *O.E. Hom.* I. 283 Nu raise þai up þe rode. *a* **1300** *Cursor M.* 22548 (Edinb.), þe tres forcastin sal þaim payn For to riht þaim op ogayn. **1387** TREVISA *Higden* (Rolls) V. 399 þey arered up þe baner of þe cros. **1530** TINDALE *Gen.* xxviii. 18 Iacob..toke the stone..and pitched it vp an ende. **1598** MARSTON *Sco. Villanie* II. vi. (1599) 201 Capro reads,..Strokes vp his haire. **1608** TOPSELL *Serpents* 117 The tayle is very long, at the end and turning vp like a Vipers tayle. *a* **1732** T. BOSTON *Crook in Lot* (1805) 152 God will..remove the weight..and let them get up their back long bowed. **1784** J. POTTER *Virtuous Villagers* I. 51 She now and then bridled herself up a little in the..style of an old maid. **1837** MARRYAT *P. Keene* i, The honourable spinster bridled up with indignation. **1850** *Tait's Mag.* XVII. 342/2 The Doctor..drew himself up in offended dignity.

b. Upon one's feet from a recumbent or reclining posture; *spec.* out of bed.

Also from a recumbent to a sitting posture: see GET *v.* 80 a, SIT *v.* 27 a, c. With reference to the rising of the dead there may be an admixture of sense 3 b.

(*a*) *c* **900** tr. *Baeda's Hist.* v. xii. (1899) 613/2 On dagunge he eft acwicode & sæmnunga upp [*v.r.* up heh] asæt. *c* **1200** ORMIN 8363 He ras up & toc þe child,..& for till Israæless land. *c* **1205** LAY. 6495 þat deor up astod and ræsde o þene stede. *a* **1250** *Owl. & Night.* 731 Clerekes, munekes, & canunes..Arisep vp to middelnyhte. *c* **1325** *Spec. Gy Warw.* 251 Vp he ros þe þridde day. **1382** WYCLIF *Matt.* ii. 13 The aungel of the Lord apperide in sleep to Joseph, sayynge, Ryse vp,..and flee in to Egipt. *a* **1400-50** *Alexander* 5055 Sone as þe day-rawe rase he risis vp belyue. *c* **1400** *Laud Troy Bk.* 5779 Menescen was feld, but op he ros. **1535** COVERDALE *2 Esdr.* ii. 12, I gat me vp in ye night season. *a* **1550-** [see GET *v.* 80 a]. **1590-** [see RISE *v.* 3 b]. **1629** WADSWORTH *Pilgr.* iii. 14 Euery morning the fift houre summons them vp. **1671** MILTON *P.R.* II. 282 Lightly from his grassy Couch up rose Our Saviour. **1719** DE FOE *Crusoe* II. (Globe) 363 Being thus gotten up, he look'd out. **1803** *Med. Jrnl.* 520 The patients..endeavoured to get up, and to remain out of bed. **1865** L. OLIPHANT *Piccadilly* (1870) 317, I went to bed, and did not get up till the lamps were being lighted in Piccadilly.

(*b*) **971** *Blickl. Hom.* 157 þa ahof Drihten hie up & hie þa cyste. *c* **1290** *Beket* 85 in *S. Eng. Leg.* I. 109 For Ioye heo ful a-doun i-swowe... þe knaue hire op nam. *a* **1300** *Cursor M.* 25743 Penance..quen we fall vp mai vs lifte. **1470-85** [see HEAVE *v.* 1]. **1537** BIBLE *2 Sam.* xii. 17 The elders..went to him to take him vp from the erth. **1590** SPENSER *F.Q.* I. viii. 40 He found the meanes that Prisoner vp to reare. **1591-3** [see REAR *v.*[1] 2 b, 2 c]. **1663-** [see KNOCK *v.* 18 f]. **1749** FIELDING *Tom Jones* VII. xii, [They] had raised up the body of Jones, but..again let him fall. **1850** TENNYSON *In Mem.* xxxi, Behold a man raised up by Christ!

fig. **1642** T. CASE *Gods Rising* (1644) 3 It is the duty of Gods people, to pray him up, when he seems to be down.

c. So as to rise from a sitting, stooping, or kneeling posture and assume an erect attitude.

See also GET *v.* 80 a, p, HELP *v.* 6, LEAP *v.* 4, STAND *v.* 103 a. For *up and*——, see sense 33.

c **1000** *Ags. Gosp.* John viii. 7 Se hælend abeah nyþer;..þa aras he upp. *c* **1290** *Beket* 1371 in *S. Eng. Leg.* I. 145 Seint thomas wolde op arise: Men beden him sitte a-doun. *c* **1330** R. BRUNNE *Chron. Wace* (Rolls) 1803 Coryneus first vp he stirt, & wyþ a cloþ his body gyrt. **1340** *Ayenb.* 240 þo lhip op þe mayster and him keste. *a* **1400-50** *Alexander* 82 Artaxenses is..resyn vp with all his rewme to ride vs agayn. *Ibid.* 2074 þan pullis him vp þe proude kyng. **1503** HAWES *Examp. Virt.* vii. 150 With that dame Iustyce vp arose. **1526** TINDALE *Luke* xiii. 11 [The] woman..was bowed to gether, and coulde nott well lifte vp her silfe. **1535** COVERDALE *1 Chron.* xxiii. 16 Yet get the vp, and be doynge. —— *2 Esdras* ii. 20 We..are gotten vp, & are buyldinge. **1667** MILTON *P.L.* VIII. 258 Up I sprung,..and upright Stood on my feet. **1795** MACNEILL *Scotland's Scaith* v. vii, Up he bang'd; and ..Sad and silent took the road. **1802** LEYDEN *Cout of Keeldar* xiv, A wee man..Up started by a cairn. **1877** SPURGEON *Serm.* XXIII. 82 The rebel may stand up in bold defiance.

fig. **1656** COWLEY *Chronicle* iii, Till up in Arms my Passions rose, And cast away her yoke.

6. a. So as to mount or rise by gradual ascent, in contact with a surface, to a higher level or altitude; sometimes *spec.* = up-stairs.

Beowulf 2893 Heht ða þæt heaðoweorc to hagan biodan, up ofer ecgclif. *c* **900** tr. *Baeda's Hist.* I. vii. (1890) 38 þa astah se..Godes andettere mid þa menigeo on þa dune upp. **944** *Charter* in Sweet *A.S. Reader* (1908) 57 Ðonne of ðam þornum up on ða lytlan dune middewearde. **991** in Thorpe *Laws* (1840) I. 286 þeh..þa menn up ætberstan into þære byrig. *c* **1000** ÆLFRIC *Num.* xiv. 40 Sona on ærne merien [hy] astigon gewæpnode up to ðære dune. *a* **1066** in Kemble *Cod. Dipl.* IV. 221 Ðæt Urk min huskarl habbe his strand.. upp of sæ and ut on sæ. *c* **1205** LAY. 25807 Beduer..up a-stæh þene munt. **1382** WYCLIF *Matt.* v. 1 Jhesus forsothe, seynge cumpanyes, wente vp in to an hill. *c* **1386** CHAUCER *Sqr.'s T.* 378 As rody and bright as dooth the yonge sonne That in the Ram is four degrees vp ronne. *c* **1400** *Destr. Troy* 4978 Goand vp by degres þurgh mony gay Alys. **1487-8** *Rec. St. Mary at Hill* (1905) 136 To William paris for amendyng of the floores in the house vppon the steyer, and for beryng vp of ij[o] sackes sonde. **1531** TINDALE *Exp. 1 John* (1538) 76 Yf a rude fellowe shulde breake vp into the kynges priue chambre. **1565** COOPER *Thesaurus* s.v. *Accliuis*, *Trames accliuis*, a way goyng vp against a hill. **1656** M. BEN ISRAEL *Vind. Jud.* 15 He went up into a belcony in the palace. **1713** SWIFT *Jrnl. to Stella* 10 Feb., Sterne..has been often to see me, he says, but my man has not yet let him up. **1753** *World* 37 There is hardly a chambermaid that will bring me up a bottle of water into my room. **1777** SHERIDAN *Sch. Scand.* I. i, Show him up.—He generally calls about this time. **1798** COLERIDGE *Anc. Mar.* IV. x, The moving Moon went up the sky, And no where did abide: Softly she was going up. **1818** SCOTT *Hrt. Midl.* xx, Widow Butler's bullseg, that I used to see spieling up on my bed. **1844** MRS. BROWNING *Lost Bower* ii, Summer-snow of apple blossoms running up from glade to glade. **1884** *Harper's Mag.* Jan. 211/2 You keep on plunging up and up until you are worn out.

b. To a higher point on or within a river, channel, etc., or a point further from the sea. Cf. UP *prep.*[2] 2.

847 in *O.E. Texts* 434 Ðonne up on broc oð heottes dic. *c* **900** *O.E. Chron.* (Parker MS.) an. 893, On þa ea hi tugon up hiora scipu oþ þone weald. **935** in Kemble *Cod. Dipl.* V. 220 Upp andlang Ocerburnan to halelan mærscæ.

a **1550** LELAND *Itin.* (1711) II. 52 From Mineheved up along the Severne Shore to Stoke Gurcy. **1600** HAKLUYT *Voy.* II. 194 The voyage..vp into the Bay of Saint Laurence ..as farre as the Isle of Assumption. **1697** DAMPIER *Voy.* 5 We..might have gone up into the River, having a strong tyde of flood. **1764** *Pres. St. Navig. Thames* 33 The Price of Carriage thro'..Locks, up even to Wallingford, might also be adjusted. **1790** BRUCE *Source of Nile* I. 48 They border upon another large tribe..., which extends from thence up into Nubia. **1867** SMYTH *Sailor's Word-bk.* 707 *Up along*, sailing from the mouth of the channel upwards. **1881** J. HATTON *New Ceylon* v. 136 The voyage up, with the trade goods, is done in a canoe.

†**c.** On shore; from the sea; at land. *Obs.*

Beowulf 224 þanon up hraðe Wedera leode on wang stigon. *Ibid.* 1920 Het þa up beran æþelinga gestreon. *c* **893** K. ÆLFRED *Oros.* IV. x. §10 He..up comon æt Leptan þæm tune. *c* **900** tr. *Baeda's Hist.* I. xxv. (1890) 58 On þyssum ealande com upp..Agustinus. *a* **1122** *O.E. Chron.* (Laud MS.) an. 1014, Cnut..com to Sandwic, & let þær up þa gislas þe his fæder geseald wæron. *c* **1175** *Lamb. Hom.* 87 þa þe heo comen on midden þere se, þa wes þet godes folc up of þere se agan. *c* **1290** *Beket* 1796 in *S. Eng. Leg.* I. 158 At douere were knigtes gare..Sone ase he come op þere al aredi him to quelle. *Ibid.* 1799. *c* **1350-1483** [see RIVE *v.*[2]]. *c* **1400** *Destr. Troy* 2017 þai..Past into port,..Lepyn vp to þe lond, leuyn þere ship.

d. In conventional uses, esp. in contrast to DOWN *adv.* 2. (See also 26 c.)

[**1382** WYCLIF *Matt.* xx. 18 Loo! we gon vp to Jerusalem.] ? **1475** *Stonor Papers* (Camden) I. 156, I com hoppe [= to London]..and grette nede I hadde now of you. **1516-** [see COME *v.* 74 a]. **1518** in Leadam *Star Chamber Cases* (Selden) II. 129 The Inhabitauntes..sent vpp the seid John power.. to make further Sute..for Redresse. **1537** *Lett. & Papers Hen. VIII*, XII. I. 10 [They] marvel that..Sir George should ryde huppe at this time. **1610** B. JONSON *Alch.* II. vi, Shee's come vp here, of purpose To learne the fashion. **1667-8** MARVELL *Corr.* Wks. (Grosart) II. 240 Also they have sent for the Lieutenant Governor of Chester; he having writ up news that an apothecary of that town had [etc.]. **1707** *Lond. Gaz.* No. 2306/3 They came out of Ireland,..but met with a violent Storm that put them up as high as Lundy. **1719** DE FOE *Crusoe* II. (Globe) 514 The great..Gulph which goes up to Siam. **1783** LD. PERCY in G. Rose *Diaries* (1860) I. 59, I shall be three days in going up [to London]. **1794** BP. HAY in *Ushaw Mag.* Dec. (1913) 284 He took the opportunity of my company to..go up with me. His business in London [etc.]. **1820** *Examiner* No. 615. 57/2 Pope..resolved to go up to London. **1850** BROWNING *Christmas Eve* iv. 64 The thump-thump..Of the train..up from Manchester. **1853** DICKENS *Bleak Ho.* lvii, Four horses out there for the next stage up! Quick! **1857** HUGHES *Tom Brown* I. iv, Goes through it every day of my life [says the coach-guard]. Twenty minutes afore twelve down..ten o'clock up. **1861** [see GO *v.* 96 a].

e. *Naut.* To windward.

1591 RALEIGH *Last Fight Reuenge* B 2, The ships that wer vnder his lee luffing vp, also laid him aborde. **1603** BRETON *Packet Mad Lett.* xii. (1633) 6 My state being so downe the winde,..I know not how to set saile vp in the weather. **1605** SHAKS. *Temp.* III. ii. 2 Beare vp, & boord 'em. **1611** BIBLE *Acts* xxvii. 15 The ship..could not beare vp into the winde. **1633-** [see COME *v.* 74 l]. **1669** STURMY *Mariner's Mag.* I. ii. 17 He cannot put up the Helmne. **1720-** [see BEAT *v.* 19 b]. **1769** FALCONER *Dict. Marine* (1780) s.v. *Bearing*, We say, up to windward and down to leeward. **1829** MARRYAT *F. Mildmay* v, I..put the helm up. **1830** —— *King's Own* xvi, This..brought the ship up in the wind. **1841** R. H. DANA *Seaman's Man.* 78 Put the helm down and bring her up into the wind.

7. a. So as to direct the sight to a higher point or level. (Cf. 26 b.)

See also CAST *v.* 83 d, HEAVE *v.* 1, LIFT *v.* 5, LOOK *v.* 45 a.

c **900** tr. *Baeda's Eccl. Hist.* IV. ix. (1890) 290 [He] locade up in heofon. **971** *Blickl. Hom.* 123 þa hy þa up on þone heofon..locodan. *a* **1000** *Gl.* in Wr.-Wülcker 79 *Ne erigas* [*oculos tuos*], ne ðu up ne arær [ðine eagan]. *c* **1000** *Ags. Gosp.* John xi. 41 Se hælend ahof upp his eagan. *a* **1300** *Cursor M.* 21393 Constantin..lok up, and in þat sight He sagh þar cristis cros ful bright. **1388** WYCLIF *John* xi. 41 And Jhesus lifte vp hise igen, and seide [etc.]. *c* **1420** *Anturs of Arth.* 356 He gliffed vp with his eighen, þat grey were and grete. *c* **1450** *Mankind* 31 (Brandl), Be-holde not þe erthe, but lyfte yowur ey wppe. **1535** COVERDALE *Ps.* xl. 12 My synnes haue taken soch holde vpon me, that I am not able to loke vp. **1621** G. SANDYS *Ovid's Met.* v. (1626) 92 His turn'd-vp eyes. **1719** DE FOE *Crusoe* II. (Globe) 363 He could only look up, and see that it was a clear Starlight Night. **1820** KEATS *Isabella* xxv, Looking up, he saw her features bright. **1854** MRS. JAMESON *Bk. of Th.* (1877) 13 It is good for us to look up, morally and mentally. **1859** SALA *Tw. round Clock* 39 His eyes..cast up to count the peaches on the wall.

b. So as to cause sound to ascend, increase, or swell. (Cf. 11 b.)

See also GIVE *v.* 64 f, PIPE *v.*[1] 9, RAISE *v.* 13, 21, SET *v.*[1] 154 c, SPEAK *v.* 20 b.

Beowulf 128 þa wæs æfter wiste wop up ahafen, micel morgensweg. *c* **897** K. ÆLFRED *Gregory's Past C.* xv. 91 Hefe up ðine stefne sua ðes bime. *c* **1205** LAY. 11280 Scottes huuwen up muchelne ræm. *c* **1386** CHAUCER *Merch. T.* 1120 Vp he yaf a roryng and a cry. *a* **1400** *Northern Passion* 257 Ilkone kest vppe a grete cry. **1413-** [see LIFT *v.* 5 e]. *c* **1500** *Melusine* xxxvi. 283 He made hys trompettes to blow vp, that euery man shulde be armed. *a* **1548** HALL *Chron., Hen. VIII*, 76 b, Then vp blewe the trumpettes..on bothe sides. **1581** SIDNEY *Apol. Poetrie* (Arb.) 46 Who sometimes rayseth vp his voice to the height of the heauens. **1595** *Locrine* II. vi. 28 Sound drummes & trumpets, sound vp cheerfully. **1611** BIBLE *Job* iii. 8 Let them curse it.., who are ready to raise vp their mourning. **1617** SIR W. MURE *Misc. Poems* xxi. 5 Raise vp thy voice and..proclaime A greater subject. **1869**, **1890** [see GO *v.* 96 c].

II. In figurative and transferred applications.

Under the following heads are placed only those figurative uses which admit of being classified under some general concept. Further illustration will usually be found under the verbs most commonly occurring in the various phrases, together with many special uses which are confined to one or other of those verbs (see e.g. BRING *v.* 27, CAST *v.* 83, COME *v.* 74, DRAW *v.* 89, etc.). Some uncertainty attaches to the origin and development of many of these uses, the variety of which is so great that the adverb comes to present a number of highly divergent and even directly opposite senses, e.g. *to bind up* (sense 19) in contrast with *to break up* (sense 21 b).

8. a. From a lower to a higher status in respect of position, rank, or affluence. (Cf. SET *v.*[1] 154 j.)

c **825** *Vesp. Psalter* xxxvi. 34 Dryhten..hefeð up ðe þæt ðu ineardie eorðan. *c* **888** K. ÆLFRED *Boeth.* xxxix. §11 þy læs hi for longum gesælðum hi to up ahæbben. *c* **1000** *Ags. Ps.* (Thorpe) xlviii. *heading*, þæt hy hy upp ne ahofen for heora welum. *c* **1200** ORMIN 10881 Whase shall i Crisstenndom Beon hofenn upp & hadedd Till bisscopp orr till unnderrpreost. *c* **1386** CHAUCER *Monk's T.* 683 From humble bed to roial magestee Vp roos he, Iulius the Conquerour. **1387** TREVISA *Higden* (Rolls) VI. 355 He suffrede no man to stye up to..[that] manere dignitee.., but he were wel i-lettred. *c* **1440-** [see LIFT *v.* 2 b]. **1477** EARL RIVERS (Caxton) *Dictes* 142 Yf he see that fortune raise and bring up som other of lower degre. **1530** TINDALE *Practice of Prelates* B vi b, When y[e] bishopes office began..to be honorable, then the deacons ..clam vp therunto. **1530-1561** [see COME *v.* 74 f]. **1605** CAMDEN *Rem.* 223 This one steppe will not bring you vppe a steppe higher. **1658** *Trad. Mem. K. Jas.* G ij, By what steps the Puritans got up, and the old Clergy degenerated. **1685** W. CLELAND *Poems* (1697) 127 Now down with the confounded Whiggs,..for Hey Boies up go Wee. **1832** HT. MARTINEAU *Life in Wilds* vii. 99 We are getting up in the world.

b. Into (greater) repute, credit, or estimation.

1593- [see CRY *v.* 22]. **1641** J. JACKSON *True Evang. T.* I. 65 Oh how doth it cry up Christ, in the world, that he hath such servants. **1711** G. HICKES *Two Treat. Chr. Priesth.* (1847) I. 291 Instead of writing up the other Protestant Churches to the Church of England. **1741** tr. *D'Argens, Chinese Lett.* xx. 137 Men, who preach up nothing but Patience, Humility, Obedience. **1863** GLADSTONE in Morley *Life* II. 99 [Queen Victoria] spoke..of Roundell Palmer; I had a good opportunity of speaking him up. **1871** LOWELL *Study Wind.* (1886) 146 A preacher-up of Nature.

9. a. To a higher spiritual or moral level or object.

c **888** K. ÆLFRED *Boeth.* xli. §6 Se mann ana gæþ uprihte; þæt tacnað þæt he sceal ma þencan up þonne nyðer. *c* **1200** ORMIN 2749 Swa þatt hiss herrte iss hofenn upp To follghenn Godess wille. *Ibid.* 2754. **1297** R. GLOUC. (Rolls) 9342 Holdeþ vp to god..goure þogt. *a* **1340** HAMPOLE *Psalter* xxii. 6 þou has purged my hert, and liftid vp to haf þe ioy of contemplacioun. *a* **1375** *Lay Folks Mass Bk.* App. iv. 552 Hef vp gor hertes in-to heuen. **1526** *Pilgr. Perf.* (1531) 290 It heueth and lyfteth vp the spiryt to god. **1535-** [see LIFT *v.* 5 d]. **1589** R. BRUCE *Serm.* (1843) 166 To haue.. our minds lifted vp to the heavens. *a* **1708** BEVERIDGE *Thes. Theol.* (1711) III. 410 It is a good while before we can get up our hearts from earth to heaven.

b. To a state of greater cheerfulness, confidence, resolution, etc.

See also CLEAR *v.* 27, for various senses of *clear up*.

1297 R. GLOUC. (Rolls) 9336 Ʒoure herten hebbeþ vp... Hopieþ al on god. **13..-** [see PLUCK *v.* 8 a]. *c* **1430-** [see PULL *v.* 35 c]. *c* **1450** *Mirk's Festial* 65 Heue vp þyn hert, and make mery. **1572** tr. *Lauaterus' Ghostes* (1596) 108 Gabriel with comfortable wordes did lift up the blessed Virgin. **1590-** [see HEARTEN *v.* 2 b]. **1597-** [see CHEER *v.* 10]. *c* **1600** W. FOWLER *Wks.* (S.T.S.) I. 191 O thow..that rayses vp my courage and abaites. **1732**, **1875** [see BRIGHTEN *v.* 2 b]. **1894** BARING GOULD *Kitty Alone* II. 116, I really could not pluck up courage to do so.

c. Into a state of activity, commotion, excitement, or ferment.

1340- [see STIR *v.* 16]. **1535** COVERDALE *Luke* viii. 24 Then wente they vnto him [*sc.* Christ], and waked him vp. **1596** DALRYMPLE tr. *Leslie's Hist. Scot.* (S.T.S.) I. 76 Sa gret appetite and wil of beiring rule did fyre wpe, and inflame baith the peples. **1689** STILLINGFL. *Serm.* (1698) III. iii. 120 To work up a heated..Imagination to the Fancy of Raptures. **1720** OZELL *Vertot's Rom. Rep.* I. II. 118 Finding the People were blown up again to their former Animosity. **1798-1824** [see FIRE *v.*[1] 5]. **1822** SHELLEY *Chas. I*, I. 123 Their sounds..Rouse up the astonished air. **1869** PHILLIPS *Vesuv.* iii. 59 The mountain, as usual, fired up. **1901** *Scribner's Mag.* April 407/2 Work the crowds up,..but don't get caught yourselves.

d. To or at a greater or higher speed, rate, amount, etc.

See also COME *v.* 74 k, GET *v.* 80 d, RUN *v.* 81 g (*d*).

1538 ELYOT, *Equus citatus*, a horse taken vp. **1565** COOPER *Thesaurus* s.v. *Equus*, To fetch vp with the spurre. **1607** MARKHAM *Cavel.* II. (1617) 126 Whose sharpnes and torment..will so quicken your horse up..that [etc.]. **1664** H. MORE *Myst. Iniq.* 474 They gore and spurre up the Ass. **1677** *Essex Papers* (Camden) II. 130 Upon the late new letting it [*sc.* the Excise], they had..bid up very high upon the present farms. **1839** ALEX. SOMERVILLE *Hist. Brit. Leg.* xi. 236 Flogging the men up, to prevent their falling into the hands of the wandering guerillas. **1883, 1892** [see GO *v.* 96 e]. **1900** ELINOR GLYN *Visits Elizabeth* (1906) 105 Carry had better hurry up and get that house in Park Street.

10. To or towards mature age, or proficiency in some art, etc.

a **900** *O.E. Martyrol.* 21 Oct. 192 [Hilarion] wæs up cymen in Palestina. *c* **1420** *Chron. Vilod.* 1625 He was norysshut vp in þat place. *c* **1450** *Merlin* vii. 112 And so he ..put his owe sone..to be norisshed vp with a-nother woman. **1483-** [see BRING *v.* 27 b]. *c* **1530** LD. BERNERS *Arth. Lyt. Bryt.* 505 It semeth wel this people dyd never nouryssh you up. **1534** in Leadam *Star Chamber Cases* (Selden) II. 207 To take apon hym the Craftes of Bakyng and bruyng where in he was neuer brought vp. **1535-** [see GROW *v.* 13 a]. **1597** *Wills & Inv. N.C.* (Surtees, 1835) 172 My mynde is that he shalbe brought up in learnynge. **1611** BIBLE *Prov.* xxii. 6 Traine vp a childe in the way he should goe. **1730** THOMSON *Autumn* 836 Nurse of a people, in misfortune's school Train'd up to hardy deeds. **1796** H. HUNTER tr. *St.-Pierre's Stud. Nat.* (1799) II. 554 We are brought up to sense of fear only, and not of gratitude. **1839** FR. A. KEMBLE *Resid. Georgia* (1863) 11 As soon as they begin to grow up and pass from infancy to youth. **1879** MISS YONGE *Magnum Bonum* I. 290 She'll be governessed up, and kept to lessons all day. **1894** HALL CAINE *Manxman* 3 He had been brought up to no profession.

11. a. Into existence, prominence, vogue, or currency; so as to appear or prevail.

See also BLAZE *v.*[1] 3 (quot. 1878), GET *v.* 80 r, RISE *v.* 19.

(*a*) *a* **900** *Andreas* 1236 (Gr.), Storm upp aras æfter ceaster-hofum. *c* **1000** ÆLFRIC *Saints' Lives* xxx. 61 Ic eom hælende crist þe..ʒedyde þæt leoht up asprang. *c* **1055** *Byrhtferth's Handboc* in *Anglia* VIII. 306 Of þissum syx tidum aspringð up bissextus. *a* **1225** *Ancr. R.* 286 Amidde þe redunge..þeonne cumeð up a deuociun. *c* **1410** *Lanterne of Liȝt* 28 Liȝt is vp spronngen to þe riȝtwise. *c* **1449-** [see COME *v.* 74 e]. **1535** COVERDALE *Wisdom* vi. 22 As for wyszdome, what she is, and how she came vp, I wil tell you. **1556** in W. H. Turner *Select. Rec. Oxford* (1880) 246 The fire got up. **1556-** [see START *v.* 13 c]. *a* **1572** KNOX *Hist. Ref.* Wks. 1846 I. 77 Upoun what uther trifeling questionis..the war brak up, we omitt to wryte. **1591** SHAKS. *1 Hen. VI*, I. iv. 102 A holy Prophetesse, new risen vp. *a* **1679** J. WARD *Diary* (1839) 297 Round knitt capps were the auncient mode before hatts came upp. **1704** SWIFT *T. Tub* ii, Before they were a month in town, great shoulder-knots came up. **1704-** [see TURN *v.* 81 v]. **1833** A. CRICHTON *Hist. Arabia* I. 216 Sabellians, Valentinians, and a host of obscurer sects, all rose up. **1844-** [see CROP *v.* 10 b]. **1882** A. GRIFFITHS *Chron. Newgate* (1884) I. 13 As usual the difficulty of providing funds cropped up. **1902** T. W. WEBBER *Forests Upper India* xiii. 156 Dinner ready... Smyth, however, had not turned up.

(*b*) *c* **1200** ORMIN 16840 Þeȝȝ..hofenn þurrh hemm sellfenn upp..Settnessess, hu mann birrde..Godess laȝhe follȝhenn. **1393** LANGL. *P. Pl.* C. I. 37 Somme murthes to make,..And fynde vp foule fantesyes. *a* **1400-50** *Alexander* 829* Nicholas..Had rasyd vp a rode hoste. **1443** *Reg. Mag. Sig. Scot.* 86/2 To the quhilkis we..gert chese upe ane assise of the barony. **1535-** [see RAISE *v.* 1 b]. **1560** DAUS tr. *Sleidane's Comm.* 28 b, Suche as eyther Reyse up new customes, or extorte that is forboden. **1568, 1611** [see RAISE *v.* 11]. **1637** HEYWOOD *Royall King* II. iv, Cannot all this stirre his impatience up? **1645** USSHER *Body Div.* 362 That God..would raise up faithfull and painfull Ministers. **1711** ADDISON *Spect.* No. 47 ¶ 5 Stirrers up of Laughter among Men of a gross Taste. **1729** GAY *Polly* I. ix, When Kings by their huffing Have blown up a squabble. **1832** HT. MARTINEAU *Demerara* i. 10 A few..sluggards who had not put up their appearance at the proper hour. **1843** *Blackw. Mag.* LIV. 737 Why couldn't we get up a play? **1867** H. SPENCER *First Princ.* I. (ed. 2) 413 The meteorologic processes eventually set up in the Earth's atmosphere. **1870** H. KINGSLEY *Hillyars & Burtons* lxxvi, It is your grandfather's will. I..drew it up.

b. So as to be heard. (Cf. 7 b.)

a **1723** [see SPEAK *v.* 20 b]. **1748** THOMSON *Cast. Indol.* I. lxiv, As when..a burnish'd fly..Tunes up amid these airy halls his song. **1802** LEYDEN *Lord Soulis* lii, Then up bespake him, true Thomas. **1853** *Public School Matches* 10 The bell from the Pavilion strikes up.

12. a. To the notice or consideration of a person or body of persons (*spec.* of one in authority).

See also CALL *v.* 35 b, d, SHOW *v.* 4 e.

a **1122** *O.E. Chron.* (Laud MS.) an. 1052, Þær bær Godwine eorl up his mal. **1362-** [see PUT *v.* 56 h]. **1414** *Rolls of Parlt.* IV. 22 Or the Petitions biforesaid yeven up yn writing. **1439** *Ibid.* V. 9 In a Petition putte up to the Kyng. **1483-** [see BRING *v.* 27 c]. **1529** in Leadam *Star Chamber Cases* (Selden) II. 34 The byll of compleynt..put vppe to the Kynges highnes. **1559-** [see GIVE *v.* 64 e]. **1585** in *Eng. Hist. Rev.* Jan. (1914) 111 Th' acte..being then sent up by the comens to the lords. **1602** MARSTON *Antonio's Rev.* III. ii, I have a prayer or two to offer up. **1604-** [see CAST *v.* 83 i]. *c* **1633** in *3rd Rep. Hist. MSS. Comm.* 400/2 Ane paper which they send wpe to ȝour Majestie. **1641** [see PUT *v.* 56 h (*b*)]. **1709** T. ROBINSON *Vind. Mosaick Syst.* Introd. 5 It would be Folly for Men to send up Prayers to a God that is not present to hear them. **1820** BYRON *Mar. Fal.* I. ii. 12 The sentence will be sent up to the Doge. **1844** *Fraser's Mag.* XXX. 504 The writ went up to the Lords. **1884** BRIGHT in *Times* 5 Aug. 10/4 When a Bill leaves the House of Commons it has gone up to the House of Lords.

b. Before a judge, magistrate, etc.

c **1440** *York Myst.* xxxvii. 113 Calle vppe Astrotte and A To giffe þer counsaille in þis case. **1440-** [see PUT *v.* 56 i]. **1749-** [see HAVE *v.* 16 b]. **1753** *World* No. 35, I was unfortunately called up to give evidence against him. **1821** SCOTT *Pirate* xlii, Cleveland and Altamont..were brought up the first of the pirate crew. **1825-** [see PULL *v.* 35 d]. **1865-** [see HAUL *v.* 1 d].

c. So as to divulge, reveal, disclose, or let out.

1593 in *Maitl. Cl. Misc.* (1840) I. 59 That [the names of] all excommunicatis..be gevin wp this daye viij dayes. *a* **1625-** [see GIVE *v.* 64 h]. **1826-** [see SHOW *v.* 27 b]. **1880-** [see OWN *v.* 5 c]. **1884** GILMOUR *Mongols* xxiii. 285 If his two companions in accusation would not own up.

d. As a charge or accusation. (Cf. UPBRAID *v.*)

1604- [see CAST *v.* 83 i]. **1611** BIBLE *Numb.* xiv. 36 Bringing vp a slander vpon the land. **1889** *N.W. Linc. Gloss.* (ed. 2) 74 *Bring up against* [a person],..to accuse, to charge with. **1890** [see THROW *v.* 48 h].

13. a. Into the hands or possession of another.

See also DELIVER *v.* 7, GIVE *v.* 64 a, b, RESIGN *v.* 1, YIELD *v.* 10 a, 14 b, 16.

1132 *O.E. Chron.* (Laud MS.), [The king] dide him ȝyuen up ðet abbotrice of Burch. *a* **1225** *Leg. Kath.* 134 Al.. cweðen hire þe meistrie & te menske al up. **13..** *Cursor M.* 10220 (Gött.), All þair giftes þai ȝeld vp þar [*Trin.* Offerede vp her ȝiftes]. *c* **1375** *Ibid.* 15879 (Fairf.), He deliuered his maister vp. *a* **1400-50** *Alexander* 758 Opire recouyre me þi rewme or reche vp þe girdill. *c* **1400** *Brut* cl. 162 Here y resyngn op þe crone..of Engeland into þe Popis Hande. *c* **1440** *Jacob's Well* 302 And so, as tretourys, þei ȝeuyn vp þe castel of god. **1568** GRAFTON *Chron.* II. 46 After the geuyng vp of the sayd Citie. **1588-9** *Act 31 Eliz.* c. 6 §2 For the levinge or resignyng upp of the same. **1604-** [see GIVE *v.* 64 d]. **1613** SHAKS. *Hen. VIII*, II. i. 97 To th' water side I must conduct your Grace: Then giue my Charge vp to Sir Nicholas Vaux. *a* **1690** BP. HOPKINS *Exp. Lord's Prayer* (1692) 47 That his Mediatory Kingdom being fulfilled, it might be delivered up unto the Father. **1713** ATTERBURY *Serm.* (1734) II. 48 Those..who do not surrender themselves up to the Methods it prescribes. **1802** MAR. EDGEWORTH *Moral T.*, *Prussian Vase*, He..yielded himself up a prisoner. **1839** THIRLWALL *Hist. Greece* VI. 281 They were assured that no harm should befal them if they gave up Bessus. **1890** *Spectator* 30 Aug., That rich yield-up of the land that speaks of such abundant future provision.

b. So as to relinquish, abandon, or forsake.

c **1290-** [see YIELD *v.* 14 c]. **1387** TREVISA *Higden* (Rolls) V. 413 Þanne he awook and ȝalde up þe goost. **1388** WYCLIF *Matt.* xxvii. 50 Jhesus eftsoone..ȝaf vp the goost. *c* **1400** *Laud Troy Bk.* 13252 For thi wyff this werre be-gan, We ȝeue it vp here euery a man. **1457** HARDYNG *Chron.* in *Eng. Hist. Rev.* Oct. (1912) 747 Whan enmyse gafe vp pese..As lyon fell he putte hym forth in prese. **1510-** [see GHOST *sb.* 1]. **1530-** [see CAST *v.* 83 h]. **1558-** [see GIVE *v.* 64 b, c, h]. **1596** in *Spalding Club Misc.* I. 88 James Low..said, in his last wordis, befoir he gef wp his braitht [etc.]. **1621-42** [see TURN *v.* 80 p]. **1653** H. MORE *Antid. agst. Ath.* III. ii. (1712) 89 For his unserviceableness he was..turned up loose in the pasture. **1678-** [see THROW *v.* 48 g]. **1885-93** [see THROW *v.* 80 p].

14. Into a receptacle or place of storage, as for security, convenience, or use when required.

See also STORE *v.* 4 b, and for special senses, KNOCK *v.* 18 g, LAY *v.*[1] 60 c-g, PUT *v.* 56, SET *v.*[1] 154 oo.

c **1290** *St. Kenelm* 262 in *S. Eng. Leg.* I. 352 Þis writ was wel nobleliche i-wust and up i-do. **13..** *Coer de L.* 6770 He ..stablede up hys destrers. **1340** *Ayenb.* 232 Þeruore ssel þet tresor by..well y-do op, þet his ne by uorlore. ? *a* **1366** CHAUCER *Rom. Rose* 184 Gret tresouris vp to leyne. *a* **1368-** [see PUT *v.* 56 n, o, p]. *c* **1470** *Golagros & Gaw.* 1123 Thai.. Put up thair brandis sa braid, burly and bair. **1539** CRANMER *Matt.* vi. 19 Laye not vp for your selues treasure vpon earth. **1567** *Gude & Godlie B.* (S.T.S.) 93 Thy gudness and beningnitie..; Thow lay thame vp with me in stoir. **1604** SHAKS. *Oth.* I. ii. 59 Keepe vp your bright Swords, for the dew will rust them. **1629** PARKINSON *Parad.* 470 The flowers of Marigolds,..pickled vp against winter. **1631** GOUGE *God's Arrows* II. §12. 148 God doth sometimes treasure up the sinnes of predecessours. **1692** E. WALKER *Epictetus' Mor.* Praise of Ep. iv, Riches,..Which Knaves hoard up. **1706** PHILLIPS (ed. Kersey), *Rusca Butyri*, a Tub, or Barrel of Butter salted up. **1721** BRADLEY *Philos. Acc. Wks. Nat.* 50 Then they are reckon'd in a right State for Barrelling up for the Markets. **1800-** [see PUT *v.* 56 n (*d*)]. **1867** H. SPENCER *First Princ.* (ed. 2) I. 301 Those highly-compounded nitrogenous molecules in which so much motion is locked up. **1879** H. GEORGE *Progr. & Pov.* I. ii. 36 The heat of the sun is stored up in coal.

ellipt. **1760-72** H. BROOKE *Fool of Qual.* (1809) III. 138 May we not order your horses up [= to be stabled]? You must not think of going.

15. Into one's possession, charge, custody, etc.

See also GET *v.* 80 o, PICK *v.* 21 c, TAKE *v.* 90 d, l.

a **1400-50** *Alexander* 760 Þan set þai þam..a day.., And þar-to tuke vp þaire trouthis. **1479** *Cely Papers* (Camden) 15, I am avysyd to take oppe at London as meche as I schall nede. **1482** *Ibid.* 122 To lette hym [= a horse] ron in a parke tyll Hallowtyd and then take hym wpe. **1659** W. GUTHRIE *Chr. Gt. Interest* viii. (1724) 88 A Man may take up his gracious State by his Faith, and the Acting thereof on Christ. **1674** *Pennsylv. Archives* I. 33 Permission is hereby granted..for to take vp a certaine peice of land for himself and his heires. **1697** PRIOR *Ep. to Sheppard* 21 Now, as you took me up when little, Gave me my Learning, and my Vittle. **1710** STEELE *Tatler* No. 204 ¶6 He has taken up a Resolution. **1711** SWIFT *Jrnl. to Stella* 27 Feb., To get up his debts abroad. **1751** JORTIN *Serm.* (1771) I. iii. 45 His servants..being employed in gathering up the Tares. **1752-3** A. MURPHY *Gray's Inn Jrnl.* No. 21, After having gleaned up all I could..at School. **1802** MAR. EDGEWORTH *Moral T.*, *Forester* xv, One of his boys was taken up amongst the rioters. **1844, 1876** [see GET *v.* 80 t].

16. Into the position or state of being open.

Originally implying the raising of a gate, barrier, etc. For the fig. use of *open up*, see OPEN *v.* 24.

c **1205** LAY. 1704 Vp heo duden heora castels ȝaten. *c* **1300** *K. Horn* 1115 (Laud MS.), Horn gan to þe yate turne, And þe wyket op spurne. **1375** BARBOUR *Bruce* XVII. 778 He.. gert all wyde set vp the ȝet. *c* **1386** CHAUCER *Miller's T.* 615 And vp the wyndowe dide he hastily. *a* **1400-50** *Alexander* (Dublin) 783* Þe wy..Brades vppe þe brade ȝate. *c* **1400** *Gamelyn* 311 Gamelyn ȝede to þe ȝate & lete it vp wide. *c* **1450** *Le Morte Arth.* 1839 The chamber dore he sette vp ryght. **1513** DOUGLAS *Æneid* VII. xi. 32 He that..Thyr ȝettis suld vp oppin and warp wyd. **1523-** [see BREAK *v.* 57 j]. *c* **1600** W. FOWLER *Wks.* (S.T.S.) I. 183 Blist be that houer ..that opned vp the wyndowes to disdayne. **1639** SIR E. VERNEY in *V. Papers* (1853) 233, I have broaken upp my packett againe to insert this letter. **1792** A. WILSON *Watty & Meg* xix, Up the door flew—like a fury In came Watty's scawling wife. **1825** JAMIESON *Suppl.* s.v., Set up the door.

17. a. Into an open or loose condition of surface.

See also BREAK *v.* 57 f, g, CUT *v.* 60 e, DIG *v.* 14 c, PLOUGH *v.* 9 e, RIP *v.*[1] 3, TURN *v.* 80 f.

1377 LANGL. *P. Pl.* B. VI. 109 Dikeres & delueres digged vp þe balkes. *c* **1440** *Pallad. on Husb.* II. 74 The lond vnclene al doluen up mot be. **1577** TUSSER *Husb.* (1878) 83 In January, husband..will break vp his laie. **1588** SHAKS. *Tit. A.* IV. ii. 87 Sooner this sword shall plough thy bowels vp. **1721** STRYPE *Eccl. Mem.* I. xxviii. 197 To endure the more pain when they should be cut down and ripped up. **1799** J. ROBERTSON *Agric. Perth* 247 He directs the moss to be *delved* or dug up with spades. **1801** *Farmer's Mag.* Nov. 484 An Essay..upon the question of breaking up Grass Land. **1894** *Times* 21 May 4/4 A gang of men was sent..to pick up and relay the part. **1895** *Ibid.* 5 Feb. 8/2 That would mean taking up all the streets in South London.

b. So as to sever or separate, esp. into many parts, fragments, or pieces.

See also BREAK *v.* 2 b, 57 a, CHOP *v.*[1] 3, CUT *v.* 60 b. In OE. a similar use occurs in *upp forlætan*, to divide (a river).

14.. *Voc.* in Wr.-Wülcker 563 *Anatene*, up cuttynge. **1530** in Leadam *Star Chamber Cases* (Selden) II. 50 To breke vppe or caste downe eny dyche or hedge. **1573** BARET *Alv.* s.v. *Cut*, Cut vp, or winne these partriges. **1611** SHAKS. *Wint. T.* III. ii. 132 Breake vp the Seales, and read. **1827** FARADAY *Chem. Manip.* ii. (1842) 47 The tube itself being broken up and disregarded. **1849** D. CAMPBELL *Inorg. Chem.* 295 Hydrosulphide of ammonium..dissolves it up. **1857** HUGHES *Tom Brown* I. vii, Engaged in tearing up old newspapers..into small pieces.

18. To or towards a state of completion or finality. (Frequently serving merely to emphasize the import of the verb.)

a. With verbs denoting consuming or destroying.

See also BURN *v.* 8 b, EAT *v.* 18, KILL *v.* 2 b, SLAY *v.* 5 b, SPEND *v.* 13, STIFLE *v.* 1 (quot. 1582).

a **1300** *Cursor M.* 6634 Slas vp yon caitefs al bidene! *c* **1374** CHAUCER *Troylus* v. 1470 She made vp frete here corn. **1390** GOWER *Conf.* I. 81 Thei..brenden up the remenant. *c* **1400** *Sowdone Bab.* 414 Destroye vp bothe man and place. **1481** *Cely Papers* (Camden) 80 Schepe dys [= dies] wpe in Englelonde. **1546** BALE *Eng. Votaries* I. (1560) 7 The murthering vp of them whiche hathe done it. *a* **1555** PHILPOT *Apology*, etc. (1555) B 4 b, Lyke humbledories, eating vp the hony of the bees. **1594** NASHE *Unfort. Trav.* C ij b, I heard where they dyde vp all in one Familie, and not a mothers childe escapde. **1609-10** *Act 7 Jas. I*, c. 20 The Sea hath..surrounded and drowned up much hard groundes. **1636** WINTHROP *Hist. New Eng.* (1825) I. 388 The Indians killed up all their swine, so as Capt. Lovell had none. **1647** VICARS *England's Worthies* (1845) 63 The Royalists resolving..to gird up Gloucester..on all sides to tire and starve it up if it might be. **1793** PELLEW in Osler *Life* (1835) 89 We dished her up in fifty minutes, boarded, and struck her colours. **1803-** [see DO *v.* 52 d, e]. **1872** SPURGEON *Treas. Dav.* Ps. lxxix. 7 The oppressor would quite eat up the saints if he could. **1894** HALL CAINE *Manxman* 419 The spendthrift had..sold up the remainder of his furniture.

b. With other verbs, denoting progress to or towards an end.

1307 *York Memo. Bk.* (Surtees) I. 181 Oute taken girdels that er fully wroght upp. *c* **1400** *Laud Troy Bk.* 14614 Thei ..heled him vp with medycyns. *c* **1407** LYDG. *Reson & Sens.* 2681 She shal performe vp of ryght Al that euer I haue behight. *c* **1440** *Jacob's Well* 207 Tyl þou haue vp full þi cost & þin expensis. **1480** *Cely Papers* (Camden) 48 Y understond Lombardys has bowght ytt [*sc.* the wool] up yn Ynglond. *c* **1540** in J. R. Boyle *Hedon* (1875) App. 67 Yf any ..offycers die..then the common of burgesis to choise other to occupye upe that yeare. **1560** DAUS tr. *Sleidane's Comm.* 298 He will commaunde the fathers..to finish up their work begon. **1601** R. JOHNSON *Kingd. & Commw.* (1603) 114 By husbandry..they dry vp and drain fenny and vnholsome places. **1639** T. DE GRAY *Compl. Horsem.* 322 Therefore heale him up with sweet butter. **1682** DRYDEN *Medal* Ep. Whigs ¶3 Whatever the Verses are, buy 'em up I beseech you. **1726** BERKELEY *Let.* Wks. 1871 IV. 120 It is an infinite shame that the debts are not cleared up and paid. **1771** MRS. HAYWOOD *New Present for Maid* 158 Beat up the yolks of three eggs. **1791** SMEATON *Edystone L.* 121 Lime wetted up in large heaps for use. **1809** MALKIN *Gil Blas* III. ix. ¶1 The establishment was paid up and discharged. **1821** BYRON *Juan* III. lxiii, Cloves..were boil'd Up with the coffee. **1873** *Punch* 18 Jan. 21/1 They liquor up despondently. **1882** MISS BRADDON *Mount Royal* III. 195 Could there not be some kind of institution..to force parents to cash up. **1896** *Pall Mall G.* 19 Aug. 5/1 Prices have subsequently firmed up in many instances.

c. With vbs. denoting cleaning, putting in order, or fixing in place.

See also CLEAN v. 3, CLEAR v. 27 c, DECK v. 2 b, DO v. 52 b, DRESS v. 7 d, FIT v.[1] 6, GET v. 80 l, m, MAKE v. 96 i, POLISH v. 3, REDD v.[2] 6 a, RIG v.[2] 1 b, TACKLE v. 1, 3, TRIM v. 7.

1419–20 *York Memo. Bk.* (Surtees) I. 199 Pro purgacione (*anglice* clensyng uppe) unius centene [arcuum]. *c* **1440** *Pallad. on Husb.* I. 406 Polish al vp thy werk in goodly tyme. **1500–20** DUNBAR *Poems* xliii. 28 Ȝour ladeis grathit vp gay. **1605** CHAPMAN *All Fools* I. i. 73 Spung'd up, adorn'd, and painted. **1706** POPE *Lett.* (1735) 26 To paint your Shop, and ..to brush You up like your Neighbours. **1766** GOLDSM. *Vicar* xi, They can do up small cloaths. **1768** STERNE *Sent. Journ.* (1778) II. 199 The beds..were fixed up..near the fire. **1827** SOUTHEY *Hist. Penins. War* II. 762 The rear-guard of cavalry..remained bridled up all night. **1878** W. S. GILBERT *H.M.S. Pinafore* 1, I polished up the handle of the big front door. **1900** *Daily News* 4 June 2/4 We have cleaned up for the month of May,..760 tons.

19. a. By way of summation or enumeration.

See also CAST v. 83 j, COUNT v. 1 c, MAKE v.[1] 96 j, RECKON v. 1 b, 2 e, RUN v. 81 j (*b*), SUM v. 1 (*b*), TOTAL v. 2.

13.. *E.E. Allit. P.* B. 2 Clannesse who-so kyndly cowþe comende, & rekken vp alle þe resounz þat ho by riȝt askez. *c* **1450** *Bk. Curtasye* 540 in *Babees Bk.*, Tyl countes also þer-on ben cast, And somet vp holy at þo last. **1621** *Stat. Reg.* (Arber) IV. 23 Compendious tables for the speedy casting vp of anie some. **1686** tr. *Chardin's Trav. Persia* 252 Relicks ..among which they number up the Veronique. **1727** THOMSON *To Mem. Newton* 132 But who can number up his labours? **1802** MAR. EDGEWORTH *Moral T., Forester* xiii, Hours..spent in casting up and verifying accounts. **1871** R. H. HUTTON *Ess.* (1877) I. 4 If..you numbered up the acts of trust. **1875** JOWETT *Plato* (ed. 2) I. 130 All my years when added up are many.

b. To a final or total sum or amount.

c **1200** ORMIN 11310 Seofenn siþe sexe gan, Ȝiff þatt tu willt hemm sammnenn, Upp inntill fowwerrtiȝ & twa. **1482** *Monk of Evesham* (Arb.) 49 Y addyd.. as mony dayes..as wold make vppe the noumbre of the dayes of lente. **1583** STUBBES *Anat. Abus.* II. (1882) 32 Promising them..that they shall pay no more rent yeerelie, till the same be runne vp. **1601** SHAKS. *Jul. C.* IV. iii. 208 The Enemy, marching along by them, By them shall make a fuller number vp. **1629** J. COLE *Of Death* 195 His deceased children were alive still in heaven; and the ten more given him here, make them up twenty. *a* **1700** [see RUN v. 81 g]. **1719** [see MAKE v. 96 c *b*]. **1741** in C. F. Jenkins *Tortola* (1923) 86 Next Week we purpose a Monthly Meeting, here being three little Meetings to make it up. **1837–** [see KNOCK v. 18 e]. **1895** *Westm. Gaz.* 9 May 5/3 Hearne..had hit up 8 runs when he lost Wright.

20. a. Into a close or compact form or condition; so as to be confined or secured.

See also BIND v. 6, 11 b, BUNDLE v. 1, 2, COIL v.[3] 3 c, DOUBLE v. 8 (quot. 1893), FOLD v. 1 (quots. 1621, 1712), GATHER v. 16 b, ROLL v.[2] 8 b, SHUT v. 19 f, TIE v. 11 a, TRUSS v. 1, 6.

c **1374** CHAUCER *Troylus* III. 517 There as..al þis heigh matere Towchyng here loue were at þe fulle vp bounde. *c* **1386** —— *Prol.* 681 But hood..wered he noon, For it was trussed vp in his walet. *c* **1475** *Golagros & Gaw.* 224 Thai turssit vp tentis and turnit of toun. **1490** CAXTON *Eneydos* li. 144 He made hys thye to be dressed and bounden vp. **1535** COVERDALE *Song Sol.* vii. 5 The hayre of thy heade is like the kynges purple folden vp in plates. **1590** SHAKS. *Mids. N.* III. i. 206 Tye vp my louers tongue, bring him silently. *c* **1600** —— *Sonn.* xii, Sommers greene all girded vp in sheaues. **1639** T. DE GREY *Compl. Horsem.* (1656) 373 Rope up all his legges to the body, not suffering him to lie down. **1693** *Humours Town* 44 He is fairly trust up according to his deserts. **1802** MAR. EDGEWORTH *Moral T., Forester* viii, Forester..tied up a small bundle of linen. **1825** LAMB *Elia* II. *Wedding*, Visitors huddled up in corners. **1861** O. W. HOLMES *Elsie V.* xxviii, Old Sophy..bound up her long hair for her sleep. **1876** GROSS *Dis. Bladder*, etc. (ed. 3) 21 The limbs are drawn up as in acute enteritis.

b. Into a closed or enclosed state; so as to be shut or restrained.

See also CLOSE v. 21 a, DAM v.[1] 1, 2, 2 b, PEN v.[1] 2, PEND v.[2], PENT *ppl. a.* 1 b, TIE v. 11 b, d.

c **1489–** [see SHUT v. 19 c]. **1528** in Leadam *Star Chamber Cases* (Selden) II. 20 Mulso..hath vnlawfully enclosyd vppe ageyn the sayd comon grownde. **1565–** [see LAY v. 60 d]. **1568** GRAFTON *Chron.* II. 528 The Englishmen that were shut up in the Castel. **1615** W. LAWSON *Country Housew. Gard.* (1626) 12 Take heede of a doore or window ..: yea, though it be nailed vp. **1622** *Reg. Mag. Sig. Scot.* 130/2 The damyng up of the said watter. **1642** *Action before Cyrencester* 4 The streets were barricadoed up with chaines, harrowes and waggons. **1727** THOMSON *Britannia* 244 Her merchants scatter'd wide; Her hollow shops shut up. **1769** MRS. RAFFALD *Eng. Housekpr.* (1778) 323 Mix them all exceedingly well in your cask, close it well up.

c. So as to cover or envelop. Also in fig. context.

13.. *E.E. Allit. P.* A. 434 Knelande to grounde [ho] folde vp hyr face. **1577** HARRISON *England* III. i. (1877) II. 11 Ech peece [of the boar] is wrapped vp..with bulrushes. **1589** [? LYLY] *Pap w. Hatchet* B 4 b, Hee woulde not smoother vp sinne. **1593–** [see FOLD v. 8]. **1602–** [see ROLL v.[2] 9 b]. **1719** DE FOE *Crusoe* I. (Globe) 56, I..wrapt it up Parcel by Parcel in Pieces of the Sails. **1792** *Munchhausen's Trav.* x. 34 The sentinels were wrapped up in the arms of Morpheus. **1837** P. KEITH *Bot. Lex.* 151 If the wound is covered closely up. **1872–** [see COVER v. 22].

21. a. Into a state of union, conjunction, or combination; so as to bring together.

See also GET v. 80 o, MAKE v. 96 f *e*.

c **1450** LOVELICH *Merlin* 6117 Thus thanne was knyt vpe the pes. **1553–** [see GATHER v. 16 b, c, d]. **1577** HOLINSHED *Chron.* I. *Descr. Irel.* 7/2 How sagely Ireneus claspeth vp all the whole controuersie. **1599** SHAKS. *Hen. V*, IV. Prol. 13 With busie Hammers closing Riuets vp. **1627** EARL OF MANCHESTER in *Buccleuch MSS.* (Hist. MSS. Comm.) I. 267 Therefore the remain [of the loan] must needs be got up, which is not past 50,000 *l.* **1638** R. BAKER tr. *Balzac's Lett.* (vol. II) 19 If yours were not bound up in one volume with them. **1693** *Humours Town* 16 Those wretched Compounds which make up all your Lives. **1724** WATTS *Logic* II. ii. §6 A Compound Proposition is made up of two or more Subjects. **1759** STERNE *Tr. Shandy* I. x, That he could draw up..a hole in his breeches. **1820** BYRON *Mar. Fal.* III. i. 43 Your fame, your name, all mingled up in mine. **1846** CARPENTER *Man. Phys.* 8 These substances..being made up of three or four elements. **1869** MRS. WHITNEY *We Girls* v. (1874) 101 She could only stitch up a straight slant.

b. So as to supply deficiencies, defects, etc.

a **1568–** [see MAKE v. 96 c *a*]. **1586–** [see PIECE v. 8]. **1589** PUTTENHAM *Eng. Poesie* II. xii. (Arb.) 128 A sillable ouerplus to annexe to the word precedent to helpe peece vp another foote. **1596–** [see FILL v. 17]. **1605** B. JONSON *Volpone* III. vi, My dwarf shall dance, My eunuch sing, my fool make up the antic. **1755** JOHNSON, To *Supply*, to fill up as any deficiencies happen. **1774–** [see PATCH v. 1].

22. a. To or towards a person or place; so as to approach or arrive.

1362– [see COME v. 74 b]. *c* **1420** *Anturs of Arth.* 345 Ho raykes vp..bifor þe rialle, And halsed sir Arthur. **1599** HAKLUYT *Voy.* II. 287 Vp comes toward them the other frigat. **1607** SHAKS. *Cor.* I. ii. 29 If they set downe before 's: for the remoue Bring vp your Army. **1659–** [see GET v. 80 c]. **1669** in *Buccleuch MSS.* (Hist. MSS. Comm.) I. 429 He rid up to meet him. **1719** DE FOE *Crusoe* I. (Globe) 298 We all mended our Pace, and rid up as fast as the Way..would give us leave. **1730** THOMSON *Autumn* 439 Hot-steaming, up behind him comes again Th' inhuman rout. **1780** *Mirror* No. 108, The train of Sir Edward brought up their master in the condition I have described. **1797** COLERIDGE *Christabel* I. 22 The Spring comes slowly up this way. **1841** DICKENS *Barn. Rudge* lix, She thought..how he would have rode boldly up, and dashed in among these villains. **1878** T. HARDY *Ret. Native* IV. iii, Leave me before they come up.

b. To or towards a particular point or line.

1513 DOUGLAS *Æneid* XI. xvi. 58 [She] hir hornit bow has bent, Quharin onon the takyll vp is stent; Syne halis vp in ire and felloun haist. **1605–** [see DRAW v. 89 f]. **1864–** [see LINE v. 8 b]. **1865** BUSHNELL *Vicar. Sacr.* Introd. 16 As if He [*sc.* Christ] were engaged to even up the score of penalty. **1901** *Munsey's Mag.* XXV. 371/1 To even up my account with his people.

c. To or into later life.

1535 COVERDALE *Luke* xviii. 21 All these haue I kepte fro my youth vp. **1596** DALRYMPLE tr. *Leslie's Hist. Scot.* (S.T.S.) I. 235 Frome his barneheid vpp, he was brocht vpp be S. Columba. *c* **1800** WORDSW. *Excurs.* I. 53 We were tried Friends: I from my Childhood up Had known him. **1890** *Review of Rev.* II. 427/2 It has been so from his youth up.

d. So as to find, come upon, overtake, or keep on the track of. (Cf. LOOK v. 45 g–j.)

a **1622–** [see FETCH v. 21 g]. **1657–** [see RUN v. 81 h]. **1791** W. BARTRAM *Carolina* 488 They enter..with a view of.. hunting up the sturdy bear. **1794–** [see FOLLOW v. 22]. **1817** J. BRADBURY *Trav.* 265 It sometimes happens that he is two days in 'hunting them [*sc.* stray hogs] up'. **1868** *Field* 18 July 49/1 Failing to get quite up, [he] was beaten cleverly by three parts of a length. **1879** F. POLLOK *Sport Brit. Burmah* II. 204, I..hit off the tracks of a large herd of bison and followed them up.

23. To a stop or halt.

See also BRING v. 27 f, g, DRAW v. 89 e, FETCH v. 21 i, PULL v. 35 d, f.

1623 in Birch *Crt. & Times Jas. I* (1848) II. 392 A man, thinking nothing, pulled up his coach, and so made the horse start a little. **1769** FALCONER *Dict. Marine* (1780), *To Bring-up*, a provincial phrase peculiar to the seamen in the coal-trade, signifying to anchor, &c. **1857** LD. DUFFERIN *Lett. High Lat.* (ed. 3) 14 At Kylakin we were obliged to bring up for the night. **1891** C. ROBERTS *Adrift Amer.* 214 When the river is foggy, the boats have to bring up at night. **1902** *Westm. Gaz.* 26 May 7/3 If all goes well it should fetch up at Sheerness..to-morrow morning.

III. With a preposition following.

24. up against ——. *to knock* or *run up against*, to come across, to fall in with.

1886 *Pall Mall G.* 4 Aug. 3/1 Our extradition treaty with the United States has run up against its first snag. **1886** [see RUN v. 61 b]. **1887–** [see KNOCK v. 18 a].

25. up till ——. = *up to* (in various senses).

c **1200** ORMIN 1281 Ȝiff þatt tu forrlangedd arrt To cumenn upp till Criste. *Ibid.* 11318. *c* **1250** *Gen. & Ex.* 1606 Iacob..slep and saȝ,..fro ðe erðe up til heuene bem, A leddre stonden. **1599** SHAKS. *Pass. Pil.* 382 She, poor bird, as all forlorn, Lean'd her breast up-till a thorn.

1845 R. BUCHANAN in Howie *Scots Worthies* p. xix, Up till that time they had still continued to attend public worship. **1886** *Manch. Exam.* 13 Jan. 4/7 Up till now Greece has altogether disregarded the..admonitions.

26. up to ——. a. (*a*) As high or as far as (a specified height or altitude) by ascent or extension.

944 *Charter* in Sweet *A.S. Reader* (1908) 58 Andlang dic to ðam weȝe þe scytt up to ðam hricgge. *c* **1000** ÆLFRIC *Saints' Lives* xxvi. 183 Heofonlic leoht ofer þæt ȝeteld astreht stod up to heofonum. *a* **1122** *O.E. Chron.* (Laud MS.) an. 1070, Hi..clumben upp to þe stepel. *c* **1200** *Vices & Virtues* 119 He..bar up to heuene ure loac. *a* **1300** *Cursor M.* 22569 (Edinb.), Op to þe lift ris sal þe se. **13..** *Coer de L.* 4171 The pytte..was feld and fordytte, Up to the bank maad al playn. **1390** GOWER *Conf.* I. 137 A tree..Whos heihte straghte up to the hevene. *Ibid.* 273 He styh up to his fader. *c* **1430** HOCCLEVE *New Ploughman's T.* 114 Shee vp to heuene ascendid up and sty. *c* **1450** *Merlin* i. 15 So it was cristened Merlyn, and was delyuered to the women vpe to the wyndowe to the moder. **1526** TINDALE *John* iii. 13 Noo man hath ascended vppe to heven, butt he that cam doune from heven. *a* **1586** SIDNEY *De Mornay* i. ¶5 Like as from the Earth wee have styed up too the Ayre. **1623** GOUGE *Serm. God's Provid.* §15 A partition..which reached up to the floore of the garret. **1667** MILTON *P.L.* v. 198 Ye Birds, That singing up to Heaven Gate ascend. **1684** BUNYAN *Pilgr.* II. (1900) 173 Let the most blessed be my guide..Up to his Holy Hill. **1799** G. S. CAREY *Balnea* (ed. 2) 178 Whatever way you approach Ludlow, you find an ascent up to the market-place. **1842** LOUDON *Suburban Hort.* 491 When the cuttings get up to the glass,..the outer pot can be changed. **1850** ROSSETTI *Blessed Damozel* vii, The souls, mounting up to God.

(*b*) As high or as far as (a certain part of the body, containing vessel, penetrating weapon, etc.).

For the figurative import of the phrases *up to the ears*, etc., see the sbs. Other figurative phrases denoting completeness or fullness are illustrated under HUB[1] a, KNOCKER 2 c, NINE *sb.* 6 b, NOTCH *sb.* 1 b.

c **950** *Lindisf. Gosp.* John ii. 7 Ðefyldon ða ilca uið to briorde up. *c* **1175** *Lambeth Hom.* 47 Ieremie þe prophete stod..in þe uenne up to his muðe. *a* **1250** *Owl & Night.* 96 Hi fuleþ hit vp to þe chynne. *c* **1305** *Land Cokayne* 181 He mot wade..up to þe chynne So he schal þe londe winne. **13..** *Gaw. & Gr. Knt.* 1594 For þe mon..Hit hym vp to þe hult. *c* **1386** CHAUCER *Knt.'s T.* 802 Vp to the Anclee foghte they in hir blood. **1388** WYCLIF *John* ii. 7 Fille ȝe the pottis with watir. And thei filliden hem, vp to the mouth. *c* **1450** *St. Cuthbert* 1641 With in þe se Vp to þe nek naked stode he. **1470–85** MALORY *Arthur* I. xvii. 61 Her horses went in blood vp to the fytlokys. *a* **1553** [see EAR *sb.*[1] 1 c]. **1590** W. WEBBE *Trav.* (Arb.) 32 She might haue gone vp to the mid leg in.. mire. **1599** [see HILT *sb.* 1 b]. **1601** SHAKS. *Jul. C.* III. i. 107 Let vs bathe our hands in Cæsars blood Vp to the Elbowes. **1607** DEKKER & MARSTON *Northw. Hoe* IV. ii, Weele draw all our arrowes of reuenge vp to the head. **1616** [see CHIN *sb.*[1] 1 d]. **1648** HEXHAM II, *Tot den Hecht toe*, up to the Haft. **1662** J. DAVIES tr. *Mandelslo's Trav.* 64 They go bare-breasted, and bare-arm'd up to the Elbows. **1687–** [see HILT *sb.* 3]. **1790** BRUCE *Source of Nile* I. v, The girls..stand up to their knees in the water for a considerable time. **1808** ANDREW SCOTT *Poems* (ed. 2) 101 Up to the haft at ilka stroke Some clash their hooks. **1825** COBBETT *Rur. Rides* (1830) I. 67 With white aprons and bibs..going from the apron up to the bosom. **1883** A. ROBSON *Dead Letter* II. v, Up to our Elbows making Damson Jam. **1884–9** [see EYE *sb.*[1] 2 e].

(*c*) Raised or short so as to leave uncovered.

1835 LADY DUFFERIN *Charming Woman* 22 Her shoulders are rather too bare, And her gown's nearly up to her knees. **1868** LOUISA M. ALCOTT *Little Women* iv, Sometimes she is so bad, her frock is up to her knees.

b. Up towards; aloft in the direction of.

c **900** tr. *Baeda's Hist.* I. vii. (1890) 38 Albanus..his eaȝan ahof upp to heofonum. **971** *Blickl. Hom.* 227 He..mid his eaȝum up to heofenum locade. *c* **1000** ÆLFRIC *Gen.* iv. 10 Þines broðor blod clypað up to me of eorðan. *c* **1220** *Bestiary* 187 Deme ðe noȝt wurdi, ðat tu dure loken up to ðe heuene-ward. **1297** R. GLOUC. (Rolls) 9342 Ȝoure riȝt honden holdeþ vp to god. *c* **1375** *Sc. Leg. Saints* v. (*John*) 566 Hevand his handis vpe to þe hevyn. *a* **1425** *Cursor M.* 19468 (Trin.), Vp to heuen he helde his honde. *a* **1626–** [see LOOK v. 45 d]. **1719** WATTS *Ps.* cxxi. 1 Up to the hills I lift mine eyes. **1845** BAILEY *Festus* (ed. 2) 171 Oh! my heart was lift to thee Like a glass up to a star. **1852** MRS. STOWE *Uncle Tom* xxvii, But oh, if mas'r could only look up..—up to the dear Lord Jesus!

c. (*a*) So as to reach or arrive at (a particular place or person).

The precise force of *up* varies in accordance with sense 6.

(*a*) **1516** in E. Lodge *Illustr. Brit. Hist.* (1791) I. 15 If I shulde com up to London the next terme. **1518** in Leadam *Star Chamber Cases* (Selden) II. 150 Oder evill disposed persones..ben commyn vp to hym to maynteyn hym. **1592** *Arden of Feversham* I. i. 531, Ile vp to London straight. **1695** WOODWARD *Nat. Hist. Earth* I. (1723) 41 When I first brought my Collection of these Things up to London. **1774** ABIGAIL ADAMS in *Fam. Lett.* (1876) 48 Mr. Hill's father had some thoughts of removing up to Braintree. **1810** in Milner *Suppl. Mem. Eng. Cath.* (1820) 153 To wait..until Bishop Gibson should come up to town. **1821** J. H. NEWMAN *Lett.* (1891) I. 56 Coming up to Oxford to study. **1889** 'J. S. WINTER' *Mrs. Bob* xxvi, In time to catch the next train up to Town.

(*b*) **1555** R. THOMSON in *Hakluyt's Voy.* (1600) III. 448 Wee did vnbarke our selues and went on land vp to the citie or head towne. **1599** NASHE *Lenten Stuffe* D j, The three riuers that vagary vp to her. **1659–** [see GET v. 80 c]. **1684** BUNYAN *Pilgr.* II. (1900) 173 When Christina came up to the Slough of Dispond. **1694** *Lond. Gaz.* No. 3023/1 He.. could not get up again to the Fleet. **1709** *Tatler* No. 114 ¶1 When he came up to me, he took me by the Hand. **1726** SWIFT *Gulliver* I. viii, I was forced to swim till I got up to it [*sc.* the boat]. **1806** A. DUNCAN *Nelson* 46 He could not get the bomb vessels up to the point of attack. **1823** SOUTHEY *Hist. Penins. War* I. 171 A carriage with six mules drew up to the guard-house. **1888** F. HUME *Mme. Midas* I. xii, They will never catch up to that horse.

(*b*) As far as (a specified point).

1832 L. HUNT *Poems* 193 With green up to the door. **1865** EARLE *Sax. Chron.* p. xiii, Back into the mists of high mythology,..and so up to Adam. **1875** *Encycl. Brit.* III. 637/1 Up to the book of Joshua all three [narratives] run side by side. **1881** *Phil. Trans.* CLXXIII. 483 The rostrum is very uniform up to near the front end.

(*c*) Till, until (a specified time).

In frequent use from *c* 1835. Cf. UP-TO-DATE.

1803 M. VENZEE *Fate* 187 Up to the present time. **1834–6** *Encycl. Metrop.* (1845) VIII. 415/2 Up to 1750, he had made about two hundred tons [of zinc]. **1849** ROCK *Ch. of Fathers* I. ii. 125 Up to the present day is still kept..this very rubric. **1864** LEWINS *H. M. Mails* 311 Government letters..may be posted, without extra fee, up to the latest moment. **1891** MEREDITH *One of our Conq.* xxvi, A comprehensible pride.. keeps the forsaken man silent up to death.

ellipt. **1851** MRS. BROWNING *Casa Guidi Wind.* I. 993 By councils,—from Nicaea up to Trent.

(*d*) *colloq.* Before (one's face).

1862 TROLLOPE *Orley F.* II. 111 She told me so, up to my face.

(*e*) As a task or responsibility upon (a person). Cf. UP *adv.*[2] 19 d.

1908 'FRANK DANBY' *Heart of Child* xviii, We'll let them know what is going on, and put it up to them to take action.

d. (*a*) So as to reach or attain (a specified point or stage) by action directed to an end.

See also ACT v. 9 e, COME v. 74 h, KEEP v. 57 i, LIVE v.[1] 4 f.

1611 SHAKS. *Wint. T.* IV. iv. 544 Your discontenting Father striue to qualifie And bring him vp to liking. **1629** EARLE *Microcosm.* (Arb.) 81 A verse or some such worke he may sometimes get vp to, but seldome aboue the stature of an Epigram. **1688** DRYDEN tr. *Life Xavier* I. 10 To Exhort them to live up to the Rules of Christianity. **1748** *Biog. Brit.* II. 1305 He was not unacquainted with the antient rules of Poetry, nor was he incapable of writing up to them. **1751** F. COVENTRY *Pompey the Little* II. v. 166 A Country Gentleman, who had lived, as it is called, up to his Income. **1827** FARADAY *Chem. Manip.* iv. (1842) 128 Boiling at different temperatures will, of course, communicate heat up to their boiling points. **1834** J. H. NEWMAN *Par. Serm.* (1837) I. xx. 313 Such men do not practise up to their knowledge. **1855** *Poultry Chron.* II. 538/2 Without it amateurs scarcely know what points to breed up to. **1908** *Animal Managem.* 69 Where horses are called on to work up to their rations.

(*b*) So as to reach by progression or gradual rise.

17.. RAMSAY *Birth of Drumlanrig* vii, Your Prince, who late Up to the state of manhood run. **1772** *Regul. H.M. Service at Sea* 5 The youngest Officer shall vote first, proceeding in Order up to the President. **1793** JEFFERSON *Writ.* (1830) IV. 482 Money being so flush, the six per cents run up to twenty-one and twenty-two shillings.

(*c*) As many or as much as; including all below (a specified number, etc.).

1892 *Photogr. Ann.* II. p. cl, The sizes..up to and including 9 inches focus. **1910** T. A. JOYCE *Handbk. Ethnogr. Coll. Brit. Mus.* 259 Good canoes..carrying up to thirty-six men.

e. Bridge. *to lead up to*: to lead in a manner which allows (a particular card or suit) to be played from the third or fourth hand. Also after the sb.

1911 L. LEIGH *Blue Bk. Bridge & Auction* iii. 97 In a trump deal, if the lead has been a low card the suit cannot be more than moderately strong, and the third hand..may lead up to a weak holding in Dummy's hand. **1927** L. HATTERSLEY *Auction & Contract Bridge Clarified* xxv. 251 The Queen should *never* be led up to the Ace with the vain idea of making a finesse. **1950** G. S. COFFIN *Learn Bridge* iv. 26 He must lead a ◇ away from his king up to dummy's ace-queen. **1964** R. L. FREY *Official Encycl. Bridge* 655/2 The old maxim recommending a lead 'up to weakness' is valid but not very helpful. **1973** REESE & DORMER *Compl. Bk. Bridge* xvii. 223 He leads up to and not away from dummy's high cards.

27. up until——. = *up to*——, sense 26 c (*c*). Cf. *up till*——, sense 25.

1938 *Tablet* 28 May 698/2 Up until the time when *Mit Brennender Sorge* and the associated Encyclicals appeared, there was indeed some reason for believing that the idea of Catholic Action was to be interpreted more or less in such a manner. **1971** *Sci. Amer.* Oct. 118/3 Up until the past few years all the pictures we saw of that world..seemed less photographic, for all their authenticity, than maplike.

28. up with ——. (Cf. 32.) **a.** So as to reach.

1659 *Nicholas Papers* (Camden) IV. 95, 3 Spanish men of warre..who..came vp with vs and fired at vs. **1678-** [see COME *v.* 74 c]. **1719** DE FOE *Crusoe* I. (Globe) 17 Finding the Pirate..would certainly come up with us in a few Hours, we prepar'd to fight. **1761** *Ann. Reg., Chron.* 156/2 At five A.M. we got almost up with the chace. **1795** NELSON in Nicolas *Disp.* (1845) II. 13 As he drew up with the Enemy. **1795** *Ann. Reg.* I. 15 The Russians..came up with his rear.

b. ***to put up with***: see PUT *v.*[1] 56 p (*b*).

c. *to draw* or *take up with*: see DRAW *v.* 89 i, TAKE *v.* 90 z.

IV. In elliptic uses.

29. a. Used imperatively (with ellipse of verb), as a command or exhortation to action, activity, rising from bed, movement, etc. Cf. UP *v.* 4.

a **1300** *Cursor M.* 2819 Vp loth,..þat ȝee ne be tint wit þis cite. **1535** COVERDALE *Judges* iv. 4 Debbora sayde vnto Barak: Vp, this is the daie wherin [etc.]. **1579** SPENSER *Sheph. Cal.* Nov. 47 Then vp I say,..Let not my small demaund be so contempt. **1595** SHAKS. *John* II. i. 295 Vp higher to the plaine, where we'll set forth In best appointment all our Regiments. **1612** DRAYTON *Poly-olb.* iii. 1 Up with the jocund lark (too long we take our rest). **1617** HIERON *Wks.* II. 315 Dauid..was the first which said, 'Vp, let vs flie!' **1625** SANDERSON *Serm.* I. 131 Up then with the zeal of Phinehas, up for the love of God and of His people. **1669** STURMY *Mariner's Mag.* I. ii. 18 Up alaft [*sic*] to the Top-mast-head, and look abroad. **1733** W. ELLIS *Chiltern & Vale Farm.* 5 These with the Thistles, and many others when they get the Dominion, is, up Weed and down Corn. **1798** WORDSW. *Tables Turned* 3 Up! up! my Friend, and quit your books;..Up! up! **1816** SCOTT *Paul's Lett.* 181 'Up, Guards, and at them,' cried the Duke of Wellington. **1827** KEBLE *Chr. Y., Advent Sunday* ii, Awake!..Up from your beds of sloth for shame.

b. With auxiliary or other verbs: To go or come up; to rise. Also rarely without verb.

An OE. instance occurs in *Genesis* 497.

1535 COVERDALE *Ps.* xi[i]. 6, I wil vp (sayeth the Lorde). **1590** SHAKS. *Mids. N.* IV. i. 114 We will..vp to the Mountaines top. *c* **1630** SANDERSON *Serm.* II. 280 He would up therefore to a higher..Judge; and that was the Lord. **1637** R. ASHLEY tr. *Malvezzi's David Persecuted* 205 The great favorites of Princes..fall headlong, they are gone, they cannot up againe. **1647** N. BACON *Disc. Govt. Eng.* I. lix. 184 Perceiving that the Kings spirit would up againe. **1678** LUTTRELL *Brief Rel.* (1857) I. 2 On the 9th the king came.. and sent for the house of commons up. **1727** SWIFT *Imit. Hor.* Wks. 1755 III. II. 48 Lewis, the dean will be of use; Send for him up, take no excuse. **1816** MUIR *Minstrelsy* 27 (E.D.D.), Up they till't like twa game cocks.

30. Followed by a noun in objective relationship to a verb omitted (e.g. *hold, raise, pull*, etc.). Orig. only with imperative force; now freq. in other uses and tending to assume the function of a verb. (Cf. UP *v.* 3–4.)

c **1384** CHAUCER *H. Fame* II. 1021 Now vp the hede for alle ys wele. **1628** RUTHERFORD *Lett.* (1664) 425 Courage, up your heart. *a* **1751** in A. Whitelaw *Bk. Sc. Song* (1866) 29 She rants up some fule-sang, like, Up your heart, Charlie! **1823** SCOTT *Quentin D.* xxii, Up heart, master, or we are but gone men. **1828** COL. HAWKER *Diary* (1893) I. 343, I 'up gun' and down came a bird. **1853** KANE *Grinnell Exped.* xxx. (1856) 264 When the weather is very cold, I up hood. **1854** F. W. MANT *Midshipman* 88 So that I am free to up stick and away. **1891** KIPLING *Light that Failed* viii, He wants to up-stakes and move out.

Naut. **1829** MARRYAT *F. Mildmay* xxiii, We agreed to up helm. **1832** —— *N. Forster* x, As soon as the jolly-boat comes on board we'll up anchor. **1834** —— *P. Simple* III. 286 She up courses and took in her topgallant sails. **1840**, **1859** [see HELM *sb.*[2] 1 c]. **1859** BARTLETT *Dict. Amer.* (ed. 2), *To up jib*, to be off. A sailor's phrase. **1867** SMYTH *Sailor's Word-bk.* 707–8 Up anchor... Up boats!.. Up courses!.. Up screw! **1893** MCCARTHY in *Westm. Gaz.* 9 March 5/1 That moment he and his companions would up steam and make for the shores of Gloria.

31. *ellipt.* for *up with*— (sense 32 e). *colloq.*

1937 S. BECKETT in A. Chisholm *Nancy Cunard* (1979) xxiii. 241 Up the Republic! *a* **1966** 'M. NA GOPALEEN' *Best of Myles* (1968) 330 'Up the Prince of Wales' or something, I suppose. **1980** M. MCMULLEN *My Cousin Death* (1981) xi. 131 Conor's taken him off... Up Conor, I say.

32. up with (also †**mid**) **—.** (Cf. 28.)

a. Denoting the raising of a weapon, the hand, etc., esp. so as to strike. (Cf. UP *v.* 8 b.)

c **1275** LAY. 23931 Arthur vp mid his spere..and pungde vppen Frolle. **1387** TREVISA *Higden* (Rolls) IV. 355 Judas.. up wiþ a stoon and smoot Ruben on þe hede. *c* **1400** *Gamelyn* 535 Gamelyn vp with his staff..And girt him in þe nek. *c* **1450** *Knt. de la Tour* xix. 27 Her husbonde up with his fust, and gaue her .ij. or .iij. gret strokes. **1584** in *Cath. Rec. Soc. Publ.* V. 82 The Earle..up with his fiste and gave the poore man a great blowe upon the face. **1610** HEALEY *St. Aug. Citie of God* XVIII. xiv. 688 Hercules..one time vp with his harpe and knockt out his maisters braynes. **1689** HICKERINGILL *Ceremony-Monger* Concl. iii, He up with his foot, and kick't it off from the King's Head. **1704** SWIFT *T. Tub* xi, He would down with his knees, up with his eyes, and fall to prayers. **1885** STEVENSON *Pr. Otto* I. ii, Otto..up with his whip and thrashed him. **1893** *Daily Tel.* 17 July 6/4 She 'up with her fist'.

b. Denoting erecting, raising, drawing or pulling up, etc. Chiefly in imperative use. Also ***up with you!*** = rise, get up.

c **1377** in *Minor Poems Vernon MS.* 718/99, I ou rede..þat vch a Mon vp wiþ þe hede, And mayntene him boþe heiȝe and lowe. *c* **1460** *Towneley Myst.* xxiii. 215 Vp with the tymbre [= cross]. **1594** SHAKS. *Rich. III*, V. iii. 7 Vp with my Tent, heere wil I lye to night! *a* **1596** *Sir T. More* II. iii. 24 Vpp with the drawbridge, gather som forces To Cornhill. **1645** J. FARY *Gods Severity* 26 Can it..be endured that a tree should stand, yeelding no increase?.. No, the good husband-man will up with it. **1816** BYRON *Siege of Cor.* xxii, Alla Hu! Up to the skies with that wild halloo! **1857** HUGHES *Tom Brown* I. vi, 'Let's toss two of them together.'.. 'Up with another one.' **1863** A. YOUNG *Naut. Dict.* (ed. 2) 432 Up with the helm.

(*b*) **1809** MALKIN *Gil Blas* VI. i. ¶9 Up with you! up with you! was the alarum of..Ambrose. **1846** MRS. A. MARSH *Father Darcy* II. iii. 81 Up, up, with you, my master, and it please you.

c. To drink off, consume.

1542 UDALL *Erasm. Apoph.* 30 He demaunded, how that medeicine was to bee taken?.. The seruaunte had aunswered, that he must vp with it all at a draught.

d. To 'come out' with, to utter or sing (something).

1594 NASHE *Unfort. Trav.* A 3 b, He bad me declare my minde... I vp with a long circumstaunce..and discourst vnto him what [etc.]. **1688** R. L'ESTRANGE *Erasm. Colloq.* 190 Then Fawn up with his story, and tells him [etc.]. **1766** GOLDSM. *Vicar* xvii, 'He has taught that song to our Dick.' ..'Then let us have it:..let him up with it boldly.'

e. Denoting support or advocacy of a person or thing. † *to be up with*, to commend, praise, laud, extol. *Obs.*

1592 NASHE *P. Pennilesse* D i, They..run their words at random,..and are vppe with this man and that man. **1599** —— *Lenten Stuffe* D 4 b, One is vp with the excellence of the browne bill and the long bowe: another [etc.]. **1643** TRAPP *Comm. Gen.* xxxi. 44 Laban likewise talks a great deal here; and is up with the more, and down with the less, (as they say). *a* **1792** in *Statist. Acc. Scotl.* II. 436 That song, 'Up with the souters of Selkirk, and down with the Earl of Hume'. **1815** SCOTT *Guy M.* vi, After some clubs had drunk Up with this statesman, and others Down with him.

Comb. **1902** G. K. MENZIES *Prov. Sk.* 105 A 'down-with-the-Lords' young man, An up-with-myself young man.

33. a. up and —, denoting the act of rising or starting up, accompanied by subsequent action.

13.. *Sir Orfeo* 96 (A.), Ac euer sche held in o cri, And wold vp and owy. *c* **1374** CHAUCER *Troylus* III. 548 Pandare vp and..straught a morwe vn-to his nece wente. **1542** UDALL *Erasm. Apoph.* 180 b, Achilles..vp and gaue hym suche a cuff on the eare, that he slewe hym. **1682** BUNYAN *Holy War* 240 At the sound of their feet he would up and run, and meet them half way. **1838** DICKENS *O. Twist* xxxi, Why didn't you up, and collar him? **1894** ASTLEY *50 Years Life* II. 258 Refreshed, I up and plod on again.

b. With verbs of speaking or saying, implying a sudden or open declaration.

1548 UDALL, etc. *Erasm. Par. Luke* xxiv. 13–24 Thei..vp & declare at large vnto Jesus the summe of al yᵉ wholle matier. **1562** T. WILSON *Rhet.* (ed. 2) 79 The Italian vp and tolde him all. **1611** MIDDLETON & DEKKER *Roaring Girle* I 1, He forswore all, I vp and opened all. *a* **1639** W. WHATELEY *Prototypes* II. xxxi. (1640) 111 For the man..up and told them all that had fallen out. **1702** W. J. tr. *Bruyn's Voy. Levant* xlvi. 181 Whereupon she up and told him all that had passed between them. **1836–7** DICKENS *Sk. Boz, Mr. W. Tottle* ii, He seed her several times, and then he up and said he'd keep company with her. **1880** MRS. R. O'REILLY *Sussex Stories* I. 279 She'll up and speak to the gentry themselves. **1891** 'R. BOLDREWOOD' *Sydney-side Sax.* Introd., I wonder what he would say if I up and asked him for Miss Cissie.

up (ʌp), *adv.*[2] Forms: 1–6 uppe, 3–6 vppe (5 wppe), 3 *Orm.*, 5 upp (7 vpp), 6– up (7 upe, vpe); 4 ope, oppe, 4–5, 9 *dial.* op. [OE. *uppe*, = OFris. *uppa* (*oppa*, *opa*), OS. *uppa*, MDu. *oppe* (*uppe*), ON. *uppe*, *uppi* (Icel. *uppi*, Norw. and Sw. *uppe*, Da. *oppe*), f. *upp* UP *adv.*[1]

Also in part representing OE. *up*, *upp* UP *adv.*[1], which is occasionally used in place of *uppe*.]

I. In senses denoting position in space.

1. a. At some distance above the ground or earth; high in the air; on high; aloft.

c **897** K. ÆLFRED *Gregory's Past C.* xvi. 101 He ȝeseah ane hlædre standan æt him on eorðan. Oðer ende wæs uppe on hefenum. **975** *O.E. Chron.* (Parker MS.), And þa wearð ætywed uppe on roderum steorra on staðole. *c* **1000** *Ags. Ps.* (Thorpe) cxiii. 11 Ys ure se halȝa God on heofon-dreame, uppe mid englum. *c* **1200** ORMIN Ded. 259 Sannt Johan.. sahh upp inn heffne an boc. *c* **1300** *K. Horn* 1171 (Laud MS.), Ayol was op in toure. *c* **1375** *Cursor M.* 3148 (Fairf.), Vp hey a-pon ȝone felle sal þou bren þi sone for me. **1593** SHAKS. *Rich. II*, V. v. 112 Mount, mount, my soule, thy seate is vp on high. **1603** —— *Meas. for M.* II. ii. 152 True prayers, That shall be vp at heauen, and enter there Ere Sunne rise. **1634** J. LEVETT *Ordering of Bees* 23 The ringing of basons,.. which I haue often heard when a swarme is up, or in rising. **1788** DIBDIN *Poor Jack* ii, There's a sweet little cherub that sits up aloft, To keep watch for the life of poor Jack. **1815** SCOTT *Guy M.* v, A flag that's up yonder in the garret. **1842** TENNYSON *Lady Clare* i, The time when..clouds are highest up in air.

b. Of the heavenly bodies: Risen above the horizon; ascended into the sky.

a **1000** in *Narrat. Angl. Conscr.* (1861) 29 Næs se mona þa ȝyt uppe. *c* **1000** *Sax. Leechd.* III. 272 On winterlicre tide hi [*sc.* the Pleiades] beoð on niht uppe & on dæȝ adune. *c* **1380** WYCLIF *Sel. Wks.* II. 222 Sunne of riȝtwisnesse is uppe. **1481** CAXTON *Godfrey* lxxii. 116 In the morne whan the sonne was vp. **1526** TINDALE *Matt.* xiii. 6 When the sun was vppe hitt..wyddred awaye. **1599** *Broughton's Let.* v. 15 If the Sunne were vp..he was punished. **1650** B. *Discolliminium* 32 If the Sun be down though the Stars be up. **1719** DE FOE *Crusoe* II. (Globe) 494 Tho' the Moon was up. **1728** CHAMBERS *Cycl.* s.v. *Honey* ¶5 The Bees only gather it after the Sun is up. **1812** BYRON *Ch. Har.* II. xxi, The moon is up; by Heaven, a lovely eve! **1844** WILLIS *Contempl.* 1 They are all up—the innumerable stars.

transf. **1595** SHAKS. *John* V. v. 21 The day shall not be vp so soone as I.

2. On high or (more) elevated ground; more inland; further from the coast or sea.

In OE. also 'on shore; on land; inland'. Cf. UPALAND, UPONLAND.

Beowulf 566 Hie..on merȝenne..be yðlafe uppe læȝon. *c* **897** K. ÆLFRED *Gregory's Past. C.* xxviii. 197 Ða Saul hine wolde secean uppe on ðæm munte. *a* **900** *Baeda's Hist.* III. xxiii. (1890) 230 Se biscop..him stowe ȝeceas mynster to ȝetimbriȝenne in heawum morum uppe. *a* **1050** *O.E. Chron.* (MS. D) an. 1016, Ða se kyning ȝeahsade þæt se here uppe wæs, þa ȝesamnade he..ealle Engla þeode.

c **1560** A. SCOTT *Poems* ii. 38 For Sym wes bettir sittin, Nor Will, Vp at the Drum that day. **1697** DAMPIER *Voy.* 218 The City..is 20 mile up in the Country. **1710** *Tatler* No. 254 ¶7, I proposed a visit to the Dutch cabbin, which lay about a mile further up in the country. **1825** SCOTT *Betrothed* xxiii, The Red Pool..lies up towards the hills. **1846–8** LOWELL *Biglow P.* I. Poems (1912) 223 Recollect wut fun we hed..Up there to Waltham plain last fall. **1855** BROWNING *Up at a Villa* ii, Up at a villa one lives, I maintain it, no more than a beast.

3. a. In an elevated position; at some distance above a usual or natural level.

c **897** K. ÆLFRED *Gregory's Past C.* xxxiii. 222 Swæ swæ iu ..wæron ða lac forbærndu uppe on ðæm altere. *a* **1000** *Rood* 8 (Gr.), Ðimmas..fife wæron uppe on þam eaxleȝespanne. *a* **1200** *Vices & Vertues* 95 Ðe postes þat sculen beren up ðis weorc. *c* **1200** ORMIN 1169 All þatt Judewisshe lac þatt ȝuw her uppe iss shæwedd. *c* **1275** LAY. 17495 He bar þare his croune heȝe vppe on his heued. *c* **1275** *Doomsday* 51 in *O.E. Misc.* 167 Heo schule iseon þene kyng..vppe on þe rode myd stronge pyne abouhte. **1377** LANGL. *P. Pl.* B. VII. 91 As wilde bestis with wehe [ȝe] worthen vppe and worchen. *a* **1400–50** *Alexander* 198 Quen he was semely vp set with septour in hand. *Ibid.* 977 (D.), Alexander hys ayre vppe in hys awne trone. **1526–** [see STAY *v.*[2] 1 c]. **1596** *Edward III*, III. iii. 134 Edwards great linage,..Fiue hundred yeeres hath helde the scepter vp. **1667** PEPYS *Diary* 22 July, In my Lord's roome,..where all the Judges' pictures hung up. **1669** STURMY *Mariner's Mag.* v. xii. 68 As you hale him out, keep him up that you may bring no Powder out with the Ladle. **1764** FOOTE *Patron* I. Wks. 1799 I. 337 He never brought them..a birth till the christening was over; nor a death till the hatchment was up. **1799** *Hull Advertiser* 13 April 2/1 Cutter-built sloop,..measures up aloft thirty-two feet. **1819** W. TENNANT *Papistry Storm'd* (1827) 48 At anes the bells baith up and under Begoud to rattle on like thunder. **1855** BAIN *Senses & Int.* II. ii. §6 An object seems to us to be up or down, according as we raise or lower the pupil of the eye in order to see it. **1899** *Daily News* 6 Nov. 4/5 The accommodation is limited to one room down and two up.

b. In fig. phrases or expressions.

c **1386** CHAUCER *Knt.'s T.* 675 As doon thise loueres in hir queynte geres.., Now vp, now doun, as boket in a welle. *c* **1430** *Pilgr. Lyf Manhode* I. lxxviii. (1869) 46 So michel þow didest, what up what doun, þat to mariage þow haddest hire. **1579** TOMSON *Calvin's Serm. Tim.* 758/1 Wee must..be readie to forgoe all: wee must alwayes haue one foote vp. **1741** RICHARDSON *Pamela* (ed. 3) I. 199 There I stood, my Heart up at my Mouth. **1749** WALPOLE *Let. to Mann* 23 March, Ned's envy, which was always up at high-water-mark. **1828** CARR *Craven Gloss.* s.v., I can find him nayther up-ner-down; *i.e.* I can find him no where.

c. Of an adjustable (esp. sliding) device or part: Raised.

1599 SHAKS. *Hen. V*, II. i. 55 Pistols cocke is vp, and flashing fire will follow. **1600** FAIRFAX *Tasso* VI. xxvi, Her ventall vp so hie, that he descride Her goodly visage. **1610**

R. VAUGHAN *Water-workes* P4b, Vnlesse..my seruants suffer the Sluces to be vpp when they should be downe. **1708** MRS. CENTLIVRE *Busie Body* IV. ii, He has escap'd out of the Window, for the Sash is up. **1764** MRS. E. CARTER *Let. to Miss Talbot* 3 Feb., The glasses [of the coach] were up and broke to shivers. **1796** SOUTHEY *Joan of Arc* II. 488, I saw him.. Riding from rank to rank, his beaver up. **1799** LAMB *Lett.* (1888) I. 112 Travelling with the coach windows sometimes up. **1838** J. F. COOPER *Excurs. Italy* I. 57 We were closely curtained and had the glasses up [in the travelling-carriage]. **1879** MEREDITH *Egoist* i, The visitor carried a bag, and his coat-collar was up. **1892** *Photogr. Ann.* II. 407 It closes itself either way, with the piston up or down.

d. *colloq.* On horseback; riding. Also *fig.*

1812 J. H. VAUX *Flash Dict.* s.v., A man who is 'in swell-street', that is, having plenty of money, is said to be 'up in the stirrups'. **1856** H. DIXON *Post & Paddock* vi. 93 His running in a sweepstakes, when Sam [the jockey] was not 'up'. **1857** G. LAWRENCE *Guy Liv.* iii, A match for £50, 10 st. 7 lb. each. Owners up. **1886** in *Fores's Sporting Notes* III. 6 To pace the paddock when Archer's up.

e. Of a woman's hair: worn tied or pinned on top of or at the back of the head, not hanging down; *spec.* as an indication of entry into adult society.

1911 BEERBOHM *Zuleika D.* xiv. 207 Her hair, tied back at the nape of her neck, would very soon be 'up'. *a* **1976** A. CHRISTIE *Autobiogr.* (1977) IV. i. 166, I was now ready to 'come out'. My hair was 'up', which at that period meant.. large knots of curls high up on the head.

†**4.** Of a gate, door, etc.: Open. *Obs.*

13.. *Cursor M.* 24423 (Gött.), All vp [*Cott.* opind] war þair grauis sene. **1340** *Ayenb.* 255 Yef hi vyndeþ þe gate oppe, hi guoþ in liȝtliche. **1390** GOWER *Conf.* III. 336 The dore is up, and he in wente. *c* **1480** HENRYSON *Twa Mice* xxi, Bot in he went, and left the dure vp wyde. **1550** CROWLEY *Epigr.* 118 In seruice tyme no dore standeth vp, Where such men are wonte to fyll can and cuppe.

5. a. High, in respect of the river-bank or shore.

1387 TREVISA *Higden* (Rolls) II. 51 Seuarne is ofte vppe and passeþ þe brynkes. **1546** *Yorks. Chantry Surv.* (Surtees) 209 At such tyme when the waters be uppe. **1720** DE FOE *Capt. Singleton* xiii. (1840) 221 The tide was up. **1844** W. H. MAXWELL *Wand. Highl.* xxxvii, The sea was up. **1882** 'MARK TWAIN' *Roughing It* vii. 35 The Platte was 'up', they said—which made me wish I could see it when it was down.

b. Out of the stomach, etc.

1579 GOSSON *Sch. Abuse* (Arb.) 65 If I giue them a Pil to purge their humor, they neuer leaue belking till it bee vp.

c. On or above the surface of the ground or water.

1835 *Trans. Zoological Soc.* I. 234 By remaining perfectly quiet when the animal is 'up' the spectator is enabled to attain an excellent view of its movements in the water. **1854** RUSKIN *Let. to Miss Mitford* 7 Aug., The soldanella..is.. distinguished for its hurry to be up in the spring. **1865** G. MACDONALD *A. Forbes* viii, She was as lonely as if she had anticipated the hour of the resurrection, and was the little only one up of the buried millions. **1883** GRESLEY *Gloss. Coal-m.* 268 *Up*, on the bank, or on the surface.

6. a. In a standing posture; on one's feet; standing (and delivering a speech).

(*a*) **1297** R. GLOUC. (Rolls) 3828 Is suerd he drou þere Vor to asaile him þerwiþ, ac þe oþer was vp ere. *a* **1300**, **1398** [see BEAR *v.* 18]. *c* **1440** *Generydes* 44 An hert was fownde.., And vppe vppon his fete he was a non. *c* **1450** *Mankind* 29 (Brandl), O ȝe souerens, þat sytt, and ȝe brotherne, þat stonde ryghte wppe. **1595** SHAKS. *John* III. iv. 137 He that stands vpon a slipp'ry place, Makes nice of no vilde hold to stay him vp. **1613** WITHERS *Abuses Stript* I. v, They..are so quickly up in a *bravado*. **1682** BUNYAN *Holy War* 164 They were not able without staggering to stand up under it. **1787** 'G. GAMBADO' *Acad. Horsem.* (1809) 34 The standing up in your stirrups, whilst trotting.., has a most elegant and genteel effect. **1860-** [see HOLD *v.* 44 f]. **1888** J. H. STIRLING in A. H. Stirling *Life* (1912) 310 The student up was just translating in the ordinary slip-slop, unthinking fashion.

(*b*) **1657** *Burton's Diary* (1828) I. 319, I only stood up first, to speak to the orders of the House. But now I am up, I desire [etc.]. **1762** FOOTE *Orator* III. Wks. 1799 I. 220 Silence, gentlemen;..A worthy member is up. **1778** *Ann. Reg., Hist.* 133/2 The Minister concluded a long..speech, which kept him full two hours up. **1835** DICKENS *Sk. Boz, Parl. Sketch*, Members arrive..to report that 'The Chancellor of the Exchequer's up'. **1899** *Daily News* 24 March 2/1 He had a comparatively small audience, augmenting in numbers as news went round that he was up.

b. In an upright position.

Also *bolt, right, straight up*: see these words.

1669 PEPYS *Diary* 3 March, My Lord Mayor did retreat out of the Temple by stealth, with his sword up. **1727-** [see SIT *v.* 25 c]. **1859** TENNYSON *Geraint & Enid* 546 Bound on a foray..[the earl] Came riding with a hundred lances up. **1884** *Lillywhite's Cricket Ann.* 60 He kept up his wicket until the finish.

c. Erected, built.

1613-39 I. JONES in Leoni *Palladio's Archit.* (1742) I. 70 Part of this Building..is finish'd, but the rest have some part of the Basement up only. **1742** LEONI *Ibid.* II. 69 Of the Rings for Races... A third is yet up.., though half-ruined.

d. *Baseball.* At bat.

[**1862** *N.Y. Sunday Mercury* 13 July 6/1 Crane came up to open the inning.] **1896** *Sun* (N.Y.) 13 May 4/1 At the beginning of the tenth inning the score was a tie. Van Haltren was the first New Yorker up. **1909** R. H. BARBER *Double Play* xvii. 208 The fourth man up chose a ball to his liking and sliced it down the first-base line. **1942** P. GALLICO *Lou Gehrig* viii. 97 Koenig was up next, a precision machine at getting a man along to second with hit or sacrifice. **1976** E. BLACKWELL in *Baseball between Lines* 52 They got a man in scoring position with two out and Buddy Kerr up.

7. a. Out of bed; risen.

a **1375** *Joseph Arim.* 234 In þe morwe he was vppe and roises þis oþure. *c* **1400** *Laud Troy Bk.* 16992 The sonne is rysen & schynes bryght, And thei are vppe & redi dyght. **1470-85** MALORY *Arthur* VIII. xxv. 311 Take youre rest and loke that ye be vp by tymes. **1523** FITZHERB. *Husb.* §149 Go to thy bedde and slepe, and be vppe betyme. **1581** MULCASTER *Positions* 19 Those people..be drousie when they are vp, for want of their sleepe. **1607** DEKKER *Westw. Hoe* II. i, We..must be vp with the lark. **1641** in *10th Rep. Hist. MSS. Comm.* App. I. 78, I vas upe this morninge be two a cloacke. **1693** DRYDEN *Juvenal* III. 218 In vain we rise, and to their Levees run; My Lord himself is up, before, and gone. **1719** DE FOE *Crusoe* II. (Globe) 363 Another..asked, who it was that was up? **1771** MRS. HAYWOOD *New Present for Maid* 255 When the family is up, she should set open the windows of the bed-chambers. **1854** R. S. SURTEES *Handley Cr.* li, Mrs. Jorrocks,..and Benjamin, were up with the lark. *a* **1873** LYTTON *Ken. Chillingley* xiv, One of the young ladies who attended..to the dairy was already up.

b. Not gone to bed; not yet abed.

a **1535** FISHER *Wks.* (1875) 367 Peraduenture he was late vp the night before. **1550-** [see SIT *v.* 25 b]. **1622** J. TAYLOR (Water P.) *Shilling* B 5, Whilst all the Drawers must stay vp and waite Vpon these fellowes be it ne're so late. **1763** G. WILLIAMS in Jesse *Selwyn & Contemp.* (1843) I. 250 While Lord March and I are up half the night with people of a profligate character. **1779** WARNER *Ibid.* (1844) IV. 274, I was in hopes that some of the servants were still up. **1834** MAGINN in *Blackw. Mag.* XXXV. 748 My eye caught a light in the window... Seeing that the old fellow was up, I determined to step over. **1852** DICKENS *Bleak Ho.* lviii, The corporation of servants are dismissed to bed (not unwilling to go, for they were up all last night). **1855-** [see WAIT *v.*[1] 7 f].

c. Of game: Roused, started.

1611 SHAKS. *Cymb.* III. iii. 117 Hearke, the Game is rows'd... The Game is vp.

d. In various colloq. phrases: ***up and about, around***, active, moving about, esp. of a person who has been ill, no longer in bed; ***up and doing***, busy and active.

1817 H. GRANVILLE *Let.* in B. Askwith *Piety & Wit* (1982) vii. 103 We are all much better for her presence—it says 'up and doing', she looks so reviving. **1893** 'MARK TWAIN' in *Century Mag.* Dec. 234/2 She was up and around the same day. **1901** *Daily Chron.* 17 Dec. 3/2 She was..the most up-and-doing woman of all her generation. **1909** *Dialect Notes* III. 385 *Up and about*,..used in expressing moderate health. **1927** G. HUNTING *Vicarion* xxi. 350 It required another week for him to get up and about. **1946** K. TENNANT *Lost Haven* (1947) 3 Steamy rains wash..from men's minds all desire to be up and doing. **1978** *Lancashire Life* Sept. 88/2 It was not unusual to hear her up and about in the middle of the night, checking on a seriously ill patient.

8. a. Further away from the mouth towards the source of a river, the inner part of a bay, etc.

1600 HAKLUYT *Voy.* II. 194 Wee..arriued in the Easter-side thereof some ten leagues vp within the Bay. **1697** DAMPIER *Voy.* 7 We..rowed up to the head of the Creek, being about a mile up, and there we landed. **1766** GOLDSM. *Vicar* iii, By taking the current a little farther up, the rest of the family got safely over. **1816** TUCKEY *Narr. Exped. R. Zaire* vi. (1818) 223 At day-light sent off all..the people who had been up with me, to the transport. **1862** KINGSLEY in *Lett.*, etc. (1877) II. 139, I never saw such a river, though there are very few salmon up.

b. Pointing or directed to the stream.

1821 *Acc. Peculations Coal Trade* 7 Then he recollects there is a punt head up in Mill-hole tier.

c. Towards a place or position; forward; advanced in place.

1613 SHAKS. *Hen. VIII*, V. iv. 92 *Porter.* Make way there... *Man.* You great fellow, Stand close vp. **1806** SURR *Winter in London* II. 133 'Is my chariot up?' said the captain. 'Next to the duchess's, sir.' **1867** SMYTH *Sailor's Word-Bk.* 368 *Hard up*, the tiller so placed as to carry the rudder close over to leeward of the stern-post. **1868** *Field* 18 July 49/2 Viscount lying second, and the others in close order well up. **1903** WARNER in Hutchinson *Cricket* 65 If the ball is a half-volley or well up.

d. At or in a place of importance (*spec.* London).

1845 CARLYLE *Cromwell* (1871) III. 126 'Dick Cromwell and his Wife' seem to be up in Town on a visit. **1866** TROLLOPE *Claverings* iv, You'll be up in London by the 10th of next month. **1886** C. E. PASCOE *London of To-day* ii. (ed. 3) 37 Literary parsons 'up' for a week or two's reading at the British Museum.

e. *colloq.* At or in school or college. Cf. sense 16 below.

1847 TENNYSON *Princ.* Prol. 175 We seven stay'd at Christmas up to read. **1866** *Routledge's Ev. Boy's Ann.* 197 The boys were still 'up', that is, in school [= Eton]. **1886** *Law Times' Rep.* LIII. 664/2 The permission to remain up during the vacation.

f. Of a foxhound or a follower of the hunt: keeping pace with the fox; present at its death.

1839 'HARKAWAY' *Jrnl.* 4 Jan. in E. A. Pease *Cleveland Hounds* (1887) iii. 63 Sly Reynard ran down the lane a field's length, and then took the fields. This gave the leaders a sob and the second-raters time to get up. **1889** F. MASON *Flowers of Hunt* 199 Ride as they might, the pace was so great that only a select few were on anything like terms with the hounds. 'Only eight of us up!' remarked Tom Chirpington. **1908** *Punch* 8 Apr. 267/1 Biggest ole dog-fox what ever I see!.. Nobody up but the Master an' me! **1972** *Daily Tel.* 21 Nov. 19 On the second occasion the pack accounted for a brace of foxes, but the Princess's party was not up at either kill.

9. In miscellaneous uses: **a.** Facing upward.

1683 DRYDEN & LEE *Dk. of Guise* v. i, The world's..better now, 'tis downside up. **1852** MORFIT *Tanning & Currying* (1853) 289 The skin is stretched over this, with the grain side up. **1891** *Anthony's Photogr. Bull.* IV. 65 The tissue should be completely immersed, face up.

b. Off the ground; in store; in a proper place or receptacle.

to keep up: see KEEP *v.* 57 a, k. *to lie up* (= in bed, etc.): see LIE *v.*[1] 29.

1865 TROLLOPE *Belton Est.* iii. 26 Our hay has been all up these three weeks.

c. With the surface broken or removed.

1886 *Daily News* 14 Oct. (Encycl. Dict.), Streets that are up. **1891** C. JAMES *Rom. Rigmarole* 1 A great deal of road-way was 'up'. **1908** *Times* 28 July 2/6 There was a good deal of traffic in the road, part of which was up for repairs.

II. In figurative senses.

10. a. In a state of disorder, tumult, revolt, or insurrection; risen in rebellion. Also const. *in* (mutiny, etc.).

13.. *E.E. Allit. P.* B. 834 Fro þe seggez haden souped.., Er euer þay bosked to bedde þe borȝ was al vp. *c* **1420** *Contin. Brut.* 358 And anon come tydyngez þat Harry of Bolyngbroke was vp with a strong power of pepill. **1487** *Cely Papers* (Camden) 166 The comens of the town..hawe ben upp onys or twyse allredy. *a* **1548** HALL *Chron., Edw. IV*, 208 b, All the Realme was vp, and by open Proclamacion commaunded to make warre against hym. **1593** MARLOWE *Edw. II*, I. iv, 'Tis treason to be vp against the king. **1655** *Nicholas Papers* (Camden) II. 298 The Levellers wilbe spedily vpp against Cromwell. **1688** WOOD *Life* (O.H.S.) III. 284 Lord de la Mere up in Cheshire with forces and crie 'No bishops!' **1695** C. HATTON in *H. Corr.* (Camden) II. 216 For thes 2 nights a great mob have been up in Holborn and Drury Lane. **1849** MACAULAY *Hist. Eng.* ix. II. 529 The eastern counties were up. **1889** C. DOYLE *Micah Clarke* 58, I had heard that Monmouth was up, and I knew that you would not lose a night ere starting.

(*b*) **1656** EARL MONM. tr. *Boccalini's Advts. fr. Parnass.* II. xi. (1674) 150 People that are up in commotion. **1844** P. HARWOOD *Hist. Irish Rebellion* 137 The British fleet was then up in mutiny.

b. ***up in arms***, risen, levied, or marshalled as an armed host. Also *fig.* (see ARM *sb.*[2] 4 b).

c **1590** *Sir T. More* I. iii. 77 A number poore artificers are up In arms. *c* **1595** CAPT. WYATT *Dudley's Voy.* (Hakl. Soc.) 47 On a soden yow shall have all quarters up in armes. **1690** C. NESSE *O. & N. Test.* I. 278 All created beings are up in arms to reduce the rebels. **1704** [see ARM *sb.*[2] 4 b]. **1812** CRABBE *Tales* v. 249 Be not a Quixote, ever up in arms To give the guilty and the great alarms. **1879** J. D. LONG *Æneid* x. 321 Ascanius, cooped in by wall and ditch, The Latins up in arms, fights hand to hand. **1893** FORBES-MITCHELL *Remin. Gt. Mutiny* 108 The public-house keepers..were up in arms to raise as much opposition as possible.

c. Actively stirring or moving about. Also *fig.*

c **1460** *Wisdom* 518 in *Macro Plays* 52 'Farewell,' quod I; 'þe deuyll ys wppe'. **1611** BEAUM. & FL. *Philaster* I. i, This earth you tread upon..was not left..To your inheritance, and I up and living. **1838** LONGF. *Psalm of Life* ix, Let us, then, be up and doing. **1855** MACAULAY *Hist. Eng.* xxii. IV. 714 They pursued him: the hue and cry was raised:..the whole country was up. **1872** SPURGEON *Treas. Dav.* Ps. lxxvii. 6 He was up and at it, resolutely resolved that he would not tamely die of despair. **1922** JOYCE *Ulysses* 295 Bob's a queer chap when the porter's up in him.

d. In a state of agitation, excitement, exaltation, or confidence.

1470-85 MALORY *Arthur* X. lxxv. 546 What,..is your herte vp? yester daye ye ferd as though ye had dremed. **1576** NEWTON *Lemnie's Complex.* 18 When theyr rage is vp, they will not easily be pacifyed. **1589** R. HARVEY *Pl. Perc.* (1590) 7 Now the blood is vp. **1602** MARSTON *Ant. & Mel.* II. Wks. 1856 I. 19 My stomack's up... The match of furie is lighted. **1691** HARTCLIFFE *Virtues* 21 Our Passions,..when they are up, and would hurry us into evil Actions. **1741** RICHARDSON *Pamela* III. 40 It was a nice Part to act; and all his Observations were up, I daresay, on the Occasion. **1766** GOLDSM. *Vicar* xvii, Let us have a bottle of the best gooseberry wine, to keep up our spirits. **1805** WORDSW. *Prelude* III. 18 My spirit was up, my thoughts were full of hope. **1824** SCOTT *St. Ronan's* xiii, His pluck was up, and finding himself in a fighting humour, he [etc.]. **1859** DICKENS *T. Two Cities* II. v, Up one minute and down the next; now in spirits and now in despondency. **1891** E. PEACOCK *N. Brendon* I. 111 When his temper is up he might do anything.

e. Bound *for* (a place); ready *for* (something). Cf. 19 a (*d*).

1870 LONGF. *John Endicott* ii, On board the Swallow,.. Up for Barbadoes. **1894** BLACKMORE *Perlycross* 131 Christie was quite up for it. She loved a bit of skirmish.

11. a. In a state of prevalency, performance, or progress. (In later use mainly with *keep* v.)

c **1290** *Beket* 229 in *S. Eng. Leg.* I. 113 þis Ercedekne.. stifliche heold op hire riȝte. *Ibid.* 404 þou auȝtest more to holden op þane to with-seggen mi power. **1362** LANGL. *P. Pl.* A. IV. 58 Bot ȝif Meede make hit þi Mischef is vppe. **1399** —— *Rich. Redeles* I. 29 þey..cowde no mysse amende whan mysscheff was vp. **14..** *Siege Jerusalem* 295 Now is ȝour sorow vppe. **1513-** [see KEEP *v.* 57 f]. **1537-** [see HUNT'S-UP]. **1582-** [see HOLD *v.* 44 g]. **1670-** [see KEEP *v.* 57 e].

†**b.** In power or force. *Obs.*

1541 in W. H. Turner *Select. Rec. Oxford* (1880) 163 He shold se er he died friers and monks uppe agayn. **1607** SHAKS. *Cor.* III. i. 109 To know, when two Authorities are vp,..How soone Confusion May enter. **1641** J. JACKSON *True Evang.* T. II. 89 They are such beasts as while the Law was up,..furnished Gods Altar with Sacrifices.

c. Much or widely spoken of, whether favourably or (latterly) unfavourably.

Cf. the OE. sense 'disclosed, made known', and ON. and Icel. *uppi*, noted, remembered.

1618 BOLTON *Florus* (1636) 265 The name of Caius Cæsar was up, for eloquence, and spirit. **1680** V. ALSOP *Mischief of Imposit.* vii. 41 His name being up, he may lie abed till noon. **1766** G. WILLIAMS in Jesse *Selwyn & Contemp.* (1843) II. 33 [He] has again taken to his bed, and now, since his name is up, there he may lie. **1789**, **1809** [see NAME *sb.* 5]. **1812** *Sporting Mag.* XXXIX. 283 He observed his name was up there, and he should be suspected. **1824** MRS. CAMERON *Pink Tippet* III. 16 Your name's up in the town.

d. *colloq.* Occurring (as a special, unusual, or undesirable event); taking place, going on; amiss, wrong. (Very freq. from *c* 1850.)

1838 MRS. GASKELL *Let.* 19 Aug. (1966) 37, I did not mention a word to Lucy but she must have guessed something was 'up'. **1849** ALB. SMITH *Pottleton Legacy* ix.

75 He saw something was 'up'. 1851 MAYHEW *Lond. Labour* I. 21 A shout in answer from the other asks, 'What's up?' 1908 *Times* 29 May 15/6 We constantly thought that something was going to be up.

e. Amiss or wrong *with* a person, etc.

1887 RIDER HAGGARD *Jess* vii, There's something up with that girl.

f. Of food, drink, etc.: ready, served; freq. (*tea up!*, etc.) as an indication that something is ready to be served, eaten, or drunk. *colloq.*

1941 J. SMILEY *Hash House Lingo* 55 *Up.* This is usually added to another as 'coffee up' 'waitress up' or 'bread up' and designates the want or approach of a person or thing. 1950 'D. DIVINE' *King of Fassarai* xxi. 177 They heard her voice, 'Chow up!' 1972 J. PORTER *Meddler & her Murder* xi. 138 Grub's up!.. Them as wants forks can fetch 'em! 1981 J. WAINWRIGHT *All on Summer's Day* 14 'Tea up.' Wooley ..carrying a steaming pot.

12. In senses denoting completion.

a. Of a period of time, etc.: Completed, ended, expired, over. (Cf. UPHALIDAY.)

Cf. the same sense of ON. and Icel. *uppi*, LG. *up*, Du. *op*, G. *auf*.

c 1400 *Destr. Troy* 7207 When the tyme was ourtyrnyt, and þe tru vp, Agamynon þe grekys gedrit in þe fild. 1596 DALRYMPLE tr. *Leslie's Hist. Scot.* (S.T.S.) II. 86 The king ..commandis..to lat him pas frie,..or vp trues, against thame he sal proclayme weiris. *Ibid.* 235. 1688 MIÈGE *Gt. Fr. Dict.* II. s.v., The Quarter is up. 1776 in Sparks *Corr. Am. Rev.* (1853) I. 310 Whose time of enlistment will be up in a few days. 1840 R. H. DANA *Bef. Mast* xxix, He should want a second mate before the voyage was up. 1865 CARLYLE *Fredk. Gt.* XIX. viii. (1873) VIII. 240 So that the Ball is up; dress-pumps and millineries getting all locked into their drawers again. 1878 H. C. ADAMS *Wykehamica* xv. 268 As soon as morning school was up, there was a general rush.. to breakfast. 1889 'J. S. WINTER' *Mrs. Bob* xxi, As his leave was nearly up, he..would be off in the morning.

b. Of an assembly: Risen; adjourned; over.

1632 MASSINGER & FIELD *Fatal Dowry* I. ii, The court is vp; make way. 1647 CLARENDON *Hist. Reb.* IV. §255 The Duke said..that..all men being upon their feet, and out of their places, he conceiv'd the house had been up. 1711 SWIFT *Jrnl. to Stella* 7 May, Yet perhaps it may not be till Parliament is up. 1773 FOOTE *Bankrupt* III. Wks. 1799 II. 126 As both the Houses are up, I shall adjourn..till their meeting again. 1825 HONE *Every-day Bk.* I. 492 After parliament's up. 1853 DICKENS *Bleak Ho.* xxxix, The Chancellor is, within these ten minutes, 'up' for the long vacation. 1881 J. HATTON *New Ceylon* Pref., There was much bustle of departing travellers. Parliament was up.

c. (At) the number or limit agreed upon as the score or game.

1667 DRYDEN *Sir M. Mar-all* I. i, Which most mads me, I lose all my sets when I want but one of up. 1680 COTTON *Compl. Gamester* (ed. 2) 30 Of Trucks... The Game, because it is sooner up than Billiards, is Nine, and sometimes Fifteen. 1685 TATE *Cuckolds-Haven* II. ii. 15 Security and his Wife playing at Putt.. *Sec.* There's up, Wynny, there's up; Come give me my Winnings. 1740 RICHARDSON *Pamela* II. 259, I had four Honours the first time, and we were up at one Deal. 1873 BENNETT & CAVENDISH *Billiards* 5 The game was twelve up. 1876 *Encycl. Brit.* IV. 180/2 (Bowls), The game..is 'up' or won when the number of casts agreed on have been obtained by the winning side.

d. Come to a fruitless or undesired end; 'played out'. Usu. with *game*.

1787 JEFFERSON *Writ.* (1859) II. 283 Are we to suppose the game already up? 1800 *Aurora* (Philadelphia) 17 Dec. (Thornton), As the Baltimore paper says, 'The Jigg's up, Paddy'. 1838 DICKENS *O. Twist* xxxiv, He feared the game was up. 1848- [see JIG *sb.*[1] 5]. 1867 FREEMAN *Norm. Conq.* vi. I. 558 Godwine might well think that the game was up.

e. *all up*, completely done or finished; quite over. Also *all U P* (juː piː). (See also U 5.)

1825 C. M. WESTMACOTT *Eng. Spy* I. 322 That's all up now. 1854 WARTER *Last of Old Squires* ix, Now corrupted into the simpler saw, 'It's all U P—up!' 1860 WHYTE MELVILLE *Market Harb.* 94 Consequently, when you drop into a run, he goes as long as he can, and it's all U P!

f. Const. *with*, in previous sense.

1829 P. EGAN *Boxiana* 2nd Ser. II. 243 When time was called, it was 'all up' with Bob, and Jem was declared the winner. 1833 DISRAELI *Cont. Fleming* II. vi, It is all up with him by this time. 1837 COL. HAWKER *Diary* (1893) II. 121 It appears now to be 'all up' with coast gunning. 1854 R. S. SURTEES *Handley Cr.* xxxvi Crikey! they're past! and it's U P with old Pug. 1888 McCARTHY & PRAED *Ladies' Gallery* I. ix. 221 It was all but up with me.

g. In other applications.

1883 GRESLEY *Gloss. Coal-m.* 268 A stall or heading is said to be *up* when it is driven or worked up to a certain line.., beyond which nothing further is to be worked. 1909 *Cent. Suppl.* s.v., *Up*,..in *printing*, finished; noting completion of a task: as, the chapter is up; the paper is up.

13. a. Higher in the ascending scale in respect of position, rank, fortune, etc.; in a position of affluence or influence. Also *fig.* (quot. 1791).

1509 BARCLAY *Shyp Folys* 17 b, He that lyeth on hye [is] Nowe vp, nowe downe, vnsure as a Balaunce. 1611 SHAKS. *Cymb.* I. v. 39 Which first (perchance) shee'l proue on Cats and Dogs, Then afterward vp higher. 1791 MME. D'ARBLAY *Diary* 4 June, I shall be apt to be rather up in the world, as the folks say, if I tope on at this rate! 1877 TENNYSON *Harold* I. i, For in our windy world What's up is faith, what's down is heresy. 1905 in *Eng. Dial. Dict.* s.v.

b. Increased in power, force, strength, or vigour; actually blowing; ready for action. Also (in *Computing*), in working condition. Freq. in phr. *up and running*. Cf. UP TIME and DOWN *adv.* 17 c.

1547 BOORDE *Introd. Knowl.* 127 Yf the winde be any thyng vp. 1570 FOXE *A. & M.* (ed. 2) III. 2197/1 The winde was somwhat vp, and it caused the fire to be ye fiercer. 1601 SHAKS. *Jul. C.* v. i. 68 The Storme is vp, and all is on the hazard. 1659 PELL *Impr. Sea* 500 His often hushing of the winds, when they are up. 1742 R. BLAIR *Grave* 32 The wind is up: hark! how it howls! 1833 I. TAYLOR *Fanat.* i. 16 What shall be the movements of the deep..when the winds are up! 1848 J. MITCHEL *Jail Jrnl.* 27 May, A Government steamer ..lay in the river, with steam up. 1889 GUNTER *That Frenchman* xxi. 298 Steam is up, and the boat is soon ready to leave her dock. 1978 *Computing* 9 Feb. 1/1 British Steel's giant private packet-switched network is up—and running successfully. 1978 *Nature* 24 Aug. 746/1 The host computer had just broken down, forcing a delay until it could be brought up again. 1983 *Austral. Personal Computer* IV. 106/3 A lot of other facilities need to be available to make a complete up-and-running software package.

c. Advanced, increased, or high in number, value, or price.

1546 in Ellis *Orig. Lett.* Ser. II. II. 175 Th' exchaunge is vp agen above xxiiijs. 1722 DE FOE *Plague* (1884) 165 The Bill was up at 2785. 1801- [see KEEP *v.* 57 c]. 1855 BAGEHOT *Lit. Stud.* (1879) I. 3 A head full of sums, an idea that tallow is 'up'. 1887 A. BIRRELL *Obiter Dicta* Ser. II. 93 The price of £100 stock was up to £340. 1891 *Science-Gossip* XXVII. 51/1 Six shillings a couple for ducks, and four for teal, as they're up now.

d. Advanced *in* years.

a 1822 SIR A. BOSWELL *Old Beau* iii, Though up in life, I'll get a wife. 1834 *Tait's Mag.* I. 417/1 An Irishman, rather up in years. 1884 T. SPEEDY *Sport Highl.* ii. 13 Gentlemen who are somewhat up in years.

e. (So many points, etc.) in advance of a competitor.

1894 *Times* 19 July 7/2 They were two up at the third hole. 1900 J. DOE *Bridge Man.* 61 When the adversaries are 28 up. 1903 *Times* 6 Feb. 7/6 The former pair winning by three up and two to play.

fig. 1919 J. B. MORTON *Barber of Putney* vi, It's one up to 'im for stickin' it.

f. At a high or lofty pitch.

1902 O. WISTER *Virginian* ix, All the ladies thought the world of her, and McLean had told him she was 'away up in G'. 1905 ELINOR GLYN *Viciss. Evangeline* 81 He has a giggle right up in the treble.

14. a. Before a magistrate, etc., in court. (Cf. UP *adv.*[1] 12 b.)

b. Offered or exposed publicly.

1921 *Conquest* Sept. 480/1 His business is to set a value on the teas up for sale.

III. With a preposition following.

15. up against—, faced or confronted by (difficulties, etc.). *colloq.* (orig. *Amer.*).

1896 ADE *Artie* i. 7, I saw I was up against it. 1901 S. CRANE *Monster*, etc. 231 All he's up against is a case of grand larceny. 1910 *Chambers's Jrnl.* April 232/1 In Canadian phraseology, we were 'up against it' with a vengeance!

16. up at—, attending (a specified college or university). Cf. sense 8 e.

1873 TROLLOPE *Lady Anna* (1874) I. viii. 96 The grand idea that young Jack Bluestone, who was up at Brasenose, should marry the Lady Anna. 1926 J. BUCHAN *Dancing Floor* I. i. 11 It's old Milburne. He's up at Magdalen with me.

17. up for—. a. Liable to, having to submit to, due to receive; under consideration for, having been proposed for.

1918 L. E. RUGGLES *Navy Explained* 52 Down for a shoot, ..or up for a shot are all the same. It means that a man has been placed on the report and will have to appear at the mast before the captain. 1921 [see sense 14b]. *a* 1936 KIPLING *Something of Myself* (1937) ii. 29 The Prefects..were all of the 'Army Class' up for the Sandhurst or Woolwich Preliminary. 1979 A. SCHOLEFIELD *Point of Honour* 34 She said he was up for a medal... And a few weeks later there was the announcement of the VC.

b. *up for grabs*: see GRAB *sb.*[2] 1 b.

18. up in —, expert or versed, well informed or instructed, in a subject, matter, work, etc. *colloq.*

In frequent use from *c* 1860.

1838 DICKENS *Nich. Nick.* xxiii, 'Intrigue', and 'Ways and Means', you're all up in; so we shall only want one rehearsal. 1856 MISS YONGE *Daisy Chain* I. xxx, As to the examination ..the very subjects had been chosen in which he was most up. 1885 'F. ANSTEY' *Tinted Venus* 100, I did think Potter was better up in his work.

19. up to —. a. (*a*) Able to perform, do, or undertake; fit or qualified for; capable of.

In frequent use from *c* 1850. For phrases involving this or one of the following senses see also SLUM *sb.*[1] 5, SNUFF *sb.*[2] 3 a, THING *sb.*[1] 14 f, TRAP *sb.*[1] 5.

1785 TRUSLER *Mod. Times* I. 88 He was up almost to any villainy. 1792 PAINE *Rights of Man* II. ii. 17 Man, naturally as he is, with all his faults about him, is not up to the character. 1801 F. LEIGHTON *Let. to J. Boucher* 15 May (MS.), I hope you will have no strangers with you... I am not up to that. 1820 *Examiner* No. 659. 761/2 An old..hardy Highland Chieftain was up to no such mawkish sentiments. 1856 MRS. CARLYLE *Lett.* (1883) II. 282, I was up to nothing but lying on the sofa all the evening. 1890 'R. BOLDREWOOD' *Col. Reformer* (1891) 225 The 'fence..is barely up to the weight of six hundred bullocks..at a high degree of momentum. 1898 'H. S. MERRIMAN' *Roden's Corner* xvii. 179 To provide situations for elderly men who are no longer up to their work.

(*b*) 1855 SMEDLEY *H. Coverdale* i, Two showy saddle-horses, the best being up to fifteen stone with any hounds. 1861 E. YATES in *Temple Bar* II. 473 A cob 'well up to fourteen stone'.

(*b*) Well aware of and prepared for; competent to deal with; a match for.

1785 GROSE *Dict. Vulgar T.* s.v., Up to their gossip. 1806 LADY S. LENNOX *Lett.* (1901) II. 202 To be up to all the wiles and arts used to entrap them. *c* 1830 MRS. SHERWOOD *Houlston Tracts* III. lxxxi. 10 To use a vulgar phrase very common with us servants at that time, I was so far up to Anne Simpson, that..I would not be put upon by her. 1864 H. AINSWORTH *John Law* v. ix, Sir Patrick and I are both wide awake,..so we shall be up to their tricks. 1890 'R. BOLDREWOOD' *Col. Reformer* (1891) 321 It takes a smart man to be up to chaps of their sort.

(*c*) Thoroughly acquainted with; expert or versed in; possessing a thorough knowledge of.

In frequent use from *c* 1840.

1800 LAMB *Let. to Manning* 3 Nov., He does not want explanations..when you make an assertion; up to anything; down to anything. 1823 MRS. SHERWOOD *H. Milner* III. v. 88 Sam is not up to many things about a horse. 1853 KANE *Grinnell Exped.* xxii. (1856) 171 They are a..well-educated set of men, thoroughly up to the history of what has been done by others.

(*d*) Ready for. (Cf. 10 e.)

1849 THACKERAY *Pendennis* xxiv, She was up to any party of pleasure by whomsoever proposed. 1893 MISS YONGE *Girl's Little Bk.* 23 Boys fancy they like a jolly girl up to anything,..but they do not respect her.

b. (*a*) Equal in quality or quantity to (something specified); on a level with.

See also KEEP *v.* 57 i, and the phrases under DICK *sb.*[5], KNOCKER 2 c, NINE *sb.* 6 b.

1809 WINDHAM *Let.* in *Sp.* (1812) I. 114 Though I am considerably above my rate of London health, I am..not quite up to that which residence here ought to have given me. 1821- [see MARK *sb.*[1] 12 c]. 1826 DISRAELI *V. Grey* II. xiv, The Baronet is not up to the nineteenth century. 1862 THOREAU *Excursions* viii, Of course no flavors are thrown away; they are intended for the taste that is up to them. 1883 *Manch. Guard.* 22 Oct. 5/5 The harvest of this year was up to a full average.

(*b*) *not up to much*, of no great ability, importance, or worth.

1863 MISS BRADDON *Aurora Floyd* xxi, The new chap warn't up to mooch. 1884 SALA *Journ. due South* I. ix, The shoes were not, to use a vulgarism, 'up to much'.

(*c*) *dial.* Even with (a person). Cf. 20 b.

1853 MRS. GASKELL *Cranford* xiv, But I'll be up to her... I'll make her a pudding, and a pudding she'll like, too. 1854 MISS BAKER *Northampt. Gloss.* 371 'I'll be up to you'; i.e. I'll retaliate.

c. Engaged in or bent on (some activity, esp. of a reprehensible nature); occupying or concerning oneself with; doing or planning.

1837 DICKENS *Pickw.* xxvii, What's the old 'un up to, now? 1853 —— *Bleak Ho.* xxxix, They are still up to it, sir,..still taking stock, still examining papers. 1875 W. S. GILBERT *Tom Cobb* I, That Whipple's up to some bedevilment. 1890 R. C. LEHMANN *H. Fludyer* 84, I suppose you've been up to some of your games again.

d. *colloq.* Obligatory or incumbent upon. orig. *U.S.*

From the game of poker; in common use from *c* 1913.

1896 ADE *Artie* ii. 11 Up to me—see! 1901 S. CRANE *Monster*, etc. 212 It's up to us to whirl in an' git some of it. 1902 GREENOUGH & KITTREDGE *Words* 56 So with the poker terms 'ante up' and 'it is up to you'. 1908 *Westm. Gaz.* 21 Feb. 4/2 It was 'up to him', then, as an American would put it, to say that he had done this thing.

e. In phr. *to be up to* (a master), to be tutored by (him). *Public school colloq.* (chiefly *Eton College*).

1874 C. M. YONGE *Life J. C. Patteson* I. ii. 19 The lower remove of the fourth form..was then 'up to' the Rev. Charles Old Goodford, *i.e.* that was he who taught the division so called in school. 1910 A. HUXLEY *Let.* 15 Feb. (1969) 33 This half we are all up to that ignorant creature Heygate. I have successfully proved his ignorance. 1927 H. E. WORTHAM *Oscar Browning* vii. 99 Curzon was subsequently 'up to him'. 1977 A. J. AYER *Part of my Life* ii. 36 In the official language of the school..to be in a master's division was to be up to him.

20. up with —. (See also 11 e, 12 f.)

a. On a level with (a person, place, etc.).

1623 JOBSON *Golden Trade* 8 When the day appeared we were up with the Iland of Launcerot. *a* 1633- [see KEEP *v.* 57 j]. 1669 STURMY *Mariner's Mag.* I. ii, We have a stearn-Chase, but we shall be up with her presently. 1858 THACKERAY *Virginians* xxxviii, She makes for the vestry... The two whiskeyfied gentlemen are up with her, however. 1893 SIR G. CHESNEY *Lesters* II. xxi, Lionel..was the only one quite up with the hounds at the last.

fig. 1785 BURNS *To W. Simpson* ix, We'll gar our streams an' burnies shine Up wi' the best. 1899 WERNER *Capt. of Locusts* 41 But I don't worry myself to keep up with things, as people say.

b. Even with; quits with. Now *dial.*

1741 RICHARDSON *Pamela* III. 308 Let me turn myself about, and I'll be up with you, never fear, Madam. 1778 [W. MARSHALL] *Minutes Agric.* 3 Feb. 1775, But I will certainly be up with him to-morrow. 1800 LATHOM *Dash of Day* IV. i, I'll be up with her for her deceit, I am determined. 1825 JAMIESON s.v., I'se be up wi' him for that. 1899 *Cumberland Gloss.* 351.

IV. 21. *Comb.* in phrases used attributively, as ***up-all-night***, ***up-and-at-'em***, etc. Cf. UP-AND-COMING *a.*

1857 DICKENS *Dorrit* I. xx, A curious *up-all-night air about it. 1891 S. MOSTYN *Curatica* 158 Chimney tops, and *up-all-night-looking window blinds. 1909 O. H. BALL *Their Oxford Year* 193 It was always the *up-and-at-'em aspect of things that appealed to him. 1933 DYLAN THOMAS *Let.* 25 Dec. (1966) 82 You like the..'up-&-at 'em'.. shoutings of Mr. Kipling. 1848 CLOUGH *Bothie* II. 59 A sort of unnatural *up-in-the-air balloon-work. 1898 *Westm. Gaz.* 4 June 7/1 The mere *up in the roof ventilation. 1893 K. SANBORN *S. California* 4 In that brilliant and *up-with-the-times city.

† **up** (ʌp), *prep.*[1] *Obs.* Forms: α. 1–2 uppan, 1–3 uppon (2 huppon), 2–3 uppen, vppen (2 upen, 4 vpen). β. 3–4 vppe, 2–3, 5 uppe (4 oppe), 2–4 upe, 3–6 vpe (4 ope). γ. 3–5 vp (4 op, 5 wp), 3–5 up. [OE. *uppan*, *uppon* (in earlier use *on uppan*

ANUPPE *prep.*), = OFris. *uppa* (*oppa*), OS. *uppan*, f. *upp* UP *adv.*[1] Cf. OHG. *ûfan*, *ûffan* (MHG. *uffen*).

By gradual loss of the ending (perhaps also by simple assimilation) the prep. finally acquired the same form as the adverbs. A similar reduction (or substitution of the adverbial form) appears in Du. and WFris. *op*, NFris. *üp* (*üb*), LG. *up*, G. *auf*.]

I. Denoting motion or direction.

1. So as to reach, or be on, by ascension.

c **1000** *Ags. Gosp.* Matt. xxvi. 30 Þa ferdon hiȝ uppan Oliuetes dune. *a* **1122** *O.E. Chron.* (Laud MS.) an. 1083, Sume of ðam cnihtan ferdon uppon þone uppflore. *c* **1205** LAY. 26005 Heo..stiȝen up þan hulle. **1297** R. GLOUC. (Rolls) 4179 Þo he com vpe þe hul an hey. **1422** YONGE tr. *Secreta Secret.* 166 The Philosofre lepid vp the mule.

b. Denoting arrival upon (a coast, etc.) from sea.

c **1205** LAY. 13970 Heo droȝen heore scipen uppe þe lond. **1297** R. GLOUC. (Rolls) 362 Þo he was iwar þat such folc was ariued..vp his londe.

2. On or upon. (In various contexts.)

c **960** *Rule St. Benet* lviii. (Schröer) 100 Sona swa he þæt ȝewrit uppan ðam altare lecge, beginne þis fers. *c* **1000** *Ags. Gosp.* Matt. xxi. 44 Se þe fylð uppan þysne stan, he byð tobrysed. *c* **1175** *Lamb. Hom.* 35 [þe] saule..ne mei abeoren alla þa sunne þe þe mon uppon hire deð. *c* **1200** *Trin. Coll. Hom.* 21 Þe holie gast wile cumen uppen þe. *c* **1205** LAY. 6504 And þet deor he smat a-nan uppe þat hæued-bæn. *Ibid.* 13257 Þe crune he nom an honden; he setten heo vppe Costance. *a* **1225** *Ancr. R.* 286 Slep go uppe þe ase þu lokest þeron [*sc.* holy reading]. *c* **1250** *Owl & Night.* 1625 Me may vppe [*v.r.* up one] smale sticke Me sette a wude in þe þikke. **1297** R. GLOUC (Rolls) 3624 Þo þe niȝt vpe hom com. *a* **1325** *Prose Psalter* lii. 3 God loked fram heuen vp mennes sones. *Ibid.* liv. 4 Drede of deþ fel vp me. *Ibid.* cxviii. 135 Liȝt þi face vp þi seruant. **1340** *Ayenb.* 210 Ssete þe dore ope þe. **1377** LANGL. *P. Pl.* B. XI. 203 For-þi loue we as leue bretheren shal and vche man laughe vp other. *c* **1391** CHAUCER *Astrol.* II. §1 Rekene..which is the day of thi monthe & ley thi reule vp that same day. **14..** *Cron. Eng.* (Caxton) ccxxiii. 222 Thousandes fell to the ground eche vp other in to a hepe.

b. Denoting desire: After, for.

a **1200** *Vices & Virtues* 51 Alle ȝe Adames children ðe bieð lustfull uppe newe wastmes.

3. a. In hostile encounter with or attack on; in active opposition to.

a **1122** *O.E. Chron.* (Laud MS.) an. 1086, Þa hæðenan men..herȝodan uppon þam Xpenan mannan. *c* **1205** LAY. 10563 Carrais..bigon ræuinge uppen Basian þene kinge. **1297** R. GLOUC. (Rolls) 5054 Vor naȝt we abbeþ so ofte vpe hom ywonne þat lond. *Ibid.* 8987 þe erl..bigan to rere worre vpe þe king of france. *c* **1330** *Arth. & Merl.* 6680 (Kölbing), Þe king of þe hundred kniȝtes Com hem vp þo forþ riȝtes.

b. Against (as an accusation, penalty, etc.).

a **1122** *O.E. Chron.* (Laud MS.) an. 1094. Hi..ealne þone bryce uppon þone cyng tealdon. *c* **1200** *Trin. Coll. Hom.* 51 Þermide [hie] brohten godes wraðe uppen hem. *Ibid.* 105 Werpeð þat gilt uppen ure drihten. *a* **1250** *Owl & Night.* 1683 (Cott.), Schille ich an utest uppen ow grede. *c* **1290** *Beket* 1466 in *S. Eng. Leg.* I. 148 Mo luþere dedene þe king bi-þouȝte ȝeot ope seint thomas. *a* **1325** *MS. Rawl. B.* 520 fol. 54 That..Bissopes ȝeuen þe grete sentense ope alle þulke þat aȝen the foreseide chartres goz. **1393** LANGL. *P. Pl.* C. II. 159 Vp man for hus mysdedes þe mercement he taxeþ.

II. Denoting rest or location.

4. On or upon. (In various contexts.)

α. *c* **1000** ÆLFRIC *Gen.* xlix. 32 He feold his fet uppan his bed. *c* **1000** *Ags. Gosp.* John vi. 19 Þa ȝesawon hiȝ þone Hælend uppan þære sæ gan. *a* **1175** *Cott. Hom.* 243 Cnihtscipe is mannes lif upen eorðe. *c* **1175** *Lamb. Hom.* 147 Þa þe he hefde uppen his hefde þornene helm. *c* **1205** LAY. 23985 Uppen þan gras-bedde his gost he bi-læfde. *a* **1225** *Ancr. R.* 242 Ȝe beoð ouer þisse worldes see, uppen þe brugge of heouene. *c* **1250** *Prov. Ælfred* 262 in *O.E. Misc.* 118 For he schal vppen eorþe dreori i-wurþe.

β. *a* **1175** *Cott. Hom.* 239 Alse fele unþeawes alse [he] hade upe him and sennenn. *c* **1200** *Trin. Coll. Hom.* 93 Ðe asse þe ure helende uppe set. *c* **1250** in *O.E. Misc.* 164 Moni of þisse riche þat..rideþ uppe stede and uppen [*v.r.* uppon] palefrai. **1297** R. GLOUC. (Rolls) 6559 Vppe a chaere he sat adoun al vpe þe se sonde. *c* **1315** SHOREHAM II. 176 Ase þou þoledest, lord, for me Ope caluaryes doune. **1340** *Ayenb.* 180 þe wedercoc þet is ope þe steple.

γ. *a* **1250** *Owl & Night.* 494 Euerich vp oþer rideþ. *c* **1275** LAY. 25758 Noht hii ne funde cwic vp þan hulle. **1297** R. GLOUC. (Rolls) 6299 King edmond..lenede vp is sseld. *c* **1300** *K. Horn* 1344 (Laud MS.), Op þe scheld was drawe A crowch of ihesu cristes lawe. *a* **1325** *Prose Psalter* xlvi. 8 God shal sitten vp his holy sege. **1377** LANGL. *P. Pl.* B. I. 12 Þe toure vp þe toft. *Ibid.* IX. 99 Lesyng of tyme..Is moste yhated vp erthe of hem þat beth in heuene. **1422** YONGE tr. *Secreta Secret.* 184 Thay mete wyth kynge Gurgnynce vp the See. **1470–85** MALORY *Arth.* IX. xli. 408 What sygnefyeth this kynge and this quene, and that knyght standynge vp bothe their hedes?

b. So as to be suspended from or supported on.

c **1175** *Lamb. Hom.* 41 Uppon þan treon he him sceawede þe wrecche saulen a-honge. *c* **1205** LAY. 26475 Alle heo sculleð heongien heȝe uppen treouwe. *c* **1275** *Ibid.* 5863 Of ȝoure hors a-liþteþ and vp ȝoure feot stondeþ. *c* **1280** *Christ on Cross* 23 in *E.E.P.* (1862) 21 Man bi-hold what ic for þe þolid up þe rode tre. **1297** R. GLOUC. (Rolls) 7734 He wolde him sulf vp is fot..Liȝtliche ssete. *c* **1350** *Will. Palerne* 2809 þe hert & þe hind..ferden ferst on foure fet & seþþe vp tweyne. *c* **1485** *Digby Myst.* (1882) I. 273 This ferdell of gere I ley vp my bakke.

c. In transferred or figurative uses.

α, β. *c* **1200** *Vices & Vertues* 31 Ðat liht of his ansiene is ȝemarked riht uppen us. *Ibid.* 71 Bereð min ȝoc uppe ȝeu. **1297** R. GLOUC. (Rolls) 5032 Þo vel he in siknesse & sorwe vpen oþer. *a* **1325** *MS. Rawl. B.* 520 fol. 48 b, Þat he..vsurpede some fraunchises ore occupiede ope þe kinge ore his predecessours. *c* **1340** *Ayenb.* 54 Þo þet habbeþ þe lhordssip ope þe bodyes. *c* **1340–70** *Alex. & Dind.* 861 Whan a wolf wanteþ his fode,..he ne fundeþ no flech to feden him vppe.

γ. *c* **1250** *Gen. & Ex.* 2320 Vp quam ðu it findes witterlike. *a* **1325** *Prose Psalter* xl. 3 Our Lord be to hym helpe up þe charge of his sorowe. *Ibid.* xlvi. 8 God shal regne vp men. **1382** WYCLIF *2 Cor.* xi. 21 Vp vnnobley [L. *secundum ignobilitatem*]. **1422** YONGE tr. *Secreta Secret.* 129 Ther-for god..granted hym mervellous victori vp his enemys.., Namly vp the morthes.

5. a. *up(þe) land*, = UPONLAND *adv.*

?*c* **1000** *Ags. Letter* in *Engl. Stud.* VIII. 62 Þu byst uppan lande mid wimmannum oftor þonne ic beo. *a* **1122** *O.E. Chron.* (Laud MS.) an. 1086, To ælcen cyrcean uppe land. *c* **1250** *Owl & Night.* 733 Preostes vpe londe singeþ. *c* **1330** *Arth. & Merl.* 698 (Kölbing), Al þe men..Boþe vp lond & in cite. **1514** BARCLAY *Cyt. & Uplondyshman* v. Prol. 44 Well he noted the madde enormyte, Enuy,..Whiche reygne in cytes; therfore he ledde his lyfe Up londe in vyllage. **1596** SPENSER *F.Q.* v. x. 25 They came vnto a Citie farre vp land.

b. On the bank or brink of; close beside.

c **1205** LAY. 7 He wonede..at æðelen are chirechen, vppen Seuarne staþe. *Ibid.* 28544 Uppe þere Tambre heo tuhte to-somne. **1340** *Ayenb.* 251 Ope þo welle þe herte resteþ efter þe trauayl of guode workes. *Ibid.*, He him zette and restede ope þe welle. **14..** in *Hist. Coll. Citizen London* (Camden) 96 The kyng made a grete justysse be-syde Kyngys towne uppe Temys.

6. a. On or upon, in respect of belief, etc.

c **1200** *Trin. Coll. Hom.* 11 Cursed be þe man þe leueð upen hwate. *Ibid.* 93 Þo forsineȝede þe hauen al here þonc uppen eorðliche richeise. *a* **1240** in *O.E. Hom.* I. 213 Þu..lettest me al iwurden wið þeo þet ich truste uppon. *a* **1300** *X Commandments* 23 in *E.E.P.* (1862) 16 Hi..þat liuiþ op goddis mo þan one. *c* **1369** CHAUCER *Dethe Blaunche* 922 So frendely, and so wel y-grounded, Vp al resoun so wel y-founded. *c* **1380** WYCLIF *Sel. Wks.* III. 88 Up trust of absolucioun. **1393** LANGL. *P. Pl.* C. x. 333 Vp trist of ȝoure tresour tryennels to haue. **1462** *Paston Lett.* II. 114 Up trust that the same John Paston shuld founde there a college.

b. According to; in accordance or agreement with; to the extent of.

1297 R. GLOUC. (Rolls) 5137 Ac vpe godes wille it is, wanne it ssal be. *Ibid.* 5657 He..vpe is poer destruede..cristendom. *c* **1300** *K. Horn* 456 (Laud MS.), And helpe þou me to knicte Oppe þine myȝte. **1382** WYCLIF *Matt.* ix. 29 Vp ȝour feith be it don to ȝou. **1388** —— *2 Sam.* xxii. 21 The Lord schal ȝelde to me vp my riȝtfulnesse.

c. By (chance, guess, etc.).

c **1350** *Will. Palerne* 2722 So brod was þe see þat sayle hem bihoued holliche al a niȝt & vp happe wel more. **1377** LANGL. *P. Pl.* B. v. 421, I nam nouȝte shryuen..tweies in two ȝere and þanne vp gesse I schryue me. *c* **1380** WYCLIF *Wks.* (1880) 375 But vp hap þu art a clerke or a religious man. *a* **1508** *Gest Robyn Hode* 49 Wayte after some vnkuth gest Vp chaunce ye may them mete.

d. In comment on or explication of; concerning.

1340 *Ayenb.* 187 Ase zayþ a glose ope the sautere. **1393** LANGL. *P. Pl.* C. XI. 113 Þre daies to-gederes we ȝeoden, Disputynge vp dowel daye after oþere. *c* **1400** *Three Kings Cologne* 39 After þe glose þat is made vp þis tixt. **1422** YONGE tr. *Secreta Secret.* 123 Wp whych matyer, Arystotle answerid in this maner. *Ibid.* 202 Vp this texte Saynte Austyn sayth thus.

7. a. On or upon (oath, condition, etc.).

a **1122** *O.E. Chron.* (Laud MS.) an. 1095, Forþam se cyng him naþer nolde ne ȝislas syllan, ne uppon trywðan ȝeunnon þæt he..cumon moste. *a* **1200** *Vices & Virtues* 11 Ic habbe ..uppe mine lahfulnesse ofte him behet, þat ic næure eft him neȝelæste. **13..** *K. Alis.* (W.) 228 'Dame,' he saide, 'beo thou nought loth, Y am y-come to telle up oth'. *c* **1369** CHAUCER *Dethe Blaunche* 750 (Fairf.), I telle hyt the vp a condicioun. *c* **1400** *Gamelyn* 411 Vp suche forward..I wil do þerto alle þat in me is. **1422** YONGE tr. *Secreta Secret.* 175 The tyraunt hit grauntid vp that covnantte.

b. Upon pain or under penalty of; on.

Freq. *c* 1380–*c* 1430, esp. with *pain*, *peril*.

(*a*) *c* **1205** LAY. 500 Þat come to hirede,..vppen lif & uppen leomen al þes londes folc. **13..** *Coer de L.* 3875 He..bad hys folk, up lyff and leme, Noo good off hem for to neme. *c* **1350** *Will. Palerne* 2378 Helpes hastily, hende men i hote, vp ȝour liues! *c* **1425** *Eng. Conq. Ireland* 120 He..vp mansynge, forbed lered & lewed, that non [etc.]. *c* **1430** LYDG. *Min. Poems* (Percy Soc.) 38 A confortatife And remedye I shal make, up my life.

(*b*) *c* **1205** LAY. 5118 Al comen to Lundene uppe wit of feowerti punden. *c* **1380** WYCLIF *Wks.* (1880) 24 Þat þei ben holden to vp peyne of lesynge of here lordischipe. *c* **1386** CHAUCER *Sompn. T.* 563 And ye shul seen, vp peril of my lyf, ..That [etc.]. **1393** LANGL. *P. Pl.* C. v. 128 Neiþer graue ne vngraue of gold ne of suluer, Vp forfeture of þe fee. **14..** *Cron. Eng.* (Caxton) ccxxi. 213 That they shold smyte of syr edmondes heede..vp payne of lyf and lymme. **1474** *Cov. Leet Bk.* 389 Vp þe peyn of vj s. viij d. at euery defalt.

8. More than; above.

a **1325** *Prose Psalter* l. 8 Y shal be made whyȝte vp snowe. *Ibid.* li. 3 Þou louedest malice up blisfolhede. **1340** *Ayenb.* 39 Þer byeþ zuo uele oþre maneres.., þet long þing hit were to zigge, ac zome byeþ y-contined, ope þan þet byeþ yzed.

III. In respect of time.

9. After (a specified time). Cf. OVER *prep.* 16.

c **1000** *Ags. Gosp.* John x. 11 *marg.*, On sunnan dæȝ feowertyne nyht uppan eastron. *a* **1122** *O.E. Chron.* (Laud MS.) an. 1095, Uppon Eastron on sancte Ambrosius mæsse niht, þæt is .ii. no. Apr. [etc.]. *Ibid.* an. 1103, On morȝen uppon sancte Laurentius mæsse dæȝ. *c* **1205** LAY. 6405 Þa hit wes muchel uppe non, þe king þene duc ouer-com. *Ibid.* 22309 Seouen niht uppen Æstre. *c* **1275** *Ibid.* 2632 Vppen one stunde þe sipes i-maked were. *c* **1290** *Beket* 1123 in *S. Eng. Leg.* I. 138 Þene moruwe ope seint lucus day, tiwesdai it was þo [*sc.* 19 Oct.], he departede fram þe kingus court.

10. At; upon (a stated time).

a **1200** *Vices & Virtues* 123 Ȝif mann ware..uppen his deaðe, and he prest ne mihte habben. *c* **1290** *Beket* 825 in *S. Eng. Leg.* I. 130 Alle..seide þo þat..ope þe pointe he was to beon i-cast In prisone. *c* **1315** SHOREHAM v. 151 Ope þe heȝe eȝtynde day He order-ȝede þe gywen lay. *c* **1374** CHAUCER *Troylus* IV. 1153 Here woful spirit from his propre place, Right with þe word, alwey vp poynt to pace.

up (ʌp), *prep.*[2] [Elliptical use of UP *adv.*[1], by omission of a preposition, as *against*, *along*, *through*, etc. Cf. the earlier use of *adown* and *down* as prepositions.]

I. Denoting or implying movement.

1. a. From a lower to a higher point on or along (an ascent); so as to ascend or mount (a stair, slope, etc.).

1509 HAWES *Past. Pleas.* XXVII. (1555) Q iij, After that they brought me vp a stayre Into a chambre. **1530** PALSGR. 828/1 Up the hyll and downe the vale. **1593** SHAKS. *2 Hen. VI*, IV. viii. 1 Vp Fish-streete, downe Saint Magnes corner,..throw them into Thames. **1602** —— *Ham.* IV. iii. 39 As you go vp the staires into the Lobby. **1607** MARKHAM *Cavel.* VI. 9 Hee may eyther runne..vp hils, or down hils. **1697** DRYDEN *Virg. Georg.* III. 552 The Sun..When up the Skies he shoots his rosie Head. **1730** THOMSON *Autumn* 701 The..exhalations, check'd As up the middle sky unseen they stole. **1786** BURNS *On Dining w. Ld. Daer* i, Sae far I sprackled up the brae. **1807** J. BARLOW *Columb.* I. 190 A heaven-illumined road; That..Reach'd o'er the hills, and lengthen'd up the sky. **1828** LYTTON *Pelham* II. xviii, If your way is up Pall Mall, I have no objection to join you. **1851** *Offic. Catal. Gt. Exhib.* 366 By which the weight on the horse's back is regulated in going up or down hill. **1867** MORRIS *Jason* I. 208 Who, up the temple steps, beneath the weight Of precious things went bending.

Comb. **1732** E. ERSKINE *Wks.* (1791) 598/2 This phrase..implies, that religion is an up-the-hill work and way.

fig. **1824** WILSON in *Blackw. Mag.* Aug. 242 Abusing the Germans up-hill and down-dale. **1844** DICKENS *Mart. Chuz.* xxxv, All this time, Martin was cursing Mr. Pecksniff up hill and down dale.

b. Extending upwards on.

1574 *Southampton Court Leet Rec.* (1905) I. 101 The Raylles vpe the steares goynge vpe vnto the Wache towere. **1730** THOMSON *Autumn* 679 The vineyard..Spreads o'er the vale; or up the mountain climbs. **1756** *Constat* in *L.T.R. Particulars for Leases* 4974 (P.R.O.), The dimensions up one pair of Stairs are only Thirty one Feet.

c. Up into. *U.S. local.*

1774 P. V. FITHIAN *Jrnl.* 16 July (1900) 209 She then retired up chamber. **1833** [S. SMITH] *Lett. J. Downing* xxiv. (1835) 98, I..walked straight up chamber. *Ibid.* 150 When they undertook to cum up-chamber,..it was time to snub 'em. **1893** S. HALE *Let.* 22 May (1919) 282 Louise..is now carrying some new pails up garret.

d. *vulgar.* Of a man: having sexual intercourse with.

1937 PARTRIDGE *Dict. Slang* 926/2 *Up*,..in coïtion with (a woman): low: late (? mid-) C. 19–20. **1973** 'J. PATRICK' *Glasgow Gang Observed* xii. 108 We've aw been up her. **1977** C. WATSON *One Man's Meat* viii. 74 The younger man said to the older: 'I'd rather be up her than up in Newcastle.'

2. Along (a river, etc.) in a direction from the mouth towards the source.

1513 *Acc. Ld. High Treas. Scotl.* IV. 465 To ane bot [going] wp the watter with cabillis,..xiiij s. **1560** DAUS tr. *Sleidane's Comm.* 360 b, They brought in vitayle both vp the streame and down. **1600** *Reg. Mag. Sig. Scot.* 384/1 Haldand up the said burne to the inver of the burne of Auldclachrie. **1659** *Nicholas Papers* (Camden) IV. 95 Alexandria, from whence I went up the Riuer Nilus to Cairo. **1698** FRYER *Acc. E. India & P.* 38 All the Factories on the Coast..as far as the Bay of Bengala, and up Huygly River. **1738** *Voy. up the Thames* 15 It was propos'd we should take a Voyage up its Banks. **1814** SCOTT *Diary* 3 Sept., in *Lockhart*, With the purpose of running up the loch to see Londonderry. **1849** MACAULAY *Hist. Eng.* ii. I. 191 The Dutch fleet sailed up the Thames. **1877** MISS A. B. EDWARDS (*title*), A Thousand Miles up the Nile.

3. a. Towards the inner or upper end of; into or towards the interior of. Also *transf.*

1596 SPENSER *F.Q.* v. ix. 23 His name was Awe; by whom they passing in Went vp the hall. *a* **1700** in *Orpheus Caledonius* (1725) 28 The wooer he step'd up the House. **1745** P. THOMAS *Jrnl. Anson's Voy.* 63 The Treasure..being sent up the Country..out of our Reach. **1818** *Sketches of Character* (ed. 2) I. 44 Lady Aucherly..sauntered up the room with her three disconsolate nieces. **1849** MACAULAY *Hist. Eng.* ix. II. 482 William's army began to march up the country. **1863** MAYNE REID *Croquet* i. (1865) 25 A ball croque'd beyond the boundaries is sent to 'Hong Kong', or 'up the country'.

b. ***up yours***, an exclamation of contemptuous rejection, often used *imp.* (and accompanied by an impolite gesture) [shortened f. *up your arse* (or a similar expression): cf. SHOVE *v.*[1] 10 e]. *coarse slang.*

1956 'E. MCBAIN' *Cop Hater* ii. 18 'How's the graft these days?'.. 'Up yours,' Carella answered drily. **1969** B. MALAMUD *Pictures of Fidelman* vi. 208 Fidelman blew a..green horse for Beppo..'Up yours,' said the glass blower. **1970** A. TOFFLER *Future Shock* viii. 154 The upraised finger—the 'up yours' gesture—appears to be gaining greater respectability. **1975** J. SYMONS *Three Pipe Problem* xviii. 208 She made a V sign at the audience, said distinctly 'Up yours'. **1978** J. HYAMS *Pool* xi. 168 'Up yours, Richie Lesser,' Freda said without malice. 'I'm smarter than you are any day.'

4. In a direction contrary to; against.

1611 COTGR., *Prendre le vent*, to goe vp, or against, the wind. **1618** BRETON *Court & Country* A 4, For one that goes up the weather a number goe downe the winde. **1674** N. COX *Gentl. Recreat.* (1677) 77 The Huntsman [should]..then draw round apace, first down the Wind, though usually Deer go up the Wind. **1719** D'URFEY *Pills* III. 269 The Fox has broke Covert,..she runs up the Wind. **1816** SCOTT *Bl. Dwarf* ii, I gaed a mile round to get up the wind to them. **1838** [see UP-WIND *adv.*].

5. Along (in a horizontal direction or straight course).

up street (dial.), along the street or village.

1669 STURMY *Mariner's Mag.* I. ii. 20 Port, edge towards him [*sc.* a ship]. We will run up his Side. **1683** [see GO *v.* 66].

1719 De Foe *Crusoe* I. (Globe) 156, I went up the Shore and down the Shore, but..could see no other Impression. **1758** Johnson *Idler* No. 92 ¶6 He..walks up a bye-street. **1851** Mrs. Browning *Casa Guidi Wind.* II. 742 The sun strikes, through the windows, up the floor. **1883** *Harper's Mag.* Oct. 718/1 It is approached up an avenue. **1886** Froude *Oceana* 63 After breakfast we went up the town.

II. Denoting location.

6. a. In that part of (a place) which is (regarded as) higher than another, or is more remote from the chief centre.

1667 Pepys *Diary* 8 Sept., Nova Scotia..hath a river 300 miles up the country, with copper mines. **1750** Gray *Elegy* 112 Nor up the lawn, nor at the wood was he. **1795** T. Wilkinson *Wandering Patentee* III. 244 She turned quite round up the stage, (though not in character) as much as to say, kiss—. **1799** *Hull Advertiser* 12 Oct. 1/1 All those five tenements up the yard. **1810** Scott *Lady of Lake* II. xxxvi, Far up the lake, 'twere safest land. **1885** Jerome *On the Stage* 43 Mind you all keep well up the stage ('up' the stage means towards the back). **1890** *Cent. Mag.* Aug. 634/1 The man who abandoned a farm up the Hudson.

Comb. **1815** Scott *Guy M.* l, We're just plain up-the-country folk. **1897** *Outing* XXIX. 424 Up-the-creek natives.

b. *U.S.* Up in (the), up at. Cf. sense 1 c.

1845 S. Judd *Margaret* II. ix. 344 You will find..in the bottom of my chest, up garret, five dollars and a quarter. **1862** M. D. Colt *Went to Kansas* 274 My nephew is..teaching among the Indians up Lake Superior. **1884** 'Mark Twain' *Huck. Finn* xxvi. 237 Up garret was a little cubby with a pallet in it. **1923** R. Frost *Two Witches in New Hampshire* 66 Then we asked was there anything Up attic that we'd ever want again.

c. Up at. *colloq.* and *dial.*

1960 M. Spark *Ballad Peckham Rye* vi. 122 Collie Gould up the Elephant with young Leslie. **1967** J. Burke *Till Death us do Part* xi. 165 'Where you been? That's what I want to know.' 'Up the pictures.' **1975** A. Drummond *Thames Jrnls. Vicesimus Lush* 23 Vicesimus Lush..was living in a cottage near the Hape mine—'up the Hape' in the local speech.

7. a. At the top of. **b.** At some distance up on or in. (Cf. uphill *a.*, upstairs *adv.* 2.)

For fig. expressions see gum-tree 2, tree *sb.* 7, sleeve *sb.* 2 b, spout *sb.* 4 b.

1645 Rutherford *Tryal Faith* xxiii. 261 Heaven.., when sight [of faith] faileth us, [is] toylesome and up the mount. **1714** Arbuthnot, etc. *Mem. M. Scribl.* Introd., His lodging was in a small chamber up four pair of stairs. **1833** Moore *Trav. Ir. Gentl. Search Relig.* I. 1 As I was sitting alone in my chambers, up two pair of stairs, Trinity College. **1846** Tennyson *Golden Year* 4 We that day had been Up Snowdon. **1860** Geo. Eliot *Mill on Fl.* I. ii, He'll..sleep up three pair o' stairs—or four, for what I know. **1890** [see sleeve *sb.* 2 b].

U P, U. P.: see up *adv.*² 12 e and U 5.

U. P. (= United Presbyterian): see U 4.

up-, *prefix*, representing OE. *up-*, *upp-* (see below) and corresponding to OFris. *op-*, *up-* (WFris. *op-*, NFris. *üp-*, *ap-*), MDu. and Du. *op-*, OS., MLG., and LG. *up-*, OHG. and MHG. *ûf-* (G. *auf-*), ON., Icel., and Norw. *upp-*, MSw. *up-*, *upp-* (also *op-*, *opp-*), Sw. *upp-*, MDa. and Da. *op-*.

The prefix is identical with the adverb up¹, from which in OE. it becomes clearly separable only when prefixed to nouns and adjs. In the cognate languages there is much variation in the extent to which it is employed with different parts of speech. In OS. and OFris. it occurs with verbs and nouns, in OHG. with verbs, nouns, and a few adjs., in ON. chiefly with nouns, in MHG., MLG., MDu., MSw. and MDa. with both verbs and nouns, and occasionally adjs. In the later and modern forms of these languages the use of the prefix has increased as in English, and parallel formations are very common; these are cited only when the Eng. compound is important enough to appear as a main word.

Of the numerous formations with *up-* which have been employed in English, only a limited number are of a permanent character. A large proportion consists of forms employed for nonce, especially for metrical reasons, and the same compound may recur several times without any historical continuity; such isolated occurrences, indeed, are often separated by an interval of several centuries. A number of these are given in the following sections, as illustrations of the various uses of the prefix in the different periods of the language.

I. In comb. with sbs. (except as in 7, 8).

1. a. In OE. *up-* occurs freely with sbs. in the sense of 'occupying a higher position', 'upper', 'superior', as *up-eard*, *-ende*, *-engel*, *-flór*, etc. Some of these, however, are only found in poetry. In ME. this type practically disappears, and in later use is chiefly represented by upland *sb.*² and upside, with an occasional rare formation, as *upwold*.

b. With the sense of 'in a supported state', *up-* occurs with nouns in OE. *upheald*, ME. *uphald*, uphold, ME. *uptie* (naut.), and the modern *upkeep*.

2. a. In the sense of 'upwards' OE. had compounds of *up-* with nouns, mainly derived from intransitive verbs, as *up-cyme*, *-færeld*, *-ryne*, *-spring*, *-stiȝe*, rarely from transitive, as *upwearp*. Of these only *upspring* and *upsty* survived in ME., but a number of new formations were added, as the obsolete *uparist*, *-brixle*, *-brud*, *-ras*, *-rist*, and the surviving *upbraid*, *-come*, *-rise*, *-set*. Between 1450 and 1800 new formations are rare, the chief being *upcast* and *upstir* in the 16th cent., with *upskip* and *upstart* (as designations of persons) from the same period; also *upshot* (with variants *-shoot* and *-shut*), in which the force of the *up-* is not clear. After 1800 the type reappears and subsequently becomes common. A considerable number of the examples are of sufficient importance to be entered as main words in their alphabetical places, as *upbeat*, *-break*, *-burst*, *-flow*, *-growth*, *-heaval*, *-lift*, etc. Others of more recent origin or less currency are ***upblaze***, ***-climb***, ***-cry***, ***-curl***, ***-curve***, ***-draw***, ***-drift***, ***-flutter***, ***-glance***, ***-gush***, ***-haul***, ***-heave***, ***-jet***, ***-jump***, ***-liftment***, ***-reach***, ***-shine***, ***-slip***, ***-sweep***. In *upset*, as in the corresponding verb, the prefix is employed in an unusual sense.

1920 *Blackw. Mag.* July 69/2 The lonely halts of the long *upclimb. **1677** *Sec. Packet of Advices to Men of Shaftesbury* 55 They are better at *Up-cry, and Out-cry, and Down-cry. **1929** O. F. Dudley *Masterful Monk* viii. 88 There would undoubtedly be an upcry from Rome. **1928** *Nation* 27 June p. iii/3 Our circulation is on the *up-curve. **1950** Fraser & Thomson *Honest Bread* vii. 64 The upcurve in public drinking. **1912** J. London *Son of Sun* I. ii. 23 Grief, with a quick *updraw of his knees to the other's chest, broke the grip and forced him down. **1876** Meredith *Beauch. Career* xxvi, It suggested an arrow-head in the *up-flight. **1929** D. H. Lawrence *Pansies* 35 And then the geese scuttled in.. and round the ring they went..then doubled, and back, with a funny *up-flutter of wings. **1860** Hawthorne *Marb. Faun* xvi, The shifting..*up-gush and downfall of water. **1981** *Sunday Express Mag.* 14 June 24 (*caption*) *Uphaul line with knots, used to pull sail up from water. **1984** *Times* 25 Aug. 11/2 Taking all the weight on my legs I eased the sail out of the water using the uphaul and paused for it to drain. **1860** Vivian *Deb. Coal Clause* (1861) p. xv, The 'Great Lower Veins', varying from 50 feet on the Northern to 100 feet on the Southern outcrop, and upwards of 70 feet on the Central *upheave. **1817** *Sporting Magazine* L. 128 He received some dreadful *up-hits in his throat. **1850** 'H. Hieover' *Pract. Horsemanship* 129 The moment he does this, give him an *up-pull. **1926** D. H. Lawrence *David* xiii. 100 So the *upreach of his love fails him. **1934** F. Scott Fitzgerald *Tender is Night* II. iv. 176 The *upshine of a street-lamp. **1876** *Whitby Gloss.*, **Upshow*,..display.

b. More rarely, *up-* is employed in the sense of 'upwards', with other nouns than those of action, e.g. OE. *upweȝ*, early mod.E. *upway*, and the recent *up-grade*, *-road*, *-shaft*, *-wave*.

1926 *N.E.D.*, Up-road. **1938** X. Herbert *Capricornia* (1939) xiii. 185 Up-road guests may come by special train.. at excursion rates. **1984** *Times* 18 July 19/2 'Footsie' started on the uproad.

II. **3.** *Up-* is rarely employed in combination with adjs.; *upheaded* (16th cent. and mod. dial.), *upstraight* (17th cent.), *upfingered*, *uphearted*, *upnosed*, and *upsighted* (19th cent.) are unusual types, as also are *upspring* and *upstart* (16th cent.) employed as adjs., but retaining the form of the noun or verb.

III. With verbs, participles, verbal substantives, and agent-nouns.

4. In OE. the placing of *up* immediately before a verbal form was determined by the syntactical principles which have been explained in the article on out-. The number of verbs with which *up* was commonly employed in this way is not large; it includes *ábrecan*, *áhebban*, *áræran*, *árísan*, etc., *gán*, *hebban*, *rǽcan*, *springan*, *spryttan*, *stiȝan*, *yrnan*. It is difficult to determine in how many of these the adverb had become a real prefix, but apparently it had attained this function in some forms, as *upáhebban* and *uphebban*. In ME. the use of the prefix is thoroughly established, though it is not always possible to distinguish between real compounds and simple precedence of the adverb on metrical or rhetorical grounds. A number of these uncertain examples may be found under various senses of up *adv.*¹ Of those established compounds which require separate entry some occur as early as the 13th century, as *upbraid*, *-break*, *-bring*, *-come*, *-go*, *-nim*, *-stand*, etc., and many more are found from about 1300 onwards, as *upbear*, *-call*, *-cast*, *-draw*, *-give*, *-heave*, *-hold*, *-leap*, etc. Others have been constantly added during the following centuries, so that even with the disappearance of earlier instances the type has been well maintained down to the present day. A considerable proportion, however, occur only in poetry, and are simple substitutions for the verb followed by the adverb, although they are regarded as real compounds and written as one word.

In the OE. collocations or compounds the prefix has regularly the sense of 'upwards'. In ME. it also assumes various transferred or figurative senses of the adverb, and latterly may have any meaning which has attached to this in connexion with a verb, e.g. *upbind* to bind up; *up-pen* to pen up; *upspeed*, to speed up, etc. The same variety of meaning naturally occurs also in combination with participles and verbal nouns.

In addition to those which are entered as main words, the following examples illustrate the tendency to employ the prefix in place of the adverb. The first group contains examples earlier than 1650, the second those of more recent origin (mostly after 1800); where no definition is added, the meaning is that of the simple verb in conjunction with *up*.

The earlier group could be considerably enlarged by the inclusion of examples from Scottish poets of the 16th cent., esp. Douglas, who freely employs such forms as *upblese* (= blaze), *-flow*, *-glide*, *-hese* (= raise), *-kindle*, *-rax* (= stretch), *-rive*, *-sprent*, *-stend*, *-stour*, *-strike*, *-swak*, *-warp*, *-wrele*. Instances from other authors are *upbrace*, *-keek*, *-lese* (= gather), *-sit*, *-skail*, *-spread*, *-sprinkle*, *-win* (= rise).

a. upa'rise [OE. *up-árísan*], **up'bend**, *intr.*; **up'burst**, **-'call**, **-'delve**, *trans.*; **up'dive**, *intr.*; **u'peat**, *trans.*; **up'find**, *trans.* to invent; **up'fly**, *intr.*; **up'fo**, *trans.* to receive; **up'get**, *intr.* to rise up; **up'grave**, *trans.* to dig up; **up'harbour**, **-'harrow**, *trans.*; **up'head**, *trans.* to cover in; **up'heal**, *intr.*; **up'hebbe** [OE. *up-hebban*], *trans.* to raise up, exalt; **up'hilt**, *trans.* to plunge up to the hilt; **up'keep**, *trans.* to support; **up'kever**, *intr.* to recover; **up'knit**, *trans.*; **up'lope**, *intr.* to spring up; **up'pen**, **-'prop**, *trans.*; **up'rape**, *intr.* to rise hastily; **up'reek**, *intr.*; **up'render**, **-'rent** (= rend), **-re'store**, **-'rid**, *trans.*; **up'ripe**, *trans.* to search out; **up'run**, *intr.*; **up'screw**, **-'shear**, **-'sheath**, **-'shore**, *trans.*; **up'smite**, *intr.*; **up'snatch**, *trans.*; †**up'soup**, *trans.* to swallow up; **up'spar**, **-'spear**, *trans.* to close up; **up'speed**, *trans.*; **up'spire**, *intr.* to shoot up; **up'staunch**, *trans.*; **up'stock**, *trans.* to dig up; **up'sup**, *trans.*; **up'thrive**, *intr.*; **up'truss**, **-'tuck**, **-vomit**, *trans.*; **up'waff**, *intr.* to begin to blow; **up'wall**, *trans.*; **up'wax**, *intr.*; **up'weigh**, *trans.* to lift up; **up'weir**, *trans.* to defend; **up'wend**, *intr.* to go up; **up'wrap**, **-'wring**, *trans.*

1340 *Ayenb.* 186 Al ase þe oyle *op arist ine þe lompe alle þe oþer woses. **1649** F. Roberts *Clavis Bibliorum* 43 Them that against thee up-arose Thou utterly didst over-throw. *c* **1440** *Pallad. on Husb.* I. 1087 First floore it ij feet thicke enclynynge softe The fourneis ward, so that the flaume *vpbende. **1596** Spenser *F.Q.* VI. xi. 43 But Calidore..The dores assayled, and the locks *vpbrast. *c* **1340** Hampole *Pr. Consc.* 4963 Alle men þai sal þan *up-calle And byd þam cum til þe dome alle. *c* **1400** *Northern Passion* (H.) 468 When he saw þai sleped all, Peter first he gan vp call. *c* **1440** *Pallad. on Husb.* IX. 92 Ther as they growe, *vpdelue..v foote into the grounde. **1603** J. Davies (Heref.) *Microcosmos* Wks. (Grosart) I. 81/2 Plunge thee ore head and eares in Helicon, ..Thence make thy fame *vp-dive. **1630** Drumm. of Hawth. *Shadow of Judgement* 247 In Townes, the liuing doe the dead *vp-eate. *c* **1440** *Pallad. on Husb.* Prohem. 85 What thynge engyne *vpfynde, or reson trie And iustifie. *a* **1542** Wyatt *Complaint upon Love* in *Tottel's Misc.* (Arb) 49, I gaue him winges, wherwith he might *vpflie To honor, and fame. **1600** Fairfax *Tasso* XIX. xviii, But he..Let go his hold, and on his feete vpflew. *a* **1300** *E.E. Psalter* cxvii. 13, I am turned, þat i suld falle; And lauerd *vpfange [*v.r.* onfonge; L. *suscepit*] me with-alle. **1582** Stanyhurst *Æneis* I. (Arb.) 27 Æneas..With Phœbus rising *vpgot. *a* **1340** Hampole *Psalter* vii. 16 þe lake he oppynd and *vp grofe it [L. *effodit*]. *Ibid.*, He vpgraues it when he waitis all þat he may [etc.]. **1563** Sackville in *Mirr. Mag.* 131 b, Such heapes of harmes *upharbard in his brest..my honour to deface. **1582** Stanyhurst *Æneis* III. (Arb.) 86 You rest in fre quiet, thee seas you need not *vpharrow. **1519** *Extr. Aberd. Reg.* (1844) I. 96 Alexander Galloway..promittit..to big and *vpheid..ane chapell and oratour. *c* **1440** *Pallad. on Husb.* XI. 239 Yf a tender tree Me kitte,..in oon yeer *vpheleth hit attonys. **1340** *Ayenb.* 217 Arere we..oure honden to god þet *ophebbeþ oure benes be guode workes. **1582** Stanyhurst *Æneis* II. (Arb.) 61 His blad he with thrusting in his old dwynd carcas *vphilted. *c* **1412** Hoccleve *De Reg. Princ.* 4930 A bridil, Which þat an hors *vpkepeth fro fallyng. *c* **1350** *Will. Palerne* 2759 For al þat sterne strok stifli he *vp-keuerede, & swam swiftili awei. **1596** Spenser *F.Q.* IV. vi. 30 Glauce thus gan wisely all *vpknit; Ye gentle Knights [etc.]. *a* **1600** Montgomerie *Misc. Poems* iii. 33 The cadger clims,..And ladds *vploips to lordships all thair lains. **1600** Fairfax *Tasso* XVI. xxxiii, What letharge hath in drowsinesse *vppend Thy courage thus? **1601** Donne *Progr. Soul* 386 Himselfe he *up-props, on himselfe relies. **13..** *Seuyn Sages* (W.) 1620 The wretche stiward ne might nowt slape; Ac in the moreweing he gan *uprape. *c* **1250** *Gen. & Ex.* 3465 Smoke *up-rekeð and munt quakeð. **1551** Robinson tr. *More's Utopia* (Arb.) 43 That they..shal..yelde, and *vprender the possession therof. *c* **1620** Robinson *Mary Magd.* 48 Blind Cupid seem'd to shoote, and tender hearts *vprent. *a* **1560** Phaer *Æneid* VIII. (1562) Bb iiij b, And seruice left since yesterdaye He gladly *vprestores. **1581–2** *Catal. Anc. Deeds* (1906) V. 484 [They shall] stocke, brushe, *uppe ridde and carie away [all] breers, brembles [etc.]. ? *a* **1400** *Morte Arth.* 3940 The riche kynge ransakes..And *vp-rypes the renkes of alle the Rownde Tabylle. *c* **1440** *Pallad. on Husb.* XII. 598 And next to hem xvj [feet] *vprenneth sone. **1646** G. Daniel *Poems* Wks. (Grosart) I. 18 Let petty Sphæres their heightned Peggs *vp-Scrue, To rival with the greater. **1430–40** Lydg. *Bochas* III. 5107 So of that lynage he hath the weed *up-shorn. **1614** Gorges *Lucan* II. 47 Let thy vaine rage his sword *vp-sheath. *c* **1557** Abp. Parker *Ps.* cxix. 364 Yere after yere me then *upshore with thy good helping hand. **1446** Lydg. *Two Nightingale Poems* ii. 39 The bawmy vapour of grassis gan *vp-smyte In-to myn hede. *a* **1566** R. Edwards *Damon & Pithias* C iv, Snap yᵉ Tipstaffe..came and *vpsnatched him. **1382** Wyclif *Ps.* cxxiii. 4 Per auenture water hadde *vp sopen vs [1388 sope vs vp; L. *absorbuisset*]. **1630** *Tinker of Turvey* 35 His eyes were..

sparkling like the starres, When the day her light *up sparres. 1538 BALE *Johan Baptystes* ad fin., Adam, by hys pryde, ded paradyse *vp speare. 1338 R. BRUNNE *Chron.* (1810) 77 Saynt Cutberte's clerkes..At Geruans set þer merkes, a hous þei gan *vpspede. 1558 PHAER *Æneid* U j, Whan..stickes are kindled fast, and flame with noyse doth close *vpspyre. c1440 *Pallad. on Husb.* VI. 125 Ek skyn and strynges seryng so tenfire *Vpstauncheth blood. *Ibid.* 46 If ther be treen, *vpstocke hem by the roote. 1537 SURREY in *Tottel's Misc.* (Arb.) 14 The whiche [tears] as sone as sobbyng sighes..*Vpsupped haue, thus I my plaint renewe. c1440 *Pallad. on Husb.* II. 446 The seueth [hour] as v, and eight as iiij *vpthrive. c1340 HAMPOLE *Pr. Consc.* 5567 Silver and gold..þe whilk þai had in hurde *uptrust. a1529 SKELTON *E. Rummyng* 419 Her kyrtell she did *vptucke. 1582 STANYHURST *Æneis* II. (Arb.) 54 Theire steed hath *vp-vomited from gorge a surfet of armdmen. 13.. *E.E. Allit. P.* B. 949 To wakan wederez so wylde þe wyndez he callez, & þay wroþely *vp-wafte & wrastled togeder. c1440 *Pallad. on Husb.* I. 435 When that is drie, *vpwalle hit euery side. 1340 *Ayenb.* 75 Þer *opwexeþ alle guodes, uayrhede, richesse, worþssipe, blisse. 1513 DOUGLAS *Æneid* VI. vii. 62 The new mone quhen first wpwaxis sche. a1593 MARLOWE *Hero & Leander* I. 450 They..At his..feet the engins layd, Which th' earth from ougly Chaos den *vp-wayd. a1586 MAITLAND *Theivis of Liddisdail* 63 Sum grit men..That..will *vp-weir þair stollin geir. c1200 *Trin. Coll. Hom.* 23 Þo he steah to heuene swo þat his apostles..bihielden hwu he *upwende. a1400 *Isumbras* 510 With wery bones the knyghte up-wenede In to that haythene stede. 1600 FAIRFAX *Tasso* X. lxx. 193 The wilie dame In other foldes our mischiefes would *vpwrap. a1560 PHAER *Æneid* IX. (1562) Ff i, The gate..at last he shutts, and bolts *vpwrings.

b. up'buoy, -'crane, -'drag, -'hand, -'harrow, -'heel, -'knit, -'prick, 'rend, -'shoulder, -'snatch, -'speed, -'spew, -'spin, -'stamp, -'stir, -'sway, -'thrust, -'whirl, *trans.*; **up'blacken, -'blaze, -'blow, -'bubble, -'creep, -'curve, -'flame, -'flee, -'flower, -'jet, -'kindle, -'knit, -'move, -'pop, -'rein, -'rouse, -'run, -'spire, -'steam, -'step, -'tend,** *intr.*

1818 MILMAN *Samor* VIII. 43 The rocks..*Upblacken to the sky. 1839 HOOD *Nocturnal Sketch* ii, The gas *up-blazes with its bright white light. 1798 COLERIDGE *Anc. Mar.* V. xi, The ship mov'd on; Yet never a breeze *up-blew. 1865 E. CASWALL *May Pageant* ii. 25 Close to where St. Oswy's ancient well *Up-bubbles from its arch'd and mossy cell. 1954 L. MACNEICE *Autumn Sequel* xxvi. 160 Wells of words Upbubble. 1652 BENLOWES *Theoph.* I. lxviii, Pow'rs cannot poets, as they pow'rs *up-buoy. a1850 ROSSETTI *Dante & Circle* II. (1874) 296 Nor once from her did show of love up-buoy This passion. 1816 *Monthly Mag.* XLI. 527 To heave aboard the stores, *Upcrane the cannon, roll the water casks. 1874 R. BUCHANAN *Poet. Wks.* III. 234 On thy shore he sinks in death, And thy still tides *upcreep. 1885 B. HARTE *Maruja* iii, Then something like a light ring of smoke *up-curved from the saddle before him. 1847 TENNYSON *Princ.* IV. 347 She..stoop'd to *updrag Melissa. 1826 CARRINGTON *Dartmoor* 87 To Jupiter *upflamed The human hecatomb. 1810 SOUTHEY *Kehama* XVIII. vi, He started,..and to his head His hands *up-fled. 1894 MRS. A. WEBSTER *Mother & Daughter* (1895) 31 My youth *upflowers with hers. 1865 KINGSLEY *Herew.* iv, To high heaven, all so softly, The angels *uphand him. 1795 MACNEILL *Scotland's Skaith* IV. v, A' thy gentle mind *upharrows—Hate, revenge, and rage uprears. 1877 *The Sea* 1 Dec., The ship was beginning to sink; a sudden breeze springing *upheeled her still more. 1860 TENNYSON *Sea Dreams* 52 With ground-swell, which ..*upjetted in spirits of wild sea-smoke. 1857 HEAVYSEGE *Saul* (1869) 189 Why in your eye *upkindles no fierce joy At coming-on of battle? 1889 RIDER HAGGARD *Cleopatra* II. iii, Does the half-death of sleep..thus *upknit the cut thread of human kinship? 1805 *Poet. Register* 178, I reach a cot; the friendly latch *upmoves. 1855 SINGLETON *Virgil* I. 359 So many tongues, Mouths just so many babble, she *uppricks So many ears. 1812 W. TENNANT *Anster F.* I. xxvi, The churlish spirit..*up-popp'd from sea, a tangle-tassel'd shape. 1883 R. W. DIXON *Mano* I. xvii. 57 By his cottage this bold knight *upreined. 1830 TENNYSON *Poems* 126 Music, borne abroad By the loud winds, though they *uprend the sea. 1812 J. BAILLIE *Orra* III. i, *Uprouse ye, then, my merry men! 1791 COWPER *Iliad* XVIII. 543 A son..[who] like a luxuriant plant *Upran to manhood. 1844 KINGLAKE *Eothen* (1845) 104 A high struggling ridge that *upshouldered itself from out of the wilderness of myrtles. 1844 MRS. BROWNING *Lost Bower* xliv, Mystic Presences of power Had *up-snatch'd me to the Timeless. 1872 J. PAYNE *Songs of Life & Death* 9 In his stead there was *upsped A grisly Death from Hell. 1714 [CROXALL] *Original Canto Spenser* xxi, 'Till from their inly Maw their Loads they did *upspew. 1925 E. BLUNDEN *English Poems* 27 The darkening room by use well knows Each thread of life that these upspin. 1854 J. D. BURNS *Vision of Prophecy* 165 The temple, like a glorious dream, *upspires Into the lucid air. 1791 COWPER *Iliad* V. 598 A dusty cloud..which steeds..*Up-stamp'd into the brazen vault of heaven. 1812 CARY *Dante, Parad.* VIII. 75 The vapoury cloud..Bituminous *upsteamed. a1828 *Hynd Horn* xx. in Child *Ballads* I. 207/1 Straight to them ye will *upstep. 1833 MRS. BROWNING *Stanzas Passage Emerson's Jrnl.* VI, As when the war-trump of the wind *Upstirs our dark blue sea. 1811 SCOTT *Don Roderick* II. xvi, That right-hand giant 'gan his club *upsway. a1711 KEN *Christophil* Poet. Wks. 1721 I. 420 She, as to Heav'n each Syllable *uptends, From Syllable to Syllable descends. a1893 CHR. G. ROSSETTI *Poems* (1904) 215/1 As seeds their proper bodies all *upthrust. 1845 MANGAN *German Anthol.* I. 40 The maelstrom..*upwhirled and up-bore me to daylight at length.

5. The use of *up* with past pples., originally syntactical, gave rise to compounds of which several had already so far established themselves in OE. that derivatives in *-nes* and *-líce* were formed from them. Examples are *up(á)hafen, upáhefed, up(á)sprungen, upástigen, upcumen.* In ME. a number of new formations appear; among the earlier of these are *upborne, -drawn, -folden, -hung, -laid, -lifted, -reft, -risen, -set.* In the 16th and 17th cent. there are also frequent examples, and the type is still usual, but at all periods these forms have been mainly employed in verse. When used attributively the stress is normally on the prefix, but metrical instances frequently retain it on the stem.

The following are illustrations of casual examples of earlier and later date; a few others are used by Scottish writers of the 16th cent., esp. Douglas.

(*a*) †**upaheven** [OE. *up-áhafen*], lifted up, uplifted; †**upbounden**, tied up; **upbred, -framed;** †**upgraven**, dug up; †**uphoist**, lifted up; **upled;** †**uplent**, arrived on high; **uploughed, -puffed, -pulled, -reft, -rent, -ripped,** †**upsete(d**, oppressed; †**upshet**, shut up, enclosed; **upshut, -soaked,** †**-soaken, -stalled;** †**upstreyht, upstretched; upsucked, -trailed,** †**-whelmed, -wrapped, -wrought.**

a1225 *Juliana* 58 To þonken godd wið honden *upaheuene. a1225 *Leg. Kath.* 2373 Heo biheold upward, wið upaheuen heorte. c1440 *Pallad. on Husb.* III. 514 Now stakid & *vpbounden wol they be. 1590 SPENSER *F.Q.* III. ix. 20 Her golden locks, that were in tramels gay Vpbounden. 1577 HOLINSHED *Chron.* I. *Hist. Scotland* 126 As those that were no Brytaynes borne, but straungers vnto them, being both borne and *vpbred in a forraine countrey. a1560 PHAER *Æneid* VIII. (1562) Bb iij b, A towne there is with aunciaunt stones *vpfraamed. *Ibid.* IX. Ee ij b, A towre.. then stood, with skaffolds large of length In place vpframyd fit. a1340 HAMPOLE *Psalter* lxxix. 17 Kyndild at þe fire and *vpgrafen [L. *suffossa*]. c1557 ABP. PARKER *Ps.* ii. G iij b, Lyke dust or chaffe they bee *Uphoyst by winde. 1568 T. HOWELL *Arb. Amitie* (1879) 68 So I vphoyst by wyffling windes..Doe bide the brunt of bitter blastes. 1667 MILTON *P.L.* VII. 12 *Up led by thee Into the Heav'n of Heav'ns. c1450 *Songs, Carols*, etc. (E.E.T.S.) 71/83 For þat mayst þou joy, man, þat þi cownt is *vplent, Wher God..his body doth present. 1610 G. FLETCHER *Christ's Vict.* I. lxxi, The *up-plowed heart, all..wounded by it selfe. 1573 TUSSER *Husb.* (1878) 147 His looke like a coxcombe, *vp puffed with pride. 1658 A. FOX *Würtz' Surg.* IV. ii. 316 Such wounds, where there appeareth an up-puffed swelling. c1440 *Pallad. on Husb.* X. 166 With roote a plaunte *vppuld & sett, wol springe. a1300 *Cursor M.* 20950 *Vp-reft he [*sc.* Paul] was to thrid heuen. 1584 HUDSON *Du Bartas' Judith* III. (1611) 33 Their Crosbowes were *vprent with yron Racks. 1653 HOLCROFT *Procopius, Goth. Wars* IV. 130 These Barbarians ..made a new fashioned Ram, using no timbers *upript, nor lying a crosse. 1390 GOWER *Conf.* III. 283 For of the false Moabites..The poeple of god was ofte *upsete. 1549 LYNNE *Briefe Collection* (title-p.), Yᵉ most blessed..of them that be vpseted wyth sycknes and other visitations of God. c1440 *Pallad. on Husb.* I. 993 [With] water myxt the grount, ..*Vpshette aboute, and trampled with catel. c1485 in *E.E. Misc.* (Warton Club) 52 Where are thy bestes, good sone?.. They be now up-schete. 1658 A. FOX *Würtz' Surg.* I. viii. 35 That *up-shut moisture will stir at the changing of weathers. 1582 STANYHURST *Æneis* II. (Arb.) 55 Lyke rauening woolfdams *vpsoackt and gaunted in hunger. *Ibid.* III. 77 Theire face wan withred in hunger, With famin *vp-soaken. 1430–40 LYDG. *Bochas* VIII. 208 Domycian.. Proudli comaundid, in his estat *up stallid, Of all the world he sholde a god be callid. 1569 E. HAKE *Newes Powles Churchyarde* (1579) F 5 These ranckly feede the pamperd Swyne vpstalled in their nest. c1425 *Orolog. Sapient.* iii. in *Anglia* X. 348/1 To go pruwdelye with an *vp-streyht nekke. 1560 B. GOOGE tr. *Palingenius' Zodiac* II. (1561) D viij, *Vpsuckt the floudes from out the seas, the whyrlwyndes vp doe beare. c1440 *Pallad. on Husb.* I. 290 But vines may ha vices worthy blame: To longe or brode, *vptrailed or extendid. 1568 T. HOWELL *Arb. Amitie* (1879) 38, I rage and rewe.., *Vp-whelmde in woes full sore. 1642 H. MORE *Song of Soul* II. I. i. 2 A Meteor,..Whose inward hidden parts ethereall Ly close *upwrapt in that dull sluggish fime. c1400 *Destr. Troy* 1542 The walles *vp wroght, wonder to se.

(*b*) **upbrightened, -broken, -brushed, -choked, -conjured, -covered, -cushioned, -flung, -followed, -girt, -hoisted, -led, -lighted, -looped, -mixed, -perched, -pointed, -poised, -propped, -ridged, -shouldered, -shoved, -spouted, -starched, -steamed, -stiffed, -swollen, -swung, -trilled, -wrenched, -wrought, -yoked.**

1861 *Macm. Mag.* IV. 132/1 Russet and green *upbrightened with white. 1833 MANGAN *Poems* (1903) 124 When the *up-broken dreams of boyhood's span..Come down like night upon the feelings. 1894 W. J. LOCKE *At Gate of Samaria* (1895) viii. 87 A shapely neck, on which clustered coquettishly a few tiny madcap curls below the smooth, *upbrushed, fair hair. 1968 *Guardian* 24 July 7/1 He was responsible for the 'up-brushed' coiffures. 1785 BURNS *Winter Night* ii, While burns, wi' snawy wreeths *up-choked, Wild-eddying swirl. 1833 WORDSW. *At Sea off Isle of Man* 5 Suddenly *up-conjured from the Main, Mists rose to hide the Land. 1857 HEAVYSEGE *Saul* (1869) 419 An old man,..*upcovered with a mantle. 1828 CARLYLE *Misc.* (1857) I. 142 The throne's *upcushioned lordliness. 1828 ATHERSTONE *Fall of Nineveh* I. 11 Arms *upflung, and swaying heads. 1903 R. KIPLING 5 *Nations, The Destroyers*, Nearer the up-flung beams that spell The council of our foes. 1818 KEATS *Endym.* I. 163 After them appear'd, *Up-follow'd by a multitude,..a fair wrought car. 1890 *Atlantic Monthly* July 35 The braider stands With loin *upgirt. 1768 CHATTERTON *Bristowe Tragedie* 193 Whatte tho', *uphoisted onne a pole, Mye lymbes shalle rotte ynne ayre. 1872 BLACKMORE *Maid of Sker* (1881) 159 Horses..with their tails uphoisted. 1845 WORDSW. '*Forth from a jutting ridge*' 7 *Up-led with mutual help. 1794 —— *Guilt & Sorrow* xlvi, The bag-pipe dinning..In barn *uplighted. 1887 BOWEN *Æneid* I. 320 Bare at the knee, and her fluttering folds *uplooped for the chase. 1821 ATHERSTONE *Poems* 26 In the turbid rain-streams, thick *upmix'd With ashes hot. 1818 KEATS *Endym.* I. 828 The nightingale, *up-perched high. 1830 ATHERSTONE *Fall of Nineveh* II. 102 The threatening spear *Up-pointed, harmless as a wand became. 1864 BRYANT *Constellations* 45 Thine eyes..would see..the Swan *uppoised On gleaming wings. 1784 COWPER *Task* II. 116 Never such a sudden flood, *Upridg'd so high.., Possess'd an inland scene. 1879 G. MACDONALD *Sir Gibbie* ix, The..river, flowing..through *upshouldered fields of wheat. 1837 CARLYLE *Fr. Rev.* III. v. vi, The Citoyens, with *upshoved *bonnet rouge*, or with doffed bonnet. 1789 COWPER *Queen's Visit to London* 19 The ocean..*Up-spouted by a whale in air. 1922 *Upstarched [see SAMBO]. 1805–6 CARY *Dante, Inf.* XXX. 99 Sharp fever drains the reeky moistness out, In such a cloud *up-steam'd. 1922 JOYCE *Ulysses* 39 In a Greek watercloset he breathed his last: ..stalled upon his throne, with *upstiffed omophorion, with clotted hinderparts. 1774 GRAVES *Spir. Quix.* (ed. 2) II. 198 The Rector, in sleek surcingle.., With eyes *up-swoln, and shining double-chin. 1882 G. MACDONALD *Weighed & Wanting* III. xviii. 254 She saw on Amy's neck a frightful upswollen wale. 1868 GEO. ELIOT *Sp. Gipsy* 323 He saw above The form of Father Isidor *upswung. 1799 COLERIDGE *Lines in Concert-room* ii, The long-breathed singer's *uptrill'd strain. 1808 MRS. ILIFF *Poems* (1818) 98 A rocky fragment, from the ground *upwrenched. 1784 COWPER *Task* II. 111 Ocean.., *upwrought To an enormous and o'erbearing height,..invades the shore Resistless. 1837 WHITTOCK *Bk. Trades* (1842) 407 (*Smith*), Afterwards appeared the beer-man with his cans '*up-yoked'.

6. a. The use of *up* before present participles, and forming possible combinations with these, is somewhat rare in OE.; the chief examples which occur are *up(á)stígende, upstandende,* and *upyrnende.* ME. furnishes a few instances, as *uparising, -hanging, -looking, -springing, -tempering;* but this type of formation becomes common only after 1500. In the following illustrations of casual forms the earlier examples are separated from those occurring after 1700.

(*a*) **uparising, -belching, -blowing, -botching, -creeping, -floating, -hasping** (= closing), **-hoising, -leaning, -peaking** (PEAK *v.*²), **-plucking, -riving, -seizing,** †**-souping** (= swallowing), †**-sparpling** (= scattering), **-steaming, -tempering.**

c1325 *Prose Psalter* xvii. 43 Þou put out þe *vparisand [L. *insurgentes*] ȝaines me. 1576 NEWTON *Lemnie's Complex.* 142 Their Chawes rammishe, And throate *vpbelching fulsome breathes. 1590 SPENSER *F.Q.* III. iv. 13 Till that at last The watry Southwinde from the seabord cost *Vp-blowing, doth disperse the vapour lo'st. 1582 STANYHURST *Æneis*, etc. 95 Theese thre were *vpbotching, not shapte,.. A clapping fyerbolt. 1626 *Parallel Pelag. Error* A 4 b, An euill *vpcreeping since his death. 1582 STANYHURST *Æneis* I. (Arb.) 21 Soom wights *vpfloating on raisd sea wyth armor apeered. *Ibid.* IV. 103 Hee causeth sleeping and bars: bye death eyelyd *vphasping. *Ibid.* 21 Thee northern bluster..Thee sayls tears tag rag, to the sky thee waues *vphoysing. 1588 SPENSER *Virg. Gnat* 154 Whilst thus his carelesse time This shepheard driues, *vpleaning on his batt. 1590 —— *F.Q.* III. ii. 42 With that vpleaning on her elbow weake [etc.]. 1582 STANYHURST *Æneis* III. (Arb.) 76 Thee fourth day..thee shoare, neere setled, apeered And hils *vppeaking. *Ibid.* II. 52 Hee..sighs *vpplucking from brest ful deepelye, thus answerd. 1621 G. SANDYS *Ovid's Met.* IX. (1626) 179 Oft should you see him..solid trees *vp-riuing. c1550 BALE *K. Johan* 1737, I wyll kepe this crowne in myn owne hande, In the Popes behalfe *upseasyng Ynglond. 1582 STANYHURST *Æneis* III. (Arb.) 84 Charybdis On left hand swelleth..In to gut *vpsouping three tymes thee flash water angrye. a1560 PHAËR *Æneid* IX. (1562) Ee iiij, A yong stere whyte as snow,..which with his fete *vpsparpling spredes the dust. a1560 *Ibid.* VIII. Bb ij b, An Yle there is..where smoke from stones to starrs *vpsteaming sties. c1440 *Pallad. on Husb.* VII. 243 This flouris smale..*vptempuryng, forsake Noman for hem to make.., As of rosate is taught.

(*b*) **upblazing, -bounding, -bracing, -breaking, -brimming, -bristling, -bubbling, -burning, -charioting, -coiling, -crawling, -flaming, -gaping, -gliding, -heaping, -knelling, -ridging, -rousing, -scaling, -slanting, -snatching, -spearing, -splashing, -stretching, -swarming, -sweeping, -thundering, -tracing, -wreathing.**

1801 SOUTHEY *Thalaba* VI. viii, Now its wavy point *Up-blazing rose, like a young cypress tree. 1840 MANGAN *Poems* (1903) 136 The startled soul, *upbounding from the mire Of earthliness. c1833 WHITTIER *Randolph of Roanoke* 102 His gaunt frame *upbracing. 1859 TENNYSON *Guinev.* 388 Sheets of hyacinth That seem'd the heavens *upbreaking thro' the earth. a1861 CLOUGH *Ess. Class. Metres, Alcaics* 5 The fury of winds, that all night *Upbrimming, sapping slowly the dyke,..Fall through the breach. 1898 T. HARDY *Wessex Poems* 163 When her dreams were upbrimming with light. 1852 W. WICKENDEN *Hunchback's Chest* 16 Like a wild boar *upbristling for the fight. 1874 R. BUCHANAN *Poet. Wks.* III. 58 The spring *Upbubbling faintly seemeth as a sound. a1865 TENNYSON *Mystic* 45 The last [circle],.. with a region of white flame..into a larger air *Upburning. 1812 W. TENNANT *Anster F.* II. ii, The sun, *upcharioting from Capricorn. 1803 WORDSW. *Yew-trees* 18 A growth of inter-twisted fibres serpentine *Up-coiling. 1896 KIPLING 7 *Seas, Derelict*, The..weed Folds me and fouls me, strake on strake *upcrawling. 1805 SOUTHEY *Madoc in W.* I. 34 Many a fire *Up-flaming, stream'd..Red lines of lengthening light. 1832 L. HUNT *Dryads* 19 Yellow bills, *up-gaping for their food. 1805–6 CARY *Dante, Inf.* XXV. 7 Another [serpent] to his arms *Upgliding, tied them. 1888 R. BUCHANAN *City of Dream* VIII. 158 And in its inmost shrine the priests of Baal Are not *upheaping gold. 1845 MANGAN *German Anthology* II. 108 Then hear I music sweet *upknelling From many a..phantom-band. 1791 COWPER *Odyssey* XIX. 555 *Upridging high His bristly back.., he sprang Forth from the shrubs. 1830 ATHERSTONE *Fall of Nineveh* II. 16 With firm tread The thronging echos

..*Uprousing as he passed. **1882** ARMSTRONG *Garland fr. Greece* 226 *Upscaling steep and rough to cross the Pass. **1876** C. WELLS *Joseph & Brethren* I. v. 73 The thorns that ye have cast *Upslanting in my path. **1828** ATHERSTONE *Fall of Nineveh* I. 241 The fallen reins *Upsnatching then, .. o'er the field The Assyrian looked. **1784** COWPER *Task* v. 23 The bents And coarser grass, *up-spearing o'er the rest, .. now shine Conspicuous. **1871** R. ELLIS *Catullus* lxiv. 128 She .. Now to the brine ran forth, *upsplashing freshly to meet her. **1815** HOGG *Poet. Mirror* Wks. 1866 II. 111 Two long ears *upstretching perpendicularly. **1791** COWPER *Iliad* XII. 541 They .. *upswarming show'd On the high battlement their glittering spears. *c* **1873** J. ADDIS *Eliz. Echoes* (1879) 94 Th' uncertain hum Of hosts *upsweeping from the subterrene. **1796** COLERIDGE *Ode Departing Year* viii, Central fires through nether seas *up-thundering. **1846** PROWETT *Prometh. Bound* 21 Hollow tones, From Hades' sullen realm upthundering. **1727** THOMSON *Summer* 1100 *Up-tracing, from the vast Inane, The Chain of Causes and Effects to Him. **1849** LONGF. *Building of Ship* 187 Around it columns of smoke, *up-wreathing, Rose.

b. In the earlier periods of the language these forms in *-ing* were not employed attributively. Examples of this use begin to appear in the 16th century, but are not common before the 19th. As adjectives, such compounds would normally have the main stress on the prefix, and a secondary stress on the stem (e.g. *'up,bearing*, *'up,creeping*), but in verse the full stressing of the stem is frequently retained. The following illustrations of rarer forms are divided into earlier and later instances.

(*a*) **upcreeping, -flinging, -running, -sprouting, -sticking.**

1611 COTGR. s.v. *Eschalas*, A Vine or any other weake-branched, *vp-creeping .. Plant. **1566** DRANT *Horace, Sat.* ii. F 2 When with grosse *upflyngyng fumes, your syght is masde and dull. **1527** ANDREW *Brunswyke's Distyll. Waters* H ij, The same is good for the *upronnyng pymples of the face. **1563** WINȜET *Wks.* (S.T.S.) II. 18 The snairis of the *wpsprouting hæretikis. **1611** COTGR., *Bricot*, .. an *vp-sticking stub of a late cut shrub or tree.

(*b*) **upbearing, -bounding, -breaking, -bursting, -cocking, -cropping, -crowding, -flashing, -flowing, -gushing, -pouring, -quivering, -reaching, -sprouting, -stealing, -stretching, -striving, -struggling, -tearing, -tilting.**

1830 TENNYSON *Isabel* iii, A leaning and *upbearing parasite, Clothing the stem. **1845** MANGAN *German Anthology* I. 60 Then *upbounding Life .. Unto all that died the Sun shall bring. **1822** J. WILSON *Lights & Shadows* 124 A sort of glimmer, like that of an *upbreaking and disparting storm, gathered about him. **1818** KEATS *Endym.* II. 56 Now he is sitting by a shady spring, And elbow-deep .. Stems the *upbursting cold. **1879** STEVENSON *Trav. Cevennes* 159 The roof fell in and the upbursting flames discovered his retreat. **1804** COLLINS *Scripscrap.* 58 A Brainless young Crimp, with an *upcocking snout. **1898** B. GREGORY *Side Lights Confl. Meth.* 249 An occasional *up-cropping consciousness. *c* **1870** M. ARNOLD *Obermann once more* ad fin., The domed Velan, with his snows, Behind the *upcrowding hills. **1813** SHELLEY *Q. Mab* VII. 231 Showers of gore from the *upflashing steel Of safe assassination. **1801** SOUTHEY *Thalaba* II. xxvi, No eye beheld the spring Of that *upflowing Flame. **1845** MANGAN *German Anthology* II. 18 Drink at Life's *upgushing wells! **1858** HAWTHORNE *Fr. & It. Note-bks.* I. 145 An artificial lake with upgushing fountains. **1842** R. FORD in Shorter *Borrow & Circle* (1913) 253 Just dash down the first genuine *uppouring idea and thoughts in the plainest language. **1851** HAWTHORNE *Ho. Sev. Gables* x, One of those *up-quivering flashes of the spirit. **1894** *Outing* (U.S.) XXIV. 151 Where the black *up-reaching ledge Holds high its moss-hung turrets. **1898** CLODD *Tom Tit Tot* iv. 41 Persephone, whom Demeter seeks .., to find her with the *upsprouting corn. **1859** *Roses & Thorns* 254 The *up-stealing shadows of evening. **1827** CARLYLE *Misc. Ess., Richter*, This *upstretching aurora of a morning. **1855** LYNCH *Lett. Scattered* ii. (1872) 26 One *upstriving flame of prayer. **1835** CARLYLE in Froude *Life in London* (1884) I. 46 One glorious *up-struggling ray .. which perished, .. in a lax, languid, impotent character. **1817** J. SCOTT *Paris Revisit.* (ed. 4) 219 Broad rugged tracks, which seemed as if they had been swept by some fiery *up-tearing stream. **1841** H. MILLER *O.R. Sandst.* vi. 107 The strata .. have been un-packed and arranged by the *uptilting agent.

7. In OE. the combination of *up-* with a verbal substantive is limited to *uphebbing*, perhaps directly formed from *uphebban*. In ME. a number of instances occur, the earliest being *upastying* (= ascending), *-casting*, *-coming*, *-covering* (= recovery), *-nimming*, *-rising*, *-stying*, and *-taking*. In the 16th c. the type becomes common, and again in the 19th. Earlier and more recent formations of a casual nature are illustrated in the following groups.

(*a*) **†uparising, †-astying, -bolstering, †-crying, -passing, †-receiving, -sealing, -twinkling, -tying, †-weening.**

1340 *Ayenb.* 213 At yestre [= Easter], his *oparizinge, hou he aros uram dyaþe to liue. *a* **1200** *St. Marher.* 1 Efter ure lauerdes .. ariste of deað, ant efter his *up astihunge. **1610** J. ROBINSON *Justif. Separation* 258 The Churches vngodly connivency, and *vpboulstring them in their scandalous sinns, makes them nothing the better. **1651** *Burgh Rec. Stirling* (1889) II. 306 To John Wordie for reading the ordoures annent *upcrying the money. **1533** GAU *Richt Vay* (S.T.S.) 49 Ye maner of his [*sc.* Christ's] *vppassing. **1572** *Reg. Privy Council Scot.* II. 145 In thair uppassing and douncuming. **13..** *Castel of Love* (H.) 1665 The cursede shull in erthe byn .., wyth the *up-receyveng they shulle agryse. **1563** MAN *Musculus' Commonpl.* 281 b, That grace ..the token, sacrament and *upsealinge [L. *obsignatio*] whereof is in Baptisme. **1597** *Pilgr. Parnass.* IV. 425 To see A puritane *up-twinckling of his eye. **1614** P. FORBES *Comm. Revelation* 217 Then his *vptying is to bee counted, when .. hee is perfectly made fast. **1340** *Ayenb.* 21 Þe þridde boȝ of prede is arrogance þet me clepeþ *opweninge oþer opniminge.

(*b*) **upbubbling, -flickering, -gushing, -lighting, -piling, -pouring, -ripping, -squatting, -streaming, -summing, -surging, -swelling, -winding, -working.**

1888 *Daily News* 26 May 5/8 To watch the *upbubbling of the flashing .. waters. **1881** *Cornh. Mag.* XLIV. 481 The last *up-flickering of his dying intelligence. **1846** HAWTHORNE *Mosses* II. iii. 50 The *upgushings and outpourings of these initiated souls. **1860** J. H. STIRLING *Crit. Ess., Macaulay* (1868) 122 The *up-lighting of the 'age of reason'. **1844** BLACKIE in *Class. Mus.* I. 339 A more cumbrous *up-piling of erudite blunders. **1918** W. STEVENS in *Others* Dec. 9 A deep *up-pouring from some saltier well Within me, bursts its watery syllable. **1859** SALA *Tw. round Clock* (1861) 121 The *upripping of his unhappy coat-collar. **1840** BARHAM *Ingol. Leg.* Ser. I. *Ghost*, The Gorgon's head Was but a type of Nick's *up-squatting in the bed. **1880** GEIKIE *Phys. Geog.* (1885) 46 A constant *upstreaming of warm moist air. **1884** J. PARKER *Apost. Life* III. 23 The all but infinite prudence which forecasts totalities and *upsummings. **1883** *Century Mag.* XXVI. 130 The *upsurging .. of nobler and better feelings. **1899** *Edin. Rev.* Apr. 317 *Upwellings of molten basalt. **1837** LOCKHART *Scott* IV. i. 22 A better *upwinding of the plot of the Black Dwarf. *a* **1834** COLERIDGE *Notes & Lect.* (1849) I. 230 A wild *up-working of love .. is perceptible throughout.

8. The use of *up-* with agent-nouns first appears in ME. in the 14th century, the earliest examples being *upstyer* and *uptaker*, with *upbearer*, *-holder*, and *-raiser* following a little later. Similar forms occur in the 16th cent. (but chiefly Sc.), as *upbigger* (= builder), *-closer*, *-creeper*, *-lifter*, *-looker*, *-putter*, *-setter*, and a few in the 17th, as *upbringer*, *-giver* (Sc.), *-riser*. Later formations are mainly from the 19th cent., as *upbuilder*, *-climber*, *-shutter*, *-stander*.

-up, *suffix*. The adverb UP appended to vbs. (sbs., etc.) as a suffix forming substantival or adjectival compounds (usu. derived from a simple vbl. phr.: see UP *adv.*[1] II), implying an instance or spell of an activity, an abundance or abuse of something, characterized by the action of the specified vb., etc. Such combinations are typically disyllabic and stressed on the first element: e.g. *balls-*, *beer-*, *booze-*, *brush-*, *foul-*, *fuck-*, *mop-*, *nosh-*, *show-*, *sign-up*, see at main element; *blow-*, *break-*, *build-*, *call-*, *clean-*, *close-*, *cock-*, *cover-*, *dust-*, *flare-*, *hold-*, *jam-*, *knees-*, *lay-*, *link-*, *make-*, *mark-*, *mock-*, *muck-*, *mug-*, *pick-*, *pile-*, pin-, *press-*, *pull-*, *punch-*, *push-*, *round-*, *run-*, *set-*, *shape-*, *smash-*, *speed-*, *stack-*, *stand-*, *stick-*, *tip-*, *tune-*, *walk-*, *warm-up*, see as main entries.

'up-a-daisy, *int.* Now *dial.* or *colloq.* Also 8 -dazy, 8-9 -daisey. [f. UP *adv.*[1]: cf. UPSIDAISY and dial. *upaday*. For the ending, cf. *lackadaisy* and (*a*)*lack-a-day*.] An exclamation made to a child on encouraging or assisting it to rise from a fall, etc., or to surmount an obstacle, or when raising it in the arms or jerking it into the air.

1711 SWIFT *Jrnl. to Stella* 5 Feb., Come stand away, let me rise... Is there a good fire?—So—up a-dazy. **1756** TOLDERVY *Hist. 2 Orphans* II. 24 'Up-a-daisey,' said Miss Bella, and then .. gave him a push behind. **1854** MISS BAKER *Northampt. Gloss.* 370 *Up-a-daisy*, a fondling expression of a nurse to a child whilst lifting it from the ground, encouraging it to assist itself in rising. **1899** G. FORD *'Postle Farm* ix. 43 'Up-a-daisy!' said Annie, as the fat little legs struggled to mount the steps.

u'paithric, *a.* [f. Gr. ὑπαίθρ-ος + -IC: see HYPÆTHRAL *a.* and cf. HUPAITHRIC *a.*] Open to the air; having no roof; hypæthral.

1819 SHELLEY *Ess. & Lett.* (1852) II. 155 Their temples were mostly upaithric; and .. the stars .. were seen above. **1851** [J. FANE] *Poems Early Years* 24 A vast upaithric fane.

†upaland, Sc. var. of *upoland* UPONLAND *adv.* (with further reduction of the prep.; cf. ALAND *adv.*). *Obs.*

1500-20 DUNBAR *Poems* l. 19 At feistis and brydallis wpaland, He wan the gre. **1560-1** *1st Bk. Discipl. Ch. Scot.* (1621) 40 If it be upaland where the people convene to the doctrine but once in the week. **1572** *Satir. Poems Reform.* xxxiii. 158 Ȝe do not ȝour office, For vpaland thay haue not dew seruice. *a* **1600** MONTGOMERIE *Sonn.* xxv. 3 This is no lyfe that I live vpaland.

b. *Jock upaland*, a rustic. Also allusively.

a **1568** *Bannatyne MS.* (Hunter. Club) 268 Thus said Jok vpalland. **1637-50** Row *Hist. Kirk* (Wodrow Soc.) 463 Many are gaping for it [*sc.* a church], and using moyen at Court to gaine it, but it will be Jok up-a-land.

Hence **†upalands** *a.* = UPLANDS *a.*

1535 LYNDESAY *Satyre* 4040, I leirit ȝow merchants mony ane wyle, Vpalands wyfis for to begyle. **1595** DUNCAN *App. Etym.* (E.D.S.), *Pero*, vpalands shoone.

up-along, *adv. dial.* Along in a particular or specified direction; in the world at large; in or towards a larger community outside an isolated region. Freq. in Cornish speech: up North, uphill. Also as *sb.*

a **1552** J. LELAND *Itinerary* (1721) IV. 89 The Beauty of Bermingham .. is one Street going up alonge almost from the left Ripe [= bank] of the Brooke. **1905** E. PHILLPOTTS *Secret Woman* III. ii. 249 'I wish I had the mastery of the Word that man hath.' 'Very fine,' said Mr. Tapp, 'but I hate fog—whether 'tis up-along or in church. The man goeth in a mist, an' his landmarks fail him.' **1908** K. GRAHAME *Wind in Willows* ix. 199 'Nice little farm,' replied the wayfarer briefly. 'Upalong in that direction'—he nodded northwards. **1913** H. S. WALPOLE *Fortitude* I. iv. 45 Well, 'ere's the end of yer as yer are... Up along they'll change yer. **1959** *Coast to Coast 1959–60* 136 Wish she'd stop going then. Where we heading? Up-a-long or down-a-long? **1963** C. BERRY *Portrait of Cornwall* (1984) iii. 54 'Coming up-along, are 'ee?' asks a West Cornwall man of his friend at the foot of the hilly street. **1966** J. AIKEN *Trouble with Product X* vii. 128, I said as how you'm taking Miss Whatname upalong to hospital. **1972** *Even. Telegram* (St. John's, Newfoundland) 29 June 3/1 If you have some of your people down from upalong, keep a modest bearing and don't go boasting. They may say, in their curious mainland accents: 'Waal, gee! Will ya look at all those birds. Why, this is incredible!'

‖**Upanayana** (upa'na:jana). Also **Upanayan, Upanayanam.** [a. Skr. *upanayana*, f. *upa* towards + *nayana* leading, bringing (f. *nī* to lead).] An initiation ceremony, one of the rites undergone by Hindu boys of the three higher castes between the ages of eight and sixteen.

1817 tr. *Dubois' Descr. People of India* II. i. 92 The children of Brahmans are invested with the Cord when they come to the age of seven or nine years... The ceremony .. is called *Upanayana*, or, *the Introduction to the Sciences*. *Ibid.*, I had some difficulty in bringing myself to detail the whole of this ceremony of the Upanayana, it is so filled with minute and trifling superstition. **1877** J. N. WILSON *Indian Caste* I. v. 188 The *Upanayana* (or sacrificial endowment with the string) of a Bráhman should take place in his seventh year. **1919** S. CAVE *Redemption Hindu & Christian* iv. 97 The three higher castes alone can perform the *upanayana* ceremony, they alone can qualify themselves for the study of the Veda. **1935** L. S. S. O'MALLEY *Pop. Hinduism* iv. 112 For the twice-born castes the most essential is the *upanayan* or investiture with the sacred thread, which takes place in a boy's eighth, eleventh or twelfth year according to his caste. **1950** M. K. GANDHI *Hindu Dharma* lv. 91 The *upanayanam* ceremony, though I have discarded it myself, it has .. a deep meaning. The sacred thread is a sign of new birth, a regeneration. **1971** *Illustr. Weekly India* 4 Apr. 11/1 Among all the sixteen *sanskars*, the *upanayana* is the most important. It signifies the practice of making over a boy to a learned religious teacher for education.

up-'anchor, *v.* [UP *adv.*[1] 1 d.] *intr.* To weigh or heave up the anchor.

1889 'MARK TWAIN' *Connecticut Yankee* xi. 137, I was all complete and ready to up anchor and get to sea. **1897** KIPLING *Capt. Cour.* 185 At last she cleared decks, .. up-anchored and began to move.

up-and-'coming, *a.* [UP *adv.*[2] 21.] **a.** *U.S.* Active, alert, wide-awake, energetic.

1889 *Harper's Mag.* Dec. 146/2 Can't you hear just how up an' comin' it was? **1901** *Harper's Mag.* CII. 678/1 She had an up and coming kind of way with her. **1926** F. N. HART *Bellamy Trial* i. 10 Redfield's pretty up and coming for a place of its size. **1946** R. LEHMANN *Gipsy's Baby* 59 They are of course admitting the blond curls of my brother; perhaps the juicy, up and coming appearance of all the four. Jolly-looking family. **1954** WODEHOUSE *Jeeves & Feudal Spirit* ii. 20 His attitude towards me had been that of an official at Borstal told off to keep an eye on a more than ordinarily up-and-coming juvenile delinquent.

b. Promising, making progress, beginning to achieve success. orig. *U.S.*

1926 R. HUGHES in *Hearst's Internat.* Feb. 44/1 The up-and-coming young prize-fighter 'Curly' Boyle. **1950** G. HACKFORTH-JONES *Worst Enemy* i. 19 Next to Meriton I would have placed Peters (on his reports) as a most up-and-coming youngster. **1959** 'R. SIMONS' *Houseboat Killings* vi. 67 'He's one of our up-and-coming young men.' 'Oh. So he is a successful artist?' **1977** B. PYM *Quartet in Autumn* xviii. 161 Their fashionable little house in that up-and-coming district by the common.

Hence **up-and-'comer**, an up-and-coming person; **up-and-'comingness.**

1890 *Advance* (Chicago) 24 April, There is about our Methodist brethren .. an up-and-a-comingness .. that [is] .. delightful. **1944** *Gen* 9 Sept. 24/2 I've named only a few of the up-and-comers. **1968** T. STOPPARD *Real Inspector Hound* (1970) 40 Ah—yes—well, I like to give young up and comers the benefit of my—er—of course, she lacks technique as yet—. **1982** 'W. HAGGARD' *Mischief-Makers* vi. 77 He's one of their up-and-comers.

up and down, *adv.*, *prep.*, *a.*, and *sb.* [f. UP *adv.*[1] and *adv.*[2] + DOWN *adv.*]

A. *adv.* **1. a.** Alternately on or to a higher and a lower level or plane. Also in fig. context.

c **1205** LAY. 14276 He bi-heold þene wal up and dun ouer al. *a* **1300** *Cursor M.* 2238 Þat ai quen we se ani chesun, Freli [we] may climb vp and dun. *c* **1340** *Ayenb.* 246 Þe lheddre .. huerby þe angles .. cliue op and doun. *c* **1400** MAUNDEV. (Roxb.) xxxi. 139 Fendez .. fliez vp and doune in þe aer with grete thunders. *c* **1485** *Digby Myst.* (1882) III. 1669, I fel ytt ster In my wombe vp and down. **1559** W. CUNNINGHAM *Cosmogr. Glasse* 29 Then rayse vp and downe the ruler .. vnto the sonne. **1583** HOLLYBAND *Campo di Fior* 27 Washe your mouth, and do the water up and downe in your throate. **1633** P. FLETCHER *Purple Isl.* XII. lii, Tost up and down in waves of worldly floud. **1680** in W. Hacke *Coll. Voy.* (1699) III. 7 Which Ebbs and Flows here two Fathom up and down. **1712** J. JAMES tr. *Le Blond's Gardening* 192 The short Cilinder .. is moved up and down in the Barrel of the Pump. **1820** BYRON *Juan* v. lxxviii, Wrestling both his arms into a gown, He paused, and took a survey up and down. **1889-91** [see STARE *v.* 2 c]. **1892** *Photogr. Ann.* II. 402 The action is up and down, without vibration.

fig. *c* **1374** CHAUCER *Troylus* II. 659 She..gan to casten and rollen vp and down with-inne here þought his excellent prowesse. *c* **1450** *Mirour Saluacioun* (Roxb.) 149 Sekeing oft vp and doune of deth fande thay cause none rightwise. **1513** DOUGLAS *Æneid* X. ii. 100 All the hevynly wychtis dyd quhyspir and roun, In opynyonys full diuers, wp and doun. **1584** D. FENNER *Def. Min.* (1587) 121 Although he knewe..the meaning of them, yet he turneth them vppe and downe as if they were riddles. **1974** M. BIRMINGHAM *You can help Me* iv. 106 Robin had been exceptionally quiet at lunch... He usually showed off in front of visitors. Still, he did go up and down.

b. *fig.* With variation of success or fortune.

1430–40 LYDG. *Bochas* I. 2718 Ay the tribut & seruage off the toun Procedith foorth, thei constreyned wer so sore, Lich as ther lott turned up and down.

c. *fig.* (In predicative use, passing into adj.) Varying, changeable, unstable. Now also often in sense 'of varying quality'.

1643 CARYL *Sacr. Covt.* 36 It is..most unsutable..for us to be up and downe, forward and backward, likeing and disliking, like that Double-minded man. **1645** RUTHERFORD *Tryal & Tri. Faith* 16 Men naturally beleeve, though they be but up and down with Christ, yet Christ doth so bear them at goodwill, as [etc.]. **1650** BAXTER *Saint's R.* iv. 38 His Love to thee will not be as thine was..to him, seldom and cold, up and down. **1945** C. S. LEWIS *Let.* 28 May (1966) 207 Mrs. Moore is up and down; very liable..to fits of bad jealousy.

2. Hither and thither; to and fro; backward and forward.

a **1200** *Moral Ode* 240 in *O.E. Hom.* I. 175 Ho..walkeð weri up and dun, se water deþ mid winde. **1297** R. GLOUC. (Rolls) 11513 Wiþ him to wende aboute, to sywe him vp & doun. **1303** R. BRUNNE *Handl. Synne* 4034 He ȝede yn hys celle vp and down. *c* **1386** CHAUCER *Nun's Pr. T.* 359 On hise toos he rometh vp and doun. *c* **1440** *Cast. Persev.* 2519 Up & doun þou take þe wey. **1508** DUNBAR *Gold. Targe* 84 There saw I May..Within the gardyng walking vp and doun. **1582** N. LICHEFIELD tr. *Castanheda's Conq. E. Ind.* 93 b, The enymyes were scouring up and downe in the Sea. **1659** PELL *Impr. Sea* 55 Many of you walk up and down in the ships you have command of. **1692** R. L'ESTRANGE *Fables* (1694) 251 You are so..given to squirting up and down, and chattering, that [etc.]. **1713** ADDISON *Cato* III. i, Life wanders up and down Through all her Face, and lights up ev'ry Charm. **1741** RICHARDSON *Pamela* (ed. 3) I. 187 She is up and down so much, that I am afraid of her surprising me. **1811** BYRON *Hints fr. Hor.* 478 And boys shall hunt your bardship up and down. **1872** TENNYSON *Last Tourn.* 647 Pacing moodily up and down.

3. a. Here and there; at various points; *esp.* in several or diverse places throughout a district, country, etc.

In very frequent use from *c* 1635 to 1700.

a **1300** *Cursor M.* 11444 Þai..spird him efter vp and dun. *c* **1374** CHAUCER *Compl. Mars* 210 What availeth suche a longe sermon Of auentures of love vp and dovne. **1601** B. JONSON *Poetaster* I. ii. (1905) 18 He..liu'd obscurely vp and downe in boothes, and taphouses. **1680** R. L'ESTRANGE *Citt & Bumpkin* (ed. 3) 3 We had our Agents at all Publick Meetings,..all the Schools up and down. **1712** BUDGELL *Spect.* No. 277 ¶13 With several Ribbons stuck up and down in it. **1760** C. JOHNSTON *Chrysal* (1822) III. 37 A few of the eldest..gathered up and down into little sets. **1855** BROWNING *Fra Lippo Lippi* 41 Brother Lippo's doings, up and down, You know them?

b. Throughout the works of an author or authors.

1668 H. MORE *Div. Dial.* IV. ix. 31 Intimated up and down in the Gospels by our Blessed Saviour. **1698** T. HEARNE *Duct. Hist.* (1714) I. 35 To relate all the Witticisms scattered up and down in the Books of the Cabalists, about this Word. **1699** BOYER *Fr. Dict.*, *Centon*,..a Poem made up of several Pieces pick'd up and down from the Works of others.

4. Upside-down; topsy-turvy. Also *fig.* Now *s.w. dial.*

1591 PERCIVALL *Sp. Dict.*, *Trastornadura*, ouerthrowing, turning vp and downe. **1600** W. WATSON *Decacordon* Pref. (1602) A 3 b, The Germaines (where the imperiall triple Crowne of Caesar yet remaines vp and downe). **1634** *Malory's Arthur* I. cxiv. Z 4 b, Syre launcelot charged so sore vpon him that his horse reuersed vp and downe. **1888–92** in Somerset and Devon dialect (*Eng. Dial. Dict.* s.v.).

5. In or into a vertical position; vertically.

1669 STURMY *Mariner's Mag.* II. 80 Set the end of the Cross-Staff to the outside of the Eye,..holding it right up and down. **1697** DAMPIER *Voy.* I. x. 298 A long Yard that peeks up and down like a Mizen-yard. **1748** *Anson's Voy.* II. i. 112 We hove the cable right up and down. **1791** SMEATON *Edystone L.* §132 The..cable..had been hawled in so tight as to keep the swivel from striking the ground, when right up and down. **1867** SMYTH *Sailor's Word-bk.* 574 In anchor work, when the cable is in that condition, the boatswain calls, 'Up and down, sir'. *Ibid.* 707.

6. a. In every respect; entirely, thoroughly, completely. Now *dial.*

1542 UDALL *Erasm. Apoph.* 291 b, He was even Socrates up and down in this pointe.., yͭ noman ever sawe hym either laugh or wepe. **1579–80** NORTH *Plutarch* (1595) 170 His eloquent tongue, and ready vtterance,..in those he was Pisistratus vp and downe. **1620** MIDDLETON *Chaste Maid* III. ii, It has the mother's mouth. The mother's mouth up and down. **1649** MILTON *Eikon.* xi, This is the Pharisee up and down, 'I am not as other men are'. **1832** J. BARRINGTON *Personal Sk.* III. 224 God bless him, up and down, wherever he goes, here or hereafter! **1878–89** in dialect glossaries, etc. (Cumbld., Lanc., Linc.).

†**b.** Altogether; in all. *Obs.*⁻¹

1562 J. HEYWOOD *Prov. & Epigr.* (1867) 215 What comth our meate to? foure shyllyngs vp and downe.

7. *U.S. colloq.* In a straightforward or blunt manner; acting in this way. (Cf. C. 2 b).

1854 'O. OPTIC' *In Doors & Out* 29, I told her, up and down, that she was not what she used to be when she lived with you. **1869** MRS. STOWE *Oldtown Folks* xx, Talk about coddling! it's little we get o' that, the way the Lord fixes things in this world... He's pretty up and down with us, by all they tell us. **1891** *Cent. Dict.* s.v. *Up*, To handle a matter up and down; to talk up and down.

B. *prep.* **1. a.** Backward and forward in; to and fro along or upon.

1412–20 LYDG. *Chron. Troy* I. 1575 Þe halle in soth sche walkyth vp and down. **1553** T. WILSON *Rhet.* 31 You shall haue a pretie litle boye, runnyng vp and doune youre house. **1568** GRAFTON *Chron.* II. 334 The Lordes counsayled the king..to rowe vp and downe the ryuer. **1645** PAGITT *Heresiogr.* (ed. 2) 32 They wandred up and downe the Countreyes without staves. ? **1676** LADY CHAWORTH in *12th Rep. Hist. MSS. Comm.* App. V. 34 She..is pulled up and down the ponds in them [*sc.* sledges] every day. **1711** STEELE *Spect.* No. 96 ¶3, I was strolling up and down the Walks in the Temple. **1745** P. THOMAS *Jrnl. Anson's Voy.* 230 Every Person of any Account goes up and down them [*sc.* streets] either on Horseback or in a Chair. **1820** SOUTHEY *Wesley* I. 405 Under such feelings he wandered up and down the fields. **1855** MACAULAY *Hist. Eng.* xiii. III. 269 Accompanying James in his last walk, up and down the Mall. **1896** *Law Times Rep.* LXXIII. 615/1 A red light was automatically shown up and down the line.

b. Here and there in or upon; in several parts of or diverse places throughout.

1597 SHAKS. *2 Hen. IV*, II. i. 113 She sayes vp & downe the town, that her eldest son is like you. **1640** H. SPELMAN in *Lett. Lit. Men* (Camden) 164 They that to prevent my election, published up and downe some Colledges that..[I] had declined the choice. **1675** BROOKS *Gold. Key* Wks. 1867 V. 309 They have frequently acknowledged it to be an everlasting covenant, as is evident up and down the Scripture. **1711** STEELE *Spect.* No. 11 ¶4 Sprinkled up and down the Writings of all Ages. **1834** MEDWIN *Angler in Wales* I. 33 The eyes..in some insects amount to six or seven thousand, and spread up and down the body as on the spider. **1849** MACAULAY *Hist. Eng.* ix. II. 444 Early in August hints..were whispered up and down London. **1894** *Times* 4 June 6/2 To gather into one collected whole statements scattered at present all up and down your columns.

2. Alternately on or to a higher and lower plane in or upon.

1665 HOOKE *Microgr.* 202 A certaine white substance..may be observ'd to fly up and down the Air. **1726** SHELVOCKE *Voy. round World* 250 The danger..of carrying a load up and down mountains. **1741** RICHARDSON *Pamela* (ed. 3) I. 201 The Maid Nan..asked if any thing was the matter, that I was so often up and down stairs? **1855** [J. R. LEIFCHILD] *Cornwall* 153 Along levels, and up and down winzes (ventilating openings), the air is coursing. **1859** F. E. PAGET *Curate of Cumberworth* 62 The whole herd, tearing up and down the hill side.

C. *adj.* (Now usually hyphened.)

1. a. Directed, occurring, or taking place, alternately upward and downward.

1616 CHAPMAN tr. *Musæus* D 6 b, With vp and down-lookes, whetting his desire. **1795** *Phil. Trans.* LXXXV. 587 The up-and-down motion in walking. **1834** *Encycl. Metrop.* (1845) VIII. 748/2 The up-and-down action is communicated to this machine by chains. **1839** URE *Dict. Arts*, etc. 1110 These faller wires..are guided truly in their up-and-down motions..by a cleaner-plate. **1874** BEDFORD *Sailor's Pocket Bk.* v. 121 To insure getting an 'up and down cast' [of the lead]. **1883** *Black's Guide Devon.* (ed. 11) 175 From here to Brendon Church..is 2½ miles of very up-and-down travelling.

transf. **1808** VANCOUVER *Agric. Devon* 100 Farming tenantry..rent..from 200 to 300 acres of land, the greater part of which is subject to a system of up-and-down husbandry.

b. Adapted or used for hauling up and down.

1794 *Rigging & Seamanship* II. 281 A chain, called an up-and-down span. **1860** NARES *Seamanship* 37 What tackles are used? A luff and an up-and-down. **1867** SMYTH *Sailor's Word-bk.* 708 Up-and-down tackle.

c. Of persons: That hauls, goes, works, etc., up and down.

1851–61 MAYHEW *Lond. Labour* III. 247/1 'Up-and-down men', or coalwhippers, as they are usually called. **1897** *Westm. Gaz.* 10 April 2/1 A man, a cook-housemaid, an up-and-down girl.

d. *fig.* Alternately rising and falling; presenting variations comparable to movement up and down.

1812 BYRON *Waltz* Ep., A d—d see-saw up-and-down sort of tune. **1819** *Metropolis* I. 104 Uneven measures, sportiveness and fancy must lead them [*sc.* poets]..an up and down dance. **1889** *Spectator* 14 Dec. 839 Even the free-living artist Fra Lippo Lippi talks in Browning's sudden, impatient, up-and-down style.

2. a. Perpendicular; straight up, erect; very steep.

c **1710** CELIA FIENNES *Diary* (1888) 232 Its such an Enclosed Country, and such up and down steep hills. **1817** H. T. COLEBROOKE *Algebra*, etc. 15 Repeat the operation till the up and down line contain but two quantities. **1894** C. N. ROBINSON *Brit. Fleet* 278 The *Warrior* and *Defence* classes had plain up and down cutwaters. **1897** *Daily News* 21 Sept. 3/2 With clothes hanging in folds upon her up-and-down figure.

b. *U.S.* Direct, straightforward, downright.

1836 HALIBURTON *Clockm.* Ser. I. xxxvi, No strong-minded, straight-a-head, right up and down man does that. **1869** MRS. H. B. STOWE *Oldtown Folks* xxiv, A well-preserved, up-and-down, positive, cheery, sprightly maiden lady. **1896** *Peterson Mag.* Jan. 94/2 The two women folks..finally had an up-and-down row.

3. a. Having an uneven or irregular surface; consisting of ups and downs.

1775 S. J. PRATT *Liberal Opin.* cxxiii. (1783) IV. 133 Very few gentlemen..come to such a d—m—d up-and-down place as this. **1830** COLMAN *Random Records* 202 Durham,..a strange up-and-down Episcopal City. **1853** DICKENS *Bleak Ho.* vi, [My room] was of this kind, with an up-and-down roof. **1898** A. AUSTIN *Lamia's Winter Quarters* 49 He lived in an up-and-down hamlet among the hills.

b. *fig.* Marked by alternations of success, etc.; changeful, variable. Also, of a person: subject to alternating or changing moods.

1907 A. RANSOME *Bohemia in London* 200 It is an up-and-down-life, my friends. **1960** I. CROSS *Backward Sex* 125 She had always been an up-and-down sort of person, depressed one minute and elated the next.

4. Taking place to and fro or backward and forward; spent in moving about.

1824 MISS MITFORD *Village* Ser. I. I. 111 She has, in the course of an up-and-down life, met with a good many authors. **1876** PREECE & SIVEWRIGHT *Telegraphy* 292 What is called *up* and *down* working; that is,..each station sending alternately one or several messages. **1884** SALA *Journ. due South* II. i, The perpetual up-and-down flowing of the crowd.

5. In collocations arising from an ellipse of the sb. after *up*: **a.** *Pugilism.* (See quots.)

1840 BLAINE *Encycl. Rural Sports* 1218 That species of contest, called up and down fighting, that is, when a man is got down he is kept down and punished till incapable of motion. **1863** KINGSLEY *Water-Bab.* iv, They were fighting; savage, desperate, up-and-down fighting. **1867** [T. WRIGHT] *Some Habits Working Classes* 124 Up-and-down fights, in which..the men fight both up and down.

b. Of or pertaining to 'up' and 'down' trains.

1890 *Daily News* 16 Sept. 6/4 Two complete sets of up and down lines run out of that station. **1898** *Engineering Mag.* XVI. 73 Acting as through stations for the main up-and-down traffic.

c. *Watchmaking.* (See quot.)

1884 F. J. BRITTEN *Watch & Clockm.* 276 [An] up and down Indicator..[is] mechanism for indicating when a watch or chronometer requires winding.

D. *sb.*

I. Pl. uses (occas. hyphened), **ups and downs.**

1. a. Undulations or irregularities on the surface of ground, etc. Also in fig. context.

1682 *Whitelock's Mem.* Pref., There are flats..as well as ups and downs and precipices. **1687** A. LOVELL tr. *Thevenot's Trav.* I. 159 The Street being full of ups and downs, they make it..smooth from end to end. **1698** T. FROGER *Voy.* 110 The town is nothing throughout but up's and downs and..consequently carriages are very impracticable there. **1717** BERKELEY *Tour in Italy* Wks. 1871 IV. 563 After our ascent through a difficult path, many ups and downs, stony, narrow and uneasy, among shrubby mountains, etc. on foot. **1821** COBBETT *Rur. Rides* (1853) 10 The ups and downs of sea in a heavy swell. **1859** TENNYSON *Marriage of Geraint* 236 Geraint..rode, By ups and downs, thro' many a grassy glade. **1879** HARE *Story of my Life* (1900) V. xx. 169 All the ups and downs of the ground.

b. Undulatory motions, tracings, etc. Also *fig.*

1860 W. H. RUSSELL *Diary India* II. 227, I did not find it easy to sleep in the palkee, with its ups and downs. **1860–70** STUBBS *Lect. Europ. Hist.* (1904) 8 Charles's wars with Francis are a regular seesaw. The Pope is generally the person who pulls the ups and downs. **1888** R. ABERCROMBY *Weather* ii. 30 If we look at the barometer-trace.., the 'ups' and 'downs' suggest the analogy of waves.

2. a. Vicissitudes, variations, or alternations in respect of fortune, success, etc. Also const. *of* (life, fortune, etc.).

In frequent use from *c* 1850.

1659 BUNYAN *Law & Grace Unf.* Wks. 1855 I. 553 The very saints of God have..many ups and downs in this their travel towards heaven. **1680** C. NESSE *Ch. Hist.* 99 The church..continued 450 Y[ears] in its Vps and Downs. **1727** P. WALKER *Remarkable Passages* (1827) I. 293 He..had many Ups and Downs in his Case, warm Blinks and Clouds. **1793–4** AIKIN & MRS. BARBAULD *Even. at Home* (1805) IV. 5, I have had my ups and downs in the world. **1807** SOUTHEY *Espriella's Lett.* II. 178 The ups and downs of commercial Speculation. **1809** MALKIN *Gil Blas* x. ii. ¶7 The ups and downs in the lottery of my own life. **1859** THACKERAY *Virgin.* lxxxi, They had their ups and downs of fortune. **1875** HELPS *Soc. Press.* xx. 297 His life is a life of ups and downs, the ups and downs not being of exceeding magnitude.

b. Alternations in respect of condition, quality, etc.; vagaries, variations.

1855 BRIMLEY *Ess., Westw. Ho!* 301 The ups and downs, the fortunes and emotions, of a passion. **1882** MRS. OLIPHANT *Lit. Hist. Eng.* I. 368 The ups and downs of a mind so precariously balanced. **1899** *Allbutt's Syst. Med.* VI. 897 The ups and downs met with in the course of the disease.

II. Singular uses (usually hyphened).

†**3.** A swing-boat. *Obs.*

1813 *Sporting Mag.* XLII. 20 There were the usual swings, ups-and-downs, and roundabouts. **1816** in Hone *Every-day Bk.* (1825) I. 572 Up-and-downs, merry-go-rounds [at fairs]. **1825** HONE *Ibid.* 1228 There is an 'up and down', or swing, of..woodwork.

4. a. Alternate rise and fall, esp. *fig.* in respect of position, fortune, etc.; variation of condition, lot, or circumstances.

1775 S. J. PRATT *Liberal Opin.* cviii. (1783) IV. 29 [The present world] is in itself one general up-and-down: the human soul abhors sameness. *a* **1838** C. MORRIS *Lyra Urban.* (1840) II. 338 What an up-and-down is this? A shift from palace to cot. **1867** LOWELL *Biglow P.* Ser. II. Introd., Poems (1912) 287/2 The regular up and down of the pentameter churn. **1876** S. LANIER *Clover* 71 Th' incalculable Up-and-Down of Time Made plain before my eyes.

b. Fluctuation or vacillation *of* passion, etc.

1905 STOPFORD BROOKE *Ten Plays Shakesp.* 88 The up-and-down of his bewildered passion has passed away.

5. An irregularly undulating surface, lineation, etc.

1856 MRS. BROWNING *Aur. Leigh* I. 1109 Such an up and down Of verdure,—nothing too much up or down, A ripple of land. **1888** *Encycl. Dict.* s.v. *Tonic*, The 'up and down' of pitch is not represented to the eye as on the staff.

6. A rapid or cursory survey or perusal; the 'once-over'. *rare.*

1923 WODEHOUSE *Inimitable Jeeves* x. 102 'Read this letter.' He gave it the up-and-down.

Hence **up-and-'downishness; up-and-'downy** *a. nonce-words.*

1853 R. S. SURTEES *Sponge's Sp. Tour* xliv, The up-and-downy, wavy piece of road. **1873** A. J. ELLIS in *Trans. Philol. Soc.* 130 Such wonderful up-and-downishness does not shew much declamatory taste.

up-and-'downer. *slang.* Also **up-and-a-downer, upper and downer.** An up-and-down fight or argument (UP AND DOWN *a.* 5 a); a violent quarrel.

1927 *Daily Tel.* 6 Sept. 7/7 My daughter's young man wants to be king of the castle,.. and the trouble is that the missus thinks more of him than she does of me. We has a bit of an up-and-a-downer last night, and he has the cheek to fetch a policeman. **1932** P. MACDONALD *Rope to Spare* xii. 174, I 'appened to hear them in a proper up-and-downer. **1955** M. GILBERT *Sky High* v. 71 Regular upper-and-downer you seemed to be having with Miss Palling. **1978** D. WILLIAMS *Treasure up in Smoke* viii. 73 I've just had the most glorious up-and-downer with my brother.

up-and-'over, *a.* [UP *adv.*[1] + OVER *adv.*] Denoting a type of garage door which opens by moving horizontally as it is raised.

1959 *Motor Manual* (ed. 36) ix. 221 Up-and-over doors, which are counterbalanced and swing away into the roof space.. are gaining popularity. **1968** P. MARLOWE *Hire me a Hearse* xii. 169 The garage up-and-over door.. had a tendency to rattle on its pulleys. **1979** J. COOPER *Class* xi. 197 The Weybridged house has.. an up-and-over garage door.

up and 'under. *Rugby Football.* [f. UP *adv.*[1] + UNDER *adv.*] A high kick intended to give the kicker and some other members of his team time to reach the point where the ball will come down. Also *up-and-under kick.*

[**1949** D. M. DAVIN *Roads from Home* ii. 28 'Up and under,' their captain cried and Star forwards.. raced ahead to be under it when it fell.] **1960** V. JENKINS *Lions down Under* 208 An early tackle when he followed through after kicking an up-and-under. **1960** *Times* 18 Nov. 22/2 Oxford regained the lead from a high up-and-under kick. **1979** J. P. R. WILLIAMS *JPR* i. 32 Up on Lock's Common the wind is at its strongest; this is where dad chose for his barrage of up and unders for us all to catch.

Upanishad (uː'pænɪʃæd). [a. Skr. *upa-nishád*, f. *upa* near to + *ni-shad* to sit or lie down.] In Sanskrit literature, one or other of various speculative treatises chiefly dealing with the Deity, creation, and existence, and forming a division of the Vedic literature.

1805 COLEBROOKE in *Asiatic Researches* VIII. 446, I shall here quote, from this Upanishad, a single dialogue. **1816** R. ROY *(title)*, Translation of the Céna Upanishad, one of the chapters of the Sáma Véda. **1861** MAX MÜLLER *Lect. Sci. Lang.* 145 Dárá.. became a student of Sanskrit, and translated the Upanishads.. into Persian.. in the year 1657.

Upani'shadic, *a.* Also **Upaniṣadic, Upnishadic.** [f. UPANISHAD + -IC.] Of or pertaining to the Upanishads.

1921 M. A. BUCH *Philos. Shankara* 1 All the main ideas of Shankara's theory are anticipated by the Upnishadic seers. **1927** BELVALKAR & RANADE *Hist. Indian Philos.* II. vii. 242 *(heading)* A critical exposition of Upanishadic texts. **1937** *Mind* XLVI. 407 Witness his cogent criticism of Zeller and Burnet on Parmenides and his comments on the Upaniṣadic theories of self-consciousness. **1954** A. L. BASHAM *Wonder that was India* vii. 332 The great Śaṅkara himself.. maintained the rigid Upaniṣadic doctrine of salvation by knowledge. **1964** *Language* XL. 112 A series of studies of Vedic and Upanishadic problems of interpretation.. preluded his inheritance of Bloomfield's projected Vedic variants.

up'arch, *v. Geol.* [f. UP- 4.] *trans.* To raise (strata, etc.) to form a broad dome or anticline. Hence **up'arching** *vbl. sb.*, the raising of strata into an anticlinal form; the structure so produced.

1877 G. K. GILBERT *Rep. Geol. Henry Mountains* iv. 95 So soon as the lava can uparch the strata it does so, and the sheet becomes a laccolite. **1911** *Ann. Assoc. Amer. Geographers* I. 43 The present form and altitude of the range is therefore not due to the monoclinal displacement of the compound mass.. but to the broad and simple up-arching of a much later date. **1954** *Jrnl. Glaciol.* II. 420 In a small quarry.. I again photographed up-arching of granite. **1970** R. J. SMALL *Study of Landforms* iii. 94 The strong tensional forces arising from uparching produce structural weaknesses.. at the crest of an anticline. **1979** *Prof. Papers U.S. Geol. Survey* No. 1127. 1/1 A regional north-south compression.. uparched several east-trending anticlines in central Washington.

upard, obs. f. UPWARD *adv.*

uparise, -arising, -arist: see UP- 2 b, 4, 6, 7.

‖**upas** ('juːpəs). Also 9 oopas. [a. Malay *ūpas* poison, in the comb. *pōhun* (or *pūhun*) *ūpas* poison-tree.

In senses 1 and 2 correct usage would require the compound *upas-tree*. The full Malay name has been used by some writers in the inexact forms *bohon, bohun, bopon, bon*, and *boa upas*.]

1. A fabulous tree alleged to have existed in Java, at some distance from Batavia, with properties so poisonous as to destroy all animal and vegetable life to a distance of fifteen or sixteen miles around it.

The account given in the *London Magazine* of 1783, from which Erasmus Darwin adopted and gave currency to the fiction, professed to be translated from one written in Dutch by Mr. Foersch (who was a surgeon at Samarang in 1773), but was app. the invention of George Steevens. The history of the fable is fully traced in Yule and Burnell's *Hobson-Jobson*, s.v. *Upas*.

α. **1783** *London Mag.* 513/1 They are asked.., whether they will go to the Upas tree for a box of poison? **1819** WIFFEN *Aonian Hours* 58 His life was like the Upas-tree, The curse of all his kind! **1841** THACKERAY *Misc. Ess.* (1885) 401 Avoid tobacco as you would the upas plant.

β. **1783** *London Mag.* 516/2, I have been convinced, that the gum of the Upas is the.. most violent of all vegetable poisons. **1789** E. DARWIN *Loves of Plants* III. 238 Fierce in dread silence on the blasted heath Fell Upas sits, the Hydra-Tree of death. **1815** HELEN M. WILLIAMS *Pres. St. France* iv. 68 Held in as much abhorrence as if they had shed the poisons of the Upas. **1858** SEARS *Athan.* ii. 89 The Upas of the desert, and the nightshade of the jungles.

attrib. and *Comb.* **1838** RUSKIN *Scythian Banquet Song* iv, Nor deemed [I] my love, like Upas dew, A plague. **1845** FORD *Handbk. Spain* II. 724 Such is its upas-like atmosphere. **1847** EMERSON *Mithridates* 19 Swing me in the upas boughs, Vampyre-fanned, when I carouse.

b. *fig.* A baleful, destructive, or deadly power or influence.

α. **1801** SOUTHEY *Thalaba* IX. II. 200 From that accursed venom springs The Upas Tree of Death. **1824** *Westm. Rev.* April 464 That Upas tree, which has since borne all the bitter fruits of Turkish oppression. **1839** FR. A. KEMBLE *Resid. in Georgia* (1863) 90 This tremendous soil, where one grain of knowledge may spring up a gigantic upas-tree. **1885** E. GARRETT *At Any Cost* iv. 64 This failure.. lies about the very root of many upas-trees of human life.

β. **1818** BYRON *Ch. Har.* IV. cxxvi, This uneradicable taint of sin, This boundless upas, this all-blasting tree. **1865** PARKMAN *Huguenots* viii. (1875) 138 Thus did Spain.. crush the upas of heresy in its germ. **1876** FARRAR *Marlb. Serm.* xxxvi. 359 This is the sole resemblance between the tree of life and the upas of evil.

attrib. **1832** [R. CATTERMOLE] *Beckett*, etc. 169 Even Despotism's dark upas-root For us a blessing bore. **1853** KINGSLEY *Hypatia* I. p. xi, Was not the Empire trying to extend over the Church itself that upas shadow with which it had withered up every other form of human existence?

2. *Bot.* The Javanese tree *Antiaris toxicaria*, yielding a poisonous juice. (Cf. ANTIAR.)

1814 T. HORSFIELD in *Thomson's Ann. Philos.* IX. 202 An Essay on the Oopas, or Poison Tree of Java. **1834** *Penny Cycl.* II. 98/2 There is such a tree as the upas, and its juice, if mixed with the blood.., is speedily fatal. *Ibid.* 420/2 The Upas tree of Java. **1872** OLIVER *Elem. Bot.* II. 234 The celebrated Upas.. is a native of Java. The juice.. was formerly used by the natives to poison their arrows.

attrib. **1857** MILLER *Elem. Chem., Org.* 287 Strychnia.. is one of the active constituents of the upas poison.

3. The poison obtained from the upas-tree.

1783 *London Mag.* 515/2 To suffer death by a lancet poisoned with Upas. *Ibid.* 516/1, I.. procured.. some grains of Upas. **1814** T. HORSFIELD in *Thomson's Ann. Philos.* IX. 207 One of the experiments.. was made with the oopas prepared by myself. **1830** LINDLEY *Nat. Syst. Bot.* 95 An order [of plants] which contains the most deadly poison in the world, the Upas of Java. **1860** MAYNE *Expos. Lex.* s.v.

up-'banding, *vbl. sb.* (App. an error for *up-bending*: see UPBEND *pa. pple.*)

1620 QUARLES *Jonah* H 2, 'Tis not your Mimmick mouthes,.. Nor prodigall vp-banding of thine eyes, Whose gashfull balls doe seeme to pelt the skyes.

'up-bank, *adv.* and *a.* [UP *prep.*[2]]

1. *adv.* Upwards. *north. dial.*

1760- in *Eng. Dial. Dict.* **1808** [see BANK *sb.*[1] 2 b].

2. *adj.* (See quot.)

1883 R. H. SCOTT *Elem. Meteor.* 213 The well-known phenomenon of 'up-bank thaw', when it thaws on the hills, while the frost is unbroken in the valleys below.

up'bear, *v.* [UP- 4 + BEAR *v.*[1] 18, 21. Cf. MSw. *upbära* (Sw. *uppbära*), MDa. *upbære*. Freq. in pa. pple. *upborne*: see UP- 5.]

1. *trans.* To bear up, support, sustain; also, to lift up, raise.

a **1300** *Cursor M.* 7258 Þe post þat al þat huse vpbare Wit bath his handes he it scok. **13..** *K. Alis.* 5163 Swiþe wiȝtlych hij.. swymme, Of þe water þat hij were inne Vpberande faire chynne. **1390** GOWER *Conf.* III. 296 He that alle thing mai kepe.. broghte him sauf upon a table, Which to the lond him hath upbore. *c* **1440** *Promp. Parv.* 508/1 Vbberyn, or vpberyn, *supporto*. *c* **1470** HENRY *Wallace* IX. 1632 A thourtour bande, that all the drawcht wpbar, He cuttyt it. *a* **1550** LYNDESAY *Syde Taillis* 23 Thocht thare Rob Royallis be vpborne, I think [etc.]. **1582** STANYHURST *Æneis*, etc. (Arb.) 136 Earst the flud, vpbearing thee ship, now the cartwheele vpholdeth. **1590** SPENSER *F.Q.* II. vii. 43 Many great golden pillours did vpbeare The massy roofe. **1667** MILTON *P.L.* II. 408 Who shall.. spread his aerie flight Upborn with indefatigable wings Over the vast abrupt. **1725** POPE *Odyssey* v. 542 A monst'rous wave up-bore The Chief. **1784** COWPER *Task* I. 20 Joint-stools were then created; on three legs Upborne they stood. **1831** E. IRVING *Exp. Rev.* I. 60 Upbearing His person as Aaron and Hurr upbore the hands of Moses. **1870** MORRIS *Earthly Par.* II. III. 352 A chief's gold ring his left arm did upbear. **1891** ATKINSON *Moorland Par.* 64 Slabs of stone of sufficient solidity to upbear any loaded vehicle.

2. *fig.* To support or sustain; to exalt.

a **1300** *E.E. Psalter* lxxvii. 76 He ches Dauyd, hyne hisse; And vp-bare him all with blisse. *Ibid.* cxxx. 1 Vphouen es noght mi hert, Ne vpborn er mine eghen in quert. **1303** R. BRUNNE *Handl. Synne* 7159 He.. loueþ alle þat sothfast es; Alle godenes he vp berep. *c* **1384** CHAUCER *H. Fame* 818 Euerych ayre other stereth More and more, and speche vp-bereth. **1412-20** LYDG. *Chron. Troy* I. 4424, I wil,.. vp-born with support of ȝour grace, Forþe a-complische, as I vndertook. *a* **1586** SIDNEY *Ps.* xxx. ii, I.. was from ev'l by thee upborne. **1590** SPENSER *F.Q.* II. vii. 65 Food, and sleepe, which two vpbeare, Like mightie pillours, this fraile life of man. **1630** DRUMM. OF HAWTH. *Flowres Sion* viii, A Virgine Maide A weakling did him beare, who all vpbeares. **1829** I. TAYLOR *Enthus.* ix. 248 A.. proof of the intrinsic power of Christianity, upbearing so ponderous a mass of error. **1876** LOWELL *Among my Bks.* Ser. II. 325 His own language rarely rises above it, except when it is upborn by the thought.

†**up'bearer.** *Obs.* [UP- 8. Cf. prec.] A supporter, sustainer.

1386 *Rolls of Parlt.* III. 225/1 Nichol Brembre, wyth his upberers. *c* **1400** tr. *Secreta Secret., Gov. Lordsh.* 101 Þe wyt of a kynge ys helpyd by his vpberers. *c* **1440** *Promp. Parv.* 512/2 Vpberere, *supportator*. **1513** DOUGLAS *Æneid* VI. xiii. 89 The wpberar of the hevin, Atlas. **1624** BP. MOUNTAGU *New Gagg* 306 Vasquez himself.., that great Upbearer of Roman Idolatry.

up'bearing, *vbl. sb.* [UP- 7. Cf. UPBEAR *v.*] The action of carrying, raising, taking or holding up; support, sustaining.

a **1340** HAMPOLE *Psalter* cxxx. 1 Vpberyng of een withouten is signe of pryde. *a* **1400** *Prymer* (1891) 23 Wonderful been the upberynges of the se. *c* **1440** *Promp. Parv.* 512/2 Vpberynge, *supportacio*. **1501** *Acc. Ld. High Treas. Scot.* II. 114 The chekker.. passit to Schir Adam Crechtonis hous, for upbering of the rollis. **1513** JAS. IV *Let.* in Hall *Chron., Hen. VIII* (1548) 30 The greate wronges.. quhilk we haue suffred this long time in vpberyng, maynsweryng, noun-redressyng of Attemptates. **1878** SPURGEON *Treas. Dav.* V. 48 A most fitting accompaniment to the upbearing of the ark. **1885** *19th Cent.* June 967 The patient upbearing against hardship.

upbearing, *ppl. a.*: see UP- 6 b.

'upbeat, *sb.* [UP- 2.]

1. *Mus.* 'The beat of a bar at which the hand is raised; an unaccented beat' (Stainer and Barrett).

1869 OUSELEY *Counterp.* iii, The up-beat may be either a concord or a discord. **1874** —— *Musical Form* 63 The second phrase concludes with the third of the tonic, but at the up-beat.

2. *Pros.* **a.** An anacrusis. **b.** An arsis or stressed syllable.

1883 H. M. KENNEDY tr. *Ten Brink's E.E. Lit.* 194 Orm reproduced the foreign metre with pains-taking accuracy. The up-beat (*auftakt, anacrusis*) never fails. **1899** D. HYDE *Lit. Hist. Irel.* xxxviii. 532 If we take it for granted that the syllables in which rhyme or alliteration appear must also bear the accent or up-beat of the voice. **1942** J. C. POPE *Rhythm of Beowulf* 49 Anacrusis derives its effect.. from being placed in the up-beat or arsis. **1948** S. O. ANDREW *Postscript on Beowulf* 120 Anacrusis is an introductory unstressed up-beat.

3. *fig.* An optimistic or positive mood, development, etc.; a pleasant occurrence.

1950 C. MCCULLERS in *Theatre Arts* Apr. 28/1 The publisher says this character must not die and the book should end on an 'up beat'. **1955** *N.Y. Times Mag.* 1 May 28 *(heading)* Upbeat for modern dance. **1969** H. WAUGH *Young Prey* xiii. 118 Breakfast with a pretty airlines hostess.. was Frank Sessions' only upbeat of the morning. **1976** *National Observer* (U.S.) 31 July 17/6, I don't think he's going to end tragically—he's in the classic sense a comic character, on the upbeat rather than the down.

upbeat, *a.* [f. the sb.] *colloq.* (orig. and chiefly *U.S.*). Cheerful, happy; hopeful, optimistic, positive; lively, vigorous.

1947 *N.Y. Herald-Tribune* (U.S.) 26 Sept. 16 *(heading)* Dizzy Gillespie, Yardbird Parker, Thelonius Monk get nod in up-beat set. **1952** *Variety* 2 Jan. 5, '51 was 'Up-beat' but '52 looms as 'Challenge Year'. **1961** *John o' London's* 25 May 591/3 Diana Sands as Beneatha brings a much-needed touch of up-beat comedy. **1965** *Punch* 25 Aug. 275/2 Like Queen Victoria I am inordinately cheered up by the delivery of pieces of upbeat information, not merely about my own luck, but about others, even. **1977** C. MCFADDEN *Serial* (1978) xxvi. 58/2 I'm feeling a lot more upbeat about Gregor now. **1984** *Times* 27 Mar. 10/2 *(heading)* Upbeat mood as Hongkong talks start again.

upbeild, obs. Sc. variant of UPBUILD *v.*

up'bigged, *pa. pple. Sc.* [UP- 5 + BIG *v.* 4.] Built up. Also **up'bigger; up'bigging** *vbl. sb.*

c **1425** WYNTOUN *Cron.* v. vii. 1280 Ierusalem in hys tyme gert he Weill agane vpbiggit be. **1514** *Extr. Aberd. Reg.* (1844) I. 91 Dikkis.. to be vpbiggit apoun the expensis of the land. **1563** *Reg. Privy Council Scot.* I. 247 Ordanis all paroche kirkis.. quhilkis ar decayit.. to be reparit and upbiggit. *a* **1897** in R. Murray *Hawick Songs* (ed. 3) 65 Till it seems.. A whole fairy city, upbiggit wi' stars. **1562** WINȜET *Wks.* (S.T.S.) II. 3 The.. *wpbigare of the wallis of Ierusalem. **1525** *Extr. Aberd. Reg.* (1844) I. 113 The reparat[i]oun and *upbiging of thair portis. **1562** WINȜET *Wks.* (S.T.S.) II. 6 To be a faythful souldiour.. in the wpbigging of thir haly wallis.

up'bind, *v.* [UP- 4. Cf. Du. *opbinden*, Da. *opbinde*, Sw. *uppbinda*, G. *aufbinden.*] *trans.* To bind up.

1590 SPENSER *F.Q.* III. iv. 40 His griesly wound:.. which hauing well vpbound, They pourd in soueraine balme. **1596** *Ibid.* IV. xi. 52 [They] haue the sea in charge to them assinde, ..To bring forth stormes, or fast them to vpbinde. **1650** *Metr. Ps. Ch. Scotl.* cxlvii. 3 Their painfull wounds he tenderly up-bindes. **1746** COLLINS *Ode to Peace* iii, O Peace, thy injur'd robes up-bind.

upblaze, -blazing: see UP- 4, 6.

† **up'blowing**, *vbl. sb. Obs.* [UP- 7.] Inflation.
1527 ANDREW *Brunswyke's Distyll. Waters* F ii, In lyke wyse synketh the great..upblowynge of the tongue. **1562** TURNER *Baths* 8 It is good for them that have..windines or upblowyng of the bellye.

upblowing, *pres. pple.*: see UP- 6.

up'blown, *pa. pple.* and *ppl. a.* [UP- 5.] Blown up; *esp.* inflated, puffed up.
1590 SPENSER *F.Q.* I. iv. 21 His belly was vp-blowne with luxury. **1596** *Ibid.* v. i. 17 He, whose spirit was with pride vpblowne. **1810** CRABBE *Borough* xvi. 44 With wine inflated, man is all upblown, And feels a power which he believes his own. **1828** TENNYSON *Lover's T.* II. 175 One morning when the upblown billow ran Shoreward.

up'boil, *v.* [UP- 4.] **a.** *intr.* To boil up; *fig.* to rise up hotly. † **b.** *trans.* To cause to boil. *Obs.*
1435 MISYN *Fire of Love* 79 Behald, myn inhir partis has vpbolyd [L. *efferbuerunt*], & þe flawme of charite..has wastyd. *c* **1440** *Pallad. on Husb.* x. 188 Vpboile hit thenne And stere hit vntil honythicke it renne. **1555** *Lydgate's Chron. Troy* II. xiii. I iv/1 She wepeth..With wawes vpboyled from her eyen clere. *a* **1902** E. F. TAYLOR *Æneid* XII. 1099 Then terribly Æneas' wrath upboils.

up'boiling, *vbl. sb.* (UP- 7. Cf. prec.)
1794 COLERIDGE *Fall Robespierre* I. 88 He feels The dire upboilings of the storm within him.

upborne: see UPBEAR *v.*

'upbound, *a.* and *adv. U.S.* [UP *prep.*² 2.] Going upstream.
1884 'MARK TWAIN' *Huck. Finn* xii. 99 We watched the..up-bound steamboats fight the big river in the middle. **1976** *Advance News* (Ogdensburg, N.Y.) 18 July 9/1 The Britannia, Royal Yacht of Queen Elizabeth II and Prince Philip of England, is due to transit the Dwight D. Eisenhower Locks upbound on the St. Lawrence Seaway.

upbounden, -bounding, -bracing: see UP- 5, 6, 7.

† **up'braid**, *sb. Obs.* Forms: α. 3 upbreid, -bræid, 4 -breyd(e, 4-5 -breide; 3- upbraid (5 *Sc.* upbrad), 4-6 upbraide, 5-7 upbrayde (6 -brayed). β. 4 vbbreid(e, obbrayd, 6 obbraid, obrayd, 7 ubbrayd. [f. UP- 2 + BRAID *sb.* 1. Cf. the verb, also UMBRAID *sb.* and UPBRUD.]

1. With *a* and pl. A reproach or reproof.
α. *a* **1200** *Vices & Virtues* 41 [Job was assailed] mid maniȝe euele upbreides..of his auene frienden. *a* **1300** *Cursor M.* 5673 Moyses for þis vp-braid Was stonand in his hert. **1338** R. BRUNNE *Chron.* (1810) 219 In ȝow a faute men fynde, & is an ille vpbraid, þat ȝe ere nere blynde. *c* **1449** PECOCK *Repr.* II. xvi. 247 Alle the vpbreidis and alle the reproues which Holi Writ ȝeueth to the worschipers of tho ymagis. **1482** *Monk of Evesham* (Arb.) 106 Vexyd with tormentys and vpbraydys of seche wekyd folke. **1549** COVERDALE, etc. *Erasm. Par. 1 Tim.* 11 Not onely any naughtye faulte but also any false feyned vpbrayed. **1575** *Brieff Disc. Troub. Franckford* (1846) 84 They coulde haue nothing with owte bytter upbraids. **1641** *Vind. Smectymnuus* 9 It is no envious upbraid to parallell ours with the former Bishops. **1677** tr. *Groeneveldt's Treat. Stone* 61 Moved at length by the upbraids of the Parents,..he made incision in the groin.
β. **1325** *Metr. Hom.* in *Herrig's Archiv* LVII. 243/1 Of fendes hedde I mony vbbreide. **1575** LANEHAM *Let.* (1907) 17 With spitefull obrayds and vncharitabl chaffings alweiz they freat. *a* **1603** T. CARTWRIGHT *Confut. Rhem. N.T.* (1618) 575 Which..you your selues without the ub-brayd of a lie by your own conscience, cannot deny.

2. Without article: Reproach, reproof; evil speaking.
α. *c* **1205** LAY. 26036 þa nolde Arður on slepen na wiht hine areppen, leste he an uferre daȝe up-bræid iherde. *c* **1275** in *Hist. Holy Rood-tree*, etc. 78 Skoarn, upbraid, and schome speche. *c* **1330** R. BRUNNE *Chron. Wace* (Rolls) 7996 Bytwyxt to þer a stryf þey herde, Of grete vpbreide ilk oþer onswerde. *a* **1400-50** *Alexander* 1800 Lettis neuire it broȝt be on brade for vpbraide of schame. *c* **1460** J. RUSSELL *Bk. Nurture* 395 As it is showed afore, beware of vpbrayde. **1591** SPENSER *M. Hubberd* 2 For disdaine of sinfull worlds vpbraide. **1596** —— *F.Q.* IV. ix. 24 Through lewd vpbraide Of Ate and Duessa they fell out.
β. *c* **1325** *Spec. Gy Warw.* 537 ȝif þi neiheboure misdoþ þe, ..Or in dede, or in vbbreid. *a* **1400** *New Test.* (Paues) Heb. xi. 26 Trowynge þe obbrayd of Crist grettour rychesse þan þe tresour of Egypcyenes. **1548** PATTEN *Exped. Scotl.* Pref. b iv b, So maye the subiect without obbraid of benefites, recount the bounty of hys Princes larges.

upbraid (ʌp'breɪd), *v.* Forms: α. 1 upbredan, 3-4 upbreyde (5 -dyn), 4 -breide(n; 4-7 upbrayde (6 wp-), -braide, 4- upbraid (7 -brayd), 5 uppe-, 6 upbrade; *pa. t.* and *pa. pple.* 3, 6 op-, 6-7 upbraid (4 -brayde, 5 -brayd, -brayed), 3-4 upbreide, 4-5 -breyde. β. 5 vbbreydyn, 6 obbrayd, -braid; 5 (*pa. t.*) obreide, 6-7 obrayde, 7 obraid. [OE. *upbreȝdan*, f. *up-* UP- 4 + *breȝdan* BRAID *v.*¹: cf. MSw. *up-*, *op-*, *o(b)- brygdha*. See also BRAID *v.*², ABRAID *v.*¹ and *v.*², EMBRAID *v.*¹, IMBRAID *v.*, and UMBRAID *v.*
The orig. strong pa. t. (*upbraid*) gave rise to the reduced form UPBRAY *v.*]

I. † **1.** *trans.* To bring forward, adduce, or allege (a matter), as a ground for censure or reproach. Orig. const. with dative of person, later with *to* or *against*. *Obs.*
For the use of *up-* in this connexion cf. the Scottish and northern *to cast up to* (one), CAST *v.* 83 i, the modern *to bring up against* (one), and the dial. *to throw up against*.
α. *c* **1000** WULFSTAN *Hom.* 248 þæt þu þæt god ȝefylle, þe þu canst, þe læs þe [*v.r.* eow] God upbrede þone godspellican cwide [etc.]. *a* **1225** *Ancr. R.* 426 þe ancre neuer more þer efter þene ilke gult ne upbreide hire. *a* **1250** *Owl & Night.* 1414 Ne schal no mon wymman bigrede & fleysses lustes hire vpbreyde. *c* **1290** *Beket* 1748 in *S. Eng. Leg.* I. 156 Wel ofte þe king him opbraid þat he dude him er of guode. **1542** UDALL *Erasm. Apoph.* 240 Lest the others might thynke niggardship to bee upbraided unto hym, and cast in his teeth. **1583** GOLDING *Calvin on Deut.* clxxii. 1068 It shall bee vpbraided vs that wee haue turned our heartes backe. **1625** BACON *Ess., Envy* (Arb.) 513 It doth vpbraid vnto them their owne Fortunes; And pointeth at them. **1631** GOUGE *God's Arrows* III. §60. 294 This is not upbraided to David as a crime. **1672** DRYDEN *Defence of Epilogue* ¶2 It was upbraided to that excellent poet, that he was [etc.]. **1718** PRIOR *Solomon* I. 293 May they not justly to our Climes upbraid Shortness of Night, and Penury of Shade.
β. **1581** J. BELL *Haddon's Answ. Osor.* 343 That we purge ourselves of the cryme of novelty, falsly obbraydid agaynst us by Osorius. **1602** R. T. *Five Godlie Serm.* 143 First reproouing them of errour, and afterwards obraiding against them the cause thereof.

b. Without personal const.: To censure, find fault with, carp at.
c **1290** *S. Eng. Leg.* I. 61/271 For ȝwane ani Man opbraid is pouerte, he was in gret deliȝt. **1303** R. BRUNNE *Handl. Synne* 672 þey scorne Ihesu, and vpbreyde hys pyn. **1382** WYCLIF *Ecclus.* xx. 15 Fewe thingus he shal ȝyue, and manye thingus he shal vpbreiden. *a* **1586** SIDNEY *Arcadia* II. x, How much doth thy kindnesse upbraide my wickednesse? **1591** SPENSER *Ruines of Time* 215 His hope is faild,..And euill men, now dead, his deeds vpbraid. **1655** JOHN SERGEANT *Schism Disarm'd* 331 On all occasions you are still up[b]raiding the liberty given to Papists. **1667** MILTON *P.L.* VI. 182 Thy self not free,..Yet leudly dar'st our ministring upbraid. **1719** YOUNG *Busiris* II. i, What far transcends my merit, and for ever Must silently upbraid my little worth. **1741** RICHARDSON *Pamela* IV. 105 Mr. Clermont then upbraids her Guilt. **1792** WORDSW. *Descrip. Sk.* 251 There doth the maiden watch her lover's sail Approaching, and upbraid the tardy gale. **1821** JOANNA BAILLIE *Metr. Leg., Lady of B.* Introd. 22 For who can these as meaner times upbraid, Who think of Saragossa's valiant maid? **1867** EMERSON *May-day* 621 Who can, like thee, our rags upbraid?
β. **1591** G. FLETCHER *Russe Commw.* 66 The Chrim..sent to the Russe Emperour a knife:..obbraiding this losse, and his desperate case. **1635** HABINGTON *Castara* I. (ed. 2) 58 Why are their rimes So steept in gall? Why so obrayde the times?

† **c.** To insult. *Obs.*⁻¹
1678 SOUTH *Serm.* (1679) 173 The case is so plain, that I shall not upbraid any mans understanding by endeavouring to give it any farther Illustration.

2. To reproach, reprove, censure (a person, etc.). Occas. const. *for*, or *that*.
α. *a* **1300** *Cursor M.* 16718 þe theif þat biside him hang.. him can vp-braid. *a* **1340** HAMPOLE *Psalter* xxxiv. 8 Outrageusly þai vpbraidid my saule. *c* **1374** CHAUCER *Troylus* v. 1710 O Pandarus, that in dremes for to triste Me blamed hast, and wont art ofte vp breyde. *c* **1412** HOCCLEVE *De Reg. Princ.* 3500 A sad wys knyght of his with lokkes greye..seide Vnto his lord, and þus he hym vp breyde. **1482** *Monk of Evesham* (Arb.) 72 Sche vsyd inpacyently to scolde and vpbrayde hem that dyd her wronge. **1530** PALSGR. 784 Yet to upbrayde hym afore folkes is none honestye. **1590** SHAKS. *Mids. N.* IV. i. 55, I did vpbraid her, and fall out with her. **1600** *1st Pt. Sir J. Oldcastle* I. ii. 6 Grieuous complaints haue past betweene the lippes Of enuious persons to vpbraide the Cleargy. **1665** MANLEY *Grotius' Low C. Wars* 291 Queen Elizabeth recall'd all her Souldiers,..not without upbraiding the States. **1697** DRYDEN *Virg. Georg.* IV. 507 He sadly stands,..Upbraiding Heav'n from whence his Lineage came. *a* **1721** SHEFFIELD (Dk. Buckhm.) *Wks.* (1753) I. 267 Has she spread wit and learning thro' the world,..And is she now upbraided? **1782** MISS BURNEY *Cecilia* VII. ix, All present were upbraided as if accomplices in the disaster. **1841** LANE *Arab. Nts.* I. 109 On hearing these words, I abstained from upbraiding her. **1872** DARWIN *Emotions* vii. 186 As she upbraided him, her eyebrows became extremely oblique.
refl. **1789** BOSWELL *Lett.* (1924) 373, I cried bitterly and upbraided myself for leaving her. **1831** SCOTT *Ct. Rob.* xxxiv, She upbraids herself that..she had also survived Irene.
β. *c* **1412** HOCCLEVE *De Reg. Princ.* (Roxb.) 62 Pharao clept Abraham, & hym obreide [*v.r.* ubreyde]. *c* **1440** *Promp. Parv.* 508/1 Vbbreydyn, or vpbreydyn, *impropero*. **1648** J. HOWELL tr. *Venice Looking-glass* 8 He might well..have obraided her in the same words as Henry the 3. did upbraid Paris.

b. Const. †*of* or *with* (the cause of censure).
(*a*) *a* **1250** *Prov. Alfred* 279 in *O.E. Misc.* 118 Heo ne scholde þe forþ vp-breyde of þine baleu-syþes. **1303** R. BRUNNE *Handl. Synne* 724 þe pyne, he suffred for þy gode, And þou vpbreydyst hym of þe rode. *c* **1330** —— *Chron. Wace* (Rolls) 11665 þey vpbraide vs of our auncessours. *c* **1374** CHAUCER *Anel. & Arc.* 118 Lest he of eny vntrouthe her vpbreyde. **1584** LODGE *Alarum* Wks. (Hunter. Cl.) I. 28 Trust not to straungers, for they will vpbraide you of their benefite.
(*b*) *c* **1440** *Alph. Tales* 318 þis preste..tolde hur cowncell, & vpbrayed hur þerwith. **1482** *Monk of Evesham* (Arb.) 67 The mynystrys and wykyd angellys of the deuylle vpbraydyn me with the same. **1581** J. BELL *Haddon's Answ. Osor.* 346 This nickname of newe Gospellers (wherewith the Catholickes doe obbrayd us). **1596** WARNER *Alb. Eng.* x. liv. 244 Yeat not her Infancie should be vpbraided with the blood Of many thousand slaughtred Soules. **1640** HABINGTON *Edw. IV*, 150 Obrayding the King with inglorious sloath. **1679** J. GOODMAN *Penit. Pard.* III. iv. 317 It is said..Cæsar's thoughts continually upbraided him with the great exploits Alexander had effected. **1719** DE FOE *Crusoe* II. (Globe) 503, I began to upbraid them with the just Retribution of Heaven in this Case. **1774** J. BRYANT *Mythol.* I. 141 Peor, the same with whose rites the Israelites are so often upbraided. **1843** BETHUNE *Sc. Fireside Stor.* 100 [He] upbraided her with a wish to bring him to an ignominious death.

c. *absol.* To speak reproachfully.
a **1340** HAMPOLE *Psalter* xli. 14 Whils my banes ere brokyn, [they] vpbrayded til me. **1382** WYCLIF *Jas.* i. 5 God, the which ȝiueth to alle men largeli, and vpbraydith not. *c* **1410** *Lanterne of Liȝt* 10 þanne þis enviouse man sclaundriþ, vpbreidiþ, reproueþ. **1596** SPENSER *F.Q.* v. vii. 32 Proud Radigund,..thus vpbrayding, said. *a* **1628** PRESTON *Mt. Ebal* (1638) 28 He giveth liberally, and obraideth not. **1715** POPE *Iliad* II. 311 Have we not known thee,..The man who acts the least, upbraids the most? **1797** S. & HT. LEE *Canterb. T.* (1799) I. 185, I come not to upbraid. **1856** O. W. HOLMES *Birthday of D. Webster* xvi, In vain the envious tongue upbraids; His name a nation's heart shall keep.

II. † **3.** To cast, pull, or set up. *Obs.*
c **1205** LAY. 16519 And seoððe he hine up bræid, swulc he hine to-breken wolde. **13..** *Gaw. & Gr. Knt.* 781 þe bryge was breme vp-brayde. *c* **1450** HOLLAND *Houlate* 680 The Falcoune..Bad birnis burdis vp braid, with a blyth cheir.

† **4.** *intr.* To come out of a swoon; to start up, spring up. *Obs.*
14.. *Chaucer's Sqr.'s T.* 477 (Petworth MS.), After þat she of swowne gan vpbreide. **1448-9** J. METHAM *Wks.* (1916) 69/1869 And with þat word bothe deede bodyis vp-brayd. **1513** DOUGLAS *Æneis* I. iv. 36 Quhill al in flamb the bleis of fyir upbradis.

† **5.** *trans.* To give utterance to. *Obs.*⁻¹
1587 FLEMING *Contn. Holinshed* III. 1016/2 This woman ..beginneth to vpbraid in the open church verie hard and vnseemelie speeches concerning religion.

6. Of food: **a.** To make uneasy with repletion or indigestion. Now *dial.*
1599 NASHE *Lenten Stuffe* F iv b, Because, in the boyling or seathing of it in his maw, he felt it commotion a little and vpbraide him. **1601** B. JONSON *Poetaster, Apol. Dial.* 24 Their spight..who..Haue nothing left, but the vnsau'ry smoake Of their blacke vomit, to vpbrayd themselues. **1664** J. C. *Praxis Lat. Syntax* 118 The fried egge and bacon that I did eat..upbraideth my stomach. **1841** R. W. HAMILTON *Nugae Lit.* 340 The grossness of the food..upbraids him. **1866-** in dial. glossaries (Yks., Linc.).

b. *intr.* To rise in the stomach. Now *dial.*
Cf. earlier quots. s.v. UPBRAIDING *vbl. sb.* 3.
1604 R. CAWDREY *Table Alph.* **1787** GROSE *Provinc. Gloss.* s.v., My dinner upbraids. **1824-** in dial. use (Yks., Linc.).

Hence **up'braided** *ppl. a.*
1700 DRYDEN *Wife of Bath's T.* 458 If Poverty be my upbraided Crime. —— *Ilias* I. 490 His upbraided Mother. **1748** RICHARDSON *Clarissa* II. 305 The upbraider..is in some sense a superior; while the upbraided, if with reason upbraided, must make a figure as spiritless as conscious.

up'braider. [f. UPBRAID *v.*] One who upbraids; a reprover.
1636 B. JONSON *Discov.* Wks. (1641) 106 The latter hath no upbraiders. **1700** N. ROWE *Amb. Step-Moth.* IV. i. 1718 This Rebel Son! This insolent Upbraider. **1748** [see prec.]. **1751** SMOLLETT *Per. Pic.* xxxi, Assuring the upbraider that he considered her as an object of compassion. **1877** D. M. WALLACE *Russia* xxv. 392 'We are quite ready,' they said to their upbraiders, 'to admire your great works as soon as they appear'.

up'braiding, *vbl. sb.* [f. as prec.]

1. A reproach or reproof.
c **1205** LAY. 19117 þenne nabbeoð ure æfterlinges nane upbreidinges. *a* **1300** *E.E. Psalter* lxxxviii. 49 Mined be, lauerd, of vpbraidinges of þi hine. *c* **1449** PECOCK *Repr.* II. xvi. 247 Certis..alle her vpbreidingis mad ben iust. **1590** SHAKS. *Com. Err.* v. i. 73 Thou saist his meate was sawc'd with thy vpbraidings. **1611** SPEED *Hist. Gt. Brit.* IX. viii. 496/2 When..hee snebs the King for comminatory obraydings, and contumacious malepartnesse. **1627** SANDERSON *Serm.* I. 270 The horrors and upbraidings of a condemning heart. **1712** STEELE *Spect.* No. 448 ¶6 You your self cannot..but allow the Justice of the Upbraidings of Your Injured Friend. **1773** MRS. CHAPONE *Improv. Mind.* (1774) I. 174 If jealousy is expressed by unkind upbraidings. **1844** THIRLWALL *Greece* VIII. 320 He was there received with..upbraidings, and reproaches. **1894** J. D. CAMPBELL *Life Coleridge* 46 Coleridge then broke out in extravagantly-worded upbraidings.

2. The action of reproaching or reproving.
a **1300** *E.E. Psalter* cxviii. 22 Bere fra me vpbraidinge and forhoghte. **1303** R. BRUNNE *Handl. Synne* 766 But ȝe leue ..ȝoure vnkynde vpbreydyng, ȝe shul go a deueyl weye. *a* **1340** HAMPOLE *Psalter* ii. 5 þat speche sall be vpbraydynge þat þai wild noght doe his biddynge. *c* **1410** *Lanterne of Liȝt* 124 At alle tyme he schal be cursid & worþi vpbreiding. **1526** *Pilgr. Perf.* (W. de W. 1531) 241 b, Without ony exprobracyon, upbraydyng or rebukyng. **1599** HAKLUYT *Voy.* I. 562 A thing foolish and vaine,..deuised for the vpbrayding of our nation. **1656** BRAMHALL *Replie to S. W.* 70 For in my discourse there is nothing either of repining or upbraiding. **1749** FIELDING *Tom Jones* VIII. xiv, He received nothing but scorn and upbraiding from me. **1775** SHERIDAN *Rivals* III. ii, I had come resolved to wear a face of coolness and upbraiding. **1825** SCOTT *Talism.* xvii, Without a word of upbraiding, she attended upon the Queen. **1878** MISS BRADDON *Eleanor's Vict.* iii, No word of upbraiding had ever crossed those tender lips.

† **b.** An object of reproach or censure. *Obs. rare.*
a **1300** *E.E. Psalter* xxi. 5, I am worme, and man nathing; Mennes vpbraiding, of folk outkasting. *Ibid.* xxxviii. 12.

† **3.** Eructation of food; regurgitation. *Obs.*
1533 ELYOT *Cast. Helthe* (1541) 73 It tourneth also norishement vnto corrupcion, whiche maketh vpbraidynges fumishe or sharpe. **1561** HOLLYBUSH *Hom. Apoth.* 2 The payn of the head commeth..by yᵉ vpbraything of yᵉ stomak into the head. **1574** NEWTON *Health Mag.* 21 When throughe drinkinge of wine there is any upbraidinge and

mordication in the stomacke. **1611** COTGR., *Remors de l'estomac*, the vpbraiding of the stomacke.

up'braiding, *ppl. a.* [f. UPBRAID *v.* + -ING².] Reproachful, reproving.

a **1300** *E.E. Psalter* xliii. 18 Steuen of vpbraidand and forspekand. *c* **1449** PECOCK *Repr.* II. xvi. 247 Alle tho reprouyng and upbreiding processis vpon ydolatrers ben trewe. **1568** GRAFTON *Chron.* II. 101 You haue written to vs againe after a threatning sort, and vpbrayding manner. *a* **1618** SYLVESTER *Epist.* vii. 31 Th' upbraiding blurr of my young Muse's rape. **1625** T. GODWIN *Moses & Aaron* I. iii. 12 They vsed no vpbraiding termes towards them. **1663** *Extr. St. Papers Friends* Ser. II. (1911) 183 Mr. Knight returned me this scornfull and vpbraiding answer. **1732** BERKELEY *Alciphr.* v. §30 This being spoke with..an upbraiding air. **1810** SCOTT *Lady of L.* II. vi, 'Twas thus upbraiding conscience said. **1822** J. WILSON *Lights & Shadows* 143 The Minister looked,..with an upbraiding countenance, on the young man. **1848** BUCKLEY *Iliad* 397 But him..Diana sharply rebuked, and uttered this upbraiding speech.

up'braidingly, *adv.* [f. prec.] In an upbraiding manner; with reproach or reproof.

1593 NASHE *Christ's T.* Riij, Any man..that is vpbraidingly dyscontent. **1653** R. SANDERS *Physiogn.* 257 Neither should we upbraidingly be accused for our negligence. **1679** PRANCE *Addit. Narr. Pop. Plot* 9 Upbraidingly telling him, That he should be a Prisoner there. **1748** RICHARDSON *Clarissa* (1768) IV. 173 Afraid, as the women upbraidingly tell me, that I should find it there. **1825** SCOTT *Talism.* viii, 'I never knew thee before hesitate for fear of life,' said Richard upbraidingly. **1861** MEREDITH *Evan Harrington* III. ix. 147 Its absence was upbraidingly mentioned.

†**up'bray**, *sb. Obs.* [Cf. next.] = UPBRAID *sb.* 1.

1590 SPENSER *F.Q.* III. vi. 50 Faire Psyche to him lately reconcyld, After long troubles and vnmeet vpbrayes.

up'bray, *v. Obs.* exc. *dial.* Also 6 ob-, 7 ubbray. [Erroneous back-formation from *upbrayd*, obs. pa. t. of UPBRAID *v.*]

1. = UPBRAID *v.* 1, 2.

1581 J. BELL *Haddon's Answ. Osorius* 337, I my selfe have heard the Jewes obbraying us christians with the same faults. **1590** SPENSER *F.Q.* II. iv. 45 Vile knight, That knights and knighthood doest with shame vpbray. **1602** W. BASSE *Sword & Buckler* lxi. (1893) 25 You needlesly ubbray our haire. **1642** H. MORE *Song of Soul* I. ii. 27 The hearts do ne're agree But felly one another do upbray. **1898** R. BLAKEBOROUGH *Wit, etc. N. Riding Yorks.* 466.

†**2.** = UPBRAID *v.* 5. *Obs.*⁻¹

a **1600** in *Sidney's Arcadia*, etc. (1922) II. 368 Yet not of women judginge as he sayd. But first with rage, his rage on them [he] upbrayde.

†**3.** = UPBRAID *v.* 6. *Obs.*⁻¹

1598 MARSTON *Sco. Villanie* III. x, Vpbray'd by Capons greace, consumed quite By eating stewes, that waste the better spright.

Hence **up'braying** *vbl. sb.*

1585 PARSONS *Chr. Exerc.* I. v. 45 Consider the intollerable vpbraying of the wicked infernal spirits.

'upbreak, *sb.* [UP- 2. Cf. next.]

1. An eruption or outburst.

1856 MRS. BROWNING *Aur. Leigh* VII. 54 Through all The upbreak of the fountains of my heart. **1871** E. F. BURR *Ad Fidem* xiv. 277 A furious upbreak of unbelief.

2. A breaking-up or dissolution.

1882 *Macm. Mag.* XLV. 496 The upbreak of the Catholico-Feudal System.

upbreak (ʌp'breɪk), *v.* [UP- 4. Cf. WFris. *opbrekke*, (M)Du. *opbreken*, (M)LG. *upbreken*, LG. *upbräken*, MHG. *ûfbrëchen* (G. *aufbrechen*), Da. *opbrække*.]

†**1.** *intr.* To break out; to begin to speak. *Obs.*

c **1205** LAY. 5431 Þeo hit [alles] up bræc, hit wes god þat he spec. *c* **1320** *Castel Love* 457 So þat Pees a-last vp-breek, And þus to hire Fader speek.

2. *trans.* To break up; to break open.

1382 WYCLIF *Gen.* xix. 9 Now nyȝ it was that thei shulden vp breke [L. *effringerent*] the ȝatis. *a* **1400** *Octouian* 190 The emperour tho..gan vp-breke The dore. *c* **1440** *Pallad. on Husb.* VIII. 1 At Iuyl the lond vpbroken in Aprile Is eft to plowe. **1582** STANYHURST *Æneis* I. (Arb.) 24 Thee stags vpbreaking they slit to the dulcet or inchepyn. **1855** LYNCH *Rivulet* VIII. i, As a field Is by the plough up-broken for the corn. **1885–94** R. BRIDGES *Eros & Psyche* May iv, The sun ..Upbroke the grey dome of the morning sky.

3. *intr.* To force or make a way upward or to the surface.

1859 TENNYSON *Guinevere* 391 They..rode..over sheets of hyacinth That seem'd the heavens upbreaking thro' the earth. **1887** *Cornhill Mag.* Aug. 214 When from the gloom Of the dark earth upbreaks the tender bloom.

up'breaking, *vbl. sb.* (UP- 7. Cf. prec.)

1493 *Acta Auditorum* (1839) 171/1 For þe vpbreking of þe said Johnnis Compt burdis. **1578** LYTE *Dodoens* 683 It stoppeth vomitinges, and the vpbreakynges of the stomacke. **1830** CROLY *George IV*, 283 The general upbreaking of society. **1876** K. O'MEARA *F. Ozanam* xxi. 298 The upbreaking of terrible destructive forces through the calm surface.

up'breathe, *v.* [UP- 4.] *trans.* To send up as a breath.

1606 MARSTON *Trag. Sophonisba* III. i, To you corruptlesse hunny, and pure dew, Upbreathes our holy fire. **1844** MRS. BROWNING *Rhyme Duchess May* xc, Straight as if the Holy name did upbreathe her as a flame..She upsprang. **1880** S. LANIER *Hymns of Marshes, Sunrise* 5 Up-breathed from the marshes, a message..Came to the gates of sleep.

†**up'bring**, *v. Obs.* [UP- 4. Cf. OFris. *opbringa* (WFris. *opbringe*), (M)Du. *opbrengen*, MLG. *upbringen* (LG. *upbrengen*), MHG. *ûfbringen* (G. *aufbringen*), later Da. *opbringe*, Sw. *uppbringa*.]

1. *trans.* To bring up or forth; *fig.* to utter.

a **1250** *Owl & Night.* 200 Þo hule one wile hi biþoȝte, & after þan þis word up-broȝte. *c* **1250** *Gen. & Ex.* 3190 Ðor he doluen,..and hauen up-broȝt ðe bones ut of ðe erðe.

2. To bring up, to rear. (Cf. UPBROUGHT.)

1297 R. GLOUC. (Rolls) 9334 Ʒe stalwarde kniȝtes þat þe king henry vp broȝte & honourede. *c* **1375** *Cursor M.* 7924 (Fairf.), [A sheep] þat he had wiþ his siluer boȝt and fra a lambe hit vp-broȝt. **1559** *Mirr. Mag.* (1563) Vij, Beyng one whom earst I had upbrought Euen from his youth.

3. To bring forth, produce.

c **1440** *Pallad. on Husb.* I. 1005 Right as chaff and donge is profitable On rootis, and vpbryngith breed & wynys. *Ibid.* IV. 681 They oned thus, fruyt of dyuers colour Vpbrynge.

4. To raise up, exalt.

1513 DOUGLAS *Æneid* VII. ii. 167 Sic ane air [= heir], Quhilk sall our name abuf the sternis wpbring.

up'bringer. (UP- 8. Cf. prec. 2.)

1599 JAS. I *Βασιλ. Δωρον* (1603) 97 Honour also..your gouernours, vp-bringers, and Præceptours.

'up,bringing, *vbl. sb.* [UP- 7.]

†**1.** The action of building. *Obs.*⁻¹

1484 *Extr. Aberd. Reg.* (1844) I. 41 Johne Gray, mason,.. has takin upon him to be..diligent for the vpbringing of the said [St. Nicholas'] wark.

2. The action of bringing up young persons; the fact of being brought up while young, or the manner of this; early rearing and training. (Cf. BRINGING *vbl. sb.* 3.)

Rare in older Eng. use, but common in Scottish in the second half of the 16th c., and occasionally used by later Scottish writers. In general use only from *c* 1870.

1520 *Calisto & Melib.* C iv b, They can not well labour in dede Be cause in youth of theyr ydyll vpbryngyng. **1568** FULWELL *Like will to Like* E ij, All licenciously was my vp bringing. **1584** HUDSON *Du Bartas' Judith* IV. (1611) 45 One of the Captains..discriving, to another, her stock and vpbringing. *a* **1670** SPALDING *Troub. Chas. I* (1850) I. 139 The maisteris..of the said college, who cairfullie attendit thair callinges for vpbringing of the youth. **1678** R. BARCLAY *Apol. Quakers* v. §23. 173 Men..have the Eye of the Soul darkned or dimmed through Evil up-bringing and Learning. **1822** CARLYLE *Let.* in Froude *Life* (1882) I. 171 What have I done to..reward those that had the trouble of my upbringing? **1831** —— *Sart. Res.* II. ii, Let me not quarrel with my upbringing! **1864** BURTON *Scot Abr.* I. ii. 95 Preserving no traces of the influence of their..hard upbringing. **1873** MORLEY *Rousseau* II. 197 The theory and art of the upbringing of the young.

up'bristled, *ppl. a.* (UP- 6 b.)

c **1611** CHAPMAN *Iliad* II. 126 Zephyr's vehement gusts.. make the stiff up-bristled ears [of corn] do homage to his breath. **1885** C. J. LYALL tr. *Anc. Arab. Poet.* 113 A lion with angry mane upbristled.

†**up'brixle.** *Obs.*⁻¹ [UP- 2 (cf. UPBRAID *v.*) + ON. *brigzl*, *brigzli* reproach, shame, f. *bregða* (see BRAID *v.*²). Cf. MSw. *upbrygdhilse*, MDa. *obrygdhilse*, *opbryksel*.] Reproach, scorn.

c **1200** ORMIN 4871 Icc amm an wurrm, & nohht nan mann, Uppbrixle menn bitwenenn.

†**up'broid**, *v. Obs.*⁻¹ [UP- 4 + BROID *v.*¹] *trans.* To entangle.

1387 TREVISA *Higden* (Rolls) VII. 431 Þe kyng maked [them]..appose þe cardinales..and upbroyde [*v.r.* upbreide] hem..wiþ sotil sophyms.

up'brought, *pa. pple.* (UP- 5. Cf. UPBRING *v.* 2.)

c **1375** *Sc. Leg. Saints* xxxiv. (*Pelagia*) 291 A dekine, þat wes vpe-brocht with bischope veron. ? *c* **1470** G. ASHBY *Active Policy* 473 Also chese your servantes.., Remembryng with whom thei haue be vpbraught. **1520** *Calisto & Melib.* C iv b, As long as yong pepyll be euell vpbrought. **1596** SPENSER *F.Q.* VI. vi. 9 That same beast was bred of hellish strene, And long in darksome Stygian den vpbrought. *Ibid.* I. ix. 3, etc. **1899** in *Eng. Dial. Dict.* s.v. UP *adv.* 1.

'up-brow. *Coal-mining.* [UP- 2 b + BROW *sb.*¹ 8.] (See quots.)

1867 W. W. SMYTH *Coal & Coal-mining* 135 The bays.. will be connected with the main roads by pairs of drifts (up-brows) carried up the rise of the seam; or sometimes..by down-brows. **1883** GRESLEY *Gloss. Coal-m.* 268 *Up-brow*, an inclined plane worked to the rise.

†**upbrud.** *Obs. rare.* [f. UP- 2 (cf. UPBRAID *sb.*) + OE. *brýd*, **bryȝd*, related to *breȝdan* BRAID *v.*¹, *v.*²] Reproach.

a **1225** *Ancr. R.* 108 In his earen he hefde..al þet edwit, & al þet upbrud, & al þe schorn..þet earen muhte iheren. *c* **1230** *Hali Meid.* 33 Hit is..to al his cun schome, vpbrud in uuel muð, tale bimong alle.

upbrushed, -bubble: see UP- 5, 4 b.

up'build, *v.* (UP- 4.) Also **up'builded, -'built; -'builder; -'building.**

1513 DOUGLAS *Æneid* VIII. iv. 191 Potitius..Ʒone altar in this cuchill did vpbeild. **1570** *Satir. Poems Reform.* xxii. 43 This bailfull bird richt beinly can vpbeild..hir noysum nest. **1850** BLACKIE *Æschylus* I. 235, I will upbuild His house who honours thee. **1890** J. PULSFORD *Loyalty to Christ* I. 47 We..should be careful to..upbuild our energies, equally from God and from Nature. **1865** J. H. INGRAHAM *Pillar of Fire* xvi. 188 Each [pyramid], had not the others been *upbuilded, would have been a marvel of grandeur. **1882** *Proc. Soc. Psychical Research* I. II. 149 The science of zoology could not have been upbuilt without it. **1865** E. BURRITT *Walk to Land's End* 409 The chief *upbuilders of the place in its industrial enterprise. **1732** E. ERSKINE *Wks.* (1791) 647/2 A whole Trinity..lay themselves out..for the *upbuilding of this house. **1876** FAIRBAIRN in *Contemp. Rev.* June 138 What he terms its development or upbuilding may be termed its diseased growth. **1898** B. GREGORY *Side Lights Confl. Meth.* 379 The impression..was in a high degree..bracing and upbuilding.

up'buoyance. (UP- 2.)

? **1799** COLERIDGE *Visit of Gods* 13 Me rather, bright guests! with your wings of upbuoyance Bear aloft to your homes.

'upburst. [UP- 2.] An upward outburst or outbreak.

1843 *Penny Cycl.* XXVI. 424/2 A violent upburst of clouds of scoriæ and ashes. **1872** BP. FORBES *Kal. Sc. Saints* 290 A scarped upburst of trap-rock out of the surrounding red sandstone. **1876** MRS. WHITNEY *Sights & Ins.* II. xxxv. 642 The great upburst of gladness.

upbursting, *ppl. a.*: see UP- 6 b.

up-'by, *adv. Sc.* (and *north. dial.*). Also **up-bye.** [f. UP *adv.*² 2, 8 d + BY *adv.* 2. Cf. IN-, OUTBY.] Up there; up at (or to) a particular place (*spec.* a 'great house' or mansion).

1768 ROSS *Helenore* I. 8 Up by the lambie's lying yonder styth. **1816** SCOTT *Bl. Dwarf* ii, She sits in the neuk yonder, upbye. **1830** J. WILSON *Chr. North* (1856) III. 37 Wha can see the..cairn up-by yonder, when a' the haill heaven is ae coal-cloud? **1871** W. ALEXANDER *Johnny Gibb* xix, Inveetin' the coachman..up bye, aifter Sir Simon gaed awa'.

upcall: see UP- 4.

'up-card. *U.S.* [UP *a.*] In various card games: a card turned face up on the table; a turn-up (TURN-UP *sb.* 3 a).

1938 WOOD & GODDARD *Compl. Bk. Games* 223 The next card, called the up-card, is faced up beside the undealt cards, or stock. **1951** *Amer. Speech* XXVI. 102/1 *Up cards*, cards that are dealt face up in stud [poker]. **1964** *Life* 27 Mar. 80 Charts at top tell player how to play his hand, depending on the dealer's up card. **1974** J. SCARNE *New Compl. Guide to Gambling* 375 This example should make it clear to the reader why Black Jack experts attach so much importance to the dealer's upcard.

'upcast, *sb.* Also 9 *dial.* **upkest.** [UP- 2. Cf. MDa. *opkast* in sense 6.]

1. A chance or accident. *rare.*

1611 SHAKS. *Cymb.* II. i. 2 Was there euer man had such lucke? When I kist the Iacke vpon an vp-cast, to be hit away? **1619** DRAYTON *Legends, P. Gaveston* cvii, Only some small force..For vs to trust to, Fortune had vs left, On which our Hopes, vpon this Vpcast lay. **1897** RHOSCOMYL *White Rose Arno* 131 Pengraig..hoped that he might by some marvellous upcast succeed in overhauling the escaped scoundrel.

2. *Sc.* and *north. dial.* A reproach or taunt; a ground or occasion of reproach.

1681 R. FLEMING *Fulfilling of Script.* (ed. 3) 51 This did never occasion bitter reflexions, or was their upcast before the World. **1681** P. FORMAN in Thomson *Cloud of Witnesses* (1871) 205 Ye are an upcast to poor sufferers. **1825** BROCKETT *N.C. Gloss.* s.v. **1863** JEAN L. WATSON *By-gone Days* 124 If she will only come back again, she will never get an upcast frae me nor mine. **1878–** in *Eng. Dial. Dict.* (Sc., Cumb., N. Irel.).

3. *Mining* and *Geol.* An upward dislocation or shifting of a seam or stratum; a fault caused by this. (Cf. UPCAST *ppl. a.* 3.)

Used in contrast to DOWNCAST or DOWNTHROW.

1793 [EARL DUNDONALD] *Descr. Estate of Culross* 31 The Proprietors..found their Coals after working to a certain depth, thrown up to the north, by an up-cast, as it is commonly called. **1839** MURCHISON *Silur. Syst.* I. xxxvii. 510 The upcasts of the various coalfields. **1842** SEDGWICK in *Hudson's Guide Lakes* (1843) 200 A great cleft or 'fault'.. producing such an enormous 'upcast' towards the N.E., that the carboniferous beds..are on the other side of it. **1872** W. S. SYMONDS *Rec. Rocks* v. 148 The extraordinary upcast of Silurian rocks in Marloes Bay.

4. *upcast shaft* (or *pit*), the pit-shaft by which the ventilating air of a mine is returned to the surface.

1816 [see DOWNCAST *sb.* 2]. **1839** URE *Dict. Arts* 987 The air of the upcast pit being rarefied by the heat. **1867** W. W. SMYTH *Coal & Coal-mining* 207 If a really large volume of air be required, we must heat the full height of the column in the upcast shaft.

ellipt. **1839** URE *Dict. Arts* 971 Pit of ventilation or upcast for the smoke. **1864** A. MILLER *Rise & Progr. Coatbridge* xxv. 169 The air..is conveyed round the whole of the workings, and guided by air courses to the upcast.

b. A casting or hurling upward; a cast or throw in an upward direction.

1890 *Nature* 6 Nov. 16/1 The 'upcast' to which the air must be subject in a cyclone.

5. *Sc.* An upset.

1824 SCOTT *St. Ronan's* xxviii, What wi' the upcast and terror..my head is sair eneugh distressed.

6. Material thrown up in digging, etc.

1883 WHITELAW *Sophocles, Antigone* 250 No mattock's stroke indeed, Nor spade's upcast was there. **1891** G. NEILSON *Per Lineam Valli* 3 Outside..there lies a vast heap of promiscuous earth, the 'upcast' from the trench.

up'cast, *v.* [UP- 4. Cf. CAST *v.* 83 and MSw. *up-*, *opkasta*, Sw. *uppkasta*, (M)Da. *opkaste* in sense 3.]

†**1.** *trans.* To utter loudly. *Obs.*

Cast up also occurs in this sense in ME.

13.. *E.E. Allit. P.* B. 1574 Þis cry was vp-caste, & þer comen mony Clerkes out of caldye. *a* **1400** *Rom. Rose* 7129 The vniuersite.. Gan forto braide.. at the noys the heed vpcast.

†**2.** To open or turn up (the eyes). *Obs.*

1390 Gower *Conf.* II. 103 His slombrende yhen he upcaste, And seide [etc.]

3. To cast, throw, or toss up.

c **1386** Chaucer *Man of Law's T.* 808 (Lansd. MS.), Att þe last.. Custance and eke hir childe þe see vpkast. **1390** Gower *Conf.* III. 314 At Ephesim the See upcaste The cofre. **1608** Topsell *Serpents* 269 The female.. Out of web-breeding-belly.. vp-casting twine. **1850** Blackie *Æschylus* II. 180 This brave Capaneus.. upcasts Loud billowy boasts in Jove's high face. **1862** Lytton *Str. Story* II. 352 The atoms up-cast by the light of the moon. **1875** Morris *Æneid* I. 84 The winds.. driving down upon the sea its lowest deeps up-cast.

†**4.** *Sc.* To throw or force open (a gate). *Obs.*

c **1425** Wyntoun *Cron.* VIII. xi. 1757 All þe ȝettis þai vpkest [*v.r.* wpcast], To lat þaim entir. **1533** Bellenden *Livy* v. viii. (S.T.S.) II. 176 The portis [war] brokin and vpcassin.

5. *Sc.* and *north. dial.* To bring up against one; to cast in one's teeth; to allege as a fault.

1825 Brockett *N.C. Gloss.*, *Upcast*, to upbraid. **1850** Blackie *Æschylus* II. 186 Thy brother too.. He whips with keen reproaches, and upcasts With bitter taunts his evil-omened name. **1865-** in *Eng. Dial. Dict.* (Sc., N. Irel., Northumb., etc.).

'upcast, *ppl. a.* [up- 5. In predicative use *up'cast.*]

1. Of the eye or look: Turned or directed upwards.

c **1402** Lydg. *Compl. Bl. Knt.* 216 Lying in a traunce. With loke up-cast. **1412-20** —— *Chron. Troy* IV. 1481 With eye vp-cast in rancour and in Ire. **1676** Dryden *State Innoc.* II. ii, Beasts with up-cast eyes forsake their Shade. **1715** Addison *To Sir G. Kneller* 61 Old Saturn too with upcast eyes Beheld his abdicated skies. **1816** Keats '*I stood Tip-toe*' 122 Lover of loneliness,.. Of upcast eye, and tender pondering! **1887** J. Ker *Serm.* Ser. II. xiv. 210 With that upcast look to Christ's face.

2. Raised up, prominent. *rare*$^{-1}$.

1658 A. Fox tr. *Wurtz' Surg.* II. x. 87 Do not stitch [the wound];.. it would cause an ugly up-cast scarr.

3. *upcast dyke* (in mining), = upcast *sb.* 3.

1810 J. Bailey *Agric. Durham* 29 They are denominated up-cast dykes, and down-cast dykes, as the strata are cast up or down, according to the direction in which the colliery is working. **1825** E. Mackenzie *View Northumbld.* (ed. 2) I. 82 When the miner finds the vein he has been working thrown below his feet, he calls it a Downcast Dike; but if it be thrown upwards it is then an Upcast Dike.

4. Cast, thrown, or tossed upwards.

1823 Joanna Baillie *Poems* 260 The mighty Geyser's up-cast stream. **1827** Carlyle *Richter, Misc.* (1840) I. 29 Close by their outer churchyards, where crumbled upcast coffin-boards were glimmering. **1892** *Pall Mall G.* 21 Sept. 6/1 The usual upcast spray of water [of a fountain].

up'casting, *vbl. sb.* [up- 7.] The action or result of casting or throwing up, in various senses.

[**1250-68** *Cockersand Chartul.* (Chetham Soc.) 899 Aliud latus prædictæ terræ jacet ad Houpcastinges terræ meæ.] *c* **1450** *Mirk's Festial* 172 But when he schuld dye, he myȝt not receue hit [*sc.* the sacrament] for vpcasting. **1808** Jamieson, *Upcasting*, the rising of clouds above the horizon, especially as threatening rain. **1819** W. Tennant *Papistry Storm'd* (1827) 185 A black up-castin' [of clouds], with ane rim o' darkness. **1882** *Proc. Berw. Nat. Club* X. I. 11 Bare.. rounded hills, with.. yellow up-castings of soil indicating the retreats of rabbits.

up'catch, *v.*, **-caught,** *pa. pple.* (up- 4, 5.)

a **1560** Phaer *Æneid* IX. (1562) Ff1b, The wynds vpcaught yᵗ stroke and Iuno quene ye daunger brake. **1590** Spenser *F.Q.* III. v. 24 He.. His bootelesse bow in feeble hand vpcaught. *a* **1711** Ken *Psyche* Poet. Wks. 1721 IV. 269 He Psyche, as he Jesus once, upcaught. **1791** Cowper *Odyssey* XII. 118 With ev'ry mouth She bears upcaught a mariner away. **1820** Wordsw. *To Enterprise* 132 Withered leaves, from earth's cold breast Up-caught in whirlwinds, nowhere can find rest.

up-'channel, *adv.* and *a.* [up *prep.*² 2.] (Moving, leading, etc.) towards the upper end of a channel.

1893 Kipling *Seven Seas* (1896) 4 Go, get you gone up-Channel with the sea-crust on your plates. **1898** *Daily News* 17 Oct. 5/4 There was a nice up Channel breeze. **1925** Belloc *Cruise of 'Nona'* 135 Anyone going up-Channel makes for the lighthouse.. for this shortens an up-Channel course. **1936** E. G. Bowen in H. C. Darby *Hist. Geogr. Eng.* i. 24 The up-Channel shift of the important trade routes. **1954** —— *Settlement Celtic Saints in Wales* ii. 45 Llanilltud ..and Nant Carban.. are.. conveniently well up-Channel to provide an easy crossing.

†**up'cheer,** *v. Obs. rare.* [up- 4.] *trans.* To cheer up, to encourage.

c **1586** C'tess Pembroke *Ps.* LV. vi, But, my ore loaden soule, thy selfe upcheare. **1596** Spenser *F.Q.* VI. i. 44 Who comming forth yet full of late affray, Sir Calidore vpcheard.

upchoked: see up- 5.

upchuck (ˈʌptʃʌk), *v. U.S. slang.* [up *adv.*¹: cf. *to throw up* s.v. throw *v.*¹ 48 b.] *intr.* To vomit. Also *trans.*

1960 Wentworth & Flexner *Dict. Amer. Slang* 561/2 *Up-chuck, upchuck*, v.i., v.t. to vomit. Since c 1925... Considered a smart and sophisticated term c 1935, esp. when applied to sickness that had been induced by over-drinking. **1967** 'T. Wells' *What should you know of Dying?* i. 19 Anyway, Natalie had to upchuck, it's that kind of bug. **1975** P. de Vries *Glory of Hummingbird* ii. 21 'Did I ever tell you about the time I got sick in Miss Haley's dancing class?' .. He.. had quite copiously up-chucked. **1981** 'A. Cross' *Death in Faculty* i. 9 She up-chucked it.. onto the bedroom floor.

up'climb, *v.* [up- 4. Cf. NFris. *upklêm*, MDu. *opclemmen, -climmen* (Du. *opklimmen*), MLG. *upklemmen*, MHG. *ûfklimmen* (G. *aufklimmen*).] *intr.* and *trans.* To climb up; to ascend. Also **up'climber, -'climbing.**

1546 Joye *Declar.* xcii b, His arrogant vpcliminge and extollinge of him selfe aboue god. **1582** Stanyhurst *Æneis* II. (Arb.) 54, I run forward.., Wheare shouts vpclymbing most rise. **1600** Fairfax *Tasso* XVIII. xci, Farre in the aire vp clombe the fortresse tall, Higher than.. church or towre. **1816** *Monthly Mag.* XLI. 527 Some promise to upclimb the light-house spire. **1845** Mangan *German Anthology* II. 133 To the topmost peak upclomb The conquerors in that bloody fray! **1878** T. Sinclair *Mount* 274 To show sincere students and upclimbers some of the footsteps of their predecessors.

up'close, *v.* [up- 4.] *trans.* and *intr.* To close up, in various senses.

c **1440** *Pallad. on Husb.* I. 921 Good is.. With affadille vp close her holis alle. *c* **1590** J. Stewart *Poems* (S.T.S.) II. 63/235 The ring scho did vpclois In till hir mouth. **1603** Bp. Hall *Kings Proph.* xiii, Eliza dyde, and with the closing yeare Her dayes vpclosde. **1868** Arnold *Lines Kensington Gardens* ix, The flowers upclose, the birds are fed. **1898** T. Hardy *Wessex Poems* 173 Now that my page upcloses,.. Never to press thy cosy cushions more.

up'closed, *pa. pple.*, **up'closer.** (up- 5, 8.)

c **1450** Lydg. *Secrees* 429, I lakke language breffly for to telle The bawme vpclosyd in your tresourye. *a* **1566** Glencairn in Knox *Hist. Ref.* (1846) I. 73 The upclosars of Heavins yett; Cankcarit corruptars of the Creid.

'up-coast, *a.* [up *prep.*²] Situated, extending, etc., further up the coast.

1882 De Windt *Equator* 38 The Resident of one of the up-coast districts. **1900** *Daily News* 16 Jan. 5/2 The column started last night by the up-coast railway line.

'upcoast, up'coast, *adv.* [up *prep.*²] Situated or travelling further up the coast.

1909 J. Masefield *Multitude & Solitude* xii. 296 He lay in his bunk in a cabin.., on his way up-coast. **1931** H. T. Concannon *St. Patrick* 241 Muirchu writes of the Saint as having sailed up-coast. **1974** W. R. Hunt *North of 53* i. 5 St Michael, just upcoast from the Yukon River delta.

'upcome, *sb.* Chiefly *Sc.* [up- 2.]

1. *Sc.* Way up, ascent. *rare.*

1375 Barbour *Bruce* VI. 167 The vpcom wes then Dittit with slayn hors and men. **1866** Gregor *Banffshire Gloss.* 204.

2. *Sc.* Outward appearance (of a person). ? *Obs.*

Jamieson (1808) suggests that the idea is 'probably borrowed from the first appearance of the.. blade after sowing'.

? *a* **1630** D. Hume *Hist. Ho. Douglas* (1644) 235 A Courtier .. cast in a word of doubting and disparaging: It is true, said he, if all be good that is up-come; meaning if his action and valour were answerable to his personage and body. **1819** [A. Balfour] *Campbell* I. 27, I hae nae doubt o' his abilities, for he promises fair according to his upcome. [**1819** Scott *Leg. Montrose* iv, 'A stout fellow,' replied Anderson, 'if all be good that is upcome'. **1823** —— *Quentin D.* vii, You should be a right man-at-arms, if all be good that is upcome.]

3. *Sc.* The final or decisive point.

1824 Scott *Redgauntlet* let. iii, My portrait is.. scandalously caricatured. *I* fail or quail in spirit at the upcome!

4. The result, yield, or produce.

c **1874** C. Patmore in Champneys *Mem.* (1900) I. 250 The upcome of a year can be reaped in one fine day. **1887** *Sat. Rev.* 11 June 821/1 The positive.. upcome of this last of Mr. Gladstone's perambulations.

up'come, *v. rare.* [up- 4. Cf. WFris. *opkomme*, MDu. *opcomen* (Du. *opkomen*), MLG. *upkomen*, MHG. *ûfkomen* (G. *aufkommen*), MSw. *up-, opkoma, -komme* (Sw. *uppkomma*), (M)Da. *opkomme.*] *intr.* To come, spring, or rise up.

c **1000** *Ags. Gosp.* Mark iv. 17 Syþþan upcymð deofles costnung. *c* **1200** Ormin 1267 ȝiff þu.. ȝeornesst tatt tu mote sket Uppcumenn inntill heoffne. *c* **1400** *Master of Game* (MS. Digby 182) xxiv, Of corne and of oþer thynges that vppe commeth of þe londe. **1828** Atherstone *Fall of Nineveh* I. 48 In a moment more, Upcame the monstrous universal shout.

up'coming, *vbl. sb.* [up- 7.]

1. The action of coming up, in various senses.

13.. *Guy Warw.* (A.) 7240 Þe best him neyed, & smot him Wiþ his vp-coming so fel & grim [etc.]. *a* **1340** Hampole *Psalter* lxxii. 19 Þai fal downe þat lang tyme had in vp-comminge. **1387** Trevisa *Higden* (Rolls) V. 229 Me dradde þe arryvynge and upcomynge of straunge men. **1535** Stewart *Cron. Scot.* (Rolls) II. 700 Of the Scrymgeouris and thair Vpcuming. *a* **1575** *Diurn. Occurr.* (Bann. Cl.) 109 In thair vpcuming my lord of Ergyle bare the croun. **1654** Wariston *Diary* (S.H.S.) II. 292 This checked me in the up-coming out of Leyth. **1746** E. Erskine *Serm.* (1755) 391 The Up-coming of the Breaker is with much awful Majesty. **1862** Carlyle *Fredk. Gt.* XIII. ix. III. 524 In his young time he had a hard upcoming. **1889** *Athenæum* 29 June 831/2 Half-lights reveal on the surface the upcoming of eddies in films from below.

†**2.** *Sc.* An ascent, an upward path. *Obs.* (Cf. upcome *sb.* 1.)

1375 Barbour *Bruce* VI. 81 Sua strate wes þe vp-cummyng, þat twa men mycht nocht sammyn thryng. *Ibid.* 170.

'up,coming, *ppl. a.* [up- 6 b.]

a. Coming up.

1848 T. Aird *Nebuchadnezzar* III. 12 Upcoming hunters on the hill appear. **1879** McCarthy *Own Times* II. 169 Personal reasons.. for particular distrust of the upcoming Emperor.

b. That is about to happen, etc., forthcoming. Chiefly *U.S.*

1959 A. Huxley *Let.* 3 Sept. (1969) 878, I am working like mad.. on my lectures for the upcoming semester. **1967** Mrs. L. B. Johnson *White House Diary* 5 June (1970) 521 Today it was work on the speeches for the upcoming trip to New England. **1971** *Publishers' Weekly* 1 Nov. 18/1 Booth and Haley did their upcoming books no harm. **1973** *Express* (Trinidad & Tobago) 27 Apr. 31/3 The up-coming contest is open to all karate associations. **1982** T. Barling *Terminate with Prejudice* IV. v. 104 An upcoming visit by a member of the Soviet Politburo. **1984** *Daily Tel.* 25 Feb. 17 No change in the law was required, the existing statute was merely being clarified and there was no need to insert a special clause in the upcoming Finance Bill.

up-con'verter. Chiefly *Electr.* [up- 8.] A device for converting a signal to a higher frequency. So **up-con'version;** also **up-con'vert** *v. trans.*, **up-con'verted** *ppl. a.*

1958 *Bell Syst. Technical Jrnl.* XXXVII. 989 (*heading*) Gain and noise figure of a variable-capacitance up-converter. *Ibid.*, In up-conversion (modulation) a power gain results, with the power added to the input signal being supplied by the beat oscillator. In down-conversion a power loss results. **1968** *Microwave Jrnl.* Aug. 52/2 The 12·4 GHz signal from the frequency up-converter is first down-converted to 160 MHz.. then upconverted to 12·4 GHz in a single frequency parametric upconverter. **1970** *New Yorker* 11 Apr. 34 A laser beam can be used to upconvert infrared light to visible light. **1972** *Physics Bull.* Jan. 18/2 Since the upconverted radiation now has a wavelength close to both the helium-neon and krypton (0·605 μm) wavelengths, an accurate interferometric comparison is much easier to perform than with the 9·3 μm line directly. **1972** Upconverter [see parametric *a.*¹ b]. **1975** D. G. Fink *Electronics Engineers' Handbk.* XIV. 72 There is a distinct advantage to up-conversion; image rejection is easily achievable by a simple low-pass filter. **1976** *Which?* Nov. 262/3 UHF signals received at the aerial are sometimes translated to VHF or even lower frequencies (HF). These VHF (or HF) signals can't be plugged directly into a UHF TV... They need either a box (called an up-converter) to turn them back into UHF signals, or a specially modified TV. **1983** E. Trundle *Beginner's Guide Videocassette Recorders* v. 91 The up-conversion process during replay involves a heterodyne system.

'up-country, up-'country, *sb.*, *a.*, and *adv.* [up *a.* and *prep.*²]

As adv. and adj. the phrase is current in English dialects (cf. quot. 1688), but the general 19th century use originated partly in India and partly in the United States; from *c* 1875 it has also been employed in, or with reference to, Australia, South Africa, etc.

1. *sb.* †**a.** An uplying or inland district. *Obs.*

1688 R. Holme *Armoury* III. 352/2 A Pit Saw in a Frame .. is not in use with us, but in the Up Countreys.

b. The inland part of a country.

Used without article, or with *the*.

(*a*) **1837** [Mrs. Maitland] *Lett. fr. Madras* (1843) 110, I continue to like 'up country,' as they call it, far better than the Presidency. **1888** [D'Avigdor] *Antipod. Notes* v. 30 Thousands from up-country make their annual business visit to the capital. **1897** P. Warung *Tales Old Regime* 162 To say good-bye before leaving for up-country.

(*b*) **1817** M. L. Weems *Let.* in *M. L. Weems: Works & Ways* (1929) III. 176, I have a number due in the up country. **1835** J. H. Ingraham *South-West* I. xxiii. 248 In the cabin are the merchants and planters of the 'up country'. **1872** De Vere *Americanisms* 163 The nearest districts became early known.. as the Up Country. **1894** *Cent. Mag.* April 849 Later generations in the up-country have applied the word to the products of corn after cooking.

2. *adj.* Situated in, belonging or relating to, etc., the inland part of a country, or a part of the country away from any town. (Now rare in the U.K.)

In this sense and as *adv.* sometimes implying 'higher in altitude'.

1810 M. L. Weems *Let.* in *M. L. Weems: Works & Ways* (1929) III. 27 Not thinking the little up-country post offices safe in matters of money [etc.]. **1831** *Canton Miscell.* V. 321 Up-country stations in India. **1835** Macaulay in Trevelyan *Life* (1876) I. 406 Any [library] which would be readily accessible at an up-country station [in India]. **1859** F. Fuller *Five Years' Residence N.Z.* xi. 233 The up-country tracks were not then marked out. **1861** Clough *Mari Magno* 29 What racy tales of Yankeeland he had! Up-country girl, up-country farmer lad. **1874** Ranken *Domin. Australia* xiii. 237 The 'up-country store-keeper'.. sells everything wholesale or retail. **1884** *Health Exhib. Catal.* p. xliii, Models.. of European up-country bungalows, and.. of a bazaar in an up-country town. **1911** C. E. W. Bean '*Dreadnought' of Darling* xx. 193 The fact that each of seven station hands *could* agree to put in £70 may throw some light upon the conditions amongst upcountry workers in Australia. **1911** W. H. Koebel *In Maoriland Bush* xxii. 284 Homely little upcountry race meetings. **1923** [see station *sb.* 13 d]. **1929** K. S. Prichard *Coonardoo* xvi. 162 Poor degraded wretches,.. drifting about the up-country towns and settlements along the coast. **1962** J. Frame *Edge of Alphabet* xviii. 102 How I would have liked to.. live in an upcountry house whose tall windows faced the mountains. **1965** B. Wannan *Fair Go, Spinner* IV. 131 The Drongo once got a job on an up-country farm. **1970** *Kenya Farmer* Feb. 9/1 One of the greatest pleasures that Kenya can offer—a weekend on an 'up country' farm. **1977** *Church Times* 29 July 6/3 A BCMS missionary nurse in upcountry Uganda. **1981** *Times* 2 Feb. 16/7 He was the first Kandyan (upcountry) Sinhalese Buddhist to be appointed Governor-

General, his predecessor having been a low country Sinhalese Christian.

3. *adv.* In or to the inland part of a country. Also, away from any town, remote.

1864 TREVELYAN *Compet. Wallah* 31 A young couple going to an appointment up-country. **1866** M. A. BARKER *Station Life N.Z.* (1870) vi. 37, I had danced with a young gentleman whose station was a long way 'up country'. **1889** 'J. S. WINTER' *Mrs. Bob* iii, Whilst we were up-country,.. we met Colonel Coles. **1891** KIPLING *Light that Failed* ii, I'm going up-country with a column. **1891** G. CHAMIER *Philosopher Dick* I. ii. 43 Here, up country, we have mostly a moving population of tramps, topers and outcasts. **1911** E. M. CLOWES *On Wallaby* iv. 86 Up-country the sundowner, or *bona fide* worker in search for a job, will find 'tucker' for the asking at any farm or station. **1911** W. H. KOEBEL *In Maoriland Bush* xiii. 183 Nature is a staunch friend to this obsolete atmosphere. Nowhere, perhaps, does it come to its aid with greater fervour than in New Zealand, up-country. **1962** J. FRAME *Edge of Alphabet* i. 14 As if his head were a secret gully somewhere up-country. **1962** *Housewife* (Ceylon) Apr. 10 Children's woollen clothes very moderately priced and ideal for wear, both up-country and abroad. **1971** *Inside Kenya Today* Mar. 48/1 Farmers.. can grow a variety of crops—just as much as their counterparts up-country could. **1980** *Word* *1979* XXX. 167 Transportation problems, levels of literacy, as well as economic factors, tend to restrict the diffusion of the newspapers up-country.

†**up'covering**, *vbl. sb.* *Obs.*⁻¹ [UP- 7 + COVER *v.*² 4. Cf. *upkever*, UP- 4.] Recovery.

a **1300** *Cursor M.* 25821 Suagat for þair wanhopping þai fall wit-vten vp-couering.

†**up'creeper.** *Obs.*⁻¹ (UP- 8.)

c **1534** *Image Hypocr.* I. 531 in *Skelton's Wks.* (1843) II. 429 Thou arte a cursed crekar, a crafty vppcrepar.

up'curl, *v.* [UP- 4.] To curl up.

trans. **1801** SOUTHEY *Thalaba* IV. xxxi, High, high in heaven upcurl'd The dreadful sand-spouts moved. **1852** M. ARNOLD *Tristr. & Iseult* III. 118 The.. furnace of the world, In whose hot air our spirits are upcurled Until they crumble. **1895** F. THOMPSON *Sister Songs* 3 Ere.. Thou disclose my flower of song upcurled..!

intr. **1838** MARY HOWITT *Birds & Flowers* 189 Where the branching ferns up-curl. **1845** MANGAN *German Anthology* II. 126 A stupendous column of sand.. upcurls.. in eddies and whirls.

up'curling, *vbl. sb.* (UP- 7. Cf. prec.)

1828 *Lights & Shades* II. 185 The up-curling of its widely-dilated nostrils.

'upcurrent, *sb.* [UP- 2.] A rising current of air.

1909 F. W. LANCHESTER in *Flight* 22 May 296/1 When a plane falls normally through a vertical path, there is set up around the edges an up-current of air. **1921** *Flight* 8 Sept. 604/1 This map brings out very clearly.. the manner in which Klemperer followed the valleys and took advantage of the gusts, up-currents, etc., which were caused by the nature of the country. **1931** *Air Ann. Brit. Empire* 30 The most elementary form of up-currents are caused by the deflection of winds over hills.. necessary for soaring flight. **1953** N. TINBERGEN *Herring Gull's World* iv. 39 The influence of the upcurrent on their flight is seen most impressively when.. one forces the gulls to make a detour out over the beach. **1979** B. L. C. JOHNSON *Pakistan* iv. 55/1 It limits the scope for upcurrents in the surface monsoon air stream to rise very high.

upcurved, *pa. pple.* and *ppl. a.* (UP- 5.)

1870 HOOKER *Stud. Flora* 183 Bracts upcurved. **1875** DARWIN *Insectiv. Pl.* xiv. 328 Covered.. near their extremities with upcurved prickles. **1893** *Athenæum* 1 April 399/2 Avocets with up-curved bills.

'up-cut. *Engin.* [UP- 2.] A cut made by a cutter rotating so that the teeth are moving upwards when cutting; so ***up-cut milling***.

1934 WEBSTER, Upcut. **1950** J. A. OATES in A. W. Judge *Machine Tools & Operations* III. ii. 113 Down-cut milling produces a dull surface, in contrast to the bright and polished type resulting from ordinary up-cut milling. **1964** S. CRAWFORD *Basic Engin. Processes* vi. 166 The normal or conventional method of milling is known as up-cut milling. **1973** J. G. TWEEDDALE *Materials Technol.* II. vi. 146 Figure 6.4c shows an 'upcut'.

upcyne: see note to UPTIE *sb.*

up'dart, *v.*, etc. (UP- 4, 5, and 6.)

1722 J. JONES tr. *Oppian's Halieuticks* III. 143 The Barbel, when encircling Seines inclose,.. O'er Battlements of Cork up-darting flies. **1791** COWPER *Iliad* xv. 102 So swift up-darted Juno to the skies. **1799** H. GURNEY *Cupid & Pschye* 42 High o'er the dragons he will tower Updarting thro' the azure air.

up'datable, *a.* [f. next + -ABLE.] That may be updated.

1976 *Business Week* 5 Apr. 44/2 Eastman Kodak Corp. and Xerox Corp. are experimenting with nonsilver imaging and updatable microfiche. **1977** *Financial Times* 19 May 17/1 GEC have developed a magnetic card which looks much like existing credit cards, but carries updatable information which frees banks from their present large central accounting systems.

up'date, *v.* orig. *U.S.* [UP- 4; cf. UP TO DATE, UP-TO-DATE *adv. phr.*] *trans.* **a.** To bring (information, esp. written material or material recorded in some other form) up to date.

1948 *Time* 11 Oct. 22/1 [The speech] had been corrected and updated after last-minute teletype reports from.. Paris. **1959** *Times Lit. Suppl.* 20 Mar. 155/2 He would streamline the production, add a chorus of dancing girls, update the lyrics, and upjazz the music. **1962** C. WALSH *From Utopia to Nightmare* 12 All current allusions have been 'updated' (as of early 1962). **1979** *Ottawa Law Rev.* XI. 815 The entry for 'Hudson's Bay Company' needs to be updated.

b. To supply (a person) with the most recent information; to bring (a person) up to date.

1952 *N.Y. Herald-Tribune* 14 Mar. 21/2 He updated me on a couple of gimmicks. **1970** J. EARL *Tuners & Amplifiers* 7 The book will have appeal, too, to the older hand, allowing him to become quickly updated without the task of researching into piles of technical literature. **1975** *Sunday Times* 16 Nov. 44/4 No doubt I'll update myself in a few weeks and emerge as a real Seventies mum.

c. Of equipment, processes, etc.

1959 *Listener* 4 June 998/1 This prescience has now been 'up-dated', as they say, by reference to nuclear warfare. **1970** *Islander* (Victoria, B.C.) 8 Feb. 7/2 Despite.. updating the equipment to include new freezing facilities.. this [whaling] venture also folded. **1977** *N.Y. Rev. Bks.* 13 Oct. 45/1 To update the 'dirty test tube' analogy, the effects of the contaminants have been estimated and found to be minor. **1984** *Daily Mail* 1 Dec. 14/1 (Advt.) This way, you can update your equipment whenever you want.

Also **up'dated** *ppl. a.*; **up'dating** *vbl. sb.*

Quot. 1910 is an isolated early British example.

1910 HARDY *Satires of Circumstance* (1914) 222 Your up-dated modern page. **1954** *Newsweek* 27 Sept. 58/1 The new research center is an updated transplant of the National Bureau of Standards world-wide radio investigations formerly based in Washington. **1959** *Spectator* 31 July 134/2 Despite the up-dating and jazzy typographical treatment, one fairly quickly perceives an enduring pattern of traditional attitudes. **1974** ADBY & DEMPSTER *Introd. Optimization Methods* iv. 96 Round-off errors in the computations of the up-dating process can lead to non-positive definitive S_k and divergence. **1978** *Jrnl. R. Soc. Arts* CXXVI. 672/1 The plan adopted is said to be a revised and updated version of an outline plan for the development of the economy produced in 1975.

'update, *sb.* orig. *U.S.* [f. the vb.] **1.** New information received or supplied; an updated version of something. Also, an account or report of the present state of affairs. *colloq.*

1967 *Britannica Bk. of Year* (U.S.) 804/3 *Update*, current information for use by a computer in order to make the calculations necessary for achieving a particular goal. **1970** N. ARMSTRONG et al. *First on Moon* v. 116 When you're ready to copy.. I've got a couple of small flight plan updates. **1975** B. GARFIELD *Hopscotch* ix. 92 Thanks for the update. Keep on it. **1976** *Physics Bull.* July 313/2 Quarterly updates are available for each course. **1977** H. GREENE *FSO-1* xiii. 119 One of his people will.. give you a full update on related problems. **1983** *Brit. Med. Jrnl.* 6 Aug. 417/1 The editors of *Harrison's Principles of Internal Medicine* have bridged the gap between the 9th and 10th editions with a series of updates. **1984** *Miami Herald* 6 Apr. 11D/1 An embarrassing update of the 1960s comedy filmed on Fort Lauderdale Beach. **1985** *Times* 5 Jan. 17/7 The new album is a high-grade Motown update, funky, sleek and packed with potential hits.

2. The action or result of updating; the supplying of new information, data, etc. Freq. in *Computers*.

1968 *Amer. Documentation* Jan. 75/1 Thus, interrogations, extractions and updates can be based upon items or subitems, but not upon units smaller than these. **1972** *Computer Jrnl.* XV. 191/2 The effect, of course, is to put the clock back to the time of the last dump and all updates made since then must be repeated. **1976** *Gramophone* Aug. 353/3 Such 'updates' as they are called, involve switching individual tracks of the tape from the 'read' to the 'write' mode. **1982** *ICL News* No. 96. 5/1 A pre-Conference session.. was followed by an overall update and presentations on latest versions of data management software.

3. *attrib.*

1969 *Sunday Times* 13 July 13/2 *Update pad*, information on spacecraft attitudes, and other data, transmitted to the crew in standard format. **1972** *Computers & Humanities* VII. 127 Working with this printout, the editor prepares data for the update module in which insignificant variants are deleted and citations added. **1983** *Word Ways* Nov. 197 It.. is supplemented by update lists which the computer automatically generates.

updelve, -dive, -drag: see UP- 4.

up-dip, *a.* and *adv.* *Geol.* [f. UP *prep.*² + DIP *sb.*]

A. *adj.* (Stressed *'up-dip.*) Situated or occurring in a direction upwards along the dip. **B.** *adv.* (Stressed *up-'dip.*) In an up-dip direction.

1916 F. H. LAHEE *Field Geol.* viii. 191 When a fault is approximately parallel to the strike of the strata, the block on the side of the fault toward which the dip of the beds is measured may be termed the down-dip block, and the other one is the up-dip block. **1957** G. E. HUTCHINSON *Treat. Limnol.* I. i. 156 The bays originated as artesian springs, which tended to migrate inland up-dip. **1965** [see LENTICULARITY]. **1974** R. D. GRACE in P. L. Moore et al. *Drilling Practices Manual* xiii. 329 It predicts up-dip deviation when drilling into softer rock.

up-do ('ʌpdu:). *colloq.* (orig. *U.S.*). Also **updo**. [f. UP *adv.*¹ + DO *sb.*¹ 2, after *hair-do.*] A style of dressing women's hair by sweeping it up and securing it away from the face and neck.

1938 *Sun* (Baltimore) 29 Nov. 9/4 The 'up-do' hair style does not click with De Paul University men students... The 'up-do' probably will go back down after movie stars get tired of it. **1966** J. S. COX *Illustr. Dict. Hairdressing & Wigmaking* 157/1 *Up-do*, a hair style dressed away from the forehead and neckline. Updo: American Spelling. **1984** *Daily Tel.* 3 Sept. 13/5 She has not appeared to be wearing anything in her hair. If Miss Resnik returns to space a second time, Mr Menchaca said he would consider putting in 'braids or an up-do'.

up'doming, *vbl. sb.* *Geol.* [UP- 7.] The upward expansion of a rock mass into a dome shape.

1964 *Bull. Vermont Geol. Survey* No. 23. 7 Updoming was the deforming mechanism of the anticlinorium. **1977** A. HALLAM *Planet Earth* 78/3 The heating of the rocks beneath the rift zone causes expansion, and this accounts.. for the updoming.

updraught. [UP- 2. Cf. DRAUGHT *sb.* 23.]

†**1.** = INDRAUGHT 3. *Obs. rare.*

14.. *Sailing Direct.* (Hakl. Soc.) 15 A south west mone makith hiest watir by the see coste, and in the updraughtis it dooth not so. *Ibid.* 19.

2. Also (chiefly *U.S.*) **updraft.** [DRAUGHT *sb.* 24.] An upward-moving current of air. Cf. DOWN-DRAUGHT 1. Also *fig.*

1909 *Daily Graphic* 26 July 10/1 While the planes are fighting against the wind their area will be comparatively small, but when floating on an up-draught they will be expanded as a fan expands. **1935** C. DAY LEWIS *Time to Dance* 31 Some aimed at a small objective but the fierce updraught of their spirit Forced them to the stars. **1953** N. TINBERGEN *Herring Gull's World* iv. 28 A north wind caused an updraught, which enabled the birds to hang motionless in the air for many minutes. **1954** R. J. SCHWARTZ *Dict. Business & Industry* 533 Updraft. *a* **1963** S. PLATH *Crossing Water* (1971) 38 A sheet of newsprint on the fire Levitating a numb minute in the updraft. **1983** D. BOGGIS *Woman they sent to FIGHT* iv. 28 Brakes off, undercarriage down.. *Slam* through the updraught off the spinney.

up'draw, *v.* [UP- 4. Cf. (M)Du. *opdragen*, MLG. *updragen, -dregen*, LG. *updragen*, MHG. *ûftragen* (G. *auf-*), MSw. *updragha* (Sw. *uppdraga*), (M)Da. *opdrage.*]

†**1.** *trans.* To pull out of the ground. Also *fig.*

c **1290** *Holy Rood* 165 in *S. Eng. Leg.* I. 6 He ne miȝte nouȝt aboute þe eorþe swinke, ne þe weodes up drawe. *a* **1300** *Cursor M.* 6330 Bot moyses.. þaa wandes durst he noght vp-drau [*Fairf.* vpdragh]. **13..** *K. Alis.* 2633 (Laud MS.), In þe grounde it stiked fast,.. non ne miȝt it vp-drawe. *c* **1449** PECOCK *Repr.* I. ii. 8 Forto meete aȝens the firste bifore spoken opinioun, and forto vnroote and vpdrawe it.

2. To draw up to a height or from a lower place; also, to draw (a bow) to the full.

c **1300** *Havelok* 932 He kam to þe welle, water vp-drow. **13..** *Seuyn Sages* (W.) 2682 Ich wil fol fawe Heghe him honge and vpdrawe. **1390** GOWER *Conf.* II. 295 Bardus with his Asse anon Him hath updrawe [*sc.* out of a pit]. *c* **1440** *Bone Flor.* 532 Ye schoulde.. close the yatys, and the brygges up drawe. **1508** DUNBAR *Flyting* 90 Thow saw the saill abuif my heid vpdraw. **1600** FAIRFAX *Tasso* XX. lxiii, Three times her angrie hand the bow vp drew. **1667** MILTON *P.L.* II. 874 She .. Forthwith the huge Portcullis high up drew. **1791** COWPER *Iliad* I. 597 Their galley they up-drew.. From the rude surge remote. **1813** HOGG *Queen's Wake, Glen-Airn* xxviii, Dawning in the air updrew From many a.. hill, Her folding robe of fairy blue.

b. *fig.* To bring up before the mind.

1828 TENNYSON *Lover's Tale* I. 634 If so be that the echo of that name.. had updrawn.. a phantasm of the form.

†**3.** To bring up, to rear. *Obs.*⁻¹

1390 GOWER *Conf.* I. 186 A knyht, whom fro childhode He hadde updrawe into manhode.

up'drawn, *pa. pple.* and *ppl. a.* (UP- 5, 6 b. Cf. prec.)

c **1250** *Gen. & Ex.* 1858 Folc of salem ðor-fore was slaȝen, wiwes, and childre, and aȝte up-draȝen. **1390** GOWER *Conf.* II. 238 Fro his lond with sail updrawe Thei wente hem forth. **1582** STANYHURST *Æneis* III. (Arb.) 79 Oure vessels vpdrawne are grapled at anchor. **1667** MILTON *P.L.* IV. 228 The rapid current,.. with kindly thirst up drawn. **1762** FALCONER *Shipwr.* II. 485 The sounding cord, Updrawn, an undiminish'd depth explor'd. **1866** LYTTON *Lost Tales Miletus, Secret Way* 6 As cloud, from purest dews Updrawn, makes sorrowful a star in heaven. **1887** M. ARNOLD *Ess. Crit.* Ser. II. (1888) 261 Alexis Karénine's updrawn eyebrows. **1901** *Daily Chron.* 26 Aug. 3/5 A tree.. has fallen, and the up-drawn roots form a bridge.

up'dress, *v.* (UP- 4.)

a **1400** *Rom. Rose* 7067 That he wolde vpdresse Engyns bothe more and lesse To cast at vs by euery side. *a* **1500** *Chaucer's Dreme* 662 Right in his wo he gan to braid, And him vp dresses for to knele. **1600** FAIRFAX *Tasso* XVI. xxiii, Her curles garland wise she did vpdresse.

up'dried, *pa. pple.* (UP- 5.) Also **up'dry** *v.*, **up'drying** *vbl. sb.*

c **1440** *Pallad. on Husb.* I. 238 Lupyne and ficchis slayn, and on their roote Vpdried, are.. londis boote. **1530** LYNDESAY *Test. Papyngo* 138 The balmy droppis of dew Tytane vpdryis. *c* **1586** C'TESS PEMBROKE *Ps.* LXVI. iii, The sea up-dried by his hand, Became a field of dusty sand. **1658** A. FOX tr. *Würtz Surg.* III. xxiii. 290 That updrying.. comes from an oppilation of that member, be that caused from what it will. **1889** F. THOMPSON in *Merry England* Sept. 306 Till Time, the hidden root of change, updries, Are Birth and Death inseparable on earth.

updrinking, *vbl. sb.* [UP- 7.] (See quot. and cf. UPSITTING.)

1819 [A. BALFOUR] *Campbell* I. 13 At the feast given on my mother's recovery, which in that part of the country was termed the up-drinking.

upeat: see UP- 4.

†**upen**, obs. var. OPEN *a.* (Cf. UPON *a.*)

13.. *E.E. Allit. P.* A. 1066 Þe ȝates stoken was neuer ȝet Bot euer more vpen at vche a lone.

up-'end, *v.* Orig. *dial.* [UP *adv.*¹]

1. a. *trans.* To set (something) on its end; to turn end upwards; *dial.* to set (also *refl.*, to get) on one's feet. Also *fig.*

1823 E. MOOR *Suffolk Words* 460 *Upinnd*, to set a cask or any thing on its end. **1868** *Rep. to Govt. U.S. Munitions War* 274 The bursting of a few shells.. tearing, up-ending, and setting fire to the planking of the latter [deck]. **1874** BEDFORD *Sailor's Pocket Bk.* 173 An approaching heavy sea may carry the boat away.. and turn it broadside on, or up-end it. **1900** H. LAWSON *Over Sliprails* 29 It crawled to the wall, against which it slowly and painfully up-ended itself. **1970** G. GREER *Female Eunuch* 37 By growing their hair they managed to up-end some strange presupposition about its sexual significance.

b. In pa. pple.: Sitting up.

1874 E. WAUGH *Chimney Corner* (1879) 123, I left him about two minutes sin' up-ended i' bed.

2. *intr.* To rise up on end; *spec.* of waterfowl: to dip the head below water and raise the tail into the air, when searching for food in shallow water.

1897 KIPLING *Capt. Cour.* 52 They up-eend thet way when they're hungry. **1902** S. E. WHITE *Blazed Trail* xxxii, A log in the advance up-ended; another thrust under it. **1927** E. SANDARS *Bird Bk. for Pocket* II. 126 [Brent Geese] sometimes when feeding at high tide, up-end like Ducks. **1954** A. W. P. ROBERTSON *Bird Pageant* i. 20 Avocets.. often when water-borne.. up-end like ducks. **1957** R. A. H. COOMBES in D. A. Bannerman *Birds Brit. Isles* VI. 266, I never saw them 'upending' in the shallows as the other geese were fond of doing.

fig. **1981** *Birds* Summer 47/2 An up-ending mallard is a feeding mallard, but this, our commonest duck, is as adaptable in its feeding technique as it is in its choice of food.

Hence **up-ended** *ppl. a.*

1880 'MARK TWAIN' *Tramp Abr.* xlvii. 488 Propping them.. with her up-ended valise. **1896** C. ALLEN *Papier Mâché* 121 The up-ended box whereon the student was perched.

upfield, *adv.* and *a.* [UP *prep.*²]

A. *adv.* (Stressed *up'field.*) **1.** *Football*, etc. In or towards the end of the field nearest the goal which the team is attacking.

1951 *Sport* 27 Apr.–3 May 8/1 The wee Scot whipped the ball upfield to the late Jack Lambert before Huddersfield had organised their ranks. **1960** *Times* 29 Feb. 3/3 France worked their way upfield again. **1976** *Evening Advertiser* (Swindon) 31 Dec. 19/4 He would not stay upfield wide on the wing and was coming back too deep.

2. *Chem.* and *Physics.* In a direction corresponding to greater field strength.

1965 *Jrnl. Chem. Physics* XLII. 636/2 The $^{205}\Pi$+ resonance is shifted upfield by a very large amount. **1976** *Nature* 29 July 424/3 The statement.. makes the dangerous assumption that no aromatic protons are shifted upfield or downfield out of this region by local ring current effects.

B. *adj.* (Stressed *'upfield.*) **1.** *Football*, etc. Directed into or occurring in a part of the field near(er) the goal attacked.

1960 *Times* 18 Nov. 22/2 Long upfield kicks by stand-off Evans. *Ibid.* 6 Dec. 18/3 Upfield support of forwards by the backs. **1983** *N.Y. Times* 30 Jan. v. 8/6 Manley is the upfield pass rusher.

2. *Chem.* and *Physics.* Situated or occurring in the direction of greater field strength.

1967 *Inorg. Chem.* VI. 1133/2 Increased metal to ligand π bonding produces an upfield coordination chemical shift. **1979** *Macromolecules* XII. 763/1 These spectra show an upfield peak separated from a smaller peak, 2·36 ± 0·1 downfield.

up'fill, *v.* [UP- 4. Cf. MSw. *upfylla* (Sw. *upp-*), MDa. *upfylle*, Du. *opvullen.*] *trans.* To fill up. Also **up'filled** *pa. pple.*

c **1440** *Pallad. on Husb.* XII. 350 So braunches fewe vpfille a huge londe. **1592** SHAKS. *Rom. & Jul.* II. iii. 7, I must vpfill this Osier Cage of ours, With balefull weedes. **1596** SPENSER *F.Q.* IV. iii. 42 A cup she hild, The which was with Nepenthe to the brim vpfild. **1861** *Macm. Mag.* June 134 A fine tree.. that upfilled a picture with cows or haymakers beneath it.

up'filling. [UP- 7. Cf. prec.] Something which serves to fill up.

1822 G. YOUNG *Geol. Surv.* 168 The red sandstone.. occupying the valleys in the form of what has been called an upfilling. **1833–4** *Encycl. Metrop.* VI. 705/2 At length the originally rugged chasm is changed by additions and upfillings into the smooth, evenly declining hollow. **1844** H. STEPHENS *Bk. Farm* III. 810 A gate to be permanent, should be.. a simple rectangular frame without upfillings.

†**up'finder.** *Obs.*⁻¹ [UP- 8.] A deviser.

1430–40 LYDG. *Bochas* IX. 482 Double of hir tunge, vpfyndere of tresoun.

'upfloor. [ad. OE. *upflór*: UP- 1.] A triforium. (In quot. 1922, *arch.* in sense 'an upper floor'.)

This special application is derived from the use of the word with reference to the church at Glastonbury in the *O.E. Chron.* (Laud MS.), an. 1083.

1879 A. TAYLOR *Guienne* 12 Our ancestors.. gave the triforium (then lately devised) the vernacular English name of 'upfloor'. **1912** C. E. POWER *Eng. Mediæv. Archit.* I. 20 The 'triforium chamber' or 'up-floor' of monastic writers. **1922** JOYCE *Ulysses* 381 Sir Leopold heard on the up-floor cry on high and he wondered what cry that it was whether of child or woman.

'upflow, *sb.* (UP- 2.)

1871 *Contemp. Rev.* XIX. 40 This incessant out-flow or up-flow (if the physicist will permit the latter word). **1890** *Philos. Mag.* Dec. 501 The final results of the upflow of air limited as to space. *Ibid.*, The strata of air surrounding the upflow.

'upfold, *sb. Geol.* [UP- 2.] = ANTICLINE.

1902 MACKINDER *Britain & Brit. Seas* vi. 80 The Mendip Range.. is a complete upfold of carboniferous limestone.

up'fold, *v.* [UP- 4. Cf. LG. *upfolden*, G. *auffalten.*] *trans.* To fold up, fold together; †to raise, push up. Also **up'folded**, †**-'folden** *pa. pple.*

13.. *E.E. Allit. P.* B. 643 Abraham, al hodlez with armez vp-folden. *a* **1460** *Lament. Virgin* in *Chester Plays* (1847) II. 206 The ston owyr hym he can upfolde,.. And wente hys wey wherso he wolde. **1600** FAIRFAX *Tasso* XVI. xiv, The gentlie budding rose.. her beauties doth vpfold In their deare leaues. **1822** J. WILSON *Lights & Shadows Sc. Life* 342 The leaves yet upfolded might almost be heard budding in the bower. **1878** E. JONES *Sens. & Event* (1879) 200 Come o'er the hills, and pass unto the wold, And all things, as thou passest, in rest upfold.

upfollowed, -framed: see UP- 5.

upfront, *adv.* and *a. colloq.* (orig. *U.S.*). Also **up-front, up front.** [f. UP *adv.*¹, *adv.*² + FRONT *sb.*] **A.** *adv.* **a.** At the front, in front.

1937 [see LATCH *v.*¹ 1]. **1954** A. FULLERTON *Bury Past* I. i. 9 In their sealed compartment up front the sound came thinly. **1968** *Listener* 25 July 107/2 'Get your parachutes on.' He added reluctantly: 'We're having a little trouble up front and you may have to jump.' **1976** *Sunday Post* (Glasgow) 26 Dec., Alloa just deserved their success because they were a bit sharper up front.

b. *transf.* Of payments: in advance; initially. Also openly, frankly.

1972 *Britannica Bk. of Year* (U.S.) 733/3 *Up front, adv.*, in advance (actors demanding $1 million *up front*). **1980** *Maledicta* III. II. 238 That is much like the 'frank' people these days who confess their inadequacies or even villainies *up front* and then are shocked when you do not cancel those things out as exculpated by admission. **1982** S. WILSON *Dealer's Wheels* xiv. 135 'How much cash did you have in mind?' 'Five thousand, up front.' 'I beg your pardon?' 'In advance.'

B. *adj.* That is in the forefront; honest, open, frank; (of money) paid in advance. **a.** *attrib.*

1967 *Time* 29 Dec. 24/2 What the up-front struggle really amounts to is an angry, private little war between two people. **1975** *New Yorker* 20 Jan. 31/1, I'd like to suggest that we get most of the people involved below the line, so we won't need much of that scarce up-front bread. **1977** *Bulletin* (Sydney) 22 Jan. 88/1 Lunch with local film people who want to buy film rights... They chat about 'up-front money' and consider whether Robert Altman or Werner Herzog would do the better job. **1980** *Fortune* 24 Mar. 70/2 The up-front problem in the division today is that it does not garner deposits. **1982** *Chicago Sun-Times* 14 Oct. 100/1 'We've never had a budget to market these properties before,' he said. 'This time we have $250,000–$300,000 in upfront money.' **1985** *Broadcast* 11 Jan. 7/1 As well as the up-front money from RAI on these two documentaries RAI Channel 1 will also be taking up to 100 hours of natural history and scientific documentaries from Horizon.. and QED.

b. *predic.*

1970 J. LENNON in J. Wenner *Lennon Remembers* (1972) 67 That game of 'Well, I'm going to be up-front because.. a few people said she'd got a lousy name in New York.' **1973** D. LANG *Freaks* 119 You might as well live in a totalitarian state that's up front with it, at least. **1978** M. PUZO *Fools Die* xxiii. 258 He would.. make them understand in a nice way that he would trade space for a piece of ass. He was that upfront about it. **1980** *Washington Star* 2 July C2 Sirois was totally 'up front', O'Malley said, in his efforts to inform and ask for help from the Caps.

up'furled, *pa. pple.* (UP- 5.)

1818 KEATS *Endym.* I. 461 Who, upfurl'd Beneath thy drowsy wing a triple hour, But renovates and lives? **1852** M. ARNOLD *Parting* 88 Where the white mists, for ever, Are spread and upfurl'd. **1867** G. MACDONALD *Disciple*, etc. 32 My roll of ill with theirs upfurled, And flung in deepest hell.

'upgang. Latterly *north. dial.* and *Sc.* [UP- 2. Cf. WFris. *opgong*, Du. *opgang*, OHG. *ûfgang, -canc* (MHG. *ûfganc*), ON. *uppgangr* (Norw. *uppgang, -gong*; MSw. *up-, opgang*, Sw. *uppgång*; MDa. and Da. *opgang*) and *uppganga* (Norw. *uppgonga*).] **a.** The act of ascending; ascension. **b.** An ascent, an upward path or way.

a **900** *Laws Alfred* I. § 25 ʒif he.. æfter sunnan upgonge þis deð, he bið mansleʒes scyldiʒ. **971** *Blickl. Hom.* 201 Hi ne mihton ofer þæt scræf.. gongan, ærðon hie ʒerymdon þone upgang. *c* **1000** *Sax. Leechd.* III. 246 þas twelf tacna.. ʒefyllað twa tida mid hyra upgange oððe nyþergange. **1375** BARBOUR *Bruce* VI. 141 His hors, that wes born doune, Cummerit thaim the vpgang to ta. *Ibid.* VIII. 38 On the south half, quhar Iames was, Is ane vpgang, ane narrow plas. **1818** SCOTT *Hrt. Midl.* xxix, Our minny here's rather driegh in the upgang. **1855** [ROBINSON] *Whitby Gloss.*, *Upgang*,.. a track up a hill, as 'Upgang', from the Mulgrave sands to the turnpike on the cliff top.

†**upganger.** *Obs.* [UP- 8.] (See quot.)

1726 J. LAURENCE *New Syst. Agric.* 198 Of Brick-Making: .. an Up-Ganger, who,.. as they become stiff, takes them [*sc.* the new bricks] up, and sets them in Wind-Rows to be dried.

up'gather, *v.* [UP- 4. Cf. Du. *opgaderen.*] *trans.* To gather up, to collect. Also **'upgathered** *ppl. a.*, **-'gathering** *vbl. sb.*

1590 SPENSER *Muiopot.* 397 Himselfe he close vpgathered more and more Into his den. **1590** —— *F.Q.* III. vi. 19 Soone her garments loose Vpgath'ring, in her bosome she comprized, Well as she might. **1807** WORDSW. *Misc. Sonn.* I. xxxiii, The winds.. are up-gathered now like sleeping flowers. **1824** *Examiner* 650/2, I must upgather to the strife the reason that remains. **1851** LONGF. *Gold. Leg.* i. ad fin., The stooping sun upgathers his spent shafts. **1883** RUSKIN in Collingwood *Life* (1893) I. 223 Any poor little piece of *upgathered silver of my own. **1884** J. PARKER *Apost. Life* III. 173 A marvellous *upgathering and focalising of information.

up'gaze, *v.*, etc. (UP- 4, 6, and 7.)

1812 BYRON *Ch. Har.* II. liv, Tired of up-gazing still, the wearied eye Reposes gladly [etc.]. **1855** SINGLETON *Virgil* I. 62 Why, Daphnis, on the ancient risings of the signs Up-gaze? **1874** R. BUCHANAN *Poet. Wks.* III. 122 The shepherds gather'd, Up-gazing dreamily Into the silent air.

†**up'give**, *v. Sc. Obs.* [UP- 4. Cf. OFris. *op-, upieva* (WFris. *opjaen*), (M)Du. *opgeven*, MLG. *upgeven* (LG. *upgäfen*), MHG. *ûfgeben* (G. *auf-*), MSw. *up(p)giva* (Sw. *uppgifva, -giva*), Da. *opgive*, Icel. *uppgefa.*]

1. *trans.* To give up, resign, abandon.

1415 *Reg. Mag. Sig. Scot.* (1882) 39/1 Huchon.. sal frely delyver and upgif to the sayd Villiam.. the sayd landis. **1499** *Munim. de Melros* (Bann. Cl.) 622 Rent.. Quhilk.. lady Jonet.. wpgaif and resignit in our handis. **1513** DOUGLAS *Æneid* XI. iii. 29 Ȝour kyng hes our confiderans vpgeve. **1606** *Munim. de Melros* (Bann. Cl.) 658 To resigne dimit surrander vpgeif and ouergeif.. þe maner place of Melrosse. **1652** Z. BOYD in *Zion's Flowers* (1855) App. 26/1 Giveing them full power to upgive the same [*sc.* goods] as if they were given by mine owne mouth. [**1840** *Origines Par. Scotiae* I. 440 They upgave to him.. the common pasture of Hauden.]

2. To declare, avow. (Cf. UPGIVING *vbl. sb.* 2.)

a **1776** *Song Outlaw Murray* lix, And gif you refuse to do that, I freely here upgive with [? *read* to] thee, There will never [etc.].

'upgiven, *ppl. a. poet. nonce-use.* [UP- 5.] Surrendered, resigned. Cf. GHOST *sb.* 1.

1947 DYLAN THOMAS *In Country Sleep* in *Horizon* Dec. 304 The upgiven ghost Of the dingle torn to singing.

†**up'giver.** *Sc. Obs.* [UP- 8. Cf. GIVE *v.* 64 e.] One who furnishes information or particulars (*of* something).

1576 in Balfour *Oppr. Orkney & Shetl.* (1859) 45 Harie Bruce and Thomas Boyne, quha was bayth the upgiffaris of the faltis. **1621** *Sc. Acts Parlt., Jas. VI* (1814) IV. 599/1 [To] caus the pairties vpgevaris of the saidis inventoures everie pairtie subscryve his awin inventar him selff. *c* **1630** SIR T. HOPE *Minor Practicks* (1726) 30 The Caution is holden to be found not by the Minor, but by the Upgiver.

up'giving, *vbl. sb. Sc.* [UP- 7.]

1. Surrender; abandonment.

c **1423** *Reg. Mag. Sig. Scot.* (1882) 45/1 For the upgiffin of hys tak of the landdis of Kyrktoun. **1492** *Acta Dom. Conc.* (1839) 246/1 For þe vpgiffing of þe charteris evidentis and all vþer richt þat he haid. **1678** J. BROWN *Life of Faith* v. (1726) 121 What could be expected next, but utter upgiving?

†**2.** Declaration, presentment. *Obs.*

1574 in C. Rogers *Three Sc. Reformers* (1874) 10 As to my Insprech.. I refer to my wifis aith and vpgeving. *c* **1630** SIR T. HOPE *Minor Practicks* (1726) 19 The omitted Benefices, which the Prelates.. omitted in the Upgiving of the Rental. *a* **1670** SPALDING *Troub. Chas. I* (1850) I. 338 [He] presentit the subscrivit rollis of the tenthis givin wp be the oath of ilk subscriver, as thay who had commissioun to receave and sie the vpgiveing of the saidis rollis.

'upglide. *Phonol.* [UP- 2 a: see next and GLIDE *sb.* 4.] An upward glide.

1930 [see DOWN-GLIDE]. **1957** *Publ. Amer. Dial. Soc.* XXVIII. 115 Normally *or* marks the division between rise and fall, itself occurring at the end of the upglide. **1972** W. LABOV *Language in Inner City* i. 9 In New York and other northern cities,.. the back upglide of *ball* and *hawk*, so characteristic of many southern areas, is rarely heard.

'upgliding, *ppl. a. Phonol.* [UP- 6 b: see prec.] Gliding towards a high(er) vowel.

1933 O. JESPERSEN *Essentials Eng. Gram.* iv. 42 The *r*, or the resulting vowel [ə], also prevents the formation of the up-gliding diphthong [ou] in words like *oar, board*, [etc.]. **1948**, **1962** [see INGLIDING *ppl. a.*]. **1970** *Publ. Amer. Dial. Soc. 1968* L. 19 An upgliding diphthong occurs sporadically. **1981** *Amer. Speech 1977* LII. 203 Variants listed as deviating from his constructed general pattern of simple, upgliding, and ingliding vowels.

'upgo, *sb. dial.* Also *Sc.* **-gae.** [UP- 2.] An ascent; *spec.* a rise in a stratum of rock.

1683 G. SINCLAIR *Misc. Obs. Hydrost.* 278 Some [strata] again making their rise much more than their course, which they call Up-gaes. **1855** *Whitby Gloss.* 185 *Upgo*, a track up a hill.

up'go, *v.* [UP- 4. Cf. MDu. *opgaen* (Du. *opgaan*), MLG. *upgân*, MHG. *ufgän, -gen* (G. *aufgehen*), MSw. *up(p)ga, op(p)ga, -gaa* (Sw. *uppgå*), MDa. and Da. *opgaa.*] *intr.* To go up; to ascend, mount.

c **1250** *Gen. & Ex.* 1608 Iacob.. saȝ.., Fro ðe erðe up.., A leddre stonden, and ðor-on Angeles dun-cumen and up-gon. *c* **1440** *Pallad. on Husb.* XI. 139 The tendir plaunte is take anoon & blyue Vpgoth. *c* **1475** *Golagros & Gaw.* 1151 He gart schir Gawyne vpga. **1513** DOUGLAS *Æneid* VIII. i. 57 Quhill in the ayr vpgois the tuynkilland lycht. **1600** FAIRFAX *Tasso* XVII. xl, He ceas'd, and then a murmur lowd vp went With noise of ioy. **1791** COWPER *Iliad* XIII. 1016 Up-went the double roar into the heights Ethereal. **1830** WORDSW. *Egyptian Maid* 183 Then up-went Into the ethereal element The Birds.

up'going, *vbl. sb.* [UP- 7.] The action of going up; *esp.* ascent, ascension.

1555 WATREMAN *Fardle Facions* App. 315 A faire vp goyng, by a slope bancque of Turfes. **1658** J. NICOLL *Diary* (Bann. Cl.) 211 Upone this accompt.. the Scottis

Commissioneris, quho wer reddy to pas to Lundoun.., wer stayed from thair upgoing. **1734** E. ERSKINE *Serm.* Wks. (1791) 697/1, I would speak a little of the solemnity of his [*sc.* Christ's] up-going. **1870** SPURGEON *Treas. Dav.* I. 422 The eye of the psalmist looked..beyond the typical upgoing of the ark of the sublime ascension of the King of glory.

'upˌgoing, *ppl. a.* (UP- 6 b.)
1859 J. LANG *Wand. India* 125 On the down-coming travellers nearing us, the bearers of us—the up-going travellers—called a halt. **1896** *Pop. Sci. Monthly* Feb. 523 The upgoing current..may increase in volume.

up'gradable, *a.* Also upgradeable. [f. UPGRADE *v.* + -ABLE.] Capable of being upgraded or raised to a higher standard; *spec.* in *Computers*, applied to (the storage size of) a system. Hence **upgrada'bility.**
1974 *Physics Bull.* Dec. 568/1 (Advt.), ND 100 has a completely solid state memory with 1K, 2K, or 4K memory capacity (field upgradeable). **1982** *Which Computer?* June 44/3 The ease of software upgradability certainly makes it attractive. **1983** *Daily Tel.* 14 June 6 (Advt.), The Exxon 8431 System features an advanced central controller with upgradeable storage up to 320 MB. **1985** *Personal Computer World* Feb. 42/2 (Advt.), Works equally well on 5¼", 3½", or 3" disks, with upgradability built-in from 100K to 2.6 Mbyte.

'up-grade, *sb.* and *adv.* Orig. *U.S.* [UP- 2 b.]
1. a. An upward slope or incline.
1873 J. H. BEADLE *Undevel. West* xv. 257 Forty miles of staging over boulder and rocky up-grade. **1888** J. PENNELL *Sent. Journey* 236 There were so many long up-grades, and the sign-posts were all wrong. **1893** KATE SANBORN *Truthf. Wom. S. California* 87, I have no taste for overtaking runaway mules on a steep and interminable up-grade.
b. *adv.* Uphill.
1899 *Lutheran* (Phila.) 6 Apr. 327 A railroad train will go for some distance upgrade after the engine is detached.
2. *on the upgrade*, ascending, rising; improving.
1892 *Daily News* 26 Sept. 2/4 In the iron trade..demand seems to be on the up grade. **1914** A. BENNETT *Price of Love* vi. 110 'Auntie still on the up-grade?' he inquired... He guessed..that Mrs. Maldon must be still better. **1926** *Ladies' Home Jrnl.* Oct. 143 Monty's been the hardest child we've had to handle,..but I believe he's on the upgrade. **1951** 'J. TEY' *Daughter of Time* iv. 55 Don't you worry. I'm on the up-grade. Even my temper has improved. **1972** *Daily Tel.* 21 Jan. 1/2 Various indices..show that the economy is now firmly on the upgrade.
3. [f. the vb.] An upgraded version. Also, an upgrading to a higher standard (chiefly, in *Computers*, to a larger and more powerful system).
1980 *Nature* 17 Apr. 599/1 The upgrade of this facility, PBFA-II, will deliver 3.5 MJ at 100 TW and will be available for experiments in 1986. **1982** *Which Computer?* June 55/2 They can reach down to the more sophisticated microcomputer user, holding out the possibility of an upgrade to a larger machine. **1983** *What's New in Computing* Jan. 30 (Advt.), PT7/s powerful local processing..allows simpler planning of mainframe upgrades.

up'grade, *v.* Also up-grade. [f. UP- 4: cf. the sb.]
1. *trans.* To increase the grade or status of (a job); to raise (an employee) to a higher grade or rank. Also *fig.*
1920 [implied at UPGRADING *vbl. sb.*]. **1928** *Daily Express* 5 Mar. 3/5 His job..has become so important that the post is being 'up-graded'. **1942** *Tee Emm* (Air Ministry) II. 130 In future they are going to be upgraded [from angels] to archangels. **1955** [see DOWN-GRADE *v.*]. **1976** *National Observer* (U.S.) 20 Nov. 14/2 The commission agreed to upgrade controllers at 32 facilities, but fewer controllers would be promoted than the union demands. **1985** *Contact* (Pre-School Playgroups Assoc.) Feb. 23/1 Teachers who underestimate the richness of children's homes decide to upgrade the children's language skills.
2. a. To raise (something, esp. equipment or facilities) from one grade to another; to improve or enhance physically.
1935 [implied at UPGRADED *ppl. a.*]. **1955** M. REIFER *Dict. New Words* 217/2 *Upgrade*, to improve the grade of a product. **1959** *Globe & Mail* (Toronto) 17 July 13/3 If Canada were to maintain and extend its capabilities in this field, it was necessary that its effective weapons be continuously upgraded. **1964** G. L. COHEN *What's Wrong with Hospitals?* vii. 143 These old places are really quite comfortable, you know; they've been up-graded out of all recognition. **1971** *Daily Tel.* 13 Sept. 10/6 The money.. would be spent on financing sewerage schemes and up-grading existing effluent treatment facilities. **1976** A. HOPE *Hi-fi Handbk.* 14 If you wish to up-grade a music centre, you can only throw it out and replace it with a better one. **1979** 'J. LE CARRÉ' *Smiley's People* xvii. 211 He booked a first-class seat and said he would upgrade his economy ticket on arrival at the airport.
b. More generally, to raise to a higher level; to improve.
1959 G. D. MITCHELL *Sociol.* 120 Generally it was found that women were more likely than men to up-grade themselves. **1962** M. MCLUHAN *Gutenberg Galaxy* 43 For until men have up-graded the visual component communities know only a tribal structure. **1977** *New Yorker* 24 Oct. 79/2 They have upgraded their criminal expertise by watching such programs as..'Kojak'. **1983** *Times* 29 Oct. 16/4 A lunch in the City..led to one broker upgrading his forecast for the year.
c. *absol.* or *intr.* (for *refl.*).
1950 *Sun* (Baltimore) 2 Oct. 9/1 Movers say that the bulk of families moving are 'upgrading'. By that they mean that they are occupying new apartments renting for much more than they have been paying. **1967** *Boston Sunday Globe* 23 Apr. B41/5 The head of a family..wants to upgrade—and usually does. **1970** J. EARL *Tuners & Amplifiers* iii. 60 This may differ slightly if we already possess some items of equipment and merely wish..to upgrade by changing a particular item..for an equivalent of improved quality.
Hence **up'graded** *ppl. a.*; **up'grading** *vbl. sb.*
1920 *Glasgow Herald* 19 Aug. 8/3 The government proposals for..the upgrading of the unskilled labourers.. were rejected by the operatives. **1935** *Times* 1 Oct. 4/4 The rates on the upgraded stretch and the 1 in 22½ Dashwood Hill were 15 and 50 and 30 and 44 m.p.h. **1938** *Encycl. Brit. Bk. of Year* 214/1 The Burnham Committee..dealt with the up-grading and down-grading of Elementary Schools for the assessment of Head Teachers' salaries. **1959** *Times Lit. Suppl.* 9 Oct. 579/1 The danger of 'escalation'—the upgrading of the size of the weapons in reply to the apparent use by the enemy of bigger types. **1976** P. R. WHITE *Planning for Public Transport* viii. 186 A preliminary study suggests that investment in an upgraded rail link may provide net benefits as high as for a parallel road scheme.

†**'upground.** *Obs.*$^{-1}$ [UP- 1.] Higher ground; ground above the beach.
a **1550** LELAND *Itin.* (1768) I. 34 The Shore and upground from Trent Ripe..to Gainesborough is al sandy.

up'grow, *v.* [UP- 4. Cf. MDa. *opgro.*] *intr.* To grow up, spring up; *fig.* to increase.
c **1430** LYDG. *Min. Poems* (Percy Soc.) 246 In his encrees up-growynge as a flour. *c* **1440** *Pallad. on Husb.* VII. 77 Yf me wete Her lond, vpgroweth now this herbis sete. **1513** DOUGLAS *Æneid* XI. xi. 14 Ne this luf..of layt in Dyanis breist vpgrew. *Ibid.* XII. viii. 116 Than mair in greif and ire vpgrewis he. **1667** MILTON *P.L.* IV. 137 Over head up grew Insuperable highth of loftiest shade. **1791** COWPER *Iliad* II. 810 Tlepolemus spear-famed Had scarce up-grown to manhood's lusty prime. **1848** CLOUGH *Amours de Voy.* III. 90 The cypress-spires..Withering still at the sight which still they upgrow to encounter. **1867** LD. HOUGHTON *Ess. Reform* 56 Disappointment was not the soil from which a desire for further change upgrew.

up'growing, *vbl. sb.* (UP- 7.)
1430-40 LYDG. *Bochas* II. 2627 The cedre is strong.., In his vpgrowyng riht as any lyne. *a* **1618** RALEIGH *Invent. Shipping* Wks. 1751 II. 87 There are five manifest Causes of the Upgrowing of the Hollanders and Zelanders.

'upˌgrowing, *ppl. a.* (UP- 6 b.)
1863 MRS. WHITNEY *Faith Gartney's Girlh.* ii. 14 The flower of the upgrowing world. **1895** CLIVE HOLLAND *Jap. Wife* vii, The responsibilities of a rapidly upgrowing daughter.

up'grown, *pa. pple.*, **'upgrown,** *ppl. a.* [UP- 6, 6 b.] Grown up.
1667 MILTON *P.L.* IX. 677 So standing, moving, or to highth upgrown The Tempter all impassiond thus began. **1671** —— *P.R.* I. 140 This man born and now up-grown,.. henceforth I expose To Satan. **1827** G. HIGGINS *Celtic Druids* 99 The contests..are only worthy of up-grown babies. **1848** WHEWELL in Todhunter *Acc. Writ.* (1876) II. 348 A great up-grown body of knowledge. **1895** K. GRAHAME *Golden Age* 46 To them the inhabited world is composed of..children and upgrown people.

'upgrowth. [UP- 2.]
1. The process or fact of growing up; origination, development.
1844 S. WILBERFORCE *Hist. Prot. Episc. Ch. Amer.* i. 2 The up-growth of such a body amongst institutions so unlike our own. **1869** A. W. HADDAN *Apost. Succession* v. 104 The speedy upgrowth..of contentions and schisms.
2. That which has grown up; a result of growth or development.
1845 TRENCH *Huls. Lect.* ii. 26 The parts of it being the upgrowth of a single age. **1873** MANNING *Serm. Eccl. Subj.* III. p. lxxxiv, The International is a new creation or upgrowth from beneath.
b. *spec.* A raised growth or process.
1870 ROLLESTON *Anim. Life* 11 The..sixth and seventh [lateral processes] have prominent upgrowths. **1893** BOWER in *Phil. Trans.* B. CLXXXV. 504 Evidence..of the origin of upgrowths (sporangiophores) which would raise the sporangia beyond the surface.

upgush, -gushing: see UP- 2, 6, 7.

†**up'hale,** *v. Obs.* [UP- 4. Cf. (M)Du. *ophalen*, (M)LG. *uphalen*, MHG. *ûfholn* (G. *aufholen*), (M)Da. *ophale*, Sw. *upphala.*] *trans.* To pull or draw up; *fig.* to drink up. Also **up'haled** *pa. pple.*
14.. in *Pol., Rel., & L. Poems* (1903) 247 The rote of an erbe I sholde vp hale, Men call it chastite. *c* **1540** *Dr. Doubble Ale* 154 in Hazl. *E.P.P.* III. 311 Our Doctour Doubble Ale, Whose countenaunce is neuer pale, So wel good drinke he can vphale. **1582** STANYHURST *Æneis* (Arb.) 19 This Queene..Downe swasht theyre nauy, thee swelling surges vphaling. *c* **1620** Z. BOYD *Zion's Flowers* (1855) 3 They turn like mist uphaled by the sunne.

'Uphaliday, Up-Helly-'Aa. *Sc. Obs.* exc. *Shetl. dial.* Also 5–6 **vphaly** (6 **-ye**) **da(y)**, 6 **ouphalliday, uphaldy;** 6 **vphelly,** 9 **uphellie,** *Shetl.* **uphelya, -hellia (day), -helly-a,** 20 **Up-Helly-A'.** [f. UP *adv.*[2] 12 a (see quot. 1884) + *haliday* HOLIDAY. Also with omission of *-day* in *uphelly even, night*, and in mod. Shetl. forms, in which the final *-a* may stand for *all* adj.]
1. a. The festival of the Epiphany (Jan. 6, Twelfth-day), as the end of the Christmas holidays.
In quot. 1884 the reckoning is by a combination of Old and New Style.
1478 *Acta Dom. Conc.* (1839) 20/1 Þe lordis continewis þe mater to þe morne efter vphalyday nixt tocum. **1501** *Acc. Ld. High Treas. Scot.* II. 77 The vj day of Januar, Uphalyday, to the Kingis offerand, thre Franch crounes. **1535** *Burgh Rec. Edinb.* (1871) II. 71 Evin sang in the haly dayes of Yule, New Yeir day, and Vphaly day. **1588** A. KING in *Cath. Tractates* (S.T.S.) 175 Vphaliday when Christ vas reueled first to the gentiles. **1609** SKENE *Reg. Maj., Burrow Lawes* 135 Ane decreit given..vpon Mononday, after Vphaliday. **1884** *Gd. Words* 747 Uphelya, the twenty-fourth day after Yule, and that on which the Holy or holidays are supposed to be 'up'.
b. So *Uphalimass* in the same sense.
1532 *Acc. Ld. High Treas. Scot.* VI. 39 For the doune putting of thare bassyngis at New ȝear Daye, Uphalymes and Pasche. **1556** *Burgh Rec. Edinb.* (1871) II. 260 The festuall dayis of Yule, New-yeir-mes, and Vphellymes.
c. **Up-Helly-Aa** (ˌʌphɛlɪ'ɑː). (A revival of) a traditional midwinter fire-festival held at Lerwick in the Shetland Islands (see quots.).
1872 *Saturday Herald & Shetland Gaz.* (Kirkwall) 10 Feb. 1/3 Monday night was what is here [*sc.* in Lerwick] called 'Up-haly a', and the youths here indulged in their savage sports of tar-barrel burning. **1901** *Shetland News* 5 Jan., The principal Festival of the season to Lerwegians, namely 'Up-helly A',..is now celebrated with..Norse galleys, torch-light processions, and guizing galore. **1934** W. MOFFAT *Shetland* 129 Up-Helly-Aa night was the twenty-fourth night of the Helli or Holy Days, and that period of feasting, drinking, singing and rejoicing concluded with a great flare-up on Up-Helly-Aa night. **1948** C. E. MITCHELL *Up-Helly-Aa* 2 Up-Helly-Aa is the final day of the Jola Bød or Yule Period which commenced on the fifth day of January, old style, and ended twenty-four days later in a climax of revelry. **1955** *Shetland Times* 28 Jan., When a man is elected to the Up-Helly-A' Committee he can expect to become Guizer Jarl according to his seniority. **1972** *Guardian* 15 Jan. 14/5 The fire festival of Up-Helly-A in the Shetlands, which celebrates the passing of midwinter with ..torchlight processions..and a lifesize longboat that goes up in flames.
2. *uphali(day) even*, the eve of the Epiphany; *uphaly night*, the night of Jan. 6.
1506 *Acc. Ld. High Treas. Scot.* III. 178 The fift day [of January], Uphaldy evin, to the men that brocht the sensouris. **1582** *Rec. Elgin* (1903) I. 164 That scho in na times to cum sall ring bessingis, brassin nor irn morteris,.. within this burgh upon Vphelly ewin. **1881** S. R. MACPHAIL *Relig. Ho. Pluscardyn* xix. 155 The thirteenth night o' Eel [= Yule] was called 'uphellie nicht'.

†**up'hance,** *v. Obs.* In 4–5 vphauns(e. [UP- 4 + HANCE *v.*] *trans.* To lift up, raise.
a **1375** *Joseph Arim.* 515 Þer weoren hedes vn-huled, helmes vphaunset. *c* **1400** *Apol. Loll.* 31 Crie, cese not, vphauns þi vois os a trompe. *c* **1410** *Lanterne of Liȝt* 28 Liȝt ..is vp spronngen, & meke loweli ben vphaunsid.

up'hand, *a.* [UP- 3.] Operated, or performed, by raising the hand or hands.
1677 MOXON *Mech. Exerc.* i. 4 The Uphand Sledge, used by under-Workmen when your work is not of the largest;.. they use it with both their hands before them, and seldom lift their Hammer higher than their Head. **1688** HOLME *Armoury* III. 321/2 The third is termed the up-hand Hammer, or up-hand sledge, of some termed the Fore-Hammer. **1835** J. D. CARRICK, etc. *Laird of Logan* 85 (E.D.D.), Girzie..was apt to enforce her commands with uphand emphases.

up'hang, *v.* [UP- 4. Cf. (M)Du. *ophangen*, MLG. *uphangen*, G. *aufhangen*, MSw. *up-, op(p)hängia* (Sw. *upphänga*), MDa. *uphængie* (Da. *ophænge*).] **a.** *intr.* To hang on high. **b.** *trans.* To hang up, suspend. Also **up'hanged** *pa. pple.*, **up'hanging** *vbl. sb.*
c **1440** *Ps. Penit.* (1894) 32 Thu were offred uphongyng, For mannes sake on rode tre. **1555** *Lydgate's Chron. Troy* I. 2242 Thus she stode in doubtfull Jeopardy, Of loue and shame.., Full euenly vphanged in balaunce. **1591** SPENSER *Visions Bellay* vi, Soone on a tree vphang'd I saw her spoyle. **1742** SHENSTONE *Schoolmistress* xiv, How Israel's sons.., untuning ev'ry string, Uphung their useless lyres. **1789** T. RUSSELL *Sonn.*, etc. 1 Stern Chivalry her idle spear uphung. **1860** LD. LYTTON *Lucile* II. v. §4. 10 When soft stars were brightly uphanging the night. **1861** *Macm. Mag.* June 128 To build a stone-pier for the uphanging of great coats or hats.

†**up'hap,** *adv. Obs.* [UP *prep.*[1] 6 c + HAP *sb.*[1] 4 b.] Perhaps, possibly.
c **1350**, *c* **1380** [see UP *prep.*[1] 6 c]. **1387-8** T. USK *Test. Love* I. viii. (Skeat) l. 132 Therin thou lesest..uphap thy renome everlasting. *c* **1450** CAPGRAVE *Life St. Aug.* 46 Vphap it semeth a bischop for to were swech on, þouȝ it semeth not ..a pore man.

upharbour, -harrow, -hasping: see UP- 4, 6.

up'headed, *a. north. dial.* [UP- 3.] Of cattle: Having upright horns.
1549 *Knaresb. Wills* (Surtees) I. 55 One whie of foure yeres olde, uppheded. **1582-3** *Durham Wills* (Surtees) II. 99 A browne upheaded stot goinge in the northe feild. **1828** CARR *Craven Gloss.*, *Up-heeaded*, having the horns growing up nearly perpendicularly.

up'heap, *v.* [UP- 4. Cf. WFris. *opheapje*, MDu. *ophopen* (Du. *ophoopen*), MLG. *uphupen*, MHG. *ûfhufen* (G. *aufhäufen*).] *trans.* To heap up.
1469 *Plumpton Corr.* (Camden) 21, I could nott gett it windowd before it went to the ship,..therefore I upheaped with a quarter, xxi quarters for xx quarters. **1483** *Cath. Angl.* 404/2 To Vppehepe, *consarcire*.., *cumulare*. **1641** BEST *Farm. Bks.* (Surtees) 103 First we poore in the meale, and upheap the bushell; then doe wee..thrust it downe.

up'heaped, *pa. pple.* (UP- 5. Cf. prec.)

c **1380** WYCLIF *Wks.* (1880) 370 þe same malyce in kynde he schal fynde, ȝhe uphepid, in our byschopis. *c* **1440** *Pallad. on Husb.* III. 819 Of peres sowre..yf that they be Ytake & kepte vphepid daies thre. **14..** *W. of Henley's Husb.* (1890) 50 Be wele ware off mesuryngc off your bushell þat is vphepide. **1549** COVERDALE, etc. *Erasm. Par. 2 Peter* 16 Let brotherly charitie be augmented and upheaped with love. **1560** B. GOOGE tr. *Palingenius' Zodiac* II. (1561) D v b, Thy barnes vpheaped & hugy mowes of corne. **1596** H. CLAPHAM *Brief of Bible* 95 Their Sinne vpheapt, God sendeth them away To Babylon. **1777** *A. Hunter's Georg. Ess.* I. 416, I.. laid on 167 chaldrons of lime, 32 bushels, upheaped, to the chaldron. **1807** CRABBE *Par. Reg.* I. 489 Whose board is high up-heap'd with generous fare. **1828** CARR *Craven Gloss.* II. 228 Excellent measure, not only up-heaped, but pressed down.

fig. **1862** [C. C. ROBINSON] *Dial. Leeds* 4 Shoo said he wur a rascal upheaped and downthrussen. [Cf. UPHEAP *v.*, quot. 1641.]

up'heaped, *ppl. a.* (UP- 5. Cf. prec.)

1549 COVERDALE, etc. *Erasm. Par. 1 Pet.* iv. 12 God..shal repaye a with vpheaped mesure. **1565** in Picton *L'pool Munic. Rec.* (1883) I. 86 That the old upheaped mete be.. allowed and none other. *a* **1619** FOTHERBY *Atheom.* I. xi. §4 (1622) 116 He maketh such vpheaped piles of dishes. **1641** BEST *Farm. Bks.* (Surtees) 103 Wee have allwayes of a stricken bushell of corne an upheaped bushell of meale. **1821** COLERIDGE *Lett., Convers.*, etc. I. 183 An upheaped love and devotion to her admirable husband. **1850** BLACKIE *Æschylus* II. 159, I alone Must bear the up-heaped murmurings of the whole. **1891** FARRAR *Darkn. & Dawn* lxvi, Amid the upheaped corpses the blood..hissed and bubbled.

up'heaping, *vbl. sb.* (UP- 7.)

c **1374** CHAUCER *Boeth.* II. pr. iii. (1868) 37 It deliteþ me to comen now to þe singuler vphepyng of þi welefulnesse.

up'heaping, *pres. pple.*: see UP- 6.

up-'hearted, *a.* [UP- 3.] Of good heart; not readily discouraged.

1862 TROLLOPE *Orley F.* xxix, He was cheery and up-hearted, but at the same time gentle.

up'heaval. [UP- 2.]

1. *Geol.* The action of raising, or fact of being raised, above the original level, esp. by volcanic action.

1838 LYELL *Man. Geol.* v. 96 Very extensive regions.. have been undergoing slow and gradual upheaval. **1862** G. P. SCROPE *Volcanoes* 429 The upheaval of the latter strata. **1886** WINCHELL *Walks Geol. Field* 112 This is the general plan of a mountain of upheaval.

b. An instance of this; an upward displacement of some part of the earth's crust.

1849 DANA *Geol.* xvii. (1850) 675 Some of the upheavals the country has experienced, may have opened fissures. **1876** PAGE *Adv. Text-bk. Geol.* ii. 39 Upheavals and subsidences occasioned by..volcanic convulsions. **1897** E. B. NICHOLSON *Golspie* 252 These upheavals took place after ..the great Ice Age.

c. In general use.

1890 CLARK RUSSELL *Ocean Trag.* III. xxviii. 74 A volcanic upheaval of flame. **1908** S. E. WHITE *Riverman* iv, Constantly the logs shifted, and..the men shifted also, avoiding the upheavals.

2. *fig.* A strong agitation or convulsion of society, etc.; a sudden or violent alteration.

1850 MCCOSH *Div. Govt.* II. iii. 250 There have been times of upheaval in the moral world, similar to those periods which geologists describe. **1867** C. H. PEARSON *Hist. Eng.* I. 89 It was a general upheaval of peoples. **1887** LOWELL *Democr.* 13 There had also been social upheavals before the Reformation.

Hence **up'heavalist**, an advocate of the theory that geological changes are due to upheaval.

1862 G. P. SCROPE *Volcanoes* 201 Lyell, in his.. examination of the question, decided it against the upheavalists.

upheave, *sb.*: see UP- 2.

up'heave, *v.* [UP- 4. Cf. OE. *uphebban*, ME. *uphebbe*, = OFris. *op-*, *upheva* (WFris. *opheevje*), (M)Du. *opheffen*, MLG. *upheven*, LG. *upheffen*, OHG. *ûfhevan* (MHG. *ûfheben*, G. *aufheben*), MSw. *uphäfia*, *ophävia*, etc. (Sw. *upphäfva*, *-häva*), (M)Da. *ophæve*.]

1. *trans.* To heave or lift up; to raise; †to exalt.

a **1300** *E.E. Psalter* iii. 3 Lauerd, mi fanger art þou in lande, Mi blisse, and mi heued vpheueande [L. *exaltans*]. *Ibid.* cxliv. 1, I sal vpheue þe, god. *c* **1375** *Sc. Leg. Saints* xliii. (*Cecilia*) 94 þe ald his handis..Vphewit to þe hewine rycht þare. *c* **1386** CHAUCER *Knt.'s T.* 1570 Arcita anon his hand vp haf. **1513** DOUGLAS *Æneid* XIII. x. 21 The fader Eneas..His handis bayth vphevis towartis hevin. **1563** *Mirr. Mag.* R iv, Vp heauing to the skyes Her wretched handes. **1592** SHAKS. *Ven. & Ad.* 482 Her two blew windowes faintly she vpheaueth. **1620** QUARLES *Feast for Worms* §12 No sooner Titan had vp-heau'd his head From off the pillow. **1676** HOBBES *Iliad* I. 429 Chryses pray'd with hands to Heaven upheaved. **1736** GRAY *Statius* I. 15 Another orb upheaved his strong right hand. **1791** COWPER *Iliad* IV. 504 The waves by Zephyrus up-heaved. **1817** *Monthly Mag.* XLIII. 237 Couch'd on the shore his head and shoulders twain, Upheaves a giant shape. **1850** BLACKIE *Æschylus* II. 69 Let the sea upheave her billows! **1855** BROWNING *Saul* xiv, While Hebron upheaves The dawn.. on his shoulder.

b. *esp.* To toss or throw up with violence; *spec.* in *Geol.*

1708 J. PHILIPS *Cyder* I. 202 Th' infernal winds..from beneath the solid mass Upheav'd. **1809** WORDSW. *Poems Nat. Indep.* II. xvi, War upheaved The ground beneath thee with volcanic force. **1813** BAKEWELL *Introd. Geol.* (1815) 234 Some great convulsion has upheaved from their foundations ..the whole mass of the chalk rocks. **1867** LADY HERBERT *Cradle L.* vii. 194 There are masses of stone and brick.. lying about as if upheaved and overturned by some tremendous earthquake.

fig. **1835** I. TAYLOR *Spir. Despot.* i. 16 Let the infidel and the Dissenter join hands in upheaving the Church. **1854** J. S. C. ABBOTT *Napoleon* (1855) I. i. 23 The portentous rumblings of that approaching earthquake, which soon uphove both altar and throne.

†**2.** = UPLIFT *v.* 4, RAISE *v.*[1] 13. *Obs.*

a **1300** *E.E. Psalter* xcii. 4 Þai vphoue, louerd, stremes euen, Vphoued stremes þair steuen. *a* **1593** MARLOWE *Ovid's Elegies* III. v. 52 The bold floud..his hoarse voice vpheau'd Saying, [etc.].

3. *intr.* To rise up.

1649 LOVELACE *Lucasta* (1904) 99 The July-flow'r.., But for one look of her, upheaves. *a* **1826** J. HYATT in Spurgeon *Treas. Dav.* IV. 108 To represent human nature as upheaving under its load. **1850** B. TAYLOR *Eldorado* I. 170 The surface of the bay..upheaved with a slow, majestic movement. **1893** *Scribner's Mag.* XIII. 92/1 Along the west it upheaves into the fine Valles range.

4. *trans.* To support, sustain. *rare*$^{-1}$.

1729 SAVAGE *Wanderer* IV. 170 Pillars..Which, nodding, just up-heave their crumbling load.

Hence **up'heaved** *ppl. a.*, **up'heavement**, **up'heaver**, **up'heaving** *vbl. sb.* and *ppl. a.*

1847 EMERSON *Ode to Channing* 30 If earth fire cleave The *upheaved land, and bury the folk. **1859** R. F. BURTON *Centr. Afr.* in *Jrnl. Geog. Soc.* XXIX. 10 The upheaved sea beach..which forms the esplanade. **1866** G. MACDONALD *Ann. Q. Neighb.* xiii, Each like one million-petalled flower of upheaved whiteness. **1841** TRIMMER *Pract. Geol.* 56 It was the agent employed in the *upheavement of chains of mountains. **1864** *Reader* 5 March 301/3 After the last upheavement of the Alps, great fissures or basins of lakes were left there. **1597** A. M. tr. *Guillemeau's Fr. Chirurg.* 7 b/1 An Elevatorium [*marg.* or *vpheaver], to lift vp the bullet and drawe him therout. **1872** SPURGEON *Treas. Dav.* Ps. lxv. 6 Philosphers..too much engrossed with their laws of upheaval to think of the Upheaver. **1892** *Graphic* 18 June 731/3 The pullers up of streets and the upheavers of footways. **1830** LYELL *Princ. Geol.* I. 231 Great *upheavings of the coast. **1856** STANLEY *Sinai & Pal.* i. 23 The traces of igneous action on the granite rocks belong to their first upheaving. **1863** —— *Jew. Ch.* xiii. 285 The Conquest was over, but the upheavings of the conquered population still continued. **1880** MCCARTHY *Own Times* xli. III. 226 All over the world there seemed to be an unheaving of old systems. **1821** ATHERSTONE *Poems* 72 Ocean monsters, from their beds..Torn by th' *upheaving billows to the day. **1853** KANE *Grinnell Exp.* xxxii. (1856) 282, I mounted the upheaving ice, and rode upon the fragments. **1881** W. STEPHENS *Chichester* 158 [They] could not foresee what mighty and upheaving changes were at hand.

uphebbe: see UP- 4.

'upheld, *ppl. a.* (UP- 5.)

1870 MORRIS *Earthly Par.* III. IV. 189 One maiden..Bore in her gleaming upheld skirt Fair silken balls. **1883** JEFFERIES *Story of My Heart* xi. 168 The upheld finger of light.

†**uphelder**, obs. var. UPHOLDER 1.

1356 in Riley *Mem. London* 282 Stephen Basham, lockyer, and Adam Wayte, upheldere.

uphellie, -helly, Up-Helly-Aa: see UPHALIDAY.

†**uphend**, *v. Obs.* [UP- 4. Cf. MDa. *ophente.*] *trans.* To catch or snatch up; to take up, raise.

a **1300** *Cursor M.* 12183 Leui..a yeird vp-hint, And gaf him in þe heued a dint. **13..** *Seuyn Sages* (W.) 3133 Vnto the lady the ring he cast... The lady has the ring uphent. *c* **1420** *Sir Amadace* (Camden) lxvii, Then Sir Amadace a squrd vppe-hente. **1513** DOUGLAS *Æneid* v. viii. 63 Acestes ..has wphint in feild His friend Entellus. *Ibid.* XI. i. 49 [Let] the ensenȝeis and baneris be vphynt. **1600** FAIRFAX *Tasso* XII. lxxii, He would not leaue the corses faire in field But in their armes the soldiers both vphent.

upher, variant of UFER (fir-pole).

†**uphigh**, *v. Obs.* Chiefly *Sc.* [UP- 4. Cf. Du. *ophoogen*, G. *aufhöhen*, MSw. *uphöghia*, *ophöia*, etc. (Sw. *upphöja*), (M)Da. *uphøge* (Da. *ophøje*), Norw. *upphøgja*.] *trans.* To exalt; to raise up.

13.. *Prose Psalter* (1891) 190 Heȝe [*v.r.* uphie] him in þe worldel! *c* **1470** HENRYSON *Mor. Fab.* v. *Parl. Beasts* xxi, The lawest heir I can full sone vp hie. **1508** DUNBAR *Poems* vii. 5 Onto the sterris vpheyt is thyne honour. **1513** DOUGLAS *Æneid* VIII. i. 72 Tyburinus, furth of the styll river, ..hymself vpheis. **1563** WINȜET *Wks.* (S.T.S.) II. 58 Be zeris it mot be strenthit,..and be aige vpheit.

'uphill, *sb.* and *a.* Also up-hill. [UP *prep.*[2] Cf. next.]

A. *sb.* **1.** An ascent; a high or steep rise.

1548 UDALL *Erasm. Par. Luke* iii. 28 b, That countrey is full of vphilles and downhilles, & almost no parte of it euen, or plain chaumpian ground. **1611** CORYAT *Crudities* 54 [The traveller has] no euen way, but continually high vp-hils and steepe down-hils til he commeth to Tarare. **1631** A. TOWNSHEND *Albion's Triumph* B, There is no vp-hill in the skyes; Clouds stay not feathered feete. **1671** tr. *Frejus' Voy. Mauritania* 54 Built on very high ground, but..we come insensibly to the Town, without perceiving any up-hill. **1883** C. HOWARD *Roads Eng. & Wales* (ed. 3) 81 From here is a long stiff uphill along the coast.

†**2.** *Gaming.* (See quots.) *Obs.*

a **1700** B. E. *Dict. Cant. Crew*, *Uphils*, high Dice. **1785** GROSE *Dict. Vulgar T.*, *Uphills*, false dice that run high. **1824** *Hist. Gaming* 41 To the landlord..he taught the art of ..cutting the broads right, and throwing uphills.

B. *adj.* **1.** Situated on high ground; elevated.

1613 PURCHAS *Pilgrimage, India* (1614) 481 Ouer Balaguate, or the vp-hill Countrey (for *Bala* in the Persian Language signifieth the toppe, and *Guate* a Hill). **1701** O. HEYWOOD *Diaries*, etc. (1885) IV. 176 My last and best journey will be to the up-hill city. *a* **1716** *Gonzanga* III. i. in *New Brit. Theatre* III. 121 My passage to the up-hill seat of power. **1853** *Public School Matches* 12 Whatever you do, throw up full from the uphill side.

b. Grown on high ground.

1892 *Daily News* 7 Dec. 6/1 It was a well-known fact that up-hill hay was much the best.

2. Leading or directed towards higher ground; going upwards, esp. steeply.

1622 BACON *Hen. VII*, Ep. Ded., And it is with Times, as it is with Wayes. Some are more Up-hill and Down-hill, and some are more Flat and Plaine. **1684** BUNYAN *Pilgr.* II. 65 They love not to take Pains, up-hill way is unpleasant to them. **1728** YOUNG *Love Fame* v. 99 Yet, as immortal, in our up-hill chace We press coy fortune with unslacken'd pace. *c* **1854** FABER *Hymn, 'The Light must win'* vi, The Church, the Sacraments, the Faith, Their uphill journey take. **1875** JOWETT *Plato* (ed. 2) III. 234 But before virtue the gods have set toil, and a tedious and uphill road. **1891** T. HARDY *Tess* xxvii, An up-hill and down-dale ride of twenty-odd miles.

b. Presenting difficulties; carried on against difficulties or opposition; arduous, hard.

Used esp. with *battle*, *fight*, *game*, *task*, *work*.

1622 [see prec.]. **1659** TREVOR in *Burton's Diary* (1828) IV. 348, I move not to bring it into question whether it be up-hill or down-hill. **1741** LD. LYTTELTON in *Athenæum* 23 Feb. (1895) 251/3 It was an uphill piece of work considering the difficulties he lies under. **1748** RICHARDSON *Clarissa* (1768) IV. 149 What an up-hill labour! **1849** COBDEN *Speeches* 8 We had an up-hill battle, but we succeeded. **1850** J. H. NEWMAN *Diffic. Anglic.* v. 107 This misfortune is nothing new; we always reckoned on an uphill game. *a* **1860** ALB. SMITH *Med. Student* (1861) 119 The up-hill struggles ..of his laborious future career. **1886** T. FROST *Remin. Country Journalist* xxi. (1888) 245 'It was up-hill work to establish it [*sc.* a newspaper],' he told me.

c. Contending against difficulties. *rare.*

1821 HAZLITT *Table-T.* Ser. I. *Indian Jugglers*, He was the best *up-hill* player in the world. **1885** TENNYSON *Ancient Sage* 279 Lay thine uphill shoulder to the wheel, And climb the Mount of Blessing.

3. ***uphill and downhill***, alternately cheerful and depressed.

1681 R. CROMWELL *Let.* in *Eng. Hist. Rev.* (1898) 96, I hope shee will find..a better account of the goodness of the Lord then what we meet with by your uphill and downhill letters.

up'hill, *adv.* Also up-hill, up hill. [f. UP *prep.*[1] Cf. HILL *sb.* 1 c. In early use unhyphened.]

1. Towards the top of the hill or high ground; in an upward direction on a (steep) slope. Also in fig. contexts.

α. **1607** TOPSELL *Four-f. Beasts* 311 The Persians.. accustome their Horsses to run both down hil, and vp hil. **1687** A. LOVELL tr. *Thevenot's Trav.* I. 10 The Streets..are incommodious, in that one is always going either up hill or down hill. **1737** [S. BERINGTON] *Mem. G. di Lucca* 112 These Men..were approaching to the Line,..and supposing the Structure of..the Earth to be Spheroidal, went up Hill all the way. **1746** in *10th Rep. Hist. MSS. Comm.* App. I. 440 As we march'd, all the way up hill, and over very uneven Ground. **1779** G. KEATE *Sketches fr. Nat.* (ed. 2) I. 67 The successors of Saint Peter..trotted them up hill, and down hill,..just as they pleased to lead the way. **1824** SCOTT *St. Ronan's* iv, Mr. Winterblossom..would gladly have been the personal representative of the company ..—but it [*sc.* the walk] was up hill.

β. **1712** J. JAMES tr. *Le Blond's Gardening* 118 To be constantly going Up-hill, or Down-hill. **1748** *Anson's Voy.* II. i. 122 The dogs..ran up-hill with great alacrity. **1818** HAZLITT *Eng. Poets* v. 178 Thomson's blank verse..seems always labouring up-hill. **1877** HUXLEY *Physiogr.* 17 To do that the water would have to run up-hill. **1879** F. POLLOK *Sport Brit. Burmah* I. 79 He could only go up-hill backwards.

fig. **1682** SIR T. BROWNE *Chr. Mor.* (1716) 109 To offer at iniquities, which have so little foundations in thee, were to be vitious up hill, and strain for thy condemnation. **1876** BANCROFT *Hist. U.S.* VI. 340 We are always working up-hill.

2. To or on the upper side *of*.

1922 'CLAXON' *Heather Mixture* xii. 246 The huntsman was riding..on Dicky's left, working to get uphill of the pack.

up'hillward, *adv.* and *a.* [f. prec.] **a.** *adv.* In an uphill direction. **b.** *adj.* Leading uphill.

c **1655** MILTON *To C. Skinner* Wks. 1738 I. 59 Nor bate a Jot Of Heart or Hope, but still attend to steer Uphillward. **1876** FARRAR *Marlb. Serm.* xii. 112 The path of life is narrow and uphillward. **1877** —— *Eternal Hope* (1892) 90 The difficulty of..virtue's uphillward path.

up'hoard, *v.* [UP- 4.] *trans.* To hoard or heap up.

1582 STANYHURST *Æneis* III. (Arb.) 72 Thee gould thee traytor vp hurdeth. **1591** SPENSER *Teares Muses* 553 Heapes of huge words vphoorded hideously. **1602** SHAKS. *Ham.* I. i. 134 If thou hast vp-hoorded in thy life Extorted Treasure in the wombe of Earth. **1652** BENLOWES *Theoph.* III. xlv, Eusebia truth for her uphords.

uphoising, -hoist, -hoisted: see UP- 5, 6.

'uphold, *sb.* Chiefly *Sc.* and *north. dial.* Also *Sc.* 5–6 vp- (6 wp-, oup-), uphald, 8 uphad, 9 uphadd, -haud, uppal; 9 *north.* uphod. [OE. *uppheald* (f. UP- 1 b + *heald* HOLD *sb.*[1]), = ON. *upphald* (Norw. *upphald*; MSw. *up-*, *ophald*, *-hold*, MDa. and Da. *ophold*), MLG. *upholt*, MDu. *ophout*;

MHG. *ûfhalt* (G. *aufhalt*) stop, delay; also MSw. *uppe-*, *oppehald* (Sw. *uppehåll*).]

1. A support or stay.

a **1066** in Kemble *Cod. Dipl.* (1846) IV. 232 Ic eom ðæs mynstres mund and upheald. *c* **1200** ORMIN 9217 Crist, Godess Sune,.. Hælennde, & hellpe, & god upphald Till þa þatt he shall chesenn. **1559** KNOX *First Blast* App. (Arb.) 58 So is the testimonye of a clean conscience to me a stay and vphold. **1596** DALRYMPLE tr. *Leslie's Hist. Scot.* (S.T.S.) II. 45 O cruel creatures, quha dang doune sa strong a stay, piller, and vphald of the Realme! **1791** J. LEARMONT *Poems* 142 Deckit wi' French flutteration, Stap forth the uphads o' the nation. **1825** JAMIESON s.v. *Uppal*, The death o' wives, and the luck o' sheep, are a puir man's uppal. **1894** A. REID *Sangs Heatherland* 16 Wha'll cast the end gin aince ye try To pu' oor uphauds doon?

2. The support, sustenance, or maintenance *of* a person, estate, etc. Also without const.

α. **1439** *Sc. Acts, Jas. II* (1814) II. 54/2 þe said princesse ..has..assignit..to þe uphald of our said soueryn lord and his sistris..iiij^m markis. **1456** SIR G. HAY *Govt. Princes* Wks. (S.T.S.) II. 153 The gudis ar the uphald of the lyf. *c* **1500** *Cartul. St. Nicholai Aberdon.* (New Spald. Cl.) I. 259 Sextene bredir singaris and abill men to ye vphald of devin service. **1552** LYNDESAY *Tragedy* 191, I wes the cause of mekle more myschance, For vphald of my glore and dignitie. **1597** *Sc. Acts, Jas. VI* (1814) IV. 154/2 Oure said souerane Lord..Annexis..to þe same citye..for þe better vphald þerof the foirsaidis liberteis. *a* **1598** D. FERGUSSON *Coll. Sc. Prov.* (S.T.S.) 84 Pride and sweirnesse wald have meikle uphald. **1808** JAMIESON s.v. *Uphald*, *Uphadd*, support.

β. **1483** in Rymer *Fœdera* (1711) XII. 174/1 To the upholde, maynteyne and encrease of their both Estatis. **1582** in *Archaeologia* (1846) XXX. 166 Those..placed here for the uphold and maintenance of the peace. **1680** in *Proc. Soc. Antiq. Scot.* XLV. 241 The broad curse of God is on ministers and professors, for your joyning for their uphold.

b. The maintaining *of* a building, etc., in proper repair.

1471 in *Charters, &c. Edinb.* (1871) 133 For the vphald, reparatioun and bigging of the sammyn [port]. **1527** *Extr. Aberd. Reg.* (1844) I. 116 The biging of the brig of Dee, and ..the gret offeris..be his lordschip, for the vphald of the samyn. **1588** *Exchequer Rolls Scot.* XXI. 403 Payit yeirlie.. for uphald of the brig of Tay.

c. *north. dial.* Personal maintenance (in respect of food, etc.).

1855- in dial. glossaries (Cumb., Yks.).

up'hold, *v.* Forms: *α.* 3–4 **upholden**, 4–6 **vp-**, 5–6 **upholde**, 5–7 **vphold**, 5– **uphold** (6 **upphold**); *north. dial.* 8–9 **uphowd** (8 **upphoud**), 9 **uphod**. *β.* 4 **vp-haldene**; *north.* and *Sc.* 5 **vpp-**, **uppehalde**, 4, 6 **vp-**, **uphald**, 9 **-uppal**, 8–9 **uphaud**, 9 **uphadd**. [UP- 4. Cf. OFris. *op-*, *uphalda* (WFris. *ophâlde*), MLG. *upholden* (LG. *upholden*, *-hollen*), (M)Du. *ophouden*, MSw. *up-*, *ophalda*, *-halla*, *-holda*, etc., Da. *opholde*, MHG. *ûfhalten* (G. *aufhalten*); also MSw. *uppe-*, *oppehalda* (Sw. *uppehålla*).]

1. *trans.* To support or sustain physically; to keep from falling or sinking.

a **1300** *Cursor M.* 538 Hijs fete him bers up fra fall, Als þe erth vp haldes all. **13..** *Gaw. & Gr. Knt.* 2079 þe heuen was vp halt, bot vgly þer vnder. **1390** GOWER *Conf.* I. 75 He hire in hise armes fast Uphield. *c* **1440** *Pallad. on Husb.* IV. 82 A lighter vyne is with a lesse Stakyng vpholde. **1483** *Cath. Angl.* 404/2 To Vpphalde, *sustentare*, *supportare*. **1515** BARCLAY *Eclogues* iv. (1570) C vi b/1 With marble pillers the building to vpholde, About be turrets of shape moste excellent. **1590** SPENSER *F.Q.* I. viii. 40 Whose feeble thighes, vnhable to vphold His pined corse, him scarse to light could beare. **1610** HOLLAND *Camden's Brit.* I. 697 An Altar..which I saw there, vpholding now the Staires of an house. **1663** BP. PATRICK *Parab. Pilgr.* xxxvii, The winds that blew, and the rough waves.., were no less subject to that power which upheld him, than [etc.]. **1726** LEONI *Alberti's Archit.* I. 52 Coverings..must..be sufficient for upholding themselves, and their burthens. **1763** MILLS *Pract. Husb.* IV. 359 Poles were extended between them, and these were up-held by props. **1807** CRABBE *Par. Reg.* III. 938 No more his span-girth shanks..Upheld a body of smaller size. **1849** MACAULAY *Hist. Eng.* I. 47 The leading strings, which preserve and uphold the infant. **1880** JEFFERIES *Gt. Estate* 33 The slender stems uphold the cup-like flowers two or three inches above the surface.

2. To support, sustain, maintain, by aid or assistance; to preserve unimpaired or intact.

a **1225** *Ancr. R.* 140 Teke þis, heo mot ȝete þuruh hire uorbisne..ȝiuen oðre strenðe, & upholden ham, þet heo ne uallen iðe dunge of sunne. *a* **1250** *Prov. Alfred* 171 For nys no w[u]rt..þat euer mvwe þas feye furþ vp-holde [*Trin. Coll. MS.* þe lif up helde]. *c* **1320** *Cast. Love* 609 A child þer is i-boren to vs,..þat schal vp-holden his kynedome. **1389** in *Eng. Gilds* (1870) 110 The gilde bretherun..that this gilde furst begonne, and lengest sal vp-haldene. **1462–3** *Pol. Poems* (Rolls) II. 268 Falshode, myschyef, secret synne upholdyng, Whiche hathe caused..endelez langoure. **1488** *Act 4 Hen. VII*, c. 12 §2 The housbondrie..wherby the Chirche of Engleind is upholden. **1542–3** *Act 34 & 35 Hen. VIII*, c. 10 §1 The Citie..hathe been mainteyned and upholden by divers and sundrye handye craftes there used. **1593** SHAKS. *3 Hen. VI*, III. iii. 106 While Life vpholds this Arme, This Arme vpholds the House of Lancaster. **1647** N. BACON *Disc. Govt. Eng.* I. i. 2 Though great Nations may be upholden by power. **1671** MILTON *Samson* 892 An impious crew Of men conspiring to uphold thir state By worse than hostile deeds. **1725** DE FOE *Voy. round World* (1840) 328 They had..some comforts however which might a little uphold their spirits. **1781** COWPER *Retirem.* 89 Thine, and upheld by thy paternal care, This universal frame. **1838** THIRLWALL *Greece* xxxv. IV. 377 Rather to take the lead in a revolution, than steadily to uphold the established order of things. **1877** FREEMAN *Norm. Conq.* (ed. 3) II. App. 666 Malcolm continued to be powerfully upheld by English help.

absol. **1560** BIBLE *Isaiah* lxiii. 5, I loked, & there was none to helpe, & I wondered that there was none to vpholde.

†**b.** To carry out, succeed in. *Obs.*$^{-1}$

c **1450** *Cov. Myst.* (Shaks. Soc.) 214 He wyl us werke ryght mekyl shame, His fals purpos if he upholde.

c. To maintain at the same level or standard.

1523 FITZHERB. *Husb.* §66 That he rere two oxe-calues, and two cowe-calues,..to vpholde his flocke. **1832** CHALMERS *Pol. Econ.* (1849) II. 60 Such a high style of husbandry cannot possibly be upholden. **1875** *Economist* 27 Feb. 260/1 Beans and peas..firmly uphold their value. **1883** *Manch. Exam.* 26 Nov. 4/2 The demand for yarns..has been very dull, but quotations have nevertheless been upheld.

d. To sustain spiritually.

1820 J. J. GURNEY in Reid *Life W. E. Forster* (1888) I. 33 Both William and his wife were marvellously upheld. **1824** SCOTT *St. Ronan's* xxxvii, God send she may not have been left to hersel'!—God send she may have been upholden! **1864** TENNYSON *En. Ard.* 783 Uphold me, Father, in my loneliness A little longer!

3. †**a.** To furnish or provide, to perform or discharge, regularly. *Obs.*

a **1417** *York Memo. Bk.* (Surtees) I. 221 The whilk vj.s. viij.d...sall be keped..to upholde and releve a lyght to be borne..on Corpus Cristy day. **1444** *Extr. Aberd. Reg.* (1844) I. 12 Williame Mathouson..sal vphald the ladymesse with uoce..ilke owke for a yher. **1539** in *Abst. Protocols Town Clerks of Glasgow* (1897) IV. 118 The said maister to uphald and fynd ane pryckat of wax nychtlie byrneand.

b. To maintain in good condition or in a proper state of repair.

1511 *Reg. Privy Seal Scotl.* I. 344/2 That the saidis landis salbe uphaldin and keipit unharmit or skaithit. **1535** *Act 27 Hen. VIII*, c. 22 §1 If any Owner..shuld..occupie any suche mese or land..he shulde..uphold and susteyne the same. **1563** *Reg. Privy Council Scot.* I. 246 The Abbottis.. wer accustomat.., upoun thair expenssis, to uphald and big the wallis. **1631** WEEVER *Anc. Funeral Mon.* 333 This Church is vpholden in wondrous good repaire. **1701** in W. O. Blunt *Ch. Chester-le-Street* (1884) 104 Paid Thos. Pearson for upholding ye bell wheels for 7 yeare. **1753** *Scots Mag.* Apr. 164/2 Provided that the city be obliged to uphold the..buildings in repair. **1816** SCOTT *Antiq.* i, It's Jamie Martingale that furnishes the naigs on contract, and uphauds them. **1833** *Stat. 3 & 4 Wm. IV*, c. 46 §101 Every person..shall uphold and keep in proper repair the fences aforesaid. **1894** *Westm. Gaz.* 3 May 2/3 He was also bound by a covenant in the lease to 'uphold' the premises.

c. To provide with sustenance; to support with food, etc. Now *dial.*

1546 *Reg. Cupar Abbey* II. 36 [He] sall vphald honestlie in meit and claytht..the said Jhone Alane. **1574** *Satir. Poems Reform.* xlii. 380 Rentis sufficient to vphauld Ane gude number of sic Studentis. **1615** MARKHAM *Country Contentm.* I. viii. 101 The best generall foods for the ordinarie vpholding of a dogge in a good state of body. [**1684** J. S. *Profit & Pleas. United* 163 The best Food for upholding a dog.] **1863** MRS. TOOGOOD *Spec. Yorks. Dial.* (MS.), I kept my brother some time, but he was so wasteful I couldn't uphod him any longer.

4. To support by advocacy or assent; to sustain against objection or criticism.

1485 CAXTON *Paris & V.* (1868) 12 Other knyghtes rise vp that mayntened and vpheld the beaute of Vyenne. **1525** LD. BERNERS *Froiss.* II. xlv. 153 This worde was vpholden and obserued. **1530** PALSGR. 769/1 Sythe he hath sayde it, I wyll upholde it. **1598** R. BERNARD tr. *Terence, Andria* IV. iii, See that thou be readie to answer and vphold my talke. **1753–4** RICHARDSON *Grandison* III. xxvi. 309 He does nothing but hop, skip, and dance about me, grin and make mouths; and every-body upholds him in it. **1781** BURKE *Corr.* (1844) II. 451 Perhaps I have wished to uphold with enthusiasm the honour and dignity of the community I belong to. **1818** CRUISE *Digest* (ed. 2) I. 522 The owner of the inheritance, who was interested in upholding it [*sc.* an arrangement]. **1869** J. MARTINEAU *Ess.* II. 57 This plea..upholds a practice essentially unjust. **1890** *Law Times' Rep.* LXIII. 733/2 He refused to answer that question, and was upheld in his refusal by the learned judge. **1893** *Ibid.* LXVIII. 444/1 On appeal to the County Court Judge..the decision of the registrar was upheld.

b. To maintain (a statement), to warrant or guarantee (a fact). Now chiefly *north. dial.* and *Sc.*

Orig. with complementary object or clause. In later usage freq. in loose construction, esp. in dialect forms (see *β* and *Eng. Dial. Dict.* s.v.). Also with indirect personal dative.

α. **1530** PALSGR. 769/1, I upholde a ware or marchaundyse to be good. *Ibid.*, I wyll upholde hym for as sounde a horse as any is in Englande. **1583** GOLDING *Calvin on Deut.* Pref. Ep. 2 The other side upholdeth..that it is a vilainous defiling of religion. **1653** BLITHE *English Improver Impr.* 86, I dare uphold one Acre would be as good as divers now are in many parts of it. **1821** SCOTT *Kenilw.* xxix, I know that shall make Varney uphold me sober. **1853** MISS YONGE *Heir of Redclyffe* xli, He always upheld that you acted for his good. **1897** RHOSCOMYL *White Rose Arno* 274 Your names'll do for Chapel, I'll uphold.

β. **1787** GROSE *Prov. Gloss.*, *Uphowd*, to warrant. **1793** T. SCOTT *Poems* 357 I'se uphaud ye Owr the lugs i' love to be. **1807** R. ANDERSON *Cumbld. Ball.* 121, I'll uphod ye, we's 'gree. **1820** SCOTT *Monast.* Introd. Ep., 'I'se uphaud him a scholar,' answered David. **1861** WAUGH *Birtle Carter's T.* 8 Yo'd raytheer ha' loaf-brade, aw'll uphowd yo. **1891** BARRIE *Little Minister* iii, It was no sport to them, Susy, I'se uphaud.

5. To raise or lift up; to direct upwards.

a **1400** *Isumbras* 52 The knyghte felle on his knes..And bothe his handis uphelde. *c* **1400** *Destr. Troy* 8760 With a noble sword..naked in his hond, Vp holdand on high as he þat wold stryke. *c* **1450** *Songs, Carols*, etc. (E.E.T.S.) 6/39 Vphold the flowr of gud Jesse, And worship it for ay bewte. *c* **1480** HENRYSON *Fables, Lion & Mouse* 188 Scho..baith hir handis vnto the heuin vpheld. **1513** DOUGLAS *Æneid* Concl. 8 The bettir part of me sal be vpheild Abuif the starnis perpetualy to ryng. **1618** ROWLANDS *Sacred Mem.* 24 With eyes vpheld To heauen, he did blesse. **1681** DRYDEN *Abs. & Achit.* I. 595 His Hand a Vare of Justice did uphold. **1891** FARRAR *Darkn. & Dawn* xxxix, They upheld their clenched hands..to plead for mercy.

up'holdatory, *a.* (f. UPHOLD *v.*)

1829 *Moore's Mem.* (1854) VI. 6 Lord L. showed me..a letter..from Lord Anglesey... One word in it rather an odd coinage: 'upholdatory of his government'.

up'holden, *ppl. a.* (UP- 5. Cf. UPHOLD *v.*)

1817 KEATS *Sleep & Poetry* 143 Some with upholden hand and mouth severe. **1838** MRS. BROWNING *Seraphim* II. Wks. (1904) 87 The creature's and the upholden's sacrifice!

up'holder. Also 4–5 **vpholdere**, 6 **opholder**; 4, 6 *Sc.* **uphalder**, 5 *north.* **uppalder**. (See also UPHELDER.) [f. UPHOLD *v.* (in sense 1 app. in the sense of 'to keep in repair'). Cf. MDa. *op(pe)holdere* in sense 2.]

1. †**a.** A dealer in small wares or second-hand articles (of clothing, furniture, etc.); a maker or repairer of such things. *Obs.* **b.** = UPHOLSTERER. Now *rare.*

1333 *Will of Robert de Reppes* 18 June, Quod perquisivi de Thoma Drie upholdere. **1362** LANGL. *P. Pl.* A. v. 168 A Ropere, a Redyng-kyng, and Rose þe disschere,..And of vp holders an hep. **1377** *Rolls of Parlt.* III. 9 A null Mercer, Coteller, Jualer, Uphalder, ne a nul autre denszein ne forein. **1417** *York Memo. Bk.* (Surtees) I. 183 That na uppalder wyrk in Girdelecrafte. *c* **1440** *Promp. Parv.* 512/2 Vpholdere, þat sellythe smal thyngys, *velaber*. **1495** *Act 11 Hen. VII*, c. 19, To the..greate rebuke and disclaunder to the seid Crafte of Upholders. **1598** STOW *Survey* 154 [In] this lane.., in the raigne of Henry the sixt, had ye for the most parte dwelling Fripperers or Upholders, that solde olde apparell and housholde stuffe. **1688** R. HOLME *Armoury* III. 449/2 Such..was of old the Vpholders, or Vpholsteres Arms of Chester. **1711** *Act 10 Anne* c. 19 §84 All ..Drapers, Mercers, Upholders,..having..any Stock of.. Silks. *a* **1766** MRS. F. SHERIDAN *Sidney Bidulph* (1767) III. 126, I did not like the furniture,..so I..have bespoke new of an upholder. **1807** SOUTHEY *Espriella's Lett.* I. 155 An upholder just now advertises Commodes, Console-tables,.. and Chiffoniers. **1812** *Ann. Reg.*, *Chron.* 121 Messrs Wilkinsons, upholders,..having of late been frequently robbed of feathers. **1881** *Instr. Census Clerks* (1885) 53 Upholstery:..Stuffer. Upholder. Upholsterer's Spring Maker. **1910** *Daily Chron.* 9 March 4/7, I have seen 'Carpenter and Upholder' on the signboard of a shop in a Surrey village.

c. An undertaker. *Obs.* in general use.

1709 STEELE *Tatler* No. 99 ¶4, I..shall give my good Friends the Company of Upholders, full Power to bury all such Dead as they meet with. **1714** GAY *Trivia* II. 347 Th' Upholder, rueful Harbinger of Death, Waits with Impatience for the dying Breath. **1724** SWIFT *Reasons agst. Exam. Drugs* ¶5 The company exercising the trade and mistery of upholders. **1903** *Daily Chron.* 8 April 5/2 A large glass sign describing the owners as 'upholders', whereas other evidence shows them to be 'undertakers'.

2. A supporter, sustainer, or maintainer (*of* a thing or person).

c **1403** LYDG. *Temple of Glas* 468 To ȝov my ladi, vpholder of my life, Mekeli I þanke. **1439** *Coventry Leet Bk.* 191 They ordeyn that..suche maner vpholders..be pursewed as they were persones sole. **1536** *Stories & Proph. Script.* M ij b, The Lorde lyueth, and blessyd be myne opholder. **1547** BALE (*title*), The first Examinacyon of Anne Askewe latelye martyred in Smythfelde, by the Romysh popes vpholders. **1590** NASHE *Pasquil's Apol.* I. B iv b, I wyll not be theyr vpholder which lye sleeping and snorting in their charges. **1642** R. CARPENTER *Experience* III. iii. 12 For God leaveth many things undone,..to preach this doctrine that creatures are not his upholders. **1691** WOOD *Ath. Oxon.* I. 581 The said Duke..was an upholder of him and his unworthy doings. **1710** SWIFT *Poems, Atlas* 22 When the weight of kingdoms lies Too long upon his single shoulders, Sink down he must, or find upholders. **1809** COLERIDGE *Friend* 87 Intellect, and Thought alone can be our Upholder and Judge. **1840** J. H. NEWMAN *Par. Serm.* (ed. 2) V. x. 152 When was the power of the world an upholder of God's truth? **1879** FARRAR *St. Paul* II. 229 A reverence for him far deeper than that of his upholders.

b. Of things: A support, stay, or prop.

1398 TREVISA *Barth. De P.R.* v. liv. (Bodl. MS.), It nedeþ to haue so many vndursettinges and vpholders þat suche a beeste may þe [more] ablelich..meue and goo. **1571** GOLDING *Calvin on Ps.* lxi. 8 Gentlenesse and faithfulnes are ye trew upholders of kingdomes. **1617** WOODALL *Surg. Mate* Wks. (1639) 80 Wheat flower..is the principall naturall upholder of the life and health of man. **1730** SOUTHALL *Bugs* 40 Two Upholders drove into the Wainscot or Wall. **1884** A. ROSS *Talk upon Hair* 21 A thick Indiarubber ankle upholder, over which is worn the boot and sock.

up'holding, *vbl. sb.* [UP- 7.]

†**1.** Sustenance; support in necessaries. *Obs.*

c **1375** *Sc. Leg. Saints* iii. (*Andrew*) 965 þu sal hafe þi vphalding with honeste in al thinge In myn dioce. **1535** COVERDALE *2 Macc.* iii. 10 Money layed vp for the vpholdinge of weddowes and fatherlesse children. **1667** *D. Fergusson's Coll. Sc. Prov.* No. 707, Pride and sweerness would have meikle upholding.

2. Maintenance in regular use or in proper condition.

a **1350** in *Facsimiles Nat. MSS. Scotland* II. (1870) 14 Ad ..sustentacionem [*glossed* vphalding] dicti molendini. **1453** *Extr. Aberd. Reg.* (1844) I. 20 For the vphaldyng and eikyng of Godis seruice to be done in the paroche kirk. **1486** in *Exchequer Rolls Scotl.* X. 100 For the uphalding and bering of the..chargis of the said office. **1521** *Lincoln Wills* (1914) 104 To the upholdyng of Notyngham briges. **1522** *Ibid.* 106 To the upholdyng of the forsaid churche. **1543** *Richmond. Wills* (Surtees) 47, I bewhethe other twenty shelyngs..for the upholdyng of one seirge of waxe yerly. **1612** in *Essex*

Rev. XVII. 105 The upholdinge and perfectinge of the companies in good strength and number. **1631** WEEVER *Anc. Funeral Mon.* To Rdr. 6 For the repairing and vpholding.. of that..building. **1842** J. AITON *Clerical Econ.* 112 It must have separate houses, which,..in upholding, must cost disproportionally dear. **1894** C. N. ROBINSON *Brit. Fleet* 62 No sacrifice can therefore be too great for the upholding of our fleet.

3. The action of sustaining or supporting by aid or influence.

1599 SANDYS *Europæ Spec.* (1605) 8 The vpholding of their wordly power and glorie of their Order. **1607** HIERON *Wks.* I. 226 The inquirie..how we haue striuen and fought for the vpholding and maintenance of Gods truth. **1637** *Documents agst. Prynne* (Camden) 95 This was my Lord of Lincolne's case in his upholding the creditt of Prydean. **1691** BLOUNT *Law Dict.* (ed. 2), *Maintenance*, signifies the upholding or maintaining of a Cause or Person. **1818** MILLMAN *Samor* v. 209 If this life Be worthy thy upholding. **1863** J. COLDSTREAM in Balfour *Biog.* (1865) v. 195 We sensibly felt the 'upholding' graciously vouchsafed. **1872** SPURGEON *Treas. Dav.* III. 10 He asked..for deliverance, and here he returns thanks for upholding.

4. The action of maintaining in argument.

1587 GOLDING *De Mornay* ix. 144 What els then is his vpholding of the world to be eternal, than a turning of yͤ whole world vpside downe?

5. The action of raising or holding up.

1574 in *Maitl. Cl. Misc.* (1840) I. 111 He..forder obleist him with uphalding of his hand, that he suld be ane trew sugget. **1598** in J. Ronald *Landmarks Old Stirling* (1899) 338 They promised solemnlie be uphaulding of their hands. **1866** J. G. MURPHY *Comm., Exod.* xvii. 12 Aaron and Hur joining in the upholding of Moses's hands.

up'holding, *ppl. a.* [UP- 6 b.] Supporting, sustaining.

1553 POYNET *Short Catech.* 43 [The] church, which Paul calleth the piller, and vpholding stay of truth. **1561** T. N[ORTON] tr. *Calvin's Inst.* III. xxi. 239 The vpholdyng stay of sounde affiance. **1674** BOYLE *Excell. Theol.* I. i. 27 Though the soul of man, by the continuance of his ordinary and upholding concourse, may survive the body. **1724** E. ERSKINE *Wks.* (1791) 122/1 His quickening, strengthening, and upholding presence may be withdrawn. **1784** COWPER *Task* III. 658 Flow'rs..expect th' upholding aid Of the smooth-shaven prop. *c* **1830** BRYANT *Forest Hymn* 67 The indwelling Life,..the upholding Love, That are the soul of this wide universe. **1890** 'L. FALCONER' *Mlle. Ixe* vi, She.. would have fallen, but for the timely aid of two upholding arms.

Hence **up'holdingly** *adv.* (nonce poet. formation).

1934 KIPLING *Non nobis Domine* in *Verse* (1940) 512 O Power by whom we live—Creator, Judge and Friend, Upholdingly forgive.

†**up'holster**, *sb. Obs.* Also 5 upholdester, 5, 7–8 upholdster, 6 *north.* uphaldster. [f. UPHOLD *v.* + -STER.] = UPHOLDER I.

α. **1411** *Close Roll 12 Hen. IV* (dorso), Johannes Dryuer, upholdester. **1479** *Paston Lett.* III. 271, iij girdels Staunton. j girdel upholdester. *c* **1481** CAXTON *Dialogues* 2 Of tayllours and vpholdsters. **15..** *York Memo. Bk.* (Surtees) I. 64 Every uphaldster that sellis eny furrez within this citie. **1647** LILLY *Chr. Astrol.* xii. 74 Upholdsters, Limners, Glovers. **1660** PEPYS *Diary* 9 Oct., I found..part of our chambers hung to day by the upholdster. **1722** E. WARD *Parish Gutt'lers* 37 Once on a time he turn'd Upholdster, And slily dealt in Bed and Bolster.

β. **1483–5** *Rec. St. Mary at Hill* 123 Richard Crick, vpholster, for o quarter. **1491** CAXTON *Vitas Patr.* (W. de W. 1495) 144 Whan the chaunger..knewe his gowne that heng at the Vpholsters dore and all redy was there to selle, he was sore wrothe. *c* **1515** *Cocke Loreli's B.* 10 Harpe makers, leches, and upholsters. **1573** in Feuillerat *Revels Q. Eliz.* (1908) 209 Upholster for pendentes of burnished golde for the Maskers garmentes. **1614** in *10th Rep. Hist. MSS. Comm.* App. I. 43 As for a resting chyre.., I did enquyre at an upholster the pryce of itt. **1666** PEPYS *Diary* 22 Aug., My closett is doing by upholsters, which I am pleased with. **1677** WYCHERLEY *Pl. Dealer* III. i, Your Bookseller is properly your Upholster; for he furnishes your Room, rather than your Head. **1725** *Brice's Weekly Jrnl.* 27 Aug. 4 Any Person, having Occasion to imploy an Upholster, may be faithfully serv'd by Ann Hutchins. **1764** H. WALPOLE *Let. to Dalrymple* 31 Jan., Our booksellers..are little more or less than upholsters.

fig. **1593** G. HARVEY *Pierce's Super.* 151, I..looue not to be an Vpholster of stuffed, and bombasted malice in other. **1614** J. COOKE *Greene's Tu Quoque* H 1 b, When thou art growne to bee An old Vpholster vnto Venerie. **1660** W. SECKER *Nonsuch Prof.* 156 As for flatterers they may be stiled the Devils Upholsters.

†**b.** Used spec. with reference to the making and selling of beds and bedding. *Obs.*

1554 in W. H. Turner *Select. Rec. Oxford* (1880) 218 George Bedder..to occupy the bedders craft,..to sell upholsters wares wythyn the lybertyes of thys Cytye. **1576** GASCOIGNE *Steele Gl.* (Arb.) 80 When vpholsters sel fethers without dust. **1622** BRETON *Fantastickes* Wks. (Grosart) II. 10/1 The Poulters feathers make toward the Upholster. **1647** TRAPP *Comm., 1 John* iii. 7 These are the devils.. upholsters that sow such pillows. **1688** *Secr. Serv. Money Chas. & Jas.* (Camden) 186 To John Poictvin, upholster,.. for making two bedds and furniture for the Queen.

up'holster, *v.* Orig. *U.S.* [Back-formation from UPHOLSTERER or UPHOLSTERY. Cf. next.]

1. *intr.* To do upholstery work.

1861 MRS. STOWE *Pearl Orr's Isl.* 21 Miss Roxy and Miss Ruey..could upholster and quilt.

2. *trans.* **a.** Of materials: To cover after the manner of upholstery.

1864 LOWELL *Fireside Trav.* 45 The dull weed upholstered the decaying wharves. **1873** J. E. TAYLOR *Half Hours in Green Lanes* x. 292 Several species have already upholstered the rough bark with..delicate shades of velvety green.

b. To furnish or trim with, or as with, upholstery. Also *fig.*: in quot. 1873, to provide with (fine or smart) clothes, to dress; cf. UPHOLSTERED *ppl. a.* b.

1873 'MARK TWAIN' *Gilded Age* xxxiii. 300 It had cost something to upholster those women. **1877** —— *Mississippi Pilot* 24 The bar keeper had been barbered and upholstered at incredible cost. **1890** C. DIXON *Ann. Bird Life* 85 All [ducks] upholster their nests in the same singular manner. **1891** *Lancet* 24 Jan. 218/1 The whole thorax hollow is now laid bare and upholstered with the skin-muscle flap.

up'holstered, *ppl. a.* [f. as prec. + -ED.]

a. Furnished or fitted with upholsterer's work.

1837 CARLYLE *Misc.* (1840) V. 167 Farewell, thou old Château, with thy upholstered rooms. **1866** *Lond. Rev.* 6 Jan. 4/1 Sofa-divans, and..arm-chairs all comfortably upholstered with national colours. **1889** MRS. E. KENNARD *Landing a Prize* i, The drawing-room [is] rosewood, upholstered in red damask.

b. *fig.* and *transf.* Esp. of persons (*euphemistically*): (well-)dressed; plump, stocky. See also WELL-UPHOLSTERED *ppl. a.*

1892 W. H. MALLOCK *Human Document* xviii, Considered by others as an article essential to a decorously upholstered mind. **1924** WODEHOUSE *Leave it to Psmith* iii. 60 This sumptuously upholstered young woman. **1929** D. H. LAWRENCE *Pansies* 31 The upholstered dead that sit in deep arm-chairs. **1958** S. J. PERELMAN *Most of S. J. Perelman* 21 Where are those big, jolly, upholstered girls one used to see? **1976** R. LEHMANN *Sea-Grape Tree* 6 British travellers.. stoutly upholstered middle-aged couples from the Midlands.

upholsterer (ʌpˈhəʊlstərə(r)). Also 8 **uphoulstarer, upholdsterer.** [f. UPHOLSTER *sb.* + -ER[1] 3.] A tradesman or shopkeeper whose business is the making, finishing, or repairing of articles of furniture and other house-furnishings in which woven or similar fabrics, or materials used for stuffing these, are employed.

1613 MARSTON *Insatiate Countesse* C j b, The fault's in my Vpholsterer, Lady. **1653** W. RAMESEY *Astrol. Restored* 132 If thou makest the childe..a Perfumer,..Glover or Upholsterer. **1677** *Lond. Gaz.* No. 1233/4 Mr. Cooke an Upholsterer next door to the Star. **1722** DE FOE *Plague* (1754) 111 Upholdsterers, Joyners, Cabinet-makers. **1776** ADAM SMITH *W.N.* II. i. I. 334 Upholsterers frequently lett furniture by the month or by the year. **1823** BENTHAM *Not Paul* 85 Tent-making: an art, in which the operations of the architect and the upholsterer are combined. **1875** W. S. HAYWARD *Love agst. World* 6 Painters, decorators, upholsterers,..were immediately set to work.

fig. **1642** T. TRESCOT *Zeal. Magist.* 14 Better to meet with sound Reprovers,..than the Devills Vpholsterers. **1779** HERVEY *Nav. Hist.* II. 459 This led the prince of Conti to call Luxembourg 'The Upholsterer of Notre Dame'.

b. *transf.* Applied to certain bees and birds. Also *attrib.*

1830 J. RENNIE *Insect Archit.* 53 The leaf-cutting bees.. may be denominated more generally 'upholsterer-bees', as there are some of them which use other materials beside leaves. **1840** WESTWOOD *Introd. Mod. Classif. Insects* II. 272 They have been termed..upholsterer bees;..the upholsterers employ in the construction of their cells portions of leaves. **1890** C. DIXON *Ann. Bird Life* 84 Upholsterers.—The birds which come into the present group comprise the Ducks and Geese.

upholsteress, var. of UPHOLSTRESS.

up'holstering, *vbl. sb.* [f. UPHOLSTER-ER, -Y.] Upholstery. Also *attrib.*

1807 SOUTHEY *Espriella's Lett.* III. 272 The women of the family in which she then worked at the upholstering business. **1896** *Daily News* 15 Dec. 2/2 The velvet upholstering and pile carpets.

up'holstering, *ppl. a.* [f. as prec.] Serving to upholster.

1828 LYTTON *Pelham* III. xvii, All that especial neatness of upholstering paraphernalia. **1859** SALA *Tw. round Clock* 210 The march of upholstering intellect is there in its entirety.

up'holsterous, *a.* [f. as prec.] Given to the use of upholstery.

1887 W. CORY *Lett. & Jrnls.* (1897) 523 Since then our educated people have been less happy, though more upholsterous. **1894** T. PINKERTON *Blizzard*, etc. 101 He was not at all upholsterous.

up'holstery. [f. UPHOLSTER *sb.*] Upholsterer's work or materials; *spec.* the fabrics and materials used in the covering and stuffing of furniture; the collective use of these in a room or house.

1649 J. TAYLOR (Water P.) *Western Voy.* 13 In the Mount I saw a craggy rugged seat, of Rocky Upholstery, which the old fabulous rumour calls St. Michaels Chair. **1653** *Ordin. Contin. Excise* 17 Mar. 111 Linnens fine and course, Upholstery, Haberdashery [etc.]. **1756** W. OWEN *Bk. Fairs* (1788) 62 Hacheston, Suffolk, Nov. 12., for boots, shoes, upholstery, and joiners. **1859** THACKERAY *Virgin.* iv, Mantel-pieces, carved cornice-work,..carpets and costly upholstery. **1882** MISS BRADDON *Mt. Royal* I. vi. 147 The bedrooms had been improved by modern upholstery.

transf. **1850** LD. OSBORNE *Gleanings W. Irel.* 86 There were drills, and carts, and other farm upholstery.

fig. **1862** CARLYLE *Fredk. Gt.* XIV. viii. III. 737 Fantastic Bielfeld..becomes positively wearisome, chanting the upholsteries of Life.

b. *attrib.* and *Comb.*

1803 SHERATON *Cabinet Dict.* (title-p.), The Terms used in the Cabinet, Chair and Upholstery Branches. **1844** M. F. OSSOLI *Wom. in 19th C.* (1862) 99 She..is, in short, always spoken and thought of upholstery-wise. **1858** HAWTHORNE *Fr. & It. Note-bks.* II. 123 Their whole charm is..in no degree of the upholstery kind. **1866** *Lond. Rev.* 15 Sept. 287/2 Those upholstery authors..whose books have the run at Mudie's.

Hence **up'holsterydom.** *rare*$^{-1}$.

1860 SALA in *Cornh. Mag.* I. 572 He went on painting, in spite of all the Morrises in upholsterydom.

up'holstress. Also **-holsteress.** [f. UPHOLSTER(ER).] A female upholsterer.

1859 *Edin. Rev.* CIX. 321 The London dress-makers.. and the upholstresses. **1884** *Pall Mall G.* 2 Aug. 6/1 The Secretary of the Upholsteresses' Society.

†**up'hoven**, *pa. pple. Obs.* [UP- 5. Cf. UPHEAVE *v.*] Raised up, exalted.

c **1200** ORMIN 12148 To beon abufenn alle menn Upphofenn heȝhe & wurrþedd. *Ibid.* 17389. *a* **1300** *E.E. Psalter* lxxiv. 11 Up-hoven ben hornes of rightwys.

uphroe, var. EUPHROE (fir-pole).

up'hung, *pa. pple.* Also 4 uphang, 6 *Sc.* -hing. [UP- 5. Cf. OE. *up-hangen.*] Hung up, suspended.

a **1300** *Cursor M.* 20912 Vphang his fette, his hed don, Naild on þe rod he was. *c* **1440** *Pallad. on Husb.* IV. 875 Take brawny bodied [foals],..Smale ballockyng, and euere short vphonge. **1513** DOUGLAS *Æneid* VIII. xii. 116 On the proud pillaris..[he] maid [them] thar be vp hing. **1757** DYER *Fleece* III. 170 Oft the wet web is steep'd..: then uphung On rugged tenters,..Its level surface..it expands. **1805–6** CARY *Dante, Inf.* VIII. 3 Our eyes Its height ascended, where we mark'd uphung Two cressets. **1867** M. ARNOLD *Bacchanalia* ii, Uphung the spear, unbent the bow.

up'hurl, *v.* [UP- 4.] *trans.* To hurl up, throw aloft. Also **up'hurled** *pa. pple.*

1582 STANYHURST *Æneis* II. (Arb.) 63 Thee wals God Neptune, with mace threeforcked, vphurleth. **1845** MANGAN *German Anthology* II. 128 From thousand smoke-enveloped cones, Colossal blocks..Are night by night uphurled in air. **1860** BORROW *Sleeping Bard* 40 For all the ills by hell uphurl'd It has a remedy. **1898** MEREDITH *Poems, Hard Weather* II. 111 Her passion for old giantkind, That scaled the mount, uphurled the rock.

up Jenkins (ʌp ˈdʒɛŋkɪnz). [f. UP *adv.*[1] + the surname *Jenkins.*] The name of a parlour game resembling tip-it.

1889 K. GREENAWAY *Bk. Games* 25 *Up Jenkins.* The company divide into two parties and sit round a table. One party then puts their hands under the table and a shilling or other small article is placed in one of the palms. The other side then calls out: 'Up Jenkins!' and the players whose side has the shilling concealed must all place their closed hands on the table. The opposite side must then guess in which hand the shilling is concealed. **1916** D. H. LAWRENCE *Twilight in Italy* 193 Afterwards we played 'Up, Jenkins'. **1928** E. WAUGH *Decline & Fall* III. iv. 255 'I must ask you both to put your hands on the table in front of you,' said the warden. 'Like Up Jenkins,' said Margot faintly. **1933** S. JAMESON *Day Off* 83 They played Up Jenkins, in which a button is passed frenziedly from hand to hand. **1946** L. P. HARTLEY *Sixth Heaven* viii. 164 They..pressed their hands on the table as if for 'Up Jenkins'. **1951** S. SPENDER *World within World* iii. 144 Sometimes he would play childish games such as 'Up Jenkins'. **1981** P. THEROUX *Mosquito Coast* xvi. 212 We played Up Jenkins on the Gallery floor.

upjet, -keep, *vbs.*: see UP- 4.

'upkeep, *sb.* [UP- 1 b. Cf. KEEP *v.* 57 d.] Maintenance in good condition or repair; also, the cost of such. (Freq. from *c* 1885.)

1884 *Pall Mall G.* 10 May 10/2 Arrangements..for continuing the up-keep and in-gathering of the crops in Mauritius and Ceylon. **1887** MRS. DALY *Digging & Squatting* 171 The Northern Territory depends very much upon the gold revenue for the upkeep and support of the settlement. **1893** DK. ARGYLL *Unseen Found. Soc.* v. 145 The constant upkeep of innumerable canals.

So **'upkeeping** *vbl. sb.* (UP- 7.)

1899 *Westm. Gaz.* 26 June 7/1 Premises which took £150 a year for up-keeping. *Ibid.*, The up-keeping of the premises.

upkever, -kindle, -knit: see UP- 4.

up'laid, *pa. pple.* [UP- 5. Cf. UPLAY *v.*]

1. Laid up; put away or in place.

c **1400** *Northern Passion* (H.) 872 Ilka man said..What þai suld with þe siluer do,..þat it suld sauely be vp laid. *c* **1425** WYNTOUN *Cron.* v. vii. 1262 Quhen þe chesabill is vplaid Befor the eleuatioun.

†**2.** Upturned, overthrown. *Obs.*$^{-1}$

1582 STANYHURST *Æneis* II. (Arb.) 63 Then dyd I marck playnely thee castel of Ilion vplayd, And Troian buyldings quit topsy turuye remooued.

†**'upland**, *sb.*[1] and *a.*[1] *Obs.* Also 1, 4 uppe-, 3 upe-, 4 oppe-, 6 uplande. [Subst. and adj. use of the phrase *uppe land*, in the country: see UP *prep.*[1] 5 a, and cf. UPONLAND *adv.*]

A. *sb.* The parts of a country outside the towns; the rural districts.

a **1122** *O.E. Chron.* (Laud MS.) an. 1087, Se cyng..bead þæt ælc man..sceolde cuman to him..of porte & of uppelande. **1209** in *Eng. Hist. Rev.* Oct. (1901) 720 Altres gens et numeement cil de upelande. **1303** R. BRUNNE *Handl. Synne* 1315 Ȝyf þou do any man yn prysun,..Or bynde yn upland or in burgh. **1346** *Little Red Bk. Bristol* (1900) II. 14 Drap qest fulee sur oppelande. *c* **1350** *Cron. London* (Camden) 46 En cele temps fut le vj.^{me} dener de bienz levé en Loundres et en autres cytés en Engletere, et sure upelond le x.[me] denier. **1377** *Ann. Barber Surgeons* (1890) 36 [Barbers from] uppelande. *c* **1500** *World & Child* 579 Poore men that come from vplande. *c* **1510** BARCLAY *Mirr. Gd. Manners* (1570) G iv, Forbidding great building sumptuous..in Countrey or uplande. [**1864** SIR F. PALGRAVE *Norm. & Eng.* IV. 43 Rufus renewed his general summons to his English lieges. From..town and from upland they were called.]

B. *adj.*

1. Living out in the country; rustic, rural.

14.. in *Sc. Acts Parlt.* (1844) I. 339 Of þe borowyng of uplande mannis pundis. **1598** HAKLUYT *Voy.* I. 485 Taking away with him the vpland, or countrey people that should haue tilled the ground. **1599** NASHE *Lenten Stuff* E j b, Other engrating vpland cormorants will grunt out [etc.]. **1615** CHAPMAN *Odyss.* I. 315 Kept alive Within an isle by rude and upland men. **1670** MILTON *Hist. Eng.* II. 48 In peace the Upland Inhabitants besides hunting tended thir flocks and heards.

Comb. *c* **1611** CHAPMAN *Odyssey* IX. 308 This heape of fortitude [*sc.* the Cyclops], That so illiterate was, and vpland rude.

2. Characteristic of the country; of rustic form or make. *rare*⁻¹.

1666 *Despauterius' Gram. Inst.* (1677) C j, *Pero, peronis*, an upland shooe.

'upland, *sb.*[2] and *a.*[2] [f. UP *a.* 1 + LAND *sb.*[1], perhaps partly suggested by prec. Cf. ON. *Upplǫnd* pl., the name of the eastern inland counties of Norway; MSw. *Upland* (Sw. *Uppland*), a district in central Sweden; MDa. *Opland* Sweden, Norw. *uppland*, Da. *opland* the inland country.]

A. *sb.* **1.** The part of a country lying away from the sea; the interior or high-lying districts. Also *pl.* Now *arch.*

1579–80 NORTH *Plutarch* (1595) 687 He determined to draw these pirats from the sea into the vpland. **1615** G. SANDYS *Trav.* 12 Smal watch-towers, which..do giue knowledge vnto one another (and so to the vpland) of suspected enemies. **1618** BOLTON *Florus* III. vi. (1636) 193 Who transplanted this brood of Mariners..out of the very ken of the sea, and, as it were, teddred them fast in the uplands [L. *mediterraneis agris*]. **1825** JAMIESON *Suppl.*, *Upwark*, apparently, labour in the *inland*, or *upland*, as distinguished from employment in fishing. **1857** HUGHES *Tom Brown* I. i, Leaving their mark in American forests and Australian uplands.

2. An area or stretch of high ground; a piece of high, hilly, or mountainous country. Usually in *pl.*

1566 *Act 8 Eliz.* c. 13 §1 Beakons..in suche Place or Places of the Sea Shores and Uplandes neere the Sea costes. **1589** FLEMINGE *Virg. Eclogues* vi. 18 You the nymphs of woods, Close in the uplands [L. *claudite saltus*] of your woods. **1617** BRATHWAIT *Law of Drinking* 147 Their Long Acres, Uplands and Downe-lands shall flie in a trice to retaine thee. *a* **1676** HALE *Prim. Orig. Man.* II. vii. (1677) 192 The Downs or Uplands of Cammington in Huntingdonshire. *Ibid.* 200 The Up-lands in England yield strong, sinewy, hardy Men. **1724** DE FOE *Tour Gt. Brit.* (1742) I. 9 They generally chose to leave their own Lasses to their Neighbours out of the Marshes, and went into the Uplands for a Wife. **1764** GOLDSM. *Trav.* 107 Its uplands sloping deck the mountain's side. **1787** G. WHITE *Selborne* i, At the foot of this hill, one stage or step from the uplands, lies the village. **1807** J. BARLOW *Columb.* I. 298 How slope their up-lands to the morning sun! **1825–9** MRS. SHERWOOD *Lady of Manor* I. vi. 176 A blue upland in the remotest distance finished this exquisite picture. **1879** FARRAR *St. Paul* I. 414 He was working with Paul alone on the wild uplands of Lycaonia.

b. In sing. with *the*, or without article.

1699 DAMPIER *Voy.* II. II. 111 The whole Country, the Up-land I mean, seems to be much the same [kind of soil]. **1784** COWPER *Task* v. 197 As a shepherd separates his flock, These to the upland, to the valley those. **1813** SCOTT *Rokeby* v. ii, The eve, that slow on upland fades, Has darker closed on Rokeby's glades. **1856** MERIVALE *Rom. Emp.* xxxviii. IV. 359 They had emerged..from the woods, and had gained the open upland of swamp and moor. **1891** T. HARDY *Tess* viii, Their present speed on the upland being by no means slow.

3. High ground, as opposed to meadow or marsh; ground not liable to flooding; a stretch of this. Chiefly *local* and *U.S.*

1572 *Kent & Surrey Sewers Comm.* (1909) 115 Alle the vpp lande betwin Newington and Lambeth Sewinge to the same sluce. **1580** TUSSER *Husb.* (1878) 51 New broken vpland..for wheat is not best. **1598** *Archdeaconry of Essex Minutes* (MS.) fol. 49 Being sessed by the acar..at i[d] the acre of vpland and ii[d] the acre for marshe. **1639** in Coffin *Hist. Newberry, Mass.* (1845) 29 All the upland and meadow and marish between us and Ipswich. **1696** AUBREY *Misc.* 11 This Marsh-land..was never worth one Farthing to me, but very often eat into the Rents of the Up-land. **1708** *Lond. Gaz.* No. 4489/3, 46 Acres of Uplands, or Side-hill-Lands. **1763** *Museum Rust.* I. 307 If it was sowed in up-land,..you could not get the timothy-grass out of it. **1774** GOLDSM. *Nat. Hist.* I. 159 A large upland, with its houses, its corn, and cattle,..loosened from its place. **1833** TENNYSON *Lady of Shalott* I. 34 The reaper weary, Piling sheaves in uplands airy. **1841** N. P. ROGERS in *Whittier's Prose Wks.* (1889) II. 227 The Pemigewasset,..meandering from upland to upland through the meadows.

4. *ellipt.* in *pl.* Upland cotton. (Cf. B. 2 c.)

1858 HOMANS *Cycl. Comm.* 448 Cotton..[exported from] Florida. To foreign ports—Uplands, 30,880 bales. **1880** C. R. MARKHAM *Peruv. Bark* 468 Species of cotton... New Orleans or 'Uplands'... 'Uplands' grown in India.

B. *attrib.* or as *adj.*

1. Of districts or places: Lying away from the sea or in the higher parts of a country; inland, remote.

1575 *Russia* (Hakl. Soc. No. 20) 9 The uplande countries of Russia..stretchethe exceding large and long. **1582** BATMAN *Barth. De P.R.* XVIII. lxxxi. 376/2 The want of tillage..decayes villages, hamlets, and vpland townes. **1601** R. JOHNSON *Kingd. & Commw.* (1603) 14 The vpland townes are fairer and richer, then those that stand nearer the sea. **1632** MILTON *L'Allegro* 92 Som times with secure delight The up-land Hamlets will invite. **1829** SCOTT *Old Mort.* Introd., The little upland village of Balmaclellan, in the Glenkens of Galloway. **1872** A. DE VERE *Leg. St. Patrick* 73 Fire takes the little cot beside the mere, And leaps upon the upland village.

b. Living inland.

1716 B. CHURCH *Hist. Philip's War* (1865) I. 92 Some.. Narraganset Indians, and some other Upland Indians, in all about 300. **1870** BURTON *Hist. Scot.* lxvi. VI. 345 Among the upland folk of Scotland there were strong prejudices against all attempts to settle in distant wilds.

2. Lying higher than the surrounding country; forming part of an elevated area; situated on high ground.

1610 NORDEN *Spec. Brit., Cornw.* (1728) 20 Their haye groweth comonly in the vplande and drye groundes. **1707** MORTIMER *Husb.* 12 The worst of Up-land Meadows is that they often need mending or feeding. **1731** MILLER *Gard. Dict.* s.v. *Ranunculus*, Take a Quantity of fresh Earth from a rich up-land Pasture. **1795** SOUTHEY *Joan of Arc* IX. 292 Dark on the upland bank The hedge-row trees..Rose on the grey horizon. **1843** LYTTON *Last Bar.* I. i. 23 The twin green hills..with the upland park and chase. **1879** A. R. WALLACE *Australasia* ii. 15 These highlands generally present the appearance of hilly upland plains.

b. Living on, or frequenting, high ground. (In modern use freq. in specific names of birds, etc.)

1622 J. TAYLOR (Water P.) *Farewell to Tower Bottles* A 4, When Vpland Trades-men thus dares take in hand A wat'ry buis'nesse, they not vnderstand. **1695** E. GIBSON tr. *Camden's Brit.* 408 Fenmen, a sort of people..of brutish unciviliz'd tempers, envious of all others whom they term Upland men. *a* **1825** [see UPLANDER]. **1859** DARWIN *Orig. Spec.* vi. 185 There are upland geese with webbed feet which rarely or never go near the water. **1867** MORRIS *Jason* IV. 2 The upland sheep Must guard themselves..Against the wolf. **1872** COUES *N. Amer. Birds* 260 Upland Plover. Field Plover. **1878** A. POPE (*title*), Upland Game Birds and Water Fowl of the United States.

c. Growing upon high ground; belonging to species growing or developed on high ground. ***upland cotton***, a class of short-stapled cotton. Also (of minerals, etc.), found on high ground.

1639 T. DE GRAY *Expert Farrier* 309 Fine upland hay, which was cut about midsummer. **1759** MILLER *Gard. Dict.* (ed. 7) s.v. *Pasture*, The best Sort of Upland Hay Seeds, taken from the cleanest Pastures. **1789** T. WRIGHT *Meth. Watering Meadows* (1790) 43 The hay of watered meadows is by no means equal in value to upland hay. **179.** NEMNICH *Polyglot Lex.* s.v., Upland willow. The red willow. **1796** KIRWAN *Elem. Min.* (ed. 2) II. 173 Upland Argillaceous Iron Ore. **1832** MCCULLOCH *Dict. Commerce* 409 The upland or bowed Georgia cotton forms the..best portion of the short stapled class. **1833** G. B. WOOD & BACHE *Dispensatory* (1865) 710 *Rhus glabrum*.., called variously smooth sumach, Pennsylvania sumach, and upland sumach. **1858** HOMANS *Cycl. Comm.* 436/1 The upland cotton is a different species from the sea-island. **1894** *Yellow Book* I. 189 Where the upland hay..stretched thirstily up to the clouds.

d. Flowing down from higher ground.

1653 BLITHE *Eng. Improver Impr.* 56 Cleer from any Land-floods, or up-land waters running through them. **1707** MORTIMER *Husb.* 18 Fenny Lands..drowned by Upland-floods and great Rains.

†**upland**, *adv.*[1] *Obs.* [Later form of *up land*, *uppe lande*, etc.: see UP *prep.*[1] 5 a.] Out in the country: = UPONLAND *adv.*

c **1380** WYCLIF *Wks.* (1880) 176 To..helpe here pore neiȝeboris..& parische chirchis vplond. *c* **1400** *Found. St. Bartholomew's* (1923) 20 Hit ys tolde of a Richemanne vplond dwellyng that come to this Chirche. *c* **1449** PECOCK *Repr.* I. vi. 28 Men of the cuntre vplond bringen into Londoun in Mydsomer eue braunchis of trees..and flouris. **1551** BALE *Eng. Votaries* II. 67 b, In most places they dwelt vplonde.

b. *Jack* (*John*) *Upland*, used as a name for a rustic. (Cf. UPALAND *adv.* b.)

1402 in Wright *Pol. Poems* (Rolls) II. 16, I, Jacke Upland, make my mone to very God. *Ibid.* 40 A frere..aresoneth Jak Uplonde. **1529** LYNDESAY *Compl.* 407 Ihone Upeland bene full blyith, I trow, Because the rysche bus kepis his kow.

upland, *adv.*[2] *rare*⁻¹. [f. UP *prep.*[2] 6 + LAND *sb.*[1]] In the higher or inner part of a country.

a **1674** MILTON *Hist. Moscovia* ii. Wks. 1851 VIII. 483 Further up-land they have also built other Cities of Wood.

'uplander. [f. UPLAND *sb.*[2] Cf. Da. *oplænder.*] An inhabitant or native of an upland part or district.

1699 BOYER, Uplander, *montagnard*. **1706** PHILLIPS (ed. Kersey), *Uplander*, one that lives in the High Grounds; an High-lander. **1773** JOHNSON (ed. 4) s.v. *Upland*, Probably because the uplanders, having less commerce, were less civilised. *a* **1825** FORBY *Voc. E. Anglia* II. 365 *Uplander*, *Uplandman*, an inhabitant of the uplands. **1868** MORRIS *Earthly Par.* I. I. 14 But fifty knew the shipman's gear, The rest were uplanders. **1888** OMAN *Hist. Greece* xi. (1901) 103 These Uplanders occupied the arid hills of the interior.

up'landish, *a.* and *sb.* Also 4–5 **vplondische**, **-isshe**, **-ysche**, **-ysshe**, 6 **vplandis(s)he**, **-ys(s)he**, etc. [f. UPLAND *sb.*[1] and [2] + -ISH. Cf. OE. *uplendisc*, MDa. *oplændisk* 'Swedish' (Da. *oplandsk* uplandish), MSw. *upländsker*, *uplenzsker*, etc. (Sw. *uppländsk*) of Uppland (also = Swedish), Icel. *upplenzkr* of Upplönd in Norway.]

†**1.** Of persons: = UPLAND *a.*[1] 1. *Obs.*

Very common in the 16th c., freq. in the sense of 'rustic, rude, uncultivated, boorish'.

1387 TREVISA *Higden* (Rolls) II. 159 Vplondisshe men [L. *rurales homines*] wil likne hym self to gentil men. **1398** —— *Barth. De P.R.* XIV. xlix. (Tollem. MS.), Of þis name *rus* þe uplondische men haue þat name and ben clepid *rustici*. *c* **1440** *Promp. Parv.* 512/2 Vplondysche mann, *villanus*. **1490** CAXTON *Eneydos* Prol. A ij, This present booke is not for a rude vplondyssh man to laboure therin..but onely for a clerke. **1529** MORE *Dyaloge* IV. Wks. 257/2 Now was thys doctrine in Almaine of the comen vplandishe people.. plesauntly harde. **1542** UDALL *Erasm. Apoph.* 167 The fair flatte truthe, that the uplandyshe or homely and plain clubbes of y[e] countree dooen use. **1592** GREENE *Upst. Courtier* C 1 b, Shamste thou not vplandish vpstart to heare me discourse thy imperfections? **1603** KNOLLES *Hist. Turks* (1621) 155 The Grecians.., especially that rusticall and uplandish companie, began to flie. **1647** WARD *Simple Cobler* 76 An uplandish Rusticke [may speak] more in one word than himselfe..understands.

†**b.** Characteristic of, pertaining to, rustics. *Obs.*

1534 WHITINTON *Tullyes Offices* II. (1540) 113 Glory and fame before rychesse: customes..of cyties before uplandisshe customes. **1565** STAPLETON tr. *Bede's Hist. Ch. Eng.* 147 The vnsemely dwelling and vplandish rudenesse of the inhabitants.

†**c.** Of bees: Wild. *Obs.*⁻¹

1608 TOPSELL *Serpents* 65 Others [*sc.* bees] againe are altogether wilde, vplandish, and agrestiall.

2. Of places: = UPLAND *a.*[2] 1. Now *rare*.

c **1380** WYCLIF *Sel. Wks.* I. 197 No drede Crist wente to smale uplondishe touns, as to Bethfage and to Cana. **1513** *Life Hen. V* (1911) 110 All other were lodged in vplandish cots, such as they coulde finde. **1568** WITHALS *Dict.* 37 b/2 The vplandish house or dwelling place, *villa*, *tugurium*. **1589** PUTTENHAM *Eng. Poesie* III. iv. (Arb.) 157 In any vplandish village or corner of a Realme, where is no resort but of poore rusticall or vnciuill people. **1622** CALLIS *Stat. Sewers* (1647) 66 In Towns and Villages which be in the high uplandish Countries. **1642** *Declar. Lords & Com. Stat.* 5 *Hen. IV*, 4 All such as do lodge strangers in uplandish Towns. [**1784** CULLUM *Hawsted* 220 *note*, These [districts] used to be called *uplandish*, a term that implied an inferiority in civilization.] **1906** GASQUET *Eng. Mediæval Parish Life* ii. 41 A small, uplandish, remote parish..on the borders of Exmoor.

†**3.** Of ground: = UPLAND *a.*[2] 2. *Obs.*

1551 ROBINSON tr. *More's Utopia* II. (1895) 118, xv. myles space of vplandyshe grounde, where the sea had no passage. **1582** STANYHURST *Æneis* III. (Arb.) 88 Then far of vplandish we doe view thee fird Sicil Ætna.

†**b.** = UPLAND *a.*[2] 2 b, 2 c. *Obs.*

1545 ASCHAM *Toxoph.* (Arb.) 128 Whether there be any difference, as concernynge the fether of..a fennye goose, or an vplandish goose. **1623** MARKHAM *Cheap Husb.* (ed. 3) 53 For his hay, you shall see that it be dry short vplandish hay.

†**4.** Outlandish, foreign. Also as *sb.*, foreign speech. *Obs.*

1586 FERNE *Blaz. Gentrie* II. 23 You chop so much vplandish in your tale that by my troth, I scantly vnderstand the halfe of it. **1589** *Rare Tri. Love & Fort.* IV. (Roxb. Cl.) 122 *Bomelio.* You are de runaway from your ma'ter... *Lentulo.* I a runnaway, sirra? goe with your uplandishe, goe. **1607** HEYWOOD *Faire Maide Exch.* E 4, He had..made some scuruy quaint collection Of fustian phrases, and vplandish wordes. **1609** W. M. *Man in Moone* C 3, Natiue apparell will not content him, he flieth for vplandish fashions.

Hence **up'landishness**. *rare*⁻⁰.

1530 PALSGR. 285/2 Uplandysshnesse, *ruralite*.

†**'uplands**, *a.* *Obs.* Chiefly *Sc.* [f. UPLAND *sb.* (either possessive sing. or the plur. used attrib.), or Sc. var. of prec.] = UPLANDISH *a.*

c **1330** *Arth. & Merl.* 5077 (Kölbing), The vplondismen, þat hadden ladde Cartes & somers. *Ibid.* 5271, 6776. **14..** in *Sc. Acts Parlt.* (1814) I. 333 Ilke burges may punde ane unplandis man. *c* **1450** HOLLAND *Howlat* 218 Held he na houss; Bot in wplandis townis..Cryand full crowss. **1500–20** DUNBAR *Poems* xiii. 1 Ane mvrlandis man of vplandis mak. **1585** JAS. I *Ess. Poesie* (Arb.) 63 Gif zour purpose be of landwart effairis, [take heed] To vse corruptit and vplandis wordis.

up'lay, *v.* [UP- 4. Cf. Du. *opleggen*, G. *auflegen*, and UPLAID *pa. pple.* 1.] *trans.* To lay up, store up.

1591 SPENSER *Ruins of Time* 212 All is with him dead, Saue what in heauens storehouse he vplaid. *c* **1600** DONNE *To R. Woodward* 32 We..may, If we can..thrive, uplay Much, much deare treasure for the great rent day. **1609** —— *Annunc. & Passion* 45 This treasure then, in grosse, my Soule uplay. *a* **1850** ROSSETTI *Dante & Circle* I. (1874) 239 As he who evermore uplays That heavenly wealth which the worm cannot waste.

'upleap, *sb.* [UP- 2.]

1. An upward leap or spring.

1876 MISS BROUGHTON *Joan* I. xxxiii, The fire giving one sudden upleap,..plays upon his face. **1885** E. F. BYRRNE *Entangled* III. II. xviii. 140 This upleap of wild regret..was not dependent upon reason.

2. *Mining.* (See quot.)

1883 GRESLEY *Gloss. Coal-m.* 268 *Up-leap*, a fault which appears as an up-throw.

up'leap, *v.* [UP- 4. Cf. OE. *uphléapende* pres. pple. and WFris. *opljeappe*, Du. *oploopen*, MSw. and Sw. *upplöpa*, MDa. and Da. *opløbe*, G. *auflaufen*.] *intr.* To leap or spring up or upwards.

c **1205** LAY. 1882 Ofte heo up lupan [*c* **1275** vp leopen], alse heo fleon wolden. *a* **1300** *Cursor M.* 5193 Israel wit þis vp-lepp þat moght noght forwit strid a step. *c* **1350** *Will. Palerne* 3283 þe stede..vp-leped, & faire wiþ his fore fet kneled doun to grounde. *a* **1560** PHAER *Æneid* IX. (1562) F fi, The wyld seas meeting mixe, and darkning skyes vpleapes ye sands. **1600** FAIRFAX *Tasso* III. xlix, But now Rinaldo from the earth vp lept. **1805** WORDSW. *Prelude* v. 441 And, now and then, a fish up-leaping snapped The breathless stillness. **1888** R. BUCHANAN *City of Dream* VIII. 152 The sable steed upleapt And bounded on.

up'leaping *vbl. sb.* and *ppl. a.* (UP- 6 and 7.)
1867 'OUIDA' *Idalia* xxxiii, A sudden upleaping of the vivid life within him. **1885–94** R. BRIDGES *Eros & Psyche* Dec. xxvi, Its little rill is an upleaping jet Of cold Cocytus.

upled, -lent: see UP- 5.

'uplift, *sb.* [UP- 2. Cf. next.]
1. a. The fact of being raised or elevated.
a **1845** WILLIS *David's Grief for Child* 28 His brow Had the inspired up-lift of the king's. **1890** STANLEY *Darkest Africa* I. xvi. 413 There was uniform uplift and subsidence of the constantly twirling spear blades.
b. *spec.* An elevation or rise in level, esp. of a portion of the earth's surface.
1853 KANE *Grinnell Exp.* xvii. (1856) 128 The false horizon, which I had selected as an index of the uplift. **1856** —— *Arct. Expl.* II. vii. 82 Indicative of secular uplift of coast. **1878** WHITTIER *Seeking Waterfall* xix, The grand uplift of mountain lines. **1882** *U.S. Rep. Prec. Met.* 619 The assumption of an uplift or elevation of the Sierra Nevada.
2. *fig.* An elevating effect, result, or influence in the sphere of morality, emotion, physical condition, etc.
In very common use after 1890.
1873 HOLLAND *A. Bonnic.* i. 22 But it is impossible that he could know what an uplift he gave to the life to which he ministered. **1885** E. F. BYRRNE *Entangled* II. II. viii. 255 The uplift of the heart..towards a sterner and more austere allegiance to duty. **1889** *Lancet* 28 Sept. 661/1 The rapidity of the uplift in health in many of the cases. **1893** K. L. BATES *Eng. Relig. Drama* 195 The uplift and the glory of conception melted and were gone.
3. The support or lift gained from a garment that raises part of the body, esp. the bust; the (part of the) garment which achieves this.
1929 *Radio Times* 8 Nov. 435/3 A supporting stocking... Its gentle uplift massaging action has a beneficial effect upon the varicose veins. **1934** *Times* 22 June 17/6 The skirt covers neatly fitting trunks and clings closely to the figure; the top has a knitted uplift. **1955** J. P. DONLEAVY *Ginger Man* xxv. 297 Bras the uplift of which will put a new lust into the hearts of these citizens. **1957** *Daily Mail* 25 Oct. 10/4 When the vulgarity of too much uplift, too much emphasis on the female form finally overwhelmed us Dior sensed it before we did. **1959** *Housewife* June 22 The bra that gives a natural uplift.
4. An increase (in prices, wages, etc.).
1949 *Times* 26 Oct. 5/5 The whole conception of uplift.. assumes that the manufacturer of consumer goods has..two prices, one for sales to the wholesaler and one for direct sale to the retailer. **1952** *Sunday Express* 15 Nov., These appliances are given an uplift of 100% between the maker and the public. **1955** *Canadian Tax Jrnl.* III. 99 If the price of the transaction differed [from normal]..an uplift would be applied to the actual sale price to determine price for tax purposes. **1962** E. GODFREY *Retail Selling & Organization* xv. 158 If goods normally purchased through a wholesaler are bought at a lower price direct from a manufacturer, they may be subject to uplift. **1979** *Daily Tel.* 1 Dec. 21 The Ford agreement..consists of a 20·5 p.c. uplift in wages plus an extra 1 p.c. to cover an increase in the supplementary payment.
5. *attrib.* **a.** In sense 2.
1915 *Sphere* 23 Jan. 110/2, I find in an American paper a scornful reference to one of the 'uplift' magazines. **1930** J. BUCHAN *Castle Gay* ii. 32 Thomas was beginning to be much in request by uplift societies. **1940** R. S. LAMBERT *Ariel & all his Quality* ii. 50 The 'uplift' experiment..fell between.. the professors of adult education..and the broadcasting experts. **1977** P. JOHNSON *Enemies of Society* ix. 122 Schneider and Dornbusch identified four common characteristics in the religion idealized in these uplift books: activism, optimism, individualism and pragmatism.
b. uplift bra(ssière), a brassière that provides uplift (sense 3 above).
1932 *Week-End Rev.* 1 Oct. 373/1 An 'up-lift' brassière would make you look rounder, of course. **1949** M. MEAD *Male & Female* iv. 80 Far enough removed from the up-lift bras and the way Grandfather looks when Grand-daughter wears one of them. **1957** J. D. MACDONALD *Executioners* (1959) vii. 134 She wore nothing under pants and blouse except an uplift bra. **1977** E. J. TRIMMER et al. *Visual Dict. Sex* (1978) iv. 51 The flavour of that era of uplift bras and pencil-skirts is still nostalgically preserved.

up'lift, *v.* [UP- 4. Cf. MSw. *uplypta, -lyfta*, etc. (Sw. *upplyfta*), MDa. *oplyfte* (Da. *opløfte*), and UPLIFT(ED *pa. pples.*]
1. a. *trans.* To elevate in rank, honour, estate, or estimation. Also *absol.* Now *rare*.
1338 R. BRUNNE *Chron.* (1810) 72 þe Londreis..Him for þai kyng vplift, his name was kald Edgar. *a* **1340** HAMPOLE *Psalter*, etc. 501 Lord makis pore and he makis riche: he mekis and he vpliftis. **1390** GOWER *Conf.* I. 27 Alisaundre put hem under,..So that the Monarchie lefte With Grecs, and here astat uplefte. **1554–9** *Songs & Ball. Phil. & Mary* (Roxb.) 3 For of balefull branches and fyere brandes of hel To be members of mersye he hathe us up lyfft. **1611** SHAKS. *Cymb.* v. iv. 103 Your low-laide Sonne, our Godhead will vplift. **1860** PUSEY *Minor Prophets* 593/1 He uplifts ordinary things, that they too should be sacred. **1863** KINGLAKE *Crimea* I. p. x, That which will uplift the repute of the far-famed Russian infantry.
†**b.** To support, assist. *Obs.*⁻¹
1338 R. BRUNNE *Chron.* (1810) 55 þei said he did inouh, þe erle alle vplift, þe kyng forgaf his wraþe.
c. *Sc.* To make proud. (Cf. UPLIFTED *ppl. a.* 3.)
1863 JEAN L. WATSON *By-gone Days* 176 Though she was sae bonny, that never seemed to uplift her.
d. To elevate morally. (Cf. UPLIFTED *ppl. a.* 2.)
1883 FAIRBAIRN *Stud. Relig. & Theol.* (1910) 94 The regeneration that changes the man and uplifts the life. **1890** J. PULSFORD *Loyalty to Christ* I. 53 That He may be able to uplift and bless men.
2. To lift up to a higher level or more erect position; to raise, rear, erect.
a **1340** HAMPOLE *Psalter* ci. 11 Vpliftand þou downsmate me. **1390** GOWER *Conf.* I. 48, I uplifte Min hefd with that. *a* **1400–50** *Alexander* 805 þen Alexander in ane ire his arme vp-liftis. *c* **1440** *Ipomydon* 1911 Hys swerd in bothe handis he toke..And hertely be dyd it vplyfte. **1582** STANYHURST *Æneis* IV. (Arb.) 102 Theese woords, vplifting both his hands, he toe Iuppiter vttred. **1590** SPENSER *F.Q.* II. i. 46 The gentle knight her soone with carefull paine Vplifted light, and softly did vphold. **1606** SHAKS. *Ant. & Cl.* v. ii. 211 Slaues..shall vplift vs to the view. **1667** MILTON *P.L.* VI. 646 They pluckt the seated Hills.., and by the shaggie tops Up lifting bore them in thir hands. **1757** DYER *Fleece* II. 234 Soon..the huge stone Up-lifting to the deck, [they] unmoor'd the bark. **1784** COWPER *Task* IV. 274 The glowing hearth..With faint illumination, that uplifts The shadow to the ceiling. **1820** SHELLEY *Prometh. Unb.* I. 159 At thy voice her pining sons uplifted Their prostrate brows. **1846** HAWTHORNE *Mosses* I. i. 7 The boy uplifted his axe. **1887** *Spectator* 7 May 626/1 Some internal force has up-lifted the earth's crust along a certain line.
Fig. **1594** SPENSER *Amoretti* lxxxii, I..shall all be spent, in setting your immortall prayses forth. Whose lofty argument vplifting me, shall lift you vp vnto an high degree. **1846** MANGAN *Poems* (1903) 24 On thy knees Uplift thy soul to God alone.
3. a. *Sc.* To collect, levy (rents, etc.); to draw (wages).
1508 *Reg. Privy Seal Scot.* I. 256/2 The males, proffitis and dewiteis to rais, uplift and inbring. **1553** *Reg. Privy Council Scot.* I. 139 Under the pane of xl lib., to be upliftit and takin of every Provest. **1617** *Extr. Aberd. Reg.* (1848) II. 354 Vnder the paines following, to be vplifted of the contravenar as oft as they be..convict. **1646** Z. BOYD in *Zion's Flowers* (1855) App. 31/1, I..give the..Colledge full power to uplift the same. **1710** in *Nairne Peerage Evid.* (1874) 44 Since we have uplifted two thousand of the three thousand merks due to him. **1753** *Stewart's Trial* 250 That Glenure..had employed him to uplift the rents from the other tenants. **1869** *Act 32 & 33 Vict.* c. 116 §7 A power.. to enter..the lands disponed in security, and uplift the rents thereof. **1895** CROCKETT *Cleg Kelly* xii, He endeavoured to uplift his week's wage before it was due.
b. More generally, to collect or pick up (something other than money); *spec.* of a bus: to take up (passengers). Chiefly *Sc.*
1961 *Alexander's (Midland) Bus Timetable, Falkirk* 171 Only passengers who are travelling beyond Milngavie Cross will be uplifted between Glasgow (Buchanan Street) and Milngavie Cross. **1967** E. RUDINGER *Wills & Probate* 109 The court is asked to confirm that the executors who have sworn the inventory are the persons entitled to up-lift and administer the various items of estate listed in the inventory. **1968** 'S. JAY' *Sleepers can Kill* xvii. 175 Somebody..has left a message for Felson. The objective is to uplift the message without being detected. **1976** *Buses* XXVII. 421 Near-empty SBG buses, none allowed to uplift potential passengers, glide into town. **1982** G. HAMMOND *Game* xii. 129 The letter was waiting at the airport for him. I checked up yesterday, and the letter was uplifted.
4. a. = RAISE *v.* 13.
1816 SCOTT *Bl. Dwarf* xiii, When he first uplifted the psalm in presence of those persons. **1847** EMERSON *Dæmonic & Celest. Love* 26 New flowerets bring, new prayers uplift. *a* **1850** BRYANT *Earth* 43 Earth Uplifts a general cry for guilt and wrong. **1887** BOWEN *Æneid* VI. 174 All now..uplift their voices in grief.
b. = RAISE *v.*[1] 34. Cf. sense 4 of the sb.
1962 E. GODFREY *Retail Selling & Organization* xv. 158 The Inland Revenue Department uplifts the price to what the goods would have cost had they been purchased through a wholesaler. **1971** *Timber Trades Jrnl.* 14 Aug. 45/2 Devaluation of sterling..technically should have had the effect of uplifting import prices by 16·7%.

up'lift, *pa. pple.* and *ppl. a.* [UP- 5. See LIFT *v.*] = UPLIFTED.
1303 R. BRUNNE *Handl. Synne* 7086 Almes..ys a ȝyfte; And for þe ȝyuyng, man ys vplyfte. **13..** *E.E. Allit. P.* B. 987 Wyth lyȝt louez vplyfte þay loued hym swyþe. **1667** MILTON *P.L.* I. 193 Satan talking to his neerest Mate With Head up-lift above the wave. **1748** RICHARDSON *Clarissa* VI. 63 How many..admirers, with up-lift hands, I should have! *a* **1822** SHELLEY *Fragm. Unf. Drama* 239 O friend, sleep was a veil uplift from Heaven. **1841** KINGSLEY *Palinodia* 2 Torrent-furrowed slopes, And bare and silent brows uplift to heaven. **1868** GEO. ELIOT *Sp. Gipsy* I. 60 A figure lithe, ..now stood With ripened arms uplift and regal head.

up'liftable, *a.* *Sc. rare*⁻¹. [f. UPLIFT *v.* 3.] Leviable.
1670 in Paterson *Hist. Regality Musselburgh* (1857) 26 An annual rent of 2400 merk upliftable furth of the said toun.

up'lifted, *pa. pple.* and *ppl. a.* [UP- 5. Cf. UPLIFT *v.* and *pa. pple.*]
1. Raised, elevated, held up; also *fig.*, exalted in estate.
a **1300** *E.E. Psalter* xxxvi. 37 Vphouen I saw þe wicked man And lifted [*H.* uplifted; L. *elevatum*] als cedre of Yban. *Ibid.* lxxxvii. 16, I am up-lifted [L. *exaltatus*], I am meked. *c* **1410** *Lanterne of Liȝt* 129, I haue sen þe vnpitiouse.. enhaunsid & vplifted as þe cedre trees of Liban. **1593** SHAKS. *Rich. II*, II. ii. 50 The banish'd Bullingbrocke..with vp-lifted Armes is safe arriu'd At Rauenspurg. **1630** MILTON *Solemn Music* 11 Where the bright Seraphim..Their loud up-lifted Angel trumpets blow. **1667** —— *P.L.* I. 347 Th' uplifted Spear Of their great Sultan waving to direct Thir course. **1725** POPE *Odyss.* II. 424 The matron with uplifted eyes Attests th' all-seeing Sovereign of the skies. **1748** RICHARDSON *Clarissa* VII. 125 This dame in effigie, with uplifted head and hand. **1822** SCOTT *Nigel* xiv, 'Now, Heaven bless you, my lord,' said Richie Moniplies, with uplifted eyes. **1868** *Rep. U.S. Commissioner Agric.* (1869) 225 These table-lands..are the uplifted beds of an ancient ocean. **1887** BOWEN *Æneid* IV. 246 The uplifted crest and the proud Slopes of the age-worn Atlas.
fig. **1595** SPENSER *Col. Clout* 816 So we him adore With humble hearts to heauen vplifted hie. **1805** WORDSW. *Prelude* v. 226 Yet I..will pour out Thanks with uplifted heart.
b. Exalted in fame; renowned.
1596 SPENSER *F.Q.* VI. Prol. vi, Yet so from low to high vplifted is your name. **1885** TENNYSON *Balin & Balan* 491 A name..Which our high Lancelot hath so lifted up, And been thereby uplifted.
2. Elevated intellectually, morally, or spiritually.
c **1454** PECOCK *Folewer* 15 þe more a man..takiþ into him of kunnyng, þe more is his resoun vp liftid. **1548** GESTE *Pr. Masse* H ij b, With our myndes eleuate and vplifted. **1818** SHELLEY *Eugan. Hills* 360 The winds whose wings rain balm On the uplifted soul. **1839** BAILEY *Festus* 46 Are they not worthy of a deathless state; A boundless scope; a high uplifted life? **1890** J. PULSFORD *Loyalty to Christ* I. 116 Ye gladdened and uplifted ones, come ye aside also awhile with Jesus.
3. Elated; rendered proud. Now *Sc.* and *north. dial.*
1606 SHAKS. *Tr. & Cr.* III. ii. 175 Or that perswasion could but thus conuince me,..How were I then vp-lifted. **1747** *Mem. Nutrebian Crt.* II. 82 Maillan, excessively up-lifted with the imagined advancement of his daughter. **1823** SCOTT *Quentin D.* xvi, He said, that..they were uplifted in heart because of their wealth and their privileges. **1897** W. BEATTY *Secretar* xli, Being so uplifted at the part I was like to play.
4. Raised in utterance.
1828 ATHERSTONE *Fall of Nineveh* I. 114 Them..with proud uplifted voice, Thus Azareel bespake. **1863** MISS BRADDON *Aurora Floyd* xiii, Did the unlucky speculators.. hide themselves while the uplifted voices were rejoicing?
Hence **up'liftedness**.
1893 *Scribner's Mag.* Sept. 387/1, I hate the coldness and upliftedness of religion.

up'lifter. [f. UPLIFT *v.*]
†**1.** *Sc.* A collector (of rents, etc.). *Obs.*
1585–6 *Reg. Privy Council Scot.* IV. 47 The upliftaris of the said taxt. **1641** *Kirkcudbr. War-Comm. Min. Bk.* (1855) 159 He hes constituted the said James Montgomerie uplifter thairof [*sc.* of the king's rents].
2. One who raises or elevates.
1650 *Metr. Psalms Ch. Scot.* iii. 3 Yet thou my shield, and glory art, th' uplifter of mine head. **1884** TENNYSON *Becket* I. i, Henry the King hath been..mine uplifter in this world. **1890** J. PULSFORD *Loyalty to Christ* I. 57 Henceforth he should be a man of influence, and a great uplifter of men.
3. *N. Amer.* One engaged in social reform; a 'do-gooder'.
1923 [see DO-GOOD]. **1935** S. LEWIS *It can't happen Here* xvii. 191 Social workers, both amateurs and long-trained professional uplifters. **1971** J. H. GRAY *Red Lights on Prairies* iv. 97 As the publisher of the paper explained when uplifters complained..it was no part of the responsibility of a newspaper to police the morals of its tenants.

up'lifting, *vbl. sb.* [UP- 7, or f. UPLIFT *v.*]
1. The action of raising or lifting up; an instance of this. Also *fig.*
1548 GESTE *Pr. Masse* H iv, Can ther be made to god..an effectual prayer withoute an vplyftinge of oure hartes vnto hym? **1650** *Metr. Psalms Ch. Scot.* cxli. 2 Let..the uplifting of my hands [be] as th' evening sacrifice. **1834** *Tait's Mag.* I. 693/1 An uplifting of the horse's hind heels. **1844** KINGLAKE *Eothen* xv, There was an uplifting of arms, and a repeating of words. **1886** HALL CAINE *Son of Hagar* I. v, With an eloquent uplifting of the hand.
b. *Geol.* Elevation in level; an upheaval.
1833–4 J. PHILLIPS *Geol.* in *Encycl. Metrop.* (1845) VI. 685/2 The uplifting of the Western Alps. **1855** *Orr's Circ. Sci., Inorg. Nat.* 51 The uplifting and dislocation of strata. **1881** *Q. Rev.* July 102 Upliftings and downcasts of strata.
2. *Sc.* Collection, levying (of rents, etc.).
1594 in *Spalding Club Misc.* I. 9 All receaving vplifting vptacking or intrometting with off ony maillis. **1640** *Kirkcudbr. War-Comm. Min. Bk.* (1855) 128 Unless your lordship caus hasten the uplifting and peyment of all that is dew. **1706** in J. J. Vernon *Parish of Hawick* (1900) 201 Collectors for the uplifting and inbringing of the stent.
3. The action of the verb, in various senses.
1824 SCOTT *Redgauntlet* ch. xii, There was heard within the uplifting of a Scottish psalm. **1826** —— *Woodst.* v, A crowning mercy—a vouchsafing—an uplifting. **1899** A. C. BENSON *Life E. W. Benson* II. 232 They excluded a source of sacred pleasure and divine uplifting from their lives.

up'lifting, *ppl. a.* [UP- 6 b. Cf. UPLIFT *v.*] That uplifts or elevates. Chiefly *fig.*
1818 SHELLEY *Homer's Hymn Sun* 20 The light vest.. Glows in the stream of the uplifting wind. **1881** [see UPLOOKING]. **1889** E. W. BENSON in *Life* (1899) II. 290 A friendship..of which every hour was uplifting. **1896** in *Daily News* 24 Feb. 3/3 To-day it [*sc.* the Salvation Army] is one of the greatest uplifting forces in the country.

up'liftment. Chiefly *Black* and *Indian English*. [f. UPLIFT *v.* + -MENT: see UP- 2.] The action or process of improving or raising to a new standard; *spec.* amelioration of economic or social conditions; the result of this.
1926 *Brit. Weekly* 15 Apr. 46/3 Native women of the educated class might be potent influences in the upliftment and betterment of their people. **1973** *Caribbean Contact* Feb. 11/3 A company of West Indians formed for the

economic upliftment of the people of the region. **1976** *Nigerian Chron.* 18 Aug. 12/2 Mr Onette congratulated the people of Osomba..for their initiative towards educational up-liftment in their community. **1979** P. NIHALANI et al. *Indian & Brit. Eng.* I. 187 The upliftment of the rural areas should be a top priority for the government. **1984** *Times* 25 Aug. 5/2 His immediate priorities would be the economic and educational upliftment of his people.

ˈuplight. [UP- 2.] = next.
1982 *Program 1982/83* (Erco trade catal.) 56 Up-lights are the free-standing version of downlights. They illuminate the ceiling. **1983** *Homes & Gardens* Mar. 92/2 We decided to have uplights to cast light on to the fabric.

ˈuplighter. [UP- 2.] A light placed or designed to throw illumination upward.
1969 *Queen* 17–30 Sept. 96/2 Rotaflex uplighters in plain black cans, shining on, say, a picture. **1974** *Habitat Catal.* 116/1 Uplighter..to stand on the floor or a low table to light a strategically placed plant or shapely object. **1978** J. KRANTZ *Scruples* iii. 67 He installed three ten-foot-tall Kentia palms he got wholesale at Kind's, lit them from underneath with uplighters. **1983** *Homes & Gardens* Nov. 137 Best lighting for watching television comes from an uplighter placed behind the set; it cuts down glare and avoids reflections on the screen.

ˈuplink. [UP- 2.] A communication link for transmissions from the earth to a satellite, weather balloon, etc. Freq. *attrib.*
1968 W. M. GRIGGS *AMSS Prototype Radiosonde* (Rep. AD-680-409) 4 The radiosonde is designed to perform two functions... As a transponder, it must receive the uplink range tones. **1975** *Sci. Amer.* June 127/1 Since its launch in late 1972 it has offered a repeater service open to all, with an uplink at two meters and a downlink at 10. **1982** *New Scientist* 9 Sept. 682/1 These 'uplink' signals are at frequencies between 5·9 and 6·4 gigahertz.

upˈlock, *v.* [UP- 4 + LOCK *v.*¹] *trans.* To lock up.
1600 FAIRFAX *Tasso* XIX. xxxix, Come, come,..Thy selfe within this fortresse safe vplocke. **1611** R. BADLEY *Panegyr. Verses* in Coryat *Crudities*, Thy bitter journey..Deserv'd the sweetest wines Piemont up-locks. **1689** in Law *Hampton Court Pal.* (1891) III. 9 Then Benting up-locks His King in a box.

upˈlocked, *ppl. a.* (UP- 5. Cf. prec.)
c **1600** SHAKS. *Sonn.* lii, So am I as the rich whose blessed key, Can bring him to his sweet vp-locked treasure.

ˈuplong, *prep.*, *sb.*, and *a.* [UP *adv.* + *long* ALONG *prep.* and *adv.*] **A.** *prep.* Up along.
1762 FALCONER *Shipwr.* I. 198 Uplong the slipp'ry Masts the Yards ascend.
B. *sb.* A strengthening bar extending along the sail of a windmill.
1819 REES *Cycl.* s.v. *Windmill*, There ought to be three uplongs..to the driving, and two to the leading side,..to strengthen the lattice. **1892** P. H. EMERSON *Son of Fens* xxxii. 356 That uplong have got loose.
C. *adj.* Extending upwards.
1875 MORRIS *Æneid* IX. 244 In daily hunt, whereby we learned the river's uplong brim.

ˈuplook, *sb.* [UP- 2.] An upward look or glance.
1836 T. POWER *Impressions of Amer.* II. 235 The Virginian, tall of stature,..with an open up-look. **1869** RUSKIN *Q. of Air* §135 To all true modesty the necessary business is not inlook, but outlook, and especially *up*look. **1888** FLO. WARDEN *Woman's Face* II. xv. 112 Giving her a very straight uplook into the eyes.

upˈlook, *v.* (UP- 4. Cf. UPLOOKING *pres. pple.*)
a **1300** *Cursor M.* 1820 Noe..fined noþeir night ne day For þat caitiue folk to prai,..Bot durst he neuer wel [*Gött.* wid eie] vp-lok. **1596** SPENSER *F.Q.* VI. iii. 11 The morrow next, when day gan to vplooke, He also gan vplooke with drery eye. **1818** MILMAN *Samor* VII. 840 But not as wont, uplooks he to the sky.

upˈlooker. (UP- 8.)
1581 MARBECK *Bk. of Notes* 661 Which thing the Greeks noted by the name of a man, calling him *Anthropos*, an vp-looker. **1895** *Expositor* April 260 Prayers that had long been flashed from the souls of these up-lookers.

upˈlooking, *pres. pple.* and *ppl. a.* (UP- 6, 6 b.)
a **1340** HAMPOLE *Psalter*, etc. 497 Thynnyd ere myn eghyn ..vplokand [L. *suspicientes*] in heghe. **1805** WORDSW. *Prel.* VI. 86 Often have I stood Foot-bound uplooking at this lovely tree. **1838** MRS. BROWNING *Cowper's Grave* vii, Wild timid hares..Uplooking to his human eyes with sylvan tendernesses. **1881** J. MARTINEAU *Ess. & Addr.* (1891) IV. 306 Two minds present with each other in uplooking and uplifting attitude.

†**upˈloper.** *Obs.* [ad. Du. *oplooper*, f. *oploopen* to leap up: see UPLEAP *v.*] A variety of pigeon resembling a pouter.
1735 J. MOORE *Columbarium* 36 To trip beautifully with his Feet..without Jumping, which is the Quality of an Uploper. **1765** *Treat. Dom. Pigeons* 104 When it approacheth the hen, [it] generally leaps to her with its tail spread, which is the reason of its being called Uploper.

ˈupˌlying, *ppl. a.* [UP- 6 b.] Situated or lying on elevated ground; upland.
1877 *Scribner's Mag.* Aug. 479/2 The favourite haunt of the wild strawberry is an up-lying meadow. **1884** *Nature* 25 Sept. 530/1 In up-lying situations,..fluxion-structures are seldom detected.

upmaist, Sc. var. UPMOST *a.*

upˈmake, *v.* *Sc.* [UP- 4 + MAKE *v.*¹ Cf. older Flem. *opmaecken*, Du. *opmaken* to use up, put up, etc., LG. *upmaken*, G. *aufmachen* to put up, etc.]
1. *trans.* To make up for (a defect or lack); to supply or fill up where there is a deficiency.
1485 *Sc. Acts Parlt., Jas. III* (1814) II. 172/1 Þe werk to be brokin, the werkman to vpmak þe avale to þe finace foresaid. **1526** *Extr. Aberd. Reg.* (1844) I. 114 To cloise the tovnn, and bred the portis of the same, and oupmak all wydis and waistis.
2. To construct, build.
1507 *Extr. Aberd. Reg.* (1844) I. 77 [He] sale..big, oupmak,..and complet the xxxiiij stallis in thar queir.

ˈupˌmaking, *vbl. sb.* [UP- 7.]
1. *Sc.* The action of making up, in various senses.
1513 *Extr. Aberd. Reg.* (1844) I. 84 The biggin and vpmakin of thar blokhouse for thair artailzerie. **1681** R. FLEMING *Fulfilling Script.* (ed. 3) 64 When they..compared their gain with their losse, their upmaking with these dayes of trial. *Ibid.* 71 They have therein found a very sensible upmaking. **1856** *Morton's Cycl. Agric.* II. 620/1 The average cost..did not exceed 15*s.* per acre.., with all necessary upmaking. **1897** MRS. OLIPHANT *W. Blackwood* II. xxii. 409 A sheet was often left for him in the 'upmaking' till the last possible moment.
2. *Shipbuilding.* (See quot. 1846.)
1846 A. YOUNG *Naut. Dict.* 357 *Upmaking*,..pieces of plank or timber piled on each other as a filling up; more especially those placed between the bilge-coads and the ship's bottom, preparatory to launching. **1883** *Scotsman* 11 July 5/2 The upmaking never showed any signs of giving way until the vessel was well clear of the standing ways.

ˈupˌmaking, *ppl. a.* *Sc.* [UP- 6 b.]
1. That makes up for a defect or lack.
1682 R. HAMILTON in M. Shields *Faithful Contendings* (1780) 40, I have found my Lord..ay the same up making, (and more than up making) portion. **1726** WODROW *Corr.* (1843) III. 269 May he, by his Spirit, be assisting, comforting, and upmaking to you! **1729** E. ERSKINE *Serm.* (1791) 336/1 Rest in him, and upon him, as our upmaking and everlasting all. [**1852** *Chr. Treasury* 405/2 God..is an upmaking portion;..he can supply the place of all things.]
2. Seeking acquaintance or intimacy.
1863 MRS. CARLYLE *Lett.* (1882) III. 166 They were very ..'up-making' to me, and pressed me to visit them.

Upmann (ˈʌpmən). The proprietary name of a make of (Havana) cigar.
[**1878** *Trade Marks Jrnl.* 16 Jan. 59 H. Upmann... Henry Upmann and William Rocholl, trading as H. Upmann and Co., Havana, Cuba; cigar manufacturers. Manufactured tobacco, cigars. **1912** *Official Gaz.* (U.S. Patent Office) 15 Oct. 770/1 H. Upmann & Co., Habana, Cuba... Cigars.] **1969** N. FREELING *Tsing-Boum* xxi. 148 He..had a cigar going, an Upmann that could have been made of tightly-rolled hundred-franc notes. **1979** A. SCHOLEFIELD *Point of Honour* 142 He was dispensing Upmanns from a humidor.

ˈupmanship. *colloq.* = *one-upmanship* s.v. ONE *numeral a.*, *pron.*, etc. 30 c.
1962 *Spectator* 23 Nov. 837/2 (Advt.), Upmanship is the art of being one up on all the others. **1967** *Ibid.* 25 Aug. 212/2 He obviously thought I was trying upmanship on him before that word had been invented. **1976** *Casper* (Wyoming) *Star-Tribune* 29 June 19/1 (*caption*) Hospital upmanship: My Doc' is better'n yours! **1980** *Brit. Med. Jrnl.* 6 Sept. 666/1 In a moment of inspired upmanship this young moonlighting casualty officer had quietly dropped the word that he was a famous specialist in exotic diseases.

ˈup-market, *a.* and *adv.* Also (esp. *adv.*) **up-ˈmarket.** [UP *prep.*²] **A.** *adj.*
1. Of merchandise, etc.: characteristic of or designed for the more expensive end of the market; superior, expensive, 'quality'.
1972 *Times* 28 June 14/4 Glass has still, apparently, a more up-market image than plastic. **1974** *Daily Tel.* 17 Sept. 6 An 'up-market' £1,950 version of the Austin Allegro, hand-finished by the Vanden Plas coachbuilders. **1976** *Daily Mail* (Hull) 30 Sept. 18/3 Sarila Kitchens are the ultimate in luxury and design. Naturally, they are also up-market in price. **1980** *National Times* (Austral.) 24 Aug. 4/3 Franchised lines, apart from the usual T-shirts, badges, posters and dolls run up to a range of $200 couturier ensembles and an upmarket line of cosmetics.
2. *transf.* and *fig.*
1976 *Listener* 6 May 584/1, I cannot allow other people to have all the most up-market remarks. **1979** *Early Music* Jan. Suppl. 13/3 Trust House Forte's up-market evenings..are presenting several early music groups in 1979. **1981** *Times Lit. Suppl.* 30 Jan. 117/5 Linguistic shamanism is respected, for there have been some distinguished practitioners. Sir Ernest Gowers was an up-market shaman. So was H. W. Fowler.
B. *adv.* Towards the more expensive end of the market. Also *transf.* and *fig.*
1975 *Daily Tel.* 12 Apr. 12/4 Lyons-Tetley go up-market a bit with their Red Label and Orange Label [tea]. **1978** *South China Morning Post* 24 Nov. 14/7 Protectionism will increase in European Common Market countries so that Hongkong will have to diversify upmarket. **1980** *Times Lit. Suppl.* 24 Oct. 1206/2 Even the secessionist New English Art Club moved up-market to become a nursery for the Academy, with its paintings of..the pleasing and the picturesque. **1983** *Daily Tel.* 14 Mar. 11/8 Slightly upmarket of the rest of the channel's evening fare, *Omnibus* (BBC-1) has settled for an Everyman figure..as presenter. **1984** W. GOLDING *Paper Men* xi. 125 To contemplate the nature of predestinate insects or, moving up-market, Lobsters and crabs.
Also as *v. trans.*, to raise the standing of (a product) in the market, esp. by advertisement or actual improvement. Hence **up-ˈmarketing** *vbl. sb.*
1972 *Times* 25 Aug. 7 Mathew Clark wants to upmarket Noilly Dry French, plugging heavily the drink's provenance compared with that of Italian Martini and Cinzano. **1975** *Listener* 4 Dec. 735/3 Leyland..decided the group's future lay in..improving its cars and charging more for them... It would take a lot of up-marketing to keep it [*sc.* Leyland] at even half its present size. **1977** *Daily Mirror* 21 Mar. 12/2 The British Sausage Bureau, in short, is trying to up-market its succulent product. **1980** *Times Lit. Suppl.* 19 Sept. 1030/4 In 1819 Harris, now joined by his son, sensed the way trade was going and boldly up-marketed his nursery books still further.

upˈmet, *pa. pple.* (UP- 5 + *met* METE *v.* Cf. UPHEAPED *pa. pple.*)
1828 CARR *Craven Gloss.*, *Up-met*, filled above the measure... Hence, the expression 'up-met and down throsten,' excellent measure... Also, 'he's a rogue, up-met and down throsten;' i.e. a complete villain.

ˈupmost, *a.* Also *Sc.* 6 vpmest, 6–9 upmaist. [f. UP *adv.*² + -MOST.]
1. = UPPERMOST *a.* (in various senses).
1560 BIBLE (Genev.) *Isaiah* xvii. 6 Two or thre beries are in the top of the vpmoste boughs. **1567** DRANT *Horace, Ep.* To Rdr. *iv, He that woulde come to the vpmoste top of an highe hill. **1599** T. M[OUFET] *Silkwormes* 62 That which lies vpmost is of least renowne. **1632** LITHGOW *Trav.* IX. 391 Sulphure streames, which haue burst forth from the vpmost tops of Ætna. *Ibid.* 418 Podalia, the vpmost Countrey of Polland. **1664** EVELYN *Kal. Hort.* 75 Taking away some of the upmost exhausted earth, and stirring up the rest. **1715** LEONI *Palladio's Archit.* (1721) II. 16 The middle of the upmost Wall ought to be perpendicular with the middle of the nethermost. **1808** SCOTT *Let. to Sharpe* 30 Dec. in *Lockhart*, You have..been upmost in my thoughts for some time past. **1859** GULLICK & TIMBS *Paint.* 163 The upmost flat surface is divided into nine compartments. **1875** LIGHTFOOT *Comm. Col.* 411/1 What was the thought upmost in the Apostle's mind..?
b. *absol.* or as *sb.*
1589 FLEMING *Virg. Georg.* III. 43 Let him skarse set his feet vpon th' upmost [*note* The superfie or vppermost part] of the sand.
†**2.** *Sc.* = UMEST *a.* 1. *Obs.*
1592 *Lyndesay's Wks.* 134–5 The Vicar..will nocht faill to tak ane kow, And vpmaist claith. **1609** SKENE *Reg. Maj.*, *Stat. Will.* 11 The forestar sall take..his vpmaist claith. **1620** *Henry's Wallace* x. i. 229 Wallace in haste gart take their upmost weed.

upˈmount, *v.* (UP- 4.)
a **1560** PHAER *Æneid* IX. (1562) Ee iv b, A clamorous noise vpmounts on fortres tops.

upˈmounted, *pa. pple.* (UP- 5.)
1616 J. LANE *Contn. Sqr.'s T.* VII. 487 Vpmounted are the greate Artilerie, on owne huge-iron-carriages. **1818** KEATS *Endym.* I. 642, I felt upmounted in that region Where falling stars dart their artillery forth.

upˈmounting, *pres. pple.* (UP- 6.)
1794 WOLCOT (P. Pindar) *Wks.* III. 221 The Moon.. upmounting slow, In solemn stillness. **1820** KEATS *Hyperion* I. 157 Like the mist Which eagles cleave, upmounting from their nest.

ˈupness. [UP *adv.*²] The quality of being elevated or raised.
1887 W. JAMES in *Mind* No. 45. 14 Rightness and leftness, upness and downness, are..pure sensation. **1902** *Yorks. Post* 28 Feb., With the..idea of height or up-ness in our minds.

†**upˈnim,** *v.* *Obs.* [UP- 4. Cf. OFris. *opnima*, *opnema* (WFris. *opnimme*), (M)Du. *opnemen*, MLG. *upnemen* (LG. *upnämen*), MHG. *ûfnemen* (G. *aufnehmen*).] *trans.* To take up.
c **1250** *Gen. & Ex.* 3024 It so bi-cam, ðat moyses askes up-nam. *c* **1290** *St. Brandan* 11 in *S. Eng. Leg.* I. 220 Bi-twene his armes seint brendan þis holie man op nam. *c* **1320** *Cast. Love* 1488 He þat from heuene com, From louh an heiȝ he vs up-nom. **1340** *Ayenb.* 143 Hi deþ ase deþ þe ilke mayde strongliche opnome of loue.
Hence †**upˈniming** *vbl. sb.* *Obs.*
1340 *Ayenb.* 22 Þe þridde kuead..ys fole opnyminge of uals strif. *Ibid.* 83 Fole op-nymynge is huer lite profit liþ, and moche cost.

upoˈ (ʌˈpəʊ), *prep.* Forms: 3, 5, 9 *dial.* uppo, 3, 8 *Sc.* upo (3–4 up-o, 4 opo), 5 vpo; 8– *Sc.* and *dial.* upo' (9 *Sc.* apo'). [f. UP *adv.*² + O, O', *prep.*¹ Cf. UPON *prep.*] = UPON *prep.*, in various senses. (In later use *Sc.* and *north. dial.*)
c **1200** ORMIN 11959 Þe deofell brohhte Jesu Crist Wiþþutenn o þe temmple Upponn an sæte uppo þe rof. *c* **1230** *Hali Meid.* 37 And eauer habben sar care,..& bringe on his moder sorhe up-o sorhe. *c* **1300** *Havelok* 2596 Helpes me and yu-self baþe, And slos up-o þe dogges swiþe. *c* **1310** in Wright *Lyric P.* xlii. 114 Fayrest fode upo loft. *c* **1330** R. BRUNNE *Chron. Wace* (Rolls) 2761 Faste þey fullen opo þem alle. *c* **1400** *Destr. Troy* 7037 The renke vp rose..And foght vpo fote as a freke noble. **1610** B. JONSON *Alchemist* II. ii, Thatch will lie light upo' the rafters, Lungs. **1721** RAMSAY *Ode to the Ph*—— vi, If they command the storms to blaw, Then upo' sight the hailstanes thud. **1772** FERGUSSON *To R. Fergusson* xii, [To] hae a charot at the door To wait upo' me. **1773** GOLDSM. *Stoops to Conq.* I. ii, *Landlord*, They have lost their way upo' the forest. **1808** A. SCOTT *Poems* (ed. 2) 101 Upo' the rig she shoor wi' Hab. **1865** G. MACDONALD *A. Forbes* xi, I never kent ony guid come o' bein' ower sair upo' bairns.

upon (əˈpɒn), *prep.* Forms: α. 3– upon (4–5, 7 up on, 6 *Sc.* uponn), 4–7 vpon (3–5 vp on, 4, 5 *Sc.* vpone, *Sc.* 5–6 wpone, 6–7 wpon), 3–7 uppon, vppon (3 *Orm.* upponn, 4 upp on). β. 3–6 opon (4 oupon, opan), 4–5 oppon. γ. 3–6, 9 *Sc.* apon (4 apan), 5 *Sc.*, 6 apone, 5–6 *Sc.* apoun, 5–7 *Sc.* appon(e, apponne. δ. 6 poun, 8–9 'pon. See also UPO'. [Early ME. *upon, uppon*, etc., f. UP *adv.*[1] and *adv.*[2] + ON *prep.*; distinct from late OE. and early ME. *uppon*, var. of OE. *uppan* UP *prep.*[1]

The compound may have partly arisen from uses of *upp on* or *uppe on* in OE. (for instances see UP *adv.*[1] and *adv.*[2]), but the date at which it appears, and the locality of the texts in which it is first prominent, suggest that it is mainly due to the influence of ON. *upp á* (MSw. *up a, op a, uppa, oppa*, etc.; Sw. *på*, Norw. and Da. *paa*), with which it agrees in laying the stress on the preposition and weakening or altogether ignoring the force of *up*. In the mod. Scand. tongues, except Icelandic and Færöese, the reduced form *på, paa*, corresponding to Eng. (colloq. or dial.) *'pon, 'po'*, has displaced the simple prep. *á, aa* = on.]

Originally denoting elevation as well as contact, the compound has from the earliest period of its occurrence so far lost the former implication, that is, it has been regularly employed as a simple equivalent of *on*, in all the varieties of meaning which that preposition has developed. The use of the one form or the other has been for the most part a matter of individual choice (on grounds of rhythm, emphasis, etc.) or of simple accident, although in certain contexts and phrases there may be a general tendency to prefer the one to the other. For ease of comparison, the following arrangement of the senses corresponds as closely as possible with that of ON. (See also HERE-, THERE-, WHERE-UPON.)

I. Of local position outside of, but in contact with or close to, a surface.

1. Above and in contact with; in an elevated position on; at rest on the upper surface of; on and supported by; = ON *prep.* 1.

In a few instances in late MSS. (e.g. Hatton Gosp. *Matt.* v. 14) OE. *up on* can be taken in this sense, but appears to be merely a scribal variant or alteration of *uppon* for *uppan* UP *prep.*[1]

c **1250** *Gen. & Ex.* 2867 Ðat..hise folc..ben ðor ȝare, In ðe deserd an stede up-on, His leue sacrifise to don. *a* **1272** *Luue Ron* 121 in *O.E. Misc.* 97 Hit stont vppon a treowe mote. *c* **1290** *St. Brendan* 368 in *S. Eng. Leg.* I. 229 At ester eue heore procuratour bad heom..heore resurrection opon þe fisches rugge make. *Ibid.* 577 Þe ston þat ich op-on sitte. **13..** *E.E. Allit. P.* A. 1054 The hyȝe trone..þe hyȝe godez self hit set vpone. *c* **1386** CHAUCER *Miller's T.* 637 Til he cam to þe selle Vpon þe flore. *c* **1440** *Pallad. on Husb.* I. 199 Vynys that vppon the hillis stonde. *c* **1489** CAXTON *Sonnes of Aymon* xxii. 486 Reynawde..was vpon the hyghe gate of Ardeyn. **1508** DUNBAR *Gold. Targe* 20 The birdis sang vpon the tender croppis. *c* **1560** A. SCOTT *Poems* i. 4 Welcum, oure rubent roiss vpoun þe ryce. **1606** SHAKS. *Ant. & Cl.* IV. xiv. 4 A forked Mountaine, or blew Promontorie With Trees vpon't. *a* **1648** DIGBY *Chym. Secr.* II. (1682) 215 Take it upon the point of a knife. **1732** BERKELEY *Alciphr.* IV. §8 The castle upon yonder hill. **1749** FIELDING *Tom Jones* XIV. ii, She's here, Mrs. Honour is upon the stairs. **1816** J. WILSON *City of Plague* I. i. 191 Wilt thou rest, old man, Upon this traveller's seat? **1825** J. NICHOLSON *Operat. Mechanic* 383 A pair of rollers upon the top of the roving-can. **1903** MRS. DE LA PASTURE *Cornelius* 7 A Crown Derby service was spread forth upon a round table.

b. Said with reference to an expanse, as of land, sea, etc.; = ON *prep.* 1 b. (Freq. from *c* 1650.)

upon a (*†the*) *level* (*with*): see LEVEL *sb.* 2, 3.

c **1250** *Gen. & Ex.* 3273 And moyses stod up-on ðe sond. *c* **1300** *Havelok* 735 Þer sat is ship up-on þe sond. **1340–70** *Alex. & Dind.* 39 Neuere werrede we wiþ wiȝth up-on erþe. *Ibid.* 739 Of swiche bestus..þei han miht vp-on molde. **1362** LANGL. *P. Pl.* A. IX. 56 Vnder a Lynde, vpon a launde leonede I a stounde. **1390** GOWER *Conf.* I. 53 He syh upon the grene gras The faire freisshe floures springe. *c* **1420** *Chron. Vilod.* 2393 Þis blessud virgyn..Twolfeȝere..in hurr tombe lay, As saffe, as hole as he vpon vrthe ȝede. *c* **1470** *Gol. & Gaw.* 312 Thai plantit doun ane pailyeoun, vpone ane plane lee. **1526** TINDALE *Mark* vi. 48 When they sawe him walkinge apon the see. **1535** FISHER *Wks.* (1876) 305 He must treade vppon the fallowes. **1568** *Durham Wills* (Surtees) III. 44 Corne..in the barne 58l., Upon the earth at 20l. **1609** BIBLE (Douay) *Ezek.* xvi. 5 Thou wast throwen forth upon the face of the earth. **1650** HOWELL *Giraffi's Rev. Naples* I. 15 Benches, Forms,..were burnt all to ashes upon the streets. **1662** J. DAVIES tr. *Olearius' Voy. Ambass.* 203 Wood and Lodging..are very scarce upon that Road. **1711** ADDISON *Spect.* No. 42 ¶3 Two or three Shifters of Scenes..make up a complete Body of Guards upon the English Stage. **1812** BYRON *Ch. Har.* I. xiii. 75 Now I'm in the world alone, Upon the wide, wide sea. **1828** LYTTON *Pelham* III. xix, I have no time..to speak of the earlier part of my life. I passed it upon the race-course. **1871** HAWEIS *Music & Morals* (1874) 7 The Painter's art lies upon the surface of the world.

c. Denoting the part of the body on which one is supported; = ON *prep.* 1 c.

See also FOOT *sb.* 27, KNEE *sb.* 3 a, TIPTOE *sb.* 1.

1390 GOWER *Conf.* I. 286 Sche began merci to crie Upon hire bare knes. *c* **1440** *Generydes* 44 Vppe vppon his fete he was a non. **1481** CAXTON *Reynard* (Arb.) 18 He satte vpon his hammes. **1601** SHAKS. *Jul. C.* II. i. 270 Vpon my knees, I charme you,..By all your vowes of Loue. **1661** EARL ORRERY *St. Lett.* (1742) 40 We are now upon our last legs. **1692** tr. *C'tess D'Aunoy's Trav.* 157 Three or four Pages..serve me upon Knee. **1712** STEELE *Spect.* No. 460 ¶7 Gallantry strutting upon his Tiptoes. **1784** COWPER *Task* IV. 546 Her tott'ring form Ill propp'd upon French heels. **1800** WORDSW. *Hart-Leap Well* I. xi, Upon his side the Hart was lying stretched. **1843** MACAULAY *Horatius* lxvi, Horatius in his harness, Halting upon one knee.

d. Indicating a means of locomotion or conveyance; = ON *prep.* 1 d.

a **1300** *Cursor M.* 894 For þou sal slid apon þi brest. *c* **1300** *Havelok* 2041 Yf he mouhte..gangen wel up-on hise fet. **13..** *E.E. Allit. P.* B. 88 Swyerez þat swyftly swyed on blonkez, & also fele vpon fote. **1393** LANGL. *P. Pl.* C. VII. 43 Strengest vp-on stede, and styuest vnder gurdell. *c* **1400** MAUNDEV. (Roxb.) i. 4 It es made sittand apon a hors. *c* **1475** *Rauf Coilȝear* 794 Vpon ane rude Runsy he ruschit out of toun. **1590** SPENSER *F.Q.* I. i. 4 She..heauie sat vpon her palfrey slow. **1648** HEXHAM II, *Een Rijdt-bane*, a Sliding place..to slide upon Schates. **1660** F. BROOKE tr. *Le Blanc's Trav.* 350 The great King, whom they carry upon a *Sindela* of cotton. **1719** DE FOE *Crusoe* II. (Globe) 345 We went on Shore upon the Tide of Flood, near high Water. **1803** SOUTHEY *Queen Orraca* IV. vii, Upon her palfrey she is set, And forward then they go. **1821** SCOTT *Pirate* xxx, She saw him flee forth of the window..upon a dragon. **1853** KANE *Grinnell Exp.* xxxii. (1856) 282, I mounted the upheaving ice, and rode upon the fragments.

e. Denoting that on which the hand is placed in taking the oath, or the basis of an oath, etc.; = ON *prep.* 1 f.

See also CONSCIENCE 9, EVANGEL[1] 3, EVANGELY 3, FAITH *sb.* 8, HONOUR *sb.* 9 b, LIFE *sb.* 3 c, REP[1], SOUL *sb.* 10 c, WORD *sb.*

c **1290** *Beket* 585 in *S. Eng. Leg.* I. 123 Þat he ne scholde nouȝt swerie op-on þe boke. *c* **1330** R. BRUNNE *Chron. Wace* (Rolls) 10468 He swor hym vpon þe bok, To holde of hym his heritage. **1398** TREVISA *Barth. De P.R.* XV. cxxxvi. (Bodl. MS.), Hoote welles þat..blindeþ þeues ȝif he swereþ vpon þe water and toucheþ heere yȝen þerewiþ. *c* **1400** *Destr. Troy* 642 Yow swiftly shall sweire vppon swete goddes, This couenaunt to kepe. *a* **1460** in *Hist. Coll. Lond. Cit.* (Camden) 119 The for sayde captaynys have sworne a-pon hyr honowre that..they shalle not makyn [etc.]. **1493** *Litt. Red Bk. Bristol* (1900) II. 134 This ys trew apon owre consciens. **1610** SHAKS. *Temp.* II. ii. 130 I'le sweare vpon that Bottle, to be thy true subiect. **1645** *Docq. Lett. Pat. at Oxf.* (1837) 268 Administring of Oathes vpon the Holy Evangelistes. **1710** ADDISON *Tatler* No. 253 ¶1 The Assistants..were all sworn upon their Honour. **1722** DE FOE *Col. Jack* (1840) 67 He would come back..and untie him, upon his word. **1776** *Trial Nundocomar* 52/1 You have sworn me upon the waters of the Ganges: how can I tell more than I remember? **1831** JAMES *Phil. Augustus* III. x, I declare that..he himself [is] worthy of death, upon my honour! **1848** DICKENS *Dombey* xxxix, Upon my word and honour,..it would be a charity.

†f. Above, more than. *Obs.* Cf. UP *prep.*[1] 8.

13.. *Guy Warw.* (A.) 359 Opon al oþer y loue þe. *c* **1430** *Syr Gener.* (Roxb.) 969 Son, vpon al thing Doo aftre Nathanaels teching.

†g. *fig.* Over (a person, etc.), in respect of rule, authority, or supervision. *Obs.*

See also REIGN *v.* 1 b, RULE *v.* 5 b, RULER 1 (quot. 1382).

c **1380** WYCLIF *Wks.* (1880) 383 Þe kyngis of heþen han lordeschip vp-on hem. *c* **1400** MAUNDEV. (Roxb.) iii. 10 Þi powere es grete apon þi subgets. **1422** YONG tr. *Secreta Secret.* 162 Oure Lord god enoyntyd Saule Kynge vppon Israell. **1477** EARL RIVERS (Caxton) *Dictes* 69 He aught to haue lawde That..hath lordship vpon his ennemyes. **1534** WHITINTON *Tullyes Offices* I. (1540) 11 A man that wolde be chefe ruler vpon the commentye.

h. Taking part in, forming a member of (an inquest, jury, etc.). Cf. ON *prep.* 1 g.

1516 *Reg. Privy Seal Scot.* I. 422/2 Thai..being apone the inqueist..in the schiref court. **1609** [see SIT *v.* 28]. **1643** *Docq. Lett. Pat. at Oxf.* (1837) 5 Consociating himselfe with his neighboring Justices in sitting upon an illegal Commission. **1676** *Office Clerk of Assize* a vj, Persons..to serve in or upon the Grand Jury. **1729** JACOB *Law Dict.* s.v. *Jury*, Clergymen, Apothecaries, &c. are exempted by Law from serving upon Juries. **1769** [see JURY *sb.* 2 b].

i. Hence in many phrases, originally denoting physical location, of which the sense has become more or less figurative; = ON *prep.* 1 h. See esp. ANVIL *sb.* 2 b, CARPET *sb.* 1 b, HAND *sb.* 32, HIGH *a.* 17 h, 18, LEVEL *sb.* 4, PAR *sb.* 1, SPOT *sb.*[1] 9, TABLE *sb.* 5 b.

2. Denoting contact with or location on a surface, etc., whatever its position; = ON *prep.* 2.

(*a*) *c* **1200** ORMIN Ded. 69 Þatt upponn all þiss boc ne be Nan word ȝæn Cristess lare. *a* **1300** *Cursor M.* 23215 Painted fire..þat apon a wagh war wroght. **1382** WYCLIF *Exod.* xxxiv. 1 Y shal write vpon hem [*sc.* stone tables] the wordes that hadden the tablis. **1535** COVERDALE *Hab.* ii. 2 Wryte the vision planely vpon thy tables. **1552** in J. O. Payne *St. Paul's Cathedral* (1893) 22 A greate clothe of redd silke..with lions of golde upon it. **1566**, **1596** [see INSCULP *v.*]. **1596–** [see RECORD *sb.* 1]. **1605** SHAKS. *Macb.* v. i. 7, I haue seene her..take foorth paper,..write vpon't, read it. *Ibid.* viii. 26 As our rarer Monsters are Painted vpon a pole. **1729** T. INNES *Crit. Essay* (1879) 74 His name is upon it, written with his own hand. **1766** [see ENGRAVE *v.* 3 a]. **1776** *Trial Nundocomar* 97/2 Did you see upon the face of the bond anything to make you suspect it? **1801** *Farmer's Mag.* Apr. 203 Which is very practicable upon paper. **1888** 'J. S. WINTER' *Bootle's Childr.* v, A gold bangle with 'Mignon' upon it..in raised letters.

(*b*) *a* **1225** *Leg. Kath.* 1187 Þe treo þer he deide upon. *c* **1290** *S. Eng. Leg.* I. 43/300 Þis ȝoungue Man sixe and þritti dawes heng up-on þe galu-treo. **1377** LANGL. *P. Pl.* B. I. 154 Was neuere leef vpon lynde liȝter þer-after. **14..** LYDG. *Min. Poems* (1911) 252 As he [*sc.* Christ] hangeth vp-on the roode tre. **1536** *Exhort. to North* in Furnivall *Ballads fr. MSS.* I. 307 The gallous apone, prepared for mardoche, hanged he was. **1596** DALRYMPLE tr. *Leslie's Hist. Scot.* I. 121 Lat him end his lyf vpon ane fork. **1605** SHAKS. *Macb.* v. v. 39 Vpon the next Tree shall thou hang. **1867** SMYTH *Sailor's Word-bk.* 411 A sail set upon the flying jib-boom. **1899** *Shetland News* 16 Dec. (*E.D.D.* s.v. *Hing*), I took aff me kjaep, an' hang her apon a nail.

(*c*) *c* **1386** CHAUCER *Prol.* 111 Vp on his arm he baar a gay bracer. *c* **1450** *St. Cuthbert* (Surtees) 813 With broches and golde opon hir arme. **1494** *Act 11 Hen. VII*, c. 23 The little Bone that sitteth upon the great Fin. **1523** FITZHERB. *Husb.* §21 A wedynge-hoke with a socket set vpon a lyttel staffe. **1547** in Feuillerat *Revels Edw. VI* (1914) 10 Th'under sleves of..Satten cut vpon Red Sarcenett. **1655** STANLEY *Hist. Philos.* II. 7 By reflection of the Sunns beams upon a thick cloud, which, not able to pierce it, are refracted upon it. **1774** J. BRYANT *Mythol.* II. 231 Upon the head of the woman is a veil. **1824** T. G. CUMMING *Rail & Tram Roads* 24 Several branches were made..with the flaunche upon the wheel, and not upon the rail. **1847** MARRYAT *Childr. N. Forest* xix, Those clothes would not look so well upon Oswald. **1889** DOYLE *Micah Clarke* 318 Monmouth must fight now, if he ever hopes to feel the gold rim upon his temples.

b. Used of immaterial relationships, or in figurative expressions.

to (*be*)*get..upon* (a woman): see BEGET *v.* 2 b, GET *v.* 26.

a **1400** *Minor Poems fr. Vernon MS.* xlii. 8 His eȝe is euere þe vppon. **1423** JAS. I *King's Q.* ii, I..toke a boke to rede apon a quhile. *c* **1450** *Mirk's Festial* I. 6 Vnsley old man, goo heþen! for I se apon þe mony meruayles. **1548–9** (Mar.) *Bk. Com. Prayer* Pref., All thynges must be read vpon the boke. **1591** SHAKS. *Two Gent.* I. i. 20 Vpon some booke I loue, I'le pray for thee. **1662** STILLINGFL. *Orig. Sacræ* II. iii. §4 That what is spoken hath the impress of Divine authority upon it. *Ibid.* v. §2 They have a clear and distinct perception of God upon their own minds. **1719** DE FOE *Crusoe* II. (Globe) 498 The Horror which was upon our Minds. **1753–4** RICHARDSON *Grandison* I. xii. 66 Every one's eyes were upon me. **1806** J. BERESFORD *Miseries Hum. Life* (ed. 4) VI. 97 Here am I..with a sort of traveller's lumbago upon me. **1832** L. HUNT *Gentle Armour* I. 142 The page returns with doubt upon his eyes. **1848** BAILEY *Festus* (ed. 3) 230 There was a tale Upon thy tongue he interrupted. **1877** SPURGEON *Serm.* XXIII. 669 It is absurd upon its very face.

c. By means of; with. Now *dial.*

c **1440** *York Myst.* xix. 212 Þe knyght vppon his knyffe Hath slayne my sone. **1590** SHAKS. *Mids. N.* II. i. 244 To die vpon the hand I loue so well. **1742** *Phil. Trans.* XLII. 266 The Perfection of Smelling in the Inhabitants of the Antibes, who can run a Man upon the Nose like an Hound. **1751** LABELYE *Westm. Bridge* 71 Explaining before them, upon a working Model, the Method I proposed. **1790** BOSWELL *Lett.* (1924) 388, I intended to have printed it upon what is called an English letter. **1865** R. HUNT *Pop. Rom. West Eng.* I. 105 Which eye can you see me upon?

d. Used in reference to an axis, pivot, or base; = ON *prep.* 1 e. (Cf. RAISE *v.* 8 b, TURN *v.* 3.)

1570 BILLINGSLEY *Euclid* I. i. 8 A triangle..set or described vpon a line. **1593** FALE *Dialling* 14 Upon E make a halfe circle from H by G. **1679** MOXON *Math. Dict.* s.v. *Circle*, The Circle..is described upon the Centre A. **1728** CHAMBERS *Cycl.* s.v. *Triangle*, A Triangle is equal to a Parallelogram upon the same Base, but half the Altitude. **1796** *Instr. & Reg. Cavalry* (1813) 149 Each describing the portion of a circle upon (P) as a center. **1830** TENNYSON *Mariana* vi, The doors upon their hinges creak'd. **1832** *Prop. Reg. Instr. Cavalry* III. 47 Two contiguous points given as a Base, upon which a body of troops is to march or form. **1877** HUXLEY *Anat. Inv. Anim.* vi. 309 The next four somites..cease to be moveable upon one another.

3. a. On the bank of (a river or lake); on the shore of (the sea); on the borders of (a territory, etc.); close by, near to; bordering upon; beside or by; = ON *prep.* 3.

13.. *K. Alis.* 4090 (Laud MS.), A Castel he had vpon þe ryue. **1387** TREVISA *Higden* V. 329 He fauȝt..aȝenst þe Saxons..uppon þe ryver Gleny. *c* **1425** *Eng. Conq. Irel.* 142 The tounes vp-on the see. **1474** *Rental Bk. Cupar-Angus* (1879) I. 197 To mak a myl..othir vpoun the gret watter or vpoun the burn. **1526** *Reg. Privy Seal Scot.* I. 514/1 Theifis and tratouris duelland apoun Levin. **1585** T. WASHINGTON tr. *Nicholay's Voy.* I. viii. 7 b, Alger..is situated vpon the Mediterane Sea. **1601** R. JOHNSON *Kingd. & Commw.* 192 Siras seated vpon the riuer Bindimire. **1662** STILLINGFL. *Orig. Sacræ* III. iv. §13 The greatest part of the Countries lying upon the Ocean and Mediterranean. **1720** DE FOE *Capt. Singleton* xiii. (1840) 226 A tract of land..seated upon some navigable river. **1747** *Col. Rec. Pennsylv.* V. 87 Upon the heads of Joniady River. **1859** TENNYSON *Marriage of Geraint* 145 Arthur..Held court at old Caerleon upon Usk.

†b. About; near; close on (a specified number, etc.). *Obs.*

In later use only with CLOSE *adv.* 1 d, NEAR *adv.*[2] 5 c, NIGH *adv.* 12 c.

1451 CAPGRAVE *Life St. Gilbert* 68 He left at his deth swech persones dedicate to God vp-on too þousand too hundred. **1477** CAXTON *Jason* 74 He cessed not to..rowe til he cam nyghe the Ile vpon a bowe shotte. **1478** J. PASTON in *P. Lett.* III. 219 A steppe modyr of hyrs, whyche is upon l. yer of age. **1482** *Cely Papers* (Camden) 102 Ther wylbe in aull with blottes apon xxvij or xxviij sarplers wholl. **1534** TINDALE *Luke* viii. 42 He had but a doughter only, apon a twelve yere of age. *a* **1548** HALL *Chron.*, *Hen. VIII*, 32 b, He had askryed a nombre of horsemen..vppon the poynct of syx thousand. **1600** HOLLAND *Livy* 177 There were upon two thousand & five hundred taken alive. **1660** *Nicholas Papers* (Camden) IV. 226 To pay mee my allowance..as it was regulated upon three years since.

4. Denoting collateral position; esp. with *side, hand, †half; beam* (of a ship), *point* (of the compass); *north, south*, etc.; *right, left*; = ON *prep.* 4.

See also BORDER *v.* 5, TOUCH *v.* 14, VERGE *v.*[1] 2 b.

(*a*) *c* **1330** R. BRUNNE *Chron. Wace* (Rolls) 7929 Southsex..& Middelsex..marchen vpon Kent. *c* **1400** MAUNDEV. (Roxb.) vi. 22 Mesopotamy also marchez apon þe desertes of Araby. **1568** GRAFTON *Chron.* II. 354 For we [Scots] are so lodged vpon England, that we may..enter which way we lust. **1586–** [see NEIGHBOUR *v.* 1, 2]. **1596** DALRYMPLE tr. *Leslie's Hist. Scot.* (S.T.S.) I. 31 Wpon the coste of the Lenox lyes Argyle. **1624** HEYWOOD *Gunaik.* II. 92 That part..which butted upon the west. **1681** DRYDEN *Span. Friar* I. i, Upon the skirts Of Arragon our squander'd troops he rallies. **1786** W. THOMSON *Watson's Philip III* (1839) 311 An island bordering upon Istria. **1842** R. I. WILBERFORCE *Rutilius & Lucius* 106 Behind they abutted upon the grounds of Milo. **1873** T. W. HIGGINSON *Oldport Days* v. 115 The house was close upon the water.

(*b*) **13..** *Gaw. & Gr. Knt.* 2069 Þe brode ȝatez [were] Vnbarred, & born open, vpon boþe halue. **1375** BARBOUR

Bruce XI. 175 Schir Gylys de Argente he set Vpon ane half, his renȝe to get. ? *a* **1400** *Morte Arth.* 3795 We are with Sarazenes be-sett appone sere halfes! *c* **1475** *Rauf Coilȝear* 291 I se the Firmament fair vpon ather syde. **1565** GOLDING *Ovid's Met.* I. 1 b, Twoo Zones do cut the Heauen vpon the righter syde. **1577** B. GOOGE *Heresbach's Husb.* II. (1586) 71 b, A rich grounde, leuell, and lying vpon the Sunne. **1644** in *Eng. Hist. Rev.* Apr. (1913) 341 My Lord Ambassador beinge plac'd..upon his left hand about three Seates distante from him. **1669** STURMY *Mariner's Mag.* I. ii. 4 Upon what Point of the Compass the Object beareth from you. **1739** LABELYE *Piers Westm. Bridge* 5 When the Wind is upon any Point of the Compass between the South and the West. **1791** SMEATON *Edystone L.* §76 A vessel steering to Foy will have the wind upon her beam. **1823** F. CLISSOLD *Ascent Mt. Blanc* 11 [It] shelved down, upon our right, in one plane of smooth rock.

transf. **1656** CROMWELL *Sp.* in Burton *Diary* (1828) I. p. clxix, It was never so upon the thriving hand. **1718** WODROW *Corr.* (1843) II. 362 May the kingdom of our Lord be upon the growing hand. **1852** BAILEY *Festus* (ed. 5) 252 To you, dear ass, upon the sire's side, To you, sir steed, I'm on the dam's allied.

b. *transf.* Indicating the side, part, cause, etc., espoused or supported by the agent.

c **1430** *Chev. Assigne* 219 'Go we forthe, fader,' quod þe childe, 'vpon goddes halfe!' **1445** in *Anglia* XXVIII. 256 [They] seyen the duke of yorke hath god vpon his side. **1595** SHAKS. *John* I. i. 34 Till she had kindled France and all the world, Vpon the right and party of her sonne. **1611** B. JONSON *Catiline* V. M 2, The least man, that falles vpon our party This day.., Shall walke at pleasure, in the tents of rest. **1821** SHELLEY *Hellas* 440 Famine, and Pestilence, And Panic, shall wage war upon our side!

c. Engaged in assailing, or about to attack.

1568 GRAFTON *Chron.* II. 291 The French men were so mingled among their enemies, that some time there was fiue men vpon one Gentleman. *c* **1670** WOOD *Life* (O.H.S.) I. 114 Captain Walter had six rebells upon him, and..fought it out so..gallantly that [etc.]. **1701** W. WOTTON *Hist. Rome* 269 The Senate heard that Severus was just upon them. **1719** DE FOE *Crusoe* I. (Globe) 270 He saw five Men upon him. **1721** —— *Mem. Cavalier* (1840) 211 We are all undone, the roundheads are upon us. **1860** *All Year Round* No. 66. 384 Certain manœuvres, which had just time to result.., when the squall was upon us. **1885** *Manch. Exam.* 10 June 4/7 The crisis..is upon us at last.

†**d.** Having a tendency to be; verging towards; bordering on. Freq. with *little*. *Obs.*

Cf. *to run upon* s.v. RUN *v.* 70 b.

1707 LD. RABY in Hearne *Collect.* (O.H.S.) II. 43 He is.. a little upon ye dirty as all ye Poles are. **1716** in *London Gaz.* No. 5438/4 Lost.., a large Brilliant.., a little upon the Blue. **1738** SWIFT *Pol. Conversat.* 180, I think he's a little upon the silly, or so. **1740** tr. *De Mouhy's Fort. Country Maid* (1741) I. 35 A Countenance much upon the Wheedler and the Devotee.

5. Within the bounds or limits of; in; = ON *prep.* 5. (Cf. UPO' *prep.*, quot. 1773.)

13.. *Sir Beues* (A.) 4180 [He] karf.. Doun riȝt þe viser wiþ is swerd And half þe her vpon is berd. **1605** SHAKS. *Lear* IV. vi. 256 Seeke him out vpon the English party. **1639** LAUD *Wks.* (1853) V. 364, I find by the bishop's certificate, that he hath constantly resided upon his episcopal houses. **1765** *Museum Rust.* IV. 449 His country seat, possessed and lived upon by his ancestors for several generations. **1824** SCOTT *St. Ronan's* xxii, Miss Clara..just sitting upon the wind of a door [= in a draught].

†**b.** Denoting ratio between two numbers, etc.; = PER *prep.* III. 2, IN *prep.* 4. *Obs. rare.*

1622 MALYNES *Anc. Law-Merch.* 195 In regarde of lecage of tenne or fifteene vpon the hundreth. **1739** LABELYE *Piers Westm. Bridge* 76 The Ascent..not being above one Foot perpendicular upon 20 Feet slope. *Ibid.* 78.

6. Denoting the day of an occurrence, regarded as a unit of time. Freq. also with *night, morn, morrow, eve(n, time,* †*tide,* †*hour, occasion,* etc. = ON *prep.* 6.

once upon a time: see ONCE *adv.* 4.

a **1300** *Cursor M.* 19810 Apon a dai at þe tid o non An angel com. **1338** R. BRUNNE *Chron.* (1810) 37 Unto Kyngeston..Com S. Dunstan, opon a Sonenday. **1390** GOWER *Conf.* I. 3 Now upon this tyde Men se the world.. so diversed, That [etc.]. ? *a* **1400** *Arthur* 539 And sone after vpon an owr He hurde of Mordred. **1424** *Stonor Papers* (Camden) I. 36 Writen at Sarum apon þe seynt Michell euen. *a* **1470** *Ibid.* 111 My wyf and y welbe with you uppon Ester. **1535** COVERDALE *Job* i. 6 Now vpon a tyme..the seruauntes of God came and stode before the Lorde. **1551** ROBINSON tr. *More's Utopia* (1895) 15 Vpon a tyme, when tidynges came [etc.]. **1631** WEEVER *Anc. Funeral Mon.* 471 Once euery yeare vpon the same day of his Anniuerse. **1663** *Extr. St. Papers Friends* Ser. II. (1911) 183 [They] were all brought before the mayor vpon the 28th of December. **1672** T. GODDEN *Cath. No Idolators* 35 Would an Impartial Reader (to use Dr. Taylor's expression upon another occasion) say [etc.]? **1711** ADDISON *Spect.* No. 164 ¶4 Upon the Day on which..their Marriage was to have been solemnized. **1771** MRS. GRIFFITH *Hist. Lady Barton* III. 285, I wrote upon the instant, but..cannot recollect what I said. *a* **1821** KEATS *Eve St. Mark* 1 Upon a Sabbath-day it fell. **1868** TENNYSON *Lucretius* 24 He..woke upon a morn That mock'd him.

†**b.** In, at, or during (any period of time); in the course of; = ON *prep.* 6 b. *Obs.*

(*a*) **1390** GOWER *Conf.* I. 314 [He] made upon the derke nyht..Gret fyr. *c* **1400** *Destr. Troy* 8684 Wyth myche dole vppon dayes & on derke nightes, Sum walt into wodenes. **1427–9** *Rolls of Parlt.* IV. 364 To make a Toure to be uppon day light a redy Bekyn. **1529** in Leadam *Star Chamb. Cases* (Selden) II. 34 Thomas..directed..the hole recordys.. vppon a yere past or more to vs..to examen the same. **1585** T. WASHINGTON tr. *Nicholay's Voy.* I. xix, Vpon the euening the fire..got into their pouder. **1603** SHAKS. *Meas. for M.* IV. i. 35 Vpon the Heauy midle of the night. **1661** *Act 13 Chas. II*, c. 9 §27 No man in or belonging to the Fleet shall sleep upon his Watch. **1673** in Picton *L'pool Munic. Rec.* (1883) I. 247 Offences committed by them the same day upon the said election. [**1820** KEATS *St. Agnes* vi, Upon the honey'd middle of the night.]

(*b*) **1591** UNTON *Corr.* (Roxb.) 103 Upon nowe advertisement is come from the Kinge. **1638** LD. DIGBY *Lett. Conc. Relig.* (1651) 19 To tell you what upon the present..occurreth to me.

†**c.** Within the space of (a specified period of time); = ON *prep.* 6 c. *Obs.*

c **1375** *Cursor M.* 510 (Fairf.), Be iournays qua ga hit may, fourty myle a-pon a day. *c* **1386** CHAUCER *Prol.* 704 Vp on a day he gat hym moore moneye Than þat the person gat in Monthes tweye. **1457–8** in *Acta Dom. Conc.* II. Introd. 15 He sall warne thame to pass to the kings chapell..apone xl dais. **1459** *Rolls of Parlt.* V. 369/2 A commaundement..to be redy to come..upon a day warnyng. ? *a* **1585** MONTGOMERIE *Misc. Poems* vii. 35 Rome wes not biggit all vpon ane day. **1674** *Reg. Privy Council Scot.* Ser. III. IV. 299 [The lords] ordaines letters of horning upon 48 houres to be direct for that effect.

d. At the point of; close on, touching on; = ON *prep.* 6 d.

Usu. with vbl. sb. or gerundive: see group (*a*). ***upon the point of***: see POINT *sb.*^{1} D. 5.

(*a*) **1426** AUDELAY *Poems* 6 Have mynd apon ȝoure endyng of the payns of helle. **1491** *Acta Dom. Conc.* (1839) 205/1, I am apone my saling and may nocht lang tary. **1530** PALSGR. 423/1, I am upon my lieng downe, as a woman that is nere her tyme. **1604** DEKKER *Honest Wh.* xii, *Wife.* Comes the Duke this way? *Pio.* Hee's upon comming, mistris. **1611** COTGR., *Emmati*,..faded, vpon withering. **1669–70** MARVELL *Corr.* Wks. (Grosart) II. 310, I intended more, but the post also is upon going. **1707** HEARNE *Collect.* (O.H.S.) II. 10 The King of Prussia is upon sending to the..Library all the..medals. *a* **1774** GOLDSM. *Hist. Greece* I. 247 The truce..was just upon expiring. **1842** C. WHITEHEAD *R. Savage* I. i, I was just upon commending them to a lower place.

ellipt. **1899** *Daily News* 12 Sept. 4/7 The new..recreation garden..is just upon finished.

(*b*) **1585** T. WASHINGTON tr. *Nicholay's Voy.* I. xix. 22 As wee were vpon our departure. **1626** BRETON *Fantasticks* D 3 b, Few that are merry, but..wenches that are vpon the mariage. **1632** MASSINGER *Maid of Hon.* V. i, Signor Adorni is return'd! now upon entrance! **1666** MARVELL *Corr.* Wks. (Grosart) II. 197 The Smyrna fleet..is upon returne. *c* **1680–** [see GO *sb.*^{1} 8 d]. **1722** POPE *Lett.* (1735) I. 274 I'm told you are all upon Removal very speedily. **1775** S. J. PRATT *Liberal Opin.* cxxxiii. (1783) IV. 206 Our old rector will make a subject by and by;..he's certainly upon the go [= dying]. **1797** MRS. M. ROBINSON *Walsingham* IV. 318 The good fellow is upon the go; his life is not worth six weeks' purchase. **1820** BYRON *Mar. Fal.* IV. ii. 66 *Doge.* How goes the night? *Ber. F.* Almost upon the dawn.

†**e.** By or for (a specified time). *Obs.*

1510 *Brasenose Coll. Doc.* (MS.) A^3 43 To make me a Dublett and a Jacket upon Crystmasse next comyng.

†**f.** For the extent or period of. *Obs.*

Cf. *upon a stretch* s.v. STRETCH *sb.* 6 a.

a **1548** HALL *Chron.*, *Hen. VII*, 49 b, Which sickenes contynued vpon fyue monethes.

7. a. On the occasion of; = ON *prep.* 7.

In freq. use *c* 1670–*c* 1825. Group (*b*) illustrates obs. usages.

See also OCCASION *sb.* 10 b, SIGHT *sb.* 4 b, 6 b, SUDDEN *sb.* 1 b, SUDDENTY 1 b, VIEW *sb.* 16.

(*a*) *c* **1440** CAPGRAVE *Life St. Kath.* I. 981 Vp-on this hir letter hath she sent. **1492** HEN. VII in G. Griffiths *Hist. Tong* (ed. 2) 224 To thentent that uppon convercacion we may shewe unto you our minde. **1515** in Leadam *Star Chamber Cases* (Selden) II. 79 The saide artificers seyne that by the grauntis made uppon their first corporacion it appereth that [etc.]. **1566** DRANT *Horace, Sat.* I. iii. B v, His maister hangs him straighte upponte. **1596** BACON *Use Com. Law* (1635) 2 If one kill another upon a suddaine quarrell. **1662** CULPEPER in *Extr. St. Papers Friends* Ser. II. (1911) 152 *note*, I haue some Quakers..in prison which I doe intend to let goe upon taking the Oath. **1698** FRYER *Acc. E. India & P.* 74 The Banyans repairing to the Suburbs upon Tattoo. **1705** COLLIER *Ess. Mor. Subj.* III. *Pain* 13 Was ever..any Fencer, worth the naming, heard to groan upon a Hit? **1712** ADDISON *Spect.* No. 369 ¶17 They..were cast into Hell upon their Disobedience. **1774** GOLDSM. *Nat. Hist.* (1776) II. 309 Upon comparing the various animals..with each other, we shall find [etc.]. **1817** MILL *Brit. India* II. 450 They retired upon the brisk advancement of the grenadiers. **1841** LANE *Arab. Nts.* I. 101 Upon which they raised their heads, and answered as before. **1890** LD. ESHER in *Law Times' Rep.* LXIII. 734/1 [He] shall be released from that obligation upon the Director undertaking the cure.

(*b*) **1510** *Reg. Privy Seal Scot.* I. 307/1 The slauchter.. committit be him apoun subdante. **1577** HOLINSHED *Chron.* I. 35/1 Cesar..writeth that immediatly vpon knowledge had ..he woulde inuade Brytaine. **1646** SIR T. BROWNE *Pseud. Ep.* 269 The Silly-how, that sometimes is found about the heads of children upon their birth. **1707** HEARNE *Collect* (O.H.S.) II. 63 Y^e sneaking Villains, like Worms upon a Rain, crawl'd out. **1726** SWIFT *Gulliver* II. v, Yet often, upon a pinch, I was forced to work like a common mariner. **1736** BUTLER *Anal.* I. iv, Persons may be betrayed into wrong behaviour upon surprise. **1763** JOHNSON in *Boswell* 25 June, He has no tenants..who will follow him to the field upon an emergency.

b. Immediately after; following on.

1390 GOWER *Conf.* II. 71 Whan that he this tale herde, Hou upon that the king ansuerde With Hercules he moste feighte. **1496** *Coventry Leet Bk.* 573 And what persones þat be absent þat day vppon warnyng shall pay xij d. **1523** LD. BERNERS *Froiss.* I. cxlviii. 177 [They] conquered..townes and castels one vpon the other by force. **1562** J. HEYWOOD *Prov. & Epigr.* (1867) 45 So soone vpon supper.., Sleepe maketh yll..digestion. **1596** SHAKS. *Merch. V.* IV. i. 384, I am content..to render it, Vpon his death, vnto the Gentleman. **1614** DAY *Festivals* ix. (1615) 268 Whether the Fault were unawares, or upon advisement. **1645** BP. HALL *Rem. Discontents* 80 After he had upon ten years siege, taken the rich City. **1688** HOLME *Armoury* II. 181/2 The bite or sting of a Scorpion is present Death if..[Swine] drink upon it. **1711** G. HICKES *Two Treat. Chr. Priesth.* (ed. 3) II. 30, I have wrote..not rashly or by chance, but upon thought. **1748** *Anson's Voy.* II. xiii. 276 Immediately upon this fortunate supply they stood to the westward. **1780** *Mirror* No. 95, I left my own house immediately upon the discovery I made. **1814** JANE AUSTEN *Mansf. Park* xi, Coming, as it generally did, upon a week's previous inactivity. **1849** MACAULAY *Hist. Eng.* V. I. 539 This plan had been dropped upon the detection of the Rye House Plot. **1883** HOWELLS in *Harper's Mag.* Dec. 79 The silence which his friend has absent-mindedly let follow upon his last words.

ellipt. **1818** COLEBROOKE *Import Colonial Corn* 183 The capital should at first be less productive if,..upon a balance, this become more fruitful.

†**c.** As soon *as*. *Obs.*$^{-1}$

1475 *Paston Lett.* III. 128, I woll, uppon as I heer from yow, come to yow in alle hast possible.

†**8.** Denoting physical arrangement, order, etc., = in (masses, a row, etc.). Cf. ON *prep.* 8. *rare.*

c **1300** *Havelok* 892 Als he lep þe kok vn-til, He shof hem alle upon an hyl. *c* **1400** *Destr. Troy* 1991 The flode..Rose vppon rockes [= in high masses] as any ranke hylles. *c* **1450** LOVELICH *Merlin* 1474 For thinges that ben past, j knowe, And thinges that ben comeng vppon a rowe. **1665** J. WEBB *Stone-Heng* 68 Nor [could] these have continued upon such a direct line, as still some of them seem to do.

9. In (a particular or specified manner, etc.); = ON *prep.* 9.

See also CROSS *sb.* 29, HEAD *sb.*^{1} 35 d, LOFT *sb.* 2 a, SLY *sb.* 2 (*a*), SQUARE *a.* 12 a, b.

c **1300** HAVELOK 468 Godard..tok þe maydnes bothe samen, Al-so it were up-on hiis gamen. **1338** R. BRUNNE *Chron.* (1810) 25 Bot þat þise lowed men vpon Inglish tellis, Right story can me not ken, þe certeynte what spellis. *a* **1400–50** *Alexander* 3300 Like to þis werke, þat þis coppis opon kell-wyse knytt in þe woȝes. *c* **1400** *Destr. Troy* 7359 There only was ordant of Ectors dethe, With all Soteltie to serche opon sere wise. *c* **1450** HOLLAND *Howlat* 828 The lordis leuch vpoun loft. *c* **1518** SKELTON *Magnyf.* 497 Chanons can not counterfet but vpon thre. **1600** SHAKS. *A.Y.L.* I. i. 2 It was vpon this fashion bequeathed me by will. **1628** FELTHAM *Resolves* II. lxxxii. 233 Though he doth forbeare to call for it, yet I beleeue, vpon the like, thou owest him. **1641** EARL MONM. tr. *Biondi's Civil Wars* III. 146 Charles de Lens..was slaine upon cold bloud.

†**b.** *upon new* = ANEW *adv.* 1. *Obs.*$^{-1}$

1399 GOWER *Praise of Peace* 315 Every dai it chaungeth uppon newe.

10. a. Occupied with; engaged in; employed on; = ON *prep.* 10 b.

For further illustration of group (*b*) see GUARD *sb.* 5 a, PATROL *sb.* 1, SENTRY *sb.* 3, WATCH *sb.* 6 b.

(*a*) **13..** *Seuyn Sages* (W.) 190 He was ever upon his bok, And to his lore tok gret kepe. *c* **1386** CHAUCER *Frankl. T.* 197 Vp on this daunce, amonges othere men, Daunced a squier biforn Dorigen. **1478** *Acta Dom. Conc.* (1839) 19/1 þe lordis ..declarit þat þai wald nocht sit apoun na summondis quhil þe said xj day. **1612** in *10th Rep. Hist. MSS. Comm.* App. I. 608 The Electour Palatine is now at the Haghe upon his voyage into England. **1634** W. TIRWHYT tr. *Balzac's Lett.* (vol. I) 154 Those who carve in Brasse or Marble waxe old upon their workes. **1659** VANE in *Burton's Diary* (1828) III. 171 Consider what it is we are upon, a Protector in the office of Chief Magistrate. **1690** LOCKE *Govt.* I. xi. §146 When Mankind were but one People,..and were upon Building a City together. **1705** HEARNE *Collect.* (O.H.S.) I. 30 He designs to carry on the work, being now upon a III^d volume. **1709** SWIFT *Adv. Relig.* Wks. 1755 II. I. 100 Neither am I at present upon a wild speculative project. **1719** DE FOE *Crusoe* II. (Globe) 563 They seemed to be upon their own affairs. **1741** RICHARDSON *Pamela* I. 163 Well, Jacob, what do you stare at? Pray mind what you're upon. **1784** in B. Ward *Dawn Cath. Revival* (1909) I. iv. 81 That they may be upon the mission all *unius moris in Domino*. **1859** DICKENS *T. Two Cities* II. i, He was never absent..unless upon an errand.

(*b*) **1577–** [see GUARD *sb.* 5 a]. **1647–8** in *Eng. Hist. Rev.* Oct. (1917) 573 There was onely townesmen upon the guarde, and those expressed great joy to see Sir Hugh. **1678** BUTLER *Hud.* III. i. 459 He was upon pursuit, To take you somewhere hereabout. **1681** V'CTESS CAMPDEN in *12th Rep. Hist. MSS. Comm.* App. V. 56 Lady Skidmore..was at Mr. Conisby's house upon a visette. *a* **1716** SOUTH *Serm.* (1717) VI. 378 No Man would spend the Night upon the Sentry, who [etc.].

b. Denoting state or condition. Cf. ON *prep.* 10.

See also BEHAVIOUR 3, BY *sb.*^{2} 2 b, CASE *sb.*^{1} 2 b, CONTENT *sb.*^{2} 2, DUTY 5 e, FRET *sb.*^{2} 6, LOAN *sb.*^{1} 3, LOOSE *a.* B. 1, OATH *sb.* 1, PAROLE *sb.* 1, TRIAL *sb.* 12. The uses placed under (*b*) are obsolete.

(*a*) *c* **1290** *S. Eng. Leg.* I. 272/39 Ich am a man opon mi seruiz, and noman serui i-nelle Bote mi louerd. *a* **1400–50** *Alexander* 42 He was wyse enoȝe wirdis to reken..of ledes opon lyfe. **1525** LD. BERNERS *Froiss.* II. lxxvii. [lxxiii.] 229 All suche..were styll in theyr owne houses vpon a redynes. *c* **1580** in *Eng. Hist. Rev.* July (1914) 517 You must kepe good wache by night and be upon your owne kepinge. **1585** T. WASHINGTON tr. *Nicholay's Voy.* I. xi. 13 b, The Caddy ..keepeth the town vpon tribute vnder the king of Alger. **1628** FELTHAM *Resolves* II. iv. 7 Their difference is neuer so much vpon the view, as then. **1657** EARL MONM. tr. *Paruta's Pol. Disc.* 35 Large Plains in Italy, wherein he might fight the Romans upon great advantage. **1683** MOXON *Mech. Exerc., Printing* xiii. ¶1 It must with the Chissel be split upon a good Blood-Red-Heat in that place. **1706** FARQUHAR *Recruiting Officer* I. i, A Granadeer..absent upon Furlow. **1769** GOLDSM. *Hist. Rome* (1786) II. 373 He never missep hitting..the fleetest animals, though upon full speed. **1788** CLARA REEVE *Exiles* I. 181 Poor Albert..had been upon the fret ever since I left him. **1801** tr. *Gabrielli's Myst. Husb.* III. 86 The kettle was just upon the boil. **1823** SOUTHEY *Hist. Penins. War* I. 686 The fate of the continent was upon the hazard.

(*b*) **1425** *Rolls of Parlt.* IV. 290 For lake of Parsons.. children have deghed uncristend..and wymen opon chyld perechyd. **1535** COVERDALE *1 Chron.* xiii. 17 Yf ye come vpon disceate, and to be mine aduersaries. **1604** SHAKS. *Oth.* I. i. 100 And now in madnesse..Vpon malitious knauerie, dost thou come To start my quiet. **1707** J. STEVENS tr. *Quevedo's Com. Wks.* (1709) 45 Finding a Door upon the jar.

a **1715** BURNET *Own Time* III. xiv. (1900) II. 357 Lord Russell.. was upon all the secret of his [*sc.* Rumsey's] going beyond sea. **1740** tr. *De Mouhy's Fort. Country Maid* (1741) I. 269, I had left the Door upon the Jarr.

c. Indicating a sphere of activity or existence.

Partly with implication of locative sense: cf. 1 b.

1487 *Cely Papers* (Camden) 159 Mony goyth now uppon the bursse at a xj^{s} iij^{d} ob. the nobull. **1589** NASHE *Pasquil's Ret.* 1, I little thought to meete thee so suddainly upon the Exchange. *c* **1645** HOWELL *Lett.* (1650) I. 26 One may hear 7. or 8. sorts of toungs spoken upon their Bourses. **1709** STEELE *Tatler* No. 48 ¶4, I was curious to observe the Reception these Gentlemen met with upon Change. **1712** —— *Spect.* No. 266 ¶2 This Creature is what they call newly come upon the Town. **1763** JOHNSON in *Boswell* 25 June, A Merchant upon the 'Change of London. **1822** W. IRVING *Braceb. Hall* vii. 59 A dashing young ensign, just come upon the town. **1838** D. JERROLD *Men of Char.* II. 255 Again was John Applejohn upon the world. **1882** PEBODY *Eng. Journalism* xi. 79 He found employment upon the *Morning Post*.

d. With sbs. denoting activity or progress.

See also GALLOP *sb.* 1, GOG², HUNT *sb.*² 1 b, LISTEN *sb.* 2, LONG RUN, SCRAMBLE *sb.* 1, TROT *sb.* 1 d.

1645 SLINGSBY *Diary* (1836) 176 Our horse, upon a Gallop without once drawing up. **1662** J. WILSON *Cheats* I. i, I was out t'other Night upon the Randan. **1678** in *12th Rep. Hist. MSS. Comm.* App. V. 50 Lord Rochester hath bin att the gates of death, and so penitent that he is upon an amendment. **1728** VANBR. & CIB. *Prov. Husb.* v. i, You will every Day see hundreds as fast upon the Gallop, as she is. **1768** GOLDSM. *Good-n. Man.* I. i, Everything upon the waste. **1801** *Farmer's Mag.* Jan. 105 Grain of all kinds continues upon the advance. **1877** SPURGEON *Serm.* XXIII. 505 The leaves are just upon the turn, and the fall of the year is close at hand.

e. Denoting situation with a portion of time or space.

1632 SIR T. HAWKINS tr. *Mathieu's Unhappy Prosperitie* 76 His life was now almost wholly wasted, he is upon the last hour. **1680** R. L'ESTRANGE *20 Sel. Colloq. Erasm.* 258 Observing the Woman to Yawn and just upon her last Stretch, he put [etc.]. **1694-** [see TACK *sb.*¹ 6]. **1720** DE FOE *Capt. Singleton* xi. (1840) 187 We being then upon our starboard tack.

11. Indicating the basis or reason of reliance, trust, etc.

See also COUNT *v.* 9, DEPEND *v.* 5, HANG *v.* 13 b (quot. 1817), RELY *v.*¹ 5, REST *v.* 5 b, STAND *v.* 78 c, STAY *v.*² 2 b, 3 b, SUSPEND *v.* 9, TRIST *v.* 1, TRUST *v.* 1.

c **1200** ORMIN 16724 And wha se lefeþþ upponn himm, þatt mann iss all unndemedd. *a* **1225** *Ancr. R.* 280 Uor þet stonding is treowe trust of herdi bileaue uppon Godes strencðe. *c* **1250** *Prayer to Virgin* 18 in *O.E. Misc.* 196 Al min hope is uppon þe. *c* **1315** SHOREHAM v. 51 Four manere ioyen hy hedde here Of hyre sone so lef an dere, Wytnes opan þe godspelle. **1377** LANGL. *P. Pl.* B. I. 117 Þei leueden vppon hym þat lyed in þis manere. **1382** WYCLIF *Isaiah* vii. 2 Siria restede vp on Effraym. **1509** *Reg. Privy Seal Scot.* I. 286/2 Ony proclamatioun.. anent the intercommonyn and sitting apoun the Inglismenis assouerans. **1574** R. SCOT *Platform Hop Gard.* 2, I, for my part, relye not upon other mens opinions. **1585** T. WASHINGTON tr. *Nicholay's Voy.* I. xx. 24 [He] resolued [= relied] vppon so smal an assuraunce of the Bascha. **1604** SHAKS. *Oth.* I. iii. 295 My life vpon her faith. Honest Iago, My Desdemona must I leaue to thee. **1640** LAUD *Wks.* (1853) III. 279 His Majesty's goodness was confident upon the fidelity of his subjects. **1767** GOOCH *Treat. Wounds* I. 241 It is fallacious, and by no means to be depended upon, as a Criterion. **1796** JANE AUSTEN *Pride & Prej.* i, Depend upon it, .. I will visit them all. **1823** SOUTHEY *Hist. Penins. War* I. 715 They counted upon succour from San Juan's troops. **1850** TENNYSON *In Mem.* xxxii. 7 Then one deep love doth supersede All other, .. And rests upon the Life indeed.

b. According to; in agreement or accordance with; on the model of.

(*a*) **1390** GOWER *Conf.* II. 108, I not if that be Sompnolence, Bot upon youre conscience, Min holi fader, demeth ye. *c* **1400** *Sowdone Bab.* 105 Comaundinge hem vppon her legeaunce To come. *c* **1420** *Avow. Arth.* xxxiii, Quat is thi rawunsun opon ryȝte, The sothe thou me sayn? *c* **1440** *Jacob's Well* 66 To make amendys, fully in trewe restitucyoun, vp-on þi powere. **1516** in *Acta Parlt. Scot.* (1875) XII. 37/1 He.. behavis him swa towart.. ȝoure brothir.. that apon Ressoune na man sall be discontentit of his gyding. **1585** T. WASHINGTON tr. *Nicholay's Voy.* I. xviii. 20 b, The king.. was set at libertie, vpon an accord and alliaunce which hee made. **1664** *Extr. St. Papers Friends* III. (1912) 226, I inform'd my Lord.. that vpon my certaine knowledge a greate number would meete.. att such a house. **1698** FRYER *Acc. E. India & P.* 54 Nothing remaining of it but only what is taken upon Chronicle. **1702** VANBRUGH *False Friend* I. i, I find you much upon my taste in this matter. **1748** RICHARDSON *Clarissa* (1811) VII. 373 Here Mr. Belford gives the substance of it upon his memory. **1867** LOWELL *Fitz Adam's Story* 464 An honest cord [of wood] in Jethro still would fail By a good foot upon the Deacon's scale.

(*b*) *a* **1225** *Leg. Kath.* 994 Hwi schulde he forhohien to wurðen to þet þing þet is iwend [= formed] upon him? **1563** SHUTE *Archit.* B iv, This piller [is].. made by the Ionians vpon the Simetrie of a strong man. **1776** *Ann. Reg.* 148 A rifle gun upon a new construction. **1790** W. WRIGHTE *Grotesque Archit.* 11 The four minarets at the angles bring the plan upon a square of forty feet. **1791** SMEATON *Edystone L.* §85 Upon these ideas I drew up.. the following plan. **1863** MARY HOWITT tr. *F. Bremer's Greece* I. viii. 264 The new constitution of Greece is formed very much upon that of France. **1882** PEBODY *Eng. Journalism* xxii. 172 The Society papers.. are to some extent modelled upon the Reviews.

c. Indicating the ground, basis, occasion, or reason of an action, opinion, etc.; = ON *prep.* 11.

In very frequent use from *c* 1525. In group (*b*) with allusion to literal uses (sense 1).

(*a*) **1456** SIR G. HAYE *Law Arms* (S.T.S.) 179 A symple knycht may nocht lede a baroun.. apon his sauf condyt. *a* **1500** in C. Trice-Martin *Chanc. Proc.* (1904) 4 Uppon untrue verydyte yoven in London ther lieth none atteynt. **1515** *Reg. Privy Seal Scot.* I. 403/2 The slauchter.. committit apoun forthocht felony. **1554-5** in Feuillerat *Revels Q. Mary* (1914) 170 In a redines to serve vpon further warnynge. **1584** R. SCOT *Discov. Witchcr.* x. i. (1886) 143 Those witches that make men beleeve they can prophesie upon dreames. **1602** W. S. *Thomas Ld. Cromwell* v. iv, The great Lord Cromwell arreasted vpon treason! **1647-8** in *Eng. Hist. Rev.* Oct. (1917) 569 How.. Cholmeley came first to be imployed in the Parliament service, and upon what grounds hee quitt the same. **1697** WALSH *Life V*, ¶26 in Dryden *Virgil*, He has solv'd more Phænomena of Nature upon sound Principles, than Aristotle in his Physics. **1722** DE FOE *Plague* (1754) 14 Upon these Arguments my Brother chang'd my Resolutions again. **1747** W. GOULD *Eng. Ants* Pref., Upon this Reason my Lord Bacon does not approve of the historical Method of writing in Philosophy. **1787** WHITAKER *Mary Q. Scots Vind.* I. 62 They thus condemn the Queen.. upon letters unauthenticated by the producers. **1827** SCOTT *Chron. Canongate* Introd., Invernahyle obtained from the Chevalier his prisoner's freedom upon parole. **1846** *Chambers' Jrnl.* VI. 280/2 Upon the most insubstantial of pretexts. **1872** LIDDON *Elem. Relig.* i. 16 The most intellectual Gnostics were Sensualists; Sensualists upon a theory and with deliberation.

(*b*) *a* **1400-** [see FOUND *v.*² 4]. **1565** SIR R. MAITLAND in *Maitland Folio MS.* 23 Grund all thy doing vpon suthfastnes. **1573-** [see BUILD *v.* 6 b]. **1672** T. GODDEN *Catholicks No Idolaters* 23 This is the major Proposition of his Syllogism, and if this fail, the Charge he builds upon it, must needs fall. **1711** ADDISON *Spect.* No. 9 ¶8 Our Modern celebrated Clubs are founded upon Eating and Drinking. **1814** JANE AUSTEN *Mansf. Park* xlii, He particularly built upon a very happy.. autumn there this year. **1844** BERESF. HOPE *Ess.* 111 This.. does give us very different ground to go upon. **1878** HOPPS *Princ. Relig.* iii. 13 Upon this great truth.. we base all our hopes.

†**d.** Of (a cause of death or illness). *Obs.*

c **1420** *Brut* 344 Mony a worthi man yn þat viage deid vpon þe Flix. **1510** in Leadam *Star Chamber Cases* (Selden) II. 73 Vppon the seid enprisonement the same John.. deyed within xij howres. **1600** HOLLAND *Livy* 1264 Upon which fracture he died thirtie daies after. **1645** SLINGSBY *Diary* (1836) 163 Y^{e} Gentlewoman y^{t} had lived in it dead upon Grief. **1696** A. TELFAIR *New Confut. Sadd.* 10 Which frightned him so much, that he fell sick upon it immediately.

e. Indicating means of subsistence or existence, or an article of food furnishing sustenance.

Sometimes = 'after having taken or consumed': see (*c*).

(*a*) **1457** HARDING *Chron.* in *Eng. Hist. Rev.* Oct. (1912) 747 His lyfelode exceded noght all clere An hundreth marke to leue vpon in dede. *c* **1489** CAXTON *Sonnes of Aymon* iii. 98 We have loste our store of vytaylles, so that we have noo thynge to lyve upon. **1564** *Child-Marr.* 125 Aspshawe is a very poore man, and liveth apon his neibours. **1583-** [see LIVE *v.*¹ 2]. **1599** B. JONSON *Ev. Man out of Hum.* Descr. Char., A Thred-bare Sharke. One that.. lives upon lendings. **1600** J. PORY tr. *Leo's Africa* v. 249 Monasteries.. maintained vpon the common beneuolence of the citie. **1625** BURGES *Pers. Tithes* 45 All liuing vpon Fishing. **1713** [see LIVE *v.*¹ 3]. **1884** *Pall Mall G.* 9 Sept. 3/1 The lady did not indeed say that she lived *with* her father and mother, but she lived *upon* them. **1885** *Law Times Rep.* LII. 651/1 He earned nothing, and he lived upon some money of mine.

(*b*) *c* **1440** *Pallad. on Husb.* x. 76 Til May hit wol suffice vppon to feede. **1571** DIGGES *Pantom.* Pref. Bj, Suche two footed Moules and Todes whom.. nature hath ordayned to .. suck vpon the muck. **1600** PORY tr. *Leo's Africa* VI. 276 They liue vpon the flesh of Ostriches and camels. **1678** WANLEY *Wond. Lit. World* v. i. §94. 467/2 'Tis thought he surfeited upon Melons. **1713** STEELE *Guard.* No. 34 He.. breakfasted upon toast and ale. **1743** P. FRANCIS tr. *Horace, Sat.* II. iii. 124 While Moths upon his rotting Carpets fed. **1818** G. S. FABER *Horæ Mosaicæ* II. 281 If the Dominical Supper be a feast upon a sacrifice. **1832** HT. MARTINEAU *Life in Wilds* ii. 26 The grass it fed upon. **1885** *Manch. Exam.* 16 June 5/1 M. Henze fed his prize oxen upon silage.

ellipt. **1717** PRIOR *Alma* III. 243 Was ever Tartar fierce or cruel, Upon the Strength of Water-Gruel. **1737** BRACKEN *Farriery Impr.* (1757) II. 109 A young Horse may look pretty sleek upon Hay only. **1897** MEREDITH *Amazing Marriage* i, The clergyman, .. renouncing strong drinks, because he found that he 'cursed better upon water'.

(*c*) **1663** BOYLE *Usef. Exp. Nat. Philos.* II. vi. 185 Though .. [it] did make her sickish, especially, when she slept upon it. **1829** SCOTT *Jrnl.* 5 July, So to roost upon a crust of bread and a glass of small beer, my usual supper.

†**f.** At (an expense, cost, etc.). *Obs.*

c **1400** *R. Gloucester's Chron.* (Rolls) 3799 Al þe bachelerie .. he nom in is compaynie.. vp [*v.rr.* vp on, vppon] is coust. **1476** *Acta Auditorum* (1839) 49/1 Þare to remain apoun þare awin expenss. **1513** BRADSHAW *St. Werburge* II. 1157 Many shyps were made vpon the kynges cost. **1563** *Ref. Privy Council Scot.* I. 239 To commande thame to warde, to remane thairin upon thair awne expense. **1577** HANMER *Anc. Eccl. Hist.* 396 He had buylded vpon his owne costes and charges the sepulchres and tumbes. **1674** *Reg. Privy Counc. Scot.* IV. 278 A mudwall rowme.. built upon his owne coast. **1711** in *10th Rep. Hist. MSS. Comm.* App. V. 124 Each company.. was subsisted upon the cost of every captain for three months.

g. Denoting security of a loan, etc.

1474 CAXTON *Chesse* (1883) 121 The besant.. was holden & gaged vpon an ymage. **1562** J. HEYWOOD *Prov. & Epigr.* Bb i b, No man will one peny lende upon it. **1611** BIBLE *Neh.* v. 4 Wee haue borrowed money.. vpon our lands and vineyards. **1677** YARRANTON *Eng. Improv.* 7 Moneys lent upon Goods at very easie Interest. **1707** *Lond. Gaz.* No. 4333/8 They will.. Lend Money upon Tallies or other good Securities, at 5 l. per Cent. **1742** KAMES *Decis. Crt. Sess.* (1799) 40 The money is secured.. upon land. **1791** BOSWELL *Johnson* (1904) I. 328 Security being taken upon the property. **1861** M. PATTISON *Ess.* (1889) I. 36 He assigns 1000 marks.. to his son's wife, secured upon the Swiss possessions of his house. **1868** ROGERS *Pol. Econ.* iv. 43 If [a banker].. issues notes upon no property at all, the issue is fraudulent. **1885** *Act 48-49 Vict.* c. 54 §11 Any mortgage or charge duly created.. upon the profits of any benefice.

†**h.** On condition of. *Obs.*

1516 *Reg. Privy Seal Scot.* I. 422/2 The kingis grace dischargis thaim apone thair remaining in ward for the said errour. **1591** SHAKS. *1 Hen. VI*, IV. v. 36 Vpon my Blessing I command thee goe. **1626** in Picton *L'pool Munic. Rec.* (1883) I. 199 Maister Lappage doth.. promise that hee will continew his ministry.. upon true payment and receivinge the afforesaid allowance. **1662** STILLINGFL. *Orig. Sacræ* III. III. §5 If it were suitable to Gods nature to promise life to man upon obedience.

†**i.** Out of; with; by the use of. *Obs. rare.*

1553 T. WILSON *Rhet.* (1580) 42 He did not make the wife vppon the same claie, whereof he made man. **1683** MOXON *Mech. Exerc., Printing* ii. ¶2 That his Letter be Cast upon good Mettal, that it may last the longer.

j. In many phrases, as *upon.. accord, account* (*of*), *composition, condition, design, distrust, envy, foot, fraud, head, lease, matter, purpose, score, shame, suspicion, trust, whole*, for which see the sbs.

12. At the risk or with the certainty of incurring or suffering (a pain, penalty, etc.); on peril of; = ON *prep.* 12.

See also PAIN *sb.*¹ 1 b, PENALTY *sb.* 2 d.

c **1384** CHAUCER *H. Fame* III. 1570 That he shuld fast goon Vpon the peyn to be blynde. *c* **1420** *Contin. Brut* 384 Þe King commaunded to.. late hem passe yn pees, vpon deth. *Ibid.* 385[He] chargyd ham, vpon her lyf, to kepe wel the toun and þe Castell. **1480** CAXTON *Descr. Brit.* 9 Walsshmen shold not passe that dyche with wepen vpon a grete payne. **1540** *Acts Privy Council* (1837) VII. 21 To temperate his tongue hereafter upon adventure of further punishement. **1553** W. CHOLMELEY *Req. & Suite* 19 in *Camden Misc.* (1853) II, Commaundyng.. the Aldermen, upon the losse of their auctoritie and office, .. to see [etc.]. **1596** *Edward III*, I. i. 70 With threats, Vppon a penaltie, inioynd to come. **1603** PARSONS *2nd Pt. Three Convers. Eng.* xii. 625 The Duke protesteth the contrary (vpon his death). **1656** EARL MONM. tr. *Boccalini's Advts. fr. Parnass.* 126, I have, .. upon severe punishment, inhibited the translation of my Alcheron. **1699** BENTLEY *Phal.* 439 He order'd every man upon the pain of death to bring in all the money he had.

13. Indicating that which forms the basis of revenue, profit, fines, taxation, lending, etc.; = ON *prep.* 13.

See also RETIRE *v.* 1 e (quot. 1806), TAX *sb.*¹ 1.

1466 *Acta Auditorum* (1839) 4/2 [He] sall.. resaue þe soume of mone aucht till him vppoun þe said annuel. **1495** *Act 11 Hen. VII*, c. 43 *Preamble*, So that the seid Erle upon his seid leasses.., do reserve asmuch rentis.. as be nowe usuell. **1535** COVERDALE *Neh.* v. 3 Let vs borowe money of the kinge vpon vsury. **1554** in Leadam *Star Chamber Cases* (Selden) II. 217 They so offending to be payned opon a certen some of money. ? **1677** PETTY *Pol. Arithm.* (1699) 272 Such a part of the full value of their Commodities, as may possibly be lost upon the sale of them. **1719** D'URFEY *Pills* I. 333 Five hundred Pounds upon the brown Bay still. **1798** *Hull Advertiser* 24 Mar. 2/3 Insurance upon.. outhouses, and upon unthreshed stock therein. **1845** R. W. HAMILTON *Pop. Education* x. 278 How can the State raise the amount? Is it not to be raised upon the people? **1892** *Law Times* XCIV. 104/1 A commission of over 60 per cent. upon the sums received.

II. Of motion or direction towards a position, thing or person, state, etc.

14. Upward so as to place or be on a surface, point, etc. Cf. ON *prep.* 14.

c **1200** ORMIN 11959 Þe deofell brohhte Jesu Crist Wiþþutenn o þe temmple Upponn an sæte uppo þe rof. *c* **1250** *Gen. & Ex.* 3899 Moyses ðor made a wirme of bras, And henget heȝe up-on a saft. *c* **1300** *Havelok* 1942 He lep up on a stede lith. **13..** *Seuyn Sages* (W.) 2318 Vpon his palfrai lep Catoun. **1375, 1470-85** [see START *v.* 1]. **1470-85** MALORY *Arthur* IX. xxx. 384 They came vpon sir launcelot sodenly and vnnethe he myght putte vpon hym his helme. **1535** COVERDALE *Joel* ii. 9 They shal clymme vp vpon the houses. **1627** DRAYTON *Nymphidia* xvii, Flye Cranion her Chariottere, Vpon the Coach-box getting. **1639** S. DU VERGER tr. *Camus' Admir. Events* 130 He leapes upon his Mule. **1725** *Fam. Dict.* s.v. *Pears*, Mount them one upon another Steeplewise. **1847** TENNYSON *Princ.* III. 208 To lift the woman's fall'n divinity Upon an even pedestal with man. **1854** H. MILLER *Sch. & Schm.* xxi. 446 A large loligo .. had thrown itself high and dry upon the beach.

b. To or towards a position on a surface, etc.; = ON *prep.* 14.

Group (*b*) corresponds to sense 1 c; group (*c*) illustrates non-physical uses.

(*a*) *c* **1200** ORMIN 14667 Sniþ itt, alls itt wære an shep, & leȝȝ itt upponn allterr. *c* **1250** *Gen. & Ex.* 3186 On an gold gad ðe name god Is grauen, and leid up-on ðe hod. *Ibid.* 3949 Vp-on hise ase his sadel he dede. *a* **1300** *Cursor M.* 8894 Vnwarli sco sett hir don Apon þis ilk tre. *c* **1386** CHAUCER *Knt.'s T.* 921 Some drope of pitee.. Vp on vs wrecched wommen lat thou falle. *c* **1391** —— *Astrol.* II. §7 Ley thi label vp-on the same degree of the sonne. *c* **1400** *St. Alexius* (Cotton) 257 They hylde water wppon hys hede. *c* **1430** *Two Cookery Bks.* 42 Þan take fayre pecez of Brede.. vppe-on þe Eyroun. **1602** MARSTON *Antonio's Rev.* IV. iii, Her head sunk down upon her breast. *a* **1655** SIR T. MAYERNE *Archimag. Anglo-Gall.* No. 84 (1658) 58 Lay this froth upon your sullibub as high as you can. **1697** DRYDEN *Virg. Georg.* IV. 611 The various God.. draws a Rock upon his dark Abode. **1728** CHAMBERS *Cycl.* s.v. *Triangle*, If a Perpendicular be let fall upon the Base of an oblique angled Triangle. **1808** SCOTT *Marm.* II. i, Upon the gale she stooped her side. **1844** J. JACK *Hist. of St. Monance* xi. 74 The skipper placed upon the table a large wooden caup or platter. **1870** ANDERSON *Missions Amer. Bd.* IV. xxvi. 63 The mob rushed forward and trampled spitefully upon it.

ellipt. *c* **1450** *Mirk's Festial* I. 5 Sle, sle, opon þe broche, rost hote.

(*b*) **1303** R. BRUNNE *Handl. Synne* 952 Syttyþ dowun vppon ȝoure knees. *c* **1400** *26 Pol. Poems* 149/233, I set me doune apon my kne. **1486** *Bk. St. Albans* b iv b, Softe and layserly fall oppon yowre kneys. **1535** COVERDALE *Mark* xv. 19 [They] fell vpon the kne, & worshipped him. *a* **1578** LINDESAY (Pitscottie) *Chron. Scot.* (S.T.S.) I. 209 The said preist..kneillit doune wpoun his knie. **1611** SHAKS. *Cymb.* IV. ii. 288 Come on, away, apart vpon our knees. **1837** SIR F. PALGRAVE *Merch. & Friar* iv. (1844) 176 The Chancellor, dropping off the Woolsack upon his bended knees. **1876** F. K. ROBINSON *Whitby Gloss.* 208, 'Up-end yourself,' get upon your legs.

(*c*) *c* **1325** *Spec. Gy Warw.* 995 And anon god putte his fuisoun Vp-on hire mele. **1382** WYCLIF *Job* xxv. 3 Vp on whom shyneth not the li3t of hym? **1461** *Rolls of Parlt.* V. 463/2 Takyng upon hym..the Coroune and name of Kyng. **1535** COVERDALE *Num.* vi. 25 The Lorde make his face to shyne vpon the. **1656** EARL MONM. tr. *Boccalini's Advts. fr. Parnass.* II. vi. 210 Whereby they had put themselves..upon great difficulties. **1697** DRYDEN *Virg. Georg.* IV. 773 The Nymphs, Companions of th' unhappy Maid, This Punishment upon thy Crimes have laid. **1765** STERNE *Tr. Shandy* VIII. xxi, I fell in love all at once..it burst upon me ..like a bomb. **1768** BOSWELL *Lett.* (1924) 145, I am thrown upon the wide world again. **1793** T. BEDDOES *Demonstr. Evid.* 79 The magnitudes, being doubled upon themselves, increase so, that [etc.]. **1816** BYRON *Prisoner of Chillon* x, A light broke in upon my brain.

c. Denoting incidence, seizure, hold, etc.; = ON *prep.* 14 b.

c **1250** *Gen. & Ex.* 2339 Ðo cam iosep swilc rewðe up-on, he dede halle ut ðe toðere gon. **1398** TREVISA *Barth. De P.R.* XVII. cxv. (Bodl. MS.), Ripe & igadered ere corrupcioune oþer rostinge falle vpon whete. **1530** PALSGR. 748/2, I take holde apon one, *jempoygne.* **1535** COVERDALE *Ps.* cxiv. 3 The paynes of hell gat holde vpon me. **1535–** [see LAY *v.*[1] 22]. **1546–** [see SEIZE *v.* 9]. **1632** LITHGOW *Trav.* VII. 303 The Venetian Factor seased vpon all. **1665** *Extr. St. Papers Friends* III. (1912) 240 There was a full congregation of quakers and the like seised vppon by Sir Francis Clarke sunday last. **1880** J. PAYNE *New Poems* 259 A deadly terror got A sudden hold upon her. **1892** H. LANE *Differ. Rheum. Dis.* (ed. 2) 67 It seems to have taken a firm hold upon the public.

d. Of the incidence of a blow, stroke, etc.; = ON *prep.* 14 c.

c **1300** *Havelok* 2734 He..smot him so up-on þe crune, þat [etc.]. **13..** *Guy Warw.* (A.) 2368 Þan hastiliche þe ost ichon Opon Segyn þat smiten anon. **1470–85** MALORY *Arthur* x. lx. 516 Sir Tristram gaf hym suche a buffet vpon the helme. **1507** in Leadam *Star Chamber Cases* (Selden) 253 He sawe..Irton being hurt vppon the hed. **1562** *Aberd. Kirk Sess. Rec.* (Spalding Cl.) 6 To be puneist with ane palm vpone the hand for ilk falt. **1594** *Selimus* 1447 Dart Thy smouldring flame Vpon the head of cursed Acomat. **1611** BIBLE *Exod.* vii. 17 Behold, I will smite with the rod..vpon the waters. **1711** ADDISON *Spect.* No. 9 ¶11 His Neighbour may give him a Kick upon the Shins. **1737** WHISTON *Josephus, Hist.* I. xxi. 13 Many..have stood amazed..when they saw him..shoot the arrow upon the mark. **1813** SCOTT *Rokeby* VI. xxv, One stroke, upon the Castle bell, To Oswald rung his dying knell. **1844** MRS. BROWNING *Drama Exile* 64 This is the Eden lost By Lucifer!..this the sword..That smote upon the forehead. **1881** BESANT & RICE *Chapl. of Fleet* I. viii, The cruel cat falling at every step upon their.. bleeding shoulders.

e. In phrases of the type ***harm upon harm, torment upon torment***, denoting cumulative addition or repetition; = ON *prep.* 14 d.

c **1320** R. BRUNNE *Medit.* 865 þey wounded here, and heped harm vp on harmes. *c* **1380** WYCLIF *Sel. Wks.* III. 346 And so servauntis upon servantis weren char[g]ious to þis hous. *c* **1485** *Digby Myst.* (1882) IV. 1336 He had torment opon torment. **1529** S. FISH *Supplic. Beggers* (1871) 13 The capteyns of his kingdome..haue heped to him benefice vpon benefice. **1596** SHAKS. *Merch. V.* III. i. 91 Why, thou losse vpon losse! **1599** —— *Much Ado* II. i. 252 Hudling iest vpon iest, with..impossible conueiance vpon me. **1613** PURCHAS *Pilgrimage* (1614) 152 Which heaped vpon them Anathema vpon Anathema. **1699** EVELYN *Acetaria* App. P 4, Cover the Bottom of the Jar with some Dill,..then a Bed of Nuts; and so *stratum* upon *stratum.* **1864** KINGSLEY *Roman & T.* 137 Dietrich had had to write letter upon letter. **1882** 'OUIDA' *Maremma* I. 90 Centuries upon centuries of carnage ..have laid the land bare. **1884** C. F. WOOLSON in *Harper's Mag.* Feb. 371 Millions upon millions of violets.

f. On (a voyage, expedition, mission, etc.); = ON *prep.* 14 e.

1426 LYDG. *De Guil. Pilgr.* 648 Or I myhte make my passage To gynnen vp-on my pylgrymage. *c* **1430** —— *Min. Poems* (Percy Soc.) 12 The kyng procedyng forthe upon his way, kome to the Condyte. **1596** SHAKS. *1 Hen. IV*, I. iii. 150 When the vnhappy King..did set forth Vpon his Irish Expedition. **1711** ADDISON *Spect.* No. 55 ¶1 A young Fellow..sent upon a long Voyage. **1712** W. ROGERS *Voy.* 324 To encourage our South Sea Company..to go upon some Discovery that way. **1817** KIRBY & SP. *Entomol.* xvii. II. 77 The rufescent ants do not leave their nests to go upon these expeditions..till [etc.]. **1839** BAILEY *Festus* 232 As on they sped upon their starward course.

15. Into contact or collision with, esp. by way of attack; against; = ON *prep.* 15.

See also COME *v.* 51 b, FALL *v.* 70 b, FLY *v.*[1] 8 b, GO *v.* 67 a, LAY *v.*[1] 32 a, SET *v.*[1] 132 a.

a **1300** *Cursor M.* 24461 Me-thoght moght it [*v.r.* i] apon him rine,..I suld ha ben all hale. **13..** *Guy Warw.* (A.) 1996 Þou schalt 3if þe first asaut Opon þe Almaundes. *c* **1385** CHAUCER *L.G.W.* 1327 *Dido* (Fairf.), On a nyght sleping he let hir lye, And staal a-wey vpon [*v.r.* vnto] his companye. *c* **1400** *Sc. Trojan War* II. 444 Russhande wpone the altare. *c* **1450** *Merlin* iii. 56 Whan Vter saugh..the Danes assembled, he sette vpon hem as vigorously or more. *c* **1500** *Melusine* lix. 348 Go we vpon our enemyes to helpe & socoure our frendes. **1535** COVERDALE *1 Sam.* xvii. 35 And when he wolde haue bene vpon me, I toke him by his beerde. **1585** T. WASHINGTON tr. *Nicholay's Voy.* I. xix. 22 The Turkes.., vpon whom they of the Castle..gaue an assault. **1622** MABBE tr. *Aleman's Guzman d'Alf.* II. 48, I stumbled ..vpon a great dung mixen. **1631** PELLHAM *Gods Power* 2 Wee eight men..were bound for this Greenland aforesaid, to make a voyage upon Whales or Sea-horse. **1711** ADDISON *Spect.* No. 299 ¶2 He drew his Sword upon me before he was nine years old. **1782** COWPER *Royal George* 20 She ran upon no rock. **1801** STRUTT *Sports & Past.* III. i. 130 The two combatants..were thereby prevented from running their horses upon each other. **1857** T. HUGHES *Tom Brown* i. ix, [They] run plump upon one of the masters as they emerge into the High Street.

ellipt. c **1450** *Merlin* iii. 56 The kynge seide to his peple, 'Now vpon hem in all that we may'. **1535** COVERDALE *2 Sam.* xviii. 14 Not so, I wil vpon him before thy face. **1588** SHAKS. *L.L.L.* IV. iii. 367 Aduance your standards, & vpon them Lords. **1821** BYRON *Sardanap.* IV. i, Upon them! (Trumpet sounds again.)

fig. **1535–** [see RUSH *v.*[2] 6 b, 3 a]. **1887** 'L. CARROLL' *Game of Logic* i. 36 Let them Rush upon their Fate!

16. In the direction of; towards; = ON *prep.* 16.

a. In respect of looking, etc.

See also CAST *v.* 7, FRONT *v.*[1] 1, GAPE *v.* 3, GAZE *v.* 1 b, GLARE *v.* 2, LAUGH *v.* 4, LOOK *v.* 1, PORE *v.* 1, SEE *v.* 21, SMILE *v.* 2 a, SQUINT *v.* 2.

a **1225** *Ancr. R.* 56 To kesten kang eien upon 3unge wummen. *c* **1250** *Gen. & Ex.* 2661 Ðor quiles he seweden [= looked] him up-on, Mani dede bileph un-don. *c* **1340** HAMPOLE *Pr. Consc.* 5024 Þair bodys sal alle unsemely be,.. and ugly, opon to se. *c* **1386** CHAUCER *Knt.'s T.* 219 He cast his eye vpon Emelya. **14..** in *E.E.P.* (1862) 144 Dame ypocryte loke vp-on a boke. **1526** TINDALE *1 John* i. 1 That which..we have loked apon, and oure hondes have handled. **1581** [see TURN *v.* 48]. **1632** LITHGOW *Trav.* I. 38 Arthur looked vpon me, and I laughed vpon him. **1710** STRYPE *Life & Acts of E. Grindal* vii. 70 These Unsuccesses were justly looked upon to proceed from the punishing Hand of Heaven. **1790** BRUCE *Source of Nile* I. 5 We pointed our prow directly..upon Alexandria. **1799** WORDSW. *Two April Mornings* 19 Matthew..fixing still his eye Upon the eastern mountain-top. **1845** S. AUSTIN *Ranke's Hist. Ref.* II. 357 The fears of some, the hopes of others, and the attention of all, were now turned upon the young emperor. **1874** FARRAR *Christ* I. 472 He turned His back for a time upon His native land. **1884** MRS. OLIPHANT *Sir Tom* iv, Her gray eyes absolutely flamed upon him.

b. In respect of movement, etc.

? *a* **1400** *Morte Arth.* 262 Thow countez no caas, ne castes no forthire, Bot hurles furthe appone heuede, as thi herte thynkes. *c* **1400** *Destr. Troy* 6258 If any stert vpon stray, strike hym to dethe! **1511** *Guylforde's Pylgr.* (Camden) 21 After .viij. dayes..he come vpon [= appeared to] theym ayen. **1634** SIR T. HERBERT *Trav.* 11 [We] were driuen to lee-ward a hundred leagues vpon the Coast of Brazil. **1697** COLLIER *Ess. Mor. Subj.* I. B 1, Unless you point directly upon his Vice. **1716** *Lond. Gaz.* No. 5455/3 Our Fleet.. bore down upon them. **1828** in Concanen *Rowe* v. *Brenton* (1830) 28 To sink a shaft upon the lode. **1829** NAPIER *Penins. War* II. 142 The hospitals..of Salamanca being evacuated upon Lamego, that town was crowded.

17. †**a.** In or into (pieces); = ON *prep.* 17 b.

c **1400** *Sege Jerusalem* 699 Twey apys..þat renten þe rawe flesche vpon rede peces.

b. Into, as by penetration; = ON *prep.* 17 a.

1738 HERRING in J. Duncombe *Lett.* (1773) II. 137 The sea, which here indents upon the country.

18. Unto, to (a person): in reference to descent or (*Sc.*) marriage; = ON *prep.* 18.

1492 *Acta Dom. Conc.* (1839) 254/2 His faider..maryit him apoun his sister dochter incontrare his band. **1536** BELLENDEN *Cron. Scot.* (1821) I. 127 The eldest of hir dochteris wes married upon..Marius. **1596** BACON *Use Com. Law* (1635) 32 If this inheritance descend upon a woman. **1667** [see DESCEND *v.* 9]. **1821** GALT *Ann. Parish* i, My marriage upon my own cousin, Miss Betty Lanshaw. **1893** STEVENSON *Catriona* xxi, She was married..upon my Uncle Robin.

19. Into, to, or on (some action, occupation, course, or condition); = ON *prep.* 19.

a **1300** *Cursor M.* 15580 Alle þe apostels þan bi-gan to fal a-pon a gret. **1390** GOWER *Conf.* I. 30 Thanne upon dissencioun Thei felle. **1435** [see SET *v.*[1] 114]. **1483** in *Acta Dom. Conc.* II. Introd. 103 The said schiref put apone the said inquest..persons quhilk war suspect of the law. *a* **1513** FABYAN *Chron.* 351 A quest of .xii. Knyghtes of Myddlesex, sworne vpon a iurye. **1581–** [see RUN *v.* 70 d]. **1607** T. ROGERS *39 Art.* Pref. §5 Wee set vpon the building of Gods house. **1625–** [see FALL *v.* 70 d]. **1658** ALLESTREE *Whole Duty Man* XIV. §22. 300 It puts the child upon shifts, and tricks. **1709** STRYPE *Ann. Ref.* I. xxi. 240 Some while..after the entrance of Queen Elizabeth upon her government. **1750** JOHNSON *Rambler* No. 1 ¶1 The perplexity of being forced upon choice. **1764** FOOTE *Mayor of G.* I. Wks. 1799 I. 165 I advised him to pull off his spurs before he went upon action. **1813** *Examiner* 17 May 320/1 It put the Church upon the alert. **1847** WORDSW. in *Mem.* (1851) I. 14 When at school, I..was put upon reading the first six books of Euclid.

20. Indicating the person or thing that action, feeling, etc., is directed towards or against, or that is influenced or affected by it; = ON *prep.* 20.

Construed with many verbs, as *attend, await, bear, bespit, bestow, breathe, call, charge*, etc. See also FIE *int.* 1–2, OUT *int.* 2, SHAME *sb.* 16 b.

c **1200** ORMIN 1750 Þa bedess, þatt te Laferrd Crist Forr hise þeowwess biddeþþ Uppnn hiss faderr heofennking. *Ibid.* 6119 Þe birrþ þin rihhte swinnkess winn Uppnn 3uw alle nittenn. *a* **1225** *Leg. Kath.* 130 Ah se sone ha..wende hare wiheles, upon ham seoluen. **1297** R. GLOUC. (Rolls) 3167 Þe king ek in is syde is herte up on him caste. *c* **1320** *Cast. Love.* 1482 Þat muche wo ve brou3te vppon. *c* **1400** tr. *Secreta Secret., Gov. Lordsh.* 106 He hadde greuously synned vpon him. **1473** WARKW. *Chron.* (Camden) 8 The Kynge..losyde his gonnys of his ordynaunce uppone them. *c* **1500** *Melusine* lix. 360 Be ye he that wyl take the trybute vpon my Fortresse? **1533** *Acc. Ld. High Treas. Scot.* VI. 156 To Johne Drummondis childer wirkand upoune the hagbute stokkis. **1585** T. WASHINGTON tr. *Nicholay's Voy.* I. xviii. 21 We will not leaue the following on vpon our purpose. **1633** MARMION *Fine Companion* I. iii. (1875) 114 They can doe no more good upon me, than a young pittifull Lover upon a mistress that has the sullens. **1656** EARL MONM. tr. *Boccalini's Advts. fr. Parnass.* II. v. 206 He..had made their places be conferred upon men void of counsel. **1680** *Laws Nevis* iii. (1740) 6 If the said Offenders are not able to pay..then to be compelled to work it out upon the Forts. **1737** WHISTON *Josephus, Antiq.* XVI. iv. §3 The father may have a suspicion upon all his sons. **1796** *Ann. Reg., St. Papers* 297 The constitution..is sacredly obligatory upon all. **1805** tr. *Lafontaine's Hermann & Emilia* I. 261 Nothing is more detestable than to offer one's self upon a young man. **1850** ROBERTSON *Serm.* Ser. III. (1857) 7 Persecution is that which affixes penalties upon views held, instead of upon life led. **1896** *Peterson Mag.* Jan. 102/2 The intruded-upon young lady turned her back upon him.

b. Denoting the object of regard, desire, etc.; = ON *prep.* 20 b.

See also DOTE *v.*[1] 3, EAGER *a.* 6, KEEN *a.* 6 b, MAD *a.* 4, RUN *v.* 70 b, SET *v.*[1] 37.

c **1330** R. BRUNNE *Chron. Wace* (Rolls) 7604 Opon þat meyden he wax al mad. **1382** WYCLIF *Psalm* xxxix. [xl.] 17 Ful out io3e thei, and glade vpon me, alle that sechen thee. *c* **1449** PECOCK *Repr.* II. xx. 267 He schal haue miche gretter affeccioun vpon the seid freend. **1470–85** MALORY *Arthur* x. lvi. 508 Louers..soo mad and soo soted vpon wymmen. *a* **1578** LINDESAY (Pitscottie) *Chron. Scot.* (S.T.S.) I. 169 The king..was covatous wpoun money. **1598** BARCKLEY *Felic. Man* I. 51 A young man..that was..enamoured vpon an Image of marble. **1614** BP. HALL *Recoll. Treat.* 982 In this case, Moses should have beene..cast downe..; yet how hot is hee uppon justice. **1711** ADDISON *Spect.* No. 106 ¶3 When he is pleasant upon any of them, all his Family are in good Humour. **1843** *Fraser's Mag.* XXVIII. 619 O'Connell is bent upon the disruption of the British empire.

†**c.** Among (a number of sharers, etc.). *Obs.*

1492 in *10th Rep. Hist. MSS. Comm.* App. V. 323 Distributers of the same upon the commynes. **1526** TINDALE *Rom.* xv. 26 To make a certayne distribucion apon the poore sanctes. **1598** DALLINGTON *Meth. Trav.* K 3, Hee diuideth the Lands vpon his horsemen, to each his portion.

d. Indicating the person by whom a cheque, draft, order, etc., is payable, or the bank on which it is drawn; = ON *prep.* 20 c.

See also CHEQUE *sb.* 3, DRAUGHT *sb.* 35, DRAW *v.* 65.

1660 *Nicholas Papers* (Camden) IV. 226 Mr. Fox hauing giuen mee a note upon Mr. Shaw to pay me my allowance. *a* **1722** FOUNTAINHALL *Decis.* (1759) I. 12 The bill upon his wife for £200. **1722** DE FOE *Col. Jack* (1840) 216 He shows me a bill upon me, drawn by my wife. **1798** in *Ushaw Mag.* Dec. (1913) 287 An order upon Mr. Wright for £12 as the price of the book sent you. **1843** *Blackw. Mag.* LIV. 736 It may be quite as well..to draw upon the bank.

21. Indicating a person or thing towards whom or which hostile or adverse action or language is directed; against; = ON *prep.* 21.

See also (*a*) BLOW *v.* 30, COMPLAIN *v.* 6 b, CRY *v.* 21 b, DESIGN *sb.* 1 b, LIE *v.*[2] 1 b, PEACH *v.* 2, RAGE *v.* 2 b, RAIL *v.*[4] 1 b, STEAL *v.* 5 e; (*b*) GO *v.* 67 a, MAKE *v.* 81, SEEK *v.* 17.

(*a*) *c* **1200** ORMIN 415 Þatt fand mann nan þing uppon hemm To wre3enn, ne to tælenn. *a* **1225** *Leg. Kath.* 2204 Þa Porphire iseh feole, þet me seide hit upon,..dreien to deaðe. *c* **1275** *Passion Our Lord* 241 in *O.E. Misc.* 44 A ueole kunne wise hi lowen him vp-on. *c* **1430** LYDG. *Hors, Shepe & G.* 151 He cryethe affter peasse, compleynnythe vppon þe werres sore. *c* **1440** *Alph. Tales* 12 Þis abbatis..forgaff þaim all þai had saide vppon hur. **1560** DAUS tr. *Sleidane's Comm.* 10 He declareth howe grevously he is complained upon unto the Duke. **1642** LAUD *Diary* 2 Dec., They were sufficiently railed upon in the streets. **1651** H. MORE *Second Lash* in *Enthus. Tri.*, etc. (1656) 253, I now forgive thee heartily for all thy abuses upon me. *a* **1715** BURNET *Own Time* III. (1900) II. 84 The court carried every question.., though with..a protestation made upon every step that was carried. **1737** WHISTON *Josephus, Hist.* v. xiii. §1 He also jested upon him. **1753** MISS COLLIER *Art Torment.* II. ii. (1811) 130 Nor need you be apprehensive of the others telling tales upon you. **1861** F. TEMPLE *Serm.* 274 The unhappy man who has not courage to tell upon himself. **1891** *Law Times* XC. 441/2 The judges..must accept criticism upon their order.

(*b*) *c* **1200** ORMIN 7155 Forr þatt he wennde þatt tatt follc Uppon himm cumenn wære..for to niþþrenn himm. *c* **1230** *Hali Meid.* 17 Leccherie..secheð earst upon hire, nebbe to nebbe. *c* **1300** *Havelok* 65 Was non so bold..þat durste upon his menie bringhe Hunger. **13..** *K. Alis.* 4875 (Laud MS.), Euermore hij beþ werrende, And vpon oþer conquerrende. *c* **1386** CHAUCER *Monk's T.* 537 The peple roos vp-on hym on a nyght. **1393** LANGL. *P. Pl.* C. VII. 106 Ich am wratthe,..wol gladliche smyte Boþe with ston and with staf, and stele vp-on myn enemy. *c* **1450** *Merlin* ii. 24 The hethen assembled a grete oste vpon hem. **1475** *Bk. Noblesse* (Roxb.) 5 They bring assailours uppon this lande. **1518** in Leadam *Star Chamber Cases* (Selden) II. 137 Afterwardes they sought vpon hym at hys boothe with ij clubbys. **1535** COVERDALE *1 Esdras* i. 27, I am not sent..to fight agaynst yᵉ, for my warre is upon Euphrates. **1608** *Yorksh. Trag.* vii. 17 It shall be my charge To raise the towne vpon him.

(*c*) **1476** *Acta Auditorum* (1839) 55/2 Elene Tulloch..wes marijt þe tim þat þe said det wes recouerit apon hir. **1482** *Cely Papers* (Camden) 85 To see the hurtes and harms he dyd yow uppon your goodes. **1598** BARRET *Theor. Warres* 28 He is to haue great care that his soldiers grow not licencious vpon their poore hosts. **1647** in *Crawford Proclam.* (1910) II. 55/1 Robberies committed by the tories and rebels upon the protestants. **1678** WANLEY *Wond. Lit. World* v. i. §98 Encroachments upon his Dominions. **1748** *Anson's Voy.* II. v. 176 The most eligible situation on that coast for cruising upon the enemy. **1754** A. MURPHY *Gray's-Inn Journal* No. 102 ¶2 A Design upon one another's Pockets..was introductory of another Crime. **1772** in *Eng. Hist. Rev.* Jan. (1915) 30 He places a number of..sepoys upon them and their families. **1883** *Harper's Mag.* Aug. 448/2 The disadvantages are..unreliability in stays.., hardness upon helms.

b. On or against (a person), by way of vengeance or the like.

a **1300** *Cursor M.* 5862 Þat suerd apon hus tak na wrak. *c* **1400** *Pilgr. Sowle* (Caxton, 1483) III. viii. 55 They alwey hauen sought vengeaunce.., to be wroken vppon tho that ought haue mysliked them. **1470–85** MALORY *Arthur* x. lv. 506 Soone we shold haue ben reuenged vpon the fals knyghtes. **1526–** [see REVENGE *v.* 1–2]. **1535** COVERDALE *Isaiah* i. 23, I must ease me of myne enemies, and a venge me vpon them. **1595** *Locrine* II. v. 86 Reuenge my death vpon his traiterous head. **1860** HOOK *Lives Abps.* I. vii. 377 Edwy had the power to avenge himself upon Dunstan.

ellipt. c **1485** *Digby Myst.* (1882) I. 322 A shamefull deth I aske vpon herowde. **1535** COVERDALE *Ps.* lviii. 10 God letteth me se my desyre vpon myne enemies.

c. So as to close in or confine.

1382 WYCLIF *2 Kings* iv. 5 The woman wente, and closede the dore vpon hir silf and vpon hir children. **1535** COVERDALE *Num.* xvi. 33 They wente downe quycke in to the hell..And the earth closed vpon them. —— *Ps.* lxix. 15 That..the pitte shut not hir mouth vpon me. **1633** T. ADAMS *Exp. 2 Pet.* ii. 5 The Lord..himselfe shut the doore of the Arke upon Noah. **1701** PRIDEAUX *Direct. Ch.-wardens* (1712) 10 If they shall meet..with the Doors lock'd, barred, or bolted upon them. **1844** DICKENS *Mart. Chuz.* xlviii, Softly turning the key upon him as they went out.

22. With respect or regard to; in reference to; touching, concerning; as to; = ON *prep.* 22.

See also AGREE *v.* 10 b, COMPLIMENT *v.* 3, CONCLUDE *v.* 13, CONSULT *v.* 1, INSIST *v.* 3, LOT *sb.* 1, MATTER *sb.* 25 c, PRIDE *v.* 4, TREAT *v.* 2 a, VALUE *v.* 6.

1382 WYCLIF *Ecclus.* xxii. 11 A litil weep vp on the deade, for he restede. **1390** GOWER *Conf.* I. 110, I finde upon Surquiderie, How that..be olde daies was a King [etc.]. *c* **1400** *Contin. Brut* 321 In þe whiche parlement was treted ..how he myȝte best oppon his wrong be avenged. **1439** *Cases bef. King's Council* (Selden) 105 The Kyngis counsaillours examined the persones..upon the ryot. **1484** *Surtees Misc.* (1888) 43 Surmising none othere upon hyme. **1515** in Leadam *Star Chamber Cases* (Selden) II. 85 Two seuerall Writtes..to theym directed to enquere and examyn vpon certen Interrogatoriez. **1584** COGAN *Haven Health* xc. 81 If you will not be at cost vppon spices, you may make a verie sweete water thus. **1609** BIBLE (Douay) *1 Kings* xxx. 6 The soule of everie man was bitterly affected upon their sonnes, and daughters. **1680** MOXON *Mech. Exerc.* xiii. 227 Having such good Success upon Brass, I improv'd the Invention so, as to make it serve for Wood also. **1710** STEELE *Tatler* No. 150 ¶4, I could name Two, who..fell out and parted Beds upon the boiling of a Leg of Mutton. **1760** *Imposters Detected* III. vii, [She] was not in the least vain or proud upon the encomiums..from every mouth. **1826** *Art of Brewing* (ed. 2) 9 Opinions and practices..completely at variance upon the subject of mashing. **1843** *Blackw. Mag.* LIV. 209, I shall set you at ease..upon that point. **1885** SIR H. C. LOPES in *Law Reports 14 Q.B.D.* 921 This case raises a novel point upon which there is no authority.

b. Denoting the object to or towards which mental activity is directed; = ON *prep.* 22 b.

See also CONSIDER *v.* 11 b, MEDITATE *v.* 4 b, MIN *v.*[2] 3 b, MIND *sb.*[1] 7 (quot. 1589), PUT *v.* 27 c, REFLECT *v.* 13, REMEMBER *v.* 4 c, RUN *v.* 70 c, STUDY *v.* 1, 2, THINK *v.*[2] 3 b, TREAT *v.* 2.

a **1300** *Sarmun* xxxvi. in *E.E.P.* (1862) 5 And þench þos wordis her ispoke; for-ȝite ham noȝt ac þench apan. *a* **1300** *Cursor M.* 112 In hir wirschip wald I bigyn A lastand warc apon to myn. **1390** GOWER *Conf.* I. 14 To studie upon the worldes lore Sufficeth now withoute more. *a* **1400** *Isumbras* 427 Sir Ysambrace hym umbithoghte Appone a horse that coles broghte. *c* **1450** *Merlin* iii. 49 The moste remembraunce that I shall haue, shall be vpon yow, and on yowre nedes. **1463** *Bury Wills* (Camden) 34 A remembraunce to thinke vpon me. **1582** N. T. (Rhem.) *Matt.* vii. 28 The multitude were in admiration vpon his doctrine. **1611** BIBLE *1 Tim.* iv. 15 Meditate vpon these things. **1655** EARL ORRERY *Parthen.* I. VIII. 418 Did you reflect upon it with an vnprejudicate opinion. **1719** DE FOE *Crusoe* I. (Globe) 226, I ask'd him what it was he study'd upon. *Ibid.* II. (Globe) 379 But now the Admiration was turn'd upon another question. **1871** W. ALEXANDER *Johnny Gibb* xlvi, It has a closin'-in heid-piece concern that min's me..upon a mutch that my wife hed ance. **1899** W. J. LOCKE *White Dove* 3 S—— was at last able to reflect upon the entire unexpectedness of his presence.

c. Denoting the subject of speech or writing; = ON *prep.* 22 c.

Freq. with verbs, as *rave, talk, write*; AMPLIFY *v.* 7 b, CRITICIZE *v.* 1 b, DISTINGUISH *v.* 8 c, SPEAK *v.* 15.

(*a*) *a* **1390** *Wycliffite Bible* (1850) IV. 303 An other [prologue] vpon Romaynus. **1390** GOWER *Conf.* II. 65 Laodomie his lusti wif..Upon a thing wherof sche dradde A lettre..sende him. **1525** LD. BERNERS *Froiss.* II. Preface, My Preface vpon the fyrst volume of this cronycle. **1533** FRITH *Answ. More* E iij b, The mynde and exposition of the olde Doctours vpon the wordes of Chrystes maundye. **1557** *Tottel's Misc.* (Arb.) 113 Vpon the deceas of W. Ch. **1605** SHAKS. *Macb.* II. i. 23 We would spend it in some words vpon that Businesse. **1697** DE FOE *Ess. Projects* Pref., I wou'd not adventure to appear in Print upon that Subject. **1709** STEELE *Tatler* No. 114 ¶1 Our Discourse chanced to be upon the Subject of Death. **1758** BOSWELL *Lett.* (1924) 6 From 1 to 2, [I] attend a college upon Roman Antiquities. **1801** *Farmer's Mag.* Jan. 66 A series of animadversions.. published upon it in a provincial paper. **1824** BYRON *Juan* XVI. xlvii, She..Made epigrams..Upon her friends. **1893** STEVENSON *Catriona* xii, He engaged the goodwife..with some compliments upon the rizzoring of our haddocks.

†(*b*) **1483** CAXTON *G. de la Tour* 107 Now I shalle telle yow upon this matere of a good lady. **1528** in Roy *Rede me*, etc. (Arb.) 152 Austyne sayeth vppon the psalter, ye clargy occupyeth the secular lordshyppe secularly. **1574** R. BRISTOW *Treatise* 47 Vpon these two, Christ..and his Church, ronneth al the Scriptures. **1581** FULKE in *Confer.* III. (1583) Q ij b, I wil not vouchsafe to replie vpon this answere. **1605** CAMDEN *Rem.* 143 But he repaied him with this re-allusion vppon the name. **1710** STEELE *Tatler* No. 14 ¶1 My Design of observing upon Things. **1748** RICHARDSON *Clarissa* (1811) I. 185, I..am the less solicitous ..to amplify upon the contents of either.

(*c*) **1481** in Blades *W. Caxton* (1882) 231 The polytyque book..whiche that Tullius wrote vpon the disputacons [etc.]. *c* **1600** W. FOWLER *Wks.* (S.T.S.) 9 A Fvneral Sonet, written vpon the death of..Elizabeth Dowglas. **1709** ADDISON *Tatler* No. 163 ¶3 The Sonnet..was written upon a Lady. **1776** JOHNSON in *Boswell* (1904) I. 647 A man who has never been engaged in trade himself may undoubtedly write well upon trade. **1791** 'G. GAMBADO' *Ann. Horsem.* (1809) 55 Had they spent as much time in riding upon turnips, as they have in writing upon them.

III. In other senses.

†**23.** From (a person or persons), esp. by means of hostile attack; = ON *prep.* 23. *Obs.* (Cf. 21.)

Const. with verbs, as *make, nim, recover, take, win*; also CONQUER *v.* 2 b, GAIN *v.*[2] 4.

1338 R. BRUNNE *Chron.* (1810) 22 Uppon Saynt Edmunde Northfolk he nam. **1387** TREVISA *Higden* (Rolls) VI. 291 Egbertus..took Chestre uppon þe Britouns. **1412–20** LYDG. *Chron. Troy* III. 3423 Troyens han wonne a-geyn her londe Vp-on Grekis. **1483** in *Acta Dom. Conc.* II. Introd. 114 Quhilk some was recoverit be..Dure apone the said Schir Johne. *a* **1533** LD. BERNERS *Huon* 527 A ryche shyp, the whiche was wonne vpon the sowdans men. **1568** GRAFTON *Chron.* II. 194 They wanne dayly and yerely vpon the sayd Turkes, so that they had..much of the landes. **1643** PRYNNE *Doom Cowardice & Treach.* 6 At last by such forcible assaults the said Towne was taken upon the said Robert. **1654** BRAMHALL *Just Vind.* i. (1661) 2 Whatsoever the Popes of Rome gained upon us. **1660** *Nicholas Papers* (Camden) IV. 187 The prizes made by the Ostenders upon the Kings subjects. **1742** LEONI *Palladio's Archit.* II. 66 The Spoils made upon Pyrrhus King of Epirus.

†**24.** In respect of; = ON *prep.* 24. *Obs.*

a **1310** in Wright *Lyric P.* v. 26 He is blosme opon bleo brihtest under bis. **13..** *Cursor M.* 2034 (Gött.), He lis here vte, cum se þu sal, Naked apon his limes all.

25. On (a musical instrument).

c **1384** CHAUCER *H. Fame* III. 110 Ther herd I pleyen vpon an harpe..Orpheus ful craftely. **1524** *Reg. Privy Seal Scot.* I. 499/1 Playing apoun organis in the Kingis chapell. **1552** in Feuillerat *Revels Edw. VI* (1914) 89, I haue provided one to plaie vppon a kettell drom. **1621** BRATHWAIT *Nat. Embassie* Ded., Able to play vpon an oaten pipe. **1683** KENNETT tr. *Erasm. on Folly* 68 No more skill..than a Pig playing upon the Organs. **1709** MRS. MANLEY *Secret Mem.* I. 149 A great many of 'em..can toot, toot, toot, it upon a Pipe. **1804–6** SYD. SMITH *Mor. Philos.* (1850) 175 Any air.. performed upon such an instrument as the bagpipe. **1842** TENNYSON *Locksley Hall* 2 When you want me, sound upon the bugle-horn. **1876** GRANT *Burgh Sch. Scot.* II. 380 Discoursing laments upon the Bagpipes.

26. Denoting advance from or improvement on some standard, etc.

See also IMPROVE *v.* 8, IMPROVEMENT 6 b, REFINE *v.* 10.

1662 EVELYN *Chalcogr.* 50 Which afterwards Sebastian Serli refining upon composed the better part of that excellent book of his. **1711** ADDISON *Spect.* No. 44 ¶6 The French have therefore refin'd too much upon Horace's Rule. **1782** PRIESTLEY *Corrupt. Chr.* I. III. 301 An improvement was made upon this doctrine. **1843** *Blackw. Mag.* LIV. 197 Mr. Collins has improved greatly upon his last year's exhibition. **1859** GLADSTONE *Glean.* (1879) II. 171 If he continues to advance upon himself as he has advanced heretofore.

†**u'pon,** *adv.* *Obs.* (exc. *arch.* in sense 1 b). [Ellipt. use of prec.]

1. a. On it; on or upon the surface.

1307 *York Memo. Bk.* (Surtees) I. 181 Lether with the here apon. **1382** WYCLIF *Ecclus.* xxxiii. 6 An hors courser.. vnder eche man vpon sittende neȝeth. **1547** in Feuillerat *Revels Edw. VI* (1914) 13 Changeable Taffita stripyd vpon with blewe golde dornix. **1567** in *Rep. Hist. MSS. Comm.* (1907) IV. 90 A clothe of blacke and redd wroughte with goulde vpon. **1596** SHAKS. *Merch. V.* II. vii. 57 A coyne that beares the figure of an Angell Stampt in gold, but that's insculpt vpon.

b. On one's person, as an article of apparel. Phr. ***clothed upon***, after biblical use (see quot. 1611.) Cf. CLOTHE *v.* 9.

a **1366** CHAUCER *Rom. Rose* 364 A chapelet, so semly oon, Ne werede neuer mayde vpon. *c* **1386** —— *Friar's T.* 84 He [*sc.* a gay yeoman] hadde vp-on a courtepy of grene. **1390** GOWER *Conf.* II. 246 And sche..hir scherte dede upon And caste on hire a mantel clos. **1446** LYDG. *Two Nightingale P.* ii. 123 Whan Crist Ihesu was for mankynd dede And had vpon a garnement ful newe. **1513** BRADSHAW *St. Werburge* I. 1301 His gloues, his gyrdell, the kynge had vpon. **1611** BIBLE *2 Cor.* v. 2 Desiring to be clothed vpon with our house, which is from heauen. **1643** CARYL *Expos. Job* 1885 Those bodies of Saints..shall be cloathed upon with a house which is from Heaven. **1895** L. JOHNSON *Poems* 34 Old ramparts, gray and stern; But comely clothed upon With wealth of moss and fern. **1930** *Month* Mar. 230 Ancient stones, like Ezekiel's dry bones, need to be clothed upon.

2. a. Into or to a position on a surface or object; so as to be put or placed on the thing in question.

1382 WYCLIF *Num.* xvii. 2 Of echon the name thow shalt vpon write [L. *superscribes*] to his ȝerde. *c* **1400** *Lanfranc's Cirurgie* 219 Make it abrood upon a cloop & leie it vpon hoot. *c* **1440** *Pallad. on Husb.* VII. 106 Do donge vppon and vmbe on euery side. **1534** TINDALE *Luke* xx. 18 But on whosoever it faul vpon, it wyll grynde him to powder.

b. In a direction towards something indicated or specified.

c **1400** *Apol. Loll.* 2 þer for, if we wil, we mai calle bischoppis, locars up on. **1593–1611** [see LOOK *v.* 46].

3. On or upon that (in time or order); thereafter, thereupon. Esp. coupled with *anon, near, soon.*

See also HEREUPON, THEREUPON, WHEREUPON *advs.*

14.. *Lydgate's Bochas* v. 2898 Afftir whos deth anon vpon [*MS. Harl.* 1245 vpon anoon] suyng, To Euergetes..She was ageyn ioyned in mariage. *c* **1440** *Generydes* 1926 Thanne came the prince of Cesare sone vppon. *Ibid.* 6632 Kyng auferius fell seke anon vppon. **1523** FITZHERB. *Husb.* §12 So that they be sowen ere the begynnynge of Marche, or sone vpon. **1602** SHAKS. *Ham.* I. ii. 179 *Ham.* I thinke it was to see my Mothers Wedding. *Hor.* Indeed my Lord, it followed hard vpon. **1603** —— *Meas. for M.* IV. vi. 14 The..Citizens Haue hent the gates, and very neere vpon The Duke is entring. **1606** —— *Tr. & Cr.* IV. iii. 3 It is great morning, and the houre prefixt..Comes fast vpon.

4. By way of addition, increase, etc.

a **1485** FORTESCUE *Wks.* (1869) 487 Why will God put uppon newe turments ovir the travaile of ther labour?

†**upon,** obs. var. OPEN *a.* (Cf. UPEN *a.*)

13.. *E.E. Allit. P.* B. 453 þenne wafte he vpon his wyndowe. **14..** *Sir Beues* (E.) 87/1691 Anon þe gate he vpon look.

†**uponland,** *adv.* *Obs.* Also 3–4 vp o londe, 5 *Sc.* upolande; 5–6 vp of land, and UPALAND. [f. *uppe* UP *adv.*[2] + ON *prep.* 1 b (O *prep.*[1]) + LAND *sb.*[1] Cf. UPLAND *adv.*[1]] In the country, as opposed to the town.

a. *a* **900** in Thorpe *Anc. Laws* (1840) I. 118 Be ciepemonna fore uppe on londe. *c* **1386** CHAUCER *Prol.* 702 A poure person dwellynge vp on lond. **1430–40** LYDG. *Bochas* Prol. 84 Folkis that duellyn vp-on lande. *c* **1480** HENRYSON *Twa Mice* i, The vther [mouse] wynnit vponland. —— *Sheep & Dog* xviii, Ane schireff stout, Quhilk..dytis all the pure men vpon land [**1568** *Bann. MS.* vp of land].

β. *c* **1300** *Havelok* 763 Gode paniers..to beren fish inne, Vp o-londe to selle and fonge. **14..** *Burgh Laws Scotland* xxxiv, It is for to wyt that men upolande may borow thair pundis thryis.

γ. *c* **1440** *Alph. Tales* 173 On a tyme he was lugid on a night in a howse vp of land. **1568** [see *a.* above].

b. ***John Uponland***, a rustic. (Cf. UPALAND b.)

a **1568** in *Bannatyne MS.* (Hunter. Club) 269/26 This said Johnne vponland.

†**uponlandis,** obs. Sc. var. UPLANDS *a.*

c **1480** HENRYSON *Fables* heading (Harl. MS.), The Taill of the vponlandis Mous and the burges Mous.

†**uponon(e,** *adv.* *Obs. rare.* Also uponan. [f. UPON *prep.* + ONE *pron.* 32 f.] = ANON *adv.* 4.

c **1400** *Destr. Troy* 2418, I onswaret hym esely euyn vp-onon. *Ibid.* 6712 Polidamas..can fight, With his Enmeis full egurly, euer vpon-one.

'up-patient. [UP *a.*; cf. UP *adv.*[2] 7 a.] An in-patient in hospital no longer confined to bed.

1952 'R. GORDON' *Doctor in House* xi. 119 Two up-patients, dressing-gowned old gentlemen. **1959** *Manch. Guardian* 19 Aug. 5/6 Topham is an up-patient... We started him with a couple of hours up each morning. **1976** J. GRENFELL *Joyce Grenfell requests Pleasure* (1977) xi. 163 Up-patients sat on the grass on grey army blankets.

†**uppe,** *v.* *Obs.* Forms: 1 yppan, 2 ippen, 3 uppen. [OE. *yppan* (also *ȝeyppan*), f. *upp* UP *adv.*[1], giving southern ME. *üppen*, midland *ippen*. Cf. ON. *yppa* (MDa. *yppe*), and OHG. *ûffan* (MHG. *ûffen, ûfen*, obs. G. *aufen*).] *trans.* To display or make manifest; to bring to notice; to make known.

c **897** K. ÆLFRED *Gregory's Past. C.* lix. 451 Ðæt we hit.. forðy yppen ðæt mon God herige. *c* **900** tr. *Baeda's Hist.* IV. xxv. (1890) 352 Se Godes mon..þa unrotnesse his heortan ..ypte & cyðde. *a* **1000** *Colloq. Ælfric* in Wr.-Wülcker 102 Ic ne deor yppan þe diȝla ure. *c* **1200** *Trin. Coll. Hom.* 165 Here wombe is here crist, and all iuele forbisne hie ippen of hem seluen. *a* **1225** *Ancr. R.* 146 Hercneð nu..hu hit is to uppen & ȝelpen of god dede. *Ibid.*, Ancre þet was iwuned.. wel uorte wurchen, & seoððen..uppede hit & scheawede.

uppen: see UP *prep.*[1]

'uppen, *v.* *E. Angl.* ? *Obs.* [f. UP *adv.*[1] + -EN[5]. Cf. UPPE *v.*] *trans.* To bring up, mention, disclose.

1565 GOLDING *Ovid's Met.* III. 344 When that after mickle talke..Joves name was upned. **1567** *Ibid.* XII. 179 Every wyght Delyghts too uppen oftentymes..The perills and the narrow brunts. **1583** —— *Calvin on Deut.* xxi. 125/2 It woulde not haue booted at all to haue vppened neuer so many thinges by parcellmeale. **1823** E. MOOR *Suffolk Words* 460 Yeow didnt uppen it did ye?

up-'pent, *pa. pple.* (UP- 5.)

1600 FAIRFAX *Tasso* x. xlii, With this siege, if we be long vp pent, Famine I doubt. **1614** GORGES *Lucan* I. 18 A proud Courser..in the stable close vp-pent. **1870** A. O'SHAUGHNESSY *Poems, Neglected Harp* 15 These wondrous melodies up-pent And languishing in me.

'upper, *sb.*[1] [From UPPER *a.*]

1. a. That part of a boot or shoe above the sole and welt. Usu. pl.

1789 G. PARKER *Life's Painter of Variegated Characters* v. 36 If the top and leg of a jack-boot were joined to a dog-skin upper and a buff sole. **1845** J. COULTER *Adv. in Pacific* ix. 112 My shoes were..only held together by passing straps of goat-skin under the soles, over the uppers. **1862** *Catal. Internat. Exhib., Brit.* II. No. 4769, Grained leather; machine-closed uppers. **1880** *Times* 21 Sept. 4/4 Forcing the needle through the outer sole, the edge of the upper, and the insole.

attrib. **1875** KNIGHT *Dict. Mech.*, *Upper-machines*,..those for cutting out or preparing the uppers of boots or shoes.

b. *U.S.* A cloth gaiter for wearing above the shoe over the ankle (*Cent. Dict.* 1891).

c. In fig. phr. (***down***) ***on one's uppers***: in poor or reduced circumstances; having hard luck; also formerly ***to walk*** (etc.) ***on one's uppers.*** *colloq.* (orig. *U.S.*).

1886 *Lantern* 8 Sept. 4/3 The Royal Street actors who are walking on their uppers, must mourn..when they..hear of some of the boys spending 200 a week yachting. **1891** *Cent. Dict.* s.v. **1895** ROBERTS & MORTON *Adv. Arthur Roberts* xi. 143, I know two actors who were left, as the term goes, 'on their uppers', in a town in the heart of the Midlands. **1899** 'J. FLYNT' *Tramping with Tramps* I. v. 117 I's been a moocher, an' now I's shatin' on me uppers. **1901** *Munsey's Mag.* XXV. 432/1 The rumor whirled about the Street that Greener was in difficulties. Financial ghouls..said ..'Greener is on his uppers'. **1903** *Judy* 9 Dec. 577/1 'What would you do if you were in my shoes?' 'Eh? Oh, then I should be fairly down on my uppers.' **1905** R. Marsh *Spoiler of Men* xxv. 227 'I'm on my uppers... I want money.' 'So do we all.' **1918** *Blackw. Mag.* May 602/2 We are pretty well down on our uppers as regards transport. **1985** D. Williams *Wedding Treasure* ii. 31 My guess is the swine's on his uppers... He's going for the ten thousand a year.

2. a. An upper jaw, dental plate, tooth, etc.

1878 C. Hunter *Mech. Dentistry* 79 In the case of edentulous or nearly edentulous uppers or lowers. **1900** *Hutchinson's Arch. Surg.* XI. 222 On the backs of both uppers..there are now peculiar changes. **1904** F. P. Dunne in *Westm. Gaz.* 14 Oct. 1/3 He [*sc.* a child] has two uppers an' four lowers.

b. *ellipt.* for upper deck, storey, berth, etc.

1938 'Giraldus' *Merry Matloe Again* 179 Just sit down opposite the hatch and contemplate your new shipmates as, one by one, they troop on the 'upper'. **1955** F. O'Connor *Wise Blood* i. 17 The man in the station..had sold him a berth..an upper one... A sign said to get the porter to let you into the uppers. **1968** *Globe & Mail* (Toronto) 13 Feb. 30/6 (Advt.), Well located duplex with extra large upper. **1969** *Down Beat* 17 Apr. 16/1 Two chartered sleeping cars carried the men across the United States like royalty—and nobody ever had to take an upper.

3. *U.S.* A log or piece of sawed lumber of superior grade.

1877 *Lumberman's Gazette* 24 May, The finest stock of uppers to be found in the country.

4. a. *Public school slang.* A pupil of the upper school.

1929 J. Buchan *Courts of Morning* ii. viii. 379 The Eton Beagles in the fields beyond Slough, and himself and Lariarty, both newly become uppers, struggling desperately to keep up with the field. **1937** [see pi-jaw *sb.*].

b. *colloq.* An upper-class person.

1955 T. H. Pear *Eng. Social Differences* iii. 90 While many people use 'person' indiscriminately, some 'uppers' employ it chiefly in a derogatory sense. **1967** [see lower *a.* (*sb.*) 3 a]. **1968** *Economist* 27 Apr. p. v/1 The genuine uppers' genuine feeling of superiority.

'upper, *sb.*[2] *slang* (orig. *U.S.*). [f. up *v.* + -er[1]; cf. up *a.* 5.] **1.** A drug (esp. an amphetamine), often in the form of a pill, which has a stimulant or euphoric effect.

1968 *Current Slang* (Univ. S. Dakota) Fall 50 *Upper*, type of drug that makes you feel active. Amphetamine is a commonly used stimulant of this kind. **1969** Fabian & Byrne *Groupie* (1970) xix. 133, I wasn't used to so many uppers all at once. **1976** 'R. Rostand' *D'Artagnan Signature* vii. 45 The trained-down leanness..likely came from epsom salts and uppers. **1981** 'D. Shannon' *Murder most Strange* ii. 52, I want all your pills, man, all the uppers and downers you got.

2. *transf.* and *fig.*

1973 *Time* 1 Jan. K2 It certainly is a relief to know that State 2 is an upper; but by that time, who cares? **1976** *National Observer* (U.S.) 27 Nov. ii. 22/3 Shorty's alchemy with rum and other potions produces something called a Goombay Smash that is a definite upper. **1977** *Time* 18 Apr. 45/2 Singing is a real upper. It makes me feel dizzy and energetic.

upper ('ʌpə(r)), *a.* Also 4–6 vpper, 5–7 vper; 6 hoper. [f. up *a.* + -er[3]. Cf. MDu. *upper* (Du. and Flem. *opper*), LG. *upper, üpper*, MSw., Norw. *yppare*, older Da. *yppere*, better.] Comparative of up *a.*, and signifying 'higher', 'over', 'loftier', 'top' (in contrast to *lower, nether, under*). In some senses replacing the earlier uver, over *adjs.*

I. 1. a. Occupying, comprising or consisting of, rising or more elevated ground (and usu. further in the interior). Freq. in proper names of districts, etc.

13.. *K. Alis.* 5691 (Laud MS.), þe kyng þennes went forþ ..in to ynde in þe norþ, þat is ycleped..þe vpper ynde. **1526** Tindale *Acts* xix. 1 Paul passed thorow the vpper costes and cam to Ephesus. **1598** Grenewey *Tacitus, Ann.* xii. vii. (1622) 163 About the same time vpper Germany quaked with feare. **1601** Shaks. *Jul. C.* v. i. 3 You said the Enemy would..keepe the Hilles and vpper Regions. *a* **1660** *Contemp. Hist. Irel.* (Ir. Archæol. Soc.) I. 160 Either to Vper Ormond or the countie of Clare. *a* **1676** Hale *Prim. Orig. Man.* (1677) 219 If Inundations prevailed in Greece and those upper Countries, Egypt..could not easily escape them. **1728** Chambers *Cycl.* s.v. *Nimbis*, The Nimbis is seen on the Medals..of the upper Empire. **1791** Geo. III in *Ann. Reg., St. Papers* 124* His majesty thinks..that..his province of Quebec..should be divided into two separate provinces, to be called the province of Upper Canada, and the province of Lower Canada. **1849** Eastwick *Dry Leaves* 22 My vessel being an Upper Sindh boat. **1863** Lyell *Antiq. Man* 43 For the river to bring down from the upper country so large a quantity of earthy matter. **1864–** [see ward *sb.*[2] 20].

b. Of peoples: Occupying a higher or more inland district.

1617 Moryson in C. L. Falkiner *Illustr. Irish Hist.* (1904) 215 The Iberni, called the upper Irish, inhabiting about Beer-haven and Baltimore. *c* **1790** *Encycl. Brit.* (ed. 3) V. 484/1 The Lower and Upper Cossacks,..and a part of the Don Cossacks.

c. Situated in, located on, a higher or loftier position, high ground, etc.; more elevated or lofty; higher in altitude.

Freq. in the proper names of hamlets, villages, etc.

1467 *Rolls of Parlt.* V. 586/2 Landes and Tenementes in Netherburneham, Upperburneham, West Wode. **1509** Hawes *Past. Pleas.* xxxii. (Percy Soc.) 159 After this, dame Correccion..first..led me to the upper ward. **1611** Bible *Joshua* xv. 19 He gaue her the vpper springs, and the nether springs. **1687** Miège *Gt. Fr. Dict.* ii. s.v., The Upper Region of the Air. **1708** Watts *Poems* (1743) ii. 160 Around the golden Streets they rove, And bless the Mansions of the upper Skies. **1778** *Encycl. Brit.* (ed. 2) III. 1604/2 The bason [of the lock] being filled with water by an upper sluice to the level of the waters above, a vessel may ascend thro' the upper gate. *Ibid.* 1605/1 So that the water in the lock may rise to a level with the water in the upper canal. **1796** Mme. D'Arblay *Camilla* V. 296 [She] thought herself in the upper regions, where happiness..consisted of perpetual admiration. **1819** Shelley *Peter Bell 3rd* ii. vii, Each had an upper stream of thought. **1857** Hawthorne *Eng. Note-bks.* (1870) II. 414 Those misty upper-depths seemed almost to be hung with clouds. **1862** J. Brown *Minchmoor* (1864) 11 You can get a glimpse of the upper woods of Abbotsford. **1873** Geikie *Phys. Geog.* §89 [These] clouds..are driven along by upper currents of air. **1883** *Good Words* Aug. 529/2 Those plants and animals which live in the 'upper littoral'.

fig. **1647** N. Bacon *Disc. Govt. Eng.* i. lvii. 166 To make him yet more bold, he had the upper ground of the heire.

d. Occupying or forming (part of) the higher or highest portion or division of a building.

1522–3 *Rec. St. Mary at Hill* 317 A chest in the vpper vestry. **1557** Bible (Genev.) *Acts* i. 13 They went vp into an vpper chamber. **1597** J. Payne *Royal Exch.* 15 The thrid sort be retaylers in the vpper shopps. **1611** Florio, *Soprastanza*, an vpper-lodging. **1665** in *Verney Mem.* (1907) II. 247 A lower and an upper chamber. **1764** Harmer *Observ.* iii. §1. 89 An upper-story, which is flat on the top. **1779** *Mirror* No. 9, Some of the upper boxes were filled with ladies. **1846** Mrs. A. Marsh *Father Darcy* II. xiv. 254 He used to lie..upon the floor of his little upper room.

fig. **1647** Trapp *Comm. 2 Cor.* v. 1 In the wonderful frame of man's body the bones are the timber work, the head the upper-lodging. **1699–** [see story *sb.*[2] 1 c]. **1796** [see garret *sb.*[1] 3]. **1870** Brewer *Dict. Phrase & Fable* 924/1 'Ill-furnished in the upper story'; a head without brains. **1877** *Holderness Gloss.* 152/1 He's a bit wake (weak) iv his upper-garret.

Comb. **1667** Dryden *Æneis* Ded. e 3 b, Our Upper-Gallery Audience in a Play-House.

2. a. With partitive terms, esp. *end, part, side.*

Occas. hyphened or as one word, as †*upperhand, upperside.*

1484 Caxton *Fables of Æsop* v. vii, He to whome men purposen to doo somme euylle tourn, syth men holden hym at auauntage, men muste putte hym self at the vpper side of hym. *c* **1489** —— *Blanchardyn* xlvi. 178 The noble mayden ..ryght fyersli..began to loke vpon hym, drawyng herselfe to the vpperhande of hym. **1526** *Pilgr. Perf.* (W. de W. 1531) 3 b, The vpper parte of this foresayd ymage. **1568** *Freiris Berwik* 22 The tovne,..the castell and the land, The he wallis vpoun the vpper hand. **1570** Billingsley *Euclid* xi. xxix. 341 Lines..which ioyne together the angles of the vpper and nether bases. *a* **1600** in Child *Ballads* II. 245/2 A grave, a grave,..to put these lovers in; But lay my lady on the upper hand. **1674** Hooke *Animadv.* 52 The upper side thereof must be plained exactly smooth and flat. **1731** P. Miller *Gard. Dict.* s.v. *Melo*, The Upperside of the Hot-beds where your early Melons..are planted. **1769** Falconer *Dict. Marine* (1780), *Down-haul*,..a rope..tied to the upper-corner of the sail. **1778** Miss Burney *Evelina* xxi, Driving us to the upper end of Piccadilly. **1805** R. Jameson *Char. Min.* (1816) 204 When..[the crystal] has upon its upper and under parts, faces that alternate with each other. **1868** *Rep. U.S. Commissioner Agric.* (1869) 360 The well and the opening in the upper side [of the road]. **1886** J. Barrowman *Sc. Mining Terms* 69 The upper portion of a [coal] seam.

b. Of surfaces. †*upperface*, = superficies.

1583 Stubbes *Anat. Abus.* ii. B 3, Then came there fire.. and consumed them all, from the vpper face of the earth. **1594** Blundevil *Exerc.* iii. (1597) 128 b, Superficies or vpper-face, is that which onely hath length and breadth. **1596** *Edward III*, i. ii. 152 Where the vpper turfe of earth doth boast His..party coloured cost, Delue there. **1611** Cotgr., *Rez*,..the superficies, or vpper face of a plaine, or leuell peece of ground. **1728** Bradley *Dict. Bot.* s.v. *Marrubium*, Leaves..smooth and woolly underneath.., but somewhat..rugged on the Upperside. **1733** Tull *Horse-hoeing Husb.* 404 The Upper-surface of the Fore-end of the Beam. **1826** Kirby & Sp. *Entomol.* III. 364 *Facies*,..the upper surface of the head. **1884** Coues *Key N. Amer. Birds* 110 The upper and under surfaces of the wing.

3. a. That forms the higher of a pair of corresponding things or sets. Also occas. = uppermost. Hence *fig.* in phr. (*crushed*, etc.) ***between the upper and the nether millstones***, between two irreconcilable opposing forces.

upper-case, Printing (quots. 1683–): see case *sb.*[2] 9.

c **1460** [*upper crust*: see 13 a]. **1524** *State Papers Hen. VIII*, II. 117 He shall endevour hymself to cause the Kynges subjectes..to have the upper berdes to be shaven. **1530** Tindale *Deut.* xxiv. 6 No man shall take the nether or the vpper milstone to pledge. **1533** *MS. Rawl. D.* 776 fol. 157 b, The vpper fflowryng of the same wharffe. **1609** Bible (Douay) *Exod.* xii. 22 Sprinkle the uppertransome of the doore therwith. *Ibid.* 23 The bloud on the uppersil, and on both the postes. **1611** Cotgr. s.v. *Espée*, The vpper boords of a Vine-presse. **1683** Moxon *Mech. Exerc., Printing* ii. §3. 19 The Whole Vpper-Case is divided into Ninety eight square Boxes. **1726** Swift *Gulliver* ii. vii, I first mounted to the upper step of the ladder [= a movable pair of stairs]. **1833** Loudon *Encycl. Archit.* § 691 The two upper branches or rails of the trunk, or upright piece. **1852** Seidel *Organ* 37 A couple of bellows..consist first of an upper and under board. **1867** Smyth *Sailor's Word-bk.* 708 *Upper masts*, the top-mast, topgallant-mast, and royal-mast. **1873** *Routledge's Yng. Gentl. Mag.* July 503/1 An upper-iron being screwed on to the lower one to turn the shaving back a little.

fig. **1788** *New London Mag.* 264 One blow well told to the upper tire (the head), tells better than three below. **1902** G. B. Shaw *Mrs Warren's Profession* Pref. p. xxi, Thus am I crushed between the upper millstone of Mr Redford, who thinks me a libertine, and the nether popular critic, who thinks me a prude. **1921** L. Strachey *Queen Victoria* v. 167 His position, crushed between the upper and the nether millstones, grew positively unbearable. **1948** F. R. Cowell *Cicero & Roman Republic* vii. 131 [A] Consul..was a link between Senate and People, responsible to both, an unenviable situation between an upper and a nether millstone. **1950** A. Bryant *Age of Elegance* ii. 40 Not only were the French Armies of Portugal and the North.. marching to the fortress's relief, but Soult and Joseph with 60,000 men were threatening Madrid from Valencia. The British were in Danger of being crushed between the upper and nether millstones.

Comb. **1738** Chambers *Cycl.* s.v. *Letter*, Printers distinguish their letters into capital..or upper-case letters, ..and..small, or under-case letters. **1771** Luckombe *Hist. Print.* 261 [These letters] are not reckoned..among Upper-case Sorts.

b. *spec.* in *Anat.*, etc. (Cf. superior *a.* 11.)

1546 [see 18 a]. **1548** Vicary *Anat.* v. (1577) F ij b, The bones or bony partes, fyrste of the Cheekes be two;..of the vpper Mandible, two. **1610** Healey *St. Aug. Citie of God* 335 [The] crocodile..moueth his vpper chappe. **1646** Sir T. Browne *Pseud. Ep.* 108 It conveyeth it into the duodenum or upper gut, thence into the lower bowells. **1728** Chambers *Cycl.* s.v. *Maxillæ*, The..Upper Jaw, is immoveable in Man. **1774** Goldsm. *Nat. Hist.* V. 274 The upper chap [of the parrot], as well as the lower, are both moveable. **1826** Kirby & Sp. *Entomol.* III. xxxiii. 374 The Upper or Primary Wings. **1838** *Penny Cycl.* X. 141/2 When the upper lid [of the eye] is raised. **1850** J. F. Cooper *Ways of Hour* I. 104 His front upper teeth were all gone. **1884** Coues *N. Amer. Birds* 110 The upper Primary coverts, or coverts of the primaries.

Comb. **1879** Ruskin *St. Mark's Rest* Suppl. ii. 20 The man's thigh and upper-arm bones. **1896** *Godey's Mag.* April 430/1 His upper-limb muscles.

c. ***Upper Bench***, the name during the exile of Charles II of the King's Bench. Now *Hist.*

1649 *Acts Interregnum* (1911) II. 108 Three or more of the Justices of the upper Bench. **1651** in *Kitchin's Jurisdictions* (1653) 579 The most Vsual Writs which have been used in the Kings Bench, and are most like to continue in that Court, now called the Vpper-Bench. *a* **1675** Whitelocke *Mem.* (1682) 375 Voted [on 12 Feb. 1649] that the Kings-Bench Court should be called the Upper Bench.

d. ***orange upperwing***, a European noctuid moth, *Hoporina croceago*.

1832 Rennie *Brit. Butterfl. & Moths* 85 The Orange Upperwing..appears in September;..first pair [of wings] golden orange..; second pair white. **1869** E. Newman *Brit. Moths* 373/1.

4. † a. ***upper-stock***: (see stock *sb.*[1] 40). Usu. pl.

1535 in *Archaeologia* IX. 251 A paire of upper stockis of purple veluette,..also..a newe paire of nether stockis. **1542** *Nottingham Rec.* III. 220 One peyr blacke hoys, the upper stokes blake velvet. *c* **1570** *Pride & Lowl.* (1841) 19 His upper stockes of sylken grogerane. **1606** G. W[oodcocke] *Hist. Ivstine* xxxviii. 118 He conueyed a dagger in the vpperstock of his hose. [**1821** Scott *Kenilw.* xxxi, His upper stocks of white velvet, lined with cloth of silver.]

b. That covers or clothes an upper part of the body, esp. the chest or shoulders. (Cf. 5 a.)

Freq. from 1579 to 1625 in ***upper body***.

1579 *Aldeburgh Rec.* in *N. & Q.* 12th Ser. VII. 328/2 An upper bodye and lyninge and a neckercher for hir. **1587** in *Antiquary* (1896) XXXII. 76 For an upper body and lace, xxiij d. **1625** Fletcher *Fair Maid* ii. ii, Nothing but her vpper bodies. **1871** S. Mateer *Land of Charity* xxi. 278 A cloth or scarf laid over the shoulder, called the 'upper cloth,' as worn by the Súdra women. **1895** C. Silvester Horne *Story of L.M.S.* 298 In 1858, the 'upper cloth' riots broke out again.

5. a. Of garments, etc.: Worn above or outside another; outer, exterior; = over *a.* 1 b. (Cf. 4 b.)

1526 Tyndale *John* xiii. 4 Iesus..layde a syde hys vpper garments. **1547** in Feuillerat *Revels Edw. VI* (1914) 10 Thupper & nether Baces & thunder sleves of clothe of golde. **1598** Florio, *Sourafodro*, a false vpper scabbard. **1611** ——, *Soprabenda*, an vpper scarfe. **1615** Sandys *Trav.* 14 Their arme-pits: from whence the skirts flow loosely, fringed below; the vpper shorter than the neather. **1645** Rutherford *Tri. Faith* 305 Christ clothed with love,..and yet his upper garment is vengeance. **1686** *Lond. Gaz.* No. 2193/4 A brown coloured upper Coat. **1759** Johnson *Rasselas* xxxviii, When my upper vest was taken off. **1778** Clara Reeve *Old English Baron* 84 You may take off her upper garments, and any thing of value. **1796** *Grose's Dict. Vulgar T.* (ed. 3), *Upper Benjamin*, a great coat. **1812** J. H. Vaux *Flash Dict.*, *Upper-Ben, Upper-Benjamin, Upper-Tog*, a great coat. **1819** Scott *Ivanhoe* ii, The upper dress of this personage resembled that of his companion in shape. **1850** Thackeray *Pendennis* iii, A white upper-coat ornamented with cheese-plate buttons.

fig. *a* **1634** Chapman *Bussy d'Ambois* v. (1641) 65 Note what he wants? He wants his upper weed, He wants his life, and body.

Comb. **1840** Thackeray *Pict. Rhapsody* Wks. 1899 XIII. 350 A hideous dress, with upper-Benjamin buttons.

b. Furthest removed from the door or entrance; innermost. Usually with *end* (cf. 2).

1590 Spenser *F.Q.* ii. ix. 27 Thence she them brought into a stately Hall... At th' upper end there sate..a comely personage. *a* **1613** Overbury *Newes* Misc. Wks. (1890) 191 The best company makes the upper end of the table, and not the salt-cellar. **1667** Milton *P.L.* x. 446 His high Throne.. at th' upper end Was plac't in regal lustre. **1711** Steele *Spect.* No. 109 ¶1 We were now arrived at the Upper-end of the Gallery. **1819** Scott *Ivanhoe* iii, The walls of this upper end of the hall.

fig. *a* **1672** Wilkins *Nat. Relig.* 331 So only those at the upper end of the world are capable of being counted rich. **1714** R. Fiddes *Pract. Disc.* ii. 157 Sometimes the most profligate sinners are seated at the upper end of the world.

6. a. Said of the surface of the earth and things upon it, in contrast to the under or nether regions.

1667 Milton *P.L.* x. 422 For those Appointed to sit there, had left thir charge, Flown to the upper World. **1679** C. Nesse *Antichrist* Ded., You may improve this upper-ground whereon you stand. **1697** Dryden *Virg. Georg.* iv. 699 The lovely Bride In safety goes,..Longing the common Light again to share, And draw the vital breath of upper Air. **1815** Wordsw. *Artegal & Elidure* 53 Of Arthur,—who, to upper light restored,..Shall lift his country's fame above the polar star! **1822** Byron *Vis. Judgem.* xii, He's dead—and upper earth with him has done; He's buried. **1887** BROWNING *Apollo & Fates* 10 *The Fates.* (Below. Darkness.).. We.. Deal to each mortal his dole of light On earth—the upper, the glad, the bright.

Comb. **1862** SMILES *Engineers* III. 9 The upper-ground workmen employed at the coal-pits.

b. Constituting or forming a stratum, layer, bed, etc., lying nearer the earth's surface or formed later in time; *spec.* of stratifications of more recent formation than another of that character and name.

See also 13 b, GREENSAND 1, OOLITE 2–3, SILURIAN *a.* 2 b. **1696** WHISTON *The. Earth* 77 Our upper strata.. being generally factitious, or acquir'd at the Universal Deluge. **1733** TULL *Horse-Hoeing Husb.* 251 The.. Hills whereof the Upper-Stratum (or Staple) is Mould. *c* **1775** in *Encycl. Brit.* (ed. 2) IV. 2526/1 If a ditch.. penetrate through the upper stratum of clay. **1839** MURCHISON *Silur. Syst.* xlv. 605 The Ludlow and Wenlock Formations, or Upper Silurian Rocks. **1852** SEDGWICK in *London Lit. Gazette* 338/3 A part of my Upper Cambrian series. **1873** DAWSON *Earth & Man* iv. 56 The Lower Silurian is the Upper Cambrian of Sedgwick. **1873** E. HULL *Coal-fields Gt. Brit.* (ed. 3) 192 The strata overlying the 'Upper-foot', or 'Bullion-coal'. **1886** J. BARROWMAN *Sc. Mining Terms* 69 *Upper-leaf*, the upper portion of a seam which is separated by a parting into two portions.

fig. **1859** G. MEREDITH *R. Feverel* xix, Tossed into the upper stratum of civilized life. **1877**, **1890** [see STRATUM 6].

Comb. **1865** LUBBOCK *Preh. Times* 299 The height at which the upper-level gravels stand above the present water-line. **1890** *Science-Gossip* XXVI. 146 The upper limestone masses.

7. Occurring or taking place in, directed towards, a higher or the highest position. ***upper cut***: (*a*) in *Pugilism* (see quot. 1897); also as *v. trans.*; (*b*) in *Cricket*, a cut that sends the ball up (*obs.* exc. *humorously*).

1607 TOPSELL *Four-f. Beasts* 402 An vpper attaint or ouer-reach vpon the backe sinnew of the shanke. **1728** CHAMBERS *Cycl.* s.v. *Attaint*, The Farriers distinguish upper Attaints, given by the Toe of the Hind-foot upon the sinew of the Fore-leg,—And nether Attaints. **1815** J. SMITH *Panorama Sci. & Art* II. 135 The further admission of steam to that side during the upper stroke [of the piston]. **1842** *Spirit of Times* 17 Sept. 339/2 Giving him a sharp upper cut as he fell. **1856** *Sat. Rev.* II. 658/2 Resorting to means of defence against which cross-buttocks and upper-cuts.. will do very little good indeed. **1850** in *Mem. T. Sayers* (1858) 21 Sayers.. hit short at Collins with his left, who upper-cut him sharply, and slipped down. **1865** *F. Lillywhite's Guide to Cricketers* 128 [He] has.. made some good scores this year, his 'upper cut' being particularly effective. **1867** SMYTH *Sailor's Word-bk.* 708 *Upper transit*, the passage of a circumpolar star over the meridian above the pole. **1872** *Baily's Mag.* June 44 Smith's plucky innings was considerably helped by hits known as 'upper cuts'. **1897** *Encycl. Sport* I. 139 *Upper cut*,.. a counter, delivered upwards with either hand, when an opponent leads off or rushes in with his head down. **1898** A. M. BINSTEAD *Pink 'Un & Pelican* 237 She wouldn't 'old her tongue the other night, an' so.. I uppercuts her with the right. **1955** A. ROSS *Australia 55* 133 Two upper-cuts sent second and third slip on futile chases to the boundary.

II. 8. a. Occupying a higher (or the highest) position, station, or rank; superior in authority, place, etc. Cf. UPSTAIRS *a.* c.

1477 *Extr. Aberd. Reg.* (1844) I. 36 That Alexander.. be continevit vpper and principale maister of wark. **1526** TINDALE *Acts* xxii. 26 The vnder captayne.. went to the vpper captayne, and tolde hym. **1561** in *Maitl. Club Misc.* III. 209 We hawe command of ye vppir poweris to put the same in executione. **1647** *Bury Wills* (Camden) 195 At the disposing of.. God, whoe is the onely supreme and vpper Lord of all. **1710** STEELE *Tatler* No. 180 ¶4 The Abatement which they suffer when paid, by the Extortion of Upper Servants. **1771** LUCKOMBE *Hist. Print.* 86 He was upper-warden of the Stationer's Company. **1776** J. WOODFORDE *Diary* 3 June (1924) I. 182 One of them is to be an upper servant and she lived very lately with Mr. Howes. **1783** *Ibid.* 24 Mar. (1924) II. 65 Betty, my Upper Maid stayed at home being Washing Week. *a* **1817** JANE AUSTEN *Persuasion* (1818) III. vi. 102 Her upper-housemaid and laundry-maid. **1836–9** DICKENS *Sk. Boz, Gt. Winglebury Duel*, I am the upper-boots..; the other man's my man, as.. does odd jobs. **1847** C. BRONTË *J. Eyre* v, One of the upper teachers.. installed herself at the top of one table. **1862** TROLLOPE *Orley F.* II. 248, 'I was housemaid at Orley Farm.' 'Were you upper or under there?' **1872** [see QUAVER *v.* 3 b]. **1958** R. WILLIAMS *Culture & Society* III. 329 That kind of confidence which will enable the upper servants to supervise and direct the lower servants.

b. Higher or highest in respect of influence, wealth, office, or dignity; wealthy, aristocratic, influential.

Freq. since *c* 1890, esp. with *class* (cf. CLASS *sb.* 2). Also used to indicate finer gradations in the social scale, as ***upper-lower, -middle, -upper, -working*** (class); see also UPPER-MIDDLE-CLASS *a.* and *sb.* as main entry. Also ***upper bourgeois***.

1825 J. WILSON in *Blackw. Mag.* March 373, I wad aiblins introduce the upper ranks intil the wark. **1837** CARLYLE *Fr. Rev.* I. VII. ii, The best-informed Upper-Circles. **1839** —— *Chartism* v, The oppressing or neglecting upper classes. **1844–** [see 20 a]. **1856** EMERSON *Eng. Traits, Universities*, These seminaries are finishing schools for the upper classes, and not for the poor. **1907** M. BERENSON *Let.* 6 Mar. (1983) 139 So you aren't a 'County Family'.. 'not knowing yet' whether you're Upper Middle or only Middle. **1938** E. BOWEN *Death of Heart* III. vi. 420 Oh, shut up, darling... Don't be so upper class. **1940** HARRISSON & MADGE *War begins at Home* v. 103 The response was best from the upper and middle classes; whilst the upper-working or artisan class supplied its quota. **1955** T. H. PEAR *Eng. Social Differences* iii. 88 Radio-copies of lower-middle, upper-lower and middle-lower speech. **1964** T. B. BOTTOMORE *Elites & Society* iv. 82 The postwar reforms of recruitment to the French higher civil service.. have changed the ethos of education for the administrative elite—have made it more 'managerial' and less 'upper class'. **1964** C. BARBER *Ling. Change Present-Day Eng.* ii. 18 The general pattern of usage is as follows: *pudding* (upper and upper-middle), *sweet* (middle), [etc.]. **1967** M. ARGYLE *Psychol. Interpersonal Behaviour* iv. 83 A development in the British class system during the 1950s was the emergence of an upper working class. **1974** H. WAUGH *Parrish for Defence* (1975) xxxix. 182 You're closer to where it's at if you're only upper middle class than if you're upper upper.

Comb. **1837** CARLYLE *Fr. Rev.* II. v. ix, The riband-cockade, as a sympton of Feuillant Upper-class temper. **1890** *Spectator* 3 May, The upper-class Arabs and Turks. **1897** MARY KINGSLEY *W. Africa* 318 This aristocracy has sub-divisions, the M'pongwe of Gaboon are the upper-circle tribe. **1955** *Caribbean Quarterly* IV. II. 109 The 'upper-upper' French Creoles who number under 200 consider all the rest to be of mixed ancestry. **1970** P. DICKINSON *Seals* vi. 123 The harryings of ninety sets of upper-bourgeois parents.

absol. **1898** G. MEREDITH *Odes Fr. Hist.* 12 They, the triumphant tonant towering upper, were under; They, violators of home, dared hope an inviolate home. **1967** N. FREELING *Strike out where not Applicable* 74 She was too much upper to say cheers.

c. ***upper-bracket*** adj., belonging to or characteristic of the higher section of a (social) scale; upper-class, wealthy, influential; cf. (*income*) *bracket* s.v. BRACKET *sb.* 5 c; also ***upper-income*** adj.

[**1943** Upper bracket: see BRACKET *sb.* 5 c.] **1945** S. LEWIS *Cass Timberlane* 157, I go there all the time, to shave the upper-bracket crooks when they got too big a hang-over to walk. **1957** O. NASH *You can't get there from Here* 130 And, should upper-bracket dreamers wake, Squab o' Neptune, and Plankton Steak. **1960** N. MITFORD *Don't tell Alfred* ix. 98 He's all set for the upper-income group—tax free of course. **1973** J. ROSSITER *Manipulators* xiv. 138 Luckhurst's overcoat and suit had been expensively tailored, the watch on his wrist an upper-bracket Rolex. **1978** *Detroit Free Press* 16 Apr. 8A/1 The migration of middle and upper-income whites out of the central cities has become a headlong flight.

9. a. Consisting of or including more advanced studies or more proficient students; having a higher place or standing in studies or learning.

1629 WADSWORTH *Pilgr.* iii. 15 The Students of the three vnder schooles, go vp to those of the vpper. **1740** J. CLARKE *Educ. Youth* (ed. 3) 209 The Boys of the upper Classes may be admitted. **1749** FIELDING *Tom Jones* II. iii, His scholars were divided into two classes, in the upper of which was a young gentleman [etc.]. **1857** HUGHES *Tom Brown* I. viii, Three unhappy fellows.. whom the Doctor and the master of the form were always endeavouring to hoist into the Upper school.

b. With an ordinal number. (*a*) Designating the senior division of a class or form at school, as ***upper sixth (form)***, etc. (*b*) ***upper second***, the upper division of a second-class honours degree.

1856 C. M. YONGE *Daisy Chain* I. ix. 90 They are a low, ungentlemanly lot just now, about sixth and upper fifth form. **1858** J. A. SYMONDS *Let.* 6 June (1967) I. 145 Bosanquet is an Upper Sixth Boy and nearly a Monitor. **1905** R. BROOKE *Lett.* (1968) 29, I decided that Swinburne would be a great aesthetic blessing to the starved Upper Sixth. **1935** C. ISHERWOOD *Mr. Norris changes Trains* i. 7 An incident.. To do with the upper fourth form classroom. **1981** E. NORTH *Dames* ii. 24 The form previously called Middle Five B would now be known as Upper Fifth. **1982** *Oxford Times* 25 June 11/3 He decided he wanted to see America, after graduating at Oxford with an Upper Second in Geography.

10. a. Of a higher, better, more excellent, or more comprehensive quality; superior.

a **1586** SIDNEY *De Mornay* ii. ¶1 We reduce the particulars too an vnderkind, the vnderkinds to an vpperkind, and the vpperkind to a most generall. As for example, we reduce all particular humane persons vnder the terme of man. **1587** GOLDING *Ibid.* x. 163 If the mixture of the Elements cannot make the forme whereby the vpperkyndes differ from one another, as the sencelesse things from the things that haue sence. **1831** CARLYLE *Sart. Res.* II. ix, Here, then, as I lay in that Centre of Indifference; cast, doubtless by benignant upper Influence, into a healing sleep [etc.]. **1895** MARIE CORELLI *Sorrows Satan* iv, [Genius] is.. an 'upper' thing, beyond earthly smells and savours.

†**b.** ***upper fortune***, the upper hand (cf. 16).

1613 FLETCHER *Honest Man's Fort.* I. ii, Since You have the upper fortune of him, 'twill Be some dishonor to you to bear your self With any pride or glory over him.

11. Constituting or producing a higher tone, note, or notes.

1843 *Penny Cycl.* XXVI. 418/2 The upper or female voice part of the scale. *Ibid.* 419/1 The extreme upper notes of the falsetto. **1880** *Grove's Dict. Music* II. 654/1 The difficulty of hearing the upper partial tones. **1895** *Funk's Stand. Dict.*, *Upper-keyboard*, the right-hand side of the keyboard. **1896** A. J. HIPKINS *Pianoforte* 122 *Upper Partial*, any partial or simple division of a compound vibrating string that is above the first, or Fundamental.

III. Special collocations.

12. upper air = *upper atmosphere*; **upper atmosphere**, the upper part of the earth's atmosphere; now *spec.* that above the troposphere; **upper berth** *U.S.*, the higher of two bunks set one above the other, usu. in a boat, sleeping-car, etc.; **upper circle**, the tier of seats above the dress circle in a theatre; cf. CIRCLE *sb.* 11 b; **upperclassman** *U.S.*, a junior or senior student in school or college (as opp. FRESHMAN).

[**1877** *Q. Jrnl. Meteorol. Soc.* III. 447 It would not.. do to imagine that every cloud in the rear of another cloud was cirrus, and yet it might be a distinct upper air current.] **1895** *Ibid.* XXI. 182 The scheme of exploring the upper air by means of small balloons was first proposed by Geheimrat A. Meydenbaur. **1957** *Encycl. Brit.* XXII. 883B/1 In meteorology the exploration of the upper air, using instruments carried by balloons, kites or aircraft, is an important part of observational technique. **1979** G. B. NAVARRA *Atmosphere, Weather & Climate* x. 357 Aircraft provide a highly mobile way of gathering data in the upper air. **1895** *Q. Jrnl. R. Meteorol. Soc.* XXI. 182 The Upper Atmosphere.—On July 7th, 1894, Dr. Assmann set free at Charlottenburg a balloon, equipped with self-registering apparatus for the determination of meteorological data in the higher regions of the atmosphere. **1933** *Discovery* Dec. 359/2 There is a monthly sequence of intense magnetic activity when wireless waves are absorbed and not reflected by the upper atmosphere. **1976** *Physics Bull.* Dec. 554/2 The author looks at the earth's upper atmosphere, taking the tropopause as its lower boundary. **1894** F. M. CRAWFORD upper berth. **1917** J. HUSBAND *Story of Pullman Car* 29 The upper berth might be closed in the day time and also serve as a receptacle for bedding. **1829** *Harlequin* 20 June 46 The upper circle and lower gallery were reserved for company to view the entertainment. **1889** *Theatre* May 292 The house consists of four tiers, pit and stalls, dress circle, upper circle, and gallery. **1926** A. CONAN DOYLE in *Liberty* 18 Dec. 9/1 Amberley.. had taken two upper-circle seats at the Haymarket Theater. **1871** L. H. BAGG *4 Years at Yale* 70 Only a few upper-class men will be found there. **1897** FLANDRAU *Harvard Episodes* 202 If they happened to be upper classmen. **1933** F. SCOTT FITZGERALD *Let.* 26 June (1964) 502 Insofar as upperclass-men are concerned I saw a rather depressed runt at the Yale game. **1978** J. IRVING *World according to Garp* ii. 48 He befriended Garp in a very decent fashion while he was an upperclassman at Steering and Garp was just starting out.

13. upper crust: **a.** The top crust of a loaf. Also *transf.* †**b.** The exterior or surface layer of the earth. **c.** *slang.* The human head; a hat. **d.** *dial.* (See quot.) **e.** (See quot. 1848.) *colloq.* (orig. *U.S.*). Freq. *attrib.* or as *adj.* **f.** Hence **upper-crusty** *a.*, aristocratic, (socially) superior.

a. *c* **1460** J. RUSSELL *Bk. Nurture* 342 Kutt þe vpper crust [of the loaf] for youre soueravne. **1542** BOORDE *Dyetary* xi. (1877) 261 Wherfore chyp the vpper crust of your breade. **1591** A. W. *Bk. Cookrye* 10 b, Put therto a peece of vpper crust of white bread. **1768** W. DONALDSON *Life B. Sapskull* II. 108 The upper-crust of that building [the Mansion-house] is thought too heavy for the simple ingredients of an aldermanic pasty. **1823** J. BADCOCK *Dom. Amusem.* 32 Alum throws up a flowery paleness upon the whole upper crust. **1868** FURNIVALL *Babees Bk.* 271 *margin*, The upper crust of a fine loaf.

b. **1555** EDEN *Decades* 234 An other kynde of Rubies.. found in the mountaynes in the vpper crust or floure of the earth. **1669** WORLIDGE *Syst. Agric.* (1681) 230 It.. doth not bury the upper-crust of the ground so deep as usually is done by digging. **1696** WHISTON *The. Earth* 53 Such an Upper Crust or Shell of Earth on the face of the Abyss. **1762** MILLS *Syst. Pract. Husb.* I. 39 When the upper crust of the earth is removed, all that can be seen, or dug, is marle.

c. **1826** *Sporting Mag.* XVIII. 253 Tom completely tinkered his antagonist's upper-crust. **1829** P. EGAN *Boxiana* 2nd Ser. II. 461 Ward.. threw his upper-crust into the ring. **1832** —— *Bk. Sports* (Farmer), Sam's nob had been in pepper alley, and his upper crust was rather changed. **1851** *Household Words* II. 320/1 A highly-polished Parisian upper-crust.. smashed under the weight of a carter's slouch.

d. **1854** MISS BAKER *Northampt. Gloss.* 371 'Mrs. Upper Crust,' a fictitious designation for any female who assumes unauthorised superiority.

e. **1836** HALIBURTON *Clockm.* xxviii, It was none o' your skim-milk parties, but superfine uppercrust real jam. **1843** —— *Sam Slick in Eng.* xxiv, I want you to see Peel,.. Macaulay, old Joe, and so on. These men are all upper crust here. **1848** BARTLETT *Dict. Amer.* 370 *Upper crust*, the aristocracy, the higher circles. **1850** J. F. COOPER *Ways of Hour* vi. I. 186 Those families.. are our upper crust—not upper ten thousand, as the newspapers call it, but upper hundred. **1863** G. DU MAURIER *Let.* May in *Young G. du Maurier* (1951) 204 All Millais' [paintings] are upper crust. **1878** W. S. GILBERT *H.M.S. Pinafore* II. 31 Two tender babes I nussed: One was of low condition, The other, upper crust, A regular patrician. **1898** *Daily News* 14 Feb. 2/7, 55 magistrates, 46 of whom belonged to what.. [is] sometimes called 'the upper crust'. **1957** *New Statesman* 19 Oct. 1/2 Views which are commonplace in upper-crust circles. **1966** D. FRANCIS *Flying Finish* vii. 82 One particular horse from an upper crust stud. **1973** M. AMIS *Rachel Papers* 116, I stalked up to the door and rapped, with an upper-crust rap, on the knocker.

f. **1977** *Time* 26 Dec. 1/1 The politicians' wives, looking upper-crusty. **1980** *TWA Ambassador* Oct. 77/3 We lived in Garden City, the upper-crusty part.

14. upper deck, the highest continuous deck of a ship. (Orig. the higher of two decks, in contrast to the *lower*.)

1591 RALEIGH *Last Fight Reuenge* B 3, Sir Richard.. was neuer so wounded as that hee forsooke the vpper decke. **1598** FLORIO *Dict.* To Rdr. 9, I was but one to sit at sterne, to pricke my carde, to watch vpon the vpper decke. **1626** CAPT. SMITH *Accidence Yng. Seamen* 10 The vpper Decke should be layd with so many beames as are fitting with knees to bind them. *a* **1687** PETTY *Treat. Naval Philos.* I. i, The Hull under the said upper Deck is divided into the Cavity or Hold [etc.]. **1758** J. BLAKE *Plan Mar. Syst.* 2, It is proposed, that.. guns run out on the upper deck only. **1769** FALCONER *Dict. Marine* (1780) s.v. *Deep-waisted*, To leave a vacant space, called the waist, on the middle of the upper-deck. **1846** A. YOUNG *Naut. Dict.* 98 That part of the upper-deck which is between the forecastle and poop.. is termed the Main-deck. **1889** E. C. STEDMAN in *Life W. Sharp* (1910) ix. 155 You looked down upon its members from the Servia's upper-deck.

fig. *a* **1613** OVERBURY *Characters, Saylor* Wks. (1890) 75 Nothing but hunger and hard rockes can convert him, and then but his upper decke neither; for his hold neither feares nor hopes.

attrib. **1709** *Lond. Gaz.* No. 4521/2 Upon whom we fired ..our Upper-deck..Guns. **1892** E. Reeves *Homeward Bound* 129 To give third-class passengers a little breathing upper-deck space.

15. upper dog. [After underdog.] The victorious party in a contest; the one who has the upper hand or a position of superiority. Cf. overdog. *rare.*

1903 G. Bowles in *Parl. Debates* 18 Feb. 224 If it came to a question of force, we should always be the 'upper dog' in Persia. **1940** 'G. Orwell' *Inside Whale* 82 One has got to change sides when the underdog becomes an upperdog. **1971** *Daily Progress* (Charlottesville, Va.) 30 Mar. 4/2, I am for the upperdog—the achiever, the succeeder.

16. upper hand: **a.** The mastery, control, or advantage (*of*, or *over*, a person, people, etc.); predominance, rule, or dominion. Usu. const. with verbs, as *attain*, *gain*, *get*, *have*, *obtain*. Cf. the earlier over-hand *sb.*, uver-hand. (Freq. *c* 1560–*c* 1600.) **b.** A person or party in power or authority. **c.** The place of authority or honour; preference, precedence. (Usu. with *give* or *take*.)

a. 1481 Tiptoft *Tulle of Old Age* (Caxton) g viij b, Marcus Attilius..had the vppirhande and victorye of the men of cartage. **1535** Coverdale *Ps.* ix. 19 Vp Lorde, let not man haue the vpper hande. **1576** Gascoigne *Steele Gl.* (Arb.) 64 Downe goeth al, where they [*sc.* soldiers] get vpper hand. *a* **1616** Beaum. & Fl. *Little Fr. Lawyer* I. i, I have seen fools, and fighters, chain'd together, And the Fighters had the upper hand, and whipt first, The poor Sots laughing at 'em. **1690** Somers *Vind. Proc. Late Parlt.* 10 The Jacobites, and the Malecontents..might perhaps get the upper hand, if not prevented in time. **1742** Young *Nt. Th.* III. 479 Where ev'ry ranger of the wilds, perhaps Each reptile, justly claims our upper hand. **1743** Pococke *Descr. East* I. 177 When the Greeks got the upper hand,..they treated them with great rigour. **1838** Dickens *O. Twist* xv, I've got the upper-hand over you. **1861** Ld. Brougham *Brit. Const.* xiii. 195 They blindly followed the dictates of the faction which had the upper-hand. **1865** Mrs. Carlyle *Lett.* (1883) III. 303, I decided to take the upper hand with her, and keep it.

transf. (of things). **1535** Coverdale *Wisdom* x. 5 Whan wickednes had gotten yᵉ vpper-hande, so yᵗ the nacions were puft vp with pryde. **1546** Bp. Gardiner *Detect. Devil's Sophistrie* 16 Whiles the bely hath the vpperhande amonge a greate many. **1579** G. Harvey *Letter-bk.* (Camden) 87 Summer gettith the upperhande of wynter, and wynter agayne of summer. **1622** Peacham *Compl. Gent.* xv. 186 Hereby the minde getteth the dominion and vpperhand. **1712** Pope *Spect.* No. 408 ¶3 If a Man suffers them [*sc.* the passions] to get the upper hand. **1796** Mme. D'Arblay *Camilla* I. 289 Sir Hugh..said it never broke out from him but by accident, which..should never get the upper hand again. **1873** Mrs. Oliphant *Innocent* III. 160 The natural honesty to which he had appealed gained the upper hand. **1885** *Manch. Exam.* 29 June 5/1 The worst tendencies of the party will gain the upper hand.

b. 1548 Hall *Chron., Hen. VI*, 126 The poore inhabitauntes..were..compelled to yeilde and rendre theimselfes, to the more power, and vpper hande. **1606** *Sir G. Goosecappe* I. iv, One of these painted communities, that are rauisht with Coaches, and vpper hands.

c. 1580–3 Greene *Mamillia* Wks. (Grosart) II. 49 If by chaunce the Vestal virgins walkt abroad, the Senators would giue them the vpper hand. **1598** Hakluyt *Voy.* I. 68 They ..gaue vs and Duke Ieroslaus the vpper hand, when we were abroad in their companie. **1662** J. Davies tr. *Olearius' Voy. Ambass.* 9 The *Priestaf* gave the Ambassadours the upper Hand, and conducted them to the Inn. **1663** Pepys *Diary* 25 Jan., A late dispute between my Lord Chesterfield ..and Mr. Edward Montagu..who should have the precedence in taking the Queen's upper-hand abroad out of the house. **1715** *Lond. Gaz.* No. 5329/1 The Empress..gave the upper Hand to the [Dowager] Empress Amalia. **1746** Francis tr. *Hor., Sat.* II. v. 26 Yet wait upon him, at his least command, And always bid him take the upper hand. **1809** Malkin *Gil Blas* VII. ii. ¶9 [At] the second table..the whole household..insisted on giving me the upper hand.

fig. **1594** Shaks. *Rich. III*, IV. iv. 37 If ancient sorrow be most reuerent, Giue mine the benefit of signeurie, And let my greefes frowne on the vpper hand.

d. *adv.* (See quots., and cf. underhand *adv.* 2 c.)

1771 Luckombe *Hist. Print.* 333 The Nut and Spindle, and the Toe of the Spindle, are all to be well oiled; that they may all perform their several offices the easier..; both Upper and Under hand. **1808** Stower *Printer's Gram.* 530 When the spindle goes soft and easy,..it goes well upper hand or above hand. **1888** Jacobi *Printers' Vocab.* s.v.

e. Hence **upperhandism**. *nonce-word.* [-ism 2 b.]

1845 E. B. Barrett *Lett. to R. Browning* (1899) I. 26 The curious thing in this world is not the stupidity, but the upperhandism of the stupidity.

17. upper house, a higher house of deliberation or legislation, esp. the House of Lords.

1532–3 *Act 24 Hen. VIII*, c. 12 §4 The Spirituall Prelatez and other Abbottes and Priours of the upper House assembled..in the Convocacion. *a* **1577** Sir T. Smith *Commonw. Eng.* II. ii. (1584) 38 Besides the Chauncelor, there is one in the vpper house who is called Clarke of the Parliament. **1640** Yorke *Union Hon.* 66 Which was concluded in the upperhouse of Parliament. *a* **1670** Hacket *Abp. Williams* II. (1693) 180 The Bishops..intended that this Petition..should be preferred to the King..in the Upper House of Parliament. **1708** J. Chamberlayne *St. Gt. Brit.* II. (1710) 481 A List of the Members of the Upper-House of Convocation. **1728** Chambers *Cycl.* s.v. *Convocation*, Things are first usually propos'd in the upper House; then communicated to the lower. **1818** Bentham *Ch. Eng.* p. x, The Lower House was indeed untaxable. But the Upper House..taxed themselves. **1849** Macaulay *Hist. Eng.* iii. I. 325 The abolition of the monasteries deprived the Church..of her predominance in the upper house of parliament. **1859** W. Swainson *New Zealand* xi. 289 The Legislative Council, or Upper House. **1885** Lowe *Bismarck* I. 293 The Lower Chamber would not yield an inch to the Crown and the Upper House.

attrib. **1610** Bolton *Elem. Armories* 150 Or should I not doe wrong to Campes, and Parliaments, robbing souldiers, and vpper-house men of their colour?

18. upper leather: **a.** Leather forming the upper of a boot or shoe; also, = upper *sb.*[1] 1. **b.** Sheet-leather suitable or prepared for such.

a. 1528 Roy *Rede me* (Arb.) 82 *Jef.* To mangill their good shues so, Me thynketh it but folisshnes. *Wat.* They cutt but the vpper ledder. **1603–4** *Act 1 Jas. I*, c. 22 §23 The upper Leather of any Shoes, Startups, &c. **1708** Ockley *Saracens* I. 142 Those who had strong Boots on,..had the Soals torn off from the Upper-Leathers. **1759** *Phil. Trans.* LI. 39 With that shoe struck off, and its upper-leather torn. **1841** *Penny Cycl.* XXI. 410/2 The lasting or tacking of the upper-leather to the in-sole. **1846** Thackeray *Laman Blanchard* Wks. 1899 XIII. 467 Persons who..polish their upper-leathers as well as they can. **1872** T. Hardy *Under Greenw. Tree* II. ii, The upper-leather of a Wellington-boot.

fig. **1647** N. Ward *Simple Cobler* (title-p.), Willing to help 'mend his Native Country, lamentably tattered, both in the upper-Leather and sole.

b. 1629 *Leather* 12 The..strongest, which might..serue both for sooling leather and vpper leather. *Ibid.* 15 The Market is full of excellent Leather (strong Backes, and good vpper Leathers). **1885** *Harper's Mag.* Jan. 278/1 Upper-leather..is sold by the foot or pound.

19. upper lip: **a.** The lip on the upper side of the mouth; the superior lip of a person, animal, or insect. **b.** The higher of the two edges of an organ-pipe mouth. **c.** *Bot.* The superior or upper division of a bilabiate corolla or calyx. **d.** *spec.* (See underlip 1 b.)

a. 1546 J. Heywood *Prov.* (1867) 77 He can yll pype, that lacth his vpper lyp. **1596** Spenser *State Irel.* Wks. (Globe) 635/1 That noe man shall weare his bearde but onely on the upper lipp like muschachoes. **1611** Bible *Lev.* xiii. 45 The leper..shall put a couering vpon his vpper lip. **1670** Milton *Hist. Eng.* VI. 304 The English then useing to let grow on their upper-lip large Mustachio's. **1704** *Dict. Rust.* s.v. *Rules buying Horses*, If his Upper-Lip will not reach his Nether. **1748** Richardson *Clarissa* VI. 387 Which made John's upper-lip..rise to his nose. **1758** J. S. tr. *Le Dran's Observ. Surg.* (1771) 42 It possessed the whole Upper-Lip. **1815** *Massachusetts Spy* 14 June 4/4, I kept a stiff upper lip, and bought license to sell my goods. **1826** Kirby & Sp. *Entomol.* III. xxxiii. 355 *Labrum* (the Upper-lip), a usually moveable organ; which..is situate between the Mandibulæ. **1833–** [see lip *sb.* 2, stiff *a.* 11]. **1836** Yarrell *Brit. Fishes* I. 378 [The loach] with four barbules or cirri..on the upper lip in the front. **1849** C. Bronte *Shirley* xxiii, He had the shorter nose and longer upper-lip of his sister.

b. 1728 Chambers *Cycl.* s.v. *Organ*, Over this Aperture is the Mouth..; whose upper Lip.., being level, cuts the Wind as it comes out at the Aperture. **1852** Seidel *Organ* 78 The upper lip..forming, together with the under lip, the mouth of the pipe. **1875** Knight *Dict. Mech.* 1709/2 The lower edge of the leaf is termed the upper lip.

c. 1731 Miller *Gard. Dict.*, *Salvia*..hath a labiated Flower, consisting of one Leaf, whose Upper-lip is sometimes arched. **1793** Martin *Lang. Bot.*, *Galea* (an helmet), the upper lip of a ringent corolla. **1796** Withering *Brit. Plants* (ed. 3) III. 555 *Digitalis purpurea*... Segments of the calyx egg-shaped, acute:..upper lip nearly entire. **1807** J. E. Smith *Phys. Bot.* 434 *Ajuga* [has] scarcely any upper lip at all.

20. a. upper ten, the upper classes; the aristocracy. *colloq.* Orig. (*U.S.*) ***upper ten thousand.***

(*a*) **1844** N. P. Willis in *Even. Mirror* (N.Y.) 11 Nov. 2/1 At present there is no distinction among the upper ten thousand of the city. **1861** Lever *One of Them* xix. 149 The Peerage,..the bulky volume that records the alliances and the ages of the 'upper ten thousand'. **1871** *Punch* 15 May 187/2 There was no grievance on the part of the 'upper ten thousand'.

(*b*) **1846** A. J. H. Duganne *Daguerreotype Miniature* 20 Major Peyton Florence was held in great reverence by the 'upper ten'. **1848** Bartlett *Dict. Amer.* 370 *The upper ten thousand*, and contracted, *the upper ten*,..the upper circles of our large cities. **1860** W. H. Russell *Diary in India* I. 119 Petty jealousy and 'caste' reigned in the Residency; the 'upper ten' with stoical grandeur would die the 'upper ten'. **1886** C. E. Pascoe *Lond. of To-day* xxxii. (ed. 3) 294 Clubs of some note..patronized by the 'upper ten'. [**1890** Rider Haggard *Beatrice* xi, Plenty of carriages, and other needful things, including of course the *entrée* to the upper celestial ten.]

transf. **1879** Jefferies *Wild Life* 160 Neither is he [*sc.* the robin] a favourite with the upper class of cottagers—for there is an 'upper ten' even among cottagers.

b. Hence **upper-tendom** = *upper ten.* Chiefly *U.S.*

1848 F. A. Buck *Yankee Trader in Gold Rush* (1930) 13, I suppose you and those other families left out constitute an *Upper Ten-dom*, in the place. **1855** *Doesticks* xvi. 131, I did go to a ball for the benefit of the poor—a two-dollar commingling of upper-tendom with lower-twentydom. **1863** N. Hawthorne *Our Old Home* II. 199 All the girls, whether daughters of the uppertendom, the mediocrity, the cottage, or the kennel. **1887** [W. F. Rae] *Miss Bayle's Romance* I. 253 This countess belongs to the real upper tendom.

21. upper works: **a.** That part of a vessel which is above water-level when it is ready or laden for a voyage; = dead-work 1. (Also †*upper work.*) **b.** The higher portion of a structure. **c.** *slang.* The head; the mental capacity.

a. 1591 Raleigh *Last Fight Reuenge* B 3 b, The mastes all beaten ouer board,..her vpper worke altogither rased. **1627** Capt. Smith *Seaman's Gram.* xi. 52 She is brought in narrow to her vpper workes. **1693** *Lond. Gaz.* No. 2865/1 The French Man of War..who fought the Berkeley Castle ..being very leaky,..and all her upper Work torn to pieces. **1745** P. Thomas *Jrnl. Anson's Voy.* 270 To caulk the Ship's Upper-Works and Decks. **1769** Falconer *Dict. Marine* (s.v.), Upper-work. **1798** Nelson in Nicolas *Disp.* (1845) III. 106 The Sérieuse was set on fire to burn her upper works which were above water. *c* **1850** *Rudim. Navig.* (Weale) 157 *Upper works*,..all that part which may be considered as separated from the bottom by the main wale. **1898** Kipling *Fleet in Being* i. 7 The battleships overtook us, their white upperworks showing like icebergs as they topped the sea-line.

fig. **1751** Smollett *P. Pickle* vi, I'd have you take care of your upper works; for if once you are made fast to her poop, egad, she'll..make every beam in your body crack with straining.

b. 1791 Smeaton *Edystone L.* §60 The object was to repair or restore the Upper Works.

c. 1809 Malkin *Gil Blas* III. iii. ¶12 Arsenia and Florimonde are not strong in their upper works; but then they have a facility in their vocation which is more than all the wit in the world. **1818** *Sporting Mag.* July 167 Neate gave Oliver..a..hit on his mouth, that his *upper works* were in a complete state of *chaos.* **1860** J. P. Kay-Shuttleworth *Scarsdale* II. 299 Oi'm i' gradely fettle..i' th' upper warks.

ˈupper, *adv.* Now *rare.* [f. up *adv.*[1] or *adv.*[2] + -er[3].] To or in a loftier place or position; higher, further up.

c **1384** Chaucer *H. Fame* II. 884 With this word, vpper to sore He gan. *c* **1391** —— *Astrol.* II. §12 As the sonne clymbith vppere & vppere. *c* **1550** Cheke *Matt.* xxiii. 12 Whosoever abaseth himself schal be set vpper. *a* **1552** Leland *Itin.* (1711) III. 6 A litle Foreland about a Mile upper then Kenor on Severn. **1901** *Punch* 21 Sept. 224/1 We go up, up, up, up, and upper, upper,..skirting..precipices.

†upper-bodying, *vbl. sb. Obs.* (See upper *a.* 4 b.)

1502 *Priv. Purse Exp. Eliz. York* (1830) 22 For upper bodyeng sleving and lynyng of a gowne.

upper crust(y), upper-cut: see upper *a.* 13, 7.

ˈupperest, *a.* Now *rare.* Also 4 **uppurest**, 4–5 **uppereste**, 5 **-ist**; 6 **upperst**. [A superlative form on upper *a.* Cf. MDu. *upperst* (Du. and Flem. *opperst*), LG. *upperst*, *üpperst*, Sw. and older Da. *ypperst*, Norw. *ypparst*, *yppast* best, choicest.] Most high in situation, position, or rank; uppermost, highest, loftiest; †outermost.

In modern use rare for *uppermost*.

13.. *K. Alis.* 7068 (MS. Linc.), Þeose seresys..Vppurest folk buþ of ynde. *c* **1374** Chaucer *Boeth.* I. pr. i. 2 (Camb. MS.), By whiche degrees men myhten clymbyn fro the nethereste lettre to the vppereste. **1387–8** T. Usk *Test. Love* I. x. (Skeat) l. 32 We men, that..holden the upperest degree, under god, of benigne thinges. **1483** Caxton *Gold. Leg.* 62 b/1 Moyses..made hym upperist bysshop for his fader Aaron. *Ibid.* 76 b/1 She wente up in the upperist cubicle of the hows. *a* **1548** Hall *Chron., Hen. VIII*, 2 b, His grace ware in his vpperst apparell, a robe of Crimosyn Veluet. **1874** M. Collins *Frances* III. 212 An American of the very upperest five hundred. **1880** W. Morris in Mackail *Life* (1890) II. 15 Above the Round House, on what might be called the upperest Thames.

b. *absol.* The uppermost or highest point.

1484 Caxton *Fables of Æsop* III. iii, He that..is atte vpperest of the whele of fortune, may wel falle doune.

†ˈupperest, *adv. Obs. rare.* In 5 up(p)rest. [f. upper *adv.*] In the highest place or position.

1481 *Cely Papers* (Camden) 71, vij packes..lying be afte the maste, j pack lyeth upprest. *Ibid.* 72 A few broken felles and pesys..lyeth uprest nexte the maste.

upper-flapped, *a.* (upper *a.* 3 a.)

1850 'H. Hieover' *Pract. Horsemanship* 107 The Shaftoed upper-flapped, and stuffed lower-flapped saddle.

upper hand(ism): see upper *a.* 16 (also 2).

upper leather, lip: see upper *a.* 18, 19.

upper-middlebrow, *sb.* (*a.*) [upper *a.* 8 b.] One whose cultural interests lie between those of the middlebrow and those of the highbrow. Also *attrib.* or as *adj.*

1956 R. Conquest *New Lines* p. xiv, A sort of upper-middle-brow equivalent of the horror-comic. **1959** *Economist* 28 Feb. 787/1 Magazines for upper middle-brows. **1974** *Country Life* 14 Mar. 588/2 The middle to-upper-middle brow range that Chichester programmes now generally encompass. **1977** *Listener* 11 Aug. 170/1 In *Life* magazine, nearly 30 years ago, an American critic said: What culture and civilized living we have today is provided by the interaction of..the aesthetic radical highbrow and the somewhat more conservative upper-middlebrows.

upper-middle-class, *a.* and *sb.* [upper *a.* 8 b.]

A. *adj.* Of, pertaining to, or characterized by the class of polite society next below the upper class.

1872 *Times* 26 Dec. 5/4 Upper and upper middle-class society is represented in all its grades. **1906** Galsworthy *Man of Property* I. i. 3 Those privileged to be present at a family festival of the Forsytes have seen..an upper middle-class family in full plumage. **1949** W. L. Warner in M. Fortes *Social Structure* 4 Excerpts from the Total Configuration of an upper-middle-class doctor illustrate how this technique is used. **1967** M. Argyle *Psychol. Interpersonal Behaviour* iv. 80 English upper-middle-class speech includes considerable understatement; a person who fails to follow this convention is regarded as boastful. **1982** 'W. Haggard' *Mischief-Makers* ii. 20 Willy's skin was the colour of coal... He thought of himself as an upper-middle-class Englishman.

B. *sb.* **1.** Usu. unhyphened. This class itself, or its members.

c **1885** M. Darwin *Let.* in G. Raverat *Period Piece* (1952) vi. 98 The upper middle class think they are acting rightly by over-protecting their daughters. **1891** H. D. Traill in *National Rev.* Mar. 15 The great body of the upper middle classes. **1903** G. Gissing *Private Papers H. Ryecroft* 210 A lad whose education ranks him with the upper middle class. **1923** A. Bennett *Riceyman Steps* I. ii. 5 He had the air neither of a bookman nor of a member of the upper-middle class. **1955** H. Roth *Sleeper* xii. 99 Stamford, Connecticut, is a typical transplanting ground of the upper middle class. **1965** R. Williams in *Tribune* 5 Mar. 1/5 The English upper-middle class.

2. *ellipt.* as ***upper-middle***, a member of the upper middle class. Usu. in *pl.*

1955 [see *middle-middle* s.v. middle *a.* 6]. **1967** *Economist* 18 Feb. 607/2 In Birmingham, Manchester, Liverpool, the upper-middles do not choose to live in the city. **1978** R. Westall *Devil on Road* xv. 111 When my parents quarrel, they..fight in hoarse whispers. But like a lot of upper-middles..Derek and Susan let it all hang out.

'uppermore, *adv.* and *a.* Now *dial.* Also 5 **vppyr-, vppermare, vpher more**, 6 *Sc.* **vppermair, -mer, vppirmer**, 7 **vppermere**, 9 *north. dial.* **uppermer.** [f. upper *adv.* and *a.* + -more. Cf. older Da. *yppermere.*]

A. *adv.* Higher locally; further up; at or to a greater altitude. (In later use *Sc.*)

c **1400** Maundev. (Roxb.) xiv. 63 Vppermare amanges þe mountaynes es a faire citee. c **1410** *Master of Game* (MS. Digby 182) xxi, þat þe flewe be iii. or iiii. fyngres vppermore þanne þe heed. **1435** Misyn *Fire of Love* I. x. 20 Bettyr it is ..þat criste..to vs say, 'frende, cum vppyrmare'. **1501** Douglas *Pal. Hon.* III. v, Weil I considderit na vppermair I micht, And to discend sa hiddeous was the hicht, I durst not auenture. **1596** Dalrymple tr. *Leslie's Hist. Scot.* (S.T.S.) I. 30 Abone or vppirmer, vpon Leuin, is the toune. **1616** *Barbour's Bruce* (Hart) II. 440 To that word they assented all, And from them walloped vppermere.

B. *adj.* That is the more elevated (of two); higher, upper.

c **1400** Maundev. (Roxb.) xx. 90 Bathe þe emisperies, þe vppermare and þe nedermare. a **1425** tr. *Arderne's Treat. Fistula*, etc. 44 After þat þe vppermore iuncture of þe bone of þe fynger was drawen out. **1869-** in north. dialect use (*Eng. Dial. Dict.*).

'uppermost, *adv.*, *a.*, and *sb.* Also 5 **wpwr-, wppwrmwste**, 6 *Anglo-Ir.* **uppermuste**; 5 **wpwr-**, 6 **vp(p)ermoste** (6 **vppermooste**), 5–7 **vper-**, 6–7 **vppermost.** [f. as prec. + -most.]

A. *adv.* **1.** In or to the highest, upmost, or most elevated position or place.

1481 *Cely Papers* (Camden) 74 A packe lyes wpwrmwste apon Dawlttons behynde the maste. *Ibid.* 75 Thay ly behynde the maste wpwrmoste. **1617** J. Taylor (Water P.) *Observ. & Trav. fr. London to Hamburgh* E 1 b, A good featherbed vndermost,..and another featherbed vppermost. **1622** Sir R. Hawkins *Observ. Voy. S. Sea* 3 With a storme..shee was turned topse-turvie, her Kele vppermost. **1668** Bp. Hopkins *Serm., Vanity* (1685) 76 His hand turns all things here about like so many wheels;..the same part is now uppermost, and anon lowermost. **1712** Addison *Spect.* No. 281 ¶11, I..shall therefore only take Notice of what lay first and uppermost. **1747** Wesley *Prim. Physick* (1762) 55 Lie with that Ear uppermost. **1814** Scott *Diary* 7 Aug. in *Lockhart*, This man being uppermost on the cord,..called out to his brother who was next to him. **1842** Loudon *Suburban Hort.* 263 Care must be taken that the upper end of the cutting..be kept uppermost. **1860** Tyndall *Glac.* I. xvi. 118 In making this effort the spike of my axe turned uppermost.

fig. **1866** G. Macdonald *Ann. Q. Neighb.* vii. (1878) 117 If the wine hadn't got uppermost.

b. In the first or foremost place in respect of precedence, station, rank, or the like.

1526 Tindale *Matt.* xxiii. 6 They..love to sytt vppermooste at feastes. **1530** Palsgr. 713/2, I set hyest, or upper moste in a companye. **15..** *Bk. Precedence* i. 14 All Dukes daughters shall goe all-one with a nother, soe that alwayes the Eldest Dukes Daughter go vpermost. **1628** [see C. 1 b]. **1850** J. F. Cooper *Ways of Hour* I. 317 It is the people today;..some prince to-morrow; and by the end of the week we may have..a Robespierre uppermost.

c. *fig.* In the chief place or predominancy.

1805 Wordsw. *Prelude* IX. 389 We..saw..generous love ..Uppermost in the midst of fiercest strife. **1850** Robertson *Serm.* Ser. III. (1857) 125 A mourning in which self is ever uppermost. **1885** 'M. Rutherford' *Deliv.* i. 11 Every now and then, when the subject was uppermost.

2. Foremost in, most prominently in or into, the mind, thoughts, conversations, etc.

In frequent use from c 1830.

1693 *Humours Town* 54 Perpetual Chat on whatever comes uppermost. **1719** De Foe *Crusoe* II. (Globe) 316 It was uppermost in all my Thoughts. **1723** *Pres. St. Russia* II. 151 It was always my Way to say what came uppermost. **1802–12** Bentham *Ration. Judic. Evid.* Wks. 1843 VII. 172 Any one word that comes uppermost is sufficient. **1848** Thackeray *Van. Fair* xli. Ever since she had left them she had not ceased to keep them uppermost in her thoughts. **1860** Trollope *Framley Parsonage* xxvi, To speak out what came uppermost to her tongue.

B. *adj.* **1.** Occupying the highest position or place; loftiest, topmost, highest in place; furthest up (on a river, etc.).

c **1500** *Melusine* lix. 358 He yede vp to the vpermost stage of the donjon. **1526** Tindale *Luke* xi. 43 Ye love the vppermost seates in the sinagoges. a **1548** Hall *Chron., Hen. VIII*, 226 b, One of the officers demaunded his vpper garment for his fee, meanyng his goune, and he [*sc.* Sir Thomas More]..tooke him his cappe, saiyng it was the vppermoste garment that he had. **1623** Bingham *Xenophon* 133 Xenophon..encamped in the vppermost village neere the mountaines. **1657** Hobbes *Absurd. Geom.* 3 Perhaps you mean that the uppermost quantitie 0 + 1 is equal to the uppermost quantity 1. **1702** *Post Man* 8–11 Aug. 2/1 Inquire at the uppermost House..in the said Buildings. **1764** *Museum Rust.* IV. 19, I preserve only two of the new shoots, the uppermost and its opposite. **1844** Kinglake *Eothen* x, The golden juice ascended from..the cellar to the uppermost brains of the friars. **1886** J. A. Brown in *Q. Jrnl. Geol. Soc.* May 196 There had been a manufactory of Palæolithic implements on this uppermost floor. **1896** A. Sterry *Tale Thames* (1903) 43/1 One the most attractive portions of what may be called the Uppermost Thames.

b. Outermost; most external.

a **1548** [implied in quot. under 1 above]. **1560** *First Bk. Discipl.* (1621) 48 The uppermost claith, corps-present; clerk maile, the Pasche-offering. **1567** Maplet *Gr. Forest* 69 The Adder..casteth off yearely his uppermost skin or coate. **1861** J. R. Greene *Man. Anim. Kingd., Cœlent.* 103 An expanded bulb, above which are disposed..the various appendages... Of these the hydrocysts are uppermost, or external.

†**2.** Maximum, utmost. *Obs.*⁻¹

1579 in *10th Rep. Hist. MSS. Comm.* App. V. 430 If any [person]..steallinge of any..wares, do..restore the thing or thinges so taken or the uppermuste vallue thereof.

3. Highest in respect of rank, importance, precedence, etc.; chiefest, first.

1680 Walton in Aubrey *Lives* (1898) II. 15 He was in.. the vpermost fforme in Westminster scole. **1699** Bentley *Phal.* 188 The Thought [was] so very obvious and uppermost. **1780** Warner in Jesse *Selwyn & Contemp.* (1844) IV. 398 In the Westminster [election] struggle Rodney is to-day got uppermost. **1876** Miss Yonge *Womankind* xii, This entire seclusion from all means of reaching the poor..is seldom found in the uppermost classes. **1885** *Manch. Exam.* 6 Apr. 5/2 The weather is, in view of the approaching holiday, the uppermost subject of concern.

b. Having the chief power, control, or authority; predominant, supreme; most influential.

1691 Wood *Ath. Oxon.* I. 887 In the time of the rebellion he sided with those that were uppermost. **1693** *Humours Town* 42 The Violence of those that are uppermost. **1732** Berkeley *Alciphr.* II. §21 Where heavy heads are lowest, and men of genius uppermost. **1818** Scott *Br. Lamm.* xxvii, Uniform adherents to the party who are uppermost. **1855** Macaulay *Hist. Eng.* xiv. III. 445 The politician whose practice was always to be on the side which was uppermost.

C. *sb.* †**1.** The highest part or portion. *Obs.*

1484 Caxton *Fables of Æsop* v. xiii, Yf an Egle were at the vppermost of the heuen. **1613–39** I. Jones in Leoni *Palladio's Archit.* (1742) II. 49 The uppermost of the highest Cornice, is of large Tyles. **1646** J. Gregory *Notes & Obs.* 11 For so they call Τὰ μετέωρα τῶν οἰκημάτων, the uppermosts of their Houses.

b. The highest place or position.

1628 R. H. *J. Owen's Epigr.* II. liv. 11 Let me set alwayes vppermost at boord, The vppermost in bed I'le you afoord.

†**2.** That which is highest, most predominant, etc. *Obs.*

1687 *Good Advice* 60 It is certain that two predominant Religions, would be two Uppermosts at once. a **1753** Bp. Berkeley in Fraser *Life* (1871) 477 Wᵗ judgement would he make of uppermost and lowermost who had always seen through an inverting glass?

†**3.** The upper hand; superiority or dominion.

1718 *Entertainer* No. 43. 302 If ever they get the Uppermost, after their long Struggles for Superiority.

†**upperplus.** *Obs.*⁻¹ [f. upper *a.*, substituted for *sur-* in *surplus.*] Surplus, balance.

1578 *Surrey & Kent Sewers Comm.* (1909) 286 To sell the same and satisfye the chardge and make restitucion of the vpperplus.

†**upper-stocked**, *a.* *Obs.* (See upper *a.* 4 a.)

1535 in *Archaeologia* IX. 250 Two paire of hoose,..the one paire upperstocked with yalowe damaske.

upper ten, works: see upper *a.* 20, 21.

Upper 'Voltan, *a.* and *sb.* [f. *Upper Volta* (see def.) + -an: cf. upper *a.* 1.] **A.** *adj.* Of or pertaining to Upper Volta, an inland republic in West Africa (a former French colony whose independence was recognized in 1960, now called Burkina). **B.** *sb.* A native or inhabitant of Upper Volta. Cf. Voltaic *sb.* and *a.*²

1972 *N.Y. Times* 28 Nov. 2/4 Horsemen from the Upper Voltan fringes of the Sahara called out, 'Pa! Pa! Pompidou!' **1975** *Congress. Q.: Editorial Research Rep.* (Daily Service) 7 May, For many Upper Voltans the real villain of the piece is not Mali but France. **1976** *Facts on File* 17 Apr. 269/3 Upper Voltan trade unions had welcomed the formation of the new government. **1983** *Times* 25 Jan. 6/1 There are more than 500,000 immigrants from Niger, as well as..Togolese, Beninese, Upper Voltans and Chadians.

uppie ('ʌpɪ). *slang.* [-y⁶, -ie.] = upper *sb.*²

1966 *Sunday Times* (Colour Suppl.) 13 Feb. 35/4 *Uppies and downies*, pep pills and tranquillisers. **1975** J. F. Burke *Death Trick* (1976) ii. 22 There's nothing in the box but a few uppies. I haven't got a regular prescription.

up-'piled, *pa. pple.* and *ppl. a.* (up- 5.)

1600 Fairfax *Tasso* XIX. xxx. 342 There vnderneath th' vnburied hils vppilde Of bodies dead, the liuing buried lie. **1742** Collins *Ode Poet. Char.* 55 High on some cliff, to heav'n up-pil'd. **1796** Coleridge *To Yng. Friend* 2 A green mountain variously up-piled. **1818** Keats *Endym.* II. 288 He cannot see.., up pil'd, The cloudy rack slow journeying in the west. **1855** Singleton *Virgil* I. 88 Thrice the Sire in ruins laid The up-piled mountains with his flash. **1873** Symonds *Grk. Poets* i. 28 With Homeric games and pyres up-piled to heaven.

†**'upping**, *vbl. sb.*¹ *Obs.* [OE. *ypping*, f. *yppan* uppe *v.*] Manifestation, making known.

c **950** *Rit. Durham* 195 *Epiphania, manifestatio*, ypping. a **1225** *Ancr. R.* 148 God dede idrawen uorð nis nout one uorloren þuruh þet uppinge, auh þuncheð ȝet atelich biuoren Godes eien.

'upping, *vbl. sb.*² [f. up *v.*]

1. The action of catching and marking swans. (See up *v.* 1, and cf. swan-hopping, -upping.)

1560–1 in W. H. Turner *Select. Rec. Oxford* (1880) 285 For upping of half game in cowemeade, iiij d. **1570–1** *Ibid.* 338 For upping of swans, viij s. **1593** Buckhurst in Kempe *Losely MSS.* (1836) 306 That the upping of all those swans ..may be upped all in on day wᵗ the upping of the Tems. **1892** *Pall Mall G.* 2 Aug. 2/1 The operation of 'upping' is performed by the Crown and the Companies' swan-masters together.

attrib. **1572–3** in W. H. Turner *Select. Rec. Oxford* (1880) 350 Chargys aboute the swanes..at the syttynge tyme and uppynge tyme. **1584–5** *Order for Swans*, His Dinner and Supper free, on the vpping day.

2. The action of getting up; only *attrib.* in ***upping-block, -stock, -stone***, a horse-block, a mounting-stone.

Also in dial. use with *-chock, -steps.*

1796 *Grose's Dict. Vulgar T.* (ed. 3), *Upping block, steps for mounting a horse. **1826** Cobbett *Rur. Rides* (1830) 529 Houses..with large stone upping-blocks against the walls of them. **1883** *Trans. Amer. Philol. Soc.* 55 *Upping-block*, 'a horse-block,' in common use in West Virginia. a **1691** Aubrey *Nat. Hist. Wilts* (1847) 26 At the foot of Shotover-hill, near the *upping-stock. **1820** *Sporting Mag.* VI. 159 An itinerant preacher on the upping-stock at the back of my house. **1856** G. Roberts *Soc. Hist. Eng.* 560 Upping stocks and horse blocks were necessary when double horses were in use. **1809** Hazlitt in *The Hazlitts* (1911) I. 433 A conception of the ladder which I learned from the *upping stone on the down.

3. *dial.* The end, issue, or upshot of a matter.

1828- in Yks. and Lanc. glossaries.

uppish ('ʌpɪʃ), *a.* Also 8–9 **upish.** [f. up *adv.*² + -ish.]

†**1. a.** Flush of money. *Obs.*

1678 in Pollock *Popish Plot* (1903) App. B. 382 The one saying to the other that..he would treat him..with wine and oysters, whereupon the other replied..: 'What you are uppish then, are you?' a **1700** B. E. *Dict. Cant. Crew*, *Uppish*, rampant, crowing, full of Money. *He is very Uppish*, well lined in the Fob; also brisk.

†**b.** Elevated in station. *Obs.*

1797 *Hubbub* 7 No sooner did he get a little uppish in the world, than [etc.].

2. †**a.** Elated; in high spirits; cock-a-hoop.

Common in the early years of the 18th century, freq. const. *upon.* Johnson (1755) defines as 'proud; arrogant' and adds 'A low word'.

a. a **1704** T. Brown *Wks.* (1720) I. 173 Half-pay Officers at the Parade very uppish upon the Death of the King of Spain. **1708** T. Cockman in *Ballard MSS.* XXI. 81 Ye Brittish Papists were mighty uppish upon ye attempt made upon Scotland. **1722** Wodrow *Corr.* (1843) II. 643 The Jacobites are uppish, and very big in their hopes. **1746** in *10th Rep. Hist. MSS. Comm.* App. I. 289, I fear the Victory will have very bad consequences, if it render the Ministry uppish and secure.

β. **1710** *Wentworth Papers* (1883) 122 The Torys are very upish and expect all to come in for Places. **1712** Swift *Jrnl. to Stella* 25 Jan., I find Dingley smelled a rat; because the Whigs are upish; but if ever I hear that word again, I'll uppish you. **1802** A. Carlyle *Autobiog.* (1861) 154 He agreed with me that they [*sc.* the Jacobites] had less ground for being so sanguine and upish than they imagined.

†**b.** Elevated with drink. *Obs.*⁻¹

1728 Vanbrugh *Journey to London* III. i, *Lady Head.* Not so drunk, I hope, but that he can drive us? *Serv.* Yes, yes, Madam, he drives best when he's a little upish.

c. Ready to take offence; short-tempered, peevish. Now *dial.* or *Obs.*

1778 Miss Burney *Evelina* lv, Miss is so *uppish* this morning, that I think I had better not speak to her again. **1785** Grose *Dict. Vulgar T.*, *Uppish*, testy, apt to take offence. **1823** E. Moor *Suffolk Words* 460 A man prone to take offence is said to be *uppish*:—or *pepperish*; apt to be hot. **1863** Mrs. C. Brock *Margaret's Secret* ii. 31 When I used to find fault he would get uppish with me, and answer back rudely.

d. Inclined to be 'stuck up'; putting on airs; aiming at gentility.

1789 O'Keefe *Farmer* I. ii, Must bounce a few, Betty's so upish—likely wou'dn't have me else. **1823** *Blackw. Mag.* XIII. 365 It is according to human nature to feel uppish on preferment. **1858** Trollope *Dr. Thorne* xxxiv, You think he's an uppish sort of fellow, I know, and you don't like to trouble him. **1886** Besant *Childr. Gibeon* II. xxxii, She's uppish you know,..and he's only a working-man.

e. *dial.* (See quots.)

1841 Hartshorne *Salop. Ant.* Gloss. 605 *Uppish*, pert, proud, impudent. **1854** Miss Baker *Northampt. Gloss.*, *Uppish*, captious, pert, self-opinionated, tenacious of opposition.

3. Characterized by presumption or affectation of superiority.

a **1734** North *Exam.* (1740) 48 It seems [that] daring to rail at Informers..and Officers was not uppish enough, but his Lordship must rise so high as daring to limit the Power ..of the Crown. **1808** Eliz. Hamilton *Cottagers of Glenburnie* ii. 37 Besides, she is getting uppish notions, from sitting up like a lady from morning to night. **1864** J. H. Newman *Apol.* 100 Discouraging and correcting whatever was uppish or extreme in our followers.

4. Slightly elevated or directed upwards.

1862 *Morn. Star* 9 June, Hayward sends a long uppish hit. **1887** *Daily News* 1 July 6/4 After two uppish strokes Mr.

Scott hit remarkably well. **1895** *Westm. Gaz.* 2 March 5/1 Peel was there to hold the uppish ball.

Hence **'uppishness.**

1716 N. HOUGH in Thoresby *Corr.* (1832) II. 341 The uppishness and indiscretion..of some..in the West Riding. *a* **1832** BENTHAM *Chrestom.* Tab. i, Uppishness a probable result of the distinctions thus obtained. **1867** *Gard. Chron.* 16 Nov. 1180/1 The uppishness, the insolence, and the lawlessness of some of the young men. **1896** J. H. WYLIE *Hist. Eng. Hen. IV*, III. 468 The staid authorities resented his uppishness; but his spirit was irrepressible.

'uppishly, *adv.* [f. UPPISH *a.* + -LY[2].]

a. *Cricket.* Of the ball, etc.: in a slightly upward direction, esp. so as to give some chance of a catch.

1904 P. F. WARNER *How we recovered Ashes* 109 Just after he had passed his hundred, he sent one uppishly through the slips. **1955** A. ROSS *Australia 55* 137 Hutton..then turned Archer a shade uppishly through the short-legs. **1963** *Times* 11 Jan. 10/6 Guest..drew one false stroke out of Dexter which went uppishly past gully.

b. In an uppish (sense 2 d) manner.

1911 G. B. SHAW *Blanco Posnet* Pref. 307 The majority of the Committee began by taking its work uppishly and carelessly. **1960** M. SPARK *Ballad Peckham Rye* vii. 141 'Miss Merle Coverdale, one of my unofficial helpers,' Dougal said uppishly. **1981** *Times Lit. Suppl.* 26 June 727/2 Rowland Lacy, wooer of the uppishly poised Rose.

uppity ('ʌpɪtɪ), *a. colloq.* (orig. and chiefly *U.S.*). [f. UP *adv.*[1] + *-it-* + -Y[1]: cf. BIGGITY *a.*] Above oneself, self-important, 'jumped-up'; arrogant, haughty, pert, putting on airs. Cf. UPPISH *a.* 2 d. **a.** *attrib.*

1880 J. C. HARRIS *Uncle Remus* 86 Hit wuz wunner deze yer uppity little Jack Sparrers, I speck. **1933** *Times Lit. Suppl.* 9 Nov. 776/2 Grammy is living contentedly enough with an 'uppity' young creature named Penny. **1952** F. L. ALLEN *Big Change* II. viii. 130 The effect of the automobile revolution was especially noticeable in the South, where one began to hear whites complaining about 'uppity niggers' on the highways, where there was no Jim Crow. **1982** B. CHATWIN *On Black Hill* v. 28 He had a head for figures and a method for dealing with 'uppity' tenants.

b. *predic.*

1932 *Sun* (Baltimore) 23 Aug. 6/2 [She] could have plenty o' friends. The trouble with her is she thinks folks too common to bother with unless they're too uppity to bother with her. **1947** 'N. SHUTE' *Chequer Board* 68 They've been here alone too long, and they've got uppity. **1955** F. O'CONNOR *Wise Blood* v. 89, I reckon you ain't as uppity as you was last night. **1966** D. BAGLEY *Wyatt's Hurricane* i. 27 The Navy is trying to build up Cap Sarrat as a substitute for Guantanamo in case Castro gets uppity and takes it from them. **1973** P. WHITE *Eye of Storm* viii. 381, I came prepared to rough it... It's Dorothy who grows uppity if all the cons aren't mod.

Hence **'uppitiness,** the quality of being 'uppity'; an instance of this.

1935 H. L. DAVIS *Honey in Horn* x. 145 Clay's bravery and uppitiness had done nothing. **1966** *Listener* 27 Oct. 622/1 She had decided that Joyce was 'pretentious' and 'underbred'... But who was Virginia Woolf to talk (in this purely literary sense) of 'uppitiness'? **1975** *Ibid.* 9 Oct. 479/1 Few delegates seemed versed in *Private Eye* nomenclature and would, anyway, disapprove of such uppityness. **1982** R. BARNARD *Death & Princess* ii. 17 Joe may appreciate my couthness..but he can sniff out uppitiness.

up'plucked, *pa. pple.* (UP- 5. Cf. *upplucking* UP- 6 (*a*), and Du. *opgeplukt.*)

c **1440** *Pallad. on Husb.* VII. 61 Now benys,..vpplucked sone, Maad clene, and sette vp. *c* **1449** PECOCK *Repr.* I. x. 51 In this wise..is vnrootid and vppluckid..the firste of the iij. opinions. **1582** STANYHURST *Æneis* III. (Arb.) 71 When an oother wicker is vp pluckt..From that stub.

uppon, var. UP *prep.*[1] *Obs.*; obs. f. UPON *prep.*

up-pouring: see UP- 7(*b*).

up-'pricked, *pa. pple.* (UP- 5.)

1592 SHAKS. *Ven. & Ad.* 271 His eares vp prickt..; His nostrils drinke the aire. **1777** MASON *Eng. Gard.* II. 343 The coward hare..Will..steal, with ear Up-prick'd, to gnaw the toils.

'up-push. *rare.* [UP- 2.] A pushing upwards.

1910 J. W. GREENE *Clin. Course Dental Prosthesis* 46 There is now a little general up-push all along the yielding line. **1940** *Sun* (Baltimore) 5 Apr. 23/1 (*heading*) Rails continue up-push in bonds. **1960** R. W. MARKS *Dymaxion World B. Fuller* 28/1 If such a man took the proper head-long attitude, with respect to air resistance, the amount of up-push required to keep him plummeting forward should be no more than that supplied by his leg muscles to give him his initial altitude.

'up-put. *Sc.* [UP- 1 b, 2.]

1. 'The power of secreting' (Jam.).

a **1689** CLELAND *Poems* (1697) 101 Tho he can swear.. And lye, I think he cannot hide... They are not fitt For Stealth, that want a good up-put.

2. = UP-PUTTING *vbl. sb.* 2.

1866 GREGOR *Banffshire Gloss.* 204. **1893** STEVENSON *Catriona* xix, Ye'll can leave your horse here and your bags, for it seems we're to have your up-put.

†**'up-,putter.** *Sc. Obs.* [UP- 8.] One who raises or erects.

a **1578** LINDESAY (Pitscottie) *Chron. Scot.* (S.T.S.) I. 194 Thair promovearis or vpputaris to that he estait. **1623** *Extr. Aberd. Reg.* (1848) II. 385 The wpputter thairoff,..that wald hawe the said windo reedifiet,..sall reedifie and put wp the said windo. **1721** in Gordon *Chron. Keith*, etc. (1880) 97 As upputters at the first and proprietors of the sd. loft.

'up-,putting, *vbl. sb. Sc.* [UP- 7.]

†**1.** The action of erecting or setting up. *Obs.*

1513 *Extr. Aberd. Reg.* (1844) I. 86 For vpputting of the weddercok of Sanct Nicholace stepill,..v lib. **1597** *Ibid.* II. 158 The perfyting, ending, and vpputting of ane dyell..one the tolbuyith. **1642** in Cramond *Ann. Cullen* (1888) 41 Anent upputting and edifeing the tolbuith. *a* **1670** SPALDING *Troub. Chas. I* (1840) I. 313 To tak doun the portrait of our blissid virgyn Marie..that had stand since the vpputting thairof.

2. Accommodation, lodging. (Cf. PUT *v.* 56 o.)

1815 SCOTT *Guy M.* ix, You, who have free upputting—bed, board, and washing. **1831** MRS. CARLYLE *Lett. & Mem.* (1903) I. 37 We succeeded to realising a much better up-putting..in the house of a Mrs. Miles. **1895** CROCKETT *Men of Moss-hags* xxxviii, In the wild country..was no provision for the up-putting of young..maids.

up'raisal. [UP- 2.] = UPHEAVAL 1.

1865 JEVONS *Coal Quest.* ii. 25 The upraisals, the downfalls, the dislocations,..which rocks have suffered.

'upraise, *sb. U.S. Mining.* [UP- 2.] A shaft made by working upwards.

1877 RAYMOND *Statist. Mines & Mining* 158 A drift..has been run through the..ground, and an upraise commenced. **1882** *U.S. Rep. Prec. Met.* 98 At the end of this [tunnel] they are pushing an upraise, finding the rock a little softer as they go up.

up'raise, *v.* [UP- 4. Cf. MSw. *up-, opresa, -reesa* (Sw. *uppresa*), MDa. *uprese, oprese, opreise* (Da. *oprejse*).]

†**1.** *trans.* To raise from the dead. *Obs.*

a **1300** *Cursor M.* 14363 Son oueral þis tiþand ras O lazar þat vpraisid was. *c* **1340** HAMPOLE *Pr. Consc.* 4325 He sal alswa dede men uprays. **1382** WYCLIF *Matt.* x. 8 Hele ȝe seke men, vpreyse ȝee dead men. **1533** GAU *Richt Vay* 29 He sal wpraisz agane al thayme to the euerlestand lyff.

2. †**a.** To raise by laudation; to extol. *Obs.*

a **1300** *Cursor M.* 27584 We agh ilk man upraise, And in vr hert vrself dispraise. **1595** SPENSER *Col. Clout* 355 By wondring at thy Cynthiaes praise,..thy selfe thou mak'st vs more to wonder, And her vpraising, doest thy selfe vpraise.

b. To raise (or direct) to a higher level; to lift up or elevate; *fig.* to exalt.

In the 19th c. the pa. pple. after the noun is common, as 'with hand upraised'.

a **1300** *E.E. Psalter* xxxvi. 37 (E.), I saw þe wicked man.. vpraised als cedre of Yban. *c* **1385** CHAUCER *L.G.W.* 1163 *Dido*, Whan that the mone vp reysed hadde his lyght. **1430–40** LYDG. *Bochas* IX. 2351 Lik as Phebus passeth a litil sterre, Hiest vpreised in his mydday speere. **1563** *Mirr. Mag.* V iv, Dead laye his corps,..Tyil swellyng syghes.. Upraysde his head. **1748** THOMSON *Cast. Indol.* II. lxvii, The sick up-rais'd their heads, and dropp'd their woes awhile. **1788** WOLCOT (P. Pindar) *Brother Peter* Wks. 1816 I. 380 This lord..uprais'd his convert chin. **1791** COWPER *Odyssey* IX. 624 Then pray'd the Cyclops..With hands upraised toward the starry heaven. **1821** CLARE *Vill. Minstr.* II. 61 Cowslips,..upraise your loaded stems. **1830** LYELL *Princ. Geol.* I. 458 Both these accounts..agree in expressly stating, that the sea retired, and one mentions that its bottom was upraised. **1874** SPURGEON *Treas. Dav.* Ps. xcv. 5 He bade the isles upraise their heads.

fig. **1828** ATHERSTONE *Fall of Nineveh* I. 238 The fire-eyed priest Upraised his voice, and called upon the Gods.

c. To raise from a prostrate, low, or dejected state; to assist, encourage, or cheer.

a **1340** HAMPOLE *Psalter* cxliv. 15 Lord vpraysis all þat fallis. *c* **1440** *Wycliffite Bible* 1 Sam. ii. 8 (MS. Bodl. 277), He upreisiþ a nedy man fro poudre, and upreisiþ a pore man fro dritt. **1533** GAU *Richt Vay* 105 The vangel or ioiful tithandis ..throw the quhilk he wesz wprasit in his hart. **1600** FAIRFAX *Tasso* I. ii, O heauenly muse,..Inspire life in my wit, my thoughts vpraise. **1610** FLETCHER *Faithf. Sheph.* V. i, Once again upraise Her heavy Spirit that near drowned lyes In self consuming care. **1667** MILTON *P.L.* x. 946 He.. thus with peaceful words uprais'd her soon. **1723** *Briton* No. 18 (1724) 76 It help'd the Distressed, uprais'd the Heavy-hearted. **1746** FRANCIS tr. *Hor., Sat.* II. viii. 80 Sure he had wept,..But wise Nomentane thus up-rais'd his Friend. **1809–14** WORDSW. *Excurs.* IV. 574 Furnished thus, How can you droop, if willing to be upraised? **1818** MILMAN *Samor* VII. 409 Oh, Monarch,..to repentant deeds of mightiest fame Heaven can upraise the farthest sunken. **1850** BLACKIE *Æschylus* II. 120 They with Mercy's vote upraised us From the prostrate woe.

d. To excite, rouse. *rare.*

a **1600** *Flodden F.* iv. (1664) 40 Their courage keen now was uprais'd. **1667** MILTON *P.L.* II. 372 This would..our Joy upraise In his disturbance.

3. To erect, set up, build.

1338 R. BRUNNE *Chron.* (1810) 78 Þe kastelle of Bamborgh þe walles he did vpreise. *c* **1400** *Laud Troy Bk.* 4658 Thei ran alle..To sette vp tentis, Pauylons to bylde;..Many a tent was ther vp-reysed. **1513** DOUGLAS *Æneid* XI. vi. 47 That sammyn douchty hand..Quhilk now..Vprasit hes the cite Argyripas. **1582** STANYHURST *Æneis* I. (Arb.) 26 Romulus..towne wals statelye shal vpraise..Of Rome.

'upraised, *ppl. a.* [UP- 5. Cf. prec.]

1. a. Raised or lifted up; elevated.

c **1400** tr. *Secreta Secret., Gov. Lordsh.* 117 Vpraysyd shuldren bytoknys sharpe nature. **1785** WILKINS *Bhagvat* xi. 90 The mighty compound..being Haree, having..thus spoken, made evident..his..heavenly form; of many a mouth and eye;..many an up-raised weapon. **1796** MME. D'ARBLAY *Camilla* V. 476 The upraised arm of the form before her dropt. **1853** KANE *Grinnell Exp.* xxii. (1856) 173 The thickness of the upraised tables. **1890** 'R. BOLDREWOOD' *Col. Reformer* (1891) 204 He saw Hutkeeper leap at him, with upraised tomahawk. **1898** *Allbutt's Syst. Med.* V. 611 Osseous material..beneath the upraised periosteum.

b. *spec.* in *Geol.* Raised by upheaval.

1835 LYELL *Princ. Geol.* (ed. 4) II. 342 Near Uddevalla.. we find upraised deposits of shells. **1863** —— *Antiq. Man* 45 These upraised strata..form a terrace. **1877** HUXLEY *Physiogr.* 212 The upraised deposits of silt which skirt the estuary of the Clyde.

2. Directed upwards.

1707 E. SETTLE *Siege of Troy* I. ii. 9 Hail, beauteous goddess, all divine, Our up-rais'd eyes and hearts all thine. **1817** COLERIDGE *Biog. Lit.* II. xxiv. 309 The upraised Eye views only the starry Heaven. **1851** D. JERROLD *St. Giles* xii. 124 The big tears that rolled from her upraised eyes.

3. Sounded aloud.

1871 S. B. JAMES *Duty & Doctrine* (ed. 3) 173 Penitence.. must mingle with the upraised notes of gladness.

up'raiser. [UP- 8.] One who raises up.

c **1440** *Wycliffite Bible* 2 Sam. xxii. 3 (MS. Bodl. 277), þe horn of myn helþe, myn upreiser [L. *elevator*], and my refuyt. *c* **1440** *Jacob's Well* 59 Alle comoun baratours, vprayserys of vnryȝtfull batayles. **1533** GAU *Richt Vay* 88 Iesus christus..is..the veray wprayser of al marcie and grace.

up'raising, *vbl. sb.* (UP- 7. Cf. ON. *uppreising, -reisning*, MSw. and MDa. *up-, opresning.*)

c **1400** LOVE *Bonavent. Mirr.* (1908) 179 Thou art.. Resurreccioun or vpreysynge and lyf. *c* **1454** PECOCK *Folewer* 15 His witt schal þerbi take in maner now seid a greet vpreisyng. **1611** COTGR., *Resource*,..a recouerie, vpraising, rising againe. **1839** URE *Dict. Arts* 839 The successive upraising of the roof of a gallery. **1926** *Daily Colonist* (Victoria, B.C.) 19 Jan. 17/4 The upraising going on in the underground working is progressing very satisfactorily. **1936** BELLOC *Battle Ground* xi. 225 Some said he was Elias, come back to the up-raising of men.

up'raising, *ppl. a.* (UP- 6 b.)

1609 DANIEL *Civ. Wars* VII. lxxii, Think whether this poore State..Stands not in need of some vp-raysing hand. **1860** ELLICOTT *Life Our Lord* v. 229 The upraising hand of the great Healer.

uprape: see UP- 4.

†**upras.** *Obs.* [a. ON. *upprás*, f. *upp-* UP- 2 + *rás* RACE *sb.*[1]] Resurrection.

a **1300** *Cursor M.* 17784 Yow thinc selcut..O iesus vp-ras. *Ibid.* 18683 Sant thomas..of his up-ras..was in were.

up'rate, *v.* [UP- 4.] *trans.* To raise to a higher standard, to upgrade; *spec.* to improve the performance of (a mechanical device or process); to increase the value of (a commodity, grant, etc.).

1965 *National Observer* (U.S.) 8 Feb. 15/1 The first stage of the Saturn 1-B is similar..except that its engines have been uprated to produce more power. **1968** *Listener* 1 Aug. 159/1 At a time when petrol prices were rather unstable, Esso uprated their Extra..to super or five-star grade. *a* **1974** R. CROSSMAN *Diaries* (1976) II. 372 Every two years we uprate pensions in order to see that they don't lose their purchasing power. **1980** 'D. RUTHERFORD' *Turbo* ii. 29 The [car] springs had been uprated to carry the extra weight. **1984** *Daily Tel.* 25 Jan. 17/4 Government plans to uprate early leavers' pensions by up to 5 p.c.

Hence **up'rated** *ppl. a.*, **up'rating** *vbl. sb.* and *ppl. a.*

1967 *Jane's Surface Skimmer Systems 1967–68* 116/2 More recent models are fitted with the uprated..version of this marine diesel. **1968** *Listener* 1 Aug. 159/1 The recent mass switch to five-star petrol may..be partly due to the uprating of Extra. *a* **1974** R. CROSSMAN *Diaries* (1976) II. 372, I can tell you we should now expect a pension up-rating Bill to be published within the next fortnight. **1981** *Sunday Express* (Colour Suppl.) 14 June 21 An uprated sports suspension makes sure that all this extra power is kept under control.

†**up'raught,** *pa. pple. Obs.* [UP- 5 + REACH *v.* Cf. OHG. *ûfrahta.*] Drawn up, raised.

c **1375** *Sc. Leg. Saints* i. (*Peter*) 717 For þu art richt and vpracht [L. *excelsus et altus*], and of our-selfe haf we na maucht. **1563** SACKVILLE *Mirr. for Mag.* 128 These rockes upraught, that threatned most our wreck We seemde to sayle much surer in the streame.

‖**uprava** (u'praːva). [Russ., = authority.] In Imperial Russia: the executive board of a municipal council.

1870, 1886 [see DUMA]. **1918** G. A. BIRKETT in R. Beazley et al. *Russia* III. iii. 432 Thirty-four provinces of European Russia..received self-government under the law of 1864. Each district had its own zémstvo council, which elected an executive board (*uprâva*) sitting constantly and reporting to the annual meeting of the council. **1954** G. VERNADSKY *Hist. Russia* (ed. 4) x. 221 The representatives elected a board known as the *uprava* for a term of three years. **1967** H. SETON-WATSON *Russ. Empire 1801–1917* xi. 385 Every city was to have a municipal council..and they elected from their number an executive board (*uprava*).

up'rear, *v.* [UP- 4. Cf. OE. *upræ̂rend* pres. pple.]

1. *trans.* To raise up, elevate, erect, etc.

a **1300** *E.E. Psalter* cxliv. 14 Lauerd raises alle þat doune falle, And þe hurt he vprers [L. *erigit*] alle. *c* **1400** *R. Gloucester's Chron.* (Rolls) 6509 (MS. α), He..chirchen let vprere þat were arst as uorlore. **1563** *Mirr. Mag.* R ij b, The Percian kyng..With his huge host that..Dismounted hilles, and made the vales vprere. **1596** SPENSER *F.Q.* IV. x. 50 Next to her sate goodly Shamefastnesse, Ne euer durst her eyes from ground vpreare. **1597** BEARD *Theatre God's Judgem.* (1612) 80 Ieroboam..as he had..vpreared a new kingdome, so..vpreared also a new religion. **1638** JUNIUS *Paint. Ancients* 67 The great Lampe of light up-rearing his flaming head above the earth. **1667** MILTON *P.L.* I. 532 Then [he] strait commands that..be upreard His mighty Standard. **1718** ROWE tr. *Lucan* I. 259 So in the field.. Uprears some antient Oak his rev'rend head. **1748** THOMSON *Cast. Indol.* I. xxxi, Ah! how shall I for this uprear my moulted wing? **1818** BYRON *Ch. Har.* IV. xlv, For Time

hath .. up-rear'd Barbaric dwellings on their shatter'd site. **1842** BORROW *Bible in Spain* xxvi, Millions of maize plants upreared their tall stalks. **1898** WATTS-DUNTON *Aylwin* v. ii, A cobra uprearing its head to spring at her.
refl. **1616** R. C. *Times' Whistle* (1871) 36 When she doth vprear Her selfe vpon her feet.
fig. **1840** MANGAN *Poems* (1903) 185 See the palace-dome its pride uprearing One fleet hour!

b. To raise in dignity; to exalt.
1382 WYCLIF *Isaiah* xxxiii. 10 Now I shal ben enhauncid, now I shal ben vp rered [L. *sublevabor*]. *c* **1400** *Cato's Morals* in *Cursor M.* App. iv. 192 Wiþ lernyng & teyching growes graiþ kunnyng, & mani man vp-rered. **1566** STERNHOLD & H., etc. *Ps.* cxii. 2 His seede on earth God wil vp-reare. **1592** KYD *Sp. Trag.* II. i, Yet might she loue me to upreare her state. **1872** TENNYSON *Last Tourn.* 122 My realm, uprear'd, By noble deeds at one with noble vows.

2. To bring up, tend in growing.
13.. *E.E. Allit. P.* B. 561 Hym rwed þat he hem vprerde & raȝt hem lyflode. *c* **1440** *Pallad. on Husb.* III. 303 To thicke vppon the tre do not the vyne, And yf on folde vprere another tre. **1833** HT. MARTINEAU *Fr. Wines & Pol.* iv. 67 Here were .. little children upreared by their mothers amidst the fire and smoke.

3. To rouse, stir up, excite.
1486 *Bk. St. Albans* e iiij, How many maner beestys as with the lymere Shall be vpreryde in fryth or in felde. *a* **1600** *Flodden F.* iv. (1664) 40 His rancor old it was up-rear'd. **1795** MACNEILL *Waes o' War* II. v, Is it nature, vice, or folly, .. Hate, revenge, and rage uprears?

4. *intr.* To rise up.
1828 ATHERSTONE *Fall of Nineveh* I. 48 Myriads of bright harnessed steeds Were seen uprearing. **1868** MORRIS *Earthly Par.* I. I. 274 A great black fold against him did uprear.

up'reared, *pa. pple.* and *ppl. a.* [UP- 5 or f. prec.]
†**1.** Excited in feeling; angry. *Obs.*
1382 WYCLIF *Prov.* xv. 18 A man .. who is pacient, swageth the vprered [L. *suscitatas*].
2. Raised up, elevated, erected, etc.
1422 YONGE tr. *Secreta Secret.* 222 A grete breste and brode, vprerid and sumwhate fatte. *Ibid.* 223 Shamel[e]s men [have] hey vprerid shuldris. *c* **1430** LYDG. *Min. Poems* (Percy Soc.) 5 His swerd upreryd, proudly gave manace. *a* **1593** MARLOWE & NASHE *Dido* III. iv, I .. vow .. Neuer to leaue these newe vpreared walles, Whiles Dido liues. **1597** HALL *Sat.* I. iii. 11 On crowned kings .. Or some vpreared, high-aspiring swaine. **1602** MARSTON *Antonio's Rev.* IV. iii, With innocent upreared armes to Heaven. **1798** LANDOR *Gebir* I. 228 The long moon-beam on the hard wet sand Lay like a jaspar column half uprear'd. **1848** A. CLOUGH *Amours de Voy.* III. 14 Where, over fig-tree and orange .., Garden on garden upreared, balconies step to the sky. **1870** MORRIS *Earthly Par.* III. IV. 330 In front of me An upreared changing dark bulk did I see.

up'rearing, *vbl. sb.* (UP- 7. Cf. UPREAR *v.*)
1551 BALE *Eng. Votaries* II. 54 b, About the ouerthrowe of pryncely autoryte, and vprearynge of Antichristes tyranny. **1853** KANE *Grinnell Exp.* xxvi. (1856) 212 This uprearing of the ice is not a slow work. **1892** *Daily News* 10 March 2/3 The uprearing of the new fabric of British citizenship.

upreceiving, -reek, -reft, etc.: see UP- 4–7.

up'rend, *v. rare.* [UP- 4.] *trans.* To pull or tear up; to uproot.
1911 CHESTERTON *Ballad White Horse* I. 9 Earthquake swallowing earthquake Uprent the Wessex tree. **1932** *Sphere* 10 Dec. 435/1 (*caption*) A 130 + m.p.h. gale .. uprent the expedition's wireless mast.

up'rest. [var. of UPRIST.] Uprising.
1600 W. WATSON *Decacordon* Pref. (1602) A 2 b, Not onely physicall or naturall, but also morall and politicall cadences and vp-rests. **1817** SHELLEY *Rev. Islam* III. xxi, The uprest Of the third sun brought hunger.

uprestore, -rid, -ridge, -ridging: see UP- 4–7.

upright ('ʌpraɪt, ʌp'raɪt), *a.* and *sb.* Forms: 1 upp-, 1, 3–4 upriht, 4–5 vpriht, 4 up-, 5 vpryht; 3–5 up-, vpriȝt (4 op-), 4 upriȝte, 5 vpryȝt, vp-ryȝht (vpryȝth); *Sc.* 5 vpe-, 6 vprycht, vpricht, 6– upricht; 3–7 vpright (4–6 vprighte, 5 vpperight), 4–6 vpryght (4 vpperyght, 4–5 vpryghte), 5 upryght (upperyghte, 6 upryghte, upperyght); 4– upright (6 uprighte, 7 uprite). [OE. *up-, uppriht* (f. *up* UP *adv.*[1] + *riht* RIGHT *a.*), = OFris. *upriucht* (WFris. *oprjucht*), MDu. *oprecht, opregt* (Du. *oprecht*), MLG. *uprëcht, upricht* (LG. *upricht, uprecht, upregt*), OHG. (MHG.) *ûfrëht* (G. *aufrecht, -richt*), ON. *upréttr* (Da. *opret*, Sw. *upprät*).]

A. *adj.* **I.** *pred.* **1.** Erect on the feet or end; in or into a vertical position; perpendicular to the ground or other surface. (Cf. 3.)

a. With verbs, as *go, rise, sit, stand, walk.*
In OE. the advb. form *uprihte* is occas. used.
Beowulf 2092 Hyt ne mihte swa syððan ic on yrre uppriht astod. *c* **1250** *Gen. & Ex.* 3248 Ðe water up-stod .. On twinne half, also a wal up-riȝt. **1297** R. GLOUC. (Rolls) 5868 Þis holi man sat vpriȝt, & ysei is deþes wounde. **1340** *Ayenb.* 56 Huanne þe glotoun geþ in to þe tauerne ha geþ opriȝt. **1388** WYCLIF *Acts.* xiv. 9 Rise thou vp riȝt on thi feet. *c* **1400** *Anturs of Arthur* l, The king stode vp righte And commaunded pes. **14..** *Sir Beues* (M.) 4184 Sir Beues was wery .. That vnnethe he myght sitt vp-right. **1535** COVERDALE *Lev.* xxvi. 13, I haue broken the cepter of youre yocke, and caused you to go vp right. **1582** N. LICHEFIELD tr. *Castanheda's Conq. E. Ind.* I. xxxii. 79 b, Many Noble men .. all standing upright vppon theyr feete. **1607** *Merry Devil Edmonton* Induct. 3 My stiffned haire stands vpright on my head. **1697** DRYDEN *Virg. Georg.* III. 121 Upright he walks, on Pasterns firm and straight. **1703** [R. NEVE] *City & C. Purchaser* 278 A Man likewise standing firmest when he stands uprightest. **1782** MISS BURNEY *Cecilia* X. x, Supported by pillows, she sat almost upright. **1821** LAMB *Elia* Ser. I. *My Relations*, He .. has a spirit, that would stand upright in the presence of the Cham of Tartary. **1847** MRS. CARLYLE *Lett.* (1883) I. 391, I .. can hardly sit upright. **1892** *Photogr. Ann.* II. 419 The films are thick enough to place in racks to wash, or to stand upright to dry.

b. With other verbs (or *ellipt.*).
a **1300** *Cursor M.* 3804 Þe stan his heued lai on þat night, In takning, he it sett vp right. *c* **1391** CHAUCER *Astrol.* II. §28 Thise signes arisen more vpriht, & they ben called eke souereyn signes. *a* **1400** *Northern Passion* 143/158 Sodanly þir launces thre .. With outt mannys helpe war raysed vppe ryght. *c* **1450** LOVELICH *Merlin* 2698 Bothe dragowns .. thanne tornen .. hem bothe with gret myht, and meveth al the erthe evene vpryht. **1496** *Cov. Leet Bk.* 575 Maister Meire, hold vp-right your swerde. **1523** FITZHERB. *Husb.* §24 His forkes and rakes .. wolde be .. beyked, and sette euen, to lye vpryght in thy hande. **1622** J. TAYLOR (Water P.) *Farew. to Tower-bottles* A 2 b, 'Twas my chance in Bacchus spight, To come into the Tower vnfox'd vpright. **1667** MILTON *P.L.* I. 221 Forthwith upright he rears from off the Pool His mighty stature. **1700** DRYDEN *Theodore & Honoria* 146 Stood Theodore .. With chatt'ring Teeth, and bristling Hair upright. **1747** WESLEY *Prim. Physick* (1755) 30 The Apoplexy... Rub the Head,.. and let two strong Men carry the Patient upright. **1807** WORDSW. *White Doe* I. 245 A vault where the bodies are buried upright. **1900** L. B. WALFORD *One of Ourselves* xiv, A tall figure reared itself upright at her approach.

c. In figurative uses.
a **1225** *Ancr. R.* 266 Herdi bileaue makeð ou stonden upriht. *c* **1340** HAMPOLE *Pr. Consc.* 1298 Þe mare .. þat we wax upright In welthe, and in worldly myght. **1390** GOWER *Conf.* I. 8 [They] With good consail on alle sides Be kept upriht in such a wyse, That hate [etc.] **1399** —— *Praise of Peace* 6 The worschipe of this lond, which was doun falle, Now stant upriht. *c* **1412** HOCCLEVE *De Reg. Princ.* 537 O engelond! stande vp-ryght on thy feet! *c* **1421** *26 Pol. Poems* xxi. 147 Of erþe ȝe ben cleped 'salt' .. ; Go vp-riȝt and be not halt. **1551** CROWLEY *Pleas. & Pain* 590 Al men should walk in their callynge vpryght. **1570–6** LAMBARDE *Peramb. Kent* 105 While the honour of the Britons stood vpright. **1609** HOLLAND *Amm. Marcell.* XV. v. 38 Most wished it were to be, that our fortune alwaies continued upright. **1644** MILTON *Divorce* (ed. 2) II. iii. 40 The justice of God stood upright ev'n among heathen disputers. **1670** COTTON *Espernon* III. XII. 601 Yet did he ever keep himself upright from manifesting his sorrow. **1822** LAMB *Elia* Ser. I. *Dream Children*, Pain .. could never bend her good spirits, or make them stoop, but they were still upright. **1900** *Westm. Gaz.* 14 June 2/1 To 'keep the country upright' should be .. the first aim of the British Government.

†**d.** *Cant.* (See quot.) *Obs.*
a **1700** B. E. *Dict. Cant. Crew* s.v., *Go Upright*, said by Taylers and Shoemakers, to their Servants, when any Money is given, .. and signifies, bring it all out in Drink, tho' the Donor intended less.

†**2.** Lying or so as to lie at full length, flat or recumbent, on the back and with the face upwards; supine. Usu. with *lie* v. *Obs.*
a **1100** in Napier *O.E. Glosses* 58/1 *Supinus*, upriht, astreht. **1297** R. GLOUC. (Rolls) 8635 He pulte him mid is vot & adoun vpriȝt him caste. *c* **1300** *Beket* 93 This maide ful upriȝt iswoȝe tho heo him iseȝ. **13..** *St. Cristofer* 651 in Horstm. *Altengl. Leg.* (1881) 462 In his chayere he welte vpryghte. *c* **1386** CHAUCER *Prioress' T.* 159 Ther he with throte ykoruen lay vpright. *c* **1400** *Pilgr. Sowle* (Caxton, 1483) III. vi. 54 They leyen euen vpright gapyng. *c* **1450** *Mirk's Festial* I. 172 He saue eche tre full of bryddes lying vpryȝt dede. **1539** ELYOT *Cast. Helthe* 48 Lienge vpright on the backe is to be vtterly abhorred. **1555** WATREMAN *Fardle Facions* I. vi. 88 Leaste he should giue vp the ghoste lieng vpright. **1620** VENNER *Via Recta* (1650) 303 Sleeping upright upon the back be not healthfull. **1627** DRAYTON *Nymphidia* vii, And Mab .. Bestrids young Folks that lye vpright.

II. 3. a. Having the chief axis or distinctive part perpendicular to a surface; set or placed in a vertical position, posture, etc.; pointing or directed upwards; not inclined or leaning over (Cf. 1 b.)
pred. **1398** TREVISA *Barth. De P.R.* v. viii. (Bodl. MS.), An erbe þat growiþ in hard londe is litel and vpright. **1563** GOLDING *Cæsar* (1565) 73 Theyr foredecks wer very streight vpright, and so were also theyr sternes. **1597** GERARDE *Herball* III. 1226 Another kind of *Myrtus* .. groweth vpright vnto the height of a man. **1611** BIBLE *Jer.* x. 5 They [*sc.* idols] are vpright as the palme tree. **1666** *Act 18 & 19 Chas. II*, c. 8 §12 That all Lights .. made into any of them [*sc.* cellars] be .. made upright. **1719** DE FOE *Crusoe* I. (Globe) 128 It cost me a Month to shape it .. to something like the Bottom of a Boat, that it might swim upright. **1759** R. BROWN *Compl. Farmer* 112 'Tis a grass that grows very upright. **1787** BEST *Angling* 3 Such [fish] as swim with their backs upright, or at right angles to the horizon.
attrib. **1420** *Searchers Verdicts* in *Surtees Misc.* (1890) 16 William of Alne hafes a upperyghte gavell. **1517** in *Archaeologia* (1883) XLVII. 312 For makyng of an upright steyer of assheler. **1570** BILLINGSLEY *Euclid* XII. prop. 18. 382, I call that an vpright cone, whose axe is perpendicular to his base. **1640** PARKINSON *Theat. Bot.* 755 This Violet groweth about a foote high or more, with hard upright stalkes. **1668** R. STEELE *Husbandm. Calling* vii. (1672) 189 No creature upon earth hath an upright countenance as man hath. **1714** YOUNG *Force Relig.* I. 290 When the winds .. descend, The fair and upright stem is forc'd to bend. **1784** COWPER *Task* I. 355 The upright shafts of .. [the] tall elms. **1855** *Poultry Chron.* II. 602 Formed of upright bars of stout wire. **1870** LUBBOCK *Orig. Civiliz.* vi. (1875) 294 The custom of marking boundaries by upright stones.
fig. **1600** HOLLAND *Livy* 1359 During the upright and flourishing state of Rome.

b. In specific names of plants, etc. (see quots.).
1597 GERARDE *Herbal* I. 24 Vpright Dogs grasse or Quich grasse. *Ibid* II. 705 The vpright Pancie. **1597** [see CLAMBERER]. **1640** PARKINSON *Theat. Bot.* 755 *Viola surrecta purpurea*, Vpright Violets. *Ibid.* 1462 Vpright Woodbinde or Hony suckle. **1731** MILLER *Gard. Dict.* s.v. *Malva*, China Upright Mallow, with small white Flowers. **1760** J. LEE *Introd. Bot.* App. 319 Upright Fir Moss, *Lycopodium*. **1822** *Hortus Anglicus* II. 92 *S. Recta.* Upright Stachys. **1830** *Baxter's Libr. Agric. Knowl.* 256 *Nardus stricta*, Upright mat grass. *Ibid.*, *Agrostis stricta*, Upright bent. **1855** MISS PRATT *Flower. Pl.* VI. 105 Upright Brome-grass. **1882** *Garden* 11 March 166/2 The upright Acacia (*fastigiata*), a tree quite as erect in growth as the Lombardy Poplar.

c. *spec.* and *techn.* (See quots.)
upright pianoforte: see PIANOFORTE.
1610 GUILLIM *Heraldry* III. xxii. 167 Fishes are borne after a diuers manner, viz. Directly, Vpright, Imbowed [etc.]. **1611** COTGR., *La montée d'vn bastiment*, th'vpper part of a building; or, a representation, or modell thereof, called the vpright plot of a building. **1638** S. FOSTER *Art of Dialling* 12 Of upright declining Plaines. Those Plaines are upright, which point up directly into the Zenith. **1704** J. HARRIS *Lex. Techn.* I. s.v., *Upright South Dyals.* See Prime Verticles. [*Prime Verticals*, or Direct Erect North or South Dyals, are those whose Planes lie parallel to the Prime Vertical Circle.] **1727** BAILEY (vol. II), *Upright* (with Heralds) is a Term used of Shell-fishes, when they stand so in a Coat of Arms. **1795** STODART in *Abridgm. Specif. Patents, Mus.* (1871) 29 An upright grand piano in the form of a bookcase. **1802** LOUD *Ibid.* 44 Improvements in the construction and action of upright pianofortes. **1875** KNIGHT *Dict. Mech.* 2684/1 *Upright*, .. a term .. applied to a boiler whose hight is greater than its width. *Ibid.*, *Upright*, .. a term applied to a molding-machine whose mandrel is perpendicular. **1884** *Ibid.* Suppl. 915/1 *Upright drill*, a term applied to a drill whose mandril is vertical. *Ibid.*, Upright molding machine. **1887** *Golfing* 96 A club is said to be 'upright' when its head is not at a very obtuse angle to the shaft. **1888** JACOBI *Printers' Vocab.* 150 *Upright flues*, the main flue or shaft which carries the smoke from the furnace beyond the housetop. **1896** A. J. HIPKINS *Pianoforte* 122 *Upright Grand Piano*, accurately a grand piano placed vertically upon a stand; .. applied in the present day to the better kinds of the cottage piano. **1898** STAINER & BARRETT *Dict. Mus. Terms* 359/2 The upright spinet and harpsichord.

d. Marked by perpendicular position or attitude; characterized by vertical bearing; erect.
An OE. instance occurs in Ælfric's *Hom.* I. 276.
1634 MILTON *Comus* 52 Circe .. Whose charmed Cup Who-ever tasted, lost his upright shape. **1658** PHILLIPS, *Orthography*, .. in Architecture or Fortification, .. is taken for the upright erection of any work. **1774** GOLDSM. *Nat. Hist.* (1776) VI. 157 The anal fin .. serves to keep the fish in its upright or vertical situation. **1791** MRS. RADCLIFFE *Rom. Forest* ii, It being impossible to preserve it in an upright situation. **1871** W. H. G. KINGSTON *R. Kiffin's Ward* v, Although .. more than seventy, he still walked with an upright carriage. **1877** TENNYSON *Har.* III. ii. 39, I have lost Somewhat of upright stature thro' mine oath. **1878** B. TAYLOR *Deukalion* I. ii. 22 His eyes that met the sun, his upright tread.

4. a. Of persons: Erect in carriage. (Chiefly *pred.*)
c **1386** CHAUCER *Miller's T.* 78 She was .. Long as a Mast and vprighte as a bolt. **1430–40** LYDG. *Bochas* III. 4457 Folk in ther pouerte .. Ben .. lusti preuid at a neede, Vpriht of lymes ther iournes for to speede. **1588** SHAKS. *L.L.L.* IV. iii. 89 O most diuine Kate, .. As vpright as the Cedar. **1597** —— *2 Hen. IV*, II. ii. 91 Away, you horson vpright Rabbet. **1758** JOHNSON *Idler* No. 13 ¶ 11 When these [spinning] wheels are set upon a table .., they will .. keep the girls upright. **1840** DICKENS *Barn. Rudge* x, He was .. past the prime of life, yet upright in his carriage. **1865** KINGSLEY *Herew.* iii, Hereward, bleeding, but still active and upright, broke away. **1905** 'GUY THORNE' *Lost Cause* i, Hibbert was an upright, soldierly-looking man.

†**b.** *Cant.* Of vagrants: Big, strong, or sturdy. Applied spec. to one of the higher classes of vagabonds. Usu. ***upright-man***. *Obs.*
1561 AWDELEY *Frat. Vacab.* (1869) 4 An Vpright man is one that goeth wyth the trunchion of a staffe. **1567** HARMAN *Caveat* (1869) 31 A vpright man, the second in seote .. of these rainginge rablement of rascales. **1608** DEKKER *Belman of London* Wks. (Grosart) III. 92 This band of Vpright-men seldome march without fiue or six in a company. **1622** FLETCHER *Beggar's Bush* II. i, Come Princes of the ragged regiment, .. Prig my most upright Lord. **1641** BROME *Jov. Crew* II. G 1 You, .. That never yet with man did Mell; Of whom no Upright man is taster. *a* **1700** B. E. *Dict. Cant. Crew*, *Dells*, .. young bucksome Wenches .. [that] have not lost their Virginity, which the 'vpright man' pretends to, and seizes. [**1815** SCOTT *Guy M.* xxviii, Johnny Faa, the upright man.]

5. a. = PERPENDICULAR *a.* 1 b, RIGHT UP *a.* 1.
1596 DANETT tr. *Comines* (1614) 295 We mounted vp such a maruellous steepe and vpright hill. **1599** DALLAM in *Early Voy. Levant* (Hakl. Soc.) 12 This mountayne is verrie upryghte on bothe sides. **1861** WHYTE MELVILLE *Good for Nothing* iii, Another time do not ride so fast at an upright leap.

†**b.** Perpendicular *to* a surface. $Obs.^{-1}$
1678 MOXON *Mech. Exerc.* iv. 65 Exactly even and upright to the edges of the Board.

c. Of a rectangular superficies: Having the height greater than the breadth.
1888 JACOBI *Printers' Vocab.*, *Upright*, a page or job set or cut to an upright size—the reverse of oblong. **1892** *Photogr. Ann.* II. 523 The remaining portion .. permits of upright or oblong pictures being taken.

†**6. a.** Of shoes: That may fit either foot; straight. (Opposed to 'right' and 'left'.) *Obs. rare.*
1608 DAY *Hum. out of Br.* II. ii, A paire of vpright shooes, that gentlemen weare .. now of one foote, then of another. **1621** BURTON *Anat. Mel.* II. ii. VI. i, He that weares an vpright shooe, may correct the obliquity. **1642** FULLER *Holy & Prof. St.* IV. v. 262 An upright shoe may fit both feet.

†**b.** Straight in respect of grain. $Obs.^{-1}$

1776 G. SEMPLE *Building in Water* 115 The..Braces.. ought to be made of sound hearty upright Oak.

7. Taking place in a vertical direction; upward.

1650 ROW *Hist. Kirk* (Wodrow Soc.) 431 Everie christian should be an hawk; his course should be upward and upright, or right up. **1837** P. KEITH *Bot. Lex.* 248 An upright growth of six inches in the year. **1876** STAINER & BARRETT *Dict. Mus. Terms* 352/2 The upright action was invented for the purpose of constructing pianofortes [etc.].

III. *fig.* 8. a. Of persons: Adhering to or following correct moral principles; of unbending integrity or rectitude; morally just, honest, or honourable.

1530 PALSGR. 328/2 Upright, indifferent bytwene party and party, and nat affectionate, *indifferent,..juste.* **1560** BIBLE *2 Chron.* xxix. 34 The Leuites were more vpright in heart to sanctifie them selues, then the Priests. *Ibid., Ps.* xi. 2. **1605** CAMDEN *Rem.* 7 That goodly, vpright, provident,.. and reasonable creature. **1656** EARL MONM. tr. *Boccalini's Advts.fr. Parnass.* II. xi. (1674) 149 The uprightest and most experienced Senator. **1700** DRYDEN *Pref. Fables* Wks. (Globe) 499, I have..been an upright judge betwixt the parties in competition. *a* **1720** SEWEL *Hist. Quakers* (1795) I. II. 142 They were found upright in their dealing. **1742** POPE *Dunc.* IV. 208 So upright Quakers please both Man and God. **1828** LYTTON *Pelham* III. xiv, I have always thought him the most upright and honourable of men. **1856** FROUDE *Hist. Eng.* (1858) I. ii. 173 [He] bore through England the reputation of an upright and virtuous king. **1904** *Verney Mem.* II. 296 She had been upright in her life.

absol. **1560** BIBLE *Prov.* xxviii. 10 The vpright shal inherit good things. —— *Ps.* vii. 10 God..preserueth the vpright in heart. **1786** *Paraphrases Ch. Scotland* xxi. 1 Th' upright in heart alone have hope.

b. Of the mind, qualities, actions, etc.: Marked or characterized by integrity or probity; having conformity or accordance with moral rectitude.

1538 STARKEY *England* I. ii. 43 Settyng themselfe in relygyouse housys, ther quyetly to serue God and kepe theyr myndys vpryght. **1549** COVERDALE, etc. *Erasm. Par. 1 Cor.* 53 That we both may..haue therwith an vpryght harte to God. **1560** BIBLE *Ps.* xxxvii. 14 To slay suche as be of vpright conuersation. **1579** W. WILKINSON *Confut. Fam. Love* B ij, That we might serve..God..with an vpright righteousnes and holynes. **1623** *Extr. Aberd. Reg.* (1848) II. 388 They sall giwe wnto thame thair trew and upricht counsall whan the same salbe askit. **1667** MILTON *P.L.* I. 18 Thou, O Spirit, that dost prefer..th' upright heart and pure. **1700** T. BROWN *Amusem. Ser. & Com.* 31 Have you any Use in your Country for Upright Honesty? *a* **1721** PRIOR *Vicar of Bray & More* Wks. 1907 II. 259 An upright and unprejudiced Conscience. **1781** COWPER *Conversat.* 682 Those hearts should be reclaim'd, renew'd, upright. **1782** MISS BURNEY *Cecilia* VIII. vi, Now I see the fair promise of his upright youth. **1818** CRUISE *Digest* (ed. 2) II. 458 Fair or upright dealing. **1844** H. H. WILSON *Brit. India* III. 473 The diligent and upright discharge of the duties. **1904** *Verney Mem.* I. 415 His upright chivalrous conduct.

Comb. **1654** ALLEN in Thurloe *St. Papers* (1742) II. 214 The honour God hath put uppon him,..I mean that of upright-heartedness to the Lord. **1818** SCOTT *Hrt. Midl.* xliii, The best and most upright-minded men. **1836** [MRS. CHEAP] *Going to Service* xii. 140 An upright-minded girl.

†9. a. *Sc.* True; undoubted; rightful; = RIGHT *a.* 16. *Obs.*[−1]

c **1480** HENRYSON *Cock & Fox* xi, ȝe ar ȝour Fatheris Sone and air vpricht.

†b. In good condition; in proper order; correct. *Obs.*

1526 SKELTON *Magnif.* 651 Fansy and I, we twayne,.. counterfeted our names we haue, Craftely all thynges vpryght to saue. **1557** TUSSER *Husb.* (1878) 232 Good husbandes that laye, to saue all things vpright: for Tumbrels and cartes, haue a shed redy dight. **1630** SHERLEY in Bradford *Plymouth Plantation* (1856) 270 If it should please God yᵉ one should faile.., yet yᵉ other would keepe both recconings, and things uprighte.

†c. Plain; straightforward; unambiguous. *Obs.*

1587 HARRISON *Descr. Brit.* I. i. in *Holinshed* I. 2/1 My purpose is to..deliuer such things as I intreat of in distinct and vpright order. **1607** DEKKER *Knt.'s Conjur.* (1842) 56 He had bin in vpright tearmes an vsurer.

10. a. Stable, equable. b. *dial.* Sound in respect of health.

1551 ROBINSON tr. *More's Utopia* II. M iij b, The quiete and vpright state of the bodye. **1905** *Eng. Dial. Dict.* VI. 327/2 My horse is quite upright.

B. *sb.* †1. a. A vertical front, face, or plane. *Obs.*

1563 SHUTE *Archit.* C iv b, This is the foundacion through the whiche we knowe and finde all the measures and vprightes belonging to the pillor. **1663** GERBIER *Counsel* 12 Shun too much carved Ornaments on that upright. *Ibid.* 15 Contracting the Balconies within the upright of a Column. **1679** MOXON *Mech. Exerc.* viii. 141 You design the Balcony to project beyond the Upright of the Front. **1703** [R. NEVE] *City & C. Purchaser* 11 The springing of the Arch is skew'd back from the upright of the Jambs. **1726** LEONI *Alberti's Archit.* I. 55 The vacuities..left between the back of the sweep of the Arch, and the upright of the Wall it is turn'd from,..shou'd be fill'd up.

†b. = ELEVATION 11, ORTHOGRAPHY 2 b. *Obs.*

1603 B. JONSON *K. Jas.'s Entertain.* ¶1 The scene presented it selfe in a square and flat upright like to the side of a citty. **1620–50** I. JONES *Stone-Heng* (1655) 56 The groundplot, with the uprights, and profyle of the whole work. *Ibid.* 61 The upright of the work, as when entire. **1712** J. JAMES tr. *Le Blond's Gardening* 216 You may judge by the Upright, of the handsome Effect this Cascade would make. **1782** H. WALPOLE *Vertue's Anecd. Paint.* (ed. 3) I. Suppl. T. 1, There are not many uprights, but several ground plans of some of the palaces. **1842** GWILT *Archit.* Gloss. 1049 *Upright*..; a term rarely used.

†c. A very steep declivity. Cf. PERPENDICULAR *sb.* 2. *Obs.*[−1]

1712 HENLEY tr. *Montfaucon's Antiq. Italy* vii. 108 The Lake runs..thro' the Mountain, till it comes to an upright, where there is a mighty Fall.

2. a. An upright or vertical position; the perpendicular.

1683 MOXON *Mech. Exerc., Printing* xix. 297 So that the Tympan may stand..towards an upright. **1851** LAXTON *Builder's Price Bk.* 133 Plasterer's Work... Dubbing out.. not to be allowed unless the work is out of an upright. **1883** in Elworthy *W. Somerset Word-bk.* (1888) 791 Thick there wall's a little bit out of an upright. **1905** *Times* 30 Sept. 8/1 The mullion was much out of upright, and had..an iron stay.

b. That which lies immediately above a thing.

1768 BLACKSTONE *Comm.* III. 217 Every man may do what he pleases upon the upright or perpendicular of his own soil.

3. a. Something set or standing upright, erect, or vertical; a perpendicular stone, post, part, etc.

In frequent use from *c* 1790.

1742 *De Foe's Tour Gt. Brit.* (ed. 3) I. 259 By which means the Uprights [of Stonehenge] are less liable to fall or swerve. **1776** G. SEMPLE *Building in Water* 131 The upright of c. has a square Hole in the upper End of it. **1786** ABERCROMBIE *Gard. Assist.* 54 Uprights or growing stakes. **1794** *Rigging & Seamanship* 140 Vessels in harbour..have uprights [for awnings]. **1794** BURNS *Caledonia* 46 Rectangle-triangle the figure we'll choose, The upright is Chance, and old Time is the base. **1845** J. SAUNDERS *Cabinet Pict. Eng. Life* 19 A beam laid cross-wise upon two uprights. **1854** AINSWORTH *Flitch of Bacon* IV. iii, A magnificent staircase of many turnings... The uprights on each landing were decorated with rampant nondescripts. **1883** MISS BROUGHTON *Belinda* III. iii, One of the spiked iron uprights of the gate. **1886** FURNIVALL in Shaks. *Ven. & Ad.* (1st Qo. facsimile) p. xix, 'Hooke-nosoe', should be 'hook-nosde'; the upright of the d unluckily failed to print.

b. *spec.* One of the vertical members of a framing, etc.

a **1700** EVELYN *Diary* 27 Aug. 1666, We plumb'd the uprights in several places. **1791** SMEATON *Edystone L.* §34 The outside timbers (since called the uprights) were seventy-two in number). **1807** PIKE *Sources Mississ.* I. (1810) App. 46 Part of the houses are framed, and..there are small logs let into mortises made in the uprights. **1851** RUSKIN *Stones Ven.* (1874) I. i. 18 Timbers attached to uprights on the top of the nave pillars. **1870** MORRIS *Earthly Par.* III. IV. 61 The greasy blackened wood Of the hall's uprights.

(*b*) *spec.* in *Football*, a goalpost (as opp. to the crossbar).

1910 *Glasgow Herald* 14 Feb. 12/6 Barr..had little difficulty in placing the ball between the uprights. **1927** W. E. COLLINSON *Contemp. Eng.* 24 There were all the 'Kennings' in the sporting columns... Sphere for football, the uprights or sticks for the goalposts. **1951** *Sport* 27 Apr.–3 May 4/1 Bill rapped the upright with a penalty-kick. **1954** J. B. G. THOMAS *On Tour* 72 Morkel hit an upright with his conversion attempt. **1977** *Irish Press* 29 Sept. 18/2 Mick Lawlor's 24th minute left-footed drive..hit the bottom part of the upright and rebounded into play.

c. (See quots.)

1856 'STONEHENGE' *Brit. Rur. Sports* I. x. 82/2 The Spire [has] a brow antler, and half-developed beam, called *uprights*; a Staggart, brow, tray, and uprights. **1878** in Elworthy *W. Somerset Word-bk.* 792 A male deer of one year old has..one straight horn each side only, which we term his *upright*.

d. An upright pianoforte (see PIANOFORTE).

1860 *Builder* 15 Sept. 588/1 The best grands and uprights of the present day. **1894** S. FISKE *Holiday Stories* (1900) 118 The baby grands nestled between the larger instruments. The uprights looked..out of place.

e. A kind of fly-hook.

1878 W. NASH *Oregon* vi. 135 The lawyer put on a 'black palmer' and a 'blue upright'. **1892** *Daily News* 14 April 3/1 The comparatively large uprights and browns are as fatal as ever to the smallest trout.

f. *Basketry.* A plane used for shaving skeins to a required width.

1842 *Encycl. Brit.* IV. 429/1 In order to bring the split into a shape still more regular, it is passed through another implement called an upright, consisting of a flat piece of steel, each end of which is fashioned into a cutting edge. **1907** *Jrnl. Soc. Arts* 11 Jan. 190/1 For finer work the rod is split into three or more skeins by a cleaver; the splits are then successively drawn through a shave to remove the central pith and through an upright to render them uniform in width. **1929** A. G. KNOCK *Fine Willow Basketry* 37 For most skein work the skeins can be used after being shaved, but for ..extra fine skein work of other kinds they are made uniform in width and as narrow as required by being drawn through the upright. **1961** L. G. ALLBON *Basic Basketry* iii. 18 Two specialized planes complete the process. The shave skims away the pith and renders the skein of even thickness; the upright straightens up the sides of the skein to an even width. **1981** T. W. BAGSHAWE *Basket Making in Bedfordshire* 16 (*caption*) Uprights for shaving to uniform width.

g. In a crossword puzzle, one of the clues whose solution is to be entered vertically in the frame.

1917 M. T. HAINSSELIN *Grand Fleet Days* xv. 96 How far have you got? Only as far as the 'uprights'—Belgium and Berlin. **1967** *Sci. Amer.* Sept. 268/2 The first stanza gives clues for two words, called the uprights, that are spelled vertically by the initial and final letters of the words to which clues are given by the numbered stanzas.

4. An upright stratum; = ARRECT *sb.*

1811 PINKERTON *Petral.* II. 158 A mountain of a most regular structure; the arrects, or uprights, having their planes parallel to its great axis.

5. *slang.* (See quot.)

1796 *Sporting Mag.* VIII. 107 [They] drank 57 quarts of *upright*, viz. a quart of beer with a quartern of gin in it.

'upright, *adv.* [f. prec. Cf. OE. *uprihte.*]

1. = UPRIGHTLY *adv.* 1.

1509 HAWES *Conv. Swearers* ix, I sende you gretynge..& grace Right wel to gouern vpright your dominion. **1577** B. GOOGE *Heresbach's Husb.* I. (1586) 2 All seeke to lyue, but none to liue upryght. **1591** in *10th Rep. Hist. MSS. Comm.* App. I. 76 That thay may leif togidder in luif, upricht to God. **1624** J. DAVIES *Ps.* xiv, Not one doth good, not one doth well, vpright.

†b. In a just manner; correctly. *Obs.*[−1]

1601 HOLLAND *Pliny* II. 585 In truth, if we will consider this pageant upright, we must needs confesse [etc.].

2. In a vertical direction; vertically upwards.

1590 WEBBE *Trav.* (Arb.) 22 Ye wonderfull..swelling of the water vpright..to ye height of a huge mountaine. **1591** J. DEE *Diary* (Camden) 38 Wownded on his hed by his own wanton throwing of a brik-bat upright, and not well avoyding the fall of it. **1605** SHAKS. *Lear* IV. vi. 27 For all beneath the Moone would I not leape vpright. **1664** BUTLER *Hud.* II. III. 437 That Cannon-Ball,..shot in th' Air point-blank, upright. **1715** DESAGULIERS *Fires Impr.* 12 As for the Rays that go upright, nothing can hinder them from getting out at top of the Chimney. **1736** GRAY *Statius* I. 45 Nor tempts he yet the plain, but hurl'd upright, Emits the mass.

Comb. **1842** LOUDON *Suburban Hort.* 352 In the case of upright-grown plants. *Ibid.* 549 The pear is grafted or budded on stocks raised..from any strong upright-growing kind.

3. *dial.* Independently; on one's own means.

1823 E. MOOR *Suffolk Words* 460 A live upright on 'a's forten. **1896** *Westm. Gaz.* 28 April 2/1, I shall be able to retire and 'live upright', as the butler said.

'upright, *v.* Also 5 *Sc.* vp-, wpricht. [f. as prec. Cf. MDu. *uprichten* (Du. *oprigten*), Flem. (Kilian) *oprechten*, OHG. (MHG.) *ûfrihten* (G. *aufrichten*).]

1. *trans.* To raise to an upright or vertical position; to erect. Also *fig.* and in fig. context.

a **1340** HAMPOLE *Psalter* cxii. 6 He vprightis þe pore out of þe fen of fleyssly lust. *Ibid.* cxlv. 7 Lord vprightys þe smytyn down. **1590** SIR J. SMYTH *Disc. Weapons* 30 They all vpright their piques. **1591** —— *Instruct.* (1595) 22 Then are they to saie to the first ranke Vpright your piques. **1609** DANIEL *Civ. Wars* VII. lxxii, It rests within your iudgements, to vp-right..the Land. **1890** *Standard* 5 April 6/3, I..assisted to upright the boat, which was baled out. **1893** *Westm. Gaz.* 16 Sept. 4/1 As soon as he had uprighted his machine [= bicycle].

†2. *Sc.* To make reparation to or for; to compensate. *Obs.*

1463 *Extr. Aberd. Reg.* (1844) I. 26 The forsaide Thomas til sek til his warande gif he hafe ony til vpricht him. **1480** *Ibid.* 411 That the saids persons acht til wpricht and assith him for hir. **1492** *Ibid.* 420 To amende and vpricht the skaitht done.

†uprighten, *v. Obs.* [f. prec. + -EN[5].] *trans.* = prec. 1.

1617 AINSWORTH *Annot. Ps.* cxlv. 14 Iehovah upholdeth all that fall: and up-righteneth, all that are crooked.

up'righteously, *adv. rare*[−1]. [Cf. next.] In an upright manner.

1603 SHAKS. *Meas. for M.* III. i. 205 You may most vprighteously do a poore wronged Lady a merited benefit.

up'righteousness. [Cf. UPRIGHT *a.* and RIGHTEOUSNESS.] The quality of being upright.

1549 LATIMER *4th Serm. bef. Edw. VI* (Arb.) 110 The vpryghteousnes of hys cause. **1550** THOMAS *Ital. Dict.*, *Dirittura*, vprightwisenesse. **1570** *Satir. Poems Reform.* x. 349 Not only lufit he vprychteousnes, Bot als he hatit vice. **1623** COCKERAM II, *Vprighteousnes*, Sinceritie. **1904** *Daily News* 26 Aug. 6 Respectability and conscious uprighteousness oozing from his every pore.

'uprighting, *vbl. sb.* [f. UPRIGHT *v.*] The action of making upright; *spec.* the process of ensuring uprightness of position. Also *attrib.*

1884 F. J. BRITTEN *Watch & Clockm.* 153 Bad pivots, bad uprighting,..are responsible for much of the trouble experienced in position timing. *Ibid.* 279 An uprighting tool.

'uprightish, *a. rare.* [f. UPRIGHT *a.* + -ISH[1].] Somewhat upright.

1806 J. GALPINE *Brit. Bot.* 112 Stems uprightish:..calyx-teeth setaceous, elongated.

'uprightly, *adv.* [f. as prec. + -LY[2].]

1. In a just or upright manner; with strict observance of justice, honesty, or rectitude; sincerely, justly. (Freq. *c* 1560–*c* 1590.)

1549 COVERDALE, etc. *Erasm. Par. Acts* xxiii. 75 Bearyng my selfe vpryghtely and with a good conscience. **1583** STUBBES *Anat. Abus.* II. (1882) 32 In times past when men dealt vprightly, and in the feare of God. **1624** BEDELL *Lett.* x. 129 Iudge now vprightly if this be indifferent dealing. **1649** DAVENANT *Love & Hon.* IV. iii. 27 If you uprightly love her and the prince. **1668** DRYDEN *Dram. Poesy* Ess. (ed. Ker) I. 89 Betwixt the extremes of admiration and malice, 'tis hard to judge uprightly of the living. **1755** JOHNSON, *Honestly*,..uprightly; justly. **1838** ARNOLD *Hist. Rome* I. 296 The first decemvirs..governed uprightly and well. **1847** S. AUSTIN *Ranke's Hist. Ref.* III. 39 A man who would rule uprightly. **1855** MACAULAY *Hist. Eng.* xiv. III. 454 He was sure, he said, that they had acted uprightly.

†b. Candidly; straightforwardly. *Obs.*

1565 *Reg. Privy Council Scot.* I. 340 To declair planelie and uprychtlie the wordis and brute..of the said allegeit conspiracie. **1579** E. K. *Gloss. to Spenser's Sheph. Cal.* Aug. 53 By Perigot who is meant, I can not vprightly say. **1598** J. MELVILL *Diary* (Wodrow Soc.) 439 All sic as stud uprightlie for the established discipline and fredome of the Kirk. **1620** BP. ANDREWES *Serm.* (1629) 130 Besides (to speake vprightly) one might..complaine of the privatenesse of the Angells appearing. **1630** *R. Johnson's Kingd. & Commw.* 13

To speak uprightly, from these Nations .. have tortures of more exquisite device taken their originals.

2. In an upright position; vertically, perpendicularly. Also *fig.* and in fig. context.

1601 HOLLAND *Pliny* I. 159 He .. shall live in this world uprightly and in even ballance, without enclining more to one side, than unto another. **1639** J. TAYLOR (Water P.) *Part Summers Trav.* 46 You were never known to be drunke, and though you never walke uprightly, yet you never stumbled. *a* **1718** PARNELL *Poems* (1758) 9 The waters were afraid; .. In heaps uprightly plac'd they learn to stand. **1751** HARRIS *Hermes* I. v. (1765) 84 These Pronouns .. assumed a peculiar Accent of their own, which gave them the name of ὀρθοτονουμέναι, or Pronouns uprightly accented. **1826** in A. C. Hutchinson *Pract. Obs. Surg.* (ed. 2) 173 But I have watched him,—have seen him .. walk .. as uprightly as you can walk. **1868** LOCKYER *Elem. Astron.* §168 We found that the Sun was not floating uprightly in our sea, the plane of the ecliptic.

'uprightness. [f. as prec. + -NESS.]

1. The state or condition of being sincere, honest, or just; equity or justness in respect of principle or practice; upright quality or conduct; moral integrity or rectitude.

1541 ELYOT *Image Gov.* xii. 22 He loued syncerytie, vulgarly called vprightnesse. **1571** *Act 13 Eliz.* c. 11 §2 Any .. Subjectes using upryghtnes and trueth in the barrelling of such Fishe. **1591** SAVILE *Tacitus, Agricola* 242 Agricola .. caryed himselfe easily with great vprightnes and iustice. **1628** WITHER *Brit. Rememb.* VII. 1553 They of my uprightnesse judge amisse. **1668** OWEN *Indwelling Sin* vi. 72 Accordingly his design is to walk before God, and his frame is sincerity and uprightness therein. **1736** BUTLER *Anal.* I. v. 92 Those who preserve their Uprightness .. raise themselves to a more secure State of Virtue. **1766** AMORY *Buncle* (1770) III. 210 A canted uprightness and seeming piety. **1820** SHELLEY *Liberty* vii, Many a deed of terrible uprightness By thy sweet love was sanctified. **1855** MACAULAY *Hist. Eng.* xi. III. 60 Veracity, uprightness, and manly boldness were then, as now, qualities eminently English. **1879** R. K. DOUGLAS *Confucianism* iii. 72 The Sage .. maintains a perfect uprightness and pursues the heavenly way without the slightest deflection.

b. Const. *of* (conduct, etc.).

1560 BIBLE *1 Kings* iii. 6 He walked .. in vprightnes of heart with thee. **1576** FLEMING *Panopl. Epist.* 22 Modestie of life and uprightnesse of manners. **1592** CHETTLE *Kind-harts Dr.* A 4, Diuers of worship haue reported his vprightnes of dealing. **1644** MILTON *Divorce* (ed. 2) II. iv, The uprightnesse of his ways. **1651** HOBBES *Leviath.* II. xxvii. 152 Cleared by the Uprightnesse of his own Intention. **1775** ADAIR *Amer. Ind.* Ded., The uprightness of my intentions as to the information here given. **1795** *Gentl. Mag.* 543/1 Integrity of heart and uprightness of intention. **1831** SIR J. SINCLAIR *Corr.*, etc. II. 393 [He] was distinguished by .. great uprightness of conduct.

2. The state or character of being erect, vertical, or upright; erect or vertical attitude; erectness.

1645 WALLER *To Chloris* Poems 180 So the fayre tree .. In stormes from that uprightnesse swerves. **1706** STEVENS *Span. Dict., Derechura*, straightness, uprightness. **1782** V. KNOX *Ess.* lxxix. (1819) II. 114 The uprightness of the pilaster. *c* **1815** JANE AUSTEN *Persuasion* vi, Mrs. Croft .. had a squareness, uprightness, and vigour of form. **1853** KANE *Grinnell Exp.* xix. (1856) 143 The poor things had lost their uprightness. **1889** *Pall Mall G.* 9 Mar. 7/1 The rigid uprightness of his collars.

† uprights, *adv. Obs.* [f. UPRIGHT *adv.* + -S[1].]

1. In an upright position; perpendicularly.

c **1350** *Will. Palerne* 1789 Tvo white beres .. went on alle four .., & whan þei wery were þei went vp-riȝttes. **1390** GOWER *Conf.* I. 140 Than scholde he stonde ayein uprihtes. *c* **1400** MAUNDEV. (Roxb.) xxxi. 143 Þai .. gase on fete nere-hand vprightes. *c* **1410** *Master of Game* (MS. Digby 182) xii, Men shull take suche an Hounde and holde hym faste and vpreghtes [*v.r.* fast vpryȝtes].

2. Upon one's back and with the face upwards.

c **1420** LYDG. *Sege Thebes* 3911 Many on lay slayen at the gate, Gapyng vprightys. *Ibid.* 4481 Thorgh-girt with many wounde .. [they lay] stark vpriȝtes.

upripe, etc.: see UP- 4–7.

up'risal. [UP- 2.] Uprising.

1871 *Daily News* 7 March, The danger of a sudden uprisal of the north-eastern quarters of Paris. **1889** HERRING & ROSS *Irish Cousin* I. xiv, The sudden uprisal .. of an abnormally lengthy dachshund.

uprise (ʌp'raɪz, 'ʌpraɪz), *sb.* [UP- 2. Cf. ON. *upprisa* (MSw. *uprisa*, Sw. *uppresa*), rising up, resurrection.]

† 1. Resurrection. *Obs.*

a **1300** *Cursor M.* 1479 Wit þair vpris fra ded to lijf. *Ibid.* 18571 Þan bigan þai to bede þam hightes For to lei of his vp-rise.

2. a. Rising (of the sun, etc.); dawn (of day).

1588 SHAKS. *Tit. A.* III. i. 159 A Larke, That giues sweet tydings of the Sunnes vprise. **1600** S. NICHOLSON *Acolastus' After-witte* A 4, Faire Queene Aurora, .. Whose blithsome vp-rise makes Nights prisoners blest. **1635** HEYWOOD *Hierarchy* III. Comm. 183 Because the Sunne in his mornings vprise looketh red and blushing. **1674** J. W[RIGHT] *Seneca's Thyestes* 71 Father of gods and men, at whose Uprise Night doth her beauty loose. **1794** SOUTHEY *Elinor* 11 When in better years poor Elinor Gazed on thy glad uprise with eye undimm'd By guilt. **1818** SHELLEY *Eugan. Hills* 73 The pæan With which the legioned rooks did hail The sun's uprise majestical. *a* **1851** MOIR *Poems, Mine Own* i, Alike at orient day's uprise, And pensive shut of night.

† b. The act of rising from bed. *Obs.*

1633 P. FLETCHER *Purple Isl.* XII. iv, Musick and base flattering tongues, Which wait to first-salute my Lords uprise.

c. The act of rising to a higher level; ascent.

1690 C. NESSE *O. & N. Test.* I. 126 The dreadful downfal, as well as up-rise, of the waters. **1817** SHELLEY *Rev. Islam* XII. xvi, A blood-red gleam Burst upwards... I heard the mighty sound Of its uprise. **1882** GEIKIE *Text-bk. Geol.* VI. v. 900 An intermittent uprise of the land.

d. The beginning of an ascent; an ascending shaft in a mine.

1875 BROWNING *Aristophanes' Apol.* 334 Now bound For Dorion, at the uprise .. Of Mount Pangaios. **1877** RAYMOND *Statist. Mines & Mining* 174 Fifty feet in from the mouth of the tunnel an uprise was made.

3. a. Ascent to power or dignity; rise to wealth or importance.

1810 JANE PORTER *Scot. Chiefs* x, At the fall of Dunbar .. he again founded his uprise on the ruins of this country. **1877** *N.W. Linc. Gloss.* 265 The uprise o' that family was th' inclosures.

b. The act of coming into existence or notice; origination.

1817 SHELLEY *Rev. Islam* VII. ii, Awakened from that dreamy mood By Liberty's uprise. **1844** THACKERAY *Wks.* (1886) XXIII. 205 The young painters .. whose uprise this Magazine and this critic were the first to hail. **1862** F. HALL *Hindu Philos. Syst.* 241 The uprise of a new .. affection of the internal organ. **1875** WHITNEY *Life Lang.* vi. 107 The uprise of the class of prepositions.

uprise (ʌp'raɪz), *v.* [UP- 4. Cf. WFris. *oprize*, MDu. *oprisen* (Du. *oprijzen*), MLG. *uprisen* (LG. *uprîsen*), MHG. *ûfrîsen*.]

1. *intr.* To rise to one's feet; to assume a standing posture.

a **1300** *Cursor M.* 2733 Quen þai war rest wel vp-ras þai. **13..** *E.E. Allit. P.* C. 378 He radly vp-ros & ran fro his chayer. *c* **1385** CHAUCER *L.G.W.* 1743 *Lucrece*, She anoon vp roos with blysful chere And kyssed hym. **1448–9** METHAM *Amoryus & Cl.* 1867 Hole and sound, with-owte wemme off yowre woundys, Nowe vp-ryse. ? *a* **1550** *Freiris of Berwik* 341 (*Maitland Folio*), Þan the freyr uprais, And tuk his buik and to the flure he gayis. **1590** SPENSER *F.Q.* I. iv. 16 Suddein vpriseth from her stately place The royall Dame. **1715** POPE *Iliad* I. 95 Uprising slow, the venerable sage Thus spoke the prudence and the fears of age. *a* **1800** COWPER *Odyssey* (ed. 2) XXIV. 496 Soon as on full seats The whole assembled senate sat, uprose Eupithes first. **1858** MERIVALE *Rom. Emp.* liii. VI. 216 Then uprose Sabinus to advance his charges. **1870** BRYANT *Iliad* I. I. 14 Now up-rose Nestor, the master of persuasive speech.

fig. *a* **1300** *E.E. Psalter* xxvi. 6 If vprise ogaine me fight, In þat sal i hope in might. **1812** BYRON *Ch. Har.* I. lxxxi, Ere War uprose in his volcanic rage. **1837** *Mag. Nat. Hist.* I. 134 The whole neighbourhood uprose in arms, till every bird of them was killed.

b. To rise from bed.

13.. *Seuyn Sages* (W.) 3181 Opon the morn the knyght vprase. *c* **1386** CHAUCER *Reeve's T.* 329 Aleyn vprist and thoughte, er þat it dawe I wol go crepen In by my felawe. **1503** DUNBAR *Thistle & Rose* 29 Quhairto .. sall I vprys at morrow? **1513** BRADSHAW *St. Werburge* I. 2544 She wolde vp-ryse at an houre conuenyent. **1526–*a* 1628** [see DOWN-LIE *v.*]. **1725** POPE *Odyss.* VI. 59 Uprose the virgin with the morning light. **1878** *Masque Poets* 95 It was a wicked Nephew bold Who uprose in the night.

2. Of the sun: To rise.

The Chaucerian *uprist* (= upriseth) has by archaizing writers been taken as a past tense.

c **1350** *Will. Palerne* 1791 Al þat long niȝt, til it dawed to day & sunne to vp-rise. *c* **1374** CHAUCER *Compl. Mars* 4 For when the sunne vprist then wol they sprede. **1471** RIPLEY *Comp. Alch.* II. xii. in Ashm. (1652) 138 For there the Son wyth Day-lyght doth upryse In Somer. **1513** DOUGLAS *Æneid* VII. iii. 56 First as the son wprysis. **1729** T. COOKE *Tales*, etc. 136 The Critic took his Way, Slow pacing, home-ward, and uprose the Day. **1798** COLERIDGE *Anc. Mar.* II. iv, Nor dim nor red, .. The glorious Sun uprist. **1818** MILMAN *Samor* x. 417 The sun uprising sees the dusk night fled Already from tall Pendle. **1880** W. S. BLUNT *Love Sonn. Proteus* ci, Ere yet the sun uprist.

3. To rise from the dead.

a **1300** *Cursor M.* 203 How he vprais, how he upstey, Many man on stod and sey. *c* **1340** HAMPOLE *Pr. Consc.* 5026 Alle þat er gude þan and rightwyse, Þat sal be save, sal first up-ryse. *c* **1440** *York Myst.* xxxvii. 31, I schall .. on the thirde day ryght vprise. **1553** POYNET *Short Catech.* 21 b, The third daye after, he vprose agayne, a lyue in bodye also. **1567** *Gude & Godlie B.* (S.T.S) 78 Christ maid us Iust quhen he vprais. **1879** ARNOLD *Light of Asia* I. 3 The dead that are to live, the live who die, Uprise, and hear, and hope!

b. To come from the underworld.

? *a* **1550** *Freiris Berwik* 524 (Bann. MS.), I coniure the, That thow vprys and sone to me appeir. *a* **1743** SAVAGE *On False Historians* 32 The devil .. The sorcerer us'd to raise, the parson lay, When Echard wav'd his pen, .. The parson conjur'd, and the fiend uprose. **1816** SHELLEY *Dæmon* II. 21 Erebus With all its banded fiends shall not uprise To overwhelm .. The dauntless.

4. To rise or ascend to a higher level; to rise into view.

a **1300** *Cursor M.* 21074 Þat erth .. Men seis vprisand fra þe grund. **13..** *Anticrist* 547 Þe dals [sal] uprise, þe fells dunfalle. *c* **1400** *Secreta Secret., Gov. Lordsh.* 89 For þou seez it [*sc.* an enchanted stone] vprys vpon waterys whenne þay rynne with þe wyndes. **1842** TENNYSON *Vis. Sin* 208 Once more Uprose the mystic mountain range. **1858** LONGF. *M. Standish* v. 1 As the mists uprose from the meadows. **1867** TENNYSON *Victim* 71 The rites prepared, the victim bared, The knife uprising toward the blow.

fig. *a* **1300** *Cursor M.* 17474 All fals sal far þat ilk wise, And euer sal rightwisnes vprise. **1513** DOUGLAS *Æneid* X. ix. 44 Be that gude beleif quhilk thou has eyk Of Ascanyvs vprysyng to estait. **1568** CHARTERIS *Pref. to Lyndesay's Wks.* (1871) 13* Cum, all degreis, in Lurdanerie quha lyis, .. And lerne in vertew how for to vpryis!

b. To become erect.

1796 SCOTT *Wild Huntsman* xliv, Uprose the Wildgrave's bristling hair. **1827** PRAED *Red Fisherman* 77 'Twas a sight to make the hair uprise.

5. To ascend as a sound.

1503 DUNBAR *Thistle & Rose* 176 The commoun voce vprais of birdis small. **1838** DICKENS *O. Twist* l, The crowd grew light with uncovered heads, and again the shout uprose. **1850** BLACKIE *Æschylus* I. 235 How shall my hymn uprise to bless thee? **1890** [see HALE *sb.*[4] 1].

6. To come into existence.

1471 RIPLEY *Comp. Alch.* v. viii. (MS. Ashm. 1445), So ther shulde no frute be vprysinge. **1562** WINȜET *Cert. Tractatis* Wks. (S.T.S.) I. 25, I being drery and dolorus for the schisme .. in Godis Kirk, and apperand temporal calamiteis to vpryse tharthrou. **1584** SOUTHWELL *Wks.* (1828) II. 150 So infinite [are] the sects .. into which it hath spread, besides new ones daily uprising. **1820** SHELLEY *Prometh. Unb.* I. 82, I had clothed, since Earth uprose, Its wastes in colours not their own. **1880** *Libr. Univ. Knowl.* IX. 300 But now up-rise some marvelous phenomena.

up'risen, *pa. pple.* and *ppl. a.* [UP- 5. Cf. ON. *upprisinn* and prec.] Risen up; arisen.

13.. *Cursor M.* 17384 (Gött.), Fra dede to lijf vp-resen es he. *a* **1400** *Sir Perc.* 977 Up-resyne es a sowdane, Alle hir landes hase he tane. **1446** LYDG. *Nightingale* 401 Hell despoiled, & slayn oure mortall foo, Oure lord vpryse with palme of hye victorie. **1600** FAIRFAX *Tasso* XII. xxxv, These flames vprisen to forestall my way, Perchance more terrour far than danger bring. **1621** BP. MOUNTAGU *Diatribæ* 283 Those new vp-risen brethren *Roseæ Crucis*. **1682** BUNYAN *Holy War* (1905) 345 He is up-risen, and is departed from them. **1849** ROCK *Ch. of Fathers* I. ii. 127 Christ's Body is not only up-risen, but has passed into an incorruptible .. state.

up'riser. (UP- 8.)

1656 [S. HOLLAND] *Don Zara* III. ii. 144 *marg.*, The number of Inhabitants, up-risers and down-lyers in this mighty City. **1823** *Blackw. Mag.* XIV. 692 The uprisers have not mixed wisdom with their cry for freedom.

up'rising, *vbl. sb.* In sense 7 'uprising. [UP- 7.]

1. The action of rising from death or from the grave; resurrection. Now *rare*.

c **1250** *Creed* in Maskell *Mon. Rit.* (1882) III. 251 Hy troue .. forȝifnes of sinnes, uprisinge of fleyes. *c* **1290** *S. Eng. Leg.* I. 416/453 A-sonenday, .. Þe day of mine oprisingue. **1297** R. GLOUC. (Rolls) 8530 Bi þe vprisinge of god Robelin me ssal ise .. stalwarde kniȝt be. **1340** *Ayenb.* 227 Ine þe oprisinge ne ssel by non spousynge. *c* **1400** *Pepysian Gosp. Harmony* (1922) 73 Þo asked Jesus ȝif þat sche leued it þat he was vprising and lyf. *c* **1440** *Alph. Tales* 195 Ane heresye þat þan began at rise in þaim þat trustid not in vprysyng of flessh. *c* **1450** *Cov. Myst.* (Shaks. Soc.) 371 Of his uprysyng he dede us lere Whan he walkyd with us in fere. *c* **1550** CHEKE *Matt.* xxii. 30 In ye vprising noyer schal men mari nor women be maried. *c* **1555** HARPSFIELD *Divorce Hen. VIII* (Camden) 38 By the death and uprising of Christ. **1648** HERRICK *Hesper.*, *'Here down'* 11 At my up-rising next, I shall .. thank ye all. **1852** ROCK *Ch. of Fathers* I. ix. III. 322 The life, the death, the uprising of her divine Son.

2. a. The action of rising from bed.

a **1300** *K. Horn* 844 Horn .. cam to þe kinge At his vp-risinge. *c* **1430** *Syr Gener.* (Roxb.) 574 Ful erly in the morning The king made his vprising. **1518** H. WATSON *Hist. Oliver of Castile* (Roxb.) D 4 b, Erly in ye mornynge his seruauntes came to his chambre for to be at his vprysynge. **1578** H. WOTTON *Courtlie Controv.* 240 Hee .. prayed them to goe vnto the kings vprising, and giue hym good morrowe. *a* **1628** PRESTON *New Cov.* (1630) 80 How many there are at vprising and down-lying from day to day. **1675** HAN. WOOLLEY *Gentlew. Comp.* 211 You ought .. to .. keep due hours for their [*sc.* children's] up-rising and going to bed. **1827** KEBLE *Chr. Y., Morning* vi, New every morning is the love Our wakening and uprising prove. **1863** GEO. ELIOT *Romola* I. Introd. 2 The faint light [of dawn] .. fell .. on the hasty uprising of the hard-handed labourer.

b. The action of rising from a sitting, kneeling, or recumbent posture.

1521 CLERK in Ellis *Orig. Lett.* Ser. III. I. 265 The Master of the ceremonyes .. causyd me to kysse his foott, and att myn vprising .. his Holynes toke me by the sholders. **1535** COVERDALE *Ps.* cxxxviii. 2 Thou knowest my downe syttinge & my vprisynge. **1865** *Sat. Rev.* 5 Aug. 177 The down-sittings and uprisings of each day. **1893** A. S. ECCLES *Sciatica* 78 Uprising from the couch is performed by the attendant grasping the patient's extended hands.

† c. *spec.* The rising of a woman after confinement. *Obs.*

1611 COTGR., *Relevailles d'une femme*, th' vprising, or vp-sitting, also the Churching, of a woman. *a* **1693** URQUHART *Rabelais* III. xli. 336 An uprising or Women Churching Treatment. [**1899** *N. & Q.* 9th Ser. III. 212 Child-Bed pew, another name for this was 'uprising seat'.]

3. The action of rising after a fall. Also *fig.*

a **1300** *Cursor M.* 11363 Þis child .. Sal be to fel men in dun fall, And to fell in vprising. *c* **1330** *Arth. & Merl.* 9906 (Kölbing), Often þai made dounfalleing, & when þai miȝt, vpriseing. *a* **1375** *Cursor M.* 25821 (Fairf.), Squa-gate for þaire wanhoping þai falle wiþ-outin vprising. *a* **1555** LATIMER in Foxe *A. & M.* (1563) 1310/1 For remembraunce of that fal and vprisyng kepeth vs in our fal from dispairing.

4. The rising of the sun; †also (quot. 1535), the quarter in which the sun rises.

c **1330** *Arth. & Merl.* 3865 (Kölbing), In þe sonnes vpriseing Bigan, certes, þis rideing. *c* **1400** *Three Kings Cologne* (1886) 50 Þei come .. in to Ierusalem .. in þe vpperisyng of þe sunne. **1412–20** LYDG. *Chron. Troy* IV. 2050 Þe Grekis han, at Phebus vp-rysynge, I-armed hem with gret dilligence. **1471** RIPLEY *Comp. Alch., Rec.* iv. in Ashm. (1652) 187 There is the uprysyng of the Son apperyng whyt and bryght. **1535** COVERDALE *2 Esdras* xv. 20 All the kynges of ye earth which are from the vprysinge. **1598** HAKLUYT *Voy.* I. 59 The terrible noise, which the Sunne made at his vprising. **1665** SIR. T. HERBERT *Trav.* (1677) 64 Ecbar .. gives those Rebels battel at the Suns first up-rising.

5. Advancement in place or power; improvement in position or circumstances.

1430–40 LYDG. *Bochas* VIII. 467 Aftir tryumphes and ther uprisinges, What folwith aftir, hir [Fortune's] wheel telle can. **1629** PRYNNE *Anti-Armin.* 52 Who know no other passage to their owne secure vp-rising but by religions downefall. **1868** ATKINSON *Cleveland Gloss.*, *Uprising*, a prosperous rise in one's circumstances and condition; a getting on in the world.

6. A rise or ascent; a swelling; a welling-up.

1588 SHAKS. *L.L.L.* IV. i. 2 Was that the King that spurd his horse so hard, Against the steepe vprising of the hill? **1611** COTGR., *Bosse*,..any round swelling, vprising, or puffing vp. **1874** T. HARDY *Far fr. Mad. Crowd* lvi, Something big came into her throat and an uprising to her eyes.

†**b.** *Arch.* Elevation. *Obs.*⁻¹

1669 tr. *Scamozzi's Mirr. Archit.* 23 The half of the building on the ground... The other half with the up-rising.

7. (ˈ*uprising*.) An insurrection; a popular rising against authority or for some common purpose.

1587 HOLINSHED *Chron.* III. 37/2 It was a greefe to him still to be vexed with such tumults and vprisings as they dailie procured. **1861** M. PATTISON *Ess.* (1889) I. 45 The great communistic uprising under Wat Tyler in 1381. **1871** FREEMAN *Norm. Conq.* xvii. IV. 54 Liable to be driven out whenever the whole nation should join together in one sudden and vigorous uprising.

8. The process or fact of coming into existence or notice.

1587 GOLDING *De Mornay* xxxiii. 618 If they iudge it by the first vprysing of the Christian Religion. *a* **1591** H. SMITH *Gods Arrow* iv. (1593) I 1 b, The beginning of Mahomets vprising, and of his Sect. **1634** SIR M. SANDYS *Prudence* 251 Death is but.. The uprising of Consolation, and the downe-setting of Perturbation. **1657** J. WATTS *Vind. Ch. Eng.* 101 The uprising of bloody Wars, and throwing down of Order. **1851** BRIMLEY *Ess.*, *Wordsw.* 110 The uprising of a new aristocracy of wealth and intellect. **1871** BLACKIE *Four Phases* i. 27 The notable uprising of national spirit and of popular power.

upˈrising, *ppl. a.* [UP- 6 b.] That rises up, in various senses.

a **1300** *E.E. Psalter* xxxiv. 13 Vprisand witnes, swikel ware ai. **1585** FOXE *Serm. 2 Cor. v.* 48 Some be repentant and uprysing sinners, some be unrepentant. *a* **1593** MARLOWE *Ovid's Elegies* I. xiii. 28 How oft wisht I, night would not giue thee place, Nor morning starres shunne thy vprising face. **1633** FORD *Love's Sacr.* I. i, My seruice shall pay tribute in my lownesse, To your vprising vertues. **1727** P. WALKER *Life W. Smith* (1827) II. 88 To transmit a tearful Remembrance of them to the up-rising and following Ages. **1819** MRS. BROWNING *Battle of Marathon* III. ad fin., When the uprising morn extends her light. **1884** PROCTOR in *Longm. Mag.* April 597 Uprising streams of aqueous vapour.

†**upˈrist,** *sb. Obs.* [UP- 2 + *-rist* rising: see ARIST *sb.* Cf. OIcel. *uppreist*, MSw. *uprest.*]

1. Rising from the dead; resurrection.

c **1250** *Song Passion* 79 in *O.E. Misc.* 199 Grante ous, crist, wit þin uprist to gone. *a* **1290** *St. Eustace* 173 in Horstm. *Altengl. Leg.* (1881) 215 Euere he þouhte on Jhesu Crist On his deþ, on his ouprist. *c* **1315** SHOREHAM v. 188 Þe prydde ioye þat com of cryste Hadde oure leuedy of hys opryste Fram deaþes harde bende. *c* **1400** *Pepysian Gosp. Harmony* (1922) 111 Þe deciples..assembleden hem in a soleer..vpe þe fourtiþe day after his vpryst. *a* **1425** *Cursor M.* 14264 (Trin.), Ihesus seide I am vpriste [*earlier MSS.* vpris, -ras] & lif. *c* **1450** *Mirk's Festial* I. 80 Forto be wyttenes of his [*sc.* Christ's] vprist wyth vs.

2. The rising of the sun.

a **1300** *K. Horn* 1436 Tofore þe sunne vpriste His schup stod vnder ture. *c* **1386** CHAUCER *Knt.'s T.* 193 In the gardyn at the sonne vpriste She walketh vp and doun. *c* **1430** LYDG. *Min. Poems* (Percy Soc.) 23 When the larke.. Salveth the uprist of the sonne shene. ? *a* **1444** *Ibid.* 153 Geyn Phebus uprist syngen wyl the quaylle. **1555** WATREMAN *Fardle Facions* I. iv. 43 Certeine of theim worshippe the Sonne at his vprijste. **1625** LISLE *Du Bartas, Noe* 132 Both at the suns uprist, and where he goes to bed.

3. The act of rising out of bed.

13.. *Seuyn Sages* (W.) 1649 Out of mi lond I rede thou flee,..For, abide thou min uprist, Thou be honged! **1390** GOWER *Conf.* I. 116 At his upriste Men tolden him how that it ferde.

uprist, *pa. pple.*, archaizing var. UPRISEN.

1579 SPENSER *Sheph. Cal.* Mar. 18 Flora..bids make ready Maias bowre, That newe is vpryst from bedde. **1887** C. MACKAY in *Temple Bar Mag.* June 178, I could trace their pallid features In the moonlight, new up-rist.

†**upˈrive,** *v. Obs. rare.* [UP- 4 + RIVE *v.*²] *intr.* To arrive on shore; to land.

1338 R. BRUNNE *Chron.* (1810) 1 In þe ȝere after..Kom.. Ini & Iuore, In schip out of Irelond, in Wales gan þei vp-ryue. *c* **1425** WYNTOUN *Cron.* VII. x. 3275 Quhare þai mycht wit him till vprif, Thare þai suld meit him þan belif.

up-river (ˈʌpˌrɪvə(r)), *a.* and *sb.* orig. *U.S.* [UP *prep.*² 2, 6.]

1. *adj.* **a.** Belonging to, situated, etc., farther up, or towards the upper end of, a river.

1774 I. LITCHFIELD *Jrnl.* 19 Apr. in W. J. Litchfield *Litchfield Family in Amer.* (1906) I. 334, I..ordered them to meet at upriver meeting house by the Sun an hour high Compleat in arms with 4 Days provision. **1857** *Trans. Mich. Agric. Soc.* VIII. 732 Charming villages are also rapidly springing into existence along the up river bank of the Grand River in this country. **1877** *Encycl. Brit.* VII. 648/1 The fine 'up-river' quality [of cocoa]. **1886** *Pall Mall G.* 17 April 5/2 The advantages offered by the up-river docks. **1899** KEANE *Man Past & Pres.* 241 The forest and up-river Dyaks.

b. Leading or directed towards the source of a river.

1836 *Southern Lit. Messenger* II. 698/1, I had never imagined that any thing half so grand..awaited us on our up-river jaunt. **1857** W. CHANDLESS *Visit to Salt Lake* I. i. 1, I passed a few days there, waiting for an up-river boat. **1890** 'R. BOLDREWOOD' *Col. Reformer* (1891) 319 Wending his way along the 'up-river' road. **1893** D. J. RANKIN *Zambesi Basin* vi. 95 We proceeded on our up-river journey.

2. *sb.* The district lying farther up a river.

1902 S. E. WHITE *Blazed Trail* xix, If the men from up-river come by.

up-ˈriver, *adv.* [UP *prep.*² 2.] Towards or in the direction of the source of a river.

1848 THOREAU in *Union Mag.* Nov. 220/2 Only a few axe-men have gone 'up river' into the howling wilderness which feeds it. **1887** *Harper's Mag.* Apr. 667/1 Logs were usually cut and hauled in summer-time to the banks of streams, often a long distance 'up-river'. **1929** BELLOC *Joan of Arc* ii. 38 He had been all day up-river in the marshes shooting quail. **1981** M. NABB *Death of Englishman* I. i. 25 Upriver the ghost of the Ponte Vecchio..was straddling nothing.

uproar (ˈʌprɔə(r)), *sb.* Also 6 uprour(e, 6–7 uprore (9), -roare. [ad. Du. *oproer* or MLG. *uprôr* (MHG. *ûfruor*, G. *aufruhr*), f. *op-*, *up-* UP- 2 + *roer*, *rôr* ROAR *sb.*² Cf. also WFris. *oproer*, *oproar*, Da. *oprør*, Norw. *upprør*, Sw. *up(p)rör*. In sense 2 associated with ROAR *sb.*¹

First used by Tindale and Coverdale in passages in which Luther's Bible has *aufruhr*. In the same passages the Dutch version of 1563 has *oproer*, which in that of 1531 appears only as a marginal variant to 2 Kings xi. 14.]

1. An insurrection or rising of the populace; a serious tumult, commotion, or outbreak of disorder among the people or a body of persons. Also without article. Now *rare*.

α. **1526** TINDALE *Acts* xxi. 38 That Ægipcian whych.. made an vproure, and ledde out into the wildernes about iiij. thousande men. **1535** COVERDALE *2 Kings* xi. 14 Athalia rente hir clothes, & sayde vproure, vproure. **1555** WATREMAN *Fardle Facions* II. xi. 247 Among them is no mutinyng, no vproures, no sturres. **1560** DAUS tr. *Sleidane's Comm.* 13 b, Who shall represse the sodayne insurrections and civile vprours [L. *motus*]?

β. *a* **1548** HALL *Chron., Hen. VI*, 169 b, The beginner of this temerarious commocion, and sodain vprore. **1561** DAUS tr. *Bullinger on Apoc.* lxxvi. 524 Al wise men haue greuously condemned seditions, which we are wonte to calle tumultes or vprores. **1595** DANIEL *Civ. Wars* III. xix, Least the realme might chance indure Some new reuolt, or any fresh vprore. **1606** G. W[OODCOCKE] *Hist. Ivstine* XXXIV. 112 That the kingdome should remaine in more safety, and lesse vprore. **1628** COKE *On Litt.* 109 b, Keeping the king's peace in time of sudden uprores.

γ. *a* **1586** C'TESS PEMBROKE *Ps.* LXV. iv, When stormy uproares tosse the peoples brayn. **1607** DEKKER *Wh. Babylon* C 2 b, Confusion, tyranie, vproares will shake all. **1677** HUBBARD *Narrative* II. 84 These late Uproars amongst the Indians. **1702** CALAMY *Life Baxter* vi. 76 To avoid Uproars of this kind, he was advis'd to withdraw a while from Home. **1748** *Anson's Voy.* III. vi. 347 The officers found it difficult for some time to appease the uproar. **1905** J. H. MCCARTHY *Dryad* 258 There was nothing so wonderful in the crushing of such an uproar as that of the Catalan Grand Company.

b. In fig. uses.

1593 SHAKS. *Lucr.* 427 His eye, which late this mutiny restrains, Unto a greater uproar tempts his veins. **1602** MARSTON *Ant. & Mel.* I, The rocks gron'd At the intestine uprore of the maine.

2. Loud outcry or vociferation; noise of shouting or tumult.

1544 BETHAM *Precepts War* I. clxiii. H vj, The souldiours ..cannot take anye counsayle of thynges to be doone in suche vprore and wepynges [of women]. **1590** SPENSER *F.Q.* II. ii. 20 That all on vprore.. The house was raysd, and all that in did dwell. **1613** PURCHAS *Pilgrimage* (1614) 386 The King was receiued into the house.., where without any vproar he slew seuentie. **1667** MILTON *P.L.* x. 479 Night and Chaos wilde..fiercely oppos'd My journey strange, with clamorous uproare Protesting Fate supreame. **1718** *Free-thinker* No. 63. 52 A Field of War, stained with Blood, and filled with Uproar and Confusion. **1820** KEATS *Hyperion* III. 1 Thus in alternate uproar and sad peace, Amazed were those Titans utterly. **1852** MRS. STOWE *Uncle Tom's C.* xxxv. 317 The sound of wild shrieking,..mingled with the barking of dogs and other symptoms of general uproar.

transf. **1726** THOMSON *Winter* 190 Wild Uproar lords it wide; the Clouds commixt, With Stars, swift-gliding, sweep along the Sky. **1820** KEATS *Eve St. Agnes* xl, The arras.. Flutter'd in the besieging wind's uproar.

b. With article (*an* or *the*) and in pl.

1572 FORREST *Theophilus* 1057 Although to his shame yt make an uprore Of admyration before the worldes sight. **1623** BINGHAM *Xenophon* 98 We heard vpon the sudden a great vprore and cry, Strike, strike, throw, throw. *a* **1670** HACKET *Abp. Williams* II. (1693) 187 The daily Uproars about his Palace of Whitehall, which did emperil and threaten his Life. **1760** G. COLMAN *Polly Honeycombe* 19 There's always an uproar in the family about marrying the daughter. **1794** MRS. RADCLIFFE *Myst. Udolpho* xxx, It was the wild uproar of riot, not the cheering gaiety of tempered mirth. **1832** DOWNES *Lett. Cont. Countries* I. 291 Hearing.. a prodigious uproar in the street, we hastened to the window. **1849** C. BRONTË *Shirley* xv, His uproars are all sound and fury, signifying nothing. **1897** HENTY *On the Irrawaddy* 152 The uproar of the advancing crowd was prodigious. Every man was yelling, at the top of his voice.

3. *in (an) uproar*, in a state of tumult, commotion, or excitement.

(*a*) **1548** UDALL, etc. *Erasm. Par. Mark* Pref. C iv b, To haue all the worlde in an vprore, and inquieted with warres. **1596** DANETT tr. *Comines* (1614) 55 Those that escaped put all the country in an vprore as they went. **1635** *Life & Pranks Long Meg of Westm.* viii. 16 The street was in such an uproar. **1778** MISS BURNEY *Evelina* xl, For some minutes the room seemed quite in an uproar [of laughter]. **1831** [HARE] tr. *Tieck's Old Man of Mount.* 40 His head is in an uprore, his heart throbs tumultuously. **1848** L. HUNT *Jar of Honey* 188 Thus it was at Alcamo, where the streets seemed to be in an uproar till after midnight. **1853** KANE *Grinnell Exp.* (1856) 522 Ice in an uproar.

(*b*) **1597** BEARD *Theatre God's Judgem.* (1612) 68 Whereat heauen grieuing, clad it selfe in blacke: But earth in vprore triumpht at their wracke. **1630** *R. Johnson's Kingd. & Commw.* 573 All Persia was in uprore about the election of a new Prince. *a* **1700** EVELYN *Diary* 16 Aug. 1650, As we pass'd St. Denis the people were in uproar.

ˈuproar, *v.* [f. prec.]

1. *trans.* To throw into confusion. *rare*.

1605 SHAKS. *Macb.* IV. iii. 99 Nay, had I powre, I should ..Vprore the vniuersall peace, confound All vnity on earth. **1811** W. R. SPENCER *Poems* 48 The demon rage which uproared Europe's peace.

2. *intr.* To make an uproar.

1831 CARLYLE *Sart. Res.* III. viii, Do not we..uproar (*poltern*), and revel in our mad Dance of the Dead? **1837** —— *Fr. Rev.* III. VI. ii, Danton was not prone..to act or uproar for his own safety. *Ibid.* vii, All men accuse, and uproar, and impetuously acclaim.

†**uproarer.** *Obs.* [f. UPROAR *sb.*] A creator of uproar; a turbulent person.

1628 GAULE *Pract. The.* (1629) 212 So doe these rude Vproarers snatch and hale Christ..to their High Priests House. **1647** HEXHAM I, An uprorer, or a seditious fellow, *een oproermaker*.

upˈroariness. [f. **uproary*, adj. f. UPROAR *sb.*] = UPROARIOUSNESS.

1806 SURR *Winter in Lond.* II. 112 Like the uproariness of our gallery gods, the rudeness of these rogues must perhaps be tolerated. **1834** M. SCOTT *Cruise Midge* x, The excess of her joy, and the uproariness of her laughter.

ˈuproaring, *vbl. sb.* [f. UPROAR *sb.* or *v.*] A tumult or disturbance.

1827 CARLYLE *Germ. Rom.* III. 285 Every time a conversion happens,..there is an uproaring and a shooting.

upˈroarious, *a.* [f. UPROAR *sb.*]

1. Making, or given to making, an uproar.

1819 *Blackw. Mag.* IV. 717 The trio..is altogether so cheerful.., so uproarious, if we may be allowed the expression. **1858** DORAN *Crt. Fools* 101 The bachelor and uproarious Court of William Rufus. **1871** JOWETT *Plato* I. 182 A somewhat uproarious young man.

2. Characterized by uproar; noisy.

1818 LADY GRANVILLE *Let.* 12 Aug. (1894) I. 135 We arrived here to dinner and found Hart in uproarious spirits. **1849** MRS. CARLYLE *Lett.* (1882) II. 42 We dined. After that, very youthful and uproarious sports till twelve! **1874** GREEN *Short Hist.* viii. §7. 531 The King..paused..at Oxford, where he was received with uproarious welcome. **1885** *Manch. Exam.* 10 Nov. 4/7 The proceedings were very uproarious.

3. *fig.* Disordered, unkempt.

1836 JAS. GRANT *Random Recoll. Ho. Lords* xiv. 316 The uproarious condition of his dark grey hair.

Hence **upˈroariously** *adv.*, **-ness**.

1838 DICKENS *O. Twist* ix, At which Mr. Charles Bates laughed *uproariously. **1871** L. STEPHEN *Playgr. Eur.* iii. 147 We should..have been uproariously triumphant over our victory. **1847** L. HUNT *Men, Women, & B.* II. xi. 265 His delight at having his head patted by Lord Clarendon, and his honest *uproariousness. **1898** 'H. S. MERRIMAN' *Roden's Corner* xxxii. 340 In jail..for intoxication and uproariousness.

†**uproarish,** *a. Obs.* [f. UPROAR *sb.*] Turbulent, unruly. Hence †**uproarishly** *adv. Obs.*

1550 W. LYNNE *Curious Cron.* 180 b, The Poles drew into their faction the vprouryshe kynde of men called Thaborites. **1647** HEXHAM I, Vprorish, seditious, or tumultuous. *Ibid.*, Vprorishly or seditiously.

upˈroll, *v.* [UP- 4. Cf. WFris. *oprôlje*, Du. *oprollen*, G. *aufrollen*, Sw. *upprulla*, Da. *oprulle*.]

1. *trans.* To impel upwards by rolling.

1513 DOUGLAS *Æneid* VI. ix. 4 Hir rosy chariot the fresche Aurora..Begouth for till wproll and rais on hie. **1743** FRANCIS tr. *Horace, Epodes* xvii. 24 Sisiphus, with many a Groan, Uprolls, with ceaseless Toil, his Stone. **1855** SINGLETON *Virgil* I. 88 Thrice they essayed..on Ossa to uproll Leaf-fraught Olympus.

2. To roll or wind up. Also const. *in*.

1613 DRUMM. OF HAWTH. *Cypress Grove* ¶7 A swift.. wheele, which twinneth forth and againe vprolleth [1630 vpwindeth] our life. **1623** —— *Flowers Sion* xxv, I am that Monarch whom all Monarches feare, Who hath in Dust their farre-stretch'd Pride vproll'd.

b. *intr.* To concentrate by rolling; to form a roll.

1805–6 CARY *Dante, Inf.* XXIV. 102 The dust again Uproll'd spontaneous, and the self-same form Instant resumed. **1818** MILMAN *Samor* VI. 17 But far and wide,.. Venomous and vast the clouds uproll. **1887** STEVENSON *Mem. & Portraits* xiii. 224 How the congregated clouds themselves uproll, as stiff as bolsters!

ˈuproll, *sb. rare.* [UP-2.] A rolling movement upwards.

a **1885** G. M. HOPKINS *Poems* (1967) 192 Moist..With the uproll and the downcarol of day and night delivering Water. **1984** A. PRICE *Sion Crossing* v. 83 David must have been.. not quite senior enough to have sighted the gun and pulled the lanyard on the uproll—?

up'rolled, *pa. pple.* and *ppl. a.* [UP- 5. Cf. UPROLL *v.*] Rolled up; brought together by rolling. Also const. *in*.

1592 WYRLEY *Armorie, Ld. Chandos* 79 Then I call My banner for, vproled I hit bring Vnto my prince. **1600** FAIRFAX *Tasso* IX. lxxxi, The sweat..Seem'd pearles.., The dust therein vprold, adorn'd his haire. **1667** MILTON *P.L.* VII. 291 Thither they Hasted,..uprowld As drops on dust conglobing from the drie. **1762** FALCONER *Shipwr.* III. 406 High o'er the poop th' audacious seas aspire, Uproll'd in hills of fluctuating fire. **1821** SHELLEY *Boat on Serchio* 16 Day had..clothed with light..The mists in their eastern caves uprolled. **1844** EMERSON *Ess., Nat.*, The uprolled clouds and the colours of morning and evening. **1864** E. SARGENT *Peculiar* III. 98 The lids of the eyes hung loosely over the uprolled balls.

'uproot, *sb.* [f. next.] An uprooted tree.

1891 E. ROPER *By Track & Trail* iii. 33 Stumps and logs and fallen trees, uproots and old dead weeds.

up'root, *v.*[1] [UP- 4 + ROOT *v.*[1]: cf. UPROOTED *pa. pple.*] *trans.* To tear up by the roots; to remove from a fixed position.

1695 CONGREVE *Taking of Namur* viii, Uprooting Hills.. To form the High and Dreadful Scale. **1771** BEATTIE *Minstrel* I. xxiv, The river..Down the vale thunders, and..Uproots the grove. **1796** MORSE *Amer. Geog.* I. 475 Storms and hurricanes sometimes happen, which..uproot trees. **1836–7** DICKENS *Sk. Boz, Tales* iv, Mr. Cymon..uprooted the chairs, and removed them further back. **1860** TYNDALL *Glac.* I. xxv. 185 We were powerfully shaken, but had no fear of being uprooted. **1877** HUXLEY *Physiogr.* 171 The stalks are not uprooted and carried across the field.

b. *fig.* To remove as by tearing up; to eradicate, exterminate, destroy.

a **1620** J. DYKE *Worthy Commun.* (1640) 193 Before wee can be rooted in Christ, we must be unrooted and uprooted in regard of our natural condition. **1743** FRANCIS tr. *Hor., Odes* III. xxiv. 52 Tear forth, uprooted from the youthful Breast, The Seeds of each deprav'd Desire. **1813** SHELLEY *Q. Mab* IX. 191 [To] uproot The germs of misery from the human heart. **1868** FREEMAN *Norm. Conq.* viii. II. 173 That he acted on any settled scheme of uprooting the nationality, the laws, or the language of England is an exploded fable.

Hence **up'rootal**; **up'rooter**; **up'rooting** *vbl. sb.* and *ppl. a.*

1861 *Macm. Mag.* V. 22 He would have shrieked like a mandrake at *uprootal. **1890** CLARK RUSSELL *Shipmate Louise* II. 285 The sudden uprootal and crash of their one mast and sail. **1828** CAMPBELL *On Battle of Navarino* 10 No! your lofty emprise was to fetter and foil The *uprooter of Greece's domain! **1882** *Blackw. Mag.* CXXXII. 102/2 War..—that remorseless and violent uprooter of ordinary life. **1775** ASH s.v., *Uprooting. **1847** MANGAN *Poems* (1903) 223 But the end of all is Sadness,..Spoliation and Uprooting! **1858** O. W. HOLMES *Aut. Breakf.-t.* x. 95 The uprooting of the ancient gravestones in..our city burial-grounds. **1818** BYRON *Ch. Har.* IV. clxxiii, The *uprooting wind which tears The oak from his foundation. **1880** MEREDITH *Tragic Com.* (1881) 265 Should there come no preternatural uprooting tempest.

up'root, *v.*[2] [UP- 4 + ROOT *v.*[2]] *trans.* To grub up.

1726 POPE *Odyssey* XVIII. 36 Those teeth.., Like some vile swine's, that..Uproots the bearded corn. **1889** A. R. WALLACE *Darwinism* 16 Some [herbivorous mammals] uproot and devour the buried tubers.

up'rooted, *pa. pple.* and *ppl. a.* [UP- 5, or f. UPROOT *v.*[1]] Rooted up; eradicated. Also *fig.*

a **1593** MARLOWE tr. *Lucan* I. 4 We sing..Armies alied, the kingdoms league vprooted. **1667** MILTON *P.L.* VI. 781 At his command the uprooted Hills retir'd. **1737** GLOVER *Leonidas* IX. 294 With prostrate glories lie the stately oak.. And elm uprooted. **1743** FRANCIS tr. *Hor., Odes* III. xxv. 22 The Bacchanalian Maids..Tear from the bursting Glebe th' uprooted Tree. **1809** J. BARLOW *Columb.* x. 257 For him no more..Uprooted mountains sweep the dark profound. **1844** KINGLAKE *Eothen* viii, One man above all others (he is now uprooted from society) she blasted with her wrath. **1861** GEO. ELIOT *Silas M.* iii, Almost as helpless as an uprooted tree.

up'rootedness. [f. UPROOTED *ppl. a.* + -NESS.] The state of being uprooted; a condition of severance from one's natural origins. Chiefly *fig.*

1927 J. LAVRIN *Russ. Lit.* v. 29 The negative features of a romantic type: uprootedness, fear and hatred of reality. **1954** KOESTLER *Invisible Writing* xxii. 247 What a refugee craves most is relief from his permanent feeling of uprootedness. **1974** O. COOK *Eng. Country House* i. 7 The contrast..between our uprootedness and the continuity and stability of the life led in the great mansion.

uproused, *pa. pple.* and *ppl. a.* (UP- 5.)

1592 SHAKS. *Rom. & Jul.* II. iii. 40 Thy earlinesse doth me assure, Thou art vprous'd with some distemprature. **1796** SCOTT *Wild Huntsman* xxii, Again uproused, the timorous prey Scours moss and moor. **1802** J. BAILLIE *2nd Pt. Ethwald* I. ii, What, meanst thou this? Uprous'd again unto this dev'lish pitch? **1848** THACKERAY *Van. Fair* xviii, Cried out this uproused British lion. **1871** HAWTHORNE *Sept. Felton* (1872) 36 To prevent the uproused people from coming..close to the main body.

'uprush, *sb.* Also (older) **up'rush.** [UP- 2.] An upward rush or flow. (Common in recent use.)

1871 BROWNING *Balaustion's Adventure* 31 In the fire-flash of the appalling sword, the uprush and the outburst. **1873** B. STEWART *Conserv. Force* iv. 108 The up-rush of air through the chimney. **1877** G. F. CHAMBERS *Astron.* (ed. 3) I. i. 5 The uprushes of incandescent gas and metallic vapours.

up'rush, *v.* [UP- 4.] *intr.* To rush up.

1818 MILMAN *Samor* x. 338 Uprush'd the giant fire, Piercing the dim heavens with its blazing brow. **1826** N. T. CARRINGTON *Dartmoor* 17 Years have flown Sweet Lara, yet thy bank uprushes still With the old charm. **1872** A. DE VERE *Leg. St. Patrick* 119 She knelt, and unto God..Uprushed the strength of prayer, as when the cloud Uprushes..From billowy deep unseen.

up'rushing, *ppl. a.* (UP- 7.)

1801 SOUTHEY *Thalaba* XII. xvii, But ever the uprushing wind Inflates the wings above. **1869** J. PHILLIPS *Vesuv.* iii. 93 From the source came up continual jets of uprushing incandescent stones. **1895** *Edin. Rev.* Oct. 413 The uprushing, glowing material of sun-flames.

'up,saddle, *v. S. African.* [ad. Du. *opzadelen*, f. *op-* UP- 4 + *zadelen* SADDLE *v.*] *intr.* To saddle a horse.

1838 in W. B. Boyce *Notes S. Afr. Affairs* vi. 148 Dingaan ..inveigled them within an enclosure..just as they were up-saddling to depart, and massacred..every living soul of them. **1863** W. C. BALDWIN *Afr. Hunting* vi. 181 We up-saddled and went in pursuit. **1887** RIDER HAGGARD *Jess* xxx, At midday they offsaddled their horses for an hour... Then they upsaddled and went on.

†**up-sail.** *Obs.* [UP *adv.*[1]] A hoisted sail.

1637 RUTHERFORD *Lett.* (1664) 303 The Devil and the lusts of a deceiving world and sin, are upon horse-back, and follow with up sails. *Ibid.* 346, I wait on..till the Lord send a full sea, that with up-sailes I may lift up Christ.

‖**upsara** ('ʌpsərə). *Indian Mythol.* Also **apsaras.** [Hindi *apsarā*, f. Skr. *apsarās*.] A celestial nymph, one of the wives of the Gandharvas (heavenly minstrels).

[**1846** J. T. THOMPSON *Dict. Hindee & Eng.* 17/2 *Upsura* .., a female dancer or courtezan in *Swurg*, the hindoo paradise.] **1865** [see *Vedaic* adj. s.v. VEDA]. **1879** J. DOWSON *Class. Dict. Hindu Mythol. & Relig.* 20 The Apsarases..are fairylike beings... They are the rewards in Indra's paradise held out to heroes who fall in battle. **1892** KIPLING *Barrack-Room Ballads* 105 Above the dark *Upsaras* flew, beneath us plashed the blood. **1932** F. M. ATKINSON tr. H. de Wilman-Grabowska in J. Hackin et al. *Asiatic Mythol.* 113 The Apsarases are the recognized courtesans of the sky. **1968** B. WALKER *Hindu World* II. 143 In Hindu mythology the celestial nymph or *apsarā* (ap-sara, wet-flow) is a personification of the mists or clouds in the form of a beauteous damsel.

'upscale, *a. U.S.* [UP *prep.*[2]] At the higher end of a (social) scale; superior, of a high quality; 'up-market'.

[**1945** *Newsweek* 2 Apr. 68/2 The Mullikin selling method, which he called 'upscaling', aimed to build up the idea that prefabricated houses were rich-looking, comfortable and permanent.] **1966** *One Hundred Basic Media Terms Defined* (Batten, Barton, Durstine & Osgood Inc. Media Dept.) 15 Downscale is a term used to describe a market or audience with above-average representation at the lower end of the socio-economic scale. Its opposite is 'upscale'. **1975** *New Yorker* 1 Dec. 44/1 A lot of advertising people don't think jazz fans have that all-important rage to consume. They don't think the jazz audience is 'up-scale' enough. **1977** P. STREVENS *New Orientations Teaching of English* xiii. 163 The *up-scale* lab has all typical facilities, plus full remote control of each student machine. **1983** *Chicago Sun-Times* 24 Nov. 110 '20-20' generally finishes behind 'Hill Street', whose up-scale audience it shares. **1984** *Christian Science Monitor* 2 Mar. 10/4 He cites Chi-Chi's Mexican restaurants as appealing to customers who want a bit more upscale atmosphere.

upse-, var. of UPSY *Obs.*

upsedoun, -down, obs. ff. UPSIDE DOWN.

†**upseed.** *Sc. Obs.*[−1] [UP *adv.*[2] 5 c.] ***upseed time***, harvest.

1678 [see STREEKING *vbl. sb.* 2].

†**up'seek**, *v. Obs.* [UP- 4. Cf. WFris. *opsiikje*, Du. *opzoeken*, MSw. *up-*, *opsökia* (Sw. *uppsöka*), Da. *opsøge*.] *trans.* To seek or search out; to search through.

c **1315** SHOREHAM I. 1581 Þanne aȝte..wyues nauȝt aȝens men Non on-wrestnesse werche,..And nauȝt onwrest opsechen hy. *c* **1400** *Destr. Troy* 12010 Grete palis of prise [þai] put into askys,..And all the Cite vp soght to þe sad walles. *a* **1500** *Coventry Corpus Chr. Pl.* i. 809 All the chylder of that age dy the[y] mvst nede; Now with all my myght the[y] schall be vpsoght. **1615–6** BOYS *Wks.* (1630) 462 That we should not expect vntill other vpseeke vs, but that we should seeke and serue them.

†**up'seeking**, *vbl. sb. Obs.*[−1] [UP- 7.] A seeking after.

1594 LYLY *Mother Bombie* v. iii, *Accius.* We shall haue good chere these foure dayes. *Lucio.* And be fooles for euer. *Sil.* Thats none of our vpseekings.

up'seeking, *ppl. a.* (UP- 6 b.)

1801 SOUTHEY *Thalaba* XII. xxxii, Upseeking eyes suffused with tears devout. **1846** KEBLE *Lyra Innoc.* 58 Or chanced the Thorny Crown her first upseeking glance to win?

upsees. *pseudo-arch.* Also **up seyes.** (A misuse of *upsee* UPSY.)

1810 SCOTT *Lady of L.* VI. v, Off with thy liquor, Drink upsees out, and a fig for the vicar! **1821** —— *Kenilw.* xx, Here goes it, up seyes—to Varney and Leicester! **1842** D. VEDDER *Poems* 184 And there was wassail in the court, And upsees in the hall.

'upsend, *sb.* [UP- 2.] An upward discharge.

1842 *Blackw. Mag.* LII. 409 So soon as the rolling cannonade is over, there is an upsend from the mines beneath.

up'send, *v.* [UP- 4. Cf. Du. *opzenden*.] *trans.* To send up; to discharge upwards.

1667 MILTON *P.L.* I. 541 At which the universal Host upsent A shout that tore Hells Concave. **1791** COWPER *Iliad* XVIII. 257 As when some island..Upsends a smoke to heaven. **1816** *Monthly Mag.* XLI. 144 Huge bonfires first their cones of flame upsend. **1854** S. DOBELL *Balder* v. 33 Sudden the universal host upsent Impotent rage.

†**upserve**, obs. variant of OBSERVE *v.*

1539 in Ellis *Orig. Lett.* Ser. II. II. 145 Commanding all hys..subjettes to upserve and keype all manner of holly sacrementes.

'upset, *sb.* [UP- 2.]

I. †**1.** *Sc.* An insurrection, revolt. *Obs.*

c **1425** WYNTOUN *Cron.* v. xii. 3634 (Cott. MS.), His lufftennandis þai slew þar..In to þat vpset richt fellon. *Ibid.* VIII. iv. 699 þat vpset..þat Chore agayne Moyses wroucht.

†**2.** *north.* and *Sc.* The fact of setting up in business as a master, or of becoming a freeman in a particular trade; also, the sum paid to the guild on this occasion. *Obs.*

1463–4 in *York Memo. Bk.* II. (Surtees) 207 Every foreine walker commyng to this citie..and wil sett up as a maister, ..he shall paie at his upsett xiijs. iiijd. **1505** in A. Pennecuik *Blue Blanket* (1756) 46 Persons..admitted frie men or master to the saids Crafts,..shall pay at his entrie for his upset, Five pounds. **1598** in J. M. Lambert *2000 Years Gild Life* (1891) 255 The moytie of all Upsettes, incomes, or other receites..accrewinge..to the said Companie. **1639** *Rec. Burgh Lanark* (1893) 133 That nae persone..be admittit..frieman for any les wpsett nor is abone wryttin. **1687** in J. R. Boyle *Hedon* (1875) App. 192 Every apprentice .., his yeares beinge ended, shall pay for his upp sett two shillings to the said Company.

3. †**a.** A curved part of a bridle-bit, fitting over the tongue of the horse. *Obs.* (Cf. UPSET *ppl. a.* 1 b.)

1607 MARKHAM *Cavel.* II. 64 Others..haue added, from the eye of the byt to the outside of the vpset, a strong trench. *Ibid.*, The fashion of which vpsets..you shall behold in these figures. **1611** COTGR., *Col d'oye*, the port, or vpset of some Bits. **1611** FLORIO, *Suenata briglia*, a bit with an open mouth as ports or upsets. *c* **1720** GIBSON *Farrier's Guide* II. lxii. (1722) 218 The usual Method of Cure is to open the Horse's Mouth with the Upset.

b. *Mining.* (See quots.)

1883 GRESLEY *Gloss. Coal-m.* 268 *Upset*, a bolt hole or thirl put through between two levels in edge coals. **1886** J. BARROWMAN *Sc. Mining Terms* 69 *Upset*, a short working place driven to the rise.

c. *Basketry.* Usu. **upsett.** The first section of waling, which sets the stakes firmly in place.

1907 T. OKEY in *Jrnl. Soc. Arts* 11 Jan. 191 (*caption*) It will be seen that the bye-stakes are merely inserted in the upsett. **1946** N. WYMER *Eng. Country Crafts* vii. 73 He then lets in the stiff 'uprights' and fastens them securely by working in several willows together to form the 'upset'. **1977** B. MAYNARD *Basketry* 19/2 You may like to start the upsett with one round of 4-rod wale.

4. = UPSHOT *sb.* 4.

1821 J. W. CROKER *Diary* 9 June, The upset, however, is that all is at a stand. **1901** F. E. TAYLOR *Folk-sp. S. Lancs.*, *Upset*, the upshot.

5. a. A rendering or translation.

1828 T. C. CROKER *Fairy Leg. S. Irel.* II. 71 It would be a thousand pities not to give you his verses; so here's my hand at an upset of them into English.

b. A rough draft.

1841 H. GREELEY in *Corr. R. W. Griswold* (1898) 102 Having got the right sort of a letter from Burleigh, I have set right down and written you an upset of it.

II. 6. a. The overturning of a vehicle or boat; the fact of being overturned. (Cf. OVERSET *sb.* b.)

1804 MOORE *Mem.* (1853) I. 162 Driving through mud and filth,..and risking an upset at every step. **1840** B. HALL *Patchwork* (1841) III. vii. 130 At this..moment, when an upset was obviously inevitable, the horses slackened their pace. **1852** MANSFIELD *Paraguay*, etc. (1856) 112 The Major ..was afraid of the possible consequences of an upset of the canoe. **1880** L. STEPHEN *Pope* iv. 90 He had good-naturedly lent his own chariot to a lady who had been hurt in an upset.

b. An overturning or overthrow *of* ideas, plans, etc. Also const. *to*.

1822 *Blackw. Mag.* XI. 453 The revolution and the upset of opinions..created a new order of..taste. **1827** SOUTHEY in *Corr. W. C. Bowles* (1881) 119 What a strange upset of old principles and old measures! **1886** *Manch. Exam.* 9 June 5/2 The result was a complete upset of all the predictions of the prophets.

c. A physical or (more commonly) mental disturbance or derangement.

1866 CHR. G. ROSSETTI *Prince's Progr.* xxv, Some old volcanic upset must Have rent..and blackened the crust. **1892** HUXLEY in *Life* (1900) II. 320 My wife got an awful dose of neuralgia and general upset. **1899** *Allbutt's Syst. Med.* VIII. 301 The poor and hard-working are subject to mental upset..in much larger numbers than the well-off.

d. A quarrel, a misunderstanding.

1887 G. R. SIMS *Mary Jane's Mem.* 75 They were always getting at each other and both trying to bring me into their upsets. **1895** *Daily News* 31 Oct. 9/1 We had only one upset there. I happened to hit the defendant.

up'set, *v.* [UP- 4. Cf. WFris. *opsette*, MDu. *opsetten* (Du. *opzetten*), (M)LG. *upsetten*, MHG. *ûfsetzen* (G. *aufsetzen*), MSw. *upsätia*,

-*sättia* (Sw. *uppsätta*), (M)Da. *opsætte* in sense 1. With senses 4–6 cf. OVERSET *v.* 3–4.]

I. 1. *trans.* †**a.** To set up, raise up, erect. *Obs.* (Cf. UPSET *pa. pple.* 1.)

c **1440** *Pallad. on Husb.* I. 395 Bordis of cipresse Playn & direct, vpsette hem in their kynde A foote atwyn. **1513** DOUGLAS *Æneid* XI. i. 15 Ane akin tre..Apone a motys hycht vpset hes he. **1608** TOPSELL *Serpents* 26 The serpent fierce ..rough scales vpsetteth that were deiected.

†**b.** To establish. *Obs.*⁻¹

1559 in R. Keith *Hist. Ch. & St. Scot.* (1734) 111 To advance the Glory of God, by maintaining and upsetting true Preachers of the Word.

c. *techn.* To force back the end of (a metal bar, etc.) by hammering or beating, esp. when heated.

1677 MOXON *Mech. Exerc.* i. 11 You may Up-set it, that is, take a Flame Heat, and set the heated end upright upon the Anvil, and hammer upon the cold end till the Heated end be beat or up-set into the Body of your Work. **1688** HOLME *Armoury* III. 88/2 *Up-set*, is when at a heat the Iron is beaten back into the Body of the work. **1841** *Penny Cycl.* XX. 156/2 Wire ropes may be..secured at their ends by passing them through the small end of a conical collar, and doubling up, or upsetting, the ends of the wires. **1869** SANDBERG tr. *Styffe's Iron & Steel* 11 The author 'upset' or stubbed the bars at the ends. **1884** C. G. W. LOCK *Workshop Receipts* Ser. III. 286/2 A pick should never be 'upset', or hammered endwise.

d. *Agric.* To ridge up.

1764 *Museum Rust.* III. 321 Fifth ploughing, sowing earth, up-set it, and harrowing.

e. Usu. **upsett.** (Pa. t. and pa. ppl. also **upsetted.**) (*a*) To bend upwards (a stake) plaited into the base of a basket to form part of the frame for the side; (*b*) to form the 'upset' of (a basket); also *absol.*

1875 *Encycl. Brit.* III. 423/1 Osiers..are forced or 'scallumed', between the rods of the bottom from the edge towards the centre, and are turned up, 'upset', in the direction of the sides. **1907** T. OKEY in *Jrnl. Soc. Arts* 11 Jan. 190/2 If a foot is needed it is now put on by inserting the tops cut off from the stakes alongside the upsetted stakes. **1912** —— *Art of Basket-Making* vi. 33 Very coarse work.. is upsetted with a pair instead of a wale. **1945** H. J. MASSINGHAM *Wisdom of Fields* v. 94 My basketer..after 'scalluming' the foreign rods..proceeded to wale up the sides, 'upsetting' as it is called, that is to say, building up the frame. **1977** B. MAYNARD *Basketry* 19/2 Stake up with the 40 side stakes, nip them at the edge of the base and tie them together tightly at the top... Upsett with six rounds of waling with No. 6 cane keeping the sides quite vertical.

2. †**a.** *Sc.* To make good, make up for; to get over, recover from (a loss, etc.). *Obs.*

1513 DOUGLAS *Æneid* Direct. 33 God grant I may amend it, With grace and space to vpset this tynsell. **1557** *Extr. Aberd. Reg.* (1844) I. 305 Gif ony dampnage cumis thairthrow,..that the said Gilbert be..obleist to vpsett the same. **1593** *Sc. Acts, Jas. VI* (1816) IV. 26/2 þe said morowing gift, sa faithfullie..promesit to be vpsett and maid guid. **1606** ROLLOCK *Lect. 2 Thess.* 53 The lose thou getst by deceite wil neuer be vpset. **1806** A. DOUGLAS *Poems* 123 Folk as stout an' clever..Hae gotten skaith they never Upset for mony year.

b. To restore to good or usual condition. *Obs.* exc. *dial.*

a **1652** BROME *City Wit* III. i. (1653) C 8, When she failes by diseases or paine, The Doctor new Vamps and upsets her againe. **1905** in *Eng. Dial. Dict.* s.v., *Cor[nwall]*. Two men went up the hill upsetting [= reviving] the fire.

3. *intr.* Of a cylindrical bullet: To become bent.

1859 'STONEHENGE' *Shot-Gun* 306 A pointed cylinder soon 'upsets', as it is termed, and is then at once rendered useless as a projectile. [Cf. UPSETTING *vbl. sb.* 1 e.]

II. 4. *intr.* To be overturned or capsized.

Said of a vehicle, boat, etc., or of persons in it.

1799 T. KNIGHT *Turnpike-gate* II. iii, If the horses had not run so fast we should not have upset. **1820** MOORE *Mem.* (1853) III. 116 If there came the slightest breath of wind, they would upset with so many on board. **1889** JEROME *Three Men in Boat* iii, The boat..will not be so liable to upset.

5. a. *trans.* To overturn; to capsize; to knock over.

In this or the next sense called 'a low word' by Todd (1818).

1803 REES *Cycl.*, *Capsize*, in Naval Language, to upset or turn over anything. **1808** JAMIESON s.v., To upset a cart, boat, &c. **1813** SOUTHEY *Nelson* I. 15 It was with the utmost difficulty that the crew could prevent them from staving or upsetting her. **1852** MRS. STOWE *Uncle Tom's C.* vii. 45 One luckless wight contrived to upset the gravy. **1871** JOWETT *Plato* II. 43 The light active boxer upsetting two stout gentlemen.

fig. **1883** *Pall Mall G.* 26 Oct., If the Control had done more it might have upset the apple-cart altogether.

b. To involve (persons) in the accidental overturning of a vehicle or boat. Chiefly in *passive.*

1807 SOUTHEY *Espriella's Lett.* II. 192 Had we been.. overtaken by storms and upset in the lake. **1819** MOORE *Mem.* (1853) II. 345 Very nearly upset by the horse backing down the hill. **1832** A. W. FONBLANQUE *Eng. under 7 Administr.* (1837) II. 206 'He then built him another [vessel], ..which he succeeded in setting afloat.'..'Aye, and it nearly upset him..at sea.' **1867** P'CESS ALICE *Mem.* (1884) 176 Mme. d'Usedom..was lately upset with her carriage off the road.

c. *fig.* To overthrow, undo, put out of joint.

1818 MOORE *Mem.* (1853) II. 221 Very natural, but very likely to upset the whole concern. **1859** W. COLLINS *Q. of Hearts* iii, She..upset every one of our calculations on the first day of her arrival. **1884** SIR H. COTTON in *Law Times Rep.* LI. 277/1 A witness who is coming..to assist the plaintiff in upsetting..a fraudulent scheme.

6. a. To throw into mental disorder or discomposure; to trouble or distress.

1805 BLACKWOOD in Nicolas *Nelson's Disp.* (1846) VII. 224, I never was so shocked or so completely upset as..to find that Lord Nelson was even then at the gasp of Death. **1857** TROLLOPE *Barchester T.* III. 116 Eleanor..was a good deal upset, as people say, and could not at the moment collect herself. **1885** *Law Times* 7 Feb. 270/2 Deceased appeared very irritable upon the morning in question, but witness knew of nothing to upset him.

b. To disorder physically.

1845 BUDD *Dis. Liver* 261 A young person, delicate, and easily upset by any imprudence in diet. **1889** MRS. E. KENNARD *Landing a Prize* x, The least thing upset his liver.

Hence **up'setment; up'settable** *a.*; **up'settal.**

1893 *Standard* 10 Mar., For this *upsetment too, nothing would be gained. [Cf. w. Somerset (1888) *upsotment*, 'disturbance, break up'.] **1890** *Sat. Rev.* 4 Oct. 386/1 Persons *upsettable..at their own peril. **1890** *Graphic* 11 Oct. 406/1 Never a little finger did I put to help in his *upsettal.

up'set, *pa. pple.* and *ppl. a.* [UP- 5. Cf. prec. and WFris. *opset*, Norw. *uppsett*, Da. *opsat*, Sw. *uppsatt*.]

1. a. Set up, erected, raised up, etc.

1838 R. BRUNNE *Chron.* (1810) 70 Now is he in þe see with saile on mast vpsette. **1390** GOWER *Conf.* II. 204 Ther scholde be tofore his bed A bord upset and faire spred. *c* **1400** tr. *Secreta Secret., Gov. Lordsh.* 108 Trees þat hauyn yu hem many braunches and rotes, and þe stoke vpsette. **1430–40** LYDG. *Bochas* IX. 23 Ful of idoles upset on hihe stages. **1513** DOUGLAS *Æneid* II. iii. 53 Scharslie the statw was in thair temple wpset, Quhen all hir membris bittir teris swet. **1658** A. FOX *Würtz' Surg.* III. xii. 253 An upset hand is sooner bowed, than a hand which hangeth down, to be set upright. **1824** MACTAGGART *Gallovid. Encycl.* 362 Puir Girzey, wi' her upset chin.

†**b.** *upset mouth*, = UPSET *sb.* 3 a. *Obs.*

1580 BLUNDEVIL *Art of Riding* III. xxvii. 54 The square ports, otherwise called vpset mouthes. **1607** MARKHAM *Cavel.* II. 52 He..for a more libertie to the tongue, giueth allowance to the cannon, with the vpset mouth. *Ibid.* 64 Others to these vpset mouthes, haue added..a strong trench.

2. Of price: Stated as the lowest sum for which property exposed to auction will be sold; named as the sum from which bidding may start. Orig. *Sc.* and *U.S.*

1814 *Act. 54 Geo. III*, c. 137 §42 The Price..shall not be less than the last upset Price at which it had been exposed to public Sale. **1815** SCOTT *Guy M.* xiv, Mr. Glossin offered the upset price for the lands and barony of Ellangowan. **1834** *Spectator* 8 Nov. 1066/1 The price at which land [in U.S.] is..sold, varies from the upset price to many pounds sterling per acre. **1866** VENESS *El Dorado* App. 178 All Crown lands [in S. Australia] are open to purchase at the upset price of £1 per acre. **1884** *Public Opinion* 3 Oct. 434/2 The mansion, park, and home farm..were bought in, the highest bid..being considerably under the upset price.

3. Overturned, capsized. *upset race* (see quot. 1876).

1842 C. WHITEHEAD *R. Savage* (1845) I. x. 135 He..threw him over the upset table. **1876** *Encycl. Brit.* IV. 812/2 Canoes for 'upset races' (where the canoeist has to jump out, tow his boat while swimming, and then get in). **1882** *Daily News* 3 July 5/2 An upset hansom is a rare thing.

4. Physically disordered: said esp. of the stomach.

1973 C. LEACH *Send-Off* iii. 26 All you get is a burned back and an upset tummy. **1980** J. GARDNER *Garden of Weapons* III. iii. 249 Hoffer had sent him back because of his upset stomach.

up set down, obs. form of UPSIDE DOWN.

upsete: see UP- 5.

up'settable, *a.* [f. UPSET *v.* + -ABLE.] Capable of being upset.

1930 R. C. HUTCHINSON *Thou Last Devil* xii. 167 He was, of course, in an upsettable mood. **1958** J. CANNAN *And be a Villain* vi. 145 'Hugh is..the most upsettable.' 'Couldn't agree more,' said Laura, 'thirteen's too young for funerals.' **1973** J. ELSOM *Erotic Theatre* iii. 53 In the dialogue, he tiptoes around the subject with the clumsy concern of Bertie Wooster, surrounded by upsettable coffee tables.

up'setter. [UP- 8. Cf. UPSET *v.*]

†**1.** *Sc.* One who 'sets up' as a master workman. (Cf. UPSET *sb.* 2.) *Obs.*⁻¹

1518 *Perth Hammermen Bk.* (1889) 2 He sall pay..till his upset six markis. And gif the upsetter be ane outman he sall pay sex markis.

2. †**a.** *Sc.* One who posts up a placard. *Obs.*⁻¹

1567 *Sc. Acts, Mary* (1814) II. 552/1 The first Inventar, writtar, tynar, and vpsettar of the samin.

†**b.** *Sc.* A founder or establisher. *Obs.*

1581 HAMILTON in *Cath. Tractates* (S.T.S.) 84 Thir Caluinian ministers, quha louit so heichlie thair vpsetters. **1581** BURNE *Ibid.* 162 The hail hous of the Hamiltonis..was the cheif vpsettar, and protector of his hæresie.

c. A repairer of stocking-frames.

1839 URE *Dict. Arts* 653 A set of men employed in this [hosiery] trade, and distinguished by the name of upsetters.

d. Part of a tire-shortening machine.

1875 KNIGHT *Dict. Mech.* 2581/2 A machine for upsetting, cutting, and punching tires. The upper figure shows the upsetter.

†**3.** *Sc.* A support or prop. *Obs.*

1628 *Maitl. Cl. Misc.* III. 371 For sex knopis to the gairden ȝettis with sevin upsetteris to the ordinance. **1644** *Papers Army Solemn League & Cov.* (S.H.S.) 34 Stanes for upsetters twelve.

4. One who upsets, overturns, disarranges, etc.

1836 DICKENS *Sk. Boz, Our Parish* xviii, The volunteer driver of the hackney coach..and the involuntary upsetter of the whole party. **1859** MEREDITH *R. Feverel* xxix, The upsetter of ordinary calculations. **1886** MACQUOID *J. Wentworth* xviii, Willie had usually been the upsetter of her peace.

up'setting, *vbl. sb.* [UP- 7. Cf. UPSET *v.*]

I. †**1. a.** The action of setting up or erecting. *Obs.*

c **1449** PECOCK *Repr.* II. iv. 156 The hauyng, and the vpsetting of ymagis. **1507** *Acc. Ld. High Treas. Scotl.* III. 261 For prenes to the pailȝoun and upsetting of it, x d. **1525** *Reg. Mag. Sig. Scot.* 96 Ilk man of the said craft that settis up ane buth sall pay 40 schillingis at thare buth upsetting.

†**b.** *Sc.* The action of raising to, or establishing in, position or power. *Obs.*

1470 in Ellis *Orig. Lett.* I. 133 He..confessed that he was cawser of the upsetynge of the Kynge of England that now is. **1560** *Maitl. Cl. Misc.* III. 224 For avancement and upsetting of the Kingdome and glorie of God. **1570** BUCHANAN *Admon.* Wks. (1892) 27 In doun putting of thevis and upsetting of justice. **1669** R. FLEMING *Fulfill. Script.* (1671) I. 151 The Roman empire mouldred down for Antichrist's upsetting. **1748** E. ERSKINE *Serm.* (1755) 327 What a pleasant Upsetting of Christ, and his Kingdom, would it be, to see him [etc.].

c. *Agric.* (See quot.)

1785 A. YOUNG *Annals Agric.* II. 442, I saw them ploughing their fallows;..they do not ridge up, what is called up-setting in some parts, that is, raising the centers much higher than the furrows.

d. *techn.* (See quots. and UPSET *v.* 1 c.)

1815 J. SMITH *Panorama Sci. & Art* I. 11 When it is required to thicken any part of a bar of iron without welding, the operation called upsetting must be resorted to. **1831–3** *Encycl. Metrop.* (1845) VIII. 24 Having heated his iron rod, and thickened it by a process..called *upsetting.* **1875** KNIGHT *Dict. Mech.* 2684/1 Shortening [a] tire, to enable it to bind the fellies more firmly, is called upsetting.

e. (See quot. and UPSET *v.* 3.)

1859 'STONEHENGE' *Shot-Gun* 306 By upsetting is to be understood the turning sideways of an elongated ball.

f. The action of raising or building up. *nonce-use.*

1882 BESANT *All Sorts* xxviii. (1898) 191 The younger men..were quite sure.. that with a little more upsetting and downpulling the balance would be set right.

g. *Basketry.* = UPSET *sb.* 3 c; the formation of this.

1924 C. CRAMPTON *Canework* 13 *Upsetting*, the three or four rows [of weaving] worked at the commencement of the side..to 'set' the stakes in order. **1937** A. H. CRAMPTON *Raffia Wk. & Basketry* II. ii. 44 The first row of upsetting is worked with four canes, each passing in front of three stakes and behind one. **1953** A. G. KNOCK *Willow Basket-Wk.* 20 The number of rounds of waling forming the upsetting should, in fine basket-work, never be less than two, and seldom less than three. **1964** H. HODGES *Artifacts* x. 146 Waling was frequently used at the base of baskets in order to hold the upright stakes securely..in which case it is.. referred to as upsetting.

†**2.** = UPSITTING *vbl. sb.* 1. Also *attrib. Obs.*

1501 *Acc. Ld. High Treas. Scotl.* (1900) II. 41 Giffin to the Maister Cuke that he bocht in Edinburgh to the ladyis upsetting fest,..viijs. **1676** COLES, *Up-setting-time*, when the Child-bed woman gets up. **1746** *Exmoor Courtship* (E.D.S.) 380 You werent so skittish..up to Darathy Vuzz's Up-setting. **1814** *Monthly Mag.* Sept. 126/2 *Upsetting*, christening... [A word] peculiar to Exmoor.

†**3.** The action of setting up in a trade or occupation. *Obs.*

1569 *Wills & Inv. N.C.* (Surtees, 1835) 301 Eyther at ye daye of his upsetting to his science or at the daye of his mariaidge. **1640** [SHIRLEY] *Capt. Underwit* IV. v, The musick at a Convocation of Catts upon a witches upsetting.

4. *Sc.* An attempt to set oneself up above others; undue assumption of superiority or superior airs.

1821 GALT *Ann. Parish* xxix, Partly with upsetting, and partly by the eating rust of family pride. **1823** —— *Entail* lxiv, I declare if e'er I heard the like of sic upsetting.

II. 5. a. The action of overturning, or fact of being overturned.

1819 MOORE *Mem.* (1853) III. 85 Two men on each side of our carriage all the way, to keep it from upseting. **1820** WORDSW. in C. Wordsw. *Mem.* (1851) II. 103 Of these, one ..was drowned..by the upsetting of a boat in a storm. **1860** *Builder* 14 Jan. 31/2 Brickwork..thrown down by the accidental upsetting of a water-tank. **1873** MRS BROOKFIELD *Not a Heroine* I. 218 It was an accident—the upsetting of a cart.

b. The action of overthrowing, demolishing, etc.

1827 WORDSW. in C. Wordsw. *Mem.* (1851) II. 21 The upsetting of so diabolical a system as Buonaparte's. **1841** S. WARREN *Ten Thousand a Year* I. vi, The dismal upsetting of his hopes. **1860** GEN. P. THOMPSON *Audi Alt. Part.* III. cxli. 121 All the danger attending the upsetting a nest of thieves.

c. A dislocation, disturbance, upset.

1847 HALLIWELL, *Upsetting*, a disagreement; a quarrel. *South.* **1881, 1887** in Isle of Wight and Kent glossaries. **1884** *Manch. Exam.* 25 Nov. 5/2 We have two or three agitations and upsettings when one would have sufficed.

up'setting, *ppl. a.* [UP- 6 b. Cf. UPSET *v.*]

1. *Sc.* Presumptuous; unduly aspiring, ambitious, or forward.

1818 SCOTT *Rob Roy* xxxvi, That lang-tongued, conceited, upsetting serving-man o' yours. **1822** GALT *Provost* xlii, He was by nature and inclination one of the

upsetting sort. 1854 ['SARAH TYTLER'] *P. Millar* 151 Their poor upsetting attempts at gentility.
Comb. 1824 MISS FERRIER *Inher.* lxvi, He's a proud, upsetting-like puppy.

2. Overturning, overthrowing, disturbing, etc.
1872 BAGEHOT *Physics & Pol.* v. 163 A new idea..is, as common people say, so 'upsetting'. 1899 *Westm. Gaz.* 8 June 2/2 A most upsetting amendment to the Service Franchise Bill.

up'settingly, *adv.* [f. UPSETTING *ppl. a.* + -LY².] In an upsetting manner; distressingly.
1926 'L. MALET' *Dogs of Want* vi. 155 Barbara Heritage's graceful silhouette had, somehow, become interchangeable with that of the Margate peroxide blonde of ten years back. Most upsettingly, but, also, most unjustifiably so. 1981 *Washington Post* 26 Apr. H9/1 To traditionalists it is upsettingly disheveled chaos.

up'settingness. [f. as prec. + -NESS.] The quality of being upsetting or disturbing.
1922 *Glasgow Herald* 23 Feb. 6/8, I have heard an old man speak with asperity of the 'upsettingness' of one who had adopted 'Mac', which his father had not used. 1949 G. RYLE *Concept of Mind* iv. 93 The degrees of upsettingness..are ordinarily characterised as degrees of violence. 1977 'M. INNES' *Honeybath's Haven* xviii. 167 He had taken the reason to have been simply the general upsettingness of Melissa's turning up on them in that restaurant in Rome.

upsey-: see UPSY.

'upshift, *sb.* Chiefly *U.S.* [UP- 2.] A movement upwards (esp. in various devices); *spec.* a change to a higher gear in a motor vehicle.
1839 URE *Dict. Arts* 833 The line over s, represents the down-shift, and d' the up-shift [of a vein]. 1951 W. K. TOBOLDT et al. *Automatic Transmissions* iv. 129 The point of upshift from second to third and from third to fourth is excessively high. 1967 D. G. HAYS *Introd. Computational Linguistics* iv. 65 In standard paper-tape machines, a single capital letter is represented by three frames of tape, one for *upshift*, one for the character, and one for *downshift*. 1978 L. PRYOR *Viper* (1979) ix. 175, I missed one upshift and smashed gears.

'upshift, *v.* Chiefly *U.S.* [UP- 4.] *intr.* To change into higher gear in a motor vehicle. Also used of the gear itself. Cf. SHIFT *v.* 12e. Hence **'upshifting** *vbl. sb.*
1956 W. H. CROUSE *Automotive Mechanics* (ed. 3) xxiv. 513/2 If the brake band is released and at the same time the clutch is applied, the planetary set upshifts or goes into direct drive. *Ibid.* 515/2 Upshifting is controlled by both throttle opening and car speed. 1979 *Truck & Bus Transportation* 31 July 25/2 The flexibility..covers up an out-of-sequence ratio gap between 3rd and 4th gears. It is not at all apparent when upshifting..but it is noticeable when changing down.

'upshoot, *sb.* [UP- 2.]
1. = UPSHOT *sb.* 4. *Obs.* exc. *dial.*
1588 SHAKS. *L.L.L.* IV. i. 138 Then will shee get the vpshoot by cleauing the pin. 1603 HOLLAND *Plutarch's Mor.* 258 That the chife point of cunning and perfection was in the up-shoot and end of all. 1624 HEYWOOD *Captives* II. i, Hee no questione, That sett mee on to compasse this my will, May when the up-shoote comes assist mee still. 1887 *S. Cheshire Gloss.* 418 Th' upshoot on [= of] it.
2. The act of shooting up or the result of this; an upward rush (*of* something).
1850 W. HOWITT *Year-Bk. of Country* iv. 172 His oaks and elms in his park..what are they but the towering upshoots of his prejudices? 1866 ALGER *Solit. Nat. & Man.* I. 25 A palm, in its resistless upshoot, cleaving altar and image. 1890 *Nature* 9 Jan. 228/2 If the individual is the mere ..upshoot from the continuous root of ancestral plasm. 1898 *Columbus* (Ohio) *Dispatch* 29 Mar. 12/4 The upshoot of flame..was well forward.

up'shoot, *v.* [UP- 4. Cf. WFris. *opsjitte*, Du. *opschieten*, LG. *upschêten*, G. *aufschiessen*.]
1. *intr.* To spring or grow up. Also **up'shooting** *pres. pple.*
1590 SPENSER *F.Q.* II. xii. 58 The painted flowres, the trees vpshooting hye. 1841 CAMPBELL *Child & Hind* iv, Where Elysian meadows smile, And noble trees upshoot. 1842 TENNYSON *Day-Dream, Sleeping Palace* vi, All round a hedge upshoots. 1876 BLACKIE *Songs Relig. & Life* 4 Like a star in strength upshooting.
2. *trans.* and *refl.* To send or raise up.
1804 W. L. BOWLES *Spir. Discov.* IV. 332 A beauteous tree upshoots amid the glade Its trembling top. 1856 HAWTHORNE *Eng. Note-bks.* (1870) II. 166 A beautiful sheet of water, and a fountain upshooting itself. 1872 BLACKIE *Lays Highl.* 89 Here erect..The Buchail More upshoots his Titan cone.

'up,shooting, *ppl. a.* (UP- 6b. Cf. prec.)
1869 J. PHILLIPS *Vesuv.* ix. 265 The often expanding stream of upshooting stones.

upshore: see UP- 4.

'upshot, *sb.* [UP- 2. Cf. UPSHOOT *sb.* 1, -SHUT.]
†1. A final shot in a match at archery; chiefly *fig.*, a closing or parting shot. *Obs.*
1531 *Privy Purse Exp. Hen. VIII* (1827) 143 Item [paid] to the same Coton for one up shotte that he wanne of the kinges grace, vj s. viij d. 1575 LANEHAM *Let.* (1871) 54 Wel, to this number of biniteez, take ye one mo for an vpshot, & heer an eend. 1589 NASHE *Anat. Absurd.* Ep. Ded. 4 Euery man shotte his bolte, but this was the vpshot, that England afforded many mediocrities. 1597 HOOKER *Eccl. Pol.* v. lxv. §12 As for their last vpshot of all towards this marke, they are of opinion [etc.]. 1614 JACKSON *Creed* III. i. §13 As it were for an vp-shot to all the fooles thunderbolts they had let flie before. 1618 BOLTON *Florus* (1636) 56 That event which vertue was about to have given heere, for an upshot, or clozing Victory, fortune gave.
†2. A mark or end aimed at. *Obs.*
1591 SPENSER *M. Hubberd* 770 The onely vpshot whereto he doth ayme. 1595 *Locrine* III. ii. 45 Our regall minde, Which aimes at nothing but a golden crowne, The only vpshot of mine enterprises. 1610 HEALEY *St. Aug. Citie of God* A 3b, They could not come to the vpshotte of their desires but in the time of warre. 1660 H. MORE *Myst. Godl.* IV. ix. 121 The Ephesians erecting the Image of Hercules.., which is a sign that Pagan Idolatry was the upshot of the plot. 1754 SHERLOCK *Disc.* i. 21 The Upshot of all Religion is to please God.
†3. An end, conclusion, or termination. *Obs.*
*c*1580 STANYHURST *Æneis*, etc. (Arb.) 152 Vertuus he liued, through grace that vertuus eended. What may be then better, than a godly and gratius vpshot? 1595 SOUTHWELL *St. Peter's Compl.*, etc. 55 Death cals her vp, shame driues her out, Despaires her vp-shot make. *a*1617 BAYNE *On Eph.* (1658) 70 Through fear of death the upshot of evils. 1639 S. DU VERGER tr. *Camus' Admir. Events* 73 To cast him into his grave, and to make a ridiculous upshot of his life. 1662 HIBBERT *Body Divinity* II. 113 They were sung at the departure of the people out of the temple, for an upshot to their divine service.
†b. The climax or completion *of* something.
1586 T. B. *La Primaud. Fr. Acad.* I. 17 For the upshot and perfection of all happines and felicitie in this world.
c. The extreme limit. Also *attrib.*
1669 BOYER *Dict. Royal* II. s.v., A gay Coat and a Grimace is the upshot of what he can pretend to. 1838 DE QUINCEY *Wks.* (1890) XII. 158 We account it frailty that threescore years and ten make the upshot of man's pleasurable existence. 1864 *Field* 23 July 62/1 The odds in this instance were of a more moderate character than those ventured at Liverpool, 4 to 1 being her upshot price.
4. The result, issue, or conclusion (*of* some course of action, etc.).
In very frequent use from *c* 1830.
1604 SHAKS. *Ham.* v. ii. 395 So shall you heare..Of accidentall iudgements,..And in this vpshot, purposes mistooke. 1620 VENNER *Via Recta* iv. 82 You shall commonly see..a dropsey to be the vpshot of all their outragious drinkings. 1649 MILTON *Eikon.* xviii. 166 Hee sought them onely, as by the upshot appeard, to get opportunities. 1680 C. NESSE *Church Hist.* 323 The upshot of all was, our Lord vanquished the devil. 1737 WHISTON *Josephus, Wars* v. xi. 6 The Jews..prevented the upshot of the battle, and retired into the city. 1782 MISS BURNEY *Cecilia* v. xii, Suppose a man was to talk in that manner when he's doing business, what would be the upshot? 1834 PRINGLE *Afr. Sk.* xi. 341 The upshot was, that I found myself overwhelmed with debts. 1856 MERIVALE *Rom. Emp.* xlvi. V. 289 The senators had been growing uneasy, not knowing what upshot to anticipate. 1887 T. A. TROLLOPE *What I remember* I. xvii. 347 A council..was called, the upshot of which was that our two..allies decided to return to Dover.
b. The conclusion resulting from the premises of an argument.
1639 F. B. tr. *Balzac's Lett.* (vol. IV) 174 This is the upshot of all,..that you must lay a foundation of Bounty. 1677 W. HUGHES *Man of Sin* III. iv. 142 The Upshot..must necessarily come to this, that The Pope is certainly the Man of Sin. 1710 BERKELEY *Princ. Hum. Knowl.* §75 Yet the upshot of all is—that there are certain unknown Ideas in the mind of God. 1768 FOOTE *Devil* III. Wks. 1799 II. 269 Putting that and t'other together, my notion of the upshot is, that..you must have been born there. 1799 KIRWAN *Geol. Ess.* 496 The upshot of my argument was simply this.
5. In phrases: **a.** *in* (rarely *at*, †*upon*) *the upshot*, in the end, at last. †Also const. *of*.
(*a*) 1577 HARRISON *England* III. vii. (1878) II. 28 He..killed them [*sc.* deer] with his hands in the vpshot of that exercise and end of his recreation. 1600 HOLLAND *Livy* XXI. xiv. 401 A cruell commaundement,..but yet needfull, as afterwards it was well seene in the end and upshot of all. 1634 W. TIRWHYT tr. *Balzac's Lett.* (vol. I) 130 We shall in the upshot see them remove mountaines. 1675 ALSOP *Anti-Sozzo* 695 We may be sure that all come to this in the Up shot. 1732 BERKELEY *Alciphr.* VII. §24 In the upshot, I apprehend you will find it impracticable to destroy all sense of religion. 1768 TUCKER *Lt. Nat.* (1834) I. 37 The service I may do will rise to the same amount in the upshot. 1837 LOCKHART *Scott* I. v. 145 Good for the higher faculties themselves in the upshot. 1854 DE QUINCEY *Wks.* (1889) II. 184 In the upshot, this conclusion *eventuated* (to speak Yankeeishly), that purely on principles of..universal philanthropy could Coleridge have meditated..the insult.
(*b*) 1617 MORYSON *Itin.* II. 118 It was probable that the King of Spaine would doe something now at the vpshot. *a*1628 PRESTON *Mt. Ebal* (1638) 48 They shall pay deere for it at the last upshot. 1714 POPE *Let.* 13 July, Wks. 1751 VII. 204 At the upshot, after a life of perpetual application, you reflect [etc.]. 1823 BENTHAM *Not Paul* 81 To apprehend him for the purpose of trying him, and probably at the upshot killing him.
(*c*) 1699 BOYER, Upon the upshot,..*aprés tout.* 1709 O. DYKES *English Proverbs* 145 Malice, Spite, and Envy, are always Self-Murderers upon the Upshot. 1796 CHARLOTTE SMITH *Marchmont* I. 207 Upon the upshot it appears..that he was deeper in for it than any body thought for.
b. *to bring, come*, etc., *to the* (or *an*) *upshot*, to bring to, arrive at, a final or decisive point.
*a*1600 EDMONDS *Observ. Cæsar's Comm.* (1604) 35 To the end he might bring the matter to a speedy vpshot. 1601 SHAKS. *Twel. N.* IV. ii. 76, I cannot pursue with any safety this sport to the vppeshot. 1646 TRAPP *Comm. John* vii. 50 How far had Judas outstripped Nicodemus till it came to the upshot! 1728 EARL OF AILESBURY *Mem.* (1890) 463 When it came to the upshot he..had all burnt.
†**c.** *at an upshot*, at an end. *Obs.*
1653 tr. *Stegmann's Brevis Disq.* i. 1 If they once obtain that their Church..is such a Judge..., the whole businesse is at an upshot.
6. †**a.** *slang.* ? A riotous frolic. *Obs.*
1811 *Lexicon Balatronicum* Pref., They may..abuse their less spirited companions, who prefer a good dinner at home to a glorious up-shot in the highway, without the hazard of a cudgelling.
b. *dial.* A merry-making, a feast.
1837 *Penny Cycl.* VIII. 223/2 Cumbrian peasantry have various festive meetings, called the *kirn*,..sheep-shearing, merry nights, and upshots.

upshot, *ppl. a.* (UP- 5a.)
1847 SURTEES *Hawbuck Grange* xi. 211 Breaking an upshot column of smoke against his hat brim.

up'shots, *adv.* [Cf. UPSHOT *sb.* and UPSIDES *adv.*] (*to be*) *upshots* (*with*), = UPSIDES *adv.* a.
1877 H. SMART *Bound to Win* I. iii. 61 A rigid resolve to be upshots with Jim Laceby should the opportunity be vouchsafed him.

'upshut, obs. or dial. var. UPSHOT *sb.*
1620 FORD *Linea V.* 69 This King of men is substitute to his King with this vpshut [etc.]. 1658 A. FOX tr. *Würtz' Surg.* I. ii. 3 In the upshut it proveth meerly an accustomed thing. 1887 *S. Cheshire Gloss.* 418 The form *upshut* is still used in Dorset.

up'shutter. (UP- 8.)
1809 in *Spirit Pub. Jrnls.* XIII. 81 Thou foe to all fun, thou up-shutter of shops.

upsidaisy ('ʌpsə,deɪzɪ), *int. colloq.* Also **oops-a-daisy, ups(e)y-daisy** (*dial.* **upsa daesy**), **ups-a-daisy, upsy daisy**, etc. [A fanciful variant of the earlier UP-A-DAISY.] (See quot. 1862.) Also in extended use.
1862 [C. C. ROBINSON] *Dial. Leeds* 442 *Upsa daesy!* a common ejaculation when a child, in play, is assisted in a spring-leap from the ground. 1904 *Sat. Rev.* 4 June 713/2 There is little Freddy waiting..to be lifted—'upsidaisy'—into his perambulator. 1912 J. SANDILANDS *Western Canad. Dict. & Phrase-Bk.*, *Ups-a-daisy*, the tender words of the fond father when engaged in baby-jumping. 1934 D. L. SAYERS *Nine Tailors* I. ii. 61 Hoops-a-daisy, over she goes! 1940 *Horizon* Mar. 204 Come on, sonny, that's the way! Upsy-daisy! 1948 'P. QUENTIN' *Run to Death* xx. 153 'Upsy-daisy.' I picked her up, swung round and dumped her in the bath-tub. 1953 C. S. FORESTER *Hornblower & Atropos* 76 'There baby', said the landlady. 'Daddy's going to play with you. Oops-a-daisy, then.' 1967 PARTRIDGE *Dict. Slang* Suppl. 1277/2 *Oops-a-daisy!*, a c.p. [*sc.* catch phrase] of consolation as one picks up a child that has fallen. 1969 'I. DRUMMOND' *Man with Tiny Head* vii. 92 'Upsidaisy,' said Jenny. 'No time to waste.' 1970 K. GILES *Death in Church* viii. 190 'Ooops a-daisy,' said the gunman and the Inspector was hurled to the twelve-feet-high ceiling. 1974 N. FREELING *Dressing of Diamond* 173 He..smacked Colette lightly on the bottom, and said, 'Oops-a-daisy, girl: half-time.' 1976 *South Notts Echo* 16 Dec. 6/5 Only a series of oops-a-daisy mishaps, how-ever, persuaded him to slim down in time. 1984 *New Yorker* 13 Feb. 125/1 The Great Rudner is..given the most labyrinthine acrobatic choreography—a tortuous series of slithers, blind leaps, upsy-daisy lifts, and ass-over-heels floorwork.
Hence *ellipt.* as **'upsa** (and varr.) *int.*
1922 JOYCE *Ulysses* 491 Hoopsa! Don't fall upstairs. 1928 E. M. FORSTER *Life to Come* (1972) 141 'Upsa! Take care!' 'Upsa!' were some drops of brandy, which Conway had spilt.

'upside. Also **up-side.** [UP- 1. Cf. Da. *opside.*]
1. The upper side or surface (*of* a thing); the upper half or part.
1611 COTGR., *Reboursant*,..turning, or standing inside outward, or the vpside downe. 1654 in E. B. Jupp *Carpenters' Co.* (1887) 316 Two foote 6 inches from the vpside of the trusse to the vpside of the floore. 1678 MOXON *Mech. Ex.* iv. 65 Till the whole upside of the Stuff be Plained. 1706 SWIFT *Baucis & Philemon* 59 With the upside down, to show Its inclination for below. 1833- [see DOWNSIDE *sb.*]. 1842 J. AITON *Clerical Econ.* 177 It should then be..put into a dry cloth with the upside down. 1867 MRS. WHITNEY *L. Goldthwaite* v, This glass is in such a horrid light! I don't seem to have but half a face, and I can't tell which is the upside of that!
2. *upside of*, above, beyond.
1890 *N. & Q.* 26 July 73/1 People whose ages are up-side of forty.
3. (See UP *a.* 2b.) Also *attrib.*
1880 *Daily News* 13 Dec. 6/7 The upside road [of the railway]..was quite clear. 1898 *Westm. Gaz.* 11 Nov. 7/3 The crowd that thronged the up-side of the station.
4. *Comm.* An upward movement of share prices, etc.; also = *upside potential.* Also as *adj.*, esp. ***upside potential***, the possibility of (gain from) such a rise in value.
1961 in WEBSTER. 1969 *Punch* 5 Feb. 206/1 The share price..needs to improve by only 50 per cent... Likewise, your original upside potential would be considerably higher. 1977 R. E. MEGILL *Introd. Risk Analysis* xvi. 175 Most parameters have up-side and down-side possibilities in addition to a most probable value. 1983 *Sunday Tel.* 27 Feb. 20/7 The share price..is vulnerable to even the most modest of bear rumour and..the downside substantially exceeds the upside. 1983 *Observer* 29 May 19/1 Could Pilkington Brothers..be poised to meet that dream investment criterion—downside risk low; upside potential high? 1984 *Times* 18 June 17/3 The upside should again be approximate yield parity with the equity market.
5. Quasi-*adv.* (or *prep.*): ***upside*** (one's) ***head***, ***knot***, (of a blow) on the head; esp. ***to go upside*** (someone's) ***head***, etc., to strike on the head; to attack or fight. Chiefly *U.S. Blacks'.*
1970 H. E. ROBERTS *Third Ear* 14/2 *Upside one's head*, to fight someone. 1971 *Black Scholar* Apr.-May 35/2 This is until a white cop comes up and go upside your knot. 1973 E. BULLINS *Theme is Blackness* 6 The TV slap of a pigstick upside some sister's head in front of an Alabama courthouse. 1976 *New Yorker* 8 Mar. 33/3 There is a further penalty of a hit upside the head for stiffing the toll collector. 1978 J.

WAMBAUGH *Black Marble* iv. 28 When I busted her old man that time he went upside her head with a meat mallet.

,upside 'down, *adv.*, *sb.*, and *a.* Forms: *α.* 4–5 up (5 upe, uppe) so doun (don, doune; 4 *north.* up swa doune), 4–6 up so down (5–6 downe). *β.* 4 upsa-, 5 opsadoun; 4–6 upsedoun (5 -done), 5–6 -downe. *γ.* 6 up set doune; up (uppe) set (sette) downe. *δ.* 6 upsyde downe, upside doune (downe), 6– upside down. *ε.* 6–7 vpsidown(e, 6 upsidowne, 6 upsy(e)downe, 6 (9) upsydown. [Originally *up so* (northern *swa*) *doun*, frequently reduced to *upsa-*, *upse-*, and subsequently altered to *upset* and *upside down*, in the endeavour to make the phrase more intelligible. The use of *so* is peculiar, the only appropriate sense being that of 'as if' (so *adv.* 17 c), and the phrase has no parallel in the cognate languages. It is possible that *up to doun*, occurring in R. Glouc. 6831 (with *up so doun* as a later variant) may be the more original form.]

A. *adv.* **1.** So that the upper part or surface becomes the under or lower. Freq. in phr. ***to turn upside down***; also in pred. use = inverted, overturned.

α. **13..** *Seuyn Sages* (W.) 788 The cradel and the child thai found Up so doun upon the ground. *c* **1340** HAMPOLE *Pr. Consc.* 7230 þarfor it es ryght and resoune, þat þai be turned up-swa-doune. *c* **1400** *Lanfranc's Cirurg.* 67 Hise iȝen in his heed weren turned vp so doun. *c* **1440** *Pallad. on Husb.* I. 275 The lond aboute a roote is to be moued Al vpsodoun. *c* **1500** *Melusine* v. 25 Raymondyn..wold haue smytte hym betwene the foure legges, For he leye vpsodounne the bely vpward. **1532** HERVET *Xenophon's Househ.* (1534) 48 b, He also must..turne vp so downe and styr the grounde. **1538** ELYOT *Dict.*, *Procello*,..to turn vp so downe.

β. **1382** WYCLIF *Matt.* xxi. 12 He turnyde vpsadoun [**1388** vpsedoun] the bordis of chaungeris. *c* **1400** *Brut* I. 253 Wherwiþ þe gode man awoke..and turnede his body opsadoun. *c* **1440** *Promp. Parv.* 512/2 Upsedowne, ..*eversus, subversus.* **1523** LD. BERNERS tr. *Froiss.* I. 356 He toke kyng Dampeter by the legge and turned hym vpsedowne.

γ. *c* **1520** BARCLAY *Jugurth* (1557) 18 Transuersed or turned vp set downe. **1532** HERVET *Xenophon's Househ.* 55 Lyke this greke lettre, *Y*, turned vp set downe.

δ. *c* **1490** *Liber Pluscardensis* XI. xi. (Bodl. MS.), Iustice makis ryche bath realme & ceteys,..Quhar lak of law bryngis all this vp sid doun [*v.r.* vpsadon]. **1535** COVERDALE *Judg.* vii. 13 Whan it came to the tente, it..ouerthrew it, and turned it vpsyde downe. **1570** FOXE *A. & M.* (ed. 2) 2307/2 The wagon also beyng cast vpsidedowne. **1600** PORY tr. *Leo's Africa* III. 155 Deepely deluing into the earth, they turne vpside downe the foundations of houses. **1669** STURMY *Mariner's Mag.* v. 66 Every Fortnight..turn all the Barrels,..turn them upside down. **1706** LONDON & WISE *Retir'd Gard'ner* I. x. 289 Stick into the Ground a Stake.., put at Top of it a Mug upside down. *c* **1791** *Encycl. Brit.* (1797) VII. 374/1 Others think, that the waters of the sea.. turned the whole surface of the earth upside down. **1841** MRS. MOZLEY *Lost Brooch* II. xxi. 154 They will come and search the house, and all our things will be turned upside down. **1889** JEROME *Three Men in Boat* xv, We..decided that the bottom was the top, and set to work to fix it upside-down.

ε. **1569** W. HUBBARD *Ceyx & Alcione* A vij, The boisterous windes..our ship on Seas did tosse.., Vntill it was turnd upsidowne. **1590** SPENSER *F.Q.* II. vii. 4 In his lap a masse of coyne he told, And turned vpsidowne, to feede his eye. **1848** ALB. SMITH *Chr. Tadpole* xiv. 131 [The sand-glass] topples over upsy-down and runs back again.

2. *fig.* In, or into, a state of overthrow, reversal, or disorder. Chiefly with *turn.*

α. *c* **1327** *Pol. Songs* (Camden) 335 Thus is the ordre of kniht turned up-so-doun. *c* **1374** CHAUCER *Boeth.* v. pr. iii. 156 How fer fro þe soþe and how up so doun is þis þing þat we seyn. **1390** GOWER *Conf.* I. 282 Al up so doun my joie it casteth. *c* **1430** LYDG. *Min. Poems* (Percy Soc.) 151 The wourld is tournyd almoost up so doun. *a* **1450** *Knt. de la Tour* vi. 9 Atte the yongest doughtres hous it was turned up-so-doun, and alle unthrifti. **1508** FISHER 7 *Penit. Ps.* vi. Wks. (1876) 12 The wounde of a mannes conscyence..stereth vpsodowne the memory. **1559** *Mirr. Mag.* Bj, By reason kynge Richarde,..By synister aduyse, had tourned all vpsodowne.

β. **13..** *Minor Poems Vernon MS.* lv. 103 For he may turne kuyndes vpsedoun, þat alle kuyndes made of nouȝt. **1426** LYDG. *De Guil. Pilgr.* 17064, I ha tournd the vp-se-doun.. With my trouble and with my wo. ? **1450** in *3rd Rep. Hist. MSS. Comm.* 279/2 Who but antichrist coude turne the treuthe upsedone? **1568** GRAFTON *Chron.* II. 625 To chaunge all things, and tourne the world upsedowne.

γ. **1509** BARCLAY *Shyp of Folys* 135 A foole..tournynge the lawes vp set downe By vyle rewardes. **1540** MORYSINE *Vives's Introd. Wysd.* Biij b, Many [things]..have loste their ryghte estimation and are chaunged uppe sette downe. **1569** J. SANFORD tr. *Agrippa's Van. Artes* 89 They disquiet and turne the earth upset downe.

δ. **1535** COVERDALE *Ps.* cxlv[i]. 9 As for the waye of yᵉ vngodly, he turneth it vpsyde downe. **1579** KNEWSTUB *Confut.* Ep. Ded. *4 b, H. N. turneth religion vp side downe, and buildeth heauen heere vpon earth. **1627** H. LESLY *Serm. bef. Majesty* 23 Our nature..must be turned up-side-downe, cast into a new mould. **1712** ADDISON *Spect.* No. 305 ¶15 These young Machiavils will, in a little time, turn their College upside-down with Plots and Stratagems. **1817** KEATINGE *Trav.* I. 33 The walls of this town exemplify to us ..the world turned upside down. **1855** KINGSLEY *Westw. Ho!* iv, Mr. Frank..would have..turned her poor little flighty brains upside down for ever. **1883** STEVENSON *Treas. Isl.* xxx, Why, your liver, man, is upside down. Did you take that medicine?

ε. **1549** LATIMER *Fifth Serm. bef. Edw. VI* (Arb.) 137 Iosias..tourned al vpsydowne, he would suffer no Idolatrye to stand. **1579** G. HARVEY *Letter-bk.* (Camden) 73 Your delicacy would haply have delighted your self in overturning ye proverbe upsyedowne. **1601** R. JOHNSON *Kingd. & Commw.* (1603) 19 By remaining full of French soldiers all things were turned vpsidowne. **1876** BESANT & RICE *Gold. Butterfly* II. 254 It's a story without an end, it's a story told upsy-down.

†**B.** *sb.* An overturning. *Obs.*

1593 G. HARVEY *Pierce's Super.* 84 A fewe resolute Aphorismes; that..roundly determine all with an Vpsy-downe. No reformation without an Vpsy-downe.

C. *adj.* Turned upside down; inverted.

Written with hyphen (*upside-down*) or as one word.

1866 G. STEPHENS *Runic Mon.* I. 84 Twisted runes, upside-down runes, and such like. **1882** BESANT *All Sorts* xxviii, The same upsydown, topsy-turvy, one-sided.. perverseness. **1883** W. S. GILBERT *Foggerty's Fairy*, etc. (1890) 238 She was..an industrious little girl, and, as far as I could judge by her upside-down reflection, neat in her dress.

Hence **'upside-,downism.**

1861 F. METCALFE *Oxonian in Iceland* vii. (1867) 106 The Demons of Misrule and Upside-downism.

'upside 'downward(s, *advs.* [f. prec. + -WARD, -WARDS.] = prec. A.

1611 COTGR., *Enverser*,..to turne vpside-downeward, or the inside outward. *Ibid.* s.vv. *Reboursé, Revers.* **1672** BLAKESTON *Lazarillo* II. xiii. T 4 b, She made the peeces of my Cloak to be stiched one to another, and for very hast they put them upside downwards. **1781** C. JOHNSTON *Hist. J. Juniper* II. 131 On his arrival he found the town turned, as we say, upside downwards. **1826** DISRAELI *V. Grey* VI. i, As he tossed, with a careless hand, the great horn upside downwards. **1845** —— *Sybil* II. ix, I think the world is turned upside downwards in these parts.

up'sides, *adv.* [f. UPSIDE *sb.* Cf. MSw. *upsidhis*, *-es* by the side (of), alongside.]

1. ***upsides with***, even, equal, or quits with (a person) by means of retaliation or successful rivalry. *dial.* (orig. *Sc.*) or *colloq.*

1746 LD. LOVAT in Williams *Hist. Rec. 11th Hussars* (1908) 47, I..am still in good spirits, and hope to be upsides with the barbarous villains who have used me so. **1752** in *Scots Mag.* (1753) Sept. 454/1 He did not care though he should be up-sides with him. **1816** SCOTT *Antiq.* xxi, It's best no to be rash;..I'se be upsides wi' him ae day. **1853** R. S. SURTEES *Sponge's Sp. Tour* xxx, He considered it his duty to be 'upsides' with him, and tell the servants all he knew about him. **1891** ATKINSON *Last of Giant-killers* 65 He did want to be upsides with that insulting little jackanapes.

2. *colloq.* On a level *with*; alongside *of.*

1883 *Standard* 12 Feb. 2/6 Baron Farney must finish at least upsides with his then conqueror. **1894** ASTLEY *50 Years Life* II. 210 Never [to] let any horse get upsides of him if he could help it.

†**upsie-turvy**, *adv. Obs.* [var. of TOPSY-TURVY, influenced by *upsie-down.* Cf. *upside-turvy* in mod. dial. (s. Linc.).] Topsy-turvy.

a **1592** GREENE *Jas. IV*, III. iii, I came to court... There found I all was vpsie turuy turnd.

†**'upsight.** *Obs. rare.* [In sense 1 prob. ad. older Du. and Flem. *opsicht* (mod. *opzicht*); in sense 2 f. UP- 2.]

1. View, inspection.

1515 *St. Papers Hen. VIII* II. 14 Nowe, after the upsyght hereof, he maye pretende no manner ignoraunce. **1648** HEXHAM II, *Opsichtigh*, which hath Regard or Vpsight.

2. Height as viewed from below.

a **1560** PHAER *Æneid* IX. (1562) Ee ij b, A towre of stepe vpsight [L. *vasto suspectu*] there stood, with skaffolds large of length.

up'sighted, *a. s.w. dial.* [UP- 3.] Having eyes which cannot readily look downward.

1847 HALLIWELL. **1903** 'Q' (QUILLER COUCH) *Hetty Wesley* I. viii, An angle which gave an 'up-sighted' expression to his small eyes.

upsiloid, var. HYPSILOID *a.*

1889 *Buck's Handbk. Med. Sci.* VIII. 156/1 A upsiloid (U-shaped), depressed line with lateral branches.

upsilon (juːpˈsaɪlən, ˈʊpsɪlɒn). [a. Gr. ὖ ψιλόν 'slender u', the adj. having reference to its later sound (y).]

1. The Greek letter *Υ*, *υ* (originally **V, Y**) representing the vowel *u* (see U, V, and Y). Also *attrib.*, = having the form of this letter.

1642 HOWELL *For. Trav.* xi. (Arb.) 56 In some places of the Morea..they confound these three leters *η*, *ι*, *υ* (Eta, Iota, Upsilon). **1693** DRYDEN *Persius, Sat.* iii. 109 *note*, Pithagoras of Samos made the allusion of the Y, or Greek Upsilon, to Vice and Virtue. **1763** *Ann. Reg., Misc.* 194/1 The last notes..(pronounced as the Greek upsilon, or the French u). **1799** TOWNSON *Tracts & Observ. Nat. Hist.* 75 The upsilon Cartilage. **1820** T. S. HUGHES *Trav. Sicily* I. 245 The only people who pronounce the letter *upsilon* like the Italian *u*. **1854** BUSHNAN in *Orr's Circ. Sci., Org. Nat.* I. 121 The hyoid bone is described as having the shape of the Greek upsilon.

2. *Ent.* A species of moth (see quot.).

1832 RENNIE *Brit. Butterfl. & M.* 59 The Upsilon (*Orthosia Upsilon*, Ochsenheimer) appears in July,..the stigmata pale, between which is a black mark resembling a Y or V.

3. *Particle Physics.* A meson with a mass of about 9·4 GeV that is thought to consist of a *b* quark and its antiquark; also ***upsilon particle.*** Freq. designated by *Υ.*

[**1976** *Daily Tel.* 7 Feb. 10/4 Upsilon was discovered by a team of scientists from Columbia University, New York, the Fermi Laboratory and the State University of New York. **1976** D. C. HOM et al. in *Physical Rev. Lett.* 24 May 1239/2 We suggest the name *Υ* (upsilon) be given either to the resonance at 6 GeV if confirmed or to the onset of high-mass dilepton physics.] **1977** S. W. HERB et al. in *Ibid.* 1 Aug. 255/2 Following ref. 1 [*sc. prec. quot.*], a reasonable designation for this enhancement is *Υ*(9·5). **1979** *Nature* 7 June 482/2 The more recently discovered upsilon T [? *read* *Υ*]..should provide an even better system for investigating QCD effects as the coupling strength for that very massive quark system is even smaller. **1980** *TWA Ambassador* Oct. 61/3 Dr. Charles had told me about Truth and Beauty—that is, the quarks given those names—and the discovery in 1977 of the upsilon particle, which seems to be a meson consisting of a beauty quark and a beauty antiquark.

Hence **up'silonism**, tendency to use the letter *u*.

1879 T. F. SIMMONS *Lay Folks Mass Bk.* Introd. p. lvi, The perpetual upsilonism of our West-Midland text E.

†**'upsitten**, *ppl. a. Sc. Obs.* [UP- 5.] Inactive, indifferent, callous.

1682 PEDEN *Lord's Trumpet* (1739) 16 The Lord..hath been crying to You in these Lands (and namelie to thee upsitten Scotland) to watch with him. **1728** P. WALKER *Life Peden* (1827) Pref. 27 These backslidden, upsitten, lukewarm Ministers, Elders and Professors. *Ibid.* 61 The Indulged, Backslidden and Upsitten Ministers of Scotland. [**1896** STEVENSON *Weir of Hermiston* v, The sister of the gardener..had shown herself 'upsitten'.]

up'sitting, *vbl. sb.* [UP- 7.]

1. The occasion of a woman's first sitting up to receive company after a confinement. *Obs.* exc. *dial.* (Cf. UPSETTING *vbl. sb.* 2.)

1572 J. JONES *Bathes of Buckstone* 9 b, Some in forme of Cakes, as at weddings; some Rondes of Hogs, as at vp-sittings. **1603** DEKKER *Bachelor's Banquet* C 3, It is your vpsitting, and a fortnight at the least since you were brought to bed. **1641** BROME *Joviall Crew* II. (1652) F 2 b, We will have such..A Christning; such up-sitting and Ghossipping! **1688** R. HOLME *Armoury* III. 12/2 This is a kind of dress which Women in Child-bed usually wear, when they are for Christnings, and up-sittings. **1746** *Exmoor Scolding* (E.D.S.) 24 'Twas thee roil'st upon me to Daraty Vogwill's Upzitting. **1828–** in dialect glossaries (Yks., Som., Dev.).

†**2.** The fact of sitting up again after an illness.

1646 FULLER *Wounded Consc.* xix. 140, I must..rejoyce at thy upsitting, whom God hath raised from the bed of despaire. **1742** RICHARDSON *Pamela* IV. 303, I am once more..enabled to dedicate to you the first Fruits of my Penman-ship, on my Upsitting.

†**3.** *Sc.* Inactivity, indifference. *Obs.*

1680 STEWART in Howie *Cloud of Witnesses* (1778) 74 The Lord hath rubbed shame on all our faces, because of many backslidings and upsitting in duty. **1709** WODROW *Corr.* (1842) I. 55 There is a remarkable upsitting among us in mutual freedom one with another.

4. *S. African.* The practice of sitting up during the night as a method of courtship. (After Du. *opzitten.*) Also *attrib.*

1863 W. C. BALDWIN *Afr. Hunting* vi. 165 When two upsittings have been going on, at opposite corners of a large room. *Ibid.*, The upsitting business I consider about the best of their old customs. **1896** *Westm. Gaz.* 20 Jan. 1/3 The nocturnal courtship, or 'upsitting'.

up-'sitting, *pres. pple.* (UP- 6.)

1753 G. WEST tr. *Pindar* I. 242 On his Couch up-sitting all Night long. **1776** *Maiden Aunt* II. 148, I..found her up-sitting.

†**'up-skip.** *Obs.* [UP- 2.] An upstart.

1549 LATIMER *2nd Serm. bef. Edw. VI*, E j, Heare menes suetes your selfe..& put it not to the hearing of these veluette cotes, these vp skippes.

'upslope, *sb.*, *a.*, and *adv.* [UP *prep.*²] **A.** *sb.* An upward slope; rising ground.

1920 D. H. LAWRENCE *Lost Girl* v. 63 The eye would instinctively wander..to the long upslope opposite. **1929** —— *Escaped Cock* II. 58 Inland, the steep grooved upslope was dark, to the long wavering outline of the crest against the translucent sky. **1973** *Times* 6 Mar. 2/7 He walked up the main up-slope for a closer inspection. **1977** *New Yorker* 8 Aug. 55/2 The ball, after landing on the upslope to the green, hopped through the opening between the two front bunkers and curled directly toward the pin.

B. *adj.* Caused by, occurring, or acting upon an upward slope; esp. as ***upslope fog*** (see quot. 1956).

1941 [see ADVECTION]. **1956** J. C. SWAYNE *Conc. Gloss. Geogr. Terms* 146 *Upslope fog*, fog formed when moist air blows over hilly ground and is cooled adiabatically until its dew point is reached and condensation takes place. **1970** R. J. SMALL *Study of Landforms* vi. 215 Upslope factors are considered to be of virtually no importance in Penck's theory. **1973** *Nature* 9 Feb. 394/1 If the grain size were halved instead of doubled the up-slope fluid drag on each grain would be reduced to a quarter.

C. *adv.* At or towards a higher point on a slope.

1956 A. G. GARNETT in D. L. Linton *Sheffield* 53 Temperatures in the bottom of Edale..are..colder than at points only a few hundred feet up-slope. **1970** R. J. SMALL *Study of Landforms* vi. 214 In time an almost infinite number of new units, each of gentler gradient than the next unit above it, will be formed at the foot of the slope and undergo migration upslope. **1979** *Sci. Amer.* July 110/1 Walcott returned to the spot the following year to search upslope for the shale stratum that had been the source of his fallen rock.

up'soar, *v.* [UP- 4.] *intr.* To soar upwards. Also **up'soaring** *pres. pple.*

1582 STANYHURST *Æneis* I. (Arb.) 29 Thow shalt shortlye see townwals, And citty vpsoaring..to skytoppe. **1725** POPE *Odyss.* xv. 565 On the right up-soar'd in air The hawk. **1743** FRANCIS tr. *Hor., Odes* III. iii. 11 Thus to the flamy Towers above, The vagrant Hero.. Upsoar'd. **1855** BROWNING *Saul* II. x, As when..upsoareth the cherubim chariot. **1865** TRENCH *Poems* 480 How like a swan.. The voice upsoars of thy triumphant song.

up'soaring, *vbl. sb.* (UP- 7. Cf. prec.)
1846 HAWTHORNE *Mosses* II. v, Higher upsoarings and baser degradations of the soul. **1876** FAIRBAIRN in *Contemp. Rev.* XXVII. 955 The sudden upsoaring of the revived national spirit.

up'soaring, *ppl. a.* (UP-^{1} 6 b.)
1818 MILMAN *Samor* VII. 259 Mysterious union of upsoaring spirits.

† **up'solve**, illiterate for ABSOLVE *v.* 6.
1598 B. JONSON *Ev. Man in Hum.* I. iv, You are a scholler, vpsolue me that, now.

up'speak, *v.* [UP- 4.] *intr.* To speak up; to begin to speak.
1819 W. TENNANT *Papistry Storm'd* (1827) 103 Let him up-speik as best he may. *a* **1842** W. MAGINN *Homeric Ball.* (1850) 251 They all agreed, and then upspoke the chief of many a wile. **1888** R. BUCHANAN *City of Dreams* VII. 130 But soon the host upspake, and sought to spread A feeble cheer.

upspin: see UP- 4 b.

'upspring, *sb.* [UP- 2.]
† **1.** Rising *of* the sun; dawn *of* day. *Obs.*
c **1000** *Rule of Chrodegang* xviii, Fram þæs dæȝes upspringe to halsungtiman. *c* **1000** *Sax. Leechd.* III. 274 Easterne wind.. blæwð fram ðære sunnan upspringe. **1471** RIPLEY *Comp. Alch.* VII. vi. (MS. Ashm. 1486), Thus ye vii gate.. In ye vpspryng is of ye soone requyrede. **1562** TURNER *Herbal* II. 50 The.. parte of the worlde toward the vpspryng of the son.
2. The action of springing up into existence; beginning of growth or development; origin; †generation.
c **1000** ÆLFRIC *Gen.* v. 10 Æfter þes upspringe, he leofode .viii. hund ȝeara. **13..** *Cursor M.* 9283 (Gött.), A mayden sal brede, of his hup-spring [*Cott.* ox-spring]. **1554** KNOX *Faythf. Admon.* C 3 b, From the beginning of the late vpspryng of the Gospel in England. **1585** T. WASHINGTON tr. *Nicholay's Voy.* III. iii. 73 Hauing.. giuen amply.. to vnderstand the vpspring of the Asamoglans. **1651** R. CHILD in *Hartlib's Legacy* (1655) 63 You ought to sow them.. in March, April, or May, when frosts are.. not so sharp.. as to endanger their up-spring. **1825** COLERIDGE *Aids Refl.* 40 A state.. favourable to the germination and up-spring of a nobler seed.
† **3.** A kind of dance. *Obs.*$^{-1}$
For Shaks. *Ham.* I. iv. 9 see note to UPSPRING *a.*
a **1634** CHAPMAN *Alphonsus* III. (1654) 33 We Germans have no changes in our dances, An Almain and an upspring, that is all.

† **'upspring**, *a. Obs.* [UP- 3.] Upstart; newly arisen or come in.
In quot. 1602 *upspring* has also been interpreted as sense 3 of the sb., *reels* being taken as a verb with cognate object.
1591 HORSEY *Trav.* (Hakl. Soc.) 258 The patriarcke,.. bishops and friers, and other the new upspringe nobillitie. **1602** SHAKS. *Ham.* I. iv. 9 The King doth wake to night, and takes his rouse, Keepes wassels and the swaggering vpspring reeles [= revels].

up'spring, *v.* [UP- 4. Cf. WFris. *opspringe*, (M)Du. *opspringen*, MLG. *upspringen*; MHG. *ûfspringen* (G. *aufspringen*); MSw. *up-*, *opspringa* (Sw. *upp-*), (M)Da. *opspringe*.]
1. *intr.* Of plants, etc.: To spring up, to grow.
c **1000** *Ags. Gosp.* Matt. xiii. 5 Sume feollon on stænihte.. and hrædlice upsprungon. *c* **1200** ORMIN 10543 Allswa summ corn & chaff Uppspringenn off an rote. *c* **1374** CHAUCER *Former Age* 10 But corn vp-sprong vnsowe of mannes hond. **1471** RIPLEY *Comp. Alch.* V. viii. (MS. Ashm. 1479), So ther shuld ther of no frute vp spring. **1865** EMERSON *Sphinx* 18 Erect as a sunbeam, Upspringeth the palm. **1876** BLACK *Madcap Violet* ii, Far away.. the subtle fire of the earth upsprang in pale primroses.
b. *fig.* To arise, come into being.
c **1386** CHAUCER *Clerk's T.* 884 Fro Boloigne is this Erl of Pavyk come, Of which the fame vp sprang to moore and lesse. *a* **1500** *Ratis Raving* I. 1428 Gud dissert will nocht vpspring, But hail purpos. **1562** WINȜET *Cert. Tractatis* Wks. (S.T.S.) I. 6 Pryde and auarice, of the quhilkis.. hes vpsprung the electioun of vnqualifeit bischopis. **1596** DALRYMPLE tr. *Leslie's Hist. Scot.* (S.T.S.) I. 325 Frome him the hous and clann of the Cumeinis first vpsprang. **1667** MILTON *P.L.* VII. 462 These [cattle] in flocks Pasturing at once, and in broad Herds upsprung. **1744** THOMSON *Winter* 641 Up-springs the Dance along the lighted Dome. **1821** BYRON *Heav. & Earth* iii. 869 The forests' trees (coeval with the hour When Paradise upsprung). **1842** BORROW *Bible in Spain* xliv, Here upsprang, in Spain's better days, a little city. **1890** J. PULSFORD *Loyalty to Christ* I. 7 The joy of eternity begins to upspring in our bosoms.
2. To rise, to ascend; to spring or leap upwards; to start to one's feet.
c **1374** CHAUCER *Compl. Mars* 14 Er sunne gan vp sprynge. **14..** in *Anglia* XXVII. 286 We saw his stern in þe est spedily vpspryng. **1500–20** DUNBAR *Poems* xii. 2 Airly as did the day vpspring, Thus sang ane bird. **1563** SACKVILLE *Induct. Mirr. Mag.* lxvi, The flames vpspring, and.. crepe From walle to roofe. **1729** SAVAGE *Wanderer* IV. 138 The trout.. Up-springs, and sunward turns its crimson stains. **1760** BEATTIE *Ode to Hope* 22 Startled at the heavenly ray, With speed unwonted Indolence upsprings. **1806** J. GRAHAME *Birds of Scot.* 12 When flush, the game upsprings. **1848** LYTTON *K. Arthur* VI. lv, Upsprung the host, upsprung the guests in ire—Upsprung the gentle dames, and fled affrighted. **1885–94** R. BRIDGES *Eros & Psyche* June vi, Upsprang she then, and kiss'd them and embraced.

up'springing, *vbl. sb.* (UP- 7. Cf. prec.)
c **1400** tr. *Secreta Secret., Gov. Lordsh.* 92 If þou take seuen graynes.. and breke hem yn þe vpspryngynge of lucyfer and venus. **1851** MRS. BROWNING *Casa Guidi Wind.* I. 5 The upspringing Of such a nimble bird. **1868** MORRIS *Earthly Par.* I. II. 633 The white upspringing of the spurts of spray.

up'springing, *ppl. a.* (UP- 6 b. Cf. UPSPRING *v.*)
c **1400** tr. *Secreta Secret., Gov. Lordsh.* 112 Stable þou þe mountant, or þe vpspryngand, yn þe tokenynge of þe Lyon. **1551** BALE *Eng. Votaries* II. 95 The vpspryngynge braunches of Sodome. **1845** HIRST *Com. Mammoth*, etc. 111 The downy wing Of some up-springing bird. **1873** B. HARTE *Fiddletown* 52 By the upspringing light he saw the figure of Kate. **1883** MISS BURNE *Shropsh. Folklore* xxv. 344 Men implored a blessing upon their land and its upspringing crops.

up'sprung, *pa. pple.* (UP- 5. Cf. UPSPRING *v.*)
c **1000** *Ags. Gosp.* Matt. xiii. 6 Soþlice upsprungenre sunnan hiȝ adruwudon. *c* **1250** *Gen. & Ex.* 3050 Trees it for-brac, and gres, and corn, ðat was up-sprungen ðor biforen. **1400** tr. *Secreta Secret., Gov. Lordsh.* 99 He hadde no sterre vp-sprongyn þat was euyl no contrary. **1563** WINȜET *Wks.* (S.T.S.) II. 12 Be the negligence.. of zour Hienes forebearis.. al this perturbatioun, trible, and hie interpryseis.. ar wp-sproung. **1729** SAVAGE *Wanderer* II. 415 Up-sprung, such weed-like Coarseness it [*sc.* the grain] betrays, Flocks on th' abandon'd Blade permissive graze. **1826** E. IRVING *Babylon* I. II. 78 We are not to suppose that the ten.. were all up-sprung before the little horn appeared. **1876** F. K. ROBINSON *Whitby Gloss.* 209 *Upsprung*, adj., sprung up in all senses.

† **upspurner.** *Obs.*$^{-1}$ [UP- 8 + SPURN *v.*^{1} 5 b.] ? One who treats with disdain.
1545 JOYE *Exp. Dan.* iv. 59 b, Howe wretchedly Pompeius that vpspurner of the erth perisshed, Lucanus describeth it.

upstage, *adv.*, *a.* (and *sb.*). [UP *prep.*^{2} 6.]
A. *adv.* (Stressed *up'stage.*) At or in the direction of the back of the stage; on that part of the stage furthest from the audience. Also *fig.*
1870 O. LOGAN *Before Footlights & Behind Scenes* xxxv. 500 And in one minute.. has been convulsed with laughter at a side-speech given 'up stage' and as a sort of sequel to the sentiment delivered to the audience. **1923** J. AGATE *At Half-Past Eight* 209 You remember how Marcus and Mercia.. with the lions roaring up-stage, kept a steadfast face to their admirers. **1938** C. MACKENZIE *Windsor Tapestry* xx. 418 At this point the dapper figure of Mr Anthony Eden crosses upstage. **1946** A. CLARKE *Second Kiss* 11 Columbine enters, right, upstage, hesitant, and as if in fear. **1967** T. STOPPARD *Rosencrantz & Guildenstern are Dead* I. 23 Rosencrantz and Guildenstern occupy the two downstage corners looking upstage. **1976** *Listener* 1 Apr. 404/2 The Wallace family felt able to emerge from its bailiff-proof bolt-hole in SE4, and move upstage a bit to Clarence Gate Gardens, by Baker Street.
B. *adj.* (Stressed *'upstage.*) **1.** Superior or aloof in manner; 'stuck-up'. Chiefly of persons.
1918 F. HUNT *Blown in by Draft* 287 As doggy as the military police, as upstage as the Engineers.. the Field Signal Battalion has the additional point of being of strangest birth. **1927** *Sunday Express* 8 May 10 Although Costello.. had definite ideas.. in connection with his art, as he took pictures seriously, he was never in the least bit 'up stage' with us youngsters. **1938** *Sun* (Baltimore) 3 Oct. 8/3 Even without 'Cotton Ed's' upstage behavior, this plea would have been unimpressive. **1947** N. MARSH *Final Curtain* xii. 188 All upstage and county! **1966** 'J. HACKSTON' *Father clears Out* 84 He was a little patronizing to me, upstage in his bearing.
2. That is situated or occurs at or towards the rear of the stage. Also as *sb.*, the back of the stage, furthest from the audience.
1933 P. GODFREY *Back-Stage* i. 14 The up-stage O.P. flood. **1959** [see DITHER *v.* 1]. **1974** F. WARNER *Meeting Ends* I. viii. 30 Hanging on upstage side of pump.. are a brightly coloured towel and a black shawl.

up'stage, *v.* [f. the adv.] **1.** *trans. Theatr.* To move upstage of (another actor), forcing him to face away from the audience; to divert attention from (a fellow performer) to oneself, to 'steal the scene' from.
1933 [implied in UPSTAGER, UPSTAGING *vbl. sb.*]. **1958** B. NICHOLS *Sweet & Twenties* 200 Miss Tempest always 'upstaged' her—.. she slowly pushed her chair to the rear so that.. Miss X was obliged to turn away from the audience. **1958** *New Statesman* 6 Sept. 302/2 So if Strether's 'tragedy' seems.. rather trivial, that is partly because the hero has been upstaged by the backdrop. **1972** *Islander* (Victoria, B.C.) 18 June 6/3 While Gracie was singing her famous aspidistra song, a stray dog wandered onto the stage and upstaged her. **1976** *Early Music* Oct. 400/1, I would hesitate before *telling* an Aeneas that he is being literally upstaged during his climactic high F.
2. *fig.* To put (a person, etc.) at a disadvantage; to outshine. Also, to treat in a haughty or snobbish manner. *colloq.*
1921 H. C. WITWER *Leather Pushers* x. 268 Nada Nice has upstaged the Kid.. at your orders. **1946** 'BRAHMS' & 'SIMON' *Trottie True* v. 103 The Duchess stood there exerting her personality to its most ducal extent... 'Blast,' said Trottie under her breath. 'Upstaged.' **1967** *Daily Tel.* 10 Apr. 10/6 My sister.. didn't get on with the other debs —she was more beatnik. They were rude and kept upstaging her. **1974** 'R. TATE' *Birds of Bloodied Feather* iii. 57 It was the only occasion in Edward's life that he had been upstaged by his younger brother.
So **up'stager**; **up'staging** *vbl. sb.* and *ppl. a.*
1933 P. GODFREY *Back-stage* iii. 40 With the chronic upstager the only remedy for the other actors is to withhold their speech until they have deliberately taken up a position favourable to themselves. *Ibid.*, 'Crowding' and 'upstaging' are tricks of the selfish actor... 'Up-staging' is to take up a position nearer to the back of the scene than the other players. This forces them to turn three-quarter-back to the audience when speaking to the up-stage actor. **1968** M. WOODHOUSE *Rock Baby* v. 46 I'd been running a bright, upstaging little war with Driver and McKellar and patting myself on the back. **1982** P. LOVESEY *False Inspector Dew* II. iii. 29 With her dramatic training, she knew all about upstaging.

'up-ˌstage: see UP *a.* 2.

'upstair, *adv.* and *a.* [UP *prep.*^{2} 1, 7.]
1. *adv.* = UPSTAIRS *adv.* 1.
1627 DRAYTON *Moon Calf* 165 When vp-stayre one, downe-stayre another hies.
2. *adj.* = UPSTAIRS *a.*
1814 HEYNE *Tracts India* 277, I staid in an upstair room with him for many hours. **1849** ROCK *Ch. of Fathers* I. iii. 230 Many of such upstair-chapels are still to be seen in.. Gloucester cathedral. **1861** FLOR. NIGHTINGALE *Nursing* ii. (ed. 2) 27 But do these people know the up-stair habits of this class [*sc.* young ladies]? **1885** *Fortn. in Waggonette* 18 An upstair sitting-room.

upstairs, *adv.*, *sb.*, and *a.* [UP *prep.*^{2} 1, 7.]
A. *adv.* (ʌp'stɛəz). **1. a.** So as to ascend a flight of stairs; to the floor at the top of a staircase.
Stressed *'upstairs* when contrasted with *downstairs*.
1596 SHAKS. *1 Hen. IV*, II. iv. 112 His industry is vpstaires and down-staires, his eloquence the parcell of a reckoning. **1658** E. PHILLIPS *Myst. Love & Eloquence* 75 Up stairs we nimbly creep, And find the Sluts asleep. **1661** in Jamieson *Sc. Dict.* s.v. *Breadberry*, Tripping up stares and down stares with a posset or berry for the laird or lady. **1722** DE FOE *Plague* (1896) 127 Some [running] down stairs and some up stairs. **1767** *Woman of Fashion* I. 244 Shew the Lady up Stairs. **1797** S. & HT. LEE *Canterb. T.* (1799) I. 152 He abruptly walked up stairs, and.. opened the door. **1839** DICKENS *Nickleby* lxii, He made his way up stairs into the room. **1876** T. HARDY *Ethelberta* vii, I think that after the women had gone upstairs the others turned their thoughts upon you again.
b. *fig.* (See KICK *v.* 5 b.)
c **1697** BURNET *Orig. Mem.* (1902) 145 He [Halifax] had said he had known many kicked down stairs, but he never knew any kicked up stairs before. **1821** [see KICK *v.* 5 b].
c. (*a*) *Parliament.* In phr. ***to send (a bill) upstairs***, to refer (a bill) for its committee stage from the floor of the House to a standing committee. Cf. COMMIT *v.* 4.
1835 *Mirror of Parl.* 17 June 1399/2, I rise to suggest, that if this Bill requires mature deliberation with respect to its details, it should be referred to a Committee up-stairs, and not to the Registration Committee. **1907** *Hansard Commons* 11 Apr. 419 Was it the intention of the Government that such a Bill as the Army Bill should go upstairs? **1931** *Economist* 31 Jan. 215/2 In spite of the Government's majority, it is clear that the Bill will emerge from Committee in a very different form from the one in which it is sent upstairs. **1959** *Daily Tel.* 13 Nov. 13/3 For detailed consideration, the Bill will be sent to a Committee 'upstairs', consisting of about 45 M.P.s. **1975** J. P. MORGAN *House of Lords & Labour Govt.* ii. 54 All Public Bills usually have their Committee Stage in the Lords on the Floor of the House... In response to the pressure of legislation in 1968 the Lords tried the experiment of taking some Bills 'upstairs' for their Committee Stage.
(*b*) Hence more generally, (i) to a more influential position (sometimes *ironical*); (ii) to a higher authority (of a matter referred for judgement). *colloq.*
1965 [see PLENUM 2]. **1977** D. BAGLEY *Enemy* xi. 75 I'll have to push it upstairs for a ruling. **1978** S. BRILL *Teamsters* vii. 289 The Pressers get him another job with the Joint Council or the statewide union. You know, he gets thrown upstairs.
d. *Aeronaut.* Up in or into the air. In phr. ***to go (climb, etc.) upstairs***, to become airborne. *colloq.*
1908 *Punch* 10 June 429/2 Climbing upstairs over Richmond Park [in a balloon] in search of conducive current. **1919** C. P. THOMPSON *Cocktails* 250 We hauled the plane from the trees where she had been pushed out of sight.. and.. went upstairs at speed.
2. a. At the top of, on a floor or in a room reached by, a flight of stairs; in one of the upper stories of a house.
1781 COWPER *Table T.* 151 To be the Table Talk of clubs up stairs. **1796–7** JANE AUSTEN *Pride & Prej.* lv, Her mother.. was sitting up stairs with Kitty. **1844** KINGLAKE *Eothen* xvi, It is upstairs—on the first floor. **1882** MISS BRADDON *Mt. Royal* III. ii. 28 You would rather dine upstairs, I dare say.
b. quasi-*sb.*
1842 LOVER *Handy Andy* xiv, The ogre's voice from upstairs. **1898** WATTS-DUNTON *Aylwin* XII. iii, As I spoke I heard a noise... It seemed to come from upstairs.
c. As *sb.* An upper story or floor. Also *transf.*, a person or persons living on an upper floor.
1872 E. EGGLESTON *End of World* i. 19 They say, he has all up-stairs full of books. **1884** in *Proc. Soc. Psychical Research* Dec. (1885) 329, I was.. present on the day when Mr. Coulomb gave the charge of the upstairs to our party. **1896** *Westm. Gaz.* 23 April 2/3 The magistrate could not discriminate whether upstairs or down-stairs began [the fight].
d. *Aeronaut.* In the air; in flight; aloft. *colloq.*
1918 H. A. BRUNO *Flying Yankee* v. 77 Cold as the devil upstairs. *Ibid.* xii. 193 'Upstairs' a stiff breeze was blowing. **1934** V. M. YEATES *Winged Victory* II. v. 232 There won't be any Huns about upstairs [on] a day like this. **1940** N. MONKS *Squadrons Up!* 252 Dashing about 'upstairs' in stratospherical aloofness. **1967** W. LORD *Incredible Victory* 94 By 5:30 the weather was clearing 'upstairs'. **1981** I. ST.

JAMES *Balfour Conspiracy* v. 138 The R.A.F. are upstairs now..at about seventy thousand feet.

e. Mentally, 'in the head'. Chiefly in phrases indicating weak (or abundant, etc.) mental capacity. *slang.*

1932 J. FARRELL *Young Lonigan* i. 44 Aw, she's all vacant upstairs. **1945** A. KOBER *Parm Me* 179 '*Meshugeh* upstairs!' Jennie laughed and drummed on her forehead. **1952** G. W. BRACE *Spire* xxvii. 322 He just ain't right upstairs. **1962** A. HUXLEY *Island* xi. 184 'One may be very stupid upstairs.' She patted the top of her head. **1974** P. DE VRIES *Glory of Hummingbird* (1975) v. 63 Assurances that my progress here would be well lubricated by my having 'plenty upstairs'.

f. ***the Man Upstairs***, euphem. and slang for 'God'. Cf. UP THERE 1. *U.S.*

1961 J. HELLER *Catch-22* xviii. 184 'When you talk to the man upstairs,' he said, 'I want you to tell Him something for me.' **1971** *Guardian* 8 Oct. 9/4 Everything that's happened to me has been very much because of the Man Upstairs. **1976** H. KEMELMAN *Wednesday Rabbi got Wet* xix. 129 I'd just lost my wife, see. I guess the Man Upstairs wanted her.

B. *adj.* (ˈʌpstɛəz). **1. a.** Situated on an upper story or at the top of a flight of steps.

1782 *Jrnl. Yng. Lady of Virginia* (1871) 46 Nancy had a fire made up in one of the up-stairs rooms. **1850** *Household Words* I. 206/1 In upstairs Infirmary wards. **1879** MRS. A. E. JAMES *Ind. Househ. Managem.* 35 A bungalow has rarely any upstairs rooms.

b. Belonging to, connected with, the upper rooms or parts of a house.

1839 HOOD *On Completing Forty-Seven* iv, I hear the up-stairs bell. **1848** THACKERAY *Van. Fair* xvi, At the usual hour..the upstairs maid knocked at the door of the..bed-chamber. **1894** ELIZ. BANKS *Camp. Curiosity* 10 The up-stairs duties of a first-class lodging-house.

c. *fig.* Of, pertaining to, or characteristic of life 'above stairs' (i.e. in private rooms of a household, as opp. to the servants' quarters) (chiefly *Hist.*); refined, genteel, privileged. Freq. in phr. ***upstairs-downstairs*** adj., denoting the social contrast between employer and domestic servant.

1942 'M. INNES' *Daffodil Affair* I. ii. 13 Almost might she be said, in upstairs language, to be receiving. [**1971** *TV Times* 9 Oct. 6/2 A six-part series, *Upstairs, Downstairs* (or Secrets of an Edwardian Household), starting Sunday, lovingly, critically examines life at that time through one family.] **1974** D. FRANCIS *Knock Down* i. 6 To one side of the sale ring, and built to a specification as Upstairs as the wooden circle was Downstairs, was a magnificent turn of the century stable yard. **1975** *New Society* 6 Nov. 305/2 Our system is too monolithic, based as it is on an upstairs-downstairs view of music. Upstairs people choose the classics on Radio Three... Downstairs, people listen to pop. **1978** G. MITCHELL *Mingled with Venom* i. 4 She had been taken on as kitchen-maid... She was..a ready learner of upstairs speech and manners. **1980** E. BEHR *Getting Even* i. 18 The lady in black with white lace cap and apron, a real upstairs-downstairs figure.

2. Having more than one story.

1840 E. E. NAPIER *Scenes & Sports For. Lands* II. v. 163 Old B—— possessed one of the few up-stairs houses in the cantonment, in the lower part of which he had his shop.

upstalled: see UP- 5.

ˈupstand, *sb.* [UP- 2.] An upstanding thing; an upright structure or part; *spec.* a turned-up edge of any flat surface or sheeting, esp. in a roof space where it meets the wall; also *attrib.* (see quot. 1963).

1847 HALLIWELL, *Upstands*, marks for boundaries of parishes, estates, &c., being live trees cut off about breast high. *Kent.* **1880** LOMAS *Alkali Trade* 33 A 14-in. lead up-stand, flanged upon the floor. **1955** *Archit. Rev.* CXVII. 283/3 It [*sc.* a roof tile]..is readily adapted to different plan shapes having an easy repertoire of trimming details at eaves, verges and upstands. **1956** *Ibid.* CXX. 10 The steel box frames forming the turbine-house rooflights make a self-contained rigid frame with sliding joints supported on concrete upstand curbs from the main roof. **1963** *Gloss. Building Terms* (*B.S.I.*) 16 *Upstand beam*, a beam projecting above an adjoining slab. **1974** W. E. KELSEY *Building Construction* viii. 141 It [*sc.* a damp-proof course] is best placed where the upstand or skirting of the roof covering is turned into a mortar joint. **1983** *Ideal Home* June 69 An upstand at the back of the worktop will make it easier to clean and more hygienic—no crumbs or food waste can get trapped in the gap at the back.

upˈstand, *v.* [UP- 4. Cf. OS. *upstandan*, WFris. *opstean*, MDu. *opstaen* (Du. *opstaan*), MLG. *upstân*, MHG. *ûfstân*, *-stên* (G. *aufstehen*), MSw. *upstanda*, *op(p)sta* (Sw. *uppstå*), MDa. *opstande*, *opsta* (Da. *opstaa*).]

†**1.** *intr.* To stand erect or upright. *Obs.*

c **1205** LAY. 1650 Þa þe castel vp-stod he wes strong & swiðe god. *c* **1250** *Gen. & Ex.* 3247 Ðe water up-stod..On twinne half, also a wal up-riȝt. *c* **1340** HAMPOLE *Pr. Consc.* 4762 Þe se sal ryse,..And in his stede even upstande, Als an heghe hille dus on þe lande. *c* **1440** *Pallad. on Husb.* III. 310 A dight vine in prouyntial manere That lyke a busshe vpstont. **1513** DOUGLAS *Æneid* IX. v. 50 O kyndly goddis.. Vndre quhais myghtis all tyme Troy vpstandis. **1552** LYNDESAY *Monarche* 5465 The sey..sall nocht spred ouir the land, Bot, lyke ane wall, ewin straycht vpstand.

2. To rise to one's feet; to stand up. Also *fig.*

a **1300** *E.E. Psalter* ii. 2 Vpstode kinges of þe land,.. Ogaine þair lauerd þai come on ane. **13..** *Guy Warw.* (A.) 1599 When he of swoning vp stod, His feren he biheld wiþ drery mod. *a* **1400** *Isumbras* 324 Whenne the wounded knyght myght up-stande,..Wepande awaye went hee. **1513** DOUGLAS *Æneid* XI. vii. 93 Ane Drances tho vpstud, and speke began. **1596** SPENSER *F.Q.* IV. vi. 23 But die or liue for nought he would vpstand. **1653** MILTON *Psalm* ii. 2 Why do ..the Kings of th' earth upstand With power? **1667** —— *P.L.* VI. 446 In th' assembly next upstood Nisroc. **1791** COWPER *Yardley Oak* 173 The father of us all,..moulded by his Maker into man At once, upstood intelligent. **1896** in *Westm. Gaz.* 27 May 6/1 With all dignity..Alexandra Feodorovna upstood from her throne.

3. *fig.* To stand up *for* something. *rare*$^{-1}$.

1722 W. HAMILTON *Wallace* IX. i. (1816) 154 In the defence or righteous royal blood, For which thou always loyally up-stood.

upˈstander. [UP- 8. Cf. Icel. *upp-standari.*] *spec.* One of two upright posts on a sledge.

1856 KANE *Arct. Expl.* II. x. 98 It has two standards, or, as we call them, 'upstanders'. **1903** PEARY in *McClure's Mag.* Feb. 419/2, I had scarcely time to seize the upstanders when my dogs were off.

upˈstanding, *vbl. sb.* [UP- 7.] The action of standing (up), or rising to one's feet; the fact of remaining in place.

Some dialect uses are recorded in the *Eng. Dial. Dict.*

1535 COVERDALE *Isaiah* xxxiii. 3 Graunte..that at thy vpstondinge the Gentiles maye be scatred abrode. **1538** LATIMER in Nichols *Hist. Leics.* (1800) III. 1065/2 He wold be an humble sewter..for the upstandynge of his forsayd howsse. **1861** J. EDMOND *Children's Ch. at Home* xi. 166 There were many feelings expressed in that upstanding and applause. **1886** SPURGEON *Treas. Dav.* Ps. cxxxvi. 6 The original upheaval and perpetual upstanding of the habitable land.

upˈstanding, *pres. pple.* [UP- 6.]

1. Standing up; erect; on one's feet.

c **1375** *Lay Folks Mass Bk.* (MS. B.) 261 Saye pater-noster, ȝit vp-standande. *c* **1440** *Pallad. on Husb.* XII. 601 Mydday & ouernoon..A mydde is noon vpstondyng right. **1596** SPENSER *F.Q.* V. vii. 20 With long locks vp-standing, [he] stifly stared. **1628** MAY *Virg. Georg.* III. 99 The water-snakes, with scales up-standing, dy. **1828** ATHERSTONE *Fall of Nineveh* I. 142 Toward the Median camp, Upstanding in his car, himself looked out. **1861** *Illustr. Lond. News* 1 June 505/1 A white-headed clergyman was called upon to say prayers, which he did upstanding. **1884** LADY BRASSEY *Egypt after War* IV. 17 Feb., In the court outside are two obelisks, one still upstanding.

2. *fig.* Remaining in good estate, intact, or in the same condition. *north. dial.*

c **1450** *Lay Folks Mass Bk.* 70 We sall pray..for all lande tyllande, þat god..maynteyn þame so, þat þai may be up-standand. **1649** W. G. *Surv. Newcastle upon Tine* 24 All his stock upstanding, he living all that time of the Profit that his ground yeelded. **1855** [ROBINSON] *Whitby Gloss.*, *Upstanding*, remaining as heretofore.

3. *Mining.* (See quot.)

1883 GRESLEY *Gloss. Coal-m.* 269 *Up-standing*, the condition of a goaf when such portions of the pillars are worked away as still to leave the roof supported.

upˈstanding, *ppl. a.* [UP- 6 b.]

1. Standing up; erect.

c **1000** *Sax. Leechd.* I. 332 Aho on upstandende twiȝ. *c* **1000** ÆLFRIC *Gloss.* in Wr.-Wülcker 154 *Pira*, upstandende herebeacn. *c* **1384** CHAUCER *H. Fame* 1389 She Had also fele vpstondyng eres And tonges, as on bestes heres. **1590** SPENSER *F.Q.* II. ix. 13 Staring with hollow eyes, and stiffe vpstanding heares. **1611** COTGR. s.v. *Rasibus*, The top of an open, and vp-standing Hogs-head. **1628–9** in *Maitl. Club Misc.* III. 370 To lay fyre to the upstanding Craig at the greine. **1805** SOUTHEY *Madoc* I. vii. 87 Round the helm A coronal of high upstanding plumes. **1883** *Times* 11 June 4/5 A pigeon is perched upon each of the two upstanding handles. **1898** *St. James's Gaz.* 14 Nov. 13/1 A close round black toque and upstanding feathers.

2. Of animals (esp. horses) or persons: Having an erect carriage; well set up.

(*a*) **1835** SIR G. STEPHEN *Adv. Search Horse* xv. 191 Very superior, well-bred,..up-standing..seasoned horses. **1877** *J. Coleman's Sheep & Pigs* 36 The latter are white and clean in both, and more, what are generally called *upstanding* sheep. **1883** R. GROOM *Gt. Dane* 13 A large, upstanding dog, of noble presence.

(*b*) **1882** MISS BRADDON *Mt. Royal* III. vi. 106 A well-grown upstanding young woman. **1894** *Strand Mag.* VIII. 156 The Marquis was a tall, upstanding man of spare figure. **1901** *Longm. Mag.* Dec. 147 The Nolans were all fair and big, upstanding men and women.

b. *fig.* Of persons: Of open, honest, or independent bearing; straightforward, down-right.

1863 R. S. HAWKER in Byles *Life* (1905) 462 He found the Miners and the Fishermen an upstanding rollicking courageous people. **1889** 'R. BOLDREWOOD' *Robbery under Arms* (1890) 2 A lot of game upstanding chaps, that acted like men. **1890** —— *Col. Reformer* (1891) 169 As good a specimen of the thoroughbred upstanding pirate as any..in print.

3. ***upstanding wage***, a regular or fixed wage in contrast to one dependent on circumstances.

1888 W. E. NICHOLSON *Coal-Trade Gloss.* 103 *Upstanding Wage*, a certain weekly wage. **1897** *Railway Review* 1 Jan. (E.E.D.), The Company are prepared to arrange a suitable upstanding-wage.

†**upstantial**, illiterate var. SUBSTANTIAL *a.*

1589 R. HARVEY *Pl. Perc.* (1590) 16, I will take it vpon the credit of my selfe, an vpstantiall yeoman.

upstarched: see UP- 5 (*b*).

upˈstare, *v.* (UP- 4. Cf. next and Spenser *F.Q.* III. xii. 36.)

1886 DOWDEN *Shelley* I. viii. 372 These wild locks upstared more wildly.

upˈstaring, *pres. pple.* [UP- 6.]

†**1.** Of hair: Standing on end. *Obs.*

1590 SPENSER *F.Q.* I. ix. 22 They might perceiue his.. curld vncombed heares Vpstaring stiffe. **1610** SHAKS. *Temp.* I. ii. 213 The Kings sonne Ferdinand With haire vp-staring.

2. Gazing upwards.

For 'vp-staring' in Marlowe's *Hero & L.* II. 200 the true reading is prob. 'vp-starting', as in some later edd.

1835 RUSKIN *Tour France* x. Wks. 1903 II. 400, I stood, upstaring at the lofty steeple.

upstart (ˈʌpstɑːt), *sb.* and *a.* [UP- 2, 3.]

A. *sb.* **1.** One who has newly or suddenly risen in position or importance; a new-comer in respect of rank or consequence; a parvenu; = START-UP *ppl. a.* and *sb.*[1] 1.

1555 *Instit. Gentl.* C iiij b, These gentlemen are nowe called vpstartes, a terme lately inuented by such as pondered not yᵉ groundes of honest meanes of rising or commyng to promocion. **1577** B. GOOGE *Heresbach's Husb.* I. 46 b, The newe vpstart; that takes vpon him the name of a gentleman. **1592** GREENE *Vpst. Courtier* B 4, Mary gyp goodman vp-start, who made your father a gentleman? **1641** MILTON *Reform.* II. 74 Then shall the Nobles possesse all the Dignities..without the improper mixture of Scholastick and pusillanimous upstarts. **1691** HARTCLIFFE *Virtues* 39 An Upstart was to bear himself otherwise in his Petition, than..an ancient Nobleman. **1747** RICHARDSON *Clarissa* (1768) I. xl. 270 None but the prosperous upstart Mushroom'd into rank..was arrogantly proud of it. **1777** J. ADAMS *Fam. Lett.* (1876) 307 There are rascally upstarts in trade, I doubt not, who have made great fortunes in a small period. **1825** MACAULAY *Ess., Milton* ¶43 Gods..compared with whom Jupiter himself was a stripling and an upstart. **1858** FROUDE *Hist. Eng.* III. xiii. 167 The Duke of Norfolk ..disdained the dictation of an unknown upstart. **1888** BRYCE *Amer. Commw.* III. lxxxvii. 161 The Greeks thought that the old families ruled their households more gently than upstarts did.

transf. **1613** PURCHAS *Pilgrim.* (1614) 319 If it seeme strange, that the Turkish Religion (a newer vpstart) be declared before those former. **1647** N. BACON *Disc. Govt. Eng.* I. xlvii. 123 The Empire perceiving..the youthfull courage of this upstart, was glad to enter mutuall league with it. **1791** COWPER *Yardley Oak* 134 Yonder upstarts of the neighb'ring wood, So much thy juniors. **1834** *Tracts for Times* No. 29. 5 All the meetings [= Dissenting sects] are.. in one sense, upstarts.

2. †**a.** An upward start or spring. *Obs.* exc. *poet.*

1645 RUTHERFORD *Tryal & Tri. Faith* vi. 43 The upstarts and boylings of corruption and the flesh that are mixed with our Prayers. **1923** [see *round-barred* s.v. ROUND *a.* 16 a].

b. *dial.* (See quot.)

a **1825** FORBY *Voc. E. Anglia*, *Upstart*, the deep impression of a horse's foot in a clayey soil, soon filled up with water, which, when another horse happens to tread in the very same place, starts upwards and plentifully bespatters the rider.

c. *Gymnastics.* On the horizontal, parallel, or asymmetric bars: a series of movements by which the gymnast swings to a position with the body supported by the arms above the bar, esp. at the start of a routine.

1909 A. MOSS *Horizontal Bar Exercises* 22 *Upstart.* Stand about three feet from the bar, then jump and catch it..force the legs well to the front with a swing, and bring them to the bar. Kick them outwards and downwards; at the same time pull, so that you rise above the bar. **1931** E. LINKLATER *Juan in Amer.* III. v. 246 Saturdays were more strenuously occupied with up-starts, long arm balancing, vaulting, and similar exercises. **1956** KUNZLE & THOMAS *Freestanding* v. 58 *Agility.* This group of movements includes the upstarts, headspring and handspring. **1972** P. PRESTIDGE *Women's Gymnastics for Performer & Coach* viii. 55 The upstart..is one of the most important movements for the gymnast to master, for a complete routine cannot be composed without upstarts.

†**3.** Upspring, origin. *Obs.*$^{-1}$

1669 PENN *No Cross* xi. (1682) 219 All Men and Families ..have had their Upstarts, that is, their Beginnings.

4. *Sc.* A stick forming a support for a thatched roof. ? *Obs.*

1811 W. AITON *View Agric. Ayrs.* 114 (Jam.), Over these were hung sticks..called cabbers; and smaller ones set on the top of the wall were termed upstarts.

5. The meadow-saffron, *Colchicum Autumnale.*

1852 E. HAMILTON *Flora Homœopath.* I. 199 Common Meadow Saffron, Tuber Root,..Upstart. **1863** PRIOR *Plant-n.* 232 *Upstart*, from its flowers starting up suddenly from the ground without putting out leaves first.

B. *adj.* **1. a.** Of things: Lately come into existence or notice; new-fangled.

1565 STAPLETON *Fortr. Faith* 9 The grounde and foundation of all your vpsterte ghospell. *Ibid.* 94 Their small secret, and late vpstert congregation. **1593** BILSON *Govt. Christ's Ch.* 286 This up-start fansie is far from God's ordinance. **1607** J. NORDEN *Surv. Dial.* I. 18 Surveying..is an upstart arte found out of late. **1654** H. L'ESTRANGE *Chas. I* (1655) 5 Not daring to infuse into so solid a judgement their up-start and erroneous fancies. **1697** J. POTTER *Antiq. Greece* I. iv. 19 All their Laws were repeal'd, and the upstart Form of Government utterly dissolv'd. **1720** SWIFT *Right of Precedence* 23 Physick is as old as the Occasion of it;.. which can by no means be said of the other, in comparison, Upstart Profession. **1772** PRIESTLEY *Inst. Relig.* (1782) II. 62 Christianity was despised as..an upstart thing. **1851** HAWTHORNE *Twice-told T.* i, Now, the old aristocratic edifice hides its time-worn visage behind an upstart modern building. **1878** BOSW. SMITH *Carthage* 365 The upstart naval power of Rome in the West.

b. Characteristic of upstarts.

a **1593** MARLOWE *Edw. II*, I. iv. 336 Think you that we can brooke this vpstart pride? **1603** B. JONSON *Sejanus* v. viii, It is a note Of vpstart greatnesse, to..watch For these poore trifles. **1665** MANLEY *Grotius' Low C. Wars* 687 His Death was..rejoyced at by those who envyed his new and upstart

Rising. 1727 GAY *Fables* I. xxiv, How insolent is upstart pride! 1788 GIBBON *Decl. & F.* xlvii. IV. 550 He dreaded their upstart ambition. 1817 COBBETT *Pol. Reg.* 25 Jan. 99 The upstart pride of those who call themselves the gentlefolk of Manchester. 1822 HAZLITT *Table-t.* Ser. II. iv. 66, I do not desire to be driven out of my conclusions.. merely to make way for his upstart pretensions.

2. Of persons, families, etc.: Lately or suddenly risen to prominence or dignity.

1566 STAPLETON *Ret. Untr. Jewel* I. 8 Your late vpstert masters of Germany and Geneua. 1586 FERNE *Blaz. Gentrie* 260 He will.. passe vp and downe the streates of London in a side gowne, like vnto some newe vp-start Legist. 1615 CROOKE *Body of Man* 88 It is more safe to side with the old Legions led by Galen,.. then with new and vpstart Nouices. 1665 MANLEY *Grotius' Low C. Wars* 383 The Covenants.. were found fault with by malitious and upstart People. 1687 DRYDEN *Hind & P.* I. 175 Some Authors thus his Pedigree will trace, But others write him of an upstart Race. 1740 RICHARDSON *Pamela* (1824) I. 123 Ours is no upstart family; but is as ancient as the best in the kingdom. 1791 BURKE *App. Whigs* Wks. VI. 19 Scorn and contumely of their upstart masters. 1836 THIRLWALL *Greece* II. xiii. 166 An obscure and upstart race of shepherds. 1879 TOURGEE *Fool's Err.* xxxviii. 271 When reproved.. by an upstart superior, he had the boldness [etc.].

†3. Rising on end. *Obs.*$^{-1}$

1590 SPENSER *F.Q.* III. x. 54 He.. ran away,.. With vp-start haire, and staring eyes dismay.

Hence 'upstartism, 'upstartness. *nonce-words.*

1838 *Blackw. Mag.* XLIII. 311 That spirit of upstartness which.. characterises all French youth. 1881 *Nat. Rev.* Oct. 406 These latter [ballads] are all broad satires on up-startism.

up'start, *v.* [UP- 4.]

1. *intr.* To start or spring up: *esp.*, of persons, to spring to one's feet. Also *fig.*

With the earlier unhyphened examples, cf. UP *adv.*[1] 5 c.

1303 R. BRUNNE *Handl. Synne* 5601 Þys man vp sterte, and toke þe gate. *c* 1386 CHAUCER *Wife's T.* 190 (Lansd. MS.), Wiþ þat worde vpstert [*v.rr.* vp sterte, vp stirte] þis olde wif. *c* 1400 *Tourn. Tottenham* iv, Upsterte the gadlyngs with thaire lang staues. 1412–20 LYDG. *Chron. Troy* IV. 919 Anoon Dispeir in a rage vp-sterte And cruelly cauȝte hym by þe herte. *a* 1529 SKELTON *Col. Cloute* 646 Sodaynly vpstarte From the donge carte, The mattocke and the shule, To reygne and to rule. 1554 in Strype *Eccl. Mem.* (1721) III. 139 The suffragan.. upstert to the Pulpit. 1590 SPENSER *F.Q.* I. i. 16 Their dam vpstart, out of her den effraide, And rushed forth. 1602 *2nd Pt. Return Parnass.* II. v. 908 At last he [*sc.* the hart] vpstarted at the other side of the water. 1700 DRYDEN *Ovid's Met.* XIII. 3 To these the Master of the sevenfold Shield Upstarted fierce. 1725 POPE *Odyssey* XIV. 569 Upstarted Thoas strait, Andræmon's son. 1816 WORDSW. *Ode Morn. Gen. Thanksgiving* 147 As from a forest-brake Upstarts a glistering snake. 1859 TENNYSON *Merlin & V.* 421 The beauteous beast Scared by the noise upstarted at our feet.

b. Of the hair: To rise on end.

1513 DOUGLAS *Æneid* IV. vi. 2 Wpstert his hair, the voce stak in his hals. 1563 *Mirr. Mag.* P iv b, While my heares vpstarted with the sight, The teares out streamde.

c. To spring up by growth; to come into existence.

1573 TUSSER *Husb.* (1878) 49 Much wetnes.. makes thistles a number foorthwith to vpstart. 1581 J. BELL *Haddon's Answ. Osor.* 363 b, As one errour doth commonly engender another: there upstart another whelpe of the same litter. 1875 MORRIS *Æneid* VIII. 637 There for the sons of Romulus the sudden war upstarts With Tatius.

d. To rise suddenly into view.

1874 R. BUCHANAN *Poet. Wks.* I. 4 O wondrous Faces that upstart In this Strange Country. 1880 BROWNING *Pan & Luna* 22 Peak to base, Upstarted mountains.

2. *trans.* To cause to start up.

1892 TOWNDROW *Garden* 47 Where the moor-hen shyly pushes Into darkness when upstarted.

up'started, *ppl. a.* (UP- 5. Cf. prec.)

1602 MARSTON *Ant. & Mel.* III. E 2, Gastly amazement, with vpstarted haire, Shall.. vsher vs. 1613 CHAPMAN *Rev. Bussy D'Ambois* I. B 3 b, What thoughts the many headed-beast.. breathes out concerning me, My ends, and new vpstarted state in Brabant.

Hence **up'startedness**. *rare.*

1642 HEYLIN *Hist. Episc.* II. 93 Undertaking.. to make known the new upstartedness of their Assemblies.

up'starting, *vbl. sb.* (UP- 7.)

[1775 ASH.] 1845 S. AUSTIN *Ranke's Hist. Ref.* I. 27 This continual upstarting of refractory powers.

up'starting, *pres. pple.* and *ppl. a.* (UP- 6, 6 b. Cf. UPSTART *v.*)

1581 HANMER *Jesuites Banner* B 2 b, This new found order and vpstarting Jesuites. 1592 GREENE *2nd Pt. Conny Catch.* A 2 b, Such vpstarting suckars that consume the sap from the roote of the Tree. 1596 SPENSER *F.Q.* V. v. 13 By this vpstarting from her swoune, she star'd.. about her. 1784 COWPER *Task* III. 521 Then rise the tender germs upstarting quick. 1812 J. WILSON *Isle of Palms* II. 70 As to the touch of fairy-hand Upstarting dim the nameless land Extends its mountain line. *c* 1830 PRAED *Poems* (1864) II. 308 Lo, they will weep.., Upstarting from their broken prayer. 1893 MCCARTHY *Dictator* xxvi, She had.. slept a little in a fitful, upstarting sort of way.

up'startle, *v.* (UP- 4.)

a 1849 POE *Whipple*, etc., Wks. 1864 III. 388 Multitudinous thunders that upstartle aghast the echoes. 1870–4 J. THOMSON *City Dreadf. Nt.* xx. vii, A louder crash upstartled me in dread.

up'startled, *ppl. a.* (UP- 5.)

1812 CARY *Dante, Parad.* XXVI. 72 The upstartled wight loathes that he sees. 1846 J. H. STIRLING in A. H. Stirling *Life* (1912) v. 89 Silence, like an upstartled hound, skulked sulkily to its place again.

'upstate, *adv.*, *a.*, and *sb.* orig. and chiefly *U.S.* Also up-State, up State, etc. A. *adv.*

1. In that part of a state which is (regarded as) higher than another, or is more remote from the chief centre. Freq. with reference to the State of New York.

1901 in *N. Amer. Rev.* Feb. 162 American girls.. imported from small towns up-State. 1938 J. DANIELS *Southerner discovers South* 247, I heard about it upstate. 1958 *Economist* 8 Nov. 504/2 Confident.. that he would do well in the city.., Mr Harriman had concentrated his efforts upstate. 1977 *New Yorker* 5 Sept. 29/3 He was coming upstate Friday, and staying for the weekend. 1985 *Village Voice* (N.Y.) 8 Jan. 3/1 At that time, the remaining six projects located upstate with 175 beds will be under construction.

2. *U.S. slang.* In prison.

1934 T. V. WILDER *Heaven's my Destination* 23 You get the strait-jacket.. upstate. 1977 'E. MCBAIN' *Long Time no See* xi. 177 She got married while I was upstate doing time.

B. *adj.* Of, pertaining to, or characteristic of, an area upstate; situated upstate, rural; also, designating part of a State remote (esp. north) from a large city, as *upstate New York.*

1901 *Daily Chron.* 16 Sept. 3/7 All the up-State constituencies. 1904 *Collier's* 16 July 16/1 The crews of the up-State college [Cornell]. 1935 *Amer. Speech* X. 107 Pronunciation in upstate New York... Upstate speech has been studied.. by three previous investigators. 1949 *Southern Weekly* 16 Nov. 3/2 This is the figure with complete returns from Greater New York and 19 up-State districts missing. 1969 *Wall St. Jrnl.* 30 Sept. 28/3 Five days at an upstate New York county fair. 1978 J. UPDIKE *Coup* vi. 219 Not a metropolis, but a small industrial city, of the type you call.. upstate. 1983 'W. HAGGARD' *Heirloom* i. 6 He had taken her back to up-State New York.

C. *ellipt.* or as *sb.* An upstate region; a rural area.

1965 *Economist* 23 Jan. 323/1 It was the Democrats from 'upstate' (outside the city) who swung behind Mr Kennedy at once. 1972 *Village Voice* (N.Y.) 1 June 78/2 The Liberal Socialists, who came down every week from upstate for meetings. 1974 *Progress* (Easley, S. Carolina) 24 Apr. II. 8/4 Many of us in the upstate do not appreciate the value of the Tidelands.. to our environment.

Hence **'upstater**, one who lives or comes from upstate.

1944 E. A. HOLTON *Yankees were like This* xvii. 202 The Cape Codder and the Up-Stater are blood brothers with only the difference in the backdrops of sea or mountain. 1965 *Economist* 23 Jan. 323/1 Now, around the figure of Senator Kennedy,.. the upstaters have begun to develop some strength. 1975 *New Yorker* 10 Feb. 106/3 In a move to put upstaters' minds at ease about one thing, Carey.. assured them, 'The capital of this state is not New York City or elsewhere.'

up'stay, *v.* [UP- 4.]

1. *trans.* To sustain by material support; to prop up.

1590 SPENSER *F.Q.* III. xii. 21 Those two villeins, which her steps vpstayd. 1596 *Ibid.* IV. i. 37 They reared him on horsebacke, and vpstayd. 1642 H. MORE *Song of Soul* I. II. xxvii, An uggly cloven foot this monster doth upstay. 1667 MILTON *P.L.* VI. 195 The tenth on bended knee His massie Spear upstaid. 1793 WORDSW. *Descriptive Sk.* 252 Bare steeps, where Desolation stalks,.. by a blasted yew upstay'd. 1814 —— *Excurs.* VII. 678 The Child.. by some friendly finger's help upstayed. 1873 R. BRIDGES *Elegy on Lady Poems* (1912) 239 Each on high a torch upstaying.

2. *fig.* To sustain, support.

1600 FAIRFAX *Tasso* XVII. xliii, For by the sword, the scepter is vpstaid. 1619 DRAYTON *Legends* iv. 338 That Atlas, which the gouernement vpstay'd. 1820 WORDSW. *River Duddon* xxviii. 11 Glad meetings, tender partings, that upstay The drooping mind of absence. 1851 CLOUGH *Relig. Poems* vii. 10 A hand that is not ours upstays our steps. 1883 R. W. DIXON *Mano* I. i. 2 If God.. still with life upstay The hand that writes.

upsteamed, -steaming: see UP- 5, 6.

†**upsteaming**, *pres. pple.* *Obs.*$^{-1}$ [UP- 6 + *steam* STEM *v.*[4]] Rising up.

1582 STANYHURST *Æneid* II. 28 Two serpents.. Whose brests vpsteaming [L. *arrecta*],.. Hygh the sea surmounted.

up'steer, *v.* Now *dial.* [UP- 4.] *trans.* To stir up; to throw into turmoil or disorder.

1557 PHAER *Æneid* VI. (1558) S j, What slaughters wyld shall they vpsteere? 1570 *Satir. Poems Reform.* xi. 38 Wa worth the wit that first began This deir debait for to vpsteir. 1596 DALRYMPLE tr. *Leslie's Hist. Scot.* (S.T.S.) I. 273 His Nobilis.. he vpsteiris to take Weapounis. 1889 *N.W. Linc. Gloss.* (ed. 2) 589 All th' rooms was upsteer'd.

Hence **up'steerer**. *rare*$^{-1}$.

1596 DALRYMPLE tr. *Leslie's Hist. Scot.* (S.T.S.) II. 413 That ȝe suld be the.. author and vpsteirer of thir tumultes.

upstick, *adv. phr.* (See STICK *sb.*[1] 7, and UP *adv.*[1] 30.)

1904 A. GRIFFITHS *50 Yrs. Pub. Serv.* 81 The Naval Agent .. dying to be upstick and away.

up stick(s, verbal phrase: see STICK *sb.*[1] 7, and UP *adv.*[1] 30.

upstiffed: see UP- 5.

'upstir. Now *dial.* Also 6 upstirre, upsturre. [UP- 2 + STIR *sb.*[1] Cf. MDa. *opstyr*, Norw. *uppstyr* riot, tumult, disturbance.] A disturbance or commotion.

1549 CHEEKE *Hurt Sedit.* (1569) D j b, Better redresse was entended, then your vpstirres and vnquietnesse coulde obtaine. 1550 HARINGTON tr. *Cicero's Bk. Friendship* (1562) 26 Tiberius Graccus.. made an vp sturre in the common wealth. 1847 HALLIWELL. 1849– in general dialect use (*Eng. Dial. Dict.*).

up'stirred, *pa. pple.* (UP- 5. Cf. next.)

1663 BLAIR *Autobiog.* ii. (1848) 10, I was not a little refreshed and upstirred.

up'stirring, *vbl. sb.* [UP- 7.] The action of stirring up or arousing; stimulation; incitement, encouragement.

1613 P. FORBES *Comm. Rev.* v. (1614) 30 The singing of the rest should serue the Church for a new vpstirring to insist in his praise. *a* 1653 BINNING *Serm.* (1735) 634/1 There is no up-stirring to Faith among us. 1671 [R. MACWARD] *True Nonconf.* 393 We are to emulat the grace and principle of zeal.. for our upstirring to acts in like manner. 1730 T. BOSTON *Mem.* xi. (1899) 353 The which practice I found useful to my upstirring. 1826 E. IRVING *Babylon* II. 414 The upstirring of infidel principles. *a* 1861 SIR G. SCOTT *Lect. Archit.* (1878) I. 142 It was a period of deep-seated mental excitement, of a prodigious upstirring of the human intellect.

up'stirring, *ppl. a.* [UP- 6.] Stimulating, rousing.

1751 R. SHIRRA in *Rem.* (1850) 182 Sacred biography is very upstirring to the godly reader. 1834 D. SMITH *Mem. Rev. John Brown of Whitburn* 57 Only as viewed in promises are they sanctifying and upstirring.

'upstoop. *Mining.* (See quots.)

1883 GRESLEY *Gloss. Coal-mining* 269 When a heading is driven to a point at which another should be put in or meet it at right angles.., the first-named heading is called *up-stoop.* 1886 J. BARROWMAN *Sc. Mining Terms* 69 A working room is *up stoop* or *in stoop* when its length is equal to the side of the pillar to be formed.

†**upstraight**, *a.* *Obs.* [UP- 3. Cf. ME. *upstreyht* (= upstretched), UP- 5.] Erect, upright.

1598 FLORIO, *Trisciato*, smooth, vp-straight, smug. 1642 H. MORE *Song of Soul* I. III. I, For that old crumpled wight gan go upstraight.

up-stream, *adv.* (*sb.*) and *a.* Also up stream, upstream. [UP *prep.*[2] 2, 6.]

A. *adv.* 1. a. In a direction contrary to the flow of a stream; higher up or along a stream.

Common from *c* 1890. Properly as two words, stressed *up-'stream*, except when contrasted with *down-stream*. In recent use also const. *of* or *from* (a place).

1681 ROBERTSON *Phraseol. Gen.* 1282 To go up stream, *adverso flumine navigare.* 1839 LONGF. *Hyperion* I. viii. (1844) 58 The rising tide bears against the rushing torrent up stream, and pushes back the hurrying waters. 1849 CUPPLES *Green Hand* xvi, The sound of a loud rush of water up-stream broke upon us. 1889 JEROME *Three Men in Boat* ix. 142 Three or four miles up stream is a trifle, early in the morning.

b. quasi-*sb.* A position or place further up a stream.

1891 *Nature* 18 June 152/2 From upstream of it are derived three main trunk canals. 1915 I. H. EVANS in *Man* XV. 25 A spot some two miles to the up-stream of the Tamu ground.

2. In the oil and gas industries: at or towards the source of production; *spec.* at a stage in the process of extraction and production before the raw material is ready to be refined.

1973 *Auckland Star* 10 Feb. 18 The most natural way the oil producers can spend their vast wealth.. is in developing the industry itself. Huge investment is needed 'upstream'. 1983 *Business Week* 21 Feb. 61/1 KPC has not neglected foreign activities upstream. It wants to expand exploration in the U.S.

B. *adj.* (*'up-stream*) 1. Situated farther or higher up a stream.

1838 *Civil Eng. & Arch. Jrnl.* I. 150/1 The up-stream angles of the dam. 1843 *Ibid.* VI. 88/1 [A] deposit accumulated largely on the up-stream side. 1875 KNIGHT *Dict. Mech.* 1084/2 The up-stream end of a canal-lock.

2. Directed, taking place, up-stream.

1826 J. F. COOPER *Mohicans* iii, They call this up-stream current the tide. 1889 *Science-Gossip* XXV. 209/2 There is an up-stream migration of elvers in the spring. 1894 *Field* 9 June 832/1 Many experienced anglers do not like an up-stream wind for.. dun hatchings.

3. *U.S.* Difficult, troublesome. *rare*$^{-1}$.

1847 J. BROWN in *Boston Public Library Bulletin* May (1900) 177, I do not wish any upstream measure taken to supply funds.

4. Relating to the stages in the production of oil and gas before the raw material is ready for refining.

1965 WILLIAMS & MEYERS *Oil & Gas Terms* (ed. 2) 429 Gathering activities are.. ended when gas reaches a central point... Facilities used before this point of demarcation are upstream facilities. 1981 *Times* 3 Apr. 17/1 Upstream activities.. are overshadowed by the comfortable world supply position while downstream, weak demand is making it more difficult to recoup rising operating costs.

up'streaming, *pres. pple.* and *ppl. a.* (UP- 6, 6 b.)

1849 M. ARNOLD *Resignation* 62 There [it] winds, upstreaming slowly still Over the summit of the hill. 1884 GEIKIE *Phys. Geog.* (ed. 2) 87 A zone, in which the currents would meet and ascend as an upstreaming mass of air.

'upstreet, *adv. colloq.* and *dial.* [UP *prep.*² 5.] Up or along the street; in, into, or towards the higher part of a town, etc.

1828, etc. [see DOWN-STREET *adv.* (*a.*)]. **1933** [see PIE *sb.*² 4 a].

upstretched, *pa. pple.* and *ppl. a.* (UP- 6, 6 b.)

1563 C'TESS HERTFORD in Ellis *Orig. Lett.* Ser. II. II. 278 The Queens..graceous pardon.., wych wyth upstretched hands..most humbly I crave. **1642** H. MORE *Song of Soul* II. ii. III. xxii, So must it be upstretch'd unto the skie. **1860** O. W. HOLMES *Elsie V.* v, Two meeting-houses stood on two eminences,..looking..as if they would..crow out of their upstretched steeples.

†up-striked, *pa. pple. Obs.*⁻¹ [UP- 5.] Struck up, arranged.

1677 F. SANDFORD *Genealog. Hist. Kings Eng.* 130 So 'tween Sister and this Prince, The marriage was up-strik'd.

†up-striker. *Obs.* [UP- 8.] (See quot.)

1726 J. LAURENCE *New Syst. Agric.* 198 Of Brick-making. .. An Up-striker, a Boy, that lays the Earth upon the Table, and cuts it out for the Moulder.

'up-stroke. Also upstroke. [UP- 2 + STROKE *sb.*¹]

1. *dial.* The upshot, end, or conclusion.

1828- in *Eng. Dial. Dict.* (Yks., Lancs., Derby, Linc.).

2. A stroke delivered upwards.

1828 *Gardener's Mag.* III. 30 The air which enters from the valves by the up-stroke of the bellows. **1883** *Encycl. Brit.* XVI. 447/2 When the up-stroke is being made..the piston is forced to make part of a revolution.

3. The upward stroke of a pen, etc.

1848 DICKENS *Dombey* lix, [She] clutches the money tight until a receipt..is duly signed, to the last up-stroke. **1856** MRS. BROWNING *Aur. Leigh* I. 847 Some upstroke of an alpha and omega. **1898** *Allbutt's Syst. Med.* V. 822 In the irritable heart of young adults the upstroke in the sphygmogram is brisk and high.

4. *Physiol.* The part of a nerve impulse when the action potential is becoming more positive.

1974 *Nature* 4 Jan. 69/2 The upstroke of the action potential is considered the result of a Hodgkin cycle. **1979** *Sci. Amer.* Sept. 65/2 The depolarizing upstroke of the action potential is produced mainly by the inflow of sodium ions into the terminal.

†upsty, *sb. Obs.*⁻¹ [Cf. next and OE. *upstiʒe*, OHG. *ûfstîc*, ON. *upp-stiga.*] Ascension (of Christ).

c **1300** *Cursor M.* 20831 (Edin.), Aftir þe upsteich [*Cott.* vpstei, *Gött.* vpsti] of þat driʒtine.

†up'sty, *v. Obs.* Forms: 1 **upstiʒan**, 3-4 **vpstiyhe**, 5 **up-stiʒe, vpsty**; 3-4 **vpsteghe, vpstei**, 4 **upstey**, 4-5 **vpstey**. [OE. *upstíʒan* (UP- 4), = WFris. *opstige*, MDu. *opstigen* (Du. *opstijgen*), OHG. *ûfstîgan* (G. *aufsteigen*), ON. *uppstíga* (MSw. *up-*, *opstigha*, Sw. *uppstiga*, Da. *opstige*).] *intr.* To rise or mount up; to ascend.

a **900** CYNEWULF *Crist* 464 Ærþon upstiʒe ancenned sunu. *c* **1000** *Ags. Gosp.* John i. 51 ðe ʒeseoð.. Godes englas up-stiʒende & nyþer-stiʒende ofer mannes sunu. *a* **1300** *E.E. Psalter* ciii. 9 Vpsteghes hilles, and feldes doun gas. *a* **1300** *Cursor M.* 203 How he [*sc.* Christ] vprais, how he vpstey, Many man on stad and sey. **1382** WYCLIF *Gen.* xxxii. 26 Leeue me, forsothe now vpsteyeth the morewetide. *c* **1400** LOVE *Bonavent. Mirr.* iii. (Gibbs & Sherard MSS.), þe syght of hier sone myghtyly to heuene upstyynge.

Hence **†up'stying** *vbl. sb. Obs.*

a **1300** *E.E. Psalter* ciii. 3 [He] þat settes þin vpsteghing kloude [*v.r.* upstiying þine þe kloude]. *a* **1325** *Prose Psalter* lxxxviii. 18 Our vp-steiʒeing ys of our Lord. *c* **1400** tr. *Secreta Secret., Gov. Lordsh.* 86 After good constellacioun of þe mone, & his remuynge fro nusant sterrys, and his prosperyte of his vpstiyng. *c* **1450** *Mirk's Festial* I. 152 Yn þys vpsteyng þat ys callet þe assencyon.

†up'styer. *Obs.*⁻¹ [UP- 8, or f. prec. Cf. ON. *uppstígari.*] One who mounts; a rider.

c **1340** HAMPOLE *Pr. Consc.* 4180 þe Dan..sal þe nedder be,..And sal byte þe hors by þe hufe harde, And mak þe up-stegher fal bakwarde.

†up-sun, *adv. phr. Obs.* [UP *adv.*² 1 b. Cf. SUN-UP.] **a.** *with up-sun*, at sunrise. **b.** *Sc.* Between sunrise and sunset.

a **1400-50** *Wars Alex.* 4067 þe secund day with vp son he with his sowme neʒes. **1703** FOUNTAINHALL *Decis.* (1761) II. 189 The precise question was, If an ejection may be executed in the night-time,..or if it must be done with up-sun. **1825** JAMIESON, *It was upsun*, the sun was not set. Galloway.

'upsurge. [UP- 2.] **1.** A sudden rise or increase of feeling.

1928 *Catholic Times* 11 May 11/5 His books are an upsurge of primitive passion. **1944** D. WELCH *Jrnl.* 20 June (1973) 123, I remember..saying, 'That's a wonderful poem,' and his vital upsurge of agreement. **1958** *Times* 28 June 9/3 There has been a great upsurge of interest in recent years in regal pelargoniums. **1971** *Times* 22 Feb. (Canada Suppl.) p. vii/2 More recently there has been a noisy upsurge of English-Canadian nationalism in Toronto.

2. An uprising, an insurrection.

1930 *Aberdeen Press & Jrnl.* 4 Feb. 7/5 The beginnings of a widespread revolutionary upsurge..are visualised in a proclamation issued by the Red International. **1937** E. LYONS *Assignment in Utopia* (1938) II. ii. 68 The Chinese heritage asserted itself. [Eugene] Chen traveled to the land of his forebears and, without knowing its language, became a leader in the revolutionary upsurge. **1963** *Ann. Reg. 1962* 291 Political machinery for collective leadership to guarantee the revolutionary upsurge.

3. A sharp rise in economic activity, demand, prices, etc.

1935 *Sun* (Baltimore) 22 Apr. 8/2 A sharp upsurge in the postal receipts at Denver. **1955** *Times* 14 July 13/1 It was hardly to be expected that the paint industry could fail to share in the general upsurge of industrial activity over the past 18 months. **1962** *Listener* 7 June 980/2 The speediest possible upsurge in the production of meat and milk. **1974** *Guardian* 25 Jan. 14/1 An upsurge in exports this year has boosted the national output by 6·9 per cent. **1985** *Times* 8 Jan. 17/2 Distillers Co...was another to fail to join the upsurge.

4. A rapid growth in number or size.

1955 A. L. ROWSE *Expansion of Elizabethan Eng.* 161 The sudden upsurge..is witnessed precisely by Hakluyt. **1974** *Sunday Post* (Glasgow) 31 Mar. 9/1 In this year of strife there's been an upsurge of Scots wanting to emigrate.

5. *lit.* A surging upwards.

1969 *Daily Tel.* 5 Feb. 1/8 There was such an upsurge of gas that 14 surplus workmen were evacuated by helicopter. But then the safety valve clicked in.

up'surgence. [f. prec. + -ENCE, after *resurgence*, etc.] = UPSURGE.

1934 in WEBSTER. **1945** *Sun* (Baltimore) 5 Feb. 40/2 Mr. Harry L. Hopkins' view of what is needed to keep the Germans and Japanese from new upsurgences is certainly not a frivolous one. **1958** *Church Times* 22 Aug. 3/4 He emphasized the great dangers of the upsurgence of non-Christian religions in the Eastern world—particularly Buddhism. **1971** I. G. GASS et al. *Understanding Earth* xii. 160/1, I have mentioned the possible effect of plant upsurgence during the Carboniferous.

up'swallow, *v.*, etc. (UP- 4, 5, 6.)

1591 DRAYTON *Harmonie of Church, Song Jonah* 8 Mighty wallowing waves..Have with their power up-swallowed me. **1618** H. AINSWORTH *Ps.* cvii. 27 All their wisdom is upswallowed quight. **1850** BLACKIE *Æschylus* II. 176 And the greedy spear upswallowing, Man by man, its gory food. **1853** F. W. NEWMAN *Odes of Horace* 97 Some, victims to stern-gazing Mars The Furies give: and sailors The greedy sea upswallows.

up'swarm, *v. trans.* (UP- 4.)

1597 SHAKS. *2 Hen. IV*, IV. ii. 30 You haue taken vp..The Subiects of Heauens Substitute, my Father, And..Haue here vp-swarmed them.

upswarming, -sway: see UP- 4, 6.

'upsweep. [UP- 2.] **1.** An upward movement in a long, sweeping curve; a raising or lifting up. Also *fig.*

1898 W. J. LOCKE *Idols* xx. 285 'Who knows?' said Minna, with an insolent upsweep of her lazy lashes. **1954** M. OLIVER *Failing Wine* xxvii. 100 But what are we to say of the upsweep of the moral curve? **1976** *Daily Tel.* 2 Aug. 10 As a result I believe we would see an upsweep in the morale of the whole country.

b. *spec.* An upswept hair-style.

1946 'P. QUENTIN' *Puzzle for Fiends* (1947) xxi. 151 She moved out of the room..absently patting the stray hairs of her upsweep. **1978** J. UPDIKE *Coup* iii. 105 The trim Dacron skirt and jacket, with secretarial upsweep and..dearth of bangles.

up'swell, *v.* [UP- 4 + SWELL *v.* Cf. MDu. *opswellen* (Du. *opzwellen*), MLG. *upswellen*, MHG. *ûfswellen* (G. *aufschwellen*).]

1. *intr.* To swell up; to rise up by or as by swelling. Also *fig.*

c **1386** CHAUCER *Prioress' T.* 108 The serpent Sathanas, That hath in Iues herte his waspes nest, Vp swal [*Petworth MS.* vpswal] and seide [etc.]. **1582** STANYHURST *Æneis* II. (Arb.) 52 His feet ar vpswelling with raynes of bridil ybroached. **1740** DYER *Ruins of Rome* 135 The num'rous porticoes and domes upswell, With..columns interpos'd. **1816** WORDSW. *Ode, 1814*, 14 The azure sea upswelled upon the sight. **1828** J. STERLING *Ess.*, etc. (1848) II. 62 The tall ash which..upswells to and waves amid the skies. **1875** MORRIS *Æneid* XII. 666 In his heart upswelled a mighty flood Of..maddening grief.

2. *trans.* To increase the volume of (something) by or as by swelling.

1582 STANYHURST *Æneis* II. (Arb.) 56 As a trauayler.. whips backward from woorme, with poysoned anger Vp-sweld. **1793** WORDSW. *Descr. Sk.* 563 Alps overlooking Alps their state upswell. **1845** MANGAN *German Anthology* I. 48 The rain..dashes earthwards in floods, Upswelling the deluging fountains.

upswelled, *ppl. a.* (UP- 5. Cf. prec.)

1878 LE CONTE *Elem. Geol.* 246 These lines of upswelled and folded strata.

up'swelling, *vbl. sb.* (UP- 7.)

1548 BODRUGAN *Epit. King's Title* 248 In tempestious vp-swellynges of water. **1658** A. FOX *Würtz' Surg.* III. xiv. 260 That water..filleth up that place.., wherby [it]..is enforced to an up-swelling. **1878** LE CONTE *Elem. Geol.* II. v. 253 The amount of upswelling..is fully adequate to account for the upheaval of the greatest mountain-chains.

up'swelling, *ppl. a.* (UP- 6 b.)

1855 BRIMLEY *Ess.* (1858) 74 The personal unhappiness, the private wrong,..give way before the upswelling sympathy.

'upswept, *a.* Also (older) up'swept. [UP- 5 (*b*).]

1. Swept up.

1791 COWPER *Iliad* XI. 375 The foam Upswept by wand'ring gusts fills all the air.

2. Applied to (a style of) hair brushed up and fastened at the top of the head; = *swept-up* s.v. SWEPT *ppl. a.* 1.

1938 *Vogue* 15 June 34 Those toy-size doll hats..on many French heads already—and what a fine solution they are to up-swept hair. **1939** M. B. PICKEN *Lang. Fashion* 160/3 *Up-swept*, term applied to style of hairdress with smooth, high-swept back and small curls on top of head. **1946** 'P. QUENTIN' *Puzzle for Fiends* (1947) xvii. 119 Her rakish upswept hair-do. **1959** *News Chron.* 12 Aug. 3/6 Two oval faces, with smooth up-swept hair. **1976** J. GRENFELL *Joyce Grenfell requests Pleasure* xiii. 182 Lynn showed me how to achieve a fold at the back of my up-swept hair. **1981** A. LURIE *Lang. Clothes* iii. 72/1 Her upswept hairdo, puffed out over pads of wire and horsehair.

3. More generally, having an upward sweep, curved upwards.

1960 *News Chron.* 16 Sept. 1/7 The woman the police are seeking..wears glasses with blue upswept frames. **1961** *Shropshire Mag.* Apr. 43/1 (Advt.), New spectacle frames... Two-tone 17/-; Upswept 20/-. **1961** WEBSTER s.v., Upswept rear fenders. **1984** *Washington Post* 9 July C7/1 There he is, with his striped pantaloons and upswept conquistador hat.

'upswing. [UP- 2.] **1.** *Golf.* = *back-swing* s.v. BACK- A. II. *rare.*

1922 WODEHOUSE *Clicking of Cuthbert* vi. 145 His up-swing was shaky, and he swayed back perceptibly.

2. a. *Econ.* An upward movement or trend in economic conditions; a (period of) improvement in trading activity. Freq. in advb. phr. ***on the upswing***.

1934 *Sun* (Baltimore) 20 Oct. 1/2 Reflecting a sharp upswing in retail trade throughout the country, data on current employment and pay roll trends were made public today. **1946** [see DOWN-SWING]. **1953** *Times* 31 Oct. 1/11 They do not..reflect the vigorous upswing in the industrial output this year, as revealed by the monthly Treasury indices. **1967** *N.Y. Herald Tribune* (Internat. ed.) 11-12 Feb. 7/7 (*heading*) Market closes on upswing; color TV comes into demand. **1973** 'R. MACLEOD' *Burial in Portugal* iv. 90 When he'd bought in, Consolidated had already been shading at 130 and Maltsters had been on the upswing at 146. **1983** *Daily Tel.* 20 Oct. 21/2 The latest batch of cyclical indicators suggest that the upswing in the economy will continue well into 1984.

b. *transf.* and *fig.*

1947 *Ann. Rev. Microbiol.* I. 351 The seasonal upswings of influenza A or B are much less uniform in time than those of other diseases such as diphtheria, measles, or chickenpox. **1951** *Sunday Pictorial* 21 Jan. 12/5 There is a general upswing in your affairs. **1963** 'E. MCBAIN' *Ten Plus One* (1964) ii. 27 Gang violence..seemed to enjoy an upswing during the summer months. **1976** A. CASSORLA *Skateboarder's Bible* 13 The Sport was once again on the up-swing.

upswollen: see UP- 5.

†upsy, *prep. phrase. Obs.* Forms: 6-7 **vpsy**, **vpsey, vpse, vpsie**, 7 **vpsee**; 7 **upsy, upsi, upse, upzee**, 7-8 **upsey**. [ad. Du. *op zijn* (= op SEI), lit. 'on his (her, or its)', used in such expressions as *op zijn Vriesch*, 'in the Frisian fashion'.] In the ..fashion; after the..manner.

A. In the phrases *upsy Friese*, *Dutch*, *English*, 'after the Frisian, German (or Dutch), English fashion', used originally with reference to modes or habits of drinking.

I. upsy Friese. 1. *adv.* Deeply, heavily, to excess.

The phrase also occurs as the name of a tune (*a* 1627) in *Historie of Fryer Bacon*. The reason for the addition of *crosse* in quot. 1592 is not clear.

1592 NASHE *P. Penilesse* E iv, He is no body that cannot drinke *super nagulum*, carouse the Hunters hoop, quaffe *vpsey freze crosse*. **1601** [? MARSTON] *Jack Drums Entert.* II. D 4 b, Powre Wine,..Drinke Duch like gallants, lets drinke vpsey freeze. **1606** DEKKER *Sev. Sins* I. (Arb.) 12 They.. were drunke, according to all the learned rules of Drunkennes, as Vpsy-Freeze, Crambo, Parmizant, &c. **1635** HEYWOOD *Philocoth.* 65 To drinke Vpse-phreese.

b. Thoroughly; entirely; quite.

1598-9 B. JONSON *Case is Altered* IV. iii, Tut, no more of this surquedry; I am thine own *ad unguem*, upsie freeze, pell mell.

2. *sb.* A mode of drinking or carousing.

1590 LODGE *Euphues Gold. Leg.* D 2, After they had feasted and frolickt it twise or thrise with an vpsey freeze. **1600** NASHE *Summer's Last Will* F j b, *A vous, mounsieur Winter*, a frolick vpsy freese, crosse, ho, *super nagulum*. **1608** DEKKER *Dead Term* A 4 b, At his [*i.e.* the Dutchman's] owne weapon of Vpsie freeze will they dare him.

b. Intoxicating liquor. *rare.* (Cf. C.)

1648 *Canterburie March* B 3 Fill me a cup of upsy-frize To joy our Friends.

3. *adj.* Inclined or addicted to carousing. *rare*⁻¹.

1631 J. DONE *Polydoron* 105 The Saylor is reasonable at Sea and cannot abide Whistling; but at Land they [*sc.* soldiers and sailors] are both upzeefreeze.

Hence **upsy-'friese** *v.*, to drain or empty (a pot of liquor); **upsy-'friesy** *a.*, addicted to drinking deeply.

1617 J. TAYLOR (Water-P.) *Trav. to Hamburgh* B 2, My company and my selfe went to a Dutch drinking-schoole, and..vpsefreez'd foure pots of boone beere. **1622** MASSINGER & DEKKER *Virg. Martyr* II. i, Bacchus..grand patron of rob-pots, upsy-freesy tipplers, and super-naculum takers.

II. upsy Dutch. 1. *adv.* = prec. 1.

1607 DEKKER *Knt.'s Conjur.* (1842) 29 He..swore he could find in his heart to goe presently (hauing drunk vpsy

Dutch). **1622** FLETCHER *Beggar's Bush* III. i, Sit downe Lads, And drink me upsey-Dutch. *a* **1634** CHAPMAN *Alphonsus* III. i. (1654) 30 We'l spend this evening lustie upsie Dutch, In honour of this unexpected league. **1670** DAVENANT & DRYDEN *Tempest* IV. 62, I will pledge your Grace Up se Dutch.

b. In general use.

a **1634** CHAPMAN *Alphonsus* II. ii. (1654) 18 Then kiss your hand three times upsy Dutch. **1721** D'URFEY *Athenian Jilt* Operas, etc. 165 And now do's upsey Dutch endeavour To make himself more valu'd be By bragging of his Family.

2. *adj.* Suggestive of having drunk too deeply; heavy.

1610 B. JONSON *Alch.* IV. vi, I doe not like the dulnesse of your eye: It hath a heauy cast, 'tis vpsee Dutch, And say's you are a lumpish whore-master.

III. upsy English (cf. *upsy Friese* 2 b).

1622 FLETCHER *Beggar's Bush* IV. iv, *Prig.* I for the structure, Which is the bowl. *Hig.* Which must be up-sey English, Strong, lusty London beer.

B. In other uses.

1. ***upsevant muff*** [cf. Du. *want* mitten, and MUFF *sb.*[1], *sb.*[2]], ? like a fur cap.

1591 NASHE *Introd. Sidney's Astr. & Stella* A iv b, An Asse is no great stateman in the beastes common-wealth, though he weare his eares *vpseuant muffe*, after the Muscouy fashion.

2. As *adj.* or *adv.* Extreme(ly), ultra.

1650 A. B. *Mutatus Polemo* 10 He that even now was upsie Cavaleer high Royalists. **1694** LOCKE in Ld. King *Life* (1830) I. 383 He that reads this act [for licensing printing] with attention will find it upse ecclesiastical.

3. As *prep.* In or after the manner of.

1663 KILLIGREW *Pars. Wedding* IV. i, Yes, faith, they have treated her upsey Whore, lain wth her.

†**'uptails.** *Obs.* Also up-tails. [UP *adv.*[1] + TAIL *sb.*[1] 1, 5.]

1. ***up tails all***, the name of an old song and its tune. Also used allusively (see TAIL *sb.*[1] 5, 5 c).

1598 B. JONSON *Ev. Man in Hum.* I. iii, Hang sorrow, care will kill a cat, vp-tailes all, and a poxe on the hangman. **1607** SHARPHAM *Fleire* (1610) F j b, Shee euerie day sings Iohn for the king, and at Vp-tailes all, shees perfect. **1610** R. VAUGHAN *Water-Workes* K 2, Though I am no Poet yet I can make Ballads, To the tune of vp-tayls-all. **1648** HERRICK *Hesper.*, *Up tailes all*, For love he doth call For his Uptailes all; And that's the part to be acted. **1697** VANBRUGH *Prov. Wife* v. iii, *Mademoiselle.* Why, what be de matter? *Rasor.* The matter? Why, uptails all's the matter..My lady has cuckolded my master.

2. a. (With *all*.) A jovial fellow; a reveller.

1602 DEKKER *Satyrom.* I 2 b, Feele (my light-vptailes all) feele my weapon.

b. A woman.

1671 CROWNE *Juliana* III. 26 How I shall laugh to see the little pretty uptails come to make a home-thrust at a man.

3. A card-game.

1694 *Poor Robin* Dec. B 7 b, Whisk, Uptails, Sant, New-Cut,..With other Games besides, the which I know not.

'uptake, *sb.* Also *Sc.* uptak', *north. dial.* uptack. [UP- 2. Cf. ON. and Icel. *upptak* neut., *upptaka* fem.]

1. The action of, or capacity for, understanding; comprehension. Usu. in phr. ***quick*** (***slow, gleg*** (*Sc.*), etc.) ***on*** (***at, in***) ***the uptake***. Orig. *Sc.*

1816 SCOTT *Old Mort.* vii, Everybody's no sae gleg at the uptake as ye are yoursell. **1847** W. E. AYTOUN *Dreepdaily Burghs* iv, 'I really do not understand you, gentlemen.' 'Troth, then, ye're slow at the uptak.' **1871** ALEXANDER *Johnny Gibb* x, I'm nae sayin' 't Benjie hisna a better uptak' nor the like o' him. **1878** A. PAUL *Random Writ.* 112 Children are very quick in the uptake. **1911** E. M. CLOWES *On Wallaby* vi. 162 They..are not so 'smart', so quick in the up-take, as themselves. **1927** H. A. VACHELL *Dew of Sea* 259 For a moment the chieftain was puzzled. But he was fairly quick at the up-take, replying after a pause. **1931** D. L. SAYERS *Five Red Herrings* viii. 92 A good girl..but slow in the uptake. **1940** R. S. LAMBERT *Ariel & all his Quality* viii. 190 No one was 'quicker on the uptake'; no one responded quicker to a nod or a wink. **1949** *Here & Now* (N.Z.) Oct. 13/1 An energetic, likeable, cockily pugnacious figure, but slow, almost Neanderthally slow, on the uptake. **1957** H. NICOLSON *Journey to Java* vi. 106 Being quick at the uptake, he then realized that the flat had been visited by house-breakers. **1980** K. CROSSLEY-HOLLAND *Norse Myths* p. xxvi, He was..a bit slow in the uptake, but immensely strong and dependable.

2. = TAKE-UP *sb.* 4.

1839 R. S. ROBINSON *Naut. Steam Eng.* 129 The uptake, communicating from each boiler, in the common funnel. **1859** W. RANKINE *Steam-Engine* 451 A chamber called the smoke box, or uptake, in which the various flues terminate. **1887** *Encycl. Brit.* XXII. 499/1 The uptakes from both ends converge to the funnel base above the centre of the boiler's length.

3. A ventilating shaft by which foul air ascends.

1889 WELCH *Text Bk. Naval Archit.* xii. 132 Advantage is taken of the hollow towing bollards..to utilise these also as uptakes. **1908** *Animal Managem.* 248 Permanent air funnels ..should be arranged in pairs,..thus furnishing an up-take and down draught (outlet and inlet).

4. An upward draught or current of air.

1887 R. ABERCROMBY *Weather* 79 To assume that the ascensional uptake in front of the main body of the shower is as unsteady as the surface-wind. *Ibid.* 126 Where the uptake is less strong.

5. Absorption or incorporation by a living system. Also *transf.*

1931 W. O. JAMES *Introd. Plant Physiol.* vi. 156 (*heading*) The uptake of water. **1956** *Nature* 28 Jan. 192/1 The uptake of potassium ions by disks of red beet root tissue. **1971** *Country Life* 8 July 119/1 Between 1968 and 1975 the textile industry's uptake of wool would fall by 23 per cent. **1974** [see *photoscan* s.v. PHOTO- 2].

up'take, *v.* [UP- 4. Cf. TAKE *v.* 90, MSw. *up-, upptaka*, etc. (Sw. *upptaga*), MDa. (and Da.) *optage* in sense 3.]

†**1.** *trans.* To perform or pursue (a flight) upwards. *Obs.*

c **1250** *Gen. & Ex.* 277 Min fliȝt..ic wile up-taken, Min sete norð on heuene maken. *a* **1711** KEN *Hymnotheo* Poet. Wks. 1721 III. 226 Saints Self-jealous will their Flights uptake, We'll follow of the first the radiant Wake.

†**2.** To deliver up, to surrender. *Obs.*[−1]

1297 R. GLOUC. (Rolls) 7949 þe king him made þuder wende, mid is owe folc, to make þe folc þat þer inne was þen castel him vp take [*v.r.* optake].

3. To pick or take up; to raise from the ground, etc.; to lift. *Obs.* or *arch.*

a **1300** *E.E. Psalter* xvii. 19 He sent fra hegh, and vptoke me; Fra many watres me nam he. **13..** *K. Alis.* 7579 (Laud MS.), He was vptaken of gentil men And ysette on heiȝe benche. *c* **1340** HAMPOLE *Pr. Consc.* 5142 Ihesu Crist þat here es uptane Fra yhow, til heven. *c* **1420** *Anturs of Arth.* 656 (Douce MS.), Boþe þes trauayled mene þey truly vp take; Vnnethe miȝte þo sturne stonde vp riȝte. *c* **1440** *Pallad. on Husb.* XI. 291 Of see quyete vptaketh they maryne Water purest. **1587** TURBERV. *Trag. T.* 89 b, Then willd he all the Ladies limmes..To be vptaken, peece by peece. **1596** SPENSER *F.Q.* IV. ii. 25 It..befell, That Satyran a girdle did vptake, Well knowne to appertaine to Florimell.

fig. **1590** SPENSER *F.Q.* III. ii. 9 The word gone out, she backe againe would call,..But that he it vp-taking ere the fall, Her shortly answered. **1654** GAYTON *Pleas. Notes* II. ii. 37 But Sancho (wise) uptakes That matter, and..Desires with bread and cheese to pacifie His great distemper.

†**b.** *fig.* To raise from distress or straits; to take into one's care or protection. *Obs.*

Only in or after Biblical usage, usually tr. L. *suscipere*.

a **1300** *E.E. Psalter* xxvi. 16 Mi fader and mi moder me for-soke þai; Lauerd sothlike vptoke me ai. *a* **1340** HAMPOLE *Psalter* xvii. 38 þi righthand vptoke me. **1388** WYCLIF *Isaiah* xli. 10 Y coumfortide thee..; and the riȝthond of my iust man vp took thee. *c* **1400** *Prymer* (1895) 84 Uptake þou me bi þi word, & y schal lyue. *c* **1450** *Cov. Myst.* (Shaks. Soc.) 127 Israel for his childe up-toke he to cum. **1551** STERNHOLD & H. *Ps.* vi. 4 Lord turne thee to thy wonted grace, my sely soule vp take [**1584** vptake].

†**c.** To raise up, exalt. Also *absol.* *Obs.*

c **1340** HAMPOLE *Pr. Consc.* 8247 þai salle þan se..Whi ane es uptane tylle a kyngdom, And ane other es putted in-tylle thraldom. *c* **1460** *Towneley Myst.* xxiv. 380 As fortune assyse men wyll she make; hir manners ar nyse, she can downe and vptake.

†**4.** To take possession of; to occupy. *Obs.*

c **1425** WYNTOUN *Cron.* IV. ix. 1173 All þe cete þus fand þai With þare fais neire vptane. **1452** *Reg. Mag. Sig. Scot.* 131/2 My gudis..to be frely ressavit, uptakyn, governit and fullely disponit at the will..of the saide Walter. **1513** DOUGLAS *Æneid* III. ii. 108 The lugeingis [were] void and reddy to thair fais, The sete left waist till ony it wptais.

†**5.** To reprove, rebuke. *Obs.*[−1]

c **1440** *Psalmi Peniten.* (1894) 1 Lord, yn thin anger, uptake [L. *corripias*] me nought.

†**6.** To receive hospitably. *Obs.*[−1]

a **1470** HARDING *Chron.* IX. i, Winde theim droue..Into Affrique, where..Thei welcomed wer and worthely vptake.

†**7.** *Sc.* To obtain, get, or exact by way of tax, contribution, or payment; to levy; = UPLIFT *v.* 3.

1493 *Reg. Cupar Abbey* I. 244 Dewiteis of the samyn [lands] to rais and vptak. **1534** *Acc. Ld. High Treas. Scot.* VI. 221 To help the said John Perdovin to uptak the said movable gudis. *c* **1560** A. SCOTT *Poems* i. 133 Teindis ar vptane be testament transgressouris. **1592** *Excheq. Rolls Scot.* XXII. 236 The maillis of the castellandis..intromettit and uptaikin be Johnne, lord Maxwell. **1640–1** *Kirkcudbr. War. Comm. Min. Bk.* (1855) 58 The Committie ordaines him to uptak the pryce according to the feirs of the yeir.

8. *Sc.* (and *north. dial.*). To take into the mind; to comprehend, understand.

1726 *Fleming's Fulfill. Script.* (ed. 5) Table Scots Phr., *Uptake*, to understand a thing. **1829** BROCKETT *N.C. Gloss.* (ed. 2). **1839** R. M. M'CHEYNE in Bonar *Mem.* (1844) 195 Have you really and fully uptaken Christ as the gospel lays him down? **1898** C. SPENCE *From Braes of the Carse* 32 What a pity the Laird is so dull!.. For certes he doesna uptak' what I mean.

up'taken, *pa. pple.* [UP- 5. Cf. prec.] Taken up, captivated, or charmed *with* something.

1605 in Sylvester *Du Bartas* B 2 b, Hence itching Eares with Toyes and Tales vp-taen. **1876** *Whitby Gloss.* 209/1.

†**uptaker.** *Obs.* [UP- 8, or f. UPTAKE *v.*]

1. One who sustains or supports another; a helper.

a **1340** HAMPOLE *Psalter* iii. 3 þou lord is myn vptakere. [Also xvi. 3, xli. 12, lviii. 10.] **1388** WYCLIF *Ps.* xlv. 8 God of Jacob is oure vptakere. [Also liii. 6, lxxxviii. 27.]

2. *Sc.* One who collects or levies taxes, etc.

1576 *Rec. Sheriff Crt. Aberdeen.* (1904) 242 Uptaker of the multur and knaifschipe of the tounes and lands. **1596** DALRYMPLE tr. *Leslie's Hist. Scot.* (S.T.S) II. 444 Faithful vptakeris of the lyueng and gathereris of the rentis.

3. *Sc.* A leader of psalmody; a precentor.

1620 *Extr. Burgh Rec. Stirling* (1887) 153 Teacher of musik, and uptaker of the psalmes in the kirk. **1662** *Ibid.* 241 The offices of a readder in the kirk,..and uptaker of the psalmes.

up'taking, *vbl. sb.* Chiefly *Sc.* [UP- 7, or f. UPTAKE *v.*]

In Sc. use also with stress *'up,taking*.

†**1.** The source of a stream. *Obs.*[−1]

Probably after ON. *upptaka* in the same sense.

1241–51 *Cockersand Chartul.* (Chetham Soc. 56) 854 Terram quæ jacet inter Arkelbec et stagnum molendini ad huptaking et est longitudo a le huptaking usque ad terram Margeriæ.

†**2.** The action of sustaining; sustenance, support. *Obs.*

a **1300** *E.E. Psalter* lxxxviii. 18 For of lauerd es oure vptakinge [L. *adsumptio*]. **1388** WYCLIF *Ps.* cvii. 9 Effraym is the vptaking [L. *susceptio*] of myn heed. **1447** BOKENHAM *Seyntys* (Roxb.) 46 The uptakyng of oure frele nature Whiche wyth synne was almost schent.

†**3.** *Sc.* **a.** = UPLIFTING *vbl. sb.* 2. *Obs.*

1471 in *Charters, &c. Edin.* (1871) 134 In the rasing, vptakin and paying of the said custumes. **1512** *Reg. Privy Seal Scot.* I. 374 That ȝe ceis fra all intrometting and uptaking of the saidis thre lastis of salmond. *a* **1578** LINDESAY (Pitscottie) *Chron. Scot.* (S.T.S.) I. 164 The rowmes and rentis quhilk they war in wse and possessioun affoir of wptaking thairof. **1594** [see UPLIFTING *vbl. sb.* 2]. *a* **1670** SPALDING *Troub. Chas. I* (1850) I. 78 They fell in sum wordis about the vp-taking of this fyne. *Ibid.* 133 Quhilk bred gryte truble in vptaking of the rentall.

†**b.** The levy or raising of forces. *Obs.*[−1]

a **1578** LINDESAY (Pitscottie) *Chron. Scot.* (S.T.S.) II. 243 The laird..passit..to Dundie.. for vptaking of men of weir.

†**c.** (See DITTAY.) *Obs.*[−1]

1609 SKENE *Reg. Maj., Stat. Alex. II*, 15 Vptaking of dittay and pvnissing of malefactours.

†**4.** *Sc.* ? Drawing together, gathering. *Obs.*[−1]

1503 *Acc. Ld. High Treas. Scot.* II. 203 For ane elne lynnyne to the platis uptaking of the crammesy cote, xiiij d.

5. *Sc.* A raising, picking, or lifting up.

1495 *Acta Dom. Conc.* (1839) 394/2 þe wrangwis.. vptaking of þer merchis and stanis. **1503** *Acc. Ld. H. Treas. Scot.* II. 356 For uptaking of certane treis..and carying of thaim to Strivelin. **1513** DOUGLAS *Æneid* IX. vi. 116 Behind thame, for vptakyng quhayr it lay, Mony brycht armour rychly dycht thai left. **1576** in Balfour *Oppr. in Orkney & Shetl.* (1859) 69 The allegeit uptaking of ane pece see-drewin tre. **1613** P. FORBES *Comm. Revelation* xii. (1614) 103 The exalting of the childe, is the deiecting of the Dragon from heauen: and the deiection of the Dragon, is the vptaking of the childe. **1888** C. P. BROWN *Cotton Manuf.* 168 *Up-taking*, Sc. for the take-up motion.

†**6.** *Sc.* The action of leading the psalm; precenting. *Obs.*

1579 *Burgh Rec. Edin.* (1882) IV. 126 His yeirlie stepend for vptaking of the psalmes in the kirk. **1599** *Extr. Aberd. Reg.* (1848) II. 204 To Patrik Walter for the vptacking of the psalme in the new kirk. **1618** *Extr. Burgh. Rec. Stirling* (1887) 150 The soume of ten merkis in feall for uptaking of the psalmes.

7. *Sc.* A receiving into or grasping with the mind; comprehension, conception, understanding.

1614 W. COWPER *Dikailogie* 85 Your errour proceeds from the wrong vptaking of the question. **1663** BLAIR *Autobiog.* ii. (1848) 32, I was thereby much satisfied and confirmed by his uptaking of the nature and notion of faith. **1730** T. BOSTON *Mem.* v. (1899) 59 My preaching..by degrees..ripened into a more clear uptaking of the doctrine of the gospel. *a* **1749** E. ERSKINE *Wks.* (1791) 683/1 It has in it a knowledge and uptaking of a God in Christ. **1811** CHALMERS *Let.* in Hanna *Life* (1851) I. 228 Aunty Jean tries to help out the matter by the uptakings of her quick and confident discernment. **1839** R. M. M'CHEYNE in Bonar *Mem.* (1844) 195 How many that have no uptaking of Christ, and are yet cold-hearted and at ease?

'up,taking, *ppl. a. Sc.* [UP- 6.] **a.** Engrossing, absorbing. **b.** Quick in understanding; intelligent.

1737 J. WILLISON *Afflicted Man's Comp.* i. (1744) 13 This should be the great and uptaking Business of every Man. **1756** MRS. CALDERWOOD in *Coltness Collect.* (Maitl. Cl.) 148 Though they [the Dutch] have no vivacity, yet I think they are..smarter, a great deall, than the English, that is, more uptaking.

up'tear, *v.* [UP- 4 + TEAR *v.*[1] Cf. UPTORN.] *trans.* To pull up by the roots or from the foundation; to rend up, tear out.

1593 *Sidney's Arcadia* Wks. 1922 II. 240 The laborer which cursed earthe uppteares With sweatye browes. **1667** MILTON *P.L.* VI. 663 The rest in imitation to like Armes Betook them, and the neighbouring Hills uptore. **1786** BURNS *To Mountain Daisy* v, But now the share uptears thy bed, And low thou lies! **1803** LEYDEN *Scenes Infancy* III. xxii, The forest bull, that..the ground uptore. **1850** BLACKIE *Æschylus* II. 195 He from their socket roots uptore His eyes. **1855** SINGLETON *Virgil* I. 126 Hence it nor storms, nor gusts, nor showers uptear.

fig. **1847** C. BRONTË *J. Eyre* xxvii, What good would it do if I bent, if I uptore, if I crushed her? **1850** BLACKIE *Æschylus* II. 61 Such wedlock even now He blindly broods, as shall uptear his kingdom.

up 'tempo, *a.*, (*adv.*) *Mus.* [UP *a.*] Of music, etc.: characterized by or played at a fast tempo.

1948 *Down Beat* 19 May 13 'Sleeps' is an up tempo thing by Norvo. **1958** A. MORGAN in P. Gammond *Decca Bk. Jazz* xii. 139 None..has achieved the same degree of tension.., a feeling which is more obvious in such up-tempo excursions as *Cherokee*. **1961** *Down Beat* 19 Jan. 31 'Sesame', in particular, is swift-moving and taken up-tempo. **1968** *Times* 22 Nov. 9/3 The flip side of Hey Jude was an up-tempo song called Revolution. **1976** *New Musical Express* 17 Apr. 19/6 It's uptempo with a rather slight melody.

uptene, obs. Sc. f. OBTAIN *v.*

'upter, *predic. adj. Austral. slang.* Also upta. [A corruption of *up to putty* (see PUTTY *sb.* 3 b), or some similar phr.] Bad or worthless; no good.
1919 W. H. DOWNING *Digger Dialects* 52 *Up to putty*, bad; useless; ineffectual. *Upter*, a corruption of 'up to putty'. **1949** J. CLEARY *You can't see round Corners* xxvi. 169 'How are you going?' 'Upta. I've lost on every race so far.' **1953** 'CADDIE' *Sydney Barmaid* xxxviii. 219 Dadda made some derogatory remark about the tucker. 'If it's upter why don't you 'ave a go?'

up there, *adv. phr.* [UP *adv.*^{2}] **1.** Above the earth; in heaven; *spec.* with reference to God. Cf. ABOVE *adv.* 1 b.
1938 M. MUGGERIDGE *In Valley of this Restless Mind* xvi. 145 Don't imagine..that the old gentleman up there is going to interfere... He doesn't exist. **1969** P. THEROUX *Murder in Mount Holly* iii. 44 You had to..really believe in that Big Man Up There. **1977** J. MCVEAN *Bloodspoor* xx. 260 Sometimes I almost get to feel someone up there must be pitching for us.
2. Up on a level *with* (something else highly rated). *colloq.*
1970 *Globe & Mail* (Toronto) 25 Sept. 6/1 The Post Office, which among things to have, rates right up there with athlete's foot. **1977** *Gay News* 7–20 Apr. 32/1 It is necessary to her kind of survival not to make an impression, either as an award-laden superstar (up there with Streisand..and Fonda) or even as an actress.

upthrow ('ʌpθrəʊ), *sb.* Also 9 up-throe. [UP- 2. Cf. next.]
1. *Geol.* and *Mining.* An upward dislocation of a stratum or seam.
1807 J. HEADRICK *View Arran* 66 A high rock, caused by what is called an up-throe of the metals. *Ibid.*, This up-throe running westward, forms a sort of ridge. **1883** [see UPLEAF *sb.* 2]. **1888** J. PRESTWICH *Geol.* II. 95 An elevation of the strata on one side, and..depression on the other, which are called by the miners the upthrow and the downthrow.
attrib. **1839** URE *Dict. Arts* 965 Dikes and faults are denominated upthrow or downthrow, acording to the position they are met with in working the mine. **1872** *Proc. Amer. Philos. Soc.* XII. 444 A fine upthrow fault..in East Tennessee. **1882** GEIKIE *Geol. Sk.* 282 A true fault with an upthrow and downthrow side.
b. Amount of upward displacement.
1889 *Hardwicke's Sci. Gossip* XXV. 228/1 A small fault, with five feet upthrow.
2. *Geol.* An upheaval of part of the earth's crust or surface; an uplift.
1833 LYELL *Princ. Geol.* III. 338 The sudden upthrow of another system of parallel chains of mountains. **1863** DANA *Man. Geol.* 727 By the upthrow, rocks of the Lower Silurian have been carried up to the level of those of the Subcarboniferous. **1884** GEIKIE in *Nature* 13 Nov. 31 In the great upthrow, it is this sandstone platform which has been pushed over the limestones.
3. An outburst or manifestation.
1855 M. PATTISON in *Oxford Ess.* 274 The Wycliff movement,..that last upthrow of Latin philosophy.
4. The action of throwing up or casting upwards.
1898 *Daily News* 23 Sept. 2/3 The up-throw with which a marksman jerks his rifle from his shoulder after a successful shot.

upthrow (ʌp'θrəʊ), *v.* [UP- 4. Cf. THROW *v.*^{1} 48.]
1. *trans.* To throw or cast upwards; to toss or fling up.
c **1614** SIR W. MURE *Dido & Æneas* II. 276 Both heards of Hart and Hinde..with feet the dust vpthroe. **1748** THOMSON *Cast. Indol.* I. xxvii, The fountain..That in the middle of the court up-threw A stream. **1750** COLLINS *Superstit. Highlands* 144 A Pigmy-folk..Whose bones the delver with his spade upthrows. **1819** BYRON *Juan* II. xxix, Fifty tons of water were upthrown By them per hour. **1875** MORRIS *Æneid* x. 844 [He] forth his hands upthrew Toward heaven.
†**b.** To cast up (the eyes). *Obs.*$^{-1}$
1600 FAIRFAX *Tasso* XVII. lxxv, Of Almerike the image.. that vpthrew His eies, like one that vs'd to contemplate.
†**2.** = UPTEAR *v.* *Obs.*$^{-1}$
1627 DRAYTON *Moon-Calf* 168 The Tempest so outragious grew, That it whole hedgerowes by the roots vp threw.

up'throwing, *vbl. sb.* (UP- 7. Cf. prec.)
1825 JAMIESON, *Upthrowin*, the vulgar name for puking. **1844** [R. CHAMBERS] *Vestiges Nat. Hist. Creation* 73 An era of local up-throwing of the primitive..matter of our planet.

'upthrust, *sb.* [UP- 2.]
1. a. The action of thrusting or fact of being thrust upwards, esp. by volcanic action.
1846 *Mem. Geol. Surv. Gt. Britain* I. 228 The upthrust of the Cornish and Devonian granites. **1862** G. P. SCROPE *Volcanos* 129 Serpentine and even granite may be..in course of formation and upthrust..at the present day. **1895** *Pop. Sci. Monthly* Mar. 580 A crater of this sort is formed by the upthrust of the masses of lava.
b. The upward force that a liquid exerts on a body in it.
1916 ALLEN & MOORE *Text-bk. Pract. Physics* 54 The resultant supporting force may be termed the upthrust. **1982** J. J. WELLINGTON *Physics for All* vii. 46 A heavy ship needs a very large upthrust on it to make it float.
2. An upthrust body of rock or the accompanying fault.
1942 M. P. BILLINGS *Structural Geol.* viii. 154 Upthrusts are high angle faults along which the relatively uplifted block has been the active element. **1977** G. SCOTT *Hot Pursuit* viii. 75 Mountains run the whole length of the North Island of New Zealand, great upthrusts of grey-wacke and jointed sandstone. **1982** T. HILLERMAN *Dark Wind* (1983) viii. 46 The plane..had struck an upthrust of basalt which jutted from the floor of the wash.

up'thrust, *pa. pple.* and *ppl. a.* (UP- 5.)
1845 BROWNING *Time's Revenges* 36 Some creature..to be down-torn, Upthrust and outward-borne. **1873** LONGF. *Wayside Inn* III. *Poet's T., Interl.* 40 Then flash of brazen armour bright,..and spears up-thrust. **1890** *Q. Jrnl. Geol. Soc.* May 216 An upthrust portion of the old crystalline floor.

up'thrusting, *vbl. sb.* [UP- 7.]
1924 A. GEIKIE *Long Life's Work* vii. 229 He was greatly interested in the proofs of the stupendous upthrusting of the strata. **1931** J. S. HUXLEY *What dare I Think?* vi. 183 This generation's multifarious upthrustings of the religious spirit. **1984** W. GARNER *Rats' Alley* xi. 235 Antequera, an upthrusting of castle, belfries and white walls.

up'thrusting, *ppl. a.* [UP- 6.]
1951 A. L. ROWSE *England of Elizabeth* 314 Monastic buildings that could be made into comfortable country houses for up-thrusting families. **1958** T. EDWARDS *Worlds Apart* x. 205 Upthrusting granite crags polished by sun and wind.

'up-tick. Chiefly *U.S.* [UP- 2.] An upward trend; an increase in rate.
1970 *Time* 27 Apr. 84/1 The Government reported upticks in three key indicators. **1975** *Newsweek* 10 Feb. 30/1 A modest uptick would begin around the end of the year, and..produce real growth of 4.8 per cent. **1977** *Time* 18 July 44/3 Less cheering was an uptick in the unemployment rate. **1982** *Times* 20 May 17/8 A further up-tick in interest rates offers little encouragement to London's bulls.

'uptie, *sb. Naut. Obs.* Forms: 3–4 **upteye**, 4 **vpteigh, vpteygh, vptieghe, vptihe,** 5 **vptie (huptie).** [UP- 2 + TIE *sb.*] = TIE *sb.* 2.
1295 *Acc. Exch. K.R.* 5/7 In vj. cables et in uno uptey emptis ix. li. xij. s. *Ibid.* 5/12 Pro aliis diversis cordis..que dicuntur listinges upteys et steyes. **1336** *Ibid.* 19/31 m. 4 In xl petris cordis de canabo..pro duobus upteyes inde faciendis. **1359** in *Pipe Roll 38 Edw. III*, m. 47 b, iiij. haunsers, .ij. vptieghes, j boterope, j wyndyngrope. ? *a* **1400** *Morte Arth.* 3675 Vptyes [*text* Vpcynes] eghelynge þay ochene þare-aftyre; With þe swynge of þe swerde sweys þe mastys. **1420** in *For. Acc. 3 Hen. VI*, H j b, In j. salierd, ij haliers ij. hupties j Cople ȝerderopes. **1424** *Ibid.* 59 m. 22 d j haunser pro upteyes.

up'tie, *v.* [UP- 4 + TIE *v.* 11.]
1. *trans.* To tie, bind, or fasten up.
1590 SPENSER *F.Q.* I. iv. 31 An hatefull Snake, the which his taile vptyes In many folds. *Ibid.* II. ii. 15, VI. iv. 24. **1714** [CROXALL] *Orig. Canto Spenser* xx, The Chain, Which did her tender Limbs to th' Rock upty.
fig. **1590** SPENSER *F.Q.* II. ii. 1 When Sir Guyon with his faithfull guide Had..The end of their sad Tragedie vptyde.
†**2.** To enclose or confine. *Obs.*$^{-1}$
1600 FAIRFAX *Tasso* XIV. x, A narrow roome our glorie vaine vp-ties, A little circle doth our pride containe.
So **up'tied** *pa. pple.*, **up'tying** *pres. pple.*
c **1450** *Cov. Myst.* (Shaks. Soc.) 217 My breche be nott ȝett welle up-teyd, I had such hast to renne away. **1654** GAYTON *Pleas. Notes* III. x. 131 (Deny'd accesse, and tongues up ty'd) To Paper Stratagems we turn'd. **1818** KEATS *Endym.* II. 803 Every eve saw me my hair uptying With fingers cool as aspen leaves.

up'tight, *a. colloq.* and *slang* (orig. *U.S.*). [UP- 3.] **1. a.** Of a person: in a state of nervous tension or anxiety; inhibited, worried, 'on edge'; angry, 'worked up' (*about* something).
Quot. 1934 is an isolated early example.
1934 J. M. CAIN *Postman always rings Twice* xvi. 190 I'm getting up tight now, and I've been thinking about Cora. Do you think she knows I didn't do it? **1966** *Sunday Times* (Colour Suppl.) 13 Feb. 35/4 *Up tight*, tense. **1968** *Mad* LXXVII. 30 'Uptight' means, like, a bad scene. It's when you're hung up, or wigged out, or you can't make it. We all get 'uptight' once in a while. **1969** C. YOUNG *Todd Dossier* 38 He looked worried. Really worried. As the kids say, he was up-tight. **1973** E. CALDWELL *Annette* (1974) VI. ii. 137 I'd guess you'd gotten so uptight from being denied motherhood that you were ready to leave home. **1975** D. LODGE *Changing Places* ii. 83 You're feeling all cold and uptight and wishing you hadn't come. **1977** M. EDELMAN *Political Lang.* v. 90 To the uptight policeman everyone is a potential offender. **1981** P. P. READ *Villa Golitsyn* II. iv. 112, I was afraid you might be a little uptight about that sort of thing.
b. *fig.* Characteristically formal in manner or style; correct, strait-laced.
1969 *Manch. Guardian Weekly* 28 Aug. 18 Who would have thought that an uptight institution like the august Oxford University Press would have done a thing like this? Here is a..spirited and supine piece of autobiography.. served up as a book. **1970** E. M. BRECHER *Sex Researchers* ix. 253 They tended to swing in the same socially corrrect, formal, 'up-tight' style they followed in their other activities. **1976** *Chatelaine* (Montreal) Jan. 73/3 In the morning, the apartment looked curiously uptight to Meredith.
2. In approbation: that reaches the desired standard; excellent, fine.
1962 *Down Beat* Aug. 20/2 *Jazz* Gene Ammons *Up Tight!* **1966** [see OUT-OF-SIGHT *adj. phr.* (*sb.*) 2]. **1969** *Courier-Mail* (Brisbane) 31 May 11/7 Disc jockeys..talk in a kind of sub-English..as in 'All right baby sock-it-to-me it's allright uptight yeah.'
3. Short or out of money; 'broke'.
1967 *Time* 6 Jan. 18/3 'Up tight' can mean anxious, emotionally involved or broke. **1968** *Esquire* Apr. 160/3 The expression 'uptight', which meant being in financial straits, appeared on the soul scene in the general vicinity of 1953.
Hence **up'tightness**.
1969 FABIAN & BYRNE *Groupie* vi. 46 The paranoia and savage uptightness which comes from three such guys living on top of each other and attempting to lead very together type lives while being stoned most of the time. **1974** A. LASKI *Night Music* 95 It hadn't made him any looser..that rigid uptightness was still in him. **1976** *New Yorker* 8 Mar. 57/3 In [*The Entertainer*]..Archie contrasted the uptightness of the British who don't make 'a fuss' with a fat black woman he once heard in America who sang 'her heart out to the whole world'.

uptilted, *pa. pple.* and *ppl. a.* (UP- 5.)
1849 H. MILLER *Footpr. Creat.* i. 2 Its various deposits.. have been uptilted from the bottom. **1872** W. S. SYMONDS *Rec. Rocks* ii. 33 Metamorphosed, uptilted, denuded, and formed into a ridge. **1887** SMILES *Life & Labour* 189 The sharp uptilted nose, which has run through the family.

'uptime. *Computers.* [UP *adv.*^{2}] Time when a computer or similar device is 'up' or able to function. Cf. UP *adv.*^{2} 13 b.
1958 *Communications Assoc. Computing Machinery* June 23 Uptime is based on productive time vs scheduled time. **1970** *IEEE Trans. Reliability* XIX. 24/1 Expressions are given in the literature for the availability, mean-time-between-failures, mean uptime, and mean downtime for systems consisting of a number of identical modules in redundancy. **1982** *What's New in Computing* Nov. 5/4 The document transport system has been designed for maximum reliability and uptime.

up to date, 'up-to-,date, *adv. phr.* and *a.* [UP *adv.*^{1} 26 c (*c*). See DATE *sb.*^{2} 7.]
A. *adv. phr.* **1.** Right up to the present time, or the time of writing.
1868 W. M. BAKER *New Timothy* xiii, So of Solomon in reference to Rehoboam, and of every father in reference to his son, up to date. **1882** *Imperial Dict.* s.v. *Post* v., To make the requisite entries on [a book] up to date. **1899** PLUMMER *Saxon Chronicles* II. p. xxvii, But up to 1001 the Winchester monks kept it up to date.
2. In a condition abreast of the times in respect of qualities, style, knowledge, presentation of facts, etc.
1889 SIMS & PETTITT (*title*), Faust Up to Date. Burlesque Opera. **1890–** [see DATE *sb.*^{2} 7]. **1892** *Photogr. Ann.* II. 293 The improvements for this season render this camera quite 'up to date'. **1892** *Bookseller* 8/2 The..information seems.. to be as accurate and as well up to date as ever. **1894** *Daily News* 9 June 5/2 Why, then, should Lord Salisbury sharpen his faculties and keep them, as the odious modern phrase is, up to date?
B. *adj.* **1.** Extending to the present time; presenting or inclusive of the latest facts, details, etc.; employing or involving the latest methods or devices.
1888 *Academy* 4 Feb. 73/2 In the absence of a good up-to-date English work on the islands. **1890** *Sat. Rev.* 16 Aug. 209/2 A complete and up-to-date summary of Demosthenic scholarship. **1892** *Pall Mall G.* 8 Feb. 2/1 Providing Malta dockyard with proper and up-to-date salvage and pumping apparatus. **1894** SALA *London up to Date* 30 Juvenility of appearance and general up-to-date smartness.
2. a. *pred.* Of persons: Having or employing the latest information, facts, or methods; keeping or being abreast of the times.
1889 W. S. GILBERT *Gondoliers* I, A Grand Inquisitor is always up to date. **1892** *Spectator* 5 March 339/1 The young farmer is thoroughly up to date, to use the modern catch-word. **1896** *Pall Mall Mag.* March 397 Jimmy is up to date, and much too clever for me.
b. *attrib.* Having tastes, style, manners, etc., regarded as prevailing at or characteristic of the present time.
1891 *Star* 16 Dec. 3/4 Up-to-date damsels, and eighteenth century belles. **1897** MCCARTHY *Own Times* V. v. 99 The 'up-to-date' reader, to use a vile slang phrase of the present day, does not much care about classics.
Hence **up-to-'datedness** (*rare*$^{-1}$); **up-to-'dately** *adv.* (*rare*$^{-1}$); **up-to-'dateness** (freq. in recent use); **up-to-'datish(ness; up-to-'datism.**
1891 *Bicycling News* 21 Feb. 113/2 Their list..suggests cheapness and up-to-dateness. **1893** *Educat. Rev.* May 423 His up-to-dateness..in the right view of handling history in class. **1893** *Pall Mall Mag.* I. 75 The terrible well-informedness and alarming up-to-datism. **1902** *Westm. Gaz.* 14 July 2/3 And this, they keep saying, is 'up-to-datishness'. **1903** *Chr. Endeavour Times* 5 Nov., *The Academy*, under its new editor, is decidedly more up-to-datish. **1928** *Daily Express* 23 Mar. 5/4 Furnish and equip her studio charmingly..and above all up-to-dately. **1931** A. HUXLEY *Music at Night* IV. 224 The public is taught that up-to-datedness is one of the first duties of man.

up top, *adv. phr.* [UP *adv.*^{2}]
1. *Mil. slang.* **a.** Above decks. **b.** Of an aircraft: in the sky.
1917 'TAFFRAIL' *Off Shore* 36 'Up top there!' bellowed James... 'Help!' James shouted. **1934** V. M. YEATES *Winged Victory* I. xix. 154 Then he saw the Fokkers. Where were the people up top? **1942** G. HACKFORTH-JONES *One-One-One* ix. 88 'What's going on up top?' he asked after he had received the Commander's message.
2. *fig.* In a position of authority or influence.
1967 WODEHOUSE *Company for Henry* iv. 66 It doesn't do any harm if she lends a hand herself. Can't leave everything to the men up top. **1979** *N.Y. Times Mag.* 30 Sept. 33/1 Sonny had friends up top in all these places—people he'd take to race-track junkets, or to theater outings.

uptorn, *pa. pple.* and *ppl. a.* (UP- 5. Cf. UP-TEAR *v.*)
a **1586** SIDNEY *Certaine Sonets* Wks. 1922 II. 303 Time haste my dying hower: Place see my grave uptorne. **1729**

SAVAGE *Wanderer* v. 192 Her Tombs wide-shatter'd, and her Dead up-torn. **1784** COWPER *Task* IV. 438 The gardener's pale, the farmer's hedge.. Uptorn by strength,.. he bundles up the spoil. **1818** KEATS *Endym.* III. 499 [She was] seated upon an uptorn forest root. **1841** *Dublin Rev.* May 344 The broken window and uptorn brass. **1877** L. MORRIS *Epic Hades* II. 121 The humble homes uptorn To gain one poor fair face.

up'toss, *v. intr.* and *trans.* (UP- 4.)
1828 CAMPBELL *Death-boat of Heligoland* 22 Now surf-sunk for minutes, again they uptossed. *a* **1851** MOIR *Graves of Dead* iv, When.. the groaning Tempest uptosses the forests. **1890** *St. Nicholas* Aug. 866/1 The noble steed uptossed his head.

up to the 'minute, *adv.* (and *adj.*) *phr.* [UP *adv.*[1]] Right up to the present time; in the latest fashion (see MINUTE *sb.*[1] 1 b). Chiefly *attrib.* or as *adj. phr.* (hyphened), as up to date as possible; completely modern; most recently available. Similarly ***up-to-the-moment, -second*** adj. phrs.
1909 R. A. WASON *Happy Hawkins* xxvii. 322 They had stopped for over a month with his friends in England, an' was posted up to the minute. **1922** S. LEWIS *Babbitt* vi. 69 Babbitt, the.. efficient, up-to-the-minute and other-wise perfected modern. **1933** J. B. PRIESTLY *Wonder Hero* v. 185 A very bright, up-to-the-minute sort of room. **1937** [see MINUTE *sb.*[1] 1 b]. **1938** *Times* 3 May 13/2 Feminine dress, new and old, is here displayed—up-to-the-moment gowns of British design. **1950** 'S. RANSOME' *Deadly Miss Ashley* iv. 44 Her black hair-do was smartly plain to set off her up-to-the-minute face. **1956** [see MINUTE *sb.*[1] 1 b]. **1967** *N.Y. Daily News* 13 Oct. 17 Dr. Frank Field.. brings you up-to-the-second weather reports. **1979** A. HAILEY *Overload* I. i. 6 This place with its up-to-the-second information. **1980** *Radio Times* 25 Nov.–5 Dec. 102/3 It's important to look up-to-the-minute, but clothes are too costly to be bought for just one appearance. **1985** *Broadcast* 11 Jan. 19/3 A lot of what you see about Poland is the latest up-to-the-minute riot or government move. There's very little that is reflective.
Hence **up-to-the-'minutely** *adv.*; **up-to-the-'minuteness.**
1940 D. A. LORD *Our Lady in Modern World* iii. 141 They proclaim their up-to-the-minuteness. **1959** *Listener* 2 Apr. 600/1 The heart of his ambition was to be.. as smartly and up-to-the-minutely American as possible.

'up-to-then, *adv. phr.* [UP *adv.*[1]] Before a given point in time; until then.
1959 P. BULL *I know Face* ix. 152, I did get my revenge by calling him Audrey instead of Aubrey, in the up-to-then famous dinner-table scene. **1976** *Brit. Jrnl. Sociol.* XXVII. 345 [National liberation struggles] in fact shook the up-to-then facile dominance of the developmentalists in the academy.

up'tower, *v. intr.* and *trans.* (UP- 4.)
1848 B. D. WALSH *Aristoph., Clouds* I. iv, There uptowers the Holy Temple. **1850** BLACKIE *Æschylus* I. 224 They their tents Against these high-towered infant walls uptowered. **1872** A. DE VERE *Leg. St. Patrick* 102 The mitred brow Uptowered sublime.

up-'town, *adv.*, **'up-town,** *a.* (Also without hyphen.) [UP *prep.*[2]]
1. *adv.* In, to, or into the higher or upper part of a town, or (*U.S.*) the residential portion of a town or city.
1802 J. COWLES *Diary* 8 Apr. (1931) 65 Mama went uptown today. **1839** C. F. BRIGGS *Harry Franco* I. xiii. 96 The rain was pattering against the windows, and the house was far uptown. **1855** CLARKE, *Uptown*, up the town. **1861** DICKENS *Gt. Expect.* vii, I had heard of Miss Havisham up town. **1883** *Century Mag.* Oct. 856/2 The current of domestic life.. then flowed onward up-town. **1899** J. L. WILLIAMS *Stolen Story*, etc. 30 Two.. told me about it uptown at dinner.
2. *adj.* Situated or dwelling up-town; of or pertaining to the upper (also, *U.S.*, residential) part of a town.
1838 J. L. STEPHENS *Trav. Greece* I. 83 Even I,.. a quondam speculator in 'up-town lots'. **1859** *Habits of Gd. Society* v. 192 So universal is insolence in America,.. even in what is called good society—the 'up-town' sets. **1883** *Century Mag.* Oct. 857/2 The course of the up-town movement at first included Broadway.
3. as *sb.* The higher or upper part of a town or city, *spec.* the residential or more prosperous area. *U.S.*
1946 R. BLESH *Shining Trumpets* vii. 160 New Orleans' downtown is the old quarter north of Canal Street. Uptown is the district around the nucleus of the American Quarter. **1975** J. GORES *Hammett* vii. 50 The frisk.. was for show, to impress high-rollers from uptown out for a night of slumming.
Hence **'uptowner**, a person from 'uptown'.
1924 [see HIGH-HAT *v.*]. **1981** P. MALLORY *Killing Matter* xii. 129 The area had.. its own rough charm, but it was as remote as Mozambique.. to your educated Uptowner.

up train: see UP *a.* 2.

up'trained, *pa. pple.* (UP- 5.)
1569 PRESTON *Cambyses* D j b, The King himselfe was godly vp trained. **1590** SPENSER *F.Q.* II. x. 27 Three faire daughters, which were well vptraind. *a* **1711** KEN *Hymns Festiv.* Poet. Wks. 1721 I. 282 In Jesus Love the Saint uptrain'd, Wou'd humble Deacon be ordain'd.

'uptrend. Chiefly *U.S.* [UP- 2.] An upward tendency; *spec.* in *Econ.*, a rise in value over a period of time.
1926 *Daily Colonist* (Victoria, B.C.) 23 Jan. 17/3 A fair demand at the opening of the [stock market] session influenced a temporary up-trend. **1934** *Sun* (Baltimore) 1 Dec. 17/1 The mercantile agency finds the irregular increases in factory operations.. have been 'transferred into a steady uptrend'. **1961** *Times* 29 Nov. 11/5 The uptrend is of less significance. **1979** *Arizona Daily Star* 5 Aug. D 1/2 Schrikker's charts show both the U.S. dollar and the pound sterling in important uptrends. **1984** *Times* 23 Nov. 19/5 AGD Research went back on an uptrend as market men heard whispers of good news from America.

† up tro, *adv. phr. Obs.*[−1] [a. LG. *up troe* (Du. *op trouw*). Cf. TROW *sb.*[1]] In good faith; really.
1654 GAYTON *Pleas. Notes* IV. xxv. 282 To gather up the arms Came Sancho up tro, or revenge Don's harmes?

'uptrunk. *nonce-wd.* [UP- 2.] Punning reference to a brass musical instrument and the trunk of an elephant.
1922 JOYCE *Ulysses* 280 Tuning up... That's music too. Brasses braying asses through uptrunks.

'upturn, *sb.* [UP- 2.]
1. a. An upturned or upthrown part.
1868 KINGLAKE *Crimea* IV. v. 90 A little upturn of the soil with a few Turks standing behind it.
b. A portion of the material of a garment turned up, e.g. at the end of a leg. *rare.*
1923 *Daily Mail* 11 Aug. 1 (Advt.), Shorts have good upturns for lengthening. **1926** *Minister's Rep. of Fashion for Gentlemen* Feb. 8/2 Trousers for wear with morning coats and dressy lounges are, of course, finished with plain bottoms, but for general wear the permanent up-turn still holds the field.
2. *fig.* = UPHEAVAL 2.
1864 *Gd. Words* 231/1 The upturns and the overthrows of war. **1873** SYMONDS *Grk. Poets* viii. 239 That idea of world-destruction, of that total upturn and Titanic revolution in the universe. **1883** *19th Cent.* May 796 There has been no greater revolution and upturn of all preconceived notions.
3. An improvement or upward turn, esp. in economic conditions; a rise in rate or value.
1930 *Daily Express* 6 Sept. 2/6 The turnover.. remained light, the upturn reflecting an extreme scarcity of sellers rather than any considerable number of buyers. **1932** *Sun* (Baltimore) 5 Nov. 14/7 Helping to hoist wheat prices were upturns in securities and cotton. **1940** [see DOWN-TURN *sb.*] **1944** [see *split-up* s.v. SPLIT-]. **1958** *Spectator* 13 June 783/2 There will be no quick upturn in the economy. **1971** LD. ROBBINS *Against Inflation* (1979) x. 51 Certainly I think that the measures which the Chancellor of the Exchequer and the Government have taken could produce.. some upturn, provided that confidence is restored. **1981** *Daily Tel.* 9 July 1/6 It is less sanguine about an imminent upturn in the economy.
4. *Linguistics.* A rise in pitch.
1964 [see DOWN-TURN, DOWNTURN *sb.*]. **1967** D. STEIBLE *Conc. Handbk. Linguistics* 132 *Upturn*, a term designating a rise in pitch, most noticeable as the terminal rise on the last syllable of an interrogative construction.

up'turn, *v.* [UP- 4. Cf. TURN *v.* 81.]
† 1. *trans.* To overthrow, subvert, or cause to fall.
a **1340** HAMPOLE *Psalter* cxvii. 13, I am put and vpturnyd [L. *eversus sum*], þat i had fallyn: and þe lord resayued me. *a* **1400** *Wycliffite Bible* Titus i. 11 Ther ben manye.. the whiche subuerten [*v.r.* vpturnen; L. *subvertunt*] alle housis.
2. To turn, throw, or tear up; to cast or turn over.
1567 DRANT *Horace, Ep.* xiv. E v, The countrye clownes when they see me vnfitte Vpturning cloddes,.. theill stande, and lawghe at it. **1667** MILTON *P.L.* x. 700 Boreas and Cæcias.. rend the Woods and Seas upturn. **1725** POPE *Odyss.* VIII. 218 Fierce from his arm th' enormous load he flings;.. Down rushing, it up-turns a hill of ground. **1762** FALCONER *Shipwr.* II. 156 Th' approaching squall.. Upturns the whitening suface of the deep. **1855** SINGLETON *Virgil* I. 74 Come then, the soil Of earth.. Let straight upturn stout bullocks. **1881** *Fortn. Rev.* Feb. 209 He.. then with a backward heave upturns the whole.
† 3. To turn upside down. *Obs.*[−1]
1610 HOLLAND *Camden's Brit.* I. 3 Where Driver, hight Arctophylax, doth his drie waine up-turn [L. *resupinat*].
4. To direct or cast (the eye, face, etc.) upwards.
1667 MILTON *P.L.* x. 279 The grim Feature.. upturn'd His Nostril wide into the murkie Air. **1744** THOMSON *Winter* 131 With broaden'd Nostrils to the Sky upturn'd, The conscious Heifer snuffs the stormy Gale. **1789** E. DARWIN *Bot. Gard.* (1791) II. 33 Vallisner sits, up-turns her tearful eyes. **1828** ATHERSTONE *Fall of Nineveh* I. 32 With brazen throats upturned,.. ten thousand [trumpets] spake again. **1838** MRS. BROWNING *To Bettine* i, Upturning worship and delight With such a loving duty To his grand face, as women will.
5. *intr.* To turn or move up or upwards.
1805 WORDSW. *Prelude* IV. 448 Up-turning, then, along an open field, We reached a cottage. **1818** BYRON *Ch. Har.* IV. li, Laid on thy lap, his eyes to thee upturn.

'upturned, *ppl. a.* [UP- 5. Cf. prec.]
1. Turned or directed upwards: **a.** Of the eye, face, etc.
1592 SHAKS. *Rom. & Jul.* II. ii. 29 The white vpturned wondring eyes, Of mortalls that fall backe to gaze on him. **1797** MRS. RADCLIFFE *Italian* i, The thousand upturned faces of the gazing crowd. **1835** LONGF. in *Life* (1891) I. 213 How strange looked the upturned faces.. in that glare! **1837** CARLYLE *Fr. Rev.* I. I. ii, With upturned awestruck eye. **1863** GEO. ELIOT *Romola* Proem *ad. fin.*, Upturned living faces and lips moving to the old prayers for help.
b. In general use.
1839 DE LA BECHE *Rep. Geol. Cornwall*, etc. v. 140 It may .. even rest upon the edges of upturned strata. **1865** TYLOR *Early Hist. Man.* 48 The upturned hands seem to expect some desired object to be thrown down.
2. Turned upside-down; inverted, overturned, capsized; turned up by digging, etc.
1816 WORDSW. *Ode, 1815*, 31 The upturned soil receives the hopeful seed. **1849** C. BRONTE *Shirley* xxvii, You knelt on the floor with.. your upturned box before you. **1895** *Daily News* 14 May 2/5 The body of a young man had been found, together with an upturned canoe.
3. Turned upwards at the point, extremity, or end; curved.
1843 LYTTON *Last Bar.* I. iv, Solomon in pointed upturned shoes. **1847** W. C. L. MARTIN *The Ox* 73/2 A fine and some-what up-turned muzzle. **1876** BRISTOWE *Th. & Pract. Med.* 571 The nose.. broad at the root, and upturned. **1885** J. E. TAYLOR *Brit. Fossils* 225 A perforation in the upturned beak.

up'turner. (UP- 8. Cf. UPTURN *v.* 2.)
1870 *Contemp. Rev.* XIV. 618 A field.. that would repay with interest an intelligent upturner and cultivator.

up'turning, *vbl. sb.* [UP- 7. Cf. UPTURN *v.*] The action of turning or causing to turn upwards; an instance of this.
[**1775** ASH.] **1846** DANA *Zooph.* (1848) 131 An upturning of the margin. **1855** J. PHILLIPS *Man. Geol.* 388 The upturning of the strata through an arc of 90°. **1869** E. A. PARKES *Pract. Hygiene* (ed. 3) 583 There has been much upturning of the soil. **1873** BLACK *Pr. Thule* vii, A quick upturning of the face.
fig. **1864** TREVELYAN *Compet. Wallah* ix. 309 The general up-turning of society occasioned by the rebellion.

up'turning, *ppl. a.* (UP- 6 b.)
1762 FALCONER *Shipwr.* II. 81 Th'upturning points his ponderous bulk sustain.

upupa (ʊ'puːpə). Now *rare* exc. as the name of a genus. [L.] = HOOPOE.
1601, etc. [see HOOP *sb.*[3] 1]. **1677** [see HOOPING *ppl. a.*[2]]. **1688** [see HOOPOE]. **1922** JOYCE *Ulysses* 407 Agendath is a waste land, a home of screechowls and the sandblind upupa. [**1979** P. MATTHIESSEN *Snow Leopard* i. 53 Then the first ray of sun in days strikes the harlequin feathers of a hoopoe, and I smile. Like many of the foothill birds, *Upupa* is a bird of Africa, but I saw one much more recently—last month, in fact—in the mountains of Umbria, in Italy.]

'upvaluation. *Econ.* [UP- 2.] A revaluation upwards, esp. of one currency in relation to others on a common standard.
1953 *N.Y. Times* 12 Jan. 26/3 Why suppose that the situation would be bettered by a new up-valuation of gold, with its invitation to a new round of inflation? **1958** *Spectator* 18 July 92/1 The disruptive rumours of an up-valuation of the German mark have disappeared. **1962** *Punch* 28 Mar. 508/1 The upvaluation of the guilder.. must have had some effect. **1976** *Economist* 10 Apr. 18/1 The French have taken the franc out of the snake, and the weedy reptile that remains may soon be killed by an overdue upvaluation of the German mark.
Hence (as a back-formation) **'upvalue** *v. trans.*, to raise the value of (a currency, etc.) on a scale.
1968 *Guardian* 23 Nov. 8/1 The refusal of the Germans to upvalue their D-mark. **1974** *Times* 9 Mar. 15/7 Sterling could have been upvalued and inflation reduced.

up'waft, *v. poet. rare.* (UP- 4.) *trans.*
1757 DYER *Fleece* III. 309 Chimney-tops.. up-wafting to the clouds The incense of thanksgiving. **1944** BLUNDEN *Shells by Stream* 20 The winds up-waft The smoke of an enchanter's fire.

up'wafted, *pa. pple.* (UP- 5.)
1791 COWPER *Iliad* VIII. 635 From the plain, Upwafted by the winds the smoke aspired. **1817** MOORE *Lalla R., Par. & Peri* 85 Ev'ry breath Upwafted from the innocent flow'rs. **1874** R. BUCHANAN *Poet. Wks.* I. 242 Unto your dim distance My soul upwafted is on wings.

upwafting: see UP- 6.

up'wake, *v. rare.* [UP- 4. Cf. MDu. *opwaken*, (M)LG. *upwaken*, Da. *opvaage*, G. *aufwachen.*] *intr.* and *trans.* To wake up.
c **1250** *Gen. & Ex.* 3466 Slep ðor non ðe ða ne up-wakeð. **1535** *Goodly Primer, Evensong* Ps. iii, I myself shall up-wake me. **1842** MANGAN *Poems* (1859) 121 Mine inner sense upwakes to see The Ghostworld's.. wondrous Deep. **1845** —— *German Anthology* I. 105 An earthquake shout upwakes the North: Forward!

upwall: see UP- 4.

upward ('ʌpwəd), *adv.*, *prep.*, *a.*, and *sb.* Forms: α. 1 **upweard** (2 **uppweard**), 2– **upward** (3 *Orm.* **uppward**), 3–7 **vpward** (4–5 **opward**), 4–6 **vp-**, 6 **vpp(e)warde**; 3 (9 *Sc.*) **upwart**, 5, *Sc.* 6 **vpwart** (5 *Sc.* **wp-**). β. 3–4, *dial.* 9 **uppard**, 4 **vppard**, 3–4 **vpard**, 4 **opard**; 3 **uppart**, 5 *Sc.* **vpart**. [OE. *upweard*, f. *up* UP *adv.*[1] + *weard* -WARD. Cf. MLG. *upwart, -wort*, MDu. *opwaert, -wert, -werd*, etc. (Du. *opwaart*), MHG. *ufwart, -wert.* See also UPWARDS.]
A. *adv.* **I. 1.** To or towards a higher position or plane; from a lower to a loftier level or object; in an ascending course or direction: **a.** In reference to movement or extension through space.
Occas. ***upward and downward***, = UP AND DOWN *adv.* 1.
α. *a* **900** CYNEWULF *Elene* 805 (Gr.), He mid bæm handum .. upweard plegade. *c* **1000** ÆLFRIC *Hom.* II. 548 Ða ʒewende eal se sang upweard to heofenum. *c* **1200** ORMIN 12826 ʒe shulenn sen.. Godess enngless Uppwarrd & dunnwarrd baþe upponn þe manness Sune stiʒhenn. *a* **1225** *Ancr. R.* 72 Ase ʒe muwen iseon þe water, hwon me punt hit, .. þeonne is hit ined aʒein uor to climben upward. **1297** R.

Glouc. (Rolls) 6564 þe water uaste wax vpward hei & wide. **1303** R. Brunne *Handl. Synne* 5272 þe fendys þat were yn þe pytte Smote vpwarde. *c* **1374** Chaucer *H. Fame* II. 236 Fire or sovne Or smoke..Alwey..seke vpwarde on hight. *c* **1400** *Pilgr. Sowle* (Caxton, 1483) v. i. 69 Now..fle we vpward, as fast as we may! **1481** Caxton *Reynard* (Arb.) 33, I will helpe that the ladder be sette vp, that he may goo vpwart theron. **1500–20** Dunbar *Poems* x. 42 Now spring vp flouris fra the rute, Reuert ȝow vpward naturaly. **1598** B. Jonson *Ev. Man in Hum.* III. v, He voided a bushell of soot yesterday, upward and doneweard. **1620** Venner *Via Recta* i. 21 Because it fumeth vpward, it causeth drowsinesse. **1697** Dryden *Virg. Georg.* I. 499 Watchful Herons,..mounting upward with erected Flight,..soar above the Sight. **1706** Prior *Ode to Queen* v, Upward the Noble Bird directs his Wing. **1771** J. S. *Le Dran's Observ. Surg.* (ed. 4) 172 Mr. Morand..dilated the Part upward and downward. **1823** Byron *Island* III. i, Sulphury vapours upward driven Had left the earth. **1876** Tennyson *Harold* I. i, Like a spirit in Hell who..cannot scape the flame..Steam'd upward from the undescendible Abysm.

fig. and *transf.* **1297** R. Glouc. (Rolls) 2957 As sone as eldol him ysey is herte vpward drou. **1766** Goldsm. *Vicar* xxviii, Thus to..fling those curses upward that must soon descend to crush thy own grey head..! **1850–1** Longf. *Golden Leg.* IV. Cloisters 15 Upward steals the life of man, As the sunshine from the wall.

β. *c* **1200** *Trin. Coll. Hom.* 105 Ech god ȝiue..cumeð of heuene dunward, and ech idel, and unnit and iuel, neðen uppard. *a* **1225** *Leg. Kath.* 1964 (Bodl. MS. 17), Hwenne þe twa walden keasten uppart þing þet ha chahten. **13..** *R. Gloucester's Chron.* (1724) 321 So þat þe water vaste waxe vppard hey & wyde. ? **13..** *Geburt Jesu* 181 in Horstm. *Altengl. Leg.* (1875) 75 Heo ne bi heold after fader ne moder, þo heo vppard steiȝ.

b. In reference to aspect, attitude, or direction.

a **1000** *Boeth. Metr.* xxxi. 23 Nis þæt ȝedafenlic þæt se modsefa monna æniȝes niðerheald wese, & þæt neb upweard. *c* **1175** *Lamb. Hom.* 59 þene Mon he lufede and welbiþohte, and for-þi his neb upward he wrohte. *a* **1225** *Leg. Kath.* 2372 Heo biheold upward, wið upaheuen heorte. **1303** R. Brunne *Handl. Synne* 6664 He loked vpwarde with hys yne. **1362** Langl. *Piers Pl.* A. v. 262 A þousent of Men ..Criȝinge vpward to Crist..To haue grace [etc.]. **1390** Gower *Conf.* I. 64 Upon his brest..he leith His hond, and cast upward his yhe. **1484** Caxton *Fables of Æsop* v. x, He loked and byheld vpward to the heuen. **1565** Cooper s.v. *Resupinus*, He standeth vpright with his clawes or nayles vpwarde to heauen. *a* **1586** Sidney tr. *De Mornay* i, If yee looke upward, yee see there infinite bodies. **1646** Sir T. Browne *Pseud. Ep.* IV. i. 181 To gape or looke upward with the eye. **1697** Dryden *Æneis* v. 687 Acestes,..shooting upward, sends his shaft. **1703** Pope *Thebais* 644 His sad companions upward gaze. **1789** Wordsw. *Evening Walk* 25 Impatience, pointing upward, showed, Through passes yet unreached, a brighter road. **1812** J. Wilson *Isle of Palms* II. 79 Upward when he turns his sight. **1818** Shelley *Rosal. & Helen* 1155 His countenance Raised upward, burned with radiance. **1850** *Household Words* I. 229/1, I saw him looking upward.

fig. *a* **1670** Hacket *Abp. Williams* II. (1693) 194 They.. look't downward upon those dishonourable Actions, not upward upon his Vertues. **1836** W. Irving *Astoria* I. 29 To these were added an aspiring spirit that always looked upward; a genius [etc.].

c. *fig.* To or towards a loftier stage, level, or standard, in respect of thought, feeling, life, distinction, excellence, etc.

c **1200** Ormin 6014 God mann riseþþ aȝȝ uppwarrd In alle gode dedess. *a* **1225** *Ancr. R.* 132 [They] þencheð uppard, of þe blisse of heouene. *c* **1449** Pecock *Repr.* III. x. 337 The chirche grewe vpward bothe in kunnyng and in lyuyng. *c* **1510** More *Picus* Wks. 2/2 Whose mind should alway as the fyre aspire vpward to heauenlye thinges. *a* **1535** —— *Rich. III*, Ibid. 68/1 Sir James Tyrell..had an high heart and sore longed vpwarde. **1605** Shaks. *Macb.* IV. ii. 24 *Rosse.* Things at the worst will cease, or else climbe vpward, To what they were before. **1692** Dryden *Eleonora* 152 Now 'tis Faith ascends, Now Hope, now Charity, that upward tends. **1732** Pope *Ess. Man* I. 173 What would this Man? Now upward will he soar, And little less than Angel, would be more. **1849** Thirlwall *Rem.* (1878) III. 352 Upward hearts—upward, above all paltry, sordid, grovelling aims and desires. **1898** Illingworth *Divine Immanence* i. 9 Every form of conscious life, from the lowest sensitive organism upward.

d. Higher in respect of price or value, etc.

1874 *Times* 12 Jan. 6/5 The trade was very firm, with a strong inclination upward in price. *Ibid.*, There appears to be a strong tendency upward [in the price of corn].

e. Sociol. ***upward mobility***, movement from a lower to a higher social level. Hence ***upward-mobile*** adj. phr., possessing upward mobility.

1949 *Amer. Jrnl. Sociol.* LIV. 519/2 These children were learning attitudes and habits leading to upward social mobility. **1964** Gould & Kolb *Dict. Soc. Sci.* 434/2 A change in social class position..is called vertical mobility, with the sub-classes of upward mobility and downward mobility. *Ibid.* 604/2 A hungry rat may be rewarded by food, an upward-mobile person by a symbol of prestige. **1969** J. & S. Baratz in T. Kochman *Rappin' & Stylin' Out* (1973) 14 The price of integration for the upward-mobile black man has been continuous tension and anxiety. **1978** J. Updike *Coup* (1979) vii. 259 Her hard-packed determination to achieve, with her husband Bud, upward mobility.

2. a. Up along the course of a stream, etc.; further into the interior of a country; to or towards a centre, metropolis, source, etc. Also in fig. context.

a **1122** *O.E. Chron.* (Laud MS.) an. 1013, Sweȝen cyning mid his flotan..wende..to Humbran muðan, & swa upp weard andlang Trentan. *c* **1205** Lay. 9298 Hamun arnde upward & oðer while adunward. **1387** Trevisa *Higden* (Rolls) II. 73 þanne vpward aboue þat is þe ilond Farne. *c* **1450** Capgrave *Life St. Aug.* 3 In þis same Numedie stant ..Tagatenses..sumwhat upward mor on-to Cartage. **1505** in Leadam *Star Chamber Cases* (Selden) 223 Euery Trow or Cobull passing vpward vndre the seide Brugge. **1568** Grafton *Chron.* II. 765 The yong kyng..he conueyed vpwarde towarde the Citie of London. **1697** Dryden *Virg. Georg.* IV. 408 An ancient Legend I prepare to sing, And upward follow Fame's immortal Spring. **1709** Pope *Ess. Crit.* 127 Be Homer's works your study,..And trace the Muses upward to their spring.

b. Towards the body or head. (Cf. 3 b, 5.)

1600 Shaks. *Hen. V*, II. iii. 19 (Q. 1), I felt to them [*sc.* his feet],..And to his knees,..and so vpward, and vpward. **1647** N. Bacon *Disc. Govt. Eng.* I. xlvii. 123 The vast body of the Roman Empire like a body wasting with age, died upward.

3. a. In, occupying, or so as to occupy a higher or the highest position or place.

a **1300** *Cursor M.* 23316 þai sal be sett in þair prisun, Vpward þair fete, þair hefdes dun. *c* **1375** *Sc. Leg. Saints* i. (*Peter*) 688 It is myn will one þe croice to be festnyt swa, myn fet vp-wart. *c* **1440** *Pallad. on Husb.* III. 787 Vpwarde The bottom, do this vessel closid so. *c* **1450** *Two Cookery-bks.* 101 Ley the pike in a charger, the wombe side vpward. **1523** Fitzherb. *Husb.* §16 The plough..tourneth the roote vpwarde, that it maye not growe. *a* **1548** Hall *Chron., Hen. VIII*, 40 They make of hym an Image paynted reuersed with his heles vpwarde. **1601** Shaks. *Jul. C.* v. iii. 93 *Messa[la].* Titinius face is vpward. *Cato.* He is slaine. **1613**, **1641** [see invert *v.* 1]. **1667** Milton *P.L.* VI. 649 Coming towards them..they saw The bottom of the Mountains upward turn'd. **1755** Johnson, *Supination*, the act of lying with the face upward. **1809** in *Naval Chron.* XXI. 369 Puncheons..were placed end-upward. **1849** Ainsworth *Lanc. Witches* II. iii, [He has nailed] a horse-shoe..to t'threshold.., heel uppard.

b. In respect of the upper part or parts, esp. of the body.

c **1400** Maundev. (1919) xxx. 178 Sum men seyn þat þei [*sc.* griffins] han the body vpward as an Egle, and benethe as a Lyoun. **1426** Lydg. *De Guil. Pilgr.* 1704 Tak exaumple off thy staff Wych Grace Dieu vn-to the gaff: Thogh the poynt be sharp & kene, Yt ys vpward pleyn, smothe & clene. **1575** Laneham *Let.* (1907) 54 Fyrst, oour too feet, too legs, too kneez, so vpward: and abooue, too shoolderz [etc.]. **1607** *Puritan* I. iv. 75 Hee lookes like a Monkey vpward, and a Crane downe-ward. **1667** Milton *P.L.* I. 463 Dagon his Name, Sea Monster, upward Man And downward Fish.

†4. Upright; erectly. *Obs. rare.*

c **1290** *S. Eng. Leg.* I. 82/11 A wei þer was of scharpe stones: and opward stoden echon. **1297** R. Glouc. (Rolls) 7186 He sat him vpward vp is bed.

5. With (vertical) extension *from* a point or part (esp. of the body) to another expressed or implied.

1387 Trevisa *Higden* (Rolls) V. 209 A child..þat hadde tweie bodyes from þe navel upward. *c* **1400** Maundev. (Roxb.) ii. 5 þai made þat peece þat went fra [*ed.* 1839 from] þe erthe vpward..of cypresse. *Ibid.* vii. 24 It had..fra þeine vpward þe schappe of a gayte. *c* **1440** *Wycliffite Bible* 1 Sam. ix. 2 (MS. Bodl. 277), Fro þe schuldre and upward he appeeride ouer þe peple. *c* **1450** *Mirk's Festial* I. 97 Fendes token vp þe body, and beten hyt wyth brennyng scorgys from þe nauell vpward. *c* **1511** *1st Eng. Bk. Amer.* (Arb.) p. xxxiii/2 The whyche ben fro the myddel vpward lyke men. **1539** Bible *Ezek.* i. 27 As it had bene all of fyre within from hys loynes vpward. **1592** *Soliman & Pers.* IV. ii. 41 His skin is but pistol profe from the girdle vpward. **1600** Shaks. *Much Ado* III. ii. 36 (Q. 1), A Spaniard from the hip vpward. **1642** Howell *For. Trav.* (Arb.) 57 It is well known the Habassines are Jacobites and Christians from the girdle upward.

6. *Comb.*, as (sense 1) ***upward-climbing, -curving, -gazing, -rushing, -shooting, -stirring, -striving***; ***upward-parted, pointed***; (sense 2) ***upward-bound***.

1710 *Lond. Gaz.* No. 4681/3 The *upward-bound Ships for the Eastward. **1800** *Hull Advertiser* 18 Oct. 3/2 The upward-bound..are at anchor. **1920** Kipling in Kipling & Graves tr. *Horace's Odes* v. 17 For fierce she-Britons, apt to smite Their *upward-climbing sisters down. **1963** *Times Lit. Suppl.* 8 Mar. 168/3 Upward-climbing iambics. **1922** Joyce *Ulysses* 24 He walked along the *upwardcurving path. **1871** Palgrave *Lyr. Poems* 64 As some still *upward-gazing lake. **1865** G. M. Hopkins *Poems* (1967) 151 A brush of trees Rounded it, thinning skywards by degrees, With parallel shafts,—as *upward-parted ashes. **1821** Atherstone *Poems* 6 With *upward pointed hands, these pray'd aloud. **1871** Tennyson *Last Tournament* 440 An ever *upward-rushing storm and cloud Of shriek and plume. **1857** Dufferin *Lett. High Lat.* (ed. 3) 328 The *upward shooting fluff of seas. **1844** Emerson *Ess.* II. viii, In countless *upward-striving waves The moon-drawn tide-wave strives.

II. 7. Backward in order of time; continuously into the past.

c **1055** *Byrhtferth's Handboc* in *Anglia* VIII. 327 Swa fela daga tell þu fram martius monðes ende upweard. *c* **1175** *Twelfth Cent. Hom.* 34 Lucas tealde þanon..upweard to Adame seofen & hund-seofentiȝ mæȝða. *c* **1200** Ormin 2056 Cristess kinn Onn eorþe, o moderr hallfe, Bi weppmann shollde reccnedd ben Uppwarrd & dunnwarrd baþe. **1611** Bible *Haggai* ii. 18 Consider now from this day, and vpward,..euen from the day that the foundation of the Lords Temple was laid, consider it. *Ibid.* 15.

8. a. To or into later life. Cf. up *adv.*[1] 22 c.

c **1530** Tindale *Num.* viii. 24 From .xxv. yere vppwarde they shall goo in to wayte [etc.]. **1531** Elyot *Gov.* I. xvi, Children..from the age of xiiii. yeres upwarde. **1711** Steele *Spect.* No. 136 ¶2, I am, and ever have been from my Youth upward, one of the greatest Liars. **1875** Jowett *Plato* (ed. 2) V. 54 He was a soldier from his youth upward. **1890** J. Pulsford *Loyalty to Christ* I. 123 From childhood and upward, our ears have been..thronged with the jargon of idolaters.

b. ***and*** (also *or*) ***upward*** = upwards *adv.* 6 b.

(*a*) **1555** Eden *Decades* (Arb.) 369 Children of th[e] age of .xii. or .xiii. yeares or vppewarde. **1595** Platt *Discov. Eng. Wants* A 3, Seacoale..at the rate of 8s the chawdren or vpwarde. **1596** Harington *Anat. Metam. Ajax* L iij b, A Cesterne containing a barrell [of water] or vpward. **1708** *Lond. Gaz.* No. 4479/8 A black Cart Gelding, about 15 hands high, or upward.

(*b*) **1560** Daus tr. *Sleidane's Comm.* 422 He was xxxii. yeares olde and vpwarde. **1608** *Relat. Trav. W. Bush* E j b, To the number of two thousand people and vp-ward. **1796** H. Hunter tr. *St.-Pierre's Stud. Nat.* (1799) I. 162 A series of a hundred and fifty leagues in length, and upward.

c. To a higher number or amount. *rare*$^{-1}$.

1575 Laneham *Let.* (1907) 54 So az all..numbrings from too vntoo three, and so vpward, may well be counted numberz.

9. ***upward of*** = upwards *adv.* 8.

1613 Shaks. *Hen. VIII*, II. iv. 36, I haue beene your Wife, in this Obedience, Vpward of twenty yeares. *a* **1628** F. Grevil *Sidney* (1652) 199 The builders of any ships upward of so many hundred Tuns. **1864** *Intellectual Observer* VI. 282 A good swarm..containing at the lowest estimate upward of 40,000.

10. ***upward compatibility***, the property of computer software and hardware by virtue of which software written for a less capable machine can be used on a more capable one; so ***upward-compatible*** adj. phr., exhibiting upward compatibility.

1964 *Computer Bull.* June 44/2 The IBM SYSTEM/360 is available in six models... IBM is developing an additional, very high performance system to be upward-compatible with these models. **1965** *Ibid.* June 20/1 In addition to upward compatibility the Compatibles/100 offer users the protection of a more complete range of software. **1976** *Aviation Week* 6 Sept. 155/1 All software in the series is upward-compatible. **1979** *Business Week* (Industr. Ed.) 27 Aug. 83 The new system is aimed at providing the current users of GSD's systems with a more powerful, upward-compatible system. **1982** *Computerworld* 15 Mar. 4/1 The system is upward-compatible with both the Harris 1600 and Harris 9200 series processors. **1983** *Australian Personal Computer* Oct. 49/2 There are..rumours that IBM will soon release an in-house developed DOS..which will be more upward compatible to IBM disk operating systems. **1983** *Pop. Computing* Nov. 15 Instruction sets for the micro-processors are 'upward compatible', that is, a program written for the original Z80 will also work on the faster Z80A, Z80B, or Z80H, but the reverse is not necessarily true. **1984** *Computerworld* 16 Apr. 47 Version 4.0 provides full upward compatibility for Template Version 3.0 applications programs.

†B. *prep.* Up; along the line of ascent of. *rare.*

c **1485** *Digby Myst.* (1882) v. 388, I se hym now com vpward the hill. **1818** Keats *Endym.* I. 266 Whether to surprise The squatted hare..; Or upward ragged precipices flit To save poor lambkins.

C. *adj.* (Cf. OE. *upweard* adj.)

†1. Facing upwards; lying on the back; supine; = upright *a.* 2. *Obs.*

A few examples occur in OE.

1607 Topsell *Four-f. Beasts* 465 A certaine herbe.. which..maketh him to fall presently vpon his backe & lye vpward without stirring. **1615** Crooke *Body of Man* 268 The position or manner of lying of the sickeman, eyther prone that is downeward, or supine that is vpward. **1646** Sir T. Browne *Pseud. Ep.* 194 Women drowned float prone,.. but men supine or upward, is an assertion wherein the.. point it selfe is dubious.

2. a. Directed towards a higher or loftier point, place, or plane; having a vertical or ascensional course or direction; taking place or inclined upwards; ascending.

1607 Shaks. *Timon* IV. iii. 190 Common Mother [= the earth],..Teeme with new Monsters, whom thy vpward face Hath to the Marbled Mansion all aboue Neuer presented. **1634** Milton *Comus* 98 The slope Sun his upward beam Shoots against the dusky Pole. **1700** Dryden *Theodore & Hon.* 315 So spread upon a Lake, with upward Eye, A plump of Fowl behold their Foe on high. **1704** Prior *Let. to Boileau* 174 The Eagle..directs her upward Flight. **1718** —— *Solomon* III. 875 The Angel said; With upward Speed His agile Wings He spread. **1784** Cowper *Tiroc.* 383 The exalted prize demands an upward look. **1839** Bailey *Festus* 334 The last high upward slant of sun on the trees. *a* **1842** Wordsw. *Misc. Sonn.* III. xxxi, She stands.., One upward hand..lying softly on her breast. **1890** J. Pulsford *Loyalty to Christ* I. 104 The upward slopes of the new life are delightful, and the prospects enrapturing. **1899** *Allbutt's Syst. Med.* VIII. 81 The movement and discomfort in the hands may be relieved..by very gentle upward rubbing.

transf. **1843** *Penny Cycl.* XXVI. 419/1 The speech-note on the word 'pale' will consist of an upward movement of the voice.

spec. **1875** Knight *Dict. Mech.* 2684/1 *Upward filter*, a filter in which the flow of the liquid is upward.

b. Having a trend, course, drift, etc., which indicates advance, progress, or increase.

1596 Shaks. *3 Hen. VI*, v. iii. 1 Thus farre our fortune keepes an vpward course. **1852** *Lawson's Merchant's Mag.* July 236 A change..in the weather..has checked the upward tendency in quotations [of grain]. **1870** *Pall Mall G.* 23 Sept. 9/2 Where there is any change [in the Stock Markets] it is in the upward direction. **1914** *Eng. Hist. Rev.* Jan. 135 The upward movement which raised the lower labouring classes.

c. Having lofty aims or purpose.

1850 Tennyson *In Mem.* XLI. vi, Tho' following with an upward mind The wonders that have come to thee.

3. Situated or lying aloft or above; higher in place or position; lofty.

1622 Boys *Wks.* 957 Troubles in this world (quoth Austin) are an vpward hell. **1815** Shelley *Alastor* 278 A swan..with strong wings Scaling the upward sky. **1819** W. Tennant *Papistry Storm'd* (1827) 79 Barns spy'd, frae his upwart place,..George's face.

4. †a. (See quot.) *Obs.*

1729 Boyer *Dict. Royal* II. s.v., Upward Goods, or Merchandize, (so inland Traders call Goods designed for London).

b. Directed, moving, etc., up along a stream or river; taking place up-stream.

1731 in *Extr. Navig. Rolls Thames* (1772) 22 The Master or chief Boatman of any upward Boat or Barge. **1816** TUCKEY *Narr. Exped. R. Zaire* iv. (1818) 134 Running directly on the rocks, and forming a strong upward eddy on its west side. *Ibid.* 144 Our upward view of the river. **1818** M. BIRKBECK *Notes Journ. Amer.* (ed. 4) 80 The upward navigation of these streams. **1887** *Field* 31 Dec. 985/3 In regard to other migratory fish..the same weirs have the effect..of..arresting their upward migration.

†**5.** Going backward in time. *Obs.*$^{-1}$

1603 B. JONSON *Panegyre* 90 She then remembered to his thought..the vpward race Of kings, præceding him in that high court.

D. *sb.* †**1.** The top part; the crown or summit.

1605 SHAKS. *Lear* v. iii. 136 From th' extremest vpward of thy head, To the discent and dust below thy foote.

2. Upward movement. Also *fig.*

1898 MEREDITH *Odes Fr. Hist.* 30 Not singing the spirally upward of rapture, the downward of pain Rather, the drop sheer downward from pressure of merciless weight.

'upwardly, *adv.* [f. prec. + -LY².]

1. In an upward direction; upwards.

1816 L. HUNT *Rimini* IV. 387 There lay she praying, upwardly intent. **1835** BROWNING *Paracelsus* v. 883 All tend upwardly though weak, Like plants in mines which never saw the sun. **1844** MRS. BROWNING *Brown Rosary* III. xxii, She glanced upwardly mute. **1875** KNIGHT *Dict. Mech.* 2706/1 The pistons..were fitted with upwardly opening valves.

2. Special collocations: ***upwardly compatible*** adj. phr. = *upward-compatible* adj. phr. s.v. UPWARD *adv.* 10; ***upwardly mobile*** adj. phr. = *upward-mobile* adj. phr. s.v. UPWARD *adv.* 1 e.

1981 *Electronics* 24 Mar. 8 In 1976 J. L. Wagener suggested 'structured Fortran—an evolution of standard Fortran' as an extended upwardly compatible compiler. **1984** *Austral. Micro Computerworld* Feb. 28/1 Macintosh is the bottom-end system of the Apple 32 Supermicro family comprising Macintosh, a bridge product, Lisa II, Lisa II/5 and Lisa II/10. These machines are upwardly compatible. **1964** *Sunday Times* 23 Aug. 10/2 The barriers within that structure..can be crossed by upwardly-mobile Jews. **1967** A. LURIE *Imaginary Friends* vi. 68 Suppose she were to..marry some upwardly mobile local boy. **1973** *Publishers Weekly* 3 Sept. 50/2 Son of upwardly mobile parents, his youth has been a series of movings—from apartment to ever better apartment. **1981** *Times* 22 May 14/2 The Liberal voter.., the upwardly mobile, ex-working-class malcontent. **1984** *New Yorker* 13 Feb. 39/1 A purely personal prejudice, this, and not to be taken seriously by upwardly mobile executives.

'upwardness. [f. UPWARD *a.* + -NESS.]

1. Tendency or proclivity to rise or mount upwards; the quality of suggesting upward movement.

1614 LATHAM *Falconry* 21, I haue reclaimed an outragious, vnstaied hawke;..shee hath falne cleane from her vpwardnesse and high flying. **1618** *Ibid.* II. 117 If by nature there were euer any vpwardnesse or high flying in her. **1860** W. J. C. MUIR *Pagan or Christian* 62 The lancet-headed windows, arches, niches, all are in harmony of upwardness. *Ibid.* 88 This entire upwardness of composition [in Gothic architecture]. **1877** BLACKIE *Wise Men* 305 They by natural upwardness Remount to earth.

2. The quality of being upward; relative altitude.

1896 DK. ARGYLL *Philos. Belief* 122 We cannot shake off the conception of high and low, of upwardness and downwardness.

upwards ('ʌpwədz), *adv.* and *prep.* Forms: 1 up-, uppweardes, 2, 5-6 upwardes (6 upp-), 5, 6 vpwardes, 6-7 vp-, 7- **upwards** (7 upp-); 6 *Sc.* **vpwartis**, 9 *dial.* up-, uppards, etc. [OE. *up-, uppweardes*, f. *upweard* UPWARD *adv.* + *-es* of adv. genitive: see -WARDS. Cf. OS. *upwardas*, MLG. *upwordes*, MDu. *op-, upwaerts, -werdes*, etc. (Du. *opwaarts*), MHG. *ufwertes* (G. *aufwärts*).]

A. *adv.* **I. 1. a.** = UPWARD *adv.* 1 a.

†*to make upwards* (quot. 1575): see MAKE *v.*¹ 45.

c **888** K. ÆLFRED *Boeth.* xxxiv. §10 þæt he onȝinð of þæm wyrtrumum & swa upweardes grewð oð ðone stemn. *c* **1000** *Boeth. Metr.* xiii. 62 Sio sunne..stihð a upweardes, oð hio eft cymeð þær hire yfemesð bið eard ȝecynde. *c* **1410** *Master of Game* (MS. Digby 182) xiii, þe tayle..streight and a litell crompynge vpward [*MS. Reg.* vpwardes]. **1575** TURBERVILE *Faulconrie* 158 To make a high fleeing Hawke vpwards. *Ibid.*, It hapneth oftentimes that a hawke..wil yet be long before she be made upwards. **1578** BANISTER *Hist. Man* v. 76 The vretarie vessels..also prohibite that vpwardes none [*sc.* urine] may returne agayne. **1613** BIBLE *Gen.* vii. 20 Fifteene cubits vpwards [**1611** vpward], did the waters preuaile. **1647** COWLEY *Mistr., My Fate* i, Go bid the Stones a journey upwards make. **1711** ADDISON *Spect.* No. 62 ¶5 His ambitious Love is a Fire that naturally mounts upwards. **1786** PINKERTON *Anc. Sc. Poems* I. p. lxvii, Their shoulders are moved upwards and downwards. **1815** J. SMITH *Panorama Sci. & Art* II. 189 A dry glass rod or tube, rubbed ..upwards and downwards with a dry hand. **1827** FARADAY *Chem. Manip.* iv. (1842) 89 Another..mode..is to continue the furnace upwards by a deep ring. **1858** GLENNY *Gard. Every-day Bk.* 230/2 These..trailing plants..are more frequently trained upwards.

fig. **1828** LYTTON *Pelham* II. xvi, Men..who join ignorance of every principle of legislation to indifference for every benefit to the people:..who level upwards, and trample downwards. **1905** FORSYTH in *Contemp. Rev.* Oct. 581 The Christ needs the apostle, the preacher. The Mediator upwards needs mediators downwards.

transf. **1907** J. H. PATTERSON *Man-Eaters of Tsavo* viii. 87 Lions always begin at the tail of their prey and eat upwards towards the head.

Comb. **1844** NOAD *Electricity* (ed. 2) 272 The upwards bent platinum wire.

b. = UPWARD *adv.* 1 b.

c **890** WÆRFERTH tr. *Gregory's Dial.* 286 þa færinga locode heo uppweardes,..& ȝeseah þone hælend þider cuman to hire. *c* **1000** *Sax. Leechd.* III. 38 Nim mid þinum twam handum uppweardes. *c* **1175** *Lamb. Hom.* 59 Neb upwardes he him [*sc.* man] wrohte. *c* **1400** *Pepysian Gosp. Harmony* (1922) 70 Jesus..wiþstoode and bihelde hym vpwardes. **1648** HEXHAM II, *Opwaerts sien*, to See upwards, or to Looke on high. **1709** T. ROBINSON *Vind. Mosaick Syst.* 112 Man..hath his Head upwards towards Heaven. **1795-6** WORDSW. *Borderers* II. 988 Upwards I cast my eyes. **1805** —— *Prelude* VII. 200 Behold, turned upwards, a face hard and strong In lineaments. **1817** SHELLEY *Rev. Islam* v. xlix, She paused, and pointed upwards. **1860** TYNDALL *Glac.* I. ii. 21 Looking upwards we saw a series of coloured rings.

c. *fig.* = UPWARD *adv.* 1 c.

1557 in Lodge *Illustr. Brit. Hist.* (1791) I. 274 Prisoners.. of the degree of a Baron, or uppwardes. **1605** in *Archaeologia* (1800) XIII. 321 The lorde who beeinge an earle or upwardes,..is to have..a cloathe of estate. **1732** BERKELEY *Alciphr.* v. §33 The army; wherein the tendency is always upwards from lower posts to higher. **1855** *Poultry Chron.* II. 423 The character of the..fowls proves that their progress is upwards in quality.

attrib. **1849** ROBERTSON *Serm.* (1863) 160 Not mere change, but true, ever upwards progress.

d. = UPWARD *adv.* 1 d.

1874 *Times* 1 Jan. 7/6 Coffee.—A strong demand prevails, with few sellers, and the market still tends upwards. **1875** *Economist* 2 Jan. 5/2 Straits tin..after a moderate reaction upwards fell to 92*l* 5*s* in August.

2. = UPWARD *adv.* 2.

1513 DOUGLAS *Æneid* VIII. ii. 65 Bayth nycht and day ilk man..Can spend in routh..Our slidand fast vpwartis the river. **1538** in *Lett. Suppress. Monast.* (Camden) 245, I am cumyng upwardes [= to London] as fast as my sekenes will suffre me. **1598** W. PHILLIP tr. *Linschoten* I. x. 19 First Daman, from thence fifteene miles vpwardes..the towne of Basaün. **1601** HAKLUYT *Galvano* 90 From thence vpwards.. he went along the coast of the Abassins. **1662** R. VENABLES *Exper. Angler* x. 99 In small Brooks you may angle upwards. **1801** *Rusher's Reading Guide* 7 The Mail Coaches to and from Bath, Bristol, &c. pass upwards and downwards every night. **1869** TOZER *Highl. Turkey* I. 184 We followed this stream upwards. **1893** *Field* 17 June 904/3 For years the labourers have been in the habit of going 'upwards'—that is, up round London—for mowing and haymaking.

fig. **1805** WORDSW. *Prelude* XI. 177 This..Soured and corrupted, upwards to the source, My sentiments.

3. = UPWARD *adv.* 3.

1548 VICARY *Anat.* vii. (1577) I i, The brode end..[of the heart] is vpwardes, and the sharpe ende is downewardes. **1599** SHAKS. *Much Ado* III. ii. 71 Shee shall be buried with her face vpwards. **1658** ROWLAND tr. *Moufet's Theat. Ins.* 928 The mouthes or passages of their cells are..altogether downward; and they very providently place the bottom of their cels upwards, that [etc.]. **1668** MOXON *Mech. Dyalling* 18 Holding the Center A upwards, so as the Plumb-line play free in the Grove. *Ibid.* 31 If this Dyal were turned with its Center upwards. **1733** TULL *Horse-Hoeing Husb.* 304 The Share, turn'd Bottom upwards. **1839** TIMPERLEY *Dict. Printers* 104 He..then puts a quantity of the worked off sheets on it, taking care to have the printed side upwards. **1848** BAILEY *Festus* (ed. 3) 228 For the Infinite is upwards, and above The highest thing created—upwards aye. **1875** SIR T. SEATON *Fret-Cutting* 91 Take a set of gouges, stand the largest of the set edge upwards.

b. = UPWARD *adv.* 3 b. *rare*$^{-1}$.

c **1400** MAUNDEV. (1919) xix. 110 þerfore make þei the halfondel of ydole of a man vpwardes, & the toþer half of an ox dounwardes.

4. = UPWARD *adv.* 5.

1599 HAKLUYT *Voy.* II. I. 224 These men goe naked from the girdle vpwardes. **1634** SIR T. HERBERT *Trav.* 187 They ..goe naked from the waste vpwards. **1855** *Orr's Circ. Sci., Inorg. Nat.* 106 One genus (*Belemnites*), very common.. among all the secondary rocks, from the lias upwards.

5. ***upwards of***, at or to a higher level than; above.

1853 G. JOHNSTON *Nat. Hist. E. Bord.* I. 140 Upwards of this, the hill is well-covered with..turf and heather.

II. 6. a. To a higher aggregate, figure, or the like.

1523 in Ellis *Orig. Lett.* Ser. I. I. 221 The goods to paye jˢ of the li. from xxˡⁱ upwards. **1617** *Eastland Co.* (Camden) 21 Deales from Eighteene foote longe uppwards. *Ibid.*, Greate masts from fifteene hand upwards the peece. **1910** *Stage Year Bk.* 47 First-class hotel accommodation..for two and a half or three guineas a week, upwards.

b. Usu. ***and upwards, or upwards***. Freq. = somewhat more or rather above a specified age, number, value, size, etc. = UPWARD *adv.* 8 b.

(*a*) **1570** FOXE *A. & M.* (ed. 2) 2268/2 *Hussy.* How old art thou? *Eliz.* Forty and vpwardes. **1612** SIR D. CARLETON in *10th Rep. Hist. MSS. Comm.* App. I. 572 Diverse companies to the number of 700 men and upwards. **1693** R. LYDE *Acc. Retaking of The Friend's Adventure* Title-p., Their Majesties Customs of the said ship amounted to 1,000*l.* and upwards. **1717** in *Nairne Peerage Evidence* (1874) 31 Robert Robertson..aged ffifty years and upwards. **1729** T. INNES *Crit. Essay* (1879) 315 Within these last hundred years and upwards. **1818** [S. WESTON] *La Scava* 25 Eighty whetstones and upwards..have been found. **1839** TIMPERLEY *Dict. Printers* 105 All above 52 Pica ems, upon Small Pica and upwards. **1887** *Daily Chron.* 17 Jan. (Encycl. Dict.), Some of them worth as much as £30 and upwards.

(*b*) **1593** *Tell-Troth's N.Y. Gift* A3, Ioyning..their daughters of twentye yeares olde or vnder, to rich cormorants of threescore or vpwards. **1687** MIÉGE *Gt. Fr. Dict.* II. s.v., It amounts to ten Pounds, or upwards. **1709** *Lond. Gaz.* No. 4502/2 A Ship of 70 Guns, or upwards. **1857** MILLER *Elem. Chem., Org.* 74 A solution of soda.. which contains two per cent. or upwards of alkali. **1861** *Brit. Postal Guide* 1 Jan. 28 Messengers, whose weekly wages.. are..8*s.* or upwards.

c. To later life; = UPWARD *adv.* 8 a.

1805 WORDSW. *Prelude* VIII. 348 Even then, And upwards through late youth, until not less Than two-and-twenty summers had been told. **1851** DIXON *W. Penn* 252 The great idea which he had nursed from his youth upwards. **1874** FARRAR *Christ* xv. 166 Might they not have understood that, from childhood upwards, He had not lived by bread alone?

7. Backwards in time; into the past.

a **1654** SELDEN *Table-T.* (Arb.) 69 Some of them are asham'd upwards, because their Ancestors were too great. **1729** T. INNES *Crit. Essay* (1879) 142 [He] pronounced this genealogy..from Fergus, son of Erch, to Fergus, son of Ferchar, and upwards. **1887** SKEAT *Princ. Eng. Etym.* I. 52 English should be traced downwards as well as upwards. **1890** GRINDLESTONE *Foundations of Bible* 19 History of the art of writing, from the days of Nehemiah upwards [to the time of Moses].

8. ***upwards of***, (rather) more than; = UPWARD *adv.* 9.

In frequent use from *c* 1760.

1721 PERRY *Daggenh. Breach* 17 A large Chest or Machine, upwards of eighty Foot long. **1753-4** RICHARDSON *Grandison* III. xvi. 227 He..kept his word till he was upwards of seventy. **1841** BORROW *Zincali* II. xi. III. 109 Considerably upwards of a century. **1885** *Law Rep. 29 Chanc. Div.* 538 The estate..was found liable for upwards of £5,000. **1893** J. PULSFORD *Loyalty to Christ* II. 321 Upwards of three thousand years ago.

b. Used erron. for: Somewhat less than (a specified amount); nearly, not quite. Chiefly *dial.*

1902 *Yorks. Post* 28 Feb., Thus 'upwards of a hundred' would mean nearly, or well on to a hundred. **1902-** in colloquial use, Linc. to Devon (*Eng. Dial. Dict.*).

†**B.** *prep.* Up along the course of; = UP *prep.*² 2. *Obs.*

1601 HAKLUYT *Galvano* 72 He went into Arabia, Persia, and vpwards the riuer Euphrates.

†**'upwark.** *Sc. Obs.* [UP *adv.*² 12 a + *wark* WORK *sb.*] Cessation of work.

15.. *Aberdeen Reg.* XXI. (Jam.), Upwark, quhen the fysching wes done. **1570** *Rec. Inverness* (New Spalding Club) I. 197 [He] alse protestis for ane sufficient oxe of sex yeiris auld at vpwark.

'upwarp. *Geol.* [UP- 2.] A gentle, extensive elevation of part of the earth's surface. Hence **up'warping** *vbl. sb.*, the raising of part of the earth's surface to form an upwarp.

1917 *Prof. Papers U.S. Geol. Survey* No. 93. 109/1 Synclines and anticlines, both broad and narrow, sharply delineated monoclines, and domical upwarps follow one another in succession. **1952** *Geol. Mag.* LXXXIX. 130 Three domal upwarps superimposed on the simple anticlinal structure. **1954** W. D. THORNBURY *Princ. Geomorphol.* ix. 223 Intermittent upwarping took place, but there were periods of relative stillstand which are marked by erosional surfaces and terraces. **1974** *Nature* 23 Aug. 684/1 Owing to large scale Plio-Pleistocene up-warpings of the South African coastal margins, many rivers show substantially steeper gradients along their lower courses than in higher reaches. **1977** A. HALLAM *Planet Earth* 78/2 An important feature of rift valleys is that they follow the crests of long, low upwarps of the Earth's crust.

'upwash. [UP- 2.] **1.** A wash of a wave up a beach. *rare*$^{-1}$.

1923 D. H. LAWRENCE *Kangaroo* v. 93 Then suddenly he saw Jack running across the sand in a bathing suit, and entering the shallow rim of a long, swift upwash.

2. *Aeronaut.* The upward deflection of an airstream by an aerofoil. Cf. DOWNWASH.

1936 *Aircraft Engin.* VIII. 251/3 With highly tapered wings there is an upwash at the wing tip. **1974** *Sci. Amer.* Mar. 79/2 The flow field in the vortex wake can be viewed as an induced upwash at the outer edge. **1979** *Nature* 20/27 Dec. 778/2 Beyond the wing there is an upwash, which is very intense near the wingtip.

upwax: see UP- 4.

'upway. *rare*$^{-1}$. [UP- 2 b. Cf. OE. *upweȝ*, WFris. *opwei*, Du. *opweg*, LG. *upweg*.] Ascent.

1616 CHAPMAN tr. *Musæus* D 8 b, Hopelesse, dangerous The bar'd vp-way is to a Virgins bed.

upways, *adv. rare*$^{-1}$. [f. UP *prep.*²] In an upward direction; upwards (*from*).

1890 *Telegr. Jrnl.* 28 Nov. 653/1 Distance measured upways from OA indicates roughly the degree of hardness.

upweening, -weigh: see UP- 4, 7.

up'well, *v.* [UP- 4.] *intr.* To well up; *spec.* of liquid, esp. seawater: to surge upwards. Also *fig.*

1885 R. BRIDGES *Eros & Psyche* x. xix, Out of the topmost stone Of yonder hill upwells a fountain head. **1886** *National Rev.* Apr. 229 As when, up-welling from his fountain deeps, The Infant River leaves his native snows. **1913** R. KANE *Good Friday to Easter Sunday* 29 A fresh warm tear..is born,..silently upwelling. **1938** *Nature* 29 Oct. 778/1 Atlantic water..is rich in phosphate because it contains water that has upwelled at the edge of the continental shelf. **1973** C. SAGAN *Cosmic Connection* xvi. 115 Hot molten rock, called lava, upwells through tubes in the upper layers of the Earth. **1979** *Nature* 8 Feb. 470/2 Most meltwater from icebergs may spread laterally rather than upwell along the sides.

up'welled, *ppl. a.* (UP- 5; cf. prec.)

1938 *Jrnl. Marine Res.* I. 161 The upwelled water will in turn be carried away from the coast. **1957** G. E. HUTCHINSON *Treat. Limnol.* I. v. 280 Recently upwelled water rich in plankton. **1970** *Sci. Amer.* Feb. 32/3 The upwelled strips of basalt are distinguishable from one another by differences in the direction of their magnetic polarity.

up'welling, *ppl. a.* (UP- 6 b.)
1854 WHITTIER *Hermit of Thebaid* 1 O strong, upwelling prayers of faith. **1875** HELPS *Social Pressure* i. 4, I foresee a source of enjoyment,..a very constant and up-welling source. **1884** *Century Mag.* XXIX. 108 Blushing deeply with upwelling patriotism and bashfulness. **1936** *Discovery* Aug. 259/1 The cold up-welling polar waters. **1964** *Oceanogr. & Marine Biol.* II. 348 The muscle band..may act as a reflector for upwelling luminescence.

up'welling, *vbl. sb.* [UP- 7.] **1.** *gen.* A welling upwards.
1868 J. H. NEWMAN *Verses on Various Occasions* 309 The fresh upwelling of thy tranquil spirit. **1896** MRS. H. WARD *Sir G. Tressady* II. xx. 462 Strange up-wellings of feelings long trampled on and suppressed. **1976** J. WHEELER-BENNETT *Friends, Enemies & Sovereigns* v. 164 Truman derived his own keen perception from within himself, through an upwelling of his own inner consciousness.
2. *spec.* The rising of water from the depths of the ocean, often bringing with it a renewed source of nutrients; also, the water thus risen.
1912 *Internat. Rev. der gesamt. Hydrobiol. und Hydrographie* V. 250 Holway..attributed the cold surface water to an upwelling of bottom water. **1922** W. G. KENDREW *Climates of Continents* 11 This is a cool current..partly owing to the upwelling of cold water along the coast. **1963** G. L. PICKARD *Descriptive Physical Oceanogr.* iv. 39 Upwelling is important in replenishing the surface layers. **1967** *Oceanogr. & Marine Biol.* V. 57 This gives rise along the south coast of New Guinea to a violent upwelling whose existence is evident only during this month. **1973** *Sci. Amer.* June 22/3 The concentration of nutrients in the Peru upwelling is many times greater than that in the open ocean.

upwent, pa. t. of UPGO *v.*

upwhelmed: see UP- 5.

up'whirled, *pa. pple.* (UP- 5.)
1667 MILTON *P.L.* III. 493 All these upwhirld aloft Fly.. Into a Limbo large and broad. **1821** WORDSW. *Eccles. Sonn.* II. *Reflect.* 8 The 'trumpery' that ascends in bare display.. Upwhirled, and flying o'er the ethereal plain.

up'whirling, *vbl. sb.* (UP- 7.)
1877 G. F. CHAMBERS *Astron.* (ed. 3) x. ii. 828 The up-whirling of the glowing gases.

up'whirling, *ppl. a.* (UP-[1] 6.)
1801 SOUTHEY *Thalaba* v. xl, The upwhirling flood received Mohareb, then..Engulph'd him in the abyss.

upwind (ʌp'waɪnd), *v.* [UP- 4. Cf. UPWOUND *pa. pple.*, and (M)Du. *opwinden*, MLG. *upwinden*, MHG. *ûfwinden* (G. *aufwinden*), MSw. *op-*, *upvinda* (Sw. *uppvinda*), Da. *opvinde*.]
†**1. a.** *intr.* To fly up. *Obs.*$^{-1}$
c **1250** *Gen. & Ex.* 2988 He smot..on ðe lond, And gnattes hird ðor ðicke up-wond.
†**b.** *trans.* = UPTAKE *v.* 1. *Obs.*$^{-1}$
c **1250** *Gen. & Ex.* 3084 A suðen wind is fliȝt up-wond, And blew ðat day and al ðat niȝt.
†**2.** To finish up; to complete. *Obs.*$^{-1}$
c **1440** *Pallad. on Husb.* VII. 47 Thus shal an ox in dayes fewe vpwynde An heruest al.
3. To wind, coil, or roll up (something).
1560 *Nice Wanton* 51 *Barn.* Learne..to spyn and sowe... *Ism.* Spyn, quod ha? Yea, by the masse, and with youre heles vp-wynd. **1613** DRUMM. OF HAWTH. *Cypress Grove* Wks. (S.T.S.) II. 71 The motion of a swift & euer-whirling wheele, which twinneth forth and againe vp-windeth our life?
b. To raise or hoist by winding.
1600 FAIRFAX *Tasso* XV. vii, Her anchors she vpwound, And lanched foorth to sea her pinnesse flit.
4. *intr.* To become coiled up.
1616 J. LANE *Contn. Sqr.'s T.* XI. 256 Speckd snakes.. which turninge round, out sprange at length, and in againe vpwound.
5. To wind upwards.
1880 LANIER *Sunrise* 103 Low multitudinous stirring Upwinds through the woods.

up-wind (ˌʌp'wɪnd), *adv.* and *adj.* Also **upwind.** [UP- *prep.*[2] 4.]
A. *adv.* Contrary to the course of, against, the wind.
1838 SCROPE *Deer-stalking* 17 Deer..always run up wind. **1861** WHYTE MELVILLE *Market Harb.* 7 Here their fox had made his point good up-wind. **1897** HINDE *Congo Arabs* 202 They always started up-wind from our quarters.
B. *adj.* Occurring in a direction against the wind.
1942 *Tee Emm* (Air Ministry) II. 95 The aircraft should always be ditched on the upwind slope of the swell. **1943** [see PRANG *v.* 2]. **1980** *Yachts & Yachting* 29 Feb. 651/1 For upwind work, we chose to use a Navik vane.

up'wing, *v. poet. rare.* [UP- 4.] *intr.* To soar or fly up; to rise. Occas. *trans.*, to fly above.
1885 *Nineteenth Cent.* Aug. 262 Anon with joy it singeth, Vie with the lark it will, And praising God upwingeth Full many a holy hill. **1927** K. MACLEOD *Road to Isles* 212 Gold the morn at dawn upwingeth. **1964** H. E. G. ROPE *Dream Holiday* 10 Amid the kindled altar lights upwings The voice of many martyrs she hath slain.

'upwith, *adv.*, *prep.*, *sb.*, and *a.* Chiefly *Sc.* ('ʌpwɪθ) and now *rare.* [UP *adv.*[1] + WITH.]
A. *adv.* In an upward course or direction; upwards. Also *fig.*
1513 *Acc. Ld. High Treas. Scot.* IV. 515 Tua drawyn towis to keip hir [*sc.* a cannon] at upwith and dounewith. **1535** STEWART *Cron. Scot.* (Rolls) II. 548 The Danis..Traistand the Scottis vpwith to the hill, Suld tyre ilkone than or tha come thame till. *a* **1598** D. FERGUSON *Prov.* (S.T.S.) 10 As meikle upwith, as meikle down with. **1858** M. PORTEOUS *Souter Johnny* 30 Ye'll wi' a braindge Jirk aff the mune, an' upwith whud Far furth to range. **1864** LATTO *Tam. Bodkin* xxiii, They..durstna mount upwith to the riggin'.
B. *prep.* Up along the course of.
1504 in *Reg. Mag. Sig. Scot.* (1888) 239/2 Ascendand up-with the said swaill quhill it cum to the littill stane calsay.
C. *sb.* Upward course. Also *fig.*
1508 DUNBAR *Tua Mariit Wemen* 401 All is bot frutlese his effeir, and falȝeis at the vp-with. **1607** MARKHAM *Cavel.* VI. 9 If the fierce horse haue in his skelping course, either vpwithes..or downewithes, which is, that hee may eyther runne..vp hils, or down hils. **1808** JAMIESON s.v., *To the upwith*, taking a direction upwards.
b. An ascent or rising ground. *rare*$^{-1}$.
1819 *St. Patrick* II. 91 Will ye see how the[y]'re spankin' along the side o' that green upwith?
D. *adj.* Having an upward inclination, tendency, or slope; rising.
1864 A. WALLACE *Sc. Tales, M. Lauder* 37 It was a good bit upwith gate, so she would give her a tankard of ale to make her climb the brae the better. **1875** W. ALEXANDER *Ain Folk* 99 They'll be an upwith market shortly, or it chates me.

'upwold. (UP- 1.)
1875 KINGLAKE *Crimea* V. vi. 90 The upwold, or high level part of the neck [of the isthmus]. *Ibid.* 92 The spine of the upwold.

upwound (ʌp'waʊnd), *pa. pple.* (UP- 5. Cf. UPWIND *v.*)
1590 SPENSER *F.Q.* I. i. 15 Her huge long taile..was in knots and many boughtes vpwound. **1610** G. FLETCHER *Christ's Vict.* I. xii, Pale Sicknes, with his kercher'd head upwound. **1642** H. MORE *Song of Soul* II. III. ii. 6 The lowest is not awake, Therefore the midst lies close in sleep upwound.

upwrap, -wrapt, -wreathing, etc.: see UP- 4, 5, 6.

upya ('ʌpjə), *int. slang* (chiefly *Austral.*). Also **upyer.** [Corruption of *up you*: see UP *prep.*[2] 3 b.] (See quots.)
1941 BAKER *Dict. Austral. Slang* 79 *Upya!*, a contemptuous ejaculation. **1955** D. NILAND *Shiralee* 101 No, he said, I won't truckle to you. Upya for the rent. **1966** 'L. LANE' *ABZ of Scouse* II. 112 *Upyer!*, a term of defiance and/or contempt, but often made jocularly.

†**up'-yield**, *v. Obs.* [UP- 4.] *trans.* To yield or deliver up; to resign.
1297 R. GLOUC. (Rolls) 7406 þat lond þat him was iȝiue, þat he ssolde him vp ȝelde. *c* **1315** SHOREHAM II. 114 þe soule he gan op-ȝelde. *c* **1350** *Lybeaus Disc.* 517 To syr Lybeaus they gon up-yelde..har sperys. *c* **1380** *Sir Ferumb.* 4016 Fayne y wolde þe croune op-ȝelde. **1502** in *Antiq. Rep.* (1808) II. *321 Our King Henry..to..Arthure hadde the seid londs remysed and uppyelden.

ur (ɜː(r)). Also **urh.** [Echoic. Cf. HURR *v.*] An inarticulate sound, uttered instead of a word that the speaker is unable to remember or bring out.
1846 O. W. HOLMES *Rhymed Lesson* Poems (1896) 50/2 When you stick on conversation's burs, Don't strew your pathway with those dreadful urs. **1891** *Pall Mall G.* 13 June 2/1 The only pauses are the pauses of rhetoric, and the hesitating 'urh, urh' is never heard.

ur, obs. or dial var. OUR *pron.*

‖**ur-** (ʊər), *prefix*, repr. G. (also MHG., OHG.) *ur-*, denoting 'primitive, original, earliest,' as *ur-Hamlet*, *-origin*, *-stock*, etc. See also URHEIMAT, URSCHLEIM, URSPRACHE, URTEXT.
G. *ursprache* (= primitive language) has been freq. used in recent English philological works.
[**1864** MAX MÜLLER *Lect. Sci. Lang.* (1871) II. 133 The most troublesome of all vowels, the neutral vowel, sometimes called *Urvocal*, better *Unvocal*.] **1889** JACOBS *Caxton's Aesop* I. 37 Any light he can throw on the Ur-origin of the Fables. **1901** BOAS *Kyd's Wks.* p. xlv, The *Ur-Hamlet* may have contained a number of these borrowings. **1926** A. MØLLER tr. *Pedersen's Israel* I. I. 245 The word *shēm* is found in all Semitic languages and belongs to the absolutely certain ur-semitic components. **1927** A. H. MCNEILE *Introd. to Study of New Testament* iii. 50 It was an *Ur-Evangelium*, a primitive written Gospel, some say in Hebrew, some in Aramaic, on which our Gospels were based. **1937** O. JESPERSEN *Analytic Syntax* 142 Some well-known students of language who even call this [*sc.* 'S is P'] the 'urform' of sentences. **1943** V. NABOKOV in *Atlantic Monthly* May 69/2 The dreadful vulgarity, the Ur-Hitlerism of those ludicrous but vicious organisations. **1947** AUDEN *Age of Anxiety* (1948) ii. 46 For Long-Ago has been Ever-After since Ur-Papa gave The Primal Yawn that expressed all things. **1949** F. FERGUSSON *Idea of Theater* i. 26 An enactment of the Ur-Myth of the year-god. **1950** *Psychiatry* XIII. 168/2 The concept of ur-language and ur-symbolism is of particular importance in Freud's thought. **1964** C. S. LEWIS *Discarded Image* iv. 54 Plato's ur-Freudian doctrine of the dream as the expression of a submerged wish. **1966** *Punch* 9 Nov. 718/2 Above is Leonardo da Vinci's design for an ur-tank. **1971** *Astrophysics & Space Sci.* X. 363 (*heading*) Orientation of galaxies and a magnetic 'urfield'. **1977** *Listener* 31 Mar. 416/1 The importance of the folk example which he [*sc.* Bartók] argued to be one of the ur-sources of music. **1979** *Ibid.* 14 June 831/1 Sir Nikolaus Pevsner's ur-history, *Pioneers of Modern Design*. **1983** *Sunday Tel.* 13 Mar. 14/6 Russell Hoban is an ur-novelist, a maverick voice that is like no other.

uracan, -ano, obs. varr. HURRICANE.

'urachal, *a.* [f. URACH-US + -AL[1].] Of or pertaining to, affecting or found on, the urachus.
1890 BILLINGS *Med. Dict.* **1905** H. D. ROLLESTON *Dis. Liver* 251 Various abdominal cysts, such as pancreatic, omental, chylous, urachal, mesenteric cysts.

‖**urachus** ('jʊərəkəs). *Anat.* [mod.L., ad. Gr. οὐραχός urinary canal of a fœtus.] A fibrous cord binding the apex of the bladder to the anterior abdominal wall and the peritoneal folds.
[**1578** BANISTER *Hist. Man* v. 83 b, Out of the higher part and middest of the bottome of the bleddar a way springeth ..called Vrachos.] **1615** CROOKE *Body of Man* (1631) 213 The ligament of the bladder cald Vrachus. **1646** [see ALLANTOIS]. **1661** LOVELL *Hist. Anim. & Min.* Introd. b 5 b, To the urachus the umbilicall arteries are joyned. **1728** CHAMBERS *Cycl.* s.v. *Umbilical*, The Urachus is only plainly found in Brutes. **1788** *Encycl. Brit.* (ed. 3) I. 742 These fibres have been considered as the urachus, though without having been ever found pervious. **1804** *Med. Jrnl.* XII. 14 From their uniting part arose the umbilical vessels, meeting as usual the urachus. **1890** *Retrospect Med.* CII. 336 An enormously dilated urachus.

uracil ('jʊərəsɪl). *Biochem.* [a. G. *uracil* (R. Behrend 1885, in *Ann. d. Chemie* CCXXIX. 11), of unknown origin (perh. f. Eng. UR(EA + G. *acetsäure* acetic acid + *-il*).] A pyrimidine base, $C_4H_4N_2O_2$, which is a constituent of RNA.
1890 ROSCOE & SCHORLEMMER *Treat. Chem.* (ed. 2) III. 387 Behrend has succeeded in preparing..compounds, which are derivatives of a hypothetical substance, to which he has given the name uracil. **1907** *Jrnl. Biol. Chem.* III. 187 The uracil dissolved completely on warming. **1944** [see OROTIC *a.*]. **1959** *Times* 12 June 15/7 It has been calculated ..that a thousand-unit polynucleotide chain consisting of a coded repeat of only four different components—adenine, guanine, cytosine, and uracil—in the same ratio as exists in tobacco mosaic virus nucleic acid could form about 10^{57} different arrangements. **1975** *Sci. Amer.* May 25/2 Poliovirus RNA is a single chain of about 7,500.. nucleotides, each of which consists of a ribose sugar component and one of four organic bases: adenine, uracil, guanine and cytosine.

uraconite ('jʊərəkɒnaɪt). *Min.* [f. URA-NIUM + Gr. κον-ία dust, etc.: see -ITE[1] 2 b.] 'Sulphate of uranium, found as a lemon-yellow powder' (Chester).
1868 DANA *Min.* 668 Uraconite. Uranochre. **1888** *Cassell's Encycl. Dict.*, *Uraconite*,..a mineral..occurring in exceedingly minute scales, or earthy, on uraninite..at Joachimsthal, Bohemia.

‖**uræmia** (jʊ'riːmɪə). *Path.* Also **uremia.** [mod.L., f. Gr. οὖρ-ον urine + αἷμα blood. Cf. It. *uremia*, F. *urémie*.] A morbid condition resulting from the presence in the blood of urinary constituents, which are normally eliminated by the kidneys.
1857 DUNGLISON *Med. Lex.*, *Uræmia*.., a condition of the blood in which it contains urine or urea. **1867** A. FLINT *Princ. Med.* 84 An excess of uric acid..in the blood constituting a condition differing from uræmia. **1886** *Buck's Handbk. Med. Sci.* II. 253/1 The respirations..are slow in the coma of compression and uræmia.

uræmic (jʊ'riːmɪk), *a. Path.* Also **uremic.** [f. UREM-IA + -IC. Cf. F. *urémique*.]
1. Of or pertaining to, marked or characterized by, uræmia.
1855 W. D. MOORE tr. *Heller's Chem. Urine* 85 Uremic vomitus occurs in connexion with other uremic phenomena. **1871** A. MEADOWS *Man. Midwifery* (ed. 2) 367 The influence of the uræmic poisoning on the central nervous system. **1886** *Buck's Handbk. Med. Sci.* II. 535/1 In chronic uræmic dropsies. **1890** CAGNEY tr. *Jaksch's Clin. Diag.* 51 Uræmic blood shows an increased quantity of urea and extractives.
2. Of persons: Affected by uræmia.
1890 BILLINGS *Med. Dict.* **1905** H. D. ROLLESTON *Dis. Liv.* 226 The patient becomes more drowsy and uræmic.

‖**uræus** (jʊ'riːəs). *Egyptian Antiq.* Pl. **uræi** (jʊ'riːaɪ). [A modern Latinization of οὐραῖος, given by Horapollo as the Egyptian name for the cobra (now transliterated as *ı͗'r·t*), perhaps influenced in form by the Gr. adj. οὐραῖος, f. οὐρά tail.] A representation of the sacred asp, snake, or serpent, or of its head and neck, employed as an emblem of supreme power, sometimes *spec.* as worn on the headdress of ancient Egyptian divinities and sovereigns.
1832 G. LONG *Egypt. Antiq.* I. xi. 254 The snake called Chnuphis or Uræus, the symbol of royalty found so often on the monuments of Egypt. **1847** LEITCH *C. O. Müller's Anc. Art* §232. 205 The Sun-god..with the head of a hawk..with the sun's disc, upon it an uræus. **1890** RIDER HAGGARD & A. LANG *World's Desire* I. vi, I will..stake the sacred circlet upon my brow, against the Royal uraeus on thine. **1904** BUDGE *3rd & 4th Egypt. Rooms Brit. Mus.* 116 A canopy of a bier..ornamented with a row of uræi wearing disks.
attrib. **1858** BIRCH *Anc. Pottery* I. 20 Figures of vultures, of the uræus serpent, and a scarabæus. *Ibid* 89 The crocodiles of Sabak, uræi or cobra-capella snakes, emblems of the gods. **1889** RIDER HAGGARD *Cleopatra* II. ix, The sceptre in her hand, and on her brow the uræus diadem of gold.

Ural[1] ('jʊərəl). [See def.] **a.** The name (more freq. *Urals*, *Ural mountains*) of a mountain-chain forming the north-eastern boundary of

Europe with Asia, used attrib. in various specific appellations of birds, animals, etc., native to or found in that region, as ***Ural duck, lizard***, etc. (see quots.).

1785 LATHAM *Gen. Synop. Birds* VI. 514 *Ural Duck, *anas mersa*,..is a trifle bigger than the common Teal. **1881** LYELL *Pigeons* 81 The smooth-legged chequered or spangled ones are known in this country as *Ural ice[-pigeons]. **1802** SHAW *Gen. Zool.* III. 252 *Ural Lizard, *Lacerta Uralensis*,..moves with great swiftness. **1781** LATHAM *Gen. Synop. Birds* I. 148 *Ural Owl, *Stryx Uralensis*,..is very full of feathers. **1824** STEPHENS *Shaw's Gen. Zool.* XII. II. 218 *Ural Scoter (*Oidemia Leucocephala*), ..Ural Duck [of Latham],..is particularly abundant in Russia, Livonia, and Fionia.

b. Ural-Altaic *a.*, pertaining or belonging to the region including the Ural range and the Altaic mountains (in central Asia), its inhabitants, or their speech. Also *absol.*, the family of agglutinative languages spoken in eastern Europe and northern Asia; Turanian; Finno-Tartar.

1853 C. BUNSEN *Let.* 2 Aug. in Max Müller *Chips* (1873) III. 482 Therefore, for Turanian = Ural-Altaic, or the north-eastern branch. **1854** —— *Outl. Philos. Universal Hist.* I. 291 In the Ural-Altaic languages..we have *one* declension and *one* conjugation, and only a very small number of irregular forms. **1855** MAX MÜLLER *Lang. Seat of War* 96 The third or Turkic branch of the Ural-Altaic division. **1880** SAYCE *Introd. Sci. Lang.* viii. II. 194 It seems to have been a possession of the undivided Ural-Altaic community. **1888** A. H. KEANE in *Encycl. Brit.* XXIV. 1/2 Hence it is that the roots..in Ural-Altaic are always in evidence.

ural[2] (ˈjʊərəl). *Med.* [Irreg. f. UR-ETHANE.] A preparation of chloral hydrate and urethane, used as a hypnotic; chloral-urethane; = URALIUM.

1891 *Cent. Dict.* **1895** *Buck's Handbk. Med. Sci.* IX. 922/2 Ural has no advantage over chloral, and has the inconvenience of being soluble in water.

uralborite (jʊərəlˈbɔəraɪt). *Min.* [ad. Russ. *uralborit* (S. V. Malinko 1961, in *Zap. Vsesoyuznogo Min. Obshchestva* XC. 673), f. the name of the *Ural* Mountains: see -ITE[1].] A basic calcium borate, CaB_2O_4, occurring as colourless monoclinic crystals.

1962 *Amer. Mineralogist* XLVII. 1482 Uralborite occurs in radiating-fibrous aggregates of columnar crystals up to 0·5–0·7 cm. **1971** [see NIFONTOVITE]. **1977** *Soviet Physics —Doklady* XXII. 279/1 The most interesting feature of uralborite is the $[B_4O_4(OH)_8]^{4-}$ 'island' groups..which are overlapped by the Ca deltadodecahedra forming a three-dimensional cationic skeleton.

‖**urali** (ʊˈrɑːlɪ). [var. of OORALI. Cf. WOORALI.] The urari-plant (*Strychnos toxifera*), or the poison obtained from this. Also *attrib.*

1843 MILL *Logic* I. III. vii. 446 If we knew nothing of the Indian arrows but their fatal effect, accident alone could turn our attention to experiments on the urali. **1862** in Veness *El Dorado* (1867) 131 The well-known Urali Poison is prepared from the bark of the Urali (*Strychnos toxifera*?). **1883** IM THURN *Among Indians Guiana* 311 In Europe it is variously called..urari, urali, and ourali.

Uralian (jʊˈreɪlɪən), *a.* [f. URAL[1] + -IAN. Cf. F. *ouralien.*] Of or pertaining to, dwelling in or near, the Ural mountains; also, Ural-Altaic.

[**1797** *Encycl. Brit.* XVIII. 691 Urallian Chain..of mountains.] **1801** *Ibid.* Suppl. II. 757/1 The Uralian Cossacs are all enthusiasts for the ancient ritual. **1866** *Chamb. Jrnl.* 28 Apr. 257/1 Some malachite specimens of doors, vases, and clocks, contributed by the emperor of Russia. These were for the most part Uralian, I believe. **1875** MAINE *Hist. Inst.* 65 That portion of..mankind which has lately been called Uralian, the Turks, Hungarians, and Finns.

Uralic (jʊˈrælɪk), *a.* and *sb.* [f. as prec. + -IC.] Of or belonging to the Ural mountains, or the peoples living in or near them. Also as *sb.*, esp. a sub-family of the Ural-Altaic family of languages.

1861 MAX MÜLLER *Lect. Sci. Lang.* 302 It is generally supposed that the original seat of the Finnic tribes was in the Ural mountains, and their languages have been therefore called Uralic. **1880** SAYCE *Introd. Sci. Lang.* viii. II. 191 The Finno-Ugric or Uralic dialects. *Ibid.* 192 The civilization and migrations of the primitive Uralic tribes. **1959** [see OSTYAK]. **1963** E. A. SEEMAN in *Current Trends in Linguistics* I. 392 (*heading*) Uralic. **1972** [see OSTYAK]. **1975** G. F. CUSHING tr. *Hajdú's Finno-Ugrian Lang. & Peoples* 1. 32 Finno-Ugrian and Samoyed are themselves descendants of a common language called Uralic.

uralite[1] (ˈjʊərəlaɪt). *Min.* [ad. G. *uralit* (1831), f. *Ural* (mountains) + -ITE[1] 2 b. Cf. F. *ouralite.*] 'Pyroxene altered to amphibole' (Chester).

1835 *Penny Cycl.* III. 85/2 The uralites of [Professor G.] Rose appear to be its natural consequence. **1849** MURCHISON *Siluria* App. C. 538 Hypersthene and diallage are partly changed into uralite. **1888** RUTLEY *Rock-Forming Min.* 180 The well-known paramorphic conversion [of augite] into hornblende, the result being termed Uralite.

b. ***uralite-porphyry, -syenite***: (see quots.).

1868 *Watts' Dict. Chem.* V. 940 *Uralite-porphyry*, an aphanite-porphyry occurring in the Ural, containing uralite, and sometimes also crystals of labradorite. **1888** *Cassell's Encycl. Dict.* VII. 382 *Uralite-syenite*, a variety of syenite.. which contains uralite.

Uralite[2] (ˈjʊərəlaɪt). [Etym. unknown.] A proprietary name for an asbestos-based building material.

1899 *Trade Marks Jrnl.* 30 Aug. 1050 *Uralite*... Compounds of asbestos and silica, being manufactures for building and decoration. The British Uralite Company, Limited,..London; manufacturers. **1902** *Chambers's Jrnl.* Nov. 748/1 A demonstration was recently given at the factory at Higham, Kent, of a fireproof material called uralite... Its principal ingredient is asbestos, which is combined with chalk, water-glass and other materials. **1967** 'M. HUNTER' *Cambridgeshire Disaster* v. 33 Prefabricated Uralite billets. **1978** J. MATSON *Dear Osborne* xxi. 133 The buildings..were prefabricated in sections clad with a material called Uralite.

uralitic (jʊərəˈlɪtɪk), *a. Min.* [f. URALITE[1] + -IC.] Of or pertaining to, containing or consisting of, uralite.

1845 tr. *Humboldt's Cosmos* I. 268 Melaphyre, Augitic, Uralitic, and Oligoglassic [*sic*] Porphyry. **1879** RUTLEY *Stud. Rocks* xii. 218 A little hornblende occurs, which..is generally of a uralitic character.

uralitization (ˌjʊərəlɪtaɪˈzeɪʃən). *Petrol.* [f. URALITE[1] + -IZATION.] The alteration of a pyroxene, esp. augite, to form an amphibole, esp. actinolite. Hence **ˈuralitized** *ppl. a.*

1888 J. P. IDDINGS tr. *Rosenbusch's Microsc. Physiogr. Rock-Making Minerals* 241 The alteration of augite into a hornblende mineral, uralitization, is very common. **1909** *Q. Jrnl. Geol. Soc.* LXV. 378 The uralitized pyroxenes..have not been transformed into true nephrite. **1954** H. WILLIAMS et al. *Petrography* vi. 112 Also to be ascribed to deuteric action is the widespread uralitization of the augite seen in many monzonites. **1970** *Nature* 23 May 692/1 The rocks.. retain much of their original structure and texture, the basalts being uralitized or chloritized.

uralium (jʊˈreɪlɪəm). *Med.* [See URAL[2] and -IUM.] = URAL[2].

1889 *Brit. Med. Jrnl.* 16 March 609/1 Gustavo Poppi, a medical student of Bologna, recently described..the effects of a new hypnotic, which he proposes to call 'uralium'. *Ibid.*, Uralium induces sleep more quickly..than any other known hypnotic. **1891** *Lancet* 3 Jan. 46/1 Uralium or chloral-urethane..has recently been carefully tested.

Uralo- (jʊˈreɪləʊ), combining form of URAL[1], occurring in a few terms, as ***Uralo-Altaic*** (= URAL[1] b); ***Uralo-Caspian***, pertaining to or situated near the Ural river and the Caspian sea; ***Uralo-Finnic***, of or pertaining to the ethnically-allied Ural-Altaic and Finnic peoples.

1867 *Chambers' Encycl.* IX. 670/1 The Uralo-Caspian deserts. **1876** J. B. MITCHELL *Dates & Data* 76 The Uralo-Finnic dialects of the present day. *Ibid.* 77 The Uralo-Finnic speaking people. **1877** A. H. KEANE tr. *Hovelacque's Sci. of Lang.* vi. 308 In Central Asia other Uralo-Altaïc [*sic*] tribes have..adopted Persian. **1879** *Encycl. Brit.* IX. 219/2 It is maintained by some that the Finnic languages represent the oldest forms among the Uralo-Altaic groups.

uramil (jʊˈræmɪl). *Chem.* [G. *uramil*, f. UR-EA or UR-IC *a.* + AM-MONIA (or -IUM) + *-il* -YL.] Dialuramide; amido-barbituric acid; murexan.

1839 R. D. THOMSON in *British Ann.* 378 Uramil. **1841** BRANDE *Chem.* (ed. 5) 1381 Uramil..a product of the decomposition of thionuric acid. *Ibid.*, Uramil is soluble in sulphuric acid. **1878** C. M. TIDY *Handbk. Mod. Chem.* 717 Boiling uramil and mercuric oxide in a weak solution of ammonia.

u'ramile. *rare.* [-ILE.] = prec.

1843 T. THOMSON *Chem. Animal Bodies* 118 Uramile is soluble in potash ley. *Ibid.*, The constituents of uramile. **1866** ODLING *Anim. Chem.* 137 Mesoxalic Mon-ureides [include] Uramile.

uramilic (jʊərəˈmɪlɪk), *a. Chem.* [f. URAMIL + -IC 1 b.] Obtained or derived from uramil. Usu. ***uramilic acid.***

1839 R. D. THOMSON in *British Ann.* 382 Uramilic acid. **1841** BRANDE *Chem.* (ed. 5) 1383 Uramilic acid forms soluble crystallizable salts with ammonia, and with the fixed alkalis. **1856** WATTS tr. *Gmelin's Handbk. Chem.* X. 191 Uramilic acid dissolves in cold nitric acid without evolution of gas.

uran- (ˈjʊərən), combining form of URANITE, URANIUM, occurring in a few terms, as **uranatemnite**, etc. (see quots.).

Cf. G. *Uran-ocher, -oxyd, -vitriol*; F. *uranochre.*

1843 E. J. CHAPMAN *Min.* 104 *Uranatemnite. (Pitchblende.)..Sk. black; no cleavage. **1843** *Penny Cycl.* XXVI. 40/1 Carbonate of Uranium, *Uran Bloom. **1805** *Phil. Trans.* XCV. 348 If this mineral be the *Uran-glimmer [=uran-mica]. **1837** DANA *Min.* 246 Uranite. *Uranalus Quadratus*...Chalcolite-Uranglimmer. **1816** JAMESON *Syst. Min.* (ed. 2) III. 553 Uranium. This Order contains three species, viz. Pitch-ore, *Uran-mica, and Uran-ochre. **1855** *Orr's Circ. Sci., Geol.*, etc. 548 *Autunite.*—Yellow Uranite, Uran-mica, Phosphate of Uranium. **1812** SIR H. DAVY *Chem. Philos.* 424 Uranium..may be procured from the ores called Pechblende, and *Uranochre. **1855** *Orr's Circ. Sci., Geol.*, etc. 506 *Pechuran.*—Pitch Blende, Uran Ochre, ..Oxide of Uranium. *c* **1840** *Encycl. Metrop.* (1845) VI. 518/2 Pitchblende. *Uran-pitch-ore. **1850** ANSTED *Elem. Geol., Min.*, etc. §492 Johannite, *Uran vitriol, sulphate of uranium.

ura'nalysis. *Med.* [f. UR-INE *sb.* + ANALYSIS. Cf. URINALYSIS.] Chemical analysis or examination of urine.

1894 C. W. PURDY (*title*), Practical Uranalysis and Urinary Diagnosis.

uranate (ˈjʊərənət). *Chem.* [f. URAN-IC + -ATE[1] 1 c. Cf. F. *uranate.*] A salt produced by the action of uranic oxide upon a base.

1842 T. GRAHAM *Elem. Chem.* 644 The alkaline and earthy uranates. **1868** *Watts' Dict. Chem.* V. 947 Uranate of Ammonium... Uranate of Barium. *Ibid.* 948 Uranate of Zinc. **1878** C. M. TIDY *Handbk. Mod. Chem.* 337 Uranic oxide can act both as base and acid, forming in the latter case the compounds called uranates.

urang-utang, var. ORANG-OUTANG.

‖**Urania** (jʊˈreɪnɪə). [L. *Urania* (the muse of astronomy), ad. Gr. Οὐρανία 'the Heavenly One', fem. of οὐράνιος heavenly, f. οὐρανός heaven. Cf. F. *Uranie* (Du Bartas) in sense 1.]

1. As the title of a book or poem dealing with celestial or astronomical themes, etc.

?**1614** DRUMMOND OF HAWTH. *Poems* 66 b, Vrania, or Spirituall Poems. **1615** J. TAYLOR (Water P.) *title*, Vrania, or His Heauenly Muse. **1621** LADY M. WROTH (*title*), The Countesse of Mountgomeries Urania. **1754** J. HILL (*title*), Urania: or, a compleat view of the Heavens. **1880-** (*title*), Urania: a Monthly Journal of Astrology, Meteorology, and Physical Science.

2. *Astr.* One of the planetoids or asteroids.

1865 *Chambers' Encycl.* VII. 577.

Uranian (jʊˈreɪnɪən), *a.*[1] and *sb.*[2] [f. URANI-A + -AN.]

A. *adj.* **1.** Pertaining to or befitting heaven; celestial, heavenly. (Freq. from *c* 1890.)

1600 TOURNEUR *Transf. Metam.* lxxv, He bent his mind to pure Vranian vses. **1619** A. GARDEN *Bp. Elphinston* (Hunt. Cl.) 680 That concord, loue, and peace,..Ar suirlie.. Uranian and Diuine. **1818** SHELLEY *Prose Wks.* (1880) III. 21 Surrounded by sculptures of divine workmanship, he sees the earthly image of Uranian Love. **1854** S. DOBELL *Balder* xxiii. 90 That old Italian whose Uranian pride, When his great prince had forfeited the skies, Built him another heaven. **1893** F. THOMPSON *Poems* 21 And parting from her, in me linger on Vague snatches of Uranian antiphon.

b. As a distinctive epithet of Venus (or Aphrodite): Heavenly, spiritual. (Cf. the etym. note to PANDEMIC.)

1768 TUCKER *Lt. Nat.* III. 301 Genuine Liberty, offspring of all-protecting Jove, and sister of Uranian Venus. **1847** TENNYSON *Princ.* I. 239 O'er his [*sc.* Cupid's] head Uranian Venus hung. **1904** L. TRACY *Rainbow Island* viii, One might almost fancy her ladyship the Moon appearing on the scene as a Uranian Venus.

c. Homosexual (from the reference to Aphrodite in Plato's *Symposium*). Cf. URANISM, URNING.

1893 J. A. SYMONDS in *Spirit Lamp* III. II. 29 Thou standest on this craggy cove, Live image of Uranian Love. **1898** O. WILDE *Let.* *c* 18 Feb. (1962) 705 To have altered my life would have been to have admitted that Uranian love is ignoble. **1914** E. CARPENTER *Intermediate Types among Primitive Folk* 11 Inversion in some form was regarded as a necessary part of social life, and the Uranian man accorded a certain meed of honour. **1975** P. FUSSELL *Gt. War & Mod. Memory* viii. 294 The effect of the revision is to efface indications of the poem's Uranian leanings, to replace the pretty of 1913 with the nasty of 1917.

2. Pertaining, belonging, or dedicated to Urania.

1656 EARL MONM. tr. *Boccalini's Advts. fr. Parnass.* II. iii. (1674) 136 Euclide..was set upon by some under the Uranian Porch. **1820** SHELLEY *Milton's Spirit* 2, I dreamed that Milton's spirit rose, and took From life's green tree his Uranian lute. **1885** BLACKIE *Lett. to Wife* (1909) 333, I paid worship to the Uranian muse.

3. Of or pertaining to astronomy; astronomical.

1761 *Ann. Reg., Chron.* 194/2 Crabtree, whom Horrox had, by letter, invited to this Uranian banquet [= observing the transit of Venus, 1639]. **1832** FROST (*title*), Uranian Guide; or, Outline Celestial Atlas. **1839** (*Broadside title-p.*), Uranian Society is established for the advancement of Astronomical Science.

B. *sb.* A homosexual.

c **1908** 'X. MAYNE' *Intersexes* vii. 173 An appreciable influence in developing early Uranism is the fact that the tutor..may be an Uranian of pederastic inclinations. **1909** E. CARPENTER *Intermediate Sex* i. 13 One may safely say that the defect of the male Uranian, or Urning, is *not* sensuality —but rather *sentimentality*. **1947** E. RICKWORD *Coll. Poems* 58 When blessed parthenogenesis arrives and he-uranians can turn honest wives. **1975** P. FUSSELL *Gt. War & Mod. Memory* viii. 283 A less respectable..tradition of homoeroticism was that of the so-called Uranians, a body of enthusiastic pedophils.

Uranian (jʊˈreɪnɪən), *a.*[2] and *sb.*[1] [f. URAN-US + -IAN.]

A. *adj.* Of or pertaining to the planet Uranus.

1844 SMYTH *Cycle Celestial Objects* I. 205 The Uranian astronomer must be well stationed for watching comets. **1866** LOCKYER *Guillemin's Heavens* 263 The simultaneous presence or absence of these bodies from the Uranian sky. **1870** PROCTOR *Other Worlds than Ours* vii. 167 During the long Uranian year. **1885** AGNES CLERKE *Pop. Hist. Astron.* 114 No further Neptunian or Uranian satellites can be perceived.

B. *sb.* An inhabitant of Uranus.

1870 PROCTOR *Other Worlds than Ours* vii. 168 For upwards of 20 years..the Uranians—if there are any—never see the small Uranian sun. *Ibid.*, The year of the Uranians lasts 84 of our years.

†**u'raniate.** *Chem. Obs. rare.* [f. URANI-UM + -ATE[1] 1 c.] A salt produced by the action of uranium trioxide on a base.

1825 T. THOMSON *First Princ. Chem.* II. 30 The uraniate of potash. *Ibid.* 37 The uraniate of barytes, when pure, is a sesqui-uraniate. **1826** HENRY *Elem. Chem.* II. 81 The decomposition of uraniate of lead by exposing the anhydrous salt, ignited, to hydrogen gas.

u'ranic, *a.*[1] Also ouranik. [f. L. *ūran-us*, Gr. οὐραν-ός heaven, + -IC 1. Cf. med.L. *ūranic-us.*] Astronomical, celestial.

?*c* **1860** CARLYLE (Webster), Drawing accurately his meridian line, on I know not what telluric or uranic principles. **1883** R. BROWN *Eridanus* 44 There is another ouranik and doubtless preconstellational stream, namely the *Via Lactea.*

uranic (jʊ'rænɪk), *a.*[2] *Chem.* [f. URAN-IUM + -IC 1 b. Cf. F. *uranique.*] Formed from, or related to, the higher oxide of uranium.

1837 DANA *Min.* 246 Uranic Ochre, *Uranalus Ochraceus.* **1842** FRANCIS *Dict. Arts* s.v., Uranic acid, peroxyde of uranium, or the sesquioxyde of uranium. **1866** ROSCOE *Elem. Chem.* 203 The uranous salts are green, whilst the uranic compounds are yellow. **1868** *Watts' Dict. Chem.* V. 942 Uranic nitrate, or Nitrate of Uranyl. *Ibid.*, Uranic sulphate, or Sulphate of Uranyl. **1873** RALFE *Phys. Chem.* 196, 1 C.C. of the uranic oxide solution.

u'ranic, *a.*[3] *Anthropol.* [f. Gr. οὐραν-ός palate (sky, etc.: see URANO-[1]) + -IC 1.] Pertaining or relating to the palate. Freq. ***uranic index.***

1901 F. RUSSELL in *Amer. Anthrop.* III. 38.

†**u'ranical,** *a. Obs.* [f. med.L. *ūranic-us* celestial (cf. URANIC *a.*[1]) + -AL[1].]

a. Astronomical. **b.** Astrological.

a. 1595 J. BLAGRAVE *Astrol. Uran.* (title-p.), An Instrument or generall Astrolabe..called the Vranicall Astrolabe. **1619** J. BAINBRIDGE *Descr. Late Comet* 3 Tycho Brahe, of whose admirable Vranicall instruments many honourable witnesses are still suruiuing. **1716** M. DAVIES *Athen. Brit.* II. 341 Captain Hally, whose method of taking Uranical Observations had been..question'd.

b. 1671 SALMON *Syn. Med.* To Rdr. *4 The Uranical Precepts are more subtile and pure; whose Sublimity is Heaven it self. *Ibid.* *5 In our Uranical Disquisitions, even through all the three Books.

Urani'centric, *a. rare*[−1]. [f. URAN-US.] Having Uranus as the centre.

1867 G. F. CHAMBERS *Astron.* 152 Their [*sc.* Uranus' satellites] Uranicentric motion is retrograde.

†**u'ranics,** *sb. pl. Obs.*[−1] [See URANIC *a.*[1] and -IC 2.] Astrological matters; astrology.

1671 SALMON *Syn. Med.* To Rdr. *4b, So much as Spiritual and Heavenly things exceed Natural and Earthy, so much do the Uranicks exceed the Physicks.

ura'nidiform, *a.* [f. mod.L. *Uraniidæ* (see def.).] Having the form characteristic of the *Uraniidæ*, a family of lepidopterous insects.

1859 *Ann. Rep. Smithsonian Instit. 1858*, 186 Uranidiform larvæ will be found possibly..in Florida.

uraniferous (jʊərə'nɪfərəs), *a.* [f. URAN- + -IFEROUS.] Containing or yielding uranium.

1912 [see BETAFITE]. **1957** G. E. HUTCHINSON *Treat. Limnol.* I. xv. 831 Judson and Osmand..have recorded.. much higher values from ground waters in uraniferous localities. **1977** A. HALLAM *Planet Earth* 149 In zones where water has percolated down through uraniferous deposits, torbernite..may occur.

'uranile, obs. var. URANYL. (Cf. -ILE.)

1855 J. SCOFFERN in *Orr's Circ. Sci., Chem.* 484 Some chemists regard sesquioxide of uranium as really the protoxide of a radical termed uranile.

uraninite (jʊ'rænɪnaɪt). *Min.* [f. URANIUM + -IN[1]: see -ITE[1] 2 b.] Pitchblende.

1879 *Amer. Jrnl. Sci.* Ser. III. XVIII. 153 The masses contain in many cases, a nucleus of uraninite. **1897** L. FLETCHER *Introd. Study Min.* 89 Uraninite, or Pitchblende, consists almost entirely of oxygen and uranium.

u'ranious, var. URANOUS *a.*

1912 *Archaeol.* LXIII. 107 The uranious sand employed by the ancient glass-maker.

ura'nisco-, comb. form of mod.L. *uraniscus* (ad. Gr. οὐρανίσκος 'roof of the mouth'), occurring in a few medical and surgical terms, as *uranisconitis, -plastic, -plasty* [cf. F. *uraniscoplastie*], *-rraphy.* (1848- in medical dicts., etc.)

uranism ('jʊərənɪz(ə)m). *rare.* [ad. G. *uranismus*, f. L. *Urania*, ad. Gr. Οὐρανία, an epithet of Aphrodite: see URANIA, -ISM.] Homosexuality. Hence **'uranist**, a homosexual. Cf. URANIAN *a.*[1] 1 c, *sb.*[2], URNING.

1895 *Jrnl. Compar. Neurol.* V. 33 The education of congenital inverts (or uranists, to employ a word invented by a famous invert) has not yet been undertaken. *Ibid.* 34 The causes of uranism..are probably as mysterious as those of the difference of sex. **1899** [see MASOCHISM]. *c* **1908** [see URANIAN *sb.*[2]].

uranite ('jʊərənaɪt). [a. G. *uranit* (Klaproth, 1789), or F. *uranite*, f. URAN-IUM + -ITE[1] 2 b, 4.]

†**1.** *Chem.* = URANIUM 1. *Obs.*

1794 G. PEARSON *Table Chem. Nomencl.* 20 One new Metal, the Uranite, was discovered by Klaproth in 1790 [*sic*]. **1796** KIRWAN *Elem. Min.* (ed. 2) II. 301 Uranite..is soluble in the nitrous acid. **1821** URE *Dict. Chem. & Min.*, *Uranite* or *Uranium*, a new metallic substance, discovered by the celebrated Klaproth in the mineral called Pechblende.

2. *Min.* An ore or mineral composed largely of uranium, and consisting of the two varieties autunite and torbernite.

1802 *Paris as it was* II. lxix. 385 A collection of tin ore, cobalt, uranite, &c. from Saxony. **1815** A. AIKIN *Mineralogy* (ed. 2) 138 Uranite, Uran glimmer *W.*,..occurs crystallized in rectangular prisms and tables. **1839** URE *Dict. Arts* 1263 A double phosphate of uranium and copper, called green uranite, and uran mica, occurs in Cornwall. **1866** ROSCOE *Elem. Chem.* 203 Uranium..existing combined in two somewhat rare minerals, pitchblende and uranite.

ura'nitic, *a.* [f. prec. + -IC.] Of, pertaining to, or containing uranite (or uranium).

1796 KIRWAN *Elem. Min.* (ed. 2) II. 302 Uranitic Calx is insoluble in alkalis. *Ibid.* 469 Crystals of uranitic vitriol. **1819** BRANDE *Man. Chem.* 265 The uranitic ore, called by the Germans *uran glimmer*, is a hydrate of the yellow oxide. **1836** *Ibid.* (ed. 4) 733 The mineral called uranitic ochre is generally considered as a hydrated peroxide.

uranium (jʊ'reɪnɪəm). [mod.L. (Klaproth, *c* 1790), f. the name of the planet URAN-US + -IUM.]

1. a. A rare, heavy, grayish metallic element, found esp. in pitchblende and uranite. (Now important as fissile material in nuclear reactors and atomic bombs.) Also with following (arabic) numeral, denoting the mass number of the isotope concerned; and with following (usu. Roman) numeral or capital letter denoting an isotope of uranium or one formed by the decay of uranium.

uranium I, uranium 238; ***uranium II***, uranium 234; ***uranium X*** or X_1, thorium 234 (the decay product of uranium I); ***uranium*** X_2, metastable protactinium 234 (the decay product of uranium X_1); ***uranium Y***, thorium 231 (a decay product of uranium 235); ***uranium Z***, protactinium 234 in its ground state.

In first quot. erron. identified with *pitchblende.*

1797 *Encycl. Brit.* (ed. 3) XVIII. 691 *Uranium*, a fossil found..in Saxony, and..in Bohemia, and is, by the miners, called *Pechblend.* **1805** *Phil. Trans.* XCV. 348 The solution ..contained oxide of uranium. **1842** E. A. PARNELL *Chem. Anal.* 169 Both the peroxide and protoxide of uranium are precipitated from their solutions by ammonia. **1843** *Penny Cycl.* XXVI. 39/2 Uranium is very combustible;..it burns with a remarkably white and shining light. **1857** MILLER *Elem. Chem., Org.* x. §1. 592 Salts of uranium. **1868** WATTS *Dict. Chem.* V. 940 Péligot, in 1840, showed that the body previously regarded as metallic uranium was really the protoxide (UO); he likewise obtained the true metal. **1875** VOGEL *Chem. Light* xvi. 267 Uranium itself is a rare metal whose combinations play a great part in colouring materials. **1900** W. CROOKES in *Proc. R. Soc.* LXVI. 418 The new body must have a name. Until it is more tractable I will call it provisionally UrX—the unknown substance in uranium. **1903** *Phil. Mag.* V. 442 It was shown in 1900 by Sir William Crookes (*Proc. Roy. Soc.*, 1900, vol. lxvi. p. 409) that the activity of uranium to a photographic plate is caused by the presence of a minute amount of a foreign substance to which he gave the name Uranium X. **1911** G. N. ANTONOFF in *Ibid.* XXII. 425 The period of the new product deduced from the curve is 1·5 days... It is proposed to call the new product uranium Y (UrY). **1912** GEIGER & NUTTALL in *Ibid.* XXIII. 444 It enables us to calculate the period of ionium and of the second product in uranium (uranium II.) with greater certainty than has hitherto been possible. Uranium I. therefore..emits α particles of range 2·5 cm. in air.. and is followed by another α-ray product, uranium II., which.. emits α particles of range 2·9 cm. **1950** tr. *Hahn's New Atoms* 109 The element 93 remains in bulk in solution—free from uranium, uranium X and the fission products. **1950** GLASSTONE *Sourcebk. Atomic Energy* xiv. 401/2 The non-fissionable uranium-238..constitutes over 99·2 per cent of ordinary uranium. **1960** W. T. L. NEAL in J. C. Collins *Radioactive Wastes* ii. 25 Reactors are operated for three purposes—for fuel production (e.g. production of plutonium-239 from uranium-238, or uranium-233 from thorium-232), for power production and for research. **1962** *Newnes Conc. Encycl. Nucl. Energy* 659/1 Uranium II, U^{234}, is a decay product of natural uranium, being formed by beta decay of uranium X_2 and uranium Z.

b. *attrib.*, esp. in the names of salts, ores, etc., as ***uranium acetate, fission, fuel, nitrate, -ore, oxide, phosphate, vitriol***; also *Comb.*, as ***uranium-bearing, -prepared***; **uranium bomb**, an atomic bomb in which uranium is the fissile material; **uranium hexafluoride**, a whitish crystalline hygroscopic compound, UF_6, which sublimes at 56°C and is the form in which uranium isotopes are separated by gaseous diffusion; **uranium lead**, (*a*) the isotope lead 206, = *radium G* s.v. RADIUM 1 b; (*b*) used *attrib.* (with hyphen) to designate a method of isotopic dating, and the results obtained with it, based upon measurement of the relative amounts in rock of uranium 238 and 235 and of their ultimate decay products lead 206 and 207; **uranium series**, the series of isotopes produced by the radioactive decay of uranium 238, each member resulting from the decay of the previous one.

Various other examples have appeared in special Dicts., as ***uranium-bloom, -green, -ochre, -orange, -yellow*** (1868 *Watts' Dict. Chem.* s.v.).

1890 CAGNEY tr. *Jaksch's Clin. Diagn.* 269 Uranium acetate or nitrate is added in solution. **1941** in M. Gowing *Britain & Atomic Energy 1939–1945* (1965) 394 We have now reached the conclusion that it will be possible to make an effective uranium bomb..which would be equivalent as regards destructive effect to 1,800 tons of T.N.T. **1955** *Times* 14 June 6/5 Information appears to be coming to light here which confirms that the so-called hydrogen bomb exploded at Bikini last year was a uranium bomb involving a triple process of fission-fusion-fission. **1964** M. GOWING *Britain & Atomic Energy 1939–45* i. 38 As war began there was much speculation about Hitler's supposed 'secret weapon' and..the uranium bomb was among the candidates for this title. **1942** POLLARD & DAVIDSON *Applied Nucl. Physics* x. 187 The answer lies in the discovery of uranium fission by Hahn and Strassman. **1955** J. LINDHARD in W. Pauli *Niels Bohr* 193 Through the discovery of uranium fission it became possible to investigate the penetration of highly charged nuclear fragments. **1956** A. H. COMPTON *Atomic Quest* 321 Uranium fuel must compete economically with such energy sources as coal. **1899** *Collective Index Trans. & Abstr. Chem. Soc. 1873–1882* 629/1 Uranium *hexa*-fluoride. **1941** in M. Gowing *Britain & Atomic Energy 1939–45* (1964) 395 Work on a fairly large scale is needed to develop the chemical side for the production in bulk of uranium hexafluoride, the gaseous compound we propose to use [for the manufacture of ^{235}U]. **1971** Uranium hexafluoride [see HEX *sb.*[2]]. **1984** *Times* 27 Aug. 1/6 The ship's owners identified the material as uranium hexa-fluoride, a radioactive gas. **1914** *Phil. Mag.* XXVIII. 825 The equation for the complete disintegration of uranium is U→8He + Radium G (uranium lead). **1955** [see *thorium lead* s.v. THORIUM 2]. **1955** *Bull. Geol. Soc. Amer.* LXVI. 1141/1 (*heading*) Uranium-lead age of the granite. **1977** A. HALLAM *Planet Earth* 184/2 Isotopic age measurements by the uranium-lead and rubidium-strontium methods on most meteorites have yielded a solidification age close to 4600 million years. **1873** RALFE *Phys. Chem.* 237 The solution of Uranium Nitrate. **1837** DANA *Min.* 372 Pitchblende. *Uranius amorphus.* Uncleavable Uranium-Ore. **1890** CAGNEY tr. *Jaksch's Clin. Diagn.* 269 A solution of uranium oxide. **1862** *Catal. Internat. Exhib., Brit.* II. No. 3054, Developments of uranium-prepared papers. **1909** *Chem. News* 26 Mar. 146/2 (*heading*) A new radio-active product of the uranium series. **1973** Uranium series [see *thorium series* s.v. THORIUM 2]. **1850** WATTS tr. *Gmelin's Handbk. Chem.* IV. 175 Monosulphate. Found native as Uranium-vitriol.

2. *ellipt.* A solution of a salt or nitrate of uranium. Chiefly *attrib.* and *Comb.*

1878 ABNEY *Photogr.* 155 Printing with iron and uranium compounds. **1890** *Anthony's Photogr. Bull.* III. 361 The uranium intensifier..in my own practice has proved the simplest and best of all intensifiers. **1892** *Photogr. Ann.* II. 422 Carbutt's Positive Films..are amenable to uranium toning. **1900** J. A. HODGES *Pract. Enlarging* xiii. (ed. 4) 98 The appearance of a uranium-toned print.

urano-[1] ('jʊərənəʊ), combining form of Gr. οὐρανός sky, heaven(s), roof of the mouth, occurring in: **a.** †**ura'nognosy** (see quot.); **ura'nolatry**, worship of the heavenly bodies; **urano'mania, -pathy, -pho'tography, -pho'tometer, -'scopian** (a fish of the family *Uranoscopidæ*), **-theism** (see quots.). **b. uranosto-ma'toscopy**, examination of the hard palate and back of the mouth; also URANOPLASTIC *a.*, -PLASTY.

Recent Dicts. give ***uranoplegia, -rrhaphy, -schisis, -staphylplasty, -staphylorraphy.***

a. *a* **1831** BENTHAM *Logic* App., Wks. 1843 VIII. 286/2 By *Uranognosy, rather than Astronomy, may that branch of Topography, taken in its largest sense, which remains after the substraction of Geography be designated. **1877** W. H. RULE *Oriental Rec., Mon.* 6 *Uranolatry was grown into a system, and the Chaldean or Babylonian astronomy had become a science. **1890** BILLINGS *Med. Dict.* II. 723 **Uranomania*, monomania involving the idea of a divine or celestial origin or connection; a species of megalomania. **1868** W. CORY *Lett. & Jrnls.* (1897) 246 That crenopathy and *uranopathy, that yielding of ourselves to running water and to still clouds. *a* **1909** WOODBURY *Encycl. Photogr.* 304 **Urano-photography*, the photography of celestial spaces. **1876** *Nature* 21 Dec. 170/1 The diffuse light of the sky..has recently been a subject of study by M. Wild,..who has endeavoured to measure it with a somewhat complicated instrument devised by him and named a '*uranophotometer'. *c* **185.** *Sir J. Richardson's Mus. Nat. Sci.* II. 120/1 *Urano-scopians, or Sky-gazers. **1801** *Monthly Mag.* XI. 646 *Urano-theism, or the worship of sun, moon, thunder, and meteors.

b. *a* **1891** *Medical News* XLIX. 559 (Cent.), Phrenopathic uranostomatoscopy.

'urano-[2], combining form of URAN-IUM, occurring, usu. in the sense 'containing, composed or having the structure of, uranium', in various (chiefly mineralogical) terms (some of which have little or no real currency in the language, but are mere borrowings from German sources), as ***urano-ammonic, -chalcite, -circite, -niobate, -phane, -phyllite, -pilite, -pissite, -sphærite, -spinite, -tantal(ite, -thallite, -thorite, -til(e.***

1850 WATTS tr. *Gmelin's Handbk. Chem.* IV. 184–5 Urano-ammonic Carbonate,..Urano-ammonic Sulphate. **1850** ANSTED *Geol. & Min.* 220. **1855** *Orr's Circle Sci., Geol.* 531. **1867** BRANDE & COX *Dict. Sci.* III. 905. **1868** DANA *Min.* **1868** *Watts' Dict. Chem.* V. 186, 949. **1883** *Encycl. Brit.* XVI. 407, 425, 427. **1896** CHESTER *Dict. Min.* 278–9.

uranography (jʊərə'nɒgrəfɪ). Also 7–8 (9) ourano-. [ad. Gr. οὐρανογραφία: see URANO-[1] and

-GRAPHY. Cf. F. (1762) *uranographie*, Sp. and Pg. *uranografia*.]

†**1.** A description of heaven. *Obs. rare.*

1650 FULLER *Pisgah* II. v. i. 189, I found the Canaan by him described no Geography, but Ouranography, no earthly truth, but mysticall prediction. **1710** B. JENKS (*title*), Ouranography, or, Heaven opened. The Substance of Cardinal Bellarmine's Five Books concerning the Eternal Felicity of the Saints.

2. The science of describing or delineating the sidereal heavens; a description or delineation of the stars. Also *transf.*

α. **1675** SHERBURNE *Manilius' Sphere* a ii, Constellations.. are distinguished into prophane and Sacred Figures or Morphoses, according to the different Uranography of the Antient Ethnicks. **1699** HOWE *Redeemer's Dominion* Wks. 1724 II. 85 When our Lord is said to have ascended far above all Heavens,..whose Uranography [will suffice] to describe how far that is? **1715** tr. *Gregory's Astron.* I. 310 From hence did he [*sc.* Hevelius] deduce his Uranography or Tables of all the Stars. **1833** HERSCHEL *Astron.* 159 So in uranography, any conspicuous star may be selected as an initial point. **1890** *Science-Gossip* XXVI. 102/1 An Uranography, or brief description of the constellations visible in the Northern Hemisphere..illustrated by star maps.

β. **1684** in Birch *Hist. Royal Soc.* (1757) IV. 272 The ingenious Mr. Hooke, in his animadversions on Hevelius's ouranography. **1881** tr. *Verne's Fur Country* 17 He had rendered great services to ouranography.

Hence **ura'nographer**, one who practises or studies uranography; **urano'graphic(al** *adjs.*, of or pertaining to uranography; **ura'nographist**, = URANOGRAPHER.

1686 GOAD *Celest. Bodies* II. xi. 316 He is as great as the Greatest *Uranographer can make him. **1861** G. F. CHAMBERS *Astron.* 313 Many of the above smaller constellations are..rejected by modern uranographers. **1715** tr. *Gregory's Astron.* I. 310 These *Uranographic Schemes of the Constellations are delineated in *Plano.* **1855** *Tallis's Crystal Palace* II. 245 Detouche and Houdin (France) exhibited a uranographic apparatus. **1882** R. BROWN *Law Kosmic Order* 52 A remarkable conical black Babylonian Stone.., which, though not strictly zodiacal, is certainly uranographic in character. **1833** HERSCHEL *Astron.* 179 The *uranographical effect of aberration. **1844** *N. Brit. Rev.* I. 394 His whole stores of ouranographical and astronomical knowledge. **1861** G. F. CHAMBERS *Astron.* 273 The determination of the exact uranographical position of a star. **1731** BAILEY (vol. II), **Ouranographist*,..an astronomer, or one who describes the heavens. **1812** SOUTHEY *Omniana* II. 142 The great Swedish Ouranographist [*sc.* Swedenborg], whose discoveries were not always confined to heaven.

u'ranolite. *rare.* [See URANO-[1] a and -LITE.] An aerolite or meteoric stone.

1815 *Monthly Mag.* XXXIX 299 The name of *uranolite* has long appeared to me to be better suited to bodies.. which tend towards the earth through that boundless space in which the stars move. **1860** WORCESTER (citing Hutton).

So **u'ranolith.** [-LITH.]

1889 C. A. YOUNG *Gen. Astron.* xviii. 430 The pieces which fall from it are called..uranoliths (heaven-stones), or simply meteoric stones.

ura'nology. Also 9 ouran-. [See URANO-[1] a and -(O)LOGY. Cf. Pg. *uranologia*.]

1. The study of the sidereal heavens; astronomy.

1735 B. MARTIN *Philos. Gram.* 10 Cosmology or Uranology..treats of..the Universe in general, and particularly of our solar System. *Ibid.* 107 Of Uranology, or the Doctrine of the heavenly Bodies. **1740** —— *Bibl. Techn.* xvii. 325 Uranology..may be considered under the following branches: Heliography;..Astrography. **1792** SIBLY *Occult Sci.* I. 53 Uranology is a science which treats of the natural body of Heaven. **1816** BENTHAM *Chrestom.* Table, Wks. 1843 VIII. 13/1 Acquaintance with Uranology, more frequently termed Astronomy.

b. A treatise or discourse on the sidereal heavens; a system of astronomy.

1736 BAILEY (folio) Pref., *41. Uranology*,..a Treatise or Discourse of the..celestial Regions and the Bodies in them contained. **1854** OWEN in *Orr's Circ. Sci., Org. Nat.* I. 261 One must not strive to make an ouranology out of a system of metaphysics.

2. Doctrine as to heaven. *rare*[−1].

1866 *Reader* No. 170. 317/1 Angelology and uranology.

So †**ura'nologer**, an astronomer; ˌ**urano'logical** *a.*, of or pertaining to uranology.

1686 GOAD *Celest. Bodies* II. i. 129 The Words of that great Uranologer John Kepler. **1816** BENTHAM *Chrestom.* 55 Uranological Geography. **1851** tr. *Humboldt's Cosmos* III. 29 The uranological portion of the physical description of the world. *Ibid.*, The uranological..domain of the Cosmos.

†**uranomancy.** *Obs.*[−1] [See URANO-[1] a and -MANCY.] Divination by the stars; astrology.

1657 G. STARKEY *Helmont's Vind.* 16 All other natural practical Arts, as Geometry, Astronomy, Uranomancy, Geography, Arithmetick, and the like.

‖ˌ**urano'metria.** [mod.L. *uranometria* (Bayer, 1603).] = URANOMETRY.

1882 *Pop. Sci. Monthly* XX. 700 Uranometria of the Southern Heavens. **1885** *Encycl. Brit.* XVIII. 841/1 Sir John [Herschel]..did not go on to the formation of a complete 'uranometria'.

ˌ**urano'metrical,** *a. rare*[−1]. [See next and -ICAL.] Relating or pertaining to uranometry.

1652 CHARLETON *Darkn. Atheism Dispelled* 327 The simple and demonstrable Uranometrical observations and Axioms of Antiquity.

ura'nometry. [ad. mod.L. *uranometria* URANOMETRIA: see URANO-[1] a and -METRY. Cf. F. (1776) *uranométrie*, Sp. and It. *-metria*.]

1. A work descriptive of the heavens and esp. the fixed stars, showing or recording their magnitudes, relative positions, etc.

1715 tr. *Gregory's Astron.* I. 310 He says that Bayer, who, in his Uranometry, attempted the contrary, thoughtlesly inverted all the Stars. **1879** NEWCOMB & HOLDEN *Astron.* 435 The uranometries of..Heis and Gould give the lucid stars..laid down on maps. **1898** W. PECK *Observer's Atlas* Pref., Thanks to the various modern Uranometries,.. accurate maps of the star sphere can now be produced.

2. The measurement of the real or apparent distances of heavenly bodies.

1792 SIBLY *Occult Sci.* I. 53 Uranometry..is a science that points out the magnitude, measure, and motion of the heavens. **1849** HERSCHEL *Outl. Astron.* 71 The problems of uranometry..consist in the solution of a variety of spherical triangles. **1883** C. PRITCHARD in *Mem. R. Astron. Soc.* XLVII. 367 The aims of these observers have not been especially directed to Uranometry.

ˌ**urano'plastic,** *sb.* and *a.* [f. URANOPLASTY + -IC 2.] **a.** *sb. pl.* = URANOPLASTY. **b.** *adj.* Of or pertaining to uranoplasty.

a. 1861 *Medical Times* 20 July 70/1 He had the opportunity of performing uranoplastics on a patient. **b. 1890** BILLINGS *Med. Dict.* s.v. **1903** *Med. Record* 30 May 884 (Cent. Suppl.).

'**uranoˌplasty.** *Surg.* [a. F. *uranoplastie*: see URANO-[1] b and -PLASTY.] Plastic surgery of the hard palate.

1846 BRITTAN tr. *Malgaigne's Man. Oper. Surg.* 370 Uranoplasty... The ligatures being placed as in Staphyloplasty,..the operator detaches..the layer of soft parts. **1862** *N. Syd. Soc. Year-Bk. Med.* 248 Uranoplasty by detachment of the Mucous-peritoneal Covering of the Palate. **1872** COHEN *Dis. Throat* 200 [An] operation of uranoplasty for cleft of the hard palate.

†**u'ranoscope.** *Obs.* [a. F. (16th c.) *urano-, ouranoscope*: see URANOSCOPUS.] = URANOSCOPUS.

1591 SYLVESTER *Du Bartas* (1605) I. v. 232 Th' Vranno-scope [*margin* Vrano-Scopus], so, hid in mud, doth put Out of his gullet a long limber gut. **1753** *Chambers' Cycl.* Suppl. s.v. *Trachinus*, This is the uranoscope, or *Trachinus* of authors, called also *callionymus*. Artedi.

ˌ**urano'scopic,** *a. rare.* [f. Gr. οὐρανοσκόπ-ος observing the heavens.] **a.** Pertaining to the study of the heavens. **b.** Directed towards the heavens.

1816 BENTHAM *Chrestom.* Wks. 1843 VIII. 86 Uranoscopic Physiurgics has for its single-worded synonym the adequately expressive appelative Astronomy. **1854** *Fraser's Mag.* L. 203 Till his uranoscopic eyes warn him that the..fishes..are within gulp of his open sepulchre of a throat.

‖**ura'noscopus.** *Ichth.* 6 -ascapos, -oscopos. [L. *ūranoscopus*, or ad. Gr. οὐρανοσκόπος: see prec.] = STAR-GAZER 2.

α. **1584–7** GREENE *Carde of Fancie* Wks. (Grosart) IV. 143 The Fish called Vranascapos. **1594** T. B. *La Primaud. Fr. Acad.* II. 552 One fish..hath the eyes set in the top of the head, and therefore it is called by the Græcians *vranoscopos.*

β. **1591** [see URANOSCOPE]. [**1623** COCKERAM *Eng. Dict.* III. Hence in PHILLIPS.] **1753** *Chambers' Cycl.* Suppl. s.v., The situation of the eyes of the *Uranoscopus*. **1774** GOLDSM. *Nat. Hist.* VI. 306 The *Uranoscopus*,..the mouth flat; the eyes on the top of the head;..an inhabitant of the Mediterranean Sea. **1803** SHAW *Gen. Zool.* IV. I. 130 The Weever was by Artedi considered as not generically distinct from the Uranoscopus. **1854** BADHAM *Halieut.* 127 The name of this fish, *uranoscopus*, or 'sky-gazer', is derived from the position of the eyes, which are singularly planted on the crown of the head.

uranoscopy. *rare.* Also ourano-. [ad. mod.Gr. οὐρανοσκοπία: see prec. and -Y[3]. Cf. It. *uranoscopia*.] (See quots.)

1656 BLOUNT *Glossogr.*, *Uranoscopy*, (Gr.) a speculation or view of the Heavens. [**1658-** Phillips, Bailey, and later Dicts.] **1681** R. WITTIE *Οὐρανοσκοπία*, etc. 73 Of which I have been discoursing more at large in my *Ouranoscopy*, or *Survey of the Heavens.*

ura'noso-, combining form of URANOUS *a.*, occurring in a few chemical terms, as **uranoso-ammonic, -potassic, -uranic.**

1850 WATTS tr. *Gmelin's Handbk. Chem.* IV. 181–7 Uranoso-uranic oxide,..uranoso-ammonic Carbonate,.. uranoso-ammonic sulphate,..uranoso-potassic Sulphate. **1868** —— *Dict. Chem.* V. 941 Pitchblende..consists of impure uranoso-uranic oxide. *Ibid.* 946.

uranous ('jʊərənəs), *a. Chem.* [f. URAN-IUM + -OUS c. Cf. F. *uraneux*.]

1. Formed from or related to the lower oxide of uranium.

1842 T. GRAHAM *Elem. Chem.* 643 The uranous sulphate yields, by evaporation, green prismatic crystals. **1866** ROSCOE *Elem. Chem.* 203 There are two oxides which form salts, viz., uranous oxide, UO, and uranic oxide, U_2O_3. **1868** *Watts' Dict. Chem.* V. 942 Uranous Bromide. *Ibid.*, Uranous chloride. **1894** G. S. NEWTH *Inorg. Chem.* 617 Uranium dioxide..yielding the unstable uranous salts, such as uranous sulphate.

2. Of or pertaining to, typical of, uranium.

1878 ABNEY *Photogr.* 159 This is reduced to the uranous state by the action of light in the presence of organic matter.

uran-outang, obs. f. ORANG-OUTANG.

1853 J. CUMMING *Scripture Reading Genesis* ii. 18 The absurdity of supposing such a similarity between..an uran-outang and man.

Uranus ('jʊərənəs, jʊ'reɪnəs). *Astr.* [a. L. *Ūranus*, a. Gr. Οὐρανός husband of Gæa (Earth) and father of Cronos (Saturn).] The most remote but two of the planets, situated between Saturn and Neptune.

Discovered in 1781 by Sir Wm. Herschel, who named it 'the Georgium sidus', 'the Georgian planet'. The name *Uranus* was first proposed by Bode, in conformity with other planetary names from classical mythology.

1802 O. GREGORY *Treat. Astron.* 128 By some astronomers it is called *Herschel*, in honour of the discoverer; though among almost all foreigners, it has acquired the name of *uranius* [sic], which it is likely to retain. **1822** *Encycl. Metrop.* (1845) III. 498/1 Both these appellations are, however, now nearly become extinct, that of *Uranus* being almost universally adopted. **1860** OLMSTED *Mech. Heavens* 267 Uranus was the remotest known planet .., until the discovery of..Neptune.

uranyl ('jʊərənɪl). *Chem.* [f. URAN-IUM + -YL.] A radical (UO_2) held to exist in many compounds of uranium.

1850 WATTS tr. *Gmelin's Handbk. Chem.* IV. 181 Chloride of uranyl. **1863** —— *Dict. Chem.* I. 797 Carbonate of Uranyl and Ammonium. *Ibid.*, Uranyl, U^2O^2, is a diatomic radicle which may be supposed to exist in the uranic salts, e.g. uranic nitrate. **1884** FRANKLAND & JAPP *Inorg. Chem.* 708 Salts in which the dyad radical uranyl ($U^{vi}O_2$) plays the part of a dyad metal.

b. ***uranyl chloride, oxide, phosphate, salts***: (see quots.).

1865 MANSFIELD *Salts* 285 The so-called 'Uranyl' Salts of Peligot, supposed to be of the form U_2O_2. **1878** C. M. TIDY *Handbk. Mod. Chem.* 337 Uranic oxide (sesquioxide) or Uranyl oxide. **1888** *Encycl. Brit.* XXIV. 7/2 Solutions of uranyl salts (nitrate, &c.). **1888** *Cassell's Encycl. Dict.* VII. 384 *Uranyl-chloride*, Uranic-oxychloride. **1903** *Amer. Jrnl. Sci.* Ser. IV. XVI. 237 The filtering of a precipitate of ammonium uranyl phosphate through a Gooch crucible.

Hence **ura'nylic** *a.* (See -IC 1 b.)

1884 FRANKLAND & JAPP *Inorg. Chem.* 708–711 Uranylic chloride,..bromide,..fluoride,..nitrate,..sulphate,.. pyro-sulphate,..sulphide.

‖**urao** (ʊ'rɑːəʊ). *Min.* [Native name. So F. *urao*.] = TRONA.

1839 URE *Dict. Arts* 1263 Urao, is the native name of a sesquicarbonate of soda found at the bottom of certain lakes in Mexico. **1863** *Watts' Dict. Chem.* I. 796 Tetrasodic Carbonate or Sesquicarbonate of Sodium..occurs..as *urao* at the bottom of a lake in Maracaibo, South America. **1889** *Amer. Nat.* XXIII. 814 The composition of urao, a mineral ..from Venezuela.

‖**urari** (ʊ'rɑːrɪ). Also urary, urare; ourari, oorara. [See CURARE, and cf. URALI, OORALI, WOORALI.] (See quots. 1859, 1866.)

α. **1838** in *Annals Nat. Hist.* (1841) VII. 417 The whole of the Urary is poured by degrees through the small funnel. **1876** *Daily News* 21 June 2 The prohibition of the use of urari as an anæsthetic.

β. **1859** A. S. TAYLOR *On Poisons* (ed. 2) 771 The poison known under the name of..Woorali, Oorara, and Curara. **1866** *Treas. Bot.* 1106 *Strychnos toxifera* also yields a frightful poison called Ourari.., employed by the natives of Guiana.

b. *attrib.* and *Comb.*, as ***urari-house, -maker, poison***; **urari bark**, bark of the **urari plant**, *Strychnos toxifera.*

1838 in *Annals Nat. Hist.* (1841) VII. 416, I was fortunate enough in purchasing a quake or basket of Urary bark. *Ibid.*, The much-famed Urary poison. *Ibid.* 417 Other fire than that made by the Urary-maker is not allowed to come under the roof of the Urary-house. **1841** *Ibid.* 415 The pure bark of the Urari plant, *Strychnos toxifera.* **1862** MILLER *Elem. Chem., Org.* (ed. 2) 502 The Urari or woorara poison of South America.

Urartian (ʊ'rɑːtɪən), *sb.* and *a.* Also **Urartæan, Urartean.** [f. the name of *Urart(u*, an ancient kingdom in eastern Asia Minor + -IAN.] **a.** = KHALDIAN b. **b.** A native or inhabitant of Urartu.

1934 WEBSTER, Urartaean *a.* and *n.* **1939** [see KHALDIAN]. **1939** A. TOYNBEE *Study of Hist.* VI. 62 Rediscovered language..Sumerian, Akkadian, Elamite, Urartian,..and so on. **1950** H. L. LORIMER *Homer & Monuments* v. 176 Though the early history of the Urartians is obscure, they are believed to have come eastward to Lake Van from Anatolia. **1964** G. ROUX *Ancient Iraq* xiv. 192 Their language [*sc.* that of the Hurrians]..is neither Semitic nor Indo-European, but belongs to the vague so-called 'Asianic' group, its nearest relative being Urartian, the language spoken in the country of Urartu (Armenia) in the first millennium BC. **1965** J. PUHVEL *Evidence for Laryngeals* 84 The Urartean *Kulḫai* may correspond to the later city of Κολχίς in Armenia. **1972** W. B. LOCKWOOD *Panorama Indo-Europ. Lang.* 175 The I[ndo-E[uropean] immigrants imposed their language on both Hurrians and Urartians and doubtless the non-IE people are ultimately responsible for many of the peculiar and unexplained features of Armenian. *Ibid.* 263, Hurrian is a non-IE language which has affinities with Urartian, the language of the kingdom of Urartu ('Ararat'), centred on the area between the lakes Van, Urmia and Sevan. **1977** *Antiquaries Jrnl.* LVII. 264 The Copenhagen cauldron can be regarded as Greek work of Urartian inspiration in the eighth or seventh centuries B.C.

‖**u'raster.** [a. mod.L. *uraster* (Agassiz).] The common star-fish, *Asterias rubens.*
1863 *Intell. Observer* Nov. 251 The commoner Urasters, found everywhere between tide-marks, are examples of the five-rayed form.

‖**ura'tæmia.** *Path.* [mod.L., f. URATE + Gr. αἷμα blood.] A morbid condition due to accumulation of urates in the blood. Cf. URÆMIA.
1897 *Allbutt's Syst. Med.* III. 162 A condition which may be termed uratæmia prevails.

urate ('jʊərət). *Chem.* Also **urat.** [a. F. *urate*: see UR-IC *a.* and -ATE¹ 1 c.] A salt produced by the action of uric acid on a base.
1800 tr. *Lagrange's Chem.* II. 404 The urate of potash may be decomposed by the muriatic acid. **1811** HENRY in *Manchester Soc. Mem.* (1813) II. 403, I have examined the properties of each individual urate. **1826** —— *Elem. Chem.* II. 462 Uric acid, urate of ammonia, and phosphate of lime. **1844** G. BIRD *Urin. Deposits* 88 Uric acid and urates may occur in great abundance in the urine. **1869** TANNER *Clin. Med.* (ed. 2) 330 Being made up of urates of lime, magnesia, soda.
attrib. **1877** HUXLEY *Anat. Inv. Anim.* vii. 441 The granules..probably consist of urate of ammonia (Kölliker). Hence the cells of the layer which contain them are termed by Schulze the 'urate cells'. **1886** *Buck's Handbk. Med. Sci.* II. 258/2 Urate concretions..are especially common as renal calculi in children. **1890** F. TAYLOR *Man. Pract. Med.* (1891) 924 Urate deposits in gout.

uratic (jʊ'rætɪk), *a.* [f. prec. + -IC 1 b.] Of or pertaining to, containing or consisting of, a urate or urates. ***uratic diathesis***: (see quot. 1885).
1876 BRISTOWE *Th. & Pract. Med.* 618 Scanty urine with abundant uratic deposit. *Ibid.* 885 These results being due ..to uratic infiltration. **1885** *Encycl. Brit.* XVIII. 388/2 The peculiar liability from uric acid is sometimes called the uric-acid or uratic diathesis or constitution. **1897** *Brit. Med. Jrnl.* 27 March 769 Uratic crystals forming only in necrosed and never in healthy tissues.

‖**ura'tosis.** *Path.* [f. as prec. + -OSIS.] A morbid condition of health resulting from the deposit of urates in the tissues or fluids of the body.
1890 SIR W. ROBERTS in *Lancet* 29 Nov. 1162/1 He ventured to suggest that uratic precipitation..should be known by the name of 'uratosis'. **1897** *Allbutt's Syst. Med.* II. 981 He [Sir Wm. Roberts] believes that both the gouty diathesis and lead poisoning have the same tendency (for which he has coined the word 'uratosis') to precipitate crystalline urates in the tissues or fluids of the body. *Ibid.* III. 167 Uratosis cannot occur, so far as is known, without co-existing uratæmia.

†**uraught.** *Anglo-Irish. Obs.* Also **uriaght.** [a. Irish *oireacht* faction, party, clan.] An Irish petty chief.
1586 *Treaty[se] of Ireland* in *MS. Bodl.* Add. c 39 fol. 49 b, McGuyer is one of Oneills Uraughts. *Ibid.*, Ochan is chefe of Oneylls Uraughts. **1601** Q. ELIZ. *Let.* in Moryson *Itin.* (1617) II. 201 If our Armes must be accompanied with any ..mercy, rather to imploy the same in receiuing the secondary members and Vriaghts from him. **1603** *Ibid.* 280, I doe absolutely renounce all challenge or intermedling with the Vriaghts..or exacting any blacke rents of any Vriaghts (or bordering Lords).

urban ('ɜːbən), *a.* and *sb.* [ad. L. *urbān-us* (whence It., Sp., Pg. *urbano*), f. *urb-s* city. Rare before the 19th cent.; cf. next.]
A. *adj.* **1. a.** Pertaining to or characteristic of, occurring or taking place in, a city or town.
1619 A. GARDEN *Bp. Elphinston* (Hunt. Cl.) 2239 Vrban and tunishe [= townish] turns, For for the land's effairs,.. his wit Him fit for all declairs. *c* **1770** ERSKINE in *Encycl. Brit.* II. 912 Predial servitudes are divided into rural servitudes, or of lands; and urban servitudes, or of houses. **1821** LAMB *Elia* I. *Valentine's Day*, I include all urban and all rural sounds. **1845** R. W. HAMILTON *Pop. Educ.* iii. 42 It is contended that urban labour is engrossing, unhealthy, and demoralising. **1867** W. L. NEWMAN in *Quest. Reformed Parl.* 121 The progressive forces of urban and agricultural life. **1877** GLADSTONE *Glean.* (1879) I. 157 We..are apt to say that the influence of money..is a considerable element in the strength of urban Toryism.
b. Constituting, forming, or including a city, town, or burgh, or part of such.
1841 W. SPALDING *Italy & It. Isl.* II. 309 One uniform system of municipal government, embracing all districts, rural as well as urban. **1867** A. O. RUTSON *Ess. Reform* 297 The activity of mind and the zeal for improvement which belong to urban constituencies. **1872** *Act 35–36 Vict.* c. 79 §3 Such urban and rural sanitary districts. **1888** BRYCE *Amer. Commw.* II. lxi. 433 A 'town' in New England..is a rural and not an urban area. **1894** *Act 56–57 Vict.* c. 73 §21 Urban sanitary authorities shall be called urban district councils, and their districts shall be called urban districts.
2. a. Exercising authority, control, supervision, etc., in or over a city or town.
Used by Howell in place of his usual *urbane.*
1651 HOWELL *Venice* 16 All Magistrats are either Urban or Forren, viz. of Town or Countrey. *a* **1704** T. BROWN *Walk Lond. & Westm.* Wks. 1720 III. 317 The pathetick Harangue of that Urban Magistrate a R——r. **1815** J. C. HOBHOUSE *Substance Lett.* (1816) II. 17 The national guard of Paris,..that urban guard whose patriotism and approved zeal [etc.]. **1872** *Act 35–36 Vict.* c. 79 §4 Urban sanitary authorities shall be the several bodies of persons specified [etc.]. **1886** *Encycl. Brit.* XX. 145/2 The Urban Quæstors.
b. Residing, dwelling, or having property in a city or town.
1837 C. LOFFT *Self-formation* I. 40 His urban, or sub-urban brother, the man of the multitude, the unit of the mob. **1849** ALISON *Hist. Eur.* I. ii. 225 Government has.. found a counterpoise to the vehemence of urban democracy. **1873** MORLEY *Struggle Nat. Educ.* 95 The brutalising lives that are led by the rural and urban poor in their crowded hovels. **1889** *Spectator* 14 Dec. 834 How do they justify the absorption of the increment of value from urban landholders alone?
3. Special collocations: ***urban blight***, the gradual unfolding or existence of slum areas, waste land, ghettos, etc., within a city or town (cf. BLIGHT *sb.* 4 b); ***Urban District*** (*Hist.*): see DISTRICT *sb.* 3 b; ***Urban District Council***, the local council of an Urban District; abbrev. *U.D.C.*; ***urban guerrilla***, a guerrilla operating in cities or towns and involved in kidnapping, etc.; also *attrib.*; ***urban guerrilla warfare***, irregular kidnapping, bombing, etc., by urban guerrillas; ***urban renewal*** (orig. *U.S.*), the clearance and redevelopment of slum areas, waste land, ghettos, etc., within a city or town; also *attrib.* and *fig.*; ***urban-rural*** adj., of or pertaining to both town and country; ***urban sprawl***, the uncontrolled expansion of urban areas; ***urban village***, a small self-contained district or community within a city or town (= VILLAGE *sb.* 1 e); so ***urban villager***, an inhabitant of an urban village.
1938 M. L. WALKER (*title*) Urban blight and slums. **1975** M. BRADBURY *History Man* i. 14 A real town of urban blight and renewal, social tensions, discrimination. **1894** Urban district council [see sense A. 1 b]. **1973** *Whitaker's Almanack 1974* 617/2 Urban district councils are also highway authorities. **1967** G. JACKSON *Let.* 31 Jan. in *Soledad Brother* (1971) 106, I have made inroads into political economy.. and when I can get hold of them some of the works on urban guerrilla warfare. **1972** *Guardian* 17 Jan. 11/2 The army.. is claiming only that it has the measure of the urban guerrilla in Belfast. **1979** G. SEYMOUR *Red Fox* iii. 44 The threat.. posed by the rash of urban guerrilla groups. **1955** *Statutes at Large U.S.A.* LXVIII. I. 622 The heading of title I of the Housing Act of 1949..is hereby amended to read Title I —Slum Clearance and Urban Renewal. *Ibid.*, A fund.. known as the 'Urban Renewal Fund', shall be available for advances, loans and capital grants to local agencies for urban renewal projects. **1961** E. A. POWDRILL *Vocab. Land Planning* iii. 55 'Urban renewal' can be defined as a generic expression or term which comprises the elements of redevelopment (demolition and rebuilding), rehabilitation (repairing, altering and remodelling), and conservation (the preservation of buildings or groups of buildings). **1966** H. NIELSEN *After Midnight* (1967) iv. 61 He heads some extremist group... Sort of an urban renewal project of the Ku Klux Klan. **1977** D. M. SMITH *Human Geogr.* v. 104 Some change such as urban renewal or the construction of a new hospital has the capacity to shift the welfare frontier. **1984** *Times* 24 Apr. 13/4 Our delegation visited and discussed urban renewal. **1953** A. E. SMAILES *Geogr. of Towns* ii. 33 There is no longer either socially or physically a simple clear-cut dichotomy of town and country; rather it is an urban-rural continuum. **1970** R. STAVENHAGEN in I. L. Horowitz *Masses in Lat. Amer.* vii. 256 There may be those who see in this situation only an ecologic relation, an 'urban-rural' conflict. **1958** *Listener* 25 Sept. 448/2 The result is a disturbing incidence of crime, juvenile delinquency, road accidents, congestion, urban sprawl, ignorance, and ugliness. **1979** *Monitor* (McAllen, Texas) 8 July 8D/3 Houston's urban sprawl is greater than that of Los Angeles. **1962** H. J. GANS *Urban Villagers* i. 4 The West End was an urban village, located next to Boston's original and once largest skid row area, Scollay Square. **1974** *Times* 15 Apr. 2/4 A device to create an 'urban village' in a predominantly middle-class area. **1962** H. J. GANS (*title*) Urban villagers.
B. *sb.* **1.** One who belongs to or lives in a town or city.
1891 *Cent. Dict.* Also in recent use (1922).
2. = *urban district council* (see sense A. 3 above). *rare.*
1952 M. LASKI *Village* ii. 40 'What do you think of this proposal to bring us under Walbridge Urban?'.. 'Well, I suppose it might mean some street lighting.'
Hence **'urbanism,** urban character; town-planning; town-life; urbanization. [Cf. F. *urbanisme.*]
1889 *Universal Rev.* Oct. 210 The local colour or detail, the sentiment or the social life, the provincialism or urbanism of the story. **1929** *Times* 16 July 17/6 In all the opening speeches..the newly coined word 'urbanism' was prominent. It denotes town-planning, [etc.]. **1934** A. HUXLEY *Beyond Mexique Bay* 258 Many primitive virtues are obviously incompatible with urbanism and industrialism. **1952** GERTH & MARTINDALE in *Weber's Anc. Judaism* p. xviii, Weber saw the civic society of Palestine as a variation of ancient Mediterranean urbanism. **1977** *Ecologist* VII. 52/3 The dynamic of urbanism as we know it makes inevitable the syndrome of violence, alienation, high crime rates and delinquency that we associate with our cities. **1980** *Times Lit. Suppl.* 26 Sept. 1061/5 The discussion of the Capitol's urbanism and topography.

urbane (ɜː'beɪn), *a.* [ad. F. *urbain* (14th c.), or L. *urbān-us* URBAN *a.* For the difference, in form and stress, between *urban* and *urbane*, cf. *human* and *humane.*]
1. Of or pertaining to, characteristic of or peculiar to, a town or city. Now *arch.* or *Obs.*
1533 BELLENDEN *Livy* I. xx. (S.T.S.) I. 114 Siclike vrbane & civil laubouris. *Ibid.* v. v. II. 161 Thus had al þe romane tentis almaist bene replete of seditioun vrbane. **1570** LEVINS *Manip.* 19 Vrbane, *vrbanus.* **1607** R. C[AREW] tr. *Estienne's World Wond.* 233 They see greater cunning and dexteritie, and a more ciuill and vrbane kind of life. **1681** STAIR *Inst. Law Scot.* XVII. 343 Negative Urbane Servitudes, do chiefly concern the light view or prospect of Tenements. **1788** *Trifler* No. 26. 344 In the simple beauty of the country the once wealthy merchant of Bassora lost the recollection of urbane magnificence. **1809–14** WORDSW. *Excurs.* VIII. 71 A poor brotherhood who walk the earth,..Raising..savage life To rustic, and the rustic to urbane.
†**b.** Exercising jurisdiction over, dwelling or residing in, a town or city. *Obs.*
1651 HOWELL *Venice* 16 Among the Urbane or Cittie Magistrats the Judges are rankd. **1652** GAULE *Magastrom.* 373 M. Æmilius, the urbane prætor. **1658** J. HARRINGTON *Oceana* Introd. Bjb, The Urbane Tribes of Rome consisting of the Turbaforensis [etc.]. **1681** H. NEVILE *Plato Rediv.* 61 The Rustik Tribes being twenty seven, and the Vrbane nine.
c. Following the pursuits, having the ideas or sentiments, characteristic of town or city life.
1698 FRYER *Acc. E. Ind. & P.* 54 The Citizens are urbane, being trained up to Commerce. **1870** LOWELL *Study Wind.* (1871) 177 The same combination of circumstances produced Béranger, an urbane or city poet.
2. Having the manners, refinement, or polish regarded as characteristic of a town; courteous, civil; also, blandly polite, suave.
1623 COCKERAM I, *Vrbane*, ciuill, courteous. **1656** BLOUNT *Glossogr.*, *Urbane*,..civil in curtesie,..pleasant in behaviour and talk. **1796** T. HOLCROFT tr. *Stolberg's Trav.* lxii. I. 483 The urbane youth..gave due praise to the country of Menelaus. **1827** LYTTON *Pelham* xv, We took advantage of our acquaintance with the urbane Frenchman to join his party. **1873** DIXON *Two Queens* IV. 139 In Eustace Chapuys, master of requests, he had a man of law,..urbane, alert, unscrupulous. **1882** STEVENSON *Mem. & Portr.* xi. (1887) 170, I feel never quite sure of your urbane and smiling coteries.
b. Characterized by urbanity, courtesy, or politeness.
1679 MARG. MASON *Tickler Tickled* 2 To treat a Lady of Mrs. Ellen Rigby's Quality, with the name of Bitch-Fox,.. is not at all Urbane. **1800** W. TOOKE *Cath. II*, III. 105 *n.*, A man remarkable for his talents and urbane manners. **1832** W. IRVING *Alhambra* II. 289 His manners were gentle, affable, and urbane. **1860** W. COLLINS *Wom. in White* II. 279 Stepping forward in the most urbane manner. **1871** BROWNING *Balaust.* 1839 To guests, a servant should not sour-faced be, But do the honours with a mind urbane.
3. Refined in expression; politely expressed.
1806 W. L. BOWLES *Pope's Wks.* I. 298 The latter part of it [*sc.* an epistle] is certainly urbane, elegant, and unaffected. **1876** LOWELL *Among my Bks.* Ser. II. 139 We miss the point, the compactness, and above all the urbane tone of the original.
Hence **ur'banely** *adv.*; **ur'baneness** (Bailey, 1727).
1822 *Monthly Rev.* XCVII. 540 This taste is so finely polished and so urbanely expressive. **1881** 'RITA' *My Lady Coquette* xiii, 'I am going to the wood,' he answers urbanely.

'Urbanist¹. [f. the Papal name *Urban* (see defs.) + -IST. Cf. F. *Urbaniste* in sense 2.]
1. An adherent of Pope Urban VI (1378–89), the opponent of anti-pope Clement VII. Also *attrib. rare.*
1523 LD. BERNERS *Froiss.* I. ccccxxx. 305 b, All the flemynges be as good Urbanystes as we be. **1855** MILMAN *Lat. Chr.* VI. 17 As Clement's party drew back, the Urbanists took up the cry. **1926** S. F. SMITH *Great Schism of West* 22 To say..that the urbanist succession was valid is by no means the same as [etc.].
2. A nun of a branch of the Poor Clares, following the rule as mitigated by Pope Urban IV in 1264.
1687 MIÈGE *Gt. Fr. Dict.*, *Urbanistes*,..Vrbanists, a sort of Nuns. **1756–9** A. BUTLER *Lives Saints, B. Colette*, She.. took the habit of..the mitigated Clares, or Urbanists. **1806** *Archaeol.* XV. 93 They were also called Urbanists, from Pope Urban IV, who mitigated the rigour of their rules as originally drawn up by St. Francis. **1884** *Catholic Dict.* 667/1 The order [of nuns of St. Clare] was thus divided into two branches, the larger being known by the name of Urbanists, the latter by that of Clarisses.

'urbanist². [f. URBAN *a.* and *sb.* + -IST.] A specialist in or advocate of town-planning.
1930 *Times Lit. Suppl.* 11 Sept. 708/4 To do so would be to entrust the fate of a city to the technical urbanist. **1964** *Economist* 5 Sept. 917/1 The 'urbanists' fight for more railways to revive the city's heart. **1979** *Jrnl. R. Soc. Arts* Nov. 776/1 The Urbanist's rôle is to design fragments of the city which reflect the culture and ideals of these groups while contrasting them with other orders—pragmatic or architectural.
Hence **urba'nistic** *a.*, **urba'nistically** *adv.*
1959 *Listener* 12 Feb. 289/1 Though he [*sc.* Le Corbusier] has derived so much from the study of the city, his own urbanistic achievements are scarcely to be considered to rank alongside his architectural ones. **1975** *Times Lit. Suppl.* 13 June 660/2 Urbanistically, there is no Middle America. **1983** *Listener* 21 Apr. 7/3 An international competition was held for an urbanistic plan for the Sassi.

urbanite ('ɜːbənaɪt). [f. URBAN *a.* and *sb.* + -ITE¹.] A dweller in a city or town.
1897 *Advance* (Chicago) 29 Apr. 542/1 They will capture streets.., will say to urbanites and suburbanites, 'Stand and deliver.' **1927** *Irish Rosary* July 508 All comes from splendid organizing, bringing peasants, villagers, townsmen and urbanites to meet..and work with bishops, priests, university men. **1960** *Twentieth Cent.* Apr. 347 The urbanite's usual excessive enthusiasm for the beauties of nature. **1979** *Church Times* 29 June 10, I was..only doing what hundreds of thousands of other Londoners do every day, as do urbanites in other big cities.

urbanity (ɜːˈbænɪtɪ). [a. F. *urbanité* (13–14th c.), or ad. L. *urbānitāt-*, *urbānitās*, f. *urbān-us* URBAN *a.* Cf. It. *urbanità*, Sp. *urbanidad*, Pg. *urbanidade*.]

1. The character or quality of being urbane; courtesy, refinement, or elegance of manner; refined or bland politeness or civility.

In frequent use since *c* 1825.

1535 STEWART *Cron. Scot.* (Rolls) II. 328 Ane man he wes of greit vrbanitie. **1547** BOORDE *Brev. Health* (1557) Prol., Egregious doctours,.. of your Urbanitie exasperate not youre selfe agaynst me. *a* **1566** R. EDWARDS *Damon & Pithias* (1906) 46 A right courtier is virtuous, gentle and full of urbanity. **1606** BRYSKETT *Civ. Life* 245 The meane which teacheth the tempering of those excesses, called the vertue of Vrbanitie, a Latine name, which in English we cannot better. **1693** DRYDEN *Juvenal* (1697) p. lxii, His Urbanity, that is, his Good Manners, are to be commended. **1713** *Guardian* No. 36 ¶11 The Virtue called Urbanity by the Moralists, or a Courtly Behaviour. **1746** *Gentl. Mag.* 7/2 Urbanity is a certain impression of politeness and goodness, which appears in the mind, conversation and sentiments of a person. **1777** W. DALRYMPLE *Trav. Sp. & Port.* vii, He was all urbanity and good humour. **1814** SCOTT *Wav.* xi, If you have no respect for the laws of urbanity. **1849** MACAULAY *Hist. Eng.* iv. I. 439 That exquisite urbanity, so often found potent to charm away the resentment of a justly incensed nation. **1878** PATER *Child in House* (1894) 15 A kind of comeliness and dignity, an *urbanity* literally, in modes of life, which he connected with the pale people of towns.

transf. **1616** J. LANE *Contn. Sqr.'s T.* IX. 152 Cambuscan ..eyenge Giant Horbills iollite, rann at his tassant plumes vrbanitie.

b. Const. *of* (manners, etc.)

1793 V. KNOX *Let. Yng. Nobleman* v, Wks. 1824 V. 10 You cannot read and taste his beauties, without improving your urbanity of manners. **1798** S. & HT. LEE *Canterb. T.* II. 129 From the moment they quitted France, urbanity of manners vanished. **1808** *Med. Jrnl.* XIX. 258 The late Dr. Purcell,.. whose urbanity of manners..will long be remembered. **1816** SCOTT *Old Mort.* xxxv, The gentleness and urbanity of his general manners.

c. *pl.* Civilities, courtesies.

1646 SIR T. BROWNE *Pseud. Ep.* I. vi. 23 The passages of societie and daily urbanities of our times. **1822** GALT *Provost* xlii, There is a surprising difference, in regard to the urbanities in use among those who have not yet come to authority. **1866** FELTON *Anc. & Mod. Gr.* II. v. 71 In the urbanities of social life,..Athens was without an equal, without a second.

†**2.** Conversation characteristic of well-bred townspeople; cheerful, witty, or pleasant talk; polished wit or humour. *Obs.*

a **1566** R. EDWARDS *Damon & Pithias* (1571) Bib, Then grudge not at all, if in my behauiour, I make the Kinge mery, with pleasant vrbanitie. **1640** BP. REYNOLDS *Passions* xxi. 214 Men are delighted..with Elegancies, Tests, Vrbanity, and Flowers of wit. **1656** E. REYNER *Rules Govt. Tongue* 223 Use Recreational speeches;..this is urbanity, or pleasantness of speech. **1693** DRYDEN *Juvenal* (1697) p. liv, Moral Doctrine, says he, and Urbanity, or well-manner'd Wit,..constitute the Roman Satire.

3. The state, condition, or character of a town or city; life in a city; town-life.

In freq. use from *c* 1898.

1549 *Compl. Scotl.* vi. 43 Tha detestit vrbanite, and desirit to lyue in villagis. **1789** BELSHAM *Ess.* I. xvii. 328 The serenity, the elegance and urbanity of Paris. **1877** R. MARTINEAU tr. *Goldziher's Mythol. Heb.* iv. 83 This trait of glorification of the old-fashioned Beduin-life, to the disparagement of the free urbanity of the townsmen. **1898** MAITLAND *Township & Borough* 13 A difference between.. urbanity and rusticity. **1900** A. JESSOPP in *Birm. Weekly Post* 14 April 5/3 A glimpse of the world of streets and the docks and the seamy side of 'urbanity'.

ˌurbaniˈzation. [f. next + -ATION.] The process of investing with an urban character; the condition of being urbanized.

Freq., esp. in journalistic use, since 1904.

1888 *Advance* (Chicago) 8 Mar. 152 One of the most remarkable characteristics of the time is 'the urbanization of the country'. **1904** *Parl. Rep. Comm. Phys. Degeneration* 16 The 'urbanization' of the population cannot have been unattended by consequences prejudicial to the health of the people.

urbanize (ˈɜːbənaɪz), *v.* [f. URBANE or URBAN *a.* + -IZE, or (in sense 2) ad. F. *urbaniser* (1873). Cf. Pg. *urbanisar* in sense 1.]

1. *trans.* To render urbane or civil; to make more refined or polished.

1642 HOWELL *For. Trav.* (Arb.) 14 Those more refined Nations, whom Learning and Knowledge did first Vrbanize and polish. **1785** *Hist. & Antiq. York* II. 2 In order to cultivate a better Understanding of human Nature amongst them, and urbanize their savage Disposition.

2. To make of an urban character; to convert or transform into a city.

Freq. in journalistic use since *c* 1900.

1884 [see the *ppl. a.*]. **1888** *Boston* (Mass.) *Jrnl.* 4 Feb. 2/3 It is impossible to urbanize the country.

3. To accustom to life in a city or town. Chiefly as *pa. pple.* (or *ppl. a.*).

1948 *Rep. Native Laws Commission 1946–48* (Dept. Native Affairs, S. Afr.) 19/1 There are large numbers of Natives in a transitional state, who are partly urbanised but have not yet broken their ties with the Reserves. **1963** *Daily Tel.* 18 Jan. 15/3 Robins are becoming more 'urbanised'..and will now take crumbs from the hand at the cafeteria. **1969** *Ibid.* 9 Sept. 13/2 The 'good old Mother Earth' myth..can turn the most urbanised of people into horticultural maniacs.

Hence **ˈurbanized** *ppl. a.* Also, in recent use (1923), **urbanizing** *ppl. a.*

1884 *Western Morn. News* 17 July 4/5 The Government will..then appeal to the urbanised counties. **1974** *Times* 22 Apr. 7/3 What about the eight million urbanized blacks living in white cities?

urbanology (ɜːbəˈnɒlədʒɪ). [f. URBAN *a.* and *sb.* + -OLOGY.] The study of cities or towns and their problems. So **urbaˈnologist**.

1967 *Time* 28 July 11 The 'urbanologist' aspires to be a student of the entire city,..whose concerns go beyond brick and mortar to budgets and laws, souls and sensibilities. Just as the word urbanology is a cross between Latin and Greek, the science..is a mélange of disciplines. **1972** *Daily Colonist* (Victoria, B.C.) 27 Apr. 33/1 The solution as some urbanologists see it is to come up with a new concept in automotive packaging. **1972** *New Yorker* 16 Sept. 124/2 A landscape that transcends all the nickel-and-diming defeats of our urbanology. **1975** M. BRADBURY *History Man* iii. 51 The local council, now impressed with Howard's urbanology, have accepted this scheme;..the surviving houses in the terrace will ultimately be restored.

urˈbarial, *a. rare.* [f. G. *urbari-um* register of landed property, f. MHG. *urbar* (revenue from) landed property.] Of or pertaining to, based or founded on, the register of landed property.

1849 *Blackw. Mag.* LXV. 622 The projected reform of the Urbarial code [in Hungary]. *Ibid.* 629 The lands held by urbarial tenure. **1852** *Times* 26 June 6/4 The draught of indemnification for the loss of urbarial [*printed* urbanal] rights in Hungary has been completed.

ˈurbian, *a. rare*$^{-1}$. [f. L. *urbi-s*, *urbs* a city + -AN. Cf. SUBURBIAN *a.*] Of or pertaining to a city.

1710 *Brit. Apollo* No. 85. 3/1 Urbian Piles advanc'd their tow'ring head.

ˈurbic, *a. rare.* [ad. L. *urbic-us*, f. *urbs* a city.] †**a.** = URBICARY *a.* **b.** Of or pertaining to a city.

1664 OWEN *Vind. Animad. Fiat Lux* iv. 67 She failed under the just hand of God, when the persons of that Vrbick Church were extirpated..by Totilas. **1855** *Fraser's Mag.* LI. 261 Nor, if sufficiently opulent to have maintained a mint, would some urbic, or other district coin, have failed [etc.].

†**urbiˈcarian**, *a. Obs.* [f. L. *urbicāri-us* (see next) + -AN.] Of or belonging to a city, esp. the City of Rome.

1654 H. HAMMOND *Answ. Animadv. Ignat.* v. §1. 121 Rome the Metropolis of the Roman Province, or Urbicarian region. **1656** BLOUNT *Glossogr.*, *Urbicarian*, belonging to a City.

†**ˈurbicary**, *a. Obs.* [ad. L. *urbicāri-us*, f. *urbicus* URBIC *a.*] (See quots. and SUBURBICARY *a.*)

1683 CAVE *Govt. Anc. Ch.* 261 The Roman Bishop began to extend his jurisdiction commensurate to the urbicary diocess, within which his metropolitical was swallowed up. **1725** tr. *Dupin's Eccl. Hist. 17th C.* I. v. 151 They gave the Name of Urbicary or Suburbicary, to all the Provinces which depended upon the Jurisdiction of the Vicar of Rome. **1728** CHAMBERS *Cycl.* (1738) s.v. *Suburbicary*, Those provinces of Italy, &c., which composed the antient diocese, or patriarchate, of Rome,..were also sometimes called urbicary provinces.

urbicide (ˈɜːbɪsaɪd). [f. L. *urbis*, *urbs* a city + -CIDE 2.] The destruction of a city or its character.

1966 *Harper's Mag.* May 94/1 This fearful instrument of urbicide will be not only the tallest, but unquestionably one of the ugliest buildings in the world. **1972** *N.Y. Times* 15 Oct. IV. 14 It does no good to speculate at what point real estate becomes art, or history, or a talisman of place. When it does, it enters the public domain. To destroy it is an act of urbicide.

urbiculture (ˈɜːbɪkʌltjʊə(r)). [f. L. *urbis*, *urbs* a city + CULTURE *sb.*] **a.** The development of cities and towns and urban life; the cultivation of urban interests. **b.** = *rurbanization* s.v. RURBAN *a.*

1954 *Daily Progress* (Charlottesville, Va.) 26 July 16/1 A bill introduced by Rep. J. Arthur Younger..to create a U.S. Department of Urbiculture. **1959** [see RURBANIZATION].

Hence **ˌurbiˈculturist**.

1977 *Sat. Rev.* (U.S.) 23 July 48/1 The urbiculturists—give a multimillion-dollar skyscraping enclave or two—move now not to knock down and build anew, but to make over or, to use today's mot juste, to recycle.

‖**urbi et orbi** (ˈɜːbɪ ɛt ˈɔəbɪ), *adv. phr.* [L.] Of papal proclamations, blessings, etc.: to the city (of Rome) and to the world. Also *transf.*, for general information or acceptance; to everyone.

1867 *Chambers's Encycl.* IX. 671/2 *Urbi et Orbi*.., a form used in the publication of papal bulls, for the purpose of signifying their formal promulgation to the entire Catholic world, as well as to the city of Rome. **1876** MRS. TAIT tr. *Klaczko's Two Chancellors* viii. 268 These were the expressions contained in an official document of incontrovertible authority, a diplomatic manifesto which announced *urbi et orbi* the lofty thoughts of the Imperial Government of France. **1889** M. S. VAN DE VELDE *Cosmopolitan Recoll.* II. v. 165 The Conclave met; the election of Camerlingo Pecci was foreseen, it was voted without opposition, and at one p.m., March 3rd, announced *urbi et orbi* from the *loggia* of St. Peter. **1907** G. W. E. RUSSELL *Pocketful of Sixpences* 21 On the eve of the General Election of 1880 she [*sc.* Lady Burdett-Coutts] issued a proclamation, *urbi et orbi*, enforcing the need for a 'strong government'. **1924** J. O. FIELD *Uncensored Recoll.* xiii. 239 The great pose of Morès..was a deep-rooted hatred of England, to which sentiment he was always giving very loud and dramatic utterance, *urbi et orbi*. **1958** *Listener* 27 Nov. 861/1 The familiar figure dressed in white..giving his benediction *urbi et orbi* from the loggia of St. Peter's. **1961** *Times* 7 Jan. 9/3 The voice of the poet addressing himself *urbi et orbi*. **1973** M. BENCE-JONES *Palaces of Raj* v. 105 One of the nobles, whose bard would, every two hours of the night, proclaim *urbi et orbi*..his titles and honours. **1980** *Times* 27 Dec. 3/6 The Pope's traditional Christmas homily *Urbi et Orbi* (to the city and the world).

Urbino (ɜːˈbiːnəʊ). Name of a city in the province of Le Marche, Italy, and of a former duchy, used *attrib.* to designate (items of) majolica made there from the fifteenth to the seventeenth centuries.

1881 C. C. HARRISON *Woman's Handiwork* II. 104 An Urbino drug-pot, or a Delft plaque. **1883** J. W. MOLLETT *Illustr. Dict. Art & Archæol.* 331/1 *Urbino ware*, made at Urbino, under the patronage of its Duke. **1924** RACKHAM & READ *Eng. Pottery* iv. 47 Another class of Italian motives is the strange brood of caryatids, sphinxes, winged beasts, dragons, and semi-monstrous birds... The seed of this kindred may have come in some cases from some piece of Urbino maiolica. **1940** *Burlington Mag.* Aug. 64/2 A large Urbino dish in the Musée de Cluny. **1952** B. RACKHAM *Italian Maiolica* v. 24 A dish at Cambridge..interesting as an example of Urbino ware with lustre enrichment added by Maestro Giorgio at Gubbio—is now considered to be the work of the son. **1973** *Times* 3 Nov. 2/2 The sale also contained an Urbino majolica dish painted with the murder of Amphiarus by Francesco Xanto.

ˈurceiform, *a.* [f. L. *urce-us* water-pot + -(I)FORM. Cf. Sp. *urceiforme*.] Having the form of a vase or goblet.

1840 *Penny Cycl.* XVIII. 366/1 *Polypiaria dubia*. Animals urceiform, provided with long..tentacula. **1860** MAYNE *Expos. Lex.* 1321.

†**ˈurcelle.** *Obs.*$^{-1}$ [a. OF. *urcel* (12th c.), or med.L. *urcell-us* (Dief.), = L. *urceolus* URCEOLUS.] A little pitcher.

1483 CAXTON *Gold. Leg.* 247 b/2 Thenne Romayne brouȝt an urcelle or a cruse with water..and receyued baptysme of hym.

urˈceolar, *a. Bot.* [ad. L. *urceolāris*, f. *urceolus* URCEOLUS.] = URCEOLATE *a.* 1.

1860 R. FOWLER *Med. Vocab.* s.v.; and in later Dicts.

urceolate (ˈɜːsiːələt), *a.* [ad. mod.L. *urceolatus*, f. L. *urceolus* URCEOLUS.]

1. Having the shape of an urn or pitcher; *esp.* in *Bot.*, *Anat.*, etc.

a. 1760 J. LEE *Introd. Bot.* III. xxii. (1765) 229 The Corolla is *Urceolate*, Pitcher-shaped, when it is inflate and gibbous on all Sides, after the Manner of that Vessel. **1776** MARTYN *Lett.* xxvi. (1785) 408 An urceolate or pitcher-shaped stigma. **1821** W. P. C. BARTON *Flora N. Amer.* I. 14 Calix regularly urceolate. **1832** LINDLEY *Introd. Bot.* 104 They thus form a single urceolate body. **1887** W. PHILLIPS *Brit. Discomycetes* 216 Hymenium urceolate, black; stem short.

b. 1826 KIRBY & SP. *Entomol.* III. 423 In the *Rutelidæ*, the *labium* is urceolate. **1847** *Todd's Cycl. Anat.* IV. 4/1 Capsule Animalcules..; body..covered with a univalve urceolate or scutellate shell. **1867** MURCHISON *Siluria* ix. (ed. 4) 203 The glabella has only two pairs of furrows and is long and urceolate.

c. 1823 *Christie's Catal. Grk. Vases of Englefield* 18 A small Vase (urceolate) with triply-scalloped lip. **1833** *Christie & Manson's Catal. Grk. Pottery*, etc. 8 A one-handled urceolate vase.

2. 'Provided with or contained in an urceolus, as a rotifer' (*Cent. Dict.*, 1891).

ˈurceolated, *a. Zool.* [f. as prec. + -ED^1 2.] = URCEOLATE *a.* 1.

1752 HILL *Hist. Anim.* 107 The extremity of the body is terminated by a kind of rattle, formed of a series of urceolated articulations. **1822** J. PARKINSON *Outl. Oryctol.* 64 The cells, rather membranous, urceolated, ventricose [etc.]. **1840** *Penny Cycl.* XVIII. 366/1 *Polypiaria membranacea*. Animals very short, urceolated.

ˈurceole. *Eccl. rare.* [ad. L. *urceolus* URCEOLUS. Cf. obs. F. *urceolle*.] = CRUET 2.

After Fuller (*Ch. Hist.* IV. 157), who thus uses *urceolum*. **1824** SOUTHEY *Bk. of Ch.* I. 353 The candlestick, taper, and urceole were taken from him as acolyte. [**1865** BONAR *Last Days Martyrs* (ed. 2) v. 125 The alb and maniple were next removed; then the candlestick, taper, and urceole.]

‖**urceolus** (ɜːˈsiːələs). [L., dim. of *urceus* pitcher.] (See quots. 1866–86.)

1832 LINDLEY *Introd. Bot.* 104 The true nature of the urceolus. **1845** *Encycl. Metrop.* XXV. 1006/1 Corolla [of *Vahia*] urceolate; ovarium girded by an entire urceolus. **1866** *Treas. Bot.* 1193/2 *Urceolus*, the two confluent bracts of *Carex*; any flask-shaped or cup-shaped anomalous organ. **1886** *Encycl. Brit.* XXI. 4/2 Several genera [of *Rotifera*] present an external casing or sheath or tube which is termed an 'urceolus'. *Ibid.* 5/1 The urceolus serves as a defence.

urchin (ˈɜːtʃɪn). Forms: α. 4 vrchun, 4–5 vrchon (5 nurchon, norchon), 4–6 urchone, 5 vrchone, vrchoun(e, 6–7, 8–9 *dial.* urchon, 7 urchan. β. 5–7 urchen, 6 vrchen, vrchyn, 6–7 vrchin (7 -ine, urching), 7– urchin; 5 norchen, 6, 9 *dial.* orchen. γ. 5 vrchion (9 *dial.* urchion), 6 vrcheon, 5, 7, 9 *dial.* urcheon. δ. 7 orchant, ourchant, 9 *dial.* urchint, -ont, -ant, -unt. [var. of HURCHEON and

IRCHIN, agreeing in vowel with the former, and with the latter in the dropping of *h*.]

A. *sb.* **1. a.** = HEDGEHOG 1.

α. *a* **1340** HAMPOLE *Psalter* ciii. 19 The stone fleyng til vrchuns [L. *petra refugium herenacijs*]. **1382** WYCLIF *Lev.* xi. 5 An vrchon, that chewith kude,..is vnclene. *c* **1400** *Rom. Rose* 3135 Like sharp vrchouns his here was growe. **1480** CAXTON *Chron. England* 53 b, Till that his body Stykked as full of arewes as an vrchone is full of prikkes. *a* **1500** in *Rel. Ant.* I. 81 A norchon by tho fyre rostyng a greyhownde. **1530** PALSGR. 285/2 Urchone a beest, *herysson*. **1676** GREW *Musæum, Anat. Stomach & Guts* ii. 8 The Gulet of an Urchan enters the Stomach towards the middle. **1683** in W. S. Banks *Walks Yorks.* (1871) 43 To March lad for one urchon, [£]o o 2. **1750** J. COLLIER (Tim Bobbin) *Lanc. Dial.* Wks. (1862) p. xxxvii, Od rottle the; whot seys to? Hes to foryeat'n th' Tealier finding th' Urchon; an th' Rimes? **1876–** in Westm., Yks., and Lancs. dialect use (*Eng. Dial. Dict.*).

β. *c* **1425** *St. Christina* x. in *Anglia* VIII. 123/28 In þe maner of an vrchyn þe lumped body 3ode to þe owne shappe. **14..** *Nom.* in Wr.-Wülcker 700 *Hic urunacius*,..a urchen. **1556** J. HEYWOOD *Spider & Fly* iii. 32 To grounde he shranke Like an vrchyn vnder an aple tree. **1591** SYLVESTER *Du Bartas* I. vii. 683 Thou Sluggard,..Go learn the Emmet's and the Urchin's Art. **1624** BURTON *Anat. Mel.* (ed. 2) II. iii. VII. 291 As a Tortoise in his shell,..or an Vrchin round... I decline their fury and am safe. *a* **1653** G. DANIEL *Idyll* v. 98 Stript Porcupine May to an Vrchin, of his wants complaine; Well-thatcht, gainst Winter's Stormes. **1698** FRYER *Acc. E. India & P.* 290 However here are Salmon.., and the Urchin..under the Hedges and Trees of an Orchard. **1779** *Gentl. Mag.* 350 The poor persecuted creature to which I allude is the Hedge-hog or Urchin. **1813** BINGLEY *Anim. Biog.* (ed. 4) I. 349 Urchins..feed, for the most part, on roots, worms, and the larvæ of insects. **1863** ATKINSON *Stanton Grange* 218 Sae, I reckon, it is with the urchin. **1867** EMERSON *May-day* 306 The pebble loosened from the frost Asks of the urchin to be tost.

γ. **14..** in *Rel. Ant.* I. 51 Tak the grees of an urcheon, and the fatte of a bare. *c* **1475** *Cath. Angl.* 404/2 Vrchion, *erecius, erinacius*. **1522** SKELTON *Why not to Court* 163 They are.. Lyke vrcheons in a stone wall. **1895** J. K. SNOWDEN *Web of Weaver* x, We had no more to liven us than an urcheon has in winter-time.

δ. **1665–6** *Ormskirk Churchw. Acc.* (Lanc. & Chesh. Hist. Soc.) Ser. III. VI. 174 Paid Thos. Mawdsley for one orchant and one kyde [= kite], oolb. o1s. o6d. **1682** in W. S. Banks *Walks Yorksh.* (1871) 43 Paid for 21 ourchants and 7 fylomots, [£]o 5 10. **1883** *Almondbury Gloss.*, *Urchint*, a hedgehog. **1891** *Sheffield Gloss.* Suppl. 62 *Urchont*, a hedgehog.

b. Applied allusively to persons (see quots.).

1593 G. HARVEY *Pierce's Super.* 12 But Agrippa was an urcheon, Copernicus a shrimpe, Cardan a puppy,.. Cuiacius a bable to this Termagant. **1594** *Selimus* K 1, Enter Selimus..at one door, and Acomat.., Vizier, and their soldiers at another. *Sel.* What are the vrchins crept out of their dens, Vnder the conduct of this porcupine? **1632** HEYWOOD *2nd Pt. Iron Age* I. i. B 2 b, *Ther*[*sites*]. By the gods Wee haue two meeting soules: be my sweete Vrchin. *Syn*[*on*]. I will, And thou shalt bee mine vgly Toade.

†**c.** A goblin or elf. (From the supposition that they occas. assumed the form of a hedgehog.)

1584 R. SCOT *Discov. Witchcr.* VII. xv. 122 They have so fraied us with bull beggers, spirits, witches, urchens, elves, ..that [etc.]. **1592** NASHE *Four Lett. Confut.* K j b, The Fairies and night Vrchins. **1594** —— *Terrors of Night* H j b, An old wiues tale of diuells and vrchins. **1598** SHAKS. *Merry W.* IV. iv. 49. **1614** *Hawking*, etc. 7 in T. Ravenscroft *Briefe Disc.*, By the moone we sport and play;..Trip it, little Vrchins all, Lightly as the little little bee.

2. *transf.* †**a.** Applied to the porcupine. *Obs.*

c **1400** MAUNDEV. (Roxb.) xxxi. 143 Þere ben also vrchounes als grete as wylde swyn here; wee clepen hem *Porcz de Spyne*.

b. A sea-urchin or sea-hedgehog; = ECHINUS 1.

1601 HOLLAND *Pliny* I. 253 Of the same sort that the Crabs be, are the Vrchins of the sea called Echini. **1661** LOVELL *Hist. Anim. & Min.* 230 *Urchin*... The ashes of the shells help sordid ulcers. **1796** H. HUNTER tr. *St.-Pierre's Stud. Nat.* II. 381 The violet-coloured urchins, armed with points and spears. **1845** GOSSE *Ocean* vi. (1849) 277 The irregular movements of the spined urchins. **1853** ANNE PRATT *Common Things Sea-Coast* v. 308 The Purple-tipped Urchin (*Echinus miliaris*). *Ibid.*, Heart urchins, and Fiddle-heart urchins, and Cake urchins; names all expressive of the shape.

†**c.** *U.S.* = URSON. *Obs. rare.*

1796 MORSE *Amer. Geog.* I. 201 The Urchin, or Urson,.. is commonly called Hedgehog or Porcupine, but differs from both those animals.

3. One who is deformed in body; a hunchback. Now *dial.*

1528 ROY *Rede me*, etc. (Arb.) 43, I trowe the vrchyn will clyme To some promocion hastely. **1607** TOPSELL *Four-f. Beasts* 278 In English, a Hedghog, or an vrchine: by which name also we call a man that holdeth his Necke in his bosome. **1706** PHILLIPS (ed. Kersey), *Urchin*,..a Dwarf. **1821** SCOTT *Kenilw.* ix, A queer, shambling, ill-made urchin, who, by his stunted growth, seemed about twelve or thirteen years old. **1824** BYRON *Def. Transf.* I. i, *Bert.* Out, hunchback! *Arn.* I was born so, mother!.. *Bert.* Out, urchin, out! **1891** *Sheffield Gloss.* Suppl. 62 *Urchont*, a hump-backed person.

4. a. A pert, mischievous, or roguish youngster; a brat.

c **1530** *Calisto & Melib.* B i, Come hydyr, thou lytyll fole let me see the:..What lytyll vrchyn hast forgotyn me? **1599** BRETON *Miseries Mauillia* Wks. (Grosart) II. 37/1 Come on, you urchen, you will never come to good. **1726** SWIFT *Gulliver* II. iii. 125, I could not tell to what extremity such a malicious urchin might have carried his resentment. **1828** CARR *Craven Gloss.* s.v., Thou lile urchin thou!

b. *poet.* Applied to Cupid.

1709 PRIOR *Venus Mistaken* ii, Who's blind now Mamma? the Urchin cry'd. **1713** SWIFT *Cadenus & Vanessa* 515 The urchin..Took aim, and shot with all his strength A dart. **1799** SOUTHEY *Love Elegies* III. v, From you, sweet locks! he wove the subtile line Wherewith the urchin angled for my Heart. **1805** ANDREW SCOTT *Poems* 184 Cupid, blind urchin.

5. a. A little fellow; a boy or youngster; †a child or infant.

In frequent use from *c* 1780. Often applied with commiserative force to children poorly, raggedly, or untidily clothed.

1556 J. HEYWOOD *Spider & Fly* C ij, Will ye have this urchin, of eyght weekes olde? It is a babling brat above all other. **1600** NASHE *Summers Last Will* E ij, Learne of him, you deminitiue vrchins, howe to behaue your selues in your vocation. **1648** J. BEAUMONT *Psyche* IX. cxlv, As for thy Lord, He term'd him Josephs Brat, The silly Carpenter's poor Urcheon. **1683** KENNETT *Erasm. on Folly* 82 Looking big upon the trembling Urchins. **1790** COWPER *Let. to Mrs. Throckmorton* 10 May, He sent an urchin (I do not mean a hedgehog,..but a boy, commonly so called). **1799** SHERIDAN *Pizarro* II. i, The little darling urchin robs me, I doubt, of some portion of thy love, my Cora. **1812** BYRON *Ch. Har.* II. xviii, And well the docile crew that skilful urchin guides. **1839** FR. A. KEMBLE *Resid. in Georgia* (1863) 11 The tone of insolent superiority assumed by even the gutter urchins over their dusky companions. **1892** STEVENSON & L. OSBOURNE *Wrecker* iii. 42 [He] took a fancy to the urchin [and] carried him on with him in his wandering life.

†**b.** Applied to a literary production. *Obs. rare.*

1589 [? LYLY] *Pappe w. Hatchet* E ij, This is the Epistle which he woonders at himselfe, and like an olde Ape hugges the Vrchin so in his conceipt, as [etc.]. **1813** H. & J. SMITH *Horace in London* 89 Then may new Drury's widely yawning pit O'erwhelm thy urchin, and engulph thy muse.

†**c.** *transf.* An offspring *of* hell, etc. *Obs. rare.*

1584 HARSNET *Serm. Ezek.* (1658) 129 How can he but hate him?..the childe of Darkness,..the Urchin of Hel? **1648** J. BEAUMONT *Psyche* x. xxix, Unhappy Saturninus, how hast thou Prov'd thine own selfe an urcheon of Damnation!

†**6. a.** An ugly or uncomely woman; a hag. *rare.*

1657 THORNLEY tr. *Longus' Daphnis & Chloe* 203 It is incredible that of such an old Churle, and such an Urchin as his Wife, there should come a child so fair.

†**b.** A girl or young woman, esp. of an ill-tempered or roguish disposition. *Obs.*

1534 MORE *Comf. agst. Trib.* II. Wks. 1182/2 What eyleth this gyrle? that eluish vrchin weneth I wer a diuell I trow. **1768** GOLDSM. *Good-n. Man* II. i, You did indeed dissemble, you urchin you; but where's the girl that won't dissemble for a husband? *a* **1777** —— *Epilogue to 'The Sisters'* 23 The little urchin smiles, and spreads her lure, And tries to kill, ere she's got power to cure.

7. *techn.* (See later quots.)

1835 URE *Philos. Manuf.* 167 By this repeated transfer from one cylinder-card or urchin to another..the filaments become separated and expanded. **1839** —— *Dict. Arts* 348 Some cards consist entirely of cylinders, the central main cylinder being surrounded by a series of smaller ones called urchins or squirrels. **1875** KNIGHT *Dict. Mech.* 2684/1 *Urchin*, one of a pair of rapidly revolving small card cylinders, arranged around the periphery of a large card drum.

8. a. *attrib.* and *Comb.*, as (sense 1 c) †*urchin blast*, †*show*; (sense 7) *urchin card*, *cylinder*; *urchin-like* adj., *-snouted* ppl. a.; †**urchin cockle** (see quot.); †**urchin crowfoot**, the ranunculus, *R. arvensis*; **urchin cut**, a short style of haircut for women; also as *ppl. adj.*, and *urchin hair-cut*; **urchin fish**, (*a*) the sea-urchin; (*b*) the porcupine-fish or sea-porcupine; **urchin-form**, the form or form-type of an echinus; †**urchin lump-fish**, †**mushroom**, †**rind**, †**star-fish**, †**-worm** (see quots.).

1634 MILTON *Comus* 845 Helping all *urchin blasts, and ill luck signes That the shrewd medling Elfe delights to make. **1851** GORDON *Art Jrnl. Illustr. Catal.* p. iv**/2 The large card-drum is generally surmounted by *urchin or squirrel cards instead of tops. **1688** HOLME *Armoury* II. 339/1 *Concha Echinata*,..a Cockle covered or set with pricks. An *Urchin Cockle. **1578** LYTE *Dodoens* 420 White Crowfoote, or *Urchin Crowfoote. **1951** *Urchin cut [see CUT *sb.*[2] 17 a]. **1958** *Woman's Own* 4 June 9/1 She was long-limbed, slender, her shining hair urchin-cut. **1958** *Woman* 11 Oct. 32/3 She was small and boyish, with urchin-cut hair. **1979** N. FREELING *Widow* v. 26 A small girl with an urchin face and an urchin-cut. **1835** URE *Philos. Manuf.* 168 When the fibres have been thus thoroughly teazed out by..*urchin cylinders. **1566** DRANT *Horace, Sat.* iv. G 8 b, Whence purple coloure flowes..from Micen *vrchen fishe. **1688** HOLME *Armoury* II. 343/2 The Globe Star fish..is by some Authors termed the Urchin fish, or Sea Urchin. **1773** *Gentl. Mag.* 220 The Urchin or Hedgehog Fish. **1863** WOOD *Illustr. Nat. Hist.* III. 337 The Urchin-Fish or Sea Hedgehog is a good example of the genus Diodon, or Two-toothed fishes. **1878** F. J. BELL *Gegenbaur's Comp. Anat.* 198 The decrease in size of the antambulacral surface..will give us the *Urchin-form. **1958** 'E. DUNDY' *Dud Avocado* I. vii. 132 A lot of rather gorgeous..girls floating around with *urchin hair-cuts. **1708** KERSEY, **Urchin-like Rind*, the outward Husk of the Chesnut. **1855** GOSSE *Man. Marine Zool.* I. 63 Round depressed urchin-like disks. **1688** HOLME *Armoury* II. 337 The *Urchin, or Hedghog Lump fish, hath its skin set with more sharper and longer pricks. *c* **1711** PETIVER *Gazophyl.* x. xcii, *Urchin Mushroom:..From its roughness underneath. **1688** R. HOLME *Armoury* II. 85/1 The *urchin rind, is the cover of the Chestnut. [Cf. *urchin-like*.] **1610** SHAKS. *Temp.* II. ii. 5 But they [*sc.* spirits] 'll nor pinch, Fright me with *Vrchyn-shewes, pitch me i' th mire [etc.]. **1592** —— *Ven. & Ad.* 1105 This foule, grim, and *vrchin-snowted Boare. **1688** HOLME *Armoury* II. 349/2 An *Urchin Star-fish; this is a Star-fish of five long and slender Rays. **1668** CHARLETON *Onom.* 53 *Echini*,..*Vrchin-Worms.

b. Appositive or as adj., as *urchin article*, *bitch*, *deity*, *messenger*, *prince*.

1534 MORE *Comf. agst. Trib.* III. xxiv. (1553) T vij, I feare me when I here once that vrchin bitche bark, I shal..forgeat altogether. *a* **1670** HACKET *Abp. Williams* II. (1693) 91 Our Bishop..made himself merry with the Conceit, how easie it was to stride over such Urchin Articles. No man would find leisure to read the whole 36, they are so frivolous. **1818** HAZLITT *Eng. Poets* ii. (1870) 53 The triumph of Cupid at the mischief he has made is worthy of the malicious urchin deity. **1826** SCOTT *Woodst.* xxxii, The urchin messenger entered the hall, making several odd bows. **1830** LD. LYTTELTON in *Lady L.'s Corr.* (1912) 259 The two urchin Princes..in little Hussar dresses.

Hence '**urchiness**, a female urchin (= sense 4 above); '**urchinly** *a.*, of the nature of, resembling, an urchin.

1852 *Househ. Words* V. 378/2 Many were the names of urchins and *urchinesses..which decked the plaster walls of Broad-Bumble school. **1654** *New Brawle* 11 Like a feeble *Vrchinly Rascall as thou art. **1834** *Fraser's Mag.* IX. 741 Applying a foot to the part of his urchinly person corresponding with that particular department of Sir John Doyle.

urdee, *a. Her.* Also 7 **urde**, 9 **urdé**. [Of obscure origin: possibly due to a misreading and misunderstanding of F. *vidée* in the phrase *croix aiguisée et vidée*.]

1. Of a cross: Having the extremities drawn to a sharp point instead of being cut at right angles to the beam; pointed.

1562 LEGH *Armory* 61 b, He beareth Tenne, a crosse vrdee, Or. **1572** BOSSEWELL *Armorie* 26 Crosses enuecked, entrayled,..Batune, formye, vrdee, pomelle. **1688** HOLME *Armoury* I. 49/1 He beareth Gules, a Cross Urdee (or champain) Or. *Ibid.* IV. xii. (Roxb.) 509/1 Charged with a crosse vrdee voided at each point a pommell. *c* **1828** BERRY *Encycl. Her.* I. s.v., A cross, urdée, is the same as that which French heralds call clechée. **1882** CUSSANS *Handbk. Her.* viii. (1893) 126 *Aiguisé*, or *Urdé*: used by French and the early English Heralds to signify pointed.

2. Of a bend, etc.: Having the margin or containing line broken into a series of parallel pointed projections. Also of a line broken in this fashion.

1688 HOLME *Armoury* I. 32/1 He beareth Argent, a Bend Urdee, or Champaine, Vert. *Ibid.* 75/1 He beareth party per Bend Urde, Gules and Or. *Ibid.* 93 He beareth party per Pale, Barry of six contrary Urdee... Some term it..Barry of 6 Urdee at the ends, or contrary champion at the sides. **1722** A. NISBET *Syst. Her.* I. 23 The other Line is blazoned Urdee or Champagne by Ferne. Upton calls it Vere; because its Points are formed like Pieces of Vair.

urdeur, obs. f. ORDURE.

'**urdite.** *Min.* [a. Da. *urdit* (1855), f. the local Norwegian place-name *Urd-a* (= 'the scree'): see -ITE[1] 2 b.] = MONAZITE.

1868 *Watts' Dict. Chem.* V. 949 *Urdite*, a mineral of unknown composition, occurring in the orthoclase of Notteröe in Norway. **1908** *Athenæum* 16 May 609/2 The rare element scandium..only occurs terrestrially in a few uncommon minerals, such as urdite.

Urdu ('ʊəduː, 'ɜːduː), *sb.* and *a.* Also 8–9 Oordoo. [a. Hindustani (Pers.) *urdū* camp (ad. Turkī *ordu*, etc.: see HORDE *sb.*), ellipt. for *zabān-i-urdū* 'language of the camp'.]

A. *sb.* Formerly, = HINDUSTANI *sb.* 2; in recent use distinguished from Hindustani (the lingua franca) and designated as the official language of Pakistan.

1796 J. B. GILCHRIST *Gram. Hindoostanee Lang.* 261 The Rekhtu,..that mixed Dialect, also called Oordoo..or the polished language of the Court. **1813** J. SHAKESPEAR *Gram. Hindustani Lang.* 1 The dialect most generally used in India, especially among the Muhammadan inhabitants,..is called *Urdū* (camp) or *Urdū zabān* (camp-language). **1824** HEBER *Jrnl.* 6 Sept., The boys read Oordoo, Persian, and English. **1847** W. YATES *Hindustani Dict.* Pref., The Hindustáni or Urdú is peculiarly the language of the Muhammadan population of Hindústán. **1872** BEAMES *Comp. Gram. Aryan Lang.* I. 39 By a curious caprice, Hindi, when it uses Arabic words, is assumed to become a new language, and is called by a new name—Urdu. **1878** [see HINDUSTANI *sb.* 2].

Comb. **1880** *Encycl. Brit.* XI. 849/2 A collection of stories ..in mixed Urdū-Hindī.

B. *adj.* Of or pertaining to, printed, written, or composed in, Urdu.

1845 J. T. THOMPSON (*title*), An English and Oordoo, and Oordoo and English Dictionary. **1847** W. YATES *Hindustani Dict.* Pref., In good Urdú writing or conversation. **1880** *Encycl. Brit.* XI. 847/2 The origin of Urdū literature. *Ibid.* 848/1 The earliest Urdū authors.

urdy, Anglicized form of URDEE *a.* 2.

1688 HOLME *Armoury* I. 75/1 He beareth party per Bend Urde, Gules and Or. *Ibid.*, There is a difference between Urde, and Urdee or Urdy; the first being of a single number, the other signifies many. **1831** *Encycl. Metrop.* (1845) V. 600/2 *Palissy*, or *Urdy*, is an imitation of the palisading of a trench.

†**ure**, *sb.*[1] *Obs.* [a. AF. **eure*, = OF. *uevre*, *euvre*, *evre* (13th cent.; F. *œuvre*):—L. *opera* OPERA *sb.*]

I. *in ure*: **1. a.** In or into use, practice, or performance. Often with vbs., as *bring*, *come*, *have*, and esp. *put* (freq. *c* 1510–*c* 1630). Also rarely with *into*.

(*a*) *c* **1420** LYDG. *Assembly of Gods* 1448 Whom folowyd Dethe, whych wold nat tary Hys feruent power there to put in vre. *c* **1440** *Pallad. on Husb.* I. 215 And elder than oon yeer, no grayn in vre Thou putte, in drede hit die. *c* **1500** MEDWALL *Nature* (Brandl) 815 He hath shewed me a praty whyle [= wile], If I may put yt in vre. **1522** MORE *De Quat. Noviss.* Wks. 76/2 Y[t] this only lesson wel learned & busily putte in vre, must nedes leade vs to heauen. **1591** SYLVESTER *Du Bartas* I. vi. 1031 Even as a Surgeon..before in ure he put His violent Engins on the vicious member. **1627** HAKEWILL *Apol.* (1630) 287 Would God men would be pleas'd to put this course in ure. **1682** *New News fr. Bedlam* Postscr., You have put his jealous Pen in Ure. **1702** R. L'ESTRANGE *Josephus, Antiq.* XVI. i. 444 That was the Course therefore, they resolved to put in Ure.

(*b*) **1563** SHUTE *Archit.* F i, They maye be practised and brought in vre to diuers vses. **1581** PETTIE tr. *Guazzo's Civ. Conv.* I. (1586) 26 b, Perchaunce they haue brought in ure both publikelie and priuatlie vices far more pernitious than this. *a* **1604** HANMER *Chron. Ireland* (1633) 175 If hee dyed seised during that time, his wife shall not be indowed of the same land as came late in ure. **1606** HOLLAND *Sueton.* 97 Martiall discipline he required most sharply, bringing again into ure and execution certaine..chastisements.

(*c*) *c* **1475** *Partenay* 3722 My goddoughter I may calle hir in vre. **1494** in *Househ. Ord.* (1790) 112 The sitting of all Dukes, Earles, and Barons sonnes.., such things hathe beene well had in ure. *c* **1530** *Remedy of Love* xxiii, But this am I sure, Moche lyke thyng I haue had in vre. *a* **1542** WYATT *Poet. Wks.* (1913) I. 11 Trouth is tryed where craft is in ure. **1545** ASCHAM *Toxoph.* (Arb.) 57 What thing a man in tender age hath most in vre. **1577** HANMER *Anc. Eccl. Hist.* 128 Neither had it any agreement with that which is in vre among vs. **1613** W. BROWNE *Brit. Past.* I. v, The staires of rugged stone, seldome in ure.

b. With dependent infinitive.

a **1530** HEYWOOD *Love* (Brandl) 33 No tonge can attayne to put in vre Her to discryue. **1575** GASCOIGNE *Glasse of Govt.* II. vi, Greate the paines which teachers put in ure, To trade them still, in verteous qualities. **1598** MARSTON *Sco. Villanie* II. (1599) 175 [To] dare put in ure To make Jehoua but a couverture To shade ranck filth.

c. With reference to statutes, etc.: In or into effect, force, or operation. Chiefly with vbs., esp. *put*.

1454-5 in Bolton *Stat. Irel.* (1621) 23 All the Statutes.. against Escheators shall be put in ure, and be of force. *a* **1513** FABYAN *Chron.* VII. 505 To the entente that they shulde see y[e] sayde proclamacyon put in vre. **1539** *St. Papers Hen. VIII*, I. 597 My letters to the said Depute shall not nede to be put in ure. **1581** LAMBARDE *Eiren.* I. xviii. 165 Ye statute of Northampton..is now..put in vre for the punishment of Forcible Entries. **1610** HOLLAND *Camden's Brit.* I. 420 They ment to bring..S. Edwards lawes and liberties againe In ure. **1614** BACON *Draft of King's Speech* Wks. 1869 V. 30 His Majesty could wish the ancient statutes were put in ure. *c* **1670** HOBBES *Dial. Com. Laws* (1681) 141 That the Diocesan hath Jurisdiction of Hersesie, and that so it was put in ure in all Queen Elizabeths reign. **1701** ATTERBURY *Add. to 1st Ed. Rights Convocation* 48 They would not Enact, put in Ure, Promulge, or Execute any New Canons. **1711** G. HICKES *Two Treat. Chr. Priesth.* (ed. 3) II. 79 Without any retrospection to old Principles, the King's Ecclesiastical Supremacy in Virtue of these Laws, was put in Ure.

d. In remembrance or recollection. Only ***to have..in ure***.

1432-50 tr. *Higden* (Rolls) I. 347 The peple..sayethe.. Gurmunde..to have made those dyches, hauenge not Turgesius in vre or in remembraunce. *c* **1450** *Harl. Contin. Higden* (Rolls) VIII. 452 The kynge havynge not in ure of the seide promisse.

e. In or into a state of prevalence or existence. Chiefly with vbs., as *come*, *draw*, *put*.

1470 in Ellis *Orig. Lett.* Ser. II. I. 134 Towchinge the tyme whene the Mariage shalbe put in ure. **1477** *Paston Lett.* III. 191 For th'enconvenyence that I have knowe let in ur in case lyke, and yit enduryth in Kente. *a* **1547** SURREY in *Tottel's Misc.* (Arb.) 15 Like as when, rough winter spent, The pleasant spring straight draweth in vre. **1548** UDALL *Erasm. Par. Luke* xxii. 167 b, What thyng Petur did, the same would the other disciples also haue dooen, if lyke necessitee had cum in vre. **1549** PROCTOR *Fall of late Arrian* R iij b, Touchynge the dispensacion of the flesh, and the misterye nowe in force and vre, Christ shalbe subiected vnto the father. **1638** FARLEY *Emblems* H 3, This waxen torch is able to endure The winds, when Æolus puts them in ure.

2. Of persons, their faculties, etc.: In or into the regular exercise or practice of a particular pursuit. Usu. with verbs, as *fall*, *put*, and chiefly (esp. *c* 1580–*c* 1685) *keep*.

(*a*) *c* **1460** J. RUSSELL *Bk. Nurture* 1173 Y haue shewed the, & brought þe in vre, to know þe Curtesie of court. **1513** MORE *Rich. III.* (1883) 18 Himself had bene al his dayes in ure therwith. *a* **1548** HALL *Chron., Edw. IV*, 217 To put his people in vre, that thei might bee the more ready to fight. **1571** CAMPION *Hist. Irel.* II. i. (1633) 69 Sundry times came Lacy to quicken his labourers, full glad to see them fall in ure with any such exercise. **1594** PLAT *Jewell-ho.* 42 Till they have brought their hande in ure with the shape and fashion of the Letters. **1677** MIÉGE *Gt. Fr. Dict.* s.v., To put himself in ure, *s'accoûtumer*.

(*b*) **1539** LATIMER *Serm. & Rem.* (Parker Soc.) 416, I pray you, keep your hand in ure. **1577** tr. *Bullinger's Decades* 84 Hee..by the Crosse doth keepe our patience in vre. **1611** SPEED *Hist. Gt. Brit.* IX. xxiv. 351 To keepe in vre and exercise, the skill and valour of her English. **1627** BP. HALL *Epist.* III. viii. 329 To keepe the heart in vre with God is the highest taske of a Christian. **1627** —— *Art. Divine Medit.* xxxi, The minde is by turnes depressed and lifted vp:.. which order doth best hold it in vre, and just temper. **1690** W. WALKER *Idiomat. Anglo-Lat.* 254 He lies to keep his tongue in ure. **1692** R. L'ESTRANGE *Fables* 92 Keeping his hand in Ure with somewhat of Greater Value.

II. 3. ***out of ure***: **a.** Out of use; disused; obsolete.

1553 BRENDE *Q. Curtius* Q vi, Oure naturall toungue throughe the conversation of straunge nacions is gone out of ure. **1567** JEWEL *Def. Apol. Ch. Eng.* V. v. §1. 524 Al these thinges are woorne nowe out of vre, and nighe deade. *a* **1600** HOOKER *Eccl. Pol.* VII. xiv. §2 The mention of contrary orders worn so many ages since quite and clean out of ure.

b. Out of practice. *rare*$^{-1}$.

1625 BACON *Ess., Simulation* (Arb.) 509 Which..maketh him practise Simulation in other things, lest his Hand should be out of vre.

III. 4. Custom or habit on the part of persons; wont *to* do something. *rare*.

c **1425** *Cast. Persev.* 3629 in *Macro Plays* 185 þe vij dedis of mercy, who-so hadde vre to Fylle. **1506** *Kalender of Sheph.* A iv b, I Nouembre wyll not abyde behynde, To shewe my kyndly worthynes and vre. **1556** ABP. PARKER *Ps.* cvii. 316 Ryght oft is hys vre by loue to allure. **1557** F. SEAGER *Sch. Virt.* 716 in *Babees Bk.* (1868) 344 And sure it is taken by custome and vre, whyle yonge you be there is helpe and cure. *c* **1600** SYLVESTER *Miracle of Peace* xxv, Or (if you cannot leave your wonted ure) Leave (at the least) all mutinous alarmes.

5. *Sc.* Work; labour. *rare*$^{-1}$.

a **1510** DOUGLAS *K. Hart* I. 2 King Hart, into his cumlie castell strang Closit about with craft and meikill vre.

†**ure**, *sb.*[2] *Sc. Obs.*$^{-1}$ [App. repr. OE. *ór* beginning, front, van, taken in the sense of *ord* point, front, beginning.] The point of a weapon.

1432 *Sc. Acts Parlt., Jas. I* (1814) II. 21 Gif he hurtis or defoulis with fellon assailȝeing with ege or vre, he sal remayn in preson.

†**ure**, *sb.*[3] *Obs.* Also 7 **owre**. [a. OF. *ure* (16th c.), or ad. L. *ūrus* URUS. Cf. OE. *úr*, OHG. (MHG.) *ûr*, ON. *úrr*.] = URUS, AUROCHS.

1563 GOLDING *Cæsar* (1565) 163 Ures..are of bignes somwhat lesse than Elephantes, in kind and color and shape like a Bull. **1577** HARRISON *England* III. iv. (1878) II. 29 As for the plowing with vres (which I suppose to be vnlikelie) and alkes. **1600** FAIRFAX *Tasso* III. xxxii, The swift Vre by Volgaes rolling flood. **1668** CHARLETON *Onomasticon* 6 *Urus Jubatus*, the Owre. [**1706** PHILLIPS (ed. Kersey), *Owre*, a kind of wild Bull. (Hence in Bailey and some later Dicts.)]

ure (ør), *sb.*[4] *Orkney* and *Shetland*. Forms: 6–7 **uris-**, 6 **wyris-**, **uyerris-**, 7 **vrs-**, 8 **urs-**, **erys-**, 9 **eris-**; 8– **ure** (9 **eure**). [ad. ONorw. *øyrir* (Norw. *øyre*, *øre*), = MSw. and Sw. *öre*, MDa. and Da. *øre*, Icel. *eyrir*, ounce of silver (also denoting a standard value and latterly a coin), ad. L. *aureus* a gold solidus (taken at its value in silver); the original vowel remains unmutated in the ON. pl. *aurar*. Cf. ORA[1] and ORE[4].]

1. In genitive combinations (ON. *øyris-*, *eyris-*). **a.** ***uris-land*** [ON. *øyrisland*, MSw. *örisland*], land giving the rent of one-eighth of a mark; an ounce-land. (From the feu-duty formerly paid to the superior.) *Obs.* exc. *Hist.*

1534 in *Orkney & Shetl. Rec.* (1907) 64 Quhatsumevir that pertenis..to ws..wythin the half wyris land of Sabbaye. **1589** in *Reg. Mag. Sig. Scot.* (1890) 460/1 The landis of Trosnes extending to ane urisland. **1592** *Ibid.* (1892) 117/2 My 6 merk land and 2 uyerris land of Kildabuster. **1627** in Peterkin *Rentals of Orkney* (1820) III. 94 Lying in the vrs-lands off Brabister. **1772** G. GIFFORD in Low *Orkney* (1879) 144 Our Ure or Ursland..contains 18 Pennylands. **1795** *Statist. Acc. Scot.* XIV. 323 Every Erysland of 18 penny land had one [chapel] for matins and vespers. **1805** BARRY *Orkney* 220 The entries are first by islands and parishes,..and lastly by marklands, erislands [*printed* erls-] or ounce-lands.

b. ***uris-cop*** [ON. *øyris-*, *eyris-kaup*], = prec.

1609 *Reg. Mag. Sig. Scot.* 128/2, 6 lie uriscoppis in Glenna, cum lie quoyis. *Ibid.*, 9 lie uriscoppis de Mo.

†**c.** ***uris-thift***, stolen goods to the value of an ounce of silver. *Obs.*$^{-1}$

1602 *Shetland Law Rep.* in *Scotsman* (1886) 29 Jan. 7/1 Gif he beis apprehendit with the walor of an uristhift.

2. ***ure of land***, = 1 a. [So MSw. *öre*.]

[**1624** *Reg. Mag. Sig. Scot.* (1894) 212/1, 2 merc. 5 lie uris terrarum de Brabister.] **1799** *Statist. Acc. Scotl.* XXI. 278 In these parishes there are 1618 merks 4 ures of land. **1821** SCOTT *Pirate* i, Scarce a merk—scarce even an ure of land. **1884** *Scotsman* 26 July 3/1 (Shetland advt.), Three Merks, One Ure and One-Third of an Ure of Land.

ellipt. **1774** G. GIFFORD in Low *Orkney* (1879) 145, 8 Ures make 1 Mark [of Land]. **1799** *Statist. Acc. Scotl.* XXI. 278 An ure is the eighth part of a merk. **1822** HIBBERT *Descr. Shetl. Isl.* 179 *note*, The division of a mark of land into Ures, appears to have been first introduced..in the year 1263.

attrib. **1814** SHIRREF *Agric. Surv. Orkn.* 31 The lands in Orkney had been early divided into ure or ounce lands. **1822** HIBBERT *Descr. Shetl. Isl.* 179 *note*, [Hacon] divided the islands into Eurelands or Ouncelands.

ure, *sb.*[5] *local Sc.* [a. ON. *úr* drizzling rain.]

1. A damp mist.

1818 *Edinburgh Mag.* Sept. 155/1 The mune be this was shinan clearly abune a' the ure. *a* **1824** in Mactaggart *Gallovid. Encycl.* 333 Glowring at the azure sky, And loomy oceans ure.

2. An atmospheric haze, esp. of a coloured nature. Freq. ***dry ure***.

a **1824** in Mactaggart *Gallovid. Encycl.* 455 The east was blae, dry ure bespread the hills. **1824** MACTAGGART *Ibid.* 455 *Ure*, a kind of coloured haze, which the sun-beams make in the summer time. **1875** J. VEITCH *Tweed & other Poems* 49 The dry ure glow of sky-enkindled flame.

ure, var. EURE *sb.* and *v. Obs.*; obs. f. EWER[2] (pitcher, etc.); var. EWER[3], YURE (udder) *dial.*; obs. f. HOUR; obs. var. ORE[2].

†**ure**, *v.*[1] *Obs.*$^{-1}$ [ad. OF. *urer*, *ourer*, *orer*:—L. *ōrāre* to pray.] *intr.* To pray.

a **1225** *Ancr. R.* 286 Ofte, leoue sustren, ȝe schulen vren [*v.r.* preyen] lesse uorte reden more.

†**ure**, *v.*[2] *Obs.*$^{-1}$ [var. of EURE *v.*] *intr.* To have good fortune.

c **1440** *Pallad. on Husb.* III. 845 In hillis is to cure To sette hem on the south, yf they schal vre.

†**ure**, *v.*[3] *Obs.* [f. URE *sb.*[1]] *trans.* = INURE *v.* 1.

a **1500** *Chaucer's Dreme* C.'s Wks. (1598) 356/1 And in my selfe I me assured, That in my body I was well vred. **1530** PALSGR. 769/2 And he be ones ured to it, he wyll do well ynoughe. **1551** ROBINSON tr. *More's Utopia* I. (1895) 49 The Frenche souldiours..haue byne practysed and vrede in feates of armes. **1596** *Edward III*, I. i. 159 Thou must begin Now to..vre thy shoulders to an Armors weight.

ure, obs. var. OUR *pron.*

-ure (jʊə(r)), a suffix, repr. F. *-ure*, L. *-ūra* (hence It., Sp., Pg. *-ura*), occurring in many words of F. or L. origin. In L. *-ūra* primarily denoted action or process, hence result of this, office, etc.; after further development in F., the use was extended in Eng., and denoted action or process, the result or product of this (e.g. *enclosure*, *figure*, *picture*, *scripture*), function, state, rank, dignity, or office (e.g. *judicature*, *prefecture*, *prelature*), a collective body (e.g. *legislature*), that by which the action is effected (e.g. *clausure*, *closure*, *ligature*, *nouriture*), etc. Many words were adopted from F. at an early date, as *figure* (*a* 1225–), *scripture* (*a* 1300–), *nouriture* (*c* 1374–), *censure*, *closure*, *investiture*, *juncture*, *pressure*, *tonsure* (1380–), *fissure*, *scissure* (*c* 1400–), etc.; while a few others, as *clausure* (1398), *plicature* (1578), *mercature* (*a* 1620), *aperture* (1649–), were directly adapted from L. The suffix was also added to Eng. stems of L. origin, giving *composure* (1599–), *disposure* (1569–), *exposure* (1605–), or to true L. stems, whence *vomiture* (1598), †*beneplaciture* (1662), *ructure* (1657–69), *unigeniture* (1659–); and was further used with stems of Romance origin, as in †*bankrupture* (1617–22), †*disembogure* (1653), †*praisure* (1622), and with native or other bases, as in †*clefture* (1545, 1596), †*raisure* (1613, 1677), and *wafture* (1601–).

To this form various F. suffixes (as *-eure*, *-ir*, *-or*, *-our*) have been assimilated in Eng., as in *pleasure*, *soilure*, †*trap(p)ure* (TRAPPER *sb.*[1]), *treasure*, *velure*.

urea (juːˈriːə, ˈjʊərɪə). *Chem.* [ad. (with Latinized ending) F. *urée* (1803), f. Gr. *οὖρον* urine, or the verb *οὐρέω*. Cf. It., Sp., Pg. *urea*.]

1. a. A soluble crystalline compound, forming an organic constituent of the urine in mammalia, birds, and some reptiles, and also found in the blood, milk, etc.; carbamide, $CO(NH_2)_2$.

1806 *Phil. Trans.* XCVI. 374 A decomposition of a portion of urea. **1819** BRANDE *Chem.* 446 Urea is the principle which confers upon urine its chief peculiarities. **1862** HUXLEY *Lect. Working Men* 72 Urea..forms one of the waste products of animal structures. **1878** KINGZETT *Anim. Chem.* 190 Urea was discovered by Boerhaave before 1720, and was called by him the essential salt of urine.

b. A urea-formaldehyde plastic or resin.

1935 *Economist* 7 Dec. 1142/2 Phenolic plastics are used for various mouldings, urea is translucent plastic. **1961** H. R. SYMONDS *Source Bk. New Plastics* II. ii. 32 A new urea especially prepared for the bonding of particle board. **1969** L. K. ARNOLD *Introd. Plastics* vi. 83 The ureas are somewhat more expensive [than the phenolics] but have the advantage of being available in a wide range of light colors.

2. *attrib.* and *Comb.*, as ***urea excretion***, ***-formation***, ***-residue***; **urea-formaldehyde**, used *attrib.* and *absol.* to designate plastics, resins, etc., made by condensation of urea with formaldehyde; **urea nitrate**, **oxalate** (see quots. 1873); **urea resin**, a synthetic resin derived from urea; a urea-formaldehyde resin.

1866 ODLING *Anim. Chem.* 129 The assumption of pre-existent urea-residues in uric acid. **1873** RALFE *Phys. Chem.* 83 Urea oxalate ($2CN_2H_4O,C_2H_2O_4$): the crystals form long, transparent, tufted laminæ. *Ibid.*, Urea nitrate (CN_2H_4O,HNO_3): the crystals form shining, rhombic plates. **1897** *Allbutt's Syst. Med.* IV. 292 Observations on the urea excretion. *Ibid.* 72 Pointing to the liver as the chief seat of urea-formation. **1928** *Brit. Patent 291,473* 3/2 When using urea-formaldehyde resins, alkaline catalysts may be used to obtain the intermediate condensation product. **1933** [see *phenolformaldehyde* s.v. PHENOL c]. **1937** R. S. MORRELL et al. *Synthetic Resins* ii. 52 Tootal, Broadhurst, Lee Company Limited have patented the use of urea resins to prevent the crushing of cellulosic fabrics. **1975** M. P. STEVENS *Polymer Chem.* xii. 329 Decorative interior plywood is normally glued with urea resin because the dark-colored phenolic resins can stain the veneer. **1976** *Milton Keynes Express* 9 July 14/4 The majority of houses have cavity walls and these can be insulated by filling the cavity with..a foaming resin called urea formaldehyde. **1984** *Christian Science Monitor* 2 Mar. 23/1 The safety of urea-formaldehyde insulation..has been a subject of debate for years.

urea-, combining form of UREA, occurring in a few terms, as **ure'ameter**, **-metry** (see quots. and cf. UREO-).

1890 CRUISE in *Lancet* 22 March 643/2 The importance of ureametry is far greater than testing for albumen. *Ibid.* 644/2, I venture to draw attention to this very simple ureameter. **1895** C. J. Mayhew *Ibid.* 10 Aug. 334/1 A new ureameter which I have designed.

ureal (ˈjʊərɪəl), *a.* [f. ure-a + -al¹.] Of or pertaining to, of the nature of, urea; characterized by excessive urea.

1848 Dunglison *Med. Lex.* (ed. 7) 266/1 D[iabetes] Ureal. **1864** E. A. Parkes *Pract. Hygiene* 154 With no excess of ureal excretion. **1869** *Ibid.* (ed. 3) 340 The formation of ammonium carbonate from ureal decomposition. **1891** *Cent. Dict.* s.v., A ureal solution.

ureaplasma (jʊərɪəˈplæzmə). *Biol.* Pl. -plasmas. [f. urea + plasma.] A micro-organism of the genus *Ureaplasma*, formerly included within the genus *Mycoplasma* (cf. mycoplasma), which is characterized by the ability to metabolize urea.

[**1974** M. C. Shepard et al. in *Internat. Jrnl. Syst. Bacteriol.* XXIV. 160 It is reasonable to propose establishing a new, separate genus in the family *Mycoplasmataceae* in which to classify the T mycoplasmas isolated from man and lower animals. The name *Ureaplasma* is proposed for this new genus, which at present contains a single human species.] **1975** *Jrnl. Med. Microbiol.* VIII. 528 Mouse mastitis is suggested as being a suitable small animal model for studying ureaplasma infections. **1981** *Annales de Microbiol.* CXXXII. B. 172 Ureaplasmas were isolated first from the human genito-urinary tract.

urease (ˈjʊərɪeɪz). *Biochem.* [f. ure(a + -ase.] An enzyme produced in bacteria and certain plants which converts urea into carbon dioxide and ammonia.

1892 *Jrnl. R. Microsc. Soc.* 515 M. P. Miquel describes a new diastase which according to the nomenclature of Duclaux is called urease. **1926** *Jrnl. Biol. Chem.* LXIX. 437 The jack bean appears to contain a very large amount of urease. **1967** M. E. Hale *Biol. Lichens* iv. 58 These lichens often contain urease enzyme systems. **1982** T. I. Diamondstone in T. M. Devlin *Textbk. Biochem.* xi. 544 The source of this ammonia is urea, which, being freely diffusible, finds its way into the large intestine, where it is acted upon by bacterial urease.

urech, obs. southern var. freck *a.* (greedy).

Urecholine (jʊəriːˈkəʊliːn, -ɪn). *Pharm.* Also ure-. [f. ure(a + choline.] A proprietary term in the U.S. for the preparation of carbaminoyl-β-methyl choline chloride, $C_7H_{17}ClN_2O_2$, a quaternary ammonium compound used as a parasympathomimetic agent to stimulate bowel or bladder muscle activity.

1941 *Official Gaz.* (U.S. Patent Office) 29 Apr. 1104/2 Merck & Co., Inc.... *Urecholine* for medicinal preparation for the treatment of disorders of the peripheral circulatory system and for stimulation of the para-sympathetic nervous system. **1954** S. Duke-Elder *Parsons' Dis. Eye* (ed. 12) v. 70 Two drugs are sometimes employed which combine the direct and indirect methods of stimulation—doryl..and urecholine (carbaminoyl-β-methyl-choline chloride). **1961** A. Goth *Med. Pharmacol.* iv. 51 Bethanechol (Urecholine) and methacholine (Mecholyl) have many of the actions of acetylcholine on glands. **1981** Gerald & O'Bannon *Nursing Pharmacol. & Therapeutics* vii. 64/2 Bethanechol (Urecholine), possessing relatively specific effects on the smooth muscle of the gastrointestinal tract and urinary bladder, is clinically employed to restore parasympathetic tone and relieve postoperative abdominal distention and urinary retention.

uredine (jʊˈriːdaɪn), *sb.* and *a.* *Bot.* [f. the pl. uredines (in place of the correct sing. uredo), or mod.L. *Uredine-æ*, f. L. *ūrēdin-is*, *ūrēdo*.]

1. *sb.* A fungus of the N.O. *Uredineæ* of minute ascomycetal fungi (including mildew, rust, smut, etc.), parasitic upon and frequently injurious to living plants.

1889 Plowright *Brit. Uredineæ* i. 2 According to the nature of the Uredine under examination. *Ibid.* ii. 7 The mycelium of a Uredine. **1895** [see uredosporous *a.*].

2. *adj.* Pertaining or belonging to the uredines.

1889 Plowright *Brit. Uredineæ* iii. 15 The Uredine yeast-spore falls to the bottom of the fluid. *Ibid.*, Uredine spermatial cultures. **1902** *Nature* 20 Nov. 72/2 The Uredine Fungus *Pucciniæ dispersa*.

ureˈdineous, *a.* [f. mod.L. *Uredine-æ* (see prec.) + -ous.] Pertaining or belonging to the uredines; affected by uredo; uredinous. (1891– in Dicts.)

‖**uredines** (jʊˈriːdɪniːz). *Bot.* [L.: see uredo. Cf. F. *urédinés*.] Species of fungi parasitic upon and injurious to plants, etc. Cf. uredo.

1753 *Chambers' Cycl.* Suppl. s.v. *Blast*, That species called *uredines*, or fire-blasts. **1836** Berkeley *Fungi* in *Smith's Eng. Flora* V. ii. 6* Many entophytal parasites, such as *Uredines*, &c. **1843** *Penny Cycl.* XXVI. 47/2 The whole three plants were branded with myriads of Uredines. **1858** Irving *Handbk. Brit. Pl.* 156 One of these [sub-orders] contains the *Uredines* (Cornbrands). **1860** Berkeley *Outl. Brit. Fungology* xiii. 87 In the same way the relations of *Tremellini* to *Uredines* are clear, if [etc.].

uredinium (jʊərɪˈdɪnɪəm). *Bot.* Pl. -inia. [f. L. *ūrēdin-*, *ūrēdo* uredo + *-ium*.] A cluster or sorus of uredospores and the hyphæ which bear them. So **ureˈdinial**, **ureˈdinoid** *adjs.*

1900 B. D. Jackson *Gloss. Bot. Terms* 283/1 Uredinial. **1905** J. C. Arthur in *Bot. Gaz.* XXXIX. 221 For the sorus of the second spore-stage,..I propose *uredinium*..; derivatives *uredinial*, *urediniospore* or if preferred *uredospore*, etc. **1916** *Mycologia* VIII. 182 Since the development of the uredinial stage is supposed to be subepidermal as a rule, this deviation seems worthy of note. **1929** J. C. Arthur et al. *Plant Rusts* i. 13 Less easily recognized as aecia, with spores borne singly on pedicels and usually without peridia or paraphyses, are the stylosporic or uredinoid aecia. **1970** J. Webster *Introd. Fungi* ii. iv. 375 Rusts with uredinoid aecia. **1974** G. W. Burns *Plant Kingdom* ix. 168 (*caption*) Diagrammatic section through a uredinium. *Ibid.* 169 The uredinia begin their development beneath the epidermis of the host. **1982** Hiratsuka & Sato in Scott & Chakravorty *Rust Fungi* i. 12 The uredinial state is the most destructive spore state of such rusts as wheat stem rust..and poplar leaf rust.

uredinous (jʊˈriːdɪnəs), *a.* [f. L. *ūrēdin-* (see uredo and uredine) + -ous.]

1. *Bot.* Of the nature of a uredine; belonging to the *Uredines*.

1865 M. C. Cooke *Microscopic Fungi* 122 One of the most showy of uredinous fungi. **1889** *Athenæum* 20 April 509/3 Affected with a parasitic disease due to a uredinous fungus.

2. *Path.* Affected with, of the nature of, nettle-rash. (1891– in Dicts.)

uredium (jʊˈriːdɪəm). *Bot.* Pl. uredia. [mod.L., f. uredo.] = uredinium. Hence **uˈredial** *a.*

1937 *Nature* 8 May 800/2 Forty-four days after the inoculation was made, we observed small uredia on the upper surface of several of the pustules. **1937** Uredial [see æcium]. **1949** B. B. Mundkur *Fungi & Plant Dis.* vii. 155 Towards the end of the growing season the formation of uredia ceases and teliospores begin to appear. **1967** *Trans. Brit. Mycol. Soc.* L. 192 Aecia usually result from a fertilization process..but they may also originate from aeciospores and, thus, can be a repeating spore form (uredial aecia as in *Cronartium* and *Coleosporium*). **1970** J. Webster *Introd. Fungi* ii. iv. 369 A single uredium may contain from 50,000 to 400,000 spores.

‖**uredo** (jʊˈriːdəʊ). *Bot.* [L. *ūrēdo* (pl. *ūrēdinēs*) blight, blast, itch, f. L. *ūrĕre* to burn.]

1. A form of blight, = brand *sb.* 7. *rare.*

1706 Phillips (ed. Kersey), *Uredo*, the blasting of Trees or Herbs. **1728** Chambers *Cycl.* s.v. *Disease*, Diseases of Plants... 9. Uredo, or Scorching, of which there are two Kinds. **1832** Lindley *Introd. Bot.* 299 *Albigo*, *ferrugo*, and *uredo*, commonly called mildew, smut, rust, brand, and other names, are diseases caused by the presence of myriads of minute fungi.

2. A name for various fungi (popularly called *rust*, *smut*, *mildew*, etc.) parasitic on grain and certain other plants; formerly regarded as a distinct genus, but now known to be only the intermediate stage of the *Uredineæ* or rust fungi (cf. uredospore). Usu. with capital.

1836 M. J. Berkeley *Fungi* 369 The specimens are referred by Klotzsch to *Uredo*. **1843** *Penny Cycl.* XXVI. 47/1 The wheat became attacked with Uredo. **1889** Plowright *Brit. Uredineæ* 125 The Uredo and Uromyces frequently attack the petioles.

b. A species or plant of this.

1836 M. J. Berkeley *Fungi* 375 Elongated Uredo... Parallel Uredo. **1843** *Penny Cycl.* XXVI. 47/1 He diffused the granules of a Uredo in water. **1849** *Lancet* 17 Nov. 531/2 The uredo is studded all over with sharp points. **1889** *Berwick. Nat. Club's Proc.* XII. 488 A brown *Uredo* or *Puccinia* of the Common Mallow.

c. A receptacle or hymenium in which uredospores are formed. *rare*⁻¹.

1879 *Encycl. Brit.* IX. 831/2 Again, in a few days, this mycelium forms a new kind of receptacle, the uredo.

3. *attrib.*, as ***uredo-form***, ***-patch***; **uredo-fruit**, a group of uredospores; **uredo stage**, the summer stage of certain rust fungi.

1875 Bennett & Dyer tr. *Sachs's Bot.* 248 While the Fungus is multiplying..during the summer in its *uredo-form, the production of a new form of spores begins in the older *uredo-fruits. **1887** Bentley *Man. Bot.* (ed. 5) 380 These uredo-fruits consist of a dense mycelium [etc.]. **1887** Hillhouse tr. *Strasburger's Pract. Bot.* 265 The haulm of an oat which is infected with rusty *uredo-patches. **1880** Bessey *Bot.* 316 Later in the season..the *uredo stage begins to make its appearance..upon the leaves. **1895** M. C. Cooke *Study Fungi* xx. 246 In this group [sc. *Pucciniopsis*] of species the uredo stage is deficient.

uredosorus (jʊˌriːdəʊˈsɔərəs). *Bot.* Pl. -sori. [f. uredo + sorus¹.] = uredinium.

1905 *Bot. Gaz.* XXXIX. 221 The structure which arises from a single, fertile hyphal mass, or hymenium, either with or without a peridium, now usually called spermogonium, aecidium, uredosorus, teleutosorus, or kindred names. **1930** *N.Z. Jrnl. Sci. & Technol.* XII. 126 The term 'uredosorus' is applied to sori in which the spores are borne singly on distinct pedicels. **1973** *Nature* 17 Aug. 463/1 The majority of plants in the plot were infected, some severely (500–2,000 uredosori per plant).

uˈredospore. *Bot.* Also ureˈdiniospore, uˈrediospore. [f. uredo + spore. cf. uredinium.] One or other of the peculiar summer spores developed during the uredo stage in rust fungi.

1875 Bennett & Dyer tr. *Sachs's Bot.* 248 These uredo-spores are dispersed after the rupture of the epidermis. **1882** Bentley *Man. Bot.* (ed. 4) 372 From which vertical branches shoot upwards bearing at their extremities oval granular spores, the uredospores. **1905** Urediniospore [see uredinium]. **1937** *Nature* 8 May 801/1 The urediospores germinate normally and readily infect wheat seedlings. **1970** J. Webster *Introd. Fungi* ii. iv. 368 The urediospores [*ed.* 2 (1980): urediniospores] are detached by wind and blown to fresh wheat leaves upon which they germinate. **1978** *Bio Systems* X. 32/1 The first method..has been seen only in two related species of *Uromyces*, although it is the standard means of urediniospore separation as far back as the fern rusts.

Hence **uˌredoˈsporic** *a.*, 'of or pertaining to a uredospore' (*Cent. Dict.*, 1891); **uˌredospoˈriferous** *a.*, bearing uredospores; **uˌredoˈsporous** *a.*, characterized by uredospores.

1895 M. C. Cooke *Study Fungi* xx. 242 The uredosporiferous sori are variously coloured. *Ibid.* xx. 248 Species of uredosporous Uredines.

ureide (ˈjʊərɪaɪd). *Chem.* Also ureid. [f. ure-a + -ide, -id⁴.] A derivative of urea containing acid radicles.

1857 Miller *Elem. Chem.*, *Org.* 617 Urea likewise gives rise to the formation of a class of compounds analogous to the amides, forming substances which have been called ureides. **1867** Bloxam *Chem.* 620 They are, therefore, sometimes styled ureides, and sometimes compound ureas. **1884** *Encycl. Brit.* XVII. 519/2 Ureids are a class of bodies which are related to urea as amido-bodies are to ammonia.

ureilite (ˈjʊərɪlaɪt). *Geol.* [ad. Russ. *ureĭlit* (Erofeev & Lachinov 1888, in *Zhurnal Russ. fiziko-khim. Obshchestva pri Imper. St. Petersburgsk. Univ.* XX. 213), f. the name of Novo-*Ureĭ*, a village near Penza, in the vicinity of which a meteorite belonging to this class fell.] Any of a group of calcium-poor achondrite meteorites that consist mainly of olivine and pigeonite.

[**1889** *Jrnl. Chem. Soc.* LVI. 225 The authors find, after comparison with known classes of aerolites, that the meteorite described above differs from all of them in many points, and propose to name this form ureïlithe.] **1916** *Mineral Mag.* XVIII. 38 The ureilites consist of a coarsely crystalline aggregate of olivine and monoclinic pyroxene cemented together by a film of nickel-iron and carbonaceous matter. **1962** B. Mason *Meteorites* 111 The ureilites form a unique group of three meteorites, quite distinct from all other achondrites. **1971** I. G. Gass et al. *Understanding Earth* viii. 116/1 The presence of diamond in the small group of ureilites appears to be due to extraterrestrial shock effects.

ureisun, obs. f. orison.

ureit, obs. Sc. var. writ *sb.*, write *v.*

uremia, -ic, varr. uræmia, uræmic.

ˈ**urent**, *a. rare.* [a. L. *ūrent-*, *ūrens*, pres. pple. of *ūrĕre* to burn. Cf. It. and Sp. *urente*.] Burning; causing a burning sensation.

1656 Blount *Glossogr.* **1777** S. Robson *Brit. Flora* 6 *Urent*, beset with venomous stings, as in Nettles. **1863** J. G. Wood *Illustr. Nat. Hist.* III. 741 The cables retain their urent property long after they have been detached from the animal.

ureo- (ˈjʊərɪəʊ), combining form of ure-a, occurring in a few words, as **ureo-carbonate**, **-carbonic**, **ureomer**, **ureometry**: (see quots. and cf. urea-, uro-¹).

1852 Watts tr. *Gmelin's Handbk. Chem.* VII. 377 It is resolved into alcohol and a *ureo-carbonate of the alkali. *Ibid.*, The constituents of vinic ether and of hypothetically anhydrous *ureo-carbonic acid. **1876** J. G. Blackley in *Jrnl. Chem. Soc.* II. 467 A modification of Russell and West's *ureometer. **1884** Knight *Dict. Mech.* Suppl. 915/1 In Hüfner's new ureometer,..the exact methods for the determination of urea in organic liquids are..complex and tedious. **1901** *Lancet* 9 March 697/1, I have examined the urine with Martindale's ureometer. **1876** J. G. Blackley in *Jrnl. Chem. Soc.* II. 447 The operation of *ureometry.

ureotelic (jʊərɪəʊˈtɛlɪk), *a.* *Biochem.* [ad. It. *ureotelico* (A. Clementi 1916, in *Atti della R. Accad. dei Lincei: Rendiconti* XXV. i. 366), f. *ureo-* + Gr. τελικός final.] Of an animal or its metabolism: producing nitrogenous waste chiefly in the form of urea.

1924 [see uricotelic *a.*]. **1972** M. S. Gardiner *Biol. Invertebrates* xiii. 500 Animals are conveniently classified as ammonotelic, ureotelic, or uricotelic.

ure-ox (ˈjʊərɒks). [ad. MHG. *ûr-ochse* (G. *urochs* urochs, *auerochs* aurochs), or f. ure *sb.*³ + ox.] = urus.

1607 Topsell *Four-f. Beasts* 722 Their large bodies and manes..it is not vnfit to attribute..also to the Vre-Oxe. *Ibid.* 723 In Malonia neer Lituania..those Vre-oxen are kept as it were in parkes and chases. **1611** Cotgr., *Ure*, the huge-bodied, bulch-backed, short-horned, and red-eyed wild Oxe, called the Vre-oxe. **1661** Lovell *Hist. Anim. & Min.* 23 Bull, *Taurus*... Hereto may be referred the Bison; and Vre-oxe.

1887 tr. *Hahn's Wand. Plants & Anim.* 495 The ure-ox and wisent of the German forests. **1888** E. Gerard *Land beyond Forest: Transylvania* II. 11 Whoever..let himself be lured into quaffing mead from her ure-ox drinking horn, was effaced.

urerythrine (jʊərəˈrɪθraɪn). *Chem.* [f. ur-ine + erythrin.] (See quots.)

1858 Thudichum *Urine* 321 Ureythrine occurs in fresh urine generally in a dissolved state. **1878** Kingzett *Animal Chem.* 238 Urerythrine is a substance first described by Proust under the name of rosacic acid.

ures, obs. f. ours.

ureson, uresun, obs. ff. ORISON.

-uret (jʊərɛt), *Chem.*, a suffix, ad. mod.L. *-urētum*, *-orētum*, added to a stem or truncated word to form names of simple compounds of an element with another element or a radical. First used (after F. words in *-ure*) about 1790 in *azoturet*, *hydruret*, *phosphuret*, *sulphuret* (from *azote*, *hydr-ogen*, *phosph-ure*, *sulph-ure*), it was extended to other terms, as *carburet*, *nitruret* (1794), *ioduret* (1816), *seleniuret* (1818), and (more recently) *arseniuret*, *bromuret*, *chloruret*, *cyanuret*, *floruret*, *hydroguret*, *telluret*, etc. It is now largely replaced by -IDE, q.v.

The French school of chemists in 1787 proposed the suffix *-urētum*, *-orētum*, in mod.L. terms (as *phosphorētum*, *sulphurētum*); but in F. words they preferred the suffix *-ure* (1787 De Morveau, etc. *Méthode de Nomenclature Chimique* 207, 231, etc.).

† **'uretary**, *a.* and *sb.* *Obs. rare.* Also 7 **uritary**. [ad. F. *uretaire* (16th c.), f. *uretère*: see next.] **a.** *adj.* Of, pertaining to, or constituting the ureters. **b.** *sb.* = URETER.

1578 BANISTER *Hist. Man* v. 75 b, The extreme endes of the vretarie vessels, which both giue passage to the vrine discendyng into the bleddar. **1650** EARL MONM. tr. *Senault's Man bec. Guilty* IV. v. 213 That which Divine Justice shews in the sicknesses of the earthly Monarches when by a grain of sand he stops the uritaries [F. *vretaires*].

ureter (jʊ'riːtə(r)). *Anat.* Also 6–7 **vretere**, **vreter**, 7 **uriter**. [a. medical L. *ūrētēr*, a. Gr. οὐρητήρ, f. οὐρεῖν to make water. Cf. F. *uretère* (1541), It. and Pg. *uretere*, Sp. *urétere*.] Either of the fibro-muscular tubes or vessels which convey the urine from the pelvis of the kidney to the bladder; a urinary duct.

1578 BANISTER *Hist. Man* v. 78 b, From this veyne springeth a vessell called *Vreter*. **1591** JAS. I *Poet. Exerc.*, *Furies* 862 A Stone, which stops.. The sliddrie vreter, carier of Salt vrine. **1615** CROOKE *Body of Man* (1631) 190 The paine of the Stone is.. acute when it mooueth into or toward the Vreter. **1725** *Fam. Dict.* s.v. *Stone*, To make use of his Probe, and to thrust it [*sc.* the stone] thro' the Ureter into the Bladder. **1800** *Med. Jrnl.* IV. 392 On the left side of the bladder, near the termination of the ureter. **1835–6** *Todd's Cycl. Anat.* I. 348/1 The ureter [in birds].. has the same structure as in the mammalia. **1875** HUXLEY & MARTIN *Elem. Biol.* 198 The duct [of the frog]—ureter (female) or genito-urinary canal (male)—running.. to the cloaca. **1893** *Brit. Med. Jrnl.* 7 Jan. 11/2 A calculus impacted in the lower end of the ureter.

attrib. **1601** HOLLAND *Pliny* II. 72 The juice of Mallows.. enlargeth the Vretere conduits. **1898** *Brit. Med. Jrnl.* 5 Nov. 1412/2 The ureter catheters.. must be used with aseptic precautions.

b. More usually in pl.

1578 BANISTER *Hist. Man* v. 83 b, Two other passages.. deducyng Urine from the reynes, and called Vreteres. **1594** T. B. *La Primaud. Fr. Acad.* II. 372 Two other passages, called vreteres or vrine pipes. **1625** HART *Anat. Ur.* I. ii. 30 They shew forth the disposition.. of the kidneyes, vreters, or vrine-pipes, and the bladder. **1653** H. MORE *Conject. Cabbal.* 156 Fishes, and.. birds,.. are both also destitute of Vreters. **1707** FLOYER *Physic. Pulse-Watch* 346 This shews the Constitution of the Veins and Ureters, by which we may understand the phlegmatic Temper. **1755** *Gentl. Mag.* XXV. 416 The ureters.. are situated near the seminal vessels on each side of the spine. **1808** BARCLAY *Muscular Motions* 556 The urine.. is propelled by the successive muscular action of the ureters into the bladder. **1848** CARPENTER *Anim. Phys.* 282 In all Mammalia, and in others, we find the ureters.. dilated at their lower extremity into a bladder. **1876** *Clin. Soc. Trans.* IX. 26 Both ureters were full of thick yellow pus.

u'reteral, *a.* *Anat.* [f. prec. + -AL¹.] Of or pertaining to, affecting or connected with, a ureter.

1883 DUNCAN *Clin. Lect. Dis. Women* (ed. 2) x. 76 The similar condition of the urine in hysteria.. and in ureteral fistula. **1894** *Ann. Surgery* Sept. 267 The treatment of the ureteral wound.

u,rete'rectomy. *Surg.* [f. as prec. + Gr. ἐκτομή: see -TOMY.] Surgical removal of a ureter.

1893 *Brit. Med. Jrnl. Epit.* 1 Apr. 49/3 Ureterectomy. Reynier.. reports a case in which he removed the whole of one ureter. **1897** *Allbutt's Syst. Med.* IV. 437 Ureterectomy for diseases of Ureter.

ureteric (jʊəriː'tɛrɪk), *a.* [f. as prec. + -IC. Cf. F. *urétérique*.] Pertaining to, affecting, or occurring in a ureter or the ureters.

1822 GOOD *Study Med.* IV. 444 Ureteric stoppage of urine. **1890** BILLINGS *Med. Dict.* s.v., Superior,.. middle,.. and inferior ureteric arteries. *Ibid.*, Ureteric calculus,.. Ureteric fold.

ureteritis (jʊriːtə'raɪtɪs). *Path.* [f. as prec. + -ITIS. Cf. F. *urétérite*, It. *ureterite*.] Inflammation of a ureter.

1823 CRABB *Dict. Technol.* II. s.v. *c* **1840** *Encycl. Metrop.* VII. 653/2 Ureteritis and cystitis rarely co-exist with diseases of other parts. **1889** *Buck's Handbk. Med. Sci.* VIII. 560/2 A simple uncomplicated ureteritis probably never occurs. **1898** *Lancet* 1 Jan. 17/2 If the ureter is found to be .. in a condition of tuberculous ureteritis.

uretero- (jʊ'riːtərəʊ), combining form of URETER, occurring in various surgical and medical terms, as **ureterocele** [Gr. κήλη tumour, rupture], an outward protrusion of the wall of a ureter; **urete'rography**, radiography of the ureters; **ureterosigmoi'dostomy** [-STOMY], the operation of implanting the ureters into the sigmoid flexure of the colon; also **uretero-cystoneostomy**, **-cystostomy**, **-enterostomy**, **-lithotomy**, **-stomy**, **-tomy** *sbs.*; **uretero-genital**, **-uterine**, **-vaginal**, **-vesical** *adjs.*

Many other instances occur in recent Dicts., etc., as ***ureterodialysis***, ***-lith***, ***-lithic***, ***-lysis***, ***-nephrectomy***, ***-plasty***, ***-pyelitis***, ***-pyosis***, ***-rrhaphy***, ***-stenosis***, ***-ureteral***.

1913 *Interstate Med. Jrnl.* XX. 346 On close observation of the right ureter orifice.. during urinary excretion, a considerable cystic dilation was noticed and the condition was diagnosed as a *ureterocele. **1976** *Lancet* 11 Dec. 1302/1, I would have appreciated more information about those boys with radiological abnormalities who did not undergo surgery, the one with a right ureterocele,.. and the 8-year-old with grade-III reflux. **1893** *Medical Press* 15 Nov. 503/2 *Uretero-Cystoneostomy,.. that [operation] of placing a severed ureter in communication direct with the bladder. **1903** *Med. Record* 13 June 958 (Cent. Suppl.), *Ureterocystostomy. **1893** *Brit. Med. Jrnl. Epit.* 4 Mar. 34/1 Any attempt at *uretero-enterostomy would.. be contraindicated in cases of atonic or relaxed condition of the lower orifice of the ureter. **1887** *Lancet* 3 Sept. 496/1 (*heading*), *Uretero-genital fistulæ. **1912** STEDMAN *Med. Dict.* (ed. 2) 961/2 *Ureterography. **1926** YOUNG & DAVIS *Young's Pract. Urol.* II. xiii. 241 Ureterography.—The contour of the ureter may be shown by filling it with various shadowgraphic media and taking the *x*-ray film or plate in the same manner as described for pyelography. **1977** *Proc. R. Soc. Med.* LXX. 187/1 Mr Hendry.. has described the methods by which today an accurate and precise diagnosis may be made by early high-dose urography and ureterography. **1893** *Brit. Med. Jrnl.* 7 Jan. 11/2 Case III. *Uretero-Lithotomy... The patient was placed in the lithotomy position [etc.]. **1934** WEBSTER, *Ureterosigmoidostomy. **1940** A. I. DODSON *Urol. Surg.* xxxix. 600 If this fails, muscle transplants or ureterosigmoidostomy should be done, depending upon the extent of the deformity. **1977** *Proc. R. Soc. Med.* LXX. 536/2, 2 teenage girls with bladder exstrophy and previous bilateral ureterosigmoidostomy performed in childhood. **1901** *Lancet* 6 April 1034/1 The operations of ureterotomy and lumbar *ureterostomy. **1885** *Ibid.* 14 Feb. 296/2 Removal of the calculus impacted in the ureter by intra-peritoneal *ureterotomy is feasible. **1894** *Ann. Surgery* Sept. 289 This case was one in which *uretero-ureterostomy might have been performed with advantage. **1887** *Lancet* 3 Sept. 496/2 Conditions similar to those which give rise to *uretero-uterine fistulæ. *Ibid.*, *Uretero-vaginal fistulæ. **1893** *Brit. Med. Jrnl. Epit.* 4 March 34/1 The *uretero-vesicle [*sic*] sphincter.. is only relaxed to give issue from time to time to a jet of urine.

urethane ('jʊərɪθeɪn, jʊ'rɛθeɪn). *Chem.* Also **-an**. [a. F. *uréthane*: see UR-EA and ETHANE; coined by J. B. A. Dumas 1833, in *Ann. d. Chim. et Physique* LIV. 236.]

1. a. Ethyl carbamate; valued as an anæsthetic.

1838 T. THOMSON *Chem. Org. Bodies* 600 The specific gravity of the vapour of urethan. **1844** FOWNES *Man. Chem.* 386 Urethane is a white, solid, crystallizable body, fusible below 212°. **1885** *Lancet* 19 Dec. 1167/2 He had slept comfortably by the aid of urethan.

b. Any ester of carbamic acid. **c.** By extension, any compound which includes the group –NH·CO·O– in the molecule.

1856 *Jrnl. Chem. Soc.* VIII. 276 Butylic urethane.. forms beautiful nacreous scales. **1876** *Encycl. Brit.* V. 578/1 The neutral ethereal salts of carbamic acid are known as urethanes. **1926** *Jrnl. Amer. Chem. Soc.* XLVIII. 2176 It was decided.. to prepare the mono- and dicarbethoxy-guanidines... The compounds may be regarded as urethans. **1954** C. H. FISHER et al. in G. S. Whitby *Synthetic Rubber* xxv. 926 The diisocyanate reacts with the terminal hydroxyls of the polyester, forming urethane linkages. **1968** R. O. C. NORMAN *Princ. Org. Synthesis* xiv. 447 The isocyanate is converted into an amine or a urethane. **1976** A. L. TERNAY *Contemporary Org. Chem.* xxii. 688 Urethanes have high melting points, making them useful as derivatives of phenols.

2. = POLYURETHANE; also *attrib.* and *fig.*

1956 [see PROCESSABLE *a.*]. **1969** *Jane's Freight Containers 1968–69* 463/2 Construction: Aluminium extrusion and sheet,.. urethane foam, laminated wood. **1971** *Cabinet Maker & Retail Furnisher* 1 Oct. 14/2 Children's stools made of ICI's new solid urethane plastic are being supplied to infant and primary schools. **1976** A. CASSORLA *Skateboarder's Bible* 9 The past can be shrouded by the translucent urethane gauze of the present. **1979** *Arizona Daily Star* 8 Apr. A3/3 (Advt.), Madly flattering sandals of soft kid urethane, with flexible, easy going soles.

urethra (jʊ'riːθrə). *Anat.* [a. late L. *ūrēthra* (whence F. *urèthre*, *urètre*, It., Sp., Pg. *uretra*, Pg. *urethra*), a. Gr. οὐρήθρα, f. οὐρεῖν to urinate.] The membranous tube or canal through which the urine is discharged from the bladder.

1634 JOHNSON tr. *Paré's Wks.* XIX. i. 723 There bee some who have the Urethra or passage of the yard obstructed by budding caruncles. **1638** A. REID *Anat. Body of Man* 215 There is no conspicuous passage, by the which the seed passeth into the urethra. **1682** T. GIBSON *Anat.* xix. (1684) 127 In Men it [*sc.* the neck of the bladder] is longer and narrower, and.. opens into the Urethra. **1732** ARBUTHNOT *Rules of Diet* iv (1736) 428 In the Urethra, or Passage of the Urine from the Bladder. *c* **1790** *Encycl. Brit.* (ed. 3) V. 271/2 The urethra.. terminates in the podex. **1840** G. V. ELLIS *Anat.* 584 The urethra.. reaches from the bladder to the extremity of the penis in the male, or to the vulva in the female. **1880** *Lancet* 24 Jan. 119/1 The urethræ of men differ in calibre. **1884** W. PYE *Surg. Handicraft* 465 Normal urethras differ greatly in their calibre.

attrib. and *Comb.* **1875** KNIGHT *Dict. Mech.* 2684/2 *Urethra-cutter*.., an instrument for enlarging the urethral canal.. in case of stricture. *Ibid.*, *Urethra-syringe*,.. a syringe with a long nozzle.

urethra-, combining form of URETHRA (cf. URETHRO-), occurring in a few terms, as **u'rethragraph**, **-tome**, **ure'thrameter** (see quots.).

1875 KNIGHT *Dict. Mech.* 2684/2 *Urethratome*,.. a knife for dividing strictures of the urethra. **1883** G. HERSCHEL in *Lancet* 2 June 943/2 The instrument which I have devised, and to which I propose to give the name of *urethragraph. *Ibid.*, Every surgeon who habitually makes use of the *urethrameter. **1885** *Brit. Med. Jrnl.* 11 July 54/2 Having found out the number, situations, and sizes of the contractions [of the urethra].. by the urethrameter.

urethral (jʊ'riːθrəl), *a.* [ad. mod.L. *ūrēthrāl-is*, or f. URETHR-A + -AL¹. Cf. F. *uréthral*, Pg. *urethral*, *uretral*.]

1. *Anat.* Of or pertaining to the urethra; constituting the urethra.

1835–6 OWEN in *Todd's Cycl. Anat.* I. 354/1 There is no true urethral canal [in birds]. *Ibid.* 355/2 Prostatic or other urethral glands. **1857** SIR H. THOMPSON *Dis. Prostate* (1861) 16 The urethral mucous membrane. **1884** —— *Tumours of Bladder* 25 For which purpose the small urethral incision suffices.

2. *Path.* Affecting or occurring in the urethra; resulting from operating on the urethra.

In frequent use since *c* 1875.

1843 R. J. GRAVES *Syst. Clin. Med.* xxv. 309 The running and urethral inflammation. **1845** *Encycl. Metrop.* VII. 600/2 Urethral hæmorrhage is a flux of blood from the urethra. **1884** W. PYE *Surg. Handicraft* 466 This urethral fever, or urethral shivering,.. is generally transient.

3. Adapted for, used in, operating on the urethra.

1852 *Lancet* 7 Feb. 144/1 The prompt removal of strictures of the urinary canal with the urethral guide and tubes. **1861** ERICHSEN *Surg.* (ed. 3) 1028 Urethral lithotrite. **1884** KNIGHT *Dict. Mech.* Suppl. 263/2 The urethral divulsor for obliterating strictures. *Ibid.* 551/2 Urethral forceps... Urethral scoop.

ure'thralgia. *Path.* [f. URETHR-A + Gr. ἄλγος pain.] A painful affection of the urethra.

1859 *New Syd. Soc. Yearbk.* 195 A case of urethralgia.. yielded to frictions of chloroform liniment.

ure'threctomy. *Surg.* [f. URETHR-A + Gr. ἐκτομή: see -TOMY.] Surgical removal of the urethra or part of it.

1893 *Medical Press* 29 March 324/1 Urethrectomy as a method for radical treatment of rupture of the urethra, fistula, or organic stricture. **1898** *Brit. Med. Jrnl.* 11 June 1556/1 A case of urethrectomy for impermeable stricture with retention of urine.

urethritis (jʊəriː'θraɪtɪs). *Path.* [f. URETHR-A + -ITIS. Cf. F. *uréthrite*.] Inflammation of the urethra.

1823 CRABB *Dict. Technol.* II. s.v. **1843** R. J. GRAVES *Syst. Clin. Med.* xxvii. 347 The extension of urethritis sympathetically or by metastasis. **1888** *Lancet* 14 Jan. 58/1 The condition commonly known as chronic granular urethritis.

Hence **ure'thritic** (-'ɪtɪk), *a.* (*a*) Arising from, due to, urethritis; (*b*) Affected with urethritis.

(*a*) **1860** MAYNE *Expos. Lex.* 1313 Urethritic or gonorrhœal prostatitis.
(*b*) **1891** *Cent. Dict.*

urethro- (jʊ'riːθrəʊ), combining form of URETHRA, occurring in various surgical and pathological terms, as **urethrocele**, **-gram**, **-graph**, **-meter**, **-plasty**, **-rrhaphy**, **-scope**, **-scopy**, **-stenosis**, **-stomy**, **-tome**, **-tomy** *sbs.*; **urethro-genital**, **-metric**, **-plastic**, **-rectal**, **-scopic**, **-sexual**, **-vaginal**, **-vesical** *adjs.*; **ure'thrography**, radiography of the urethra.

Various other terms appear in recent or special Dicts., as ***urethrobulbar***, ***-cystitis***, ***-penile***, ***-perineal***, ***-phraxis***, ***-plastic***, ***-scopical***, ***-spasm***, ***-tomic***, etc. (Cf. F. *uréthroplastie*, *-rrhagie*, *-rrhaphie*, *-rrhée*, *-scope*, *-scopie*, *-tome*, *-tomie*.)

1873 *Lancet* 7 June 811/2 Such a *urethrocele proved extremely inconvenient to a married lady. **1885** *Buck's Handbk. Med. Sci.* I. 519/1 Urethrocele.. affects the posterior wall a few millimetres above the orifice. **1840** G. V. ELLIS *Anat.* 452 The *urethro-genital portion of the perinæal space. **1893** *Medical Press* 8 Feb. 144/1 The Urethrometer.—B shows the mechanism which takes a *urethrogram by the pencil points A writing on a sliding slip of paper. **1884** G. HERSCHEL in *Lancet* 5 April 608/1 A technical description of my *urethrograph. **1933** R. M. LECOMTE *Man. Urol.* i. 38 *Urethrography. This is done by filling the urethra with a radiopaque solution and taking an x-ray film. **1974** J. D. MAYNARD in R. M. Kirk et al. *Surgery* viii. 157/1 Urethrography. Micturating cystograms do not produce satisfactory radiographs of the urethra. **1884** ERICHSEN *Surg.* (ed. 8) II. 1092 For the purpose of measuring these slight strictures, Otis, of New York, has invented an instrument which he calls the '*urethrometer'. **1895** *Arnold & Sons' Surg. Instrument Catal.* 572 Urethrometer (Mac Munn's), automatic. **1884** KNIGHT *Dict. Mech.* Suppl. 916/2 **Urethrometric Sound*, an olivary sound in a canula. **1856** *Lancet* 4 Oct. 378/2 Delpech.. performed a *urethroplastic operation. **1845** *Ibid.* 25 Jan. 83/2 (*heading*), *Urethro-plasty. **1861** ERICHSEN *Surg.* (ed. 3) 1095 Urethroplasty may in such cases be advantageously practised. **1857** *Lancet* 5 Sept. 247/2 Followed by the formation of a *urethro-rectal fistula. **1883** *Holmes' Syst. Surg.* (ed. 3) III. 682 *Urethroraphy is performed by refreshing the edges of the fistula [etc.]. **1893** *Lancet* 13 May 1135/2 The above cases of circular urethrorraphy. **1868**

Ibid. 12 Dec. 768/2 A very simple *urethroscope. 1886 *Buck's Handbk. Med. Sci.* II. 659 The Urethroscope in position. 1895 *Arnold & Sons' Surg. Instrument Catal.* 573 *Urethroscopic Tube (Otis's). 1899 *Brit. Med. Jrnl.* 2 Dec. 1544 Urethroscopic examination showed the presence of a simple gonorrhœa. 1890 BILLINGS *Med. Dict.* II. 725 *Urethroscopy. 1901 *Lancet* 31 Aug. 599/1 The illumination..by a source of light from the outside, reflected into the tube, is as old as urethroscopy itself. 1835–6 OWEN in *Todd's Cycl. Anat.* I. 348/1 The same segment of the cloaca..is therefore termed the *urethro-sexual cavity. 1841 *Penny Cycl.* XXI. 161/1 The urethro-sexual canal. 1848 DUNGLISON *Med. Dict.* (ed. 7) 874 **Urethrostenosis*, stricture of the urethra. 1900 R. HARRISON *Vasectomy* 44 Remote results of structural lesions in urethro-stenosis. 1900 *Brit. Med. Jrnl. Epit.* 28 April 66/2 Perineal *Urethrostomy:..In this operation, the first stage of which is an ordinary external urethrotomy, the exposed urethra is cut across. 1849 CRAIG s.v., *Urethrotome. 1860 *Lancet* 21 July 58/2 Two cases of stricture of the urethra successfully treated by the urethrotome dilator. 1874 *Ibid.* 13 June 830/2 Along this the tunneled eye of the urethrotome is threaded. 1848 DUNGLISON *Med. Dict.* (ed. 7) 874 *Urethrotomy. 1852 *Lancet* 28 Aug. 204/2 Who invented urethrotomy on a grooved staff as a cure for stricture? 1867 *Biennial Retrospect* (New Syd. Soc. XXXII) 321 Internal urethrotomy is more prompt in execution. 1853 ERICHSEN *Surg.* 864 *Urethro-vaginal fistulæ are..of most common occurrence. 1885 *Buck's Handbk. Med. Sci.* I. 519/1 The whole thickness of the urethro-vaginal wall. 1873 *Lancet* 15 Nov. 699/2 *Urethro-vesical calculus.

urethylane (jʊˈrɛθɪleɪn). *Chem.* [f. UR-EA: see ETHYL and -ANE 2 b.] Methyl-urethane; methyl carbamate.

1844 FOWNES *Man. Chem.* 417 It yields with dry ammonia a solid crystallizable substance, called urethylane. 1852 WATTS tr. *Gmelin's Handbk. Chem.* VII. 292 Urethylane crystallizes in tables derived from an oblique rhombic prism. 1863 *Watts' Dict. Chem.* I. 751 Carbamate of Methyl. Urethylane.

u'retic, *a.* (and *sb.*) [ad. late L. *ūrētic-us*, a. Gr. οὐρητικός, f. οὐρεῖν to urinate. Cf. obs. F. *uretique* (1581), *ourétique*.] †**a.** *uretic acid*, phosphoric acid (1857 Mayne *Expos. Lex.* 847/1). *Obs.* **b.** Diuretic (1849 Craig; hence in later Dicts.).

u'rette. [f. UR-INE *sb.* + -ETTE.] (See quot.)

1840 J. BUEL *Farmer's Comp.* 72 Urette is animal urine, absorbed and rendered dry by mixture with calcareous earth.

Urfirnis (ˈʊəfɜːnɪs). [Ger., f. *ur-* UR- + *firnis* varnish, veneer.] A form of early Greek pottery (see quots.).

1912 WACE & THOMPSON *Prehist. Thessaly* ii. 21 Urfirnis Ware..was first found..at Orchomenos... The whole vase is covered with a thin semi-lustrous wash which varies in colour from red-brown to..black... The Orchomenos Urfirnis naturally occupies a middle position between the Tirynthian and that from Lianokladhi. 1928 PEAKE & FLEURE *Steppe & Sown* x. 126 Into this mixed population [around Corinth] came the Cycladic traders with their characteristic *Urfirnis*, or primitive glazed pottery. 1939 J. D. S. PENDLEBURY *Archaeol. Crete* ii. 75 The pottery, peculiar to Vasilike, is a highly specialized form of 'Urfirnis' ware—the pottery covered with a lustrous black or brown wash—which develops in Greece and the Islands, no doubt with an ultimate Anatolian origin. 1957 V. G. CHILDE *Dawn Europ. Civilization* (ed. 6) v. 65 Besides self-coloured wares a light fabric was made and covered all over with shiny brown or black paint. This ware, termed 'neolithic urfirnis', looks like an attempt to reproduce the appearance of black burnished ware in kiln-fired vases, but is said to begin in Middle Neolithic times in Corinthia. 1970 BRAY & TRUMP *Dict. Archaeol.* 245/2 *Urfirnis*, a characteristic ware of the Early Helladic II period of Greece. It has a buff fabric decorated partly or all over with a dark lustrous slip, often loosely called a glaze.

urge (ɜːdʒ), *sb.* [f. next.] The action of urging or fact of being urged or prompted; an impelling motive, force, pressure, etc.

In frequent use from *c* 1910.

a 1618 SYLVESTER *Forgive us our Trespasses* xxvii, O may it please thy heavenly grace,..That we may pray without all urge; Forgive us, Lord, our debts. 1884 WHITMAN *Leaves of Grass* 324 O I am sure they really came from Thee, The urge, the ardor, the unconquerable will. 1886 R. W. GILDER *Lyrics, Recognition*, i, Creation,..With swift, concentric, never ceasing urge, Resolving gradual to one disk of fire. 1914 J. L. PATON *J. B. Paton* xviii. 317 Every good deed is bound to grow. There is an inward urge that forces it upwards.

urge (ˈɜːdʒ), *v.* Also 6 urdge. [ad. L. *urgē-re* to press, drive, compel, etc. (whence It. *urgere*, Sp. and Pg. *urgir*).]

I. 1. *trans.* To bring forward, present, or press upon the attention (a fact, reason, argument, etc.) in an earnest or urgent manner; to plead with or by way of argument or excuse; to allege, affirm, or state, esp. in justification, extenuation, or defence.

In frequent use from *c* 1685.

1560 DAUS tr. *Sleidane's Comm.* 315 b, The Emperour..aunswered him plainly that he could not..praise the same decree, and still vrged his promesse and couenaunt. 1565 CALFHILL *Answ. Martiall* 155 Ye vrge a miracle, for euery..splinter of the Crosse, inasmuch as a Church..was preserued from burning by it. 1596 *Edw. III*, II. i. 447, A spatious field of reasons could I vrge. 1655 FULLER *Ch. Hist.* I. 8 This..were an argument (as K. Iames did once pleasantly urge it) to prove our Old stile before the New. *a* 1695 J. SCOTT *Chr. Life* II. Wks. 1718 I. 419 The Apostle urges our having a compassionate High Priest in Heaven to intercede for us. 1713 BERKELEY *Hylas & Phil.* II. Wks. 1871 I. 314, I am at a loss what more to urge. 1784 COWPER *Task* VI. 56 The few.., seeking grace t'improve the prize they hold, Would urge a wiser suit than asking more. 1798 S. & HT. LEE *Canterb. T.* II. 164 [He] urged his weak health, as rendering it necessary he should travel very leisurely. 1816 J. SCOTT *Paris Revisit.* (ed. 3) 321 Canova appeared as a claimant in behalf of Rome, which had only her venerable name to urge. 1855 *Poultry Chron.* III. 242/2 The most fastidious can urge no objection. 1864 D. G. MITCHELL *Sev. Stor.* 279 The Count urged the scandal which would grow out of such a measure.

b. Const. *on, upon*; *to*, etc.; also *against*.

1593 SHAKS. *Rich. II*, II. i. 299 Vrge doubts to them y^t feare. 1607 —— *Cor.* IV. vii. 19 He knowes not What I can vrge against him. 1654 BRAMHALL *Just Vind.* iii. 35 Yet three things are urged against it. 1667 MILTON *P.L.* VI. 622 The terms we sent were terms of weight,..and full of force urg'd home. 1749 FIELDING *Tom Jones* VII. xv, So far from being an Advocate for the present Prisoner, she urged his Guilt to his Officer. 1841 A. COMBE *Physiol. Digestion* (ed. 3) 304, I shall..urge upon him the necessity of rendering our knowledge more complete. 1872 TENNYSON *Gareth & Lynette* 1313 Lancelot on him urged All the devisings of their chivalry.

c. With clause as object, either introduced by *that* or directly quoted.

(*a*) 1560 DAUS tr. *Sleidane's Comm.* 227 The French men..especially vrged that the Scotes myght be comprised in the peace. 1596 DRAYTON *Legends* i. 352 Further to urge what she before had said. 1638 JUNIUS *Paint. Ancients* 2 Wee doe therein urge somewhat further, that [etc.]. 1672 H. STUBBE *Justif. Dutch War* 24 The Queen urged, that..she was to be Arbitress. 1817 JAS. MILL *Brit. India* II. IV. v. 217 It was urged..that the servants..ought not to be deprived of such precious advantages. 1885 'MRS. ALEXANDER' *At Bay* ix, I urged that the disappearance of the..money..would tell against him.

(*b*) 1689 PRIOR *Epistle to Fleetwood Shephard* 78 So Atoms dancing round the Center, They urge, made all Things at a Venture. *a* 1743 OZELL tr. *Brantome's Sp. Rhodom.* (1744) 67 M. de Lansac urged, It was absolutely necessary. *a* 1792 SIR J. REYNOLDS *Journ. Flanders & Holland* Wks. 1797 II. 124 There is lightness, airiness, and facility in Rubens, his advocates will urge. 1838 DICKENS *Nickleby* vi, 'Father,' urged the maiden [to the monk],..'our daily alms have been distributed.' 1865 —— *Mut. Fr.* III. i, 'Don't break out, Lammle,' urged Fledgeby, in a submissive tone. 1884 tr. *Lotze's Logic* 424 We are left after all, it will be urged,..walled in within the all-embracing delusions of those ideas.

2. To advocate or advise earnestly (some course of action, etc.); to press with importunity, claim or demand pressingly.

1595 SHAKS. *John* IV. ii. 204 Why vrgest thou so oft yong Arthurs death? 1596 WARNER *Alb. Eng.* IX. xlvi. (1602) 217 Then proudly pricke the mounted Sers, the Harrolds..vrging fees to gentellize their name. 1601 SHAKS. *Jul. C.* IV. iii. 261, I should not vrge thy duty past thy might. 1661 *Reg. Privy Council Scot.* I. 5 The Lord Chancellour..is to urge of them the oath of supremacie. 1682 DRYDEN *Medal* 187 What vengeance will they urge, Whose Ordures neither Plague nor Fire can purge. 1805 *Med. Jrnl.* XIV. 206, I thought it my duty to urge the operation. 1816 SCOTT *Old Mort.* xxxiii, He hath ever urged peace with the malignants. 1831 JAMES *Phil. Augustus* II. v, The many, which were all eager to urge a course that..he would have been the first to follow, but [etc.].

b. With impersonal subject.

1592 KYD *Sp. Trag.* III. i. 61 Embassadour, What news hath vrg'd this sodain entrance? *Ibid.* IV. iv. 87, I see your lookes vrge instance of these wordes. 1605 SHAKS. *Lear* V. i. 52 The Enemy's in view, draw vp your powers;..your hast Is now vrg'd on you. 1667 MILTON *P.L.* IX. 250 For solitude somtimes is best societie, And short retirement urges sweet returne. 1872 GEO. ELIOT *Middlem.* lxxxvi, A past error may urge a grand retrieval.

II. 3. To entreat or plead with (a person) pertinaciously; to importune, press, or ply with arguments or strong persuasion; to prompt, solicit, or request earnestly. Also, with impersonal subject: To incite or impel strongly.

1568 BIBLE (Bishops') *Luke* xi. 53 The lawyers and the pharisees began to vrge hym vehemently, and to prouoke hym to speake many thynges. 1586 DAY *Eng. Secretorie* II. (1625) 25 To vrge me as you doe, may but breed that which neither of vs may returne pleasing. 1595 SHAKS. *John* II. i. 475, I see a yeelding in the lookes of France;..vrge them while their soules Are capeable of this ambition. 1640 HABINGTON *Queen of Arragon* II. 366, I urg'd Them with the memory of their former deedes. 1667 MILTON *P.L.* IX. 588 Hunger and thirst at once,..quick'nd at the scent Of that alluring fruit, urg'd me so keene. 1692 DRYDEN *St. Euremont's Ess.* 24 Urged with an apprehension of their ruine, [they] abandoned themselves to the Conduct of Xantippus. 1717 POPE *Iliad* X. 135 Strong necessity our toils demands,..and urges all our hands. 1814 J. AUSTEN *Mansf. Park* xv, Do not urge her, madam... It is not fair to urge her in this manner. 1847 HELPS *Friends in C.* I. v. 83 Men..cannot be moved in masses as of old. At one time chivalry urged all men—then the Church. 1853 J. H. NEWMAN *Hist. Sk.* (1873) I. 183 The barbarian..moves when he is urged by appetite.

b. Const. *to* with inf.; also with advs. (as *on*, *onward*) and preps.

(*a*) 1565 COOPER *Thesaurus* s.v. *Insto*, Vrge me not, or presse me not to iudge. 1613 SHAKS. *Hen. VIII*, IV. ii. 157 Vrge the King To do me this last right. 1671 MILTON *Samson* 1677 A spirit of phrenzie..Who..urg'd them on with mad desire To call in hast for thir destroyer. 1753–4 RICHARDSON *Grandison* II. xxiii. 167 Should she engage without waiting for his consent; as she was urged to do, by Letters. 1816 SCOTT *Bl. Dwarf* xviii, His patriotism urged him to serve his country abroad. 1891 FARRAR *Darkn. & Dawn* xxix, Seneca..urged the Emperor to summon him into his presence.

(*b*) 1600 *1st Pt. Sir J. Oldcastle* IV. ii. 9 Pardon, my Lord; my conscience vrg'd me to it. 1776 PAINE *Com. Sense* 9 Hunger in the mean time would urge him from his work. 1791 COWPER *Iliad* V. 904 Venus..and the Archer..have urged, themselves, to this The frantic Mars. 1832 LYTTON *Eugene A.* I. v, They urge us onward, yet present no limit to our progress. 1846 MRS. A. MARSH *Father Darcy* II. iv. 98 He was not urging others to a course in which he never intended to venture himself. 1871 *Leisure Hour* 480/1 Two guineas paid to..his clerk, to urge him on with the works.

†**c.** To charge strongly *with* something. Also with *that* and clause. *Obs.*

1599 THYNNE *Animadv.* (1875) 54 Speakinge to his wyfe, he urgethe her that she cannott denye yt. 1628 SIR W. MURE *Spir. Hymne* 144 Thou of our innocence the ground, for vs, with guilt was vrgde. 1689 WOOD *Life* (O.H.S.) III. 310 Speed's daughter told the bishop of it and the bishop urg'd him with it. 1703 ROWE *Fair Penit.* V. i, Thou com'st to urge me with the wrongs I ha' done thee.

4. a. To serve or act as a constraining influence on (something); to bear pressingly on; to spur, actuate, or constrain.

1576 FLEMING *Panopl. Epist.* 62 More I may say to you, then any mans mynde is urged to accomplishe. 1592 KYD *Sp. Trag.* III. iv. 14 A guiltie conscience, vrged with the thought Of former euils, easily cannot erre. *Ibid.* IV. iv. 145 But loue of him..Did vrge her resolution to be such. 1633 BP. HALL *Hard Texts, O.T.* 620 Yee have extreamely urged the patience of the Lord. 1823 SCOTT *Quentin D.* ii, I..will pay fitting respect to your age, if you do not urge my patience with mockery. 1843 NEALE *Hymns for Sick* 23 Give me when those last trials urge Thy Very Flesh and Blood. 1878 *Masque Poets* 42, I was wrong to urge your will And wrong to mar your life.

†**b.** To treat (a mineral, etc.) with great heat.

1758 REID tr. *Macquer's Chym.* I. 69 If the calx of Tin be urged by a strong fire. 1828–32 WEBSTER s.v., To urge an ore with intense heat.

III. 5. To hasten or press forward (a proceeding, enterprise, etc.); to prosecute with effort, energy, or vigour; to push forward.

1565 COOPER *Thesaurus* s.v. *Insto, Instabit huic loco*,..He shall vrge this, or be earnest in this. 1583 STUBBES *Anat. Abus.* I. H 4, [It] bringeth death before nature vrge it,..or age require it. 1598 HAKLUYT *Voy.* I. 145 Swandepolcus..affirming that himselfe neuer prospered so long as he vrged warre against them. 1667 BOYLE *Orig. Formes & Qual.* 430 This Substance..will..(if the Distillation have been urg'd far enough) [be] brittle. 1684 EARL ROSCOM. *Ess. Transl. Verse* 238 Urge your Success, deserve a lasting Name. 1697 DRYDEN *Æneis* V. 273 The Crew of Mnestheus,..with elated Minds, Urge their Success. *Ibid.* VII. 660 While Turnus urges thus his Enterprise. 1713 ADDISON *Cato* III. v, Why wilt thou urge the fate Of wretched men? 1781 COWPER *Table-T.* 214 The peasants urge their harvest. 1789 E. DARWIN *Bot. Gard.* II. 79 When..wither'd Famine urged the work of death. 1855 PRESCOTT *Philip II*, I. viii. I. 239 Henry obstinately urged his fate, and compelled the count..to take the saddle. 1855 MACAULAY *Hist. Eng.* xii. III. 213 The bills which the Commons were urging forward. 1885 *Daily Tel.* 11 Sept. (Encycl. Dict.), Urging the carnage, and eyeing with pleasure all the horrors of war.

transf. 1857 RUSKIN *Pol. Econ. Art* 110 Every kind deed..in relieving distress..would..open and urge, in a thousand unforeseen directions, the sluices of commerce and the springs of industry.

6. To press forcibly in some direction; to force or impel forward or onward; to drive. Also with preps. or advs., as *against*, *away*, *down*, *through*.

1594 KYD *Cornelia* V. 188 Now we of our side vrge them to retreate, And nowe before them we retyre as fast. 1634 SIR T. HERBERT *Trav.* 87 The first walke is set with pipes of Lead and Brasse, through which the water is vrged. 1693 T. CREECH *Juvenal* XIII. 93 Rivers chang'd to Blood Roul wond'rous Waves, or urge a Milky Flood. 1742 POPE *Dunc.* IV. 592 From Stage to Stage the licens'd Earl may run,..The Senator at Cricket urge the Ball. 1791 COWPER *Iliad* V. 70 For Menelaus..the spear urged through his breast. 1813 BYRON *Corsair* III. xv, The blue waves sport around the stern they urge. 1827 FARADAY *Chem. Manip.* xvi. 395 The latter [*sc.* air] being urged away from the tube by a force proportionate [etc.]. 1862 CALVERLEY *Verses & Tr.* 16 Still I see you..Urge, towards the table's centre,..the squail.

transf. 1737 POPE *Imit. Hor., Ep.* II. ii. 253 Heir urges heir, like wave impelling wave. 1821 SHELLEY *Adonais* xxi, As long as skies are blue,..Evening must usher night, night urge the morrow.

fig. 1870 BRYANT *Iliad* II. I. 77 The fates Decreed their early death and urged them on.

b. To cause to move, hasten, or gather speed; to accelerate the pace of; to speed up. Usu. with advs. (as *forward*, *on*) or preps.

a 1721 PRIOR *Journey to Copt-Hall* 12, I mount, and..With unarm'd kick urge on my horse. 1760 FAWKES tr. *Anacreon, Ode* lix. 8 With tighten'd Rein, I'll urge thee round the dusty Plain. 1821 SHELLEY *Epithalamion* 20 Nay, return, Vesper! urge thy lazy car! 1846 MRS. A. MARSH *Father Darcy* II. xix. 317 Their wearied horses..gave evidence of the fierce desperation with which they had been urged forward. 1902 VIOLET JACOB *Sheep-Stealers* x, Coachmen were urging their horses up to the door.

refl. 1805 BINGLEY *Anim. Biog.* (ed. 2) II. 159 [Birds] urge themselves forward in the air by means of wings.

c. To press or pursue (one's flight, way, the chase); to hasten or accelerate (one's pace, etc.).

1697 DRYDEN *Virg. Georg.* III. 75 High Epidaurus urges on my speed, Fam'd for his hills, and for his horses' breed. 1703 POPE *Thebais* 558 Hapless Tydeus..Thro' the thick deserts headlong urg'd his flight. 1735 SOMERVILLE *Chase* III. 543 He..up the Breeze Urges his Course with eager Violence. *a* 1763 SHENSTONE *Elegies* xvi. 94 Led by their beams I urg'd the pleasing chase. 1801 M. G. LEWIS *Tales of Wonder, Sir Hengist* ii, Sir Hengist urged his courser's pace. 1804 W. L. BOWLES *Spir. Discov.* IV. 579 With De Quiros to the South Still urge thy way. 1840 THIRLWALL *Greece* VII. 61 He had several motives to urge his progress. 1854 H. MILLER *Sch. & Schm.* xvi. 340, I should have to urge my way through the works of our best writers.

7. a. To stimulate to expression or action; to provoke or excite; to increase or intensify.

1594 *1st Pt. Contention* (1843) 24 Forbeare ambitious Prelate to vrge my griefe. **1594** Kyd *Cornelia* I. 166 The wrath of heauen (though vrg'd) we see is slow In punishing the euils we haue done. **1616** W. Browne *Brit. Past.* II. iv. 516 Anger and pitty, in his manly brest, Urge, yet restraine his teares. **1800** tr. *Lagrange's Chem.* I. 401 Then urge the fire gradually, bring the crucible to a white heat. **1820** Shelley *Prometh. Unb.* I. 42 While from their loud abysses howling throng The genii of the storm, urging the rage Of whirlwind. **1839** Ure *Dict. Arts* 1124 The heat having been briskly urged for a short time. **1865** J. M. Neale *Hymns on Paradise* 28 All his spite my Tempter urges.

b. To provoke to anger; to irritate or annoy. Also with clause (quot. 1593). Now *dial.*

1593 Lodge *Will. Longbeard* E 3 This is it that urgeth me that I fall into his hands. **1655** [see urging *ppl. a.* 1 b]. **1876–** in dialect use (*Eng. Dial. Dict.* s.v. *Urge v.*¹ 2).

8. To ply vigorously; to use, work, or employ briskly or diligently.

1697 Dryden *Æneis* v. 301 Both urge their Oars. *a* **1760** I. H. Browne *Fireside Poems* (1768) 126, I urge the gay flask With a set of old friends. **1820** Shelley *Fragm. Satire on Sat.* 25 Follow his flight with winged words, and urge The strokes of the inexorable scourge.

IV. *intr.* **9.** To press by inquiry or statement; to adduce or bring forward arguments, allegations, etc. Also const. *to* with inf.

1592 *Soliman & Pers.* III. i. 73 Erastus, ile not yet vrge to know the cause That brought thee hether. **1613** Shaks. *Hen. VIII*, v. iii. 48, I doe beseech your Lordships, That..my Accusers..may stand forth face to face, And freely vrge against me. **1804** *Something Odd* I. 130 When she had no company at home, he would urge to go and seek it abroad. **1818** Shelley *Julian* 616, I urged and questioned still, she told me how All happened.

b. To press solicitously, make a strong claim, *for* something.

1607 Shaks. *Timon* III. ii. 13 One of his men..vrg'd extreamly for't [*sc.* money], and shewed what necessity belong'd too't. **1660** Sharrock *Vegetables* 67 Infinite storyes of strange conjunctions which urge earnestly for credit. **1726** Swift *Serm. Martyrd. K. Chas.* Wks. 1765 XV. 134 That wicked faction.., not content with all those marks of his justice.., urged still for more. **1753–4** Richardson *Grandison* II. ix. 60 He again urged for her hand, and for a private marriage. **1769** Goldsm. *Hist. Rome* I. 183 The tribunes..began once more to urge for the removal.

†**c.** To strive *for* (mastery). *Obs.*⁻¹

1691 tr. *Emilianne's Frauds Rom. Monks* (ed. 3) 302 His lovely Countenance, where the Lilly and the Rose did urge for Mastery.

10. To press, push, or hasten on. Esp. with advs., as *along*, *on*, *onward*, *upward*.

1605–8 Donne *To Sir H. Goodyere* 8 A Palace..decayes: But hee which dwels there, is not so; for hee Strives to urge upward, and his fortune raise. **1653** Milton *Psalm* vii. 21 Rise Jehovah in thine ire, Rouze thy self amidst the rage Of my foes that urge like fire. **1692** Prior *Ode, Imit. Horace* v. 31 Darius flies, young Ammon urges on. **1712** Steele *Spect.* No. 374 ⁋1 Those behind him, if he does not urge on, will tread him down. **1821** Clare *Vill. Minstr.* II. 27 Thou hast heard the thorn's in flower, And childhood's bliss is urging on. **1857** Susanna Winkworth tr. *Life Tauler* ix. 247 Through all this he shall urge onward, till [etc.]. **1907** *Westm. Gaz.* 19 Oct. 3/1 A woman.., moaning inarticulately, urges wearily along.

11. To act as an impelling or prompting motive, stimulus, or force; to incite or stimulate; to exercise pressure or constraint.

1645 Waller *Poems* 142 Let Brutes..that cannot thinke, So far as drought and Nature urges, drinke. **1656** Smith *Pract. Physick* 147 Since two things do urge, either Malignity or the Feaver; if that urge, most Antidotes are necessary. *a* **1660** *Contemp. Hist. Irel.* (Ir. Archæol. Soc.) I. 157 There-fore thriued your precept may vrge, but your example is not souldierlike. **1667** Milton *P.L.* I. 66 Hope never comes That comes to all; but torture without end Still urges. **1698** Fryer *Acc. E. India & P.* 172 The present Occasions urging, and [they] being willing to blind themselves. **1716** Pope *Iliad* VI. 453 The combat urges, and my soul's on fire. **1752** Hume *Pol. Disc.* viii. 138 Necessity calls, fear urges, reason exhorts. **1791** Cowper *Iliad* v. 848 The time Urges, and need appears that we ourselves Now call to mind the fury of our might. **1805–6** Cary *Dante's Inf.* IV. 21 Our length of way Urges to haste.

†**b.** To be of weight or importance. *Obs.*

1654 Z. Coke *Logick* 145 A Syllogism leading to absurdity, much urgeth in disputing.

Hence **urged** (ɜːdʒd) *ppl. a.*

1595 Daniel *Civ. Wars* IV. lxxxiv, Whilst looking onely on the vrged crime Vnto the farther drift they take no heed. *c* **1611** Chapman *Iliad* XVI. 264 Remember you express Your late-urged virtue. **1628** Feltham *Resolves* II. lxv. 186 Gifts are the greatest Vsurie; because a two-fold retribution is an vrged effect, that a Noble nature prompts vs to. **1786** Burns *On W. Chalmers* ii, I am nae stranger to..his warm-urged wishes. **1883** Duncan *Clin. Lect. Dis. Women* (ed. 2) ii. 8 And such urged passing [of uterine bougie] induces spasms.

urgence (ˈɜːdʒəns). [a. F. *urgence* (1572), or f. urgent *a.*: see -ence.]

1. Earnest or pressing solicitation; importunity; = urgency 2.

c **1592** Marlowe *Jew of Malta* Prol., This all that he intends, (And that too, at the vrgence of some friends). **1624** Heywood *Gunaik.* II. 100 His urgence overcame the silence of the Oracle. **1634** —— *Maidenh. well lost* I. C 2, At my vrgence He promis't you a parley. **1879** Howells *L. Arosstook* 166 She tried to remember at his urgence, something of her childhood. *Ibid.* 219 'Oh I give you the right,' he cried with passionate urgence. **1893** F. Adams *Egypt* 255 At the united urgence of France and England.., [he] resigned.

2. Urgent need; pressing necessity or importance; = urgency 1.

c **1605** Bodley in *Trecentale Bodleianum* (1913) 44 The Keeper may sometimes, vpon Vrgence of buisnesse,..desire a dispensation for his personal absence from his charge. **1610** Heywood *Gold. Age* IV. i, Urgence calls me hence To an enforced absence. **1639** Davenport *New Trick* I. i, His businesse craves dispatch, And is of serious urgence.

3. Quickness, expedition, haste.

1612 J. Cotta *Dang. Pract. Physic* I. viii. 60 Drunkennesse, whose ordinarily knowne effects are..in some imaginations..quicke and readie, in some with as apparent vrgence, yet senselesse. **1868** Geo. Eliot *Sp. Gipsy* 72 Late despatches sent With urgence by the Count of Bavien. **1869** Blackmore *Lorna D.* x, We found good reason for the urgence and melancholy of the duck-birds.

4. Impelling force; = urgency 5.

1874 S. Lanier *Poems, Corn* 13 Expirations strong Throb from young hickories..With stress and urgence bold of prisoned spring. **1876** Geo. Eliot *Dan. Der.* v. xxxvi, A shrinking finally overcome by the urgence of poverty. **1876** Dowden *Poems* 2 The lapsing waters tell The urgence uncontrollable Which makes the trouble of their breast.

urgency (ˈɜːdʒənsɪ). [f. next (see -ency), or ad. late L. *urgentia*. Cf. It. *urgenza*, Sp. and Pg. *urgencia*, and prec.]

I. 1. a. The state, condition, or fact of being urgent; pressing importance; imperativeness.

1540 *Act 32 Hen. VIII*, c. 48 §6 If the importaunce or urgency of the cause..so require. **1594** Hooker *Eccl. Pol.* I. viii. §8 Only in case of so great vrgency. **1624** *Impeachm. Dk. Buckhm.* (Camden) 129 Alleadgeing the urgency of the present service. **1686** tr. *Chardin's Trav. Persia* 63, I told him the Urgency of my Occasions. **1793** Jefferson *Writ.* (1859) IV. 96 The ascertaining of this point becomes a matter of present urgency. **1797** Mrs. Radcliffe *Italian* xi, The urgency of your circumstances. **1833** I. Taylor *Fanat.* i. 7 There are..motives..of far greater force, and these..have a peculiar urgency in reference to the present moment. **1866** Geo. Eliot *F. Holt* xxv, I will not wait for the urgency of necessity. **1877** Erichsen *Surg.* I. 13 The four cases of extreme surgical urgency.

b. *spec.* (See quot. 1884.)

1881 E. W. Hamilton *Diary* 14 Mar. (1972) I. 116 In consequence of these tactics on the part of the Tories, the Government of course failed this afternoon to get the necessary majority to vote urgency. **1883** May *Treat. Parlt.* (ed. 9) 383 By the aid of these rules of urgency, a serious political crisis had been overcome. **1884** *Imp. Dict.* IV. 529 In parliament, *urgency* is when, by a vote of three to one in a house of not less than 300 members, a measure is declared urgent in the interest of the state.

2. Pressure by importunity or entreaty; urgent solicitation; insistence.

1611 Cotgr., *Importunite*, importunitie, vrgencie, earnestnesse. **1735** Swift *Gulliver's Let. to Simpson* ⁋1 By your great and frequent urgency, you prevailed on me to [etc.]. **1782** Miss Burney *Cecilia* VII. iv, This confession..was torn from her by..[Delville's] impetuous urgency. **1828** Lytton *Pelham* III. x, In spite of all the urgency and entreaties of my letters for a reply. **1882** T. Mozley *Remin. Oriel College*, etc. I. Introd. 4 At his encouragement and urgency I stood for a Fellowship.

3. Stress *of* wind, weather, etc.

1660 Burney *Κέρδ. Δῶρον* (1661) 12 There was never any tender nightingale so preserved in the urgencie of the weather. **1859** W. M. Thomson *Land & Book* I. 66 Neither heavy weights.., nor the importunate urgency of the wind, can sway it [*sc.* a palm-tree] aside from perfect uprightness.

4. Persistence, eagerness. *rare*⁻¹.

a **1677** Barrow *Serm.* xvi. Wks. 1686 III. 184 And why with less expedition or urgency should we persue the certain means of our present security?

5. Impelling or prompting force or quality.

1816 Scott *Antiq.* xxxvi, What she has told you..from no apparent impulse but the urgency of conscience. **1858** J. Martineau *Stud. Chr.* 281 The urgency of desire and devotion. **1863** Geo. Eliot *Romola* II. xxx, The new urgency of this habitual thought brought a new suggestion.

II. 6. An urgent need or situation.

1647 May *Hist. Parl.* II. i. 11 Collections through the Kingdom being too slow for such an urgency. **1695** Locke *Further Consid. Value Money* 58 The accidental difference ..is sometimes (but rarely) two pence in five shillings, or somewhat more in great urgencies. **1820** Keats *Isabella* xxix, With sudden speed,..Because of some great urgency and need In their affairs. **1832** *Rolls of Parlt.* Index 467/2 Agrees to respite the Levy..for Two Years,..unless any Urgency should arise.

7. A driving or constraining impulse or motive.

1664 H. More *Myst. Iniq.* xx. 76 Pinched betwixt the sense of poverty and quick urgencies of Devotion. **1822** Good *Study Med.* I. 343 The patient..will still perhaps be tormented with..a perpetual urgency to expulsion. *c* **1830** Chalmers *Lect. Romans* lxix. (1840) 346 Evil might ensue from unbridled and unreasonable urgencies of talk upon this subject. **1883** D. C. Murray *Hearts* viii, A superstitious reverence for his guest's genius, and its various urgencies.

8. *pl.* Earnest representations or entreaties; importunities.

1823 Jefferson *Writ.* (1830) IV. 376 We..met, and after the urgencies of each on the other, I consented to undertake the task. **1877** 'H. A. Page' *De Quincey* xvii. II. 40 Books.. to be returned, in answer to the urgencies of librarians. **1883** Miss Broughton *Belinda* III. v, Belinda,..despite the warm urgencies of the..strangers, retires in favour of her visitors.

III. 9. *attrib.*, as ***urgency order***, ***pledge***, ***rate***, etc.

1881 E. W. Hamilton *Diary* 14 Mar. (1972) I. 116 Another piece of news which took one by surprise was Sir S. Northcote's manifesto deprecating resort to the urgency rules of which Mr. Gladstone had given notice for supply this evening. **1883** May *Treat. Parlt.* (ed. 9) 383 It became necessary to revive the urgency resolution of the 3rd February 1881. **1890** *Lunacy Act* §11 In cases of urgency where it is expedient..that the alleged lunatic should be forthwith placed under care and treatment, he may be received and detained..upon an urgency order. **1891** *Pall Mall G.* 7 April 5/2 It is said Mrs. Cathcart is confined under an urgency order. **1898** Morley in *Daily News* 14 Feb. 3/7 The Press agencies..paid what is called an urgency rate—that is about, I think, twenty or thirty times higher than the ordinary Press rate. **1906** R. Whiteing *Ring in the New* 47 Taking in urgency pledges after the closing of the pawn-shops.

urgent (ˈɜːdʒənt), *a.* [a. F. *urgent* (14th c.), a. L. *urgent-*, *urgens*, pres. pple. of *urgēre* to urge. Cf. It., Sp., Pg. *urgente*.]

I. 1. Pressing, impelling; demanding or calling for prompt action; marked or characterized by urgency. (Freq. from *c* 1800.)

In earliest use with *cause* or *necessity*.

1496 *Rolls of Parlt.* VI. 515/1 Towarde the.. mayntenaunce of the Armye aforsaid, and urgent causes concernyng the same. **1526** *Pilgr. Perf.* (W. de W. 1531) 162 b, But onely whan cause vrgent, & very necessite compelleth. **1558** Bp. Watson *Sev. Sacram.* xix. 119 Where the Sacrament is excluded by vrgent necessitye. *a* **1586** Sidney *Arcadia* III. iv, The more I stirre about urgent affaires. **1604** Thornborough *Discovrse* (title-p.), The euident vtilitie and vrgent necessitie of the desired happie Vnion. **1660** Milton *Free Commw.* Wks. 1851 V. 451 To the retarding..oft times of thir Counsels or urgentest occasions. **1676–7** Marvell *Corr.* Wks. (Grosart) II. 521 The true remedy of the urgent condition of this poore Nation. **1712** Swift *Jrnl. to Stella* 25 Feb., I have no urgent business upon my hands. **1755** Young *Centaur* vi. Wks. 1757 IV. 282 With only this additional, and still more urgent,..motive for reformation. **1772** W. Buchan *Dom. Med.* (ed. 2) 278 Unless these symptoms are urgent, it is safer to let it alone. **1816** J. Scott *Paris Revisit.* (ed. 3) 117 They were soon forced to separate to attend to their respective urgent duties. **1843** R. J. Graves *Syst. Clin. Med.* xx. 239 What may be done by simple means in relieving an urgent disease. **1866** Rogers *Agric. & Prices* I. xxi. 528 The necessity not being so urgent as it is now.

b. Of commands, messages, etc., by which a matter is strongly pressed upon a person's attention.

1611 Bible *Dan.* iii. 22 The Kings commandement was vrgent. **1779** *Mirror* No. 32, The remonstrances of his man of business, aided by very urgent requests from me. **1816** Bentham *Chrestom.* 262 Other objects, for the illustration of which the demand..is accordingly still more urgent. **1856** Stanley *Sinai & Pal.* iv. 205 This summons was as urgent as words can describe. **1883** O. W. Holmes *Pages fr. Old Vol. Life* 63 A second telegraphic message..so direct and urgent that I should be sure of an answer to it. **1886** Baring-Gould *Court Royal* xxxviii, 'Papa,' said Lady Grace in urgent tones.

2. Of a feeling, etc.: That constrains, impels, or prompts. Also const. *of*.

1559 *Reg. St. Andrews Kirk Session* (S.H.S.) I. 18 Giue thei be vexed and urnet with ustioun and urgent appetites of the flesche. **1566** Drant *Hor., Sat.* II. i. E vij b, Yf I haue suche vrgent luste, and lykyng to indite. **1641** Milton *Ch. Govt.* I. vii, The miseries of Ireland are urgent of a speedy redress. **1748** G. White *Serm.* (MS.), If people will not follow nature in her most urgent affections, and importunate Requests. **1873** Morley *Rousseau* (1905) II. 34 When men are beginning to feel the urgent spirit of a new time.

3. Of persons: Pressingly solicitous; importunate, insistent. Also with preps., as *for*, *in*, *on*, †*unto*.

1548 Elyot, *Premo,..premere*,..to be vrgent or instante vpon. **1565** Cooper *Thesaurus* s.v. *Premo*, I was not more vrgent or instant on any pointe, then, &c. *a* **1593** Marlowe & Nashe *Dido* III. i, All these..Haue been most vrgent suiters for my loue. **1611** Bible *Exod.* xii. 33 The Egyptians were vrgent vpon the people that they might send them out of the land in haste. **1698** Collier *Immor. Stage* 107 Oedipus is..Urgent for an account of Particulars. **1732** Lediard *Sethos* II. x. 355 The officers of his fleet were urgent in offering their services. **1778** Miss Burney *Evelina* ii, The advice and entreaties of all his friends, among whom I was myself the most urgent. **1820** W. Irving *Sketch Bk.* II. 149 His family have been very urgent for him to make an expedition to Margate. **1883** *Law Times* 20 Oct. 408/1 The public and the Profession were alike urgent in calling for sweeping reforms.

b. Eagerly desirous *to* do something.

1753–4 Richardson *Grandison* II. xxviii. 227, I never knew him to be so very urgent to know my heart. **1798** S. & Ht. Lee *Canterb. T.* II. 181 [It] made him..urgent to set out for England. **1826** Galt *Last of Lairds* xxxiv. 302 Mr. Loopy..had been calling, urgent to see me. **1846** Mrs. A. Marsh *Father Darcy* II. 243 He is very urgent to see him.

II. 4. Impelling, pressing, or bearing onwards.

1546 *Yorks. Chantry Surv.* (Surtees) 209 When as the waters of Rothere and Downe are so urgent, that the curate of Rotherham cannot to them repayre. **1876** R. Bridges *Growth of Love* v, Her launched passion when she sings Wins on the hearing like a shapen prow Borne by the mastery of its urgent wings. **1879** —— *A Passer-by* i, Whither, O splendid ship, thy white sails crowding, Leaning across the bosom of the urgent West.

†**5.** Oppressive; severe; heavy. *Obs.*

1545 Brinklow *Compl.* ii. 10 b, An vrgent dammage to the common welth. **1600** Hakluyt *Voy.* III. 49 During the two houres of those two dayes the heat is very vrgent. **1606** Shaks. *Ant. & Cl.* I. ii. 187 Not alone The death of Fuluia, with more vrgent touches, Do strongly speake to vs. *a* **1699** J. Beaumont *Psyche* III. 147 Which Jesus seeing, He upon him threw The urgent yoak of an express Injunction.

†**6.** Of time: Pressing; passing quickly. *Obs.*

1611 Shaks. *Wint. T.* I. ii. 465 Please your Highnesse To take the vrgent houre. **1791** Cowper *Iliad* I. 74 But time is urgent; haste we to consult Priest, prophet, or interpreter of dreams.

Hence ˈ**urgentness**, urgency. *rare*.

1598 BARRET *Theor. Warres* II. i. 25 The vrgentnesse of the cause doeth deepely require it. **1727** BAILEY (vol. II), *Pressingness*, Urgentness.

'urgently, *adv.* [-LY[2].] In an urgent manner.
1548 UDALL, etc. *Erasm. Par. John* xix. 108 b, Therfore the Jewes called more vrgentely vpon the matter. **1611** COTGR., *Importunément*, importunately, vrgently, earnestly. **1789** in C. F. Jenkins *Tortola* (1923) 90, I thank thee for thy kind advice thou hast so urgently given me. **1840** THIRLWALL *Greece* VII. 303 His attention..was urgently claimed by the danger which now threatened him. **1871** A. MEADOWS *Man. Midwifery* iii. (ed. 2) 361 Prompt action is urgently necessary.

urger ('ɜːdʒə(r)). [f. URGE *v.* + -ER[1].]
1. a. One who urges or incites. Also with *on.*
1598 FLORIO, *Scongiuratore*, a conspirer, a coniurer, an vrger. **1605** W. BRADSHAW *Eng. Puritanism* v. 29 They hould that such an ooth (on the vrgers part) is most damnable. **1659** F. OSBORN *Misc. Ess.*, etc. 149, I confesse Necessity cannot onely abate the Edge of these Reasons; but turne their Poynts against the Urger. **1704** D'URFEY *Heir Adopted* lxx, 'Twas past all Bounds before, And needed not an urger on. **1753** RICHARDSON *Grandison* (1781) II. xxix. 276 If the urger suspects not the fitness of his addresses. **1837** B. D. WALSH *Aristoph., Knights* IV. i, The urgers-on of nimble steeds. **1892** *Temple Bar Mag.* Dec. 496 Scott..was the tempter and urger in a ruinous policy. **1903** T. HARDY *Dynasts* I. VI. iii, The Eternal Urger, pressing change on change.
b. A man who obtains money illegally or discreditably, esp. as a tipster at a racecourse. *Austral. slang.*
1919 V. MARSHALL *World of Living Dead* 69 The truly light-fingered gentry, the racecourse urger (tip slinger), the magsman..never hesitate to express their contempt for the more roughly inclined of the profession. **1934** *Bulletin* (Sydney) 21 Mar. 40/3 He was a tout or an urger, I gathered. 'Mixed up in racecourses,' was the way she put it. **1960** A. KIMMINS *Lugs O'Leary* v. 74 'An urger,' explained Lugs patiently, 'is a man who looks around for suckers like you and tips each one a different horse. Someone's *got* to win.'
2. An instigator or advocate, an earnest supporter or presenter, *of* something. Now *rare.*
In frequent use *c* 1620–*c* 1670.
1575 *Brieff Disc. Troub. Franckford* 215 From whose.. pennes, the vrgers of theis [letters] receiued first the light off the gospell. **1632** LE GRYS tr. *Velleius Paterc.* 39 Marcus Cato, the perpetuall urger of the destruction thereof. **1640** in Rushw. *Hist. Coll.* (1692) I. 114 The Author and Urger of some Particular Changes. **1678** CUDWORTH *Intell. Syst.* 209 The Urgers of the forementioned Objection. **1847** COVENTRY DICK in Brown *Horæ Subs.* (1882) 406 Nought detains the urger of these pleas, But dinners.

'urging, *vbl. sb.* [f. as prec. + -ING[1].] The action of the verb; an instance of this.
1590 SHAKS. *Com. Err.* v. i. 359 Her vrging of her wracke at sea. **1615** HIERON *Wks.* I. 606 It is by such vrgings as this, which..it pleaseth Him to make effectuall. **1651** HOBBES *Leviath.* II. xxv. 133 [It] is manifest enough, by the long and vehement urging. **1721** BAILEY, *Importunity*, an eager pressing or urging. **1838** LYTTON *Alice* x. iv, After repeated conferences and urgings. **1876** GEO. ELIOT *Dan. Der.* xlv, A painful urging of something vague and difficult. **1897** RHOSCOMYL *White Rose Arno* 82 One whose vigorous urgings to immediate action had [etc.].

'urging, *ppl. a.* [f. as prec. + -ING[2].]
1. That serves as a motive or impelling cause; that constrains, or actuates; inciting, spurring, stimulating, strongly prompting; compelling.
1612 SELDEN *Illustr. Drayton's Poly-olb.* VI. 106 If it be the same with *Lyra*, as some think, although urging reason and authority are to the contrary. **1668** OWEN *Indwell. Sin* ii. 16 It is..an inbred, working, impelling, urging Law. **1678** DRYDEN *Limberham* I. i, How stand thy Affections to her, thou lusty Rogue? *Wood.* All o'fire: A most urging Creature! **1723** *Pres. St. Russia* II. 273 Causes..weighty and urging enough for Russia to begin a War. **1728** SWIFT *Let. to Abp. of Dublin* ¶ 22 We shall..sacrifice all honesty to the present urging advantage. **1802** WOLCOT (P. Pindar) *Isl. Innocence* 63 The sportive fry,..leaping oft as urging hunger calls, Meet the dropp'd crumb. **1870** TYNDALL *Fragm. Sci.* (1871) 322 It is a useful urging force.
b. *dial.* Of words: Taunting, irritating.
1655 *N. Riding Rec.* (1887) V. 191 A Sumersides yeoman [tried] for giving scandallous, urginge and provoking words.
c. Strongly operative or active.
1658 SIR T. BROWNE *Hydriot.* iii. 43 How slender a masse will remain upon an open and urging Fire of the carnall composition.
†**2.** Characterized by urgency; urgent. *Obs.*
1647 COTTERELL *Davila's Hist. Fr.* I. 49 It would be very easie, this urging necessity once past, to moderate..the.. power of the Duke of Guise. **1683** HOWE *Union among Prot.* Wks. 1863 IV. 261 The case was at that time urging and important. **1683** KENNETT *Erasm. on Folly* 150 If at any time some urging occasions require them to become entangled in secular affairs.
Hence **'urgingly** *adv.*
c **1882** 'MARK TWAIN' *Speeches* (1923) 104, I say it beseechingly, urgingly. **1893** *Temple Bar* XCVII. 524 She instinctively and urgingly clapped her hands to a faster tune.

Ur'gonian, *a. Geol.* [ad. F. *Urgonien* (D'Orbigny, 1852), f. *Orgon* (see def.).] Forming or belonging to a series of massive limestones of the Lower Cretaceous system as developed at Orgon in the Durance valley.
1856 *Quart. Jrnl. Geol. Soc.* XII. 69 M. d'Orbigny's Urgonian series, or upper division of the Neocomian group. **1888** DAWSON *Geol. Hist. Plants* 282 These beds are regarded as Lower Cretaceous (Urgonian).

‖**Urheimat** ('uːrhaimat). [Ger., f. *ur-* UR- + *heimat* home, homeland.] The place of origin of a people or of a language.
1934 PRIEBSCH & COLLINSON *German Lang.* i. 17 The 'cradle' or primeval home (*Urheimat*) of the Indo-Europeans and their physical characteristics are still matters of controversy. **1950** J. R. FIRTH *Papers in Linguistics 1934–51* (1957) xiv. 178 The more romantic theorists who enjoy Indo-European fantasies and from *Ursprache* go on to speculate on the *Urvolk* and the *Urheimat.* **1976** D. R. SNOW in W. Cowan *Papers 7th Algonquian Conf.* 339 (*heading*) Archaeological implications of the Proto-Algonquian Urheimat.

-uria ('jʊərɪə), a second element in Latin form (cf. DYSURIA, ISCHURIA), derived from Gr. -ουρία, employed in various pathological terms denoting morbid conditions of the urine, as *albuminuria, glycosuria, hæmatinuria, hæmaturia, hæmoglobinuria, oxaluria, planuria, polyuria, pyuria.*

Uriah Heep (jʊ'raɪə hiːp). The name of a character in Dickens's *David Copperfield* (1850) used allusively for a man who is hypocritically humble. Also *attrib.* Hence **Uriah Heepish** *a.*, reminiscent of Uriah Heep.
1876 [see ANANIAS]. **1915** J. WEBSTER *Dear Enemy* 77 The Uriah Heepish attitude toward trustees that characterized Mrs. Lippett's manners. **1947** I. BROWN *Say the Word* 106 Uriah Heepish creatures. **1974** *Listener* 4 Apr. 438/1 'If I may—' often issues from the lips of the Uriah Heeps. **1976** A. J. RUSSELL *Pair Hemlock* v. 57 A Uriah Heep kind of guy named Logan.

urial ('ʊərɪəl). Also oorial. [a. Punjabi *ūrial.*] A wild sheep, a subspecies of *Ovis orientalis*, having a reddish coat and long, curved horns, found in northern India and other parts of central Asia.
1860 P. L. SCLATER in *Proc. Zool. Soc.* XXVIII. 127 The Koch, or Oorial of the Sulimani Range, has already been well described. **1887** *Athenæum* 31 Dec. 897/3 The Secretary..exhibited..a pair of horns of the oorial. **1898** *Contemp. Rev.* Dec. 878 Oorial and snow leopards abound on the mountains. **1898** R. LYDEKKER *Wild Oxen* 172 The urial, as this sheep is termed in the Salt Range and other districts of the Punjab, is not entitled to specific separation from the sha of Astor and Ladak. **1912** R. LYDEKKER *Sheep & its Cousins* xiii. 263 The range of the urial is very wide. **1928** V. G. CHILDE *Most Anc. East* ix. 201 The foot-hills to the north and west are still the haunts of wild urial sheep. **1950** T. LONGSTAFF *This my Voyage* ix. 180 We were astonished to see a herd of urial. **1969** J. FISHER et al. *Red Bk.* 168/1 The group of sheep known as Asiatic mouflon, red sheep, and urial are all forms of *Ovis orientalis.* **1977** G. B. SCHALLER *Mountain Monarchs* ix. 227 Urial ewes, as well as urial lambs, differed from the others in being almost passive.

uric ('jʊərɪk), *a. Chem.* Also 8–9 ouric. [a. F. *urique*, f. *ur-ine* URINE *sb.*[1]: see -IC 1 b.]
1. ***uric oxide***: (see quot. 1860).
1797 PEARSON in *Phil. Trans.* LXXXVIII. 37 It will be necessary to give a name to this urinary animal oxide... I trust that philological critics will find the name ouric or uric oxide perfectly appropriate. **1803** FESSENDEN *Poet. Petition* 12 Such a man..May view this uric oxyd's basis, And tell exactly what the case is. **1844** *Lancet* 19 Oct. 129/1 It is clear that uric oxide differs from uric acid simply in containing two atoms less of oxygen. **1860** MAYNE *Expos. Lex.* 1314 *Uric Oxide*...a substance constituting a very rare ingredient in vesical calculi, and otherwise termed urous oxide, and xanthic oxide.
2. ***uric acid***, a crystallizable acid, $C_5H_4N_4O_3$, found in the urine of man, certain animals, reptiles, and birds, being produced in the metabolism of nitrogenous bodies, and excreted by the kidneys.
1800 tr. *Lagrange's Chem.* II. 404 To separate the uric acid from the latter salts. **1803**- [see LITHIC *a.* 1]. **1826** HENRY *Elem. Chem.* II. 467 It is in those organs..that a new acid, the uric, is generated. **1872** HUXLEY *Physiol.* v. 106 Urea and uric acid are both composed of the elements carbon, hydrogen, oxygen, and nitrogen.
ellipt. (and *attrib.*). **1822** GOOD *Study Med.* IV. 508 The uric calculi..are of a yellowish or reddish-brown colour. **1846** G. E. DAY tr. *Simon's Anim. Chem.* II. 460 One minute calculus passed at the same time with others of pure uric, had a nucleus of oxalate of lime.
b. *attrib.* and *Comb.*, as ***uric acid calculus, diathesis, -excreting, excretion, gravel***, etc.
1819 *Rees' Cycl.* XXXVII. 3 X/2 Lithic or Uric Acid Calculus. **1843** *Penny Cycl.* XXVI. 52/1 Uric Acid Crystals. **1845** *Encycl. Metrop.* VII. 552 A gouty or rheumatic state of the constitution, or uric acid diathesis. **1864** GARROD *Mat. Med.* (ed. 2) 108 In cases of uric acid gravel. **1866** ODLING *Anim. Chem.* 128 The uric acid group of compounds. **1880** *Encycl. Brit.* XI. 7/2 The uric-acid-excreting function of the kidneys.
c. uric-acidæmia, = URICÆMIA; **uric-acidity**, the condition of containing an excess of uric acid.
1893 *Brit. Med. Jrnl.* Suppl. 26 Aug. 33 Nervous conditions depending upon *uric acidæmia. **1897** *Lancet* 15 May 1338/2 Symptoms..which would seem to depend upon uricacidæmia. **1893** A. S. ECCLES *Sciatica* 30 The *uric-acidity of the blood and tissues.

uricæmia (jʊərɪ'siːmɪə). *Path.* Also urichæmia. [mod.L., f. *uric-us* URIC *a.* + Gr. αἷμ-α blood.] = LITHÆMIA.
1867 A. FLINT *Princ. Med.* 84 An excess of uric acid (in the form of urates) in the blood constituting a condition differing from uræmia; it is desirable to distinguish it by a name... I would propose *uricæmia.* **1900** *Lancet* 25 Aug. 572/1 The relation of urichæmia to the different symptoms of the malady.
Hence **uri'cæmic** *a.*, = LITHÆMIC *a.*
1900 *Lancet* 25 Aug. 571/2 These urichæmic states in no degree determine gout, renal function being adequate.

uricase ('jʊərɪkeɪz). *Biochem.* [a. F. *uricase* (Battelli & Stern 1909, in *Compt. Rend. des Séances & Mem. de la Soc. de Biol.* LXVI. 412): see URIC *a.* and -ASE.] An enzyme which promotes the conversion of uric acid into allantoin and is found in certain insects and most mammals other than primates.
1910 *Jrnl. Biol. Chem.* VII. 172 If we limit the use of this term..to the oxidizing enzyme which produces allantoin and CO_2 from uric acid, and appreciate there may possibly exist other enzymes which destroy uric acid.., we find that either the kidney or the liver of every animal investigated, except man..possesses uricase. **1934** *Times Lit. Suppl.* 19 Apr. 286/1 The preparation of soluble uricase from ox kidney. **1956** *Nature* 31 Mar. 622/2 It was also possible to demonstrate the presence of the uricase enzyme in those fungi. **1977** D. E. METZLER *Biochem.* xiv. 883/2 Injection of the uric acid-hydrolyzing enzyme uricase has been tested experimentally.

Uriconian (jʊərɪ'kəʊnɪən), *a. Geol.* [f. *Uriconi-um*, name of Roman town at Wroxeter, + -AN.] Consisting of, pertaining to, a series of volcanic rocks such as constitute the Wrekin in Shropshire.
1886 C. CALLAWAY in *Q. Jrnl. Geol. Soc.* XLII. 481 In the Uriconian series itself I had found conglomerates full of rounded pieces of granitoid and gneissic rocks. *Ibid.* 483 The Charlton conglomerates are of Uriconian age. **1893** GEIKIE *Text Bk. Geol.* (ed. 3) 710 The Uriconian volcanic group..is probably pre-Cambrian.

uricosuric (ˌjʊərɪkəʊ'sʊərɪk), *a. Med.* [f. URIC *a.* + -O + -*s*- + URIC *a.*] Causing or characterized by an increased excretion of uric acid or urate in the urine.
1948 *Amer. Jrnl. Med.* IV. 774/1 This effect is similar to that produced by other drugs..all of which produce a simultaneous increase in minute excretion of urate and a decrease in plasma urate concentration. This pattern of pharmacologic actions has been termed the 'uricosuric effect'. **1961** *Lancet* 19 Aug. 430/2 All phosphate levels were estimated before starting, or at least one month after finishing, uricosuric therapy. **1974** M. C. GERALD *Pharmacol.* xiv. 269 High doses of aspirin, about 5 g, have a uricosuric action. **1980** *Brit. Med. Jrnl.* 17 May 1212 An orally active diuretic with uricosuric properties.

uricotelic (ˌjʊərɪkəʊ'tɛlɪk), *a. Biochem.* [ad. It. *uricotelico* (A. Clementi 1916, in *Atti della R. Accad. dei Lincei: Rendiconti* XXV. I. 366), f. *urico* URIC *a.* + Gr. τελικός final.] Of an animal or its metabolism: producing nitrogenous waste chiefly in the form of uric acid or urates, as in certain insects, birds, and reptiles, rather than urea.
1924 *Proc. R. Soc.* B. XCVII. 227 Clementi enunciated the doctrine that arginase is present in the livers of all those animals which have what he calls a 'ureotelic' metabolism —a metabolism, that is, in which urea is the final product of protein degradation—and absent from the livers of those in which protein metabolism is 'uricotelic'—ending in uric acid. **1934** *Biochem. Jrnl.* XXVIII. 1390 The uricotelic character of the metabolism of this gastropod is supported by new *in vitro* experiments. **1954** *New Biol.* XVII. 45 The uricotelic nitrogen metabolism of insects..is economical of water since uric acid can be excreted without much water loss. **1979** *Jrnl. Compar. Physiol.* CXXXIII. 211/2 Xeric adapted arboreal frogs of at least two genera..excrete nitrogen predominantly in the form of urate (uric acid), in proportions and amounts similar to uricotelic reptiles.

'uride. *Chem.* [f. UR-IC *a.* + -IDE.] A compound of uric acid with another element, or with a radical. Also *attrib.*
1887 A. M. BROWN *Anim. Alkaloids* 68 A body apparently of the uride family. *Ibid.* 90 He had obtained from normal urines a uride, allantoine.

uridine ('jʊərɪdiːn). *Biochem.* [ad. G. *uridin* (Levene & Jacobs 1910, in *Ber. d. Deut. Chem. Ges.* XLIII. 3152), f. *ur-acil* URACIL: see -IDINE.] A pyrimidine nucleoside, $C_5H_9O_4{\cdot}C_4H_3N_2O_2$, in which the base is uracil and the sugar ribose, and which is a constituent of RNA and various intermediates in cell metabolism.
1911 *Jrnl. Chem. Soc.* C. I. 96 Nitrous acid effects the quantitative elimination of the amino-group from cytidine, and uridine is obtained. **1946** [see NUCLEOSIDE]. **1970** R. W. MCGILVERY *Biochemistry* xx. 477 Uridine triphosphate can be used for nucleic acid synthesis or in the formation of metabolic intermediates such as uridine diphosphate glucose. **1976** *Sci. Amer.* Feb. 33/2 RNA..differs from DNA in that all the thymidine units are replaced by uridine.

uri'drosis. *Path.* [mod.L., f. Gr. οὖρ-ον URINE *sb.*[1] + ἱδρόω I sweat: see -OSIS.] A morbid excretion of certain urinary constituents in the perspiration; urinous sweating.
1857 DUNGLISON *Med. Dict.* 947. **1860** MAYNE s.v. **1899** *Allbutt's Syst. Med.* VIII. 736 Uridrosis. A minute amount of urea is normally present in sweat.

uridylic (jʊərɪ'dɪlɪk), *a. Biochem.* [f. URIDINE + -YL + -IC.] ***uridylic acid***: the phosphoric acid ester, $C_5H_8O_3(PH_2O_4)\cdot C_4H_3N_2O_2$, of uridine, one of the four nucleotides present in RNA.

1933 *Jrnl. Biol. Chem.* CI. 529 Cytidine is readily transformed into uridine, having properties identical with those of the uridylic acid. **1946** [see NUCLEOSIDE]. **1975** *Sci. Amer.* May 25/2 There are four kinds of nucleotide, named for their bases: adenylic acid, uridylic acid, guanylic acid and cytidylic acid, better known as *A*, *U*, *G* and *C*.

-urient ('jʊərɪənt), *suffix*, ad. L. -*ūrient*-, pres. pple. stem of desiderative verbs, occurring first in a few direct adoptions from L., as *parturient* (1592), †*micturient* (1654), *esurient* (*a* 1672), and hence occas. added to L. stems to form adjs. with the meaning 'desiring, characterized by a desire, (to do something)', as in †*novaturient* (1679), *nupturient*, †*vomiturient* (1666).

1878 *Eagle Mag.* (St. John's Coll. Camb.) X. 81 The vapid concourse of dangling men and nupturient maids.

‖**urim** ('jʊərɪm). [a. Heb. *ūrīm*, pl. intens., referred to *ōr* 'light', pl. *ōrīm*, and by some taken as = lights, φωτισμοί 'illuminations' (Symmachus).]

1. Certain objects, the nature of which is not known, worn in or upon the 'breast-plate' of the Jewish high-priest, by means of which the will of Jehovah was held to be declared.

Used chiefly in the collocation *Urim and Thummim* (once *Thummim and Urim*), occurring five times in the O.T. In the earlier English versions rendered after the Vulgate *doctrina et veritas* (from the LXX δήλωσις καὶ ἀλήθεια), whence Wyclif 'doctryne [l.v. techyng] and trewthe'; Coverdale has 'light and perfectnesse', following Luther's *licht und recht*, but in the 'Great' Bible of 1539 and in later versions the words are left untranslated.

(*a*) **1537** BIBLE (Matthew's) *Num.* xxvii. 21 Eleazar yᵉ preast..shal aske councell for him after the iudgement of Urim before the Lorde. *Ibid. 1 Sam.* xxviii. 6 Nether by dreame nor by Urim nor yet by prophetes. **1598** SYLVESTER *Du Bartas* II. ii. *Babylon* 400 That never Vrim, Dream, or Vision sung Their Oracles, but all in Isaak's tongue. **1641** MILTON *Ch. Govt.* I. v, The Priests..had the Oracle of Urim to consult with. **1659** J. HARRINGTON *Lawgiving* II. ii. 38 When God was enquired of by Urim, he gave his Oracle by the shining of certain stones or jewels in the breastplate of the high priest. **1737** WHISTON *Josephus, Antiq.* III. viii. §9 *note*, The very last instance of any thing like the prophetic Urim among the Jewish nation.

(*b*) **1537** BIBLE (Matthew's) *Exod.* xxviii. 30 Thou shalt put in the brestlappe of iudgement vrim and Thumin. **1560** BIBLE (Genev.) *Deut.* xxxiii. 8 Let thy Thummim and thine Vrim be wᵗ thine holy one. **1595** W. CLERKE *Polimanteia* I 4, Concerning the reuelation done by Vrim and Thummim. **1613** PURCHAS *Pilgrimage* (1614) 198 Lord, doe it for [Aaron] the Priest, with Vrim and Thummim. **1671** MILTON *P.R.* III. 14 Thy Counsel would be as the Oracle Urim and Thummim, those oraculous gems On Aaron's breast. *a* **1763** SHENSTONE *Ess. Men & Mann.* Wks. 1768 II. 229 An illiterate stupid preacher discoursing upon Urim and Thummim, and beating the pulpit cushion. **1768–74** TUCKER *Lt. Nat.* (1834) II. 343 In the course of the Levitical law,..answers by urim and thummim..gradually ceased. **1874** GEO. ELIOT *Coll. Breakf.-P.* 144 An oracular gem in price beyond Urim and Thummim lost to Israel. **1877** C. GEIKIE *Christ* I. 393 'The..prophet', who should bring back the lost Urim and Thummim.

b. *transf.* and *fig.*

1618 BP. HALL *Contempl., N.T.* I. i. How little were the Jews better for this, when they had lost the Urim and Thummim, sincerity of doctrine and manners! *a* **1652** J. SMITH *Sel. Disc.* v. 134 Whenever we look upon our own soul.., we shall find an Urim and Thummim there, by which we may ask counsel of God himself. *a* **1670** HACKET *Abp. Williams* I. (1693) 164 Conscience and Honour, the Urim and Thummim, with which the Noblest..should consult in all things. **1760–72** H. BROOKE *Fool of Qual.* (1792) III. 19 Every mechanic professed, like Aaron, to carry a Urim and Thummim about him. **1825** J. NEAL *Bro. Jonathan* II. 193 He stood and spoke..like one to whom old age is..the sign of wisdom and power—the urim and thumim of survivorship. **1851** KINGSLEY *Yeast* x, The heart ..enshrines the priceless pearl of womanhood,..the 'Urim and Thummim', before which gross man can only inquire and adore. *a* **1886** W. B. ROBERTSON *Dream Foolish Virgin* (1898) 17 And stars repeat it.., The Urim and the Thummim on the breastplate of the night.

2. *Mormon Ch.* (See quots.)

1843 H. CASWALL *Proph. of 19th Cent.* v. 77 The mystic Urim and Thummim, which appeared in the form of two transparent stones, set in the rim of a bow, like a pair of spectacles, and fastened to a golden breastplate. **1864** *Chambers's Encycl.* VI. 569/2 Along with the records was found a curious instrument, called by Smith 'Urim and Thummin'... By means of these stone spectacles [etc.].

'urinable, *a. rare*⁻¹. [f. URINE *v.* + -ABLE.] Capable of being excreted in the urine.

c **1900** *Buck's Handbk. Med. Sci.* III. 543 (*Cent. Suppl.*).

uri'næmia. *U.S. Path.* Also -emia. [mod.L.: see URINE *sb.* and cf. URÆMIA.] A morbid condition due to retention in the blood of certain constituents normally eliminated in the urine.

1860 R. FOWLER *Med. Voc.* s.v. **1871** HAMMOND *Dis. Nervous Syst.* 46 Epilepsy, urinæmia, stomachal vertigo.

urinal ('jʊərɪnəl, jʊə'raɪnəl), *sb.* Forms: 3–7 vrinal, 4–6 -all(e, 4–5 vrynal, 4–6 -all(e, 6–7 urinall (6 -alle, 7 -ell), 7– urinal; 5 orinal, orynal; also 3 vrnal, 6 vrnall. [a. OF. *urinal* (12th c.; also *orinal*, pl. *orignaulx*), a. L. *ūrinal*, f. *ūrina* URINE *sb.*[1] Cf. Pr. *urinal*, Pg. *ur-*, *ourinol*, It. *orinale*, Pr. and Sp. *orinal*.]

†**1.** A glass vessel or phial employed to receive urine for medical examination or inspection. *Obs.*

c **1275** LAY. 17724 He nam his vrinal [*c* 1205 glæs-fat] anon, an þe king meh þar on; one wile after þan þe vrnal an honde he nam. **13..** *Seuyn Sages* (W.) 1049 The yonge man ..taketh an vrinal for to sen. *c* **1386** CHAUCER *Pard. Prol.* 19 Thyne vrynals and thy Iurdones. *c* **1440** *Promp. Parv.* 370/1 Orynal, or vrynal, *urinale*. **1495** *Nottingham Rec.* III. 284, ij vrinalles, price iiij d. **1548** RECORDE *Urin. Physick* iv. 14 b, The Vrinall..shulde be of pure clere glasse, not thyck, nor greene in colour. **1596** NASHE *Saffron Walden* R 3 b, Then shee neuer need to haue her water cast in an vrinall for the greene sicknes. **1642** FULLER *Holy & Prof. St.* II. ii. 53 Reasons drawn from the urine alone are as brittle as the urinall. **1685** BOYLE *Effects of Motion* Suppl. 142 Thin Vessels of Glass, especially Urinals, to be diligently made clean with Sand. **1737** *Phil. Trans.* XLI. 707 The *Capillamenta*, whilst in the Urinal, and till the Urine was decanted. **1757** *Keysler's Trav.* IV. 19 While her maid is stirring a medicine in a spoon, and the physician looking into the urinal. **1858** THUDICHUM *Urine* 19 In some hospitals the ancient urinal is still in use.

fig. c **1645** HOWELL *Lett.* (1650) II. 2 When I found those letters..which he sends as urinals up and down the world, to look into his water for discovery of the crazie condition of his body. **1663** SIR G. MACKENZIE *Religious Stoic* 19 There ye shall know by the Urinal of his eyes, and the water standing therein, what convulsion-fits his soul suffers.

transf. **1688** HOLME *Armoury* III. xiv. (Roxb.) 10/2 He beareth Argent, a vrinall Azure.

†**2.** *Alchemy.* (See quot. 1738.) *Obs.*

c **1386** CHAUCER *Can. Yeom. T.* 73 Sondry vessels maad of erthe and glas, Oure vrynals and our descensories. **1559** MORWYNG *Evonym.* 1 Men call it a receiver or a urinall. *Ibid.* 212 If ij urinals be set together. **1584** R. SCOT *Discov. Witchcr.* XII. xvii. (1886) 212 Take a glasse viall full of holie water... On the mouth of the viall or urinall, two olive leaves must be laid. **1667** BOYLE *Orig. Forms & Qual.* 298, I took two parcels of Gold,..and having cast each of these in a distinct Urinal,..I caus'd [etc.]. **1738** CHAMBERS *Cycl.*, *Urinal*, in chemistry, is an oblong glass vessel, used for making solutions.

3. A chamber-pot.

c **1475** *Cath. Angl.* 405/1 (A.), An Vrynalle, *vrinaria*,..*vbi* Jordane. **1519** HORMAN *Vulg.* 168 b, Se that I lacke nat by my beddis syde a chayer of easement:..and an vrnall bye. **1542** UDALL *Erasm. Apoph.* 212 b, His groome whose dayly office it was to geve unto hym his urinall in his chaumbre. **1622** MABBE tr. *Aleman's Guzman d'Alf.* I. 232 Not finding any of his Pages there, he..tooke the Vrinall himselfe, which stood at his beds head. **1642** MILTON *Apol. Smect.* 13 Some Politicians..lyable to a night-walking cudgeller, or the emptying of a Urinall. **1695** CONGREVE *Love for L.* II. iii, [To] warm your Bed, and..set the Candle and your Tobacco-Box, and your Urinal by you. **1739** R. BULL tr. *Dedekindus' Grobianus* p. viii, He finds Occasion to inspect the Urinal and the Bed-pan. *a* **1774** GOLDSM. tr. *Scarron's Com. Romance* (1775) I. 35 Pray reach me the chamber-pot, quoth Rancour... The other..took up the urinal, and gave it to Rancour. **1822** GOOD *Study Med.* IV. 540 Forming red sand on the surface, as it probably would otherwise have done in the bladder or the urinal. **1875** H. C. WOOD *Therap.* (1879) 342 The use of chloral to keep free from odor the urinals of paraplegics.

transf. a **1700** B. E. *Dict. Cant. Crew*, *Urinal of the Planets*, Ireland,..because of its frequent and great Rains.

4. A vessel or reservoir with conductor worn on the person for incontinence of urine.

1855 OGILVIE *Suppl.* **1895** *Arnold & Sons' Catal. Surg. Instrum.* 707 Urinals for Invalids, Travellers, etc. The best quality of Urinals are all made of specially prepared Ætherized India-rubber. **1899** *Allbutt's Syst. Med.* VIII. 244 The wearing of indiarubber urinals, and other means of avoiding 'accidents'.

5. A building, erection, or enclosure for accommodating persons when requiring to pass urine.

1851 J. H. STIRLING in A. H. Stirling *Life* (1912) vi. 106, I had put my back to one of the urinals. **1869** E. A. PARKES *Pract. Hygiene* (ed. 3) 319 Earthen-ware or slate urinals should be used, with water running through them. **1898** G. B. SHAW *Plays* II. *Candida* 29 A vast district..well served with ugly iron urinals.

6. *attrib.* and *Comb.*, as *urinal-glass* (= sense 1), *-like*, *metal*; † **urinal cherry** (see quot. 1629); †**urinal monger**, †**quack**, †**shaker**, a quack doctor who diagnoses by inspecting the urine.

1611 COTGR., *Vrinaire*,..vrinall-like. **1629** PARKINSON *Parad.* 572 The Vrinall Cherrie..is long and round, like vnto an Vrinall. **1641** COWLEY *Guardian* II. v, That damn'd Urinal-monger..has not so much physick as would cure the toothach. **1651** FRENCH *Distill.* i. 37 Put upon it another urinall-glasse inverted. *a* **1652** BROME *Queenes Exch.* IV. E 4 b/2 He thinks my skull's made but of urinal mettal. **1663** COWLEY *Cutter Coleman St.* II. viii, *Wor.* He's a kind of Grave-maker, *Cut.* A Urinal Shaker. **1763** J. CLUBBE *Physiognomy* 7 How came this art into reputation?.. By the same means that Urinal Quacks and Conjurors have had a run here. **1881** *Instr. Census Clerks* (1885) 99 Urinal Cleaner, Attendant, &c.

urinal, *a.* ? *Obs.* [a. F. *urinal* (16th c.), ad. late L. *ūrīnāl-is*, f. *ūrīna* URINE *sb.*[1]]

1. a. Of or pertaining to, consisting or characteristic of, urine.

1541 R. COPLAND *Guydon's Quest. Chirurg.* I iv, Wherby receyueth the bladder the superfluite vrynal of the kydnees? **1653** URQUHART *Rabelais* I. xxxvi, The pisse of that Urinal flood ran glib away. **1703** T. H. (*title*), Compleat Treatises of Urines, shewing the right Method of Urinal Prognostication. **1743** *Lond. & Country Brew.* IV. (ed. 2) 285 Though it be of an Urinal Taste.

b. Marked by immoderate discharge of urine.

1822 GOOD *Study Med.* IV. 459 Both [kinds of diabetes] were named indifferently diabetes,..urinary diarrhœa, urinal dropsy, and..water-flux.

2. = URINARY *a.* 1.

1615 CROOKE *Body of Man* (1631) 212 The Pipe or Canale of the yarde which in greeke they call οὐρήθρα, the vrinal pipe. **1620** VENNER *Via Recta* vii. 154 They..purge the reines, and vrinall passages. *a* **1651** *Recorde's Urin. Physick* To Rdr. A 2 b, The Urine..returneth back again in the veines, to the liver and urinall vessels. **1803** *Med. Jrnl.* X. 512 The effects of..cantharides to the urinal system.

†**'urinalist.** *Obs.* [f. URINAL *sb.*] A urinologist.

1631 DEKKER *Match me in London* 111, I..bid him..To keepe my health from falling, which I felt Tottering.., but my Vrinalist..left no Artery Vnstretcht vpon the Tenters.

uri'nalysis. *Med.* [Irreg. f. L. *ūrīn-a* URINE *sb.*[1] + ANALYSIS.] = URANALYSIS.

1889 *Buck's Handbk. Med. Sci.* VII. 416/1 Processes to be found in large works on urinalysis. **1897** *Columbus* (Ohio) *Dispatch* 18 June 5/2 He..was familiar with the term urinalysis. **1971** *Nature* 12 Mar. 113/1 All subjects had a routine physical check-up, including complete blood counts, urinalysis, chest X-ray, [etc.]. **1980** *Daily Tel.* 15 Oct. 19/6 A post-fight urinalysis showed the presence in Ali of opiates and the drug Phenothiazine.

'urinant, *a. Her.* [ad. L. *ūrīnant-*, *ūrīnans*, pres. pple. of *ūrīnārī* to dive.] Borne with the head downward, and the tail erect.

1688 HOLME *Armoury* II. xiv. 327/1 He beareth Gules, a Dolphin reversed, Argent; (or else a Dolphin with the tail erected;) but more properly a Dolphin Urinant. *c* **1828** BERRY *Encycl. Her.* I. Gloss., *Diving*, or *Urinant*, is said of a dolphin or other fish, borne with the head downwards. **1863** BOUTELL *Her. Hist. & Pop.* xi. 67 A fish is..urinant when its head is in base.

'urinary, *sb.* ? *Obs.* [ad. med.L. *ūrīnāri-um*, f. L. *ūrīnāre* to URINE. Cf. F. *urinoir*.] †**a.** (See first quot.) *Obs.*⁻⁰ **b.** = URINAL *sb.* 5.

1828–32 WEBSTER, *Urinary*, *Urinarium*,..a reservoir or place for the reception of urine, &c., for manure. **1836** J. M. GULLY *Magendie's Formul.* (ed. 2) 135 The chlorurèt of lime may also be..used in the disinfection of water-closets, urinaries,..hospital-wards, &c.

urinary ('jʊərɪnərɪ), *a.* [ad. med.L. **ūrīnāri-us* (whence It., Sp., Pg. *urinario*, It. *orinario*, F. *urinaire*), f. *ūrīna* URINE *sb.*[1]]

1. Affording passage to, effecting or assisting in the secretion and discharge of, urine.

1578 BANISTER *Hist. Man* v. 83 The begynnyng of the Urinarie passage. **1600** SURFLET *Countrie Farme* II. xxvi. 235 The decoction..casteth out grauell contained in the vrinarie vessels. **1625** HART *Anat. Ur.* II. i. 52 A stoppage of the Liuer, kidneyes, and the vrinarie vessels. **1688** [see 3 a]. **1728** CHAMBERS *Cycl.* s.v. *Bladder*, From whence it takes various Denominations, as Urinary-Bladder, Gall-Bladder, &c. **1732** ARBUTHNOT *Rules of Diet* in *Aliments*, etc. I. 358 Everything which drives the Blood into the Urinary Canals. **1794** G. ADAMS *Nat. & Exp. Philos.* I. xi. 488 The alkaline solution..is apt..to prove irritating to the urinary passages. **1843** *Penny Cycl.* XXVI. 50/1 Indicating..the state of the urinary system. **1864** GARROD *Mat. Med.* (ed. 2) 93 It is desirable to keep uric acid in solution during its transit through the urinary organs. **1877** ROSENTHAL *Muscles & Nerves* (1881) 98 The urinary duct, in which each drop of urine leaving the kidneys produces a wave which propagates itself..to the urinary bladder.

2. Of the nature of urine; excreted as urine.

1646 SIR T. BROWNE *Pseud. Ep.* v. v. 239 Whereby it [*sc.* the bladder] dischargeth the waterish and urinary part of its aliment. **1822** GOOD *Study Med.* IV. 500 The urinary secretion in a state of health is one of the most compound fluids of the animal system. **1872** HUXLEY *Physiol.* v. 105 The urinary fluid flows..into the bladder. **1874** GARROD & BAXTER *Mat. Med.* (ed. 4) 129 Citrate of potash sits easily upon the stomach, and..slightly increases the urinary water.

†**b.** = URINOUS *a.* 1. *Obs.*⁻¹

1819 *Rees' Cycl.* XXXVII. s.v., Some urinary salts crystallize when precipitated.

3. a. Adapted for using on the urinary passage.

1688 HOLME *Armoury* III. xx. (Roxb.) 237/2 The Lapidillum..ia a spoon..; with it the stone is taken out of the Urinary passages. Some call it the Urinary Probe.

b. Adapted for receiving or containing urine.

1822 GOOD *Study Med.* IV. 494 In incontinence of urine .., the patient will find it very convenient to be provided with a light urinary receptacle.

4. a. Lodged or formed in the urinary organs or bladder; excreted in the urine.

c **1793** *Encycl. Brit.* (ed. 3) XI. 91/2 Urinary calculi. **1797** WOLLASTON in *Phil. Trans.* LXXXVII. 386 On Gouty and Urinary Concretions. **1808** *Nicholson's Jrnl.* XX. 317 Analysis of a Urinary Calculus. **1845** *Encycl. Metrop.* VII. 580 Of Urinary Deposits. *Ibid.*, Precipitable substances.. which..form urinary sediments. **1857** DUNGLISON *Med. Lex.* 427/2 Diabetic, Urinary, and Hepatic sugar. **1887** A. M. BROWN *Anim. Alkaloids* 65 The urinary alkaloid obtained by Pouchet.

b. Of or pertaining to, affecting or occurring in, the urinary system or organs.

1822 [see URINAL *a.* 1 b]. **1828–32** WEBSTER s.v., Urinary abscesses. **1845** G. E. DAY tr. *Simon's Anim. Chem.* I. 59 Laws of much importance in urinary pathology. **1874** VAN BUREN *Dis. Genit. Org.* 1 Its urinary function is purely secondary. **1875** H. C. WOOD *Therap.* (1879) 478 When lessened urinary excretion is purely functional in its origin. **1890** *Lancet* 14 June 1295/1 Urinary fever is believed by some to be neurotic in its origin.

urinate ('jʊərɪneɪt), *v.*[1] [f. med.L. *ūrīnāt-*, ppl. stem of *ūrīnāre* to pass water, f. L. *ūrīna* URINE *sb.*[1]]

1. *intr.* To discharge urine; to make water; to micturate.

1599 A. M. tr. *Gabelhouer's Bk. Physicke* 170/2 When the Patient vrinateth in the bath. **1831** J. DAVIES *Mat. Med.* 208 Diuretics (διουρεω, I urinate), act upon the general system in the same manner as stimulants. **1845** *Lancet* 25 Jan. 83/2 The patient now urinates very freely. **1879** DUNCAN *Clin. Lect. Dis. Wom.* x. 110 A hysterical woman, when she is under the influence of that condition, urinates frequently.

2. *trans.* **a.** To wet or saturate with urine.

1768 [see URINATED *ppl. a.*]. **1885** H. O. FORBES *Nat. Wand. E. Archip.* 116 The adjags first urinate all the grass.

b. To pass as or after the manner of urine.

1915 *Evid. before Bryce's Committee German Outrages* 142 During this journey..about 20 of the men..urinated blood.

Hence **'urinated** *ppl. a.*

1768 [W. DONALDSON] *Life Sir B. Sapskull* II. ix. 74, I was swaddled in my urinated blankets.

† **urinate,** *v.*[2] *Obs.*[−0] [f. L. *ūrīnāt-*, ppl. stem of *ūrīnārī* (ante-class. *ūrīnāre*).] *intr.* (See quot.)

1623 COCKERAM I [following Cooper], *Vrinate*, to diue or swimme vnder water.

urination[1] (jʊərɪ'neɪʃən). [a. med.L. **ūrīnātiōn-*, **ūrīnātio*, noun of action f. *ūrīnāre* to URINATE. Cf. F. *urination.*] The action of passing water; micturition.

1599 A. M. tr. *Gabelhouer's Bk. Physicke* 176/1 The Milte of a yonge Goate..causeth gentle, and easye vrinatione. **1699** G. HARVEY *Van. Philos. & Physick* xi. 93 Infrequent Urination, or making of Water. **1857** DUNGLISON *Med. Dict.* 948/1 *Urination*, micturition. **1868** T. G. THOMAS *Dis. Women* (1869) 100 If the effusion reaches the urethra, there is obstruction to urination. **1897** *Allbutt's Syst. Med.* III. 545 The patients..complain only of increased thirst and increased urination.

† **uri'nation**[2]. *Obs.*[−1] [f. L. **ūrīnātiōn-*, **ūrīnātio*, noun of action f. *ūrīnārī* URINATE *v.*[2]] The action of diving.

1697 EVELYN *Numism.* viii. 281 Those also who have perfected the way of Diving and Urination.

† **'urinative,** *a.* *Obs.*[−1] [ad. med.L. type **ūrīnātīv-us* (cf. It. *ur-, orinativo*), f. *ūrīnāre* to URINATE.] Provoking or stimulating urination.

1626 BACON *Sylva* §43 Medecines Urinative do not work by Rejection and Indigestion, as Solutive do.

† **'urinator.** *Obs.* [a. L. *ūrīnātor*, agent-noun f. *ūrīnārī* to dive.] One who dives under water; = DIVER I.

In frequent use from *c* 1655 to *c* 1685.

1648 WILKINS *Math. Magic* II. v. 183 It is observed, that a barrell or cap..will not serve a Urinator or Diver for respiration. **1682** BEALE *Let.* in *Boyle's Wks.* (1772) VI. 446 His majesty's urinator, Mr. Curtis, published in the Gazette, how he had practised. *Ibid.*, Which minds me how easy it were..for our merchants, in all their voyages, to be furnished with such urinators. **1691** RAY *Creation* I. (1692) 73 All those Relations of Urinators belong only to those places where they have dived.

urine ('jʊərɪn, 'jʊəraɪn), *sb.*[1] Forms: α. 4–5 vryne, 4–6 uryne, 4–7 vrine, 4– urine; 4–5 ureyne, 5 vreyne. β. 4–6 vryn, 4–7 vrin, 7 urin; 5 uren. [a. OF. *urine* (12th c.), ad. L. *ūrīna* (whence It., Pr., Pg. *urina*, Pg. *ourina*, It. and Sp. *orina*, OF. *orine*, Du. *urine*, G., Da., Sw. *urin*), related to Gr. οὖρον.]

1. a. The excrementitious fluid secreted from the blood by the kidneys in man and the higher animals, stored in the bladder, and voided at intervals through the urethra; = WATER *sb.* 18.

Also freq. in *Path.* with qualifying terms, denoting morbid condition.

α. *c* **1325** in *Pol. Songs* (Camden) 333 He wole wagge his urine in a vessel of glaz. **13..** *Seuyn Sages* (W.) 1571 In vrine he segh he mighte libbe. *c* **1400** *Lanfranc's Cirurg.* 60 Vreyne of a ȝong man wiþ nitre. **14..** LYDG. *Daunce of Machabree* 417 Maister of Phisike, which on your vryne So looke and gase and stare agaynst the sunne. **1484** CAXTON *Fables of Alfonce* i, Whan the medecyns had sene..his vryne also, they sayd that he had no bodyly sekeness. **1509** HAWES *Past. Pleas.* XVI. (Percy Soc.) 67 A physycyen, truely, can lyttel descerne Ony maner sekenes wythout syght of uryne. **1584** B. R. tr. *Herodotus* I. 34 Mandâne: whom hyr father on a night dreamed to haue let her vryne in..great aboundance. **1601** HOLLAND *Pliny* I. 217 Their urine (after it is made) congealeth into a certain ycie substance. **1662** H. NEWCOME *Diary* (Chetham Soc.) 74 My urine gave mee some alarm, & so yᵉ Dʳ seeinge it [etc.]. **1732** ARBUTHNOT *Rules of Diet* in *Aliments*, etc. I. 248 Cucumbers are useful in bloody Urine. **1787** WINTER *Syst. Husb.* 58 Human and animal urine are composed of water, oil, and salt. **1803** FESSENDEN *Poet. Petition* 10 For bottled urine has, no doubt, In public mails, been frank'd about. **1819** J. G. CHILDREN *Chem. Anal.* 308 The sugar of diabetic urine. **1873** RALFE *Phys. Chem.* 188 Healthy human urine is a clear, transparent, amber-coloured fluid. **1897** *Allbutt's Syst. Med.* II. 1075 If chylous urine is passed into a urine glass. **1897** [see SMOKY *a.* 6].

β. *c* **1330** R. BRUNNE *Chron. Wace* (Rolls) 9011 He tasted his pous, saw his vryn. **13..** *Coer de L.* 3030 Rychard bad his men seche For some wys clerk..For to loke hys uryn. *a* **1400–50** *Alexander* 3826 Sum of his awen vryn & sum on Iren lickid. *c* **1440** *Pallad. on Husb.* I. 950 Oil dregges and oxe uren. **1548** VICARY *Anat.* (1888) 76 The more that the bladder is filled with vrin. **1663** BOYLE *Usef. Exp. Nat. Philos.* II. App. 324 Vrin is a Body, which, as homely and despis'd as 'tis wont to be, may [etc.]. **1691** RAY *N. Co. Words* (ed. 2) 52 *Netting*, Chamber-Lee, Urin.

b. With *an*, etc., and pl.

1483 *Cath. Angl.* 404/2 An Vryn, *vrina*..; *vbi* pissynge. **1525** R. BANKES *Seynge of Vryns* (title-p.), Here begynneth the seynge of vryns,..with medycynes annexed to euery vryne. **1541** ELYOT *Castel of Helth* IV. ix. 82 The most common iudgement in sicknes is by vrines. **1625** HART *Anat. Ur.* I. iv. 39 The vrines of women with child alter almost euery day. **1656** R. SHORT *Drinking Water* 95 They ..that will not vought-safe to look upon an urine. **1707** FLOYER *Physic. Pulse-Watch* 312 Black Vomits, Spits, or black Urines or Stools. **1728** CHAMBERS *Cycl.* s.v., The Author establishes two kinds of Urines. **1840** *Cat. MSS. Brit. Mus.* I. 10/1 Receipts..; with rules for the discerning of urines. **1887** A. M. BROWN *Anim. Alkaloids* 64 The existence of kreatinine in urines.

† **2.** [Partly f. the vb.] The action of passing urine; urination. *Obs. rare.*

1561 in H. B. Wilson *Hist. Merchant-Taylors' Sch.* (1814) 17 Unto their uryne the schollers shall goe to the places appointed them. **1638** RAWLEY tr. *Bacon's Life & Death* (1650) 54 The quantity of..drink, which a man..receiveth into his body, is..much more than he voideth again..by urine, or by sweating. **1662** R. MATHEW *Unl. Alch.* 43 It drank with White-wine..oft-times at urine sends forth like jags of cloath. *Ibid.* 57 Losing his blood at Urine. *Ibid.* [He] meets with my Pills..and..quite stopt his Urine of Blood.

3. a. *attrib.* and *Comb.*, as ***urine analysis***, †*-bladder*, *-cistern*, *drainage*, *expulsor*, *-gutter*, *-monging*, *pigment*, *-provoking*, *-soaked*, *-sodden*, etc.; **urine battery** (see quot.); **urine-cart**, one for conveying urine; **urine fever** (see quot.); **urine-glass**, = URINAL *sb.* 1; † **urine-lake**, *poet.* the contents of the bladder; † **urine leader**, † **urine-pipe**, a ureter; † **urine probe** (see quot. and cf. URINARY *a.* 3 a); † **urine-river**, *poet.* urine passing through a ureter; **urine-salts**, salts of urine; **urine sugar**, urinary sugar.

1884 THOMPSON *Tumours of Bladder* 6 The whole subject of *urine analysis. **1884** KNIGHT *Dict. Mech.* Suppl. 916/2 **Urine battery*, (Electricity). The plates are immersed in a trough through which urine flows. **1738** CHAMBERS *Cycl.* s.v. *Bladder*, From whence it takes various denominations, as *urine-bladder, gall-bladder, &c. **1837** *Flemish Husb.* 92 in *Husb.* (L.U.K.) III, The carrots,..by the help of the *urine-cart, soon swell to a good size. *Ibid.* 90 His *urine-cistern is twenty feet square, and seven feet deep. **1888** R. HARRISON in *Lancet* 14 Jan. 57/2 Cases where it was impossible to obtain perfect *urine drainage. **1597** A. M. tr. *Guillemeau's Fr. Chirurg.* 48 b/2 The *urine expulsors, or urine-provoking remedyes. **1888** R. HARRISON in *Lancet* 14 Jan. 57/2 An aguish form of pyrexia, which I shall speak of henceforth as *urine fever. **1880** *Ibid.* 15 May 771/1 *Urine-glasses with glass or vulcanite stop-cocks at the bottom to draw off the sediment have been made. **1844** H. STEPHENS *Bk. Farm* II. 443 Have every particle of filth removed daily from..the *urine-gutters. **1633** P. FLETCHER *Purple Isl.* II. xxv, The *Urine-lake..By little swells, and fills his stretching sides. **1615** H. CROOKE *Body of Man* (1631) 149 The Vreters or *vrine leaders or vessels of Vrine. **1623** HART *Arraignm. Ur.* (title-p.), The manifold errors and abuses of ignorant *Vrine-monging Empirickes. **1625** —— *Anat. Ur.* I. ii. 15 The ordinarie sort of vrine-monging Physitians. **1860** P. MUNK in *New Syd. Soc. Year-bk.* 108 On *Urine Pigment. **1863** W. O. MARKHAM tr. *Anal. Urine*, etc. 371 The quantity of urine pigment is considerably increased in all acute febrile diseases. **1594** T. B. *La Primaud. Fr. Acad.* II. 372 Two other passages, called vreteres or *vrine pipes. **1625** HART *Anat. Ur.* II. ix. 107 This suppression is.. procured by the obstruction..of the Kidneys and Vrine-pipes. **1688** HOLME *Armoury* III. 429/2 The Catheter, or *Urine probe,..is a long pipe with some few holes at one end. **1597** A. M. tr. *Guillemeau's Fr. Chirurg.* 48 b/2 *Vrine-prouoking remedyes. **1633** P. FLETCHER *Purple Isl.* II. xxiv, Into a lake the *Urine-river falls. **1846** G. E. DAY tr. *Simon's Anim. Chem.* II. 141 If the *urine-salts froth very much upon being treated with an acid. **1876** ROBERTS *Urinary Dis.* 485 Marked symptoms of deranged *urine-secretion. **1908** *Animal Managem.* 77 A dirty, damp, *urine-soaked mass. **1912** *Man. Elem. Milit. Hygiene* (War Office) x. 62 The front of the latrine rapidly becomes a *urine-sodden quagmire. **1944** *Public Health* LVII. 137/1 Nauseating odours assail one's nostrils on entry, and the source is usually located in some urine-sodden faecal-stained mattress in an upstairs room. **1876** *Clin. Soc. Trans.* IX. 37 The *urine sugar still continuing to be very copious. **1837** *Flemish Husb.* 83 in *Husb.* (L.U.K.) III, The whole being swept into the *urine-tank below. **1873** T. H. GREEN *Introd. Pathol.* (ed. 2) 319 The interstitial growth..produces.., in the kidney, compression of the *urine-tubes. **1839** URE *Dict. Arts* 675 The *urine vat is prepared by digestion of the ground indigo in warmed stale urine.

b. **urine** †**-caster**, **-doctor**, **-inspector**, †**-monger**, †**-prophet**, one who diagnoses diseases by inspection of the urine.

1625 HART *Anat. Ur.* I. iv. 38 Who told these *vrine-mongers that the wombe daunced attendance on the bladder? **1654** WHITLOCK *Zootomia* 82 Admirers of Urine-prophets. [Cf. PISS-PROPHET.] **1763** *Brit. Mag.* IV. 116 Tenant, an urine caster. **1815** KIRBY & SP. *Entomol.* iv. (1816) I. 141 The prescription of a famous urine-doctor. **1843** *Penny Cycl.* XXVI. 50/1 In former times, the Uromantes, or Urine-casters, pretended [etc.]. **1863** W. O. MARKHAM tr. *Anal. Urine*, etc. 281 Dozens of specimens of urine were sent daily..to a female urine-inspector.

† **urine,** *sb.*[2] *Obs. rare.* [Of obscure origin; perh. an error for *grine* GRIN *sb.*[1] 1.] In *Hawking*: (see quots.).

1486 *Bk. St. Albans* a ij b, Who so will take hawkes he must haue nettis wich ben kalled vrines and tho must be made of good small threde. [**1621** MARKHAM *Hunger's Prevent.* xii. 150 You shall take a paire of those Nettes which Faulkoners commonly doe call Vrines or Vrnes.]

urine ('jʊərɪn, 'jʊəraɪn), *v.* ? *Obs.* [f. URINE *sb.*[1], or ad. F. *uriner* (16th c.), ad. med.L. *ūrīnāre* (whence It. *urinare*, *orinare*, Pr. and Pg. *urinar*, Pg. *ourinar*, Sp. *orinar*, OF. *oriner*) to URINATE.]

1. *intr.* To pass or make water; to urinate.

In freq. use from *c* 1645 to *c* 1700.

1605 B. JONSON *Volpone* IV. i, By the way, I cheapend sprats: and at Sᵗ Markes, I vrin'd. **1629** MASSINGER *Roman Actor* II. i, This hopefull youth Vrines vpon your monument. **1638** FORD *Fancies* I. ii, I will..urine in thy bason. **1705** *Phil. Trans.* XXV. 2111, I ask'd him..whether he found any ease when he did either Vomit, Sweat or Urined. **1757** *Gentl. Mag.* Aug. 364/2 [He] felt for the first time a difficulty in urining. **1796** 'A. PASQUIN' *New Brighton Guide* 18 As to grinning when jobbernowls urin'd upon me, 'Tis false. **1817** JAS. MILL *Brit. India* I. II. iv. 154 When a man spits on another, when he urines on him. **1828** FLEMING *Hist. Brit. Anim.* 11 [The dog] urines sidewise, lifting his hind leg.

2. *trans.* To cause to pass *out*, as urine.

1662 R. MATHEW *Unl. Alch.* 44 This man..did drink without measure, but could not urine it out.

Hence **'urining** *vbl. sb.* Also *attrib.*

1668 WILKINS *Real Char.* 241 Urining,..make water. *Ibid.* Alph. Dict., *Ureter*,..Urining Vein.

uri'nette. [pseudo-Fr., f. URIN(E *sb.*[1] + -ETTE.] (See quot. 1967.)

1954 J. PUDNEY *Smallest Room* 35 The 'urinettes' have always been there. **1967** *Gloss. Sanitation Terms (B.S.I.)* 58 *Urinette*, a urinal like an elongated W.C. pan, for female use.

uri'niferous, *a.* *Anat.* [ad. mod.L. *ūrīniferus*: see URINE *sb.*[1] and -(I)FEROUS, and cf. F. *urinifère.*] Conveying urine. Usu. with *duct*, *tubule*, or (most freq.) *tube*.

1744 tr. *Boerhaave's Inst.* III. 151, I therefore concluded ..that the Blood..had dilated the uriniferous Ducts of the Kidneys. **1831** R. KNOX *Cloquet's Anat.* 799 The inner [membrane]..even introduces itself into the uriniferous tubes. **1857** G. BIRD *Urin. Deposits* (ed. 5) 142 A uriniferous tubule. **1880** BRADY *Copepoda* III. 18 The hinder portion of the alimentary canal is perhaps also uriniferous.

uri'niparous. *a.* *Anat.* [f. as prec. + -PAROUS. Cf. F. *urinipare.*] Secreting urine.

1857 DUNGLISON, *Uriniparous*,..an epithet for tubes in the cortical portion of the kidney, which prepare the urine. [Hence in Webster (1864), and later Dicts.]

urino- ('jʊərɪnəʊ), combining form of L. *ūrīn-a* URINE *sb.*[1], occurring in various terms, as **ˌurino'genitary**, = URINOGENITAL *a.* 1; **uri'nologist**, a urologist; **uri'nology** (see quot. and cf. UROLOGY b); **'urinomancy**, diagnosis of diseases by examination of the urine; **ˌurinopyk'nometer** (see quot.); **ˌurino'scopic**, of or pertaining to the inspection of urine as a means of diagnosing diseases (*Cent. Dict.*, 1891); **uri'noscopist**, **-scopy**, = UROSCOPIST, -SCOPY.

1878 F. J. BELL *Gegenbaur's Comp. Anat.* 523 The vasucular system, and *urino-genitary organs. **1897** *Columbus* (Ohio) *Dispatch* 18 June 5/2 The doctor was again summoned to..produce urine in the presence of the *urinologist. **1900** *Nature* 17 May 53/2 The book should be of value to urinologists. **1860** R. FOWLER *Med. Voc.*, **Urinology*, the branch of Medicine which treats of the urine. [Hence in various Dicts.] **1904** G. S. HALL *Adolescence* I. 116 The many centuries when *urinomancy and urinoscopy vied with astrology. **1905** *Brit. Med. Jrnl.* 1 July 27 The *urino pyknometer..is serviceable for making a rough clinical estimate of the specific gravity of small quantities of urine. **1836** R. FURNESS *Astrologer* II. Poet. Wks. (1858) 146 Let some one..Take Thor's first morning water in a phial, And give the *Urinoscopist a trial. *Ibid.* 150 Volumes of *Urinoscopy. **1839** SPILLAN tr. *Schill's Outl. Pathol. Semeiology* 7 With that exception, ignorance and superstition prevailed in this half of the second period. Urinoscopy occupied the place of semeiology. **1904** [see *urinomancy* above].

ˌurino'genital, *a.* [f. prec. + GENITAL *a.*]

1. = UROGENITAL *a.*

1836 *Penny Cycl.* VI. 249/1 A specific effect will be exerted on the urino-genital organs. **1879** E. P. WRIGHT *Anim. Life* 12 The urino-genital opening. **1881** F. BALFOUR *Compar. Embryol.* II. 599 The urethra and vagina open independently into the common urinogenital sinus.

2. Affecting or occurring in the urogenital organs.

1846 G. FRANKS *Urino-genital Diseases* 45 It is a fruitful source of stricture, impotence, and general deranged state of the urino-genital functions.

‖ **urinoir** (yrinwar). [Fr.] A public urinal.

1955 G. GREENE *Quiet American* II. iii. 147 The old women gossiped as they had always done, squatting on the floor outside the urinoir. **1962** *Spectator* 16 Nov. 770 A wrought iron urinoir in Holborn.

uri'nometer. [f. URINO- + -METER. Cf. F. *urinomètre.*] An instrument for determining the specific gravity or weight of urine.

Also, in recent Dicts. (1891–), *urino'metric*, *-'ometry*.

1843 *Penny Cycl.* XXVI. 55/1 [The] Urinometer..is constructed on the principle of a common hydrometer. **1858** THUDICHUM *Urine* 34 Which, when destined to be used for the urine only, should be called urogravimeter, but has been wrongly styled urinometer. **1898** *Allbutt's Syst. Med.* V. 426 A urinometer possessing a somewhat extensive scale of graduations.

attrib. **1898** *Allbutt's Syst. Med.* V. 426 Chloroform and benzol are mixed in an ordinary urinometer glass.

† **uri'nose**, *a.* *Obs.*$^{-1}$ [ad. mod.L. *ūrīnōs-us*: see next.] Of the nature of urine.

1692 RAY *Creation* II. 64 In the Kidneys there should be such innumerable..Tubes conveying the Urinose Particles to the Pelvis and Ureters.

urinous ('jʊərɪnəs), *a.* [ad. mod.L. *ūrīnōs-us* (whence It. and Pg. *urinoso*, It. and Sp. *orinoso*), f. L. *ūrīna* URINE *sb.*^{1} Cf. prec., F. *urineux* (1611), and the earlier MERDURINOUS *a.*]

1. Possessing or partaking of the essential properties of urine.

In frequent use from *c* 1670 to *c* 1700.

1644 G. PLATTES in *Hartlib's Legacy* (1655) 217, 1. Nitrous Salt, 2. Urinous Salt, in which are comprehended, 3. all Dungs, Horns, Shreads, and the like. **1663** BOYLE *Usef. Exper. Nat. Philos.* II. 200 What an Acid Menstruum dissolves, an Alcalizate, or an Urinous will precipitate. *Ibid.* 201 Volatile and Urinous Spirits, as Spirits of Urine it self. **1698** W. KING tr. *Sorbière's Journ. Lond.* 33 As Meat rots, it becomes more Urinous and Salt. **1708** J. KEILL *Anim. Secretion* 74 Lime does strongly attract Urinous Salts. **1763** W. LEWIS *Comm. Phil.-Techn.* 95 A mixture of the vitriolic acid with the same urinous spirit. **1819** *Rees' Cycl.* XXXVII. s.v., Urinous Salts are the same with what we otherwise call alkaline salts, or alkalies.

b. Characteristic or suggestive of that of urine.

In frequent use from *c* 1800.

1670 H. STUBBE *Plus Ultra* 135 The former in that mixture lost its urinous smell. **1677** PLOT *Oxfordsh.* 38 A salt of a urinous tast. **1742** *Lond. & Country Brew.* III. (ed. 2) 235 It will certainly give the Beer..an urinous Taste. **1758** *Ann. Reg., Extraord. Adv.* 280/2 A urinous volatile effluvia came from the prison. **1786** *Phil. Trans.* LXXVI. 136 An exceeding sharp urinous smell. **1813** J. THOMSON *Lect. Inflam.* 355 The urinous smell of the perspiration. **1837** WHITTOCK *Bk. Trades* (1842) 179 Soap..would give the liquor a 'urinous' taste. **1863** W. O. MARKHAM tr. *Anal. Urine*, etc. 291 The 'urinous-odour' (as it is called) of patients, depending chiefly upon the presence of this salt.

c. Obtained or derived from urine. *rare*$^{-1}$.

1663 BOYLE *Usef. Exp. Nat. Philos.* II. v. vii. 180 By tempering the Urinous extract with a convenient quantity of good Wood Ashes.

2. Of fluids, etc.: Of the nature of urine.

1669 W. SIMPSON *Hydrol. Chym.* 74 Which should separate from the blood an urinous latex. **1728** CHAMBERS *Cycl.* s.v. *Urine*, The serous or urinous Parts [are there] secreted [from the blood]. **1753** N. TORRIANO *Midwifry* 22 Which second Evacuation some have supposed..to have been urinous. **1788** tr. *Swedenborg's Wisd. Angels* § 341 Excrementitious and stercoraceous, rancid and urinous matters. **1847–9** *Todd's Cycl. Anat.* IV. 462/1 A urinous fluid was passed off from the stomach by vomiting. **1860** MAYNE *Expos. Lex.*, *Uridrosis*,..urinous sweat. **1876** W. ROBERTS *Urin. & Renal Dis.* III. viii. (ed. 3) 487 Sometimes the organic urinous matters only exist in traces.

3. Marked by the presence or prevalence of urine.

1788 tr. *Swedenborg's Wisd. Angels* §341 Wherefore those Hells have their Names from thence, and some are called.. stercoraceous, some urinous, and so on. **1851** S. NOBLE tr. *Swedenborg's Heaven & Hell* §488 Those who have applied divine truths to promote their own loves,..love urinous substances and places.

Hence **'urinousness**, 'urinous quality'.

1727 BAILEY (vol. II).

uris, obs. var. OURS.

urisk ('ʊərɪsk). Also ‖**uruisg**. [a. Gaelic *ùruisg*, *uirisg*.] In the Highlands of Scotland: A supernatural being supposed to frequent lonely places; a brownie.

1806 P. GRAHAM *Scenery Perthshire* 19 The Urisks were a sort of lubberly supernaturals, who..could be gained over by kind attentions, to perform the drudgery of the farm. **1853** C. ROGERS *Week at Bridge of Allan* (ed. 3) 330 The Urisks, a species of beings of which the existence was long credited in the upland and secluded districts of Scotland. **1885** *Chamb. Jrnl.* 371 The urisks..acted the part ascribed to the brownies of England.

urison, -soun, -sun, obs. ff. ORISON.

uritary, var. URETARY *Obs.*

† **urith**, = *vrith*, s. dial. var. FRITH *sb.*^{2} 3.

1671 SKINNER, *Urith*, vox in Com. Wilts usitatissima. [Hence in Bailey (1721), etc.]

† **uritive**, *a.* *Obs.*$^{-1}$ [f. L. *ūr-ĕre* to burn: see -IVE.] Dry, parching.

a **1425** tr. *Arderne's Treat. Fistula*, etc. 82 Vertegrese is ful mich penetratife, dissolutiue, pungityue, vrityue, and liquefactyue.

† **uritory**, variant of URETARY *a.* *Obs.*

1657 W. COLES *Adam in Eden* cxcix, To wash the Reines and Uritory parts from Gravell or Stones gathered therein.

† **uriture**, obs. variant of URETER.

1662 R. MATHEW *Unl. Alch.* 4 If the defect be amongst the Uritures, Kidneys, Reins or Bladder.

urke, obs. var. IRK *a.*

1460 *Paston Lett.* Suppl. (1901) 64, I am urke of variaunces.

Urkey ('ɜ:kɪ). [Origin unknown.] A local name of a children's game (see quot.). Also, the person who is 'it' in this game. As *v. trans.*, to defeat in this game. Cf. LERKY.

1938 E. THOMAS *Childhood E. Thomas* iii. 53 The best game was an evening one, called Urkey. One boy who was Urkey stood still by a tin can while the others hid. When a shout told that they had found a hiding place he went in search of them. His object was to see one and run home to the can, crying 'I Urkey Johnny Williams.'

url(e, obs. ff. EARL.

‖**urlar** ('ʊəlɑ:(r)). [Gael.] (See quots.)

1889 *Cent. Dict.* s.v. *Pibroch*, It consists of a ground-theme or air called the *urlar*, followed by several variations, ..the whole concluding with a quick movement called the *creanduich*. **1900** C. S. THOMASON *Ceol Mor* 5 The Ground or *Urlar*, which corresponds to the *Thema* or Theme of ordinary modern music. **1925** J. P. GRANT *Piobaireachd* 27 All that appears is the Urlar and a Doubling. The first and third lines of the Urlar correspond with Angus Mackay's MS. **1962** A. MACLEOD *Eighth Seal* iv. 44 Flora had been working out the *urlar*, the groundwork or theme of her pibroch. **1977** *Meanjin* (Austral.) XXXVI. I. 80 *Urlar* and *Siubhal*..are respectively the 'ground' and 'variations' in classical pipe music.

urle, obs. var. ORLE.

† **urle**, *sb.*^{1} *Obs.*$^{-1}$ [Of obscure origin.] A tare.

1659 C. HOOLE tr. *Comenius Visible World* xvii. 37 Pease, Beans, Vetches, and those that are lesse than these, Lentils and Urles (or Tares) [L. *lentes et cicera*].

† **urle**, *v.*^{1} *Obs. rare.* [ad. OF. *ourle-r* (13th c.), or med.L. *url-are*, f. OF. *ourle*, *urle*: see ORLE.] *trans.* To provide with a border; to border or trim *with* something.

c **1330** R. BRUNNE *Chron. Wace* (Rolls) 12463 [Ryton ordered Arthur to] flowe of his owen berd,..For he wolde vrle his pane wyþ-al Aboute wiþ a ffylet smal. *Ibid.* 12472. **1599** THYNNE *Animadv.* (1875) 35 The kinges dalmaticall garmente of the same samitte..vrled or bordrede..withe orfreyes.

urle, *v.*^{2} *north. dial.* [See URLING^2.] *intr.* (See quots.)

1683 G. MERITON *Yorksh. Dial.* (1684) 48 What ails our Tibb, that she urles seay ith Neauke? **1684** —— *Yorksh. Ale* Gloss. 112 To *Vrle*, is to draw ones self up on a heap. **1781** W. HUTTON *Tour to Caves* (ed. 2) Gloss., *Url*, to look sickly, or to go back in health. **1828** [CARR] *Craven Gloss.*, *Url*, to be pinched with cold.

urled, *ppl. a. north. dial.* [f. prec. + -ED^1.] Stunted in growth; dwarfed, dwarfish, ill-thriven.

1691 RAY *N. Co. Words* 78. *a* **1800** PEGGE *Suppl. Grose* s.v. **1828-** in dialect glossaries (n. Cy., Cumbld., Westm., Yks., Lancs.).

† **'urling**^{1}. *Obs.*$^{-1}$ [See URLE *v.*^{1} and -ING^1; cf. ORLE.] The border, hem, or edge of a garment.

a **1300** *E.E. Psalter* cxxxii. 2 Als þe smerle..þat doune falles in vrlinge [L. *in ora*] Of him, þat es þe klethinge.

'urling^2, north. dial. variant of WIRLING.

1691 RAY *N.C. Words* 78 An *Urling*, a little dwarfish person. **1807** J. STAGG *Poems* 91 Thou's a menceless urlin ista. **1824-** in Yks. dial. glossaries, etc. **1881** SARGISSON *Joe Scoap's Jurneh* 107 He turnt on t'urlin noo at ah still held be t'neck.

urn (ɜ:n), *sb.* Also 5 vrn (6 *Sc.* wrn), 4–7 vrne, 5 uryn, 7 urne. [ad. L. *urna* (whence It., Sp., Pg. *urna*, F. *urne*), f. *ūrĕre* to burn.]

1. An earthenware or metal vessel or vase of a rounded or ovaloid form and with a circular base, used by various peoples esp. in former times (notably by the Romans and Greeks) to preserve the ashes of the dead. Hence vaguely used (esp. *poet.*) for 'a tomb or sepulchre, the grave'.

In frequent use from *c* 1640.

1374 CHAUCER *Troylus* v. 311 The poudre..prey I þe þow take and it conserue In a vessel, þat men clepeþ an vrne, Of gold. **14..** LYDG. *Bk. Life of our Lady* (Caxton) i vi b, The pyece..Was by an aungel in an vrne of golde To charlis brought. **1420–2** —— *Thebes* III. 4575 Some of hem with vrnes made of gold, whan the asshes fully weren made cold, Tenclosyn hem. **1591** SHAKS. *1 Hen. VI*, I. vi. 24 When she is dead, Her Ashes, in an Vrne..Transported, shall be at high Festiuals. **1595** —— *Hen. V*, I. ii. 228 Lay these bones in an vnworthy Vrne, Tomblesse, with no remembrance ouer them. **1607** DEKKER *Hist. Sir T. Wyatt* A 3, Alasse, how small an Vrne containes a King! **1658** SIR T. BROWNE (*title*), Hydriotaphia, Urne-Buriall, or, a Discourse of the Sepulchrall Urnes lately found in Norfolk. **1685** DRYDEN *Thren. August.* xiii, So, rising from his Fathers Urn, So Glorious did our Charles return. **1702** ECHARD *Eccl. Hist.* III. iv. 376 Ordering his Urn to be brought,..[Severus] said 'Little Urn, thou shalt now contain what the whole World could not before'. **1750** GRAY *Elegy* xi, Can storied urn or animated bust Back to its mansion call the fleeting breath? **1824** BYRON *Juan* XVI. xviii, As you turn Backward and forward.., voices from the urn Appear to wake. **1838** [J. MURRAY] *Econ. Vegetation* iii. 76 The capsule of the poppy ..seems to have been adopted as the pattern of the cinerary urn. **1875** W. EASSIE *Cremation* 16 In both ancient Greece and Rome the dwelling-house was made the repository of the funeral urns. *Ibid.* 123 Urns of gold and silver were not uncommon in ancient times, and are even yet used in Siam.

2. a. A vessel for holding voting-tablets, lots, or balls, in casting lots, voting, etc. Chiefly *Roman Antiq.*

1513 DOUGLAS *Æneid* VI. i. 46 The deidlie vrne.., Out of the quhilk the lottis warrin draw. *Ibid.* vii. 18 The fatale wrn and ballance. **1601** B. JONSON *Poetaster* v. iii, Come, We of the bench Let's rise to the vrne, and condemne 'hem. **1658** J. HARRINGTON *Oceana* 72 The number of the Ballottants at either Urn. **1703** PRIOR *Ode Memory G. Villiers* 92 When th' Infernal Judges dismal Pow'r From the dark Urn shall throw Thy destin'd Hour. **1720** OZELL *Vertot's Rom. Rep.* II. xii. 235 To draw out of the Urn none but the Names of such Tribes. **1781** J. MOORE *View Soc. Italy* I. xi. 121 Each elector..throws a little billet into an urn... On this billet is inscribed the person's name. **1825** FOSBROKE *Encycl. Antiq.* 201 Urns for the Ballot... These urns were of two kinds. **1838** DE MORGAN *Ess. Probab.* 54 A white ball has been drawn, and from one or other of the two following urns. **1884** tr. *Lotze's Logic* 368 Suppose we put in an urn..3 white balls, in a second urn..4 white balls.

† **b.** *in the urn*, not yet discovered; unknown.

1658 SIR T. BROWNE *Hydriot.* i. 2 That great Antiquity America lay buried for a thousand years, and a large part of the earth is still in the Urne unto us.

c. A ballot-box.

1888 *Times* (weekly ed.) 21 Dec. 6/1 Nearly 75 per cent. of the..voters appeared at the urns. **1892** *Nation* (N.Y.) 8 Dec. 428/1 Since the extension of the suffrage [in Italy], the attendance at the urns has considerably fallen off.

3. a. A hollow (esp. earthenware) vessel or pot of an oviform or rounded shape, and having a circular base; used for various purposes. Also in fig. context.

a **1639** CAREW *Poems* (1651) 8 Vesta is not displeas'd if her chast urn Doe with repayred fuell ever burn. **1648** WILKINS *Math. Magick* II. x. 234 As a rustick was digging the ground ..he found an Urne..in which there was another urne, and in this lesser, a lamp clearly burning. **1656** COWLEY *Mistr.*, *Dialogue* iv, Like Tapers shut in ancient Urns. **1754** GRAY *Progr. Poetry* 109 Bright-eyed Fancy..Scatters from her pictured urn Thoughts, that breathe. **1827** POLLOK *Course T.* VIII. 633 He put A penny in the urn of poverty. **1851** NEALE *Med. Hymns* 102 Here the urn of manna standeth.

transf. **1857** HEAVYSEGE *Saul* (1869) 234 [A] song.. Falling as faintly and as dewlike down Into the urn of my night-opened ear.

fig. *a* **1854** H. REED *Lect. Brit. Poets* xiv. (1857) II. 171 The steady orb of a planet, its golden urn filled at the fountain of the sun. **1857** EMERSON *Ode sung in Town Hall* 2, O tenderly the haughty day Fills his blue urn with fire. **1860** SANGSTER *Hesperus* 26 Morn on the mountains lights his urn of fire.

b. A sculptured ornament resembling or shaped like a vase, water-pot, or cinerary urn.

1653 in *Verney Mem.* (1907) I. 530 Her statue..set uppon an Urne or Pedestall. **1658** SIR T. BROWNE *Hydriot.* Ep. Ded., Theatrical Vessels, and great Hippodrome Urns in Rome. **1728** CHAMBERS *Cycl.*, *Urn*,..a kind of Vase,..used ..as Ornaments over Chimney-pieces, a-top of Buildings, Funeral Monuments, &c. **1767** JAGO *Edge-hill* I. 472 Nor the lone Hermit's Cell, or mournful Urn Build on the sprightly Lawn. **1842** TENNYSON *Day-Dream* 29 Soft lustre bathes the range of urns On every slanting terrace-lawn. **1849** C. BRONTË *Shirley* xi, The cedar on the lawn,..and the granite urns on the garden wall. **1885** J. B. FLEMING *Let. to Dr. W. G. Blackie* 20 March (MS.), The Draped Urn of Monumental Sculpture. *Ibid.*, Draped or Monumental Urns.

4. a. An oviform pitcher or vessel for holding water, etc.; a water-pitcher, water-pot.

1613 R. CAWDREY *Table Alph.* (ed. 3), *Vrne*, a pot or pitcher. **1649** OGILBY *Æneis* VII. (1684) 286 There Argus watch'd, lest to her shape she [*sc.* Io] turn, By Inachus pouring from a graven Urn. **1688** HOLME *Armoury* III. 205/2 Temperance hath a Cup in the one hand, and a Bottle Urn in the other, pouring Wine thereout. **1725** POPE *Odyssey* II. 398 But by thy care twelve urns of wine be fill'd. **1747** SPENCE *Polymetis* 172 Aquarius..holds the cup or little urn in his hand, inclined downwards. **1796** H. HUNTER tr. *St.-Pierre's Stud. Nat.* I. 252 Some very ancient medals, in which rivers were represented by figures leaning on an urn. **1821** SHELLEY *Adonais* xi, One from a lucid urn of starry dew Washed his light limbs. **1846** KEBLE *Lyra Innoc.* (ed. 3) 280 The wedding guests are met, The urns are duly set. **1867** MORRIS *Jason* IV. 460 To turn the mill, and carry forth the urn Unto the stream.

fig. and *transf.* **1720** POPE *Iliad* XXIV. 663 Two urns by Jove's high throne have ever stood;..From thence the cup of mortal man he fills, Blessings to these, to those distributes ills. **1781** COWPER *Charity* 436 When one, that holds communion with the skies, Has fill'd his urn where these pure waters rise. **1838** LYTTON *Alice* I. iii, Her simplicity of thought was daily filled, from the urns of invisible spirits. *a* **1866** B. TAYLOR *Summer Camp* 13 Shadelike dew Poured from the urns of twilight.

b. The source of a stream, river, etc.; a spring or fountain. Also, the course of a stream.

From the practice of representing river gods or nymphs in sculpture or painting as holding, leaning upon, or pouring water from, an urn.

[**1692** PRIOR *Ode Imit. Hor.* x, Where-e'er old Rhine his fruitful Water turns, Or fills his Vassals Tributary Urns.] **1728** YOUNG *Love Fame* VII. 207 From the rich store one fruitful urn supplies, Whole kingdoms smile, a thousand harvests rise. **1767** JAGO *Edge-hill* I. 209 From many a subterraneous Reservoir,..the rocky Urns..their liquid Stores discharge. **1781** COWPER *Retirem.* 76 Ten thousand rivers poured..From urns that never fail. **1810** T. L. PEACOCK *Genius of Thames* 10 The streams roll on, nor e'er return To fill again their parent urn. **1824** LONGF. *Woods in Winter* iv, From their frozen urns, mute springs Pour out the river's gradual tide. **1830** TENNYSON *Ode to Mem.* 61 The brook..Drawing into his narrow earthen urn..The filter'd tribute of the rough woodland.

c. A bottle or vase for holding tears (freq. with *lachrymal*). Also *transf.*

1753 *Chambers' Cycl.* Suppl. s.v., Another kind of Urns were those which they called *lachrymales*, or the tear-Urns. These were contrived to receive the tears of the friends of the deceased. **1771** MRS. GRIFFITH *History of Lady Barton* III. 46, I opened the little trunk,..which may properly be called the lachrymal urn of the unfortunate Maria. **1837** *Popular Encycl.* VI. 764 Little vessels have occasionally been found in ancient tombs, denominated lachrymal urns.

d. *Astr.* The constellation of Aquarius.

1633 P. FLETCHER *Pisc. Ecl.*, etc. *To W. R.* iv, The sunne, which yet in fishes hasks, Or wat'ry urn, impounds his fainting head. **1697** CREECH *Manilius* II. 65 The Fish oppose the Maid, the watry Urn With adverse Fires sees raging Leo burn. **1770** AKENSIDE *Odes* I. xvi. 1 With sordid floods the wintry Urn Hath stained fair Richmond's level green.

5. Short for *tea-urn*, TEA *sb.* 9 c.

1781 W. HAYLEY *Tri. Temper* IV. 120 No smoke arises from the silver urn, And the blank tea-board..Only supplied the paper of the day. **1784** COWPER *Task* IV. 38 The bubbling and loud-hissing urn. **1834** DICKENS *Sk. Boz, Boarding-ho.* ii, James brought up the urn, and received an unlimited order for dry toast and bacon. **1880** MISS BRADDON *Just as I am* xxi, Miss Blake presided over the urn and teapots.

6. a. *Bot.* The spore-case or capsule of urn-mosses.

1840 *Penny Cycl.* XVI. 9/2 The urn (*sporangium*, or *theca*) in which the spores, or seed-like bodies, are generated. **1858** CARPENTER *Veg. Phys.* §736 The fructification of Mosses.. consists of a capsule or urn, borne at the top of a long foot-stalk, which grows out from the centre of a cluster of leaves. **1890** *Nature* 20 Feb. 379 The mosses unfold the delicate lacework of their dainty urns.

b. *Biol.* An urn-shaped process or part.

1877 HUXLEY *Anat. Inv. Anim.* xi. 655 An infusoriform, bilaterally symmetrical embryo, which consists of an urn, a ciliated body, and two refractive bodies. **1883** H. DRUMMOND *Nat. Law in Spir. W.* 370 No power on earth can make these little urns of the *Polycystinæ* except Life.

7. *attrib.* and *Comb.*, as (sense 1) ***urn-burial***, ***-graveyard***, ***-niche***; (sense 5) ***urn-room***, ***-stand***; (sense 2 c) ***urn-system***; ***urn-burying***, ***-cornered***, ***-like***, ***-maker***, ***-shaped***, etc.; **urn animalcule**, **-flower**, **-moss** (see quots.); **urnfield**, a cemetery of individual cremation graves with remains in pottery urns, *esp.* as used by North European peoples from *c* 1200 B.C. onwards; also *attrib.*, esp. designating peoples using this rite or their cultures.

1847 T. R. JONES in *Todd's Cycl. Anat.* IV. I. 11 The Trichodinæ, or *Urn animalcules,..are provided with a fasciculus or circlet of cilia situated in front of their bodies, which are disc-shaped, bowl-shaped, or conical. **1658** *Urn-burial [see sense 1]. *a* **1796** in *Gentl. Mag.* LXVI. I. 41/1 The latter [*sc.* Danish] people used urn-burial, and burnt their dead. **1836** *Archaeol.* XXVI. 370 Evidence..that urn burial had been disused at length by the Romans. *a* **1682** SIR T. BROWNE *Tracts* (1683) 154 They might be erected..before the term of *Urn-burying or custom of burning the dead expired. **1895** K. GRAHAME *Golden Age* 45 Terrace after terrace of shaven sward, stone-edged, *urn-cornered. **1889** *Soc. Antiquaries, Notice of Meeting* 5 Dec., Celtic Pottery from an ancient British *urn-field. **1928** V. G. CHILDE in *Antiquity* II. 37 On the continent as in Britain the later phases of the Bronze Age are marked by the spread of large cremation cemeteries generally termed urnfields. One of the several groups of urnfield cultures in Central Europe occupies such a pre-eminent position that it may even claim to be the parent of all the rest. It is known as the Lausitz or Lusatian culture. **1958** T. G. E. POWELL *Celts* 38 The dead were generally cremated, and the broken bones placed in an urn for burial in a flat cemetery. Many of these cemeteries ..have been called urnfields so that the descriptive labels 'Urnfield Period' and 'Urnfield Culture' have come into use. **1968** A. POWELL *Military Philosophers* iv. 177, I walked up the road.., leaving them [*sc.* Welshmen] to move eastward towards the urnfields of their Bronze Age home. **1979** B. CUNLIFFE *Celtic World* 15/1 This period, generally referred to..as the Urnfield period, is typified by the appearance of large cremation cemeteries, the ashes of the dead interred in urns. The tradition took form in Hungary sometime in the thirteenth century B.C. and was rapidly adopted further west. **1891** *Cent. Dict.*, *Urceolina pendula* and *U. latifolia* are border plants from Peru, known in cultivation as **urn-flower*. **1888** R. BROWN *Our Earth & its Story* II. 264/1 A separate kind of burial-place are the *urn-graveyards. *a* **1661** HOLYDAY *Persius* (1673) 295 The hollow womb Of his..*urn-inclosing tomb. **1826** GALT *Last of Lairds* xxxii. 281 A tall *urn-like china-pot. **1830** LINDLEY *Nat. Syst. Bot.* (1836) 407 *Thecæ*, hollow urn-like cases seated upon a seta or stalk. **1881** *Instr. Census Clerks* (1885) 46 Tray Maker. *Urn Maker. **1846** LINDLEY *Veg. Kingd.* 66 *Urnmosses are found in all parts of the world where the atmosphere is humid. **1866** *Treas. Bot.* 1194/2 *Urn-Mosses*, ..the *Bryaceæ* or true Mosses. **1848** J. GRANT *Adv. of Aide-de-camp* xii, The dismal aspect of the place—its dark walls and darker *urn-niches. **1901** *Guinness Trust, Fulham P. Rd.* 6 The *urn room..is fitted with a series of copper kettles. **1857** in W. Eassie *Cremation* (1875) 127 Burning the Dead, or *Urn-Sepulture..generally considered. **1796** WITHERING *Brit. Plants* (ed. 3) I. 211 Nectary concave, *urn-shaped. **1875** BENNETT & DYER tr. *Sachs' Bot.* 246 The spermogonia..are urn-shaped receptacles. **1862** *Catal. Internat. Exhib., Brit.* No. 5773, Marble chess-table and *urn-stand. **1901** *Westm. Gaz.* 7 Mar. 6/1 The *urn system existing in the French Chamber. **1839** BAILEY *Festus* 54 An *urn-topped column.

† **urn**, *v.*[1] *Sc. Obs.* Also 7 uren, 9 ern. [Of obscure origin.]

1. *trans.* To cause pain or anguish to (a person); to pain, irritate. Also *absol.*

c **1470** HENRY *Wallace* v. 384 So bett I am with strakis sad and sar; The cheyle wattir vrned me mekill mar. **1559** *Reg. St. Andrews Kirk Session* (S.H.S.) I. 18 Give thei be vexed and urnet with ustioun and urgent appetites of the flesche. *a* **1600** MONTGOMERIE *Misc. Poems* xl. 58 Let furious Faits be fearce; Let absence vrne; let Cupids arrou peirce. *a* **1614** J. MELVILL *Autob. & Diary* (Wodrow Soc.) 270 When he died, I mervelit at my awin hart that was so urened and moved with it. **1808** JAMIESON, *To urn the ee*, to pain the eye, as a mote or a grain of sand does. **1825** —— *Suppl.* s.v. *Ern*, Nae sae muckle as would ern your ee.

2. *intr.* To feel or suffer pain. *rare*[−1].

a **1600** MONTGOMERIE *Sonn.* xxxvi. 4, I vrne for anger, ȝit I haif no yre.

urn (ɜːn), *v.*[2] [f. URN *sb.* Cf. INURN *v.*] *trans.* To deposit (ashes, or bones) in a cinerary urn; to enclose in or as in an urn. Also *transf.*

1612 *Two Noble K.* I. i. 47 He will not suffer us..To urne their ashes. **1651** W. BARKER in Cartwright *Poems* b 7, Their scatter'd Ashes are rak't up and Urn'd. **1744** YOUNG *Nt. Th.* VII. 830 When horror universal shall descend, And heav'n's dark concave urn all human race. **1849** J. WILSON in *Blackw. Mag.* LXVI. 380 Nature has, during a season, cased and urned its torpid and death-like repose. **1855** SINGLETON *Virgil* II. 87 The gathered bones In a bronze casket Corinæus urned.

† **b.** To place in a tomb; to bury. *Obs.*[−1]

1649 G. DANIEL *Trinarch., Hen. V*, xli, Richard, whose Bones..Slept in a Cottage; Harry doth remove To better lodging; vrnes him, like a King.

urn, obs. f. EARN *v.*; s.w. dial. var. RUN *v.*

ˈ**urnal**, *a.* ? *Obs.* [f. URN *sb.* + -AL[1]. Cf. L. *urnālis* containing an urn (of liquid measure).]

1. Of the nature of a cinerary urn; also, sepulchral.

1573 TWYNE *Æneid* XI. Hhj b, The Ashes heapes which there confused lay, In urnal pottes they put. **1631** in Habington *Surv. Worcs.* (Worcs. Hist. Soc.) I. 376 Baynham still longes to wayte uppon her to thys nocturnall urnall den.

2. Effected in a sepulchral urn.

1658 SIR T. BROWNE *Hydriot.* iii. 48 Urnall enterrments and burnt Reliques lye not in fear of worms. **1761** *Ann. Reg.* II. 154/2 The reduction of the body to ashes, the urnal inclosure of those ashes.

† **urnal, urnell**, varr. ORNEL *Obs.*

1348 *Acc. Exch. K.R.* 471/1 m. 3 Pro iiijxx. xj. pedibus de Asshelere emptis pro predicta posterna;..pro .ijc. pedibus de Vrnal emptis pro eodem. **1365** in Brayley & Britton *Hist. Anc. Pal. Westm.* (1836) 187 [5675 feet of stone called] urnell.

urnare, obs. var. RUNNER.

† **urnary.** *nonce-use.* [f. URN *sb.*: cf. -ERY 2.] The designing or making of urns.

1750 LADY LUXBOROUGH *Let. to Shenstone* 14 Feb., I do not yet know what to say about the inscription to the urn. Mr. Alley is vastly against its being in English... I find it is against rule, if rules there be in *Urnary*.

urne, dial. var. OURN *poss. pron.*

urne, s.w. dial. var. RUN *v.*

urned (ɜːnd), *a.* [f. URN *sb.* + -ED[1].]

1. Deposited or buried in an urn. Also *fig.*

1631 EARL MANCH. *Al Mondo* 25 Many times..the vrned bones doe meete with foule hands. **1849** CARLYLE in Reid *Life Houghton* (1890) I. 435, I know no more urned books than his. It is like the writing of a ghost.

2. Of the nature of, effected in, a cinerary urn.

1909 A. REID *Regality Kirriemuir* i. 3 Urned cists, a crannog, and canoes, are among the recorded 'finds'. **1911** J. WARD *Rom. Era Brit.* viii. 138 Cremation was supplanted by inhumation, but not suddenly, the skeleton followed by an urned interment implying an overlap.

urnement, obs. var. ORNAMENT.

urnest, obs. f. EARNEST *sb.*[1]

ˈ**urnful.** [-FUL.] The fill of an urn.

1820 *Monthly Rev.* XCIII. 539 Here is another such urnfull of posthumous remains. **1864** WEBSTER.

urning (ˈɜːnɪŋ). Now *rare.* Also Urning. [a. Ger., coined by K. H. Ulrichs ('Numa Numantius') in 1864.] A homosexual. Cf. URANIAN *a.*[1] 1 c, *sb.*[2], URANISM.

1883 *Jrnl. Nervous & Mental Dis.* Apr. 200 For himself and fellow-Urnings there was nothing left but this unnatural love. **1892** C. G. CHADDOCK tr. *Krafft-Ebing's Psychopathia Sexualis* 255 The urning loves and deifies the male object of his affections. **1896** J. A. SYMONDS *Probl. Mod. Ethics* vii. 91 Man, Woman, and Urning—the third being either a male or a female in whom we observe a real and inborn, not an acquired or a spurious inversion of appetite. **1909** E. CARPENTER *Intermediate Sex* (ed. 2) 135 According to the information of De Joux..the number of Urnings in all Europe is about five millions.

uro-[1] (ˈjʊərəʊ), combining form of Gr. οὐρο-ν urine, used in many terms of physiological chemistry, etc., which denote esp. (*a*) pigments present in or derived from urine, as ***uroˈcyanin***, ***-cyˈanogen***, ***-ˈmelanin***, ***-ˈphæin***(*e*, ***-ˈpittin***(*e*, ***-ˈrhodin***, ***-theoˈbromin***(*e*; (*b*) a morbid condition of the urine (or urinary organs), as ***urocyˈstitis***, ***-ˈplania***; (*c*) instruments for investigating the urine, as ***urograˈvimeter***, ***uˈrometer***, = URINOMETER; also used in various adjs., as ***uroˈleucic*** (*acid*); ***uroˈphanic***, appearing in the urine; ***uˈrophanous***, passing into the urine; ***uroˈsexual***, urogenital; etc. The more important or earlier examples will be found below, as UROBENZOATE, -CHROME, -GENITAL, etc.

Also (in medical or some recent Dicts.) *urocele*, *-cyst(ic*, *-genous*, *-lith*, *-lithic*, *-lithology*, *-phthisis*, *-rrhagy*, *-rrhœa*, *urosis*, etc. (Cf. F. *urocyanine*, *-cystite*, *-mètre*, *-planie*.)

1820 GOOD *Nosology* 451 *Paruria erratica*..has often been described under the name of uroplania. **1852** *Todd's Cycl. Anat.* IV. II. 1244/1 The urethra, or uro-sexual canal. **1855** W. D. MOORE tr. *Heller's Chem. Urine* 15 Heller's urometer. *Ibid.* 25 Kreatin and kreatinin..occur in the flesh of muscle, and are urophanous. **1858** COPLAND *Dict. Pract. Med.* III. 1196 Chronic uro-cystitis is often..a consequence of stricture of the urethra. **1858** THUDICHUM *Urine* 34 Urogravimeters..made of..glass or metal. *Ibid.* 131 This denomination may be considered as corresponding to Heller's urophæine. *Ibid.* 380 Urophanic Organic Acids. **1868** *Watts' Dict. Chem.* V. 963 Urorhodin,..uromelanin, ..uropittin. **1883** C. A. MCMUNN in *Brit. Med. Jrnl.* 1 Dec. 1060/2 The various colouring matters which I have met with in urine..are normal and febrile—urobilin, urohæmatin, urolutein,..urohodin, and others without names. **1888** KIRK in *Brit. Med. Jrnl.* 4 Aug. 233/1 The finest specimens have been of an opaque, almost milk-white, hue; and from this circumstance we would propose to call this body 'urolcucic acid'. **1900** *Lancet* 6 Jan. 36/1 Urotropine.. appears to be a compound produced by the action of formaldehyde on ammonia and is known shortly as formin.

b. **urodyˈnamics**, the branch of medicine concerned with the containment and flow of urine in the body; hence **urodyˈnamic** *a.*; **uroliˈthiasis**, lithiasis in the bladder or urinary tract; **uroˈthelium** [EPI)THELIUM], the epithelium of the urinary tract, esp. the bladder; hence **uroˈthelial** *a.*; **uroˈtropine** (-piːn), † **-in** [ad. G. *urotropin* (A. Nicolaier 1895, in *Deut. med. Wochenschr.* 22 Aug. 541/1): see -TROPIC, -INE[5]] = ***hexamethylenetetramine*** s.v. HEXA-.

1963 *Jrnl. Urol.* XC. 730/2 Practical application of electromanometric urodynamic studies depends upon additional information. **1981** *Brit. Med. Jrnl.* 23 May 1706/3 The clinical and urodynamic evaluation of incontinence in elderly patients. **1954** D. M. DAVIS in *Ann. Surg.* CXL. 839 (*heading*) The hydrodynamics of the upper urinary tract (urodynamics). **1977** *Lancet* 13 Aug. 335/2 The past decade has witnessed an enormous step forward in our knowledge and understanding of the mechanisms involved in incontinence in women and consequently of the principles of management. The new science that has evolved is that of urodynamics. **1865** W. ROBERTS *Pract. Treat. Urinary & Renal Dis.* II. iii. 209 (*heading*) Gravel and calculus. (Urolithiasis.) **1926** YOUNG & DAVIS *Young's Pract. Urol.* I. vi. 388 Urolithiasis is one of the four important and serious conditions causing hematuria. **1966** *Lancet* 31 Dec. 1455/2 The prevalence of urolithiasis in Arad was lower than in the Beersheba settlers, and the urinary output was higher. **1977** *Ibid.* 26 Mar. 684/2 Close similarities between Balkan nephropathy and urothelial tumours with respect to geographical clustering, age, and sex. **1954** P. A. NARATH in M. Campbell *Urology* I. I. iii. 88 Absorption is accomplished by the urothelium which lines the tract. **1977** *Proc. R. Soc. Med.* LXX. 413/2 In patients with bacterial infections of the lower urinary tract it is possible that small amounts of nitrosamines may be produced which could initiate neoplastic or preneoplastic changes in the urothelium. **1895** *Amer. Practitioner & News* XX. 486 The name urotropin was applied to hexamethylenetetramin owing to the changes which its administration brought about in the urine. **1897** *Lippincott's Med. Dict.* 1097/2 Urotropine. **1898** *Therapist* VIII. 115/1 (*heading*) Administration of urotropine and its effects upon the urine. **1940** [see *hexamethylenetetramine* s.v. HEXA-]. **1967** J. A. SIMMONS et al. in H. S. Pieser *Crystal Growth* (Jrnl. Physics & Chem. Solids Suppl.) 270/1 In the cases of urotropine and arsenolite the growth forms change when the crystal starts with disturbed growth.

uro-[2] (ˈjʊərəʊ), combining form of Gr. οὐρ-ά tail, occurring in many terms of comparative anatomy, etc. (of which the more important are entered in their places below), designating or relating to a posterior, caudal, or tail-like part, region, segment, or process, as ***urogaster***, ***-mere***, ***-pod***, ***-pteran***, ***-some***, ***-somite***, ***-steon***, ***sternite*** sbs.; ***urochordal***, ***-gastric***, ***-podal***, ***-pyloric***, ***-sacral***, ***-stylar*** adjs.

Various other examples are entered in some special Dicts., as *uromeric*, *-platoid*, *-somatic*, *-stegal*, *-stege*, *-stegite*, *-sthene*, *-sthenic*, etc.

1825 *Encycl. Metrop.* XVII. 595/1 *Decapoda.* The hinder part of the body, which Latreille calls the post-abdomen, or *Urogaster*, but which is usually though erroneously called the tail. [Hence in Mayne, etc.] **1842** BRANDE *Dict. Sci.*, etc. 1278 Uropterans, *Uroptera*,..a family of Amphipodous Crustaceans, including those in which the tail is terminated by enlarged appendages in the shape of fins. **1877** HUXLEY *Anat. Inv. Anim.* vi. 319 A strong calcified urocardiac process. **1884** COUES *N. Amer. Birds* 114 Urosacral or false tail-bones. **1896** CALMAN *Deep-Sea Crustacea* 19 The outer plate of the uropod. **1898** A. S. PACKARD *Text-book of Entomology* 163 We have designated the abdomen, as the urosome; the abdominal segments of insects..as uromeres, and the sternal sclerites as urosternites.

uroˈbenzoate. *Chem.* [a. F. *urobenzoate*: see next and -ATE[1] 1 c.] = HIPPURATE.

c **1845** MILLER in *Todd's Cycl. Anat.* III. 800/2 Solutions of the urobenzoates furnish a cinnamon brown precipitate. **1860** MAYNE *Expos. Lex.* 1315 *Urobenzoate*,..a combination of urobenzoic acid with a salifiable base.

urobenˈzoic, *a.* *Chem.* [ad. mod.L. *urobenzoicus*: see URO-[1] and BENZOIC *a.*] ***urobenzoic acid***, hippuric acid.

1836 BRANDE *Chem.* (ed. 4) 1179 The urine of the rhinoceros:..the clear portion,..on the addition of muriatic acid, deposits urobenzoic acid. **1858** COPLAND *Dict. Pract. Med.* III. 1204 Urobenzoic acid exists chiefly in the urine of herbivorous animals.

urobilin (jʊərəʊˈbaɪlɪn). *Chem.* Also -ine. [f. URO-[1] + L. *bīl-is* bile: see -IN[1], and cf. F. *urobiline*; coined as G. *urobilin* by M. Jaffe 1869, in *Arch. f. Path. Anat. & Physiol.* XLVII. 406.]

A brownish resinous pigment found in the urine, and occas. in the blood.

1876 tr. *Wagner's Gen. Path.* (ed. 6) 638 The urine of man constantly contains a red pigment—urobilin. **1887** *Brit. Med. Jrnl.* 17 Sept. 645/2 Urobiline exists in the urine either alone, or associated with bilary pigments.

urobilinogen (jʊərəʊbaɪˈlɪnədʒən). *Biochem.* [f. prec. + -OGEN.] Any of a group of colourless tetrapyrrole compounds produced by the reduction of bilirubin, esp. by bacterial action in the gut, and forming urobilin upon subsequent oxidation.

1893 A. EICHHOLZ in *Jrnl. Physiol.* XIV. 331 Reserving the name urochromogen for the body isolated from urine, one may perhaps adopt the name urobilinogen for this artificial product. **1947** *Radiology* XLIX. 303/2 This excessive destruction of red cells is also indicated by a maintained increase in excretion of fecal urobilinogen and urinary bilirubin. **1974** R. M. KIRK et al. *Surgery* vi. 97 Jaundice... The kidneys excrete conjugated bilirubin.. and urobilinogen.. so that the urine is dark.

ˌurobiliˈnuria. *Path.* [f. UROBILIN + Gr. οὖρ-ον urine: see -IA¹.] A morbid condition characterized by excess of urobilin in the urine.

1887 *Brit. Med. Jrnl.* 17 Sept. 645/2 Urobilinuria is always met with in the period of asystolia, in cardiac diseases. **1897** *Lancet* 27 March 884/1 That trional would give rise to excessive urobilinuria.

uroboros (jʊərəʊˈbɒrəs). Also ouroboros, uroborus. [ad. Gr. οὐροβόρος, also οὐρηβόρος, devouring its tail (freq. connected with δράκων).] The symbol, usu. in the form of a circle, of a snake (or dragon) eating its tail.

1940 H. G. BAYNES *Mythol. of Soul* vi. 221 Thus the *uroborus* symbol represents our psychic continuity with the immemorial past. *Ibid.*, Geber, or Jabir, the most famous of the Arabian alchemists, who lived in Kufa about A.D. 776, used the *uroborus* to represent a closed system or magic ring, denoting the idea of an eternal process. **1953** R. F. C. HULL tr. *Jung's Psychol. & Alchemy* in *Coll. Wks.* XII. III. v. 357 The alchemical parallel.. is the double nature of Mercurius, which shows itself most clearly in the Uroboros, the dragon that devours, fertilizes, begets, and slays itself and brings itself to life again. **1957** N. FRYE *Anat. Criticism* 157 Alchemical symbolism takes the ouroborus and the hermaphrodite.. in this redemptive context. **1975** HUGHES & BRECHT *Vicious Circles & Infinity* Fig. 11 The ouroboros, the snake with his tail in his mouth, is the prototype of the vicious circle... The 'Endless Snake' depicts an ouroboros who has become one with himself. It has fallen into the mathematical sign for infinity.

urochloralic (jʊərəʊklɔəˈrælɪk), *a.* *Biochem.* [tr. G. *uro-chloralsäure* urochloralic acid (von Mering & Musculus 1875, in *Ber. d. Deut. Chem. Ges.* VIII. 666), f. URO-¹: see *chloralic* adj. s.v. CHLORAL.] *urochloralic acid*: a metabolite formed in the body after chloral has been administered (see quot. 1977).

1875 *Jrnl. Chem. Soc.* XXVIII. 1040 The authors propose to give it the provisional name of urochloralic acid. **1882**, etc. [see GLYCURONIC *a.*]. **1931** *Chem. Abstr.* XXV. 349 (*heading*) The pharmacology of urochloralic acid with special regard to the diuretic action of the sodium salt of this acid. **1977** *Martindale's Extra Pharmacopoeia* (ed. 27) 753/2 Chloral hydrate is.. excreted slowly in the urine as trichloroethanol and its glucuronide (urochloralic acid).

urochord (ˈjʊərəkɔːd). *Zool.* [f. URO-² + CHORD *sb.*]

1. The notochord of ascidians and tunicates, regarded as corresponding to the primordial spinal column in vertebrates.

1877 HUXLEY *Anat. Inv. Anim.* x. 595 The appendage.. may be termed the *urochord*. *Ibid.* 598 A ganglion.. passes along one side of the urochord to its extremity. **1880** A. WILSON in *Gentl. Mag.* Jan. 46 Among the sea-squirts, the 'urochord' persists throughout life.

2. One of the *Urochorda*, a branch consisting of ascidians or tunicates.

1885 F. J. BELL *Comp. Anat.* 313 Amphioxus has no external skeleton, nor have those Urochords that are tailed throughout life.

ˈurochrome (-krəʊm). *Chem.* [f. URO-¹ + Gr. χρῶμα CHROME *sb.* Hence F. *urochrome.*] A yellow, amorphous pigment found in the urine.

1864 THUDICHUM in *Brit. Med. Jrnl.* 5 Nov. 513/1, I consider that there is one colouring matter in the urine, to which I appropriate the name of Urochrome. **1900** *Lancet* 10 Nov. 1329/2 To urochrome itself a place must be assigned among the derivatives of hæmoglobin.

‖**urochs** (ˈʊər-, ˈjʊərɒks). [G., var. of *auerochs* AUROCHS. Cf. URE-OX.] (See quots.)

1839 *Penny Cycl.* XIV. 54/2 An animal peculiar to Lithuania is the urochs, or bison. **1864** J. HUNT tr. *Vogt's Lect. Man* xii. 335 The bones found belonged to.. the now extinct 'urochs' (*Bos primigenius*);.. the Lithuanian Bison, or Auerochs (*Bos urus*, or *Bison Europæus*).. is a distinct species. **1881** *Nature* XXIII. 296 Post-tertiary animals (such as mammoth, rhinoceros, urochs).

urodæum, -eum (jʊərəʊˈdiːəm). *Zool.* Pl. -æa, -ea. [mod.L., irreg. f. URO-¹ + Gr. ὁδαῖος on or by the way.] The part of the cloaca into which the urinary ducts open.

1888 H. GADOW in *Phil. Trans. R. Soc.* B. CLXXVIII. 28, I propose to designate the typical urino-genital and fæcal chambers the Urodæum and Coprodæum in accordance with Professor E. Ray Lankester's terms Stomodæum and Proctodæum. **1897** PARKER & HASWELL *Text-bk. Zool.* II. xiii. 368 The cloaca is a large chamber divided into three compartments, the coprodæum.., the urodæum.., and the proctodæum. **1959** W. ANDREW *Textbk. Compar. Histol.* xi. 444 Urine formed in the kidney is concentrated in the cloacal chambers (urodeum and coprodeum) where water is absorbed through the walls. **1975** *Nature* 17 Jan. 217/2 At the other end, the proctodeum opens into urodeum leading to the coprodeum.

uroˈdelan, *sb.* *Zool.* [f. next + -AN.] = next.

1872 HUMPHRY *Myology* 3 In Urodelans.. the movements of the bony pieces are restricted, or nearly so, to one plane. **1879** NICHOLSON *Palæont.* (ed. 2) II. 175 The *Palæosiren* of Geinitz.. is from the Lower Permian, and is believed by its discoverer to be a Urodelan.

urodele (ˈjʊərədiːl), *sb.* and *a.* *Zool.* [a. F. *urodèle*, usu. pl. *urodèles* (Duméril), or ad. mod.L. *Urodēla*, neuter pl. of **ūrodēlus*, f. Gr. οὐρ-ά URO-² + δῆλος evident.]

A. *sb.* A member of the order *Urodela* of amphibians, in which the larval tail persists in adult life; a Urodelan.

1842 BRANDE *Dict. Sci.*, etc. 1278 Urodeles, *Urodelæ*,.. that tribe of Caducibranchiate Batracian reptiles which preserve the tail through all stages of their existence. *c* **1850** *Todd's Cycl. Anat.* IV. II. 1254 The amphibious *Urodeles*. **1874** MIVART *Frog* 42 The largest existing Urodele—the gigantic Salamander (*Cryptobranchus*)—is found in Japan.

B. *adj.* Belonging to the *Urodela* (see prec.).

1874 MIVART *Common Frog* 49 The world's surface may be divided according to its Urodele population into three legions. **1875** HUXLEY in *Encycl. Brit.* I. 762/1 No urodele amphibian has more than four digits in the manus.

Hence **uroˈdelous** *a.*, pertaining to, having the characteristics of, the *Urodela*.

c **1844** *Todd's Cycl. Anat.* III. 448/2 The urodelous kinds of Caducibranchiates. **1861** R. E. GRANT *Tabular View Rec. Zool.* 14 Noctilionida... With distinct tail (urodelous). **1881** A. S. PACKARD *Zool.* 479 A step higher in the Urodelous scale is the *Menopoma*.

uroeˈrythric, *a.* *Chem.* [f. next: see -IC 1 b.] Derived from uroerythrin.

1871 WATTS tr. *Gmelin's Handbk. Chem.* XVIII. 408 Uroerythric acid [is obtained] by mixing urine with half its volume of hydrochloric acid.

uroeˈrythrin. *Chem.* Also -ine. [f. URO-¹ + ERYTHRIN.] A reddish pigment found in the urine of persons suffering from fevers, esp. rheumatic fever.

1845 G. E. DAY tr. *Simon's Anim. Chem.* I. 216 Uroerythrin, in all probability, owes its origin to the hæmatin of the blood-corpuscles. **1863** W. O. MARKHAM tr. *Anal. Urine*, etc. 49 Uroerythrine is the pigment which gives to sediments of uric acid and urate of soda their brick or rosy red colour. **1889** *Buck's Handbk. Med. Sci.* VII. 416 Its oxidation [*i.e.* of urochrome] gives rise to a red pigment called uroerythrin.

urogastrone (jʊərəʊˈgæstrəʊn). *Biochem.* [f. URO-¹ + GASTR(IC *a.* + -ONE; cf. *enterogastrone* s.v. ENTERO-.] Any of a number of closely related humoral agents in mammalian urine which retard gastric secretion and motor activity.

1940 J. S. GRAY et al. in *Proc. Soc. Exper. Biol. & Med.* XLIII. 228 Until such time as the gastric inhibitory factor is definitely identified, we propose to call it urogastrone. **1946** *Nature* 31 Aug. 305/1 (*heading*) Urease in the gastric mucosa and its increase after a meat diet, soya bean flour diet or urogastrone injections. **1966** WRIGHT & SYMMERS *Systemic Path.* I. xiv. 494/1 Extracts of normal urine contain a substance, urogastrone, that inhibits the action of pepsin and hydrochloric acid. **1975** *Nature* 25 Sept. 325/1 The two urogastrones were shown to be water-soluble polypeptides of relatively low molecular weight and the difference between them could be shown by various physical techniques including acrylamide gel electrophoresis.

uroˈgenital, *a.* (and *sb.*). *Comp. Anat.* [f. URO-¹ + GENITAL *a.* Cf. F. *urogenital* and URINO-GENITAL *a.*]

1. *adj.* Pertaining or belonging to the urinary and genital products or organs; genito-urinary.

1848 *Quain's Elem. Anat.* II. 1278 Transformation of the uro-genital sinus. **1870** ROLLESTON *Anim. Life* p. xlvii, All Mammalia have a urogenital canal independent.. of the termination of the intestine. **1883** E. R. LANKESTER in *Encycl. Brit.* XVI. 693/2 In the *Ostrea edulis* fertilization of the eggs is effected at the moment of their escape from the uro-genital groove.

2. *sb.* A urogenital organ. Usu. *pl.*

1891- in various Dicts.

So **uroˈgenitary** *a.*

1883 *Lancet* 19 May 875/2 Co-existent defects of uro-genitary organs.

uroglaucin (-ˈglɔːsɪn). *Chem.* Also -ine. [a. G. *uroglaucin*: see URO-¹ and -IN¹, and cf. GLAUCOUS *a.*] A blue pigment found in the human urine during certain diseases, as scarlet fever.

1846 G. E. DAY tr. *Simon's Anim. Chem.* II. 523 The existence of a large quantity of uroxanthin in urine is indicated.. by the presence of the products of its oxidation, uroglaucin and urrhodin. **1863** W. O. MARKHAM tr. *Anal. Urine*, etc. 45 Uroglaucine presents itself in the form of a blue powder. **1889** *Buck's Handbk. Med. Sci.* VII. 417/1 Uroglaucin (blue) and urrhodin (red) are closely related to indigo blue and indigo red.

urography (jʊˈrɒgrəfɪ). *Med.* [f. URO-¹ + -GRAPHY.] Radiography of the urinary tract.

1925 W. F. BRAASCH in *Jrnl. Urol.* XIV. 631 The present widespread employment of urography as an aid in the diagnosis of surgical conditions affecting the urinary tract merits careful consideration. **1962** *Lancet* 19 May 1049/1 Excretory urography showed that both kidneys were functioning well. **1977** *Proc. R. Soc. Med.* LXX. 187/1 An accurate and precise diagnosis may be made by early high-dose urography and bulb ureterography.

Hence **uroˈgraphic** *a.*; also **ˈurogram**, a radiogram of the urinary tract.

1925 W. F. BRAASCH in *Jrnl. Urol.* XIV. 632 The personal equation may be a large factor in interpreting the urogram. *Ibid.* 634 That it is often the cause of obscure abdominal pain.. is not borne out by pathologic, urographic or clinical evidence. **1940** P. S. PELOUZE *Office Urol.* xii. 520 Every patient in whom a movable kidney is felt or suspected should be subjected to urographic study. **1980** *Nature* 17 Apr. 619/1 The success of transplantation and the cross-sectional area of the kidneys were demonstrated on excretory urograms.

urohæmatin (jʊərəʊˈhiːmətɪn). *Chem.* Also -hematin(e. [f. URO-¹ + HÆMATIN.] A variety of hæmatin forming the colouring matter or pigments of the urine.

1863 W. O. MARKHAM tr. *Anal. Urine*, etc. 43 Dr. Harley calls this body urohæmatine. **1865** *N. Syd. Soc. Year-bk. Med.* 161 An excessive excretion of uro-hæmatin. **1878** KINGZETT *Anim. Chem.* 239 Under the name of Urohæmatine, Proust, Scherer, Harley, Heller, Marcet, constituted the colouring principles of urine.

urohyal (-ˈhaɪəl), *a.* and *sb.* *Comp. Anat.* [f. URO-²: see HYOID *a.* and -AL I.] **a.** *adj.* Forming or relating to a median posterior process or part of the hyoid arch in fishes or birds. **b.** *sb.* The bone forming this.

1835-6 OWEN in *Todd's Cycl. Anat.* I. 345/1 The superior larynx [in birds].. rests upon the uro-hyal element of the os hyoides. **1848** —— *Archetype & Homol. Vertebr. Skel.* 69 In most others [*sc.* fishes] there is.. another.. bone, which expands vertically as it extends backwards, in the middle line, from the basihyals; this is the 'urohyal'. **1888** ROLLESTON & JACKSON *Anim. Life* 93 A thin median bone, the basi-branchiostegal (= urohyal of Huxley).

urokinase (jʊərəʊˈkaɪneɪz). *Biochem.* and *Pharm.* [f. URO-¹ + KINASE.] An enzyme which catalyses the conversion of plasminogen to plasmin and is used in the treatment of blood clots.

1952 G. W. SOBEL et al. in *Amer. Jrnl. Physiol.* CLXXI. 768/2 Normal human and dog urine contains.. a potent activator of profibrinolysin (plaminogen). The activator.. we have designated urokinase. **1977** *Daily Colonist* (Victoria, B.C.) 23 Oct. 10/5 Urokinase is used in the treatment of blood clots and scientists said it has the potential of preventing 50,000 deaths per year in the United States alone. **1983** DAVIES & MCNICOL in *Oxf. Textbk. Med.* II. xix. 132/2 Urokinase is produced naturally by cells in the kidney and is present in human urine, probably to aid maintenance of ureteric patency.

urolagnia (jʊərəʊˈlægnɪə). *Psychol.* [f. URO-¹ + Gr. λαγνεία, act of coition, lust.] Sexual pleasure derived from urination. Hence **uroˈlagnic** *a.*

1906 H. ELLIS *Stud. Psychol. Sex* V. iii. 47 These [functions] are sometimes termed the scatalogical group, with the two subdivisions of urolagnia and coprolagnia. *Ibid.* 62 So far we have been concerned with the urolagnic.. variety of scatalogical symbolism. **1940** HINSIE & SHATZKY *Psychiatric Dict.* 545/1 *Urolagnia*.., pleasure connected with urine... Some individuals gain gratification in watching others urinate. **1980** *Spectator* 5 July 20 Was it his mother's fault that he suffered from urolagnia?

urology (jʊˈrɒlədʒɪ). Also 8 (9) ourology. [f. URO-¹ + -LOGY. Cf. F. *urologie* (1877) and URINOLOGY.] †**a.** A treatise or discourse on urines. *Obs.* **b.** The scientific study of urine, its secretion and constituents.

1753 *Chambers' Cycl.* Suppl. s.v., The chemists have given us treatises on the analysis of urine, and the preparations of it, such as the phosphorus, &c. under the name of *ourologies*. **1855** DAY in *British & For. Medico-Chirurg. Jrnl.* July 71 Contributions to Urology. **1895** *Lancet* 12 Jan. 99/2 Now there are many works on urology.

Hence **uroˈlogical** *a.*, pertaining to or dealing with urology; **uˈrologist**, one versed or skilled in urology.

1855 DAY in *Brit. & For. Medico-Chirurg. Jrnl.* July 89 The various causes.. are discussed.. by Beneke in his Urological Studies. **1889** *Lancet* 15 June 1216/1 Professor Heller.. had a high reputation as a urologist. **1913** *Times* 9 Aug. 4/1 The Surgical and Urological Sections [of the Congress of Medicine].

†**ˈuromancy.** *Obs.* [ad. mod.L. *uromantia*: see URO-¹ and -MANCY, and cf. F. *uromancie*, Sp. *uromancia.*] = URINOMANCY.

1569 J. SANFORD tr. *Agrippa's Van. Artes* lxxxiii. 145 b, For this cause Scatomancie, Oromancie [*sic*], Drymimancie, be called the diuinations or Prognostications of Phisitians, gathered by ordures and vrines. **1625** HART *Anat. Ur.* I. v. 47 This Parson being.. reputed famous in vromancie. [**1721** BAILEY. **1823** CRABB.]

†**uroˈmantical,** *a.* *Obs.*⁻¹ [f. mod.L. *uromantia* (see prec.) + -ICAL.] Of or pertaining to urinomancy.

1623 HART *Arraignm. Ur.* v. 70 A certaine Physitian of no small account and fame for his supposed uromanticall skill.

‖**uro'mastix.** *Zool.* [mod.L.: see URO-² and -MASTIX.] One or other species of a genus (*Uromastix*) of thorn-tailed, agamoid ground-lizards, native to parts of the Old World and Australia.

In earlier use only as the generic name.

[**1681** GREW *Musæum* 46. **1753** *Chambers' Cycl.* Suppl. s.v. *Cordylus.* **1838** *Penny Cycl.* XII. 441. **1840** *Cuvier's Anim. Kingd.* 275.] **1860** TRISTRAM *Gt. Sahara* 406 *Uromastix Spinipes*, Geoff.; the dabb (common uromastyx).

uronic (jʊ'rɒnɪk), *a. Chem.* [f. URO-¹ + *-n-* + -IC 1 b, or f. GLYC)URONIC *a.*] ***uronic acid***: any derivative of a monosaccharide in which the $-CH_2OH$ group has been oxidized to a $-COOH$ group.

1925 D. R. NANJI et al. in *Jrnl. Soc. Chem. Industry* 253 T/2 Lactose oxidised by bromine in presence of calcium carbonate yields a dicarboxylic acid from which galacturonic acid can be obtained on hydrolysis, whilst sucrose under similar treatment yields glycuronic acid. We shall refer to these compounds as 'uronic' acids. **1946** *Nature* 24 Aug. 271/1 The viscosity of solutions containing the 'recovered' sodium alginate is..higher..than that of solutions of salts of low molecular uronic acids. **1982** N. B. SCHWARTZ in T. M. Devlin *Textbk. Biochem.* viii. 430 The long heteropolysaccharide chains are made up largely of disaccharide repeating units, in which one sugar is a hexosamine and the other a uronic acid.

uroo. Var. of EURO.

uropod ('jʊərəʊpɒd). *Zool.* [f. URO-² + Gr. πούς, ποδ- foot.] Orig., any abdominal appendage of a crustacean; now *spec.* each of the sixth and last pair of abdominal appendages of malacostracan crustacea, which together form part of the tail fan in lobsters.

[**1884** A. SEDGWICK tr. *Claus's Elem. Text-bk. Zool.* x. 454 The three posterior pairs of abdominal feet (uropoda) are well developed and often much elongated.] **1893** T. R. R. STEBBING *Crustacea* iv. 46 In Amphipoda the fourth and fifth pairs [of abdominal appendages] are more or less adapted for springing, and bear the name of uropods, or tail-feet. This name is also given to the appendages of the twentieth segment whenever they are present. **1933** R. H. WOLCOTT *Animal Biol.* xiii. 251 The appendages of the last abdominal segment [of the crayfish] are broad and flat and are called uropods. **1974** *Encycl. Brit. Macropædia* V. 547/1 In hermit crabs the uropods are modified into structures that help to hold the abdomen of the crab in the gastropod shell in which it lives.

uropoietic (jʊərəʊpɔɪ'ɛtɪk), *a.* Also 8 -poetic. [ad. mod.L. *uropoietic-us*: see URO-¹ and POIETIC *a.*, and cf. F. *uropoétique.*] Concerned with, of or pertaining to, the secretion of urine; secreting or excreting urine.

1783 H. WATSON in *Med. Commun.* I. 234 The uropoetic viscera were not..diseased. **1793** T. BEDDOES *Calculus* 37 Such an action of the uropoietic organs. **1839–47** *Todd's Cycl. Anat.* III. 366/1 The uropoietic system.. communicates with the respiratory cavity. **1877** HUXLEY *Anat. Inv. Anim.* i. 62 Uropoietic organs..are probably represented by the water-vascular system and segmental organs of the worms.

uroporphyrin (jʊərəʊ'pɔːfɪrɪn). *Biochem.* [ad. G. *urinporphyrin* (H. Fischer 1915, in *Zeitschr. f. physiol. Chem.* XCV. 34): see URO-¹ and PORPHYRIN.] Any of a group of porphyrins, occurring esp. in the urine during certain types of porphyria, in which each of the pyrrole rings has one acetate and one propionate side chain.

[**1915** *Chem. Abstr.* IX. 2884 Methyl ester..prepd. by the action of MeOH-HCl upon urinoporphyrin.] **1924** *Ibid.* XVIII. 2720 For uroporphyrin and coproporphyrin..the spectra are now shown to be quite distinct. **1939**, etc. [see PORPHOBILINOGEN]. **1955** [see next]. **1958** *New Biol.* XXV. 75 The African plantain-eaters [*sc.* a family of birds]..are unique in possessing two uroporphyrin pigments, green turacoverdin and the turacin. **1978** A. R. BATTERSBY in Porter & Fitzsimons *Further Perspectives Org. Chem.* (CIBA Symp. No. 53) 37 M. Thompson mixed the protiomethyl ester of uroporphyrin-II with the corresponding deuteriomethyl ester.

uroporphyrinogen (jʊərəʊpɔːfɪ'rɪnədʒən). *Biochem.* [a. G. *uroporphyrinogen* (Fischer & Zerweck 1924, in *Zeitschr. f. physiol. Chem.* CXXXVIII. 242): see prec. and -OGEN.] Any porphyrinogen in which the pyrrole rings have side chains as in a uroporphyrin.

1924 *Chem. Abstr.* XVIII. 3063 (*heading*) Uroporphyrinogen heptamethyl ester and a new conversion of uro- into coproporphyrin. **1955** *Science* 17 June 878/2 Uroporphyrins and very small amounts of coproporphyrins have been recovered after incubation of uroporphyrinogen I or III..with *Chlorella* preparations. **1982** T. M. DEVLIN *Textbk. Biochem.* xxii. 1077/1 This enzyme acts on the side chains of the uroporphyrinogens to form the coproporphyrinogens.

uropygial (-'pɪdʒɪəl), *a.* and *sb. Ornith.* [a. F. *uropygial*: see UROPYGI-UM and -AL¹.]

1. *adj.* Situated on, belonging to, the rump or uropygium. Usu. ***uropygial gland.***

1870 ROLLESTON *Anim. Life* 16 The crop and the uropygial gland are peculiar to, though not universally found in Birds. **1884** COUES *N. Amer. Birds* 86 This is a two-lobed..gland, saddled upon the 'pope's nose', at the root of the tail, and hence sometimes called the uropygial or rump gland. **1891** *Cent. Dict.* s.v., Uropygial feathers.

2. *sb.* A rump-feather.

1886 NEWTON in *Encycl. Brit.* XX. 180/2 The middle feathers of the tail, ordinarily concealed..by the uropygials, are black.

‖**uropygium** (-'pɪdʒɪəm). *Ornith.* [med.L. *ūropygium* (Diefenb.), ad. Gr. οὐροπύγιον. Cf. It. and Pg. *uropigio.*] The rump in birds.

1771 G. WHITE *Let.* in *Selborne* (1789) xxxv. 92 The trains of those magnificent birds [*sc.* peacocks]..growing not from their *uropygium*, but all up their backs. **1813** BINGLEY *Anim. Biog.* (ed. 4) II. 235 The brilliant train of the Peacock..not growing from the *uropygium* (or rump,) but upon the back. **1835–6** OWEN in *Todd's Cycl. Anat.* I. 349/1 A gland which is situated above the coccyx or uropygium. **1886** P. L. SCLATER *Catal. Birds Brit. Mus.* XI. 17 Cap, uropygium, and upper wing-coverts shining blue.

uroscopy (jʊ'rɒskəpɪ). Also 7 ouroscopie, 9 -scopy. [ad. mod.L. *uroscopia*: see URO-¹ and -SCOPY, and cf. Sp. *uroscopia*, F. *uroscopie.*]

1. The scientific examination of urine, esp. as a means of diagnosing diseases; = URINOSCOPY.

1646 SIR T. BROWNE *Pseud. Ep.* To Rdr. A 4, Composed by snatches of time, as medicall vacations and the fruitlesse importunity of Vroscopy would permit us. [**1656** BLOUNT. **1658** PHILLIPS.] **1804** *Edin. Rev.* III. 415 Uroscopy has, in some measure, given way to cranioscopy. **1863** W. O. MARKHAM tr. *Anal. Urine*, etc. 281 The progress of Organic Chemistry, and the general study of the microscope, first gave its scientific value to uroscopy. **1888** *Libr. Mag.* (N.Y.) Mar. 252 As a physician he was skilful in dietetics and uroscopy.

†**2.** Divination by inspection of the urine; = UROMANCY. *Obs. rare.*

1650 H. BROOKE *Conserv. Health* 209 The Vanities and Deceits of Vroscopy, or Devination by Vrin. **1651** WITTIE *Primrose's Pop. Err.* To Rdr., Many of them doe by Ouroscopie or Chiromancie undertake to tell Fortunes. **1857** MAYNE *Expos. Lex.* 847 *Ouroscopia*,..ouroscopy.

Hence **uro'scopic** *a.* [F. *uroscopique*], = URINOSCOPIC *a.* (*Cent. Dict.*, 1891); **'uroscopist**, one skilled or versed in uroscopy.

1889 *Buck's Handbk. Med. Sci.* VII. 403/2 Actuarius, the 'Uroscopist' of the Byzantine court, described in the minutest detail the visible changes of urine in health and in disease.

uro'stealith. *Chem.* [ad. G. *urostealit* (Heller, 1845), f. *uro-* URO-¹ + Gr. στέαρ fat + *-lit* -LITH.] A peculiar fatty substance found in certain urinary calculi.

1846 G. BIRD *Urin. Deposits* (ed. 2) 314 The urine, in the only case in which urostealith has been hitherto found. **1858** THUDICHUM *Urine* 415 Urostealith was found dissolved in the urine.

attrib. **1872** BRYANT *Pract. Surg.* 523 The uro-stealith, and the siliceous formations. **1883** *Holmes' Syst. Surg.* (ed. 3) III. 250 The uro-stealith calculus is another of the pseudo-forms.

So **uro'stealite.** [Cf. -LITE.]

1854 R. D. THOMSON *Cycl. Chem.* 511/2 *Urostealite*, an urinary calculus insoluble in water. **1868** *Watts' Dict. Chem.* V. 968.

'urostyle. *Biol.* [f. URO-² + Gr. στῦλος pillar.] The posterior unsegmented portion of the vertebral column in certain fishes and amphibians.

1875 HUXLEY & MARTIN *Elem. Biol.* 183 The commencement of the canal of the urostyle. *Ibid.* 204–6. **1878** F. J. BELL *Gegenbaur's Comp. Anat.* 433 A long dagger-shaped bony piece..ordinarily known as the urostyle. **1888** ROLLESTON & JACKSON *Anim. Life* 94 The last or terminal caudal vertebra..has the centrum prolonged into the urostyle.

uro'toxic, *a.* [See URO-¹ and TOXIC *a.*] Of or pertaining to the toxicity or toxic materials of the urine.

1890 BILLINGS *Med. Dict.* s.v. **1897** *Allbutt's Syst. Med.* IV. 330 By comparing the amount of urine injected with the weight of the animal he established what he [*sc.* Bouchard] called urotoxic equivalents. **1898** [see next].

'urotoxy. [Cf. prec.] The toxic quality or substance of the urine; a unit of urine in respect of its toxicity.

The fuller form ***urotoxicity*** is sometimes used.

1890 G. M. GOULD *Med. Dict.* 452/2 *Urotoxy*, a term invented by Bouchard to denote the standard of toxicity of urine necessary to kill a kilogramme of living substance. **1898** V. C. VAUGHAN *Ptomaïns*, etc. 125 The term urotoxy has been employed to designate the relative toxicity of the urine in various conditions. *Ibid.* 127 The urotoxic coefficient is the number of urotoxies which 1 kgm. of man forms in twenty-four hours.

urouer, urour(e, south. var. FROVER *sb. Obs.*

†**'urous,** *a. Chem. Obs.* [f. UR-INE *sb.*¹ + -OUS c.] ***urous acid, oxide***: (see quots.).

1855 DUNGLISON *Med. Dict.*, *Urous acid*, uric oxide. **1860** MAYNE *Expos. Lex.* 1314 *Uric Oxide*,..otherwise termed urous oxide, and xanthic oxide. **1878** KINGZETT *Anim. Chem.* 206 Xanthine..is known in old publications also as uric oxide and urous acid.

urous, var. EUROUS *a. Obs.*

urox, anglicized f. UROCHS. (Cf. URE-OX.)

1879 J. TODHUNTER *Alcestis* 19 Uroxen from the mountains..Lashing their lazy tails. [**1879–** in various Dicts.]

u'roxanate. *Chem. rare*⁻¹. [f. UROXAN-IC *a.* + -ATE¹ 1 c.] A salt of uroxanic acid.

1868 WATTS *Dict. Chem.* V. 969 After several weeks or months, tabular crystals of potassic uroxanate are formed.

uroxanic (jʊərɒk'sænɪk), *a. Chem.* [f. UROXAN-THIN + -IC 1 b.] Of an acid: Obtained by oxidation of uric acid in alkaline solution.

1854 R. D. THOMSON *Cycl. Chem.* 512/1 Uroxanic Acid ..; obtained by allowing a solution of uric acid in excess of potash to stand, when this acid is deposited along with urate of potash. **1868** *Watts' Dict. Chem.* V. 969 A yellowish hygroscopic substance is left,..having the composition of uroxanic anhydride, $C^5N^4H^8O^5$ (which is also that of dialurate of ammonium). **1884** ROSCOE & SCHORLEMMER *Treat. Chem.* III. II. 297 Uroxanic Acid, $C_5H_8N_4O_6$, is formed when a solution of uric acid in caustic potash is exposed for some months to the action of air free from carbon dioxide.

uro'xanthin (jʊərə'zænθɪn). *Chem.* Also -ine. [a. G. *uroxanthin* (Heller): see URO-¹ and XANTHIN(E. Cf. F. *uroxanthine.*] = INDICAN.

1846 G. BIRD *Urin. Deposits* (ed. 2) 73 Heller has lately given the name of uroxanthin to the reputed pigment, but which he has not succeeded in separating. **1858** THUDICHUM *Urine* 4 The lemon-yellow colour, sometimes met with in cholera, or in spinal disease, is due to the presence of an excess of uroxanthine. **1889** *Buck's Handbk. Med. Sci.* VII. 416/2 Urine indican (Heller's uroxanthin and the indogen of Thudichum) is not a pigment.

‖**urraca.** Also uraca. [Sp. *urraca* magpie.] (See quots.)

1882 E. W. WHITE in *Proc. Zool. Soc.* 619 *Guira piririgua* (Vieill.)..The native name of this noisy bird is 'Uraca'; and it is found abundantly all over the [Argentine] Republic. *Ibid.*, The Uracas are sometimes tamed and kept in houses to rid them of insects. **1894–5** LYDEKKER *Roy. Nat. Hist.* III. 321 The urraca jay (*Cyanocorax chrysops*) is a well-known Brazilian species.

urre, var. IRRE *sb. Obs.*

urrhodin ('jʊərədɪn). *Chem.* Also -ine. [ad. G. *urorhodin* (Heller), f. *uro-* URO-¹ + Gr. ῥόδ-ον the rose + -IN¹.] A red colouring matter or pigment found in the urine in certain morbid conditions.

1846 G. E. DAY tr. *Simon's Anim. Chem.* II. 522 Uroglaucin and urrhodin occur in diseases..similar in one [character]—the presence of an excess of urea in the blood. **1863** W. O. MARKHAM tr. *Anal. Urine*, etc. 45 In an amorphous state, urrhodine forms rosy-red granules. **1889** [see UROGLAUCIN].

Hence **urrhodinic** (-'ɪnɪk) *a.*, pertaining to or derived from urrhodin.

1886 R. KIRK in *Brit. Med. Jrnl.* 27 Nov. 1018/2 We would propose to call it, from its source and from its colour, Urrhodinic acid. *Ibid.*, The crystals of urrhodinic acid.

†**urring tanye,** obs. var. ORANGE-TAWNY *sb.*

1575 G. HARVEY *Letter-bk.* (Camden) 143 Yᵉ small inamled ring with a ribben of urring tanye.

urry. *dial.* ? *Obs.* [Of obscure origin.] (See quots.)

1669 WORLIDGE *Syst. Agric.* 24, I have seen much of the blew Clay which they call Urry that's digged out of Coal-mines, and lyes neer the Coal, laid on Meadow, and Pasture-lands, to a very considerable advantage. [Hence in *Dict. Rust.*, Kersey, *Fam. Dict.*, etc.] **1712** J. MORTON *Nat. Hist. Northampt.* 119 The black Earth call'd Urry.

urrysone, urs, obs. ff. ORISON, OURS.

urs (ʊəs). Also 'urs, Urs. [a. Arab. *'urs*, lit. 'marriage ceremony'.] A ceremony celebrating the anniversary of the death of a Muslim saint. Also *attrib.*

1839 T. J. NEWBOLD *Straits of Malacca* I. v. 252 There is no particular day..on which they congregate to perform the Urs, or pilgrimage. **1885** T. P. HUGHES *Dict. Islam* 655/2 *'Urs*..., the ceremonies observed at the anniversary of the death of any celebrated saint or *murshid*. **1974** *Encycl. Brit. Macropædia* IX. 920/1 The Muslim masses also celebrate the death anniversaries of various saints in a ceremony called *'urs* (literally, 'nuptial ceremony'). The saints, far from dying, are believed to reach the zenith of their spiritual life on this occasion. **1975** *Bangladesh Observer* 18 July 8/1 Five hundred Muslims from Bangladesh and 150 from Pakistan were among about one lakh devouts who attended the urs. **1979** *Morning News* (Karachi) 24 May 3/4 An exquisite silver embroidered velvet green 'Chadar'..will be flown..from Lahore for laying at the Mazar of Hazrat Khwaja Moeenuddin Chishti during the Urs celebrations starting at Ajmer Sharif from May 28.

‖**Ursa** ('ɜːsə). [L. *ursa* bear (esp. she-bear), Great Bear constellation. Cf. URSE, and Pr. and Pg. *ursa*, It. *orsa*, Sp. *oso.*]

1. *Astr.* = sense 2.

c **888** K. ÆLFRED *Boeth.* xxxix. §13 Ne se steorra þe we hataδ Ursa ne cymδ næfre on þam westdæle. *c* **1374** CHAUCER *Boeth.* IV. met. vi. (1868) 143 þe sterre yclepid þe bere... þe same sterre vrsa. **1791** COWPER *Iliad* XVIII. 606 The might Of huge Orion, with Him Ursa call'd, Known also by his popular name, the Wain, That spins around the pole.

2. ***Ursa Major***: **a.** *Astr.* The northern constellation also called the Great Bear.

1398 TREVISA *Barth. De P.R.* VIII. xxiii. (Bodl. MS.), þe taille of þe figure that hatte vrsa maior. **1412–20** LYDG. *Chron. Troy* I. 710 Amongis sterrys..sche is stallyd, And Vrsa Maior is of clerkys callyd. **1553** EDEN *Treat. Newe Ind.* (Arb.) 22 Being not farre from *Vrsa maior*, called charles wayne. **1605** SHAKS. *Lear* I. ii. 141 My Natiuity was vnder

Vrsa Maior, so that it followes, I am rough and Leacherous. **1728** CHAMBERS *Cycl.* s.v. *Constellation*, Thus, Hevelius, *v.g.* between Leo and Ursa Major, makes Leo Minor;.. under the Tail of Ursa Major, Canes Venatici, &c. **1843** CARLYLE *Past & Pr.* III. xi, The huge Winds, that sweep from Ursa Major to the Tropics. **1868** LOCKYER *Elem. Astron.* §341 One of the most striking circumpolar constellations is Ursa Major,.. the Plough, or Charles' Wain, as it is otherwise called.

b. † (*a*) One whose sign or symbol is a bear (see first quot.). *Obs.* (*b*) A person (regarded as) having a very bearish disposition or appearance.

a **1635** NAUNTON *Fragm. Reg.* (Arb.) 31 There were others that steered and stood at the Helm besides himself [Burleigh], and more Starres in the Firmament of her grace [Q. Eliz.] than *Vrsa major*, or the Bear with the ragged staffe. **1773** BOSWELL *Tour Hebrides* 6 Nov., My father's opinion of Dr. Johnson may be conjectured from the name he afterwards gave him, which was *Ursa Major*. **1788** BURNS *Fête Champetre* i, Or him [*sc.* Jas. Boswell] wha led o'er Scotland a' The meikle Ursa-Major. **1893** CROCKETT *Stickit Min.* 273 Strong, stalwart, unkemp, John Bradford,.. Minister of the Queen, strode over the Galloway heather in his rough home-spun. 'Ursa Major' they called him in the House.

3. ***Ursa Minor***, the Little Bear constellation.

[**1597** G. HARVEY *Trim. Nashe* G 2 b, At last louing like.. the two sisters *Vrsa maior* and *Vrsa minor*, wee may bee carried vp to heauen together, and there translated into two starres. **1638** CHILMEAD *Treat. Globes* iii. (Hakl. Soc.) 50 The first [northern constellation] is called in Latine Ursa Minor,.. that is to say, the lesser Beare.] **1728** CHAMBERS *Cycl.* s.v. *Septentrio*, A Northern Constellation, more usually call'd *Ursa minor*, or the little Bear. **1843** *Penny Cycl.* XXVI. 55/1 Ursa major and Ursa Minor.. [are] two of the most remarkable constellations of the northern hemisphere. **1868** LOCKYER *Elem. Astron.* §341 The northern celestial pole lies in Ursa Minor.

'ursal, *a.* [f. L. *urs-a* or *urs-us* bear + -AL[1].] Resembling a bear in disposition or characteristic features; hence *fig.*, bearish. (Cf. URSINE *a.* 3.)

1837 *Fraser's Mag.* XVI. 201 The subsequent encouragement of these ursal authorities was generally referable to military commanders. **1840** tr. *Cuvier's Anim. Kingd.* 100 The Otaries [include].. The Ursal ..(*Arctocephalus ursinus*..)—Eight feet long, no mane, varying from brown to whitish. **1848** MAUNDER *Treas. Nat. Hist.* 718/2 *Ursal*, [applied to] a species of Seal,.. It is said to be.. most pugnacious and ferocious.

‖**Urschleim** ('uːrʃlaɪm). [Ger., f. *ur-* UR- + *schleim* slime.] In early biology, the original form of life; protoplasm.

1921 G. B. SHAW *Back to Methuselah* p. xxix, Lorenz Oken.. defined the original substance from which all forms of life have developed as protoplasm, or, as he called it, primitive slime (*Urschleim*). **1958** *Times Lit. Suppl.* 15 Aug. 454/4 When first it was investigated a belief arose in a plain of *Urschleim* on the ocean bed, a protoplasmic half-living matter, in which the process of creation was still at work.

†**urse**. *Sc. Obs. rare.* [ad. L. *urs-a* or *urs-us* bear. Cf. URSA.]

1. *pl.* The Great and Little Bear constellations.

1513 DOUGLAS *Æneid* XIII. Prol. 67, I se the poill, and eik the Ursis brycht. **1536** BELLENDEN *Cron. Scot.* (1541) A i b, Abone our heid wes the vrsis twane.

2. A bear.

1600 COLVILLE *Palinod* (1604) A 5, As the wounded Vrse or wyldegoat seeking his Origane.

ur-seluen, obs. f. OURSELVES.

'ursicidal, *a.* [f. L. *ursi-*, *ursus* bear: see -CIDE 2 and -AL[1].] Of or pertaining to the killing of bears.

1857 *Fraser's Mag.* LVI. 146/2 Various ursacidal [*sic*] schemes to be put in practice at Jan Mayen. **1901** *Daily News* 8 March 4/7 It greatly disturbed the mental balance of the brown bear. Ursicidal mania was his complaint.

'ursicide. [f. as prec. + -CIDE I.] One who kills a bear.

a **1861** T. WINTHROP *Life in Open Air* x. (1863) 75 Vain hope! I was not to be an ursicide.

ursid ('ɜːsɪd), *a.* and *sb.* [a. mod.L. family name *Ursidæ*, f. L. *ŭrsus* bear, adopted as a generic name by Linnæus (*Systema Naturæ* (1735)): see -ID[3].] **A.** *adj.* Of, pertaining, or belonging to the family Ursidæ. **B.** *sb.* A mammal of this family.

1921, 1973 [see PROCYONID *sb.* and *a.*]. **1976** *Nature* 22 Apr. 700/1 They have revealed.. the ursid nature of the giant panda. **1979** *Ibid.* 12 July 138/1 Groups thus added to the Sahabi faunal assemblage include primates, ursids, [etc.].

'ursiform, *a.* [f. L. *ursi-* (see URSICIDAL *a.*) + -FORM. Cf. Pg. *ursiforme*.] Having the form or appearance of a bear.

c **1793** SHAW *Naturalist's Misc.* III. C c, The Ursine Bradypus, or Ursiform Sloth. **1798** [PENNANT] *View Hindoostan* II. 258 A new and most singular animal, the Ursiform Sloth.

ursine ('ɜːsaɪn, -ɪn), *a.* [ad. L. *ursīn-us* (whence Sp. and Pg. *ursino*, It. *orsino*, Pr. *orsin*, Fr. *oursin*), f. *ŭrsus* bear.]

1. Of or pertaining to, characteristic of, due to, a bear or bears.

c **1550** *Clariodus* IV. 1063 Full corpolent he was with breist ursyne,.. and sperit leonine. **1656** BLOUNT *Glossogr.*, *Ursine*,.. of or belonging to a Bear. **1841** HOR. SMITH *Moneyed Man* I. x. 290 Quotations from Scripture as to the ursine fate of prophet-mockers. **1851** KINGSLEY *Yeast* xiii, The ursine howls of the new-comer. **1880** HARTING *Brit. Anim. Extinct* I. 14 Portions of ursine skeletons.

2. Of the nature of, resembling or having the essential characteristics of, a bear; consisting of bears.

1833–4 J. PHILLIPS *Geol.* in *Encycl. Metrop.* (1845) VI. 695/2 Bones of ursine.. animals.. are rare. **1859** SALA *Tw. round Clock* 132 Any fierce or ancient member of the ursine tribe. **1870** FREEMAN *Norm. Conq.* (ed. 2) I. App. 768 The bear.. had also, it would seem, known ursine descendants.

b. In specific names of animals: (see quots.).

1802 BINGLEY *Anim. Biog.* (1805) I. 64 The *Ursine Baboon. These animals.. are found in great numbers among the mountains at the Cape. **1834** PRINGLE *Afr. Sk.* viii. 274 The ursine or dog-faced baboon.. is covered with shaggy hair, of a greenish brown colour. *c* **1793** SHAW *Naturalist's Misc.* III. Cc. pl. 58, The *Ursine Bradypus, or Ursiform Sloth. *c* **1842** *Todd's Cycl. Anat.* III. 259/1 *Dasyurus* [*ursinus*]... The *Ursine Dasyure or Devil of the Tasmanian Colonists. **1884** *Imp. Dict.* IV. 530 *Ursine howler, the *Mycetes ursinus*. **1800** SHAW *Gen. Zool.* I. II. 504 *Ursine Opossum. *Didelphis Ursina*... The largest of all the Opossums:.. Native of New Holland. **1839** *Penny Cycl.* XIV. 454/2 The Ursine Opossum utters a kind of hollow barking. *c* **1842** *Todd's Cycl. Anat.* III. 262/2 The *Ursine and other Phalangers. **1778** COOK *Voy. Pac. Ocean* IV. v. (1784) II. 377 From the colour and shagginess of the hair,.. we judged it might probably be.. the large male *ursine seal. or sea-bear. **1802** BINGLEY *Anim. Biog.* (1805) I. 193 The Ursine Seals live in families. Every male is surrounded by a seraglio of from eight to fifty mistresses. **1849** *Sk. Nat. Hist., Mammalia* III. 195 The skin of the ursine seal is very thick. **1800** SHAW *Gen. Zool.* I. I. 159 *Ursine Sloth. *Bradypus Ursinus*... Black Sloth, with very long shaggy hair. **1867** BRANDE & COX *Dict. Sci.*, etc. III. 910/1 The labiated bear, commonly called the ursine sloth.

3. Suggestive of that or those of a bear; bear-like. Also *transf.* (cf. BEARISH *a.* 2).

1837 SOUTHEY *Lett.* (1856) IV. 522 Whatever remarkable persons have been noted for ursine manners. **1858** CARLYLE *Fredk. Gt.* IV. v. (1872) I. 307 An ursine man-of-genius. **1899** *Westm. Gaz.* 13 Dec. 11/1 To the joy of all, from the Governor of the Bank of England down to the gambler in mining shares—always excepting the ursine fraternity.

Hence † **'ursinal** *a. Obs.*[−1]

a **1693** *Urquhart's Rabelais* III. xlii. 344 His Dam.. put his Members into that.. shape which Nature had provided for those of an.. Ursinal kind.

ursinia (ɜː'sɪnɪə). [mod.L. (J. Gaertner *De Fructibus et Seminibus Plantarum* (1791) II. 462), f. the name of John *Ursinus* (1608–66), German botanist + -IA[1].] An annual or perennial aromatic herb of the genus of this name, belonging to the family Compositæ, native to South Africa, and bearing orange, yellow, or white flowers.

1928 *Gardeners' Chron.* 7 July 9/1 This Ursinia remains open until dark. **1959** *Listener* 26 Mar. 572/1 For the cool greenhouse ursinias make lovely pot plants. **1976** *Hortus Third* (L. H. Bailey Hortorium) 1140/1 The annual ursinias of the flower garden are grown from seeds planted indoors or directly in the open.

urson ('ɜːsən). *Zool.* [a. F. *ourson* (1549), dim. of *ours* m., bear. Cf. It. *ursone*, Pg. *ursão*.] The Canada porcupine, *Erethizon dorsatus*.

1774 GOLDSM. *Nat. Hist.* IV. 114 The urson.. is a native of Hudson's Bay... Several of the trading Americans depend on them for food, at some seasons of the year. **1833** *Penny Cycl.* I. 443/2 The urson.. is the only species of porcupine.. which appears to have the power of climbing trees. **1891** E. ROPER *By Track & Trail* xvii. 253 There are several kinds of grouse,.. wolves, ursons.

ursone ('ɜːsəʊn). *Chem.* [f. L. (*ūva*) *urs-i* (see UVA) + -ONE.] A crystalline principle obtained esp. from the leaves of the bearberry.

1866 WATTS tr. *Gmelin's Handbk. Chem.* XVII. 361 Ursone burns with a yellow smoky flame. **1885** *Buck's Handbk. Med. Sci.* I. 482/1 Ericolin.. is an amorphous, yellowish glucoside, yielding with diluted acids sugar, and an essential oil—ursone. **1892** C. E. A. SEMPLE *Mat. Med.* 318 Two crystallisable principles, Ursone ($C_{20}H_{32}O_2$) and Arbutin ($C_{12}H_{16}O_7$).

‖**Ursprache** ('uːrʃpraːxə). Also ursprache. Pl. -en. [Ger., f. *ur-* UR- + *sprache* speech: see note s.v. UR-.] = PROTO-LANGUAGE.

1908 T. G. TUCKER *Introd. Nat. Hist. Lang.* ix. 163 The Semitic Ursprache (or common parent). **1922** O. JESPERSEN *Language* iii. 85 The basis of the whole was not an artificially constructed nebulous *ursprache*, but the familiar forms and words of an historical language. **1937** *Science & Society* I. 158 The term 'Indo-European school' is.. applied.. to all scholars using the general methods employed in the study of these languages (for instance, the building of *Ursprachen* on the basis of detailed comparisons in surviving languages). **1950** [see URHEIMAT]. **1964** R. H. ROBINS *Gen. Linguistics* viii. 319 The 'starred forms'.. give reasons for assuming the existence of an earlier relatively unitary stage of I[ndo]-E[uropean] (or any other family established in this way), the so-called Ursprache, or parent language; but they do not constitute it, or represent word forms in it or any other language. The evidence for the earlier existence of an Ursprache is not the same as bits of the Ursprache itself. *a* **1975** A. TOYNBEE *Greeks & their Heritages* (1981) 122 Greek, Latin and Sanskrit.. are all close enough in structure to their common progenitor, the *Ursprache*, to have retained the *Ursprache*'s principal characteristic.

Ursuline ('ɜːsjʊlaɪn, -ɪn, -iːn), *sb.* and *a.* [f. St. *Ursul-a*, name of a legendary early British virgin-martyr, + -INE.]

A. *sb. pl.* A religious order of nuns, established under the rule of St. Augustine in 1572 from a company founded at Brescia in 1537, for the teaching of girls, nursing of the sick, and the sanctification of the lives of its members.

1693 *Emilianne's Hist. Monast. Orders* 248 They are called Urselines, from a holy Virgin called Ursula.. who suffered Martyrdom.. near Colen. **1701** in *Cath. Rec. Soc. Publ.* VII. 88 We were.. afterwards at yͤ Grand Ursulines. **1797** MRS. RADCLIFFE *Italian* xiii, A convent of Ursulines, remarkable for their hospitality to strangers. **1823** SCOTT *Quentin D.* xxxv, These it is my purpose to dedicate to Heaven in the convent of the Ursulines. **1884** ADDIS & ARNOLD *Cath. Dict.* (1897) 912 The Ursulines do not now increase so rapidly as in former times.

B. *adj.* Pertaining or belonging to the Ursulines.

1739 GRAY *Lett.* (1900) I. 17 We went also to the chapels of the Jesuits and Ursuline Nuns. **1804** MARY LAMB *Lines Picture Two Females* 2 The Lady Blanch.. To the Urs'line convent hastens. **1815** MILMAN *Fazio* 45 Our convent gates are rude,.. Our Ursuline veils of such a jealous woof [etc.]. **1894** T. C. UPHAM *Life Mme. Guyon* i. 2 She was placed at the Ursuline Seminary.

urter, dial. form of HURTER[2] I.

1616 *Vestry Bks.* (Surtees) 72 For thre gudgions and thre vrters and a windband.

‖**Urtext** ('uːrtɛkst). Also urtext. [Ger., f. *ur-* UR- + *text* TEXT *sb.*[1]] An original text; the earliest version. Also *attrib.* or as *adj.*

1932 *Times Lit. Suppl.* 14 July 511/3 In these volumes.. we have the nearest thing possible in Chopin's case to an *Urtext*. **1959** *Cambr. Rev.* 6 June 598/2 Authoritative editions allegedly based on urtexts. **1963** S. WEINTRAUB *Private Shaw & Public Shaw* iv. 119 The earlier version still retains advocates, because of its more complete, ur-text quality, and the comfortable feeling that no Procrustean games were played with its vocabulary and sentence structure. **1974** *Early Music* Oct. 259/1 The edition is *urtext*, with prefatory staves, showing the original clefs and signatures. **1982** *Times* 2 Apr. 14/2 An *urtext* edition of the 21 Schubert piano sonatas. **1983** *London Rev. Bks* 7–20 July 21/4 Elaborate versions often point back to the gospel of Mark as a kind of cryptic *Urtext*.

urth(e, obs. varr. EARTH *sb.*

‖**urtica** ('ɜːtɪkə, ɜː'taɪkə). [L. *urtīca* nettle (whence It. *ortica*, Sp. *ortiga*, Pg. *urtiga*):—*ūrĕre* to burn.]

† **1.** = SEA-NETTLE. *Obs. rare.*

a **1682** SIR T. BROWNE *Norf. Fishes* Wks. 1835 IV. 333 Sea stars in great plenty,.. whether they be bred out of the urticas [*printed* urticus], squalders, or sea jellies, as many report, we cannot confirm. **1753** *Chambers' Cycl.* Suppl. s.v., The *Urtica*.. is obliged to throw out the shell fish alive again.

2. (With capital initial.) A genus of apetalous plants, typical of the Nat. Order *Urticaceæ*, including the true nettles; also, a plant of this, a stinging-nettle.

The original stressing *ur'tica* (cf. quots. 1764–89) is retained in some modern dictionaries. Ash (1775), however, gives *'urtica*, and this is usual in Dicts. from 1888-.

1706 PHILLIPS (ed. Kersey), *Urtica*, the Nettle, an Herb so call'd because it raises Blisters. **1764** GRAINGER *Sugar Cane* II. 505 The fring'd urtica spreads her purple form To catch the gale. **1789** E. DARWIN *Bot. Gard.* II. 103 Wide o'er the mad'ning throng Urtica flings Her barbed shafts. **1840** *Penny Cycl.* XVI. 163/1 The Nettle-trees.. having leaves resembling those of some kinds of Urtica. **1899** *Allbutt's Syst. Med.* VIII. 489 Certain species of urtica or nettle.

urticaceous (ɜːtɪ'keɪʃəs), *a. Bot.* [f. mod.L. *Urticace-æ* (see prec.) + -OUS.] Belonging to, consisting of, the *Urticaceæ*; resembling that of, having the character of, a nettle.

1836 LINDLEY *Nat. Syst. Bot.* (ed. 2) 175 Batis has a common Urticaceous fruit. **1842** BRANDE *Dict. Sci.*, etc. 1273/1 *Ulmaceæ*.. are apetalous Exogens, nearly allied to the Urticaceous order. **1846** LINDLEY *Veg. Kingd.* 261 The old Urticaceous Order.

urtical ('ɜːtɪkəl, ɜː'taɪkəl), *a.* and *sb. Bot.* [f. L. *urtīc-a* URTICA + -AL[1].]

1. *adj.* Typified by the genus *Urtica* of stinging-nettles; pertaining or belonging to the sting-nettles.

1846 LINDLEY *Veg. Kingd.* 258 The plants of the Urtical Alliance. *Ibid.* 259 Urtical Exogens, with 2-lobed anthers splitting vertically.

2. *sb.* An exogenous plant belonging to the genus *Urtica*.

1846 LINDLEY *Veg. Kingd.* 258 Natural Orders of Urticals. *Ibid.* 273 Euphorbials may be regarded then as a higher form of Urticals.

'urticant, *a.* [a. med.L. *urticant-*, ppl. stem of *urtīcāre* to URTICATE. Cf. F. *urticant*.] Adapted for stinging; producing an itching sensation.

1870 J. H. BENNET *Winter Medit.* (ed. 4) I. vi. 151 A crowd of polyps armed with urticant filaments.

‖**urticaria** (ɜːtɪ'kɛərɪə). *Path.* [mod.L., f. L. *urtīca* URTICA.] = NETTLE-RASH.

1771 *Encycl. Brit.* III. 59/1 *Exanthemata*, or eruptive fevers; comprehending.. 7. Scarlatina; 8. Urticaria. **1800** *Med. Jrnl.* IV. 201 Diseases admitted under the Care of the

Physicians..[included] Urticaria, 1 [case]. **1842** T. H. BURGESS *Man. Dis. Skin* 52 Urticaria is one of the few cutaneous eruptions which can be traced distinctly to its source. **1880** *Lancet* 4 Sept. 406/1 The urine shortly becomes scanty and of a deep orange tint, and the urticaria then appears. **1899** *Allbutt's Syst. Med.* VIII. 484 The name urticaria was applied to this affection because a process of wheal-formation..is often a conspicuous clinical feature.

attrib. and *Comb.* **1881** *Lancet* 18 June 990/2 Evanescent urticaria wheals and tubercles. **1899** *Allbutt's Syst. Med.* VIII. 609 Every prurigo papule has an urticaria-like basis.

urti'carial, *a. Path.* [f. prec. + -AL[1].] Of or pertaining to, appearing in, or characteristic of urticaria. Also *Comb.*

1883 *Lancet* 16 June 1044/2 The lesion is of an urticarial nature. **1886** *Ibid.* 22 May 968 An urticarial rash. *Ibid.*, Urticarial asthma. **1899** *Allbutt's Syst. Med.* VIII. 559 Even urticarial-like rashes may appear.

urti'carious, *a. Path.* [f. as prec. + -OUS.]

1. Appearing in, characteristic of, urticaria.

1849-52 *Todd's Cycl. Anat.* IV. 1154/2 An individual, licking an urticarious eruption. **1897** *Allbutt's Syst. Med.* III. 50 The erythemas occur chiefly in children, in marginate, papular, or urticarious forms.

2. Resembling, or showing the symptoms of, urticaria.

1899 *Hutchinson's Arch. Surg.* X. 176 A peculiar form of persistent Urticarious Dermatitis.

urticate ('ɜːtɪkeɪt), *v.* [a. med.L. *urtīcāt-*, ppl. stem of *urtīcāre* (Dief.), f. L. *ŭrtīca* URTICA.]

1. *intr.* To sting, as or like a nettle; to affect with a tingling pain or stinging sensation.

1843 [see URTICATING *ppl. a.*]. **1855** OWEN *Lect. Compar. Anat.* (ed. 2) ix. 167 An oval capsule from which a stiff bristle-like spine protrudes: these do not urticate. **1882** SALA *Amer. Revis.* I. xix. 271 The Brush-fiend..not only urticates, he hurts. **1899** *Allbutt's Syst. Med.* VIII. 469 Various 'rashes'..which may urticate or vesicate.

2. *trans.* To flog with fresh stinging-nettles; also *gen.*, to flagellate, whip.

1861 *Illustr. Lond. News* 5 Jan. 10/1 Those who are partial ..to being urticated with laurel rods. **1873** M. COLLINS *Miranda* III. 206 The one at the end of it shall be urticated. .. I mean that..the worst man on the list shall be flogged with sting-nettles.

b. To produce urtication in or on (a part of the body, etc.); to affect with a stinging pain.

1862 *Temple Bar Mag.* VI. 335 Do I urticate my back hair with two brushes? **1882** SALA *Amer. Revis.* I. xix. 270 With an ordinary implement made of bristles..he brushes you 'off'; and while he urticates you he utters a low crooning murmur. **1899** *Allbutt's Syst. Med.* VIII. 480 That scratching urticates the lesions is undoubted.

3. To irritate *to* indignation, etc.; to goad, nettle.

1873 M. COLLINS *Squire Silchester* II. xvi. 195 Urticated to unwonted indignation, it is thought he swore—slightly.

Hence **'urticating** *ppl. a.*, causing or producing urtication.

1843 OWEN *Lect. Compar. Anat.* ix. 102 This stinging or urticating property..procured for the 'Radiares Mollasses' of Lamarck the name of Acalephæ. **1855** *Ibid.* (ed. 2) 176 The urticating tentacles. **1861** HULME tr. *Moquin-Tandon* II. IV. i. 235 The ancients employed urticating caterpillars in the formation of Sinapisms. **1877** *Nature* 4 Oct. 475/1 Urticating Organs of Planarian Worms.

'urticate, *a.* [ad. med.L. *ŭrtīcāt-us*: see prec.] Presenting the appearance characteristic of urticaria.

1899 *Allbutt's Syst. Med.* VIII. 469 The macular, urticate, centrifugally enlarging, and figured eruptions so commonly seen after poisoning by tinned food.

urtication (ɜːtɪ'keɪʃən). [a. med.L. *ŭrtīcātiōn-*, *ŭrtīcātio*, n. of action f. *ŭrtīcāre* to URTICATE. Cf. F. *urtication*, It. *orticazione*, Pg. *urtic-*, *urtigação*.]

1. The action or function of urticating or stinging like or as a nettle; a stinging operation.

1655 JER. TAYLOR *Unum Necess.* v. §3. 253 A body may be said to be lustful though it be asleep, or eating, without the sense of actual urtications and violence, by reason of its constitution. **1858** LEWES *Sea-side Stud.* 146 Certain minute organs found in all Polypes, and variously styled 'thread-capsules', 'filiferous capsules', or urticating cells, are organs of urtication or stinging. *Ibid.* 148 Here, then, we have the organ, without any corresponding function; 'urticating cells', but no urtication!

b. A burning or pricking sensation suggestive of stinging with nettles.

1859 HUXLEY *Oceanic Hydrozoa* 94 The mucus which produces the well-known urtication of the human skin. **1899** *Allbutt's Syst. Med.* VIII. 483 So that..urtication..may be excited in them [i.e. elements of a certain eruption] by mechanical irritation or heat.

2. The flogging or pricking of a benumbed part or paralytic limb with green nettles, so as to restore sensation, etc.

1837 J. G. MILLINGEN *Curios. Med. Exper.* II. 55 A case of obstinate lethargy was cured..by repeated urtication of the whole body. **1870** J. G. BERTRAM *Flagellation* xxii. 207 Elidœus Paduanus recommends whipping with nettles, or urtication,..for assisting the development of the eruption in exanthematic diseases. **1873** M. COLLINS *Miranda* III. 206 Urtication is the best cure for rheumatism.

urti'cose, *a.* ? *Obs.* [ad. mod.L. *urticos-us*, f. L. *ŭrtīca* URTICA.]

1. 'Full of nettles' (Bailey, 1721).

2. *Path.* Marked or characterized by minute red, itching pimples.

1822 GOOD *Study Med.* IV. 553 Most of these remarks apply equally to the urticose variety [of lichenous rash].

‖**urubu** (uːruː'buː). [a. Brazilian (Tupi) *urubú.*] The black vulture *Cathartes foetens* or *atrata*, native to the southern United States and South America.

a **1672** WILLUGHBY *Ornith.* (1676) 68 The Brasil Vulture called Urubu. **1753** *Chambers' Cycl.* Suppl. *App.* s.v. *Vultur*, The Brasilian, white-legged vultur, called by some authors *urubu* and *aura*. In size it is equal to the common kite. **1834** MCMURTRIE *Cuvier's Anim. Kingd.* 119 The Urubu or carrion crow of the south. **1870** GILLMORE tr. *Figuier's Reptiles & Birds* 604 In these countries the Urubus perform the whole duty of cleansing the public streets from all kinds of filth and garbage. **1884** F. WHYMPER in *Girl's Own Paper* 28 June 613/1 Note..hard by, the sociable vulture,..the urubu of South America.

‖**urucu** (uːruː'kuː). Also 8 uruca, 9 uruku. [a. Brazilian (Tupi) *urucú* anatta. Cf. ROUCOU.]

†**a.** Anatta; = ROUCOU 2. *Obs.* **b.** The anatta-tree, *Bixa orellana*; = ROUCOU 1.

1613 PURCHAS *Pilgrimage* (1614) 840 The women..are well faced, painted red with Vrucu, which growes in a cod like a beane. **1666** J. DAVIES tr. *Rochefort's Caribby Isles* 43 The Roucou is the same tree which the Brasilians call Urucu. **1681** GREW *Musæum* II. §ii. i. 217 The Fruit of the Urucu. **1753** *Chambers' Cycl.* Suppl., *Orleana*, in the materia medica, the name of the arnotto, or uruca. **1863** BATES *Nat. Amazon* I. 222 The red [tints are made] with the seeds of the Urucú, or anatto plant.

attrib. **1894** *Nation* (N.Y.) 14 June 451/3 A red oil made of the uruku-plant.

‖**urucuri** (uːruː'kuːrɪ). [a. Brazilian (Tupi) *urucurí* palm.] The Brazilian palm-tree, *Attalea excelsa* (also *A. funifera*); rarely (*collect.*), the nuts obtained from this.

1860 [see INAJÁ]. **1863** BATES *Nat. Amazon* I. 342 The broad-leaved Murumuru and Urucuri, the slender Assai. **1880** C. R. MARKHAM *Peruv. Bark.* 457 The milk is subjected to the smoke of the *urucuy* [sic] or nuts of the *Atholea excelsa* palm.

attrib. **1863** BATES *Nat. Amazon* II. 168 A quantity of the Urucuri plums. **1866** *Treas. Bot.* 1063/2 Burning the nuts of the Urucuri palms. **1882** BENTLEY *Man. Bot.* (ed. 4) 705 The Coquilla nuts of commerce..are also termed urucuri nuts.

Uruguayan (jʊərə'gwaɪən, ʊər-, -gweɪ-), *a.* and *sb.* [f. *Uruguay*, the name of a republic in eastern S. America + -AN.] **A.** *adj.* Of or belonging to Uruguay or its inhabitants; produced in or characteristic of Uruguay. **B.** *sb.* A native or inhabitant of Uruguay.

1869 *Jrnl. R. Geogr. Soc.* XXXIX. 340 A piece of solid gold weighing over 1 lb..has been taken out of the quartz on the surface, and is in the hands of the Uruguayan minister of war. **1889** *Cent. Dict.*, *Uruguay..a.* and *n.* **1912** *20th Cent. Impr. of Uruguay* 225/2 The Uruguayan soil contains the necessary chemical components for the general run of agricultural farming. **1923** R. SETON *Memories Many Years* 113 There I met the Uruguayan idling about. **1972** *Daily Tel.* 11 Apr. 13/8 While duelling is perfectly within Uruguayan law, there are one or two ways in which the authorities seek to discourage it. **1976** *Nature* 22 July 243/2 The Uruguayans in their zeal to stamp out the Tupamaro guerillas seem to have 'processed' an extraordinarily large proportion of the population.

Uruk ('ʊrʊk). The Sumerian name of an ancient city in southern Iraq (mod. Warka), used *attrib.* in ***Uruk period*** to designate a phase in Sumerian-Akkadian culture.

1932 *Antiquity* VI. 198 The Jemdet Nasr culture is preceded at Uruk (Warka)..by an older urban civilization in which writing was being developed, that is termed the URUK I culture. *Ibid.* 522 (Index), Uruk culture. **1934** V. G. CHILDE *New Light Most Anc. East* vi. 146 The next phase is..best known as a result of the excavations so meticulously conducted and so promptly published by the Germans at Erech. It is accordingly designated the Uruk period (Uruk is just the Babylonian form of the Hebrew Erech). **1947** D. DIRINGER *Alphabet* i. 41 The earliest extant written cuneiform documents, consisting of over one thousand tablets and fragments, discovered mainly at Uruk or Warka, the Biblical Erech, and belonging to the 'Uruk Period' of the Mesopotamian pre-dynastic period, are couched in a crude pictographic script and probably Sumerian language. **1958** L. COTTRELL *Anvil of Civilisation* vii. 94 Phase Two, the so-called 'Uruk' period, [was discovered] by the Germans at Warka.

‖**urus** ('jʊərəs). *Zool.* Pl. ‖**uri** (uruses). [a. L. *ūrus*, = Gr. οὖρος, OTeut. **ūrus*: see AUROCHS. Cf. URE *sb.*[3], URE-OX.]

1. = AUROCHS, URE-OX.

1601 HOLLAND *Pliny* II. 323 Those Neat or Buffles called Vri and Bisontes. **1688** HOLME *Armoury* II. 130/2 Such as have Horns, and chew the Cud, as..Goat, Elk, Urus, Bison, etc. **1752** J. HILL *Hist. Anim.* 583 The bull, in it's wild state; ..Authors have called it..Urus, as if of a different species. **1766-** [see AUROCHS]. **1791** SMELLIE tr. *Buffon* VI. 171 The urus, or aurochs, is the same animal with the common bull in its natural and wild state. **1829** SCOTT *Anne of G.* ii, One of those huge horns made out of the spoils of the urus, or wild bull. **1841** *Penny Cycl.* XX. 237/1 The forest of Bialoviza..is the only place where the *urus* is still found. **1888** E. GERARD *Land beyond Forest* II. 176 The ibex and urus have completely died out, the last urus known of in Transylvania having been killed..in 1775.

2. Applied to species of fossil or prehistoric oxen.

1823 BUCKLAND *Reliq. Diluvianæ* 63 The horn of a very large urus..found at a considerable depth in digging away the diluvium. **1869** LUBBOCK *Preh. Times* (ed. 2) vi. 198 The urus, or great fossil ox, is now altogether extinct. **1874** J. GEIKIE *Gt. Ice Age* 405 Associated with this ancient peat-moss are found the bones of the Asiatic elephant,..the urus or great ox.

‖**urushi** (u'ruːʃi). Also 8 urusi. [Jap.] The Japanese lacquer tree, *Rhus verniciflua*; also, Japan lacquer, used for coating Japan ware.

1727 [see *Japan varnish (tree)*]. **1881** *Encycl. Brit.* XIII. 590/2 The varnish tree is of several kinds, and the *Urushi* tree growing in Japan..supplies, it is said, a finer gum than any other of the same species. **1909** *Cent. Dict.* Suppl., *Urushi*,..Japanese lacquer; varnish. **1965** W. SWAAN *Jap. Lantern* x. 120 Lacquer is made from the sap of the *urushi* or lac tree. **1983** *New Scientist* 21 Apr. 149/1 Far Eastern lacquer, or *urushi*, is a poisonous exudate from the stems of the lacquer tree, or varnish sumach.., which can be tapped like those of rubber trees.

urushiol (ə'ruːʃɪɒl). *Chem.* [f. Jap. *urushi* (see prec.) + -OL.] An oily phenolic liquid causing skin irritation which is present in various plants and is the main constituent of the lacquer obtained from the Japanese lacquer tree.

1908 *Chem. Abstr.* II. 2307 According to the author [*sc.* K. Miyama] the main constituent of the lac is a polyhydrophenol with unsaturated radicles in the side chains, the name Urushiol is proposed for it. **1945** *Jrnl. Amer. Med. Assoc.* 7 Apr. 920/2 It is highly probable that urushiol is the irritant common to ivy, sumac and the lac trees. **1974** J. E. UNDERHILL *Wild Berries Pacific Northwest* 95 Sumach is closely related to Poison Ivy..and Poison Sumach... It lacks the poisonous oil, urushiol, that makes them such a hazard.

urycan, obs. f. HURRICANE.

†**uryn**, obs. var. ARAIN (spider).

c **1450** *Mirk's Festial* I. 181 An adyrcope þat somme men callyn an vryn.

urysone, urysoun, obs. ff. ORISON.

us (ʌs), *pers.* and *refl. pron.* Forms: *α.* 1-2 ús, 3-5 (9 *dial.*) ous, 4-5 ows; 3- us (3 *Orm.*, 7 uss, 4 os, 6 *Sc.* usz), 3-7 vs (5 vsse, 7 vss), 4 vus, 4-6, *Sc.* 7 ws (6 *Sc.* wsz), 9 *north. dial.* uz. *β.* 2-5, 9 *north. dial.* hus (5 huse), 9 *north. dial.* and *Sc.* huz. See also 's 3. [Common Teutonic: OE. *ús*, = OFris. *ûs* (WFris. *ús*, NFris. *üüs*), OS. (MLG.) *ûs* (LG. *ûs*, *üs*), ON. and Icel. *oss* (Norw., Sw., Da. *os*); these forms have lost an *n* which appears in MDu. (and Du.) *ons*, OHG. (MHG. and G.) *uns*, Goth. *uns* (and *unsis*); the stem represents the weak grade of Indo-Eur. **nes*, retained in Skr. *nas*.] The objective case of the pronoun WE, repr. the OE. accusative and dative.

I. With reference to two or more persons.

1. a. Accusative, as direct object of a verb.

c **825** *Vesp. Ps.* xliii. 26 Aris dryhten ȝefultume us & ȝefrea us. *c* **975** *Rushw. Gosp.* Matt. vi. 13 Ne ȝelaet us ȝelaede in costnungae ah ȝelese us of yfle. *c* **1175** *Lamb. Hom.* 53 þe feder, and þe sune,..iscilde us þer wið. *c* **1205** LAY. 26490 Nimeð heom, slæh heom: Iscend heo us habbeoð. **1297** R. GLOUC. (Rolls) 1886 Vor godes loue bring us of þis wrechede. *c* **1300** *Cursor M.* 12622 Leue sun, qui has þou gloppend hus? *c* **1315** SHOREHAM I. 711 Hys blod he let os drynke. *c* **1330** R. BRUNNE *Chron. Wace* (Rolls) 11785 Auaunce now boþe þy self & ous. *c* **1386** CHAUCER *Prol.* 748 To the soper sette he vs anon And serued vs with vitaille. *c* **1460** *Towneley Myst.* xx. 189 Here is oone of his men That thus vnwynly gars vs wake. **1480** *Cely Papers* (Camden) 43 Jhesu kepe you and huse. **1526** *Pilgr. Perf.* (W. de W. 1531) 6 Vnto the tyme it hath brought vs to our iourneys ende. **1581** CAMPION in R. Simpson *Life* (1907) 435 In condemning us you condemn all your own ancestors. **1632** MILTON *L'Allegro* 117 Towred Cities please us then. **1665** SIR T. HERBERT *Trav.* (1677) 174 The Sultan..ushered us to our lodging. **1712** STEELE *Spect.* No. 374 ¶1 If our past Actions reproach us. **1766** GOLDSM. *Vicar* iv, These rufflings..will only make us hated. **1802** WORDSW. *Milton* 7 We are selfish men; Oh! raise us up. **1877** LOWELL *Bankside* 7 The same shadows on the water lean, Outlasting us.

b. Dative, as indirect object, = To us.

α. *c* **825** *Vesp. Ps.* iv. 6 Hwelc oteaweð us god? *c* **888** K. ÆLFRED *Boeth.* xix. §1 Behealde he..hu neara þære eorðan stede is, þeah heo us rum þince. *c* **1000** ÆLFRIC *Hom.* II. 124 Us ȝedafenað þæt we Godes swingle.. ondrædan. *c* **1055** *Byrhtferth's Handboc* in *Anglia* VIII. 306 Us com nu to mode hu se arwurða abbud [etc.]. *c* **1200** ORMIN Ded. 175 Off all þiss god uss brinngeþþ word. *c* **1205** LAY. 25577 Lauer sæi us þi sweuen. *c* **1275** *Ibid.* 902 þis vs þincheþ wel idon. **1297** R. GLOUC. (Rolls) 1081 Gret vilte þou askest ous. *a* **1310** in Wright *Lyric P.* xxv. 73 Jesu, my soule bidde y the, Everemore wel us be. **1340-70** *Alex. & Dind.* 447 þanne is vs grayþed no graue in þe grounde doluen. *c* **1386** CHAUCER *Prol.* 785 Vs thoughte it was noght worth to make it wys. *c* **1386** —— *Can. Yeom. Prol. & T.* 393 Vs moste putte oure good in auenture. **1393** LANGL. *P. Pl.* C. I. 175 We myȝte be lordes aloft and lyue as vs luste. *c* **1440** *Pallad. on Husb.* I. 8 Tilynge is vs to write of euery londe. *c* **1450** *Mirk's Festial* I. 1 God..ȝif vs all his blessyng. **1508** DUNBAR *Tua Mariit Wemen* 153 Confese ws the treuth. **1535** COVERDALE *1 Chron.* xiii. 19 It mighte cost vs oure neckes. **1611** DONNE *Anat. World* 21 Enough is us to praise them. **1659** MRQ. NEWCASTLE in *Nicholas Papers* (Camden) IV. 125 God sende vss a good meetinge att Whit Hall. **1668** MARVELL *Corr.* Wks. (Grosart) II. 258 Lord Bellasis writ the letter.. and red us it over. *a* **1700** in *Cath. Rec. Soc. Publ.* VIII. 25 This year the widdow Belt gave us 12 Gennis. **1743** BULKELEY & CUMMINS *Voy. S. Seas* 20 It had almost cost us our Lives. **1819** SHELLEY *Cenci* III. i. 328 Give us clothes, father! Give us better food! **1847** TENNYSON *Princess* IV. 396 Unless you send us back Our son, on the instant, whole.

β. *a* **1175** *Cott. Hom.* 223 God hus for-bead þes trowes westm. *a* **1300** *Cursor M.* 114 For to do man knaw hir kyn, þat hus scli wirschip cum to wyn. *c* **1300** *Havelok* 1217 Wel is hus we sen þe on lyue. *a* **1400–50** *Wars Alexander* 3518 So sall I gete hus ay þe gree. *c* **1460** *Towneley Myst.* iii. 46 Oyle of mercy he hus hight. **1828** CARR *Craven Gloss.* s.v. *Huz*, Shoe gavv huz ten words for yan.

c. As object of a prep. (or other governing word or phrase). ***one of us***: see ONE *numeral a., pron.*, etc. B. 15 b.

c **825** *Vesp. Ps.* iv. 7 Ʒetacnad is ofer us leht ondwlitan ðines dryhten. **971** *Blickling Hom.* 115 And æghwonon þes middanȝeard flyhþ from us mid mycelre biternesse. *c* **1100** *O.E. Chron.* (MS. D) an. 1052, Betwyx us sylfum to mycclum forwyrde. *a* **1175** *Cott. Hom.* 229 He com to us, þat he wolde for hus deað þrowian. *c* **1205** LAY. 25288 þu art hæxt ouer us. *a* **1300** *Cursor M.* 4533 Aiþer of hus a drem we sau. *c* **1315** SHOREHAM IV. 124 No longeþ noþyng to ous. **1390** GOWER *Conf.* I. 1 Good is that we also..among ous hiere Do wryte of newe som matiere. **1405** *Lay Folks Mass Bk., Bid. Prayer* ii. 66 At sche pray for hus. *c* **1475** *Golagros & Gaw.* 323, I rede we cast ws betuene, How best is to done. **1508** DUNBAR *Gold. Targe* 197 The bataill broucht on bordour hard vs by. **1584** ALLEN in *Cath. Rec. Soc. Publ.* V. 116 The whole worlde did runne from Christe..after Edwarde the vj[th] with us into Zwynglianisme. **1659** *Nicholas Papers* (Camden) IV. 95, 3 Spanish men of warre..came vp with vs and fired at vs. **1712** STEELE *Spect.* No. 374 ¶1 So most of us take Occasion to sit still. **1748** RICHARDSON *Clarissa* (1768) I. 173 We have but one mind between us. **1815** SCOTT *Antiq.* xv, He hasna settled his account..wi' huz for sax months. **1845** J. COULTER *Adv. in Pacific* xiii. 184 Our enemy numbers three times us. **1880** TENNYSON tr. *Battle Brunanburh* v, Fiercely we hack'd at the flyers before us.

d. With participles in absolute construction.

1549 COVERDALE, etc. *Erasm. Par. Acts* 24 b, Vntill he ascended vp (all vs beholdyng hym) to heauen. **1667** MILTON *P.L.* VII. 142 This inaccessible high strength,..us dispossest, He trusted to have seis'd.

e. In ethical dative. *Obs.* exc. *arch.*

1685 TRAVESTIN *Siege Newheusel* 48 They also killed us Captain Feluck. **1711** *Lond. Gaz.* No. 4864/1 They wounded us only one Man.

f. Persons like ourselves; ordinary citizens, as opp. to those in authority.

1948 *Observer* 17 Oct. 5/2 The 'whistle stops'..break down the difference between 'them' and 'us'. **1957**, etc. [see THEM *pers. pron.* 1 e]. **1962**, etc. [see THEM *pers. pron.* 3 c]. **1984** *Times Lit. Suppl.* 26 Oct. 1206/1 The Chinese awareness of 'us and them' is intense, pervasive and hard to break down.

2. Reflexive, = Ourselves. (Also †***us selven***: see SELF A. 3.) †**a.** Accusative, as direct object of a verb. *Obs.*

971 *Blickl. Hom.* 37 Ʒeþencean we ȝeornlice þæt we us healdan on þas tid, & on ælce, wiþ þa heafodlican leahtras. *c* **1175** *Lamb. Hom.* 69 And halde we us from uniwil. *c* **1200** ORMIN 7542 ȝiff we wolldenn shunenn ass To fillenn uss wiþþ esstess. *a* **1300** *E.E. Psalter* xcix. 3 And he vs made, and our-self noght vs. *c* **1386** CHAUCER *Merch. T.* 597 For we han leue to pleye vs by the lawe. *c* **1430** *Hymns Virgin* (1867) 19 For we may not hide us from þin iȝe. **1526** *Pilgr. Perf.* (1531) 26 We may lerne how to prepare vs towarde our iourney. **1594** KYD *Cornelia* IV. i. 160 Shall we..Submit vs to vnurged slauerie. **1625** PURCHAS *Pilgrims* I. II. 1133 We made vs fast to the stones of them. **1719** DE FOE *Crusoe* II. (Globe) 552 We stopp'd..to refresh us. **1729** LAW *Serious C.* xvi. 289 We must not let this hour pass, without presenting us to him.

b. Dative, as indirect object, or as object of a prep. *Obs.* exc. *dial.*

c **1000** *Ags. Gosp.* Luke iii. 8 We habbað us to fæder abraham. *c* **1175** *Lamb. Hom.* 65 Her is swiþe ufel bone, ȝif we hietieð us bitwene. *c* **1500** *Yng. Children's Bk.* 27 in *Babees Bk.* 19 Fore oure mete, & drynke, & vs, Thanke we owre lord Ihesus. **1596** SHAKS. *Merch. V.* II. iv. 5 We haue not spoke vs yet of Torch-bearers. **1600** —— *A.Y.L.* II. i. 21 Come, shall we goe and kill vs venison? **1605** —— *Macb.* IV. iii. 214 Let's make vs Med'cines of our great Reuenge. **1861** O. W. NORTON *Army Lett.* (1903) 35 We..then took possession of a stack of wheat and made us good beds and slept well. **1907** S. E. WHITE *Arizona Nights* x. 166 We got us timbers, and made a scow. **1928** 'M. CHAPMAN' *Happy Mountain* 42 We'll make us a heap o' cash money. **1942** *Sat. Even. Post* 22 Aug. 42/3 Le's go and wake us up a preacher.

c. After some verbs of motion or posture. Now *arch.* or *dial.*

c **1350** *Will. Palerne* 4594 þus sped we vs out of spayne. **1526** *Pilgr. Perf.* (W. de W. 1531) 72 b, These thynges..we shall spede vs..to declare. **1587** [see HIE *v.*[1] 3]. **1599** *George a Greene* B 2 b, Let vs hye vs to Wakefield. **1641** [see HIE *v.*[1] 3]. **1781** COWPER *Expost.* 289 The cry..is still the same—Speed us away to battle and to fame. **1892** in *Eng. Dial. Dict.* s.v., We sat us dahn on a wall top.

†**3.** Each other. *Obs. rare.*

13.. *Guy Warw.* (A.) 4575 Ouer alle oþer we loueden ous. *c* **1400** T. CHESTRE *Launfal* 108 But, syr meyr,..May y take with the sojour? Som tyme we knewe us yore.

4. In restricted use with defining term added.

c **1400** *Brut* I. lxxx. 81 To maken oppen werr and contak aȝeyns vs of Rome. *a* **1547** SURREY *Æneid* II. 252 Us caitifes then a far more dredful chaunce Befell. **1596** SHAKS. *1 Hen. IV*, II. ii. 89 Bacon-fed Knaues, they hate vs youth. **1612** R. CH. *Olde Thrift newly revived* 38 The true state and dislike of vs Husband-men and Farmers. **1641** in A. H. Matthew *Convers. Sir T. Matthew* (1904) 176 Concerning the loyalty of us Catholics. *a* **1680** T. GOODWIN *Wks.* (1861) I. 152 None of us creatures had ever come into this after-account. *a* **1718** PRIOR *Epilogue to Phædra* 5 To let Us Moderns know How Women lov'd two thousand years ago. **1814** *Spaniards* II. ii, Thou 'rt..fond to pass The inventions..As real facts upon us simple men. **1825** SCOTT *Talism.* xxv, Thou art ever prompt to pleasure us poor women. *c* **1850** LOWELL *Interview M. Standish* x, They understand us Pilgrims! **1871** JOWETT *Plato* I. 154 None of us unskilled individuals can..become physicians.

5. a. Used as a nominative, in place of WE. Now *dial.*

1607 DEKKER & WEBSTER *Sir T. Wyat* B j, Come my Lords, shall vs march? **1699** O. HAIG in J. Russell *Haigs* xi. (1881) 339 May us and all our posterity be thankful to Heaven. **1737** DYCHE *Dict.*, *We*, ourselves, us that are present. *a* **1775** *Dick o' the Cow* ii. in Child *Ball.* III. 464 England and us has been long at a feed. **1846–** in general dialect use (*Eng. Dial. Dict.*). **1880** MRS. PARR *Adam & Eve* II. 25 Us'll have down the big Bible and read chapters verse by verse. **1904** [see UP *v.* 4].

b. With sb. or adj. numeral in apposition.

c **1489** CAXTON *Sonnes of Aymon* ix. 212 None other shall knowe the same, but oonly we, vs thre. **1611** SHAKS. *Cymb.* v. iv. 70 For this..we came, our Parents, and vs twaine. **1663** PEPYS *Diary* 8 June, Mr. Coventry and us two did discourse with the Duke. **1814** MOORE *Mem.* (1853) II. 36 A thing us men ought..to bless God for. **1840** THACKERAY *Barber Cox* May, What enjoyments us aristocracy used to have! **1853** DICKENS *Bleak Ho.* vii, Us London lawyers don't often get an out. **1889** 'R. BOLDREWOOD' *Robbery under Arms* xxxv, Only us five were in possession of the secret.

c. In continuative or exclamatory clauses introduced by *and*.

1848 DICKENS *Dombey* xlvi, And him so rich..And us so poor!

d. In the predicate after the verb *to be*.

Common in dialect and colloquial use, and occasionally employed in writing.

1883 STEVENSON *Treas. Isl.* xxx, It's us must break the treaty when the times come. **1890** W. JAMES *Princ. Psychol.* I. 291 Our bodies themselves, are they simply ours, or are they *us*? **1897** *Westm. Gaz.* 25 Sept. 8/2 That is one of the things we all take for granted—because the Empire is Us.

e. As *adj.*, suited to or representative of our tastes, personality, etc.; appropriate for us. Usu. *predic.*

1940 M. DICKENS *Mariana* viii. 312 'How could you know I'd like something like this?'..'It just looked absolutely us, somehow.'

6. The word *us*.

1748 RICHARDSON *Clarissa* (1768) VII. 18 If by thy *We's* and *Us's* thou meanest thyself or me.

7. *Naut.* = Our vessel.

1622 R. HAWKINS *Voy S. Sea* 66 We had taken the Vice-admirall, the first time shee bourded with vs. **1719** DE FOE *Crusoe* II. (Globe) 519 They crowded after us, and endeavoured to come under our Stern, so as to board us. *c* **1800** in *N. & Q.* 12th Ser. XI. 42 Gen[era]l Bowls..happened to be on board of us, taking his passage..to Jamaica.

II. With reference to a single person.

8. a. Used by a sovereign or other potentate or magnate. Cf. WE *pron.* 2 a. Also quasi-*sb.* (quot. 1863).

In older Sc. also used for *we* before the name of a person.

1258 HENRY III *Proclam.* 4 And we hoaten alle vre treowe in þe treowþe þæt heo vs oȝen. **1425** *Reg. Mag. Sigilli Scot.* 11/1 Be it kend tel al men throwch thir present letteris ws Archibald Erle of Douglas [etc.]. **1436** K. HENRY VI in *Rep. Hist. MSS. Comm.*, *Var. Coll.* IV. 200 That he may wythoute delay certefie Us of the same. **1477** JAS. III in *Excheq. Rolls Scotl.* VIII. 403 *note*, Landis..the quhilkis umquhile Cuthbert Colvile had of ws of before. **1579** Q. ELIZ. in Nicolas *Hatton* (1847) 106 Such Princes as..have sought us in way of marriage. **1585** JAS. VI in *Spalding Club Misc.* I. 3 Send the samen extract attentiklie subscriuit be the shireff clerk to ws. **1601** Q. ELIZ. in Moryson *Itin.* II. (1617) 151 Tell Our Army from Vs, that [etc.]. **1708** *Royal Proclam.* 18 Jan., in *Lond. Gaz.*, They shall be liable to be Impress, except the Watermen belonging to Us. **1710** in *Nairne Peerage Evidence* (1874) 151 Be it kend to all men by thir present letters Us William lord Nairne..Forasmuch as we considering it [etc.]. **1823** SCOTT *Quentin D.* xxvii, Should our host murder us on this spot—us, his King and his kinsman. **1850** CDL. WISEMAN *Pastoral* 7 Oct., His Holiness was pleased to raise us..to the rank of Cardinal Priest of the Holy Roman Church. **1863** 'OUIDA' *Held in Bondage* i, I did know his family—the royal-sounding 'Us'.

b. In editorial or authorial use.

1835 J. POOLE *Sk. & Recoll.* I. 87 Respecting the subscriptions..to his weekly balls, it is not for *us* to speak. **1895** *Westm. Gaz.* 9 May 2/2 The man chosen to do it was the one public man who is supposed never to read Us.

9. *dial.* and *colloq.* Me; to me.

1828 CARR *Craven Gloss.* s.v., 'Give us some bread,' i.e. give me some bread. **1854–** in dialect use (*Eng. Dial. Dict.*). **1857** HUGHES *Tom Brown* I. iv, Tell us something more about the pea-shooting.

us, obs. f. USE *sb.*

†**-us**, phonetic var. *as*, *es* HIS *pers. pron.*[2] ('them').

c **1420** *Chron. Vilod.* 1916 Bot whethen he cometh & houdere he wolle þou shaltus not knawe.

usable ('juːzəb(ə)l), *a.* Also **useable**. [a. OF. *usable* (1311), f. *user*: see USE *v.* and -ABLE. Cf. It. *usabile*, Pr. *uzable*.] That may or can be used; capable of use.

Somewhat rare *a* 1800 (not in Johnson). Freq. from *c* 1840.

1382 WYCLIF *Exod.* xxxix. 36 Thei offerden vp..the candel-stik, lanterns, and the vsable thingis of it. —— *Ps.* cxlviii. 10 Bestis, and alle vsable bestis. *c* **1449** PECOCK *Repr.* II. xviii. 259 Forwhi no vntrewe speche..is alloweable and vsable. *c* **1454** —— *Folewer* 26 þe werk and office..not resonable to be excercible and vseable bi eny of þe wittis bifore seid. **1619** *Time's Storehouse* 756/1 If it be neither vseable, nor beneficiall. **1666** J. SMITH *Old Age* 82 How much service they [*sc.* the grinders] do to man while usable. **1768–74** TUCKER *Lt. Nat.* (1834) II. 636 Every wood is usable for some good purpose. **1801** *Monthly Mag.* II. 289 There is a difference..between words used and words useable. **1832** COLERIDGE *Lett.* (1895) 761 This tract is a very treasure, and never more usable as a medicine for our clergy. **1848** MILL *Pol. Econ.* I. 53 The books, or other useable or saleable articles. **1893** *Cosmopolitan* XIV. 462/2 The synonym is shorter, more usable.

Hence **usa'bility**, **'usableness**.

1842 *Blackw. Mag.* LII. 730 It is not the utility, but the useability of a thing which is in question. **1872** H. W. BEECHER *Pop. Lect. Preaching* iv. 110, I do not know anything that can compare in facility of usableness with phrenology. **1888** *Standard* 26 Jan. 2/4 They had a right to half the 'usability', if he might use the term, of the line.

usage ('juːzɪdʒ, 'juːsɪdʒ), *sb.* Forms: 3–7 vsage, 4– usage (5 osage, 6 uzag, yousage, usaige); 6 vsadge, 6–7 usadge (7 usadg, usidge, 9 *dial.* yousetch). [a. AF., OF. *usage* (OF. also *usaige*), = Pr. *uzatge*, Sp. *usage*, It. *usaggio*, med.L. *ūsāticum*, f. L. *ūs-us* USE *sb.*]

1. a. Habitual use, established custom or practice, customary mode of action, on the part of a number of persons; long-continued use or procedure; custom, habit. (= USE *sb.* 7, 9.) In group (*b*), coupled with cognate terms, esp. *custom.*

13.. *K. Alis.* 1286 (Laud MS.), Comeþ messagers..And asken of Philipp trovage, Of wood, & water, & londe, by vsage. **1387–8** T. USK *Test. Love* III. i. (Skeat) I. 111 Custome is of commen usage by length of tyme used; and custome nat writte is usage. *c* **1440** *Partonope* 332 He brente hys bonus in grette haste, That was the vsage of that contre. **1456** SIR G. HAYE *Law Arms* (S.T.S.) 73 The usage was that thai suld enter in barras. *c* **1530** LD. BERNERS *Arth. Lyt. Bryt.* (1814) 422 Accordinge to the vsage y[t] was than in y[t] country. **1581** PETTIE *Guazzo's Civ. Conv.* II. (1586) 65 Yet they are content in speaking to followe the common usage. **1680** PRIDEAUX *Lett.* (Camden) 78 The liberty of printeing by long usage, and..granted by charter till the time of K. Charles y[e] 1st, whose grant recites the sayd usage. **1697** W. WALSH *Life Vergil* in *Dryden's V*, (1721) I. 44 Every one should serve the Gods after the Usage of his own Country. **1709** PRIOR *Henry & Emma* 67 Usage confirm'd what Fancy had begun. **1768** BLACKSTONE *Comm.* III. 108 Laws..corrected, altered, and amended by acts of parliament and common usage. **1785** PALEY *Mor. Philos.* VI. xii. 642 The greater part [of the rules] have grown insensibly into usage. **1809** COLERIDGE *Friend* 225 Reasoners, who argue for a change in our government from former usage and from Statutes still in force. **1849** MACAULAY *Hist. Eng.* v. I. 573 The custom house officers..had gone on board according to usage. **1888** BRYCE *Amer. Commw.* II. xl. 83 The charter contained a sort of skeleton constitution, which usage had clothed with nerves.

(*b*) *c* **1400** MAUNDEV. (Roxb.) xiii. 58 Thurgh comoun custom and vsage þat þai er wont vnto. *c* **1444** PECOCK *Donet* 176 þe peple schulen be brouȝt into vsage and custom..forto attende into þe doctryne. *a* **1548** HALL *Chron.*, *Hen. VIII*, 189 Ther awne lawes and constitucions..the spiritualitie sore defended..by prescription and vsage. **1558** in *10th Rep. Hist. MSS. Comm.* App. V. 417 The costome and usadge of the contry beinge evidently knouin. **1728** CHAMBERS *Cycl.* (1738) s.v. *Usance*, The usage and custom of the places whereon they [*sc.* bills of exchange] are drawn. **1759** FRANKLIN *Ess.* Wks. 1840 III. 378 They alleged, usage and custom against reason and justice ought to have but little weight.

†**b.** In predicative use without article. *Obs.*

c **1330** *Arth. & Merl.* 727 In þis lond was þo vsage, Who so [etc.]. **13..** *Sir Beues* (A.) 3470 Ase hit was lawe & riȝt vsage. **1390** GOWER *Conf.* II. 386 To bidde..unto thymage Of Venus, as was thanne usage.

†**c.** ***by usage***, customarily; usually. *Obs.*

c **1374** CHAUCER *Former Age* 4 The fructes..Whiche þat the feldes yaue hem by vsage.

2. a. With *a* and pl.: An established or recognized mode of procedure, action, or conduct; a custom or practice; *spec.* one which has force in law.

1297 R. GLOUC. (Rolls) 3945 Vor hii hulde þe olde vsages, þat men wiþ men were Bi hom sulue & wymmen bi hom sulue. **13..** *E.E. Allit. P.* B. 710 Now haf þay skyfted my skyl & scorned nature, & henttez hem in heþyng an vsage vnclene. *a* **1400** in *Eng. Gilds* (1870) 349 þese ben þe olde vsages of þe Cite of Wynchestre. *c* **1450** *Mirk's Festial* I. 241 Wherefor ȝeet yn the lond of Surry ys an vsage þat when þe gospell schall be red, anon yche knyght..draweth out his sword. **1473** *Rolls of Parlt.* VI. 66/1 Dyvers Privileges, Liberties and free Usages. *a* **1568** GRAFTON *Chron.* II. 330 There was and is an vsage in England in many places, that the noble men..hauing Fraunchises ought to haue seruices of the commons. **1630** *R. Johnson's Kingd. & Commw.* 29 Three other usages have we had in England, which have kept our people in spirit and valour. **1680** [see CUSTOM *sb.* 2]. **1724** S. KNIGHT *Life J. Colet* 60 Colet thought some Usages in the Church were intolerable. **1734** tr. *Rollin's Anc. Hist.* I. Pref. p. xxxi, All I have here related was a receiv'd usage. **1766** BLACKSTONE *Comm.* II. 263 If there be a usage..that all the inhabitants of that parish may dance on a certain close, at all times,..(which is held to be a lawful usage) this is strictly a custom. **1811** *Regul. & Orders Army* 25 Well versed in the Usages and Customs of the Service. **1867** SMYTH *Sailor's Word-bk.* 708 Besides the general laws of merchants, there are certain commercial and seafaring usages which prevail in particular countries with the force of law. Underwriters are bound by usages. **1883** VILLARI *Machiavelli* IV. 117 Recommending every usage of the Romans. **1884** A. R. PENNINGTON *Wiclif* ix. 285 Every ecclesiastical usage should rest on Scriptural grounds.

b. ***the Usages***, in *Ch. Hist.* (see quot. 1855).

1718 SPINCKES *No Sufficient Reason* 2 The Pleas brought for the Essentiality of the Usages now contended for. **1788** SKINNER *Eccl. Hist.* II. [623 Many of the ejected clergy..wished to revive these ancient usages..in the eucharistic service. *Ibid.*] 633 On the 9th. of July 1724, there was a general meeting of them all at Edinburgh, where, after much communing and reasoning about the Usages, the following stipulations were agreed to. *Ibid.* 634 On the commencement of the dispute about the Usages. **1855** PROCTER *Hist. Bk Com. Pr.* 145 The ceremonies revived in the new Communion Office were, The mixing of Water with the Wine, Prayer for the Dead, Prayer for the descent of the Holy Spirit on the elements, and the Prayer of Oblation. These were called The Usages, and those who practised them were called Usagers. **1887** ABBEY *Eng. Ch. & Bps.* I. 191 A little before Hickes's death, in 1715, they were hotly at variance among themselves on the subject of the 'usages'.

c. *local.* A right-of-way.

1829 T. FAULKNER *Chelsea* (ed. 2) I. 40 Charles Street,.. Crooked Usage,.. Chapel Row. **1884** *N. & Q.* 23 Feb. 148/1 Crooked Usage is a narrow lane..[in] Chelsea. **1902** *Academy* 12 July 56/1 The straight strips of ground between the various holdings of land were known as usages.

3. The body of rules or principles followed by a particular set of persons, or recognized in a particular craft, occupation, etc. Const. *of*.

c **1340** HAMPOLE *Pr. Consc.* 3790 For þe lovyng of God principaly And for usage of haly kyrk. *c* **1386** CHAUCER *Prol.* 110 Of woodecraft wel koude he al the vsage. **1489** CAXTON *Faytes of A.* IV. vii, More ought men to obey therunto, than to the vsage of armes. **1548–9** (Mar.) *Bk. Com. Prayer, Confirm.* Pref., It is agreeable with the vsage of the churche. **1585** T. WASHINGTON tr. *Nicholay's Voy.* III. xv. 99 b, Sonnets, compounded after the vsage of their rime. **1787** J. A. PARK *Law Marine Insur.* 13 Provided the usage of the trade..sanctions it. **1827** JARMAN *Powell's Devises* II. 357 If she had been married to him according to the usage of the church of England. **1878** MACLEAR *Celts* x. 163 Adamnan was won over from the Celtic to the Catholic usage.

4. a. Manner of (ordinarily) bearing or comporting oneself; usual conduct or behaviour.

a **1300** *Cursor M.* 28456, I..has hade it in myn vsage, O mete and drink to do vtrage. *c* **1386** CHAUCER *Clerk's T.* 729 Among al this after his wikke vsage This Markys yet his wyf to tempte moore..haþ [etc.]. *c* **1400** *St. Alexius* (Laud 622) 86 Men þat ȝeden in pilerinage.. was his vsage Often forto fede. *c* **1440** *Jacob's Well* 31 þey hadde leuere fulfyllen here malyce,..þan for to leue þat malyce,..& here fals vsage, for to gon to heuene. **1548** COVERDALE, etc. *Erasm. Par. Rom.* vii. 17 b, My synful vsage was not onely not restrayned, but also seemed quyckened. **1574** WHITGIFT *Def. Aunsw.* i. 71 What opinion they had of their vsage in their offices. **1606** *Arraignem. & Execution of Late Traitors* 3 (Hindley II), The little shew of their sorrow, their usage in prison, and their obstinacy to their end. **1848** DICKENS *Dombey* viii, Mrs. Wickam, agreeably to the usage of some ladies in her condition, pursued..the subject without any compunction.

b. A practice or habit on the part of a person or persons.

1303 R. BRUNNE *Handl. Synne* 7669 Comunly, þat men done yn ȝenkþe, Yn age haunte þey hyt on lenkþe; And mowe nat leue þat foule vsage þat þey toke yn ȝouþe. **14..** *Chaucer's Rom. Rose* (Thynne) 293 Enuye..ne loked but awrie Or ouertharte al baggyngly And she had a foule vsage. *c* **1440** *Ipomydon* 1498 To the tayle was turnyd his visage; They bad hym lerne a new vsage. **1523** LD. BERNERS tr. *Froiss.* I. xiv. 14 They put in wrytynge all the dedis of the kyng..and all his vsages, and euyll behauyngis. **1587** A. DAY *Daphnis & Chloe* (1890) 16 Of these [they] found diuers pastimes wherewith to occupie them selues togethers. Their vsages were holie. **1655** JER. TAYLOR *Golden Grove* 88 O let us never..by unworthy usages profane thy holy Name.

†**c.** *of usage*, as a habit or custom; regularly. *Obs. rare.*

c **1381** CHAUCER *Parl. Foules* 15 Of vsage what for lust & what for lore On bokis rede I ofte. **1525** LD. BERNERS *Froiss.* II. cxvi. [cxii.] 333 And of usage his bedde was wont to be chafed with a bason with hote coles.

†**5.** The fact of accustoming or being accustomed to do or employ something. *Obs.*

c **1374** CHAUCER *Boeth.* I. pr. i. (1868) 6 þei holden þe hertes of men in usage, but þei ne delyuere not folk fro maladye. **1456** SIR G. HAYE *Law Arms* (S.T.S.) 84 A knycht is usit in harnes.., the quhilk usage makis him hardy and expert. **1585** T. WASHINGTON tr. *Nicholay's Voy.* IV. xvi. 130 b, They haue also the commoditie & vsage to speake and vnderstand all other sortes of languages.

6. a. The action of using something; the fact of being used; use, employment.

c **1374** CHAUCER *Boeth.* IV. pr. vi. (1868) 140 þe vsage & exercitacioun of pacience. *c* **1385** —— *L.G.W.* 2337 *Philomene*, He..kepte hire to his vsage & his store. *c* **1400** *Cato's Morals* 315 in *Cursor M.* App. iv. 1673 If þou haue carlis boȝt to serue þe in þi poȝt, to þine vsage. **1490** CAXTON *How to Die* 18 Thou haste the vsage of reason. **1509** HAWES *Past. Pleas.* I. (Percy Soc.) 5, I myght not slake Of my great musyng..of these two wayes so muche in usage. **1548** UDALL, etc. *Erasm. Par. Mark* i. 6 The world had far swarued from the right vsage of the law of nature. **1574** in Feuillerat *Revels Q. Eliz.* (1908) 242 Paper for patternes..& such other necessary uzag in thoffice. **1609** *Manch. Crt. Leet Rec.* (1886) II. 248 A doore which fformerlie did open and leade vnto the vsage of a barne. **1617** WOODALL *Surg. Mate* (1639) 8 Incision sheeres..are..scarce once in a mans life worth the usage. **1688** HOLME *Armoury* III. 317/2 The Coopers Axe..is contrary to all other Workmens Axes both for shape and usage. **1782** PRIESTLEY *Corrupt. Chr.* I. I. 94 The constant usage of the form of baptism. **1844** *Fraser's Mag.* XXX. 429/1 The usage of hops was entirely unknown to the ancient Gauls. **1870** F. R. WILSON *Ch. Lindisf.* 127 The parish register..has suffered from time, damp, and usage. **1885** TENNYSON *Anc. Sage* 270 Nor thou be rageful, like a handled bee, And lose thy life by usage of thy sting.

†**b.** The use *of* something as an article of food or drink. *Obs.*

1542 BOORDE *Dyetary* xxix. (1870) 292 Beware of the vsage of fruytes. **1585** T. WASHINGTON tr. *Nicholay's Voy.* IV. xxvii. 146 They forbade him the vsage of any kind of meat. *Ibid.* xxix. 150 [He] taught the Thebans to plant the vines and the vsage of wine.

7. Action, behaviour, or conduct towards a person, etc.; manner of using or being used; treatment. Also const. *of*, †*to* (= of). **a.** With qualifying adjs.

In freq. use (esp. during 17th c.) from *c* 1600.

1563–4 CLOUGH in Burgon *Life Gresham* (1839) II. 48 Here is suche talke of the ill yousage of owre offysers. **1582** STANYHURST *Æneis* III. (Arb.) 87 This loa..bringeth firme hoape for peaceable vsadge. **1588** SIR E. RADCLYFFE in Ellis *Orig. Lett.* Ser. II. III. 142 Her Majestie hath..comforted many of us with her most gratious usage. **1621** in Foster *Eng. Factories Ind.* (1906) 233 For kinde usadge ore refreshinge for sick men. **1687** A. LOVELL tr. *Thevenot's Trav.* I. 229 Another Saycot seeing this..came..and surrendred of her own accord, in hopes of better usage. **1706** E. WARD *Wooden World Diss.* (1708) 95 Bad Usage makes him as dull and useless as an old Razor. **1784** P. WRIGHT *New Bk. Martyrs* 794/2 The barbarous usage of those poor people. **1840** R. H. DANA *Bef. Mast* xxiii, On the whole, there was good usage on board. **1892** *Photogr. Ann.* II. 563 Without fear of their being injured by the roughest usage during transit.

transf. **1675** T. HOWARD in Lady Newdegate *Cavalier & Puritan* (1901) 74 The severe usage of the gout making me unfit to appear in any company.

b. Without adj.

1605 SHAKS. *Lear* II. iv. 26 Resolue me..which way Thou might'st deserue, or they impose this vsage, Comming from vs. **1614** LATHAM *Falconry* II. iv. 88 When you haue a Hawke.., you must be very carefull in her vsage. **1666** EARL ORRERY *St. Lett.* (1742) 197 Our usage in England amazes me. They will not only wound our estates, but our titles. *a* **1700** EVELYN *Diary* Sept. 1646, He..was..displeas'd at the usage we received. **1717–8** HEARNE *Collect.* (O.H.S.) VI. 153 She justifyeth her Usage to [= of] the Queen of Scots. **1766** GOLDSM. *Vicar* xxvi, To try how you may like the usage of another master. **1799** S. FREEMAN *Town Officer* 75 To inquire into the usage of children legally bound out. **1849** J. J. G. WILKINSON *Swedenborg* II. 191 He complained that he had met with usage the like of which had been offered to none since the establishment of Christianity in Sweden.

8. Established or customary use or employment of language, words, expressions, etc.

1697 DE FOE *Ess. Projects* 236 The Voice of this Society should be sufficient Authority for the Usage of Words. **1785** PALEY *Mor. Philos.* III. 158 All senses of all words are founded upon usage, and nothing else. **1818** CRUISE *Digest* (ed. 2) VI. 384 To make words stand for ideas, in opposition to the sense which usage had put upon them. **1845** *Encycl. Metrop.* I. 132/1 When we speak of nouns and verbs, we only conform to the established usage. **1875** WHITNEY *Life Lang.* xii. 231 As to the common name by which they shall be called, usage is very diverse.

†**9.** Interest on money lent; rate of interest; = USANCE 4 b. *Obs.*

1822 SCOTT *Nigel* v, The money, meanwhile, lying at the ordinary usage. **1824** —— *St. Ronan's* xxxix, Some debts.. have been paid up by Mr. Touchwood, who contented himself with more moderate usage.

10. *attrib.*, as (sense 8) ***usage guide, label, labelling.***

1972 R. D. WALSHE in G. W. Turner *Good Austral. Eng.* xi. 241 There is a need for up-dating. This is true of most of the 'usage guides' which editorial offices and printeries use in order to impose a consistency of style. **1980** *Amer. Speech* LV. 134 Readers of these usage guides too often take them as gospel truth. **1967** F. CHRISTENSEN in P. B. Gove *Role of Dict.* 24/2 The new dictionary has dropped the usage label *colloq*...altogether. **1981** *Dictionaries* II.–III. 75 Usage-label treatment is just as important to the composition student as treatment of synonyms. **1977** *Computers & Humanities* XI. 89/2 In this kind of usage labeling, 'label' is not to be taken literally. **1982** *Papers Dict. Soc. N. Amer.* 1977 66 The first of these anxieties gives weight to the need for rather particular status-labelling—and this term (used in Webster's) also seems..preferable to 'usage-labelling'.

†**usage**, *v. Obs. rare*$^{-1}$. [a. OF. *usager* (15th c.), *usagier* (1289), f. *usage* USAGE *sb.*] *trans.* To habituate or accustom (a person).

1530 PALSGR. 769/2 Whan a man is nat usaged in a thyng, it is no marvayle though he can nat do it.

usager ('ju:zɪdʒə(r)). [f. USAGE *sb.* In sense 1 perh. a. F. *usager*.]

†**1.** One who has the usufruct of something. *Obs.*$^{-1}$

1596 DANIEL *Civ. Wars* III. lxxxviii, He consum'd the common Treasurie: Whereof he being the simple vsager.. Did alien at his pleasure.

2. *Ch. Hist.* A member of that section of non-jurors which observed 'the usages' in celebrating Holy Communion. See USAGE *sb.* 2 b.

1788 J. SKINNER *Eccl. Hist.* II. 623 Bishop Jeremy Collier, the laborious Church-historian,..appeared keenly at the head of the Usagers, as we shall now call them. **1845** LATHBURY *Nonjurors* 291 Mr. Peck went to Scotland in 1718, on behalf of..the Usagers, as they were designated. **1877** A. J. ROSS *Mem. A. Ewing* xiii. 179 'Usagers' was the designation of a certain party in the Scottish Episcopal Church.

usance ('ju:zəns). Also 4–7 vsance (6 *Sc.* vsans), 5–6 vsaunce (5 hew-, 6 ewsaunce). [a. OF. *usance* (1271 in Godef.), = Pr. *uzansa*, Sp. and It. *usanza*, Pg. *usança*, med.L. *ūsancia*, *-zia*, f. *ūsant-*, *ūsans*, pres. pple. of *ūsāre* to use.]

1. Habit, custom, wont; = USAGE *sb.* 1.

c **1380** *Sir Ferumb.* 2217 Wat doþ ȝour men of fraunce; Of hure disport & ek hure play, what is ȝour mest vsaunce? *c* **1385** CHAUCER *L.G.W.* 586 *Cleopatra*, For to conqueren regnes and honour Vnto the tovne of Rome, as was vsaunce. **1456** SIR G. HAYE *Law Arms* (S.T.S.) 159 Efter the custum of the contree, and the usaunce of the weris. **1489** CAXTON *Faytes of A.* IV. vii, To doo suche a thinge, it is vsaunce of armes. **1513–4** *Act 5 Hen. VIII*, c. 7 Accordyng to the olde usance and custome. **1568** GRAFTON *Chron.* II. 134 By meane of which Proclamation, nothing was taken..but it were streight payed for.., which vsance continued but a while. **1620** E. BLOUNT *Horæ Subs.* 49 That must bee referred to publike vsance, not to Cæsars power. **1656** EARL MONM. tr. *Boccalini's Advts. fr. Parnass.* I. lxxii. (1674) 90 Obsolete Proclamations and Edicts, which have lost their validity by contrary usance. **1715** M. DAVIES *Athen. Brit.* I. 224 The same different Martyrologe usance obtain'd here in England. **1825** *New Monthly Mag.* XIII. 19 Ruffs..were confined by special usance to the fair sex. *a* **1839** PRAED *Poems* (1864) II. 194 By established usance, Miss Gravity is quite amiss [etc.]. **1878** J. J. AUBERTIN tr. *Camoens' Lusiad* IX. 1, The Nereids' beauteous choir..grouped together move, In graceful dances, as of usance old.

b. With *a*, *this*, or plural.

c **1475** *Pol. Poems* (Rolls) II. 285 In thyse dayes ther is a hewsaunce, That puttyth the pore pepylle to grett hynderaunce. **1583** STOCKER *Civ. Warres Lowe C.* IV. 40 Laudable and auncient Customes, Usances, and.. particuler Rightes. **1606** DANIEL *Queen's Arcadia* 2568 Custome..inchaines our iudgements and discourse Vnto the present vsances. **1658** OSBORNE *Q. Eliz.* Ep. A 3 b, Strangers to the Usances of the Ancients. **1673** RAY *Journ. Low C., Venice* 197 In our time this usance is not observed. **1860** BUCKLE in Huth *Life* (1880) II. 33, I have in this way heard something of the prospects and usances of teachers.

c. Habit or custom on the part of the individual. Also with *a*, = USAGE *sb.* 4 b.

1470–85 MALORY *Arthur* X. xvii. 440 This is a shameful custome and a vylaynous vsaunce for a Quene to vse. *a* **1568** in *Bannatyne MS.* (Hunterian Club) 195/42 In yowtheid vse the to temprance, And so begin the with vsance. **1862** SALA *Acc. Addresses* 226, I tried to recollect the things to which we have grown so accustomed.., that usance has begotten familiarity.

2. = USAGE *sb.* 6. Now *arch.*

c **1460** *Wisdom* 658 in *Macro Plays* 57 Lust ys in so grett vsance. *Ibid.* 1031 Lo, wakynge ys a holy thynge! þer yt ys hade with goode vsance, Many gracys of yt doth sprynge. *a* **1470** HARDING *Chron.* CXII. i, He a nonne had rauyshed to his vsaunce. *c* **1489** CAXTON *Blanchardyn* vii. 30 She fell doune dyuerse tymes in a swoune..or euer thusaunce of speche was in her restored. **1502** *Ord. Crysten Men* I. iv. (W. de W. 1506) E i, As sone as he cometh to haue dyscrecyon & vsaunce of vnderstandinge. **1591** SPENSER *Daphn.* 503 Riches, beautie,..nought of them is yours, but th' onely vsance Of a small time. **1615** T. ADAMS *Mystical Bedlam* 59 But why doe you call this benefit made of our money, vsurie ..? It is but vsance, and husbandring [*sic*] of our stocke. **1659** FULLER *App. Inj. Innoc.* I. 50 What was wanting..hath since sufficiently been supplyed..by usance thereof to Gods Service only. **1869** LD. LYTTON *Poems* (1894) 128 Life is good;..so is beauty. Mere stuff Are all these for Love's usance.

†**3.** Enjoyment by use. *Obs.*$^{-1}$

1483 CAXTON *Gold. Leg.* 306/1 Therto ben thre thynges necessarye:..Soueranye loue,..parfyght knowlege,..and perpetuel fruycion or usaunce.

†**4.** The practice or fact of lending or borrowing money at interest. Cf. USE *sb.* 5. *Obs. rare.*

1570 FOXE *A. & M.* (ed. 2) I. 356/1 To borrow vppon vsance, to make the money which was required. **1585** SIDNEY *Let. to Walsingham* 1 Dec., I have takne up three hundred powndes of Hans Barnard at usance. **1596** SHAKS. *Merch. V.* I. iii. 109 Many a time and oft In the Ryalto you haue rated me About my monies and my vsances. **1611** R. FENTON *Usury* I. ii. 4 They will not call it Vsurie... But it shall be termed Vse or Vsance in exchange.

b. = INTEREST *sb.* 10, USE *sb.* 5 b. Also *fig.*

The use in the 19th cent. is a literary revival.

1584 LODGE *Alarm agst. Usurers* D ij, My stocke might lye without vsaunce to my vtter vndooing. **1592** G. HARVEY *Four Lett.* iii. 48 Vse heauenly Eloquence indeede: and employ thy golden talent with amounting vsance indeede. **1596** SHAKS. *Merch. V.* I. iii. 46 He..brings downe The rate of vsance here. **1615** MELLIS *Recorde's Gr. Arts* 211 Sir, this is yet within the compasse of some reasonable vsance.

1823 BYRON *Let. to Kinnaird* 18 Jan., Make an investment of any spare monies as may render some usance to the owner. **1862** T. A. TROLLOPE *Marietta* I. 30 The old Catholic doctrine that no usance whatever could be unsinfully received for the use of money. **1890** HATTON *By Order of Czar* I. iv, He..had made money by dint of saving his profits and lending them at fair usance.

c. A document acknowledging a loan of money.

1843 CARLYLE *Past & Pr.* II. iv, One almost hopes he.. had his [*sc.* a Jew's] usances and quittances and horseleech papers summarily set fire to!

5. The time or period (varying in respect of different countries) allowed by commercial usage or law for the payment of a bill of exchange, etc., esp. as drawn in a foreign or distant land.

Orig. in the phrase ***at usance***: see below.

1617 MORYSON *Itin.* I. 278 Touching the exchange from London to Venice farther distant, by the word vsance three moneths are signified, and by double vsance six moneths. **1651** MARIUS *Advice Bills of Exchange* 20 You must not count every 30 Days a Usance,..but a moneth by denomination. **1682** SCARLETT *Exchanges* 101 Sometimes Usance is taken for some certain time after the date of the Bill, some-times for some certain time after sight. **1728** CHAMBERS *Cycl.* (1738) s.v., At London, usance is a calendar month; and double usance, two months. **1732** *De Foe's Eng. Tradesman* (ed. 3) I. 361 Usance from Antwerp or Amsterdam, payable to Venice, is two Months, payable in bank. **1759** CHESTERF. *Let.* 2 Feb., The Specie, the Banco, Usances, Agio, and a thousand other particulars. **1834** MCCULLOCH *Dict. Commerce* (ed. 2) 560 The usance and days of grace for bills drawn upon some of the principal commercial cities. **1875** JEVONS *Money* 246 Government bonds..differ..in the fact that they have very long, or even interminable, usance.

b. In the phr. *at usance*; *at..usance(s)*.

1487 *Cely Papers* (Camden) 159, I hawe made yow ower be exchaunge..an ciiij^{xx} nobulles ster: payabull at usuance [*sic*]. **1572** T. Wilson *Disc. Usury* 120 b, It shal go at vsance, which is a moneths time, at xxiiii.s. iiii.d. and at double vsance, which is ij. moneths time, at xxiiii.s. viii.d. **1617** Moryson *Itin.* I. 278 Our Merchants write their bils of exchange..to bee paid, at sight, at vsance, at halfe vsance, and at double vsance. **1682** Scarlett *Exchanges* 25 At Usance, Pay this my first Bill of Exchange..to Mr. N. W. or his Order. **1704** *Lond. Gaz.* No. 4070/8 A Bill of Exchange of 50l..., drawn at double Usance, on Monsieur Kesterman. **1716** *Ibid.* No. 5472/4 A First Foreign Bill of Exchange.., payable to Tho. Ellis at two Usance. **1849** Freese *Comm. Class-bk.* 73 A bill drawn in London upon Hamburg at usance, signifies..one month after it is dated; if at two usances, two months after date. **1878** *Encycl. Brit.* VIII. 795/1 No bills are now drawn in London at usance, and the practice is being gradually dropped in other countries.

†usant, *a.* *Obs.* Also vsant(e, vsaunt. [a. OF. *usant*, pr. pple. of *user* to use.] Accustomed or wont *to* do something; addicted *to* some practice.

c **1380** *Sir Ferumb.* 3296 In þat sche may sche ys vsaunt to do þe yule to spede. *c* **1386** Chaucer *Pars. T.* ¶821 He that is vsant to this synne of Glotonye. **1412–20** Lydg. *Chron. Troy* IV. 1629 His ȝonge knyȝtes..Swyche as he was vsant for to lede. *a* **1470** H. Parker *Dives & Pauper* (W. de W. 1496) II. iv. 113/2 Be not vsaunt in swerynge to medle the with sayntes names.

b. Habitual. *rare*$^{-1}$.

a **1470** H. Parker *Dives & Pauper* (W. de W. 1496) II. vi. 115/2 Comonly grete swerers & vsaunt swerers ben full false.

Hence **†usantly** *adv.*, habitually. *Obs.*$^{-1}$

a **1470** H. Parker *Dives & Pauper* (W. de W. 1496) II. x. 119/2 Yf he do it [*i.e.* swear] with auysement or vsauntly it is dedely synne.

†usation. *Obs.*$^{-1}$ [ad. med.L. **ūsātiōn-*, *ūsātio*, noun of action f. *ūsāre* to use. Cf. Sp. *usacion*.] Customary action; established usage.

1556 J. Heywood *Spider & Fly* xxxvii. 25 If..the flies do here pike That quarell to spiders, in customes vsacion. That is tit for tat.

Usbeck, Usbeg, etc., varr. Uzbek.

uschaw, uschay, obs. Sc. variants of issue *sb.*

usche, var. ush *v.*^{1} *Sc. Obs.*

uschew, -u, obs. north. varr. issue *sb.* and *v.*

†uscova, obs. variant of usquebaugh.

1632 Lithgow *Trav.* x. 431 Gentlemen..reserue euer in their houses, Spanish Sack, and Irish Vscoua.

use (juːs), *sb.* Forms: α. 3–5 vs (4–5 vss), 4, 7 *Sc.* us (3–4 hus, 4–5 uss), 5 ws (5 owse, 5–6 *Sc.* wss), 5–7 vse (5 vce, *Sc.* 5–6 wse), 4– use (5 uce, 6 usse). β. *Sc.* and *north.* 4 oise, 4–5 oys, oyse, 5 oysse, ois, 6 oiss; 4 vice, 5 vys, 5–6 vyss. [a. AF. and OF. *us*, *uus*, *hus* m. (also *use* f.):—L. *ūsus*, f. the ppl. stem of *ūtī* to use.]

I. Act of using, or fact of being used.

1. a. The act of employing a thing for any (esp. a profitable) purpose; the fact, state, or condition of being so employed; utilization or employment for or with some aim or purpose, application or conversion to some (esp. good or useful) end.

α. *a* **1225** *Ancr. R.* 16 Þis word habbeð muchel on vs & i muðe euch time þet ȝe muwen. **1297** R. Glouc. (Rolls) 2211 Ne conne ȝe noȝt lerni þing þat ȝe ne dude neuer er; Change ȝoure hond & to þe vs of suerd & lance is [? *read* it] do. **1340** *Ayenb.* 55 Ine þe greate bysihede þet hy habbeþ, to porchaci. .. Efterward, mid grat lost þet hy habbeþ ine þe us. **1382** Wyclif *Coloss.* ii. 22 Nether ȝe schulen touche, nether taste, nether trete with hondis tho thingis, the which alle ben into deeth by the ilke vss. *c* **1440** *Promp. Parv.* 335/1 Mesure, in vse of..nedefulle thyngys,..*frugalitas*. **1558** in Feuillerat *Revels Q. Mary* (1914) 251 To lend me the vse of one of your maskes. **1599** B. Jonson *Cynthia's Rev.* v. i, Denying to the world the precious vse Of hoorded wealth. **1605** Verstegan *Dec. Intell.* i. (1628) 23 The Picards..are said first to haue gotten that name of their great and most accustomed use of pikes. **1646** Sir T. Browne *Pseud. Ep.* I. vii. 26 In..Law and History, there is..a frequent and allowable use of testimony. **1690** Locke *Hum. Und.* III. x. §1 The obscurity and confusion that is so hard to be avoided in the Use of Words. **1729** T. Innes *Crit. Essay* 444 The ancient use of letters among the Irish. **1753** Challoner *Cath. Chr. Instr.* Pref. p. vi, What the Doctor has alledged against the Use of Incense. **1782** Miss Burney *Cecilia* VIII. viii, Is the gift of speech only granted us to pervert the use of understanding? **1831** Scott *Ct. Rob.* xi, His excellence in the use of the French language. **1860** Warter *Sea-board* II. 436 Certainly use and abuse are very different things. **1891** Sir A. Wills in *Law Times* XCI. 232/2 Massey..lent the use of his name to Kensington in order to oblige him.

β. **1375** Barbour *Bruce* XVII. 252 For in Scotland..The oys of thame [*sc.* cannon] had nocht beyn sene. *c* **1425** Wyntoun *Cron.* I. 1310 As þe makaris had daynte Off þa bestis and delyte Be freyte or oysse, or be profyte.

b. In legal phr., coupled with *occupation* (or *occupancy*).

1738 *Act 11 Geo. II*, c. 19 §14 In an Action on the case, for the Use and Occupation of what was so held or enjoyed. **1772** Buller *Introd. Law Nisi Prius* (1775) 139 In Case for Use and Occupation of an House by Permission of the Plaintiff. **1808** W. Selwyn *Law Nisi Prius* II. 1180 Chap. xxxvii.—Use and Occupation. **1918** *Nation* (N.Y.) 7 Feb. 165/1 A percentage..will be paid on a pro-rata basis for each day of lost use and occupancy.

c. Freq. *to make* or *take* (..) *use of*.

1591 Shaks. *Two Gent.* II. iv. 67 Sir Protheus..Made vse, and faire aduantage of his daies. **1606** Chapman *M. D'Olive* I. i, At my chamber, where we may take free use of our selves, that is, drinke sack, and talke Satyre. **1663** Gerbier *Counsel* 55 Those that mind the making use of Chalk in their walls. **1711** Addison *Spect.* No. 62 ¶5 The Words Fire and Flame are made use of to signify Love. **1774** Goldsm. *Nat. Hist.* (1776) V. 264 This bird's making use of the bed or nest of another to deposit its own brood in. **1823** P. Nicholson *Pract. Build.* 420 Plate-glass is the most beautiful glass made use of. **1862** Tyndall *Mountaineer.* ii. 16 We made use of all our strength. **1897** T. Hardy *Well-Beloved* I. vi, Perhaps she had only made use of him as a convenient aid to her intentions.

†d. *your* (*their*, etc.) *use*, = use of you (them, etc.). *Obs.*

1596 Shaks. *1 Hen. IV*, I. iii. 21 When we need Your vse and counsell, we shall send for you. **1667** Milton *P.L.* IX. 750 Thy praise hee also who forbids thy use, Conceales not from us. **1691** T. H[ale] *Acc. New Invent.* 37 The Ingredients..being Forraign, such has sometimes been the scarcity thereof here, (even when their use has been most wanted).

2. a. In various prepositional phrases (with *in*, *to*, *into*, *out of*, *for*, *of*).

(*a*) *a* **1340** Hampole *Psalter* cxviii. 48 For of mykil thynkynge of þe comandmentis cumys in oyse goed werke. *c* **1400** *Lanfranc's Chirurg.* 306 Þe .i. instrument þat is comoun & moost in vss, is clepid nodulum. **1558–9** *Act 1 Eliz.* c. 2 §13 That suche Ornamentes of the Churche and of the Ministers therof shall bee reteyned and bee in use as was in this Churche of Englande. **1568** Grafton *Chron.* II. 345 Gonnes were first in vse, which were inuented by one of Germany. **1631** Gouge *God's Arrows* IV. Ded. p. v, I remember a Proverbiall speech in use among the Iewes. **1691** T. H[ale] *Acc. New Invent.* 5 To apply themselves forthwith to the putting in use this Invention upon some of his own Ships. **1711** Steele *Spect.* No. 36 ¶8 All the fashionable Phrases and Compliments now in use. **1755** Johnson, *To Quarry*,..to prey upon. A low word not in use. **1801** *Med. Jrnl.* XXI. 83 Every plan of cure at present in use. **1885** *Manch. Exam.* 10 July 5/2 Those [lamps] now in use. **1890** Sir N. Lindley in *Law Times Rep.* LXIII. 690 These two forms of order..are in constant use in the Chancery Division.

(*b*) **1388** Wyclif *Neh.* x. 31 The puplis..that bryngen in thingis set to sale, and alle thingis to vss. *a* **1425** tr. *Arderne's Treat. Fistula*, etc. 89 Be it kept to vse in ane erþen potte. *c* **1460** Fortescue *Abs. & Lim. Mon.* vi. (1885) 120 It nedith þat ther be lyvelode asseigned ffor the payment therof; wich lyvelode be in no wyse putte to no other vse. **1552–3** in Feuillerat *Revels Edw. VI* (1914) 112 By him bought and prouided and spent to the vse aforesaid. **1570** Billingsley *Euclid* II. prop. ii. 63 Which oftentimes serueth to great vse in working. **1590** Shaks. *Com. Err.* III. ii. 97, I know not what vse to put her too. **1628–***a* **1700** [see put *v.*^{1} 18]. **1748** Chesterf. *Let.* 16 Feb., Every moment may be put to some use. **1893** *Nat. Observer* 7 Oct. 536/1 The gallows were put to real use.

(*c*) *c* **1444** Pecock *Donet* 51 Or ellis he takiþ into vse alle kyndis of hem [*sc.* goods]. **1688** Miége *Gt. Fr. Dict.* II. s.v., To put a Thing into Use. **1728** North *Mem. Music* (1846) 55 Instruments..invented, and brought into common use. **1835** *Penny Cycl.* IV. 398/1 At what time..bills of exchange were first brought into use is a matter..not..satisfactorily ascertained. **1879** M. J. Guest *Lect. Hist. Eng.* I. 508 Two wonderful instruments had lately come into use. **1890** *Sat. Rev.* 8 Feb. 175/2 This word came into use to express [etc.].

(*d*) **1538** Elyot, *Exoletus*, he that is passed growynge..olde, or out of vse. **1579** E. K. *Spenser's Sheph. Cal.* Epist., Such good and naturall English words, as haue ben long time out of vse. **1603** G. Owen *Pembrokeshire* iii. (1891) 36 And soe was the English growne out of use..and used only amonge the basest sorte of people. *a* **1700** Evelyn *Diary* 18 March 1649, The blessed Sacrament, now wholly out of use in the Parish Churches. **1710** Steele *Tatler* No. 174 ¶3 A broken Limb will recover its Strength by the sole Benefit of being out of Use. **1892** *Monthly Packet* Oct. 430 The name ..had in some way gone out of use.

(*e*) **1548** Elyot, *Vsualis*,..vsuall, that serueth for our vse. *a* **1648** Digby *Chym. Secr.* II. (1684) 195 Make it up into Balls..and keep them for Use. **1697** Dryden *Virg. Georg.* III. 480 The Fleece, when drunk with Tyrian Juice, Is dearly sold; but not for needful use. **1742** Young *Nt. Th.* II. 154 Since Time was giv'n for use, not waste. **1807** Crabbe *Par. Reg.* I. 81 There pious works for Sunday's use are found. **1896** Lucas *Cyclealities* 117 A small Hold-all for use with handle-bar carriers.

(*f*) **1611** Bible *Transl. Pref.* ¶1 Thus it is apparent, that these things..are of most necessary vse. **1648** Sanderson *Serm.* (1653) 6 Words..of very frequent use in the New Testament. **1833** Holland *Manuf. Metal* II. 285 Articles of such universal use and importance. **1839** Fr. A. Kemble *Resid. in Georgia* (1863) 18 Implements..of household use. **1880** J. Britten *Old Words* p. xiv, Others [*sc.* words] apparently of general use.

†b. *in the use of*, making use of. *Obs.*

1594 *Southampton Court Leet Rec.* (1906) II. 296 Robert Russell, william cortney, John grant nowe in the vse of Thomas heths brewary.

†c. *of use*, used, employed. *Obs.*$^{-1}$

1634 Sir T. Herbert *Trav.* 183 [The jacks] boyld giue food no lesse pleasant..then doe the Date-stones of vse in Persia.

3. In special senses: **a.** The act of using or fact of being used as food, etc.; consumption.

1586 Day *Eng. Secretorie* I. (1595) 27 A kind of graine growing in great cods, whereby we sometimes obtaine (though not the naturall) yet some vse of bread. **1588** Kyd *Househ. Philos.* Wks. (1901) 259 The Nurses shoulde not be so narrowly forbidde the often vse of wynes. **1697** Dryden *Virg. Georg.* IV. 231 They..hoard, for Winter's Use, the Summer's Gain. **1708** Ockley *Saracens* I. Table, *Sawik*, a sort of Food in Use among the Arabians. **1725** N. Robinson *Th. Physick* 290 The Patient should be exhorted not to leave off the Use of the Bark too soon. **1772** W. Buchan *Dom. Med.* (ed. 2) 255 Wholesome food, and a moderate use of generous liquors. **1836** A. Combe *Physiol. Digestion* (ed. 2) 319 Many persons imagine that spirits..cannot be injurious, because they feel no immediate bad effects from their use. **1862** *Chambers's Encycl.* III. 552/2 Certain substances [*i.e.* tobacco, tea, and coffee] which..may fairly be considered, from the universality of their use, to exert a definite influence on the organism.

b. Employment or maintenance for sexual purposes. (See also quot. 1841.) Cf. use *v.* 10 b.

1565 Cooper *Thes.* s.v. *Fruor*, He hath the vse of hir, &c. **1607** Tourneur *Rev. Trag.* II. ii, I cannot honor her [*ante* my mother],..Her tongue has turnd my sister into vse. **1647** A. Ross *Mystag. Poet.* viii. (1675) 176 His step-mother desired the use of his body. *Ibid.* ix. 225 [Ixion] began to fall in love with Juno, desiring the use of her body. **1676** R. Dixon *Two Testaments* 551 A wife, not a Concubine, might be taken by use; for a whole un-interrupted year without usurpation. **1748** *Earthquake Peru* iii. 247 Two ancient Ways of marrying still subsist in this Country; that of keeping a Mistress is very answerable to that which was call'd by Use. **1841** Hartshorne *Salop. Ant.* Gloss. 606 A mare is said to be 'in use' when she is under the influence of certain appetites or affections. **1894** *Nature's Method in Evol. Life* iii. 45 The bulls [are] put to use about twelve months old. *Ibid.*, Stallions are commonly in use long before they are full grown.

4. *Law.* **a.** The act or fact of using, holding, or possessing land or other property so as to derive revenue, profit, or other benefit from such.

1535–6 *Act 27 Hen. VIII*, c. 10 §6 Concernyng such right, title, use, interest, or possession as they..have clayme or pretende to have. **1579** Rastell *Termes de la Ley* 183 b/2 The stat. of An. 27. H. 8. c. 10 prouided..that who hath the vse of the lande, the same hath ye possession therof by vertue of that estatute. **1596** Bacon *Max. & Use Com. Law* II. (1635) 57 They conveyed their full estates of their lands in their good health, to friends in trust,..and this trust was called, the use of the land. **1642** tr. *Perkins' Prof. Bk.* viii. §528. 231 Before the statute of West. 3,..there was no use of lands or of houses if not that it were expressed upon the delivery of the estate. **1681** Stair *Institut.* xvi. 327 Usufruct is the power of disposal of the use and fruits, saving the Substance of the thing. **1706** Stanhope *Paraphr.* III. 334 The longest Inheritance and Descent, is in truth but the longest Use, but not so much as a Lease or Tenant-right. **1734** Pope *Hor. Sat.* II. ii. 165 'Pity! to build, without a son or wife:'..Well, if the use be mine, can it concern one, Whether the name belong to Pope or Vernon? **1766** Blackstone *Comm.* II. 137 The property or possession of the soil being vested in one man, and the use, or profit thereof, in another. **1818** Cruise *Digest* (ed. 2) I. 474 No use would have resulted to the father, because blood was a sufficient consideration to have vested the use in the son. **1888** *Encycl. Brit.* XXIII. 596/1 The conveyance of an estate to a friend on the understanding that they should retain the use, *i.e.*, the actual profit and enjoyment of the estate.

b. A trust or confidence reposed in a person for the holding of property, etc., of which another receives or is entitled to the profits or benefits.

1535 *Act 27 Hen. VIII*, c. 10 §1 Fraudulent feoffementes, fynes, recoveryes, and other assurances craftely made to secrete uses, intentes, and trustes. *Ibid.* §12 Any person.. seasid of or in any Landes, Ten[emen]tes, or Hereditamentes to any use, trust, or confydence. **1579** Rastell *Termes de la Ley* 183 b/2 Vses of Land had beginning after that the custome of propertie began among men. **1628** Coke *On Litt.* 272 b, An Vse is a Trust or Confidence reposed in some other. **1759** Sterne *Tr. Shandy* I. xv, By force and virtue of the statute for transferring of uses into possession. **1765** Blackstone *Comm.* II. 335 This is sometimes called a secondary, sometimes a shifting, use. **1766–** [see springing *ppl. a.* 8]. **1845** Williams *Law Real Prop.* 124 A doctrine was laid down, that there could not be a use upon a use. **1882** F. Pollock in *Macm. Mag.* XLVI. 365 The Statute of Uses (A.D. 1535) was passed in order to prevent the severance of legal from beneficial ownership. **1888** *Encycl. Brit.* XXIII. 596/1 The feoffee to uses, as he was called, or the person seised to the use of another.

c. In the phrase *in use* or *to* (..) *use*.

1491 *Act 7 Hen. VII*, c. 2 §5 They and their feoffes to the use of every of theym. **1535** *Act 27 Hen. VIII*, c. 10 §1 Any Honoures, Castelles,..Remaynders or other Hereditamentes, to the use, confidence or trust of any other ..parsones or of anye bodie polytike. *Ibid.*, In suche lyke estates as they had or shall have in use, trust, or confidence of or in the same. **1596** Shaks. *Merch. V.* IV. i. 383 So he will let me haue The other halfe in vse, to render it Vpon his death, vnto the Gentleman. **1606** —— *Ant. & Cl.* I. iii. 44 But my full heart Remaines in vse with you. **1720** T. Wood *Inst. Laws Eng.* 436 Where no Uses are Declared, the Feoffment, Fine or Recovery shall enure to the Use of the Feoffor, Cognizor, etc. **1818** Cruise *Digest* (ed. 2) V. 525 Supposing the Earl of Derby a feoffee to use,..still the grant ..was free and gratuitous. **1888** *Encycl. Brit.* XXIII. 596/1 This alienation of land in use was looked upon with great disfavour by the common law courts.

5. a. The fact of using money borrowed or lent at a premium.

1603 Holland *Plutarch's Mor.* 283 [They] choose..to pawn them for to borrow money thereupon & pay for use. **1607** Harington *Nugæ Ant.* (1804) II. 232 Sending some present, enough perhaps to pay for the use of 1000 li. **1641** *Aldeburgh Rec.* in *N. & Q.* 12th Ser. IX. 146/2 Rec[ei]^{vd} of Mr. John Blowers for one yeeres use of 40 li. 2[li.] 16. 00. **1729** Jacob *Law Dict.* s.v. *Usury*, Reasonable Interest may be taken for the Use of Money at this Day. **1767** Blackstone *Comm.* II. 454 When money is lent on a contract to receive..an increase by way of compensation for the use. **1862** [see usance 4 b].

b. Premium on money lent to another; interest, usury. Now *dial.* or *arch.* Freq. *to †take* or *pay use*.

In frequent use from *c* 1612 to *c* 1690.

1611 Rich *Honest. Age* (Percy Soc.) 60 Therefore, (sayth the Vsurer), we may take vse of him that is rich. **1655** Stanley *Hist. Philos.* III. (1687) 104/2 If the Moon Ne'r rise again, I'm bound to pay no use... 'Cause use you know is paid by th' Month. **1690** CHILD *Disc. Trade* 207 With them . . there is not any Use for Money tollerated, above the rate of Six in the Hundred. **1728** T. SHERIDAN tr. *Persius* vi. 93 Do not you . . advise me, to live upon the Use of my Money. **1747** *Mem. Nutrebian Crt.* I. 55 On whom he settled the use of 20,000 crowns for her life. **1825** JAMIESON. **1869-** in dialect use (*Eng. Dial. Dict.*). **1872** TENNYSON *Foresters* IV, 'Here be one thousand marks.' . . 'Ay, ay, but there is use, four hundred marks.'

fig. **1599** SHAKS. *Much Ado* II. i. 286 Hee lent it [*sc.* his heart] me a while, and I gaue him vse for it, a double heart. **1628** EARLE *Microcosm., Vniuersitie Dunne* (Arb.) 74 The sole place to supply him is the Butterie, where hee takes grieuous vse vpon your Name. **1648** J. BEAUMONT *Psyche* VI. ccxxiii, The Serpent, whose illustrious skin Plaid with the Sunne and sent him back his beams With glorious Use. **1784** COWPER *Task* III. 364 Human life Is but a loan to be repaid with use. **1874** HARDY *Far fr. Mad. Crowd* xli, You'll never see Fanny Robin no more—use nor principal—ma'am.

transf. **1637** in *Verney Mem.* (1907) I. 104 He threatens to make him pay use for his barn.

c. In the phr. ***at, to, †upon*** ***(. .) use.*** Now *dial.*

(*a*) **1598** E. GUILPIN *Skial.* (1878) 21 As heresie he shuns all merriment, And turn'd good husband, puts forth sighs to vse. **1631** MASSINGER *Emperor East* I. ii, I, alas! Lend out my labouring brains to use, and sometimes For a drachma in the pound. **1642** D. ROGERS *Naaman* 158, I would not put my mony to use; but that it is against a Common wealth to keepe it. **1680** R. L'ESTRANGE *Erasm. Colloq.* (1725) 248 They Buy, they Sell, they take to Use, they put to Use. **1700** ASTRY tr. *Saavedra-Faxardo* II. 149 We read, that Pompey put out his Money to Use. **1738** tr. *Guazzo's Art Convers.* 43 Two Florentine Brethren, who let out their Money to Use. **1785** CUMBERLAND *Natural Son* v. (ed. 2) 82 You are my own son;—you have put my money out to use already.

(*b*) **1618** *Barnevelt's Apol.* C 4 *b*, Our last borrowed money is . . at vse at sixteene. **1656** EARL MONM. tr. *Boccalini's Advts. fr. Parnass.* 95 One Menalcas . . took up money at use. **1727** SWIFT *To Earl of Oxford* Wks. 1755 III. II. 47 Is your money out at use? **1784** R. BAGE *Barham Downs* I. 172, I had three hundred pounds at use. **1814** SCOTT *Wav.* xlii, If his honour had mair ready siller . . he could put it out at use . . at great profit. **1841** HARTSHORNE *Salop Ant.* Gloss. 606 Money out at use. **1849-** in dialect use (*Eng. Dial. Dict.* s.v.).

(*c*) **1622** MABBE tr. *Aleman's Guzman d' Alf.* II. 251 Let him but take vp so much vpon Vse. **1630** *R. Johnson's Kingd. & Commw.* 353 Some doe give voluntarily, others doe lend frankly, or upon light use. **1667** DUCHESS OF NEWCASTLE *Life Duke of N.* (1886) II. 146 The loss of my Lord's estate, in plain rents, as also upon ordinary use.

†d. ***use upon*** (also ***on***) ***use***, compound interest; excessive interest. Also *fig. Obs.*

[**1591** SYLVESTER *Du Bartas* I. iii. 521 You City-Vipers, that (incestious) joyn Use vpon use, begetting Coyn of Coyn!] **1620** SANDERSON *Serm.* (1632) 111 Your vse vpon vse, that doubleth the principall in seven yeares, is nothing to it. **1651** CLEVELAND *Smectymnuus* 70 No Eccho can improve the Author more, Whose lungs paies use on use to half a score. **1682** SIR T. BROWNE *Chr. Mor.* (1756) 15 To famish in plenty, and live poorly to die rich, were multiplying improvement in madness, and use upon use in folly.

6. Employment or usage resulting in, or such as to cause, impairment, wear, etc.

c **1440** *Promp. Parv.* 522/2 Weryn or wax olde and febyl by vse, . . *veterasco, vetero, invetero.* **1670** SIR SACKVILLE CROW in *12th Rep. Hist. MSS. Comm.* App. V. 15 Theire ordnary designes [in tapestry] . . with a whiles use will soone loose theire luster. **1697** DRYDEN *Virg. Georg.* III. 6 All other Themes that careless Minds invite, Are worn with Use. **1755** JOHNSON, *To wear*, . . to waste with use or time. **1840** DICKENS *Old C. Shop* xvii, Everything told of long use and quiet slow decay. **1848** MILL *Pol. Econ.* I. 44 Although deteriorated in some small degree by each use, it does not do its work by being deteriorated. **1904** *Verney Memoirs* I. 68 The wear and tear of even holiday use.

II. Habit of using.

7. a. With *the.* The habitual, usual, or common practice; continual, repeated, or accustomed employment or exercise; habit, custom. (Cf. 9.)

1297 R. GLOUC. (Rolls) 9402 þe wone & hus [*v.r.* vse] þat ȝe abbeþ euere ibe aboue þat aȝte make ȝou abbe to fiȝte þe betere loue. *a* **1400-50** *Alexander* 2950 Sen þe vse is here vn-honorable here I þam lefe. *c* **1480** HENRYSON *Sheep & Dog* ii, By the vse, and cours, and commoun style On this maner [he] maid his Citatioun. **1565** COOPER *Thesaurus* s.v. *Usus*, To suche a one as was nowe paste the vse and custome of lewde doeynge. **1577** B. GOOGE *Heresbach's Husb.* II. 66 The vse of sowing of them is best. **1594** MARLOWE & NASHE *Dido* I. i, It is the vse for Turen maides to weare Their bowe and quiuer in this modest sort. **1604** JAS. I *Counterbl. to Tobacco* To Rdr., The vile vse (or other abuse) of taking Tobacco. **1637** EARL MONM. tr. *Malvezzi's Romulus & Tarquin* 209 The use of seeing dead men takes mercy totally away. **1656** —— tr. *Boccalini's Advts. fr. Parnassus* II. xxviii. 271 The use of being drunk, being rather a piece of publick cunning amongst the Dutch, then [etc.]. **1720** OZELL *Vertot's Rom. Rep.* (1740) II. xi. 170 Metellus Pius commanded them, as a Proconsul, according to the Use of those Days. **1725** POPE *Odyssey* x. 551 The cause remov'd, habitual griefs remain, And the soul saddens by the use of pain. **1825** SCOTT *Betrothed* xxi, One not in the use to speak before his purpose was fixed. **1854** C. WORDSW. *Misc.* (1879) I. 104 The use is inveterate, and it would be difficult to reform it. **1877** MRS. OLIPHANT *Makers Flor.* iv. 112 The painter following the religious use and wont of his time.

b. In the phr. ***as the use is***, etc. Cf. 9 b.

1432 in *15th Rep. Hist. MSS. Comm.* App. VIII. 44 The saidis Jone and Elisabeth sall be handfast, as the oys is, in haly Kirk. *c* **1475** *Harl. Contin. Higden* (Rolls) VIII. 441 That men electe to be bischoppes . . may . . be confermede of theire metropolitans as the vse was afore. **1535** COVERDALE *Judith* xvi. 20 The people was ioyfull, as the vse is. **1611** BIBLE *2 Macc.* xii. 39 Vpon the day following as the vse had bene, . . his company came to take vp the bodies. **1633** P. FLETCHER *Purple Isl.* I. v, Wake thy . . Muse, And thank them with a song, as is the use. **1871** W. ALEXANDER *Johnny Gibb* xxxv, They fixed it [*sc.* the settlement of the minister], as the use and wont is, for a week day.

c. With limiting genitive or possessive pron.

1390 GOWER *Conf.* I. 15 Upon the hond to were a Schoo . . Acordeth noght to the behove Of resonable mannes us. *c* **1400** *Destr. Troy* 6426 Nay, warloghe wolfe, . . þat neuer of forray art full, with þi foule vse. *c* **1425** *Cast. Persev.* 774 in *Macro Plays* 100 Messenger, do now þyne vse! *Ibid.* 949 Do now wel ȝoure olde owse whanne ȝe com to Mankynde! **1432** *Rolls of Parlt.* IV. 404/1 Eny clothis . . made aftre the use of the Countrey. **1535** COVERDALE *2 Macc.* xi. 25 That they maye lyue acordinge to the vse & custome of their forefathers. **1568** GRAFTON *Chron.* II. 89 His vse was to ride with a thousande horses continually. *c* **1600** SHAKS. *Sonn.* lxxviii, So oft haue I inuok'd thee for my Muse, . . As euery Alien pen hath got my vse. **1609** DEKKER *Gull's Horn-bk.* v. 22 Let it be your vse to repaire thither some halfe houre after eleuen. **1612** SHELTON *Quix.* I. iv. (1620) 24 It is the vse of Cowards to doe that which thou dost. **1670** WALTON *Lives* II. 126 After his customary publick Devotions, his use was to retire into his Study. **1800** WORDSW. *Michael* 155 Not alone For pastime and delight, as is the use Of fathers. **1836** HUSENBETH *Faberism Exposed* v. 528 The use and practice of the Catholic Church . . of reordaining clerical converts from the Anglican Church. **1864** TENNYSON *Aylmer's F.* 566 The gentle creature shut from all Her charitable use, . . slowly lost . . her hold on life.

8. A custom, habit, or practice.

c **1350** *Lybeaus Disc.* 752 In fyghtyng he hath an us Knyghtes to begyle. *c* **1425** WYNTOUN *Cron.* II. v. 376 In till Egipt . . That vys is kepit to þis day. *c* **1450** *Mirk's Festial* I. 113 þou marterys me by a foule vse and custom of sweryng. *c* **1489** CAXTON *Sonnes of Aymon* ix. 200 Be not dismayed for no thynge, for this is but an vse of werre; suche a thyng befalleth often to many one. **1542** BOORDE *Dyetary* (1870) 252 Englande hath an euyll vse in syttynge longe at dyner. **1587** R. HOVENDEN in *Collect.* (O.H.S.) I. 217 We never let our woods but once and that by great oversight: this one tyme we trust your Lordship will not count an use. **1601** HAKLUYT *Galvano's Discov. World* 15 It was a vse also . . to passe to India by land. **1613** PURCHAS *Pilgrimage* (1614) 749 They haue a filthy and detestable vse in marrying their Maidens. **1721** KELLY *Scot. Prov.* 272 An ill Use ought to be early broken off. **1728** CHAMBERS *Cycl.* (1738) s.v., Uses and Customs of the sea. **1819** SHELLEY *Cenci* IV. iv. 177 She knows not yet the uses of the world. **1875** GLADSTONE *Glean.* (1879) VI. 124 When such an use came in, it was thought to be like a sign of the double superlative in High Churchmanship.

9. a. Without article. Accustomed practice or procedure; habit, usage, custom, wont. (Cf. 7.) Also (*b*) coupled with synonymous term, esp. *wont.*

(*a*) *c* **1340** HAMPOLE *Pr. Consc.* 7634 Planetes . . styk noght fast, als smale sternes dose, Ilk ane his course mase thurgh use. **1340-70** *Alex. & Dind.* 720 ȝe schullen bi ordre of vse offren to venus A ful derworþe douue. **1390** GOWER *Conf.* I. 133 The which to comun us is strange. *c* **1440** *Alph. Tales* 273 Opon þe day of his translacion it was vse to bere his bonys furth of þe kurk. *c* **1480** HENRYSON *Fox & Wolf* 173 Use drawis Nature swa in propertie Of beist and man, that neidlingis thay man do As thay of lang tyme hes bene hantit to. **1565** COOPER *Thesaurus* s.v. *Usus*, Vse, the inuentour of woordes. **1585** FETHERSTONE tr. *Calvin on Acts* vi. 2 Vse is the father of wisedome. **1651** HOBBES *Leviath.* II. xxvi. 138 Long Use obtaineth the authority of a Law. **1697** DRYDEN *Virg. Georg.* II. 366 So strong is Custom; such Effects can Use In tender Souls of pliant Plants produce. **1733** SWIFT *Apology* Wks. 1755 IV. I. 212 Madam, the mighty pow'r of use Now strangely pleads in my excuse. **1781** COWPER *Convers.* 189 To rush into a fixt eternal state, . . Whatever use may urge, or honour plead, On reason's verdict is a madman's deed. **1812** CARY *Dante, Parad.* XXVI. 135 In mortals, use Is as the leaf upon the bough: that goes, And other comes instead.

(*b*) **1526** *Pilgr. Perf.* (W. de W. 1531) 162 b, Let vs not come to yͤ chirche by vse and custome, as the oxe to his stall. **1609** SKENE *Reg. Maj.* 44 He craues onelie na other service, bot vse and wont. **1689** in *Acts Parlt. Scotl.* (1875) XII. 58/2 þat the maltmen þer be lyable for the excyse according to use and wont. **1728** CHAMBERS *Cycl.* s.v. *Language*, 'Tis Use and Custom is the Rule of a Language. **1762** in *Nairne Peerage Evidence* (1874) 95 Priviledges belonging to the said lands conform to use and wont. **1805** WORDSW. *Prelude* XIV. 158 The tendency . . Of use and custom to bow down the soul Under a growing weight of vulgar sense. **1825** R. WILSON *Sk. Hist. Hawick* 190 This tax, . . by the law of 'use and wont', . . has become part and parcel of the system. **1850** TENNYSON *In Mem.* xxix. 11 Make one wreath more for Use and Wont, That guard the portals of the house.

attrib. **1845** CARLYLE *Cromwell* (1871) IV. 42 Constitutional Presbyterian persons, Use-and-wont Neuters. **1885** PATER *Marius* I. 131 A careless, half-conscious, 'use-and-wont' reception of our experience.

b. *Sc.* In the phr. ***as use is***, etc. Cf. 7 b.

c **1375** *Sc. Leg. Saints* xviii. (*Egipciane*) 126 Syne, as oyse was, þai entryt in þare oratore. **1423** in *Charters, &c. of Edinburgh* (1871) 55 Payand of the chaldre as vse and custume is and as thai war wont to pay [etc.]. **1549** *Reg. Aberdon.* (Maitl. Cl.) I. 434 As vse euer hes beyne in tyme bygane. **1557** *Reg. Cupar Abbey* II. 140 Payand ȝerle . . ten merkis money . ., as vse and wont wes. **1697** *Jedburgh Fleshers' Book* (MS.), [He] has payed all dewes as use is.

c. Freq. in the phr. ***in (. .) use.*** Also (chiefly *Sc.*), ***to be in use of***, or ***to*** (do something).

(*a*) *c* **1450** *Mirk's Festial* I. 45 Mony fals opynyons of wyche-craft . . þe whech ben noght to telle among crysten men, lest þay wer drawen yn vse. **1565** COOPER *Thesaurus*, *Increbuit consuetudo*, the custome did grow in vse. **1579** SPENSER *Let. to Harvey* Poet. Wks. (1912) 635/2 As for the two worthy Gentlemen, . . they haue me . . in some vse of familiarity. **1662** STILLINGFL. *Orig. Sacr.* II. vii. §9 The reason of the ceremoniall precepts did respect the customs in use when they were given.

(*b*) **1504** *Munim. de Melros* (Bann. Cl.) 601 That the said schirref was in vse of calling of the said landis . . in thare courtis. **1574** *Reg. Privy Council Scot.* II. 389 He has bene in use of pament of the soume of fourtie pundis yeirlie. **1581** *Ibid.* III. 399 They wer nevir in use of setting of new takkis befoir the expyring of the auld. **1800** A. CARLYLE *Autobiog.* (1860) 44, I was in use of going to my father's on Saturdays.

(*c*) **1566** *Reg. Privy Council Scot.* I. 492 The Personis of Glasgow hes alwayis bene in use to furneis breid. *c* **1630** SIR T. HOPE *Minor Practicks* (1726) 26 The Executors . . are in Use . . to protest that [etc.]. **1759** ROBERTSON *Hist. Scot.* (1761) II. 77 The respect, with which the Scots were in use to receive her ministers. **1780** *Mirror* No. 101, He too had been in use to talk of feeling and of sentiment. **1829** BENTHAM *Justice & Cod. Petit.* 82 A multitude of distinguishable sources, out of which complexity is in use to arise. **1862** *Chambers's Encycl.* III. 608/2 The emperors were in use expressly to confer upon the universities the right of appointing doctors of laws.

†d. Ordinary or usual experience. *Obs.*$^{-1}$

1588 KYD *Househ. Phil.* Wks. (1901) 266 One should so helpe another as wee see by vse in our owne bodies; when the one leg is weary we can rest it on the other [etc.]. **1601** SIR W. CORNWALLIS *Ess.* II. xxxii, But to my vse, we leaue our women ignorant, and so leaue them fearefull.

10. Const. *of.* **a.** Opportunity, occasion, habit, or practice of using. Chiefly ***to have the use of.***

a **1340** HAMPOLE *Psalter* lii. 2 Thai ere brokyn fra oyse and strenght of reson. *c* **1380** WYCLIF *Wks.* (1880) 453 As seyntes þat ben in heuene han vss of alle þes worldly godis. *Ibid.*, þis is þe freest vss þat men han off worldly godis. **1565** COOPER *Thesaurus*, *Ususfructuarius*, . . he that hath the vse and fruite of a thyng, but not the proprietie. **1577** HOLINSHED *Chron.* I. *Hist. Scotl.* xiv. 21/2 The Pict (saith Herodian) hath generally no vse of apparell. **1590** SIR J. SMYTH *Disc. Weapons* 42 b, The weapon of all others that God hath put into the hearts of men, to deuise and vse . . to chasten . . other such Nations, as . . had the perfect vse of the same. **1656** H. PHILLIPS *Purch. Patt.* (1676) 137 Men, who have daily use hereof, have tables and lines upon their Rulers. **1698** T. FROGER *Voy.* 75 Not having the use or knowledge of iron. **1715** LEONI *Palladio's Archit.* (1742) I. 82 The Ancients not having had the Use of Stirrups. **1774** J. BRYANT *Mythol.* I. 341 They had the use of the sphere, and were acquainted with the zodiac. **1780** *Mirror* No. 81, I was never allowed the use of my limbs, because I could afford a coach. **1814** WORDSW. *Excurs.* v. 849 Nature's . . higher creatures born and trained To use of reason. **1826** GALT *Last of Lairds* ix. 85 Considering the use ye have had of his money.

b. The power of using some faculty, etc.; ability to use or employ.

1483 CAXTON *Gold. Leg.* 432/1 Fyue wymmen . . recouerd the use of goyng whiche they had loste by dyuers sekenesse. **1539** ELYOT *Cast. Helth* (1541) 64 Passions of the mynde . . bryng a man from the vse of reason, and somtime in the displeasure of almightye God. **1585** T. WASHINGTON tr. *Nicholay's Voy.* Ep. Ded., He had the exquisite vse of two and twenty sundry tongues. **1592** in J. Morris *Troubles Cath. Forefathers* (1877) 30 Another Catholic, that had but the use of one of his hands. **1610** SHAKS. *Temp.* III. iii. 38 People . . expressing (Although they want the vse of tongue) a kinde Of excellent dumbe discourse. *a* **1654** GATAKER *Antid. Errour* Ep. Ded. (1670) A 3 b, If God had granted him a little longer use of light [= life]. **1711** STEELE *Spect.* No. 36 ⁋8 How hard a thing it is for those to keep Silence who have the Use of Speech. **1753** CHALLONER *Cath. Chr. Instr.* 23 Till a Person is come to the Use of Reason. **1859** TENNYSON *Merlin & V.* 495 She lay as dead, And lost all use of life. **1860** MRS. CARLYLE *Lett.* (1883) III. 51 'Little darling' has lost the use of an arm and hand by paralysis.

11. The act of accustoming or fact of being accustomed by repeated exercise, employment, application, etc.; habituation, practice.

1382 WYCLIF *1 Sam.* xvii. 39 Thanne Dauid . . began to asaye if armyd he myȝte goo . . . And Dauid seide to Saul, I may not thus goo, for and vse I haue not. *c* **1440** *Promp. Parv.* 508/1 Vse, oftyne tymys, þat ys callyd excersyse, . . *exercicium.* *c* **1470** HENRY *Wallace* VIII. 1259 Lang ws in wer gert thaim desyr thair will. **1529** MORE *Dyaloge* I. Wks. 144/2 Howe far so euer his people fal from the vse of vertue. **1551** T. WILSON *Logike* C viii, When men can by muche vse, leape, wrastle, or cast the barre, better then any other. *a* **1586** SIDNEY *Astroph. & Stella* cvii, Giue thy lieuetenancie To this great cause, which needes both use and art. **1680** MOXON *Mech. Exerc.* xii. 203 Use has made the Mawl more handy for them. *a* **1774** GOLDSM. tr. *Scarron's Com. Romance* (1775) I. 154, I frequented all the fencing-schools to keep my hand in vse. **1788** GIBBON *Decl. & F.* xli. IV. 130 The infantry . . yielded to the more prevailing use and reputation of the cavalry. **1805** WORDSW. *Prelude* VII. 332 Ere we have learnt by use to slight the crimes And sorrows of the world. **1819** SHELLEY *Cenci* III. i. 173 Should the offender live? . . and make, by use, His crime Thine . . element.

12. *Eccl.* **a.** The distinctive ritual and liturgy, form of service or public worship, that prevailed or obtained in a particular church, province, diocese, community, etc. Now *Hist.*

c **1380** WYCLIF *Sel. Wks.* III. 202 To seie matynes and masse and evensong bi Salisbury uss. *Ibid.* 482. *c* **1450** *St. Cuthbert* (Surtees) 7549 Of monkys vse þai saide þair houres. *c* **1470** HENRY *Wallace* x. 1006 Salysbery oyss our clerkis than has tan. **1527** *Prymer* (title-p.), This prymer of Salysbury vse. **1548-9** (*title*), The Booke of the Common Prayer . . after the vse of the Churche of England. *Ibid.* Pref., Some folowyng Salsbury vse, some Herford vse, some the vse of Bangor, some of Yorke, and some of Lincolne. *Ibid.*, From hencefurth, all the whole realme shall haue but one vse. **1590** in Fuller *Ch. Hist.* (1655) IX. 198 The said Thomas Cartwright . . conformed himself in both to the use and form of some other forraign Churches. **1636** PAGITT *Christianogr.* III. 95 The Popes Legates . . brought in the Roman use or service into Ireland. **1643** BAKER *Chron., Hen. V*, 58 In his third yeare, the order of Church Service . . was changed from the use of Pauls to the use of Salisbury. **1849** ROCK *Ch. of Fathers* I. v. (1903) I. 321 Almost the whole of the Salisbury Use had been printed while this country was still Catholic. **1878** SIMMONS *Lay Folks Mass Bk.* 89 The Order of Mass for Trinity Sunday, according to the use of York. *Ibid.* 354 A comparative calendar and index of fixed feasts, so necessary in the identification of uses.

b. Religious rite or ceremony observed in particular services of the church; a customary form of religious observance or service.

1382 Wyclif *Exod.* xxvii. 19 Alle the vessels of the tabernacle, into alle vsis and serymonyes,.. thow shalt make of brasse. *c* **1425** Wyntoun *Cron.* II. 715 His body.. Was put in honest sepulture, Wiþ swylk oysse and solempnyte As þat tyme was in þat cuntre. **1560** Daus tr. *Sleidane's Comm.* 34 He him selfe.. cannot tell what time this accustomed vse of masse.. came vp. **1877** A. J. Ross *Mem. A. Ewing* 180 Some very remarkable 'uses'.., such as mixing water with the wine in the Holy Communion. **1889** Pater *G. de Latour* (1896) 39 This mother of churches, which had also its own picturesque peculiarities of 'use'. **1897** *Daily News* 12 April 6/7 The revived 'use' of the Victorian era in the Anglican Church.

13. a. The custom, usage, or practice obtaining or prevailing in a particular country, community, etc.

1432–50 tr. *Higden* (Rolls) I. 401 The vse of that cuntre differrethe from the rite of Englonde in clothenge,.. and in mony other thynges. *c* **1450** Capgrave *Life St. Augustine* 47, I trowe þat he had þe vse of Itaile whilles he studied þere, and coude not litly out of þe same vse, for þei ete not mech at onys. *c* **1500** *Melusine* xxvi. 207 The halle was hanged nobly with ryche clothes after the vse of the land. **1582** N. Lichefield tr. *Castanheda's Conq. E. Ind.* I. lxxvi. 155 His night gowne was.. after the French use laced about, with lase of golde. **1885** Dunckley in *Manch. Weekly Times* 23 May 5/6 The proper pronunciation.. was handed down by oral tradition and by the use of the synagogue.

†**b.** *Sc.* Accustomed manner of life. *Obs.*

c **1425** Wyntoun *Cron.* VII. 1218 His awyn oysse to lif wertual, May mirroure and ensampil be Til alkyn statis. *c* **1470** Henry *Wallace* VII. 1279 In wtlaw oys he lewit thar but let.

III. Manner of using.

14. Manner or mode of employing, applying, turning to account, etc.: **a.** With qualifying adjs.

c **1325** *Metr. Hom.* 3 That wisdom.. That God hauis giuen us for to spend, In god oys til our liues end. *a* **1340** Hampole *Psalter* lxxvii. 14 He gifis þaim.. riches, and þai dispend þaim in ill oyse. *c* **1340** —— *Prose Tr.* 11 All maner of wilfull pollusyone procurede one any maner agaynes kyndly oys. **1390** Gower *Conf.* III. 136 Loke wel that he ne schifte Hise wordes to no wicked us. **1526** Tindale *Romans* i. 27 Lyke wyse also the men lefte the naturall vse of the woman. **1563** *Homilies* II. *Use of Ch.* II. Cc iij, Concernyng the right vse of the temple of god. **1592** Wyrley (*title*), The True Vse of Armorie, shewed by Historie. **1667** Milton *P.L.* IV. 204 [He] perverts best things To worst abuse, or to thir meanest use. **1781** Cowper *Retirem.* 170 Nor these alone prefer a life recluse, Who seek retirement for its proper use. **1804** *Med. Jrnl.* XII. 433 The result of the advantageous use of that remedy.

b. Without qualification.

1624 E. Gunter (*title*), The Description and vse of the Sector. The Crosse-staffe and other instruments. **1669** Sturmy *Mariner's Mag.* I. ii. 5 So have you made the Mariner's Sea-Compass. The Use shall be shew'd in its place. **1703** Moxon *Mech. Exerc.* 348 The use of the Line of Chords. As its use is very easie, so its convenience is very great.

15. With *a* and pl. A manner or method of using, utilizing, or employing; an instance of this. ***to make a*... *use of***: cf. 1 c.

1386 *Rolls of Parlt.* III. 226/1 The whiche comune wronge uses [of the king's power], and many other if it lyke to yow mowe be shewed. **1611** Bible *Transl. Pref.* ¶4 But what mention wee three or foure vses of the Scripture? **1634** Sir T. Herbert *Trav.* 154 If they casually finde a piece of paper that has his [*sc.* Jesus'] name in it, they preserue it from all bad uses. **1651** J. Reading *Guide to Holy City* xxxv. 428 To make a more thankfull, prudent, and holy use thereof [*sc.* of health]. **1725** Watts *Logic* (1736) 359 There is a proper Use to be made of large Paraphrases. *Ibid.*, There is also a Use of shorter Hints. **1774** Goldsm. *Nat. Hist.* (1776) VI. 250 With respect to their [*sc.* animals] uses indeed,.. they differ much. **1819** Shelley *Cenci* IV. iii. 55 Thou wert a weapon in the hand of God To a just use. **1825** Scott *Talism.* xii, A use of the weapon, sometimes.. resorted to, when a missile was necessary. **1849** Macaulay *Hist. Eng.* vi. II. 64 He.. made so dexterous an use of the influence of that cabal that [etc.]. **1875** Jowett *Plato* (ed. 2) IV. 157 Some of these uses of the word are confusing.

IV. Purpose served by the thing used.

16. a. A purpose, object, or end, esp. of a useful or advantageous nature.

c **1340** Hampole *Pr. Consc.* 3674 Yhit may it availle to a gude use. **1382** Wyclif *Titus* iii. 14 Forsothe and oure men lerne for to be bifore in good werkis, to necessarie vses, that thei be not vnfruytouse. *c* **1425** Wyntoun *Cron.* II. 246 He ordaynyt þe iugis set [= seat] To be for þat oysse þe market. **1495** Glanvil *Trevisa's Barth. De P.R.* v. lxiv. (W. de W.) 182 Skynnes of beestes ben graunted to men for ryght many maners and dyuerse vses. **1552–3** in Feuillerat *Revels Edw. VI* (1914) 104 Prouided for lynyng of.. his officers garmentes and like vses. **1597** Hooker *Eccl. Pol.* v. lxxix. §1 If we.. convert some small contemptible portion thereof to charitable uses. **1623** J. Taylor (Water P.) *Discov. by Sea* B 8 b, At his death perhaps.. he will giue.. a little money to Pious vses. **1669** Sturmy *Mariner's Mag.* II. vi. 67 This is sufficient for that Use, to shew you the difference between the true Compass and the Steering Compass. **1726** Swift *Gulliver* I. viii, I had the tallow.. for greasing my boat, and other uses. **1736** *Act 9 Geo. II*, c. 36 Many large.. Alienations or Dispositions made by.. Persons, to Uses called Charitable Uses. **1818** Shelley *Julian & Maddalo* 100, I.. saw.. A building on an island; such a one As age to age might add, for uses vile. **1842** Tennyson *Day-Dream* 201 To what uses shall we put The wildweed-flower that simply blows?

b. With limiting genitive phr. or poss. pron.

1382 Wyclif *Exod.* xxx. 37 Siche a makynge ȝe shulen not make into ȝoure owne vses. **1535** Coverdale *Baruch* vi. 10 The prestes.. take the golde and syluer from them, and put it to their owne vses. **1550** *Extr. Aberd. Reg.* (1844) I. 277 That tha may caus mak inuintour thairof to be keipit to the vsis of the altaragis thairof in tymes cuming. **1600** Shaks. *2 Hen. IV*, II. i. 127 (Q. 1), You haue.. made her serue your vses both in purse and in person. **1654** *Nicholas Papers* (Camden) II. 43 There is some oweing to me, that I have layd out for his Highnes uses. **1673** Ray *Journ. Low C.* 36 To cast the Rain Water.. into a large Cistern, where it is kept for the uses of the House.

†**c.** The provision, supplying, or maintenance *of* something. *Obs. rare.*

1382 Wyclif *2 Sam.* xxiv. 22 Hast thou.. a wayn, and ȝockis of oxen into the vse of trees [**1388** in to vss of wode]. **1427** *Cov. Leet Bk.* 110 Dyuers somes.. to go to þe vce of vestments of þe Trinite chirche. **1496** *Ibid.* 572 Euery other person [to pay].. xx d. to þe vse of þe Cundith. **1497** *Ibid.* 587.

†**d.** A part of a sermon or homily devoted to the practical application of doctrine. *Obs.*

1631 Massinger *Emperor East* III. ii, I am so tir'd With your tedious exhortations, doctrines, vses, Of your religious morality. **1641** Brome *Joviall Crew* Ded., I will winde up all, with a Use of Exhortation. **1679** South *Serm.* 43, I proceed now to the Uses which may be drawn from the Truths delivered. **1734** Watts *Relig. Juv.* (1789) 81 In his last sermon he had an use of reproof, for some vices which were practised.. in his parish. **1816** Scott *Old Mort.* xvii, A.. devout, Christian woman, whom many thought as good as himself at extracting a doctrine or an use. *Ibid.* xviii, The discourse.. was divided into fifteen heads, each of which was garnished with seven uses of application.

fig. **1632** Massinger *Maid of Hon.* I. i, When you had been Cudgell'd well twice or thrice, and from the doctrine Made profitable uses.

e. *Forging.* (See quots. 1861 and 1875.)

1783 H. Cort in *Patents Manuf. Iron* (1858) 10 Peculiar method.. of preparing, welding, and working various sorts of iron, and of reducing the same into uses by machinery. **1861** Sir W. Fairbairn *Iron* 102 The forging of 'uses,' that is,.. those peculiar forms so extensively in demand for steam-engines, steam-boats, railway carriages, and other works. **1863** *Appleby's Handbk. Mach. & Iron Work* 49 Forgings.. Boss Uses. **1875** Knight *Dict. Mech.* 2685 *Use*,.. a slab of iron welded to the side of a bar near the end, to be drawn down by the hammer in prolongation of the length of the bar.

17. The fact or quality of serving the needs or ends *of* a person or persons.

Catch-phr. — ***for the use of***, with the obj. of *of* preposed.

a **1340** Hampole *Psalter* iv. 8 Whet, wyne and oile.. ere mast nedful til mannys oise. **1375** Barbour *Bruce* XIX. 196 [They] distroyit the men ilkane, And till thar oys thar gude has tane. *c* **1400** Maundev. (Roxb.) xviii. 84 Of þe whyte peper sell þai bot lytill,.. bot kepez it till þair awen vse. *c* **1450** Lovelich *Merlin* 946 (Kölbing), God to his ws hath taken it, trewly. *c* **1480** Henryson *Pract. Medecyne* 47 This vntment is rycht ganand for ȝour awin vs. **1522** in *Ripon Ch. Acts* (Surtees) 357 To the use and behowe of Cecill my wiffe. **1560** Bible *Judith* xii. 15 Her maide.. spred for her skinnes.. which she had receiued of Bagoes for her daily vse. —— *Wisdom* xv. 7 The potter.. facioneth euerie vessel with labour to our vse. **1617** J. Taylor (Water P.) *Observ. & Trav. fr. London to Hamburgh* F 2, Hares.. killed.. and carried to the markets by cart-loads, and sold for the vse of the honourable owners. **1657** Milton *Lett. State* Wks. 1851 VIII. 387 Rice, Sugar, and Coffee.. for the use of the Grand Seignior. **1713** Berkeley *Hylas & Phil.* I. Wks. 1871 I. 273 Common language.. is framed by and for the use of the vulgar. **1774** Goldsm. *Nat. Hist.* (1776) I. 230 We shall never know whether the things of this world have been made for our use. **1821** Scott *Pirate* ii, A bargain of rock-cod, purchased.. for the use of the family. **1895** Scully *Kafir Stories* 106 Food for the use of the Zulus on the journey would be provided.

1959 [see Mallaby-Deeley]. **1971** D. Francis *Bonecrack* iv. 44 There was.. an armchair of sorts, visitors for the use of.

18. *Law.* The advantage *of* a specified person or persons in respect of profit or benefit derived from lands or tenements, etc.

In AF. the original *us* (also *use*) was later replaced by the unrelated forms *oes, eus, eups, ops, oeps*: see oeps.

1393 in *Collect. Topogr.* (1836) III. 256 A rente charge paiable to the vs and profit of his chanterie there. **1429** *Rolls of Parlt.* IV. 344/1 Any of the seide Lordes shal,.. to thair use or behove, receyve or take any astate, feffement, or possession of landys.. that standith.. in debate. **1442** *Ibid.* V. 57/1 The said Feffees haue no title ner interest therynne, but only upon trust, and to his use, to execute his will. **1487** *Act 3 Hen. VII*, c. 4 All dedes of gyfte of goodes and catalles.. made of trust to thuse of that persone or persones that made the same dede of gyfte. **1535–6** *Act 27 Hen. VIII*, c. 10 §4 Where.. purchase of any Landes.. shalbe made.. to any other person or persones.. to the use and behove of the seid Husbond and Wife or to the use of the wife. **1599** in *Roxb. Ball.* (1886) VI. p. xxvi, The somme of sixteene poundes of myne Restinge in the handes and keepinge for me and to my use of Richard Oringe. **1729** Jacob *Law Dict.*, *Cestui que Use*.. signifies him to whose Use any other Man is enfeoffed of any Lands or Tenements. **1766** Blackstone *Comm.* II. 271 The lands were granted.. to nominal feoffees to the use of the religious houses. **1818** Cruise *Digest* (ed. 2) I. 338 If the heir refuses to come in.., the Lord.. may seize the estate to his own use. **1843** *Penny Cycl.* XXVI. 65 If a feoffment had been made to A for life to his own use, with remainder to B in fee for the use of C.

19. Office; function; service.

1509 Hawes *Past. Pleas.* xxiv. (Percy Soc.) 108 This is the use of the eyene intere, To se all thynges. **1560** Bible (Genev.) *1 Chron.* xxviii. 15 For the candlestickes of siluer,.. and the lampes thereof, according to the vse of euerie candlesticke. *a* **1718** Prior *Alma* ii. 398 Observe but in these Neighb'ring Lands, The diff'rent Use of Mouths and Hands. **1729** Law *Serious C.* iv. 47 Things may, and must differ in their use. **1811** A. T. Thomson *Lond. Disp.* (1818) 442 The use of the sand in these processes is to prevent the amber.. from passing over into the receiver. **1858** Sears *Athan.* xviii. 161 It performs its use in the grand economy.

20. a. The character, property, or quality which makes a thing useful or suitable for some purpose; capability for securing some end; usefulness, utility; advantage, benefit.

1598 Manwood *Lawes Forest* To Rdr., The necessarie vse and common good, that may arise.. by the publishing of this Treatise. **1628** Prynne *Cens. Cozens* 40, I would willingly learne but this much..: what vse there is of these Deuotions.. in our Church or State? **1667** Milton *P.L.* VII. 346 God made two great Lights, great for thir use To Man. **1700** Locke *Hum. Und.* (ed. 4) IV. vii. §14, I may have reason to think their use is not answerable to the great Stress which seems to be laid on them. **1712** Steele *Spect.* No. 492 ¶2 Here's a little Country Girl that's very cunning, that makes her use of being young and unbred. **1759** Johnson *Rasselas* xxxi, He that has built for use, till use is supplied, must begin to build for vanity. **1780** Bentham *Princ. Legisl.* (1789) p. ccxcv, A few words, for the purpose of giving a general view of the method of division here pursued,.. may have their use. **1853** Kane *Grinnell Exp.* xxix. (1856) 248 Her position changes so constantly that there is little use of recording it. **1878** T. Hardy *Ret. Native* II. ii, Is there any use in saying what can do no good, aunt? **1880** Mrs. Forrester *Roy & V.* I. 3 What is the use of making up my mind.

b. In the phr. ***to*** or ***of*** (***no, little,*** etc.) ***use***.

(*a*) **1382** Wyclif *Wisdom* xiii. 13 To noon vse, a crokid tree.. he maketh. **1542** Udall tr. *Erasm. Apoph.* 157 b, Denying the arte of geometrie.. to bee to veraye litle use or purpose. **1611** Bible *Tobit* vi. 6 To what vse is.. the gall of the fish? **1643** Cromwell *Lett. & Sp.* (1871) II. 288 It is to no use any man's saying he will do this or that. **1868–** in Yks. and Oxford dialect use (*Eng. Dial. Dict.*).

(*b*) **1627** J. Taylor (Water P.) *Armado, or Navy of Land Ships* C 1, The Snarle, a small dogged Pinnace, of more vse then profit. **1634** Sir T. Herbert *Trav.* 35 A Castle planted with great Ordnance and Ammunition, but of small vse. **1663** Bp. Patrick *Parab. Pilgr.* xxxvi, It is a thing of great Use, and great Value. **1711** Addison *Spect.* No. 121 ¶2 Beasts and Birds.. that are of Assistance and Use to Man. **1735** Johnson *Lobo's Abyssinia* Voy. iv. 27 Some pieces of Callicoe, which were of the same Use as Money. **1810** Crabbe *Borough* xx. 322 To be of use Would pleasant thoughts and heavenly hopes produce. **1859** F. E. Paget *Curate Cumbersworth* 354, I had good reason to hope that I was being of use at Roost. **1880** Geikie *Phys. Geog.* ii. 83 Snow is of great use in winter, as it protects vegetation from being nipped by severe frost.

c. With ellipse of prep.

1820 Shelley *Let. to Maria Gisborne* 222 Alas! it is no use to say, 'I'm poor!' **1837** J. H. Newman *Lett.* (1891) II. 230 From their thinking it no use doing good, unless it is talked about. **1874** Dasent *Half a Life* III. 46 Fifty years before it might have been some use to him. **1886** 'H. Conway' *Living or Dead* xxv, Rothwell [tried].. to look as much at his ease as possible. But it was no use.

21. a. Need or occasion for using or employing; necessity, demand, exigency. Freq. ***to have use for*** (or †***of***).

1604 Shaks. *Oth.* III. iii. 319 Giue it [*sc.* a handkerchief] me... I haue vse for it. **1607** Norden *Surv. Dial.* 213 For there is no Country.. but hath vse of timber. **1633** Bp. Hall *Hard Texts, N.T.* 95 Not out of any necessity or use of nature.. he took that fish. **1672** *Mede's Wks.* (ed. 3) *Life* p. xxxvi, A Book of Mathematicks which he had great use of, and had long thirsted after. **1695** Dryden *Parallel Poetry & Paint.* Ess. (ed. Ker) II. 140 Our author calls them figures to be let; because the picture has no use of them. **1826** Andrew Scott *Poems* 39 The warld will still have use for you and me. **1854** H. Miller *Sch. & Schm.* vii, There was no use, they said, for being in the Devil's Cave so late.

b. In the phr. ***to have no use for***, to be set against; to wish to have nothing to do with; to dislike. Orig. *U.S.*

1872 *Harper's Mag.* June 158/2 He was an obstinate fellow.. and moreover, he 'had no use for' the defendant any way. **1887** *Trans. Amer. Philol. Assoc.* XVII. 46, I have no use for him—don't like him. **1896** *Harper's Mag.* XCII. 771/1 Bülow.. spoke his mind freely to his adjutant. 'I have no use for Bernadotte,' said he. **1903** 'H. S. Merriman' *Last Hope* xl, The Marquis had.. spoken in French, and the Captain had no use for that language.

V. 22. *attrib.* and *Comb.*, as *use-value*; *use-established*, *-making*, *-trampler*; **use-forge** (see 16 e and forge *sb.*); **use immunity** *U.S. Law* (see quot. 1972); **use-inheritance** (see quot. 1890); **use-life**, useful life. Also use-man, -money.

1608 Dod & Cleaver *Expos. Prov.* ix–x. 15 A profitable use-making of the undeserued favour.. shewed unto them. **1617** Hieron *Wks.* (1620) II. 290 The well vnderstanding and right vse-making of these. **1873** *Iron* 5 Apr. 356/1 A use forge with a 45-cwt. double-acting Nasmyth's steam hammer. **1887** Browning *Parleyings, Apollo & Fates* 61 What if we granted—law flouter, use-trampler—His life at the suit of an upstart? **1887** tr. *Marx' Capital* I. 2 The utility of a thing makes it a use-value. *Ibid.*, Use-values become a reality only by use or consumption. **1890** W. P. Ball *Effects Use & Disuse* 23 The increasing difficulty of complex evolution by natural selection is no proof whatever of use-inheritance. [*Note.*] I venture to coin this concise term to signify the direct inheritance of the effects of use and disuse in kind. **1897** *Month* April 364 'Mass,' in the honest, use-established sense, means the Roman Mass. **1950** *Chambers's Jrnl.* Mar. 191/2 It is now reported that the magnesium type of dry-cell has a 'use-life' of about thirty hours. **1972** *Computers & Humanities* VII. 87 Interactive systems on today's scale are very recent; for the program designer there are obstacles of rapid change, little standardization, and relatively high development expenses in relation to the probable use-life of the programs. **1972** *New Yorker* 25 Mar. 86/3 The suggested revision, known as 'use immunity', would prevent anyone who was compelled to testify from being prosecuted on the basis of that testimony. **1976** *Ibid.* 19 Apr. 42/3 Under use-immunity law, however, people who were compelled to testify could later be prosecuted as long as the government did not base its case against them directly or indirectly, on their own testimony.

use (juːz), *v.* Forms: α. 3–4, 7 vsen (5 vsyn, vson), 3–4 usen (5 usyn), 4–7 vse (3–4 vsi, 4 vsy, 4–5 vsie, *Sc.* 5–6 wse, 6 ws, vsz), 4– use (4 usy, 8 ues); 5 ouse, yowese, 6 (9 *dial.*) youse, 9 *dial.* yuse, 5 (9 *dial.*) hewse, 6 euse (9 *dial.* ewse). β. *north.* and *Sc.* 4 oise, 4–6 oys, oyse, 5–6 oyss (5 oysse, os, ose), 6 oiss; 4 wyse, 5 vyse, 6 vise. [ad. OF. *user* (also F.), *useir, usser, uiser*, etc. (= Sp. and Pg. *usar*, It. *usare*, med.L. *ūsāre*), f. L. *ūs-*, ppl. stem of *ūtī*: see prec.]

I. 1. a. *trans.* To celebrate, keep, or observe (a rite, custom, etc.); to pursue or follow as a custom or usage.

a **1240** *Lofsong* in *O.E. Hom.* I. 207 Þurh alle þe oðre sacremenz þet holi chirche foluweð and useð. *c* **1290** *Beket* 518 in *S. Eng. Leg.* I. 121 Customes here weren bi-fore i-vsed, ich onder-stonde. **1340** *Ayenb.* 48 Vor alle þe sacremens of holi cherche me sael vsi clenliche. **1387** TREVISA *Higden* (Rolls) IV. 351 Þat manere is ȝit i-used in the chirche of Rome. *c* **1400** *Destr. Troy* 9097 Þen ordant was..a fynerall fest, þat frekes þen vset. ? *a* **1450** *Compend. Treat.* in Roy *Rede me*, etc. (Arb.) 183 The lettre of the ceremonies of ye olde lawe sleyth the Iewes and them that nowe vsen them. *c* **1450** *St. Cuthbert* (Surtees) 2076 Þai vsed customes vnstabill. **1504** in Leadam *Star Chamber Cases* (Selden Soc. 1911) II. 286 Contrare to ther costomez out of tyme of mynde vsed. *c* **1592** MARLOWE *Jew of Malta* IV. ii, *Bar.* No, 'tis an order which the Fryars vse. **1622** J. TAYLOR (Water P.) *Farew. Tower-bottles* A 2 b, So..did Customes change: The Ancient vse, vs'd many yeares before, Was solde. **1625** PURCHAS *Pilgrims* II. 1132 The like custom is vsed throughout the Dominions of Mutezuma. *a* **1648** LD. HERBERT *Hen. VIII* (1683) 7 That the Crown might be put on the King's Head with that Solemnity, which in former times was used. **1889** MEIKLEJOHN *New Hist. Eng.* I. 11 Many noble Britons assumed and used the Roman toga,..and the customs and manners of their conquerors.

†**b.** (*to be*) *used*, to constitute a use, usage, or custom; to be usual or customary. Also (*b*) with *to* (and inf.), or *that* (and clause). *Obs.*

13.. *Gosp. Nicodemus* (G.) 122 Of Emperoures þat are had bene þis was used in þat land. **1387** TREVISA *Higden* (Rolls) V. 145 It was i-ordeyned þe Lente fastynge of Crist..schulde bygynne and dure as it is now i-used. **1422** YONGE tr. *Secreta Secret.* 247 Aftyr the..houre of the day y-custumet or vset. **1550** CROWLEY *Last Trumpet* 1231 Thou shalt not fynd that thou maiest..leauy a great fine More then hath bene vsed alwayes. **1582** STANYHURST *Æneis* I. (Arb.) 28 Of Tyrian virgins too weare thus a quiuer is vsed [L. *mos est*]. **1648** GAGE *West Ind.* 88, I thought..of Indians turned into the shape of beasts (which amongst some hath been used). **1650** in W. S. Perry *Hist. Coll. Amer. Col. Ch.* (1860) I. 2 It shall be lawful, as it hath been used heretofore, to make Probates of wills..in the Colony.

(*b*) **1377** LANGL. *P. Pl.* B. XVIII. 377 It is nouȝt vsed in erthe to hangen a feloun Ofter þan ones. *c* **1450** in *Surtees Misc.* (1890) 62 It is usyd that the sayd Burgese schall chese ..two ale tastars. **1487** *Sc. Acts, Jas. III* (1814) II. 182/2 Ane vthir to..haue thare feis as wes vsit to be gevin to.. changeoures in ald tymes. **1523** FITZHERB. *Husb.* §15 It is vsed in many countreys, the husbandes to haue an oxe-harowe..made of sixe smal peces of timbre. **1548** HALL *Chron., Hen. VII*, 50 b, It was also vsed that he..shoulde likewise..be..committed to the Bishoppes pryson. **1577** FULKE *Answ. True Christian* 42 From the beginning it was not vsed to praye for the deade. **1621** BP. MOUNTAGU *Diatribæ* 531 It was in old times vsed..for men to shaue themselues. **1642** tr. *Perkins' Prof. Bk.* ii. §119. 53 Forasmuch as it is commonly used to write a deed before it be sealed.

†**2.** To observe or comply with (a law, rule, etc.); to enforce or put into practice. *Obs.*

a **1300** *Cursor M.* 9478 Þis es bot lagh..Vsed in curth þis ilk dai. *c* **1320** *Cast. Love* 240 In þe kynges court ȝit vche day Me vseþ þulke selue lay. *c* **1350** *Will. Palerne* 5240 Alle luþer lawes þat long hadde ben vsed. **1440** *Paston Lett.* I. 40 The Duk..hath made his oath upon the Sacrement, and usyd it, never for to bere armes ayenst Englond. *c* **1450** *St. Cuthbert* (Surtees) 2076 To vse þair reule þai [*sc.* monks] had na wille. *Ibid.* 3706 Our haly faders statutes,..Vyse ȝe þaim besyly as ȝow aghte. **1526** TINDALE *1 Tim.* i. 8 We knowe that the lawe is god, yf a man vse it lawfully. **1609** SKENE *Reg. Maj.* 3 Al Barons sall receaue, and vse the lawes, as they are vsed in the Kings court.

3. To prosecute or pursue (some course of action); to do, perform, carry on. Now *rare.*

α. *a* **1352** MINOT *Poems* (ed. Hall) ii. 30 Þe Skotte..vses all threting with gaudes and gile. **1444** *Rolls of Parlt.* V. 121 The seid Co[mun]alte..may use accion of the somes of money accorded to the payd to the seid Co[mun]alte, ayeinst him. **1454** *Ibid.* 255 That all manere of persones..use thaire continuel abood uppon thaire said Office. **1547** BOORDE *Introd. Knowl.* 217 They be lyght fyngerd and vse pyking. **1573** TUSSER *Husb.* (1878) 113 Use now in thy rie, little raking or none. **1648** GAGE *West Ind.* x. 35 The chiefest Market place, where all the buying and selling was used. **1670** NARBOROUGH *Jrnl.* in *Acc. Sev. Late Voy.* I. (1694) 52 They use bathing and stuping those places. **1765–8** ERSKINE *Inst. Law Scot.* II. ix. §4 The superior's consent is presumed, from his not using acts of interruption. **1873** W. STOKES *Rapid Writing* 100 The Art of using writing should be.. inculcated by all teachers.

β. **1375** BARBOUR *Bruce* x. 565, I oysit lang that travalling, So that I can that rod ga richt. *c* **1425** WYNTOUN *Cron.* VII. x. 3528 In Ingilwode and Bernnysdaile þai oyssit al þis tyme þar trawale. *c* **1450** *St. Cuthbert* (Surtees) 7008 At his graue he vysit praying. **1513** DOUGLAS *Æneid* XII. xiv. 110 Oys furth thy chance: quhat nedis proces mar?

†**4. a.** To ply or carry on (an occupation, profession, etc.); to follow or exercise; to discharge the functions of (an office). *Obs.*

1375 BARBOUR *Bruce* XII. 414 Men that oysis thai mysteris. **1382** WYCLIF *1 Chron.* xxiv. 2 Eleasar vsede presthode, and Ythamar. *c* **1440** *Generydes* 1176 Wherefore they calle vs noo good lauenders, And we haue vsid it thus many yerez. **1495** *Acta Dom. Conc.* (1839) 415/1 In caise..Alexander haid remanit..nocht within þe said toune nor vsand þe Course of merchandise þerintill. **1542** *Reg. Cupar Abbey* II. 22 We will at nane hant nor vs the office of brewing, bakin, selling of wyne [etc.]. **1556** *Rec. Inverness* (New Spald. Cl.) I. 2 Aganis the law the sayd Thom..dispresit him wsand his office. **1585** T. WASHINGTON tr. *Nicholay's Voy.* II. viii. 42 [If] she will continue in that occupation, she..may vse it at her pleasure. **1611** BIBLE *1 Tim.* iii. 10 Then let them vse the office of a Deacon, being found blamelesse. **1652** NEEDHAM tr. *Selden's Mare Cl.* 197 Merchants..using Commerce in the very Sea with the Inhabitants. **1665** in De Foe *Plague* (1754) 48 That no Searcher..be permitted to use any public Work or Employment. **1721** PERRY *Daggenh. Breach* 115 Commanders of Ships, particularly those who use the Southern Trade. **1773** *Life N. Frowde* 75 An Implement Nr. M'Namara had worn ever since he used the Mediterranean Trade.

transf. **1730** *Lett. to Strickland rel. Coal Trade* 16 A Number of Ships crouded into the [Coal] Trade, that did not use it before.

†**b.** To follow or pursue (a manner or course of life). *Obs.*

c **1340** HAMPOLE *Prose Tr.* 25 Our Lorde forto stere som forto vse this medlid liffe toke [etc.]. *a* **1450** *Knt. de la Tour* (1868) 12 [She] used the blessed lyf that any woman might. **1483** CAXTON *Gold. Leg.* 195 b/1 Whan she had lyued and usyd thys lyf fyfty yere. **1578** *Scot. Poems 16th C.* (1801) II. 125 The wicked life that I did vse. **1821** SCOTT *Pirate* xxxi, I am determined to turn honest man, and use this life [*sc.* piracy] no longer.

c. To spend or pass (a period of time) in a certain way. (Now only as implying sense 7.)

1477 EARL RIVERS (Caxton) *Dictes* 5 He is happy that usith his dayes in doyng couenable thinges. *a* **1533** LD. BERNERS *Huon* lxxxii. 256 In grete doloure & payne I haue vsyd my youth. **1538** STARKEY *England* I. i. 24 So now also vse your tyme..to the mayntenance..of the same. **1607** SHAKS. *Timon* III. i. 39, I haue obserued thee alwayes for..one that knowes what belongs to reason; and canst vse the time wel. **1613** *Sidney's Arcadia* III. 390 Now me thinks it time To goe vnto the Bride, and vse this day. **1873** W. STOKES *Rapid Writing* 43 Use your spare moments in practising Writing.

†**d.** To frequent (another's company). *Obs.*

1547 BOORDE *Brev. Health* cccxxix. C vij, Fyrste lyue out of syn..and than vse honest myrth and honest company. **1564** *Child-Marriages* (1897) 101 As report is, she hath vsid the evill Companie of William Gallimour. **1599** SHAKS., etc. *Pass. Pilgr.* 422 They that fawn'd on him before Use his company no more.

5. a. To engage in, practise (a game, etc.).

1320–30 *Horn Ch.* 42 To harpe wele, and play at ches, And al gamen that used is. *c* **1380** *Sir Ferumb.* 2225 Summe þay vseþ a maner of play to caste wel a spere. **1557** NORTH *Gueuara's Diall Pr.* I. ii. (1568) 163 They agree to their scollers to vse some pastyme. **1581** *Southampton Court Leet Rec.* (1906) II. 221 Dennys Edwardes..comenly vssethe vnlawffull games. **1626** BACON *Sylva* §299 Use not Exercise and a Spare Diet;..if much Exercise, then a Plentifull Diet. *c* **1636** A. STAFFORD *Just Apol.* (1860) p. xxxix, To shoote in ..Cross-Bowes, and to vse diverse other Recreations. **1764** in Willis & Clark *Cambridge* (1886) III. 539 A..corpulent Man, who lived freely and used no Exercise. ? **1770** T. BRIDGES *Homer* 11 Let discord cease, Use War abroad, at home use Peace. **1794** S. WILLIAMS *Vermont* 83 In such a situation, he uses no exercise. **1801** STRUTT *Sports & Past.* II. ii. 74 In old time,..wrestling was more used than it has been of later years.

†**b.** To have experience, or be engaged, in (war).

c **1440** *Alph. Tales* 76 Alde knyghtis þat..vsyd batels & cuthe gyff gude cowncell. **1474** CAXTON *Chesse* II. iv. (1883) 44 He had longe tyme vsid the warre. **1523** LD. BERNERS *Froissart* I. cclxxv. 167 b/2 He had long tyme vsed the warre, and sene great experience therin.

6. a. To put into practice or operation; to carry into action or effect.

In very freq. use, with a variety of objects, *c* 1340–*c* 1610.

α. **13..** *Gaw. & Gr. Knt.* 2106 He is a mon methles, & mercy non vses. **13..** *Coer de L.* 4670 Yiff thou it [*sc.* clemency] use, Thou dedest nought as I the bad. *c* **1400** *Ywaine & Gaw.* 36 For trowth and luf es al bylaft, Men uses now another craft. *c* **1440** *Alph. Tales* 353 He vsid robborie, avowtrie, inceste. **1483** CAXTON *G. de la Tour* e vj b, He.. vsed all euyl dedes whiche he couthe ymagyne to doo. **1542** BRINKLOW *Lament.* 1 Certayne greate vyces vsed therin [*sc.* in London]. **1550** BALDWIN *Mor. Philos.* N vi, To vse vertue is perfecte blessednesse. **1589** GREENE *Menaphon* (Arb.) 88 Twas a good world when such simplicitie was vsed, sayes the old women of our time. **1616** R. C. *Times' Whistle* (1871) 50 All lawyers I cannot heerof accuse, For some there are that doe a conscience vse. **1644** MILTON *Areop.* (Arb.) 37 The like severity no doubt was us'd. *a* **1680** BUTLER *Rem.* (1759) I. 15 She [Nature] affects so much to use Variety, in all she does. **1710** W. KING *Heathen Gods & Heroes* 41 Her other Brother Neptune used the same Freedom with her. **1758** S. HAYWARD *Serm.* p. xiv, It is certainly a minister's duty..to use plainness and faithfulness. **1839** FR. A. KEMBLE *Resid. in Georgia* (1863) 76 They consider it the lowest degradation in a white to use any exertion. **1898** *Scribner's Mag.* Dec. 690 It was her regular smile, the one she used every evening.

β. *a* **1340** HAMPOLE *Psalter*, etc. 497 Oysand sorow for my syn. *c* **1375** *Sc. Leg. Saints* xii. (*Matthias*) 108 Quhen na man mycht se, þane wald he oyse sic cruelte. **1447** BOKENHAM *Seyntys* (Roxb.) 167 For þe facundye wych she oysyd þere. *c* **1500** *Lancelot* 1699 To mych to oys familiaritee Contempnyng bryngith one to hie dugre.

b. To practise or exercise towards, against, or upon others.

1387 TREVISA *Higden* (Rolls) VII. 17 He wolde have i-used þe strengþe of religioun, but þe cruelte of Gascoyns wolde nouȝt suffre it. **1388** WYCLIF *Matt.* xx. 25 Thei that ben gretter, vsen power on hem. *c* **1460** FORTESCUE *Abs. & Lim. Mon.* ii. (1885) 111 Vsing vppon thaim the lordshippe that is callid *dominium regale tantum*. **1470** HENRY *Wallace* VI. 895 Sic salusyng I oyss till Inglis men. **1542** UDALL in *Lett. Lit. Men* (Camden) 4 It maye please your maistership to use towardes me sum moderacion. **1598** R. BERNARD tr. *Terence, Andria* Prol., I pray you..use not parcialitie, and diligently weigh the matter. **1632** MASSINGER & FIELD *Fatal Dowry* V. i, Therefore use a conscience..To me. **1653** HOLCROFT *Procopius, Goth. Wars* I. 6 The Goths..had used hostility upon Gratiana. **1656** EARL MONM. tr. *Boccalini's Advts. fr. Parnass.* I. xv, Ingratitude which moral Philosophers were daily seen to use towards their benefactors. **1702** *Eng. Theophrast.* 124 The violences we commit upon our selves are oftentimes more painful, than those which other people use towards us. **1737** WHISTON *Josephus, Antiq.* VI. iii. §4 The ungrateful conduct they have used towards me. **1822** SHELLEY tr. *Calderon* III. 78 Tell me all, what poisonous Power Ye use against me.

II. 7. a. To make use of (some immaterial thing) as a means or instrument; to employ for a certain end or purpose.

α. *c* **1315** SHOREHAM I. 532 Wel bet may god to oure prou Dyuerse formes vsy. *c* **1340** HAMPOLE *Pr. Consc.* 3503, I rede ilk man..þat he use þa ten thinges sere þat fordus.. Alle veniel syns. *c* **1375** *Sc. Leg. Saints* iii. (*Andrew*) 946 Vndir ȝour proteccione to luf in contemplacione, and warldly thingis to refuse and hewinly thing sine to wse. *c* **1400** *St. Alexius* (Laud 622) 672, I graunt wel þat it be so, þine bedes ȝif þou wilt ouse. *c* **1410** *Lantern of Liȝt* 132 Þat helpe may cum of vsing Goddis word. **1464** *Rolls of Parlt.* V. 561/2 The preferment of labour and occupacion, such as hath been used by the makyng of the seid Cloth. **1537** CROMWELL in Merriman *Life & Lett.* (1902) II. 107 That vsing your effortes ernestly..in other pointes of your charche & comission you schalbe playne with the said depute. **1568** GRAFTON *Chron.* II. 52 He so vsed the matter with Adrian the fourth.., that he was by him dispensed of his aforesayde othe. **1592** *Arden of Feversham* I. i. 256 As sharpe witted Poets..Vse humble promise to their sacred Muse. **1614** T. DAVIES (Heref.) *Eclogue* 198, I nill vsen any skill so mytch..as this so nice, and free. **1671** MILTON *P.R.* II. 380 And who withholds my pow'r that right to use? **1732** BP. BERKELEY *Alciphr.* v. §35 Freedom is either a blessing or a curse as men use it. **1766** GOLDSM. *Vicar* xxi, His generous patron..judged it highly expedient to use dispatch, lest [etc.]. **1819** SHELLEY *Cenci* I. i. 127 The third of my possessions! I must use Close husbandry, or gold..Falls from my withered hand. **1877** SPARROW *Serm.* xiv. 183 The blessings of this life generally, he says, the good man uses but does not serve. **1884** tr. *Lotze's Metaph.* 433 Using the images of processes which themselves spring from it in a way we cannot explain.

β. *a* **1340** HAMPOLE *Psalter* Prol. (1884) 4 He spekis of crist ..in þat at he oises þe voice of his seruantes. *c* **1375** *Sc. Leg. Saints* xxvi. (*Nicholas*) 730, I pray ȝou þat ȝe wil oys it [*sc.* the legend] dewotly. *a* **1400** in *Hampole's Wks.* (Horstm.) I. 261 Þan awe it maste of alle othire Orysouns to be Oysede in all-haly kyrke.

b. With *to* (and inf., or sb. denoting purpose).

c **1275** LAY. 24293 Moche hii vsede þat craft [= astronomy] to lokie in þan lufte. **1377** LANGL. *P. Pl.* B. x. 129 Þo þat vseth þis haueloune to blende mennes wittes. **14..** *Lydgate's Horse, Shepe & G.* 507 in *Pol., Rel., & L. Poems* (1903) 36 Vse her yiftes & her prerogatives To that same eende. **1486** *Bk. St. Albans* c v, That an hauke use hir craft all the seson to flye or lefe. **1551** in Feuillerat *Revels Edw. VI* (1914) 56 In the meane tyme to vse soche dilligence to his furnyture, as shall seme to you expedyent. **1578** TIMME *Calvin on Gen.* 109 Sacrifices were used of the holy fathers, to celebrate the benefits of God. **1644** *Direct. Publique Worship* 32 Endeavours ought to be used to convince him. **1728** VENEER *Sincere Penitent* Pref. p. x, The emperor was obliged to use all his authority to make him leave Antioch. **1798** S. & HT. LEE *Canterb. T.* II. 3 The arguments used by Lady Lettingham to detain her brother. **1821** SCOTT *Kenilw.* xxxviii, Until she had used her own efforts to have her rights acknowledged by him. **1874** GREEN *Short Hist.* vii. 409 Elizabeth used the daring blow to back her negotiations for peace.

c. To employ (a standard, type, etc.).

a **1300** *Cursor M.* 27274 Vsand oþer weght or mette Again þe lagh in land es sett. *Ibid.* 28437 Again þe lagh..Haf i wysed fals weght and mette. **1387** TREVISA *Higden* (Rolls) I. 37 Þey haueþ a ȝere of apperynge þat þey vseþ in calculynge and in cronicle. **1563** SHUTE *Archit.* B j b, Afterwardes vsing then the measures of the forsayde Pillours. **1662** STILLINGFL. *Orig. Sacræ* I. i. §20 They might use the form of the Phœnician Letters. **1706** *Act 6 Anne* c. 11 §17 That.. the same Weights and Measures shall be used throughout the United Kingdom. **1826** JAS. VEITCH *Tables*, etc. 7 The weight used for Hay..contains 22 pounds..in the Stone.

8. a. To employ or make use of (an article, etc.), esp. for a profitable end or purpose; to utilize, turn to account.

1303 R. BRUNNE *Handl. Synne* 2391 Ȝif þe be leyde a borde to wedde,..ȝif þou hit vse aȝens hys wylle, holy cherche seyþ þat þou dost ylle. *a* **1340** HAMPOLE *Psalter* Prol. (1884) 4 Þis boke of all haly writ is mast oysed in halykyrke seruys. *c* **1400** *Cato's Morals* 152 in *Cursor M.*, Þat þou has gitin to þe, vse hit in honeste, & be noȝt calde niþing. *c* **1450** *St. Cuthbert* (Surtees) 1098 In swete mylk sethe floure of wheete, And vyse it whils it hase þe heete. **1486** *Bk. St. Albans* e iv b, At holyrode day he gooth to Ryde, And vsith the bit When he may gete hit. **1556** *Rec. Inverness* (New Spald. Cl.) I. 2 The serwandis quhā wes wyrkand and wssand the bot on the loch. **1585** T. WASHINGTON tr. *Nicholay's Voy.* I. xviii. 21 Vpon high places they vse cesternes, but vppon the plaine.. they haue many welles. **1680** MOXON *Mech. Exerc.* x. 187 When the Wheel is used, its Edge stands athwart the Cheeks of the Lathe. **1736** BAILEY *Housh. Dict.* s.v. *Acorns*, Both the Acorn and husk, are us'd in many astringent medicines. *a* **1815** in A. T. Thomson *Lond. Disp.* 524 It is necessary that all the vessels,..which are used, be of glass. **1833** J. HOLLAND *Manuf. Metal* II. 36 In the manufacture of surgeons' instruments.., the very best steel..should be exclusively used. **1900** *Longm. Mag.* March 435, I received for answer that the first flower used felt cooler than the second one.

b. To wear as an article of apparel.

c **1375** *Cursor M.* 2048 (Fairf.), Na breke was vsed þan in lande. *c* **1375** *Sc. Leg. Saints* vii. (*James Minor*) 59 Na claþs of sylk he wald nocht were, bot lenyne clath he oysit ay. *a* **1450** MYRC *Par. Pr.* 1032 Hast þou ben prowde of any gyse Of any þynge þat þou dedust vse, Of party hosen, of pykede schone. **1593** MARLOWE *Hero & Leander* I. 31 Buskins of shels all siluered vsed she. *a* **1660** *Contemp. Hist. Irel.* (Ir. Archæol. Soc.) I. 183 How the Councell used vizards. **1857**

R. M. Ballantyne *Coral Island* iv, As they [*sc.* boots] fitted his large limbs and feet, he consented at last to use them. **1885** Dillon *Fairholt's Costume* II. 302 A cloak with a hood, used when travelling. **1889** [see 1].

c. To make use of (land, ground, etc.) by working, tilling, or occupying.

1573 Tusser *Husb.* (1878) 17 To get good plot to occupie, and store and vse it husbandlie. **1604** E. G[rimstone] *D'Acosta's Hist. Indies* iv. 209 Although there be..many mines..as at the Indies, yet they vse none but those of gold and silver. **1641** *Aldeburgh Rec.* in *N. & Q.* 12th Ser. IX. 146/2 Of Robt. Fowler for a yeeres fearme for the shopp he useth. *Ibid.*, Recᵈ: of Henry Lawrence for usinge the Towne ground. **1736** Pegge *Kenticisms* (E.D.S.) 54 He uses it [*sc.* land for farming] himself. *Ibid.*, Who uses this or that farm?

9. To work, employ, or manage (an implement, instrument, etc.); to manipulate, operate, or handle, esp. to some useful or desired end.

13.. *K. Alis.* 5256 The glevmen useden her tunge; The wode aqueighte so hy sunge. **1340–70** *Alex. & Dind.* 439 Vs ne likeþ no lome in oure land vse. **1446** Lydg. *2 Nightingale Poems* i. 305 The fende..Leying hys lynes and with mony a bayte Wsynge his hokes. **1474** Caxton *Chesse* ii. iv. (1883) 44 That he had longe tyme vsid..armes. **1539** Bible (Great) *Numb.* x. 2 That thou mayst vse them [*sc.* trumpets] to call ye congregacion together. **1582** N. Lichefield tr. *Castanheda's Conq. E. Ind.* i. iii. 8 b, The people..using the selfe same sorte of darts. **1596** Shaks. *Merch. V.* ii. ii. 5 Good Launcelot Iobbo, vse your legs,..run awaie. **1611** Bible *Jer.* xxiii. 31, I am against the prophets..that vse their tongues. **1613** Purchas *Pilgrimage* (1614) 62 In their festiuals they vsed..musical instruments. **1733** Tull *Horse-Hoeing Husb.* 295 A Farmer who uses this Plow, may Till in all Weathers. **1765** A. Dickson *Treat. Agric.* (ed. 2) 154 Of the instruments used in tillage. **1828** Scott *F.M. Perth* ii, While I form armour and weapons for others, I cannot myself withstand the temptation of using them. **1859** Tennyson *Geraint & Enid* 900 [I have] wrought too long with delegated hands, Not used mine own. **1880** *Encycl. Brit.* XI. 504/2 In these investigations he..used a *perspicillum* or simple lens.

10. a. To employ (a person, animal, etc.) in some function or capacity, esp. for an advantageous end.

1382 Wyclif *2 Macc.* iv. 40 The cumpanyes aȝein rysynge,..Lysymacus almest three thousand aarmyd wickid hondis bygan for to vse, [by] sum tyrauant duyk. *c* **1470** Henry *Wallace* v. 27 In Gyllisland thar was that brachell brede, Sekyr off sent to folow thaim at flede. So was scho vsyt on Esk. **1526** *Pilgr. Perf.* (W. de W. 1531) 299 Vpon the asse, whiche of no man before had ben vsed ne exercised. **1541** Wyatt *Declar.* Wks. 1816 II. 281, I used Weldon and Sworder..to be spies over Brancetour. **1598** Florio s.v. *Mulatiere*, The carriers..driue mules, and vse them to carrie. **1600** W. Watson *Decacordon* (1602) 214 He had better haue vsed his friend in another matter. **16..** Middleton, etc. *Old Law* i. i, If you want money, to-morrow use me. **1671** Milton *Samson* 1499 Were not his purpose To use him further yet in some great service. **1706** *Act 6 Anne* c. 16 §6 If any Person..shall keep or use any Greyhounds..to kill and destroy the Game. **1802** James *Milit. Dict.* s.v., He used his choicest troops on that decisive day. **1875** Jowett *Plato* (ed. 2) V. 54 They used and honoured all the talent which they could find. **1897** A. Lillie *Croquet* 170 In making your break use your partner in preference to your adversary.

transf. *c* **1600** Breton *Daffodils & Primroses* Wks. (Grosart) I. 20/1 Some will saie (that many muses vse) There are but nyne, that euer vsde to wryte.

b. To have sexual intercourse with. *Obs.* exc. *dial.* (Cf. use *sb.* 3 b.)

13.. *Gaw. & Gr. Knt.* 2426 Alle þay were biwyled With wymmen þat þay vsed. **1382** Wyclif *Prol. Bible* iii. 6 Thei that han..newly weddid a wyf, and not vsid hir. **1411–2** Hoccleve *De Reg. Princ.* 1583 For þise causes thow hire vse muste, And for non othir. **1541** *Act 33 Hen. VIII*, c. 21 If the queene or wife of the prince..stirre any person..to vse or haue carnal knowledge with them. **1565** *Child-Marriages* (1897) 201 Hit hath bene told this deponent, that they have vsid either other at bed and board, as man and wief. **1584** R. Scot *Discov. Witchcr.* iv. v. (1886) 63 Manie are so bewitched that they cannot use their owne wives. **1611** Cotgr., *Accommoder vne femme*, to vse a woman. **1650** Bulwer *Anthropomet.* 197 Bels of gold,..which they put in when they are of age to use Women. **1889** *N.W. Linc. Gloss.* (ed. 2) 590 *To use women*, to commit fornication or adultery.

11. a. To take or partake of as food, drink, etc.; to consume by eating or drinking. Also *fig.*

13.. *E.E. Allit. P.* B. 11 Þay teen vnto his temmple & temen to hym seluen,..þay hondel þer his aune body & vsen hit boþe. **1382** Wyclif *Exod.* xxx. 38 Eche man that doth lyik thing, that he ful vse [L. *perfruatur*] the smel [**1388** odour] of it, he shal peryshe fro his puplis. **1390** Gower *Conf.* III. 23 For who that useth that [food] he knoweth Ful selden seknesse on him groweth. *a* **1450** Myrc *Par. Pr.* 1940 Ȝef any flye, gnat, or coppe Doun in-to þe chalys droppe,..Vse hyt hol alle i-fere. *c* **1480** Henryson *Lion & Mouse* xiii, Quhilk vsis daylie meittis delitious. **1542** Boorde *Dyetary* xxvi. (1870) 289 And vse these thynges, Cowe mylke, Almon mylke, yolkes of rere egges. **1585** T. Washington tr. *Nicholay's Voy.* iv. xix. 134 [In] Lent they doe fast.., vsing none other food, then..hearbs, frutes, and certaine leane pottages. **1613** Purchas *Pilgrimage* (1614) 483 They drinke not wine, nor vse vinegar, but onely water. **1632** Lithgow *Trav.* iii. 102 Lemmons..the Turkes vse at their meate, as we doe the Verges. **1859** Tennyson *Merlin & V.* 462 Yea! Love..carves A portion from the solid present, eats And uses, careless of the rest.

(*b*) Now *esp.*, to take or consume (an alcoholic drink, a narcotic drug) regularly or habitually.

1902 Kipling *Traffics & Discoveries* (1904) 15, I don't use rum as a rule, but I did then, because I needed it. **1906** W. Churchill *Coniston* i. ix. 104 Unlike Jethro, he 'used' tobacco. **1921** J. Buchan *Path of King* xiv. 276 It's curious that a man who don't use tobacco or whisky should be such mighty good company. **1929** D. Hammett *Dain Curse* xiv. 149 He..picked up the morphine paper... 'What do you suppose this is doing here?' he asked. 'She uses it.' **1942** J. D. Carr *Seat of Scornful* iv. 43 'Not that I've got any objections to 'em,' Mr. Morell assured him, alluding to the tobacco and the spirits. 'Just don't use 'em.' **1962** H. Burn *Drugs, Med. & Man* x. 106 The best known drugs of addiction are morphine, heroin and cocaine. Somewhat less well known are cannabis..and pethidine. These are the main drugs, other than alcohol, which are used by addicts. **1982** J. Wainwright *Anatomy of Riot* 31 Okay, a little hash here an' there. He sold it. Maybe he used it. Okay, he used it.

†**b.** To partake of (the sacrament); to take or receive (the eucharist). *Obs.* (Chiefly *absol.*)

c **1450** *St. Cuthbert* (Surtees) 7074 Þe sacrement..At þe last he..vsed and toke. **1567** *Gude & Godlie B.* (S.T.S.) 17 Quha vsis it vnworthilie Ressauis deide eternallie.

absol. *a* **1375** *Joseph Arim.* 660 Þenne com Ihesu crist..; He vsede of Goddes bord & a writ brouhte. **1389** in *Eng. Gilds* (1870) 14 From þe leuacioun of cristis body sacrid in til þat þe preest haue vsed. **14..** *Pol., Rel., & L. Poems* (1906) 122 When þe preste hath don his masse, Vsed, & his hondes wasche. *c* **1450** *St. Cuthbert* (Surtees) 7058 When he [*sc.* a priest] suld vse, In to þe chalys lokes he.

12. To expend or consume (a commodity, etc.) by use; to exhaust by employment.

c **1440** *Promp. Parv.* 522/2 Weryn, or vson, as clothys and other thyngys.., *vetero.*

1699 Boyer *Fr. Dict.* s.v. *User*, They use, waste or burn a great deal of Wood in that House. **1747** Mrs. Glasse *Cookery* p. ii, A Cook that used six Pounds of Butter to fry twelve Eggs. **1791** R. Mylne *2nd Rep. Thames Navig.* 11 The Millers..were using all the Water as fast as possible. **1849** Soyer *Mod. Housewife* 357 [As] the cream..rises in a froth,.. place it on the sieve; continue till all is used.

13. *to use up*: **a.** To consume (a commodity or stock) by use; to exhaust the supply of.

1785 Grose *Dict. Vulgar T.*, *Used up*, killed; a military saying, originating from a message sent by the late general Guise, on the expedition to Carthagena [etc.]. **1811** Ld. Brougham in Bentham *Wks.* (1843) X. 462, I cannot possibly better use up (as the housewives say) this little credit. **1847** *Illustr. Lond. News* 10 July 27/3 To see if there were anything there that had not yet been used up. **1875** Merivale *Gen. Hist. Rome* li. 406 The genuine Roman race must have been almost used up in the desperate warfare.

b. To dispose or 'make an end' of (a person). Orig. *U.S. colloq.*

1833 Jas. Hall *Leg. West* 38 It's a mercy, Miss, that the cowardly varments hadn't used you up body-aciously. **1863** in *Southern Hist. Soc. Papers* XII. 220 If you advance..on them in front while I attack them in flank I think we can use them up.

c. *colloq.* To exhaust with fatigue, overwork, etc.; to overtire, wear out.

1850 Smedley *F. Fairlegh* x, I saw you were getting used up. **1882** Besant *All Sorts* xxviii. (1898) 199 The girls grow up narrow-chested, stooping, consumptive. They are used up wholesale. **1884** 'Edna Lyall' *We Two* v, Even if it should use me up, what then? **1887** *Daily Tel.* 5 March (Encycl. Dict.), We have used up no fewer than six Irish Secretaries in little more than as many years.

14. *to use off* or *out*, = sense 13 a.

1812 Southey *Omniana* II. 2 An obscure..periodical publication, which has long since been used off as 'winding sheets for herrings'. **1849** Froude *Nemesis of Faith* 109 The heart will have used out its own power, and thoughts..will be unreal still.

15. *to be able to use*, to be in need of, to be in a position to benefit from, to want. *colloq.*

1956 'N. Shute' *Beyond Black Stump* viii. 217 But I could use a river, and the sight of snow on a mountain. **1958** V. Scott *Savage Affair* ix. 152 Listen..they said they might see their way to an advance. Two-fifty apiece. You could use two hundred and fifty dollars, couldn't you? **1961** R. Godden *China Court* 258/1 'I could use a gin,' said Bella. **1976** *Ulverston* (Cumbria) *News* 3 Dec. 1/6 The tarn is the most beautiful part of the village and The Landings can use some cleaning up. **1977** *Oxford Diocesan Mag.* July 18/1 We could have used more time to explore this avenue.

III. 16. a. To speak or converse in (a language); to write or talk.

c **1275** Lay. 10068 Folk gan to vsi Yrlondes speche. *c* **1330** *Arth. & Merl.* 23 Freynsche vse þis gentilman, Ac euerich Inglische Inglische can. *c* **1500** *Droichis Part of Play* 111 For never in land quhair Eriche was vsit, To dwell had I dellyte. **1547** Boorde *Introd. Knowl.* i. (1870) 120 In England is vsed all maner of languages and speches of alyens in diuers Cities. *Ibid.* xxxv. 210 Where Laten is most vsed. **1628** Milton *Vac. Exerc.* 8 Hail native Language,..Here I salute thee and thy pardon ask, That now I use thee in my latter task. **1668** Wilkins *Real Char.* 3 The Language used in Denmark. **1819** Scott *Ivanhoe* ii, The Prior..using the lingua Franca, or mixed language, in which [etc.]. **1821** —— *Kenilw.* xxxvi, Can falsehood use thus boldly the language of truth? **1888** Jessopp *Visit. Norwich* p. xxxix, [He] should be able to use Latin, not merely to understand it.

b. To employ or give utterance to (words, phrases, etc.); to say, utter.

a **1340** Hampole *Psalter* lxxiii. 23 Na wise man oysis gret athis, in þe whilke werid men vpbraydis god of his mercy. *c* **1374** Chaucer *Boeth.* ii. pr. ii. (1868) 33, I wolde plete wiþ þee a fewe þinges, vsynge þe wordes of fortune. *a* **1425** *Cursor M.* 12050 (Trin.), Teche him..Blessyng to vse & not to ban. **1484** Caxton *Fables of Æsop* i. Pref., Esope..techeth also to be humble and for to vse wordes. *a* **1500** in *Ratis Raving*, etc. 98 Oys fare langage in alkyne thinge. **1539** Bible (Great) *Ecclus.* xxiii. 11 A man yᵗ vseth moch swearing. **1596** Harington *Metam. Ajax* (1814) 24 [When] such phrases..are used to ribaldry. **1621** Bp. Mountagu *Diatribæ* 14 Euery where, either directly, or indirectly, you doe, to use your owne phrase, Cry downe that right. **1655** Stanley *Hist. Philos.* i. (1687) 27/2 Using speeches, the effect whereof, he afterwards thus exprest in Verse. **1728** Chambers *Cycl.* s.v. *Viscera*, This Word is also frequently used singularly, *Viscus*, to express some particular part of the Entrails. **1729** T. Innes *Crit. Essay* (1879) 295 Nennius ..uses promiscuously the names of Scythæ and Scoti for the same people. **1793** Martyn *Lang. Bot.* s.v. *Leaflets*, For the same reason, if we use *leaf*, we must not use *foliole*. **1820** Shelley *Orpheus* 100 Nature must lend me words ne'er used before. **1838** Lytton *Leila* ii. i, Thou usest plain language, my friend. **1875** Jevons *Money* (1878) 250 We use a great many words with a total disregard of logical precision.

17. a. To resort to (a place) frequently or habitually; to frequent or haunt; also, to dwell in. Now *rare*.

c **1400** Maundev. (1839) xxxi. 307 Ȝif the Merchauntes useden als moche that Contre as thei don Cathay. *c* **1440** *Promp. Parv.* 512/2 Vsyn, or hawntyn, *frequento*. **1528** in Leadam *Star Chamber Cases* (Selden) II. 175 All iiij [have] eusyd & occupyd the market and inhaunsyd the pryse of grayne. **1535** Coverdale *Jer.* ii. 23 Like a wilde Asse, that vseth the wildernesse. **1603** Shaks. *Meas. for M.* iii. ii. 231 [I am] Not of this Countrie, though my chance is now To vse it for my time. **1611** in B. Camm *Benedictine Martyr in Eng.* (1897) 268 The other was Mr. Somers, alias Wilson, who used London altogether. **1658** Cokaine *Obstinate Lady* i. i, Poems (1874) 55 Use the Tavern once or twice a day. **1686** tr. *Chardin's Coronat. Solyman* 143 Forty large Barques, such as use the Caspian Sea. **1708** *Lond. Gaz.* No. 4427/16 He useth the Queen's-head Ale-house. **1725** Sloane *Jamaica* II. 320 It uses more the low sandy inland parts than the plovers, snipes, &c. **1848** Thackeray *Van. Fair* xxxviii, He did not fail to tell everybody who 'used the room'. **1867** *Cornh. Mag.* Apr. 449 Doubtless also in his sojourn here.. he used this house, as our expressive phrase has it. **1884** *Good Words* June 399/2 Your ordinary thief..may..lord it in the public-houses he 'uses'.

b. *to use the sea* (†*seas*), to practise the calling of a sailor. Cf. follow *v.* 9.

a **1634** Isaacson *Andrewes* in Fuller *Abel Rediv.* (1867) II. 156 His father, having most part of his life used the seas. **1681** R. Knox *Hist. Ceylon* 124 These many years..have I used the seas. **1728** Morgan *Algiers* II. ii. 223 Rais was then about thirty, and had used the Sea full ten years. **1773** *Life N. Frowde* 24 His Name was George White,..who had used the Seas from my own Age. **1791** Smeaton *Edystone L.* §314 John..continued for some time to use the sea. **1894** *Pall Mall Mag.* Sept. 4 He had used the sea for above thirty years, had built, owned and commanded ships.

†**c.** To associate with (a person). *Obs.*⁻¹

1594 in *Cath. Rec. Soc. Publ.* V. 262 At my being there I could not heare or perceyue he used any Inglishman much.

18. a. To treat or deal with (a person or thing) in a specified manner; to behave or act towards (another) in a particular way.

In frequent use from *c* 1550 to *c* 1730.

1483 Caxton *G. de la Tour* g v, They wold use her of an enorme and ouer foule faytte. **1542** Udall *Erasm. Apoph.* 171 Many noble menne vsen their frendes none other wyse. **1568** Grafton *Chron.* II. 804 Then he that tolde him the tale vsed him with good wordes. **1590** Marlowe *Edw. II*, v. ii, Vse Edmund friendly, as if all were well. **1639** in *Verney Mem.* (1907) I. 106 My Collonel useth me with very greate courtesy. **1680** Otway *Orphan* ii. iv, But use me gently like a loving Brother. **1709** Steele *Tatler* No. 11 ¶4, I am used by some People as if Isaac Bickerstaff..was no Body. **1756** C. Smart tr. *Hor., Sat.* ii. ii, When years shall approach, and feeble age require to be used more tenderly. **1768** Sterne *Sent. Journ., Translation*, 'Tis..using him worse than a German. **1859** Tennyson *Merlin & V.* 534 So used as I, My daily wonder is, I love at all. **1863** Kinglake *Crimea* I. 311 They won France. They used her hard. **1888** 'J. S. Winter' *Bootle's Childr.* iv, I didn't use poor Bill any too well.

b. *refl.* To conduct or comport (oneself). †Also, to resort or repair (cf. sense 23).

Freq. from *c* 1530 to *c* 1590.

c **1470** Henry *Wallace* xi. 1031 Yhe haiff so lang her oysyt yow allane, Quhill witt tharoff is in till Ingland gane. **1496–7** *12 Hen. VII*, c. 6 §1 Every persone frely to use theym self to his moost avauntage, without exaccion. **1513** Bradshaw *St. Werburge* i. 2354 He folowed saynt Werburge counsell, Vsynge hym after her swete ghostly doctryne. **1547** Boorde *Brev. Health* ccvii, Thus vsynge my selfe, I thanke God I dyd make my selfe whole. **1590** *Southampton Court Leet Rec.* (1906) ii. 285 Being called before vs, [they] vsed themselves contemtuously. **1621** Lady M. Wroth *Urania* 307 Who comming to my fathers house, vsed himselfe.. insolently. *a* **1648** Ld. Herbert *Hen. VIII* (1683) 295 He used himself more like a Fellow to your Highness, than like a Subject. **1653** *Nissena* 108 Excusing himself for that he had not before used himself with such obsequiousness towards them as he ought. **1860** Miss Yonge *Hopes & Fears* I. 387 Her eyes were on the alert to judge how he had been using himself in the last half-year.

IV. 19. a. To make (a person, etc.) familiar or accustomed by habit or practice; to habituate, accustom; to inure. Freq. const. †*in* or *with* (something).

In later use *Sc.*, and chiefly in pa. pple.; cf. c below.

c **1305** *St. Edmund Conf.* 78 in *E.E.P.* (1862) 73 In penance he was so wel yused & þeron ȝung ibroȝt þat..hit ne greuede him riȝt noȝt. *a* **1340** Hampole *Psalter* cxviii. 71 It is profetabil till me, þat þou oysid me in sere temptacioun. **1387** Trevisa *Higden* (Rolls) VI. 289 He þat was idel..meoveþ hym to batayle þat is i-used in dedes of armes. *c* **1425** *Eng. Conq. Ireland* 22 Throgh kynd of Fraunce, we ben vsed in wepene. **1489** Caxton *Faytes of A.* i. viii. B ij b, To see his men vsed & wel taught in the said art and fait of armes. *a* **1500** *Ratis Raving* 32 With wordis of lawte vs thi twnge. *c* **1586** C'tess Pembroke *Ps.* lxxvii. xii, A path whereon thy crew As shepherds use their sheep. **1587** Holinshed *Chron.* (ed. 2) II. *Hist. Scotl.* 391 This man had accesse unto the queene to plaie at cards, and to use hir with other courtlie pastimes. **1606** Chapman *Gentl. Usher* v. ii, Using thy husband in those vertuous gifts For which thou first didst choose him. **1711** *Countrey-Man's Lett. Curat* 85 Many..had been used with the English Liturgie..at London. **1815** Scott *Guy M.* lv, The like o' them's used wi' graves and ghaists. *a* **1826** in Child *Ball.* IV. 98/1 She took my gay lord frae my side, And used him in her company. **1835** D. Webster *Orig. Sc. Rhymes* 115, I had little been used wi' sic resolute foes.

refl. **1534** in Leadam *Star Chamber Cases* (Selden) II. 211 Compleynaunt hathe vseyd hymselfe in exercysyng the fete of bakyng. **1560** Becon *New Catech.* Wks. 1564 I. 320 This verye selfe same bodye.. whiche vseth it selfe here with the soule in all maner of good workes.

b. Freq. with *to* (and sb. or inf.).

c **1386** Chaucer *Pars. P.* ¶245 For to vsen a man to doon goode werkes. **1535** Coverdale *Ecclus.* xxiii. 13 Vse not thy mouth to vnhonest and fylthye talkynge. **1560** Daus tr. *Sleidane's Comm.* 231 b, That they do eschew all.. idle talke, and vse their familie to do lykewyse. **1585** T. Washington tr. *Nicholay's Voy.* iv. i. 114 b, [Hunting being] an argument & occasion to vse men to ryse betimes. *c* **1643** Ld. Herbert *Autobiog.* (1824) 70 You shall do well also to use your Horse to Swimming. **1688** Shadwell *Sqr. Alsatia* ii. i, Some moderate skill in it will use a man to reason closely. **1740** Chesterf. *Lett.* Oct., To use your ear a little to English verse. **1769** Goldsm. *Hist. Rome* (1786) I. 402 Having used his body much to antidotes, the poison had but little effect. **1783** Justamond tr. *Raynal's Hist. Indies* VII. 91 It is not.. surprising that the seal.. should use her little ones to live under water. **1814** Scott *Wav.* liv, He wanted to use her by degrees to live without meat. **1873–** in dialect use (*Eng. Dial. Dict.*). **1877** Mrs. Lear tr. *Fenelon's Spiritual Lett.* 240 So as to wean you like a child, and use you to dry bread instead of milk.

refl. *c* **1305** *St. Edmund Conf.* 44 in *E.E.P.* (1862) 72 So longe hi hem vsede þerto. *a* **1450** *Knt. de la Tour* (1868) 9 For suche lyff-as ye wille contynue, use you to in youre youthe. *a* **1568** Ascham *Scholem.* ii. (Arb.) 88 For translating, vse you your selfe.. to chose out some Epistle.. of Tullie. *a* **1568** in *Bannatyne MS.* (Hunter. Cl.) 195 In yowtheid vse the to temprance. **1615** tr. *De Montfort's Surv. E. Indies* 39 Those who have us'd themselves to Tobacco. **1697** Dryden *Virg. Georg.* i. 63 Use thyself betimes to hear and grant our Pray'rs. **1719** De Foe *Crusoe* i. (Globe) 211 Using himself to them [*sc.* garments], at length he took to them very well. **1753** L. M. *Accompl. Woman* II. 213 We may use ourselves to fear as well as to be bold. *a* **1818** M. G. Lewis *Jrnl. W. Ind.* (1834) 296 Mithridites used himself to poisons. *a* **1850** Keble *Lett.* (1870) 104 Using themselves when they wake in the night to rise and say the fifty-first Psalm.

c. More usu. in pa. pple. (Const. *to* or †*of*.)

For the pronunc. of *used to*, see note at sense 21 a.

c **1480** Henryson *Fables, Two Mice* 58 To tender meit my stomok is ay vsit. **1483** Caxton *G. de la Tour* e iv b, So were the seuen Cytees brenned.. by cause that they were moche vsed of the fylthe and ordure of lechery. **1526** *Pilgr. Perf.* (W. de W. 1531) 94 b, Wherby man.. be accustomed & vsed to chose.. yᵉ thynge that is of lesse goodnes. **1555** Eden *Decades* i. x. (Arb.) 104 Suche as haue byn vsed to owr breade made of wheate. **1607** Topsell *Four-f. Beasts* 80 It is requisite that they bee alwaie vsed to hand. *c* **1645** Howell *Lett.* (1678) 48 This City was us'd to fetch all those Spices. **1682** Lister *Godartius Of Insects* 54 The Catterpillar.. as soon as it perceives any thing it is not us't to. **1720** Mandeville *Free Thoughts* (1729) 276 St. Poinct.. was used to ask, whether the farce.. was ready to be acted. **1796** Mme. D'Arblay *Camilla* IV. 329 I'm not used to be used in this manner! **1833** Disraeli *Cont. Fleming* vi. vi, The friar smiled, and was evidently used to this raillery. **1850** Thackeray *Pendennis* li, A person.. used to making sacrifices. **1888** 'J. S. Winter' *Bootle's Childr.* xi, Which.. had stirred Terry's heart just as it had been used to stir it years and years ago.

V. *intr.* **20.** To do a thing customarily; to be in the habit of so acting or doing; to be wont to do. (Chiefly in clauses introduced by *as*, and now only literary.) **a.** Of persons.

c **1380** Wyclif *Sel. Wks.* III. 434 And so shulde perish makyng of prests and doyng of sacraments, as holy Chirche usiþ. *c* **1400** Maundev. (1839) v. 40 Clothed in.. the Sarazines guyse, and as the Sarazines usen. **1473** *Reg. Cupar Abbey* I. 182 Tha sal tak iijˣˣ of fuderis of petis quhar thair oysit befor. **1533** in Leadam *Star Chamber Cases* (Selden) II. 205 The boucher.. grevyd shall signifie.. the name.. of any such person.. that so vsith. **1596** Spenser *State Irel.* Wks. (Globe) 645/1 To manure and husband it as good farmors use. **1616** J. Lane *Contn. Sqr.'s T.* x. 388 This familiar Dove twixt yond twoe kinges went boldlie to and fro, as vsen frendes. **1663** Butler *Hud.* i. i. 632 We should, as learned Poets use, Invoke the Assistance of some Muse. **1720** Ozell *Vertot's Rom. Rep.* (1740) II. xii. 237 In the sight of all the Citizens, as the Censors use, when they [etc.]. **1748** *Earthquake Peru* ii. 161 To kill animals in the same Manner as they always had used. **1791** Smeaton *Edystone L.* §267 We had got up our stones.. as we had used from the beginning. **1816** Wordsw. '*A little onward*' 30 To push forth His arms, as swimmers use, and plunge.. into the 'abrupt abyss'. **1852** T. L. Peacock *Misc.* Wks. 1875 III. 364 First, as the truly pious always use, Approach with prayer. **1875** Browning *Aristoph. Apol.* 365 Die at good old age as grand men use.

†**b.** Of things. *Obs. rare.*

1656 tr. *T. White's Peripat. Inst.* 152 It varies its figure with every motion as fire uses. **1676** *Phil. Trans.* XI. 773 In the same manner as the trunk of the lymphaticks uses.

21. With *to* and inf.: To be accustomed or wont *to* do something.

In very frequent use from *c* 1400, but now only in pa. t. *used to*, with pronunc. (ju:st tu:, 'ju:stʊ), and *colloq.* in *did* (*not*) *use* (or *used*) *to*: see also usen't, useter; *used to could*: see can *v.*[1] A. 7.

α. **1303** R. Brunne *Handl. Synne* 691 For ryche men vse comunly Sweryn [*v.r.* to swere] grete oþys grysly. *Ibid.* 2661 *c* **1385** Chaucer *L.G.W.* 787 *Thisbe*, For olde payenys that Idolys heryed Vsedyn tho in feldys to ben beryed. *c* **1386** —— *Reeve's T.* 20 A theef he was,.. a sly, and vsaunt [*v.r.* usand] for to stele. *c* **1440** *Gesta Rom.* v. 12 His modir vsith euery day gretly to sorowe. **1464** *Rolls of Parlt.* V. 563/2 Dyvers persones have gretely used to shippe woll.. oute of this Reame. **1542** Udall *Erasm. Apoph.* 43 Such as the beggerye philosophiers.. usen to weare. **1550** *Southampton Court Leet Rec.* (1905) i. 14 Thomas Casberd hathe vsid to sett his carte in the streate. **1596** Spenser *F.Q.* v. viii. 17 Her name Mercilla most men vse to call. **1612** Webster *White Devil* i. ii. 202 Your silke-worme useth to fast every third day. **1625** J. King *David's Strait* 15 As we vse to maligne a Bayliue. **1670** Milton *Hist. Eng.* vi. 304 The English then useing to let grow on their upper-lip large Mustachio's. **1728** Gay *Begg. Op.* ii. iv, You are not so fond of me, Jenny, as you use [*sic*] to be. **1767** *Woman of Fashion* II. 26 How did we all use to admire her! **1837** Lockhart *Scott* I. iv. 122 He used to get all the copies of these ballads he could. **1873** C. M. Yonge *Pillars of House* II. xvi. 105 Did Alda use to be nice, or is it love? **1884** W. C. Smith *Kildrostan* 53 You used to be a leal, true-hearted girl. **1925** S. Lewis *Arrowsmith* xviii. 192 Didn't we used to have fun. **1927** E. Hemingway *Men without Women* 154 He certainly did used to make the fellows he fought hate boxing. **1935** E. Farjeon *Nursery in Nineties* iii. i. 124 Mama, did you use to be a flirt? **1963** V. Nabokov *Gift* ii. 117 And now I continually ask myself what did he use to think about in the solitary night. **1974** *Radio Times* 28 Feb. 25, I suppose I did use to be a prophet of doom.

β. *c* **1375** *Lay-Folks Mass-Bk.* (MS. B) 401 A litel belle men oyse to ryng. *c* **1425** Wyntoun *Cron.* i. 1265 Tebany þai oysse to calle In to Grece þe Thebis all. *c* **1470** Henry *Wallace* v. 760 Now thow sall feyll how I oys to lat blude.

b. Predicated of things.

In frequent use from *c* 1620 to *c* 1675.

1445 in *Anglia* XXVIII. 267 Al goddesses.. Haue ioyned her dauncys within thi breste, which vsid hem to receive. **1547** *Homilies* i. *Salvation* iii. ¶7 Therfore scripture vseth to saie, that faithe without woorkes doeth iustifie. **1586** J. Chilton in Hakluyt *Voy.* (1589) 588 Where the ships vse to ride, made fast to ye said wal, with their cables. **1609** Holland *Amm. Marcell.* 333 What time folkes minds.. use to be dull and dead. **1662** Stillingfl. *Orig. Sacræ* ii. i. §6 Jewels do not use to lie upon the surface of the earth. **1684** *Contempl. St. Man* ii. ix. (1699) 231 Temporal Felicity uses often to end in Eternal Misery. **1726** Leoni *Designs* 5 b, In that Season of the Year when the Water uses to be lowest. **1778** *Hist. Eliza Warwick* I. 260 Alas! his absence.. did not use thus to affect me! **1810** Scott *Lady L.* i. xxi, Yet seemed that tone.. Less used to sue than to command. **1839** Fr. A. Kemble *Resid. in Georgia* (1863) 245 It is now.. the rule, though it used not to be so formerly. **1857** C. M. Yonge in *Monthly Packet* Jan. 34 'Things didn't use to be so stupid when Ned was there!' sobbed Gilbert. **1884** F. M. Crawford *Rom. Singer* I. 35 They used to be only a baiocco apiece. **1983** *Listener* 10 Feb. 31 (*heading*) Adrenalin sports are big. TV didn't used to be one.

†**c.** In passive construction. *Obs.*

1523 Fitzherb. *Husb.* §132 If a tree be heeded, and vsed to be lopped and cropped. **1607** Shaks. *Cor.* iii. iii. 25 He hath bene vs'd Euer to conquer. *a* **1648** Ld. Herbert *Hen. VIII* (1683) 399 As concerning Annates used to be paid. *a* **1706** Evelyn *Hist. Relig.* (1850) I. 402 Nor were they used of old to be read in churches. **1737** Waterland *Eucharist* 393 Prayer was then used to be offered up for that Purpose. **1788** *London Mag.* 399 The Tuilleries, where boats were used to be found.

22. †**a.** To act, conduct oneself or one's affairs, in a particular or specified manner. *Obs. rare.*

a **1325** *Prose Psalter* lxxvi. 12 Y shal þenchen in alle þyne werkes, and y shal vse [L. *exercebor*] in alle þy fundynges. *c* **1375** *Cursor M.* 24931 (Fairf.), Bot now men vsis on oþer wise, þer is mare of hir seruise. **1523** Ld. Berners *Froiss.* I. xv. 15 Kyng Edward.. and yᵉ quene his mother.. vsed moche after yᵉ counsell of syr Thomas Wage. **1579** Tomson *Calvin's Serm. Tim.* 181/1 And therfore we haue to vse of our selues modestly.

b. *Sc.* To accustom oneself, become accustomed or habituated, get used, *to* something.

1836 Carlyle *Let.* in *Atlantic Monthly* Sept. (1898) 295/1 'You will use, you will use,' and get hefted to the place, as all creatures do. **1842** Mrs. Carlyle *Lett.* (1883) I. 158 If I do not use to the noise. **1894** Crockett *Raiders* 284 So soon does one use to the sight.

23. a. To go frequently, to resort or repair customarily, to a place or person; to frequent or haunt a place. Freq. with advs. (as *thither*, *where*), or with preps. (esp. in earlier use with *to*). Latterly *dial.* (Eng. Dial. Dict. s.v.) and *U.S.*

(*a*) *c* **1470** Henry *Wallace* i. 209 Into the toun he wsyt everilk day. *Ibid.* ii. 290 He wsyt offt to that religious place. **1590** in *Cath. Rec. Soc. Publ.* V. 181 [They] be good witnesses.. howe many severall persons have vsed to the saienge of masses. **1599** Sir R. Wrothe in Ellis *Orig. Lett.* Ser. ii. III. 181 Sertaine lewde fellowes.. doe frequente and use aboute Layton heath. **1602** Breton *Mother's Blessing* Wks. (Grosart) I. 6/1 Presumptuous fooles, and irreligious Iewes, Emong the Nobler sort should neuer vse. *a* **1613** Overbury *Characters, Ord. Widdow*, Shee uses to cunning women to know how many husbands she shall have. **1653** Holcroft *Procopius, Pers. Wars* ii. 51 Then shall you by our Countrey have the conveniencie of using to Roman Seas. **1663** *Extr. St. Papers Friends* Ser. ii. (1911) 168 When he is in London he vseth frequently at Mr. Lawries howse. **1834** J. Hall *Kentucky* II. 40 'But you seem acquainted with these woods.' 'Yes, I use about here some.' **1884** 'M. Twain' *Huckleberry Finn* vi, If he didn't quit using around there she would make trouble for him.

(*b*) **1470–85** Malory *Arthur* xviii. xxii. 765, I am a gentilwoman that vseth here in this forest huntynge. **1592** in J. Morris *Troub. Cath. Forefathers* Ser. ii. (1875) 54 Cotton did use thither divers times. **1596** Spenser *F.Q.* vi. Prol. ii, Conduct me well In these strange waies, where neuer foote did vse. *a* **1700** B. E. *Dict. Cant. Crew, Flash-ken*, A House where Thieves use. **1848** Bartlett *Dict. Amer.* 372, I can see where the deer used. **1851** Mayhew *Lond. Labour* II. 475/2 The master of the hotel or the gents that uses there.

transf. **1591** Sylvester *Ivry* 370 Even as a Galley, in smooth Sea subdues The tallest Ship that in the Steights doth use. **1637** Milton *Lycidas* 136 Ye valleys low where the milde whispers use, Of shades and wanton winds.

†**b.** To inhabit, reside, or dwell in or at a place.

a **1585** Montgomerie *Cherrie & Slae* 97 Musis that vsis At fountaine Helicon. **1610** Fletcher *Faithf. Sheph.* iii. i, I will give thee for thy food, No Fish that useth in the mud. **1628** May *Virg. Georg.* iii. 93 Snakes that use within the house for shade, Securely lurk. **1707** Sloane *Jamaica* I. p. xviii, This is known by the places where they [*sc.* fish] use.

†**c.** To associate (or cohabit) *with* a person. *Obs.*

1382 Wyclif *John* iv. 9 Jewis vsen not with Samaritans. **1559** Bercher *Nobylytye Wymen* (Roxb.) 141 The daughters of Lot, which vsed carnallye with their ffather. **1566** Sternhold & H. *Ps.* xxvi. 4, I do not lust to haunt or vse, with men whose deedes are vayne.

†**24. a.** To make use *of* some thing. *Obs.*

c **1500** *Melusine* xx. 110 As long that ye shall vse of feythfulnes. **1542** Udall *Erasm. Apoph.* 44 For in the same solemnitees men usen of a custom. **1704** N. N. tr. *Boccalini's Advts. fr. Parnass.* II. 171 He us'd of all the Rhetorick he had, to praise that Vice.

†**b.** Similarly with *with*. *Obs. rare.*

a **1400–50** *Alexander* 3594 Olyfauntis.., As ilkane vsyd with in ynde vmquile with to fiȝte. **1502** *Ord. Crysten Men* (W. de W. 1506) iv. xxi. X vj, He ought iustely to vse with his puyssaunce and not in abusynge.

25. To take drugs. *slang.*

1953 W. Burroughs *Junkie* (1964) x. 104 The reason it is practically impossible to stop using and cure yourself is that the sickness lasts five to eight days. Twelve hours of it would be easy, twenty-four possible, but five to eight days is too long. **1960** C. Cooper *Scene* 15 Why don't you bust a cap with me? It's choice. I used this morning and I'm still nice. **1962** 'K. Orvis' *Damned & Destroyed* xi. 71 Almost twenty-four hours.. since I've had a fix... Are you the only one?.. You forget I use, too.

used (ju:zd), *ppl. a.* [f. use *v.* + -ed[1].]

I. 1. †**a.** Customarily employed, experienced, or met with; accustomed, usual, wonted. *Obs.*

c **1374** Chaucer *Boeth.* i. met. v. (1868) 22 þe euesterre esperus.. comeþ eft aȝeynes hir vsed cours. *c* **1440** Capgrave *St. Kath.* iv. 1719 These too natures in oure lord ihesu were.. coupled to-geder ageyn vsed kynde. **1445** in Willis & Clark *Cambridge* (1886) I. 343 Thei shall ocupye with all maner of cariagez.. the vsed way within the ground. **1449** Pecock *Repr.* v. ii. 489 These now had and vsid religiouns in the chirche. **1480** *Wardr. Acc. Edw. IV.* (1830) 150 A pane of scarlet furrid with used ermyns. **1579** E. K. *Spenser's Sheph. Cal.* Gen. Argt. ¶2 To call them by the vsed and best knowen name. **1650** Howell *Giraffi's Rev. Naples* i. 2 Forcing him [*sc.* Gensericus] to bid a us'd farewell to fair Italie. **1655** Moufet & Bennet *Health's Improv.* xxix. 272, I perswade strong and indifferent stomachs to continue their used Diet.

b. That is or has been made use of; utilized. *spec.* (*a*) (esp. of a vehicle) = second hand, second-hand B. 2; also in hyphenated attrib. phr.; (*b*) of paper currency: not in mint condition.

1594– [see well-used]. **1758** B. Franklin *Poor Richard* (1890) 270 The used Key is always bright. **1864** E. A. Parkes *Pract. Hygiene* 157 The used surfaces of the teeth begin to bear a square mark. **1885** J. W. Palmer *Bric-à-Brac* 27 Papering a room with used stamps. **1931** *Punch* 3 June 589/2 It seems there is little demand nowadays for used cars. People find they can get all the walking exercise they need without buying a second-hand car. **1932** L. N. Wright *Links of Old Family Tree* x. 184 She was tempted to go into the business of dealing in used furniture. **1938** [see repossession 1]. **1955** F. O'Connor *Wise Blood* iv. 67 By six-thirty, he was down town, looking for used-car lots. **1960** I. Jefferies *Dignity & Purity* i. 12 He gave me five hundred quid in used ones. **1966** J. B. Priestley *Salt is Leaving* i. 12 Albert is doing quite nicely in the used-car business. **1970** 'D. Halliday' *Dolly & Cookie Bird* vii. 109 Nine thousand used dollar bills.

2. †**a.** Established by usage; customary. *Obs.*

c **1450** tr. *De Imitatione* iii. xiii. 81 The olde used custom wol wipstonde, but it shal be ouercomen by a better custom. **1603** Florio *Montaigne* ii. xv. 358 An auncient custome, and vsed cerimony.

b. *used and wont*, that is usual or customary; according to use and custom. *Sc.*

1510 *Reg. Privy Seal Scotl.* I. 315/2 Payand thairfor ȝerelie four pundis thre s. usuale money,.. with all maner of dewiteis usit and wount. **1562** *Reg. Cupar Abbey* I. 362 Item, to the convent.. for ane part of thair sustentatioun vsit and wont. **1609** Skene *Reg. Maj.* ii. Table 63 Bot the fourt heire sall make service vsed and wont. **1718** in *Nairne Peerage Evidence* (1874) 34 With the rights rents and services.. used and wont. **1814** Scott *Wav.* l, [He] claimed permission to perform.. the service used and wont. **1864** *Jedburgh Council Rec.* 31 Oct. (MS.), With all ceremonies used and wont.

3. Experienced (*in* something); expert. Latterly *Sc.*

c **1425** *Eng. Conq. Ireland* 23 Throgh kynde of Fraunce, we ben wsyd in wepyn. *c* **1470** Henry *Wallace* iii. 379 For thai war wicht, and weill wsyt in wer. **1786** Burns *Epist. to J. Rankine* ix, Some auld us'd hands had taen a note, That [etc.]. **1824** Scott *St. Ronan's* iii, Dick.. was an auld used hand.

II. used up. 4. *U.S.* Discussed thoroughly; talked of, or written about, critically.

1839 Mrs. Kirkland *A New Home* xxxv, 237 After tea the poor Brents were completely 'used up', to borrow a phrase much in vogue with us, and the next day I was.. asked.. if I had heard that Mr. and Mrs. Brent were going to 'part'. **1848** Poe *J. R. Lowell* Wks. 1895 VIII. 5 The various criticisms, in which we have been amused (rather ill-naturedly) at seeing Mr. Lowell 'used up'.

5. *slang* or *colloq.* **a.** Thoroughly exhausted by physical exertion or hardship; tired out, 'done up'.

1839 H. McLeod *Let.* 18 Jan. in *Papers M. B. Lamar* (122) II. 423, I will come down in a few days with Genl Rusk, but I am really so 'used up' now, that I cannot undergo the fatigue. **1840** R. H. Dana *Bef. Mast* xxviii, [He was] barefooted..; 'cleaned out' to the last real, and completely 'used up'. **1850** Smedley *F. Fairlegh* xlvii, Why, the perspiration is pouring down your face,—you look regularly used-up. **1888** J. C. Harris *Free Joe*, etc. 226 It was a five-mile excursion; and he returned, as Mrs. Haley expressed it, 'a used-up man'.

b. Knocked up by excess.

1890 GUNTER *Miss Nobody* xiii, My heavens! what a head I have accumulated over night! .. I wonder if Avonmere is used up likewise?

6. a. Worn out, debilitated, rendered useless, as with hard work, age, dissipation, etc.

1848 DICKENS *Dombey* x, A smoke-dried, sunburnt, used-up, invalided old dog of a Major, Sir. 1862 CALVERLEY *Poems* 57 What is coffee, but a noxious berry, Born to keep used-up Londoners awake? 1863 W. C. BALDWIN *Afr. Hunting* vi. 214 An old used-up brute [*sc.* horse]. 1871 ELEANOR GROVE tr. *Ebers' Egypt. Princess* I. Preface (Tauchn.) p. xv, In days when a used-up man of the world, like Antony, could desire in his will that [etc.].

transf. 1852 C. B. MANSFIELD *Paraguay*, etc. (1856) 369 The more respectable people here .. have a sort of used-up look, which is not inviting. 1853 DICKENS *Bleak Ho.* liii, The cousin .. yawns, 'Vayli'—being the used-up for 'very likely'. 1871 EARLE *Philol. English Tongue* i. 106 The extreme oddity of our sound of *U* comes out under a used-up or languid utterance. 1875 J. GRANT *One of the '600'* iii, The used-up bearing of those .. who affect to act as if .. life itself was a bore.

b. Emotionally exhausted; blasé.

1845 C. J. MATHEWS *Used Up* I. i. 8 Here I am, at thirty-three, completely blazé—a man literally 'used up!' 1853 MRS. GASKELL *Ruth* xxiii, He was pleased to feel jealous again. He had been really afraid he was too much 'used-up' for such sensations.

7. Reduced, exhausted, or consumed by using; rendered unserviceable by use.

1855 DELAMER *Kitchen Garden* 179 In short, make a general clearance of used-up things [in a garden]. 1881 SHAIRP *Asp. Poetry* 132 The accumulations of used-up verbiage, which had so long choked the sources of inspiration. 1896 *Allbutt's Syst. Med.* I. 312 The contaminated or used-up air.

Hence †**'usedly** *adv.*, commonly; **'usedness**. Also **used-upness** (*nonce-use*).

1561 T. NORTON *Calvin's Inst.* IV. 81 But it was .. vsedly the custome .. to shorten their iourney. 1680 BAXTER *Answ. Stillingfl.* xxxiii. 48 If Usefulness and Usedness .. may afford us a Prognostick. 1871 MRS. WHITNEY *Real Folks* xiii, You would notice instantly the consummate usedness to the world. 1891 'L. KEITH' *Halletts* II. 220 There was a good deal of used-upness about Spenceley, though .. the world had still certain points open to his combativeness.

'used-to-be, *sb.* [USE *v.* 21.]

1. A person whose time of popularity or efficiency is past; also = EX *sb.*^{1} *U.S.*

1853 [see HAS-BEEN *sb.*]. 1911 [see *never-was* s.v. NEVER *adv.* 8]. 1942 L. HUGHES *Shakespeare in Harlem* 50, I want to tell you 'bout that woman, My used-to-be—She was de meanest woman I ever did see.

2. (See quot.) *nonce-use*.

1883 J. W. RILEY *Poems Here at Home* (1893) 21 There lies a land, long lost to me, The land of Used-to-be.

u'see. *U.S.* [f. USE *v.* + -EE^1.] 'A person for whose use a suit is brought in the name of another' (*Cent. Dict.*, 1891).

use-fruyt, Sc. var. USUFRUIT *Obs.*

useful ('ju:sfʊl), *a.* and *sb.* [f. USE *sb.* + -FUL.]

Implied in the one early instance (1483) of *usefulness*, but app. not current till *c* 1600; cf. USELESS *a.*

A. *adj.* **1. a.** Of persons: Having the ability or qualities to bring about good, advantage, benefit, etc.; helpful for any purpose; serviceable. Also of animals (cf. 2).

1595 SHAKS. *John* v. ii. 81, I am too high-borne to be propertied, .. Or [a] vsefull seruing-man. 1646 *Verney Mem.* (1907) I. 343 Women were never soe usefull as now. 1671 MILTON *Samson* 564 Now blind, disheartn'd, .. quell'd, To what can I be useful? ? *a*1700 *Tak your Auld Cloak about ye* ii. in Ramsay *Evergreen*, My Cromie is a useful cow. 1708 J. C. *Compl. Collier* (1845) 19 Especially when such an Adventurer is so useful to the Publick. 1776 GIBBON *Decl. & F.* ii. (1782) I. 49 If he had any opportunity of rendering himself either useful or agreeable. 1831 SIR J. SINCLAIR *Corr.* II. 349 Baron Itzenplitz .. wishes [to see] his children .. useful for their country. 1861 WHYTE MELVILLE *Market Harb.* ix, Useful horses; .. and seem pretty fit to go. *Ibid.*, Very like hunters: remarkably useful horses indeed! 1887 RUSKIN *Præterita* II. 422 [He] was benevolently useful, as a landlord should be, in his county.

b. *Theatr.* (See quot.)

1824 W. IRVING *T. Trav.* II. (1848) 187, I was enrolled among the number of what are called *useful men*; those who enact soldiers, senators, and Banquo's shadowy line.

c. Applied to an odd-job man. *Austral. colloq.*

1866 R. HENNING *Let.* 16 May (1966) 219 There are three men employed about the place [*sc.* a logging business]. The bullock-driver, the punt-man and a 'generally useful' man. 1900 H. LAWSON *Middleton's Peter* in *Stories* (1964) 1st Ser. 293 There were two rooms .. attached to the stables. One was occupied by a man who was 'generally useful'.

2. Of things, actions, etc.: Having the character or quality to be of use or utility; suitable for use; advantageous, profitable, beneficial.

1606 SHAKS. *Ant. & Cl.* IV. xiv. 80 With a wound I must be cur'd. Draw that thy honest Sword, which thou hast worne Most vsefull for thy Country. 1634 SIR T. HERBERT *Trav.* 183 Food no lesse pleasant and vsefull to Kine. 1644 MILTON *Educ.* 99 The usefullest points of grammar. 1669 STURMY *Mariner's Mag.* II. x. 76 How to make a most useful Instrument of the Stars. *c*1737 SWIFT *Corr.* (1913) V. 435, I cannot doubt of your being willing to encourage all useful inventions. 1752 HUME *Pol. Disc.* iv. 67 Every thing useful to the life of man, arises from the ground. 1780 *Mirror* No. 80, They .. publish useful information to mankind. 1846 LANDOR *Imag. Conv.* Wks. I. 197/2 We are not always to consider in our disquisitions what is pleasantest, but sometimes what is usefullest. 1871 JOWETT *Plato* IV. 309 Exercises .. useful both in peace and war. 1875 R. F. MARTIN tr. *Havrez's Winding Mach.* 8 We thus see that .. the useful load exceeds the half of the total load. 1890 'R. BOLDREWOOD' *Col. Reformer* (1891) 337 A steady reader in her own line, which she denominated 'useful'.

absol. 1802 C. FINDLATER *View Agric. Peebles* 55 Admirers of the curious, as much as of the useful, in farming. 1818 J. FOSTER *Contrib. Eclectic Rev.* (1844) I. 482 The useful was to him the *summum bonum*. 1836–8 [see USELESS 1]. 1892 ZANGWILL *Bow Mystery* 157 A man who has always preached the Useful day and night.

b. *useful load* (Aeronaut.), the difference between the maximum permitted weight of an aircraft and its weight when empty, including cargo, passengers, crew, fuel and (with some writers) fixed equipment such as radios also; similarly *useful weight*.

1909 A. BERGET *Conquest of Air* II. iv. 205 A 'useful weight' in the form of fuel and oil to the extent of 80 kilogrammes. 1914 *Sphere* 7 Mar. 298/2 The most remarkable of the new aeroplanes is the Sikorsky... It can carry a useful load of over a ton. 1978 D. B. THURSTON *Design for Flying* ix. 112 If the airplane is intended for the .. private market, thin skin could be used and the weight saved converted to useful load.

c. Of a performer or performance: reasonably effective, fairly successful.

1955 *Amer. Speech* XXX. 23 A horse with a seemingly excellent racing background will be described as good; and a horse the record of which .. would seem good will be described as useful. 1959 *Listener* 23 July 129/1 He .. played a useful game of cricket .. with a local league side. 1971 N. STACEY *Who Cares?* i. 19, I had been a useful school sportsman and got into the first eleven at most sports at Dartmouth.

d. Of a woman's dress; practical, unostentatious; suitable for a variety of occasions.

1963 *Observer* 3 Nov. 33/1 In the dress trade, 'a useful little dress' means one with no distinguishing characteristics; 'romantic' means 'cleft to the waist'. 1968 M. JONES *Survivor* i. 22 The dinner was arranged... She had dressed with restraint in a 'useful' black dress.

B. *sb.* **1.** A useful article. *rare*$^{-1}$.

1662 PETTY *Taxes* 21 Metals, cloth, linen, leather, and other usefuls.

2. An odd-job person. *Austral colloq.*

1898 A. JOYCE *Homestead Hist.* (1969) 41 Our friends had met with a trained carpenter in town, whom with his wife they had hired for £20 a year, the man as general useful, .. and his wife as cook. 1935 K. TENNANT *Tiburon* 37 Roman stepped out of the room next to the laundry of O'Brien's Hotel, where he was barman, yardman and general useful. *a*1963 J. FOUNTAIN in 'B. James' *Austral. Short Stories* (1963) 277 Every boy .. knew the .. circumstances of .. Maggie's affair with the useful from the hotel.

Hence **'usefullish** *a.*, somewhat useful. *rare*$^{-1}$.

1848 CARLYLE in Froude *Life in London* (1884) I. 421, I seem to them a desperate half mad, if usefullish fireman.

'usefully, *adv.* [f. prec. + -LY^2.] In a useful manner; so as to be of use; to a useful end; beneficially, profitably, serviceably.

1634 MASSINGER *Very Woman* III. ii, Serve usefully, Serve all with diligence. 1656 COWLEY *Davideis* III. 281 How the kind Sun usefully comes and goes. 1711 STEELE *Spect.* No. 145 ¶2 You cannot employ yourself more usefully. 1781 GIBBON *Decl. & F.* xxx. III. 175 Whose arms would have been more usefully employed to maintain the Roman limits. 1807 G. CHALMERS *Caledonia* I. III. v. §3. 357 The notices of topography come in here, usefully, to illustrate the obscurity of history. 1868 KINGLAKE *Crimea* III. 144 It was hardly one which could be usefully submitted to a numerous assembly.

'usefulness. [f. as prec. + -NESS.]

†**1.** The advantage or benefit *of* (a place). *Obs.*$^{-1}$

1483 DUKE GLOUCS. in R. Davies *Extr. Munic. Rec. York* (1843) 147 For the wele and usefullnes of þe realme.

2. The state or condition of being useful or serviceable; utility, serviceableness.

1617 WOODALL *Surg. Mate* (1639) B 3 b, The goodnesse and usefulnesse thereof, for the preserving of mens lives. 1662 STILLINGFL. *Orig. Sacræ* III. i. §16 The peculiar usefulness of the several parts of mans body. 1749 BERKELEY *Word to Wise* Wks. 1871 III. 437 We are all agreed about the usefulness of meat, drink, and clothes. 1760 'PORTIA' *Polite Lady* x. 28 The usefulness and importance of all the different parts of education. 1835 *Penny Cycl.* IV. 398/1 *Bill of Exchange*, a well-known mercantile instrument, of great and extensive usefulness. 1860 RUSKIN *Unto this Last* (1862) 125 In accurate terms, usefulness is value in the hands of the valiant. 1871 JOWETT *Plato* IV. 19 The preliminary sciences .. are to be studied partly with a view to their practical usefulness.

b. With pl.: A good, benefit, or advantage. *rare*.

1664 H. MORE *Exp. 7 Epist.* Pref. c iv b, And these .. are main Usefulnesses discoverable in the Interpretation. 1668 —— *Div. Dial.* I. To Rdr. a j b, The particular Vsefulnesses of the Creation.

usel, obs. variant of ISEL (ashes, etc.).

useless ('ju:slɪs), *a.* [f. USE *sb.* + -LESS.]

1. Of things, actions, etc.: Destitute of useful qualities; serving no good end or profitable purpose; not answering or promoting the proposed or desired end; unserviceable, ineffectual, inutile.

In frequent use from *c* 1650.

1593 SHAKS. *Lucr.* 859 The aged man .. like still-pining Tantalus .. sits, And useless barns the harvest of his wits. *a*1623 FLETCHER *Love's Cure* I. i, Let your deeds Make answer to me: useless are all words Till you have writ performance with your swords. 1645 STAPYLTON tr. *Musæus* C 3 b, The giddy Seas their uselesse drinke bestow'd. 1697 DRYDEN *Virg. Georg.* III. 833 Useless to the Currier were their Hides. 1729 T. INNES *Crit. Essay* (1879) 56 An useless as well as an endless discussion. *Ibid.* 206 It became quite useless towards supporting Buchanan's schemes. 1776 GIBBON *Decl. & F.* ii. (1782) I. 55 According to the useless rhetoric of that age. 1825 SCOTT *Betrothed* xvii, He .. fell .. ere Raoul could afford him his support, useless as that might have proved. 1855 MACAULAY *Hist. Eng.* xix. IV. 271 The six thousand waggons which had accompanied the French army were useless. 1890 *Retrospect Med.* CII. 177 Physicians, almost without exception, give nearly useless doses of arsenic.

absol. 1836–7 SIR W. HAMILTON *Metaph.* i. (1859) I. 4 What is a utilitarian? Simply one who prefers the Useful to the Useless. 1838 *Penny Cycl.* XI. 345/2 To distinguish good from evil, the useful from the useless.

b. For which there is no present use.

1745 *Transl. & Paraphr.* 50 They'll lay the useless Trumpet by, and study War no more.

2. Of persons: Destitute of competence or capacity; of inadequate or insufficient ability; inefficient.

1670 COVEL in *Early Voy. Levant* (Hakl. Soc.) 135 With great courage .. [he] turn'd upon the Rogues, who were uselesse, and thought they had him safe. 1710 W. KING *Heathen Gods & Heroes* vi. (1722) 12 [Prometheus] brought Men out from the Caves where they liv'd useless, and like Beasts. 1783 BURKE *Rep. Aff. India* Wks. 1842 II. 52 That Mr. Hastings .. had recalled a useless officer. 1810 CRABBE *Borough* xx. 331, I lost my sight, and my employment gone, Useless I live. 1840 THIRLWALL *Greece* VII. 180 He .. sent the baggage and all his useless people to Melitæ. 1855 LONGF. *Hiaw.* x. 29 Bring not here a useless woman.

'uselessly, *adv.* [f. prec. + -LY^2.] In a useless or fruitless manner; ineffectually; †so as to become of no use.

1615 G. SANDYS *Trav.* III. 151 The grasse wast-high, vnmowed, vneaten, and vselessly withering. 1690 LOCKE *Hum. Und.* II. i. §15 To be so idlely and uselesly employ'd. 1765 *Museum Rust.* IV. 371, I would not so uselesly misapply .. your time. 1774 PENNANT *Tour Scot. in 1772*, 272 My money had been so uselessly laid out. 1831 SCOTT *Cast. Dang.* vi, You have been long, and I hope not uselessly, my pupil. 1880 MCCARTHY *Own Times* lxvi. IV. 506 He had thrown away his life uselessly in a quarrel.

'uselessness. [f. as prec. + -NESS.] The quality of being useless; futility, inutility.

1690 LOCKE *Hum. Und.* III. iv. §10 Another Peripatetick definition .. which .. betrays its Uselesness and Insignificancy. 1733–4 BP. BERKELEY in Fraser *Life* (1871) vi. 217 The impropriety and uselessness of .. going to Cloyne. *a*1768 SECKER *Serm.* (1771) VI. 69 The Revelation of St. John is accused of Obscurity, and consequently of Uselessness. 1845 JAMES *Arrah Neil* v, The uselessness of remonstrance or opposition. 1889 S. LANGDON *Appeal to Serpent* i. 23 These vast monuments of laborious uselessness.

†**'usell**, *a.* *Obs.* [a. ON. *ú-sæll* unhappy (MSw. *usal*, Sw. *usel*, Da. *ussel*, miserable, pitiful), f. *ú-* UN-^{1} + *sæll* happy.] Wretched, miserable. Hence †**'uselldom**, wretchedness. *Obs.*$^{-1}$

*c*1200 ORMIN 891 Forr baþe leddenn usell lif I metess & i claþess. *Ibid.* 3668 Unnorne & wrecche & usell child Inn ure mennisscnesse. *Ibid.* 3708 To libbenn her onn eorþe Full wrecchelike inn uselldom Off metess & off claþess.

†**use-man.** *Obs. rare.* [f. USE *sb.* 5, 16 d.]

1. A usurer.

1633 HEYWOOD *Eng. Trav.* III. i, If I can aswell put off my Vse-man This day, I shall be maister of the field.

2. (See quot. and USE *sb.* 16 d.)

*a*1716 SOUTH *Serm.* (1717) V. 34 To give those Doctrine and Vse-men, those Pulpit-Engineers their due.

'use-money. Now *dial.* [f. USE *sb.* 5 b.] = INTEREST *sb.* 10. Also *fig.*

1616 HEALEY *Theophrastus* 66 When he coms to his debtors for his vsemony. 1626 MIDDLETON *Anything for Quiet Life* I. i, Never did any man thrive that purchased with use-money. 1656 TRAPP *Comm.* (ed. 2) *Matt.* v. 26 All that wicked men suffer here is but a paying the use-money required for that dreadful debt, that must be paid at last. 1700 T. BROWN *Amusem. Ser. & Com.* 29 There sneaks a Hunger-starv'd Usurer in quest of a Crasie Citizen for Use and Continuance-Money. 1849– in dialect use (Durham, Cumbld., Yks., Lincs., Somerset). 1874 T. HARDY *Far fr. Mad. Crowd* viii, When the use-money is gied away to the second-best poor folk.

usen't, colloq. shortening of *used not*.

*c*1863 T. TAYLOR in M. R. Booth *Eng. Plays of 19th Cent.* (1969) II. 96, I usen't to mind unkind looks and words much once. 1907 G. B. SHAW *Major Barbara* III. 255 That is a new accomplishment of Andrew's, by the way. He usent to drink. 1929 'H. H. RICHARDSON' *Ultima Thule* III. v. 279 Usen't Richard to say that it was etiquette in the profession to treat a patient's relatives .. as so many cretins?

user^1 ('ju:zə(r)). Also 6 *Sc.* usar. [f. USE *v.* + -ER^1. Cf. OF. *useur*.]

1. a. One who has or makes use of a thing; one who uses or employs anything.

*c*1400 LOVE *Bonavent. Mirr.* (1908) 70 So ofte þe maker and þe vsere offendeth god. *a*1425 tr. *Arderne's Treat. Fistula*, etc. 8 þe forseid [counsels] .. shal giffe a gracious going to þe vser to þe hiȝte of worship. 1467 in *Eng. Gilds* (1870) 387 That it be so stopped by the doers or vsers therof. 1579 NORTHBROOKE *Dicing* (1843) 177 God graunt that .. the magistrates .. may .. set sharpe punishment for the vsers and teachers thereof. *c* **1600** SHAKS. *Sonn.* ix, But beauties waste hath in the world an end, And kept vnvsde the vser so destroyes it. **1626** DONNE *Serm.* (1640) 675 As he [*sc.* God] sees him a good or bad user of his graces. **1683** TRYON *Way to Health* 223 These Superfluities..are become as it were Essential to the Nature of the Users. **1711** *Countrey-Man's Lett. Curat.* 58 What tho' all our Reformers had been users and readers of the English Service? **1738** WARBURTON *Div. Legat.* I. 84 The utmost Consumption may be made.. without Injury to the User. **1846** GREENER *Sci. Gunnery* p. vii, The safety of the user of guns. **1846** MOZLEY *Ess.* (1878) I. 251 He is a user of Puritanism. **1862** *Cornh. Mag.* VI. 608 A moderate user of tobacco. **1876** WHITNEY *Language & its Study* iii. 74 It seeks..to save time and labour to the users of language.

b. A person who takes narcotic, etc., drugs. orig. *U.S.*

1935 A. J. POLLOCK *Underworld Speaks* 129/2 *User*, a person addicted to any of the poisonous habit forming drugs; a hop-head; dope fiend. **1953** W. BURROUGHS *Junkie* (1964) vi. 58 The owner knew Tony had been a user and had told him to stay off the stuff or get another job. **1969** *Guardian* 3 Dec. 9/1 She was taking six grains of heroin a day... She had been a user for about six months. **1975** H. WHITE *Raincoast Chron.* (1976) 144/2 There had always been users around in the shadowy back streets. **1983** *Easyriders* Feb. 111/4 Harley man, 29..seeks lady 5'7" or under for friend, lover, and partner... No boozers or heavy users.

c. *spec.* A person or organization that makes use of a computer. Freq. *attrib.* and *Comb.* (cf. sense 5 below).

1967 [see *user-assigned* adj., sense 5 below]. **1973** C. W. GEAR *Introd. Computer Sci.* iv. 151 The software makes it possible for a user to prepare procedures and have them executed by the computer with a minimum of effort. **1984** *Which Micro?* Dec. 8/1 Micro breakdown..drives users to despair.

†**2.** *Sc.* One who puts a writ, etc., in force or execution. *Obs.*

1576 in *Excheq. Rolls Scotl.* XX. 504 David Fowlar,..usar of the said precept, declarit that he deliverit [it]..to John Kellie. **1609** SKENE *Reg. Maj., Forme of Proces* 122 The wreit or evident is declared to be fals;..And the vser thereof, is punished capitallie. *c* **1630** SIR T. HOPE *Minor Practicks* (1734) 242 If the King..give a Letter of Regress;..when the Order of Redemption is used and declared, the User of the Redemption is immediately seased, upon the Sight of the Regress.

†**3.** A usurer. *Obs.*[1]

1566 DRANT *Horace, Sat.* I. ii. A viij b, What soeuer cums by vsers skylle, to get, and gender more.

4. *north. dial.* A useful animal.

1828 CARR *Craven Gloss.* s.v., A cow is said to be a good *user*, when she yields abundance of milk, &c. **1863** MRS. TOOGOOD *Yorks. Dial.* (MS.).

5. *attrib.* and *Comb.*, (esp. in sense 1 b) as ***user benefit, charge, cost, fee, group***; ***user-assigned, -supplied*** adjs.; ***user-processing***; **user-definable** *a. Computers*, having a function or meaning that can be specified and varied by a user; so **user-defined** *a.*; **user-friendly** *a. Computers*, easy to use; designed with the needs of users in mind; also *transf.*; hence **user-friendliness**; **user interface**, the means by which a person is enabled to use a computer; **user-orientated, -oriented** *adjs.*, designed with the user's convenience given priority; **user-programmable** *a. Computers*, capable of being programmed or assigned a function by the user.

1967 COX & GROSE *Organization & Handling Bibl. Rec. by Computer* 84 The valves DCN, DATE, DAY, etc. are the user-assigned names for the bibliographic date fields. **1972** *Computers & Humanities* VI. 303 We will study the cost-effectiveness of stripping away various features..with least prejudice to user-benefit. **1945** *Sun* (Baltimore) 29 Sept. 3/2 John J. Pelley, president of the Association of American Railroads, urged..that 'user charges' be levied against highway, waterway and airway carriers. **1976** *Times* 29 Nov. 12/2 It is possible to raise only one cheer for user charges as a means of avoiding the dilemma of cutting public services or increasing taxes. **1936** J. M. KEYNES *Gen. Theory Employment* vi. 70 We have defined the user cost as the reduction in the value of the equipment due to using it as compared with not using it. **1969** D. C. HAGUE *Managerial Economics* (1971) II. v. 103 The cost of servicing and repairs is part of what economists call 'user cost', the cost of using the car (or any other asset) instead of leaving it idle. **1972** *IBM Technical Disclosure Bull.* XIV. 3553 (*heading*) Representation of tree data structures as matrices suitable for user-definable traversing. **1983** *MicroComputer Printout* Sept. 69/1 A programmable character set (also called user-definable) may let you design your own characters—mathematical symbols, or foreign alphabets. **1985** *Personal Computer World* Feb. 133/1 The number of user-definable characters that you can enter at the Model 4 Keyboard in this way is limited to 20. **1968** *Simulation* XI. 304/2 User-defined functions. **1984** *Which?* July 302/1 In rating graphics..we looked at..the range of graphics features provided with the computer-graphics characters,..sprites, ...user-defined graphics (shapes you can set up yourself) and so on. **1984** *Personal Software* Winter 26/2 The program will allow you to have up to fifty user defined commands. **1980** *Tucson* (Arizona) *Star* 4 Mar., He sees no reason why 'user fees'..should not be charged for libraries. **1984** *Gainesville* (Florida) *Sun* 2 Mar. 12A/5 It is clear that (Proposition 1) fails to allow for increased demand on government-owned utilities and other user-fee services resulting from population increases and other causes. **1979** *Interfaces* May 72 User friendliness is a term coined by Harlan Crowder to represent the inherent ease (or lack of ease) which is encountered when running a computer system. **1982** *Daily Tel.* 7 Dec. 2 (Advt.), The system has been very well received—a credit to the HP 3000's user-friendliness. **1977** BIRSS & YEH *Set Theoretic Data Structures* (*STDS*) 31 STDS-I does not provide the user with a sufficiently 'user-friendly' interface to allow noncomputer scientists to easily work with a data base. **1982** *New Scientist* 30 Sept. 931/1 The program it works from is 'user-friendly' insofar as the commands are based on initials such as CV for 'centre vertically' and FD for 'forms design'. **1984** *Which Micro?* Dec. 3 (Advt.), Every computer manufacturer now claims its products are 'user friendly'. **1984** *Listener* 13 Dec. 38/1 No TV show (not even the news) could close without reference to this user-friendly family of dolls. **1972** *Accountant* 26 Oct. 518/2 To satisfy the information needs of entrepreneurs, investors, and other outside user-groups is to guarantee a full and active future for the accountant. **1983** *Lebende Sprachen* XXVIII. 48/1 Language mediators represent one of the largest user groups of terminology. **1968** *Proc. Internat. Fed. Information Processing* (1969) I. II. 570 Three levels of user interface are defined for the information retrieval language. **1983** *Byte* Feb. 36/1 The company's first task was to devise a new user interface—that is, a new and better way for humans to interact with the computer. **1985** *Personal Computer World* Feb. 137/2 The operating system, GSX and GEM Services bind together to form the programmer interface, but they do not provide the user interface directly. **1969** *Computer Aided Design* Winter 5/2 The plea for more languages.. which are specific to particular problems, and in this sense 'user-orientated'. **1978** *Hi-Fi News* Sept. 218 (Advt.), There's a low distortion equaliser, tape duplication switch ....plus a host of user-orientated features. **1964** *Communications Assoc. Computing Machinery* VII. 290/1 (*heading*) An experiment in a user-oriented computer system. **1979** *Dictionaries* I. 110 User-oriented service programs..could put the student in immediate contact with a wealth of lexicographic information. **1958** *Newnes Compl. Amat. Photogr.* 283 Kodak Ltd. propose eventually to market processing kits..for the user-processing of Kodacolor Film. **1976** *Scientific & Technical Aerospace Rep.* XIV. XXII. 2927/1 To fulfil all desired capabilities, a user programmable communication device is required. **1983** *What's New in Computing* Jan. 60/1 The full alphanumeric and function key keypad..includes..eight user-programmable keys. **1969** *Computers & Humanities* III. 130 It contains the ability to perform, *inter alia*, the following tasks:... Generate reports of extracted data according to user-supplied format.

'user[2]. *Law.* [a. F. *user* to USE, or inferred from NON-USER. Cf. the earlier ABUSER[2], DISUSER.] Continued use, exercise, or enjoyment of a right, etc.; presumptive right arising from use.

1835 CROMPTON, MEESON & ROSCOE *Rep. Cases* I. 418 *marg.*, No right having been acquired by user or length of possession. **1858** LD. ST. LEONARDS *Handy-bk. Prop. Law* xxv. 191 That there should be an user proved every year during the period. **1888** *Pall Mall G.* 29 Feb. 1/1 An open space in which the public has an uninterrupted right of user for purposes of public meeting.

transf. **1875** BLACKMORE *Alice Lorraine* II. xvi. 207 A crust of mud, as if some underground duct were anxious to maintain user of its right of way.

attrib. **1897** *Westm. Gaz.* 16 June 4/2 In which [judgement] there was only one slight reference to the user question.

userer, -y, etc., obs. varr. USURER, USURY.

useter ('ju:stə(r)). Also **useta**, **uster**. Repr. an informal or uneducated pronunc. of *used to* (see USE *v.* 21).

1890 *Dialect Notes* I. 69 When it rains and wets our old rooster, He don't look like he useter. **1898** J. D. BRAYSHAW *Slum Silhouettes* 215 I've just seed Liz Dukeson,..her that Cocky uster cart abaht. **1921** E. O'NEILL *Emperor Jones* v. 185 Is you sellin' me like dey uster befo' de war? **1935** in Z. N. Hurston *Mules & Men* (1970) I. viii. 172 Naw, dat's Uncle Yistiddy, he's a useter-be! **1937** D. L. SAYERS *Busman's Honeymoon* i. 57 You mind the little cottage down by the river..where old Blunt useter live? **1952** M. STEEN *Phoenix Rising* vi. 134 Dey say she gone to Harlem... Useta teach school. **1978** L. BLOCK *Burglar in Closet* (1980) i. 8, I useta beg her to keep some of that stuff in a safe-deposit box. **1982** A. TAYLOR *Caroline Minuscule* x. 79 'He said it'd be all right for me to doss down here... He useter—' 'Liar. He couldn't have done.'

ush, *sb. Sc.* Also 5–6 **vsche**, 5 **wsche**. [See next and ISH *sb.*]

†**1.** = ISH *sb.* 1, EGRESS *sb.* 1. *Obs.*

1429 *15th Rep. Hist. MSS. Comm.* App. VIII. 10 [He] sall haf fre vsche and entre in to the said castell. **1534** *Munim. de Melros* (Bann. Cl.) 628 To be haldin..in houssis,.. pastouris, lesouris, fre vsche and entray.

†**2.** = ISH *sb.* 2, ISSUE *sb.* 2.

1463 *Extr. Aberd. Reg.* (1844) I. 23 To fynd the childe of the brok of his gudis to the vsche of fyue yeris. **1472** *Rental Bk. Cupar-Angus* (1879) I. 164 The sade John Sperk entrand at the vsche of his [*sc.* Cant's] tak. **1489** *Sc. Acts, Jas. IV* (1814) II. 215 þat a proclamacioune be maid at the vsche of this parliament.

†**3.** A fine or amerciament; = ISSUE *sb.* 7 b. *Obs.*

1417 *Reg. Aberdon.* (Maitland Cl.) I. 215 þe kyrk..is in possession of þe tend penny of all wardis, relefis, and mariagis, vscheis of courtis, eschetis.

4. = ISSUE *sb.* 9. *rare.*

a **1900** *Caithness Words* (E.D.D.), *Ush*, the entrails of a slaughtered animal.

ush, *v.*[1] *Sc.* (†and *north.*). Also 5 **vssh(e**, 5–6 **wsch**, 6 **vsche**, 7, 9 **ushe**. [var. of ISH *v.*[1]]

†**1.** *intr.* To issue, come *out* (or *forth*). *Obs.*

c **1420** *Avow. Arth.* lxiv, On a day we vsshet oute. *c* **1470** HENRY *Wallace* v. 1050 Thai..wsched furth upon the secund day. *Ibid.* VIII. 116 Erll Patrik wschyt, for bid him wald he nocht. ?**1550** *Freiris Berwik* 130 (*Maitland MS.*), He had ane preuie postroun..That he micht vsche [*Bann.* ische] quhen [that] him list vnknawin. *a* **1578** LINDESAY (Pitscottie) *Chron. Scot.* (S.T.S.) II. 11 Certaine of the castell men wschit out. *a* **1614** J. MELVILL *Diary* (Wodrow Soc.) 273 Hendrie Hamilton ushes out of a hous, where he lay in wait for bloode.

†**b.** To go or come *in*; = ENTER *v.* 1. *Obs.*

a **1400** *Sir Degrev.* 1078 (1062), þey vschen in with banere, v. hunderyd knyȝtus.

†**2.** *trans.* To clear (a place) of people; to expel or drive out (occupants). *Obs.*

a **1578** LINDESAY (Pitscottie) *Chron. Scot.* (S.T.S.) II. 83 [[They] dang out the portar ffrome the ȝett and wschit all the rest of the place. *a* **1614** J. MELVILL *Diary* (Wodrow Soc.) 317 The King, taking me asyde, caussit ushe the Cabinet. *a* **1639** SPOTTISWOOD *Hist. Ch. Scot.* VI. (1655) 374 Presently the roomes were ushed, and the Earl with his company went forth. **1685** *Acts of Sederunt* (1790) 163 The Lords.. recommends to the Ordinary..to order the house to be ushed and cleared.

b. To empty, cleanse.

1887 *Suppl. Jamieson* 257/1 To ushe the belly.

ush, *v.*[2] *dial.* or *colloq.* [Back-formation from USHER *sb.*]

1. *trans.* To guide, escort, or lead.

a **1824** in C. K. Sharpe *Ballad Bk.* (1824) 11 Three valets, ...To beir my tail up frae the dirt, And ush me throw the toun.

2. *intr.* To act the usher. (USHER *sb.* 1 d.) *U.S.*

1890 *Harper's Mag.* Dec. 160/2 The six gentlemanly cow-boys..swore that whoever should prove to be the lucky man, the others would ush for him at the ceremony. **1910** *Ibid.* Mar. 613/1 Man alive, you've crossed half a continent to 'ush' at that wedding!

ushabti (u:'ʃæbtɪ). *Egyptology.* Also **ushebte, ushebti.** Pl. **ushabtis, -iu.** [a. Egyptian *wšbty* answerer.] A figurine of a deceased person, made of faience, stone, wood, etc., and placed in an ancient Egyptian tomb to act as a substitute for the dead person in any work he might be called upon to do in the afterlife. Also ***ushabti-figure***. See also SHABTI, SHAWABTI.

1885 E. A. W. BUDGE *Dwellers on Nile* viii. 164 The figures placed with the dead were called *ushabtiu*, and were inscribed with the name of the deceased and the sixth chapter of the Book of the Dead. **1894** H. M. TIRARD tr. *Erman's Life in Anc. Egypt* xiii. 317 Besides these models of servants and of sailors which replaced the earthly domestics of the departed, there were many other figures of a different kind... These are the so-called funerary statuettes, or as they are termed in Egyptian the Ushebte, *i.e.* the *answerers*. **1910** *Encycl. Brit.* V. 709/1 This polychrome faience was also now [*sc.* in the Eighteenth Dynasty] used for the *ushabti* figures which were placed in the tombs; hitherto they had been made exclusively of stone or wood..the plain blue and black of the ordinary vases was adopted. The *ushabtis* of King Seti I...are fine specimens of this type. **1925** *Glasgow Herald* 27 July 8 The ushabtiu figures..were deposited either in the coffin itself or near to it. **1933** A. W. SHORTER *Everyday Life in Anc. Egypt* viii. 175 The actual meaning of the word *ushabti* is not known for certain, one explanation being that the word is derived from the verb *usheb* 'to answer', and therefore means 'answerer'—i.e. one who comes at the summons of the deceased. *Ibid.* 176 The *ushabti*..represents the deceased himself in mummy form. .... The *ushabti*-figures of the Eighteenth Dynasty..are made of wood or stone... The manufacture of faïence *ushabtiu*, however,..became popular. **1957** L. DURRELL *Justine* I. 57 The air was all at once full of..tear-bottles, Ushabti, and Sèvres. **1961** A. H. GARDINER *Egypt of Pharaohs* iii. 32 The tombs of the well-to-do often yield hundreds of small statuettes mostly of faience or wood now generally known by their later name of *Ushabti* figures or 'answerers'..; the earlier writing Shawabti is of doubtful meaning. **1979** H. EVANS *Mystery of Pyramids* ii. 62/2 To make this everlasting life as comfortable as possible, the spirit called upon the magical aids and implements provided in its earthly tomb. These facilities even included model figures, *ushabtis*, that could act as substitutes if the gods called for workers in the fields.

Ushak ('ʊʃæk). Also **Ouchak, Oushak.** [ad. Turk. *Uşak.*] The name of a town in W. Turkey used *attrib.* or *ellipt.* to denote a type of antique rug made there.

1901 J. K. MUMFORD *Oriental Rugs* iv. 35 For rugs of the heavier quality, such as the ponderous Oushaks and Anatolians, the sheep of the Asia Minor Plains produce a wool that is adequate in length, and..soft to the touch. **1905** M. C. RIPLEY *Oriental Rug Bk.* xv. 115 In Turkish carpets of large size many styles are grouped under the trade name "Ouchak" in which modern methods are observable. **1922** KENDRICK & TATTERSALL *Hand-Woven Carpets, Oriental & European* I. II. i. 100 The carpets of Asia Minor, of the kind called Ushak, which date from the fifteenth to the seventeenth centuries, are invariably woven with the Ghiordes knot. **1931** A. U. DILLEY *Oriental Rugs & Carpets* Pl. 45 (*caption*) Ushak prayer rug, late sixteenth century. **1952** B. MIALL tr. *Jacoby's How to know Oriental Carpets & Rugs* 106 From the very first the Ouchaks differed very perceptibly, in colour and design, from the Persian carpets. **1975** 'E. LATHEN' *By Hook or by Crook* xvi. 152 We should list some of our best rugs... Or just mention the Ushak. **1977** *Times* 12 Feb. 14/6 (*heading*) Rare Ushak carpet is sold for £42,000. **1984** *Times* 1 June 12 (*caption*) Charles Sternberg with the large Ushak (or Mahal) for which he paid ££48,600.

usher ('ʌʃə(r)), *sb.* Forms: 4–5 **vsscher, usscher, uscher,** 5 **vschere, vshure,** 6 **vscher;** 4–5 **vssher** (5 **-ere**), 4–6 **ussher** (5 **-ere**), 6 **vsher,** 5– **usher** (7 **ushier**); 4 **oyschere,** 5 **oischer;** *Sc.* 5 **isscheare,** 5–6 **ischar,** 6 **ischair, -ear,** 7 **isher.** [a. AF. *usser* (12th c.), OF. *ussier, uissier, uscier*, var. of *huisier*, etc., HUISHER *sb.* Cf. OSTIAR(Y.]

1. An official or servant who has charge of the door and admits people to a hall, chamber, etc.;

a door-keeper; in later use esp. an officer in a court of justice, or an attendant who conducts people to seats in a church, public hall, or place of amusement.

c 1386 Chaucer *Sqr.'s T.* 293 The vsshers and the squiers been ygoon, The spices and the wyn is come anoon. a 1400–50 *Boke of Curtasye* 30 in *Babees Bk.* 300 Whille marshalle or vssher come fro þe dore, And bydde the sitte, or to borde the lede. c 1400 *Northern Passion* (H.) 617 Saint iohn spak to visscher þan. c 1410 *Sir Cleges* 287 The vsscher at the hall dore was Wyth a staffe stondynge. a 1470 H. Parker *Dives & Pauper* (W. de W. 1496) vi. xi. 249/1 She dyd hyr offyce, for she was usshere and keper at the dore. 1525 Ld. Berners *Froiss.* II. xcvi. 110b/1 Than the squyer..called the vssher to open the dore. c 1610 in [T. Maude] *Verbeia or Wharfdale* (1782) App. 43 The Usher's Wordes of Directions. First,..he must go before them thro' the hall [etc.]. 1677 *Govt. Venice* 121 He disposes of the little Offices about the Palace, as the Ushers and others. 1694 E. Chamberlayne *Pres. St. England* I. III. 681 Chelsea College. .. There are several other..Servants, as..Sexton, Usher, Porters [etc.]. 1728 Chambers *Cycl.* (1738) s.v., The ushers of the inquisition..think themselves highly honoured, by only looking to the doors of the sacred tribunal. 1799 *Report Comm. Courts of Justice* 29 Usher of the Court. *Ibid.* 31 The Court of King's Bench..[Officers include] Usher and Cryer. Deputy Cryers. Deputy Ushers. 1868 Dickens *Let.* 3 Jan., He met one of the 'ushers' (who show people to their seats) coming in with Kelly. 1898 A. M. Binstead *Pink 'Un & Pelican* 181 Like the legal gent.., asked to define the duties of the ushers in the law courts.

b. *fig.*, *transf.*, and in fig. context.

c 1380 Wyclif *Sel. Wks.* II. 163 Crist..haþ resoun of many þingis; for he is dore, he is ussher. 1387 Trevisa *Higden* v. xvii. (MS. Cott. Tib. D. vii.) fol. 188 Seþþe..so meny..priueleges..were ygrauntet to petur y dare no3t wiþsygge [so] grete and soche an oyschere and porter. 1573 Tusser *Husb.* (1878) 20 Make eie to be vsher, good vsage to haue, make bolt to be porter. 1594 *Zepheria* v. B 3, Feare, Centinell of sad discretion,..Cares Vsher, Tenant to his owne oppression. 1630 Prynne *Anti-Armin.* 258 Arminianisme is but a Bridge, an Vsher vnto grosse Popery. 1638 T. Whitaker *Blood of Grape* 4 As if Satiation were the Usher of diseases. 1709 Steele & Swift *Tatler* No. 67 ¶10 In this chamber of Fame..no historians are to be admitted at any of these tables; because they..are to be made use of as ushers to the assemblies. 1878 Stewart & Tait *Unseen Univ.* i. §5. 27 Being the usher of souls in their passage to the future state.

c. Const. *of* (the hall, chamber, etc.).

a 1400–50 *Bk. Curtasye* 432 in *Babees Bk.*, Speke I wylle a lytulle qwyle Of vssher of chambur, with-outen gyle. [Description of his duties follows.] ? 1436 *Pol., Rel., & L. Poems* (1903) 13, I was put to þe Soudenys house & was made vssher of halle. 1480 *Acta Dom. Conc.* (1839) 49/1 Sir Johne of Culquhone..vschare in þe tyme of oure souerane lordis chawmer durre. 1503 *Acc. Ld. High Treas. Scot.* II. 311 John Knox ischar of the hall. 1538 Elyot, *Admissionales*, vshers of the chambre. 1623 Cockeram II, An Vsher of a Hall, *atrict.* 1728 Chambers *Cycl.* (1738) s.v., In the French Court there are two ushers of the ante-chamber, or hall where the king dines in public.

fig. a 1500 *Assemb. Ladies* in Skeat *Chaucerian Pieces* (1897) 383, I am..Of her [*sc.* Loyalty's] chambre her ussher. 1501 Douglas *Pal. Hon.* III. lviii, Humanitie and trew Relatioun Bene ischaris of his chalmer.

d. *U.S.* One who performs the functions of an usher (sense 1) at a wedding.

1895 *Outing* (U.S.) XXVII. 181 He sent the young lady a beautiful Colport cup and saucer,..at the same time breathing a prayer that Elliott would not ask him to be usher.

2. An officer at court, in a dignitary's household, etc., whose duty it is on occasion to walk or go before a person of high rank; also, a chamberlain. ***Usher of the Black Rod, Green Rod***: (see Black Rod, and quot. 1869).

1518 H. Watson *Hist. Oliver of Castile* (Roxb.) N 2b, There came dyuers kynges and herauldes of armes, and after came the Vsshers. 1553 *Rutland Papers* (Camden) 118 The Duke of Northfolke..claymethe to be highe vssher the daye of the coronacion. 1641 *Sc. Acts Chas. I* (1870) V. 332/1 Commandit.. to goe befoir the king as Ischear with ane rod in his hand. 1678 Phillips (ed. 4) s.v., Usher of the Black-rod. 1689 *Breviate St. Scot.* 10 The Second Great Heritable Offices in the Kingdom, are The Lord High Constable,.. The Heritable Usher. 1718 Echard *Hist. Eng.* III. 622 The Usher of the Black-Rod commanded their Attendance in the House of Lords. 1721 Ramsay *Poems* I. List of Subscribers, Usher of the Green Rod, and daily Waiter to his Majesty. 1850 Marsden *Early Purit.* 402 The king sent down the usher of the House of Lords with a message. 1869 Cussans *Her.* 235 The Officers attached to this Noble Order [of the Knights of the Thistle] are: The Dean;..and the Usher of the Green Rod.

fig. 1641 Milton *Reformation* 2 Faith needing not..the Senses, to be either the Vshers, or Interpreters, of heavenly Mysteries. 1673 A. Walker *Leez Lachrymans* 18 When he is pleased to send this usher of the Black-Rod, Death,..a white-staffe is too weak to make Resistance.

transf. 1577 B. Googe *Heresbach's Husbandry* III. 116 A Colt..passeth bridges, not tarriing for an vsher, nor fearing the Ise. 1606 Shaks. *Ant. & Cl.* III. vi. 44 The wife of Anttony Should haue an Army for an Vsher. 1626 T. H[awkins] *Caussin's Holy Crt.* 37 Anciently Pearles were called Vshers, because they made way for Ladyes, who were attyred with them. 1726 Pope *Odyssey* xvii. 251 The good old proverb how this pair fulfill! One rogue is usher to another still. 1763 Churchill *The Ghost* IV. 37 A downright Usher to admit New-Comers to the Court of Wit.

†**b.** A male attendant on a lady. *Obs.*

1621 Fletcher *Wild-G. Chase* III. i, If she want an Usher; such an implement; One that is throughly pac'd; a clean made Gentleman; Can hold a hanging up. 1649 Davenant *Love & Honour* I. i, Consumptive Ushers that are decay'd In their Ladies service. 1664 Butler *Hud.* II. i. 96 She call'd for Hood And Usher, Implements abroad Which Ladies wear. 1749 Smollett *Gil Blas* I. xvi, A lady who..was squired by an old usher [F. *écuyer*], and a little black moor carried her train. 1809 Malkin *Gil Blas* I. xvi. ¶2 She released her sweet hand from the custody of the usher [F. *écuyer*].

3. One who precedes or arrives before another, esp. a higher dignitary or personage; a precursor. Also *transf.* Cf. harbinger *sb.* 3.

1548 Udall *Erasm. Par. Matt.* iii. 28 By his ussher and messenger John. c 1550 N. Smyth tr. *Herodian* III. 40 b, He had certayne Usshers going before him, which commaunded euerye man to auoyde the stretes. 1641 J. Jackson *True Evang. T.* II. 151 That other lesson..[Christ] suffered his Ushers that went before him to teach. 1847 Emerson *Initial Love* 75 Heralds high before him [*sc.* Cupid] run, He has ushers many a one.

b. *transf.* That which precedes or gives intimation of the approach or advent of a person or thing.

c 1586 C'tess Pembroke *Ps.* L. i, God comes,..His guarde huge stormes, hot flames his ushers goe. 1599 Sir J. Davies *Hymns of Astræa* 5 Early, chearfull, mounting Larke, Lights gentle Vsher. 1633 P. Fletcher *Elisa* I. xxviii, Ah death!.. Thou one meals fast, usher to endlesse feasting. 1640 J. Gower *Ovid's Festiv.* II. 32 In comes the Lecher bold;..His groping hands his warie ushers were. 1645 Stapylton tr. *Musæus* C j b, Leander..Expecting the sad Torch, and to be led By that bright Vsher to his private bed.

fig. a 1586 Sidney *Arcadia* II. xxvii, Stretching out his hand, and making vehement countenances the ushers to his speches. 1597 Hooker *Eccl. Pol.* v. lxxii. §18 Fasts haue beene set as Vshers of festiuall dayes. 1607 Shaks. *Cor.* II. i. 173 [Stage direction] A showt, and flourish. *Volum.* These are the Vshers of Martius. 1632 tr. *Bruel's Praxis Med.* 58 Troublesome dreames are vshers to this disease. c 1670 M. Bruce *Gd. News in Evil Times*, etc. (1708) 26 They make the Sabbath, as it were, Mr. Usher to their Visiting of Christ.

c. *Ent.* A species of moth.

1819 Samouelle *Entomol. Compend.* 360 *Geometra leucophearia*, The Spring Usher. *Ibid.*, [G.] *nigricaria*, The dark-bordered Usher. 1832 Rennie *Brit. Butterfl. & Moths* 102 The Spring Usher (*Anisopteryx leucophearia*, Stephens) appears in oak woods the end of February. *Ibid.*, The Wall Usher (*A. Æscularia*).

4. An assistant to a schoolmaster or head-teacher; an under-master, assistant-master. Now *rare*. Also in fig. context.

1512 *Nottingham Rec.* (1885) III. 453 To..establisshe one free schole of one Schole Maister and one Vssher. 1561 in H. B. Wilson *Hist. Merchant-Taylors' Sch.* (1814) 15 Yff both the maister and the usshers be sick at once (as God defend) then let the schoole cease for that while. 1581 J. Bell *Haddon's Answ. to Osorius* 259 b, Who hath made you usher I pray you, or prepositour of Ciceroes schoole? 1632 D. Lupton *London & Countrey carbonadoed* 119 Country Vshers..are vnder the Head-maister, equall with the chiefe Schollers, and aboue the lesser boyes. 1653 Baxter *Worc. Petit. Def.* 6 We are but Ushers, and Christ is the..chief Master of the School. 1669 E. Chamberlayne *Pres. St. Eng.* II. 483 This Colledge consists of a Master.., a Chaplain,.. A Master and Usher to instruct 44 Scholars. 1687 Wood *Life* (O.H.S.) III. 247 He being usher to a Presbyterian scholemaster. 1711 Hearne *Collect.* (O.H.S.) III. 205 Tollet is made IId Master, he being before a chief Usher. 1791 Boswell *Johnson* an. 1732, He accepted of an offer.. as usher in the school of Market-Bosworth. 1818 Scott *Hrt. Midl.* xxvii, Conning over a few pages of Horace or Juvenal with his usher. c 1868 in Hughes *Tom Brown* (ed. 6) Pref., Persecution..he can't stop; no more could all the ushers in the world. 1876 *Scheme C.C. 8 governing Foundation Thetford School Hosp.* 6 From the same date..the present usher of the said School shall cease to hold his office as such Usher.

†**b.** *transf.* A teacher or preceptor acting under another. *Obs.*

1533 More *Confut. Tindale* Wks. 585/2 Oure sauiour.. sent him [*sc.* Judas] forth..for one of hys vsshers to teache in his owne time. 1577 Hanmer *Anc. Eccl. Hist.* VI. xiv. 105 He ordained Heraclas..his fellowe helper, and Usher,.. committing vnto him the instruction of the inferiour sort. 1613 Purchas *Pilgrimage* I. iv. 16 Nature was his Schoole master; or if you will rather, Gods Usher.

c. = provost *sb.* 8.

1545 [see provost *sb.* 8]. 1699 Boyer I, *Prevost de sale d'armes*, the Provost, or Usher of a Fencing-School. 1765 Angelo *Sch. Fencing* 52 When an usher..has finished his apprenticeship under an able master,..he is obliged to fence with several masters.

†**5.** ***Usher of the Coins, Change***, or ***Exchange***, an officer of the Mint. *Obs.*

1485 *Cal. Patent Rolls* (1914) 49 [The] controller,..clerk and ussher of the coynes. 1485 *Rolls of Parlt.* VI. 365/2 The Office of Usher of the Exchaunge of oure said Soveraigne Lord, within his Towre [of London].

6. *attrib.* and *Comb.*, as ***usher life, -like***.

1580 Fulke *Martiall Confut.* iv. 164 An other foolish brable and vsherlike construing, he maketh of Cyprians words. 1873 W. Cory *Lett. & Jrnls.* (1897) 341 The eight years I had then gone through of usher life.

Hence **'usherdom**, the office or status of an usher; **'usheress**, a female usher; **u'sherian**, of or pertaining to an usher or ushers; **'usherism**, conduct or comportment characteristic of ushers.

1846 Worcester (citing *Qu. Rev.*), *Usherdom. 1905 A. C. Benson *Upton Lett.* 106 The ugly slough of usherdom. 1879 *Ch. Times* 5 Sept., An appointment..as an '*usheress' in a big establishment. 1826 Disraeli *V. Grey* I. iv, Certain powers were..delegated to..beings called Ushers... The *usherian rule had, however, always been comparatively light at Burnsley Vicarage. 1869 Ellis *E.E. Pronunc.* I. vi. 625 That kind of pedantic self-sufficiency which is the true growth of half-enlightened ignorance, and may be termed '*usherism'.

usher ('ʌʃə(r)), *v.* [f. prec. Cf. huisher *v.*]

1. a. *trans.* To act as usher to (a person or persons); to admit ceremoniously; to conduct, attend, or introduce with ceremony *from*, *to* or *unto* or esp. *into* (a place), etc.; to announce, introduce, or bring *in* as an usher.

In frequent use from c 1820. In group (*b*) with advs.

(*a*) 1596 Warner *Alb. Eng.* XII. lxxv. 312 Vnto their Lodging Stafford did the Ladies Vsher then. 1632 J. Hayward tr. *Biondi's Eromena* A 3 b, Excuse my boldnesse in ushering her Excellencie..into so excellent a presence. 1725 Pope *Odyss.* xvii. 447 My Lords! this stranger..The good Eumæus usher'd to your court. 1773 *Cook's Voy S. Pole* II. ii. (1777) I. 202 An old gentleman came along-side, who..was some king or great man. He was accordingly, ushered on board. 1821 Scott *Kenilw.* xiv, The hall..to which Tressilian was ushered by one of the Earl's attendants. 1844 Disraeli *Coningsby* III. iii, Whose gracious lot it was to usher them from the apartment. 1891 Farrar *Darkn. & Dawn* xxv, The tribune ushered her into the Emperor's chamber.

(*b*) 1749 Fielding *Tom Jones* XIV. x, He..ushered his visitant up stairs. 1760 in Doran *Mann. & Manners* (1876) II. 63 For which purpose I set forth in a Coach and Six, and ushered him in. 1835 Dickens *Sk. Boz, Parish* i, Simmons bows assent, and ushers the woman out. 1853 C. Bronte *Villette* xli, Ushering me in, he shut the door behind us.

b. Predicated of things. Also *transf.*

1623 T. Scot *Tongve-Combat* 63 This brauerie..vshers them into the company of best princes. 1697 Luttrell *Brief Rel.* (1857) IV. 311 Boats having mett them with divers sorts of musick to usher them into that harbour. 1807–8 W. Irving *Salmag.* (1824) 169 The piece opens with a gentle *andante affetuoso*, which ushers you into the Assembly-room.

c. *fig.*, *transf.*, and in fig. context.

1594 [Southwell] *Mary Magd. Funeral Tears* 69 b, As desire is euer vshered by hope, and waited on by feare. 1612 Drayton *Poly-olb.* iii. 3 Yet the blushing dawn out of the chearful east Is ushering forth the day. 1623 Cockeram III, *Nusculus*, a friendly fish to the Whale, it vshers him from rocks, shelues, and shores. a 1661 Fuller *Worthies*, *Leic.* II. (1662) 130 Sir Tho. Lake may be said to have ushered him [*sc.* Villiers] to the English Court. 1715 Rowe *Lady Jane Gray* IV. i, As if his traitor father's haggard ghost, And Somerset,..had usher'd him to ruin. 1749 Fielding *Tom Jones* IV. i, [The hero] is generally ushered on the Stage by a large Troop of..Scene-shifters. 1790 Burke *Fr. Rev.* 6 That mode of signature to which you have thrown open the folding-doors of your presence chamber, and have ushered into your National Assembly. 1806 J. Beresford *Miseries Hum. Life* (ed. 4) II. xiii, A furious wind which ushers the dust into your eyes. 1867 H. Macmillan *Bible Teach.* vi. 109 A new class of objects is now ushered upon the scene. 1891 Farrar *Darkn. & Dawn* lxvi, Those whom we ushered into the reader's presence at the beginning of this book.

refl. 1812 *Ann. Reg., Chron.* 47 This singular person ushered himself into public notice in London, by [etc.].

d. *absol.* To act as or after the manner of an usher.

1612 Donne *Progresse of Soule, 2nd Anniversary* 156 Yet Death must usher, and unlocke the doore. Thinke further on thy selfe, my Soule. 1657 F. Cockin *Div. Blossomes* 4 For to insinuate into his will, And usher, thorough his Judgment to 's Affection..That he may give to Thee all due subjection.

(*b*) *spec.* to act as an usher in a cinema. *U.S.*

1973 *Publishers Weekly* 27 Aug. 243/1 A 13-year-old boy who ushers in a movie house. 1980 M. Gordon *Company of Women* (1981) I. i. 26 It was teen-agers who flocked to see that kind of movie. Mary Rose had to usher at those movies now.

2. a. To precede, escort, or go before (a dignitary) ceremonially as an usher.

1612 in *10th Rep. Hist. MSS. Comm.* App. I. 599 All his equippage was ushered by certaine officers in ritche coates. 1665 Brathwait *Comment Two Tales* (1900) 47 If I at any time use him for the Squire of my Body, or to Usher me in the streets. 1676 *Office Clerk of Assize* E vij, His Bayliffs, with their white wands in their hands, do usher the Justices from the Court, to the place where they dine. a 1700 Evelyn *Diary* 23 April 1667, His Majesty went to Chappell with the Knights of the Garter.., usher'd by the Heraulds.

†**b.** To precede (a person, esp. of higher rank) as a forerunner or harbinger. Also in fig. context.

1629 Gaule *Pract. The.* A 5, You shall see your Sauiour at once Vshered, Afforded, Humbled, and Exalted: Vshered by his Prophets, afforded in his Person. 1639 Fuller *Holy War* III. vi. 118 [Richard I] set forth [to the Crusade] with many of our nation, which either ushered or followed him. 1646 G. H[ils] *Odes of Casimire* Pref., Juno and Venus ushered by chaste love Through..Flora's banks here move.

c. *fig.* and *transf.*

1599 T. Storer *Life & D. Wolsey* H j b, Who follow'd me, but Fortune was at hand, To follow him? or, if she went before, To vsher him? 1602 Marston *Ant. & Mel.* III. E 2, Gastly amazement..Shall hurry on before, and vsher vs. 1609 B. Jonson *Sil. Wom.* IV. i, Nor will it bee out of your gaine to make loue to her too, so shee follow, not vsher, her ladies pleasure. 1621 Brathwait *Nat. Embassie*, etc. (1877) 203 My friends..Wish'd that all good successe might vsher mee. a 1668 Davenant *Play House to let* III. i, Wilt thou now guided be By that bright Star which ushers me.

d. To precede, come or happen immediately before, in order of time; to lead up to. (Cf. 7 c.)

1607 *Merry Devil Edmonton* I. ii. 55 In and feed, And let that vsher a more serious deed. c 1611 Chapman *Iliad* v. 864 Pitchy tempests threat, Usher'd with horrid gusts of wind. 1616 B. Jonson *Epigrams* ci, Some better sallade Vshring the mutton. 1647 Clarendon *Hist. Reb.* VII. §282 Such an application to Court as usually ushered those promotions. 1821 Shelley *Adonais* xxi, Evening must usher night, night urge the morrow. 1821 Byron *Sardanap.* v. i, The day at last has broken. What a night Hath usher'd it!

†3. To wait at (a banquet) as an usher. *Obs.*⁻¹

1602 DEKKER *Satirom.* K 3 b, Euen thus the Mercury of Heauen Vshers th' ambrosiate banquet of the Gods.

4. To introduce (something uttered); to preface. (Cf. 7 e.)

1635 A. STAFFORD *Fem. Glory* 55 She made two pawses usher her answer. **1637** C. DOW *Answ. to H. Burton* 159 Divine offices..must not bee curtall'd..by..any new-devised formes of praier, either ushering, or following them. **1717** POPE *Eloisa to Abelard* 32 Oh name for ever sad!.. Still breath'd in sighs, still ushered with a tear.

†**5.** To lead, conduct, or direct (a thing) to some point. *Obs. rare.*

1668 CULPEPPER & COLE tr. *Barthol. Anatomy* II. x. 120 The External [membrane].. sticks close to the intermediate Ligaments.., and ushers along the recurrent Nerves. **1791** COWPER *Iliad* II. 649 Skill In ushering to its mark the rapid lance.

6. To introduce or bring *into* the world.

1679 C. NESSE *Antichrist* 6 Harbingers..to usher him into the world. **1713** STEELE *Englishm.* No. 1. 5 The Jest..is ushered into the World by the loudest Laughter. **1756** H. JOHNSON in J. Duncombe *Lett.* (1773) III. 38 You have done a great favour to the world in ushering so noble..a work into it. **1835** MARRYAT *J. Faithful* i, It was about a year after the loss.., that I was ushered into the world. **1855** BREWSTER *Newton* II. xviii. 172 The theory he ushered into the world.
transf. **1835** MARRYAT *J. Faithful* v, I am very nearly ushered into the next World.

7. to usher in: (see also 1). **a.** To bring in (a banquet, meat, etc.) with ceremony.

1613 HEYWOOD *Silver Age* II. i, Vsher me in a costly banquet straight To entertaine my Lord. **1706** E. WARD *Wooden World Diss.* (1708) 94 The Captain's Bell calls him to usher in the Apple-dumplins. **1829** S. H. CASSAN *Lives Bps. Bath & Wells* 262 The meat was ushered in.

b. To inaugurate or bring in (a period of time).

c **1600** SHAKS. *Sonn.* cxxxii, That full Starre that vshers in the Eauen. **1656** S. WINTER *Serm.* 147 That so he might usher in the eternitie of the world. **1698** FRYER *Acc. E. India & P.* 276 The Morning being ushered in with..Music. **1781** COWPER *Hope* 717 If chance..A tempest usher in the dreaded morn. **1791** SMEATON *Edystone L.* §306 The year 1762 was ushered in with stormy weather. **1827** LONGF. *Life* (1891) I. viii. 121 The day was 'ushered in', as the newspapers say, by the firing of cannon. **1850** TENNYSON *In Mem.* lxxii, Dim dawn,.. Who usherest in the dolorous hour With thy quick tears. **1872** YEATS *Techn. Hist. Comm.* 298 The French Revolution ushered in a new era of taste.

c. = sense 2 d.

1641 MAISTERTON *Serm.* 18 An anteambulo to usher in a thousand pains. **1663** SOUTH *Serm.* (1717) V. 89 Every Fast portended some Villany, as still a Famine ushers in a Plague. **1695** J. EDWARDS *Perfect. Script.* 414 The Lord, who was to be usher'd in by Elijah the prophet. **1707** *Curios. in Husb. & Gard.* 44 Flowers..appear only to usher in the Fruit, or the Seed; afterwards they fade. **1712** ADDISON *Spect.* No. 363 ¶18 That vision of Lewdness and Luxury which usher in the Flood. *a* **1721** PRIOR *Many Daughters have done well* 10 How welcome did that light appear Which usher'd in a form all Heav'nly fair.

d. To mark the introduction, beginning, or occurrence of (an event, etc.); to introduce.

1646 J. HALL *Horæ Vac.* 8 They generally usher in uproares in the State. **1650** R. STAPYLTON *Strada's Low C. Wars* VII. 49 These punishments seemed only to usher in the Death of the two Counts. **1697** DAMPIER *Voy.* (1729) I. 394 A convenient place to usher in a Commerce with the neighbouring country. **1784** COWPER *Task* IV. 23 But oh th' important budget! usher'd in With..heart-shaking music. **1801** *Med. Jrnl.* V. 231 Increased heats..already described as ushering in the hæmorrhage. **1843** R. J. GRAVES *Syst. Clin. Med.* x. 106 The symptoms..bear a very strong analogy to those which usher in typhus. **1870** FREEMAN *Norm. Conq.* (ed. 2) I. 738 The event of 1018..was ushered in by a comet.

e. = sense 4.

1662 STILLINGFL. *Orig. Sacr.* II. vi. §5 Their deliverance by Cyrus..he ushers..in with this preface that [etc.]. **1673** *True Worship of God* 8 These Sacrifices not only accompanying their Confessions..; but their Hymns and Doxologies also,..to usher them in with more acceptance. **1699** BENTLEY *Phal.* 222 He would have usher'd the Word in with some kind of introduction. **1757** GRAY *Let.* Poems (1775) 252 All that ushers in the incantation from 'Try we yet..', I am delighted with. *a* **1763** W. KING *Lit. & Polit. Anecd.* (1819) 154 He was..so unfortunate as to usher in his criticisms with [etc.]. **1814** CHALMERS *Evid. Chr. Revel.* II. ii, The quotation is..ushered in by the general words, 'As it is written'.

Hence **'ushering** *ppl. a.*

1628 [A. LEIGHTON] *Appeal to Parliament* 145 Why breaketh out the fearfull wrath of God..among us, but because of Baal-peor his ushering Ceremonies..? **1634** MILTON *Comus* 279 Could that [*sc.* darkness] divide you from neer-ushering guides? **1820** CLARE *Rural Life* (ed. 3) 32 That rural call..All noises now to silence lulls, In soft and ushering sounds.

†**'usherage.** *Obs. rare.* [f. prec. + -AGE.] The act of ushering or introducing; insertion.

1661 HICKERINGILL *Jamaica* 28 [An interstice] admitting not so much as the intermediate or usherage of a twig. **1662** —— *Apol. Distressed Innoc.* Wks. 1716 I. 298 If the usherage of Sanctity cannot hand in their black deformities of Rapine.

†**'usherance.** *Obs.* [f. as prec. + -ANCE.] The action of introducing or bringing in; introduction.

1711 SHAFTESB. *Charac.* III. 190 Our Author's First Letter..occasion'd the revival of this abortive Piece, and gave Usherance to its Companions.

'usherer. [f. USHER *v.* + -ER¹.] One who or that which ushers in; an usher or harbinger. Also with *in.* Occas. *fig.*

1598 MARSTON *Scourge of Villanie* II. v. E 4 b, Codrus my well-fac'd Ladies taile-bearer, (He that some-times play'th Flauias usherer). **1640** REYNOLDS *Passions* xxxv. 424 The Usherers in, or Attendants and followers on the Grave, Age, Infirmity, Sicknesse. *c* **1645** HOWELL *Lett.* IV. xxix. (1890) 607 True spiritual Pride, the usherer-in of all Confusions. **1824** GALT *Rothelan* II. III. ii. 16 The Past is usherer to the Future. **1892** WALT WHITMAN in *Harper's Mag.* April 709/2 Thee [*sc.* Death], envoy, usherer, guide at last of all.

ushe'rette. [f. USHER *sb.* + -ETTE.] A female usher in a cinema or theatre.

1925 *College Humor* Aug. 66/2 The obese usherette in the toney movie house who has to wear a different fancy dress costume every week. **1926** *Bulletin* 27 Feb. 2 Thirty beautiful girls..will receive visitors to..the Plaza, at its opening on Tuesday. They will be called 'usherettes'. **1948** *Times* 24 Feb. 7/4 Will the usherette hush the little fellow crying in the stalls. **1960** M. SPARK *Ballad Peckham Rye* vii. 136 She's an usherette at the Regal from six-thirty to ten-thirty. **1980** R. BUTLER *Blood-Red Sun at Noon* (1981) II. i. 129 Nothing in her career as theatre usherette, conjuror's assistant and night-club hostess had prepared her for this kind of life.

'ushering, *vbl. sb.* [f. as USHER *v.* + -ING¹.] The action of the verb, in various senses. Also with *in.*

1588 SHAKS. *L.L.L.* v. ii. 328 Nay he can sing A meane most meanly, and in Vshering Mend him who can. *a* **1613** OVERBURY *Characters, A Fine Gentleman,* Afterwards he maintaines himselfe an implement of houshold, by carving and ushering. *a* **1693** *Urquhart's Rabelais* III. xxx. 247 At the ushering in [F. *l'apport*] of the Second Service, Panurge ..[made] a low Reverence. **1850** O. WINSLOW *Inner Life* x. 273 The ushering in of that great event. **1851** GALLENGA *Italy* i. 21 The ushering in of a new political phasis. **1866** TROLLOPE *Claverings* ii, Even though he had earned that money by 'ushering' for the last two years.

'usherless, *a.* [f. USHER *sb.* + -LESS.] Lacking an usher, herald, or harbinger. In earlier use *fig.*

1598 SYLVESTER *Du Bartas* II. i. IV. *Handy-crafts* 88 Where Usher-lesse, both day and night, the..windes enter and goe forth. **1604** MARSTON *Malcontent* IV. v. G j, There Vsherlesse the ayre comes in and out. **1815** MILMAN *Fazio* 80 Who art thou thus usherless and unbidden Scarest my privacy? **1883** J. PAYN *Thicker than Water* II. xxix. 217 On the great staircase he met Mrs. Sotheran coming up usherless.

'usherment. *rare*⁻¹. [f. USHER *v.* + -MENT.] The fact of being prefaced, introduced, or ushered in.

1887 SAINTSBURY *Hist. Elizab. Lit.* ii. 46 These last..do not come in with the somewhat ostentatious usherment and harbingery, which for instance laid the even more splendid bursts of Jeremy Taylor open to the sharp sarcasm of South.

'ushership. [f. USHER *sb.* + -SHIP.]

1. The office or functions of an usher.

1580 FULKE *Martiall Confut.* iv. 165 Yᵉ Priestes are appointed to vse those signes, which if Martials Vshership will not admit, [etc.]. **1631** T. POWER *Tom of all Trades* 44 To leape into instantly, and imediately out of a Ladies vshership. **1740** LD. HARRINGTON in *10th Rep. Hist. MSS. Comm.* App. I. 275 The Ushership of the Exchequer. **1788** COWPER *Let.* Wks. 1836 VI. 201 When I was under his ushership at Westminster. **1825** T. HOOK *Sayings* Ser. II. III. 93 To assume the ushership of the black rod at Montgomery Place. **1881** *Daily News* 1 Aug. 5/3 In Algeria ..his years of ushership had been the most wretched of his life.

2. A post or position as a (school-) usher.

1788 W. COWPER *Let.* 30 Nov. (1982) III. 233, I was under his ushership at Westminster. **1825** HONE *Every-day Bk.* I. 79 The son..being put to school, obtained successive usherships. **1880** R. K. DENT *Old & New Birmingham* 79 Johnson having found the drudgery of an ushership..too irksome for him.

ushewe, obs. f. ISSUE *sb.*

†**ushing,** var. ISHING *vbl. sb. Obs.* (Cf. USH *v.*¹)

1375 BARBOUR *Bruce* VI. 363 (E.), Hys wyt schawyt hym the strait entre off the furd, and the uschyng alsua.

‖**usine** (yzin, ju:'zi:n). [F. *usine* factory, (in early use) water-mill.] A factory; esp. in later use, a West Indian sugar factory.

In first quot. the word is misapplied.

1798 W. ETON *Turk. Empire* 216 Their furnaces are of *usine,* which is particularly adapted to the casting of iron. **1858** SIMMONDS *Dict. Trade* 396 *Usine,* a glass-house; an iron-work. **1878** *Times* 10 May 4/3 Furnaces and vast usines. **1888** *Daily News* 13 April 5/4 Of these usines, or crushing factories, there are already several in Trinidad, St. Lucia, and British Guiana.

using ('ju:zɪŋ), *vbl. sb.* [f. USE *v.* + -ING¹.]

1. The action of making use of something, or the fact of being used.

a **1340** HAMPOLE *Psalter* liv. 2, I am made sary in myn vsynge. **1387–8** T. USK *Test. Love* III. vi. l. 60 They han as wel dyvers aptes and dyvers maner usinges. *c* **1400** *Cursor M.* 29369 (Cott. Galba), þat oþer [case] es of..portere, in vsyng of þaire awin mistere. **1422** YONGE tr. *Secreta Secret.* 247 Vsynge of honementys aftyr the tyme and complexcione. *c* **1445** PECOCK *Donet* 50 Mesurable and resonable vsing of worldly goodis. **1526** *Pilgr. Perf.* (W. de W. 1531) 45 In iust commutacion & vsyng of these thynges. **1560** BIBLE (Genev.) *Col.* ii. 22 Which all perishe with the vsyng of them. **1656** EARL MONM. tr. *Boccalini's Advts. fr. Parnass.* II. li. (1674) 202 The using of the same severities which Augustus..practised. **1690** LOCKE *Hum. Und.* III. x. §2 The using of Words, without clear and distinct Ideas. **1705** *Lond. Gaz.* No. 4114/4 A fine Coach lined with Velvet, little the worse for using. **1774** GOLDSM. *Nat. Hist.* III. 315 His teeth wear, like those of most other animals, by using. **1826** *Art of Brewing* (ed. 2) 94 The twelve principal houses have..disclaimed the using of any material in their Beer, except malt and hops. **1893** C. C. KING in *Social Eng.* I. 43 Of..arrow-heads as missile weapons there are none that seem worth the using.

†**b.** The celebration of the Eucharist. *Obs.*

1452 *Paston Lett.* I. 237 The seid servaunts..knelyng to see the usyng of the Masse. **1454** *Ibid.* 280. *c* **1500** *Langforde's Meditacyons* in Wickham Legg *Tracts on Mass* (1904) 28 From the sacryng vnto the vsing be done, you may remember..the Passyon and deith of our sauyour.

c. The action of accustoming *to* something.

1702 *Eng. Theophrast.* 212 It goes a great way towards Felicity, the using of our selves to other Peoples Follies.

2. Manner of usage or employment.

1388 WYCLIF *Rom.* Prol., Thei weren brouȝt in to the lawe and profetis, that is, in to cerymonyes..acordynge with tho cerymonyes, which vsyng is contrarie now to the treuthe.. of Cristis gospel. **1553** T. WILSON *Rhet.* 114 b, iii. The placing of these Images, is like vnto wordes written. iiii. The vtteraunce and vsing of them, is like vnto readynge. **1669** in *Buccleuch MSS.* (Hist. MSS. Comm.) I. 32 Extolling the King of England's using of people. **1726** LEONI *Alberti's Archit.* I. 62 b/2 For the right using of these benefits, the Fathers may provide by Laws and Statutes. **1827** KEBLE *Chr. Y., Palm Sunday* v, As in this bad world below Noblest things find vilest using.

3. *using-up,* consumption or exhaustion *of* a commodity, etc.

1863 JAS. SANDERSON *Agric. Berw. & Roxb.* 32 The using-up of the manure is the preferable mode. **1889** HAMERTON *French & English* I. i. 14 The decline caused by industrialism and the rapid using-up of life in large cities.

4. Special Comb.: **using-file,** a file affixed to the work-bench (instead of being held in the hand), for having the work rubbed upon it; **using-ground** *U.S.,* the haunt of wild-fowl; †**using stone** (see quot. 1688).

1683 MOXON *Mech. Exerc., Printing* xii. ¶2 The Using-File..is about nine or ten Inches long, and three or four Inches broad... The two broad sides must be exactly flat and straight. **1688** HOLME *Armoury* III. 303/1 The using File..; the teeth not half so rough as the common File. *Ibid.* 382/1 The Using Stone [of jewellers]..is a flat smooth Stone shooting out into two angles or points on each side. **1893** *Harper's Mag.* Oct. 681/2 The 'using-grounds' of the coveys are generally known or suspected by the farmer.

'usitate, *a.* [ad. L. *ūsitāt-us,* pa. pple. of *ūsitārī* to use often.] **a.** Customary, usual. **b.** Much used *of* (= by).

1885 DIXON *Hist. Ch. Eng.* xx. III. 462 The usitate dignities of rural deans and archdeacons. **1890** *Sat. Rev.* 27 Sept. 383/1 A form of punishment usitate of French novelists.

'usitative, *a. rare.* [f. as prec. + -IVE.] That denotes customary action.

1849 ALFORD *Gk. Testament* I. 19 Not the usitative aorist, but declarative of the definite past εὐδοκία of the Father in Him. **1939** [see CONSUETUDINAL *a.* and *sb.*].

†**usker.** *Obs. rare*⁻¹. [a. Irish *usgar.*] An ornament or jewel. In quot. *collect.*

1536–7 *Act 28 Hen. VIII,* in Bolton *Stat. Irel.* (1621) 130 That also no woman vse or weare any kyrtell, or cote.. couched ne layd with vsker, after the Irish fashion.

usle, obs. var. ISEL (ashes, etc.).

'usnate. *Chem.* [f. USN-IC + -ATE¹ 1 c.] A salt produced by a combination of usnic acid with a base.

1866 WATTS tr. *Gmelin's Handbk. Chem.* XVII. 50-51 Usnate of Ammonia,..Usnate of Potash,..Usnate of Soda, ..Usnate of Baryta,..Usnate of Copper. **1868** *Watts' Dict. Chem.* V. 970 The usnates of the alkali-metals are soluble in water.

‖**Usnea** ('ʌsnɪə). Pl. usneas, usneæ. [med.L. (12th cent.), ad. Arab. and Pers. *ushnah* moss. Hence F. *usnée* (1530).] A genus of gymnocarpous lichens, typical of the family *Usneidæ;* a species or plant of this.

1597 GERARDE *Herbal* III. clvi. 1369 *Muscus quernus;*..the Arabians and the Apothecaries call it *Vsnea.* **1693** tr. *Blancard's Phys. Dict.* (ed. 2), *Usnea,* Moss which grows upon Bones or Trees. **1706** PHILLIPS (ed. Kersey), *Usnea,* a kind of green Moss..which is us'd in Physick. **1753** *Chambers' Cycl.* Suppl., *Usnea,*..of this genus of plants there are nineteen known species: 1. The stringy-tree moss, or common *Usnea* of the shops. *Ibid.,* 19. The smallest of all the *Usneas*..grows on the barks of old trees. **1857** M. J. BERKELEY *Introd. Crypt. Bot.* 417 *Usneæ,* finally, when well-grown, are perhaps the most beautiful of Lichens. **1857** THOREAU *Maine W.* ii. (1867) 155 The spruce still grows shaggy with usnea. **1861** M. MACMILLAN *Footn. fr. Page Nat.* 109 So late as the seventeenth century, some of the filamentous lichens were sold in the shops of barbers and perfumers under the name of Usnea.
attrib. **1854** THOREAU *Walden* 137 The single spruce stands hung with usnea lichens. **1878** H. M. STANLEY *Dark Cont.* II. vii. 204 From many of the branches depended the Usneæ moss in graceful and delicate fringes.

'us-ness. [-NESS.] The fact of being or feeling united in mind, feeling, or purpose; the fact of forming a unity.

1927 *Glasgow Herald* 7 Mar. 6 In a magazine story... 'It's Us-ness that makes love,' the heroine of the tale is made to say to the hero, 'it's being two of you together against the world.' **1958** *Listener* 27 Nov. 874/1 One of the dangers of

'The Method' is that it tends to reduce everything to us-ness, if I may so put it. **1966** P. J. KAVANAGH *Perfect Stranger* vii. 77 There was a pleasant feeling of 'us-ness' in the unit. Were the prisoners 'us' or had they comfortably become 'them'? **1976** *Christian* III. 167 This has the effect of buttressing and reinforcing the me-ness of me (insistently individual) as part of the intensified us-ness of us (compellingly corporate).

'usnic, *a. Chem.* Also usneic. [f. USN-EA + -IC 1 b.] ***usnic acid***, carbusnic acid; usnin.

1847 W. GREGORY *Handbk. Org. Chem.* (ed. 2) 502 Usnic Acid..is found in many lichens,..and in many species of *Usnea* [etc.]. **1848** FOWNES *Elem. Chem.* (ed. 2) 514 The *Usnea barbata* and several other lichens contain usneic acid. **1861–7** [see USNIN].

usnin ('ʌsnɪn). *Chem.* Also -ine. [f. USN-EA + -IN[1].] Usnic acid.

1861 H. MACMILLAN *Footn. fr. Page Nat.* 82 Alpine lichens generally are more or less of a brown or black colour. This peculiarity seems to be owing to the presence of usnine or usnic acid. **1867** BRANDE & COX *Dict. Sci.*, etc. III. 912/2 Usnin or Usnic Acid..forms yellow crystals, which with great difficulty are fused like a resin.

‖**uso.** *Obs.* [It. or Sp. *uso.*] = USANCE 5, 5 b.

1704 *Lond. Gaz.* No. 3992/4 Two first Bills of Exchange, ..payable to Jean Voordagh or Order, at 2 uso 8 days. **1740** W. DOUGLASS *Disc. Curr. Brit. Plant. Amer.* 4, Notes of Hand payable in Silver at certain Uso's or Periods.

†**'usque.** *Sc. Obs.* Also 8 usquæ, husque, usky (cf. WHISKY *sb.*[1]). Short for USQUEBAUGH.

1728 RAMSAY *Friends in Ireland* 10 Drinking roundly rum and claret, Ale and usquæ. *c* **1730** BURT *Lett. N. Scotl.* (1754) I. 188 This drink [common ale] is of itself apt to give a Diarrhea, and therefore..they interlace it with Brandy or Usky. **1739** A. NICOL *Poems* 76 Good ale and Usque ga'd about In Healths.

attrib. *c* **1730** BURT *Lett. N. Scotl.* (1754) II. 83 My Merchants..mov'd the Usky Vessels before 'em. *Ibid.* 84 The Usky Men were my Companions.

‖**usque ad nauseam** ('ʌskweɪ æd 'nɔːzɪæm). Also **ad nauseum usque.** [L., = 'right up to sickness'.] = AD NAUSEAM.

1616, 1693 Ad nauseam usque [see AD NAUSEAM]. **1819** T. MOORE *Tom Crib's Memorial* p. xxxi, That person has already been exhibited, perhaps, 'usque *ad nauseam*', before the Public.

usquebaugh ('ʌskwɪbɔː). Forms: α. 6 vskebeaghe, 7 vsque-ba'he, vskebah (uskkiba), 7–9 usquebah (7 usquabah), 7 vsquebach; 7 vsque-, 7- usquebagh, 7 vsce-, usce-, uskabagh; 6 vscough-, 7- usquebaugh. β. 7 vsque-, usque-, husquo-, uskebath. γ. (Chiefly *Sc.*) 6 iskie-bae, 7 usquebay, 8–9 usquebae (8 usquabae). [a. Irish and Sc. Gaelic *uisge beatha* (*uisci-betha* in Ann. Loch Cé, an. 1405), lit. 'water of life' (cf. AQUA-VITÆ), f. *uisge* water, and *beatha* life. The latter word is differently pronounced in Irish and Scottish Gaelic, approximately (bɑː) and (bɛː). Cf. WHISKY(BAE.] = WHISKY *sb.*[1]

With α-forms, in very freq. use from *c* 1610.

α. **1581** DERRICKE *Image Ireland* F ij, She filles them then with Vskebeaghe. **1600** SIR R. CECIL *Lett.* (Camden) 33 Remember..the Lord Threasurer with a couple of pugges or some vscough baugh. **1610** BEAUM. & FL. *Scornf. Lady* II. i, A bottle of Usquebaugh. **1658** ROLAND tr. *Moufet's Theat. Ins.* 913 The Irish prepare a distilled Oenomeli made with Honey, Wine and some herbs, which they cal Vsquebach. **1682** *Lond. Gaz.* No. 1776/4 There is right Irish Usquebagh to be sold..at the Rein-Deer in Tuttle-street,..By one from Ireland. **1706–7** FARQUHAR *Beaux' Strat.* I. i, An honest Gentleman that came this way from Ireland, made her a Present of a dozen bottles of Usquebaugh. **1762** FOOTE *Orators* III. 61 Usquebaugh..is an exhilirator of the bowels, and a stomatic to the head. **1818** HAZLITT *English Poets* vii. 260 The last long precious draught of his favourite usquebaugh. **1882** MISS BRADDON *Mt.-Royal* I. iv. 118, I wonder whether she had a strong brogue, and a sneaking fondness for usquebaugh.

attrib. **1630** RANDOLPH *Aristippus* 24 Are you there you Vsquebaugh Rascall, with your Metheglin iuyce?

β. **1621** S. WARD *Life of Faith* 33 Vsing it [*sc.* faith] as Vsquebath and strong Waters for swones and heart qualmes onely. **1681** T. DINELEY *Jrnl. Tour Irel.* in *Trans. Kilkenny Archaeol. Soc.* Ser. II. II. 25 As thou did not want Usquebath Oat cakes,..How is it then that thou diedst? **1713** TYLDESLEY *Diary* (1873) 117 Hee gave us two drames of uskebath.

γ. **1583** *Leg. Bp. St. Androis* 1062 And George Gipsones iskie bae Had all the wyte he womit sae. *a* **1689** W. CLELAND *Poems* (1697) 12 A Tupe Horn fill'd with Vsquebay. **1715** RAMSAY *Christ's Kirk Gr.* II. viii, Another gill Of usquebae. **1791** BURNS *Tam O'Shanter* 108 Wi' usquabae, we'll face the devil! **1819** SCOTT *Leg. Montrose* iv, A flask of usquebæ, designed for the refreshment of Lord Menteith. **1840** R. BREMNER *Excurs. Denmark*, etc. II. 211 Morning drinkers of usquebae.

ussay, usscha, usscho, usse, obs. Sc. varr. ISSUE *sb.*

us self, etc.: see SELF A. 3–4.

ussell, obs. or dial. var. OUZEL.

usshe, obs. form of USH *v. Sc.*

usshew, ussu, etc., obs. varr. ISSUE *sb.*

ussingite ('ʌsɪŋaɪt). *Min.* [ad. Da. *ussingit* (O. B. Bøggild 1913, in *Meddelelser om Grønland* (1914) LI. 103), f. the name of N. V. Ussing (1864–1911), Danish mineralogist: see -ITE[1].] A triclinic basic sodium aluminosilicate, $Na_2AlSi_3O_8OH$, found as reddish-violet crystals.

1914 *Chem. Abstr.* VIII. 3170 (*heading*) Ussingite, a new mineral from Kangerdluarsuk, Greenland. **1975** *Jrnl. Geol.* LXXXIII. 763/1 In both localities, ussingite is late-stage in character, occurring as a pegmatitic mineral in Lovozero [in the Kola Peninsula, USSR].., and as a hydrothermal vein mineral, in the Ilimaussaq intrusion [in Greenland].

ustad ('uːstɑːd). Also **Ustad.** [Pers., Urdu.] A master, esp. of music.

1903 M. A. STEIN *Sand-Buried Ruins Khotan* viii 125 The few 'ustads' (masters) who cared to attend to my orders. **1967** V. MEHTA *Portrait of India* 40 He is Hindustani music's unrivalled *ustad* (Urdu for 'master'). Actually, '*ustad*' is a sort of Muslim counterpart of '*guru*'. **1971** *Femina* (Bombay) 16 Apr. 8/3 She was able to become the pupil of the well-known Ustad Atah Khan of Patiala.

Ustashi (uː'stɑːʃɪ), *sb. pl.* (also taken as *sing.* with pl. *-s*). Also **-chi, -ci, -sha, -ša, -še, -si.** [a. Serbo-Croatian *Ustaše* pl., *Ustaša* sing., insurgent rebel.] (Members of) a party and separatist movement of Croatians; the soldiers and supporters of the autonomous Croatian régime between 1941 and 1944: as *sing.*, a member or supporter of the Croatian separatist movement. Also *attrib.*

1932 *Times* 8 Oct. 11/6 The Ustasi move in small groups from village to village and organize their adherents, train them in shooting, and disappear as suddenly as they came. **1943** C. HOLLINGWORTH *German just behind Me* xiii. 258 There are also the terrorist societies such as the Croat *Ustashi.* **1946** A. M. HYAMSON *Dict. Internat. Affairs* 334 *Ustaci, The*, the party of Croatian Fascists who, under Pavelitch and subject to the overriding veto of Germany and Italy, governed Croatia after its conquest in 1941 by Germany. **1949** KOESTLER *Promise & Fulfilment* II. i. 217 The Arab troops in this region were..reinforced by..Croat Ustachis. **1949** F. MACLEAN *Eastern Approaches* III. iii. 334 The independent State of Croatia..was a kingdom, but its King, the Italian Duke of Spoleto, had wisely omitted to take up his appointment and power was in the hands of Ante Pavelič and his Ustaše, supported by the Wehrmacht. *Ibid.*, Orthodox churches were..burned down with the screaming congregation inside them (an Ustaše speciality, this). **1961** E. WAUGH *Unconditional Surrender* III. i. 210 There are five or six divisions of Cetnics and Ustachi..the Serb and Croat Quislings. **1972** *Guardian* 28 Jan. 11/2 If Ustashi activists.. planted a bomb on board the Yugoslav airliner..it will be their biggest outrage since the war. **1973** *Nation Rev.* (Melbourne) 24–30 Aug. 1405/1 Frequent statements that the Ustasha exists in Australia and that the croatian community..condones terrorist acts. **1976** *New Yorker* 22 Mar. 64/2 Two Croatian nationalists—members of Ustaša, the party that ran an 'autonomous' Croatian state for the Nazis during the Second World War, killed hundreds of thousands of other Yugoslavs, and operates now as a secret terrorist society—tortured and then murdered the Yugoslav ambassador to Sweden. **1976** J. COLVILLE *Footprints in Time* xxxvii. 213 The fanatic Croat Ustasi. **1978** 'G. VAUGHAN' *Belgrade Drop* vii. 46 The caves where the Ustaše, the Croat fascists whose fanaticism in Hitler's cause had rivalled that of the SS, had butchered the Partisans. **1980** *Listener* 28 Feb. 265/3 The Ustashas were Croat Fascist collaborators.

uste, obs. Sc. var. HOST *sb.*[4] 2.

ustel-, ustilement, etc., obs. ff. HUSTLEMENT.

†**usterosis,** obs. var. HYSTEROSIS.

a **1661** FULLER *Worthies, Bedford.* I. (1662) 121 Mean time we take notice of an *Usterosis*, beholding R. Basset (though first named) as his Under-Sheriff.

ustilagineous (ʌstɪlə'dʒɪnɪəs), *a. Bot.* [f. mod.L. *Ustilagine-æ* (see def.) + -OUS.] Of or pertaining to the *Ustilagineæ* (brand fungi).

1889 PLOWRIGHT *Brit. Uredineæ* x. 60 One peculiarity of most of the Ustilagineous mycelia. **1900** B. D. JACKSON *Gloss. Bot. Terms* 283 *Usterophyte*,..Berkeley's name for one of the Ustilagineous Fungi.

ustilaginous (ʌstɪ'lædʒɪnəs), *a. Bot.* [f. mod.L. *Ustilagin-*, USTILAGO + -OUS.]

1. Resembling, belonging or allied to, *Ustilago.*

1857 M. J. BERKELEY *Introd. Crypt. Bot.* 323 Besides the Ustilaginous species, there are others. **1900** B. D. JACKSON *Gloss. Bot. Terms* 283.

2. 'Affected with ustilago; smutty' (*Cent. Dict.*).

‖**ustilago** (ʌstɪ'leɪgəʊ). *Bot.* Pl. **ustilagines** (-'eɪdʒɪniːz). [Late L. *ūstilāgo*, app. a kind of thistle; in mod.L. applied to smut on account of its burned or blackened appearance: cf. next.] Smut on oats, barley, or other grain, etc.; also *spec.*, a genus of parasitic fungi, typical of the N.O. *Ustilagineæ* (brand fungi).

1578 LYTE *Dodoens* 471 *Vstilago* is a certayne disease, or infirmitie, that happeneth vnto..ebare eares, but especially vnto Otes. *Ibid.*, This barren and vnfruitefull herbe is nowe called *Vstilago*, that is to say, Burned, or Blighted. *a* **1722** LISLE *Husb.* (1757) 130, I could find little ustilago in my oats. *Ibid.*, The ustilago is common to the ears of grass as well as of corn. **1822–7** GOOD *Study Med.* (1829) II. 118 Wheat which is..infested with albigo (mildew), ustilago (smut), and clavus (ergot or spur). **1857** M. J. BERKELEY *Introd. Cyrpt. Bot.* 323 Scarcely ever so much a to make them disagreeable objects like the Ustilagos. **1866** *Treas. Bot.* 1197/2 *Ustilago*, smut, a disease in which the natural tissue is replaced by black powder. **1895** M. C. COOKE *Study Fungi* xxi. 251 It was..customary to associate the Ustilagines with the Uredines.

†**'ustion.** *Obs.* [a. OF. *ustion* (13th c., = Sp. *ustion*, It. *ustione*, Pg. *ustão*), ad. L. *ūstiōn-em*, noun of action f. *ūst-us*, pa. pple. of *ūrĕre* to burn. Cf. ADUSTION, INUSTION.]

1. The action of burning, or fact of being burnt.

1567 MAPLET *Gr. Forest* 10 Likewise Incision..kepeth the place of vstion, free and cleare from yll smelling and rancoring. **1617** WOODALL *Surg. Mate* (1639) 274 Vstion is a preparation of things..by burning them in a crucible, or in the fire. **1673** *Phil. Trans.* VIII. 6132 All these to be further examined by..Arefaction, Assation, Ustion, Calcination. **1728** CHAMBERS *Cycl.* s.v., The Ustion of Minerals, is a more imperfect kind of Calcination. **1778** PRYCE *Min. Cornub.* 241 It may be worth enquiry, whether..Ores..may not be advanced in value by a previous ustion. **1802** *Trans. Soc. Arts* XX. 209 Another [cause of the fetid smell]..is ustion or burning the [fish-] oil.

2. The action of searing; cauterization.

1588 J. READ tr. *Arcæus' Meth. curing Woundes* 60 That imperfection..cannot bee holpen without vstion or burning. **1638** A. READ *Chirurg.* ii. 14 Wee ought not, but upon great necessitie, to have recourse to ustion. **1651** BIGGS *New Disp.* ¶256 They..have stoutly played the Vulcans, and have appointed also Arabick ustions..for the sciatica. **1684** tr. *Bonet's Merc. Compit.* XIX. 712 The ustion of the Ioynts that was grown out of use, has been restored. **1737** BRACKEN *Farriery Impr.* (1756) I. 319 Ustion or Burning was the Remedy most used.

b. A place or surface presenting the appearance of being seared or cauterized.

1607 TOPSELL *Four-f. Beasts* 255 The roote of the greater Siler..cureth those cold vstions in the flesh or belly, when the place looketh blacke or looseth sence.

3. *fig.* Concupiscence; libidinous desire. *rare.*

1559 [see URN *v.*[1] 1]. **1624** SANDERSON *Serm.* I. 228 Marriage,..the sole allowed remedy against..burning lusts; by the apostle..commanded in case of ustion to all men.

†**'ustive,** *a. Obs. rare.* [f. L. *ūst-us* (see prec.) + -IVE.] **a.** Caustic. **b.** Adapted for a burn.

1597 A. M. tr. *Guillemeau's Fr. Chirurg.* 22 b/2 Causticke or vstive medicamentes, a Aqva fortis. **1599** —— tr. *Gabelhouer's Bk. Physicke* 332/1 Linteseede-oyle..is an excellent ustive oyntment.

†**u'storious,** *a. Obs.*[−1] [See prec. and -ORIOUS.] Characterized by the faculty or power of burning.

1724 WATTS *Logic* I. vi. §3 It is by an ustorious Quality in the Mirrour or Glass,..arising from a certain unknown substantial Form in them.

†**'ustulate,** *v. Obs.*[−0] [ad. L. *ūstulāt-*, ppl. stem of *ūstulāre* to burn.] *trans.* (See quots.)

1623 COCKERAM, *Vstulate*, to curle or burne. **1656** BLOUNT *Glossogr.*, *Ustulate*, to burn or sear a thing [so Cooper s.v. *Vstulo*]; also to frizel or curle. **1775** ASH, *Unustulated*,..not ustulated; not burnt.

ustulate ('ʌstjʊlət), *a.* [a. L. *ūstulāt-us*, pa. pple.: see prec.] (See quots.)

1826 KIRBY & SP. *Entomol.* IV. xlvi. 289 *Ustulate*,..so marked with brown as to have the appearance of being scorched. **1840** PAXTON *Bot. Dict.* 325/2 *Ustulate*, blackened. [Hence in later works.]

ustulation (ʌstjʊ'leɪʃən). [ad. med.L. *ūstulātiōn-*, *ūstulātio*, noun of action f. L. *ūstulāre* to burn.]

1. The action of burning or fact of being burnt; *spec.* in later use, torrification, roasting.

1658 tr. *Porta's Nat. Magic* x. xii. 267 To extract Oyl by Descent..is common and vulgar to all; for it is done by Ustulation. **1667** SPRAT *Hist. R. Soc.* 296 The ustulation or affriction between the Nave and the Axel-tree. **1753** *Chambers' Cycl.* Suppl., *Ustulation*,..the roasting or torrefying of humid or moist substances over a gentle fire, so as to render them fit for powdering. **1780** J. T. DILLON *Trav. Spain* (1781) 262 Melting and ustulation of the mercurial ores. **1811** *Self Instructor* 534 Blacking lies in the iron, and particularly in its ustulation. **1839** URE *Dict. Arts* 820 The combustion must be so conducted as..to prolong the ustulation, and let the whole mass be equably penetrated with heat.

†**2.** *fig.* = USTION 3. *Obs. rare.*

1660 JER. TAYLOR *Ductor* III. iv. rule 20 §13 A state of cœlibate exposes us to a perpetual ustulation. *Ibid.* §16 It is not certain that they took the better part when they chose ustulation before marriage.

ustyl(l)ment, obs. varr. HUSTLEMENT.

†**usuable,** obs. var. USABLE *a.*

1544 in Leadam *Sel. Cases Crt. Requests* (Selden) 112 By the olde vsuable custome of the seyd manoyr.

†**usuage,** obs. var. USAGE *sb.*

1641 in *Verney Mem.* (1904) I. 203 Contrary to the custom & usuage of Parliment. **1708** *Brit. Apollo* No. 50. 1/1 So customary an Usuage. *a* **1744** T. INNES in *Spalding Club Misc.* (1842) II. 365 These usuages of Sarum were.. confirmed by the rescripts..of popes.

usual ('juːʒuːəl, -ʊəl), *a.* Forms: 4–7 vsual, -all (6 vsial, wsuall), 6– usual (6–7 -all, 7 usewal); 4–7 vsu-, usuale; 4–5 vsu-, usuell. [a. OF. *usual* (1298 in Godef.), *usuel* (F. *usuel*), or ad. L. (post-class.) *ūsuāl-is* (whence It. *usuale*, Sp. and Pg. *usual*, Pr. *uzual*), f. *ūsus* USE *sb.*]

1. That is in ordinary use or observance; having general currency, validity, or force; commonly observed or practised; current, prevalent.

1396 in *Scottish Antiq.* XIV. 218, xix. marcis of vsuale moneth. **1396–7** in *Eng. Hist. Rev.* (1907) XXII. 296 Oure usuel presthod þe qwich began in Rome. *c* **1450** *Godstow Reg.* 553 Robert yaf to him xij. shillings of vsuall money. **1495** *Act 11 Hen. VII*, c. 43 *Preamble*, Noe gretter fees..but such [as] at this tyme be usuell. **1523** Fitzherb. *Surv.* 36 b, F. G...payeth vnto the lordes at the termes their vsuels sixtene shillynges. **1575** *Extr. Aberd. Reg.* (1848) II. 24 Fortie markis wsuall money of Scotland. *a* **1577** Sir T. Smith *Commw. Eng.* II. xii. (1589) 67 In this court [of Chancery] the vsuall and proper forme of pleading of England is not vsed. **1620** *Extr. Aberd. Reg.* (1848) II. 368 Tua vsuall termis in the yeir, Witsonday and Martimes. **1687** A. Lovell tr. *Thevenot's Trav.* I. 278 He never goes up thither but at the usual hours, unless it be [etc.]. **1747** Berkeley *Lett.* Wks. 1871 IV. 315 Pray give him the usual fee for the best lawyer. **1848** Wharton *Law Lex.*, *Usual terms*, a phrase in the common law practice, which means pleading issuably, rejoining gratis, and taking short notice of trial. **1855** *Poultry Chron.* II. 580/2 At half the usual rates of charge. **1897** *Daily News* 10 April 7/2 Stay of execution for a fortnight upon 'the usual terms'.

†**2. a.** Of a year: Solar. *Obs. rare.*

1387 Trevisa *Higden* (Rolls) I. 37 For þe Iewes in tretys and couenauntes haueþ a ȝere vsual, and bygineþ in Ianuarie. **1398** —— Barth. De P.R. IX. iii. (Tollem. MS.), Some ȝere is clepid usuale, as is þe ȝere of þe sonne.

†**b.** Of a month: Calendar. *Obs.*⁻¹

1594 Blundevil *Exerc.* III. I. xlv. (1597) 172 b, The vsuall month is that number of daies which are set downe in our common Kalenders.

3. a. Ordinarily used; constantly or customarily employed; in common use; ordinary, customary.

c **1444** Pecock *Donet* 34 He must take þe eukarist, not as oþire comoun or vsual meete and drynk. *a* **1479** Caxton *Epil. Boeth.* 92 b, Maister Geffry Chaucer hath translated this sayd werke oute of latyn in to oure vsual and moder tonge. **1532** More *Confut. Tindale* Wks. 621/1 He turned the vsuall englyshe woordes of churche, priest, and penaunce, to congregacyon, senior, and repentaunce. **1550** Bale *Eng. Votaries* II. 40 A Consuetudynary or vsuall boke of the churche. **1579** Fulke *Refut. Rastel* 781, Thou perhaps wilt say, my bread is common and vsual bread. **1610** Holland *Camden's Brit.* I. 673 From whence there is an usuall passage over into Ireland. **1641** J. Jackson *True Evang. T.* I. 37 Earth-quakes, which (according to the usuall scandall)..were ascribed as a punishment to the Christians. **1671** Milton *P.R.* IV. 316 They..Rather accuse him [*sc.* God] under usual names, Fortune and Fate. **1729** T. Innes *Crit. Essay* (1879) 236 He reforms the bard Forchern's story of it (according to the usual custom of posterior bards). **1776** *Trial Nundocomar* 24/2 What was Selabut's usual method of attesting papers as a witness? **1797** *Monthly Mag.* III. 549 The sheriff shall make..proclamations..at or near to the most usual door of the church, or chapel. **1836** W. Irving *Astoria* II. 31 He began by the usual expressions of friendship. **1860** Tyndall *Glac.* I. ix. 61 We reached the place by the usual route. **1883** *Manch. Exam.* 30 Oct. 8/4 Beer in the usual stately German flagons with pewter covers.

(*b*) Freq. in ***usual channels*** [channel *sb.*¹ 8]; ***usual office***(*s*: see office *sb.* 9 b.

1905 *Hansard Commons* 16 May 500 In reply to the Question of the hon. Member for Waterford, I have to ask him to communicate with my right hon. friend near me through the usual channels. **1946** *Erskine May's Law of Parl.* (ed. 14) xii. 245 The Government Chief Whip.. together with the Chief Whips of the other parties, constitutes what is known as the 'usual channels', through which communications pass as to business arrangements and other matters which concern the convenience of Members as a whole. **1975** J. P. Morgan *House of Lords & Labour Govt.* viii. 213 The usual channels had collapsed and, in the absence of the customary arrangements, the Government could only hope that they might limit discussion by imposing a guillotine.

†**b.** Habitually done or made. *Obs. rare.*

1576 Fleming *Panopl. Epist.* A ij b, Often reading, and usual marking the epistles of Tullie. *Ibid.* 2 Sundry Gentlemen, that haue usual resort to my house. **1577** Harrison *England* II. iii. (1877) I. 81 One thing onlie I mislike in them, and that is their vsuall going into Italie.

c. Of persons: Commonly employed or serving in a particular capacity.

1590 Shaks. *Mids. N.* V. i. 35 Where is our vsuall manager of mirth? *Mod.* He sent the money by his usual messenger. Our usual postman did not come to-day.

4. a. That ordinarily happens, occurs, or is to be found; such as is commonly met with or observed in ordinary practice or experience; common, wonted.

1577 *Misogonus* IV. i, Gods providence in shewinge mercye to his servauntes is alwayes vsiall. **1579** Tomson *Calvin's Serm. Tim.* 248 It was a verie vsuall thing in the East countrie, for a man to haue two or three wiues. **1638** Junius *Paint. Anc.* 8 So is it likewise an usuall thing in..our life, that we..study alwayes to [etc.]. **1651** Hobbes *Leviath.* II. xxii. 122 The usuall meeting of men at Church, or at a publique Shew, in usuall numbers. **1759** R. Brown *Compl. Farmer* 91 The usual signs that precede their swarming. **1784** Cowper *Task* II. 61 And th' old..earth has had her shaking fits More frequent, and forgone her usual rest. **1831** James *Phil. Augustus* III. v, A table groaning under a repast not very usual on the boards of a prison. **1855** J. Phillips *Man. Geol.* 204 The usual hardening of sandstone and shale, carbonization of coal, &c., occur.

b. Customary on the part of a person or persons *to* do something.

1605 Verstegan *Dec. Intell.* ix. 310 It hath..grown somwhat vsuallin England, to giue vnto children..the surnames of their Godfathers. **1630** *R. Johnson's Kingd. & Commw.* 183 It is usuall with all the Gauls..to constraine Travellers (though unwilling) to stay. **1716** Addison *Freeholder* No. 10 ¶5 It was usual for him to shew the Delicacy of his Taste by [etc.]. **1719** London & Wise *Compl. Gard.* 312 It is very usual to meet with those. **1825** *Encycl. Metrop.* (1845) XVII. 36/1 In most Pigeon-houses it is usual to have a Salt-cat. **1839** Hallam *Hist. Lit.* IV. vii. 506 *note*, It is not usual for..[a] woman to turn it into drollery.

c. Common or habitual *to* a person or thing.

1665 Mrq. Worcester *Cent. Inv.* §18 Several shapes and effects usual to Fountains of pleasure. **1693** Congreve *Old Bach.* I. i, Why truth on't is, these early Sallies are not usual to me.

d. ***as*** (or ***than***) ***usual***, as (or than) is or was customary or habitual. (Cf. usually *adv.* 1 b.) ***as per usual***: see per *prep.* III. 1.

[**1617** Moryson *Itin.* I. 114 Liuing things cast into that caue, and held there for longer time then is vsuall.] **1716** Addison *Freeholder* No. 22 ¶2 Our Conversation opened, as usual, upon the Weather. **1725** *Fam. Dict.* s.v. *Pulse*, When the Strokes are much smaller than usual. **1795** *Gentl. Mag.* 539/2 The blights were this year..more destructive than usual. **1854** *Poultry Chron.* II. 348/2 The poultry department was, as usual, the principal attraction. **1865** Dickens *Mut. Fr.* I. xiv, The huddled buildings looked lower than usual. **1876** [see usualness].

†**5.** ***usual fruit***, = usufruit, usufruct. *Sc.*

1558 Knox *First Blast* (Arb.) 46 God wold not suffer that the commoditie and vsuall frute..shulde passe to an other [tribe].

†**6. a.** Of persons: Customary, regular. *Obs.*

1579 *Southampton Crt. Leet Rec.* (1906) II. 167 Owen symons is a vsuall convayor of wood beyond the seas.

†**b.** Habitually resorting. *Obs.*⁻¹

1597 J. Payne *Royal Exch.* 27 The devill perswades sum carnall and viciouse parsons that there tyme ys well spent, beinge vsuall in the taverne.

7. *absol.* **a.** ***the*** (***his***, etc.) ***usual***, what is usual, customary, or frequent (esp. with a person or persons).

1876 Geo. Eliot *Dan. Deronda* V. xxxv. III. 22 To be an unusual young man means for the most part to get a difficult mastery over the usual. **1892** E. Reeves *Homeward Bound* 189 Nothing in Naples is so clean as the horses' harness, and to-day the drivers outdid their usual. **1897** *Daily News* 23 Dec. 3/5 Coroner: How much whisky did he drink?—Witness: Eighteen half quarterns a night..was his usual.

b. *colloq.* Customary state of health.

1887 Annie S. Swan *Gates of Eden* xx, Aunt Susan is in her usual, I know.

Hence **'usualness**.

1653 H. More *Antid. Ath.* I. x. 30 The usualnesse of such dangers have made them loose the sense of the danger. **1705** Clarke *Evid. Nat. & Rev. Relig.* xiv. (1716) 297 'Tis only usualness or unusualness that makes the distinction. **1727** Bailey (vol. II), *Frequentness*, oftenness; usualness. **1876** Mrs. Whitney *Sights & Ins.* II. ix. 405 They had been two days together, as usual; the usualness is a great power.

usually ('juːʒuːəlı, -ʊəlı), *adv.* [f. prec. + -ly².]

1. In a usual or wonted manner; according to customary, established, or frequent usage; commonly, customarily, ordinarily; as a rule.

In frequent use from *c* 1600.

1477 *Rolls of Parlt.* VI. 191/2 All the Membres usuelly called to the forseid Parlementes. **1485** *Yorks. Archaeol. Soc., Record Ser.* XLI. 1 [He] awaytid vpon hym thyder according as he vsually dyde. **1526** *Pilgr. Perf.* (W. de W. 1531) 17 The moost vyle meet that is vsually ordeyned for beestes. **1587** *Southampton Crt. Leet Rec.* (1906) II. 262 Emery lake doth vsually delyver his key of the lynnen hawle to straungers at all dayes. **1613** Purchas *Pilgrimage* (1614) 331 b, Through their excellencie in horsemanship they vsually made the victorie..to be certaine. **1634** W. Tirwhyt tr. *Balzac's Lett.* (vol. I) 203 If thy letters be so short, as usually they are. **1682** Norris *Hierocles* 10 The Keeper of this observation was usually call'd..by the mystical Name Oath. **1709** Steele *Tatler* No. 17 ¶2 The Ornaments which are usually given to the Actions of the Great. **1766** Goldsm. *Vicar* xii, One of those observations I usually made to impress my wife. **1825** Scott *Betrothed* xv, The blessings which are usually bestowed on a departing kinswoman. **1840** *Penny Cycl.* XVII. 174/1 Palms are woody plants, usually trees, with simple stems. **1878** Jevons *Prim. Pol. Econ.* 66 Even a successful strike usually occasions loss.

b. In the phr. ***than usually*** (now only as in quot. 1875), †***as usually***. Cf. usual *a.* 4 d.

a **1700** Evelyn *Diary* 18 Jan. 1645, A very large payr of stayres, round, without any stepps as usualy. **1713** Derham *Phys. Theol.* I. iii. 22 The Summer of 1708, part of which.. was much colder than usually. **1749** Fielding *Tom Jones* XV. iii, The Company behaved as usually on these Occasions. **1805** *Med. Jrnl.* XIII. 107 It absorbs this substance more eagerly from the surface of the body than usually. **1875** Jowett *Plato* (ed. 2) IV. 38 The mind of man has been more than usually active in thinking about man.

†**2.** In a regular manner; regularly. *Obs. rare.*

1573 Tusser *Husb.* (1878) 17 To walke thy pastures vsuallie To spie ill neighbours subtiltie. **1605** Camden *Rem.* 233 He would not have so weighty a matter tumultuously and rashly done, but vsually and orderly.

usuary ('juːzjuːərı). *Roman Law.* [ad. late L. *ūsuāri-us* sb., f. *ūsuārius* a., f. L. *ūsus* use *sb.*] One who has the use but not the ownership of a thing.

1871 Poste *Gaius* IV. 507 As the usufrutuary has no possession, it follows a fortiori that the usuary has no possession.

usu'capient. *Roman Law.* [ad. L. *ūsūcapient-*, pres. pple. stem of *ūsū-capĕre*: see usucapion.] One who has acquired, or claims title to, property by usucapion.

1875 Poste *Gaius* (ed. 2) II. 192 The possession of the usucapient must be based on a justa causa or titulus. **1880** Muirhead *Gaius* Dig. 457 A thing delivered to the usucapient by one who was not its owner.

usucapion (juːzjuː'keıpıən). [a. L. *ūsū-capiōn-*, *ūsu-capio* (whence F. and Sp. *usucapion*, It. *usucapione*, Pg. *-capião*), f. *ūsū-capĕre* to acquire ownership by prescription. Cf. usucaption.] In *Roman* and *Civil Law*, the acquisition of ownership by long use or enjoyment; prescription in virtue of continuous undisturbed possession. Also *fig.*

1606 Birnie *Kirkburial* xix, The vnion is so indissoluble, that neyther prescription of tyme, vsucapion of person, nor boutgate of circumstance can giue a regresse. **1617** Collins *Defence Bp. of Ely* II. x. 471 The name Catholike appertaining thereunto, by vsucapion forsooth, by plaine prescription, as Campian dreameth. **1681** Stair *Instit.* xxii. I. 433 Prescription which is short in Moveables, is commonly called Usucapion. **1765–8** Erskine *Inst. Law Scot.* III. vii. §14 Thus things sacred or public could not by the Roman law be acquired by usucapion. **1841** *Penny Cycl.* XX. 117/2 Without affecting to give him ownership, which the law alone could give him by virtue of usucapion. **1855** Lorenz tr. *Van der Keessel's Select Theses* ccvii, By no means opposed to the usucapion of a movable thing in three years. **1871** Poste *Gaius* II. 153/2 The Senate..decreed that such usucapions are revocable.

attrib. **1875** Poste *Gaius* (ed. 2) IV. 641 Possession..is transformed by a certain lapse of time into dominion; and is called Usucapion-possession.

Hence **usu'capionary** *a.*, in virtue of usucapion.

1880 Muirhead *Gaius* Dig. 585 By completing his usucapionary possession, he cured the defect.

usucapt ('juːzjuːkæpt), *v.* *Roman Law.* [ad. L. *ūsū-capt-*, past pple. stem of *ūsū-capere*: see usucapion.] *trans.* To acquire ownership of or title to (a property, etc.) by usucaption. Also *absol.*

1880 Muirhead *Gaius* II. §93 A usufructuary cannot usucapt. **1886** —— in *Encycl. Brit.* XX. 692/2 Upon him who had usucapted by possession the greater part of a deceased person's estate.

Hence **usu'captable, -ible** *adjs.*, capable of being held by usucaption; **usu'captor**, = usucapient.

1880 Muirhead *Gaius* Dig. 582 The land was not usucaptable. *Ibid.* II. §57 Such usucapions may be revoked, and the heir recover from the usucaptor. **1886** —— in *Encycl. Brit.* XX. 690/2 Any citizen..holding movables as his own, provided they were usucaptible.

usu'caption (juːzjuː'kæpʃən). *Roman Law.* [a. OF. *usucaption*, *-cion*, or med.L. *ūsūcaptiōn-*, ad. L. *ūsū-capiōn-* usucapion.] = usucapion.

1656 Blount, *Usucaption* (*usucaptio*), prescription or long possession or the attaining a thing thereby. **1728** Chambers *Cycl.* s.v., Some make a Difference between Prescription and Usucaption, maintaining that the latter is only used with regard to Moveables, and the former with regard to Immoveables. **1760** tr. *Vattel's Law of Nations* II. xi. 166 Usucaption is the acquisition of domain founded on a long possession, uninterrupted and undisputed. **1826** G. Spence *Orig. Laws Mod. Europe* p. xvii, Modes of acquiring property or ownership in individual things: Of usucaption and prescription. **1853** Whewell *Grotius* I. 276 The right of usucaption, by which a thing long used becomes the property of the possessor. **1874** Motley *Barneveld* I. 283 Rather by usucaption than usurpation, Holland had..come to consider herself..the Republic itself.

attrib. **1871** Poste *Gaius* IV. 501 Possession,..which we will call usucaption-possession.

usufruct ('juːzjuːfrʌkt), *sb.* [a. late L. *ūsūfruct-us* (whence Sp. and Pg. *usufructo*, It. *usu-*, *usofrutto*, Pr. *usufrug*), ad. L. *ūsus-fructus* (abl. *ūsū-fructū*). Cf. usufruit.]

1. *Law.* The right of temporary possession, use, or enjoyment of the advantages of property belonging to another, so far as may be had without causing damage or prejudice to this. Also *transf.*

c **1630** Sir T. Hope *Minor Practicks* (1734) 252 After the Usu-fruct is once lawfully constitute by a Seasin. **1681** Stair *Instit.* xvi. 327 Usufruct is the power of disposal of the use and fruits, saving the Substance of the thing. **1710** J. Harris *Lex. Techn.* II. s.v. *Services*, Services Personal, are those due from a Thing to a Person, and of these they account..Usufruct, Use and Habitation. **1766** Blackstone *Comm.* II. 105 A subject therefore hath only the usufruct, and not the absolute property of the soil. **1839** Carlyle *Chartism* x. 176 Lawsuits in chancery for some short usufruct of a bit of land. **1853** J. H. Newman *Hist. Sk.* (1873) I. I. ii. 74 They held it [*sc.* Sogdiana] in possession.. for 90 or 100 years; they came into the usufruct and enjoyment of it. **1868** Browning *Ring & Bk.* II. 211 He owned some usufruct, had moneys' use Lifelong.

fig. **1863** Patmore *Angel in Ho.* I. II. ii, Could eternal life afford That tyranny should thus deduct From this fair land ..A year of the sweet usufruct.

b. An office of which one is usufructuary. *rare.*

1848 Hallam *Suppl. Notes Hist. Mid. Ages* 116 M. Guérard..is of opinion that, though benefices were ultimately fiefs, in the first stage of the monarchy they were only usufructs.

2. *gen.* Use, enjoyment, or profitable possession (*of* something).

1811 Lamb *Elia* I. *Bachelor's Compl.*, In the rich man's houses and pictures..I have a temporary usufruct at least. **1835** Greswell *Parables* IV. 490 No more than preliminary to the usufruct of the Kingdom itself. **1863** Kinglake *Crimea* I. 41 Which of the rival Churches should have the control and usufruct of every holy shrine.

b. *esp.* Beneficial use or enjoyment of land. Also *fig.* and *transf.*

1864 MARSH *Man & Nat.* 35 Man has too long forgotten that the earth was given to him for usufruct alone, not for consumption. **1870** HUXLEY *Lay Serm.* xii. 313 Depriving man of the usufruct of one of the most fertile fields of his great patrimony, Nature. **1898** HARCOURT in *Times* 30 March 8/2 The 'usufruct' of Port Arthur and Ta-lien-wan had been granted to Russia. 'Usufruct' appears to be a new word [in this connection].

3. *attrib.*, as ***usufruct discipline***, ***right***.

1845 R. W. HAMILTON *Pop. Educ.* iv. 69 A sordid, utilitarian, usufruct, discipline of the youthful mind. **1881** 'H. H.' *Century of Dishonor* 115 The usufruct right of the Indians to the lands occupied by them.

Hence **usu'fruction**, = sense 2 b.

1846 *Congressional Globe* 27 May 862/3 They saw..that they could..get the whole [boundary-line], at least for a long time, under our own delusive project of joint usufruction.

'usufruct, *v.* [f. prec. Cf. med.L. *ūsūfructāre*, *-uāre*, It. *usufruttare*, *-uare*, Sp. *usufructuar*.] *trans.* To hold (property) as a usufructuary; to possess in or subject to usufruct. Also *absol.*

1880 MUIRHEAD *Gaius* II. §14 It is.. the right of usufructing, and the right under the obligation that is incorporeal. **1886** —— in *Encycl. Brit.* XX. 709/2 Property usufructed should revert unimpaired to the owner.

Hence **'usufructed** *ppl. a.*

1880 MUIRHEAD *Gaius* II. §94 Whether we can possess and usucapt through a usufructed slave.

† **usufructuar**, obs. Sc. variant of next.

1531 *Dunfermline Reg.* (Bann. Cl.) 362 Legat of scotland and vsufructuar of þe abbay of dunfermeling.

usufructuary (juːzjuː'frʌktjuːərɪ), *sb.* [ad. late L. *ūsūfructuāri-us*, f. *ūsūfructu-s* USUFRUCT *sb.* Cf. Pg. *usufructuario*, It. *usufruttuario*.]

1. *Law.* One who has the temporary use and reaps the fruits or profits of an estate, benefice, office, etc., legally belonging to another or others; one who enjoys the usufruct of a property, etc.

a **1618** RALEIGH in Gutch *Coll. Cur.* I. 72 The ordinary *ususfructus* is determined by the death of the usufructuary. **1658** BRAMHALL *Consecr. Bps.* viii. 186 He held all these Bishopricks..as an Vsufructuary not as a true owner. **1692** WASHINGTON tr. *Milton's Def. Pop.* vi. 158 He, that has but the Crown, and the Revenues that belong to it, as an Usufructuary. **1710** PRIDEAUX *Draught of a Bill, Reasons* 2 The Ministers are only the usufructuaries to receive the annual income. **1726** AYLIFFE *Parergon* 86 The Parsons of Parishes are not in Law accounted Proprietors, but only Usufructuaries. **1790** FRANCIS in Burke *Corr.* (1844) III. 166 The Church..whose property its usufructuaries very wisely said it would be sacrilege to invade. **1820** *Ann. Reg.* II. 718 The land-tax is not taken into account except for the proprietor or usufructary [*sic*]. **1868** BROWNING *Ring & Bk.* III. 159 A certain yearly sum,—our Pietro being,..an usufructuary,—Dropped in the common bag as interest Of money, his till death. **1881** DISRAELI in *Daily Tel.* 27 April, That all books..[be] properly preserved by..the usufructuary thereof for the time being.

b. *transf.* and *fig.*

a **1638** MEDE *Wks.* (1672) 121 Because the whole land was holy, and God's land, and they but Usufructuaries. **1648** SANDERSON *Serm.* II. 24 God hath entrusted us with the..culture of our own hearts..: the fruits wholly accrue to us, as usufructuaries. **1652** NEEDHAM *Selden's Mare Cl.* 483 What advantages..are made by others, who of Usufructuaries [of the sea] by permission, have in design now to make themselvs absolute Lords of the Fee. **1702** J. HOWE *Self Ded.* 27 God indeed is the only Proprietor, Men are but usufructuaries. **1768–74** TUCKER *Lt. Nat.* (1834) II. 150 We do not possess in property but only as usufructuaries, and we know the lading will be taken off our backs..at the end of our journey through life. **1866** ALGER *Solit. Nat. & Man* IV. 370 [To conform] to the will of God ..as its grateful executives and usufructuaries.

2. In general use: One who has the use or enjoyment *of* something.

1621 BACON in Spedding *Lett.*, etc. (1874) VII. 226, I have ..ever..counted myself but an usufructuary of myself, the property being yours. **1622** MABBE tr. *Aleman's Guzman d'Alf.* I. 125 The Vsufructuarie, and free inioyer of thy life. **1652–3** LEICESTER in Collins *Lett. & Mem. State* (1746) II. 680 If the Gift be of your self..you shall be but an Usufructuary of yourself. **1794** J. GIFFORD *Reign Louis XVI*, 425 We are but usufructuaries of life. **1839** HALLAM *Hist. Lit.* III. iv. 359 That the supreme power or sovereignty ..does not reside in the chief magistrate, but in the people themselves, and that no other is proprietor or usufructuary of it. **1886** W. GRAHAM *Soc. Problem* 458 The present usufructuaries of the blessings of civilisation.

usu'fructuary, *a.* [ad. late L. *ūsūfructuāri-us* (whence Sp. and Pg. *usufructuario*, It. *usufruttuario*, F. *usufructuaire*): see prec.]

1. Pertaining or relating to usufruct; of the nature of usufruct.

1710 PRIDEAUX *Orig. Tithes* i. 17 To receive and enjoy them in a usustructuary [*sic*; **1736** usufructuary] tenure under him. **1810** COLERIDGE *Jer. Taylor* Wks. 1838 III. 245 The ordinary graces bequeathed by Christ to his Church as the usufructuary property of all its members. **1880** MUIRHEAD *Gaius* II. §30 So that the cessionary shall have the usufructuary right, he himself retaining the bare property.

†**2.** Holding or enjoying an office, etc., by usufruct. *Obs.*⁻¹

1728 CHAMBERS *Cycl.* s.v. *Usufruit*, The Incumbents of Benefices are only Usufructuary.

† **usufruictor, -uor**, obs. varr. USUFRUCTUARY.

1689 *Def. Liberty agst. Tyrants* 107 At the least we may esteem him [*sc.* the king] Usufruictuor of the Kingdom, and of the Demean; nay, truly we can allow him to have the Usufruit for being Usufrictor [*sic*].

† **'usufruit.** *Obs.* Also 5 *Sc.* **vse-fruyt**, 7 **usufrute.** [a. OF. (and F.) *usufruit* (13th c.), ad. late L. *ūsū-fructus* USUFRUCT *sb.*] = USUFRUCT *sb.* 1.

1478 *Acta Dom. Conc.* (1839) 13/1 Robert nor nane vþeris ..has þe vse fruyt of þer wifis propir landis for þer life tyme. **1547** *Bk. of Marchauntes* d iiij, Possession was..adiugged to hym in herytage wyth yᵉ vsufruits of the tres growing ther. *a* **1577** SIR T. SMITH *Commw. Eng.* III. viii. (1589) 134 The husband shal haue the vsufruite of her landes. **1604** E. G[RIMSTONE] *D'Acosta's Hist. Indies* IV. xi. 240 The vsufruite was adiudged to him by sentence as the dicoverer [of the mine]. **1689** [see prec.]. **1728** CHAMBERS *Cycl.* s.v. *Substitution*, Certain Persons, who are likewise to have the Usu-fruit in their Times, but never the Property.

† **usu'rarious,** *a. Obs. rare.* [f. L. *ūsūrāri-us* (see USURARY *a.*) + -OUS.] Usurious.

1623 R. CARPENTER *Conscionable Christian* 14 Usurarious extorting State-spoyling money-mongers. **1646** J. BENBRIGGE *Vsura Accom.* 4 Such lending ought to be praised ..and in no case conceived to be Usurarious. **1660** JER. TAYLOR *Ductor* I. v. rule vi. §1 All usurarious contracts. *Ibid.* II. ii. rule vii. §7 If a common-wealth permits an usurarious exchange or contract.

† **'usurary,** *sb. Obs. rare.* [ad. med.L. *ūsūrāri-us* (Diefenb.): see next.] A money-lender.

c **1440** *Alph. Tales* 524 Som tyme in Colayn þer was ane vsurarie. *Ibid.* 526 All þies vsuraries rase and went oute confusid.

† **'usurary,** *a. Obs. rare.* [ad. L. *ūsūrāri-us* (whence It., Sp., Pg. *usurario*, F. *usuraire*), f. *ūsūra* USURY *sb.*] Marked by the payment of interest; on which excessive interest is paid.

1649 BP. HALL *Cases Consc.* i. 7 How odious..usurary contracts have been in all times. *Ibid.* 13 Every increase by loan of money is not usurarie. **1678** SIR G. MACKENZIE *Crim. Laws Scot.* I. xxiv. §7 (1699) 124 That the Usurary Bond or Contract shall be reduced. **1693** STAIR *Instit.* (ed. 2) II. x. 331 That if it [*sc.* a lease] were in the Terms of the old Act, Parl. 1449. cap. 19. far within the true Avail, it were usurary and null.

† **usure,** *sb. Obs.* Also 4–5 **vsere**, 5 **vsur**, **usur.** [a. OF. *useure* (13th c.), *usure* (also AF. and F.), ad. L. *ūsūra* (whence It., Sp., Pg. *usura*, Pr. *uzura*), n. of action f. *ūs-us*: see USURY *sb.*]

1. The fact or practice of lending money at interest. Cf. USURY *sb.* 1.

a **1325** *Prose Psalter* liv. 11 Usure [L. *usura*] and trecherie ne failed nouȝt in his waies. [**1382, 1388** WYCLIF *Ibid.*] *c* **1380** WYCLIF *Wks.* (1880) 277 Þat þe sotil vsure of riche clerkis & marchaundes be hurled out of lond. *c* **1400** MAUNDEV. (1919) iii. 12 Men of Grece..sey also þat vsure is no dedly synne. **1436** *Pol. Poems* (Rolls) II. 176 Thus they lyve..wyth suche chevesaunce That men calle usure, to oure losse and hinderaunce. **1456** SIR G. HAYE *Law Armes* (S.T.S.) 70 Thair digniteis, that thai have gottyn wrangwisly throu usur, scisme, or symony. *c* **1530** *Pol., Rel. & L. Poems* (1903) 60 What is vsure, but..a lawfulle thefe that tellyth ys entent. **1533** BELLENDEN *Livy* II. xi. (S.T.S.) I. 167 Þis dett..was ay duplyit on him be vsure and okkir. **1605** B. JONSON *Volpone* I. i, I turne no moneys, in the public bank; Nor vsure priuate.

Personif. **1362** LANGL. *P. Pl.* A. II. 66 Hit witen..þat I, Fauuel, feffe Fals to þat mayden Meede,..With þe Yle of vsure And Auarice þe False. **1390** GOWER *Conf.* II. 274 Upon the bench sittende on hih With Avarice Usure I sih.

b. A usurious act or practice.

a **1325** *Prose Psalter* lxxi. 14 He shal raunsoun her soules fram vsures and wickednes. **1382** WYCLIF *Ibid.* *c* **1440** *Alph. Tales* 472 With myne vsuris I grevud God bothe day & nyght. **1456** SIR G. HAYE *Law Arms* (S.T.S.) 188 Usuris and barat, subtilitee and trechery.

2. = INTEREST *sb.* 10, USURY *sb.* 2. Also occas. ***at, to usure.***

Freq. in Wyclif (1382), occas. in plural, tr. L. *usuræ*.

1338 R. BRUNNE *Chron.* (1810) 224 Þe chartres & þe scris þat noied Cristen men, þat lay for vsure in pris elleuen als for ten. ? *a* **1366** CHAUCER *Rom. Rose* 185 That is that for vsure Leneth to many a creature. **1377** LANGL. *P. Pl.* B. VII. 83 For beggeres borwen euermo and her borghe is god almyȝti, To ȝelden hem þat ȝiueth hem and ȝet vsure more. **1382** WYCLIF *Lev.* xxv. 37 Thi money thow shalt not ȝyue to him to vsure. *c* **1400** *Rom. Rose* 7026 If a wight, out of mesure, Wolde lene his gold, and take vsure. **1483** CAXTON *Gold. Leg.* 431 b/1 That no Justycer shold..constrayne them that were bounden to the Jewes..to paye or yelde to them theyr vsure or growyng. *a* **1513** FABYAN *Chron.* VII. 353 As a Iewe wolde haue forced a Cristen man to haue gyuen to hym more than .ii.d. for the vsure of .xx.s. for a weke.

† **usure,** *v. Obs.* [ad. OF. *usurer* (13th c.), ad. med.L. *ūsūrāre* (whence Sp. and Pg. *usurar*), f. L. *ūsūra*: see prec.]

1. *intr.* To practise usury; to lend at interest. Also *fig.*

c **1380** WYCLIF *Sel. Wks.* II. 207 Þus God usuriþ for oure prow, for alle þingis..he ȝyveþ us for þis eende. **1382** —— *Prov.* xix. 17 He vsureth to the Lord, that hath reuthe of the pore. —— *Jer.* xv. 10. **1530** PALSGR. 769/2 If our charyte were utterly parfyte, one christenned man shulde nat usure with an other.

2. *trans.* To lend (money) at a premium. *rare*⁻¹.

1620 BRATHWAIT *Five Senses* ii. 24 Oppresse I cannot, when I heare the Orphans teare... Vse my money, but vsure it I will not.

usurer ('juːzjʊərə(r)). Forms: α. 3–7 **vsurer**, 4–5 **-ere**, 5, *Sc.* 6 **-ar**; 5 **usurere**, 6– **usurer.** β. 4–6 **vserer**, 5 **-ere**, 6–7 **userer** (6 **uss-**). [a. AF. *usurer*, *userer*, = OF. *usureor*, ad. med.L. *ūsūrārius* USURARY *sb.* Cf. USURIER, and Sp. *usurero*, Pg. *usurario*, It. *usurajo*.] One who practises usury or lends money at interest; a money-lender, esp. in later use one who charges an excessive rate of interest.

α. *c* **1290** *St. Magdalena* 117 in *S. Eng. Leg.* I. 465 An vsurer was ȝwilene, þat hadde dettores tweyne. **1303** R. BRUNNE *Handl. Synne* 2611 Whan any vsurere was dede, þe chercheȝerde þey hym forbede. **1377** LANGL. *P. Pl.* B. XI. 275 If prestes weren parfyt þei wolde..nouȝte [take] her mete of vsureres. *c* **1410** *Lantern of Light* 132 In þis chirche ben vsureris, okureris, iourours. *a* **1450** *Knt. de la Tour* (1906) 53 Other..ben bawdes and theues, usureres, bariters. **1551** T. WILSON *Logike* G ij, No Christian is an vsurer. **1584** LODGE *Alarum agst. Usurers* B iij, The Broker in this matter, getteth..thousand thankes of this diuellish Vsurer. **1606** DEKKER *Sev. Sins* VI. (Arb.) 39 These are Vsurers: who for a little money..bring yong Nouices into a fooles Paradice till they haue sealed the Morgage of their landes. **1677** WOOD *Life* (O.H.S.) II. 395 Mʳ Deane, the old usurer. **1742** YOUNG *Nt. Th.* II. 270 As all-rapacious usurers conceal Their doomsday-book from all-consuming heirs. **1781** GIBBON *Decl. & F.* xvii. II. 70 The usurer, who derived from the interest of money a silent and ignominious profit. **1839** DICKENS *Nickleby* i, This promising lad commenced usurer on a limited scale at school. **1874** RUSKIN *Fors Clav.* xliv. 129, I know myself to be an usurer as long as I take interest on any money.

β. **1303** R. BRUNNE *Handl. Synne* 2453 Cauuarsyns and vserers, þys are, Lucyfer, þy peres. *c* **1440** *Promp. Parv.* 206/2 Gowlare, or vserere, *usurarius*. *c* **1450** *Merlin* xxiii. 434 The riche vserer that deliteth in his richesse. **1581** *Southampton Crt. Leet Rec.* (1906) II. 221 Edwardes..is an extreme usserer. **1588** *Marprel. Epist.* (Arb.) 32 He beareth ..to vserer Haruies good chear and money bags. **1616** R. COCKS *Diary* (Hakl. Soc.) I. 198 This man is a greate userer; and the King of Firando oweth hym much money. **1699** in E. W. Dunbar *Soc. Life Moray* (1865) 31 Under the certificating of being pursued as Occurrers or Userers.

b. *attrib.* and *Comb.*, as ***usurer class***, ***-like.***

1729 BOYRE *Dict. Royal* I, *Usurairement*, usurer-like. **1892** *Pall Mall G.* 23 April 7/1 The usurer-ridden peasantry and overworked operatives. **1902** *Fabian News* May 20/1 The landlord and usurer classes of India.

'usuress. *rare.* [f. USUR-ER + -ESS.] A female usurer.

1641 BRATHWAIT *Eng. Gentlew.* 300 A religious divine comming to a certaine usuresse,..told her [etc.]. **1648** HEXHAM II, *Een Woeckeresse*, an Usuresse, or a woman Usurer. **1898** *Daily Tel.* 28 May 7/3 The defendants.. evinced no little hostility to the usuress.

† **usurier.** *Obs.*⁻¹ [a. OF. (F.) *usurier*, ad. med.L. *ūsūrārius* USURARY *sb.*] A usurer.

c **1481** CAXTON *Dialogues* 2 Of paintours and vsuriers.

† **'usuring,** *ppl. a. Obs.* Also 6 **usering.** [f. USURE *sb.* or *v.* + -ING².]

1. Of persons: Practising or given to usury; usurious.

1593 MUNDAY *Def. Contraries* 37, I shall see no more..the vsuring Geneway, nor the boasting Modenan. **1622** MABBE tr. *Aleman's Guzman d'Alf.* I. 178 My Vsuring Merchant had hanging at his girdle a paire of kniues. **1681** COLVIL *Whigs Supplic.* (1751) 22 The fatherless and widows portion, Which usuring fathers lent to lairds. **1710** *Brit. Apollo* II. No. 105. 3/1 Streight to a Usuring Dog I hurry'd.

fig. and *transf.* **1598** MARLOWE & CHAPMAN *Hero & Leander* VI. 266 Filthie vsering Rocks that would haue blood, Though they could get of him no other good. *a* **1640** J. DAY *Parl. Bees* x. (1881) 60 Fenerator, Or the Vsuring Bee.

2. Looking for ample return or increase; causing cost without return. *rare.*

1607 SHAKS. *Timon* IV. iii. 516 Is not thy kindnesse subtle, couetous, If not a Vsuring kindnesse, and..Expecting in returne twenty for one? **1609** HEYWOOD *Brit. Troy* VII. viii, The barraine fieldes deceive the Plow-mans trust, The usuring seede is molded unto dust.

usurious (juː'zjʊərɪəs), *a.* [f. USURY *sb.* + -OUS. Cf. next.]

1. Characterized by, of the nature of or involving, usury or excessive interest.

1610 HOLLAND *Camden's Brit.* 748 Vsurious contracts, voluptuous and vicious life. **1611** FENTON *Vsurie* 21 If it be a gaine couenanted meerely in respect of loane, it is condemned as vsurious. **1678** R. L'ESTRANGE *Seneca's Mor.* II. xii. 154 We have found out wayes,..by Bloody Usurious Contracts, to undoe one another. **1729** JACOB *Law Dict.* s.v. *Usury*, A Bond..shall not be avoided by a corrupt usurious Agreement between others. **1784** COWPER *Task* III. 798 An usurious loan To be refunded duely, when his vote..shall have earn'd its worthy price. **1840** HOOD *Kilmansegg, Marriage* xxix, Fruits obtained before they were due At a discount most usurious. **1855** MILMAN *Lat. Chr.* IX. vii. IV. 125 The Jews were especially to be compelled..to abandon all their usurious claims. **1869** SPURGEON *Treas. Dav.* I. 209 To lend money even at the lowest interest to their fellow farmers [*sc.* Jews] in times of poverty would have been usurious.

b. Of interest, etc.: Charged by way of, acquired by virtue of, usury; exorbitant, excessive. Freq. with *interest*.

1611 COTGR., *Vsuraire*, vsurious; taken, or giuen for interest or vse. **1729** JACOB *Law Dict.* s.v. *Usury*, It is not material, whether the Payment of the Principal and the usurious Interest, be secured by the same, or by different Conveyances. **1776** ADAM SMITH *W.N.* I. ix, The same usurious interest which is usually required from bankrupts. **1812** CRABBE *Tales* xiv. 160 If thus he grasp'd at such usurious gains. **1847** C. BRONTE *J. Eyre* iv, A usurious rate of interest—fifty or sixty per cent. **1880** L. OLIPHANT *Gilead* x. 291 To lend money on mortgage..at a reasonable rate, instead of at the usurious percentage at present charged.

transf. **1634** RAINBOW *Labour* (1635) 41 Pile up thine house with obligatory parchment,..farme out th' usurious time..and let each day redouble thine hundreds.

2. a. Practising usury; taking or charging excessive interest on loaned money; exacting in respect of interest. Also *transf.*

a **1631** DONNE *Love's Usury* 2 For every houre that thou wilt spare mee now, I will allow, Usurious God of Love, twenty to thee. **1635** QUARLES *Embl.* III. xv. 183 Plead not; Vsurious Nature will have all, As well the Int'rest, as the Principall. **1836** J. ABBOT *Way to do Good* iii. 96 The most hard-hearted usurious creditor. **1870** MACDUFF *Mem. Patmos* x. 136 The usurious vendors dealing out a stinted penny-worth to the famishing. **1870** H. SMART *Race for Wife* iv, Even a usurious solicitor is possessed of pride of some kind.

b. Characteristic of a usurer.

1727 BAILEY (vol. II), *Usuriousness*, usurious or extortioning Quality or Disposition. **1832** *Rolls of Parlt.* Index 958 The usurious Conduct of Peter de Appelby. **1862** J. SMALL *Eng. Metr. Hom.* p. vii, The knight, whose usurious feelings suddenly returned, proposed to the beggar to leave the grain.

†**3.** Liberal, abundant. *Obs.*⁻¹

1780 BURKE *Sp. at Bristol* Wks. III. 376, I shall..pay ample atonement and usurious amends to..humanity for my unhappy lapse.

Hence **u'suriously** *adv.*; also **u'suriousness** (*rare*⁻⁰).

1670 SIR T. CULPEPER *Necess. Abating Usury* 38 Finding ..nothing sweet but summes usuriously improved. **1727** Usuriousness [see USURIOUS *a.* 2b]. **1798** COLERIDGE in Cottle *Early Recoll.* (1837) I. 311 To make the present moment act fraudulently and usuriously towards the future time. **1808** HAN. MORE *Cœlebs* xii. I. 152 She flatters egregiously and universally, on the principle of being paid back usuriously in the same coin.

† **'usurous**, *a. Obs. rare.* [f. USURE *sb.* + -OUS.] = USURIOUS *a.*

1605 CHAPMAN, etc. *Eastw. Hoe* II. B 4, I am now loose, to get more children of perdition into my vsurous bonds. **1616** B. JONSON *Ev. Man out of Hum.* v. v. Wks. 165, I referre mee to your vsurous Cannibals, or such like. *c* **1624** CHAPMAN *Batrach.* 270, I can by no means th' usurous darner move To let me have the mantle to restore. **1738** tr. *Guazzo's Art Convers.* 53 The usurous Contracts he made with certain poor Men. **1794** W. BLAKE *Songs of Exper., Holy Thursday* i, Babes. Fed with cold and usurous hand.

† **u'surp**, *sb. Obs.*⁻¹ [f. next.] Usurpation.

a **1647** HABINGTON *Surv. Worcs.* (Worcs. Hist. Soc.) I. 540 The Normans, who overcame them with the vsurp of the Crowne.

usurp (juː'zɜːp), *v.* [ad. OF. *usurper* (14th c.), ad. L. *ūsūrpāre* (whence It. *usurpare*, Pr., Sp., Pg. *usurpar*) to seize for use, to use, employ.]

I. 1. *trans.* To appropriate wrongfully to oneself (a right, prerogative, etc.). †Also const. *against*, *upon*.

a **1325** *MS. Rawl. B.* 520 fol. 56 b, ȝif þe Eir mid wronge vsurped þe seisine of Eldere þoru deseisine. **1399** LANGL. *Rich. Redeles* III. 257 To vsurpe þe service þat to sages bilongith, To be-come conselleris er þey kunne rede. **1569** J. SANFORD tr. *Agrippa's Van. Artes* 154 b, Apicius more then all others haue vsurped yᵉ glory and fame of this arte. *a* **1578** LINDESAY (Pitscottie) *Chron. Scot.* (S.T.S.) I. 18 [He] sould have usurpat all honnour riches and authoritie. **1596** *Edward III*, I. i. 80 Tell him, the Crowne that hee vsurpes is myne. **1607** COWELL *Interpr., Quo Warranto*, is a writ that lyeth against him, which vsurpeth any Frawnchis or libertie against the king. **1656** EARL MONM. tr. *Boccalini's Pol. Touchstone* (1674) 277 That pretence of Right, which the violence of the Sword hath usurp'd upon other mens Estates. *a* **1680** BUTLER *Rem.* (1759) I. 346 They were fain to usurp the Right of his Cause, to justify their own. **1709** STRYPE *Ann. Ref.* I. xiv. 187 The people by a great consent usurped them [*sc.* favours] to themselves. **1791** COWPER *Iliad* I. 624 Him with shame The King of men hath overwhelm'd, by force Usurping his just meed. **1813** SHELLEY *Q. Mab* VI. 223 The almighty Fiend Whose name usurps thy honours. **1838** LYTTON *Leila* I. ii, My uncle usurped my birthright.

fig. and *transf.* *a* **1586** SIDNEY *Arcadia* II. vii, So ougly a darkenesse..usurped the dayes right. **1634** FORD *Perk. Warbeck* II. iii, Tis our pleasure To giue our Cosen Yorke for wife our kinswoman the ladie Katherine: Instinct of soveraigntie Designes the honor, though her peevish Father Vsurps our Resolution.

b. *esp.* To intrude forcibly, illegally, or without just cause into (some dignified or important office, position, etc.); to assume or arrogate to oneself (political power, rule, authority, etc.) by force; to claim unjustly.

1440 *Jacob's Well* 28 þo þat vsurpyn of newe tyme þe kepyng or þe amonicyoun of ony cherch in tyme of voydaunce. **1447** BOKENHAM *Seyntys* (Roxb.) 28 Andronicus..be tyranny Usurpyd the pryncehood of that plas. *a* **1513** FABYAN *Chron.* IV. xx. 49 He..vsurpyd the Rule and domynyon of the lande. **1538** TONSTALL *Serm. Palm Sund.* (1823) 5 Wherfore he [*sc.* Christ] dyd not vsurpe equalitie vnto god, but [etc.]. **1598** BARRET *Theor. Warres* IV. i. 103 To vsurpe the preheminence, which onely is due to the Camp-Master. **1651** HOBBES *Leviath.* II. xxviii. 162 The acts of power usurped,..are not acts of publique Authority. **1681** H. NEVILE *Plato Rediv.* 34 Either to usurp Tyranny over his own Country, or to lead men forth to..subdue another. **1729** T. INNES *Crit. Essay* (1879) 32 Carausius.. usurped the empire in Britain towards the end of the third century. **1751** JOHNSON *Rambler* No. 166 ⁋ 5 Eager to usurp the station to which he has no right. **1836** THIRLWALL *Greece* III. 245 Cleon..did not wish to usurp the functions of Nicias. **1844** H. H. WILSON *Brit. India* III. 280 To set aside the local government, and usurp an independent and paramount authority. **1891** *Pall Mall G.* 9 Oct. 2/1 Mr. Parnell repeated..—'You attempted to put the resolution and usurp my authority as chairman'.

fig. and *transf.* **1603** SHAKS. *Meas. for M.* III. ii. 99 To.. vsurpe the beggerie hee was neuer borne to. **1667** MILTON *P.L.* XII. 421 So he dies, But soon revives, Death over him no power Shall long usurp. **1722** WOLLASTON *Relig. Nat.* 24 The bridle will be usurped by those appetites which it is a principal part of all religion..to curb. **1781** COWPER *Conversat.* 745 The world grown old,..Usurps God's office, lays his bosom bare. **1799** SICKELMORE *Agnes & L.* II. 195 In the silent hours of retirement reflection usurped the empire of the leaden god. **1839** SIGOURNEY *Lett. to Mothers* xv, The worldly and common trains of thought, which usurp dominion over us. **1857** TOULMIN SMITH *Parish* 119 Too much inter-meddling from the Home Office has been allowed to be gradually usurped.

2. To seize or obtain possession of (territory, land, etc.) in an unjust or illegal manner; to assume unjust rule, dominion, or authority over, to appropriate wrongfully. Also const. *on*, *upon* (= against), *over*.

c **1400** MAUNDEV. (1839) 145 He..usurped the Lond, and helde it to himself, and cleped him Emperour of Trapazond. **1432–50** tr. *Higden* (Rolls) II. 103 The Danes vsurpede the realme of Estenglonde. **1483** CAXTON *Gold. Leg.* 224 b/1 By cause that he wold usurpe to hym self hys heritage. **1507** *Reg. Privy Seal Scotl.* I. 208/2 Gif ony of thaim occupiis and usurpis ony part of the kingis propir lands. **1579** FENTON *Guicciard.* 358 To reconquer to the sea Apostolike, all those places..that had bene vsurped vpon the Church. **1598** HAKLUYT *Voy.* I. 147 The cities adhearing vnto the king vsurped diuers Castles belonging to the Master, tooke certain..knightes. **1653** H. COGAN tr. *Pinto's Trav.* iv. 11 Having usurped the town of Goa upon him. **1687** A. LOVELL tr. *Thevenot's Trav.* I. 223 That Church..was usurped by the Turks, and serves them..for their chief Mosque. *a* **1721** PRIOR *Dial. Dead, Cromwell & Porter* Wks. 1907 II. 267 The three Kingdoms You Usurped. **1809** BAWDWEN *Domesday Bk.* 2 Walden usurped two houses of Ketel the priest.

fig. and *transf.* **1592** SHAKS. *Ven. & Ad.* 591 Whereat a sudden pale..Usurps her cheek. **1592** *Arden of Feversham* I. 99 Sweete Mosbie is the man that hath my hart: And he vsurpes it. **1633** G. HERBERT *Temple, Bunch of Grapes* i, One aire of thoughts usurps my brain. *a* **1700** EVELYN *Diary* 3 Aug. 1656, Blasphemous and ignorant mechanics usurping the pulpets every where. **1726** POPE *Odyssey* xx. 430 Universal night usurps the pole! **1807** J. BARLOW *Columb.* II. 210 Ere..Memphian pyramids usurp'd the skies. **1841** EMERSON *Ess., Love* ⁋ 4 The proportion which this topic of personal relations usurps in the conversation of society.

b. *transf.* To occupy or take the place of, physically; to encroach or trench upon.

1635 QUARLES *Embl.* I. ii. 10 The white-mouth'd Water now usurpes the Shore. **1687** DRYDEN *Hind & P.* III. 863 A just Reprise would only be Of what the Land usurped upon the Sea. **1764** GOLDSM. *Trav.* 290 The firm connected bulwark [= dyke of Holland] seems to grow; Spreads its long arms amidst the watery roar,..and usurps the shore. **1817** BYRON *Manfred* III. iv, Ivy usurps the laurel's place of growth. **1841** T. R. JONES *Anim. Kingd.* 730 The placenta completely usurps the place of the allantois.

c. Of feelings, passions, etc.: To take possession of, occupy, or assume predominance in (the mind, bosom, etc.).

1749 SMOLLETT *Regicide* v. viii, Distemper'd passion.. Usurped my troubled bosom. **1798** FERRIAR *Illustr. Sterne*, etc., *Genius* 282 When frenzy and imposture usurp the regard. **1824** CAMPBELL *Theodric* 490 Alarm..now usurp'd his brain. **1853** KANE *Grinnell Exp.* xviii. (1856) 138 The object which seemed to usurp the undivided attention of our party.

d. *to usurp the place of*, in fig. uses.

1573 BARET *Alv.* K k i, Concerning I consonant, which oftentimes vniustly vsurpeth the sounde and place of g. **1739** BUTLER *Serm.* Wks. 1874 II. 229 True religion takes up that place in the mind, which superstition would usurp. **1781** COWPER *Table-t.* 320 When tumult..usurp'd authority's just place. **1863** HOLLAND *Lett. Joneses* xix. 271 The love of party has always usurped the place of the love of Country. **1879** H. PHILLIPS *Notes Coins* 5 Copper began to usurp the place of other metals.

†**3.** To take or hold possession of (something belonging to another or others) by sleight or force; to appropriate by ruse or violence; to steal.

c **1412–20** LYDG. *Chron. Troy* v. 73 þat he þis relik reioisshe shulde of riȝt, Be sleiȝte wonne.., And vsurpeth, be maner of avaunt. **1484** CAXTON *Fables of Æsop* II. xviii, I beleue wel that thow hast vsurped and robbed som thynge. **1560** DAUS tr. *Sleidane's Comm.* 242 b, The reuenewes of some they haue vsurped already. **1620** BRENT tr. *Soave's Hist. Counc. Trent.* I. 100 The Ecclesiasticall goods should not be vsurped. **1643** BURROUGHES *Exp. Hosea* vii. 375 As a man that hath his goods taken away from him usurped.

fig. and *transf.* *a* **1425** tr. *Arderne's Treat. Fistula*, etc. 30 Any oþer witty man perceyuyng his werk mow vsurpe it to hymself. **1602** SHAKS. *Ham.* I. i. 46 What art thou that vsurp'st this time of night? **1605** —— *Lear* IV. ii. 28 To thee a Womans seruices are due, My Foole vsurpes my body. *a* **1637** B. JONSON *Discov.* Wks. (Rtldg.) 747/2 Their own fox-like thefts..are so rank, as a man may find whole pages together usurped from one author.

4. To make use of (something not properly belonging to one or one's estate); to use or employ wrongfully.

c **1412** HOCCLEVE *De Reg. Princ.* 440 Certes to blame ben þe lordes grete,..þat hir men lete Vsurpe swiche a lordly apparaille. *a* **1548** HALL *Chron., Hen. VI*, 114 Beside this, she vsurped a cote of arms. **1578** LYTE *Dodoens* 727 The barke of..Sorbus..is in some places wrongfully vsurped.. for the diseases of the milte. **1601** SHAKS. *All's Well* IV. iii. 119 His heeles haue deseru'd it, in vsurping his spurres so long. **1661** SPARROW *Bk. Com. Prayer* (ed. 2) A 6, Learned Jews from that time, usurp the same partition of Chapters on the Old Testament. **1713** ADDISON *Cato* IV. i, Who's this that dares usurp The Guards and Habits of Numidia's Prince? **1831** SCOTT *Ct. Rob.* iii, A portrait of Alexander, in executing which, some inferior dauber has usurped the pencil of Apelles.

fig. and *transf.* **1598** B. JONSON *Ev. Man in Hum.* (Q.) v. i. 307 Which suit..I put on, and vsurping your mans phrase and action, caried a message to Signior Thorello in your name. **1744** *Harl. Misc.* I. 66 To Prince and People, that usurp unlawful Methods to accomplish their unjust Intentions. **1781** COWPER *Table-T.* 637 [To] claim the palm for purity of song, That lewdness had usurp'd and worn so long. **1813** SHELLEY *Q. Mab.* IX. 100 The old thorn.. Usurped the royal ensign's grandeur.

b. To assume or claim (a name or title) unduly as one's own; to arrogate or take to oneself. Also simply, to assume, bear.

1549 W. THOMAS *Hist. Italie* 15 b, Theyr owne priuate capitaines enterprised many tymes not onely to rebell, but also to vsurpe the name of emperours. **1577** HOLINSHED *Chron., Hist. Eng.* I. 202/1 Euery one..sought..to usurp yᵉ title of King. **1592** SHAKS. *Ven. & Ad.* 794 Call it not love, for Love to heaven is fled, Since sweating Lust on earth usurp'd his name. **1610** HEYWOOD *Gold. Age* F 4, Let that Clime henceforth Be cal'd Arcadia, and vsurpe thy name. **1675** DRYDEN *Aurengz.* v. (1676) 81 The noble Arimant usurp'd my name. **1776** GIBBON *Decl. & F.* I. 58 The name ..of Orator was usurped by the sophists. **1781** COWPER *Retirem.* 319 He that has not usurp'd the name of man. **1883** F. POLLOCK in *Proc. Roy. Instit.* X. 381 The name of claymore (commonly usurped by the much later basket-hilted pattern).

c. To take (a word or words) into use; to borrow or appropriate from another language, source, etc.; to employ, use.

1531 ELYOT *Gov.* I. xxii, Of them two [*sc.* 'celeritie' and 'slownesse'] springeth an excellent vertue where unto we lacke a name in englisshe. Wherfore I am constrained to usurpe a latine worde, callyng it *Maturitie*. **1559** W. CUNNINGHAM *Cosmogr. Glasse* 56 [The word] stadium..is vsurped, for a place where men exercise ther horse, ronnyng a rase. **1573** DAUS tr. *Bullinger on Apoc.* (ed. 2) 254 b, And these wordes haue more grace in ours and other straunge languages, vsurped than translated. So haue remayned in the Church, Osanna, Amen [etc.]. **1601** B. JONSON *Poetaster* III. i, 'White' is there vsurpt for her brow. **1649** MILTON *Eikon.* 126 He usurps a common saying, That it is kingly to doe well and heare ill. **1690** LEYBOURN *Curs. Math.* 347 *ddd* is..there usurped for *ggc*. **1859** SIR W. HAMILTON *Lect.* (1877) I. xi. 197 The[se] Latin terms..were very rarely usurped in their present psychological meaning.

†**5.** To exercise, practise, or inflict (injury, cruelty, etc.); to put into act, impose. Occas. const. *on*, *towards*. Also *transf.* *Obs. rare.*

1456 SIR G. HAYE *Law Arms* (S.T.S.) 134 It is..honest to oppos..all injure or violence unlauchfully usurpit. **1583** STOCKER *Civ. Warres Lowe C.* III. 103 b, Usurping on them all kinde of crueltie, and warlike licence. **1625** [? SKINNER] tr. *Montanus Inquis.* 89 Certaine penalties and punishments vsurped towards offenders. *a* **1700** DRYDEN *Sigism. & Guisc.* 419 [State laws] are usurp'd on helpless Woman-kind, Made without our Consent, and wanting Pow'r to bind.

6. To supplant, oust, or turn out (a person); †to deprive (one) *of* possessions. Also *refl.* *rare.*

a **1325** *MS. Rawl. B.* 520 fol. 56 þoru þat he him vsurpede bi-þoute iugement þoru his oune propre auctorite. **1512** *Helyas* in Thoms *Prose Rom.* (1828) III. 91 The erle.. wyllynge to usurpe her of her duchy. **1601** SHAKS. *Twel. N.* I. v. 198 *Vio.* Are you the Ladie of the house? *Ol.* If I do not vsurpe my selfe, I am. **1622** MABBE tr. *Aleman's Guzman d'Alf.* I. 194 No man shall dare or presume, to vsurpe or defraud one another in this kinde. **1890** *Pall Mall G.* 9 Oct. (1891) 2/1 'How dare you, sir, attempt to usurp me in the chair?' he [*sc.* Mr. Parnell] exclaimed.

transf. **1821** SHELLEY *Hellas* 260 O miserable dawn, after a night More glorious than the day which it usurped!

II. †**7.** *intr.* To claim or make pretensions, to assume or attempt arrogantly, *to* be or do something. *Obs.*

c **1391** CHAUCER *Astrol.* Prol., I ne vsurpe nat to haue fownde this werk of my labour. **1430–40** LYDG. *Bochas* VIII. 772 This Karansynvs..Proudli vsurped to be ther gouernour. *Ibid.* IX. 125 He gadred peeple, gan wexe a werreiour, Ageyn Heraclius,..And vsurped to ride in tho cuntres. **1483** CAXTON *Gold. Leg.* 204/4 To be crucyfyed upryght I haue not usurped. **1521** in Ellis *Orig. Lett.* Ser. II. I. 282 The said Dukes fader tooke upon hym and usurped to be king ageinst his elder broder.

8. To act or play the usurper; to rule or exercise authority as a usurper. Also const. *over*, *against*. Now *rare.*

c **1425** WYNTOUN *Cron.* v. x. 2476 He..hald him of his part content, Vsurpand nocht oure his extent. **1477** NORTON *Ord. Alch.* v. in Ashm. (1652) 67 When he usurpeth above equality. *a* **1513** FABYAN *Chron.* IV. lxxiv. 51 Whenne he had reygned, or more verely vsurped, by the terme of iiii. yeres. *c* **1585** [R. BROWNE] *Answ. Cartwright* 83 If any do usurpe, as traitors, against her maiesty. **1592** KYD *Sol. & Pers.* III. iv, Your Lord vsurps in all that he possesseth. **1596** [see USURPATION 4]. **1640** HABINGTON *Edw. IV*, 224 The house of Lancaster usurping against Edward. **1653** HOLCROFT *Procopius, Vandal Wars* I. 9 Basiliscus..attempted to usurp, and prevailed... And Basiliscus usurped a year and eight months. *a* **1733** RAYMOND *Reports* (1743) 954 Though he afterwards usurp and die, and the advowson descend to his heir.

fig. **1667** MILTON *P.L.* IX. 1132 Sensual Appetite.. Usurping over sovran Reason claimd Superior sway. *Ibid.* XI. 823 All fountaines of the Deep Broke up, shall heave the Ocean to usurp Beyond all bounds. **1827** KEBLE *Chr. Year, Sexagesima Sunday* vi, Chaining to earth..Hearts that would highest else aspire, And o'er the tenderer sex usurping ever most.

9. *to usurp on* or *upon*: **a.** To practise usurpation upon, to commit illegal seizure or action against (a person or persons).

1470–85 MALORY *Arthur* I. iii. 39 Kyng Vther felle seke.., And in the meane whyle hys enemyes Vsurpped vpon hym. **1530** PALSGR. 769/2 Howe longe it is sythe he began first to usurpe upon you. **1576** *Southampton Court Leet Rec.* (1905) I. 138 His breethren doo vssurpe vppon the Comers vnto of this towne. **1640** HABINGTON *Edw. IV*, 21 Women who usurpe on their husbands. **1677** *Govt. Venice* 250 Popes.. have usurped upon Seculars in the very power of suppressing of Heretical Books. **1701** WATSON *Clergyman's Law* 85 If any other Person.. doth usurp upon the Lessee. **1760–72** H. BROOKE *Fool of Qual.* (1809) III. 36 When any of the three estates have usurped upon the others. **1889** LOWELL *Latest Lit. Ess., Walton* (1891) 77 When he speaks of himself he never seems to usurp on other people.

fig. **1603** FLORIO *Montaigne* III. x. 606 The motions of love, which I felt to vsurpe vpon me. **1608** SHAKS. *Per.* III. ii. 82 (Q. 1), Death may vsurpe on Nature many howers, and yet The fire of life kindle againe the ore-prest spirits.

b. To encroach or infringe upon (a right, privilege, etc.); to arrogate to oneself unjustly.

1493 *Acta Dom. Conc.* (1839) 287/1 Vsurping apon þe fredomez & priuilegis of þe said burghe. **1531** *Dialogues on Laws Eng.* xxvi. 58 That they vsurpe vpon the popes auctorite. **1594** O. B. *Quest. Profit. Concern.* 31*b, Such destroying fathers vsurped vpon the right. **1598** DALLINGTON *Meth. Trav.* L2b, The Noblesse of Athens hauing vsurped vpon the Democratie of that City. **1643** S. MARSHALL *Copy of Let.* 25 It is most apparent that they have not usurped upon His Majesties Prerogative. **1684** T. BURNET *Theory Earth* I. Ep. to King, Those that would usurp upon the fundamental priviledge and birth-right of mankind. **1720** GORDON & TRENCHARD *Independ. Whig* (1728) 153 It is.. the highest Sacrilege to usurp upon this great Authority. **1771** GOLDSM. *Hist. Eng.* II. 141 The commission.. had usurped upon his authority. **1822** *Monthly Mag.* LIII. 333 This would.. suffer Sweden and Prussia gradually to usurp on its Baltic ascendancy. **1868** MANNING in *Ess. Relig. & Lit.* Ser. III. (1874) 12 The Saxon and the Norman kings gradually usurped upon the freedom of the Church by customs. **1879** M. PATTISON *Milton* 123 Many matters, in which the old prelatic church had usurped upon the domain of the state.

transf. **1599** B. JONSON *Ev. Man out of Hum.* Charac. Persons, Shift, a thread-bare shark:.. He vsurps vpon cheats, quarrels, and robberies which he neuer did. **1654** G. GODDARD in *Burton's Diary* (1828) I. 83 Whensoever any advantage offers itself, the one will usurp on the other, and .. strive totally to subvert it. **1670** H. STUBBE *Plus Ultra* 137 To prevent the Virtuosi from usurping upon my discoveries and intendments. **1840** DE QUINCEY *Style* Wks. 1859 XI. 175 This tendency in political journals to usurp upon the practice of books. **1870** LOWELL *Study Wind.* 212 The unclean rites of Baal.. usurp on the worship of the one only True and Pure.

c. To seize, intrude or lay hold upon (land, property, etc.) without right or just cause; to assume authority or domination over, to become superior to.

1630 *R. Johnson's Kingd. & Commw.* 576 The Moores or Arabians,.. usurping upon the maritime coasts of the Country, have built them places and Cities. *a* **1674** CLARENDON *Surv. Leviath.* (1676) 160 When he usurp'd upon France with equal Tyranny. *a* **1700** EVELYN *Diary* 18 March 1649, The parish churches, on which the Presbyterians and fanatics had usurp'd.

fig. and *transf.* **1588** SHAKS. *Titus A.* III. i. 268 This sorrow is an enemy, And would vsurpe vpon my watry eyes. *a* **1613** BREREWOOD *Lang. & Relig.* (1614) 10 At this day, the Greek tongue is very much decayed:.. in.. the west, the natural languages of the countries have usurped upon it. **1622** WALLER *On Danger his Majesty escaped* 86 The loud winds usurping on the main. **1633** MARMION *Antiquary* I. i, Usurp then on the proffer'd means, Show yourself forward in an action. **1709** MRS. MANLEY *Secret Mem.* (1720) II. 263 Her killing Eyes now seem'd to lay aside their Darts: Languishments usurp'd upon the Fire. *a* **1859** DE QUINCEY *Posth. Wks.* (1893) II. 42 The heart of stone had usurped upon the heart of flesh.

d. To encroach upon physically. (Cf. 2 b.)

1658 CLEVELAND *Rustick Rampant* (1687) 447 The honest Husbandmen.. repairs the Banks, but does not usurp upon the Stream.

†**10.** To take possession *of* a thing by usurpation; to become participator *of*. *Obs.*

a **1513** FABYAN *Chron.* VII. (1811) 429 He had vsurpyd of the comon grounde of yͤ cytie, in settynge of the said towre. **1609** BIBLE (Douay) *Joshua* vii. 1 The children of Israel transgressed the commandment, and usurped of the anathema.

†**u'surpant**, *a. Obs. rare.* [a. L. *ūsūrpānt-*, pple. stem of *ūsūrpāre*: see USURP *v.*] That usurps; guilty of or inclined to usurpation.

1461 in Halliwell *Lett. Kings Eng.* (1846) I. 126 Harry late usurpant king of our said realm. **1473** *Rolls of Parlt.* VI. 92/2 For takyng of Henry late usurpaunt uppon our magistee Roiall. **1659** GAUDEN *Tears Ch.* 473 Some factious.. Presbyters ventured to be extravagant and usurpant.

†**usurpate**, *v. Obs.*⁻¹ [ad. L. *ūsūrpāt-*, pa. pple. stem of *ūsūrpāre.*] *trans.* = USURP *v.* 1 b.

1542 in Halliwell *Lett. Kings Eng.* (1846) I. 382 The princes of Christendom, whose powers he euer practiseth to usurpate.

†**usurpate**, *a. Obs.* [ad. L. *ūsūrpāt-us*: see prec.] Characterized by, based upon, usurpation or unwarranted encroachment.

1560 ABP. PARKER in J. Ware *Hunt. Romish Fox* (1683) 116 By our Reformation, and denying of unlawful Demands, which be proud and usurpal [*sic*] of the Bishops of Rome. **1598** W. WATSON in *Archpriest Controv.* (Camden) I. 96 Their malice.. towards priests is in nothing more plaine, then managing oute yͭ vsurpate archpriest. **1600** —— *Decacordon* (1602) 15 The vsurpate pretend of Iesuiticall esteeme. *Ibid.* 32, 168, 360. **1612** T. JAMES *Jesuits' Downef.* 44 The most egregious, tyrannicall, vsurpate, intrusiue auctoritie of the Iesuits.

Hence †**usurpately** *adv. Obs.*⁻¹

1536–7 *Ir. Act 28 Hen. VIII*, c. 12 (1621) 113 The said Proctors.. doe.. vsurpitly take vpon themselues to be parcell of the body. **1537** *Orig. & Sprynge of Sectes* I The Byshop of Rome (that vsurpatly called hymselfe Pope).

usurpation (juːzɜːˈpeɪʃən). [a. OF. and AF. *usurpacion* (F. *usurpation*), ad. L. *ūsūrpātiōn-*, *ūsūrpātio*, n. of action f. *ūsūrpāre*: see USURP *v.* Cf. It. *usurpazione*, Sp. *usurpacion*, Pr. *-cioun*, Pg. *usurpação*.]

I. 1. Claim or assertion that is unwarranted or unauthorized; unjustified assumption, arrogation, or pretension.

1387–8 T. USK *Test. Love* I. ix. (Skeat) l. 117 Their name of godliheed, they [*sc.* devils] han by usurpacion, as the prophete sayth [etc.]. **1426** LYDG. *De Guil. Pilgr.* 17716 Fyrst, ageynes al resoun, I wolde, by vsurpacioun, Fro poynt to poynt in ech degre, The zodyak sholde obeye me. **1622** MALYNES *Anc. Law-Merch.* 4 The Customes of Merchants concerning trafficke,.. when they are not truely obserued in some places, by some errour or misprision,.. loose their names, and are called Vsurpation. **1650** BULWER *Anthropomet.* 203 She might the better conceal her usurpation and counterfeit manhood. **1727** DE FOE *Syst. Magic* I. i. (1840) 20 As he usurped divine honours, so he made a figure suitable to his usurpation. *a* **1854** H. REED *Lect. Brit. Poets* i. (1857) 18 The sovereignty of even Homer or Shakspeare could hold no exclusive usurpation.

2. The action of usurping, illegally seizing, or wrongfully occupying some place or property belonging to a person or persons; unlawful encroachment upon or intrusion into the office, right, etc., of another or others; unjust or illegal possession. Also *personif.*

c **1420** LYDG. *Assembly of Gods* 661 Vsurpacion, with Horryble Vengeaunce, Came alther last of that company. **1480** *Acta Dom. Conc.* (1839) 74/2 þe vsurpacion and purprisioun done in þe takin vp of þe malis of þe samyn landis. **1573** *Extr. Aberd. Reg.* (1848) II. 10 The usurpatioune of the preuilegeis of the burght. **1597** HOOKER *Eccl. Pol.* v. lxii. §22 Considering that the worke of externall ministerie in Baptisme is only a preeminence of honor, which they that take to themselues.. doe,.. by meanes of such vsurpation, incurre the iust blame of disobedience to the Law of God. **1654** BRAMHALL *Just Vind.* i. (1661) 2 Whatsoeuer the Popes of Rome gained upon us.. was meer tyranny and usurpation. **1692** DRYDEN *Disc. Satire* Ess. (ed. Ker) II. 88 The usurpation of that prince upon their freedom. **1766** J. Z. HOLWELL *Orig. Princ. Anc. Bramins* II. iv, [Men] do, by the force of their tyrannic usurpation, labor to make their [*sc.* the animals'] state more miserable. **1784** COWPER *Task* v. 760 Ye will not find.. A liberty like his, who, unimpeach'd Of usurpation, and to no man's wrong, Appropriates nature as his father's work. **1817** JAS. MILL *Brit. India* II. IV. v. 199 The servants of the Company were now vested with a right to that plentiful source of gain, in which they had hitherto participated only by usurpation. **1819** SCOTT *Ivanhoe* xliv, I will appeal to Rome against thee .. for usurpation on the immunities and privileges of our Order. **1837** HT. MARTINEAU *Soc. Amer.* II. 80 The United States having furnished the means by which the usurpation of Texas has been achieved.

fig. and *transf.* **1655** in *Verney Mem.* (1907) II. 24 There is a soveranity in honour which noe usurpation can depose. **1900** 'J. DOE' *Bridge Man.* 18 If the usurpation of your right to double make no difference to the original lead.

b. *esp.* The unlawful or forcible seizure or occupation of a throne, sovereign power, etc.; wrongful assumption of supreme authority.

1470 *Rolls of Parlt.* V. 456/2 Edward.., late by usurpacion Kyng of England. **1485** *Ibid.* VI. 276/1 Callinge and nameinge hymself, by usurpacion, King Richard the IIIᵈ. **1578** T. N. tr. *Conq. W. India* 77 Those Princes began their usurpation by way and colour of Religion. **1595** SHAKS. *John* II. i. 9 To rebuke the vsurpation Of thy vnnaturall Vncle, English Iohn. **1610** HOLLAND *Camden's Brit.* I. 725 The violent usurpation of Henry the Fourth. **1683** *Brit. Spec.* 64 This Power he got by Usurpation, and not by any Election of.. the People. **1729** T. INNES *Crit. Essay* (1879) 402 This leaves no room for his expedition.., either before or after his usurpation. **1776** GIBBON *Decl. & F.* xii. I. 330 Florianus shewed himself unworthy to reign, by the hasty usurpation of the purple, without expecting the approbation of the senate. **1791** BURKE *Corr.* (1844) III. 282 The assembly cannot annihilate the constitutional states. It is itself an usurpation, and its acts are void. **1844** H. H. WILSON *Brit. India* III. 189 He also calculated upon.. the co-operation of a strong party inimical to the usurpation. **1856** *N. Brit. Rev.* XXVI. 289 This government of generals, successively ruling.. by forcible usurpation. **1877** FROUDE *Short Stud.* (1883) IV. I. ii. 19 The usurpation of Stephen had left behind it a legacy of disorder.

c. With *a* and pl.: An act of usurping another's rights, privileges, etc.; an instance of encroachment *on* or *upon* (liberty, etc.).

16.. ROWLEY *Birth Merl.* IV. iii. 14 *Vort.* The Saxons which thou broughtst To back thy usurpations, are grown great. **1638** R. BAKER tr. *Balzac's Lett.* (vol. II) 3 This so tyrannical an usurpation upon the liberty of mens spirits. **1679** C. NESSE *Antichrist* 213 The corruptions and usurpations of Antichrist. **1721** BOLINGBROKE in *Swift's Lett.* (1766) II. 41 Exercising an insolent and cruel usurpation over their brethren. **1757** in *10th Rep. Hist. MSS. Comm.* App. I. 217 What he called Our Usurpations in America. **1771** GOLDSM. *Hist. Eng.* III. 250 The depression of the nobility as a necessary consequence of the popular usurpations on the crown. **1823** *Tonstall's Serm. Palm Sund.* Pref. 2 The bondage of a baneful and preposterous usurpation on the liberties of mankind. **1863** H. COX *Instit.* I. vii. 82 Usurpations of unconstitutional powers by the House of Commons.

d. *transf.* Physical encroachment on sea or land. *rare.*

1553 BRENDE *Q. Curtius* 41 b, The Tyrians deuined that Neptune reuenging the vsurpacion that the Macedons had made vpon the sea, would shortely destroy the worcke. **1597** SHAKS. *Hen. IV*, I. i. 63 So lookes the Strond, when the Imperious Flood Hath left a witnest Vsurpation.

3. *Eccl. Law.* The action on the part of a stranger of dispossessing a lawful patron of the right of presenting a cleric to a benefice.

1596 BACON *Max. Com. Law* (1630) 2 So if I be seised of an advouson in gross, and an vsurpation bee had against mee, and at the next avoidance I vsurpe arere, I shall be remitted. **1628** COKE *On Litt.* 277 b, When an estranger that no right hath presenteth to a Church, and his Clarke is admitted and instituted, hee is said to bee an vsurper, and the wrongfull act.. is called an Usurpation. **1701** W. WATSON *Clergyman's Law* 89 By Usurpation the rightful Patron may be divested of the possession of his Advowson. *a* **1733** RAYMOND *Reports* (1743) 953 If a purchaser of an advowson in fee-simple, before any presentment, suffer an usurpation. **1768** BLACKSTONE *Comm.* III. 242 Another species of injury, called usurpation; which is an absolute ouster or dispossession of the patron. **1877** F. G. LEE *Gloss. Liturg. & Eccl. Terms* 432 No usurpation can displace the estate or interest of any patron, nor turn it to a mere right.

†**4.** Usurpatory rule or power. *Obs. rare.*

1654 tr. *Scudery's Curia Pol.* 125 To re-conquer Amuraths Usurpation, and attain to the King my Fathers Throne. **1667** MILTON *P.L.* II. 983 If I that Region lost, All usurpation thence expell'd, reduce To her original darkness and your sway. **1761** HUME *Hist. Eng.* II. xxiii. 67 The duke .. attempted to overthrow that usurpation which he himself had so zealously contributed to establish.

b. ***the usurpation***, the period of the Commonwealth (COMMONWEALTH 4).

[**1664** G. FELL in *Extr. St. Papers Friends* Ser. III. (1912) 227 Seduced into that Phanatique opinion of the Quakers in the late time of Vsurpation.] **1682** in *Scottish Antiq.* July (1901) 4 The tyme of the late rebellione and wsurpatione. **1727** SWIFT *Lett. Eng. Tongue* Wks. 1755 II. I. 187 During the usurpation, such an infusion of enthusiastic jargon prevailed in every writing, as [etc.]. **1782** PENNANT *Journ. Chester to Lond.* 235 On the usurpation, he had the meanness to sit in Cromwell's mock parlement. **1829** SCOTT *Hrt. Midl.* Note R, He afterwards advanced £20,000 for the service of King Charles, during the usurpation.

†**5.** *Roman Law.* Interruption of usucapion.

1676 R. DIXON *Two Testaments* 551 A wife: not a Concubine, might be taken by use; for a whole uninterrupted year without usurpation.

II. 6. The action of taking into use or making use of a thing; acceptance or agreement in the use of anything; usage, employment.

1583 FULKE *Def. Tr. Script.* 160 Which worde [*sc.* priests] is taken vp by common vsurpation, to signifie sacrificers. **1589** PUTTENHAM *Eng. Poesie* III. xix. (Arb.) 250 By common vsurpation, nothing is wiser then the Serpent, more couragious then the Lion, more bewtifull then the Angell. **1611** GUILLIM *Heraldry* VI. v. 269 No man had his Badge set on a Wreath vnder the degree of a Knight: But.. time and vsurpation concurring with prescription, hath so much preuailed, as that [etc.]. **1659** PEARSON *Creed* 252 There can be no kind of certainty in any such observations of the Articles, because the Greeks promiscuously often use them, or omit them, without any reason of their usurpation or omission.

†**b.** A special use of a word or expression. *Obs.*

1644 BULWER *Chirol.* To Rdr. A 6 b, Humane literature, wherein.. I shall lay claime to all metaphors, proverbiall translations or usurpations.

Hence **usur'pationist**, one who advocates usurpation. Also *attrib.*

1899 R. WALLACE *G. Buchanan* iii. 58 A principle.. subversive of the despotic doctrine of the Divine right of Kings, so prevalent in usurpationist quarters in that day.

usurpative (juːˈzɜːpətɪv), *a.* [ad. late L. *ūsūrpātīv-us*, f. L. *ūsūrpāre*: see USURP *v.*] Of the nature of, marked or characterized by, usurpation; arbitrary.

1797 J. PINKERTON *Hist. Scot.* I. 10 Pretensions, which now strike as vague or usurpative. **1811** *Monthly Rev.* LXVI. 470 Laurence was of a less usurpative and more tolerant disposition. **1827** G. S. FABER *Sacr. Calend. Prophecy* (1844) II. 64 A clear usurpative invasion of the.. co-equal independence of all the other Patriarchs. **1879** TOURGEE *Fool's Err.* xx. 115 The foolish usurpative acts of the President. **1908** *Amer. Naturalist* XLII. 16 The usurpative control of their nutrition by the fungus suggests [etc.].

Hence **u'surpatively** *adv. rare*⁻¹.

1838 G. S. FABER *Inquiry* 334 Let him not dare usurpatively to administer any divine sacrament, until [etc.].

†**usurpator.** *Obs.* Also 6 -our. [ad. OF. (F.) *usurpateur* (14th c.), or a. late L. *ūsurpātor*, agent-n. f. L. *ūsurp-āre*: see USURP *v.* Cf. It. *usurpatore*, Pr., Sp., Pg. *usurpador*.] A usurper.

1529 RASTELL *Pastyme* (1811) 63 Tirantis and usurpatours of the empyre. **1549** *Compl. Scot.* ix. 79 The inglismen var violent vsurpatours of al scotland. **1654** HOWELL *Parthenop.* II. 37 Under the Iron yoak of Usurpators.

usurpatory (juːˈzɜːpətərɪ), *a.* [ad. late L. *ūsurpātōri-us*, f. *ūsurpātor* USURPATOR. Cf. F. *usurpatoire*.] Marked or characterized by usurpation; usurping.

1847 WEBSTER. **1864** *Daily Tel.* 16 July, To let it [= an assembly] alone while harmless, to prorogue it when mischievous, and to bring it to book when usurpatory. **1906** *Times* 26 Dec. 7/3 A usurpatory claim that can no longer be admitted.

†**usurpatrix.** *rare*⁻⁰. [a. late L. *ūsurpātrix*, fem. of *ūsurpātor* USURPATOR.] = USURPRESS.

1611 COTGR., *Vsurpatrice*, an usurpatrix.

usurpature (ˌjuːzɜːˈpeɪtjʊə(r)). *poet.* [f. L. *ūsurpāt-*, ppl. stem of *ūsurpāre* to usurp, + -URE.] Usurpation. Also *transf.*

The stressing (*u'surpature*) given in various Dicts. from 1884 is not borne out by the quots.

1845 BROWNING *Flight of Duchess* xiv, Her step kept pace with mine nor faltered, As if age had foregone its usurpature. **1860** LD. LYTTON *Lucile* II. iv. §7. 65 Something superior;..from my innermost nature Not wholly expell'd by the world's usurpature. **1869** BROWNING *Ring & Bk.* XII. 5 Up and up roared and soared A rocket, till the key o' the vault was reached, And wide heaven held..In brilliant usurpature.

u'surped, *ppl. a.* [f. USURP *v.* + -ED¹.]

1. Seized, obtained, held, etc., by usurpation or force; possessed unjustly or illegally; arrogated wrongfully.

c **1375** *Sc. Leg. Saints* xxi. (*Eugenia*) 135 Sen vsurpyt pouste has mad me ȝoure lady be. *c* **1430** LYDG. *Min. Poems* (Percy Soc.) 158 No vengable herte shal..Extort power nor fals usurpyd myhte. **1477** *Rolls of Parlt.* VI. 191/1 A pretensed Parlement..by usurped auctorite summoned..by your Rebell and Enemye. **1504** ATKYNSON tr. *De Imitatione* I. xxiv. 175 Than shalbe more allowable a constant pacience than all vsurped power. *a* **1548** HALL *Chron., Hen. V*, 34 b, Gregory..did put doune hymself of his owne propre mocion from his foolishe usurped name and Popishe dignitee. **1569** T. KNELL *Epit. Boner* A iiij, *Sus* taught *Mineruam* there to long, Which held vsurped place. **1590** SPENSER *F.Q.* III. iii. 47 That from the Danishe Tyrants head shall rend Th' vsurped crowne. **1629** MILTON *Hymn Nativity* xviii, Th' old Dragon under ground..Not half so far casts his usurped sway. **1672** SOUTH *Serm.* (1717) V. 294 A Nation under an usurped Government. **1746** LD. HARDWICKE in Harris *Life* (1847) II. 305 This usurped power was audaciously made use of. **1759** STERNE *Tr. Shandy* I. xviii, The many other usurped rights which..the constitution was hourly establishing. **1831** JAMES *Phil. Augustus* I. xi, The resistance he meditated to the usurped authority of the pope. **1861** PALEY *Aeschylus, Agam.* (ed. 2) 1447 *note*, That the..usurped female authority over them, is intolerable to bear.

fig. **1781** COWPER *Conversat.* 462 Yet fashion, leader of a chatt'ring train,..Holds an usurp'd dominion o'er his tongue.

b. Marked or characterized by usurpation.

1430-40 LYDG. *Bochas* I. 2990 In ther fals vsurped tirannye To holde peeplis in long subieccioun. **1461** *Rolls of Parlt.* V. 467/2 The usurped reigne of the same Henry. **1464** *Ibid.* 511/2 The same Humfrey..traiterously adhered unto the seid Henry.., and..in his fals and usurped quarell,..toke hoole and full parte. **1597** HOOKER *Eccl. Pol.* v. lxii. §13 His vsurped actions haue in him the same nature. **1771** GOLDSM. *Hist. Eng.* I. 216 Henry was now resolved..to dispute..Stephen's usurped pretensions. *c* **1850** *Fullarton's Gaz. Scotl.* I. 135/1 During the usurped and military possession of Scotland by Edward I of England.

†**2.** Of persons: Holding office, exercising authority, by virtue of usurpation. *Obs.*

1569 L. AVALE (*title*), A Commemoration or Dirige of Bastarde Edmonde Boner,..vsurped Bisshoppe of London. **1790** BURKE *Fr. Rev.* 84 Another revolution, to get rid of this illegitimate and usurped government.

†**3.** Used or employed without due justification or warrant; appropriated, borrowed. *Obs. rare.*

a **1548** HALL *Chron., Hen. V*, 34 b, Gregory the .xij...did put doune hymself..from his foolishe usurped name. **1611** SHAKS. *Twel. N.* v. i. 257 *Vio[la]*. This my masculine vsurp'd attyre. **1673** J. FALDO *Quakerism* Title-p., A Key, for the understanding their sense of their many usurped and unintelligible words and phrases.

†**b.** False, counterfeit. *Obs. rare*⁻¹.

1604 SHAKS. *Oth.* I. iii. 346 Come, be a man:..follow thou the Warres, defeate thy fauour, with an vsurp'd Beard.

Hence **u'surpedly** *adv.*

1545 BRINKLOW *Compl.* 47 b, His accustomyd pollagys, which vsurpedly he had out of this reame. **1556** J. HEYWOOD *Spider & Fly* lxv. Ee ij, This spider hath vsurpedlie growne To potentate state. **1647** LILBURNE & OVERTON *Out-cryes Oppr. Commons* I The Lords..now sitting at Westminster, who have usurpedly..assumed..a power in criminall causes.

usurper (juːˈzɜːpə(r)), *sb.* Also 5 usurpur, 6 *Sc.* -ar. [a. OF. *usurpeur* (1321), or f. USURP *v.* + -ER¹. Cf. USURPOR, and Pr. *usurpaire.*]

1. One who usurps a crown or throne; one who seizes or arrogates supreme power or authority without right or just cause.

In frequent use from *c* 1700.

1414 EARL OF CAMBRIDGE in Ellis *Orig. Lett.* Ser. II. I. 45 Harry of Lancastre usurpur of Yngland. **1477** *Rolls of Parlt.* VI. 193/2 His enemies mortall, the usurpers, laboryng..to exclude hym..from the Regalie. **1520** *Caxton's Chron. Eng.* v. 62 b/1 He..slewe Leo the vsurper of his realme. **1574** *Homilies* II. *Rebellion* VI. 609 That forraigne false vsurper the Bishop of Rome. **1587** *Mirr. Mag., Porrex* x, Vsurpers may perswade themselues a while There is no God, no lawes of sacred crowne. **1627** P. FLETCHER *Locusts* I. xxi, They crowne Usurpers with a wreath of lead. **1663** SOUTH *Serm.* (1717) V. 95 They sounded the first Trumpet to Rebellion, ..courting and recognizing an Usurper [*sc.* Cromwell]. **1727** DE FOE *Syst. Magic* I. iii. (1840) 68 If the Devil, the ancient usurper of his throne, had not been at work again to step up in his room. **1790** BURKE *Fr. Rev.* 32 But King James was a bad king with a good title, and not an usurper. **1831** JAMES *Phil. Augustus* II. ii, The barons of England adhered to an usurper..rather than to their legitimate prince. **1869** J. BALDWIN BROWN *Misread Passages* ix. 124 Who would recognise an usurper because he occupies the palace and assumes the signet of the rightful king? **1882** J. RHYS *Celtic Britain* v. 189 Macbeth was not a mere usurper.

attrib. and *Comb.* **1670** DRYDEN *1st Pt. Conq. Granada* III. i, Too well I know her blandishments to gain, Usurper-like, till settled in her reign. **1877** W. R. COOPER *Egypt. Obelisks* xii. 66 The power of the half usurper king of Egypt.

b. One who illegally or unjustly seizes, appropriates, or intrudes into any office, property, rights, etc. Also const. *upon.*

c **1425** LYDG. *Assembly of Gods* 682 There were bosters, braggars, & brybores,..Wrong vsurpers, with great extorcioners. **1567** *Reg. Privy Council Scot.* I. 547 Gif he [*sc.* a discharged custom-house officer] forder intromettis, he salbe repute ane usurpar to our Soverane Lordis authoritie. **1599** T. STORER *Life & D. Wolsey* D 4, Victorious Iosuah that in armes subdued Prophane vsurpers of their hallowed things, And smote their leaders. **1628** [see USURPATION 3]. **1697** DRYDEN *Virg., Past.* VIII. 62 In Desarts thou wert bred; And at the Dugs of Salvage Tygers fed: Alien of Birth, Usurper of the Plains. **1713** GIBSON *Codex* 782/2 If the Incumbency be by Usurpation, and the Usurper and Ordinary Confirm the Parson's Lease. **1769** ROBERTSON *Chas. V*, x. Wks. 1813 III. 214 Compelled..to submit to the jurisdiction of magistrates whom they detested as usurpers. **1771** GOLDSM. *Hist. Eng.* III. 19 They represented him as.. an unjust usurper upon the privileges of the council. **1818** COBBETT *Pol. Reg.* XXXIII. 237 The tyrant usurpers of our rights. **1840** HOOD *Up Rhine* 47 'The end was, I got my bed.' 'And what excuse..did the usurper offer for his intrusion?'

c. *fig.* and *transf.*

a **1628** F. GREVIL *Cælica* xcvi. (1633) 244 Pleasure is chosen as a Goddesse fit, The wealth of Nature freely to impart;..Which faire Vsurper runnes a Rebel's way. **1632** LITHGOW *Trav.* v. 186 The vsurpers of Gods word.. maintaine..that famous Kingdome, being but one thousand and fifty Turkes in all. **1847** EMERSON *Repr. Men, Napoleon* ¶4 [He] becomes..actually a monopolizer and usurper of other minds. **1898** TALMAGE *Serm.* in *Chrn. Herald* (N.Y.) 12 Jan. 24/3 That man has made that which might be a healthful recreation an usurper of his affections. **1900** 'J. DOE' *Bridge Man.* 9 If a player deals out of turn he may be stopped.., but if he completes his deal, the deal holds good, and the usurpers make the declaration.

†**2.** A conqueror or vanquisher *of* something.

1509 *Parl. Devylles* lxiv, I [*sc.* Christ] am lorde and kynge of blysse, Usurper of dethe, myghty in fyght.

Hence **u'surpership.** *rare*⁻¹.

1781 BP. WATSON in Farquhar *Bps. of Dunkeld* (1915) iii. 18 As if the Lord's Day had been equally the institution of his [George III's] present usurpership.

†**u'surper**, *v.* *Obs.*⁻¹ [f. prec.] *intr.* (with *it*). To play the usurper.

1656 S. H. *Gold. Law* 57 He invades, and evades Law, and ..yet neither Usurpers nor Arbytraters it.

u'surping, *vbl. sb.* [f. USURP *v.* + -ING¹.] The action of the verb; usurpation; an instance of this. Also in fig. context.

1521 LD. DACRE in Ellis *Orig. Lett.* Ser. II. I. 282 The Dukes fader..in the tyme of his usurping made diverse knightes. **1550** CROWLEY *Inform. & Petit.* 1 The vsurpyng of tenthes to priuate commoditie. **1595** SHAKS. *John* II. i. 119 Excuse it is to beat vsurping downe. **1649** LOVELACE *Lucasta* Poems (1904) 37 Dropping December shall come weeping in, Bewayle th' usurping of his Raigne. **1656** EARL MONM. tr. *Boccalini's Advts. fr. Parnass.* I. lxxi. (1674) 89 The injurious usurping the Countries liberty. *a* **1667** JER. TAYLOR *Pol. Disc.* (1674) b 4, To secure the inclosures of the Clerical orders from the usurpings and invasions of.. unhallowed spirits.

u'surping, *ppl. a.* [f. as prec. + -ING².]

1. That usurps, in various senses. Also in fig. context.

1574 *Homilies* II. *Rebellion* VI. 611 [To] blesse the cursynges of suche wicked vsurpyng bishops and tyrantes. **1586** MARLOWE *1st Pt. Tamburl.* IV. iii, That such a base vsurping vagabond Should..weare a princely crowne. **1596** *Edward III*, III. iii. 35 The vsurping King of Fraunce. *a* **1642** GODOLPHIN in *Caroline Poets* II. (1906) 247 Hear an usurping soule doth dwell. **1659** *Nicholas Papers* (Camden) IV. 164 'Tis a reasonable..demaunde, specially as to new and vsurpinge lords. **1707** NORRIS *Treat. Humility* vii. 313 God is jealous of his glory;..he makes war against the proud man, as an usurping invader of it. **1715** POPE *Iliad* II. 242 That worst of tyrants, an usurping crowd. **1818** BYRON *Ch. Har.* IV. cliii, I have..survey'd Its [*sc.* St. Sophia's] sanctuary the while the usurping Moslem pray'd. **1833** J. H. NEWMAN *Arians* II. i. 160 To expel an usurping idol from the house of God. **1901** GLOVER *Life & Lett. in 4th Cent.* Introd. 9 Usurping and suspicious Emperors.

b. *transf.* Of things.

1588 SHAKS. *L.L.L.* IV. iii. 259 It mournes, that painting vsurping [= false] haire Should rauish doters with a false aspect. **1590** —— *Com. Err.* II. ii. 180 If ought possesse thee from me, it is drosse, Vsurping Iuie, Brier, or idle Mosse. **1634** MILTON *Comus* 337 If your influence be quite damm'd up With black usurping mists. *a* **1661** FULLER *Worthies* III. (1662) 226 It follows not that the Usurping Tulip is better then the Rose.

c. *fig.* Of emotions, qualities, etc.

1633 G. HERBERT *Temple, Love* II. iii, Thou shalt recover all thy gods in kinde, Who wert disseized by usurping lust. **1659** W. CHAMBERLAYNE *Pharon.* I. III. 319 By that flood To wash usurping grief from off that part Where most she reigned. **1698** W. CHILCOT *Evil Thoughts* vi. 165 There are none more apt to grow usurping and ungovernable..than these [thoughts]. **1747** JOHNSON *Winter* ii, The ling'ring hours prolong the night, Usurping Darkness shares the day.

2. Characterized by usurpation.

1809 WORDSW. '*O'er the wide earth*' 8 In these usurping times of fear and pain.

Hence **u'surpingly** *adv.*

1589 *Hay any Work* 25 Many other causes, which you bishops..do usurpingly take from the ciuill magistrate. **1621** T. WILLIAMSON tr. *Goulart's Wise Vieillard* 76 Either for that their children misgouerne themselues, or their wiues behaue themselues vsurpingly. **1661** *Sir H. Vane's Politicks* 3 It skills not much whether lineally descended, or usurpingly advanced. **1827** POE *Tamerlane* 32 The fever'd diadem on my brow I claim'd and won usurpingly.

†**u'surpious**, *a.* *Obs.*⁻¹ [See USURP *v.* and -IOUS.] Exercising or practising usurpation.

1606 WARNER *Albion's Eng.* xv. xcvii. 387 From Rome vsurpious, bloodie, proud, hereticall then seuer Ye Creatures of Hers.

†**u'surpment.** *Obs. rare.* [f. USURP *v.* + -MENT.] Usurpation. Also *attrib.*

a **1470** HARDING *Chron.* ccx. *heading*, The kynge sayde at hys deathe..nought of repentaunce of [his] vsurpement of the realme. **1660** *Extr. St. Papers Friends* Ser. II. (1911) 123 Ashfeild..took no oath or covenant under the late usurpment powers.

†**u'surpor.** *Obs. rare.* Also 5-6 -our. [a. AF. *usurpor*: see USURP *v.* and -OR 2.] = USURPER.

1474 *Rolls of Parlt.* VI. 119/2 Harry the sext late usurpour. **1563** *Mirr. Mag., Hastings* xciii, The vsurpour Boare, that hellyshe freak. **1586** FERNE *Blaz. Gentrie* 303 If the Vsurpor haue enemies that compasse his death.

†**u'surpously**, *adv.* *Obs.*⁻¹ [f. USURP *v.*: see -OUS and -LY².] By usurpation; usurpingly.

1461 *Rolls of Parlt.* V. 463/2 Takyng upon hym usurpously the coroune and name of kyng.

usurpress (juːˈzɜːprɪs). [f. USURPER + -ESS¹.] A female usurper.

1640 HOWELL *Dodona's Gr.* 26 She is a double Vsurpresse, in detaining not only Elaiana from her right, but [etc.]. *c* **1650** *Don Bellianis* 210 Faint not, Usurpress of anothers heart, but animate yourself. **1658** CLEVELAND *Rustic Rampant* 122 She had seized the Kingdome as an Usurpresse by Tyrannie. **1805** *Pennant's London* 245 An innocent usurpress [*sc.* Lady Jane Gray] succeeded to her apartments in 1553. **1873** DIXON *Two Queens* I. viii. I. 56 The Austrians..detested Isabel as a usurpress.

usury (ˈjuːzjʊərɪ), *sb.* Forms: α. 4-6 vsurye, 5-6 usurye, 7 -ie, 5-7 vsury, -ie, 6 -ee, 5- usury. β. 4-5 vsery(e, 4, 6 vserie, 6-7 usery. [a. AF. **usurie*, ad. med.L. *ūsūria*, f. L. *ūs-us*, pa. pple. of *ūtī* to use. Cf. USURE *sb.*]

1. The fact or practice of lending money at interest; esp. in later use, the practice of charging, taking, or contracting to receive, excessive or illegal rates of interest for money on loan.

1303 R. BRUNNE *Handl. Synne* 2417 To whom þat vsery ys lefe, Gostely he ys a þefe. **1377** LANGL. *P. Pl.* B. II. 175 Lat sadel hem with siluer owre synne to suffre, As auoutrie.. and derne vsurye. *c* **1445** PECOCK *Donet* 68 Siþen in vseri þe leener..compelliþ þe borewer to..paie a summe of his owne good bisidis þe summe borewid. **1487** *Act 3 Hen. VI*, c. 6 That all unlefull Chevysaunces and Usurye be dampned, and none to be used, upon payne [etc.]. **1514** BARCLAY *Cyt. & Uplondyshman* (Percy Soc.) 23 Some lyve by rapyne,.. and some in usury. **1595** MOSSE (*title*), Arraignment and Conviction of Vsurie. That is, the Iniquitie, and Vnlawfulnes of Vsurie, displayed in sixe Sermons. **1643** MILTON *Divorce* 33 The Christian Magistrate permits usury. **1663** in *Verney Mem.* (1907) II. 195, I hate this rack-renting; 'tis worse than usury. **1711** STEELE *Spect.* No. 114 ¶1 His Estate is dipped, and is eating out with Usury. **1754** ERSKINE *Princ. Sc. Law* (1809) 520 The crime of usury, before the Reformation, consisted in the taking of *any* interest for the use of money; and now in taking an higher rate of interest than is authorised by law. **1787** BENTHAM *Def. Usury* ii. 7, I know of but two definitions that can possibly be given of usury: one is, the taking of a greater interest than the law allows of... The other is the taking of a greater interest than it is usual for men to give and take. **1801** *Farmer's Mag.* Aug. 338 The criminality of usury ..[consists] in exacting more than the usual rate of the market. **1858** LD. ST. LEONARDS *Handy-bk. Prop. Law* xiv. 87 The statutes against usury..are repealed, so that you may take for your money whatever amount of interest you can get.

Personif. *c* **1420** LYDG. *Assembly of Gods* 644 Pety capteyns .., As..Vsury, Periury, Ly, and Adulacion. *c* **1430** —— *Min. Poems* (Percy Soc.) 172 Usurye lyethe fetrede in dystresse. **1606** DEKKER *Sev. Sins* II. (Arb.) 22 Thou doest likewise Lye with Vsury. **1615** BRATHWAIT *Strappado* (1878) 28 O vsurie.., how much haue we Occasion to proscribe thee from our land.

attrib. **1813** (*title*), A Treatise on the Usury Laws with Disquisitions on the Arguments adduced against them by Bentham.

2. Premium or interest on money (or goods) given or received on loan; †gain made by lending money. Now *arch.*

c **1440** *Alph. Tales* 472 Þer was ane vsurar þat wolde neuer restore his vsurie agayn. **1555** EDEN *Decades* (Arb.) 365 With increase of dowble vsurie. **1567** *Termes Laws* (1579) 184/1 *Vsurie* is a gayne of any thing aboue the principal, or that which was lent, exacted onely in consideration of the loane, whether it be of corne, meat,..or such like, as money. **1600** HOLLAND *Livy* 262 Albeit the Vsurie was well eased by bringing it downe from twelve to one. **1621** CULPEPPER *Tract agst. Usury* 8 For Vsury going at ten in the hundred, if a man borrow fiue pounds [etc.]. **1690** CHILD *Disc. Trade* 209 The rate of Usury is the measure by which all men Trade,..or any other ways bargain. **1729** FRANKLIN *Ess.* Wks. 1840 II. 273 This may bring down the common usury to the pitch it is determined at by law. **1746** P. FRANCIS tr. *Horace, Sat.* I. ii. 14 *note*, The Laws allowed an Usury.. which doubled the capital Sum in an hundred Months.

b. *fig.* and in fig. context. Freq. ***with usury.***

1549 COVERDALE, etc. *Erasm. Par. 1 Pet.* 2 That you may waxe riche in the encreasing vsury of good workes, more and more. **1590** SPENSER *F.Q.* I. viii. 27 Behold what ye this day haue done for mee, And what I cannot quite, requite with vsuree. **1595** —— *Col. Clout* 39 Of good passed newly to discus, By dubble vsurie doth twise renew it. **1606** B. JONSON *Hymenæi* C 4 Haste, therefore,..and call, Away: The gentle Night is prest to pay The vsurie of long delights, She owes to these protracted rites. **1661** RUST *Origen's Opin.*

66 What is it then..which they may not have with usury and advantage in a body of purer Consistence? **1695** PEPYS in *Academy* 9 Aug. (1890) 111/1, I repay you with usury yor kinde Wishes. **1732** LEDIARD *Sethos* II. IX. 342 The motive of taking Siga has been accomplish'd with usury. **1750** JOHNSON *Rambler* No. 48 ¶10 [He] must not only pay back the hours but pay them back with usury. **1790** BURKE *Fr. Rev.* 117 Learning paid back what it received..with usury. **1813** SHELLEY *Q. Mab* IV. 209 They have three words:—well tyrants know their use, Well pay them for the loan, with usury. **1842** TENNYSON *Talking Oak* 196, I would have paid her kiss for kiss, With usury thereto.

c. In the phrases *at, to, on, upon usury*.

13.. *Prose Psalter* xiv. 6 (Dublin MS.), He þat ȝaf mony to vsurye ne toke noȝt ȝiftes vp on innocentes. **1535** COVERDALE *Deut.* xxiii. 20 Vnto a straunger thou maiest lende vpon vsury. **1579** G. HARVEY *Letter-bk.* (Camden) 62 Lett me borrow them both upon tolerable usurye. **1603** HOLLAND *Plutarch's Mor.* 283 That it might not be lawfull for those to borrow upon usurie. **1651** HOBBES *Leviath.* I. viii. 35 Taking mony at usurie, for the present payment of interest. **1702** *Eng. Theophrastus* 332 'Tis lending on Usury, under the pretence of giving freely. **1844** tr. *M. T. Asmar's Mem. Babylonian Princess* II. 105 If I put it [*sc.* corn] at usury, shall not my bones howl from my grave. **1888** *Encycl. Brit.* XXIV. 17 The man who does not..lend his capital upon 'usury' is..lacking in his duty to himself or his family.

†**3.** *pl.* Instances or kinds of usury. *Obs.*

1603 HOLLAND *Plutarch's Mor.* 284 Their rootes of debts ..bring foorth infinite troubles and intolerable usuries. **1603** SHAKS. *Meas. for M.* III. ii. 7 Since of two vsuries the merriest was put downe, and the worser allow'd by order of Law. **1611** —— *Cymb.* III. iii. 45 Did you but know the Citties Vsuries, And felt them knowingly.

†**4.** *transf.* Increase, augmentation; advantage.

1576 FLEMING *Panopl. Epist.* 352 Howe bountifull a seruitour is the earthe, to the husbandeman? what vsurie doeth it pay for that which it borroweth? **1599** T. M[OUFET] *Silkwormes* 71 Diuine we hence, or rather reckon right, What vsury and proffit doth arise, By keeping well these.. creatures white. **1613** HEYWOOD *Silver Age* III. G 3, With full sickles You shall receiue the vsury of their seeds. **1624** —— *Gunaik.* 31 The profitable usurie arising from agriculture.

†**5.** The use or employment of anything. *rare.*

1607 TOURNEUR *Rev. Trag.* IV. ii, To prostitute my brest to the Dukes sonne: And put my selfe to common vsury. **1625** GILL *Sacr. Philos.* II. 127 That thou mightest inioy the usury of this aire but for the time.

Hence †**'usury** *v. trans.*, to give *out* (favours), with a view to advantageous return. *Obs.*

1654 WHITLOCK *Zootomia* 368 We usury out, not bestow our Favours, each Curtesie being a Designe not so much of doing, as receiving good, with unconscionable Advantage.

usward ('ʌswəd), *adv.* Now *arch.* [f. US. See -WARD, TOWARD, and cf. HER-, HIM-, MEWARD.] Orig. (and chiefly) *to usward*, = toward us. Also *from usward*.

(*a*) *c* **1391** CHAUCER *Astrol.* I. §17 Thanne bygynnyth the sonne to come agayn to vs-ward. **1420** in Rymer *Fœdera* (1709) IX. 907/1 The Letters..enseled undir the Grete Seel of our said Fader to usward, and under Ours to hymward. **1451** *Paston Lett.* I. 202 The baly..knewe not..what myn unkyll was to us ward. **1529** FRITH *Pistle to Chr. Reader* 4 b, In kindnes to vsward thorow Christ Jesus. **1611** BIBLE *Ps.* xl. 5 Many..are..thy thoughts, which are to vs ward. **1642** J. EATON *Honey-comb Free Justif.* 344 Mystically to us-ward, and inwardly and spiritually to God-ward. **1650** *Metr. Psalms Ch. Scotl.* cxvii. 2 For great to us-ward ever are his loving kindnesses. **1779** J. BROWN in R. Mackenzie *Life* (1918) 220 How kind His thoughts to usward! **1809** COBBETT *Pol. Reg.* 22 April 618 To us-ward, both Parties are as much alike as two peas. **1881** SWINBURNE *Mary Stuart* I. ii, From France our friends Lift up their heads to usward.

(*b*) **1603** J. DAVIES *Microcosm.* 37 Sol..makes vs heavie going from vs-ward. **1902** *Westm. Gaz.* 8 Aug. 1/3 She went her way from usward.

b. With ellipse of prep.

1871 SWINBURNE *Songs bef. Sunrise, Eve Revolution* 70 Thy vesture wrought of ages legendary Hides usward thine impenetrable sleep.

uszza, ussza ('ʌzə), *int.* [App. a mere exclamation, but cf. HUZZA *int.*] A shout of anger or effort.

1913 D. H. LAWRENCE *Sons & Lovers* ii. 30 As he sat on his heels, or kneeled, giving hard blows with his pick, 'Uszza-uszza!' he went. **1914** —— *Widowing of Mrs. Holroyd* II. 36 Let me smash that bloody door in. Come out —come out—ussza!

ut (ʊt, ʌt), *sb. Mus.* [L. *ut* 'that': see note on GAMUT. Cf. F., Sp., Pg., and It. *ut*.] The first note in Guido's hexachords, and of the octave in modern solmization, now commonly DO *sb.*[2]; the note C in the natural scale of C major.

Cf. also EFFAUT, GAMUT, G-SOL-RE-UT.

c **1325** in *Rel. Ant.* I. 292 Sol and ut and la. *c* **1550** *Armonye of Byrdes* 185 in Hazl. *E.P.P.* III. 194 Chaungyng their key From ut to rey. ? **1596** BATHE *Brief Introd.* A v b, The next thing necessary to be knowne for the right naming of notes, is the place where that note standeth which is named Ut. **1645-** [see MI *sb.*]. *c* **1656** LOVELACE *To T. S.* iv, Poems (1904) 172 But yet the Spoaks by which they scal'd so high, Gamble hath wisely laid of Ut Re Mi. **1754-** [see DO *sb.*[2]]. **1797** *Encycl. Brit.* (ed. 3) XII. 547/2 From the adjuncts of the mode, that is to say, the modes of its two fifths, which for *ut* are *fa* and *sol*. **1801** BUSBY *Dict. Mus.* s.v., Ut and do are always the tonic, or key-note, of the major-mode, and the ..third of the minor mode. **1890** [see FA].

b. *ut, re* etc.: the notes of the gamut; also *transf.*, the 'gamut' or elements *of* something.

1588 SHAKS. *L.L.L.* IV. ii. 102 Olde Mantuan, Who vnderstandeth thee not loues thee not, *vt re sol la mi fa*. **1599** B. JONSON *Cynthia's Rev.* II. i, Your courtier elementary, is ..as it were in the alphabet, or *ut-re-mi-fa-sol-la* of courtship. **1728** CHAMBERS *Cycl.* s.v. *Note*, Of the seven musical Notes, ut, re, mi, fa, sol, la, si, the first six are ascribed to Aretine.

ut, utal, obs. ff. OUT *adv.*, UDAL.

‖**uta** ('juːta). [Jap., poem, song, f. *utau* to sing.] A Japanese poem; *spec.* = TANKA[2].

1855 R. HILDRETH *Japan* xxxiv. 335 He found out certain words which he brought together into an *Uta*, or verse. **1897** *Japan Times* 23 Mar. 2/6 The collection of the *uta* of the old school being a riddle to the ordinary reading public. **1911** *Encycl. Brit.* XV. 169/1 Such couplets [which admitted Chinese words] were called *shi* to distinguish them from the pure Japanese *uta* or *tanka*.

utas[1] ('juːtæs). Now *Hist.* Also 5 **vtaus, vtauce, vtase** (*Sc.* **wtast, wtes**), 5–7 **vtas** (7 **outas**), 6 **utais**, 7 **vtis**. [Reduced form of the pl. *utaves*: see OCTAVE *sb.*] **a.** = OCTAVE *sb.* 1 a. **b.** = OCTAVE *sb.* 1 b.

1387, *c* **1420** [see OCTAVE *sb.* 1]. *c* **1430** *Pilgr. Lyf Manhode* III. xx. (1869) 146, I selle it by dayes, and bi wookes, bi vtases and bi quinsimes, bi monethes, and bi yeeres. **1463-93** [see OCTAVE *sb.* 1]. **1563** BECON *Reliques* 175 b, For ..euery day of the Vtas an hundred days of pardon in remission of al their sinnes. **1599, 1610** [see OCTAVE *sb.* 1]. **1657** SPARROW *Bk. Comm. Prayer* 178 It was the custome of our fore-fathers to observe the Octave or Vtas of their high and principall Feasts. **1672** MANLEY *Cowell's Interpr.*, *Utas*, ..is the eighth day following any Term or Feast,..and any day between the Feast and the Octave, is said to be within *the utas*. **1701** HODY *Hist. Councils* 368 The Octaves or..the Utas of S. Martin. **1762** *Gentl. Mag.* 567 These Octaves or Uta's [*sic*], as they are often called. **1810** *Stat. Realm* I. 390/1 This present Parliament holden..at the Utas of the Holy Trinity [1369]. **1833** NICOLAS *Chronol. Hist.* (1838) 102 The Octave or Utas of each Feast..is always the seventh day after it occurs; or the eighth day, if the day of the Festival be included.

attrib. **1453** *Paston Lett.* I. 257 Wretyn at Norwych, on the Utas day of Peter and Powll.

c. *transf.* A period of festivity; = OCTAVE 1 c.

1597-1602 [see OCTAVE 1 c].

'utas[2]. Also 9 *dial.* **utis.** [Later var. OUTAS.]

†**1.** = OUTAS. *Obs.*[−1]

1600 HOLLAND *Livy* 134 The Romanes were in dread of your *utas* and outcries.

2. *dial.* Clamour, din.

1875 A. PORSON *Quaint Words* 26 The hounds were here this morning and kicked up a deuce of a utis. **1910** *19th Cent.* May 901 She complains of a *utis* after the village club-feast or merrymaking—a loud, riotous noise.

ut-borewe, etc., obs. ff. OUTBORROW.

ut-draȝen, ME. var. OUTDRAW *v.*

†**ute**, *v. Obs.* Forms: 1 **utun**, 1–2 **uton, utan**, 2–3 **uten, ute, vte** (3 **oute**). [Later form of OE. *witon*, *wuton*, originally subj. (= 'let us go') of OE. *ȝewitan* I-WITE *v.*[2]] An interjectional form used with an infinitive verb, having the force of a subjunctive, with the sense 'Let us ——'.

c **888** K. ÆLFRED *Boeth.* xxxiv. §7 Uton lætan þonne bion þa spræce. *c* **1000** *Ags. Gosp.* Matt. xvii. 4 Ʒyf þu wylt, uton wyrcean her þreo eardung-stowa. *a* **1175** *Cott. Hom.* 241 Ute we nu isi wice bioð ure ifo. *a* **1200** *Moral Ode* 333 Vte we us bi-werien wid þes wrecches worldes luue. *c* **1205** LAY. 20635 Uten we heom to liðe. *c* **1275** *Passion of our Lord* 173 in *O.E. Misc.* 42 Ariseþ vp..and vte we heonne go.

Ute (juːt), *sb.*[1] and *a.* Also 9 **Eutaw, Utaw**, etc. [Shortening of *Utah*, a. Sp. *Yuta* an unidentified Indian language.] **A.** *sb.* **a.** A Shoshonean Indian people inhabiting parts of Colorado, Utah, and New Mexico; a member of this people. **b.** The language of this people. **B.** *adj.* Of or pertaining to the Ute or their language.

1826 in D. M. Frost *Notes on General Ashley* (1960) App. B. 136 The Eutaws and Flatheads..express a great wish that the Americans should visit them frequently. **1846** G. R. GIBSON *Jrnl.* 13 Oct. in *S.W. Hist. Ser.* (1935) III. 252 About fifty Ute Indians came in and held a council with Colonel Doniphan. **1846** M. B. EDWARDS *Jrnl.* 2 Nov. in *Ibid.* (1936) IV. 212 Major Gilpin..made a long and arduous journey through the country of the Ute and Navajo. **1885** D. G. BRINTON in *Pennsylvania Mag.* Apr. 30 The simple form of the verb may convey three different ideas, as in Ute, where the word for 'he seizes' means also 'the seizer'. **1907** *Univ. Calif. Publ. Amer. Archaeol. & Ethnol.* IV. III. 67 The Ute vocabulary was obtained, also in 1900, among the Uintah Ute. **1933** [see PAIUTE *sb.* b]. **1958** L. C. PRITCHETT *Cabin at Medicine Springs* (1959) xxii. 199 Tha's talk of herdin' all the Utes out of Colorado. **1973** A. H. WHITEFORD *N. Amer. Indian Arts* 93 Plains lazy-stitch sewing is characteristic of the work of..the Ute of the Plateau. **1979** C. MCCARRY *Better Angels* III. iii. 180 Woolen socks, hand-knitted by Ute women.

ute (juːt), *sb.*[2] Colloq. (chiefly *Austral.* and *N.Z.*) abbrev. of UTILITY 4 b.

1943 HUNT & PRINGLE *Service Slang* 68 *Ute*, short for Utility truck, a light van used by the Army. **1951** E. LAMBERT *Twenty Thousand Thieves* 178 He gets pissed one night, pinches a ute from the transport lines. **1961** J. DANVERS *The Living Come First* I. 17 I'd like you to take the ute and drive in to Alice. The wire we ordered has arrived. **1971** *N.Z. Listener* 8 Nov. 15/5 Wind whipped at the ute and rocked it on the road's sharp corners. **1981** *National Times* (Austral.) 25–31 Jan. 23/4 We used to help load Teddy into the back of the ute. **1984** *NZ Farmer* 12 Apr. 39/1 Now Nissan has followed it with a tough new 4 × 4 ute, known at this stage just as the 720.

ute, var. OUTE *adv. Obs.*

utebrast, etc.: see OUTBURST *v.*, etc.

utemest, etc., obs. ff. UTMOST *a.*

utenn wiþþ, obs. var. OUTWITH.

utensil (juː'tɛnsɪl), *sb.* Forms: *α.* 5 **vtensele, utensyle**, 6 **-cyle, vtensyle**, 6–7 **sile**, 7 **utensile.** *β.* 5 **vtensyl**, 6 **-sylle, utensille**, 7 **vtensil**, 7–8 **utensill**, 7– **utensil**; 5–6 *Sc.* **vtensel**, 6 **-cell, utencell**, 7 **vtensell(e.** [a. OF. *utensile*, etc. (14th c.; F. *ustensile*), a. med.L. *ūtēnsile* sb., f. L. *ūtēnsil-is* adj., fit for use, useful. Cf. It. *utensile*, Sp. and Pg. *utensilio*.

The stressing *'utensil*, evidenced by metrical examples down to *c* 1800, is corroborated by Johnson and some later Dicts. down to 1835; but the present stressing appears in Bailey's Dict. (1730), and is supported by Ash, Todd, etc.]

†**1.** *collective sing.* Vessels or instruments for various domestic uses. Chiefly *Sc. Obs.*

c **1375** *Sc. Leg. Saints* xlvi. (*Anastasia*) 170 In it [*sc.* the prison] for to kepe vmquhile Of þe kechine ves vtensel [L. *coquinæ utensilia*]. **1411** *E.E. Wills* (1882) 18 Y be-qweythe to lucye my wyfe..alle þe vtensyl of myn hows, þat ys to say, in halle, in Chambre, in Pantrie and Botrie, in larder and Kechyn. **1428** *Reg. de Aberbrothoc* (Bann. Club) II. 58 Hal chawmyr kechyng and butre with swilk vtensele as the said John Vernour vsis. **1535** STEWART *Cron. Scot.* (Rolls) III. 222 Mony come him till,..With wyffe and barne, and all thair vtencell, As tha in Scotland euir mair sould duell.

2. Any article useful or necessary in a household; a domestic implement, vessel, or article of furniture; now *esp.*, an instrument or vessel in common use in a kitchen, dairy, etc.; †freq. *pl.*, = household goods.

α. **1484** CAXTON *Fables of Poge* i, He gaf to her all new utensyles to kepe houshold. *c* **1510** MORE *Picus* Wks. 6/1 Much siluer vessel and plate, with other..costly vtensiles of houshold. **1575** LANEHAM *Let.* (1871) 48 Kenelworth Castl ..so fully furnisht of rich apparell, & vtensilez apted in all pointes to the best. **1611** COTGR., *Vtensile*, an vtensile; any implement,..or household stuffe. **1648** MASY in Nightingale *Ejected of 1662* (1911) 922 The enemie hath.. spoyled my house, windowes, dores & all utinseles [*sic*].

β. **1542** *Test. Ebor.* (Surtees) VI. 160 All the utensilles nowe beinge at Snape. **1546** in *Eng. Gilds* (1870) 199 Certen other plate..with diuerse vtensylles. **1610** SHAKS. *Temp.* III. ii. 104 He ha's braue Vtensils..Which when he ha's a house, hee'l decke withall. *a* **1661** FULLER *Worthies, Yorks.* III. (1662) 186 Small utensils, as Salt-cellars, and the like. *c* **1710** CELIA FIENNES *Diary* (1888) 141 Ye stands, table, and fire utensills. **1767** A. YOUNG *Farmer's Lett. to People* 218 No expences are calculated for the dairy, such as wood, utensils, &c. **1771** SMOLLETT *Humph. Cl.* To Lewis 11 Oct., There was no furniture but the utensils of the kitchen. **1836** W. IRVING *Astoria* III. 47 The culinary utensils of the party. **1865** DICKENS *Mut. Fr.* I. vi, The tap and parlour..were provided with comfortable fireside tin utensils. **1904** *Verney Mem.* I. 550 Household utensils were apt to run short in the families of the English planters.

b. Any vessel (†article, implement, etc.) serving a useful end or purpose.

1502 *Ord. Crysten Men* IV. (W. de W. 1506) X iij b, Vtensyles as vesturs made of lynen cloth or wollen, flesshe, corne, & wyne. **1551** in Feuillerat *Revels Edw. VI* (1914) 62 Instrumentes vtensiles and other furniture..appertaynynge to the Lorde of Mysrule. **1554-5** —— *Revels Q. Mary* (1914) 173 Hedpeces wepons and other vtensiles for maskes. **1660** WATERHOUSE *Arms & Arm.* 11 Coat-armours and other portable utensiles which we call *Insignia*. **1671** MILTON *P.R.* III. 336 Waggons fraught with Utensils of war. **1689** 'PHILOPOLITES' *Grumble. Crew* p. ii, Gibbets you know, are Utensils of State. **1705** W. DERHAM in *Lett. Lit. Men* (Camden) 316 The utensils for observing the Quantities of Rain which fall. **1751** ELIZA HEYWOOD *Betsy Thoughtless* IV. 227 She..made her wearing apparel be also disposed of in proper utensils. **1805** *Act 45 Geo. III*, c. 30 §10 By melting any metal..in any pot, crucible, or other utensil. **1858** HAWTHORNE *Fr. & It. Notebks.* (1871) I. 2 A foot-warmer (a long, flat tin utensil, full of hot water) was put into the carriage.

transf. **1657** W. RAND tr. *Gassendi's Life Pieresc* II. 246 A large Library, and other literary utensils. **1691** RAY *Creation* I. (1692) 62 Fire..is..a Subject or Utensil of..various and inexplicable use. **1705** HEARNE *Duct. Hist.* (ed. 2) I. 190 The Reader will find plenty of necessary Utensils for the improvement of his Manners.

c. *esp.* An implement or tool useful to or used by an artisan, mechanic, farmer, etc.

1604 R. CAWDREY *Table Alph.*, *Vtensils*, things necessary for our use..in a trade. **1659** W. CHAMBERLAYNE *Pharon.* IV. v. 337 The straitened 'prentice..Changes the baser utensils of trade For burnished arms. **1669** WORLIDGE *Syst. Agric.* 277 *Utensils*, Instruments used in any Art, especially Husbandry. **1693** EVELYN *De la Quint. Compl. Gard.* II. 178 If we find the Walks..kept neat and clean, and no Garden Tools or Utensils any where neglected. **1708** J. C. *Compl. Collier* (1845) 15 [In] sinking a Coal-Pit, what Utensils are requisite? **1774** *Act 14 Geo. III*, c. 71 §1 The exportation of the several tools or utensils made use of in preparing..the Cotton and Linen Manufactures. **1791** SMEATON *Edystone L.* §212 *note*, The tools and utensils contrived or adapted to the Edystone works. **1841** W. SPALDING *Italy & It. Isl.* III. 378 Agricultural implements, and utensils of trade. **1848** LYTTON *Harold* I. i, That tablinum..was now filled with.. faggots, and farming utensils.

†**d.** *Mil.* In *pl.* = FREE-QUARTER. *Obs.*[−0]

1702 *Milit. & Sea Dict.* (1711), *Utensils*, the Necessaries due to every Soldier, and to be furnish'd by his Host where he is quarter'd. They are, a Bed with Sheets, a Pot, a Glass or Cup to drink out of, a Dish, a Place at the Fire, and a Candle. [Hence in Phillips (1706) and James (1802).]

3. †**a.** A part of the human frame serving a special purpose. *Obs. rare.*

1601 Shaks. *Twel. N.* I. v. 264, I will giue out diuers scedules of my beautie. It shalbe Inuentoried and euery particle and vtensile labell'd to my will. **1664** Power *Exp. Philos.* I. 67 The whole Body, and all the Organs and Utensils therein. **1675** Baxter *Cath. Theol.* II. VIII. 156 Is not the whole frame of Humane Nature (and our Utensils) put into the hand and power of Christ the Redeemer.

b. One who is made use of; a useful person. *rare.*

1678 Otway *Friendship in F.* v. i, A Sot, a Beetle, a Droan of a Husband, a mere Utensil. **1692** E. Walker tr. *Epictetus' Mor.* xxx, I thus shall useless grow To those I love,.. Nor raise them to be Utensils of State. [**1794** Wolcot (P. Pindar) *Remonstrance* 69 Yet is a King a utensil much wanted—A screw.. to keep together The ship's old leaky sides in stormy weather.] **1896** T. Healy in *Daily News* 14 Feb. 2/4 The first use the Unionist Government made of their Viceregal utensil.

4. A sacred vessel, furnishing, etc., belonging to, and esp. used in the services of, a church, temple, or other place of worship.

1650 Hobbes *De Corp. Pol.* 150 All the Utensils of sacrifice and other holy Things, were ordered by Moses. **1660** Jer. Taylor *Ductor* III. iv. rule vi. §20 The Rulers office.. may extend to sumptuousness, to ornaments of churches, to rich utensils, to splendor, to majesty. **1701** Prideaux *Direct. Ch.-wardens* (1712) 30 What are not fixed to the Freehold of the Church, but are of the moveable Goods belonging thereto, are called the Utensils of the Church. **1751** *Affect. Narr. of Wager* 155 The Jesuits Church.., the Utensils of which are exceedingly valuable. **1805** Foster *Ess.* IV. iv. 164 Consecrated utensils stolen out of a temple. **1836** Thirlwall *Greece* II. 52 In certain solemn processions.. they were compelled to bear a part of the sacred utensils. **1877** J. D. Chambers *Div. Worship* 249 The forms for Benediction of the Sacramental Utensils.

5. A stool for evacuation; a chamber-pot. Spec. ***chamber utensil.***

1699 Garth *Dispens.* II. 24 The Springs of Life their former Vigour feel, Such Zeal he had for that vile Utensil. **1731** Swift *Strephon & Chloe* 173 The nymph.. brings a vessel into bed: Fair utensil, as smooth and white As Chloe's skin. **1768–74** A. Tucker *Lt. Nat.* (1834) II. 147 If Alexander and Cæsar could never be easy off the stool, I would not deny them that needful utensil. **1834** *Westm. Rev.* XX. 494 On being waked by her house on fire, [she] laid hold of the chamber utensil and rushed out. **1861** Flor. Nightingale *Nursing* (ed. 2) 16 Any chamber utensil without a lid.

†**utensil,** *a. Obs.* In 6 vtensel, -sile, 7 utensile. [ad. L. *ūtēnsil-is*: see prec.] Necessary for use, esp. in a household.

1490 *Acta Dom. Conc.* (1839) 148/2 Johne.. sall restore.. certane gudis vtensill and domicill. **1549** *Compl. Scot.* xvii. 145 Mettellis var meltit to mak vtensel veschel necessair to serue ane houshald. **1552** Huloet, Utensile or necessarye to be vsed, *vtensilis*. **1617** Moryson *Itin.* III. 219 The gift of vtensile goods made to the husband. *Ibid.*, In Misen the wife hath not the vtensile goods, which [etc.].

†**utensilies,** *sb. pl. Obs.* [ad. L. *ūtēnsilia* things for use.] Utensils, esp. of a household.

1496–7 *Act 12 Hen. VII*, c. 13 §12 Implementis of Houshold.. and utensilies of the same. **1509** *Bury Wills* (Camden) 109 All my ostylmentys, vtensiliez, and joell that to my hows bylonge. **1531** More *Dyaloge* (ed. 2) I. 8b, Christ was serued with syluer & gold in the vessels vtensylys and ornamentes of his chyrche. **1602** *2nd Pt. Return Parnass.* I. ii. 128 If my kitchen want the vtensilies of viands.

†**utensilment.** *Obs.*⁻¹ [-MENT; after *ustil-*, HUSTLEMENT.] = UTENSIL *sb.* 2.

1428 *E.E. Wills* (1882) 78 All the vtensilmentes longyng to my kechyn.

uter, -ast, obs. ff. UTTER, UTTEREST *adjs.*

uterage, obs. form of OUTRAGE *sb.*

†**uterine,** *sb.*¹ *Obs.*⁻¹ [ad. med.L. *uterīnus*, f. late L. *uterinus* adj.: see next.] *pl.* Children or offspring of the same mother.

1432–50 tr. *Higden* (Rolls) V. 29 Thei were [not] uterynes or childer of oon woman.

uterine ('juːtəraɪn, -ɪn), *a.* and *sb.*² Also 5–6 uteryne, 7 uterin. [a. OF. *uterin*, *-ine* (F. *utérin, -ine*), or ad. late L. *uterīnus* (whence It., Sp., Pg. *uterino*), f. L. *uterus* UTERUS.]

A. *adj.* **1.** Having the same mother, but not the same father. Also in fig. context.

1432–50 tr. *Higden* (Rolls) V. 295 Medardus.. and Gildardus,.. bothe breþer uteryne, borne in oon day. **1447** Bokenham *Seyntys* (Roxb.) 45 Melchy.. Pantars brother.. Weddyd iacobes modyr & gat ely. So iacob & ely wer bretherne vteryne. *c* **1555** Harpsfield *Divorce Hen. VIII* (Camden) 174 To be taken not only of the brother by father and mother but of the uterine and half brother also. **1600** W. Watson *Decacordon* (1602) 359 Saint Peter was the onely vterine, and germane brother to saint Andrew. *c* **1629** Donne *Serm.* (1640) 621 If Sodome and Jerusalem were Sisters, Babylon and we may be so too; uterin sisters of one wombe. *a* **1695** Wood *Ath. Oxon.* (1721) II. 1094/2 Walter Pope, uterine Brother to Dr. Joh. Wilkins. **1703** Quick *Dec. Wife's Sister* 19 His uterine Sister. **1765–8** Erskine *Inst. Law Scot.* III. viii. §8 Brothers or sisters of the deceased by the mother only, who are called *uterine*. **1844** W. K. Kelly tr. *Michelet's Hist. France* I. 561 The uterine sister of Henry III. **1860** Emerson *Cond. Life* i. 11 People are born with the moral.. bias—uterine brothers with this diverging destination.

b. Related by blood through the mother. *rare.*

1632 Lithgow *Trav.* x. 503 Whose Vterine blood he is, and present Brother.. sprung from one Mother. **1816** Tuckey *Narr. Exped. R. Zaire* iv. (1818) 161 The property.. devolves to his brothers or uterine uncles. **1888** *N. & Q.* 7th Ser. V. 493/2 The direct lineal ancestress in the female line, or what is sometimes termed umbilical or uterine ancestress.

c. (See quot.) *rare*⁻¹.

1882 A. Macfarlane *Consanguinity* 11 The uterine system, that is, the system resulting from tracing kinship through females only.

2. *Surg.* Adapted for using or operating on or in the uterus or womb.

1615 Crooke *Body of Man* 239 Wee must proceede by the guide of a vterine probe. **1849** *Lancet* 29 Dec. 609/2 Dr. Routh exhibited to the Society three uterine scarificators. **1857** Dunglison *Dict. Med. Sci.* 851/2 *Sound, Uterine*, Uterine bougie. **1865** *Lancet* 29 April 465/1 The uterine tents made from dried stem of sea-tangle. **1875** Knight *Dict. Mech.* 2685 Uterine dilator,.. elevator, redressor, scarificator, speculum.

3. Of, pertaining or belonging to, the uterus; situated in, connected with, the womb.

1646 Sir T. Browne *Pseud. Ep.* VII. vii. 352 In hot climates and where the uterine parts exceed in heat. **1728** Chambers *Cycl.* s.v., From a Turgescency or Inflation of the Uterine Vessels. **1788** *Encycl. Brit.* (ed. 3) I. 744/2 The Fallopian or uterine tubes, which open into the cavity of the uterus. **1800** *Med. Jrnl.* IV. 191 In the fœtus, we note several contrivances for the uterine state. **1834** J. Forbes tr. *Laennec's Dis. Chest* (ed. 4) 665 The only arteries in which it can be supposed to be produced are the hypogastric, iliac, and uterine. **1838** *Lancet* 7 July 497/2 The diseases of the uterine organs. **1877** W. Turner *Hum. Anat.* II. 519 A uterine venous plexus is arranged on and in the wall of the uterus.

b. Affecting, occurring or taking place in, the uterus.

uterine souffle: see SOUFFLE, and cf. PLACENTAL 1.

a **1661** Fuller *Worthies, Somerset.* III. (1662) 20 Our Bath-waters.. are good for uterine effects, proceeding from cold and windy Humours. **1669** W. Simpson *Hydrol. Chym.* 77 This exotick acidity coagulating the blood.. is the author of most of their uterine infirmities. **1728** Chambers *Cycl.* s.v., Maids that were.. seiz'd with the Uterine Fury. **1752** Smellie *Midwifery* 142 Vomiting,.. in a few,.. prevails during the whole time of uterine gestation. **1771** *Encycl. Brit.* III. 163/1 Of the Immoderate Flux of the Menses, or Uterine Hæmorrhage. **1838** *Penny Cycl.* X. 333/2 The embryo.. during the rest of its uterine life has been denominated the fœtus. **1839** C. West tr. *Naegele's Auscultation* 13 The uterine sound varies in its intensity.. within a very short time. **1851** E. Hamilton *Flora Homœop.* I. 111 Boerhaave.. employed it in uterine diseases. **1889** *Buck's Handbk. Med. Sci.* VII. 448/1 This congestion causes.. painful uterine contractions.

c. Suitable or adapted for remedying or aiding the uterus.

1771 *Encycl. Brit.* III. 163/1 Uterine cathartics are aloes, myrrh, bryony, colocynthus [etc.]. **1849** *Lancet* 22 Dec. 661/2 A new uterine supporter. **1875** Knight *Dict. Mech.* 2685/1 *Uterine douche*, a form of irrigator for the uterus.

4. Of the nature of a uterus.

1841 T. R. Jones *Anim. Kingd.* 201 The exact nature of the uterine sacculus.. is imperfectly understood.

5. Of vellum: Prepared from the skin of a fœtal or abortive calf or lamb.

1870 Rock *Text. Fabr.* p. cxxxv, That now rare kind of vellum called, among manuscript collectors, 'uterine'.

†**B.** *sb.* A medicine or herb remedial in uterine affections. *Obs.* Cf. UTERINE *a.* 3 c.

1661 Lovell *Hist. Anim. & Min.* 460 Uterines, in.. flux, inflammation, scirrhus and ulcers of the womb. **1697** Floyer *Eng. Baths* i. 18 In the *Mola Uteri*, let Women swim in salt Water, or apply the Steam of it in which Uterines are boyl'd. **1718** Quincy *Compl. Disp.* 81 Some commend it as a good Uterine.

‖**uteritis** (juːtə'raɪtɪs). *Path.* [mod.L., f. UTERUS + -ITIS.] Inflammation of the womb; metritis.

c **1840** *Encycl. Metrop.* (1845) VII. 771/1 Parts secondarily.. affected in the female [in gonorrhœa]. Inguinal glands producing Bubo. Uterus producing Uteritis.

utero- ('juːtərəʊ), comb. form of L. *uter-us* UTERUS, occurring in various medical and surgical terms esp. with the sense 'of or pertaining to the womb and —', as **ˌutero-ab'dominal** *a.*, relating to, suitable for, the uterus and the abdomen. **ˌutero-in'testinal** *a.*, affecting or occurring in the uterus and the intestines. **ˌutero-o'varian** *a.*, of or pertaining to the uterus and the ovary. **ˌutero-perito'neal** *a.*, pertaining to, connecting, the uterus and the peritoneum. **ˌutero-pla'cental** *a.*, pertaining to the uterus and the placenta. **ˌutero-'sacral** *a.*, pertaining to, connecting, the uterus and the sacrum. **'uterotome,** an instrument for incising the uterus. **ute'rotomy,** surgical incision of the uterus; hysterotomy. **ˌutero-'tractor** *U.S.*, a kind of 'tractor' or forceps used in operating for vaginal hysterectomy. **ˌutero-'vaginal, -va'ginal,** *a.*, pertaining to, connected with, the uterus and the vagina. **ˌutero-'vesical** *a.*, of or pertaining to the uterus and the bladder.

Various other terms are given in recent American or medical Dicts., as ***uterocervical, -copulatory, -deferent, -fixation, -lith, -mania, -pelvic, -pexy, -tubal.***

1838 *Lancet* 21 April 125/2 The *utero-abdominal supporter. **1896** *Nomencl. Diseases* 199 Fistula. *a.* Utero-vesical. *b.* *Utero-intestinal. **1896** *Lancet* 4 Jan. 33/1 Rheumatoid arthritis was neither the cause nor the effect of *utero-ovarian disturbance. **1872** *Ibid.* 18 May 680/1 Case of *utero-peritoneal fistula. **1857** Dunglison *Med. Dict.* 721 The *utero-placental veins. **1859** *Todd's Cycl. Anat.* V. 707/1 As high up as the level of the *utero-sacral ligaments. **1863** Weiss *Catal. Surg. Instr.* Pl. xxix, Sim's *Uterotome.. and Caustic Holder. **1846** Brittan tr. *Malgaigne's Man Oper. Surg.* 559 Incision of the Neck of the Uterus, or Vaginal *Uterotomy. **1890** *Retrospect Med.* CII. 111 A small, but important, detail is not to introduce the *utero-tractor into the uterine cavity. **1856** *Lancet* 2 Feb. 129/1 New *utero-vaginal plug. **1897** *Allbutt's Syst. Med.* II. 1092 The long combined utero-vaginal passage. **1822** Good *Study Med.* IV. 153 *Utero-vesical Prolapse. **1891** Mouillin *Surg.* 1346 The uterovesical pouch of peritoneum.

ˌutero-ge'station. [See prec. and GESTATION.] The progressive development of the embryo in the womb from conception till birth.

1775 A. Hamilton *Pract. Midwifery* 70 During the whole term of Utero-Gestation. **1836–9** *Todd's Cycl. Anat.* II. 436/1 Utero-gestation in the Mammalia is terminated by parturition or the birth of the young. **1888** *Brit. Med. Jrnl.* 14 April 800/1 Acute intestinal obstruction complicating utero-gestation.

‖**uterus** ('juːtərəs), Pl. ‖uteri ('juːtəraɪ). [L.; whence F. *utérus* (Paré). Cf. It., Sp., Pg. *utero.*]

1. In the primates: The organ in which the young are conceived, developed, and protected till birth; the female organ of gestation; the womb.

1615 Crooke *Body of Man* IV. xiii. (1631) 222 It is called *Vterus* properly in women. **1638** A. Read *Man. Anat. Body of Man* 239 The hypogastricall veins,.. as soone as they come to be implanted into the substance of the uterus,.. lose their owne coats. **1702** Drake in *Phil. Trans.* XXIII. 1236 The Observation and Experiment being made on the Uterus of a Cow. **1728** Chambers *Cycl.* s.v. *Matrix*, The Cavity of the Uterus. **1770** *Med. Observ.* (1772) IV. 388 The History of a fatal Inversion of the Uterus. **1834** Owen in *Phil. Trans.* CXXIV. 333 A Description of the Impregnated Uterus of the Kangaroo. **1837** Baly tr. *Müller's Physiol.* 1580 An examination of recently impregnated uteri. **1871** Darwin *Desc. Man* I. iv. 123 In all mammals the uterus is developed from two simple primitive tubes.

transf. **1728** Chambers *Cycl.* s.v. *Generation*, Every Herb and Tree bears its Seed..; which being thrown into the Earth, as into its Uterus, spreads forth its Roots.

b. In the lower female animals, fishes, or birds: The matrix; the ovary.

1753 *Chambers' Cycl.* Suppl. s.v., Uterus of Fishes. **1839** *Penny Cycl.* XIII. 383/2 Leeches are oviparous. The ova remain in the uterus for some time. **1877** Huxley *Anat. Inv. Anim.* 178 The outer, or vaginal, end of the uterus [in *Turbellaria*]. **1878** F. J. Bell tr. *Gegenbaur's Comp. Anat.* 182 Special portions of the oviduct [in *Vermes*] function as a Uterus, by which name parts, very different morphologically, are known. **1880** Günther *Fishes* 166 The ends of the uteri open.. into the cloaca.

c. (See quot.)

1841 T. R. Jones *Anim. Kingd.* 200 The vulva [in leeches].. leads into a pear-shaped membranous bag, which is usually, but improperly, named the uterus.

2. *Bot.* **a.** = PERICARP.

1676 Grew *Anat. Flowers* vii. *heading*, The Time, in which the Uterus or Fruit and Seed-Case are formed. **1677** —— *Anat. Fruits* III. v. §1 The Fruit, strictly so called, is, A Fleshy Uterus, which grows more moist and Pulpy, as the Seed ripens. But the Seed-Case.. is, A Membraneous Uterus.

†**b.** (See quot.) *Obs. rare*⁻¹.

1776 J. Lee *Introd. Bot.* 396 *Stygma*, the female Uterus, at the Top of the Pistil, furnished with a moist Humour.

c. In Fungi: (see later quots.).

1829 Loudon *Encycl. Plants* 981 *Angiogastres.* Uterus finally bursting forth, separate from the receptacle. **1836** M. J. Berkeley *Fungi* in *Smith's Eng. Flora* V. II. 19 *Uterus* sessile, bursting irregularly, marbled internally with anastomosing veins. **1866** *Treas. Bot.* 1197/2 *Uterus*, the volva or receptacle of certain fungals. **1895** M. C. Cooke *Study Fungi* 356/2 *Peridium*, the enveloping coat of a sporophore, or receptacle in which the spores are developed in a closed cavity. In Gastromycetes sometimes called the uterus, the contents being the gleba.

†**3.** A hollow or cavity. *Obs.*⁻¹

1693 Ray *Three Disc.* 137 The *Tophus* it self must have vegetated, containing a cavity or *uterus* of the shape of the Tooth, into which an osseous humour,.. filling the cavity of the *Uterus*, must there have coagulated.

ute-tan, etc., obs. ff. OUT-TAKEN, etc.

utface, var. OUTFACE (surface) *Obs.*

utfangthef(e, -theif, etc., varr. OUTFANGTHIEF. *Obs.*

uth, obs. f. YOUTH.

uthail, -ale, -all, obs. ff. UDAL.

†**uthe.** *Sc. Obs.*⁻¹ [For earlier **ōth*, a. ON. *óð-r* poetry, melody.] Harmony.

c **1465** *Liber Pluscardensis* XI. xi, Rycht as [all] stringis ar reulit in a harp In ane accord, and tunyt al be an uth. [Rhyming with *suth* 'sooth' and *muth* dull = MOTHE *a.*]

uthe, obs. f. YOUTH.

uþe: see UNNE *Obs.*

uðe, var. YTHE (wave) *Obs.*

uthel(ler, obs. ff. UDAL(LER.

uther, etc., obs. f. OTHER, etc.; obs. or dial. f. UDDER.

uthes, var. OUTAS *sb. Obs.*

†**uþwite.** *Obs.* [OE. *úþwita*, f. *úp-* (Goth. *unþa-*) away, beyond + *wita* one who knows, WITE *sb.*] A wise man; a sage.

*c***888** K. ÆLFRED *Boeth.* xxxiii. §4 Swa swa ure uðwita sæde, Plato. *c* **1000** *Menologium* 166 in *O.E. Chron.* (1892) I. 278 Swa hit foregleawe ealde upþwitan æror fundan. *c* **1200** ORMIN 7083 Þa þatt sohhtenn Jesu Crist Wæren Magy ȝehatenn, .. Uþwitess swiþe wise.

†'**utible**, *a.* [ad. L. *ūtibilis*, f. *ūtor* to use, employ.] That may be used; useful, serviceable.

1623 COCKERAM, *Vtible*, profitable. **1656** BLOUNT *Glossogr.* ? **1711** (*title*), Proposals by the Utible Society, for the Insurance on Marriages, by a weekly Dividend.

utile ('juːtaɪl), *a.* Now *rare.* Also 5–6 **vtyle**, 6 **vtyll, utyle, utille.** [a. OF. (F.) *utile* (13th c.), ad. L. *ūtilis*, f. *ūtī* to use. Cf. It. *utile*, and OF., Pr., Sp., Pg. *util.*] Useful, profitable, advantageous. Also const. *to, unto.*

1484 CAXTON *Fables of Æsop* I. x, Theyre felauship [*sc.* of evil folk] is not good ne vtyle. **1518** H. WATSON *Hist. Oliver of Castile* (Roxb.) B 4, To whome it semeth good and vtyll for the prosperyte of bothe partyes. *c* **1532** DU WES *Introd. Fr.* in *Palsgr.* 1072 Of all meates the best and most utille to the body of man is of capons. **1578** BANISTER *Hist. Man* v. 74 The most pure and vtile substaunce. **1653** H. COGAN tr. *Pinto's Trav.* lxx. 284 To shew that the conquest thereof would have been far more utile unto us. **1678** GALE *Crt. Gentiles* IV. III. 5 Means utile and conducible to the promoting of Divine glorie. **1839** J. ROGERS *Antipopopr.* i. 69 An order that He has given .. to employ our energy in the utile pursuit of following. **1894** *Advance* (Chicago) 24 May, There is the cost value... There is the productive or utile value.

absol. **1685** COTTON tr. *Montaigne* (1711) III. 2 Wherein he quitted the utile for the honest.

utile ('juːtɪlɪ), *sb.* [a. the specific epithet of the tree's Latin name: see UTILE *a.*] The timber of a large West African forest tree, *Entandrophragma utile*, of the family Meliaceæ; also, the tree itself.

1956 *Handbk. Of Hardwoods* (Forest Prod. Res. Lab.) 228 Utile reaches a height of 150 ft or more. *Ibid.*, In structure and general appearance utile resembles the closely allied sapele .. and is somewhat more open in texture. **1970** *Timber Trades Jrnl.* 21 Mar. 54/1 There are now signs of weaker prices for utile. **1980** *Yachts & Yachting* 29 Feb. 680/2 As nice a piece of red utile as you'll see this side of a stereo cabinet.

Utilidor (juː'tɪlɪdɔə(r)). *Canad.* Also u-. [f. UTILITY *sb.* + *-dor* ad. Gr. δῶρον gift. For the formation cf. CUSPIDOR, HUMIDOR, and THERMIDOR.] The proprietary name of a system of enclosed conduits used esp. for carrying water and sewerage in regions of permafrost.

1957 *Maclean's Mag.* 14 Sept. 92/2 At many outposts such as Churchill, Norman Wells and Frobisher ingenious insulated conduit boxes called 'utilidors' are used to convey water, sewage and heating pipes to their destinations. The idea is that the warmth from the heating pipes is just enough to keep the other two pipes from freezing. **1969** *Official Gaz.* (U.S. Patent Office) 15 Apr. TM 112 Ric-Wil, Incorporated, Barberton, Ohio. Filed June 12, 1967. *Utilidor.* For prefabricated conduits used in under-ground services... First use at least as early as Apr. 30, 1950. **1977** *Islander* (Victoria, B.C.) 21 Aug. 14/3 Each year one expects to pay $5000 for utilities hooked to each house by the famous utilidor.

†**u'tilious**, *a. Obs.*⁻¹ [f. L. *ūtili-s* UTILE *a.* + -OUS.] Useful.

1652 F. KIRKMAN *Clerio & Lozia* 190 This Treason was so utilious to this Barbarian, and so prejudicial to ours, that he .. retook the Towns.

utilitarian (juːtɪlɪ'tɛərɪən), *sb.* and *a.* [f. UTILIT-Y, after sbs. and adjs. in *-arian.* Hence Pg. and It. *utilitario*, F. *utilitaire.*]

A. *sb.* One who holds, advocates, or supports the doctrine of utilitarianism; one who considers utility the standard of whatever is good for man; also, a person devoted to mere utility or material interests.

1781 BENTHAM *Let.* Wks. 1843 X. 92/1 He is a utilitarian, a naturalist, a chemist, a physician. **1821** GALT *Ann. Parish* xxxv, I thought they had more sense than to secede from Christianity to become Utilitarians. **1835** WORDSW. *Yarrow Revisited*, etc. 326 A right in the people (not to be gainsaid by utilitarians and economists) to public support when [etc.]. **1860** MAURY *Phys. Geog.* (Low) iv. 268 The utilitarian who compares the water-power that the falls of Niagara would afford if applied to machinery. **1875** JOWETT *Plato* (ed. 2) IV. 29 We are therefore justified in calling Socrates the first utilitarian.

B. *adj.* **1.** Of philosophy, principles, etc.: Consisting in or based upon utility; *spec.* that regards the greatest good or happiness of the greatest number as the chief consideration or rule of morality.

1802 BENTHAM *Let.* Wks. 1843 X. 390 A new religion would be an odd sort of a thing without a name: accordingly there ought to be one for it—at least for the professors of it. Utilitarian .. would be the more *propre.* **1814** *New Brit. Theatre* I. 50 The sublime ideas of the utilitarian philosophy. *Ibid.* 227 The philanthropy of the true utilitarian principles. **1841** GLADSTONE *State in Relat. Ch.* (ed. 4) I. 107 A reason quite irreconcilable with the utilitarian theories. **1861** MILL *Utilit.* iv. (1863) 51 The utilitarian doctrine is, that happiness is .. the only thing desirable, as an end. **1869** LECKY *Europ. Mor.* I. 18 They were at once profoundly antipathetical to Utilitarian morals.

b. Of or pertaining to utility; relating to mere material interests.

1830 *Westm. Rev.* Jan. 3 So far from its being proscribed by Utilitarian notions, they demand its existence. **1853** KANE *Grinnell Exp.* x. (1856) 77 Their application to the fishing grounds .. would be a matter of large utilitarian interest. **1859** W. S. COLEMAN *Woodlands* 58 Turning from the picturesque or romantic, to the utilitarian view of this tree. **1873** MRS. BROOKFIELD *Not a Heroine* I. 23 From a utilitarian point of view.

c. In quasi-depreciative use: Having regard to mere utility rather than beauty, amenity, etc.

1847 H. MILLER *First Impr. Eng.* xvi. 294 For the hill-top cottage .. I found a modern hard-cast farm-house, with a square of offices attached, all exceedingly utilitarian, well kept, stiff, and disagreeable. **1876** MISS BRADDON *J. Haggard's Dau.* I. 29 A good garden of the old-fashioned utilitarian type.

2. Of persons: Holding or advocating utilitarian views, principles, etc.; aiming at, supporting, or advancing utilitarianism; also, preferring mere utility to beauty or amenity.

1802 [see 1]. **1828** BENTHAM *Let.* Wks. 1843 XI. 2/2 The accomplished utilitarian statesman. **1834** K. H. DIGBY *Mores Cath.* v. x. 360 The favour of utilitarian philosophers, or of self-interested reformers. **1862** SIR B. BRODIE *Psychol. Inq.* II. i. 32 The mere utilitarian philosopher, having his views limited to some immediate practical result. **1873** MILL *Autobiog.* 79 [In the winter 1822–3] the name I gave to the society I had planned was the Utilitarian Society. It was the first time that any one had taken the title of Utilitarian; and the term made its way into the language from this humble source.

3. Of times: Marked or characterized by prevalence of utilitarian doctrine, principles, or views. (Freq. with *age.*)

1828 CARLYLE *Goethe* ¶16 In these hard, unbelieving utilitarian days. **1839** *Morn. Herald* 3 Sept., The cold 'philosophy' of a money-getting utilitarian age. **1854** *Poultry Chron.* II. 251/1 In these utilitarian days, every thing seems to .. play its proper part.

Hence **utili'tarianly** *adv. rare*⁻¹.

1878 *Fraser's Mag.* XVII. 665 A new tower .. built, utilitarianly, of common yellow brick.

utili'tarianism. [f. prec. + -ISM. Hence F. *utilitarianisme* (1885).] Utilitarian doctrine, principles, theories, or practices; *spec.* in *Philos.*, the doctrine that the greatest happiness of the greatest number should be the guiding principle of conduct.

1827 G. S. FABER *Sacr. Cal. Prophecy* (1844) I. 202 Intent only upon the present, .. men will .. devote themselves .. to a life .. of sordid godless Utilitarianism. **1839** DICKENS *Nickleby* xxxvi, But knockers may be muffled for other purposes than those of mere utilitarianism. **1861** MILL *Utilit.* ii. (1863) 16 Utilitarianism, therefore, could only attain its end by the general cultivation of nobleness of character. **1878** W. H. DALL *Later Preh. Man* 31 The growth of sentiment (as opposed to savage utilitarianism), which is characteristic of the human mind in all ages.

utili'tarianist. *rare*⁻¹. [f. as prec. + -IST.] A utilitarian.

1882 H. J. GAMBLE *W. Dalton* 20 A distinguished utilitarianist of the present day.

utili'tarianize, *v. rare.* [f. as prec. + -IZE.] *trans.* To turn to a utilitarian end or purpose; to invest with a utilitarian character.

1852 MRS. C. MEREDITH *Home in Tasmania* I. 143 The colonists, sad matter-of-fact people that they are! who utilitarianize everything. **1907** *Jrnl. Educ.* Oct. 671/1 Utilitarianize your secondary education.

utility (juː'tɪlɪtɪ), *sb.* Also 5–6 **vtilite** (6 **-ie**), 6 **utillitie** (7 *Sc.* **vtillatie**), **utilite**, 7 **-ie.** [a. OF. *utilitei, utelite* (1291), *utilitet* (12th c.), etc. (F. *utilite*), ad. L. *ūtilitāt-, ūtilitās*, f. *ūtili-s* UTILE *a.* Cf. Sp. *utilidad*, Pg. *-idade*, It. *utilità.*]

1. a. The fact, character, or quality of being useful or serviceable; fitness for some desirable purpose or valuable end; usefulness, serviceableness.

In frequent use *c* 1540–*c* 1650, and from *c* 1755. The constructions in the two earliest quots. are obsolete.

c **1391** CHAUCER *Astrol.* II. §26 The vtilite to knowe the Assenciouns in the rihte cercle. *a* **1425** tr. *Arderne's Treat. Fistula* 55 Maners of curacions .. to be noted vnder compendiousnez to þe vtilite of helyng. *c* **1440** *Gesta Rom.* xciv. 424 (Add. MS.), I clad my seruaunte, that is, my manhode, nought but to vtterly vtilite and necessite. **1528** R. THORNE in Hakl. *Voy.* (1589) 251 The commoditie and vtilitie of this Nauigation. *c* **1566** J. ALDAY tr. *Boaystuau's Theat. World* S ij, The wonderfull Invention, Utilitie and Dignitie of Printing. **1603** HOLLAND *Plutarch's Mor.* 19 Where .. the attractive pleasure and sweetenesse of speech, is not without some fruit nor void of utilitie. **1651** HOBBES *Leviathan* IV. xliv. 349 The utility of Prayer for the Dead. **1758** JOHNSON *Idler* No. 93 ¶1 He discussed the utility .. of the Islington turnpike. **1762–71** H. WALPOLE *Vertue's Anecd. Paint.* (1786) II. 266 The circular court is a picturesque thought, but without meaning or utility. **1801** S. & HT. LEE *Canterb. T.* IV. 418 A cottage .. more calculated for utility than ornament. **1841** ELPHINSTONE *Hist. Ind.* II. 71 The extent and utility of his public works. **1871** MOZLEY *Univ. Serm.* vi. (1876) 124 The older poetical view brought in more the utility and active force of nature. **1878** JEVONS *Prim. Pol. Econ.* 15 Everything which forms a part of wealth must be useful, or have utility.

b. In the phrase *of* (..) *utility.*

c **1440** *Pallad. on Husb.* III. 524 Rootys smale of noon vtilite Cutte of. **1514** BARCLAY *Cyt. & Uplondyshman* (Percy Soc.) 5 Fayre warkes of grete utylyte. **1598** BARRET *Theor. Warres* V. i. 139 Which thinke you to be of most vtilitie in the warres? **1759** ROBERTSON *Hist. Scot.* II. ¶32 This victory .. was of no real utility. **1778** *Learning at a Loss* II. 11 Five thousand other Instruments of Equestrian Utility. **1801** S. & HT. LEE *Canterb. T.* IV. 424 Those in whose hands .. [life] is an engine of either private or public utility. **1831** D. E. WILLIAMS *Life & Corr. Sir T. Lawrence* II. 42 The habit .. is of the greatest utility. **1857** RUSKIN *Pol. Econ. Art* 11 The two great objects of utility and splendour.

c. *Philos.* The ability, capacity, or power of a person, action, or thing to satisfy the needs or gratify the desires of the majority, or of the human race as a whole.

1751 HUME *Princ. Mor.* v. 73 In common Life .. the Circumstance of Utility is always appeal'd to. **1780** BENTHAM *Princ. Legisl.* i. (1789) p. iii, An action then may be said to be conformable to the principle of utility .. when the tendency it has to augment the happiness of the community is greater than any it has to diminish it. **1785** PALEY *Moral & Pol. Philos.* I. vi, Or must we give up our princple, that the criterion of right is utility? **1830** MACKINTOSH *Progr. Eth. Philos.* vi. Wks. 1846 I. 194 A theory founded on Utility .. requires that we should cultivate .. those other habitual dispositions which we know .. to be generally the source of actions beneficial to ourselves and our fellows. **1861** MILL *Utilit.* ii. (1863) 9 The creed which accepts as the foundation of morals, Utility, or the Greatest Happiness Principle. **1883** H. SIDGWICK *Pol. Econ.* I. iii. 77 There is another difficulty lurking in the conception of Utility as a measure of wealth.

d. The intrinsic property of anything that leads an individual to choose it rather than something else; in game theory, that which a player seeks to maximize in any situation where there is a choice; the value of this, as (actually or notionally) estimated numerically.

1881 F. Y. EDGEWORTH *Math. Psychics* p. vi, It is argued from mathematical considerations that the basis of arbitration between contractors is the greatest possible utility of all concerned. **1934** *Economica* Feb. 53 Suppose .. that we have a utility function given; that is to say, we know, for the individual in question, how much utility he would derive from any given set of quantities of the goods on the market. **1944** VON NEUMANN & MORGENSTERN *Theory of Games* i. 16 We feel .. that one part of our assumptions at least—that of treating utilities as numerically measurable quantities—is not quite as radical as is often assumed in the literature. **1948** *Jrnl. Polit. Econ.* LVI. 280/1 Choices among riskless alternatives are explained in terms of maximization of utility: individuals are supposed to choose as they would if they attributed some common quantitative characteristic —designated utility—to various goods and then selected the combination of goods that yielded the largest total amount of this common characteristic. **1960** A. RAPOPORT *Fights, Games, & Debates* iv. 64 The more he worked, the more he would get and so the more utility would accrue to him on that account. The more he worked, however, the more tired he would get and the more *negative* utility would accrue to him on that account. **1965** *Papers Regional Sci. Assoc.* XV. 162 The individual will tend to locate himself at a place whose characteristics possess or promise a relatively higher level of utility than in other places which are conspicuous to him. **1968** G. OWEN *Game Theory* vi. 133 This cannot be determined simply by measuring the increase and decrease of utility which this action causes to the two individuals, for .. the units of utility scales are arbitrary and thus cannot be used for interpersonal comparisons. **1973** *Proc. R. Soc.* B. CLXXXIV. 421 In such a calculus [of medicine] it is necessary to assume that it is possible to attach a measure of worth or value to any state of health, and for this measure we use the word utility. **1980** A. J. JONES *Game Theory* iv. 178 If you assign a utility of −50 to the loss of $10, then it will not pay you to engage in this gamble if your utility for a gain of $20 is less than 75. *Ibid.* 180 One alternative possesses a larger utility than another because it is preferred, not the other way round.

†**2.** The quality of being advantageous or profitable, profit, advantage, use. Freq. const. *of* (a person, etc.). *Obs.*

In frequent use *c* 1535–*c* 1580, esp. coupled with *profit.*

c **1440** *Pallad. on Husb.* III. 485 This wey is light and more vtilite. **1455** *Paston Lett.* I. 365 Charges born and payd .. for the avauncement of his conquest, the good and utilite of hym, of his seyd royaume and duchie forseid. **1471** CAXTON *Recuyell* (Sommer) 120 This is ayenst your prosperite and utilite. **1509** HAWES *Past. Pleas.* VI. (Percy Soc.) 25 You shall, quod she, my scyence wel lerne, In tyme and space, to your gret utilite. **1533–4** *Act 25 Hen. VIII*, c. 9 §1 To the greate profete and vtilitie of a greate number of the Kynges Subjectes. **1576** LAMBARDE *Peramb. Kent* Ded. ¶iii b, What vtilitie foloweth the studie of Hystories. **1657** *Rec. Old Aberd.* (New Spalding Club) I. 94 The hundreth merkis .. left in legacie be .. George Clerk .. for the vse and vtillatie of the said cittie. **1698** KEILL *Exam. Th. Earth* 63 Choosing such .. positions of things as bring with them the greatest good and utility to the Universe. **1752** J. LOUTHIAN *Form of Process* (ed. 2) 238 Circuit Courts was [*sic*] introduced for the manifest Utility of the Lieges.

3. a. A useful, advantageous, or profitable thing, feature, etc.; a use. Chiefly in pl.

1483 CAXTON *Cato* a viij b, By the comyn wele of a londe is saued all synguler proufftytes and utylytes. **1489** —— *Faytes of A.* I. vi. 14 For the regarde of somme particuler vtilite. **1502** ARNOLDE *Chron.* Index (1811) 6 That money .. to be chosen .. for necessites and vtylites of the same cite. **1541** COPLAND *Guydon's Quest. Chirurg.* B iij b, The scyence of the Nathomy is .. nedefull to the Cyrurgyen for .iiij. vtylyties. **1586** A. DAY *Eng. Secretorie* I. (1595) 142 Iudge by your owne decernment .. howe greatlie you are ledde awrie, in thus careleslie roaming vpon others vtilities. **1604** E. G[RIMSTONE] *D'Acosta's Hist. Indies* VII. i. 496 If therefore there were no other fruite in the Historie .. of the Indians, but this common vtilitie. **1659** PEARSON *Creed* i. 34 Which no man who considereth the uses and utilities of every species can deny. **1688** BOYLE *Final Causes Nat. Things* iii. 82 Of several of his creatures, whereof men..make some uses, they shall hereafter discover other utilities. **1775** HARRIS *Philos. Arrangem.* ix. 196 The Knowledge of Nature, and the Utilities of common Life. **1800** W. TAYLOR in Robberds *Mem.* (1843) I. 355 Genius never was remarkable for teaching the practical utilities. **1876** HOLLAND *Seven Oaks* xii. 169 It had lifted him above the bare utilities of a house, so that he could see the use of beauty. **1908** S. E. WHITE *Riverman* xxviii, Heinzman wanted the improvements..sold as a public utility to the highest bidder.

b. *Pol. Econ.* (See quots., and cf. 1 c.)

1848 MILL *Pol. Econ.* I. iii. I. 56 What we produce..is always..an utility. Labour is not creative of objects, but of utilities. **1904** R. T. ELY & WICKER *Elem. Princ. Economics* 81 A good or utility is anything which can satisfy a human want.

c. ***public utility***: see PUBLIC *a.* 2 i. Also simply *utility*. Hence, a company providing such a service or supply. In *pl.* also shares in such a company. chiefly *N. Amer.*

1930 *Daily Express* 6 Sept. 2/6 Utilities joined in the forward movement, which gathered considerable momentum in the final dealings, and the closing was strong. **1935** *Economist* 26 Jan. 195/1 Steel shares were merely steady, but utilities were inclined to take fresh heart... Mayor La Guardia indeed turned his attention this week from power utilities to the transit companies. **1936** L. C. DOUGLAS *White Banners* iii. 46 It was a new..sensation to be free of bill-collectors... You would have thought him another person than the..apologizer..who had abased himself before..the credit departments of the stores and the utilities. **1942** *Sun* (Baltimore) 7 Mar. 20 Additional housing..within the limits of existing utilities..is immediately desirable. **1957** [see DOW-JONES]. **1968** *Globe & Mail* (Toronto) 17 Feb. 5/1 Toronto Hydro's request for a 700-foot smokestack on the..steam heating utility. **1974** *N.Y. Times* 8 Dec. IV. 3/1 American Electric Power Co., the nation's largest privately owned utility.

4. a. Short for *utility actor* (sense 5 a). Also, the activity of a utility actor, the taking of any small part.

1803 T. WILKINSON *Let.* in A. Mathews *Mem. C. Mathews* (1838) I. xvii. 359, I take it for granted in very full plays you will..not object to pantomime utility, being a lord mayor, a witch, &c. **1846** G. A. A'BECKETT *Quizziology of Brit. Drama* 10 The heavy man, who is paid thirty shillings a week for doing the 'respectable utility'. **1885** JEROME *On the Stage* 80 A 'lead' may get three pounds.., and a young 'utility' thinks himself very well off indeed on a guinea. **1889** H. B. BAKER *London Stage* II. 168 She was playing utility, that is to say, going on for anything, at the Park Theatre.

b. A utility vehicle (see sense 5 c (a) below). chiefly *Austral.* and *N.Z.*

1944 *Coast to Coast 1943* 162 They walked..to where a fairly new utility was parked with one or two other cars and an old truck. **1949** *Automobile & Carriage Builders' Jrnl.* Nov. 34 (*caption*) Two views of an Alvis Fourteen utility. **1960** *Guardian* 28 Dec. 2/3, I bought a 1949 Jowett Bradford utility two years ago. **1961** D. STUART *Driven* iv. 40 He had come to the well in the utility and found the footmen washing their clothes. **1968** K. WEATHERLY *Roo Shooter* 101 As he passed the bore he noticed a very battered looking utility parked there. **1971** *N.Z. Listener* 8 Nov. 15/5 He got in the utility by Honi, who waited with the motor running. **1984** *Auckland Star* 2 Mar. A3/7 A 54-year-old Southland man..died in a four-wheel drive utility accident.

c. A utility suit (see sense 5 c (c) below).

1945 J. B. PRIESTLEY *Three Men in New Suits* ii. 12 His clothes were rather like yours. He must have been dressed in his best Utility. **1957** J. BRAINE *Room at Top* xviii. 164 The suit was my demob Utility.

d. *Computers.* Short for *utility program* (see sense 5 a below).

1972 *Computers & Humanities* VI. 277 There are..a number of natural-language utilities available, but often they do not fit exactly the user's research design. **1983** *Daily Tel.* 30 Apr. 25/3 Commodore..has now produced a utility, called 'SIMONS BASIC' which is both delightful and infuriating to use.

e. Short for *utility room* (see sense 5 a below).

1976 *Field* 18 Nov. 948 (Advt.), Drawing room, dining room, study, cloakroom, kitchen, utility, etc.

5. *attrib.* passing into *adj.*: **a.** ***utility value***; (sense 3 c) ***utility bill, company, executive, pole, wire***; (sense 4 a) ***utility-business***; **utility actor**, an actor of the smallest speaking-parts in a play; **utility area**, a part of a house set aside for general use rather than for habitation; **utility curve**, a graph of a utility function; **utility function**, a mathematical function which ranks alternatives according to their utility to an individual; **utility man**, (*a*) a utility actor; (*b*) *U.S.*, a substitute capable of taking any position in a baseball team (Webster, 1911); **utility program** *Computers*, one for carrying out routine tasks associated with the use of a computer; **utility room**, a room set aside for domestic appliances such as a boiler for a central heating system, a washing machine, etc., and for the storage of other equipment; **utility routine** = *utility program* above.

1860 *Cornh. Mag.* II. 748 Known respectively as 'eccentric comedian' and 'utility actor'. **1969** 'E. LATHEN' *Murder to Go* (1970) xiv. 135 The new Hedstrom house..consisted of one spacious common room and assorted bedrooms, serviced by tiny utility areas. **1978** *Morecambe Guardian* 14 Mar. 24/2 (Advt.), Accommodation comprises: entrance hall, lounge, dining room, kitchen, 2 bedrooms, bathroom/WC. Utility area. **1976** *National Observer* (U.S.) 24 Jan. 13/3 Warmer-than-usual weather has reduced the schools' projected utility bills. **1984** *New Yorker* 30 Jan. 48/1 Whether it's utility bills or telephone bills or taxes or health costs or heating costs, it seems that the cost of the average family raising their family is going up. **1879** *Era Almanack* 46 The drudgery of 'utility' business. **1926** *Daily Colonist* (Victoria, B.C.) 1 Jan. 18/3 The progress and prosperity of a community naturally is reflected in the fortunes of the utility companies whose duty it is to supply such essentials as light, water, power, [etc.]. **1980** *Amer. Speech* LV. 54 Presumably, the utility companies..specify certain hours of the day as the peak hours. **1948** *Jrnl. Pol. Econ.* LVI. 297/1 A single prize will be the optimum..if.. every chord from the utility curve at the current income to the utility of a higher income is everywhere above the utility curve. **1969** Utility curve [see INDIFFERENCE 8]. **1931** F. L. ALLEN *Only Yesterday* iii. 59 Book-censors, Jew-haters, Negro-haters, landlords, manufacturers, utility executives, upholders of every sort of cause,..all wrapped themselves in Old Glory and the mantle of the Founding Fathers. **1979** *Time* 8 Jan. 39/1 Says a utility executive in Iowa: 'People have been had too many times.' **1934** Utility function [see sense 1 d above]. **1977** *Dædalus* Fall 84 Models now start from mathematical representations of personal choice (utility functions) where work and leisure stand in the 'correct' relationship to each other and where mathematics imposes a 'correct' income and substitution effect. **1849** *Theatrical Mirror* 1 Oct. 37/1 He is a great friend of the utility-man's. **1851** MAYHEW *Lond. Labour* I. 383/1 At one of the theatres,..I eventually rose to a 'general utility man', at 12*s*. per week. **1860** *Cornh. Mag.* II. 748 The leading lady ..and the utility man will all act in the same way. **1961** in *Webster*, His car sideswiped a utility pole. **1973** *Advocate-News* (Barbados) 15 Feb. 4/2 The car fell into a three-foot gully and came to rest against a utility pole which kept it from overturning. **1964** T. W. MCRAE *Impact of Computers on Accounting* i. 24 Utility programmes have been devised for the same reason as the autocodes. **1980** S. HOCKEY *Guide Computer Applications in Humanities* ii. 29 Most computer centres have a utility program which makes copies of magnetic tapes. **1953** C. ARMSTRONG *Catch-as-catch-Can* xviii. 153 They were in a small lumber room, utility room, the Californian equivalent of a cellar. **1959** *Housewife* Oct. 69/1 The utility room is fitted with a sink and drainer and also houses the fuel store and gas boiler. **1964** G. L. COHEN *What's Wrong with Hospitals?* vi. 115 A partial answer comes from North America, where the treatment and utility rooms are increasingly made up of movable partitions. **1978** *Cornish Guardian* 27 Apr. 14/7 (Advt.), The accommodation comprises..rear hallway, wash house/utility room, [etc.]. **1962** Utility routine [see HOUSEKEEPING *sb.* 5]. **1980** M. S. WU *Introd. Computer Data Processing with BASIC* ix. 188 If an installation frequently receives data from various locations on small reels of magnetic tape, a utility routine may be written to combine the data from the short reels onto one large reel of tape prior to processing. **1926** A. E. TAYLOR *Plato* xvi. 431 Our question is not what 'art' has the..greatest utility-value, but simply which sets up the most severe standard of truth and accuracy. **1974** B. PEARCE tr. *Amin's Accumulation on World Scale* I. i. 64 It is impossible to 'measure' statistically the advantage (or disadvantage) that the underdeveloped countries derive from international exchange, whether one looks at the matter from the angle of labor value or from that of utility value. **1968** *Listener* 22 Aug. 235/1 Ugly poles carrying utility wires. **1973** *Sunday Advocate-News* (Barbados) 25 Feb. 18/6 We experience a lot of damage done to roofs by overhanging trees over-hanging verandahs and low-hanging utility wires.

b. Of a dog, fowl, etc.: That is bred, reared, or kept to serve a useful end or object as distinct from purposes of beauty, display, show, etc.

1877 STABLES *Pract. Kennel Guide* 96 The Points of Utility Dogs, including the Newfoundland, the Collie [etc.]. **1903** H. FRANCKLIN (*title*) Incubating and Rearing Utility Fowls. **1904** *Daily Chron.* 10 Feb. 3/2 The utility poultry keeper.

c. Intended for use; generally useful; (passing into) merely functional; *spec.*: (*a*) of a motor vehicle: designed for carrying both passengers and goods; (*b*) of a player in a team game: able to play competently in more than one position (cf. *utility man* in sense 5 a above); (*c*) during and in the aftermath of the war of 1939–45, designating clothes and household goods made in a standardized form in accordance with an official allowance of materials (cf. AUSTERITY 4 b).

1895 *Montgomery Ward Catal.* Spring & Summer 585/1 Combination Barrel and Utility Cart... Cart will pick up barrel or body in a moment. **1908** *Westm. Gaz.* 29 Sept. 4/2 A utility vehicle..good for ten or even fifteen years' hard service. **1911** WEBSTER, Utility man. **1911** *Daily Colonist* (Victoria, B.C.) 25 Apr. 20/2 (Advt.), 1000 Yards Utility Cloth, fast colors..Per yard, 20¢. **1920** *Car* 3 Nov. 225/1 No greater mistake could be made than in the assumption that America's resources are limited to the production of 'utility' motor vehicles. **1942** *Daily Express* 24 Mar. 4/1 (*caption*) Frankly, Meadows, can you see *me* in a utility suit? **1943** *Ann. Reg. 1942* 32 Exempting so-called 'utility' cloth and clothing and boots and shoes from purchase tax. **1943** *Archit. Rev.* XCIII. 3 An exhibition has recently been held of utility furniture and utility pottery. **1944** F. CLUNE *Red Heart* 11 A utility truck stood at the edge of the landing-ground. **1947** *Jane's Fighting Ships 1946–47* 57 *Savage* and ships of 5 later groups have been described officially as a 'utility' type. **1948** *Observer* 8 Feb. 5/3 The dental profession..will..refuse to enter a service which..will lower the present high standard of dental treatment to a utility level. **1949** *Automobile & Carriage Builders' Jrnl.* Nov. 49/1 The utility car, estate wagon or shooting brake has been standardized by some motor manufacturers. **1950** *RAC Guide & Handbk. 1950–51* 52 The utility vehicle, shooting brake, or station wagon is not a class of vehicle known as such to the law. **1952** M. LASKI *Village* i. 14 Mrs. Wilson made the tea and then they both sat down on their camp-beds and sipped it out of thick white Utility cups. **1959** W. GOLDING *Free Fall* iv. 100 No, madam, I'm sorry, we don't supply them at that price. This is a utility model. **1963** *Daily Tel.* 13 Nov. 25 (*heading*) 'Utility' state opening without the Queen..Peers and M.P.s in ordinary dress. **1970** *Times* 2 Nov. 14/8 They would be the centres, with Davies (a centre last year) on the right wing and Linnecar, a utility player, on the left. **1971** *E. Afr. Standard* (Nairobi) 10 Apr. 2/2 Kadir, an intelligent utility half-back. **1974** *Country Life* 26 Sept. 828 Utility clothes, furniture and household goods..were the wartime government's solution. **1976** *National Observer* (U.S.) 16 Oct., Pickup trucks and four-wheel-drive utility vehicles have jumped in popularity in the West and may bid for a national status rivaling the van's. **1978** *Early Music* Oct. 587/2 The selection of illustrations..ranges from fine illuminated manuscripts to simple 'utility' articles. **1984** *NZ Rugby News* 9 May 2/2 Utility Laurie Holmes has shifted to Sydney.

'utilizable, *a.* Also **-isable.** [a. F. *utilisable*, or f. UTILIZE *v.* + -ABLE.] Capable of being utilized.

1881 'FORTIOR' *Fair Trade Cry* 13 The utilizable lands of America. **1889** J. A. BERLY tr. *Reynier's Voltaic Accumulator* 138 The mean utilisable fall of potential in normal discharge.

utilization (juːtɪlaɪˈzeɪʃən). Also **-isation.** [a. F. *utilisation* (1812): see next and -ATION.]

1. The action of utilizing; the fact of being utilized.

1847 WEBSTER. **1864** LOWELL *Fireside Trav.* (1909) 57 A man of genius, but of genius that evaded utilization. **1881** SIR W. THOMSON in *Nature* XXIV. 434 The utilisation of tidal energy. **1894** GRANT ALLEN in *Westm. Gaz.* 12 June 2/1 The whole history of the human race on earth is a continuous history of successive utilisations.

2. *Comb.*, as **utilization factor**, the proportion of a given resource which is being used or is available for use.

1921 A. P. TROTTER *Elem. Illumination Engin.* viii. 81 The ratio of the flux of light which reaches the working plane, whether directly or by reflection, to the whole flux of light from a lamp, is called the utilization factor, or coefficient of utilization. **1982** *IEEE Jrnl. Solid-State Circuits* XVII. 671/1 A gate utilization factor of ~ 95 percent has been achieved in programming the gate array.

utilize (ˈjuːtɪlaɪz), *v.* Also **-ise.** [ad. F. *utiliser* (1792), ad. It. *utilizzare* (1760), f. *utile* UTILE *a.*: see -IZE, and cf. Sp. *utilizar*, Pg. *-isar*.]

1. *trans.* To make or render useful; to convert to use, turn to account.

Rare before 1858. '*Utilize* is fast antiquating *improve*, in the sense of "turn to account"' (1873 F. Hall *Mod. Eng.* 167).

1807 J. BARLOW *Columbiad* IX. 683 [To] Improve and utilise each opening birth, And aid the labors of this nurturing earth. **1824** *Westm. Rev.* April 454 Izmail and Kilia..are respectively able to nullify or to utilize the northern mouth of the Danube. **1860** RUSKIN *Mod Paint.* V. IX. xi. §22 Let all physical exertion..be utilized. **1882** PITMAN *Mission Life in Greece & Pal.* 123 Her services could not be utilised for missions.

2. *intr.* To make oneself of use. *rare*$^{-1}$.

1883 HOWELLS *Register* i, Come in here and sympathize a little!.. *Miss S.* No; you come out here and utilize a little.

Hence **'utilized** *ppl. a.*, **'utilizing** *vbl. sb.*

1859 in *N. & Q.* 3rd Ser. VI. 306/1 Odd proposals for the utilising of power. **1881** P. GEDDES in *Nature* XXIV. 524 The application of the utilised matter and energy by the given society.

'utilizer. Also **-iser.** [f. prec. + -ER[1].] One who or that which utilizes.

1873 DAWSON *Earth & Man* xv. 380 Man was..to be..a care-taker and utiliser..of the things given to him. **1883** *Standard* 21 Nov. 5/3 Not a man of science, but only a utiliser of scientific results. **1884** *Health Exhib. Catal.* 66/1 Register Stove fitted with the Oxford Heat Utilizers.

‖**'utinam.** *Obs.* [L. *utinam* oh that! would that!, f. *uti* (*ut* conj.) + *nam* indeed.] An earnest wish or fervent desire.

1643 SIR T. BROWNE *Relig. Med.* §24 'Tis not a melancholy *Utinam* of mine owne, but the desires of better heads. **1646** —— *Pseud. Ep.* I. x. 38 Nor can the will which hath a power to runne into velleities..have any *utinam* of this. **1718** *Entertainer* No. 9. 56 Our Religion is pure and undefiled... A Glance or a *Utinam*, in Christianity, are Criminal.

†**'uting,** *vbl. sb. Obs.* [Later var. of *yowting*, *yeoting*, YOTING *vbl. sb.*] The action of steeping grain in the process of brewing. Only attrib. in *uting-fat*, *-room*, *-vat*.

1610 R. VAUGHAN *Water-Workes* E 4, Vting-rooms, Garnars, Matting-roomes [etc.]. *Ibid.* K 3, The water from my Vting-vats will doe the like. **1702** *Act 1 Anne* Stat. 2, c. 3 §3 All Cisterns Uting-Fats Utensils and other Vessels. **1720** *Lond. Gaz.* No. 5864/3 Corn..steeped in any Cistern or Uting-Fat. **1800** *Act 41 Geo. III*, c. 6, Every Maltster.. should wet or steep his Barley..in the Cistern, [or] Uting-fat.

‖**uti possidetis** (ˈjuːtaɪ pɒsɪˈdiːtɪs, juːtɪ pɒsɪˈdeɪtɪs). [late L., = as you possess, f. *uti* (*ut* conj.) + *possidētis* 2nd pers. pl., pres. indicative, of *possidēre* to possess.] (See quot. 1980.)

1681 [see INTERDICT *sb.* 2 a]. **1763** J. BELL *Trav. from St. Petersburg* I. II. vi. 307 All matters were soon accommodated ..on the footing of *uti possidetis*; i.e. each of the parties [*sc.* Russia and China] retaining the people and territories that then belonged to them. **1780** BURKE *Let. Affairs Ireland* 20 The six resolutions were to be considered as a sort of *uti possidetis*. **1823** BYRON *Don Juan* x. xlv. 75 A sort of treaty or negotiation, Between the British cabinet and Russian,.. Something about the Baltic's navigation, Hides, train-oil, tallow, and the rights of Thetis, Which Britons deem their 'uti possidetis'. **1905** *Cambr. Mod. Hist.* (1907) III. xxi. 709 In 1593 a truce had been arranged on the *uti possidetis* basis. **1934** A. TOYNBEE *Study Hist.* I. 381 He made peace..on a basis of *uti possidetis.* **1980** *Oxf. Compan. Law* 1269/1 *Uti possidetis*, in the Roman law, an interdict whereby the colourable possession of real property by a *bona fide* possessor was continued until the rights of parties were finally determined. The phrase is sometimes referred to as a principle under which property not expressly provided for in a treaty terminating hostilities is to remain in the hands of the party who happened to have possession of it when hostilities ended.

utis, variant of UTAS.

†**'utlagary.** *Obs.* [a. AF. *utlagarie, -erie*: see OUTLAWRY.] = OUTLAWRY 1.

1440 *Paston Lett.* I. 41 As the seide utlagare was certyfyed. **1567** *Lanc. Wills* (Chetham Soc.) II. 82, I have byn divers tymes wrongfullye sued and brought to the poynt of utlagari. **1642** tr. *Perkins Prof. Bk.* i. §27. 12 Attainder of Felony..by utlagery, by verdict and by confession. **1660** *Act 12 Chas. II*, c. 12 ¶ 12 Any person..whose Conviction, Utlagary or Attainder is by this Act discharged.

utlagh(e, -laȝe, -lahe, -law(e, obs. ff. OUTLAW.

utlarie, -y(e, -lawry(e, obs. ff. OUTLAWRY.

utleden, var. OUTLEAD *v. Obs.*

†**utle'gation.** *Obs.*[−1] [ad. med.L. *utlagātion-*, n. of action f. *utlagāre*: see OUTLAW *v.*] The legal process by which a person was outlawed. (Cf. OUTLAWRY 1.)

1678 BUTLER *Hud.* III. i. 1521 When to a Legal Utlegation You turn your Excommunication.

utlepe, -leph, -lete, obs. ff. OUTLEAP *sb.*, etc.

†**utmer, utmore,** *a. Obs. rare.* [f. *utm-est* UTMOST *a.*, with comparative ending: see -MORE, and cf. OUTMER *a.*] = OUTER *a.* 1.

1382 WYCLIF *Ezek.* xlvi. 21 That thei bere not out in to the vtmer house [1388 to the outermere halle]. —— *Matt.* xxii. 13 Sende ȝee hym into vttermore [*v.r.* vtmore, vtmer] derknessis. *Ibid.* viii. 12.

utmost ('ʌtməʊst, 'ʌtməst), *a.* and *sb.* Forms: α. 1 ute-, **utmest** (*Northumb.* **wut-**), 3 **ute-**, 4 **ut-**, 5, 6 *Sc.* **vtmest**; 5 *north.* and *Sc.* **vtmast**, *Sc.* 6 **vt-**, 9 **utmaist**; 4–7 **vt-**, 5–6 **vtte-**, 7– **utmost** (6 **vtmoste, vtmoost**). β. 3–4 **otemost**, 4–5 **ottemoste**; 4 **ot-, ottemeste**. [OE. *útemest, útmest* (rare, and chiefly northern, variants of the usual *ýte-, ýtmest*), a double superlative (cf. FOREMOST, INMOST) from *úte* or *út* OUTE, OUT *advs.* + *-m-est*: see -MOST. Cf. the later OUTMOST *a.*

In Layamon 11023 *utemæste* prob. represents OE. *ýtemeste*. The ME. forms with *ote-, otte-, ot-* seem to imply an earlier *ŭte-* with shortened vowel (as in Icel. *ŭtan* from *ūt*). The shortening in *utmost* may be partly due to the double consonant, and partly to the influence of UTTER *a.*]

I. 1. a. Situated farthest from the centre; occupying, lying at, or dwelling in the extreme bound or bounds; most external or remote in position or location; outermost, uttermost; OUTMOST *a.* 1.

α. *c* **950** *Lindisf. Gosp.* Matt. xxii. 13 Sendas hine in ðiostrum ðæm utmestum. *c* **1100** *Ælfreds Boeth.* xix. (Bodl. MS.), þeah hit nu ȝebyriȝe þæt ða utemestan ðioda eowerne naman up ahebban. *c* **1320** *Sir Orfeo* 357 (Auchinleck MS.), Al þe vtmast wal Was..schine as cristal. *c* **1400** *Destr. Troy* 5487 Beyten is out in the orient the vtmast syde. *c* **1425** WYNTOUN *Cron.* III. i. 8 Ane of his tais with The vtmast endis be þe lith Quyt wes smyttyn of þaim. *c* **1450** *Godstow Reg.* 106 His ende vttemost toward the tenement of the forsaid Vincente Menge. **1526** TINDALE *Matt.* viii. 12 The children of the Kingdom shalbe cast out in to the vtmoost dercknes. **1590** SPENSER *F.Q.* II. x. 12 Corineus had that Prouince vtmost west To him assigned. **1618** LAWSON *New Orchard* (1623) 46 We admit without the fence, of Walnuts in most plaine places, Trees middle-most, and..Elmes vtmost. **1660** BARROW *Euclid* I. prop. 21 The utmost points of one side of a triangle. **1697** DRYDEN *Æneis* IX. 221 Where the foes their utmost guards advance. **1729** T. INNES *Crit. Ess.* (1879) 63 The utmost extremities of the north of Britain. **1798** S. & HT. LEE *Canterb. T.* II. 326 The utmost limit of creation! **1820** SHELLEY *Prometh. Unb.* IV. 372 It..doth pass Into the utmost leaves and delicatest flowers. **1859** TENNYSON *Elaine* 525 Knights of utmost North and West. **1877** RUSKIN *St. Mark's Rest* iv. (1894) 50 The entire tablet varied to its utmost edge.

fig. **1667** SOUTH *Serm.* (1715) II. 24 Which surely must reach the utmost Thoughts of any Atheist whatsoever.

β. **1297** R. GLOUC. (Rolls) 11433 þe castel hii asailede,..& brake þe otemoste wal. **1387** TREVISA *Higden* (Rolls) I. 303 In þe vttermeste (MS. *a.* otmeste) ende of all þe erþe. *a* **1390** *Wycliffite Bible* Num. xxii 36 (MS. Bodl. 959), [A] toun..sette in ye otemost coostys of Arnon. **1398** TREVISA *Barth. De P.R.* XV. clv. (Bodl. MS.), þe ottemoste norþe..of Germania. *c* **1450** *M.E. Med. Bk.* (Heinrich) 93 Pile þe barke þe ottemoste [*v.r.* ottemoste rynde] awey.

†**b.** Of garments: Outermost; exterior. *Obs.*

1553 *Respublica* 1774 Doe of your vtmoste robes eche one. **1584** T. HUDSON *Du Bartas' Judith* IV. (1611) 47 Her vtmost robe was colour blew Cœlest.

c. Furthest extended; greatest in extent, length, measure, etc.

1709 FELTON *Diss. Classics* (1718) 12 To put forth Your Hand to the utmost Stretch, and reach whatever You aspire at. **1746** FRANCIS tr. *Horace, Epist.* I. xvi. 108 Death is..That utmost Course, where human Sorrow ends. **1791** COWPER *Odyss.* XI. 454 A night of utmost length. **1844** KINGLAKE *Eothen* xvii, All the whole earth that I could reach with my utmost sight and keenest listening was still.

2. That is of the greatest or highest degree; of the largest amount, number, etc.; extreme.

Somewhat rare before 1590; in freq. use since 1710.

a **1325** *Prose Psalter* lvii. 6 God shal defoulen her teþe..; our Lord shal breke þe uttemast [*Dublin MS.* ottermast] tuels of þe wicked. *c* **1375** *Sc. Leg. Saints* xii. (*Mathias*) 113 Scho let hym wyt þe vtmast thinge, þat he wes but a fundlynge. **1482** *Monk of Evesham* xxli. (Arb.) 53 He was takyn..to the vtmest peynys and ponissement of dethe. **1526** *Pilgr. Perf.* (W. de W. 1531) 2 b, The vttemost perfeccyon that man may attayne to. **1586** MARLOWE *1st Pt. Tamburl.* II. iii, With amitie we yeeld Our vtmost seruice to the faire Cosroe. **1610** *Chester's Triumph* B 4, What e're our more then strained vtmost-All Can possibly performe, performe we shall. **1628** MAY *Virg. Georg.* III. 84 Her temptations make Two stubborne Bulls..with their Hornes to try their utmost deedes. **1667** MILTON *P.L.* I. 103 His utmost power with adverse power oppos'd In dubious Battel. **1704** EVELYN *Diary* 7 Sept., This day was celebrated the thanksgiving..with the utmost pomp and splendour. **1782** MISS BURNEY *Cecilia* v. iv, Her mind was now in a state of the utmost confusion. **1805** WORDSW. *Waggoner* II. 73 The utmost anger of the sky. **1833** HT. MARTINEAU *Brooke Farm* iii. 35 The utmost profit of a cow. **1876** GEO. ELIOT *Dan. Der.* I. vii, His antigropelos, the utmost approach he possessed to a hunting equipment.

3. Latest in order or time; last, final. Now *rare*.

c **1460** *Towneley Myst.* xxv. 248 Mary, me mynnys, thi moder hight, the vtmast ende of all thy kyn. **1526** TINDALE *Matt.* v. 26 Till thou have payed the vtmost [1611 vttermost] farthing. **1590** SPENSER *F.Q.* II. i. 49 In these sad words she spent her vtmost breath. **1591** —— *Ruins of Time* 45 From their first vntill their vtmost date. **1642** MILTON *Apol. Smect.* 41 Many wise men have miscarried in praising great designe before the utmost event. **1670–1** MARVELL *Corr.* Wks. (Grosart) II. 367 Censure..against those who, after an utmost day set, shall persist to absent themselves. **1672** DRYDEN *Conq. Granada* II. i, 'Till I have found the last and utmost Foe. **1691** SWIFT *Ode Athenian Society* xi, When the sad melancholy muse Stays but to catch his utmost breath. **1772** PRIESTLEY *Inst. Relig.* (1782) I. 82 They prolong life to the utmost term of nature. **1809–12** MAR. EDGEWORTH *Absentee* iv, He would use it [*sc.* the power] to obtain the utmost penny of his debt. **1818** BYRON *Juan* I. lxxx, I..hear these freedoms form the utmost list Of all o'er which such love may be a ranger. **1856** KANE *Arct. Expl.* I. xv. 171 Grating it down nicely,..and adding the utmost oil as a lubricant.

II. *absol.* and as *sb.*

In *Lindisf. Gosp.* Mark v. 23 *in utmestum* is used to render the L. *in extremis* (= at the point of death).

4. That which is most outward, distant, or remote; the farthest part, district, limit, etc., *of* an extent or area. Now only *arch.*

c **825** *Vesp. Psalter* cxxxviii. 9 In ðem utmestan sæs. *a* **950** *Ritual Dunelm.* (Surtees) 55 Oð to vtmeste earðes. **1382** WYCLIF *Job* xxxvi. 30 The vtmost of the se he shal couere. **1382** —— *Acts* i. 8 ȝe schulen be witnessis to me..to the vtmeste [*v.r.* vttermest] of erthe. **1614** W. B. *Philosopher's Banquet* (ed. 2) 43 The utmost of the taile is poyson. **1615** G. SANDYS *Trav.* 177 A City..on the utmost of the ridge of a hill. **1887** MORRIS *Odyssey* XI. 13 At last unto the utmost of the Ocean-stream we came.

†**b.** *sb. pl.* Remotest parts *of* the earth, etc. *rare*.

1382 WYCLIF *Ps.* cxxxiv. 7 Bringende out cloudis fro the vtmostis [*v.r.* vttermostis] of the erthe. **1382** —— *Isaiah* vii. 18 The fleȝe, that is in the vtmostes [*v.r.* vttermostis] of the flodus of Egipt.

5. That which is greatest or of the highest degree; the most or greatest possible or attainable in respect *of* force, skill, etc.; the utmost point, extreme limit or degree, *of* something.

1472 *Cov. Leet Bk.* 377 Thei..seid thei wold abyde with the Maire..to the vtmost of herr goodes in that mater. **1526** TINDALE *Acts* xxiv. 22 When Lisias..is come, I will know the vtmost of youre matters. **1594** *1st Pt. Contention* C 4, To morrow we will ride to London, And trie the vtmost of these Treasons forth. **1596** SPENSER *F.Q.* VI. i. 38 Thinking the vtmost of their force to trie. **1622** MABBE tr. *Aleman's Guzman d'Alf.* II. 346 The Painter..shew'd therein the vtmost of his skill. **1667** EARL ORRERY *St. Lett.* (1742) 331 The utmost I aimed at..was to tell your grace what others told me. **1752** HUME *Ess. & Treat.* (1777) I. 95 The utmost we have to boast of are a few essays. **1764** REID *Inquiry* i. 75 The utmost which the human faculties can attain. **1805** J. SPAULDING *Universalism* 129 That the damned suffer the utmost of their desert. **1838** THIRLWALL *Greece* V. 153 Thebes had accomplished the utmost she could now reasonably aim at. **1855** BAIN *Senses & Int.* I. ii. §23 The utmost that can be said in the present state of our knowledge.

b. With possessive adjs.: The highest, greatest, or best of one's ability, power, etc.; the very most. Freq. with *do*.

c **1611** CHAPMAN *Iliad* II. 119 Come then,..and fly to our loved home; for now, nor ever, shall Our utmost take in broad-wayed Troy. **1646** GAULE *Cases Consc.* 118 Their utmost is but to produce a..false species of things. **1660** SOUTH *Serm.* (1715) IV. 23 Nor will it suffice..to rally up all one's little Utmost into one Discourse. **1690** LOCKE *Hum. Und.* IV. xix. §15 A Man, having..done his utmost to inform himself in all Particulars,..may [etc.]. **1708** ADDISON *Pres. State of War* 26 Let us perform our utmost,..and we shall overwhelm 'em. **1785** BURNS *To Rev. John M'Math* xvi, [One who] to his utmost would befriend Ought that belang'd ye. **1818** COBBETT *Pol. Reg.* XXXIII. 633 Will you do your utmost to obtain justice? **1856** MISS YONGE *Daisy Chain* I. xviii, His work, after he goes to Oxford, will be doing his very utmost—and you know what an utmost that is. **1887** P. MCNEILL *Blawearie* 136 It taxed to its utmost the ingenuity of the rival wooers.

c. As *sb.* An extreme amount, degree, or limit.

1856 [see prec. sense]. **1863** JEAN INGELOW *Poems* 24 Forever yawns before our eyes An utmost—that is veiled.

6. The end, finish, or issue *of* something.

1603 SHAKS. *Meas. for M.* II. i. 36 See that Claudio Be executed;..let him be prepar'd, For that's the vtmost of his pilgrimage. **1666** BOYLE *Orig. Forms & Qual.* 264 An Accident robb'd me of my Glasse, before I could see the utmost of the Event. **1674** [see UTTERMOST *a.* 6].

7. *to the utmost*, to the extreme or uttermost degree, extent, capacity, or limit. Also const. *of* (one's power, etc.).

c **1450** *Mirk's Festial* I. 91 Gracyously he woll þat a man be demed wyth mercy and not to þe vtmast here. **1526** TINDALE *1 Thess.* ii. 16 For the wrath off God is come on them, even to the vtmost. **1613** SHAKS. *Hen. VIII*, V. iii. 146 Some of ye ..Would trye him to the vtmost, had ye meane. **1685** BOYLE *Enq. Notion Nat.* vii. 266, I grew weary before I had prosecuted it to the utmost. **1738** WESLEY *Ps.* v. vi, Thy wrath on the rebellious Race Shall to the utmost come. **1756** C. LUCAS *Ess. Waters* III. 307 Let us pursue our enquiries to the utmost. **1834** HT. MARTINEAU *Demerara* iv. 46 He was sure to..torment the animal to the utmost. **1860** MOTLEY *Netherl.* ii. I. 59 He would keep his pledge to the utmost. **1873** F. HALL in *Scribner's Monthly* VI. 465 The sages..have certainly consulted his comfort to the utmost.

(*b*) **1596** *Edward III*, IV. v. 86 That same man..keepes it [*sc.* his word] to the vtmost of his power. **1659** *Nicholas Papers* (Camden) IV. 147, I shall to the vttmost of my power constantly endeauour to doe him right. **1729** LAW *Serious C.* vi. 90 So sure is it, that we are to do them to the utmost of our power. **1802** MRS. E. PARSONS *Myst. Visit* II. 245 The good woman..fortunately succeeded to the utmost of her wish. **1875** MANNING *Mission H. Ghost* xii. 346 Let us to the utmost of our power, submit our will to the will of God.

8. ***at the utmost*** (†*at utmost*), at the very most in respect of time, quantity, etc. Cf. MOST *a.* 6.

1619 in Foster *Eng. Factories India* (1906) I. 143, 15 dayes stay there, or 20 at uttmost. **1643** TRAPP *Comm. Gen.* xi. 7 [He] beautified it, or, at utmost, inlarged it. **1722** WHISTON *The. Earth* III. iii. 247 The Modern Age of Men at the utmost is not 80. **1753** *Chambers' Cycl.* Suppl. *App.* s.v. *Vultur*, The head..has, at the utmost, only a downy matter on it. **1818** CRUISE *Digest* (ed. 2) II. 418 At the utmost it was in the discretion of the Court.

Hence †**'utmostness.** *nonce-use.*

1674 N. FAIRFAX *Bulk & Selv.* 7 With all that earnestness of threatning, that may beget in man the utmostness of dread.

utnemis: see OUTNEME *a.* and *adv.*

utnume(nn, -liȝ: see OUTNUMEN(LY.

Uto-Aztecan (ˌjuːtəʊæz'tɛkən), *sb.* and *a.* Also **Uto-Aztekan, Utaztekan.** [f. UTE *sb.*[1] and *a.* + -O + *Aztecan* adj. s.v. AZTEC *sb.* and *a.*] **A.** *sb.* A family of languages spoken in central America and western North America. **B.** *adj.* Of or pertaining to this language family.

1891 D. G. BRINTON *Amer. Race* 44 Different bands of the same linguistic stock were found, some on the highest, others on the lowest stages of development, as is strikingly exemplified in the Uto-Aztecan family. *Ibid.* III. i. 118 Of all the stocks on the North American Continent, that which I call the *Uto-Aztecan* merits the closest study. **1913** E. SAPIR in *Jrnl. de la Société des Américanistes de Paris* X. II. 384 Southern Paiute has developed a number of secondary forms of the original Uto-Aztekan vowels and consonants. *Ibid.* 422 In..Ute-Chemehuevi pre-nominal elements occur as suffixes..not prefixes, as ordinarily in Uto-Aztekan. **1935** *Amer. Anthropologist* XXXVII. 608 Are there any traits that distinguish 'Shoshonean' from the rest of Uto-Aztecan? If there are, I do not know what they are. **1937** J. R. FIRTH *Tongues of Men* vii. 93 The Uto-Aztekan group of related languages, spoken by the Indians of Utah, Arizona, California, and Mexico. **1968** *Occas. Papers Idaho State Mus.* XXII, (*title*) Utaztekan prehistory. **1979** I. DAVIS in Campbell & Mithun *Lang. Native Amer.* 409 The differences between Uto-Aztecan and Kiowa-Tanoan both in phonology..and grammar are striking.

Also **'Uto-Aztec** *a.* and *sb.*

1932 W. L. GRAFF *Lang.* xi. 430 The Uto-Aztec group comprises the three branches of Shoshonean, Pima-Sonoran, and Nahuatl. **1956** J. WHATMOUGH *Lang.* (Map facing p. 22) Uto-Aztec.

†**utole,** var. OUT-TOLL *Sc. Obs.* (Cf. OUT-PENNY.)

1742 in Kilkerran *Decisions Crt. Sessions 1738–52* (1775) 504 The resignation of an annual-rent out of a tenement in Aberdeen in the year 1720, being made with the symbol of a penny utole.

Utopia (juː'təʊpɪə). [mod.L. (More, 1516), f. Gr. οὐ not + τόπ-ος a place: see -IA[1], and cf. EUTOPIA. Hence It., Sp., Pg. *Utopia*, F. *Utopie*.]

1. An imaginary island, depicted by Sir Thomas More as enjoying a perfect social, legal, and political system.

1551 (*title*), A fruteful and pleasaunt Worke of the beste state of a publyque weale, and of the newe yle called Utopia; written in Latine by Syr Thomas More knyght [publ. 1516], and translated into Englyshe by Raphe Robynson. **1570** FOXE *Bk. Martyrs* (ed. 2) 1156/2, I do not..thinke, that..there is any such fourth place of Purgatory at all (vnles it be in M. Mores Vtopia). **1607** A. BREWER *Lingua* II. vi, I remember in the Country of Utopia, they use no other kind of artillery. **1625** BACON *Ess., Usury* (Arb.) 544 So as that Opinion must be sent to Vtopia. **1685** CROWNE *Sir C. Nice* I. Dram. Wks. 1874 III. 270 He will find it is a dream fit for nothing but Utopia. **1692** BENTLEY *Boyle Lect.* 66 Once upon a time,..in the land of Utopia, there was a dialogue between an oak and a cedar. **1725** [MRS. E. HAYWOOD] (*title*), Memoirs of a certain Island adjacent to the Kingdom of Utopia. **1751** J. BROWN *Shaftesb. Charac.* 65 But of this infallible race I know none, except the inhabitants of Utopia. **1818** [see CACOTOPIA]. **1837** MACAULAY *Ess., Lord Bacon* (1897) 402 An acre in Middlesex is better than a principality in Utopia. **1895** LUPTON *More's Utopia* 115

Plate, Reduced facsimile of the woodcut of the Island of Utopia.

transf. **1802–12** BENTHAM *Ration. Judic. Evid.* Wks. 1843 VI. 206 The law is an Utopia—a country that receives no visits, but [etc.].

b. *transf.* Any imaginary, indefinitely-remote region, country, or locality.

1610 TH. TH[ORPE] *Healey's St. Augustine's City of God* Ded., Then [in translating Hall's *Mundus Alter et Idem*, he treated] of a deuised Country scarse on earth, now of a desired Citie sure in heauen; then of Vtopia, now of Eutopia. **1646** SIR T. BROWNE *Pseud. Ep.* III. xii. 132 Some say it liveth in Æthiopia, others in Arabia, some.. in Utopia, for such must that be which is described by Lactantius. **1684** J. P. tr. *J. Ludolphus' Hist. Ethiopia* (ed. 2) 46 Ignorant where this River rises,.. whether in Asia, in Africa, or in Utopia. *a* **1779** WARBURTON *Div. Legat.* II. §4 Wks. 1788 I. 206 A fabulous relation of a voyage to the imaginary island of Panchæa, a kind of ancient Utopia.

2. A place, state, or condition ideally perfect in respect of politics, laws, customs, and conditions.

1613 PURCHAS *Pilgrimage* (1614) 708 The reports of this his voyage savour more of an Vtopia, and Plato's Commonwealth, then of true Historie. **1642** CHAS. I in Rushw. *Hist. Coll.* (1692) I. 727 That new Vtopia of Religion and Government into which they endeavour to transform this Kingdom. **1691** NORRIS *Pract. Disc.* 177 To contemplate all this not.. as an uncertain Reversion, or imaginary Vtopia, but as a state that will shortly and certainly be. **1738** WARBURTON *Div. Legat.* I. 272 No romantic impracticable Utopia. **1760–72** H. BROOKE *Fool of Qual.* (1792) II. 113 But the law-suits.. will not permit me to go in search of my Utopia. **1818** SHELLEY *Julian* 179 'Aye, if we were not weak—and we aspire How vainly to be strong!' said Maddalo: 'You talk Utopia.' **1871** MORLEY *Condorcet* in *Crit. Misc.* Ser. I. 78 To find adequate gratification in the artificial construction of hypothetical utopias. **1883** *Manch. Exam.* 22 Nov. 5/2 Ingenious speculators who hope to reach Utopia by the nationalisation of the land.

b. An impossibly ideal scheme, esp. for social improvement.

a **1734** NORTH *Lives* II. 364 Young men, for want of experience,.. create Utopias in their own imagination, and calculate according to their present fancy. **1843** MARRYAT *M. Violet* xliii, These are not the wild utopias of a heated imagination. **1869** LECKY *Europ. Mor.* I. 180 Averse to all enthusiasm, mysticism, utopias, and superstition.

3. *Comb.*, as ***Utopia-maker, -monger.***

1821 *Edin. Rev.* XXXV. 320 The fantastic brain of some Utopia-monger. **1901** GLOVER *Life & Lett. in 4th C.* 362 The general satire,.. no doubt a fling at the Utopia-makers.

Hence **U'topia-ize** *v. intr.*, to conceive or form impossibly ideal schemes. *nonce-word.*

1853 MRS. GORE *Dean's Daughter* III. 57 A Virginia Hargreave, born to Utopia-ise over a Bostonian tea-table, concerning triumphs to be achieved.

Utopian (juːˈtəʊpɪən), *a.* and *sb.* [ad. mod.L. *Utopian-us* (More, 1516): see prec. and -AN.]

A. *adj.* **1.** Of or belonging to the imaginary island of Utopia or its people.

1551 ROBINSON *More's Utopia* Ep. (1895) 1 This boke of the vtopian commen wealth. **1556** *More's Utopia* Printer to Rdr. (Arb.) 168 The Vtopian Alphabete. **1622** J. TAYLOR (Water P.) *Sir G. Nonsence* Wks. (1630) Aa j b, He.. began to declare in the Vtopian speech, what I haue here.. Translated. **1633** ROWLEY *Match at Midn.* v. I 1 b, Two Vtopian Trunks, full of gold and Iewels. **1681** (*title*), A Pleasant Battle between two Lap-dogs of the Utopian Court. **1808** CAYLEY tr. *More's Utopia* II. 7 That I should anticipate him in what belongs to the Utopian Commonwealth. **1895** LUPTON *More's Utopia* 117 On this and other repellent features of the Utopian character, as drawn by More.

†**b.** Having no known location; existing nowhere. *Obs. rare.*

1609 in Capt. Smith *Wks.* (Arb.) 637 It hath beene to the Spaniards more fearefull then an Vtopian Purgatory. **1678** CUDWORTH *Intell. Syst.* 60 They must be imagined to subsist in certain intermundane spaces and Utopian regions without the world. **1689** SWIFT *Ode to Sir W. Temple* i, Search out this Utopian ground, Virtue's *terra incognita.*

†**c.** Having no assigned diocese or sphere of work. *Obs.*$^{-1}$

1709 BINGHAM *Antiq.* IV. vi, The Nullatenenses of latter Ages, as Panormitan calls Titular and Utopian Bishops.

2. Possessing or regarded as having impossibly or extravagantly ideal conditions in respect of politics, customs, social organization, etc.

In this and next sense occas. with small letter.

1613 PURCHAS *Pilgrimage* (1614) 520 Yea, no Vtopian State comparable to theirs. **1647** *Mercurius Anti-pragmaticus* No. 6. 4 They are like to wander forty yeeres.. ere they arrive in their Utopian Paradise. **1651** C. WALKER *Hist.* III. 14 To these.. they entrust the Administration of this Utopian Commonwealth. **1768** TUCKER *Lt. Nat.* (1834) II. 302 The introduction of an Utopian state. **1782** H. WALPOLE *Vertue's Anecd. Paint.* IV. 284 When he was laying out so magnificent, charitable, and philosophic an Utopian villa. **1855** KINGSLEY *Westw. Ho!* xix, When we have babbled together of Utopian governments in days which are now dreams to me. **1856** H. ROGERS *Ess.* II. viii. 380 Considered as a possible political structure.. Plato's 'Republic' deserves to be considered the most Utopian that ever entered the mind of man.

b. Involving, based or founded on, imaginary or chimerical perfection; impossibly ideal, visionary.

1621 BURTON *Anat. Mel.* To Rdr. 58 Vtopian parity is a thing to be wished for rather then effected. **1643** PRYNNE *Sov. Power Parl.* App. 1 A new Utopian absolute Royall Prerogative.. not bottomed on the Lawes of God or the Realm. **1646** J. COOK *Vind. Law* 28 Thats but a Vtopian consideration, a possibility which never comes into Act. **1659** BP. WALTON *Consid. Considered* 72 This, I doubt, will prove an Utopian conceit. **1762** KAIMES *Elem. Crit.* ii. (1774) I. 35 For confuting such Utopian systems without the fatigue of reasoning. **1798** FERRIAR *Illustr. Sterne* iii. 59 He indulges himself in an Utopian sketch of a perfect government. **1806** H. SIDDONS *Maid, Wife, & W.* III. 6 The sentiments which inspired me may be laughed at as Utopian. **1849** C. BRONTE *Shirley* ix, Marriage! I cannot bear the word: it sounds so silly and utopian. **1877** BURROUGHS *Taxation* 22 They have regarded any attempt to practise absolute equality as Utopian.

3. Of persons: That belongs to or dwells in a Utopia. *rare*$^{-1}$.

1620 J. TAYLOR (Water P.) *Jack a Lent* Wks. (1630) 113/2 As Nymshag an ancient Vtopian Philosopher declares.

b. That conceives, proposes, or advocates impracticably ideal projects or schemes for social welfare, etc.; believing in or aiming at the perfecting of polity or social conditions.

1597–8 DONNE *Let. to Sir H. Wotton* 46 If men.. Durst looke for themselves.. They would like strangers greet themselves, seeing than Utopian youth, growne old Italian. **1661** COWLEY *Cromwell* Wks. 1906 II. 373 You are.. a Theoretical Common-wealths-man, an Utopian Dreamer. **1680** BUTLER *Characters* (1908) 24 A Republican is a civil Fanatic, an Utopian Senator. **1691** BAXTER *Nat. Ch.* xii. 52 As capable of Governing one Kingdom, as an Utopian College of Bishops (that some dream of). **1857** W. SMITH *Thorndale* v. iii. (1858) 427 An Eclectic and Utopian Philosopher. **1868** PEARD *Water-farm.* xi. 114 We are not so Utopian as to assert that [etc.].

B. *sb.* **1.** A native or inhabitant of Utopia; a dweller in some Utopia. Also *Comb.*

1551 ROBINSON tr. *More's Utopia* II. (1895) 218 The wyttes therefore of the Vtopians.. be maruelous quycke. **1597** HOOKER *Eccl. Pol.* v. xxxvi. §4 Such suttle opinions as few but Vtopians are likely to fall into. **1614** RALEIGH *Hist. World* III. viii. §1 They liued Vtopian-like, saue that they vsed no other occupation than Warre. **1684** BURNET tr. *More's Utopia* Pref. A 7 The precaution used in Marriages among the Utopians. **1771** J. ADAMS *Diary* 10 Nov., The good humor,.. and wisdom of the Utopians, is charming. **1857** W. SMITH *Thorndale* IV. v. (1858) 312, I know not precisely how his Utopians intend to deal with war. **1905** *Edin. Rev.* Oct. 426 The admiration of the Utopians.. was by no means confined to the strictly classical authors.

2. One who conceives, proposes, or introduces schemes supposed or intended to bring about improved or perfect social and political conditions, etc.; an advocate of social reform.

a **1873** LYTTON in *Life* (1883) I. 101 My grandfather.. in youth.. was a Utopian, and remained to the last much more than a 'Whig'. **1878** SEELEY *Stein* II. 363 Stein.. was never the utopian here described. **1887** J. C. MORISON *Serv. Man* p. xxiv, He looks with coldness on Utopians who are equally ignorant of capital, labour, or hard work.

Hence **U'topianist**, = UTOPIAN *sb.* 2.

1854 J. S. C. ABBOTT *Napoleon* (1855) II. xxix. 556 What seemed a crime to the eyes of Utopianists. **1876** *Contemp. Rev.* xxviii. 447 Neither abandoned nor disregarded by a few devoted Utopianists.

Utopianism (juːˈtəʊpɪənɪz(ə)m). [f. prec. + -ISM.]

†**1.** A Utopian idea or condition. *Obs.*$^{-1}$

a **1661** HOLYDAY *Juvenal* (1673) 194 Plato indeed would have his cittizens ambidexters:.. this was but one of his vtopianismes.

2. The body of views, aims, or tenets of Utopians; impossibly ideal schemes for the amelioration or perfection of social conditions, etc.

1802–12 BENTHAM *Ration. Judic. Evid.* (1827) IV. 69 Such an improvement that the stamp of Utopianism.. threatens to render the acceptance of it next to hopeless. **1833** CHALMERS *Const. Man* (1835) I. vi. 237 The abortive enterprises of wild yet benevolent Utopianism. **1879** KAUFMANN *Utopias* 258 The superiority of the most recent forms of Utopianism over previous schemes of social improvement.

Utopianize (juːˈtəʊpɪənaɪz), *v.* [f. as prec. + -IZE. Cf. UTOPIA-IZE *v.*]

1. *trans.* To render Utopian; to form a Utopia of.

1834 [implied in *Utopianizer* below]. **1913** *Public Opinion* 26 Dec. 715/1 The international aspect of Utopianising the modern world.

2. *intr.* = *Utopia-ize* vb. s.v. UTOPIA.

1905 H. G. WELLS *Mod. Utopia* ii. 62, I pass.. from Utopianising altogether, to ask the question that.. Schopenhauer failed completely to answer. **1911** —— *New Machiavelli* I. iv. 141 We planned, half in earnest and half Utopianizing, a League of Social Service.

Hence **U'topianizer**, one who projects or conceives a Utopian state or polity.

1834 SOUTHEY *Doctor* ccxli, Like most Utopianisers the legislator of this Columbia had placed his Absolute King and his free People under.. strict laws.

U'topiast. [f. UTOPIA + -(I)ST.] = UTOPIAN *sb.* 2.

1854 tr. *Lamartine's Celebr. Char.* II. 384 The visionary Utopiasts, who advocate a purely metaphysical form of government. **1887** *Westm. Rev.* Jan. 130 It is the weakness of Utopiasts.. to place themselves outside the pale of their own system.

utopiate (juːˈtəʊpɪeɪt). [Blend of UTOPIA and OPIATE *sb.*] A drug which induces fantasies of a utopian existence; a euphoriant.

1964 R. BLUM (*title*) Utopiates: the use and users of LSD 25. *Ibid.* XIV. 292 The movement promises much—a return to paradise, a Utopia of the inner life—and so LSD-25 becomes, if one may be allowed a neologism, a 'Utopiate'. **1983** *Guardian* 11 Aug. 18/3 The typical recruit for drug addiction is the young, weak, inadequate person for whom the drug is a 'utopiate', an escape from the problems of reality.

†**utopical**, *a. Obs. rare.* [f. UTOP-IA + -ICAL.] Impracticable; chimerical.

1620 BP. HALL *Hon. Marr. Clergy* III. xiii. 805 King Edgars Vtopicall decree. *c* **1628** —— *Beauty & Unity of Ch.* (1634) II. 368 Let no idle Donatist.. dreame hence of an Utopicall perfection. **1628** —— *Rem. Wks.* (1660) 20 There is no freedom with these unquiet dispositions, but in.. their own utopical prescriptions.

Utopism (ˈjuːtəpɪz(ə)m). [f. as prec. + -ISM.] = UTOPIANISM 2.

1888 *Cycl. Political Sci. & U.S. Hist.* III. 258/2 It is utopism to believe that the state will have more unity, more harmony,.. because [etc.]. **1901** *Field* 19 Oct. 606/2 What remains of impracticable Utopism that may cling to this new project.

Utopist (ˈjuːtəpɪst). [f. as prec. + -IST. Cf. F. *utopiste* (1857), It., Sp., Pg. *Utopista*, and UTOPIANIST.] = UTOPIAN *sb.* 2.

1845 LEWES *Hist. Philos.* I. 100 Like the Utopists of modern days, he [*sc.* Plato] has developed an *à priori* theory of what the State should be. **1881** MORLEY *Cobden* xxix. II. 268 Men.. who.. thought that the existing government.. was better than the anarchy of utopists, anarchists, and talkers. **1898** *Salesian Bulletin* 15 Feb. 404 The indefatigable utopist of abandoned youth.

†**'utouth**, *prep.* and *adv. Sc. Obs.* Forms: 4–6 ututh, -outh, 5 -owth, 6 utoth; 4–6 vt-, wtouth (5 vttouth), 5 vtouthe, 6 vtowth; 4–5 otouth (5 otow, otowth, outhouth), 5 oututh, 6 -outh; 5 vteuthe, 6 uteucht, utewcht (6 wtew). [Sc. var. of OUTWITH.]

A. *prep.* **1.** Without, outside of, in respect of position.

c **1375** *Sc. Leg. Saints* xxviii. (*Margaret*) 68 Scho.. gefine wes to fostir & fede wtouth the towne. **14..** *Burgh Laws* vii. in *Sc. Acts Parlt.* I. (1844) 334/2 He sall noch mote ututh þe burgh. **1478** *Acta Auditorum* (1839) 59/2 [He] nocht being lauchfully warnit to his defenss and seruit vteuthe þe schire. **1536** [see OUTWITH *prep.* 1]. **1557** *Peebles Burgh Rec.* (1872) 237 Vnfremen that duellis.. vtouth the burgh.

2. Out of, out or away from, throughout, in respect of motion.

1375, *c* **1375** [see OUTWITH *prep.* 1 b]. **1530** *Burgh Rec. Edinb.* (1871) II. 37 The said seiknes.. spreddis vtouth the toun in diuers placis. **1534** BELLENDEN *Livy* II. vi. (S.T.S.) I. 147þai durst put na thing vtouth þe wallis.

B. *adv.* Without; on the outside; outwardly.

1375 BARBOUR *Bruce* II. 299 Till thaim wtouth send thai sone, And bad thaim herbery thaim that nycht. *c* **1375** *Sc. Leg. Saints* xxxii. (*Justin*) 170 A lytil vngument he hym tacht, & bad hyme ga.. & þe wallis oututh ennoynt. **1398** *Munim. de Melros* (Bann. Cl.) 489 My demaynis.. with al þe appourtenaunce vtouth and enovth. **1455** in *Charters* &c. *Edinb.* (1871) 80 Baith in the watter and vtouth. **1491** *Cartular. St. Nicholai Aberdon.* (New Spald. Cl.) I. 255 Nay chaplane of the College nor vtouthe. **1512** *Acc. Ld. High Treas. Scot.* IV. 348 Ane coup.. nettit with gold of florising utewcht. **1532** *Reg. Privy Seal Scot.* II. 190/2 Assemblies to be had within our realme or utouth.

transf. **1453** *Dunfermline Reg.* (Bann. Cl.) 341 þe quhilkis.. I will all vtrali be excludit and neuer to be herd in jugement na vtouth. **1496** *Acta Dom. Conc.* II. 23 Decerning the sammyn to be of nane availe.. in tyme tocum in jugment nor utouth.

utrack, etc.: see OUTRAKE, etc.

†**u'trality.** *nonce-word.* [f. L. *uter, utr-*, which (of two), after NEUTRALITY.] Tendency to favour both sides; inclination towards either party.

1642 W. PRICE *Serm.* 2 Apostacy and neutrality, or rather utrality (if you will pardon the word).

utraly, obs. Sc. var. UTTERLY.

utraquism (ˈjuːtrəkwɪz(ə)m). [f. as next + -ISM.]

1. *Hist.* (With capital initial.) The doctrine or tenets of the Utraquists.

1861 LD. ACTON *Lett.* (1906) 186 In Bohemia Utraquism was the national faith. **1892** *Athenæum* 2 Jan. 10/1 From the dawn of Utraquism to its eclipse.. in the disaster of the White Mountain in 1620.

2. The use or employment of two languages on an equal footing. *rare*$^{-1}$.

1897 *Speaker* 10 April 392/2 The [Austrian] concession.. [*sc.* of officially recognising Czech] is spoken of as sanctioning 'the *utraquism* of German and Czech'.

utraquist (ˈjuːtrəkwɪst), *sb.* and *a.* With capital initial in specific uses. [ad. mod.L. *Utraquista*, f. L. *utraque* each, both (in the phrase *sub utrāque speciē* 'under each kind': see SPECIES *sb.* 2, KIND *sb.* 13 b). Cf. -IST, and F. *Utraquiste.*]

A. *sb.* **1.** *Hist.* = CALIXTIN 1.

1836 *Pop. Encycl.* I. 814/1 *Utraquists*, a sect of Hussites in Bohemia. **1855** MILMAN *Lat. Chr.* VI. 248 They were called the Utraquists, as insisting on the Eucharist in both elements. **1881** STANLEY *Chr. Instit.* v. 95 When the Bohemian Utraquists fought with desperate energy to recover the use of the cup.

2. 'One who composes in both Latin and the vernacular' (Webster, 1911).

B. *adj.* **1.** *Hist.* Belonging to the Utraquists; demanding, insisting on, or advocating the receiving the Communion in both kinds.

1894 F. I. ANTROBUS tr. *Pastor's Hist. Popes* III. 214 The Utraquist Clergy. **1900** *Pilot* 27 Oct. 539/1 The Hussites.. were pre-eminently utraquist.

2. Speaking or using both or two languages.

1867 *Chambers's Encycl.* IX. 686/1 The name Utraquist is still applied to certain districts or villages in Bohemia and Moravia..to convey that..*both languages*, Bohemian and German, are spoken.

Hence **'utraquistic** *a.*

1894 F. I. ANTROBUS tr. *Pastor's Hist. Popes* III. 216 This oath was thoroughly Catholic, and left no room for any Utraquistic interpretation.

Utrecht ('juːtrɛkt, 'ytrɛxt). Also *Sc.* 5 **Vtt-, Out-, Owtrecht, Outrech, -rik,** 7 **Utrik.** The name of a town and province in Holland, used attrib. in the sense 'coined, made, etc., at Utrecht', as † ***Utrecht gulden, noble.***

1494 *Halyburton's Ledger* (1867) 52 An Vttrecht gudlyn and a Gentis gudlyn. **1497** *Ibid.* 125 Item lent hym..7 Outrecht guldynis. **1604** *Extr. Burgh Rec. Stirling* (1887) 108 Aucht haill Utrik nobles.

†**b.** *ellipt.* or as *sb.* A Utrecht gulden. *Obs.*

1493 *Halyburton's Ledger* (1867) 31 Item resauit fra him.. 3 Outrikis, price 4s. **1498** *Ibid.* 249 Gyffyn the Archden..at his partyn, 10 Outrech... Som of thir Owtrechtis, 2 li. 1s. 8.

c. Utrecht velvet, a strong, thick kind of plush made of worsted, mohair, or mohair and cotton, used in upholstering furniture, carriages, etc.; furniture plush.

1848 H. R. FORSTER *Stowe Catal.* 252 Armchairs, covered with Utrecht velvet. **1897** *Daily News* 14 June 6/6 Green Utrecht velvet upholstered oak furniture.

†**'Utrechted,** *pa. pple. Obs.*$^{-1}$ [f. prec. + -ED.] Having its seaward defences destroyed, as stipulated in the Treaty of Utrecht (1713).

1748 H. WALPOLE *Lett.* (1846) II. 217 Dunkirk to remain as it is, on the land side; but to be Utrecht'd again to the sea.

utrely, obs. Sc. f. UTTERLY *adv.*

†**'utricide.** *Obs.*$^{-1}$ [ad. L. *ūtricīda*, f. *ūtri-s, ūter* leathern bottle, vessel of skin: see -CIDE 1.] One who stabs an inflated vessel of skin.

1566 ADLINGTON *Apuleius* 30 That I, after the slaughter of so many enemies,..might embrace..not an homicide but an utricide. [**1879** LEWIS & SHORT, *Utricida*, one who cuts skins or bags in pieces, a skin-slayer, utricide.]

utricle[1] ('juːtrɪk(ə)l). [ad. F. *utricule* (18th c.), or L. *ūtriculus* UTRICULUS[1].]

1. *Bot.* A small sac or bladder-shaped body; a bottle-shaped part or structure.

primordial utricle: see PRIMORDIAL *a.* 4 b.

a. 1731 MILLER *Gard. Dict.* s.v. *Sap*, All Male Flowers that have Utricles at the Bottom of the Petala. **1793** MARTYN *Lang. Bot.* s.v. *Vessels*, Utricles, or little Bags; usually full of a green pulp. **1816** KEITH *Phys. Bot.* I. 349 The structure of the utricles of the tree is also said to be different from that of the utricles of the herb. **1875** DARWIN *Insectiv. Pl.* xvii. 419 The spherical glands were still white but their utricles were broken up.

b. 1826–34 *Encycl. Metrop.* (1845) VII. 50/1 An utricle is a membranous, elastic pericarp. **1861** BENTLEY *Man. Bot.* 314 The Utricle is a superior, one-celled, one or few-seeded fruit.

c. 1849 [see PRIMORDIAL *a.* 4 b]. **1857** HENFREY *Elem. Course Bot.* 495 The primordial utricle is a layer of substance of a dense mucilaginous consistence.., applied intimately to the inner surface of the cell-membrane of young cells [etc.]. **1875** BENNETT & DYER *Sach's Bot.* 62 The hydrostatic pressure which the vacuole-fluid exercises on the protoplasm [**1882** primordial] utricle.

d. 1858 IRVINE *British Pl.* 240 The Carex Tribe... Fruit without hairs at the base, enclosed in a peculiar envelope (utricle). **1897** WILLIS *Flower. Pl.* II. 126 The axil of a second glume (the utricle) which closely enwraps it.

e. 1874 COOKE *Fungi* 49 After the spores have become ripe, the free point of the utricle bursts.

f. 1875 DARWIN *Insectiv. Plants* xviii. 451 Found within the utricle or neck of one leaf.

2. *Anat.* and *Biol.* A small cell, sac, or bladder-like process.

1822 GOOD *Study Med.* IV. 603 Those utricles, or minute bladders of the cuticle containing a watery fluid. **1836–9** TODD *Cycl. Anat.* II. 413/2 Utricles floating loosely in the abdominal cavity. **1899** *Allbutt's Syst. Med.* VIII. 905 Microbacillus of the 'peladic utricle'.

b. The larger of the two sacs in the membranous labyrinth of the ear.

1837 *Penny Cycl.* IX. 239/1 The utricle, or sinus of the vestibule [in birds]. **1857** HOLDEN *Hum. Osteol.* (ed. 2) 252 The utricle occupies the upper half of the vestibule. **1886** *Buck's Handbk. Med. Sci.* II. 563/2 The vestibular membranous labyrinth is divided into sacs: (1) the oblong utricle or..common sinus [etc.].

3. *gen.* A small bladder-like body; a globule.

1858 GRAHAM & WATTS *Elem. Chem.* (ed. 2) II. 681 Vapour of sulphur, when it comes in contact with cold bodies, condenses in the form of *utricles*, that is to say, of globules composed of a soft external pellicle filled with liquid sulphur... This utricular condition has also been observed in selenium.

'utricle[2]. *Anat.* [ad. F. *utricule*, or L. *utriculus* UTRICULUS[2].] A small cul-de-sac in the prostatic portion of the urethra in man; the prostatic vesicle.

1861 SIR H. THOMPSON *Dis. Prostate* (ed. 2) 28 The Utricle..is a small sac..opening on the anterior aspect of the verumontanum. **1888** *Cassell's Encycl. Dict.* s.v., There is a utricle of the male urethra.

b. In the cat: (see quot.).

1881 MIVART *Cat* 242 A small, ridge-like prominence, called the *verum montanum*, in the midst of which is a narrow, slit-like depression, named the utricle.

utricular (juː'trɪkjʊlə(r)), *a.*[1] [f. L. *ūtricul-us* small leathern bag, UTRICULUS[1] + -AR[1]. Cf. F. *utriculaire.*]

1. Of the nature of, resembling or like, a utricle.

1760 J. LEE *Introd. Bot.* III. xviii. (1765) 211 *Utricular*, like little Bottles. **1775** ELLIS in *Phil. Trans.* LXVI. 8 The Gorgonia..has no series of utricular vessels, as the transverse vessels of wood are called by Malpighi. **1822** J. PARKINSON *Outl. Oryctol.* 92 The bottle encrinite, possessing a utricular form. **1856** W. CLARK *Van der Hoeven's Zool.* I. 184 Body utricular, roundish, marked with transverse rugæ. **1858** [see UTRICLE[1] 3]. **1881** BENTHAM in *Jrnl. Linn. Soc.* XVIII. 367 A single utricular glume enclosing the flower.

2. Composed of utricles or small bladders.

1835 LINDLEY *Introd. Bot.* (ed. 2) 5 Cellular, Utricular, or Vesicular tissue, generally, consists of little bladders.. adhering together in masses. **1849** HENFREY in *Rep. & Papers Bot.* (Ray Soc.) 163 In such cases the cavities appear like utricles. This utricular structure [etc.].

u'tricular, *a.*[2] [f. L. *utricul-us* little womb, etc. (UTRICULUS[2]) + -AR[1]. Cf. F. *utriculaire.*] Of or pertaining to the uterus or abdomen; uterine.

1827 J. FORBES tr. *Laennec's Dis. Chest* (ed. 2) 58 The entrance and escape of the air through the wound gave rise to an extremely distinct utricular buzzing. **1857** BULLOCK *Cazeaux' Midwif.* 180 The utricular glands also become visibly enlarged. **1871** A. MEADOWS *Man. Midwifery* (ed. 2) 21 the lining membrane of the uterus..appears to be made up of a countless number of small tubes, the utricular glands or follicles.

‖**Utricularia** (juːtrɪkjʊ'lɛərɪə). Pl. **-ariæ.** [mod.L. (1737), f. L. *ūtricul-us* UTRICULUS[1].] A genus of scrophulariaceous plants, characterized by bearing small bladders at the margins of their leaves; bladderwort, hooded (water) milfoil; a species or plant of this.

1753 *Chambers' Cycl.* Suppl., *Utricularia*,..the name of a plant used by Linnæus for..hooded water milfoil. **1793** MARTYN *Lang. Bot.* s.v. *Folliculus*, Follicles..are vessels distended with air: as at the root in *Utricularia.* **1819** *Rees' Cycl.* XXXVII. 4 F 2/2 Almost every morning's walk afforded them a new Utricularia. *Ibid.*, Twenty-four Utriculariæ, natives of New Holland alone. **1863** T. W. HIGGINSON *Out-Door Papers* 278 The slender Utricularia, a dainty maiden whose light feet scarce touch the water.

utriculate (juː'trɪkjʊlət), *a. rare.* [ad. mod.L. *ūtriculāt-us*, f. L. *ūtriculus* UTRICULUS[1].] (See quots.)

1860 MAYNE *Expos. Lex.* 1318/1 *Utriculatus*, Bot. having the form of a small leathern bottle..: utriculate. **1864** DANA in *Webster's Dict.* 1457/2 *Utriculate*, a., swollen like a bladder; inflated; utricular.

'utricule. *Bot. rare*$^{-1}$. [a. F. *utricule*: see UTRICLE[1].] A small bladder-like sac or body.

1830 LINDLEY *Nat. Syst. Bot.* 240 The reservoirs of oil in the leaves of Labiatæ..are little utricules having an open orifice.

u'triculoid, *a. rare*$^{-0}$. [f. L. *ūtricul-us* UTRICULUS[1] + -OID.] Resembling a bladder; utricular.

1864 DANA in *Webster's Dict.* 1457. [Hence in later Dicts.]

utriculoplasty (juː'trɪkjʊləʊ,plæstɪ). *Surg.* [f. UTRICUL(US[2] + -O + -PLASTY.] An operation to reduce the size of the uterus by removing part of the uterine wall.

1910 *Practitioner* June 788 The operation of utriculoplasty as carried out by Howard Kelly. **1911** V. BONNEY in *Proc. R. Soc. Med.* IV. (Obstetr. & Gynecol. Sect.) 272, I have ventured to apply to it the term 'utriculoplasty' as best describing its object. **1974** PASSMORE & ROBSON *Compan. Med. Stud.* III. xxviii. 68/2 Plastic repair of a bicornuate uterus (utriculoplasty) may be indicated in cases of recurrent abortion.

‖**utriculus**[1] (juː'trɪkjʊləs). [L., dim. of *ūter* leathern bag or bottle: see -CULUS. Cf. Pg. *utriculo.*]

1. *Bot.* (See quots. and UTRICLE[1] 1.)

1753 *Chambers' Cycl.* Suppl. s.v., The leaves of trees, whose cuticle has been eat off on one side by small insects, sometimes afford views of these *Utriculi.* **1793** MARTYN *Lang. Bot.*, *Utriculi*,..utricles; reservoirs to secrete and receive the sap. **1838** *Penny Cycl.* XI. 346/1 Fruit [of grasses]..occasionally an utriculus. **1857** HENFREY *Bot.* 428 (Sedges), A single erect anatropous ovule, forming in fruit an utriculus. **1866** *Treas. Bot.* 1197/2 *Utriculus*,..the two confluent glumes of *Carex.* **1885** GOODALE *Physiol. Bot.* 346 Utricularia, a genus named from the utriculi or little bladders found on the dissected leaves of some of its species.

2. *Anat.* Of the ear; = UTRICLE[1] 2 b.

1847 TODD & BOWMAN *Phys. Anat.* II. 82 As the osseous canals open into the vestibule, so the membranous ones open at both ends into the utriculus. **1878** F. J. BELL *Gegenbaur's Comp. Anat.* 535 The sacculus and utriculus contain otoliths.

‖**u'triculus**[2]. *Anat.* [L., dim. of *uterus* UTERUS: see -CULUS.] = UTRICLE[2].

1848 *Brit. & For. Med.-Chirurgical Rev.* I. 271 A canal, originating by the usual opening on the utriculus. *c* **1848** *Todd's Cycl. Anat.* IV. 152/1 That the utriculus is a male uterus. **1893** D. J. CUNNINGHAM *Man. Pract. Anat.* I. 609 This [small recess] is the *sinus pocularis* or the *utriculus.*

utriform ('juːtrɪfɔːm), *a. rare.* [ad. mod.L. *ūtriform-is* (whence F. *utriforme*), f. L. *ūtri-s, ūter* bag, bottle, etc.: see -FORM.] Having the shape of a leathern bottle.

1860 MAYNE *Expos. Lex.* 1318/2 *Utriformis*, ..swoln out and without apparent pedicle, as in the *Lycoperdon utriforme*: utriform. **1889** *Quart. Jrnl. Geol. Soc.* XLV. 566 The zooecia..have the exsert parts conical, or, again, they may be leathern-bottle-shaped (utriform).

utrique(ing, varr. OUTREIK(ING *Sc. Obs.*

‖**'utrum.** *Obs.* or *Hist.* [L. *utrum*, neut. sing. of *uter* which, whether.] A writ authorizing the holding of an assize to decide the status of a property (see quot. 1728) Usu. in ***assize of utrum.***

c **1290** BRITTON (1865) II. 206 La quarte assise est de *Utrum. Ibid.* 207 Le bref de *Utrum* pur le clerc.

1592 RASTELL *Law Terms*, *Vtrum* is a writ and it lyeth when the right of any Church is aliened and holden in lay fee. **1728** CHAMBERS *Cycl.* [following Cowell s.v. *Assise de utrum*], *Assize of Utrum*, lies for a Parson against a Layman, or a Layman against a Parson, for Land or Tenement, doubtful whether it be in Lay-fee, or Free-alms. **1865** NICHOLS *Britton* II. 207 *margin*, *Utrum*, the parson's writ of right. *Ibid.* 208 *margin*, No assize of *Utrum* for land belonging to cathedral or convent. **1881** TWISS *Bracton* (Rolls) IV. 622 [Assise] of Utrum may not be brought by a vicar for a small pension paid to a religious house. *Ibid.*, Assise of utrum can never be taken upon a previous assise of utrum.

‖**ut supra** (ʊt 's(j)uːprə). [L., f. *ut* as + *suprā* SUPRA *adv.*, (*a.*), *prep.*] As previously, as before (in a book or writing), as above. Also shortened **ut sup.**

c **1450** in J. Stainer *Early Bodl. Music Sacred & Secular Songs* (1901) I. no. lxii, Chorus. vt supra What tydynges. **1520** R. ELYOT in T. Elyot *Governour* (1880) I. 310 And the prest vid to synge ut supra. **1526** [see SUPRA 1]. **1651** T. IRELAND *Abridgment Rep. Sir J. Dyer* 202 The going at large *ut supra*, is not an escape. **1668** [see SUPRA 1]. **1875** PALEY & SANDYS *Select Private Orations Desmosthenes* I. 164/1 He let the arbitrators give judgment against him by default (compare Mid. *ut sup.*) and then moved for a new trial. **1959** E. POUND *Thrones* xcviii. 43 That the books you read shall be Cheng King Ut supra.

utt, utter, obs. ff. OUT, UDDER.

'utter, *sb. Mech.* [See quot. 1879.] *pl.* Indentations or marks made on a surface by the vibration or too great pressure of a tool.

1853 O. BYRNE *Artisan's Handbk.* 351 Excessive pressure ..only fills the work with furrows, or produces an irregular indented surface, which by workmen is said to be full of utters. **1879** HOLTZAPFFEL *Turning* IV. 342 Fine lines or striæ, also called 'utters',..from the sound emitted by the work when in vibration against the tool.

utter ('ʌtə(r)), *a.* Forms: *α.* 1 **utera, uterra, utra,** 4–6 **vter,** *Sc.* 6 **vtir, utyr,** 6, 9 **uter.** *β.* 2 **uttera, uttra,** 3, 6 **uttre,** 4–6 **vttre,** 4– **utter** (4–6 **uttir,** 5 **uttere);** 4–7 **vtter** (4 **otter,** 5 **outter, vttere,** 6–7 *Sc.* **wtter),** 4–6 **vttur,** 5 **vtture, vttir,** 4 **vttyr.** [OE. *útera, úterra, úttra*, etc. (also *ýtera, ýtra, ýttra*) adj. (comparative formed on *út* OUT *adv.*), = OFris. *ûtera, uttera, uttra*, MLG. *ūtere, uter* (LG. *ûter, üter*), MDu. *utere* (Du. *uiter-*), OHG. *ûzero, ûzaro* (MHG. *ûzer*, G. *äusser*), also ON. *ytri*, MSw. *ytre*, etc. (Sw. *yttre*), Norw. *ytre*, Da. *ydre.* Cf. OUTER *a.*

Shortening of the original *ū* of the stem is normal before the group *ttr*, which in OE. was regularly developed from *tr.*]

I. 1. a. That is farther out than another (implied or distinguished as *inner*); forming the exterior part or outlying portion; relatively far out, outward, external, exterior; also, indefinitely remote. Cf. OUTER *a.* 1. Now only *poet.*

In very frequent use from *c* 1400 to *c* 1620. App. in disuse *c* 1670–*c* 1825, except in ***utter bar, barrister*** (see BAR *sb.*[1] 24, BARRISTER[1]).

α. *a* **901** ÆLFRED *Laws* c. 44 § 1 Ʒif ðæt uterre [*v.rr.* utre, uttere] ban bið þyrel. **13..** [see 1 b]. **1507** *Acc. Ld. High Treas. Scot.* III. 292 The Kingis offerandis in the utir kyrk. **1535** STEWART *Cron. Scot.* (Rolls) III. 48 Suppois than of that toun The vter wallis win war and put doun. **1592** *Reg. Mag. Sig. Scot.* 753/1 Lie uter port de Halyrudhous. **1887** *Jamieson's Suppl.* 257/2 The uter door.

β. *c* **1125** [see *a*]. *c* **1374** CHAUCER *Troylus* III. 664 (Camb. MS.), In þis vttir [*v.rr.* vtter, outter] hous. *a* **1400–50** *Bk. Curtasye* 444 in *Babees Bk.* 313 For lordys two beddys schalle be made, Bothe vtter and inner. *c* **1435** *Chron. London* (Kingsford, 1905) 40 By the hemme off the kyngis cote, vndir his vttir garnement. **1471** *Paston Lett.* III. 20 Opyn the cofyr that standyth in the utter chambyr. **1526** TINDALE *Matt.* xxv. 30 Cast that vnprophetable servaunt into vtter dercknes. **1542** BOORDE *Dyetary* iv. (1870) 239 If there be an vtter courte made. **1578** LYTE *Dodoens* 752 An ounce of the utter barke taken with wine. **1614** SYLVESTER *Little Bartas* 432 Earth's but a Point, compar'd to th' upper Globe; Yet, who hath seen but half her utter Robe? **1661** P. GORDON *Diary* (Spalding Club) 49 Whilst my servants were cleansing the inner room, he breake downe the oven in the utter roome. **1667** MILTON *P.L.* VI. 716 Drive them out From all Heav'ns bounds into the utter Deep. **1827** POLLOK *Course T.* IX. 1180 They heard, Afar to left, among the utter dark, Hell rolling o'er his waves of burning fire. 1848 Bailey *Festus* (ed. 3) 107 From Time's last orb which eyes The inner and the utter infinite. 1870 J. Payne *Masque of Shadows* Ded., Whoso is fain To enter in this shadow-land of mine, He must forget the utter summer's shine.

fig. 1608 B. Jonson *Masques* Wks. (1616) 934 I,.. who haue neuer touch'd so much as to the barke, or vtter shell of any knowledge. 1877 L. Morris *Epic Hades* II. 147 So high a strain arose As trembled on the utter verge of being.

b. Freq. with partitive terms, as †*deal*, *end*, *part*, †*party*, and esp. *side*. Also *fig.* Now *rare*.

a1300 *Cursor M.* 9912 þis castell..es painted a-bute þe vtter [*Gött.* vter] side. c1340 Hampole *Pr. Consc.* 4815 þe world sal bryn on ilk syde,.. Until þe utter end of alle helle. 1387 Trevisa *Higden* (Rolls) I. 59 For betynge of veynes is bettre i-knowe in þe vttre parties of bodies þan ynward. *Ibid.* VI. 251 þe utter deel of his oost. c1400 *Beryn* 3928 [He] had a mantell..; The vttir part of purpill. 1457 *Cov. Leet. Bk.* 298 The newe Crosse vppon the heth at the vtter syde of theyre fraunchice. 1508 *Bk. Keruynge* A iv, The vtter ende of the clothe on the vtter syde of the table. 1526 Tindale *Matt.* xxiii. 25 Ye make clene the vtter side off the cuppe, and off the platter. 1577 B. Googe *Heresbach's Husb.* I. 21 b, A little rayne falling, hath but wette the vtter part, and not gone deepe. 1629 Sir W. Mure *True Crucifixe* 485 Like painted Tombs who clense the vtter side, [Cf. Matt. xxiii. 27]. 1637 Rutherford *Lett.* (1671) 183 For two feathers or two straws of the devil's painted pleasures, onely lustred in the utter side. 1848 Bailey *Festus* (ed. 3) 59, I have looked down upon the utter side Of such thoughts from the leeming room of reason.

†**2. a.** = outer *a.* 2. *Obs.*

c900 tr. *Baeda's Hist.* IV. xiii. (1890) 304 þæt heo seolfe wæron ȝe on þæm nearran [*v.r.* inneran] godum, ȝe on þæm utteran [*v.r.* uttran] mid heofonlice ȝife ȝewelȝade. c1000 *Ags. Ps.* (Thorpe) xv. 7 þeah he me þara uterrena ȝewinna ȝefreode, þeah winnað wið me þa inran unrihtlustas. a1225 *Ancr. R.* 92 Hwo se ȝemeleasliche witeð hire uttre eien,.. heo ablindeð in þe inre eien. 1357 *Lay Folks' Catech.* (L.) 330 The be-houys to know þy fyue wyttys þe vttyr and þe ynnyr. c1386 Chaucer *Sec. Nun's T.* 498 (Camb. MS.), Teere lakkyth no thyng to thyn vtter Iyen. 1398 Trevisa *Barth De P.R.* III. ix. (1495) 54 The vtter wytte conteyneth the syghte,.. taastynge and towchynge. c1450 tr. *De Imitatione* III. xiv. 82 For þe utter enemy is sonner ouercomen, if þe ynner be destroied.

†**b.** *utter man*, = outward *a.* 2 c. (Cf. outer *a.* 2 b.) *Obs.*

a1050 *Liber Scintill.* x. (1889) 53 þæt ys fullfremed & ȝesceadwislic fæsten þænne ure mann uttra fæst, se inra ȝebitt. a1340 Hampole *Psalter* ix. 20 þat..þe utter man haf noght maistry of þe inere. c1380 Wyclif *Sel. Wks.* I. 53 þis is bifore spiritual joy, as utter man is bifore spiritual. 1388 —— *2 Cor.* iv. 16 Thouȝ oure vtter man be corruptid. 1565 Jewel *Reply Harding* 430 Simple folke, beinge not hable to discerne, what thinges they be in the Holy Scriptures, that are to be applied to the Inner Man, and what to the Vtter.

†**3.** = outward *a.* 4. *Obs.*

a1225 *Ancr. R.* 4 Ye schullen alle weis.. wel witen þe inre & þe uttre [*sc.* riwle] vor hire sake. a1275 *Ibid.* 420 *note* (Cotton MS.), Understondeð þet of alle þeose þinges nis nan hest ne forbot; for alle ha beoð of þe uttere riwle, þet is lute strencðe of. 1526 Tindale *John* vii. 24 Judge not after the vtter aperaunce. 1548 Hoby in Strype *Eccl. Mem.* (1721) II. App. Y. 80 He.. is even now.. as content to the utter shew, as he was at any time of his most prosperity. 1558 Bp. White *Ibid.* III. App. lxxxi. 279 You in time of divine service, do ..both in heart and utter gesture..adore the same flesh. 1563 *Homilies* II. *Place & Time of Prayer* 282 Straightly to obserue and kepe the vtter ceremonyes of the Saboth-day. 1593 Nashe *Christ's T.* R 4 b, Lyke the Geometritians, they square about poynts and lynes, and the vtter shew of things.

II. 4. a. Going to the utmost point; extreme, absolute, complete, entire, total.

In very frequent use from c 1515.

c1430 *Generides* (Roxb.) 3040 This wer to vs..an vttir shame for euermore. 14.. *Lydgate's Thebes* 4122 (MS. Laud Misc. 557, fol. 58), It were to hem a perpetuall shame, An vtter [*v.r.* outre] hyndryng vnto Grekes name. a1511 Fabyan *Chron.* VI. clxxxix. 191 To the..vtter displeasure of the Kynge. 1550 Crowley *Epigr.* 1241 Ambition was punished wyth vtter exile. 1562 Winȝet *Cert. Tract.* Wks. (S.T.S.) I. 7 Ane manifest confusion and vter exterminion of this realme. 1606 Dekker *News fr. Hell* Wks. (Grosart) II. 143 Burning Riuers In which..are [*sic*] no vtter danger. 1662 Stillingfl. *Orig. Sacræ* I. ii. §1 We have seen already an utter impossibility of having any ancient Records among them. 1718 Prior *Poems* Dedication b j, Two Things which were his utter Aversion. 1778 Miss Burney *Evelina* xxi, I saw they were in utter amazement. 1812 J. Wilson *Isle of Palms* III. 535 A graceful calm is seen All foreign to this utter solitude. 1849 Ruskin *Sev. Lamps* vii. §11. 184 Restraint, utter and unrelaxing, can never be comely. 1871 Tylor *Prim. Cult.* I. 277 Her utter belief that in her vision she had really seen this bright being. 1889 Clark Russell *Marooned* xii, The arrest of his movements could not have been more spasmodic and utter.

b. Freq. said of destruction, ruin, loss, etc.

1412-20 Lydg. *Chron. Troy* IV. 2443 He him [Agamemnon] had brouȝt in gret distresse, To outter meschef and confusioun. ?1456- [see undoing *vbl. sb.*[1] 3 c]. 1523 *Act 14 & 15 Hen. VIII*, c. 1 §1 The utter ruyne, decaye, impoverysshyng and undoyng of a great nombre of the Kynges owne naturall Subjectes. 1560 Daus tr. *Steidane's Comm.* 40 To the vtter destruction of the common wealthe. 1591 Shaks. *1 Hen. VI*, v. iv. 112 The vtter losse of all the Realme. 1667 Milton *P.L.* III. 308 Thou hast.. quitted all to save A World from utter loss. 1674 *Jackson's Recant.* B 1 b, Turn'd out of Doors, to their utter ruin and destruction. 1772 Priestley *Inst. Relig.* (1782) I. 408 The utter ruin of their city..was foretold. 1827 Keble *Chr. Y.*, *11th Sunday after Trinity* v, Full many a soul..To utter death that hour shall sweep. 1841 Miss Mitford in L'Estrange *Life* (1870) III. viii. 125 Dark depression and utter failure of intellect. 1846 Mrs. A. Marsh *Father Darcy* II. xxi. 359 The utter destruction of all reverence for the unseen.

c. Of answers, decisions, etc.: Given without reserve or qualification; unmodified, decisive, definite. In early use chiefly *Sc.*

1456 Sir G. Haye *Law Arms* (S.T.S.) 173 As for utter ansuere to this questioun,..lawe and gude faith avidis that ..he is behaldin [etc.]. 1472 *Stonor Papers* (Camden) I. 126 But and [= if] ye..conceyve þat shee hath yoven you an utter nay. 1515 Q. Marg. in Ellis *Orig. Lett.* Ser. I. I. 127 Send me ȝour uter mynd and ansuer in all thyng. 1560 Rolland *Seven Sages* 33 This is my vtter minde and will, That ȝe prepair [etc.]. a1600 Montgomerie *Misc. Poems* xxxii. 86 Ȝour vter ansueir courteously I crave. 1647 Clarendon *Hist. Reb.* VIII. §15 The utter refusal of the auxiliary regiments of London and Kent to march farther. 1828-32 Webster s.v., An utter refusal or denial.

d. Of darkness, etc.: Complete, absolute.

1596 Shaks. *1 Hen. IV*, III. iii. 42 But thou..wert indeede, but for the Light in thy Face, the Sunne of vtter Darkenesse. 1814 Wordsw. *Excurs.* VII. 357 Then, shall the slowly-gathering twilight close In utter night. 1825 Scott *Talism.* v, They blew out their lights at once, and left the knight in utter darkness. 1830 Tennyson *Confess. Sens. Mind* 95 What if Thou..seest me drive Through utter dark a full-sailed skiff Unpiloted. 1868 —— *Lucretius* 70 Then, from utter gloom stood out the breasts..of Helen.

e. Pure; unalloyed. *rare*[−1].

1875 Morris *Æneis* IX. 262 Two cups of utter silver wrought.

f. As a trivial emphasizer.

1898 G. B. Shaw *You never can Tell* IV. 308 Certainly not. It's utter bosh. Nothing can be in better taste. 1914 —— *Misalliance* 33 You are the only really clever..man I know who has given himself away to me by making an utter fool of himself with me. 1930 N. Coward *Private Lives* III. 78 You're talking utter nonsense! 1956 *Times* 3 Jan. 3/6 Professor Richard van der Riet Woolley, the newly appointed Astronomer Royal, said..that the prospect of interplanetary travel was 'utter bilge'.

5. a. Of persons: That is such to an absolute degree; out-and-out, complete, 'perfect'.

In early use, usu. with 'enemy'; in 19th c., freq. with 'stranger'.

c1420 Lydg. *Assembly of Gods* 594 He hathe be euer myn vtter enemy. 1555 J. Bradford in Strype *Eccl. Mem.* (1721) III. App. xlv. 131 That he shoulde be..the Kinges utter enemye. 1560 Daus tr. *Sleidane's Comm.* 82 b, Their moste vtter and mortall ennemie. 1633 G. Herbert *Temple*, *Method* vii, Those Who heare not him, but quickly heare His utter foes? 1662 Trenchfield *Chr. Chym.* 39 Julius Cæsar having taken..the Cabinets of Pompey and Scypio his utter enemies. 1678 Bunyan *Pilgr.* I. 163 Ye be utter strangers to me; I know you not. 1828 Scott *F.M. Perth* xiii, Some of them are yet utter heathens. a1845 Hood *Lamia* vi. 80 And thou wilt..say the outer woman is utter woman, And not a whit a snake! 1849 Lever *Con Cregan* xviii, To win some acknowledgment of confidence from an utter stranger. 1875 Jowett *Plato* (ed. 2) III. 70 The persons..are utter rogues.

b. *ellipt.* (in affected use).

1881 W. S. Gilbert *Patience* 11, (The Officers have some difficulty in maintaining their constrained [æsthetic] attitudes.)..*Ang.* Oh, Saphir, are they not quite too all-but? *Saph.* They are indeed jolly utter. 1882 H. S. Leigh *Strains fr. Strand* 5 You and I have been together Dining up at Eaton Square. Pretty creature, tell me whether All was not 'quite utter' there. *Ibid.* 131 My wife has gone 'utterly utter'.

†**6. a.** Uttermost, utmost. *Obs.*

Freq. in Sc. use in 16th cent., with *power*.

1513 Douglas *Æneis* IX. ix. 16 Quham to assailȝe,..all the Italianis At vtir power ombeset atanis. 1533 Bellenden *Livy* I. iv. (S.T.S.) I. 30 þare husbandis wald gif þare vter besines..to recovir baith [etc.]. 1576 Fleming *Panopl. Epist.* 59 My request, which yt you wold accomplish to my utter expectation, we..beseech you most earnestly. 1590 *Hecuba's Mishaps* in T. Fenne *Frutes* Ff 2 b, When that I had ..shewed my utter might.

†**b.** Ultimate, original. *Obs.*[−1]

1634 Sir T. Herbert *Trav.* 144 They haue neuer altered the Dialect [of Persia] from its vtter sence, at this day being cald *Pharsee*.

†**7.** Final; last. *Obs.*[−1]

1558 Phaer *Æneid* II. D iii b, Our vtter houre is comen alas, fell destinies death hath brought.

8. *the utter*, that which is utter or extreme; = uttermost *a.* 7, utmost *a.* 5, 5 b. *rare*.

1584 Raleigh *Let.* in Aubrey *Lives* (1898) II. 192 Readie to countervaile all your courtesies to the utter of my power. 1894 *Athenæum* 29 Sept. 418/1 Nothing suits him but the utter. His heroine is 'beautifully modelled' [etc.].

III. †**9.** *Combs.* (hyphened, or as one word): **utter-bark**, **-brass**, **-court**, **-deal** (deal *sb.*[1] 1 d), **-end**, **-gate**, **-room**, **-shape** (see sense 3), **-side**; **utterward** (see ward *sb.*[2] 14 c); also *fig.* (quot. c1440); **utter-wit**, knowledge of things external to one.

1398 Trevisa *Barth De P.R.* v. xxx. (Bodl. MS.), þe vtterdele þereof is clene and bright. c1440 *Jacob's Well* 222 As þou hast v. watyrgatys in þe vttere-warde, owtward in þe pytt of þi body. c1450 *Brut* II. 545 The vtterward of the castell of Chestre. 1483 Caxton *Gold. Leg.* 309/2 The towne ..in the utterende of Dalmace. 1485 *Rolls of Parlt.* VI. 353 The Uttergate of the Castell of Flynte. 1495 *Trevisa's Barth. de P.R.* III. vi. c viij/1 Felynge, bodyly wytte and Ymagynacyon arne sytuate in the soule that he is onid to the body, and yeue it lyfe, & Innerwytte & vtterwytt to perfeccion of the body. c1530 Ld. Berners *Arth. Lyt. Bryt.* (1814) 139 One [bed]..ye vtterbrasses therof were of grene jasper. 1530 Palsgr. 286/1 Utterbarke of a tree, *escorche*. *Ibid.*, Uttercourt, *basse court*. a1550 Leland *Itin.* (1769) VII. 118 Estward to the utterward of the Chyrch. 1567 Drant *Horace, Sat.* iii. G 4 To folow showes, and uttershapes,..Is folie leude. 1577 Harrison *England* II. xii. (1877) I. 236 The vtterside of their mansions. 1603 Daniel *Def. Rhime* H 6, When we heare musicke, we must be in our eare, in the vtter-roome of sense. 1675 Hobbes *Odyssey* XXI. 258 [He] shut the utter-Gate.

†**utter**, *adv.* *Obs.* Forms: 1 utor, 6 *Sc.* uter; 1 uttor, 2, 7, 9, utter, 3-5 uttere (6 *Sc.* uttir), 4-7 vtter (5 vttir, vttyr), 4-5 vttere. [OE. *útor*, *úttor*, *útter* (compar. of *út* out *adv.*), = MLG. *uter*, G. *ausser*, ON. *útarr*.]

1. Farther out, away, or apart; out, outside, without.

c888 Ælfred *Boeth.* xxxiv. §12 Nabbað hi nan god ofer þæt to secanne, ne hi nanwuht ne maȝonne ufor ne utor findan. c1000 *Ags. Gosp.* Matt. xx. 28 þonne byþ ðe arwurðlicor þonne þe man uttor scufe. c1200 *Trin. Coll. Hom.* 73 [He] ne dar his sinnes seien þe prest leste hit uttere cume þat hie tweien witen. 13.. *E.E. Allit. P.* B. 42 He schulde be halden vtter, With mony blame ful bygge,.. Hurled to þe halle dore. 13.. *Gaw. & Gr. Knt.* 1565 þer he ..made hym, maw-gref his hed, forto mwe vtter. 1399 Langl. *Rich. Redeles* III. 232 þe portir with his pikis þo put him vttere. c1440 *Pallad. on Husb.* v. 112 In wynter to his codde an heep of stonys Is good, that in the somer vtter don is. c1450 *Mirk's Festial* I. 258 þys man..set to þe roches his schuldyr, and bade hom..sterte vttyr. c1500 *World & Child* 527 Stonde vtter, felowe! Where doest thou thy curtesy preue. a1529 Skelton *E. Rummyng* 535 A strawe, sayde Bele, stande vtter.

2. From among others; = out *adv.* 1 e. Cf. out-try *v.* 1. *rare*[−1]

c1440 *Pallad. on Husb.* II. 294 In Nouember kitte of the bowes drie, Superfluent & thicke ek vtter trie.

3. To an utter degree; quite, altogether.

1611 Beaum. & Fl. *King & No K.* IV. i, I know they will deny me gracious Madam, Being..So utter empty of those excellencies That tame Authority. 1652 G. Sandys *Trav.* (ed. 5) 47 It utter [*earlier edd.* utterly] excludes his former excuse of an allegory. 1816 Accum *Chem. Tests* (1818) 139 Exposed in an utter dark place, to a brisk current of air.

4. *utter-fine*: **a.** Of metals: Superfine. *Sc.*

1562-3 *Reg. Privy Council Scot.* I. 232 Fourtie five unce of uter fyne silvir. 1641 in Cochran-Patrick *Rec. Coinage Scot.* (1876) I. Introd. 31 Vtter fynne gold. 1641 *Reg. Mag. Sig. Scot.* 366/2 Per ferramenta trium petrarum purissimi lie utter fyne argenti.

b. *ellipt.* A superfine make or quality of cloth. *Sc.* (Freq. c 1537-50.)

1529 *Acc. Ld. High Treas. Scot.* V. 365 Ane eln tua quarteris, and ane half of uterfyne to be tua pair of hois. 1537 *Ibid.* VI. 351 Ten elnis utter fyne to be ane goun. 1564 *Reg. Privy Council Scot.* I. 309 Sevintene cairsayis and fyve stekis of uttir fyne.

utter ('ʌtə(r)), *v.*[1] Forms: α. 5 outer, outre (ottre, *Sc.* vtre), 6 vter, outter. β. 5 utterne, uttren, 5-7 vtter (6-7 *Sc.* wtter), vttre, 5 vttyr, 6 vttar; 5- utter, 6-7 uttre. [Partly from out *adv.* or *v.* (with shortening of the vowel as in utter *adv.*), partly ad. MDu. *uteren* (also *uyteren*, Du. *uiteren*, WFris. *uterje*) to drive away, announce, speak, show, make known, or MLG. *üteren*, *ütern* to turn out, sell, speak, demonstrate, etc. (LG. *ütern*), = MHG. *ûzeren*, *ûzern*, *iuzern* (G. *äussern* to speak, declare, †bring forth); Da. *ytre*, *yttre*, Sw. *yttra*, Norw. *ytra*, are from LG. The AF. *uttrer* (1463), Anglo-L. *utterare* (1551) are obviously from the English word.

For the earlier *oute(n*, *owten*, in Chaucer *Wife's Prol.* 521 and *Canon Yeom. Prol. & T.* 281, two later readings are respectively *outer*, *vttren*.]

I. †**1. a.** To put (goods, wares, etc.) forth or upon the market; to issue, offer, or expose for sale or barter; to dispose of by way of trade; to vend, sell. *Obs.*

In very frequent use from c 1540 to c 1655.

α. ?c1400 *Chaucer's Wife's Prol.* 521 (Petw. MS.), With daungere outer [*v.rr.* oute, outen, owten] we al oure chaffare. 1423 *Rolls of Parlt.* IV. 255/1 Swiche warkes ..[they] kepen and senden unto the fayres.., and ther thei outre hem. 1483 in J. H. Glover *Kingsthorpiana* (1883) 43 Yf any man brewe for the avayle of the Churche, that all other brewers cesse for the tyme uppon lefulle warnynge tyll that be outred.

β. 1425 *Rolls of Parlt.* IV. 307/2 þat your said Commens may utter and sende her Corn, Bestus and Merchaundise over the see, into the parties abovesaid. 1436 *Pol. Poems* (Rolls) II. 175 At Venice of them men wol it bye, Then utterne [*v.r.* Thei utter] there the chaffare be the payse. c1450 *Harl. Contin. Higden* (Rolls) VIII. 450 These men of Flaundres commynge to londe to utter theire merchandyse. 1523 *Act 14 & 15 Hen. VIII*, c. 1 §1 Yf any person..doo nat ther or elles where bargayne utter and sell the sayed Clothe. 1570 Foxe *A. & M.* (ed. 2) 1206/1 Seeing good wyne nedeth no tauerne bushe to vtter it. 1607 Middleton *Michaelmas Term* IV. ii. 13 Do they [*sc.* traders] not thrive best when they utter most? 1649 Bp. Hall *Cases Consc.* III. vii. 296 When they gathered their Frankincense, none of it might be uttered till the Priest had the tithe of it. a1668 Lassels *Voy. Italy* (1698) I. 68 Besides they utter a world of Taffataes, Velvets,..and other things of value. 1735 Berkeley *Querist* §544 Whether she [*sc.* Lyons] doth not receive and utter all those commodities. 1764 Burn *Poor Laws* 243 To keep a common ale-house.., and to utter and sell therein victuals. 1825 Scott *Betrothed* xxiii, Where other men are admitted that have wares to utter. [1863 H. Cox *Instit.* I. xi. 279 Booksellers were, by statute.., prohibited from uttering Tindal's translation of the Bible.]

fig. and in fig. context. c1430 Lydg. *Poems* (Percy Soc.) 150 Uttre nevir no darnel with good corn, Begyn no trouble whan men trete of pees. 1588 Shaks. *L.L.L.* II. i. 16 Beauty is bought by iudgement of the eye, Not vttred by base sale of chapmens tongues. 1613 J. Taylor (Water P.) *Watermen's Suit* Wks. (1630) 174/1 [The waterman's] worke and ware is seene and knowne, and hee vtters it with the sweat of his browes. 1624 Quarles *Job* v. 60 Earth's black babbling Daughter (she that heares, And vents alike, both Truth and Forgeries, And vtters, often, cheaper then she buyes). **1828** SCOTT *F.M. Perth* vi, The devil has factors enough to utter his wares.

absol. **1600** CORNWALLIS *Ess.* ii. C 5, Let vs receiue, and vtter, be capable, and returne increase of this fruite.

b. To announce for sale; = CRY *v.* 5 b. *rare.*

1806–7 J. BERESFORD *Miseries Hum. Life* (1826) IV. i, The infernal dialects in which their goods are *uttered*.

†**c.** *intr.* Of goods: To find purchasers; = SELL *v.* 6. *Obs.*⁻¹

1611 COTGR., *Marchandise d'emploicte*, ware that sells well, that vtters quickly.

2. a. To give currency to (money, coin, notes, etc.); to put into circulation; *esp.* to pass or circulate (base coin, forged notes, etc.) as legal tender.

c **1483** *Chron. London* (1827) 110 Every man, because of the said newe exchange, outred gold, and kept sylver. *c* **1550** *Disc. Common Weal Eng.* (1893) 78 Strangers haue conterfeted oure coine,..and heare vttered it, as well for oure gold and silver, as for oure chefe commoditie. **1554–5** *Act 1–2 Philip & Mary* c. 1 To the intent to utter or make paiment withe the same [*sc.* counterfeit foreign coin] within this Realme. **1602** FULBECKE *1st Pt. Parall.* 86 To utter or cause to be uttered false mony knowing it to be false. **1697** EVELYN *Numism.* i. 16 Tokens which every Tavern.. presumed to stamp and utter. **1718** S. SEWALL *Diary* 21 Sept., Found Guilty of uttering Counterfeit Bills of Credit. *c* **1740** FIELDING *Ess. Char. Men* Wks. 1784 IX. 417 Uttering great number of promissory notes. **1780** H. WALPOLE in Jesse *Selwyn & Contemp.* (1844) IV. 317 Last night I saw a proof-piece of seven-shilling pieces... I know they were not uttered, but could you get me one from the Mint? **1825** W. O. RUSSELL & RYAN *Crown Cases* 455 The prisoner was.. convicted..of the offence of uttering and publishing, as true, a forged promissory note. **1848** AKERMAN *Introd. Study Anc. & Mod. Coins* i. 2 The earliest coins..bearing the symbol of the state by which they were uttered. **1861** *Act 24–25 Vict.* c. 99 §9 Whosoever shall tender, utter, or put off any false or counterfeit Coin.

absol. **1863** STEPHEN *Blackstone's Comm.* (ed. 5) IV. 227 The punishment of forging, uttering, and the like at common law. **1905** *Daily Chron.* 22 May 5/7 Charged with being in the possession of counterfeit coins and plant for making them, and..accused also of 'uttering'.

b. *fig.* and *transf.* Also *absol.*

1588 KYD *Househ. Philos.* Wks. (1901) 274 Memory,.. imprinting in it selfe al the Images and formes of visible.. things, could not vtter them in time conuenient..vnlesse it had so ordered. **1609** B. JONSON *Sil. Wom.* IV. vi, Mavis was more deceiu'd then we; 'twas her commendation vtter'd 'hem [*ante* 'these adulterate knights'] in the colledge. **1800** ADDISON *Amer. Law Rep.* 44 Misner was indicted..for uttering this assignment. **1839** BAILEY *Festus* 145 The great bards Of Greece, of Rome,..Men who have forged gods —uttered—made them pass.

c. To issue by way of publication; to publish. Now *arch. rare.*

1561 in Haynes *Cecil Papers* (1740) 368 Sondry Bookebynders and Stationers do utter certen Papers, wherein be prynted the Face of hir Majesty. *c* **1567** STOWE in *Surv.* (1908) I. p. li, Ye same [book] was well vtteryd by ye printar. **1584** *Star Chamb. Decree Printers & Stationers* (1863) 9 Bokes printed in England are uttered no where els. **1977** 'M. INNES' *Honeybath's Haven* iv. 37 He..placed on the seat beside him his hat, his gloves, and the handsomely illustrated brochure uttered by the proprietors of Hanwell Court to their prospective clients (or inmates).

3. †**a.** To send out; *esp.* to issue or give out from or as from a store. *Obs. rare.*

1529 MORE *Dyaloge* III. Wks. 213/2 To by [= buy] many of the same suyte.., whiche were by them vttred to diuers yonge scolers such as thei founde properly witted. **1578** in *Househ. Ord.* (1790) 272 All those [pieces] that have beene uttered out of the store.., for the supplie of the fortes. **1617** MORYSON *Itin.* II. 243 Such victuals as are..vnfit to be vttered to the souldier.

b. To put or thrust forth, shoot or urge out; to discharge, emit, eject, exhale. Also with *forth, out.* Now *dial.*

1536 LATIMER in Strype *Eccl. Mem.* (1721) I. 260 God prosper you, to the uttering all hollow harts of England. **1565** COOPER *Thesaurus, Tortuosa vrina*, vrine vttered with payne. **1579** SPENSER *Sheph. Cal.* March 15 Thilke same Hawthorne studde.. beginnes to budde, And vtter his tender head. **1607** BRETON *Murmurer* Wks. (Grosart) II. 10/1 His Tongue like the sting of a Serpent, which vttereth nothing but poison. **1673** R. HEAD *Canting Acad.* 168 He that utters his Stomach in his next fellows Boots. **1820** W. IRVING *Sketch Bk.* (1821) I. 69 The sage Nicholas Vedder, with his..fair long pipe, uttering clouds of tobacco smoke. **1821** LAMB *Elia* I. *Old Benchers*, The little cool playful streams those exploded Cherubs uttered [*sc.* from Lincoln's Inn Square fountain]. **1905** *Eng. Dial. Dict.* s.v., The spouts couldn't utter the water.

transf. **1881** P. BROOKS *Candle of Lord* 14 Every candle of the Lord must utter its peculiar light.

fig. *a* **1586** SIDNEY *Arcadia* II. iv, Shee might give passage to her thoughts, and so as it were utter out some smoke of those flames. **1588** SHAKS. *Tit. A.* v. iii. 12 My tongue may vtter forth The Venemous Mallice of my swelling heart.

†**c.** To produce or yield; to send out, supply, or furnish. Also in fig. context. *Obs.*

1547 *Homilies* I. *Faith* Biiij b, They that..doe lyue in sinne.., not vttering the frutes that do belong to suche an high profession. **1603** OWEN *Pembrokeshire* (1892) 54 The cheeffest and greatest comoditie that this sheere vttereth. *Ibid.* 57 It also vttereth yerelie great store of oysters. **1620** MARKHAM *Farw. Husb.* 8 The mixt Earth, which vtters Whynnes, Bryars [etc.].

†**4.** *intr.* Of a horse: To go out of the lists or course at a tournament. *Sc. Obs. rare.*

1550 LYNDESAY *Sqr. Meldrum* 506 Bot Talbartis Hors, with ane mischance, He outterit, and to ryn was laith. *a* **1578** LINDESAY (Pitscottie) *Chron. Scot.* (S.T.S.) I. 234 Schir Patrickis horse wtterit witht him and wald on nowayis reconter his marrow.

II. 5. a. *trans.* To send forth as a sound; to give out in an audible voice; to give vent or expression to (joy, etc.); to burst out with (a cry, yell, etc.).

c **1400** [see UTTERING *vbl. sb.*]. **1530** PALSGR. 769/2, I utter ..my voyce, *je profere.* **1560** DAUS tr. *Sleidane's Comm.* 215 b, He vttereth great gladness. **1611** SHAKS. *Wint. T.* IV. iv. 185 Hee singes seuerall Tunes, faster then you'l tell money: hee vtters them [etc.]. **1612** BRINSLEY *Lud. Lit.* iii. 15 They [*sc.* vowels] being rightly vttered. **1621** J. TAYLOR (Water P.) *Sir G. Nonsence* Wks. (1630) Aa 1 b, Three sighs, smilingly vttered in the Hebrew Character. **1667** MILTON *P.L.* III. 347 A shout..sweet As from blest voices, uttering joy. **1712** STEELE *Spect.* No. 468 ¶1 Dictating to a Set of young Players, in what Manner to speak this Sentence, and utter t'other Passion. **1786** tr. *Beckford's Vathek* 209 She uttered a tremendous yell. **1800** WORDSW. *Michael* 347 When I heard thee.. First uttering, without words, a natural tune. **1815** STEPHENS in *Shaw's Gen. Zool.* IX. I. 18 The male has a very melancholy note..which is..uttered.. while the female is sitting. **1833** COLERIDGE *Table Talk* (1884) 253 Man only can utter consonants. **1863** W. C. BALDWIN *Afr. Hunting* ii. 49 One lion..uttered a fierce roar.

fig. and *transf.* **1590** SHAKS. *Mids. N.* IV. ii. 44 And most deare Actors, eate no Onions, nor Garlicke; for wee are to vtter sweete breath. **1874** R. BUCHANAN *Poet. Wks.* III. 106 Unto me all seasons utter'd pleasure.

b. With advs., esp. *forth.* Also *transf.*

1594 SPENSER *Amoretti* xlviii. 10 To vtter forth the anguish of his hart. **1603** SHAKS. *Meas. for M.* III. i. 87 There my fathers graue Did vtter forth a voice. **1728** ADDISON '*The Spacious firmament*' iii, In reason's ear they [*sc.* stars] all rejoice, And utter forth a glorious voice. **1827** POLLOCK *Course T.* VI. 86 What harp of..exhaustless woe, Shall utter forth the groanings of the damned? **1872** TENNYSON *Gareth & Lynette* 1053 [When] birds..utter forth May-music growing with the growing light.

6. a. To give utterance to (words, speech, a sentence, etc.); to speak, say, or pronounce. Occas. with advs., as *forth, out.*

In frequent use from *c* 1840.

c **1400** *Destr. Troy* 12215 Then answard Vlixes, & vtterit his speche. *c* **1444** LYDG. in *Pol. Poems* (Rolls) II. 215 Yiff thow art feerffulle to ottre thy language. *c* **1475** *Partenay* 3570 For that heuy word he was ther outring. **1509** HAWES *Past. Pleas.* XII. (Percy Soc.) 48 Utterynge the sentence Wythout..intellygence. **1587** in Feuillerat *Revels Q. Eliz.* (1908) 392 For them that are to utter certeine speches. **1598** *Mucedorus* Induct. 48 Giue me the leaue to vtter out my play. *c* **1614** SIR W. MURE *Dido & Æneas* II. 832 Her latest words scarce heard, nor vtt'red right. **1651** HOBBES *Leviath.* III. xlii. 298 While he was uttering the words of Consecration. **1711** ADDISON *Spect.* No. 1 ¶3, I scarce uttered the Quantity of an hundred Words. **1793** COWPER *To Mary* 22 Like language utter'd in a dream. **1796** H. HUNTER tr. *St.-Pierre's Stud. Nat.* IV. 197 She began to sob and weep without uttering a single word. **1816** SCOTT *Bl. Dwarf* xiv, The phrase which..she had compelled herself to utter. **1890** *Retrospect Med.* CII. 137 Voices of different qualities uttering sentences.

b. To give expression to (a subject, theme, one's thoughts, etc.); to express, describe, or report in words; to speak of or about.

In very frequent use *c* 1560–*c* 1600, and from *c* 1820.

to utter one's stomach, etc.: see STOMACH *sb.* 6 b.

α. *c* **1449** PECOCK *Repr.* IV. ix. 471 This thing..Crist expressith and outrith in a larger and generaler fourme. *c* **1475** *Partenay* 1233 All is trouth that I outre you or say.

β. *c* **1445** PECOCK *Donet* 6 It is honest ynouȝ a man to speke and write aftir oon of þo opynyouns, and an oþire tyme to vttre þe oþire opinioun. **1526** *Pilgr. Perf.* (W. de W. 1531) 216 b, In vttrynge his malycyous mynde. **1565** HARDING *Answer Jewell's Chalenge* 169 The wordes of Hilarius the Pope vtter the same doctrine. **1590** WEBBE *Trav.* Ep. to Rdr., I haue undertaken in this short discourse, to vtter vnto thee ye most part of such things. **1611** BIBLE *Isaiah* xxxii. 6 His heart will worke iniquitie,..to vtter errour against the Lord. **1616** SIR W. MURE *Misc. Poems* xvii. 6 A mourning mynd, Quhich fain wold wtter.. Thir latest dutyes of a dulefull hert. **1667** MILTON *P.L.* I. 626 Th' event was dire, As this place testifies, and this dire change Hateful to utter. **1710** STEELE *Tatler* No. 2 ¶3, I must not prostitute the Liberal Sciences so far, as not to utter the Truth in cases which [etc.]. **1755** YOUNG *Centaur* iii. Wks. 1757 IV. 181 His terrified imagination uttered horrors not to be repeated. **1816** J. WILSON *City of Plague* II. i. 115, I have many a heavy thought to utter. **1841** LANE *Arab. Nts.* I. 110 If, at my grave, you utter my name. **1888** A. K. GREEN (Mrs. Rohlfs) *Behind Closed Doors* ii, This acknowledgment was uttered with emphasis.

fig. **1560** BIBLE *Ps.* xix. 2 Daie vnto daie vttereth the same [**1611** speech]. **1850** L. HUNT *Autobiog.* III. xxiii. 205 Flowers utter their beauty and their fragrance, as much as birds utter their songs.

c. With clause as object, introduced by *what, how*, etc., or with words directly quoted.

c **1449** PECOCK *Repr.* I. xvi. 90 And therfore..for drede of God..y write and outre what y now haue outrid. **1530** TINDALE *Answ. More* Wks. (1573) 293/2 He vttereth how fleshly mynded he is. **1539** BIBLE *2 Macc.* iii (ch. heading), Symon vttereth what treasure is in the temple. **1582** STANYHURST *Æneis* I. (Arb.) 32 O wights most blessed, whose wals be thus happelye touring, Æneas vttred. **1611** SHAKS. *Wint. T.* I. ii. 104 Then didst thou vtter, I am yours for euer. **1781** COWPER *Conversat.* 381 Yes ma'am, and no ma'am, utter'd softly. **1818** SCOTT *Hrt. Midl.* xv, 'The newborn infant was barbarously murdered,' he uttered in a low ..voice. **1859** TENNYSON *Elaine* 1173 Lancelot kneeling utter'd 'Queen, Lady, my liege'.

†**7. a.** To disclose or reveal (something unknown, secret, or hidden); to make manifest; to declare, divulge. *Obs.*

In frequent use from *c* 1525 to *c* 1590.

1444 *Rolls of Parlt.* V. 74/1 He nethir uttered ne communed of the specialite of the matiers concernyng..the said Tretie of peas. **1477** EARL RIVERS (Caxton) *Dictes* 11 Uttre not the secretes of thy hert but to them that thou hast preued. **1530** PALSGR. 769/2 He that uttereth my counsayle ones, I wyll never truste hym whyle I lyve. **1548** UDALL, etc. *Erasm. Par. Mark* 33 Jesus..woulde not vtter her by name, lest [etc.]. **1575** *Record's Gr. Artes* Ee viij b, As my erroure hath vttered my follye, so it hath procured mee better vnderstanding. **1614** RALEIGH *Hist. World* III. x. 125 Silanus the Sooth-sayer, who had vttered Xenophons purpose. **1670** WALTON *Lives* III. 209 With what gravity..his Tongue and Pen uttered Heavenly Mysteries. **1677** TEMPLE *Let. to Sir J. Temple* Wks. 1720 II. 459 The Prince,..uttering his whole Heart, told me [etc.].

†**b.** To show, display; to bring to light.

1542 HEN. VIII *Declar. Scots* in *Compl. Scot.* App. i. 200 After this homage done the Scottis vttered some piece of their naturall disposition. **1548** UDALL *Erasm. Par. Matt.* xiii. 59 b, At length the cockelles growynge vp together (their vnlykenes vtteryng or shewyng them,) began to appere. **1575** LANEHAM *Let.* (1871) 12 Dauncing of Lordes and Ladiez..vttered with..liuely agilitee & commendabl grace. **1582** STANYHURST *Æneis* I. (Arb.) 32 The Princesse Theare the pate, in digging, or an horse intractabil vttred.

refl. **1548** UDALL, etc. *Erasm. Par. Luke* xvii. 132 Yet did he hyde within hym a secrete power of the nature of the godhed, whiche than & neuer before vttred it self. **1574** WHITGIFT *Def. Answ. to the Admonition* 135 When doe.. sinister affections more vtter themselues, then when an election is committed to many?

†**8. a.** To declare, reveal, make known, or set forth the character or identity of (a person or thing). *Obs.*

1526 TINDALE *Mark* iii. 12 He streyghtly charged them that they shulde not vtter him. —— *2 Thess.* ii. 6. 8. **1534** MORE *Treat. Passion* Wks. 1305/2 John, whome Christe so tenderly loued, that..to hym secretely he vttred the false dissimuled traytour. **1548** GESTE *Pr. Masse* A vi, Yf they wold, [they] could handle and vtter hyr [*ante* 'this pryvate masse'] accordingly.

refl. *c* **1530** TINDALE *Gen.* xlv. 1 Ioseph..commaunded.. that there shuld be no man with him, whyle he vttred him selfe vnto his brethern. **1565** STAPLETON tr. *Bede's Hist. Ch. Eng.* 137 If he wold playing utter and shewe himselfe, what he was. **1587** GOLDING *De Mornay* v. 54 God hath voutsafed to vtter himselfe vnto vs in his Scriptures.

†**b.** Const. *to* (be or do something). *Obs. rare.*

1548 UDALL *Erasm. Par. Matt.* xxvi. 104 Thy speche doth vtter the to be a Galilean. **1560** DAUS tr. *Sleidane's Comm.* 134 The kyng..stroke of her heade, and whan she was dead, vttered her to haue played the whore. **1562** LEGH *Armorie* 205 He vtterith him self yᵉ better to be yᵗ officer, whose name he beareth.

9. *refl.* To express (oneself) in words.

1600 HOLLAND *Livy* 35 The Consul was..so much surprised..that he had no power to speak. But, soon after, when he began to utter himself [etc.]. **1655** tr. *Sorel's Com. Hist. Francion* VIII. 18 He beheld a Man upon the Bed, who ..uttered himself in a thousand contumelious words to a Woman. **1711** ADDISON *Spect.* No. 119 ¶5 Several..utter themselves often in such a manner as a Clown would blush to hear. **1845** T. W. COIT *Puritanism* 129 His only refuge is to utter himself to One who is never prejudiced. **1860** HAWTHORNE *Marble Faun* xliii, Straying with Hilda.., he meant, at last, to utter himself upon that theme. **1881** SHAIRP *Asp. Poetry* 132 Each [English] poet..uttered himself in his own way,..as native passion prompted.

fig. **1824** W. IRVING *T. Trav.* II. 9 My feelings refused to utter themselves in rhyme.

transf. *a* **1648** *Ess. on Death* in *Bacon's Remaines* 9 An excellent Musician..cannot utter himself upon a defective instrument. **1878** FR. A. KEMBLE *Rec. Girlhood* II. 18 She [*sc.* an actress] remained to utter herself in Juliet to the English public. **1913** JANE E. HARRISON *Anc. Art & Ritual* iv. 91 So this intense desire uttered itself in the..[rite] of his resurrection.

10. a. *intr.* To exercise the faculty of speech; to speak. Also (rarely) const. *of, on.*

In the first quot. app. with indirect object.

? *a* **1400** *Morte Arth.* 418 The kyng in his concelle, curtaise and noblee, Vtters þe alienes, and ansuers hyme seluene. *c* **1440** *Alph. Tales* 532 When þai come aforn hym..he was compellid to vttyr. *c* **1475** *Partenay* 1024 To whome ful suetly outred she and sayd, 'Now vnderstandith' [etc.]. *Ibid.* 3156 Of Gaffray..I shall you outre and say. **1576** G. BAKER *Gesner's Jewell of Health* 101 b, Bellonius, uttering and wryting of those medycines.., affirmeth [etc.]. **1587** GOLDING *De Mornay* vi. 94 The highest God commaundeth, the second ordereth, and the third vttereth or publisheth. **1774** *Francis Lett.* (1901) I. 236 My trembling was so great for a few minutes that I could not utter. **1820** CREEVEY in *C. Papers* (1904) I. 338 Western..is close by my side, but has not uttered yet—such is his surprise. **1867** BP. WILBERFORCE in *Life* (1882) III. 226, I think it probable we shall utter now on the Vestments of the Minister. **1870** MISS BROUGHTON *Red as Rose* I. 141 You may sit by a person for hours and never utter to them! **1898** *Westm. Gaz.* 27 Aug. 2/1 Not a word was, of course, spoken by the men save *àpropos* of golf.., and as for the women.., they never uttered at all.

transf. **1873** MISS THACKERAY *Old Kensington* ii, Sacred voices that will utter to her through life.

b. Of words, etc.: To be spoken; to undergo utterance.

1792 CHARLOTTE SMITH *Desmond* II. 36 Could you have seen the countenance of Geraldine, while this speech was uttering! **1850** WORDSW. *Prelude* v. 110 While this was uttering,..I wondered not. **1857** J. HAMILTON *Lessons fr. Gt. Biog.* 314 Wishes that cannot be understood, and words that will not utter.

Hence **ˈuttering** *ppl. a.*

1818 KEATS *Endym.* III. 475 That my words not burn These uttering lips, while I in calm speech tell [etc.].

†**utter**, *v.*² *Obs. rare.* [a. OF. *utrer, outrer, oultrer*, etc. (AF. *ultrer*), to cross, traverse, excel, vanquish, f. *outre* prep., ad. L. *ūltrā* beyond.]

1. *trans.* To vanquish, conquer, or overcome.

c **1400** *Destr. Troy* 5819 Philmene.., with a fell dynt, Vttrid Vlixes vne in the place;..And he gird to þe ground. *Ibid.* 7076 Honerable Ector..That holly the herhond hade at his wille, And haue vttred his Enmyes angur þat tyme.

c **1532** Du Wes *Introd. Fr.* in *Palsgr.* 951 To hurte, *oultrager*; to utter, *oultrer*.

2. *refl.* To exclude *from* some privilege, etc.

a **1450** *Knt. de la Tour* (1868) 162 They lyue in blame.. and outre hem self from the grace of God [F. *en oultre l'amour et la grace de Dieu*].

utterable (ˈʌtərəb(ə)l), *a.* [f. UTTER *v.*[1] + -ABLE.]

†**1.** That may be disposed of by sale. *Obs.*

1581 Mulcaster *Positions* xxxix. 210 Some gainefull commoditie verie vtterable abroade. **1611** Cotgr., *Marchandise Latine*,..the best, or most vtterable commodities.

2. Capable of being uttered or expressed in words.

1648 Saltmarsh *Spark. Glory* 168 That is, the speakings or manifestations of the Spirit of God are not so utterable by the flesh or voice of man. **1735** Dyche & Pardon *Eng. Dict.* s.v. *Effable*, Whatever is utterable, or capable of being expressed. **1782** Miss Burney *Cecilia* x. viii, When his woe became utterable, he wrung his hands. **1826** *Q. Rev.* XXXIII. 397 And then she touches in utterable words upon unutterable things. **1846** De Quincey in 'H. A. Page' *Life* (1877) I. xv. 326 All this wretchedness, not utterable to any human ear. **1893** *Nat. Observer* 15 April 534/1 Dividing all things utterable into things which are, and things which are not.

absol. **1873** Carlyle *Lett.* (1913) I. 497 While he was discoursin' the utterable concernin' all sorts o' high topics. **1896** *Edin. Rev.* Oct. 302 The vision of the utterable passes into the vision of the unutterable.

Hence **uttera'bility**, capability of being uttered; also *pl.*, things that may be uttered.

1851 Carlyle *Sterling* II. vi, He flashed..into a subject; gathered it up into organic utterability, with truly wonderful dispatch. **1858** —— *Fredk. Gt.* IV. i. I. 389 He learned also to clothe his bits of notions, emotions, and garrulous utterabilities, in the French dialect.

utterance[1] (ˈʌtərəns). Forms: 5- utterance (5-6 -aunce), 5-7 vtterance (5-6 -aunce, 6 -ans), 5 vttrawnce (6 -ance), vttr-, 8 utt'rance; 5 ottyrance, oterauns, uter-, 6 vteraunce. [f. UTTER *v.*[1] + -ANCE.]

I. †**1. a.** The disposal of goods, commodities, etc., by sale or barter. *Obs.*

1436 *Rolls of Parlt.* IV. 499/1 If it seme come to, that utterance and sale of the seid Wolle..be so escarse. **1461** in *10th Rep. Hist. MSS. Comm.* App. V. 300 If ony citsaine.. wil gyve the utterance of ony marchandise..unto a strangere. a **1513** Fabyan *Chron.* VII. 630 Theyr vtteraunce of clothe of golde and sylkys to the..lordes of the realme. **1579** *Southampton Court Leet Rec.* (1906) II. 176 The fishe-mongers should have shoppes..built in the ffishe marcket for the..vtterance of the same. c **1630** T. Mun *Eng. Treas.* (1664) 18 We must..sell as cheap as possible..rather than to lose the utterance of such wares. **1632** in *10th Rep. Hist. MSS. Comm.* App. V. 478 The greate losse which husbandmen receive for want of utterance for their corne.

†**b.** In the phr. *to have* or *make* (...) *utterance*.

1502 Arnolde *Chron.* (1811) 129 The said peper is so musty..your said suppliant as yet can haue non vttraunce therof. *Ibid.*, He is neuer lyke to haue ani vttiraunce of the said peper heraftir. **1577** Harrison *England* II. v. (1877) I. 136 By ridding their worke to make speedie vtterance of their wares. **1600** Hakluyt *Voy.* (1810) III. 594 There hee had reasonable vtterance of his English commodities. **1622** Mabbe tr. *Aleman's Guzman d' Alf.* II. 313 Having no such vtterance of her Ware. **1675** *Machiavelli's Prince* Wks. 258 Towards the Sea-side they have no utterance for any thing.

†**2.** The action of giving out of a store; issue. *Obs. rare.*

a **1483** *Liber Niger* in *Househ. Ord.* (1790) 57 That ye take ..suche oversights of all..stuffe, comprised within your charge,..that the utterance of it be guyded to the King's most worship and profitt. **1603** Breton *Packet Mad Lett.* xliii, Usurers are halfe mad, for lacke of vtterance of their mony. **1757** Jos. Harris *Coins* 86 Coining only ascertains the quantity of metal contained in the several pieces, at their utterance out of the mint.

fig. c **1585** *Fair Em* I. iv. 24 Nature vniust, in vtterance of thy arte, To grace a pesant with a Princes fame!

3. a. The action of uttering with the voice; vocal expression of something; speaking, speech. Also with *of*.

Also freq. from c 1667 in the phrase *to give utterance* (*to* something).

c **1456** Pecock *Bk. of Faith* (1909) 130 A publisching or a nakid uttraunce, telling, or denouncing. **1474** Caxton *Chesse* II. iii. (1883) 38 Oftetymes they selle as welle theyr scilence as theyr vtterance. **1489** *Cov. Leet Bk.* 536 For disclosure & vtteraunce of certain seducious langage. **1553** T. Wilson *Rhet.* 4 Utterance therefore is a framyng of the voyce, countenaunce, and gesture, after a comely maner. a **1589** Palfreyman *Baldwin's Mor. Philos.* (1600) 156 The holinesse and cleannesse of the mouth, standeth in the utterance of rightnesse and truth. **1589** Greene *Menaphon* (Arb.) 51 Samela..seeing his vtterance full of broken sighes. **1642** Milton *Apol. Smect.* 47 In vaine therefore do they pretend to want utterance in prayer, who can finde utterance to preach. **1648** Wilkins *Math. Magic* II. iv. 176 The utterance of articulate sounds. **1667** Milton *P.L.* IX. 1066 Adam..At length gave utterance to these words constraind. **1703** Rowe *Fair Penit.* I. i, Utterance all is vile; since I can only Swear you reign here, but never tell how much. **1784** Cowper *Task* VI. 339 The total herd..resolv'd..To give such act and utt'rance as they may To ecstasy. **1794** Mrs. Radcliffe *Myst. Udolpho* xxix, Her courage failed as often as she attempted utterance. **1839** Dickens *Nickleby* xii, With such energy of utterance as might have been.. mistaken for rapture. **1847** Mrs. S. Austin *Ranke's Hist. Ref.* III. 141 These protests were only the utterance of the feeling that France yielded to force. **1861** Geo. Eliot *Silas M.* ix, The Squire was purple with anger.., and found utterance difficult.

transf. **1602** Shaks. *Ham.* III. ii. 378 These [*sc.* recorder stops] cannot I command to any vtterance of hermony, I haue not the skill. **1842** Tennyson *Love & Duty* 61 We.. to the want..Gave utterance by the yearning of an eye. a **1854** H. Reed *Lect. Brit. Poets* i. (1857) 14 The souls of mighty poets finding utterance in the music of English words.

b. The action of expelling breath.

1844 W. Upton *Physioglyphics* 186 This primary reference..of *a r*, to the utterance of the breath with earnestness.

4. The faculty or power of speech; manner of speaking.

1474 Caxton *Chesse* III. v. (1883) 119 The gracious speche and vtterance of rethorique. **1480** —— *Trevisa's Higden* (1482) 140 He..was connyng in crafte of fayre vtteraunce. **1526** *Pilgr. Perf.* (W. de W. 1531) 30 To some persones is gyuen syngular good vtteraunce of eloquence. **1553** Wilson *Rhet.* 116 b, Hauing a good tongue,..he shall be thought to passe all other, that haue the like utteraunce. **1602** *2nd Pt. Return Parnass.* III. i. 1151 It remaines to try whether you bee a man of good vtterance. **1667** Milton *P.L.* III. 62 All the Sanctities of Heaven..from his sight receiv'd Beatitude past utterance. **1676** Dryden *Aureng Z.* Ep. Ded. A 2 b, 'Tis onely because God has not bestow'd on them the gift of utterance. **1709** Steele *Tatler* No. 27 ¶5 She has naturally a very agreeable Voice and Utterance. **1782** Miss Burney *Cecilia* v. iv, All utterance seemed denied her. **1828** D'Israeli *Chas. I*, I. ii. 21 The King's difficult utterance rendered his addresses..painful to himself and the Parliament. **1848** Dickens *Dombey* xxiii, A deep, gruff, husky utterance. **1871** Tylor *Prim. Cult.* I. 45 A king of Singhalese patois, peculiar in dialect and utterance.

fig. **1702** Steele *Grief à-la-Mode* III. i. 43 Her Charms are Dumb, they want utterance.

5. That which is uttered or expressed in words; a spoken (or written) statement or expression; an articulated sound.

Freq. from c 1865, esp. with *an* and pl.

c **1454** Pecock *Folewer* 103 Suche wordis, countenauncis, gesturis and vttrauncis. **1596** *Edw. III*, II. i, I might perceiue..His eare to drinke her sweet tongues vtterance. **1667** Milton *P.L.* IV. 410 Eve..turnd him all eare to heare new utterance flow. **1817** Shelley *Rev. Islam* VII. xxxii, Sweet melodies Of love..I caught,..when thy dear eyes Shone through my sleep, and did that utterance harmonize. **1831** Carlyle *Sart. Res.* I. iii, To hear a whole series and river of the most memorable utterances. **1860** Geo. Eliot in Cross *Life* (1884) III. 131 The 'Mill on the Floss' be it then! .. The title is rather a laborious utterance. **1871** Blackie *Four Phases* i. 97 Let us attempt to analyse this utterance. **1887** Bowen *Æneid* IV. 280 Horror bristles his locks, on his lips all utterance dies.

b. Freq. in *Linguistics*, spoken or written words forming the complete expression of a thought. (Used with varying degrees of technicality.)

1932 A. H. Gardiner *Theory of Speech & Lang.* iv. 206 Under the term 'utterance' writing must be included. **1951** Z. S. Harris *Methods in Structural Linguistics* ii. 14 An utterance is any stretch of talk, by one person, before and after which there is silence on the part of the person. The utterance is, in general, not identical with the 'sentence'. **1955** J. L. Austin *How to do Things with Words* (1962) v. 61 Written utterances are not tethered to their origin in the way spoken ones are. **1964** M. A. K. Halliday et al. *Linguistic Sci.* iv. 95 The utterance, the smallest institutional unit of language activity. **1966** Y. Bar-Hillel in *Automatic Transl. of Lang.* (NATO Summer School, Venice, 1962) 17, I have already suggested..to distinguish artificially between them *qua* technical terms and use 'utterance' for observational entities and 'sentence' for theoretical ones.

II. †**6.** A place of egress; an outlet. *Obs.*

1662 Chandler *Van Helmont's Oriat.* 222 In what part the Stomach layeth open at top,..is called its Orifice or mouth: But its utterance beneath [L. *infernus vero ejus exitus*], is named the *Pylorus* or Porter.

III. 7. *attrib.* and *Comb.*, as *utterance-type*; *utterance-final*, *-initial*, *-interior*, *-medial* adjs.; *utterance-finally* adv.

1953 C. E. Bazell *Linguistic Form* 5 The most common English utterance-type. **1957** in *Amer. Speech* 1972 (1975) XLVII. 229 Even assuming there may be for some speakers certain contrasts in utterance-interior positions which might require both /č/ and /tš/ in the inventory, surely there are no such contrasts in utterance-initial and utterance-final sequences. **1964** W. Jassem in D. Abercrombie et al. *Daniel Jones* 346 Voiced stops do not occur utterance-finally in Polish. **1970** *Language* XLVI. 80 Even in his speech the laryngeal is lost in utterance-medial positions. *Ibid.* 82 For the nasal consonants, the variant which occurs in utterance-initial syllable onset before nasal vowels is taken to be basic. **1977** *Ibid.* LIII. 318 The optional utterance-final particle *-o* may be added to both imperatives and vocatives. **1978** C. Hookway in Hookway & Pettit *Action & Interpretation* 32 The notion of utterance type is itself translational, as Wallace puts it.

utterance[2]. Now *lit.* or *arch.* Forms: 5-7, 9 utterance, 6 -aunce, 5 vtterauns(e, -ans, 5-6 -aunce, 6-7 -ance, 5 uttraunce, 6-7 -ance, 5-7 vttraunce, 5-6 -anse; 5 vtraunce, 6 vterance, -aunce, *Sc.* vtyrrans, wterance. [ad. OF. *oultrance*, *outrance*: see OUTRANCE.]

†**1.** A degree which surpasses bounds or goes beyond measure in respect of severity, vehemence, etc.; immoderate force or violence; excess, the uttermost. *Obs.*

c **1400** *Destr. Troy* 5130 Þen Vlixes, with vtterans vne vpponone, The derfe wordis of Diamede dullit with speche. *Ibid.* 5808 Vlixes with vtterauns vnder his shild Mony stithe in stoure stroke on þere helmes. **1430-40** Lydg. *Bochas* IX. 3221 In tokne that God his quarel wolde auaunce, Disconfiture was maad on that partie, Vpon King Iohn be violent vttraunce. **1470-85** Malory *Arthur* VII. v. 218 It doth me good to fele your myght and yet my lord I shewed not the vtteraunce. a **1513** Fabyan *Chron.* I. xv. (1811) 15 The Circumstaunce of the vtterans of yᵉ vnkyndnesse of his .ii. doughters. **1590** Greene *Royal Exch.* B 1 b, Anie..that had [not] doone some exployte before in some battaile of vtteraunce.

2. a. *to* (*unto, into*) *the* (*such*, etc.) *utterance*, to an extreme degree; to the bitter end; to the last or utmost extremity. Freq. (*b*) with *fight*, etc. Now *lit.* or *arch.* (revived in 19th cent.).

c **1400** *Destr. Troy* 7981 Þat all the deire of the ded be done on vs two, To vttranse & yssue vne at this tyme. c **1450** Lovelich *Merlin* 10088 So that they sworen..thereon to ben avenged jnto þe vttrawnce. **1470-85** Malory *Arthur* VII. xii. 230 Thenne will I haue adoo with hym to the vtteraunce. **1525** Ld. Berners *Froiss.* II. xlviii. 163 No frensshmen wolde vndertake to kepe it [*sc.* a town] to the vtteraunce, for it was not stronge ynoughe. **1567** Paynell tr. *Treas. Amadis of Gaule* 239, I must take the sword by the way of the armes betwene you and me onely unto the utterance of your life or mine. **1587** Greene *Euphues* Wks. (Grosart) VI. 158 To make a counterpoyse of discourtesie to the vtteraunce. **1601** Holland *Pliny* I. 428 Corne steeped in water, whereof they will drinke to the utterance, and be drunke. **1605** Shaks. *Macb.* III. i. 72 Come Fate into the Lyst, And champion me to th' vtterance.

1860 Motley *Netherl.* iv. I. 130 The champion to the utterance against Spain, stood there with lance in rest. **1907** McCarthy *Needles & Pins* xi, She had loved him well and proved it to the utterance.

(*b*) **1475** *Bk. Noblesse* 77 To doo armes in liestis to the utteraunce. **1512** *Helyas* in Thoms *Prose Rom.* (1828) III. 93 Here is my gauge to sustain it to the utteraunce. **1550** J. Coke *Eng. & Fr. Heralds* §59 Heralde the usurper fought the battayle to th' utteraunce. **1578** H. Wotton *Courtlie Controv.* 7 Thus the Gentlemen..skirmished to the vtterance. **1600** Holland *Livy* 1126 He prepared warre with all his power to the utterance. **1606** —— *Sueton.* 16 At the saide solemnity of sword-plaiers, there fought to the uttrance..Fvrivs Leptinvs..and A. Calpenvs.

1821 Southey *Exped. Orsua* 56, I will fight him to the utterance upon this quarrel. **1834** Sir H. Taylor *Artevelde* II. v. ii, The Lower Lis They to the utterance will dispute. **1837** Browning *Strafford* v. ii, I fought her [*sc.* England] to the utterance, I fell, I am hers now, and I will die.

†**b.** *to bring* or *put to* (or *unto*) *utterance*, to overcome completely, vanquish thoroughly; to bring to ruin or subjection, put to death. *Obs.*

1430 Lydg. *St. Margaret* 324 Thou hast me brought shortly to vttraunce, I am venquysshed. c **1430** —— *Min. Poems* (Percy Soc.) 135 Whan Amelech was brouhte unto uttraunce. c **1477** Caxton *Jason* 138 Whan his complices apperceyued that he was put to vtteraunce. **1509** Barclay *Shyp of Folys* 185 If thy iustyce sholde put vs to vttraunce, We sholde be damnyd for our mysgouernaunce. a **1533** Ld. Berners *Huon* xvii. 47 He hath brought his enemy to vttranse, and slayne hym. **1596** Z. J. tr. *Lavardin's Hist. Scanderbeg* 92 The Christians increasing still in fury..did on all parts put them to utterance.

fig. **1509** Barclay *Shyp Folys* 226 Assaynge for to put our fayth to harde vttraunce.

†**3.** *at* (*the*) *utterance*: **a.** With the highest degree of energy or vigour; with the utmost force or violence; to the last or uttermost degree. Freq. with verbs, esp. *fight.* (Cf. 2 a.)

1480 Caxton *Chron. Eng.* ccxlii. 148 b, Than thees two worthy lordes comen..and weren redy in the place for to fight at vtteraunce. **1485** —— *Chas. Gt.* 62 They lete theyr horses renne wyth a grete courage for to Iuste at vtteraunce. *Ibid.* 142 Þe pylers of marble & other stones bygonnen to brenne & make fyre at vtteraunce. a **1548** Hall *Chron.*, *Rich. III*, 26 He woulde fighte with hym at the vtteraunce. **1600** Holland *Livy* 684 Corbis and Orsua made profession to trie the title at the utterance by dint of sword. **1611** Shaks. *Cymb.* III. i. 73 Of him, I gather'd Honour, Which he, to seeke of me againe, perforce, Behooues me keepe at vtterance. a **1630** D. Hume *Hist. Ho. Douglas & Angus* (1644) 30 Hee used them so gently, which he would not have done if he had taken it [*sc.* the castle] at utterance.

†**b.** To the utmost *of* (one's power). *Obs.*

1513 Douglas *Æneid* XII. ix. 124 Euery man..At the vtyrrans of all his fors gan fycht.

†**c.** At the last extremity. *Obs. rare*⁻¹.

1525 Ld. Berners *Froiss.* II. xxiv. 26/1 A varlet..stode by and sawe the batayle... And whan he sawe his maister almost at vttraunce, he was sorie.

'utterancy. *rare*⁻¹. [f. UTTER *v.*[1] + -ANCY. Cf. UTTERANCE[1].] The action of uttering or expressing.

1827 Coleridge *Improvisatore* Poems (1907) 356 A constitutional communicativeness and *utterancy* of heart and soul.

uttered (ˈʌtəd), *ppl. a.* [f. as prec. + -ED[1].] To which utterance has been given; expressed by the voice.

a **1586** Sidney *Apol. for Poetry* (Arb.) 27 The faulte is.. not in the sweet foode of sweetly vttered knowledge. **1593** *Sidney's Arcadia* IV. (1922) II. 112 Overwayed with her so wisely uttred affection. **1594** Hooker *Eccl. Pol.* II. iv. §1 The name of faith..must needs haue reference vnto some vttered word. **1801** Southey *Thalaba* IX. x, She wakes as from a dream, She asks the utter'd voice. **1820** Keats *Eve St. Agnes* xxiii, No utter'd syllable, or, woe betide! **1858** Carlyle *Fredk. Gt.* IX. i, Uttered intellect is not what permanently makes way, but unuttered.

utterer (ˈʌtərə(r)), *sb.* Also 6 *Sc.* -ar. [f. as prec. + -ER[1].]

†**1.** One who sells; a seller, vendor. *Obs.*

1542-3 *Act 34 & 35 Hen. VIII*, c. 6 The Penaltie..shall oonelie extende to the Utterer and Seller of the saide Pynnes. **1593** *Brief Note Obs. Fish-Days* ¶6 Net-makers, Saile-makers,..and Vtterers of Fish, maintained chiefly by fishing. **1653** *Ordin. Contin. Excise* 17 Mar. 110 For all Spirits.., upon every Gallon, to bee paid by the Utterer and Seller thereof, one shilling.

b. One who utters counterfeit coin, forged notes, etc.

1731 *Flying Post* 24 June 2/1 The Utterer of the forged Bank-notes. **1796** COLQUHOUN *Police Metropolis* 107 This sort of counterfeit coinage is..the least profitable to the Dealer, who..disposes of it to the utterers, vulgarly called Smashers. **1859** H. KINGSLEY *G. Hamlyn* xiii, We could lay our hands on the utterer of the [forged] cheques at any moment. **1862** H. MARRYAT *Year in Sweden* II. 241 Coiners and utterers of base money. **1887** *Pall Mall G.* 19 March 3/2 The coiners manufacture, and the utterers buy and distribute.

2. One who utters, speaks, or expresses in language.

1509 HAWES *Past. Pleas.* XII. (Percy Soc.) 47 Whan the utterer, wythout impediment,..Dothe his tale unto them tretably. **1567** DRANT *Horace, Ep.* To Rdr. *iiij, To be able vtterers of the gospell. **1594** HOOKER *Eccl. Pol.* II. iv. §1 Things are made credible, either by the knowne Condition and qualitie of the Vtterer, or [etc.]. **1613** W. BROWNE *Brit. Past.* I. ii. 35 Barre I those lips? fit to be th' vttrers, when The heauens would parly with the chiefe of men. **1672** DRYDEN *Assignation* III. i, For Beatrix, she's a meer Utterer of Yes and No. **1785** HOLCROFT *Tales of Castle* (ed. 2) I. 69 Falsehood..sooner or later..brings dishonour on its utterer. **1841** S. WARREN *Ten Thousand a Year* II. iv, A single successful speech..opens before its utterer the shining doors of fashion. **1846** MAURICE *Relig. World* II. ii. (1861) 170 He feels and confesses himself to be only a reflection of the divine Light, an utterer of the divine Voice. **1893** LIDDON *Life Pusey* I. iv. 84 The utterer of maxims..useful to bear in mind.

†**b.** One who discloses, reveals, declares, or publishes. *Obs.*

1549 COVERDALE, etc. *Erasm. Par. Rom.* 18 The lawe is not authour of synne, but the vtterer and apeacher therof. **1560** DAUS tr. *Sleidane's Comm.* 101 That holy spyrit (vtterer of all truthe). **1587** HOLINSHED *Chron.* (ed. 2) III. 1132/1 The vtterer of which conspiracie was one White. **1590** SPENSER *F.Q.* II. ix. 25 Vtterers of secrets he from thence debard.

† '**utterer**, *a. Obs. rare.* [A double comparative, f. UTTER *a.* + -ER^3.] Situated farther out.

c **1410** *Lantern of Light* 73 Crist seide..sende him in to þe vttirar dercknes.

utterest ('ʌtərɛst), *a.* (*sb.*). Also 3 **uttrest**, 5 **otter(e)st**, **vttyreste**, **vterrest(e**, **vttrest(e**, **-ist**, **utteres**, *Sc.* **uterast**. [f. UTTER *a.* + -EST. Cf. OFris. *ûterst*, *utterst*, *utrest*, etc., OLG. *ûtrist*, MDu. *uterst* (Du. *uiterst*), OHG. *ûzar-*, *ûzzar-*, *ûzorosto*, etc. (MHG. *ûzzer-*, *-ûzereste*, G. *äusserst*), ON. *útarst* adv. (Da. *yderst*, Norw. *ytrast*, *yttarst*), MSw. *yterst*(*e*, *ytärsta*, etc. (Sw. *ytterst*), a superl. formed on a comparative: cf. OUTEREST *a.*]

Now rare, the usual form being *uttermost*.

I. †**1.** Most outward; = UTMOST *a.* 1. *Obs.*

c **1200** *Vices & Virtues* 17 Ðanne clepeð he his pineres, & hat hem me nemen,..& werpen me in ðe uttreste þiesternesse. *Ibid.*, þe uttreste is se þiesternesse of helle. *c* **1350** *Leg. Rood* 69 Þai fell In-to þe vtterest end of hell. *c* **1374** CHAUCER *Boeth.* I. pr. i. (1868) 7 Þo come sche nere and sette hir doun vpon þe vterreste corner of my bedde. **14..** *M.E. Med. Bk.* (Heinrich) 93 Doo away the vttrest barke. **1464** *Rolls of Parlt.* V. 568/2 Your seid Town is sette in the utterest place of this youre Reame. **1491** CAXTON *Vitas Patr.* (W. de W. 1495) I. xvi. 19 b 1 He had dwellyd in thutterest of last desertes of Heracleos.

2. a. Extreme; = UTMOST *a.* 2. Now *rare.*

c **1386** CHAUCER *Clerk's T.* 787 (Camb. MS.), His wif to tempte more To the vttyreste priue of hire corage. *c* **1400** *Pilgr. Sowle* III. iv. (Caxton, 1483) 53 Doyng yow to wite, that ye ben now wretchid poure Caitifs at the vtterest meschyef. *c* **1444** PECOCK *Donet* 90 Gloriose benefetis of god ..ben in her vtterist goodnes and felicite. *a* **1470** H. PARKER *Dives & Pauper* (W. de W. 1496) II. ii. 120/2 Punysshed with the uttrest payne & torment. **1481** *Cely Papers* (Camden) 67, I schall do my best in sayelles [*sc.* sales] to my otterst poyer. **1530** BAYNTON in *Palsgr.* p. xii, He..may..in a brefe tyme attayne to his utterest desyre. **1883** J. PARKER *Tyne Ch.* 89 The utterest darkness of the wintriest night.

b. Of persons: That is such to a superlative degree; greatest.

1593 NASHE *Christ's T.* 8 If you should denie it,..the diuill (my vttrest enemy) would confirme it. **1873** 'OUIDA' *Pascarèl* II. 140 The utterest fool..in all the universe.

†**3.** Last, final; = UTMOST *a.* 3. *Obs.*

c **1400** LOVE *Bonavent. Mirr.* xxxvi. (1908) 184 He wolde ..myȝtily suffre the malice of his pursueres in to the vttereste ende. *c* **1440** *Promp. Parv.* 513/1 Vttrest, and laste of alle,..*extremus, novissimus.* **1456** SIR G. HAYE *Law Arms* (S.T.S.) 272 Till all gude resoun of uterast conclusioun of understanding of this poynt. *c* **1470** G. ASHBY *Active Policy* 371 Thaugh your wytt excelle & be more hable To discerne the vtterest Iugement In any case to your appurtenent.

II. *absol.* or as *sb.*

†**4.** Extreme limit, part, etc.; = UTMOST *a.* 4.

a **1300** *E.E. Psalter* cxxxiv. 7 Fra vttrest of erthe kloudes ledand. *Ibid.* cxxxviii. 8 If i..cerde in vtrest of þe se. *a* **1325** *Prose Psalter* cxxxviii. 8 Ȝif þat y take my liȝtynges..and wonne in þe vtterest [*Dublin MS.* vttermast] of þe see.

†**5.** The very most; = UTMOST *a.* 5, 5 b. *Obs.*

c **1410** *Lantern of Light* 122 We must do oure vttirest to conforme oure wille to þis. **1450** *Paston Lett.* I. 156 That wyll sette hym verely to do the utterest ayens yow. **1481** CAXTON *Reynard* (Arb.) 109, I haue not yet shewde the vtterist of my myght on yow. **1571** FORTESCUE *Forest* 145 b, Defending theim selues to their vtterest, from the force of any other. **1577** HELLOWES *Gueuara's Chron.* 41 Traiane did vtter and expend the vtterest of his skill, deuice, and policie, to take him.

6. ***to the utterest***, = UTMOST *a.* 7.

c **1400** MAUNDEV. (Roxb.) xxiv. 111 Þe emperour.. destruyd þam to þe vtterest. ? *c* **1430** *Brut* II. 437 Thei two floughten togederis, armyd at all poyntis, to the vtterist. **1474** *Stonor Papers* (Camden) I. 150 He seith hit..wolbe sued to the utterest accordyng to your title. **1481** CAXTON *Reynard* xlii. (Arb.) 115 Neuer for noman wold I torne fro yow, But abyde by yow to the utterist. **1571** FORTESCUE *Forest* 129 Paulus Emilius..did his paine to the vttereste, that his children should be like hym. **1884** J. PAYNE *Tales fr. Arabic* I. 302 She was distinguished to the utterest for chastity.

(*b*) **1513** W. SABYN in *Lett. & Papers War France* (1897) 142, I do yt to the utterest off my power. **1540** CROMWELL in Merriman *Life & Lett.* (1902) II. 272 To the utterest of my Remembraunce. **1549** COVERDALE, etc. *Erasm. Par. Rom.* 41 Jesus Christe, whose worke I labour in, to the vtterest of my power.

†**7.** ***at (the) utterest***: **a.** = sense 6. *Obs.*

c **1420** *Brut* II. 355 Þeze ij worthi lordez comyn yn to þe ffelde, clene armed.., and were yn the place redy to fiȝt at þe vttrest. *c* **1449** PECOCK *Repr.* I. xvii. 99 If eny man dare not ..suffre his feith and hise othere opiniouns be brouȝt into liȝt..to be at uttrist examyned.

†**b.** At the utmost limit or latest period of time. *Obs.*

c **1425** *Orolog. Sapient.* v. in *Anglia* X. 361/24 To-morowe or atte þe vtterist with-in þis seuen-nyȝte. **1487** *Cely Papers* (Camden) 169 Wythyn viij or x days wee schall knowe at the uttrest.

'**uttering**, *vbl. sb.* [f. UTTER *v.*^{1} + -ING^1.] The action of the verb, in various senses.

c **1400** *Found. St. Bartholomews* 45 For defawtynge of his hert, the vtteryng of his voice begane to breke. **1428** in *Surtees Misc.* (1890) 3 He gart forge yt in shapp of osmundes for uttering of his iren so into Iseland. *c* **1449** PECOCK *Repr.* I. xvi. 89 Bi greet kunnyng of preching and bi sauory vttring therof. **1530** PALSGR. 286/1 Uttryng or sellyng of ware, *uente.* **1579** SPENSER *Let. to Harvey* Wks. (1912) 635/1, I was minded for a while to haue intermitted the vttering of my writings. *a* **1586** SIDNEY *Arcadia* I. ii, An eloquence as sweete in the uttering, as slowe to come to the uttering. **1616** R. C. *Times' Whistle* (1871) 43 Daily each one, in vttering of his wares, Cosens his chapmen. **1633** T. STAFFORD *Pac. Hib.* II. iv. 157 Monies of this new Standard of Ireland, after their first uttering. **1648** in Rushw. *Hist. Coll.* III. (1692) I. 221 The Proclamation for the sole composition and uttering of Tabaco. **1742** *Act 15 Geo. II*, c. 28 The uttering of false Money, knowing it to be false, is a Crime. *a* **1777** in Evans *Old Ballads* I. 59 Nor fears [he] the blasting of his iron, Nor uttering of his wares. **1835** *Penny Cycl.* IV. 404/1 The uttering of any such forged bill or indorsement with a knowledge of the forgery, is a felony. **1887** *Pall Mall G.* 19 March 3/2 The coining and the uttering are generally two distinct branches.

utterless ('ʌtəlɪs), *a.* [f. as prec. + -LESS.]

1. Incapable of being uttered; unutterable.

1643 MILTON *Divorce* 45 To endure a clamouring debate of utterles things. **1820** KEATS *Hyperion* II. 120 How he means to load His tongue with the full weight of utterless thought. **1840** LOWELL *The Moon* 12 Its only voice a vast dumb moan, Of utterless anguish speaking. *a* **1893** CHR. G. ROSSETTI *Poems* (1904) 271/2 Pangs of utterless desire.

b. Incapable of being expressed or described; inexpressible.

1832 MOIR in *Blackw. Mag.* XXXI. 238 Cold were the heart, and bigoted indeed, Which..Could destine all that differ'd from his creed To utterless perdition. **1850** S. DOBELL *Roman* i. 14 By thine eternal youth, And coeternal utterless dishonour.

2. Incapable of utterance; speechless. *rare*$^{-1}$.

1854 S. DOBELL *Balder* xxiii. 100 As a trusting maid who waits Her far false lover,..Chilled with the bitter day where love is not, Blighted and mute,..Stands utterless.

† '**utterlike**, *adv. Obs.*$^{-1}$ [f. UTTER *a.* + -LIKE 2 b. Cf. UTTERLY *adv.*] = OUTWARDLY *adv.* 2.

c **1200** ORMIN 16510 Fele..Bigunnenn sone anan onn himm To lefenn..Acc nohht wiþþ innwarrd herrte ȝet, Ne nohht wiþþ fulle trowwþe, Acc utterrlike.

† '**utterly**, *a. Obs. rare.* Also 3 **-liche**. [f. UTTER *a.* + -LY^1. Cf. MHG. *ûterlîk*, MDu. *ûterlic* (Du. *uiterlijk*), MHG. *ûzerlîch* (G. *äusserlich*), Da. *yderlig*, Sw. *ytterlig*, extreme, excessive.]

1. Open, manifest; = OPENLY *a.*

12.. *Ancr. R.* 344 To eueriche preoste mei ancre schriuen hire of swuche openliche [*v.r.* utterliche] sunnen.

2. Absolute, extreme; final.

c **1440** *Gesta Rom.* xciv. 424, I clad my seruaunte, that is, my manhode, nought but to vtterly vtilite and necessite. **1553** GRESHAM *Let.* in *S.P. For. Edw. VI*, XII. fol. 37 (P.R.O.), Plenttye of merchauntes wythe-owght exsperyence and substaunce ys the vttyerly [*sic*] distruccioune of anny Realme.

utterly ('ʌtəlɪ), *adv.* Forms: α. 3– **utter-**, 3–6 **vtter-** (5 *Sc.* **wtter-**), 4–6 **vttir-**, 4–5 **uttir-**, 5–6 **uttur-**, 6 **ottorly**; also 3–5 **-liche**, 4–5 **-lich**, **-li** (5 **-le**), 6–7 **-lie**, **-lye**. β. 4–5 **vterliche**, 4 **uter-**, 4–5 **vterly** (6 **-lie**), 4 **vtyrly** (*Sc.* **wtirly**), 6 **vtirlie**, **-ly**, **vturlie**; 4–5 **vtrely**, **-li**, *Sc.* **wtrely**, 5 **wttrely**, 4–5 **wtraly**, 5 **vtraly**, **vtt-**, **wtt-**, **uttraly**. [f. UTTER *a.* + -LY^2. Cf. MLG. *uterlike*, *-liken*, MDu. *uterlike*, *-lijc*, *-lic* (Du. *uiterlijk*), MHG. *ûzerliche*, *-lich* (externally, etc.), ON. *útarliga* (far out); also ALL-UTTERLY, OUTERLY *advs.*]

†**1.** Without reserve or extenuation; sincerely, truly, plainly; straight out, straightway. *Obs.*

a **1225** *Ancr. R.* 206 Ine ȝuweðe me deð wundres: gulche hit ut ine schrifte, utterliche. *Ibid.* 314 Ȝif he nefde iseid utterliche þet ilke þing þet he dude ine childhode, he were idemed among þe uorlorene. *c* **1330** *Arth. & Merl.* 8615 (Kölbing), Ich ȝou sigge vterliche, þei in þis warld war non oþer swiche [etc.]. *c* **1380** WYCLIF *Wks.* (1880) 213 Whanne it is reserued to þe holy gost to ȝeue vtterly conseil in special poyntis. **1450** FASTOLF in *Paston Lett.* I. 155 Yff the wydow wolle sylle it.., sendyth me utterly word, for I wolle not melle of it ellys thus avysed. **1539** BIBLE *Luke* iv. 23 Ye wyll utterly saye unto me this proverbe. **1558–9** *Act 1 Eliz.* c. 1 §9, I A. B. doo utterly testifie and declare in my Conscience, that the Quenes Highnes is [etc.].

†**b.** Truly, verily, indeed. *Obs. rare.*

c **1400** *Beryn* 848 For vtterlich to have a child was al hir delite. **1526** TINDALE *1 Cor.* vi. 5 Ys there vtterly no wyse man amonge you? *Ibid.* 7.

2. In a complete or utter manner; to an absolute or extreme degree; altogether, entirely, absolutely; fully, thoroughly, out and out.

In very frequent use from *c* 1400 with α-form.

α. *c* **1374** CHAUCER *Troylus* II. 710 If I wolde vttirly his sight fle. *c* **1380** WYCLIF *Wks.* (1880) 280 Þat is vterly aȝenst goddis biddynge. *a* **1400–50** *Alexander* 1472 We er vtterly vndone. *c* **1430** *Syr Tryam.* 271 Marrok thoght utturly To do the quene a velanye. *c* **1489** CAXTON *Sonnes of Aymon* xxiv. 514 The persans shall be now vtturli discomfyted. **1528** ROY *Rede me* c ij, Par case they will nott admitt But vtterly make resistence. **1568** GRAFTON *Chron.* II. 283 They with in the Towne perceauing they were vtterly without reliefe. **1593** *Sidney's Arcadia* IV. (1922) II. 117 Ah of all sides utterly ruined Philoclea, said she. **1615** G. SANDYS *Trav.* 92 The suburbes..are vtterly razed. **1651** HOBBES *Leviath.* II. xxvi. 150 The Common-wealth faileth, and is Utterly dissolved; as a building whose Foundation is destroyed. *a* **1700** EVELYN *Diary* 23 March 1688, The French Tyrant..utterly taking away their estates, and their children. **1706** POPE *Let. to Wycherley* 10 April, Pray let me know your mind in this, for I am utterly at a loss. **1766** GOLDSM. *Vicar* xxviii, They will not be utterly forsaken. **1844** KINGLAKE *Eothen* v, The lowly grave..has closed over all his rich fancies... He is utterly married! **1865** KINGSLEY *Herew.* xxxvi, Torfrida turned herself utterly to serve the Lady Godiva. **1871** TYLOR *Prim. Cult.* I. 370 Men who so utterly believe that [etc.]. **1883** WHITELAW *Sophocles, Ajax* 519 My life hangs utterly on thee.

β. **1375** BARBOUR *Bruce* III. 196 Then wtraly wencusyt is he. *c* **1375** *Sc. Leg. Saints* xii. (*Mathias*) 115 Quhene he vyst wtrely, þat it wes swa. *c* **1425** WYNTOUN *Cron.* I. xvi. 1556 (Cott. MS.), Men may trow ful werraly, And mystrow þis ful vttraly. *c* **1470** HENRY *Wallace* XI. 1377 So wttraly it suld beyn at his will. *c* **1520** M. NISBET *N. Test. in Scots* (S.T.S.) III. 269 And vtralie the fire tuichet nocht thame. **1596** DALRYMPLE tr. *Leslie's Hist. Scot.* (S.T.S.) I. 51 The fatt syde..hes throuch leinnes bene vtirlie deformet.

b. Freq. with verbs of perishing, refusal, etc.

(*a*) *c* **1375** *Sc. Leg. Saints* iii. (*Andreas*) 430 Þat thinge restoryt is but wene, þat uterly periste has bene. *c* **1380** WYCLIF *Last Age Ch.* (1840) 29 Petir þe Apostle..myȝte not uttirly distrie Symoun Magus, but bi helpe of Poul. *a* **1400** *Chast. Goddes Chyld.* 20 They falle in to perylle of deth or elles utterly they lityll and deye. **1456** SIR G. HAYE *Law Arms* (S.T.S.) 175 That he be in perile to be maid outhir crepill,..or to dee utterly. **1538** STARKEY *England* 19 Ther be men wych..affyrme..euery one in hys secte to be sauyd, and non to perysch vtturly. **1577** B. GOOGE *Heresbach's Husb.* II. (1586) 69 b, It vtterlie destroyeth them. **1611** BIBLE *2 Peter* ii. 12 They..shall vtterly perish in their owne corruption. **1631** GOUGE *God's Arrows* III. §1. 181 Gods purpose against Amalek..was utterly to root him out. **1711** ADDISON *Spect.* No. 124 ¶2 Millions of Volumes, that would be utterly annihilated. **1816** SHELLEY *Dæmon* 562 For what thou art shall perish utterly. **1860** TYNDALL *Glaciers* I. 98 It would be utterly destroyed before reaching the bottom. **1874** GREEN *Short Hist.* vi. §3. 287 Literature indeed seemed ..to have died as utterly as freedom itself.

(*b*) **1422** YONGE tr. *Secreta Secret.* 188 Thou shalt wythstonde a losengeoure vtreli. *c* **1450** tr. *De Imitatione* III. xxxvii. 107 Sonne, þou maist not haue parfit liberte, but þou denye þiself utterly. **1477** EARL RIVERS (Caxton) *Dictes* 66 He refused hit utterly. *a* **1513** FABYAN *Chron.* VII. (1811) 370 But peas was to theym vtterly denyed. **1558–9** *Act 1 Eliz.* c. 1 §9 Therfore I doo utterly renounce and forsake all forraine Jurisdiccions. **1655** FULLER *Ch. Hist.* IX. 163 Whitgift..in the presence of the Queen utterly refused it. **1695** LD. PRESTON *Boeth.* III. 145 Fire doth utterly refuse any such Division. **1801** *Med. Jrnl.* V. 571 By utterly denying their origin from dentition, he has equally departed from truth. **1855** KINGSLEY *Westw. Ho!* xxvii, She refused utterly to sing anything but the songs and psalms.

c. Qualifying adjs. (Freq. from *c* 1660, esp. with words implying negation, defect, or opposition).

1395 PURVEY *Remonstr.* (1851) 24 [It] is vttirli vnleful. **14..** in *Hist. Coll. Citizen London* (Camden) 123 Every subgett..shall be utterly fre. *c* **1489** CAXTON *Blanchardyn* 138 His suster..was vttyrly fayre. **1553** EDEN *Treat. New Ind.* (Arb.) 5 One not vtterlye ignoraunt hereof. *a* **1586** SIDNEY *Arcadia* III. xviii, The one [knight] was utterly unable to defend himselfe. **1641** J. JACKSON *True Evang. T.* III. 206 That all warres were utterly unlawfull. **1662** STILLINGFL. *Orig. Sacr.* II. ii. §1 It was utterly impossible. **1728** MORGAN *Algiers* II. iv. 274 That of which he was utterly ignorant. **1777** R. WATSON *Philip II* (1793) II. XIV. 23 The limitations..were utterly repugnant to Philip's temper. **1815** SHELLEY *Alastor* 660 When heaven remained utterly black. **1844** THIRLWALL *Greece* VIII. lxii. 173 An utterly hollow pretext. **1871** B. TAYLOR *Faust* (1875) I. I. v. 69 There the utterly deepest bottom is. **1879** F. HARRISON *Choice of Bks.* i, It is..of utterly no importance.

†**uttermore**, *a.* and *adv. Obs.* Forms: 4–5 **vtter-**, etc., **vtirmere** (6 *Sc.* **-maire**), 5–6 **-mer**; 4–7 **-more**, 5 **vttermor**. [f. UTTER *a.* + -MORE. Cf. ON. *útar meirr*, MSw. *yttermere* (Sw. *-mera*, Da. *ydermere*), and OUTERMORE *a.*]

A. *adj.* **1.** More outward, remoter, farther removed; exterior, outer (opp. to *inner*).

1382 WYCLIF *Matt.* xxii. 13 His hondis and feet bounden, sende ȝee hym into vttermore derknessis. **14..** *Wycliffite Bible* Ezek. xlvi. 21 Wher thei shuln say sacrifice, that thei bere not out in to the vtmer [*v.r.* vttermore] house. *c* **1520** M. NISBET *Matt.* viii. 12 [They] salbe castin out into vtirmaire mirknessis. **1565** *Raynald's Byrth Mankynde* p. li, The seconde or vttermer infolder of the bottome of the matrix. *a* **1608** DEE *Relat. Spirits* I. (1659) 249 The foresaid letter,..and moreover..the Copy of the Emperour's letter, all in one uttermore paper closed (Letter like). **1610** HOLLAND *Camden's Brit.* I. 701 The two Pyramides in the middest..did almost touch one another: the uttermore stand not far off.

2. Very great; utmost. *rare*⁻¹.

1382 WYCLIF *Exod.* xx. 18 Al the puple..ferde and smitun togidere with vttermore drede.

3. External; secular; lay. *rare*⁻¹.

1395 PURVEY *Remonstr.* (1851) 138 It were bettere to him that ertheli dedes constreyniden him to deth, vndir vttirmore other worldli abide.

4. = OUTWARD *a.* 4. *rare*⁻¹.

a **1420** *Wycliffite Bible* Prov. iii. 3 *margin*, Temperaunce and oneste in vtirmere conuersacioun.

B. *adv.* Farther outward. *rare*⁻¹.

1414 *26 Pol. Poems* 58 Whanne ȝe han made pes wiþ-ynne All ȝoure reme in vnyte, Vttere-more ȝe mot bygynne.

uttermost (ˈʌtəməst), *a.* (*sb.*). Forms: see UTTER *a.*; also 4- **-most**, 5-7 **-moste**, 6 **-moost**; 4-5 **-mest**, **-meste**, 4-6 **-mast**, 5-6 **-maste**, 6 *Sc.* **-maist**; 4-5 **vttre-**, 5 **vttrmest**, 6 **uttirmuste**, *Sc.* **utermost(e**, **vtermast**. [f. UTTER *a.* + -MOST. Cf. OUTERMOST *a.*]

I. 1. Outermost; farthest out or off; remotest; = UTMOST *a.* 1 a, OUTMOST *a.* 1.

In frequent use *c* 1385-*c* 1630. Now somewhat *rare*.

13.. *Coer de L.* 2911 [He swore] But yff it were i-brought adoun Be noon, the uttermeste wall, He scholde hym hew to peses small. **13..** *Prose Psalter* cxxxiv. 7 (Dublin MS.), þe ottermast endes of þerþe. **1398** TREVISA *Barth. De P.R.* III. xx. (1495) 67 The vttermest sydes and partyes of the tongue. **1486** *Bk. St. Albans* a viij, The vttermest Clees ye shall call the Pety Sengles. **1585** LUPTON *Thous. Notable Th.* (1660) 37 The uttermost or last joint of the tail. **1632** LITHGOW *Trav.* I. 23 It reacheth..to the vttermost bounds of the Dutchy of Ferrara. **1651** HOBBES *Leviath.* III. xxxviii. 248 From the uttermost parts of the Earth. **1667** MILTON *P.L.* VII. 266 To the uttermost convex Of this great Round. **1819** SHELLEY *Mask of Anarchy* lxvii, From the corners uttermost Of the bounds of English coast. **1872** BLACKIE *Lays Highl.* Introd. 49 To indulge in the flight to uttermost Unst.

†**b.** Of garments or other coverings: = UTMOST *a.* 1 b. *Obs. rare.*

c **1471** FORTESCUE *Wks.* (1869) 452 If it be a pore Cote under their uttermost Garment. **1532-3** *Act 24 Hen. VIII*, c. 13 Their Gownes, Cootes with Sleves or other uttermost Garmentes. **1545** RAYNALD *Byrth Mankynde* I. ii. (1552) 1 b, Of the which [coats] the first and vttermost is called the skyn.

c. Greatest in extent; longest. *rare.*

a **1586** SIDNEY *Apol. Poetrie* (Arb.) 63 The vttermost time presupposed in it, should be..but one day. *a* **1586** —— *Arcadia* III. xviii, [He] stood..with..his shield at the uttermost length of his arme.

2. Extreme; = UTMOST *a.* 2.

13.. [see UTMOST *a.* 2]. **1429** *Rolls of Parlt.* IV. 352/1 To the uttermast distruction and anientisment of the said Merchantz. **1468** SIR J. PASTON in *Paston Lett.* II. 329 The uttermost pryse had not passyd v. mark. **1544** in Leadam *Star Chamber Cases* (Selden) II. 306 As they will answere.. for the same att their uttermost perilles. **1556** OLDE *Antichrist* 59 The best..that shoulde lye in his uttermost possible power to doo. **1607** NORDEN *Surv. Dial.* III. 88 You that haue bene here presently sworn to performe your uttermost duties. **1676** HALE *Contempl.* II. 212 Thou.. may'st most justly expect from the children of Men our uttermost Love, and Fear. **1702** H. DODWELL *Apol.* § 1 in S. Parker *Cicero's De Finibus*, The time wherein Philosophy.. received its uttermost Perfection. *a* **1796** in Morse *Amer. Geog.* I. 91 His friendships are..faithful to the uttermost extremity. **1807** WORDSW. *White Doe* III. 91 A voice of uttermost joy. **1856** RUSKIN *Mod. Paint.* IV. 74 To speak with uttermost truth of expression. **1890** HALLETT *Thous. Miles on Elephant* 430 It is in the uttermost degree unlikely.

†**b.** Of persons: = UTTEREST *a.* 2 b. *Obs.*

1572 FORREST *Theophilus* 743 Howe happened thee to goe ..Vnto his enemye moste vttermoste..? **1606** G. W[OODCOCKE] *Hist. Ivstine* XXII. 82 They were solde..to the uttermost enemy of their estate.

†**3.** Last in time; final. Cf. UTMOST *a.* 3. *Obs.*

c **1440** *York Myst.* xxxvii. 232 And Marie me menys þi modir hight, þe vttiremeste ende of all þi kynne. **1463** *Paston Lett.* II. 133 For..the Sunday was the uttermest day. **1470-85** MALORY *Arthur* X. lxxxvi. 567 To the vtter-mest dayes of my lyf. **1549** COVERDALE, etc. *Erasm. Par. 2 Tim.* 20 He..is hable ynoughe to kepe vnto the vttermost daye, the thing that [etc.]. **1593** *Sidney's Arcadia* IV. (1922) II. 111 The uttermost instant is scope enough for him, to revoke every thing. **1600** HOLLAND *Livy* V. xxii. 195 b, The finall end and fall of Veij,..which even in this last and utter-most [L. *ultimus*] calamitie shewed her mightinesse.

b. Last of a series, store, etc. Chiefly in ***uttermost farthing***.

1553 LATIMER *Sermon on Lord's Prayer* (1562) 51 b, The lord..caste him into prison, there to lye till he had paied the vttermost farthing. **1611** BIBLE *Matt.* v. 26 Thou shalt by no meanes come out thence, till thou hast payd the vttermost farthing. **1622** BACON *Hen. VII*, 183 Vowing not to leaue him, till the vttermost drop of their bloud were spilt. **1630** *R. Johnson's Kingd. & Commw.* 446 The first borne is heire to all, even to the uttermost farthing. **1821-2** SHELLEY *Chas. I*, II. 77 The uttermost Farthing exact from those. **1837** CARLYLE *Fr. Rev.* III. II. viii, His accounts lie all ready, correct in black-on-white, to the uttermost farthing.

II. *absol.* or as *sb.*

4. External limit, part, etc.; = UTMOST *a.* 4.

13.. [see UTTEREST *a.* 4]. **1382** WYCLIF *Deut.* vi. 15 Lest eny tyme the woodnes of the Lord..doo thee awey fro the vttermoost of the erthe. *c* **1520** M. NISBET *Acts* i. 8 In al Judee,..and into the vtermast of the erd. **1563** SHUTE *Archit.* D iv, From the vttermost of the Abacus. **1851** LONGF. *Gold. Leg.* III. *Nativity* iii. 43 The Angel of the uttermost Of all the shining, heavenly host.

b. *sb. pl.* = UTMOST *a.* 4 b. *Obs. rare.*

a **1390** *Wycliffite Bible* Isaiah xlii. 10 (MS. Douce 369), Singiþ..his praisynge fro þe vttermostis of þe erþ [L. *ab extremis terræ*]. (See also UTMOST *a.* 4 b.)

†**5.** The very most; = UTMOST *a.* 5, 5 b. *Obs.*

a **1425** tr. *Arderne's Treat. Fistula*, etc. 83 For þe vertu of þam aboute fire is þe vttermoste of strenght. ? **1477** *Stonor Papers* (Camden) II. 34 You schalle vnderstonde the vttermeste of my stomake. *a* **1513** FABYAN *Chron.* VII. (1811) 645 For the encrece & augmentacion thereof, to the vtter-moost of theyr powers. **1526** *Pilgr. Perf.* (W. de W. 1531) 37 He wolde haue done his vttermost. **1578** H. WOTTON *Courtlie Controv.* 40 In doing wherof, you shall bynde me with the vttermoste of my seruice to acknowledge the honoure. *c* **1590** MARLOWE *Faustus* iii, But be resolute, And trie the vttermost magicke can performe. **1604** SHAKS. *Oth.* III. iv. 167 Ile moue your suite, And seeke to effect it to my vttermost. **1610** R. FIELD *Fifth Bk. Ch.* lvii. 466 The vttermost therefore that our Aduersaries can say, is [etc.]. **1638** JUNIUS *Paint. Ancients* 228 The uttermost on either side is vicious. **1668** SANDERSON *Cases* 75 Let the Daughters disobedience deserve all this uttermost of punishment, from the offended Father.

†**6. a.** End; issue; = UTMOST *a.* 6. *Obs. rare.*

1470-85 MALORY *Arthur* VII. vii. 223 Aweye wille I not tyl I see the vttermest of this Iourneye. **1593** *Sidney's Arcadia* III. (1922) II. 4 Zelmane..had now looked to the uttermoste [*ed.* **1674** utmost] of it, and established her minde upon an assured determination.

b. The extreme or furthest limit (in time). *Obs.*⁻¹

1601 SHAKS. *Jul. C.* II. i. 213 *Bru.* By the eight houre, is that the vttermost? *Cin.* Be that the vttermost, and faile not then.

7. ***to the uttermost***, = UTMOST *a.* 7. Now *rare* or *Obs.*

c **1400** *Pilgr. Sowle* (Caxton, 1483) IV. xxix. 61 Ne he ne shalle nought ben of power..for to descryuen to the utter-most, be it good or badde. **1470-85** MALORY *Arthur* IV. vii. 128 To doo the bataille to the vttermest. **1526** *Pilgr. Perf.* 13 b, All the appetites of man shalbe replenysshed with all goodnes, and saciat with glory, to the vttermoste. **1588** A. KING tr. *Canisius' Catech.* 51 The sonne of god..hes sufferit all things to the vttermaist. **1598** R. BERNARD tr. *Terence* (1607) *Andria* IV. i, To labour to the vttermost with might and maine. **1605** *London Prodigal* III. ii, Her loue will then be tried to the vttermost. **1622** R. HAWKINS *Voy. S. Sea* 120 The cause that every man forceth himselfe to the vttermost, to doe the labour of two men. **1772** COOK *First Voyage* III. i. (1773) III. 493 They..seemed resolved to defend their coast to the uttermost. **1844** MRS. BROWNING *Lost Bower* lxxiii, The prayer preserves it greenly, to the last and uttermost. **1846** TRENCH *Mirac.* xxvii. 359 Now the Scribes were pressing the advantage which they had gained..to the uttermost. **1871** FREEMAN *Norm. Conq.* xviii. IV. 139 To withstand the stranger to the uttermost.

(*b*) **1489** *Rolls of Parlt.* VI. 424 True and faithfull service to the uttermost of his power. **1557** *Order of Hospitalls* E 4 b, To the best and uttermost of your wits and powers. **1593** *Sidney's Arcadia* v. (1922) II. 158 To the uttermost of my skill. **1594** HOOKER *Eccl. Pol.* II. i. § 1 That..we defend, to the vttermost of that habilitie which he hath giuen. **1611** BIBLE *Translators to Rdr.* ¶ 3 To haue care of Religion,..yea to promote it to the vttermost of their power. **1638** *Hamilton Papers* (Camden) 32 The Couenanters haue..labored to the uttermost of ther power to procure the rescinding. **1725** DE FOE *Voy. round World* (1840) 183 The natives..will generally be..kind also to the uttermost of their power.

8. †**a.** ***at the uttermost*** (also ***at uttermost***), = UTMOST *a.* 8. *Obs.*

1530 in W. H. Turner *Select. Rec. Oxford* (1880) 87 For every pott iij^s, or at the uttermuste iiij^s. **1535** LAYTON in *Lett. Suppress. Monast.* (Camden) 72 On Wedinsday by nyght, at utermoste. **1577** B. GOOGE *Heresbach's Husb.* I. 30 b, Within three monethes, or foure at the vttermost after they are sowen. **1582** N. LICHEFIELD tr. *Castanheda's Conq. E. Ind.* I. ii. 6 b, Not aboue thirtie leagues distaunt from thence at the vttermost.

b. ***at one's uttermost***, at the utmost point of test or danger. *rare*⁻¹.

1859 TENNYSON *Marr. Geraint* 502 But if I live, So aid me Heaven when at mine uttermost, As I will make her truly my true wife.

ˈutterness. [f. UTTER *a.* + -NESS.] The condition or quality of being utter, absolute, or complete; absoluteness.

1827 LYTTON *Falkland* II. 113, I have started to find the utterness of my desolation! **1871** *Daily News* 1 Mar., The utterness of her collapse. **1904** *Westm. Gaz.* 9 Nov. 2/1 He tried it on Catherine—with a resulting utterness of failure.

utterquidaunce, var. OUTRECUIDANCE *Obs.*

†**ˈutterward**, *adv.* and *a.* *Obs. rare.* [f. UTTER *a.* or *adv.* + -WARD.]

A. *adv.* Outside; outwardly, externally.

1436 *Pol. Poems* (Rolls) II. 157 The trewe processe of Englysh polycye, Of utterwarde to kepe thys regne in rest Of oure England. **1538** in *Lett. Suppress. Monast.* (Camden) 228 The state of the howse bothe inwardely and utterward.

B. *adj.* Of confession: Made to a member of a religious house by a non-member.

c **1535** T. BEDYLL in G. J. Aungier *Syon Mon.* (1840) 88 To know his pleasire..towching the muring up of the howses of utterward confessions. [Cf. UTTWARD (quots. *c* 1535).]

utteward, utward, obs. varr. (with shortened vowel) of OUTWARD *adv.*

a **1425** tr. *Arderne's Treat. Fistula*, etc. 12 Vpon þe aposteme, forsoþe, vtward be putte a gode emplastre. **1428** in *Surtees Misc.* (1888) 9 For other occupacions that he had to doo utteward.

uttrage(ouss, obs. ff. OUTRAGE(OUS.

uttward, utward, etc., obs. varr. (with shortened vowel) of OUTWARD *a.*

1503-4 *Act 19 Hen. VII*, c. 4 Preamble, Honour & Victorie..goten agayne utwarde enymyes. **1526** TINDALE *2 Cor.* iv. 16 Though oure vttward man perisshe. *c* **1535** T. BEDYLL in G. J. Aungier *Syon Mon.* (1840) 87 The place where thes frires haue beene wont to hire uttward confessiouns of al commers. *Ibid.*, Hering of utward confessions hath beene the cause of muche evyl. [Cf. UTTERWARD *a.*]

‖**utu** (ˈʊtʊ). *New Zealand.* [a. Maori *utu* return for anything, satisfaction, reward, reply.]

a. Recompense, satisfaction, return or price paid for injuries received.

1828 in W. Colenso *Papers* (typescript) III. 18 Until another chief has been killed as an utu or payment. **1840** J. S. POLACK *Manners & Customs N. Zealand* II. 63 Utu or payment is invariably expected for any injustice committed [by the Maoris]. **1852** MUNDY *Antipodes* x. II. 89 'Utu', (which may be freely translated,) 'blood for blood', is with him [*sc.* the Maori] a sacred necessity. **1890** J. M. MOORE *N. Zealand* iii. 49 The utu, or satisfaction for murder (*lex talionis*), theft, or any other crime,..was rigorously carried out among the Maoris.

b. *transf.* (See quot.)

1902 *Webster's Suppl.* 226/3 *Utu*,..any compensation, as for services rendered; reward, payment, wages; often corrupted to *hoot*.

utward(e, ME. varr. OUTWARD *adv.*

utwit, utwith, obs. forms of OUTWITH.

uuen (in *on uuen*): see ANOVEN *adv.*

uuenan, -en, -on, varr. OVENON, -AN *Obs.*

uut-yede, obs. pa. t. of OUTGO.

uva (ˈjuːvə). Pl. **uvæ** (ˈjuːviː). [L. *ūva* grape, uvula, etc. (whence It., Pr., Sp., Pg. *uva*, F. *uve*).]

†**1.** (See quot.) *Obs. rare*⁻¹.

App. an error for, and misunderstanding of, UVEA.

1562 TURNER *Herbal* II. 67 Oliue..is good for the diseases of the ey called vua, and for wheles. [Hence in Langham *Garden of Health* (1579) 439.]

2. *Bot.* A grape or raisin; a grape-like fruit.

1670 EVELYN *Sylva* (ed. 2) 25 Nor may we here omit to mention the Galls, Misletoe, Polypod, Agaric (us'd in Antidots) Vuæ, Fungus's to make Tinder. [Hence in Mortimer *Husb.* (1707) 327.] **1753** *Chambers' Cycl.* Suppl., *Uva*, Grape. See the article *Grape*. **1862** M. C. COOKE *Man. Bot. Terms* 87 *Uva*, (Lat. a grape), applied to such succulent indehiscent fruits as have a central placenta. [Hence in *Imp. Dict.* (1884), and later Dicts.] **1892** C. E. ARMAND SEMPLE *Elem. Mat. Med.* 225 *Uvæ*—Raisins.—The ripe fruit of Vitis Vinifera.

3. ***uva ursi*** (ˈjuːvə ˈɜːsaɪ), the bearberry, *Arctostaphylos Uva-ursi*, a trailing plant valued as furnishing an astringent tonic.

1753 *Chambers' Cycl.* Suppl. s.v., There is only one known species of the *Uva Ursi*, which is the plant called.. the whortle-berry. **1786** ABERCROMBIE *Arrangem.* 39 in *Gard. Assist.*, Evergreen Trees and Shrubs [include]..Uva ursi, or bearberry. **1820** GOOD *Nosology* 454 The powder of the uva *ursi*,..recommended by Linnéus as [a] valuable lithontriptic. **1822** *Encycl. Metrop.* (1845) XIV. 742 As a remedy the Uva-Ursi was used by the ancients. **1873** BENTLEY *Man. Bot.* (ed. 3) 562 Trailing Arbutus.—The leaves and stems possess similar properties to Uva-Ursi.

b. *Med.* The leaves of the bearberry, or an infusion of these.

1805 *Med. Jrnl.* 465 A combination of such medicines with the uva-ursi, was..administered. **1842** BRANDE *Dict. Sci.*, etc. 138 The leaves of this plant, under the name *uva ursi*, are used as an astringent and tonic in medicine. **1892** C. E. ARMAND SEMPLE *Mat. Med.* 318 Uva ursi may also be used for gleets.

Hence †**ˈuval** *a.*, = UVEAL *a.* 1. [Cf. F. *uval*.]

1656 BLOUNT *Glossogr.*, *Uval*,..pertaining to a Grape or Vine.

uvala (ˈuːvələ). *Physical Geogr.* Also **ouvala**. [a. Serbo-Croat *uvala* hollow, depression.] A depression in the ground surface occurring in karstic regions (see quots.).

1902 *Geogr. Jrnl.* XX. 429 Dr. Cvijič's researches have led him to consider the uvala (Karstmulde) as an intermediate form between doline and polye. The uvala is a large, broad sinking in the karst with uneven floor, formed by the breaking down of the wall between a series of dolines. **1921** *Geogr. Rev.* XI. 600 As time goes on, the divisions between neighboring dolines are broken down; and larger depressions, called 'uvalas' or 'ouvalas', are created. **1922** *Geol. Mag.* XIX. 401 Several of the smaller..poljes of Southern Herzegovina..appear to result from the collapse of underground watercourses. To such depressions it would perhaps be better to restrict the use of the local Bosnian term 'uvalas'. **1954** W. D. THORNBURY *Princ. Geomorphol.* xiii. 323 The Bosnian term uvala is most commonly applied to the larger depressions resulting from the collapse of extensive roof sections over underground watercourses. What have been designated above as compound sinkholes are sometimes called uvalas, but this usage of the term does not seem justified. **1970** R. J. SMALL *Study of Landforms* iv. 152 In many areas closely adjoining sotchs have amalgamated, through lateral extension, to give larger depressions comparable with the 'uvalas' of the Karst proper.

uvarovite, (uːˈværəvaɪt). *Min.* Also **ouw-, uwarowite; ouw-, ouvarovite**. [Named in 1832 by G. H. Hess, after Count S. S. *Uvarov*,

President of St. Petersburg Academy: see -ITE[1] 2 b.] An emerald-green variety of garnet.
1837 DANA *System Mineralogy* 353 Ouwarowite..occurs in transparent emerald-green dodecahedrons. 1855 *Orr's Circ. Sci., Geol.*, etc. 526 Uwarowite.—Chrome and Lime Garnet... Translucent;..infusible. Found in the Ural. 1897 L. FLETCHER *Introd. Study Min.* 102 Uvarovite is a green chrome-garnet.

†**uve.** *Obs.* [ad. L. *ūva* UVA.] = UVULA 1.
c 1530 *Judic. Urines* II. vii. 29 b, Epiglotum is moost parte all waye calleth in Phisike & in gramer also, vua or vuula, *anglice* y^e vue, or y^e vuule.

‖**uvea** (ˈjuːvɪə). *Anat.* [med.L. *uvea* (whence It., Sp., Pg. *uvea*, F. *uvée*), f. L. *ūva* UVA.]
†**1.** The posterior coloured surface or choroid coat of the eye. *Obs.*
1525 tr. *Jerome of Brunswick's Surg.* B j b/2 The vtter most [part of the coat]..is named vuea, & hath the hole of the ball of the iye. 1543 TRAHERON *Vigo's Chirurg.* Interpr. Words s.v., One of the skynnes of the eye is called vuea bycause it is lyke the stone of a grape. 1615 CROOKE *Body of Man* (1631) 555 Figure 4 sheweth the Vuea or Grapy coate with a portion of the Opticke Nerue. 1676 *Phil. Trans.* II. 746 Where he considers, why the Uvea or Choroides is black in Men, but of divers colours in Brutes. 1685 [see PUPIL *sb.*[2] 1 β]. 1728 CHAMBERS *Cycl.* (1738) s.v. *Eye*, The crystalline [humour], situate immediately under the aqueous, behind the uvea, opposite to the pupil. 1797 MRS. M. BRYAN *Syst. Astron.* 156 The uvea commences where the choroides divides from the sclerotica, from which part..the pupil is called the iris.
2. A layer of pigmented cells forming the posterior covering of the iris; the middle coat or vascular tunic of the eye, composed of the choroid, iris, and ciliary body; the uveal tract.
1745 R. JAMES *Med. Dict.* s.v. *Iris*, The generality of Anatomists call that Membrane, which I have spoke of under the Name of Iris, the Uvea. c 1760 A. MONRO *Anat. Nerves* Wks. (1781) 349 Small fibres..running along the choroid coat on the outside of the retina in their course to the uvea or iris. 1771 *Encycl. Brit.* I. 289/2 This portion [of the coat of the eye] goes commonly by the particular name of uvea..and..has likewise got the name of iris. 1838 *Penny Cycl.* X. 139/2 A vertical section of the globe, showing the ciliary body and processes with the uvea.

uveal (ˈjuːvɪəl), *a.* [f. UVE-A + -AL[1].]
†**1.** (See quot. and cf. UVAL *a.*) *Obs. rare*$^{-0}$.
1658 PHILLIPS, *Uveal*, belonging to a Grape, like a Grape.
2. Pertaining or belonging to, constituting or consisting of, the uvea.
uveal tract, = UVEA 2.
1658 PHILLIPS s.v. *Tunicle*, The Uveal, the Vitreal or glassy, and the Christalline [tunicles of the eye]. 1869 J. S. WELLS *Dis. Eye* iii. 144 The whole forming, in reality, one tissue, the uveal tract. 1891 *Lancet* 21 March 678/1 A glandular apparatus by which the aqueous humour is secreted. Dr. Nicati names it the 'uveal gland'. 1894 D. J. CUNNINGHAM *Man. Pract. Anat.* II. 624 The portion on the deep surface of the iris forms its posterior uveal pigmentary layer.
b. Affecting or occurring in the uvea.
1896 *Lancet* 15 Feb. 422/2 A case of Uveal Cysts in the Iris in a man aged forty-seven.

‖**uveitis** (juːviːˈaɪtɪs). *Path.* [mod.L., f. med.L. *uve-a* UVEA + -ITIS. Cf. F. *uvéite.*]
Inflammation of the uvea.
1848 DUNGLISON *Med. Dict.* s.v. [Hence in later Dicts.] 1889 WALSHAM *The. & Pract. Surg.* (ed. 2) 499 Plastic uveitis is characterized by a great tendency to deposition of lymph.

uvel(e, obs. ff. EVIL *a.* and *sb.*

uvelien, ME. var. EVIL *v.* *Obs.*

ˈ**uvelloid,** *a.* [f. mod.L. *ūvell-a*, dim. of L. *ūva* UVA, + -OID.] Like or resembling a small cluster of grapes.
1880 W. SAVILLE-KENT *Man. Infusoria* I. 190 Similar, but detached, uvelloid clusters. *Ibid.* 191 The propagation of the species by the detachment of entire uvelloid masses.

†ˈ**uvemest,** *a.* *Obs.* Forms: 1 **ufemest, -myst,** 3 **ufenmeste;** 3 **uue- (huue-), uvemest, vuemest(e, uuemaste.** [Late OE. *ufemest, -myst* (rare for *yfemest, yfemyst*), superl. of *ufera* (comparative, UVER *a.*), f. root *uf-*: see OVEMEST *a.*, and cf. UMEST *a.*] Uppermost; topmost; highest.
c 1000 ÆLFRIC *Hom.* II. 76 On midne dæȝ bið seo sunne on ðam ufemestum ryne stiȝende. c 1000 —— *Genesis* xl. 17 (Laud MS.), On þam ufemystan windle wære maneȝra cynna ȝebæc. c 1200 [see OVEMEST *a.* a]. c 1205 LAY. 6085 Vp heo hine duden heȝe an ufenmeste þan turre. c 1220 *Bestiary* 775 Vp he ros..and steȝ to heuene uvemest. a 1225 *Ancr. R.* 328 Heo hudet eke hore ihole cloðes, & doð an alre vuemeste [a 1275 *Cotton MS.* uueward] on viterokes al to torene.

uveoparotid (ˈjuːvɪəʊpəˌrɒtɪd), *a.* *Med.* [f. UVE(A + -O + PAROTID *a.* and *sb.*] Affecting or involving the uvea and the parotid gland. So ˌ**uveoparoˈtitis,** inflammation of the uvea and the parotid.
1917 *Brit. Jrnl. Ophthalmol.* I. 619 He came to the conclusion that..uveo-parotid fever is nothing more than atypical mumps. *Ibid.* 620 The case for mumps as the sole cause for uveo-parotitis is as yet, 'not proven'. 1961 *Lancet* 16 Sept. 614/1 In 5 out of 13 patients who have uveoparotitis the pulmonary disease..has led to severe fibrosis. 1967 [see LYMPHOGRANULOMA]. 1974 PASSMORE & ROBSON *Compan. Med. Stud.* III. xv. 1/1 A generation ago textbooks gave accounts of Hutchinson's disease, Besnier's disease, Boeck's disease, lupus pernio and uveoparotid fever... All these conditions..are different expressions of the disorder now known as sarcoidosis. 1975 *Brit. Med. Jrnl.* 27 Dec. 731/2 Two middle-aged sisters, living separately, developed sarcoidosis with bilateral uveoparotitis and cranial palsies within six months of each other.

†ˈ**uveous,** *a.* *Obs.* [a. late or med.L. *uveus* (Quicherat): see UVE-A and -OUS.] = UVEAL *a.* 2.
1691 RAY *Creation* ii. (1692) 25 The Uveous Coat or Iris of the Eye. 1696 J. EDWARDS *Demonstr. Exist. God* II. 31 A round hole in the middle and forepart of this uveous membrane. 1710 J. CLARKE tr. *Rohault's Nat. Philos.* (1729) I. 281 The Rays..are hindred from going any further by the Uveous Tunick.

ˈ**uver,** *a.* Now *dial.* Forms: 1 **uferra, ufera, ufara,** 2–3 **ufere,** 3 **uferre, vfere, vuere, uuere;** *Sc.* 4, 6 **uvyr,** 6 **uuir,** 5 **wuyr, vuir,** 5–6 **vuer,** 6, 9 **uver, uvir,** 9 **iver, ever;** *dial.* 8–9 **uvver,** 9 **uvvor.** [OE. *uferra, ufera, ufara* (also *yferra, yfera*), = OS. *oƀarro*, MLG. *overe*, OHG. *obaro, obero*, etc. (MHG. and G. *obere, ober*); cf. ON. *øfri* (Icel. *efri*), MSw. *öfre, öffre* (Sw. *öfre*), Da. *øvre* (Norw.) *øver*. See also OVER *a.*]
1. a. That is higher or loftier in position; upper; = OVER *a.* 1.
c 825 *Vesp. Psalter* ciii. 3 Ðu biðeces in wetrum ða uferran his. c 897–c 1275 [see OVER *a.* 1 a]. 1372 *Reg. Mag. Sig. Scot.* 151 Baronia de Uvyrcrelyne. 1424 in *Antiq. Aberd. & Banff* (1862) IV. 388 Terras de..Nethirbulgny, Wuirbulgny, Midilmast Bulgny. 1495 *Ibid.* 439 Terrarum de Vuer Towiis, Nethir Towiis. 1511 *Reg. Privy Seal Scotl.* I. 342/2 Litera..super terris de le Uver part de Lany. 1550 *Abstr. Protocols Town Clerks of Glasgow* (1894) I. 18 The foir uvyr hows, viz., hall, chalmer and wairdrop, with the peis waist. 1596 DALRYMPLE tr. *Leslie's Hist. Scot.* I. 14 In vuir Clydisdale and in nethir Clidisdale. 1703 THORESBY *Let. to Ray, Uvver*, for *upper*, or *over*. 1808 JAMIESON s.v. *Ouer*. 1824 [CARR] *Craven Gloss.* 8 Th' uvver side o' th' Gill. 1828– in Yks., Derby, Leics., Northampt., and Shropsh. dialect use (*Eng. Dial. Dict.* s.v. OVER *a.* 21).
b. ***uver lip***, the upper lip; = OVER-LIP.
1027–34 *Laws of Cnut* in *Liebermann* 334 Þonne do man ut his eaȝan, & ceorfan of..his earan & þa uferan lippan. 1788 [see OVER-LIP]. 1854 MISS BAKER *Northampt. Gloss.* 373. 1864 B. PRESTON *Poems* 10 (E.D.D.), His hair..spraated aht fro' t' uvvor lip. 1876 *Whitby Gloss.* 209.
c. ***uver hand***, the 'upper hand'; the superiority or mastery; = OVER-HAND *sb.*
c 1205 LAY. 18325 Þa wes hit swa ufel idon, þæt þat hæðene uolc þa ufere hond hafeden. 1562 WINȜET *Wks.* (S.T.S.) I. 50 *margin*, The wicket hes the vuir hand. 1808 JAMIESON s.v. *Ouer, The uvir hand*, the upper hand. 1828 *Craven Gloss.* II. 25 To have the..uvver-hand. 1891 *Sheffield Gloss.* Suppl. 42 He's got t' uvver hand of him.
†**2.** Later; after; future; = OVER *a.* 5. *Obs.*
Beowulf 2200 Eft þæt ȝe-iode ufaran dogrum. c 1000, c 1205 [see OVER *a.* 5]. c 1205 LAY. 26035 Þa nolde Arður on slepen na wiht hine areppen, leste he an uferre daȝe upbræid iherde.

†ˈ**uver-mar,** *adv.* *Obs.*$^{-1}$ In 3 **uferr-mar.** [f. OE. *ufor* higher, highest + *-mar* -MORE. Cf. ON. *ofar meir*, MSw. *öwermeer, öffuermere.*] Higher up; above.
c 1200 ORMIN 1715 All þiss icc seȝȝde ȝuw littlær Her uferr mar a litell.

ˈ**uvermost,** *a.* Now *dial.* In 6 *Sc.* **uvirmest,** 9 *dial.* **uvvermost, -must.** [f. UVER *a.* + -MOST.] Uppermost; highest.
1549 *Burgh Rec. Stirling* (1887) 55 Anent the tua uvirmest lychtis. 1841 C. H. HARTSHORNE *Salopia Antiqua* 606 Gwon to th' uvvermost leasow. 1880 MISS JACKSON *Shropshire Word-bk.* 463 Keep the Maister's collars uvvermost.

†ˈ**uveward,** *a.* *Obs.* In 1 **ufeweard, ufawærd, ufweard,** 3 **uueward.** [OE. *ufe-, ufweard*, etc., f. root *uf-* (see OVEMEST *a.*) + *-weard* -WARD 2. Cf. OE. *ufanweard*, ON. *ofan-verðr.*] Upper, higher; forming the upper part. Also *absol.*
c 897 K. ÆLFRED *Gregory's Past. C.* i. 28 Forðon ða eaȝan bioð on ðæm lichoman foreweardum & ufeweardum. c 950 *Lindisf. Gosp.* Matt. xxvii. 51 And heonu waȝhrahel temples ..tosliten wæs..from ufawærd wið to nioðaweard. a 1000–c 1200 [see NETHEWARD *a.*] a 1275 [see UVEMEST *a.*].

†ˈ**uvid,** *a.* *Obs. rare.* [ad. L. *ūvid-us* damp, etc.] Moist, wet.
1656 BLOUNT *Glossogr., Uvid*, moist, or wet. [Hence in PHILLIPS (1658).] 1762 *Gentl. Mag.* 544 On land, their uvid locks new grace acquire.

†ˈ**uviferous,** *a.* *Obs.*$^{-0}$ [f. L. *ūvifer-us* bearing grapes (f. *ūv-a* UVA) + -OUS.] (See quot.)
1656 BLOUNT *Glossogr., Uviferous*,..that bears Grapes or Vines.

uvrou, -ow: see EUPHROE, YUFFROUW.

‖**uvula** (ˈjuːvjʊlə). Forms: 5–7 **vuula,** 6 **uuula,** 6–7 **vvula,** 7– **uvula;** 6 **euuela, uuila, vuola, vuala.** [a. med.L. *ūvula* (whence Sp. and Pg. *uvula*, It. *uvola, ugola*, OF. *uvule, uvele, huvele* UVULE), dim. of L. *ūva* UVA.]
1. *Anat.* The conical fleshy prolongation hanging from the middle of the pendent margin of the soft palate in man and some other primates.
c 1400 *Lanfranc's Cirurg.* 261 Aboue þis instrument is vuula þat is þe palet of þe mouþ & helpiþ for to make soun. *Ibid.*, Sumtyme vuula wexiþ to long. 1525 tr. *Jerome of Brunswick's Surg.* B ii/2 Tonge, rowfe, and vuula, ye whiche is a lytell deme hangynge in ye throte lyke the spynne. 1569 ANDROSE *Alexis' Bk. Med.* III. 33 Against the falling of the Vuola, and swelling of the Pallate. 1607 TOPSELL *Four-f. Beasts* 495 Good and ready helpes for the sorenes of the vuula which is in the Horses mouthes. c 1645 HOWELL *Lett.* II. i. (1650) 1 The same defluxion..fell..into my throat in Oxford, and distilling upon the uvula impeached my utterance a little. 1676 WISEMAN *Surg.* IV. vii. 333 An Elongation of the Uvula through the abundance of salivous Humour flowing upon it. 1705 *Phil. Trans.* XXV. 1984 The Uvula..is moved by three pair of Muscles. 1724 RAMSAY *Health* 183 When th' uvula has got its mortal wound. 1753 TORRIANO *Gangr. Sore Throat* 4 After having examin'd her, they found the Uvula much lengthened. 1805 *Med. Jrnl.* XIV. 150 On inspecting the throat, the tonsils and uvula were not observably altered. 1831 R. KNOX *Cloquet's Anat.* 597 The uvula..forms the inferior edge of the velum palati into a double arch. 1866 HUXLEY *Physiol.* vi. 146 The soft palate, or velum—the middle of which is produced into a prolongation, the uvula. 1902 HUGHES & KEITH *Man. Pract. Anat.* III. 368 The uvula is connected with each tonsil by the furrowed band, to be seen when the uvula is pulled gently aside.
b. A small eminence forming the apex of the trigone, and projecting into the urethral orifice.
1835–6 *Todd's Cycl. Anat.* I. 386/1 The uvula in the child is the most depending part of the bladder. 1861 SIR. H. THOMPSON *Dis. Prostate* (ed. 2) 7 The mucous membrane and submucous tissues around the internal meatus, particularly those forming the uvula or luette vesicale. *Ibid.* 26 A faint whitish line directly in front of the uvula.
c. A lobe or triangular elevation situated between the two tonsils of the cerebellum.
1848 DUNGLISON *Med. Lex.* (ed. 7) 887 The inferior vermiform process..consisting of three portions—the pyramid, the uvula, and the nodulus.
†**2.** *ellipt.* Inflammation of the uvula; uvulitis.
1539 ELYOT *Cast. Helthe* (1541) 69 b, Whereby are ingendred Catarres or reumes, the uuula, the cough, and the stytche. 1570 T. WILSON *Demosth. Orat., Life* 133 Troubled with the Vvula being a swelling in the throte.
3. *attrib.* and *Comb.*, esp. in the names of surgical instruments for operating on the uvula, as ***uvula elevator, scissors, spoon***, etc.; also **uvula-cushion** (see quot. 1884); **uvula trill** (see quot. 1908); †**uvula-wort,** the nettle-leaved bell-flower, *Campanula Trachelium*.
1597 GERARDE *Herbal* II. ii. 366 [It] is called..in English ..Throtewoort or *Vuula* woort, of the vertue it hath against the paine and swelling thereof. 1678 PHILLIPS (ed. 4), *Uvula-spoon*..is an Instrument to be held right under the Uvula. 1710 [see UVULAR *a.* 1]. 1728 BRADLEY *Dict. Bot.* s.v., Uvula Wort; see Throat-wort. 1869 ELLIS *E.E. Pronunc.* I. 8 *R r* uvula trill, F. *r* provençal or grasseyé. *Ibid.* 198 A sharp uvula rattle without any moisture. 1875 KNIGHT *Dict. Mech.* 2685/2 Uvula-scissors with claws. 1876 tr. *Ziemssen's Cycl. Pract. Med.* IV. 43 The instrument..called the uvula-holder. *Ibid.* 67 A uvula elevator. 1884 M. MACKENZIE *Dis. Throat & Nose* II. 253 Beneath the septum the base of the uvula containing the azygos muscle forms a slight projection, called the 'uvula-cushion'. 1895 *Arnold & Sons' Catal. Surg. Instrum.* p. xlv, Uvula Hook, Scissors, Twitch. 1908 SWEET *Sounds of English* 40 The 'burred *r*' is a uvula-trill; the uvula..is driven upwards by the force of the outgoing air [etc.].

uvular (ˈjuːvjʊlə(r)), *a.* (*sb.*). [ad. mod.L. *ūvulār-is* (whence also F. *uvulaire*), f. med.L. *ūvula* UVULA.]
1. Used in disorders of the uvula. *rare*$^{-1}$.
1710 T. FULLER *Pharm. Extemp.* (1719) 480 Uvular Powder..Let the Powder be blown upon the Uvula with a Pipe or Uvula Spoon.
2. Pertaining or belonging to the uvula.
1843 WILKINSON *Swedenborg's Anim. Kingd.* I. ii. 67 The palatine and uvular glands. 1848 DUNGLISON *Dict. Med. Sci.* (ed. 7) 878 *Uvular glands*, are small follicles, belonging to the mucous membrane covering the uvula. 1891 *Cent. Dict.* s.v., Uvular muscle.
3. Produced by vibration of the uvula.
1873 MURRAY *Dialect So. Counties* 241 The uvular trill in French Paris. 1884 *Schaff's Encycl. Relig. Knowl.* III. 2155 The Semitic alphabet is..characterized by fulness of guttural, uvular, and spirant consonants. 1889 ELLIS *E.E. Pronunc.* v. 642 The German uvular *r*.
b. As *sb.* A uvular consonant.
1884 *Schaff's Encycl. Relig. Knowl.* III. 2155 In the several [Semitic] dialects, the movement has been towards a diminution of the number of gutturals and uvulars.
Hence ˈ**uvularly** *adv.*, with a thick obstructed utterance, as when the uvula is unduly long.
1860 DICKENS *Uncomm. Trav.* iii, Number Two laughed (very uvularly), and the skirmishers followed suit.

‖**uvularia** (juːvjʊˈlɛərɪə). *Bot.* [early mod.L. *ūvulāria*, f. med.L. *ūvula* UVULA.]
†**1.** The S. European shrub *Ruscus Hypoglossum*.
1706 PHILLIPS (ed. Kersey), *Uvularia*, the Herb Horse-tongue.
2. One or other species of *Uvularia*, a small liliaceous genus typical of the tribe *Uvulareæ* of melanthaceous plants.
1829 LOUDON *Encycl. Plants* 271 A plant like an Uvularia in habit. 1846 LINDLEY *Veg. Kingd.* 199 Uvularias are said to be simply astringent. 1850 MISS WARNER *Wide Wide World* xl, Wild columbine, the delicate corydalis, and more uvularias, which she called yellow bells.

uvulatome (ˈjuːvjʊlətəʊm). [f. UVULA + Gr. *τομ-ός* cutting. Cf. UVULOTOME.] An instrument for cutting or removing the uvula.
1872 COHEN *Dis. Throat* 145 An uvulatome..renders the operation very easy of performance. 1880 M. MACKENZIE

Dis. Throat & Nose I. 13 The uvulatomes..in use in this country at the end of the eighteenth century were of very rough construction.

uvulatomy (juːvjʊˈlætəmɪ). [See prec. and -TOMY. Cf. UVULOTOMY.] The operation of cutting or excising the uvula.

1887 *Lancet* 7 May 935/2 Uvulatomy gives very various results in the subsequent degree of discomfort during cicatrisation. **1890** BILLINGS *Nat. Med. Dict.* II. 731. [Hence in recent Dicts.]

†**uvule.** *Obs.* Also 6 vuels. [a. older F. *uvule* (also OF. *uvele, huvele*), or ad. med.L. *ūvula* UVULA.]

1. *Anat.* = UVULA I.

c **1530** *Judic. Urines* II. vii. 30 A sekenes yᵗ is called..casus vuule, yᵗ is no more for to say but sekenes of vuule. **1547** BOORDE *Brev. Health* xxvi. 16 Metyng with reume at the vuels in the rough [= roof] of the mouth. *Ibid.* ccclxxviii. 121 In Englyshe it is named vuels the whiche doth lye in the roufe of the mouthe lyke lytle longe teetes.

2. (See quot.) *rare*⁻¹.

1589 J. BANISTER *Antidotary* (1633) 87 A Gargarisme for them that be roofe-fallen, commonly called the Vvule.

‖**uvulitis** (juːvjʊˈlaɪtɪs). *Path.* [mod.L., f. med.L. *ūvul-a* UVULA + -ITIS. Cf. F. *uvulite.*] Inflammation of the uvula.

1848 DUNGLISON *Med. Dict.* (ed. 7) 187 *Cionitis*, inflammation of the uvula; uvulitis. **1880** M. MACKENZIE *Dis. Throat & Nose* I. 18 [In] Uvulitis..the uvula.. becomes intensely red, swollen, and elongated. **1897** *Allbutt's Syst. Med.* IV. 733 Chronic uvulitis is usually associated with chronic pharyngitis.

uvulotome (ˈjuːvjʊlətəʊm). [f. *uvulo-*, used as comb. form of UVULA, + Gr. τομ-ός cutting.] = UVULATOME.

1897 *Allbutt's Syst. Med.* IV. 734 In performing uvulotomy..the tip of the uvula—unless the uvulotome be used—should be..gently drawn forward.

uvuˈlotomy. [See prec. and -TOMY.] = UVULATOMY.

1889 *Buck's Handbk. Med. Sci.* VII. 505/2 At the present day uvulotomy is practised with an increasing degree of discretion. **1897** [see prec.].

uwing, obs. Sc. f. OWING *ppl. a.*

uxorial (ʌkˈsɔərɪəl), *a.* [f. L. *ūxōri-us* UXORIOUS *a.* + -AL¹.]

1. Of or pertaining to a wife or wives.

1800 A. GEDDES *Crit. Rem. Script.* 172 The speech [of Zipporah (Exodus iv. 25)] is not a speech of reproach or indignation, but of uxorial endearment. **1837** BP. WILBERFORCE *Let.* in Ashwell *Life* (1880) I. 105 All your uxorial connections living in the neighbourhood. **1853** LYTTON *My Novel* IV. i, The beauty of wives—the uxorial beauty. **1896** *Parl. Papers, Turkey* No. 3 (1897) CI. 23 The rather generous uxorial laws of Islam.

2. = UXORIOUS *a.* 2.

1853 LYTTON *My Novel* VIII. xii, Riccabocca..melted into absolute uxorial imbecility at the sight of that mute distress. **1872** F. W. ROBINSON *Bridge of Glass* II. xx, 'Waiting for your wife!' exclaimed Lady Coedstown. 'Uxorial, is it not?' he asked.

Hence **uxoriˈality**, the condition of being a wife; wifehood. *rare*⁻¹.

a **1832** BENTHAM *Deontol.* (1834) I. 235 Maritality, uxoriality, paternity, maternity, filiality.

uxoricide¹ (ʌkˈsɔərɪsaɪd). [ad. mod.L. **ūxōricīd-a*, f. L. *ūxor* wife: see -CIDE I.] One who murders his wife.

1860 WORCESTER. **1889** *Macm. Mag.* Jan. 237/2 Henry.. the tyrant and uxoricide. **1894** *Columbus* (Ohio) *Dispatch* 13 Oct. 6/5 To-day the uxoricide was arrested.

uˈxoricide². [ad. med.L. *ūxōricīd-ium*: see prec. and -CIDE 2.] The murder of one's wife.

1854 *Fraser's Mag.* xlix. 307 Such a detail of premeditated murders, suicides,..uxoricides, and fratricides. **1861** GOLDW. SMITH *Doctr. Hist. Progress* 39 They can embrace ..the butcherly vagrancy laws of a Tudor King, his brutal uxoricides, his persecutions. **1887** *Fortn. Rev.* Nov. 659 Adultery, incest, uxoricide, usually by poison, prostitution, are terribly frequent [in Sicily].

Hence **uˈxoricidal** *a.*, of, pertaining or tending to, uxoricide.

1891 *Cent. Dict.* (citing *Cornhill Mag.*).

uxorilocal (ˌʌksɒrɪˈləʊkəl), *a. Anthrop.* [f. L. *uxōri-us* (f. *ūxor* wife) + LOCAL *a.*] Applied to or denoting residence after marriage in the area of the wife's home or community. Cf. MATRILOCAL *a.*; RESIDENCE *sb.*¹ I d; VIRILOCAL *a.*

1936 R. FIRTH *We, the Tikopia* xvi. 596 The greater tendency to uxorilocal settlement at marriage. **1948** L. ADAM in *Man* Jan. 12/2 The adjectives 'patrilocal' and 'matrilocal' do not fulfil these requirements [of accuracy and clarity]... I therefore propose adoption of the adjectives 'virilocal' and 'uxorilocal' to indicate whether a married couple shares the domicile with the family of the husband or of the wife. **1958** *Man* Apr. 69/1 Marriages are about equally virilocal and uxorilocal. **1974** A. P. WOLF *Relig. & Ritual in Chinese Soc.* 156 When a family has no sons who survive to marry, they ordinarily must arrange an uxorilocal marriage for a daughter or an adopted daughter.

Hence ˌ**uxoriˈlocally** *adv.*

1963 *Brit. Jrnl. Sociol.* XIV. 24 So that now you may read about individual couples 'marrying avunculocally' or 'living uxorilocally'. This seems to me an abuse of terminology. **1974** A. P. WOLF *Relig. & Ritual in Chinese Soc.* 148 From her father's point of view, a daughter is an outsider. She can achieve the right to a place on his altar only by marrying a man who agrees to reside uxorilocally.

uxorious (ʌkˈsɔərɪəs), *a.* [f. L. *ūxōri-us* (f. *ūxor* wife): see -OUS.]

1. Of persons: Dotingly or submissively fond of a wife; devotedly attached to a wife.

1598 BP. HALL *Sat.* IV. vi, Whose mannish housewives.. make a drudge of their uxorius mate. **1609** B. JONSON *Sil. Wom.* IV. i, Hee's an asse that will be so vxorious, to tie his affections to one circle. **1649** MILTON *Eikon.* 64 Effeminate and Uxorious Magistrates, govern'd and overswaid at home under a Feminine usurpation. **1680** C. NESSE *Ch. Hist.* 178 Whom, being an uxorious man, Jezabel his wife stirred up. **1730** FIELDING *Rape upon Rape* Wks. 1775 II. 39 You are not the only wife who would give her husband this advice... Were all men so uxorious to take it, Tyburn [etc.]. **1782** W. F. MARTYN *Geog. Mag.* I. 218 The uxorious monarch [*sc.* Solomon]. **1822** T. ATTWOOD in C. M. Wakefield *Life* (1885) vii. 89, I am a little what vulgar folks call uxorious, and am never truly eloquent upon any subject but my wife and children. **1836–7** DICKENS *Sk. Boz, Charac.* vii, A living warning to all uxorious old boys. **1899** *Allbutt's Syst. Med.* VIII. 150, I have found that uxorious men..may bring themselves into a somewhat similar state of debility.

transf. **1708** PRIOR *Turtle & Sparrow* 417 Uxorious Inmate, Bird obscene, Dar'st thou defile..These silent Seats of faithful Loves?

b. *fig.* (of inanimate objects, etc.).

1634 CARTWRIGHT *Ordinary* I. iv, We have got One that will doe more good with 's tongue that way Than that uxorious showre that came from Heaven. **1719** D'URFEY *Pills* (1872) VI. 196 Weary Ploughmen cursed the Stay Of the too Uxorious Day. **1743** FRANCIS tr. *Hor., Odes* I. ii. 19 Th' uxorious River glides away,..smooth-winding to the Sea. **1813** H. & J. SMITH *Horace in London* 19 Sir Francis.. To father Thames commits his fate. In secret the uxorious tide Safe bears him to the Surrey side. **1863** CONINGTON tr. *Horace, Odes* I. ii. 20 Old Tiber,..spite of Jove, his banks o'erflows, Uxorious flood.

2. Of actions, etc.: Marked or characterized by excessive affection for one's wife.

1623 B. JONSON *Time Vind.* ad fin., The Boy..hath plots upon you all. A Pensioner unto your wives, To keepe you in uxorious gives. **1631** WEEVER *Anc. Fun. Mon.* 13 Husbands ..were wont to straw..vpon the graues..of their deceased deare wiues,..diuers purple flowers: by which vxorious office, they did..lessen the griefe of their hearts. *a* **1704** T. BROWN *Dial. Dead* Wks. 1711 IV. 29 My dotage on her Charms had bred in me..a fond, blind, uxorious Vice. **1739** EARL ORRERY in *O. Papers* (1903) I. 269 My Hours..at Caledon..slide away in uxorious happiness, and rustic Joys. **1813** *Edin. Rev.* XXI. 199 The..uxorious propensities of the dynasty. **1835** DICKENS *Sk. Boz, Mr. Watkins Tottle* i, A rather uncommon compound of strong uxorious inclinations, and an unparalleled degree of anti-connubial timidity. **1879** F. W. FARRAR *St. Paul* I. 309 Claudius..with all his pedantic and uxorious eccentricity was not devoid.. of kindness.

Hence **uˈxoriously** *adv.*

1647 STAPYLTON *Juvenal* 87 If thou'lt uxoriously to one adhere, Submit thy willing necke the yoke to beare. **1693** DRYDEN tr. *Juvenal, Sat.* VI. 292 If thou art thus Uxoriously inclin'd, To bear thy Bondage. *a* **1721** SHEFFIELD (Dk. Buckhm.) *Wks.* (1753) II. 152 Uxoriously led by the nose all your life. **1827** SOUTHEY *Lett.* (1856) IV. 70 A foolish wife, of whom he was uxoriously fond. **1903** *Sat. Rev.* 28 Feb. 261/1 She is quite worthy to have plays written uxoriously round her.

uˈxoriousness. [f. prec. + -NESS.] The character or quality of being uxorious; doting or submissive fondness of one's wife.

1626 DONNE *Serm.* 24 Feb. 12 If he satisfied her, and his owne Vxoriousnesse, any satisfaction is not nothing. **1688** PENTON *Guardian's Instruction* 26 You may manage your uxoriousness more warily than I have done. **1775** H. DOWNMAN *Infancy* II. 308 Courage may be changed To brutal force;..and tender Nuptial Love To mean Uxoriousness. **1830** D'ISRAELI *Chas. I*, III. vii. 120 Charles ..is accused by all parties of..spiritless uxoriousness and subserviency to his Queen. **1859** TENNYSON *Marriage of Geraint* 60 A prince whose manhood was all gone, And molten down in mere uxoriousness.

uxtar, obs. Sc. form of HUCKSTER *sb.*

uylie, Sc. var. OIL *sb.*¹

†**uyre**, obs. northern var. ORE².

1530–1 *Durham Househ. Bk.* (Surtees) 47 In every lode 60 stone of uyre and 12 lb. of leyde to yᵉ ston.

uz, dial. f. US *pron.*

Uzbek (ˈʊzbɛk, ˈʌz-). Also formerly **Usbeck, Usbeg, Uzbeg,** and other varr. [Russ.] One of a Turkic people of central Asia, forming the basic population of the Uzbek SSR (Uzbekistan), and also living in Afghanistan; the language of this people. Also *attrib.* or as *adj.*

1616 T. ROE *Let.* 17 Jan. in *Embassy to Court of Gt. Mogul* (1899) II. 113 The King..intendeth the conquest of the Vzbiques, a Nation between Smarchand and him. **1715** J. STEVENS *Hist. Persia* xxii. 221 To make war on the Usbecks. **1788** GIBBON *Decl. & F.* VI. lxiv. 292 A descendant of Zingis, who reigned over the Usbeks of Charasm, or Carizme. **1834** A. BURNES *Bokhara* I. viii. 262 We now found ourselves among the Uzbeks. **1841** J. WOOD *Personal Narr. Journey to River Oxus* xiv. 215 Murad Beg, the head of this Uzbek state. **1876** E. SCHUYLER *Turkistan* I. iii. 106 The Uzbeks are the descendants of the Turkish tribes who ..migrated to this part of Asia [*sc.* Tashkent], both before and since the time of Tchinghiz Khan. **1889** G. N. CURZON *Russia in Central Asia* vi. 153 The huge sheepskin bonnets ..disappeared in favour of the capacious white turban of the Uzbeg or the Tajik. **1891** A. CONSTABLE tr. *Bernier's Trav. in Mogul Empire* 120 There are probably no people more narrow-minded, sordid or uncleanly, that the Usbec Tartars. **1900** 'ODYSSEUS' *Turkey in Europe* iii. 101 Uzbek also is not strictly a linguistic name, but political, and denotes the Turks who are, or were, the ruling faction in the Khanates of Khiva, Bokhara, and Kokand. **1927** *Glasgow Herald* 15 Aug. 13 Agitation has been set on foot among the Uzbek people, on the southern banks of the Oxus, who now demand affiliation with their Soviet kinsmen across the river. **1929** [see JAGATAI]. **1933** L. BLOOMFIELD *Language* iv. 68 The Turkish..family of languages..Turkish, Tartar, Kirgiz, Uzbeg, Azerbaijani. **1957** H. BOWER *Short Guide Soviet Life* 7 Constituent Republics (SSR) are with capitals in parenthesis..Turkmen SSR (Ashkhabad) Uzbek SSR (Tashkent) Tadzhik [etc.]. **1961** [see *Iranize* vb. s.v. IRANIAN *sb.* 2]. **1964** G. WHEELER *Mod. Hist. Soviet Central Asia* ix. 212 Firqat (1858–1909)..did the first translation of a Russian classic—Tolstoy's *What Men Live By*—into Chagatay, or old Uzbek, as it is now called, in 1877. **1974** T. P. WHITNEY tr. *Solzhenitsyn's Gulag Archipelago* I. I. ii. 59 On the Volga Canal construction site newspapers were published in four national languages: Tatar, Turkish, Uzbek, and Kazakh. **1976** *Times* 3 Nov. 16/5 A dark-haired agronomist from an Uzbek collective farm.

Uzi (ˈuːzɪ). Also (*erron.*) **Uzzi.** Shortened f. the name of Uziel Gal, Israeli army officer, used *attrib.* or *absol.* to designate an Israeli type of sub-machine gun designed by him.

1959 E. O'BALLANCE *Sinai Campaign* ii. 73 The personal small arms of the man was either the Mauser rifle or the Uzi sub-machine-gun. *Ibid.*, The Uzi is one of the finest guns of this type I have ever handled. **1966** L. DAVIDSON *Long Way to Shiloh* xi. 156 Too many men and too many Uzzis which were much too easy to fire. **1971** *Scope* (S. Afr.) 19 Mar. 17/2 A loaded Uzzi sub-machine-gun..is always within reach. *Ibid.* 22/1 The Uzzi..fires a clip of 9 mm bullets in double-quick time and is accurate up to 100 metres. **1976** G. SEYMOUR *Glory Boys* viii. 94 Two other young men, both of whom had been issued with licences..to carry Uzi sub-machine-guns. **1981** C. R. LAJEUNESSE *Dead Man Running* lxii. 177 Cyril was cut in two by bullets from Weasel's Uzi.

uzzard, variant (now dial.) of IZZARD.

a **1697** (*Bodl.*) *MS. Eng. Bib. c. 3* fol. 37 Uzzard, Z.

uzzle, dial. var. OUZEL.

V

V (viː), the 22nd letter of the modern English and the 20th of the ancient Roman alphabet, was in the latter an adoption of the early Greek vowel-symbol **V**, now also represented by U and Y (q.v.), but in Latin was employed also with the value of the Greek digamma (viz. *w*), to which it corresponds etymologically. When not purely vocalic, it still denoted this sound at the time when the earliest Latin loan-words were adopted in the Teutonic languages; consequently such words beginning with *v* appear in Old English with *w*. Under the Empire, however, the semi-vocalic sound gradually changed to a bilabial consonant, and finally became the labio-dental voiced spirant now denoted by the letter in English and various other languages. This development did not take place in Old English; and no *v*, whether bilabial or labio-dental, occurred initially in the older Teutonic languages, although the sound was common in other positions (in OE. denoted by *f*, in early texts by *b*).

In OE. dictionaries there is thus no set of words with initial V, one or two Latin words adopted at a late period usually appearing with *f*, as *fann*, *fers* (but also *vers*), from L. *vannus*, *versus*. The first appearance of V-words is found in those ME. texts which begin to show a distinct French influence, as the *Ancren Riwle*; even early writers like Orm and Laȝamon, while not free from the use of French words, do not employ any beginning with *v*. The number of such words steadily increases in later texts, and is subsequently greatly reinforced by direct adoptions from Latin, by new formations on Latin stems, and by adoptions from other Romanic languages. The other sources of initial V are of minor importance. The change of *w* to *v*, which took place in the middle period of the Scandinavian languages, is represented in a few words, as *Valhalla*, *valkyrie*, *viking*, but otherwise the words with this initial are chiefly derived from languages not directly related to English. A small number of words, however, as *vat*, *vixen*, exemplify the voicing of *f*- peculiar to southern (now only south-western) dialects. This change is not indicated in OE. spelling, and how far it had developed in speech is uncertain, but in southern ME. texts all native words (rarely those of French or Latin origin) beginning with *f* may appear with *v*- (or its equivalent *u*-); the more important variant forms due to this cause are entered in their places below. Conversely words properly having *v*- are occasionally written with *f*-, and there is evidence that this is not merely graphic, but represents an actual pronunciation. ('Euen so oure Englishmen vse to speake in Essexe, for they say fineger for vineger, feale for veale, & contrary wyse a voxe for a foxe, voure for foure, etc.' 1546 Langley, tr. *Pol. Verg. de Invent.* I. vi. 14.)

When not initial, *v* occurs freely in native words as well as in those of Latin or other origin. In the former it represents OE. *f* when voiced, as in *ǽfen* even, *drīfan* drive, *lufu* love. The use of *f* (or *ff*) in such words was partly retained in ME. (and especially in Sc. down to the 16th century); but even in late OE. *u* is frequently substituted, and in early ME. (as in med.L. and OF.) *u* and *v* come into general use to denote the sound in all positions. It was only in the 17th century that these two letters, both of which had been employed in a double function (see U), were finally distinguished as vowel and consonant; and down to the 19th century words beginning with either letter continued to form one series in dictionaries.

In some ME. (chiefly northern) manuscripts, and in many Scottish texts of the 15th and 16th centuries, *v* is more or less frequently written in place of *w*, while conversely *w* is freely written instead of *v*. These forms are merely graphic, and do not imply a phonetic interchange of *w* and *v* (though in mod. north-eastern Sc. *wr*- has become *vr*-). In south-eastern English dialects the change of *v*- to *w*- does occur, and older representations of Cockney speech exhibit a converse change of *w*- to *v*-, which recent investigators have been unable to verify as still existent. The latter change is illustrated in the following quotations.

1803 Pegge *Anecd. Eng. Lang.* (1814) 77 Villiam, I vants my vig... Vitch vig, Sir?.. Vy, the vite vig in the vooden vig-box, vitch I vore last Vensday at the westry. **1824** *Spirit Publ. Jrnls.* (1825) 37, I vas valking by the Admirallity in my vay home. **1837** Dickens *Pickw.* xxxiii, Ve got Tom Vildspark off.. ven all the big vigs.. said as nothing couldn't save him.

Elision of *v* when not initial has taken place extensively in dialects, especially those of the North and Scotland, as in *deil* devil, *shule* shovel, *hairst* harvest. In standard English this is represented by such words as *hawk*, *head*, *lark*, *lord*, and is specially indicated in a few archaic or poetic forms, as *e'en* even, *e'er* ever, *ne'er* never, *o'er* over.

I. 1. Illustrations of the use of the letter or of its name. †***double V*** [i.e. *U*], = W.

?**1460** in *Archaeol.* (1842) XXIX. 331 There was an V and thre arres to-gydre. **1530** Palsgr. 440 A byfore V. **1552** Huloet s.v., There is a diuersitie betwene the single V. and the dowble W., therfore the alphabete of them shalbe set diuersly. **1593** G. Harvey *Pierces Super.* Wks. (Grosart) II. 211 He that can tickle Mar-prelate with taunts, can twitch double V. to the quicke. **1636** B. Jonson *Eng. Gram.* iii, V ..is, like our *i*, a letter of a double power. **1668** Wilkins *Real Char.* 16 Some Letters of the same name and shape are used sometimes for Vowels, and sometimes for Consonants; as J, V, W, Y. **1676** Grew *Anat. Pl.*, *Anat. Fl.* iv. 154 An Angle, twice as big as that of a V Consonant. **1728** Chambers *Cycl.* s.v. *U*, Besides the Vowel U, there is a Consonant of the same Denomination, wrote *V*, or *U*. **1736** Ainsworth ii. s.v., Our Saxon ancestors, who commonly substitute *f* in the place of *v*. **1808** Jamieson, *V*, in some of our old printed books, is invariably used for *W*. **1888** Jacobi *Printers' Vocab.* 151, V is not used as a signature in the printer's alphabet. **1901** *Scotsman* 9 Oct. 11 The letter for the ensuing year was directed to be changed to V Gothic.

2. Used with reference to the shape of the letter; an object having this shape; a V-shaped, acute-angled formation. Cf. vee a.

1832 [see *V-pug* below]. **1835** *Court Mag.* VI. p. xiii/1 The corsage draped in the form of a V on the bosom. **1863** Tyndall *Heat* (1870) iv. §131 The water.. is first brought into one arm of the V. **1894** *Outing* XXIV. 45/2 The first geese of the season will wing their way in lines and V's from the south. *a* **1917** W. De Morgan *Old Madhouse* (1919) ii. 14 Until you've seen her in a low neck, or at least a V, you really can't tell. **1930** *Sat. Even. Post* 13 Dec. 11/3 Midway, the range was cleft from summit to base by a V more than 2000 feet deep. **1958** E. Birney *Turvey* vii. 78 The V of Ashanti spears above the fireplace. **1985** J. Melville *Death Ceremony* xxi. 156 A pulsing at her throat above the V of her delicate silk under-kimono.

b. *attrib.*, as ***V-form***, ***shape***; freq. in the sense 'shaped like the letter V', as ***V anvil***, ***-blouse***, ***body***, ***edge***, ***-formation***, ***-front***, ***girder***, ***hut***, ***slide***, ***thread***, ***tool*** (in fret-cutting), ***-trough***, etc.; **V aerial**, **antenna**, an aerial in which the conductors form a large horizontal V that transmits principally along its axis; **V-belt**, a belt which is V-shaped in cross-section in order to give better traction on a pulley; **V-block**, a metal block with a V-shaped recess cut in it to hold a cylindrical object while it is being worked on; **V-eight**, an internal combustion engine with eight cylinders arranged in two rows of four at an angle to each other, forming a V-shaped cross-section; freq. *attrib.* and written **V-8**; also, a motor vehicle with such an engine; so **V engine**; **V-neck**, a garment neckline in the shape of a V; freq. *attrib.*; also *absol.*, a garment, as a pullover etc., with a V-shaped neckline; **V-pug**, a species of moth (see quot.); **V-thread**, a screw thread which is V-shaped in profile. Cf. vee b.

1961 *Amat. Radio Handbk.* (ed. 3) xiii. 385/2 The *V aerial produces one major beam along its axis, together with a rather complex pattern of minor lobes. [**1931** *Proc. IRE* XIX. 1822 Fig. 41 is a polar diagram showing the power distribution for a *V* wire, having sides equal to one wave, in the plane of the wires.] **1932** *Ibid.* XX. 1033 These [curves] were taken during the process of adjustment of a *V antenna system in which both antenna and reflector units each consisted of 2 V wires one above the other. **1959** K. Henney *Radio Engin. Handbk.* (ed. 5) xx. 60 V antennas are arranged to utilize this main lobe from all wires of the system. **1861** Sir W. Fairbairn *Iron* 125 The *V anvil, fig. 43, the natural offspring of the steam-hammer. **1911** C. S. Lake *Motor Cyclist's Handbk.* viii. 116 The most common form of transmission on a motor cycle is that of a '*V' belt. **1973** A. Parrish *Mech. Engineer's Ref. Bk.* xiii. 7 One of the problems associated with V belts.. is the variation in velocity ratio which occurs from time to time. **1901** *Shop & Foundry Pract.* (Colliery Engineer Co.) II. §10.45 Cylindrical parts are usually supported on *V blocks. **1971** B. Scharf *Engin. & its Lang.* viii. 54 V-blocks are usually made in pairs so that they can support a long tube. **1915** *Contemp. Rev.* Sept. 370 Quaker maidens now wear tucks or *V-blouses or anything else that is the fashion. **1885** 'Mrs. Alexander' *Valerie's Fate* iv. 69 That black satin and lace costume.. with the clear sleeves and a *V body. **1930** *Autocar* 2 May 841/2 It is said.. that the *V eight.. is superior as regards compactness of build. **1936** *Motor Man.* (ed. 29) ii. 40 The V-eight engine comprises two blocks, each containing four cylinders, which are set at right angles on a single crankcase. **1942** G. R. Gilbert in D. M. Davin *N.Z. Short Stories* (1953) 252 Lena would giggle and look pleased as though she had Prince Charming waiting in a V8 outside the kitchen door. **1959** I. Jefferies *Thirteen Days* x. 162 A V-8 pick-up was parked, with a pair of Haganah in the back. **1963** Bird & Hutton-Stott *Veteran Motor Car* 57 Often claimed to be the first V-eight to be marketed. **1982** *Times Lit. Suppl.* 5 Mar. 249/4 The comparison between the purist Bugatti engine.. and an American V-8 engine of thirty years later. **1924** *Motor Man.* (ed. 25) i. 19 An eight-cylinder *V engine. **1967** *Economist* 29 July 425/3 Berliet has a range of v-engines due to appear soon. **1844** H. Stephens *Bk. Farm* III. 794 A rod passing.. through a *V-form brace of iron. **1949** Koestler *Insight & Outlook* xi. 163 The *V-formation of migrating geese. **1974** 'J. Graham' *Bloody Passage* i. 10 A flight of Brent geese drifted across the sky.. in a v formation. **1895** *Montgomery Ward Catal.* Spring & Summer 92/1 Men's Rutland *V front collars. **1919** *Brit. Manufacturer* Nov. 24/1 The output of 'T', '*V', and lattice girders of all gauges. **1851** *Lyttelton* (N.Z.) *Times* 1 Feb. 3 One *V hut was blown away. **1857** R. B. Paul *Lett. Canterbury* 57 The form is that of a V hut, the extremities of the rafters being left bare. **1879** C. L. Innes *Canterbury Sk.* 20 A 'V' hut.. is exactly as if you took the roof off a house and stood it on the ground. **1910–11** *T. Eaton & Co. Catal.* Fall & Winter 20/1 Women's coat sweater... The *V-neck and fronts have wide, plain knitted border. **1921** [see *house-dress* s.v. house *sb.*[1] 19]. **1949** O. Nash *Versus* 62 They lose their rubbers and store their V-necks. **1970** T. Lewis *Jack's Return Home* 127 He had on a white shirt.., a bottle green V-neck, twill trousers. **1978** *Detroit Free Press* 5 Mar. 30 (Advt.), T-shirts or V-neck shirts. **1832** J. Rennie *Consp. Butterfl. & M.* 132 The *V. Pug [*Eupithecia V. ata*]... Wings.. marked with a black V behind the middle. **1869** Rankine *Machine & Hand-tools* Pl. N 2, A pair of opposite dies of a *V shape. **1844** *Civil Eng. & Arch. Jrnl.* VII. 88/1 A rectangular or oblong table of iron.. upon two *V slides. **1869** *Routledge's Ev. Boy's Ann.* 479 The *V supports may now be secured in their places. *a* **1877** Knight *Dict. Mech.* III. 2061/2 *(caption)* *V-thread. **1887** D. A. Low *Machine Draw.* (1892) 14 The Whitworth V thread.. is the standard form of triangular thread used in this country. **1939** [see *square thread* s.v. square *a.* 15 a]. **1971** B. Scharf *Engin. & its Lang.* xi. 101 A distinction is also made between V-threads and square threads, according to their cross-section. **1875** Sir T. Seaton *Fret-Cutting* 8 The *V tool is the most difficult of all tools to sharpen. **1862** *Catal. Internat. Exhib., Brit.* II. No. 2983, *V-trough for funnel and subterranean wires. **1842** Francis *Dict. Arts*, **V tube*, a glass tube, in the form of the letter V.., to show the decomposition of a neutral salt by galvanism.

c. *Comb.* in ***V-shaped*** adj., *spec.* designating or pertaining to a valley having such a cross-section, esp. when contrasted with a U-shaped valley; also in *Comb.* with other adjs., ppl. adjs., and sbs., as ***V-cut***, ***-fronted***, ***-like***, ***-necked***, ***-type***, ***-winged*** adjs. Cf. vee b.

1912 S. Ford *Shorty McCabe's Odd Numbers* 107 Maybe Cornelia will have some plans of her own, thinks I, as I gets into my silk faced dinner jacket and V-cut vest. **1977** H. Kaplan *Damascus Cover* iv. 36 She wore a V-cut peasant blouse. **1927** *Blackw. Mag.* Jan. 76/1 They stamp the snow from their V-fronted high-heeled jackboots. **1929** E. Linklater *Poet's Pub* xxiv. 258 A cattle-track.., branching V-like off the road. **1971** V-necked [see signature *sb.* 4 b]. **1835–6** *Todd's Cycl. Anat.* I. 202/1 A fissure or triangular V-shaped notch. **1843** *Penny Cycl.* XXV. 423/2 Tools.. generally double-angular or V-shaped. **1872** Coues *N. Amer. Birds* 103 A V-shaped black mark on side of head. **1894** V-shaped [see *U-shaped* s.v. U 2 a]. **1907** *Bull. Geol. Soc. Amer.* XVIII. 355 Downstream from the glacial region the valley ceases to be U-shaped. It becomes narrow and V-shaped, and the terraces die out. **1937** [see hypsograph]. **1970** R. J. Small *Study of Landforms* i. 6 On the resultant maps.. the forms of valley floors (whether V-shaped, rounded, or flat-bottomed).. [are] shown. **1967** *Technology Week* 20 Feb. 35/1 The 'V' type antenna is used because it can be designed to give good performance even if distorted. **1876** G. M. Hopkins *Poems* (1967) 178 Through the velvety wind V-winged.. To the nest's nook I balance and buoy.

d. as *v. intr.* Of geese: to fly forming the shape of a horizontal V. Cf. *V-formation*, sense 2 b above and V 2 a (quot. 1894).

1907 *Canad. Mag.* XXIX. 21/1 Then across his senses came the nearing doom—the honk, honk of wild geese V-ing their way along the shadow trail of the night sky. **1970** R. Lowell *Notebk.* 245 The usual autumn Flight of Canada geese V above it, moonborne. **1972** J. Gores *Dead Skip* ii. 14 Another batch of kids.. their cries as full of spring as geese V-ing north.

3. Used to denote serial order, as V Battery, MS. V, or as a symbol of some thing or person, a point in a diagram, etc. ***V-agent***, any of a group of organophosphorus nerve gases having anticholinesterase activity; ***VX***, a type of

V-agent, O-ethyl *S*-2-diisopropylaminoethyl methylphosphonothiolate.

1964 Kirk & Othmer *Encycl. Chem. Technol.* (ed. 2) IV. 874 Aerosolized V agents also are quite lethal by inhalation. **1975** *Nature* 10 Jan. 82/3 The nerve gas codenamed VX is the most toxic of a family of V-agents produced by British chemical warfare scientists since World War Two. **1966** *New Statesman* 16 Dec. 900/1 The Americans..have also produced less volatile gases called V agents, particularly a liquid called VX. **1980** *Sci. Amer.* Apr. 36/1 Some 5,000 tons of VX were made between 1961 and 1967.

II. 4. The Roman numeral symbol for: Five (†or fifth).

13.. *K. Alis.* 1851 Anon he doþ his bemen blowe, v c. on a þrowe. **1340** *Ayenb.* 23 þe v. boȝ of predc. *c* **1449** Pecock *Repr.* I. v. 23, v. Chapiter. The v^{e}. principal argument..is this. **1484** Caxton *Fables of Æsop*, *Alfonce* iii, [Of the x tonnes] v were ful of oylle, & the other v were but half ful. **1530** Palsgr. 58 As appereth in the III chaptre and the v rule of the same. **1535** Coverdale *Job* i. 3, v. C. yock of oxen, v. C. she asses. **1636** B. Jonson *Eng. Gram.* ii, Our numeral letters are, I for 1, V for 5. **1788** Gibbon *Decl. & F.* xlviii. V. 6 A single chapter will include, III. The Bulgarians, IV. Hungarians, and, V. Russians. **1842** *Civil Eng. & Arch. Jrnl.* V. 151/2 With an Engraving, Plate V. *Ibid.* 197/1 Lecture V.

b. ***V***, ***V-spot***, ***V-note***, a five-dollar note. *U.S.*

1837 *Knickerbocker Mag.* IX. 96 My wallet..[was] distended with V's and X's to its utmost capacity. **1849** Lowell *Biglow P.* Ser. I. viii. 57, I vow my holl sheer o' the spiles wouldn't come nigh a V spot. **1864** Browning *Dram. Personæ* Wks. 1896 I. 603 Sixty Vs must do. A trifle, though, to start with! *Ibid.*, A poor lad..hears the company Talk grand of dollars, V-notes, and so forth.

III. 5. Abbreviations.

a. Of various Latin words or phrases: **v.** = *verso* 'the back of the leaf', *versus* 'against', *vide* 'see'; **v.g.** = *verbi gratia*; **vs.** = *versus*.

1678 Phillips, *V.G.* an usual character or abbreviation of the words *verbi gratia*, *i.e.* namely, or to instance in a word. **1690** Locke *Hum. Und.* II. xxx. §5 [Ideas] made up of such collections of simple ideas as were really never united..: v.g. [etc.]. **1738** Chambers *Cycl.* (1751) s.v. *Angle*, *V.* Phil. Trans. N°. 420. p. 147. **1767** R. Burn *Eccl. Law* (ed. 2) IV. Cc, A Table of the Cases adjudged;..Acton *v.* Smith... Adams *v.* Rush [etc.]. **1827** Jarman *Powell's Devises* II. 311 It is to be observed that Maddison *v.* Andrew, and Mills *v.* Norris, were decided at a period when the rule..was not so well settled. **1865** *Reader* 28 Jan., Rime *v.* Rhyme. **1889** *Cent. Dict.*, *vs*, an abbreviation of *versus*. **1949** E. Pound *Pisan Cantos* lxxix. 74 Kumasaka vs/ vulgarity. **1967** *Boston Sunday Herald* 26 Mar. VI. 4/7 It has developed a way of seeing Europe that seems the perfect answer to the group vs. non-group argument. **1970** *Jrnl. Gen. Psychol.* LXXXIII. 133 Conditions..are optimal for divergent *vs.* convergent tasks.

b. Of English words and phrases: **V.**, various proper names, as Victoria, Vincent, Violet, etc.; **V.**, the chemical symbol of Vanadium; **V**, victory, *spec.* used as the symbol of allied victory in the war of 1939–45 (cf. *V-Day* below; VE, VJ, V-sign); **V, v**, volt; **v.**, verb; **v.**, verse; **v.**, very (in various phrases, as *v.g.* very good, *v.h.c.* very highly commended, etc.); **v.**, vision (in *Med.*); **VA** (*U.S.*), Veterans' Administration; **V.A.**, Vicar-Apostolic; **V.A.**, Vice-Admiral; **V.A.**, visual acuity; **V.A.D.**, (a member of a) Voluntary Aid Detachment; **V. and A.**, Victoria and Albert Museum; **VASCAR**, **Vascar**, visual average speed computer and recorder; **V-bomber** (see quot. 1955); **V.C.**, Vice-Chancellor; **V.C.**, Victoria Cross, a holder of the Victoria Cross; **VC** (orig. and chiefly *U.S.*) = Viet Cong *sb.* and *a.*; **V.C.H.**, Victoria County History (or Histories); **V.C.O.**, Viceroy's Commissioned Officer; **VCR**, videocassette recorder; **v.d.**, various dates; **V.D., v.d.**, venereal disease; freq. *attrib.*; **V.D.**, Volunteer Decoration (formerly awarded in the Territorial Army or the Royal Naval Volunteer Reserve); **V-Day**, **V-day**, **V Day**, Victory Day, used variously with reference to allied victory in the war of 1939–45 (cf. *VE-day* s.v. VE; *VJ-day* s.v. VJ); also *transf.* and *fig.*; **VDT**, video (or visual) display terminal; **VDU**, **vdu**, visual (or video) display unit; **V.F.** (*R.C.Ch.*) = *vicar foran*(*e*) s.v. vicar 4c; **V.F.A.** (*Austral.*), Victorian Football Association; **V.F.L.** (*Austral.*), Victorian Football League; **V.F.R.**, visual flight rules; **VFW** (*U.S.*), Veterans of Foreign Wars; **V.G.** = vicar general (sense 2); **VHD**, video high density (system); **VHF**, **vhf**, very high frequency: applied to radio waves with a frequency between 30 and 300 MHz; **VHS**, Video Home System; **VIP**, vasoactive intestinal (poly)peptide; **VISTA**, Volunteers in Service to America; **VLA** (*Astron.*), very large array (system of radio telescopes in the U.S.); **VLBI** (*Astron.*), very long baseline interferometry (method of measuring signals from a radio astronomical source); **VLCC**, very large crude (oil) carrier; **VLDL** (*Biochem.*), very low-density lipoprotein; **VLF**, very low frequency: applied to radio waves with a frequency between 10 and 30 kHz; **V.L.R.**, very long range; **VLSI** (*Electronics*), very large scale integration (*or* integrated); **V.M.**, Virgin Mary; **V-Mail** (*U.S.*), victory mail (see quot. 1966); **VOA**, Voice of America; **VOR**, VHF omnirange (cf. *omnirange* s.v. omni-); **VP**, verb phrase (in Transformational Grammar); **V.P.**, Vice-President; **V.P.P.** (*India*), value payable post (see quot. 1975); **v.r.**, variant or various reading; **V.S.**, veterinary surgeon; **V.S.O.**, Voluntary Service Overseas; a member of the organization thus called; **V.S.O.P.**, very special old pale (brandy); **V-STOL**, **V/STOL**, **VSTOL**, vertical and short take-off and landing; **VTO(L)**, vertical take-off (and landing); **VTR**, video tape recorder; **VU**, **vu** (*Electronics*) [prob. abbrev. of *volume unit*: cf. quots. for this s.v. volume 10c, where it is implied to be so], a unit in which some types of volume indicator are calibrated, a sine wave with a power of 1 mW being assigned the reference value of 0 VU (see quot. 1940 and cf. *volume indicator* s.v. volume 10c); freq. *attrib.*, esp. in ***VU meter***, any volume indicator employing the VU scale; **v.y.**, various years. See also (as main entries) VAT, VE, Veejay, V.I.P., VJ, V-sign.

1866 F. H. Wilson *Our Father* (1869) 122 Placards with the lion and unicorn at the top, the letter *V at the one side and R at the other. **1863** *Q. Rev.* Jan. 159 It is said also, that the prisoners have been known to make an example of a warden who was not in their opinion sufficiently liberal with his *V.G.'s ('Very Good,' as marked in the accounts). **1901** *Essex Weekly News* 8 Mar. 3/4, I have been 'good, bad, and indifferent' and I have been 'v.g.' **1901** *Scotsman* 9 Oct. 10/2, v.h.c. in the cheese fair. **1891** W. S. Churchill *Let.* 1 Jan. in R. S. Churchill *Winston S. Churchill* (1967) I. Compan. I. v. 219 V-happy V. well. **1941** C. Milburn *Diary* 20 July (1979) 104 The *V campaign (... —) was launched by Mr Churchill today. V for victory, the opening notes of Beethoven's V (fifth) symphony. **1973** D. Westheimer *Going Public* iv. 67 She raised her hand in a peace sign... He realized it was not the peace sign at all. To those of the old woman's generation it was V for Victory. **1889** W. P. Maycock *Pract. Electr. Notes & Definitions* II. 23 Comparison of various E.M.F.s... Continuous dynamo = 10*V to 500V. **1943** C. L. Boltz *Basic Radio* x. 166 Mains valves..can be operated with 200V, 300V, and even 400V on the anode. **1966** *Wireless World* July (Advt. section) 83 Power pack kits. Fully smoothed output 250 v. 60 mA. H.T. and L.T. 6·3 v. 1·5 amps. **1945** *Newsweek* 16 Apr. 40/2 Last week..unfavourable publicity hit the *VA. **1976** N. Thornburg *Cutter & Bone* xii. 275 He spent a long time with the shrinks in VA hospitals. **1787** in Milner *Suppl. Mem. Eng. Cath.* (1820) 48 The ecclesiastical government by *V.V.A. is by no means essential to our religion. **1820** Milner *Ibid.* 252 The Prelate who did publish the Resolutions was the Western V.A. **1794** R. F. Greville *Diary* 23 Aug. (1930) 300 We near'd the *Minotaur*, on which *V.A. McBride took that Opportunity of hoisting out His barge. **1915** W. S. Churchill 23 Jan. in M. Gilbert *Winston S. Churchill* (1972) III. Compan. I. 444 In the absence of Adl Carden, Adl de Robeck will have a temporary rank of V.A. **1932** *Optician* LXXXIII. 398/2 No effect on the peripheral *V.A. of one half of an eye was noted when the other half was illuminated. **1982** M. Urvoy et al. in François & Maione *Paediatric Ophthalmol.* 399/2 For a subjective measurement of V.A., we have four groups of tests. **1915** G. Bell *Let.* 10 Feb. (1927) I. xiv. 359 She is a *V.A.D. part of a detachment which is going up as orderlies to the Cross Hospital at G.H.Q. **1916** *Lancet* 18 Mar. 651/1 Whether he had received any complaints from the V.A.D. hospitals as to the strict nature of the regulations governing the movements of convalescent wounded. **1980** 'M. Yorke' *Scent of Fear* x. 85 In that earlier war she had become a VAD nurse. **1937** Partridge *Dict. Slang* 929/1 **V. and A., the*..The Victoria and Albert Museum: museum-world coll.; late C. 19–20. **1958** *Listener* 28 Aug. 317/1 At the V. and A. both the Morris dining-room and the magnificent Poynter grill room ..have gone. **1977** J. Aiken *Last Movement* vi. 115 He sold them [*sc.* pictures] all to the V & A. **1966** *N.Y. Times* 1 Oct. 39/5 Trademarked *Vascar, the instrument divides the time a car takes by the distance it travels, and shows the answer in miles an hour. **1967** *Traffic Digest & Rev.* May 3/2 VASCAR is a device which allows an operator by measuring quantities of distance and time to compute the speed of vehicles on a highway. The chief advantage of VASCAR, according to its inventor, Arthur N. Marshall of Richmond, Virginia, is that the officer in a car equipped with VASCAR can maintain regular patrol and still clock the speed of other vehicles on the road. **1973** *Times* 13 Aug. 4/3 Essex police are..to introduce a new speed detection device. Known as VASCAR—visual average speed computer and recorder—it has been tested in the country for two years. **1983** *Times* 24 Feb. 3/8 He had decided to make a Vascar speed check with the equipment fitted in his vehicle, which meant choosing two fixed features on the road—this case a large tree and a bridge. **1955** *Britannica Bk. of Year* 489/2 Concentration on air-power was reflected in terms like **V-Bomber* (the initial referring to the types, Victor, Vulcan and Valiant). **1958** *Spectator* 10 Jan. 59/1 This weapon is the natural armament of the 'V' bombers. **1975** in R. Crossman *Diaries* I. 57 Mr Wilson proposed to replace the M.L.F. with an Atlantic nuclear force, which would include American Polaris submarines, British V-bombers, 'some kind of mixed-manned, jointly owned elements' and the British Polaris submarine that Labour was not going to scrap after all. **1715** in Bodleian MS. Ballard 49 f. 154, We the *V.C. & Heads of Houses & Professors think it incumbent on Us to make this publick Declaration of our Utmost Abhorrence & Detestation of Such Offences. **1866** *Law Rep.* (Chancery Appeal Cases) I. 66 V.C. *Wood* held that the Plaintiff's having come to the nuisance did not disentitle him to equitable relief. **1883** J. A. H. Murray *Let.* 8 Nov. in K. M. E. Murray *Caught in Web of Words* (1977) xii. 227 The V.C. had to rush off in a cab. **1953** M. Davidson *Medicine in Oxford* ii. 26 It seems not unlikely that the latter may have consulted the V.-C. about Francis's migration. **1971** *Rayden's Pract. & Law of Divorce* (ed. 11) I. iii. 43 Sir Richard Kindersley V.-C., nevertheless said [etc.]. **1859** A. Thackeray *Let.* in H. Ritchie *Lett. A. T. Ritchie* (1924) v. 111 Papa gave us a letter to read..from Edward Thackeray's colonel recommending him for a *V.C. **1872** Lever *Ld. Kilgobbin* lxxix, It's a case for the V.C. **1929** *Daily Express* 7 Nov. 13/5 Mr. Thomas Dinesen, the Danish V.C., and the only foreigner to win the decoration, arrived at Liverpool-street Station. **1964** *N.Y. Times* 16 Sept. 4 *V.C.—They are of course the Vietcong, the enemy. But when a private displeases his sergeant, he may hear 'you knucklehead V.C.!' **1965** *Punch* 11 Aug. 214/1 Some of them [*sc.* GIs] responded to a professional sergeant's claim that they were..eager to get to grips with the 'VCs', as the Viet Cong are now known in the trade. **1968** *Listener* 23 May 656/3, I felt rather anxious that the patrol might have disappeared and left me in the empty suburb with Mr Van and the VC snipers. **1977** *N.Y. Rev. Bks.* 23 June 6/3 A nineteen-year-old Marine is discovered cutting the ears off a dead VC. **1931** *Times Lit. Suppl.* 10 Sept. 683/1 Thornton Riseborough, according to the *V.C.H., appears always with a double title after the twelfth century. **1965** *Listener* 8 Apr. 531/3 The V.C.H., as it is known to all its users, is a great work of reference, but it is unreadable. **1945** C. J. Auchinleck *Let.* 24 Nov. in Mansergh & Moon *Transfer of Power* (1976) VI. 531 Officers, *V.C.O.s, and I.O.R.s who became officers in the I.N.A. **1977** 'D. MacNeil' *Wolf in Fold* ii. 15 The acting squadron commander's a VCO—a *risaldar* named Jalala Khan. **1971** *New Scientist* 26 Aug. 469/1 So that the television does not have to be adapted to take the recorder, the *VCR is put between the TV and its aerial. **1983** *Listener* 12 May 3/1 VCRs whirred away as people took advantage of watching the latest movies. **1984** *What Video?* Aug. 5/4 The cassette is totally incompatible with British VCRs and TV sets. **1863** Hotten *Hand-bk. Topogr.* 195/2 Cuttings from Newspapers [etc.]..*V.D. **1920** *Ann. Rep. Chief Med. Officer, Ministry of Health* II. iii. (*caption facing* p. 163), *V.D. clinic. Suggested plan of arrangement of a..hut. **1920** F. Fox *G.H.Q.* vi. 87, I do not know where the idea sprang from that v.d. was very common in the Army. **1962** E. Snow *Other Side of River* (1963) xxxv. 262, I didn't spend my old man's money learning to become a V.D. quack for a gangster society. **1978** 'L. Black' *Foursome* ii. 15, I don't do it for money—only with men I like the look of. And I haven't got VD. **1901** T. F. Fremantle *Bk. of Rifle* p. v, The Hon. T. F. Fremantle, *V.D. **1946** *Jrnl. R. United Service Institution* XCI. 129 Captain C. A. R. Shillington, V.D., R.N.V.R. **1941** *Newsweek* 28 July 22/3 Encouraged by the success [of the V propaganda campaign], Britain proclaimed July 20 as '*V Day'. **1942** *Time* 16 Mar. 11/1 We at Hercules are eager to learn of any new material, process, or equipment..which can enable us to create more employment after V-Day. **1945** *Times* 5 Apr. 5/2 To-day the battle still rages with loss and peril in Europe. On V Day it will still go on over great stretches of land and water in the Far East. **1949** Koestler *Promise & Fulfilment* I. xiii. 146 It was Jewry's V-day—the first since the time of the Maccabeans. **1967** A. Christie *Endless Night* xxiii. 211 'Well,' said Greta with a deep satisfied sigh, 'we've made it.' 'V-Day all right,' I said. **1975** *Nature* 16 Oct. 557/1 If reporters can operate typewriters with the accuracy necessary for an OCR reader they can probably operate keyboards producing punched tape for the computer or sophisticated visual display terminals (*VDTs) on-line to the computer. **1979** *Globe & Mail* (Toronto) 20 Feb. 9/1 Mr. Brown described himself as not very mechanically minded, but said he has worked hard to become knowledgeable about the video display terminals—known as VDTs. **1982** A. Clements *Microcomputer Design & Construction* ii. 236 The main output device..of many microprocessor systems is the video display terminal (VDT). **1968** *Brit. Med. Bull.* XXIV. 192/2 The data-terminal..may consist of a 'video display unit' (*VDU), in effect the combination of a television-like display tube with a keyboard. **1970** *Computer Management* Nov. 52 (*caption*) Entering data via the keyboard of the VDU. **1976** *Liverpool Echo* 24 Nov. (Advt.), Hardware consists of an ICI 1900 mainframe linked to mini-computers with disc storage, local printers and VDUs. **1982** *What's New in Computing* Nov. 5/3 Because the entire unit is stalk mounted, the vdu angle can be adjusted for best visibility. **1985** *Personal Computer World* Feb. 195/2 Designs published to date have concentrated on putting the intelligence in the node controller which then allows operation of the system through an ordinary VDU. *a* **1912** W. T. Rogers *Dict. Abbrev.* (1913) 197/1 *V.F., Vicar Forane. **1922** Joyce *Ulysses* 312 The rev. John Lavery, V.F. **1936** *Age* (Melbourne) 1 May 7/8 (*heading*) *V.F.A. Seconds. **1969** *Melbourne Truth* 12 July 24/1 Dandenong and Preston meet in the most tension packed VFA game of the season. **1936** *Age* (Melbourne) 1 May 7 (*heading*) *V.F.L. Season opens on Saturday. **1969** *Melbourne Truth* 12 July 2/6 The new kicking out-of-bounds rule introduced by the VFL this season. **1949** *Jrnl. R. Aeronaut. Soc.* LIII. 967/2 Under *V.F.R. (Visual Flight Rules) it appears that communication takes place between the ground and the aircraft for an aggregate time of about 60 seconds. **1974** L. Deighton *Spy Story* xv. 146 This aircraft's electronics were primitive. Flying V.F.R. meant he'd have to put it down before dark. **1981** *Pilot* Jan. 13/1 A special VFR clearance. **1920** *Foreign Service Mag.* Dec. 12/1 The *V.F.W. is an organization for service. That is the purpose of its existence. **1977** C. McFadden *Serial* (1978) xlviii. 103/2 You're gonna get all those calls again from people who want you to sing 'God Bless America' at VFW conventions. **1871** *Tablet* 14 Oct. 502/1 Very Rev. Dr. O'Shea, P.P., *V.G. **1922** Joyce *Ulysses* 312 The rt rev. Mgr M'Manus, V.G. **1980** *New Scientist* 13 Nov. 442 In the US, *VHD will face stiff competition from Philips's laser-reading (VLP) system. **1984** *What Video?* Aug. 11/1 The juke boxes use Thorn EMI VHD disc players and discs (not available for the home). **1932** *Admiralty Handbk. Wireless Telegr. 1931* p. ii, The range of frequencies of the æther waves used in wireless communication is now subdivided as follows:..Above 30,000 kc./s... Very high Frequencies (*V.H.F.). **1951** 'N. Shute' *Round Bend* ii. 50 A small V.H.F. radio set. **1955** *Times* 29 July 5/4 The present system of amplitude modulation in the v.h.f. maritime services should be changed to one of frequency modulation. **1956** *B.B.C. Handbk. 1957* 134 The introduction of very high frequency transmissions, with frequency modulation (VHF/FM) in several parts of the country, was the major development of the year in sound broadcasting. **1974** Harvey & Bohlman *Stereo F.M. Radio Handbk.* ii. 9 Also, at v.h.f., there was sufficient bandwidth available for hi-fi quality. **1982** *Daily Tel.* 30 July 3/5 (Advt.), Simple to use *VHS recorder with 10-day timer. **1984** *What Video?* Aug. 10/2 SKC..is also launching a range of high grade cassettes in standard lengths in VHS and Beta formats. **1972** *Bioorganic Chem.* II. 30 (*heading*) Synthesis of the vasoactive intestinal peptide (*VIP). *Ibid.* 87 Information on partial sequences of VIP became available recently. **1983** R. G. LONG et al. in *Oxf. Textbk. Med.* I. xii. 50/1 VIP secretion has been demonstrated after direct neural stimulation. **1964** *Amer. Forests* Oct. 13/1 The act provides for establishment of the Volunteers In Service To America (*VISTA)—a sort of domestic peace corps. **1980** *New Age* (U.S.) Oct. 42/2 NOFA..sponsored VISTA workers to help set up farmers' markets in New Hampshire and Vermont. **1974** *VLA [see OPTICAL *a.* 2a]. **1978** PASACHOFF & KUTNER *University Astron.* xxvi. 669 When fully operational..the VLA will make pictures of a field of view a few minutes of arc across, with resolutions comparable to the 1 arc sec of optical observations from large telescopes, in about 10 hours. **1969** *Sci. Jrnl.* Aug. 63/2 This interferometer system which is called the very long baseline interferometer (*VLBI) is unusual in that there is no connection between the receiving elements. **1982** *Sci. Amer.* May 85/3 The VLBI maps now being made are as good as the maps made with linked telescopes 10 years ago. **1968** *Punch* 24 Apr. 612/3 The introduction of *VLCCs (very large crude carriers, supertankers of up to 200,000 tons) will cut transport costs dramatically. **1974** *Nature* 19 Jan. 196/1 In December 1969 three VLCCs had serious explosions in one of their centre tanks during tank cleaning. **1975** *Times* 30 June 16/5 Tanker rates continued to increase..as Very Large Crude Carrier (VLCC) premiums moved up. **1977** *Time* 21 Nov. 40/1 Among the largest and lightest of these globules are the very-low-density lipoproteins (*VLDL). **1938** *Admiralty Handbk. Wireless Telegr. 1938* I. (Nomenclature of Waves), On the basis of a recent C.C.I.R. recommendation, promulgated in French; a suitable nomenclature, likely soon to be accepted internationally, may be given in English as follows:—Below 30 kc/s... Very Low Frequencies (*V.L./F.). **1962** L. DEIGHTON *Ipcress File* xx. 136 There was a V.L.F. (very low frequency) radio wave-length and a compass bearing. **1983** *New Scientist* 13 Jan. 93/1 Scientists in California have discovered that the Earth's magnetic field can act as a giant neutral amplifier for very low-frequency (VLF) radio waves. **1943** W. S. CHURCHILL in *Hansard Commons* 8 June 566 We took the measures which have thrown the long-range aircraft—the very long-range aircraft—the *V.L.R., as they are called—, effectively in to the anti U-boat struggle. **1946** *Happy Landings* July 7/3 In April, 1945 [he] became A.O.A., Tiger Force (V.L.R.), Bomber Force for the bombing of Japan. **1978** *World Book Year Bk.* 309/1 In 1977..the semiconductor segment of the industry was virtually on the threshold of a new frontier—very large scale integration (*VLSI). **1979** W. J. CAELLI *Microcomputer Revolution* p. xvii, VLSI—Very Large Scale Integration. This term flows on from the LSI designation and refers to component densities of well over 1000 components. **1983** *Listener* 25 Aug. 25/2 The amount of VLSI (Very Large Scale Integrated) circuitry needed to enable them to sync Autocue clichés with corny visuals is as great as that employed in the space shuttle. **1984** *Ann. Rep. Racol Electronics PLC* 6/1 The collaborative development of a microelectronic very large scale integrated (VLSI) process. *Ibid.* 7/1 The design of VLSI chips. **1670** COVEL in *Early Voy. Levant* (Hakluyt Soc.) 111 A pretty little picture of the *V.M. **1942** *N.Y. Times* 13 June 17/6 The new *V-Mail for United States overseas forces, patterned after the British microfilm postal system, was started when letters were delivered to President Roosevelt today. **1943** R. VANCE *They made me a Leatherneck* 44 'George never lets up on V mail to that female,' Weber observed. **1966** *Sunday Times* (Colour Suppl.) 4 Dec. 73/4 [GI jargon.] *V-Mail*, letters to or from home, reproduced photographically to conserve shipping space. **1949** *Bull. U.S. Dept. of State* 27 Mar. 396/2 The second part [of a broadcast] originating in the *VOA offices in New York, will include news. **1975** *New Yorker* 26 May 28/3 The basic problem is that V.O.A. has been placed at the intersection of journalism and diplomacy: the practice of one of these disciplines negates the practice of the other. **1955** *Times* 17 Aug. 6/4 There was controversy earlier this year over how soon—if at all—Tacan should replace *VOR/DME..as the standard air navigation system in the United States for civil as well as military aircraft. **1982** T. BEATTIE *Diamonds* xviii. 157 'Could you confirm your VOR is monitoring?' 'Freetown roger... The VOR is unserviceable.' **1972** HARTMANN & STORK *Dict. Lang. & Linguistics* 249/1 In transformational-generative grammar, the verb phrase is that constituent of a sentence which contains the predicate (or complement or adjunct)... The abbreviation *VP is used in phrase structure rules. **1976** *Word 1971* XXVII. 248 The main verb or an auxiliary verb, if there is one, is placed in the final position of a verb phrase in German deep structure while it occupies the initial position of a VP in surface structure. **1887** *Irish Times* 30 Nov. 5/3 Sir Andrew Hart, *V.P., T.C.D. **1925** C. S. LEWIS *Let.* 14 Aug. (1966) 103 When the V.P. [of Magdalen College, Oxford] laid a red cushion at his feet I realized.. that this was going to be a kneeling affair. **1978** M. PUZO *Fools Die* xxvii. 310 With his bosses, like the VP in charge of production at Wartberg's Tri-Culture International Studios,..he was much more frank, more human. **1888** KIPLING *Barrack-Room Ballads* (1892) 112 How he met with his fate and the *V.P.P. **1975** C. ALLEN *Plain Tales from Raj* viii. 93 With VPP or Value Payable Post, you paid the postman the value of the goods in the parcel. **1952** A. M. SULLIVAN *Last Serjeant* xiii. 139 The ancient claimant to the degree of *V.S. was a little more learned but often a little less skilful than the country cow doctor. **1960** *Voluntary Service Overseas* 4 Volunteers give their service free... This leaves *V.S.O. with the task of raising funds to cover the cost of travel and insurance. **1962** *Times Lit. Suppl.* 28 Dec. 1007/3 Mrs. Dickson's husband was largely responsible for initiating the scheme, known as Voluntary Service Overseas (VSO). **1965** *Listener* 7 Jan. 21/2 He was the first British V.S.O. to come to Libya. **1967** *Guardian* 30 May 5/5 The conflict came to a head shortly before my VSO year came to an end. **1980** *Jrnl. R. Soc. Arts* Jan. 111/1 She has a VSO working with her and six or seven dedicated staff. **1981** E. NORTH *Dames* xiii. 256 Your children will..work for V.S.O. and Amnesty International. **1907** *Yesterday's Shopping* (1969) 99/2 J. and F. Martell's..*V.S.O.P.—108/0. **1951** R. POSTGATE *Plain Man's Guide to Wine* ix. 125 Five Stars should indicate a good brandy; higher-up the various firms have their own indications: X.O., V.S.O.P., Cordon bleu, and so forth. **1982** M. O'DONNELL *Devil's Prison* II. i. 88 The waiters had left them alone with a jug of coffee and a bottle of VSOP. **1960** *Aeroplane* XCVIII. 234/1 In the United States, NASA applies the STOL appelation to any fixed-wing type capable of operating from a 500-ft. strip surrounded by 50-ft. obstacles. This is sufficiently drastic, however, to eliminate all but a handful of experimental aircraft, which may more accurately be described as *V-STOL (very short take-off, etc.) types. **1961** *New Scientist* 23 Feb. 462/2 Construction of economical V/STOL aircraft ..is..a much more urgent and profitable line of development than supersonic aircraft will ever be. **1977** *R.A.F. News* 30 Mar.–12 Apr. 13/2 The future of military VSTOL would seem to be assured in a maritime context. **1954** *Aviation Week* 26 Apr. 30/2 New approaches to the problems of developing vertical-rising aircraft are being explored... NACA has been doing basic research in the *VTO field for more than a decade. **1955** *Sci. Amer.* Apr. 106/3 V.T.O. aircraft (vertical take-off) are being developed vigorously in both England and the U.S. **1963** *Ann. Reg. 1962* 390 Bristol-Siddeley had produced a prototype supersonic VTO fighter. **1955** *Wall St. Jrnl.* 4 Feb. 3/4 Bell Aircraft Corp. announced it has built and flown the first jet-propelled vertical rising airplane which takes off and lands without needing a runway. The test *VTOL (vertical take-off and landing) airplane weighs about 2,000 pounds, is 21 feet long, has a wing span of 26 feet, and carries only the pilot. **1958** *Times* 1 Mar. 7/3 V.T.O.L. designs are as yet in their infancy. **1979** N. SLATER *Falcon* i. 24 The basic [plane] design owed much to the VTOL Harrier. **1954** *Britannica Bk. of Year* 638/1 *VTR (video tape recorder). **1968** *Globe & Mail* (Toronto) 17 Feb. 51 (Advt.), Minimum of two years experience preferably in colour telecine and Ampex VTR. **1982** J. GARDNER *For Special Services* xii. 109 Each [cabin] had a large sitting room with television, stereo and VTR. **1940** H. A. CHINN et al. in *Proc. IRE* XXVIII. 14/2 It was thought..that there would be less confusion in adopting the new standards if a new name were coined for expressing the measurements. The term selected is '*vu', the number of vu being numerically the same as the number of decibels above or below the new reference-volume level. **1944** *Ibid.* XXXII. 601/1 A key located to the left of the VU meter should be used. **1959** K. HENNEY *Radio Engin. Handbk.* (ed. 5) xiii. 19 The A scale emphasizes the VU markings and has an inconspicuous voltage scale. **1976** *Canad. Jrnl. Linguistics* Spring 70 The speaker made every attempt to maintain equal intensity across syllables by monitoring his output on a VU meter.

c. In music an abbrev. of various Italian words, as *verte* 'turn', *violino* 'violin', *voce* 'voice', *volta* 'time'.

1724 *Short Explic. For. Wds. in Mus. Bks.* 1 The Letter *V* is often used as an Abbreviation of the Word *Violino*. *Ibid.*, The Letters *VS* at the Bottom of a Leaf are often used as an Abbreviation of the Words *Volti Subito*. **1753** *Chambers' Cycl.* Suppl., *V*, in music, is often used to shew that a piece is designed for the violin; and VV, for two violins, or more.

d. Of German words: V, *Vergeltungswaffe*, 'reprisal weapon'; used to denote German missiles of the war of 1939–45, as ***V-1*** = *flying bomb* s.v. FLYING *vbl. sb.* 3; hence ***V-bomb***; ***V-2***, a type of rocket bomb; hence ***V-weapons***; **VW**, Volkswagen.

1944 *Times* 30 June 3/5 For two weeks London has now been subjected to ceaseless bombardment by the German weapon V1. **1944** *Life* 21 Aug. 17/1 It seems probable..that the V-2, successor to the V-1 robot bomb, will be a heavy rocket. **1944** *Evening Sun* (Baltimore) 13 Sept. 1/6 The Germans, after toning down their 'V' weapons threat for a few days, are now making new threats. **1944** *Sun* (Baltimore) 20 Nov. 3/4 Lord Vansittart found no substance in objections that German V-bombs debar a Big Three meeting in Britain. **1952** M. ALLINGHAM *Tiger in Smoke* ii. 43 Night. V2 time... Remember V2's?.. Suddenly, no warning, no whistle, wallop! **1962** F. I. ORDWAY et al. *Basic Astronautics* ii. 23 The modern space carrier vehicle is a direct descendant of the V2 guided missile developed by the German army during World War II. **1978** D. KYLE *Black Camelot* x. 156 Hitler remains confident he can win the war. .. The V-weapons, I suppose. **1982** T. FITZGIBBON *With Love* II. viii. 155 After D-Day, 6 June 1944, a new horror arrived..the pilotless flying bombs, called V1s and known ..as 'doodle-bugs'... In September..the first rockets (V2s) reached London. **1958** S. ABBEY *Bk. of Volkswagen* v. 45 It is possible to improve the performance of the VW by a standardized engine tuning process... The VW owner is saved the cost of several accessories which are desirable. **1962** A. LURIE *Love & Friendship* vii. 135 Maybe it's just the fellow feeling of his Volkswagen for my Renault; he would be equally helpless if the VW broke down. **1977** C. MCFADDEN *Serial* (1978) iii. 13/1 She..extricated Kat Vonnegut..from the rear of her VW bus.

e. Of French words: **V.D.Q.S.**, *vin délimité de qualité supérieure*, a wine of superior quality from amongst the wines of a limited area.

1962 *Wine Mag.* Sept.–Oct. 253/2 Next in order of quality are the V.D.Q.S. wines, or, to give them their full title, the *Vins Delimités de Qualitié Supérieure*. **1966** P. V. PRICE *France: Food & Wine Guide* 135 Below the A.C. wines come those marked V.D.Q.S.—*vins délimités de qualité supérieure*. **1974** *Times* 2 Dec. (Suppl.) p. ii/1 The VDQS stamp..[is] a stamp of quality awarded by the French Government. VDQS stands for 'Vins Délimités de Qualité Supérieure'.

IV. Symbolic uses.

6. *Particle Physics.* **V** is used to designate the heavy unstable particles that produce characteristic V-shaped tracks when they decay (***V-events***), now identified as hyperons and kaons. *Obs.* exc. *hist.*

1950 P. M. S. BLACKETT *Let.* 12 July (MS.), We have been discussing here the question of nomenclature and I would like to ask your views about the following suggestion. This is that we should call the special type of track that you and we have observed v-tracks and the particle or particles which make them v-particles. The advantage of this seems to be that the letter v is reasonably unallocated and that the name has strong mnemonic values as, in fact, the tracks are v shaped. **1951** *Nature* 31 Mar. 503/1 Six charged *V*-tracks are due to the decay of new unstable particles. *Ibid.* 503/2 Two schemes are suggested to explain the photographs: $V^0 \to p^+ + \pi^-$..; $V^0 \to \pi^+ + \pi^-$. **1952** *Sci. Amer.* Jan. 26/2 The V-particles appear to be somewhat more massive than a proton or neutron, because in some instances a proton is a decay product. **1968** M. S. LIVINGSTON *Particle Physics* v. 98 If an incident neutral particle has an interaction leading to two charged particles, the vertex of the V event shows the location, and the balance of transverse momenta identifies the incoming direction of the neutral particle. **1974** FRAUENFELDER & HENLEY *Subatomic Physics* vii. 170 By about 1952, many *V* events had been seen, and a mystery had developed: the *V* particles were produced copiously but decayed very slowly.

Hence **V-d** *pa. pple.*, cut with a V-shaped incision.

1881 GREENER *Gun* 380 The sight consists of a steel spring screwed on to the top rib, with one end set at right angles and V-d to form the sight.

va, southern ME. var. FOE *sb.*; obs. Sc. f. WAY *sb.*, WOE *sb.* and *a.*

Vaad Leumi (ˈvaːaːd ləˈʊmiː). [Heb. *waʿaḏ* committee + *lə'ummī* national.] A national committee of Palestine Jews, serving as their official representative during the period of the British Mandate from 1920 to 1948.

The form *Vaad Haleumi* in the 1926 example includes the definite article.

1926 *Zionist Rev.* Feb. 127/2 The Second Jewish National Assembly appoints a Vaad Haleumi composed of 38 members. **1932** *Palestine Post* 4 Dec. 1/2 Mr I. Ben Zevi, a member of the Vaad Leumi Executive. **1941** *Contemp. Jewish Rec.* IV. 428/2 The threat of Nazi occupation caused the Agency Executive..to ratify an agreement between the Vaad Leumi and the Right bloc. **1949** KOESTLER *Promise & Fulfilment* I. xv. 169 On March 1 the *Vaad Leumi* met in Tel Aviv. **1963** *Times* 24 Apr. 16/1 He later became one of the founders of the General Council for Palestine Jews (*Vaad Leumi*), the executive body of the Jewish community, and served as chairman or president from 1931 until it was dissolved with the establishment of the State of Israel. **1971** *Encycl. Judaica* XVI. 49 The Va'ad Le'ummi represented the *yishuv* in its relations with the Mandatory government and the Arab leaders and dealt with internal matters (such as the school system) which were delegated to it by the Zionist Executive.

vaalhaai (ˈfɑːlhaɪ). *S. Afr.* Also Vaalhai. [Afrikaans, f. Du. *vaal* pale + *haai* shark.] A local name for the tope, *Galeorhinus galeus*; = TOPE *sb.*[2] Also *attrib.*

1947 K. H. BARNARD *Pict. Guide S. Afr. Fishes* 10 Tope; Vaal-haai... This medium-sized (6 feet) cosmopolitan shark has recently become of considerable economic importance in South Africa for the extraction of vitamins from its liver-oil. **1949** *Cape Times* 24 Sept. 1/6 Any person capturing a Vaalhaai shark shall land it in a whole state. **1958** *Cape Argus* 14 June 13/4 The vaalhaai..grows to about 6 ft. and is harmless to man. **1973** *Stand. Encycl. S. Afr.* IX. 603/2 In South Africa that [*sc.* the liver] of the liver-oil shark *Galeorhinus* (vaalhaai) is especially rich, and from 1940 to 1955 this species was specially hunted for it.

vaalite (ˈvɑːlaɪt). *Min.* [f. the *Vaal* River, S. Africa, + -ITE[1] 2b; named by Maskelyne.] A variety of vermiculite.

1874 MASKELYNE in *Geol. Soc. Lond.* XXX. 409 Vaalite.. occurs in hexagonal prisms, the angles of which are nearly 60° and 120°.

‖**vaaljapie** (ˈfɑːljɑːpɪ). *S. Afr.* Also **Vaal Japie.** [Afrikaans, lit. 'tawny Jake', f. as Du. *vaal* pale + *japie* dim. of the name *Jaap* f. *Jakob*.] Rough young wine, inferior wine.

1945 *Cape Times* 21 May, What I say is 'Come quick, go quick,' and Vaal Japie is my best friend. **1949** L. G. GREEN *Land of Afternoon* 59 Young wine, not matured but about six months old, is known as Vaaljapie... It takes its name from its tawny colour though some varieties are red. **1958** *Cape Times* 29 Nov. 1/5 Some woodcutters..made him drunk on *vaaljapie* and called the police while he was asleep. **1968** D. J. OPPERMAN *Spirit of Vine* 242 Brandy and vaaljapie have always had an irresistible attraction for these people. **1975** *Stand. Encycl. S. Afr.* XI. 464/2 The wine ration given by farmers to their labourers..is referred to as 'boys' wine', or 'vaaljapie'.

‖**Vaalpens** (ˈfɑːlpɛns). *S. Afr.* Pl. **-pens, pense(n).** Also with lower-case initial in attrib. use. [Afrikaans, f. as prec. + *pens* paunch, belly.]

a. A name for a member of the Ba-Kalahari tribe. **b.** *colloq.* A nickname for a Transvaaler.

1871 J. MACKENZIE *Ten Years North of Orange River* iii. 53 Their fellow-countrymen to the south..sometimes call them 'Vaalpensen', which is the Dutch for Bakalahari, the ill-favoured and lean vassals of the Bechuanas. **1899** *Eastern Province Herald* (Port Elizabeth) 6 Dec. 3/4 A South African Dutchman writes us a somewhat bitter letter... He writes as a Dutch Afrikander, a Vaalpens in fact. **1900** A. H. KEANE *Boer States* iii. 32 Here [in the Bosch Veld] is also the true home of the Vaalpens, most degraded of all the South African aborigines. **1916** *Eastern Province Herald* (Port Elizabeth) 28 Sept. 3 The Vaalpens reported that one of our oxen had been mauled... We saddled up and with three Vaalpens soon found where the lion had caught the ox. **1934** *Star* (Johannesburg) 1 May 13/1 For the past 50 years and more Free Staters have been known among Dutch-speaking South Africans as Blikore (tin ears) and Transvaalers as Vaalpense, the latter so called after a certain native tribe of that name who lived in the Transvaal. *a* **1936** E. MARAIS *Soul of Ape* (1969) iii. 92 Here in Waterberg..a case of 'homing' in a descendant of the so-called 'vaalpens pygmies' that at one time inhabited the Bushveld of the northern Transvaal. **1970** *Personality* Competition, The 'Vaalpens' are very scarce in South Africa nowadays.

vaat, obs. form of VAT.

‖**va banque** (va bɑ̃k). *Gambling.* [Fr., lit. 'go bank'.] In baccarat and chemin-de-fer, a bet against the whole of the banker's stake. (In quots., *fig.*) Cf. BANCO *int.*

1946 A. J. P. TAYLOR *Course of German Hist.* ii. 38 Both dynasties desired the defeat of Napoleon; but the Hohenzollerns, having nothing more to lose, were ready to bid *va banque*—the Habsburgs were not. **1966** *Economist* 12 Nov. 683/3 Disraeli..was an adventurer who played the great game *va banque* with a courage and effrontery that commanded, perhaps even deserved, success.

vac[1] (væk), abbrev. (chiefly in Univ. colloquial use) of VACATION *sb.*

1709 *Brit. Apollo* No. 55. 3/2 It was very hard in the *Vac.* without Gains. **1864** BP. CREIGHTON in Mrs. Creighton *Life* (1904) I. ii. 11, I shall have all the rest of the Vac. to perpend and meditate on that point. **1871** M. LEGRAND *Camb. Freshm.* 365 When I was a boy at Harrow, I always hated going home for the 'vacs'. **1906** *Catholic Weekly* 18 May 7 Others lectured to working men in the vacs.

vac[2], colloq. abbrev. of VACUUM *v.*

1942 N. LAST *Diary* 23 July in *Nella Last's War* (1981) vii. 212, I hurried home to bake my bread, vac the dining-room and dust. **1970** J. WAINWRIGHT *Prynter's Devil* iii. 50 Vac the room first, kiddo. Then start the repaint job. **1971** *Guardian* 26 Nov. 11/5 Little ladies in nylon overalls were noisily vaccing the deep red carpet. **1981** J. WAINWRIGHT *Urge for Justice* II. i. 100 My cleaning lady..vacs and polishes around.

vac[3], colloq. abbrev. of *vacuum cleaner* s.v. VACUUM 4.

1974 P. WRIGHT *Lang. Brit. Industry* xvii. 164 The brave new indoor world of *vacs, mixers, mincers* and all the rest. **1976** *Star* (Sheffield) 20 Nov. (Advt.), Cash paid for Washers, Vacs and Fridges in good condition. **1979** *Arizona Daily Star* 1 Apr. (Advt. Suppl.), Wards has jiffy vacs priced low as 22.88.

vac, abbrev. VACANT *a.*: see *sit(s) vac* s.v. SIT *sb.*[2]

†**vacabond.** *Obs.* Forms: α. 5–6 **vacabound(e**, 5 **wayka-**). β. 5–6 **vacabund(e**. γ. 5–6 **vacabond(e**, 6 **vaco-, vaka-**). δ. 6 **vacabo(u)n, wacabone.** [a. OF. *vacabonde* (*vacquabonde, vaccabon*), app. an alteration of *vagabond(e* VAGABOND under the influence of L. *vacāre* (F. *vaquer*) to be unoccupied or idle.

The form survives in northern F. dialects, and in the 17th century Chifflet gives *vacabond* as the pron. of *vagabond* (Littré). In Anglo-L. of the 15–16th cent. *vacabundus* occurs in place of *vagabundus*.]

1. A person having no settled means of living or no fixed home; a vagabond.

α. **1404** in Ellis *Orig. Lett.* Ser. II. I. 37 Al men of the forsaede shirs exepte fowre or five gentilmen & a fewe vacaboundis, woldin faene cum to pees. **1472** *Presentments of Juries* in *Surtees Misc.* (1890) 24 John Bek is a vacabound. **1483** *Ibid.* 28 One Wrodyngton, a waykabound. **1530–1** *Act 22 Hen. VIII*, c. 12 It shall be leful to the constables..to arest the sayde vacaboundes and ydell persones. **1578** WHETSTONE *Promos & Cass.* II. IV. i, Fetche me in all ydle vacaboundes.

β. **1453** *Rolls of Parlt.* V. 270/1 Thomas Watkynson.. Yoman and Robert Withes late of Salley in the shire of York Vacabunde. **1495** *Coventry Leet Bk.* 568 All maner vacabundes & beggers myghty in body within þis Citie. **1530** PALSGR. 183 *Vngz piegz*, a payre of stockes to punysshe vacabundes. **1552** *Nottingham Rec.* IV. 103 Any vacabunde, suspect person, or nowghty people. **1584** *Mirr. Mag.* 16 b, He commaunded, that vnto a nomber of yong diseased vacabunds, there shuld be ministred a thin Diet, an excessiue labor, and cleanly lodging.

γ. **1472** *Presentments of Juries* in *Surtees Misc.* (1890) 24 Thomas Dransfeld..liffez as a vacabond. *a* **1533** LD. BERNERS *Huon* xxviii. 85 There was no begger, vacabonde, nor rybault..but by grete flockys they came. **1563** in Turner *Select. Rec. Oxford* (1880) 303 Beggers or vakabondes do come into the Cytye. **1588** GREENE *Perimedes* Wks. (Grosart) VII. 39 Hast thou these fourteen yeeres gone as a vacabonde about the world vnknowen and despised?

δ. **1556** *Nottingham Rec.* (1889) IV. 113 He dothe harber wacabones. **1567** HARMAN *Caveat* 19 Vagarantes and sturdy vacabons. **1571** R. EDWARDS *Damon & Pithias* E iij b, Betten with a codgell like a Slaue, a Vacaboun, or a lasie Lubber.

2. *attrib.* or as *adj.* (Cf. VAGABOND *a.*)

1538 ELYOT, *Errabundus*, moche wanderynge, or vacabunde. **1550** J. COKE *Eng. & Fr. Heralds* § 190 The true beginning of the Frenchmen was by a vacabunde captayne named Marcomyrus. **1552** HULOET, Vacabund parson, *erro.* **1591** SAVILE *Tacitus, Hist.* II. viii. 57 Adjoining vnto him certaine fugitiue and beggerly vacabond persons.

†**vacabuncy.** *Obs.*$^{-1}$ [irreg. f. *vacabund* VACABOND. Cf. VAGABUNCY.] Vagabondage.

1535 *Act 27 Hen. VIII*, c. 25 Euery stronge and valiant begger and vacabound, after he were whipped for his vacabuncie and idelnes.

vacance (ˈveɪkəns). Chiefly *Sc.* Also 6 **wacance, vacans,** 9 **vacanse.** [ad. L. *vacantia* (see next), or a. F. *vacance* (1642).]

†**1. a.** A vacant period. *Obs.*$^{-1}$

1533 BELLENDEN *Livy* I. vii. (S.T.S.) I. 43 This gouernance..was callit the Interregne, That is to say, þe vacance betuix the deith of ane king to þe electioun of ane vthir.

†**b.** Cessation or suspension *of* laws. *Obs.*

1533 BELLENDEN *Livy* III. ii. (S.T.S.) I. 247 þe vacance of lawis [L. *justitium*] was commandit. *Ibid.* 249 At the returnyng of quintius to rome, the vacance of lawis ceissit.

†**2.** The fact of becoming vacant; the vacation *of* an office. *Obs.*

1579 *Reg. Privy Council Scot.* III. 177 Upoun the vacance of ony prelacie the kirkis thairof salbe disponit to qualifiit ministeris in titill.

3. = VACATION 2. Now *rare.*

1563–7 BUCHANAN *Reform. St. Andros* Wks. (S.T.S.) 10 Heir efter..thair may be gevin sum vacans on to the first day of October. **1567** *Sc. Acts, Jas. VI* (1814) III. 32/2 The Lordis of counsell and sessioun hes bene in vse..to haue vacance at ȝule, Fastingis euin, Pasche, & Witsonday. **1609** in Seton *Life A. Seton* (1882) 9 The Yule vacance to be and continue from the 24th December to the 6th January *inclusivé*. **1678** SIR G. MACKENZIE *Crim. Laws Scot.* II. xii. §ii. (1699) 207 Neither the Sheriff, nor Barrons, can hold Courts *in feriat*, or close, time of Vacance. **1695** SIBBALD *Autobiog.* (1834) 129, I past the Bajon yeer under Mr. James Wyseman, who died the vacance thereafter. **1752** J. LOUTHIAN *Form of Process* (ed. 2) 28 These Letters pass upon a Bill signed by three Lords in Time of Vacance, and four in Time of Session. **1826** J. WILSON *Noct. Ambr.* Wks. 1855 I. 242 The fates o' the laddies at the Edinburgh Military Academy, on the Saturday before their vacanse. **1835** *Blackw. Mag.* XXXVIII. 154 We have angled ten hours a-day for half-a-week (during the vacance). **1901** TROTTER *Gall. Gossip* 338 Give them vacance to-morrow.

attrib. *a* **1712** FOUNTAINHALL *Decis.* (1759) II. 345 It was just and necessary to arrest him, and make him answer, though in vacance-time. *a* **1774** FERGUSSON *Poems* (1789) II. 46 Their stamack's aft in tift In vacance-time.

†**4.** In Eng. use: Leisure, relaxation. *Obs. rare.*

1609 BIBLE (Douay) *Ecclus.* xxxviii. 25 *comm.*, The wisdom of a scribe in the time of vacance. *a* **1760** J. H. BROWNE *Poems* (1768) 141 Nor thou disdain Fit hour of Vacance with the Muses' train.

5. *poet. nonce-use.* A rendering of Fr. *absence* in the original.

1930 T. S. ELIOT tr. *St.-J. Perse's Anabasis* viii. 53 To the scale of our hearts was such vacance completed!

vacancy (ˈveɪkənsɪ). Also 6 **vacantie,** 7 *Sc.* **vaccancy.** [f. VACANT *a.* (see -ANCY), or ad. late and med.L. *vacantia* (Sp. and Pg. *vacancia*, It. *vacanza*), f. *vacant-, vacans* vacant. Cf. prec.]

I. 1. a. = VACATION 2. Also in *pl.* Now *arch.*

c **1580** W. SPELMAN *Dial.* (1896) 6 There I contynued my sute untill the tyme of ther vacantie in the Lawe. **1633** W. ROBINSON in Rigaud *Corr. Sci. Men* (1841) I. 18 He is to come this vacancy into Lincolnshire about business of his own. **1679** *Trials of White & other Jesuits* 62 *Joseph.* He was [absent] in the time of the Vacancy... *L.C.J.* When are the Vacancies? *Joseph.* In August, my Lord. **1702** MARWOOD *Diary* in *Cath. Rec. Soc. Publ.* VII. 134 To-day the Vacancys of the lower Classe began, and end at St Luke. **1703** in Ritchie *Churches of St. Baldred* 128 He must not grant the vacancie without acquainting the session. **1780** STILES *Diary* (1901) II. 409 At the End of the Vacancy 1744 Mr. Reed carried his 3 pupils..to enter into Harv[ard] College. **1876** GRANT *Burgh Sch. Scot.* II. v. 182 Besides the half and occasional holiday two annual 'plays', or 'vacancies', have of old been granted to the scholar. **1876** in Hare *Story Life* (1896) IV. 412 They are having their vacancies.

†**b.** Without article. *Obs. rare.*

1643 in *Fasti Aberd.* (1854) 421 The porter..shall attend the colledge for saving the fabrick, both in tyme of play and vacancie. **1691** tr. *Emiliane's Observ. Journ. Naples* 15 Every year in Autumn they have two Months of vacancy.

†**2. a.** Temporary freedom or cessation from business or some usual occupation. Also const. *from.*

1599 *Broughton's Let.* vii. 21 His assiduous reading in any vacancie from busines. **1602** SEGAR *Honour Mil. & Civ.* IV. xxi, For he that hath been longest vacant may take place before him that is lesse ancient in Vacancie. *c* **1630** MILTON (*title*), On the University Carrier who sickn'd in the time of his vacancy, being forbid to go to London, by reason of the Plague. **1663** BP. PATRICK *Parab. Pilgr.* xxix. (1668) 337 He did not find so much vacancy as his heart desired for private Prayer. **1775** JOHNSON *Lett.* (1788) I. 291 Air, and vacancy, and novelty, would..afford all the relief that human art can give.

†**b.** Free or unoccupied time; leisure. *Obs.*

1606 SHAKS. *Ant. & Cl.* I. iv. 26 If he fill'd His vacancie with his Voluptuousnesse. *a* **1628** PRESTON *Breastpl. Love* (1631) 114 So occupied with outward things abroad, that they have no vacancie to feed their souls within. **1656** BLOUNT *Glossogr.* To Rdr., This Work..has taken me up the vacancy of above Twenty years.

†**c.** An interval of leisure or unoccupied time.

1654 WHITLOCK *Zootomia* 305 Daies of nothing, but Riots, visits..and such like Exiles from themselves, and vacancies from the businesse of life. **1676** HALE *Contempl.* I. *Redempt. Time* 21 An industrious Husband-man, Trades-man, Scholar, will never want business for occasional vacancies and horæ subcisivæ. **1690** LOCKE *Hum. Und.* IV. xx. §3 There are none so enslav'd to the necessities of life, who might not find many vacancies that might be husbanded to this advantage of their knowledg. **1748** in *Welsh Rev.* Feb. (1892) 350 Filled in ye vacancies of ye day with work.

3. a. The state or condition of being free from or unoccupied with work, business, or action; absence of occupation; idleness; inactivity.

Freq. in the 17th c.; now *rare.*

1615 G. SANDYS *Trav.* I. 64 Chesse,..a sport that agreeth well with their sedentary vacancie. **1651** HOBBES *Govt. & Soc.* xii. §10 They who are least troubled with caring for necessary things..are invited by their vacancy sometimes to disputation among themselves concerning the Common-weal. **1670** COTTON *Espernon* Pref., Having about three Years since, and in the Vacancy of a Country Life, taken this Volume in hand. **1782** W. HEBERDEN *Comment.* xiii. (1806) 78 Nor does the vacancy of a Bath life suit complaints. **1818** COLERIDGE in *Lit. Rem.* (1836) I. 200 The source of the common fondness for novels of this sort rests in that dislike of vacancy and that love of sloth..inherent in the human mind. **1818** BYRON *Ch. Har.* IV. vi, Such is the refuge of our youth and age, The first from Hope, the last from Vacancy.

†**b.** Const. *from.* (Freq. in 17th cent.) *Obs.*

1615 JACKSON *Creed* III. Pref. A 3 b, God..blesse me outwardly with that measure of health, of vacancy from other businesse [etc.]. **1631** BYFIELD *Doctr. Sabb.* 143 A precise vacancy from all worke..is morall. **1690** NORRIS *Beatitudes* (1692) 80 Implying, that a Vacancy from Wrath is a necessary Qualification for Prayer. **1712** *Spect.* No. 408 ¶8 An absolute Indifference and Vacancy from all Passion.

†**c.** Freedom from mental preoccupation. *Obs.*

1752 JOHNSON *Rambler* No. 204 ¶13 Nor was he able to disengage his attention, or mingle with vacancy and ease in any amusement. **1796** MME. D'ARBLAY *Camilla* V. 293 Her pliant mind, in this state of vacancy, had readily been bent to the new pursuit. **1837** CARLYLE *Fr. Rev.* I. I. iii, 'Every evening at six'..[they] walk majestically out again, to embroidery, small-scandal, prayers, and vacancy. **1856** AYTOUN *Bothwell* II. i, The fishers..whistle o'er their lazy task In happy vacancy.

d. Absence of any determining influence or factor. *rare*$^{-1}$.

1754 EDWARDS *Freed. Will* II. vii. (1762) 64 The Will's Freedom consists in..this Vacancy and Opportunity that is left for the Will itself to be the Determiner of the Act.

II. †**4.** An unoccupied period or interval; a time of absence *of* some activity. *Obs.*

1601 SHAKS. *Twel. N.* V. i. 90 For three months before, (No int'rim, not a minutes vacancie,) Both day and night did we keepe companie. **1625** T. GODWIN *Moses & Aaron* I. (1641) 2 In these vacancies or distances of time, between Iudge and Iudge. **1663** HEATH *Flagellum* (1672) 32 In so long an interval and vacancy of War, from which this Nation had been blessed.

5. a. The fact or condition of an office or post being, becoming, or falling vacant; an occasion or occurrence of this.

1607 in *Hist. Wakefield Gram. Sch.* (1892) 59 Within foure daies of the vacancie knowen. **1665** MANLEY *Grotius' Low C. Wars* 197 They began a new Custom, which was, That they would in Vacancies, name the Captains, and other inferiour Officers under their Pay. **1765** BLACKSTONE *Comm.* I. ii. 172 No candidate shall, after the date..of the writs, or after the vacancy, give any money or entertainment to his electors. **1818** CRUISE *Digest* (ed. 2) III. 35 A sale of an advowson, the church being actually void, was simoniacal and void in respect to the then present vacancy. **1896** *Law Times Rep.* C. 408/1 With reference to the vacancy among the Chancery taxing masters.

b. Const. *of* (an office, position, etc.).

1610 G. CARLETON *Jurisdict.* 2 That power whereby we succeed the Emperour in the vacancie of the Empire. **1659** H. L'ESTRANGE *Alliance Div. Off.* 321 As did the Clergy of Rome also in the vaca[n]cy of that Sea determine. **1687** A. LOVELL tr. *Thevenot's Trav.* I. 77 *note*, Zornesan Mustapha Basha made Keeper of the Seal during the vacancy of the Charge of Grand Visier. **1726** AYLIFFE *Parergon* 129 In the Vacancy of a Bishoprick, the Guardian of the Spiritualities was summon'd to Parliament in the Bishop's Room. **1765** BLACKSTONE *Comm.* I. 152 The vacancy of the throne was precedent to their meeting without any royal summons.

c. An instance or occasion of land, a tenancy, etc., being or becoming vacant. *rare.*

1809 CHRISTIAN in *Blackstone's Comm.* II. 9 It cannot be said that in such a case there is ever a vacancy of possession. **1845** POLSON *Eng. Law* in *Encycl. Metrop.* II. 827/1 The maxim..that the tenancy of the land should always be filled, and that the tenant could make no disposition of his interest likely to involve a vacancy in the same tenancy.

6. a. A vacant or unoccupied office, post, or dignity.

1693 LUTTRELL *Brief Rel.* (1857) III. 81 Mounsieur Catinat..has sent 250 officers to throw themselves into the towne to supply the vacancies of those that were sick and dead there. **1706** E. WARD *Wooden World Diss.* (1708) 21 He shall force a Rupture with some one of his Lieutenants to make a Vacancy for him. **1769** *Junius' Lett.* iii. (1788) 46 His military cares have never extended beyond the disposal of vacancies. **1849** MACAULAY *Hist. Eng.* x. II. 638 How could there be an election without a vacancy? **1858** FROUDE *Hist. Eng.* IV. 286 More than twenty vacancies in the order of the Golden Fleece were placed by him at Henry's disposal.

b. A church without an incumbent or minister.

1867 J. MACFARLANE *Mem. T. Archer* I. 17 The 'vacancies' sought after him.

c. A vacant room in a hotel, guest-house, etc. Usu. *attrib.* as ***vacancy sign***, a signboard advertising available accommodation, or in *pl.*

1953 'R. MACDONALD' *Gone Girl* in *Lew Archer, Private Investigator* (1977) 24 The first motel I came to..was decorated with a vacancy sign. **1970** R. H. GREENAN *Nightmare* iv. 15 The place..is a bit sleazy... There's a vacancy sign out. **1972** *Guardian* 17 May 12/3 Hotels are replacing the 'Vacancy' signs with hoardings saying 'For Sale'. **1973** *Value Added Tax Tribunals Rep.* I. 165 Students have at their choice, provided vacancies are available, three types of accommodation. **1982** M. BABSON *Death beside Seaside* xiii. 111 Most of the trippers will be leaving this afternoon. There'll be plenty of vacancies.

7. Absence or lack *of* something. *rare.*

1650 FULLER *Pisgah* II. xiii. 269 Jordan, in the vacancy of the inhabitants, having got violent possession, fenced and fortified himself in the slime pits. **1805** FOSTER *Ess.* III. i. II. 11 With this cast of significance, and vacancy of sense, it is allowed to depreciate without being accountable.

III. 8. Empty or void space.

1602 SHAKS. *Ham.* III. iv. 117 Alas, how is't with you? That you bend your eye on vacancie, And with the incorporall ayre do hold discourse. **1606** —— *Ant. & Cl.* II. ii. 221 Th' ayre: which but for vacancie, Had gone to gaze on Cleopater too, And made a gap in Nature. **1813** BYRON *Corsair* I. xv, The tender blue of that large loving eye Grew frozen with its gaze on vacancy. **1827** Syd. Smith *Wks.* (1867) II. 134 To roar and bellow No Popery to Vacancy and the Moon. **1854** J. S. C. Abbott *Napoleon* (1855) II. x. 164 Folding his arms upon his breast, with his eyes fixed upon vacancy, he stood in gloomy silence. **1899** F. T. Bullen *Way Navy* 79 Meanwhile the 'Mersey' came up out of vacancy at her best speed.

9. a. A vacant, unfilled, or unoccupied space; an open space between objects or things, or in a row or series; a breach, gap, or opening; †an unoccupied or uninhabited piece of ground.

1652 Needham tr. *Selden's Mare Cl.* 18 In the case of those who first inhabited Vacancies; or who became possess't by right of War and Conquest. **1670** W. Perwich *Desp.* (1903) 90 As soon as ever he passed the great vacancy, he went to see the Cittadell. **1690** Leybourn *Curs. Math.* 901 In measuring of Roofing, seldom any deductions are made for..the Vacancies for Lutheren Lights, and Sky-Lights. **1726** R. Bradley *Country Gentl. Monthly Director* 3 In places where there are Vacancies in Hedges, set Truncheons, or Twigs of the White Sallow. **1744** M. Bishop *Life & Adv.* 209 It [i.e. gun-fire] soon broke us in a terrible manner, though our Vacancies were quickly filled up. **1779** Forrest *Voy. N. Guinea* 20 Their saddles have in the middle a vacancy, which must make it easy for the horse. **1820** Scoresby *Acc. Arctic Reg.* I. 55 Small vacancies in the ice would not prevent the journey. **1858** Hawthorne *Fr. & It. Note-bks.* (1872) I. 20 This great arch..with the lofty vacancy beneath it. **1905** *Westm. Gaz.* 26 Jan. 1/3 The closing of the fontanelle, or the 'vacancy' in the infant cranium.

b. *transf.* A blank, gap, or deficiency.

1759 Johnson *Rasselas* i, Every one..in the valley was required to propose whatever might contribute to fill up the vacancies of attention, and lessen the tediousness of time. **1846** Landor *Imag. Conv.* Wks. I. 2 Visions of reluctant homage from crowned heads..have passed away from me, and leave no vacancy. **1856** Dove *Logic Chr. Faith* v. ii. 317 Without revelation there would be a distinct vacancy in the scheme of knowledge.

c. *Cryst.* A defect in a crystal lattice consisting of the absence of an atom or ion from a position where there should be one.

1951 *Physical Rev.* LXXXII. 551/1 The experiments described below seem to be the most direct evidence, to date, that diffusion in close-packed metals occurs, predominantly, through the movement of vacancies. **1958** [see Schottky 2]. **1967** A. H. Cottrell *Introd. Metallurgy* xx. 365 The quench..produces a supersaturated solution of vacancies and..these vacancies agglomerate to form dislocation rings or other defects which harden the metal by acting as obstacles to gliding dislocations. **1971** *New Scientist* 25 Mar. 664/2 The interstitial migrates by jumping from one site to another, while the vacancy migrates as a result of a neighbouring atom jumping into the vacant hole. **1974** *Encycl. Brit. Macropædia* V. 334/1 Theoretical considerations require that all crystals have vacancies except at absolute zero temperature.

10. a. The state or condition of being vacant, empty, or unoccupied; emptiness.

1788 Gibbon *Decl. & F.* xlv. IV. 453 He contemplated with horror the vacancy and solitude of the city. **1796** Mme. D'Arblay *Camilla* I. 214 Such is the vacancy of dissipated pleasure, that..an opening always remains for something yet to be tried. **1817** J. Scott *Paris Revisit.* (ed. 4) 52 The dullest country town in England can afford no idea of the stillness and vacancy of the several noble-looking cities. **1823** Scott *Quentin D.* xix, Quentin felt a strange vacancy and chillness of the heart. **1878** Stewart & Tait *Unseen Univ.* i. §12. 31 When David or Hezekiah shrank from the gloomy vacancy of the grave.

b. Lack of intelligence; inanity; vacuity.

1841 Dickens *Barn. Rudge* v, Where in his face there was wildness and vacancy, in hers there was..patient composure. **1866** —— *Boy at Rugby* Christm. Stories (1874) 332 He is a smiling piece of vacancy.

†**'vacand**, *ppl. a.* and *sb. Sc. Obs.* Also 5 **wacande**, 5-6 **wacand**, 7 **vaicand**, **vacane**. *β.* 5 **wak-**, **vakande**, 5-6 **vakand**, 6 **vaken**. [Sc. pres. pple. of vake *v.* The usual spelling with *c* follows that of L. *vacant-*: see next.]

A. *ppl. a.* = vacant *a.* (esp. in sense 1).

a. **1405** in Fraser *The Lennox* (1874) II. 57 With the gyffing and the patronage of the said Kirk..alse often as it happinys to be vacand. **1458** *Burgh Rec. Peebles* (1872) 126 Sir Wilyam of Fulop chapellane sal be present..to the first service that sal hapyn vacand in thair gouernans. *c* **1470** Henry *Wallace* x. 531 As Bruce at the palȝoun So entryt in, and saw wacand his seit. **1500-20** Dunbar *Poems* lxxi. 26 Couatyce ringis into the spirituall state, Ȝarnand banifice the quhilk ar now vacand. *a* **1578** Lindesay (Pitscottie) *Chron. Scot.* (S.T.S.) I. 286 He gaue him the pryorie of Coldinghame..quhilk was wacand in his handis at that tyme. **1609** Skene *Reg. Maj.* 26 After the deceis of the husband, the Dowrie of his wife named be him, is vaicand (possessed be na man) or nocht vaicand. **1649** Lamont *Diary* (Maitl. Club) 11 He [the minister] was excommunicate, and his church declared vacane.

β. *c* **1425** Wyntoun *Cron.* viii. 27 Qwhil þus þe kynrik was wakande, Off Inglande þe kynge was þan thynkande [etc.]. **1456** *Extr. Aberd. Rec.* (1844) I. 21 That chapelnary of Saynt Nichallis altar was than vakande. **1513** Douglas *Æneid* (1710) xiii. x. 119 With this the Kyng Latinus can deceis, And left the sceptoure vakand to his hand.

B. *sb.* **1.** One who is free to take a mate.

1508 Dunbar *Tua Mariit Wemen* 206 Ȝe speik of berdis on bewch: of blise may thai sing, That, on sanct Valentynis day, ar vacandis ilk ȝer.

2. A vacant office; a vacancy.

1567 *Burgh Rec. Peebles* (1872) 306 Nixt vaken that fallis within the towne of Peblis, that the said Thomas sones sall haif the samin.

vacant ('veɪkənt), *a.* and *sb.* Forms: 3-6 **vacaunt** (5 **vacavnt**), 4- **vacant**, 5-7 **vacante**. [a. OF. (also mod.F.) *vacant* (= It., Sp., Pg. *vacante*), or ad. L. *vacant-*, *vacans*, pres. pple. of *vacāre* to be empty, etc.: cf. prec. In early senses the evidence is scanty until the latter part of the 16th century or later.]

A. *adj.* **1. a.** Of a benefice, office, position, etc.: Not filled, held, or occupied; in respect of which a successor to the previous incumbent or holder has not been appointed.

Freq. of ecclesiastical benefices (see first group of quots.).

(*a*) *c* **1290** *S. Eng. Leg.* I. 72/51 Þe bischopriche of wiricestre vacaunt was and lere. **1338** R. Brunne *Chron.* (1810) 110 Þer Steuen..suore, þat if a bisshopriche vacant wer þe se, þe kyng, no non of his, suld chalange þat of fe. **1560** Daus tr. *Sleidane's Comm.* 237 b, Many churches lye vacant. **1577** Holinshed *Chron.* I. 223/1 The Pope had accursed the english people, bicause they suffred the Bishops seas to be vacant so long a time. **1611** in *10th Rep. Hist. MSS. Comm.* App. I. 546 There hath fallen vacant a benefice annexed to ye vicariat. **1671** J. Davies (*title*), The Ceremonies of the Vacant See: or a True Relation of what passes at Rome upon the Pope's Death. **1803** Nelson *Let. to R. Suckling* 23 Mar., Mr. Horace Suckling..is very anxious that you should present him to the vacant living. **1849** Macaulay *Hist. Eng.* vi. II. 95 The archbishopric of York was vacant. **1887** *New York Independent* 8 Sept. 16 One sixth of its churches are 'vacant', meaning of course, without pastors.

(*b*) **1432-50** tr. *Higden* (Rolls) IV. 381 That he myȝhte haue reioycede an oþer tetrarchye, beenge vacante þat tyme. *c* **1440** *Promp. Parv.* 507/2 Vacavnt, not occupyyd, *vacans.* **1560** Daus tr. *Sleidane's Comm.* 303 b, Yet hath no man hetherto desyred the same places..as common & vacant to be geven them. **1607** Shaks. *Timon* v. i. 145 Speciall Dignities, which vacant lye For thy best vse and wearing. **1681** Prideaux *Lett.* (Camden) 87 You may be assured y^t as soon as this or any other place is vacant you shall be put in into it. **1805** *Med. Jrnl.* XIV. 192 Dr. Arneman..has undertaken to superintend the foreign department of the Medical and Physical Journal, vacant by the decease of the late Dr. Noehden. **1849** Macaulay *Hist. Eng.* x. II. 634 If the throne was vacant the Estates of the Realm might place William in it. **1907** *Verney Mem.* I. 115 Three places had fallen vacant.

†**b.** Const. *of* (an incumbent or holder). *rare.*

1297 R. Glouc. (Rolls) 9697 Þe vifte was þat bissopriches & abbeies al so þat vacauns were of prelas in þe kinges hond were ido. **1432-50** tr. *Higden* (Rolls) II. 109 Northumbrelonde was vacante of a kynge viij^{the} yeres.

†**c.** Having no owner or possessor. *Obs.*

1560 Daus tr. *Sleidane's Comm.* 16 The goodes of the Empire, whiche shall chaunce to be vacant, he shall geve away to no man. **1730** Bailey (fol.), *Vacant Effects* (in *Law*) are such as are abandoned for want of an Heir, after the Death or Flight of their former Owner.

2. a. Devoid of all material contents or accessories; containing, or occupied by, nothing; unfilled, empty, void.

a **1400-50** *Alexander* 4774 For, fra it droȝe to þe derke ay till it dawid eftir, It was bot vacant & voide as vanite it were. [*c* **1450** *Godstow Reg.* 417 One voide place of ther owne lond.] *Ibid.* The forsaid vacant place of lond. **1634-5** Brereton *Trav.* (Chetham Soc.) 15 In the middle a square vacant place, wherein the moulded brick is disposed. **1671** Milton *Samson* 89 The Moon, When she deserts the night, Hid in her vacant interlunar cave. **1730-46** Thomson *Autumn* 329 The billowy plain..floats wide; nor can evade ..its [the blast's] seizing force; Or whirl'd in air, or into vacant chaff Shook waste. **1753** Hogarth *Anal. Beauty* 8 The vacant space within the shell. *Ibid.* 91 It fills up the vacant angle under the arm. **1791** Cowper *Iliad* xxiii. 472 Instant to his aid The Goddess hasted, to his vacant hand His whip restored. **1817** Jas. Mill *Brit. India* II. v. ix. 714 From that very moment, complaint was extinguished; and the voice of praise..occupied the vacant air. **1858** Glenny *Everyday Bk.* 76/2 All the plants that are strong enough.. may be planted in vacant places.

transf. *a* **1822** Shelley *Death* i. 6 All dead! those vacant names alone..remain. **1875** Jowett *Plato* (ed. 2) IV. 233 Philosophy was becoming more and more vacant and abstract.

b. Devoid of an occupant; not taken up by any one. Also *fig.*

1599 Shaks. *Much Ado* i. i. 304 But now..that warre-thoughts Haue left their places vacant, in their roomes Come [etc.]. **1602** Marston *Ant. & Mel.* ii. i, There's not a vacant corner of my heart, But all is fild with deade Antonios losse. **1667** Milton *P.L.* vii. 190 Instead Of Spirits maligne a better Race to bring Into thir vacant room. **1713** Young *Last Day* iii. 220 Satan's accurs'd desertion to supply, And fill the vacant stations of the sky. **1780** Burke *Œcon. Reform.* Wks. III. 279 The bleak winds..howling through the vacant lobbies, and clattering the doors of deserted guard-rooms. **1850** Tennyson *In Mem.* xx, To see the vacant chair, and think 'How good! how kind! and he is gone'. **1887** Ruskin *Præterita* II. 247 There was a spacious half of seat vacant in my little hooded carriage.

c. Of land, houses, etc.: Uninhabited, unoccupied, untenanted. Also, of a room: Not in use, disengaged.

1518 *Star Chamber Cases* (Selden) II. 146 About viij c howsesholdes in the same Towne desolate, vacante, and decayed. **1610** Holland *Camden's Brit.* iii, Let the old souldiers..enter upon the vacant lands. **1785** Paley *Mor. Philos.* (1818) II. 383 The new settlers will naturally convert their labour to the cultivation of the vacant soil. **1847** Helps *Friends in C.* (1851) I. 2 A house which had long been vacant in our neighbourhood. **1891** S. C. Scrivener *Our Fields & Cities* 140 There are at least a million and a-half acres likely to be vacant every autumn.

d. Marked or characterized by the absence of life, activity, or sound.

1791 Cowper *Iliad* ii. 68 Amid the stillness of the vacant night. **1850** Tennyson *In Mem.* xxxiv. 16 To drop head-foremost in the jaws Of vacant darkness and to cease. **1894** Hall Caine *Manxman* iii. iv. 136 Somewhere in the dead and vacant dawn Philip went to bed.

e. Of water: Free from ice; open.

1853 Kane *Grinnell Exp.* x. (1856) 71 In the morning of the 7th, a large vacant sheet of water showed itself to the westward.

3. a. With *of*. Devoid or destitute of, entirely lacking or free from, something.

a **1400-50** *Alexander* 5116 We at ere voide ay of vice & vacant of syn. *a* **1450** tr. *De Imitatione* iii. xxxii. 101 If þe state of þe herte be vacant of a riȝt fundement. **1613** Shaks. *Hen. VIII*, v. i. 125 My person, which I waigh not, Being of those Vertues [truth and honesty] vacant. **1634** Milton *Comus* 718 That no corner might Be vacant of her [i.e. Nature's] plenty. **1663** Bp. Patrick *Parab. Pilgr.* xxxii. (1687) 391 A company of select friends, vacant of business, and full of chearfulness, met together at one table. **1751** Franklin *Essays* Wks. 1840 II. 319 Was the face of the earth vacant of other plants, it might be sowed and over-spread with one kind only. **1784** R. Bage *Barham Downs* II. 7 The hour being vacant of business, he got upon his legs. **1842** Tennyson *Locksley Hall* 175, I, to herd with narrow foreheads, vacant of our glorious gains! **1910** Fairbairn *Stud. Rel. & Theol.* ii. ii. ii. 292 How could men vacant of good have affinities with Him [etc.]?

ellipt. **1582** N.T. (Rheims) *2 Peter* i. 8 They shal make you not vacant [L. *vacuos*], nor without fruite.

†**b.** Empty-handed; destitute. *Obs. rare.*

1430-40 Lydg. *Bochas* iv. vi. (MS. Bodl. 263), They banished hym neuer to come agayne: And so this tiraunt, vacant, wente in veyn Aboute the world as a fals Fugityff. **1576** in Collier *Illustr. E.E. Pop. Lit.* No. 16. 44 So that none of us went vacant away, But of one of the parties had honestly our paye.

4. a. Of time: Free from, unoccupied with, affairs, business, or customary work; leisure. Also const. *from* (an action or occupation).

Freq. from *c* 1550 to *c* 1750; now *Obs.* or *rare.*

(*a*) **1531** Elyot *Gov.* i. viii, Puttyng one to hym..in vacant tymes from other more serious lernynge. *Ibid.* xviii, Alexander, in tymes vacaunt from bataile, delyted in that maner huntinge. *a* **1548** Hall *Chron., Rich. III* (1550) 34 Such euyl persones as wyl not leue one houre vacant from doyng and exercysing crueltie. **1631** Byfield *Doctr. Sabb.* 80 *Feriarum*, that is, dayes vacant from pleading and labour.

(*b*) **1548** Udall, etc. *Erasm. Par. Luke* xiv, He wil with good laisure at a vacaunt time sitte down [etc.]. **1593** G. Harvey *Pierces Super.* To Rdr., Such scriblings are hardly worth the vacantest howers. **1605** Bacon *Adv. Learn.* i. ii. §7 The most active or busy man that hath been or can be, hath ..many vacant times of leisure. **1631** Gouge *God's Arrows* v. §9. 419 Vacant houres cannot better be spent then in the Artillery Garden. **1712** Addison *Spect.* No. 471 ¶3 The Memory relieves the Mind in her vacant Moments. **1781** Gibbon *Decl. & F.* xviii. (1787) II. 104 Chosroes.. consumed his vacant hours in the rural sports of hunting and hawking. **1805** T. Lindley *Voy. Brasil* (1808) 34 The females, who fill up their vacant hours with this elegant amusement. **1815** Jane Austen *Emma* I. iii. 35 Any vacant evening of his own blank solitude.

†**b.** Of persons: Not engaged or employed in (one's usual or regular) occupation or work; disengaged or free *from* labour or toil; at leisure; also, having nothing or little to do. *Obs.*

(*a*) **1600** Palfreyman *Bauldwin's Mor. Philos.* i. xliv. 28 When he was vacant from his labor, he wold write most eloquent..Comedies. *a* **1628** Preston *New Covt.* (1634) 152 Those that are vacant from such things are at rest.

(*b*) **1631** Byfield *Doctr. Sabb.* 154 They may be vacant as Christians. **1671** Milton *P.R.* ii. 116 For Satan with slye preface to return Had left him vacant. **1697** Potter *Antiq. Greece* i. xxvi. (1715) 158 If he can produce any vacant Person richer than himself. *a* **1763** Shenstone *Elegies* xix. 4 Another spring renews the soldier's toil, And finds me vacant in the rural cave. **1782** *Encycl. Brit.* (ed. 2) IX. 6933/2 In such excursions those vacant people [Laplanders] find a luxurious and ready repast in these fish.

absol. **1753** Smollett *Ct. Fathom* Ded., To instruct the ignorant, and entertain the vacant.

c. Characterized by, arising or proceeding from, absence of occupation, leisure, or idleness; undisturbed by business or work.

1615 Sandys *Trav.* 256 Here vacant Life, here Peace her empire keepes. **1630** Wotton *Lett.* (1907) II. 332 A great natural principle, that the vacantest thoughts are everywhere the worst. **1662** Gunning *Lent Fast* 202 A season of vacant attendance on fasting and prayer. **1766** Goldsm. *Vicar* v, Every morning waked us to a repetition of toil; but the evening repaid it with vacant hilarity. **1777** Macpherson *Ossian* Introd. 10 That poetical enthusiasm, which is better suited to a vacant and indolent state. **1866** R. Chambers *Ess. Fam. & Hum.* Ser. ii. 89 An idle and vacant life..is not calculated to be a happy one.

d. At leisure to devote oneself *to* some object. Also of things, open or accessible *to* some influence, etc. Now *rare* or *Obs.*

1631 Byfield *Doctr. Sabb.* 151 How much more ought Christians to bee vacant to God alone on the Lords day? **1660** H. More *Myst. Godl.* v. xiv. 172 Grotius,..who by reason of his Political emploiments could not be so entirely vacant to the searching into so abstruse a Mystery. **1685** Baxter *Paraphr. N.T.* 1 Tim. v. 13 Those that are taken up with Family Business of their own are not so vacant and liable to these Crimes. **1751** Johnson *Rambler* No. 111 ¶5 When the heart is vacant to every fresh form of delight. **1763** —— *Let. to Boswell* 8 Dec., Vacant to every object, and sensible of every impulse. **1838** Sir J. Stephen *Eccl. Ess.* II. 184 So long as they shall be vacant to record..contrite reminiscences of a desire for roasted goose.

†**e.** At leisure *for* something. *Obs.*$^{-1}$

1647 Clarendon *Hist. Reb.* viii. §147 Sir John Berkely,.. who was the more vacant for that service by the reduction of Barnstable.

5. a. Of the mind or brain: Devoid of or unoccupied with thought or reflection. Chiefly *poet.*

1579 Spenser *Sheph. Cal.* Oct. 100 The vaunted verse a vacant head demaundes, Ne wont with crabbed care the

Muses dwell. **1599** SHAKS. *Hen. V*, IV. i. 286 The wretched Slaue: Who with a body fill'd and vacant mind, Gets him to rest. **1770** GOLDSM. *Des. Vill.* 122 The loud laugh that spoke the vacant mind. **1781** COWPER *Retirem.* 624 Absence of occupation is not rest, A mind quite vacant is a mind distress'd. **1818** MISS FERRIER *Marriage* xv, The demon of ennui again took possession of her vacant mind. **1855** TENNYSON *Daisy* 106 Perchance, to lull the throbs of pain, Perchance, to charm a vacant brain.

†**b.** Abstracted or disengaged *from* (the body, etc.) in contemplation or reverie. *Obs.*⁻¹

1680 H. MORE *Apocal. Apoc.* 5, I was in the spirit on the Lord's day,..my mind being vacant from this earthly body, and external senses.

†**c.** Free from care or anxiety. *Obs. rare.*

a **1639** WOTTON in *Reliq.* (1685) 171 The Duke..even in the midst of so many diversions, had continually a very pleasant and vacant face (as I may well call it) proceeding no doubt from a singular assurance in his temper. **1723** STEELE *Conscious Lovers* II. i, Why so much Care in thy Countenance?.. You, who used to be so Gay, so Open, so Vacant!

6. a. Characterized by, exhibiting, or proceeding from, absence of intelligence or thought; expressionless, meaningless; inane.

1712 STEELE *Spect.* No. 515 ¶4 The vacant look of a fine Lady is not to be preserved, if she admits any thing to take up her Thoughts but her own dear Person. **1780** COWPER *Progr. Error* 205 Yet folly ever has a vacant stare. **1819** SHELLEY *Cenci* III. i. 277 Let me mask Mine own [looks] in some inane and vacant smile. **1830** J. G. STRUTT *Sylva Brit.* 31 The loud laugh of the woodpecker, joyous and vacant. **1841** JAMES *Brigand* i, His eyes gazed upon the scene, but with somewhat of a vacant aspect. **1878** B. TAYLOR *Deukalion* II. i. 56 Vacant are thine eyes, Cold thine insulted brow and mute thy lips.

b. Empty-headed, unthinking. *rare.*

1879 FROUDE *Cæsar* xii. 163 Metellus was a vacant aristocrat, to be depended on for resisting popular demands, but without insight otherwise.

7. a. *Comb.*, as ***vacant-eyed, -looking, -minded, -seeming*** adjs.; ***vacant-heartedness, -mindedness.***

1796 MME. D'ARBLAY *Camilla* III. 219 We all heard he was engaged to your beautiful vacant-looking cousin. **1836** POE in *Southern Lit. Messenger* Apr. 339/2 Not a broad, forced, loud vacant-minded joke, but a quiet, pungent, sly, laughter-moving conceit. **1846** MRS. GORE *Eng. Char.* (1852) 49 If they have formerly figured as beauties, the fickle voice of fashion now proclaims that they are 'pretty, certainly, but silly and vacant-looking'. **1879** HOWELLS *L. Aroostook* xviii, Her frivolity—her not so much vacant-mindedness as vacant-heartedness. **1883** J. MACKENZIE *Day-dawn Dark Places* 272, I have been saddened by the vacant-minded pupil. **1922** D. H. LAWRENCE *Aaron's Rod* xiii. 186 It was a large, vacant-seeming, Empire sort of drawing-room. **1936** L. H. MYERS *Strange Glory* II. ix. 150 A boy of about ten.., ill-nourished and vacant-eyed. **1965** J. A. MICHENER *Source* (1966) 59 From the shores of Morocco..came frightened, dirty, pathetic Jews, illiterate, often crippled with disease and vacant-eyed.

b. In phr. ***vacant possession***, with reference to premises (esp. those offered for sale): available for occupation by the purchaser, not occupied by the vendor or a tenant or tenants.

The legal interpretation of the term can be modified in certain circumstances by agreement between the vendor and the purchaser.

1825 H. ROSCOE *Treat. Law of Actions relating to Real Property* I. 546 Ejectment cannot be maintained, as on a vacant possession, where there is any thing left by the tenant on the premises, however trifling. **1883** *Wharton's Law-Lexicon* (ed. 7) 287/1 In case of vacant possession the writ may be served by posting a copy on some conspicuous part of the property. **1927** *Daily Tel.* 24 May 4/7 Vacant possession at Michaelmas will be given of the Manor Farm, 428 acres, at Oxwick. **1946** *Law Rep.* (King's Bench) 264 A vendor who leaves chattels of his own on property sold by him to an extent depriving the purchaser of the physical enjoyment of part of the property has failed to give vacant possession. **1973** *Country Life* 15 Mar. 713/1 The average price of vacant-possession farms in England is £273 an acre. **1976** *Morecambe Guardian* 7 Dec. 28/1 (Advt.), Three bedroom semi-detached house with vacant possession.

B. *sb.* †**1.** *Sc.* A vacant estate. *Obs.*⁻¹

c **1475** *Rauf Coilȝear* 758 And als the nixt vacant..That hapnis in France, quhair sa euer it fall, Forfaltour or fre waird..I gif the heir heritablily.

†**2.** One who has held office but is for the time being unemployed or in retirement. *Obs. rare.*

[**1602** SEGAR *Hon. Mil. & Civ.* IV. xxi. 236 These diuers degrees were in the Emperiall Court called Administrantes, Vacantes, and Honorarii.] *Ibid.* 237 Note likewise that the Officers whom we call Vacants are of two sorts.

†**3.** *pl.* A vacation. *Obs.*⁻¹

1647 MAY *Hist. Parl.* I. iii. 35 The next Terme, after the ordinary vacants, to be held at the Burgh of Dendie.

†**4.** *poet.* A vacant space; a vacuum. *Obs. rare.*

1712 BLACKMORE *Creation* v. 248 Ready by Turns to rise or to descend, Nature against a Vacant to defend. *Ibid.* VII. 355 Thou in the Vacant didst the Earth suspend.

Hence †'**vacant** *v.*, (*a*) *trans.* to render vacant, in various senses; to vacate; (*b*) *intr.* to take a vacation. *Obs. rare.*

1649 RAINBOW *Funeral Serm.* 29 May 30 She applyed her self vigorously to the setling of all things, which concerned the secular affairs of her Family, that so she might totally and wholly be vacanted to God. **1674** [Z. CAWDREY] *Catholicon* 18 Which Sacredness they know may be presently vacanted by the Prevalency of a greater opposite Power. **1752** *Scotland's Glory* 57 For getting Yule kept up Our highest courts vacanted.

vacantie, obs. var. VACANCY.

vacantly ('veɪkəntlɪ), *adv.* [f. VACANT *a.* + -LY².] In a vacant manner; †in freedom from business or work.

1615 SANDYS *Trav.* 288 Great is the difference between leading thy life vacantly and leading it slouthfully. **1817** SHELLEY *Rev. Islam* v. 1915 Its sculptured walls vacantly to the stroke of footfalls answered. **1839** DICKENS *Nickleby* xv, The back parlour sat with her mouth wide open staring vacantly at the collector, in a stupor of dismay. **1897** RHOSCOMYL *White Rose Arno* 322 Striding over to the place he laughed vacantly as he heard the story.

†'**vacantry.** *Obs.*⁻¹ [f. as prec. + -RY.] Vacancy, idleness, inoccupation.

1606 CHAPMAN *Hero & Leander* VI. 132 So serious is his trifling companie In all his swelling ship of vacantrie.

‖**vacat.** *Obs.* [L., 3rd sing. pres. ind. of *vacāre* to be vacant. Cf. VACATUR.] An annulment or abrogation.

1592 *Child-Marriages* 160 To thend that the Recognizaunce thereof may be Adnihilated and voyd, and a vacat therevpon to be entred. **1643** R. BAKER *Chron., Edw. II* 145 The want of his fathers blessing..without which a Vacat is set upon the labours of men. *a* **1672** TWYSDEN in *Spelman's Hist. Sacrilege* (1698) Add. 21, Matt. Paris.. having written that Marriage to have been *Contra Consilium Episc. Edmundi*, [he] did afterwards make a Vacat of it.

va'catable, *a.* [f. VACATE *v.* + -ABLE.] That may be vacated; capable of becoming vacant.

1895 *Westm. Gaz.* 16 May 2/1 The number of Liberal seats vacatable in England and Scotland.

†**vacate,** *pa. pple. Obs.*⁻¹ [ad. L. *vacātus*, pa. pple. of *vacāre*: see next.] Annulled, made legally void.

c **1688** *Vind. Proc. H.M. Eccl. Comm.* 54 The statute is Obsolete,..and must be esteemed as if it had been vacate and null.

vacate ('veɪkeɪt, və'keɪt), *v.* [ad. L. *vacāt-*, ppl. stem of *vacāre* to be empty, free, etc.]

1. a. *trans.* To make void in law; to deprive of legal authority or validity; to annul or cancel.

Very common in the 17–18th c. Now only in legal use.

1643 PRYNNE *Sov. Power Parl.* II. (ed. 2) 53 The King calling a Parliament at Winchester, utterly repealed and vacated those former Ordinances. **1677** MARVELL *Corr.* Wks. (Grosart) II. 538 If any one should spend before the day of election above ten pound,..it shall be accounted bribery, and vacate his choice. **1709** *Lond. Gaz.* No. 4538/1 All Entries..shall be vacated and cancelled. **1750** CARTE *Hist. Eng.* II. 158 Her relations..incited him [Hen. VIII] to remove the obstacles to his happiness, by vacating his marriage with Anne of Cleves. **1790** in Dallas *Amer. Law Rep.* I. 120 The court will confirm the Judgment as to one, and vacate it as to the other. **1817** W. SELWYN *Law Nisi Prius* (ed. 4) II. 1141 Such omission on the part of the officer will not vacate the contract. **1855** MACAULAY *Hist. Eng.* xxiii. V. 35 The opposition asked leave to bring in a bill vacating all grants of Crown property which had been made since the Revolution. **1883** *Law Times Rep.* XLIX. 133/1, I ..declare the deed to be void, and that it ought to be cancelled and the registration vacated.

b. *transf.* To deprive of force, efficacy, or value; to render inoperative, meaningless, or useless. Now *Obs.* or *rare.*

1655 GURNALL *Chr. in Arm.* (1669) 584/1 The Christians Creed doth not vacate the Ten Commandments. **1698** CHILCOT *Evil Thoughts* i. (1851) 4 Endeavouring to vacate the obligation of the fifth commandment. **1711** in G. Hickes *Two Treat. Chr. Priesth.* (1847) I. 323 A punctilio;..as such it is vacated by the universal practice of the Church. *a* **1791** WESLEY *To Servants* Wks. 1811 IX. 103 The character of the master..does not vacate the duty of the servant. **1802** PALEY *Nat. Theol.* I. i. §3. 6 These superfluous parts..would not vacate the reasoning which we had instituted concerning other parts. **1827** R. HALL *Wks.* (1832) VI. 414 They.. inculcated the obligation of circumcision,..thereby vacating and superseding the sacrifice of Christ. **1895** 'MARK TWAIN' in *N. Amer. Rev.* July 3 In the 'Deerslayer' tale this rule is vacated.

c. To remove or withdraw (a record).

1769 BLACKSTONE *Comm.* IV. 128 Imbezzling or vacating records..is a felonious offence against public justice.

2. a. To make or render (a post or position) vacant; to deprive of an occupant or holder.

1697 J. LEWIS *Mem. Dk. Glocester* (1789) 80 As a Garter was vacated by the death of Lord Strafford. **1751** T. SHARP in *Lett. Lit. Men* (Camden) 375 Some of the Bishopricks vacated by the deprivation of the Nonjur. Bishops. **1765** BLACKSTONE *Comm.* I. 152 Suppose..that the whole royal line should at any time fail, and become extinct, which would indisputably vacate the throne. **1828** LYTTON *Pelham* I. xxv, One of the seats in your uncle's borough..is every day expected to be vacated. **1871** FREEMAN *Norm. Conq.* (1876) IV. xxi. 678 Hadrian de Castello sought the death of Pope Leo in order to vacate the throne which, when it was vacated, was filled by Hadrian of Utrecht.

b. To leave (an office, position, etc.) vacant by death, resignation, or retirement; to give up, relinquish, or resign the holding or possession of.

1850 THACKERAY *Pendennis* lxv, Pen..promised that he would give his election dinner there, when the Baronet should vacate his seat in the young man's favour. **1875** M. ARNOLD *Ess. Crit.* (ed. 3) Pref. p. x *note*, When the above was written the author had still the Chair of Poetry at Oxford, which he has since vacated.

c. *absol.* To give up an office or position.

1812 in *Examiner* 30 Nov. 763/1 As soon as the forms of the House will admit of a Member vacating, in consequence of a double return. **1894** BOASE *Exeter Coll.* (O.H.S.) p. lxxix, A Devonshire fellowship was given to Maurice Ley,.. but Ley soon vacated.

3. a. To leave or withdraw from (a place, seat, etc.); to quit or give up.

1791 MRS. RADCLIFFE *Rom. Forest* iv, It was most probable that if the officers..found the abbey vacated, they would quit before morning. **1832** G. DOWNES *Lett. Cont. Countries* I. 172 The English ladies..had caused their servant to insult one of the collegians..in the hope that they would vacate the premises. **1856** KANE *Arct. Expl.* II. v. 61, I have determined..to remove him to the berth Riley has vacated.

b. *absol.* To give up possession or occupancy of a house, etc.

1854 THOREAU *Walden* 48, I to pay four dollars and twenty-five cents to-night, he to vacate at five to-morrow morning. **1856** MISS MULOCK *J. Halifax* xiv, So we vacated; and all that long Sunday we sat in the parlour lately our neighbour's.

4. *intr.* †**a.** To devote one's time, to give oneself up, *to* something. *Obs. rare.*

1685 EVELYN *Mrs. Godolphin* (1888) 7 Prescribeing to herselfe a constant method of devotion,..that she might the better vacate to holy dutyes. *a* **1706** —— *Hist. Relig.* (1850) II. 260 There must be deacons and deaconesses,..so that the preachers may wholly vacate to the Word.

†**b.** To withdraw oneself *from* (a task). *Obs.*⁻¹

1665 G. HARVEY *Adv. agst. Plague* 1, I might justly vacate from this task, having so lately amused my self about a Tract of the French Contagion.

c. *U.S.* To give up work for a time; to take a holiday or vacation.

1836 *Knickerbocker* VII. 15 Ned and I were vacating..at his father's charming residence. **1885** *Advance* (Chicago) 23 July 476 One thing he [a Chinaman] can never learn, and that is how to vacate.

Hence **va'cated** *ppl. a.*

1791 *On Relig. Fashionable World* 114 It is the very genius of christianity to extirpate all selfishness, on whose vacated ground benevolence..plants itself. **1831** I. TAYLOR *Edwards' Freed. Will* Prefat. Essay p. xxxix, They find a deserted city and vacated palaces. **1863** DANA *Man. Geol.* 727 Leaving the rock either side of the vacated space to be pressed together. **1903** W. BRIGHT *Age of Fathers* II. xxx. 94 The priest Eugenius..was rewarded by promotion to the vacated see.

vacating (və'keɪtɪŋ), *vbl. sb.* [f. VACATE *v.*]

1. The action of annulling, making void, or depriving of legal authority or validity.

1648 (*title*), A Declaration of the Commons of England,.. expressing their reasons for the Adnulling and Vacating of these Ensuing Votes. **1691** T. H[ALE] *Acc. New Invent.* p. xcvii, How..several Lord Mayors..prosecuted the vacating of Patents that they judged entrenching on the Conservacy. **1764** T. HUTCHINSON *Hist. Mass.* ii. (1765) 229 From the restoration until the vacating the charter. **1818** CRUISE *Digest* (ed. 2) V. 227 Such a method as the vacating a statute long before extinguished.

2. The action of giving up, leaving, or relinquishing.

1820 SOUTHEY *Wesley* I. 121 He therefore looked upon himself to be fully discharged from that cure by the vacating of his primary design. **1855** BREWSTER *Newton* I. iv. 98 The expected vacating of his Fellowship. **1905** *Sat. Rev.* 23 Sept. 397/2 The vacating of a Warden's residence.

vacating (və'keɪtɪŋ), *ppl. a.* [f. VACATE *v.* + -ING².] That is retiring from office, etc.

1921 *Act 11 & 12 Geo. V* c. 21 Sched. 1. 6 Where the unexpired portion of the term of office of the vacating member is less than one year. **1981** *N.Y. Times* 18 Jan. XI. 20 Mrs. Kennelly suggested that the leader of the Senate or the House from the party of the vacating member be able to appoint a substitute legislator.

vacation (və'keɪʃən), *sb.* Forms: 4–5 **vacacioun**, 5 **vacacyone, -cione, -cyoun, wacacion(e**, 5–6 **vacacion** (6 **-cyon**), 6 **vacatione**, 5– **vacation.** [a. OF. (also mod.F.) *vacation* (= It. *vacazione*, Sp. *vacacion*, Pg. *vacação*), or ad. L. *vacātiōn-*, *vacātio* (med.L. also *vacācio*), f. *vacāre*: see VACATE *v.*]

I. 1. a. Freedom, release, or rest *from* some occupation, business, or activity.

c **1386** CHAUCER *Wife's Prol.* 684 Whan he hadde leyser and vacacioun From oother worldly occupacioun. **1531** ELYOT *Gov.* I. ii, What vacacion had they from the warres? **1575** LANEHAM *Let.* (1871) 12 The forenoon occupied..in quiet and vacation from woork. **1621** BRATHWAIT *Nat. Embassie* (1877) 156 Admit of no vacation, saue onely vacation from vice. **1690** R. LUCAS *Humane Life* 245 The life of the sluggish is but a waking dream, a vacation from all business. **1865** W. G. PALGRAVE *Arabia* II. 165 Especially during the days of vacation from ordinary business.

b. Without const. Freedom or respite from work, etc.; time of rest or leisure.

c **1425** WYNTOUN *Cron.* v. iv. 777 Bot þai war til Sancte Petyr ay Helparis in his lattyr day, Qwhen he gaf his vacacion Al hail til his deuocion. **1548** UDALL, etc. *Erasm. Par. John* viii. 58 A secrete place, or some vacacion is conuenient for preachers of the gospell. **1570** T. NORTON *Nowel's Catech.* (1853) 129 When, resting from worldly business.., and as it were having a certain holy vacation. **1610** HEALEY *St. Aug. Citie of God* XII. xvii. (1620) 435 His vacation is not idle, sloathfull nor sluggish. **1655** FULLER *Ch. Hist.* I. iv. 20 The Primitive Confessours were so taken up with what they endured, they had no vacation largely to relate their own or other Sufferings.

transf. **1639** FULLER *Holy War* II. xii. (1840) 66 After the tempest of a long war,..king Baldwin had a five years vacation of peace in his old age.

†**c.** Leisure for, or devoted to, some special purpose; hence, occupation, business. *Obs*

c **1450** tr. *De Imitatione* III. lviii. 135 Put þe vacacion of god [L. *Dei vacationem*] before all oþer þinges. **1549** *Compl. Scot.* vi. 45 Ther principal vacatione vas on the neuresing of bestialite. *Ibid.*, Ther is na faculte, stait, nor vacatione.. that can be conparit til oure stait. **1603** FLORIO *Montaigne* II. xii. 308 She [Philosophy] ascribeth no other consultation [to the Gods], nor imputeth other vacation vnto them. **1627** W. SCLATER *Exp. 2 Thess.* (1629) 2 Charity, which is the vtmost pretended aime of single life, and wilfull pouertie, whole Vacation to the Contemplation of the glorious Deitie. **1654** HAMMOND *Fundam.* xi. Wks. 1674 I. 298 The inestimable benefit of peace, and quiet and vacation for piety.

†**d.** Absence from duty or from some usual post; also, a sum paid for absence or exemption.

1461-83 in *Househ. Ord.* (ed. 4) 32 Savynge the right of the countynghouse in chekking them for theire vacations or for lak of recordes. **1472-3** *Rolls of Parlt.* VI. 57/1 Sommes of money.. abated of the fees.. of any of the said Souldeours ..for the vacations and absence oute of the said Toune. **1583** MELBANCKE *Philotimus* Q ij b, Parmenio his tongue was very fine and voluble to run ouer his masters whole life this time of vacation from his mistris. **1591** SAVILE *Tacitus, Hist.* I. lviii. 33 Vitellius.. paies the vacations to the Centurions out of his cofers.

2. a. A period during which there is a formal suspension of activity; one or other part of the year during which law-courts, universities, or schools are suspended or closed; holidays.

c **1456** PECOCK *Bk. of Faith* (1909) 228 Hou myche labour is maad in ynnes of Court in Loundoun, bi tymes of vacacioun, aboute the reding.. of the Kingis Statutis. *c* **1460** FORTESCUE *Abs. & Lim. Mon.* xv. (1885) 148 How mony owres off the day this counsell shall sytt, when thai shall haue any vacasion. **1529** *Sel. Cases Star Chamber* (Selden) II. 36 We dyd apoynte them there to mete ageyne at the vacacion of Christmas last past. **1600** SHAKS. *A.Y.L.* III. ii. 349 [Time stays] With Lawiers in the vacation: for they sleepe betweene Terme and Terme. **1617** MORYSON *Itin.* III. 10, I judge Lawyers and Officers more happy, who have their Termes to live in the City, and their Vacations to returne into the Countrey. *a* **1668** DAVENANT *Play-ho. to be Let.* I. i, We are standing Properties of the Play-house, which, in Vacation, lye in pawn for the Rent. **1722** DE FOE *Plague* (Rtldg.) 29 It being in the Time of the Vacation. **1771** *Phil. Trans.* LXI. 324 The young nobleman,.. whom I accompanied to his seat from the university, during the Christmas-vacation. **1796** BURKE *Let. Noble Lord* Wks. VIII. 35 Every honest father of a family.. will pray that there may be a very long vacation in all such schools. **1818** CRUISE *Digest* (ed. 2) V. 216 For no other reason, perhaps, but because the fine was levied in the vacation, and was dated as of the preceding term. **1829** LYTTON *Disowned* vi, To this house Algernon was constantly consigned during his vacations from school. **1904** MRS. CREIGHTON *Life Bp. Creighton* I. x. 308 In the Easter Vacation we went for a short walking tour in Norfolk.

transf. **1642** FULLER *Holy & Prof. St.* IV. i. 242 Wherefore in the midst of the Term of his businesse he makes himself a vacation to speak with them. *c* **1656** USSHER *Ann.* (1658) 814 The King of Kings forbore his hunting and feasting of the Nobles, which is a Kinde of Vacation among the Parthians.

b. *long vacation* (see LONG *a.*[1] 18).

a **1601** SIR T. FANSHAWE *Pract. Exch.* (1658) 160 In every long vacation all the bills.. and other pleadings are to be taken from the common files. **1631** T. ADAMS in *Lett. Lit. Men* (Camden) 150 The arabick Lecture.. to be entred upon after that long vacation following. **1693** [see LONG *a.* 18]. **1706** HEARNE *Collect.* (O.H.S.) I. 215 In ye Long-Vacation [he] made an Excursion. **1825-** [see LONG *a.* 18]. **1882** H. C. MERIVALE *Faucit of B.* v, When season, reading-party, and long vacation were all over,.. much distressed was the Oxford world [etc.].

c. A holiday. Chiefly *U.S.*

1878 *Masque of Poets* 177 At Saratoga, where you meet all grades of well-dressed people spending short vacations. **1888** A. K. GREEN (Mrs. Rohlfs) *Behind Closed Doors* vi, She went away for a short vacation a few days ago.

d. *attrib.*, as *vacation-exercise*, *-task*, *-time*, etc.

1628 MILTON (*title*), At a Vacation Exercise in the Colledge. *a* **1668** DAVENANT *Play-ho. to be Let* Wks. (1673) 75 Good, Sir, no French translation till the Tearm; It is too precious for Vacation-ware. **1721** AMHERST *Terræ Fil.* No. 47 (1726) 251 Every monday throughout the year, in vacation-time as well as in term-time. **1797** in Fowler *Hist. C.C.C.* (O.H.S.) 298 This Vacation exercise, the subject of which will be communicated to him at the usual time. **1828** LYTTON *Pelham* II. xiii, It is now vacation time, and I have come to town with the idea of holding lectures on the state of education. **1844** TALFOURD (*title*), Vacation Rambles and Thoughts. **1894** LD. COLERIDGE in *Life* (1904) II. xii. 382, I am smitten once more with the fate of Vacation Judge. **1904** 'M. Y. HALIDOM' *Weird Transform.* x. 84 What with his walks and his vacation tasks, small danger was apprehended.

3. †**a.** A state or period characterized by the intermission or absence *of* something. *Obs.*

1567 ALLEN *Def. Priesth.* Pref., In this pitifull vacation and long lacke of the practise of priesthoode. **1630** LENNARD tr. *Charron's Wisd.* (1658) 31 Whereby followeth a kind of intermission and vacation of the actions. **1677** TEMPLE *Let. to Hyde* Wks. 1720 II. 474 We have had since Monday last, a perfect Vacation of all Affairs. *a* **1711** KEN *Preparatives* Poet. Wks. 1721 IV. 115 Sleep's a Vacation of our Pow'rs, And innocently wastes our Hours.

†**b.** A cessation *from* something.

1617 in *Buccleuch MSS.* (Hist. MSS. Comm.) I. 184 This day is here Good Friday, and such a dead vacation from all kind of business, as I can now add little to this letter. *c* **1770** ELIZ. CARTER *Lett.* (1808) 96 That dead vacation from all present hopes and fears that stupifies the retirement of a convent.

c. A state or period of inactivity.

1644 BULWER *Chiron.* 116 The inconvenience of this cold vacation in the Hand, gave being to that Axiome in Rhetorique [etc.]. **1660** BOYLE *New Exp. Phys. Mech.* Pref. p. viii, The occasional vacations of the Press, by reason of Festivals, or the absence of the Corrector. **1862** STANLEY *Jew. Ch.* (1877) I. iv. 75 The city was in a state of comparative desolation;.. a vacation of centuries had passed over it.

4. A time of freedom, release, or respite (*from* something).

1614 RALEIGH *Hist. World* III. xii. 125 The Mantinæans, finding the war to be carried from their wals,.. would use the commodity of that vacation. **1639** FULLER *Holy War* I. vi, The longest vacation from persecution they enjoyed was when Charles was Emperor of the West. **1670** COTTON *Espernon* I. iv. 189 Giving himself a vacation from the hardships of War. **1714** R. FIDDES *Pract. Disc.* II. 100 Such times should be vacations from the common business and affairs of human life. **1748** tr. *Vegetius Renatus* 244 Let.. a Vacation from Labour be given him.

II. †**5. a.** The fact of an office or post becoming or being vacant; the time during which the vacancy lasts. *Obs.*

Chiefly in ecclesiastical use: see (*a*).

(*a*) *c* **1425** WYNTOUN *Cron.* VIII. xxxiii. 5897 In til a wacacione þai walde noucht mak electione Twys. **1454** *Rolls of Parlt.* V. 247/1 Of all.. voidaunce of Bisshopriches, Abbeys and Prioryes, tyme of vacation [etc.]. **1533-4** *Act 25 Hen. VIII*, c. 21 §16 All.. licences.. shall (during the vacation of the same see) be.. graunted vnder the name and seale of the gardiane of the spiritualities. **1560** DAUS tr. *Sleidane's Comm.* 366 b, Bishopprickes aboute lxxxxvi, by the vacations whereof, as they terme it, is caried to Rome a wonderful some of gold. **1602** SEGAR *Hon. Mil. & Civ.* IV. xxiv. 244 If it fall out that the Archbishop of Canterburie be not there, by the vacation of his See, then the Archbishop of Yorke is to take his place. **1655** FULLER *Ch. Hist.* IX. 71 Certain lands assumed by the Queen from some Bishopricks during their vacation. **1709** STRYPE *Ann. Ref.* I. vi. 98 All arrearages of subsidies and tenths past in the days of their predecessors, and in times of vacation.

(*b*) **1542** HEN. VIII *Decl. War Scots* D ij, All castels & holdes were surrendred to him as to the superior lord in the tyme of vacation. **1560** DAUS tr. *Sleidane's Comm.* 16 That he shall ratifie that which was done in the vacation of thempire, by the countie Palatine. **1614** RALEIGH *Hist. World* II. xxii. 475 But we are now arrived at a meere vacation, wherein the Crown of Juda lay voyd eleven whole yeares. **1632** LITHGOW *Trav.* III. 89 This commonly they practise in euery such like vacation, which otherwise, they durst neuer attempt.

†**b.** A vacant post; a vacancy. *Obs.*

1535 CROMWELL in Merriman *Life & Lett.* (1902) I. 398, I hertely desyre & pray you.. to graunt vnto the said Robert the next vacacion of one of the iiii Clarkes of that your courte.

†**6.** The fact of a house being unoccupied or untenanted; loss of rent due to this. *Obs.*

1479-81 *Rec. St. Mary at Hill* (1905) 96 Vacacions. In primys, syr Rafis chambyr, voyde by ij quarters, the quarter at ij s iij d. *Ibid.* 192 Item, ffor the wacacion of the howse that Wylliam Raynsford dwellyd in, for iij quarters, xx s.

†**7.** Empty space; vacuity. *Obs.*[−1]

1743 *Lond. & Country Brew.* III. (ed. 2) 211, I am of Opinion nothing less than four or five Feet high Vacation ought to be allowed.. in order to break the Force of such an Ebullition, by thus giving it Room enough to expand.

III. †**8.** The action of voiding or evacuating.

1607 MARKHAM *Cavel.* VII. (1617) 33 From fulnes, as from surfeit of meate or drink, or the want of vacation of humors.

9. The action of vacating, of leaving (or being left) vacant or unoccupied.

1860 *Players* 14 Apr. 121 Since Mr Kean's vacation of the Princess's, Miss Murray has joined the present company at the St. James's Theatre. **1876** CLARK RUSSELL *Is he the Man?* II. 2 The servants were ignorant of the true reason of old Mrs. Ransome's sudden vacation of the house. **1884** *Manch. Exam.* 29 May 5/2 The Viceroyalty of India.. will then be on the point of vacation by the Marquis of Ripon. **1892** *Sat. Rev.* 22 Oct. 465/1 Seats chosen for vacation by the Gladstonians themselves.

IV. 10. *Comb.*, as **vacation home** *U.S.*, a house used by the owner for holidays or at weekends (cf. *holiday home* (*b*) s.v. HOLIDAY *sb.* 4 a); **vacation job**, paid employment for a student during vacation from a university, polytechnic, etc.; **vacation-land** *U.S.*, an area attracting holiday-makers.

1969 'E. LATHEN' *When in Greece* xiii. 146 The whole area is honeycombed with vacation homes. **1978** D. WILLIAMS *Treasure up in Smoke* iv. 40 A big-spending visitor who maintained a vacation home. **1971** *Guardian* 23 July 6/7, 24,400 students registered for vacation jobs. **1977** D. JAMES *Spy at Evening* x. 68, I had.. managed to get a vacation job as reserve stoker in a block of flats. **1927** *Scribner's Mag.* Apr. 100 The glories of Yellowstone Park take on new meaning this year with our discovery of Gallatin Gateway! It is the great sensation of vacation-land. **1977** *Chicago Tribune* 2 Oct. IV. 18/1 The region is a vacationland of great variety. There are spas, county fairs, antiques and crafts shows, [etc.].

Hence **va'cation** *v. intr.*, to take a vacation or holiday; **va'cationing** *ppl. a.* and *vbl. sb.* (*U.S.*); **va'cationer**, (*a*) orig. *U.S.*, a holiday-maker; (*b*) a vacation-student; **va'cationist**, = prec. (*a*); **va'cationless** *a.*, having no vacation or holidays.

1896 *Advance* (Chicago) 27 Aug. 273 Despite hard times, people will go *vacationing. **1890** *Advance* (Chicago) 28 Aug., The 'swallows homeward fly'; and so, by sea and land, do *vacationers and tourists. **1898** *Atlantic Monthly* LXXXII. 491/1 It did my vacationer's heart good to see men so cheerfully industrious. **1904** *Middle Temple Rec., Min. Parlt.* I. 389 The following vacationers are fined 20s. each for absence from Mr. Daston's reading. **1961** *Times* 28 Nov. 13/7 The organized and the individual vacationers. **1967** *Idle Moments* (Austral.) Sept. 27/3 The vacationer's body also will have reduced metabolic needs which may take two or three weeks for adjustment. **1926** *Scribner's Mag.* Aug. 7/2 Advice to *vacationing young folks: In the dog days, don't be too Sirius. **1976** *National Observer* (U.S.) 24 Jan. 8/2 (Advt.), *Off-the-Beaten Path* names the really low cost Florida retirement and vacationing towns. **1978** *Detroit Free Press* 16 Apr. (Parade Suppl.) 13/1 Increasingly, vacationing Americans are taking to the woods, mountains, deserts and seashores. **1885** *Field* 18 Apr. 511 The *vacationist in quest of bracing air.. will find in Tyrol many places to suit him. **1892** *Ibid.* 2 July 25/2 Rivers.. attractive to the summer vacationist. **1891** *Advance* (Chicago) 25 June, I dislike to go away leaving people *vacationless who deserve an outing more than I do.

‖**va'catur.** *Obs.* [L. *vacātur*, 3rd sing. pres. ind. pass. of *vacāre*: cf. VACAT.] An annulment.

1682 *Lond. Gaz.* No. 1739/3 Whether Your Majesty will be pleased to order a *Vacatur* to be entred upon the Enrollment of the Charter now surrendred. **1811** in *Rep. Commis. Publ. Rec. Irel.* (1815) 71 For every Vacatur—(This seldom happens, not one having occurred these six years back), £2. 17. 11.

'vaccarage. *rare.* [See next and -AGE. Cf. also med.L. *vaccagium*.] = next.

1895 *Linc. N. & Q.* IV. 131 The vaccaria, vaccarages, or cow-pastures attached to the Abbey.

vaccary ('vækərɪ). Now only *Hist.* Also 5-6 **vaccarie**, 6 **vacchari**e, 7 **vacharie**. [ad. med.L. *vaccaria*, f. L. *vacca* cow. Cf. VACHERY, and Pg. *vacaria* herd of cows.] A place where cows are kept or pastured; a dairy-farm.

1471 in *Archaeol.* XLVII. 195 Th'issues, prouffites, and revenues coming.. of the ferme of the vaccarie of Sleigholme. **1545** *Act 37 Hen. VIII*, c. 16 One parcell of lond called the Vaccharie, conteyninge by estimacion threscore Acres. **1594** CROMPTON *Jurisd.* 194 Without warrant no subiect may haue within the forest a vaccarie. **1656** BLOUNT *Glossogr.*, *Vaccary*, alias *vacharie*, seemes to be a house to keep kine or cowes in. [Hence in Phillips, etc.] **1815** DICKSON *Lancashire* 13 The Forest of Wyersdale.. being distributed into twelve different tracts.. which still retain the ancient title of *vaccaries* or cow-pastures. [**1863** J. R. WALBRAN *Mem. Fountains Abbey* (Surtees) 343 *note*, To render annually of the profits of the vaccary twenty six stones eight pounds of butter.]

vacche(n, southern ME. var. FETCH *v.*

vacci- ('væksɪ), combining form of L. *vacca* cow, as in **'vaccicide**, the killing of a cow; **vacci'mulgence**, milking of cows.

Also, in recent Dicts., *vaccigenous* (for **vaccinigenous*) adj., 'producing vaccine'.

1796 COLERIDGE *Biog. Lit.* (1845) II. 381 Will you try to look out for a fit servant for us,.. scientific in vaccimulgence? That last word is a new one. **1900** M. C. WILSON *Irene Petrie* xi. 249 In Kashmir vaccicide is a capital crime.

†**'vaccin.** *Obs.*[−1] [ad. L. *vaccīn-ium*.] (See VACCINIUM.)

1589 FLEMING *Virg. Georg.* x. 38 What then, if Amint bee Both blacke (and swart) so violets and vaccins too are blacke.

'vaccinable, *a.* [f. VACCIN-ATE *v.*] Capable of being successfully vaccinated.

1899 in *Syd. Soc. Lex.*

vaccinal ('væksɪnəl, væk'saɪnəl), *a.* [f. VACCINE *sb.* + -AL[1], or a. F. *vaccinal* (1812).] Of or pertaining to, connected with, vaccine or vaccination.

1888 *Encycl. Brit.* XXIV. 26/2 The vaccinal eruption, especially on the scalp. *Ibid.* 27/1 Epidemics of vaccinal sore arms. **1899** *Daily News* 6 March 8/5 An inspector comes down to inquire into the vaccinal condition of the sufferers.

vaccinate ('væksɪneɪt), *v.* [f. VACCINE *a.* Cf. F. *vacciner* (*a* 1803), It. *vaccinare*, Pg. *vaccinar*, Sp. *vacunar*.]

1. a. *trans.* To inoculate with the virus of cow-pox as a protection against smallpox.

1803 RING *Treat. Cow-pox* II. 1026 A French physician.. having vaccinated the son of the English Consul. *Ibid.* 1027 A number of those who were vaccinated in New England. *c* **1825** S. M. LLOYD *Tommy Sole* 2 When her only child, Tommy, was at a proper age, Mr. Howard proposed to vaccinate him. [*Foot-note*, To inoculate him with the cow-pox.] **1856** MISS MULOCK *J. Halifax* xxv, Rather against Ursula's wish, I vaccinated the children.

fig. **1809** SOUTHEY in *Q. Rev.* I. 212 It might be supposed their ablutions at the cow's tail vaccinated them against the contagion of any other religion. **1872** O. W. HOLMES *Poet Breakf.-t.* x, There are teachers.. who vaccinate the two childhoods with wholesome doctrine. **1892** ZANGWILL *Child. Ghetto* II. 3 Who will vaccinate him against free-thinking as I would have done?

b. *transf.* To inoculate with a vaccine.

1882 E. KLEIN in *11th Ann. Rep. Local Govt. Board* in *Parl. Papers* (C. 3337. 1) XXX. II. 509 In Pasteur's case the sheep inoculated with such bacilli.. are not killed by anthrax, but 'vaccinated', and protected. **1904** *Brit. Med. Jrnl.* 10 Sept. 574 By vaccinating animals.. with a strongly neurotoxic poison. **1955** [see POLIO 1]. **1983** *Oxford Times* 3 June 18/2 Women are being urged to check that they have been vaccinated against German measles after a serious outbreak of the disease.

2. *intr.* To perform or practise vaccination.

1837 MACAULAY *Ess., Ld. Bacon* (1897) 404 The Baconian takes out a lancet and begins to vaccinate. **1843** MARRYAT *M. Violet* xviii, As I have before mentioned, the Shoshones vaccinate. **1878** [see VACCINE *sb.* 2].

3. *trans.* To inject by or in vaccination.

1868 SEATON *Handbk. Vaccination* 22 When lymph raised in cows by retro-vaccination is vaccinated back to the human subject.

Hence **'vaccinated** *ppl. a.*, **'vaccinating** *vbl. sb.* and *ppl. a.*

1808 REECE *Med. Dict.* s.v. *Cow-pox*, The proportion of *vaccinated persons. **1876** BRISTOWE *Th. & Pract. Med.* (1878) 177 Sometimes a roseolous rash spreads over the vaccinated limb. **1888** *Encycl. Brit.* XXIV. 29/1 Do the vaccinated escape in an epidemic? **1867** *Chambers's Encycl.* IX. 688/2 The method of *vaccinating and the phenomena of cow-pox. **1868** BALLARD *Vaccination* 355 The puncture of the vaccinating lancet. **1897** *Allbutt's Syst. Med.* II. 715 An active vaccinating material.

vaccination (væksɪ'neɪʃən). [f. VACCINE *a.* Cf. F. *vaccination* (*a* 1803), It. *vaccinazione* (1809), Pg. *vaccinação*, Sp. *vacunacion*.]

1. a. The action or practice of inoculating with vaccine matter as a preventative of smallpox.

1800 R. DUNNING (*title*), Some observations on vaccination, and the inoculated cow-pox. **1802** *Rep. Committees, Ho. Commons* XIV. 187 Vaccination has justly called forth their particular attention. **1813** *Examiner* 26 April 264/2 Prior to the introduction of vaccination, several hundreds annually died of the small pox. **1846** BRITTAN tr. *Malgaigne's Man. Oper. Surg.* 60 Vaccination comprises the modes of collecting the vaccine, and of inoculating. **1876** BRISTOWE *Th. & Pract. Med.* (1878) 178 Small-pox has died out..in exact proportion as efficient vaccination has been generalised.

b. The inoculation of an individual with any vaccine in order to induce or increase immunity. [The use of the term for diseases other than smallpox is due to Pasteur (*Trans. 7th Session Internat. Med. Congr.* (1881) I. 90).]

1891 *Nature* 3 Sept., To the old dangerous method.., Pasteur had added the less dangerous one of preventive inoculation by means of an attenuated virus, to which he had applied the term vaccination. **1896** *Lancet* 19 Sept. 809/2 These anti-cholera inoculations have served as a pattern for the typhoid vaccinations. **1897** *Allbutt's Syst. Med.* II. 711 The vaccination [with anti-rabic fluid] is usually made into the subcutaneous connective tissues of the sheep. **1955** *Sci. Amer.* Apr. 44/3 Tests show that antibody persists for an appreciable time after vaccination with the killed-virus vaccine. **1978** T. R. BOWRY *Immunol. Simplified* iv. 14 Cholera vaccination is still required for travel to a few countries.

2. *attrib.*, as ***vaccination act, defaulter, law, mark, officer, scar***, etc.

1867 *Chambers's Encycl.* IX. 690/1 In 1841, the Vaccination Act was passed. **1888** *Encycl. Brit.* XXIV. 28 To make the vaccination law more stringent. *Ibid.* 30 To certify to the vaccination officer the fact of vaccination. **1897** *Daily News* 18 Sept. 3/3 Inflicting repeated penalties on vaccination defaulters. **1897** *Allbutt's Syst. Med.* II. 627 Any case of cancer affecting the vaccination scar. **1899** A. E. HOUSMAN in *Univ. College Gaz.* 22 Mar. 34/2 Vain his laced boots, and vain his eyebrow dark, And vain, ah! vain, his vaccination mark. **1914** D. H. LAWRENCE *Widowing of Mrs. Holroyd* III. 92 And such arms on 'im! Look at the vaccination marks, Lizzie. **1983** *N.Y. Times* 20 Mar. 13/1 Her face was as powdered and pitted as the vaccination mark on her arm.

Hence **vacci'nationist**, a believer in the efficacy of vaccination.

1885 *Pall Mall G.* 24 Mar. 2/1 This and similar allegations form the sheet-anchor of the vaccinationist.

vaccinator ('væksɪneɪtə(r)). [f. VACCINATE *v.* Cf. F. *vaccinateur*, It. *vaccinatore*, Pg. *vaccinador*, Sp. *vacunador*.]

1. One who performs, practises, or advocates vaccination.

1808 REECE *Med. Dict.* s.v. *Cow-pox*, How the vaccinators account for this, I am at a loss to conjecture. **1863** *Times* 25 Apr., Many public vaccinators, it is said, are wholly incompetent to perform their duty. **1897** *Allbutt's Syst. Med.* II. 590 In another case the vaccinator..died of erysipelas.

2. An instrument used in performing vaccination.

1875 in KNIGHT *Dict. Mech.* 2686/1. **1897** *Allbutt's Syst. Med.* II. 633 Cases of..septic infection have been known to follow the use of some mechanical vaccinator.

Comb. **1885** HARRIES tr. *Warlomont's Anim. Vaccination* 124 [An] apparatus which we have called the vaccinator-trephine.

'vaccinatory, *a. rare.* [f. VACCINATE *v.*] Used for, connected with, vaccination; vaccine.

1828 *Blackw. Mag.* XXIV. 834 Quassia might be distributed gratis at Apothecary's Hall, as vaccinatory matter is at the Cow-pox Hospital. **1880** *Daily News* 25 May 5/7 Pus just as efficacious for vaccinatory purposes as the lymph habitually used.

vaccine ('væksiːn, -ɪn, -aɪn), *sb.* [f. as next, or a. F. *vaccine* (1800) cow-pox, vaccination, *vaccin* (1812) vaccine matter, = It. and Pg. *vaccina*, Sp. *vacuna*.]

†**1.** Vaccination. *Obs.*⁻¹

1803 tr. *P. Le Brun's Mons. Botte* III. 110 Is it to them the world owes inoculation, which they so long opposed; or the vaccine, which they still oppose?

2. a. Vaccine matter used in vaccination.

1846 [see VACCINATION 1]. **1851** LEADAM *Homœopathy* 361 A child..totally insusceptible of the influence of vaccine. **1864** *Spectator* 375 As ordinary Englishmen say, the vaccine took. **1878** T. BRYANT *Pract. Surg.* I. 94 It would be also well, for the purpose of keeping up a good supply of vaccine, occasionally to vaccinate direct from the heifer.

fig. **1861** GEN. P. THOMPSON *Audi Alt.* cliv. III. 155 Impressing the advantages of industry, with the chance of acting as a vaccine to the habits of thieves.

attrib. **1889** *Buck's Ref. Handbk. Med. Sci.* VII. 518 Ume's vaccine-scarificator consists of four blades fixed upon a horizontal axis.

b. A preparation of the causative organism or substance of a disease (or its products) that has been specially treated for use in vaccination (see also quot. 1983).

1882 E. KLEIN in *11th Ann. Rep. Local Govt. Board* in *Parl. Papers* (C. 3337. 1) XXX. II. 509, I have not yet succeeded in discovering the method employed by M. Pasteur..for the production of 'vaccine' protective against anthrax. **1892** *Brit. Med. Jrnl.* 28 May 1157/2 M. Pasteur has for some years directed his attention to the treatment of epilepsy by antirabic vaccine. **1894** *Daily News* 15 Jan. 3/1 Graduated solutions of what for want of a better word may be called the vaccine. **1911** *Lancet* 16 Sept. 814/1 The treatment of hay fever by hypodermic inoculations of pollen vaccine. **1931** W. T. VAUGHAN *Allergy & Appl. Immunol.* xxix. 328 While the use of immune sera has not been successful in the treatment of typhoid fever, the vaccine has more than demonstrated its efficiency as a preventive. **1962** J. H. BURN *Drugs, Med. & Man* xii. 132 Evidence concerning the value of whooping-cough vaccine to protect children against whooping-cough. **1980** D. J. RAPP *Allergies & your Family* xiii. 220 Measles vaccine should be avoided by children who are receiving steroids. **1983** *Sci. Amer.* Feb. 48/2 There has been increasing interest in the preparation of synthetic vaccines, which is to say vaccines containing not intact viruses but merely peptides..that have been constructed in the laboratory to mimic a very small region of the virus's outer coat.

3. Special Combs.: **vaccine-damaged** *a.*, harmed, esp. seriously, as a result of being vaccinated; also *absol.*; **vaccine therapy**, (G. B. Shaw) **vaccinetherapy**, treatment of a disease with an appropriate vaccine.

1976 *S. Wales Echo* 22 Nov. 8/8 As a parent of a vaccine-damaged daughter who is classed as severely subnormal I can say every word Mr. Peter Ellershaw wrote was true. **1980** *Times* 15 Jan. 4/1 (*heading*) New campaign to win state help for the vaccine-damaged. **1907** *Jrnl. Infectious Dis.* IV. 313 (*heading*) The opsonic index and vaccine therapy of pseudodiphtheric otitis. **1911** G. B. SHAW *Doctor's Dilemma* p. lxxxviii, The theory and practice of securing immunization from bacterial diseases by the inoculation of 'vaccines' made of their own bacteria: a practice incorrectly called vaccinetherapy (there is nothing vaccine about it). **1974** *Mycopathologia et Mycol. Applicata* LIII. 25 (*heading*) Pompholyx of the hands and feet. Its etiology, pathogenesis and specific vaccine therapy.

vaccine ('væksiːn, -ɪn, -aɪn), *a.* [ad. L. *vaccīn-us* (f. *vacca* cow), esp. in *variolæ vaccinæ* cow-pox (Dr. Jenner, 1798). Cf. It. *vaccino*.]

1. ***vaccine disease, pock***, = COW-POX.

1799 *Med. Jrnl.* I. 281 The certainty that the having suffered the vaccine disease, will prove a preservative from the infection of the small-pox. **1802** *Ibid.* VIII. 169, I found the Vaccine-pock so safe and mild a disease..that I became a convert. **1851** LEADAM *Homœopathy* 360 When the system has been satisfactorily infected by the vaccine disease.

b. Appearing in, characteristic of, the disease of cow-pox.

1800 *Med. Jrnl.* V. 28 Matter taken from a vaccine pustule. **1816** SOUTHEY in *Q. Rev.* XVI. 383 It might be supposed that, like the vaccine infection, it secured the system against a stronger poison. **1845** *Encycl. Metrop.* VII. 755/1 The vaccine cicatrix is round, deep, radiated, and puckered. **1888** *Encycl. Brit.* XXIV. 26/2 Ulceration of the vaccine vesicle..is one of the commoner forms of 'bad arm'.

2. ***vaccine lymph, matter, virus***, the characteristic virus of cow-pox (obtained directly or from human subjects) which is employed in vaccination.

1799 *Med. Jrnl.* II. 25 Manifestly arising from absorption of vaccine matter into the system. **1799** JENNER *Further Obs. Var. Vaccinæ* (Crookshank, 1889) II. 188 Mr. Henry Jenner ..inserted the vaccine virus into the arm of a child. **1813** D. MILNE in *Home Papers* (Hist. MSS. Comm.) 159, I gave his phial of vaccine matter to a Dr. Staunton. **1880** *A. Flint's Princ. Med.* 1043 The vesicles..contain a transparent, viscid liquid called the vaccine lymph. **1897** *Allbutt's Syst. Med.* II. 644 Essential constituents of vaccine lymph.

3. ***vaccine inoculation***, = VACCINATION 1.

1799 *Med. Jrnl.* II. 310 Extracts of Letters on the Vaccine Inoculation. **1802** *Ann. Reg., Hist. Europe* 182/2 Dr. Jenner, the discoverer of the vaccine inoculation. **1806** R. WILLAN (*title*), On Vaccine Inoculation.

b. Connected with vaccination.

1812 *Examiner* 21 Sept. 597/2 The National Vaccine Establishment has..published its report. **1816** J. RING (*title*), A caution against vaccine swindlers and impostors.

4. Derived from, pertaining or relating to, cows.

1804 *Med. Jrnl.* XII. 242 We have milk.., butter,.. cheese. All this is vaccine matter. **1864** *Daily Tel.* 10 June, Cows..executed a kind of comic vaccine war dance. **1881** S. R. MACPHAIL *Relig. House of Pluscardyn* ii. 51 When any animal about the farm became ill, there was generally to be found some skilled person who professed vaccine medical knowledge.

'vaccine, *v. rare*⁻¹. = VACCINATE *v.* 1.

1803 MAR. EDGEWORTH *To-morrow* Wks. 1832 V. 355, I think we had better have him vaccined.

vaccinee (væksɪ'niː). [Cf. prec. and -EE¹.] One who is, or has been, vaccinated.

1889 *Buck's Ref. Handbk. Med. Sci.* VII. 518 Vaccinees of twelve or more years. **1897** *Allbutt's Syst. Med.* II. 594 The three groups of vaccinees (vaccinated on the same day) to which these children belonged. **1970** *Nature* 24 Oct. 307/1 Some of the vaccinees might unknowingly be pregnant. **1977** *Lancet* 20 Aug. 400/1 First results were obtained from 20 sera of vaccinees.

‖**vaccinia** (væk'sɪnɪə). *Path.* [mod.L., f. L. *vaccīn-us* VACCINE *a.*] Cow-pox.

Recent Dicts. also give *vaccinella* and *vacciniola* as names of spurious or secondary eruptions sometimes following upon vaccination.

1803 *Med. Jrnl.* IX. 357 The Small-pox will never be extirpated till every parent is in the habit of inserting the vaccinia in the arm of his child. **1842** BURGESS *Dis. Skin* 129 Genuine vaccinia is sometimes developed on the hands of ostlers. **1878** T. BRYANT *Pract. Surg.* I. 52 In other cases it precedes an attack of smallpox, attends vaccinia, and is common in children.

Hence **vac'cinial** *a.*

1897 *Allbutt's Syst. Med.* II. 572 A generalized vaccinial eruption has been produced in children who had sucked their vaccination pocks.

vaccinide ('væksɪnaɪd). *Path.* [a. F. *vaccinide*, f. *vaccine* VACCINE *a.*] (See quot. 1889.)

1889 CROOKSHANK *Hist. Vaccination* II. 552 The Lyons Commission is unwilling to admit the existence of generalized vaccinal eruptions, or vaccinides. **1897** *Allbutt's Syst. Med.* II. 571 The only decisive test whether an eruption following vaccination be a true 'vaccinide' or not.

vaccinifer (væk'sɪnɪfə(r)). [f. VACCINE *sb.*] A person (esp. a child) acting as the transmitter of vaccine virus.

1868 BALLARD *Vaccination* 355 The admixture of blood from the vessels of the syphilitic vaccinifer. **1878** T. BRYANT *Pract. Surg.* I. 94 When the blood of a syphilitic vaccinifer is transferred..to a non-syphilitic subject. **1888** *Encycl. Brit.* XXIV. 24/2 The circumstance that the calf..becomes the vaccinifer, instead of the child.

Hence **vacci'niferous** *a.*

1885 HARRIES tr. *Warlomont's Anim. Vaccination* 23 The vacciniferous property of 'the grease'.

vac'ciniform, *a. Path.* [f. VACCINIA.] Resembling cow-pox.

(In recent Dicts.)

'vaccinine. Also -in. [Cf. VACCINE *sb.* and *a.*, VACCINIA.] 'The specific contagion of cow-pox.'

(In recent Dicts.)

vacciniola: see note to VACCINIA.

vaccinist ('væksɪnɪst). [f. VACCINE *sb.* or *a.* + -IST. Cf. *anti-vaccinist* (1822).] A vaccinator; a supporter or advocate of vaccination.

1847 WEBSTER, *Vaccinist*, one who inoculates with the cow-pox. **1883** *Vaccination Inquirer* IV. 189 The most insolent and fanatical vaccinist on the Metropolitan bench. **1898** *Daily News* 2 Apr. 4 From the point of view of the strict vaccinists and from that of the anti-vaccinists.

‖**vaccinium** (væk'sɪnɪəm). *Bot.* [L. *vaccīnium* bilberry (?).] **a.** A large genus of plants, chiefly belonging to the northern hemisphere, many species of which bear edible berries. **b.** One or other species of this genus; *spec.* a bilberry.

1706 PHILLIPS (ed. Kersey), *Vaccinium*, a Black-berry, a Bilberry, or Hurtle-berry; also a Violet-flower. **1753** *Chambers' Cycl.* Suppl., *Vaccinium*, in botany, a name by which some authors have called the great bilberry, or *vitis idæa magna* of other writers. **1796** WITHERING *Brit. Pl.* (ed. 3) II. 372 In structure [this is] certainly different from the other Vacciniums. **1819** STEPHENS in Shaw's *Gen. Zool.* XI. II. 269 It feeds upon the berries..of the vaccinium. **1882** *Garden* 29 Apr. 292/2 Vacciniums mix well with American plants. **1894** FENN *In Alpine Valley* III. 36 The dense mass of tender leaved vaccinium.

vaccinization (ˌvæksɪnaɪ'zeɪʃən). [a. F. *vaccinisation*, f. *vaccine* VACCINE *sb.*] Vaccination continued or repeated until the vaccine virus has no effect.

1889 *Buck's Ref. Handbk. Med. Sci.* VII. 515 In Holland, a modified vaccinization has been practised for a long time, ten insertions being made upon each subject.

'vaccino-, combining form of VACCINE *sb.* or *a.*, or of VACCINIA, as in ***vaccinophobia*** (1899), ***vaccino-syphilis, vaccino-syphilitic*** adj.

1868 BALLARD *Vaccination* 362 The dread of performing a vaccino-syphilitic inoculation. **1878** T. BRYANT *Pract. Surg.* I. 94 Vaccino-syphilis may be transferred by means of vaccination. **1885** HARRIES tr. *Warlomont's Anim. Vaccination* 78 The most pronounced case of vaccino-syphilis.

vaccino'genic, *a. rare.* [f. VACCINE *sb.*] Producing vaccine; vaccinal.

1889 CROOKSHANK *Hist. Vaccination* II. 585 According to some, the vaccinogenic eruption is never spontaneous in the cow.

So **vacci'nogenous** *a.* (1899 *Syd. Soc. Lex.*)

'vaccinoid, *sb.* or *a. Path.* [f. VACCINE *sb.* or *a.*, or VACCINIA. Cf. F. *vaccinoïde* vaccinide.] (See quots.)

[**1880** *A. Flint's Princ. Med.* 1044 Incomplete vaccinia, *vaccinoid*, as it was termed by Trousseau.] *Ibid.* 1045 Partial success, as shown by imperfect or vaccinoid vesicles, is still more common.

‖**vac'ciola.** *Obs.* [mod.L. (Stokes), f. *vacca* cow.] Cow-pox; vaccinia.

1801 *Med. Jrnl.* V. 454 The incised part bore the characteristic marks of pure Vacciola. **1804** *Ibid.* XII. 440 Small-pox inoculation after vacciola.

† **'vacciolate**, *v. Obs.* [f. prec.] *trans.* To vaccinate. So **vaccio'lation**, **'vacciolator**.

1804 *Med. Jrnl.* XII. 242 The French inaccuracy, which many of our most eminent vacciolators so complaisantly adopt. *Ibid.* 440, I know many who..have by design vacciolated themselves after the small pox. *Ibid.* 441 The effect of vacciolation (inoculation of vacciolous matter).

‖ **vac'ciolous**, *a. Obs.* [f. as prec.] = VACCINE *a.* 2.

1804 *Med. Jrnl.* XII. 242 Vacciolous matter is matter of vacciola or cow-pock.

vach, obs. Sc. f. WATCH.

vache, obs. f. VETCH.

‖ **vacherin** (vaʃrɛ̃). [Fr.] **a.** A kind of cheese (see quot. 1936). **b.** A confection of meringue and whipped cream.

1936 A. L. SIMON *Catechism concerning Cheeses* 44 *Vacherin.* A French Savoy and Swiss cheese made during the winter. **1960** E. DAVID *French Provincial Cooking* 34 We were then beguiled into eating a sweet called a *Vacherin glacé.* This turned out to be..ice-cream, glacé fruits, frozen whipped cream, and meringue. **1965** A. ROUDYBUSH *Season for Death* (1966) xxiii. 133 An impromptu supper of.. venison baked in wine and great vacherin meringues was served. **1969** R. & D. DE SOLA *Dict. Cooking* 231/1 *Vacherin,* Swedish cheese used as a spread, creamy and aromatic. **1979** *N.Y. Times* 18 May c14/4 A vacherin of nutted meringue layers with whipped cream and strawberries.

† **'vachery**. *Obs.* Also 4 **vacherie**, 5 **-erye**, **-yre**. [a. OF. (also mod.F.) *vacherie*, f. *vache* cow.] = VACCARY. Also *attrib.*

a **1325** *MS. Rawl. B. 520* fol. 28 Recouerer..þoru forme þat him is i-graunted þoru acheson of wind mulle, bercherie, vacherie, auoiting of his curt. **14..** *Voc.* in Wr.-Wülcker 618 *Vaccarium,* a vacherye. *c* **1440** *Promp. Parv.* 507/2 Vacherye, or dayrye, *vaccaria, armentarium.* **1450** *Rolls of Parlt.* V. 191/1 Of the two Vachyres called Brenand and Whytledale. **1650** in *Sussex Archæol. Coll.* (1871) XXIII. 296 The vachery lands..are not included in the valluacon. *Ibid.,* [The] litle stone gate below the vachery.

vacht, obs. Sc. form of WAUGHT *v.*

vacillancy ('væsɪlənsɪ). Now *rare.* [f. next. See -ANCY and cf. It. *vacillanza.*] Vacillation.

1668 H. MORE *Div. Dial.* I. xviii, That Vacillancy in humane Souls, and such Mutations as are found in corporeal matter. **1678** SIR G. MACKENZIE *Crim. Laws Scot.* I. i. §v. (1699) 8 The committing these Crimes may be occasioned by levity and vacillancy of judgment in minors. *a* **1680** GLANVILL *Sadducismus* I. 95 That the weakness and vacillancy of this Method may yet more clearly appear. **1811** CHALMERS in Hanna *Mem.* (1849) I. x. 253 My mind was in a state of vacillancy and discomfort.

vacillant ('væsɪlənt), *a.* [ad. L. *vacillant-, vacillans,* pres. pple. of *vacillāre*: see next. So F. *vacillant* (14th c.).]

1. Uncertain, hesitating, wavering.

1521 *Bradshaw's St. Werburge, Ball. to St. Werburge* 2 With hert contrite accepte my supplicacion, Aydynge my fraylete and lyfe vacillaunt. **1662** H. MORE *Philos. Writ.* Pref. Gen. (1712) p. v, Because the reason of Universal Nature, and of Man, ought to stand firm on all sides, and to be no where vacillant. **1901** *Blackw. Mag.* Nov. 715/1 The vacillant, magnanimous, simple-hearted Levin.

2. *Ent.* Unsteady; swaying readily.

1860 MAYNE *Expos. Lex.* 1319/1 *Vacillans,* applied to anthers when they are oblong, attached by the middle of their length, and mobile; vacillant.

'vacillate, *ppl. a.* [Cf. next and -ATE^{2}.] Vacillating, unsteady.

1830 W. PHILLIPS *Mt. Sinai* I. 74 With purpose vacillate, and changed resolve, He follow'd Israel.

vacillate ('væsɪleɪt), *v.* [f. L. *vacillāt-,* ppl. stem of *vacillāre* to sway, stagger, totter, etc., whence also F. *vaciller* (1314), It. *vacillare,* Pg. *vacillar,* Sp. *vacilar.*]

1. *intr.* To swing or sway unsteadily; to be in unstable equilibrium; to stagger.

1597 A. M. tr. *Guillemeau's Fr. Chirurg.* cj b, Those which are too longe doe vacillate, and turne this way and that way in the hand. **1721** BAILEY, *To Vacillate,* to..stagger, waggle, or shake. **1757** *Phil. Trans.* L. 505 Whether the earth, during the agitation of the waters, does rock and vacillate,.. is what I shall leave to future inquiry. **1802** PALEY *Nat. Theol.* xxii, When a spheroid..turns upon an axis which is not permanent,..it is always liable to shift and vacillate from one axis to another. **1888** STEVENSON *Black Arrow* 175 Lawless, vacillating on his feet, and still shouting the chorus of sea-ballads, took the long tiller in his hands.

b. To vary; to hover doubtfully.

1841 D'ISRAELI *Amen. Lit.* (1867) 231 The fate of books vacillates with the fancies of book-lovers. **1873** EARLE *Philol. Eng. Tongue* (ed. 2) §186 Among the words which still vacillate between the two sounds of EA, is the word *break.*

c. To fluctuate; to produce varying results.

1835 SIR J. ROSS *Narr. 2nd Voy.* xv. 235 In the course of these attempts at discovering and maintaining the best temperature, it [an apparatus for condensing the vapour] was found to vacillate.

2. To alternate or waver between different opinions or courses of action.

1623 COCKERAM I, *Vacillate,* to wauer, to be inconstant. **1661** R. BURNEY *K. Chas. presented* 9 His Majesties wrath.. causes the spirit of the ill-affected to vacillate. **1830** D'ISRAELI *Chas. I,* III. ii. 19 In his last years he stood alone, and never less vacillated in his conduct. **1846** RUSKIN *Mod. Painters* II. III. iii. §2. 179 *note,* He may pause, but he must not hesitate,—and tremble, but he must not vacillate. **1891** BP. CREIGHTON in Mrs. Creighton *Life* (1904) II. i. 22 You can judge if you look within; you vacillate if you look without.

b. Freq. const. *between.*

1827 J. F. COOPER *Prairie* II. xiii. 217 His looks appeared to be strangely vacillating between hope and fear. **1850** MᶜCOSH *Div. Govt.* II. ii. (1874) 212 The superstitious man vacillates..between hope and fear, between self-confidence and despondency.

'vacillating, *ppl. a.* [f. prec.]

1. Of persons: Given to vacillation.

a **1814** WORDSW. *Excurs.* IV. 309 The bad Have fairly earned a victory o'er..The vacillating, inconsistent good. **1844** *Mem. Babylonian Princ.* II. 57 This vacillating man.. wrote a second time. **1860** PUSEY *Min. Proph.* 86 The vacillating sinner,..impelled by his sufferings, yet presenting a passive resistance. **1872** YEATS *Growth Comm.* 232 The vacillating monarch restored the fishing privilege.

2. Of conduct, etc.: Marked by vacillation.

1828 D'ISRAELI *Chas. I,* II. v. 132 [The] address..throws a clear and steady light on the vacillating conduct of Charles the First. **1856** FROUDE *Hist. Eng.* (1858) I. iii. 255 Very unwillingly..he was compelled to act his vacillating part to England. **1863** GEO. ELIOT *Romola* xli, The vacillating expression of a mind unable to concentrate itself strongly.

3. Of things: **a.** Varying, changeful. **b.** Unsteady, swaying.

1822 SCOTT *Peveril* i, Following the vacillating and unhappy fortunes of his master. *a* **1827** M'ARTHUR in Good *Study Med.* (1829) II. 180 Pulse quick, generally full and strong, in some cases quick, low, and vacillating. **1834** LYTTON *Pompeii* IV. v, He..rushed with swift but vacillating steps down the starlit streets.

Hence **'vacillatingly** *adv.*

a **1849** POE *Marginalia* Wks. 1864 III. 565 He has made successful and frequent incursions, although vacillatingly, into the domain of the true Imagination.

vacillation (væsɪ'leɪʃən). Also 5 **-acion**. [ad. L. *vacillātio,* noun of action f. *vacillāre* VACILLATE *v.* So F. *vacillation* (1512), It. *vacillazione,* Pg. *vacillação,* Sp. *vacilacion.*]

1. The action or quality of alternating or wavering in respect of opinion or conduct; hesitation, uncertainty.

c **1400** *Pilgr. Sowle* (Caxton 1483) IV. xxx. 80 Tho that ben naturelle of the same countre withouten vacillacion wille done theyr deuoyre. **1623** COCKERAM I, *Vacillation,* inconstancy, wauering. *a* **1649** DRUMM. OF HAWTH. *Hist. Jas. III,* Wks. (1711) 40 That the friendship begun might continue without all vacillation. **1697** BURGHOPE *Disc. Relig. Assemb.* 101 This vacillation of thoughts is in some the consequent of their very constitution. **1791** BOSWELL *Johnson* (Oxf. ed.) I. 204 Christopher Smart, with whose unhappy vacillation of mind he sincerely sympathised. **1828** D'ISRAELI *Chas. I,* I. iii. 34 In the vacillation of the disputants, victory hung on the subtilty of an argument. *a* **1853** F. ROBERTSON *Serm.* Ser. IV. vii. (1876) 49 There is such an indecision, such a vacillation about the man. **1874** GREEN *Short Hist.* vii. §3. 365 Elizabeth..screened her.. statesmanship under the natural timidity and vacillation of her sex.

b. An instance of this.

1828 D'ISRAELI *Chas. I,* I. v. 116 The agents on both sides were shocked at the vacillations of their own Cabinets. **1879** CHURCH *Spenser* 22 When all about her [Elizabeth] were dismayed both at the plan itself and at her vacillations.

2. The action, or an act, of swaying or swinging unsteadily to and fro.

Quot. 1633 is a rendering of St. Augustine *De Rect. Cath. Conv.* §5, where the reading *vacillationes* is doubtful.

1633 PRYNNE *1st Pt. Histrio-m.* 27 To prohibit the vse of all diabolicall Enterludes, Vacillations, and songs of the Gentiles. **1635** H. VALENTINE *Sea-Serm.* 57 The second effect of a tempest is the vacillation, staggering, and trepidation of their bodies. **1711-2** DERHAM *Phys.-Theol.* v. ii. (1739) II. 667 To keep the Body upright, and prevent its falling, by readily assisting against every Vacillation thereof. **1802** PALEY *Nat. Theol.* xi. §5. 220 The bones of the feet.. are put in action by every slip or vacillation of the body, and seem to assist in restoring its balance. **1837** *Blackw. Mag.* XLII. 233 For this cause did the intelligent creature repose (though not indeed without vacillation) on the lower perch.

3. Variation between extremes. *rare*$^{-1}$.

1768 *Phil. Trans.* LVIII. 160 We shall then have..the double menstrual parallax, or vacillation, arising from the whole diameter of the epicycle, 14″.

vacillator ('væsɪleɪtə(r)). [f. VACILLATE *v.*] One who vacillates or wavers.

1890 *Spectator* 30 July, If we win,..the vacillators will flock over to the Unionist standard. **1902** *Sat. Rev.* 8 Nov. 590/2 He..is now but a querulous vacillator.

vacillatory ('væsɪlətərɪ), *a.* [f. VACILLATE *v.*]

1. Marked by vacillation.

a **1734** NORTH *Examen* I. i. (1740) 25 If ever such vacillatory Accounts of Affairs of State, Kings and Monarchies, were given in Print before, I am mistaken. *a* **1835** MᶜCULLOCH *Attributes* (1837) xlii. III. 89 The details are far too numerous or obscure or vacillatory to admit of a place here. **1851** HAWTHORNE *Twice-told T.* II. viii. 118 My political course, I must acknowledge, has been rather vacillatory.

2. Of persons: Tending to vacillate.

1854 MILMAN *Lat. Chr.* VII. iii. III. 183 Hildebrand..for the first time..is vacillatory, hesitating, doubtful. **1876** TROLLOPE *Amer. Senator* xxxiv, The Postmaster, half vacillatory, in his desire to oblige a neighbour produced the letter.

vacive, *a. rare*$^{-0}$. [ad. L. *vacīvus.*] 'Empty, void' (1656 Blount *Glossogr.*). Hence **va'civity**, 'emptiness' (1721 Bailey).

vacky ('vækɪ). *colloq. abbrev.* Also **vaccy**, **vakky**. [f. EVACUEE: cf. -Y^{6}.] An evacuee, *esp.* a child evacuated from the city to the country esp. at the beginning of the 1939–45 war.

1940 *John o' London's Weekly* 3 May 147/1 These little vackies and their country friends. **1940** J. CARY *Charley is my Darling* ii. 16 There are only eight vackies in the place. **1949** E. COXHEAD *Wind in West* iii. 66, I was a vakky. My home's in Clapham really, but our school was sent to Bedfordshire. **1962** M. DUFFY *That's how it Was* viii. 71 The Wortbridgers distrusted the vaccies with their quick ways and sharp, pinched faces. **1979** *Bookseller* 25 Aug. 832/2 A 'must' book for all ex-'vaccies, and their parents, and their children. **1982** J. AIKEN *Whisper in Night* 151 The Welsh landscape had changed..since he was a Vakky, sent here for safety from the Birmingham bombs.

† **'vacuate**, *pa. pple. Obs.*$^{-1}$ [ad. L. *vacuātus,* pa. pple. of *vacuāre*: see next.] Made empty.

1432-50 tr. *Higden* (Rolls) III. 339 Philippus..scholde destroye sone the cite if that hit were vacuate and voide of discrete men.

† **'vacuate**, *v. Obs.* [f. L. *vacuāt-,* ppl. stem of *vacuāre* (hence It. *vacuare*) to empty, clear, free, f. *vacuus*: see VACUUM *sb.*]

1. *trans.* **a.** To clear out; = EVACUATE *v.* 5.

1572 J. JONES *Buckstones Bathes Benefyte* 15 b, Galen willeth to vacuat, clense, or empty, that which is euill. **1607** WALKINGTON *Opt. Glass* 49 That so the superfluous humidity of his stomach may be vacuated. **1657** TOMLINSON *Renou's Disp.* 165 Senny, Rhabarb..vacuate flegm also. **1760** *Ann. Reg.* I. 158/2 We have..portable ventilators which are continually employed in vacuating the foul air from our hold.

b. To empty; = EVACUATE *v.* 1.

1651 WITTIE tr. *Primrose's Pop. Err.* IV. vi. 239 If he that hath been once abundantly vacuated, must necessarily relapse into the same disease. **1684** *Bonet's Merc. Compit.* III. 84 When the Heart-burn is violent, we must not vacuate the whole Body. **1765** *Phil. Trans.* LV. 84 Its so well vacuated by boiling the quicksilver in the tube, that I depend on its being luminous after being carried so far.

2. To annul, cancel, abrogate, set aside; = EVACUATE *v.* 4.

1654 GAYTON *Pleas. Notes* III. x. 129 Toboso too was flesh and blood; and how If some great Prince should vacuate her vow? **1681** HICKERINGILL *Black Non-Conf.* xiii. Wks. 1716 II. 104 Which Law vacuates and makes null and void all Laws of Man, ipso facto, that are made to the contrary. **1709** MRS. MANLEY *Secret Mem.* (1720) II. 234 There can be no Laws contrived..but what they can vacuate.

Hence † **'vacuating** *vbl. sb. Obs.*

1684 *Col. Rec. Pennsylv.* I. 125 They may act Eregularly, to ye Vacuating and Insecurity of such acts and Judgments of ye said Courts.

† **vacu'ation**. *Obs.* [ad. med.L. *vacuātio,* f. L. *vacuāre* VACUATE *v.* So It. *vacuazione,* Pg. *vacuação.*]

1. A vacuity or hollow part.

1541 R. COPLAND *Guydon's Quest. Chirurg.* D 2 [Of bones] They that haue the embossynges and vacuacyons be they that make the ioyntes.

2. = EVACUATION 1 a, 1 b.

1590 BARROUGH *Meth. Physick* 54 Through abundant swets, and all other immoderate vacuations. **1607** TOPSELL *Four-f. Beasts* 284 The vacuation of blood & seede, is a dubble charge to nature. **1635** A. READ *Tumors & Vlcers* 197 The vacuation of the humor impacted in the part. **1657** TOMLINSON *Renou's Disp.* 45 Which distinction is taken from the manner of excretion or vacuation. **1721** BAILEY, *Vacuation,* an emptying.

3. Emptiness. *rare.*

1611 FLORIO, *Vacuatione,* emptinesse, vacuation, vacuity, voidnesse. *a* **1660** *Contemp. Hist. Irel.* (Ir. Archæol. Soc.) I. 103 They very joyfull handlinge the same [a trunk], found it promisinge noe vacuation, but verie heavy.

† **'vacuative**. *Obs. rare*$^{-1}$. [f. VACUATE *v.*] = EVACUATIVE *sb.*

1656 RIDGLEY *Pract. Physick* 318 The vital spirits..are consumed by heat, malignity, vacuatives, grief.

va'cuefy, *v.* [f. VACUUM *sb.*, after L. *vacuēfacĕre* to make empty.] To produce a vacuum.

1727 BAILEY (vol. II), *To Vacuefy,* to make void or empty. **1828** D. CRAIGIE *Path. Anat.* 175 Vacuefying apparatus.. found in the upper surface of the head of the sucking fish.

† **'vacuist**. *Obs.* [ad. mod.L. *vacuista,* f. *vacuum* VACUUM *sb.* So It. and Sp. *vacuista,* F. *vacuiste.*] One who maintains the possibility of a vacuum in nature.

1660 BOYLE *New Exp. Phys.-Mech.* xvii. 122 Those spaces which the Vacuists would have to be empty, because they are manifestly devoid of Air, and all the grosser bodies. **1664** POWER *Exp. Philos.* II. 132 The second Hypothesis 's of the Vacuists. **1682** CREECH *Lucretius* (1683) Notes 14 Mr. Hobs adds another Argument, which is of no force against the Vacuists.

† **va'cuitous**, *a. Obs.*$^{-1}$ [f. next.] Having the nature of a vacuum; empty of matter.

1766 G. CANNING *Anti-Lucretius* III. 172 Where'er a spot vacuitous is found, There you must own that Matter feels a bound.

vacuity (væ'kjuːɪtɪ). Also 6 **vacuytee**, 6–7 **vacuitie**, 7 **vacuety**. [ad. L. *vacuitās* empty space, vacancy, freedom, etc., f. *vacuus*: see

VACUUM *sb.* So F. *vacuité* (1314), It. *vacuità*, Sp. *vacuidad*, Pg. *vacuidade*.]

I. 1. Absolute emptiness of space; complete absence of matter.

1546 LANGLEY tr. *Pol. Verg. de Invent.* I. ii. 4 b, Epicurus ..putteth two Causes Atomos or Motes and Vacuitie or emptinesse. 1597 MIDDLETON *Wisd. Solomon* i. 2 For him.. The Horizons and hemespheres obay, And windes the fillers of vacuitie. *c* 1626 DONNE *Serm.* Wks. 1839 IV. 20 Water will clamber up hills and Air will sink down into Vaults rather than admit Vacuity. 1644 DIGBY *Nat. Bodies* iii. (1658) 24 Aristotle..hath demonstrated that there can be no motion in vacuity. *a* 1700 KEN *Hymnotheo* Poet. Wks. 1721 III. 294 Some Dotards dream'd..That Atoms..Should rise from nothing in Vacuity. 1728 CHAMBERS *Cycl.* s.v. *Vacuum*, But mere Space, or Vacuity, is suppos'd to be extended; therefore it is material. 1829 *Chapters Phys. Sci.* 231 A large portion of interspersed vacuity is sufficient for all purposes. 186. G. OUTRAM *Law Lyrics, The Annuity* viii, She beats the taeds that live in stanes An' fatten in vacuity.

b. With *a*, *no*, etc. (Passing into 8.)

1603 HOLLAND *Plutarch's Mor.* 1021 There is no voidnesse or vacuity in nature. 1660 R. COKE *Power & Subj.* 54 So the laws of nature will admit of many things contrary to nature, rather then endure a vacuity. 1704 RAY *Creation* I. 83 Nature's abhorrence of a Vacuity.

transf. a 1631 DONNE *Select.* (1840) 244 In the first vacuity, when thou wast nothing he sought thee so early as in Adam. 1655 FULLER *Hist. Cambr.* (1840) 237 To prevent a vacuity, (the detestation of nature,) a new plantation was soon substituted in their room.

2. Emptiness consisting in the absence of solid or liquid matter.

1579 G. BAKER *Guydo's Quest.* 12 Some [bones] are embossed for to enter, and other haue vacuity that receiueth. 1651 BIGGS *New Disp.* 156 The vacuity of the depleted veins doth attract the blood beneath. 1822 GOOD *Study Med.* II. 10 This vacuity of the arteries upon death, was one of the objections urged very forcibly by the ancients against the circulation of the blood.

b. Absence of any of the visible objects usually occupying certain spaces; complete emptiness in respect of things or persons.

1660 F. BROOKE tr. *Le Blanc's Trav.* 268 Leading him to a dark deep well,..but terrified with the vacuity and darknesse, he retired. 1759 JOHNSON *Rasselas* xv, The princess and her maid,..seeing nothing to bound their prospect, considered themselves as in danger of being lost in a dreary vacuity. 1775 —— in *Boswell* (1816) II. 424 Madam, I do not like to come down to vacuity. 1818 SCOTT *Rob Roy* xx, Such sunbeams as forced their way through the narrow Gothic lattices..and..lost themselves in the vacuity of the vaults behind. 1842 H. ROGERS *Introd. Burke's Wks.* 67 The grim spectres..who stalk from desolation to desolation, through the dreary vacuity..of chill and comfortless chambers. 1891 T. HARDY *Tess* (1900) 139/1 As he gazed, a moving spot intruded on the white vacuity of its perspective.

c. The fact of being unfilled or unoccupied.

1664 EVELYN *Sylva* 41 But 'tis cheaper to supply the vacuity of such accidental decays by a new plantation. 1844 MRS. BROWNING *Drama of Exile* 168 To fill the vacant thrones of me and mine, Which affront Heaven with their vacuity.

3. The quality or fact of being empty, in various fig. senses.

1603 FLORIO *Montaigne* II. xii. (1632) 247 To make them feele the emptiness, vacuity, and no worth of man. 1640 BP. REYNOLDS *Passions* xvi. 169 The most generall [cause of desire]..is a Vacuity, Indigence, and selfe-insufficiency of the Soule. 1690 C. NESSE *Hist. Myst. O. & N.T.* I. 289 They have the most light to discover to themselves their own vacuity and nothingness. 1806 A. KNOX *Rem.* I. 21 It would follow that..the great central appetite of intellectual man.. was abandoned to the self-torture of irremediable vacuity. 1850 CARLYLE *Latter-d. Pamph.* vi. (1872) 202 Here is an abyss of vacuity in our much-admired opulence. 1885 PATER *Marius* II. 144 It was an experience which came in the midst of a deep sense of vacuity in things.

b. Emptiness (in fig. senses) as a condition or state having a kind of real existence.

a 1711 KEN *Christophil* Poet. Wks. 1721 I. 429 Thou all-sufficient art, and I Am nothing but vacuity. 1751 JOHNSON *Rambler* No. 141 ¶9 Think on the misery of him who is condemned to cultivate barrenness and ransack vacuity. 1776 —— *Let. to Mrs. Thrale* 30 Mar., I know that a whole system of hopes, and designs, and expectations, is swept away at once, and nothing left but bottomless vacuity. 1819 WIFFEN *Aonian Hours* (1820) 25 The drear Vacuity of sorrow on thee lay. 1840 CARLYLE *Heroes* vi. (1904) 245 Having once parted with Reality, he tumbles helpless in Vacuity. 1888 P. FITZGERALD *Fatal Zero* iv, In my lonely blue chamber, there is a sort of vacuity for thought, the world is shut out.

4. Complete absence of ideas; vacancy of mind or thought.

1594 HOOKER *Eccl. Pol.* I. vi. §1 Men..are at the first without vnderstanding or knowledge at all. Neuerthelesse from this vtter vacuitie they grow by degrees. 1661 K. W. *Conf. Charac., Meere Polititian* (1860) 27 Which will availe him little; but to be an indicium of his own vacuity and emptiness of all sollidity. 1707 FLOYER *Physic. Pulse-Watch* 363 The Pulse,..if it be weak,..indicates Vacuity and Fear. 1773 HAN. MORE *Search after Happ.* ii, Though more to folly than to guilt inclined, A drear vacuity possess'd my mind. 1818 MISS FERRIER *Marriage* xv, Imputing to fatigue of body, what in fact was the consequence of mental vacuity, he proposed returning home. 1854 MARION HARLAND *Alone* xvii, She heard and saw all that passed; but in place of heart and sense, was a dead vacuity. 1885 CLODD *Myths & Dr.* I. i. 9 We cannot so far lull our faculty of thought as to realise the mental vacuity of the savage.

b. Const. *of* (eye, mind, thought).

1760 STERNE *Tr. Shandy* III. i, That perplexed vacuity of eye which puzzled souls generally stare with. 1784 COWPER *Task* IV. 297 'Tis thus the understanding takes repose In indolent vacuity of thought. 1829 COBBETT *Adv. Young Man* v. 247 A great fondness for music is a mark of..great vacuity of mind. 1863 COWDEN CLARKE *Shaks. Char.* xx. 507 He frequents low dissolute haunts from no graver cause than idleness and vacuity of mind. 1879 FARRAR *St. Paul* I. 183 We may be sure that the vacuity of thought in which most men live was for Saul a thing impossible.

5. Complete absence or lack *of* something.

1601 SIR W. CORNWALLIS *Ess.* II. xlv. (1631) 251 Which vacuitie of vertue at that time will breede more terrour to him then darknesse to children. 1642 D. ROGERS *Naaman* 172 Christ is a sufficient store to a poore soule in the vacuity of other things. 1698 J. COCKBURN *Bourignianism Detected* i. 7 She..was in an admirable vacuity of all Desire of knowing. 1782 MISS BURNEY *Cecilia* IV. vi, When he is quite tired of his existence, from a total vacuity of ideas, he must affect a look of absence. 1792 A. YOUNG *Trav. France* 118 There is as much character in his air and manner as there is vacuity of it in the countenance of..St. Etienne. 1822 GOOD *Study Med.* III. 46 To contemplate the body and mind..at birth ..as consisting equally of a blank or vacuity of impressions.

†6. Complete freedom or exemption *from* something. *Obs.*

a 1619 FOTHERBY *Atheom.* I. xii. §1 The soule cannot haue in it, any true ioy,..vnlesse the same be founded, both in security, and in confidence, and in tranquillity. All which do imply a vacuity from feare. 1648 SANDERSON *Serm.* (1681) II. 246 By the Evenness of the Mind and the Vacuity from those secret lashes..that haunt a guilty Conscience. *a* 1665 J. GOODWIN *Filled w. the Spirit* (1867) 429 A well-grounded vacuity or freedom from all troublesome, distracting, and tormenting fears and cares.

7. †a. Leisure *for* some pursuit. *Obs.*$^{-1}$

1607 *Scholast. Disc. agst. Antichrist* I. iii. 137 From this preposterousnesse of the Crosse setting the sense before the spirite, come wee to his Vacuitie for his inwarde Devotion.

b. Lack of occupation; idleness.

1817 JAS. MILL *Brit. India* I. II. ix. 389 A whole race of men..whom the pain of vacuity forced upon some application of mind. 1875 A. R. HOPE *My Schoolboy F.* 72 The hours of thoughtful vacuity I had spent.

II. 8. A hollow or enclosed space empty of matter; *esp.* a small internal cavity or interstice of this kind in a solid body.

1541 R. COPLAND *Guydon's Quest. Chirurg.* D ij, Some [bones] are enbossed for to entre, and other haue vacuytees that receyueth. 1607 TOPSELL *Four-f. Beasts* 330 That so those places being emptied..the vacuety may be replenished with better blood. 1659 HAMMOND *On Ps.* lxv. 10 The earth..sinks down and fills up the vacuities. 1677 GREW *Anat. Pl.* (1682) 300 There are Vacuities in Water. That is to say, that all the parts of Water are not contiguous. 1731 MEDLEY *Kolben's Cape G. Hope* II. 95 Those pieces become as hard as flints, and altogether as smooth and solid; not the least vacuity or interstice being to be seen. 1770 *Phil. Trans.* LX. 422 Every particle of light that issues from the sun, must leave a spherical vacuity of one millionth of one millionth of an inch diameter. 1800 *Ibid.* XC. 235 A wad was placed over the powder, dry sand superadded, to fill all vacuities. 1840 *Jrnl. Engl. Agric. Soc.* I. III. 355 Water in descending seeks the nearest vacuity. 1872 DANA *Corals* i. 38 The polyp has..no blood-vessels but the vacuities among the tissues.

b. A cosmic space empty of matter.

1643 SIR T. BROWNE *Relig. Med.* I. §49 When this sensible world shall be destroyed, all shall then be here as it is now there, an Empyreall Heaven, a quasi vacuitie. 1667 MILTON *P.L.* II. 932 That seat soon failing, [he] meets A vast vacuitie. 1685 BOYLE *Enq. Notion Nat.* 75 Whilst their numberless Atoms wildly rov'd in their infinite Vacuity. 1795 W. BLAKE *Bk. Los* iv, The Deep fled away On all sides, and left an unform'd Dark Vacuity.

9. An empty space left or contrived in something, esp. in some composite work or structure.

1624 WOTTON *Archit.* (1672) 26 To place the Columnes precisely one over another, that so the solid may answer to the solid, and the vacuities to the vacuities. 1655 FULLER *Hist. Waltham Abbey* (1840) 257 The great pillars thereof are wreathed with indentings; which vacuities, if formerly filled up with brass,..added much to the beauty of the building. 1726 LEONI *Alberti's Archit.* I. 55/2 The vacuities which are left between the back..of the Arch, and the upright of the Wall. 1775 JOHNSON *West. Isl.* Wks. X. 509 Round which there are narrow cavities or recesses formed by small vacuities or by a double wall. 1823 P. NICHOLSON *Pract. Build.* 425 Rooms are the interior vacuities or habitable parts of a building. 1845 *Florist's Jrnl.* 67 An ingeniously contrived trap for earwigs,..leaving a vacuity for the reception of the insects. 1870 ROLLESTON *Anim. Life* 8 By a vacuity in the skull walls for the blood to pass out from the lateral sinus.

b. An open space, gap, or interval left between or among things. *rare.*

1658 SIR T. BROWNE *Gard. Cyrus* ii. ¶12 Whereby the Elephants passing the vacuities of the *Hastati*, might have run upon them. 1757 BURKE *Abridgm. Eng. Hist.* I. iv, The Scots and Picts..rushed with redoubled violence into this vacuity. 1863 HAWTHORNE *Our Old Home* (1879) 152 The market-place..of the town is a rather spacious and irregularly shaped vacuity.

c. An empty space due to the disappearance or absence of some special thing.

1822–7 GOOD *Study Med.* (1829) III. 227 He has also seen others..reproduce a smaller or larger number of teeth to supply vacuities progressively produced in earlier life. 1849 MRS. SOMERVILLE *Connex. Phys. Sci.* xxxvii. 415 Those dark vacuities called 'coal sacks' by the ancient navigators, which are so numerous between α Centauri and α Antaris. 1867–77 G. F. CHAMBERS *Astron.* VI. iv. 519 The central vacuity is not quite dark.

10. An emptiness, an empty space, a blank, in various fig. uses.

a 1631 DONNE *Select.* (1840) 5 A filling of all former vacuities, a supplying of all emptinesses in our souls. 1651 BAXTER *Inf. Bapt.* 325 In this age, when men may say any thing if they have but Rhetorick to fill up the Vacuities. 1682 W. OWTRAM *Serm.* 342 Our Saviour..filled up the vacuities that Moses had left in moral duties. 1732 POPE *Ess. Man* II. 286 Each want of happiness by hope supply'd, And each vacuity of sense by pride. 1776 ADAM SMITH *W.N.* II. ii. (1869) 303 Whatever vacuities this excessive circulation occasioned in the necessary coin of the kingdom. 1841 EMERSON *Ess.* Ser. I. x, But yesterday I saw a dreary vacuity in this direction in which now I see so much. 1850 KINGSLEY *A. Locke* i, Oh those Sabbaths..when there was nothing to fill up the long vacuity but books of which I did not understand a word.

11. An empty or inane thing.

1648 J. BEAUMONT *Psyche* XI. lxviii, That with those huge ador'd Vacuities, Which puff the World up with their frothy flood, Ev'n massy Gold must counted be. 1665 MANLEY *Grotius' Low C. Wars* 511 The Prince, by the Concessions of these Honorary Vacuities, redeeming the War from delay. 1843 CARLYLE *Past & Pr.* I. iv, Thou for one wilt not again vote for any quack, do honour to any edge-gilt vacuity in man's shape.

‖**vacuo** (in the phrase *in vacuo*): see IN (Latin prep.) 20.

vacuolar ('vækju:ələ(r)), *a.* [ad. F. *vacuolaire*, f. *vacuole* VACUOLE.] Of or pertaining to, of the nature of, a vacuole or vacuoles.

1852 *Zoologist* X. 3406 He [Huxley] next mentioned appearances which he terms vacuolar thickenings. 1859 J. R. GREENE *Protozoa* 45 In some specimens the central cavity is replaced by an aggregation of large vacuolar spaces. 1877 HUXLEY *Anat. Inv. Anim.* iii. 141 The interior of these frequently contains vacuolar spaces.

So **'vacuolary** *a.*

1897 *Allbutt's Syst. Med.* II. 907 Ehrlich says that changes are to be found in the hepatic cells—a 'vacuolary' degeneration.

'vacuolate, *a.* = next.

1890 *Q. Jrnl. Microsc. Sci.* XXX. 6 In some cases the stalk has a vacuolate structure.

vacuolated ('vækju:əleɪtɪd), *ppl. a.* [f. VACUOLE: cf. VACUOLATION.] Rendered vacuolar; modified or altered by vacuolation.

1859 HUXLEY *Oceanic Hydrozoa* 84 The cavity of the base of the involucrum appears to become filled up by vacuolated tissue. 1878 F. J. BELL *Gegenbauer's Comp. Anat.* 24 There are often vacuolated spaces in the cells, which are filled with a fluid. 1896 *Allbutt's Syst. Med.* I. 211 Cell invaginations, the protoplasm of which is highly vacuolated.

vacuolating ('vækju:əleɪtɪŋ), *ppl. a. Med.* [Back-formation from VACUOLATION: see -ING[2].] ***vacuolating agent*** or ***virus***: a papovavirus, orig. obtained from rhesus monkey kidney tissue, which is capable of causing tumours in animals and animal tissue cultures; also called *SV 40* (cf. *SV* s.v. S 4 a); also, a virus related to this.

1960 SWEET & HILLEMAN in *Proc. Soc. Exper. Biol. & Med.* CV. 420/1 This agent has been called the 'vacuolating virus' by us because of the prominent cytoplasmic vacuolation seen in infected cell cultures... The discovery of this new virus, the vacuolating agent, represents the detection..of a hitherto 'non-detectable' simian virus of monkey renal cultures. 1965 *Listener* 11 Mar. 369/2 A remarkable situation is also presented by..vacuolating virus or simian virus 40. This virus..was accidentally given to millions of human subjects with early batches of polio vaccine. 1977 *Jrnl. Virology* XXI. 179/1 Papovaviruses of the simian virus 40 (SV 40)-polyoma subgroup..occur in the mouse.., the rabbit (rabbit kidney vacuolating virus [RKV]), [etc.].

vacuolation (ˌvækju:ə'leɪʃən). [f. next: cf. VACUOLATED *ppl. a.* and -ATION.] The formation of vacuoles; change to a vacuolar state.

1858 CARPENTER *Veg. Phys.* §318 In other cases it would appear that a number of cells are formed by a process of vacuolation. 1881 MIVART *Cat* 329 Vacuolation—denoting the spontaneous resolution of part of a more or less dense structure in such a way as to give rise to a cavity or cavities within it. 1899 *Allbutt's Syst. Med.* VI. 508 Vacuolation of the nerve-cell is peculiarly frequent in senile brain atrophy.

vacuole ('vækju:əʊl). [a. F. *vacuole* (Dujardin), f. L. *vacu-us* empty.]

1. A small cavity or vesicle in organic tissue or protoplasm, freq. containing some fluid.

a. *Zool.* and *Anat.* 1853 *Ray Soc. Bot. & Physiol. Mem.* 534 All these properties had already been observed by Dujardin;..the aqueous spaces or hollows he named 'Vacuoles', regarding them as the most characteristic feature of the substance. 1859 HUXLEY *Oceanic Hydrozoa* 10 The structure of the villi and vacuoles in *Athorybia*. 1897 *Allbutt's Syst. Med.* II. 224 Into the vacuoles or loculi of this net-work the serum exudes.

b. *Bot.* 1875 DARWIN *Insectiv. Plants* xv. 351 Two or three vacuoles or small spheres appeared within some of the larger globules. 1885 GOODALE *Physiol. Bot.* (1892) 280 In numerous succulents the vacuoles of the assimilating cells frequently contain a thin mucus.

attrib. 1882 VINES tr. *Sachs' Bot.* 585 The centre of the sac is filled in the unripe seed with a clear vacuole-fluid.

2. An empty or open space (in a comet).

1881 *Science* II. 317 In this envelope was a curious oval vacuole, behind the nucleus, but on the preceding side of the axis of the tail.

ˌvacuoli'zation. [f. prec. Cf. VACUOLIZED = vacuolated.] = VACUOLATION.

1882 *Jrnl. Microsc. Sci.* Jan. 4 What is the nature of the vacuolisation? 1897 *Allbutt's Syst. Med.* VII. 168 Small and large neuroglia cells,..in a state of vacuolisation and progressive liquefaction.

vacuolized ('vækju:əlaɪzd), *ppl. a.* [f. VACUOLE + -IZE + -ED[1].] = VACUOLATED *ppl. a.*

1910 *Ann. Bot.* XXIV. 733 These bands and masses may be homogeneous or vacuolized. **1961** *Lancet* 2 Sept. 525/2 The cells were enlarged and their cytoplasm was vacuolised.

vacuome ('vækju:əʊm) *Cytology.* [a. F. *vacuome*, f. L. *vacu-us* empty: see -OME.] The vacuoles of a cell collectively (see quot. 1976).

1926 [see PLASTIDOME]. **1936** *Nature* 20 May 914/2 The vacuome and chondriome systems can be distinguished by their behaviour to vital stains. **1947** *Ann. Rev. Microbiol.* I. 9 In the dinoflagellate, *Polykrikos schwartzi*,.. mitochondria, Golgi material, vacuome, fat globules and glycogen have been described. **1959** W. ANDREW *Textbk. Compar. Histol.* v. 146 As it [*sc.* the food particle] approaches the vacuome (Golgi substance), particles from this structure are attracted to its surface. **1960** L. PICKEN *Organization of Cells* vi. 235 According to a theory elaborated by Parat and Painlevé.. all cells contain two systems, unrelated though of profound importance in cell economy: the chondriome—a lipoidal 'phase' manifested as isolated mitochondrial networks; and the vacuome—a dispersed phase of aqueous droplets staining with neutral red, to be equated with the Golgi apparatus. **1976** R. RIEGER et al. *Gloss. Genetics & Cytogenetics* (ed. 4) 564 *Vacuome*, originally, a system comprising a variety of inclusions of plant cells, from the highly hydrated tonoplast to the dense aleuron granules, all with the common ability to stain vitally with neutral red. Today, all the membrane-bounded spaces of the cell with the exception of the mitochondria and the plastids which make up the chondriome.. and the plastome respectively. **1981** *Jrnl. Ultrastructure Res.* LXXVI. 317 Multivesicular bodies seen in section of the unicellular green alga *Scenedesmus obtusiusculus* are profiles of a continuous cisternum, the vacuome.

vacuous ('vækju:əs), *a.* [f. L. *vacu-us* empty, void, free, clear, etc. (cf. VACUUM *sb.*) + -OUS.]

†**1.** Not properly filled out or developed. *Obs.*[−1]

1651 SMALLWOOD *Commend. Verses to W. Cartwright's Wks.*, False Vacuous Births in every street we see: But seldome, true and ripen'd, such as He.

2. Empty of matter; not occupied or filled with anything solid or tangible.

1655–60 STANLEY *Hist. Philos.* (1687) 374/1 It were impossible for one body to make another to recede, if the triple dimension.. were vacuous. **1677** GALE *Crt. Gentiles* IV. 226 Wil they say that these Atomes were introduced or produced in this vacuous space in time? **1794** R. J. SULIVAN *View Nat.* IV. 3 He contended, that thunder or sound would not be able to pass through walls,.. unless there were some vacuous spaces in those bodies. **1813** T. BUSBY *Lucretius* II. VI. Comm. p. xxiii, He notices many natural circumstances which.. demonstrate the vacuous nature of all substances. **1860** TYNDALL *Glac.* II. xxiv. 356 The water.. is not able to fill it, hence a vacuous space must be formed in the cell.

b. Empty of air or gas; in which a vacuum has been produced.

1669 BOYLE *Contin. New Exp.* II. (1682) 158, I put Pears bruised into a vacuous Reciever. **1842** E. A. PARNELL *Chem. Anal.* (1845) 490 The difference between its weight when containing the gas, and when vacuous. **1862** GROVE *Corr. Phys. Forces* (ed. 4) 59 No air is given off from the bubbles, so they seem to be vacuous. **1892** *Photogr. Ann.* II. 233 In incandescent lamps the electric current heats up a carbon filament inclosed in a vacuous globe.

c. *Bot.* Not containing some part or feature usually present.

1866 *Treas. Bot.* 1199/2 Bracts which usually support flowers are said to be vacuous when they have no flower in their axils.

d. Empty of any visible object.

1877 MORLEY *Crit. Misc.* Ser. II. 255 As the flies of a summer day dart from point to point in the vacuous air.

3. Empty of ideas; unintelligent; expressionless. Cf. VACANT *a.* 5.

1848 THACKERAY *Bk. Snobs* x, A vacuous, solemn.. Snob. **1883** *Standard* 2 Jan. 5/2 The absence of anxiety.. leaves their minds vacuous. **1889** *Times* 26 Oct. 9/1 That gift of oppressive familiarity which by some vacuous people is taken to indicate.. sterling sense.

Comb. **1895** 'H. S. MERRIMAN' *Grey Lady* I. iii. (1899) 28 He was rather a vacuous-looking young man.

b. Indicative of mental vacancy.

1855 THACKERAY *Newcomes* II. 25 With that vacuous leer which distinguishes his lordship. **1858** O. W. HOLMES *Aut. Breakf.-t.* vi. 55 These negative faces with their vacuous eyes and stony lineaments. **1873** BLACK *Pr. Thule* xx. 320 There was a cheery, vacuous, smiling expression on his round face.

Comb. **1879** MCCARTHY *Own Times* v. I. 116 A huge white-headed, vacuous-eyed man was to be seen.

4. Devoid of content or substance.

1870 SWINBURNE *Ess. & Stud.* (1875) 56 The vacuous monotonous desire and discontent, the fitful and febrile beauty of Alfred de Musset. **1879** HOWELLS *L. Aroostook* (1883) I. 45 Mrs. Erwin wrote an epistolary style exasperatingly vacuous and diffuse.

5. Unoccupied, idle, indolent; not filled up with any (profitable) employment or activity.

1872 MORLEY *Voltaire* 334 It cannot for ever be tolerable that the mass should wear away their lives in unbroken toil without hope or aim, in order that the few may live selfish and vacuous days. **1897** *Review of Rev.* 37 There are many rich people who.. lead such mean and vacuous lives.

Hence '**vacuously** *adv.*; '**vacuousness**.

1648 W. MOUNTAGUE *Devout Ess.* I. 352 In that vacuousness the winds and vapors of tediousness and displicence rise. **1816** J. GILCHRIST *Philos. Etym.* 226 The mistiness and vacuousness of abstract expression. **1860** *All Year Round* No. 88. 283 He had.. a broad fair face, rather vacuously good natured in its ordinary expression. **1880** *Daily Tel.* 14 Feb., So there he stood, with his hands in his pockets,.. gazing vacuously at the fighting and rough play.

vacuum ('vækju:əm), *sb.* Pl. vacua and vacuums. [L. *vacuum*, neut. of *vacuus* empty: cf. VACUOUS *a.* So F. *vacuum*, It., Sp., Pg. *vacuo*.]

1. Emptiness of space; space unoccupied by matter. Now *rare* or *Obs.*

1550 CRANMER *Lord's Supper* 21 Naturall reason abhorreth *vacuum*, that is to say, that there shoulde be any emptye place, wherin no substance shoulde be. **1570** DEE *Math. Pref.* 35 This Arte is very proffitable: to proue, that *Vacuum*, or Emptines is not in the world. **1626** BACON *Sylva* §83 The more gross of the Tangible Parts do contract and serve themselves together.. to avoid *Vacuum*. **1657** TRAPP *Ezra* ix. 6 For beyond the moveable Heavens, Aristotle.. saith there is neither body, nor time, nor place, nor *vacuum*. **1676** *Poor Robin's Intell.* 30 May–6 June 1/1 Having his head as ful of Vacuum as his small proportion of brains was capable of. **1795** W. BLAKE *Bk. Los* i, Round the flames roll,.. mounting on high Into Vacuum, into nonentity, Where nothing was. **1843** *Penny Cycl.* XXVI. 76/1 The astronomical argument, therefore, in favour of *absolute* vacuum has fallen.

2. a. A space entirely empty of matter.

1607 A. BREWER *Lingua* IV. i. H i b, First shall the whole Machin of the world.. returne to.. Chaos, then the least vacuvm be found in the vniuerse. **1638** WILKINS *New World* I. (1684) 23 To dispute against Democritus, who thought, that the World was made by the casual concourse of Atoms in a great *Vacuum*. **1714** *Let. from Layman* (ed. 2) 7 A Government can't rightfully restrain a Man's professing the Belief of a *Vacuum*, or a *Plenum*. **1763** JOHNSON in *Boswell* 21 July, There are objections against a *plenum*, and objections against a *vacuum*; yet one of them must.. be true. **1865** J. GROTE *Plato* I. i. 80 Proceeding upon his hypothesis of atoms and vacua as the only objective existences. **1884** F. TEMPLE *Relat. Relig. & Sci.* i. (1885) 8 The reasons why.. Nature abhors a vacuum were discovered.

b. A space empty of air, esp. one from which the air has been artificially withdrawn.

sing. **1652** FRENCH *Yorksh. Spa* ii. 7 So much air being spent, there would of necessity follow a *vacuum*. **1660** BOYLE *New Exp. Phys. Mech.* Proem 2 The Interest of the Ayr, in hindring the descent of the Quick-silver, in the famous Experiment touching a *Vacuum*. **1713** DERHAM *Phys.-Theol.* 8 *note*, The Ear-wig.. and some other Insects would seem unconcerned at the Vacuum a good while, and lie as dead; but revive in the Air. **1758** REID tr. *Macquer's Chym.* I. 299 The air contained therein is condensed, and leaves a *vacuum*, which the external air.. tends to occupy. **1829** *Nat. Philos., Heat* I. ii. 2 (L.U.K.), Count Rumford proved the passage of heat through a Torricellian vacuum, that is, the space left at the top of a barometer by the mercury falling. **1860** MAURY *Phys. Geog.* i. §6 At the height of 80 or 90 miles there is a vacuum far more complete than any which we can produce by any air-pump. **1872** J. P. COOKE *New Chem.* 17 Alcohol expands more slowly into the aqueous vapor than it would into a vacuum.

pl. **1777** *Phil. Trans.* LXVII. 679 That the vacua be as nearly as possible compleat. **1832** BREWSTER *Nat. Magic* x. 262 The plates, being raised or depressed by the voluntary muscles, form so many vacua.

c. *ellipt.* for *vacuum cleaner*, sense 4 below. *colloq.* (orig. *U.S.*).

1910 *Judge* 9 Apr. 8/2 A vacuum was the only thing she could be trusted to handle with safety. **1922** *Hotel World* 25 Mar. 14/1, I have three vacuums going all day. **1960** *Farmer & Stockbreeder* 8 Mar. (Suppl.) 10/1 Is it better to have a *powerful* or a *handy* cleaner? That has always been a problem when choosing a 'vacuum'. **1977** *New Yorker* 24 Oct. 88/3 Green Haven's dep [*sc.* deputy superintendent] of administration was preoccupied with the size of the wet-dry vacuums being used to clean the prison kitchen.

3. a. An empty space; a portion of space (left) unoccupied or unfilled with the usual or natural contents.

1589 NASHE in *Greene's Menaphon* (Arb.) 12 The Scythians, who.. swaddle themselues streighter, to the intent no *vacuum* beeing left in their intrayles [etc.]. *a* **1635** T. RANDOLPH *Poems, Parley with his Empty Purse* (1640) 113 Unnatural vacuum, can your emptinesse Answer to some slight questions? **1700** T. BROWN tr. *Fresny's Amusem.* viii, He made a Dive into my Pocket, but encountring a Disappointment, Rub'd off, Cursing the *Vacuum*. **1758** J. S. *Le Dran's Observ. Surg.* (1771) 141, I discovered a *Vacuum* upon the intercostal Muscles, from whence about a Spoonful of.. Matter was discharged. **1791** H. WALPOLE in *Miss Berry's Jrnl.* I. 328, I shall fill my vacuum with some lines that General Conway has sent me. *a* **1838** C. MORRIS *Lyra Urban.* (1840) II. 97 The Dandy's head, A vacuum dead, Ne'er tries for thought to seek!

b. In various fig. uses.

1617 MIDDLETON *Fair Quar.* II. D iij b, I cannot see that *vacuum* in your bloud. **1630** LENNARD tr. *Charron's Wisd.* vii. 33 It were a *vacuum*, a defect, a deformitie too absurd in nature.. that betwixt two extreames.. there should be no middle. *a* **1670** HACKET *Abp. Williams* I. (1692) 10 Commonly they misspent that triennial probation, and left upon that place a *vacuum* of doing little or nothing. **1710** PALMER *Prov.* 384 'Tis infinitely pleasing to observe there has been no *Vacuum* in our Life. **1772** *Phil. Trans.* LXII. 317 It should therefore seem that the larks from the more adjacent parts croud in to supply the vacuum occasioned by the London Epicures. **1829** MARRYAT *F. Mildmay* ix, The.. vacuum occasioned by my mother's death. **1846** GROTE *Greece* (1862) I. xvi. 294 They filled up the vacuum of the unrecorded past. **1879** R. H. ELLIOT *Written on Foreh.* I. 140 So Martin Kerr.. was left with a sheer, hopeless vacuum to fill up as best he could.

4. *attrib.* and *Comb.*, as ***vacuum-brake***, ***cleanser***, ***disk***, ***distillation***, ***engine***, ***-pan***, ***-pump***, ***-vessel***; ***vacuum-jacketed***, ***-made*** adjs.; **vacuum activity** (see quot. 1981); **vacuum aspiration**, a method of induced abortion in which the contents of the uterus are removed by suction through a tube passed into it via the vagina; **vacuum bottle** = *vacuum flask* below; **vacuum chamber**, a chamber designed to be emptied of air; **vacuum cleaner**, an electrical appliance for removing dust (from carpets and other flooring, soft furnishings, etc.) by suction; also *transf.* and *fig.*; hence (as a back-formation) **vacuum-clean** *v. trans.*, = VACUUM *v.*; so **vacuum-cleaning** *vbl. sb.*; **vacuum deposition**, deposition of a substance by allowing it to condense from the vapour in what is otherwise a vacuum; so **vacuum-deposit** *v. trans.*, **-deposited** *ppl. a.*; **vacuum extraction** *Obstetr.*, the application of suction to a baby's head to assist its birth; so **vacuum extractor**, a cup-shaped appliance for achieving this; **vacuum-fitted** *a.*, of a railway car: furnished with a vacuum brake; **vacuum flask**, a vessel with a double wall enclosing a vacuum so that liquid in the inner receptacle retains its temperature (cf. THERMOS); also *transf.* in *attrib.* use; **vacuum fluctuation** *Physics*, a fluctuation in field strength in a nominally field-free vacuum, occurring in consequence of the quantization of any radiation field; **vacuum forming**, a type of thermoforming in which a vacuum is used to draw the plastic into the mould (see quot. 1974); **vacuum grease**, a grease which because of its low vapour pressure is suitable for sealing joints in a vacuum apparatus; **vacuum packaging**, (*a*) = *vacuum-packing* vbl. sb. s.v. VACUUM-PACK *v.*; (*b*) the vacuumized container used in vacuum-packing; **vacuum polarization** *Physics*, the spontaneous appearance and disappearance of electron-positron pairs in a vacuum; **vacuum pump**, a pump for evacuating a container of air or other gas; **vacuum-tight** *a.* = AIR-TIGHT *a.*; **vacuum wax** = *vacuum grease* above.

Also ***vacuum-apparatus***, ***-cylinder***, ***-filter***, ***-gauge***, ***-shunt***, ***-valve*** (Knight, 1875–84).

1953 N. TINBERGEN *Herring Gull's World* iv. 35 It is possible.. this was just a kind of '*vacuum activity' due to the accumulation of the urge to paddle. **1981** *Oxf. Compan. Anim. Behaviour* 579/1 Vacuum activities occur in the apparent absence of the external stimuli that normally elicit the activity. **1967** *Obstetrics & Gynecol.* XXX. 28 (*heading*) A critical view of *vacuum aspiration: a new method for the termination of pregnancy. **1974** PASSMORE & ROBSON *Compan. Med. Stud.* III. xlii. 7/2 Before the 12th week it is customary and simplest to evacuate the uterus via the vagina by vacuum aspiration. **1978** F. WELDON *Praxis* ii. 13 If by mistake they fall pregnant, they abort by vacuum aspiration. **1910** *Chambers's Jrnl.* June 413/2 The *vacuum-bottle has entered so extensively into the domestic circle as to become regarded almost as indispensable. **1976** *Daily Colonist* (Victoria, B.C.) 6 Mar. 19/5 Use lunch buckets or vacuum bottles to keep foods hot or cold. **1875** KNIGHT *Dict. Mech.* 2686/1 **Vacuum-brake*, a form of steam-operated car-brake. **1889** G. FINDLAY *Eng. Railway* 168 The train is fitted throughout with vacuum brakes. *a* **1877** KNIGHT *Dict. Mech.* III. 2687/2 Huffer.. claims the use of exhaust steam from an engine to condense in a *vacuum-chamber, and so raise water to turn a wheel. **1971** *Materials & Technol.* II. v. 230 A certain amount of water is evaporated from the clay as it passes through the vacuum chamber. **1912** *Sci. Amer.* 22 Nov. 442/2 (*caption*) *Vacuum-cleaning an automobile. The exhaust gases of the motor create the suction. **1924** KIPLING *Debits & Credits* (1926) 149 The organ-bench, whose purple velvet cushion was being vacuum-cleaned on the floor below. **1956** *Good Housek. Home Encycl.* (ed. 4) 316/2 Wicker-work.. requires to be brushed or vacuum-cleaned regularly. **1973** *Physics Bull.* Feb. 110/3 These.. could then be scraped and vacuum cleaned from the carpet. **1977** J. R. L. ANDERSON *Death in City* i. 10 A team.. did the rooms,.. vacuum-cleaning floors. **1983** *Daily Tel.* 8 Apr. 16/3 Soviet spies are vacuum cleaning the West for its industrial and scientific secrets. **1903** *Hardwareman* 23 May 395 A decision of.. serious import as regards the operations of the *Vacuum Cleaner Co. **1907** *Yesterday's Shopping* (1969) 113/1 The 'Witch' Dust Extractor is a vacuum cleaner suitable alike for carpets, upholstery, clothing, &c. **1962** A. LURIE *Love & Friendship* i. 12 She.. did not hear the noise of the vacuum cleaner sucking its way up the stair carpeting. **1972** *World Bk. Sci. Ann. 1971* 342 The vacuum cleaner is actually a hydraulic pump designed to lift as much as 400 tons of material from the sea floor daily. **1976** *Times* 1 Mar. 13/3 The conservation of fish stocks.. in the face of over-developed world fishing fleets and 'vacuum cleaner' techniques of fishing. **1902** *Let.* 20 Oct. in *Goblin Story* (Goblin Ltd.) (1969) 9, I have submitted the subject of the *Vacuum Cleaning Company's operations to the King. **1916** J. WEBSTER *Dear Enemy* 71 'Well?' said she, her tone implying that I was a vacuum-cleaning agent. **1939** *Country Life* 11 Feb. p. vi (Advt.), Vacuum cleaning plant. **1903** *Westm. Gaz.* 30 May 5/3 There is a machine at work, called the '*vacuum cleanser', which gives them all, in turn, a thorough 'spring cleaning'. **1946** *Nature* 14 Dec. 862/1 Mollwo reported on the density of *vacuum-deposited salt layers. **1960** *McGraw-Hill Encycl. Sci. & Technol.* X. 596/2 Fabrication of printed resistors by vacuum deposition is an expensive process and there has been no general application of this technique except for precision resistive elements. **1982** *Jrnl. Colloid & Interface Sci.* XC. 335 When certain materials such as Se or Sn are vacuum-deposited onto heated polymers under appropriate conditions, a most unusual structure can form. *Ibid.* 337/1 The structure of the monolayer assemblies formed by vacuum deposition is almost independent of the deposition rate. *Ibid.*, The vacuum deposited structure is little altered if the system pressure during deposition is allowed to rise. **1860** TYNDALL *Glac.* I. xxiii. 163 Sometimes the *vacuum disks were parallel to the veins [of the glacier]. **1899** tr. *R. von Jaksch's Clin. Diag.* v. (ed. 4) 170 Still better for this purpose is the method of *vacuum distillation. **1825** J. NICHOLSON *Operat. Mechanic* 670 The application of Mr. Brown's pneumatic, or *vacuum engine. **1961** *Lancet* 22 July 189/2 They concluded that *vacuum extraction does not distress the fœtus. **1975** I. ILLICH *Med. Nemesis* vii. 120 The vacuum extraction method has rendered the interruption of pregnancies safe, cheap and simple. **1954** T. MALMSTRÖM in *Acta Obstetrica et Gynecologica Scandinavica* XXXIII. Suppl. No. 4. 5 The *vacuum extractor ad modum Dr Malmstrom is constructed and manufactured in co-operation with R. Soderberg & Co, Gothenburg, Sweden. **1960** *Proc. R. Soc. Med.* LIII. 749/1 The vacuum extractor consists of a flattened round metal cup with bulging sides. **1980** S. KITZINGER *Pregnancy & Childbirth* 260 Sometimes a vacuum extractor, or ventouse, is used instead of forceps. **1937** *Vacuum-fitted [see *passenger train* s.v. PASSENGER 7 a]. **1968** *Listener* 15 Aug. 210/1 We..have a brake which is known as the vacuum brake, and our wagons are known as vacuum-fitted. **1917** *Harrods Gen. Catal.* 946/3 The 'Icy-Hot' *Vacuum Flasks, improved designs, will keep liquids hot for 24 hours or cold for 3 days. **1926** *Daily Colonist* (Victoria, B.C.) 20 Jan. 5/1 This vacuum flask will keep things hot for you indefinitely. **1958** *New Statesman* 23 Aug. 214/2 Investigation in person will clearly have to wait until travellers are provided with armour-plated vacuum-flask suits. **1978** M. BABSON *Tightrope for Three* vi. 39 She..filled the kettle..and..the vacuum flask as well. **1955** L. ROSENFELD in W. Pauli *Niels Bohr* 88 The '*vacuum' fluctuations of the field variables. **1973** *Nature* 14 Dec. 397/1 The laws of physics place no limit on the scale of vacuum fluctuations. The duration is of course subject to the restriction $\Delta E\Delta t \sim h$. **1979** J. C. POLKINGHORNE *Particle Play* v. 74 Buffeted by vacuum fluctuations the elementary particle has a pretty rocky ride. This is the origin of the infinities which people found when they first tried to calculate with quantum field theories. **1946** J. SASSO *Plastics Handbk. for Product Engineers* v. 308 In the *vacuum-forming process the plastic sheet is heated to approximately 250F. **1974** *Encycl. Brit. Macropædia* XIV. 521/1 In simple vacuum forming, the plastic sheet is clamped over an airtight box, from which air is exhausted, rapidly drawing the heated plastic down on a 'former' within the box, thus reproducing its shape. **1946** *Jrnl. R. Aeronaut. Soc.* L. 393 Connection to the vacuum system is made by a ground metal joint sealed with *vacuum grease. **1977** *Vacuum* XXVII. 431/1 There are three factors involved in choosing a vacuum grease—cost, convenience, and its effect on the vacuum system. **1946** *Nature* 20 July 105/1 The best way to carry methane on motor-vehicles is as a liquid in *vacuum-jacketed tanks. **1970** *Sci. Jrnl.* Aug. 82/3 The 'lagged storage tank' for LNG would need to be vacuum jacketed. **1853** URE *Dict. Arts* (ed. 4) II. 879 *Vacuum-made liqueurs. **1954** L. C. BARAIL *Packaging Engineering* xx. 249 The cans filled with the whole products are then sealed by means of vacuum machines, a process known as *vacuum packaging. **1982** R. MANHEIM tr. *Grass's Headbirths* iv. 65 The cut in the vacuum packaging could be patched up. **1839** URE *Dict. Arts* 1208 An apparatus inserted air-tight into the cover of the *vacuum-pan. **1857** MILLER *Elem. Chem., Org.* 66 The syrup..is boiled down again in the vacuum pan, and is obtained in the form of..crushed sugar. [**1935** *Physical Rev.* XLVIII. 55/2 The existence of [such] an induced charge corresponds to a polarization of the vacuum.] **1951** *Ibid.* LXXXI. 664/1 We shall illustrate this assertion by applying such a gauge invariant method to treat several aspects of the problem of *vacuum polarization by a prescribed electromagnetic field. **1979** CHENG & O'NEILL *Elementary Particle Physics* iii. 82 The two dominant processes that modify the electron's interaction with the proton.., resulting in the Lamb shift, are the vertex correction and vacuum polarization. **1858** SIMMONDS *Dict. Trade*, **Vacuum-pump*, a pump attached to a marine steam-engine. **1882** *Chem. News* 27 Oct. 192/1 In the machine in question the refrigeration is effected simply by the evaporation of water under a special vacuum-pump. **1979** J. MATLEY *Fluid Movers* v. 267/1 A good seal between the inlet and outlet sides is essential in all mechanical vacuum pumps. **1927** *Brit. Jrnl. Radiol.* XXIII. 143 The glass is directly sealed to a chromium-iron alloy which is perfectly *vacuum-tight. **1946** *Nature* 23 Nov. 756/2 Vacuum-tight seals through hard glass with bare tungsten wire are difficult to make. **1964** M. GOWING *Britain & Atomic Energy 1939–1945* viii. 219 New techniques had to be developed for ensuring that the machinery was..exceptionally vacuum-tight. **1899** *Edin. Rev.* Apr. 323 Professor Dewar's coils and *vacuum-vessels. **1926** J. H. SMITH tr. *L. Dunoyer's Vacuum Practice* iii. 142 *Vacuum waxes. Golaz wax has been in use since Regnault's time. **1971** *Sci. Amer.* Aug. 108/1 The joint was sealed with Apiezon W-100 vacuum wax.

vacuum ('vækju:əm), *v. colloq.* (orig. *U.S.*). [f. the sb.] *trans.* To clean (a room, carpet, etc.), or to remove (dust, etc.) with a vacuum cleaner. Also *fig.* and *absol.* Occas. *intr.* for *pass.*

1922 *Hotel World* 25 Mar. 14/1, I have every room in the hotel vacuumed every week, furniture and all. **1934** in WEBSTER. **1950** *Sun* (Baltimore) 28 Apr. 36/7 Apparently electrocuted when she stepped on a metal furnace grating while vacuuming the floor. **1959** *Times* 11 Feb. 12/6 Why could not..the whole establishment be dusted one day, vacuumed another, and so on? **1961** *Time* (Atlantic ed.) 20 Jan. 17 Her retentive mind vacuums odd details from the newspapers. **1967** D. FRANCIS *Blood Sport* xv. 179 'He says the whole place is *covered* in flour.'..'It'll vacuum quite easily, won't it?' **1974** J. IRVING *158-Pound Marriage* (1980) ix. 203 Together we vacuumed fragments from every crevice. **1978** M. DICKENS *Open Bk.* xv. 141 In the living room, the carpet was so old, it came up in dusty shreds if you vacuumed. **1980** *Daily Tel.* 6 Feb. 18 Toads are hungry creatures: no-one better to vacuum a garden of slugs and other pests. **1985** *Listener* 21 Mar. 25/2 'Syd'..watered his milk, left fat on his lamb chops, and vacuumed when he was listening to symphonies on the radio.

Hence '**vacuuming** *vbl. sb.*

1953 L. KUPER *Living in Towns* ii. 16, I try to do my vacuuming quickly. **1972** J. PORTER *Meddler & her Murder* xii. 160 The lounge could do with the usual dusting and vacuuming. **1979** *Tucson Mag.* Apr. 62/3 One owner..has worked out his own vacuuming routine over the years. **1984** A. BROOKNER *Hotel du Lac* i. 14 After ten o'clock..all household noises had to be silenced; no vacuuming was heard.

vacuumize ('vækju:əmaɪz), *v.* [f. VACUUM + -IZE.] *trans.* To create a vacuum in (something); to seal (a container) from which air has been artificially withdrawn. Hence '**vacuumized** *ppl. a.*; so '**vacuumizing** *vbl. sb.*

1909 *Chambers's Jrnl.* July 478/1 Vacuumising is effected by means of a hand-wheel, or the machine can be worked by power if desired. **1939** R. S. LYONS *Wonders of Modern Industry* xi. 131 To preserve the cigarettes in fresh condition, each tin has a vacuum created inside it before being sealed. The method of vacuumizing is as ingenious as it is simple. *Ibid.* 132 It sometimes happens that some of the tins are not quite vacuumized. **1942** *N.Y. Times* 13 Feb. 18/5 The glass industry 'has always had equipment for vacuumized products'. **1980** *Cement & Concrete Res.* X. 853 The press-method of concrete compaction with simultaneous vacuumizing makes it possible to add an increased volume of mix water to concrete mix. **1983** *Mod. Metals* Jan. 66/1 Made of either tinplate or tin free steel, the TAB-E end can be applied to vacuumized, pressurized or still-filled cans.

'**vacuum-pack**, *v.* [f. VACUUM + PACK *v.*^{1}] *trans.* To pack (something) in an air-tight container from which the air has been withdrawn; to pack (such a container).

1951 *Good Housek. Home Encycl.* 416/2 Coffee that is both freshly ground and freshly roasted (or vacuum-packed). **1954** L. C. BARAIL *Packaging Engineering* xx. 249 Whether the cars have been sealed after exhausting or vacuum packed without being exhausted, they have to be processed in order to destroy microorganisms.

Hence '**vacuum-packed** *ppl. a.*; also *fig.*; '**vacuum-packing** *vbl. sb.*

1955 *Hebrew Union College Annual* XXVI. 108 No longer can we assume that Greece is the hermetically sealed Olympian miracle, any more than we can consider Israel the vacuum-packed miracle from Sinai. **1960** *Farmer & Stockbreeder* 19 Jan. (Suppl.) 41/3 The final processing involves..draining, swabbing and then vacuum-packing in transparent film bags. **1962** *Spectator* 4 May 602/3, I was at a testing of vacuum-packed bacon. Vacuum-packing is likely to spread, because it is so convenient for the handlers. **1975** *Times* 18 Feb. 13/2 The vacuum-packed fine arts sector. **1984** *Listener* 5 Apr. 10/2 The girl said it came vacuum-packed.

vacuum tube. 1. An evacuated tube or pipe, esp. one along which vehicles or other objects can be propelled by allowing air to enter behind them.

1784 in *Pall Mall Mag.* (1896) Aug. 586 Grand Vacuum Tube Company. Direct to Bengal. **1846** *Patent Jrnl.* 4 July 90/1 Fig. 1 is a..section of a railway carriage and traction tube. Fig. 2 is a cross section..showing the communication between the carriage and the piston. The traction or vacuum tube..is the same as generally used. **1920** D. H. LAWRENCE *Touch & Go* 7 A system of vacuum tubes for whooshing Bradburys about from one to the other. **1972** *Daily Tel.* 30 Dec. 6/5 The explanation, it is believed, is that while it was being scooped up it became mixed with the dark grey soil usually found on the Moon. It could not have changed as a result of exposure to the Earth's atmosphere, because it is stored in vacuum tubes. **1973** *Times* 15 Oct. 6/3 High-speed surface systems should be studied as an alternative to air travel, including advanced systems such as the gravity vacuum tube, which would give high speeds for amazingly low energy consumption. **1974** [see *people mover* s.v. PEOPLE *sb.* 8].

2. An evacuated tube (sense 2 g) (orig. a glass cylinder); *spec.* one used as a thermionic valve.

1859 *Phil. Trans. R. Soc.* CXLVIII. 15 The direct discharge is that which is visible when taken from two wires hermetically sealed in a vacuum tube. **1880** *Rep. Brit. Assoc. Adv. Sci. 1880* 260 The band-spectrum of nitrogen... It was first observed by Plücker (1858) in a vacuum tube. **1901** *Engineer* 17 May 507/2 One of the most interesting exhibits was a number of electric vacuum-tube lamps. **1915** W. H. ECCLES *Wireless Telegr. & Teleph.* 376 A. Langmuir has applied his vacuum tube with third electrode (the 'pliotron') in a manner different from those just described. **1923** *Electr. Communication* II. 157/2 No single advance has contributed so largely to change our whole picture of art as the advent of the thermionic valve or vacuum tube as it is designated in America. **1931** MOYER & WOSTREL *Radio Handbk.* VI. 317 The increased use of vacuum tubes for other than radio services has made it necessary to design vacuum tubes which will be suitable for handling much larger currents. **1957** K. R. SPANGENBERG *Fund. Electron Devices* xi. 235 The transistor is, like the vacuum tube, a device that owes its amplifying characteristics to electric-field control of current within the device. **1972** *Sci. Amer.* June 52/2 It produces a television-like image without the cumbersome vacuum tube, electron beam and high voltage required by conventional television systems.

attrib. **1923** *Electr. Communication* II. 157/2 The vacuum tube telephone repeater has made possible telephonic transmissions over practically unlimited distances. **1929** K. HENNEY *Princ. Radio* xiv. 343 Such vacuum tube voltmeters are useful at all audio and nearly all radio frequencies, and can be made to read d.-c. voltages. **1950** [see INSTRUMENT *sb.* 2].

vad, southern ME. var. FADE *a.*^{2}; obs. Sc. f. WED *sb.*, WOAD.

†'**vadable**, *a. Obs. rare.* Also vadeable. [ad. med.L. *vadābilis* (f. *vadāre* to wade through) or a. Sp. *vadeable* (Pg. *vadeavel*, OF. *vadable*).] Fordable.

1555 WATREMAN *Fardle Facions* Pref. 11 To the ende thei [*sc.* the rivers] might not onely be vadable, but passed also with drie foote. **1578** T. N. tr. *Conq. W. India* 65 After hee had iourneyed three leagues, hee came to a faire vadeable Riuer. **1611** FLORIO, *Vadoso*, vadable, or foardable.

vadam, southern ME. var. FATHOM.

Vaddah, obs. form of VEDDA.

†**vade**, *sb. Obs.*$^{-1}$ [ad. L. *vadum.*] A shallow place in a river.

1538 LELAND *Itin.* (1769) V. 94 Irwel is not navigable but in sum Places for Vadys and Rokkes.

†**vade**, *v.*^{1} *Obs.* [var. of FADE *v.*^{1}, chiefly used in fig. senses (very common *c* 1530–1630) and app. to some extent associated with L. *vādĕre* to go: see next, to which some of the quotations placed under 3–3 c may really belong.

This association may be the real explanation of the form, but see the note to FADE *a.*^{2}]

1. *intr.* Of colour: = FADE *v.*^{1} 4.

1471 RIPLEY *Comp. Alch.* Pref. in Ashm. (1652) 127 Colour whych wyll not vade. *c* **1532** DU WES *Introd. Fr.* in *Palsgr.* 956 To vade, *ternir*. *a* **1586** SIDNEY *Astr. & Stella* (1622) 578 How doth the colour vade of those vermillion dies. **1594** PLAT *Jewell-ho.* III. 45 As soone as the beautiful hew of the leaues begin to vade. **1613** *Answ. Uncasing Machiav.* E iv b, Whose colours never vade. **1647** C. HARVEY *Schola Cordis* xvii. 4 The staines of sin I see Are vaded all, or di'd in graine.

2. Of flowers, etc.: = FADE *v.*^{1} 1.

1492 [see 3 b]. *c* **1532** DU WES *Introd. Fr.* in *Palsgr.* 894 Rose that can nat vade, *rose immarcessible*. **1578** LYTE *Dodoens* I Small grayish leaves..the whiche do perish and vade in winter. **1593** SHAKS. *Rich. II*, I. ii. 20 One flourishing branch of his most Royall roote..Is hackt downe, and his summer leafes all vaded. **1621** LADY M. WROTH *Urania* 22 Do not the flowers vade, and grasse die for her departure?

3. To pass away, disappear, vanish; to decay or perish; = FADE *v.*^{1} 6.

1495 *Trevisa's Barth. De P.R.* XVI. xxxvi. 564 Aege that passyth & vadyth chaungyth tymes of thynges. *a* **1548** HALL *Chron., Hen. IV* (1550) 4 When he departed, the only shelde, defence and comfort of the common people was vadid and gone. **1568** T. HOWELL *Arb. Amitie* (1879) 19 Forme is most frayle,..it vadth as grasse doth growe. **1607** MIDDLETON *Fam. Love* I. i, I know how soon their love vadeth. **1641** BRATHWAIT *Eng. Gentlew.* 324 Where..beauty never fadeth, love never faileth, health never vadeth. *a* **1678** MARVELL *Poems, Clorinda & Damon* (1681) 12 Grass withers; and the Flow'rs too fade. Seize the short Ioyes then, ere they vade.

b. Const. *from*, *into*, *to*.

1492 RYMAN *Poems* lxxxiv. 2 in *Archiv Stud. neu. Spr.* LXXXIX. 253 As medowe floures..Vadeth to erthe.. Likewise richesse and grete honoures Shall vade fro euery creature. *c* **1537** *Thersites* D ij, The cowherd of Comertowne, with his croked spade, Cause frome the the wormes soone to vade. **1596** SPENSER *F.Q.* V. ii. 40 How euer gay their blossome or their blade Doe flourish now, they into dust shall vade. **1663** CANE *Ep. to Author of Animad. Fiat Lux* 96 All your talk in this your eighteenth chapter vades into nothing.

c. With *away*.

1530 *Proper Dyaloge* in *Roy's Rede me*, etc. (Arb.) 133 Affermynge that oure loue shuld a-way vade Without any memory of them at all. **1587** M. GROVE *Pelops & Hipp.* (1878) 38 The time thus doth consume & wear, the night doth vade away. **1625** PURCHAS *Pilgrims* II. 1761 The bankes of sand doe fleet and vade away out of the river.

†**vade**, *v.*^{2} *Obs.* [ad. L. *vādĕre* to go; cf. prec.]

1. To go away, depart. *rare.*

1569 ELVIDEN *Pesistratus & Catanea* (Bynneman), Then proclamation made That Pisistrate to proper soile should vade. **1638** BRATHWAIT *Barnabees Jrnl.* II. (1818) 67 Beauty feedeth, beauty fadeth, Beauty lost, her lover vadeth.

2. To proceed, advance.

a **1660** *Contemp. Hist. Irel.* (Ir. Archæol. Soc.) II. 5 You are too yonge to vade unto these graue matters.

vade, obs. Sc. form of WADE *v.*

†**vadelect**. *Obs.* Also 6 -lict. [ad. Anglo-L. *vadelectus*, *vadlectus* (13th c.), ad. AF. *vadlet*, var. OF. *vaslet*, *vallet*, *varlet*: see VALET *sb.* and VARLET.] A servant, serving-man.

1586 FERNE *Blaz. Gentrie* 161 The same French king, for want of a Hereald.., was constrained to subbornate a vadelict, or common seruing-man. **1628** COKE *On Litt.* 156 But if the sherife be a Vadelect of the crowne or other meniall seruant of the King, there the challenge is good. **1661** BLOUNT *Glossogr.* (ed. 2), *Vadelet* or *Vadelect*.. signifies a servant, and is used in the accounts of the Inner Temple, for a Benchers Clerk or Servant.

So **vadelet**, **vadlet**. *arch.*

1661 [see prec.]. **1813** WILLIAMS *Law of Clergy* 398 The King as founder of..many religious houses had a corrody for his vadelets, and a pension for a chaplain. **1861** RILEY tr. *Carpenter's Liber Albus* 40 As soon as the Sheriffs are sworn, all the Servants of their office—clerks, serjeants and their vadlets..—shall also be sworn.

‖**vade-mecum** ('vɑ:deɪ 'meɪkəm, 'veɪdɪ 'mi:kəm). Also **vade mecum**, **vademecum**. [L., *vāde* imper. sing. of *vādĕre* to go + *mēcum* with me. So F., Sp., Pg. *vademecum* (Pg. also *-meco*).]

1. A book or manual suitable for carrying about with one for ready reference; a handbook or guidebook. (Sometimes used as the title of such a work.)

1629 (*title*), Vade Mecum: A Manuall of Essayes Morrall, Theologicall. **1649** F. ROBERTS *Clavis Bibl.* 405 Among the very Ethiopians this book was in such repute, that the Ethiopian Eunuch made it his (Vade mecum) his companion in his journey. **1679** (*title*), A Vade-mecum for the Lovers of Musick. **1731** FIELDING *Grub St. Op.* Introd., It is a sort of family Opera. The husband's vade-mecum; and is very necessary for all married men to have in their houses. **1797** *Monthly Mag.* III. 128 The Odéon shall possess a literary journal,.. to be a valuable vade-mecum for such persons as are not in the habit of deciding on the merits of theatrical performances. **1818** BYRON *Juan* I. cci, Aristotle's rules, The *Vade Mecum* of the true sublime, Which makes so many poets, and some fools. **1880** MUIRHEAD *Gaius* Introd. p. xv, It is the remains.. of a handbook for the practitioner; a *vade mecum*, as modern law-writers would call it. **1927** *New Republic* 12 Oct. 216/1 His little book, indeed, is a religious document, and might well serve as a *vade mecum* for all those disillusioned moderns who think that, because they cannot have all, they must be content to accept nothing. **1963** *Times* 2 May 15/3 In 1935, someone *did* collect James's prefaces together into what *has* become a vade-mecum for practitioners ('required reading' for students). **1977** *Amer. N. & Q.* XV. 108/1 From the standpoint of the non-expert buyer.., it is a singularly useful and dependable vademecum. **1983** *Archæology* Jan.-Feb. 72 This is the book that all of us have been looking for: a reasonably complete vade mecum to every worthwhile site in mesoamerica.

fig. *a* **1631** DONNE *Select.* (1840) 51 His *vade mecum*, the abridgment of all nature, and all law, his own heart, and conscience.

2. A thing commonly carried about by a person as being of some service to him.

1632 LITHGOW *Trav.* VIII. 355 Gold.. was my continuall vade Mecum. **1654** WHITLOCK *Zootomia* 71 Whose Vade mecum is an Aqua vitæ Bottle. **1678** *Yng. Man's Call.* 50 You may safely take it [a maxim] as your *vade mecum* along with you, in reference to the things of this life. **1774** 'J. COLLIER' *Mus. Trav.* App. 23 To write a pamphlet against the use of a medicine which had been his *vade mecum* in all his journies. **1966** C. MACKENZIE *Paper Lives* iv. 55 A fellow Jacobean called Horner had won £77 in what are called the Pools and this sum was being used as the financial *vade mecum* for their escapade.

vader, southern ME. variant of FATHER.

vadiation (veɪdɪˈeɪʃən). *Law. rare.* [ad. med.L. *vadiātio*, f. *vadiāre* to give security.] The action of requiring or giving surety or pledges.

1753 *Chambers' Cycl.* Suppl. s.v., Vadiation, *Vadiatio*, in the civil law. **1802–12** BENTHAM *Ration. Judic. Evid.* (1827) IV. 557 *note*, Remedy against.. sequestration, or vadiation in this or that shape.

†**vadimony.** *Obs.* Also 6 vady-, 7 **vademony.** [ad. L. *vadimōnium*, f. *vad-*, *vas* bail, surety.] A pledge or recognisance.

1502 ARNOLDE *Chron.* (1811) 2 That they haue ther vadymonies [*printed* -memes] and weddes: the xiiii. artycle. *c* **1620** A. HUME *Brit. Tongue* (1865) 22 The accent in the fourth syllab from the end; as in mátrimonie, pátrimonie, vádimonie. **1654** WARREN *Unbelievers* 48 His Obligation was arbitrary and voluntary; not arising from the guilt of.. sin, but by way of vadimony, and susception. **1699** J. BARRY *Reviv. Cordial* (1802) 80 In this work,.. which he himself, as vademony and surety for God's elect, hath undertaken to.. perform.

†ˈ**vading,** *vbl. sb. Obs.*⁻¹ [f. VADE *v.*¹] The action or process of disappearing, declining, etc.

1570 FOXE *A. & M.* (ed. 2) I. 254/2 Yᵉ lyke vadyng of water happened also in the floode of Medeway.

†ˈ**vading,** *ppl. a. Obs.* Also 7 **vaid-.** [f. as prec.] Fading, passing away, fleeting, transitory.

1566 ADLINGTON *Apuleius* Ep. Ded., The vaine and soone vadynge beautie of the worlde. **1577** GRANGE *Golden Aphrod.*, etc. R j, My Lady fayre whose shape doth shine And glyster in my vading sighte. **1596** WARNER *Alb. Eng.* II. lxv. (1612) 279 What els is Forme but vaiding aire? **1615** BRATHWAIT *Strappado* (1878) 53 Thy form's Diuine, no fading, vading flower. **1661** *Sir A. Haslerig's Last Will & Test.* 2 What a vading breath, or light blast is this flash of Honour.

vadlet: see VADELET.

vadmal, -mel, varr. (after mod.Scand. forms) of WADMAL.

[**1797** *Stat. Acc. Scot.* XIV. 326 The old men and women .. continue to wear good strong black clothes without dying, called by the ancient Norse, Vadmell.] **1851** THORPE *Northern Myth.* I. 112, I am Kraka, Coal-black in vadmel! **1881** DU CHAILLU *Land Midnight Sun* II. 78 The tent was made of coarse heavy vadmal.

vadome, southern ME. variant of FATHOM *sb.*

vadose (ˈveɪdəʊs, -z), *a. Physical Geogr.* [f. L. *vadōs-us*, f. *vadum* shallow piece of water: see -OSE¹.] Of, pertaining to, or designating underground water occurring above the water-table. Cf. PHREATIC *a.*

1894 F. POSEPNY in *Trans. Amer. Inst. Mining Engineers* XXIII. 213 For that part of the subterranean circulation, bounded by the water-level, and called the vadose or shallow underground circulation, the law of a descending movement holds good. **1909** [see PHREATIC *a.* 2]. **1954** [see PHREATIC *a.*]. **1973** *Sci. Amer.* Apr. 48/2 Of the total amount of underground water, vadose water (water present in soils) accounts for only ·066 × 10^{15} cubic meters. **1977** A. HALLAM *Planet Earth* 108 (*caption*) Vadose cave formed by the waters of the Quashies River, Jamaica.

†**vaˈdosity.** *Obs.*⁻¹ [f. L. *vadōs-us*, f. *vadum* ford.] The fact of being fordable.

1658 BURTON *Comm. Itin. Antoninus* 224 The word Ford, by reason of the vadosity of the River there, being added.

ˈ**vady,** *a. south-w. dial.* [Of obscure origin.] Damp, moist.

1880 MRS. PARR *Adam & Eve* xiii. 188 The grass was too 'vady' for him to sit down upon.

‖**væ** (vaɪ). Also 6 ve. [L. *væ* alas!]

†**1.** A denunciation or threatening of woe. *Obs.*

1559 ABP. PARKER *Corr.* (Parker Soc.) 79 We should.. deserve the wrathful *væ* and vengeance of God. **1584** LODGE *Alarm agst. Usurers* F iiij, The Lord shal place you among the goates, and pronounce his Ve against you. **1602** W. WATSON *Quodl. Relig. & State* 9 With how many *væs* and woes to you Scribes and Pharisees did he come vpon them? *a* **1636** WESTCOTE *View Devonsh.* (1845) 61 There was a *væ* or woe pronounced against them in these words,—'Woe unto you Piltonians, that make cloth without wool'.

2. *væ victis* [Livy *Hist.* V. xlviii. 9]. **a.** *int.* Woe to the vanquished. **b.** *sb. phr.* The humiliation of the vanquished by their conquerors; the phrase as a maxim or utterance.

1612 J. SELDEN in Drayton *Poly-Olbion* viii. 124 Whence, vpon a murmuring complaint among the Romanes, crying væ victis, came that to be as prouerbe applied to the conquered. **1792** BURKE *Let.* 3 Jan. in M. Arnold *Lett., Speeches & Tracts on Irish Affairs* (1881) 259, I cannot say *væ victis*, and then throw the sword into the scale. **1819** SCOTT *Ivanhoe* I. ii. 39 The *vae victis*, or severities imposed upon the vanquished. **1856** M. BERNARD in *Oxford Ess.* II. ii. 90 The stonecutter has laboured to produce a vigorous representation of the *vae victis*—of triumphant pride and abject humiliation. **1904** G. K. FORTESCUE in *Cambr. Mod. Hist.* (1907) VIII. xvi. 512 *Vae victis* was one of the few unchanging revolutionary maxims. **1936** J. NEHRU *Autobiogr.* l. 401 *Vae victis* seems to run like a thread through these utterances. **1944** S. BELLOW *Dangling Man* 112 Life is hard. *Vae victis!* The wretched must suffer.

væder, væie, vælde, væle, væren,værne, væx, væʒer, southern ME. varr. FATHER, FEY *a.*, FIELD *sb.*, FELE *a.*, FERE *v.*¹, FERN *sb.*, FAX, FAIR *a.*

vaesite (ˈveɪzaɪt). *Min.* [f. the name of J. F. *Vaes*, 20th-c. mineralogist in the Belgian Congo + -ITE¹.] A mineral of the pyrite group, ideally nickel sulphide, NiS_2, found as grey isometric crystals.

1945 P. F. KERR in *Amer. Mineralogist* XXX. 483 Material approaching NiS_2 in composition and having a pyrite type of lattice has been found in the Kasompi mine of the Belgian Congo. This mineral is tentatively called vaesite. **1962** W. A. DEER et al. *Rock-Forming Minerals* V. 132 They suggest that many of the natural bravoites are actually vaesite solid solutions or two phase mixtures of nickel-rich pyrite and iron-rich vaesite. **1978** *Mineral. Abstr.* XXIX. 80/2 The first occurrence of vaesite in Japan is described from the Kuroko-type deposits of the Kosaka mine... It contains small amounts of Fe, Cu, and Co.

‖**va-et-vient** (va e vjɛ̃). [Fr., lit. 'goes-and-comes'.] Coming and going, toing and froing; commerce, exchange; bandying (of argument).

1919 R. FRY *Let.* 3 Nov. (1972) II. 465 There is.. a considerable *va et vient* of Paris artists. **1933** G. ARTHUR *Septuagenarian's Scrap Book* 18 For a large percentage of women life, day in day out, is a happy *va-et-vient*, sometimes rich in excellent results of practical value, sometimes only resolving itself into a flutter of delicious nothings. **1959** C. SPRY *Favourite Flowers* iii. 28 Looking back over the quite gentle *va-et-vient* of this argument I know that really we are in agreement. **1966** *Guardian* 19 Mar. 7/4 All the well-intentioned wordy *va-et-vient* about Capote's book. **1978** *N.Y. Rev. Bks.* 23 Feb. 8/3 In one university which has an art school, a history of art department, and a school of architecture and planning within five hundred yards of one another, the influence of one upon the other, or even the *va et vient* among the three, is virtually nonexistent. **1981** *Times Lit. Suppl.* 22 May 563/2 His whole teasing *va-et-vient* between the past and the present, at one moment restricting himself to 'period' viewpoint.., at the next speaking as from the 1970s.

vafand, vaffand, obs. Sc. ff. *waving* WAVE *v.*

vafroun, var. WAFRON *Sc. Obs.*

†ˈ**vafrous,** *a. Obs.* Also 6 **vaffrous.** [f. L. *vafer*, *vafr-* + -OUS.] Sly, cunning, crafty, shifty.

a **1548** HALL *Chron., Hen. VII*, 11 Thinkyng surely that they.. would neuer.. longe agree with the Englishmen, accordyng to their olde vaffrous [1550 crafty] varietie. **1630** *R. Johnson's Kingd. & Commw.* 17 Divine providence.. adjudged it best.. not to bestow.. upon subtle and vafrous people, Courage, and Strength of body. **1650** B. *Discolliminium* 17 These are subtle, and vafrous Men, who are never solidly, nor honestly Wise. **1664** H. MORE *Myst. Iniq.* 106 This vafrous and bloudy Treason against the holy Majesty of Christ. **1721** in BAILEY.

vag, *sb.*¹ *Devon. dial.* [Cf. FAG *sb.*²] Dried turf or peat used as fuel; a piece of this.

1796 W. H. MARSHALL *W. England* II. 6 Towards the Mountains, Turf (provincially 'Vags') and Peat (provincially 'Turf'). **1889** *Portfolio* Jan. 11/2 In the winter he may turn many an honest penny by the sale of 'vags'. **1895** G. MORTIMER *Tales Moors* 224 You can cut as much vag—or peat, as you calls it up country—as you'm a mind to.

vag, *sb.*² *Austral.* and *N. Amer. slang* abbrev. of **a.** VAGRANT *sb.* **b.** VAGRANCY. Phr. *on the vag*, on a charge of vagrancy.

1859 G. W. MATSELL *Vocabulum* 94 *Vag.* Vagrant. 'Done on the vag', committed for vagrancy. **1868** *Daily Territorial Enterprise* (Virginia City, Nevada) 1 Feb. 3/1 The authorities have a big crowd of 'vags' spotted, and are determined to make them travel. **1877** T. E. ARGLES *Pilgrim* ii. 21 She had got three months 'on the vag' for making a sleeping place of a prominent doorstep. **1919** [see HUM *sb.*² 2]. **1931** 'D. STIFF' *Milk & Honey Route* 189 He's pulled for a vag, his excuse won't do. 'Thirty days,' said the judge. **1959** K. S. PRICHARD *N'Goola* 148 Was you on the game, love? Or did they get you on the vag? **1963** H. GARNER in R. Weaver *Canad. Short Stories* (1968) 2nd Ser. 41 Who would listen to a harvest stiff in the middle of the tobacco country? I'd end up on the wrong end of a vag charge myself. **1965** X. HERBERT *Larger than Life* 40 'We got a prisoner, eh?' The servant grunted. 'Just a vag.' **1976** 'TREVANIAN' *Main* (1977) vi. 122 Either we go right now.. or you start ten days of a vag charge.

vag (væg), *v. Austral.* and *N. Amer. slang.* [f. prec.] *trans.* To charge with vagrancy.

1876 L. HEARN in *Cincinnati Commercial* 27 Aug. 6/3 If you keep on this way, Dolly,.. I'll 'vag' you. **1891** C. ROBERTS *Adrift Amer.* 169, I was arrested as a vagrant. As the popular expression went, I got 'vagged'. **1908** W. G. DAVENPORT *Butte & Montana* 46 If the Kalispel police had done their duty she would have been 'vagged' years ago. **1930** *Bulletin* (Sydney) 9 July 28 We can't have the public's mind polluted by abusive language. You're vagged. **1953** K. TENNANT *Joyful Condemned* xxi. 203 If you have no visible means of support you can be vagged. **1975** B. GARFIELD *Death Sentence* v. 31 The cops go right on vagging prostitutes and shaking down store-keepers.

vag, dial. var. FAG *v.*²; obs. Sc. f. WAGE *sb.*

vagabond (ˈvægəbɒnd), *a.* and *sb.* Forms: 5–6 **vagabound(e, -bunde,** 5–6, 8 **-bund,** 5–7 **-bonde,** 7– **vagabond;** 6 *Sc.* **wagabund, -bond;** 7, 9 *dial.*, **vagabone,** 9 *dial.* **-bon.** [a. OF. *vagabond* (14th c.) or ad. L. *vagābund-us*, f. *vagārī* to wander. Cf. mod.F. *vagabond*, It. *vagabondo*, Sp. and Pg. *vagabundo*, *vagamundo*; also G. *vagabund*, *-bond*, Sw. *vagabond*, Du. *vagebond*. As a sb. the form finally takes the place of the earlier VACABOND.]

A. *adj.* **1.** Of persons, etc.: Roaming or wandering from place to place without settled habitation or home; leading a wandering life; nomadic.

a. In predicative use.

1426 LYDG. *De Guil. Pilgr.* 16842 O thow blyssed Lady, hyde hem that flen vnto the for helpe, and they that be vagabonde, dyscoure hem nat. **1533** BELLENDEN *Livy* I. xii. (S.T.S.) I. 71 Mony of þir pepill vagabound and ouresett with pouerte tuke wagis of þe sabynis. *a* **1578** LINDESAY (Pitscottie) *Chron. Scot.* (S.T.S.) I. 322 He staw away.. and ȝeid wagabund dissagyssit ane lang quhill. **1838** STEPHENS *Trav. in Russia* 96/1 Dispersed and vagabond, exiled from their native soil and air, they wander over the face of the earth.

fig. *c* **1430** LYDG. *Min. Poems* (Percy Soc.) 256 My look, myn eyen, unswre and vagabounde. **1667** MILTON *P.L.* XI. 16 To Heav'n thir prayers Flew up, nor missd the way, by envious windes Blow'n vagabond or frustrate.

b. In attrib. use (occas. hyphened).

1555 EDEN *Decades* I. IX. (Arb.) 97 Owre men suppose them to bee a vagabunde and wanderinge nacion lyke vnto the Scythians. **1602** MOUNTJOY *Letter* in Moryson *Itin.* (1617) II. 233 How, as a Vagabond Woodkerne hee may preserve his life,.. I know not. **1640** tr. *Verdere's Rom. of Rom.* III. 31, I have for my brother and Soveraign, the Prince of Greece, whom but even now I beheld to be a vagabond Girle. **1691** tr. *Emiliane's Observ. Journ. Naples* 226 They become soon weary of it, and then turn Vagabond-Hermits. **1726** AYLIFFE *Parergon* 181 A vagabond Debtor may be cited in whatever Place or Jurisdiction he is found. **1784** COWPER *Task* I. 559 A vagabond and useless tribe there eat Their miserable meal. **1819** SCOTT *Ivanhoe* xxix, Those ballads which vagabond minstrels sing to drunken churls. **1857** HUGHES *Tom Brown* i, We are a vagabond nation now.

transf. **1606** SHAKS. *Ant. & Cl.* I. iv. 45 This common bodie, Like to a Vagabond Flagge vpon the Streame, Goes too, and backe. **1638** WILKINS *New World* xii. (1707) 98 The Concourse of many little Vagabond Stars, by the union of their Beams. **1868** LOCKYER *Guillemin's Heavens* (ed. 3) 299 Those vagabond bodies, the comets.

†**c.** *spec.* Of soldiers or sailors. *Obs.*

1748 LIND *Lett. Rel. Navy* (1757) ii. 85 If they are to be set at liberty, who are accused of perjury, how is a vagabond seaman to be found, when he comes to England? **1813** WELLINGTON in Gurw. *Desp.* (1838) X. 519, I do not know what measures to take about our vagabond soldiers.

†**2.** (See quot. and cf. EXTRAVAGANT *a.* 2.) *Obs.*

1456 SIR G. HAYE *Law Arms* (S.T.S.) 258 ȝit is thare othir lawis callit lawis extravaganis, that is for to say lawis vagaboundis, that ar nocht incorporit in othir bukis of lawis of Lombardy.

3. Inclined to stray or gad about without proper occupation; leading an unsettled, irregular, or disreputable life; good-for-nothing, rascally, worthless.

1630 *Greene's Fr. Bacon* II. i. (Q.²), Where be these vagabond [1594 vacabond] knaues, that they attend no better on their Master? **1682** BURNET *Rights Princes* ii. 66 Some idle vagabond Clarks that had procured themselves to be put in Orders. **1741–3** WESLEY *Jrnl.* (1749) 9 A clergyman came into the.. room, and ask'd aloud, with a tone unusually sharp, 'Where those vagabond fellows were?' **1777** W. DALRYMPLE *Trav. Sp. & Port.* civ, A most vagabond crew! **1836** W. IRVING *Astoria* II. 123 He took a ceremonious leave of the Crow chieftain, and his vagabond warriors. *c* **1870** B. HARTE *Coyotte* Poems (1886) 16 Lop-eared and large-jointed, but ever alway A thoroughly vagabond outcast in gray.

4. Of or pertaining to, characteristic or distinctive of, a homeless wanderer.

1585 T. WASHINGTON tr. *Nicholay's Voy.* III. xviii. 104 By suche vagabounde beggerie, they make.. beleeue, that they canne foresay and deuine. **1607** SHAKS. *Cor.* III. iii. 89 Let them pronounce the steepe Tarpeian death, Vagabond exile, .. I would not buy Their mercie. **1653** R. SANDERS *Physiogn.* 40 Voyages by Sea and Land, and a vagabond life. **1698** CROWNE *Caligula* IV. Dram. Wks. 1874 IV. 406 Rase from thy memory my sinful hours, And all my little vagabond amours. **1726** DE FOE *Hist. Devil* I. vi. (1840) 73 Satan being confined to a vagabond, wandering, unsettled condition. **1824** W. IRVING *T. Trav.* II. 27 They have the true vagabond abhorrence of all useful.. employments. **1841** BORROW *Zincali* I. i. 1. 7 Abandoning his vagabond propensities and becoming stationary. **1872** BLACKIE *Lays*

Highl. Introd. 13 This book is well-suited for your migratory needs, and vagabond habits.

5. *fig.* Roving, straying; not subject to control or restraint.

1635 QUARLES *Embl.* IV. i, My heart is a vain heart, a vagabond and unstable heart. **1643** MILTON *Divorce* Introd., The brood of Belial,..to whom no liberty is pleasing but unbridl'd and vagabond lust without pale or partition. *a* **1680** BUTLER *Rem.* (1759) II. 455 The Inconstant has a vagabond Soul, without any settled Place of Abode. **1878** MORLEY *Carlyle* 195 In that house are many mansions, the boisterous sanctuary of a vagabond polytheism.

B. *sb.* **1. a.** One who has no fixed abode or home, and who wanders about from place to place; *spec.* one who does this without regular occupation or obvious means of support; an itinerant beggar, idle loafer, or tramp; a vagrant.

α. *c* **1485** *Digby Myst.* (1882) IV. 653 Now shall all the cursinges of your lawe, Opon yow [i.e. the Jews] fall most myschevose, & be knawen of vagabundes ouer awe. **1496** LD. BOTHWELL in Ellis *Orig. Lett.* Ser. I. I. 24 Evere day throw þam þir vagabunds escapis, cummyn to Perkin. **1582** STANYHURST *Æneis* I. (Arb.) 25 And yeet theese wretched vagabunds hard destenye scourgeth.

β. **1495** *Act 11 Hen. VII*, c. 2 Every vagabounde, heremyte, or beggar able to labre, or clerk, pilgryme, or shipman. **1533** BELLENDEN *Livy* I. xii. (S.T.S.) I. 69 Gif þai suld pas as vagaboundis and vncertane pepill throw þare howsis. **1576** FLEMING *Panopl. Epist.* 354 The dogge.. defend[s] our houses from theeues, vagaboundes, lewde fellowes. **1594** R. ASHLEY tr. *Loys le Roy* 60 b, Some of them hauing bin vagabounds and beggers. **1635** *Reg. Privy Counc. Scotl.* Ser. II. VI. 5 Haveing corrupted all the equipage of the ship, who are bot vagabounds. **1706** STEVENS *Span. Dict.*, *Vagamundear*, to play the vagabound, to strole about.

γ. **1526** TINDALE *Acts* xvii. 5 The iewes..toke vnto them evyll men wich were vagabondes and gadered a company. **1575** in *Maitland Club Misc.* I. 120 All vagabondis and idill personis that hes nocht quhairupoun to sustene thame selfis. **1577** HOLINSHED *Descr. Brit.* III. v. 106 b, The third [sort] consisteth of thriftlesse poore, as..the vagabond that will abide no wheres, but runneth vp and downe from place to place (as it were seeking woorke and finding none). **1605** *London Prodigal* v. i, For shame, betake you to some honest Trade And liue not thus so like a Vagabond. *a* **1629** HINDE *J. Bruen* xxx. (1641) 94 Such assemblies are..a very randavous of all rogues, and vagabonds. **1684** BURNET tr. *More's Utopia* 22 If they do this, they are put in Prison as idle Vagabonds. **1736** *Gentl. Mag.* VI. 718/1 A Bill..for the more effectual punishing Rogues and Vagabonds. **1796** H. HUNTER tr. *St.-Pierre's Stud. Nat.* (1799) I. 376 His relations, dishonoured in the public estimation, abandon their home, and become vagabonds. **1833** HT. MARTINEAU *Three Ages* III. 95 Issuing forth as a vagabond to spread the infection of idleness and vice. **1849** JAMES *Woodman* xviii, We have more vagabonds in the forest than I like. **1873** 'OUIDA' *Pascarèl* II. III. i. 8 He was a stroller and a vagabond, so far as social status went, an idle rogue.

transf. **1602** *2nd Pt. Return Parnass.* III. iv. 1352 You grandsyre Phœbus with your louely eye, The firmaments eternall vagabond.

Comb. **1579–80** NORTH *Plutarch* (1657) 233 They were loose people and abjects..who vagabondlike wandred up and down the Countrey. **1816** TUCKEY *Narr. Exped. R. Zaire* i. (1818) 16 This corps being composed of the most ragged, bare-legged, sans-culotte vagabond-looking wretches.

δ. **1567** HARMAN (*title*), A Caueat..for Commen Cursetors Vulgarely called Vagabones. **1602** *Narcissus* (1893) 124 Wee ar noe vagabones, wee ar no arrant Rogues that doe runne with plaies about the country. [**1842** (see 2 b).] **1901** TROTTER *Gall. Gossip* 188 Rogues an vagabons.

b. A nomad. *rare.*

1756 NUGENT *Montesquieu* XX. ii. (1758) II. 3 Hospitality ..is found in the most admirable perfection among nations of vagabonds. **1837** W. IRVING *Capt. Bonneville* III. 108 They claimed..to be thorough mountaineers, and first-rate hunters—the common boast of these vagabonds of the wilderness.

c. ***vagabond's discoloration, disease, skin*** (see quots.).

1876 GREENHOW in *Trans. Clinical Soc.* IX. 46 These cases..have received the special name of 'Vogt's *Vagabonden-Krankheit*', which I have rendered into English as 'Vagabond's Discoloration'; because this discoloration of skin..is..brought on by long-continued exposure, dirty habits and the irritation of vermin. **1890** F. TAYLOR *Man. Pract. Med.* (1891) 893 The disease has then been called *prurigo senilis*, and also *vagabond's disease*. **1899** *Allbutt's Syst. Med.* VIII. 701 The vagabond's disease, or *Morbus errorum* of Greenhow. *Ibid.* 866 Excoriations, wheals and pustules are produced by scratching which, if long continued, may produce a brown, leather-like condition—the so-called vagabond's skin seen in tramps.

2. a. A disreputable or worthless person; an idle, good-for-nothing fellow; a rascal or rogue (sometimes without serious implication of bad qualities).

1686 tr. *Chardin's Trav. Persia* 178, I spoke in the mildest Terms imaginable: which nothing mov'd this Vagabond. **1848** DICKENS *Dombey* vi, No young vagabond could be brought to bear its contemplation for a moment. **1887** HALL CAINE *Son of Hagar* III. iii, I couldn't be such a vagabond of a husband. **1890** 'R. BOLDREWOOD' *Col. Reformer* (1891) 316 The dishonest, scheming vagabonds!

b. Used as a term of reproof or abuse.

1842 LOVER *Handy Andy* x, Mind, on your peril, you old vagabone, don't let them fight that badger without me. **1844** DICKENS *Mart. Chuz.* iv, You were eaves-dropping at that door, you vagabond! **1884** PAE *Eustace* 66 'What are you lying there for, you lazy vagabond?' roared Randolph.

3. In full ***vagabond hat***, = SLOUCH HAT.

1927 *Daily Express* 7 Mar. 3/4 The two greatest millinery successes of modern times, the cloche and the vagabond. **1939** R. CHANDLER *Big Sleep* vi. 38 A small slim woman in a vagabond hat. **1952** C. W. CUNNINGTON *English Women's Clothing* vii. 256 'The vagabond' felt hat, slouched over one eye.

vagabond ('vægəbɒnd), *v.* Also 7 **vagabound, -bund.** [f. VAGABOND *sb.* Cf. F. *vagabonder* (1526).] *intr.* To roam or wander (*about*) as or like a vagabond or vagrant; to vagabondize. Also with *it*.

a **1586** SIDNEY *Arcadia* IV. (1598) 414 In this sort vagabonding in those vntroden places, they were guided [etc.]. **1611** COTGR. s.v. *Rodé*, That hath roamed, wandered, vagabonded it all the countrey ouer. *c* **1614** SIR W. MURE *Dido & Æneas* III. 27 [Dido] vagabounding in ane heavy cace Through fields vnknowne, accompanyed by none. **1748** RICHARDSON *Clarissa* (1811) VI. 357 Vagabonding about from inn to inn. **1861** READE *Cloister & H.* lvi, Why is he not in my counting house at Amsterdam, instead of vagabonding it out yonder? **1901** *Westm. Gaz.* 18 Oct. 2/1 The said son went vagabonding about the world.

Hence **'vagabonding** *vbl. sb.*

a **1628** F. GREVIL *Cælica* xii, Cupid, thou naughtie Boy, when thou wert loathed, Naked and blind, for Vagabunding noted. **1925** H. L. FOSTER *Trop. Tramp with Tourists* 148 In years of vagabonding about the far corners of the earth..I have never seen [etc.].

vagabondage ('vægəbɒndɪdʒ). [f. VAGABOND *sb.* + -AGE, or a. F. *vagabondage* (1798).]

1. The state, condition, or character of a vagabond; life or conduct characteristic of or resembling that of a vagabond; idle or unconventional wandering or travelling; vagabondism.

1813 [implied in *Vagabondager*: see below]. **1823** *New Monthly Mag.* VIII. 336 That love of..bird's-nesting and vagabondage, which..is inherent in all boys. **1858** *Times* 4 Nov. 6/2 [The Ionians] have been elevated from the lowest grade of Mediterranean vagabondage. **1871** HOLME LEE *Miss Barrington* I. vii. 102 Spring arrived and he grew restless again and betook himself to vagabondage and the streets.

fig. **1863** LECKY in *Mem.* (1909) II. 34, I have been indulging in an enormous amount of literary vagabondage. **1871** MISS BRADDON *Lovels of Arden* xxii. 171 Her random sketches—some of them mere vagabondage of the pencil, jotted down half unconsciously.

2. Vagabonds collectively; persons of a vagabond class or order.

1855 [J. D. BURN] *Autobiogr. Beggar Boy* (1859) 137 One of the immediate consequences of their conduct would be, to let loose the whole vagabondage of the country. **1903** *Times* 14 Feb. 11/5 They are already bringing a good deal of rural vagabondage to London.

Hence **vaga'bondager**, one who practises vagabondage.

1813 SIR R. WILSON *Priv. Diary* (1862) II. 52 At midnight I entered my carriage, and found myself in solitude with a cheerless imagination... Thus vagabondagers pay for their temporary pleasures.

Vagabondia (vægə'bɒndɪə). *U.S. joc.* [f. VAGABOND *sb.* + -IA¹.] The realm or world of vagabonds.

1894 CARMAN & HOVEY (*title*) Songs from Vagabondia. **1908** W. STEVENS *Let.* 7 Dec. (1967) 111 And white gloves—and a proud air, the like of which was never before in Vagabondia. **1931** 'D. STIFF' *Milk & Honey Route* i. 16 You should not make the mistake of confusing Hobohemia with Vagabondia. The latter is a more ancient and less alluring realm of the Old World.

†vaga'bondial, *a. Obs.*⁻¹ In 7 -bundiall. [f. as VAGABONDAGE + -IAL.] = next.

1615 J. H. *Worlds Folly* C b, The recollection of the vagabundiall Iewes into the sheepe-fold of Iesus Christ.

vaga'bondical, *a. rare.* Also 6–7 vagabund-. [f. as prec. + -ICAL.] Roaming, wandering; vagabondish.

1576 FLEMING tr. *Caius' Dogs* (1880) 35 Dogges..which are taught and exercised to daunce in measure,..and sundry such properties, which they learne of theyr vagabundicall masters. **1658** COKAINE *Obst. Lady* II. i, He..vaticinated future Occurents by the mysterious influences of the sublime Stars, and vagabundical Planets.

a **1864** G. DANIEL *Merrie Eng.* xiv, Joe Haynes..was the hero of a variety of vagabondical adventures.

vagabonding ('vægəbɒndɪŋ), *ppl. a.* [f. VAGABOND *v.*]

1. That roams or wanders as, or in the manner of, a vagabond. Also *transf.* and *fig.*

a **1586** SIDNEY *Songs in Astr. & Stella* v. xii. (Grosart) I. 86, I now then staine thy white with vagabonding shame. **1603** FLORIO *Montaigne* III. xiii. 610 Even vagabonding roagues..have their magnificences and voluptuousnesse. **1614** DRUMM. OF HAWTH. *Wks.* (1913) I. 13, I..On euery part my vagabounding Sight Did cast. **1632** LITHGOW *Trav.* III. 111 A vagabonding Guest, Transported here and there. *Ibid.* 118 Concerning vagabonding Greekes, and their counterfeit Testimonials. **1881** *Blackw. Mag.* May 571 The sword..went fairly straight along its vagabonding road.

2. Characterized by roaming or wandering; vagabondish.

Not clearly distinct from the *vbl. sb.* used *attrib.*

a **1586** SIDNEY *Arcadia* (1622) 472 These iewels certainely with their disguising sleights, they haue pilfred in their vagabounding race. **1824** *New Monthly Mag.* X. 283 Some would spend our prime's best age In vagabonding pilgrimage. **1904** A. B. PATERSON *Poems* 92 And through our blood there runs The vagabonding love of change.

†vaga'bondious, *a. Obs.*⁻¹ [f. VAGABOND *sb.*] Vagabond, vagrant.

1661 in *MSS. Ho. Lords* (Rep. Hist. MSS. Comm.) VII. 153 [The whole trade of cardmaking and wire drawing was nearly spoiled by] vagabondious persons.

vagabondish ('vægəbɒndɪʃ), *a.* [f. as prec.]

1. Pertaining or appropriate to, characteristic of, a vagabond or vagabonds.

1805 C. WILMOT *Let.* 4 Aug. in Londonderry & Hyde *Russ. Jrnls.* (1934) II. 165 His appearance was rather *Vagabondish* at the first glimpse. **1816** J. SCOTT *Vis. Paris* (ed. 5) 97 All this has a shew of business, though of a light vagabondish kind. **1868** MISS BRADDON *Birds of Prey* II. i, There was a vagabondish kind of foppery in his costume. **1884** *Harper's Mag.* May 871 The vagabondish spirit engendered by their long..journey.

2. Of the nature of a vagabond; somewhat like a vagabond in conduct or life.

1854 GREENWOOD *Haps & Mishaps* 105 By far the larger number of those who apply to the traveller for charity are vagabondish in their instincts and indolent in their habits. **1881** *Times* 5 July 9 This vain and vagabondish mendicant.

vagabondism ('vægəbɒndɪz(ə)m). [f. as prec.]

1. = VAGABONDAGE 1.

1822 *Blackw. Mag.* II. 139 Who, after forty years of indigence and vagabondism, is admitted into the first societies. **1859** *Hist. Cant* in *Slang Dict.* p. ix, The Gypsies were not long in the country before they found native imitators. Vagabondism is peculiarly catching. **1888** *Charity Organis. Rev.* April 145 Vagabondism as a licit mode of life.

b. A rascally or knavish act. *rare.*

1840 CARLYLE *Heroes* v. (1904) 188 All errors and perversities of his, even those stealings of ribbons, aimless confused miseries and vagabondisms.

2. = VAGABONDAGE 2. *rare*⁻¹.

1872 BREWER *Eng. Studies* (1881) iv. 196 All the vagabondism of the kingdom had scented the fray.

vagabondize ('vægəbɒndaɪz), *v.* [f. as prec. + -IZE.] *intr.* To live, wander, or go about as, or in the manner of, a vagabond; to roam or travel in a free, idle, unconstrained, or unconventional manner; to play the vagabond.

a. With indefinite *it*.

1611 COTGR., *Roder*, to roame, wander, vagabondize it. **1776** *Ann. Reg., Charact.* 35/2 After thus vagabondizing it for some time, he was discovered by the consul. **1861** READE *Cloister & H.* liii, How much earlier he would have found her by staying quietly at Tergou, than by vagabondizing it all over Holland.

b. In ordinary use. Freq. with advs. and preps.

1794 MRS. A. M. BENNETT *Ellen* III. 39 No modest woman would go vagabondizing about the country. **1795** tr. *Mercier's Fragm. Pol. & Hist.* II. 223 The streets would be filled with wretches, vagabondizing round the palaces of sloth. **1832** *Westm. Rev.* July 38 Peoples among whom his fortunes cast him while vagabondizing in the remotest corners of the globe. **1868** HOLME LEE *B. Godfrey* xxvi, That ..scapegrace..had vagabondised all over Europe as a newspaper correspondent. **1894** D. C. MURRAY *Making of Novelist* 87, I..acquired a taste for vagabondising about among the poor.

fig. **1864** MISS BRADDON *Doctor's Wife* iii, The surgeon's thoughts went vagabondizing away from the little coffee-room. **1868** —— *Birds of Prey* v. iii, My thoughts went vagabondising off to Charlotte.

Hence **'vagabondizer**.

1860 *All Year Round* No. 42. 362 The itinerant traveller and poetical or artistic vagabondiser.

vagabondizing ('vægəbɒndaɪzɪŋ), *vbl. sb.* [f. prec. + -ING¹.] The action of the verb; idle or unconventional wandering; an occasion of this.

1755 C. CHARKE *Life* 223 The Aversion I had conceived for Vagabondizing..and the good Nature of my Friends in Chepstow put it strongly in my Head to settle there. **1829** SIR A. W. CALCOTT *Lett. to Chantrey* 18 Aug., A note we have had from the Phillips to join you in a vagabondizing to Hampstead. **1849** W. IRVING *Goldsmith* xviii. 203 The Continental tour..had, with poor Goldsmith, been little better than a course of literary vagabondizing. **1853** DICKENS *Bleak Ho.* xxi, Then, vagabondising came natural to you, from the beginning?

'vagabondizing, *ppl. a.* [-ING².]

1. That vagabondizes; vagabond.

1830 *Fraser's Mag.* II. 200 We have a pretty considerable ..idea of how those vagabondising ragamuffins spend the hours of the day. **1855** *Household Wds.* XII. 168 Her wicked, vagabondising, brandy-drinking..husband.

2. Characterized by, devoted or inclined to, wandering or vagabondage.

1841 *Fraser's Mag.* XXIII. 349 [They] would prefer labour to a vagabondising life. **1859** SALA *Tw. round Clock* (1861) 175 They..fade away with the dawn..and are not beheld any more till vagabondising time begins again. **1883** MISS C. F. WOOLSON *Anne* 377 July..already felt a strong affection in his capacious vagabondizing heart for the stranger.

'vagabondry. Now *rare* or *Obs.* [f. VAGABOND *sb.* + -RY.] = VAGABONDAGE 1.

1547 *Act 1 Edw. VI*, c. 3 Preamble, Idlenes and Vagabundrye is the mother and roote of all theftes. **1611** COTGR., *Maraudise*, beggerie, roguerie, idle knauerie, base vagabondrie. **1681** W. ROBERTSON *Phraseol. Gen.* (1693) 1257 A base vagabondry, *mendicimonium*. **1869** W. CORY *Lett. & Jrnls.* (1897) 257 We went through Dropmore with unusual vagabondry.

†vagabuncy, later f. VACABUNCY. *Obs.*

1549 COVERDALE, etc. *Erasm. Par. Thess.* Ded., To banysh ..ryot, idlenes, ruffianynge vagabuncie [etc.].

†**vagabundulo.** *nonce-word.* [f. *vagabund* VAGABOND *sb.*] ? A roguish trick.
1631 SHIRLEY *School of Complement* v. iii, Gorgon has had his deuices and vagabunduloes as well as the best on yee.

vagal (ˈveɪgəl), *a. Anat.* and *Path.* [f. VAG-US + -AL¹.]
a. ***vagal nerve***, the vagus or pneumogastric nerve. **b.** Of, pertaining to, or affecting this.
1854 *Orr's Circ. Sci., Org. Nat.* I. 205 The exoccipitals.. are perforated to give exit to the vagal and hypoglossal nerves. **1885** McWILLIAM in *Jrnl. Physiol.* VI. 223 The effects of vagal stimulation were frequently investigated. **1899** *Allbutt's Syst. Med.* VI. 816 The upper vagal roots are more concerned in inspiration than the lower ones.
Hence **ˈvagally** *adv.*, by, or by means of, the vagus.
1951 *Gastroenterology* XIX. 263 In dogs with vagally innervated or vagally denervated gastric pouches intravenous injections of Banthine..and of atropine.. almost completely inhibited the secretion of hydrochloric acid. **1961** *Lancet* 26 Aug. 475/1 Unconsciousness can follow irritation of vagally innervated viscera. **1978** *Nature* 28 Sept. 323/2 Vagally induced release of Ach.

ˈvagancy. *rare.* [f. VAGANT *a.*: see -ANCY.] A wandering or strolling. Also *fig.*
1641 MILTON *Ch. Govt.* I. i, That our happinesse may orbe it selfe into a thousand vagancies of glory and delight. **1641** BROME *Joviall Crew* v, *Springlove.* My humble suit is that you will be pleas'd To let me walk upon my known occasions this Sommer. *Lawyer.* Fie! Canst not yet leave off those Vagancies? **1945** A. J. MACDONALD *Episcopi Vagantes in Church Hist.* 8 The sentence of deprivation, which was intended as a means of checking episcopal vagancy, in effect only made it worse, by causing the offender to pass from being an occasional vagans into a condition of permanent vagancy.

†**ˈvagant,** *a.* (and *pres. pple.*). *Obs.* Forms: 4-5 **vagaunt,** 5-6 **-aunte,** 5-6, 8 **vagant,** 5 **-ante.** [a. OF. *vagant, vagaunt,* or L. *vagant-, vagans,* pres. pple. of *vagārī* to wander.]
1. Wandering, roaming, roving; travelling or moving from place to place; having no settled home or abiding-place. Cf. VAGRANT *a.* 3.
1382 WYCLIF *Gen.* iv. 12 Vagaunt and fer fugitif thow shalt be vpon the erthe alle the daies of thi lijf. **1432-50** tr. *Higden* (Rolls) II. 135 In the tyme of Hinguar and Hubba, Ardulphus the bischop was vagante longe with þe body of Seynte Cuthberte. **1480** CAXTON *Ovid's Met.* XIV. x, For al we haue be disparblid & longe haue be vagant on the see. **1483** —— *Gold. Leg.* 407b/1 Thus Josaphat was two yere vagaunte & erryd in deserte. **1517** WATSON *Shyppe of Fooles* A ij, I am the fyrste in the shyppe vagaunte with the other fooles. **1578** *Sc. Poems 16th C.* (1801) II. 170 Thocht vagant freirs faine wald lie, The trueth will furth.
2. Devious, erratic. *rare.*
1382 WYCLIF *Prov.* v. 6 Bi the path of lif thei gon not; vagaunt ben the goingus of hir, and vnserchable. **1708** *Brit. Apollo* No. 50. 1/1 By so Vagant a Proceedure, it is a Chance but he must hear some points of Duty..repeated.
3. Of thoughts: Wandering.
c **1450** *Myrr. our Ladye* 42 Yt can not sturre vp yt selfe from wandryng and vagant thoughtes that yt is accustomyd in. *Ibid.* 165 Also the harte oughte fulle besyly to be kepte from all vagaunte thoughtes.

‖**vagantes** (vəˈgæntiːz), *sb. pl.* [L. pres. pple. of *vagārī* to wander.] The scholar monks who travelled about Europe in the Middle Ages. Occas. in sing. form *vagans.*
1927 H. WADDELL *Wandering Scholars* p. v, The historical interest of the *Vagantes* as one of the earliest disintegrating forces in the mediaeval church has been left on one side. **1945** [see VAGANCY]. **1946** *Scrutiny* Dec. 90 Carols, nursery rhymes and the songs of the vagantes. **1973** M. BLACKETT *Mark of Maker* viii. 79 Helen began serious work on selection and translation of the lyrics of her 'vagantes'. **1982** F. CORRIGAN in H. Waddell *Songs of Wandering Scholars* 9 Her research brought her face to face with *vagantes*, wandering scholars, from the very dawn of Christianity.

vagara(u)nt, -ent, obs. forms of VAGRANT.

vagare, obs. form of VAGARY.

vaˈgarian. *rare*⁻⁰. [f. as next + -AN.] One given to vagaries or whims.
1891 in *Cent. Dict.*

vagarious (vəˈgɛərɪəs), *a.* [f. VAGARY *sb.*]
†**1.** Variable, inconstant, changing. *Obs.*⁻¹
1798 R. P. *Tour in Wales* (MS.) 36 Thus life's vagarious tenure passes on! And thus, the scenic vision glows with change!
2. Marked or characterized by, full of, subject to, vagaries; erratic.
1827 *Examiner* 70/1 The Travels of Wilhelm Meister, wild, vagarious, and disconnected as it is. *a* **1871** DE MORGAN *Budget Parad.* (1872) 153 Mr. Wirgman's mind was somewhat attuned to psychology; but he was cracky and vagarious. **1897** *Atlantic Monthly* LXXIX. 134 The work.. is free from the vagarious theorizing.
3. Wandering, roaming, roving.
1882 *Harper's Mag.* April 661 Sharp interruption from the vagarious horned enemy. **1888** *Sat. Rev.* 22 Sept. 363/2 The history of the vagarious canary, Kiki.
Hence **vaˈgariously** *adv.*
1892 *Dispatch* (Columbus) 17 Nov., An idly planned and vagariously disposed though always picturesque college retreat.

vaˈgarish, *a.* Now *rare* or *Obs.* [f. as prec.]
1. Of the eyes: Disposed to wander; wandering.
1801 WOLCOT (P. Pindar) *Tears & Smiles* Wks. 1812 V. 40 His eyes were oft vagarish. **1823** *New Monthly Mag.* VII. 230 My people's eyes were all vagarish While striving your hard phrases to conjecture.
2. Somewhat vagarious or whimsical.
1819 KEATS in Ld. Houghton *Life* (1848) II. 26 But you knowing my unsteady and vagarish disposition will [etc.].

vaˈgarisome, *a.* [f. as prec. + -SOME.] Vagarious, capricious.
1883 *Bazaar* 5 Sept. 259 Early autumn clothing is slightly vagarisome, and steady observation is necessary in order to determine what is 'worn' from what is 'put on'.

vaˈgarist. *rare.* [f. as prec. + -IST.] One who is subject to vagaries; a vagarious person.
1888 *The Voice* (N.Y.) 24 May, The Prohibition party are now free from..suspicion of being vagarists.

vagarity (vəˈgɛərɪtɪ). *rare*⁻¹. [f. as prec. + -ITY.] Capricious irregularity or variability.
1886 *N. & Q.* 7th Ser. II. 89/1 Instances of vagarity are noticeable with each Prince of Wales, many of whom seem to have ignored..the title [of Duke of Cornwall].

vagary (ˈveɪgərɪ, vəˈgɛərɪ), *sb.* Also 6-7 **vagare,** 6 **-arie.** [prob. ad. L. *vagārī* (It. *vagare*) to wander. Cf. FEGARY.]
1. †**a.** A wandering or devious journey or tour; a roaming about or abroad; an excursion, ramble, stroll. *Obs.*
Freq. in the 17th c., chiefly in verbal phrases as ***to fetch, make,*** or ***take a vagary.***
1577 STANYHURST *Descr. Irel.* in *Holinshed* (1808) VI. 24 The Irish enimie spieing that the citizens were accustomed to fetch such od vagaries,..they..laid in sundrie places for their comming. **1582** —— *Æneis* II. (Arb.) 44 Thee gates vncloased they skud with a liuely vagare. **1600** PORY tr. *Leo's Africa* I. 19 These haue often vagaries ouer the deserts vnto the prouince of Tedgear. *c* **1613** *Soc. Cond. People Anglesey* (1860) 40 To entice his neighbours wifes..to leave their husbands..and to follow him by turns, into other countreys, and after a long vagare, to return again. **1657** S. PURCHAS *Pol. Flying Ins.* I. v. 12 A hot Sun-shine..will quickly prompt them out of their Hives to take a short vagary. **1677** GILPIN *Demonol.* (1867) 320 The like did Dinah, when she made a needless vagary to see the daughters of the land. **1826** W. E. ANDREWS *Crit. Rev. Fox's Bk. Mart.* II. 413 Whether..it is likely that such a person should be permitted to make a walking vagary throughout all London.
transf. and *fig.* *c* **1630** RISDON *Surv. Devon* §225 (1810) 237 Torridge, after a long vagary, making many meanders, emptieth itself in the..sea. **1655** GURNALL *Chr. in Arm.* XVI. (1665) 359 Our hearts are soon gone away from the duty in hand, and taken a vagary to the furthest part of the world. **1759** STERNE *Tr. Shandy* I. xxii, My aunt Dinah and the coachman..led us a vagary some millions of miles into the very heart of the planetary system.
†**b.** ***to play his vagary***, of a horse, to leave or refuse to follow the proper or desired course. *Obs.*⁻¹
1580 BLUNDEVIL *Art of Riding* I. 11 If he will then play his vagarie, beate him forthwith with your wand.
c. An irregular course or distribution.
1923 *World's Work* May 566/1 Huster's attention was arrested by the uniformity in the course and distribution of nerves in comparison with the vagary of blood-vessels.
†**2.** A wandering in speech or writing; a rambling from the subject under consideration; a digression or divagation. *Obs.* (passing into sense 5).
1579 G. HARVEY *Letter-bk.* (Camden) 67 Countenauncinge oute the matter ether with tunge or penne withoute the same discoursinge vagaries. **1596** R. H. tr. *Lavaterus' Ghostes & Sp.* To Rdr. a ij, His histories seeme not idle tales, or impertinent vagaries, but very truthes. **1651** BAXTER *Inf. Bapt.* Apol. 15 When ever he was at a loss, that the people might not perceive it, he presently would fall into a wordy vagary. **1681** —— *Answ. Dodwell* iv. 54 You must talk at other rates than you have done in your tedious fallacious Vagaries. **1762** in Ellis *Orig. Lett.* Ser. II. IV. 451 Mr. Beckford..had his vagaries as usual, and gave the House a little prelude of what they were to expect.
3. a. A departure or straying from the ordered, regular, or usual course of conduct, decorum, or propriety; a frolic or prank, esp. one of a freakish nature. Now *rare* or *Obs.* (passing into sense 4).
1588 BABINGTON *Prof. Exp. Lord's Pr.* (1596) 274 A short vagare..layde a grinding griefe vpon his conscience during life. **1593** B. BARNES *Parth. & Parth.* vi, I will be His bail for this offence; and if he make Another such vagary, take of me A pawn. **1609** W. M. *Man in Moon* (1849) 21 Hee that might doe well and would not, when hee wanteth shal be unpittied ..; then shall you hear of your olde vagaries. **1667** MILTON *P.L.* VI. 614 Strait they chang'd thir minds, Flew off, and into strange vagaries fell, As they would dance. **1693** LOCKE *Educ.* §96 Would your Son engage in some Frolic, or take a Vagary, were it not..better he should do it with, than without your Knowledge? **1714** GAY *What d'ye call it* I. iv, Ye Goblins and Fairys, With Frisks and Vagarys. **1785** GROSE *Dict. Vulgar T.*, *Vagaries*, frolicks, wild rambles. *a* **1845** BARHAM *Ingol. Leg.* Ser. III. *House-Warming*, That should she incline to play such a vagary..She could turn a knight into a waggon of hay. **1862** C. STRETTON *Chequered Life* II. 100, I could not sleep: I was too much amused at the vagaries of my new acquaintances [*sc.* rats], and kept watching them.
fig. **1794** MRS. RADCLIFFE *Myst. Udolpho* i, Let us hear what vagaries fancy has been playing in your mind.
†**b.** Without article: Frolic, gambolling. *Obs.*
1791 WOLCOT (P. Pindar) *Rights of Kings* Wks. 1812 II. 401 Here—there, Up, down, she dances it; now far, now near, In mad and riotous vagary.
4. a. A capricious, fantastic, or eccentric action or piece of conduct.
1629 MASSINGER *Picture* v. iii, An old bachelor, as I am,.. is not troubled With these fine vagaries. **1711** STEELE *Spect.* No. 260 ¶1 The Vagaries of a Child are not more ridiculous than the Circumstances which are heaped up in my Memory. **1753** RICHARDSON *Grandison* (1781) IV. xxi. 162 She.., not having so great a fortune to support vagaries, would have shone..in Italy. **1831** CARLYLE *Sart. Res.* III. vi, A noble natural Courtesy shines through him, beautifying his vagaries. **1861** TULLOCH *Eng. Purit.* iv. 409 Ignorance and vanity once unbridled knew no limit to the vagaries.. into which they ran. **1888** BRYCE *Amer. Commw.* III. lxxxvi. 150 The sentiment of the nation at large..acts but slowly in restraining the vagaries..of one particular State.
b. A caprice or trick *of* fortune, fancy, the brain, a malady, etc.
1717 DENNIS *Remarks Pope's Homer* Pref. A, A vagary of fortune who is sometimes pleased to be frolicsome. **1840** HOOD *Up Rhine* 27 The vagaries of the perspective, originating in such an arrangement, were rather amusing. **1862** BURTON *Bk. Hunter* (1863) 17, I must yet notice another and a peculiar vagary of his malady. **1871** NAPHEYS *Prev. & Cure Dis.* I. iv. 123 To follow the vagaries of fashion.
5. An erratic play of fancy; a fantastic, eccentric, or extravagant idea or notion. (Cf. 2.)
1753 RICHARDSON *Grandison* (1781) VI. xxxii. 218 These ideal vagaries, which, for the time, realize pain or pleasure to us. **1771** GRAY in *Corr. w. Nicholls* (1843) 137 But by all means curb these vagaries and wandering imaginations. *a* **1806** H. K. WHITE *To Contemplation* Rem. (1825) 384, I alone, A wayward youth, misled by Fancy's vagaries, Remain'd unsettled. **1856** DOVE *Logic Chr. Faith* I. §2. 77 Every system that would land in such a conclusion is a mere logical vagary. **1882** FARRAR *Early Chr.* II. 270 *note*, But it is worse than useless to record the vagaries of Apocalyptic interpretation.

†**vaˈgary,** *v. Obs.* [Cf. prec.] *intr.* To wander or roam. Also *transf.*
1598 FLORIO, *Vagare*,..to vagarie, or range, to straie abroade. **1599** NASHE *Lenten Stuffe* Wks. (Grosart) V. 224 The marishes and lower grounds lying vpon the three riuers that vagary vp to her. **1611** COTGR., *Vaucrer*, to raunge, roame, vagarie, wander, idle it vp and downe. **1656** S. H. *Gold. Law* 60 Though he might decline Law, yet he vagari'd not therefrom. **1681** W. ROBERTSON *Phraseol. Gen.* (1693) 1257 To vagary, *vagari, palari.*

†**vaˈgation.** *Obs.* Also 4 **vagacyone,** 5-6 **-cion,** 6 **-cyon, -tione.** [ad. L. *vagātiōn-*, *vagātio*, n. of action f. *vagārī* to wander. Cf. OF. *vagation* (Godef.), Pg. *vagação.*] The action of wandering, straying, or departing from the proper or regular course; an instance or occasion of this; a wandering, rambling, roaming; an aberration. In *lit.* and *fig.* use.
c **1340** HAMPOLE *Prose Tr.* (1866) 14 Whene þe mynde es stablede sadely with-owtten changynge and vagacyone in Godd. *c* **1450** *Myrr. our Ladye* 42 For this vagacion is caused of dulnes, and of heuynes of harte. **1502** ATKYNSON tr. *De Imitatione* III. xxvii. 219 Chase fro myn hert all maner darkenes, stablysshe the great vagacions of my mynde that I suffre. **1549** *Compl. Scot.* xiii. 111 Ane of his familiar frendis inquyrit hym of the cause of his inconstant vagatione. **1597** HARVEY *Trimming T. Nashe* Wks. (Grosart) III. 53 Neuerthelesse can I accuse you of lazines; for all this time of your vagation, with you I thinke the Signe hath been in Pisces. **1652** GAULE *Magastrom.* 291 Socrates, offended at the bold and blind vagations of men, in their disputations about the measures of the sunne. **1713** DERHAM *Phys.-Theol.* IV. ii. 100 By this so curious and exact a Libration, unseemly Contortions and Vagations of the Eye are prevented. **1714** —— *Astro-Theol.* IV. v. (1769) 118 But I have myself observed a greater vagation in the third satellite.

†**vage,** *a. Obs. rare*⁻¹. [app. ad. It. *vago.* Cf. VAGISNESS.] Fine, handsome.
1604 T. WRIGHT *Passions* v. §4. 198 The finer gold, the richer stones,..the more vage and beautifull iewell.

vage, southern dial. var. FAGE *v.*; obs. f. VAGUE *sb.* and *v.*; obs. or dial. f. VOYAGE; obs. Sc. f. WAGE *v.*, WEDGE *sb.*

vageit, obs. Sc. f. WAGED *ppl. a.*

vageowr, obs. Sc. f. WAGER (soldier).

vager, obs. Sc. f. VAGUER (wanderer), WAGER (soldier).

vagging, dial. var. FAGGING *vbl. sb.*¹

vaȝ, southern ME. var. FAW *a. Obs.*

vaȝt, southern ME. var. *fought* FIGHT *v.*

vagi- (ˈveɪdʒaɪ), comb. form of L. *vagus* VAGUE *a.*, occurring in a few botanical terms, as ***ˈvagiform, vagiˈnervose*** adjs. (see quots.).
1859 MAYNE *Expos. Lex.*, *Vagiformis*,..applied by de Candolle to leaves of cellular plants when their false nervures are dispersed without order or regularity; vagiform. **1866** *Treas. Bot.* 1199 *Vaginervose*, having the veins arranged without any order.

†**ˈvagient,** *a. Obs.* [ad. L. *vāgient-em*, pres. pple of *vāgīre* to cry, squall.] Of infants, infancy, etc.: Crying, squalling, wailing.
1628 GAULE *Pract. Theo.* (1629) 417 There shall be nor vagient Youngling, nor decrepit Ageling. **1642** H. MORE

Song of Soul II. iv. III. xlii, But for the cradle of the Cretian Jove, And guardians of his vagient Infancie, What sober man but sagely will reprove? **1659** —— *Immort. Soul* (1662) 142 The vagient cries of the Infant Jupiter amidst the.. dancings of the Cretick Corybantes.

vagile ('væ-, 'veɪdʒaɪl), *a. Biol.* [ad. G. *vagil*, f. L. *vag-us* wandering, straying.] Of an organism or group of organisms: having the ability to disperse or be dispersed in a given environment. Hence **va'gility** (also *fig.*).

1903 *Amer. Geologist* XXXI. 214 Their recent descendants find it.. advantageous.. to prey upon the much richer fauna of the vagile benthos. **1937** ALLEE & SCHMIDT tr. *Hesse's Ecol. Animal Geogr.* vi. 76 The power of dispersal of an animal species may be summed up as its 'vagility'. The less the vagility of a species, the less it is able to overcome barriers.. and hence the more numerous the opportunities for independent variation. **1967** *Oceanogr. & Marine Biol.* V. 478 Many small vagile species swim in the water washing the algae. **1979** E. A. & L. D. BLOOM *Satire's Persuasive Voice* vi. 269 Eighteenth-century satire registers a widening discontent with the collapse of native culture and, conversely, a search for its own kind of moral vagility. **1981** *Science* 12 June 1291/2 Taxa with small N_e [*sc.* effective population size] due to low vagility.. are expected to experience rapid.. speciation rates.

‖**vagina** (və'dʒaɪnə). Pl. **vaginæ** (-'aɪniː), **vaginas**. [L. *vāgīna* sheath, scabbard. Cf. F. *vagin* (1762), †*vagina*, Pg. *vagina*.]

1. *Anat.* and *Med.* **a.** The membranous canal leading from the vulva to the uterus in women and female mammals.

1682 GIBSON *Anat.* 20 It has passages.. for the neck of the Bladder, and in Women for the vagina of the Womb. **1754–64** SMELLIE *Midwifery* I. 95 The upper end of the vagina is joined to the circumference of the lips of the os uteri. **1805** *Med. Jrnl.* XIV. 21 Neither could we discover by the touch any communication between the rectum and vagina. **1847** YOUATT *Horse* viii. 174 The true polypus.. is usually found in the nostrils, the pharynx, the uterus, or the vagina. **1896** tr. *Boas' Text-bk. Zool.* 490 In the Marsupials.. the two vaginæ open separately on the floor of the urinogenital sinus.

b. A canal or organ having similar form or function in other animals; a genital passage.

1826 KIRBY & SP. *Entomol.* IV. 146 This vessel, which consists of a double tunic, in the cabbage-butterfly terminates the vagina. **1871** T. R. JONES *Anim. Kingd.* (ed. 4) 358 Female generative organs of the Queen Bee:.. *e*, vagina, or common excretory duct.

c. ***vagina dentata*** (*Anthrop.* and *Psychol.*). [L. *dentata* adj., having teeth, toothed], the motif or theme of a vagina equipped with teeth which occurs in myth, folklore, and fantasy, and is said to symbolize fear of castration, the dangers of sexual intercourse, of birth or rebirth, etc.

1908 R. H. LOWIE in *Jrnl. Amer. Folklore* XXI. 108 Its variants in North America are innumerable; the most important being the crushing entrance to heaven, snapping doors,.. and the vagina dentata. **1926** J. I. SUTTIE tr. *Ferenczi's Further Contributions Psycho-Anal.* xxxii. 279 Anxiety in regard to the mother's vagina (vagina dentata = birth anxiety). **1932** *Jrnl. R. Anthrop. Inst.* LXII. 219 There is in fact one fear, the neurotic dread of sexual intercourse, which is symbolized in the same manner as *vagina dentata* by many people in many countries. **1950** [see BEAST *sb.* 4 b]. **1958** W. R. TRASK tr. *Eliade's Birth & Rebirth* iii. 51 The return [to the womb] implies the risk of being torn to pieces in the monster's jaws (or in the vagina dentata of Mother Earth). **1976** *Listener* 26 Feb. 249/3 *Vagina dentata*, that prototype male nightmare which.. always seems to crop up more often in books than real life. **1983** *Observer* 5 June 32/3 The heroes fight against being fed into the all-consuming mouth.. of a nightmarish gigantic vagina dentata.

2. a. A part or formation serving as or suggestive of a sheath; a sheath-like covering, organ, or part; a theca.

1713 DERHAM *Phys.-Theol.* VIII. iv. (1727) 363 *note*, The Female hath vaginæ prettily furrow'd; the Male smooth. *Ibid.* 365 Many of them provided with the finest Articulations, and Foldings, for the Wings to be withdrawn, and neatly laid up in their Vaginæ, and Cases. **1771** *Encycl. Brit.* I. 191/1 The fibres [of the muscles] are.. distinguished by membranous, cellular, or adipose septa, as by so many particular vaginæ. **1826** KIRBY & SP. *Entomol.* III. 361 *Vagina* (the Vagina), the jointed sheath of the *Promuscis*, representing the *Labium* in a perfect mouth.

b. *Bot.* = SHEATH *sb.*[1] 2 b.

1720 P. BLAIR *Bot. Ess.* i. 28 Sometimes they are covered with a Vagina or Sheath at the top. **1731** P. MILLER *Gard. Dict.* s.v. *Narcissus*, The Empalement, which commonly rises out of a membranous *Vagina*. **1832** LINDLEY *Introd. Bot.* I. ii. 95 Occasionally the petiole embraces the branch from which it springs, and in such cases is said to be sheathing; and is even called a sheath or vagina, as in grasses. **1857** HENFREY *Bot.* §75 The sheathing portion.. or vagina.

c. *Sculpture.* The lower part of a terminus, out of which the bust or figure appears to rise. (So F. *gaîne*.) *rare*$^{-0}$.

1728 CHAMBERS *Cycl.* s.v., The Vagina is that long Part between the Base and the Capital; and is found in divers Manners, and with divers Ornaments.

Hence **va'gina-less** *a.*

1897 *Allbutt's Syst. Med.* II. 1061, I have recently pointed out.. the process by which the embryo dracunculi quit the body of the vaginaless parent worm.

vaginal (və'dʒaɪnəl, 'vædʒɪnəl), *a.* and *sb.* [f. prec. + -AL[1]. Cf. F. *vaginal* (1762), Pg. *vaginal*.]

A. *adj.* **1. a.** *Anat.* and *Med.* Of the nature of, having the form or function of, a sheath; serving as a sheath. ***vaginal process***, a process or apophysis of the lower portion of the temporal bone, partially enclosing the styloid process.

1726 MONRO *Anatomy* 164 The Cavity between the Zygomatic, Auditory and vaginal Process. **1767** *Phil. Trans.* LVII. 295 The vaginal coat of the testicle. **1831** R. KNOX *Cloquet's Anat.* 55 A bony lamina, called the vaginal process.., which forms the posterior limit of the glenoid cavity. **1873** MIVART *Elem. Anat.* 80 A sharp ridge runs inwards and forwards from the root of the styloid process. This ridge is termed the vaginal process. **1899** *Syd. Soc. Lex.* s.v., Vaginal coat of the eye, capsule of Tenon. *Ibid.*, Vaginal tunic.

b. *Bot.* = VAGINANT *a.*

1857 HENFREY *Bot.* §75 The vaginal petiolar region is more or less distinctly evident in many Monocotyledonous leaves.

2. a. Of, pertaining to, or affecting the vagina. ***vaginal smear***: see SMEAR *sb.* 3 b.

1825 GOOD *Study Med.* (ed. 2) V. 156 *marg.*, The vaginal polypus sometimes dispersed by stimulants and astringents. **1840** E. WILSON *Anat. Vade M.* (1842) 314 The Uterine and Vaginal arteries of the female are derived from the internal iliac, or Ischiatic arteries. **1855** RAMSBOTHAM *Obstet. Med. & Surg.* 36 The vaginal canal becomes much contracted in advanced life. **1878** T. BRYANT *Pract. Surg.* I. 688 Vaginal and labial hernia may be mistaken for the mucous cysts of those parts.

b. Of instruments: Used in dealing with, or operating on, the vagina.

1875 KNIGHT *Dict. Mech.* 2687/2 Vaginal speculum. *Ibid.*, Vaginal syringe. **1895** *Arnold & Sons' Surg. Instr. Catal.* 411 Vaginal and uterine instruments.

B. *sb.* A vaginal artery or muscle.

1872 F. G. THOMAS *Dis. Women* (ed. 3) 52 Sim's instrument, on the other hand, elevates the posterior vaginal.

Hence **va'ginally** *adv.*, via the vagina; in the vagina.

1929 *Amer. Jrnl. Obstetr. & Gynecol.* XVIII. 245 We are very slow to examine primiparae vaginally. **1966** MASTERS & JOHNSON *Human Sexual Response* ix. 137 A subjective awareness of tachycardia described frequently as feeling the heartbeat vaginally. **1979** *Nature* 6 Sept. 15/1 The new compounds seem to produce fewer gastrointestinal side effects and can be given intramuscularly, vaginally or orally. **1982** 'D. SHANNON' *Motive on Record* iii. 53 She'd been raped vaginally and anally.

vaginalitis (vædʒɪnə'laɪtɪs). *Path.* [f. prec. + -ITIS.] Inflammation of the vaginal coat or tunic of the testicles.

1861 BUMSTEAD *Ven. Dis.* (1879) 134 Vaginalitis, although a very frequent, is not a constant symptom, and is always consecutive to the inflammation of the epididymis.

vaginant, *a. Bot.* [ad. mod.L. *vāgīnant-*, *vāgīnans*, f. *vāgīna* sheath. So F. *vaginant*.] = SHEATHING *ppl. a.* b.

1760 J. LEE *Introd. Bot.* III. vii. (1765) 191 *Vaginant*, forming a *Vagina* or Sheath; when the Base of the Leaf forms a cylindric Tube that invests the Branch. **1851** G. F. RICHARDSON *Geol.* vii. 203 Sessile leaves are sometimes vaginant, that is, sheathing, as in grasses.

vaginate, *a. rare.* [ad. mod.L. *vāgīnāt-us*, f. as prec.: cf. next and VAGINATED *ppl. a.*] Enclosed in a sheath or vagina; invaginate.

1849 CRAIG, *Vaginate, Vaginated*, in Botany, sheathed, invested by the tubular base of the leaf, as a stem. **1856** W. CLARK *Van der Hoeven's Zool.* I. 190 Penis vaginate simple, with a small posterior accessory part. *Ibid.* 300 Mouth.. composed of a rostellum, retractile, vaginate at the base. **1859** MAYNE *Expos. Lex.* 1320 *Vaginatus*, cased, sheathed, vaginate.

†**vaginate**, *v. Obs.*$^{-0}$ [f. L. *vāgīna*: cf. prec.] To sheathe (Blount *Glossogr.* 1656).

Phillips (1658) substitutes '*Vagination*, a sheathing'.

†**vaginated**, *ppl. a. Obs. rare.* [f. as prec. + -ED[1].] = VAGINATE *a.*

1698 *Phil. Trans.* XX. 402 Those above are wholly vaginated (or sheathed) and come trifoliate at every Joynt. **1776** *Evelyn's Silva* viii. 445 The rest of the vaginated stem touches no other part of the whole cavity. **1849** [see VAGINATE *a.*].

'**vagine**. *Obs.*$^{-0}$ [ad. L. *vāgīna* VAGINA.] A scabbard (Cockeram, 1623).

vagini-, comb. f. of L. *vāgīna* sheath (see VAGINO-) in a few scientific terms, as ***vaginiform*** adj.; **vaginiglutæus**, a muscle acting upon the sheath of the thigh; also ***vaginigluteal*** adj.; †**vaginipennous** *a.*, of beetles, having the wings covered with a sheath; coleopterous.

A few other instances of scientific or technical usage are given in some recent Dicts., as ***vaginicoline, vaginicolous, vaginiferous, vaginipennate*** adjs.

1646 SIR T. BROWNE *Pseud. Ep.* III. xv. (1686) 141 All vaginipennous or sheath-winged insects, as Beetles and Dorrs. **1656** BLOUNT *Glossogr.*, *Vaginipennous*, pertaining to such flies, which have their wings cloased as it were in sheaths or cases, as the Beetle hath. Dr Br[owne]. **1859** MAYNE *Expos. Lex.* 1320 *Vaginiformis*,.. vaginiform.

‖**vaginismus** (vædʒɪ'nɪzməs). *Path.* [mod.L. (Sims), f. *vāgīna*.] Painful spasmodic contraction of the vagina in response to physical contact or pressure; vulvismus.

1866 J. M. SIMS *Uterine Surg.* 326 By the term vaginismus I mean an excessive hyperæsthesia of the hymen and vulvar outlet. **1879** *St. George's Hosp. Rep.* IX. 443 The patient then left for two months, but was readmitted as the vaginismus still persisted. **1936** W. SHAW *Textbk. Gynæcol.* xi. 234 Typical cases of vaginismus always have a psychical basis. **1974** PASSMORE & ROBSON *Compan. Med. Stud.* III. xxxv. 35/1 Frigidity.. also includes the symptoms of those women in whom spasm of the perineal muscles (vaginismus) make the [sexual] act painful.. or impossible. **1984** *Listener* 8 Mar. 34/4 Dr Stanley gives some candid advice on premature ejaculation and vaginismus, the involuntary muscular spasm of the outer third of the vagina which prevents penetration.

vaginitis (vædʒɪ'naɪtɪs). *Path.* [f. as prec. + -ITIS. Cf. F. *vaginite*.] Inflammation of the vagina.

1846 G. E. DAY tr. *Simon's Anim. Chem.* II. 96 He found other forms of infusoria in the pus from syphilitic vaginitis. **1861** BUMSTEAD *Ven. Dis.* (1879) 187 Vaginitis is more common than any other form of gonorrhœa in women. **1879** *St. George's Hosp. Rep.* IX. 443 Spasm of sphincter vaginæ marked, with some vaginitis and endocervicitis.

vagino- (və'dʒaɪnəʊ), used as a comb. form of L. *vāgīna* in some scientific terms, as †**vagino-pennous**, = *vaginipennous*; **va'ginoscope**, an instrument for examining the vagina; **vagino-vesical**, pertaining to the vagina and the bladder.

Recent Dicts. give a number of others in *Med., Path.*, or *Surg.*, as ***vagino-fixation, vaginotomy; vagino-abdominal, -labial, -vulvar*** adjs. (Cf. F. *vaginolabial, -péritonéal, -vésical*, etc.)

1755 JOHNSON, *Ladybird*, a small red insect vaginopennous. **1825** GOOD *Study Med.* (ed. 2) V. 154 Vagino-vesical prolapse. Prolapse of the vagina dragging the bladder along with it. **1866** J. M. SIMS *Uterine Surg.* 33 Dr. Routh.. has detected pregnancy.. by means of his vaginoscope.

‖**vaginula** (və'dʒaɪnjʊlə). *Zool.* and *Bot.* Pl. **vaginulæ**. [L. *vāgīnula*, dim. of *vāgīna* VAGINA.] A little sheath or vagina; *esp.* in *Bot.* the capsule or theca enclosing the base of the seta in certain mosses.

a. 1843 WILKINSON tr. *Swedenborg's Anim. Kingd.* I. i. 18 The external.. membrane of the mouth forms a number of pyramidal and globular pouches or vaginulæ.

b. 1849 BALFOUR *Man. Bot.* §1114 Urn-shaped pistillidia.., enclosed at first within a calyptra.., which is ultimately carried up with them.., leaving often a sheath (vaginula) round the bottom of the fruit-stalk. **1863** M. J. BERKELEY *Brit. Mosses* iii. 20 In *Sphagnum* the vaginula is lifted up on a cylindrical hyaline stalk. **1882** VINES tr. *Sachs's Bot.* 360 The basal portion of the growing archegonium becomes swollen out and penetrates down into the tissue of the stem, being nourished and firmly enclosed by it (the vaginula).

vaginule. *Bot.* [Anglicizing of prec. or a. F. *vaginule*.] = prec.

1861 BENTLEY *Man. Bot.* 380 In *Jungermannia* the sporangia are elevated upon stalks arising out of the vaginule.

†**vagisness**. *Obs.*$^{-1}$ [? f. It. *vaghezza*, f. *vago* VAGE *a.*] Handsomeness, elegance.

1604 T. WRIGHT *Passions* v. §4. 197 All these [parts of the world].. are inameled with a most gratious vagisnesse, lustre, and beautie.

†'**vagit**. *Obs.*$^{-1}$ [ad. L. *vāgīt-us*, f. *vāgīre* to cry, squall.] A cry, lamentation, wail.

1627 HAKEWILL *Apol.* (1630) 294 His cruell altars with sad vagits sounde.

†'**vagitate**, *v. Obs.*$^{-1}$ [ad. med.L. *vagitāre*, f. L. *vagārī* to wander.] *intr.* To roam or travel.

1614 RALEIGH *Hist. World* I. viii. (1654) 103 Before the use of the compass was known it was impossible to vagitate a-thwart the Ocean.

vagitus (və'dʒaɪtəs). [L., f. *vāgīre* to utter cries of distress, to wail.] A cry or wail; *spec.* that of a new-born child.

1652 N. CULVERWEL *White Stone* in *Elegant Discourse Light of Nature* II. 119 Thou hast not yet the strength a well grown Christian; well, but is there the *vagitus* of an Infant? **1825** R. HOOPER *Lexicon Medicum* (ed. 5) 1237/1 *Vagitus*, the cry of young children; also the distressing cry of persons under surgical operations. **1921** *19th Cent.* July 28 The various inspired articles.. hardly went beyond the vagitus, the earliest cry of the new-born method. **1938** S. BECKETT *Murphy* v. 71 To go back no further than the vagitus, it had not been the proper A of international concert pitch,.. but the double flat of this. **1957** V. NABOKOV *Pnin* ii. 47 He actually seemed to forehear the babe's vagitus. **1977** A. SHERIDAN tr. *J. Lacan's Écrits* iii. 31 My speech was to be nothing more than a *vagitus*, an infantile cry.

vago- ('veɪgəʊ), used as comb. f. of VAGUS in a few terms of *Anat.* or *Med.* in the sense 'of or pertaining to, denoting, the vagus or pneumogastric nerve (and some other nerve or part)', as ***vago-accessory, -glossopharyngeal, -sympathetic*** adjs.; **va'gotomy** *Surg.* [-TOMY], an operation in which the vagus nerve is cut, either as a research technique or as a means of reducing the rate of gastric secretion; hence **va'gotomized** *ppl. a.*

1877 M. FOSTER *Physiol.* III. i. (1878) 392 In the mixed vago-sympathetic trunk. **1897** *Allbutt's Syst. Med.* IV. 860 Among bulbar nerves the vago-accessory is by far the most frequently attacked. **1899** *Ibid.* VI. 811 The hypoglossal root fibres lie in close proximity to those of the vago-glossopharyngeal nerve. **1906** J. R. MURLIN tr. *R. Tigerstedt's Text-bk. Human Physiol.* vi. 190 The hearts of dogs which had survived bilateral vagotomy for several months presented no anatomical changes whatsoever. **1948**

Gastroenterology X. 415 He then produced ulcers in the vagotomized animals. **1955** W. GADDIS *Recognitions* I. v. 180 You ought to go back to analysis. Or have a vagotomy. **1974** R. M. KIRK et al. *Surgery* vi. 79 Alternatively, the available gastric acid may be reduced by performing partial gastrectomy, or vagotomy and a drainage procedure if fibrous scarring has made the oesophagus too short to restore the cardia to the abdomen. **1975** *Nature* 20 Nov. 227/1 In response to isoprenaline, vagotomised rats also failed to drink normally.

vagotonia (veɪgəʊˈtəʊnɪə). *Physiol.* Also anglicized as **vagotony** (veɪ-, vəˈgɒtənɪ). [f. VAGO- + -TONIA.] The state or condition in which there is increased influence of the autonomic nervous system and increased excitability of the vagus nerve. Also **vagoˈtonus**, in the same sense.

1916, etc. [see SYMPATHICOTONIA]. **1929** A. KUNTZ *Autonomic Nervous System* xviii. 432 The clinical conception of vagotonia and sympatheticotonia was first formulated by Eppinger and Hess in 1909... They assumed that clinical cases exhibiting a functional imbalance between the sympathetic and parasympathetic nerves could be classified as vagotonic or sympatheticotonic. **1977** *Lancet* 12 Nov. 1027/2 Beta-blockers.. are probably unable to turn the situation so far towards parasympathicotony (vagotony) that more profuse lachrymation would be resumed. **1981** *Acta Astronautica* VIII. 798 Numerous disorders have been related to vagotonia.

Hence **vagoˈtonic** *a.*, displaying or promoting vagotonia.

1929 [see above]. **1977** *Proc. R. Soc. Med.* LXX. 159/1, I consider it dangerous to use a widespread sympathetic block ..combined with halothane (with its vagotonic action and myocardial depressant effect).

† **ˈvagous**, *a. Obs.* [ad. L. *vagus*: see VAGUE *a.*] Vagrant or vague, in various senses; departing from or exceeding just or ordinary bounds; irregular, inordinate; unsettled, wandering.

1660 tr. *Amyraldus' Treat. conc. Relig.* I. i. 15 We have no other assurance of it then so wild and vagous a tradition. *Ibid.* iii. 32, I know not what natural vagous and indetermin'd notion. **1684** N. S. tr. *Crit. Enq. Edit. Bible* ix. 67 The first is only a Vagous way of Disputation, propounding now one thing, now another. **1710** T. FULLER *Pharm. Extemp.* 78 The whole throng of Physicians.. crieth it up.. to.. cure vagous Pains. **1726** AYLIFFE *Parergon* 107 Such as were born and begot of a single woman, through a vagous Lust,.. were called *Spurii.* **1737** BRACKEN *Farriery Impr.* (1757) I. 319 [They] were no doubt liable to vagous and wandering Pains.

ˈvagrance. *rare.* [f. as next: see -ANCE.] Vagrancy.

1751 JOHNSON *Rambler* No. 85 ¶9 The understanding may be restrained from that vagrance and dissipation by which it relieves itself after a long intenseness of thought. **1871** B. TAYLOR *Faust* (1875) I. xxii. 197 You'll never mount the airy steep With all your tripping vagrance. **1951** W. FAULKNER *Requiem for Nun* III. i. 266 Of course, the other niggers would just be in and out over Saturday and Sunday night for fighting or gambling or vagrance or drunk.

vagrancy (ˈveɪgrənsɪ). [f. VAGRANT *a.*: see -ANCY.]

1. *fig.* The action or fact of wandering or digressing in mind, opinion, thought, etc.; an instance of this. (Cf. 3.)

1642 H. MORE *Song of Soul* II. iii. III. lxxiii, Curious men will judge't a vagrancy To start thus from my scope. **1778** JOHNSON in *Boswell* (1831) IV. 176 Of this vacillation and vagrancy of mind, I impute a great part to a fortuitous and unsettled life. **1808** HAN. MORE *Cœlebs* II. 200 Poetry.. has of late too much degenerated into personal satire,.. and caricature;.. it has exhibited the vagrancies of genius, without the inspiration. **1853** G. JOHNSTON *Nat. Hist. E. Bord.* I. 236 We can all of us apprehend the pretty vagrancy of the fancy. **1861** TULLOCH *Eng. Purit.* ii. 291 The workings of conscience helped to check the vagrancies of the heart.

2. The state, condition, or action of roaming abroad or wandering about from place to place.

a **1677** BARROW *Serm.* iv. Wks. 1686 III. 42 Therefore did he spend his days in continual labour, in restless travel, in endless vagrancy, going about doing good. *Ibid.* v. 57 Moses did not lose his affection towards his Countreymen, because he was by one of them threatned away into banishment and vagrancy. **1776** JOHNSON in *Boswell* (Oxf. ed.) II. 40 As a shepherd.. he is answerable for those that stray... But no man can be answerable.. for vagrancy which he has not authority to restrain. **1822-56** DE QUINCEY *Conf.* Wks. 1862 I. 131 Happier life I cannot imagine than this vagrancy, if the weather were but tolerable, through endless successions of changing beauty. **1829** LYTTON *Devereux* I. i, Before terminating for ever his vagrancies. **1889** B. HARTE *Cressy* i, It had been the habit of the master to utilize these preliminary vagrancies of his little flock.

transf. **1884** *Harper's Mag.* Dec. 76/2, I was struck by the wild untutored vagrancy of every growing thing.

b. *spec.* Idle wandering with no settled habitation, occupation, or obvious means of support; conduct, life, or practices characteristic of vagrants or idle beggars.

1706 PHILLIPS (ed. Kersey), *Vagrancy*, a vagrant, disorderly, or ill Course of Life. *a* **1792** BURKE *Sk. Negro Code* Wks. (Bohn) V. 544 He shall by office prosecute them for the offences of idleness.., gaming, or vagrancy. **1857** TOULMIN SMITH *Parish* 145 Vagrancy had thus everywhere a colourable excuse given to it, and soon largely increased. **1876** J. WEISS *Wit, Hum. & Shaks.* iv. 141 He ought to be taken up for vagrancy as having no visible means of support.

attrib. **1901** *Scribner's Mag.* April 406/1 The sleepy unwary are lucky if they escape the Island on a vagrancy commitment.

3. An instance or occasion of wandering or roaming; a rambling journey; a straying.

1763 LD. HARDWICKE in *Life* (1847) III. xv. 381 The runaways need not shorten their vagrancy on that account. **1799** STRUTT *Dress & Habit* II. 318 It was evidently his intention to hold up these idle vagrancies to ridicule.

vagrant (ˈveɪgrənt), *sb.* and *a.* Forms: α. 5-6 **vagaraunt(e**, 6-7 **vagarant**, 6 **-ent.** β. 6- **vagrant**, 7 **vagˈrant.** [Late ME. *vagraunt, vagaraunt*, perh. an alteration of earlier AF. *wakerant* (*wacrant, walcrant*), through association with L. *vagārī*: cf. VAGABOND. The AF. word is employed in the sense of 'vagrant' in enactments of the 14th cent.]

A. *sb.* **1.** One of a class of persons who having no settled home or regular work wander from place to place, and maintain themselves by begging or in some other disreputable or dishonest way; an itinerant beggar, idle loafer, or tramp.

Vagrants have been the subject of many legal enactments, and by the Act 5 Geo. IV, c. 83 (the Vagrancy Act of 1824, now amended), they were divided into 'idle and disorderly persons, rogues and vagabonds, incorrigible rogues and other vagrants'.

α. **1444** *Rolls of Parlt.* V. 113/1 Alle Statutes of Laborers, ..Vitaillers, Servauntz and Vagarauntz, afore this tyme made. **1583** STUBBES *Anat. Abus.* II. (1882) 75 They runne roging like vagarents vp and downe the countries like maisterlesse men. **1598** BARKCLEY *Felic. Man* (1631) 378 [Seamen] are alwaies as vagarants and in continuall exile.

β. **1452** in *Rep. Hist. MSS. Comm.* Var. Coll. IV. 201 All manere vagraunts, vacabunds and beggers begging oute of the hundred wheras they duelle. **1547** *Act 1 Edw. VI*, c. 3 §6 Yf it shall appear.. suche man.. to have been a vagraunte and vacabound or ydle parsone. **1606** WARNER *Alb. Eng.* XIV. xci. 367 Lest his Bagpipe, Sheephooke, Skrip, and Bottell.. By Vagrants, (more then many now) might suffer of their stealth. **1698** FRYER *Acc. E. India & P.* 392 These then are Vagrants, while the Husbandman fixes himself in the Villages. **1725** POPE *Odyss.* XI. 452 Vagrants who on falsehood live, Skill'd in smooth tales, and artful to deceive. **1781** GIBBON *Decl. & F.* xvii. (1787) II. 34 The præfect, who seemed to have been designed as a terror only to slaves and vagrants. **1832** HT. MARTINEAU *Ireland* 119 The listless or bold expression which characterises vagrants. **1856** FROUDE *Hist. Eng.* (1858) I. i. 75 For the able-bodied vagrant, it is well known that the old English laws had no mercy. **1884** PAE *Eustace* 57 If you dare to trespass on my grounds.. you will be treated as a vagrant or a beggar.

2. One who wanders or roams about; a person who leads a wandering life; a rover.

c **1590** GREENE *Fr. Bacon* xi, Vagrant, go roam and range about the world, and perish as a vagabond on earth! **1718** POPE *Odyss.* II. 212 Unnumber'd birds glide through the aerial way, Vagrants of air, and unforeboding stray. **1719** DE FOE *Crusoe* II. (Globe) 361 In about five Days Time the three Vagrants, tir'd with Wandring,.. came back. *a* **1770** JORTIN *Serm.* (1771) V. ix. 194 He chose the Israelites, poor vagrants who had not a foot of ground of their own. **1807** J. BARLOW *Columb.* II. 194 Why,.. if ages past Led the bold vagrants to so mild a waste,.. Why the wild woods for ever must they rove?

fig. **1612** T. TAYLOR *Comm. Titus* iii. 3 We shal not neede trauell farre to seeke instances of such vagrants out of the wayes of God.

3. A wandering or non-sedentary spider (see first quot.).

1815 KIRBY & SP. *Entomol.* xiii. (1816) I. 423 The former Walckenaer, in his admirable work on spiders, has designated by the name of *Vagrants.* **1835** KIRBY *Hab. & Inst. Anim.* II. xix. 298 There is a very common black and white spider amongst the *vagrants.*

B. *adj.* **1.** Wandering about without proper means of livelihood; living in vagrancy or idle vagabondage; of or belonging to the class of vagrants or itinerant beggars.

α. **1461** *Litt. Red Bk. Bristol* (1900) II. 127 Many.. of the Kynges liege people.. gothe vagaraunt and vnoccupied and may not haue ther labour to ther levyng. **1530** *Act 22 Hen. VIII*, c. 12 §2 Yf any suche ympotent person after the sayde Feast of Seynt Iohn, be vagarant & goo abeggyng. *Ibid.* §9 Whypped for a vagarant stronge begger. **1608** BACON *Comment. Sol.* I. Wks. 1868 IV. 91 The Indited recusant, the Non Communicant, the vagarant person. **1632** SANDERSON *Serm.* 383 Sturdy Roagues and vagarent townsend beggars.

β. **1603** KNOLLES *Hist. Turks* (1621) 160 In all which places they mustred souldiers,.. entertaining also strangers, and other vagrant and masterlesse men. **1641** BROME *Joviall Crew* II, Current and vagrant—Stockant, whippant Beggars! **1722** DE FOE *Plague* 122 Every vagrant person may, by the laws of England, be taken up. **1770** GOLDSM. *Des. Vill.* 149 His house was known to all the vagrant train. **1814-28** SOMERVILLE *Life & Times* (1861) 370 Before the general establishment of poor's-rates, the country was over-run with vagrant beggars. **1854** *Act 17 & 18 Vict.* c. 74 An Act to render Reformatory and Industrial Schools in Scotland more available for the Benefit of Vagrant Children.

fig. **1663** J. SPENCER *Prodigies* (1665) 252 If once Right Reason.. be put by its office, our inward house will soon lie ..free for every vile and vagrant Opinion to take up and dwell therein.

2. *fig.* Wandering, straying, roving, inconstant, unsettled, wayward, etc.

1522 MORE *De quat. Noviss.* Wks. 76/1 It often happeth, yᵉ the very face sheweth yᵉ mind walking a pilgrimage, in such wise yᵗ not withoute som note & reproch of suche vagaraunte mind [etc.]. **1612** T. TAYLOR *Comm. Titus* iii. 3 We haue a wandring and vagrant vaine euen after our calling, and therefore much more before. **1651** H. MORE *Enthus. Tri.* (1662) 48 His causality is more vagrant, more lax and general, then to be brought in here. **1684** BURNET tr. *Utopia* 141 They think that if they were not so strictly restrained from all vagrant Appetites, very few would engage in a married state. **1711** STEELE *Spect.* No. 143 ¶4 Ambition, Envy, vagrant Desire, or impertinent Mirth will take up our Minds. **1729** BUTLER *Serm.* Wks. 1874 II. Pref. 26 Men daily, hourly sacrifice the greatest known interest, to ..any vagrant inclination. **1755** J. SHEBBEARE *Lydia* (1769) I. 116 Pleasure skin-deep and vagrant, pain heart-felt and long-lasting! **1820** HAZLITT *Lect. Dram. Lit.* 154 We wander by forest side or fountain,.. following our vagrant fancies. **1849** MACAULAY *Hist. Eng.* v. I. 542 The offspring of a vagrant and ignoble love. **1879** DIXON *Windsor* I. xxiii. 234 A child.. with a violent and vagrant temper.

3. Leading a wandering or nomadic life; ranging or roaming from place to place; straying, straggling. Cf. VAGANT *a.* 1.

pred. **1546** *Yorks. Chantry Surv.* (Surtees) 201 They shulde here and se lernyng in the sayd college, and not to be vagrant abrode in the sayd towne. **1589** PUTTENHAM *Eng. Poesie* I. iii. (Arb.) 22 The people remained in the woods and mountains, vagrant and dispersed like the wild beasts. **1610** HEALEY *St. Aug. Citie of God* 889 [They] became vagrant through most parts of the Romaine Empire. **1649** G. DANIEL *Trinarch., Hen. IV*, lxxxii, Vagrant as a Rout Possest with feare, led by vnskillfull guides. **1728** POPE *Dunc.* I. 232 Ye shall not beg,.. Sent with a Pass, and vagrant thro' the land.

attrib. **1638** SIR T. HERBERT *Trav.* (ed. 2) 90 Fearing his vagrant sonne might grow too potent.. he rowses himselfe. **1746** FRANCIS tr. *Horace, Epist.* I. xv. 37 A vagrant Zany, of no certain Manger, Who knew not, ere he din'd, or Friend or Stranger. **1759** JOHNSON *Rasselas* xxxvii, I amused myself with observing the manners of the vagrant nations. **1781** GIBBON *Decl. & F.* xxv. (1787) II. 532 The vagrant soldiers were recalled to their standard. **1812** J. HENRY *Camp. agst. Quebec* 68 Without the path of the vagrant savage to guide us. **1849** MACAULAY *Hist. Eng.* x. II. 630 It might well be.. that.. regents would continue to administer the government in the name of vagrant and mendicant kings. **1860** HAWTHORNE *Marb. Faun* I. x. 100 They proved to be a vagrant band, such as.. all Italy abounds with.

b. Of animals, birds, etc.

1743 FRANCIS tr. *Horace, Odes* IV. iv. 4 To whom the monarch of the gods assign'd Dominion o'er the vagrant, feather'd race. **1767** *Phil. Trans.* LVII. 396 It becomes a resting place to vagrant birds. **1774** GOLDSM. *Nat. Hist.* (1776) III. 53 [The goat is] lively, capricious, and vagrant; it is not easily confined to its flock.., and loves to stray remote from the rest. **1817** WORDSW. *Vernal Ode* 90 The soft murmur of the vagrant Bee. **1855** *Poultry Chron.* III. 562 In one case two swarms, both of them vagrant swarms, took possession of the same hive.

c. Of plants: Rambling or straggling in growth or habit; straying. Also of hair.

1827 HOOD *Mids. Fairies* xlix, And sometimes we enrich gray stems, with twined And vagrant ivy. **1851** LONGF. *Gold. Leg.* ii. *A Farm*, The vagrant Vines that wandered, Seeking the sunshine, round and round. **1862** SALA *Seven Sons* I. xi. 265 She had.. a quantity of vagrant brown hair.

4. Of or belonging to a vagrant or wanderer; characterized by, peculiar to, devoted or given up to, vagrancy or wandering.

1583 STUBBES *Anat. Abus.* II. M 4 b, Doe you allow of that vagarant ministerie, which is in manie Countries.. sprong vp of late, to the discredite of the Gospell of Jesus Christ? **1598** HACKLUYT *Voy.* I. 490 The worde Turk signifieth a Shepheard or one that followeth a vagrant and wilde kinde of life. **1613** PURCHAS *Pilgrimage* (1614) 665 The Ethiopians ..liued before a vagrant life, like the *Nomades* of olde. **1659** HAMMOND *On Ps.* lvi. 8 Thou knowest the dayes of my exile, and vagrant condition. **1709** PRIOR *Henry & Emma* 304 That Beauteous Emma vagrant Courses took; Her Father's House and civil Life forsook. **1775** JOHNSON *Let.* 27 May in *Boswell*, Because it will be inconvenient to send them after me in my vagrant state. —— *Tax. no Tyr.* 22 But the age being now past of vagrant excursion. **1849** MACAULAY *Hist. Eng.* ii. I. 212 Persons whose life has been passed in vagrant diplomacy. **1867** MORRIS *Jason* XIV. 416 Keeping but vagrant life for thine own part Of what thou boastest with the Gods to share.

5. Of things: Not fixed or stationary; moving hither and thither; *spec.* in *Path.* of certain blood-cells.

1586 MARLOWE *1st Pt. Tamburl.* I. i, Ere he march in Asia, or display His vagrant Ensigne in the Persean fields. **1612** WOODALL *Surg. Mate* Wks. (1653) 226 Mercurie.. is in truth a fugitive vagrant substance. **1743** FRANCIS tr. *Horace, Odes* I. xxvi. 3 Bear them, ye vagrant winds, away. *Ibid.* xxxiv. 14 The ponderous earth, and vagrant streams. **1794** R. J. SULIVAN *View Nat.* II. 417 When we consider the motion of those vagrant worlds, the comets. **1800** MOORE *Anacreon* lviii. 10 Then I loose all such clinging cares, And cast them to the vagrant airs. **1841** DICKENS *Barn. Rudge* xv, A vagrant ray of sunlight patching the shade of the tall houses. **1857** DUFFERIN *Lett. High Lat.* (ed. 3) 203 The lofty ice mountains that wander like vagrant islands along the coast of America. **1899** *Allbutt's Syst. Med.* VI. 497 The fixed cells of the tissue to a great extent appear to supplant in its office the vagrant leucocyte.

† **b.** Of a disease or pain: Not local or confined to one particular part. *Obs.*

1656 RIDGLEY *Pract. Physick* 24 Arthritis that is vagrant is Scorbutical, and a pain of divers parts. **1684** tr. *Bonet's Merc. Compit.* IV. 126 M. N. was suddenly taken with most sharp vagrant pains.

ˈvagrant, *v. rare*⁻¹. [f. prec.] *intr.* To behave like a vagrant; to ramble or roam.

1886 MISS BROUGHTON *Doctor Cupid* I. ix. 156 The boy is out—.. vagranting after his kind.

ˈvagrantism. [f. VAGRANT *sb.* or *a.*] Inclination to, love of, vagrancy.

1908 G. S. HALL *Adolescence* I. 296 The erratic acts of these cases,.. passionate vagrantism and vagabondage, solitude and soliloquy.

ˈvagrantize, *v. rare.* [f. VAGRANT *sb.* + -IZE.] † **a.** *trans.* To arrest as a vagrant. *Obs.* **b.** To reduce to the condition of a vagrant. In quot. *absol.*

1797 MRS. A. M. BENNETT *Beggar Girl* (1813) I. 21 Set off to the next justice of the peace, for the purpose of getting the whole set vagrantized. **1893** *Liverpool Daily Post* 22 Dec. 4/10 The result is rather to permanently vagrantize—if one may coin a verb for the occasion—instead of inculcating.. independent effort.

'vagrant-like, *adv.* [f. VAGRANT *sb.*] In or after the manner of a vagrant.

1679 J. GOODMAN *Penit. Pard.* I. iv. (1713) 97 He vagrant-like wandred on in a course of dissoluteness.

vagrantly ('veɪgrəntlɪ), *adv.* Also 6 **vagrauntlie.** [f. as prec. + -LY².] As a vagrant; in a vagrant or wandering manner; †irrelevantly.

1547 *Act 1 Edw. VI*, c. 3 §6 We haue taken this bearer I. K. vagrauntlie,..going loytering idellie abowt. *a* **1603** T. CARTWRIGHT *Confut. Rhem. N.T.* (1618) 634 The contrary ..being barely and nakedly affirmed of the Iesuites, and that most vagrantly, and from the purpose. **1604** N. D. *3rd Pt. Three Conversions of Eng.* 93 Who would neither haue lands ..nor any certaine seats or habitation, but went abroade vagrantly. **1736** AINSWORTH *Lat. Dict.*, *Vage*, wandringly, scatteringly, vagrantly. **1847** WEBSTER, *Vagrantly*, in a wandering, unsettled manner. **1893** *Dispatch* (Columbus) 20 April, Come with me then, vagrantly, into a few of these lovely old home-spots of rural England.

†va'grarious, *a. nonce-word.* [Cf. next and -ARIOUS.] Vagrant, wandering.

1795 WILBERFORCE in *Life* (1830) II. 105 My health is not equal to this vagrarious kind of life.

†'vagrate, *v. nonce-word.* [f. VAGR-ANT *sb.*: see -ATE.] *intr.* To range or wander.

1807 J. BARLOW *Columb.* IX. 314 In this unbounded range, Where error vagrates and illusions change.

†'vagring, *ppl. a. Obs.*⁻¹ [f. as prec.] Vagrant, wandering; nomadic.

1619 W. SCLATER *Exp. 1 Thess.* (1629) 310 There are risen vp a scattered and vagring company, vnder color of deuotion.

vagrom ('veɪgrɒm), *a.* [Illiterate alteration of VAGRANT *a.*: cf. INGRAM *a.* In mod. use only after Shakespeare.]

1. Vagrant, vagabond, wandering.

1599 SHAKS. *Much Ado* III. iii. 26 *Dogberry*. You shall comprehend all vagrom men. **1863** G. A. SALA *Capt. Dangerous* I. x. 285 Sheep-stealers, footpads, vagrom men and women. **1874** M. COLLINS *Transmigr.* II. ii. 49 With him came the vagrom guest,..a boy almost. **1882** BESANT *All Sorts* 164 Born of a poor vagrom woman.

2. Eccentric, erratic.

1882 *Sat. Rev.* LIV. 497 Words lose their character and have their history obscured by being spelled after the vagrom devices of the phonetic people.

vagt, southern ME. var *faȝt*, pa. t. FIGHT *v.*

†vague, *sb.*¹ *Obs.* Also 6 **vage.** [Of obscure origin.] A prank or trick. Only in pl.

Freq. in the second quarter of the 16th c., esp. in the phrase ***to play one's vagues***, with which ***to take one's vagues*** appears to be synonymous.

(*a*) **1523** *St. Papers Hen. VIII*, VI. 200 Thei thought that Columpna had..takyn so his vages against the said Cardinall de Medyces..that the said Columpna dorst never have trustyd..hymself aftir in the desperat handes of the Cardinall. **1528** ROY *Rede me* (Arb.) 120 Yf they playe thus their vages, They shall not escape the plages Which to theym of Rome happened. *a* **1548** HALL *Chron.*, *Hen. VIII*, 252 b, The Scottes had some leysure to play their vagues and folowe their accustomed manier. *c* **1557** ABP. PARKER *Ps.* civ, There playth his vages Leviathan.

(*b*) **1526** *Pilgr. Perf.* (W. de W. 1531) 80 b, She despyseth all outwarde vages & vanytees, & is content to fulfyll all yᵗ her lady commaundeth. **1526** SKELTON *Magnyf.* 1968 Because of theyr neglygence and of theyr wanton vagys, I vysyte them and stryke them with many sore plagys.

vague (veɪg), *a.*, *adv.*, and *sb.*² Also 7 **vage.** [a. F. *vague* (13th c.) or ad. L. *vag-us* wandering, inconstant, uncertain, etc. (hence also It., Sp., Pg. *vago*).]

1. Of statements, etc.: Couched in general or indefinite terms; not definitely or precisely expressed; deficient in details or particulars.

1548 VICARY *Anat.* (1888) 15 Likewise a Chirurgion must take heede that he deceiue no man with his vague promises. *a* **1661** FULLER *Worthies*, *Durham* I. (1662) 298 With subtilty not light, slight, vage as air, But such as Truth doth crown. **1750** JOHNSON *Rambler* No. 76 ¶8 Men often extenuate their own guilt, only by vague and general charges upon others. **1784** COWPER *Task* II. 521 Their answers, vague, And all at random. **1844** THIRLWALL *Greece* VIII. 179 He remained inflexible, covering his refusal with the vague pretext, 'that circumstances were not in his power'. **1849** MACAULAY *Hist. Eng.* ix. II. 400 He wanted..to have, not vague professions of good will, but distinct invitations and promises of support. **1884** *Law Times Rep.* XLIX. 773/2 The statement of claim is so vague that we had to go into detail, so as to make the case clear.

2. Of words, language, etc.: Not precise or exact in meaning.

1690 LOCKE *Hum. Und.* To Rdr., Vague and insignificant forms of speech, and abuse of language, have so long passed for mysteries of science. **1744** HARRIS *Three Treat.* Wks. (1841) 2 So it was..with a thousand words beside, all no less common, and equally familiar; and yet all of them equally vague and undetermined. *a* **1781** R. WATSON *Philip III* (1793) I. III. 306 It was conceived in vague and general terms. **1796** KIRWAN *Elem. Min.* (ed. 2) I. Pref. p. xi, Its descriptive language was..arbitrary, vague and ambiguous. **1813** J. THOMSON *Lect. Inflam.* 502 By an indiscriminate use of vague terms. **1849** MACAULAY *Hist. Eng.* vi. II. 152 These vague phrases were not likely to quiet the perturbed mind of the minister. **1870** FARRAR *Fam. Speech* iii. (1873) 87 But the name Chaldee is so vague and misleading that I have purposely excluded it. **1900** E. HOLMES *What is Poetry?* 79 Vague words, then, stir emotion; exact terms repress it.

fig. **1813** SHELLEY *Q. Mab* viii. 23 Like the vague sighings of a wind at even, That wakes the wavelets of the slumbering sea, And dies on the creation of its breath.

3. a. Of ideas, knowledge, etc.: Lacking in definiteness or precision: indefinite, indistinct.

a **1704** LOCKE (J.), These vague ideas, signified by the terms, whatsoever and thing. **1753** HOGARTH *Anal. Beauty* 7 So vague is taste, when it has no solid principles for its foundation. **1792** MARY WOLLSTONECR. *Rights Wom.* v. 186 Though prudence of this sort be termed a virtue, morality becomes vague when any part is supposed to rest on falsehood. **1818** CRUISE *Digest* (ed. 2) VI. 172 The metes and bounds of property would be vague and indeterminate. **1845** BUDD *Dis. Liver* 2 To the vague and unsatisfactory state of our knowledge respecting them. *a* **1881** A. BARRATT *Phys. Metempiric* (1883) 156 Beyond this we only get a vague analogy.

(*b*) Used in superl. with ellipsis of *idea, notion*; cf. FAINT *sb.* 5 d.

1968 N. MARSH *Clutch of Constables* viii. 201 'Have you seen this particular photograph, Mr Pollock?'.. 'Haven't the vaguest.' **1981** D. UHNAK *False Witness* (1982) xi. 94 'Any particular place your customers go on Tuesday nights?' 'I haven't the vaguest.'

b. Similarly of feelings or sensations.

1797 S. & HT. LEE *Cant. T.* I. 106 [He was] trembling with a new and vague apprehension. **1837** W. IRVING *Capt. Bonneville* III. 256 Their movements not only give a vague alarm, but..will even indicate to the knowing trapper the very quarter whence danger threatens. **1845** BUDD *Dis. Liver* 387 The patient's illness begins with general disorder; ..vague pains in the belly, and sometimes with vomiting. **1868** GEO. ELIOT *F. Holt* 15 The vague but strong feeling that her son was a stranger to her. **1885** E. CLODD *Myths* I. §6. 111 Man's sense of vague wonder in the presence of powers whose force he cannot measure.

4. †a. ***vague acid*** (see quots.). *Obs.*

1741 SHAW tr. *Boerhaave's Chem.* (ed. 2) I. 112 Of the Vague Acid. The vague volatile liquid acid, found perhaps every where in mines. **1753** *Chambers' Cycl.* Suppl., *Vague Acid*, a term much used by the modern chemists, and signifying a certain volatile fluid salt or acid, supposed to be found every where in mines, and in combination with different other substances, to form many of the ordinary compound fossils. **1764** *Phil. Trans.* LIV. 45 A Belemnite, whose laminæ were in a manner dissected and laid open by the vague acid,..which every where pervades the earth, destroying some bodies, and forming others.

b. *Bot.* (See quot.)

1842 A. GRAY *Struct. Bot.* viii. (1880) 313 *Vague*, when the radicle bears no evident or uniform relation of the kind to the pericarp.

5. Lacking physical definiteness of form or outline; indistinctly seen or perceived; formless, obscure, shadowy.

1822 B. W. PROCTOR *Flood of Thessaly* I. 3 Chaos, touched with light and form, Lost its vague being. **1849** MRS. SOMERVILLE *Connex. Phys. Sci.* 433 These are in every state of condensation, from a vague film hardly to be discerned to such as have actually arrived at a solid nucleus of stars. **1879** HUXLEY *Hume* iv. 96 We travel through countries where every feature of the scenery is vague.

6. a. Of persons, the mind, etc.: Unable to think with clearness or precision; indefinite or inexact in thought or statement.

1806-20 WORDSW. *River Duddon* xxvi, Random cares and truant joys, That shield from mischief and preserve from stains Vague minds, while men are growing out of boys. **1827** CARLYLE *Misc.* (1840) I. 17 Richter has..an imagination vague, sombre, splendid, or appalling. **1847** HELPS *Friends in C.* I. viii. 142 The sharp practice of the world drives some logic into the most vague of men: women are not so schooled.

b. *poet.* Of the eyes: Devoid of expression. *rare.*

1820 KEATS *St. Agnes* viii, She danc'd along with vague, regardless eyes.

7. †a. ? Vagrant, vagabond. *Obs. rare.*

a **1627** SIR J. HAYWARD *Edw. VI* (1630) 63 The Lord Gray encouraged his men to set sharpely upon the vague villaines, good neither to liue peaceably nor to fight.

b. Of the Egyptian month or year: Beginning at varying seasons; moveable, shifting.

a **1656** USSHER *Ann.* (1658) 762 The beginnings of these years being taken from the first of the vage or moveable moneth *Thoth* of the Egyptians. **1860** R. S. POOLE in *Smith's Dict. Bible* I. 506/1 (*Egypt*), The Vague Year contained 365 days without any additional fraction, and therefore passed through all the seasons in about 1500 years. **1876** *Encycl. Brit.* IV. 665 This [Egyptian] year is called *vague*, by reason of its commencing sometimes at one season of the year, and sometimes at another.

8. a. As *adv.* Vaguely; indistinctly.

1864 LONGF. *Wind over Chimney* ix, The night-wind drear Clamours louder, wilder, vaguer.

b. In combs., as ***vague-hovering, -looking, -menacing, -sailing, -shining***, etc.

1856 R. A. VAUGHAN *Mystics* (1860) I. 238 In this wild Universe of ours, storming-in, vague-menacing, it is enough if you shall find..existence. **1871** J. HAY *Pike County Ball.* (1880) 90 Vague-hovering o'er her form..A warmer and a dearer charm. *Ibid.* 95 Vague-sailing, where the feathery clouds Fleck white the tranquil skies. **1879** DOWDEN *Southey* vii. 106 Will-o'-the-wisp, vague-shining theories that beguile night wanderers. **1904** W. H. HUDSON *Green Mansions* vi. 82 How different she seemed now; the brilliant face grown so pallid and vague-looking! **1948** WYNDHAM LEWIS *Let.* 25 Oct. (1963) 469 This super-dream..is I imagine too vague-looking to be practical.

9. a. *absol.* as *sb.*, esp. ***the vague***, the vague aspect or consideration of things. ***in the vague***, in a vague or indefinite state or condition, uncertain; without entering into details or particulars, in general.

1851 CARLYLE *Sterling* I. xii, John Mill..spoke of him.. as a gifted amiable being,..in danger of dissipating himself into the vague. **1856** MRS. CARLYLE *Lett.* II. 280 My plans are still in the vague; I feel no haste to 'see my way'. **1881** MASSON *De Quincey* 196 The meaning is all but lost in a mere vague of music. **1882** BAIN *J. S. Mill* i. 13 All this is completely in the vague. **1894** *Month* Oct. 207 We must take them rather in the vague.

b. The vague or uncertain future. *rare.*

1865 MRS. CARLYLE *Lett.* III. 260 Dr. B. is postponed into the vague.

c. The vague or undefined expanse *of* something.

1870 LOWELL *Study Wind.* 90 The great Genoese did not draw that first star-guided furrow across the vague of waters. **1875** RUSKIN *Lect. Art* vi. 169 The shadows lost or disregarded in the vague of space.

‖**vague** (vɑːg), *sb.*³ [Fr., lit. 'wave'.] A movement, trend, vogue. Cf. NOUVELLE VAGUE.

1962 *John o' London's* 19 Apr. 371/3 Here is one requisite which must be regarded as essential in any new *vague*. It must not, whatever else it is, be vague. **1970** R. LOWELL *Notebk.* 219 The *vague*, the vogue, what do they tell the critic? **1974** *Times Lit. Suppl.* 20 Dec. 1439/4 He has beautifully caught the old Hungarian *vague* of British cinema under Alexander Korda... The Hungarian *vague* also swept on to the Denham studio floor such interesting flotsam as Gabriel Pascal.

vague (veɪg), *v.*¹ Chiefly *Sc.* Now *rare* or *Obs.* Forms: α. 6–7, **vage.** β. *Sc.* 6–7, 9 **vaig,** 7 **uaige.** γ. 7– **vague.** [ad. L. *vagārī* to wander: cf. F. *vaguer*, Pg. *vagar*, It. *vagare*.] *intr.* To wander; to range, roam; to ramble idly or as a vagrant.

α. *c* **1425** WYNTOUN *Cron.* v. x. (Royal MS.) 3394 Fra land to land..he wes vagand [*v.r.* wauerande]. **1548** *Compl. Scotl.* xiii. (1872) 111 Quhen metellus hed vagit vp and doune there ane lang tyme. **1579** W. WILKINSON *Confut. Fam. Love* 2 Euill disposed persons vage and wander abroad at midnight.

β. **1587** *Sc. Acts, Jas. VI*, c. 119 ¶12 Thay sall remane within this realme..and sall not vaig thairfra. **1647** *Aberd. Rec.* in *Aberd. Jrnl. N. & Q.* (1908) I. 16/1 That all persones ..heir the word of God, and not vaig nor goe to the old toun. *c* **1657** SIR W. MURE *Ps.* cix. 10 Still vaige, and sharke, and beg about, Their bounds lay'd waist, they may. **1802** LEYDEN *Compl. Scotl.* Gloss. 379 To *vaig* is in common use, as well as *stravaig*.

γ. **1600** HOLLAND *Livy* XXIII. xlii. 503 To..suppresse these robbers that vague about our country. *Ibid.* XXXI. xxi. 785 They vagued to and fro in scattering wise up and downe the countrey a foraging. *c* **1620** Z. BOYD *Zion's Flowers* (1855) 121 Thou idle boy thus vagueing here and there. **1678** SIR G. MACKENZIE *Crim. Laws Scot.* II. xxvi. §iv. (1699) 266 If they were necessitated to vague up and down at all Courts, upon all occasions. **1766** NICHOL *Poems* 2 Thus through the country I went vaguing. **1786** in *Old Ch. Life Scotl.* (1885) 320 The profanation of this holy day by idly vaguing together. **1874** L. TROUBRIDGE *Life amongst Troubridges* (1966) 88 We vagued about until tea-time.

†b. In fig. use. *Obs.*

1567 DRANT *Horace, Ep.* Bj, Should I goe wryte at Randonne tho, and vage abroade, and raue? **1596** DALRYMPLE tr. *Leslie's Hist. Scot.* (S.T.S.) I. 289 [He] louset a brydle to thame to vaig in quhat lust or leicherie lyket thame best. *a* **1614** J. MELVILL *Diary* (Wodrow Soc.) 445 The King sould be judge if a Minister vag from his text. **1641** R. B. K. *Par. Liturgy w. Mass-bk.*, etc. 39 In these conceats all of them agree to vage.

vague (veɪg), *v.*² *rare.* [f. VAGUE *a.*] *intr.* To act or write vaguely; to be vague or indefinite.

1880 *Cornh. Mag.* Dec. 649, I have vagued away in a sort of circle round my diaries still heaped on the floor, and Josephine standing between me and the lamp. **1894** MRS. C. PRAED *Christina Chard* I. 123 I've vagued all my life—that's been my curse. *Ibid.* 128 You are to fulfil yourself. You are to 'vague' no more.

vaguely ('veɪglɪ), *adv.* [f. VAGUE *a.* + -LY².]

1. In a vague, indefinite, or indeterminate manner; with vagueness or lack of precision; in vague terms.

1781 GIBBON *Decl. & F.* xxx. (1787) III. 185 The services of Stilicho are great and manifest, his crimes, as they are vaguely stated in the language of flattery and hatred, are obscure. **1791** BOSWELL *Johnson* (1831) I. 330 Concerning the publication of which Sir John Hawkins guesses vaguely and idly. **1824** W. IRVING *T. Trav.* I. 30 When my uncle was dressing, he called vaguely to mind the visitor of the preceding night. **1855** MACAULAY *Hist. Eng.* xix. IV. 303 A motion was made so vaguely worded that it could hardly be said to mean any thing. *a* **1881** A. BARRATT *Phys. Metempiric* (1883) 104 To some such conception we are vaguely led.

b. Dimly, obscurely.

1871 TYNDALL *Fragm. Sci.* (1879) I. xxi. 494, I vaguely discerned the audience and apparatus. **1873** BLACK *Pr. Thule* xix. 316 The houses grew vaguely distinct.

2. Without attention or concentration of mind or thought; idly, vacantly.

1828 SCOTT *F.M. Perth* xxxiv, He stood..listening vaguely to what the magistrate was saying to him. **1878** T. HARDY *Ret. Native* v. v, 'No,' said Eustacia, looking vaguely through the window at the fire.

vagueness ('veɪgnɪs). [f. as prec. + -NESS.] The quality or condition of being vague; lack of distinctness or preciseness; indefiniteness.

1799 MACKINTOSH *Study Law Nat.* 8 Notwithstanding the objections of some writers to the vagueness of the language. **1829** H. NEELE *Lit. Rem.* 52 A great fault into which descriptive writers fall is the vagueness and indistinctness of their pictures. **1843** MILL *Logic* I. ii. §5 We shall have occasion to show under what conditions this vagueness may exist. **1874** L. STEPHEN *Hours in Library* (1892) I. vii. 238 A general vagueness as to the ordinary duties of mankind. *a* **1881** A. BARRATT *Phys. Metempiric* (1883) 52 The weakness of this conception is its vagueness.

b. An instance of this, a vague thing, feature, word, etc.

1838 *Lond. & Westm. Rev.* XXIX. 68 With a remark or two on those errors and vaguenesses we shall conclude. **1839** POE *Fall House Usher* Wks. 1864 I. 298 The paintings.. which grew, touch by touch, into vaguenesses at which I shuddered. *a* **1849** —— *R. H. Horne* Ibid. III. 436 Pure vaguenesses of speech abound.

'vaguer. *Sc.* Also 6 **vaigare**, 7 **va(i)ger.** [f. VAGUE *v.*¹] An idle stroller or wanderer; a vagrant.

15.. *Aberd. Reg.* (Jam.), Vaigares, adhantaris of ailhoussis. **1647** BAILLIE *Lett.* (1841) III. 15 An act against vagers from their own ministers. **1876** GRANT *Burgh Sch. Scot.* II. v. 195 They were forbidden.. to be perturbers or vaguers, wandering from place to place.

'vaguing, *vbl. sb.* Now *rare.* Also *Sc.* 6 **vaiging,** 7 **-in, vaging.** [f. as prec.] The action of the vb.; idle rambling or wandering; an instance or occasion of this. Chiefly *Sc.*

1596 DALRYMPLE tr. *Leslie's Hist. Scot.* (S.T.S.) I. 258 His wyfe.. culde nocht suffir his foull, inordinat, and voluptuous vaiging by her. **1659** A. HAY *Diary* (S.H.S.) 38 That the Lord wold reforme.. the vaigings and whorings of my heart. **1692** in Bower *Hist. Univ. Edinb.* I. 54 That thereby vaging and vice may be discouraged. **1770** J. WATT in Muirhead *Life* (1858) 203 The vaguing about the country, and bodily fatigue, have given me health and spirits. **1900** H. G. GRAHAM *Soc. Life in Scot. 18th Cent.* (1901) III. ii. 92 The vaguing or loitering idly in the streets.. was a subject of condemnation.

'vaguing, *ppl. a.* Also 7 **vaging.** [f. as prec.] Wandering, roving.

1627 W. SCLATER *Exp. 2 Thess.* (1629) 223 Men of no setled abode; vaguing, or vagabond Iewes. **1629** SIR W. MURE *True Crucifix* 2715 Sathan,.. who course doth take On wings of vaging thoughts, before to send His Messingers. **1633** STRUTHER *True Happiness* 135 Hee saw nothing beside, that could so much as draw his vaging desire to it. **1905** GUNN *Baron Crt. of Stitchill* (S.H.S.) Introd. p. xxii, The sturdy, vaguing beggar who would neither work nor want was a constant menace to the cottar and villager.

vaguish ('veɪgɪʃ), *a.* [f. VAGUE *a.* + -ISH.] Somewhat vague or indefinite.

1818 *Blackw. Mag.* III. 532 It is very clear That I into a vaguish style have got. **1853** G. J. CAYLEY *Las Alforjas* II. 146 It is a vaguish affair to have to squeeze a whole capital into a postscript, but I have no time to individualise.

vagulate ('veɪgjʊleɪt), *v. rare.* [Fanciful formation f. L. *vagul(us* nonce dim. of *vagus* wandering + -ATE³; perh. influenced by UNDULATE *v.*] *intr.* To wander in a vague manner; to waver.

Only in the writings of Virginia Woolf.

1918 V. WOOLF *Diary* 3 Nov. (1977) I. 213 Emphie vagulates in & out of the room. **1921** *Ibid.* 6 Mar. (1978) II. 97 All is too soft & emotional. Now for writing or anything I believe you must be able to screw up into a ball & pelt straight in people's faces. They vagulate & dissipate. **1930** —— *Let.* 27 June (1982) IV. 182 Poor dear Angus vagulating like some pale anemone in a cranny.

vagulous ('veɪgjʊləs), *a. nonce-wd.* [f. L. *vagulus*: see prec.] Wayward, vague, wavering.

1919 V. WOOLF *Diary* 12 July (1977) I. 291, I like Forster very much, though I find him whimsical & vagulous to an extent that frightens me with my own clumsiness and definiteness.

vagus ('veɪgəs). *Anat.* and *Path.* Pl. **vagi** ('veɪdʒaɪ). [a. L. *vagus* wandering, straying.] The pneumogastric nerve (see PNEUMOGASTRIC *a.*).

1840 E. WILSON *Anat. Vade M.* (1842) 403 The Pneumogastric Nerve (vagus) arises by numerous filaments from the respiratory tract immediately below the glosso-pharyngeal. **1876** *Trans. Clinical Soc.* IX. 96, I endeavoured to compress the right vagus at the angle of the jaw. **1899** *Allbutt's Syst. Med.* VII. 773 Some fibres of the vagus pass to the intestines.

b. *attrib.* in ***vagus nerve***, etc.

1856 TODD & BOWMAN *Phys. Anat.* II. 119 The Vagus Nerve emerges from the Medulla oblongata immediately below the glosso-pharyngeal. **1896** *Allbutt's Syst. Med.* I. 228 Atropine paralyses the vagus endings and centre. **1897** *Ibid.* IV. 631 Vagus pneumonia, as it is called, which follows section of the vagi in rabbits.

‖**vah,** *int. Obs.* Also 4 **vath.** [L. *vah* (hence Gr. οὐά); med.L. also *vath.*] An exclamation expressive of exultation, contempt, or disgust.

1382 WYCLIF *Isaiah* xliv. 16 He.. is chaufid, and seide, Vah [*v.r.* vath; *Cov.* A ha], or weel, I am hat; Y saȝ the fyr. —— *Matt.* xxvii. 40 Forsothe men passynge forth blasfemyden hym, mouynge her heuedis, and seyinge, 'Vath, or fie, to thee'. **1582** N. T. (Rhem.) *Matt.* xxvii. 40 Saying, Vah, thou that destroyest the temple of God. **1616** J. LANE *Contn. Sqr.'s T.* IV. 191 Vah, but ift bee your fortunes to goe hence, leave mee some suer gard for my weake defense! **1619** HARRIS *Drunkard's Cup* 19 Vah, vah, vah, you would sinke to see and smell. **1631** ANCHORAN *Comenius' Gate Tongues* 186 Vah, away with shame, dishonestie and lecherie!

‖**vahana** ('vɑːhana). Also **vahan.** [Skr. *vāhana*, lit. 'conveyance', f. *vah-* to carry, transport.] In Indian mythology, the mount or vehicle of a god.

1810 E. MOOR *Hindu Pantheon* 16 Lacshmi.. is with him [*sc.* Vishnu] on his *vahan*, or vehicle, Garuda. **1879** J. DOWSON *Class. Dict. Hindu Mythology* 330 *Vāhana.* 'A vehicle'. Most of the gods are represented as having animals as their vāhanas. **1891** J. L. KIPLING *Beast & Man* vi. 122 The bull receives high honours as the vâhan or steed of Shiva. **1971** *Illustr. Weekly India* 11 Apr. 11/1 (*caption*) Return of the procession after lustral rites of a Jina, with the gods and goddesses on their *vahanas.*

‖**vahine** (va'hine). Also **vahini.** [Tahitian.] A Tahitian woman or wife. Cf. WAHINE.

1950 F. H. LYON tr. *Heyerdahl's Kon-Tiki Exped.* viii. 217 They had a lively and spirited leading singer in a luxuriantly fat *vahine.* **1960** H. E. BATES *Aspidistra in Babylon* 187 Better take a *vahini*.. and settle down. *Ibid.* 227, I will build a house and live like your *vahine.* It cost nothing. I'll be your *vahine* and work for you. I'll work for you and you can love me. **1980** *London Mag.* July 24 The village of Mataiea, where Gauguin.. lived.. with his beloved *vahine* Teha'amana.

Vai (vaɪ). Also **Vei,** 9 **Vy.** [ad. a native name.] (A member of) a people of the southern coasts of Liberia and Sierra Leone; also, their language. Also *attrib.* or as *adj.*

1845 *Encycl. Metrop.* XX. 18/1 The Country near Cape Mount was anciently inhabited by the Vaï, or Faï, and Pwi Tribes. *Ibid.* 18/2 The Vaï, or Veï, were not reduced without difficulty. **1849** S. W. KOELLE (*title*) Narrative of an expedition into the Vy country of West Africa. *Ibid.* 9 The Vei language is very simple, harmonious, with scarcely any grammatical inflexions, rich in vowels. **1854** —— *Outl. Gram. Vei Lang.* p. iv, If we compare the dialects spoken by the Manis and the Veis, we discover a difference which can scarcely have arisen in less than a couple of centuries. **1923** A. L. KROEBER *Anthropol.* ix. 225 All the values of his signs were syllabic. The same holds of the West African Vei writing invented in the nineteenth century by a native. He .. fell back on syllabic signs even though this necessitated two hundred different characters. **1932** W. L. GRAFF *Language & Languages* xi. 434 Of some 435 Sudanese languages.. only five or six are written. These are Vai, of the Nigero-Senegalese group,.. [etc.]. **1936** G. GREENE *Journey without Maps* II. i. 99 Mr. Reeves was a Vai, a Mahommedan. **1949** L. D. TURNER *Africanisms in Gullah Dial.* i. 14 The Vai word for 'fat' is.. lit. 'mouth full'. **1957** M. BANTON *W. Afr. City* vii. 127 Vai territory in Sierra Leone amounts only to some twenty-five square miles on the coastline next to the Liberian frontier. There are hardly any Vai in the colony. **1965** *Sierra Leone Lang. Rev.* (*Afr. Lang. Rev.*) IV. 81 The derivations listed for these 85 terms are *prima facie* astonishing, for 63 are Mende and 21 are Vai. **1974** J. R. BAKER *Race* xxi. 411 The Mende tribe (a subdivision, like the Vai, of the Mandingo group of tribes). **1979** *Africa* XLIX. 92 The Vai script is so famous that it is surprising to realize that the language is spoken by, at most, 40,000 people. **1983** *Word* XXXIV. 136 Reading and writing Vai script was associated with certain specific skills.

vaiage, obs. Sc. f. VOYAGE.

vaick, var. VAKE *v. Obs.*

vaid, obs. Sc. f. WADE *v.*

†**vaidie.** *Obs.*⁻¹ [a. AF. *vaidye, vaidie,* = ONF. *vei(s)die,* OF. *voi(s)die,* of doubtful origin.] Subtlety, guileful cunning.

c **1325** *Metr. Hom.* 96 This said Herodes in vaidye [*v.rr.* ful coutly, full falslye], For at Crist hauid he gret enuye.

vaifer, obs. Sc. f. WAVER *v.*

vaig, obs. Sc. f. VAGUE, WAGE.

vaiȝe, southern ME. var. FEY *a.*

vaik(e, later ff. VAKE *v. Sc.*; obs. Sc. ff. WAKE *v.*, WEAK *a.* and *v.*

vail (veɪl), *sb.*¹ Now *arch.* or *dial.* Forms: *α.* 5 **vayll(e,** 5–7 **vayle;** 5 *Sc.* **waill(e, waile,** 6–7 **vaile,** 6– **vail** (6 *Sc.* **vaill**), 9 *dial.* **vaail;** 6 **veyle,** 7 **veile,** 8 **veil.** *β.* 5–9 **vale.** [f. VAIL *v.*¹ Cf. AVAIL *sb.*]

I. †**1.** Advantage, benefit, profit. *Obs.*

c **1430** LYDG. *Min. Poems* (Percy Soc.) 9 God send also unto thy most vayle.. A spiryt, a strenghte, and of good counsaylle. *c* **1450** *Mirk's Festial* 76 For, what maner vertu þat a man haue, but yf he be yn charyte, hit stondys him in no vayle. *c* **1470** HENRY *Wallace* v. 201 He wyst no waill thar langar for to bide. *c* **1500** in Denton *Eng. in 15th C.* (1888) 318 He to kepe vnder yowre tenants and haue all the vayle and thay the burdyn. *Ibid.*, [To] destroy the cherch & the towne for a lytell vayle to yowre place. **1550** CROWLEY *Epigr.* 392 At Paryse garden.. a man shall not fayle To fynde two or thre hundredes, for the bearwardes vaile.

b. *dial.* Advance, progress.

a **1847** *Isle of Wight Gloss.* (E.D.S.) s.v., Thee doesn't zim to meyak much vaail.

†**2.** *of* (..) ***vail***, of profit, value, or worth. *Obs.* Chiefly *Sc.*

c **1450** *Mirk's Festial* 262 Þeras he was wont.. to speke mony an ydull worde and of no vayle, aftyr he turnet al his speche ynto profyt. *c* **1470** HENRY *Wallace* I. 167 The byschoprykis, that war of gretast waile, Thai tuk in hand. **1475** in *3rd Rep. Hist. MSS. Comm.* 418/1 Sayand that the brocht that Master Thomas.. fand is of vayll, and the brocht that I.. fand.. is of na wayll. **1535** STEWART *Cron. Scot.* II. 136 Quhen he considderit haill The Britis war bot of sa litill vaill.

†**3.** *Sc.* Value or worth; account, estimation.

1471 *Acta Audit.* 11/1 And gif þai oxin be of mare vale, he to restor again þe Remanent. **1480** *Acta Dom. Conc.* (1839) 52/1 Henry to pay to þe said sir edward sa mekle as þe said teind was of vale. **1535** STEWART *Cron. Scot.* I. 98 Als force it is no tyme to him to faill, And lufe all thing ay efter the awin vaill. **1567** *Gude & Godlie B.* (S.T.S.) 74 Than man I .. my Goddis name manesweir, And set him at full lytill vaill.

II. 4. A casual or occasional profit or emolument in addition to salary, stipend, wages, or other regular payment, esp. one accruing or attached to an office or position; a fee or offering of this nature. Usu. in pl. Now *arch.* or *Obs.*

The pl. is occas. found construed as a sing.

c **1450** *Godstow Reg.* 648 The half of all offerynges & vayles of the auter. *Ibid.*, The offrynges & the vaylys of fowre days by the yere. *c* **1460** *Oseney Reg.* 113 A.. chapeleyne, þe which shall take all þe obuencions (or vayles) of þe Auter of þe same chapell. **1550** T. LEVER in Strype *Eccl. Mem.* (1721) II. 103 The number of the stock reserved, all manner of vails beside. **1563–70** FOXE *A. & M.* (1596) 265/2 The church of S. Helen,.. which was then esteemed woorth an hundred marks by yeere, besides other vailes and commodities belonging to the same. **1618** *Barnevelt's Apol.* F iij b, Out of the wages allowed by the citie with other veiles I could wel-nigh maintaine my family. **1645** PAGITT *Heresiogr.* (1647) 84 Our vailes for Burialls & Christenings is.. ceast. **1712** ARBUTHNOT *John Bull* (1727) 102 For he would quickly lick himself whole again by his vails. **1720** SWIFT *Fates Clergymen* Wks. 1751 II. II. 27 His revenue (besides vails) amounted to about thirty pounds a year. **1834** MACAULAY *Ess., Thackeray's Earl Chatham* (1897) 300 These ignominious vails Pitt resolutely declined.

transf. and *fig.* **1608** TOPSELL *Serpents* (1658) 627 To shew that mindes and tongues with Learnings brand, Are blest with plenty in all wordly vails. **1694** CROWNE *Regulus* v, You scorn those scorns which always are the vales Of that unlucky office [i.e. of a spy].

b. A dole or gratuity given to one in an inferior position. (Cf. 5.)

1622 J. TAYLOR (Water P.) *Very Merry-Wherry-Ferry Voy.* Wks. (1630) 13 Let Trencher-Poets scrape for such base vailes, I'l take an Oare in hand when writing failes. **1693** DRYDEN *Juvenal* I. 176 Since our Knights and Senators account To what their sordid begging Vails amount. **1863** W. W. STORY *Roba di R.* iii. 45 There are festivals and ceremonials where the people demand as of right certain vails and presents called *mancie* and *propine.*

c. A gift or present in the nature of a bribe.

1687 A. LOVELL tr. *Thevenot's Trav.* I. 253 Not reckoning a great many other Vails that are to be given every day almost to the Sous-Basha and several other knaves. **1886** C. DICK *The Model,* etc. 80 The Custom House they passed with smile and tributary vail.

5. A gratuity given to a servant or attendant; a tip; *spec.* one of those given by a visitor on his departure to the servants of the house in which he has been a guest. Now *arch.* **a.** In pl.

In the 17th and 18th centuries servants were largely paid by these gratuities, and the practice of giving them is freq. alluded to in the literature of the period. The word is recorded in various midland dialect glossaries, but usually as obsolescent.

α. **1605** *London Prodigal* II. iv, *Artichoke* [servant to Sir Launcelot]. Our yeares wages and our vailes will scarcely pay for broken swords and bucklers. **1653** MILTON *Hirelings* Wks. 1851 V. 362 Why should he, like a Servant, seek Vails over and above his Wages? **1729** SWIFT *Direct. Serv.* Wks. 1883 XI. 375, I advise you of the servants.. who expect vails, always to stand rank and file when a stranger is taking his leave. **1757** MRS. GRIFFITH *Lett. Henry & Frances* (1767) IV. 157 *note,* An Agreement entered into among the Gentlemen of several Counties in Ireland, not to give Vails to Servants. **1778** T. HUTCHINSON *Diary* II. 218 One custom they kept up, which is laid down almost everywhere else—they allow their servants to take vails. **1823** *Spirit Public Jrnls.* 107 If you tell tales, My son shall your place have, and pocket your vails. **1859** THACKERAY *Virgin.* i, The lacqueys rose up from their cards to open the door to him, in order to get their 'vails'. **1904** *Times* 20 Aug. 12/6 English visitors measure their vails.. with discretion.. in America.

fig. **1632** SANDERSON *Serm.* (1681) I. 310 These things among other the servants of God may certainly reckon upon, as the certain vails and benefits of His service. **1742** YOUNG *Nt. Th.* I. 408 Time lodg'd in their own hands is folly's vails.

Comb. **1760** (*title*), The Sentiments and Advice of Thos. Trueman, a Footman, setting forth the Custom of Vails-Giving in England. **1860** SMILES *Self Help* vii. 188 One of the minor social evils.. was the custom of what was called vails giving.

β. **1715** ADDISON *Drummer* II. i. (1722) 18 *But.* Rare News, my Lads, rare News! *Gard.* What's the Matter? hast thou got any more Vales for us? *a* **1763** SHENSTONE *Odes* Wks. (1765) 197 Phoo—how she stands—biting her nails—As tho' she play'd for half her vales. **1823** A. CLARKE *Mem. Wesley Fam.* 453 Vales to servants, that sovereign disgrace to their masters. **1878** LECKY *Eng. in 18th C.* I. iv. 571 The system of vales which made servants in a great degree independent of their masters. **1894** WEYMAN *Man in Black* 116 They expect their vales at those places.

b. In sing. *rare.*

1682 WHELER *Journ. Greece* II. 192 There are commonly Attendance, who, for a small Vale, will provide you such things as you have Occasion for. **1807** HOARE *Tour Irel.* 329 The vale or parting token, which the menial servants still in many houses expect. **1866** *Lond. Rev.* 7 April 337/2 Calling for the bill, and settling it off-hand was pleasant, but the vail to the waiter was delicious.

6. *pl.* = PERQUISITE 3 c. Now *rare.*

In early use applied to the remnants of material left over by a tailor after making a garment or suit.

1592 GREENE *Upst. Courtier* D b, He is paide for his workmanship, vnlesse by misfortune his shieres slippe awrye, and then his vales is but a shred of home spunne cloth. *Ibid.*, The vales of one veluet breech is more then twenty paire of mine. **1612** T. TAYLOR *Comm. Titus* i. 7 All that is gotten.. by stealth or vailes, whereby men vnconscionably shape out their owne commoditie out of another mans cloth. *a* **1658** Cleveland *Wks.* (1687) 75 By the same title as the upper Garment is the Vails of the Executioner. **1677** *Compl. Servant-Maid* 114 Do not covet to have the Kitching Stuff for your Vales, but rather ask the more wages. **1731** Fielding *New Way to keep a Wife* III. iii, Where ladies govern there are secrets, and where there are secrets there are vails. I lived with a lady once who used to give her cloaths away every month. *a* **1732** Gay *Fables* II. xi, A Carrier.. Would see his horses eat their corn: This sunk the hostler's vails, 'tis true; But then his horses had their due. **1821** Scott *Kenilw.* xxxvi, These tell-tale articles must not remain here—they are rather too rich vails for the drudges who dress the chamber. **1890** *Glouc. Gloss.* s.v., The malter did always get the malt-dust for his vails.

fig. **1659** Owen *Epigr.* No. 34, Things only proper unto Males, The Female Sex claim as their Vales.

†**vail**, *sb.*² *Obs.*⁻¹ [f. vail *v.*²] The going down or setting *of* the sun.

1606 Shaks. *Tr. & Cr.* v. viii. 7 Looke.. How vgly night comes breathing at his heeles, Euen with the vaile and darking of the Sunne.

†**vail**, *v.*¹ *Obs.* Forms: *α.* 4–6 vayle (4 uayle), 5–6 vaylle (5 waylle); 4–6 vaille, 4–7 vaile, 5–6 vale; 4–6 vayl, 5–6 vayll; 4–7 (9) vail (4 wail), 4–6 vaill (5–6 waill). *β. north.* and *Sc.* 4 vaily, 5 wayly; 5–6 vailȝe, valȝe, wailȝe (6 velȝe, welȝe). [ad. OF. *vail, vaill*, 1st pers. pres. indic., or *vail-, vaill-*, subj. and participial stem of *valoir* to be of value or worth:—L. *valēre*. Cf. avail *v.*]

1. *intr.* To have might or power; to prevail.

a **1300** *Cursor M.* 7375 His faas sal noght a-gain him wail [*Fairf.* vaily], For him ne his sal i noght fail.

2. To be of use or service; to avail or profit: **a.** Used impersonally with *it*.

Usu. in negative or interrogative sentences and freq. with infinitive compl.

1303 R. Brunne *Handl. Synne* 9471 Yn erytage nat long hyt vaylеþ, þe þred eyre leseþ, þat ouþer trauayleþ. **1387** Trevisa *Higden* (Rolls) VIII. 37 In a tyme an holy man blamed hym for þat dede, and it vayled nouȝt. *c* **1400** *Beryn* 3883 'What vaylith it,' quod hanybald, 'to angir or to curs?' **1426** Lydg. *De Guil. Pilgr.* 6160 Whan she sawh yt wayllede nouht Mor to maken resistence. **1509** Hawes *Past. Pleas.* 35 Where is no reason it vayleth not to chatter. **1592** W. Wyrley *Armorie* 119 What booteth it of Gentries brag to boast, What vaileth it, old ensignes foorth to show? **1601** Weever *Mirr. Mart.* Ej, What vaileth it a lion be a king Closely shut vp within this tower of stone.

b. With other subjects.

c **1340** Hampole *Pr. Consc.* 3646 Ay, whiles he is in dedly syn, His help vailles noght, bot es in vayne. **1390** Gower *Conf.* III. 89 Thurgh this science it is ful soght, Which vaileth and which vaileth noght. *c* **1430** Lydg. *Min. Poems* (Percy Soc.) 26 Withoute trouth what vailith high noblesse? **1456** Sir G. Haye *Law Arms* (S.T.S.) 178 Gif be the benefice of sauf condyte vaillis nocht, never man wald traist efter in sauf condyt. **1522** Skelton *Why not to Court* 101 Ther vayleth no resonynge, For wyll dothe rule all thynge. **1568** T. Howell *Arb. Amitie* (1879) 66 What vailes the glittering Golde, when loue is forcde to flee. **1608** Topsell *Serpents* (1658) 791 Small was the bodies band, And of the Lizards poysonous, this least in shape did vail.

c. Const. *to* (a person or thing). Cf. 3.

c **1400** *Rom. Rose* 5765 To hym not vailith his preching. **1422** Yonge tr. *Secreta Secret.* 247 To this thynges hit vaillyth moche to haue richesse and glory. *c* **1475** *Pol. Poems* (Rolls) II. 284 And yet when suche clothe ys alle ywrowte, To the maker it waylyth lytylle or nowȝtte.

d. *vail que* (or *quod*) *vail, vail that vail might* [ad. F. *vaille que vaille*], whatever may (or might) happen, at all hazards; = avail *v.* 1 c. Chiefly *Sc.*

1375 Barbour *Bruce* ix. 147 Bot gif othir wald thame assalȝe, Thai wald defend, avalȝe que valȝe [*Edin. MS.* wailȝe que wailȝe]. *c* **1475** *Partenay* 2672 Vail that vail might, the monkys brend so. **1513** Douglas *Æneid* ix. Prol. 86 Thus, vaill que vaill, ilk gude deyd helpis other. **1530** Lyndesay *Test. Papyngo* 161, I wyll, said scho, ascend, vailȝe quod vailȝe. **1550** —— *Sqr. Meldrum* 951 Now, vailȝe quod vailȝe, Upon the Ladie thow mak ane sailȝe.

3. *trans.* (Orig. with indirect object.) To be of use, advantage, or benefit to; to aid, assist, or help (a person, etc.): **a.** With *it*, or infin. clause.

a **1300** *Cursor M.* 3640 Bot þou sal do sun mi consail, Wel i wat it sal þe wail. *c* **1400** *Laud Troy Bk.* 8550 Hit hadde the vayled, hadde it be-tid. *c* **1460** Sir R. Ros *La Belle Dame* 720 What vayleth you to schew so gret rygour? **1509** Hawes *Past. Pleas.* i. (Percy Soc.) 7 It vayled not the bodye for to dispose Against the head. **1596** Lodge *Life & Death W. Longbeard* Cjb, What vailes me to compose As many verses as Homer did make? **1813** Scott *Rokeby* ii. xxviii, What 'vail'd it him, that brightly play'd The morning sun on Mortham's glade?

b. With other subjects.

a **1300** *Cursor M.* 26147 If þou be stad in suilk a nede For mikil may þe wail þis dede. *c* **1330** R. Brunne *Chron. Wace* (Rolls) 12580 þer-to algate dos ȝour trauail, & þat we may, we wil ȝow vaille. *c* **1380** *Sir Ferumb.* 877, xx^th slow he of þat rout, þat non armure ne miȝt hem vaille. *c* **1450** Lovelich *Graal* lii. 900 His defens ne vailled him not sekerly. *c* **1470** Henry *Wallace* ii. 112 The thrid he straik.. The crag in twa; no weidis mycht him waill. *a* **1510** Douglas *K. Hart* ii. 273 In all disport he may ws gritlie vaill. **1530** Palsgr. 764/2 What vayleth your rychesses you nowe? *a* **1557** Abp. Parker *Ps.* i. 2 My goodes can vayle thee nought.

4. Of persons: To be worth in respect of means or wealth.

1576 *Reg. Privy Council Scot.* Ser. i. II. 520 Ane honest man and baroun vailyeand in landis and gudis mair nor twenty thowsand pundes.

Hence †**'vailing** *ppl. a.*¹ *Obs.*

c **1470** *Gol. & Gaw.* 328 Ane sayndis-man.. Wise, vailyeing, and moist of valour.

vail (veɪl), *v.*² Now *arch.* Forms: *α.* 4–7 vale. *β.* 6–7 vayl(e, vaill, vaile, 6– vail. *γ.* 6 veile, 7–9 veil. [ad. OF. *valer* (rare), or aphetic f. avale *v.*]

I. *trans.* **1.** To lower (a weapon, banner, etc.); to cause or allow to descend or sink.

c **1330** R. Brunne *Chron. Wace* (Rolls) 12384 þat swerd he lifte wel on hey, & valede his scheld a party. **1600** Fairfax *Tasso* xx. xlii, She broke and cleft the crown; and caus'd him vaile His proud and lofty top. **1610** G. Fletcher *Christ's Vict. on Earth* xxxvi, But all so soone as heav'n his browes doth bend, Shee veils her banners, and pulls in her beames. **1864** Skeat tr. *Uhland's Poems* 234 Faint with toil, he vails his spear.

b. *spec.* To lower in sign of submission or respect.

1599 Greene *George a Greene* G ij, If any aske a reason why? or how? Say, English Edward vaild his staffe to you. **1616** J. Lane *Contn. Sqr.'s T.* v. 331 At whose approche th' whole armie veild their pikes, soldiers and officers on knees down strikes. **1651** Davenant *Gondibert* i. i. 68 They vayl'd their Ensignes as it by did move. **1687** A. Lovell tr. *Thevenot's Trav.* i. 289 The besieged begged Quarter, veiled their Standards and Colours, as a sign that they submitted to the Discretion of the Sultan.

c. To lower or cast down (the eyes); to bend, bow down (the head, etc.); to hang (the tail).

1586 Ferne *Blaz. Gentrie* 28 Which bird,.. after he hath caste downe his eyes as ashamed at the lothsomnes of his feet, vayleth his taile and plucketh downe the pride of his plumes. **1594** Kyd *Cornelia* v. 418 Valing your Christall eyes to your faire bosoms. **1646** Quarles *Hieroglyphikes* vii. 1 What dire disaster bred This change, that thus she vails her golden head? **1657** *Lust's Dominion* i. iii. in Hazl. *Dodsley* XIV. 105, I, vailing my knees to the cold earth. **1675** Plume *Life Hacket* in *Cent. Serm.* p. xlvii, The jolly Prelat .. never stoopt nor vail'd his head. **1836** Keble *Lyra Apost.* 117 Voice of the wise of old! Go.. teach proud Science where to vail her brow. **1859** Tennyson *Guinevere* 655 Here her hand Grasp'd, made her vail her eyes: she look'd and saw The novice.

†**d.** To throw down, give up or surrender (a purse). *rare*⁻¹.

1593 Peele *Edw. I*, H ij b, And this sentence is.. confirmed by our Lord Lluellen Prince of Wales, and Robin Hood of the great mountaines. So vaile your budgettes to Robin of the mountaine.

2. To doff or take off (a bonnet, hat, crown, or other head-dress), esp. out of respect or as a sign of submission. Also const. *to* or *unto* (a person, etc.).

α, β. *c* **1460** *Emare* 992 When he mette the emperour, He valed his hode with gret honour. **1528** Roy *Rede me* (Arb.) 32 In every place wheare we were presente, They vayled their bonetis and bowed a kne. **1591** Lyly *Endym.* iii. iii, Hee.. sayth, seeing it is the fashion of the world, hee will vaile bonet to beautie. **1600** Fairfax *Tasso* ii. xlviii. 29 This said, the virgin gan her beauoir vale. **1654** H. L'Estrange *Chas. I* (1655) 11 His Speech being ended, the King vailed his Crown, a thing rare in any of his Predecessors. *a* **1693** *Urquhart's Rabelais* iii. xlii, Pantagruel vayling his Cap and making a Leg with such a majestick Garb,.. farewell'd Trinquamelle the President. **1819** Scott *Leg. Montrose* viii, The bonnets, which hitherto each Chief had worn,.. were now at once vailed in honour of the royal warrant. **1843** Lytton *Last Bar.* ii. ii, The earl acknowledged their greeting by vailing his plumed cap.

γ. **1601** Holland *Pliny* II. 305 As for veiling bonnet before great rulers and magistrats, or within their sight [etc.]. **1603** Dekker *Wonderfull Year* Wks. (Grosart) I. 138 Into which [alehouse] as good lucke was,.. veiling his Bonnet, he strucke in. **1740** Somerville *Hobbinolia* ii. 279 He spake, And veil'd his Bonnet to the Crowd. **1825** Scott *Talism.* xxiv, The spiritual dignitaries, who in those days veiled not their bonnets to created being, bestowed on the King.. their blessing instead of rendering obeisance.

b. *fig.* with *bonnet*: To manifest submission; to acknowledge oneself overcome or surpassed; to yield, give way. (Cf. 3 b.)

1579 Gosson *Sch. Abuse* (Arb.) 59 If you giue but a glance to your beholders, you haue vayled the bonnet in token of obedience. **1596** *K. Edw. III*, v. 78 Copland.. with a lowly minde Doth vale the bonnet of his victory. **1609** Holland *Amm. Marcell.* 360 My heart yerneth.. to thinke how many right honourable personages in this unseemly.. manner were debased and brought to vale bonet. **1626** in Foster *Eng. Factories India* (1909) III. 138 None is made so happy but he hath cause to vale the bonnett. **1739** R. Whatley *Three Lett.* 14 After the noted rupture in St. James's Square, he had so remarkably veil'd his bonnet.

c. (As prec.) To submit or yield, to show respect, *to* some person, etc.

1587 Holinshed *Chron.* III. 297/1 All christendome must veile the bonnet to his holinesse. **1590** Nashe *Martin Marprelate* Wks. (Grosart) I. 241 All Schooles of Phylosophers shoulde haue vailed the bonet vnto God. **1611** Coryat *Crudities* 266 Shee wil very neare benumme and captivate thy senses, and make reason vale bonnet to affection. **1675** J. Smith *Chr. Relig. App.* ii. 14 Therefore we see all the Grecian Philosophy that was not founded upon Tradition.. veil'd the Bonnet to that of Pythagoras, Socrates and Plato.

†**3.** *Naut.* To lower, to let or haul down (a sail).

1553 Brende *Q. Curtius* C c iij, The waues dyd ryse so hygh and thicke.. that the shipmen beganne to vale their sayles. **1586** T. B. *La Primaud. Fr. Acad.* I. 351 In the meane while he taketh the helme into his hande, he vaileth the foresaile, and.. laboreth to come out of the darke sea. **1634–5** Brereton *Trav.* (Chetham Soc.) 3 We vailed our topsail, and.. it being answered that we were of London and bound for Rotterdam, we were dismissed.

fig. **1589** Greene *Menaphon* Wks. (Grosart) VI. 48 If he will her to keepe a low sayle, she will vayle al her sheete.

b. *esp.* To lower as a salute or in acknowledgement of inferiority. Chiefly with *bonnet* as object. Sometimes *fig.* (Cf. 2 b.)

(*a*) **1509**, *a* **1529** [see bonnet *sb.* 2]. **1560** Daus tr. *Sleidane's Comm.* 365 The french Captaine.. signified vnto them that for honoure sake, after the olde accustomed facion, they shuld vaile their bonnets, strike saile, and hailse her with shoting of their ordinaunce. **1613** Purchas *Pilgrimage* (1614) 730 Mysians, Troyans, Tyrians vaile your bonnets, strike your top-sailes to this Indian-Admirall. **1633** Sir J. Burroughs *Sov. Brit. Seas* (1651) 62 Divers Ships.. that have constantly kept the Narrow Seas, unto which all strangers even at this day vaile Bonnet in acknowlegement of this Superioritie. **1678** Marvell *Growth Popery* Wks. 1875 IV. 282 The pretended causes [of war] were made publick, which were, the not having vailed bonnet to the English yacht [etc.].

(*b*) **1631** Heywood *Fair Maid of West* i. iv, It did me good To see the Spanish Carvel vail her top Unto my maiden flag. **1653** H. Cogan tr. *Pinto's Trav.* xix. 68 In token of joy they gave a great shout, and withall vailing their top sails in shew of obedience.

†**4.** *fig.* **a.** To abase, humble, or lower (one's courage, the heart, etc.); to submit, subject, or yield (one thing) *to* (another). *Obs.*

1582 Stanyhurst *Æneis* iv. (Arb.) 98 Also let oure Dido vayle her hert too bedfeloe Troian. *c* **1592** Marlowe *Jew of Malta* v. ii, Now vaile your pride you captiue Christians. **1602** J. Davies (Heref.) *Mirum in Modum* Wks. (Grosart) I. 15/2 Vaile, vaile thy thoughts, th' imaginations vaile, Vnto the depth of all profundities. **1649** Bp. Hall *Cases Consc.* i. (1650) 2 There can be no reason why you should vail your owne just advantage to another mans excesse. **1654** Owen *Saints' Persev.* iv. Wks. 1851 XI. 211 Expressing much confidence that the world of saints.. will vail their faith and understanding to his dictates. **1827** Scott *Surg. Dau.* v, When his gold-laced hat veiled its splendour before the fresher mounted beavers of the 'prentices of Dr. Gray.

b. To strike or cast down. *rare*⁻¹.

1590 Greene *Orl. Fur.* v. i, Then maist thou think that Mars himself came down To vaile thy plumes and heaue thee from thy pompe.

II. *intr.* †**5.** To fall (*down*); to descend. *Obs.*

c **1400** *Rowland & O.* 497 A quartere of his helme a-waye gane vale, And halfen-dele his one Ere. ? *a* **1412** Lydg. *Two Merch.* 542 Thus is he valyd adoun from high degre. *c* **1570** *Henry's Wallace* viii. 1189 The donk dew doun fra the heuin did vaill. **1591** Sylvester *Du Bartas* i. iii. (1641) 23 When, through Heav'n's Vault vailing toward Spain, The Moone descendeth. *Ibid.* i. vii. 59 Here vales a Valley, there ascends a Mountain. **1624** Fletcher *Wife for Month* iii. iii, His jollity is down, valed to the ground Sir, And his high hopes .. Are turn'd tormentors to him.

†**b.** Of a swelling: To go down, subside. *Obs.*

c **1450** *St. Cuthbert* (Surtees) 4261 He laide þe hare on his eye lidd, Abouen þe bolnyng... Be fore þe mete, it vale.

†**c.** Of a storm: To abate, cease. *Obs.*⁻¹

1606 Sylvester *Tropheis* 235 Wks. (Grosart) II. 241 The Stormes that long disturb'd the State are val'd.

6. Of a bonnet or banner: To be doffed or lowered in token of respect or submission.

c **1550** *A pore helpe* 214 in Hazl. *E.P.P.* III. 260 And telles them suche a tale As makes theyr bonettes vale. **1742** Pope *Dunc.* iv. 205 His [i.e. Bentley's] Hat, which never vail'd to human pride, Walker with rev'rence took, and laid aside. **1826** Mrs. Shelley *Last Man* II. 15 The inhabitants in thousands were assembled to give him hail,.. the soldiery presented arms, the banners vailed.

†**7.** To drop or sail down stream or with the tide. Also with *down*. *Obs.*

1544 *St. Papers Hen. VIII*, X. 118 Our other shippes, which be already valed. **1553** in Hakluyt *Voy.* (1598) I. 234 We departed from Detford, passing by Greenwich.. and so valed unto Blackwall. **1598** Hakluyt *Ibid.* 367 Wee departed.. before Sunne rising and valed downe the riuer sometime sailing, and sometime rowing.

†**8.** To bow or bend down *to* the ground in obeisance or salutation. *Obs.*⁻¹

c **1593** Marlowe *Hero & Leander* i. 159 There Hero.. Vaild to the ground, vailing her eie-lids close, And modestly they opened as she rose.

III. *absol.* †**9.** *Naut.* To lower the sail. (Cf. 3.) Also in fig. context. *Obs.*

1512 in Rymer *Foedera* (1710) XIII. 330 No Vessell of the Flete vale or plukke doun his Saill unto such tyme as the Admiral hath valed. *c* **1592** Marlowe *Jew of Malta* ii. ii, Because we vail'd not to the Turkish Fleet. **1601** B. Jonson *Poetaster* iii. iv, What, will he saile by, and not once strike, or vaile to a Man of warre? **1650** Weldon *Crt. Jas. I*, 49 A Dutch Man of Warre comming by that Ship, would not vail, as the manner is, acknowledging by that, our Soveraignty over the Sea.

10. To doff or take off the cap or hat (*to* a person, etc.).

1599 B. Jonson *Ev. Man out of Hum.* v. iv, *1st Cup.* The health of that honourable countess... *2nd Cup.* I doe vaile to it with reverence. **1631** Massinger *Emperor East* i. ii, I have .. set down, To a hair's-breadth, how low a new-stamp'd courtier May vail to a country gentleman. **1648** G. Daniel *Poems* Wks. (Grosart) I. 214 Hee [Herbert] the vtmost Fame Has gain'd; and now they vaile, to heare Him Sing. *c* **1700** Pomfret *Poems, Dies Novissima* (1736) 9 Straight I finish'd —veiling low. **1753** Richardson *Grandison* II. iv. 39, I would sooner veil to such a Man as this than to a King on his throne. *a* **1845** Barham *Ingol. Leg.* Ser. iii. *Lord of Thoulouse*, Knights.. Before Count Raymond bend the knee, And vail to him.

transf. **1597** Lyly *Wom. in Moon* v. i, The Iocund trees that vald when she came neare, And.. Did seeme to say, 'Pandora is our Queene'.

11. *fig.* To submit, yield, give place *to* (or *unto*); to acknowledge the superiority or supremacy of.

In freq. use by 17th c. divines.

1610 Holland *Camden's Brit.* i. 301 All rivers else beside Vaile unto me. **1627** Hakewill *Apol.* (1630) 395 To Cæsars

Amphitheater all other workes must vaile. *a* **1677** BARROW *Serm.* (1686) I. 335 These indeed are lofty commendations thereof, yet all of them may worthily veil to this. **1706** DE FOE *Jure Divino* x. 232 Vail Satyr to the mighty Edward's Fame. **1779** T. HUTCHINSON *Diary* II. 243 The Ministry vail to every measure to humour the people. **1824** L. MURRAY *Eng. Gram.* (ed. 5) I. 525 They all vail to the English idiom, and scruple not to acknowledge its superiority over their own.

b. To do homage *to* one.

1608 SHAKS. *Per.* IV. Prol. 29 When She would with rich and constant pen Vail to her mistress Dian.

Hence **'vailing** *ppl. a.*[2]

a **1639** WOTTON in *Reliq.* (1672) 386 Where surging flouds and valing ebbs can tell That none beyond thy marks must sink or swell.

†**vail**, *v.*[3] *Obs.*[−1] In 7 vaile. [f. VAIL *sb.*[1] 5.] *absol.* To give vails or gratuities.

1598–9 B. JONSON *Case Altered* II. ii, Why, now you come near him, sir; He doth vaile, he doth remunerate.

vail, obs. f. VEIL *sb.* and *v.*

†**'vailable**, *a. Obs.* Forms: α. 4–7 **vailable**, 5–6 **vaylable**; 5 **vaill-**, 5–6 **vayllable** (6 **veyll-**); 5–6 **vaile-**, 6 **vayleable**; 5 **waleable** (*Sc.* **walable**), 6 **valeable** (*Sc.* **valabill**). β. 6 *Sc.* **vailȝieabill**, **valiabill**, **-able**, 7 *Sc.* **valliable**. [f. VAIL *v.*[1] + -ABLE. Cf. AVAILABLE *a.*]

1. Of avail, advantage, or benefit; availing, advantageous, beneficial, profitable, etc.; effectual, efficacious. **a.** Const. *for*, *to* (*unto*), or with inf.

(*a*) **1390** GOWER *Conf.* III. 136 Wordes that ben resonable, And for this art schal be vailable. *Ibid.* 198 To al the lond it is vailable Only thurgh grace of his persone. *c* **1407** LYDG. *Reson & Sens.* 948 The Ryvers..wern also ful profitable And vn-to manne ryght vayllable. **1483** CAXTON *Gold. Leg.* 88 b/2 Holy oylle..whiche is moche vayllable to thelthe of sykenesses of many men. **1530** PALSGR. 794 Every exemple is as vayllable to the lerner, as thoughe I gave a rule. **1561** *Godly Q. Hester* (1873) 57 The dayly prayer of that hole secte..Eke holy ceremonies of gods prouiseon To god is vaileable.

(*b*) **1390** GOWER *Conf.* III. 233 Thei tuo [*sc.* pity and justice] remuen alle vice, And ben of vertu most vailable To make a kinges regne stable. **1491** CAXTON *Vitas Patr.* (W. de W. 1495) I. xxxiv. 28 b/2 It is moche better & more vaylable to dispose & applie hym to folow thother gode maners & vertues of the holy faders. **1565** HARDING in Jewel *Def. Apol.* (1611) 443 For the promise with the deliuery is more vaileable to transfer my right in the horse, then my promise alone.

b. Without const.

c **1400** GOWER in *Pol. Poems* (Rolls) II. 8 Aboute a kyng good counseil is to preise, Above alle othre thinges most vailable. ?*c* **1470** G. ASHBY *Active Policy* 475 Whether thei [i.e. servants] be good or nat vailable. **1530** PALSGR. Ep. p. v, Howe soever veyllable my poore dilygence hath ben. **1544** BETHAM *Precepts War* I. cxlix. Hij b, Therefore let the capitaine be sure to haue some man vaileable in feates and strength. *a* **1577** SIR T. SMITH *Commw. Eng.* II. iv, The souldier might bee kept in more strait obedience, without which neuer Captaine can doe any thing vaileable in the warres.

c. *Sc.* Morally profitable or allowable.

1456 SIR G. HAYE *Law Arms* (S.T.S.) 301 A prince suld be amesurit to tak delytis fleschly, nocht vaillable. *a* **1500** *Ratis Raving*, etc. 3663 Kep thaim fra delyt nocht walable, And fra al deid dishonorable.

2. Legally valid or effective.

α. **1433–4** *Rolls of Parlt.* V. 437/2 In the same Parlement ..her seid demenyng of the seid Revenues of the Feoffament be declared as for good and vaillable. **1451** *Ibid.* 214/1 That the Acte made..be vaillable and stond in strengh and force. **1563–4** *Reg. Privy Council Scot.* I. 262 Grantis the samin redemptioun als valabill as gif ane decrete of the Lordis of Counsale wer gevin. **1592** WYRLEY *Armorie* 18 The law did then take the said grant to be good and vailable. *a* **1648** LD. HERBERT *Hen. VIII* (1683) 403 Whereby it doth plainly appear, that the Sentence given by the Pope to the contrary was not vailable. **1652** WADSWORTH tr. *Sandoval's Civ. Wars Spain* 9 Adriano's Commission was dated long before Don Ferdinando's deceas, therefore not valeable.

β. **1565** *Inchaffray Charters* (S.H.S.) 162 All fredomes.. be als valiable and of als greit strenth, force, and effect..as gif [etc.]. *c* **1575** *Balfour's Practicks* (1754) 456 Reversioun is vailȝieabill to redeme the landis fra ony possessour thairof.

3. *Sc.* Of sufficient means; solvent. *rare.*

1609 SKENE *Reg. Maj.* 77 Gif the debtour confessis the debt, and is not valliable in gudes and geir, to pay the samine. *Ibid.* 80 Gif the borgh may proue that the principall debtour is vailable.

†**vailance.** *Obs.* In 4 vayl-. [a. OF. *vaill-*, *vailance*: cf. next and -ANCE.] Value, worth.

1387–8 T. USK *Test. Love* II. v. (Skeat) l. 85 There the vaylance of men is demed in richesse outforth, wenen men to have no proper good in them-selfe.

†**vailant**, *a. Obs.* Forms: 4 **vaill-**, 5 **vayllaunt**, **vayl-**, **vailant**. [a. OF. *vaill-*, *vailant*, pres. pple. of *valoir* to be of use, etc.: see VAIL *v.*[1]] Of avail, advantage, or value; valid.

a **1325** *MS. Rawl. B.* 520 fol. 56 b, Þanne nere þat ȝifte noȝt vaillaunt þe wile þat a miȝtte be repeled of þe Eir. *Ibid.* 61 b, Þulke excepcion is vaillaunt ase to þe writ of possession. **1422** YONGE tr. *Secreta Secret.* 125 New Ensamplis that oryson is moch vaylant agaynys the Malice of ennemys. *c* **1450** tr. *De Imitatione* III. vi. 71 It [*sc.* love] is vailant þerfore to all þinges.

vaila(u)nt, obs. ff. VALIANT *a.*

vaile, obs. f. FAIL *v.*, VALE *sb.*[1], VEIL *sb.*

†**vailed**, *ppl. a. Obs. rare.* [f. VAIL *v.*[2]] Lowered, drooped; doffed or taken off in salutation.

1591 GREENE *Maidens Dreame* 28 A golden Hind was placed at her feet, Whose valed eares bewraid her inward greet. **1602** SHAKS. *Ham.* I. ii. 70 Do not for euer with thy veyled lids Seeke for thy Noble Father in the dust. **1621** QUARLES *Div. Poems, Esther* Wks. (Grosart) II. 53/2 Doe him honour, fitting his degree, With vayled Bonnet, and low bended knee.

†**'vailer.** *Obs. rare.* [f. as prec. + -ER[1].]

1. One who abases or brings down; a humbler.

1600 TOURNEUR *Transf. Metam.* ix, With all the force of.. fearefull thunder, vailer of Earth's pride.

2. One who vails or doffs the hat, etc. in salutation.

a **1613** OVERBURY *A Wife*, etc. E v b, If hee finds not good store of vailers, he comes home stiff and seer.

'vailful, *a.* = AVAILFUL *a.*

A conjectural reading in Shaks. *Meas. for M.* IV. vi. 4 for *vail(e full* of the Folios.

†**'vailing**, *vbl. sb. Obs. rare.* [f. VAIL *v.*[2]] The action of the vb.; a descent.

1593 MARLOWE *Edw. II*, I. ii, And happie is the man, whom he vouchsafes For vailing of his bonnet one good looke. **1624** WOTTON *Archit.* in *Reliq.* (1672) 64 The Beholder descending many steps was afterwards conveyed again by several mountings and valings to various entertainments of his sent and sight.

vaill, obs. Sc. f. VALE *sb.*; obs. var. WALE *v.* (choose) *Sc.*

vaillant, obs. f. VALIANT *a.*

vaillaunt, var. VAILANT *a. Obs.*

vailliaunce, obs. f. VALIANCE.

†**vail staff.** *Obs.*[−1] [f. VAIL *v.*[2] 1 b.] The practice of lowering a staff in token of respect or as a salute.

1599 GREENE *George a Greene* v. i, And for the ancient custome of Vaile staffe, keepe it still, Clayme priuiledge from me: If any aske a reason why? or how? Say, English Edward vaild his staffe to you.

vaimure, var. *vamure* VAUMURE *Obs.*

vain (veɪn), *a.* and *sb.* Forms: α. 4–5 **vayn** (4, 5–6 *Sc.*, **wayn**), 4–6 **vayne** (5–6 **wayne**), 4–7 **vaine** (5 *Sc.* **waine**), 4, 6– **vain** (4 **wain**). β. 4 **vein**, **veen**, 5 **veine**; 4–5 **veyn** (4 **ueyn**, 5 **weyn**), **veyne** (5 **veyyne**, **feyne**, *Sc.* **weyne**). γ. 4 **wan**, 5, 6 *Sc.*, **wane**, 5–6 *Sc.* **vane** (6 **uane**). [a. OF. *vein*, *veyn*, *vain* (F. *vain*):—L. *vānus* empty, void, idle, etc. (whence also It. and Sp. *vano*, Pg. *vão*).]

I. 1. Devoid of real value, worth, or significance; idle, unprofitable, useless, worthless; of no effect, force, or power; fruitless, futile, unavailing.

α. *a* **1300** *Cursor M.* 28332 Quen idel thoght me come and vain, Wit will i stode þam noght again. *c* **1340** HAMPOLE *Prose Tr.* 3 Na thynge..sa..dos awaye coryous and vayne ocupacyons fra vs. **1387** TREVISA *Higden* (Rolls) VII. 135 Witeþ al..men þat the power of kynges is vayne. *c* **1450** *Mirk's Festial* 64 To put away all maner worldes vanyte, and vayn murthe, and reuell. **1484** CAXTON *Fables of Æsop* I. v, For the loue of a vayn thynge men ought not to leue that whiche is certeyn. **1529** *Supplic. to King* (E.E.T.S.) 23 Such wayne, vngodly, and vnprofitable lerninge. **1560** DAUS tr. *Sleidane's Comm.* 102 b, Many woulde judge that promesse to be vayne. **1614** RALEIGH *Hist. World* II. (1634) 372 After which victorie it is said that Jephta performed the vaine vow which he made. **1662** STILLINGFL. *Orig. Sacræ* II. iii. §6 Certainly God..will never alter the course of nature, meerly for satisfaction of mens vain curiosities. **1713** STEELE *Englishm.* No. 7, Without a natural Talent, all the Acquirements of Learning are vain. **1759** FRANKLIN *Ess.* Wks. 1840 III. 525 The remainder of that day..was wasted in a vain discussion. **1802** MAR. EDGEWORTH *Moral T.* (1816) I. xiii. 103 It was vain for him to attempt any explanation. *a* **1853** ROBERTSON *Serm.* Ser. III. xiv. (1866) 178 In vain regrets for the past, in vainer resolves for the future. **1872** RUSKIN *Eagle's N.* §177 All literature, art, and science are vain, and worse, if they do not enable you to be glad.

β. **1303** R. BRUNNE *Handl. Synne* 5350 Y rede þou ȝelde hyt aȝen, Þy saluacyun ys elles alle veyn. **1390** GOWER *Conf.* Prol. I. 11 The vein honour was noght desired, Which hath the proude herte fyred. **1426** LYDG. *De Guil. Pilgr.* 1291 Thanne me sempte yt was but veyn, Mor for me to speke ageyn. *a* **1450** *Mankind* 846 in *Macro Plays* 32 Beware of weyn confidens of mercy. *c* **1500** *Lancelot* 382 Dremys..ben thingis weyn, of non affek.

γ. *a* **1450** *Mankind* 533 in *Macro Plays* 20 He xall wene grace were wane. **1500–20** DUNBAR *Poems* xii. 39 Wirk for the joy that lestis evir; For vder joy is all bot vane. **1596** DALRYMPLE tr. *Leslie's Hist. Scot.* I. 105 That rathir thay appeir nocht to be spokne of a vane ostentatione, than of the veritie.

†**b.** Of material things: Useless, worthless. *Obs.*

1578 LYTE *Dodoens* 384 Cyclaminus altera hath an unprofitable and vaine roote. **1596** SPENSER *F.Q.* IV. ii. 48 Most wretched men, whose dayes depend on thrids so vaine. **1769** SIR W. JONES *Palace Fortune* Poems (1777) 20 His spear, vain instrument of dying praise.

c. Trivial, unimportant. *rare*[−1].

1731 POPE *Ep. Burlington* 29 Imitating-Fools, Who.. Load some vain Church with old Theatric state, Turn Arcs of triumph to a Garden-gate.

†**2.** Empty, vacant, void. Also const. *of*. *Obs.*

1382 WYCLIF *Gen.* i. 2 The erthe forsothe was veyn with-ynne and void. *c* **1400** *Pilgr. Sowle* (Caxton) IV. xxix. (1859) 62 Alle folke the alouteth and abeyeth, and thou arte veyne, and voyde of al maner of vertue. **1513** DOUGLAS *Æneid* I. Prol. 19 With dull forhede and wane, With ruide engine and barrand emptive brane. **1544** *Exhort.* in *Priv. Prayers* (1851) 568 Outwardly shewing a great pretence of holiness, and being vain of true godliness inwardly. [**1822** SHELLEY tr. *Calderon's Mag. Prodig.* III. 166 Such melancholy..is Skilful in forming such in the vain air Out of the motes and atoms of the day.]

3. Of persons: Devoid of sense or wisdom; foolish, silly, thoughtless; of an idle or futile nature or disposition. Now *rare* or *Obs.*

1390 GOWER *Conf.* I. 217 Wherof he wax so proud and vein, That he his fader in desdeign Hath take. *c* **1400** *Destr. Troy* 4384 At Vaxor þe vayn pepull voidly honourit Bachian. *c* **1450** tr. *De Imitatione* I. vii. 8 He is veyne þat puttiþ his hope in men or in creatures. **1535** COVERDALE *James* ii. 20 Wilt thou vnderstonde o thou vayne man that faith with out dedes is deed? **1568** GRAFTON *Chron.* II. 106 Diuerse vaine persons bruted dayly among the Commons of the realme, that Christ had twise apered vnto him. **1590** SHAKS. *Com. Err.* III. ii. 185 This I thinke, there's no man is so vaine, That would refuse so faire an offer'd Chaine. *a* **1631** DONNE *Poems, Woman's Constancy*, Vaine lunatique, against these scapes I could Dispute, and conquer, if I would. **1663** BP. PATRICK *Parab. Pilgr.* xx. (1687) 210 If it..would make you a medler in other mens matters (as most of our vain Believers are). **1784** COWPER *Tiroc.* 754 [Art not] thou at best, and in thy sob'rest mood, A trifler vain? **1812** J. WILSON *Isle of Palms* I. 587 Hush! hush! thou vain dreamer! this hour is her last. **1819** SHELLEY *Cenci* V. iii. 36 So that our hair should sweep The footsteps of the vain and senseless crowd.

absol. *c* **1450** [see 7 a]. **1781** COWPER *Conversat.* 590 Is sparkling wit.. The fixt fee-simple of the vain and light? **1817** SHELLEY *Rev. Islam* IX. xiv, The peace of slavery, With which old times..had quelled the vain and free.

4. Given to or indulging in personal vanity; having an excessively high opinion of one's own appearance, attainments, qualities, possessions, etc.; delighting in, or desirous of attracting, the admiration of others; conceited. Also *absol.*

1692 DRYDEN *Eleonora* 101 For to be conscious of what all admire, And not be vain, advances vertue high'r. **1703** EVELYN *Diary* Feb., She..I believe carried with her out of this vain nation above £1000. **1762–71** H. WALPOLE *Vertue's Anecd. Paint.* (1786) III. 56 Perceiving the poor man to be immoderately vain, he piqued him to attempt portraits. **1832** LYTTON *Eugene A.* I. x, It might teach the vainest to forswear vanity. **1857** BUCKLE *Civiliz.* I. x. 609 The vain man, restless, insatiable, and always craving after the admiration of his contemporaries. **1884** F. M. CRAWFORD *Rom. Singer* I. 18 The heart of the vain man is lighter than the heart of the proud.

transf. **1781** COWPER *Conversat.* 366 The vainest corner of our own vain heart.

b. Const. *of*.

1697 DRYDEN *Virg. Past.* Pref., We deserve more compassion, because we are not vain of our Barbarities. **1749** FIELDING *Tom Jones* I. viii, A good, honest, plain girl, and not vain of her face. **1829** LYTTON *Devereux* I. i, Between you and me, he was not a little vain of his leg. **1848** THACKERAY *Van. Fair* xxiv, The General..sate down to pen a *poulet* (he was exceedingly vain of his French) to Mademoiselle Aménaide.

II. 5. In the advb. phrase **in vain**, to no effect or purpose; ineffectually, uselessly, vainly.

After L. *in vanum*, or OF. *en vein* (F. *en vain*, = It. *in vano*, Sp. *en vano*, Pg. *em vão*).

α. *a* **1300** *Cursor M.* 16172 Of him he wend ha signes sene, For noght, al was in vain. *a* **1340** HAMPOLE *Psalter* xx. 1 That..he spend noght his preciouse blode in vayn on vs. **1375** BARBOUR *Bruce* IV. 48 Bot þat trawaill þai maid in wayne. **1422** YONGE tr. *Secreta Secret.* 198 Thar Prayer was not in wayne. *c* **1470** HENRY *Wallace* II. 151 The more thai bad, the mor it was in wayne. **1535** COVERDALE *Job* ii. 3 Yet is it in vayne, for he contynueth still in his godlynesse. **1585** T. WASHINGTON tr. *Nicholay's Voy.* I. xvii. 20 All was in vain, for there was no remedy but to obey. **1651** HOBBES *Leviath.* II. xviii. 89 It is therefore in vain to grant Soveraignty by way of precedent Covenant. **1697** DRYDEN *Virg. Georg.* III. 394 Nor Bits nor Bridles can his Rage restrain; And rugged Rocks are interpos'd in vain. **1711** ADDISON *Spect.* No. 1 ⁋7 The secret Satisfaction of thinking that I have not Lived in vain. **1752** HUME *Ess. & Treat.* (1777) I. 157 In vain do you seek repose from beds of roses. **1836** W. IRVING *Astoria* II. 227 Here he endeavoured in vain to barter a rifle for a horse. **1849** MACAULAY *Hist. Eng.* v. I. 623 He wrote piteous letters to the king and to several courtiers, but in vain. **1864** BRYCE *Holy Rom. Emp.* vi. (1875) 76 Lewis tried in vain to satisfy his sons..by dividing and redividing.

β. **1303** R. BRUNNE *Handl. Synne* 10252 Alle here trauayle þey do yn veyn. *c* **1385** CHAUCER *L.G.W.* 1359 *Dido*, For wel I wot that it is al in veyn. *c* **1420** *Chron. Vilod.* 4173 He.. sayde, 'nowe haue y trauellede twey [= twice] in feyne'. *c* **1430** LYDG. *Minor Poems* (Percy Soc.) 65 Ye schal nat labour al in veyne, Ye shul have hevene. *c* **1500** *Lancelot* 524 The king..al this resone thinkith bot in weyne.

γ. *a* **1300** *Cursur M.* 19411 (Edinb.), Al þaire striue was bot in wan. *c* **1375** *Sc. Leg. Saints* ii. (*Paul*) 518 Ȝet wald nocht god his prayer war in wane. *c* **1480** HENRYSON *Orpheus & Eurydice* Wks. (S.T.S.) III. 37 Him to reios ȝit playit he a spryng,..Bot all in wane, þai comfort him no thing. **1483** *Cath. Angl.* 197/1 In vane, *frustra*. **1533** GAU *Richt Vay* 13 Thay that sweris in uane and thay that sweris ony fals aith. **1573** *Satir. Poems Reform.* xxxix. 140 For lake of lederis thair thay wrocht in uane. *a* **1600** MONTGOMERIE *Misc. Poems* xviii. 37 Vhen they sau they wroght in vane.

†**b.** So *for vain*. *Obs.*[−1]

1603 SHAKS. *Meas. for M.* II. iv. 12 My Grauitie Wherein ..I take pride, Could I, with boote, change for an idle plume, Which the ayre beats for vaine.

6. *to take..in vain*: †**a.** To disregard, to treat with contempt. *Obs.*

13.. *Coer de L.* 3769 Kyng Phelyp took theroff non hede, But layde thertoo a deff ear... Kyng Richardys words he took in vain. *c* **1330** R. Brunne *Chron. Wace* (Rolls) 16271 Osewy tok þy somons in veyn, To come to court he hadde disdeyn.

b. With *name* as object. To use or utter (the name of God) lightly, needlessly, or profanely; *transf.* to mention or speak of casually or idly.

A literal rendering of *assumere (nomen Dei) in vanum* in the Vulgate text of Exod. xx. 7.

13.. *Cursor M.* 25228 Len vs lord swilk mode and mayn þat we tak neuer þi name in vayn. **1382** Wyclif *Exod.* xx. 7 Thow shalt not tak the name of the Lord thi God in veyn. *c* **1450** *Mirour Saluacioun* (Roxb.) 41 The secunde thow shalle noght in vayne thi lord god name take. **1564** *Reg. Privy Council Scot.* I. 298 To sweir and tak his name in vane. **1630** W. T. *Justific. Relig. now Professed* iii. 22 His name is taken in vaine. **1731–8** Swift *Polite Conv.* 99 Who's that takes my Name in vain? **1860** Tennyson *Sea Dreams* 185 Who, never naming God except for gain, So never took that useful name in vain. **1884** Rider Haggard *Dawn* ii, I always call Chancery 'it'. I wouldn't take its name in vain for worlds.

†**7.** As *sb.* **a.** Vanity; a vain thing. *Obs.*

c **1330** *King of Tars* 71, I schal him seende such wordes to seyn, That al his thought schal torne to veyn. *c* **1450** tr. *De Imitatione* I. xx. 26 Leeue veyn [L. *vana*] to þe veyn, & take þou hede to þo þinges þat god comaundiþ þe. **1606** Sylvester *Du Bartas* II. iv. *Magnificence* 1208 All the World proclaiming Vain of Vains, Man's happinesse in God's true Fear maintains. **1628** Feltham *Resolves* I. lii. Wks. (1677) 84 The power of the Gospel, in crying down the vains of men. **1742** Young *Nt. Th.* III. 267 The fruits of dying friends survey; Expose the vain of life; weigh life and death.

†**b.** Emptiness, void space. *Obs.*

1382 Wyclif *Job* xxvi. 7 He that streccheth out the north vp on vein [L. *super vacuum*], and hangeth vp the erthe vp on noȝt. **1509** Hawes *Past. Pleas.* 105 Wythouten vayne he dyd all thyng fulfyll As astronomy doth make apparaunce.

8. In misc. adjectival or adverbial combs. or attrib. uses, as ***vain-averted, -boasting, -conceited, -headed, -hearted, -proud, -spent, -talking***, adjs.; ***vain-speaker, -struggling***.

1549 Latimer *3rd Serm. bef. Edw. VI* (Arb.) 78 There be some sclaunderouse people, vaynespeakers,.. whych I must nedes speake agaynst. **1562** Phaer *Æneid* IX. B b iij, And furst Eurialus he seeth.. Vainstruggling working much. **1562** Winȝet *Wks.* (S.T.S.) II. 28 Wanetalkand men and dissauearis, quha peruertis hail houssis. **1590** *Marlowe's Tamburl.* To Rdr., Though (happly) they haue bene of some vaine conceited fondlings greatly gaped at. **1603** Breton *Dialogue of Pithe* Wks. (Grosart) II. 17/1 If you will be vaine-headed, God helpe you, for I cannot. *a* **1618** Sylvester *Paradox agst. Liberty* 667 Wks. (Grosart) II. 61 The.. vain-proud state and port, That for the grace of Kings adorns the Courtly sort. **1633** P. Fletcher *Purple Isl.* VIII. xxii, A vagrant rout.. Strow him with vain-spent prayers, and idle layes. **1848** Buckley *Iliad* 291 O babbling and vain-boasting Ajax, what hast thou said? **1858** H. Bushnell *New Life* vi. (1861) 79 He drove Lot's family, or his vain-hearted wife, out of the city. **1871** H. King *Ovid's Metam.* VII. 523 Struggling with vain-averted eyes to shun The noontide beams.

Hence †**vain** *v. trans.*, to frustrate. *Obs.*⁻¹

1628 Feltham *Resolves* II. xii. 34 Euery good man.. must be wise and circumspect, to vaine the sleeke nauations of those that would undoe him.

vain, obs. f. vein *sb.*; southern ME. var. fain *a.* and *adv.*

vaincur, Sc. var. vainquer *Obs.*

vaine, var. wone *sb.* (hope) *Obs.*

vainess(e, obs. ff. vainness.

'vainful, *a. Obs.* exc. *dial.* Also 6 vaynfull. [f. vain *a.* + -ful.] Vain, unprofitable, useless.

1509 Hawes *Past. Pleas.* 55 They.. spende theyr time in vaynful vanyte. **1573** Tusser *Husb.* (1878) 10 Though countrie be more painfull, and not so greedie gainfull, yet is it not so vainfull, in following fansies eie. **1888** in Elworthy *W. Som. Word-bk.* 795.

Hence †**'vainfully** *adv.*, in vain, vainly. *Obs.*

1509 Hawes *Conv. Swearers* 21 Vnto the man I gaue commaundement Not to take the name of thy God vaynfully.

vaingloriness. *rare*⁻¹. [f. vainglory *sb.*] Vaingloriousness.

1820 T. Mitchell *Aristoph.* I. 4 That spirit of foppery haughtiness, and vain-gloriness.

vainglorious (veɪnˈglɔːrɪəs), *a.* Also 6–8 vain glorious, 6– vain-glorious. [f. vainglory *sb.* Cf. med.L. *vānaglōriōsus* (OF. *vana-*, *vaneglorious*), Sp. and It. *vanaglorioso*, Pg. *vanglorioso*.]

1. Filled with, given to, indulging in, vainglory; inordinately boastful or proud of one's own abilities, actions, or qualities; excessively and ostentatiously vain. **a.** Const. *of*.

c **1480** Henryson *Fables, Cock & Fox*, Nyse proud men, woid and vaneglorious Of kin and blude. **1648** Gage *West Ind.* 160 Being not a little vain glorious of what he had done with me. **1729** Law *Serious Call* xviii. (1732) 330 They think it a part of their duty to be proud, envious, and vain-glorious of their own accomplishments. **1784** Cowper *Task* III. 715 When he call'd, Vain-glorious of her charms, his Vashti forth To grace the full pavilion.

b. Without const.

c **1510** More *Picus* Wks. 6/2 Not the knowlage of the Hebrew, Chaldei, and Arabie language, beside Greke & Latin, could make him vaingloriouse. **1599** B. Jonson *Ev. Man out of Hum.* Char. Pers., A Vaine-glorious Knight, over-Englishing his travels, and wholly consecrated to singularity; the very Jacobs staffe of complement. *a* **1639** W. Whateley *Prototypes* I. xi. (1640) 88 Be not vaine-glorious, studying to doe some earthly vaine thing, for which you may be talked of farre and neere. **1651** Hobbes *Leviath.* I. xi. 49 Vain-glorious men.. delight in supposing themselves gallant men. **1713** Young *Last Day* III. 79 Look round, vain-glorious muse, and you whoe'er Devote your-selves to fame, and think her fair. **1785** Grose *Dict. Vulgar T.*, *Vain glorious*, or *ostentatious man*, one who boasts without reason. **1813** Shelley *Q. Mab* III. 139 Where is the fame Which the vainglorious mighty of the earth Seek to eternize? **1840** Ainsworth *Tower of London* (1864) 370 One of the galleries of the palace, where the vain-glorious mannikin was lingering in the hope of being admitted to the royal presence. **1881** Tylor *Anthropology* 384 Even the vainglorious scribes of Egypt would hardly venture to record events without a foundation of fact.

absol. *a* **1553** Udall *Royster D.* Prol., Our Comedie.. against the vayne glorious doth inuey. **1596** Norden *Progr. Pietie* (1847) 173 Though it please the vain-glorious for a time it will bring repentance. **1636** Featly *Clavis Myst.* viii. 101 He baiteth the hook.. for the vaine-glorious with popularitie. **1850** W. Irving *Mahomet* viii. (1853) 43 For God loveth not the arrogant and vainglorious.

transf. and *fig.* **1602** Nixon *Chr. Navy* B ij, Lofty mindes That in this world doe seeke to glister so, Blowne on this rocke by fond vaine glorious winds, Fall headlong downe. **1619** J. Taylor (Water P.) *Kicksey Winsey* Wks. (1630) 36 Itch'd with the vain-glorious worme, To write and lye.

2. Characterized by, indicative of, or proceeding from vainglory.

1533 Gau *Richt Vay* 4 Sic vane glorious tetels and namis and pouers. **1575** Gascoigne *Glasse Govt.* Wks. 1910 II. 68 Wandring.. in a vayne glorious oppinion of their owne wit. **1603** Knolles *Hist. Turks* (1621) 331 Such stately honours and vaine-glorious praises as he in his life time enioyed. **1662** Stillingfl. *Orig. Sacræ* III. iv. § 11 Whether that bee ground of that vain-glorious boast.. I here dispute not. *a* **1700** Evelyn *Diary* 25 Oct. 1667, The Vice-Chancellor's letter.. were too vaine glorious to insert. **1791** Cowper *Odyss.* IV. 610 Neptune that speech vain-glorious hearing, grasp'd His trident. **1809** W. Irving *Knickerb.* VI. ix. (1849) 376 Let not my readers imagine.. that I am indulging in vainglorious boastings. **1861** Sala *Dutch Pictures* xvi. 243 'See Naples and then die,' is the vain-glorious saying of the Neapolitans. **1896** Dk. Argyll *Philos. Belief* 268 They were the very incarnations of vainglorious pride.

vain'gloriously, *adv.* [f. prec.] In a vainglorious manner.

1545 Elyot *Dict.*, *Gloriosus*, renoumed, some tyme in the yll parte, vayneglorioussly [*sic.*], or bostynge hym selfe. **1548** Udall, etc. *Erasm. Par. Luke* iii. 31 Leat it therefore no more entre into your hertes to thynke with your selues vaingloriously. **1565** Golding *Ovid's Met.* IX. (1593) 211 Sure I meane not I To vant my selfe vaine-gloriouslie by telling of a lye. **1623** N. Rogers *Strange Vineyard* 36 When Nebuchadnezzar vaunted vainegloriously of that great Babel which he had built. **1648** Milton *Tenure Kings* 38 Which heretofore in the persuance of fame and forren dominion spent it self vain-gloriously abroad. **1702** *Lond. Gaz.* No. 3808/3 The Ambition of Spain, when it.. vain gloriously stiled its *Armado* Invincible. **1808** Edwards *Plain Pract. Plan* i. 8 A character which France can no more than vain gloriously affect to be. **1824** W. Irving *T. Trav.* I. 207, I cannot tell you how vaingloriously I walked the streets.

vain'gloriousness. [f. as prec.] The quality or character of being vainglorious.

1542 Udall *Erasm. Apoph.* 328 Their facion of makyng oracions was.. replenyshed with vauntyng.. & vaingloriousnesse. **1577** *Test. 12 Patriarchs* (1706) 25 The spirit of lying or vain-gloriousness in boasting a mans self, and in desire to fill his talk concerning his kindred and acquaintance. **1581** Pettie *Guazzo's Civ. Conv.* I. (1586) 46 b, By yᵗ meanes you see that one offendeth by arrogancie, another by obstinacie,.. another by vaingloriousnesse. **1832** L. Hunt *Sir R. Esher* (1850) 134 An amor patriæ above all our vain-gloriousness. **1844** Thackeray *Barry Lyndon* v, Led away by the vaingloriousness of youth,.. I invented a thousand stories. **1886** Tupper *My Life as Author* 355 He had repented of the vaingloriousness of those herald angels and their dome.

vainglory (veɪnˈglɔːrɪ), *sb.* Also **vain-glory, vain glory**. Forms: see vain *a.* and glory *sb.* [ad. med.L. *vāna glōria*. Cf. OF. and mod.F. *vaine gloire*, It., Sp. *vanagloria*, Pg. *vangloria*.]

1. Glory that is vain, empty, or worthless; inordinate or unwarranted pride in one's accomplishments or qualities; disposition or tendency to exalt oneself unduly; idle boasting or vaunting.

α. *a* **1300** *Cursor M.* 26933 Noght als intent o waynglori, Or als þis ypocrites dos. *c* **1340** Hampole *Pr. Consc.* 1145 Honours nuryshes, als men may se, Vayn glory, vauntyng, and vanite. **1393** Langl. *P. Pl.* C. VII. 35 Bostynge and Braggynge wyth meny bold oþes, Auauntyng vp-on my veine glorie for eny vndernymynge. *c* **1450** tr. *De Imitatione* III. xlv. 116 Verily, veyn glory is an euel pestilence & grettist vanyte. **1484** Caxton *Fables of Avian* vi, He that taketh within hym self vayne glorye of that thynge by the whiche he shold humble hym self is a very fole. **1535** Joye *Apol. Tindale* (Arb.) 22 For he that doth a thing secretly,.. how seketh he vaynglory? **1585** T. Washington tr. *Nicholay's Voy.* IV. xxxiv. 156 b, Through the.. increase of their power, they fell into such a vainglory and arrogancy. **1627** in Foster *Eng. Factories India* (1909) III. 174 Their trade.. is not augmented but deminnished by vayneglorie and unnecessarie disburcements. **1656** Earl Monm. tr. *Boccalini's Advts. fr. Parnass.* I. xxxv. (1674) 44 Tamberlan the Scythian.. had the vain-glory to be called the Emperor of the East. **1710** Norris *Chr. Prud.* vii. 309 Vainglory, whereby Men affect a great many dry and insipid Studies.. only to please others, and procure from them a blind Admiration. **1782** Miss Burney *Cecilia* VII. v, Thus have I .. acknowledged my vain-glory. **1841** Helps *Ess., Exerc. Benevolence* (1875) 34 That portion of his thinking time which he spends upon vain-glory, upon imagining, for instance, what other people are thinking about him. **1878** B. Taylor *Deukalion* III. ii. 106 The wisdom of the world? Nay: 'tis vain-glory.

β. **1390** Gower *Conf.* II. 35 Bot he such veine gloire hadde Of that he was set upon hyh. *c* **1425** Wyntoun *Cron.* IV. 2610 Til vsurpe til hym þat nayme It war bot wayne glore or defame. *a* **1500** *Ratis Raving*, etc. 3644 To schaw hire proud, at men may see, Is pryd, wanglore, and vanite. **1500–20** Dunbar *Poems* ix. 118, I synnit.. In fals vane gloir and deidis negligent.

b. In the phr. *for vainglory*.

c **1380** Wyclif *Wks.* (1880) 3 Men doon þis nouelrie for vein glorie. **1387** Trevisa *Higden* (Rolls) III. 367 Som men telleþ þat Aristotil made his bookes so schortliche and so hard for envie and for vayngloire. *a* **1548** Hall *Chron.*, *Hen. IV*, 23 He.. mervailed that the duke.. wolde nowe for vainglory under colour of doyng dedes of Armes.. violate the peace.

c. As a personal name, or in personified use.

c **1400** *St. Alexius* (Laud MS.) 1004 Hou his fader sergeauntz alle, veyn glorie gonne hym calle, And gorre on hym gonne þrowe. **14..** *Why I can't be Nun* 228 in *E.E.P.* (1862) 144 Dame sclowthe and dame veyne glory. **1596** Lodge *Wits Miserie* B ij, His first sonne is Vainglory. **1717** L. Howel *Desiderius* (ed. 3) 18 She gave him her Name, Vain-glory.

2. A vainglorious thing, action, etc. *rare*.

c **1450** in Aungier *Syon* (1840) 378 None schal take any synguler abstynence up-on her withe-oute licence of the abbes, in awnter God take it for a veyne glory. **1607** Shaks. *Timon* I. ii. 249 What needs these Feasts, pompes, and Vaine-glories? **1649** Milton *Eikon.* viii. Wks. 1851 III. 392 The Vulgar; who notwithstanding what they might know, will beleeve such vain-glories as these.

Hence **vain'glory** *v.* †(*a*) *refl.* To exalt or make much of (oneself) unduly. *Obs.* (*b*) *intr.* To indulge in vainglory. Also **vain'glorying** *vbl. sb.*

a **1637** N. Ferrar tr. *Valdes' 110 Consid.* (1638) 104, I understand, that a man being Just by his Justice, doth as much prize himselfe,.. or vain-glory himselfe, as much as the theife, who is taken from the Gallowes in the Holy Week, .. vaine-glories himselfe for his deliverance. **1882** Stevenson *New Arab. Nts.* (1884) 46 The scheme.. had involved a little vain-glorying before his acquaintance. **1887** *Westm. Rev.* July 485 It would be idle and frivolous to mention these points for the sake of vain-glorying during the Jubilee year.

†**'vainling.** *Obs. rare.* [f. vain *a.* + -ling¹ I.] A vain or vainglorious person.

1615 W. Hull *Mirr. Maiestie* Ep. Ded., Presuming himselfe (fond Vain-ling) to be of more esteeme, because he was the Nuncio and Interpreter of the Gods. *Ibid.* 134 Thus we see, he was no vaineling, who pronounced all things vnder the Sunne to bee vanitie of vanities.

vainly (ˈveɪnlɪ), *adv.* Forms: α. 4, 6 vaynly, 6–7 vainlie, 7 vaine-, 6– vainly. β. 5 veynli, -(e)ly, veinly. γ. 6 *Sc.* vanelie. [f. vain *a.* + -ly².]

1. In a vain or futile manner; without advantage, profit, or success; to no effect or purpose; in vain; uselessly, fruitlessly, ineffectually.

1382 Wyclif *James* iv. 5 Wher weenen ȝe, that veynly [L. *inaniter*] the scripture seith [etc.]. **1387** Trevisa *Higden* (Rolls) VII. 195, I folwer of evel craft.. trowed vaynly for to be defended and helped by ȝoure prayers. *c* **1450** tr. *De Imitatione* III. li. 123 Ner he shal not ioy veinly, if he be resonably excused by oþer. **1509** Fisher *Funeral Serm. C'tess Richmond* Wks. (1876) 293 This noble prynces,.. whome my purpose is not vaynly to extoll.. aboue her merytes, but to the edefyenge of other. *a* **1548** Hall *Chron.*, *Hen. VI* (1550) 23 Vitayll.. not wantonly consumed, nor vainly spent. **1607** Shaks. *Timon* v. iv. 8 Till now, my selfe and such As slept within the shadow of your power Haue.. breath'd Our sufferance vainly. **1667** Milton *P.L.* II. 811, I forewarn thee, shun His deadly arrow; neither vainly hope To be invulnerable. **1695** Ld. Preston *Boeth.* I. 12 Every one going away with that Rag which he had snatch'd, vainly believ'd that he had possess'd himself of Philosophy. **1743** Francis tr. *Hor.*, *Odes* I. xiv. 13 What though majestic in your pride you stood.., You now may vainly boast an empty name. **1781** Gibbon *Decl. & F.* xxix. (1787) III. 110 Perhaps he vainly imagined, that he laboured for the interest of an only daughter. **1808** Scott *Marm.* I. xii, There, vainly Ralph de Wilton strove 'Gainst Marmion's force to stand. **1858** Froude *Hist. Eng.* IV. xviii. 31 In the caprices of passion and humour we look vainly for any guiding principle. **1870** Bryant *Iliad* III. I. 98 From my hand The spear was vainly flung and gave no wound.

Comb. **1648** J. Beaumont *Psyche* XVI. xxviii, He.. Beyond my vainly-panting reach is plac'd.

†**2.** Foolishly, senselessly, thoughtlessly. *Obs.*

1588 *Durham Depos.* (Surtees) 330 She spoke somwhat idlie and vainlie, by reason of the extremitie of her sickness. **1596** Dalrymple tr. *Leslie's Hist. Scot.* I. 101 Nathir haue thay nochtwithstandeng now vanelie fallin frome the faith of the Catholik Kirk. **1612** Drayton *Poly-olb.* xi. 346 Ethelbald,.. though most vainly given when he was hot and young, Yet, by the wise reproofe of godly Bishops brought From those unstay'd delights by which his youth was caught. **1647** Cowley *Mistr.*, *Vain Love* 46 What Lover can like me complain, Who first lov'd vainly, next in vain! **1730** Bailey (fol.), *Inaniloquent*, talking or babbling vainly.

3. With personal vanity; conceitedly.

1602 *Ld. Cromwell* IV. i. 35 'Tis greater glorie for me, That you remember it, then of myselfe Vainlie to report it. **1650** Hobbes *De Corpore Politico* 3 How some are vainly Glorious, and hope for precedencie and superiority above their Fellows. **1692** E. Walker tr. *Epictetus' Mor.* xi, When with too much pleasure you admire Your Horse's Worth, and vainly boast his Sire. **1779** Cowper *Human Frailty* 20 A stranger to superior strength, Man vainly trusts his own.

vainness (ˈveɪnnɪs). [f. as prec. + -NESS.] The state or condition of being vain, in various senses: **a.** Futility, ineffectiveness, uselessness.

1571 GOLDING *Calvin on Ps.* xxxiii. 18 The helps of the world hold our senses entangled.. till they have given us a tryall of theyr vaynenesse. **1600** PALFREYMAN *Baldwin's Mor. Philos.* 37 The vainenes of this life is greater then the profit. **1648** W. BROWNE *Polexena* v. I. 284, I knew the vainnesse of my hopes, and the just cause Alcidiana had to punish my boldnesse. **1719** D'URFEY *Pills* (1872) IV. 303 Beauty.. shew'd the vainess of Defence, When Phillis does Invade. **1849** ROBERTSON *Serm.* Ser. I. xix. (1866) 314 Pilate, feeling the vainness.. of these pretensions. **1892** *Athenæum* 18 June 790/1 The vainness of this and that creed.

b. Vanity, esp. personal vanity or conceit. Now *rare*.

a **1586** SIDNEY *Ps.* XXVI. iii, I did not them frequent, Who be to vainesse bent. **1599** SHAKS. *Hen. V*, v. Prol. 20 Free from vain-nesse, and selfe-glorious pride. **1600** PALFREYMAN *Baldwin's Mor. Philos.* I. 12 Hee despised.. much all vainnesse of apparell. **1645** WITHER *Vox Pacifica* 19 The vices, and the vainnesse of thy tongue. **1825** COLERIDGE *Lett., Convers.*, etc. II. 179 Mr. Chance is a self-satisfied man, but of the very.. best sort... I regard such vainness but as the overflow of humanity.

†**c.** Foolishness, stupidity. *Obs.*⁻¹

1591 SPENSER *Vis. Worlds Vanitie* vi, O how great vainnesse is it then to scorne The weake.

†**vainquer.** *Obs. rare.* In 5 vaynquer, *Sc.* vaincur. [a. OF. *vainqu(i)erre*, *veinqueor*, etc. (mod.F. *vainqueur*), f. *vaincre* to conquer.] A conqueror, vanquisher, victor.

1456 SIR G. HAYE *Law Arms* (S.T.S.) 272 Thare cummys the vaincur, askand jugment of rycht. **1481** CAXTON *Godfrey* ccii. 296 Thenne made they.. moche ioye & grete, as doon the vaynquers and conquerours whan they departe theyr gayne.

†**vainqueress.** *Obs.*⁻¹ In 6 venqueresse. [a. OF. *vainqueresse*, *veinq-*: see prec.] A female conqueror or vanquisher.

a **1513** FABYAN *Chron.* VI. clxxx. (1811) 178 Elfleda that sheldes so ofte dyd rayse Agayne her enemyes, this noble venqueresse Virago and made, whose vertue can I nat expresse.

vair (vɛə(r)), *sb.* Forms: 4 veir(e, veyr(e, 5 feyre; 4, 6–8 vaire, 4, 8– vair, *Sc.* wayre, 7 vayre, 9 *dial.* vare, fare, viare, etc. [a. OF. *vair*, *veir* (also nom. *vairs*):—L. *varium*, acc. sing. masc. of *varius* parti-coloured. Cf. med.L. *varius*, also *vairus*, *vayrus*, *veyrus* (from OF.), and *vajus* (from It. *vajo*), in the same sense.]

1. A fur obtained from a variety of squirrel with grey back and white belly, much used in the 13th and 14th centuries as a trimming or lining for garments. Now only *arch.*

Cotgrave's definition of F. *vair* as 'a rich furre of Ermines powdered thicke with blue haires' is app. unsupported by evidence.

a **1300** *Cursor M.* 25466 Nu ask i noþer gra ne grene,.. Ne purperpall, nee pride o pane, Ne riche robe wit veir and grise. *c* **1330** R. BRUNNE *Chron. Wace* (Rolls) 11194 Manteles.. Of meneuer, stranlyng, veyr, & gris. *c* **1375** *Sc. Leg. Saints* vii. (*James the less*) 764 Furryt wele in wayre & grece. *c* **1382** *Pol. Poems* (Rolls) I. 265 For somme vaire, and somme gryse,.. In bagges about thai bere.

1810 SCOTT *Lady of L.* IV. xii, If pall and vair no more I wear. **1818** RANKEN *Hist. France* IV. 377 It was ordained, A.D. 1294,.. that no ecclesiastic, but dignified clergymen, should wear vair, gray, or ermine, excepting [etc.]. **1865** SWINBURNE *Poems & Ball., Laus Veneris* 266 Each man's hair Crowned with green leaves beneath white hoods of vair.

2. A weasel or stoat. Now *dial.*

Prob. due to an early misunderstanding as to the source of the fur.

1387 TREVISA *Higden* (Rolls) I. 335 Þere beeþ veyres [L. *mustelas*: Caxton *feyres*] litel of body and ful hardy and strong. **1796–** in dial. glossaries (Dev., Dorset, Somerset, Pemb., Glamorgan, Wexford, etc.) in forms *vare*, *fare*, *viare*, *vier*, *wyer*, *veer*. **1832** MRS. BRAY *Descr. Part of Devon* (1835) I. xix. 342 The stoat, vair, or vairy, is the commonest of the weasel tribe.

3. *Her.* One of the heraldic furs, represented by bell- or cup-shaped spaces of two (or more) tinctures, usu. azure and argent, disposed alternately (in imitation of small skins arranged in a similar manner and sewn together).

vair cuppa or ***tassy*** (see quot. *c* 1828 and VAIRY *a.* 1 b). ***vair-en-pal***, ***vair-en-point*** (see quot. 1766). Cf. also COUNTERVAIR.

1562 LEGH *Armorie* 132 The ninthe and last [doubling] of all, is called Vaire, which is of al coloures except these two before rehersed [i.e. azure and vert]. It may be also of three sondry colours, which.. colours must be tolde as this is blazed. **1610** GUILLIM *Heraldry* I. iv. (1611) 15 If you obserue the proportion of this vaire, you shall easily discerne the very shape of the case or skinne of little beasts, in them. **1622** PEACHAM *Compl. Gent.* xv. (1906) 194 Quarterly Gules and Vaire. **1637** *Camden's Rem.* 209 Hubert de Burgo,.. who bare for his Armes in a Shield, Gules seven Lozenges vaire, 3, 3, 1. **1728** CHAMBERS *Cycl.* s.v. *Furr*, The Heralds use two Metals,.. and two Furrs, or hairy Skins, Ermine and Vaire. **1766** PORNY *Heraldry* iii. (1777) 27 *Vair-en-point* or *Vair-en-pal*, is said when the point of a Vair is opposite to the Base of another. **1816** *Gentl. Mag.* March 223 A fesse between two chevrons Vaire. *c* **1828** BERRY *Encycl. Her.* I. Gloss., *Vair cuppa*, or *Vair Tassy*, is.. by most writers upon heraldry, considered a kind of fur, and shaped in the form of cups or goblets by divisions potent counter-potent. **1864** BOUTELL *Her. Hist. & Pop.* iv. (ed. 3) 20 Vair, Counter Vair,.. are always Argent and Azure, unless other tinctures are named in the blazon.

†**vair,** *a.* *Obs.*⁻¹ *Sc.* In 5 wayre, wa(i)re. [a. OF. *vair*, *veir*:—L. *varium*: see prec. and VARY *a.*] Varied or variegated in colour.

c **1425** WYNTOUN *Cron.* I. v. 217 The brukyd bestys and the wayre [*v.r.* ware, waire] he gert depart fra quhyt & fayre.

vair(e, southern ME. varr. FAIR *a.* and *adv.*

vaird, obs. Sc. f. WARD.

†**vaired,** *a.* *Obs.*⁻¹ [Cf. VAIR *sb.*] = VAIRY *a.*

1658 SIR T. BROWNE *Gard. Cyrus* ii, Heralds.. disposed the figures of Ermins, and vaired coats in this Quincuncial method.

†**vaires.** *Obs.*⁻¹ [perh. pl. of F. *veire* (*voire*) truth: see VEIRE.] ***in vaires***, ? in verity, truly.

13.. *Gaw. & Gr. Knt.* 1015 Wyth clene cortays carp, closed fro fylþe; & hor play was passande vche prynce gomen, in vayres.

vairhede, ME. var. FAIRHEAD.

vairloch, obs. Sc. f. WARLOCK.

vairn, obs. Sc. f. WARN *v.*

vairsta(ll, obs. Sc. ff. WARESTALL.

vairy (ˈvɛərɪ), *a.* (and *sb.*). Forms: α. 5 varri, 6–7 varrye (7 -ie), varry, 6–7, 9 varrey. β. 7–9 vairy, 8 vary. See also VERRY *a.* [a. OF. *vairy*, f. *vair* VAIR *sb.*

The mod.F. form *vairée* has been employed in some heraldic books.]

1. *Her.* Of a coat, charge, etc.: Varied or variegated with two or more colours; having divisions and tinctures like those of vair.

Some writers have drawn a distinction between *vair* and *vairy*, using the latter when tinctures other than argent and azure are blazoned.

α. **1486** *Bk. St. Albans, Her.* B iv b, Thre cootarmuris be ther called restryall in armys. Oon is whan a cootarmure is varri of dyuerse colowris to the poynt. **1562** LEGH *Armorie* 52 b, A playne crosse, varrye. *Ibid.* 131 b, The eight doubling is Varry, and is so properly called, although it be Or, and Vert, or els Vert and Or. **1592** WYRLEY *Armorie, Ld. Chandos* 97 A patie crosse of red in gold he bare On which fiue losinges varrey placed are. **1610** GUILLIM *Her.* (1611) I. iv. 15 As for the rest, *viz.* Verry and Varrye, they are meere fantasies and improper termes. **1655** FULLER *Ch. Hist.* VI. 321 Tavestock in Devon shire gave Varrey Or and Azure, on a Chiefe Or, two Mulletts. Gules. **1656** BLOUNT *Glossogr.*, *Varry*.. signifies that which is diversified with argent and azure. *c* **1828** BERRY *Encycl. Her.* I. Gloss., Varrey in point.

β. **1706** *Lond. Gaz.* No. 4217/4 The second Vary, a Canton. **1762** tr. *Busching's Syst. Geog.* V. 235 The arms of Oettingen are vairy ruby and a shield saphire. **1868** CUSSANS *Her.* iii. 53 If the field were Or, and the bells Gules, it would be blazoned as Vairy, Or and Gules.

†**b.** ***vairy-cuppy***, ***tassa*** (see quots.). *Obs.*

1610 GUILLIM *Her.* I. iv. (1611) 15 This sort of furre or doubling was.. of some old Heralds called varry cuppy and varry tassa. **1704** J. HARRIS *Lex. Techn.* I, *Vairy Coppy*, or *Potent Counter-Potent*, is a Bearing in Heraldry. **1766** PORNY *Heraldry* ii. §ii. 27 Potent-counter-potent, anciently called Vairy-cuppy, is when the Field is filled with Crutches or Potents counter-placed.

¶**2.** Furred with vair. Also used as if the name of a material.

1728 CHAMBERS *Cycl.* s.v., Vairy gowns are observed by Julius Pollux to have been the habit of the antient Gauls, as Ermins were of the Armenians. **1861** AINSWORTH *Const. Tower* (1862) 187 Wrapped in cerecloth of many folds, and in an outer cover of cloth of vairy and velvet,.. the corpse was laid out.

vairy (weasel, stoat): see VAIR *sb.* 2.

Vaisākha, var. VESAK.

vaise, dial. f. FEEZE *v.*

‖**Vaishnava** (ˈvaɪʃnavaː). [a. Skr. *vaiṣṇavá* relating, belonging, or sacred to Vishnu; a worshipper or follower of Vishnu.] **A.** *sb.* A member of one of the three great divisions of modern Hinduism, exclusively devoted to the worship of the god Vishnu as the Supreme Being. **B.** *adj.* Of or pertaining to this division of Hinduism.

1845 [see SAKTA]. **1876** [see SAIVA *sb.* and *a.*]. **1882** [see VEDISM]. **1903** *Times* 2 May 16/2 The 'holy basil' is.. planted before every Vaishnava house, and every Vaishnava wears necklaces, or armlets, and carries a rosary, made up of sections of its stalks or roots. **1944** E. THOMPSON *Robert Bridges* xi. 95 They both thought it worthless and in bad taste, as Rabindranath Tagore considered Bengali Vaishnava erotic mystical verse. **1968** *Jrnl. Mus. Acad. Madras* XXXIX. 61 To the Vaishnava devotees all over India Sri Krishna has been the Godhead for meditation.

Hence **ˈVais(h)navism** = VISHNUISM; **ˈVais(h)navite** *a.*, of or pertaining to Vaishnavas or Vishnuism.

1877 [see *S(h)aivism* s.v. SAIVA *sb.* and *a.*]. **1919** N. MACNICOL *Psalms of Maratha Saints* 5 There are one hundred and eight *tulsi* beads on the rosary worn by the Vaisnavite devotee. **1934** *Nature* 5 May 680/2 The ingrained love of life disclosed by the religions of Saktism and Vaisnavism among the Bengalis, comparable to that found among the Aryans, is a racial psychological trait to be associated with the brachycephalic Bengali castes. **1956** [see *S(h)aivism* s.v. SAIVA *sb.* and *a.*]. **1967** SINGHA & MASSEY *Indian Dances* i. 35 Of the Vaishnavite temples those at Belur and Halebid have an important significance. **1969** *Indo-Asian Culture* Oct. 70 Both Saivism and Vaishnavism were popular in Srihatta and the neighbouring region during the late Gupta and medieval times.

vaist, obs. Sc. f. WEST.

vaistie, var. Sc. WASTY *a. Obs.*

vaistour, obs. Sc. f. WASTER.

‖**vaisya** (ˈvaisja). Also 9 veisya, vaish(y)a. [Skr. *vaiśya* peasant, labourer, etc.

In Sir T. Herbert's *Trav.* (1634) 38 the form *wyses* occurs (cf. quot. 1665), and BICE from Urdu has had some currency.]

The third of the four great Hindu castes, comprising the merchants and agriculturists; a member of this caste. Also *attrib.*

1665 SIR T. HERBERT *Trav.* (1677) 53 The last Sect or Cast of Gentiles are the Wises. **1794** SIR W. JONES *Inst. of Menu* i. §31 [Brahma] caused the Brahmen, the Cshatriya, the Vaisya, and the Súdra.. to proceed from his mouth, his arm, his thigh, and his foot. **1800** *Asiat. Ann. Reg.* 53/2 Born of a Vaisya woman. **1801** R. PATTON *Asiat. Mon.* 123 The functions of the *vaisya* tribe. **1841** ELPHINSTONE *Hist. Ind.* I. 31 The practical knowledge required from a veisya is more general than that of the other classes. **1920** H. G. WELLS *Outl. Hist.* I. xx. 159/1 The four main castes seem to have been:.. The Vaisya—herdsmen, merchants, money lenders, and land-owners. **1956** R. PIERIS *Sinhalese Social Organization* v. i. 170 The existence among the Sinhalese of a system akin to the classical Hindu four-fold scheme—priestly *brahmins*, *kshatriyas* or warriors, the pastoral *vaisyas*, and the lowly *sūdras*.. is attested in the survival in Ceylon of the place-name 'brahmin village'. **1958** *Spectator* 17 Jan. 70/3 Brahmins, Kshattriyas, Vaishas and Sudras. **1971** *Illustr. Weekly India* 11 Apr. 11/1 Rishabhadeva also classified the people according to their occupations, the kshatriyas who were warriors, the vaisyas who were traders, and the sudras who made their living by manual labour. **1971** K. KENT in C. Bonington *Annapurna South Face* 309 *Vaishya*, common man or merchant.

vait, obs. Sc. f. WAIT *v.*, and *wot* WIT *v.*

vaivode (ˈveɪvəʊd). Now *Hist.* Forms: α. 6–7 vayuod(e, 7 vayvod, 7, 9 vayvode, 8 vaywode. β. 6 uai-, 7 vaiuoda; 7 vaiuod, 7–8 vaivod (7 vavoyd), 7–9 vaivode, 8 vaiwode. [Ultimately ad. older Magyar *vajvoda* (now *vajda*), representing the common Slavonic *voj(e)voda* VOIVODE. The immediate source is partly mod.L. *vayvoda* (cf. Sp., Pg., and It. *vaivoda*) or F. *vayvode*. See also WAYWODE.] A local ruler or official in various parts of south-eastern Europe (in older use esp. in Transylvania).

α. **1560** DAUS tr. *Sleidane's Comm.* 71 He had an adversarye John Sepuse, the vayuode of transsylvania. **1590** SIR J. SMYTH *Disc. Weapons* 44 b, In a great battaile fought betwixt him and that famous Vayuod Iuan Huniades Coruino. **1665** MANLEY *Grotius' Low C. Wars* 579 The one [sister], marryed to the King of Poland; the other, to Sigismund Battor, Prince or Vayvod of Transilvania. **1685** *Lond. Gaz.* No. 2070/2 The Vayvode Janco was drawing together a great Body of Morlacks with a design to attack some place in the Province of Bosnia. **1768** *Ann. Reg.* I. 19 Count Potocki, Vaywode of Kiow, had no less than ten towns, and one hundred and thirty villages, destroyed in his own territories.

fig. **1613** DEKKER *Diuels Last Will* Wks. (Grosart) III. 351 Behemah Dornschweyn,.. chiefe Vayuode of Vsury, Symony, Bribery, Periury,.. etc.

β. **1562** J. SHUTE tr. *Cambini's Turk. Wars* 7 John Uaiuoda soughte to haue al the glorie of the victorie to him selfe. **1601** R. JOHNSON *Kingd. & Commw.* (1603) 51 The Vaiuods of Valachia, Moldauia and Transiluania hold their estates by vertue of this bribery. **1696** tr. *Du Mont's Voy. Levant* xix. 242 The Government of the Cities is manag'd by Five Kinds of Officers, the Bassa, Sub-Bassa, Vaivode, Cadi and Receiver of the Customs. **1771** *W. Guthrie's Geogr.* (ed. 3) 114 Their ancient nobility were divided into knezes, or knazeys, boyars, and vaivods. **1776** *Ann. Reg.* II. 7 At Athens ..his patrimony had suffered from the extortions of a tyrannical Vaiwode. **1833** ELLIS *Elgin Marbles* I. 2 Lord Elgin then received very strongly expressed firmauns from the Porte, which were carried.. to the Vaivode of Athens and the Disdar of the Acropolis.

transf. **1618** BOLTON *Florus* II. xiv. (1636) 132 Andriscus .., delivered up into our hands by that Vaivod, or petty King, of Thrace to whom hee had fled for succour.

‖**vajra** (ˈvadʒra). [a. Skr. *vájra*.] In Hinduism and Buddhism, a thunderbolt or mythical weapon esp. one wielded by the god Indra.

1788 *Asiatick Researches* I. 241 His weapon, *Vajra*, or the thunderbolt. **1854** A. CUNNINGHAM *Ladák* xiii. 371, I should suppose that they pay especial reverence to the holy *Dorje* (*Vajra*, or thunderbolt) which descended through the air, and fell at Sera in Tibet. **1897** H. K. BEAUCHAMP tr. *Dubois's Hindu Manners* II. III. v. 638 Indra's vehicle is an elephant, and his weapon the *vajra*, a kind of sharp knife. **1980** *Catal. Fine Chinese Ceramics* (Sotheby, Hong Kong) 134 Painted with a triple band of Tibetan characters on the underside.., and with a cruciform double *vajra* tied with curling ribbons knotted under a central roundel on the interior. *Ibid.*, For the fifteenth century origin of the double *vajra* design compare the Chenghua dish in the British Museum.

vak, obs. Sc. f. WAKE *v.*

vakabonde, obs. f. VACABOND.

†**vake**, *a. Obs. rare.* [ad. L. *vac-uus.*] Empty.
1600 HOLLAND *Livy* I. xxxiii. 24 Whilest it stood void and vake, the old Latines had surprised and taken it. *Ibid.* XXIV. vii. 513 Certeine conspiratours..possessed themselves of a vake house, standing over a narrow lane.

†**vake, vaik**, *v. Sc. Obs.* Forms: α. 5 **wake**, 5–7 **vake**, 7 **veak**. β. 5 **wayk**, 5–7 **vaik**, 6 **waik**, 6–7 **vaick**, 7 **vaike**. [ad. L. *vac-āre* to be empty: cf. prec. So OF. and F. *vaquer*, Sp. and Pg. *vacar*, It. *vacare*. With the exception of quot. 1543 in 1 α the use of the word is entirely Scottish: cf. VACAND *ppl. a.*]

1. *intr.* Of a benefice, office, or position: To become or fall vacant; also, to remain vacant or unfilled.
Freq. from *c* 1550 to *c* 1650, esp. of ecclesiastical benefices.
α. *c* **1425** WYNTOUN *Chron.* v. 4110 (Cott.), Qwhen he was ded, þan dayis nyne þat se wakyt [*Wemyss MS.* vaikit]. **1456** SIR G. HAYE *Law Arms* (S.T.S.) 223 For and the Archebischopryke of Ranis or Rowan vakit, and the chanouns wald ches ane Inglisman to be archebischop. **1522** DOUGLAS in *Wks.* (1874) I. p. cx, The beneficis and grete prelaceiis that wakis. **1543** SENTLEGER in *St. Papers Hen. VIII*, III. III. 485 Ther is a Statute here [at Waterford],.. that when suche rombe shulde vake,..they shoulde then electe and chose..one Inglisheman. **1604** A. SETON in G. Seton *Memoir* (1882) iv. 57 Quhen eiuer onye place sould vake in onye maner.
β. *c* **1550** LYNDESAY *Tragedie* 361 Quhen thare doith vaik ony benefyse. **1558** KENNEDY *Comp. Treat.* in *Misc. Wodrow Soc.* (1844) 151 Gyf ane benefice vaick, the gret men of the realme wyll haue it. **1570** *Satir. Poems Reform.* xviii. 102 Sic [a lord] as..feiris God now sen the roume dois waik. **1639** MARQ. OF HAMILTON *Expl. Meaning Oath & Covenant* 16 [It] also declares, that all bishopricks vaicking, or that shall vaick, shall be only disponed to actuall preachers and ministers in the Kirk. *a* **1670** SPALDING *Troub. Chas. I* (1851) II. 204 Thus Oswall cumis bak with this ansuer, and Doctor Forbes place still vaikis. **1696** in *Home Papers* (Hist. MSS. Comm.) 271 The Justice Clerk.. disposes of the Clerk to the Justice Court his place when it vaikes.

b. Of a tack or tenancy.
1473 *Rental Bk. Cupar-Angus* (1879) I. 197 Gif it happynis..thar takis to wayk be ony maner of wa. **1542** *Records of Elgin* (New Spald. Cl.) I. 69 Failȝeand heirof the forsaidis takkis to vaik *eo facto*.

2. Of persons: **a.** To be free, to have time or leisure, for engaging in some occupation; to be occupied or busy. Const. *for*, *on* or *upon* (also, to wait or attend *upon* one), *to*.
1456 SIR G. HAYE *Law Arms* (S.T.S.) 221 The law levis all clerkis to vake in scolis and in studyis to..sciences and literature. *Ibid.* 222 Of thame quhilkis levis all richessis..to vake thareapon. **1501** DOUGLAS *Pal. Hon.* III. xviii, All thir ..on Venus seruice vaikis, In deidis of armis for thair ladyis saikis. **1566–7** *Reg. Privy Council Scot.* I. 497 Becaus the haill Lordis of Secreit Counsall may nocht weill vaik at all tymes for the ordouring thairof being occupiit with uther wechtie materis. *a* **1600** MONTGOMERIE *Misc. Poems* xli. 29 Nou Cupid compellis Our hairtis echone On Venus vha vaikis, To muse on our maikis. *a* **1614** J. MELVILL *Diary* (Wodrow Soc.) 45, I was resigned ower be my father hailelie unto him to veak upon him as his sone and servant.

b. To be at leisure or free *from* some occupation or business.
c **1470** HENRYSON *Mor. Fab.* VIII. (*Preach. Swallow*) xxxix, Esope..Quhen that he vaikit frome mair autentik werk,.. this foirsaid fabill wrait. **1596** DALRYMPLE tr. *Leslie's Hist. Scotl.* II. 107 Quhen he mycht vake fra temporal effayres, his exercise was ay in spiritual. *a* **1600** MONTGOMERIE *Sonn.* lxv. 4 Quhan I may vaik fra service of the king.

Hence †**vaked** *ppl. a.*; †'**vaking** *vbl. sb.* and *ppl. a. Obs.*
1572 J. KNOX in Calderw. *Hist. Kirk Scotl.* (Wodrow Soc.) III. 766 That all bishoprics vacand may be presented ..within a yeer after the vaiking therof. **1622** in R. M. Fergusson *A. Hume* (1899) 221 They assigne to him the first vaiking Gilbrotheris fyne that sall occur to thame. **1638** in A. Maxwell *Hist. Old Dundee* (1884) 388 Being oft times requirit, [he] would propone nothing but only ane mein [= moan] 'Vaiked Sea!' **1660** in Crookshank *Hist. Suffer. Ch. Scot.* (1749) I. 59 That hereafter vaking stipends may be intromitted with by Presbyteries.

‖**vakeel, vakil** (və'kiːl). *Anglo-Ind.* Forms: α. 7 **vakill, vekill, -ile, -ell, vikil, vicle**, 8 **vekil**, 9 **vakil, vakíl, vaquil**. β. 7– **vakeel** (7 **fakeel**), 7 **vickeele**, 7–8 **vack-, vekeel**. [a. Urdū (Pers.-Arab.) *vakīl*, *wakīl*: cf. WAKEEL.]

1. An agent or representative, esp. one representing a person of political importance either permanently or on a special occasion; a minister, envoy, or ambassador.
α. **1622** in Foster *Eng. Factories Ind.* (1908) II. 11 Two coppyes, to the Governour of this place and his owne vekile. *Ibid.* 69 Receaved two letters of Isacke Beages to Assuff Chon, and the other to his vekill. **1682** W. HEDGES *Diary* (Hakl. Soc.) I. 35 The Dutch Director's Vakill. **1687** A. LOVELL tr. *Thevenot's Trav.* II. 171 Through the bad Conduct of the Vikil, he was necessitated to reimbark. **1844** H. H. WILSON *Brit. India* II. 283 Terms..were proposed, and the Vakils returned with them to the Bai. **1870** SIR W. W. HUNTER in *Life* (1901) xi. 182 His Vakil or representative told me the story of the sunken fortunes of the family. **1906** *Contemp. Rev.* May 580 The German Ambassador there.. has become the Vaquil or Agent of the Sultan.
β. **1623** in Foster *Eng. Factories Ind.* (1908) II. 307 That hereafter the Kings people may recoure it from the vickeeles of Agha Reza. **1624** *Ibid.* (1909) III. 30 Their vackeels at Court is to acquaint the King thereof. **1691** J. OVINGTON *Voy. Suratt* 415 November the 1st, arriv'd a Pattamar or Courrier, from our Fakeel, or Sollicitor at Court. **1763** SCRAFTON *Indostan* (1770) 74 He was determined to fall on us, and turned our vacqueel out of the durbar. **1776** *Trial of Nundocomar* 24/2 He was Vakeel of Bollakey Doss, and executed whatever business he ordered. **1803** EDMONSTONE in Owen *Wellesley's Desp.* (1877) 322 Duplicates have been delivered to the Vakeels of those chiefs at the Presidency for transmission to their principals. **1878** EARL LYTTON *Lett.* (1906) II. 57 The Amir undertook to keep a *vakeel* at Peshawur.

2. A native attorney or barrister; a pleader in the Hindu law-courts.
1776 N. B. HALHED tr. *Code Gentoo Laws* iii. 105 (*heading*) Of appointing a Vakeel (or Attorney). **1850** *Directions Revenue Officers N.-W. Provinces* 230 He is allowed the assistance of the ablest Vakeel or pleader in the Court. **1858** SIMMONDS *Dict. Trade, Vakeel*, a native attorney in India. **1887** *Pall Mall G.* 12 July 13/2 An official known as the poor man's vakeel, whose duty it is to see that every prisoner.. shall be represented in court by a competent counsellor. **1890** KIPLING *City Dreadf. N.* 15 He looks like a *vakil* to the boot-heels, and..recalls memories of up-country courts.

vakin, obs. Sc. f. WAKEN *v.*

vakky, var. VACKY.

vakoof, vakuf. [Turkic var. of WAKF, WAQF.] = WAKF, WAQF.
1860 *Papers relating to Admin. Affairs in Turkey* 37 in *Parl. Papers* (1861) LXVII. 599 'Vakoof' property, which only descends..in a direct line. **1889** G. N. CURZON *Russia in Central Asia* vii. 243 It has since been suggested that a Russian class should be added compulsorily to the latter, which are already richly endowed by the *Vakufs* of deceased benefactors. **1928** *Daily Tel.* 28 Aug. 10/4 The Soviet Government has resolved to confiscate in Turkestan all landed property belonging to mosques (vakoofs).

val, southern ME. var. FALL *sb.*; obs. Sc. f. VEIL *sb.*[1], WALL *sb.*

Valachian, var. WALACHIAN.

valance ('væləns), *sb.*[1] Forms: α. 5 **valaunce**, 6–7 **valans** (6 **wal-**), 5– **valance** (8 **vol-**); 5–9 **vallance**. β. 5, 7 **valens**, 6 **valense**, 7–9 **vallens** (7 **-ins**), 6– **valence**, 6–7 **vallence**. γ. *pl.* 6 **vallanes**, 6, 8 **vallance**, 7, 9 **vallens**; 6, 9 **valence**, 7 **valens**. δ. *pl.* 6 **valandes**, 7 **vallands, -ents**, 9 **valends**. [Of obscure origin: perh. a. AF. *valance, f. *valer* = OF. *avaler* to descend (cf. *vale* VAIL *v.*[2]).
Florio (1598) gives '*Valenza, valenzana*, Say or Serge for bed-curtins or valances for beds', and '*Valenzana del letto*, valences for beds', but there is no evidence for the genuineness of these.]

1. A piece of drapery attached lengthways to a canopy, altar-cloth, or the like, so as to hang in a vertical position. Also *attrib.*
α. **1463** in *Bury Wills* (Camden) 36 The selor of cloth on loffte, with the valaunce of scripture abowte the ymage. **1494** *Househ. Ord.* (1790) 115 The ninth question; whether in the same feaste the Queens cloth of Estate shall hang as highe as the Kings or noe? answere thereunto; the Queens shall hang lower by the vallance. **1540** *Ludlow Churchw. Acc.* (Camden) 2 For wesshynge of autor clothis and albes, ..and the sowynge on of the valans of them. *Ibid.*, The walans that hangyth over the heygh auter. **1670** LASSELS *Voy. Italy* (1698) II. 22 Four stately pillars of brass bear up a canopy of the same metal..with vallances and a gilt fringe, yet all of brass. **1762–71** H. WALPOLE *Vertue's Anecd. Paint.* (1786) I. 54 A tent, striped with white and gold,..and the valance, of the same colours. **1867** BAKER *Nile Trib.* v. 106 Upon striking the tent, we found beneath the valance between the crown and the walls a regiment of scorpions. *attrib.* **1892** LOWNDES *Camping Sketches* 49 Waxing eloquent over knotted guy-ropes and missing valance-loops.
β. **1500** *Will of M. Yonge* (Somerset Ho.), Afore the ymage of our Lady within the valens of the same Chirch. *a* **1548** HALL *Chron.* (1809) 639 Sarcenet..let doune in maner of a valence before the gallery. **1577** HOLINSHED *Chron.* II. 1082/2 A rich herse,..couered with blacke veluet, with a valence fringed with golde.
γ. **1806** *Naval Chron.* XV. 231 The vallens [of the funeral canopy] were fringed with black.

2. *spec.* **a.** A border of drapery hanging round the canopy of a bed; in later use, a short curtain around the frame of a bedstead, etc., serving to screen the space underneath.
α. *c* **1450** *Bk. Curtasye* 447 in *Babees Bk.*, For lordys two beddys schalle be made..Þo valance on sylour shalle henge with wyn, iij curteyns streȝt drawen with-inne. **1480** *Wardr. Acc. Edw. IV* (1830) 132 A sperver..,conteignyng testour, celour, and valances lyned with busk. **1502** *Priv. Purse Exp. Eliz. York* (1830) 66 The seler ij yerdes dim. and the quarter long, the valance j quarter dim. depe. *a* **1593** MARLOWE in *Engl. Parnassus* (1600) 480 And as a costly vallance ore a bed, So did their garland tops the brooke orespred. **1611** COTGR., *Les pentes d'vn lict*, the Valance. **1676** COVEL in *Early Voy. Levant* (Hakluyt Soc.) 165 The vallance was of the same make. **1749** MRS. DELANY *Life & Corr.* (1861) II. 527, I think the fringe of the valance and bases should be the same depth as that on the bottom of the curtains. **1837** BARHAM *Ingol. Leg.* Ser. I. *Spectre of Tappington*, He peeped under the valance of an old-fashioned bedstead. **1861** FLOR. NIGHTINGALE *Nursing* (ed. 2) 56 An iron bedstead, (no vallance, of course), and hair mattress. **1883** F. M. PEARD *Contradictions* i. They had tucked away the scalloped valance,..and drawn back the striped curtains.
β. **1591** PERCIVALL *Sp. Dict.*, *Presilla pelada*, vallence for a bed. **1602** *Inv.* in *Collectanea Archæol.* (1863) II. 97 One bedsteede,..The vallence and frynge of curtaines of say. **1622** PEACHAM *Compl. Gentl.* xiii. (1634) 139 As we see in knops now adayes upon the Valences and Canopies of beds. **1679** *Lond. Gaz.* No. 1434/4 The Curtains and double Vallence of a red Damask Bed. **1748** RICHARDSON *Clarissa* (1811) IV. 396 She had had the presence of mind..to tear down the half-burnt vallens, as well as curtains. **1794** *Girlhood of M. J. Holroyd* (1896) 287 Mrs Maynard has made up..the Bed..with full Valences. **1831** *Remembrance* 80 The hangings of the large square bed were of yellow merino,..with plain, moth-eaten valences.
γ. **1567** HARMAN *Caveat* (1869) 67 These make laces vpon staues, purses,..and whyte vallance for beddes. **1587** *Wills & Inv. N.C.* (Surtees 1860) 317 A pare of sheates, a coueringe, a teaster, courtaynes and vallanes. **1612** WEBSTER *White Devil* III. ii. 177 Let him make Valence for his bed on't, or a demy foote-cloth. **1730** SOUTHALL *Treat. Buggs* 40 The Tester-Cloth,..to which the Head-cloth, and inside and outside Vallens are to be fixed. **1759** *Phil. Trans.* LI. 284 All the vallance were unnailed.
δ. **1512** *Test. Ebor.* (Surtees) V. 38 Two pilloo coddes with the valandes. **1590** *Shuttleworths' Acc.* (Chetham Soc.) 58 Lyttell nelles to festen valandes to bedesse, ijd. **1631** QUARLES *Hist. Samson* Wks. (Grosart) II. 161/2 My beds,.. My sheets; My vallents, and my curtaines. **1675** TEONGE *Diary* (1825) 47 The bedds..with white curtens, and vallands. **1881** BLACKMORE *Christowell* xxi. (1882) II. 50 They came from the valends of the broken down bedstead.

b. A short window-curtain. *rare.*
1726 *Adv. Capt. R. Boyle* (1768) 3 Nailing up some Vallens to the Windows in the Dining-room. **1875** KNIGHT *Dict. Mech.* 2688 *Valance*, a *lambrequin*, or drooping curtain hiding the curtain-rods of a window.

3. a. A pendant border or edging of velvet, leather, or other material.
a **1700** EVELYN *Diary* 1 Apr. 1644, The Duke of Orleans's Library;..the valans of the shelves being of greene velvet fring'd with gold. **1801** tr. *Gabrielli's Mysterious Husb.* III. 5 Nor were the valence less adorned;—indeed, they appeared to have been fashioned by a chissel. **1875** KNIGHT *Dict. Mech.* 2688 *Valance*, the drooping ledge at the parting of a trunk.
transf. **1884** W. K. PARKER *Mammalian Descent* ii. (1885) 55 *note*, In whose larval skull a similar vallance of cartilage grows copiously.

b. A flap attached to a head-dress, esp. as a protection against the sun.
1791 H. WALPOLE *Lett.* (1891) IX. 318 The hats with valences, the folds above the chin of the ladies, and the dirty shirts and shaggy hair of the young men,..have confounded all individuality. **1875** KNIGHT *Dict. Mech.* 1246 Like the cap with a valance named from the East Indian hero 'Havelock'.

c. A protective panel extending below the basic chassis construction of a vehicle.
1933 AUDEN in *Rev. Eng. Stud.* (1978) Aug. 305 A four-door sporting coupé..valances and wings in black. **1937** *Times* 11 Dec. 4/7 Here also..are..the coil on the wing valance, and the electric petrol pump on the dash. **1972** *Daily Tel.* (Colour Suppl.) 13 Oct. 27 His car incorporates a valance to hide mechanical parts underneath the body. **1979** *International Railway Jrnl.* Dec. 51/3 Underframe members are enclosed by the addition of extra panels at the front and deeper valances along the sides.

†**valance**, *sb.*[2] *Obs.*[−1] In 5 **-aunce**. [ad. F. *Valence* Valencia in Spain.] A Valencia almond.
1469 in *Househ. Ord.* (1790) 103 Item Jardens and Valaunces 330 lb.

†**valance**, *sb.*[3] *Obs.*[−1] In 6 **-aunce**. [app. ad. med.L. *valesia*, *valisia* VALISE, with ending assimilated to *sb.*[1]] A cloak-bag.
a **1562** CAVENDISH *Wolsey* (1893) 64 Byfore hyme he hadde..a gentilman that caried his valaunce, otherwyse called a clooke bage; which was made all to gether of fynne scarlett clothe, enbrodered over..with clothe of gold very richly.

'**valance**, *v. rare.* Also **vallance**. [f. VALANCE *sb.*[1]: cf. next.] *trans.* To drape or fringe with, or as with, a valance.
1857 HEAVYSEGE *Saul* 294 Butter-cups and scarlet bean Do vallance like pied beard his chin.

valanced ('vælənst), *ppl. a.* Also 6–7 **valenced** (6 **-ensed**), 7, 9 **vallanced**. [f. as prec.] Provided or furnished *with* a valance or draped edging of a specified material.
a **1548** HALL *Chron., Hen. VIII*, 9 b, The compas of the Pauilion above, enbroudered rychely, and valenced with flat golde, beten in wyre. *Ibid.* 207 b, A clothe of estate.. valanced with frettes. **1591** in *Gentl. Mag.* (1779) 121 The Canapie was of greene satten,..valenced about and fringed with greene silke and siluer. **1760** STERNE *Tr. Shandy* III. xxix, An old set-stich'd chair, valanced and fringed around with party-coloured worsted bobs. **1825** SCOTT *Betrothed* xi, [The pavilion] was of purple silk, valanced with gold embroidery, having the cords of the same rich materials.

b. *transf.* Also *ellipt.*, fringed with hair.
1602 SHAKS. *Ham.* II. ii. 403 What my olde Friend, thy face is vallanced [Q.[2] valanct'] Since I saw thee last, com'st thou to beard me in Denmarke? **1817** KEATINGE *Trav.* I. 113 Men, *barbons*, whose faces have been long vallanced, act the parts of women. **1853** G. J. CAYLEY *Las Alforjas* II. 179 A broad and nobly-cut brow, valanced with shaggy eyebrows, overhung serious, deep-set eyes. **1892** *Speaker* 29 Oct. 533/1 A tall-masted schooner rode grandly in between the Heads, valanced with foam.

†**valanche.** *Obs. rare.* [ad. F. dial. (*la*) *valanche* (for F. *l'avalanche*).] = AVALANCHE *sb.*
1766 SMOLLETT *Trav.* xxxviii, Scarce a year passes in which some mules and their drivers do not perish by the valanches.

valanea, obs. f. VALONIA.

Valanginian (vælən'dʒɪnɪən), *a. Geol.* Also †**Valenginian.** [ad. F. *valanginien* (E. Desor 1853, in *Bull. de la Soc. des Sci. Naturelles de Neuchâtel* III. 177), f. the name of the Château de *Valangin*, near Neuchâtel, Switzerland, in the vicinity of which are exposures of this series.] Of, pertaining to, or designating a stratigraphical stage, a division of the Neocomian, which forms part of the Lower Cretaceous. Also *absol.*

1885 A. GEIKIE *Text-bk. Geol.* (ed. 2) vi. 836 Valenginian—a group of limestones and marls. **1903** *Ibid.* (ed. 4) II. vi. 1197 The lowest dark marl.. indicates the emersion of these rocks at the close of the Jurassic period, and may represent the Valanginian stage. **1944** *Bull. Amer. Soc. Petroleum Geologists* XXVIII. 1141 The lower member consists of.. limestone and contains Valanginian ammonites. **1973** *Nature* 23 Nov. 211/2 The age of the oldest magnetic lineations.. is also coincident with the marine transgressions of southern Africa.. and southern Argentina during the Upper Valanginian. **1978** *Ibid.* 13 July 133/1 The fault activity of this tectonic phase lasted into Valanginian times.

valay, obs. Sc. f. VALLEY.

vald, obs. Sc. var. *would* WILL *v.*

vald(e, ME. var. FIELD *sb.*

Valdenses, -ian, varr. WALDENSES, -IAN.

Valdepeñas (vældɪˈpɛnjəs, ‖valdeˈpeɲas). Also Val de Peñas, Valdepenas, Val de Penas. [The name of a district of south central Spain.] A wine produced in this district.

1832 [see BOTA 1]. **1833** C. REDDING *Hist. Mod. Wines* vi. 181 The province of La Mancha is chiefly a wine district, and there the justly celebrated wine called Val de Peñas is made... It is grown upon a rocky or stony soil, as *Val de Peñas*, or 'Valley of Stones', indicates. **1845** R. FORD *Hand-bk. Spain* I. II. 309/1 *Valdepeñas is the* wine of Madrid.. rich, fruity. **1931** S. JAMESON *Richer Dust* v. 132 A red wine, clean, dry, strong, called Val de Penas, which they bought in La Mancha. **1963** L. DEIGHTON *Horse under Water* li. 216 In the tiny *tasoa* the marble-tops were covered in glasses of Valdepenas. **1974** *Times* 31 Aug. 9/1 Valdepeñas wines do not at all resemble the better-known Riojas.

valdinge, obs. Sc. var. WIELDING *vbl. sb.*

Valdois, obs. var. VAUDOIS.

†**val-dunk.** *Obs.*$^{-1}$ (Meaning obscure.)

1631 BRATHWAIT *Whimzies, Wine-soaker* 102 By this time his cause is heard, and now this val-dunke growne rampant-drunke, would fight if hee knew how.

vale (veɪl), *sb.*^{1} Forms: α. 4- **vale** (4-5 **vaal**), 4-5 (6 *Sc.*) **wale**. β. 5-7 **vaile** (7 **vaille**), 6 *Sc.* **vaill**, 7-8 **vail**; 5 *Sc.* **wail**, **waill(e**, 6 *Sc.* **waile**, **wayill**. [ad. OF. *val* (= It., Sp., Pg. *valle*):—L. *vallem*, acc. of *vallis*, *vallēs* valley.]

1. a. A more or less extensive tract of land lying between two ranges of hills, or stretches of high ground, and usually traversed by a river or stream; a dale or valley, esp. one which is comparatively wide and flat.

In later use chiefly *poet.* (exc. as in b), but employed as an ordinary prose word by American writers in the second half of the 18th century.

α. **13..** *E.E. Allit. P.* B. 673 For þat Cite þer bysyde was sette in a vale. *c* **1400** MAUNDEV. (Roxb.) xxxi. 138 Þare es a vale betwene twa hilles. **1426** LYDG. *De Guil. Pilgr.* 21198 Affter philisofres talys, Ther ben hylles, ther ben wales, Medwes, ryvers. **1508** DUNBAR *Goldyn Targe* 248 Suete war the vapouris,.. Halesum the vale, depaynt wyth flouris ying. **1588** SHAKS. *Titus A.* II. iii. 93 These two haue tic'd me hither to this place, A barren, detested vale you see it is. **1618** J. TAYLOR (Water P.) *Penniless Pilgr.* Wks. (1630) 136/2 Then let who list delight in Vales below, Skie-kissing Mountaines pleasure are for me. **1660** F. BROOKE tr. *Le Blanc's Trav.* 7 Towards the Tiberiade Sea there is another vale very hollow, between two hills, where the Sun is hardly ever seen. **1727-46** THOMSON *Summer* 606 [The wave] steals, at last, Along the mazes of the quiet vale. **1751** J. BARTRAM *Observ. Trav. Pennsylv.*, etc. 35 We lodged by Front Creek in a spacious vale. **1787** M. CUTLER in *Life, Jrnls., & Corr.* (1888) I. 277 At the bottom of the vale, and on the bank of the river, is a huge rock. **1835** THIRLWALL *Greece* (1839) I. 7 Into which the Spercheius.. winds through a long narrow vale. **1857** HUGHES *Tom Brown* I. i, I pity people who weren't born in a vale. I don't mean a flat country, but a vale: that is, a flat country bounded by hills. **1878** BROWNING *La Saisiaz* 8 Forth we sallied to see sunset from the vale.

transf. **1820** SHELLEY *Vision of Sea* 15 The walls of the watery vale.. are unmoved by the gale. *Ibid.* 96 The mountainous vale of the wave.

β. *a* **1400-50** *Alexander* 3980 If I be vencust in þe vaile & voidid of my lyfe. *c* **1440** *Generydes* 216 They rode in a full fayre vaile. **1535** STEWART *Cron. Scotl.* I. 14 In ane vaill that is besyde the toun, Eberieus stentit thair palȝeonis doun. *a* **1568** A. SCOTT *Poems* (S.T.S.) xiv. 16 The wallowit weidis in þe vaill. **1617** SIR W. MURE *Misc. Poems* xxi. 102 Heir wods and vails and echoes that resounds. **1770** WASHINGTON *Writ.* (1889) II. 308 The vail (through which this creek runs).. appears to be wide.

b. Const. *of* (the distinctive name of the vale).

a **1300** *Cursor M.* 2705 Abram satt his hus.. Bi-side þe wale of moat mambre. *c* **1340** HAMPOLE *Pr. Consc.* 5164 Al men sal ryse to þe dome, And in þe vale of Iosaphat come. *c* **1375** *Sc. Leg. Saints* ii. (*Paul*) 285 In þe wale of comptone [*read* campioune; L. *pugilum*]. *c* **1400** MAUNDEV. (Roxb.) viii. 30 Men schall passe thurgh þis deserte to þe vale of Elym. *c* **1425** WYNTOUN *Cron.* VIII. xxvi. 4364 A companny þat.. war walkande In til þe wail of Anande. **1560** DAUS tr. *Sleidane's Comm.* 267 By the vale of Remsie. **1577** HARRISON *England* I. xiii, The famous vales in Englande, of which one is called the Vale of white horse, another of Eouesham,.. the third of Ailesbyry [etc.]. **1667** MILTON *P.L.* XII. 266 And thou Moon [stand] in the vale of Aialon, Till Israel overcome. **1804** C. B. BROWN tr. *Volney's View* 33 West of the Allegheny, towards the vale of the Ohio, there are many remarkable hills. **1846** McCULLOCH *Acc. Brit. Empire* (1854) I. 21 The Vale of Gloucester, or that part of the Vale of Severn.. which lies in Gloucestershire.

c. Without article, occas. contrasted with *hill, mountain*, etc.

c **1402** LYDG. *Compl. Bl. Knt.* vii, The briddes.. Which on the braunches, bothe in pleyn and vale, So loude songe. *c* **1470** HENRY *Wallace* x. 999 Baith hycht and waill obeyed all till his will. **1667** MILTON *P.L.* XI. 563 Where casual fire Had wasted woods on Mountain or in Vale. ? **1786** WORDSW. '*Calm is all nature*' 6 A slumber seems to steal O'er vale, and mountain. **1822** SHELLEY *Scenes fr. Faust* II. 62 A voice.. which.. vibrates far o'er field and vale.

2. a. In fig. uses. Also const. *of* (adversity, etc.).

1412-20 LYDG. *Chron. Troy* II. 42 Sche can plonge worþi emperoures From þe hille of hiȝe prosperite In-to þe vale of aduersite. *c* **1450** *Pol., Rel., & L. Poems* (1903) 181 In the vaile of restles mynd, I sowght in mownteyn & in mede. [**1535** COVERDALE *Ps.* lxxxiii. 6 Which goinge thorow the vale of mysery, vse it for a well.] **1604** BRETON *Grimello's Fortunes* Wks. (Grosart) II. 5/2 After that I had past the great Mountaine of mishaps, I fell into a long vaile of miserie. **1784** COWPER *Task* VI. 721, I.. Have pour'd my stream of panegyric down The vale of nature. **1809** SHELLEY '*For my dagger*' 22, I dare not unveil The shadows that float o'er Eternity's vale.

b. The world regarded as a place *of* trouble, sorrow, misery, or weeping. Usu. with *this*.

14.. in *Tundale's Vis.* (1843) 123 In thys sorowfull vale Of trowbull of woo and of hevynes. **1435** MISYN *Fire of Love* 12 In þis vale of wepynge þai haue bene delityd. **1497** BP. ALCOK *Mons Perfect.* A iij/2 Y^e transytory Joye of this vale of mysery. **1500-20** DUNBAR *Poems* lxxiii. 7 Out of this vaill of trubbill and dissait. **1554** in *Maitl. Cl. Misc.* III. (1855) 65 The labilitie and breuitie of tymes.. and of men in this wale of teiris beand considerit. **1618** RALEIGH *Rem.* (1664) 113 What could you find in the vail of tears [etc.]? **1655** in *Verney Mem.* (1907) II. 12 For afflicktions whille we live in this vaille of miserey must continually be loocked for. **1781** COWPER *Conversat.* 881 Though life's valley be a vale of tears, A brighter scene beyond that vale appears. **1816** SHELLEY *Hymn Intell. Beauty* ii, Why dost thou pass away and leave our state, This dim vast vale of tears, vacant and desolate? **1911** G. B. SHAW *Shewing-Up of Blanco Posnet* 405, I thought I was a man and not a snivelling canting.. apprentice angel serving his time in a vale of tears. **1963** *Times Lit. Suppl.* 22 Feb. 130/3 It looks.. to heaven, but with no vale-of-tears morality. **1977** D. E. WESTLAKE *Enough* i. 22, I was about as safe as anybody ever is in this vale of tears.

c. The world regarded as the scene of life. With various qualifications, as *earthly*, *mortal*, etc., or const. *of* (life, etc.).

c **1446** LYDG. *Nightingale Poems* II. 351 Where-as þat god of love hym-self doth dwelle Vpon an hille ferre from the mortal vale. **1593** SHAKS. *2 Hen. VI*, II. i. 70 Great is his comfort in this Earthly Vale, Although by his sight his sinne be multiplyed. **1718** PRIOR *Solomon* I. 621 Why, whilst We struggle in this Vale beneath.., Do They more bless'd perpetual Life employ.. in Scenes of Joy? **1784** COWPER *Task* IV. 799 An unambitious mind, content In the low vale of life. **1819** SHELLEY '*A gentle Story*' 6 In this world's deserted vale. **1850** TENNYSON in Ld. H. Tennyson *Mem.* (1897) I. 309 In this vale of Time the hills of Time often shut out the mountains of Eternity.

d. *the vale of years*, the declining years of a person's life; old age.

1604 SHAKS. *Oth.* III. iii. 266 Haply,.. for I am declin'd Into the vale of yeares. **1676** D'URFEY *Mme. Fickle* IV. i, A man that has the misfortune to decline into the vail of Years. **1769** LD. HOLLAND in Jesse *Selwyn & Contemp.* (1843) II. 372 Yet I.. am weak enough sometimes to think, that if Rigby.. had pleased, I should have walked down the vale of years more easily. **1796** BURKE *Lett. Regicide Peace* Wks. VIII. 310 That venerable potentate and pontiff, issunk deep into the vale of years. **1818** SCOTT *Hrt. Midl.* ix, Mrs. Butler [was] a woman, and declined into the vale of years.

†**3. a.** One of the grooves in the beam of a hart's antler. *Obs.*$^{-1}$

c **1410** *Master of Game* (MS. Digby 182) xxiv, Alle allonge þe beames þere be smale vales, þat men clepe gotters.

†**b.** ? The notch at the back of a barbed arrowhead. *Obs.*$^{-1}$

c **1400** *Laud Troy Bk.* 7794 To that kyng he gan to hale, And drow an arwe vp to the vale.

4. *attrib.* and *Comb.* **a.** Attrib., as *vale-dweller*, *-hind*; **vale-lily**, the lily of the valley.

1822 BEDDOES *Poems, Rom. Lily* 150 My tribute shall be sweet, though small:—A cup of the vale-lily bloom. **1832** BREE *St. Herbert's Isle* 13 To mark the vale-hind ted the ripened shock. **1889** *Archaeol. Æliana* XIII. 266 The fierce pagan vale-dwellers by the North Tyne.

b. Attrib., occas. passing into *adj.*, in the sense 'of or belonging to, found, grown, or produced in, a (particular) vale', as *vale-barley*, †*-dog*, *-farmer*, *-grey* (a variety of pea), *-man*, *soil*.

1615 MARKHAM *Country Contentm.* I. viii. 98 Now the Gentlemen which dwell on the dounes and plaine grounds, to maintaine the reputation of their Dogs, affirme them to be much more nimble.. in turning, then the vale Dogs be. **1677** PLOT *Oxfordsh.* 240 When at any time they sow Peas on this Land, the best Husbandmen will chuse the Vale-gray as most proper for it. *a* **1722** LISLE *Husb.* (1757) 152 The hill-country-barley is generally better esteemed by the malsters than the vale-barley. *Ibid.*, The vale-lands are generally too wet, cold, and clayey. **1733** W. ELLIS *Chiltern & Vale Farm.* 92 The Beech will never make a good Tree in their vale, spewey, and wet Soil. *Ibid.* 221 The Vale-men in their open, low Fields,.. won't sow Peas alone. **1740** SOMERVILE *Hobbinolia* II. 7 The Vale-Inhabitants, proud, and elate With Victory. **1815** BIRKBECK *Journ. thro' France* 63 The vale farmers are busy sowing lupines.. on their wheat stubbles. **1895** *Outing* XXVII. 194/1 Those Vale farmers, no pen can ever accurately depict.

c. *Comb.*, as *vale-born*, *-buried*.

1801 MRS. ROBINSON *Sylphid* III. 24 (Jod.), Her emblems are the white rose bending in a graceful curve over the modest vale-born lily. **1808** ELEANOR SLEATH *Bristol Heiress* V. 102 The vale-buried town of Keswick.

†**vale**, *sb.*^{2} *Obs. rare.* (Erroneous var. of DALE^{3} 1, either after VALE *sb.*^{1} or by simple misprint.)

c **1635** [see PUMP *sb.*^{1} 6]. **1710** J. HARRIS *Lex. Techn.* II, *Vale of a Pump*, at Sea, is the Term for the Trough by which the Water runs from the Pump along the Ship sides, to the Scupper-holes. [Hence in later Dicts.]

‖**vale** (ˈveɪliː), *int.* and *sb.*^{3} [L., 2nd pers. sing. imper. of *valēre* to be well.]

A. *int.* Farewell; goodbye; adieu.

1550 COVERDALE tr. *Wermullerus' Treat. Death* Pref. iiij b, Vale, Loue God, leue vanitye, and lyue in Chryst. **1556** ROBINSON *More's Utopia* To Rdr. (Arb.) 20 So doynge thou shalt minister vnto me good cause to thinke my labour and paynes herein not altogethers bestowed in vaine. *Vale.* **1612** SHELTON *Quix.* To Rdr. A iij, And herewithall I bid thee farewell, and doe not forget me. *Vale.* **1656** BLOUNT *Glossogr.*, *Vale*, farewel, God be with you, God keep you in health. **1912** L. INKSTER (*title*), Vale, a Book of Verse. *Ibid.* 63 *Vale.* 'Goodbye, Goodbye!'

B. *sb.* A farewell greeting, letter, etc.; a goodbye, farewell, or leave-taking.

1580-3 GREENE *Mamillia* Wks. (Grosart) II. 86 Giuing her her *vale* with a counterfeit kind of curtesie. **1584** —— *Arbasto* Ibid. III. 211 The thankes I had for this.. was a.. churlish *vale* of the old trot Vechia. **1619** SIR S. D'EWES in *Coll. Life Jas. I* (1851) 81, I took my *vale* of him, with many thanks, and posted homewards. **1626** BRETON *Fantasticks* Wks. (Grosart) II. 6/2 The Nymphes of the Woodes in consort with the Muses sing an Aue to the Morning, and a Vale to the Sunnes setting. **1675** J. SMITH *Christ. Relig. Appeal* I. xi. §4. 103 They must bid an eternal *Vale* to their admired Law and Temple. **1814** SCOTT *Let.* in *Lockhart* (1837) III. iii. 129, I am going to say my *vales* to you for some weeks. *a* **1839** PRAED *Poems* (1865) II. 128 So instead of laughing gayly, I dropped a tear, and wrote my 'Vale'.

fig. **1631** LENTON *Charact.* C 1, He takes his *vale* for a certaine season to some sinister Sanctuary.

vale, southern ME. var. FELE *a.*; obs. f. VAIL, VEIL *sb.*^{1} and *v.*; obs. Sc. f. WALE *sb.* and *v.*, WALL *sb.*

†**valect.** *arch. Obs.* [ad. med.L. *valectus*, var. *vadelectus* VADELECT.] A personal attendant.

1610 HOLLAND *Camden's Brit.* I. 713 William de la Pole is in plaine tearmes called *Delectus Valectus*,.. that is our well beloued Valect..; now, Valect.. was in those daies an honorable title [etc.]. *a* **1661** FULLER *Worthies* (1840) III. 439 In recompence whereof the king made him his valect (equivalent to what afterward was called gentleman of the bedchamber).

†**valedatory**, variant of VALEDICTORY *a.*

App. f. L. *dat-*, *dare* to give, after the obs. phrase 'to give (one) farewell'.

1633 BRETON *Packet Mad Letters* 102 A valedatory Letter to his inconstant Mistris.

valedict, *v. rare*$^{-0}$. [ad. L. *valedict-*, *valedīcere*: see next.] *intr.* 'To bid farewell' (Bailey, 1721).

valediction (vælɪˈdɪkʃən). [ad. L. type **valedictio*, noun of action f. *vale-dīcere*, f. L. *valē* VALE *int.*, and *dīcere* to say, speak.]

1. The action of bidding or saying farewell (*to* a person, etc.); an instance of this; a farewell or leave-taking.

1614 DONNE *Lett.* li. Wks. 1839 VI. 368 For I must do this as a Valediction to the World, before I take Orders. **1654** H. L'ESTRANGE *Chas. I* (1655) 3 There [were].. such dear accollado's.. at their valediction and parting, as eye scarce ever beheld the like. **1698** FRYER *Acc. E. India & P.* 324 After a formal Valediction ashore, the next day we passed the Straits. **1796** MORSE *Amer. Geog.* II. 68 [Gustavus III] after the last valediction to the queen and prince, died. **1872** LE FANU *In a Glass Darkly* I. 158 They parted with a hurried and melancholy valediction.

2. An utterance, discourse, etc., made at (or by way of) leave-taking or bidding farewell.

1619 HALES *Gold. Rem.* II. (1673) 86, I dealt with Mr. Præses concerning a Copy of Mr. Deans Valediction to the Synod. **1641** H. L'ESTRANGE *God's Sabbath* 73 The Spirit of Comfort (which in his late valediction he promised to send his Apostles). **1658** SIR T. BROWNE *Hydriot.* 35 Their last valediction, thrice uttered by the attendants, was also very solemn. **1834** LYTTON *Pompeii* III. x, He stayed not to hear the valediction or the thanks of the witch. **1863** *Q. Rev.* July 203 The truly Yankee valediction, 'I guess we will all go home, and so, good night'.

valedictorian (vælɪdɪkˈtɔərɪən). *U.S.* [f. VALEDICTORY *a.* + -AN.] In colleges, academies, etc., the student (male or female) appointed on grounds of merit to deliver the valedictory oration on Commencement day.

1847 in WEBSTER. **1860** O. W. HOLMES *Elsie V.* (1887) 100 The last year's 'Valedictorian' of the Apollinean Institute. **1873** ELIZ. PHELPS *Trothy's Wedding Tour* 172 The valedictorian of her class in the young ladies' Star of Hope Seminary. **1887** *Lippincott's Mag.* Aug. 294 Among others.. chosen are the valedictorian of the Senior class [etc.].

valedictory (vælɪˈdɪktərɪ), *a.* and *sb.* [f. L. *valedict-um*, pa. pple. of *vale-dīcere* (see VALEDICTION) + -ORY.]

A. *adj.* **1.** Uttered or bestowed in bidding or on taking farewell; of the nature of a valediction.

1651 BAXTER *Infant Bapt.* 159 In the Pulpit in his Valedictory Oration to the People of Bewdeley. *a* **1700** EVELYN *Diary* 11 Jan. 1694, He [Dryden] read to us his

Prologue and Epilogue to his valedictory Play, now shortly to be acted. **1764** HARMER *Observ.* v. §4. 213 These valedictory songs..which the Prefetto takes notice of. **1778** STILES *Diary* (1901) II. 288 The President [of Yale] introduced the exercises in a latin Speech... Then succeeded..Valedictory Orat[ion]. Eng[lish. By] Sir Tracy. **1829** SOUTHEY *Lett.* (1856) IV. 155 The Bishop who delivered the valedictory address. **1850** IRVING *Goldsmith* iv. 70 He penned his valedictory letter to his good uncle. **1865** DICKENS *Mut. Fr.* I. xv, While delivering these valedictory observations, Wegg continually disappointed Mr. Boffin of his hand by flourishing it in the air.

2. Manifested, performed, or done by way of valediction.

1806 R. CUMBERLAND *Mem.* 166 Crowds of people,.. studious to pay to their popular chief governor every valedictory honour that their zeal and attention could devise. **1849** MRS. CRAIK *Ogilvies* xxii, All that passed between them was a valedictory bow. **1871** AINSWORTH *Tower Hill* II. xi, As he cast a valedictory look around, his eye alighted upon Dereham. **1884** *Pall Mall G.* 15 Nov. 8/1 Lord Ripon's valedictory tour..in the Punjab and North-West Provinces.

B. *sb.* **1.** *U.S.* A valedictory oration. (See quot. 1847 and cf. VALEDICTORIAN.)

1779 *New-Jersey Gaz.* (Trenton) 13 Oct. 1/1 The six young undergraduates pronounced orations; John Woodford the Salutatory in Latin and Stephen Renselaer the Valedictory in English. **1847** WEBSTER, *Valedictory*, in American colleges, an oration or address spoken at commencement, by a member of the class which receive the degree of bachelor of arts, and take their leave of college and of each other. **1884** J. QUINCY *Figures of Past* 54 An oration in English and a Latin valedictory were commonly spoken by three-year graduates.

2. A statement or speech made by way of valediction on leaving a position, person, etc.

1892 *Monist* II. 309 In his Valedictory on retiring from the Editorship. **1893** GOLDW. SMITH *United States* 296 John A. Andrew also..said in his valedictory of January the 4th, 1866, that [etc.].

Hence **vale'dictorily** *adv. rare.*

1856 CLOUGH *Poems*, etc. (1869) I. 228 Charles Norton dines with us this evening, valedictorily. **1925** F. M. FORD *No More Parades* ii. 64 He added valedictorily to Tietjens, 'I'd better..put this draft..twenty in a tent.'.. Tietjens and the colonel began to push men out of their way, going towards the door.

‖**vale-dictum.** *Obs. rare.* [L. *vale-dictum*, neut. pa. pple. of *vale-dīcere* to say farewell.] = VALEDICTION 2.

1638 SIR T. HERBERT *Trav.* (ed. 2) 23 We have said enough: let my *vale-dictum* now be this; the Land mournes [etc.]. *Ibid.* 140.

valeie, obs. f. VALLEY.

†**va'lence**^{1}. *Obs. rare.* [prob. the name of the French town *Valence* on the Rhone.] Some thin woven fabric.

c **1381** CHAUCER *Parl. Foules* 272 The remenaunt was wel keuerede to myn pay Rygh[t] with a subtyl couercheif of valence; Ther nas no thikkere cloth of no defense. *c* **1430** LYDG. *Min. Poems* (Percy Soc.) 47 Upon hir hed a kerche of Valence, Noon other richesse of counterfet array.

valence^2 ('veɪləns). [ad. L. *valentia*; see VALENCY.]

†**1.** An extract or preparation (*of* some herb) used in medicine. *Obs.*

c **1425** tr. *Arderne's Treat. Fistula*, etc. 69 Þis medicyne is called tapsi ualencia..; in þe brissing..putte in litel bi litel of oile of rose, or violet, or camamille, þat þe valence may competently imbibe it. *Ibid.* 98 Þis medyc[in]e is called Valence of scabious for þe valow of it. *Ibid.*, Valence of wormode is þus made.

†**2.** Valour, courage; = VALIANCE 1. *Obs.*

a **1604** HANMER *Chron. Irel.* (1633) 172 For his valence, he was called Cœur de Lyon, the Lyons heart.

3. *Chem.* [ad. G. *valenz* (H. Wichelhaus 1868, in *Ann. d. Chem.* Suppl. VI. 257), f. *quantivalenz* (A. W. Hofmann 1865).] = VALENCY 2. (See also quot. 1902.)

Cf. EQUIVALENCE 2 and QUANTIVALENCE.

1884 *American* VIII. 300 To what extent is the Hypothesis of 'Valence' or 'Atomicity' of Value in explaining Chemical Reactions. **1902** *Fortn. Rev.* June 1018 Meanwhile, it is clear that the 'valence', the *number* of electrical charges [in poisons], plays an important part. **1965** PHILLIPS & WILLIAMS *Inorg. Chem.* I. iv. 102 In the transition series a great number of valences are observed. **1972** [see SOLARIZATION 1 d].

4. *Psychol.* Emotional force or significance, *spec.* the feeling of attraction or repulsion with which an individual invests an object or event (see quot. 1935).

1917 C. R. PAYNE tr. *Pfister's Psychoanal. Meth.* xi. 269 They are all representations of the cottage itself and more exactly the embodiment of inhibited endeavours of high valence, the so-called libido-symbols. **1935** ADAMS & ZENER tr. *Lewin's Dynamic Theory of Personality* ii. 51 A certain object or event..is experienced as an attraction (or repulsion)... We shall say of such objects that they possess a '*valence*'. *Ibid.* iii. 81 The positive valences (+), those effecting approach; and the negative (−), or those producing withdrawal or retreat. **1952** W. SPROTT *Social Psychol.* ii. 30 The piece of chocolate is said to have 'positive valence' for the child and exercises an attractive force. *Ibid.*, A threat of punishment, and a 'negative valence' is added which alters the dynamic character of the 'field'. **1967** M. M. GLATT et al. *Drug Scene* vi. 79 His positive valences are toward the use of drugs. **1976** S. LARSEN *Shaman's Doorway* iii. 132 Its [*sc.* the religious archetype's] powerful valence is attracted to any life activity or belief which assumes a central role for an individual.

5. *attrib.* and *Comb.*, **valence band**, the energy band (range of possible energies) that contains the valence electrons in a solid and is the highest filled or partly filled band; **valence bond**, orig., a chemical bond thought of in terms of atomic valencies; in mod. use, one described in terms of individual valence electrons rather than molecular orbitals; freq. *attrib.*; **valence electron** [tr. G. *valenzelektron* (J. Stark 1908, in *Physik. Zeitschr.* IX. 85/1)], any of the electrons of an atom that are involved when it forms a bond with another atom, viz. those in the outer shell; **valence shell**, the outer shell (SHELL *sb.* 19 b) of an atom, incompleteness of which is responsible for its valency.

1956 L. P. HUNTER *Handbk. Semiconductor Electronics* ii. 7 At an intermediate temperature, therefore, the donor levels will be completely ionized..while the valence band remains practically filled. **1982** J. E. UFFENBECK *Introd. Electronics* i. 7 We can think of the valence band as containing all electrons still held by their parent atoms, while the conduction band contains all *free* electrons. **1913** *Jrnl. Amer. Chem. Soc.* XXXV. 1443 This view leads to the grouping of substances into two general classes, according as the valence bonds are chiefly polar or non-polar in nature. **1931** *Physical Rev.* XXXVII. 481 This is a homopolar valence bond, and the two electrons forming such a bond are inactive in forming further bonds, just as if they were in closed shells within a single atom. **1965** [see *molecular orbital* s.v. MOLECULAR *a.* 5]. **1978** P. W. ATKINS *Physical Chem.* xv. 493 Just as in m.o. theory, the strength of the bond according to valence-bond theory can be traced in large part to the effects of the accumulation of electron density in the bonding region between the two nuclei. **1923** KRAMERS & HOLST *Atom & Bohr Theory of its Structure* vii. 206 The last group [of electrons] is naturally of a very different nature from the first; they are 'valence electrons'. **1974** D. M. ADAMS *Inorganic Solids* i. 3 Three factors were considered as fundamental in alloy structures: (*a*) size of the atoms; (*b*) their relative electronegativities; (*c*) the valence-electron concentration. **1923** G. N. LEWIS *Valency* iv. 57 The valence shell of a free (uncombined) atom never contains more than eight electrons. **1972** R. A. JACKSON *Mechanism* v. 99 Boron compounds are unusual (in relation to most organic compounds) in having an empty valence-shell orbital.

valence, var. VALANCE *sb.*^{1}

Valencia (və'lɛnʃ(ɪ)ə). Also **Valentia**. [See def.]

1. *attrib.* Of or pertaining to, cultivated in or obtained from, Valencia, a province and town of eastern Spain.

1796 KIRWAN *Elem. Min.* (ed. 2) I. 207 The Stones commonly called Valentia garnets are..of this species... They may be the garnets of Spain, mentioned in..Raab's Catalogue. **1822** A. T. THOMSON *Dispensatory* 150 The Valentia almond is a sweet, large, flat almond, pointed at one extremity. **1858** HOMANS *Cycl. Commerce* 1477/2 In Europe, the Valencia oranges are eagerly sought after, on account of their early appearance, large size, and beautiful color.

2. Also with lower-case initial. A mixed fabric mainly employed for waistcoats, having a wool weft with a warp of silk, silk and cotton, or linen, and usually striped. Chiefly in *pl.*

1838 *Actors by Daylight* I. 8/2 (Advt.), Shawls, Valencias, Silks, and Figured Velvets of the choicest patterns, for Waistcoats. **1851** *Catal. Gt. Exhib.* 490/1 Fancy vesting called valencias or toilinets. *Ibid.* 1115/2 Toilinets and valentias. **1882** CAULFEILD & SAWARD *Dict. Needlew.* 510/1 Valentias are produced at Spitalfields, and many are showy in appearance.

3. *ellip.* in *pl.* Valencia almonds or raisins; raisins similar to those of Valencia.

1867 SIMMONDS *Dict. Trade* Suppl. 460/1 *Valencias*, raisins prepared by dipping the bunches of grapes into a hot lye made of wood ashes, oil, and lime, and then dried in the sun. **1904** *Daily News* 12 Nov. 9 This year we have some of the finest Valencias (we call all raisins Valencias, you know) from Australia.

Valencian (və'lɛnʃ(ɪ)ən), *sb.* and *a.* Also **Valentian**. [See prec. and -AN.]

A. *sb.* A native or inhabitant of the town, province, or former kingdom of Valencia in Spain. Also, the language of Valencia.

1769 ROBERTSON *Chas. V*, I. Wks. 1851 III. 517 The grievances, which the Valencians aimed at redressing. **1843** *Penny Cycl.* XXVI. 88/2 No great number of cattle or horses are kept by the Valencians. **1933** *Morning Post* 11 July 13/3 That same language, which is called Provençal, Limousin, Catalan, Valencian, or Mallorquin, according to the place.. the langue d'oc. **1937** F. BORKENAU *Spanish Cockpit* iii. 232 The anxious question 'Will they come back to-night?' remained and racked the nerves of the Valencians. **1956** J. BRODRICK *St Ignatius Loyola* ix. 242 Juan de la Peña.., like Vives, was a Valencian. **1967** *Westm. Cathedral Chron.* May 70/1 Valencian is a dialect of Catalan, but not so widely spoken.

B. *adj.* Of or belonging to Valencia (see prec.) or its people.

1753 *Chambers' Cycl.* Suppl. s.v. *Almond*, Valentian and Barbary Almonds, which are those from whence the oil is procured. **1769** ROBERTSON *Chas. V*, I. Wks. 1851 III. 399 But the Valencian nobles..considered this measure as an indignity to their country. **1843** *Penny Cycl.* XXVI. 89/1 Ribalta, Victoria,..and other painters of the Valencian school. **1845** R. FORD *Hand-bk. Spain* I. i. 69 It is called *Michi Michi*, from the Valencian *Mits e Mits*, 'half and half'. **1847** tr. *Bouterwek's Hist. Span. Lit.* 6 The author is one of the last poets who wrote in the Valencian dialect. **1937** F. BORKENAU *Spanish Cockpit* ii. 116 In Valencia there is a regional movement too, claiming..equality of rights for the Valencian dialect with the Castilian language. **1970** R. A. H. ROBINSON *Origins of Franco's Spain* ii. 81 Members were busy drawing up a statute of autonomy for the Valencian region. **1976** 'D. HALLIDAY' *Dolly & the Nanny Bird* xii. 155 A Tam lorry full of Valencian oranges passed by a grove of citrus trees.

Valenciennes (valɑ̃sjɛn). Also 8 *Sc.* **Valentians.** [See def.]

1. The name of a town in northern France, celebrated for the manufacture of lace, used *attrib.* in ***Valenciennes lace*** (see quot. 1858). Also *Comb.*

1717 LADY G. BAILLIE *Household Bk.* (S.H.S.) 214 For narow valentians lace at 11s. **1854** GREENWOOD *Haps & Mishaps* 120 There is also a class engaged in weaving Valenciennes lace, of a beautiful quality. **1858** SIMMONDS *Dict. Trade*, *Valenciennes-lace*, a rich lace which has a six-sided mesh formed of two threads partly twisted and plaited, the pattern being worked in the net. **1882** CAULFEILD & SAWARD *Dict. Needlew.* 507/2 In Belgium there are six centres for Valenciennes lace making.

2. *ellipt.* A variety of lace originally manufactured at Valenciennes; a ruffle or the like made of this.

1764 W. VAREY in Jesse *Selwyn & Contemp.* (1843) I. 270, I shall be obliged to you for four pair of Valenciennes, as good as people wear when they dress, but not too deep. **1801** MAR. EDGEWORTH *Angelina* iii, Eight and twenty [shillings] ..is really nothing for any lace you'd wear; but more particularly for real Valenciennes. **1859** READE *Love me Little* (1888) 169 'Well! does not every lady wear lace on her nightgown?.. What is that on yours, pray?' 'A little misery of Valenciennes, an inch broad.' **1905** ELIN. GLYN *Viciss. Evangeline* 99 Short sleeves ruffled with Valenciennes.

3. 'A pyrotechnic composition, usually employed as incendiary' (*Cent. Dict.* 1891).

valency ('veɪlənsɪ). Also 7 -cie. [ad. L. (ante- and post-classical) *valentia* vigour, capacity, f. *valēre* to be well or strong. Cf. Sp. and Pg. *valentia*, It. *valenza*, *valenzia*.]

†**1.** Might, power, strength. *Obs.*$^{-0}$

1623 in COCKERAM I. **1656** in BLOUNT.

2. *Chem.* **a.** The power or capacity of certain elements to combine with or displace a greater or less number of hydrogen (or other) atoms; atomicity.

Cf. EQUIVALENCY 2 and VALENCE^2 3.

1869 *English Mechanic* 19 Nov. 222/2 Any typical atom in any molecule may be replaced by another atom of similar valency, without altering the arrangement of the molecule. **1876** *Encycl. Brit.* V. 473/2 The valency of an element is usually expressed by dashes or Roman numerals placed on the right of its symbol. *a* **1881** BARRATT *Phys. Metempiric* 65, I think it will probably be eventually found that the atoms of high 'atomicity' or valency are really molecules. **1894** *Athenæum* 14 Apr. 481/1 The valencies and atomic weights in some cases need correction.

b. A unit of this capacity. Usu. in *pl.*

1869 *English Mechanic* 19 Nov. 222/1 The Molecule..is therefore a body in which all the attractions or valencies are satisfied, leaving the combined atoms to act as a whole from one centre. **1891** *Cent. Dict.* s.v., Carbon is said to have four valencies.

3. Importance, significance.

1897 *Allbutt's Syst. Med.* III. 166 These two conditions.. are by no means of identical pathological valency.

4. *attrib.* and *Comb.*, **valency electron** *Physics* = *valence electron* s.v. VALENCE^2 5.

1908 *Jrnl. Chem. Soc.* XCIV. II. 138 Two types of electrons are distinguished: the one type, arranged in the form of a ring, represents the positive electricity of the atom, and the second type consists of electrons which neutralise the positive charge of the ring and are separated from the atom when ionisation takes place, these being termed the valency electrons. **1973** J. G. TWEEDDALE *Materials Technol.* I. iv. 97 Metals tend to be good conductors of heat primarily because there is sharing of valency electrons..and so electron transfer is easy.

‖**valenki** ('valənkɪ), *sb. pl.* Also **valinki, -ky.** [Russ., pl. of *valenok* felt boot.] Felt boots of a type worn by Russians.

1943 E. M. ALMEDINGEN *Frossia* v. 201 Maria Nikolævna sat shivering,..her feet thrust into 'valenky' with many holes in them. **1951** 'A. GARVE' *Murder in Moscow* xiii. 120, I must have appeared indigenous enough in my fur hat and *shuba* and felt *valinki.* **1969** P. CHAVCHAVADZE tr. *Alliluyeva's Only One Year* 247 All of them had to get used to Russian frosts, to valenki (knee-high felt boots) and fur caps—poor unhappy birds of passage. **1975** *Country Life* 30 Oct. 1194/2 Turkish-style 'Valenki' embroidered apres ski boot £29·95. **1981** M. C. SMITH *Gorky Park* I. viii. 107 The girl..dressed in..the kind of felt boots called *valenki.*

‖**valent** ('veɪlənt), *sb.*^{1} *Sc. Law.* [L. *valent*, 3rd pl. pres. indic. of *valēre* to be of worth.]

1. Value or worth.

1765–8 ERSKINE *Inst. Law Scot.* II. v. §37 The old and new extents of lands, of which the *valent* is not known.

2. ***valent clause***, in a retour of special service, that clause in which the old and new extent of the lands are specified (W. Bell *Dict. Law Scot.*).

1752 A. MACDOUALL *Inst. Laws Scot.* IV. i. II. 460 The Valent-clause, whereby the inquest ought to have returned both the old and new extent. **1765–8** ERSKINE *Inst. Law Scot.* II. v. §38 Because annualrents arising out of lands had no distinct valuation or extent, therefore they are said in the *valent* clause of the retour, *valere seipsum.*

valent ('vælənt), *sb.*^{2} *techn.* and *dial.* [Back-formation from *valents* VALANCE *sb.*^{1}] A valance.

1794 W. FELTON *Carriages* (1801) I. 143 The pockets, the falls, and valents. *Ibid.* 204 A broad stripe of leather, welted on the edge,..which shelters the inside, and is called a vallent. **1888** ELWORTHY *W. Somerset Word-bk.* 795 *Valent*, a short curtain;..also the name of the upper or fixed part (if any) of window drapery.

†**'valent**, *a. Obs.*⁻¹ [ad. L. *valent-*, *valens*, pres. pple. of *valēre*.] Vigorous, flourishing.

1492 RYMAN *Poems* xviii. 2 in *Archiv Stud. neu. Spr.* LXXXIX. 186 A roose, a valent floure, i-wis, Crist made springe of a thorne.

-valent. [ad. L. *valent-em*, pres. pple. of *valēre* to be worth.] A formative element occurring in a few words of general currency, as *equivalent*, *prevalent* (directly f. L.), *ambivalent*, and in various scientific contexts, being used with prefixes denoting number: (*a*) in Chem., usu. with pronunc. (-'veɪlənt), forming adjs. denoting 'having a valency of the specified number' (VALENCY 2); also used in an analogous sense in Immunol. (cf. MULTIVALENT *a.* b); also with arabic number prefixed; (*b*) in Cytology (usu. with pronunc. ('-vələnt)) forming adjs. and sbs. denoting '(a meiotic structure) composed of the specified number of chromosomes' (cf. MULTIVALENT *a.* and *sb.*, QUADRIVALENT *a.* and *sb.*, TRIVALENT *a.* and *sb.*).

This suffix was first used in its Chem. sense by L. Meyer 1864, in *Mod. Theorien d. Chem.* 67.

1977 *Lancet* 25 June 1338/2 A double-blind controlled trial of a 14-valent pneumococcal polysaccharide vaccine was carried out.

va'lentia. ? *Obs.* [ad. Sp. *venencia*.] (See quots. and cf. VALINCHER.)

1688 R. HOLME *Armoury* III. 319/2 An Instrument belonging to the Vintner or Merchant, called a Valentia. The first being the Valentia is a Pipe made of Silver or Tin, round and taper, and hollow withal. **1823** E. MOOR *Suffolk Wds.*, *Valentia*, the tin machine used for lifting beer, wine, etc. out at the bung-hole of a cask, by pressing the thumb on the small hole at top... I have never heard it called Valentia out of Suffolk.

Valentia, variant of VALENCIA.

Valentian (və'lɛntɪən), *a. Geol.* [f. *Valentia*, name of a Roman province in S. Scotland + -AN.] Designating or pertaining to the earliest stratigraphical division of the Silurian in Britain, preceding the Wenlockian. Also *absol.*

1879 C. LAPWORTH in *Ann. & Mag. Nat. Hist.* III. (table facing p. 455), Silurian system... Lower division (Valentian). **1880** —— in *Ibid.* V. 47 In the south of Scotland (*Valentia*)..three subformations are recognizable... Until geologists are willing to include the Tarannon in the Llandovery it will..be best to speak of this great Scottish formation and its equivalents as the Valentian formation, its three divisions, Lower, Middle, and Upper, representing respectively the Lower Llandovery, Upper Llandovery, and Tarannon of Wales and Siluria. **1921** *Q. Jrnl. Geol. Soc.* LXXVII. 158 Some assistance in this comparison is afforded by the Valentian rocks of the Lake District. **1946** [see LUDLOVIAN *a.*]. **1974** *Encycl. Brit. Macropædia* XVI. 774/2 The oldest interval, the Llandoverian (or Valentian), saw the beginning of a sharp distinction between basin graptolitic shale facies and calcareous..shelf facies.

Valentian, variant of VALENCIAN *a.*

†**Valentide.** *Obs.*⁻¹ [f. VALEN-TINE + TIDE *sb.*] *Saint Valentide*, St. Valentine's day, or the time of the year when this falls.

1596 SPENSER *F.Q.* VI. vii. 32 On a day, when Cupid kept his court, As he is wont at each Saint Valentide.

Valentine ('væləntaɪn), *sb.* Also with lower-case initial, and 5 **valantine** (6 *Sc.* **-tene**), **valeyntyne**, 5–6 **valentyne** (6 **-tyn**); 7 **vallentyne**; 5 *Sc.*, 6 **walentyne** (6 *Sc.* **wall-**); 5 **volentyn(e**, **-antyne**, **-ontyn**. [a. OF. (also mod.F.) *Valentin*, or ad. L. *Valentīnus*, the name of two early Italian saints, both commemorated on the 14th of February.]

1. (*St.*) ***Valentine's day***, the 14th of February.

Freq. mentioned with reference to the choosing of sweethearts or the mating of birds.

c **1381** CHAUCER *Parl. Foules* 309 For this was on seynt Volantynys day Whan euery bryd comyth there to chese his make. *c* **1430** *Lydgate's Min. Poems* (1911) I. 304 A balade made..in wyse of chesing loues at Saint Valentynes day. *c* **1450** *Chron. London* (Kingsford, 1905) 127 The xiiij day of Feuerell, that is to say vpon seynt Valentyne's day, the Kyng com to London. **1523** FITZHERB. *Husb.* §137 And after saynt Valentynes daye, it is tyme to graffe both peares and wardens. **1602** SHAKS. *Ham.* IV. v. 48 To morrow is S. Valentines day. **1668** H. MORE *Div. Dial.* III. xiii. (1713) 206 As some..embrace the first they meet on Valentine's day. **1725** BOURNE in Brand *Pop. Antiq.* (1777) xviii. 209 Such is the Observation of Candlemas-Day, such is Childermas-Day, such Valentine's Day, and some others. **1822** NARES *Gloss.* 538 The number of letters sent on Valentine's Day, makes several additional sorters necessary at the Post Office in London. **1828** SCOTT *F.M. Perth* v, How blithe would she have been to see this happy Saint Valentine's morning! **1854** [see VALENTINE *v.* 2].

ellipt. **1590** SHAKS. *Mids. N.* IV. i. 144 Saint Valentine is past, Begin these wood birds but to couple now? **1714** GAY *Shepherd's Week* IV. 37 Last Valentine, the day when birds of kind Their paramours with mutual chirpings find.

b. ***St. Valentine's eve*** (*Sc. Valentine's e'en*), the eve of St. Valentine's day.

1671 *Roxb. Ball.* (1890) VII. 113 A Crew on S. Valentine's Eve did meet together. **1814–28** SOMERVILLE *Life & Times* (1861) 344 Valentine's e'en, and Hallowe'en,..used to be anniversaries observed in every house by the..young people. **1828** SCOTT *F.M. Perth* xiii, I will have no evasions, boy—Where wert thou on St. Valentine's Eve?

2. A person of the opposite sex chosen, drawn by lot, or otherwise determined, on St. Valentine's day, as a sweetheart, lover, or special friend for the ensuing year.

a **1450** *MS. Harl.* 1735 fol. 48 (Halliw.), Godys blescyng have he and myn, My none gentyl Volontyn, Good Tomas the frere. **1477** *Paston Lett.* III. 170 Unto my ryght welebelovyd Voluntyn, John Paston, Squyer, be this bill delyvered. *c* **1485** *Digby Myst.* (1882) III. 564 A! god be with my valentynes. My byrd swetyng, my lovys so dere! **1535** *Bury Wills* (Camden) 126, I gyf and bequeth to my valentyn Agnes Illyon xs. **1596** RALEIGH *Disc. Guiana* 23 After the Queens haue chosen, the rest cast lottes for their Valentines. **1623** in *Crt. & Times Jas. I* (1848) II. 395 To the great grief of his sweetheart, Mrs. Bray, my ancient valentine. **1667** PEPYS *Diary* 14 Feb., This morning came up to my wife's bedside..little Will Mercer to be her Valentine... But I am also this year my wife's Valentine. **1712** WOODES ROGERS *Voy. r. World* 359 That same Day, in Commemoration of the antient Custom in England of chusing Valentines, I drew up a List of the fair Ladies in Bristol..and sent for my Officers into the Cabbin, where every one drew. **1719** OZELL tr. *Misson's Mem. Trav. Eng.* 331 There is another kind of Valentine; which is the first young Man or Woman that Chance throws in your Way in the Street, or elsewhere, on that Day. *a* **1859** MACAULAY in *Sat. Rev.* (1863) 152 All good attend my Valentine!

transf. *c* **1750** GOLDSM. in W. Irving *Biog.* (1849) iv. 54 With submission at your shrine, Comes a heart your Valentine.

†**b.** Applied to God, or to one of the Saints, as a patron chosen by a worshipper. *Obs.*

c **1450** *Godstow Register* (1911) 14 O true valeyntyne is oure lord to me. **1500** *Will of Hewetts* (Somerset Ho.), To.. Saint Mary & to her moder Saint Anne my speciall voweis & volentyns on whoos day I was borne. **1656** BLOUNT *Glossogr.*, *Valentines*,..Saints chosen for special Patrons for a year, according to the use of the Romanists.

3. A folded paper inscribed with the name of a person to be drawn as a valentine. ***to draw valentines***, to draw lots for this or other reasons.

c **1553** *Cecil Papers* (Hist. MSS. Comm.) I. 134 There is three papers like unto walentynes put in a cap and so they draw. **1639** *Sc. Acts Parlt.* (1870) V. 604/2 Act ordaining the Commissioneris of shyris to draw lottis and valentines ȝeirlie at ilk parliament for thair places. **1725** BOURNE in Brand *Pop. Antiq.* (1777) 225 It is a Ceremony, never omitted among the Vulgar, to draw Lots, which they Term Valentines, on the Eve before Valentine day. **1774** PENNANT *Tour Scotl.* I. 141 The young people..in February draw Valentines, and from them collect their future fortune in the nuptial state. **1787** BURNS *Tam Glen* vi, Yestreen at the valentines' dealing,..thrice I drew ane without failing, And thrice it was written—Tam Glen!

b. A gift or present to a person drawn or chosen as one's especial friend on St. Valentine's day. Now only *U.S.*

c **1610** in *Heriot's Mem.* App. VII. (1822) 215 For gold, and making of a Valentine. **1621** BURTON *Anat. Mel.* III. ii. II. iv, Many such allurements there are,..tokens, favours, symbols, letters, valentines, &c. **1962** A. LURIE *Love & Friendship* ix. 167 More flowers... On the tables, on the mantelpiece, on the bookcases... All red and white, and of course it was February 14th... Would Will himself see that the whole party was a valentine for him? **1965** [see *peanut brittle* s.v. PEANUT 3 a].

c. A written or printed letter or missive, a card of dainty design with verses or other words, esp. of an amorous or sentimental nature, sent on St. Valentine's day to a person of the opposite sex; in later use also a printed sheet consisting of a more or less grotesque picture with humorous or satirical rhymes (more exactly called a ***mock valentine***).

1824 MISS MITFORD *Village* Ser. I. (1863) 42 A fine sheet of flourishing writing, something between a valentine and a sampler. **1844** ALB. SMITH *Adv. Mr. Ledbury* xxiv. (1886) 73 He had that morning received..a valentine, in a lady's hand-writing, and perfectly anonymous. **1879** *Paper & Printing Trades Jrnl.* XXIX. 20 One occasionally hears that valentines are going out. **1898** *Daily News* 15 Feb. 7/1 The Christmas card has apparently killed the valentine... Valentines are still sold, and sent, but they are chiefly of the satirical order.

d. *transf.* (Cf. VALENTINE *v.* 1.)

1847 TENNYSON *Princ.* v. 229 A song on every spray Of birds that piped their Valentines.

†**4.** *Sc.* **a.** (Meaning uncertain.) *Obs.*⁻¹

c **1450** HOLLAND *Howlat* 918 Thus wycit he the walentyne thraly and thrawin.

†**b.** 'A sealed letter from the Crown to landholders for the apprehension of persons offending against the law.' *Obs.*

1556 *Acc. Ld. High Treas. Scot.* X. 318 For inbringin of certane personis gevin in valentynis to the airis of Elgin, Banf, and Abirdene. **1561** *Reg. Privy Council Scot.* I. 169 Thir personis underwrittin:..in presence of the Quenis Grace ressavit thair valentinis of the names of the personis culpable of thift. **1587** *Sc. Acts Parlt.* (1814) III. 464/2 The kingis Maiesties clois valentynis to be send to the Maisteris, ..baillies and chiftanes of all notable lymmeris and thevis.

5. A British type of heavy tank, much used during the war of 1939–45. (So called because production was reputedly approved on 14 Feb. 1938.)

1941 *Times* 7 July 2/2 Details have now been released by the Ministry of Supply of a new British tank, officially designated as the Mark III, but now to be known as Valentine. It is a 16-ton heavy infantry tank. **1959** *Chambers's Encycl.* XIII. 451/1 Two cruiser types were in production... The Mark I (A.9) was modified..; this modified type was known as the Mark II (A.10); from it was developed the Valentine. **1960** C. BARNETT *Desert Generals* v. iii. 212 Of ninety-seven Valentines, eleven returned. **1979** D. CROW *Tanks of World War II* iii. 45/1 Infantry Tank Mark III, the Valentine, was produced in far greater numbers than any other British tank. The first Valentine, built by Vickers-Armstrongs..came off the production line in May 1940.

6. *attrib.* and *Comb.*, as ***Valentine bag***, ***card***, ***glove***, ***-writer***; **Valentine-bun** (see quot. 1854); **Valentine-day** = sense 1; **Valentine (infantry) tank** = sense 5 above.

1695 LADY G. BAILLIE *Househ. Bk.* (S.H.S.) 257 To Lisi Rainald for my Robin's vallantin gloves. **1725** BOURNE in Brand *Pop. Antiq.* (1777) 225 On the Eve before Valentine-day. **1802** (*title*), Fairburn's Annual, Original, Comic & Entertaining Valentine-writer for the year 1802. **1828** MISS MITFORD *Village* Ser. III. (1863) 505 Those that issue from the bursting Valentine-bag of our postman. **1854** MISS BAKER *Northampt. Gloss.* s.v., In Peterborough..sweet plum buns were formerly, and I believe are still, made, called Valentine buns. **1943** W. S. CHURCHILL *End of Beginning* 140 It would be wrong..to write off as useless.. the Valentine tanks. **1944** *Return to Attack* (Army Board, N.Z.) 16/2 A squadron of Valentine infantry tanks..was sent to join them. **1959** I. & P. OPIE *Lore & Lang. Schoolch.* xii. 236 Valentine cards are definitely in fashion again. **1977** *Times* 1 Feb. 8/5 Make your own Valentine card.

'valentine, *v.* [f. prec.]

1. *trans.* and *intr.* Of birds: To greet with song, to sing, at mating-time. (Cf. prec. 3 d.)

1851 MEREDITH *Pastorals*, *Poems* 104 Shall the birds in vain then valentine their sweethearts? **1885** —— *Thrush in Feb.* i, I know him, February's thrush, And loud at eve he valentines.

2. *intr.* (See quots.) *dial.*

1854 MISS BAKER *Northampt. Gloss.* 373 *Valentining*, children going from house to house, the morning of St. Valentine's day, soliciting small gratuities. **1864** *Children's Prize* Feb. 22 The little fellow had cried bitterly till she had given him leave to go 'Valentining'.

Valentinian (vælən'tɪnɪən), *sb.* and *a.* Also 7 **-ean.** [See def.]

A. *sb.* A follower of the Egyptian theologian Valentinus (fl. *c* 150), founder of a Gnostic sect.

c **1449** PECOCK *Repr.* v. iii. 497 The sect of Valentynyanys, whiche helden that Crist took no thing of Maries bodi. **1565** STAPLETON tr. *Staphylus' Apol.* 168 b, The conflictes of Irenee with the Valentinians. **1579** FULKE *Heskins' Parl.* 2 As the olde Heretiques the Valentinians did. **1616** BULLOKAR *Eng. Expos.*, *Valentinians*, certaine heretikes.. who held opinion that our Sauiour receiued not his flesh of the blessed virgin Mary. **1702** tr. *Le Clerc's Prim. Fathers* 15 The Valentinians..learned what they said concerning the Generation of their Æones, of Hesiod. **1788** GIBBON *Decl. & F.* IV. 540 *note*, The Valentinians embraced a complex, and almost incoherent, system. **1833** A. CRICHTON *Hist. Arabia* I. v. 216 Sabellians, Valentinians, and a host of obscurer sects, all rose up in the theological arena. **1874** W. R. CASSELS *Supernatural Relig.* II. II. x. 221 The Valentinians differed materially among themselves regarding certain points.

B. *adj.* Adhering or belonging to the Gnostic sect instituted by the heresiarch Valentinus; taught or disseminated by Valentinus or his followers.

1579 FULKE *Conf. Sanders* 585 Yet came that estimation of the crosse from the Valentinian heretikes. **1674** HICKMAN *Quinquart. Hist.* (ed. 2) 56, I found that there were Valentinian Anabaptists in those days. **1702** ECHARD *Eccl. Hist.* (1710) 554 And now he made many converts,.. particularly Ambrosius, noted for the Valentinian heresie. **1832** W. PALMER *Orig. Liturg.* I. 149 As a sufficient means of proving the falsehood of the Valentinian doctrines. **1874** W. R. CASSELS *Supernatural Relig.* II. II. x. 214 He calls him the most noted man of the Valentinian school.

Hence **Valen'tinianism**, the doctrine or creed of Valentinus and his followers.

1875 LIGHTFOOT *Comm. Col.* 331 *note*, The later Basilideans apparently influenced by Valentinianism superadded to the teaching of their founder. **1879** FARRAR *St. Paul* (1883) 768 The word is tainted with Valentinianism.

valentinite ('væləntɪnaɪt). *Min.* Also **-eite.** [f. the name of the alleged mediæval alchemist Basil *Valentine*; named by W. Haidinger, 1845.] White antimony; antimony bloom.

1860 *Ure's Dict. Arts* (ed. 5) I. 168 White Antimony (Valentinite) is the result of the alteration of grey antimony, native antimony, and other ores of that metal. **1863** [see ANTIMONY 3]. **1867** BLOXAM *Chem.* 379 Antimony..is also found in nature as white antimony ore or valentinite.

Valentino (vælən'tiːnəʊ). [The name of Rudolph *Valentino* (Rodolfo Guglielmi di Valentino, 1895–1926), Italian-born American film actor, particularly noted for being adored by women.] **1.** †**a.** A gigolo. *Obs.* **b.** A man having the sort of romantic good looks associated with Rudolph Valentino.

1927 *Dialect Notes* V. 466 *Valentino*, n., a handsome man kept by an oldish woman. **1930** A. P. HERBERT *Water Gipsies* ii. 12 No one could call you a Valentino, not for emotion, could they? **1961** J. H. GRIFFIN *Black like Me* 34 You have to..have your hair all slicked out and look like a Valentino. **1967** *Listener* 20 July 82/3 You expect a Rudolph Valentino? **1974** V. GIELGUD *In Such a Night* iv. 38 Her current leading man..frequently referred to as 'the contemporary Valentino'.

2. Used *attrib.* or as *adj.* to designate looks, actions, etc., associated with Rudolph Valentino.

1934 F. Stark *Valleys of Assassins* ii. 69 A young man with Rudolf Valentino looks. **1967** A. Wilson *No Laughing Matter* III. i. 206 His short black Valentino side whiskers. **1979** J. Drummond *I saw him Die* ix. 87, I saw Crozier..take her hand; very tender, very Valentino. **1981** P. Dickinson *Seventh Raven* iv. 47 That colossally handsome Valentino chappie.

'valer-, variant of valero-, employed before second elements beginning with a vowel, as ***valeraceto-nitril(e, -aldehyd(e, -aldine, -amide, -anilide.***

1848 Fownes *Chem.* (ed. 2) 542 Alkalis convert ..*valeracetonitril into valerianic and acetic acids and ammonia. **1868** Watts *Dict. Chem.* V. 972 Valeracetonitrile is a mobile colourless liquid. **1852** W. Gregory *Handbk. Org. Chem.* 236 *Valeraldehyde. **1857** Miller *Elem. Chem., Org.* 851 Valeraldehyd [= Valeric Aldehyd]. **1868** Watts *Dict. Chem.* V. 974 **Valeraldine*..An organic base, homologous with thialdine. **1852** W. Gregory *Handbk. Org. Chem.* (ed. 3) 236 When valerate of oxide of ethyle is left in contact with strong ammonia, *valeramide and alcohol are formed. **1868** Watts *Dict. Chem.* V. 974 *Valeramide*,..the primary amide of valeric acid. *Ibid.* 975 **Valeranilide*... Produced by the action of valeric anhydride on aniline.

valeral ('vælərəl). *Chem.* [f. *valer(ic)* + *al(dehyde)*: see valeric *a.*] A colourless, very mobile liquid obtained from valerianates or from amylic alcohol. Also *attrib.*

1852 W. Gregory *Handbk. Org. Chem.* 236 Valeraldehyde or valeral. **1868** Watts *Dict. Chem.* V. 972 Valeral is usually prepared by oxidising amylic alcohol with chromate of potassium and sulphuric acid. *Ibid.* 974 Valeral-ammonia melts when heated.

valerate ('vælərət). *Chem.* [f. valer-ic *a.* + -ate[1] c.] = valerianate.

1852 W. Gregory *Handbk. Org. Chem.* 236 Valerate of oxide of ethyle, or valeric ether. *Ibid.*, Valerate of Ammonia. **1857** Miller *Elem. Chem., Org.* 399 Valerate of zinc.., as well as some others of the valerates, has been used medicinally. **1868** Watts *Dict. Chem.* V. 976 Valerates are decomposed by mineral acids.

'valerene. *Chem.* [f. as prec. + -ene.] (See quots.)

1852 W. Gregory *Handbk. Org. Chem.* 237 Valerene..is obtained as one of the products of the action of zinc on iodide of amyle. **1863** Watts *Dict. Chem.* I. 626 *Borneene. Valerene* $C^{10}H^{16}$.—A liquid hydrocarbon, isomeric with oil of turpentine.

valereus, obs. Sc. f. valorous *a.*

valerian (və'lɪərɪən). Also 4-5 valirian, 5 valarian, 5-6 valeryan(e, 6 valeriane. [ad. OF. *valeriane* (mod.F. *valériane*) or med.L. *valeriana* (also It., Sp., and Pg.), app. the fem. sing. of the L. adj. *Valerianus*, f. the personal name *Valerius*.]

1. One or other of the various species of herbaceous plants belonging to the widely-distributed genus *Valeriana*, many of which have been used medicinally as stimulants or antispasmodics.

c **1386** Chaucer *Can. Yeom. Prol. & T.* 800 And herbes couthe I telle eek many oon, As egrimoigne, valirian, and lunarie. *c* **1400** *Lanfranc's Cirurg.* 269 Poudre maad of þe rotis of valarian temperid wiþ wijn. *c* **1410** *Master of Game* (MS. Digby 182) xii, An herbe..þat men calleth..in oure langage valeryane, þe whiche maketh men fnese. **1530** Palsgr. 284/1 Valeryan an herbe. **1578** Lyte *Dodoens* 339 There be two sortes of Valerian, the garden and wilde. **1597** Gerarde *Herbal* II. ccxl. 1078 Generally the valerians are called by one name. **1612** Drayton *Poly-olb.* xiii. 213 Valerian then he crops, and purposely doth stampe T' apply unto the place that's haled with the crampe. **1664** Evelyn *Kal. Hort.* 67 Flowers in Prime... Syringa's, Sedum's,.. Valerian, Veronica [etc.]. **1763** *Phil. Trans.* LIII. 199 The roots of Valerian are esteemed most medicinal, which are dug up in Oxfordshire and Glocestershire. **1782** J. Scott *Poet. Wks.* 100 Gay loosestrife there and pale valerian spring. **1822** Lamb *Elia* I. *Praise Chimney-Sweepers*, No less pleased than those domestic animals—cats—when they purr over a new-found sprig of valerian. **1866** *Treas. Bot.* 1201/1 Two Valerians are natives of this country. **1882** *Garden* 25 Mar. 204/2 Any one requiring a useful plant for some semi-wild garden ought to give the Valerian a trial.

2. With distinctive terms: **a.** Denoting varieties of true valerian, as ***garden, great, little, wild,*** etc., ***valerian.***

Many varieties are enumerated in Parkinson *Theatr. Pl.* (1640) 120-2, Bradley *Dict. Bot.* (1728), *Chambers' Cycl.* Suppl. (1753), Johnson *Gard. Dict.* (1852), etc.

1548 Turner *Names Herbes* (E.D.S.) 62 The one is growing..in moyst plasshes and in morish groundes, and it is called in englishe wylde Valerian. **1578** Lyte *Dodoens* 339 Great wild valerian. Little wild valerian. **1597** Gerarde *Herbal* II. 916 The tame or garden Valerian hath his first leaues long, broade, smooth, greene, and vndeuided. *Ibid.* 917 *Valeriana Petræa*, Stone Valerian. **1601** R. Chester *Love's Martyr* (1878) 83 Great wild Valerian and the Withie wind. **1629** Parkinson *Parad.* (1904) 386 Knobbed Mountaine Valerian. **1640** —— *Theat. Pl.* 119 The great Valerian hath a thicke short grayish roote. **1712** tr. *Pomet's Hist. Drugs* I. 42 The little Valerian has small Roots, of a good Smell. **1753** *Chambers' Cycl.* Suppl. s.v., The great garden Valerian is an alexipharmic, sudorific, and diuretic. *Ibid.*, The wild Valerian root is much more famous than this. **1790** Buchan *Dom. Med.* 427 Infusions of balm-leaves,.. the roots of wild valerian, or the flowers of the lime-tree. **1872** Oliver *Elem. Bot.* II. 192 The root of the Common Valerian possesses a strong and peculiar odour. **1890** *Science-Gossip* XXVI. 183 The handsome heart-leaved valerian (*Valeriana Pyrenaica*).

b. ***red, spur-,*** or ***spurred*** (also †***basil***) ***valerian,*** = ***Centranthus ruber.***

1597 Gerarde *Herbal* II. 551 Of Basill Valerian. Red Valerian hath beene so called of the likenesse of the flowers and spoked rundles with Valerian, by which name we had rather haue it called, then rashly to laie vpon it an vnproper name. **1640** Parkinson *Theat. Pl.* 122 This small red Valerian is very like unto the greater red Valerian. **1849** [see spurred *a.* 4]. **1855-63** [see spur *sb.*[1] 14 b]. **1866** *Treas. Bot.* 247/1 The Red Valerian, *C. ruber*, formerly known as *Valeriana rubra*, offers a good example of the genus. **1899** Bridges *Idle Flowers* Poet. Wks. (1912) 352 With red Valerian And Toadflax on the wall.

c. ***Greek*** (†***Greekish, Grecian***) ***valerian,*** Jacob's ladder, *Polemonium cæruleum.*

1578 Lyte *Dodoens* III. 340 The garden Valerian and Greeke Valerian are sowen and planted in gardens. *Ibid.*, The Greekish Valerian hath two or three holow stalkes, or moe. **1629** Parkinson *Parad.* (1904) 388 The Greek Valerian hath many winged leaues lying vpon the ground,.. very like vnto the wilde Valerian. **1682** Wheler *Journ. Greece* VI. 436 The Leaves were set upon a long stem, like to that which is called Grecian Valerian. **1785** Martyn *Lett. Bot.* xvi. (1794) 189 Greek Valerian or Jacob's-Ladder which has the corolla rather rotate. **1855** Miss Pratt *Flower. Pl.* IV. 15 Blue Jacob's Ladder or Greek Valerian. **1858** Irvine *Brit. Plants* 477 *Polemoniaceæ*, the Greek Valerian Family.

3. The drug derived from the rootstocks of the wild valerian or other species.

1794 Godwin *Caleb Williams* 29, I shall hate you as bad as senna and valerian. **1801** *Med. Jrnl.* V. 472 Internally valerian with opium [was] prescribed. **1842** *Penny Cycl.* XXII. 347/2 It is curious that the Celtic and mountain nards are also Valerians, the former being yielded by *Valeriana Celtica* and *Saliunca*. **1843** *Ibid.* XXVI. 92/2 Valerian is considered a cerebro-spinal stimulant. **1899** *Allbutt's Syst. Med.* VIII. 604 Sedatives such as bromides and valerian.. must be administered.

4. *attrib.*, as ***valerian oil, root, tea;*** **valerian family, order, tribe, -worts,** the order *Valerianaceæ.*

a. **1747** Wesley *Prim. Physick* (1762) 49 A Teaspoonful of Valerian Root. **1783** *Med. Comm.* I. 214 She had taken the drops in the valerian tea. **1868** Watts *Dict. Chem.* V. 975 Crude valerian-oil is a mixture of several substances. **1874** Garrod & Baxter *Mat. Med.* 288 Valerian Root. The root of *Valeriana officinalis*, dried.

b. **1846** Lindley *Veget. Kingd.* 698 Valerianworts are principally distinguished from Teazelworts by their want of albumen. **1849** Balfour *Man. Bot.* §906 The Valerian Family. **1855** Miss Pratt *Flower. Pl.* III. 160 The Valerian Tribe. **1857** Henfrey *Bot.* 315 The Valerian Order.

valerianaceous (vəlɪərɪə'neɪʃəs), *a.* [f. mod.L. *Valerianace-æ*: see prec.] Of or belonging to the Valerian order.

1842 Loudon *Suburban Hort.* 681 The Lamb's lettuce, or corn-salad,..is a valerianaceous indigenous annual.

valerianate (və'lɪərɪənət). *Chem.* [f. valerian + -ate[1] c.] A salt produced by the action of valeric acid on a base.

1845 W. Gregory *Handbk. Org. Chem.* 168 Hydrogen is given off, and valerianate of potash is formed. **1857** Miller *Elem. Chem., Org.* 154 Apple oil is a similar preparation of valerianate of amyl. **1876** Harley *Mat. Med.* 347 The valerianates are all soluble in water, excepting those of silver and mercury. **1899** *Allbutt's Syst. Med.* VIII. 124 Zinc, which may well be given as the valerianate.

valerianic (vəlɪərɪ'ænɪk), *a. Chem.* [f. bot. L. *Valeriana* valerian + -ic.] Derived or obtained from valerian.

1838 T. Thomson *Chem. Org. Bodies* 36 There pass over into the receiver, water and an oil; both of which contain valerianic acid. **1839** R. D. Thomson in *British Ann.* 354 Valerianic ether. **1866** W. Odling *Anim. Chem.* 6 The combination of water, valerianic aldehyd, and prussic acid. **1874** Garrod & Baxter *Mat. Med.* 288 Valerian root owes its activity to a volatile oil and valerianic acid.

valeric (və'lɛrɪk), *a. Chem.* [f. valer-ian + -ic.] = prec.

1852 W. Gregory *Handbk. Org. Chem.* (ed. 3) 236 Valerate of oxide of ethyle, or valeric ether. **1857** Miller *Elem. Chem., Org.* 128 Under the influence of spongy platinum, amylic alcohol gradually absorbs oxygen,..and valeric acid is produced. *Ibid.* 139 Valeric aldehyd... This compound may be obtained in various ways. **1868** Watts *Dict. Chem.* V. 979 Valeric bromide. *Ibid.*, Valeric chloride.

valerin ('vælərɪn). *Chem.* [f. as prec. + -in.] (See quots.)

1866 W. Odling *Anim. Chem.* 93 By combining valeric acid with glycerin we produce valerin, a constituent of whale oil. **1868** Watts *Dict. Chem.* V. 980 Valerins, glycerides produced by heating valeric acid with glycerin.

'valero-, combining form of valerian or valeric *a.*, used in a few chemical terms, as ***valerobenzoic, -glyceral, -lactic.*** (Cf. valer-.)

1854 *Fownes's Elem. Chem.* (ed. 5) 488 Anhydrous Valerobenzoic Acid. **1868** Watts *Dict. Chem.* V. 980 *Valeroglyceral*,..a compound analogous to acetal. *Ibid.* 981 *Valerolactic acid*,..syn. with ethyl-lactic acid.

valerol ('vælərɒl). *Chem.* Also -ole. [f. valer-ian + -ol.] 'The neutral oxygenated constituent of valerian-oil' (Watts).

1845 W. Gregory *Handbk. Org. Chem.* 447 When fresh, it contains no valerianic acid, but an oil, valerole. **1857** Miller *Elem. Chem., Org.* 398 The valerian root contains a compound (valerol, $C_{12}H_{10}O_2$), which by oxidation becomes converted into valeric acid. **1874** Garrod & Baxter *Mat. Med.* 289 Valerole..is a crystalline body at a low temperature. **1876** Harley *Mat. Med.* 545 Valerol is a constituent of the volatile oil of hops.

valerone ('vælərəʊn). *Chem.* Also -on. [f. as prec. + -one.] (See quots. 1852, 1868.)

1839 R. D. Thomson in *British Ann.* 362 Valeron. **1852** W. Gregory *Handbk. Org. Chem.* 237 Valerone,.. homologous with acetone, is formed when valerianic acid is heated with excess of baryta. **1868** Watts *Dict. Chem.* V. 981 Valerone is a transparent, colourless, mobile liquid, having a pleasant ethereal odour and burning taste.

valero'nitrile. *Chem.* Also -yle, -il. [f. valero- + nitrile.] Cyanide of tetryl.

1847 W. Gregory *Handbk. Org. Chem.* (ed. 2) 597 Valeronitrile..may be derived from valerianate of ammonia. **1848** Fownes *Elem. Chem.* (ed. 2) 542 Alkalis convert valeronitril into valerianic acid and ammonia. **1857** Miller *Elem. Chem., Org.* 627 If it be distilled with dilute sulphuric acid and peroxide of manganese, valeronitrile with carbonic acid and water are produced.

valerous, obs. f. valorous *a.*

'valeryl. *Chem.* Also -yle. [f. valer-ian + -yl.] 'The radicle of valeric acid and its derivatives' (Watts).

1852 W. Gregory *Handbk. Org. Chem.* (ed. 3) 236 Hydrated oxide of valeryle. *Ibid.* 237 The compounds of amyle and valeryle. **1868** Watts *Dict. Chem.* V. 981 The bromide, chloride, &c. of valeryl.

'valerylene. *Chem.* [f. as prec. + -ene.] A hydrocarbon homologous with acetylene.

1868 Watts *Dict. Chem.* V. 981 Valerylene..is a colourless very mobile liquid, which floats on water, and is nearly insoluble therein. **1873** Rolfe *Phys. Chem.* p. xviii, Quintine or Valerylene.

Valesian (və'li:ʃ(ɪ)ən). [ad. mod.L. pl. *Valesiani, Valesii*, ad. late Gr. Οὐαλήσιοι, f. Οὐάλης, L. *Valens*.] (See quots.)

1702 Echard *Eccl. Hist.* (1710) 585 There appeared a new sort of hereticks in the Church called Valesians from Valesius an Arabian. They made all their followers eunuchs. **1728** Chambers *Cycl.*, *Valesians*,..antient Sectaries, so called from one Valens, a Person unknown to Epiphanius, who makes mention of this Sect. **1808** W. Wilson *Hist. Dissenting Churches* I. 96 Others who were called heretics at that period; such as the Valesians.

valeslye, obs. var. falsely *adv.*

valet ('vælɪt, 'væleɪ), *sb.* Also 6-7 vallet (6 -ett, *Sc.* wallett), 7 valett; 8 *Sc.* vallie. [a. F. *valet*, OF. *valet, vallet, vaslet*, prob. related to vassal. Cf. vadelect, valect, and varlet.]

1. A man-servant performing duties chiefly relating to the person of his master; a gentleman's personal attendant.

1567 Fenton *Trag. Disc.* i. (1898) I. 34 Not worthy anye waye to be vallet to the worste of us. **1587** *Reg. Privy Council Scot.* IV. 181 Ane of the vallettis of the Kingis Majesteis chalmer. **1614** Selden *Titles Honor* 333 At this day, a *Diener*, seruant or vallet is both in Alemanique and Belgique called *Ein Knecht*. **1664** Butler *Hud.* II. ii. 651 Before the Dame, and round about, March'd Whiflers, and Staffiers on foot, With Lacquies, Grooms, Valets, and Pages. **1691** *Satyr agst. French* 15 That Gentleman does much himself forget, Who in his Chamber has not French Vallet. *Ibid.* 25 From hence they'd fly,..And leave not one poor Vallet here behind. **1719** Hamilton *Ep. to Ramsay* II. viii, I wad nae care to be thy vallie, Or thy recorder. **1771** Smollett *Humph. Cl.* (1815) 102 We have taken an occasional valet, whom I intend hereafter to hire as my own servant. *a* **1845** Barham *Ingol. Leg.* Ser. III. *Knight & Lady*, Thompson, the *Valet*, Look'd gravely at Sally. **1856** Sir B. Brodie *Psychol. Inq.* I. vi. 218 The rich man's valet studies his master's temper and caprices. **1885** *Athenæum* 26 Sept. 393/2 The chief characters in his plays are heavy fathers and confidential valets.

fig. **1837** Carlyle *Fr. Rev.* I. I. i, Which would not end till 'France' (La France, as she named her royal valet) finally mustered heart to see Choiseul.

2. *Mil.* A footman acting as attendant or servant to a horseman. *rare.* (Cf. varlet 1 b.)

1591 *Garrard's Art Warre* 269 There be..two quarters for horsemen, the which their vallets are to entrench with a smal trench. **1832** tr. *Sismondi's Ital. Rep.* xiii. 281 They became terror-struck when they perceived that the French caused dismounted horsemen to be put to death by their valets.

3. a. Appositive, as ***valet-courier, harquebusier, maid, -musician.***

1598 Dallington *Meth. Trav.* K 4 [A horseman] who shall quitte his horse, and serue on foot, prouided that hee haue with him a vallet Harquebusier. **1845** E. Holmes *Life Mozart* 5 The Archbishop of Saltzburg..entertained him in the capacity of valet-musician. **1867** Carlyle *Remin.* (1881) II. 32 The clever old valet maid that waited on them. **1897** 'H. S. Merriman' *In Kedar's Tents* xxii. 243 A valet-courier of taciturn habit.

b. Attributive, as ***valet judgement, service, world;*** **valet parking** *N. Amer.*, a service provided at a restaurant, etc., in which an attendant parks patrons' motor vehicles; hence (as back-formation) **valet-park** *v.*

1855 Carlyle *Misc.* (1857) IV. 354 Sublime to the valet judgment. **1983** C. Hyde *Tenth Flight* ix. 87 They valet-parked the Triumph and they made the flight with ten minutes to spare. **1960** *Britannica Bk. of Year* 558/1 *Valet parking*..referred to a system in which an attendant was responsible for parking the car. **1976** *Globe & Mail* (Toronto) 8 Nov. 16/7 A swish little marquee blinks out an offer of valet parking. **1984** *Tampa* (Florida) *Tribune* 5 Apr. 3D/5 Reservations are due for the Scholarship Night at Tampa Jai-Alai Fronton... Valet parking is available. **1939** R. STOUT *Some buried Caesar* xvi. 233 You should have put on some old clothes. The valet service here is terrible. **1981** D. BOGGIS *Time to Betray* i. 9 Rousselot wore a different pair of expensive slacks, with the abandon of a man used to valet service. **1843** CARLYLE *Past & Pres.* I. iv, It is to the sham-hero that..the valet world belongs.

Hence **'valetage**, the service rendered by a valet; **'valethood**, the state or condition of being a valet; **'valetism**, the character or spirit of a valet.

1843 CARLYLE *Past & Pres.* II. ix, The fruit of long ages of confirmed Valethood;..cloth-worship and quack-worship. **1875** HELPS *Soc. Press.* xiii. 183 To far other persons besides the valet by reason of his valetism, does the hero often cease to be a hero. **1890** *Sat. Rev.* 17 May 588/2 The vassalage or the valetage is prompted by an honest personal devotion, like that of Tom Steele to O'Connell.

'valet, *v.* [f. VALET *sb.*] **a.** *trans.* To wait upon, to attend or serve, as a valet.

1840 J. T. J. HEWLETT *P. Priggins* xx, He always comes down to college to valet me, take my things away to brush, and so on. **1861** HUGHES *Tom Brown at Oxf.* i, Fancy me waited upon and valeted by a stout party in black, of quiet, gentlemanly manners. **1886** A. GRIFFITHS *Pauper Peer* i, If he keeps no servant, the proprietor of the establishment will valet him.

refl. **1893** MCCARTHY *Dictator* i, In the most splendid days of Gloria, he had always valeted himself.

absol. **1885** G. ALLEN *Babylon* xv, But can he valet, I wonder?

b. To look after (clothes, etc.).

1931, **1951** [see VALETING *vbl. sb.*].

c. To clean (a motor vehicle).

1972 *Drive* Spring 147/1 It's not difficult to imagine an owner confining his chauffeur to valeting the car, while he hogs the driving. **1976** *Star* (Sheffield) 20 Nov. (Advt.), Young Man wanted..to serve petrol, valet cars, take forecourt enquiries.

Hence **'valeting** *vbl. sb.*

1857 HUGHES *Tom Brown* I. iii, He would have gone without nether integuments altogether, sooner than have had recourse to female valeting. **1861** MRS. CARLYLE *Lett.* III. 77, I have all the valeting to do myself. **1931** *Times* 16 Mar. 1/3 (Advt.), *Clothes valeting...* They will stand years of hard wear if you send them to us to be *turned*. **1951** *Good Housek. Home Encycl.* 296/1 Careful valeting lengthens the life of clothes. **1976** *Drive* Jan.-Feb. 11/2 The eight suggestions that, in order of importance, would contribute most to the economical running and upkeep of the average family car were: 1 regular servicing;..5 regular valeting.

valeta, var. VELETA.

‖**valetaille** (valtɑj). [F., f. *valet* VALET *sb.*] A number or retinue of valets.

1858 CARLYLE *Fredk. Gt.* VII. iii. (1872) II. 266 No end of military valetaille, chiefly 'janizaries' in Turk costume. **1862** H. MARRYAT *Year in Sweden* I. 284 The rest of the valetaille were closely incarcerated.

‖**valet-de-chambre** (valɛ də ʃɑ̃br). Also 7 **valett-**, 7–8 **valette**; 7 **vally**, 8 **vale**; 8 **valet de shamber**, 8–9 **valet de sham**, 9 **valley-de-sham.** [F., lit. 'chamber-valet'.] = VALET *sb.* 1.

α. **1646** CHAS. I *Lett. to Q. Henrietta M.* (Camden) 60 One Dubose, valett-de-chambre to the Queen Regent. **1655** *Nicholas P.* (Camden) II. 291 There finding a valet de chambre attending, the Marquis wild him to tell the prince I was there. **1711** ADDISON *Spect.* No. 106 ¶2 You would take his Valet de Chambre for his Brother. **1764** FOOTE *Patron* II. 31 It has been said, and I believe with some shadow of truth, that no man is a hero to his valet de chambre. **1782** V. KNOX *Ess.* No. 32. 147, I dare say, you remember a shrewd remark of a writer, whose name I cannot recollect, That no great man ever appeared great in the eyes of his valet de chambre. **1839** DICKENS *Nickleby* xxviii, With noiseless tread two valets-de-chambre advanced into the room. **1862** AÏDÉ *Carr of C.* III. 36 Though our *valets-de-chambre* know us to be no heroes, it is clearly their interest to make us appear such in the eyes of the world.

β. **1678** in Pollock *Popish Plot* App. B. (1903) 384 A vally de chambre to the Lord Bellasis. **1709** O. DYKES *Eng. Prov.* (ed. 2) 135 By the conversation of an illiterate Coxcomb of a Vale De Chambre. **1776** FOOTE *Capuchin* I. Wks. 1799 II. 384 His old shopman, whom he keeps as his valet de sham. **1791** O'KEEFFE *Wild Oats* I. i, I wish you hadn't made me your valet de shamber. **1853** W. IRVING *Life & Lett.* (1864) IV. 124 The door was opened by Mr. Gray's factotum and valley-de-sham Phil.

Hence **valet-de-chambreship**.

1779 J. MOORE *View Soc. Fr.* (1793) I. 14 His dexterity and intelligence in the science of valet-de-chambreship.

‖**valet-de-place** (valɛ də plas). [F., lit. 'place-servant'.] A man who acts as a guide to strangers or tourists; a cicerone.

1750 CHESTERF. *Lett.* (1774) II. xiii. 52 You will have your coach,..your own footman, and a valet de place. **1792** C. SMITH *Desmond* III. 267 A Frenchman, who had formerly served me as *valet de place*. **1818** *Gentl. Mag.* Nov. 4 6/2 We chose rather to stroll out alone, than to put ourselves under the direction of a valet-de-place. **1886** RUSKIN *Time & Tide* 62, I asked a valet-de-place at Meurice's what people were generally going to [for amusement].

valetry ('vælɪtrɪ). [f. VALET *sb.*] Valets collectively; the office or quality of a valet.

1806 W. TAYLOR in *Ann. Rev.* IV. 244 Hospitals for decayed valetry and dependents of ministerial land-owners. **1853** JAMES *Agnes Sorel* I. 191 The cutler..could not forbear some grumbling observations upon valets and valetry. **1880** SWINBURNE *Stud. Shaks.* 97 Work fitter for ushers and embalmers and the general valetry or varletry of Church and State.

†**'valetude.** *Obs. rare.* Also **valitude.** [ad. L. *valētūdo, valītūdo* state of health, f. *valēre* to be well or strong.] **a.** Good health. **b.** Condition as to health.

a **1560** ROLLAND *Crt. Venus* II. 106 Thair was worschip with welth and valitude... Thair was meiknes weil mixt with mansuetude. **1623** COCKERAM I, *Valetude*, health or sicknesse. **1657** TOMLINSON *Renou's Disp.* 261 Esula..is frequently used to the valitude of many, and the death of more.

‖**valetudinaire,** *a.* and *sb.* *rare.* [F. *valétudinaire.*] = VALETUDINARY.

1682 WARBURTON *Hist. Guernsey* (1822) 131 One, that is valétudinaire, may, in the time of his sickness, contract with any relation or stranger to take care of him. **1715** POPE *Farew. to Lond.* x, Still idle, with a busy air, Deep whimsies to contrive; The gayest valetudinaire, Most thinking rake, alive.

valetudinarian (vælɪtjuːdɪ'nɛərɪən), *sb.* and *a.* [See VALETUDINARY *a.* and -IAN.]

A. *sb.* A person in weak health, esp. one who is constantly concerned with his own ailments; an invalid.

1703 DAMPIER *Voy.* III. I. 81 Many of our English Valetudinarians have gone from Jamaica..to the I. Caimanes,..to live wholly upon Turtle that abound there. **1746** R. JAMES *Health's Improv.* Introd. 45 Such who have very strong Constitutions, are more liable to pestilential Disorders, and putrid Fevers, than Valetudinarians. **1787** *Gentl. Mag.* Dec. 1056/2 Every one knows how hard a task it is to cure a valetudinarian. **1832** J. A. HERAUD *Voy. & Mem. Midshipman* vi. (1837) 102 The hot springs and medicinal vapours..must at a very early period have excited the attention of valetudinarians. **1880** L. STEPHEN *Pope* iv. 92 Naturally, he fell into many of the self-indulgent and troublesome ways of the valetudinarian.

fig. **1712** BUDGELL *Spect.* No. 395 ¶10 These are a kind of Valetudinarians in Chastity. **1777** SHERIDAN *School for Scand.* I. i, True, madam! there are Valetudinarians in reputation as well as constitution. **1873** GOULBURN *Pers. Relig.* II. v. 81 The man becomes a valetudinarian in religion, full of himself, his symptoms, his ailments, the delicacy of his moral health.

B. *adj.* = VALETUDINARY *a.*

1713 DERHAM *Phys.-Theol.* III. iv. (1727) 72 An admirable Easement..to the valetudinarian, feeble Part of Mankind. **1740** CHEYNE *Ess. Regimen* i, The Scorbutic, Gouty, Consumptive, or Nervous Valetudinarian-low-livers. **1751** EARL ORRERY *Rem. Swift* (1752) 113 His fortune exempted him from care and sollicitude. His valetudinarian habit of body from intemperance. **1856** R. A. VAUGHAN *Mystics* (1860) II. 118 The valetudinarian devotee becomes more and more the puppet of his spiritual doctor. **1875** JOWETT *Plato* (ed. 2) III. 283 Asclepius did not instruct his descendants in valetudinarian arts.

Hence **valetudi'narianism**, the condition of a valetudinarian; tendency to be in weak health or to be much concerned about one's own health.

1839 *Fraser's Mag.* XIX. 52 Those traces of laborious valetudinarianism and nervous sensibility. **1868** W. R. GREG *Lit. & Soc. Judgm.* 490 The bolder spirits.., perhaps over-recklessly, despise such egotistic valetudinarianism. **1892** *Speaker* 30 July 141/2 The schoolmistress has had to forget her valetudinarianism and patent medicines in the struggle for existence.

vale'tudinariness. *rare*$^{-1}$. [f. VALETUDINARY *a.*] Weakness of health.

1742 CHEYNE *Regimen* III. iv. 243 If there be an habitual Thinness, Leanness, Tenderness and Valetudinariness.

†**valetudi'narious,** *a.* *Obs.* [See VALETUDINARY and -IOUS.] Having weak health; valetudinary. Also *fig.*

1648 *Petit. Eastern Assoc.* 14 Our Parliament might be somewhat valetudinarious. **1662** GURNALL *Chr. in Arm.* III. lv. 504 Valitudinarious bodies can as well spare food as physick. **1702** C. MATHER *Magn. Chr.* VI. vii. 70 About the Beginning of January he began to be very Valetudinarious, labouring under Pains that seem'd Ischiatick. **1704** S. SEWALL *Diary* 1 Apr. (1879) II. 97 Visited my valetudinarious son at Brooklin.

†**vale'tudinarist.** *Obs.* [Cf. next and -IST.] A valetudinarian.

1651 BIGGS *New Disp.* ¶204 Ere these valetudinarists arrive at the broad and pleasant way of perfect convalescence.

valetudinary (vælɪ'tjuːdɪnərɪ), *a.* and *sb.* [ad. L. *valētūdinārius*, f. *valētūdin-*, *valētūdo* VALETUDE. So It., Sp., Pg. *valetudinario*, F. *valétudinaire.*]

A. *adj.* **1.** Not in robust or vigorous health; more or less weakly, infirm, or delicate; invalid: **a.** Of the body, etc.

1581 MULCASTER *Posit.* xxx. (1887) 110 Either it is sickly, ..or it is healthy,..or it is valetudinarie, neither pure sicke nor perfit whole. **1619** DONNE *Lett.* Wks. 1839 VI. 374, I carry an infirm and Valetudinary body. **1692** BOYLE *Hist. Air* 230 Oxford..I have known to be very disagreeable to some moist splenetick and valetudinary bodies. **1836** *Fraser's Mag.* XIV. 705 His puny and valetudinary frame would not permit him.

fig. **1712** STEELE *Spect.* No. 300 ¶3 This valetudinary Friendship, subject to so many Heats and Colds.

b. Of persons. (In later use freq. implying anxious attention to the state of one's own health.)

1584 COGAN *Haven Health* cxcvii. 161 For they [students] be commonly valetudinary, that is sickely. **1646** R. BAILLIE *Anabaptism* (1647) Pref., Very small changes of the heaven and air are able to vex much a crazy and valetudinary person. **1692** BOYLE *Hist. Air* 242 Sick and valetudinary Persons used to be sent thither. **1733** CHEYNE *Eng. Malady* Pref. (1734) p. viii, A gross, full, high Diet, is [improper] for a poor, thin, low, valetudinary Creature. **1779** JOHNSON *L.P.*, *Pope* Wks. IV. 91 All the unpleasing and unsocial qualities of a valetudinary man. **1808** SCOTT in *Lockhart* (1837) I. i. 19 Though valetudinary, he lived to be nearly ninety. **1844** N. P. WILLIS *Lady Jane* I. 44 The men being old and valetudinary.

absol. **1646** SIR T. BROWNE *Pseud. Ep.* IV. xiii. 230 Preventive we call that [physic] which..preventeth sicknesse in the healthy, or the recourse thereof in the valetudinary. **1652** GAULE *Magastrom.* 139 Experience of all places, and ages tell us, that the more valetudinary, have commonly been the more vertuous. **1741** *Compl. Fam.-Piece* I. i. 2 The Tender therefore, and Valetudinary, ought cautiously to avoid all Occasions of catching Cold. **1782** *Med. Comm.* I. 11 *note*, The old and valetudinary, suffered most severely. **1823** J. BADCOCK *Dom. Amusem.* 165 The valetudinary, consumptive, and physic-taking, earliest fall victims of the ship's motion.

2. Of conditions, etc.: Characterized by weak or feeble health.

1620 VENNER *Via Recta* viii. 163 Such as are naturally infirme, and of a valetudinary state of body. **1684** tr. *Bonet's Merc. Compit.* xv. 530 No Cough nor any signs of a Valetudinary disposition of the Lungs do appear. **1701** C. WOLLEY *Jrnl. N. York* (1860) 26 A person seemingly of a weakly Stamen and a valetudinary Constitution. *a* **1776** R. JAMES *Diss. Fevers* (1778) 44 Mr. Collyer..has by that means been brought from the most valetudinary state, to one of great health and vigour. **1830** SCOTT *Demonol.* ix. 331 Apparently a man of melancholic and valetudinary habits. **1876** L. STEPHEN *Hist. Eng. Th. 18th C.* II. 386 The last thirty-six years of his long life was passed in valetudinary retirement.

B. *sb.* †**1.** An infirmary or hospital. *Obs.*

After med.L. *valetudinarium.*

1623 COCKERAM I, *Valetudinarie*, an Hospitall. **1677** W. HUGHES *Man of Sin* III. ii. 45 There lay the poor man, till being found, he was carried into the Valetudinary.

2. = VALETUDINARIAN *sb.*

1785 *Lounger* (1787) I. 200 Dr. Doddipoll was a valetudinary like myself. **1787** MME. D'ARBLAY *Diary* 15 Aug., General Grenville, a silent, reserved valetudinary, went under the same convoy. **1851** E. FITZGERALD *Euphranor* 46 It is better to die well ever so young than to grow up a valetudinary and a poltroon. **1860** *Macm. Mag.* II. 36 The painters who have shown him [Christ] as a delicate valetudinary.

†**vale'tudinous,** *a.* *Obs.*$^{-1}$ [f. L. *valētūdin-*, *valētūdo* VALETUDE + -OUS.] Invalid, weakly.

1655 FULLER *Hist. Cambridge* 128 It seemeth that soon after,..affrighted with the valetudinous condition of King Edward,..he returned to Heidelberg.

†**valeur.** *Obs. rare.* [a. OF. and F. *valeur*, later f. *valour* VALOUR.] **a.** Value. **b.** Valour.

1433–4 *Rolls of Parlt.* V. 437/2 This thaire assent and grant for to stande in strengthe, and ellus to be as voide and of noe valeure. **1456** SIR G. HAYE *Law Arms* (S.T.S.) 32 Gif the key of jurisdiccioun dois thing that it aw nocht to do,.. that suld be of lytill valeur. **1646** HOWELL *Lewis XIII*, 115 Some of the Provensall Gentlemen shew'd much Passion for the honor of their Countrey..by divers proofs of valeur.

valew, obs. f. VALUE *sb.*

†**vale-water.** *Obs.* [f. VAIL *v.*²] Ebb-tide.

1600 HAKLUYT *Voy.* III. 257 The current runneth as strong..as at London bridge vpon a vale water. **1610** HOLLAND *Camden's Brit.* I. 720 Neere unto Hunt-Cliffe and not farre from the shore there appeere aloft at a vale water certaine rocks.

valewe, southern ME. var. FALLOW *v.*¹; obs. f. VALUE *sb.*

valey, obs. f. VALLEY *sb.*

'valgous, *a.* [See next.] 'Bandy-legged; having the legs bent outward' (Craig, 1849).

‖**valgus** ('vælgəs). *Path.* [L. *valgus* bandy-legged.]

1. A variety of club-foot in which the foot is turned outwards (†or inwards).

1800 *Med. Jrnl.* IV. 195 In those diseases where the feet turn inwards, and which, I presume, Mr. Watt will call valgus. **1836–9** *Todd's Cycl. Anat. & Phys.* II. 348/2 When the foot..is turned outwards, called *valgus*. *Ibid.* 349/2 The same complication of the pes equinus with the valgus is rare. **1884** W. PYE *Surg. Handicraft* 322 The second expedient is only used for valgus, and consists in fixing a pad under the sole of the foot.

attrib. **1884** W. PYE *Surg. Handicraft* 322 Valgus pad for sole [of the foot]. **1899** *Allbutt's Syst. Med.* VIII. 15 The abductors of the foot move it into the valgus position.

2. *spurious valgus*, flat foot.

1872 BRYANT *Pract. Surgery* 1014.

Valhall, occas. variant of next.

1763 PERCY *Five Pieces Runic Poetry* 60 This place or Elizium was called *Valhall* or the hall of slaughter. **1770** —— tr. *Mallet's Northern Antiq.* I. 87 These souls were Odin's right, he received them in Valhall.

Valhalla (væl'hælə). Also **Wal-.** [a. mod.L. *Valhalla*, ad. ON. *Valhall-*, *Valhǫll*, f. *val-r* (= OE. *wæl*) those slain in battle + *hǫll* hall. Cf. G. *Walhalla*, F. *Wal-*, *Valhalla.*] In Old Northern mythology, the hall assigned to those who have died in battle, in which they feast with Odin.

α. **1768** Gray *Fatal Sisters* 79 *note*, The *Valkyriur*.. conducted them to *Valhalla*, the hall of Odin, or paradise of the Brave. **1780** *Encycl. Brit.* (ed. 2) V. 3288/1 That their great Odinus excluded all those from his *valhalla*, or paradise, who [etc.]. **1801** M. G. Lewis *Tales of Wonder, Hacho's Death Song* xvii, Soon as he gains Valhalla's gate, Eight heroes there to greet him wait. **1855** Arnold *Balder Dead* i. 19 Enough of tears, ye Gods, enough of wail! Not to lament in was Valhalla made.

β. **1851** *Expositor* 11 Jan. 171/2 A long and happy sojourn in the Walhalla.

b. *transf.* and *fig.* A place or sphere assigned to persons, etc., worthy of special honour.

c **1845** Mrs. Browning *Fourfold Aspect* ii, That this Death, then, must be found A Valhalla for the crowned. **1868** Milman *St. Paul's* 480 That St. Paul's might fitly become a Valhalla for English worthies. **1880** Ld. Acton *Lett. M. Gladstone* (1904) 56 Neither Pitt nor Peel lives in my Walhalla.

‖**vali** (va'li:). [Turk. (Arab.) *valī*. Cf. WALI.] A civil governor of a Turkish province or vilayet.

The form *valiè* occurs in the transl. of Chardin's *Coronat. Solyman* (1686) 34.

1753 Hanway *Trav.* (1762) II. v. iii. 139 Vachtanga.. ought..to have succeeded him in the dignity of vali of Georgia. **1875** R. Wilson tr. *Figuier's Hum. Race* 284 A vali and council is at the head of the administration of each government or 'vilayet'. **1897** *Outing* XXIX. 387 The *Vali*, ..like nearly all Turkish officials,..had discarded the Turkish costume. **1903** *Times* 5 Sept. 8/6 The corrupt and inefficient government of the Vali of Beirut.

Hence **va'liship**, the office or position of a vali.

1907 *Times* 17 Jan. 3/6 It may have been right to depose Kiamil from his Valiship.

valiable, obs. Sc. var. VAILABLE *a.*

valiance ('væljəns). Forms: 5 **vailliaunce, vaylliaunce**, 5–6 **valiaunce, -yaunce**, 6 **-eaunce**, 6–7, 9 **valiance**. [a. AF. *valiance* (1304), or ad. OF. *vaillance* (AF. *vayllaunce*), f. *valiant, vaillant*: see VALIANT *a.*]

1. Bravery, valour; = VALIANCY 1.

Very common in the 16th c.; now chiefly as a literary archaism.

1456 Sir G. Haye *Law Arms* (S.T.S.) 53 The mekle valiaunce of schir Cipro consul of Rome. **1475** *Bk. Noblesse* 55 For his gret trouthe, vailliaunce, and manhod..king Pirrus..offred to gyve hym the .iiij^th part of his roiaume. **1509** Barclay *Shyp of Folys* (1570) 126 These fooles them boast of deedes of valiaunce And worthy actes done by them in battayle. **1581** A. Hall *Iliad* iii. 50 When I was yong, and valiance had, and prowess. **1623** Bingham *Xenophon* 44 Let vs not expect, that other come and encourage vs to be braue and resolute, but let vs begin to excite other to valiance. **1807** G. Chalmers *Caledonia* I. iii. vii. 387 His son exerted many acts of forward valiance. **1841** Thackeray *Drum* i. v, In spite of our valiance, The victory lay with Malbrook. **1894** *Academy* 16 June 491/3 Equal to them in business capacity, superior in persevering energy, in valiance of heart and true courage.

2. A valiant act or deed; a feat of valour or bravery. Now *arch.*

1470–85 Malory *Arthur* v. viii. 173 Grete valyaunces, prowesses, and appertyces of werre were that day shewed. **1489** Caxton *Faytes of A.* i. vii. 17 By cause he had founde so many valyaunces in the romayns. **1589** Puttenham *Eng. Poesie* i. xix. (Arb.) 57 Places of assembly, where the company shalbe desirous to heare of old aduentures and valiaunces of noble knights in times past.

1879 Meredith *Egoist* I. ii. 21 Our cavalier's is the poetic leg, a portent, a valiance.

valiancy ('væljənsɪ). Forms: 6 **val(l)iauncie**, 6–7 (9) **valiancie** (7 **vall-**), 7 **valiansie**, 7– **valiancy** (7 **valiantcy**), 6–7 **valiencie**. [Cf. prec. and -ANCY.]

1. The quality or attribute of being valiant or courageous; bravery, valiantness, valour.

Freq. from *c* 1575 to *c* 1600.

1574 J. Jones *Beg. Growing & Living Things* 32 Feeblenesse of spirit, want of strength, and lacke of valiauncie. **1590** Sir J. Smyth *Disc. Weapons* 23 More to the effect of our Archers, than to anie extraordinarie valiancie of our Nation. **1605** *1st Pt. Jeronimo* ii. i, That which they lost by base Captiuitie, We may redeeme with honored valiansie. **1654** E. Johnson *Wonder-wrkg. Provid.* 30 Yet was he not minded to make triall of his peoples valiantcy in fight at this time. **1661** Morgan *Sph. Gentry* iii. v. 45 Those prizes and Crownes they had gained by their Valiancy in war.

1795 Southey *Joan of Arc* vi. 392 Though Talbot with vain valiancy Yet urged the war, and stemm'd alone the tide Of battle. **1827** Scott *Chron. Canongate* ii, Cincinnatus and the like, who fought not the common enemy with the less valiancy that their arms had been exercised in halding the stilts of the pleugh. **1850** T. H. Gill *Golden Chain of Praise* (1894) cxxxvi. viii, Turn our darkness into light; Give us valiancy for fear. **1893** F. Adams *New Egypt* 164 Would that gay valiancy be with him so long as it was with Henri IV?

b. Const. *of* (the mind, heart, spirit, etc.).

1579 Twyne *Phis. agst. Fortune* i. Ep. Ded. 3 Her flatteries haue ouercome that valiencie of mans minde. *c* **1650** *Don Bellianis* 18 Truly Prince Don Gallaneo you have plainly expressed the valiancy of your mind. **1813** Coleridge *Lect. Shaks.* in *Rem.* (1836) II. 143 This happy valiancy of style is but the representative and result of all the material excellencies so expressed. **1846** Prowett *Prometh. Bd.* 12 Or force of hands, or valiancy of heart.

c. *arch.* Used with possessive as an honorific.

1828 Scott *Fair Maid* xxiv, His blood..will flow as temperately as your valiancie's, when you stand up in your stirrups to view a field of battle.

†**2.** A valiant act or feat. *Obs.*⁻¹

1627 *Lisander & Cal.* viii. 138 Acting in the fury wherein hee was..such valiancies, that thereby he did lessen all those which heretofore hee had done.

valiant ('væljənt), *a.* (and *sb.*). Forms: α. 4 **vaillaunte, vaylaunt, vailant**, 5 **-aunt, vaillant**. β. 4, 6 **valliaunt**, 5 **valya(u)nte**, 5–6 **valya(u)nt**, 6 **waly-, valiaunt(e**, *Sc.* **valliant**, 4– **valiant** (6–7 **valient**); 6 **valeaunt(e, valeant**, *Sc.* **vaill-, wailleant**. γ. (Chiefly *Sc.*) 5–6 **vailȝeand**, 6 **vail(l)-, wailȝeant, -ȝeand, val(l)-, wal(l)ȝeand, -ȝeant, -yeant, -ieȝeand, -ieȝeant, -ieand**, etc. [ad. OF. *vaillant* (*-and*, AF. *vaylant*), *vaillant* (AF. *-aunt*), pres. pple. of *valoir* to be of worth:—L. *valēre*. Cf. It. and Pg. *valente*, Sp. *valiente*.

The comparative *valianter*, superlative *valiantest* were formerly frequent, the latter occurring occasionally in the 16th and 17th c. in the shortened forms *valiaunst, valianst, valienst*.]

1. a. Of persons: Stalwart *of* body, bone, hands.

Prob. with some implication of sense 2. In mod. Sussex dial. the sense of 'stout, well-built' is recorded.

1303 R. Brunne *Handl. Synne* 4370 Þys Conred had a seriaunt, A wys man, and of body vaylaunt. **1338** —— *Chron.* (1810) 9 So wis he was in dede, of body so valiant. *Ibid.* 144 Richer kyng is non in þis world bot ȝe, No valianter of bon in Cristendam als he. **1523** Ld. Berners *Froiss.* I. cclxxxiv. 424 Sir Moreau of Fyennes..was a right valyant man of his handes. *a* **1548** Hall *Chron., Edw. V* (1550) v, Antony Wooduile,..a wise, hardy and honourable personage, as valiaunte of handes as politique of counsayll.

†**b.** *valiant beggar*, a sturdy beggar. *Obs.*

1531 *Dial. on Laws Eng.* i. xvi. 27 b, That no man..shuld gyue any almes to any valyant begger that is well able to laboure. **1534** *Nott. Rec.* III. 373 Harberor of valyeant begers and comyn woman. **1569** J. Sanford tr. *Agrippa's Van. Artes* 104 b, The Emperoure made a streicte ordinance touching valiant beggars.

†**c.** Of things: Strong, firm. *Obs.*

1542 Becon *Pathw. Prayer* xvii. H iij, For the name of the Lorde is a stronge tower & valeaunt Bulwarke. **1603** G. Owen *Pembrokeshire* viii. (1891) 60 The Wheat and Rie endureth all the winter stormes & forces as a valiant and stout grayne. **1607** Topsell *Four-f. Beasts* 460 A Lyon hath a most valiant and strong head.

†**d.** Strong in respect of smell or taste. *Obs.*

1607 A. Brewer *Lingua* iv. iii, This, if your breath be not too valiant, will make you smell as sweet as my lady's dog. *a* **1661** Fuller *Worthies, Cornwall* (1662) i. 194 The scent thereof [i.e. garlic] is somewhat Valiant and Offensive.

2. Having or possessing courage; *esp.* acting with or showing boldness or bravery in fight or on the field of battle; bold, brave, courageous, stout-hearted.

α. **1390** Gower *Conf.* II. 56 So that these heraldz on him crie, 'Vailant, vailant, lo, wher he goth!' *c* **1400** *Ywaine & Gaw.* 541 Sir Gawayn, knyght vailaunt. *c* **1450** *Merlin* xxiii. 423 Lepe to horse many a vailaunt knyght. **1474** Caxton *Chesse* iv. v. (1883) 176 And thus is hit of euery man the more vaillant the more honoured.

β. *c* **1330** R. Brunne *Chron. Wace* (Rolls) 6952, I haue a broþer, sire Constaunt, God werrour, & man valliaunt. **1338** —— *Chron.* (1810) 9 Many tymes on Uttred Bretons bataile souht: Uttred was so valiant, he gaf of þam right nouht. ? *a* **1400** *Morte Arth.* 299 Of this grett velany I salle be vengede ones On ȝone venemus mene, wyth valiant knyghtes! **1470–85** Malory *Arthur* x. xlii. 482 The good knyghte Semound the valyaunt. *a* **1533** Ld. Berners *Huon* xcii. 296 For he is so noble and so valyaunt that he fereth no man. **1535** Coverdale *Esther* xiii. 9 O Lorde Lorde, thou valeaunt and allmightie kynge. **1578** T. Procter *Gorg. Gallery* M iij b, Wee subiect bee to griefe, eche horror feares The valiaunst harts, when death doth daunt the brest. **1600** J. Pory tr. *Leo's Africa* iv. 233 The inhabitants are valiant and warrelike people. **1634** Sir T. Herbert *Trav.* 199 Crocodiles..cruell and yet valiant. **1676** Hobbes *Iliad* vi. 144 Glaucus.., Than whom a fairer person there was not, Nor valianter in all the Land. **1706** Maule *Hist. Picts* in *Misc. Scot.* I. 39 He levies a mighty and strong army of the valiantest warriors. **1743** Francis tr. *Hor., Odes* ii. i. 33 Panting with terror, I survey The martial host in dread array, The chiefs, how valiant and how just! **1814** Scott *Lord of Isles* iv. xviii, It is the foe! Each valiant lord Fling by his bow, and grasp his sword! **1855** Macaulay *Hist. Eng.* xii. III. 204 The Englishry generally respected him as a valiant, skilful, and generous enemy. **1871** Freeman *Norm. Conq.* (1876) IV. 68 In all these castles..William placed trusty and valiant captains.

transf. ? *a* **1400** *Morte Arth.* 2573 His vesturis ryche, With the valyant blode was verrede alle ouer! **1591** Shaks. *1 Hen. VI*, iii. i. 171, I gyrt thee with the valiant Sword of Yorke. **1599** —— *Hen. V*, iv. iii. 98 Those that leaue their valiant bones in France. **1782** Highmore *Ramble Coast of Sussex* (1873) 19 The beauteous form of woman..graced with.. her smiles the feats of valiant Arms.

Comb. **1595** *Locrine* ii. iii, There might we see the valiant minded knights, Fetching carreers along the spatious plaines. **1596** Shaks. *1 Hen. IV*, v. i. 90, I do not thinke a brauer Gentleman, More actiue valiant, or more valiant young,..is now aliue.

γ. *c* **1470** *Gol. & Gaw.* 243 The king stude..maist vailyeand to se. **1500–20** Dunbar *Poems* lxiii. 7 Men of armes, and vailȝeand knychtis. **1563** Winȝet *Wks.* (S.T.S.) II. 3 The wailȝeant cheiftane of God..Nehemias. **1596** Dalrymple tr. *Leslie's Hist. Scot.* II. 9 In the weiris thay war maist valȝeant, and in peace maist faithfull.

b. Const. *of* (courage, etc.).

1338 R. Brunne *Chron.* (1810) 298 Knyghtes & sergeantz, noble men fulle couth, Of prowes fulle valiantz. **1538** Elyot, *Fortis*, valyant of corage. **1599** Shaks. *Hen. V* iv. i. 46 A Lad of Life, an Impe of Fame, of Parents good, of Fist most valiant. **1630** J. Taylor (Water P.) *Jack a Lent* Wks. (1630) L 2 b, I wish a plentifull encrease of good appetites and hungry stomackes, that euery one in their calling may proue valiant of their teeth.

c. *absol.* with *the.*

1560 Bible (Geneva) *Judges* xxi. 10 Twelue thousand men of the moste valiant. **1585** T. Washington tr. *Nicholay's Voy.* iii. ii. 71 b, [The] most valiant of the valiauntest. *a* **1668** Davenant *Poems* (1672) 335 O harmless Death! whom still the valiant brave. **1718** Prior *Henry & Emma* 80 In Tilts and Turnaments the Valiant strove..to purchase Emma's Love. **1816** Wordsw. *Ode, 1815*, 57 The valiant of this land.

†**d.** Of material things: Fine, splendid. *Obs.*

1604 Middleton *Black Book* D iij b, A valiant Buffe Doublet, stuft with Points like a Legge of Mutton with Parslye.

3. Characterized by, performed with, or exhibiting valour or courage; of a valorous character or nature.

c **1330** R. Brunne *Chron. Wace* (Rolls) 12576 Schame hit were þat eyþer ȝede Wiþouten bataille or vaillaunte dede. **1500–20** Dunbar *Poems* l. 11 He did full mony valȝeant deid In Roiss, and Murray land. *a* **1533** Ld. Berners *Huon* lv. 188 His barons stode styll to beholde his valyaunt dedes. **1568** Grafton *Chron.* II. 304 Before Winter be past I will enter into Fraunce, in puyssaunt and valyaunt maner. **1600** J. Pory tr. *Leo's Africa* ii. 75 The foresaide captaine with his armie..gaue them such a valiant onset, that the greater part of them was slaine. **1655–60** Stanley *Hist. Philos.* (1687) 750/1 The valiant Exhortation of an old Man..chang'd the minds and fortune of the whole City. **1845** Carlyle *Cromwell* (1871) I. 50 Truly with valiant patient energy..it carried its Petition of Right. **1907** *Trans. Devon Assoc.* 51 The valiant deeds of the great reign of Elizabeth.

†**4.** Of great worth or merit; worthy. *Obs. rare.*

1480 Caxton *Myrr.* i. v. (E.E.T.S.) 25 Other philosophres ther were..prudent alle and valyant, seen that they set to fore alle other thynges clergye.

†**5.** Marked or characterized by the use of strength. *Obs.*⁻¹

1531 Elyot *Gov.* i. xxvii. (1880) 289 That some be done with extending of myght, and as hit were violently, and that is called valiaunt exercise.

†**6.** Worth (a specified sum). Also const. *in* (goods or property). Cf. VAIL *v.*¹ 4. *Obs. rare.*

1590 *Reg. Privy Council Scot.* IV. 557 The said Thomas is bot ane puir man.., not valiant in substance and guidis ane hundreth pundis. **1603** *Ibid.* VI. 525 All..landit gentlemen, valiant tuentie chalderis of victuall. **1608** Middleton *Trick to catch Old One* i. i, A rich country widow, four hundred a year valiant, in woods, in bullocks, in barns and in rye-stacks.

†**b.** *Sc.* As *sb.* Value or worth. *Obs.*⁻¹

1606 *Sc. Acts, Jas. VI* (1816) IV. 286 The saidis decreittis ..may bring þe danger of the ȝeirlie violent proffeittis vpoun the persones,..thairby surmounting often tymes thair haill valient.

†**7.** *Sc.* Valid, effective, decisive. *Obs.*⁻¹

1632 Lithgow *Trav.* iv. 143 Their..definitiue sentence in Lawe or Religion is..absolutely valiant.

8. As *sb.* One who is valiant; a brave or courageous person.

1609 Bible (Douay) *Jer.* xlvi. 9 Get ye up on horses, and in chariots, and let the valiants come forth. **1611** Bible *2 Sam.* xxi. *heading*, Foure battels against the Philistines, wherein foure valiants of Dauid slay foure gyants. *a* **1722** Sewell *Hist. Quakers* Pref. (1795) A 4, For the most eminent Valiants among this People in the Beginning were not Men of Note or Learning, tho' of great Courage. **1909** *Westm. Gaz.* 25 May 4/1 Valiants of the wheel who, when they cannot drive, will tramp over the dreary marshes of Turkestan.

Hence †'**valiant** *v. trans.*, to render valiant.

1628 Feltham *Resolves* i. lxxv. (1647) 231 Sure, Virtue is a Defendress, and valiants the heart of man.

†**valiantise.** *Obs.* Forms: 4 **vaillauntise**, 4, 6 **valyauntise, valiantise**, 5 *Sc.* **vailliantis**, 6 **valy-, valiauntise**. [a. OF. *vaill-, vallantise, valiandise*, etc., f. *vaillant* VALIANT *a.*; see -ISE².]

1. Valiancy, valour.

c **1330** R. Brunne *Chron. Wace* (Rolls) 12193 He [Arthur] tristed wel..on his grete vaillauntise Ar he durst take þat emprise. **1338** —— *Chron.* (1810) 168 Now is Cipres lorn fro Isaac & hise, & to R[ichard] suorn for his valiantise. *c* **1400** *Laud Troy Bk.* 6800 Philomene sende him vnto hise, For he him wan with valyauntise. **1456** Sir G. Haye *Law Arms* (S.T.S.) 224 For suppos for grete vailliantis and honourable dede of armes a bonde man war..maid knycht in armes. **1523** Ld. Berners *Froiss.* I. cccxvii. 489 Men of armes proued well there their valyantise and prowes. **1598** Bp. Hall *Sat.* iv. iv. 31 If brabling Make-Fray, at each Fayre and Sise, Picks quarrels for to shew his valiantise.

2. A valiant act or deed. *rare.*

1513 *Life Hen. V* (1911) 11 For these and manie other valiauntises, noble feates, and victories,..the Prince was honnored.

valiantly ('væljəntlɪ), *adv.* [f. VALIANT *a.* + -LY².] In a valiant manner; with valour or courage; boldly, bravely, courageously.

α. *a* **1533** Ld. Berners *Huon* viii. 22 And hys knyghtes folowyde hym,..determynyde to do walyauntly. **1568** Grafton *Chron.* II. 296 The Erle Douglas of Scotland, who fought a season right valiauntly. **1602** Marston *Ant. & Mel.* v. Wks. 1856 I. 65 He died unforst, I trust, and valiantly. **1642** Milton *Apol. Smect.* Wks. 1851 III. 286 The Divine right of Episcopacy was then valiantly asserted. **1695** Ld. Preston *Boeth.* iv. 205 Thou must engage valiantly and fiercely against every Fortune. **1787** Burke *Sp. Fox's E. India Bill* Wks. IV. 24 This man.. was slain valiantly fighting for his country. **1879** Mrs. Hungerford *Airy Fairy Lilian* I. 104 Putting one foot into a friendly crevice, and holding on valiantly to the upper stones. **1907** *Verney Mem.* II. 219 He talked valiantly at first of military service.

Comb. **1609** DEKKER *Gull's Hornbk.* Proem. B 3, Oh what songs will I charme out in praise of those valiantly-strong-stinking breaths.

β. **1508** DUNBAR *Tua Mariit Wemen* 431 To furnyse a bancat In Venus chalmer, valȝeandly, withoutin vane ruse. **1533** BELLENDEN *Livy* II. xx. (S.T.S.) I. 210 The batall bcand in anc partc rcnewit, manilius Consul faucht na less Valeȝeantlie þan he did in ane vthir weyng. *a* **1578** LINDESAY (Pitscottie) *Chron. Scot.* (S.T.S.) I. 77 ȝe haue provin walieȝeantlie..for the defence and libertie of this realme. *a* **1600** in *Montgomerie's Poems* (S.T.S., Suppl. Vol.) 246 That I may wailȝeandle resist the fleche, þe warld, þe dewell, & hell.

ˈvaliantness. ? *Obs.* [f. as prec. + -NESS.]

1. The quality or condition of being valiant; valiancy, valour. Also *personif.*

Very common in the 16th c.

α. **1470–85** MALORY *Arthur* XII. xii. 608, I vnderstande thy valyauntnesse wel. *c* **1489** CAXTON *Sonnes of Aymon* 16 The whiche..Charlemagne by hys prowesse and valyauntnes had dyscomfyted. **1513** *Life Hen. V* (1911) 155 The Englishmen..excelled so farr the Frenchmen in there valyantnes, that they remayned conquerors in the fielde. **1540** MORYSINE *Vives' Introd. Wysd.* B v, Strengthe and valiantnesse is, to suffise and accomplyshe the exercises of vertu without werynes. **1560** DAUS tr. *Sleidane's Comm.* 25 Which honor [i.e. knighthood] in times past..was the rewarde of valeauntnes. **1603** KNOLLES *Hist. Turks* (1621) 343 Mahomet seeing this valiantnesse of the defendants, openly said [etc.]. **1672** BAXTER *Bagshaw's Scandals* i. 6 They call out for Valiantness in suffering. **1727** P. WALKER *Life of R. Cameron* in *Biogr. Presbyt.* (1827) I. 237 The Valiantness of the Four-score Priests, that withstood Uzziah.

β. **1508** DUNBAR *Poems* vii. 93 B, in thi name, betaknis batalrus;..W, valyeantnes; S, for strenewite. **1549** *Compl. Scotl.* Ep. 6 The toune of sauerne baris vytnes of his delegent vailȝeantnes. *a* **1560** ROLLAND *Crt. Venus* IV. 577 Sine Cheualrie come in with vailȝeantnes.

b. Const. *of* (courage, heart, mind, etc.).

1534 WHITINTON *Tullyes Offices* I. (1540) 7 By ryght and lawe, whereof forse & valyauntnesse of herte doth ryse. **1539** TAVERNER *Gard. Wysd.* I. 4 b, It greued moch this excellent Prynce, that so stronge an herte and valyauntnesse of nature was spent in a matter of leudenesse. **1579** TWYNE *Phis. agst. Fortune* I. xv. 16 The mightinesse of the Citie and Empire, and the valiantnesse of the peoples myndes. **1603** KNOLLES *Hist. Turks* (1621) 409 Much inferiour to this great king in wealth and number of men, but not in hautinesse of mind and valiantnesse of courage. **1736** AINSWORTH, *Magnanimitas*, valiantness of heart and courage.

2. Physical strength; robustness, sturdiness, stalwartness *of* (body). *rare.*

1553 T. WILSON *Rhet.* 104 In the Iliades are described strengthe and valeantenes of the body. **1596** DALRYMPLE tr. *Leslie's Hist. Scot.* I. 311 Bartholomew Leslie,..quhais..ablenes of mynd, valȝeantnes of body and fercenes of force, king Malcolme meruelet sa mekle.

valicot, obs. form of *walycoat* WYLIECOAT.

valid (ˈvælɪd), *a.* (and *sb.*). Also 6–7 **valide**, 8 **valed**. [ad. F. *valide* (OF. *valide*, Sp., It., Pg. *valido*) or L. *valid-us* strong, powerful, effective, f. *valēre* to be strong, etc.]

1. Good or adequate in law; possessing legal authority or force; legally binding or efficacious.

1571 *Reg. Privy Council Scot.* II. 95 Seing his said tak is valide and sufficient in the self. **1651** HOBBES *Leviath.* I. xv. 72 The nature of Justice, consisteth in keeping of valid Covenants. *a* **1688** CUDWORTH *Immut. Mor.* (1731) 2 Whatsoever is decreed and constituted, that for the time is Valid, being made so by Arts and Laws. **1726** in *Nairne Peerage Evidence* (1874) 36 Declareing if I do not exerce these faculties in my own time these presents shall remain a valed evident albeit not delivered by me. **1769** ROBERTSON *Chas. V*, IX. Wks. 1851 IV. 315 This strange tribunal founded its charge upon the ban of the empire, which..was ..destitute of every legal formality which could render it valid. **1786** BURKE *Art. agst. W. Hastings* Wks. II. 90 A claim, which they determined not to comply with but in return for the surrender of another equally valid. **1844** H. H. WILSON *Brit. India* III. 257 Those, who held rent-free lands by titles that might be declared valid. **1878** JEVONS *Primer Pol. Econ.* 128 According to law, deeds, leases, cheques, receipts, contracts, and many other documents are not legally valid unless they be stamped.

b. *Eccl.* Technically perfect or efficacious.

1674 J. OWEN *Holy Spirit* (1693) 235 So as that the Call to Office should yet be valid. *c* **1680** BEVERIDGE *Serm.* (1729) I. 28 Not but that the ordination is valid. **1876** MELLOR *Priesth.* viii. 361 No ordination is valid unless there be in the recipient of orders what is termed in the Church of Rome an habitual, or, at least, a virtual intention.

2. Of arguments, proofs, assertions, etc.: Well founded and fully applicable to the particular matter or circumstances; sound and to the point; against which no objection can fairly be brought.

a **1648** LD. HERBERT *Autobiog.* (1764) 138 The whole face of Affairs was presently changed, insomuch that neither my Reasons, nor the Ambassadors.., how valid soever cou'd prevail. **1692** BENTLEY *Boyle Lect.* iv. 115 He may admit of those Arguments as valid and conclusive. **1717** PRIOR *Alma* I. 416 For when One's Proofs are aptly chosen; Four are as valid as four Dozen. **1766** PITT in Almon *Anecd.* xxix. (1810) I. 432 The excuse is a valid one, if it is a just one. **1803** WELLINGTON in Gurwood *Disp.* (1835) II. 164 Reasons which I thought valid but which I do not think it necessary to communicate to him. **1859** MILL *Liberty* ii. 36 An objection which applies to all conduct, can be no valid objection to any conduct in particular. **1881** WESTCOTT & HORT *Grk. N.T.* Introd. §46 A generalisation obtained from one book would be fairly valid for all the rest.

b. In general use: Effective, effectual; sound.

1651 HOBBES *Govt. & Soc.* ii. §7. 23 If yet to words relating to the future, there shall some other signes be added, they may become as valid, as if they had been spoken of the present. **1774** REID *Aristotle's Logic* ii. §2. 183 This same *et cætera*..shall in any future time shew a good and valid right to a property in the subject. **1824** BYRON *Juan* XVI. xxxv, The effort was not valid To hinder him from growing still more pallid. **1860** MANSEL *Proleg. Log.* (ed. 2) 22 The only valid method of investigating the relation between thought and speech. **1875** GEO. ELIOT in Cross *Life* III. 253, I should urge you to consider your early religious experience as a portion of valid knowledge.

3. Of things: Strong, powerful. Now *arch.*

1656 BLOUNT *Glossogr.*, *Valid*, strong, mighty, puissant, able. **1667** MILTON *P.L.* VI. 438 Perhaps more valid Armes, Weapons more violent, when next we meet, May serve to better us. **1807** CRABBE *Birth of Flattery* 109 So on a dream our peasant placed his hope, And found that rush as valid as a rope. **1887** BROWNING *Parleyings* Wks. 1896 II. 692/2 What beseems a king who cannot reign, But to drop sceptre valid arm should wield? **1891** *Cornh. Mag.* Nov. 493 In addition to the strong jaws..there are three exceedingly valid hooks.

†**b.** Of malt liquor: Unduly thick. *Obs.*$^{-1}$

1742 *London & Co. Brewer* I. (ed. 4) 38 They also keep it from running into such Cohesions as would make it ropy, valid, and sour.

4. Of persons: Sound or robust in body; possessed of health and strength. Also said of health.

1652 GAULE *Magastrom.* 139 The more valetudinary have commonly been the more vertuous; and the more valid, the more vitious. **1708** MOTTEUX *Rabelais* (1737) V. 232 Thanks to Jove's Benignity you're valid. **1757** MRS. GRIFFITH *Lett. Henry & Frances* (1767) IV. 137, I much fear his excessive Grief may injure his Health, which is not very valid, at present. **1879** SALA in *Daily Telegr.* 12 June, When he was a valid man he may have had many a boxing bout with Shaw the Life Guardsman. **1899** *Daily News* 1 Dec. 7/1 The Boers have evidently put every valid male into the field.

b. Of the mind: Sane, strong. *rare.*

1854 EMERSON *Lett. & Soc. Aims, Poet. & Imag.* Wks. (Bohn) III. 139 The restraining grace of common-sense is the mark of all the valid minds.

5. As *sb.* A person in good health. Opposed to INVALID *sb.* 1.

1882 *Pall Mall G.* 20 Sept. 5 *Kuristen* and valids may alike thank Dr. Yeo for a series of highly interesting and instructive Essays.

†**ˈvalidate,** *ppl. a. Sc. Obs.*$^{-1}$ In 6 **-at**. [ad. med.L. *validāt-us*, pa. pple. of *validāre*: see next.] Valid, validated.

1586 *Reg. Privy Council Scot.* IV. 103 To be als validat ane Act of Parliament as the former.

validate (ˈvælɪdeɪt), *v.* [f. med.L. *validāt-*, ppl. stem of *validāre* (1394 in Du Cange), or after F. *valider* (1586 in Godef. *Compl.*; = Sp. and Pg. *validar*, It. *validare*): see VALID *a.* and -ATE^3. Cf. INVALIDATE *v.*]

1. a. *trans.* To render or declare legally valid; to confirm the validity of (an act, contract, deed, etc.); to legalize.

a **1648** LD. HERBERT *Hen. VIII* (1683) 209 Henry consented, that..the marriage betwixt Francis and Leonora ..should be validated and confirmed. **1659** in *Burton's Diary* (1828) IV. 435 You only establish *quantum in vobis est*, without either validating or invalidating the Acts and Ordinances for the Excise. **1706** J. SERGEANT *Acc. Chapter Bp. Chalcedon* (1853) 121 The long prescription it has enjoyed, which alone is able to validate and confirm it. **1750** CARTE *Hist. Eng.* II. 859 Pope Julius II..granted a dispensation..for validating the contract [of marriage] if it had been already made. **1801** JEFFERSON *Writ.* (1830) III. 477 It is true the treaty was not ratified; but when ratified it is validated retrospectively. **1849–50** ALISON *Hist. Europe* I. v. §49. 607 The question of the royal sanction being required to validate the acts of the legislature. **1880** MUIRHEAD *Gaius* II. §220 The legacy will be invalid by the civil law; but it will be validated by the Senatus-consult.

b. *spec.* [Now after F. *valider*.] To declare (an election) valid; to declare (a person) duly and properly elected.

1658–9 in *Burton's Diary* (1828) III. 75 Have an account brought in to validate the members for Scotland and Ireland. **1883** *Daily News* 25 June 5/3 The Chamber has validated the election for Passy of M. Cailla.

2. a. To make valid or of good authority; to confirm or corroborate; to substantiate or support.

1775 C. JOHNSTON *Pilgrim* 250 The lawyer found convenient witnesses to prove a marriage,..and every circumstance necessary to validate his scheme. **1775** S. J. PRATT *Liberal Opin.* xlviii. (1783) II. 14, I intend my memoirs shall serve as the counterpart of his; and both will indisputedly prove and validate the peculiar truth of these singular sentiments. **1803** MISS PORTER *Thaddeus* (1826) III. xvi. 341 Come, Lord Berrington, you must validate my report, for I learnt it of you. **1872** *Contemp. Rev.* XX. 395 The eschatological idea shared the fortunes of the theological, was with it materialized, spiritualized, impersonalized, validated, or dissolved.

b. To examine for incorrectness or bias; to confirm or check the correctness of.

1957 KENDALL & BUCKLAND *Dict. Statistical Terms* 309 A sample of human beings is partly validated by comparing, *inter alia*, its sex and age constitution with the known figures for the population from which it was chosen. **1963** LADEN & GILDERSLEEVE *System Design for Computer Applications* iii. 33 Because of this power of the control total to validate individual fields of data, the control total approach to the validation of a field is sometimes chosen in preference to performing some type of validation check on each field as it comes up. **1967** *Oxford Computer Explained* 20 Run 1. Reads the paper-tape Input, validates it (reporting any errors) and converts suitable records to magnetic tape. **1967** D. WILSON in Wills & Yearsley *Handbk. Management Technol.* 44 Figure 3.1 outlines the basic steps for validating (editing), processing.., and recording the output. **1979** *Sci. Amer.* Feb. 58/2 With this unique record it should be possible to construct (and validate) new, highly realistic models of atmospheric circulation. **1980** C. S. FRENCH *Computer Sci.* xxxi. 269 The transaction tape is already validated and sequenced in the order of the master file.

Hence **validated** *ppl. a.*; **ˈvalidating** *vbl. sb.*

a **1648** LD. HERBERT *Hen. VIII* (1683) 409 An act also.. was now confirmed and the Oath prescribed, for the more Validating whereof also, it was declared [etc.]. **1893** *Westm. Gaz.* 5 Dec. 7/1 Nearly all the validated deputies..voted. **1965** A. G. FAVRET *Introd. Digital Computer Applications* xii. 184 Both the master file and the validated transactions are stored on magnetic tape reels and used as input. **1965** P. CAWS *Philos. of Sci.* xxvi. 193 A validated theory requires statements which are both significant and true.

validation (vælɪˈdeɪʃən). [f. prec.: cf. F. *validation* (16th c.), Sp. *validacion*, Pg. *-ação*, It. *-azione*.] **a.** The action of validating or making valid.

1656 BLOUNT *Glossogr.* [copying Cotgrave], *Validation*, a strengthning, inforcement, confirming; an establishing or ratifying. **1847** in WEBSTER (citing Knowles). **1872** *Echo* 3 Oct. 6 Father Hyacynthe has just applied to the French tribunals for the validation of his civil marriage. **1888** *Act 51 & 52 Vict.* c. 42 §5 An instrument, the enrolment whereof is required..for the validation of an assurance. **1957** KENDALL & BUCKLAND *Dict. Statistical Terms* 309 *Validation*, a procedure which provides, by reference to independent sources, evidence that an inquiry is free from bias or otherwise conforms to its declared purpose. In statistics it is usually applied to a sample investigation with the object of showing that the sample is reasonably representative. **1967** D. WILSON in Wills & Yearsley *Handbk. Management Technol.* 44 In commercial applications the first step is normally the validation of the input data. **1967** *Oxford Computer Explained* 13 After validation, the records are converted to magnetic tape. **1980** C. S. FRENCH *Computer Sci.* xvii. 91 When data is first input to the computer, different checks can be applied to prevent errors going forward for processing. For this reason, the first computer run is often referred to as *validation* or *data vet*.

b. *attrib.*

1965 A. G. FAVRET *Introd. Digital Computer Applications* xii. 184 The 'A' type transactions are processed daily through a validation run on the computer which checks for completeness and, to some extent, for the correctness of the data. **1967** *Oxford Computer Explained* 8 All programs, except a special general purpose validation routine, would be written in Cobol. **1969** *Computers & Humanities* III. 130 Validation criteria contain limits the user places on specific items. **1973** *Jrnl. Genetic Psychol.* CXXIII. 11 A validation study..had found that among others, the IE test was correlated (negatively) with the ACL self-confidence scale. **1979** *Sci. Amer.* Sept. 99/2 All keyed entries are subjected to validation procedures, so errors are caught and corrected on the spot.

validator (ˈvælɪdeɪtə(r)). [f. VALIDATE *v.* + -OR 2.] One who or that which confirms the validity of something. Also *attrib.*

1951 R. FIRTH *Elem. Soc. Organ.* vii. 245 The prophet, the mystic, the spirit-medium are valuable interpreters and validators of religious belief. **1971** *Engineering* Apr. 31/1 Diagram showing the component parts of the coin validator mechanism. **1978** *Washington Post* 13 Jan. B2/5 The piece of equipment that accepts bills, called a validator, doesn't like cold weather. **1980** *Observer* 16 Mar. 22/7 The key is not a security device and that is that. It's a validator, to make sure that somebody hasn't made a typing error in sending the message.

validity (vəˈlɪdɪtɪ). Also 6 **valydyty(e**, 6–7 **validitie**, 7 **vallydety**, *Sc.* **validete**. [ad. late L. *validitas*, f. *valid-us* VALID *a.* Cf. F. *validité* (16th c.), It. *validità*.]

1. The quality of being valid in law; legal authority, force, or strength.

c **1550** *Life Fisher* in *F.'s Wks.* (E.E.T.S.) II. p. l, Two or three daies after, he began to discusse with him the validitie of his maryage. **1561** *Reg. Privy Council Scot.* I. 171 The questioun standis nocht upoun the validitie and invaliditie of the saising. **1608** WILLET *Hexapla Exod.* 310 Concerning the validitie of these lawes. **1651** HOBBES *Leviath.* I. xv. 72 The Validity of Covenants begins not but with the Constitution of a Civill Power. **1701** *Lond. Gaz.* No. 3715/4 A Definitive Sentence hath been..given by the Judges Delegates, for the Validity of the Last Will of John Higgs. **1769** BLACKSTONE *Comm.* IV. 315 To consider and determine the validity of appeals or indictments. **1818** CRUISE *Digest* (ed. 2) IV. 212 The validity of such a lease was established in the following modern case. **1855** MACAULAY *Hist. Eng.* xvii. IV. 77 Much as they hated him, they could not question the validity of his commission. **1884** *Law Times Rep.* L. 2/2 The plaintiff denied the validity of the transfer.

2. The quality of being well-founded on fact, or established on sound principles, and thoroughly applicable to the case or circumstances; soundness and strength (of argument, proof, authority, etc.).

a. In the phrase *of ... validity*.

1581 J. BELL *Haddon's Answ. Osorius* 488 b, Of no greater valydyty is that Argument lykewyse which they rake out of Augustines wordes. **1599** THYNNE *Animadv.* (1810) 21 This ys a mere coniecture, and of no valydytye. **1620** VENNER *Via Recta* ii. 34 Neither are their reasons of such validity. **1652** NEEDHAM tr. *Selden's Mare Cl.* 145 It remain's in the next place, that wee consider of what validitie the contrarie Opinions of Writers are. **1726** SHELVOCKE *Voy. r. World* 7 Expressions full of contempt of the Commission, making it appear as a thing of hardly any validity or consequence. **1768** *Phil. Trans.* LVIII. 222 No arguments brought in favour of absorption by the common veins appear to me of equal validity with those that can be urged against it. **1803** WELLINGTON in Gurw. *Desp.* (1835) II. 138 *note*, The assurance contained in his letter.. was of equal validity as if given by the most Noble the Governor General.

b. In general use.

1588 FRAUNCE *Lawier's Log.* I. i. 5 Artificial Logike then is the polyshing of natural wit, as discovering the validitie of everie reason. **1609** C. BUTLER *Fem. Mon.* (1634) 60 In this point the Philosopher.. seemeth to question the validity of his own arguments. **1655** FULLER *Ch. Hist.* III. 80 Something must be premised about the validity of this writing, learned men much differing therein. **1689** G. HARVEY *Curing Dis. by Expect.* i. 1 If Antiquity be capable of conferring Validity, the Art of Expectation.. may be termed equally valuable. **1716** POPE *Lett.* (1736) VI. 3 You are doubtless persuaded of the validity of that famous verse ''Tis Expectation makes a Blessing dear'. **1793** SMEATON *Edystone L.* §188 To examine the validity of the notion entertained by workmen, respecting Tarras Mortar. **1804** WELLINGTON in Gurw. *Desp.* (1835) III. 552, I do not exactly understand the validity of this objection. **1857** BUCKLE *Civiliz.* I. vii. 418 Statesmen.. who denied the validity of general principles in politics. *a* **1881** BARRATT *Phys. Metempiric* (1883) 185 That does not alter the validity of the conclusion to be ultimately arrived at.

†**3. a.** The quality or state of being physically strong or sound; robustness, strength. *Obs.*

1578 BANISTER *Hist. Man* I. 26 The shoulder blades.. putting forth a strong ridge.. not a little to the augmenting of their validitie. **1601** R. JOHNSON *Kingd. & Commw.* (1603) 148 Some men maintain great disputation, whether fortresses builte of stone, chalke or earth be of greatest validitie. **1620** MARKHAM *Farew. Husb.* II. xvii. (1668) 81 The grain wanting his true nourishment, grows withered and of no validity. **1651** WITTIE tr. *Primrose's Pop. Err.* IV. xxv. 300 If in debility of strength the bloud be lighter, and in validity of strength it be heavier.

transf. **1602** SHAKS. *Ham.* III. ii. 199 Purpose is but the slaue to Memorie, Of violent Birth, but poore validitie. **1750** JOHNSON *Rambler* No. 29 ¶13 Some pious persons who.. question the validity of their own faith, because they shrink at the thoughts of flames and tortures.

b. Physical value or capacity. *rare.*

1607 TOPSELL *Four-f. Beasts* 669 That a Bore or male swine wil not remaine of validity and good for breed past three yeare old. **1868** E. EDWARDS *Sir W. Ralegh* I. xxv. 612 No hope remained of his validity in active service.

4. Value or worth; efficacy.

Merging into sense 2, from which in some instances it is hardly distinguishable.

1593 HARVEY *New Lett.* Wks. (Grosart) I. 290 Some surmounting spirites loue to arreare a huge opinion of their excessiue validity, *pro*, or *contra*. **1595** in *Maitland Club Misc.* I. 76 To give in in writt.. the estait and validitie of the vicarage of Ruglen. **1601** HOLLAND *Pliny* II. 303 The scrapings that come of sweating in banes and hot-houses, be counted of greater validitie in all these infirmities. **1631** LENTON *Charact.* B 10b, Shee hath lately.. giuen her selfe out a brace of hundreds more then ere his estate was worth, besides his debts and legacies, wheras her validity proportionable can scarce absolue those. **1788** FRANKLIN *Autobiog.* Wks. 1840 I. 189 He had too high an opinion of the validity of regular troops. **1793** SMEATON *Edystone L.* §195 The most certain index of the validity of a limestone for Aquatic Buildings. **1809** *Med. Jrnl.* XXI. 101 The character and history of the most celebrated quacks, the ground of their popular fame, and the validity of their various pretences.

†**5.** *pl.* Valid powers or capacities. *Obs.*

1586 DAY *Eng. Secretary* I. (1625) 41 Whose spirits caried with greater efficacie of aspiring eternitie then those whose duller conceits are adapted to more terrene and grosse validities. **1597** HOOKER *Eccl. Pol.* V. lxii. §13 Nature as much as is possible inclineth vnto validities and preseruations. **1607** J. NORDEN *Surv. Dial.* II. 67 You may indeede call these things secrets, because their validities are not suddainly apprehended or found.

6. *attrib.* and *Comb.*, **validity check** *Computers*, a check that data items conform to coding requirements; so **validity checking**.

1957 *Control Engin.* May 113/2 The double entry system of book-keeping is another example of coding the work so that a validity check is readily available. **1982** *What's New in Computing* Nov. 61/1 The validity checks include field length, ranges, check digit verification and table look-up. **1960** *Communications Assoc. Computing Machinery* III. 418 (*heading*) Combining ALGOL statement analysis with validity checking.

'validless, *a.* or *adv.* *rare*$^{-1}$. [f. VALID *a.*] Without strength or force; powerless(ly).

1866 J. B. ROSE tr. *Ovid's Met.* 346 The shield and helm were cloven by the steel, Yet on the body validless it fell.

validly ('vælɪdlɪ), *adv.* [f. as prec. + -LY^{2}.] In a valid manner; with legal validity.

1637 GILLESPIE *Eng.-Pop. Cerem.* III. viii. 173 One simple Presbyter.. can not validly give Ordination. **1681** BAXTER *Answ. Dodwell* iv. 45 May a man be validly a Bishop,.. that believeth not that there is a God? **1767** CHAUNCY *Lett.* (1768) 32 They may be validly commissioned to propagate the Gospel. **1791** BOSWELL *Johnson* I. 137 A Highland gentleman.. once consulted me if he could not validly purchase the chieftainship of his family from the chief. **1863** H. COX *Instit.* I. v. 25 The Court of Exchequer decided that impositions on exports and imports might be validly made by proclamation. **1883** *Weekly Notes* 17 Nov. 170/2 He held that the Rule Committee were validly constituted and their power validly exercised.

Comb. **1848** SOAMES *Latin Church* i. 16 *note*, Nor does the tale itself necessarily imply transubstantiation.. whenever a validly-ordained consecrator intended it.

'validness. *rare.* [-NESS.] Validity.

1727 BAILEY (vol. II), *Validness*, Ability, Power; also Authentickness, &c. **1882** ARNOLD in *19th Cent.* No. 69. 718 Lucidity is the perception of the want of truth and validness in notions long current.

†**'validous**, *a.* *Obs.* [f. L. *valid-us* VALID *a.* + -OUS.] Valid, in various senses.

1603 HARSNET *Pop. Impost.* 98 Because the Consequence is so Validous wee will looke a little into these holy fireworks. *Ibid.* 100 This ranke savor was so Validous and strong that it sented through the glasse. **1611** SPEED *Hist. Gt. Brit.* IX. viii. §37. 553 The other [side urged] against Norwich, that no second election could be validous, vnlesse the former were first annulled. **1635** R. N. tr. *Camden's Eliz.* Introd., In the first Parliament which Queene Mary held.. the marriage.. was judged to be.. validous and available.

valiencie, obs. form of VALIANCY.

valient, obs. form of VALIANT.

†**'valienton.** *Obs.*$^{-1}$ [a. Sp. *valenton*, f. *valiente* valiant.] A bully, braggart.

1681 RYCAUT tr. *Gracian's Critick* 185 The Couragious, and Valientons of the World, after some few bravadoes and blustering words,.. submitted.. to the loss of Liberty.

valinch(er, velinche(r: see quots. and VALENTIA.

1823 E. MOOR *Suffolk Wds.* s.v. *Valentia*,.. I have met with the word in print, spelled *Valinch*. **1847** WEBSTER, *Valinch*, a tube for drawing liquors from a cask by the bung-hole. **1868** *Loftus' Catal. Hydrometers*, etc. 6 Velinchers for sampling casks. **1875** KNIGHT *Dict. Mech.* 2553 *Thief-tube*,.. a sampling-tube; a velinche. **1899** *N. & Q.* 4 Feb. 97/1 The nearest approach to a 'long' measure is the valincher, or valinch, used in sampling 'from the bung'.

valine ('veɪliːn). *Biochem.* [ad. G. *valin* (E. Fischer 1906, in *Ber. d. Deut. Chem. Ges.* XXXIX. 2321), f. G. *valerian-säure* valerianic acid (see VALERIANIC *a.*): see -INE^{5}.] An amino-acid that is an essential nutrient for vertebrates and a general constituent of proteins; α-aminoisovaleric acid, $(CH_3)_2CHCH(NH_2)COOH$.

1907 *Chem. Abstr.* I. 2566 Valine on heating yielded the anhydride. **1962** [see ISOLEUCINE]. **1982** T. I. DIAMONDSTONE in T. M. Devlin *Textbk. Biochem.* xii. 604/1 The diagnosis of a defect in the transamination of valine to α-ketoisovaleric acid was suspected.

valinomycin (ˌvælɪnəʊ'maɪsɪn). *Pharm.* [a. G. *valinomycin* (Brockmann & Schmidt-Kastner 1955, in *Ber. d. Deut. Chem. Ges.* LXXXIII. 57), f. *valin* VALINE (a product of its hydrolysis): see -MYCIN.] A dodecapeptide obtained from the fungus *Streptomyces fulvissimus*, which has antibiotic activity against Gram-positive bacteria and is used experimentally.

1955 *Chem. Abstr.* XLIX. 16068 *Streptomyces fulvissimus* grown in a medium.. gave 2·3g. of dry mycelium (I) per l. It.. gave an oil, which on cooling deposited valinomycin. **1969** *New Scientist* 31 July 225/1 Valinomycin is lethal to cells because it makes the membranes of mitochondria permeable to ions, particularly potassium, and stops them making energy available to all the other processes in the cell. **1979** *Sci. Amer.* Sept. 77/3 To prove that the gradient existed between the mitochondria and the surrounding cytoplasm the investigators added the drug valinomycin, which increases the rate of cell respiration and establishes an equilibrium in the concentration of potassium ions on both sides of the mitochondrial membrane.

valise (və'liːs, və'liːz). Forms: 7 **vallies, valice**, 8 **valize, valaise**, 9 *Sc.* **wal-, wallise, vallise**, 7– **valise.** [a. F. *valise* (1568), ad. It. *valigia* (Sp. *balija*), corresponding to med.L. *valisia* (1407), *valixia, valesia* (1298), of doubtful origin.

In Sandys *Travels* (1615) 115 the form *valeisa* is used.]

1. A travelling case or portmanteau, now usually made of leather and of a size suitable for carrying by hand, formerly also for strapping to the saddle of a horse. Now chiefly *U.S.*

1633 B. JONSON *Tale of Tub* II. i, I promise To keep my master's privities seal'd up In the vallies of my trust, lock'd close for ever. **1644** D. HUME *Hist. Douglas* 95 The Country people.. sometimes robbed them of their horses, sometimes of their valises and luggage. **1660** F. BROOKE tr. *Le Blanc's Trav.* 317 Poor Alari lost above two thousand franks which he had in his Valice. **1713** C'TESS WINCHELSEA *Misc. Poems* 130 Bringing their Noddles, and Valizes pack'd With Mysteries, from Shops and Taylors wreck'd. **1785** *Arab. Nts. Entert.* 576 Having brought a valaise along with him, he put as much gold into it as his horse could carry. **1797** JEFFERSON *Writ.* (1859) IV. 156 Your impatience to receive your valise and its key was natural. **1815** SCOTT *Guy M.* xxii, He drew the girths of his saddle, adjusted the walise, and put on the bridle. **1839** DICKENS *Nickleby* xiii, He packed up a few clothes in a small leathern valise. **1884** E. YATES *Rec. & Exp.* I. 46 The letters being enclosed in leather valises, which were strapped behind the post-boys.

b. *Mil.* A cylindrical cloth or leather case adapted for carrying the kit or outfit of a soldier, esp. of a cavalryman or artilleryman.

1833 *Reg. & Instr. Cavalry* I. 83 The valise being.. lightly stuffed with hay. **1851** *Ord. & Regul. R.E.* xxvii. 124 The Boxes of the Non-Commissioned Officers, and the Valises of the Men, to be placed under the foot of the Bedstead. **1877** *Field Exerc. Infantry* 410 The Officer Commanding a piquet will decide if patrols are to wear Valises or not.

2. *attrib.* in *valise dee, equipment, -lock, -saddle, strap*, etc.

1852 BURN *Milit. Dict.* II. s.v., Valise or baggage-straps. **1875** KNIGHT *Dict. Mech.* 2688/1 *Valise-lock*, a small trunk-lock. *Ibid.*, A valise-saddle is placed on each off-horse of an artillery-carriage. **1898** *Allbutt's Syst. Med.* V. 853 The modern valise equipment is less injurious to the young soldier than the old knapsack. **1898** *Daily News* 12 Dec. 9/2 The greatcoat straps will be passed downwards, through the valise dees.

Valium ('væliəm). *Pharm.* Also **valium.** [Etym. uncertain.] A proprietary name for the drug diazepam, $C_{16}H_{13}N_2OCl$, used esp. as an anti-anxiety agent, hypnotic, and muscle relaxant given orally or by injection; a tablet of this.

1961 *Official Gaz.* (U.S. Patent Office) 10 Oct. TM 50/1 Hoffmann-La Roche Inc., Nutley, N.J... *Valium* for psychotherapeutic agent. **1962** *Trade Marks Jrnl.* 10 Jan. 32/2 *Valium*... All goods included in Class 5. Roche Products Limited,.. Welwyn Garden City, Hertfordshire; manufacturers. **1972** *Guardian* 18 Sept. 14/5 She had taken an overdose of Valium after getting drunk the night before. **1976** C. BLACKWOOD *Stepdaughter* i. 59, I have been swallowing fistfuls of valium to try to calm myself. **1979** N. MAILER *Executioner's Song* (1980) I. xx. 342 Even with two Valiums to mellow her out, she felt crazy inside every time she thought about Barrett selling her car, so kept waiting for the Valium to take effect, but they didn't.

Hence **'Valiumed** *ppl. a.*, affected by taking Valium.

1973 M. AMIS *Rachel Papers* 21 My Valium-ed mother fluttered between them on the sofa. **1978** 'P. MANN' *Steal Big* ii. 16, I spent about a year this way.. Valiumed out of my skull for ten terrible days.

valk, obs. Sc. form of WAKE *v.*, WALK *v.*

valkin, -yne, obs. Sc. forms of WAKEN *v.*

'Valkyr, abbreviated form of VALKYRIE.

1841 CARLYLE *Heroes* i. (1904) 31 Of the Valkyrs and the Hall of Odin. *Ibid.*, The Valkyrs are Choosers of the Slain.

Val'kyrian, *a.* Also **Valkyriean.** [f. next.] Of or concerning the Valkyries.

1847 TENNYSON *Princ.* IV. 121 Ourself have often tried Valkyrian hymns. **1937** J. W. DAY *Sporting Adv.* 250 They came baying, like Valkyriean hounds, the skeins of brent. **1938** —— *Dog in Sport* xix. 266 On the hillside, far beyond the wood.. he lifted like a Valkyrian shadow against the clear horizon of a mountainside that had seen his kind since the birth of history. **1977** D. WILLIAMS *Treasure by Degrees* iii. 31 She opened her arms wide.. in a Valkyrian gesture. **1981** J. M. BRINNIN *Beau Voyage* (1982) 173/2 German ships.. would become.. galleries of an aspiration so Valkyrian that one would think only megalomaniacs might dally there.

Valkyrie ('vælkɪrɪ, væl'kɪrɪ). Forms: α. 8–9 **valkyria** (*pl.* **-iur**, 9 **-iæ**). β. 8–9 **valkerie** (9 **-kery**), 9– **valkyrie.** [a. ON. *valkyrja* (pl. *-kyrjur*), f. *val-r* those slain in battle + *-kyrja* chooser, f. *kur-* (:–*kuz-*), ablaut stem of *kjósa* to choose. Cf. OE. *wælcyrie* (*-ʒe, -iʒe*), *-kyrie* WALKYRIE.] In Scandinavian mythology, one or other of the twelve war-maidens supposed to hover over battlefields and to conduct the fallen warriors to Valhalla.

α. **1768** GRAY *Fatal Sisters* Note, The *Valkyriur* were female Divinities, Servants of Odin (or Woden) in the Gothic mythology. **1778** MRS. GRANT OF LAGGAN *Lett. Mount.* (1807) II. ix. 55 The prophetic Valkyria may once more say [etc.]. **1806** W. HERBERT *Sel. Icel. Poetry* I. 119 Two of the Valkyriæ or virgins of slaughter. *a* **1835** MRS. HEMANS *Sword of the Tomb* Poems (1875) 339 The far-renown'd Whom the bright Valkyriur's warning voice Had call'd to the banquet where gods rejoice.

β. **1770** PERCY tr. *Mallet's Northern Antiq.* I. 102 There are other virgins in Valhall;.. they are called Valkeries. *Ibid.* II. 99 These Goddesses are called Valkyries. **1784** JERNINGHAM *Rise Scand. Poetry* Advt. p. iii, The Valkeries are a female troop whom Odin sends to the field of battle upon invisible steeds. **1801** M. G. LEWIS *Tales of Wonder*, *Sword of Angantyr* xxxiii, 'Tis the Valkyries who sing, While they spin thy vital thread. *a* **1843** SOUTHEY *Death of Odin*, No virgin goddess him shall call;.. No Valkery for him prepare The smiling mead. **1881** DU CHAILLU *Land of Midnight Sun* II. 420 Are you Scandinavian valkyries who travel through the air?

†**vall.** *Obs.*$^{-1}$ [ad. L. *vall-is.*] A valley.

1611 CHAPMAN *Iliad* IV. 479 As from hils, raine waters headlong fall, That all waies eate huge Ruts, which, met, in one bed, fill a vall With such a confluence of streames.

vall, southern dial. var. FALL *v.*; obs. Sc. f. WALL *sb.*, WAW *sb.*, WELL *sb.*

vallal, southern dial. var. FAL-LAL *sb.*

†**va'llancy.** *Obs.*$^{-1}$ [prob. the surname *Vallancey.*] Used *attrib.* to designate a form of wig.

1674 DRYDEN *Epil. opening New House* 8 Criticks in plume and white vallancy Wig, Who lolling on our foremost Benches sit.

vallar ('vælə(r)), *a.* *Roman Antiq.* [ad. L. *vallār-is*, f. *vall-um* or *vall-us* rampart. Cf. It. *vallare*, Sp. *valar*, F. *vallaire.*] Of a crown or garland: Bestowed as a distinction on the first soldier to mount the enemy's rampart. (Cf. MURAL *a.*^{1} 1 b.)

1542 UDALL *Erasm. Apoph.* 255 Augustus used to geve golden trappour muche sooner.. then garlandes, vallares, and muralles. **1600** HOLLAND *Pliny* II. 115 The Vallare and Murall Chaplets bestowed upon brave knights and valiant soldiers, who.. mounted the wals in the assault of a citie. *a* **1660** *Contemp. Hist. Irel.* (Ir. Archæol. Soc.) II. 62 To whom shall be given now the ciuicke, murall, vallare, and nauals garlands, that the Romaines were wont to graunte theire respectiue conquerours? **1706** PHILLIPS (ed. Kersey) s.v., Vallar Crown. **1725** [see GARLAND *sb.* 3 c]. *c* **1828** BERRY *Encycl. Her.* I. Gloss.

So ˈ**vallary** *a.* Also † **vaˈllarial** *a. Obs.*

1688 HOLME *Armoury* IV. iv. (Roxb.) 294/2 He beareth for his crest, a Greyhounds head sable, out of a crowne Vallariall, Or. **1777** PORNY *Heraldry* (ed. 3) 207 The Vallary or Castrense-Crown was of gold, formed like a circle with Pales or Pallisadoes on the top of it. **1863** BURKE *Viciss. Families* Ser. III. 143 His famous attack on the..Earl of Desmond, at Kilmallock, where he won his gold spurs, and his vallary crown.

vallate (ˈvælət), *a. rare*⁻¹. [ad. L. *vallāt-us*, pa. pple. of *vallāre* to circumvallate.] Having a raised outer edge.

1878 *Ann. Nat. Hist.* 5th Ser. II. 37 In its compressed vallate character, proliferous growth, and marginal apertures, it is identical with many of the siliceous sponges.

ˈ**vallated**, *a. rare*⁻¹. [f. as prec. + -ED.] Surrounded by or as by a wall.

1888 *Science* XII. 305 The favorite but not vallated domain of literature is æsthetics in its true meaning.

vaˈllation. *rare.* [ad. late L. *vallātio*, f. L. *vallāre* (see VALLATE *a.*), f. *vallum* rampart.] A ridge, wall, or bank of earth thrown up as a defence or protection; an earthwork or fortification of this nature.

1664 EVELYN *Sylva* 112 Two hedges, with their Vallations and Trenches, will be requisite in all the Round; *viz.* one next to the Enclosure, the other about the thicket, to fence it from Cattle. **1781** WARTON *Hist. Kiddington* 70 The vallation..called Dyke-Hills, consisting of two ridges or borders with an intermediate trench,..is not Roman. **1799** R. WARNER *Walk* (1800) 12 He may..please his fancy with discriminating between the vallations of the Celtic aborigenes, and the huge mounds of their Saxon invaders.

† ˈ**vallatory**, *a. Obs.*⁻¹ [f. L. *vall-um* rampart.] Used or adapted for measuring a wall, etc.

a **1682** SIR T. BROWNE *Misc. Tracts* i. (1683) 82 With such differences of Reeds, Vallatory, Sagittary, Scriptory, and others they might be furnished in Judæa.

valle, southern ME. variant of FALL *v.*

‖**vallecula** (væˈlɛkjʊlə). Pl. **-ulæ**. [Late L. *vallecula*, var. of L. *vallicula*, dim. of *vallēs*, *vallis* VALLEY *sb.* Cf. F. *vallécule*.]

1. *Anat.* A furrow, fissure, or fossa; *spec.* = VALLEY *sb.* 6.

1859 *Todd's Cycl. Anat.* V. 883 Valley, or vallecula, of Haller. **1875** *Encycl. Brit.* I. 871/2 This lobe forms a well-defined inferior vermiform process, which lies at the bottom of a deep fossa or *vallecula*. **1897** *Allbutt's Syst. Med.* IV. 782 The spaces between these [glosso-epiglottic] folds are named the valleculæ.

2. *Bot.* A groove or channel; a sulcus or stria.

1856 HENSLOW *Bot. Terms* 211 *Vallecula*, a depressed space (interstice) between the primary 'Ridges' on the fruit of Umbelliferæ.

Hence **vaˈllecular** *a.*

1875 BENNETT & DYER *Sachs's Bot.* 376 The vallecular canals, which correspond to the furrows, arise in the fundamental tissue by separation.

† **vallente**. *Obs.*⁻¹ [app. ad. med.L. *valentia* VALENCY.] Power, might.

1475 *Bk. Noblesse* (1860) 7 [There are] v. causes principalle [for making war]: three of them bene of righte: and the other tweyne of vallente.

valler, obs. Sc. form of WALLER.

valleriite (vəˈlɪərɪaɪt). *Min.* [ad. Sw. *valleriit* (C. W. Blomstrand 1870, in *Öfversigt af K. Vetensk.-Akad. Förhandlingar* XXVII. 19), f. the name of J. G. Vallerius (1683–1742), Swedish mineralogist: see -ITE¹.] A hexagonal basic sulphide of iron, copper, magnesium, and aluminium found in high-temperature copper and iron deposits as minute cream or yellowish crystals.

1875 E. S. DANA *Dana's Syst. Min.* (ed. 5) App. II. 58 Valleriite... Massive, without a trace of crystalline texture. **1976** *Contrib. Mineral. & Petrol.* LV. 265 Chromian valleriite occurs as a replacement product of chrome spinel in the Nepean and Perseverance nickel-iron ore sulphide deposits of Western Australia.

† ˈ**vallet**. *Obs.*⁻¹ [Irreg. dimin. of VALLEY *sb.* Cf. VALL.] A small valley.

a **1647** HABINGTON *Surv. Worc.* (Worcs. Hist. Soc.) I. III. 450 In the myddest of thys vallet on a littell hyll..standethe the Churche with the Mannor house.

vallew, obs. form of VALUE.

valley (ˈvælɪ), *sb.* Forms: α. 4–5 **valeie** (4 **ualeie**), 4–6 **valei** (5 *Sc.* **walei**, **wale**, **vale**), 4 **valce**; 4–5 **valeye** (4 **ualeye**), 4–7 **valey** (4 **waley**); 4 **valleie**, 4, 6 *Sc.*, **valle**, 6 **vallei**, 6– **valley**; *Sc.* and *north.* 4 **valaye**, 4–6 **valay**, 5 **wala**, **wallay**, 6 **vallay**. β. 7 **vally**, **vallie**, *pl.* 6– **vallies**. [a. OF. *valee* (AF. pl. *valeys*), *vallee* (mod.F. *vallée*), early OF. *vallede*, = Prov. *vallada*, It. *vallata*, f. L. *vallis*, *vallēs*: see VALE *sb.*]

1. a. A long depression or hollow lying between hills or stretches of high ground and usually having a river or stream flowing along its bottom.

In ordinary use a *valley* is distinguished from a *vale* by having less width and a steeper slope on either side.

α. **1297** R. GLOUC. (Rolls) 1277 Þo he com nei kaunterburi In a valeie biside He sei þe emperours ost. **13..** *Guy Warw.* 3876 Smerteliche he dede him in þe ways, Ouer þe dounes & þe valeys. *c* **1340** HAMPOLE *Pr. Consc.* 4796 For hilles and valeis sal turned be In-til playn, and made even to se. **1375** BARBOUR *Bruce* vii. 4 In-till þe wod soyn enterit he, And held doun toward a vale, Quhar throu þe vod a vattir ran. *c* **1450** *Merlin* xiii. 195 He shewde hym the valey be the wode side. **1490** CAXTON *Eneydos* xv. 56 The reyne russhynge doun from the mountaynes descended in to the valeyes. **1535** COVERDALE *Luke* iii. 5 Euery valley shalbe fylled, and euery mountayne & hyll shalbe brought lowe. **1577** GOOGE tr. *Heresbach's Husb.* 45 Choose suche a valley, where the water can neither lye long, nor runne away to fast. **1611** SHAKS. *Wint. T.* v. i. 206 We are not (Sir) nor are we like to be: The Starres (I see) will kisse the Valleyes first. **1697** DAMPIER *Voy.* I. ii. 18 Our new Guide..crost another River, and enter'd into a large Valley of the fattest Land I did ever take notice of. **1773** COOK *1st Voy.* I. xvi. in *Hawkesw. Voy.* II. 172 To trace our river up the valley from whence it issues, and examine how far it's banks were inhabited. **1794** MRS. RADCLIFFE *Myst. Udolpho* iii, As they advanced, the valley opened. **1815** ELPHINSTONE *Acc. Caubul* (1842) I. 49 We marched up the valley, which became narrower as we advanced. **1872** RAYMOND *Statist. Mines & Mining* 247 They cannot be of large extent, as the valleys are all narrow, and without bottoms on either side.

β. **1596** MASCALL *Cattle* 253 Goats; their keeper ought for to be..bolde, for to go with them through vallies. **1625** N. CARPENTER *Geogr. Del.* II. x. 169 Plants, and Vegetalls for the most part prosper best in the vallies and plaines. **1663** S. PATRICK *Parab. Pilgrim* xxxvi. (1687) 461 Believe not me but your self..that these Vallies are watered from above. **1726** LEONI *Alberti's Archit.* I. 65/1 Hills..with..little Vallies between.., and very difficult of access thro' the narrow passes of the Vallies. **1777** W. DALRYMPLE *Trav. Sp. & Port.* ii, The verdant banks of the river, with the Indian corn in the vallies. **1827** J. F. COOPER *Prairie* i. I. 18 In the little vallies, which..occurred at every mile of their progress. **1849** JAMES *Woodman* iii, A faint, blueish mist prevented the eye from penetrating into the deeper vallies.

b. Const. *of* (the distinctive name of the valley).

c **1290** *S. Eng. Leg.* I. 5/148 Ase he in þe ualeye of Ebron leouede with teone and wo. **13..** *K. Alis.* 7027 And in þe valey of Jurdan, þey founden eddren mony on. *c* **1380** WYCLIF *Sel. Wks.* II. 405 Wheþer þat Crist shal come into þe valey of Josaphath or [etc.]. **1535** COVERDALE *Ps.* lix. 6, I wil deuyde Sichem, & mete out the valley of Suchoth. **1611** BIBLE *Ps.* lxxxiv. 6 Who passing through the valley of Baca, make it a well. **1667** MILTON *P.L.* I. 404 The pleasant Valley of Hinnom. **1726** GORDON *Itin. Sept.* 55 That eminent Ground, which bounds the Valley of Kilsyth to the Southward. **1833** LYELL *Princ. Geol.* III. 305 The valley of Kingsclere,..in Berkshire, is about five miles long and two in breadth.

c. Without article.

c **1470** HENRY *Wallace* IV. 684 Thai maid To rype the wood, bath wala, slonk, and slaid. **1667** MILTON *P.L.* IX. 116 Sweet interchange Of Hill and Vallie, Rivers, Woods and Plaines. **1784** COWPER *Task* I. 322 A spacious map Of hill and valley interpos'd between. **1859** TENNYSON *Marr. Geraint* 247 Out of town and valley came a noise. **1865** H. H. DIXON *Field & Fern* 233 Wood and valley backed up by a Cheviot hill compose a pleasant landscape.

d. The extensive stretch of flattish country drained or watered by one or other of the larger river-systems of the world.

c **1790** *Encycl. Brit.* (ed. 3) VI. 393/2 In those early ages..a certain people descended from the mountains near the cataracts into the valley overflowed by the Nile. **1843** *Penny Cycl.* XXV. 472/1 Dividing the valley of the Euphrates from the rivers which flow into the Black Sea. **1876** *Encycl. Brit.* IV. 223/2 Surface 'drift' deposits..occur..in the valley of the Amazon westward to..Peru.

e. *Geol.* (See quot. 1839.)

1833 LYELL *Princ. Geol.* III. 305 Dr. Buckland on Valleys of Elevation. **1839** G. ROBERTS *Dict. Geol.*, *Valleys of elevation*, those which seem to have originated in a fracture of the strata, and a movement of the fractured part upwards.

2. a. In figurative uses.

valley of the shadow (of death): see SHADOW *sb.* 1 b.

1382 WYCLIF *Isaiah* xxii. 1 The charge of the valey of viseoun. **1411–2** HOCCLEVE *De Reg. Princ.* 4444 The swete venym of his tonge gydeth His lord vnto þe valeie of dirknesse. **1426** LYDG. *De Guil. Pilgr.* 17447, I was engendryd fyrst in helle;..in that Valey Infernal I was begete. **1781** COWPER *Conversat.* 636 Youth has a sprightliness and fire to boast, That in the valley of decline are lost. **1822** SHELLEY *Triumph Life* 397 If..Thou comest from the realm without a name Into this valley of perpetual dream. **1851** ROBERTSON *Serm.* Ser. II. i. (1864) 18 You must be content with the quiet valleys of existence. **1882** J. PARKER *Apostolic Life* I. 78 Thou knowest how much we are in the valley, and how often we pass through dark places.

b. *valley of tears*: see VALE *sb.*¹ 2 b.

[**1382** WYCLIF *Ps.* lxxxiii. 6 In the valei of teris, in the place that he sette.] *a* **1400** *Prymer* (1891) 51 To the we syȝen gronynge and wepynge in this ualeye of teeres. *c* **1450** tr. *De Imitatione* III. xxiii. 92 In þis valey of teres þere comeþ many euell þinges. **1894** J. H. S. (*title*), The Valley of Tears... The Consolations of God.

3. *transf.* **a.** A depression or hollow suggestive of a valley; *esp.* a trough between sea-waves.

1611 SHAKS. *Wint. T.* II. iii. 100 His Fore-head, nay, the Valley, The pretty dimples of his Chin, and Cheeke. **1691** RAY *Creation* II. (1704) 298 The Eyes are sunk in a Convenient Valley. **1845** GOSSE *Ocean* iv. (1849) 164 The little Petrel flits hither and thither, now treading the brow of the watery hill, now sweeping through the valley. **1888** STEVENSON *Black Arrow* 176 The *Good Hope* swooped dizzily down into the valley of the rollers.

b. *spec.* A region of a graph which is shaped like a valley, or a set of low values of a varying quantity which would form such a region if plotted as a graph.

1935 [see HIGH FREQUENCY 1 b]. **1959** *Daily Tel.* 11 Dec. 1/1 A prompt decision by the Government is urged, that the age can be compulsorily raised in one of the three 'valley' years between 'bulges' in the number of children, 1966, 1967 and 1968. **1968** F. B. MORINIGO *tr. von Buttlar's Nucl. Physics* xiii. 103 Nuclei that can decay in two ways..are always odd-odd nuclei and lie near the bottom of the valley of stability. **1973** *Physics Bull.* Apr. 239/1 The spectrometer is claimed to provide..high resolution analysis. Its resolution is more than 10,000 with a 10% valley. **1974** ADBY & DEMPSTER *Introd. Optimization Methods* i. 16 Long curved narrow valleys are especially troublesome to simpler optimization procedures.

4. *techn.* **a.** The depressed angle formed by the meeting (at the bottom) of two sloping sides of a composite roof, or by the slope of a roof and a wall; a gutter.

1690 LEYBOURN *Curs. Math.* 901 The Bricklayer sometimes will require to have running measure for Hyps and Valleys. **1703** [R. NEVE] *City & C. Purchaser* 162 Of measuring Vallies, or Gutters in Tiling. **1782** *Phil. Trans.* LXXII. 360 In like manner the two conductors from the chimnies A and C united in the valley of the roof between them. **1833** LOUDON *Encycl. Archit.* §83 To steady and support the lower edges of slates finishing against vallies. **1866** FITZPATRICK *Sham Squire* 113 Murphy hurried Lord Edward to the roof of the warehouse, and with some difficulty persuaded him to lie in the valley. **1899** BARING-GOULD *Book of West* II. xii. 175 Here also are some quaint old slated houses; the valleys are not leaded.

b. A tile used in roofing a valley.

1833 LOUDON *Encycl. Archit.* §296 The ridge pieces, hips, and valleys, to be seven inches by one and a half inches.

† **5.** *Fr. Hist.* = PLAIN *sb.*¹ 6. (Cf. MOUNTAIN 6.)

1792 *Pref. Expl. New Terms* in *Ann. Reg.* p. xii, The *Valley*. The lower seats; and these in the middle of the hall of the Assembly.

6. *Anat.* (See quots. and cf. VALLECULA 1.)

1842 *Encycl. Brit.* (ed. 7) II. 807/2 A large hollow between the hemispheres [of the cerebellum]..is the small valley (*vallecula*) of Halley. *c* **1845** *Todd's Cycl. Anat.* III. 688/2 A deep fissure which proceeds..backwards along the median line..is called the valley.

7. a. *attrib.* and *Comb.* in sense 1 (freq. denoting 'situated in a valley'), as ***valley-bottom***, ***-cottage***, ***-dweller***, ***-fountain***, ***-gate***, ***-glacier***, ***-glade***, ***-mist***, ***-mouth***, ***-tomb***, ***-wall***, etc.; ***valley-like*** adj., ***-ward(s)*** adv.; **valley fever** *U.S.* = COCCIDIOIDOMYCOSIS; **Valley Girl** *U.S.*, a teenage girl from San Fernando Valley in southern California; also = *Valleyspeak* below; also *attrib.*; **Valleyspeak** *U.S.*, a form of slang originating among teenage girls in San Fernando Valley in southern California; **valley tan** *U.S. local*, a kind of whisky produced in Salt Lake Valley, Utah; **valley train** *Physical Geogr.*, a deposit of glacial outwash along a valley bottom.

1863 B. TAYLOR *Hannah Thurston* xxix. 373 The elms..had grown up since the *valley-bottom was cleared. **1905** A. R. WALLACE *My Life* II. 153 The little valley-bottoms were complete flower gardens. **1859** MEREDITH *Poet. Wks.* (1912) 92 For me yon *valley-cottage beckons warm. **1927** PEAKE & FLEURE *Peasants & Potters* iii. 37 It [*sc.* the wild ass] was certainly tamed by the Libyans..from whom it reached the *valley-dwellers not long after 4000 B.C. [**1937** *Jrnl. Amer. Med. Assoc.* 3 July 66/1 The disease is often diagnosed as erythema nodosum and is popularly known as 'San Joaquin Valley fever' or desert fever.] **1938** *Ibid.* 8 Oct. 1362/2 It has been found that a symptom complex like that of the first of these patients is common in the San Joaquin Valley; so common, in fact, that it is popularly known as '*valley fever' or 'desert fever'. **1979** *Tucson* (Arizona) *Citizen* 20 Sept. 1D/3 He's already a full-fledged Arizonan because Homero is recovering from a bout with valley fever. *c* **1600** SHAKS. *Sonn.* cliii, In a could *vallie-fountaine. **1535** COVERDALE *2 Chron.* xxvi. 9 Osias buylded towres..vpon the cornerporte, and on the *valley gate. **1982** *Guardian* 26 Oct. 8/7 The *Valley Girl, well-heeled with time on her hands, suburban and middle-class, is, first and foremost, a consumer. **1982** *Time* 8 Nov. 91/1 Where is the next generation of slang to come from? Not from Valley Girl, the argot made famous lately by singer Frank Zappa and his daughter. **1983** *N.Y. Times Mag.* 21 Aug. 11/1 The Brooklyn accent,..even California valley-girl slang—these are as much part of our linguistic heritage as computer jargon,..and words ending in *gate*. **1984** *Daily Mail* 20 Oct. 12/1 But the stilettoed, 10th-grade, 'Valley Girls', who stalk the West Coast Galleries..have been replaced by the Mall Girls. **1874** GEIKIE *Gt. Ice Age* (1894) 512 The *valley-glaciers becoming confluent in their lower reaches. **1820** KEATS *Ode Nightingale* viii, Now 'tis buried deep In the next *valley-glades. **1878** HUXLEY *Physiogr.* 28 Along the banks of the Thames and its tributary streams there is a bed of *valley-gravel. **1894** *Geol. Mag.* Oct. 466 The amphitheatre form of terraced land is always a *valley head. **1871** B. TAYLOR *Faust* III. (1875) II. 184 The *valley-hills That in the rear of Sparta northwards rise aloft. **1852** THOREAU *Lett.* (1865) 66 The vast *valley-like 'spore'..of some celestial beast. **1859** CORNWALLIS *New World* I. 172 A solitary moorland with valley-like undulations. **1894** *Geol. Mag.* Oct. 466 The outflow of the stream—the *valley-maker—marks ordinarily the base of the amphitheatre. **1930** BLUNDEN *Summer's Fancy* 35 Groves crouched in the deep Of *valley-mist. **1923** D. H. LAWRENCE *Birds, Beasts & Flowers* 188 The trees of the Lobo dark *valley-mouth. **1655** MOUFET & BENNET *Health's Improv.* (1746) 86 Contrariwise the *Valley People ..are ever heavy spirited, dull, and sickly. **1869** TOZER *Highl. Turkey* I. 363 The four great *valley-plains..divided by lateral spurs. **1876** T. HARDY *Ethelberta* (1890) 243 A thin young man..who arrived at the castle by the *valley-road from Knollsea. *c* **1550** ROLLAND *Crt. Venus* I. 39, I walkit furth on be ane *valay syde. **1872** INGRAHAM *Pillar of Fire* 578 Moses and the Israelites pursued their way up the cliffs of the valley-sides. **1983** *Washington Post Mag.* 23 Jan.

8 'The creative act that doesn't respond to some kind of social need isn't going to be picked up.' Clearly *Valley-speak struck a responsive chord. 1841 W. C. Bryant *Walk at Sunset* Wks. 44 Oh, let me, by the crystal *valley-stream, Wander. 1871 Palgrave *Lyr. Poems* 89 Joining then the *valley-streamlet. 1860 *Mountaineer* (Salt Lake City, Utah) 16 June 169/3 Which food do you prefer, rum, mixed drinks or *Valley Tan? 1942 *Oregon Hist. Q.* Dec. 339 Only among his cronies could he crack a quart of valley tan..with any freedom. 1930 Blunden *Poems* 290 Cause not our very joy to go Among old *valley-tombs of flesh and blood and years. 1892 *Ann. Rep. State Geologist 1891* (Geol. Survey New Jersey) 96 The drift thus deposited in a valley has sometimes been called a *valley train of sand and gravel. 1954 W. D. Thornbury *Princ. Geomorphol.* xv. 377 Study of the valley trains extending down from the Alps led Penck and Brückner to a recognition of four stages of glaciation. 1974 *Encycl. Brit. Micropædia* VII. 636/3 When confined within valley walls, the outwash deposit is known as a valley train. 1931 H. Crane *Let.* 21 Sept. (1965) 381 With the high *valley walls in the Wizard's circle. 1974 Valley wall [see *valley train* above]. 1894 *Book News* Mar. 274 Dark belts of woodland, with *valleyward the white gleam of the Froom. 1880 'Mark Twain' *Tramp Abroad* xxxv. 387 He went swinging along *valleywards again. 1962 H. R. Loyn *Anglo-Saxon England* i. 10 Native inhabitants..survived and came to terms, attracted valleywards by force or by superior agricultural technique. 1883 *Science* I. 326/1 These lakes are perhaps formed by a local depression of the *valley-way.

b. **valley-lily**, the lily of the valley.

1597 Gerarde *Herbal* II. lxxxvii. 332 The flowers of the Valley Lillie. 1766 M. Bruce *Lochleven* Wks. (1914) 206 Her breast was fairer than the vernal bloom Of valley-lily. 1818 Keats *Endymion* I. 156 Wild thyme, and valley-lilies whiter still Than Leda's love. *a*1850 Beddoes *Poems, Lily of the Valley* 201 The birthday-hours Of the valley-lily.

c. ***valley of death tree***, the Upas-tree.

1888 in *Cassell's Encycl. Dict.*

8. *attrib.* in sense 4, as ***valley-board, -gutter, -piece, -rafter.***

1823 P. Nicholson *Pract. Builder* 230 The valley-rafters of a roof. 1833 Loudon *Encycl. Archit.* §852 Proper valley boards are to be put for the lead valleys. *Ibid.* §1350 A valley-gutter between two roofs. 1842 Gwilt *Encycl. Arch.* 1049 The rafter which supports the valley is called the *valley rafter* or *valley piece*, and the board fixed upon it for the leaden gutter to rest upon is called the *valley board.*

Hence **'valleyful**, the fill of a valley; **'valleyite**, an inhabitant of a valley; **'valleylet**, a small valley.

1866 G. Greenwood *Rain & Rivers* 188 Its infinite ramification of stream and valley, streamlet and valleylet. 1890 *Longman's Mag.* July 341 A whole valleyful of appropriate plants. 1893 *Outing* XXII. 136/1 While I roamed about the burying-place of the valleyites.

'valley, *v. rare.* [f. the sb.]

1. *intr.* To form a hollow or hollows resembling a valley.

*a*1552 Leland *Itin.* (1769) V. 51 A Peace of this Roke is fallen, and valleith [*v.r.* valleyeth] after a strange fascion. 1879 Meredith *Egoist* I. xviii. 323 In the billowy white of the dress ballooning and valleying softly.

†**2.** *trans.* To adjoin as a valley. *Obs.*$^{-1}$

1635 J. Hayward tr. *Biondi's Banish'd Virg.* 36 In a deep bottome that vallied a steeper precipice.

3. To make valleys in, to furrow.

*c*1825 Beddoes *Poems, Midnight Hymn* 111 The slaves of Egypt..Vallied the unaccustomed sea.

valley, obs. var. vlei.

'valleyed, *ppl. a.* Also **vallied**. [f. valley *sb.*] Situated in a valley.

1844 *Catholic Weekly Instructor* 31 He left the sunny Italy.., and from his vallied home, wandered [etc.].

vallidom. *north. dial.* [Irreg. f. *vally* value *sb.*] The value or worth *of* a thing.

1790 Grose *Prov. Gloss., Vallidom*, the value of. 1828- in north. dial. glossaries (Yks., Durh., Cumbld., Lancs., Linc.). 1887 A. E. Barr *Border Shepherdess* iv. 57 He knew the vallidom of everything he possessed to a halfpenny.

†**vallie.** *Obs.*$^{-1}$ [f. L. *vall-um* vallum.] Rampart, wall.

1602 Warner *Alb. Eng. Epit.* (1612) 356 Seuerus his forced vallie, with other strong and huge labors and fabrications.

Vallis'caulian, *sb.* and *a.* [See def.]

a. *sb. pl.* An order of ascetic monks, forming a branch of the Benedictines, founded at Val des Choux (*Vallis Caulium*) in 1193. **b.** *adj.* Of or belonging to the Valliscaulians or their order.

1882 *Athenæum* 8 Apr. 442/1 Three priories of the Valliscaulian Order were founded in the remoter districts of Scotland during the reign of Alexander II. 1888 Rankin *Handbk. Ch. Scotl.* (ed. 4) 125 The Rented or endowed religious,..subdivided into Benedictines, Cistercians, Carthusians, Vallis-Caulians, and Trinitarians.

Vallombrosan (væləm'brəʊsən), *a.* and *sb.* [f. *Vallombrosa* near Florence, Italy + -an.]

A. *adj.* Of or pertaining to Vallombrosa; *spec.* designating a Benedictine congregation established there in the eleventh century by Giovanni Gualberto. **B.** *sb.* A monk of this congregation.

1851 E. B. Browning *Casa Guidi Windows* I. xxix. 77 The Vallombrosan brooks were strewn as thick. 1884 A. J. C. Hare *Cities Central Italy* I. xi. 297 The habit of the Vallombrosans was light grey, but the late monks wore a black cloak and a large hat when abroad. 1901 M. Carmichael *In Tuscany* 141 They were succeeded in 1793 by monks of the Vallombrosan Congregation of Benedictines. 1922 Joyce *Ulysses* 332 The monks of Benedict of Spoleto, Carthusians and Camaldolesi,.. Oratorians and Vallombrosans.

Vallon, obs. form of Walloon.

vallonia, var. valonia.

vallor, -ow, obs. forms of voller *dial.*

Vallota (væ'ləʊtə). *Bot.* [mod.L., f. the name of the French botanist Antoine *Vallot* (1594–1671).] A genus of amaryllidaceous plants, characterized by rich scarlet flowers, and consisting of but one species, *V. purpurea*, the Scarborough lily.

1837 W. Herbert *Amaryllidaceæ* 133. 1852 G. W. Johnston *Cott. Gard. Dict.* 904 A cross-seedling..obtained ..from *Cyrtanthus obliquus*, which no one could distinguish from a Vallota of the same age. 1882 *Garden* 25 Mar. 206/2 Vallotas may be increased by the quantities of offsets which they produce.

vallow, obs. form of value.

†**vallow deer**, obs. variant of fallow-deer.

1657 R. Ligon *Barbadoes* 104 Herds of Vallow Deer.

‖**vallum** ('væləm). [L., f. *vallus* stake, palisade.]

1. A wall or rampart of earth, sods, or stone, erected as a permanent means of defence; *esp.* one of those constructed by the Romans in northern England and central Scotland.

1610 Holland *Camden's Brit.* 790 Wee gather out of Bede, that the said Vallum or Rampier, was nothing else but a wall of turffes. 1699 Temple *Hist. Eng.* 38 Agricola began, and in some manner finished, a Wall or Vallum, upon that narrow Space of Land. 1726 A. Gordon *Itin. Sept.* 52 Thence the *Vallum* descends from the above-mentioned Hill, to another Brook. 1781 Warton *Hist. Kiddington* 55 The vallum or ridged bank..crossing the Ikenild-street within two miles of Ewelme. 1851 D. Wilson *Preh. Ann.* (1863) II. III. ii. 79 This British Vallum—a vast rampart of earth and stone strengthened by a fosse. 1879 Lubbock *Sci. Lect.* vi. 172 He would walk round the ancient vallum,..and wonder at the mechanical skill which could have moved such ponderous masses.

2. In Roman castrametation, a palisaded bank or mound, formed of the earth cast up from the ditch or fosse around a camp or station.

1806 *Gaz. Scot.* s.v. *Crichton*, A circular camp or intrenchment, the *vallum* of which is very distinct. 1816 Scott *Antiq.* iv, Nothing can be more plainly traced—a proper *agger* or *vallum*, with its corresponding ditch or *fossa.* 1833 Jas. Davidson *Brit. & Rom. Rem. Axminster* 13 It has been said that this intrenchment had formerly a double vallum,..but no vestiges of the inner vallum remain, if such an one ever existed. 1880 Hodgkin *Italy & Invaders* I. i. I. 120 The usual square form of a Roman camp strengthened by ditch and vallum and palisade.

transf. 1818 Lady Morgan *Fl. Macarthy* (1819) II. v. 237 A small dunghill, which usually forms the first *vallum* to the residence of an Irish peasant. 1829 Tytler *Hist. Scot.* (1864) I. 301 An inner keep or castle, surrounded by a strong wall, beyond which was a ditch or deep fosse,..and beyond this again was raised an outer vallum or rampart.

vally, dial. variant of felloe, value.

†**valoir.** *Obs.*$^{-1}$ In 6 **valoyre.** [a. F. *valoir* to be of value.] Value, worth, price.

*c*1495 *The Epitaffe*, etc. in Skelton's Wks. (1843) II. 392 Gewellys of late poysyd at grete valoyre.

valonia (væ'ləʊnɪə). Also 9 **vallonia**; 8 **valanea**, 9 **-onea**; 9 **velonia, -ea.** [ad. It. *vallonía, vallonéa*, whence also F. *vallonée, velonnée*, †*velonie* (1553), ad. mod.Gr. βαλάνια, βελάνια, pl. of βαλάνι, βελάνι acorn (anc. Gr. βάλανος).]

1. The large acorn-cups and acorns of *Quercus ægilops* (and the related *Q. vallonea*), a species of oak growing esp. in the north-eastern Mediterranean regions, valued for the abundant tannin they contain, and much used in tanning, dyeing, etc.

α. 1722 *Lond. Gaz.* No. 6040/6 Red Saunders, Shumack, Sticklack, Turnsole, Valonia. *Ibid.* 7 Valonia the Tun Weight, seven Pounds. 1812 J. Smyth *Pract. of Customs* (1821) 266 Valonia is a dying ingredient, brought from Italy and the Levant. It is the husks of the acorn, generally mixed with that fruit. 1852 Morfit *Tanning & Currying* (1853) 82 The leather made with valonia is said to be firmer and heavier than the oak-tanned. 1889 *Daily News* 12 Nov. 5/6 Another day, while I was collecting vallonia, I was assaulted by four soldiers.

β. 1775 R. Chandler *Trav. Asia M.* (1825) I. 27 The species of low oak, which produces valanea, or the large acorns used in tanning. *Ibid.* 124 The Valanea, or large acorns,..are exported, chiefly to Italy. 1867 Simmonds *Dict. Trade* s.v., In 1862, there were imported 29,720 tons of valonea. 1898 Zangwill *Dreamers Ghetto* iv. 116 Hard-headed Sephardim were busy..shipping freights of figs or valonea.

γ. *c*1835 *Encycl. Metrop.* (1845) XXIII. 743 The acorns.. are extensively used by dyers by the name of Velonea. 1849 Balfour *Man. Bot.* §1039. 1866 *Treas. Bot.* 1202/1.

b. *attrib.* and *Comb.*

1862 *Catal. Internat. Exhib., Brit.* II. No. 4628, Oak bark and valonia tanned leather. 1903 *Brighton Stand.* 27 Oct. 9/3 A..clerk in the hide and valonia business.

2. ***valonia oak***, the Levantine species *Quercus ægilops.* Also *ellipt.*

1829 Loudon *Encycl. Plants* 796 Velonia Oak. 1830 Lindley *Nat. Syst. Bot.* 98 A species known in the Levant under the name of Velonia. 1841 *Penny Cycl.* XIX. 214/2 *Q. Ægilops*, Great prickly-cupped Oak, or Valonia. 1892 Agnes Clerke *Fam. Stud. Homer* vi. 153 The tradition of acorn-eating connected with the rustic Arcadians applied evidently to the fruit of the valonia-oak.

‖**valonidi.** [ad. mod.Gr. βαλανίδι acorn-cup. Cf. F. *velanède, avelanède.*] *V. oak*, = prec. 2.

1878 Gosse *Rivers Bible* 266 The Valonidi oak, the characteristic tree of this part of the country.

valop, obs. form of wallop *sb.* and *v.*

valor ('vælə(r)). Also 6–7 **vallor**, 6 **valore**, 7 *Sc.* **walor.** [var. of valour by assimilation to, or direct adoption of, med.L. *valor.*]

†**1.** The amount in money, etc., that a thing is worth; = value *sb.* 2. *Obs.*

1496–7 *Plumpton Corr.* (Camden) 127 If hir ladyship wold send by him a token to my master, yt shall avale hir another of xx tymes the valor. 1526 *Linc. Wills* (1914) I. 179 Yerely spendyng the valore off the sayd v Roode [of land] att my forsayd yereday. *a*1577 Sir T. Smith *Commw. Eng.* (1609) 89 Thou hast stoln with force and armes an horse..to such a valor. 1676 Coles, *Valor of Marriage.* [See valour 3 d.]

transf. *c*1560 A. Scott *Poems* (S.T.S.) xxvii. 26 Will scho absent, Hyne sall I went, And at als littill valor set hir.

†**b.** In the phr. ***of*** **(*great*, etc.)** ***valor.*** *Obs.*

1467 *Mann. & Househ. Exp.* (Roxb.) 174 ȝe have..a lytel stoffe of myne for my howesold wesche [= which] is of no grete valor. 1545 in I. S. Leadam *Sel. Cases Crt. Requests* (Selden Soc.) 84 What valor they were of this deponent knoweth nott.

†**c.** The monetary value *of* (a specified sum).

1542 *Test. Ebor.* (Surtees) VI. 156 The yerlie valor of xl s. *a*1548 in Ellis *Orig. Lett.* Ser. III. II. 65 A Prebend in York ..of the yerly valor of xliiij. marks. 1602 *Shetland Law Rep.* in *Scotsman* (1886) 29 Jan. 7/1 Gif he beis apprehendit with the walor of an uris thift.

d. *Eccl.* An assessment-value set upon Church property; a list of these values.

1800 Lysons *Environs London Suppl.* 245 In the old *valors* this rectory was rated at 70 marks. 1855 Milman *Lat. Chr.* XIV. i. (1864) VI. 18 *note*, The Valor of pope Nicholas was framed by those who wished..to..lighten their taxation.

2. †**a.** Intrinsic worth or merit; = value *sb.* 6.

1580 Lodge *Sch. Abuse* Bj, All your obiections you make agaynst poetrye be of no valor. 1655 Gurnall *Chr. in Arm.* (1669) 281/1 Why! but because it hath not God to put a valor on it.

b. Power, import, significance.

1676 Collins in Rigaud *Corr. Sci. Men* (1841) II. 12, I have set down two valors of *x* to every equation. 1691 Ray *Coll. Words, Acc. Errors Alph.*, Now I come to shew that our alphabet is faulty as to the powers or valors attributed to some letters. 1808 Jebb *Corr.* (1834) I. 469 If I may make an English word to express the valor of the Greek word.

3. Courage, bravery; = valour 1 c. Now chiefly *U.S.*

1586 Hoby *Pol. Disc. Truth* xi. 36 They haue so often beene subdued by the valor of the French. 1605 *1st Part Jeronimo* III. i, Our courages are new borne, our vallors bred. 1674 tr. *Scheffer's Lapland* Pref., Where so much passive valor is necessary we may dispense with the want of active. 1757 W. Wilkie *Epigoniad* Pref. p. xli, Besides, I must have transferred, to Sthenelus, the valor, firmness, and address of Ulysses. 1782 Highmore *Ramble Coast Sussex* (1873) 19 In the days of chivalry, when the soul of valor animated every thought. 1828 Webster, *Worthy*,..a man of valor. 1874 Bancroft *Footpr. Time* i, The period of rude and restless valor among the Greeks.

valori'zation. orig. *U.S.* [See prec. and -ization.] The act or fact of fixing the value or price of some commercial commodity. Also *gen.*, evaluation, giving validity to, making valid.

1907 *Amer. Polit. Sci. Rev.* Feb. 249 (*Cent. Dict.* Suppl.), The financing of the valorization scheme is provided for by the issuing of bonds by the three coffee producing States, guaranteed by the general government. 1957 *Times* 28 Dec. 10/1 The announcement of a retention and valorization scheme by the Brazilian authorities in the spring touched off the rise in prices [of cocoa]. 1975 J. De Bres tr. *Mandel's Late Capitalism* 9 The first four chapters..deal..with..the connection between the development of capitalist technology and the valorization of capital itself. 1975 *Times Lit. Suppl.* 22 Aug. 942/1 The new structuralist model, with its valorization of the synchronic system over the older historical, genetic, diachronic modes of understanding. 1980 J. P. Farrell *Revolution as Tragedy* v. 247 A Victorian protest against the Romantic valorizations of tragedy that announce themselves in the works of Scott, Byron, and Carlyle.

valorize ('væləraɪz), *v.* [f. valor + -ize.] *trans.* To raise or stabilize the value of (a commodity, etc.) by a centrally organized scheme; *gen.* to evaluate, to make valid. Hence **'valorized** *ppl. a.*

1921 *Contemp. Rev.* July 53 It attempted both to regulate the output and to stabilise and to 'valorise' the prices. 1934 C. Lambert *Music Ho!* II. 79 Artists..have valorized the dream. 1976 T. Eagleton *Crit. & Ideology* v. 164 Criticism becomes a mutually supportive dialogue between two highly valorised subjects: the valuable text and the valuable reader. 1976 *Daily Tel.* 1 Nov. 16 Merely 'valorising' specific duties ..to recoup inflation since April would bring in £250 million. 1978 *Dædalus* Summer 48 The *Emile* and the *Contrat social* provide the explanation of the positively valorized concepts (virtue, morals, patriotism). 1984 *Christian Science Monitor* 2 Mar. B8/4 He has actually managed to suggest that the mire and blood, the 'refuse' of the embittered heart, is valorized by the poetic artifacts created from it.

valorous ('vælərəs), *a.* Forms: α. 5 **vaillerous**, 6 *Sc.* **valereus**, 7 **valerous, vallarous.** β. 5–

valorous, 7 *Sc.* val'rows, 8 val'rous. *γ.* 6–9 valourous. [ad. OF. (also mod.F.) *valeureux*, f. *valeur* VALOUR, or med.L. *valorosus* valiant, valuable, f. *valor* VALOR. Cf. It. *valoroso*, Sp. and Pg. *valeroso*.]

1. Of persons: Endowed with valour; valiant, courageous; brave, bold.

α. c **1477** CAXTON *Jason* 12 She seeing that he was..a yong gentilman..hauying a chiere of a vaillerous man receyued him into her wages as souldyour. **1600** HAMILTON in *Cath. Tract.* (S.T.S.) 221 Al the noble successeurs of this Godlie and valereus king. **1680** *Debates in Parl.* (1681) 174 A King on their side, endowed with a vallarous Spirit.

Comb. **1642–4** VICARS *God in Mount* (1844) 56 This piously valerous-hearted Gentleman.

β. **1577–87** HOLINSHED *Chron.* III. 22/1 In which voiage his valorous hart at all assaies..was most manifestlie perceiued. **1597** SHAKS. *2 Hen. IV*, II. iv. 236 Thou art as valorous as Hector of Troy. **1627** *Lisander & Cal.* I. 1 Henry, the valorous Father of our invincible Monarch. **1727** SWIFT *On cutting down the thorn at Market Hill* Wks. 1755 IV. I. 88 Sir Archibald, that val'rous knight. **1807** G. CHALMERS *Caledonia* I. III. vii. 418 Willliam invaded Scotland..with design, perhaps, to chastise, rather than subdue, a valorous people. **1879** *Sat. Rev.* 13 Sept. 324 As the valorous Swiss were some twenty in number the position of the travellers was hopeless.

Comb. **1601** WEEVER *Mirr. Mart.* D vii, They answered me I was too valorous bold.

γ. **1600** HOLLAND *Livy* XXIV. xlvi. 541 Certaine Tribunes and marshals, valourous and doubtie good men. **1647** F. BLAND *Souldiers March* 39 A token of a minde truly noble and valorous. **1807** G. CHALMERS *Caledonia* I. II. ii. 244 The Valourous Arthur of history, or the redoubtable Arthur of romance. **1841** JAMES *Brigand* xxxiii, I am about..to give you as a bride to this valourous prince.

2. Of actions, etc.: Marked or characterized by valour, courage, or bravery.

1490 CAXTON *Eneydos* Prol. 10 This present booke,..in whiche may alle valyaunt prynces and other nobles see many valorous fayttes of armes. **1590** SPENSER *F.Q.* II. x. 18 [She] gathering force, and courage valorous, Encountred him in battell well ordaind. **1612** *North's Plutarch, Epaminondas* 1125 Not able any longer to defend themselues against the valorous force of himselfe and his followers. *a* **1660** *Contemp. Hist. Irel.* (Ir. Archæol. Soc.) I. 174 The enemie..rather wonderinge at his valerous charge, then any way able to oppose it. **1813** WELLINGTON in Gurw. *Desp.* (1838) X. 532 *note*, The whole universe will acknowledge those valorous efforts. **1869** TOZER *Highl. Turkey* II. 209 Two tall peaks.., far famed for valorous deeds..of the Suliotes.

†**3.** Having value, worth, or merit; valuable.

1592 G. HARVEY *Four Lett.* iii. 19 The Hexameter verse..whereof neither Homer in Greeke, nor Virgill in Latine, (how valorous Autors!)..were ashamed. **1609** J. DAVIES (Heref.) *Humours Heaven* II. lxxxvi, Be their value ne'r so valorous Its held but base and made by nature sleight.

Hence **'valorousness**.

1727 BAILEY, *Valorousness*, Valiantness, Stoutness, Bravery. **1920** G. SANTAYANA *Character & Opinion in U.S.A.* vii. 214 Their valorousness and morality consist in their indomitable egotism. **1922** E. R. EDDISON *Worm* xxvii. 346 The Demons..by their strength and valorousness set free the Lord Goldry Bluszco.

valorously ('vælərəslɪ), *adv.* [f. prec. + -LY².] Bravely, valiantly.

1599 SHAKS. *Hen. V*, III. ii. 125 Ile pay't as valorously as I may, that sal I suerly do. c **1614** SIR W. MURE *Dido & Æneas* I. 549 The Trojans val'rowsly resist their force. **1675** tr. *Camden's Hist. Eliz.* II. 239 Which they valorously and stoutly performed, wounding James himself. **1760–72** H. BROOKE *Fool of Qual.* (1809) II. 21 [He] pushed valourously forward. **1834** PRINGLE *Afr. Sk.* viii. 287 Supposing it to be a crocodile, they valorously determined to shoot it. **1882** *Macm. Mag.* XLVI. 251 The order was valorously obeyed.

valou, obs. Sc. form of WALLOW *v.*

valour ('vælə(r)). Forms: 4– valour (5–6 *Sc.* wa-), 5 valowr, 5–6 valoure (5 *Sc.* wa-, 5–6 vo-), 6 vallour (*Sc.* wa-), 5 vallouer, 6 valouer. [a. OF. *valour* (*valur*; later and mod.F. *valeur* VALEUR), = Sp. and Pg. *valor*, It. *valore*:—late L. *valōr-*, *valor* VALOR, f. *valēre* to be strong, etc. See also VALURE.]

1. †**a.** Worth or importance due to personal qualities or to rank. *Obs.*

c **1330** *Arth. & Merl.* 3402 (Kölbing), Kay, þe steward of valour. *Ibid.* 4179 A damisel of gret valour Was þo comen to king Arthour. c **1350** *Libeaus Desc.* 140 (Ritson), He was a noble dysour, Wyth ladyes of valour, A mery man of mouthe. c **1477** CAXTON *Jason* 28 Ye that be so moche exellent and vertuous that alle my thoughtes ben torned..to you that ar of so moche hye valour. **1502** ATKYNSON tr. *De Imitatione* III. iv. 198, I am very noughte, nothynge hauynge, ne nothynge of valour. **1508** DUNBAR *Tua Mariit Wemen* 185 He lukis as he wald luffit be, thocht he be litill of valour. **1586** B. YOUNG *Guazzo's Civ. Conv.* IV. 179 b, Whereby..your valour and worthinesse maie bee deciphered, and my insufficiencie not made vnknowne.

†**b.** Worth or worthiness in respect of manly qualities or attributes. *Obs.*

13.. *Coer de L.* 4920 Yiff that he durste hym abyde, Undyr the forest off Arsour He wolde assaye hys valour. c **1375** *Sc. Leg. Saints* xxxi. (*Eugenia*) 421 Ane erle þat wes a fare man, quham for beute & waloure þe emprice luffit paramoure. *a* **1400–50** *Alexander* 2493 How Alexander in his armes all-way encreses, In valour & in victori & vertues so noble. c **1450** *Merlin* xxii. 405, I shall lete hem well wite that I am not hidde, yef in me be so moche valoure. **1508** DUNBAR *Poems* vii. 2 Renownit, ryall, right reuerend and serene Lord, hie trywmphing in wirschip and valoure.

c. The quality of mind which enables a person to face danger with boldness or firmness; courage or bravery, esp. as shown in warfare or conflict; valiancy, prowess.

1581 PETTIE tr. *Guazzo's Civ. Conv.* I. (1586) 1 Lieuetenant generall... A degree..won..by meanes of his owne valour & seruice done to the king. **1592** KYD *Sp. Trag.* I. ii. 39 Captaines stroue to haue their valours tride. **1604** JAS. I *Counterbl. to Tobacco* To Rdr., Our fortunate and oft prooued valour in warres abroad. **1654–66** EARL ORRERY *Parthen.* (1676) 54 He ow'd the Affront not to our Valours, but to his fears. **1667** MILTON *P.L.* XI. 686 In those dayes Might onely shall be admir'd, And Valour and Heroic Vertu call'd. **1715** ADDISON *Freeholder* No. 8, English Valour cannot be matched when it is animated by English Beauty. **1776** GIBBON *Decl. & F.* vi. (1782) I. 184 Valour, and the love of discipline, [became] the only qualifications for military employments. **1822** SCOTT *Peveril* vi, Real valour consists not in being insensible to danger, but in being prompt to confront and disarm it. **1857** G. LAWRENCE *Guy Liv.* ix, [She knew] that the better part of valour was advisable. **1878** MORLEY *Carlyle* 191 The same principle which revealed the valour and godliness of Puritanism.

personif. **1692** PRIOR *An Ode* i, Nor to melt at Beauties Tears, nor follow Valour's Sword.

d. Used as a personal name or (with possessives) as a quasi-title; also, a person of courage.

1606 SHAKS. *Tr. & Cr.* I. iii. 176 And at this sport Sir Valour dies; cries, O enough Patroclus. **1819** SCOTT *Ivanhoe* xl, An your valour be so dull, you will please to learn [etc.]. **1839** LYTTON *Richelieu* I. i, I,..Leading young valours..reckless as myself, Seized on the town of Faviaux. **1855** KINGSLEY *Westw. Ho!* xxvi, But the stern-gallery? How..came your valour thither?

e. *Comb.*, as *valour-breathing*, *-loving*, etc.

1605 SYLVESTER *Du Bartas* II. iii. *Law* 13 Rock-batt'ring Bumbards, Valour-murdering Guns. **1598** *Ibid.* II. i. *Furies* 35 The snares of vertue, valour-softning Hyrens. **1755** *Praises of Isis* 150 Warrior steeds, and valour-breathing knights. **1848** BUCKLEY *Iliad* 279 He sat in the tent of valour-loving Eurypylus. **1851** H. MELVILLE *Whale* xxv. I. 183 Immaculate manliness..bleeds with keenest anguish at the undraped spectacle of a valour-ruined man.

†**2.** Value or worth in material or other respects; = VALUE *sb.* 6. **a.** In the phr. *of* (..) *valour*. *Obs.*

c **1330** *Arth. & Merl.* 3265 (Kölbing), A launce he tok of gret valour. *Ibid.* 6353 His stede he smot of gret valour. c **1400** T. CHESTRE *Launfal* 984 Kyng Artour gan her fayre grete, And sche hym agayn, with wordes swete, That were of greet valour. c **1425** WYNTOUN *Cron.* lxxiv. 191 (Wemyss), In all þat land wes nane Temple standand of valoure. c **1475** *Harl. Contin. Higden* (Rolls) VIII. 511 That parliamente of kynge Ricardus was made voyde & as of noo valoure. **1526** TINDALE *Romans* iii. 23 The prayse that is off valoure before God. **1561** T. NORTON *Calvin's Inst.* I. 9 b, These hys powers,..of what valoure they be, and to what end we ought to wey them. **1631** R. H. *Arraignm. Whole Creature* ix. 69 Their Viands are of no valour, no valew without these. **1642** R. CARPENTER *Experience* II. viii. 196 If we compare his works being of infinite valour with our works.

†**b.** In other constructions. *Obs.*

1432–50 tr. *Higden* (Rolls) IV. 35 Not discordenge in eny thynge, neiþer in valoure of wordes, neither in ordre. **1502** *Ord. Crysten Men* (W. de W. 1506) II. xvii. 126 The lyfe contemplatyf excedeth in valoure and in worthynes the lyfe actyf. **1535** STEWART *Cron. Scot.* I. 559 In peice and rest..Ane small thing growis to ane greit valour. **1565** HARDING *Answ. M. Ivelles Chalenge* 220 This is the doctrine of the churche, touching the valour of the Masse. **1616** CHAMPNEY *Voc. Bps.* 307 For the effectuall applying of the merite, valour, and effect thereof vnto us.

†**3.** The amount (in money, etc.) or sum that a thing is worth; = VALUE *sb.* 2. *Obs.*

c **1350** *Libeaus Desc.* 1039 (K.), He haþ me sent þe valour Of fyfe fiȝtes four, Seþe he ferst began. c **1430** *Syr Gener.* (Roxb.) 3000 Not for the valour of al this tovn Wold I lenght thi life soo. **1456** SIR G. HAYE *Law Arms* (S.T.S.) 135 To restore agayne the thing or the valour. **1538** in Marsden *Sel. Pleas Crt. Adm.* (Selden Soc.) II. 67 Our goodes..to be solld..and of the monye that shall cum of the valour of those goodes [etc.]. **1566** PAINTER *Pal. Pleas.* (Marsh) 56 b, A verye beautifull ringe of great price and estimation, which for the valour and beautie he was very desirous perpetually to leave unto his successours. **1609** SKENE *Reg. Maj.* 97 He sall pay to his parents, the valour of his marriage. *a* **1825** FORBY *Voc. E. Anglia*, *Valour*, value.

†**b.** In the phr. *of* (*great*, *little*, etc.) *valour*.

c **1450** LOVELICH *Grail* xxvi. 332 This olde gentyl knyht..purveied him of Gold & of tresowr, and of mani a Iewel of gret valowr. **1496–7** *Plumpton Corr.* (Camden) 123 She hath in coyne in old nobles, cli,..with other goods of great valour. **1528** ROY *Rede me* (Arb.) 32 Oure fyngres shyninge with precyous stons Sett in golden rynges of ryche valoure. **1585** T. WASHINGTON tr. *Nicholay's Voy.* III. xv. 99 b, A long and large girdle of silke and gold of no small beautie and valour. **1603** KNOLLES *Hist. Turks* (1621) 439 [Zemes] caused his treasure, plate, jewels, and other things of great valour and light carriage to be trussed up.

†**c.** Const. *of.* = VALUE *sb.* 4. *Obs.*

1432–50 tr. *Higden* (Rolls) IV. 267 That euery man..scholde..offre a peny in valoure of oure x. d. usualle. c **1440** *Alph. Tales* 526 He wold not gyf þer-for þe valour of a shred clowte. c **1475** *Harl. Contin. Higden* (Rolls) VIII. 473 Londes and rentes unto the valoure of a M li. **1541** *Act 33 Hen. VIII*, c. 12 §27 Plate iewels or other goodes..of the valour of .xii. d. or aboue. *a* **1578** LINDESAY (Pitscottie) *Chron. Scot.* (S.T.S.) II. 176 The quene gaif him ane cheinȝe to the wallour of ane thowsand crounis. **1600** HOLLAND *Livy* XLIII. v. 1159 To send presents..to the valour of two thousand Asses over and above.

†**d.** *spec.* (See quot.) *Obs.*⁻¹

1607 COWEL *Interpreter*, *Valour of Mariage*..is a writ that lyeth for the Lord, hauing profered covenable mariage to the Infant, without disparidgement, against the Infant, comming to his yeares, if he refuse to take the Lords offer. And it is to recouer the value of the mariage.

4. The amount, quantity, etc., *of* (so much or so many). *rare.*

1614 B. JONSON *Barth. Fair* IV. vi, I thinke wee were best put hem in the stocks,..for the valour of an houre, or such a thing, till his worship come. *a* **1825** FORBY *Voc. E. Anglia* s.v., It might be about the valour of three hours, two miles, four acres, etc.

valouwe, southern ME. var. FALLOW *v.*¹

valpack ('vælpæk). *U.S.* Orig. (a proprietary name) **Val-A-Pak.** Also **valpac, valpak**, etc. [perh. f. elements of VALISE, PACK *sb.*¹, etc.] A type of soft zip-up travel bag.

1934 *Official Gaz.* (U.S. Patent Office) 30 Oct. 1005/2 Val-A-Pak. For Hand Bags. **1935** *Esquire* Dec. 212/1 (Advt.), Val-A-Pak hangs flat against the wall of a state-room berth or closet. *Ibid.*, By the exclusive Val-A-Pak construction, the bag whether flat or folded for carrying, always conforms to its contents. **1946** J. P. MARQUAND *B. F.'s Daughter* ix. 111 Later in his room at the Bachelor Officers' Quarters he opened his valpack and took out a packet of letter paper. **1966** E. WEST *Night is Time for Listening* ii. 45 He hung out his Valpak, removed his overcoat, and lit a cigarette. **1967** *Sat. Rev.* (U.S.) 22 Apr. 52/2 Experienced travelers in 1947 favoured the Valpack to carry clothes. It was like an Army kitbag and zipped up. **1977** E. LEONARD *Hunted* (1978) ix. 86 He threw extra clothes into a valpac.

Valpolicella (vælpɒlɪ'tʃɛlə). Also earlier **Val Policella.** The name of a valley in the western Veneto, Italy, used to designate the red or rosé wine made there.

1903 N. NEWNHAM-DAVIS *Gourmet's Guide to Europe* ix. 164 A bottle of Val Policella is exactly suited to this kind of repast. **1935** SCHOONMAKER & MARVEL *Compl. Wine Bk.* v. 130 Of the Veronese wines, the red Valpolicella is decidedly the best. **1950** E. HEMINGWAY *Across River* xii. 103 What about a fiasco of Valpolicella? **1970** A. SILLITOE *Start in Life* VI. 294 Glasses of Valpolicella not yet touched. **1979** C. CURZON *Leaven of Malice* xi. 126 *Tournedos Rossini* with salad and a reasonable Valpolicella.

valproic (væl'prəʊɪk), *a. Pharm.* [f. VAL(ERIC *a.* + PRO(PYL + -IC.] 2-Propylpentanoic acid, $C_8H_{15}OOH$, a branched-chain fatty acid; also, a salt of this. Hence **val'proate**, a salt of this acid, esp. the sodium salt, an anticonvulsant drug given orally in cases of epilepsy.

1972 *Approved Names* (Brit. Pharmacopœia Commission) Suppl. IV. 6 Valproic acid. **1974** *Brit. Med. Jrnl.* 15 June 584/1 The anticonvulsant effects of sodium dipropylacetate (sodium valproate) were first reported in France. **1977** *Lancet* 22 Oct. 860/1 The antiepileptic activity of valproic acid (dipropylacetic acid) was recognized serendipitously when the agent was administered to animals as a vehicle for a series of test compounds. **1983** F. E. DREIFUSS in Pedley & Meldrum *Rec. Adv. in Epilepsy* I. iii. 35 Clinical experience with Valproate extends over nearly 20 years. *Ibid.*, The term Valproate is used here to refer both to valproic acid and its salts (sodium or magnesium).

vals, southern ME. var. FALSE *a.*

Valsalva (væl'sælvə). *Med.* The name of Antonio M. *Valsalva* (1666–1723), Italian anatomist, used *attrib.*, in the possessive, and *absol.* to designate the action, described by him, in which an attempt is made to exhale air while the nostrils and mouth, or the glottis, are closed, so as to increase pressure in the middle ear and the chest.

1886 *Buck's Handbk. Med. Sci.* II. 577/2 To insure a proper performance of this (Valsalva's) method of inflation, it is merely requisite that the patient shall make a strong expiratory effort while holding both his mouth and his nose firmly closed. **1893** H. RICHARDS in C. H. Burnett *Syst. Dis. Ear, Nose, & Throat* I. I. 112 The patient is the operator of the Valsalva inflation. **1913** *Jrnl. Physiol.* XLVI. 186 The radial artery was released and the first rise of the Valsalva experiment was resumed. *Ibid.*, In Fig. 5 is shown another tracing of occlusion of the aberrant radial artery during Valsalva. *Ibid.* 187 The first rise in the sphygmographic curve in Valsalva's experiment is due to increased blood-pressure with increase of the calibre of the artery. **1943** *Bull. Hist. Med.* XIV. 313 Only the historian can fully realize the relative unfruitfulness of the vast amount of experimentation and of study devoted to the Valsalva. **1972** *Sci. Amer.* Feb. 85/2 In attempting to stop the heart the yogis usually performed what is called the Valsalva maneuver. **1977** *Lancet* 28 May 1140/1 In shallow diving an over-forceful Valsalva manœuvre may give rise to neuro-sensory hearing loss, with or without vertigo.

Val'salvan, *a. Med.* [f. the name of the Italian anatomist A. M. *Valsalva*; see prec.] Associated with Valsalva's researches on the organs of hearing; introduced or used by Valsalva.

1878 in *St. George's Hosp. Rep.* (1879) IX. 789 On Valsalvan inflation, the whole..bulges out into a whitish swelling. **1879** *Ibid.* 791 After some trouble, the left tympanum becomes inflated by the Valsalvan method.

valse (vɑːls), *sb.* Also 8 volse. [a. F. *valse* (= Sp. *vals*, Pg. *valsa*, It. *valzer*), ad. G. *walzer* WALTZ.] A round dance in triple time, a waltz; the music for this. Also *attrib.*

1796 *Times* 19 Feb. in Ashton *Old Times* (1885) 321 The young Ladies are particularly favourable to a German Dance, called *the Volse*. **1880** *Grove's Dict. Mus.* I. 350/1 [Chopin's] first..compositions were dances: Polonaises, Mazurkas, and Valses. **1894** E. SCOTT *Dancing* 168 The Versa, a new Valse Dance.

valse (vɔːls), *v.* [f. prec., or ad. F. *valser* (= Sp. and Pg. *valsar*).] *intr.* To dance the valse or waltz; to waltz.

1870 H. SMART *Race for Wife* i, I am quite willing to look on at your valsing for another hour. 1876 *The World* V. No. 114. 19 With whom Maud fancies herself in love because he valses so divinely.

Hence ˈ**valser**, ˈ**valsing** *vbl. sb.* (also *transf.*)

1870 MISS BROUGHTON *Red as Rose* I. 102 The gnats are dancing round and round..I wonder that that incessant valsing does not make them giddy.

valse, southern ME. var. FALSE *a.* and *v.*

valsen, -on, obs. southern varr. FAUSEN (eel).

valshede, -liche, -nesse, southern ME. varr. FALSEHOOD, -LY *adv.*, -NESS.

Valspeak (ˈvælspiːk). *U.S.* [f. VAL(LEY *sb.* + -SPEAK.] = *Valleyspeak* s.v. VALLEY *sb.* 7.

1982 *People Mag.* 13 Sept. 90/2 On the record, in pure, uncut Valspeak, Moon laments in bubbly staccato that, 'Like my mother like makes me do the dishes. It's like so *gross*.' 1982 *Guardian* 26 Oct. 8/4 Valspeak is the latest teentalk craze to surface in the real world.

valt(e, obs. ff. VAULT *sb.*[1] and *v.*[1]

valter, obs. Sc. f. WATER.

valuable (ˈvæljuːəb(ə)l), *a.* and *sb.* Also 7 **valewable**, 7-8 **valueable**. [f. VALUE *v.* + -ABLE.]

A. *adj.* **1.** Of material or monetary value; having value for use or for exchange.

1589 NASHE *Pref.* to *Greene's Menaphon* (Arb.) 8 Which being the effect of an vndescerning iudgement, makes drosse as valuable as gold. 1687 BURNET *Trav.* III. (1750) 127, I did not see the Gospel of St. Mark which is one of the valuablest Things of the Treasure. 1710 PRIDEAUX *Orig. Tithes* ii. 77 Which makes 'tithes' at least one fourth part less valueable to them, than they were to the Levitical Priesthood. 1756-7 tr. *Keysler's Trav.* (1760) IV. 53 A very valuable cabinet where the arrangement is very judicious, especially as to the coins and medals. 1776 *Trial Nundocomar* 82/2 Do you know whether he kept jewels, or other valuable effects there? 1825 MCCULLOCH *Pol. Econ.* I. i. 2 A commodity or a product is not valuable because it is useful; but it is valuable because it can only be procured by the intervention of labour. 1855 *Poultry Chron.* III. 430, I have lately lost a valuable hen from a disease which is new to me. 1863 FAWCETT *Pol. Econ.* III. xvi. 503 Gold, during the Middle Ages, was about sixteen times more valuable than the same weight of silver.

†**b.** Amounting to a reasonable sum; not merely nominal. *Obs.*

1613 *Bury Wills* (Camden) 159 Vpon trust and confidence that they..shall demise the same at a valewable rent, and to the best profite.

c. ***valuable consideration***: see CONSIDERATION 6.

1638 SANDERSON *Serm.* (1682) II. 97 Some small trifle or other: which being of very little worth or use, and so not to be taken for a valuable consideration, may therefore be called nought or nothing. 1698 in Sir H. Dalrymple *Decis.* (1792) 1 A decree..finding, that the bond was granted for no valuable consideration, and therefore discharging all execution thereupon for ever. 1766 BLACKSTONE *Comm.* II. 297 A valuable consideration is such as money, marriage, or the like, which the law esteems an equivalent given for the grant. 1818 CRUISE *Digest* (ed. 2) II. 64 Not even an alienation, for a valuable consideration, to a purchaser..will avoid it. 1898 LD. HARRIS in *Westm. Gaz.* 15 Oct. 7/1 Who will satisfy themselves that no valuable consideration has passed between the respective county clubs to bring about the transfer.

2. Having value or worth, of great use or service, *to* a person or *for* a purpose.

1647 CLARENDON *Hist. Reb.* I. §182 King James..would often say, that his access to the Crown of England was the more valuable to him, as it redeem'd him from the subjection to the ill manners..of those Preachers. 1748 *Anson's Voy.* II. iv. 164 These were the principal goods on board her, but we found besides what was to us much more valuable than the rest of the cargoe. 1851 CARLYLE *Sterling* III. iv, I..saw most of the usual wonders,—the Pæstan Temples being to me much the most valuable. 1878 JEVONS *Polit. Econ.* 96 We may say that quinine is valuable for curing fevers,..or that water is valuable for putting out fires. 1883 *Law Times* 20 Oct. 405/2 Young solicitors will find many hints valuable to them interspersed among its contents.

b. Possessed of qualities which confer value or bring into high estimation.

1638 SIR T. HERBERT *Trav.* (ed. 2) 146 Somewhat further, over heaps of stones of valewable portraictures, we mount towards the most lofty part of this Pallace. 1737 H. WALPOLE in *10th Rep. Hist. MSS. Comm.* App. I. 270, I should be glad of purchasing a good collection of yᵉ ancient Classicks, and other valuable authors. *a* 1768 SECKER *Serm.* (1770) IV. xviii. 387 Yet we never..doubt of their having a real, though unknown, Subserviency to valuable Ends. 1801 *Med. Jrnl.* V. 173 If they should accord with the spirit of your very valuable Journal, you are at full liberty to insert them. 1855 MACAULAY *Hist. Eng.* xviii. IV. 248 At such a moment the ministers could not refuse to listen to any person who professed himself able to give them valuable information. 1875 JOWETT *Plato* (ed. 2) V. 81 No instrument of education is more valuable than arithmetic.

†**c.** Of persons: Entitled to consideration or distinction; estimable. *Obs.*

1647 CLARENDON *Hist. Reb.* VI. §65 [They] appear'd to be a good Number of very valuable Men, on whose behalf he had only Authority to conclude. 1703 *Hatton Corr.* (Camden) II. 250 Mr. Pepys, who was a very valuable person,..is dead, and was yesterday buried. 1727 SWIFT *To Young Lady* Wks. 1755 II. II. 49 A lady of your acquaintance married to a very valuable person. 1730 SOUTHALL *Treat. Buggs* 3 The late Learned and truly Valuable Dr. Woodward ..approv'd the Design.

†**3.** That can be valued; capable of having the value estimated. *Obs. rare.*

1627 SANDERSON *Serm.* (1682) I. 263 That sin..from which he hath once escaped without shame, or so much as valueable loss. 1690 LOCKE *Govt.* I. ix. ¶10 We are..now speaking..of Possessions and Commodities of Life Valuable by Money.

†**4.** Capable of being compared or equated in value *with* something. *Obs.*

1646 QUARLES *Judgem. & Mercy* Wks. (Grosart) I. 86/2 Is ..a puffe of breath wee call life, valuable with his honour, in comparison of whom the very Angels are impure? 1651 HOBBES *Govt. & Soc.* ii. §14. 28 His Will..hath simply before it, for its object, a certain good valuable with the thing promised.

†**5.** Valid, sound. *Obs.*[-1]

1647 N. WARD *Simple Cobler* 8 He that will rather make an irreligious quarell with other Religions then try the Truth of his own by valuable Arguments.

B. *sb.* An article of worth or value. Usually in pl., valuable goods or possessions.

1775 in ASH. 1797 S. & H. LEE *Canterb. T.* I. 188 With such valuables and papers as he deemed most likely to secure him either impunity or revenge. 1829 LYTTON *Devereux* III. v, I did not long wrestle with my pride before I obtained the victory, and sent all my valuables to the hammer. 1842 R. I. WILBERFORCE *Rutilius & Lucius* 22 No one but had furnished himself with some valuable. 1878 BOSW. SMITH *Carthage* 123 Which the crews helped by throwing overboard their valuables.

valuableness (ˈvæljuːəb(ə)lnɪs). [f. prec.] The character or condition of being valuable.

1683 LORRAIN tr. *Muret's Rites Fun.* To Rdr. 4 Which having said with regard to the valuableness of the Subject, I shall only add [etc.]. 1721 T. THOMAS *Pref. Urry's Chaucer* p. l, The valuableness of it will appear by the use which has been made of it in the Glossary. 1768 TUCKER *Lt. Nat.* I. II. xxiv. 134 There lies a nearer way for good qualities to arrive at their valuableness. 1865 J. GROTE *Moral Ideals* vi. (1876) 71 And then it may be that the valuableness of actions varies as their usefulness.

valuably (ˈvæljuːəblɪ), *adv.* [f. as prec.]

†**1. a.** With equivalence of value. *Obs.*[-1]

1629 GAULE *Holy Madn.* 137 A great Patrimony may be valuably transubstantiated into the quantity of a little stone.

†**b.** At a high rate or value. *Obs.*

1755 JOHNSON, *Preciously*, valuably; to a great price.

2. With valuable or precious articles.

1780 *Gentl. Mag.* L. 617 Danford gained intelligence at an inn in the country of a box valuably filled. 1805 *Naval Chron.* XIII. 83 She is valuably laden.

3. In a valuable manner; so as to be valuable or highly useful.

1865 *Sat. Rev.* 5 Aug. 177/2 Mr. Palgrave's sombre picture must be treated as..valuably qualifying, not as superseding, such standard representations as that by Layard. 1895 *Review of Rev.* Aug. 167 If he had lived only to write that, he would have lived valuably. 1896 *Pop. Sci. Monthly* L. 285 Which perplex and exhaust the pupil without contributing valuably to his mental discipline.

valuate (ˈvæljuːeɪt), *v.* [Back-formation from next.] *trans.* To estimate the value of (something); to appraise.

1873 *Lond. Soc.* Feb. 140 It will be important to valuate the influence of this extraordinary man. 1892 STEVENSON & L. OSBOURNE *Wrecker* 291 The actual harm I can do I leave you to valuate for yourself.

valuation (væljuːˈeɪʃən). Also 6 **valewacion, valuacion, -atioun**, 7 **valueacion, valluacon, waluation**. [a. OF. *valuacion, -ation* (cf. mod.F. *évaluation* EVALUATION), = Sp. *valuacion*, f. *valuer* (Sp. *valuar*) VALUE *v.*]

1. a. The action of valuing; the process of assessing or fixing the value of a thing. Also *attrib.*, as ***valuation act, law, office, officer.***

1529 MORE *Suppl. Souls* Wks. 294/2 For surely it might be that he was not ware of the newe valuacion: for he ranne awaye before the valuacion changed. 1551 SIR J. WILLIAMS *Accompte* (Abbotsf. Cl.) 13 Myters, ornamentes, and other thinges received without weight or valuacion. 1577-87 HOLINSHED *Chron.* II. 313/1 The valuation of their goodes and substance, as well in cattell as in readie monie. 1672 PETTY *Pol. Anat.* (1691) 61 These Valuations were made as Parties interested could prevail upon and against one another by their Attendance, Friends, Eloquence, and Vehemence. 1737 H. WALPOLE in *10th Rep. Hist. MSS Comm.* App. I. 270, I..would give more for them on a reasonable valuation than a Bookseller would doe. 1781 GIBBON *Decl. & F.* (1787) II. 71 The secret wealth of commerce, and the precarious profits of art or labour, are susceptible only of a discretionary valuation. 1839 THIRLWALL *Greece* xlii. V. 205 A new valuation of all private property had been made. 1858 LD. ST. LEONARDS *Property Law* vii. 42 If they refuse to value the estate, or disagree in the valuation, you cannot enforce the performance of the contract.

attrib. 1855 *Statutes Gt. Brit. & Irel.* XXII. 514 Valuation (Ireland) Act Amendment; further to amend 15 & 16 Vict. c. 63 relating to the Valuation of rateable Property. 1892 *Pall Mall G.* 19 Dec. 2/1 The amendment of the valuation law. 1905 G. B. SHAW *Let.* 3 Jan. (1972) II. 503 A high official in the Valuation Office. 1925 *Act 15 & 16 Geo. V* c. 90 §55(1) It shall be lawful for rating authorities, assessment committees, and county valuation committees to appoint for the purposes of this Act such rating officers, valuation officers and other officers as they think fit. 1976 *Evening Post* (Nottingham) 14 Dec. 4/7 A spokesman for the Inland Revenue said it was customary for the valuation officers to try to reach agreement with the rate-payers. 1978 *Ryde's Rating Cases* (1979) XXI. 143 He had stated that on evidence now to hand the valuation office erred in some cases in not projecting forward the 1967/1969 rents.

b. Estimated value; worth or price as determined by deliberate estimation.

1631 WEEVER *Anc. Funeral Mon.* 816 The valuation of this religious structure..was three hundred eight pounds. 1757 WASHINGTON *Lett.* Writ. 1889 I. 437 There are many Masters of Servants yet unpaid, who are very anxious to receive their valuation. 1775 S. J. PRATT *Liberal Opin.* cxx. (1783) IV. 119 The ear-rings were no trifles in point of price .., bearing no less a valuation than 200 guineas. 1812 G. CHALMERS *Dom. Econ. Gt. Brit.* 456 The fair valuation, at which our commercial concerns might be calculated. 1844 H. H. WILSON *Brit. India* I. vii. I. 445 The money valuation of the estimated produce of the land in cultivation. 1888 ANNIE S. SWAN *Doris Cheyne* vii. 122 Mr. Hardwicke had paid the sum required for the goodwill, and had also taken the furniture at a valuation.

†**2. a.** Value or worth, esp. of a material nature.

1567 *Trial Treas.* (Percy Soc.) 6 It is not golde alwayes that doth shine, But corrupting copper, of small valuation. 1583 MELBANCKE *Philotimus* Nj b, Diuers precious Iewells .., whereof two or three Gemmes were of more valuation in his accounte, then all the rest. 1622 R. PRESTON *Godly Man's Inquisition* i. 20 If any man hath lost any matter of valuation, how diligently will they set themselues to Inquisitions. 1655 tr. *Sorel's Com. Hist. Francion* II. 44 Without receiving any considerable valuation for so precious a Jewell. 1669 WORLIDGE *Syst. Agric.* (1681) 145 Which casualties..makes their Price and valuation so uncertain, and proves so great a discouragement to the Countryman.

†**b.** *spec.* Current value (of money). *Obs.*

1551 ROBINSON tr. *More's Utopia* I. (1895) 88 One councelleth to rayse and enhaunce the valuacion of money, when the king must paye any. 1622 MALYNES *Anc. Law-Merch.* 486 By aduancing the Valuation of gold..in England, when Crowne gold was valued from fiftie fiue shillings the ounce to three pound. 1699 BENTLEY *Phal.* 454 Here are four Authorities then..for the low valuation of the Sicilian Talent. 1776 ADAM SMITH *W.N.* I. v. (1869) I. 46 No creditor could..be cheated in consequence of the high valuation of silver in coin.

†**c.** = VALUE *sb.* 7 a. *Obs.*[-1]

1636 *Recorde's Gr. Artes* 43, I may reckon them simply without any respect of their valuation or place: saying, 2 and 3 make 5.

3. Appreciation or estimation of anything in respect of excellence or merit.

1548 ELYOT, *Aestimatio*, a valuacion, consideracion, or weying of a matter. 1597 SHAKS. *2 Hen. IV*, IV. i. 189 Our valuation shall be such, That euery slight, and false-deriued Cause, Yea, euery idle..wanton Reason,..Shall, to the King, taste of this Action. 1617 MORYSON *Itin.* IV. (Roxb.) 281, I obserued in England the same superstitious neglect of Common Prayer, and excessive valution of Preaching, to haue infected some places among vs. 1650 EARL MONM. tr. *Senault's Man bec. Guilty* 256 The very Theater whereupon things are acted, serves to put a valuation upon them. *a* 1676 HALE *Prim. Orig. Man.* (1677) 356 The admirable Solution of many of those difficulties..doth give a very great valuation and esteem to the truth..of the Scriptures. 1745-6 FIELDING *True Patriot* Wks. 1775 IX. 318, I believe it is difficult to find any two persons, who place an equal valuation on any virtue, good or great quality whatever. 1884 *Manch. Exam.* 14 May 5/5 The outside public appear disposed to take Mr. Chaplin at his own valuation.

Hence **valuˈational** *a.*

1887 *Contemp. Rev.* Feb. 285 They proposed a geometrical survey, detailed and valuational.

ˈ**valuative**, *a.* [f. VALUE *v.* + -ATIVE.] Expressive of value.

1566 STAPLETON *Ret. Untr. Jewel* IV. 62 The Sacramentary off Geneua will haue the verbe *est* is, to stand for, is in value, not is in substance, and so (*est*) must not be a verbe substantiue, but a verbe valuatiue. 1946 [see APPRAISIVE *a.*]. 1958 *Listener* 12 June 983/1 Valuative disputes arise both about what is to be passed on [by education] and about the manner of passing it on.

valuator (ˈvæljuːeɪtə(r)). [f. VALUE *v.* + -ATOR, after VALUATION.] One who estimates the value of things; *esp.* one appointed or licensed to do so; an appraiser.

1731-2 SWIFT *Consid. two Bills* Wks. 1841 II. 225/1, I am therefore at a loss what kind of valuators the bishops will make use of. 1820 HOGG *Tales & Sk.* (1837) II. 197 The valuator of books made toward the door as fast as his loosened and yielding joints could carry him. 1848 *Chambers's Jrnl.* X. 423 A small daily stipend from government as a valuator of Books. 1886 C. SCOTT *Sheep-Farming* 114 The price is not always agreed upon that day; the valuators sometimes considering it advisable to wait for a time before deciding.

value (ˈvæljuː), *sb.* Forms: 4-5 **valu**, 4- **value** (4 **ualue**, 5 **walue, valwe**), 4 **valuwe**; 4, 7 **valeu**, 5 **-ieu, -eue**, 7 **valleu**; 5-7 **valewe** (5-6 **walew**, 5 **-ewe, -ywe**); 4-5 **valow(e**; 9 *dial.* **vally**. [a. OF. *value* (13th c.), *vallue* (F. dial. *vaillue*), fem. pa. pple. of *valoir* to be of worth:—L. *valēre*. Cf. med.L. *valua* (1235, from OF.), Sp. *valua*, It. *valuta*.]

I. 1. a. That amount of some commodity, medium of exchange, etc., which is considered to be an equivalent for something else; a fair or adequate equivalent or return. Phr. ***value for money*** (freq. *attrib.*).

1303 R. BRUNNE *Handl. Synne* 5966 But þou ȝyve hyt hym aȝeyn, Or þe valeu.., þou art falle þan yn þe vyce Of coueytyse. 1338 —— *Chron.* (1810) 163 Amendes I wille make... þi godes þe biken, or þe valow verray. *c* 1440 *Gesta Rom.* lxv. (Harl. MS.) 288, I saide to you þat I myȝte not selle you þe ston, no lesse þan I recyvid þerfore the trewe value. **1687** A. Lovell tr. *Thevenot's Trav.* I. 254 The other two Consuls..were not released, till their Nations..promised the Basha to pay..the value of the Ships Loadings. **1716** *Lond. Gaz.* No. 5472/4 A Bill..for Value received, for 60l. **1735** Johnson *Lobo's Abyss., Descr.* vii. 86 On Condition he paid a certain number of Cows, or the Value. **1806** Cumberland *Mem.* (1807) II. 151 We hardly could be said to have had value for our money. **1817** W. Selwyn *Law Nisi Prius* (ed. 4) II. 1286 For the recovery of the goods in question, or the value thereof, if the plaintiff cannot have the goods. **1868** Rogers *Pol. Econ.* (1876) 147 To pay at a given date..a specified sum of money, for which value has been received. **1902** W. S. Churchill in R. S. Churchill *Winston S. Churchill* (1969) II. Compan. I. 132 The first limitation is therefore the restriction of a committee on estimates to the 'merit' or 'value for money' aspect of expenditure. **1929** *Radio Times* 8 Nov. 444/3 Lissen are famed for the keen value-for-money of every component. **1951** [see promotion 1 e]. **1976** *Jrnl. R. Soc. Arts* CXXIV. 509/2 Every natural salesman knows that the true test of marketability is the subtle ratio between specification and price which even after years of anxious thought Consumers' Association can still only call 'value for money' and can still only nominate and not measure. **1977** *Management Today* July 72/2 Both in extroversion and value-for-money terms, the XJS retains the edge. **1984** *Times* 30 Apr. 25/3 The marketing manager will be impressed by an easy-to-handle, value-for-money approach.

†**b.** A standard of estimation or exchange; an amount or sum reckoned in terms of this; a thing regarded as worth having. *Obs.*

1398 Trevisa *Barth. De P.R.* vi. xvii. (Bodl. MS.), Vma is a certeyne weiȝt and valewe. *c* **1460** *Play Sacram.* 290 For so lytelle a walew in conscyence to stond bownd. **1555** Watreman *Fardle Facions* II. xi. 249 Thei game not for money, or any valewe elles. **1655** Milton *Lett. State* Wks. 1851 VIII. 333 We thought it requisite to remit beforehand two thousand Pounds of the Value of England, with all possible speed. **1754** Hanway *Trav.* vi. i. II. 146 They stripped their habitation of everything that was valuable. The Russians lost a great value [*note*, About one hundred thousand pound].

†**c.** *spec.* = valour 3 d. *Obs.*

1607 [see valour 3 d]. *a* **1631** Donne *Sat.* iii. 62 As Wards still Take such wives as their Guardians offer, or Pay valewes. **1660** *Act 12 Chas. II*, c. xxiv. §2 Values and forfeitures of marriage and all other charges incident to tenure by Knights service. **1684** Manley, *Value of Marriage* [copying Cowel: see valour 3 d].

2. a. The material or monetary worth of a thing; the amount at which it may be estimated in terms of some medium of exchange or other standard of a similar nature.

Sometimes, esp. in recent use, as the second element in combs., as *assay-*, *coin-*, *house-*, *land-value*.

1338 R. Brunne *Chron.* (1810) 83 Extendours he sette forto extend þe land... Alle þei did extend to witte þe verrey valowe. *c* **1380** Wyclif *Wks.* (1880) 414 God..wole not þat men chaffere but in þingis whoos valu þei knowen. *c* **1407** Lydg. *Reson & Sens.* 2812, I ha no konnyng dywe To declare the walywe So ryche of stonys and tresour. **1474** *Cov. Leet Bk.* 413 That ye..certifie vs as-wel of the names of all the seid gentilmen..as for þe very value of their said lyvelodes and goodes. **1552** in Feuillerat *Revels Edw. VI* (1914) 117 An Estimate of the contentes and valewe of soche parcelles and stuffe as was delyuered owte of the storehouses. *Ibid.* 118 Pantacles one paier of bridges satten in valewe iij[s] iiij[d]. **1560** Daus tr. *Sleidane's Comm.* 119b, When a benefice or prebende is fallen..what diligent inquisition is made to knowe the yearely value. **1602** *Ld. Cromwell* II. iii. 56 The King of late hath had his treasurie rob'd, And of the choysest iewelles that he had: The value of them was some seauen thousand pound. *a* **1680** Butler *Rem.* (1759) I. 53 As Metals mixt, the rich and base Do both at equal Values pass. **1771** *Encycl. Brit.* III. 255/2 Were pounds sterling, livres, florins, piastres, &c...invariable in their values. **1776** Adam Smith *W.N.* I. v. (1904) I. 43 In England..the value of all goods and of all estates is generally computed in silver. **1809** Bawdwen *Domesday Bk.* 4 In the time of King Edward the value of the city to the King was fifty-three pounds. **1859** Tennyson *Elaine* 1208 To loyal hearts the value of all gifts Must vary as the giver's. **1885** Meredith *Diana* I. 116 The value of the stock I hold has doubled.

attrib. and *Comb.* **1854** in Tomes *Amer. in Japan* 410 In Japan, as in European countries, the standard of value-weight, and that of currency-weight, differ. **1878** F. A. Walker *Money* xiii. 263 The bi-metallic theory proposes to harness two metals of somewhat diverse tendencies value-wards.

†**b.** Valuation, appraisement. *Obs.*⁻¹

c **1488** *Plumpton Corr.* (Camden) 68 It was sene by our tenants, & set to a valow what should be our charge to do, & that shall he have.

c. In phrases. ***under value***, below the proper value. † ***to good value, at a small value***, at a low or small price. ***good value*** (*colloq.*), entertaining, worth keeping company with, worth seeing, etc.

1638 Featly *Transubst.* 9 The fifth was nominated to a poore Vicaridge under vallew. **1699** Bentley *Phal.* 387 How is his Edition so scarce, that..may be purchas'd at a small value? *a* **1700** Evelyn *Diary* 14 July 1683, He..shew'd me some very rare and curious bookes, and some MSS. which he had purchas'd to good value. **1930** R. Lehmann *Note in Music* III. 102, I rather like her... She might be good value, given a chance. **1934** R. Knox *Still Dead* vii. 91 Lisbon..is really pretty good value, coming into the harbour especially. **1937** Auden & MacNeice *Lett. from Iceland* xii. 161 The geyser was better value, it went off. **1961** J. B. Priestley *Saturn over Water* vii. 104 Her eyes shone with excitement. Either the Garlettas were exceptionally good value or she was longing to get out of this house. **1979** 'S. Woods' *This Fatal Writ* 34 If it weren't for the chap's confounded habit of asking questions, he would be finding his client rather good value..because of the refreshingly casual way in which he treated..a very serious charge.

d. ***value added*** (*Econ.*), the amount by which the value of an article is increased at each stage of its production by the firm or firms producing it, exclusive of the cost of materials and bought-in parts and services; also *attrib.*, esp. in ***value added tax*** [cf. G. *mehrwertsteuer*], a tax levied on the value added to an article or the raw material forming it at each stage during its production or distribution.

1935 *Social Research* II. 161 We may call the value added tax a 'refined sales tax'. *Ibid.*, A tax which chooses as its basis of assessment the sales after deduction of all expenses for raw material and for repair or replacement of equipment, that is, a tax on the 'value added by manufacture'. **1940** *Jrnl. Polit. Econ.* XLVIII. 652 A rather imperfect form of a value-added tax was incorporated by Mr. Arthur L. Johnson in his revised old age pension bill in 1939. **1951** P. A. Samuelson *Economics* (ed. 2) xi. 236 If we insist upon decomposing the 10 cents of final product represented by the bread into the contributions of the different stages of production, we can always do so by concentrating on the so-called 'value-added' at each stage of production. **1957** J. F. Due *Sales Taxation* vii. 125 The basic intent of a value-added tax is to tax each firm on the sum of the value which it has added in the manufacturing and distribution process. **1962** *Economist* 3 Mar. 827/1 The French system of a value-added tax—that is to say, a tax on net sales, or total sales less the cost of bought-in materials and components. **1967** *Ibid.* 21 Jan. 243/2 The aids must..bring in industries with rapid growth rates and a high value-added element. **1977** M. Walker *National Front* vi. 142 A Government in mid-term (which had moreover introduced the unpopular Value Added Tax the previous month).

3. ***of value***, valuable. ***of..value***, possessed of (a specified) material or monetary worth.

c **1340** Hampole *Pr. Consc.* 9199 To precyouse stanes of vertow, And to sylver and gold and thing of valow. *c* **1400** Maundev. (Roxb.) xxvi. 124 Oile of olyfe of grete valu. *c* **1400** *Pilg. Sowle* (Caxton, 1483) IV. ix. 62 The prys of myn Appel is of suche valewe that it passeth the estymacion of ony creature. **1436** *Libel Eng. Policy* in *Pol. Poems* (Rolls) II. 162 Hit is of lytelle valeue,.. Wyth Englysshe wolle but if it menged be. **1485** Caxton *Paris & V.* (1868) 33 Not al onely these Iewelles whyche been of lytel valewe. *a* **1548** Hall *Chron., Edw. IV* (1550) 35 When he knewe the two Erles to be a praye of suche a greate value, he determined not to deliuer theim. **1556** Olde *Antichrist* 198b, So noble a garment, of more value than al y[e] treasures of golde. **1600** Pory tr. *Leo's Africa* III. 133 Their shops are full of fine earthen vessels, which are of much greater value then the things contained in them. **1628–9** Digby *Voy. Medit.* (Camden) 22 Shee [a boat] had litle of value in her. **1634** Sir T. Herbert *Trav.* 19 Gold and Siluer is of no value amongst them. **1709** T. Robinson *Nat. Hist. Westmld. & Cumbld.* vii. 37 Lead and Coal,..being of a disagreeable Nature, the one makes the other of little Value. **1771** *Encycl. Brit.* III. 260/2 The old [guineas] must be of less value still. **1861** M. Pattison *Ess.* (1889) I. 45 A tower, with a fireproof chamber for the muniments and jewels of especial value.

4. a. The equivalent (in material worth) *of* a specified sum or amount.

1362 Langl. *P. Pl.* A. xi. 34 Wolde neuer kyng ne kniht ..ȝeuen hem to heore ȝeres-ȝiue þe value of a grote! *c* **1386** Chaucer *Frankl. T.* 845 He..broghte gold vn-to this Philosophre The value of fyue hundred pound I gesse. **1412–20** Lydg. *Chron. Troy* II. 124 We trewly may aduerten ..þat for the valu of a þing of nouȝt, Mortal causes and werris first bygonne. *c* **1450** *Merlin* vii. 120 Of all the harneys that thei hade brought thider, thei hadde not with hem the valew of ij[d]. *a* **1533** Ld. Berners *Huon* xliii. 145 Thou shalt not lese the valew of one peny. *Ibid.* lxviii. 234 They left not in y[e] abbey the valew of a floren. **1613** Purchas *Pilgrimage* (1614) 652 A Bason, wherein each puts the value of twelue pence in Gold. **1771** *Encycl. Brit.* III. 260/2 If..the new guineas are below the value of a pound sterling in silver. **1839** *Penny Cycl.* XV. 322/2 A gold coin of the assayed value of 5*l.* 18*s.* 8*d.* **1887** *Whitaker's Alm.* 183 Bronze coinage..to the value of £57,563.

b. In contemptuous comparisons. Now *rare.*

c **1380** *Sir Ferumb.* 124 Ne douteþ he kyng ne Emperour þe value of a ryssche. *Ibid.* 5441 þat þe Amerel ne dredeþ hym noȝt..þe value of a kerse. *c* **1386** Chaucer *Shipman's T.* 171 He is noght worth at al In no degree the value of a flye. *c* **1400** *Laud Troy Bk.* 17506, I ȝeue right not of alle his tene, Not the value of a bene. *c* **1425** Wyntoun *Cron.* vi. xviii. 2170, I cowntyt noucht þe toþir twa Wicis þe walew of a stra. **1798** Wordsw. *P. Bell* 239 But not the value of a hair Was heart or head the better.

c. The extent or amount *of* a specified standard or measure of length, quantity, etc. Now only *dial.*

1600 Surflet *Countrie Farme* III. vi. 433 They must be sharpened like a stake for the value of the length of halfe a foote. **1731** P. Miller *Gard. Dict.* s.v. *Sap*, Flowing out very plentifully..to the Value of several Gallons in a few Days. **1764** *Museum Rust.* II. i. 10 Give each of them the value of three large table spoonfuls of the mixture for a dose. **1791** Mrs. Radcliffe *Rom. Forest* (1820) I. 67, I jogged on, near the value of a league, I warrant, and then I came to a track. **1794** —— *Myst. Udolpho* lii, They stood in the same posture for the value of a minute. **1818** Wilbraham *Chesh. Gloss.* s.v., When you come to the value of five feet deep. **1854** Miss Baker *Northampt. Gloss.* 374 There was only the vally of a bushel of apples in all the orchard. *Ibid.*, Dig down to the vally of seven or eight feet.

II. †**5. a.** Worth or worthiness (of persons) in respect of rank or personal qualities. *Obs.*

c **1330** R. Brunne *Chron. Wace* (Rolls) 4911 Alle of valow, moste & leste, Suld com to London to his feste. **1338** —— *Chron.* (1810) 100 þerfor þe duke him dight, as man of grete value. *c* **1386** Chaucer *Parson's T.* ¶ 398 Insolent is he þat dispisith in his Iugement alle oþer folk as to regard of his valieu. *c* **1400** *Brut* 248 Eueryche of ham hade ful riche ȝiftes, euery man as he was of value and of State. *c* **1425** Wyntoun *Cron.* II. viii. 721 þai þat duelt that ile wiþ in War sottis wylde of na walew. **1483** Caxton *Cato* A iiij, Thou oughtest to gyue place to hym that is gretter and more of valewe than thou arte. **1590** Greene *Mourn. Garm.* Wks. (Grosart) IX. 154 Some were Caualiers, and men of great value. *a* **1639** Wotton in *Reliq.* (1651) 484 A young Widow of value: Who lately dying..left order by Will that her body should be buried in her dwelling Parish.

†**b.** Worth or efficacy in combat or warfare; manliness, valour. *Obs.*

1590 Spenser *F.Q.* II. vi. 29 Who..his sword forth drew, And him with equall value counteruayld. **1591** Harington *Orl. Fur.* xxxiv. xii, Alceste by his value brought My father and his friends to such distress. **1614** Lodge *Seneca* 7 The Emperour..giveth a chaine of gold to some one souldier of his that approved his valew in some difficult enterprise.

6. a. The relative status of a thing, or the estimate in which it is held, according to its real or supposed worth, usefulness, or importance. In *Philos.* and *Social Sciences*, regarded esp. in relation to an individual or group; *gen.* in *pl.*, the principles or standards of a person or society, the personal or societal judgement of what is valuable and important in life.

c **1380** Wyclif *Sel. Wks.* I. 195 Oure bileve techiþ us þat God kepiþ þingis after her valu, for if ony þing be betere, God makiþ it to be betere. *c* **1385** Chaucer *L.G.W.* 602 *Cleopatra*, Loue hadde brought this man in swich a rage.. That al the world he sette at no value. **1470–85** Malory *Arthur* II. ii. 78 Your bounte..may no man preyse half to the valewe. **1584** B. R. tr. *Herodotus* I. 68 These words with Cyrus came in at one eare and went out at the other, lighter in value then the wynd in waight. **1651** Hobbes *Leviath.* I. x. 42 [Let men] rate themselves at the highest Value they can; yet their true Value is no more than it is esteemed by others. **1779** *Mirror* No. 5. 33 It unfortunately happens, that we are very inadequate judges of the value of our own discourse. **1828** Duppa *Trav. Italy*, etc. 21 These landscapes have no value but as being the earliest attempts to represent scenes from nature. **1844** H. H. Wilson *Brit. India* I. 217 Attaching to its commerce and alliance more value than belonged to either. **1884** J. Gilmour *Mongols* xvii. 205 Buddhism..tells him that each prayer repeated has a certain value in cleansing away sin. **1902** J. M. Baldwin *Dict. Philos. & Psychol.* II. 823/2 Since value is a function of desire or judgment, expressing a relation between subject and object. **1918** Thomas & Znaniecki *Polish Peasant* I. 21 By a social value we understand any datum having an empirical content accessible to the members of some social group and a meaning with regard to which it is or may be an object of activity. **1933** *Economica* XIII. 30 Like all human action social behaviour is determined..in accordance with standards of value or through conscious belief in standards assigning intrinsic value to certain types of behaviour.

pl. **1918** Thomas & Znaniecki *Polish Peasant* I. 33 Sociology..has this in common with social psychology: that the values which it studies draw all their reality, all their power to influence human life, from the social attitudes which are expressed or supposedly expressed in them. **1921** *Times Lit. Suppl.* 3 Nov. 705/4 In the effort, again, to give his characters and scenes the vivid impression of reality, the novelist, whether voluntarily or not, cannot avoid revealing not merely his powers of mind and imagination, but his spiritual and philosophical bias, his views of society, of religion, his 'values'. **1938** E. Bowen *Death of Heart* III. iv. 394 You've got a completely lunatic set of values. **1950** I. Berlin in *Foreign Affairs* XXVIII. 382 Crumbling values and the dissolution of the fixed standards and landmarks of our civilization. **1955** *Times* 10 May 8/3 Restoring to Germany the basic values of democratic civilization. **1958** *Listener* 9 Oct. 548/1 The reason..lies, I believe, in the structure of Arab society..and in its economic values. **1964** Gould & Kolb *Dict. Soc. Sci.* 744/1 Social scientists for the most part..have confined their attention to values..as empirical variables in social life whose *scientific* importance is not so much dependent on their validity and correctness as..upon the fact that they are believed..by those who hold them. **1970** N. Chomsky *At War with Asia* vi. 299 By their willingness to die, the Asian hordes..exploit our basic weakness—our Christian values which make us reluctant to bear the burden of genocide, the final conclusion of our strategic logic.

attrib. **1910** *Mind* XIX. 227 Our æsthetic, ethical and directly sensational judgments are all expressions of the fundamental value-attitude in specifically different relations. **1936** *Mind* XLV. 289 A will to maintain the society in spite of one's dissatisfaction with certain elements in its total value-pattern. **1949** G. Bateson in M. Fortes *Soc. Structure* 49 Of these differences between von Neumannian and human systems, only the differences in value scales..concern us here. *a* **1952** H. Read *Anarchy & Order* (1954) 195, I am going to assume..that 'good' and other ethical value-terms have only an emotive meaning. **1952** *Mind* LXI. 290 Attempts to construct various value-hierarchies. **1952** R. M. Hare *Lang. Morals* i. 8 'Bad' is a value-word, and therefore prescriptive. **1954** W. K. Hancock *Country & Calling* vi. 173 Myrdal saw only one remedy for it—to state explicitly the value-premises of his exploration so that writer and reader alike would always be able to distinguish the discussion of *is* from the discussion of *ought*. **1964** A. Edel in I. L. Horowitz *New Social.* 220 Some value-attitudes..are ushered into the inner sanctum of science. **1970** S. L. Barraclough in I. L. Horowitz *Masses in Lat. Amer.* iv. 123 The principal 'causes' of the agrarian problem are to be found in the population explosion,..and changing value patterns. **1977** A. Giddens *Stud. in Social & Polit. Theory* i. 91 The initial statement conceals a value premise. *Ibid.* 94 Ultimate values..involved in both the value hierarchies of individual actors, and those of overall cultures. **1977** Bullock & Stallybrass *Fontana Dict. Mod. Thought* 47/2 Any field of human discourse in which the general value-terms 'good' and 'ought' figure falls within the range of axiology. **1977** P. Howard *New Words for Old* xliii. 117 (*heading*) Value Words... The change from description to evaluation is one of the most potent agents for decaying meanings.

b. In the phr. *of* (..) *value.* (Cf. 3.)

1375 Barbour *Bruce* I. 372 Quhar it failȝeys, na wertu May be off price, na off valu. **1396–7** in *Eng. Hist. Rev.* (1907) XXII. 299 þe correlari is þe preyere of ualue spring- and out of parfyth charite. **1422** Yonge tr. *Secreta Secret.* 171 That appartenyth to a feynte herte to lowe myche a thynge of lytill walue. **1555** EDEN *Decades* (Arb.) 133 Yf this opinion bee of anye value. **1849** JAMES *Woodman* iii, There may be news of value indeed. **1855** BREWSTER *Life of Newton* II. xviii. 166 Observations of such value, that without them they could not proceed in their researches.

c. *to set a..value on* or *upon*, to estimate at a specified rate.

1651 HOBBES *Leviath.* II. xviii. 92 Considering what values men are naturally apt to set upon themselves. **1693** LOCKE *Educ.* §62 But the Backwardness Parents shew in divulging their Faults, will make them set a greater Value on their Credit themselves. *a* **1763** W. KING *Pol. & Lit. Anecd.* (1819) 101 My Lord Hardwick..who is said to be worth 800,000 *l.* sets the same value on half a crown now as he did when he was only worth one hundred. **1782** BURKE *Corr.* (1844) III. 7 You set too much value on the few and slight services, that I have been able to perform. **1842** COMBE *Digestion* 260 No one who sets any value on the lives of his horses or dogs, ever allows it to be disregarded. **1868** J. H. BLUNT *Ref. Ch. Eng.* I. 64 Wolsey set much value upon the study of Greek. **1890** *Cornhill Mag.* Oct. 365, I must see what value the kafir sets on his services.

†**d.** Estimate or opinion *of*, liking *for*, a person or thing. *Obs.*

(*a*) **1652** LOVEDAY tr. *Calprenede's Cassandra* III. 232 Thus parted those two great men, preserving in their soules such a value of one another as you may easily imagine. **1677** in *Cleveland's Poems* Ep. Ded., Such competent Judges,..in whose just value of him Clieveland shall live..the pattern of succeeding Ages.
(*b*) **1686** tr. *Chardin's Trav. Persia* 204 He has a very great Value for her by reason of her great Estate. **1709** STEELE *Tatler* No. 33 ¶5 Nay, child, do not be troubled that I take Notice of it; my Value for you made me speak it. **1749** FIELDING *Tom Jones* XIV. v, I must esteem one for whom I know Mr. Allworthy hath so much value. **1773** *Life N. Frowde* 182 In a few days she conceived a Value for me, which she expressed in the warmest Terms. **1794** MATHIAS *Purs. Lit.* (1798) 434 Men of learning have always had a proper value for the Greek language.

†**e.** *ellipt.* Esteem, regard. *Obs.*−¹

1700 DRYDEN *Fables Anc. & Mod.* Ded., I am not vain enough to boast that I have deserv'd the value of so Illustrious a Line.

f. The quality of a thing considered in respect of its power and validity for a specified purpose or effect.

1906, etc. [see *news value* s.v. NEWS *sb.* (*pl.*) 6 b]. **1933**, etc. [see *nuisance value* s.v. NUISANCE 3]. **1935** A. P. HERBERT *What a Word!* 8 To-day, instead of 'fun', we learn to speak of 'entertainment-value'. **1937**, etc. [see ENTERTAINMENT 13]. **1962** C. WINSTON *Hours Together* vi. 129 In a decade.. all this would also be a joke, and the names of these neighbourhoods..would have the same comedy value as the names he had grown up with. **1966** H. MOORE *On Sculpture* 167 These small figures, seen so much bigger, take on an extra importance and impressiveness, and are a proof that size itself has an emotional value. **1978** K. HUDSON *Jargon of Professions* 1 The solidarity-value of such nonsense-language certainly should not be underestimated. **1979** J. RABAN *Arabia through Looking Glass* v. 196 It's a synthetic soil-substitute, better than real soil by far. Its nutritional value's *much* higher.

7. a. *Math.* The precise number or amount represented by a figure, quantity, etc.

1542 RECORDE *Gr. Artes* (1575) 43 Euery Figure hathe two values: One..which it hath of his Forme, and ye other.. whiche he taketh of his Place. *a* **1680** BUTLER *Remains* (1759) II. 80 A huffing Courtier is a Cypher, that has no Value himself, but from the Place he stands in. **1715** tr. *Gregory's Astron.* (1726) I. 477 The Resolution whereof will give the Value of the Root. **1737** *Gentl. Mag.* VII. 134/2 That he can get a Value of *v* to substitute in the first Equation, to bring out the Value of *z* true. **1823** H. J. BROOKE *Introd. Crystallogr.* 255 As the value of *p* increases, the planes *b* incline more and more on the primary planes. **1867** J. HOGG *Microsc.* I. i. 2 The values of these angles..prove that the glass of the ancients differed very little from that manufactured in our own times. **1881** *Nature* No. 618. 417 So boron in the crystalline salt..has a higher atomic value than in its fluoride.

b. *Mus.* The relative length or duration of a tone signified by a note.

1662 PLAYFORD *Skill Mus.* I. vii. (1674) 25 The Semibreve ..is called the Master-Note. All the other Notes..are measured or Proportioned to its value. **1728** CHAMBERS *Cycl.* s.v. *Measure*, The Measure is regulated according to the different Quality or Value of the Notes in the Piece. **1840** *Penny Cycl.* XVI. 333/2 The value, or length in time, of the Semibreve may be considered as unity. **1869** OUSELEY *Counterp.* xix. 157 It is not allowed, in making the answer, to change the value of the notes of the subject.

c. Of cards, chessmen, or the like: Relative rank or importance according to the conventions of the game; the amount at which each (or each set) is reckoned in counting the score.

1670 COTTON *Gamester* (1680) 76 The value of the Cards [in Cribbage] is thus: Any fifteen upon the Cards is two. *Ibid.* 87 The rest of the Cards are best according to their value in pips. **1742** HOYLE *Whist* 27 Suppose you have.. four other Cards of no Value. **1850** *Bohn's Hand-Bk. Games* (1867) 152 If in cutting there be two lowest cards of a like value, the holders cut again for the deal. **1874** H. GIBBS *Ombre* (1878) 5 'French Ruff,' 'Five-cards' and other games in which the cards have the same value or nearly the same value as in Ombre.

d. *Painting.* Due or proper effect or importance; relative tone of colour in each distinct section of a picture; a patch characterized by a particular tone.

1778 SIR J. REYNOLDS *Disc.* viii. (1876) 453 A certain quantity of cold colours is necessary to give value and lustre to the warm colours. **1892** MRS. H. WARD *David Grieve* II. 312 Working [at a painting] now in the forest, now at home, the lights and values had suffered. **1896** *Daily News* 10 Feb. 3/4 The new French stamp..is printed in two impressions full and mezzo-tint, white spaces furnishing a third value.

attrib. **1902** *Academy* 12 Apr. 392/1 Replace it in the picture, it is still a vase, but quite without value relation to the other parts of the picture.

8. Special Combs.: **value analysis**, the systematic and critical assessment by an organization of design and costs in relation to realized value; also *transf.*; **value analyst**, one who undertakes a value analysis; **value calling** *Bridge*, a system of estimating bids which takes into account the scoring values of the suits; **value engineering**, the modification of designs and systems according to value analysis; **value-free** *a.*, free from criteria imposed by subjective values or standards; purely objective; = *value-neutral*; hence ***value-freedom***; **value-judgement** [cf. G. *werturteil*], a judgement predicating merit or demerit of its subject; **value-laden** *ppl. a.* = *value-loaded* ppl. adj.; hence ***value-ladenness***; **value-loaded** *ppl. a.*, weighted or biased in favour of certain values; **value-neutral** *a.*, involving no value judgements, neutral with respect to (personal or group) values; **value-orientation**, the direction given to a person's attitudes and thinking by their beliefs or standards; so ***value-oriented*** *ppl. a.*; **value-system**, any set of connected or interdependent values; **value theory**, (*a*) *Pol. Econ.*, the (Marxist) labour theory of value; (*b*) *Philos.*, axiology.

1955 K. E. BOULDING *Econ. Anal.* (ed. 3) xxxiii. 714 We can, therefore, perform something with the tools of economic analysis which might be called 'value analysis', and which should be of use in clarifying the choices involved in economic policy. **1963** *Engineering* 9 Aug. 162/1 When good engineering, manufacturing and purchasing practices are supplemented by value analysis, the cost of a product.. can be reduced by up to 25 per cent. **1977** R. HOLLAND *Self & Social Context* i. 12 It will be necessary to apply sociological techniques of value analysis in order to reach a full understanding of the theories. **1969** J. ARGENTI *Managem. Techniques* 265 Some companies establish permanent teams under a Value Analyst. **1927** *Daily Express* 8 Nov. 1/5 We do not consider that there is any general desire for the adoption of majority calling in place of value calling. **1959** *Ship & Boat Builder* Oct. 349 (*heading*) Can value engineering cut costs? **1962** *Engineering* 19 Oct. 515 Value engineering is a well-established technique in the USA... They define it as 'the systematic application of techniques and principles which aim at cutting production costs'. **1973** *Lebende Sprachen* XVIII. 73/1 *Value engineering* is a technique for reducing total cost while maintaining or improving the overall usefulness of the product or service. **1949** J. A. PASSMORE in Feigl & Brodbeck *Readings in Philos. of Sci.* (1953) 674 (*heading*) Can the social sciences be value-free? **1979** *Nature* 19 July 185/1 Science and technology are not neutral or value-free but are instruments of power, and that means political power. **1984** *Times Educ. Suppl.* 30 Nov. 3/2 Europe Singh, a maths teacher..believes maths and the sciences have wrongly been considered to be neutral and value-free. **1959** P. RIEFF *Freud* viii. 299 Scientific energies, by the facile transformation of the objectivity necessary to science into..'value-freedom', are easily enlisted to the aims of society, whatever these may be. **1892** J. ORR in *Thinker* II. 146 Two kinds of knowledge are distinguished by Ritschl—the one, religious knowledge which moves solely in the region of what he calls worth or value-judgments. **1899** GARVIE *Ritschlian Theol.* 176 The theoretical judgments cannot give an intelligible unity to the world-whole, but the value-judgments can. **1941** J. S. HUXLEY *Uniqueness of Man* xi. 229 Even in natural science, regarded as pure knowledge, one value-judgment is implicit —*belief in the value of truth*. **1961** *Listener* 30 Nov. 912/1 The decision depends on what may..be called policy considerations; that is, where the court has to make a value judgment. **1975** *Amer. N. & Q.* XIV. 53/2 Robert Frost's penchant for 'the fact' (as in 'Mowing') provides a useful measuring stick for determining the worth of value judgments about him. **1980** *Times Lit. Suppl.* 3 Oct. 1085/2 The method adopted here is a detailed interpretative analysis of poetic language and structure, liberally sprinkled with value-judgments. **1971** *Ibid.* 13 Aug. 958/4 For them, even the internal content of science is value-laden, and to some extent ideologically determined. **1977** *Jrnl. Politics* XXXIX. 24 The growing acceptance of the thesis that political science is necessarily a value-laden discipline. **1978** M. HESSE in Hookway & Pettit *Action & Interpretation* 8 A distinction between two sorts of 'value-ladenness' in social science. **1951** D. RIESMAN *Individualism Reconsidered* (1955) 33 Obviously, the very term 'masses' is heavily value-loaded. **1974** tr. *Wertheim's Evolution & Revolution* 35 To state that a given situation shows 'progress' or 'evolution'.. in relation to another situation implies the use of value-loaded criteria. **1946** GERTH & MILLS tr. M. Weber in *From Max Weber* (1947) ix. 247 Even a pirate genius may exercise a 'charismatic' domination, in the value-neutral sense intended here. **1979** *Dædalus* Winter 55 'Excellence' is not a value-neutral concept. **1951** G. W. ALLPORT in Parsons & Shils *Toward Gen. Theory Action* IV. i. 365 Prejudice is manifestly a value-orientation. **1968** W. E. LAMBERT et al. in J. A. Fishman *Readings Sociol. of Lang.* 488 In general, value orientations do not play an important role in predicting who will or will not do well in French. **1980** N. ABERCROMBIE et al. *Dominant Ideology Thesis* ii. 48 System integration is defined in terms of the processes whereby value-orientation patterns are institutionalised at the social level via the mechanism of social roles with the effect of organising the behaviour of adult members of society. **1962** N. J. SMELSER *Theory Collective Behav.* iii. 49 Behind a vast array of religious and political value-oriented movements lie the same kinds of strain. **1977** *Bull. Amer. Acad. Arts & Sci.* Oct. 16 It is at this point that value-oriented parameters for assessing progress become necessary. **1936** *Mind* XLV. 288 Persons who are not *Buerger* (citizens)..like the Jews in Nazi Germany, or the bulk of the Bantu in the Union of South Africa. For such as these, the relation to the value-system embodied in the state is of the most tenuous and indirect kind. **1969** *Listener* 3 July 3/1 Two American sociologists examined the value system of a small rural town in the American Mid-West. **1980** *Jrnl. R. Soc. Arts* June 416/2 A society in which there are overlapping different value systems which create different structures. **1887** G. B. SHAW *Let.* 17 May (1965) I. 169 Socialism does not stand or fall by the Value Theory. **1941** *Mind* L. 198 The contributions to aesthetics, value-theory, theology and Spinozistic lore have all..been published before. **1966** S. BEER *Decision & Control* x. 221 We are now in the field of value theory, the subject which attempts to bring managerial value judgments within the compass of decision theory. **1979** D. MCLELLAN *Marxism after Marx* xxiii. 309 There has been a vigorous and sophisticated defence of traditional Marxian value theory.

value ('væljuː), *v.* Forms: 5–6 **valew**, 6–7 **valewe**, 7 **vallew**; 7 *Sc.* **walow, wallow**; 6–7 **vallue**, 6– **value**. [f. the sb. Cf. Sp. *valuar*, It. *valutare*.]

I. 1. *trans.* To estimate or appraise as being worth a specified sum or amount. Const. *at*, †*to*, or with inf.

1482 CAXTON *Trevisa's Higden* VIII. i, They hadde as moche good and Jewellys, as was valewyd to fyve honderde thousand motons of Golde. **1535** COVERDALE *Lev.* xxvii. 16 It shalbe valued at fiftye Sycles of syluer. **1548** ELYOT s.v. *Aestimo*, He valewed it at iii. pence. **1627** *Rep. Parishes Scotl.* (Bann. Cl.) 2 We wallow it to be worth sex bollis off wictuall. *Ibid.* 3 Quilkis we walow at sex bollis. **1632** LITHGOW *Trav.* VIII. 355 Their Rings..were valued to a hundred Chickens of Malta. **1686** tr. *Chardin's Trav. Persia* 339, I valued it at Ten Pounds. **1734** R. SEYMOUR *Compl. Gamester* I. 27 [In the game of Codille] a Fish is generally valued at Ten Counters. **1760–72** H. BROOKE *Fool of Qual.* (1809) I. 151 The appraisers..valued the same to four pounds. **1835** *Tomlins' Law Dict.* (ed. 4) s.v. *Insurance*, After stating that the goods should be valued at so much.

†**b.** To equate in value *with* something. *Obs.*

1560 BIBLE (Geneva) *Job* xxviii. 16 Wisdome..shal not be valued with the wedge of golde of Ophir, nor with the precious onix. *Ibid.* 19.

2. To estimate the value of (goods, property, etc.); to appraise in respect of value.

1509–10 *Act 1 Hen. VIII*, c. 20 §1 Merchaundisez..to be valued after that they coste at the firste byeng or achate. **1523** FITZHERB. *Bk. Survey* j b, To value what the grasse of the gardens..be worth by the yere. **1535** COVERDALE *Lev.* xxvii. 12 Ye prest shal value it, whether it be good or bad, & it shal stonde at the prestes valuynge. **1662** J. DAVIES tr. *Olearius' Voy. Ambass.* 19 The Presents had not yet been valu'd, among which was the Cabinet.., which could not be valu'd but by them. **1755** MAGENS *Insurances* I. 197 For Labour and Wood..which has not been valued, but put at least at 25 Rixdollars. **1780** BURKE *Œcon. Reform.* Wks. III. 272, I propose to have those rights of the crown valued as manerial rights are valued on an inclosure. **1872** MORLEY *Voltaire* (1886) 206 Voltaire got his bill back, and the jewels were to be duly valued.

absol. **1667** MILTON *P.L.* VIII. 571 Weigh with her thy self; Then value.

†**b.** To rate for purposes of taxation. *Obs.*−¹

1526 TINDALE *Luke* ii. 1 All the woorlde shulde be valued.

c. With immaterial object. †Also *absol.* with *of*.

1592 GREENE *Upst. Courtier* Wks. (Grosart) XI. 228 The country swaines cannot value of my worth. **1623** HEMING & CONDELL *Ded. Shaks. Folio*, When we valew the places your H.H. sustaine, we cannot but know their dignity greater, then to descend to the reading of these trifles. **1676** HALE *Contempl.* I. 513 The Lord, who can best try, And value what is best, did pass it by.

3. To estimate or regard as having a certain value or worth: †**a.** With various constructions. *Obs.*

1589 WARNER *Alb. Eng.* VI. xxix. 129 And all their Styles together Are lesser valewed than to liue beloued of my Tuder. **1599** SHAKS. *Much Ado* III. i. 53 And her wit Values it selfe so highly, that to her All matter else seemes weake. ? **1634** EARL STIRLING *Anacrisis* ¶2, I value Language as a Conduit..: I compare a Poem to a Garden. **1661** GLANVILL *Van. Dogm.* xxiv. Apol. Philos. 247 The Swine may see the Pearl, which yet he values but with the ordinary muck. *a* **1667** JER. TAYLOR *Serm.* (1673) 124 He must by it regulate his life, and value it above secular regards. **1726** LEONI *Alberti's Archit.* I. 26/1 In India the Cypress is valu'd almost equal with the Spice Trees.

†**b.** With complementary predicate. *Obs.*

1593 SHAKS. *3 Hen. VI*, V. iii. 14 The Queene is valued thirtie thousand strong. **1619** in *Eng. & Germ.* (Camden) 107 His Master is here valued to be but a silly Jesuited soule. **1638** R. BAKER tr. *Balzac's Lett.* (vol. II) 138 He valewes himself to be worthy of an informer, and of commissioners. **1737** FRANKLIN *Ess.* Wks. 1840 II. 286 Caligula valued himself a notable dancer.

c. Const. *at* or †*of* (a specified amount). Also without prep. Usually in negative clauses.

1614 RALEIGH *Hist. World* IV. i. §1 To value at little the power of the Macedonians. **1667** DRYDEN *Sir Martin Mar-all* I. i, I will not value any man's fortune at a rush, except he have wit. **1751** LAVINGTON *Enthus. Meth. & Papists* III. (1754) 42 They don't value Ignatius of a Hair. **1754** RICHARDSON *Corr.* (1804) III. 218 If I am angry, you can't help it (as much as to say you value it not a farthing). **1848** J. GRANT *Aide-de-C.* xxiv, He would not value his ducats.. a rush. **1892** R. N. BAIN tr. *Jókai's Pretty Michal* iv. (1897) 50 He cares not a fig for muskets, and does not value his life at a boot-lace.

II. 4. To consider of worth or importance; to rate high; to esteem; to set store by.

1549 J. CHEKE in *Lett. Lit. Men* (Camden) 8 Your sight is ful of gai things abrode, which I desire not, as things sufficientli known and valewd. **1592** GREENE *Upst. Courtier* Wks. (Grosart) XI. 227 Though I am disdained of a few ouerweening fooles, I am valued as well as thy selfe with the wise. **1600** SHAKS. *A.Y.L.* I. iii. 73, I was too yong that time to value her, But now I know her. **1656** in *Verney Mem.* (1907) II. 50, I hope..that you will pries that which is most to be valewd, which is virtue. **1703** DE FOE in *15th Rep. Hist. MSS. Comm.* App. IV. 62, I value the esteem of one wise man above abundance of blessings. **1771** *Junius' Lett.* liv. (1778) 293 Perhaps the example might have taught him not to value his own understanding so highly. **1828** SCOTT *F.M. Perth* xii, Stir not your tongue,..as you value having an entire tooth in your head. **1844** LINGARD *Anglo-Sax. Ch.* (1858) II. 195 Instead of despising, he will approve and value their exertions. **1880** L. STEPHEN *Pope* iv. 94 He valued money, as a man values it who has been poor.

†**b.** To commend or praise (*to* another); to vaunt. *Obs.*

1670 R. MONTAGU in *Buccleuch MSS.* (Hist. MSS. Comm.) I. 473 That your Lordship may value it to their Ministers in England, if you find them complaining. **1672** *Ibid.* 513, I have not omitted to value to them the business of the Banquiers. *a* **1700** EVELYN *Diary* 23 Apr. 1646, In this room stands the glorious inscription of Cavaliero Galeazzo Arconati, valueing his gift to the librarie of severall drawings by Da Vinci.

†**5.** With negatives: To take account of; to heed or regard; to be concerned about; to care. *Obs.*

Freq. *c* 1630–1730 with various constructions.

1591 GREENE *Maidens Dr.* xix, But like to Scauola, for countries good, He did not value for to spend his blood. **1634** SIR T. HERBERT *Travels* 10 The foolish quality of which Bird [the booby] is to sit still, not valuing danger. **1661** in *Extr. St. Papers Friends* Ser. II. (1911) 125 My opinion is thay will not vallew their Oath. **1722** DE FOE *Plague* (1754) 84 People infected..valued not who they injur'd. **1726** SHELVOCKE *Voy. round World* (1757) 423 You are in a condition of not valuing whether the coasts are alarm'd or not. **1765** EARL HADDINGTON *Forest Trees* 19 They do not value what soil they are set in.

6. *refl.* **a.** To pride or plume (oneself) *on* or *upon* a thing. †Also *to* a person.

1667 PEPYS *Diary* 27 May, He..values himself upon having of things do well under his hand. **1699** BENTLEY *Phal.* 332 Mr. B. was not ashamed to write it, nay to value himself upon 't. *a* **1715** BURNET *Own Time* (1766) I. 20 Pierpont valued himself to me upon this service he did his country. **1748** *Anson's Voy.* III. x. 413 The calm and patient turn of the Chinese, on which they so much value themselves. **1838** LYTTON *Alice* II. ii, A sensible and frequent..speaker,..valuing himself on not being a party man. **1855** MOTLEY *Dutch Rep.* II. v. (1866) 224 Moreover.., the learned Doctor valued himself upon his logic.

b. To think highly of (oneself) *for* something.

1687 T. BROWN *Saints in Uproar* Wks. 1730 I. 75 What sort of an animal was the dragon, which thou valuest thyself so much for slaying? **1725** *Portland Papers* (Hist. MSS. Comm.) VI. 118 They value themselves here for making very fine kid gloves for ladies. **1743** J. MORRIS *Serm.* ii. 53 Those extraordinary gifts, for which the Corinthians so highly valued themselves. **1837** J. H. NEWMAN *Par. Serm.* I. xvii. 251 Every one is in danger of valuing himself for what he does.

†**7.** To give greater value to; to raise the estimation of. *Obs. rare.*

1614 RALEIGH *Hist. World* v. iii. §1. 421 Hanno..and his Partisans, being neither able to taxe the vertue of their enemies,..nor to performe the like seruices vnto the Common-weale, had nothing left, whereby to value themselues, excepting the generall reprehension of Warre. *a* **1635** NAUNTON *Fragm. Reg.* (Arb.) 16 It valued her the more,..and it took best with the people. **1673** TEMPLE *United Prov.* Wks. 1720 I. 54 The same Qualities and Dispositions do not value a private Man and a State.

III. †**8.** To equal in value; to be equivalent to. *Obs.*

1561 T. HOBY tr. *Castiglione's Courtyer* I. (1577) Gj, Seeming unto them no golde nor siluer was inough to value them. **1624** MIDDLETON *Game at Chess* III. i, This goodness Whose worth no transitory piece can value. *a* **1642** ROWLEY *Birth Merlin* IV. ii, What articles or what conditions Can you expect to value half your wrong?

†**b.** *esp.* To have the value of (so much money).

1577 HANMER *Anc. Eccl. Hist.* (1663) 12 In the Greek he writeth δραχμας, valuing six half pence a piece, the hundredth part of an Attick pound. **1611** BIBLE *Mark* xii. 15 A penny [*marg.*] Valewing of our money seuen pence halfe penie. **1634** SIR T. HERBERT *Trav.* 41 An English shilling values twentie two Pice. **1658** PHILLIPS, *Julio*, a kind of Italian coin,..valuing about six pence.

†**c.** To be worth (nothing, more, etc.). *Obs.*

1544 tr. *Littleton's Tenures* 57 The parte of that one valueth much more than the part of the other. **1602** MARSTON *Antonio's Rev.* IV. i, Whose reeling censure, if I valew not, It valewes naught. **1613** SHAKS. *Hen. VIII*, II. iii. 52 What wer't worth to know The secret of your conference? *Anne*... Not your demand; it values not your asking. **1632** LITHGOW *Trav.* III. 113 Gold..values more in purest prise, Then drosse. **1799** SOUTHEY *Lett.* (1856) I. 69 The 'Maid of the Inn' you selected for censure, and in my own mind it values little.

Hence **'valuing** *vbl. sb.*

1535 [see VALUE *v.* 2]. **1565** COOPER *Thesaurus, Aestimatio*, the prisyng or valuing of a thing. **1593** Q. ELIZ. *Boeth.* I. pr. iv. 12 The valuing of most, regardes more fortunes event, than causes merit. **1621** *Stationers' Reg.* 16 Nov. (Arb.) IV. 23 A Booke for the true valewing of anie commoditie.

valued ('væljuːd), *ppl. a.* [f. prec.]

†**1. a.** In which value is indicated. *Obs.*⁻¹

1605 SHAKS. *Macb.* III. i. 94 The valued file Distinguishes the swift, the slow, the subtle.

b. *valued policy* (see quot. 1848).

1761 in Burrow *Law Rep.* II. 1171 A valued Policy is not to be considered as a Wager Policy. **1766** *Ibid.* IV. 69. **1848** ARNOULD *Marine Insur.* I. v. (1866) I. 218 A valued policy is one in which the agreed value of the subject insured..is expressed on the face of the policy. **1903** *Daily Chron.* 25 Sept. 6/7 Let..the private individual demand a 'valued' policy, and the monopoly of the big companies collapses.

2. Estimated, appraised; to which a definite value has been assigned.

1607 MIDDLETON *Fam. Love* I. ii. 58 Art or nature never yet could set A valued price to her unvalued worth. **1613** TAPP *Pathw. Knowledge* 258 Now out of 252 li. the valued price of 12 peeces of Linnen cloth ready money, substract 46 li. [etc.] **1752** MCDOUALL *Inst. Laws Scot.* II. 333 There is no mention in the brieve or service of the Valued rent. **1798** in *Hist. Moray* (1882) I. i. 172 The valued rent is £350. **1913** R. H. GRETTON *Mod. Hist. Eng. People* I. ii. 52 Rents were refused above the 'valued rent' scale.

3. Highly esteemed or appreciated.

1665 GLANVILL *Defence Van. Dogm.* 79 Laertius sayes in his [book that] the Epicureans..were the only valued Sects of Philosophers. **1725** POPE *Odyssey* xv. 129 This silver bowl,..this valued gift be thine. **1746** FRANCIS tr. *Horace, Epist.* I. xviii. 138 You..boldly guard the injur'd Fame Of a well-known, and valued Friend. **1803** VISCT. STRANGFORD *Poems of Camoens* (1810) 107 Within my bosom's cell I bear A recent wound—a valued woe. **1841** D'ISRAELI *Amen. Lit.* (1867) 160 The exposition of a political transaction is never without some valued results. **1856** KANE *Arct. Expl.* II. xxvii. 272, I have omitted that which was its most valued characteristic. It abounded in life.

valueless ('væljuːlɪs), *a.* [f. VALUE *sb.*]

1. Destitute of value; having no value.

1595 SHAKS. *John* III. i. 101 You haue beguil'd me with a counterfeit Resembling Maiesty, which being touch'd and tride, Proues valuelesse. **1684** *Foxe's A. & M.* III. 102/1 The Sentence..might not be found faulty and valueless [*earlier edd.* valureless]. **1782** MISS BURNEY *Cecilia* VII. vi, One single obstacle has power to render them valueless. **1819** SCOTT *Leg. Montrose* vi, Take them, therefore—they are to me valueless trinkets. **1848** THACKERAY *Van. Fair* lxvii, It was found that all his property..was represented by valueless shares in different bubble companies. **1871** FREEMAN *Hist. Ess.* Ser. I. ix. 262 Like all chronicles of the kind, it is valueless alike for prophecy and for early history.

2. Priceless, invaluable. *rare*⁻¹.

1820 SHELLEY *Prometh. Unb.* IV. 281 Infinite mines of adamant and gold, Valueless stones, and unimagined gems.

Hence **'valuelessness**.

1838 *Lond. & Westm. Rev.* XXIX. 58 The valuelessness of all prior statistics of crime. **1881** BRUCE *Chief End Revelation* iv. 189 The Spinozan doctrine as to the valuelessness of miracles for the purpose of revealing God.

valuer ('væljuːə(r)). [f. VALUE *v.*] **a.** One who estimates or assesses values; a valuator. **b.** One who values, or sets a value upon something; an appreciator.

1611 COTGR., *Appreciateur*, a praiser, rater, valuer. **1638** R. BAKER tr. *Balzac's Lett.* (vol. II) 66 To say nothing more hardly of you, you are too unjust a valuer of your selfe. **1660** tr. *Amyraldus' Treat. conc. Relig.* II. viii. 266 What miserable valuers were they of its dignity. **1730** BAILEY (fol.), *Appraiser*, a Valuer of Goods. **1854** *Act 17 & 18 Vict.* c. 229 §29 To appoint a valuer to value the same. **1888** BRYCE *Amer. Commw.* I. 493 The varying scales on which valuers proceed. **1893** *The Voice* (N.Y.) 31 Aug., A chairmaker..might bring a chair, and receive from the valuer..notes for as many hours' value [etc.].

†**valure**, *sb. Obs.* Also 5 **valur, wallure**, 6 **valuer, va(l)lewer**. [app. an alteration of OF. *valur* or *valeur* VALOUR, after forms in -URE.]

1. a. Worthiness or merit; = VALOUR 1 a.

1422 YONGE tr. *Secreta Secret.* 139 What glory or what valure the may be-tyde. *c* **1440** *Ipomydon* 284 She saw also by his norture, He was a man of grete valure. *c* **1481** CAXTON *Dialogues* 4 Be swyft and redy Hym or hem first to grete, Yf he be or they be men of valure. **1577** STANYHURST *Descr. Ireland* vii. in *Holinshed*, I doubt not, but hys fame and renowme in learnyng, shall be aunswerable to his desert and valure in writyng. **1592** WYRLEY *Armorie* 65 As to the gaser well it might appeere That all the Vallewer in the world was heere.

b. Physical strength or ability; power, might. *rare.*

1574 HELLOWES *Gueuara's Fam. Ep.* (1577) 3 Of our selues we are so weake, and our abilitie so small, our valure so litle, and haue so few things, that..of our selues we haue not what to giue. **1605** WILLET *Hexapla Gen.* 440 Causing the Cananites to feare his force and valure.

c. Courage, bravery; = VALOUR 1 c.

Common *c* 1580–1610.

1577–82 BRETON *Flourish upon Fancy* Wks. (Grosart) I. 18/2 Thy valure is but vauntes, thy weapons are but wordes. **1585** T. WASHINGTON tr. *Nicholay's Voy.* IV. xii. 125 The Arabians..beleue that in valure & hardines they doe surpasse al the other nations. **1606** CHAPMAN *Gent. Usher* I. i, This is your old valure, nephew, that will fight sleeping as well as waking. **1640–1** *Kirkcudbr. War-Comm. Min. Bk.* (1855) 50 Barrones and gentilmen of good soirt..by quhas valure the kingdome hath ever been defendit.

2. Worth, importance, efficacy. Freq. in the phr. *of no valure.*

(*a*) *c* **1400** *Pilgr. Sowle* I. xxiv. (1859) 29 This excusacyon is of no valure. **1509** FISHER *7 Penit. Ps.* xxxviii. Wks. (1876) 81 Good hope,..without the whiche euery thynge that we do is of no valure. **1594** CAREW *Huarte's Exam. Wits* v. (1596) 61 We call memory a reasonable power, because without it the vnderstanding and the imaginatiue are of no valure.

(*b*) **1456** SIR G. HAYE *Law Arms* (S.T.S.) 214 For ellis war it litill of valure the privilege that the Emperour has gevin to the haly kirk. *a* **1533** LD. BERNERS *Gold. Bk. M. Aurel.* (1546) B vj b, Wordes, whiche were not mete,..rude, and least of valure. **1577** HARRISON *England* II. vi. (1877) II. 149 These [wines] are not least of all accompted of, bicause of their strength and valure. **1596** BELL *Surv. Popery* III. ix. 397 The naturall valure only of good words. *Ibid.*, The valure and just estimation of eternal life.

3. = VALUE *sb.* 2.

1453 *Rolls of Parlt.* V. 269/1 Decreas of the pris and valure of the wolles. *c* **1489** CAXTON *Sonnes of Aymon* xvi. 374 And whan Reynawde saw that that gyfte was so riche he was glad of it, bycause of yᵉ grete valure of it. **1523** *Act 14 & 15 Hen. VIII*, c. 2 [They] shall..put to such markes to every of the same wares..upon payne of forfeyture the double valure of the same wares. **1568** GRAFTON *Chron.* II. 387 Swearing vnto him that he would prouyde other for him, that should amount to as good a valure. **1588** J. MELLIS *Briefe Instr.* Ej, Putting the valure of them, how much they be, after the common price in ready money.

b. In the phr. *of* (*great*, etc.) *valure.*

1485 CAXTON *Paris & V.* (1868) 7 A shelde of crystalle of grete valure. **1491–2** *Sarum Church-w. Acc.* (Swayne) 41 Smalle peces of clene golde of litelle valure. **1523** LD. BERNERS *Froiss.* I. cccxx. 495 He reputed this aduenture of more value than v. hundred thousande frankes. **1553** EDEN *Treat. New Ind.* (Arb.) 14 Hys horse is judged to be of such valure if you respect ye price, as is one of our cities. **1599** HAKLUYT *Voy.* II. 234 There they put all their goods of any valure.

4. = VALUE *sb.* 4. Const. *of* (so much).

c **1480** *Childe of Bristowe* in Hazl. *E.P.P.* I. 124 Alle that for me thu dos pray, helpeth me not..the valure of a pese. **1485** CAXTON *Chas. Gt.* 110, I doubte the not the valure of an olde dede hounde. **1518** *Star Chamber Cases* (Selden Soc.) II. 138 Robert edward wyll spende..to the valuer of twenty markys to helpe them with all. **1534** MORE *Comf. agst. Trib.* II. Wks. 1184/1 He neuer vsed to passe vpon himselfe the valure of six pence at a meale.

5. = VALUE *sb.* 7 b.

1597 MORLEY *Introd. Mus.* Pref., With what toyle and wearinesse I was enforced to compare the parts for trying out the valure of some notes.

Hence †**valure** *v. trans.*, = VALUE *v.* 2. *Obs.* Also †**valureless** *a.*, valueless. *Obs.* †**valurous** *a.*, valuable (cf. VALOROUS *a.* 3). *Obs.*

1487 *Act 3 Hen. VII*, c. 7 §1 The nature, weight, content, or valure of all maner other merchandises used to be weyed or valured. **1563** FOXE *A. & M.* 1028/2 The sentence thereof might not be founde fautye and valureles by me. **1586** MARLOWE *1st Pt. Tamburl.* I. ii, Thy Garments shall be ..Enchast with precious iuelles of mine owne: More rich and valurous than Zenocrates.

valure, obs. variant of VELURE.

valuta (və'l(j)uːtə). Pl. **valute, valuten**. [(G. a.) It. *valuta*:—late L. **valuta*, use as sb. of fem. pa. pple. of L. *valēre* to be worth.] Foreign currency; a monetary standard, the currency constituting an acceptable medium of exchange, the valuation constituting an acceptable rate of exchange. Also *attrib.*, *transf.*, and *fig.*

1893 R. BITHELL *Counting-House Dict.* (rev. ed.) 314 *Valuta*, Russian paper money. **1921** *Glasgow Herald* 28 Oct. 11 The speculation in valute and devisen has become..ridiculous, as the great boom on the Berlin exchange proves. **1924** LUCAS & BONAR tr. *Knapp's State Theory of Money* 106 Everywhere there is a valuta or standard money. *Ibid.* 165 If there is more than one kind of money in the country, the value in valuta money is always meant. *c* **1939** E. BENN *Diary in Happier Days* (1949) xiv. 171 He doubted if the *valuten* could be found to send the Führer to England. **1954** E. H. CARR *Interregnum* i. 29 A general decree was issued 'On Valuta Operations'... It confined transactions in foreign valuta to the Exchanges. **1964** S. BELLOW *Herzog* 143 A mob broke into his house..looking for *valuta*. **1967** *Economist* 19 Aug. p. xxix/1 Russia is still the chief importer of Skoda products, but the emphasis is gradually shifting to the West and other areas. A nominal level of *valuten* income is now set. **1972** M. MUGGERIDGE *Chron. Wasted Time* I. v. 252 All were deeply moved;..as, indeed, was I, despite my valuta origins and prospects. **1979** F. E. PERRY *Dict. Banking* 262/1 *Valuta*, rate of exchange, value, currency; entries in bank books which fix charges to be made or interest charges due, such as the determination of opening and closing dates for the relative periods.

valuwen, southern ME. var. FALLOW *v.*

valva ('vælvə). *Ent.* [L.: see VALVE *sb.*¹] = VALVE *sb.*¹ 3 a, b.

1802 W. KIRBY *Monographia Apum Angliæ* I. 110 *Valvæ*. These have been frequently noticed. Swammerdam calls them *appendages of the sting*. **1826** [see VALVE *sb.*¹ 3 b]. **1924** *Ann. Entomol. Soc. Amer.* XVII. 276 The term valvæ or valves was used to denote the two lateral outer appendages. **1975** *Entomologist's Gaz.* XXVI. 198 There is in my material a further specimen..showing some variation in the valva.

'valval, *a. Bot.* [f. VALVE *sb.* 4 b.] *valval view*, that aspect of a diatom in which one of the valves is turned to the observer; the side-view.

1891– in *Cent. Dict.* and later Dicts.

valvar ('vælvə(r)), *a.* [f. VALVE *sb.* + -AR.] Of the nature of, pertaining to, a valve. In *Med.* = VALVULAR *a.* 3.

1831 MACGILLIVRAY tr. *Richard's Elem. Bot.* 420 Their calyx is superior with four or five valvar divisions. **1859** MAYNE *Expos. Lex.*, *Valvaris*,..of or belonging to a valve: valvar. **1895** *Jrnl. R. Microsc. Soc.* 669 Dr. O. Müller proposes a new terminology for diatoms... The plane which passes through the apical and the transapical axes is the valvar plane. **1946** *Nature* 26 Oct. 588/1 Division took place along the longitudinal axis in what would have been the valvar plane. **1955** *Guy's Hospital Rep.* CIV. 372 Kirklin *et al.*..have also drawn attention..to this association between valvar and infundibular stenosis. **1977** *Amer. Heart Jrnl.* XCIII. 461/1 Mitral regurgitation or other mitral valvar abnormality has been reported in four other cases. **1980** *Plant Systematics & Evolution* CXXXV. 266 (*caption*) Region of the intercalary bands seen parallel to the valvar plane.

valvassor, variant of VAVASOUR.

valvate ('vælvət), *a. Bot.* [ad. L. *valvāt-us* having folding-doors, f. *valva* VALVE *sb.*]

1. Of sepals or petals: Applied to each other by the margins only.

1830 LINDLEY *Nat. Syst. Bot.* 51 Hamamelideæ, which are known by their habit,..and also by their valvate sepals and petals. 1870 HOOKER *Stud. Flora* p. xi, Malvaceæ:.. Sepals 5, valvate.

b. Of a calyx: Composed of sepals so united.

1858 CARPENTER *Veg. Phys.* §556 The calyx of the Rhamneæ being valvate (i.e. the sepals, before expanding, having their edges in proximity with each other). 1877 HULME *Wild Flowers* I. p. xiii, Calyx five-partite, valvate in bud.

2. Of æstivation or vernation: Characterized by this arrangement of parts.

1829 LINDLEY *Synops. Brit. Bot.* 72 Calyx monophyllous, 4–5 cleft, with a valvate æstivation. 1849 BALFOUR *Man. Bot.* §186 Sometimes they are..placed so as to touch each other by their edges; thus giving rise to valvate vernation. 1861 BENTLEY *Man. Bot.* 218 The valvate æstivation may be seen in the calyx of the Lime.

valve (vælv), *sb.*[1] Also 5 valwe, 7 value. [ad. L. *valva* leaf of a door (usu. pl. *valvæ* a folding door). So F. *valve* (1611), Pg. *valva.*]

I. 1. a. One or other of the halves or leaves of a double or folding door.

1387 TREVISA *Higden* (Rolls) IV. 449 At þe laste þey brende þe valves of þe temple þat were i-heled wit gold. *c*1440 *Promp. Parv.* 508/1 Valwe, *valva, vel valve.* 1661 BLOUNT *Glossogr.* (ed. 2), *Valves*, folding doors or windows. 1718 POPE *Odyss.* I. 555 The bolt, obedient to the silken cord, To the strong staple's inmost depth restored, Secured the valves. 1834 BECKFORD *Italy* I. 326 Throwing open the valves, we entered the chapel. 1863 BARING-GOULD *Iceland* 280 The outside of the valves [of the triptych] was painted with figures of S. John the Baptist and Moses. 1871 B. TAYLOR *Faust* (1875) II. III. 164 Ye valves of yon dark iron portals!

*transf. c*1530 *Judic. Urines* I. iii. 8 For to delyuer and purge them oute by that membre, that is to say, by the matryce, and so out by the value, that is to say, by yᵉ gate of hyr body.

b. A door controlling the flow of water in a sluice.

1790 *Act 33 Geo. III*, c. 90 §65 If any Person..cause to be opened..any Lock Gate, or any Paddle, Valve, or Clough, belonging to any Lock..on the said Canal. 1847 DWYER *Princ. & Pract. Hydraul. Engin.* 74 The gate or valve of a sluice is generally made to move by machinery in a vertical position.

2. *Conch.* One of the halves of a hinged shell; a single shell of similar form; a single part of a compound shell.

1661 LOVELL *Hist. Anim. & Min.* Isagoge b 7 b, Some are covered on every side, as oisters, cocks, and tellinæ; others have but one valve, the other side sticking to rocks. 1771 *Phil. Trans.* LXI. 232, I separated the valves, and the rising part of the hinge to the edge shewed them to be shells. 1774 GOLDSM. *Nat. Hist.* (1776) VII. 69 These shells take different forms, and are often composed of a different number of valves; sometimes six; sometimes but three. 1828 STARK *Elem. Nat. Hist.* II. 80 The hollow valve of this species..was formerly used as a drinking cup. *Ibid.*, The lower valve white, and longitudinally sulcated; upper valve rufous. 1871 T. R. JONES *Anim. King.* (ed. 4) 540 The elastic ligament for opening the valves..being placed externally instead of within the shell.

3. *Ent.* **a.** = VALVULA 2.

1802 W. KIRBY *Monographia Apum Angliæ* I. 110 Linneus, in his character of *Ichneumon*, calls them the valves of the vagina of the aculeus. They are the covers of the genuine vagina. 1919 *Ann. Entomol. Soc. Amer.* XII. 277 The sternal region of segment nine is shifted.., thus bringing the bases of the dorsal and inner valvulæ into the same transverse plane with those of the ventral valves. 1969 R. F. CHAPMAN *Insects* xvii. 325 If the insect oviposits in plant or animal tissue the valves are sclerotised and lanceolate.

b. (See quot.)

1826 KIRBY & SP. *Entomol.* xxxiii. III. 390 *Valvæ* (the Valves), two lateral laminae, often coriaceous, by which the ovipositor when unemployed is covered.

c. A clasper of a male butterfly.

1864 *Trans. Linn. Soc.* XXV. 35 There remain therefore only the characters of the perfect insect, the most important of which are the anal valves in the male. These..are furnished with projecting points or spines..which serve to attach the male more firmly to the female *in copulâ.* 1883 *Ibid.: Zool.* II. 332 *C. Eubule* has a very curious valve, armed as elaborately, and as singularly, as that of many a *Papilio.* 1964 R. M. & J. W. FOX *Introd. Compar. Entomol.* iii. 109 Other orders with periphallic claspers (harpes, harpagones, valves, etc.) form them from the coxae and exite styli of the appendages of at least the ninth segment.

4. *Bot.* **a.** One of the halves or sections of a dehiscent pod, pericarp, or capsule.

1760 J. LEE *Introd. Bot.* I. vi. (1765) 13 *Siliqua*, a Pod, is a Pericarpium of two Valves, wherein the Seeds are fastened along both the Sutures or Joinings of the Valves. 1796 WITHERING *Brit. Plants* (ed. 3) I. 294 Pod long, cylindrical; ..valves 2, opening with a jerk, and the valves rolling back. 1861 BENTLEY *Man. Bot.* 452 The valves of the fruit opening longitudinally, and bearing transverse septa in their interior. 1870 HOOKER *Stud. Flora* 235 Capsule globose;..valves septiferous.

b. In various applications (see quots.).

1785 MARTYN *Lett. Bot.* xiii. (1794) 130 The inner [chaff] consisting also of two parts or valves, which you may call petals. 1796 WITHERING *Brit. Plants* (ed. 3) I. 176 Bloss[om]. 1 petal, funnel-shaped. Tube cylindrical, crooked... Mouth closed by 5 prominent, convex, approaching valves. 1812 *New Bot. Gard.* I. 23 The stamina have six filaments, subulate, inserted into the valves of the nectary. 1832 LINDLEY *Introd. Bot.* 104 The pieces of which these three classes of bracteæ are composed are called valves or valvulæ by the greater part of botanists. *Ibid.* 126 In the most common state of the anther the cells..open with two valves, by a longitudinal fissure from the base to the apex. 1870 HOOKER *Stud. Flora* 12 Anthers opening by 2 ascending lids or valves.

c. Each of the two siliceous cell walls of a diatom, similar in shape but slightly different in size, with one overlapping the other.

1852 A. PRITCHARD *Hist. Infusorial Animalcules* (rev. ed.) III. 295 Siliceous valves are deposited *exterior* to a cell-membrane. 1857 HENFREY *Bot.* §629 The cells [of Diatomaceæ]..enclosed by a membrane..impregnated with silex and separable into valves. 1898 H. C. PORTER tr. *Strasburger's Text-bk. Bot.* II. i. 313 Both valves are so strongly impregnated with silica, that, even when subjected to intense heat, they remain as a siliceous skeleton, retaining the original form and markings of the cell walls. 1973 R. G. KRUEGER et al. *Introd. Microbiol.* iii. 125/1 The newer valve of any diatom is invariably the smaller valve, because it is constructed within the confines of the older valve.

II. 5. *Anat.* **a.** A membranous fold in an organ or passage of the body (esp. in the heart, arteries, and veins), which automatically closes after the manner of a trap-door to prevent the reflux of blood or other fluid.

1615 CROOKE *Body Man* 180 In each of these passages there are Values which hinder the refluence of the choler. 1653 MORE *Antid. Ath.* Scholia II. xii. §6 As to the Fabrick of the Valves and Veins of the Heart. 1688 BOYLE *Final Causes* iv. 157 Our famous Harvey..took notice that the valves in the veins..were so placed that they gave free passage to the blood towards the heart. 1799 *Med. Jrnl.* II. 371 This foramen in the embryo..is closed by a valve which prevents the reflux of the blood. 1830 R. KNOX *Béclard's Anat.* 208 The valves..close the vein, sustain the blood, and prevent its reflux towards the capillary vessels. 1870 ROLLESTON *Anim. Life* p. xlv, The valves, which in other Vertebrata guard the entrance of the great veins into the right auricle.

b. A similar part or structure serving to close a passage for other reasons.

1805 BINGLEY *Anim. Biog.* (ed. 3) I. 97 Within each [ear] there is a kind of secondary auricle..so placed as to serve for a valve or guard to the auditory passage. 1813 *Ibid.* (ed. 4) I. 110 The ears are short, and have each a very small inner valve. 1835–6 *Todd's Cycl. Anat.* I. 322/1 The pyloric orifice of the gizzard is guarded by a valve in many birds. 1863 A. M. BELL *Princ. Speech* 192 When the Stammerer has brought the *valve* of the throat—the glottis—under due control.

fig. 1871 R. H. HUTTON *Ess.* (1877) I. 74 Animals.. have, so to say, fewer valves in their moral constitution for the entrance of divine guidance.

†6. A supposed check (similar to above) to the reflux of sap in plants. *Obs.*

1664 *Phil. Trans.* I. 30 About the Pores of bodies, and a kind of Valves in wood. 1673–4 GREW *Anat. Pl., Anat. Trunks* (1682) 126 Which..plainly shews, That in the Sap-Vessels of a Plant, there are no Valves. *a*1704 LOCKE *Elem. Nat. Phil.* ix. (1754) 35 The heat dilating, and the cold contracting those little tubes; supposing there be valves in them, it is easy to be conceived how the circulation is performed in plants. 1807 VANCOUVER *Agric. Devon* (1813) 435 These valves possess a contractile force,..whereby the regress of the moisture is prevented, and of course it is taken up by the tree.

7. a. *Mech.* A device of the nature of a flap, lid, plug, etc., applied to a pipe or aperture to control the passage of air, steam, water or the like, usually acting automatically by yielding to pressure in one direction only.

Many classes and varieties of valves are in use, and are distinguished by special epithets denoting form or purpose, as *ball-, clack-, cone-, disk-, flap-valve; air-, escape-, feed-, injection-valve*, etc. See also SAFETY-VALVE.

1659 LEAK *Waterwks.* 13 Of the Value or Suspiral. It will be also necessarie..to demonstrate the manner of the value of Copper which openeth itself by intervals. 1667 *Phil. Trans.* II. 447 A Square Woodden Bucket..on the ends of which are the moveable bottoms or Valves *EE.* 1702 SAVERY *Miner's Fr.* 68 Will not these Brass Valves..in your Engine speedily ware out? 1800 VINCE *Hydrost.* ix. (1806) 91 Each sucker has a valve opening upwards. 1839 R. S. ROBINSON *Naut. Steam Eng.* 11 The pressure shuts the valve in the neck of the air vessel, and opens the valve in the piston. 1889 WELCH *Naval Archit.* 133 Self-acting or automatic valves are fitted where watertight bulkheads..are pierced for ventilation purposes.

fig. 1830 GEN. P. THOMPSON *Exerc.* (1842) I. 295 The slightest degree of popular interference which can act as a valve to the great boiler, and prevent the whole from blowing up. 1847 DE QUINCEY *Secr. Soc.* Wks. 1863 VI. 236 There was a valve in reserve, by which your perplexity could escape. 1930 AUDEN *Poems* 56 No chattering valves of laughter emphasized..the sessile hush. 1933 E. O'NEILL *Ah, Wilderness!* IV. i. 116 Seizes this as an escape valve—turns and fixes his youngest son with a stern forbidding eye.

b. *Electronics.* = *thermionic valve* s.v. THERMIONIC *a.*

1905 J. A. FLEMING in *Proc. R. Soc.* LXXIV. 478 We have in this vacuum valve and associated mirror galvanometer a means of detecting feeble alternating electric currents or oscillations. *Ibid.* 479 This arrangement of a differential galvanometer and two valves transforms..more of the alternating oscillation into direct current than when one valve alone is used. 1924 GIBSON & COLE *Wireless of To-Day* xxiv. 307 Monster valves have now been manufactured absorbing as much as 100 kw. each, and in consequence of the tremendous heat generated, the electrodes are specially constructed permitting water to circulate within for cooling purposes. 1928 *Electr. Communication* VI. 241/2 The high-power amplifying tubes, which over here [*sc.* in Britain] we call 'valves'. 1943 C. L. BOLTZ *Basic Radio* x. 165 All battery-fed radio apparatus utilizes directly-heated valves, which need 2V on the filament. 1968 M. GUYBON tr. *Solzhenitsyn's First Circle* lxxv. 476 He was a radio engineer by training, and hadn't a box containing two valves been found during the search of his flat?

c. *Chess.* (See quot. 1930.)

1930 WHITE & HUME *Valves & Bi-Valves* 7 In chess problem terminology, the designation of a Valve has been given to any move which simultaneously opens one line while it closes another. In a broad sense, Valves include a large domain with many varied combinations of themes. There is a much narrower application of the term: Valve, and that is the particular case where not only is the move made by Black, but both of the lines affected are also Black. 1936 P. W. SERGEANT tr. *Znosko-Borovsky's Art of Chess Combination* II. v. 62 In the interception of lines one closes lines to the adversary at critical points, while here one opens lines to one's own pieces. The skilled hand deals with the valves on this side and on that.

8. *attrib.* and *Comb.* **a.** In sense 7 a, as ***valve-board, -box, casing, chest, engine, face***, etc.; ***valve governor, lifter; valve-like, -shaped*** adjs.; also in collocations used attributively, as ***valve-guide stem, valve-rod end***; also used to designate brass instruments whose range is increased by the addition of valves, as ***valve horn, trombone*** (so ***trombonist***), ***trumpet***; in sense 7 b, esp. designating apparatus employing valves, as ***valve circuit, detector, heater, -holder, oscillator, receiver, set, voltmeter***.

The number of attributive uses is very great, esp. in recent technical works.

1869 *Eng. Mech.* 24 Dec. 352/3 There is a board screwed down on the top of A. That is the *valve-board. 1885 C. G. W. LOCK *Workshop Receipts* Ser. IV. 290/2 The valve-boards are next hinged on to the feeder-boards. 1797 *Encycl. Brit.* (ed. 3) XVII. 766/2 Above..is the seat of the lower steam valve, opening into the *valve box. 1869 *Eng. Mech.* 3 Dec. 282/2 Take the high pressure valves out of the valve-box. 1839 R. S. ROBINSON *Naut. Steam Eng.* 44 The flange to which is bolted the *valve casing. 1887 D. A. LOW *Machine Draw.* (1892) 74 An elevation of the valve casing with the cover and the valve removed. 1839 R. S. ROBINSON *Naut. Steam Eng.* 62 The blow-through pipe, terminating in a *valve chest. 1889 WELCH *Naval Archit.* xi. 124 In the former, a suction-box or valve chest V is fitted beneath the pump. 1915 HAWKHEAD & DOWSETT *Handbk. Wireless Telegraphists* 119 If an E.M.F. be applied to the *valve circuit a more sensitive condition is obtained. 1934 *Times Rev. 1933* 1 Jan. p. ix/4 The Wireless Exhibition at Olympia illustrated the exceptional advances made during the year in valve and valve-circuit technique. 1915 HAWKHEAD & DOWSETT *Handbk. Wireless Telegraphists* 120 The *valve detector is used with various circuits. 1797 J. CURR *Coal Viewer* 44 The plug floor in all the common engines falls $17\frac{1}{2}$ inches below the top of the boiler, and in the *valve engine it falls 2 feet 1 inch below. 1864 WEBSTER, **Valve-face.* 1887 D. A. LOW *Machine Draw.* (1892) 70 The angle which the valve face makes with its axis is generally 45°. 1842 *Penny Cycl.* XXII. 508/2 To bring the *valve-gear within..reach of the engineer. 1835 URE *Philos. Manuf.* 27 *Valve governors, shafts, and other geering of mills. 1875 KNIGHT *Dict. Mech.* 2476/1 The *valve-guide stem has an end knob, by which its falling out is prevented. 1929 *Radio Times* 8 Nov. 443/3 Get the necessary output from a Regentone mains unit for A.C. *valve heaters. 1960 *Practical Wireless* XXXVI. 326/2 Commence wiring the valve heaters by taking a tightly twisted pair of insulated wires from V1 to V2. 1922 *Wireless World* 4 Mar. 748/1 The base..carries the *valve holder. 1960 *Practical Wireless* XXXVI. 392/2 Positions for the valve holders can be marked out from the measurements indicated in Fig. 2. 1877 *Valve horn [see *valve trumpet* below]. 1938 *Oxf. Compan. Mus.* 439/2 The valve horn has the immense advantage of..a chromatic series, for three valves add instantaneously to the air column a length corresponding respectively to a semitone, two semitones, and three semitones. 1959 *Listener* 4 June 1001/3 The more limpid yet penetrating tone of the narrower-bored French valve-horn. 1977 *Early Music* Apr. 221/2 Scores of the valve horn era. 1839 R. S. ROBINSON *Naut. Steam Eng.* 97 The eccentric rod pulled backwards and forwards by means of the *valve lifter. 1851 S. P. WOODWARD *Mollusca* (1856) 34 The in-coming and out-going currents..are kept apart by a *valve-like fringe. 1859 SEMPLE *Diphtheria* 296 A valve-like sound or a peculiar hissing noise. 1871 *Leisure Hour* 8 Apr. 222/2 The balloon had been gyrating, and the *valve-line become twisted. 1963 [see *rip line* s.v. RIP *sb.*[4] 5]. 1969 *Gloss. Aeronaut. & Astronaut. Terms (B.S.I.)* VII. 8 *Valve line*, a cord for the operation of a valve. 1935 *Discovery* Aug. 226/1 In some forms of *valve oscillator, the high-tension supply is such that only half of the wave of the a.c. feed mains is rectified. 1836–41 BRANDE *Chem.* (ed. 5) 524 A slender pipe, open at both ends, inserted into the *valve-plug. 1913 *Wireless World* Nov. 478/1 A *valve receiver of rather longer range than usual is used. 1929 *Radio Times* 8 Nov. 437/1 This popular Loud Speaker unit..gives..perfect results with any valve Receiver. 1831–3 *Encycl. Metrop.* (1845) VIII. 187/1 In this engine the working the valves is effected by eccentrics..below the *valve rods. 1861 SIR W. FAIRBAIRN *Iron* 123 To knock off the point of the trigger from the shoulder on the valve-rod. 1887 D. A. LOW *Machine Draw.* (1892) 119 Valve-rod end for a marine engine. 1841 *Civil Eng. & Arch. Jrnl.* IV. 379/2 H, the *valve-seat. 1844 *Ibid.* VII. 190/2 The next valve was composed of several triangular pieces, opening on leather joints, from the circumference of the *valve seating. 1929 *Radio Times* 397/1 Her nursery..is wired for broadcasting and..her movements or cries are now heard loud in the sitting-room ..where our *valve set is placed. 1981 S. BRIGGS *Those Radio Times* i. 28/2 By 1926..the valve set playing through loudspeakers replaced the simple crystal set. 1879 *St. George's Hosp. Rep.* IX. 365 Small *valve-shaped wound over outer side of fracture. 1844 *Civil Engin. & Arch. Jrnl.* VII. 192 It was quite clear the *valve-spindle must be of adequate strength. 1888 *Lockwood's Dict. Mech. Engin.* 397 *Valve stem*, a *valve spindle or rod. 1889 J. M. WHITHAM *Steam-Engine Design* iv. 98 If the valve..is long, the weight, friction, and diameter of the valve-stem are increased. 1970 K. BALL *Fiat 600, 600D Autobook* i. 13/1 Valve stems, once bent, cannot be straightened satisfactorily. 1883 O. COON *Harmony & Instrumentation* xxvi. 73 The *valve Trombone is often substituted for the one with a slide. **1979** *Jazz Jrnl.* XXXII. 11/1 (*caption*) Thad Jones on valve trombone. **1946** R. BLESH *Shining Trumpets* (1949) xii. 263 The *valve trombonist Brad Gowans. **1877** E. PROUT *Instrumentation* v. 81 The *valve-trumpet.. possesses, like the valve-horn, a complete chromatic scale. **1979** *Oxf. Junior Compan. Music* 331/4 The trumpet now in everyday orchestral use is the *valve trumpet*. That is to say, it has extra lengths of tubing coiled alongside its main tube, and these can be brought into action by pressing down a 'valve'. **1827** FARADAY *Chem. Manip.* xv. (1842) 373 Applying the mouth to the lower aperture of the *valve tube. **1925** *Valve voltmeter [see *slide-back* s.v. SLIDE- c].

b. In sense 4, as ***valve-flap, -lesion, segment.*** Many others occur in recent medical works.

1879 *St. George's Hosp. Rep.* IX. 433 The junction of two of the aortic valve-flaps. **1898** *Allbutt's Syst. Med.* V. 952 A deformed valve segment must.. be a strained segment. *Ibid.* 1024 In the remainder there was no valve-lesion.

c. Special Combs.: **valve head** *Mech.*, the part of a lift valve that is lifted off the valve aperture to open the valve; **valve-shell**, a gasteropod of the genus *Valvata*; **valve-tailed bat** (see quot.); **valve train** *Mech.*, in an internal-combustion engine, the gearing and linkages by which the crankshaft is caused to open and close a valve at the proper time.

1904 A. B. F. YOUNG *Compl. Motorist* (ed. 2) iv. 91 The valve-head is provided with a slot for the insertion of a tool for grinding purposes. **1971** B. SCHARF *Engin. & its Lang.* xii. 176 One also differentiates between ordinary, high lift and full lift safety and relief valves according to the distance by which the valve head is automatically raised. **1851** WOODWARD *Mollusca* I. 140 *Valvata*,.. Valve-shell. **1871** *Cassell's Nat. Hist.* I. 316 *note*, The Valve-tailed Bat.. is remarkable.. for the presence of a curious horny case, composed of two parts, which covers the extremity of the tail. **1955** W. H. CROUSE *Automotive Engines* vii. 222 The L-head engine uses a relatively simple valve train, or valve mechanism. **1981** *Pop. Hot Rodding* Feb. 31/1 A Sig Erson camshaft actuates the mildly worked valve-train, composed of Crane valve-springs, steel retainers, and TRW chrome-moly pushrods.

†**valve**, *sb.*[2] *Obs.* [perh. an error for *volve, by confusion with prec.] A turn of a bandage.

1689 J. MOYLE *Abstr. Sea Chyrurgery* I. vi. 45 Then a soft Rouler to come several turns about it, and every valve as it comes over the wound cut.. in the middle. *Ibid.* 46.

valve, *v. rare* exc. in ballooning, etc. [f. VALVE *sb.*[1]]

1. *trans.* To furnish with a valve or valves; to govern or check, to hold *back*, by a valve or similar device. Also *fig.*

1861 SMILES *Engineers* II. 160 Whilst the fresh waters should be allowed freely to escape, the sea should be valved back, and prevented flowing in upon the land. **1899** *Allbutt's Syst. Med.* VI. 512 It is probable that by these synapses the circuits of the nervous system.. are.. securely valved against regurgitation. **1960** R. W. MARKS *Dymaxion World B. Fuller* 11/1 The harnessing factor—the activity which 'valves' the mass-energy of the universe to human advantage—is inventive wisdom born of intuition and experience and put to use in a global industrial complex.

2. *intr.* To make use of a valve or valves; *spec.* in ballooning, to open a valve in order to descend.

1906 *Westm. Gaz.* 3 Oct. 8/1 All we could do was to undulate, alternately valving and ballasting. **1936** *Nat. Geogr. Mag.* LXIX. 71 Andy valved, and valved again and again! **1963** A. SMITH *Throw out Two Hands* v. 63 You valve a little. You start coming down.

3. *trans.* To discharge gas from (an airship or balloon) by opening a valve; to discharge, or let *off*, (gas) thus.

1925 *Sci. Amer.* Nov. 301/3 She was swept rapidly upwards.. Commander Lansdowne valved her freely, pointed her nose down with engines running, and she came down with.. rapidity. **1928** *Engineering* 3 Aug. 141/3 As an airship uses up its fuel, it is necessary to reduce the lift, and hitherto this has been done by simply 'valving' off some of the hydrogen used for inflation. **1928** *Daily Tel.* 18 Sept. 9/6 The extra lifting effect of the expanding gas cannot be counteracted by allowing the gas to escape, or in other words by valving the gas. **1936** *Nat. Geogr. Mag.* LXIX. 71 He opened the valves for.. another half-minute interval (which is a very long time for a balloon to be valved at low altitude).

valved (vælvd), *a.* [f. VALVE *sb.*]

1. With limiting terms: **a.** Of a door: Having (so many) leaves. *rare.*

1676 HOBBES *Iliad* 375 In the pale a high two-valved door For chars and waggons to go in and out.

b. *Bot.*, etc. Having (so many) valves.

See also *two-valved* s.v. TWO *a.*

1771 *Encycl. Brit.* I. 637/2 *Siliqua*, is a double-valved pericarpium. **1796** WITHERING *Brit. Plants* (ed. 3) III. 867 Capsule 4-valved: seeds roundish. **1831** SOUTH *Otto's Path. Anat.* 74 There are some which.. live for protection.. even in the double-valved muscles. **1847** W. E. STEELE *Field Bot.* 73 Fruit mostly a dry or fleshy capsule, 1 or many-celled and valved.

2. Provided with a valve or valves, in various senses. Also *fig.*

1793 MARTYN *Lang. Bot.*, *Valvatum petalum*, a valved petal. **1842** FRANCIS *Dict. Arts*, *Valved*, any thing that opens upon hinges or to which a valve of any kind is attached. **1852** TH. ROSS tr. *Humboldt's Trav.* I. i. 12 We made several experiments by means of a valved thermo-metrical sounding lead, on the temperature of the ocean. **1856** M. C. CLARKE tr. *Berlioz's Treatise Mod. Instrumentation* (1858) 146/2 *Valved trumpets*,—called so on account of a movable valve similar to that of the trombone, and which is moved by the right hand,—are adapted to produce the truest intervals. **1873** *Routledge's Young Gentl. Mag.* Feb. 170/1 A complete set of valved instruments, consisting chiefly of cornets, clavicors, and trombones. **1899** *Allbutt's Syst. Med.* VII. 254 The blood is returned to the heart by means of muscular movements acting on the valved veins. **1923** D. H. LAWRENCE *Birds, Beasts & Flowers* 26 To me, all faces are dark, All lips are dusky and valved. **1927** *Bull. U.S. Nat. Museum* No. 136. 51 A valved trumpet marked 'alto B flat'.. It has three rotary valves. **1970** J. EARL *Tuners & Amplifiers* 7 This book is concerned essentially with transistored equipment, for the days of the valved amplifiers and tuners have now gone for ever.

valveless (ˈvælvlɪs), *a.* [f. VALVE *sb.*] Having no valve; destitute or devoid of valves.

1830 LINDLEY *Nat. Syst. Bot.* 219 Capsule.. sometimes valveless, or dehiscing transversely. **1851** WOODWARD *Mollusca* (1856) 69 Animal and pen like Loligo in most respects;.. funnel valveless. **1881** MIVART *Cat* 216 The hepatic veins are valveless. **1884** KNIGHT *Dict. Mech.* Suppl. 919 The 'Wardwell' valveless engine.. is horizontal.

ˈ**valvelet.** *rare.* Also 9 **valvlet.** [f. VALVE *sb.* + -LET.] A small valve.

1793 MARTYN *Lang. Bot.*, *Valvula*, a.. Valvelet, or Valvule. [Hence in later Dicts.] **1870** tr. *Pouchet's Universe* 125 Two large openings, each furnished with two valves or valvlets intended to prevent the reflux of the blood.

valvifer (ˈvælvɪfə(r)). *Ent.* [f. L. *valva* VALVE *sb.*[1] + -I- + L. *-fer* (see -FEROUS).] In some insects, a modified coxa on each of the eighth and ninth abdominal segments that forms a basal plate of the ovipositor and bears a valvula.

1917 G. C. CRAMPTON in *Jrnl. N.Y. Entomol. Soc.* XXV. 236 Basal sclerite of valvula of ovipositor (Valvifer). **1935** R. E. SNODGRASS *Princ. Insect Morphol.* xix. 611 The basal apparatus consists essentially of two pairs of lobes or plates, the first and second valvifers.. which support the ovipositor shaft by the bases of the valvulae. **1981** *Animal Behaviour* XXIX. 299/1 The valvifers at its base could be seen to be moving rhythmically back and forth.

ˈ**valviform,** *a. rare.* [ad. mod.L. *valviformis* or F. *valviforme.*] Valve-shaped.

1819 SAMOUELLE *Entomol. Compend.* 268 Valviform parts of oviduct. **1859** MAYNE *Expos. Lex.* 1321.

valving (ˈvælvɪŋ), *vbl. sb.* [f. VALVE *sb.*[1] + -ING[1].]

a. A system or arrangement of valves; valves collectively. **b.** Opening and shutting in the manner of a valve; valve-like operation.

1948 *Chem. Industries* Feb. 222/1 (*heading*) Valving CC's. **1957** *Petroleum Engineer* Oct. c. 66 (*heading*) Valving critical in elaborate distribution system. **1968** *Jrnl. Dental Res.* XLVII. 1013/2 Physiologic and temporal features of oral and palatopharyngeal valving were correlated with velocity and volume of oral-nasal flow, and intraoral air pressure. **1973** *Sci. Amer.* Dec. 143/1[A giraffe's] elevated brain is supplied with oxygen by blood vessels that manage a lot of valving and pumping. **1978** *Ibid.* May 38/1 The valving [of the Newcomen steam engine] was automatic from a very early stage. **1981** *Jrnl. Air Pollution Control Assoc.* XXXI. 377 Thermal mass flowmeters, with microprocessor controlled flow and automatic valving, supply variable levels of concentrated odorant and clean dilution air to a static mixing device.

valvotomy (vælˈvɒtəmɪ). *Surg.* [f. VALVE *sb.*[1] + -O + -TOMY.] An operation in which an incision is made into a valve, esp. of the heart.

1903 *N.Y. Med. Jrnl.* LXXVIII. 296/2 The rectitis should be recognized by the general practitioner, that the rectum may be so treated that absorption of the exudate may result rather than the formation of an organized deposit rendering rigid the rectal valve—thus may valvotomy be made unnecessary. **1912** *Proctologist* VII. 155 Valvotomy is a justifiable operation, as it frequently relieves obstipation and constipation. **1962** *Lancet* 8 Dec. 1195/2, 7 days later aortic valvotomy was successfully performed. **1980** *Brit. Med. Jrnl.* 23 Feb. 563/2 We would like to plead for the continued use of closed valvotomy, notably in third world countries where large numbers of patients with mitral stenosis could overwhelm the relatively small number of surgical units equipped for open heart surgery.

‖**valvula** (ˈvælvjʊlə). *Anat.* Pl. **valvulæ.** [med. or mod.L., dim. of *valva* VALVE *sb.* Cf. L. *valvolæ* pod of legumes.] **1.** A valve or valvule.

Usually with Latin qualifying term, as *valvula coli, valvulæ conniventes.*

1615 H. CROOKE *Body of Man* (1631) 853 Some men had rather call them [*sc.* valves in the veins of the joints] *Ostiolæ* than *Valuulæ*. **1653** MORE *Antid. Ath.* II. xii. §6 You may add to these the notable contrivance of the Heart, its two Ventricles and its many *Valvulae*. **1832** [see VALVE *sb.*[1] 4 b]. **1859** *Todd's Cycl. Anat.* V. 346/2 Opposite the attached border of the *valvula*, this layer is somewhat thick.

2. *Ent.* An elongated blade-like process attached to the coxa on the eighth or ninth abdominal segments of some insects and forming part of the ovipositor; = VALVE *sb.*[1] 3 a.

1917, 1935 [see VALVIFER]. **1964** R. M. & J. W. FOX *Introd. Compar. Entomol.* iii. 106 The ovipositor is present in its fully developed form, with three pairs of valvulae, in Phasmida, Grylloblatodea, Dictyoptera, Odonata and Corrodentia. **1978** H. V. DALY et al. *Introd. Insect Biol. & Diversity* ii. 36/2 Eggs issue from the genital opening.., pass down a channel formed by the valvulae, and are deposited in the ovipositional medium.

valvular (ˈvælvjʊlə(r)), *a.* [f. prec.]

1. Having the form or function of a valve; composed or consisting of valves. Chiefly *Anat.* and *Bot.*

(*a*) **1797** M. BAILLIE *Morb. Anat.* (1807) 32 The valvular apparatus between the auricles and ventricles is also occasionally thickened. *Ibid.* 104 The œsophagus necessarily acquired a valvular communication with it. **1843** J. J. WILKINSON tr. *Swedenborg's Anim. Kingd.* I. ii. 68 Among these glands.. we observe a great number of transparent vessels, with valvular divisions. **1878** T. BRYANT *Pract. Surg.* I. 25 It may appear as a direct or as a valvular opening, depressed, or raised.

(*b*) **1829** LINDLEY *Synops. Brit. Bot.* 54 Sepals 4–5, with a valvular æstivation. **1830** —— *Nat. Syst. Bot.* 141 The calyx is valvular, and the petals only 2. **1870** HOOKER *Stud. Flora* 298 Ovary superior. Capsule valvular.

(*c*) **1876** J. J. WILKINSON *Hum. Sci. & Div. Rev.* 67 The gates of science are valvular, and open from above downwards, but cannot be opened from below upwards.

2. Furnished with a valve or valves.

1808 BARCLAY *Muscular Motions* 233 Valvular veins, when divided across, require a ligature only at the orifice which points towards the heart.

3. Of or pertaining to a valve or valves.

1866 A. FLINT *Princ. Med.* iii. 308 The structural lesions relate, in the first place, to the valves and orifices of the heart. These are known commonly as valvular lesions. **1876** BRISTOWE *Th. & Pract. Med.* 492 Valvular defects may be of two kinds; they may be obstructive,.. or such as admit of regurgitation. **1881** *Med. Temp. Jrnl.* XLVIII. 209 Valvular disease of the heart.

ˈ**valvulate,** *a. rare.* [f. as prec. + -ATE[1].] Furnished with small valves.

1888 ROLLESTON & JACKSON *Anim. Life* 564 The length of the valve is greater than its breadth, except in the form known as valvulate pedicellariae.

valvule (ˈvælvjuːl). [Anglicized f. VALVULA or a. F. *valvule.*] A small valve, in various senses.

1755 in JOHNSON. **1760** J. LEE *Introd. Bot.* I. vi. (1765) 13 The Inclosure of the Capsule, which surrounds.. the Fruit externally, is called a Valvule. **1831** T. HOPE *Ess. Orig. Man* II. 62 Their weight, pressing backwards on the parietes of the vessels, scoops these out at certain distances into bags or valvules. **1870** tr. *Pouchet's Universe* 126 In the interior of this lengthened heart larger valvules.. are folded back against the wall to let the blood pass forward. **1879** *Trans. Linn. Soc.* II. I. 31 The edge.. is not straight, but cut into a series of minute valvules, the crescentic or respiratory leaves.

‖**valvuˈlitis.** *Path.* [f. VALVULA + -ITIS.] Inflammation of the valves of the heart.

1891 in *Cent. Dict.* **1897** *Allbutt's Syst. Med.* III. 43 A grave sign indicative of serious and generally persistent or recurrent valvulitis. **1898** *Ibid.* V. 866 Endocarditis affects principally the valves of the heart, hence the name valvulitis.

valvulotomy (vælvjʊˈlɒtəmɪ). *Surg.* [f. VALVUL(E + -O + -TOMY.] = VALVOTOMY.

1916 J. F. BINNIE *Operative Surg.* (ed. 7) II. xxxi. 332 Such operations may be named internal valvulotomy. **1951** *Lancet* 21 Apr. 896/2 Valvulotomy for mitral stenosis. **1970** *New Yorker* 21 Nov. 68/2 Any two-bit surgeon who can do a valvulotomy can have a patient in this unit.

valwe, southern ME. var. FALLOW *sb.* and *v.*[2]

valx, obs. Sc. form of WAX *sb.*

valyaunce, obs. form of VALIANCE.

†ˈ**valyl(e.** *Chem. Obs.* [f. VAL-ERIAN *sb.* + -YL(E.] = BUTYL.

1850 DAUBENY *Atom. The.* viii. (ed. 2) 249 The previous discovery made by Dr. Kolbe, of a compound of carbon and hydrogen derived by electrolysis from the valerianic acid, and hence called valyle. **1857** MILLER *Elem. Chem., Org.* 195 Tetryl, Butyl, or Valyl.

ˈ**valylene.** *Chem.* [f. as prec. + -ENE.] (See quots.)

1868 WATTS *Dict. Chem.* V. 982 Valylene... This hydrocarbon is found.. among the products of the action of alcoholic potash on dibromide of valerylene. **1868** *Fownes' Chem.* (ed. 10) 564 Quintone or Valylene.

vambrace (ˈvæmbreɪs). Now only Archæol. Forms: α. 4 **vaumbras**, 4–6 **vambras** (**-brase**, 5 **uambras**, 6 *Sc.* **wambraiss**), 7 **vambrasse** (8 **-brass**). β. 4– **vambrace** (5 **wam-**, 7 **van-**). [var. of *vaunt-* VANTBRACE, through elision of *t* and change of *nb* to *mb* by assimilation.] Defensive armour for the (fore-) arm.

α. *c* **1330** R. BRUNNE *Chron. Wace* (Rolls) 10030 Vaumbras & rerbras, wyþ coters of stel. **1385–6** *Durham Acc. Rolls* (Surtees) 133, ij palets, j brestplat, vambras. **1392** *Test. Ebor.* (Surtees) I. 171 Unum bonum par cerotecarum de plate, cum vambrase et rerebrase. **1461** *Will of Benney* (Somerset Ho.), j salett garnisshed cum argento, legharnes, vambras, & rerebras. *a* **1548** HALL *Chron., Hen. IV*, 12 One sorte had the vambrases, the pace gardes, the grand-gardes.. parted with golde and azure. **1581** STYWARD *Mart. Discipl.* II. 165 To haue good.. poldrones and vambrases for their shoulders & armes. **1627** DRAYTON *Agincourt* 8 [Whether] The Vambrasse, or the Pouldron, they should prize.

β. **1411** *E.E. Wills* (1882) 19 A pare of vambrace and rerebrace. *c* **1450** METHAM *Wks.* (E.E.T.S.) 37 Thys knyghtys vambracys in coloure Alle depeyntyd with red were. **1513** *MS. Papers 5 Hen. VIII*, No. 4101 (P.R.O.), His vambraces, polvorines, ij Salettes [etc.]. **1581** STYWARD *Mart. Discipl.* I. 44 A fayre Corslet, with all the peeces appertaining to the same, that is the curats, yᵉ collers, the poldrens with the Vambraces. **1624** CAPT. SMITH *Virginia* III. ii. 47 On his arme.. an Otters skinne, or some such matter for his vambrace. **1687** A. LOVELL tr. *Thevenot's Trav.* III. 44 They have likewise the Coat of Mail, the Cuirats, the Head-piece, and a Vambrace fastened to the Sword. **1734** tr. *Rollin's Rom. Hist.* (1827) II. 379 The vambraces or greaves which covered the arms, thighs, and legs of the horsemen. **1829** SCOTT *Anne of G.* xxxii, Among gauntlets, boots, vambraces, and such like gear. **1850** BOUTELL in *Gentl. Mag.* CXX. II. 44 The arms are cased in brassarts and vambraces of plate.

transf. **1766** *Phil. Trans.* LVI. 274, I supported the arm with a vambrace, or half-canal, made of one very thin piece of wood.

'vambraced, *a. Her.* [f. prec.] Of an arm: Defended or covered by a vambrace.

1610 GULLIM *Heraldry* IV. xv. (1611) 232 He beareth Gules, three Dexter Armes Vambraced and Proper. **1688** HOLME *Armoury* III. xvii. 109/2 He beareth Gules a dexter Arme Vambraced, Or. *c* **1828** BERRY *Encycl. Her.* I. Gloss., *Vambraced*, a term which implies that the arm is wholly covered with armour. **1868** CUSSANS *Her.* vi. 92 An Arm encased in armour is Vambraced.

†**vambrash,** *v. Obs. rare.* Also **-brishe.** [Of obscure origin.] *trans.* To brandish.

1577 GRANGE *Golden Aphrod.* Nj, For Iupiter touching the heauens with his wande, caused them to thunder & vambrishe lightnings. **1593** NASHE *Christ's T.* 27b, With glistering naked swords, which..he made semblance as if hee shaked and vambrasht. **1623** COCKERAM I, *Vambrash*, to shake a staffe or launce.

vame, obs. Sc. f. WEM *sb.*, WOMB.

vamer, vameure, varr. *vamure* VAUMURE.

vamoose (və'mu:s), *v. colloq.* (orig. and chiefly *U.S.*). Also **vamos(e), vamous, vamoos, varmoose.** [ad. Sp. *vamos* let us go.]

1. *intr.* To depart, make off, decamp, disappear.

α. [**1827** W. CLARKE *Every Night Bk.* 30 They have done more foolish things in their day—but vamos.] **1834** *Knickerbocker* IV. 455 Be off, you good-for-nothing rascals—*vamos!* **1848** in Bartlett *Dict. Amer.*, Its occupants.. forthwith vamosed with their baggage. **1855** HALIBURTON *Nat. & Hum. Nat.* I. 112, I makes a spring in after him, and caught him by the hair of the head, just as he was vamosing. **1893** MCCARTHY *Red Diamonds* I. 173 The fifth name was that of Ratt Gundy, opposite to which Seth Chickering had written the one word: 'Vamosed'.

β. **1859** *Slang Dict.* 114 *Vamous*, to go, or be off. **1862** *Illustr. Lond. News* 24 May 540/3 Guess, they'd better varmoose. **1874** M. COLLINS *Frances* III. 80 If I can get money down for some of my gold bonds, we'll vamoos at once. **1892** STEVENSON & OSBOURNE *Wrecker* xvi. 254 Well, of course he can vamoose with the entire speculation, if he chooses. **1895** J. G. MILLAIS *Breath fr. Veldt* (1899) 175 The hunter was voted a fraud..and was..told to 'vamoose'. **1936** F. CLUNE *Roaming round Darling* ix. 82 The river was going downhill, and the country growing more and more similar in appearance to the Lachlan, before it vamoosed in the marshes. **1958** 'J. REEVES' *Mulbridge Manor* xii. 155 'See anyone?' asked Winston. 'Not a soul. Whoever it was has vamoosed.'

2. *trans.* To decamp or disappear from; to quit hurriedly. Freq. in phr. *to vamoose the ranch. U.S.*

1847 'M'C' *Let.* 2 Apr. in *Rough & Ready Ann.* (1848) 245 On the morning after I wrote the letter to father..they.. stacked their arms and colors, and 'vamosed the ranch'. **1852** F. MARRYAT *Gold Quartz Mining* 8 On the old Californian principle of 'making a "pile" and vamosing the ranche'. **1857** in Thornton *Amer. Gloss.*, Another pair of jail-birds have vamosed the log jail at Jacksonville. **1888** E. B. CUSTER *Tenting on Plains* I. (1893) 32, I got that far when the eyes of the old galoots started out of their heads, and they vamoosed the ranche.

Hence **va'mo(o)sing** *vbl. sb.*

1862 J. R. LOWELL *Biglow Papers* 2nd ser. v. 75 Or, when the vamosin' come, ever to find [etc.].

vamp (væmp), *sb.*[1] Forms: 3 **vaumpe,** 3, 5 **uaumpe,** 5 **vawmpe;** 4–5 **wampe,** 5 **vampe,** 6 **vamppe,** 7– **vamp.** [ad. AF. **vampé*, **vanpé* (Palsgrave *uantpié*), = OF. *avanpié* (12th c.; later F. *avantpied*), f. *avan(t)* before + *pié* foot. The final syllable is preserved in the variant VAMPEY.]

1. That part of hose or stockings which covers the foot and ankle; also, a short stocking, a sock. Now *dial.*

a **1225** *Ancr. R.* 420 Ine sumer 3e habbeð leaue uorto gon and sitten baruot, and hosen wiðuten uaumpez, and ligge ine ham hwoso likeð. **13..** *Seuyn Sages* (W.) 843 He dede his schon of-drawe, And karf his vaumpes, fot-hot, And wente him forht al barfot. **1378–9** *Durham Acc. Rolls* (Surtees) 587 Pro..j pare botarum et Wampes de Dubelsols. *c* **1425** *Voc.* in Wr.-Wülcker 654 *Hec pedana*, wampe. *c* **1440** *Promp. Parv.* 508/1 Vampe, of an hoose.., *pedana*. *a* **1562** G. CAVENDISH *Wolsey* (1893) 223 Allthoughe..that our predecessors went uppon clothe right somptiously, we do entend..to goo a foote frome thence, without any suche glory, in the vamppes of my hosyn. **1676** COLES, *Vamp*, a sock. [**1706** PHILLIPS (ed. Kersey), *Vamps* or *Vampays*, an odd kind of short Hose or Stockings that cover'd the Feet, and came up only to the Ancle, just above the Shooe.] **1880** in *E. Cornw. Gloss.*

2. The part of a boot or shoe covering the front of the foot; *U.S.*, that part between the sole and the top in front of the ankle-seams.

1654 GAYTON *Pleas. Notes* IV. iv. 192 Her Grace when she had victuall'd that grand Camp, Gave me a piece of Cheese tuff as a vamp. **1688** HOLME *Armoury* III. 14/1 Of a Shoe: ..the Vamp, is all the piece that covers the top of the foot. **1706** PHILLIPS (ed. Kersey), *Vamp*, the Upper Leather of a Shoe. **1770** *T. Hazard Son of Robt.* (1893) 288 One pair of vamps for shoes. **1785** BELKNAP in *M. Cutler's Life*, etc. (1888) II. 234 This bathing vessel..is in the form of a slipper. He sits in the Heel, and his legs go under the Vamp. **1800** MAR. EDGEWORTH *Parent's Assist.* (1854) 347 The last-maker made a last for her, and over this Mary sewed the calico vamps tight. **1845** WHITTIER *Shoemakers* ii, Now shape the sole! now deftly curl The glossy vamp around it. **1885** *Harper's Mag.* Jan. 280/1 The upper is found to consist,..in the case of a button boot, of a 'vamp' to cover the front part of the foot [etc.].

vamp (væmp), *sb.*[2] [f. VAMP *v.*[1]] Anything vamped, patched up, or refurbished; a patchwork; a book of this nature.

1884 J. F. HODGETTS *Older England* ii. 61 This name was no vamp or hybrid mixture of Latin and English. **1897** *Academy* 6 Mar. 274/1 Such vamps as the one I have analysed from Mr. Henley's notes can only be credited to him as brilliant luck brilliantly used.

b. A vamped or improvised accompaniment.

1882 in *Imp. Dict.* IV. 539.

vamp (væmp), *sb.*[3] *U.S. slang.* [Origin unknown.] A volunteer fireman.

1877 *Fireman's Jrnl.* I. 15/1 Our old friend..seems to have the run of the old vamps. **1942** BERREY & VAN DEN BARK *Amer. Thes. Slang* §850/2 *Vamp*, a volunteer fire-man.

vamp (væmp), *sb.*[4] [Abbrev. of VAMPIRE *sb.*] A woman who intentionally attracts and exploits men; an adventuress; a Jezebel; freq. as a stock character in plays and films.

a **1911** CHESTERTON *Lunacy & Letters* (1958) xxxvi. 178 Thackeray took it for granted that Mary Stuart was a vamp. **1918** *N.Y. Times* 15 July 9 Enid Bennett In a New 'Vamp' Story... 'The Vamp'..is a pleasing light comedy..in which Enid Bennett..appears as Nancy; an ingenuous wardroom girl at a musical comedy theatre where she hears sophisticated chorus girls tell how the female of the species may make the male buy her dinners and diamond bracelets by 'vamping' him... So Nancy, taking a tip from the chorus girls, 'vamps' him—and the wedding is a quick result. **1930** G. B. SHAW *Wks.* VII. 156 Ask yourself whether, if the lot in life therein described were your lot in life, you would not rather be a jewelled Vamp. **1973** *Times* 22 Dec. 9/2 Exotic red flowers like the lips of vamps. **1976** H. R. F. KEATING *Filmi, Filmi, Inspector Ghote* v. 44 She was..playing the Vamp in a film.

vamp (væmp), *v.*[1] Also 8 **vaump.** [f. VAMP *sb.*[1]]

I. 1. *trans.* To provide or furnish with a (new) vamp; to mend or repair with or as with patches; to furbish up, renovate, or restore. Also with *up*.

Some further developments in dial. use are illustrated in the *Eng. Dial. Dict.*

(*a*) **1599** [see VAMPING *vbl. sb.*[1]]. **16..** MIDDLETON, etc. *Old Law* II. i, What a time did we endure In twopenny commons, and in boots twice vamped! **1639** SHIRLEY *Gentl. Venice* III. ii, *Giovanni.* In the mean time buy thee a sword and belt, And what is fit. (*Gives him money*). *Georgio.* No more: I'll be a soldier... This will Suffice to vamp my body. *a* **1700** B. E. *Dict. Cant. Crew*, *To Vamp*, to new Dress, Licker, Refresh, or Rub up old Hatts, Boots, &c. **1844** ALB. SMITH *Adv. Mr. Ledbury* xiv. (1886) 42 Various new-footed boots..vamped and polished to the last pitch of ingenuity. **1860** EMERSON *Conduct of Life* ix. Wks. (Bohn) II. 446 Plod and plough, vamp your old coats and hats, weave a shoestring. **1884** A. GRIFFITHS *Chron. Newgate* I. i. 33 Blankets vamped in foreign parts with the hair of oxen.

(*b*) **1755** JOHNSON *Connoisseur* No. 77 ¶1 The woman of the town, vamped up for shew with paint, patches, plumpers, and every external ornament that art can administer. **1796** MME. D'ARBLAY *Camilla* V. 189 The apparel..would do well enough for herself, when vamped up, as she knew how. **1837** DISRAELI *Venetia* v. viii, Old furniture..re-burnished and vamped up. **1864** C. KNIGHT *Passages Work. Life* I. v. 219 Our old fabric..was in danger of falling,..although we had spent large sums in vamping it up. **1875** *Chambers' Jrnl.* 30 Nov. 749 Old boots and shoes are sold to men who vamp them up in such a style that their former owners would not know them.

b. *transf.* and *fig.* (Freq. with reference to literary compositions.)

(*a*) **1632** *Song* in Lyly *Sappho* II. iii. 109 To th' Tap-house then lets gang, and rore, Cal hard, tis rare to vamp a score. **1640** GATAKER *Whitaker* in Fuller *Abel Rediv.* (1867) II. 117 Let them strive to vamp Their wasted memories by another lamp. **1682** N. O. *Boileau's Lutrin* I. 1 The Argument? what needs a Proëme, To vamp a Three-half-penny Poeme? **1706** SWIFT *Baucis & Phil.* 128 He..Knew how to preach old sermons next, Vamp'd in the preface and the text. **1743** *Lond. & Co. Brewer* III. (ed. 2) 238 Vamping Malt-Liquors. —Is of late much in Practice for its excellent Service in recovering, preserving, and fining strong October and March Beers. **1795** BURNS *Address, sp. by Miss Fontenelle* 4 A Prologue, Epilogue, or some such matter, 'Twould vamp my bill, said I, if nothing better. **1800** CRABBE *Borough* xvi. 185 When on each feature death had fix'd his stamp, And not a doctor could the body vamp. **1867** EMERSON *May-Day* Wks. (Bohn) III. 417 Chemist to vamp old worlds with new. **1883** *Daily News* 8 Dec. 2/8, I meant to suggest that the Central News were parties to 'vamping' the telegram... What do you mean by 'vamping'?—Inserting matter which is not in any original telegram.

(*b*) **1741** T. BETTERTON *Hist. Eng. Stage* vi. 151 He attempted to commence Dramatic Poet, by vamping up an old Play or two of Massinger and Decker. **1752** BOLINGBROKE *Study of Hist.* v. 159 They maintained the dignity of history, and thought it beneath them to vamp up old traditions. **1825** J. FOSTER *Life & Corr.* (1846) II. 67 The expedient of vamping up an old Sermon. **1902** L. STEPHEN *Stud. Biogr.* IV. i. 21, I could not suppose that they were merely vamping up old material.

2. *transf.* To make or produce by or as by patching; to adapt, compile, compose, put together (a book, composition, etc.) out of old materials; to serve up (something old) as new by addition or alteration. Also with *up* (freq. = TRUMP *v.*[1] 5 c).

(*a*) **1644** BULWER *Chiron.* 113 This absurd motion of the armes, makes an Oratour seeme..as if he newly came from vamping his Oration. **1748** FOOTE *Knights* Pref., The three principal characters..are neither vamped from antiquated plays, pilfered from French farces, nor the baseless beings of the poet's brain. **1774** *tr. Helvetius' Child of Nature* II. 205 They consist, in general, of old characters, old incidents, and old catastrophes, vamped out in the language and dress of the day. **1827** CARLYLE *Misc.* (1840) I. 5 Well are he and Hennings of Gotha aware that this thing of shreds and patches has been vamped together for sale only. **1880** *Literary World* 17 Dec. 416 Industry worthy of the veriest drudge that vamps books together for his daily bread.

absol. **1792** A. MURPHY *Grecian Daughter* Prol., Historians..who only take Scissars and paste; cut, vamp; a book they make.

(*b*) **1692** BENTLEY *Boyle Lect.* 100 Which opinion hath been vamp'd up of late by Cardan and Cesalpinus and other news-mongers. **1760–2** GOLDSM. *Cit. W.* xxx, I set myself down, and vamped up a fine flaunting poetical panegyric. **1765** BLACKSTONE *Comm.* I. 197 The usurpers..for the most part endeavoured to vamp up some feeble shew of a title by descent. **1814** *Trewman's Exeter Flying-Post* 16 June 1 The falshood was vamped up on the authority of a pretended letter. **1850** MERIVALE *Rom. Emp.* (1865) VI. liii. 383 Forged letters were produced, a case of Majestas was vamped up. **1894** SALA *London up to date* II. i. 23, I have vamped up my description of the function from accounts which I have read.

†**b.** With personal object: To convert into, to bring forward *as*, something. *Obs.*

a **1658** CLEVELAND *Charac. Diurn. Maker* Wks. (1677) 101 It is like over-reach of Language..when a clumsie Cobler usurps the Attribute of our English Peers and is vamp'd a Translator. **1661** K. W. *Conf. Charac.* (1860) 34 For..his preferment hath metamorphosed the antient titles of his progeneters..into master, and now he is vampt a gentle-man. **1773** BERRIDGE *Wks.* (1864) 134 Some people only vamp him up as a prophet: and trample on his blood.

3. *Mus.* To improvise or extemporize (an accompaniment, tune, etc.).

1789 BURNEY *Hist. Music* III. 102 *note*, I remember very early in my musical life to have heard one of the town waits at Shrewsbury vamp a base upon all occasions. **1861** MAYHEW *London Labour* III. 191/2 As soon as I could get in to vamp the tunes on the banjo a little. **1897** SIR A. SULLIVAN in *Strand* Dec. 654/1 Then the voice parts are written out by the copyist, and the rehearsals begin; the composer..vamping an accompaniment.

b. *intr.* To improvise an accompaniment.

1876 in STAINER & BARRETT *Dict. Mus. Terms* 445/1. **1884** *B'ham Daily Post* 23 Feb. 3/5 Pianist and Vocalist; one who can vamp.

II. 4. *intr.* To make one's way on foot; to tramp or trudge. Now *dial.*

1654 GAYTON *Pleas. Notes* III. ii. 73 If my hard hearted Queen should vamp to Charon. *Ibid.* IV. xxv. 285 That is the Knight, that must be the example, That the prime horse, that with Knight-Errants vamp will. **1681** H. FOULE *Hist. Romish Treas.* 133 When Humility vamps on foot. **1705** *Wandering Spy* No. 19. 73, I Vaumpt along Cheapside, down the Poultry. **1747** *T. Hazard, Son of Robt.* (1893) 241 Our chief concern was about packing up our alls and vamping off. **1887** T. HARDY *Woodlanders* I. ii. 24, I shouldn't have vamped all these miles for any less important employer. **1891** —— *Tess* I. 12 Well, vamp on to Marlott, will ye, and order that carriage. **1893** in *Wiltshire Gloss.*

b. *trans.* To tramp or walk (the streets). *rare.*

1898 T. HARDY *Wessex Poems* 55 We vamped the streets in the stifling air.

vamp, *v.*[2] *slang. trans.* To pawn.

a **1700** B. E. *Dict. Cant. Crew* s.v., *I'll Vamp and tip you the Cole*, I'll Pawn my Cloths, but I'll raise the Money for you. [Hence in later slang Dicts.]

vamp (væmp), *v.*[3] [f. VAMP *sb.*[4]]

1. *intr.* To behave seductively; to act as a vamp, to be a vamp. *rare.*

1904 ADE *True Bills* 60 Any time that he fills in from eight o'clock to Midnight he certainly has to do some Vamping. **1922** *Observer* 1 Oct. 5/4 Trollope's Signora Neroni certainly vamped.

2. *trans.* To act as a vamp towards; to attract and exploit (a man, occas. a woman).

1918 [see VAMP *sb.*[4]]. **1927** *Observer* 20 Mar. 15/3 Her friend, Violet Usher..shamelessly vamped Randall, and he felt obliged to marry her. **1939** L. M. MONTGOMERY *Anne of Ingleside* xxv. 166 Don't try to vamp me, woman. I've paid you all the compliments I'm going to. **1973** T. PYNCHON *Gravity's Rainbow* II. 245 Eager young chaps with patent-leather hair rush about trying to vamp the ladies. **1979** D. ANTHONY *Long Hard Cure* xix. 150 Gavin's secret girl, who vamped him on the nights those four women were assaulted.

†**vampage.** *Obs.*$^{-1}$ [app. f. VAMP *sb.*[1] + -AGE; but perh. an error for *vampays* VAMPEY.] Vamps or feet (of hose).

1555 J. PROCTOR *Wyat's Rebell.* 32 Thei were driuen to.. runne awaye in the vampage of their hose.

vamped (væmpt), *ppl. a.* [f. VAMP *v.*[1] Cf. the earlier NEW-VAMPED *a.*]

1. With *up*. Mended or repaired with or as with patches; patched or furbished up; made up or composed of old materials and produced as new.

1729 J. MACKY *Journ. thro. Eng.* I. iv. 74 Women in vampt-up old Clooths. **1753** *School of Man* 18 Is this the business of a Vamped-up Maid? **1759** DILWORTH *Life Pope* 100 He justly turns into ridicule several patched and vamped up buildings. **1850** KINGSLEY *Alton Locke* v, They would not send out lying puffs of their vamped-up goods.

b. *transf.* and *fig.*

1806 SURR *Winter in London* II. 152 The hackneyed, second-hand, vamped-up hearts one meets with in common. **1812** MAR. EDGEWORTH *Manœuvring* i, A vamped-up sentimental conversation reason. **1884** *Truth* 13

Mar. 379/1 A passionate burst of vocal tragedy wedged in between an overture by S. Bennett and a violin concerto by Spohr leaves an unpleasing and vamped-up impression. **1892** B. HINTON *Lord's Return* 191 The vamped-up sentiment; the covert sneers.

c. Of a charge, story, etc.: Invented, fabricated, trumped *up*.

1802–12 BENTHAM *Ration. Judic. Evid.* (1827) IV. 170 A lawyer, who, knowing nothing about the matter, stands with a paper in his hand, containing a vamped-up story. **1871** SMILES *Charac.* xii. (1876) 361 A vamped-up charge of treason. **1874** H. R. REYNOLDS *John Bapt.* IV. §5. 260 He bade them to terrorize no one, and bring no vamped-up worthless accusation.

2. Of an accompaniment: Extemporized.

1874 in *Slang Dict.*

vamper ('væmpə(r)). [f. VAMP *v.*¹]

†**1.** A stocking. *Obs.*⁻⁰

Perhaps an error for *vampeis* or *vampeys*.

a **1700** B. E. *Dict. Cant. Crew*, *Vampers*, Stockings. [Hence in later slang dicts.]

2. One who vamps or patches. Also with *up*.

1712 *Odes of Horace* VIII. 7/1 Our Horace is a new vamper of words and borrowed this from the Greek. **1765** STERNE *Tr. Shandy* VIII. xxxvii, That in selling my chaise, I had sold my remarks..to the chaise-vamper. **1826** J. WILSON *Noct. Ambr.* Wks. 1855 I. 191, I shall use all vampers, like the great American shrike.., who sticks small singing-birds on sharp-pointed thorns. **1837** CARLYLE *Fr. Rev.* I. IV. iv, Skilfullest vamper-up of old rotten leather, to make it look like new.

3. *slang*. (See quot.)

1865 *Slang Dict.* 265 *Vampers*, fellows who frequent public-houses and pick quarrels with the wearers of rings and watches, in hopes of getting up a fight, and so enabling their 'pals' to steal the articles.

4. One who improvises music, esp. accompaniments on the pianoforte.

1884 *Yorksh. Post* 7 Nov., Lady pianist and vocalist, reader at sight, vamper. **1895** *Westm. Gaz.* 24 Sept., His education as a vamper is complete for all practical purposes.

†**vampeth**, *sb.* and *v.* *Obs.* Also **vaumped-, vampet(t.** [ad. early AF. **vamped*, later **vampé*: see next.] = VAMPEY *sb.* and *v.*

c **1430** *York Memor. Bk.* (Surtees) I. 194 Pro la vaumpedyng xij parium ocrearum. *c* **1475** *Cath. Angl.* 399/2 A vampethe [1483 vampett], *pedana, jmpedia*. To vampethe [1483 vampet], *pedanare*.

†**vampey, vampy**, *sb.* *Obs.* Also 5 **vampei, va(w)mpay, wampay.** [ad. AF. **vampé*: see VAMP *sb.*¹] = VAMP *sb.*¹ I.

c **1425** *Voc.* in Wr.-Wülcker 601 *Pedana*, a vampey. *Ibid.* 664 *Hec pedana*, wampay. *c* **1460** J. RUSSELL *Bk. Nurture* 894 [Give him] his vampeys and sokkes, þan all day he may go warme. **1485** *Rutland Papers* (Camden) 8 A pair of hosyn of crymesyn sarcenet vampeis. **1530** PALSGR. 284/1 Vampey of a hose, *auant pied*. **1592** GREENE *Upst. Courtier* Wks. (Grosart) XI. 263 Beside, you will ioin a neates leather vampy to a calues leather heele: is not heere good stuffe maister shoomaker? **1630** J. TAYLOR (Water P.) *Wks.* II. 242/2 Of the old rotten leather they make vampies for high shooes for honest country plowmen, or belts for soldiers.

Hence †**vampey, vampy** *v. trans.*, to put a vamp on, to patch. Also **vampeying** *vbl. sb.* *Obs.*

1416 *Maldon Court-Rolls* (Bundle 10, No. 6), Propter vampeyeng et solynge de vn payre de botys. *c* **1425** *Voc.* in Wr.-Wülcker 601 *Pedano*, to vampeye. **1459** *Paston Lett.* I. 487 Item, j. payre of blake vampayed withe lether. **1464** *Mann. & Househ. Exp.* (Roxb.) 255 The same day mastyr payd to hys cordwaner..for vawmpayinge of his botys, viii d. **1611** BEAUM. & FL. *Knt. Burning Pestle* v, [Her] Master wrought with Lingell and with All, And underground he vampied many a Boot.

fig. **1650** B. *Discollimin.* 19 One of my Men being well vampied in his Crowne with Ale,..rides into one of my Marishes.

'**vamping**, *sb. Mining.* (See quot.)

1881 RAYMOND *Mining Gloss.*, *Vamping*, the *débris* of a stope, which forms a hard mass under the feet of the miner.

vamping ('væmpɪŋ), *vbl. sb.*¹ [f. VAMP *v.*¹]

1. The action of the vb., in lit. and fig. senses.

1599 MINSHEU *Sp. Dict.*, *Cabeçado*,..the vamping or putting to the instops to bootes. **1680** *Vind. Conforming Clergy* (ed. 2) 50 It had certainly been a far more honest.. Employment for him to have..hired a Stall, and set himself bodily to Vamping of Boots. **1706** PHILLIPS (ed. Kersey) s.v. *Vamps*, To graft a new Footing on old Stockings is still call'd Vamping. **1773** FOOTE *Bankrupt* III, Political papers should bear vamping; like sermons, change but the application and text, and they will suit all persons and seasons. **1819** JEFFREY in Cockburn *Life* (1852) II. 187, I have just got done with another Review... I have more vamping and patching than writing. **1850** CARLYLE *Latter d. Pamph.* vii. (1872) 233 The mere vamping-together of hostile veracities. **1860** *All Year Round* No. 72. 508 No vamping of him up into a severe ancient Roman will do.

b. *attrib.* (in sense 3 of the vb.).

c **1890** (*title*), Reeves' Vamping Tutor.—The Art of Extemporaneous Accompaniment or playing by ear on the Piano. **1905** *Church Times* 30 June 842/4 Those strange, long, keyless trumpets, called vamping-horns. **1908** F. BOND *Screens & Galleries* 147 One of the strangest instruments of the old choirs is the vamping trumpet.

2. Tramping, trudging. *rare.*

1661 K. W. *Conf. Charac.* (1860) 46 His quick motion and speedy vamping from place to place..makes him smell like a traveller.

'**vamping**, *vbl. sb.*² [f. VAMP *v.*³ + -ING¹.] Seductive behaviour; acting as a vamp.

1904 [see VAMP *v.*³ 1]. **1918** *N.Y. Times* 15 July 9 Nancy tries her 'vamping' tactics on him and he confesses his crime.

'**vamping**, *ppl. a.* [f. VAMP *v.*¹] That vamps, in senses of the vb.

a **1616** BEAUM. & FL. *Bonduca* I. ii, Do you hope to triumph, Or dare your vamping valour, goodman Cobler, Clap a new soul to th' kingdom? **1737** M. GREEN *Spleen* 163 Whose easy vamping talent lies, First wit to pilfer, then disguise. **1765** STERNE *Tr. Shandy* VII. xxix, A pert, vamping chaise-undertaker..demanded if Monsieur would have his chaise refitted.

'**vampirarchy.** [f. next.] A set of ruling persons comparable to vampires.

1823 *New Monthly Mag.* VII. 144 A sceptical critic has pretended, with a degree of malice prepense against the Vampyrarchy,..that his Imperial Majesty's surgeons-major and counsellors of war might perchance be deceived in some respects.

vampire ('væmpaɪə(r)), *sb.* Also **vampyre.** [a. F. *vampire*, ad. Magyar *vampir*, a word of Slavonic origin occurring in the same form in Russ., Pol., Czech, Serb., and Bulg., with such variants as Bulg. *vapir, vepir*, Ruthen. *vepyr, vopyr, opyr*, Russ. *upir, upyr*, Pol. *upior*; Miklosich suggests north Turkish *uber* witch, as a possible source. Cf. G. *vampir, vampyr*, Da., Sw. *vampyr*, Du. *vampir*, It., Sp., Pg. *vampiro*, mod.L. *vampyrus*.]

1. A preternatural being of a malignant nature (in the original and usual form of the belief, a reanimated corpse), supposed to seek nourishment, or do harm, by sucking the blood of sleeping persons; a man or woman abnormally endowed with similar habits.

α. **1734** *Trav. three English Gent.* in *Harl. Misc.* (1745) IV. 358 These Vampyres are supposed to be the Bodies of deceased Persons, animated by evil Spirits, which come out of the Graves, in the Night-time, suck the Blood of many of the Living, and thereby destroy them. **1760–2** GOLDSM. *Cit. W.* lxxx. ¶8 From a meal he advances to a surfeit, and at last sucks blood like a vampyre. **1819** [POLIDORI] *The Vampyre* p. xx, He had been tormented by a vampyre, but had found a way to rid himself of the evil, by eating some of the earth out of the vampyre's grave. **1847** MRS. KERR tr. *Ranke's Hist. Servia* iv. 71 Speedy death was the inevitable consequence of such a visitation, and any one who so died became himself a vampyre.

β. **1796** PEGGE *Anonym.* (1809) 182 The accounts we have of the Vampires of Hungary are most incredible. They are Blood-suckers, that come out of their graves to torment the living. **1813** BYRON *Giaour* Note 38, The freshness of the face, and the wetness of the lip with blood, are the never-failing signs of a Vampire. **1846** T. WRIGHT *Ess. Mid. Ages* I. ix. 301 Walter Mapes..gives some curious stories of English vampires in the twelfth century. **1886** *Sat. Rev.* 9 Jan. 55 We would welcome a spectre, a ghoul, or even a vampire gladly, rather than meet [Stevenson's] Mr. Edward Hyde.

2. *transf.* **a.** A person of a malignant and loathsome character, esp. one who preys ruthlessly upon others; a vile and cruel exactor or extortioner. *spec.* = VAMP *sb.*⁴

1741 C. FORMAN *Obs. Revol.* 11 These are the vampires of the publick, and riflers of the kingdom. **1814** HARRIET SHELLEY in *Lett. Shelley* (1909) II. App. I. 992 In short, the man I once loved is dead. This is a vampire. His character is blasted for ever. **1844** H. H. WILSON *Brit. India* II. 174 There appeared to be no prospect of shaking off the vampires that had fastened themselves on the princes of Rajputana. **1899** F. T. BULLEN *Log of Sea-waif* 164 The vampires who supplied them with liquor had somehow obtained a claim upon all their wages. **1903** G. B. SHAW *Man & Superman* IV. 170 You lie, you vampire, you lie. **1918** *National Police Gaz.* (U.S.) 20 Apr. 4 (*caption*) Theda Bara... Vampire of the Screen. **1919** *Honey Pot* I. 42 Miss Maitland was a 'vampire' of an entirely new type. **1920** C. D. FOX *Who's Who on Screen* 301 Louise Glaum, who is credited with having given to the screen one of the most perfect vampire characterizations, was born near Baltimore. *a* **1953** E. O'NEILL *Long Day's Journey into Night* (1956) IV. 165 Made whores fascinating vampires instead of poor, stupid, diseased slobs they really are. **1968** *Word Study* Dec. 4/2 A vampire is a woman who uses sex to facilitate the acquisition of money or other signs of wealth. **1978** LD. BIRKENHEAD *Rudyard Kipling* vii. 99 A grim but authentic picture..of callow subalterns trotting beside the rickshaw wheels of faded provincial vampires.

b. *slang.* An intolerable bore or tedious person.

1862 B. TAYLOR *Home & Abroad* III. II. 215 In the German language there is no epithet which exactly translates our word 'bore', or its intensification, 'vampyre'.

c. Applied to a mosquito.

1864 GEIKIE *Life Woods* iv. (1874) 58 A sharp prick and the little vampire is drinking your blood.

3. *Zool.* **a.** One or other of various bats, chiefly South American, known or popularly believed to be blood-suckers.

α. **1774** GOLDSM. *Nat. Hist.* (1824) II. 119 An animal not so formidable, but still more mischievous than these, is the American Vampyre. **1834** *Handbk. Nat. Philos., Phys. Geogr.* 55/1 (L.U.K.), The vampyres, or blood-sucking bats, nine species of which have been mentioned. **1845** E. WARBURTON *Crescent & Cross* xvi. (1859) 168 My companion slew fifty-seven Vampyres in the few minutes.

β. **1783** *Encycl. Brit.* (ed. 2) X. 8711/2 The *vampyrus*, vampire, or Ternate bat, with large canine teeth. **1785** SMELLIE *Buffon's Nat. Hist.* (1791) V. 283 We shall call it vampire, because it sucks the blood of men and other animals when asleep. *c* **1820** WATERTON *Wand. S. Amer.* III. (1825) 154 The owls went away of their own accord... The bats and vampires remained with me. **1839** DARWIN *Voy. Nat.* ii. (1845) 22 My servant..suddenly put his hand on the beast's withers, and secured the vampire. **1893** LYDEKKER *Roy. Nat. Hist.* I. 299 The vampires are remarkable for the varied nature of their food.

b. The tarantula spider. *rare*⁻¹.

1843 MARRYAT *M. Violet* xliv, The deadly tarantula spider or 'vampire' of the prairies.

c. The devil-fish. *rare*⁻¹.

1867 *Chronicle* 5 Oct. 669 This giant of the Cephaloptera is simply a monstrous Ray; and though Sea-Devil and Vampire are assigned to it as trivial names, it..is in no way formidable save from its enormous strength and bulk.

4. A double-leaved trap-door, closing by means of springs, used in theatres to effect a sudden disappearance from the stage.

1881 W. S. GILBERT *Foggerty's Fairy* I, Where's my vampire? **1886** *Stage Gossip* 69 A 'vampire' is a trap used by the sprites, and is cut in the 'flats', and often in the stage —the sprite falling bodily through the trap.

5. *attrib.* and *Comb.*, as ***vampire bookseller, corpse, -fanned*** adj., ***legend, spell***, etc.; **vampire bat**, = sense 3 a; **vampire trap**, = sense 4.

1790 SHAW *Spec. Linn.* pl. 8, The *Vampyre Bat. Tailless Bat with the nose plain, and the flying-membrane divided between the thighs. **1807** *Phil. Trans.* XCVII. 176 The vampyre bat, which will be found to live on vegetables. **1839** DARWIN *Voy. Nat.* ii. (1845) 22 The Vampire bat is often the cause of much trouble, by biting the horses on their withers. **1875** B. TAYLOR *Faust* II. iii. iii, Like vampire-bats, they're squeaking, twittering, humming. **1788** BURNS *Poet's Progress* 29 *Vampyre-booksellers drain him to the heart. **1801** SOUTHEY *Thalaba* VIII. x, Through the *vampire corpse He thrust his lance. **1819** [POLIDORI] *The Vampyre* Introd. p. xxiii, The vampyre corse of the Arabian maid Oneiza. **1847** EMERSON *Poems, Mithridates* Wks. (Bohn) I. 410 Swing me in the upas boughs, *Vampire-fanned, when I carouse. **1855** SMEDLEY *Occult Sci.* 69 Criticism applied to the *Vampire legends by an anonymous writer. **1899** E. J. CHAPMAN *Drama Two Lives, Snake-Witch* 39 That unrest That held him with its *vampire spell. **1871** TYLOR *Prim. Cult.* II. 175 There is a whole literature of hideous *vampire stories. **1813** BYRON *Giaour* Note 37, The *Vampire superstition is still general in the Levant. **1828** *Lights & Shades* I. 42 A sort of yellowish-greenish, brownish grey —an unearthly *vampire tinge. **1846** S. F. SMITH *Theatr. Apprenticeship* viii. 63 Down I went through the trap-door (it was what actors call a *Vampire trap) before any one was aware of my intentions. **1893** *Westm. Gaz.* 29 Sept. 4/2 All his disappearances are done by means of the ordinary pantomime 'vampire' trap. **1837** A. TENNENT *Vis. Glencoe* 49 Some [of the devils] seem'd equipp'd with *vampire wing. **1831** POE *Poems* 64 Some tomb, which oft hath flung into black And *vampyre-winged pannels back.

Hence '**vampire** *v. trans.*, to assail or prey upon after the manner of a vampire; '**vampiredom**, the state of being a vampire (sense 1); the acts of a vampire; **vam'piric** *a.*, '**vampirine** *a.*, '**vampirish** *a.*, of the nature of a vampire.

1832 JEKYLL *Corr.* (1894) 306 Sotheby will not let poor Sir Walter lie quietly in his grave, but *vampires him with verses that would disgrace even the annuals. **1905** B. KENNEDY *Green Sphinx* xxi, The only wealth of the world is the produce coming from the labour of Nature... And gold insolently vampires this produce. **1933** *Times Lit. Suppl.* 28 Sept. 653/3 The more obvious literary possibilities of *vampiredom were thoroughly explored and exploited nearly forty years ago. **1972** *Daily Tel.* (Colour Suppl.) 12 May 56 There before the horrified gaze of the living was all the evidence of vampiredom—twisted position, torn shroud and blood. **1853** D. G. ROSSETTI *Let.* 17 Apr. (1965) I. 136 Such are the *vampyric notions of reciprocity. **1882** H. MERIVALE *Faucit of Balliol* II. vi, I'm not sure that you are not a ghost..of some uncomfortable vampiric order. **1963** *Listener* 24 Jan. 165/2 She [*sc.* Marilyn Monroe] had all the physical equipment of the vamp, but the spirit of the girl next door... Marilyn was never truly vampiric on the screen, and she was never a 'taker' in life. **1914** in D. McCarthy *Drama* (1940) 129 This is too much for Vanya; he explodes at the old *vampirine humbug, and..dashes from the room. **1946** BLUNDEN *Shelley* x. 135 Byron began and dropped a thriller which was becoming vampirine. **1891** A. LANG *Angling Sketches* 57 The Highland fairies are very *vampirish. **1929** *Sunday Dispatch* 13 Jan. 1/2 Among my own friends my reputation is notoriously the reverse of *vampirish, money means nothing to me. **1944** R. LEHMANN *Ballad & Source* v. viii. 300 Mother fastened vampirish eyes on her. **1981** N. TUCKER *Child & Book* vii. 198 Religious references..to the Virgin Mary behaving in a way that is distinctly vampirish have been glossed over.

vampirism ('væmpaɪrɪz(ə)m). Also **vampyrism.** [f. VAMPIRE *sb.*] The collective facts or ideas associated with the supposed existence and habits of vampires.

1794–6 E. DARWIN *Zoon.* II. 63 The supposed existence.. of witchcraft, vampyrism, animal magnetism and American tractors. **1819** [POLIDORI] *The Vampyre* Introd. p. xxii, The same measures were adopted with the corses of those persons who had previously died from vampyrism. **1855** SMEDLEY *Occult Sci.* 66 Instances of Vampirism, which chiefly occurred in Hungary. **1872** LE FANU *In a Glass* III. 262 He devoted himself to the..laborious investigation of the marvellously authenticated tradition of Vampirism.

fig. **1801** SOUTHEY *Lett.* (1856) I. 183 The Magazine exists;..the spirit having left it, I suspect vampirism in its present life. **1837** CARLYLE *Fr. Rev.* II. III. ii, Treason, delusion, vampyrism, scoundrelism, from Dan to Beersheba! **1858** O. W. HOLMES *Autocr. Breakf.-t.* ix. (1883) 175 Ah! long illness is the real vampyrism.

ˈvampirize, *v. rare.* Also **vampyrise.** [f. as prec.] **a.** *intr.* To act as a vampire. **b.** *trans.* = VAMPIRE *v.*

1819 [POLIDORI] *The Vampyre* Introd. p. xxii, That the deceased is not only doomed to vampyrise, but compelled to confine his infernal visitations solely to those beings he loved most while upon earth. **1888** MCCARTHY & PRAED *Ladies' Gallery* III. vii. 121 She took to fiction,..and vampirized Mrs. Lance when she found her own experience and imagination inadequate.

vampish (ˈvæmpɪʃ), *a.* [f. VAMP *sb.*^{4} + -ISH^1.] Suggestive or characteristic of a vamp. Hence **ˈvampishness.**

1922 S. FORD *Trilby May crashes In* iv. 60, I have got something more over the footlights than just my ankles and a few vampish hip motions. **1922** *Observer* 1 Oct. 5/4 'The Vavasour' in 'Strathmore'..out of pure vampishness makes a conquest of the hero. **1928** *Ibid.* 15 July 12/4 Not international 'stars' of vampish wiles, but hundreds of Miss Betty Balfours should be sought and cherished. **1971** *Petticoat* 24 July 24/3 At last a girl who admits that she would like to look vampish and look a 'tramp' or 'tart'. **1972** J. WILSON *Hide & Seek* ii. 36 Her crêpe dress, low-cut and forties style, very vampish and sexy. **1977** *Time* 14 Mar. 32/1 That vampish young lady in black hardly looks like the type to drive a race car or ride a bucking bronco.

vamplate (ˈvæmpleɪt). Now Archæol. Forms: α. 5 **vaun-** (**faun-**), 6 **van-**, **vantplate.** β. 6 *Sc.* **wamplat,** 6– **vamplate,** 7, 9 **vamplet.** [f. AF. *va(u)n-*, *va(u)nt-*, VANT- + *plate* PLATE *sb.*] A plate fixed on a spear or lance to serve as a guard for the hand, esp. in tilting.

α. *c* **1350** *Lybeaus Desc.* 1644 (K.), Lokeþ ȝour scheldes be strong, ȝour schaftes good and long, ȝour saket and vaunplate. **1508** *Acc. Ld. High Treas. Scot.* IV. 137 Tua vant plates, tua spere hedis, tua suordis. *a* **1548** HALL *Chron., Hen. VIII*, 78 The speres brake in the kynges hande to the vantplate all to sheuers. **1598** FLORIO, *Calce*,..a vanplate, the iron about a tilting-staffe neere the hand.

β. **1534** *Acc. Ld. High Treas. Scot.* VI. 190 For ij marekyn skynnis to lyne the twa wamplatis to the Kingis speris. *a* **1586** SIDNEY *Arcadia* III. vii. (1912) 387 Amphialus..let his staffe fall to Agenors vamplat. **1632** *Guillim's Heraldry* IV. xiii. 343 This vamplet..is of steele and is vsed for the safegard of the Tilters hand, and is taken off and put on to the staffe or speare at pleasure. **1660** in *Archaeologia* XI. 99 Vamplets for tilting staves. **1706** PHILLIPS (ed. Kersey), *Vamplate*, a Gauntlet, or Iron-Glove. *c* **1828** BERRY *Encycl. Her.* I. Gloss. **1869** BOUTELL *Arms & Armour* viii. 128 At the handle the shaft passed through a small circular shield, or hand-guard (called a vamplate), which was fixed to the shaft of the lance. **1898** VISCT. DILLON in *Archaeol. Jrnl.* V. 309 The Hatton and Prince Henry vamplates are truncated cones.

ˈvamplet. *south-w. dial.* [f. VAMP *sb.*^{1} + -LET.] A gaiter. Usu. in pl.

1842 AKERMAN *Wilts. Gloss.*, *Vamplets*, rude gaiters to defend the legs from wet. **1863** WISE *New Forest* 162 His legs are still cased..with gaiters, known as 'vamplets', or 'strogs'. **1866** BLACKMORE *C. Nowell* xlix, She wore a pair of poor Clayton's vamplets. **1875** —— *Alice Lorraine* II. xvi. 208 Instead of white stockings, he displayed gold-buttoned vamplets of orange velvet. **1883–** in dial. glossaries (Berks., Hants, Wilts.).

vampoose, vampose, erron. varr. VAMOOSE *v.*

1857 KINGSLEY *Two Years Ago* i, Has he vampoosed with the contents of a till, that he wishes so for solitude? **1857** G. H. KINGSLEY *Sp. & Trav.* (1900) 448 A 'cute Help, who had vamposed into the swamp with the family plate.

vampy (ˈvæmpɪ), *a.* [f. VAMP *sb.*^{4} + -Y^1.] That is a vamp; vampish. So **ˈvampiness.**

1928 *Sunday Express* 29 July 4 The varnished vampiness of Greto Garbo. **1949** *Richmond* (Va.) *Times-Dispatch* 7 Oct. 10 Barbara Stanwyck has come up with the statement that the vampy, predatory female makes a good wife. **1977** *Spare Rib* July 49/1 You see a lot of stilettoes, tights, revealing things, black vampy make-up.

vamure, var. VAUMURE *Obs.*

†**vamward.** *Obs. rare.* Also **vaumward, vawme-.** [var. of *vaun(t)ward* VANTWARD. Cf. VAWARD.] The vanguard of a host or army.

13.. *Coer de L.* 4025 These rydden in the vawmewarde. **1338** R. BRUNNE *Chron.* (1810) 188 He gaf him þe vamward. *Ibid.* 334 Þer vaumward was bot one dight.

van (væn), *sb.*^{1} Also 5–7 **vanne** (7 **wanne**), 7–8 **vann.** [Southern var. of FAN *sb.*^{1}, perh. partly a. OF. *van* or ad. L. *vannus*. Cf. WFlem. *van*, Du. *wan*, G. *wanne*, Sw. *vanna*.]

1. A winnowing basket or shovel; = FAN *sb.*^{1} 1 a.

Also, in mod. dial., = FANNER 2.

c **1450** [see FAN *sb.*^{1} 1 a, β]. *c* **1481** CAXTON *Dialogues* 38 Ghyselin the mande maker Hath sold his vannes,..His temmesis to clense with. **1566** ADLINGTON *Apuleius* 121 Then al the people..toke a great number of Vannes replenished with odors and pleasaunt smelles. **1598** BARCKLEY *Felic. Man* III. (1603) 246 At last he was put in a vanne,..and tossed up and downe that he might not sleepe. **1601–1791** [see FAN *sb.*^{1} 1 a, β]. **1801** RANKEN *Hist. France* I. 430 The van was a broad shovel, with which they threw the grain with force to a distance, while the light chaff fell behind. **1807** J. ROBINSON *Archæol. Græca* v. xiv. 477 To put them in vans or implements for winnowing corn. **1863** J. G. MURPHY *Comm., Lev.* vii. 30 It is used of the van in winnowing. **1880–** in south-western dial. glossaries.

b. A shovel used for lifting charcoal or testing ore.

1664 EVELYN *Sylva* 102 Your Coals sufficiently cool'd, with a very long-toothed Rake, and a Vann, you may load them into the Coal-wains. **1753** *Chambers' Cycl.* Suppl. s.v. *Vauning*, This instrument called the Vann [*printed* Vaun], is a long and moderately deep wooden shovel. **1875** KNIGHT *Dict. Mech.* 2689/2 *Van*, a shovel used in sifting ore.

c. [Cf. VAN *v.*] A process of testing ore on a shovel; the amount of metal obtained by this test.

1778 PRYCE *Min. Cornub.* 216 If the Van will cover or equal the weight of a crown piece, it is good Tin-stuff, and is termed a Crown Van. **1880** *W. Cornw. Gloss.*, *Van*, a rude process of trying tin ores by crushing and washing on a shovel. *c* **1888** *Trans. Amer. Inst. Min. Eng.* XII. 64 (Cent.), As he watched the process of making a van on a shovel, and saw the copper roll up to the highest point.

†**2.** = FAN *sb.*^{1} 1 d. *Obs.*$^{-1}$

1458 *Maldon* (Essex) *Liber B.* fol. ii b, John Dale hath in his kepynge a justyng sadel, ii vannys, and a sper.

3. A wing; = FAN *sb.*^{1} 4. Chiefly *poet.*

1667 [see FAN *sb.*^{1} 4 β]. **1671** MILTON *P.R.* IV. 583 Strait a fiery Globe Of Angels on full sail of wing flew nigh, Who on their plumy Vans receiv'd him soft. **1700** DRYDEN *Ovid's Met.* XII. 749 He wheel'd in Air, and stretch'd his Vans in vain; His Vans no longer cou'd his Flight sustain. **1791–** [see FAN *sb.*^{1} 4]. **1815** KIRBY & SP. *Entomol.* vii. (1816) I. 215 Its ample vans are calculated to catch the wind as sails, and so to carry it sometimes over the sea. **1851** D. JERROLD *St. Giles* xxxiii. 342 A carrion crow flapped its vans above the heads of man and wife. **1879** E. ARNOLD *Lt. Asia* VI. (1881) 156 Bright butterflies Fluttered their vans, azure and green and gold.

fig. **1898** G. MEREDITH *Poet. Wks.* (1912) 549 Beneath the vans of doom did men pass in.

†**4.** ? The vane of a ship. *Obs.*$^{-1}$

1698 FRYER *Acc. E. India & P.* 13 The Vans of the next Ships (though groveling with a neighbouring Wave) could not be discerned.

5. A sail of a windmill; = FAN *sb.*^{1} 6 c. (Cf. VANE 3 a.)

1837 LANDOR *Pentameron* Wks. 1846 II. 352 A sigh sets her windmill at work van over van, incessantly. **1856** MRS. BROWNING *Aur. Leigh* IV. 520 As a windmill seen at distance radiating Its delicate white vans against the sky. **1860** O. W. HOLMES *Prof. Breakf.-t.* xi, With his arms flying..like the vans of a windmill.

van (væn), *sb.*^{2} Also 7 **vann.** [Shortening of VANGUARD.]

1. The foremost division or detachment of a military or naval force when advancing or set in order for doing so.

1633 T. STAFFORD *Pac. Hib.* (1821) 420 The Van went off with few slaine. **1665** MANLEY *Grotius' Low C. Wars* 799 Spinola himself went in the Van, sending before him Scouts and Pioneers to search the ways and level them. **1667** MILTON *P.L.* II. 535 Armies rush To Battel in the Clouds, before each Van Pric forth the Aerie Knights. **1704** *Lond. Gaz.* No. 4054/1 They were very strong in the Center, and weaker in the Van and Rear. *a* **1781** R. WATSON *Philip III* (1783) v. 382 The van was led by the mareschal Lesdiguieres, the main body by the duke of Savoy, and Shomberg..brought up the rear with the artillery. **1816** SCOTT *Old Mort.* xxv, As Lord Evandale spoke, the van of the insurgents began to make their appearance. **1844** H. H. WILSON *Brit. India* II. 355 The van of the Mahratta army..had advanced to within fifteen miles of Chanda. **1879** FROUDE *Cæsar* xix. 308 Roman civilians had followed in the van of the armies.

b. Without article.

1663 BUTLER *Hud.* I. ii. 104 The Foe he had survey'd Rang'd, as to him they did appear, With Van, main Battel, Wings and Rear. **1667** MILTON *P.L.* v. 589 Standards, and Gonfalons twixt Van and Reare Streame in the Aire. **1809** WORDSW. *Hofer* 10 They stagger at the shock From van to rear. **1865** CARLYLE *Fredk. Gt.* XVIII. iv. V. 86 Van, having faced to right..and so become Left Wing, will attack Kreczor.

c. Const. *of* (war, etc.), or with possessive.

1716 POPE *Iliad* XIII. 350 But those my ship contains, whence distant far, I fight conspicuous in the Van of War. **1813** BYRON *Br. Abydos* I. vii, Another! and a braver man Was never seen in battle's van.

†**d.** *in one's van*, in front of one. *Obs.*

1724 DE FOE *Mem. Cavalier* (1840) 250 The king's army [was] in his rear, and Sir Richard Grenvil in his van.

2. The foremost portion of, or the foremost position in, a company or train of persons moving, or prepared to move, forwards or onwards.

1610 BEAUM. & FL. *Scornf. Lady* v. i, Come who leads? Sir Roger, you shall have the Van: lead the way. **1648** J. BEAUMONT *Psyche* XVI. lxxii, The gallant Pæans of His vocal Van To all the Orbs proclaim'd the Spectacle. **1674** *Jackson's Recantations* 19 in Hindley *Book Collector's Misc.* III, I..was commonly in the van, upon any desperate exploit, having the knowledge of my weapon [etc.]. **1824** W. IRVING *T. Trav.* I. 48 My aunt led the van with a red-hot poker; and, in my opinion, she was the most formidable of the party. **1850** MERIVALE *Rom. Emp.* v. (1865) I. 220 The Gauls..formed the van of the great Celtic migration. **1874** BURNAND *My Time* xxvi. 240 After the van of the procession had marched into the dining-room.

b. *fig.*, esp. in the phrases *to lead* (†*bear*, †*have*) *the van*, and *in the van*.

(*a*) *a* **1661** FULLER *Worthies* (1840) III. 115 Ratcliffe Church esteemeth it a greater grace to lead the van of all parochial, than to follow in the rear after many Cathedral Churches in England. **1683** tr. *Erasm. Moriæ Encom.* 9 Why may not I justly bear the Van among the whole troop of Gods? *a* **1708** BEVERIDGE *Thes. Theol.* (1710) I. 234 The Apostle gives us a chain of all Christian graces: wherein..faith leads the van. **1772** FLETCHER *Logica Genev.* 198 As Moses led the van of these testimonies..and St. Paul the main body, permit St. James to bring up the rear. **1838** STEPHENS *Trav. Greece* I. vii. 125, I could not follow them in their long and repeated kneelings and prostrations; but my young Greek..led the van.

(*b*) **1771** *Junius Lett.* lvii. (1788) 306 The natural resources of the crown are no longer confided in. Corruption glitters in the van. **1820** KEATS *Hyperion* I. 343 Be thou therefore in the van Of circumstance. **1843** CARLYLE *Past & Pr.* III. viii, The chief of men is he who stands in the van of men. **1879** LUBBOCK *Addr. Pol. & Educ.* iv. 87 That nothing less will suffice here if we are to maintain our position in the van of industrial nations.

3. The fore or front part of a thing. *rare.*

1727 DYER *Grongar Hill* 3 Silent Nymph!..Who..lie On the mountain's lonely van, Beyond the noise of busy man. **1762** FALCONER *Shipwr.* II. 508 While o'er the quivering deck, from van to rear, Broad surges roll in terrible career.

4. *attrib.*, as ***van-division, -ship, -squadron.***

1652 *French Occurr. Nov. 29–Dec. 6* 216 Ruttier..commanded the Van-squadron, and charged very resolutely up to us. **1795** NELSON 13 Mar. in Nicolas *Disp.* (1845) II. 14 The Admiral made the signal for the Van-ships to join him. **1796** —— 19 June *Ibid.* (1846) VII. p. lxxxii, The Admiral has honoured me with the command of the Van-Division. **1806** A. DUNCAN *Nelson* 71 He received the..fire from the van ships. **1862** MEREDITH *Poet. Wks.* (1912) 122 The day was a van-bird of summer.

van (væn), *sb.*^{3} [Shortened f. CARAVAN *sb.* 4.]

1. a. A covered vehicle chiefly employed for the conveyance of goods, usually resembling a large wooden box with arched roof and opening from behind, but varying in size (and to some extent in form) according to the use intended. Now usu., a motor vehicle with a covered rear compartment, often of shorter wheelbase than a lorry, used esp. for deliveries or service calls.

1829 LYTTON *The Disowned* I. iv. 50 Yes, Sir, we have some luggage—came last night by the van. **1855** LEIFCHILD *Cornwall* 3 The Cornish van is a conveyance both peculiar and interesting. This particular one..resembled very nearly an ordinary covered cart of some length. **1872** C. KING *Sierra Nevada* x. 213 The great van rocked, settled a little—and stuck fast. **1898** [see MOTOR *sb.* 5].

b. *felons' van, prison van* (also *ellipt.*); *police van*: see POLICE *sb.* 6. Also, a light covered vehicle employed to carry passengers.

1858 [see PRISON *sb.* 3 a]. **1863** KINGLAKE *Crimea* I. 338 The hour when the Parliament of France had been driven into the felons' van. **1895** *Daily News* 17 May 8/6 The Gaoler—There is no van between 10.30 in the morning and four in the afternoon. **1973**, etc. [see *van pool*, etc., below]. **1979** *N.Y. Rev. Bks.* 25 Oct. 7 (Advt.), Every morning, 1,441 Gulf employees who used to drive their own cars to work now make the trip in vans.

c. A gypsy caravan or one used by a showman; a holiday-maker's caravan; a camper.

1858 DICKENS *Going into Society* in *Househ. Words* Extra Christmas No., 7 Dec. 22/1 The House was so dismal arterwards, that I giv it up, and took to the Wan again. **1876** C. M. YONGE *Three Brides* II. v. 107 He was born in one of they vans, and hadn't never been to school. **1926** KIPLING *Debits & Credits* 237 You can stand at your door and mock when the gipsy-vans come through. **1952** *Motor Manual* (ed. 34) xiii. 244 The owner who wants to tow his caravan from home to some pleasant site where he can leave the van during the summer months. **1972** *Guardian* 5 Feb. 14 The trailer tent..[is] easier to tow than a full-scale trailer 'van. **1976** *Kingston* (Ontario) *Whig-Standard* 4 Aug. 25/4 In California travelling in his own van. **1979** *Observer* 15 July 2/5 Australians who fly in and buy a van to take them round Britain are finding they have to omit the extremities from their itinerary. **1980** R. HILL *Killing Kindness* vii. 62 Dave Lee had gone off in his van.

2. A closed carriage or truck used on railways for conveying passengers' luggage and the guard of the train, or in goods trains for smaller articles needing protection from the weather.

Freq. with defining terms, as *brake-, guard's, luggage van.*

1854 DICKENS *Hard Times* II. i. 143 Very heavy train and vast quantity of it [*sc.* luggage] in the van. **1868** BOYD *Less. Middle Age* 339 Emerging from the carriage door, the pilgrim..hastens to the van at the end of the train. **1885** *Law Times* LXXIX. 47/1 The portmanteau and hamper had been put into the van.

3. *attrib.* and *Comb.*, as ***van boy, dock, -driver, dweller, guard, harness, load, -man, shunter***; **van pool** *U.S.*, a group of workers sharing a van provided by their employer to transport them to work; so ***van-pooler, -pooling.***

1881 *Instr. Census Clerks* (1885) 34 *Van..Boy, Guard. **1883** *Pall Mall G.* 23 Oct. 7/2 A van boy, seventeen years of age. **1878** F. S. WILLIAMS *Midl. Railw.* 639 On the left of this platform is the '*van dock' in which the vans are standing. **1895** *Daily News* 26 Sept. 6/3 A Midland Railway *van driver. **1894** *Ibid.* 25 Jan. 2/4 The fourth annual meeting of the United Kingdom Showmen's and *Van Dwellers' Protection Association. **1921** *Dict. Occup. Terms* (1927) §723 **Van guard*..travels with and guards contents of mail vans. **1931** *Daily Express* 22 Sept. 7/3 A vanguard..was accused of being concerned with another man..in stealing a motor-car. **1862** *Catal. Internat. Exhib., Brit.* II. No. 4727, *Van harness and cart harness. **1885** *L'pool Daily Post* 23 Apr. 5/2 Countless *vanloads of happy urchins, bent on enjoying their Sunday school treat. **1881** *Instr. Census Clerks* (1885) 34 Trap Minder. *Van Man. **1891** *Daily News* 21 Sept. 2/7 Vanman of the Glasgow City Parochial Authorities. **1973** *Sunday Bull.* (Philadelphia) 7 Oct. (Parade Suppl.) 14/2 (*heading*) *Van pooling. *Ibid.*, The 3M Company in St. Paul, Minn., bought six 12-passenger vans and assigned them to workers to form 'van pools'... Van pool driver-coordinators receive free rides and can use the van during off-duty hours. **1974** *Woman's Day* (N.Y.) Oct. 138/2 Van pools are working so well at Minnesota Mining and Manufacturing's huge complex..that the company now has fifty-seven company-owned vans. **1976** *National Observer* (U.S.) 16 Oct., Van pooling is a new commuting style looking for a permanent place in transportation between private cars and mass-transit facilities. **1983** *Mass*

Transit (U.S.) Apr. 24/1 The average vanpooler saves about 400 miles of driving and 25 gallons of gas a month. **1878** F. S. Williams *Midl. Railw.* 639 The vans, as they enter the shed, are at once placed under the orders..of '*van shunters'.

van (væn), *sb.*[4] [a. Welsh *fan* (van), mutated form of *ban* height, occurring in place-names in South Wales, esp. in Brecknock.] A height or summit.

1871 Kingsley *At Last* ii, Flat 'vans' or hog-backed hills, and broad sweeps of moorland,..are as rare as are steep walls of cliff. **1905** A. R. Wallace *My Life* I. 249 The range of the great forest of Brecon, with its series of isolated summits or vans.

van (væn), *sb.*[5] *Lawn Tennis.* Abbrev. of vantage *sb.* 6.

1927 in W. E. Collinson *Contemporary Eng.* 36. **1960** N. Hilliard *Maori Girl* 47 They counted in lawn-tennis style with vans and loves. **1977** *Fremdsprachen* XXI. 125 Van in, van out: my van, your van.

van (væn), *v.*[1] Also 4 **uanni**, 5 **vane**, 5–7 **vanne**. [Southern var. fan *v.*]

1. *trans.* To winnow with a fan. ? *Obs.*

1340 [see fan *v.* 1]. *c* **1467** *Noble Bk. Cookry* (1882) 86 Tak clene whet and bet it in a mortoire and vane it clene. **1545** Elyot, *Euanno*, to van corne or other lyke thyng. **1552** Huloet, Vanne or fanne corne, *euanno*. **1611** Cotgr., *Berner*, to vanne, or winnow corne. **1631** Anchoran *Comenius' Gate Tongues* 87 Hee vanneth, winnoweth and waggeth oates with a wanne. **1648** Hexham ii, *Wt-wannen*, to Winnowe, or to Vanne out. **1706** Phillips (ed. Kersey) *Vanned*, fanned or winnowed.

fig. **14..** *Langland's P. Pl.* C. xxiii. 168 Elde..wayueth [*v.r.* vanned] away wanhope. *a* **1693** *Urquhart's Rabelais* iii. xl. 332 The Suit or Process, being well vanned and winnowed.

†**2. a.** = fan *v.* 3. *Obs.*

1565 Cooper *Thesaurus* s.v. *Ventulus*, Vanne winde saftely on hir in this maner.

†**b.** To fan; to blow upon. *Obs.*

1628 Feltham *Resolves* ii. viii. 18 Nor does the wound but rankle more, which is vanned by the publike ayre.

3. To separate and test (ore) by washing on a van or shovel. (Earlier in vanning *vbl. sb.*[1] 2.)

1839 De La Beche *Rep. Geol. Cornwall*, etc. xv. 585 We have seen a miner dexterously van pulverised iron pyrites. **1899** Baring-Gould *Bk. of West* II. v. 61 In dressing the ore the miners broke it with their hammers, and then 'vanned' it on their broad oak shovels.

van (væn), *v.*[2] *rare*[−1]. [f. van *sb.*[2]] *trans.* To go in the van of, to lead.

1852 A. Smith *Life Drama* ii, Do not the royal souls that van the world Hunger for praises?

van (væn), *v.*[3] [f. van *sb.*[3]]

1. *trans.* To send in a van.

1840 *New Monthly Mag.* LX. 167 Vanning his horses to the different meetings. **1862** H. H. Dixon *Scott & Sebright* iii. 203 When..he [a racehorse] could hardly move in his box, he was vanned down to Hermit Lodge.

2. To confine in a van.

1897 P. Warung *Tales Old Regime* 34 A convict—one of the two servants who were not 'van'd' overnight.

van, obs. Sc. pa. t. win *v.*

vanadate ('vænədət). *Chem.* [f. vanad-ium + -ate[1]. So F. *vanadate.*] A salt produced by the combination of vanadic acid with a base.

1835 *Partington's Brit. Cycl., Arts & Sci.* II. 858/2 The precipitate is vanadate of barytes or lead. **1851** Mantell *Petrifactions* iii. § 1. 145 Vanadic acid and vanadates. **1883** *Science* I. 490/1 Strontic vanadate was prepared by fusion of the acid with sodic bromide and strontic bromide. *Ibid.*, Vanadates of lead, cadmium, zinc,..were formed in the same way.

vanadian (və'neɪdɪən), *a.* *Min.* [f. vanad(ium + -ian.] Of a mineral: having a (usu. small) proportion of a constituent element replaced by vanadium.

1930 W. T. Schaller in *Amer. Mineralogist* XV. 572 Vanadium—vanadian. **1951** C. Palache et al. *Dana's Syst. Min.* (ed. 7) II. 1084 The so-called eosite from Leadhills, Scotland, apparently is a highly vanadian wulfenite.

vanadiate (və'neɪdɪət). *Chem.* [f. vanadi-um + -ate[1].] = vanadate.

1833 *Rep. Brit. Assoc. Adv. Sci. 1832–3* 470 Vanadiate of lead. **1836** T. Thomson *Min., Geol.*, etc. II. 539 Analysis of Vanadiates. The only vanadiate known at present to exist in the mineral kingdom, is the vanadiate of lead. **1849** D. Campbell *Inorg. Chem.* 301 The vanadiate of potash in the bisulphate of potash solution is boiled with hydrochloric acid. **1869** *Phil. Trans.* CLVIII. 18 Vanadiate of ammonia.

†**vanadic** (və'nædɪk, və'neɪdɪk), *a.* *Chem.* *Obs.* [f. vanad-ium + -ic. Cf. F. *vanadique.*] Of or pertaining to, derived from, vanadium; *spec.* containing vanadium in its higher valency, as opposed to vanadious *a.* Chiefly in ***vanadic acid***.

1833 *Rep. Brit. Assoc. Adv. Sci. 1832–3* 469 Vanadic acid ..in the state of powder is yellow. **1835** *Partington's Brit. Cycl., Arts & Sci.* II. 858/2 The vanadic acid is reduced to the state of salifiable oxide. **1849** D. Campbell *Inorg. Chem.* 303 Vanadic acid is a brownish powder, but when melted.. it approaches a rusty-red. **1874** Roscoe *Ess.* (Owens Coll.) II. 55 The crystalline form of a mineral contained vanadic oxide.

vanadinite (və'nædɪnaɪt). *Min.* [f. vanadium + -in + -ite.] A mineral consisting of vanadate of lead and chloride of lead, occurring in brilliant crystals of various colours.

1855 *Orr's Circ. Sci., Geol.*, etc. 532 Vanadinite... Found in Mexico, the Ural, and Dumfriesshire. **1880** Clemenshaw *Wurtz' Atom. The.* 139 The atomic weight of vanadium has been altered so that vanadinite, which is isomorphous with apotite, is represented by a similar formula.

vanadious (və'neɪdɪəs), *a.* *Chem.* [f. vanadium + -ous c.] Containing vanadium in its lower valency, as opposed to vanadic *a.*

1868 Watts *Dict. Chem.* V. 988 Vanadious phosphate and sulphate have been obtained in definite crystals. **1870** Roscoe in *Lond. Philos. Mag.* July 63 Vanadious salt.

vanadite ('vænədaɪt). *Chem. rare.* [f. as prec. + -ite. So F. *vanadite.*] (See quot.)

1835 *Partington's Brit. Cycl., Arts & Sci.* II. 859/1 Oxide of vanadium..combines with bases, and forms salts, which may be called *vanadites.* **1858** T. Graham *Inorg. Chem.* (ed. 2) II. 174 The insoluble vanadites, when moistened or covered with water, become green.

vanadium (və'neɪdɪəm). *Chem.* [mod.L., irreg. f. ON. *Vana-dís* one of the names of the Scandinavian goddess Freyja: see -ium. Named (1830) by the Swedish chemist Sefström, who found it in iron from Taberg near Jönköping.] A rare chemical element (symbol V), occurring in certain iron, lead, and uranium ores, some of the compounds of which are used in the production of aniline blacks and other dyeing materials.

The metal was detected by Del Rio in certain Mexican lead ores in 1801, and named by him *Erythronium.*

1833 *Rep. Brit. Assoc. Adv. Sci. 1832–3* 468 Vanadium.. was discovered by Sefström towards the end of 1830, in the iron from the forges of Eckersholm in Sweden. **1835** *Partington's Brit. Cycl., Arts & Sci.* II. 859/1 Vanadium dissolves readily in nitric acid and in aqua regia. **1839** Ure *Dict. Arts* 1263 Vanadium is white, and when its surface is polished, it resembles silver or molybdenum more than any other metal. **1880** *Times* 23 Oct. 6/1, I would suggest a preparation of aniline with vanadium for the tinted grounds.

attrib. **1849** D. Campbell *Inorg. Chem.* 301 The vanadium sulphide precipitates, and gathered, is..roasted in an open crucible till it becomes vanadic acid. **1869** Roscoe in *Phil. Trans.* CLVIII. 11 Vanadium dioxide, or vanadyl, V_2O_2. **1908** *Westm. Gaz.* 2 Apr. 4/2 The material used in its construction (vanadium steel, made in the company's own works).

vanadous ('vænədəs), *a.* *Chem.* [f. vanad(ium + -ous.] Of or containing vanadium, *spec.* in an oxidation state of + 2.

1850 H. Watts tr. *Gmelin's Hand-bk. Chem.* IV. 90 (*heading*) Bisulphide of vanadium.—Vanadous sulphide. **1858** T. Graham *Inorg. Chem.* (ed. 2) II. 173 Bioxide of vanadium is also capable of acting as an acid... It is hence called vanadous acid. **1887** C. M. Tidy *Handbk. Mod. Chem.* (ed. 2) xvii. 504 Preparation [of Vanadium].—By heating vanadous chloride (VCl_3) in a current of dry hydrogen, air and moisture being excluded. **1927** *Amer. Mineralogist* XII. 236 There may also be assumed to be present..:..a vanadous acmite, $Na_2O{\cdot}V_2O_3{\cdot}4SiO_2$. **1954** *Thorpe's Dict. Appl. Chem.* (ed. 4) XI. 833/1 Vanadous Oxide, VO, has not been prepared pure. **1962** H. L. Kern et al. in A. Pirie *Lens Metabolism Rel. Cataract* 386 The tubes were..gassed with N_2-CO_2 (95:5) from which the oxygen had been removed by passage through vanadous sulphate. **1980** *Jrnl. Amer. Chem. Soc.* CII. 3035/1 The change from a d^4 (chromous) to a d^3 (vanadous) ion results in a profound change in the stoichiometry.

'vanadyl. *Chem.* [f. vanad-ium + -yl.] Vanadium dioxide.

1868 Watts *Dict. Chem.* V. 987 As it enters into many vanadium-compounds.., it may be appropriately called vanadyl. **1869** Roscoe in *Phil. Trans.* CLVIII. 3 Vanadyl monochloride.

Van Allen (væn 'ælən). Also (*erron.*) **van Allen**. The name of James A. *Van Allen* (b. 1914), U.S. physicist, used *attrib.* to designate each of two regions reported by him in 1958, partly surrounding the earth at heights of several thousand kilometres and containing intense radiation and many high-energy charged particles trapped by the earth's magnetic field; also applied to similar regions around other planets.

1959 *Nature* 8 Aug. 439 (*heading*) The upper boundary of the Van Allen radiation belts. **1965** *Wireless World* Sept. 447/1 This [sensitivity to radiation damage] limits the application of junction detectors in reactor instrumentation and in the van Allen belts. **1971** *Nature* 28 May 217/2 The circular polarization of about one per cent which is emitted by the planet Jupiter indicates the presence of a field of 0·4 gauss in its van Allen belts. **1974** *Times Lit. Suppl.* 13 Sept. 968/2 It girds us Transparently like the Van Allen Belt, Simply like the tie-belt of a mac. **1983** *New Scientist* 13 Jan. 93/2 They penetrated the Van Allen radiation belt (which is contained by the Earth's magnetic field) and loosened showers of electrons.

vanaspati (və'nʌspətɪ). [Skr. *vánas-páti*, lord of the wood, forest tree.] A vegetable ghee used in India. Also *attrib.*

1949 *Food Manufacture* XXIV. 500/2 On account of the shortage of butterfat in India, the consumption of hydrogenated oils, known locally as *vanaspatis*, has recently been greatly increased. **1969** *National Herald* (New Delhi) 29 July 9/3 Oils and seeds sought lower levels following fears of nationalization of the vanaspati industry. **1973** *Indian Express* (Bombay) 29 Oct. 4/5 Several temples used vanaspati instead of ghee to keep the lamps before the deities burning. **1979** *Eastern Economist* 14 Sept. 534/1 Ensuring price stability as well as availability of vanaspati.

vanbrace, -bras, varr. vam-, vantbrace.

a **1470** H. Parker *Dives & Pauper* (W. de W. 1496) x. vi. 379/2 We sholde take with us rerebras and vanbras & gloues of plate. **1649** G. Daniel *Trinarch., Hen. V*, ccxviii, Alanzon breakes the Blow, which the King first Made... and locks his Hilt In Harrie's Vanbrace. **1816** *Monthly Mag.* XLI. 330 Their arms and legs vanbras and cuisses sheath.

Vanbrughian (væn'bruːɪən), *a.* [f. the name of Sir John *Vanbrugh* (or *Vanburgh*) (see below) + -ian.] Of, pertaining to, or characteristic of the architecture, landscaping, or plays of Sir John Vanbrugh (1664–1726). Also *ellipt.* as *sb.*, Vanbrughian style.

1947 J. Lees-Milne *Diary* 3 July (1983) 178 The windows tame Vanbrughian. **1972** *Country Life* 5 Oct. 812 The heavy Doric frieze and Vanbrughian chimneypiece. **1979** *Garden* (Victoria & Albert Mus.) 63/2 Early in the twentieth century there was..a Vanbrughian [garden] mode. **1980** *Country Life* 17 July 243/2 A tale that is..gorgeous, pyrotechnic, Vanbrughian.

vance, variant of vaunce *v.* *Obs.*

†**'vancement.** *Obs.*[−1] In 4 **vauns-**. [Aphetic f. advancement.] Advancement, preferment.

1303 R. Brunne *Handl. Synne* 5514 ȝyf þou oþer ȝaue or sent Of holy cherche to haue vaunsement.

vance-roof. *E. Angl.* Also 8–9 **vaunce-**. [f. vaunce *v.*] A garret. Also *fig.*

1655 Gurnall *Chr. in Arm.* i. vii. § 2. 256 Canst thou hide any one sin in the vance-roof of thy heart? **1657** in *Verney Mem.* (1907) II. 119 You may ges how full our hous is whan my lady and all hir faimily of women ly in the van[c]e rouff over the dining chamber. **1682–3** *MS. Lett. Norwich Quakers*, And for the vance roofes we giue 10s a weeke for those to worke in yᵉ Lodge in the hole. **1787** in Marshall *Rur. Econ. E. Norf.* **1823** in Moor *Suffolk Gloss.*

†**vanchase.** *Obs. rare.* Also **vaunchace.** [f. *van-* (see vant-) + chase *sb.*[1] Cf. vaunt-chase.] The van, front, or advanced part of the chase or hunt. So †**vanchaser**, a hound hunting in the van. *Obs.*

c **1410** *Master of Game* (MS. Digby 182) Prol., He hath ynogh at done..to loke..which houndes ben vanchasours and perfiters. *Ibid.*, He shal se, whiche houndes commeth in the vanchace [*Bodl. MS.* vaunchace] and the myddell and whiche ben perfitours.

vancomycin (væŋkəʊ'maɪsɪn). *Pharm.* [f. *vanco-*, of unkn. origin + -mycin.]

A glycopeptide antibiotic produced by the actinomycete *Streptomyces orientalis* and active against most Gram-positive bacteria.

1956 M. H. McCormick et al. in *Antibiotics Ann. 1955–6* 606 A new antimicrobial agent, vancomycin, has been isolated..from strains of *Streptomyces orientalis*, n. sp. **1974** R. M. Kirk et al. *Surgery* ii. 29/1 Vancomycin is effective against some penicillin-resistant staphylococci but is too toxic for routine use. **1982** *Brit. Med. Jrnl.* 22 May 1508/2 In the past few years..vancomycin has reemerged as a valuable antibiotic in three clinical settings: endocarditis, multiresistant staphylococcal infections, and as the first-line treatment of pseudomembranous colitis.

van-courier ('væn,kʊrɪə(r)). Forms: α. 6–7 **van-corrier**, 7 **-currier**, **-iour**. β. 7–9 **van-courier**. [Var. of *vant-* vaunt-courier.] A vaunt-courier or forerunner, in *lit.* and *fig.* senses.

α. **1581** Styward *Mart. Discipl.* i. 15 He is to appoint what bands shal watch & what vancorriers. **1652** Benlowe *Theoph.* vii. xliv, Windes are van-curriers and postilions to Thy will. **1657** Reeve *God's Plea* 147 Where is reformation to latch arrows,..to meet the Vancurriours in their march? **1687** tr. *Sallust* (1692) 287 The Vancurriers that scouted before, returning brought word, that all were friends.

β. **1670** *Caveat to Conventiclers* 1 The Van couriers appeared in number about half a score. *a* **1694** *Life M. Robinson* (ed. Mayor) 36 All the neighbouring gentlemen knew of the master's approach by these his vancouriers. **1706** Phillips (ed. Kersey), *Van-couriers*, light-armed Soldiers sent before to beat the Road, upon the approach of an Enemy. **1879** Todhunter *Alcestis* 11 What bodes this pale vancourier of fate?

vancuist, obs. Sc. pa. t. and pple. of vanquish *v.*

†**van-current**, *a.* *Obs.* [f. *van-* + current *a.*, after *van-courier*.] Forerunning, precursory.

1649 G. Daniel *Trinarch., Hen. IV*, liv, Soe van-Current feavers but Yeild to a Pestilence.

vand, obs. Sc. form of wand *sb*

Vanda ('vændə). *Bot.* [mod.L., a. Skr. and Hindī *vandā*.] A genus of epiphytal orchids, native to tropical Asia, characterized by large showy flowers borne in racemes; a plant of this genus.

1801 *Encycl. Brit.* Suppl. II. 738/1. **1844** *Florist's Jrnl.* (1846) V. 57 The Vandas, Saccolabiums, and Dendrobiums of India. **1882** *Garden* 21 Jan. 35/2, I herewith send you a dried flower of the blue Vanda, which is now flowering.

Comb. **1837** *Penny Cycl.* IX. 480/1 Dendrobiums and Vanda-like plants. **1844** *Florist's Jrnl.* (1846) V. 55 The flowers of this beautiful vanda-like plant.

Vandal ('vændəl), *sb.* and *a.* Also 6-7 **Vandale**, 7 **Vandall**, and with lower-case initial in transferred uses. [ad. L. *Vandalus*, pl. *Vandali* (also *-alii, -ili, -ilii, -uli*), whence also F. *Vandale*, It., Sp., Pg. *Vandalo*. Trevisa, in his translation of Higden (1387), uses the form *Wandales*.

The different Latin forms indicate a variation of suffix in the Germanic stem, viz. **Wandal-, -il-, -ul-*. The second of these is represented by OE. *Wendlas* (pl.), ON. *Vendill*, designating inhabitants of the north of Jutland.]

A. *sb.* **1.** A member of a Germanic tribe, which in the fourth and fifth centuries invaded Western Europe, and established settlements in various parts of it, esp. in Gaul and Spain, finally in 428-9 migrating to Northern Africa. Chiefly in *pl.*

In the year 455 their king Genseric led a marauding expedition against Rome, which he took and completely sacked. The Vandals were overthrown by Belisarius in 533 at the battle of Tricamarum.

1555 EDEN *Decades* (Arb.) 283 Chaunges..caused..by the commynge of the Gothes and Vandales, and other Barbarians into Italy. **1596** SPENSER *St. Irel.* Wks. (Globe) 627/2 The coming downe of the Gothes, the Hunnes, and the Vandals. **1605** VERSTEGAN *Dec. Intell.* ii. 44 The Gothes and the Vandalles, beeing also a people of the septentrional partes of Germanie. **1647-8** COTTERELL tr. *Davila's Hist. Fr.* (1678) 3 Famous incursions of the Vandals. **1694** DRYDEN *To Sir G. Kneller* 47 Till Goths, and Vandals, a rude Northern race, Did all the matchless Monuments deface. *a* **1743** SAVAGE *Of Public Spirit* Wks. 1777 II. 141 Rome all subdu'd, yet Vandals vanquish'd Rome. **1788** GIBBON *Decl. & F.* xli. IV. 146 The certain intelligence that the Vandal [*sc.* Gelimer] had fled to the inaccessible country of the Moors. **1842** *Penny Cycl.* XXIV. 266/1 The Slavonian tribes were subject to the Teutonic Vandals, who are often confounded with the Wends. **1888** *Encycl. Brit.* XXIV. 58/2 There does not seem to be in the story of the capture of Rome by the Vandals any justification for the charge of wilful and objectless destruction of public buildings.

2. *transf.* **a.** One who acts like a Vandal or barbarian; a wilful or ignorant destroyer of anything beautiful, venerable, or worthy of preservation.

1663 GERBIER *Counsel* 50 For who would Rob them but Goths and Vandalls. **1709** POPE *Ess. Crit.* 696 At length Erasmus..Stemm'd the wild torrent of a barb'rous age, And drove those holy Vandals [i.e monks] off the stage. **1780** COWPER *On Burning Ld. Mansfield's Library* 1 The Vandals of our isle..Have burnt to dust a nobler pile Than ever Roman saw! **1801** HELEN M. WILLIAMS *Mann. & Opin. Fr. Rep.* II. xxxv. 177 The monuments..which have escaped the fury of our modern Vandals [i.e. Jacobins]. *a* **1839** PRAED *Poems* (1864) II. 189 A horrid Vandal,—but his money Will buy a glorious coat of arms. **1895** SUFFLING *Land of Broads* 85 Stained glass, which those narrow-minded Vandals, the Puritans, took great pains to destroy.

b. *attrib.* and *Comb.*, as ***vandal-proof***, ***-resistant*** adjs.

1971 H. PACY *Road Accidents* iv. 115 A vandalproof phone, consisting of a loudspeaker and microphone sheltered behind heavy steel grids. **1977** *Linlithgowshire Jrnl. & Gaz.* 15 Apr. 3/5 We have tried to make the hall vandal-proof by introducing a number of safeguards. **1977** C. BRANDRETH *Parking Law* 50 Boston (Mass.)..have vandal-resistant meters, the coins encased in a heavy iron box.

B. *adj.* **1.** Of or pertaining to the Vandals (or a Vandal).

Vandal war, the war waged by the Roman Empire against the Vandals in Africa, 532-546.

1613 PURCHAS *Pilgrimage* (1614) 98 Procopius, in the fourth booke of the Vandale Warre. **1781** GIBBON *Decl. & F.* xxxiii. (1787) III. 346 The warlike tyrant is supposed to have shed more Vandal blood by the hand of the executioner, than in the field of battle. **1788** *Ibid.* xli. IV. 152 The chariots of state which had been used by the Vandal queen. **1842** *Penny Cycl.* XXIV. 266/1 All the names of the Vandal kings are Teutonic. **1879** LUMBY *Introd.* to *Higden* (Rolls) VII. p. xx, Gregory [VI] appealed to the emperor for help, and when an excuse of the Vandal war was made by him, the pope took the field himself against the robbers. **1888** *Encycl. Brit.* XXIV. 58/2 The Vandal occupation of this great city [i.e. Carthage]..lasted for ninety-four years.

2. Acting like a Vandal in the wilful or ignorant destruction of things of beauty or historic interest; recklessly or ruthlessly destructive; barbarous, rude, uncultured.

1700 DRYDEN *Prol.* [*Fletcher's Pilgrim*] 35 Our bold Britton..Invades the Psalms with Rhymes, and leaves no room For any Vandal Hopkins yet to come. **1798** W. T. FITZGERALD *Misc. Poems* (1801) 99 Though Europe suffers, to her foul disgrace, This second Inroad of the Vandal Race. **1889** *Science-Gossip* XXV. 34 Vandal naturalists. **1892** T. A. COOK *Old Touraine* (1894) II. 39 A certain vandal senator..irreparably destroyed a great part of the old buildings.

3. Characterized by vandalism or lack of culture; vandalic, vandalistic.

1752 H. WALPOLE *Lett.* (1846) II. 443 Some good tombs.., and a very Vandal one. **1857** LD. GRANVILLE in *Life* (1905) I. x. 260 They..are against any Vandal destruction of towns, palaces, etc. **1863** MARY HOWITT tr. *F. Bremer's Greece & Greeks* II. xii. 24 Masses of marble fragments and stones show what a work of Vandal desolation has been here.

Hence **'Vandalled** *pa. pple.*, over-run or devastated by the Vandals.

1648 WINYARD *Midsummer-Moon* 4 The whole University resembles Greece over-run by Turkes, or Italy Goth'd and Vandald.

Van'dalian, *a.* *rare*⁻¹. [Cf. VANDAL *sb.* 1, quot. 1842.] Wendish.

1730 *Hist. Litt.* I. 435 We have now an entire Translation of the Bible in the Vandalian Tongue.

Vandalic (væn'dælɪk), *a.* Also 7 **Vandallique**. [ad. L. *Vandalic-us*, f. *Vandalus* VANDAL. So F. *vandalique*. In the 15th cent. translation of Higden the form *Wandalical* occurs.]

1. Characteristic of, resembling that of, the Vandals; barbarously or ignorantly destructive; vandalistic.

1666 WATERHOUSE *Fire London* 66 This late harrass of us by a more than Gottish and Vandallique fire. **1762** WARBURTON *Doct. Grace* III. ii. Wks. 1788 IV. 704 Rash Divines might be apt to charge this holy man..with a brutal spite to Reason,—and with more than Vandalic rage against human Learning. **1801** HELEN M. WILLIAMS *Mann. & Opin. Fr. Rep.* I. xviii. 226 The vandalic fury that employed itself not only on the mutilation of statues, but destroyed the paintings of the first masters. **1865** *Ecclesiologist* XXVI. 271 Deliberate, we might say Vandalic demolition. **1887** F. R. STOCKTON *Hundredth Man* xv, In his vandalic operations Enoch had shown..fiendish ingenuity.

b. Of persons: = VANDAL *a.* 2.

1842 *Blackw. Mag.* LI. 88 The cathedral itself is ordered to be repaired, and unfortunately 'beautified', by the most Vandalic architect Paris ever was afflicted with.

2. Of or pertaining to, consisting of, the Vandals.

a **1727** NEWTON *Obs. Daniel* (1733) I. v. 34 The Burgundians, a Vandalic nation, were between the Vistula and the southern fountain of the Boristhenes. **1802** SIBBALD *Chron. S.P.* IV. p. ix, The Saxons, of Vandalic origin. **1838** G. S. FABER *Inquiry* 477 Passing thence into Germany, he long sojourned among the Vandalic States, and finally settled in Bohemia. **1853** KINGSLEY *Hypatia* II. xv. 375 Barbarians of the Vandalic race,..made insolent by success.

† **vandaliro.** *Obs.*⁻¹ [a. older Sp. *vandolera*.] = BANDOLEER 2.

a **1660** *Contemp. Hist. Irel.* (Ir. Archæol. Soc.) II. 78 The Major had noe amunition more then what the souldiers did carie in their vandaliros about them.

'vandalish, *a.* *rare.* [f. VANDAL + -ISH.] Vandalic, vandalistic.

1834 BECKFORD *Italy* II. 356 Yes, I witnessed this vandalish operation. **1839** *Blackw. Mag.* XLVI. 647 These pretended barbarians—Gothic, Vandalish, Lombard,..were in reality the restorers and regenerators of the effete Roman intellect.

vandalism ('vændəlɪz(ə)m). [a. F. *vandalisme*, first used by Henri Grégoire, Bishop of Blois, *c* 1793.] The conduct or spirit characteristic of, or attributed to, the Vandals in respect of culture; ruthless destruction or spoiling of anything beautiful or venerable; in weakened sense, barbarous, ignorant, or inartistic treatment.

1798 HELEN M. WILLIAMS *Lett. France* IV. 179 (Jod.), Those barbarous triumphs are passed and anarchy and vandalism can return no more. **1800** W. TAYLOR in *Monthly Mag.* VIII. 684 The writers, who bring against certain philosophic innovationists a clamorous charge of Vandalism. **1848** GALLENGA *Italy* 497 After several hours of that unavailing Vandalism, which set houses and palaces on fire, they were compelled to beat a retreat. *a* **1878** SIR G. SCOTT *Lect. Archit.* (1879) I. 35 Monuments, through the lapse of time and the barbarous hand of modern Vandalism, become in many cases..decayed and mutilated.

b. An instance of this; a vandalistic act.

1882 SERGT. BALLANTINE *Exper.* xxii. 218 The vandalisms that have changed the fair scene..into its present shape.

vandalistic (vændə'lɪstɪk), *a.* [f. VANDAL *sb.* + -ISTIC.] Characterized by, given to, vandalism. Hence **vanda'listically** *adv.*

1854 *Fraser's Mag.* L. 205 The authorities are Vandalistic enough to prohibit the sport. **1897** *Naturalist* 45 The most vandalistic plant-grubber. **1900** *Westm. Gaz.* 8 May 10/1 The natives..betray a vandalistic disposition towards the tablets and inscriptions. **1922** *Weekly Dispatch* 10 Dec. 7 Drew a picture of Spion Kop, of myself,..and others of the party on the table-cloth... One of the party began vandalistically to cut the square out of the cloth. **1970** J. STEER *Conc. Hist. Venetian Painting* v. 134 The *Presentation of the Virgin* [by Titian]..still hangs in the position for which it was designed, although a hole has been vandalistically cut in the left-hand side to make room for an extra door. **1980** *Times* 30 Aug. 10/3 Customers who behave so inconsiderately, not to say vandalistically.

vandali'zation. [Cf. next.] **a.** The action of rendering barbarous. **b.** An act of vandalism.

1800 W. TAYLOR in *Monthly Mag.* VIII. 684 Events thicken to accelerate the entire Vandalization of Europe. **1984** *Times* 16 June 18/8 We know one couple who finally gave in to silent local pressure to move out (five break-ins..two vandalizations).

vandalize ('vændəlaɪz), *v.* [f. VANDAL *sb.* + -IZE.] *trans.* **a.** To render Vandal in respect of culture. **b.** To deal with or treat in a vandalistic manner.

1800 W. TAYLOR in *Monthly Mag.* VIII. 684 To vandalize Europe then can have no other signification than to introduce eastern Slavonian barbarians to domination over the actual feats of culture and improvement. **1821** *New Monthly Mag.* II. 353 They are not only vandalized in style, but in sentiment. **1845** FORD *Handbk. Spain* I. 99 The noblest monuments of art and piety have been vandalized. **1905** *Chambers's Jrnl.* Dec. 17/1 A very remarkable church, spoilt and vandalised by the introduction of galleries and deal pews. **1968** *Wall Street Jrnl.* 19 Feb. 1/1 These militants roamed the campus, vandalizing the book-store and a dining hall and terrorizing students. **1971** J. WAINWRIGHT *Last Buccaneer* I. 48 He had to run more than a mile before he could find a kiosk which had not been vandalised. **1978** *Daily Tel.* 17 Aug. 2/8 Newcastle..is to incur even heavier expenditure by importing more costly American [parking] meters said to be harder to vandalise.

Hence **'vandalized** *ppl. a.*, **'vandalizing** *vbl. sb.* and *ppl. a.*

1804 FESSENDEN *Democracy Unveiled* (1806) I. 123 Direct their vandalizing ravages To make men like themselves, mere savages. **1832** *Blackw. Mag.* XXXI. 581 No..vigilance..could disarm their rude followers of ferocious and Vandalizing habits. **1971** *Oxford Times* 13 Aug. 5/7 In a two-week campaign they restored 21 vandalised kiosks to working order. **1979** U. CURTISS *Menace Within* xvi. 169 Inquiries..in connection with the vandalizing of a local school. **1984** *Times* 8 Oct. 14/3 In Minster Court, Liverpool, buyers rushed for well landscaped flats in what had been a vandalized estate.

'vandalously, *adv.* *rare*⁻¹. [f. VANDAL *sb.*] In a vandalistic manner.

1890 *Tablet* 6 Sept. 374 They were scandalously and vandalously wrong when they reviled the Mother of God.

van de Graaff (væn də grɑːf, -æ-). Also **Van de Graaff.** The name of R. J. *van de Graaff* (1901-67), U.S. physicist, used *attrib.* and *absol.* to designate a machine devised by him for generating electrostatic charge by means of a vertical endless belt which collects charge at its lower end from needle points connected to a voltage source and carries it to similar points at the top connected to the inside of a metal dome, whose potential is thereby increased; also a particle accelerator based on this machine.

1934 *Rev. Sci. Instruments* V. 18/1 The paper discusses the design and construction of a Van de Graaff electrostatic generator capable of an output of 500 microamperes and more than a million volts. **1961** G. R. CHOPPIN *Exper. Nuclear Chem.* xii. 193 Positive ions..are obtainable in cyclotrons as well as Van de Graaff and linear accelerators. **1973** *Physics Bull.* Dec. 722/1 Both tandem van de Graaffs and cyclotrons currently accelerate a variety of high quality beams. **1980** J. W. HILL *Intermediate Physics* xviii. 172 Two metal plates about 5-7 cm apart are..connected to..earth and the dome of a Van de Graaff generator.

† **vandelas.** *Obs.* Forms: 6 **vandelas**, 7 **-alas**, **-olose**, **-ulose.** [See def.] A kind of strong coarse canvas, used esp. for sails, manufactured in the district of Brittany formerly called Le Vendelais.

1571 in Feuillerat *Revels Q. Eliz.* (1908) 137 For vandelas lxvij ells di.—lxvij^{s} vj^{d}. **1572** *Ibid.* 167 For xx^{tie} peeces of Vandelas to cover the Banketting howse. **1612** *Ledger A. Halyburton* (1867) 319 Vandolose or Vitrie canves the eln, x s. **1640** in Entick *London* (1766) II. 167 Linnens,..narrow vandales, or vittry canvas. **1657** *Acts of Interregn.* (1911) II. 1213 Vandalose or Vittry Canvas.

‖ **Vandellia** (væn'dɛlɪə). [mod.L. (Linnæus), from the name of Domenico *Vandelli* (1732-), an Italian botanist, in later life resident in Portugal.] A genus of scrophulariaceous plants, some of which possess emetic or purgative properties; a plant of this genus, esp. *V. diffusa*, or a medicinal preparation of this.

1797 *Encycl. Brit.* (ed. 3) XVIII. 618/1. **1829** LOUDON *Encycl. Plants.* 530 Diffuse Vandellia. **1887** MOLONEY *Forestry W. Africa* 396 Employed in this manner the vandellia is as certain in its action as ipecacuanha.

Vandemonian (,vændɪ'məʊnɪən), *a.* and *sb.* Also **Van Diemonian, Diemenian.** [f. *Van Diemen('s Land*, the original name of Tasmania, given by its discoverer Tasman in 1642 in honour of Anthony Van Diemen (1593-1645), governor of the Dutch East Indies.]

A. *adj.* Of, belonging to, or inhabiting Tasmania.

Freq. applied to the convicts domiciled there in the early part of the 19th c.

1840 G. ARDEN *Austr. Felix* 9 A shrewd old Vandemonian colonist. **1853** S. SIDNEY *Three Colonies Austral.* (ed. 2) 171 *note*, Acts levelled against Van Diemonian expirees. **1855** W. HOWITT *Two Y. Victoria* xx. I. 367 Some of the Van Diemenian convicts.

B. *sb.* An inhabitant of Tasmania.

1852 G. C. MUNDY *Our Antipodes* III. viii. 251 The Van Diemonians, as they unpleasingly call themselves. **1867** *Cassell's Mag.* II. 440/2, 'I never wanted to leave England,' I have heard an old Vandemonian observe boastfully.

Hence **,vande'monianism**, rough or unmannerly behaviour; rowdyism.

1863 *Victorian Hansard* 22 Apr. IX. 701 (Morris), Mr. Houston looked upon the conduct of hon. gentlemen opposite as ranging from the extreme of vandemonianism to the extreme of namby-pambyism.

† **vanden.** *Obs.*⁻¹ [Humorous application of Du. *van den*, 'of the', in surnames.] Dutch.

1638 FORD *Lady's Trial* II. i, Gulls or Moguls, Tag, rag, or other, Hoger-Mogen vanden, Skip-Iacks, or Chouses.

vandendriesscheite (vændəndriːʃ(ə)aɪt). *Min.* [a. F. *vandendriesscheite* (J. F. Vaes 1947, in *Ann. de la Soc. géol. de Belgique*: *Bull.* LXX. 217), f. the name of A. *Vandendriessche*

(1914–40), Belgian mineralogist: see -ITE[1].] A hydrated oxide of lead and hexavalent uranium, $PbU_7O_{22}.12H_2O$, found as orange orthorhombic crystals.

1947 *Mineral. Abstr.* X. 146 Vandendriesscheite,.. pseudo-hexagonal barrel-shaped crystals, perfect cleavage. **1971** *Ibid.* XXII. 158/2 Among the secondary V and Th-minerals occurring in the uraninite-bearing pegmatite at Einerkilen [in Norway], the following have been identified ..: thorogummite, vandendriesscheite, [etc.].

Vanderbilt (ˈvændəbɪlt). [Name of Cornelius *Vanderbilt* (1794–1877), U.S. railway magnate, and his descendants.] One who resembles a member of the Vanderbilt family in being exceptionally rich; a millionaire. So **ˈVanderbilter**.

1885, 1910 [see ROTHSCHILD 1]. **1975** M. AMIS *Dead Babies* xv. 73 So then of course some Vanderbilters get along from Nashville and Skip starts to hang out with them.

Van der Hum (væn də ˈhʌm). Also **Vanderhum**, †**vanrhum**. [perh. a personal name.] A South African brandy-based liqueur made with nartjies.

1861 *Let.* 14 Oct. in *Cape Monthly Mag.* (1870) Oct. 225 Mrs M... has even promised to show me how to brew liqueurs, and distil 'vanrhum',—the latter a most aromatic and powerful *elixir vitæ*. **1893** KIPLING *Many Inventions* 330 Judson's best Vanderhum, which is Cape brandy ten years in the bottle, flavoured with orange-peel and spices. **1913** D. FAIRBRIDGE *That which hath Been* xxi. 240 If you want a *zoopje* there is Van der Hum on the table yonder and a bottle of old dop. **1949** A. WILSON *Wrong Set* 41 Wait..till he tasted the Van Der Hum after the meal, then he would see what the Union could do. **1966** [see NARTJIE]. **1978** K. BONFIGLIOLI *All Tea in China* xi. 141 A black, fat-bellied bottle of something called 'Van Der Hums' which he had prudently laid in at the Cape.

van der Waals (væn də ˈvɑːls). *Physics.* Also **Van der Waals**. The name of Johannes *van der Waals* (1837–1923), Dutch physicist, used *attrib.* and in the possessive to designate (*a*) an equation of state of a gas (proposed by him in 1873) that allows for intermolecular attraction and finite molecular size, viz. $(p + a/V^2)(V - b) = RT$ (where p is the pressure, V the volume, R the gas constant, T the absolute temperature, and a and b are constants); (*b*) short-range attractive forces between uncharged molecules arising from interaction between (actual or induced) electric dipole moments; so ***van der Waals attraction***, etc.

1895 C. S. PALMER tr. *Nernst's Theoret. Chem.* II. ii. 186 The equation assumes the form $(p + a/v^2)(v - b) = RT$. This is van der Waals' equation of condition. **1923** *Jrnl. Chem. Soc.* CXXIII. 3403 At the critical point in particular, Van der Waals's equation predicts that pv will be $2\frac{2}{3}$ times as great as the value given by the simple law of Boyle. **1930** *Engineering* 5 Dec. 700/3 There were, further, different types of cohesion forces. (1) Van der Waals cohesion. **1964** J. W. LINNETT *Electronic Struct. Molecules* ii. 28 No chemical bond is formed and, except for a weak van der Waals (polarization) attraction at large distances, the two atoms repel one another. **1965** P. CAWS *Philos. of Sci.* xxii. 166 The gas law..is hopelessly inadequate in most cases, and has to be replaced by Van der Waals' equation..which is itself only approximately valid. **1979** *Sci. Amer.* Dec. 145/1 If the sauce is kept cool, the colloidal particles are unlikely to touch one another with a frequency that would allow the van der Waals forces to make them coalesce into pools of butter.

vandros: see REREDOS 2 (quot. 1552).

vandscott, obs. Sc. form of WAINSCOT.

Vandyke (vænˈdaɪk), *sb.* Also 8 **Vandike**, 8–9 **Vandyck**; **Van Dyke**. [From the name of Sir Anthony *Vandyke* (Anglicized spelling of *Van Dyck*), the great Flemish painter (1599–1641).]

1. (With capital initial.) A painting or portrait by Van Dyck.

1751 H. WALPOLE *Lett.* (1846) II. 395 The whole-length Vandykes went for a song! **1888** MRS. H. WARD *R. Elsmere* 542 The ball-room, lined with Vandycks and Lelys.

2. A broad lace or linen collar or neckerchief with a deeply cut edge, in imitation of the style of collar freq. depicted in portraits by Van Dyck, forming an article of fashionable dress in the 18th century.

1755 *Gentl. Mag.* XXV. 324 Circling round her iv'ry neck Frizzle out the smart Vandike. **1769** GRANGER *Biogr. Hist. Eng., Chas. I*, I. 571 Laced handkerchiefs, resembling the large falling band worn by the men, were in fashion among the ladies: this article of dress has been lately revived, and called a Vandyck. **1838** HAWTHORNE *Amer. Note-bks.* (1868) I. 242 One of them..attempts to exchange a worked vandyke.

3. One of a number of deep-cut points on the border or fringe of an article of apparel (see quot. 1882). Usu. in *pl.*

1827 *Souvenir* I. 151/3 (Stanford), Tulle pelisse, with three vandykes on the shoulders, forming epaulettes. **1831** G. R. PORTER *Silk Manuf.* 230 The particular form required whether as vandykes, or scallops, or any other figures. **1858** *Ladies' Treasury* Sept. 185 The body has a bertha cut in vandykes. **1882** CAULFEILD & SAWARD *Dict. Needlew.* 510/1 *Vandykes*, this term is descriptive of a particular pointed form cut as a decorative border to collars and other portions of wearing apparel, and to the trimmings of dress skirts and bodices.

4. *transf.* A notched, deeply indented, or zigzag border, edging, or formation.

1846 RUSKIN *Let.* Wks. 1909 XXXVI. 64 A bridge..with this pretty vandyke outside by way of variety. **1891** *Daily News* 14 Oct. 2/8 The whole coast is a vandyke of bays and clefts and promontories.

5. *techn.* (See quot.)

1846 HOLTZAPFFEL *Turning* II. 736 (Buhl. work), Brass borders, technically known as vandykes, are worked in narrow slips.

6. = *Vandyke beard.*

1909 in WEBSTER. **1933** H. ALLEN *Anthony Adverse* III. VIII. lix. 949 A carefully trained moustache and a vandyke turning white contrived to be at once distinguished and benign. **1951** E. PAUL *Springtime in Paris* xi. 204 The 'Zazous' quarter surpasses even Oberammergau, as far as beards are concerned... The hearties have stiff whiskers, and some of the Central and South American boys sport silken Van Dykes. **1974** P. DE VRIES *Glory of Hummingbird* xvi. 252 A false mustache and Vandyke..completed the transformation. **1982** S. B. FLEXNER *Listening to Amer.* 65 The first group mainly wore short *Imperials* or waxed and pomaded *Van Dykes*.

7. Used *attrib.* or as *adj.* (with capital initial.) in designating things associated in some way with Van Dyck or his paintings, as ***Vandyke beard, border, brown, couching***, etc. (see quots. and cf. prec. senses).

1894 *Westm. Gaz.* 25 June 8/1 Everyone is now wearing a pointed V-shaped *Vandyck beard, while a few years ago the Vandyck beard was unknown. **1880** *Paper & Print. Trades Jrnl.* xxx. 29 Each page having a deep *Vandyke border. **1850** WEALE *Dict. Terms*, **Vandyke Brown*,..a species of peat or bog-earth, of a fine deep semi-transparent brown colour. **1882** CAULFEILD & SAWARD *Dict. Needlew.* 92/2 **Vandyke couching*, a Raised Couching formed with lines of whipcord laid on the linen foundation in the shape of vandykes [etc.]. **1825** MACAULAY *Ess., Milton* ¶62 His [i.e. Charles I] *Vandyke dress, his handsome face, and his peaked beard. **1757** MRS. DELANY *Life & Corr.* (1861) III. 467 Madam Godineau, in a round card cap of black lace.. and a *vandyke handkerchief of the same. **1882** CAULFEILD & SAWARD *Dict. Needlew.* 195/1 **Vandyke stitch*, a raised Couching. **1831** CARLYLE *Sart. Res.* I. v, *Vandyke tippets, ruffs, fardingales, are brought vividly before us. **1882** CAULFEILD & SAWARD *Dict. Needlew.* 499/1 **Vandyke tracery*..is worked much in the same way as Cross Tracery, and forms a zig-zag device on the open parts of leaves and other spaces. **1829** *Glover's Hist. Derby* I. 242 In 1766.. Crane manufactured a rich brocade for waistcoats,..and about two years afterwards he attempted *vandyke-work, by appending a warp-machine to a plain stocking frame.

b. (See quot.)

1889 MAIDEN *Useful Pl. W. Ind.* 99 *Panicum flavidum*, ..'Vandyke Grass' (of Bailey).

Hence **Van ˈDyckian**, pertaining to or characteristic of the paintings of Van Dyck.

1942 *Burlington Mag.* Feb. 43/2 The stage effects of court painting in the Van Dyckian vein. **1979** *N. & Q.* Feb. 71/2 The pose..is pure convention: a Van Dyckian cliché lifted from Van Dyck's etching of Pieter Brueghel the Younger.

vandyke (vænˈdaɪk), *v.* Also **Vandyck**. [f. as prec.]

1. *trans.* To furnish or provide (some dress material) with vandykes or deep-cut points, after the manner represented in Van Dyck's paintings; to cut or shape with deep angular indentations. Chiefly in pa. pple.

1800 [implied in VANDYKED *ppl. a.*]. **1828** MOIR *Mansie Wauch* vii. 65 Long muslin frockies, Vandyked across the breast. **1869** *Latest News* 5 Sept. 7 The muslin skirt is trimmed with a gathered flounce, vandyked at each edge. **1894** WEYMAN *Man in Black* 55 His dress was in the extreme of the fashion, his falling collar vandyked.

b. In general use.

1839 THACKERAY *Fatal Boots* Feb., I made the leaves of the [needle-] book, which I vandyked very nicely, out of a piece of flannel. **1868** *Fortn. Rev.* Nov. 485 A shelf of limestone..not presenting a straight face, but vandyked, as it were, into a bewildering number of zigzags. **1887** GROSART in *Lismore Papers* Ser. II. I. 4 This document is indented or vandyked along its upper edge.

c. Said of the thing forming, or helping to form, the indentations.

1854 *Chambers' Jrnl.* II. 323 Tongues of sea-sand.. vandyking its borders. **1868** LOCKYER *Guillemin's Heavens* (ed. 3) 228 It is easy to see numerous irregularities and transverse markings, vandyking and crossing the more visible features in various directions. **1898** WEYMAN *Castle Inn* 221 The peaks of three gables rose above them, vandyking the sky.

2. *intr.* To go or proceed in an irregular zigzag manner; to take a zigzag course. ? *Obs.*

1828 MOIR *Mansie Wauch* xiii. 195 It behoves me..to beg pardon..for being forced whiles to zig zag and vandyke. **1831** *Fraser's Mag.* III. 27 He discussed two bottles of old Bordeaux, and, staggering to a bye lane, vandyked to Farningham. **1845** ALB. SMITH *Fort. Scattergood Fam.* xv, Foreign gentlemen..vandyked with indecision about the quay, as they tried to recollect the name of the hotel.

vandyked (vænˈdaɪkt), *ppl. a.* [Cf. VANDYKE *v.*] Provided with vandykes; cut or shaped at the edge into deep indentations; zigzagged.

1800 *Hull Advertiser* 22 Nov. 3/3 A broad border, or rather flounce, of vandyked velvet. **1832** T. BROWN *Bk. Butterflies & M.* (1834) I. 169 The wings are of an intense black, denticulated with a vandyked border of white. **1860** SALA *Lady Chesterfield* v. 80 The vandyked morocco valance. **1892** E. REEVES *Homeward Bound* 139 The roadway is bordered by a massive stone wall..with a vandyked top, like a piece of lace.

vanˈdyking, *vbl. sb. rare.* [Cf. VANDYKE *v.*]

†**1.** *nonce-use.* ? The drawing or sketching of portraits. *Obs.*[−1]

1633 WINDEBANK in *Strafford's Lett. & Disp.* (1739) I. 161 You made many ill Faces with your Pen, (pardon I beseech your Lordship, the over free Censure of your Vandyking).

2. *concr.* Vandyked material; work shaped in vandykes or deep zigzags.

1819 [F. MAC DONOGH] *Hermit in Lond.* 170 Tiers of vandyking and quilled lace.

vane (veɪn). Also 6 **vayn**, 6–7 **veine**, 8 **vain**. [Southern var. of FANE *sb.*[1]]

1. A plate of metal, usually of an ornamental form, fixed at an elevation upon a vertical spindle, so as to turn readily with the wind and show the direction from which this is blowing; a weather-cock.

Vanes are a common addition to the tops of spires or other pinnacles of buildings.

1425 in Kennett *Par. Antiq.* (1818) II. 254 Cum ii ventilogiis, viz. vanys de Tyn emptis..ponendis super utrumque finem prædicti dormitorii. **1479–81** *Rec. St. Mary at Hill* (1905) 103 Item, for mendyng of the vane of the steple. **1483** CAXTON *G. de la Tour* Bj, Be ye not like ne semblable the tortuse ne to the Crane which wynde their hede here and there as a vane. **1532** in E. Law *Hampton Crt. Pal.* (1885) 364 A vayn servyng for the stone typis at the gabull ende of the Tennys play. **1572–3** *Sarum Churchw. Acc.* (Swayne, 1896) 287 Taking downe of the vane and mending of him. **1597** MIDDLETON *Wisd. Solomon* xiv. 17 Like as a vane is turn'd with every blast. *a* **1700** EVELYN *Diary* 13 July 1654, These were adorn'd with a variety of dials, little statues, vanes, &c. **1785** REID *Intell. Powers* II. xix. 325 When I see a spire at a very great distance there appears no vane at the top. **1826** SCOTT *Woodst.* ii, One or two..venerable turrets, bearing each its own vane of rare device glittering in the autumn sun. **1849** MRS. SOMERVILLE *Connex. Phys. Sci.* (ed. 6) xv. 138 Thus two alternations of north and south wind will cause the vane at any place to go completely round the compass. **1880** L. MORRIS *Ode of Life* 130 The old grey church, with the tall spire, Whose vane the sunsets fire.

transf. **1845** DARWIN *Voy. Nat.* i. (1873) 3 The direction of the branches was N.E. by N., and these natural vanes must indicate the prevailing direction of the trade wind. **1859** HERSCHEL in *Man. Sci. Enq.* 136 The direction of the wind, as well as its force, should be registered at each observation; and for this it is well to have a small compass with a vane of card or thin and very moveable sheet brass.

b. *fig.* An unstable or constantly changing person or thing.

1588 SHAKS. *L.L.L.* IV. i. 97 What plume of feathers is hee that indited this Letter? What veine? What Wether-cocke? ? *a* **1611** BEAUM. & FL. *Four Plays* Wks. 1912 X. 303 My desire's a vane, That the least breath from her turns every way. **1850** D. G. MITCHELL *Reveries Bachelor* 133 Who is going to shift this vane of my desires?

c. *Naut.* A piece of bunting fixed to a wooden frame, which turns on a spindle at the mast-head to show the direction of the wind. (See also DOG-VANE.)

1706 E. WARD *Wooden World Diss.* (1708) 3 Some compare her [the ship] to a Commonwealth, and carry the Allegory from the Vane, down to the Keelson. **1769** FALCONER *Dict. Mar.*, *Vane*, a thin slip of bunting hung to the mast-head, or some other conspicuous place,..to show the direction of the wind. **1863** *Rep. Sea Fisheries Comm.* (1865) II. 404/2 Do you [trawlers] carry any particular kind of vane?—Yes, until it blows away; we generally carry a red vane. **1867** SMYTH *Sailor's Word-bk.* 709 *A distinguishing vane* denotes the division of a fleet to which a ship of the line belongs, according to the mast on which it is borne.

†**2.** A metal plate having the form of a flag or banner bearing a coat of arms, esp. one supported by the figure of an animal. *Obs.*

Sometimes app. serving the purpose of a weather-cock.

1502 *Marr. Pr. Arthur* in *Antiq. Rep.* (1808) II. 260 A red lyon rampand, holdyng a vane enpeynted with the armys of Englond. *a* **1548** HALL *Chron., Hen. VIII*, 97 Ouer the gates wer arches with towers embattailed set with vanes and scutchions of the armes of the Emperor and the Kyng. **1574** in W. H. Turner *Select. Rec. Oxford* (1880) 351 For.. coloringe the beasts and the vanes and the Quenes armes.. with good colors and oyles.

3. a. A sail of a windmill.

1581 J. BELL *Haddon's Answ. Osor.* 482 All thinges are carryed about in a certaine vehement whyrling unstablenesse, as it were the fleyng vanes of a windemill. **16..** *Anc. Poems, Ball.*, etc. (Percy Soc.) 47 They have a castle on a hill, I took it for an old wind-mill, The vanes blown off by weather. **1725** *Fam. Dict.* s.v. *Windmill*, Made with vertical Sails, like the ordinary Windmils,..placed on an Axis of a proportionable length to the length of the Vanes. **1754** J. SHEBBEARE *Matrimony* (1766) I. 19 [She] took Occasion to utter three or four sighs,..each of which would have turned the vanes of a windmill. **1804** CHARLOTTE SMITH *Conversations*, etc. II. 49 The miller shewed me the machinery..and how it works the mill by the action of those vanes or sails. **1864** DASENT *Jest & Earnest* (1873) I. 182 The women with a curious cap with an erection on it like two vanes of a windmill flapping in the air.

b. A blade, wing, or similar projection attached to an axis, wheel, etc., so as to be acted upon by a current of air or liquid or to produce a current by rotation.

1815 J. SMITH *Panorama Sci. & Art* II. 17 Each axis has four or more thin arms or vanes fixed into it; the vanes are similar in all respects, except in their position. **1824** R. STUART *Hist. Steam Engine* 150 On the circumference of a wheel eight vanes or flaps are attached by joints. **1832** G. R. PORTER *Porcelain & Gl.* 38 An upright shaft furnished with arms or vanes for the purpose of agitation. **1867** W. W. SMYTH *Coal & Coal-mining* 211 Fans.—These instruments, with straight radial vanes, were abundantly used in the German mines.. about 1550.

c. A revolving fan or wheel.

1810 CRABBE *Borough* x. 248 Ev'n the poor ventilating vane, that flew Of late so fast, is now grown drowsy too. **1842** FRANCIS *Dict. Arts* s.v., Vane is also synonymous with fly or fly wheel. *Ibid.* s.v. *Vane, Electrical*, When.. the vane is placed near to it, the strength of the current will be sufficient to impel the vane forward, so that it will rotate on its centre.

4. A sight of a levelling-staff, forestaff, quadrant, or other surveying instrument.

1594 BLUNDEVIL *Exerc.* VII. xvi. 326 b, Turne both your faces, and also the vane of the Transame towardes the Sunne. **1669** STURMY *Mariner's Mag.* II. xiv. 85 Set the Vane G to a certain number of Degrees,.. looking through the Vane F,.. draw your Sight-Vane a little lower. **1674** LEYBOURNE *Compl. Surveyor* 45 Upon the longer Sight is to be placed a Vane of brass, to be moved up and down at pleasure. **1704** J. HARRIS *Lex. Techn.* I. s.v., Those Sights which are made to move and slide upon Cross-staves, Fore-staves, Davis Quadrants, &c. the Seamen call Vanes. **1748** *Anson's Voy.* III. iii. 327 The quadrant was eagerly seized, but on examination, it unluckily wanted vanes, and therefore in its present state was altogether useless. **1845** *Encycl. Metrop.* XXV. 307/1 [In] Houghton's staffs.. the vane is circular inlaid with a diamond-shaped lozenge. **1867** SMYTH *Sailor's Word-bk.* 710 The one opposite to the fore horizon-glass is the foresight-vane, the other the backsight vane.

5. The web of a feather.

1713 DERHAM *Phys.-Theol.* VII. i. 374 The Mechanism of the vanes or webs of Feathers. **1768** *Phil. Trans.* LVIII. 92 Their texture is equally extraordinary; the shafts broad and very thin; the vanes unwebbed. **1834** MUDIE *Brit. Birds* (1841) I. 14 The larger ribs of the webs or vanes of not a few are of considerable substance and strength. **1875** BLAKE *Zool.* 94 The vane consists of barbs which proceed at right angles to the shaft.

6. *attrib.* and *Comb.*, as *vane-like* adj., *-pin*, *-spindle*, *staff*, *-surmounted* adj.

1796 WITHERING *Brit. Plants* I. 91 *Versatilis*, vane-like. **1844** in Noad *Electricity* (ed. 2) 95 The balls from which arise the vane-spindles of the two churches. **1845** *Encycl. Metrop.* XXV. 306/2 The vane staff is more calculated for the purpose [than the levelling staff]. **1848** DICKENS *Dombey* ix, Then came rows of houses, with little vane-surmounted masts uprearing themselves from among the scarlet beans. **1867** SMYTH *Sailor's Word-bk.*, *Vane-spindle*, the pivot on which the masthead-vane turns. **1889** P. H. EMERSON *English Idyls* 22 She was black from stem to stern, from keel to vane-pin.

vane, southern ME. var. FAIN *a.*; obs. Sc. f. VAIN *a.*, VEIN *sb.*, WANE *sb.* and *v.*, *won* pa. t. of WIN *v.*

vaneer, obs. f. VENEER *sb.*

vanehope, Sc. var. WANHOPE.

† **vanel(l.** *Obs. rare.* Also venelle. [Anglicized f. VANILLA or VANILLE.] **a.** A vanilla pod. **b.** Vanilla.

1703 *Lond. Gaz.* No. 3891/3 The Cargo.. consisting of.. Cocoa, Venelles,.. Silk Grass,.. Ebbone and Logwood, &c. **1769** E. BANCROFT *Ess. Nat. Hist. Guiana* 101 Vanilla, or Vanells, are the fruit of a ligneous siliquose vine. **1790** BEATSON *Nav. & Mil. Mem.* I. 165 One case of vanel, sixty cases of sugar.

'vaneless, *a.* [f. VANE.] Unprovided with a vane.

1889 P. H. EMERSON *English Idyls* 25 Down the river.. came sailing the black vaneless old wherry.

‖ **va'nessa.** *Ent.* [mod.L. (Fabricius).] A genus of butterflies (including the *red admiral* and *peacock*); a butterfly belonging to this genus.

1863 BATES *Nat. Amazon* i. (1864) 10 The only Amazonian species which is at all nearly related to our Vanessas, the Admiral and Peacock Butterflies. **1903** *Spectator* 17 Jan. 84/2 Many butterflies, especially the vanessas, creep away and sleep through the winter.

va'nessid, *a.* and *sb.* *Ent.* [ad. mod.L. *Vanessidæ* (pl.), f. *Vanessa*: see prec.] **A.** *adj.* Belonging to the family of butterflies of which *Vanessa* is the type. **B.** *sb.* A butterfly of this family.

1911 *Encycl. Brit.* XVI. 467/2 The brightly coloured vanessid butterflies. *Ibid.* 469/2 The British Vanessids.

vanette (væ'nɛt). [f. VAN *sb.*[3] + -ETTE.] A small van.

1921 *Glasgow Herald* 23 July 8 A company.. were sent out from Jandola, followed.. by Lewis guns in vanettes and an armoured motor car. **1957** V. W. TURNER *Schism & Continuity in Afr. Society* v. 147 Once Mukanza was in my vanette he was my responsibility and no longer that of the village members.

van-foss(e. *Mil.* [ad. F. *avant-fossé*, after *vanguard*, etc., and FOSSE.] (See quots.)

1728 CHAMBERS *Cycl.*, *Van-Fosse*,.. a Ditch dug without the Counterscarp, and running all along the Glacis; usually full of Water. **1852** BURN *Naval & Milit. Dict.* II. 304/1 Van-foss, *avant-fossé*. **1867** SMYTH *Sailor's Word-bk.*, *Van-fosse*, a wet ditch at the outer foot of the glacis.

vang (væŋ). *Naut.* [var. FANG *sb.* 7 a.] One or other of the two ropes used for steadying the gaff of a fore-and-aft sail.

1769 FALCONER *Dict. Mar.* s.v. *Brace*, The mizen-yard is furnished with fangs, or vangs, in the room of braces. *Ibid.*, *Vangs*, a sort of braces to support the mizen gaff, and keep it steady. **1834** M. SCOTT *Cruise Midge* (1859) 486 The gaff is violently shaken by the loosened sail; for both vangs and brails are gone. **1851** *Voy. to Mauritius* i. 35 The orderly officer, seated on the bulwark, and holding on by a vang. **1881** CLARK RUSSELL *Ocean Free-Lance* III. ii. 65 He stood upon the rail.. with his arm round the vang.

vang, southern dial. and ME. var. FANG *sb.*, *v.*[1]

vangee. *Naut.* (See quots.)

1846 A. YOUNG *Naut. Dict.* 239 The pumps of a vessel are .. often worked by means of a contrivance called the vangee. [Description follows.] **1867** SMYTH *Sailor's Word-bk.* 710 *Vangee*, a contrivance for working the pumps of a vessel by means of a barrel and crank-breaks.

† **vangel.** *Obs.* Also *Sc.* 5–6 vangele, -ell; 5 wangele, -yl(e, -yll, 5–6 -ell, 6 -el. [Aphetic f. EVANGEL.] Gospel.

a **1340** HAMPOLE *Psalter* cxviii. 72 Laghe of godis mouth is þe vangel. *c* **1375** *Sc. Leg. Saints* xxvii. (*Machor*) 1401 þar þe buk of þe wangele.. he gef hyme frely in þat place. *c* **1420** *Wycliffite Bible* (1850) IV. 297 Here endith vangelis, and bigyneth a prologe on the Romayns. *c* **1425** WYNTOUN *Cron.* VI. x. 70 (Laing), He made a tysstyre in that qwhylle, Quhare-in wes closyd the Wangylle. **1473** *Rental Bk. Cupar-Angus* (1879) I. 199 Sworn apon the haly wangyl befor the Abbot and conuent. **1533** GAU *Richt Vay* 27 To prech his halie vangel to al creatur. *Ibid.*, The wangel of iesus christ. *a* **1578** LINDESAY (Pitscottie) *Chron. Scot.* (S.T.S.) I. 239 Ather of vther was sworne in the haly vangell.

attrib. *c* **1450** *Maitl. Club Misc.* III. 201 Item ane buke for the vangell lettrin.

Van Gelder (væn 'gɛldə(r)). The name of a Dutch paper-maker, used *attrib.* and *absol.* to designate a fine handmade paper with deckle edges.

1892 in G. Meredith *Jump to Glory Jane* 2 This edition is limited to an issue of 1,000 copies.. and a special issue of 100 copies on Van Gelder paper. **1928** S. J. LOOKER *Booklover's Catal.* Jan. 6 Long Ago, First American Edition,.. one of 925 copies on Van Gelder paper. **1934** H. HILER *Notes Technique Painting* iii. 224 Some good papers for practical working are cartridge, Whatman,.. Van Gelder, [etc.]. **1960** G. A. GLAISTER *Gloss. Bk.* 429/2 *Van Gelder*, one of the most famous of all hand-made papers, produced for a century or more in Holland and said to contain 100% rag. It is used by artists and publishers of fine editions. **1974** *Country Life* 17 Jan. 75/1 The.. tragic etching of 1904, *Le Repas Frugal* on van Gelder paper.

† **vangelie**, aphetic form of EVANGELY. *Obs.*

a **1390** *Wycliffite Bible, 1 Tim.* i. 11 Vp the euangelie [*v.r.* uangelie] of the glorie of blessid God. *a* **1450** LOVELICH *Grail* lii. 969 Piers.. the holy vangelye gan him vndo.

† **vangelist.** *Obs.* Also 4 wangelyst, 4–6 -ist(e. [Aphetic f. EVANGELIST.] An evangelist.

a **1330** *Roland & V.* 153 Iames þe apostel bi crist, Iones broþer, þe wangelist. *c* **1375** *Sc. Leg. Saints* xxvii. (*Machor*) 1295 þe wark of wangeliste þu do. **1533** GAU *Richt Vay* 39 And syne the wangelistis hes thairof writine. *Ibid.*, The prophetis, apostlis, and the vangelistis. **1567** *Gude & Godlie B.* (S.T.S.) 200 Wolues, quhome of my Vangelistis wryte.

vangle, dial. variant of FANGLE *sb.*[1]

‖ **vanglo.** (See quots.)

1756 P. BROWNE *Jamaica* (1789) 270 The Vanglo or Oil-plant. **1829** LOUDON *Encycl. Plants* (1836) 515 *Sesamum*... These plants were introduced into Jamaica by the Jews, and are now cultivated in most parts of the island. They are called *vanglo* or oil-plant. **1858** SIMMONDS *Dict. Trade*, *Vanglo*, a West Indian name for the teel seeds of the East (*Sesamum orientale*).

vanguard ('vængɑːd). Also *Sc.* 5 vandgard, 6 vandgarde, -gaird; 6 wangard(e, -guard, -gaird, vangart, -gard(e, -gaird. [ad. OF. *avangarde*, var. of *avantgarde*: see VANTGUARD. Cf. It. and Sp. *vanguardia*, Pg. *vanguarda*.]

1. a. *Mil.* The foremost division of an army; the forefront or van.

The Scottish examples are placed first.

(*a*) **1487** *Barbour's Bruce* XI. 164 Till renownyt erllis twa.. He gaf the vandgard in ledyng. **1513** DOUGLAS *Æneid* XII. v. 210 Alsus.. ruschis abak for feir.. In the vangart [ed. 1553 vandegarde] throw mony a poyntit glave. **1535** STEWART *Cron. Scot.* II. 224 This gude schir Loth the wangard led that da. *a* **1578** LINDESAY (Pitscottie) *Chron. Scot.* (S.T.S.) I. 270 The wandgaird was neir mearchant togither. **1596** DALRYMPLE tr. *Leslie's Hist. Scot.* I. 313 He.. obteynet the name and honour of Capitane of the kingis Vangaird.

(*b*) **1503** *Lett. Rich. III & Hen. VII* (Rolls) I. 208 The Souchyvars whiche [were] appoyncted to kepe my vanguarde avaunced tha[ym for]wardes without my knowlege. **1598** BARRET *Theor. Warres* III. ii. 63 Let the Officer of the Vanguarde draw out three rankes of the armed pikes. **1622** F. MARKHAM *Bk. War* IV. viii. 151 As soone as the head or Vanguard beginneth, that in the same time the Reare bee ready to follow. **1665** MANLEY *Grotius' Low C. Wars* 389 Villars, the Commander of the Van-Guard.., being circumvented, and taken by Fontains Army. **1693** LUTTRELL *Brief Rel.* (1857) III. 5 The landgraves vanguard pursued their rear. **1728** CHAMBERS *Cycl.* s.v., Every Army is compos'd of three Parts, a Van-guard, Rear-guard, and Main Body. **1780** *Encycl. Brit.* (ed. 2) V. 3423 Van Guard. See Advanced Guard. **1838** LYTTON *Leila* IV. i, Winding along the steeps of the mountain were seen the gleaming spears and pennants of the Moslem vanguard. **1851** LONGF. *Gold. Leg.* i. *Castle of Vautsberg*, As when the vanguard of the Roman legions First saw it from the top of yonder hill! **1875** CLERY *Min. Tact.* vi. (1877) 76 The advanced party, which may be conveniently termed the Vanguard, is composed of cavalry and infantry.

b. In fig. use. Cf. AVANT-GARDE 2.

1831 CARLYLE *Sart. Res.* I. iii, At length.. Germany and Weissnichtwo were where they should be, in the vanguard of the world. **1856** STANLEY *Sinai & Pal.* ii. 116 Palestine.. was then the vanguard of the eastern, and therefore, of the civilised world. **1878** MACLEAR *Celts* i. 12 They were to form the vanguard in the Missionary history of Europe.

attrib. **1888** *Century* XXXVI. 657 All day his vanguard spirit, flaming bright, Bore up the brunt of unavailing fight. **1958** *Times* 9 Sept. 5/1 But it was not the pretentious nonsense that so often passes for 'vanguard' culture. **1977** *Guardian Weekly* 16 Oct. 19/3 One prominent vanguard dealer in London.. had only sold one single work so far this year. **1980** *Listener* 13 Nov. 648/3 Today, vanguard art seems to have lost its 'political' role.

c. In *Communism*, the elite party cadre which, according to Lenin, would be used to organize the masses as a revolutionary force and to give effect to communist planning.

1928 E. & C. PAUL tr. *Stalin's Leninism* I. 95 As far back as 1902, foreseeing the special role of our Party, he [*sc.* Lenin] thought it necessary to point out that: Only a party guided by an advanced theory can act as vanguard in the fight. **1941** tr. *Lenin's One Step Forward* 85 The stronger our Party organizations.. the richer.. will be the influence of the Party on the elements of the working class *masses*.. guided by it. After all, the Party, as the vanguard of the working class, must not be confused with the entire class. **1952** P. SELZNICK *Organizational Weapon* 10 Only the vanguard is exposed to a full statement of communist aims and methods. **1973** C. D. KERNIG *Marxism, Communism & Western Soc.* VIII. 270/1 The vanguard proves itself both in and after the victorious proletarian revolution by taking over the leadership in all spheres of life.

d. (With capital initial.) The name of a political party in Northern Ireland, representing a secession from Ulster Unionism. Freq. *attrib.*

1972 *Times* 14 Feb. 2/4 A crowd of 1,500 attended a rally called by Mr William Craig, MP for Larne, who has founded what he calls the Vanguard Movement. *Ibid.* 13 Mar. 1/4 When it began three months ago, Vanguard was described by one Government minister as a 'comic opera'. **1973** *Times* 31 Mar. 1/2 Mr William Craig... chose the steps of Stormont to announce the formation of the Vanguard Unionist Progressive Party. **1975** BUTLER & SLOMAN *Brit. Political Facts* (ed. 4) xvi. 354 On June 28, 1973 the.. Assembly was elected; its composition was 22 Ulster Unionist.. 15 Loyalist Coalition (7 Vanguard.. 8 Democratic Unionist), [etc.]. **1982** M. WALLACE *Brit. Govt. in Northern Ireland* vii. 133 The Vanguard Unionists had decided in November 1977 to return to the official Unionist Party, while remaining a 'movement'.

2. *ellipt.* The name of a variety of peach.

1786 ABERCROMBIE *Arr.* 14 in *Gard. Assist.*, Peaches... Vanguard. **1802** W. FORSYTH *Fruit Trees* 28 To the foregoing may be added,.. Smooth-leaved Royal George, Steward's late Gallande, Vanguard. **1860** HOGG *Fruit Man.* 147 *Vanguard*.—This is a variety of the Noblesse... The only apparent difference is in the habit of the trees, which in Vanguard is much more robust and hardy than in the Noblesse.

Hence **'vanguardism**, the quality of being in the vanguard of a political, cultural, or artistic movement (cf. AVANT-GARDISM); **'vanguardist**, a person in the vanguard of a political, cultural, or artistic movement; also *attrib.* or as *adj.*; (cf. AVANT-GARDIST(E)).

1934 WEBSTER, Vanguardist. **1952** P. SELZNICK *Organizational Weapon* ii. 91 (*heading*) Vanguardism in semicolonial areas. **1964** *Spectator* 15 May 664/1 It is not true that this complex personality comes out of the same box as Rauschenberg. That vanguardist exclaims, 'Hell, what a marvellous universe.' **1971** *New Yorker* 16 Oct. 148/2 The integration of art and non-art is the essence of twentieth-century vanguardism in art. **1976** *Ibid.* 12 Jan. 22/1 Just being there must make the average armchair nihilist want to argue with his fellow-man over the merits of anarcho-syndicalism, vanguardism, and radical conformism. **1976** *Spare Rib* Nov. 21/1 After wading through some vanguardist rhetoric, and an informal discussion.. things became even more complicated. **1981** *Times Lit. Suppl.* 24 Apr. 465 (*heading*) From vanguardism to fascism.

vanhap, Sc. form of WANHAP.

† **vanil**, error for ANIL 2.

1599 WILLES in Hakluyt *Voy.* II. II. 78 Many Tartars and Mogores, that brought into China certaine blewes of great value: all we thought it to be Vanil of Cambaia wont to be sold at Ormus.

vanilla (və'nɪlə). Also 7 vaynilla. β. 7 vinello-, 8 vanello, 8–9 vanelloe (8 -eloe); 8 vanilio, -illio, 8–9 vanillo-. [In earlier use a. and ad. older Sp. *vaynilla*, now *vainilla*, dim. of *vaina* (:—L. *vāgīna* VAGINA) sheath. Subsequently a. mod. botanical L. *Vanilla*, from the same source. Cf. It. *vainiglia*, Pg. *bainilha*, *baunilha*, F. *vanille* VANILLE.]

1. A pod produced by one or other species of the genus *Vanilla* (see sense 2), esp. *V. planifolia*. Chiefly in *pl.*

α. **1662** H. STUBBE *Indian Nectar* ii. 11 They added.. the Vaynillas [to the chocolate] for the like ends, and to strengthen the brain. *Ibid.* 17 Afterwards to mix the Vaynillas, cut into pieces, and dryed. **1673** RAY *Journ. Low C.* 485 Vanillas which they mingle with the Cacao to make Chocolate.

β. **1699** DAMPIER *Voy.* 38 There grow on this Coast Vinelloes in great quantity, with which Chocolate is perfumed. **1731** ARBUTHNOT *Aliments* VI. v. (1735) 150 When.. mix'd with Vanillios, or Spices, it [chocolate] acquires likewise the good and bad Qualities of aromatick Oils. **1757** A. COOPER *Distiller* III. li. (1760) 220 Angelica-Seed, Vanellos and Mace, of each one Ounce and a half. **1758** *Elaboratory laid Open* 318 Cut the vanilloes into small pieces. **1812** J. SMYTH *Pract. of Customs* (1821) 267 Vanelloes are long flat pods, containing a reddish pulp, with small shining black seeds,.. but seldom imported. **1854**

MAYNE Expos. Lex. 311/2 The vanelloe is a long flattish pod [etc.].

2. a. The climbing orchid *Vanilla planifolia*, or other species related to this; the tropical (American) genus to which these belong.

α. 1698 T. FROGER Voy. 129 The Vanilla is a plant that creeps up along other trees, in the same manner as Ivy does. 1756 P. BROWNE Jamaica (1789) 11 Nor does the vanilla.. grow any where..in greater perfection. 1783 JUSTAMOND tr. Raynal's Hist. Indies III. 340 The vanilla is a plant which, like the ivy, grows to the trees it meets with. c1820 WATERTON Wand. S. Amer. (1825) 182 In some parts of these forests I saw the Vanilla growing luxuriantly. 1843 Penny Cycl. XXVI. 116/2 The reason of the vanilla not producing fruit in Europe when it has flowered. 1879 Cassell's Techn. Educ. I. 91/2 The vanilla is an epiphyte, or air-plant.

β. 1702 Propos. Effectual War in Amer. 19 Cacao-Trees and the Vanilio grow there [Granada in America] naturally. 1748 Phil. Trans. XLV. 160 The Vanelloe. With the Fruit of this Plant the Spaniards perfume their Chocolate. 1760 J. LEE Introd. Bot. App. 330 Vanilla, or Vaneloe, Epidendrum. 1772–84 Cook's Voy. (1790) IV. 1323 The known kind of plants to be found here are..a shrubbery speedwell, sow-thistles, virgin's bower, vanelloe.

b. With *pl.* One or other species of this genus.

1827 O. W. ROBERTS Voy. Centr. Amer. 87 Their country abounded in vanilloes and sarsaparilla. 1829 LOUDON Encycl. Plants (1836) 765 The Vanillæ shoot out roots at every joint like the Ivy. 1855 KINGSLEY Westw. Ho! xxiii, One hanging garden of crimson and orange orchids or vanillas. 1874 Athenæum 10 Oct. 488/1 La Liberté states that a wild vanilla has been introduced into commerce.

c. With distinguishing terms.

1829 LOUDON Encycl. Plants (1836) 764 Vanilla aromatica, aromatic Vanilla. [V.] planifolia, fragrant Vanilla. 1843 Penny Cycl. XXVI. 116/1 V. claviculata, Tendril-bearing Vanilla... V. grandiflora, Large-flowered Vanilla. 1866 Treas. Bot. 1204/1 Cuba Vanilla, Critonia Dalea.

3. a. The aromatic substance composed of, or obtained from, the slender pod-like capsule of *Vanilla planifolia* or related species, much used as a flavouring or perfume.

1728 CHAMBERS Cycl. s.v. Chocolate, To have the better market for their Cacao Nuts, Achiott, Vanilla, and other Drugs. 1753 Chambers' Cycl. Suppl. s.v., The pods..of the simarona, which is also called bastard Vanilla, are the smallest of all the kinds. The ley kind is the only good Vanilla. 1830 LINDLEY Nat. Syst. Bot. 265 The aromatic substance called Vanilla is the succulent fruit of a climbing West Indian plant of the order [Orchideæ]. 1852 TH. ROSS tr. Humboldt's Trav. II. xvi. 63 The English and the Anglo-Americans often seek to make purchases of vanilla at the port of La Guayra. 1870 YEATS Nat. Hist. Comm. 152 As an aromatic, vanilla is much used by confectioners for flavouring ices and custards.

b. A kind or variety of this. (See also quot. 1866.)

1753 Chambers' Cycl. Suppl. s.v., The smell of the Vanillas ought to be penetrating and agreeable. 1843 Penny Cycl. XXVI. 115/2 It does not appear that any of the Brazilian vanillas form the substance known in trade. 1866 Treas. Bot. 1204/1 Chica Vanilla, the Panama name for the fruit of a species of Sobralia. 1884 Encycl. Brit. XXIV. 67/2 None of the South American vanillas appear to be used in Great Britain for flavouring purposes.

c. A vanilla ice cream.

1955 T. STERLING Evil of Day viii. 84 You should go to Schrafft's for a plain vanilla with marshmallow sauce. 1970 Guardian 13 July 9/3 They'll have a vanilla, our Ethel, ta.

4. *attrib.* and *Comb.*, as **vanilla bean, ice(cream), orchid, pod, sugar, worker; vanilla-flavoured, -sweet** adjs.; **vanilla grass** (see quot.); **vanilla plant**, (*a*) = sense 2; (*b*) an American species of *Liatris*; **vanilla slice**, an oblong pastry containing custard flavoured with vanilla and usu. iced.

1886 American XII. 318 The aromatic principle of the *vanilla bean. 1898 19th Cent. April 644 Spices should be added, such as..cinnamon, cloves, cardamom, and vanilla bean. 1972 Harrods Christmas Catal. 59/4 French marrons in *vanilla flavoured syrup. 1974 L. DEIGHTON Spy Story xix. 207 That big vanilla-flavoured ice-cream sundae. 1856 A. GRAY Man. Bot. (1860) 574 Hierochloa borealis. *Vanilla or Seneca Grass. 1846 SOYER Cookery 553 Garnish with a custard made as for *vanilla ice. 1904 *Vanilla ice cream [see SUNDAE]. 1911 [see Neapolitan ice]. 1974 Times 6 Apr. 12/5 Serve the oranges very cold with vanilla ice cream. 1883 R. B. WHITE in Proc. R. Geog. Soc. (N.S.) V. 260 A forest..in which the trees are literally over-burdened with the *vanilla orchid. 1753 Chambers' Cycl. Suppl. s.v., The leaves of the *Vanilla plant are about a foot long, and three fingers breadth wide. 1839 URE Dict. Arts, etc. 1263 The vanilla plant is cultivated in Brazil,..and some other tropical countries. 1854 MAYNE Expos. Lex. 311/2 Epidendrum Vanilla, the systematic name of the vanelloe plant. 1856 A. GRAY Man. Bot. (1860) 185 Liatris odoratissima. Vanilla-plant... Leaves exhaling the odor of Vanilla when bruised. 1887 MOLONEY Forestry W. Africa 421 The source of the *vanilla pods of commerce. 1888 Encycl. Brit. XXIV. 66/2 The best varieties of vanilla pods are of a dark chocolate brown or nearly black colour. 1930 Radiation Cookery Book (ed. 12) vii. 119 *Vanilla Slices. Ingredients—½ lb. puff paste. A few drops vanilla, ½ pint thick custard... When the pastry is cool, spread the custard on one strip and put the second strip over the top; cover with icing, and cut with a sharp knife in strips about 2 inches wide. 1979 This England Winter 19/1 I've brought you one of your favourite vanilla slices as well! 1846 SOYER Cookery 569 Serve with whipped cream flavoured with *vanilla sugar under it. 1940 L. MACNEICE Plant & Phantom (1941) 59 All her *vanilla-sweet forgotten vaudeville nights. 1899 Allbutt's Syst. Med. VIII. 923 *Vanilla-workers sometimes manifest lichen-erythema of the face and hands.

b. Passing into *adj.*: vanilla-coloured, vanilla-flavoured. (Not clearly distinguishable from some of the uses in sense 4 a.)

1946 A. CHRISTIE Come, tell me how you Live viii. 133 A vanilla soufflé, for a wonder, goes right. 1962 Vanilla soda [see SODA[1] 4 b]. 1980 H. ENGEL Suicide Murders xviii. 121, I ordered a vanilla marshmallow sundae and a vanilla milkshake. 1982 M. RUSSELL All Part of Service iii. 23 A box of vanilla fudge. 1984 Guardian 5 Oct. 17/8 Old-fashioned vanilla sundae with hot fudge sauce.

vanille (və'niːl). Also **vanile**. [a. F. *vanille*, ad. mod.L. *Vanilla*: see prec.]

1. = VANILLA 3. Also *fig.*

a1845 SYD. SMITH in Lady Holland Mem. (1855) I. 262 Ah, you flavour everything; you are the vanille of society. 1861 BENTLEY Man. Bot. 667 Their fragrant odoriferous fruit..constitutes the Vanilla or Vanile of the shops. 1871 KINGSLEY At Last vii, And what is this delicious scent about the air? Vanille? Of course it is.

2. *vanille ice*, ice cream flavoured with vanilla essence. Also *ellipt.*

1846 MRS. GORE Eng. Char. (1852) 38 She accepts the offer of some vanille ice, which she receives over the head of a squat lady. 1856 MRS. BROWNING Aur. Leigh VII. 1184 Each lovely lady..holds her dear fan while she feeds her smile On meditative spoonfuls of vanille. 1863 MISS BRADDON Eleanor's Victory III. 235 Vanille and strawberry ices were in constant demand at Tortoni's.

va'nillic, *a.* *Chem.* [f. VANILL-A + -IC 1 b.] *vanillic acid*, vanillin, or an oxidized form of this.

1868 [see next]. 1876 HARLEY Royle's Mat. Med. 385 Vanillin..has, in fact, acid properties, and is therefore appropriately called vanillic acid. 1885 REMSEN Org. Chem. (1888) 304 Vanillic acid..is formed by oxidation of vanillin, which is the corresponding aldehyde.

va'nillin. *Chem.* Also **-ine**. [f. as prec. + -IN.] 'The neutral odoriferous principle of vanilla' (Watts).

1868 WATTS Dict. Chem. V. 994 Vanillin..was first recognised as a peculiar substance by Bley.., further examined by Gobley,..and afterwards by Stokkebye,..who designates it as vanillic acid. 1888 Encycl. Brit. XXIV. 66/2 The peculiar fragrance of vanilla is due to vanillin. Ibid., The amount of vanillin varies according to the kind. 1897 Allbutt's Syst. Med. III. 289 A solution composed of phloroglucine, 2 parts; vanilline, 1 part; absolute alcohol, 30 parts.

va'nillism. *Path.* [f. as prec. + -ISM.] A diseased condition (of the skin and general system) characteristic of workers in vanilla.

1884 St. James's Gaz. 29 Apr. 5/1 Dr. Layet has just published the results of his inquiries into the nature of a singular malady known as 'vanillism'. 1886 American XII. 269 That class of diseases in which morphinism, caffeism, and vanillism are found.

‖**vanillon.** [F., f. *vanille* VANILLE.] (See quots.)

[1839 URE Dict. Arts, etc. 1264 A third sort, which comes from Brazil, is the Vanillon, or large vanilla of the French market.] 1884 Encycl. Brit. XXIV. 67/1 In Brazil, Peru, and other parts of South America a broad and fleshy vanilla is prepared, which has an inferior odour... This variety is often distinguished as vanillon in commerce.

vanillyl ('vænɪlɪl). *Chem.* and *Biochem.* [f. VANILL(IC *a.*, -IN + -YL.] The radical, $OCH_3C_6H_3(OH)CH<$, derived from vanillin; *vanillylmandelic acid* [MANDELIC *a.*], the end-product of the metabolism of adrenaline and noradrenaline, measured to test for certain tumours; 4-hydroxy-3-methoxymandelic acid, $OCH_3C_6H_3(OH)CH(OH)COOH$.

1876 Jrnl. Chem. Soc. XXIX. 76 This body, which is still under investigation, is vanillyl alcohol. 1932 Jrnl. Pharmacol. & Exper. Therapeutics XLV. 165 The salts of vanillyl-ethylamine and methylamine were found to be quite soluble. [1957 ARMSTRONG & MCMILLAN in Pharmacol. Rev. XI. 395 Because of the cumbersome nature of the proper name for this compound..the trivial name 'vanilmandelic acid' is proposed, and the abbreviation 'VMA'.] 1961 Clin. Chem. VII. 257 The determination of 3-methoxy-4-hydroxymandelic acid, also called vanillylmandelic acid (VMA), in urine has recently come into use as a confirmatory test for pleochromocytoma. 1979 Nature 1 Mar. 41/2 Many oxidative degradations have also been carried out to break coal down into simpler species; however, isolation and identification of p-hydroxyl (IV), vanillyl (V), and syringyl (VI) groups, which are characteristic lignin oxidation products, have not yet been confirmed. 1979 Jrnl. R. Soc. Med. LXXII. 533 Twenty-four hour urinary vanillylmandelic acid (VMA) estimations were within normal limits.

va'niloquence. *rare*$^{-0}$. [ad. L. *vāniloquentia.*] (See quots.) Also **va'niloquent** *a.*; **va'niloquy** [ad. late L. *vāniloquium.*]

1623 COCKERAM I, Vaniloquence, much talke or babling. Ibid. II, Much Babling, Dicacity, Vaniloquie. 1656 BLOUNT Glossogr., Vaniloquence, vain talk, vain babling. [Hence in Phillips and Bailey.] 1727 BAILEY, Vaniloquent, talking vainly.

vanish ('vænɪʃ), *sb.* [f. the vb.]

1. Disappearance; vanishment.

1650 T. VAUGHAN Anthroposophia 58 This Vanish, or ascent of the inward Ethereall Principles doth not presently follow their separation. 1872 'MARK TWAIN' Roughing It iii. 33 He..left for San Francisco at a speed which can only be described as a flash and a vanish.

2. *spec.* A gradual cessation of a sound; a slight sound in which another ends; a glide.

1833 RUSH Human Voice (ed. 2) 319 The Drift of the downward Vanish.

vanish ('vænɪʃ), *v.* Forms: α. 4–5 **vanysche** (4 **-yȝsche**, 5 **-yssche, -yche**, 6 **-ysch**), 4–6 **vanysshe** (5 **-yssh, wanyssh-**); 4 **vanyshe**, 5 6 **vanysh**; 4, 6 *Sc.*, **vanisch** (6 *Sc.* **wanische, wenisch**), 5–7 **vanishe** (6 **-isshe**), 6– **vanish** (6 **vannish**, *Sc.* **wanish**); 4–5 **vanesche** (5 **-essche, -esshe, -esce, -eche**). β. 4–5, 6 *Sc.*, **vanys, -yss** (5 **vaynyss-**, 5–6 *Sc.* **wanys-**), 5 **wanyse**, 6 *Sc.* **vanyse**; 4–5, 6 *Sc.*, **vanis(s)-**, 6 *Sc.* **wanis(s)-**; 5 **waynes-**, *Sc.* **wanes-**, 6 *Sc.* **waneis**. γ. 4 **vansch-**, 5 **vanshe, wansh-, wanse**. [Aphetic ad. OF. *evaniss-*: see EVANISH *v.*]

1. *intr.* To disappear from sight, to become invisible, esp. in a rapid and mysterious manner:

a. With *away*; occas. with addition of *out of* or *from sight*, etc. Now *rare*.

α. 1303 R. BRUNNE Handl. Synne 8195 Wyþ þe croys she gan here blys, þan þey vanysshed aweye as swyþe. 1387 TREVISA Higden (Rolls) V. 435 Whanne þis was i-seide he vanysshed awey. c1400 Rom. Rose 2955 He vanyshide awey alle sodeynly, And I alloone lefte alle soole. c1450 Mirk's Festial 11 þen anon þys fend vanechet away wyth an horrybull stenche. 1470–85 MALORY Arthur II. viii. 85 Therwith merlyn vanysshed awey sodenly. 1545 UDALL, etc. Erasm. Par. Luke 182 b, After these woordes spoken, the Aungels vanished awaye from theyr sight. 1706 PHILLIPS (ed. Kersey), To Disappear,..to vanish away, to go out of sight. 1809 SHELLEY 'For my dagger' 17 Where the phantoms of Prejudice vanish away. 1890 DOYLE White Company xxiv, When I see the last sail..vanishing away against the western sky.

β. c1340 HAMPOLE Pr. Consc. 2269 And when þe devel herd hym þus say, Alle skomfit he vanyst oway. c1375 Sc. Leg. Saints xlii. (Agatha) 280 Away son þai vanist but ony hone, Of þar sicht wanest away, & neuire ware sene to þis day. c1440 Alph. Tales 516 When he had done, sodanlie he vanyssid away. 1456 SIR G. HAYE Law Arms (S.T.S.) 42 Na man..mycht se him, nor na bit of his body, bot vanyst fra thair sicht away. 1513 DOUGLAS Æneid III. vi. 109 The strait soundis of the mont Pelory Wanysis away pece and pece.

γ. 1375 in Horstmann Altengl. Leg. (1878) 128/1 Anon þe deuel vanschede awaye. 1387 TREVISA Higden (Rolls) V. 177 Mercurius..stiked hym in þe myddel of his body, and vansched awey. 14.. Voc. in Wr.-Wülcker 581 Euaneo, to vanshe a wey.

b. Without *away*.

α. 1377 LANGL. P. Pl. B. XII. 293 Riȝt with þat he vanesched. c1385 CHAUCER L.G.W. 1001 Dido, To Cartage she bad he shuld hym dyght And vanysshed anon out of hys syght. 14.. Tundale's Vis. 519 The angell vaneschyd and he stod stylle. 1530 PALSGR. 765/1 A spyrite wyll vanysshe and come agayne in the twynkelyng of an eye. 1582 STANYHURST Æneis II. (Arb.) 68 Fare ye wel, ô husband, oure yoong babye charely tender. This sayd, shee vannisht. 1609 DEKKER Gull's Horn-bk. 20 [This] notable Act being performed, you are to vanish presently out of the Quire. 1638 SIR T. HERBERT Trav. (ed. 2) 11 She againe deluded us, after two houres chase as a phantasma vanishing towards Goa. 1662 J. DAVIES tr. Olearius' Voy. Ambass. 261 We had hardly alighted, but our Pistols were taken away, and what was not lock'd up immediately vanish'd. 1757 GRAY Bard 104 They melt, they vanish from my eyes. 1797 MRS. RADCLIFFE Italian xi, Whose dark figures, passing without sound, vanished like shadows. 1820 W. IRVING Sketch Bk. I. 11 That land, now vanishing from my view, which contained all that was most dear to me in life. 1856 KANE Arct. Expl. I. xviii. 225 Its curved face..vanished into unknown space.

β. c1375 Sc. Leg. Saints xix. (Christopher) 267 With þat criste fra hyme wanyst, & hame he passit til his bewist. a1400–50 Alexander 1113 (Ashm.), þan waynest him þis vayne god & voidis fra þe chambre. c1480 HENRYSON Fables, Lion & Mouse xliii, And with that word he vanist, and I woke. 1490 CAXTON Eneydos xvi. 64 Mercuryus, yet spekynge, vaynyssed oute of eneas sight.

γ. 1375 in Horstmann Altengl. Leg. (1878) 132 þe addre.. vanschede out of here siȝt. 1393 LANGL. P. Pl. C. XVI. 24 Whanne he hadde seide so how sodeynlich he vanshede.

†**c.** In perfect tense with *be*; esp. *was vanished* = had vanished. *Obs.*

1390 GOWER Conf. II. 259 Thus it befell..Sche was vanyssht riht as hir liste, That no wyht bot hirself it wiste. a1400 Partonope (Univ. Coll. MS.) 826 (2568), With that worde sodenly they be Vanesshid a-way, that trewly he Wote neuer where they be become. c1425 LYDG. Assembly of Gods 1188 So sodenly As they were vanysshyd saw I neuer thyng with ey. c1480 HENRYSON Orpheus & Eurydice 113 And quhen scho wanyst was and Invisible, Hir madin wepit. a1533 LD. BERNERS Huon xxiii. 68 By that tyme they had gone a lytyll by ye ryuer syde they loste ye syght of ye castell, it was clene vanysshyd a way. a1628 F. GREVILLE Cælica xli, And I poore Ixion to my Iuno vowed, With thoughts to clip her, clipt my owne desire: For she was vanisht, I held nothing fast. 1648 HEXHAM II, Het is verstoven,..it is Vanished away as dust.

d. In fig. use.

1560 DAUS tr. Sleidane's Comm. 116 Those spirites by lytle and lytle, vanyshed cleane out of syght [i.e. in popular belief]. 1642 D. ROGERS Naaman 7 He that reads it as a bare miracle will onely vanish in a wondering humor. 1737 Gentl. Mag. VII. 292 The Epick Poets not only..immediately shew the Effects of the Inspiration they pray for,..they actually vanish from our View. 1843 CARLYLE Past & Pres. II. i, And in this manner vanishes King Lackland. 1866 G. MACDONALD Ann. Q. Neighb. xxix. (1878) 497 Straining their eyes after their brothers and sisters that have vanished in the dark.

2. To disappear by decaying, coming to an end, or ceasing to exist: **a.** With *away*.

α. c1340 HAMPOLE Prose Tr. 32 þe affeccyone of lufe es tendir and lyghtly will vanysche awaye. a1425 tr. Arderne's Treat. Fistula, etc. 88 When he seþe..þe bolnyng for to vanysh away, and þe akyng for to be cesed. 1490 CAXTON

Eneydos vii. 32 Their auncyent customes..vanysshed awaye as thei neuer had be vsed. **1530** PALSGR. 765/1 And a woman be ones fourty, her beautye wyll vanisshe awaye. **1535** COVERDALE *Isaiah* li. 6 The heauens shal vanish awaye like smoke. *a* **1600** in *Montgomerie's Poems* (S.T.S. Suppl. Vol.) 241 Bott quhat so ever waxis auld, it wenischis away. **1648** HEXHAM II, *Verdwijnen*, to Vanish away as smoake. **1804-6** SYD. SMITH *Mor. Philos.* (1850) 407 You will linger on.. after the blood, and the taste, and the sweetness are vanished away. **1839** FR. A. KEMBLE *Resid. in Georgia* (1863) 32 If the mind and soul were awakened, instead of mere physical good attempted, the physical good would result, and the great curse vanish away. **1859** FITZGERALD *Omar* lxxii, Alas, that Spring should vanish with the Rose!

β. *c* **1374** CHAUCER *Boeth.* III. pr. iv. (1868) 74 Her honours vanissen awey and þat on oon. **1513** DOUGLAS *Æneid* I. ix. 13 The clude about thame swith was brokin, And wanist tyte away amang the air.

γ. **1387** TREVISA *Higden* (Rolls) VIII. 157 But fal[s]nes i-feyned vanscheþ awey in schort tyme. *c* **1430** LYDG. *Min. Poems* (Percy Soc.) 226 His bestys dyeden in yche dyche, His katelle wanshed alle away.

b. Without adverb.

α. *c* **1350** *Will. Palerne* 639 Hit schal veraly þurth vertue do vanisch ȝour soris! *c* **1386** CHAUCER *Pardoner's T.* 404 Lo how I vanysshe, flessh and blood and skyn. **1560** BIBLE (Geneva) *Jer.* xlix. 7 Is wisdome no more in Teman?..is their wisdome vanished? **1576** FLEMING *Panopl. Epist.* 211 The benefite of the same will utterly decay and vanish. **1617** MORYSON *Itin.* II. 124 The fortifying of the Spaniards at Sligo vanished with the rumour. **1695** WOOD *Life* (O.H.S.) 13 April, The cold began to vanish and the north-east wind change. **1740** *Col. Rec. Pennsylv.* IV. 439 The Bill for Raising of Money for the use of the Crown is vanished. **1778** MISS BURNEY *Evelina* xxvii, I own my objections have almost wholly vanished. **1820** W. IRVING *Sketch Bk.* I. 42 A little while, and the smile will vanish from that cheek. **1852** H. ROGERS *Ecl. Faith* (1853) 166 Very much, indeed, that I wished to remember has vanished. **1874** CARPENTER *Ment. Phys.* I. vi. (1879) 285 Even those who had previously been most successful..found all their success vanish.

β. *γ* **1393** LANGL. *P. Pl.* C. XVI. 8 So myghte happe, þat.. vanshie [should] alle myne vertues and myne faire lockes. *c* **1440** CAPGRAVE *Life St. Kath.* I. 487 It wyll wanyse & wast, roten & be brent. **1533** GAU *Richt Vay* 31 Quhen he gettis ony aduersite or persecutione, thane it [*sc.* his faith] wanissis and wauers as ane dreyme. **1596** DALRYMPLE tr. *Leslie's Hist. Scot.* II. 239 How sune vanisses that plesure, quhilke mortall man callis felicitie.

c. Const. *into* (air, smoke, etc.).

1590 MARLOWE *2nd Pt. Tamburl.* V. iii, Weepe heauens, and vanish into liquid teares. **1609** DEKKER *Gull's Hornbk.* 27 Plaudities, and the Breath of the great Beast, which (like the threatnings of two Cowards) vanish all into aire. **1617** MORYSON *Itin.* II. 44 The ill successe of the Queenes affaires (whose great expences and Royall Army they had seene vanish into smoke). **1697** DRYDEN *Virg. Georg.* IV. 575 Surprize him first,..Then all his Frauds will vanish into Wind. **1807** HOGG *Mountain Bard, Mess John* xxiv, If the cock be heard to crow, The charm will vanish into air. **1842** LONGF. *Belfry of Bruges* iv, Wreaths of snow-white smoke ascending, vanished, ghost-like into air.

d. *Math.* Of numbers or quantities: To become zero.

1715 tr. *Gregory's Astron.* (1726) I. 190 Because the Orbits of Mercury and Venus..do almost vanish in respect of the Orbit of Saturn. **1789** *Phil. Trans.* LXXIX. 175 This series ..only differs from it by the last term S *o* not vanishing, that is, being = o. **1823** H. J. BROOKE *Introd. Crystallogr.* 201 The axis must vanish, before the planes P and P′ would reach 180°. **1840** LARDNER *Geom.* 290 The distance between them decreasing without limit, but never vanishing. **1885** WATSON & BURBURY *Math. Electr. & Magn.* I. 42 All the terms will vanish except those in which the multiples of *ϕ* are the same.

†**3.** To become worthless or vain. *Obs.*

c **1380** WYCLIF *Wks.* (1880) 419 ȝif salt vanyȝsche awey it is not worþ aftir but to be castun out. **1382** —— *Luke* xiv. 34 If salt schal vanysche [L. *evanuerit*], in what thing schal it be sauerid? —— *Rom.* i. 21 Thei vanyscheden [L. *evanuerunt*] in her thouȝtis. **1387** TREVISA *Higden* (Rolls) III. 347 Þe apostel seiþ þat suche philosofres vansched away in here þouȝtes.

4. *trans.* To cause to disappear; to remove from sight. Now chiefly with reference to conjuring.

c **1440** *Alph. Tales* 45 And with þat he vanysshid his enchawntement, & þer was oght nott lefte of all þat hym þoght he saw. **1590** MARLOWE *2nd Pt. Tamburl.* V. iii, Thus are the villaines..fled for feare, Like Summers vapours, vanisht by the Sun. **1604** *Meet. Gallants at Ordinarie* 5 Say thou'st slayne Foure hundred Silkeweauers,..vanisht As many Tapsters, Chamberlaines, and Ostlers. **1633** BP. HALL *Hard Texts, N.T.* 47 Whose bodies have been vanished into all the Elements. **1679** PENN *Addr. Prot.* II. 93 And were Liturgies..so framed,..Schisms on Opinion were utterly vanished. **1709** MRS. MANLEY *Secr. Mem.* (1736) III. 74 Whilst she was going to enquire who had sent it, the Child was dextrously vanish'd from the place. **1768-74** TUCKER *Lt. Nat.* (1834) II. 656 You might as well think of haranguing a man out of a fever, as go to vanish his scruples arising from that cause by the remonstrances of reason. **1886** *Pall Mall G.* 23 Dec. 4/1 Then he vanishes a birdcage and its occupant... Finally, he vanishes his wife. **1934** H. G. WELLS *Exper. Autobiogr.* I. v. 264 Lenin conjured government by mass-democracy out of sight, 'vanished' it as conjurors say, by his reorganization of the Communist Party. **1949** [see DISAPPEAR *v.* 3]. **1981** *Daily Tel.* 4 Jan. 6/8 Thurston..could make a girl disappear from a cage suspended in mid-air, or vanish a girl playing a piano (and the piano).

Hence **vanished** ('vænɪʃt) *ppl. a.*

1593 SHAKS. *Lucr.* 742 He runs, and chides his vanish'd, loathed delight. *c* **1600** —— *Sonn.* xxx, Then can I..mone th' expence of many a vannisht sight.

1812 BYRON *Ch. Har.* II. xl, Oft did he mark the scenes of vanish'd war. **1867** MORRIS *Jason* I. 394 Strange questions of the race of vanished men. *Ibid.* x. 554 And their hearts too, with thoughts of vanished years Were pensive. **1890** *Science-Gossip* XXVI. 108 Specimens of lifeless and shells of defunct and vanished univalves and bivalves.

'vanisher. [f. VANISH *v.*] One who, or that which, vanishes or disappears.

1864 WHITTIER *The Vanishers* iii, From the clefts of mountain rocks..Flash the eyes and flow the locks Of the mystic Vanishers.

vanishing ('vænɪʃɪŋ), *vbl. sb.* [f. the vb.]

1. The action or fact of disappearing.

c **1386** CHAUCER *Knt.'s T.* 1502 And forth sche wente, and made a vanysshynge. **1473** WARKW. *Chron.* (Camden) 22 Afore the vanyschynge therof, it apperyd in the evynynge. **1611** COTGR., *Esvanouissement*,..a vanishing out of sight. **1614** RALEIGH *Hist. World* III. (1634) 7 As where it tels of Nebuchadnezzar his owne vanishing away. **1711** ADDISON *Spect.* No. 44 ¶1 Thunder and Lightning..at the Vanishing of a Devil. **1824** BYRON *Juan* XVI. xxiv, There was no great cause To think his vanishing unnatural. **1886** *Athenæum* 9 Oct. 463/3 Amongst the vanishings and disappearances of the 'unfit'.

2. ***vanishing point***: in perspective, the point in which receding parallel lines, if continued, appear to meet; also *fig.* Similarly ***vanishing line, plane***.

1797 *Encycl. Brit.* (ed. 3) XIV. 183/2 Produce CB..and draw PV parallel to it... V is its vanishing point. **1815** J. SMITH *Panorama Sci. & Art* II. 711 Distance of a vanishing point, is the distance from the vanishing point on the picture to the eye of the spectator. **1840** *Penny Cycl.* XVII. 493 A plane W, which will be termed the vanishing plane of the original one. *Ibid.*, The vanishing line and parallel of the vertex. **1851** RUSKIN *Arrows of Chace* (1880) I. 90 In Millais' 'Mariana'..the top of the green curtain in the distant window has too low a vanishing-point. **1885** LEUDESDORF *Cremona's Proj. Geom.* 5 The point *I′*, the image of the point at infinity *I*, is called the vanishing point of *a′*. *Ibid.* 21 In every plane *σ* passing through *O* lies a vanishing line *i′*, which is the image of the point at infinity in the same plane. *Ibid.*, This plane *ϕ′*, which may be called the vanishing plane. **1913** *Times* 7 Aug. 8/2 The danger of operation, *gas* operation, is retreating to a vanishing point. **1963** *Lancet* 12 Jan. 96/2 Routine application of this test reduces to vanishing-point the mortality from air embolism during neurosurgery in the sitting position.

3. ***vanishing act, trick***.

1923 H. C. BAILEY *Mr. Fortune's Practice* vi. 160 She goes off walking at night with nothing but what she stood up in. If you ask me to believe she meant to do the vanishing act.. I can't see how it's likely. **1981** P. MALLORY *Killing Matter* vii. 79 He's chosen to pull a vanishing act just when the painting is lifted. **1973** G. SIMS *Hunters Point* xviii. 174 At the end of the path Jaeckel disappeared and it was Buchanan's turn to stop, momentarily at a loss..mystified by the vanishing trick.

vanishing ('vænɪʃɪŋ), *ppl. a.* [f. the vb.]

1. Disappearing from sight or from existence.

1434 MISYN *Mending Life* 108 So þat þou sulde..despyse abidynge þingis & to vanischynge þingis drawes. **1567** *Trial Treas.* (Percy Soc.) 18 To seke such thinges as be permanent, And not such as are of a vanishing kinde. **1571** GOLDING *Calvin on Ps.* lxi. 6 Not a vanishing prosperitie, but a stedye and substantiall gladnesse. **1607** TOPSELL *Four-f. Beasts* 124 If they remaine abroad in the aire,..they grow as light as any vanishing or softer substance. **1658** ROWLAND tr. *Moufet's Theat. Ins.* 951 The uncertainty of this vanishing life. **1760-72** H. BROOKE *Fool of Qual.* (1809) II. 75 Casting at me a vanishing glance, she was out of sight in an instant. **1833** RUSH *Human Voice* (ed. 2) 263 Of the Vanishing Stress. *Ibid.* 285 Of the Vanishing Emphasis. **1879** GEO. ELIOT *Theo. Such* vi. 129 To make the discomfort ..a vanishing quality. **1887** *Athenæum* 8 Oct. 461/1 Only a vanishing remnant lingers in the South Pacific.

2. *Math.* Becoming zero.

1823 J. MITCHELL *Dict. Math. & Phys. Sci.* s.v., We have the following rule for finding the value of vanishing fractions. **1838** *Penny Cycl.* X. 403/1 Much discussion has arisen as to whether vanishing fractions have values or not. **1892** J. EDWARDS *Diff. Calculus* (ed. 2) i. 5 When the limit of a quantity is zero.., the quantity is said to be a vanishing quantity for those values.

3. ***vanishing cream***, a cosmetic cream that is readily absorbed by the skin; also *fig.*

1916 *Daily Colonist* (Victoria, B.C.) 11 July 14/5 (Advt.), Pond's Vanishing Cream. **1923** W. A. POUCHER *Perfumes & Cosmetics* III. vi. 390 *Vanishing Creams*..consist of stearic acid, partially saponified with alkali, the bulk of the fatty acid being emulsified by the soap thus formed. *a* **1951** in M. McLuhan *Mech. Bride* (1967) 47/2 It's like your wife's vanishing cream—not greasy or sticky. **1981** E. AMBLER *Care of Time* ix. 149 If his luck holds, he's getting the defectors' vanishing-cream treatment..somewhere in North America.

Hence **'vanishingly** *adv.*

1870 tr. *Clausius* in *Lond.* etc. *Philos. Mag.* Aug. 127 The divisor *t*..must accordingly cause the term to become vanishingly small with very great values of *t*. **1881** SHAIRP *Asp. Poetry* viii. 239 Some momentary gleam..that has fleeted vanishingly over earth and sea.

'vanishment. [f. VANISH *v.*] The act of vanishing or disappearing; the state of having vanished.

1831 WILSON in *Blackw. Mag.* XXIX. 326 Mysteriously brought back from vanishment by some one single silent thought. **1851** G. S. FABER *Many Mansions* 105 His sudden vanishment from the eyes of the beholders. **1895** *Archaeol. Aeliana* XVII. 62 The usual chamfer being reduced almost to vanishment.

Vanist ('veɪnɪst). [See def. and -IST.] An adherent of Sir Henry Vane (1613–62) in respect of Antinomian principles.

1658 BAXTER *Life John Howe* Wks. 1846 Pref. p. xiii, Infidels and Papists who are very high and busy under several garbs, especially of Seekers, Vanists, Behmenists. **1664** —— *Life* (1696) 63 The Vanists, the Independants, and other Sects..was left by Cromwell to do his Business under the Name of the Parliament of England. **1825** COLERIDGE *Aids Refl.* (ed. 2) 135 Favouring the errors of the..Vanists. **1836** H. ROGERS *J. Howe* iii. 65 Here was a Vanist, pouring out his unintelligible rhapsodies.

vani'tarianism. *nonce-wd.* [f. VANITY.] The pursuit of vanities.

1849 THACKERAY *Lett.* 81 After wasting a deal of opportunities and time and desires in vanitarianism.

‖**vanitas** ('vænɪtɑːs). [L., lit. 'vanity, emptiness'.] **1.** ***vanitas vanitatum*** (from the Vulgate transl. of Eccles. i. 2): vanity of vanities, an exclamation of disillusionment or pessimism; futility.

1565 J. JEWEL *Replie unto M. Hardinges Answeare* iii. 164 This labour may well be called *Vanitas vanitatum.* **1848** THACKERAY *Vanity Fair* lxvii. 624 Ah! *Vanitas Vanitatum*! Which of us is happy in this world? Which of us has his desire? or, having it, is satisfied? **1910** CHESTERTON *G. B. Shaw* 105 In Shakespeare he saw nothing but profligate pessimism, the *vanitas vanitatum* of a disappointed voluptuary. **1978** H. SHAW in *Islands* (N.Z.) Aug. 105 Ah *Vanitas! Vanitatum!* All had been so totally suppressed, yet ..I *had* sensed certain emanations.

2. (Usu. with capital initial.) Used *attrib.* and *absol.* of a 17th-century Dutch genre of still-life painting that incorporated symbols of mortality or mutability.

1909 M. L. CLARKE tr. *Bode's Great Masters Dutch & Flem. Painting* 241 The artist [*sc.* J. Davidsz. de Heem] became a follower of the peculiar art movement of the older Leyden still-life painters, as several pictures of a 'Vanitas' show. *Ibid.* 239 The 'Vanitas' presentments required a monochrome treatment. **1942** *Burlington Mag.* Dec. 293/1 Paul..was a painter of some consequence, as shown for instance by his *Vanitas* still-life at Berlin (1636). **1947** BERGSTRÖM & TAYLOR tr. *Bergström's Dutch Still-Life Painting 17th Cent.* iv. 154 On account of its literary symbolism, often rather elaborate, the *Vanitas* occupies a special place among the forms of Dutch still-life painting. **1963** E. H. GOMBRICH *Meditations on Hobby Horse* 104 Is the spread of the genre [*sc.* still life] due to the religious appeal of the *vanitas* motif? *Ibid.*, Any painted still life is *ipso facto* also a *vanitas*. **1980** *Times* 13 Aug. 14/3 A painting by Frans Hals, 'Young Man Holding a Skull'..is a *vanitas*, a reminder of human vanity.

Vanitory ('vænɪtərɪ). orig. *U.S.* Also **vanitory**. [f. VANIT(Y + -ORY[1].] A proprietary name for a vanity unit.

1951 *Official Gaz.* (U.S. Patent Office) 13 Mar. 355/1 *Vanitory.* For combination dressing table-lavatory unit. **1958** *Trade Marks Jrnl.* 16 July 720/2 *Vanitory.* All goods included in class 11...22nd November 1957. **1960** *Spectator* 26 Feb. 300 Bathing-dressing-rooms, complete with vanitories. **1961** *Ibid.* 10 Mar. 345 The appearance of Vanitory units in the ballroom as well as the bedroom for which they were designed. **1972** *House & Garden* Dec.–Jan. 82/1 One of the bathrooms..with built in vanitory unit. **1984** *Sunday Tel.* (Colour Suppl.) 29 Apr. 40/4 A roll-out bidet which, when not in use, is neatly concealed in a vanitory unit beneath the basin.

vanitous ('vænɪtəs), *a. rare.* [f. VANITY + -OUS or ad. F. *vaniteux*.] = VAIN *a.* 4.

1900 G. MEREDITH *Let.* 12 July (1970) III. 1351 An accurate perception of foibles in those whom we love..is only a vindication of our intellect—the seeing in what way our hero or friend or beloved is a little vanitous and pretentious. **1905** *Ibid.* 30 July 1536 French criticism.. instructs without wounding any but the vanitous person. **1930** *Musical Times* 1 Mar. 210/2 It is only the very young, or the very vanitous, who think of making a world of themselves.

Hence **'vanitously** *adv.*

1939 V. WOOLF *Diary* 3 Mar. (1984) V. 207, I was pleased, vanitously, to find that Inez thinks me a poet-novelist.

vanity ('vænɪtɪ). Forms: 3–4 **uanite**, 4–5 (6 *Sc.*) **vanite** (5 **wan-**), 5–6 **vanitee**, 6–7 **vanitie** (6 *Sc.* **wan-**), 6– **vanity** (6 **-tye**); 4–6 **vanyte** (5 **wan-**, **wann-**), 4–6 **vanytee**, 6 **vanytye**, **-tie**. [a. OF. *vanite* (F. *vanité*, = It. *vanità*, Sp. *vanidad*, Pg. *vaidade*), ad. L. *vānitāt-*, *vānitās*, f. *vānus* VAIN *a.*]

1. a. That which is vain, futile, or worthless; that which is of no value or profit.

c **1230** *Hali Meid.* 27 Hare confort & hare delit, hwerin is hit al meast, bute i flesches fulðe oðer in weorldes uanite..? **13..** *E.E. Allit. P.* C. 331 Þose vnwyse ledes þat affyen hym in vanyte & in vayne þynges. *c* **1340** HAMPOLE *Pr. Consc.* 1619 Þus es þe world, and þe lyfe þare-in, Ful of vanyte and of syn. **1387** TREVISA *Higden* (Rolls) III. 431 Þonkinge of enemyes is but vanite. *c* **1450** LOVELICH *Grail* xliii. 316 Whanne alle this haddist þou seyn,..vpe thou ryse, and bethowhtest the Whethir it were soth oþer vanite. *c* **1480** HENRYSON *Abbey Walk* 51 (Bann.), Thy power and thy warldis pelf Is nocht bot verry vanitie. **1500-20** DUNBAR *Poems* xlvi. 98 This frustir luve all is bot vanite. **1611** BIBLE *Ps.* xxxix. 5 Euery man at his best state is altogether vanitie. **1691** RAY *Creation* I. (1704) 76 We see nothing in the Heavens which argues Chance, Vanity or Error. **1834** MATHEW *Serm.* ii. 44 Yet you often..are disposed to own that all in this world is vanity.

b. Vain and unprofitable conduct or employment of time.

1303 R. BRUNNE *Handl. Synne* 3346 Forsoþe hyt semeþ weyl to be Al here lyfe yn vanyte. *c* **1340** HAMPOLE *Pr. Consc.* 7228 Þai..swa mysturned here þair lyfyng In-tylle vanyte and flesschly lykyng. *c* **1374** CHAUCER *Troylus* IV. 729 But efter al this nyce vanite, They took hire leve, and hom they wente alle. *c* **1430** LYDG. *Min. Poems* (Percy Soc.) 219 Lat reson brydle thy sensualite,..Ageyn al worldly disordinat vanyte. **1514** BARCLAY *Cyt. & Uplondyshman* (Percy Soc.) 5 Men labour sorer in fruyteles vanyte, Than in fayre warkes of grete utylyte. **1567** *Gude & Godlie B.* (S.T.S.) 73, I pray the, Lord, . . All vanitie and lieand word, Full far away thow put fra me. **1607** MELTON *Sixe-folde Politician* (Arb.) 114 As the enterludes may be tearmed the Schoole-houses of vanitie and wantonnes. **1612** *Two Noble K.* II. ii. 109 All those pleasures That wooe the wils of men to vanity. **1751** *Transl. & Paraph. Sc. Ch.* xxvii. 102 In Vanity ye waste your Days.

†**c.** ***in vanity***, in vain. *Obs.*⁻¹

1509 HAWES *Conv. Swearers* 23 Ye dare not take their names in vanyte.

2. a. The quality of being vain or worthless; the futility or worthlessness *of* something.

c **1325** *Prose Psalter* li. 7 He was michel worþ in his vanite. *a* **1340** HAMPOLE *Psalter* xi. 1 A haly man þat sees þe vanyte of þe warld mutiplid. **1382** WYCLIF *Eph.* iv. 17 That ȝe walke not now, as and hethen men walken, in the vanyte of her witt. *c* **1400** *Destr. Troy* 7121 Thus curstly þat knight-hode . . Voidet þere victory for vanite of speche. **1451** CAPGRAVE *Life St. Aug.* 9 In all þis vanyte of his lif he happed to fynde a book þat Tullius Cicero mad. **1535** COVERDALE *Ecclus.* xvii. 31 He hath pleasure in the vanyte of wickednes. **1662** J. DAVIES tr. *Olearius' Voy. Ambass.* 31 A fabulous story, whereof the vanity is so much the more visible. **1674** *Essex Papers* (Camden) I. 200 This [rumour] alarmed me so much that I had little rest till Trear. spoke with King, who assured him of the vanity of it. **1711** ADDISON *Spect.* No. 159 ¶2, I fell into a profound Contemplation on the Vanity of human Life. **1741** C. MIDDLETON *Cicero* II. viii. 216 The vanity of expecting any lasting glory. **1823** SCOTT *Quentin D.* xxxiv, The Bohemian had gone where the vanity of his dreadful creed was to be put to the final issue. **1834** *Tait's Mag.* I. 699/1 The noble Lord might have anticipated the vanity of his exertions. **1864** PUSEY *Lect. Daniel* (1876) 274 The vanity of the resistance of the kings of Judah.

†**b.** The quality of being foolish or of holding erroneous opinions. *Obs.*

c **1386** CHAUCER *Miller's T.* 649 Of his vanytee He hadde yboght hym knedying tubbes thre. —— *Clerk's T.* 194 Wol nat oure lord yet leue his vanytee? Wol he nat wedde? **1578** TIMME *Calvin on Gen.* 26 Whereby their vanitie is overthrowen which think that the world was a matter alwayes without forme. **1596** DALRYMPLE tr. *Leslie's Hist. Scot.* II. 46/10 That . . [they] mycht now se thair awne daftnes, and lach or greit at thair awne vanitie. **1660** in *Extr. St. P. rel. Friends* Ser. II. (1911) 123 Your petitioner is in great dread and horrour of an oath (though hee detests the vanity of Quakers and such like giddy people).

3. a. The quality of being personally vain; high opinion of oneself; self-conceit and desire for admiration.

a **1340** HAMPOLE *Psalter* xv. 4 Synn and vnclennes þat þai ere in þat folous þaire flesch and þe vanyte of þaire blode. **1390** GOWER *Conf.* III. 166 That whil he stod in that noblesse, He scholde his vanite represse With suche wordes as he herde. *a* **1400–50** *Alexander* 1730 Be vanyte & vayne glori þat in þi wayns kindlis. *Ibid.* 1784 All þi vanyte to voide & þi vayne pride. *c* **1430** LYDG. *Minor Poems* (Percy Soc.) 65 Yowre blynde fantesies now in hertis weyve Of childisshe vanyte, and lete hem over slyde. **1596** SPENSER *St. Ireland* Wks. (Globe) 627/1 They . . through their owne vanitye . . doe therupon build . . historyes of theyr owne antiquitye. **1613** SHAKS. *Hen. VIII*, I. i. 85 What did this vanity But minister communication of A most poore issue? **1649** MILTON *Eikon.* B, The intention of this discourse was not fond ambition or the vanity to get a Name. **1705** STANHOPE *Paraphr.* I. 310 The vanity of wicked Men is scarcely more conspicuous than in the fond Imaginations they flatter themselves with. **1783** W. THOMSON *Watson's Philip III* (1839) 77 She cannot be vindicated from the imputation of female vanity, and the love of admiration on account of her exterior accomplishments. **1829** LYTTON *Devereux* I. i, His vanity was so mingled with good nature that it became graceful. **1881** LADY HERBERT *Edith* 7 To the young wife's vanity and to Mr. Gordon's pride in his choice.

b. With *a* and *pl.*: An instance of this; an occasion for being vain.

1712–4 POPE *Rape Lock* I. 52 Think not, when Woman's transient breath is fled, That all her vanities at once are dead. **1761** HUME *Hist. Eng.* II. xxxi. 203 The nobility and gentry . . who placed a vanity in these institutions. **1770** FOOTE *Lame Lover* I Wks. 1799 II. 57 To derive a vanity from a misfortune, will not I'm afraid be admitted as a vast instance of wisdom.

c. A thing of which one is vain; also *slang*, one's favourite liquor.

1854 PATMORE *Angel in Ho.* I. II. ix, She was my vanity, and oh All other vanities how vain! **1891** C. JAMES *Rom. Rigmarole* 114 It is advisable to wash it down with a long drink of the reader's particular vanity.

4. a. A vain, idle, or worthless thing; a thing or action of no value.

a **1300** *Cursor M.* 53 þat foly luue, þat uanite, þam likes now nan oþer gle. *c* **1340** HAMPOLE *Prose Tr.* 5, I satt by mine ane fleeande þe vanytes of þe worlde. *c* **1450** *Mankind* 896 (Brandl), Thynke & remembyr, þe world ys but a wanite. **1470–85** MALORY *Arthur* XXI. ix. 855, I had forsaken the vanytees of the world. **1535** COVERDALE *2 Kings* xvii. 15 They despysed his ordinaunces . . and walked in their awne vanities. **1545** BRINKLOW *Compl.* (1874) 83 Ye shuld turne from these vanitees vnto the liuinge God. **1633** in *Verney Mem.* (1907) I. 76 To run on in their sinful vanities. **1658** *Ibid.* II. 71 All I find as shee desires it for, is but to spend it uppon her vanities. **1673** CAVE *Prim. Chr.* II. ii. 33 The sights and sports of the Theatre and such like vanities. **1822** LAMB *Elia* I. *Praise Chimney-Sweepers.* A convenient spot . . at the north side of the fair, not so far distant as to be impervious to the agreeable hubbub of that vanity. **1848** THACKERAY *Van. Fair* xli, As long as we have a man's body, we play our Vanities upon it, surrounding it with humbug and ceremonies.

†**b.** An idle tale or matter; an idea or statement of a worthless or unfounded nature. *Obs.*

1340 *Ayenb.* 77 Holy wryt, þet hise clepeþ leazinges . . and metinges and uanites. *c* **1340** HAMPOLE *Pr. Consc.* 184 Many has lykyng trofels to here, And vanites wille blethly lere. *c* **1440** *Jacob's Well* 166 Whanne þou iangelyst in cherch, or thynkest vanytees. **1500–20** DUNBAR *Poems* ix. 108, I knaw me . . culpable . . In wordis vyle, in vaneteis expreming. **1560** DAUS tr. *Sleidane's Comm.* 205 The Frenche men were thought to be authors and forgers of this vanitie. **1582** N. LICHEFIELD tr. *Castanheda's Conq. E. Ind.* 37 They be great southsayers, they haue good dayes and bad dayes, . . they doe easily beleeue whatsoeuer vanitie. **1652** HEYLYN *Cosmogr.* I. 211 Turpin hath . . interlaced his Storie with a number of ridiculous vanities. **1660** F. BROOKE tr. *Le Blanc's Trav.* 391 His Poem the *Auracana* . . begins with this vanity, truely poetical and Romantick Spaniard-like. **1894** 'MARK TWAIN' in *Century Mag.* June 236/1 The claim that the knife had been stolen was a vanity and a fraud.

†**5.** Emptiness, lightness; the state of being void or empty; inanity. *Obs. rare.*

a **1400** *Stockholm Med. MS.* 127 A good oynement for þe vanyte of þe heed. *a* **1400–50** *Alexander* 4774 It was bot vacant & voide, as vanite it were. **1587** LEVINS *Pathw. Health* (1632) 6 For the Vanity of the head Take the iuice of wall-wort, . . and therewith annoint the temples.

6. *N. Amer.* **a.** = *vanity table* (see sense 7 below).

1937 'E. QUEEN' *Door Between* xiv. 148 She sat down before the vanity to cold-cream her face. **1967** 'V. SILLER' *Biltmore Call* 124 Her make-up and perfume bottles and jars were still on a kidney-shaped vanity.

b. = *vanity unit* (sense 7 below).

1967 *Boston Sunday Herald* 26 Mar. (Advt.), Classic elegance for your bathroom is yours with this 30 × 20-in. vanity.. . Vitreous china top and bowl. **1977** *Chicago Tribune* 2 Oct. XII. 8/2 (Advt.), Ceramic tile baths and vanities. **1984** *Tampa* (Florida) *Tribune* 5 Apr. (Sears Suppl.) 9/3 Start your bath remodeling with this lovely vanity.

7. *attrib.* and *Comb.*, as ***vanity-bait***, ***-giving***, ***-huckster***, ***sight***; **vanity bag**, **-box**, **-case**, a small hand-bag, etc., for ladies, fitted with a mirror and powder-puff; **vanity basin**, a wash-basin for a vanity unit; **vanity mirror**, (*a*) a small make-up mirror, *esp.* as a fitting in a motor vehicle; (*b*) a dressing-table mirror; **vanity number plate**, *U.S.* **vanity plate** (see quot. 1967); **vanity press**, **publisher** orig. *U.S.*, a publisher who publishes only at the author's expense; so ***vanity publishing***; **vanity set**, (*a*) a set of cosmetics or toiletries, (*b*) *U.S.*, a matching bath and vanity unit; **vanity table**, a dressing-table; **vanity unit**, a unit comprising a wash-basin set into a fixed dressing-table.

1907 *Yesterday's Shopping* (1969) 404/1 The Vanity Bag. Containing on one side mirror, separate pocket for powder . . with puff, . . gusset pockets . . for gold on other side, pocket for cards, papers, &c. **1946** K. TENNANT *Lost Haven* (1947) xviii. 295 The silver-beaded white vanity-bag that carried her money, her lipstick, her handkerchief. **1974** J. CLEARY *Peter's Pence* iii. 78 The note . . had said she was spending the night with Fergus.. . She had taken a small vanity bag and slipped out of the apartment. **1816** JANE AUSTEN *Emma* II. xiv. 278, I should never have expected you to be lending your sanction to such vanity-baits for poor young ladies. **1972** *House & Garden* Dec.–Jan. 84/3 'Luxe' vanity basin . . £11.25. **1912** G. R. CHESTER *Five Thousand an Hour* ii. 10 She carried her own vanity box. **1978** N. MARSH *Grave Mistake* iv. 136 A vanity box . . lay on the table. **1913** S. STORY *Spirit of Paris* 52 The exquisite *femme du monde* . . has a final glance at herself, 'vanity case' in hand. **1957** *Practical Wireless* XXXIII. 531/1 The Sky Casket by Ever Ready . . is of the vanity-case type—no controls or other external components being visible. **1979** M. McCARTHY *Cannibals & Missionaries* xi. 323 He had slipped a folded plan of the house . . into Eloise's vanity case, under her powder-puff, camouflaged by a thick layer of face-powder. **1892** *Pall Mall G.* 8 Aug. 6/3 Remembering . . that enough of our public men do eat of this vanity-giving food. **1669** PENN *No Cross* Wks. 1782 II. 205 Let such of those Vanity-hucksters as have got sufficient be contented to retreat. **1959** *Observer* 1 Mar. 21/5 Visors with vanity mirror are flush fitting. **1966** T. PYNCHON *Crying of Lot 49* i. 16 A half hour in front of her vanity mirror. **1971** 'D. HALLIDAY' *Dolly & Doctor Bird* viii. 100 The vanity mirror . . was surrounded by fourteen ormulu makeup lamps. **1983** *Listener* 27 Oct. 25/2 (Advt.), Such thoughtful touches as an illuminated vanity mirror . . and seat back map pockets are all standard. **1983** *Daily Tel.* 10 Oct. 13/4 They will sell you a personalised or 'vanity' number plate for as little as ten dollars. **1967** *Britannica Bk. of Year* (U.S.) 804/3 *Vanity plate*, an automobile license plate bearing distinctive letters, numbers, or a combination of these and usually available at extra cost. **1974** 'D. SHANNON' *Crime File* (1975) xi. 194 The drivers who wanted to pay extra . . could buy the vanity plates. **1969** C. ARMSTRONG *Seven Seats to Moon* vi. 61 Are you planning to pay that Vanity Press to publish your father's book? **1976** *N.Y. Times Bk. Rev.* 7 Mar. 12/2, I read this book with the kind of horrified fascination with which one reads vanity press confessions. **1922** HOLLIDAY & VAN RENSSELAER *Business of Writing* 138 Numerous devices are employed by the 'vanity publisher' to lead the innocent author on toward becoming famous in his own eyes and those of his friends. **1978** *Amer. N. & Q.* Nov. 45/2 There are all sorts of literary histories, ranging from the pathetic things by which vanity publishers con local authors into expenditures far beyond their means, up to the CHEL and comparable works. **1984** H. SPURLING *Secrets of Woman's Heart* 19 Ivy placed *Pastors and Masters* . . with a small firm of 'vanity' publishers called Heath Cranton in Fleet Lane, paying for publication herself. **1960** G. A. GLAISTER *Gloss. Bk.* 429/2 *Vanity publishing*, publishing on behalf of and at the expense of an author who pays for the production and often for the marketing of his book. **1981** V. GLENDINNING *Edith Sitwell* iii. 45 She had emerged from vanity publishing to the real thing.. . 'I have found a publisher.' **1930** A. P. HERBERT *Water Gipsies* xix. 285 She lightly powdered her face. Lily had . . given her a 'vanity set'. **1970** *Washington Post* 30 Sept. B11/6 (Advt.), New tub. Toilet and vanity set. **1979** D. COOK *Winter Doves* II. i. 45 He had packed dolls' Vanity Sets into boxes. *c* **1440** *Alph. Tales* 166 Sho is not transfigurd . . bod vnto þer sightis þat may be begylid with vanyte syght. **1936** L. C. DOUGLAS *White Banners* i. 9 The mirror of the vanity table. **1954** W. TUCKER *Wild Talent* (1955) xiv. 183 A vanity table likewise revealed occupied drawers. **1980** L. BIRNBACH et al. *Official Preppy Handbk.* 191/2 Women's locker rooms often boast vanity tables with combs and face powder. **1973** Vanity unit [see LIMED *ppl. a.* a b]. **1983** *Sunday Tel.* 21 Aug. 31/4 The property has modern conveniences, including . . fitted kitchen, bathroom with vanity unit and plenty of power points throughout.

8. a. Vanity Fair (after quot. 1678 below), a place or scene where all is frivolity and empty show; the world or a section of it as a scene of idle amusement and unsubstantial display.

[**1678** BUNYAN *Pilgr.* (1900) 82 The name of that Town is Vanity; and at the town there is a Fair kept, called Vanity-Fair. It . . beareth the name of Vanity-Fair, because the Town where 'tis kept is lighter than Vanity.]

1816 J. SCOTT *Vis. Paris* (ed. 5) 137 Such is the Palais Royal;—a vanity fair—a mart of sin and seduction! **1827** SCOTT *Chron. Canongate* iii, Carrying so many bonny lasses to barter modesty for conceit and levity at the metropolitan Vanity Fair. **1857** TROLLOPE *Barchester T.* III. 110 But how preach . . at all in such a vanity fair as this now going on at Ullathorne? **1861** THACKERAY *Four Georges* 72 Never was such a brilliant, jigging, smirking Vanity Fair as that through which he leads us.

attrib. **1848** THACKERAY *Van. Fair* xxv, The last scene of her dismal Vanity Fair comedy was fast approaching. *Ibid.* xli, Assuming that any Vanity Fair feelings subsist in the sphere whither we are bound.

b. Hence **Vanity-Fairian**. *nonce-wd.*

1848 THACKERAY *Van. Fair* xvii, Even with the most selfish disposition, the Vanity Fairian . . can't but feel some sympathies and regret.

'vanityless, *a. rare.* [f. the sb.] Devoid of vanity.

1854 H. STRICKLAND *Travel Thoughts* 47 [I] wonder if there is any one sane person in the whole world, utterly vanitiless.

vanjarrah, variant of *bunjarrah* BRINJARRY.

Van John. *Univ. slang.* = VINGT-UN.

1853 'C. BEDE' *Verdant Green* xi, 'Van John' was the favourite game. **1861** HUGHES *Tom Brown at Oxf.* iii, We were playing Van John in Blake's rooms till three last night. **1887** DARWIN *Life & Lett.* I. 157 A little of Gibbon's History in the morning, and a good deal of Van John in the evening.

†**vanlay**, *v. Obs.* [Cf. VAUNTLAY *sb.*] *intr.* To cast off a vauntlay (*to* a hart).

c **1410** *Master of Game* (MS. Digby 182) xxxiii, He . . shulde take goode heede þat he vanlay not, if oþer relayes be behynde, for dreede of bendynge oute fro þe relayes. *Ibid.*, When he hath be so wele ronne to and . . relayed and vanleyed to, . . þenne turneth he his heed and stondeth at abaye.

†**vanlin**, variant of VENLIN *Obs.*

1577 HOLINSHED *Chron.* II 1779/2 There were assembled fouretene Ensignes of the French footemen, .xviii. vanlins of Almains, [and] four or fiue .C. men at armes of France.

'vanmost, *a. rare*⁻¹. [f. VAN *sb.*²] Foremost.

1865 CARLYLE *Fredk. Gt.* XVIII. iv. V. 87 Ziethen, vanmost of all, finds Nadasti and his Austrian squadrons drawn across the Highway.

vann(e, obs. variants of VAN *sb.* and *v.*¹

vanner¹ ('vænə(r)). [f. VAN *sb.*¹ and *v.*¹]

1. One who winnows with a fan. *rare.*

1552 HULOET, Vanner, *uannator.* **1611** COTGR., *Vanneur*, a vanner, or winnower of corne.

2. *Mining.* One who tests the quality of ore by washing it on a shovel.

1671 *Phil. Trans.* VI. 2098 Whereby the kind, nature and quantity of the Ore is guessed at, . . without any great deception, especially if the Vanner have any judgement at all. **1875** J. H. COLLINS *Met. Mining* 12 The speed and accuracy with which a practised vanner determines the value of a sample of tin ore, fills the beholder with wonder and delight.

b. An apparatus for separating minerals from the gangue.

1882 *U.S. Rep. Prec. Met.* 71 The concentrate from the vanners is high, but the tailings rich. **1890** *Melbourne Argus* 16 June 6/2 The company . . obtained between 12 and 13 tons of pyrites from the vanners.

vanner² ('vænə(r)). [f. VAN *sb.*³] **1.** A light horse suitable for drawing a small van.

1888 *Referee* 8 April (Cassell's), Cabbers, and vanners. **1890** *Pall Mall G.* 8 Sept. 4/2 Tramway horses were keenly competed for, and, with serviceable 'vanners', fetched as an average £40 each. **1897** HAYES *Points Horse* (ed. 2) xv. 125 The light vanner belongs to a class intermediate between the light harness horse and the heavy draught horse.

2. *N. Amer.* An owner or operator of a van, *esp.* one who uses the van for recreation.

1973 *Hot Rod* Nov. 71/3 Hot Rod editor Terry Cook and art director Jervis Hill indulged their . . fantasies by forming vans into what may be the largest "Keep on Truckin'" ever created. The vanners were willing to help. **1976** *National Observer* (U.S.) 10 Apr. 15/1 Vanners . . converge on campgrounds and recreational areas every week end for van fetes all over the country. **1976** *Kingston* (Ontario) *Whig-Standard* 4 Aug. 25/3 Coming up for vanners in the area, are a few special events.

Vannetais ('væntei, ‖ vantɛ), *sb.* and *a.* [Fr., f. *Vannes* (see below).] (Designating) a dialect of

Breton spoken in the region of Vannes in Brittany.

1953 K. H. JACKSON *Lang. & Hist. in Early Britain* II. xiv. 301 He argues that the change to *-ec* took place also in Vannetais. **1967** —— *Historical Phonol. of Breton* II. i. 18 The Vannetais dialect coincides on the whole quite closely on the west with the diocesan boundary in the valley of the Ellé, as far north at least as near le Faouet. **1977** *Word 1972* XXVIII. 14 The mixed character of the Vannetais dialect of Breton is explainable by the profound influence of these early Romance dialects. *Ibid.* 19 The area now occupied by Vannetais had less chance of retaining Gaulish than did the northwestern part of Brittany.

Vannic ('vænɪk). [f. *Van*, the name of a town on the site of an ancient centre of Armenian civilization + -IC.] = KHALDIAN b. Also as *adj.* Cf. URARTIAN *sb.* and *a.*

1882 *Jrnl. R. Asiatic Soc.* 14 July 380 The Vannic inscriptions were noticed by Sir H. Rawlinson. **1888** A. H. SAYCE *Hittites* vii. 134 The language of Ararat itself, the so-called Vannic, may belong to the same family of speech. **1897** W. H. WARD in H. von Hilprecht *Rec. Res. in Bible Lands* 172 We judge that the land of the Hittites, invaded by these Vannic kings, stretched along the upper course of the Euphrates. **1908**, etc. [see KHALDIAN]. **1974** *Encycl. Brit. Macropædia* I. 832/2 The terms Chaldean and Vannic have also been used as designations for Urartian during earlier stages of research. **1977** C. F. & F. M. VOEGELIN *Classification & Index World's Lang.* 162 Vannic Haldean. .. Formerly spoken in the Mount Ararat region near Lake Van.

'vanning, *vbl. sb.*[1] [f. VAN *v.*[1]]

†**1.** The action of winnowing with a fan. *Obs.*

1552 HULOET, Vannyng, *uannatio.* **1601** HOLLAND *Pliny* I. 607 The winnowing, vanning, and laying up either of corne or pulse. **1626** BACON *Sylva* §671 The Corne which in the Vanning lieth lowest, is the best.

†**b.** The action of tossing in a winnowing-fan.

1606 HOLLAND *Sueton.* Annot. 36 Sagatio,.. that pastime with us in some place called the canvasing, and else where, the vanning of dogs.

2. The action or process of separating ore on a shovel. Also *attrib.*, as ***vanning-action, shovel.***

1671 *Phil. Trans.* VI. 2098 Vanning..is performed by pulverising the stone, or clay, or what else may be suspected to contain any mineral body, and placing it on a Vanning shovel. **1766** *Ibid.* LVI. 38, I employed a tinner dextrous in vanning (a way of breaking and trying ores, by washing them on a shovel gently with water) to try it in his usual way. **1778** PRYCE *Min. Cornub.* 223 This must be repeated, till it is cleansed from the rough gravelly parts, which may be known by vanning of it on a shovel. **1839** DE LA BECHE *Rep. Geol. Cornwall*, etc. xv. 585 Great dexterity is exhibited by the tinners in the operation termed vanning. **1875** J. H. COLLINS *Met. Mining* 11 The same principle is at the bottom of the beautiful art of 'vanning'. **1884** KNIGHT *Dict. Mech.* Suppl. 920/1 The object throughout is..to imitate the vanning action of the miner's shovel.

'vanning, *vbl. sb.*[2] [f. VAN *sb.*[3]] **a.** The action of conveying in a van. **b.** Travelling or touring in a van; caravanning.

1892 *Athenæum* 15 Oct. 509/2 In 1836 came the affair of Elis, of whose 'vanning' so much has been made, though Eclipse had been conveyed in a van..from Epsom..about fifty years before. **1910** *Times* 21 July 8/5 The 'Wanderer', ..the pioneer of 'vanning' as a pastime for health and pleasure,..is..to be sold by auction.

vanplate, obs. form of VAMPLATE.

vanquash, *v. nonce-wd.* [Jocularly f. VAN *sb.*[2] + QUASH *v.*] *trans.* To smash.

c **1626** *Dick of Devon* II. iv. in Bullen *O. Pl.* II, Nay, if you be no better in the Reare then in the Van I shall make no doubt to vanquish, and vanquash you, too, before we part.

†**vanquer.** *Obs.*[−1] [ad. F. *vainqueur*, f. *vainqu-, vaincre* VANQUISH *v.*] Conqueror.

1570 *Satir. Poems Reform.* xvi. 143 And so this Realme.. Sall now..As Aiax wes, be vanquer of the sell.

†**'vanquerer.** *Obs.*[−1] [Var. of VAN-COURIER, prob. influenced by F. *querir* to seek.] A scout.

1579 DIGGES *Stratiot.* 118 He must give order to the Scoute Mayster whyche way he shall send his Vanquerers to discover.

†**vanqueror.** *Obs.*[−1] [Cf. VANQUER and CONQUEROR.] Victor.

1583 *Exec. for Treason* (1675) 6 Neither the vanqueror nor the vanquished can haue iust cause of triumph.

'vanquish, *sb. Sc.* Also vinquish. [f. the vb.] (See quots.)

1792 *Statist. Acc. Scot.* IV. 267 The pernicious quality of a species of grass to the health of the sheep..infecting them with a disease called the Vanquish. **1793** *Ibid.* VII. 518 In one or two farms a disease also prevails termed the Vanquish. **1807** *Essays Highl. Soc.* III. 407 Change of pasture..is the best known cure for the vanquish. **1844** H. STEPHENS *Bk. Farm* III. 1122 It is quite a new disease on the Border;..nor did I ever hear its name save from Galloway, where it was called the vinquish.

vanquish ('væŋkwɪʃ), *v.* Forms: *α.* 4 vencuse, 4–5 venkus (5 wen-), 5, 6 *Sc.*, vencus (5 *Sc.* wen-), 5 -cows; 4 venkis, 5 -kes(s, wenkys; *Sc.* 5 vincuse, wyncus, 5–6 vincus(s, 6 uin-, wincus, vincous (wincows), vincuis, (win-), vancuis. *β.* 4–5 venquis (5 -quyse, -quyss, *Sc.* wenquis); *Sc.* 6 venqueis, -ques, vinqueis, winques, 6–7 winquis, 6 vanques, -quis(e, wanqueis, -ques, -quis. *γ.* 5 vencu(s)che, -cusshe, -cuȝsche, -quys(c)he, -qwysshe, -qwissh, -quissh, -quessh, 5–6 venquysshe, -quisshe; 6 vanquy(s)she, -quyche, -quishe, -quysh, *Sc.* -quhish, 6– vanquish. *δ.* 5–6 vaynquysshe (6 vayncq-, veynq-, *Sc.* waynquysse), -quesshe, -quysh, 6 vainquish, *Sc.* wainquis. [ad. OF. *vencus* pa. pple. and *venquis* pa. t. of *veintre* (:—L. *vincĕre*), mod.F. *vaincre* to conquer, overcome; the ending was finally assimilated to that of verbs from F. stems in *-iss-*: see -ISH[2]. The *δ*-forms, however, are ad. late OF. *vainquiss-*, *vainquir*, a rare variant of *vaincre*. See also VENCUE *v.*]

1. *trans.* To overcome or defeat (an opponent or enemy) in conflict or battle; to reduce to subjection or submission by superior force.

α. *c* **1330** R. BRUNNE *Chron. Wace* (Rolls) 7396 Ȝe may me vaille To vencuse þem in pleyn bataille. **1375** BARBOUR *Bruce* I. 554 He wan throw bataill Fraunce all fre; And lucius yber wencusyt he. *a* **1400–50** *Alexander* 3122 If he be fallen vndire fote..And vencust of oure violence, quat vailis him his hestis? *c* **1425** WYNTOUN *Cron.* II. xx. 23 To vincus folk he kennit sa fast That he wes vincust at þe last. **1456** SIR G. HAYE *Law Arms* (S.T.S.) 48 Thre kingis..he vencust, all halely, and put thame to the flicht. **1533** BELLENDEN *Livy* II. xvii. (S.T.S.) I. 195 How þe equis and Wolchis war diuidit amang þame self, and vincust be romanis. *c* **1550** ROLLAND *Crt. Venus* II. 232 Diuers greit Kingis in feild he did vincus. **1596** DALRYMPLE tr. *Leslie's Hist. Scot.* I. 301 Malcolme in battell first vancuist, secundly obteynes the victorie.

β. *c* **1330** R. BRUNNE *Chron. Wace* (Rolls) 5188 He auaunted hym..He venquised þe enperour alone. *c* **1386** CHAUCER *Monk's T.* 602 For þat Nichamoure and Timothee Wiþ Iewes were venqwiste mihtile. *c* **1400** *Laud Troy Bk.* 10500 For auȝt that he myȝt do,.. Thei were put vnto flyȝt, Wenkyst foule, & discomfiȝt. *c* **1470** HENRY *Wallace* III. 241 Quhen Wallace had weyle wenquist..The fals terand that had his fadyr slayne. **1549** *Compl. Scotl.* Prol. 12 Annibal,.. beand venquest be nobil scipion, past for refuge tyl anthiocus. **1596** DALRYMPLE tr. *Leslie's Hist. Scot.* I. 339 He vanquisses the King of Norway. **1609** SKENE *Reg. Maj.* 17 Gif he quha is challenged be overcome and winquised be battel.

γ. **1382** WYCLIF *2 Sam.* x. 19 Seynge alle the kyngis..hem to be vencusshid of Yrael. *c* **1386** CHAUCER *Man of Law's T.* 194 Thurgh Hanibal, That Romayns hath venquysshed tymes thre. *c* **1430** LYDG. *Min. Poems* (Percy Soc.) 97 David that sloughe Golye,..That sloughe the bere,.. venqwysshed the lyoune. *a* **1533** LD. BERNERS *Huon* lv. 185 Yf he can vanquysshe me, then he shal delyuer to thee thy nece. **1555** EDEN *Decades* To Rdr. (Arb.) 51 The Moores or Sarasens and Iewes which..yet coulde neuer before bee cleane vanquysshed vntyll the dayes of this noble and Catholyke prince. **1593** SHAKS. *2 Hen. VI*, IV. viii. 45 Wer't not a shame,..The fearfull French, whom you late vanquished, Should make a start ore-seas and vanquish you? **1635** QUARLES *Embl.* I. ii. [To] baffle hell, And vie with those that stand, and vanquish those that fell. *a* **1727** NEWTON *Chronol. Amended* i. (1728) 96 David vanquished the Ammonites. **1791** COWPER *Iliad* III. 517 Me, Menelaus, by Minerva's aid, Hath vanquish'd now, who may hereafter him. **1849–50** ALISON *Hist. Europe* VII. xlii. §21. 105 She, vanquished but not subdued, compelled to yield to necessity, followed her timid consort. **1856** KANE *Arct. Expl.* I. xxix. 394 They gnawed her feet and nails so ferociously that we drew her up yelping and vanquished.

δ. **1474** CAXTON *Chesse* 37 For by bataylle he shall not be ouercome and vaynquysshid. *c* **1489** —— *Sonnes of Aymon* xix. 428, I am vaynquysshed & overcome wythout ony stroke. **1503–4** *Act 19 Hen. VII*, c. 34 Preamble, They were rencountered, vaynquesshed, dispersed, overcome, and dyvers put to deth. *a* **1533** LD. BERNERS *Huon* xciii. 303 Syr, thanked be god we haue vaynquysshed the Emperoure. **1565** COOPER *Thesaurus*, *Debellare*, to vainquish or ouercome by warre.

b. *fig.* To overcome by spiritual power.

c **1375** *Sc. Leg. Saints* xxviii. (*Margaret*) 34 Vertuysly scho cane vincuse þe flesch, þe warld, þe fend alsa. *c* **1380** WYCLIF *Contr. Tracts* Sel. Wks. III. 439 Þe fend haþ ben many day abowte to vencushe Cristen men bi Antecristis clerkis. *c* **1440** LYDG. *Hors, Shepe & G.* 343 Bi his meknesse he.. venquysshid hath Satan. **1483** CAXTON *Cato* B ij b, Saynt Johan sayth in the pocalyps who shal vanquysshe the world. *c* **1510** MORE *Picus* Wks. 22 He it is, by whose mighty powre, The worlde was vainquished and his prince cast out. **1560** ROLLAND *Seven Sages* 44 Than speikis he to God face to face, Quhen that the Deuill he hes vincust. **1581** BURNE in *Cath. Tract.* (S.T.S.) 118 [That] the craft..of the Deuil is vinqueist and ouercum. **1671** MILTON *P.R.* I. 175 The Son of God Now entring his great duel,..to vanquish by wisdom hellish wiles.

†**c.** To expel or banish *from* a place. *Obs.*

1536 *Pilgrym's T.* in *Thynne's Animadv.* (1875) 79 Wher this man walked, ther was no farey ner other spiritis, for his blessynges..did vanquyche them from euery buch and tre. **1601** DOLMAN *La Primaud. Fr. Acad.* (1618) 374 Conspiring the reentrie of Tarquinius race unto the Kingdome of Rome, from whence they had been vanquished for wickednes and whoredome.

2. To overcome (a person) by other than physical means. Also const. *of* (= in respect of).

c **1366** CHAUCER *A.B.C.* 8 Mercyable Quene,..Hafe mercy of my Perilous langoure, Venquist has me my cruelle aduersair. *c* **1386** —— *Pars. T.* 661 Therfore saith the wise man, if thou wolt venquisch thin enemy lerne to suffre. **1477** CAXTON *Dictes* 121 He that demaundethe but reason is able to vaynquysshe & ouercome his ennemye. *a* **1500** *Bernardus de cura rei fam.* (E.E.T.S.) 122 For he is nocht ay wen-custe with þe sworde, But oft throw lufe. *c* **1530** *Pol., Rel., & L. Poems* (1903) 58 Ofte the enmy is easelyer venquysied with seruice than with stroke of swerde. *c* **1550** ROLLAND *Crt. Venus* III. 45 Hippolyte and eik Pandora sle That with hir slicht[i]s al men dois vincous. **1671** MILTON *Samson* 235, I my self, Who vanquisht with a peal of words..Gave up my fort of silence to a Woman. **1725** W. HAMILTON *To C'tess Eglinton* 22 The Fair One,..Cur'd of her scorn, and vanquish'd of her hate. **1770** GOLDSM. *Des. Vill.* 212 In arguing too, the parson own'd his skill, For e'en though vanquish'd, he could argue still. **1848** W. H. KELLY tr. *L. Blanc's Hist. Ten Y.* II. 295 At last, M. Gerard has got the upper hand; he has vanquished his colleagues, he has vanquished the king.

†**b.** To convict *of* some offence. *Obs.*[−1]

1502 *Ord. Crysten Men* (W. de W. 1506) IV. xxi. X iiij, Whan it is so that he of that was lawfully vaynquysshed or that he hath that confessed in Iugement.

3. With impersonal object: To overcome, subdue, suppress, or put an end to (a feeling, state of things, etc.).

c **1380** WYCLIF *Wks.* (1880) 435 For treuþe mut vencusche al oþer þing. *c* **1386** CHAUCER *Frankl. T.* 46 Pacience.. venquysseth.. thynges þat rigour sholde neuere atteyne. *c* **1400** *Rom. Rose* 3546 We se ofte that humilite, Bothe ire, and also felonye Venquyssheth. **1412–20** LYDG. *Chron. Troy* I. 3284 Thenfeccioun of hir troubled eyr He hath venquesched. **1474** CAXTON *Chesse* 69 And yf thou canst not vaynquysshe thyn yre than muste thyn yre ouercome the. **1513** DOUGLAS *Æneid* I. xi. 64 The flambe of torchis vincoust the dirk nycht. **1567** *Gude & Godlie B.* (S.T.S.) 122 O God, sa gude and gracious, Lat thair. Jugeing vencust be. *a* **1601** ? MARSTON *Pasquil & Kath.* (1878) II. 154 Euen then my loue shall not be vanquished. **1621** BURTON *Anat. Mel.* I. ii. I. i. (1651) 37 If the cause be removed, the effect is likewise vanquished. **1671** MILTON *P.R.* IV. 607 By vanquishing Temptation, [thou] hast regain'd lost Paradise. **1781** COWPER *Expost.* 411 To vanquish lust, and wear its yoke no more. **1819** SHELLEY *Cenci* I. iii. 110 Till it thus vanquish shame and fear. **1833** HT. MARTINEAU *Fr. Wines & Pol.* viii. 130 Charles repeatedly vanquished his resentment at the Marquis' supercilious treatment of him.

†**b.** To excel or surpass. *Obs.*[−1]

1533 BELLENDEN *Livy* I. Prol. (S.T.S.) I. 7 New authouris ..be þare crafty eloquence traistis to vincus the rude langage of anciant authouris.

†**4.** To win or gain (a battle or other contest).

a **1400** *Sir Degrev.* 1126 Sone that douȝty undur sheld Had y-venkessyd the feld. *c* **1450** *Merlin* iii. 56 Vter venquysshed the bataile, and ther ne ascaped noon of the sarazins. **1483** CAXTON *Gold. Leg.* 111/3 Thus as he demanded he vanquysshid the batayll. *a* **1548** HALL *Chron.*, *Edw. IV* (1550) 42 A gentlemanne..did demaunde of an Englisheman, how many battailes kyng Edward had vanquished.

5. *absol.* To be victorious; to have the victory.

1382 WYCLIF *1 Sam.* xiv. 47 And whidir euer he turnede hym silf, he venkusede. **1483** CAXTON *Gold. Leg.* (1892) 846 He threwe away his swerde, and judged himself better to vaynquysshe in suffering of deth. **1568** GRAFTON *Chron.* II. 756 He shall no lesse commend his wisdome where he voyded, then his manhood where he vanquished. **1596** DALRYMPLE tr. *Leslie's Hist. Scot.* I. 349 He..sa stoutlie straik and vanquist, that a noble Victorie he obteynet. **1651** *Raleigh's Ghost* 213 When he suffered his hands to fall down, Amalek vanquished.

vanquishable ('væŋkwɪʃəb(ə)l), *a.* [f. prec. + -ABLE.] Capable of being vanquished or overcome.

1555 WATREMAN *Fardle Facions* App. 309 Ye shal be of all menne moste strong and valiaunte in fight, and vanquisheable to none enemie. **1602** MARSTON *Ant. & Mel.* II, Banisht, forlorne, despairing,..vanquishable. **1654** GAYTON *Pleas. Notes* III. iv. 87 That great Gyant..was only vanquishable by the Knights of the Well. **1736** AINSWORTH I, Vanquishable, *vincibilis, superabilis.* **1831** COLERIDGE *Table T.* 25 July, I should not have wished for a more vanquishable opponent. **1866** CARLYLE *Remin.* (1881) II. 221 In which she again proved not to be vanquishable.

vanquished ('væŋkwɪʃt), *ppl. a.* Also 5–6 *Sc.* vencust, 6 *Sc.* vincust, vanquest, -queist; 6 vanquisshed, 7 vanquisht. [f. as prec.] Defeated, overcome, subdued.

1456 SIR G. HAYE *Law Arms* (S.T.S.) 272 The vencust man..suld pay to the vencusour his costis. **1513** DOUGLAS *Æneid* I. ii. 27 Cariand to Italy Thair vincust hammald goddis and Ilion. **1589** ALEX. HUME *Poems* (S.T.S.) 54 The portrators of euerie vanquest towne, Of Cittadells [etc.]. **1671** MILTON *Samson* 281 The matchless Gideon in pursuit Of Madian and her vanquisht Kings. **1710** W. KING *Heathen Gods and Heroes* x. (1722) 41 Those [arms] which Marcus Marcellus took from the vanquish'd Viridomarus. **1781** GIBBON *Decl. & F.* xxviii. (1787) III. 103 But the victors themselves were insensibly subdued by the arts of their vanquished rivals. **1849** MACAULAY *Hist. Eng.* II. 44 This plea the King considered as the subterfuge of a vanquished disputant. **1884** *Marshall's Tennis Cuts* 266 Much more they steep The vanquished soul in sweet forgetfulness.

b. *absol.* The person or persons defeated, etc.

1555 EDEN *Decades* (Arb.) 50 Greater commoditie hath therof ensewed to the vanquisshed then the victourers. **1583** STOCKER *Civ. Warres Lowe C.* I. 38 That the victors would sacke the vanquisheds houses. **1651** HOBBES *Leviath.* II. xx. 104 It is not..the Victory, that giveth the right of Dominion over the Vanquished [etc.]. **1728** ELIZA HEYWOOD tr. *Mme. de Gomez's Belle A.* (1732) II. 67 Perhaps, if Tremouille had been the vanquish'd, he could not have behaved with the same Temper, as, being Conqueror, he did. **1810** JANE PORTER *Scottish Chiefs* lxxxv, He bade that generous prince adieu, with the full belief of soon returning to find him the vanquished of Edward. **1887** BOWEN *Æneid* II. 353 One hope only remains for the vanquished—hope to resign.

vanquisher ('væŋkwɪʃə(r)). Forms: *α.* 5 *Sc.* vencusour, 6 vanquysser, *Sc.* -quisser, venquesair, vinquiesser. *β.* 5 vaynquyssheur, -our, 6 venquesshor, vanquysher, 6– vanquisher. [f. as prec.] A conqueror, subduer.

α. **1456** [see prec.]. *a* **1533** LD. BERNERS *Huon* xv. 40 Yf it fortunyd that the vanquysser sle hes enmye. **1549** *Compl. Scot.* xvii. 149 The victoree is ioyful quhen the enemeis are venqueist vitht out domage to the venquesair. **1588** A. KING tr. *Canisius' Catech.* 8 That he mycht declair him self vinquiesser ouir death and sathan. **1596** DALRYMPLE tr.

Leslie's Hist. Scot. I. 302 A certane ȝoung man,..the principal vanquisser of Cam.

β. **1474** CAXTON *Chesse* III. vii, In suffryng hym thou shalt be his vaynquysshour. **1490** —— *Eneydos* xi. 42 God forbede that it may be sayd of Eneas,..vaynquyssheur of grete bataylles [etc.]. *a* **1513** FABYAN *Chron.* II. (1811) 20 Dunwallo..was venquesshor of yᵉ other Dukes or rulers. **1577** tr. *Bullinger's Decades* (1592) 441 The Saints..are victorers and vanquishers, howsoeuer they are oppressed. **1630** J. TAYLOR (Water P.) *Gt. Eater Kent* 11 This inuincible ale victoriously vanquished the vanquisher. **1652** KIRKMAN *Clerio & Lozia* 83 This superbe Vanquisher receiving the Trophies and the Laurels. **1724** RICHERS *Hist. Roy. Geneal. Spain* 266 The Castle of Zamora soon after surrender'd to the vanquisher. **1807** G. CHALMERS *Caledonia* I. III. vii. 400 *note*, Combats, wherein they were sometimes the vanquishers, and sometimes the vanquished. **1863** J. G. MURPHY *Comm., Gen.* xxxii. 27 The secret of his power with his friendly vanquisher.

'vanquishing, *vbl. sb.* [f. as prec.] The action of overcoming or subduing.

a **1325** *MS. Rawl. B.* 520 fol. 56 Þe coniunccion ne uailleþ noȝt, so ase þe seisede mai repelen, ne þe venquissinge ne uaileþ noȝt bote ȝif hit were aioined þoru riȝt. *c* **1475** *Rauf Coilȝear* 825 For dout of vincussing they went nocht away. **1489** *Barbour's Bruce* XVIII. 206 (E.), Quhen thai of Scotland had wittering Off Schir Eduuardis wencussing. **1611** COTGR., *Victoire*, victorie, conquest, a subduing, or vanquishing. **1736** AINSWORTH I, *Debellatio*, a vanquishing, or overthrow.

'vanquishing, *ppl. a.* [f. as prec.] That overcomes or conquers.

1611 COTGR., *Vainqueresse*, a vanquishing or victorious woman. **1886** W. J. TUCKER *E. Europe* 258 Such was the dread of his vanquishing army amongst the nations of the West.

vanquishment ('væŋkwɪʃmənt). [f. as prec.] The act of vanquishing or overcoming.

1593 NASHE *Christ's T.* Wks. (Grosart) IV. 42 The vanquishment of that vglie nest of Harpies, hath beene reserued as a worke for mee, before all beginnings. **1613–8** DANIEL *Coll. Hist. Eng.* (1626) 5 He draue Valentinian to seeke ayde of Theodosius..after the vanquishment and death of his brother. **1652** GAULE *Magastrom.* 336 This he took to be an omen or presage of the vanquishment and death of Perses. **1697** POTTER *Antiq. Greece* II. xv. (1715) 328 Appearing in time of War, it signified vanquishment, and running away. **1851** I. TAYLOR *Wesley & Methodism* 26 His conversion, taking place..by successive vanquishments. **1888** B. W. RICHARDSON *Son of Star* I. 226 The princess..had gained a reputation..for her prowess and skill in vanquishment.

†vanquissant, *a. Obs.*⁻¹ [ad. obs. F. *vainquissant*, pres. pple. of *vainquir*: see VANQUISH *v.*] Victorious.

1632 J. HAYWARD tr. *Biondi's Eromena* 195 Congratulations she received not as a woman in child-bed, but as a Captaine vanquissant of a battel.

vanrhum, obs. var. VAN DER HUM.

vansire. *Zool.* [a. F. *vansire*, formed by Buffon (1765) from the Malagasy name, given by him as *vohang-* or *voangshira* (otherwise recorded as *vontsira*).] The marsh-ichneumon (*Herpestes galera*) of South Africa.

1774 GOLDSM. *Nat. Hist.* III. ix. 362 To the ferret kind we may add an animal which Mr. Buffon calls the Vansire, the skin of which was sent him stuffed, from Madagascar. **1785** SMELLIE tr. *Buffon's Nat. Hist.* (1791) VII. 222 The vansire ..is a native of Madagascar and the interior parts of Africa. **1831** *Proc. Zool. Soc.* Apr. 57 M. Goudot has brought a small carnivorous animal, which he states to be the true vansire.

Vansittartism (væn'sɪtɑːtɪz(ə)m). [f. the name of Robert Gilbert *Vansittart* (1881–1957), English diplomat + -ISM.] The foreign policy advocated by Sir Robert (later Lord) Vansittart, *spec.* with regard to the demilitarization of Germany. Also *transf.*

1941 *Economist* 27 Dec. 778/2 It is against this background that the futility of both Vansittartism and appeasement can best be judged. **1944** D. J. ENRIGHT in *Scrutiny* Spring 103 It is a fine thing to see their books published at a time when, among the circles of the learned, a kind of Vansittartism is beginning to pervade the sphere of culture. **1967** R. C. D. JASPER *George Bell* xiv. 261 Bell..had good cause to suspect that the Government had determined upon a policy of treating all Germans alike whether they were Nazis or not. .. And it was with 'Vansittartism' in mind that he wrote a letter to *The Sunday Times* on 20 January 1941. **1978** N. ROSE *Vansittart* xii. 260 A prolonged occupation by the allied forces; the complete destruction of the German army; drastic control of German heavy industry; the total disarmament of Germany; and the re-education of the German people. This was the essence of Vansittartism.

So **Van'sittartite,** a supporter of the policy of Vansittart; also *attrib.* or as *adj.*

1942 *New Statesman* 7 Mar. 166/3 Those who were once appeasers and then Vansittartites. **1973** R. W. CLARK *Einstein* xxi. 567 His..refusal to budge from an almost Vansittartite approach to Germany.

vanston(e, southern ME. varr. FONTSTONE.

vant, southern var. FONT *sb.*¹; obs. f. VAUNT *sb.* and *v.*; obs. Sc. f. WANT *v.*

vant-, *prefix*, representing AF. *vant-*, aphetic f. *avant-* AVANT-: see VANT-BRACE, -GUARD, -WARD. In a number of compounds the *t* was elided, as VANBRACE, -CHASE, -COURIER, -GUARD, etc. Before labials the *n* by assimilation became *m*, as in VAMBRACE, VAMPEY, VAMPLATE, VAMWARD; and a further reduction appears in *vamure* VAUMURE and VAWARD. The AF. variant *vaunt-* is also very fully represented in English forms: see VAUNT-CHASE, -COURIER, etc.

vantage ('vɑːntɪdʒ, -'væn-), *sb.* Also 4–7 **vauntage,** 6 **vauntadge;** 5–6 *Sc.* **wantage,** 7–8 **'vantage.** [a. AF. *vantage* (1302), var. of OF. *avantage* ADVANTAGE *sb.* Cf. It. *vantaggio*, Sp. *ventaja*, Pg. *vantagem*.]

1. a. Advantage, benefit, profit, gain. Now *arch.*

a **1300** *Cursor M.* 8015 O þam þou sal haue gret vantage, Bath to þe and to þi barnage. *c* **1380** WYCLIF *Wks.* (1880) 302 Not of leesyng of worldliche worship ne worldliche vauntage,..but of lesyng of vertues. *c* **1440** *Promp. Parv.* 508/1 Vauntage, (*K.*, or avauntage), *profectus, proventus.* *c* **1470** HENRY *Wallace* IX. 915 This wantage was, the Scottis thaim dantyt swa, Nayn Inglisman durst fra his feris ga. **1526** *Pilgr. Perf.* (W. de W. 1531) 172 b, Repute it for your singlar vauntage & wynnynge to be exercised & tossed in dyuerse temptacyons. **1555** HOOPER in *Coverdale's Lett. Mart.* (1564) 141 Such fleshe as..had great vauntage by hys word, are become his very enemies. **1576** FLEMING *Panopl. Epist.* 72, I receyued two seuerall letters from you,..Out of which..I reaped double commoditie and vauntage. **1617** COLLINS *Def. Bp. of Ely* I. i. 72 What vantage haue you now of all that is said of Peters ship to countenance Rome? **1645** *Arraignm. Persecution* 23 Shall we that have received vantage by their rejection, thus recompence them with tyranny? [**1846** LANDOR *Exam. Shaks.* Wks. II. 266 It would give..the neighbourhood much vantage, to see these two fellows good men.]

†b. Pecuniary profit or gain. *Obs.*

c **1430** *Freemasonry* (Halliw. 1840) 149 The mayster schal not, for no vantage, Make no prentes that ys outrage. *c* **1440** *Jacob's Well* 43 Iudas was wo, þat he had noȝt þat vauntage of þo xxx. pens þat was þe tythe of þe iij. hundreth pens. **1526** TINDALE *Matt.* xxv. 27 Then at my commynge shulde I have receaved my money with vauntage. **1555** EDEN *Decades* (Arb.) 340 He became a master in makynge cardes for the sea, whereby he had great vantage. **1573** TUSSER *Husb.* (1878) 90 If one penie vantage be therein to saue, of coast man or fleming be sure to haue.

†c. A perquisite. *Obs.* (Cf. VAIL *sb.*¹ 4.)

a **1470** H. PARKER *Dives & Pauper* (W. de W. 1496) VII. xxi. 308/2 That he sholde besydes his salarye take annuell or trentalle, or ony suche other, that they calle vantages. **1481** *MS. at St. Nich. Bristol* in *Clerk's Book of 1549* (Bradshaw Soc.) 70 Hit was of old vsage that the vantage of weddyngges was longgynge to the Clerke. **1558** G. CAVENDISH *Poems* (1825) II. 52 First in the privye councell was my foundacion, And cheife secretary with all vantages and fees.

†d. *Printing.* (See quots.) *Obs.*

1683 MOXON *Mech. Exerc., Printing* 393 When a White-page or more happens in a Sheet, the Compositer calls that Vantage: So does the Press-man, when a Form of one Pull comes to the Press. [**1888** JACOBI *Printers' Vocab.* 151 *Vantage*, an old synonym for the modern one of 'fat'.]

†2. a. A greater amount *of* something. *Obs.*

1398 TREVISA *Barth. De P.R.* XIV. lii. (Tollem. MS.), Therfore þese places of heremites hauen moche noye and trauayll; neþeles it haþ a vauntage [L. *plurimum*] of commodite and reste.

†b. An additional amount or sum. *for* or *to the vantage*, in addition. *vantage of bread* (see quot. 1611). *Obs.*

1529 MORE *Suppl. Souls* Wks. 331 And yet haue we for the vauntage..the boke of yᵉ kinges, the woordes of the Prophete zacharie [etc.]. **1538** *Croscombe Ch. Ward. Acc.* (Som. Rec. Soc.) 43 R. Phelyppes for the vantage of bredde, xxiid. **1604** SHAKS. *Oth.* IV. iii. 86 Yes, [there are] a dozen [such women]; and as many to th' vantage, as would store the world they plaid for. **1611** COTGR., *Le trezain du pain*, vantage of bread; the thirteenth loafe giuen by Bakers vnto the dozen. **1617** COLLINS *Def. Bp. of Ely* II. ix. 346 Supererogation there is none, where first all is not done that ought to be done, and then a vantage too, or surplus ouer. **1639** FULLER *Holy War* IV. xiii. (1647) 191 The Popes Legate and Robert Earl of Artois..would make no bargain except Alexandria..were also cast in for vantage to make the conditions down-weight. **1706** PHILLIPS (ed. Kersey), *Vantage*, that which is given over and above just Weight and Measure; Overplus.

†c. *and (a or the) vantage, with the vantage*, and above, and (a little) more. *Obs.*

1594 *Wills & Inv. N.C.* (Surtees, 1860) 244, xxj stirkes of yeare old and vantage, 18ˡ., x stirkes, of two yeares ould and vantage, 16ˡ. **1601** HOLLAND *Pliny* I. 12 But Venus ascendeth up to her station in fifteene daies and the vantage. **1621** FLETCHER *Pilgrim* I. i, She is fifteen, with the vantage, And if she be not ready now for mannage——. *a* **1656** USSHER *Ann.* (1658) 251 Of a huge stature, and a mind answerable thereunto, for it is said, that he was five cubids high, and vantage. **1708** *Lond. Gaz.* No. 4472/4 Stoln or Stray'd.., a brown bay Gelding,..14 hands and the vantage high. **1711** —— No. 4875/4 A large kindly black Mare,..two Years old, with the Vantage. **1754** J. SHEBBEARE *Matrimony* (1766) I. 4 In plain English, she had seen One and Thirty Birth-days, and a 'Vantage, as they say in the West of England.

†d. *ellipt.* = prec. *Obs.*⁻¹

1601 *Shuttleworths' Acc.* (Chetham Soc.) 124 A litle younge styre of towe yeres old vantage.

3. a. Advantage or superiority in a contest; position or opportunity likely to give superiority; vantage-ground; a vantage-point. †*upon the vantage*, at an advantage.

1523 LD. BERNERS *Froiss.* I. xvii. 18 The archers..haue noo vauntage of hym nor of his company. **1579–80** NORTH *Plutarch, Theseus* (1595) 3 The cause why they were thus shauen before, was, for that their enemies should not haue the vauntage to take them by the hayres of the head while they were fighting. *Ibid.* 4 They which by might could haue vantage ouer others, had nothing to doe with..quiet qualities. **1596** DALRYMPLE tr. *Leslie's Hist. Scot.* I. 215 Oft thay meit [in battle]: oft thay parte with lytle vantage. **1600** HOLLAND *Livy* I. xxvii. 20 When hee thought hee had gained vantage ynough, hee mounted up the hill with all his companies. **1627** E. F. *Hist. Edw. II* (1680) 117 Knowing the weakness, he esteem'd his vantage in suffering them to land. **1634** SIR T. HERBERT *Trav.* 27 A Castle, strong, and of white chalky stone, its Ordnance planted high to play in Mounts upon the vantage. **1795** SOUTHEY *Joan of Arc* VII. 345 The exasperate knight..up the steps advanced, Like one who disregarded in his strength The enemy's vantage. **1850** BLACKIE *Æschylus* II. 160 Though close hedged in by the foe, The vantage hath been ours. **1867** TROLLOPE *Chron. Barset* I. xviii. 156 The bishop found that he would thus lose his expected vantage. **1908** L. M. MONTGOMERY *Anne of Green Gables* ii. 31 It was already quite dark, but not so dark that Mrs Rachel could not see them from her window vantage. **1969** M. BRAGG *Hired Man* viii. 83 There were halloes every few minutes and the men themselves became hunters, climbing the heights in anticipation of a vantage which would give them a total view and enable them to race down when the kill was near.

b. With defining term introduced by *of*.

1523 LD. BERNERS *Froiss.* I. cxcix 97/1 The englisshemen had the vauntage of the hyll, and helde themselfe so cloose together that none coude entre into them. **1568** GRAFTON *Chron.* II. 242 Assoone as the king and his Marshalles had ordered hys battayle, he drewe vp the sayles and came with a quarter winde to haue the vauntage of the sonne. **1626** BACON *Sylva* §599 It hath been anciently practised to burne Heath, and Ling, and Sedge, with the vantage of the Wind, upon the Ground. **1805** SCOTT *Last Minstrel* v. xviii, To each knight their care assigned Like vantage of the sun and wind. **1828** —— *F.M. Perth* v, Thou wilt have better access to drive them back, having the vantage of the house. **1855** MACAULAY *Hist. Eng.* xvi. III. 621 James..consented to retreat till he should reach some spot where he might have the vantage of ground.

c. In the phrases ***coign*** (see COIGN *sb.* 1), ***place, point*** (etc.) ***of vantage.*** So also †***dice of vantage.***

c **1570** *Misogonus* II. iv. 168 (Brandl), The preistes handes ith mustardpott; the knave, throwe at an inch, Has some dise of vauntadge, myne oth I durst take. **1805–6** CARY *Dante, Inf.* XVI. 24 Naked champions..Are wont, intent, to watch their place of hold And vantage, ere in closer strife they meet. **1832–4** DE QUINCEY *Caesars* Wks. 1860 X. 55 This adoption would have been applied..as a station of vantage for introducing him to the public favour. **1860** MOTLEY *Netherl.* xvii. (1868) II. 347 It was unfortunate that the possession of Sluys had given Alexander such a point of vantage.

†4. a. With *a* and *pl.*: An advantage; a position or state of superiority. Freq. with *at* or *for*. *Obs.*

Perh. originally a wrong division of *avantage*.

c **1450** *Merlin* xxxii. 654 Petrius..cowde well fle and returne at a vauntage, and well fight with his enmyes. *c* **1489** CAXTON *Blanchardyn* liii. 204 They chased Subyon that was horsed at a vauntage better than they were. *a* **1548** HALL *Chron., Hen. VIII*, 117 Then they issued out boldly and shot coragiously as men that shot for a vauntage. *a* **1568** in *A. Scott's Poems* (E.E.T.S.) 44 Thair is nocht ane winche þat I se Sall win ane wantage of me. **1581** J. BELL *Haddon's Answ. Osor.* 268 b, Hereupon he doth conclude as it were at a vauntage that the doctrine of these men is not onely unprofitable, but also pestiferous. **1615** W. LAWSON *Country Housew. Gard.* (1626) 32 Wee may well assure our selues, (as in all other Arts, so in this) there is a vantage and dexterity, by skill. **1642** D. ROGERS *Naaman* 263 Naaman seemed humble, when he stood at Elisha his doore, but it was for a vantage.

†b. An opportunity; a chance. *Obs.*

1592 *Soliman & Pers.* I. ii, I, watch you vauntages? Thine be it then. **1611** SHAKS. *Cymb.* I. iii. 24 When shall we heare from him. *Pisanio.* Be assur'd Madam, With his next vantage. *Ibid.* II. iii. 50 You are most bound to th' King, Who let's go by no vantages, that may Preferre you to his daughter.

5. In phrases with verbs: **a.** With personal object, as ***to catch, have, hold, take*** (one) ***at*** (†***a*** or †***the***) ***vantage.***

c **1510** *Gesta Rom.* (W. de W.) A ij, At the last she had hym at a vauntage agayne, ande was afore hym. **1581** PETTIE tr. *Guazzo's Civ. Conv.* III. (1586) 156 b, You haue taken me at a vauntage. **1590** SPENSER *F.Q.* III. vii. 51 Me seely wretch she so at vauntage caught. **1596** HARINGTON *Metam. Ajax* (1814) 12 He will take a weak man at the vantage. **1827** SOUTHEY *Hist. Penins. War* II. 123 In this sort of warfare their loss was generally greater than that of the natives, who on such occasions had them at vantage. **1857** EMERSON *Poems* 153 Complement of human kind, Holding us at vantage still.

†b. With *vantage* as object, esp. ***to take.. vantage (of).*** *Obs.* (Cf. ADVANTAGE *sb.* 5 b.)

(*a*) **1573** G. HARVEY *Letter-bk.* (Camden) 2 If the vantage had bene presently takin. *c* **1585** [R. BROWNE] *Answ. Cartwright* 23 If any will take vantage, that yet their censers were holy,..let vs consider what holines this was. **1592** MARLOWE *Massacre Paris* III. i, [He] takes his vantage on Religion, To plant the Pope and popelings in the Realme. **1622** BACON *Hen. VII*, 50 Hee thought to make his Vantage upon his Parliament.

(*b*) **1591** LYLY *Endym.* II. i, You will be sure I shall take no vantage of your words. **1600** HOLLAND *Livy* I. ii. 9 The armie of the Antemnates, taking the vantage of the time,.. entred the confines of Rome. **1624** QUARLES *Job Militant* xvi. 40, I Will take no 'vantage of thy Miserie.

6. *Lawn Tennis.* = ADVANTAGE *sb.* 2.

1884 PEILE *Lawn Tennis* 50 If he lose the next stroke (he being vantage to love), the score is again called deuce. **1897** *Outing* XXX. 467/2 Then our opponents ran to deuce, and another victory made the score vantage in our favor. **1904** J. P. PARET *Lawn Tennis* 352 *Vantage-in* (or vantage server). A term used to indicate that the server has won the 'vantage' point (opposite of 'vantage-out'). *Vantage-out* (or vantage striker) [etc.].

7. *attrib.*, as (sense 2 b) †*vantage-loaf*; (sense 3) *vantage-coign, -ditch, -nook, -place, -point*; (sense 6) *vantage-game, -set*. Also VANTAGE-GROUND.

1612 in Plomer *Abstracts fr. Wills of Eng. Printers* (1903) 45 To twelve Poore people..one penny loafe and Twoe pence a peece and the vauntage loafe to the Clerke there. 1808 SCOTT *Marm.* VI. ii, Bulwark,..bastion, tower, and vantage-coign. *a*1861 CLOUGH *Relig. Poems* ii. 85 Quick seizure and fast unrelaxing hold of vantage-place. 1865 J. H. INGRAM *Pillar of Fire* (1872) 322 Terraces, house-tops,—every vantage-point—were crowded thickly with spectators. 1885 J. H. DELL *Dawning Grey, Prefatory*, Some last vantage-ditch of wrong. 1892 *Pall Mall G.* 7 July 6/3 The Londoners equalized and made another 'vantage' set necessary. *Ibid.*, The Irishmen gained the 'vantage' game every time. 1930 BLUNDEN *Summer's Fancy* 30 The many vantage-nooks That nature sets about the wooing weald.

vantage (ˈvɑːntɪdʒ, -æ-), *v.* Also 5 vauntagyn, 6 -age. [f. prec., or ad. OF. *vantager* (Palsgr.).]

1. *trans.* To profit or benefit (one). Now only *arch.* Cf. ADVANTAGE *v.* 4.

*c*1460 *Promp. Parv.* (Winch.), Forderyn,..or vauntagyn. 1530 PALSGR. 765/1 What dothe it vauntage you to go so often over-see? 1590 SPENSER *F.Q.* I. iv. 49 Needlesse feare did neuer vantage none. 1596 *Edw. III*, II. i, Yf nothing but that losse may vantage you, I would accompt that losse my vauntage to. *a*1618 SYLVESTER *Job Triumphant* IV. 227 What will it vantage mee, What shall I gain, if I from sin be free? 1825 SCOTT *Bethrothed* xxiv, To keep him as a captive might vantage them more in many degrees, than could his death. 1891 C. E. NORTON *Dante's Purgat.* xiii. 66 What hath it vantaged thee to make of me a screen?

refl. 1581 J. BELL *Haddon's Answ. Osor.* 186 They vauntage themselves nothyng by this distinction. 1598 BARRET *Theor. Warres* I. ii. 13 Thereby to aduance and vantage himselfe.

†**2.** *intr.* To make gain or profit. *Obs.*⁻¹

1563 FOXE *A. & M.* 33/1 The commen saying of..naughty wemen, which say, they vantage more in one holy day, then in L. other daies besides.

Hence ˈ**vantaged** *ppl. a.*, †increased, augmented.

1578 BANISTER *Hist. Man* Pref. 7 That..with the testimonie of a cleare conscience, we may render our vauntaged talentes vnto the high Auditour.

†ˈ**vantageable,** *a. Obs. rare.* Also 6 vantish-. [f. prec.] Advantageous, profitable.

1570 FOXE *A. & M.* 361 b/1 These Caursinites..had their debters to them bound in such sort, as was much vantishable [1596 vantageable] to them, and much iniurious vnto the other. 1610 MARCELLINI *Tri. Jas. I*, 83 And when all this had bin done, where are then his so much vantageable profits?

ˈ**vantage-ground.** [VANTAGE *sb.* 7.] A position which places one at an advantage for defence or attack.

Freq. in 19th cent., chiefly in fig. use.

1612 BACON *Ess., Of Great Place* (Arb.) 282 That cannot be without power and place; as the vantage and commanding ground. 1625 —— *Of Truth* (Arb.) 500 No pleasure is comparable, to the standing vpon the vantage ground of Truth. 1644 WALLER in *Cal. State Papers, Dom. Ser.* (1888) 301, I moved not till I had full assurance..that the enemy was clearly gone, lest it might have been but a feint to draw me from my vantage ground. 1774 BURKE *Sp. Amer. Tax.* Wks. 1842 I. 170 But I quit the vantage ground on which I stand, and where I might leave the burthen of the proof upon him. 1817 COLERIDGE *Biog. Lit.* (Bohn) 164, I am convinced that for the human soul to prosper in rustic life a certain vantage-ground is pre-requisite. 1830 HERSCHEL *Study Nat. Phil.* II. vi. 173 A means of fresh attack with new vantage ground. 1878 MACLEAR *Celts* i. 10 Making the Greek colony of Massilia..her vantage-ground.

ˈ**vantageless,** *a.* [f. VANTAGE *sb.*] Not having any advantage or superiority.

1810 SCOTT *Lady of L.* v. xii, See here, all vantageless I stand, Arm'd like thyself with single brand.

†**vantageous,** *a. Obs.*⁻¹ [f. VANTAGE *sb.*] Bringing advantage or gain.

*c*1566 T. HACKET *Treas. Amadis* D iij, It perteineth not to suche a Lord as ye are to have and to hold any such brave and vantageous purposes with me.

†**vantation.** *Obs.*⁻¹ [app. f. *vant* VAUNT *v.*] Ostentation, display.

1637 BASTWICK *Litany* III. 20 They have..scarce a sermon in the whole University; and if there be one it tends onely to vantation, and to shew the strength of lines, which indeed breatheth nothing but vanity.

ˈ**vantbrace.** Now *arch.* or *Hist.* Forms: α. 4–5 vauntbras, 6 -brasse; 6–7 (9) vantbras, 7–8 -brass. β. 5, 7, 9 vauntbrace, 6–7, 9 vantbrace. [a. AF. *vantbras*, aphetic f. *avantbras*, f. *avant* before + *bras* arm.] = VAMBRACE.

α. 1374 *For. Acc.* 49 *Edw. III*, B, In .x. bacinettis,..iij. paribus Vauntbras et rerebras. 1412 in *Somerset Med. Wills* (1901) 60 Unum basinetum cum ventale, vauntbras, rerbras [etc.]. 1416 in *Rep. MSS. Ld. Middleton* (1911) 104 Pauns, vauntbrasses,..et quysshews. 1504–6 *Acc. Ld. High Treas. Scot.* III. 90 For iij pair vantbrases. 1520 in Ellis *Orig. Lett.* Ser. I. I. 167 The King..lokythe dayly..to receive the vauntbrasse and gauntlett. 1614 SYLVESTER *Bethulia's Rescue* VI. 254 One, for his own, his Fellow's Helm puts on: One, his right Vantbras on left arm doth don. 1671 MILTON *Samson* 1121 Then put on all thy gorgeous arms,..thy broad Habergeon, Vant-brass and Greves, and Gauntlet. 1790 *Ann. Reg., Poetry* 153 On his strong vantbrass Hacon's sword descends. 1802 JAMES *Milit. Dict.*, *Vant bras*, armour for the arm.

β. 1412–20 LYDG. *Chron. Troy* III. 87 (MS. Digby 230), þat þe sleues eke so longe be þat his vauntbrace may be cured ner. 1600 FAIRFAX *Tasso* XX. cxxxix, His shield was pierst, his vantbrace cleft and split. 1622 F. MARKHAM *Bk. War* I. x. 39 As touching the Vantbrace (which armeth from the Elbow to the hand) they are not greatly materiall in this case. *a*1649 DRUMM. OF HAWTH. *Hist. Jas. V*, Wks. (1711) 105 After many..blows to the disadvantage of their casks, corslets, and vantbraces. 1801 SCOTT *Eve St. John* iii, Yet his plate-jack was braced, and his helmet was laced, And his vaunt-brace of proof he wore. 1828 HEBER *Journ. India* II. xxv. 126 Many of the others [native horsemen of Baroda] had helmets, vant-braces, gauntlets, &c.

vant-courier, -currer (-ier, -or, -our), obs. ff. VAUNT-COURIER.

vanterie, -ery, varr. VAUNTERY *Obs.*

†**vantguard,** *sb. Obs.* Forms: α. 5–6 *Sc.* wantgard, 6–7 vantgard (6 -garde), 6–8 vantguard (6–7 -guarde). β. 5–6 vauntgarde (7 vaunte-), 6–7 vauntgard, -guard. [Aphetic f. AVANT-GUARD. Cf. VANTWARD.]

1. *Mil.* = VANGUARD 1.

α. *c*1470 HENRY *Wallace* VI. 500 Wallace him selff the wantgard he has tayne. *a*1548 HALL *Chron.* (1809) 441 Bothe the vantgardes ioyned together with suche a force that it was maruell to beholde. 1587 FLEMING *Contn. Holinshed* III. 1970/2 Being lodged in the vantgard that was gouerned by monsieur de Brissac. 1598 BARRET *Theor. Warres* III. ii. 67 The one marcheth in the vantgard, and the other in the reareward. 1648 GAGE *West Ind.* x. 40 And Tupitil and Teutecatl, very principall gentlemen, had the Vant-gard with ten thousand men. 1670 COTTON *Espernon* I. III. 133 Shewing him at the same time the Duke's Vant-Guard, which began to appear upon a little eminence hard by. 1700 CHAUNCY *Hist. Antiq. Herts.* (1826) I. 39 Who..was Captain of the Vantguard of King Edward's Army in Scotland. *a*1754 CARTE *Hist. Eng.* (1755) IV. 60 His vantguard was quartered at S. Lanfranc.

β. *c*1450 *Merlin* x. 151 Now fro hens-forth may we go vpon youre enmyes, and ther-fore devise now who shall haue the vaunt garde. 1485 CAXTON *Chas. Gt.* 232 In the vaunte garde..were xx thousand crysten men. 1568 GRAFTON *Chron.* II. 124 In kepyng this course the vauntgarde encountered with the Erle of Boleyn. 1583 STOCKER *Civ. Warres Lowe C.* III. 98 b, They first appointed seuen Ensignes for the vauntguard. 1643 R. BAKER *Chron.* 94 Fauconbridge and Blunt continue the leading of the Vauntguard. 1679 BLOUNT *Anc. Tenures* 109 By condition of service to lead the Vauntguard of the Earles Army.

b. *fig.* = VANGUARD 1 b.

1598 SYLVESTER *Du Bartas* I. vi. 39 Of all the Beasts..The Elephant the Vant-guard doth command. 1623 H. SYDENHAM *Serm. Sol. Occ.* (1637) 90 Men who make a shrewd flourish in the vant-guard of Religion. 1629 N. CARPENTER *Achitophel* I. (1640) 22 Litle can true wisdome..perswade in the Reare where wicked policie commands the Vant-guard.

2. a. A breastplate, corslet. *rare*⁻¹.

1561 DAUS tr. *Bullinger on Apoc.* (1573) 120 They had also Habergions..which is a defence for the breste, called a breste plate, or a vauntgarde.

b. (See quot.)

1611 FLORIO, *Vanguardia*,..a vantguard of a helmet, of a caske or head piece.

†**vant-guard,** *v. Obs.*⁻¹ [f. GUARD *v.* after prec.] *trans.* To defend in front.

16.. T. C. C. J. *Remedy of Love* 83 (Nares), Carthage is strong, with many a mightie tower, With broad deepe ditch, vant guarding stately wall.

van't Hoff (vænt ˈhɒf). *Chem.* Also Van't Hoff. The name of J. H. *van't Hoff* (1852–1911), Dutch chemist, used *attrib.* and in the possessive to designate rules or hypotheses put forward by him with reference to:

a. Stereochemical properties of molecules.

1888 *Jrnl. Chem. Soc.* LIV. 597 (*heading*) Investigation of the second Van't Hoff hypothesis. 1979 A. BEKNAZAROV tr. *Potapov's Stereochemistry* iv. 221 In the early thirties of our century there appeared data contradicting the van't Hoff second postulate—the assumption of free rotation about single bonds.

b. The osmotic pressure of solutes in solution.

1890 *Jrnl. Chem. Soc.* LVIII. 845 (*heading*) Deductions from Van't Hoff's theory. *Ibid.* 846 The author..discusses the determination of the value of *i* for solids in solution from Van't Hoff's equation. 1926 [see LYOTROPIC *a.* 1]. 1978 P. W. ATKINS *Physical Chem.* viii. 223 The equation simplifies into the van't Hoff equation: $\Pi V = n_iRT$. The van't Hoff equation is very suggestive of the ideal gas equation.

c. The thermodynamics of chemical reactions.

1909 H. J. H. FENTON *Outl. Chem.* I. xiii. 159 Van't Hoff's 'principle of mobile equilibrium' is an application of this rule [of le Chatelier] to the case in which the imposed constraint is an alteration of temperature. 1923 *Chem. Abstr.* XVII. 2211 This [calculation] is offered as a kinetic explanation of van't Hoff's rule that for a temp. rise of 10° the speed of a reaction is doubled. 1978 P. W. ATKINS *Physical Chem.* ix. 262 This [*sc.* the Gibbs-Helmholtz equation] immediately implies the van't Hoff equation.

¶ In Du. (rarely in Eng.) written *van 't Hoff*.

vanthoffite (væntˈhɒfaɪt). *Min.* [ad. G. *vanthoffit* (K. Kubierschky 1902, in *Sitzungsber. d. Preuss. Akad. d. Wissensch. zu Berlin* XXI. 407), f. the name of J. H. VAN'T HOFF, who first synthesized the compound: see -ITE¹.]

A sulphate of sodium and magnesium, $Na_6Mg(SO_4)_4$, found as colourless, grey, or pale yellow monoclinic crystals that are transparent with a vitreous lustre and occur esp. in oceanic salt deposits.

1902 *Jrnl. Chem. Soc.* LXXXII. II. 406 The following salts are present in the mixture:..$3Na_2SO_4$, $MgSO_4$, to which the name *vanthoffite* is given. 1966 *Prof. Papers U.S. Geol. Survey* No. 550-B. 125/1 The halite rock in which the double sulfate minerals occur is medium to coarse grained...Loewite, vanthoffite, bloedite, and leonite are constituents of the ore zones.

vantishable, variant of VANTAGEABLE *a. Obs.*

vantmure, var. VAUNTMURE *Obs.*

vanton, -toun, obs. Sc. ff. WANTON *a.*

vantose, obs. var. VENTOSE *sb.*

vantour, obs. form of VAUNTER.

vantparlar, -er, etc., varr. VAUNTPARLER.

vantplate, obs. form of VAMPLATE.

vantrauth, variant of WANTROTH *Obs.*

†ˈ**vantward.** *Obs.* Also 3 vantwarde, 4–5 vauntward(e. [Aphetic form of AVANTWARD; cf. VANTGUARD. See also VANWARD *sb.*, and VAMWARD, VAWARD.] The vanguard of an army.

1297 R. GLOUC. (Rolls) 7478 Hor vantwarde was to broke, þat me miȝte wiþinne hom wende. *Ibid.* 9006 Þe vantwardes hom mette verst, as riȝt was to done. 1377 LANGL. *P. Pl.* B. xx. 94 Elde þe hore he was in þe vauntwarde, And bare þe banere bifor deth, by riȝte he it claymed. *c*1450 *Contin. Brut* II. (1908) 320 Sere Bertram Cleykyn, þat was..chyueteyn of þe vauntward of þe bataill. 1480 CAXTON *Chron. Eng.* VIII. xiii, He sette..the duc of York in the vauntward. 1557 *K. Arthur* (Copland) I. xv, Lyonses and Phariaunce had the vaunt warde. 1610 HOLLAND *Camden's Brit.* I. 794 They marched forth in the Vantward: they returned home in the Rereward.

Vanuatuan (vænwɑˈtuːən), *a.* [f. *Vanuatu* + -AN.] Of or pertaining to the Vanuatu Republic (formerly the Condominium of the New Hebrides) or any of its constituent islands.

1980 *Sunday Times* 24 Aug. 1/1 Two British soldiers of the joint military force withdrawn from the rebel Vanuatuan island of Espiritu Santo on Monday have been charged with looting. 1983 *Defense & Foreign Affairs Weekly* 28 Mar. 4 Within an hour of hoisting its flag, the Vanuatuan naval ship was being 'peaceably escorted' out of the area.

†ˈ**vanward,** *sb. Obs.* In 5 van-, 6 vawnewarde. [Reduced form of VANTWARD: cf. VANGUARD. See also VAWARD.] = VANTWARD.

In reprints of 16th cent. works *vanward* is sometimes substituted for *vauward* VAWARD, and the latter is perh. the correct reading of the MS. in quot. 1476.

1476 *Paston Lett.* III. 162 The Swechys..hathe slayne the most parte off hys vanwarde. *a*1513 FABYAN *Chron.* VI. (1516) 105 b/1 He than sette forthe his wayе; commaundynge his vawnewarde to kepe their iourney towarde Paris.

ˈ**vanward,** *a.* [f. VAN *sb.*²] Situated, having place or position, in the van or front.

1820 KEATS *Hyperion* I. 39 As if the vanward clouds of evil days Had spent their malice. 1823 DE QUINCEY *Lett. Educ.* iv. (1860) 77 Its vanward and its rearward man. 1877 PATMORE *Unknown Eros* 41 Until the vanward billows feel The agitating shallows. 1896 *Edin. Rev.* July 151 The horizon became darkened with the vanward clouds of evil days.

ˈ**vanward,** *adv.* [f. as prec.] Towards or in the front; forward. Also with *to*.

1827 HOOD *Mids. Fairies* xlvi, Then next a merry Woodsman, clad in green, Stept vanward from his mates. 1838 J. P. KENNEDY *Rob of the Bowl* ii, Vanward the same kind of enclosures..shut in a grassy court. 1888 LOWELL *Heartsease & Rue* 56 Whose brave example still to vanward shines.

vapid (ˈvæpɪd), *a.* Also 7 vappid. [ad. L. *vapid-us* savourless, insipid. Cf. obs. F. *vapide* (Cotgr.).]

1. Of liquors, beverages, etc.: Devoid of briskness; failing to produce an agreeable effect on the palate; flat, insipid.

1656 BLOUNT *Glossogr.*, *Vapid*, that gives an ill smack, that casts a vapour or ill savour, stinking. 1669 W. SIMPSON *Hydrol. Chym.* 116 A sourish, saltish, and..vapid liquor. 1676 GREW *Anat. Pl.*, *Anat. Fl.* (1682) 158 Now the Liquors, in which these are generated, do always..lose their Tast and Smell, and so become Vapid. 1707 MORTIMER *Husb.* xx. 585 Then away goes the brisk and pleasant Spirits and leave a vapid or sour Drink. 1756 C. LUCAS *Ess. Waters* II. 208 It somewhat resembled vapid French white wine. 1788 MME. D'ARBLAY *Diary* 24 July, He..made his own cold tea, and drank it weak and vapid. 1823 J. BADCOCK *Dom. Amusem.* 47 Vapid, old and worn out trees, producing vapid fruit. 1864 SALA in *Daily Tel.* 1 Nov., So are bottled mineral waters the vapidest of beverages.

fig. 1783 LD. BRISTOL A. Young *Autobiogr.* (1898) vi. 118 When you are *vapid*, if ever those *pétillant* spirits of yours are so, come and imbibe some..air at the Downhill. 1848 DICKENS *Dombey* xiii, Such vapid and flat daylight as filtered through the ground-glass windows.

b. Said of taste or flavour.

1677 GREW *Anat. Pl.* (1682) 280 A soft Taste, is either Vapid, as in Watery Bodies, Whites of Eggs, Starch,..Or Unctuous, as in Oyls, Fat, &c. 1826 *Art of Brewing* (ed. 2) 32 It gives to the beer a vapid disagreeable flavour. 1837 M. DONOVAN *Dom. Econ.* II. 337 The exhilarating effect is produced at the sacrifice of fine flavour, and with the introduction of vapid bitterness. **1859** W. S. COLEMAN *Woodlands* (1866) 118 The tempting appearance of which, however, is not borne out by their flavour, which is mawkish and vapid.

c. *Med.* Of blood: Devoid of strength or vigour; weak, inert.

1684 tr. *Bonet's Merc. Compit.* XIV. 495 In such Diseases the whole mass of Blood..is otherwise grown vappid as it were. **1744** BERKELEY *Siris* §52 Softening and enriching the sharp and vapid blood. **1834** *Good's Study Med.* (ed. 4) I. 563 *note*, Dr. Stevens thinks that the blood first loses its solid parts, and becomes thin, that it then becomes deprived of its saline principles, and turns black and vapid.

d. Of flowers: Scentless. *rare*$^{-1}$.

c **1750** SHENSTONE *Rural Elegance* 235 To rear some breathless vapid flow'rs.

2. *fig.* Devoid of animation, zest, or interest; dull, flat, lifeless, insipid: **a.** Of talk, discourse, writings, etc.

1758 JOHNSON *Idler* No. 34 ¶8 Conversation would become dull and vapid. *a* **1763** SHENSTONE *Ess.* Wks. 1765 II. 204 Vapid frivolous chit-chat serves to pass away the time. **1799** *Monthly Rev.* XXX. 211 The minute ceremonials and vapid common-place of the German theatre. **1822** HAZLITT *Table-T.* Ser. II. i, The news of the morning become stale and vapid by the dinner-hour. **1865** H. PHILLIPS *Amer. Paper Curr.* II. 112 The newspapers contained as usual vapid and lengthy essays. **1885** *Manch. Exam.* 11 Feb. 4/7 There is..a great deal of vapid declamation on this subject, but it will soon die out.

b. Of amusements, pleasures, etc.

1790 BURKE *Fr. Rev.* 16 This town..begins to grow satiated with the uniform round of its vapid dissipations. **1799** HAN. MORE *Fem. Educ.* (ed. 4) I. 98 A sophisticated little creature, nursed in these forced, and costly, and vapid pleasures. **1825–9** MRS. SHERWOOD *Lady of Manor* IV. xxviii. 399 One continued round of vapid amusements, some of which are too light and trifling even to amuse a child at a common fete. **1877** MRS. FORRESTER *Mignon* I. i, Mrs. Stratheden's 'At Homes' are very different from the general run of those vapid and dreary entertainments.

c. Of persons or places.

1784 COWPER *Task* I. 393 The languid eye, the..wither'd muscle, and the vapid soul, Reproach their owner. **1824** W. IRVING *T. Trav.* I. 197, I grew so dull, and vapid, and genteel. **1839** [MRS. MAITLAND] *Lett. fr. Madras* (1843) 272 Masulipatam was an ugly place;..nothing to be seen but wide sandy roads,..altogether, a most vapid sort of place. **1873** C. M. DAVIES *Unorth. Lond.* (1876) 119 The adoption of the most vapid young lady's perversion of her mother-tongue.

d. In miscellaneous contexts.

1796 MME. D'ARBLAY *Camilla* I. 236 A scheme of human happiness, which no time, no repetition can make vapid to a feeling heart. **1818** HAZLITT *Table-T., On Vulg. & Affect.*, It is a vapid assumption of superiority. **1847** DISRAELI *Tancred* II. vii, A smile is..in general vapid. **1861** WHYTE MELVILLE *Market Harb.* 10 The vapid demeanour and cool assurance which triumph in a ball-room. **1874** H. R. REYNOLDS *John Bapt.* viii. 515 If these pernicious views..be entertained..the renewal of humanity [is] a vapid and foolish dream.

†**3.** Of a damp or steamy character; dank; vaporous. *Obs.*

1660 BOYLE *New Exp. Phys. Mech.* xxii. 169 A vapid Air, or Water rarified into vapor, may..emulate the elastical power of..true Air. **1677** PLOT *Oxfordsh.* 18 Few (if any) vappid and stinking Exhalations can ascend from them to corrupt the Air. **1690** LEYBOURN *Curs. Math.* 449, Rheita affirms, that he observed Jupiter to be invested round with a vapid Atmosphere.

Hence **'vapidism.** *rare*$^{-1}$.

1831 CARLYLE *Schiller* in *Fraser's Mag.* III. 130 All critical guild-brethren now working diligently..in the calmer sphere of Vapidism or even Nullism.

vapidity (və'pɪdɪtɪ). [f. prec. + -ITY.]

1. The fact or quality of being vapid.

1721 BAILEY, *Vapidity*, deadness, flatness, a being palled. **1771** BURKE *Corr.* (1844) I. 256 After a violent ferment in the nation, as remarkable a deadness and vapidity has succeeded. **1822** *Examiner* 347/1 [It] threw such a gloom and vapidity over all that we never saw the beautiful opera with so little pleasure. **1863** COWDEN CLARKE *Shaks. Char.* xx. 507 Master Froth strays from the right path from sheer vapidity. **1879** FARRAR *St. Paul* II. 536 *note*, Surely such passages as these ought to be more than adequate to defend the Pastoral Epistles from the charge of vapidity.

2. A vapid remark, idea, feature, etc.

1848 *Blackw. Mag.* LXIII. 266 Their pet historian..cannot make a single speech without dragging in..some vapidity about the Revolution Settlement. **1877** C. GEIKIE *Christ* lv. (1879) 665 Teaching..so searching and practical, compared with the vapidities of the Rabbis. **1889** *Pall Mall G.* 11 May 7 Those upon whom the crudities and vapidities of the 'commission' portraits..jar.

vapidly ('væpɪdlɪ), *adv.* [f. as prec. + -LY^2.] In a vapid manner.

1847 in WEBSTER. **1880** 'OUIDA' *Moths* xx, She seemed to herself so useless, so stupidly, vapidly, frivolously useless. **1888** *Times* 24 Sept. 9/5 If they were become simply unintelligible or vapidly dull, the wonder would be less.

vapidness ('væpɪdnɪs). [f. as prec. + -NESS.] = Vapidity.

1727 BAILEY, *Vapidness*, deadness, flatness, palledness of liquors. **1820** KEATS in Rossetti *Life* (1887) 142 When once a person has smoked the vapidness of the routine of society. **1825–9** MRS. SHERWOOD *Lady of Manor* IV. xxviii. 392 The vapidness,..the languor and vexation, which accompany the life of an unconverted man. **1907** *Daily Chron.* 12 Nov. 3/5 Her work..in one or two instances sinks into vapidness.

va'pography. [Irreg. f. VAPOUR *sb.*: cf. VAPOROGRAPH.] (See quot.)

1898 *Pop. Sci. Monthly* LIII. 860 The phenomena of normal physical emanations from certain substances which have the property of influencing the sensitive plate. These phenomena have been variously labeled scotography, vapography, etc.

vapon, obs. Sc. form of WEAPON.

vapor, variant of VAPOUR.

vapora'bility. Also vapour-. [f. next.] Capacity of being vaporized.

a **1835** MCCULLOCH *Attributes* xlv. (1837) III. 184 The fluidity which its own singular nature communicates and..the vapourability dependent on that.

vaporable ('veɪpərəb(ə)l), *a.* Also 4 vapour(e)-. [ad. med.L. *vapōrābilis*: see VAPOUR *sb.* and -ABLE. Cf. OF. *vaporable*.]

1. Capable of being converted into vapour.

1398 TREVISA *Barth. De P.R.* XI. iv. (Bodl. MS.), Heete of henen..drawiþ it silfe to fulle sotellich vaporable parties of water and of erþe. **1555** EDEN *Decades* (Arb.) 357 Eyther it is not of vaporable nature, or to be of smaule quantitie. **1676** *Phil. Trans.* XI. 614 The first Beings of Embrions of mineral salts are nothing but vapours, or juices not concreted, totally vaporable. **1681** *Phil. Collect.* XII. 89 By reason of the fumes Lead usually emits, being a quick vaporable Metal. **1857** GOSSE *Omphalos* xii. 355 There would be no deposition from atmosphere if the water had not first been carried up by evaporation; and the vaporable fluid is obtained from the moistened soil. **1893** *Pall Mall G.* 12 Jan. 3/3 The vaporable parts ascending to the clear ether of heaven.

†**2.** Capable of converting substances into vapour. *Obs.*

1398 TREVISA *Barth. De P.R.* XIX. xi. (Bodl. MS.), White comeþ of vapoureable aier & watry þat is in þe membres..for white comeþ of hote aier & vaporable bestes beþ white vnder þe wombe. **1456** SIR G. HAYE *Gov. Princes* Wks. (S.T.S.) II. 118 The nature is mare vaporable and of better digestioun to corrump and bray the metis.

†**'vaporary,** *sb.* [ad. mod.L. *vaporarium*, f. L. *vapor* vapour. Cf. L. *vapōrārium* a steam-pipe in a bath.] A medical preparation used in a form of vapour-bath.

1657 TOMLINSON *Renou's Disp.* 187 A vaporary consists of the same things a semicupium is made of. **1661** LOVELL *Hist. Anim. & Min.* 504 Of a Vaporarie:..fiat decoctio..cujus vaporem excipiat. **1678** PHILLIPS (ed. 4), *Vaporary*, a Decoction of Herbs, and other ingredients, the fume whereof ascends through the hole of a Chair where the patient sits. [Hence in later edd. and other Dicts. The additional definition in Bailey (1721-) 'a stove, stew, hot-house or bagnio' follows Kersey (1706) s.v. *Vaporarium*.]

†**'vaporary,** *a. Obs.*$^{-1}$ [f. as prec.: see -ARY.] (See quot.)

1653 R. G. tr. *Bacon's Hist. Winds* 94 Let us see what may be said concerning Vaporary windes (we mean such as are engendred by vapours).

†**'vaporate,** *ppl. a. Obs.*$^{-1}$ [ad. L. *vapōrāt-us*, pa. pple. of *vapōrāre*: see next.] Vaporized.

1655 STANLEY *Hist. Philos.* (1687) 552/2 Smelling judgeth of Odors, good and ill,..putrid, humid, liquid, vaporate.

†**'vaporate,** *v. Obs.* Also 7 vapourate. [f. L. *vapōrāt-*, ppl. stem of *vapōrāre* to convert into, to become, vapour.]

1. *trans.* **a.** To convert into vapour, to vaporize.

1611 FLORIO, *Vaporabile*,..that may be vaporated.

b. To emit as a vapour.

a **1640** J. BALL *Power Godlines* (1657) 119 A boyling Sea, or Sepulchre of corruption, steeming and vaporating up continually a world of..ill-disposed imaginations. **1648** HEXHAM II, *Swademen*, to Exhale, or, to Vapourate.

2. *intr.* **a.** To rise in or as vapour.

1620 VENNER *Via Recta* vii. 111 They repress and infrigidate the hot fumes that vaporate to the head. **1643** A. ROSS *Mel Helic.* 168 If Musk, Perfume, or rosed air, Or Balm could vaporate from thee.

b. To give off vapour.

1623 COCKERAM I, *Vaporate*, to cast forth vapours.

†**vapo'ration.** *Obs.* Also 4–6 -acion, 6 -acyon, 5 vapouracioun. [ad. L. *vapōrātio*, n. of action f. *vapōrāre*: see prec. Cf. Sp. *vaporacion*, It. *-azione*.] The action of vaporizing; conversion into, production of, vapour.

1398 TREVISA *Barth. De P.R.* XIII. xxi. (Bodl. MS.), Also of vaporacion of fumosite þat he [*sc.* the sea] casteþ vpward and bredeþ myste and cloudes. **1456** SIR G. HAYE *Gov. Princes* Wks. (S.T.S.) II. 118 Tendar metis of licht and sone degestioun, and delicious thingis and of sutil vapouracioun moystis. **1528** PAYNELL *Salerne's Regim.* d ij b, Blud lettyng ..minisheth vaporation that gothe to the heed & troublethe the wyttis. **1561** HOLLYBUSH *Hom. Apoth.* 35 Make a vaporacion beneth with Rammes greace, or fat, waxe, pitche and cumin. **1623** COCKERAM I, *Vaporation*, a casting forth of vapours. **1651** FRENCH *Distill.* i. 9 It may be done..by Coroeion, By Fumigation or Vaporation. **1720** S. PARKER *Bibliotheca Biblica* I. 438 By Conflagration, and Congelation,..by Vaporation, and Evaporation: by Sublimation, and Precipitation.

†**vaporative,** *a. Obs.* Also 5 -atife, -atyf. [ad. med.L. *vapōrātīv-us*: see VAPORATE *v.*]

1. = VAPORABLE *a.*

1398 TREVISA *Barth. De P.R.* XVI. iii. (Bodl. MS.), Þinge þat is vnctuous haþ moisture in hit self, & so for bicause of þe partie þat is vaporatife hit may renne and be ymade hard bi heete. **1594** PLAT *Jewell-ho.* I. 24 The generative water became congealed, and the vaporative water passed away. **1612** WOODALL *Surg. Mate* Wks. (1653) 21* The better to receive with effect the dry or vaporative medicine.

2. Productive of vapour.

1568 SKEYNE *The Pest* (1860) 11 Quhair the ground is fat and Vaporatiue.

†**vaporatory,** *a. Obs.*$^{-1}$ In 7 vapour-. [Cf. prec. and -ATORY.] Consisting of vapour.

1683 *Weekly Mem.* 65 Amongst other things to sit in a vapouratory bath for some weeks.

vapo'rescence. *rare*$^{-1}$. [f. L. *vapōr-* vapour: see -ESCENCE.] The fact of becoming vaporous. Also **vapo'rescent** *a.*, vaporizing. (In quots. *fig.*)

1843 RUSKIN *Mod. Paint.* I. II. i. §21. 393 It is by this kind of vaporescence, so to speak, by this flat misty unison of parts, that nature [etc.]. **1872** —— *Munera P.* 47 Their vaporescent point, at which riches..'make to themselves wings'.

vaporetto (væpɒ'rɛtəʊ). Pl. -etti, -ettos. [It., dim. *vapore* f. L. *vapor* steam.] In Venice, a canal motor-boat (orig. steamboat), used as a form of public transport.

1926 C. BEATON *Diary* 25 Aug. in *Wandering Years* (1961) v. 121 We set off blindly, taking the *vaporetto*. **1941** W. GRAHAM *Night Journey* v. 62, I can catch a vaporetto from the Quay. **1956** R. MACAULAY *Towers of Trebizond* xxiv. 278, I remember it when there was nothing on the canals but gondolas, none of those horrid steamers and vaporetti. **1963** *Economist* 6 Apr. 37/1 The tourists..prefer the speed of the municipally-owned vaporettos to the romance of the older hand-driven craft [*sc.* gondolas]. **1977** *Time* 28 Nov. 30/3 Other names..soon became household words at the staid Café Florian, on every *vaporetto* water bus and in the intellectual salons of the Salute island. **1984** *New Yorker* 23 Apr. 92/3 As soon as I got off the *vaporetto*, I felt that this was where I should be.

vapo'riferous, *a.* *rare*$^{-0}$. [f. L. *vapōrifer* emitting, full of vapour + -OUS.] 'That makes or stirs up vapours' (Blount, 1656).

vaporific (veɪpə'rɪfɪk), *a.* [ad. mod.L. *vaporificus*, f. L. *vapōri-* VAPOUR *sb.*: see -FIC.]

1. Associated or connected with, producing or causing, vaporization.

1781 *Phil. Trans.* LXXI. 482 The melting, the vaporific, and shining points. **1794** G. ADAMS *Nat. & Exp. Philos.* I. ix. 375 Either in their condensed state of water, or in the state of vaporific expansion. **1799** *Phil. Mag.* III. 419 A great quantity of vaporific,..or, as it is called, latent heat. **1861** BUCKLE *Civiliz.* II. vi. 496 *note*, The statement by Dr. Thomson refers to the completion, or last stage, of the discovery, namely the vaporific combination of heat. **1886** *Daily Tel.* 8 April (Cassell's), It is the product of vaporific sublimation.

2. Vaporous.

1797 *Phil. Trans.* LXXXVII. 171 There is exhaled from it a subtile fluid in a vaporific state. **1800** tr. *Lagrange's Chem.* I. 164 During this dry slaking heat is excited, by the moisture losing its vaporific form.

fig. **1847** CARLYLE *Misc.* III. 380 With the earliest spring he has come in person,..vaporific, driven by his fixed idea.

va'poriform, *a.* [f. L. *vapōri-*, stem of *vapor* VAPOUR *sb.*: see -FORM.] Vaporous.

1860 *Ure's Dict. Arts*, etc. (ed. 5) III. 750 Steam is water in its vaporiform state. **1876** PAGE *Adv. Text-bk. Geol.* i. 36 Rock-matter in a state of vaporiform incandescence.

vapo'rimeter. [f. as prec. + -METER.] An instrument for measuring the amount of vapour.

1878 *Ure's Dict. Arts.* etc. IV. 565 The alcohol [is] determined..by Geissler's vaporimeter. **1899** tr. *Jaksch's Clin. Diagnosis* (ed. 4) vii. 355 Parlato employs the vaporimeter for the purpose.

vaporish, variant of VAPOURISH *a.*

vaporizable ('veɪpəraɪzəb(ə)l), *a.* [f. VAPORIZE *v.*] Capable of being vaporized; vaporable.

1823 J. BADCOCK *Dom. Amusem.* 108 Lead not being vaporizable, remains behind. **1848** HERSCHEL *Ess.* (1857) 343 There is probably no vaporizable body of which the atmosphere does not contain some trace. **1881** LE CONTE *Sight* 13 Unless a body is volatile or vaporizable it cannot be smelled.

vaporization (veɪpəraɪ'zeɪʃən). Also vapour-. [f. next + -ATION. Cf. F. *vaporisation*.] The action or process of converting, or of being converted, into vapour.

α. **1799** *Monthly Rev.* XXX. 560 The metal becomes oxydated during the vaporization of the sulphur. **1807** DAVY in *Phil. Trans.* XCVIII. 12 It combines with oxygene..without flame at all temperatures that I have tried below that of its vaporization. **1863** TYNDALL *Heat* xii. 442 The sun by the act of vaporisation lifts mechanically all the moisture of our air. **1878** HAMILTON *Nerv. Dis.* 38 The bichloride was necessarily discontinued, and mercurial vaporization substituted.

β. **1826** *Encycl. Metrop.* (1845) IV. 246/2 Evaporation and true Vapourisation of fluids at their boiling point. **1839** R. S. ROBINSON *Naut. Steam Eng.* 13 It is one of the most curious and important phenomena attending vapourization. **1854** RONALDS & RICHARDSON *Chem. Technol.* (ed. 2) I. 253 Application of Fuel to Vapourization.

vaporize ('veɪpəraɪz), *v.* Also 9 vapour-. [f. L. *vapōr-* VAPOUR *sb.* + -IZE. Cf. F. *vaporiser*.]

1. *trans.* To convert into smoke. *rare*$^{-1}$.

1634 SIR T. HERBERT *Trav.* 119 *marg. note*, Forty load of Tobacco vaporized.

2. To convert into vapour.

α. **1803** *Phil. Trans.* XCIII. 26 The reguline zinc, vaporized by the heat, rises from the crucible as a metallic gas. **1849** R. V. DIXON *Heat* I. 193 The vapour was projected..with a loud, whistling noise, which subsided when the liquid was all vaporised. **1878** MISS J. J. YOUNG *Ceramic Art* 81 The heat vaporizes the salt, and..the chlorine escapes.

β. **1836** SMART, *To vapourize.* **1884** J. BURROUGHS *Locusts & Wild H.* 110 The hot air vapourising the drops.

b. In fig. use.

1831 CARLYLE *Sart. Res.* II. vi, In figurative language, we might say he becomes..spiritualised, vaporised. **1866** FELTON *Anc. & Mod. Gr.* I. x. 175 They have not only vaporized her husband into a myth, but have consolidated a myth into a lover. **1888** DOWLING *Miracle Gold* III. xxvii. 15 The family estates and honours had been vapourized before that last of the Poniatowskis fell under Napoleon.

3. *intr.* To become vaporous.

1828-32 WEBSTER, *Vaporize*,..to pass off in vapour. **1855** SCOFFERN in *Orr's Circ. Sci., Elem. Chem.* 458 Zinc does not vapourize until the heat is raised to whiteness. **1872** *Athenæum* 20 Jan. 84/2 Faraday..stated..that mercury ceased to vapourize below the freezing-point. **1881** TYNDALL *Ess. Floating Matter Air* 196 The liquid within the narrow tube vaporizes.

fig. **1892** *Black & White* 2 Apr. 423/1 Money seems somehow to have vaporised away, and none knows anything about it.

4. *trans.* To spray with fine particles of liquid.

1900 O. ONIONS *Compl. Bachelor* v. 51 My hostess.. vapourised me in passing with a tiny scent fountain.

Hence **'vaporized** *ppl. a.*; **'vaporizing** *vbl. sb.* (also *attrib.*).

1839 URE *Dict. Arts* 823 Chambers into which the *vaporized substances are deposited. **1880** HAUGHTON *Phys. Geogr.* iii. 124 We must reduce the vaporised water capable of producing rain. **1888** *Daily News* 15 May 6/2 Small launches..propelled by means of vapourised spirit. **1831-3** *Encycl. Metrop.* (1845) VIII. 189/1 The valve before described, attached to the *vaporizing apparatus. **1875** KNIGHT *Dict. Mech.* 2690/2 *Vaporizing stove*, one for furnishing steam to dampen the air of apartments, conservatories, etc. **1886** *Jrnl. Education* 1 Aug. 325 Without this all theorising is empty vapourising. **1896** *Daily News* 15 July 8/4 The vaporising and condensing of ammonia.

vaporizer ('veɪpəraɪzə(r)). [f. prec.] A device or apparatus by which conversion into vapour is accomplished.

1846 in WORCESTER. **1862** *London Soc.* I. 223 Mixed with the odours of Rimmel's patent Vaporiser. **1887** *Pall Mall G.* 2 Nov. 6/1 The apparatus acts..as a vaporizer and steam generator. **1896** *Cosmopolitan* XX. 420/2 In order to start the engine a lamp is used for a few minutes to heat the vaporizer.

'vaporograph. [Irreg. f. L. *vapōr-* VAPOUR *sb.* + -GRAPH. Cf. VAPOURGRAPH.] A picture produced by vapography. Hence **vaporo'graphic** *a.*

1903 *Month* Feb. 171 Some sort of 'vaporographs' may be obtained by his methods or others that are analogous. *Ibid.* 166 The 'vaporographic' theory explaining the origin of this impression.

†**vapo'rose,** *a. Obs. rare.* [ad. L. *vapōrōs-us*, f. *vapor* VAPOUR *sb.*] Vaporous; easily vaporizing.

c **1400** *Lanfranc's Cirurg.* 16 (Addit. MS.), Woundes mowe noȝt ben y-dryȝed in a moyste eyre & a vaporose. **1661** LOVELL *Hist. Anim. & Min.* 338 The apoplexy,..if vaporose, [is cured] by abstinence, preparants,..and friction. **1731** ARBUTHNOT *Aliments* VI. vii. (1735) 204 Therefore in fat People the Use of vaporose or perspirable Food, and Exercise..are proper.

vapo'rosity. *rare.* [Cf. prec. and -ITY.] Vaporous quality or qualities.

1528 PAYNELL *Salerne's Regim.* Y iiij b, Garlyke..hurteth the eies, through it sharpenes and vaporosite. **1837** *New Monthly Mag.* XLIX. 2 As wet-paperish as St. Swithin himself, with all his *sirocco* vaporosity about him. **1837** CARLYLE *Misc. Ess., Diamond Neckl.*, He is here with his fixed-idea and volcanic vaporosity.

vaporo-sul'phureous, *a. rare*⁻¹. [Cf. VAPOROGRAPH.] Of a vaporous and sulphurous nature.

1676 *Phil. Trans.* II. 619 There are found Earths impregnated with this acid matter, being vaporo-sulphureous.

vaporous ('veɪpərəs), *a.* Also 6 **vaporouse, vaperous,** 7 **vap'rous,** 9 **vaprous;** 7-9 **vapourous.** [f. L. *vapōr-us* or ad. L. *vapōrōs-us*, f. *vapor* VAPOUR *sb.* Cf. F. *vaporeux*, It., Sp., Pg. *vaporoso*.]

†**1.** Of a bath: Consisting or composed of vapour. *Obs.* (Cf. VAPOUR-BATH.)

1527 ANDREW *Brunswyke's Distyll. Waters* P iij, Also Escume made of this herbe used in vaperous bathes dystroyeth age. **1631** JORDEN *Nat. Bathes* i. (1669) 2 These kind of watry and vaporous Bathes have been in use from all antiquity. **1706** PHILLIPS (ed. Kersey), *Balneum Vaporosum*, the Vapourous Bath, is when the Vessel that contains the Matter..is heated by the Vapours, or Steams that arise from the hot or boiling Water.

2. Emitting or exhaling vapour; †*spec.* of food in the stomach.

1544 PHAER *Regim. Lyfe* (1553) B ij b, The pacyente oughte..to forbeare all vaporous meates, as garlyke, onyons [etc.]. **1584** COGAN *Haven Health* ccxli. (1636) 269 Such things as bee most vaporous do most dispose us to sleepe. **1600** SURFLET *Countrie Farme* VI. xxii. 799 The wine is a claret,..of a thinne substance, not fuming or being vaporous. **1620** VENNER *Via Recta* viii. 181, I aduise all such ..to sup..on rosted meats, because they are lesse vaporous. **1655** MOUFET & BENNET *Health's Improv.* (1746) 392 To settle their Meat to the Bottom of their Stomach, that it may prove less vaporous to the Head. **1710** T. FULLER *Pharm. Extemp.* 20 Scorbutic Ale..restraineth the Ebullition..of the Vapourous Blood. **1731** ARBUTHNOT *Aliments* V. iv. (1735) 139 Aliment too vapourous or perspirable, will subject it to the Inconveniencies of too strong a Perspiration.

†**b.** Of the eyes: Moist with tears. *Obs.*⁻¹

1583 MELBANCKE *Philotimus* O iv b, He..at last met by chaunce with a sorcerer, to whom deploring with vaporous eyes his burdenous taske [*printed* burdurus taste] (etc.).

3. Filled with, thick or dim with, vapour; foggy, misty.

1593 SHAKS. *Lucr.* 771 O hatefull, vaporous, and foggy night,..Muster thy mists to meete the Easterne light. **1603** HOLLAND *Plutarch's Mor.* 998 Considering that mists, fogs and clouds are no congealations, but onely gatherings and thickenings of a moist and vapourous aire. **1620** VENNER *Via Recta* Introd. 5 There the aire is..seldome infected with vaporous blasts. **1665** *Phil. Trans.* I. 67 Through the Gross and Vaporous Air near the Earth. **1709** T. ROBINSON *Nat. Hist. Westmoreld.* ii. 16 The magnetick Attraction of this Ætherial Spirit of Cold, which governs the humid and vaporous Atmosphere. **1818** SHELLEY *Euganean Hills* 92 The waveless plain of Lombardy, Bounded by the vaporous air. *a* **1864** HAWTHORNE *Mother Rigby's Pipe* i, The small cottage became all vaporous. **1869** J. PHILLIPS *Vesuv.* iv. 124 The outline of the cone was plain against the illuminated vaporous atmosphere.

fig. **1600** W. WATSON *Decacordon* (1602) 334 [The Jesuits'] religious pietie in shew, is but a rainebow cloude, of atheall policie in action, drawne vp in vaporous dewes of cold congealed deuotions. *a* **1652** J. SMITH *Sel. Disc.* IX. ii. (1821) 414 To rise above that vaporous sphere of sensual and earthly pleasures, which darken the mind.

b. Covered or obscured with vapour.

a **1687** PETTY *Pol. Arith.* i. (1690) 12 Holland is a Level Country,..and by its being moist and vaporous, there is always wind stirring over it. **1818** KEATS *Endym.* II. 19 Wide sea,..Many old rotten-timber'd boats there be Upon thy vaporous bosom! **1860** TYNDALL *Glac.* I. xvi. 115 The lower cloud field—itself an empire of vaporous hills. **1885-94** R. BRIDGES *Eros & Psyche* April x, The tripod shook, and o'er the vaporous well The chanting Pythoness gave oracle.

4. Having the form, nature, or consistency of vapour. (Common in 19th cent.)

1604 E. G[RIMSTONE] *D'Acosta's Hist. Indies* III. xxv. 196 Places in th' earth, whose vertue is to draw vaporous matter, and to convert it into water. **1651** H. MORE *Enthus. Tri.* (1656) 234 How can darknesse be called a Masse? etc. No it cannot. Nor a thin vaporous matter neither. **1678** CUDWORTH *Intell. Syst.* I. v. §36. 784 Its being in Hades [is] nothing but its presiding over that Idol or enlivened vaporous Body. **1794** MATHIAS *Purs. Lit.* (1798) 136 The *virus lunare*, the vaporous drops that hang in any region of infection. [Cf. Shaks. *Macb.* III. v. 24.] **1818** ACCUM *Chem. Tests* 97 Formed from the vaporous muriatic acid. **1871** TYNDALL *Fragm. Sci.* (1879) I. iv. 119 Caused in some way by the vapourous fumes diffused in its air. **1893** SIR R. BALL *Story of Sun* 284 The photosphere must be composed of a shell of cloudy or vaporous material.

fig. **1868** GEO. ELIOT *Sp. Gipsy* 50 The westering sun That still on plains beyond streams vaporous gold.

†**b.** In older medical use applied to supposed emanations from internal organs or from substances within the body. *Obs.*

1547 BOORDE *Brev. Health* §119 A vaporous humour or fumosytie rising..from the stomake. *c* **1550** H. LLOYD *Treas. Health* C 7 From the whych ryse vaporouse spirites and move disordinatly about the brayne. **1620** VENNER *Via Recta* (1650) 49 It doth nothing lesse then offend the braine ..with vaporous fumes. **1669** W. SIMPSON *Hydrol. Chym.* 71 These vaporous steams arising from the blood.

c. *fig.* Of ideas, feelings, etc.: Fanciful, idle, unsubstantial, vain.

1605 BACON *Adv. Learn.* II. viii. §3 So whosoever shall entertain high and vaporous imaginations, instead of a.. sober inquiry of truth, shall beget hopes and beliefs of strange and impossible shapes. **1632** LITHGOW *Trav.* x. 456 O foolish pride, O suppressing ambition! and vaporous curiosity! **1796** COLERIDGE *Sybil. Leaves, Ode Departing Year* ix, The vaporous passions that bedim God's Image, sister of the Seraphim. **1820** SHELLEY *Prometh. Unb* IV. i. 321 The vaporous exultation not to be confined! **1874** MOTLEY *John of Barneveld* II. xiv. 119 But his arguments were vaporous enough and made little impression. **1876** GEO. ELIOT *Dan. Der.* II. xvi, But such vaporous conjecture passed away as quickly as it came.

d. Of fabrics or garments: Gauzy, filmy.

1863 MISS BRADDON *Eleanor's Vict.* III. xvi. 235 The most fragile and vaporous bonnets were to be seen in the Bois de Boulogne. **1881** H. JAMES *Portrait of Lady* xlii, She..kept no less anxious an eye upon her vaporous skirts. **1896** *Pall Mall G.* 11 Mar. 4/2 Full sleeves of vaporous Indian muslin.

5. Of persons or minds: Inclined to be fanciful, vague, or frothy, in ideas or discourse.

1605 BACON *Adv. Learn.* I. 9 Let him but read the fable of Ixion, and it will hold him from being vaporous or imaginatiue. **1840** R. H. DANA *Bef. Mast* xxviii, B——, the mouth-piece of the debating clubs, noisy, vaporous, and democratic. **1848** KINGSLEY *Saint's Trag.* V. ii, Shame on my vaporous brain!

6. Of state or condition: Characteristic of vapour.

1661 *Origen's Opinions* in *Phœnix* (1721) I. 53 We then find that they which steam'd forth in a vaporous Rarity..do at last fall down again in a watery Consistence. **1782** *Phil. Trans.* LXXIII. 26 The dephlogisticated marine acid, in a vapourous state, certainly acts upon it. **1815** J. SMITH *Panorama Sci. & Art* I. 7 The elevated temperature it demands to be converted into the vaporous state. **1863** TYNDALL *Heat* iii. §60 (1870) 61 We have matter in the vaporous or gaseous form.

Hence **'vaporously** *adv.*; **'vaporousness.**

1600 SURFLET *Countrie Farme* VI. xxii. 777 The most.. common annoiance that the vaporousnes of the wine doth cause, is drunkennes. *Ibid.* 781 By his vaporousnes it filleth the braine. **1757** T. BIRCH *Hist. Royal Soc.* III. 416 The warmth and vaporousness of the air at the bottom of the well. **1877** *Academy* 21 April 352 The whole thing is toned down to a pale husky vaporousness of surface. **1887** LOWELL *Democracy*, etc. 143 The thought of a god vaguely and vaporously dispersed throughout the visible creation.

vapory, variant of VAPOURY *a.*

vapour ('veɪpə(r)), *sb.* Also 5-6 **vapowre,** 6 **vapoure;** 5 **wapour,** 6 **wapure;** 6- **vapor.** [a. AF. *vapour* (OF. *vapeur*) or ad. L. *vapōr-*, *vapor* steam. Cf. F. *vapeur*, Sp. and Pg. *vapor*, It. *vapore*.]

1. Without article: Matter in the form of a steamy or imperceptible exhalation; *esp.* the form into which liquids are naturally converted by the action of a sufficient degree of heat. In mod. scientific use: cf. next sense.

c **1374** CHAUCER *Troylus* III. 11 As man, brid, best, fisshe, herbe, and greene tree The feele in tymes with vapour eterne. **1382** WYCLIF *Joel* ii. 30 Blood, and fijr, and vapour of smoke. *c* **1440** *Promp. Parv.* 588/1 Vapowre, *vapor*. **1480** CAXTON *Myrr.* II. xxv. (1913) 117 This is a moisture subtyl whiche appereth but lytyl, and is named vapour. **1565** COOPER *Thes.*, *Vaporo*, to heate or make warme with vapour. **1604** R. CAWDREY *Table Alph.*, *Vapor*, moisture, aire, hot breath, or reaking. **1610** GUILLIM *Heraldry* III. v. (1611) 97 Vapour is a moist kinde of fume extracted chiefly out of the water. **1635** SWAN *Spec. M.* v. §2 (1643) 81 If it [exhalation] come from the water or some watry place, it is Vapor. **1667** MILTON *P.L.* XI. 737 The Hills..Vapour, and Exhalation dusk and moist, Sent up amain. **1725** WATTS *Logic* (1736) 115 Snow is congealed Vapour. Hail is congeal'd Rain. **1774** GOLDSM. *Nat. Hist.* I. 199 The perpetuity of many springs, which always yield the same quantity when the least rain or vapour is afforded. **1800** tr. *Lagrange's Chem.* I. 116 A white smoke, which is azote and water in a state of vapour. **1845** *Encycl. Metrop.* IV. 246/2 Comparing a given space filled with gas, and another saturated with vapour, at a given temperature; if we suppose that space to be diminished, the gas will be compressed..but the vapour will be partly condensed. **1849** JAMES *Woodman* vi, There were large masses of heavy vapour rolling across the southern part of the horizon. **1863** E. ATKINSON tr. *Ganot's Elem. Treat. Physics* IV. i. 93 Heat..converts liquids..into the aeriform state in which they obey all the laws of gases. This aeriform state of liquids is known by the name of *vapour*, while gases are bodies which, under ordinary temperature and pressure, remain in the aeriform state. **1878** HUXLEY *Physiogr.* 40 Only when the vapour is partially condensed, and therefore ceases to be true vapour.

fig. **1597** SHAKS. *2 Hen. IV*, II. iv. 393 When Tempest of Commotion,..Borne with black Vapour, doth begin to melt. **1719** DE FOE *Crusoe* II. (Globe) 316 There is nothing but Shadow and Vapour in the Thing.

2. a. An exhalation of the nature of steam, or an emanation consisting of imperceptible particles, usually due to the effect of heat upon moisture. In mod. scientific use, a fluid that fills a space like a gas but, being below its critical temperature, can be liquefied by pressure alone.

Sometimes, esp. in poetry, loosely applied to smoky matter emitted from burning substances.

1382 WYCLIF *Ezek.* viii. 11 And the vapour, or smoke, of a cloud roos togider of the ensence. *c* **1386** CHAUCER *Melibeus* ¶23 It may nat be..þat where as gret fyre hath longe tyme endured þat þere ne dwelleth som vapour of warmnesse. *c* **1425** tr. *Arderne's Treat. Fistula*, etc. 93 Stoppe þe mouþe, þat þe vapour go noȝt out. And biry þe vessel with þe oile in moist erþe. **1535** COVERDALE *Ecclus.* xxxviii. 28 The vapoure of the fyre brenneth his flesh. **1551** TURNER *Herbal* I. A v b, The brothe of wermwood with his vapor that riseth vp from it. **1562** —— *Baths* B ij b, The hote vapores [of a bath]. **1577** GOOGE *Heresbach's Husb.* 46 Grasse..(too greene and moyst) yf it be carryed into the loft, rotteth, and the vapour being ouerheated, falleth on fyre and burneth. **1635** SWAN *Spec. M.* v. §2 (1643) 81 A Vapour hath a certain watry nature in it, and yet it is not water. **1716** POPE *Iliad* VIII. 680 Full hecatombs lay burning on the shore; The winds to Heaven the curling vapours bore. **1789** W. BUCHAN *Dom. Med.* (1790) 457 The smoke of tobacco,..the vapours of onions and garlic,..are carefully to be avoided. **1800** tr. *Lagrange's Chem.* I. 16 At the end of a certain period the bottle will be filled with red vapours. **1823** FARADAY in *Q. Jrnl. Sci., Lit., & Arts* XVI. 237 Now that we know the pressure of the vapour of chlorine, there can be no doubt that the following passage describes a true liquefaction of that gas. *Ibid.* 239 During the condensation of the gas in this manner, a liquid has been observed to deposit from it. It is not, however, a result of the liquefaction of the gas, but the deposition of a vapour (using the terms gas and vapour in their common acceptation) from it, and when taken out of the vessel it remains liquid at common temperatures and pressures. **1823** H. DAVY in *Phil. Trans. R. Soc.* CXIII. 165 The compression [of gases] resulting from their slow generation in close vessels..may be easily assisted by artificial cold in cases where gases approach near to that point of compression and temperature at which they become vapours. **1830** M. DONOVAN *Dom. Econ.* I. 337 Vapours now arise, which are concentrated acetic acid... These vapours pass over..into the cask of water. **1857** MILLER *Elem. Chem., Org.* i. 18 Vapours of ammonia will be evolved if nitrogen be present. **1883** E. ATKINSON tr. *Ganot's Elem. Treat. Physics* (ed. 11) VI. v. 312 A vapour may be defined as being a gas at any temperature below its critical point. Hence a vapour can be converted into a liquid by pressure alone, and can therefore exist in the pressure of its own liquid, while a gas requires cooling as well as pressure to convert it into a liquid. **1891** FARRAR *Darkn. & Dawn* xlvi, Then they dragged her to the bath, heated it to boiling heat, and suffocated her in the burning vapour. **1979** T. B. AKRILL et al. *Physics* xi. 141/1 It is *conventional* to use the term *vapour* to describe a gas which is at a temperature below the critical temperature for that substance, but there is no obvious difference between a vapour just below T_c.. and a gas just above T_c.

b. An exhalation rising by natural causes from the ground or from some damp place; freq., a mist or fog.

c **1386** CHAUCER *Sqr.'s T.* 385 The vapour, which that fro the erthe glood, Made the sonne to seme rody and brood. *c* **1403** LYDG. *Compl. Bl. Knt.* 24 When that the mysty vapour was agoon, And clere and feyre was the morw[e]nyng. **1508** DUNBAR *Gold. Targe* 247 Suete war the vapouris. soft the morowing. **1509** HAWES *Past. Pleas.* xvi. (Percy Soc.) 60 All abrode the fayre dropes dyd shewe, Encensynge out all the vapours yll. **1525** LD. BERNERS *Froiss.* II. cc. 252/2 Discendyng downe as in to a cellar, a certayne hoote wapure rose agaynst them. **1555** EDEN *Decades* (Arb.) 133 If.. wee shal consent that vapours are lyfted vp wherof the watery cloudes are engendred. **1604** E. G[RIMSTONE] *D'Acosta's Hist. Indies* III. viii. 143 You shall vsually see great calmes vpon the coastes, where the vapors come from the Ilands, or maine land. **1661** J. CHILDREY *Brit. Bacon.* 60 The air is not very clear because of vapors continually rising. **1698** KEILL *Exam. Th. Earth* (1734) 83 The vapours which are raised by the Sun under the Torrid Zone. **1781** COWPER *Conversat.* 50 But when the breath of age commits the fault, 'Tis nauseous as the vapour of a vault. **1820** SHELLEY *Sensit. Pl.* III. 71 And hour by hour, when the air was still, The vapours arose which have strength to kill. **1874** BLACKIE *Self-Cult.* 49 In hot countries, where insalubrious vapours in some places infest the night.

c. *fig.* Used esp. (see sense 2 a) to denote something unsubstantial or worthless.

(*a*) **1382** WYCLIF *Jas.* iv. 15 Forsothe what is ȝoure lijf? A vapour, to a litel semynge. [Similarly in Tindale and later versions.] **1579** LYLY *Euphues* (Arb.) 112 Our lyfe is but a shadow.., a vapor, a bubble, a blast. **1608** CHAPMAN *Byron's Trag.* Plays 1873 II. 311 He alters euery minute: what a vapor The strongest mind is to a storme of crosses. **1663** DAVENANT *Siege of Rhodes* Wks. (1672) 25 Let it not last, But in a blast Spend this infectious vapour, Life! **1732** LAW *Serious C.* iv. 52 Those Scriptures which represent.. the greatest things of life as bubbles, vapours, dreams, and shadows. **1781** H. WALPOLE *Lett.* (1891) VIII. 34, I am at this present very sick of my little vapour of fame. **1829** CARLYLE *Misc.* (1857) II. 78 A man to whom the Earth and all its glories are in truth a vapour and a Dream.

(*b*) **1594** SHAKS. *Rich. III*, III. vii. 164 In my Greatnesse.. to be hid, And in the vapour of my Glory smother'd. **1597** HOOKER *Eccl. Pol.* v. lxxvi. §8 Upon the Church there never yet fell tempestuous storm the vapors whereof were not first noted to rise from coldnesse in affection. **1638** R. BAKER tr. *Balzac's Lett.* (vol. II) 49, I should do wrong.. to dislustre so pure a matter with the impression of so blacke a vapour. **1818** SCOTT *Rob Roy* ix, The gleams of sense and feeling which escaped from the Justice through the vapours of sloth and self-indulgence.

3. *pl.* **a.** In older medical use: Exhalations supposed to be developed within the organs of the body (esp. the stomach) and to have an injurious effect upon the health.

1422 YONGE tr. *Secreta Secret.* 239 That the wapours that gonne vp into the hede in tyme of slepynge may haue issue. **1530** RASTELL *Bk. Purgat.* II. xviii, When the brayne is hurte so that the humours and vapours styre and move the.. phantasye. **1539** ELYOT *Cast. Helthe* (1541) 53 Of humours some are more grosse and colde, some are subtyl and hot, and are called vapours. **1639** FULLER *Holy War* IV. ii. (1840) 198 Oftentimes the head doth ache for the ill vapours of the stomach. *c* **1680** BEVERIDGE *Serm.* (1729) I. 332 Those malign vapours which by reason of over-much eating are exhaled from the stomach into the head. **1719** DE FOE *Crusoe* II. (Globe) 472 Vapours from an empty Stomach. **1868** J. F. KIRK *Chas. the Bold* III. v. ii. 375 His habit of drinking in the morning a bowl of warm barley water under the notion of expelling noxious vapors.

b. A morbid condition supposed to be caused by the presence of such exhalations; depression of spirits, hypochondria, hysteria, or other nervous disorder. Now *arch.* (Common *c* 1665–1750.)

1662 H. STUBBE *Indian Nectar* iii. 33 By the eating of those Nuts, she feels Hypochondriacal vapours.. to be instantly allayed. **1680** *Hatton Corr.* (Camden) 221 My wifes disease, I think, is vapors. *c* **1690** TEMPLE *Ess., Health & Long Life* Wks. 1720 I. 283 To all these succeeded Vapours, which serve the same Turn, and furnish Occasion of Complaint among Persons whose Bodies or Minds ail something, but they know not what. **1728** YOUNG *Love Fame* III. 136 Sometimes, thro pride, the sexes change their airs; My lord has vapours, and my lady swears. **1735–6** BAYNE in J. Duncombe *Lett.* (1773) II. 87 The dispiriting symptoms of a nervous illness commonly called vapours, or lowness of spirits. **1783** WOLCOTT (P. Pindar) *Odes to R.A.'s* v. Wks. 1812 I. 60 The World will be in fits and vapours. **1822** LAMB *Elia* Ser. I. *Praise Chimney-Sweepers*, The rake, who wisheth to dissipate his o'er-night vapours in more grateful coffee. **1822** GOOD *Study Med.* III. 146 In the First Variety, which is commonly distinguished by the name of Vapours, or Low Spirits, the patient is tormented with a visionary or exaggerated sense of pains. **1879** MEREDITH *Egoist* xx, She had a headache, vapours. They are over.

c. So *the vapours.* (Common in 18th cent.)

1711 ADDISON *Spect.* No. 115 ¶4 It is to a Neglect in this Particular that we must ascribe the Spleen, which is so frequent in Men of.. sedentary Tempers, as well as the Vapours to which those of the other Sex are so often subject. **1719** DE FOE *Crusoe* I. (Globe) 161 These things fill'd my Head with new Imaginations, and gave me the Vapours again, to the highest Degree. **1778** LADY S. LENNOX *Lett.* (1901) I. 284, I should have the vapours all day if I played an hour at cards. **1803** JANE PORTER *Thaddeus* xxviii. (1831) 251, I must drink better health to you to save myself from the vapours. *a* **1839** PRAED *Poems* (1888) 12 Don't give your Royal brain the vapours By opening Opposition papers.

†**d.** *Path.* (*sing.*) The epileptic aura. *Obs.*

1822 GOOD *Study Med.* III. 544 Professor Loeffler,.. instead of cauterising the limb from which the epileptic halitus seems to ascend, has ingeniously tied a tight ligature above the part whence the vapour issues.

4. A fancy or fantastic idea; a foolish brag or boast. Now *rare.*

1614 B. JONSON *Barth. Fair* II. iii, Let's drinke it out, good Vrs, and no vapours! *Ibid.* v, Gentlemen, these are very strange vapours! and very idle vapours! I assure you. **1657** W. MORICE *Coena quasi Κοινὴ* Def. xxvi. 264 After all their vapours what do they lymbeck out of this Text? *a* **1680** BUTLER *Rem.* (1759) II. 118 For those, whose Modesty must not endure to hear their own Praises spoken, may yet publish of themselves the most notorious Vapours imaginable. **1703** STEELE *Tender Husb.* II. i, These are mere vapours, indeed—Nothing but vapours. **1738** tr. *Guazzo's Art Convers.* 165, I have Remedies to cure them of their Arrogance, and to keep those Vapours from fuming into the Head. **1841** J. ROMILLY *Diary* 16 Apr. (1967) 214 Ray.. reminded me I had said I wd give a Guinea when the Peterhouse wall was replaced by an iron-rail:—this work is now going on:—I had forgotten this vapour; but produced the Guinea. **1940** W. B. YEATS *If I were Four-&-Twenty* iv. 8 Men whose lives had been changed by Balzac, perhaps because he cleared them of Utopian vapours.

5. *attrib.* and *Comb.* **a.** With sbs., as ***vapour-belt, -burner, -capacity, -cloud, -density***, etc.; (in sense 3 b) ***vapour-fit***; **vapour lock**, an interruption in the flow of a liquid through a pipe as a result of its vaporization; **vapour pressure**, the pressure exerted by a vapour; **vapour-proof** *a.*, impervious to vapour; **vapour tension** = *vapour pressure* above; **vapour trail**, a visible trail of condensed water vapour in the sky, in the wake of an aircraft; also *fig.*

1875 R. F. BURTON *Ultima Thule* I. 67 The *vapour-belt which girdles the mountain flanks. **1875** KNIGHT *Dict. Mech.* 2690 **Vapor-burner*, a device for burning previously vaporized liquid hydrocarbons. **1922** W. G. KENDREW *Climates of Continents* 215 The sea is then coolest relatively to the land, so that the *vapour-capacity of air blowing from the sea is increased over the land. *c* **1843** CARLYLE *Hist. Sk.* (1898) 253 Those far-spread smoke-clouds and *vapour-clouds rising up there. **1851** MAYNE REID *Scalp Hunt.* xix. 137 Vapour-clouds from the Atlantic undergo a similar detention in crossing the Alleghany range. **1862** MILLER *Elem. Chem., Org.* (ed. 2) i. §1. 25 To calculate the *vapour density of any compound. **1890** A. M. CLERKE *Syst. Stars* 54 The vapour-densities of several of these metals are significantly high. **1855** OGILVIE *Suppl.*, **Vapour-douche*, a topical vapour-bath, which consists in the direction of a jet of aqueous vapour on some part of the body. **1831–3** *Encycl. Metrop.* (1845) VIII. 188/1 Howard's steam or *vapour engine. **1839** R. S. ROBINSON *Naut. Steam Eng.* 177 Another variety of marine engine is Mr. Howard's vapour engine. **1875** KNIGHT *Dict. Mech.* 2690/1 In 1850.. M. Prospère Vincent du Trembley brought into notice what is now known as the 'binary vapor-engine, or the 'combined vapor-engine'. **1707** FLOYER *Physic. Pulse-Watch* 62 Since I find all *Vapour Fits to have the Pulse of a diary Fever, I place this Constitution next to the Fevers. **1875** KNIGHT *Dict. Mech.* 2690/1 **Vapor-inhaler*,.. one for administering vapor produced by drawing or forcing atmospheric air through a liquid, or a sponge saturated with a liquid. **1848** RONALDS & RICHARDSON *Chem. Technol.* I. 154 *Vapour lamps. **1875** KNIGHT *Dict. Mech.* 2690/2 *Vapor lamp*, see *Vapor-burner*. **1930** *S.A.E. Jrnl.* XXVII. 93/1 The more volatile a fuel, the greater will be the tendency to boil in the fuel-feed system as the engine warms up. If the fuel boils, then interruptions of flow due to *vapor lock may be expected. **1951** O. BERTHOUD tr. *P. Clostermann's Big Show* 39 My jettison-tank gave out—probably a vapour-lock in the feed pipes. **1974** *Times* 22 Mar. 15/4 Filter King is said.. to prevent carburettor flooding.. and to prevent vapour 'lock'. **1946** *Nature* 19 Oct. 562/1 A process has been developed for the preparation of motor fuel and other petroleum products by a method based on *vapour-phase cracking of the vegetable oils contained in seeds. **1964** N. G. CLARK *Mod. Organic Chem.* xxv. 515 The vapour-phase nitration of propane. **1862** SCROPE *Volcanoes* 22 The *vapour-pillar rises still higher. **1913** V. B. LEWES *Oil Fuel* 79 A horizontal cylindrical boiler with a dome from which a broad *vapour-pipe leads the distilling vapours to the condensers. **1771** SMOLLETT *Humph. Cl.* (1815) 76, I have made divers.. leaps at those upper regions; but always fell backward into this *vapour-pit. **1875** *Encycl. Brit.* III. 385/2 As regards the atmosphere, evaporation [of water] goes on until the maximum *vapour pressure for the temperature has been attained, at which point the air is said to be saturated. **1978** P. W. ATKINS *Physical Chem.* vii. 175 The vapour pressure of water at 100°C is 1 atm. **1946** *Sun* (Baltimore) 17 May 13/3 About a foot of earth was scraped away from the site and a layer of *vapor-proof material placed on the ground. **1963** *Engineering* 16 Aug. 205/1 A heat resisting gasket.. is fitted.. to render the unit vapourproof and weatherproof. **1981** *Oil & Gas Jrnl.* 20 Apr. 167/2 The recorder case is made of die cast aluminum, and it's vapor-proof. **1862** G. P. SCROPE *Volcanoes* 22 This pillar of white *vapour-puffs. [**1845** *Phil. Trans. R. Soc.* CXXXV. 169 Cyanogen.. yielded on different occasions results of vaporous tension differing much from each other.] **1864** SPENCER *Biol.* I. 18 The range.. of diffusive mobility.. appears to be as wide as the scale of *vapour-tensions. **1933** W. LINDGREN *Mineral Deposits* (ed. 4) x. 116 Sudden separation of the gaseous phase will take place.. only if the vapor tension of the solutions is greater than the external pressure. **1941** *Picture Post* 3 May 23/1 The *vapour trails are left by the R.A.F. fighters weaving in and out of the German formation. **1948** L. DURRELL *Let.* in *Spirit of Place* (1969) 98 Vapour-trails of cows on the pampas, desolation. **1977** W. MCILVANNEY *Laidlaw* xxvi. 115 The vapour trails left by interrupted conversations. **1979** C. PRIEST *Infinite Summer* 18 There, high in the blue, were several curling white vapour-trails, but no other sign of the German bombers. **1672–3** GREW *Anat. Pl., Anat. Roots* II. (1682) 67 There is yet another kind of Sap-Vessels, which may be called *Vapour-Vessels. **1862** MILLER *Elem. Chem., Org.* (ed. 2) i. §2. 46 The simplicity thus introduced into our calculations of *vapour volume. **1588** SHAKS. *L.L.L.* IV. iii. 70 Then thou, faire Sun, which on my earth doest shine, Exhalest this *vapor-vow.

b. With adjs. and pples., as ***vapour-belted, -braided, -burdened, -filled***, etc. Also ***vapour-like*** adj. and adv.

1820 SHELLEY *Witch Atl.* lvii, Many a *vapour-belted pyramid. **1855** TENNYSON *Letters* 42 Sweetly gleam'd the star, And sweet the *vapour-braided blue. **1730–46** THOMSON *Autumn* 827 Th' exhaling sun, the *vapour-burden'd air. **1894** *Outing* XXIII. 363 The dark, *vapor-filled night closed in. **1821** in Ld. Coleridge *Story Devonsh. Ho.* xvii. (1905) 280 A pair of sleek steeds that are as delicate as a *Vapour-headed Lady. *a* **1715** WYCHERLEY *Posth. Wks.* (1728) 147 If then so soon the Great and Powerful fail, And *Vapour-like, almost e'er seen, exhale. **1840** MRS. SOMERVILLE *Connex. Phys. Sci.* (ed. 5) 424 A vapour-like smoke. **1862** SPENCER *First Princ.* II. ix. §76 (1875) 227 Each portion of such vapour-like matter must begin to move towards the common centre of gravity. **1727** BAILEY (vol. II), *Vaporiferousness*, an exhaling or *vapour-producing Quality. **1832** J. BREE *St. Herbert's Isle* 68 At length the impatient hours the twilight led With *vapour-sandaled feet and rubied cheek. **1827** FARADAY *Chem. Manip.* vii. (1842) 220 The junction being made *vapour-tight.. by some glazier's putty. **1892** W. B. YEATS *Countess Kathleen* 125 Under that cold and *vapour-turbanned steep.

vapour ('veɪpə(r)), *v.* Also 5–6 **vapoure**, 6– **vapor**, 6–7 **vaper** (7 **vapr-**). [f. prec., or ad. L. *vapōrāre*: cf. VAPORATE *v.*]

1. *intr.* To rise or ascend, to be emitted or diffused, in the form of vapour. Also with *up* and *out.*

1412–20 LYDG. *Chron. Troy* I. 3921 þe bawme vapoureth vp a-lofte In-to þe eyre of þe erbes softe. **1614** T. ADAMS in Spurgeon *Treas. David* I. 190 Thick spumy mists, which vapour up from the dark and foggy earth. *a* **1647** HABINGTON *Surv. Worcs.* (Worcs. Hist. Soc.) III. 544 Annoyed with the contagion vaporinge from the water. **1655** CULPEPPER, etc. *Riverius* XV. iii. 410 Put it into a new glazed pot or pipkin, closed up.. that nothing may vapor out. **1662** R. MATHEW *Unl. Alch.* 158 Lay this lute upon the edge of thy Funnel, which will bind fast the plate and the Funnel that nothing can vapor that way.

fig. **1839** BAILEY *Festus* 154 Does not sin pour from my soul,.. And, vapouring up before the face of God, Congregate there?

b. To pass *away*, to be dissipated, in the form of vapour.

1555 EDEN *Decades* (Arb.) 357 To take such waters,.. and .. cause them to boyle and vapoure away vntyll the dregs or residence remayne in the bottome. **1594** R. ASHLEY tr. *Loys le Roy* 3 When the water is thickned, it seemes to become a stone..; when it vapoures away, to be breath or aire. **1605** TIMME *Quersit.* I. vii. 27 Whatsoeuer is aiery therein.. by the force of the heat vapoureth away. **1658** A. FOX *Würtz' Surg.* IV. iii. 138 Mingle all these well together, lute the glass body, that nothing vapour away.

fig. **1638** MAYNE *Lucian* (1664) 71 Their whole life hath vapoured away in hopes. **1638** SIR T. HERBERT *Trav.* (ed. 2) 237 The first day vapors away in Tobacco, feasts, and other ordinary feastivalls. **1685** BAXTER *Paraphr. N.T., 1 Cor.* iv. 19 For all that Men call Learning and Wisdom.. vapoureth away as Idleness and Vanity. **1751** JOHNSON *Rambler* No. 133 ¶8, I expected that their exultation would in time vapour away.

c. To pass or be dissolved *into* a state of vapour or moisture. *rare.*

1567 DRANT *Horace, Ep.* xvii. Fiij, Though he shoulde vaper into teares. **1640** WALTON *Lives, Donne* (1670) 77 In the last hour of his last day, as his body melted away and vapoured into spirit,.. he said [etc.]. *c* **1645** HOWELL *Lett.* (1650) II. To Rdr., Words vanish soon, and vapour into Ayr.

2. *trans.* **a.** To cause to rise *up* or ascend in the form of vapour. Also *fig.*

c **1407** LYDG. *Reson & Sens.* 454 Whan Phebus.. on the herbes tendre and softe The bawmy dropes siluer fair Vapoured hath vp in the ayr. **1519** *Interl. Four Elem.* (Percy Soc.) 12 Therfore by hete it is vaporyd up lyghtly, and in the ayre makyth cloudys and mystes. **1530** RASTELL *Bk. Purgat.* II. xiii, Or ellys it wyll be vapoured up by the hete of the sonne. **1627** DONNE 5 *Serm.* 45 But every Man is vapor'd up into ayre, and as the ayre can hee thinkes he can fill any place. **1795** BLAKE *Bk. Ahania* Poet. Wks. (1914) 345 Effluvia vapour'd above In noxious clouds.

b. To cause to pass *away* in the form of vapour.

1460–70 *Bk. Quintessence* (1866) 9 Putte it into a uessel of glas in þe which be putt watir tofore,.. and aftir do vapoure awey þe watir at þe fier. **1560** WHITEHORNE *Ord. Souldiours* (1588) 26 b, It must be boyled so long, till all the thinne watrinesse be vapored away, and the substaunce of the salt peter thickned. *a* **1626** BACON *Med. Rem., Baconiana* (1679) 160 Then upon a gentle heat vapour away all the Spirit of Wine. **1662** R. MATHEW *Unl. Alch.* 174 In a clean glass Vessel vapor all the Vinegar away.

fig. *a* **1600** DONNE *The Expiration* 2 So, so, breake off this last lamenting kisse, Which sucks two soules, and vapors Both away.

c. With *out* or *forth*: To evaporate.

1530 RASTELL *Bk. Purgat.* III. vii, The temperate eyer wyll .. vapour out the tartnes & sowernes of that humour. **1626** BACON *Sylva* §23 Opium leeseth some of his poisonous Quality, if it be vapoured out, mingled with Spirit of Wine, or the like. **1638** RAWLEY tr. *Bacon's Life & Death* (1650) 28 In Dissipating Medecines, some vapour forth the thinne part of the Tumours. **1674** *Govt. Tongue* 134 If he.. call me dull, because I vapor not out all my spirits into froth.

d. To convert into vapour. Chiefly with *to.*

1591 SPENSER *Ruines Time* 219 He now is dead, and all his glorie gone, And all his greatnes vapoured to nought. **1603** J. DAVIES (Heref.) *Microcosmos* Wks. (Grosart) I. 87/1 Thy soul's but a Blast, That with thy Breath is vapored to nought. **1665** *Phil. Trans.* I. 36 With more of the same Dew .. vapoured to siccity. *a* **1814** *Forgery* II. iv. in *New Brit. Theatre* I. 453 Ev'n the hot potent wine, Whose power only but a short time since Flatter'd my brain, is vapor'd all in air. **1888** DOUGHTY *Trav. Arabia Deserta* I. 79 If there runs in any water, within a while it will be vapoured to the dregs.

†3. To send *forth*, *out*, or *up*, to emit or discharge, to disperse, etc., in the form of vapour. *Obs.*

c **1430** *Pilgr. Lyf Manhode* II. cxiv. (1869) 117, I haue a special horn bi which j caste and vapoure out the wynd that j haue in my bodi. **1563** HYLL *Art Garden.* (1593) 5 Consider also the nature of the Mote.., whether the same sendeth or vapoureth forth..noisome or stinking aire. *c* **1586** C'TESS PEMBROKE *Ps.* CXLVI. ii, His strength is none, if any in his breath; Which vapor'd foorth to mother earth he goes. **1628** WITHER *Brit. Rememb.* II. 49 Ev'n when the peoples thronging, and their heat Did vapour up their breathings and their sweat, For him to swallow. **1656** [? J. SERGEANT] tr. *T. White's Peripat. Inst.* 126 The clouds of ashes (vapour'd out in Vast abundance).

fig. **1592** DANIEL *Compl. Rosamond* 803 With armes a-crosse, and eyes to heauen bended, Vaporing out sighs that to the skies ascended. **1634** SIR T. HAWKINS *Pol. Observ.* 7 He with all his might vapoured forth the smoke of his greatnesse. **1657** R. LIGON *Barbadoes* 36 He vapours out the grievousest sighs.

b. *absol.* To emit vapour.

1552 HULOET, Vapouren or cast out vapoures, *halito.* **1650** ASHMOLE *Chym. Collect.* iv. 51 Our Fire is Minerall, and vapours not, unlesse it be too much stirred up.

4. a. To expose to the moistening effect of vapour. *rare*⁻¹.

1545 RAYNALD *Byrth Mankynde* 100 The matryce..must be annoynted, perfumed, and vapored with suche thynges, the whiche maye make it more ample and large.

b. To make dim or obscure with vapour.

1875 BLACKMORE *Alice Lorraine* I. 150 One of those sudden changes, which (at less than a breath) vapour the glass of the feminine mind.

5. *intr.* To use language as light or unsubstantial as vapour; to talk fantastically, grandiloquently, or boastingly; to brag or bluster.

1628 FORD *Lover's Mel.* IV. ii, He vapours like a tinker, and struts like a juggler. **1649** MILTON *Eikon.* 145 Poets indeed use to vapor much after this manner. **1687** A. LOVELL tr. *Thevenot's Trav.* II. 180 He would suffer no body to say any thing to him, and to hear him vapour, there was no Man greater than he. **1700** S. L. tr. *Fryke's Voy. E. Ind.* 160 He vapour'd and call'd me all the Cowards he could think of. **1760** *Cautions & Adv. to Officers Army* 12, I have heard so many young Officers, vaporing and wishing to meet an Enemy. **1812** COMBE *Syntax, Picturesque* IV, Dear Mrs. Syntax, how she'd vapour, Were she to read this curious paper! **1859** W. COLLINS *Q. of Hearts* (1875) 52 You may imagine what a passion I was in when I vapoured and blustered in that way. **1884** *Pall Mall G.* 13 Mar. 1/1 Lord Salisbury has vapoured a good deal and brandished his painted sword of lath.

b. Const. *about*, *of*, or *with*.

(*a*) **1654** tr. *Scudery's Curia Pol.* 37 To strike a terrour into those who have vapoured of their owne insolencie. **1677** W. HUBBARD *Narrative* 50 Yet could the Messenger hardly forbear threatning, vapouring of their numbers and strength. *a* **1680** BUTLER *Rem.* (1759) II. 36 The Wealth of his Party, of which he vapours so much,..is no mean Motive to enflame his Zeal. **1789** J. MOORE *Zeluco* (1797) II. lxvii. 178 Some of his friends were imprudent enough to vapour a little about his determination of calling Carlostein to account. **1820** HAZLITT *Table-T.* Ser. II. xvii. (1869) 345 Strutting and vapouring about his own pretensions. **1864** THACKERAY *D. Duval* v. (1869) 65, I was..vapouring about what we would do, were we attacked. **1897** RHOSCOMYL *White Rose Arno* 185 Those dear Countesses of whom you were forever vapouring.

(*b*) **1675** *Char. Town-Gallant* (Hindley, 1872) II. 4 He.. stayed at the University long enough to..get by heart the name of his College to vapour with. **1699** BENTLEY *Phal.* 332 His Scylax, that he lately vapour'd with. **1876** J. WEISS *Wit, Hum. & Shaks.* vi. 200 The words and style which mariners and travellers brought home to vapor with to eager listeners in the taverns.

c. *trans.* To declare or assert in a boasting or grandiloquent manner. Also, in later use, with *forth* or *away*.

1658 F. OSBORNE *Trad. Mem. K. James* Wks. (1673) 470 That..vapoured he would..bring him in by the Sword. **1665** WINSTANLEY *Loy. Martyrol.* 11 An unanswerable Work, of which they will never clear themselves, brag and vapour what they please. *c* **1665** MRS. HUTCHINSON *Mem. Col. Hutchinson* (1806) 236 Plumtre..began to vapour that he would have the castle pull'd downe. **1692** BP. PATRICK *Answ. Touchstone* 258 Neither he, nor any one else (whatsoever he vapours) dare break in pieces, or tear a Crucifix, or Picture. *a* **1732** SWIFT *Sandys' Ghost* xix, To poor Ovid shall befall..A metamorphosis more strange Than all his books can vapour. **1755** WARBURTON *Apol. for two first Lett.* Wks. 1788 VII. 572 Pope gave easy credit to him, when he vapoured that he would demonstrate all the common Metaphysics to be wicked and abominable. **1848** KINGSLEY *Saint's Trag.* IV. i, Where are the high-flown fancies Which but last week..You vapoured forth? *a* **1872** MAURICE *Friendsh. Bks.* (1874) x. 279 Vapouring away patriotism is undoubtedly a very bad thing.

d. To force (a person) *into* or *out of* something, to put *down*, by talking big.

1654 WHITELOCKE *Swed. Ambassy* (1772) I. 158 Who was not to be vapoured or threatened into a conformity to their desires. **1665** GLANVILL *Scepsis Sci.* Addr. p. v, That I might not therefore be vapour'd down by insignificant Testimonies. **1829** T. L. PEACOCK *Misfort. Elphin.* ix, I am not to be sung, or cajoled, or vapoured, or bullied out of my prisoner.

6. To act in a fantastic or ostentatious manner; to show off; to swagger; to walk *in* with a swaggering air.

1652 C. B. STAPYLTON *Herodian* 127 With Pipe and Flute full often here he vapors, And round about the Altar frisks and Capers. *a* **1720** SEWEL *Hist. Quakers* (1795) I. I. 56 Some men have the nature of an horse, to prance and vapour in their strength. **1724** RAMSAY *Tea-t. Misc.* (1733) I. 89 Wow but ye will be vap'ring Whene'er ye gang to the town. **1818** SCOTT *Br. Lamm.* xxi, When you mean to vapour with your hanger and your dram-cup in support of treasonable toasts. **1842** BORROW *Bible in Spain* xl, They.. would gaze with admiring eyes upon the robbers vapouring about in the court below. **1898** J. MEADE FALKNER *Moonfleet* vi, In vapours Maskew, and with an angry glance about him makes straight for the desk.

7. *trans.* †**a.** To affect with fantastic ideas. *Obs.*

1698 COLLIER *Immor. Stage* iv. §3 (1730) 139 He was formal and fantastick, smitten with Dress and Equipage, and it may be vapour'd by his Perfumes.

b. To give (one) the vapours; to depress or bore.

1774 BERRIDGE *Lett.* xv. (1864) 386 At times, when I am very low, a letter that demands a speedy answer will vapour me as much as a large bill requiring prompt payment would a sinking tradesman. **1779** *Sylph* I. 24, I shall be vapoured to death if I stay here much longer. **1796** MME. D'ARBLAY *Camilla* III. 85 She has lost all her sprightliness, and vapours me but to look at her. **1804** *Something Odd* I. 216 His low spirits, which are indeed so very bad at times, as to bore and vapour one to death.

c. *intr.* To get the vapours. *rare*⁻¹.

1802 MARIAN MOORE *Lascelles* I. 19 The evenings are so long, that I declare I vapour every time they come for want of something else to do.

vapour-bath. Also **vapour bath.**

1. A bath consisting of vapour. (Cf. VAPOROUS *a.* 1.) Also, an apartment in which a bath of this kind is used.

1719 QUINCY *Phys. Dict.* (1722) 8 *Æstuary*, a kind of Vapour-Bath. **1766** SMOLLETT *Trav.* xxxii. II. 135 They likewise indulged in vapour-baths, in order to enjoy a pleasing relaxation. **1802** *Med. Jrnl.* VIII. 57 A machine for conveying a vapour bath to diseased limbs. **1843** SIR C. SCUDAMORE *Med. Visit Gräfenberg* 12 Some persons argue that the vapor bath is quite as useful as the blanket. **1899** *Allbutt's Syst. Med.* VIII. 579 Vapour baths help not only to remove the scales [etc.].

b. *transf.* A thing or place comparable to a bath of this kind.

1800 *Med. Jrnl.* IV. 46 This kind of internal and highly inflammable vapour-bath is ever ready to catch fire. **1838** COL. HAWKER *Diary* (1893) II. 148 The last Drawing Room of the season; so of course an awful crowd and a vapour bath. **1864** TREVELYAN *Compet. Wallah* 152 One day in August, when all Chowringhee is a vast vapour-bath.

2. *Chem.* A vessel or receptacle in which hot vapour is generated in order to heat or melt a substance.

1728 CHAMBERS *Cycl.*, *Vaporosum Balneum*, or *Vapour-bath*, in Chymistry, a Term applied to a Chymist's Bath, or Heat, wherein the Body is placed so as to receive the Fumes of boiling Water. **1844** G. BIRD *Urin. Deposits* (1857) 18 Evaporate an ounce..over a spirit-lamp without the interposition of the vapour-bath. **1891** *Science-Gossip* XXVII. 95, I have..used gelatine.., melting it like glue in a vapour bath.

Hence **vapour-bathing.**

1766 J. SYMONS (*title*), Observations on Vapor-Bathing.

vapoured (ˈveɪpəd), *ppl. a.* [f. VAPOUR *sb.* or *v.*]

1. Filled with vapour or moisture. *rare.*

1536 WYATT *Poems* (1913) I. 216 With vapourd Iyes he lokyth here and there. **1583** MELBANCKE *Philotimus* T iij b, With driueling and with vapoured eies.

2. Formed of or from vapour. *rare*⁻¹.

1559 *Mirr. Mag.* (1563) R iv, While from mine eyes The vapored teares downstilled here and there.

3. Affected with the vapours; suffering from nervous depression; low-spirited.

Freq. in the 18th cent., esp. in predicative use.

1670 COVEL in *Early Voy. Levant* (Hakluyt Soc.) 110 Instead of dull, mopish, vapour'd women..we found.. bright and airy ladyes. **1733** CHEYNE *Eng. Malady* II. iv. §3 (1734) 145 They were never vapour'd or low-spirited to any Degree. **1753** *Ess. Celibacy* 104 If a vapoured person is at one time convinced of the truth of any proposition,..at another he will adopt the opposite opinion. **1796** MME. D'ARBLAY *Camilla* III. 351 Sir Sedley..whispered: 'I am horribly vapoured!' **1810** CRABBE *Borough* ix. 137 Her have I seen, pale, vapour'd through the day, With crowded parties at the midnight play. **1824** *Blackw. Mag.* XV. 398 Write when you can do nothing else, when you are vapoured, and then I shall be sure to hear the truth.

transf. **1755** *Monitor* No. 21. I. 179 I may..give you a little respite in a vapoured day; when..your head akes.

vapourer (ˈveɪpərə(r)). Also 9 **vaporer.** [f. VAPOUR *v.*]

1. One who vapours; a bragging, grandiloquent, or fantastical talker.

1653 GAUDEN *Hierasp.* 223 This pusillanimous and frothy generation of vapourers..are the greatest enemies to..our Religion. **1665** PEPYS *Diary* 3 Dec., A fortunate, though a passionate and but weak, man as to policy,..and one that is the greatest vapourer in the world. **1771** FLETCHER *Checks* Wks. 1795 III. 238 That vapourer in favour of your perseverance, fairly and consistently builds on..the foundation of the Calvinists. **1816** J. GILCHRIST *Philos. Etym.* 214 We might show how applicable to certain rhetorical metaphysical vaporers the descriptions are. **1843** *Tait's Mag.* X. 344 Not one of your old serene metaphysical vapourers.

2. ***vapourer moth***, a British moth of the genus *Orgyia*, esp. *O. antiqua*, the male of which flies with a rapid quivering motion.

1782 W. CURTIS *Brown-tail Moth* 6 The *Phalæna Antiqua*, or Vapourer Moth, which I have seen to thrive on the deadly Nightshade and poisonous Laurel. **1832** T. BROWN *Bk. Butterflies & M.* (1834) I. 49 The following figure of the female Vapourer Moth. **1871** KINGSLEY *At Last* viii, A crawling grub, like the female of our own Vapourer moth. **1890** ORMEROD *Injur. Insects* (ed. 2) 322 The pretty and easily distinguishable caterpillar of the Common Vapourer Moth.

ellipt. **1819** SAMOUELLE *Entomol. Compend.* 418 *Bombyx gonostigmata.* The scarce Vapourer. **1861** MORRIS *Brit. Moths* I. 77 *Orgyia antiqua*, Vapourer.

ˈvapourgraph. = VAPOROGRAPH.

1903 *Sat. Rev.* 11 Apr. 457/1 These 'vapourgraphs' show the deepest stain..where the object emitting the vapour is in actual contact with the cloth.

vapouring (ˈveɪpərɪŋ), *vbl. sb.* [f. VAPOUR *v.*]

1. Emission of vapour; evaporation. *rare.*

1548 ELYOT, *Respiratio*, a breathynge, or vapourynge. **1651** FRENCH *Distill.* iii. 64 That Liquor..may be rectified by the vapouring away of the flegme.

2. The action of talking or acting in a high-flown or pretentious manner.

c **1630** SANDERSON *Serm.* (1681) II. 306 The tongue may boast great things, and talk high... We call it vapouring; and well may we so call it. **1656** EARL MONM. tr. *Boccalini's Pol. Touchstone* (1674) 269 Spanish Officers,..with their vapouring, distaste the good servants of so great a Queen. **1706** VANBRUGH *Mistake* IV. 293 Take thy satin pincushion ..thou madest such a vapouring about yesterday. **1773** JOHNSON *Lett.* 25 March (1788) I. 80 Harry will be happier now he goes to school and reads Milton. Miss will want him for all her vapouring. **1816** EARL DUDLEY *Lett.* 22 June (1840) 146 It is really amazing, that after all their vapouring ..they should not have ventured to assail him. **1840** CARLYLE *Heroes* v. (1904) 176 Consider them, with their tumid sentimental vapouring about virtue. **1879** MCCARTHY *Own Times* II. 197 The errors of which Lord Derby had been guilty and the preposterous vapourings of some of his less responsible followers.

3. *fig.* in *pl.* Vain imaginations.

1866 'MARK TWAIN' *Lett. from Hawaii* (1967) 118 All the good sound sense or point there was in his vaporings could have been boiled down into half a page of foolscap. *Ibid.* 242 The creature has got no sense, but his vaporings sound strangely plausible sometimes. **1873** DIXON *Two Queens* I. vi. I. 44 These stings of conscience..were not the vapourings of an idle fancy.

vapouring (ˈveɪpərɪŋ), *ppl. a.* [f. as prec.]

1. Acting or talking in a pretentious or high-flown manner.

1647 R. JOSSELIN *Diary* (1908) 45, 25 Troops came to quarter with us, somewhat bold and vapouring. *c* **1670** O. HEYWOOD *Diaries* (1881) II. 311 To make big of it, as if it did constitute us righteous before god, as the vapouring pharisee. **1691** *The Bragadocio* 22 'Tis that Fierce, Vapouring, Coward, Bravado, I fancy. **1794** *Manners France* 29 Prussia's fame and Glory's fled, And you're a vapouring fool. **1834** *Gentl. Mag.* CIV. I. 26 The bustling, vapouring, chattering Duke of Newcastle. **1842** THACKERAY *Contrib. to Punch* Wks. 1900 VI. 47 It is always a comfort to read of those absurd vapouring vainglorious Frenchmen obtaining a beating. **1864** C. KNIGHT *Passages Work. Life* I. i. 57 The burly Englishman regarded the vapouring little man with something like..contempt.

2. Having a fantastical, pretentious, or foolishly boastful character.

1649 tr. *Boehme's Epistles* To Rdr. (1886) 2 The frame and structure of our knowledge, which by our artificial reason we should build unto ourselves upon that foundation, would be but a vapouring motion. **1721** STRYPE *Eccl. Mem.* xvii. II. 380 They told Barnaby, in a vapouring sort, (which that Nation was then much addicted to) how little Harm England in their Wars was like to do them. **1795** BURKE in Ellis *Orig. Lett.* Ser. II. IV. 542 We shall not..employ a person capable of writing such miserable, vapouring and empty stuff. **1806** SURR *Winter in Lond.* III. 240 The vapouring vanity of one struggling against opinion, and fearing to sink in human estimation. **1859** GREEN *Oxf. Stud.* (O.H.S.) 165 In this burst of vapouring Toryism open persecution had at last reached its close. **1877** OWEN *Wellesley's Desp.* p. xxxiii, Buonaparte's vapouring letter to Tippoo and gasconading demeanour in Egypt.

3. Full of vapour; emitting or giving off a vapour.

1648 HEXHAM II, *Een domp-gat*, a smoakie or a vapouring hole. **1800** COLERIDGE *Piccolom.* II. i, Now the vapouring wine Opens the heart and shuts the eyes.

4. Of the nature of vapour; vaporous.

1821 CLARE *Vill. Minstr.* II. 192 As vap'ring clouds by summer's suns are driven. **1854** S. DOBELL *Balder* xxv. 181 Like some great vapouring cloud Topping a cumulous heaven of mysteries.

Hence **ˈvapouringly** *adv.*

1653 *Lilburn Tryed & Cast* 154 It would make a man smile, to read what hee vapouringly talks. **1767** STERNE *Tr. Shandy* IX. iii, The Corporal..gave a slight flourish with his stick—but not vapouringly. **1892** *Sat. Rev.* 20 Aug. 209/2 [He] spoke rather vapouringly..about the House of Lords.

vapourish (ˈveɪpərɪʃ), *a.* [f. VAPOUR *sb.* + -ISH.]

1. Of the nature of vapour; dim through the presence of vapour; vapoury.

1647 HEXHAM I, Vaporish, *dompigh, roockachtigh.* **1781** HAYLEY *Triumphs Temper* I. 287 To drive gross atoms from the rays of noon Or chase the halo from the vapourish moon. **1844** *Blackw. Mag.* LV. 166 The conception is generally vague, vapourish, and metaphysical. **1887** HALL CAINE *Son of Hagar* II. viii, When Greta set out, the atmosphere was yellow and vapourish.

2. Apt to be troubled with the vapours; inclined to depression or low spirits.

1716–20 *Lett. Mist's Jrnl.* (1722) I. 97 For, as most other old Maids, she is exceedingly vapourish and fanciful. **1740** RICHARDSON *Pamela* II. 315 Every one sees, that the yawning Husband, and the vapourish Wife, are truly insupportable to one another. **1782** SIR J. E. SMITH *Mem.* (1832) I. 48 It made me vapourish to see so many students going away. **1803** ANNA SEWARD *Lett.* (1811) VI. 60, I see him, with all his inherent good properties, a vapourish egotist. **1844** THACKERAY *Barry Lyndon* xix, Lady Lyndon, always vapourish and nervous,.. became more agitated than ever.

b. Of the nature of, connected with, arising from, nervous depression.

1733 CHEYNE *Eng. Malady* II. iv. §4 (1734) 148 Some Headachs..may properly enough be call'd Vapourish or Nervous. **1748** RICHARDSON *Clarissa* (1811) III. 288, I am in the depth of vapourish despondency. **1793** W. ROBERTS *Looker-on* No. 41 (1794) II. 107 Be tender of using it in this torpid and vapourish condition. **1835** MRS. CARLYLE *Lett.* I. 22 This 'very penetrating world'—as a maid of my mother's used to call it in vapourish moods. **1879** MISS BRADDON *Vixen* III. 85 His pretty,.. middle-aged wife, whose languid airs and vapourish graces were likely to pall.. after a year of married life.

3. Apt to produce vapours. *rare*$^{-1}$.

1725 *Fam. Dict.* s.v. *Flux*, He must forbear every thing that is hot and vapourish.

Hence **'vapourishness.**

1748 RICHARDSON *Clarissa* (1811) IV. 41 You will not wonder that the vapourishness which has laid hold of my heart should rise to my pen. **1860** COCKBURN MUIR *Ess., Pagan or Christ.* 116 There is a vapourishness about the design of French Cathedrals and French work generally.

'vapourized, *ppl. a.* [f. VAPOUR *sb.* 3 b.] = VAPOURED *a.* 3.

1835 MACAULAY in Trevelyan *Life & Lett.* (1883) I. 415 Our masters run from station to station at our cost, as vapourised ladies at home run about from spa to spa.

'vapourless, *a.* Also **vaporless.** [f. VAPOUR *sb.*] Destitute of, free from, vapour.

1850 B. TAYLOR *Eldorado* xxxiii. II. 99 The walls of white rock..stand out distinctly in the vaporless atmosphere. **1860** MAURY *Phys. Geog.* xi. §645 And why should these winds be almost vaporless? **1884** *Q. Rev.* April 339 The deep purple of a vapourless sky.

vapoury ('veɪpərɪ), *a.* Also 6 **vaporie,** 8–9 *U.S.* **vapory;** 7–8 **vap'ry.** [f. VAPOUR *sb.* + -Y.]

1. Of the nature or consistency of vapour; composed of, or caused by, vapour.

1598 SYLVESTER *Du Bartas* II. i. *Furies* 262 The heat, hidden in a vapoury Cloud, Striving for issue. **1598** DRAYTON *Heroical Ep., Ros. to Hen. II* (1605) M4, The waxen taper..With his dull vapory dimnesse mocks my sight. **1608** TOPSELL *Serpents* (1658) 748 A vapoury adherency..which flyeth from the strokes of hammers upon hot burning iron. **1727–46** THOMSON *Summer* 1724 They see the blazing wonder rise anew..: From his huge vapoury train perhaps to shake Reviving moisture. **1770** LANGHORNE *Plutarch* (1851) II. 1039/1 The vapoury steam is diffused over the surface of the body. **1805–6** CARY *Dante, Inf.* xxv. 84 One from the wound, the other from the mouth Breathed a thick smoke, whose vapoury columns join'd. **1824** MISS MITFORD *Village* Ser. I. (1863) 77 The clouds have gathered into one thick low canopy, dark and vapoury as the smoke which overhangs London. **1860** TYNDALL *Glac.* I. xvi. 106 The Jungfrau..had wrapped her vapoury veil around her. **1885** *Manch. Exam.* 9 Sept. 5/3 Inside the body..it is suggested that there resides a kind of vapoury form which animates it.

transf. **1748** THOMSON *Cast. Indol.* I. lxxii, On the couch ..they sighing lie reclin'd, And court the vapoury god soft-breathing in the wind.

Comb. **1796** TOWNSHEND *Poems* 65 Who wak'st the vap'ry-skirted vale To songful life.

b. *fig.* Unsubstantial, indefinite, vague.

1818 *Blackw. Mag.* II. 396 My love-fever'd spirit evolves A fair vapoury vision. **1848** MILL *Pol. Econ.* III. vii. §3 (1876) 297 The mass of vapoury and baseless speculation with which this..has in latter times become surrounded. **1874** T. HARDY *Far fr. Mad. Crowd* I. xxii. 254 His readings of her seemed now to be vapoury and indistinct.

2. Rendered dim or obscure by the presence of vapour.

1818 KEATS *Endym.* IV. 483 Leaving old Sleep within his vapoury lair. **1845** FORD *Handbk. Spain* I. 474 The vapory distant hills and the blue sea peep through vistas..of the pines. **1878** T. HARDY *Ret. Native* III. vi, The yellow and vapoury sunset..had presaged change.

3. = VAPOURISH *a.* 2. *rare*$^{-1}$.

1771 J. ADAMS *Diary* 5 June Wks. 1850 II. 269 Thirty people have been here to-day, they say;—the halt, the lame, the vapory, hypochondriac, scrofulous, &c. all resort here.

‖**'vappa.** Now *rare.* [L.] Flat or sour wine. Also *fig.*

[**1601** HOLLAND *Pliny* I. 424 Whereupon it getteth the name of Vappa, and is cleane turned to bee dead or soure.] **1629** H. BURTON *Babel on Bethel* 69 Rome or Trent hath made a dead vappa of the word of God. **1631** MASSINGER *Believe as You List* IV. i, Your viper wine [is]..But vappa to the nectar of her lippe. **1666** BOYLE *Orig. Forms & Qual.* 202 Whether Must, Wine, spirit of Wine, Vinegar, Tartar, and Vappa, be specifically distinct Bodies? **1840** DE QUINCEY *Wks.* (1862) X. 217 But how that can be, when you recollect the philosophic *Vappa* of Xenophon, seems to pass the deciphering power of Œdipus.

transf. **1753** *Chambers' Cycl.* Suppl., *Vappa*,..a peculiar state of the blood, when it is in a low, dispirited condition.

†**vappe.** *Obs. rare.* [Anglicized f. prec.]

a. = prec. **b.** *fig.* A stupid person.

1657 REEVE *God's Plea* 105 Wilt thou not at last be the meer underwit, and the grand Vappe? **1660** JER. TAYLOR *Ductor* II. iii. rule 11 §14 The Norvegians complain'd that they could very seldom get any Wine into their Country, and when it did come it was almost vinegar or vappe.

vappin, obs. Sc. form of WEAPON.

†**'vappous,** *a. Obs.*$^{-1}$ [f. L. *vappa*: see above.] Flat, insipid.

1673 *Phil. Trans.* VIII. 6021 If the boyled Must by too violent an Effervescence cast out the Lee (by which it grows vappous or dead).

'vapulary, *a. rare*$^{-1}$. [See next and -ARY.] = VAPULATORY.

1864 *Sat. Rev.* 7 May 567 Who but a hoary-headed Etonian would recur with affectionate fondness to his vapulary memories of Dr. Keate?

vapulate ('væpjʊleɪt), *v. rare.* [ad. L. *vāpulāt-*, ppl. stem of *vāpulāre* to be beaten. Cf. obs. F. *vapuler*, Sp. and Pg. *vapular.*]

1. *trans.* To beat or strike.

1603 DEKKER & CHETTLE *Grissill* 1315, I..with my ponyard vapulating and checking his engine, downe it cut mee a payre of very imperiall cloth of golde hose. **1623** COCKERAM I, *Vapulate*, to beat, to strike.

b. *absol.* To administer a flogging.

1818 J. BROWN *Psyche* 198 If they vapulate in vain.

2. *intr.* To suffer vapulation or flogging.

1783 PARR *Let.* Wks. 1828 VII. 390 Blunders for which a boy ought to vapulate.

vapulation (væpjuː'leɪʃən). *rare.* [ad. L. **vāpulātio*, n. of action f. *vāpulāre*: see prec. Cf. Sp. *vapulacion.*] A beating or flogging. Also *transf.*

1656 BLOUNT *Glossogr.*, *Vapulation*, a beating or scourging. **1706** E. WARD *London Spy* II. Wks. (ed. 3) I. 33 Like an Offender at a Whipping-Post,..the more importunate he seems for their favourable usage, the severer Vapulation they are to exercise upon him. **1791** HAMPSON *Mem. J. Wesley* III. 5 A strapping colonel interposing, the vapulation did not take place.

'vapulatory, *a. rare*$^{-1}$. [f. L. *vāpulāt-* VAPULATE *v.* + -ORY.] Of or relating to flogging.

1886 LOWELL *Wks.* (1890) VI. 163, I am not..arguing in favour of a return to these vapulatory methods.

vapyn, obs. Sc. form of WEAPON.

‖**vaquero** (və'kɛərəʊ). Also **vacero.** [Sp. (= Pg. *vaqueiro*), f. *vaca* cow. Cf. Prov. *vaquier*, F. *vacher*, and It. *vaccaro*, med.L. *vaccārius.*]

1. In Spanish America: A cowboy or cowherd; a herdsman or cattle-driver.

1826 in E. C. Barker *Austin Papers* (1924) 1483 Dⁿ Luciano..rarely has communication with any one, except his Vaceros Comes to *Town* to *Hug* his Frigoña, once a month. **1831** F. W. BEECHEY *Narr. Voy. Pacific* II. 40 Intrusting their baggage to the care of two vaqueros (Indian cattle drivers) who were to accompany them. **1837** IRVING *Adv. Capt. Bonneville* III. 86 The vaqueros, or Indian cattle-drivers. **1851** MAYNE REID *Scalp Hunters* xvii. 119, I found them in the rancho of a vaquero in the woods. **1893** K. SANBORN *S. California* xii. 152 The American vaquero—usually a short, fat man with dumpy legs, who dons a flapping sombrero.

attrib. **1880** BRET HARTE *Jeff Briggs* ii, Having caparisoned himself and charger in true *vaquero* style.

2. (See quot.)

1858 SIMMONDS *Dict. Trade*, *Vaquero*,..a jacket worn by women and children.

vaquil, variant of VAKEEL.

var (vɑː(r)). *Canad.* Also **varr.** [dial. var. of FIR.] The balsam fir, *Abies balsamea.*

1793 P. CAMPBELL *Trav. N. Amer.* 57 The men set to work, and..cut the crops of a species of ever green wood, which they call *varr* [in New Brunswick]. **1842** R. H. BONNYCASTLE *Newfoundland* II. 266 The bark of the..var.. was taken off. **1907** J. G. MILLAIS *Newfoundland* iv. 99 Trees standing clear against a brown mass of tall 'vars' and spruces. **1959** *Atlantic Advocate* Jan. 74 In the feel of drawknife in wood, smoothing a shingle out of straight-grained var, there was something that smoothed the mind. **1982** *Evening Telegram* (St. John's, Newfoundland) 8 Feb. 24 Many an axe is biting into a piece of crooked var.

var, southern dial. var. FAR *adv.*, etc.; obs. Sc. f. WAR *a.*, WARE *a.*, *were* (see BE *v.*).

var., freq. abbreviation of VARIETY.

‖**vara** ('vara). Also 7 **varra.** [Sp. and Pg. *vara* rod, yardstick:—L. *vāra* forked pole, trestle, f. L. *vārus* bent.]

1. A linear measure used in Spain, Portugal, and Spanish America, of varying length in different localities, but usu. about 33 inches long; a Spanish yard. Cf. VARE[1] 1.

1674 JEAKE *Arith. Surv.* (1696) 115 The 100 Ells of Antwerp make at Cadiz..for Cloth 81 Varras. **1748** *Earthquake of Peru* i. (ed. 2) 39 Quarters, of 150 Varas or Spanish Yards, that is 64 Fathoms square. **1811** PINKERTON *Mod. Georg.* (ed. 3) 689 A mass of native iron..about 3½ varas in length..and..half a vara in thickness. **1850** B. TAYLOR *Eldorado* xviii. (1862) 187 The minimum extent is two hundred varas square (a vara is a little less than a yard) of irrigable land.

2. *Bullfighting.* A long spiked lance used by a picador.

1932 E. HEMINGWAY *Death in Afternoon* i. 6 The picador can perform his mission with the spiked pole, or vara. **1934** R. CAMPBELL *Broken Record* 83 Trident, vara, and lance. **1967** MCCORMICK & MASCAREÑAS *Compl. Aficionado* i. 20 It [*sc.* tercio] is used both of the entire *lidia* ('bull fight'..), which is said to be divided into the tercio of the *vara* (from the picador's long pole tipped by the pic), of the banderillas; and the faena. **1968** [see MORILLO].

vara, dial. variant of VERY *adv.*

varactor (və'ræktə(r)). *Electronics.* [f. *var(iable re)actor.*] A reverse-biased *p-n* junction whose capacitance depends on the bias voltage in a definite way. Also called ***varactor diode.***

1959 PFANN & GARRETT in *Proc. IRE* XLVII. 2011/1 (*heading*) Semiconductor varactors using surface space-charge layers. **1965** *Wireless World* July 62 (Advt.), Elimination of manual tuning by a unique self-tuning system (using servo controlled varactor diodes). **1975** *Physics Bull.* Sept. 401/1 Varactor diodes are extensively used in voltage-variable tuning applications, such as in modern solid-state radio and television circuits. **1979** A. BAR-LEV *Semiconductors & Electronic Devices* xvii. 325 Varactors are also used for frequency multiplication or harmonic power generation in the microwave range.

Va'ragian, *a.* [f. mod.L. *Varagi* (pl.), ad. Old Russian *Variagi.*] = VARANGIAN *a.*

The form *Varegian* (after the mod.L. variant *Varegi*) has also been employed.

1841 *Penny Cycl.* XX. 258 A Varagian (probably Danish) freebooter of the Baltic, named Rurik.

varan ('værən). *Zool.* [ad. mod.L. *Varan-us* (Merrem, 1820), f. Ar. *waran*, var. of *waral*, monitor lizard. So F. *Varan.*] A lizard belonging to the genus *Varanus* or family *Varanidæ*; a monitor or varanian.

1843 *Penny Cycl.* XXVI. 131/1 The Heloderms have not the scales..with which they are covered surrounded by small squamous grains like the Varans. **1887** HOWORTH *Mammoth & Flood* 370 Allied to the living varans and lace-lizards of Australia.

varand, obs. Sc. form of WARRANT.

varandeisse, obs. Sc. form of WARRANDICE.

Varangian (və'rændʒɪən), *sb.* and *a. Hist.* [f. med. or mod.L. *Varang-us*, ad. med.Gr. *Βάραγγος* (pl. *Βάραγγοι*), ad. (through Slavonic languages) ON. *Væringi* (pl. *Væringjar*), app. f. *vár-* (f. pl. *várar*) plighted faith.

In the Old Russian chronicle of Nestor the name occurs as *Variagi* and *Variazi* (pl.), and survives in mod.Russ. *varyág* a pedlar, Ukrainian *varjah* a big strong man.]

A. *sb.* **1.** One of the Scandinavian rovers who in the 9th and 10th centuries overran parts of Russia and reached Constantinople; a Northman (latterly also an Anglo-Saxon) forming one of the bodyguard of the later Byzantine emperors (see B.).

1788 GIBBON *Decl. & F.* lv. V. 561 In their wars against the more inland savages [of Russia], the Varangians condescended to serve as friends and auxiliaries. *Ibid.* 562 The new Varangians were a colony of English and Danes who fled from the yoke of the Norman conqueror. **1831** SCOTT *Ct. Rob.* ii, The passengers observed to each other, that the stranger was a Varangian. **1836** *Partington's Brit. Cycl., Lit.* etc. III. 501/1 The Varangians, a race of bold pirates who infested the coasts of the Baltic. **1889** BARING-GOULD *Grettir* xliii. 379 The company called the Varangians, who acted as a bodyguard to the Emperor.

2. The language spoken by these. *rare*$^{-1}$.

1831 SCOTT *Ct. Rob.* iii, Mustering what few words of Varangian he possessed, which he eked out with Greek.

B. *adj.* Of or pertaining to the Varangians; composed of Varangians, etc.

1788 GIBBON *Decl. & F.* lv. V. 563 The primitive subjects of the Varangian chief. **1831** SCOTT *Ct. Rob.* xxx, They were to mount on horseback at the sounding of the great Varangian trumpet. **1900** HECTOR H. MUNRO *Rise Russ. Empire* ii. 17 A Varangian power..had sprung up among the tribes of the Slavic hinterland.

b. ***Varangian Guard,*** the bodyguard of the Byzantine emperors, formed of Varangians.

1831 SCOTT *Ct. Rob.* ii, This account of the Varangian Guard is strictly historical. **1845** *Encycl. Metrop.* XI. 788/2 The valour of the Varangian, or Anglo-Saxon and Danish guards, ever the firmest support of the Byzantine throne. **1889** BARING-GOULD *Grettir* xliii. 380 The order came to the Varangian guard that [etc.].

varanian (və'reɪnɪən), *sb.* and *a. Zool.* [f. mod.L. *Varan-us* VARAN + -IAN.]

A. *sb.* A lizard belonging to the family *Varanidæ* of scaled saurians; a monitor or varan.

1841 *Penny Cycl.* XX. 460/2 The Varanians form a family of scaled Saurians, including the Monitors of the Old World. **1847** T. R. JONES in *Todd's Cycl. Anat.* IV. 288/1 In the Geckos, Agamians, and Varanians, the base of the tooth is imbedded in a shallow socket.

B. *adj.* Belonging to or characteristic of the varans or monitors.

1840 OWEN *Odontogr.* I. 263 The Varanian family of squamate Saurians..includes the Monitors of the old world. **1841** *Penny Cycl.* XX. 460/2 Allied in the form of the teeth to the typical Varanian Monitors.

'varanid. *Zool.* [ad. mod.L. *Varanid-æ*, f. *Varanus* VARAN.] = VARANIAN *sb.*

1896 tr. *Boas' Text Bk. Zool.* 422 Allied [to the lizards] are the Varanids (*Varanus*), large, tropical, old-world forms with long bifid tongue.

varanus ('værənəs). [mod.L. (B. Merrem *Tentamen Systematis Amphibiorum* (1820) 58): see VARAN.] = VARAN. Cf. GOANNA, IGUANA 2, MONITOR *sb.* 5.

1934 A. RUSSELL *Tramp-Royal in Wild Austral.* viii. 60 What should come scuttling across the track but a big varanus lizard. **1953** A. SMITH *Blind White Fish in Persia* vi. 99 A Varanus in fact, a type of lizard, but it had the appearance of a Rhinegold dragon.

varble, obs. f. WARBLE *sb.*

vard, obs. Sc. f. WARD *sb.* and *v.*

vardan(e, -en, obs. Sc. ff. WARDEN.

vardanry, obs. Sc. f. WARDENRY.

varde, southern ME. var. FERD *sb.*[1]

vardel, -il, obs. Sc. ff. WORLD.

varden, southern dial. var. FARTHING; obs. Sc. f. WARDEN.

varder, southern dial. var. FARTHER; var. VERDOUR *Obs.*

†**vardingale.** *Obs.* Forms: α. 6 **verdynggale**, 6–7 **verdingale, -all.** β. 6–8 **vardingale** (6 *Sc.* **ward-**). γ. 6 **vardingard.** [ad. obs. F. *verdugale, vertugale, vertugade* (16th c.), ad. Sp. *verdugado*, f. *verdugo* rod, stick. See also VERDUGAL.] A framework of hoops formerly used by women to extend their skirts; = FARTHINGALE.

α. **1552** [see FARTHINGALE]. **1597** J. KING *On Jonas* (1618) 478 Fashion brought-in the verdingale, and carried out the verdingale, and hath againe reuiued the verdingale.., and placed it behinde, like a rudder. **1609** ROWLEY *Search for Money* (Percy Soc.) 23 Wee haue verdingales to beare up our bands, as they had to support their loose britches.

β. **1560** *Acc. Ld. H. Treas. Scot.* XI. 163 For ane wardingale to hir. **1574** in Feuillerat *Revels Q. Eliz.* (1908) 240 A hamper to pack the vard[i]ngales in. **1603** DEKKER *Wonderful Yeare* Wks. (Grosart) I. 157 The meanest that was there..was in..her vardingale, her turkie grograin kirtle. **1614** SYLVESTER *Bethulia's Rescue* v. 219 From Vardingale to Vardingale, hee flyes His brave Lievtenant, lest Hee him surprise. **1673, 1753** [see FARTHINGALE].

γ. **1578** *Inv. R. Wardr.* (1815) 230 Ane vardingard of blak taffetie the foirskirt of satine pasmentit with gold.

transf. and *fig.* **1590** R. W[ILSON] *Three Lords & Ladies London* (Roxb.) 295 Thou from Dissimulation art sent, And bring'st a gown of glosing,..A vardingale of vaine boast. **1592** GREENE *Def. Conny Catching* Wks. (Grosart) XI. 96 Blest be the French sleeues & breech verdingales, that grants them liberty to conny-catch so mightily.

vardite, -ditt, dial. or obs. forms of VERDICT.

vardle. *dial.* Also 6 **verdoll.** [Alteration of OF. *vervelle* or *vert(e)velle* in the same sense: cf. VARTIWELL, VARVEL.] (See later quots.)

1525 in *Archaeologia* XXV. 478 For hengells, verdolls, & hoks, hespes & staples, for y[e] same berne, vj s. vij d. **1787** W. H. MARSHALL *Rur. Econ. E. Anglia* Gloss., *Vardle*, a common eye or thimble of a gate, with a spike only. **1893** COZENS-HARDY *Broad Norfolk* 86 *Vardle*, bottom hinge of a gate.

vardlie, obs. Sc. form of WORLDLY *a.*

vardo. *slang.* Also **varda.** [Romany.]

A waggon; now *spec.* a gypsy caravan. Also *attrib.*

1812 J. H. VAUX *Flash Dict.*, *Vardo*, a waggon. *Ibid.*, *Vardo-gill*, a waggoner. **1934** P. ALLINGHAM *Cheapjack* vi. 59 As me brother David pointed out to me in the vardo afterwards, this 'ere finger called me a bastard—and he was right. **1940** [see READING *sb.*[2] 3]. **1977** *New Society* 29 Sept. 643/2 You know what a varda is. It's one of those painted wagons, drawn by horses, that gypsies donate to folk museums. **1980** R. HILL *Killing Kindness* xxvi. 263 Don't forget I'm pure bred Romany... To end my days sitting on the *vardo* steps puffing away at an old pipe. **1982** *Times* 30 Apr. 10/3 This 'ere Gorse Hill..was always too tiring for an 'orse after pullin' a *varda*..10 or 12 miles.

vardour, variant of *verdour* VERDOUR *Obs.*

vardy. Now *dial.* Also 8 **vardi**, 9 **vardie.** [Colloq. or dial. var. of *verdit*, obs. f. VERDICT.] Opinion, judgement, verdict.

1731–8 SWIFT *Polite Conv.* i. 15 *Lord Sp.* Well, I fear Lady Answerall can't live long; she has so much wit. *Nev.* No, she can't live... *Lady Ans.* O! Miss, you must give your Vardi too! **1796** *Grose's Dict. Vulgar T.* (ed. 3) s.v., To give one's vardy; i.e. verdict or opinion. **1825–** in dial. glossaries (N. Cy., Linc., Yorks.).

vardytt, obs. form of VERDICT.

†**vare**[1]. *Obs.* Also 7 **varre.** [ad. Sp. *vara* VARA.]

1. = VARA.

1545 *Rates of Customs* d iiij b, The Vares of Spayne:..ix. Vares makithe .viii. yardes Englysshe. **1588** PARKE tr. *Mendoza's Hist. China* 175 Certain peeces of blacke silke of twelue vares long a peece. **1599** HAKLUYT *Voy.* II. I. 273 The other measure is called a vare,..which measure is of 5 palmes or spans, and is one code and two third parts. **1604** E. G[RIMSTONE] *D'Acosta's Hist. Indies* IV. xi. 240 It extendes above foure score Varres or yardes in length.

2. A rod, staff, or wand, esp. as a symbol of judicial office or authority.

1578 T. N. tr. *Conq. W. India* 357 He tooke the Vares of Justice from the Judges and Sargeants, and incontinent restored them againe. *c* **1645** HOWELL *Lett.* I. III. xxxii, If an Alguazil..show him his Vare, that is a little white staffe he carryeth as badge of his office. **1660** F. BROOKE tr. *Le Blanc's Trav.* 48 Imposing my hand upon a Crosse held out to me upon the end of a Vare, or wand. **1681** DRYDEN *Abs. & Achit.* 595 His Hand a Vare of Justice did uphold.

†**vare**[2]. Variant of FARE *sb.*[3] *Obs.*

1653 H. APPLETON *Fight Legorn-Road* 2 At Naples I made Provision for my Squadron,..passing thence through the Vare [= Strait] of Messina.

vare, dial. var. FARE *sb.*[2]; southern ME. var. FARE *v.*; var. VAIR *sb.*[1]; obs. Sc. f. WARE *sb.*

‖**varec.** Also **varech.** [F. *varech*, *varec* (OF. *warec*, *werek*, *verec*, *vrec*, etc.), ad. old Scand. **wrek*: see WRECK *sb.*]

1. Sea-weed.

1676 *Phil. Trans.* II. 594 The Sea-Fox, in whose stomach they found a branch of the Sea-herb Varec. **1783** JUSTAMOND tr. *Raynal's Hist. Indies* VI. 294 The most ordinary of these manures is the Varec, a sea-weed which is periodically throw'n upon the coast by the sea-tide. **1836** SIR G. HEAD *Home Tour* 289, I observed large quantities of varech or sea-weed on the beach [at Robin Hood's Bay]. **1889** *Guernsey News* 1 Feb., The gathering of varech in Herm commences to-morrow.

attrib. **1873** BROWNING *Red Cott. Nt.-cap* 36 Then, dry and moist, the varech limit-line.

2. An impure carbonate of soda obtained from sea-weed.

1844 FOWNES *Chem.* 234 Carbonate of Soda... The *barilla*..is thus produced in several places on the coast of Spain... That made in Brittany is called *varec.* **1860** *Ure's Dict. Arts* (ed. 5) III. 940 *Varec*, the name of kelp made on the coast of Normandy.

varecoste, southern ME. variant of FARCOST.

varegilt (*obs. Sc.*): see WAREGILT.

vareit, Sc. variant of *waried* WARY *v.*

‖**varella.** *Obs.* Pl. **-ellaes, -ely.** [Pg. and It. *varella*, *-ela* (16th cent.), of doubtful origin.]

A pagoda.

1588 T. HICKOCK tr. *Frederick's Voy.* 33 b, They spend many of these Sugar canes in making of houses and tents which they call *Varely* for their Idoles. **1599** HAKLUYT *Voy.* II. I. 260 They consume in these Varellaes great quantity of golde; for that they be all gilded aloft. **1638** SIR T. HERBERT *Trav.* (ed. 2) 318 The Varellaes (or Temples)..are observable; each Varella farcinated with ugly (but guilded) Idolls. **1662** J. DAVIES tr. *Mandelslo's Trav.* 119 The King of Pegu..had them placed amongst the other Idols kept in a *Varella* or *Mosquee*.

†**varelle**, Anglicized form of prec. *Obs.*

1599 HAKLUYT *Voy.* II. I. 261 There is a Varelle or Pagode, which is the pilgrimage of the Pegues.

varen, southern ME. variant of FARE *v.*

vare-nut, dial. variant of FARE-NUT.

vare-widgeon. *dial.* [f. VAIR *sb.*[1]] (See quot.)

1813 MONTAGU *Ornith. Dict.* Suppl. s.v. *Smew*, The females and young birds are called in the southern part of Devonshire, Vare-Wigeon, from a supposed similitude about the head to a Weesel, which is denominated *Vare*.

†**varewort.** *Obs.*[−1] In 3 **uarewurt.** A plant of doubtful identity.

c **1265** *Voc. Plants* in Wr.-Wülcker 557 *Eptaphilos*, salerne, uarewurt.

varge, obs. or dial. variant of VERGE.

†**vargeous**, *a.* *Obs.*[−1] [f. F. *verge*:—L. *virga* rod, wand.] Resembling a rod; rod-like.

1779 *Phil. Trans.* LXVIII. 988 The same thing holds for the measure of the vargeous palets [F. *palettes de verges*], the balance wheel [etc.].

varges, -is, etc., variant of VERJUICE, etc.

vargood, dial. variant of FARGOOD.

vargueño (vɑːˈgeɪnjəʊ). [ad. Sp. *bargueño*, *vargueño* adj., of Bargas, a village near Toledo, the former place of manufacture.] A kind of cabinet made in Spain in the 16th and 17th centuries, with numerous small compartments and drawers behind a fall front which opens out to form a writing surface.

1911 E. FOLEY *Bk. Decorative Furnit.* I. 159 Prominent amid the Hispano-Moresque decorative woodwork probably made by these Moorish craftsmen is the vargueño: a box with a door in front, evolved from the chest or hucha, and mounted on a stand. *Ibid.* 160 It has been reasonably conjectured that the vargueño cabinet took its title from the small town of Vargas, near Toledo. **1923** G. L. HUNTER *Decorative Furnit.* ix. 265 The most distinctive piece of Spanish furniture is the vargueño. Like the two-story cabinets or highboys of other countries, it was a development from the chest. **1960** H. HAYWARD *Antique Coll.* 24/2 *Bargueño* or *vargueño*, Spanish cabinet with fall-front enclosing drawers and often mounted on a stand. **1975** *Oxf. Compan. Decorative Arts* 809/2 The most typical *vargueños* are in the Mudejar style... In 1568 the guilds of Mexico required a cabinet-maker to be able to make a *vargueño*..as a condition of qualification.

‖**vari.** [The first part of the Malagasy name *varikandana* or *varianda*. Cf. *varikosy* the broad-nosed lemur.] The ruffed lemur, *Lemur varius*.

1774 GOLDSM. *Nat. Hist.* (1776) IV. 241 The Vari is much larger than either of the former [i.e. mococo and mongoz]..; it has a kind of ruff round the neck, consisting of very long hair. **1785** SMELLIE *Buffon's Nat. Hist.* (1791) VII. 228 The vari is larger, stronger, and more ferocious than the maucauco. **1839** *Penny Cycl.* XIII. 420/1 The *Vari*, to which the name of *Lemur Macaco* has been applied by modern authors, is given by Linnæus as Var[iety] d. of that species.

‖**vari**, pl. of VARUS.

vari- (ˈvɛərɪ), comb. form of VARIABLE *a.* (in some words infl. by VARIATION or VARIOUS *a.*).

variability (vɛərɪəˈbɪlɪtɪ). [f. next + -ITY, or a. F. *variabilité*, = It. *variabilità*, Sp. *variabilidad*, Pg. *-idade.*]

1. The fact or quality of being variable in some respect; tendency towards, capacity for, variation or change.

1771 MRS. GRIFFITH *Hist. Lady Barton* I. 29 In her outward appearance there is a variability, that renders it almost impossible to draw an exact resemblance of her. **1796** BURKE *Regic. Peace* Wks. 1842 II. 355 His protest against binding him to his opinions, and his reservation of a right to whatever opinions he pleases, remain in their full force. This variability is pleasant, and shews a fertility of fancy. **1839** LADY LYTTON *Cheveley* III. 146 It is this atmospheric variability..that occasions the thousand little dissensions that spring from love itself. **1869** PHILLIPS *Vesuvius* viii. 246 Reasonings on the variability of the relative level of land and sea. **1885** *Contemp. Rev.* June 901 They made too little account of the variability of human nature and circumstances.

2. *spec.* **a.** The fact of, or capacity for, varying in amount, magnitude, or value.

1816 tr. *Lacroix's Diff. & Int. Calculus* 157 From this may be deduced the differential coefficient of *z*, relative to the variability of *x*. **1870** PHIPSON tr. *Guillemin's Sun* 282 The variability of a certain number of stars. **1873** H. SPENCER *Sociol.* vi. 124 The variability of the ratio..being duly conceived in terms of lines that lengthen and shorten.

b. *Biol.* Capability in plants or animals of variation or deviation from a type.

1832 LYELL *Princ. Geol.* (1835) II. 449 Variability of a species compared to that of an individual. **1859** DARWIN *Orig. Spec.* i. 40 A high degree of variability is obviously favourable, as freely giving the materials for selection to work on. **1880** WALLACE *Island Life* iv. 58 The belief in the variability of all animals in all their parts and organs.

variable (ˈvɛərɪəb(ə)l), *a.* and *sb.* Forms: 4– **variable** (5–6 **varri-**, 6 *Sc.* **vareable**), 5, *Sc.* 6, **-abill**, *Sc.* 6 **-abil** (**warieabill**), 5–6 **varyable**, 6 **-abul**, 5 **uaryabyl, veryabyll.** [a. OF. *variable* (F., Sp., and Prov. *variable*, Pg. *variavel*, It. *variabile*), ad. L. *variābilis*, f. *variāre* to VARY.]

A. *adj.* **1.** Liable or apt to vary or change; (readily) susceptible or capable of variation; mutable, changeable, fluctuating, uncertain.

a. Of the course of events, the state of things, etc.

c **1397** CHAUCER *Lack Stedf.* 8 What made this worlde to be so variable But louste þat folke haue in discencion? *c* **1400** *Rom. Rose* 5424 In a state that is not stable, But chaungynge ay and variable. **1448–9** J. METHAM *Wks.* (E.E.T.S.) 54 Thy uaryabyl squel,..O fortune! brent myght be With Pluto in helle. **1483** CAXTON *Cato* g iiij, For the goodes of thys worlde been varyable; now one is ryche and now poure. **1509** HAWES *Past. Pleas.* 51 They nothing thynke on fortune var[i]able. *a* **1548** HALL *Chron.*, *Hen. VI* (1550) 34 The Englyshe affaires..began to wauer, and waxe variable. **1609** HOLLAND *Amm. Marcell.* 119 Some joining in skirmish with the enemies, fought with variable event. **1610** —— *Camden's Brit.* 696 They had continued a doubtfull and variable fight a great part of the day.

b. Of feeling, conduct, etc.

c **1480** HENRYSON *Orpheus & Eur.* 287 Quhat art thou, lufe,..To sum constant, till othir variabil. **1555** EDEN *Decades* (Arb.) 114 So variable and vnconstant is the nature of man. **1592** SHAKS. *Rom. & Jul.* II. ii. 111 O sweare not by the Moone,..Least that thy Loue proue likewise variable. **1596** —— *Merch. V.* II. viii. 13, I neuer heard a passion so confusd, So strange, outragious, and so variable. **1667** MILTON *P.L.* XI. 92 His heart I know, how variable and vain Self-left. **1849** RUSKIN *Seven Lamps* vii. §7. 191 The decorations..might be made subjects of variable fancy. **1862** H. SPENCER *First Princ.* I. v. §29 (1875) 102 There begins to fade from the mind the conception of a special personality to whose variable will they were before ascribed.

Comb. **1618** BOLTON *Florus* IV. iii. (1636) 293 While Antonius, variable-witted,..takes upon him to be a king.

c. In miscellaneous applications.

1509 BARCLAY *Shyp of Folys* (1874) I. 126 By hir iyen clowdy and varyable vysage. **1576** FLEMING *Panopl. Epist.* 442 These beautifull shapes,..not varriable in time, not withering throughe the heate of the sunne. **1590** SPENSER *F.Q.* III. vi. 38 For formes are variable and decay, By course of kind, and by occasion. **1609** WIBARNE *New Age Old Names* To Rdr. A 4 b, If I haue omitted something in a matter so variable. **1703** MAUNDRELL *Journ. Jerus.* (1732) 63 Our Course variable between East and South. **1711** ADDISON *Spect.* No. 98 ¶1 There is not so variable a thing in Nature as a Lady's Head-dress. **1832** LEWIS *Use & Ab. Pol. Terms* Introd. 7 The variable meaning of a word. **1850** M[c]COSH *Div. Govt.* II. i. (1874) 78 This production of change is not variable or capricious, but follows certain fixed laws. **1884** tr. *Lotze's Logic* 388 Events, which..depend at once on constant and on variable conditions.

absol. **1872** BAGEHOT *Physics & Pol.* (1876) 32 We overlook and forget the constant while we watch the variable.

2. a. Of persons: Apt to change from one opinion or course of action to another; inconstant, fickle, unreliable.

1387 TREVISA *Higden* (Rolls) I. 357 þe men beeþ variable and vnstedefast, trecherous and gileful. **1393** LANGL. *P. Pl.* C. XIX. 69 Somme of ows [are] sothfast and some variable. **1402** HOCCLEVE *Min. Poems* 78 Al-be-hyt that man fynde o woman nyce, In-constant, recheles, or varriable. **1474** CAXTON *Chesse* II. iii. (1883) 37 So that they be not founde ..for enuye variable. *a* **1542** WYATT in *Tottel's Misc.* (Arb.) 37 My word nor I shall not be variable, But alwaies..firme and stable. *a* **1578** LINDESAY (Pitscottie) *Chron. Scot.* (S.T.S.) I. 135 The popularie..ar so warieabill and faccell. **1643** BAKER *Chron.* (1653) 504 Lydington was..a man of the greatest understanding,..but very variable. **1708–9** *Pennsylv. Hist. Soc. Mem.* X. 313, I am very sensible he is a variable man, and not..to be entirely depended on. **1711** ADDISON *Spect.* No. 162 ¶5 One of the most variable Beings of the most variable Kind. **1808** SCOTT *Marm.* VI. xxx, Uncertain, coy, and hard to please, And variable as the shade By the light quivering aspen made.

transf. **1484** CAXTON *Curiall* ij b, Them whom fortune the variable hath most hyely lyfte up and enhaunsed. *a* **1548** HALL *Chron., Hen. VI*, 110b, King Charles did politiquely consider, what a variable lady Fortune was.

b. Const. *in* (words, actions, etc.).

1429 *Pol. Poems* (Rolls) II. 145 In thy behestes be nat variable. *a* **1513** FABYAN *Chron.* VII. (1811) 544 See you not howe varyable the kynge is in his wordis? **1547** BOORDE *Introd. Knowl.* 214 In vsyng my rayment I am not varyable. **1562** BULLEIN *Bulwarke, Bk. Vse Sickmen* 55 Bee not variable in Religion. **1623** JAS. I in Ellis *Lett.* Ser. I. III. 139 He is in this busienesse..as variable and uncertaine as the Moone.

†**c.** Liable to alter or turn *from* (or *of*) a purpose, etc. *Obs.*

c **1400** *Beryn* 752 No mervell is, þouȝe Rome be som what variabill Fro honour & fro wele. **1412–20** LYDG. *Chron. Troy* IV. 5120 þei wil holde stable, And finally nat be variable From þe ende, platly, þat þei make. *c* **1450** *Cov. Myst.* (Shaks. Soc.) 216 If we fynde hym varyable Of his prechynge that he hath tawth. **1493** *Petronylla* 21 (Pynson), From hir entent nat founde variable.

3. a. Of the weather, seasons, etc.: Liable to vary in temperature or character; changeable.

c **1480** HENRYSON *Test. Cres.* 150 The seuin Planetis..hes power..To reull..Wedder and wind, and coursis variabill. **1631** GOUGE *God's Arrows* V. §15. 428 Peace is not like the immoveable mountaines, but rather like to the variable skie. **1722** DE FOE *Plague* (Rtldg.) 14 The Weather was temperate, variable and cool enough. **1797** *Encycl. Brit.* (ed. 3) XVIII. 493/2 The great sunshine heats of Florence, which are too variable and undetermined. **1808** *Med. Jrnl.* XIX. 569 The weather..was very variable, but upon the whole mild. **1854** *Poultry Chron.* I. 288 Exposed entirely to the vicissitudes of our ever-variable climate.

b. Of wind or currents: Tending to change in direction; shifting.

1665 BOYLE *Occas. Refl.* III. i. (1848) 146 As variable as the Wind. **1720** DE FOE *Capt. Singleton* xiii. (1840) 229 We had the wind variable. **1774** GOLDSM. *Nat. Hist.* I. 340 He who has been taught to consider that nothing in the world is so variable as the winds. **1832** DE LA BECHE *Geol. Man.* 95 There is a tendency of the surface waters to the S.E., being variable in winter. **1840** R. H. DANA *Bef. Mast* xxv. 84 The wind shifted and became variable. **1854** TOMLINSON *Arago's Astron.* 185 Much less regular in the temperate regions, they are called *variable* winds.

c. Of a star: That varies periodically in respect of brightness or magnitude.

1788 *Encycl. Brit.* (ed. 3) II. 471/2 *marg.*, Of the variable stars. **1854** BREWSTER *More Worlds* i. 7 It appears and disappears like a variable star, shewing in painful succession its spots of light and of shade. **1880** AGNES GIBERNE *Sun, Moon & Stars* 239 There are numbers of stars called Variable Stars, the light of which is constantly changing, now becoming more, now becoming less.

d. *Biol.* Liable to deviate from a type; admitting of such deviation. (Cf. VARIATION 10.)

1859 DARWIN *Orig. Species* v. 149 Beings low in the scale of nature are more variable than those which are higher. **1877** CONDER *Basis of Faith* v. 231 Species, it has been well said, are 'variable, but not mutable'. **1880** WALLACE *Island Life* 59 It is now very easy to understand how, from such a variable species, one or more new species may arise.

†**4. a.** Characterized by variation or diversity; differing, diverse, various. *Obs.*

1432–50 tr. *Higden* (Rolls) I. 239 The peple wente furthe to mete the victor with variable [L. *varia*] gladdenesse. **1509** HAWES *Past. Pleas.* XVI. (Percy Soc.) 61 For musike doth sette in all untye The discorde thynges whiche are variable. **1539** *Act 31 Hen. VIII*, c. 14 By occasion of variable and sundrie opinions..great discorde..hathe arrisen. **1576** FLEMING *Panopl. Epist.* p. iii, Flowers..delightsome to the eye, in consideration of their variable colours. **1601** HOLLAND *Pliny* II. 372 The variable transformations of Proteus. **1613** PURCHAS *Pilgrimage* (1614) 167 It were a worke..tedious to the Reader, to recite the variable opinions of Chronologers..about these points.

†**b.** Different *from* something. *Obs.*$^{-1}$

1509 BARCLAY *Shyp of Folys* (1570) 167 Thy visage chaunging by lookes manifolde:..Sometime as lead, from death scant variable.

†**c.** Variegated. *Obs.*$^{-1}$

1553 EDEN *Treat. New Ind.* (Arb.) 16 Of the coloure of boxe, somwhat variable and as it wer chekered.

†**5.** Of varying ownership. *Obs.*

1549 in *Leges Marchiarum* (1705) 80 The Land variable, common of both the People, called the Debateable Ground, which lieth between the West Marches of England and Scotland. *Ibid.* 81 The said Variable Ground.

6. a. Susceptible or admitting of increase or diminution, not remaining the same or uniform, in respect of size, number, amount, or degree.

1607 TOPSELL *Four-f. Beasts* 94 His belly is variable, now great, now small like an Oxes. **1804** *Med. Jrnl.* XII. 496 They are sold at a more reduced price, about 9s. per dozen; this, however variable,..leaves the money saved proportionably the same. **1815** J. SMITH *Panorama Sci. & Art* II. 114 The pressure of the atmosphere is variable. **1858** LARDNER *Handbk. Nat. Phil.* 281 When the quantity of heat necessary to raise a body one degree is different in different parts of the scale, the specific heat is said to be *variable*. **1882** MINCHIN *Unipl. Kinemat.* 27 If a point, *P*, moves round a circle with a velocity either constant or variable.

b. Of quantity, number, etc.: Liable to vary.

1710 J. HARRIS *Lex. Techn.* II, *Variable Quantities*, in Fluxions, are such as are supposed to be continually increasing or decreasing; and so do by the motion of their said Increase or Decrease Generate Lines, Areas or Solidities. **1743** EMERSON *Fluxions* 223 If any one of the variable Distances..be called *x*. **1763** —— *Meth. Increments* 41 Multiply the given increment by the next preceeding value of the variable quantity. **1801** *Encycl. Brit.* Suppl. II. 740/1 The abscisses and ordinates of an ellipsis, or other curve line, are variable quantities. **1828** STARK *Elem. Nat. Hist.* II. 374 A sucker composed of a variable number of scaly pieces. **1884** BOWER & SCOTT *De Bary's Phaner.* 351 Small bundles, the number of which is variable.

c. *spec.* (See quot.)

1829 *Hand-bk. Nat. Philos., Hydrost.* viii. 2 (L.U.K.), Some springs, called *variable* or *reciprocating*,..discharge a much smaller quantity of water for a certain time, and then give out a greater quantity.

d. ***variable cost*** (see quot. 1974).

1953 [see *prime cost* s.v. PRIME *a.* 9a]. **1967** A. BATTERSBY *Network Analysis* (ed. 2) xii. 200 There are other cases which more closely resemble the variable-cost control, as when the number of men allocated to a job is variable and governs duration. **1969** D. C. HAGUE *Managerial Economics* i. 15 The remainder of total cost is made up of those costs that do vary with output—with what are therefore known as variable costs. **1974** *Terminol. Managem. & Financial Accountancy* (Inst. Cost & Managem. Accounts) 24 *Variable cost*, a cost which, in the aggregate, tends to vary in direct proportion to change in the volume of output or turnover.

7. a. That may be varied, changed, or modified; alterable.

1597 HOOKER *Eccl. Pol.* v. lxii. §14 What if the minister's vocation be..not a ceremony variable as times and occasions require? **1611** BIBLE *Hab.* iii. 1 *marg.*, According to variable songs or tunes. **1875** KNIGHT *Dict. Mech.* 2690 *Variable Cut-off*, one actuated from the governor, so as to be brought into action according to the load on the engine. **1887** *Pall Mall G.* 5 Nov. 7/1 The permanent taxes..will be variable only by regular Act.

b. *Gram.* Capable of inflexion.

1891 in *Cent. Dict.*

8. *Nat. Hist.* In specific names, as ***variable cod, hare, ixalus, jacana, lemur, maple, mole, rail, tanager, toad***.

1862 *Chambers's Encycl.* III. 642/2 [The] Dorse..of the same genus with the cod..; its colour is more variable, from which it has received the name of *Variable Cod. **1896** tr. *Boas' Text Bk. Zool.* 529 The Polar or *Variable Hare (*Lepus timidus* or *variabilis*)..is white during winter in the colder regions. *c* **1880** *Cassell's Nat. Hist.* IV. 366 The *Variable Ixalus of Ceylon is..very variable in its coloration. **1785** LATHAM *Gen. Syn. Birds* III. I. 244 *Variable Jacana (*Parra variabilis*). **1896** H. O. FORBES *Handbk. Primates* I. 68 The Ruffed or *Variable Lemur derives its name from the remarkable variability of its external markings. **1833** *Penny Cycl.* I. 78/1 *Acer heterophyllum*, the *variable maple... This is the plant sold in the English nurseries under the name of *A. creticum*. **1776** P. BROWN *Illustr. Zool.* 110 *Variable Mole. **1781** PENNANT *Hist. Quad.* II. 485 Variable Mole;..color of the hair on the upper part of the body varied with glossy green and copper-color. **1824** STEPHENS in Shaw's *Gen. Zool.* XII. I. 198 *Variable Rail (*Rallus varians*). Brown Rail spotted and striated with black and white, with the body beneath and eyebrows cinereous or griseous. **1783** LATHAM *Gen. Syn. Birds* II. I. 234 *Variable Tanager..: general colour of the plumage green, very glossy and variable. *c* **1880** *Cassell's Nat. Hist.* IV. 360 The *Variable, or Green Toad, found in France, has hind limbs and feet nearly as large as those of the Frog.

9. Special collocations. **a.** In *attrib.* use, as ***variable-area, -length, -reluctance, -speed***.

1920 *Flight* XII. 5/1 Variable area or variable camber wings—or other means for reducing the landing speed of a machine. **1957** MANVELL & HUNTLEY *Technique Film Music* iii. 171 This optical wedge is caused to oscillate over a light slit by the motion of the pendulums, producing a variable-area type of sound-track. **1959** E. M. MCCORMICK *Digital Computer Primer* viii. 119 These difficulties are avoided in many business computers by organizing the storage to accommodate variable-length records. **1970** *Computers & Humanities* IV. 327 The data fields of the customer's data base in variable-length capability. **1980** C. S. FRENCH *Computer Sci.* xi. 60 Variable length records mean difficulties for the programmer but better utilisation of storage. **1959** W. S. SHARPS *Dict. Cinematogr.* 138/1 A variable-reluctance microphone is a microphone which depends for its operation on variations in the reluctance of a magnetic circuit. **1875** KNIGHT *Dict. Mech.* 2691 Olmsted's Variable-Speed Pulley. *Ibid.*, *Variable-speed Wheel*, a contrivance for obtaining alternately accelerated and retarded circular motion. **1978** P. GRIFFITHS *Conc. Hist. Mod. Music* viii. 116 Cage went further and created..his *Imaginary Landscape no. 1*, in which musicians have to perform with frequency recordings on variable-speed turntables. **1984** B. FRANCIS *AA Car Duffer's Guide* 67/2 A variable-speed fan is provided to boost the air-flow throughout the car's interior at low speeds.

b. ***variable geometry***, a configuration of component parts that can be varied; *spec.* in *Aeronaut.* = *variable sweep* below; freq. *attrib.*; ***variable-mu*** adj. (Electronics), (of a valve) having an amplification factor that can be varied; ***variable-pitch*** adj., of or pertaining to †(*a*) a propeller in which the blades are shaped so that the pitch varies along their length (see quot. 1912) (*obs.*); (*b*) a propeller, fan, etc., in which the angle of the blades with respect to the direction of air flow can be adjusted, esp. while they are in motion; ***variable sweep*** (Aeronaut.), sweep (sense 15) that can be varied during flight according to requirements; usu. *attrib.*

1957 *Jrnl. Brit. Interplanetary Soc.* XVI. 166 The design characteristics of such gliders may include..variable geometry lifting surfaces, to be very thin at high speeds and to have good lift properties at landing. **1963** *Times* 10 June 10/1 He believed that variable geometry would give a better aircraft. **1969** *Sci. Jrnl.* Apr. 48/1 The wing surface [of a bat's wing] is an elastic membrane of skin stretched between the four long fingers, with at least 11 movable joints in each wing. This very variable geometry permits a high degree of manoeuvrability and control. **1970** *New Scientist* 30 July 236 (*caption*) These drawings show the variable geometry of the air intake on the Olympus 593-3B engine. **1977** P. WAY *Super-Celeste* 39 The rival to the Super-Celeste, the variable geometry wing F-24, was airborne again. **1930** BALLANTINE & SNOW in *Proc. IRE* XVIII. 2102 (*heading*) Reduction of distortion and cross-talk in radio receivers by means of variable-mu tetrodes. **1962** [see MU 2]. **1971** E. N. LURCH *Fundamentals of Electronics* (ed. 2) v. 143 The tube employing this special grid is termed cutoff, supercontrol, or variable-mu. **1912** LEDEBOER & HUBBARD tr. *Duchêne's Mech. of Aeroplane* vii. 197 M. Drzewiecki, with the idea of getting the maximum efficiency out of every part of the propeller, varies the pitch at each point so that the actual angle of incidence is everywhere the optimum angle. Propellers of this kind are known as variable-pitch propellers, and are consequently no longer true screws. **1918** W. H. BERRY *Aircraft in War & Commerce* vii. 91 Worked in combination with a variable pitch propeller the gearbox would allow the pilot a range in power and speed. **1919** H. SHAW *Text-bk. Aeronaut.* xi. 147 In the variable pitch type, the blade angle is varied continuously from the hub outwards in such a way that the slip column of air is forced backwards with a velocity which is uniform throughout. **1952** [see *static thrust* s.v. STATIC *a.* 7]. **1971** *Daily Tel.* 4 Nov. 3 (Advt.), Variable pitch engine cooling fan. Large range to fit most popular cars. **1974** *Encycl. Brit. Micropædia* I. 375/1 Additional features have been engineered into variable-pitch propellers; first, the ability to feather..a propeller on an engine stopped in flight. **1954** *Economist* 11 Sept. 12/3 *Variable sweep.* After take-off with wings only partially swept, means are provided to sweep them back more sharply in flight. Strictly experimental. **1965** *New Scientist* 22 Apr. 217/1 The development of the variable-sweep wing in collaboration with the French might lead to a load-carrier of outstanding performance. **1966** *Economist* 22 Jan. 330/1 Massive, variable-sweep aircraft whose wings pivot around stanchions as thick as tree-trunks. **1978** D. KÜCHEMANN *Aerodynamic Design of Aircraft* iv. 120 E. von Holst flew models with various arrangements of variable sweep.

B. *sb.* **1. a.** *Math.* and *Phys.* A quantity or force which, throughout a mathematical calculation or investigation, is assumed to vary or be capable of varying in value. Cf. A. 6b and CONSTANT *sb.*

1816 tr. *Lacroix's Diff. & Int. Calculus* 4 The limit of the ratio..will be obtained by dividing the differential of the function by that of the variable. **1862** DRAPER *Intell. Devel. Europe* (1865) 173 In some mathematical expression containing constants and variables. **1882** MINCHIN *Unipl. Kinemat.* 238 In this case ϕ will also be a potential (or flow) function of the new variables (ξ, η).

b. *Computers.* A data item that can take on more than one value during or between programs and is stored in a particular designated area of memory; the area of memory itself; (also ***variable name***) the name referring to such an item or location.

1837 C. BABBAGE in B. Randell *Origins Digital Computers* (1973) 23 The number of variables which can be contained within the store will depend on the length of the rack. **1843** *Scientific Mem.* III. 666 We have..written Variable with a capital letter when we use the word to signify a *column of the engine*, and variable with a small letter when we mean the *variable of a formula*. **1957** [see SUBSCRIPT *sb.* 2b]. **1967** BECKETT & HURT *Numerical Calculations & Algorithms* i. 23 Variable names are usually limited in length because they must be coded as numbers and space is required to store these numbers... The number of characters used to define a variable is arbitrary, provided that it does not exceed a given maximum. **1972** BERGMAN & BRUCKNER *Introd. Computers & Computer Programming* ix. 288 [In FORTRAN] the data locations are divided into constants and variables... Variables are locations into which we may read numbers or place (store) numbers at execution time. **1975** H. KATZAN *Introd. Computer Sci.* v. 108 The names HOURS, RATE, and PAY are variables... A variable is an identifier that names a data item. **1979** *Sci. Amer.* Dec. 85/1 In programming languages a variable is not an item of data but a label for a location in the memory of the computer. The value of a variable at any moment is the information currently stored there. **1981** W. S. DAVIS *Computers & Business Information Processing* xiii. 234 A FORTRAN variable consists of from one to six letters or digits, the first of which must be a letter. **1982** COOPER & CLANCY *Oh! Pascal!* i. 10 The variables that computers use are like the memory keys of hand calculators—they store values... Variables can hold different types of values, including integers.., characters.., or even logical values.

c. *Logic.* A symbol whose exact meaning or referend is unspecified, though the range of possible meanings usually is.

1910 WHITEHEAD & RUSSELL *Principia Mathematica* I. i. 4 In mathematical logic, any symbol whose meaning is not determinate is called a variable. *Ibid.*, If a statement is made about 'Mr A and Mr B', 'Mr A' and 'Mr B' are variables whose values are confined to men. **1937**, etc. [see OPEN *a.* (*adv.*) 11j]. **1939** *Jrnl. Philos.* XXXVI. 702 Whereas the singular existence statement calls the alleged existent by name, e.g., 'Pegasus', the general existence statement does not; the reference is made rather by a variable '*x*', the logistical analogue of a pronoun 'which', 'something which'. **1954** A. J. AYER *Philos. Ess.* ix. 216 The range of our ontological commitments may..be reduced by our ability to recast some of our existential statements in such a way that variables which take a certain type of value disappear from them. **1969** FEYS & FITCH *Dict. Symbols Math. Logic* 6 In interpreting a formalized language it is usual to specify the respective ranges of the various variables of the language. **1978** S. HAACK *Philos. Logics* iv. 39 In general, prefixing a quantifier binding one of its free variables to an open sentence with *n* free variables yields an open sentence with *n*—1 free variables.

2. a. A variable or shifting wind; *spec.* in *pl.* (see quots. 1857, 1867).

1846 A. YOUNG *Naut. Dict.* 349 The meeting of the two opposite currents [of wind] here produces the intermediate space called the calms or variables. **1857** TOMES *Americ. in Japan* i. 31 The Variables, which are found South of the border of the South-east Trades. **1867** SMYTH *Sailor's Wordbk.* 710 *Variables*, those parts of the sea where a steady wind is not expected.

b. A variable star. (See A. 3 c.)

1868 LOCKYER *Elem. Astron.* 21 Among the acknowledged variables β *Persei* is perhaps the most interesting. **1880** *Athenæum* 11 Sept. 341/1 The period of this interesting variable is a little less than five days.

3. Something which is liable to vary or change; a changeable factor, feature, or element.

1846 GROTE *Greece* II. xxi. (1862) II. 229 The beginning and the end are here [in the Odyssey] the date in respect to epical genesis, though the intermediate events admit of being conceived as variables. **1865** MARTINEAU in *Theol. Rev.* 670 A changing scene with the variables of which he is in immediate contact. **1881** H. H. GIBBS *Double Standard* 13 Uniformity, and therefore the removal of those variables which must be an encumbrance to commerce.

'variableness. [f. prec. + -NESS.] The quality of being variable or changeable; tendency or liability to vary: **a.** Of things.

1432–50 tr. *Higden* (Rolls) II. 201 Therefore mony difference be in a man, swiftenesse of sawle, variablenesse of witte. **1569** GOLDING *Heminge's Postill.* Ded. 2 Whose interpretation being alwayes one without variablenesse. **1595** *Drake's Voy.* (Hakl. Soc.) 19 The variableness of the winde and weather. **1612** T. TAYLOR *Comm. Titus* iii. 1 The variablenes of times, places, & dispositions of churches. **1712** STEELE *Spectator* No. 478 ¶2 The Variableness of Fashion turns the Stream of Business. **1794** JONES in G. Adams *Nat. & Exper. Phil.* II. xxii. 468 *note*, The variableness in refractive power of different sorts of glass. **1820** W. SCORESBY *Acc. Arctic Reg.* I. 403 This variableness being the effect of the unequal temperature of the ice and water. **1838** ARNOLD in *Life & Corr.* (1844) II. viii. 126 With regard to the Examinations, I hear a general complaint of the variableness of the standard. **1885** *Manch. Exam.* 14 Apr. 8/6 The proverbial variableness of the Irish climate.

b. Of persons, the mind, conduct, etc.

1491 CAXTON *Vitas P.* (W. de W. 1495) II. 237 By a brother of his he hadde be Induced to soo grete varyablenesse and unstedfastnesse. **1526** *Pilgr. Perf.* (W. de W. 1531) 271 b, The varyablenesse or vnstedfastnesse of man or woman. **1576** FLEMING *Panopl. Epist.* 307 That the reading of many authors..drawe not after them the discommoditie of fickle headinesse and variablenesse. **1611** BIBLE *Jas.* i. 17 The Father of lights, with whom is no variablenesse, neither shadow of turning. **1677** HALES *Prim. Orig. Man.* I. v. 113 It being the sovereign Prerogative of Almighty God only, to be without variableness or shadow of change. **1748** RICHARDSON *Clarissa* (1811) II. xxviii. 173 The charge of variableness and inconsistency in judgment. **1782** KNOX *Ess.* xxv. I. 120 This temporary variableness of the mind. **1876** 'OUIDA' *Winter City* vi, His conduct had a variableness about it. **1882** MISS BRADDON *Mt. Royal* xi. II. 263 Is not that kind of variableness common to our poor human nature?

†**c.** Const. *from*. *Obs.*⁻¹

1614 SELDEN *Titles Honor* 1 The variablenesse of the Europeans from the Asians in Asiatique names.

variably ('vɛərɪəblɪ), *adv.* [f. VARIABLE *a.* + -LY².] In a variable, inconstant, or uncertain manner; changeably, with variation.

1590 H. BARROW *Brief Discoverie* 4 Amongst those 4 he stil contended to set vp one chief, which variably fell out, sometimes to one, sometimes to another. **1598** FLORIO, *Variamente*, changeablie,..diuerslie, variablie. **1648** HEXHAM II, *Veranderlicken*, Changeably, or Variably. **1731** BAILEY (ed. 5), *Variably*, changeably, uncertainly. **1772** C. HUTTON *Bridges* iv, The variably increased velocity. **1824** BYRON *Juan* XVI. cxxi, The blue eyes glared, And rather variably for stony death. **1852** H. ROGERS *Eclipse Faith* 372 That Nature was, within certain limits, only variably uniform. **1890** *Science-Gossip* XXVI. 275/1 The..variably-coloured Helices.

Variac ('vɛərɪæk). *Electr.* [f. VARI(ABLE *a.* + *-ac*, perh. repr. *a.c.*, alternating current.] A proprietary name for a type of autotransformer in which the ratio of the input and output voltages can be varied.

1933 *Official Gaz.* (U.S. Patent Office) 26 Dec. 874/2 General Radio Company, Cambridge, Mass... *Variac* for transformers. **1938** *Trade Marks Jrnl.* 16 Feb. 188/2 *Variac*. .. Electrical transformers (not being machines). General Radio Company.., Cambridge, State of Massachusetts. **1943** *Electronic Engin.* XV. 516/3 The movement of the sliding contact on the Variac is effected by a small reversible motor. **1945** [see INTERLOCK *sb.* 2 b]. **1983** *Sci. Amer.* Feb. 118/3, I plugged the immersion heater into a Variac so that I could experiment with the rate at which heat was released in the water.

‖**varia lectio** ('vɛərɪə 'lɛktɪəʊ). Pl. **variae lectiones**. [L., fem. of *var-ius* VARIOUS *a.* + *lectio* reading: cf. LECTION.] = *various reading* s.v. VARIOUS *a.* 8 d.

1652 N. CULVERWEL *Light of Nature* x. 81 'Tis some accurate piece that passes so many Criticks..without any *Variæ lectiones*. **1871** [see Q = *quarto* 2 s.v. Q II. 2 a]. **1969** R. RENEHAN *Greek Textual Crit.* 91 Some MSS have a *varia lectio* διακοιρανέοντα. **1980** *Times* 24 May 14/1 *The Book Collector*..is the place to read..about incunabula and ..*variae lectiones*.

†**variament.** *Obs.*⁻¹ [ad. L. type **variāmentum*, f. *variāre* to VARY.] A disagreement or difference.

1491 *Newminster Cartul.* (Surtees) 251 By reason whereof certane contraversiez, variamentez and debatez wer growen.

variance ('vɛərɪəns). Forms: 4– variance (6 *Sc.* -ans, 6 vareance), 4–6 variaunce (5 -auns); 4–7 varyaunce (5 -awnce, -anse, 6 -ance); 5 wari-, warya(u)nce; 5 veryaunce (fery-), weryauns, -ouns; 6 vari-, *Sc.* warience. [a. OF. *variance*, *-aunce*, *-ence* (= It. *varianza*), ad. L. *variantia*, f. *variāre* to VARY.]

I. 1. a. The fact or state of undergoing change or alteration; tendency to vary or become different; variation.

c **1340** HAMPOLE *Pr. Consc.* 1423 God ordayns here..Sere variaunce..Of þe tyms and wedirs and sesons, In taken of þe worldes condicions, þat swa unstable er and variande. **1398** CHAUCER *Fortune* 45 Thou born art in my regne of varyaunce. Abowte the wheel with oother most thow dryue. *c* **1400** *Brut* xxxiv, [It] was callede þe citee of Ludstan; but now þat name is chaungede þrouȝ variance of lettres, and now is callede London. *c* **1470** HENRY *Wallace* VI. 100 Bot this fals warld, with mony doubill cast, In it is nocht bot werray wariance. **1526** SKELTON *Magnyf.* 2052 She [Fortune] dawnsyth varyaunce with mutabylyte; Nowe all in welth, forthwith in pouerte. **1559** *Mirr. Mag., Duke of Glocester* v, Any man to assure, In state uncarefull of Fortunes varyaunce. **1646** SIR T. BROWNE *Pseud. Ep.* 305 It being reasonable for every man to vary his opinion according to the variance of his reason. **1762** FALCONER *Shipwr.* I. 752 By this magnetic variance is explored. **1840** *Jrnl. R. Agric. Soc.* I. III. 282 The variance in the produce of the wheats I attribute to the nature of the soil. **1859** TENNENT *Ceylon* II. VII. vii. 260 The temperature..ranges from 36° to 81° with a mean daily variance of 11°. **1888** *Harper's Mag.* Apr. 752 Even as the blood loses and replaces its corpuscles, without a variance in the volume and vigor of its current.

†**b.** Inconstancy in persons; variableness, changeableness. *Obs.*

1390 GOWER *Conf.* I. 22 Ther is deceipte in his balance, And al is that the variance Of ous, that scholde ous betre avise. *c* **1400** *Beryn* 1135 The most parte of Room held it for dotage, And had muche mervell of his variaunce. *c* **1449** PECOCK *Repr.* II. vii. 176 He spekith of a variaunce and of a chaunging..in mannis wil. *c* **1480** HENRYSON *Test. Cres.* 223 In hir face semit greit variance, Quhyles perfyte treuth, and quhyles Inconstance. **1500–20** DUNBAR *Poems* xlv. 6 Luve ..Quhilk is begun with inconstance, And endis nocht but variance.

†**c.** In the phr. ***without*** (Sc. ***but***) ***variance***. *Obs.*

The phrase occurs also in sense 3 b.

c **1430** LYDG. *Min. Poems* (Percy Soc.) 10 We say offte hert, withowte variaunce, Sovereigne lord, welcome, welcome ye be! *c* **1470** HENRY *Wallace* IV. 42 Wallace..spak to thaim with manly contenance. In fayr afforme, he said, but wariance [etc.]. **1500–20** DUNBAR *Poems* xxxi. 17 He that with gud lyfe and trewth, But varians or vder slewth,..Dois evir mair with ane maister dwell.

2. a. The fact or quality of varying or differing; difference, divergence, discrepancy.

c **1374** CHAUCER *Troylus* v. 762 For that that som men blamen ever yit, Lo, other maner folk commenden it. And as for me, for alle swich variaunce, Felicitie clepe I my suffisaunce. *c* **1380** WYCLIF *Sel. Wks.* I. 28 For alle Cristene men shulden be of oo wille, and variaunce in siche sectis makiþ variaunce in wille. *c* **1400** MAUNDEV. (Roxb.) xiii. 60 In many poyntes þai vary fra vs and fra oure faith. All þaire variaunce ware to mykil to tell. *c* **1450** *Myrr. our Ladye* 277 Ye haue not many chaunges [of service] after the varyaunce of feastes,..as the comon seruyce of the churche vseth. **1570–6** LAMBARDE *Peramb. Kent* (1826) 221 So is there variance between written storie, and common speech, touching the true place of that building. **1605** CAMDEN *Rem.* (1623) 36 Words, that in their originall are Latine, and yet (saue some small variance in their terminations) fall out all one with the French, Dutch, and English. **1839** HALLAM *Hist. Lit.* IV. ii. §12 It is evident that variance of opinion proves error somewhere. **1846** LANDOR *Imag. Conv.* Wks. I. 243 The variance of knowledge and will, where no passion is the stimulant. **1892** *Law Times* XCII. 156/1 Whether variance between the provisional and complete specification of a patent..is still a ground of invalidity.

†**b.** Variety. *Obs.*⁻¹

a **1400–50** *Alexander* 4632 Mekill variaunce of vertus enveronis oure saules.

3. a. *Law.* A difference or discrepancy between two statements or documents.

1429 *Rolls of Parlt.* IV. 346 For whiche diversite and variaunce of the seide name. *c* **1470** HENRY *Wallace* VIII. 1736 Thar may na band be maid so sufficians, Bot ay in it thai fynd a warians. *a* **1592** GREENE *Jas. IV*, v. iv, *Lawyer*. This matter craues a variance, not a speech. **1596** BACON *Max. & Use Com. Law* xxv. (1636) 98 So if I graunt you.. a way ouer my land according to a plot..whereof a table is annexed to these presents, and there be some speciall variance betweene the table and the originall plot [etc.]. **1706** PHILLIPS (ed. Kersey), *Variance*, an alteration of something formerly laid in a Plea. **1817** SELWYN *Law Nisi Prius* (ed. 4) II. 1107 Advantage cannot be taken of a variance between the plaint and the declaration in the superior court. **1827** *Bentham's Ration. Judic. Evid.* V. 598 The designation..by the name of St. Ethelburgh, instead of Saint Ethelburgha, was held to be (as lawyers term it) a fatal variance. **1835** *Tomlins Law Dict.* (ed. 4) s.v., If there is a variance between the declaration and the writ, it is error; and the writ should formerly abate.

b. In general use: A difference or discrepancy; a discriminating or divergent feature.

1497 *Naval Acc. Hen. VII* (1896) 83 The particuler variances betwene the Indentures and book of shipping. **1511** in *10th Rep. Hist. MSS. Comm.* App. V. 325 There have bene greate variaunce now of late in taking of principales. **1534** MORE *Dial. agst. Trib.* I. Wks. 1153/1 That is a ryght heauy thyng to see suche varyaunces in our belief ryse and grow among our self. **1825** NICHOLSON *Operat. Mechanic* 656 Though in the preceding statements there is an apparent variance,..the variations may have arisen [etc.]. **1860** TENNENT *Ceylon* Introd. xxxix, I have to apologise for variances in the spelling of proper names. **1884** *Law Times* LXXVII. 27/1 The variances..which have arisen between the real property law of the United States and England.

†**c.** Divergence from the truth. *Obs.*

c **1450** LOVELICH *Merlin* 706 How scholde I ȝeven the ony penaunce whanne I knowe wel thou makest variawnce. *Ibid.* 748, 958.

d. *U.S. Law.* An official dispensation from a building regulation.

1925 *New Hampshire Public Laws* xlii. 191 To authorize upon appeal in specific cases such variance from the terms of the ordinance as will not be contrary to the public interest. **1938** *Atlantic Reporter* CC. 521 A literal enforcement of the ordinance may be disregarded to permit a variance, while conditions for an exception must be found in the ordinance and may not be varied. **1973** *N.Y. Law Jrnl.* 19 July 13/7 Judgment is granted in favor of the petitioner..directing the issuance of a variance for the installation of a second kitchen in the premises. **1977** *Sat. Rev.* (U.S.) 3 Sept. 47/3 The only hotel on the island [*sc.* Bermuda] ever given a variance to be built on a hilltop. The permission took 12 years to get.

e. *Econ.* The difference between actual and expected costs, profits, output, etc., in a statistical analysis.

1964 *Times Rev. Industry* Apr. 8/2 An expression of the variation between standard cost and actual achieved cost is called 'variance'. In 1951 under manual control the variance was 31.6 per cent. **1967** D. GOCH in Wills & Yearsley *Handbk. Managem. Technol.* 145 The following example will illustrate the application of this method of variance analysis to an imaginary product. **1974** *Terminol. Managem. & Financial Accountancy* (Inst. Cost & Managem. Accountants) 13 *Variance analysis*, that part of variance accounting..which relates to the analysis into constituent parts of variances between planned and actual performance. **1978** *Accountants' Rec.* Dec. 15/1 Causal factors of the sales variance have been established by analysis... Sales variance analysis..provides data enabling management to reconsider its marketing philosophies.

4. The fact of changing, altering, or varying *from* a state, opinion, etc.; an instance of this.

1415 HOCCLEVE *To Sir J. Oldcastle* 253 Holsum to thee now were a variaunce Fro the feend to our lord god. *c* **1430** LYDG. *Min. Poems* (Percy Soc.) 45 After variaunce Fro lif to dethe. **1529** MORE *Dyaloge* IV. Wks. 271/1 In this point I assure you faythfully, there is no maner change or varyaunce from his oppinion. **1792** JEFFERSON *Writ.* (1859) III. 460 The first and only instance of variance from the former port of my resolution, I was duped into.

5. *Statistics.* The mean of the squares of the deviations of a set of quantities; the square of the standard deviation.

1918 R. A. FISHER in *Trans. R. Soc. Edin.* LII. 399 It is.. desirable in analysing the causes of variability to deal with the square of the standard deviation as the measure of variability. We shall term this quantity the Variance. **1948** *New Biol.* IV. 34 Measurements of the resting blood pressure of a group of fifty young men... We compute the mean blood pressure and the variance of the observed values, the variance being a measure of scatter of values around the mean. **1970** *Nature* 25 July 376/2 Analysis of variance gave highly significant population and fertilizer effects. **1977** R. E. MEGILL *Introd. Risk Analysis* iii. 23 Because all values are squared in the variance the standard deviation is larger than the mean deviation.

II. 6. a. The state or fact of disagreeing or falling out; discord, dissension, contention, debate. (Cf. 8 and 9.)

c **1425** LYDG. *Assembly of Gods* 409 In came Dyscord to haue made varyaunce. **1477** *Rolls of Parlt.* VI. 184/1 If variance falle betwixt any fynder, affermyng ayenst any other persone. **1490** CAXTON *Eneydos* xxiv. 89 [It] maketh theim to enterteyne well togider wythoute varyaunce. **1535** *Act 27 Hen. VIII*, c. 26 §1 Great discorde, variance, debate, ..& sedicion hath growen betwene his said subiectes. **1598** R. BERNARD tr. *Terence, Hecyra* IV. iv, When you seeke forged matter to cause strife and varience. **1639** G. DANIEL *Ecclus.* xxvii. 43 Murder attends the variance of the Proud. **1684** BUNYAN *Pilg. Prog.* II. 192 She makes Variance betwixt Rulers and Subjects, betwixt Parents and Children. **1711** BEVERIDGE *Thes. Theol.* III. 193 What is variance? A sin opposed to amity. **1760–72** H. BROOKE *Fool of Qual.* (1809) IV. 65 If any attempted to..defraud me of my property, I yielded it without variance. **1838** THIRLWALL *Greece* IV. 293 It would be necessary for a time to keep up a show of variance between them. **1855** H. REED *Lect. Eng. Lit.* v. (1878) 159 The bloody variance of a feudal nobility. **1864** MISS YONGE *Trial* II. 152, I never saw a child with such an instinct for preventing variance, or so full of tact and pretty ways.

Comb. **1552** HULOET, Variaunce makers, *litistonsores*.

b. Opposition or antagonism *to* something. *rare.*

1842 MANNING *Serm.* i. (1848) I. 16 An energetic variance of will to the mind of God. **1875** —— *Mission H. Ghost* viii. 210 We have used our wills for all manner of conscious variance to His holy will.

7. a. A disagreement, quarrel, or falling out; a dispute.

c **1425** LYDG. *Assembly of Gods* 244 Wyll ye agre that Phebe your mastresse May haue the guydyng of your varyaunce? **1453** *Rolls of Parlt.* V. 265/1 To make variaunces and commotion betwene you..and youre true people. **1473** WARKW. *Chron.* (Camden) 6 As thei went togedere..there felle in a varyaunce for ther logynge. **1541** BARNES *Wks.* (1573) 339/2 Certaine articles, for yᵉ which there is a varience in the world at this day. **1560** in W. Cotton *Elizabethan Guild* (1873) 21 Yf any variance or controversie shall at any tyme happen to ryse betwene any youre brethren. **1607** *Merry Devil of Edmonton* Induct. 84 Then thus betwixt vs two this variance ends. **1673** *Essex Papers* (Camden) I. 92 It were too long a Story to tell..yᵉ originalls and beginnings of their variances. **1782** J. BROWN *View Nat. & Rev. Relig.* IV. II. 318 No variance hath ever taken place between God and holy angels.

†**b.** *spec.* A difference or dispute leading to legal action between parties. *Obs.*

1476 *Searchers Verdicts* in *Surtees Misc.* (1890) 21 Award & jugement..of a variaunce of a ground be twix John Gilyot Alderman..and Ambrose Preston of London. **1498** *Cov. Leet Bk.* III. 595 Where-as diuerse discordes and wariaunces were late moved & had bitwen the seid parties. **1529** *Supplic. to King* (E.E.T.S.) 51 To here and iudge suche causes and varyaunces. **1562** *Reg. Privy Council Scot.* I. 203 In respect of the variance and debait standand betuix thame. **1732** POPE *Ep. Bathurst* 271 Is there a variance? enter but his door, Balk'd are the Courts, and contest is no more.

III. 8. ***in variance.*** †**a.** Forming a subject of debate, contention, or legal action. *Obs.*

1461–2 *Plumpton Corr.* (Camden) 4 He is agred..to put all thing that is in variance betwixt you & him in the said Sir John & me. **1468** *Searchers Verdicts* in *Surtees Misc.* (1890) 18 A grounde þat stode in variaunce betwix thabbot & Convent. **1534** *Star Chamber Cases* (Selden Soc.) II. 317 Suche matteres as then were in varyaunce bytwene the seid Mulsho and the seid Selby. **1559** BP. SCOT in Strype *Ann. Ref.* I. App. x. 32 Consider, I beseche you, the matters here in Varyaunce. **1588** LAMBARDE *Eiren.* IV. iv. 438 One that mooueth pleas or sutes..to the end to have part of the land, or other thing in variance. **1713** M. HENRY *Conc. Meekness Spirit* (1822) 118 If meekness rule, matters in variance may be fairly reasoned and adjusted.

†**b.** At variance; = 9 b. *Obs.*

c **1465** *Engl. Chron.* (Camden) 64 It happid that with boistez langage.. he fil in variaunce with thaym, and thay fil on him. **1523** LD. BERNERS *Froiss.* I. cccxix. 493 The realme of Englande was as then in great variance among themselfe.

9. ***at variance.*** **a.** Of persons: In a state of discord, dissension, or enmity.

1513 MORE in Grafton *Chron.* (1568) II. 757 The Lordes whome he knew at varyaunce, himselfe in his deathbed appeased. **1598** R. BERNARD tr. *Terence, Andria* III. ii, Simo and Davus are at variance about the birth of the child. **1650** T. BAYLEY *Worcester's Apophth.* 4 The Servants of his house ..were never at variance, in point of Religion. **1683** in *Verney Mem.* (1907) II. 363 Whielst the Emperor and Turke are at variance. **1710** BEVERIDGE *Thes. Theol.* II. 337 God and man naturally are at variance. *a* **1781** R. WATSON *Philip III* (1793) I. I. 60 Neither of the courts at variance seemed ..inclined to prolong the war. **1836** THIRLWALL *Greece* II. 77 The rest of the Peloponnesian allies, seeing the two kings at variance, followed the example of the Corinthians. **1870** BRYANT *Homer* I. II. 34 The powers who dwell In the celestial mansions are no more At variance.

transf. **1718** *Free-thinker* No. 73. 126, I heard a violent Noise, as if the Elements were all at Variance.

b. Const. *with, among(st* or *between, from.*

(*a*) **1528** *Star Chamber Cases* (Selden Soc.) II. 177 James hath brokyn with..his Neyburus..and is at gret waryance with them. **1593** *Bacchus Bountie* C 4, Hee falls at variance with mistris Merigodowne. **1650** *Nicholas P.* (Camden) 204 And they do their best to set this good Princess at variance with her Mother in Law. **1671** MILTON *Samson* 1585 What cause Brought him so soon at variance with him-self Among his foes? **1736** in *10th Rep. Hist. MSS. Comm.* App. I. 454 One..with whom you were at Variance. **1782** MISS BURNEY *Cecilia* VIII. ii, It is with myself only I am at variance. **1839** THIRLWALL *Greece* VI. 39 On all matters as to which he was at variance with the Athenians. **1874** GREEN *Short Hist.* iii. §5. 138 Every year found the Justiciary at greater variance with Rome.

(*b*) **1577** HOLINSHED *Chron.* I. 78/1 The Britaynes..were at variance amongst themselues. **1656** MILTON *Lett. of State* Wks. 1851 VIII. 373 We have beheld the Protestant Princes ..more and more at weakning Variance among themselves. **1867** FREEMAN *Norm. Conq.* (1877) I. 214 The Breton princes were at variance between themselves.

(*c*) **1885** *Times* (weekly ed.) 6 Mar. 11/4 A Government from which..he is totally at variance on points even more important.

c. In the phrases ***to set*** (or †***fall***) ***at variance.***

(*a*) **1526** TINDALE *Matt.* x. 35 For Y am come to sett a man att varyaunce ageynst hys father. [So in later versions.] **1535** COVERDALE *Prov.* xvii. 9 He yᵗ discloseth the faute, setteth frendes at variaunce. **1643** R. BAKER *Chron.* (1653) 541 The Spaniards set York and Stanley at variance. **1655** in *Verney Mem.* (1907) I. 557 Pale-faced envye, mixt with hatred and mallice, hath done there best indeavour to sett us att variance. **1713** ADDISON *Cato* I. iv, To disguise our passions, To set our looks at variance with our thoughts. **1755** YOUNG *Centaur* i. Wks. 1757 IV. 107 Prone to..set things at variance, which, by nature, are allies.

(*b*) **1522** MORE *De Quat. Noviss.* Wks. 89/1 Now shal ye se men fall at varyance for kissyng of the pax. *a* **1578** LINDESAY (Pitscottie) *Chron. Scot.* (S.T.S.) II. 45 The earle of Lennox and the cardinall was fallin at warience. *a* **1635** NAUNTON *Fragm. Reg.* (Arb.) 35 Mars and Mercury fell at variance whose servant he should be.

d. Of things: In a state of disagreement or difference; conflicting, differing. Usu. const. *with.*

(*a*) **1704** POPE *Spring* 60 She runs, but hopes she does not run unseen; While a kind glance at her pursuer flies, How much at variance are her feet and eyes! **1797** S. & HT. LEE *Canterb. T.* (1799) I. 72 His tongue and his countenance were a little at variance. **1826** *Art of Brewing* (ed. 2) 9 The opinions and practices of most brewers are completely at variance upon the subject of mashing. **1868** E. EDWARDS *Ralegh* I. 505 Men's opinions of the worth of what Ralegh actually did as an historian are much at variance. **1910** *Edin. Rev.* Jan. 39 The brow and the mouth are at variance.

(*b*) **1780** *Mirror* No. 84, Nature and Fashion are two opposite powers, that have long been at variance with one another. **1784** COWPER *Task* IV. 621 Arms,..in whatever cause, Seem most at variance with all moral good. **1816** SINGER *Hist. Playing Cards* I. 58 An exquisite Chinese painting is at variance with this assertion. **1849** MACAULAY *Hist. Eng.* i. I. 246 His conduct was not a little at variance with his professions. *a* **1881** A. BARRATT *Phys. Metempiric* (1883) 240 With a doctrine, like Kant's, that [etc]..., my philosophy is wholly at variance.

'variancy. *rare.* [ad. L. *variantia*: see VARY *v.* and -ANCY.] Changeability; variance.

1888 *Macm. Mag.* Oct. 475/1 The surprises there are in man, his complexity, his variancy.

variand, obs. Sc. and north. f. VARYING *ppl. a.*

variant ('vɛərɪənt), *a.* and *sb.* Also 5–6 **varyant** (5 -te), **varyaunt** (5 -te), 5 **variaunt(e.** [a. OF. *variant* (F. *variant*, = Sp., Pg., and It. *variante*), a. L. *variant-, varians*, pres. pple. of *variāre* to VARY.]

A. *adj.* **1. a.** Of persons: Changeful in disposition or purpose; inconstant, fickle. Also const. *of* or *in.* Now *rare.*

c **1386** CHAUCER *Can. Yeom. T.* 622 On his falshede fayn wold I me wreke, If I wist how, But he is heer and there, He is so variant, he byt no where. *c* **1400** *Beryn* 1974 Now þow wolt, & now þow nolt;..Now sey oon, & sith anothir; so variant of mynde! *c* **1450** *Mankind* 274 in *Macro Plays* 11 Be stedefast in condycyon! se ȝe be not varyant! **1509** HAWES *Past. Pleas.* XXVII. (Percy Soc.) 130 To be..In stable love fixt and not variaunt. **1550** BALE *Image Both Ch.* II. G viij, They are..no wher stedfast & vniforme, but euery wher variant & foolish. **1632** LITHGOW *Trav.* IV. 145 He was also deceitfull, variant, and fraudulent. **1890** 'R. BOLDREWOOD' *Col. Reformer* (1891) 360 Calm and resolute, if occasionally variant of mood.

†**b.** Acting in a changeable or fickle manner.

1387 TREVISA *Higden* (Rolls) VIII. 299 He was to large of ȝiftes,..redy to speke and variaunt of dedes.

†**c.** Dissentient, disagreeing. *Obs.*

1412–20 LYDG. *Chron. Troy* III. 3657 Sethen ȝe alle assenten and accorde, Fro ȝoure sentence I wil nat discorde, In no wyse to be variaunt.

2. a. Of things: Exhibiting variation or change; tending to vary or alter; not remaining uniform.

c **1374** CHAUCER *Boeth.* I. met. v. (1868) 22 þi myȝt attempreþ þo variauntz sesons of þe ȝere. **1387–8** T. USK *Test. Love* II. vi. (Skeat) l. 148 After the variaunt opinion in false hertes of unstable people. *c* **1400** *Pety Job* 472 in *26 Pol. Poems* 136 My thoughtes wandre wyde whare, For they ben, lorde, full variaunte. *c* **1430** LYDG. *Min. Poems* (Percy Soc.) 71 God of his grace..preserve youre variaunt brutilnesse. **1533** BELLENDEN *Livy* IV. xv. (S.T.S.) II. 103 þe cry of romanis was variant, slaw, & but curage. **1671** R. MACWARD *True Nonconf.* 136 The Ordinances..therefore were appointed..in a variant and mutable forme. *c* **1674** *Acc. Scotland's Griev. under Lauderdale's Min.* 10 It was also both inconstant in its being, and variant in its number and method. **1751** WESLEY *Wks.* (1872) XIV. 40 Nouns Variant in their gender are *dies* and *finis.*

†**b.** Of fortune, conditions, etc.: = VARIABLE *a.* 1 a. *Obs.* (In early use partly after sense 1.)

c **1412** HOCCLEVE *De Reg. Princ.* 66 So flyttyng is sche [*sc.* Fortune], and so wariant, Ther is no trust vpon hir fair lawhyng. **1470–85** MALORY *Arthur* XX. xvii. 827 But fortune is soo varyaunt, and the whele soo meuable, there nys none constaunte abydynge. **1500–20** DUNBAR *Poems* lviii. 26 So variant is this warldis rent, That nane thairof can be content. **1513** DOUGLAS *Æneid* XI. viii. 117 The variant chance Of our onstabill lyfe. **1561** *Godly Q. Hester* (1873) 58 Contente To thinke it no lyghtnes, nor wytte inconstante, But the necessytie of tymes varyant.

c. Of wind: Changing, shifting. *rare*$^{-1}$.

1847 LONGF. *Ev.* I. i. 82 Above in the variant breezes Numberless noisy weathercocks rattled.

3. a. Exhibiting difference or variety; diversified, varied; diverse, different.

c **1380** WYCLIF *Wks.* (1880) 301 These freris habitis,..þat ben þus large & variaunt as weren habitis of pharisees. *c* **1400** *Rom. Rose* 1917 The arwis were so fulle of rage, So variaunt of diversitee. *a* **1400–50** *Alexander* 5651 þai ware visid all in versis in variant lettirs. **1482** *Monk of Evesham* lvii. (Arb.) 110 A variant medelyng of melody sownyd wyth alle. **1526** R. WHYTFORD *Martiloge* (1893) 19 He was put to many varyaunt turmentes. **1585** JAS. I *Ess. Poesie* (Arb.) 33 So Iob and Ieremie..Did right descryue their ioyes, their woes and torts, In variant verse of hundreth thousand sorts. *c* **1611** CHAPMAN *Iliad* II. Comm., The decorum that some poor critics have stood upon..is far from the variant order of nature. **1632** LITHGOW *Trav.* VI. 291 They who would trauerse earths variant face. *a* **1817** T. DWIGHT *Trav. New Eng.*, etc. (1821) II. 457 The plains are of moderate extent: the surface being almost every where variant, and undulating. **1855** BAILEY *Mystic* 105 The angels ..'stablishing In variant countries various roots of men. **1858** H. BUSHNELL *Nat. & Supernat.* ix. (1864) 260 He can produce variant results through invariable causes.

†**b.** Of colours: Varied, variegated. Also of cloth or an animal in respect of colour. *Obs.*

a **1400–50** *Alexander* 4336 Nouthire..transmitte we na vebbis To vermylion ne violett ne variant littis. **1471** RIPLEY *Comp. Alch.* VI. viii. in Ashm. (1652) 163 By colors varyante aye new and new. **1473–4** *Acc. Ld. High Treas. Scot.* I. 20, vij elne of tartar of variant hewis to lyne a gowne of blac. **1502** *Ibid.* II. 346 Ane variant hors giffin to the King. **1507** *Ibid.* III. 260 Taffeti, grene, rede, blew, and variant. **1575** *Bk. Univ. Kirk Scotl.* 6 Aug., We think.. unseemly..all kinde of..licht and variant hewis in cloathing, as red, blew, ȝellow, and sicklyke. **1600** *Dr. Dodypoll* I. i, Welcome, bright Morne, that with thy golden rayes Reveal'st the variant colours of the world.

4. a. Differing or discrepant *from* something; †also const. *to* (= from).

c **1400** MAUNDEV. (1839) x. 122 And alle theise han manye Articles of oure Feythe, and to othere thei ben varyaunt. **1473–5** in *Cal. Proc. Chanc. Q. Eliz.* (1830) II. Pref. 60 The matter comprised in the side replicacion is new mater variaunt from her bill. **1534** WHITINTON *Tullyes Offices* I. (1540) 31 It is no thynge varyaunt fro the dignyte of a wyse man. **1548** GESTE *Pr. Masse* 134 Thee prieste pryvee Masse ..is not quadrant but variant to the sayd word [of God]. **1741** T. ROBINSON *Gavelkind* ii. 9 Most of the Customs of this Kingdom variant from the Common Law. **1770** *Ann. Reg., Chron.* 143/2 The publication in the papers was variant from that which he sent home. **1860** J. P. KENNEDY *Life W. Wirt* I. xxii. 355 His first impressions of him..are singularly variant from those which [etc.]. **1880** MRS. WHITNEY *Odd or Even?* xli, Words that were absurdly variant from all her present mood.

b. Without const. (Cf. VARIOUS *a.* 8 d.)

1586 FERNE *Blaz. Gentrie* To Gentl. Inner T., They shall find the interpretation thereof many wayes variant and diuers. **1865** STRANGFORD *Selection* (1869) II. 187 With a variant spelling of the body of the word. **1879** FARRAR *St. Paul* I. 373 *note*, One of the numberless instances of variant readings in the Hebrew. **1897** J. M. WHITON *Reconsid. & Reinforcem.* 23 These..are definitions not too variant to stand indifferently for synonyms of spirit.

c. *Biol.* Varying or diverging from type.

1881 *Athenæum* No. 2818. 560 'Angela' is Spielhagen's variant child. **1896** *Advance* (Chicago) 23 April 592/1 In nature a variant minority is liable to be diluted and to disappear by intermixture.

B. *sb.* **1. a.** A form or modification differing in some respect from other forms of the same thing.

1848 LAYARD *Nineveh* II. i. (1849) II. 171 *note*, Many of these [cuneiform] characters are undoubtedly what are termed 'variants'; that is, merely a different way of forming the same letter. **1862** RAWLINSON *Anc. Mon. Chaldæa* I. 143 Il, of course, is but a variant of El. **1869** ELLIS *E.E. Pronunc.* I. iv. 248 Other variants of course occur from carelessness. **1869** RAWLINSON *Anc. Hist.* 336 The names seem, however, to be chiefly variants of the general ethnic title.

b. A various reading; *spec.* a textual variation in two or more copies of a printed work (not necessarily implying reimpression).

1861 PALEY *Aeschylus* (ed. 2), *Agam.* 1116 *note*, The variants -οντο and -όντες only show that a termination was added to the original -ον. **1881** WESTCOTT & HORT *Grk. N.T.* Introd. §3 The primary work of textual criticism is merely to discriminate the erroneous variants from the true. **1927** R. B. MCKERROW *Introd. Bibliogr.* II. vi. 208 Besides these added lines, *The Devil's Charter* exhibits a very large number of striking variants in different copies, some being mere corrections of literal errors, others important alterations in wording. **1953** C. HINMAN in *Shakespeare Q.* IV. 280, I have been able to construct an instrument which ..has enabled me to collate well over a hundred folio pages a day for some months... Taking reasonable care, the investigator can hardly fail to note any variant, however minute, in two copies of the page being examined. **1972** P. GASKELL *New Introd. Bibliogr.* 357 Warner Barnes.. machine-collated an average of six copies of each of his author's eighteen primary editions... In ten of them he found possible evidence of concealed..reimpressions; in another four, variant states of the type not indicating reimpression... Most of the variants shown up by the machine were trivial.

2. A variation of the original work, story, song, etc.

1872 RALSTON *Songs Russian People* 200 There are many variants of the same song, but they do not differ materially. **1877** MISS A. B. EDWARDS *Up Nile* Pref. p. xiii, Religious books, variants of the Ritual, moral essays, maxims. **1885** CLODD *Myths & Dr.* I. iv. 70 They are the variants of stories presumably related in the Aryan fatherland.

3. *Nat. Hist.* A variant form or type.

1895 in *Funk's Stand. Dict.*

†**'variate,** *a. Obs.* [ad. L. *variāt-us*, pa. pple. of *variāre* to VARY.] **a.** Diversified, variegated. **b.** Varied in nature.

c **1440** *Pallad. on Husb.* XII. 52 Olyue is puld of colour variate. **1677** GALE *Crt. Gentiles* IV. 254 The divine effulgence and operation is one essence, both simple and impartible, and boniforme in things partible variate (as to operation).

†**'variate,** *v. Obs.* [a. L. *variāt-*, ppl. stem of *variāre*: see prec.]

1. *trans.* To produce a modification, variation, or change in (something); to alter, cause to change.

1566 PAINTER *Pal. Pleas.* I. (1569) 105 b, The perfection of that which thus doth variat and alter bothe my thoughts and passions. *Ibid.* II. 128 The examples also of sutch diversity do variate and make diverse the affections of men. **1653** GAUDEN *Hierasp.* Pref. 2 Others..study to variate and shift the extern forms and models of Religion. **1701** BEVERLEY *Praise of Glory of Grace* 45 Not Variating this Enquiry into the Multiplicity of the Lesser and more Particular Causes. **1770** BARETTI *Journ. Lond. to Genoa* I. xxi. 162 Female dress is no where variated so much as..in this country.

2. *intr.* To vary or change.

1591 SYLVESTER *Du Bartas* I. ii. 435 That which we touch, with times doth variate, Now hot, now cold.

Hence †**'variated** *ppl. a.*; †**'variating** *vbl. sb.* and *ppl. a. Obs.*

1608 J. KING *Serm.* 5 Nov. 33 What was the cause of their multiplied, variated complotments against hir? **1653** GAUDEN *Hierasp.* 22 Their shiftings and variatings from one living to another. *Ibid.* 28 Who runs like a Badger, with variating and unequal motions. **1656** *Artif. Handsom.* 43 This artificial change is but a fixation of natures inconstancy,..helping its variating infirmities.

variate ('vɛərɪət), *sb. Statistics.* [f. as VARIATE *a.*] †**a.** The value of an attribute common to a number of individuals in any one instance; an observed value of a variate (sense b). *Obs.*

1899 C. B. DAVENPORT *Statistical Methods* i. 1 A variate is a single magnitude-determination of a character... Integral variates are magnitude-determinations of characters which from their nature are expressed in integers. Such magnitudes are determined by counting; *e.g.*, the number of teeth in a porpoise. **1906** R. H. LOCK *Rec. Progress Study of Variation* iv. 90 A variate is one of the separate numerical values from which a curve of variability can be constructed; the biometrician usually deals with some such number as 1,000 variates.

b. A quantity or attribute having a numerical value for each member of a population; *esp.* one for which the values occur according to a frequency distribution.

1909 *Biometrika* VII. 97 We have, σ_1 and σ_2 being the standard deviations of the two variates and *r* their correlation, $\bar{\rho} = r\sigma_1/\sigma_2\bar{q}$. 1925 R. A. FISHER *Statistical Methods for Res. Workers* i. 5 The variable quantity, such as the number of children, is called the variate, and the frequency distribution specifies how frequently the variate takes each of its possible values. 1952 *Sci. News* XXIV. 109 The histogram gives the frequency with which the weight, a variate, takes values in a certain range in the sample. 1968 [see RANDOM *a.* 1 b]. 1971 *Brit. Med. Bull.* XXVII. 2/1 Epidemiology also has a contribution to make.. to the study of attributes (or variates, as some call them) such as intelligence.. and blood pressure.

variation (vɛərɪˈeɪʃən). Forms: 5 **varyacyoune, -cio(u)n,** 6 **-cyon;** 5 **variacioun,** 5–6 **-cion,** 6 **-cyon, -tioun,** 6– **variation.** [a. OF. *variation, -acion* (F. *variation,* = Sp. *variacion,* Pg. *variação,* It. *variazione*), a. L. *variātiōn-, variātio,* n. of action f. *variāre* to VARY.]

I. †1. Difference, divergence, or discrepancy between two or more things or persons. *Obs.*

c 1386 CHAUCER *Knt.'s T.* 1730 In al the world.. So even without variacioun Ther nere suche companyes tweye. 1426 LYDG. *De Guil. Pilgr.* 20066, I sey also.. That ther be.. Many constellaciouns And many varyaciouns. 1460 CAPGRAVE *Chron.* (Rolls) 48 Here is for to noten that their is grete variacion amongst auctoures, both of ȝeres and of Kyngis names. 1480 CAXTON *Myrr.* II. i. 65 This present fygure is.. demonstraunce certayne and trewe, without ony variacion ne doubtaunce. 1553 EDEN *Treat. New Ind.* (Arb.) 42 A clyme is a porcion of the worlde betwene South and North, wherein is variacion in length of the daye, the space of halfe an houre. 1628 T. SPENCER *Logick* 68 Health.. dissenteth from a man that is sicke, by reason of that distance, or variation, which ariseth from sicknes. *a* 1637 B. JONSON *Discoveries* Wks. 1640 II. 106 There is a great variation betweene him, that is rais'd to the soveraignity by the favour of his Peeres, and him that comes to it by the suffrage of the people.

†2. Discord, variance, dissension; an instance of this. *Obs. rare.*

c 1485 *Digby Myst.* (1882) III. 923 Be-twyx yow and me be never varyacyounes. 1523 LD. BERNERS *Froiss.* I. cccxlvi. 548 Thus the Christen realmes were in variacyon, and the churches in great dyfference, bycause of the popes.

†3. a. Uncertainty, doubt. *Obs.*⁻¹

1471 CAXTON *Recuyell* (Sommer) 28 In this sorow and in this payne and varyacion.. Vesca, Abell and the damoysel were a longe tyme.

†b. Inconstancy; variableness.

1509 HAWES *Past. Pleas* XIX. (Percy Soc.) 88 My heart shall be without variacion Wyth you present, in perfite sykernes. *c* 1530 *Crt. of Love* 1340, I.. depely swere as mine power to bene Faithful deuoide of variacion.

II. 4. a. The fact of varying in condition, character, degree, or other quality; the fact of undergoing modification or alteration, especially within certain limits.

1502 *Ord. Crysten Men* (W. de W. 1506) v. vi, In shynynge varyacyon of dyuers coloures. 1513 BRADSHAW *St. Werburge* I. 1340 This present lyfe.. How dredefull it is, full of varyacyon. 1555 EDEN *Decades* (Arb.) 45 Paralleles, are lines whereby the sonne passynge causeth variation of tyme. 1579 FENTON *Guicciard.* I. (1599) 15 Let vs looke somewhat into the variation of times and things of the world. 1637 NABBES *Microcosmus* I I, Two kisses more will cloy me; nought can relish But variation. 1674 BOYLE *Excell. Theol.* II. v. 214 According to the varying gravity of the atmosphere; which variation has.. a very considerable influence on the weather-glass. 1750 tr. *Leonardus' Mirr. Stones* 53 As is held by many learned men who have written of the variation of the air. 1785 G. A. BELLAMY *Apology* (ed. 3) I. 67 Lest you accuse me of a want of variation in the conclusion of my letters, I shall end this in the good old-fashion way. 1822 MISS M. A. KELTY *Osmond* I. 36 In this variation of feeling the morning.. wore away. 1845 G. E. DAY tr. *Simon's Anim. Chem.* I. 246 From these data, it appears, that.. the variation is the most striking with regard to the fibrin and globulin. 1885 WATSON & BURBURY *Math. Th. Electr. & Magn.* I. 96 In order to effect this object the charge upon the conductor must be capable of variation.

b. The action of making some change or alteration.

a 1704 T. BROWN *Satire Antients* Wks. 1730 I. 14 They used in other words the same variation of the letter u into i, as maxumus, maximus. 1711 in *Nairne Peerage Evidence* (1874) 133 The said parties having in order therto agreed.. in the terms of the two former contracts.. without change or variation. 1885 *Law Rep.* 29 *Chanc. Div.* 542 The powers reserved to Wilson Lomer.. to control the variation of investments. 1913 *Act 3 Geo. V,* c. 3 §1 Where a resolution is passed.. providing for the variation of any existing tax.

5. a. ***variation of the compass,*** (*†* ***lodestone,***) or ***needle,*** the deviation or divergence of the magnetic needle from the true north and south line; the amount or angular measure of this; = DECLINATION 8 b.

1556 BURROUGH in *Hakluyt* (1886) III. 126, I went on shoare and obserued the variation of the Compasse, which was three degrees. 1571 DIGGES *Pantom.* I. xxix. I ij b, Drawing a right line making an angle.. equall to the variation of the compass in your region. 1613 PURCHAS *Pilgrimage* (1614) 49 Cabot first found out the variation of the Compasse. 1679 MOXON *Math. Dict.* 160 *Variation of the Needle,* the Turning or Deviation of the Needle in the Mariners Compass [etc.]. 1687 A. LOVELL tr. *Thevenot's Trav.* II. 156 The variation of the Loadstone. 1774 M. MACKENZIE *Maritime Surv.* 62 How to find the Sun's Azimuth, and from thence to find the Variation of the Needle. 1834 MRS. SOMERVILLE *Connex. Phys. Sci.* (1840) xxix. 338 The variation of the compass. 1851 GREENWELL *Coal-trade Terms, Northumb. & Durh.* 16 The diurnal variation of the needle being far from inconsiderable.

b. *ellipt.* in the same sense.

1594 DAVIS *Seaman's Secrets* (1601) 17 If your Compasse be good and without variation. 1597 W. BARLOWE *Navigator's Supply* A 2, By the Variation is vnderstood the difference in the Horizon betweene the true and the magneticall Meridian. 1627 CAPT. SMITH *Seaman's Gram.* ii. 12 There is also.. a Compasse for the variation. 1669 STURMY *Mariner's Mag.* IV. i. 138 The Points of the Needle.. are subject to be drawn aside by the Guns.., or any Iron neer it, and liable to Variation, and doth not shew the true North. 1703 DAMPIER *Voy.* III. I. 100, I found that the Variation did not always increase or decrease in proportion to the Degrees of Longitude East or West. 1769 FALCONER *Dict. Marine* (1780) s.v., The highest variation.. appears to be 17°¼ W. and the least 16°¾ W. 1846 A. YOUNG *Naut. Dict.* 81 The variation is in practice ascertained by comparing the sun's true and magnetic amplitude or azimuths. 1878 [see DECLINATION 8].

c. ***variation of the variation*** (see last quot.).

1706 PHILLIPS (ed. Kersey), *Variation of the Variation,* is so call'd, because the Variation of the Needle is not always the same in the same Place. 1839 NOAD *Electricity* 201 The variation of the variation, that is, the fact that the variation was not a constant quantity, but varied in different latitudes, was first noticed by the discoverer of America. 1867 SMYTH *Sailor's Word-Bk.* 710 *Variation of the Variation,* is the change in the declination of the needle observed at different times in the same place.

6. The fact, on the part of the mercury, of standing higher or lower in the tube of a barometer or thermometer; the extent or range of this.

1719 QUINCY *Phys. Dict.* (1722) 11 The greatest Variation of the Height of the Mercury being 3 Inches. 1748 *Anson's Voy.* II. v. 183 The variation of the thermometer at Petersburgh is at least five times greater.. than.. at St. Catherine's. 1815 J. SMITH *Panorama Sci. & Art* II. 28 Had the tube been straight, Q would have been the limit of the scale of variation. 1858 LARDNER *Hand-bk. Nat. Phil.* 168 A rise or fall of the mercury in the tube, within the usual limits of barometric variation.

7. *Astr.* **a.** The libration of the moon; = LIBRATION 2.

1704 J. HARRIS *Lex. Techn.* I, *Variation* is, according to Tycho, the third Inequality in the Motion of the Moon. 1728 PEMBERTON *Newton's Philos.* 199 This inequality of the moon's motion about the earth is called by astronomers its variation. 1812 WOODHOUSE *Astron.* (1823) I. II. 682 The Variation is occasioned by the other resolved part, that which acts in the direction of the tangent to the Moon's orbit. 1879 NEWCOMB & HOLDEN *Astron.* 163 The disturbing action of the sun [upon the moon] produces a great number of the other inequalities, of which the largest are the evection and the variation.

b. (See quot.)

1867 SMYTH *Sailor's Word-Bk.* 43 *Annual Variation,* the change produced in the right ascension or declination of a star by the precession of the equinoxes and proper motion of the star taken together.

8. *Math.* **†a.** = PERMUTATION 3 b. *Obs.*

1710 J. HARRIS *Lex. Techn.* II, *Variation,* or Permutation of Quantities, is the changing any number of given Quantities, with respect to their Places. 1728 CHAMBERS *Cycl.* s.v. *Combination,* Suppose the Quantities 3, and the Exponent of Variation 3; the Number of Changes is found $27 = 3^3$.

b. Change in a function or functions of an equation due to an indefinitely small increase or decrease in the value of the constants.

1743 W. EMERSON *Fluxions* 3 The Velocity, Variation, or Quickness of Increase (or Decrease) of any Fluxion is called the second Fluxion. 1810 R. WOODHOUSE *Treat. Isoperimetrical Probl.* ii. 23 If problems involving merely one property, the maximum, require the variation of two, and those involving two properties, the variation of three elements [etc.]. 1843 *Penny Cycl.* XXVI. 136/2 *Variation.* Under this head comes the explanation of a part of the language of proportion which is much used... We refer to such phrases as the following:—A varies as B.—A varies inversely as B. 1847 *Cambr. & Dublin Math. Jrnl.* I. 264 We have, in this case, by Lagrange's theory of the variation of the arbitrary constants, the formulæ da/dt = [etc.]. 1885 WATSON & BURBURY *Math. Th. Electr. & Magn.* I. 6 Then.. *u* will, on arriving again at *O*, have assumed by continuous variation the value $u_0 + H$. 1918 H. C. PLUMMER *Introd. Treat. Dynamical Astron.* xii. 134 This is the foundation of Lagrange's method of the variation of arbitrary constants. 1966 H. POLLARD *Math. Introd. Celestial Mech.* iv. 91 We shall begin with the undisturbed system $\dot{x}_1 = -x_2, \dot{x}_2 = k^2x_1$, and apply the method of variation of parameters.

c. ***variation of curvature:*** (see quot. 1842).

a 1727 NEWTON *Meth. Fluxions & Inf. Ser.* (1736) 76 The Inequability or Variation of Curvature is required at any Point of a Curve. 1842 FRANCIS *Dict. Arts, Variation of curvature,* the change made on a curve, so as to occasion it to be flatter or sharper in each succeeding part.

d. *Algebra.* The following of a + sign after a − sign, or vice versa, in a row of signs.

1891 in *Cent. Dict.*

e. The difference between the values of a function at either end of a subinterval; the sum of such differences for all the non-overlapping subintervals into which a given interval is divided; the upper bound (if any) of this sum when all possible modes of subdividing the interval are considered.

1905 J. PIERPONT *Lect. Theory Functions Real Variables* I. xii. 349 An important class of limited integrable functions is formed by functions with limited variation. 1911 *Q. Jrnl. Pure & Appl. Math.* XLII. 57 Although in forming the positive (negative) variation over (*a, b*) we considered all possible sets of non-overlapping intervals, we may without loss of generality confine ourselves to sets consisting of a finite number of intervals only. 1946 H. & B. S. JEFFREYS *Methods Math. Physics* i. 23 The total variation is of interest since it is related to the condition for existence of a Stieltjes integral.. and to the determination of the total length of a curve. 1971 E. R. PHILLIPS *Introd. Anal. & Integration Theory* ix. 251 Let us assume that the set of nonnegative variations.. is bounded from above.

9. *Mus.* (See quot.)

1730 *Treat. Harmony* 34 There is another sort of Division called Variation, which may also be upon a Division.

10. *Biol.* Deviation or divergence in the structure, character, or function of an organism from those typical of or usual in the species or group.

1859 DARWIN *Orig. Spec.* i. 11 There are many laws regulating variation, some few of which can be dimly seen. 1867–8 LYELL *Princ. Geol.* III. xliii. (ed. 10) II. 488 If some modification of an organ, or instinct, be produced by what is called 'Spontaneous Variation'. 1871 TYNDALL *Fragm. Sci.* (1879) II. ix. 176 No naturalist could tell how far this variation could be carried. 1882 VINES tr. *Sachs' Bot.* 925 The characters of many of these varieties are perfectly hereditary, and all the organs show the greatest degree of variation.

III. 11. a. An instance of varying or changing; an alteration or change in something, esp. within certain limits.

Sometimes in specific senses: cf. 5–10 above.

1611 COTGR., *Muance,* change, alteration; and particularly, a variation, or change of notes in singing. 1659 PEARSON *Creed* (1839) 525 The natural course of variations in the creature. 1665 *Phil. Trans.* I. 31 A Baroscope, or an instrument to show all the Minute Variations in the Pressure of the Air. 1719 DE FOE *Crusoe* II. (Globe) 486 Variations of the Compass. 1758 JOHNSON *Idler* No. 11 ¶11 The most variable of all variations: the changes of the weather. 1786 MRS. A. M. BENNETT *Juvenile Indiscr.* IV. 231 They.. contrived to fill a long summer's day, or winter's evening, by an agreeable variation of female amusements. 1832 HT. MARTINEAU *Weal & Woe* vii. 94 Seasons are sometimes stormy and our commerce liable to variations. 1844 *Proc. Philol. Soc.* I. 196 We may therefore be disposed to consider all marked variations of dialect as evidences of difference of date. 1874 tr. *Lommel's Light* 181 The variations of light and shade are alone visible.

b. A difference due to the introduction or intrusion of some change or alteration.

1699 BENTLEY *Phal.* 36 We have the firmer ground to go upon for this little Variation. 1727 T. INNES *Anc. Inhab. Scot.* (1879) 87 Variations which the negligence as well as the ignorance of transcribers is ordinarily the cause of. 1861 PALEY *Æschylus* (ed. 2) *Supplices* 842 *note,* The other MSS. present only slight variations. 1869 TOZER *Highl. Turkey* II. 272 The.. stories have evidently come from the same original, but present curious variations in the form under which the youth is born. 1878 HUXLEY *Physiogr.* 192 In different specimens.. the lava exhibits great variations.

c. *Biol.* A slight departure or divergence from a type. (Cf. 10.)

1835 LYELL *Princ. Geol.* III. ii. (ed. 4) II. 428 The phenomenon, that some individuals are made to deviate widely from the ordinary type... How far.. may such variations extend in the course of indefinite periods of time? 1859 DARWIN *Orig. Spec.* Introd. 4 We shall see how great is the power of man in accumulating by his Selection successive slight variations. 1871 R. H. HUTTON *Ess.* I. 65 An accidental variation only means a variation of which you cannot determine the direction. 1882 VINES tr. *Sachs' Bot.* 777 Changes in these hereditary peculiarities, or variations, are never brought about by direct external influences.

d. A different form or species; a variety, variant.

1863 HUXLEY *Knowl. Org. Nat.* 99 If, by crossing a variation with the original stock, you multiply that variation, and then take care to keep that variation distinct from the original stock, and make them breed together. 1868 *Boy's Own Bk.* 593 The Matadore Game.. is a variation of All Fives. 1878 BROWNING *Poets Croisic* 5 Try a variation of the game!

12. A deviation or departure *from* something.

1647 CLARENDON *Hist. Reb.* I. §178 Besides that any Variation from it.. would make the Uniformity the less. *a* 1662 HEYLIN *Laud* I. 223 It was best to take the English Liturgie, without any variation from it. 1782 J. BROWN *Nat. & Rev. Relig.* III. ii. 246 There often befalls it a deforming variation from the original happy constitution. 1818 CRUISE *Digest* (ed. 2) I. 208 He did not think fit to make any variation from what was then determined.

13. *Math.* **a.** (Cf. 8 a.)

1728 CHAMBERS *Cycl.* s.v. *Combination,* Suppose two Quantities, *a* and *b*; their Variations will be 2; consequently, as each of those may be combined, even with it self, to these there must be added two Variations.

b. The amount by which some quantity changes in value, or the addition made to the quantity; *esp.* the change in a function when there is a small change in the variables or constituent functions of the function; ***calculus of variations,*** a form of calculus applicable to expressions or functions in which the law relating the quantities is liable to variation.

In the calculus of variations the function concerned is usu. an integral, and the aim is to find what relation between the variables in the integrand makes the integral a maximum or a minimum.

1810 WOODHOUSE (*title*), A Treatise on Isoperimetrical Problems, and the Calculus of Variations. *Ibid.* iii. 45 The general form of these equations is, $P.bg - Q.ci + R.d\delta$, $d\delta$ being a variation of the ordinate similar to the variations *bg* and *ci*. 1814 J. TOPLIS tr. *Laplace's Treat. Analytical Mech.* ii. 46 Of all the curves along which a moving body, subjected to the forces *P, Q,* and *R*, can pass from one given point to another given point, it will describe that in which the variation of the integral $\int v ds$ is nothing, and in which, consequently this integral is a minimum. 1834 [see LEAST *a.* 1 e]. 1845 *Encycl. Metrop.* II. 209 To obtain the variation of a function of *y* we must write $y + \delta y$ for *y*, and having expanded the new function according to the powers of δy, subtract from it the original function, and the first term of the difference will be the variation required. **1855** Brewster *Newton* I. xiii. 349 The calculus of variations discovered by Lagrange in 1760, was the greatest step in the improvement of the infinitesimal calculus which was made in the last century. **1861** Todhunter (*title*), A History of the Progress of the Calculus of Variations during the Nineteenth Century. **1934** W. V. Houston *Princ. Math. Physics* v. 56 The variation of the integral is defined as its value when α has the infinitesimal value δα, minus its value when α is zero. **1972** M. Kline *Math. Thought* xxiv. 578 By equating the variation of the integral to zero and by using a crude limiting process to transform the resulting difference equation, he obtained the differential equation which must be satisfied by the minimizing arc.

14. a. *Mus.* A modification with regard to the tune, time, and harmony of a theme, by which on repetition it appears in a new but still recognizable form; *esp.* in pl., embellishments in an air for giving variety on repetition after playing it in its simple form.

1801 Busby *Dict. Mus.* (1811), *Variations*, or *Var*, the name given to certain ornamented repetitions, in which, while the original notes, harmony, and modulation, are.. so far preserved as to sustain the parent subject, the passages are branched out in flourishes. **1820** Scott *Let.* in *Lockhart* (1837) IV. xi. 371 She ran a set of variations on 'Kenmure's on and awa'', which I told her were enough to raise a whole country-side. **1873** H. C. Banister *Music* 216 In some Sonatas, etc., one of the Movements is a Theme with Variations.

b. ***elegant variation***: in writing, the stylistic fault of studiedly avoiding repetition by using different words for the same thing. Also *transf.* and in ironic use.

1906 H. W. & F. G. Fowler *King's English* iii. 178 The locking of arms is.. only an elegant variation for clinging. **1926** H. W. Fowler *Mod. Eng. Usage* 131/1 It is the second-rate writers.. that are chiefly open to the allurements of elegant variation. **1947** Partridge *Usage & Abusage* 16/1 Mr Herd then picks on the device known as 'elegant variation'. 'If,' he says, 'the mayor has been mentioned, he makes further appearance as 'the civic chief', 'the leader of our official life'.. and so on.' **1981** *Guardian Weekly* 5 July 21 Most of the costumes are.. elegant variations on dancers' practice dress. **1982** *Washington Post* 7 May D2/6 ... rarely occurs less than twice per page, and often as many as five, with a 'f---' or two stuck in for elegant variation.

c. *Ballet.* A solo dance.

1912 *Dancing Times* Aug. 420/2 [Grahn's] career was interrupted by an accident while rehearsing a *variation* which she was to perform at [a] benefit. **1948** *Ballet Ann.* II. 49 She attacks the formidable difficulties of the variation and adagio with an ease and confidence. **1980** 'M. Fonteyn' *Magic of Dance* 65 He makes the preparation for his 'variation', or solo, with utmost care and accuracy.

15. *attrib.* in sense 5 b, as ***variation-chart, compass, instrument***; also **variation method** *Physics*, a method for finding an approximate solution to Schrödinger's equation by varying the trial solutions to find which gives the lowest value for the energy and is therefore closest to the true solution; **variation order**, an order authorizing a change in an original order or contract (see quots.); **variation principle** *Physics*, the principle (employed in the variation method) that the energy corresponding to an arbitrary wave function cannot be less than the actual lowest energy of the system under consideration.

1727 Bailey (vol. II), *Variation Chart*, a Chart design'd by Dr. Halley. **1748** *Anson's Voy.* Introd., A new variation-chart lately published. **1867** Smyth *Sailor's Word-Bk.* 710 The admiralty variation chart has been brought to great perfection. **1669** Sturmy *Mariner's Mag.* II. vi. 67 The Use of the Quadrant and Variation-Compass. **1769** *Phil. Trans.* LIX. 483 The variation compass.. was.. a very good one. **1837** Lloyd in *Rep. Brit. Assoc.* VI. App. 21 The variation instrument will be placed in the magnetic meridian, with respect to the theodolite. **1935** Pauling & Wilson *Introd. Quantum Mech.* vii. 182 The variation method is.. very frequently used to obtain approximate wave functions as well as approximate energy values. **1960** [see *quantum-chemical* adj. s.v. quantum 7 a]. **1974** P. W. Atkins *Quanta* 96/2 With these approximations in hand the variation method is applied to determine the best linear combination of atomic π-orbitals to describe the structure of the molecule. **1940** *Chambers's Techn. Dict.* 886 *Variation order*, .. a document giving authority for some alteration in work being done under contract. **1975** E. B. Ceadel in Barr & Line *Essays on Information & Libraries* iv. 58 Where a change is made in the contract arrangements, it is listed by the architect as a *variation order*, which is subsequently costed by the quantity surveyors. **1977** *Daily Tel.* 19 Nov. 3/2 An order was prepared.. requiring him to leave by Nov. 17... The Home Secretary.. had considered whether, instead of issuing a 'variation order', he should proceed under another provision of the Immigration Act 1971 with a view to deportation. **1923** Variation principle [see *quantum condition* s.v. quantum 7 a]. **1975** H. F. Hameka *Quantum Theory Chem. Bond* i. 28 We shall discuss the two methods of approximation that are most widely used in quantum chemistry, namely the variation principle and perturbation theory.

vari'ational, *a.* [f. prec. + -al¹.] Marked or characterized by, dealing with or concerning, variation, in various senses; *spec.* with reference to variation 13 b.

1879 Thomson & Tait *Nat. Phil.* I. i. §327 Which.. is the general variational equation of motion of a conservative system. **1888** *Encycl. Brit.* XXIV. 77/1 This succession of variational theories. **1897** *Acta Math.* XXI. 99 His substitution of the Variational Curve for the ellipse as the intermediate orbit is.. of primary importance in the Lunar Theory. **1907** *Sat. Rev.* 5 Oct. 422/1 Man.. is more variational than woman. **1937** E. C. Kemble *Fund. Princ. Quantum Mech.* iv. 130 Let J denote the integral $J[y, \lambda]$... Let δy denote the first variation in $y(x)$... Let it be required to find a function $y(x)$ and a corresponding value for the parameter λ which satisfy the variational equation $\delta J = 0$. **1957** L. Fox *Numerical Solution Two-Point Boundary Probl.* viii. 259 With a single second-order equation we were able to fix both y_0 and y_1, so that y_n was a function only of λ, and by solving a variational equation for $\partial y/\partial\lambda$ we were able to alter λ systematically until a solution was obtained. **1962** C. S. Ogilvy *Tomorrow's Math* ix. 125 Questions asking what shape, what path, or what form will yield a minimal or optimal result are known as variational problems. **1971** *Physics Bull.* Jan. 17/1 We introduce a trial wave-function ψ containing as many variational parameters as we feel to be necessary or sufficient, and then choose the values of these parameters in such a way that the Rayleigh ratio.. shall be stationary.

vari'ationist. [f. as prec. + -ist.] **1. a.** One who composes musical variations.

1901 J. Huneker *Mezzotints Mod. Music* 35 Brahms.. is not only the greatest variationist of his times, but with Bach and Beethoven the greatest of all times.

b. One who practises variation or introduces variety in anything.

1926 H. W. Fowler *Mod. Eng. Usage* 132/1 The writers are confirmed variationists. **1928** J. Y. T. Greig *Breaking Priscian's Head* 66 Mr Fowler.. pokes fun at the 'elegant variationist'. **1981** *N.Y. Times* 25 Jan. II. 25/4 Johns is by nature a variationist—someone who hates to let a good idea go while there is still something that can be done with it. *Ibid.* 2 Oct. c28/6 It works wonderfully well in terms of Mr. Judd's skill as a variationist. Every one of the 10 sections of the work has the same basic set of themes.

2. One who studies variations in usage among different speakers of the same language.

1975 *Amer. Speech 1973* XLVIII. 37 What variationists have discovered is the extraordinary stylistic and sociological importance of such variation, and the apparently remarkable consistency with which the frequency of a given alternant is patterned throughout society and throughout an individual's stylistic repertoire. **1978** *Archivum Linguisticum* IX. 48 Committed variationists .. seem to disagree on how variation is to be incorporated into the grammar of a language. **1983** *Canadian Jrnl. Linguistics* XXVIII. i. 82 It is not, however, a problem for the variationists, but for those who would arbitrarily reduce linguistics to a branch of cognitive psychology.

vari'atious, *a. rare*⁻¹. [Irreg. f. variation.] = variational *a.*

1875 Jowett *Plato* (ed. 2) II. 175 The names of Astyanax and Hector are really the same, for the one means a king, and the other is a 'holder or possessor'; 'tis all one meaning, save the phrase is a little variatious.

'variative, *a.* [f. vary *v.* + -ative.] Accompanied by or showing variation; variational.

1874 Winchell *Doctr. Evolution* B. §4. 48 The hypothesis that this variative improvement is capable of being continued indefinitely.

Hence **'variatively** *adv.* (*Stand. Dict.* 1895).

variator ('vɛərɪeɪtə(r)). [In sense 1, a. mod.L. *variātor*; in sense 2, f. variate *v.* + -or.]

†1. In University use: (see vary *v.* 5 d). *Obs.*

1749 Pointer *Oxon. Acad.* 18 The Variator opposing Aristotle, in three Latin Speeches.

2. A kind of joint, esp. used in electric subways, to compensate for variations of length in the connexions, due to changes of temperature.

1891 in *Cent. Dict.*

varicap ('vɛərɪkæp). *Electronics.* [f. *vari*(*able cap*(*acitance.*] = varactor.

1967 Aegerter & Habian in *IEEE Trans. Broadcast & Television Receivers* Nov. 103/1 A varicap is a variable capacitance diode. **1975** G. J. King *Audio Handbk.* iv. 98 Tuner-amplifiers in which varicaps are employed for tuning must also feature supply regulation. **1981** J. C. Sprott *Introd. Mod. Electronics* vi. 137 A typical varicap has a capacitance that varies over about a factor of 10 in the picofarad range.

'varicated, *a. Zool.* [f. as next.] Of a shell: Marked or furnished with varices.

1891 in *Cent. Dict.*

varication (værɪ'keɪʃən). [f. L. *varic-*, stem of *varix* varix.]

†1. *Path.* Varicose condition or formation. *Obs.*

1684 tr. *Bonet's Merc. Compit.* viii. 290 Cutting a Sinus in two places, where the varication begins, and where it ends.

2. *Zool.* The formation of a varix or varices in a shell; the form or arrangement of these.

1891 in *Cent. Dict.*

†'varice. *Obs.* [a. F. *varice* or ad. L. *varicem* varix.] A varix or varicose vein.

1541 R. Copland *Galyen's Terap.* 2 F j, Bycause of the rotten blode, or varyce (that is to say a tumyde vayne) that causeth the fluxion. **1597** A. M. tr. *Guillemeau's Fr. Chirurg.* 31/2 The Varice or bursten vayne is therunder situated.

variceal (værɪ'siːəl), *a. Med.* [f. L. *varic-*, varix + -al; *-eal* after *corneal*, *laryngeal*, etc.] Of, pertaining to, or involving a varix.

[**1947** *Jrnl. Amer. Med. Assoc.* 8 Nov. 630/1 (*heading*) Intraesophageal venous tamponage. Its use in a case of varical hemorrhage from the esophagus.] **1961** Postlethwait & Sealy *Surg. Esophagus* xii. 392/1 Others.. later used tamponade for control of variceal hemorrhage. **1981** *Brit. Med. Jrnl.* 17 Jan. 189/2 Haemorrhage from varices around an artificial intestinal stoma.. is well documented... Variceal haemorrhage from a colostomy has been less frequently reported.

‖**varicella** (værɪ'sɛlə). *Path.* [mod.L. (Vogel, 1764), irreg. dimin. of *variola* variola. Cf. F. *varicelle.*] Chicken-pox.

1771 *Encycl. Brit.* III. 59 Exanthemata, or eruptive fevers; comprehending 10 genera, *viz.* 1. Erysipelas; 2. Pestis; 3. Variola; 4. Varicella; 5. Rubeola [etc.]. **1804** *Med. Jrnl.* XII. 441 Though very much resembling variola, I remarked, [that] it might yet be found to be varicella. **1825** Good *Study Med.* (ed. 2) III. 85 While.. varicella or water-pox in all its varieties, was designated by the term variola. **1876** Bristowe *Th. & Pract. Med.* (1878) 181 Varicella has been largely confounded with small-pox, of which it has been regarded as a modified variety.

attrib. **1897** *Trans. Amer. Pediatric Soc.* IX. 131 Around many of the varicella marks.. a rapid ulceration immediately began. **1898** *Hutchinson's Arch. Surg.* IX. 369 It might be the result of.. a sequel of varicella, i.e. a varicella prurigo.

Hence **vari'cellar** *a.*, varicellous. **vari'celloid,** modified smallpox, varioloid.

1873 F. T. Roberts *The. & Pract. Med.* 186 Small-pox after Vaccination—Varioloid—Varicelloid. **1891** *Cent. Dict.*, *Varicellar.* **1899** *Allbutt's Syst. Med.* VIII. 720 When the disease is engrafted on the lesions of varicella.. it does not confine itself to the varicellar lesions.

vari'cellous, *a. Path.* [f. varicell-a + -ous.] Of or relating to, affected with, of the nature of, varicella or chicken-pox.

1822 *Edin. Rev.* XXXVIII. 333 The boy sleeping with his varicellous brother would become varicellous. **1825** Good *Study Med.* (ed. 2) III. 81 Every variety to which the small-pox can make any fair pretension, distinct, confluent, crystallized or varicellous. *Ibid.* 92 This slightness of irritability in the fluid of the varicellous vesicle. **1897** *Brit. Med. Jrnl.* 28 Aug. 33 Varicellous Laryngitis.

varices, pl. of varix.

va'riciform, *a. rare*⁻⁰. [ad. mod.L. *variciformis*, f. L. *varic-* varix.] Resembling a varix.

1849 in Craig. **1859** in Mayne *Expos. Lex.* [Recent Dicts. give *varicoid* in the same sense.]

†'varicle. *Obs.*⁻¹ [f. L. *varic-* varix: see -cle.] A varicose tumour or swelling.

1684 tr. *Bonet's Merc. Compit.* xviii. 600/1 A Nun had a very painful Varicle, and.. when I had set fire to it, it was discussed at once.

varicocele ('værɪkəʊsiːl). *Path.* [mod.L., f. L. *varic-* varix + Gr. κήλη tumour. So F. *varicocèle.*] Varicose condition or dilatation of the spermatic veins.

1736 A. Monro in *Med. Ess. & Obs.* (1742) V. i. 323 In the Vessels of a Person labouring under the *Varicocele*. **1846** Brittan tr. *Malgaigne's Man. Oper. Surg.* 469 Most authors distinguish *varicocele*, a varicose dilatation of the veins of the scrotum, from *circocele*, a varicose state of the veins of the spermatic cord; but surgeons in the present day generally understand, by *varicocele*, the varicose affection of the cord itself, which is much more common than that of the scrotum. **1874** Van Buren *Dis. Genit. Org.* 468 Varicocele is constituted by a varicose enlargement of the pampiniform plexus and veins of the cord. **1883-4** *Med. Annual* 56/1 A very successful mode of treating varicocele.

attrib. **1895** *Arnold & Sons' Surg. Instr. Catal.* 576 Varicocele Clamp,.. Spring Tractor,.. Needles,.. Ring.

varicocelectomy (ˌværɪkəʊsɪ'lɛktəmɪ). *Surg.* [f. varicocel(e + -ectomy.] An operation to remove a varicocele.

1894 Gould *Med. Dict.* 1590/1 *Varicocelectomy*.., excision of a varicocele. **1950** A. I. Dodson *Urol. Surg.* (ed. 2) xliv. 719 (*heading*) Inguinal varicocelectomy. **1980** S. J. Silber *How to get Pregnant* (1981) v. 149 The first successful case of restoration of fertility after varicocelectomy.

vari-coloured, varicoloured ('vɛərɪˌkʌləd), *a.* Also 7, 9 **vary-colour'd,** 9 **variecoloured.** [f. L. *vari-us* various *a.* + coloured *ppl. a.*] Of various or different colours; variegated in colour.

1665 Sir T. Herbert *Trav.* (1677) 115 They adorn it according to fancy; sometimes with ribbons, sometimes with streamers of varicoloured Taffata. **1684** tr. *Agrippa's Van. Arts* lxii. 184 Vary-colour'd, many-coated, canvas-wearing cloak-carriers. **1822** *New Monthly Mag.* IV. 486 The vari-coloured clouds that hang.. upon its sides. **1830** Tennyson *Arab. Nts.* 57 A walk with vary-colour'd shells. **1841** Catlin *N. Amer. Ind.* xxiv. (1844) I. 198 A profusion of vari-coloured beads. **1899** F. T. Bullen *Log Sea-waif* 73 All around the edge of the darkness ran an incessant tangle of vari-coloured lightnings.

b. *fig.* Different, diverse, diversified.

1855 Browning *Cleon* 161 My works, in all these vari-coloured kinds. **185.** Lowell *Leg. Brittany* ii. xxxii, Where fifty voices in one strand did twist Their varicoloured tones.

varicose (værɪ'kəʊs, 'værɪkəʊs), *a.* [ad. L. *varicōs-us* (hence It., Sp., and Pg. *varicoso*), f. *varic-* varix: see -ose.]

1. *Path.* or *Med.* Affected with, characterized by, of the nature of, a varix or varices.

1730 Bailey, *Varicose*, that hath the Veins puffed up and swoln more than ordinary with corrupt Blood. **1770** *Med. Observ.* (1772) IV. 377 Two Letters on the Varicose

Aneurysm, from Mr. W. White, Surgeon at York, to W. Hunter. **1808** BARCLAY *Muscular Motions* 234 Cases of disease where the distension of these veins had..produced ..that unseemly appearance which is termed varicose. **1826** S. COOPER *First Lines Surg.* (ed. 5) 180 The use of the knife, and of ligatures for the cure of varicose ulcers. **1843** *Penny Cycl.* XXVI. 185 Varicose affection of the veins of the spermatic cord constitutes the disease named varicocele. **1880** BASTIAN *Brain* 32 They then not unfrequently assume an irregular or varicose appearance.

b. Of veins: Unnaturally swollen or dilated.

'When a vein becomes varicose, it has a blue colour, becomes dilated, knotty, and irregular, and winds in a serpentine manner under the skin' (1835 *Cyclop. Pract. Med.* IV. 445).

1797 M. BAILLIE *Morb. Anat.* (1807) 357 When the enlargement of the veins is very considerable, they also become varicose. **1807** *Med. Jrnl.* XVII. 299, I have met with many instances of varicose veins on this island. **1844** G. BIRD *Urin. Dep.* (1857) 403 She had morning sickness, and the veins of her lower extremities were varicose. **1884** M. MACKENZIE *Dis. Throat & Nose* II. 56 The patient had varicose veins of the gullet.

fig. **1846** LANDOR *Imag. Conv.* Wks. I. 74 Milton has..not a sinew sharp or rigid, not a vein varicose or inflated. **1864** SALA in *Temple Bar* Feb. 337 The responsibility of originating these varicose veins in the limbs of a fair city.

2. *Ent.* and *Bot.* Unusually enlarged or swollen; resembling a varix.

1826 KIRBY & SP. *Entomol.* IV. xl. 103 These [bile-vessels] by Malpighi and the earlier physiologists..were denominated *varicose* vessels. *Ibid.* xlvi. 340 *Varicose*,.. when the nervures are disproportionably swelled in any part. **1882** VINES tr. *Sachs' Bot.* 468 The bordering cells project into the canal like varicose hairs.

3. Of appliances: Designed or used for the treatment of varicose veins.

1858 SIMMONDS *Dict. Trade*, *Varicose-stockings*, elastic or bandaged stockings for giving pressure and support to swelled veins in the legs.

Hence **vari'cosed** *ppl. a.*

1891 in *Cent. Dict.* **1900** *Brit. Med. Jrnl.* No. 2040. 248, I now saw a bright red varicosed papilla.

varicosity (værɪˈkɒsɪtɪ). [f. VARICOSE *a.* + -ITY.]

1. A varicose swelling or distension.

c **1842** *Todd's Cycl. Anat.* III. 233 Irregular dilatations or varicosities of the absorbent vessels. **1877** HUXLEY *Anat. Inv. Anim.* I. 64 These fibrils present numerous minute varicosities, and, at intervals, larger swellings. **1897** *Allbutt's Syst. Med.* II. 1078 On pricking one of these varicosities a larger or smaller quantity of fluid escapes.

2. The state or condition of being varicose or abnormally swollen; an instance or case of this.

1876 GROSS *Dis. Bladder*, etc. 157 The disease here consists either in a simple varicosity or in the development of vascular growths. **1897** *Allbutt's Syst. Med.* III. 380 Varicosity of the veins at the lower end of the œsophagus. **1898** P. MANSON *Trop. Diseases* xxxi. 462 One [type of disease] characterised by varicosity of lymphatics.

transf. **1891** RAYLEIGH in *Proc. Roy. Inst.* (1893) XIII. 264 The cylindrical [liquid] jet may be said to become *varicose*, and the varicosity goes on increasing with time.

3. The state of having varicose veins.

1879 H. P. DUNN in *Barthol. Hosp. Rep.* XV. 251 Varicosity of the lower limbs is met with in seamen.

†**'varicous**, *a. Obs.* [ad. F. *variqueux* (Paré) or L. *varicōs-us* VARICOSE *a.*] Varicose.

1597 A. M. tr. *Guillemeau's Fr. Chirurg.* 45/1 Greate Armes and great Legges, which are varicouse. **1621** BURTON *Anat. Mel.* II. iv. I. ii, Which saith that in melancholy and mad men, the varicous tumor hæmorroides appearing doth heale the same. **1634** T. JOHNSON *Parey's Chirurg.* xx. vii. (1678) 461 The swelling and blackness of the Tongue, and as it were varicous veins lying under it. **1710** T. FULLER *Pharm. Extemp.* 261 This Linament,..contracting the varicous Vessels, reduces them to their due Tenor and Size. **1782** *Med. Comm.* I. 119 The cutaneous veins were slightly varicous. **1786** *Ibid.* II. 97 [The veins had] assumed a varicous appearance.

varied (ˈvɛərɪd), *ppl. a.* [f. VARY *v.*]

1. Differing from one another; of different or various sorts or kinds.

1588 SHAKS. *Tit. A.* III. i. 86 Where like a sweet mellodius bird it sung Sweet varied notes inchanting euery eare. —— *L.L.L.* v. ii. 775 Varying in subiects as the eie doth roule, To euerie varied obiect in his glance. **1718** PRIOR *Solomon* I. 350 How shall We next o'er Earth and Seas pursue The vary'd Forms of ev'ry thing we view. **1796** H. HUNTER tr. *St.-Pierre's Stud. Nat.* (1799) II. 268 The very birds and quadrupeds, which are more beautiful, and of species more varied, in islands than any where else. **1851** HELPS *Comp. Solit.* x. 181 So varied, extensive and pervading are human distresses. **1878** STEWART & TAIT *Unseen Univ.* ii. §76. 87 That astronomy is competent to explain the varied motions of the heavenly bodies. **1880** *Grove's Dict. Music* II. 567 The art of adapting musical ideas to the varied capabilities of Stringed, Wind, Keyed, and other Instruments.

2. Marked by variation or variety; presenting different forms or qualities on this account.

1732 POPE *Ess. Man* I. 27 Observe..what other planets circle other suns, What vary'd Being peoples ev'ry star. **1748** GRAY *Alliance* 27 Howe'er opinion tinge the varied Mind. **1784** COWPER *Task* I. 172 The sloping land.. Displaying, on its varied side, the grace Of hedge-row beauties numberless. **1828** SCOTT *F.M. Perth* xiv, When I behold..this rich and varied land, with its castles, churches, ..and fertile fields. **1838** JAMES *Robber* iv, The path she followed was like a varied but a pleasant life. **1887** RUSKIN *Præterita* II. 252 Sketching the boat and her sails in their varied action.

b. *poet.* Of the Deity or persons.

a **1748** THOMSON *Hymn* 2 These, as they change, Almighty Father, these Are but the varied God. The rolling year Is full of thee. **1763** CHURCHILL *Apology* Poems I. 68 The varied actor flies from part to part.

3. Vari-coloured, variegated; *esp.* in the names of birds or animals.

1715 POPE *Iliad* IV. 225 Stiff with the rich embroider'd work around, My varied belt repell'd the flying wound. **1781** PENNANT *Hist. Quad.* I. 195 Varied Monkey. *Ibid.* II. 413 Varied Squirrel..: upper part of the body varied with black, white, and brown. **1782** LATHAM *Gen. Synop. Birds.* I. II. 568 Varied Woodpecker. **1817** STEPHENS in Shaw's *Gen. Zool.* X. II. 333 Senegal Flycatcher... Varied Flycatcher, with white eye-brows, and the outer tail-feathers half white. **1861** *Chambers's Encycl.* II. 726/1 Varied Monkey (*Cercopithecus Mona*)—an African species. **1891** *Cent. Dict.* s.vv. *Pickerel, Shrike, Thrush.*

4. *Comb.* in ***varied-coloured***, ***-winged*** adjs.

1811 SHAW *Gen. Zool.* VIII. II. 420 Varied-winged Parrakeet... Green Parrakeet, with blue crown, and wing-coverts varied with black, blue, and yellow. **1818** HERVÉ *How to Enjoy Paris* (ed. 2) 18 A little messenger of comfort, clad in varied-coloured rags. **1845** J. COULTER *Adv. in Pacific* xiv. 215 The varied-coloured bright feathers of the ground-parrot.

variedly (ˈvɛərɪdlɪ), *adv.* [f. prec. + -LY[2].] In a varied manner; diversely.

1827 CARLYLE *Germ. Rom.* I. 293 Whatever was beautiful ..these noble gentlemen had tastefully and variedly expended on the glory of that day. **1864** PUSEY *Lect. Daniel* v. 238 Good and evil are so variedly mingled in nations or individuals, that [etc.]. **1878** COX *Salv. Mundi* vii. (ed. 3) 156 We see how that law works here—how variedly and subtlely, and with what delicate complexity.

'variedness. *rare.* [-NESS.] Diversity of aspect or character.

1897 *Expositor* Oct. 281 It will flourish..by impregnating the life of the town with its own variedness.

variegate (ˈvɛərɪgeɪt, -rɪg-), *v.* Also 8 **variagate.** [f. L. *variegāt-*, ppl. stem of *variegāre* to make varied or of divers colours, f. *vari-us* VARIOUS *a.*]

1. *trans.* To diversify; to invest with variety; to enliven with differences or changes.

1653 MORE *Antid. Ath.* Ep. Ded. A3 The glorious Wisdom and Goodness of God so fairly drawn out and skilfully variegated in the sundry Objects of externall Nature. **1812** W. TENNANT *Anster F.* Pref., Ancient and modern manners are mixed and jumbled together, to heighten the humour or to variegate the description. **1813** SHELLEY *Q. Mab.* IV. 150 All the germs Of pain or pleasure, sympathy or hate, That variegate the eternal universe. **1852** H. ROGERS *Ecl. Faith* (1853) 122 The spectacle of the infinite diversities of religion, which variegate, but alas! do not beautify the world.

b. *esp.* To render varied in colour or appearance; to mark or cover with patches of different colours or objects.

a **1728** WOODWARD *Fossils* I. 20 The Shells are filled with a white Spar, which variegates and adds to the Beauty of the Stone. **1796** MORSE *Amer. Geog.* I. 620 The blended verdure of woodlands and of cultivated declivities..variegates the prospect in a charming manner. **1855** MACAULAY *Hist. Eng.* xviii. IV. 238 Where the British flag, variegated by the crosses of Saint George and Saint Andrew, hung by the side of the white flag of France. **1863** HAWTHORNE *Our Old Home* (1879) 107 Lichens..variegate the monotonous gray with hues of yellow and red.

2. To vary by change or alteration. *rare.*

1674 JEAKE *Arith.* (1696) 371 Particulars are to be divided by a Mixture of Division of Species and Compound Surds, variegated as the Case requires. **1775** ADAIR *Amer. Ind.* 69 They were not in a savage state, when they first separated, and variegated their dialects, with so much religious care, and exact art.

Hence **'variegating** *ppl. a.*

1727 POPE, etc. *Art Sinking* 93 Of tropes and figures: and first of the variegating, confounding, and reversing figures.

variegated (ˈvɛərɪgeɪtɪd, -rɪg-), *ppl. a.* [f. prec. or L. *variegāt-us*, pa. pple. of *variegāre.*]

1. a. Marked with patches or spots of different colours; varied in colour; of diverse or various colours; many-coloured, vari-coloured; *spec.* in *Bot.* (see VARIEGATION 1).

a **1661** FULLER *Worthies, Norwich* (1662) 274 The skil in making Tulips..variegated, with stripes of divers colours. **1688** BOYLE *Final Causes* ii. 46 In sawing pieces of variegated marbles. **1718** POPE *Odyss.* xv. 145 She said, and gave the veil;..The prince the variegated present took. **1748** *Anson's Voy.* II. viii. 218 The glittering of the sun on their variegated plumage. **1781** GIBBON *Decl. & F.* xviii. (1787) II. 78 A variegated flowing robe of silk. **1812** *Examiner* 24 Aug. 544/2 Some of his tradesmen..illuminated their houses with variegated lamps. **1852** *Beck's Florist* 212 This magnificent new variegated plant is a native of Java. **1876** BRISTOWE *Th. & Pract. Med.* (1878) 565 They are sometimes smooth, sometimes ribbed, upon the surface, and often variegated in colour.

Comb. **1763** MILLS *Pract. Husb.* III. 238 However, neither the yellow, nor the variegated, flowered lucerne is ever so strong as that with purple flowers. **1883** *Harper's Mag.* April 727/1 Near it is the striking foliage of the variegated-leaved althea.

b. In the specific names of animals, birds, etc.

A large number of similar uses occur in the works of Latham and Shaw.

1783 LATHAM *Gen. Syn. Birds* II. I. 99 Variegated chatterer. *Ibid.* 181 Variegated Bunting (*Emberiza principalis*). **1792** SHAW *Mus. Leverianum* 38 The Variegated Baboon. **1801** —— *Gen. Zool.* II. 17 Variegated Cavy. *Ibid.* 123 Variegated Marmot. **1802** *Ibid.* III. I. 235 Variegated Lizard. **1804** *Ibid.* V. II. 439 Variegated Sun-fish. **1814** LEACH *Zool. Misc.* I. 117 Variegated Coucal. **1840** [see SOLE *sb.*[2] 2]. **1871** *Cassell's Nat. Hist.* I. 95 The Douc, or Variegated Monkey,..is perhaps the most gaily clad of all this group. **1881** *Ibid.* V. 73 The Variegated Sole (*Solea variegata*) is rarely more than eight or nine inches long, and closely resembles the Common Sole. **1888** *Cassell's Encycl. Dict.* s.v., Variegated spider-monkey, *Ateles variegatus*, or *bartlettii*.

c. In the names of plants or shrubs.

1818 M. EDGEWORTH *Let.* 4 Oct. (1971) 107 All the varieties of trees and shrubs..he has now revealed to view —The tulip tree and acacia and variegated oak and..the variegated rhododendron. **1852** G. W. JOHNSON *Cott. Gard. Dict.* 904/2 Variegated Laurel, *Aucuba.* **1855** MISS PRATT *Flower. Pl.* V. 260 Variegated Simethis. **1859** —— *Brit. Grasses* 298 Variegated Rough Horse-tail. **1874** T. HARDY *Far fr. Mad. Crowd* II. x. 100 Boughs of laurustinus, and variegated box,..and boy's love.

d. *Min.* (See quots.)

1836 T. THOMSON *Min., Geol.*, etc. I. 622 Variegated Copper Ore. Buntkupferz—liver-coloured copper ore. **1862** DANA *Min.* 294 Erubescite.—Variegated Copper Pyrites. **1888** *Cassell's Encycl. Dict.* s.v., *Variegated copper-ore*, the same as Bornite. *Ibid.*, *Variegated-sandstone*, a name formerly given to the New Red Sandstone.

2. a. Marked or characterized by variety; of a varied character, form, or nature; diverse.

1662 STILLINGFL. *Orig. Sacræ* II. vii. 3 Therein was abundantly seen Gods πολυποίκιλος σοφία, his variegated wisdom. **1687** N. N. *Old Popery* 18 God Almighty..accepts the variegated Services of his different Creatures. **1762** FALCONER *Shipwr.* Proem 20 Ye ever-tuneful Nine! whose sacred lyres,..in softer notes, express The variegated pang of deep distress. **1775** ADAIR *Amer. Ind.* 110 The dancers prance it away, with wild and quick sliding steps, and variegated postures of body. **1798** WASHINGTON *Lett.* Writ. 1893 XIV. 57 The variegated and important duties of the Aids of a Commander-in-Chief..require experienced Officers. **1817** CHALMERS *Astron. Disc.* iv. (1852) 105 The minute and variegated details of the way in which this wondrous economy is extended. **1897** MARY KINGSLEY *W. Africa* 387, I go along the same variegated path I came by yesterday.

b. Composed of persons of various characters or kinds; heterogeneous; motley. *rare.*

1807 WORDSW. *White Doe* I. 162 A variegated band Of middle aged, and old, and young. **1863** KINGLAKE *Crimea* (1877) I. xix. 381 The variegated group which composed Lord Aberdeen's ministry.

3. Varied or diversified (in colour, appearance, etc.) *with* something.

1678 CUDWORTH *Intell. Syst.* 379 The whole World, variegated with Plants, Animals and Stars, being his [*sc.* God's] Temple. **1751** JOHNSON *Rambler* No. 156 ⁋10 No plays have oftener filled the eye with tears..than those which are variegated with interludes of mirth. **1774** GOLDSM. *Nat. Hist.* (1776) VII. 265 The colour is generally an olive brown, variegated with one that is more dusky. **1796** MORSE *Amer. Geog.* I. 180 The tract of country..is happily variegated with plains and mountains, hills and vallies. **1806** *Gazetteer Scot.* (ed. 2) 433 The surface is variegated with hills and eminences, streams of water, and fertile plains. **1845** *Florist's Jrnl.* (1846) VI. 104 Their colour is a bright-golden scarlet; the limb variegated with red and yellow. **1870** HOOKER *Stud. Flora* 287 Corolla blue variegated with white inside.

4. Characterized by variegation (of colour).

1664 POWER *Exp. Philos.* I. 7 Who does not admire the variegated diversity of colours in her [the butterfly's] expansed wings? **1835** LYELL *Princ. Geol.* III. xvi. (ed. 4) III. 271 The surface..was of a variegated colour. **1877** BLACK *Green Past.* xlii, A rich wilderness of flowers, of the most bountiful verdure and variegated colours.

5. Produced by variation; variant.

1872 LIDDON *Elem. Relig.* iv. 143 For all that disease is disease, and not a variegated form of health.

Hence **'variegatedness.**

1668 WILKINS *Real Char.* 215 Variegatedness, motly, pyed, particoloured, divers colours.

variegation (vɛərɪˈgeɪʃən, -rɪgeɪ-). [f. VARIEGATE *v.* Cf. Sp. *variegacion*, Pg. *variegação.*]

1. The condition or quality of being variegated or varied in colour; diversity of colour or the production of this; *spec.* in *Bot.*, the presence of two or more colours in the leaves, petals, or other parts of plants; also, defective or special development leading to such colouring.

1646 SIR T. BROWNE *Pseud. Ep.* 364 He..that could content himselfe..that the variegation of Birds was from their living in the Sunne. **1656** BLOUNT *Glossogr.*, *Variegation*, a garnishing with divers colours. **1758** JOHNSON *Idler* No. 64 ⁋5, I happened to catch a moth of peculiar variegation. **1775** ADAIR *Amer. Indians* 3 The variegation.. of colours among the human race. **1843** *Penny Cycl.* XXVI. 142/1 This variegation of the leaves sometimes disappears. **1861** BENTLEY *Man. Bot.* 745 Variegation in leaves must be regarded as a diseased condition of the cells of which they are composed. **1882** G. ALLEN in *Nature* XXVI. 323 When we come to consider the subject of variegation [of colours in flowers] and of reversion.

b. With *a* and pl. Also, a variegated marking.

1664 EVELYN *Kal. Hort.* 77 Plant them [tulips] in natural earth somewhat impoverish'd with very fine sand; else they will soon lose their variegations. **1725** *Fam. Dict.* s.v. *Florist's Year* (Sept.), Remembering always 'tis Nourishment is the Cause of Variegations in Plants. **1771** *Phil. Trans.* LXI. 48 The beautiful variegations in them [specimens of marble] may have probably been occasioned by the mineral vapours. **1796** KIRWAN *Elem. Min.* (ed. 2) II. 78 Its colours..passing into variegations. **1828** STARK *Elem. Nat. Hist.* I. 471 Body brown, smooth, with white variegations. **1884** BROWNING *Ferishtah* (1885) 112 And where's the gloom now?—silver-smitten straight, One glow and variegation!

2. The action or process of diversifying or rendering varied in character; an instance or occasion of this.

1668 H. MORE *Div. Dial.* LII. xxiii. 451 There being Folly and Wickedness all over the World, it is better there should be this variegation of it, then that it should be every-where in the same dress. *a* **1680** GLANVILL *Disc. Serm. & Rem.* x. (1681) 376 His attributes are but the several modes and variegations of Almighty Love. **1727** POPE, etc. *Art Sinking* 97 For variegation, nothing is more useful than the Paranomasia, or Pun. **1775** JOHNSON *West. Isl.* Wks. 1825 IX. 157 The variegation of time by terms and vacations. **1777** —— *Lett.* (1788) I. 363 Do not omit painful casualties, or un-pleasing passages; they make the variegation of existence. **1834** HT. MARTINEAU *Moral* III. 85 The diversity of production which takes place on the earth, occasioning.. a perpetual variegation and augmentation of commodities.

†**b.** Alternation *of* (one thing with another). *Obs.*

1779 JOHNSON *L.P.*, *Addison* Wks. III. 47 His.. variegation of prose and verse, however, gains upon the reader.

ˈvariegator. *rare.* [f. as prec.] One who or that which variegates.

1891 in *Cent. Dict.* **1910** DRIVER in *Expositor* Feb. 121 The 'work of the variegator' is prescribed for the screens of the Tent of Meeting.

varier (ˈvɛərɪə(r)). [f. VARY *v.*]

†**1.** *Hist.* = PREVARICATOR 4. *Obs.*

1614 [see PREVARICATOR 4]. **1665** BUCK in Peacock *Stat. Cambr.* (1841) App. B. p. lxxxii, The Proctor calleth up the Varier or Prævaricator, who, having ended his speech, is dismist by the Proctor.

2. One who varies or dissents *from* something.

1860 TENNYSON *Sea Dreams* 19 They gain'd a coast.. At close of day; slept, woke, and went the next, The Sabbath, pious variers from the church, To chapel.

varietal (vəˈraɪɪtəl), *a.* and *sb.* [f. VARIET-Y + -AL[1].] **A.** *adj.* **1.** *Biol.*, *Bot.*, and *Min.* Of or pertaining to, connected with, indicating, etc., a distinct variety of animal, plant, or mineral. Opposed to *specific* or *generic*.

1866 DARWIN *Orig. Spec.* (ed. 4) ii. 59 He is at first much perplexed in determining what differences to consider as specific, and what as varietal. **1873** DAWSON *Earth & Man* xiv. 319 The careful study of varietal forms. **1881** LEES in *Jrnl. Bot.* X. 25 Quite sufficiently distinct to merit a varietal if not a specific name. **1902** *Jrnl. R. Instit. Cornwall* XV. 123 No one can deny that it merits varietal rank. **1933** [see ŒLLACHERITE]. **1966** [see CASWELLITE].

2. Of wine: made predominantly from a single variety of grape; also, of or pertaining to the vine or grape of a particular variety. orig. *U.S.*

1941 SCHOONMAKER & MARVEL *Amer. Wines* xi. 260 The expense of.. certification could be borne by a small per-gallon tax levied upon varietal wine. *Ibid.*, Until it [*sc.* identification of the grape varieties grown in America] has been accomplished, a system of honest varietal labeling is virtually unattainable. **1955** J. STORM *Invitation to Wines* 72 The success of varietal wines in California has influenced some Eastern vintners. **1968** *Amer. Speech* 1967 XLII. 80 Varietal types of wines. **1973** *Bulletin* (Sydney) 25 Aug. 7/2 (Advt.), An aromatic wine.. with varietal flavour. **1979** A. HAILEY *Overload* III. v. 214 Among other things, Nim Goldman was a wine buff. He had a keen nose and palate and especially liked varietal wines from the Napa Valley. **1981** *Times* 2 Mar. 12/6 Limousin oak casks.. contributed another complex dimension to its distinct varietal personality.

B. as *sb.* A wine made from a single variety of grape. orig. *U.S.*

1955 J. STORM *Invitation to Wines* 72 The wines labeled according to the name of the chief informing grape are called varietals. **1977** H. FAST *Immigrants* IV. 254 There is no need for you to try to produce a varietal, which simply means a wine produced out of a single variety of grape. **1977** *Times* 15 Nov. (Italian Wine Suppl.) p. iii/3 Lambrusco, the famous wine of Modena.. is a varietal, the Lambrusco being the grape from which it is vinified. **1979** *Tucson* (Arizona) *Citizen* 28 Apr. (Weekender Mag.) 7/2 A 1977 Emerald Riesling.. displayed a high acidity that may be typical of the varietal.

Hence **vaˈrietally** *adv.*, in respect of varietal qualities; as a distinct variety.

1873 DAWSON *Earth & Man* xii. 290 Not only did man exist at this time, but man not even varietally distinct from modern European races. **1879** *Encycl. Brit.* IX. 386/2 Foraminifera.. which can be identified—not only generically and specifically, but even varietally. **1942** M. F. MABON *ABC of America's Wines* ii. 13 The majority of varietally named wines happen to be blends.

varietist (vəˈraɪɪtɪst), *sb.* [f. VARIET(Y + -IST.] One who chooses variety, esp. in the satisfaction of (sexual) desires; also *attrib.* or as *adj.* Hence **vaˈrietism**, the practice or result of such choices.

1911 G. B. SHAW *Getting Married* Pref. 153 The reassurance that man is not promiscuous in his fancies must not blind us to the fact that he is (to use the word coined by certain American writers to describe themselves) something of a Varietist. **1925** T. DREISER *Amer. Tragedy* I. I. xiii. 101 So captivated was he by this savor of sensuality and varietism that was about her. **1968** *Ann. Amer. Acad. Pol. & Social Sci.* July 65/2 Some sexual varietists.. believe that they *need* plural sex-love affairs. *Ibid.*, Such individuals manage to have their varietist inclinations fulfilled. *Ibid.* (*heading*) Sexual varietism. **1977** *N.Y. Rev. Bks.* 15 Sept. 26/2 'Free love' never meant libertinism.. but quite simply that there should be no coercion in sexual relationships... There were 'exclusivists' and 'varietists'.

variety (vəˈraɪɪtɪ). Forms: 6 **varyete, varietee, -tye,** 6–7 **-tie,** 7– **variety.** [a. F. *variété* (= It. *varietà*, Sp. *variedad*, Pg. *variedade*), or ad. L. *varietāt-*, *varietās* difference, diversity, etc., f. *vari-us* VARIOUS *a.*: see -TY.]

†**1. a.** Variation or change of fortune. *Obs.*

a **1533** LD. BERNERS *Gold. Bk. M. Aurel.* (1546) G viij, The players and gesters suffered great varietee in the empyre, according to the diuersitee of emperours. **1617** MORYSON *Itin.* II. 114 Our loose wings sometimes beating the rebels.. and sometimes being driven by them back to our Colours.. and this skirmish continuing with like varietie some three howers.

†**b.** Tendency to change; fickleness; change of purpose or plans. *Obs.*

a **1548** HALL *Chron.*, *Hen. VII*, 11 Thinkyng surely that they.. would neuer consent & longe agree with the English-men, accordyng to their olde vaffrous varietie. **1579** FENTON *Guicciard.* (1618) 312 This varietie (if it be possible to find out the truth in so great inconstancie) many attributed to his credulitie and lightnesse of beliefe.

†**c.** Dissension, division. *Obs.*[−1]

1546 BALE *Eng. Votaries* I. 68 After the decease of King Edgare,.. was a wonderfull varyete and scisme through out the whole realme.

2. Difference or discrepancy between things or in the same thing at different times.

1552 HULOET, Varietie in fourme, *dissimilitudo.* **1580** FULKE *Martiall Confut.* viii. Wks. (Parker Soc.) II. 193 The variety in time that is in the witness of the invention of the Cross. **1604** E. G[RIMSTONE] *D'Acosta's Hist. Indies* III. xix. 180 Many, according to the varietie of their opinions, attribute this to diverse causes. **1629** H. BURTON *Truth's Tri.* 245 The vulgar Latine.. hath noted in the margin.. in the variety of reading. **1654** tr. *Scudery's Curia Pol.* 165 You cannot.. but conclude.. that my reasons are valid and strong for the variety of my different Conduct in such great Affairs. **1748** *Anson's Voy.* II. x. 246 This.. occasions a very remarkable variety in the manner of equipping the ship for these two different voyages. **1774** GOLDSM. *Nat. Hist.* (1776) VI. 381 Upon examination, there will be less variety found between them than between birds that live upon land, and those that swim upon the water. **1861** PALEY *Æschylus* (ed. 2) *Prometh.* 591 *note*, There is the same variety in 601, and the latter reading necessitates the questionable lengthening of α before πρ in 612.

3. a. The fact, quality, or condition of being varied; diversity of nature or character; absence of monotony, sameness, or uniformity.

1548 UDALL *Erasm. Par. 1 Cor.* xii. 34 The diuers placying and vse is not to the member reprochful, but this varietie rather apertayneth to the welth of the whole body. **1561** tr. *Calvin's Four Godly Serm.* iii. G j, Although amonges men, there be soche a varietie & defference of myndes and desyres. **1606** SHAKS. *Ant. & Cl.* II. ii. 241 Age cannot wither her, nor custome stale Her infinite variety. **1675** R. BURTHOGGE *Causa Dei* 63 By Representing the Variety of Opinions about the thing whereon I now discourse. **1704** F. FULLER *Med. Gymn.* (1711) 3 They do not Consider the wonderful Variety of the Disorders of Nature. **1843** *Civil Eng. & Arch. Jrnl.* VI. 108/1 The powerfulness, and variety of this splendid instrument. **1856** KINGSLEY *Lett.* (1878) I. 497 The perpetual variety of work which I have been in. **1860** MOZLEY *Univ. Serm.* vii. 156 We find ourselves surrounded by the greatest variety of character in the world.

b. Without article.

1567 MAPLET *Gr. Forest* 27 b, It is to be maruelled how Dame Nature hath.. for varietie sake so manifoldly varied and multiplied yᵉ kindes of colours either simply died, and stained, or [etc.]. *a* **1633** J. AUSTIN *Medit.* (1635) 270 Therefore in Pleasures both Body and Soule desire with fulnesse of Pleasure to have fulnesse of variety. *a* **1680** BUTLER *Rem.* (1759) I. 15 And she [Nature] affects so much to use Variety, in all she does. *a* **1721** PRIOR *Ess. & Dial. Dead, Opinion* Wks. 1907 II. 196 We judge of things according to the humour we are in and that very Humour is subject to infinite Variety. **1784** COWPER *Task* II. 606 Variety's the very spice of life, That gives it all its flavour. **1826** DISRAELI *V. Grey* v. iv, Variety is the mother of enjoyment. **1859** *Habits of Gd. Society* xi. 312 A sensible man avoids variety in drinking. **1875** JOWETT *Plato* (ed. 2) V. 14 There is a want of variety in the answers.

c. As a literary, musical, or artistic quality.

1597 MORLEY *Introd. Mus.* III. 180 So that you must in your musicke be wauering like the wind, sometime wanton, sometime drooping,.. and shew the verie vttermost of your varietie, and the more varietie you shew the better shal you please. **1601** R. CHESTER *Love's Martyr* Title-p., A Poeme enterlaced with much varietie and raritie. **1622** PEACHAM *Compl. Gent.* x. (1906) 86 Varietie is various, and the rules of it so difficult [etc.]. *Ibid.*, To proceed further, were to translate Virgil himselfe; therefore hitherto of varietie. **1753** HOGARTH *Anal. Beauty* ii. 16 How great a share variety has in producing beauty. **1846** RUSKIN *Mod. Paint.* I. II. ii. §8 Variety is never so conspicuous, as when it is united with symmetry. **1870** SWINBURNE *Ess. & Stud.* (1875) 61 Variety is a rare and high quality, but poets of the first order have had little or none of it.

d. *pl.* A series or succession of different forms, conditions, etc.; variations.

1604 E. G[RIMSTONE] *D'Acosta's Hist. Indies* II. viii. 100 We see great varieties in the yeere, which proceeds from the divers motions and aspects of Planets. **1668** COWLEY *Ess., Agric., Virg. Georg.* 40 What makes the Sea retreat, and what advance: Varieties too regular for chance. **1748** *Anson's Voy.* II. v. 180, I must.. make a short digression on the heat and cold of different climates, and on the varieties which occur in the same place in different parts of the year. **1794** G. ADAMS *Nat. & Exp. Philos.* IV. xliv. 406 The great distance of.. Saturn.. [does] not permit us to distinguish the varieties of its surface. **1805** FOSTER *Ess.* I. i. 5 The varieties through which life has passed. **1849** MACAULAY *Hist. Eng.* ii. I. 167 He had passed through all varieties of fortune, and had seen both sides of human nature.

†**4.** The fact or quality of being varied in colour; variegation. *Obs. rare.*

1555 EDEN *Decades* (Arb.) 67 Hauyng theyr fethers entermengled with greene, yelowe, and purple, whiche varietie deliteth the sense not a litle. **1609** BIBLE (Douay) *Exod.* xxvi. 31 Twisted silke, wrought with imbrodered worke and goodlie varietie. —— *Ezek.* xvii. 3 A great eagle with great winges.. ful of feathers, and of varietie, came to Libanus.

5. Used as a collective to denote a number *of* things, qualities, etc., different or distinct in character; a varied assemblage, number, or quantity *of* something.

In some instances hardly distinguishable from sense 3.

a. With *the.*

1553 T. WILSON *Rhet.* (1580) 30, I might heape together the varietie of pleasures, which come by travaile. **1623** HEMINGE & CONDELL in *1st Folio Shaks.* A 3 *heading*, To the great Variety of Readers. **1634** SIR T. HERBERT *Trav.* 186 Behold the varietie of temporary blessings. **1798** S. & HT. LEE *Canterb. T.* II. 164 The variety of simple scenes.. made him delight to linger in Switzerland. **1851** CARPENTER *Man. Phys.* (ed. 2) 579 The variety of movements of which the hand of Man is capable.

b. Without article. ? *Obs.*

1575 FENTON (*title*), Golden Epistles, contayning varietie of discourse, both morall, philosophicall, and divine, gathered as well out of the remainder of Guevaraes workes, and other authors. **1602** WARNER *Alb. Eng.* XI. lxv. 278 Varietie of Men to court a Woman is her pride. **1680** MORDEN *Geog. Rect.*, *England* (1685) 21 Bravely furnished with Variety of pleasant Orchards and Gardens. *c* **1791** *Encycl. Brit.* (ed. 3) VIII. 541/1 Hindostan affords variety of beasts for carriage, as camels, dromedaries [etc.].

c. With *a*, *that*, etc.

1708 SEWEL II. s.v. *Verschiet*, There is no variety of goods; There's no choice to be had. **1728** CHAMBERS *Cycl.* s.v. *Vein*, In digging.., they meet with a Variety of Veins. **1774** GOLDSM. *Nat. Hist.* (1776) VIII. 197 He thus perceived a variety of kinds, almost equal to that variety of productions, which these little animals are seen to form. **1780** *Mirror* No. 77, From this circumstance.. a variety of remarks might be made. **1863** P. BARRY *Dockyard Econ.* 262 In consequence of the quality of the work executed, Messrs. Maudslay.. have performed a great variety of smaller operations. **1875** JOWETT *Plato* (ed. 2) I. 240 Like Proteus, he transforms himself into a variety of shapes. **1891** FARRAR *Darkn. & Dawn* xv, To Nero.. every man was sluggish and plebeian who did not care to season his recreation with a variety of vices.

d. With a plural verb.

1718 LADY M. W. MONTAGU *Let. to C'tess Bristol* 10 April, For twenty miles together.. the most beautiful variety of prospects present themselves. **1780** BENTHAM *Princ. Legisl.* xix. §24 Now of the infinite variety of nations there are upon earth, there are no two which agree exactly in their laws. **1849–50** ALISON *Hist. Europe* X. lxv. §74. 69 A variety of false attacks were immediately directed.. against the ramparts. **1887** *Science* X. 115 A variety of hooks were used for different kinds of fish and according to the time of day.

6. a. A different form *of* some thing, quality, or condition; something which differs or varies from others of the same class or kind; a kind or sort.

Also without *of*: see (*b*).

(*a*) **1617** J. TAYLOR (Water P.) *Observ. & Trav. Lond. to Hamburgh* Wks. (1630) 81/2 They haue strange torments and varieties of deaths, according to the various nature of the offences that are committed. **1639** S. DU VERGER tr. *Camus' Admir. Events* To Rdr. a vij, Some good soules.. will be glad to finde profitable admonitions.. with varieties of pleasures fitting their humour. **1784** COWPER *Tiroc.* 475 The spirit of that competition burns With all varieties of ill by turns. **1852** H. ROGERS *Ecl. Faith* (1853) 118 The distinction between the certain and the probable is felt to be too important not to be marked by corresponding varieties of speech. **1860** MOZLEY *Univ. Serm.* vii. (1877) 156 Even the varieties of good character are almost infinite. **1873** HAMERTON *Intell. Life* I. iv. 22 The two lads represent two distinct varieties of human life.

(*b*) **1643** DENHAM *Cooper's H.* 198 Nature, whether more intent to please Us or her self, with strange varieties,.. Wisely she knew the harmony of things. **1671** GREW *Anat. Pl.* Introd. 3 For beholding the Many and Elegant Varieties, wherewith a Field or Garden is adorned. **1779** *Mirror* No. 8, A good plain Mirror, intended to represent things just as they are, but with properties and varieties not to be met with in common glass. **1825** CARLYLE *Schiller* II. 77 The task of composing dramatic varieties, of training players,.. could not wholly occupy such a mind as his.

b. *Bot.* and *Biol.* A plant or animal differing from those of the species to which it belongs in some minor but permanent or transmissible particular; a group of such individuals constituting a sub-species or other subdivision of a species; also, a plant or animal which varies in some trivial respect from its immediate parent or type.

1629 PARKINSON *Parad.* xxvi. 215 Many more sorts of varieties of these kindes there are, but these onely.. are noursed vp in Florists Gardens for pleasure. **1721** MORTIMER *Husb.* (ed. 2) II. 217 To make Varieties of them, the Seeds of the best single ones.. are to be sown in September. **1721** BRADLEY *Philos. Acc. Wks. Nat.* 145 The Lady Cow, which has likewise its Varieties beautifully spotted with the gayest Colours. **1780** *Encycl. Brit.* (ed. 2) VI. 4651/2 *Tritæophya leipyria* is only a variety of the *tritæophya causus.* **1832** LANDER *Exp. Niger* II. viii. 10 Another variety of corn grows here, which has eight ears on a single stem. **1845** *Florist's Jrnl.* (1846) VI. 206 For 12 old varieties in the nurserymen's class. **1859** DARWIN *Orig. Spec.* i. 7 When we look to the individuals of the same variety or sub-variety of our older cultivated plants and animals. **1870** YEATS *Nat. Hist. Comm.* 6 A worker in wood will tell, from the texture and grain, not merely the species but the variety of tree.

attrib. **1890** *Science-Gossip* XXVI. 42 And what shall we say to some of our Latinised variety-names?

c. So in the classification of inorganic substances or of diseases.

(*a*) **1753** *Chambers' Cycl.* Suppl. s.v., The naturalists of former ages have run into great errors, in mistaking the accidental varieties of plants, animals, and minerals for distinct species. **1757** DA COSTA *Fossils* 134 The sand-stone, ..exhibited by Woodward,.. is only a variety of this kind. **1839** URE *Dict. Arts* 619 Verona green is merely a variety of the mineral called green earth. **1855** J. PHILLIPS *Man. Geol.*

204 The coal is partly 'splint',..partly of the 'cannel' or 'parrot' variety.

(*b*) **1806** *Med. Jrnl.* XV. 5 It is an inflammatory affection, but destitute of redness;..the name of phlegmasia alba, or white inflammation, will therefore sufficiently characterize this variety of it. **1876** BRISTOWE *Th. & Pract. Med.* (1878) 414 The various forms of intercurrent or secondary pneumonia, and..the lobular variety of the disease.

†7. *pl.* Articles of various kinds; odds and ends.

1624 in Foster *Eng. Factories Ind.* (1909) III. 28 Whatsoever goods or varietyes be brought in by the English.

8. *ellipt.* for variety performance (see 9 b). Also, this species of entertainment, including its presentation on radio and television.

1904 [see LEGIT., LEGIT]. **1908** *Stage Year Bk.* 26 Some provincial theatres have gone over entirely to variety. **1929** *Illustr. London News* 13 Apr. 609/1 (*caption*) Broadcasting variety from 2LO. **1967** *Stage* 2 Mar. 3/4 Variety makes a comeback to Edinburgh on Monday. **1977** J. FLEMING *Every Inch* III. v. 134 He realized..that variety was not..on the way out. It was..very much alive.

9. *attrib.* **a.** *variety shop* or *store*, one in which small goods of various kinds are sold; a general store. *N. Amer.* (orig. *U.S.*).

1768 *Boston Even.-Post* 21 Nov. 3/3 Just imported in the Bristol Packet..and to be Sold by William Jackson At his Variety Store,..Nails, Brads, and Tacks of all sorts. **1790** *Columbian Sentinel* (Boston) 15 Sept. 4/2 To be sold, at J. Brazer's Variety-store,..Holland Gin, of the best kind, in cases. **1824** A. SINGLETON (H. C. Knight) *Lett. fr. South & W.* 84 One indication of a new country is that the shops are variety-shops; each one keeping piece-goods, groceries, cutlery, porcelain, and stationary [*sic*] in different corners. **1829** in Thornton *Amer. Gloss.*, [The collected trumpery] gives the Mayor's office the appearance of a 'variety store'. **1842** MRS. KIRKLAND *Forest Life* I. 149 A 'variety store', offering for sale every possible article of merchandize, from lace gloves to goose-yokes [etc.]. **1884** *Harper's Mag.* Nov. 888/1 One of them walked gauntly down to the post-office in the corner of the variety store. **1965** H. HOOD in R. Weaver *Canad. Short Stories* (1968) 2nd Ser. 218 We proceeded to the general store, grocery store, variety store, butcher shop, what would you call it? **1975** *Weekend Mag.* (Montreal) 1 Nov. 25/1 Variety store owners just grin and bear the hockey card mania.

b. Used to designate music-hall or theatrical entertainments of a mixed character (songs, dances, impersonations, etc.). Also applied to things or persons connected with such entertainments.

1868 *Oregon State Jrnl.* 17 Oct. 3/1 Variety Troupe.—This troupe gave an entertainment in the Court House. **1878** *Appleton's Jrnl.* XIX. 36/2 A 'music-hall', a place of entertainment like that which we call a 'variety theatre' in America. **1882** [see *advance agent* s.v. ADVANCE *sb.* V]. **1886** *Referee* 25 March (Cassell's), The biggest variety company ever seen at the East-end of London. **1891** *Chambers's Jrnl.* 14 March 165/1 Music halls, or, to give them the more recent and appropriate term, variety shows, are quite modern institutions. **1892** *Daily News* 25 March 2/2 The high salaries paid to variety artists. **1894** 'M. O'RELL' *J. Bull & Co.* 200 A succession of songs and dances in costume, commonly called Variety Shows. **1895** STUART & PARK (*title*) The variety stage. **1908** *Stage Year Bk.* 26 They are now an integral part of variety performances. *Ibid.*, Theatres need the latter [licence] for the variety weeks and even extended variety seasons. **1926** G. B. SHAW *Transl. & Tomfooleries* 232 This is not a serious play: it is what is called a Variety Turn for two musicians. **1967** *Stage* 2 Mar. 3/4 A new variety-revue opens at the Palladium Theatre. **1982** C. CASTLE *Folies Bergère* ii. 60 Provincial English variety theatres before World War Two.

varifocal (vɛərɪˈfəʊkəl), *a.* [f. VARI- + FOCAL *a.*]

a. Having a focal length that can be varied.

1945 *Jrnl. Soc. Motion Picture Engineers* XLV. 466 A new positive Vari-Focal view-finder for motion picture cameras. **1962** *Jrnl. Optical Soc. Amer.* LII. 353/2 The two-lens varifocal system consists of a single movable component placed behind a fixed component. **1967** *Appl. Optics* VI. 1085 (*heading*) Stereoscopic display using rapid varifocal mirror oscillations. **1979** *Ibid.* XVIII. 5/1 We have used a varifocal lens to compensate for changes in refractive index of lens elements with wavelengths from 190 nm to 600 nm.

b. *Ophthalm.* = *omnifocal* adj. s.v. OMNI-. Also *ellipt.*

1975 L. S. SASIENI *Princ. & Pract. Optical Dispensing & Fitting* (ed. 3) xii. 373 Varifocal lenses have two areas of specified powers, for distance and reading, and an intemediate region in which the power gradually changes, from one to the other. **1982** *Ophthalmic & Physiol. Optics* II. 75 (*heading*) Theoretical aspects of concentric varifocal lenses. *Ibid.*, Substantial amounts of unwanted astigmatism in the transition zone are intrinsic to the design and to other forms of concentric varifocal.

variform (ˈvɛərɪfɔːm), *a.* Also 7 varie-form. [f. L. *vari-*, stem of *varius* VARIOUS *a.* + -FORM. Cf. It. *variforme.*] Of various forms; varied or different in form; diversiform.

1662 J. CHANDLER *Van Helmont's Oriat.* Transl. Premonit., Because every thing in its Essence and Being is good, and that, because it is one, and true; but that which is double, varie-form, seeming, or false, that it sees to be evil. **1685** COTTON tr. *Montaigne* III. 499, I..find [it] very hard properly to design them [our actions] every one by themselves by a principal quality, so ambiguous and variform they are by several lights. **1836** *Fraser's Mag.* XIII. 419 'What men call love' is a variform thing. **1845** STOCQUELER *Handbk. Brit. India* (1854) 189 Among these variform buildings, strangely interspersed, are here and there huge masses of heavy foliage. **1860** MUIR COCKBURN *Pagan or Christian* 39 It eventually becomes with its variform sculpture..a distinguishing peculiarity.

Hence **ˈvariformly** *adv.*

1891 CLARK RUSSELL *Curatica* 129 Pat was called variformly Patrick, Paddy, Patsey, or Pat.

†**ˈvariformed**, *a.* *Obs.*$^{-1}$ [f. as prec. + FORMED.] Variously formed or shaped; variform.

1578 BANISTER *Hist. Man* I. 27 The inferiour part of this shoulder bone..is..large, and variformed.

variˈformity. *rare*$^{-1}$. [f. VARIFORM *a.* + -ITY.] Variety or diversity of form.

1702 C. MATHER *Magn. Chr.* v. iv. (1852) 332 The Forms ..were not in all points the same, nor did our churches at all find that this variformity was an inconvenience.

†**ˈvarify**, *v.* *Obs.* [f. L. *vari-*, stem of *varius* VARIOUS *a.*: see -FY.] *trans.* To make varied; to vary; to variegate.

1606 SYLVESTER *Du Bartas* II. iv. *Magnificence* 661 May.. Suiting the Lawns in all her pomp and pride Of lively Colours, lovely varifi'd. **1631** J. BURGES *Answ. Rejoined* 88 So as the same Law might ever remaine firme, and vnbroken, when occasions should varifie and change particularities. **1680–90** TEMPLE *Ess., Gardening* Wks. 1720 I. 183 All the rest are either varified by Names, or not to be named with these, nor worth troubling a Garden. **1741** E. POSTON *Pratler* (1747) I. 113 You don't know what great Use a little Latin and Greek would now be of: You can't imagin the Credit and Reputation that there is in a Line, or even a Word or two, of it:..Besides, it varifies it, and makes it naturally the fitter for Entertainment.

varihued (ˈvɛərɪhjuːd), *a.* [f. HUED *ppl. a.*, after *varicoloured.*] = VARI-COLOURED, VARICOLOURED *a.*

1921 *Nat. Geogr. Mag.* Sept. 274 The varihued deposits resemble brilliant mosaics. **1950** *John o' London's Weekly* 7 July 435/1 Queer fish of another sort..make his book an aquarium of vari-hued specimens.

varily, obs. form of VERILY *adv.*

varimax (ˈvɛərɪmæks). *Statistics.* [f. VARI(ANCE + MAX(IMUM.] A method of factor analysis in which uncorrelated factors are sought by a rotation (ROTATION 1 d) that maximizes the variance of the factor loadings. Usu. *attrib.*

1956 H. F. KAISER (title of thesis, Univ. of California) The varimax method of factor analysis. **1958** —— in *Psychometrika* XXIII. 187 Dr. John Caffrey suggested the name varimax. **1969** *Language* XLV. 89 The purpose of the varimax rotation was to focus these indices on possible natural groupings of the words according to their positional characteristics. **1974** R. L. GORSUCH *Factor Analysis* x. 193 Varimax is available on virtually every computer which has any programs for factor analysis. **1977** M. MAC GRÉIL *Prejudice & Tolerance in Ireland* xv. 467 Factor No. 3 'Republican Political'..: The high varimax loadings of the four categories which constitute this cluster is akin to that of the racial cluster in Factor 1.

Varinas. [See def.] The name of a town in Venezuela used to designate a kind of tobacco (see quot. 1858). Also *ellipt.*

1747 W. DOUGLAS *Brit. Settlements N. Amer.* (1760) I. 116 Virginia tobacco, and Brazil, and Varinas tobacco, differ upon this account. **1839** J. FUME (W. A. Chatto) *Paper on Tobacco* 117 Varinas is usually imported in rolls formed of the leaves of the tobacco spun into a kind of thick twist. **1858** SIMMOND *Dict. Trade*, *Varina's* [sic] *roll*, a kind of tobacco generally plaited round a thick stick, very much like C'naster.

varing(e, obs. Sc. ff. WAIRING (spending).

vario-coupler (ˈvɛərɪəʊkʌplə(r)). *Electr.* ? *Obs.* Also variocoupler. [f. VARI- + -O + COUPLER.]

A device, consisting of two unconnected coils, one inside the other, whose relative position can be altered to vary the mutual inductance between two circuits.

1922–3 *T. Eaton & Co. Catal.* Fall & Winter 401/4 Variocouplers, built up on black fibre cylinder, with taps, fitted with lugs. **1925** P. J. RISDON *Crystal Receivers & Circuits* ii. 21 A vario-coupler..is a sort of combination of a variometer and an ordinary tapped tuning inductance. **1937** *Discovery* Feb. 54/2 (*in figure*) Vario-coupler.

‖**variola** (vəˈraɪələ). *Path.* [med.L. *variola* pustule, pox, f. L. *varius* speckled, variegated. Cf. F. *variole* and *vérole* (OF. *verole*, *vairole*), = Prov. *vairolo*, Cat. *verola*, Sp. *viruela*, It. *vajuole* fem. pl., and *vajuolo.*] The smallpox.

1771–1804 [see VARICELLA]. **1825** GOOD *Study Med.* (ed. 2) III. 85 The adjunct spurious or bastard variola. **1846** DAY tr. *Simon's Anim. Chem.* II. 282 M. Solon found the urine coagulable in five out of eleven cases of variola. **1877** F. T. ROBERTS *Handbk. Med.* (ed. 3) I. 149 Variola may be met with at any age.

Comb. **1897** *Allbutt's Syst. Med.* II. 648 Numerous strains of so called variola-vaccine lymph. **1898** *Brit. Med. Jrnl.* 7 May 1185 The measure of protection afforded these children by his variola-descended lymph.

vaˈriolar, *a.* [ad. mod.L. *variolar-is*, f. *variola*: see prec. So F. *variolaire.*] Of or pertaining to, resembling (that of), variola.

1840 in SMART. **1843** *Proc. Berw. Nat. Club* II. xi. 52 The material is a hard variety of basalt,..distinguished by a pitted or variolar aspect. **1859** in MAYNE *Expos. Lex.*

ˌ**varioˈlarioid**, *a.* [f. mod.L. *Variolaria* (see def.) + -OID.] Of or pertaining to the *Variolaria*, a spurious genus of lichens characterized by pustulate shields; pustulate, pitted.

1856 W. L. LINDSAY *Pop. Hist. Brit. Lichens* 42 This variolarioid condition is not uncommon in many crustaceous species.

variolate (ˈvɛərɪəleɪt), *v.* *Med.* [f. VARIOLA: see -ATE.] *trans.* To infect with variola; to inoculate with the virus of variola or smallpox.

c **1792** [implied in VARIOLATED ppl. a.]. **1810** *Edin. Rev.* XV. 329 The total number of those vaccinated..is perhaps not less than those variolated. **1888** *Encycl. Brit.* XXIV. 24/2 The proof being to variolate the cow on the udder. **1898** *Brit. Med. Jrnl.* 7 May 1185 He had altogether failed in attempts to variolate the cow.

Hence **ˈvariolated** *ppl. a.*

c **1792** *Encycl. Brit.* (ed. 3) IX. 246/1 The Chinese convey a pellet of variolated cotton..into the nostrils of the patient. **1801** JENNER in Ring *Treat. Cow-pox* 24 From variolated pustules one cannot be surprised to hear, that a disease has been communicated by effluvia. **1845** *Encycl. Metrop.* VII. 754/2 If the patient be exposed to a variolated atmosphere at the time he is vaccinated. **1897** *Allbutt's Syst. Med.* II. 649 The final scab on the site of inoculation is not so elevated in the variolated as in the vaccinated animals.

variolation (ˌvɛərɪəˈleɪʃən). *Med.* [f. prec.] Inoculation with the virus of smallpox.

1805 *Med. Jrnl.* XIV. 536 A remarkable coincidence of failure..of variolation as well as vaccination. **1810** *Edin. Rev.* XV. 340 It [i.e. vaccination] has been adopted by millions who never would have submitted to variolation. **1896** *Allbutt's Syst. Med.* I. 559 The practice of variolation, which was revived and introduced into Great Britain by Lady Mary Wortley Montagu.

variole (ˈvɛərɪəʊl). *rare.* [ad. med.L. *variola* VARIOLA.] Something resembling a smallpox marking or pustule in appearance or formation:

a. *Ent.* A foveole or small fovea.

1826 KIRBY & SP. *Entomol.* IV. xlvi. 270 *Variole*,..a shallow impression like a mark of the small-pox.

b. *Geol.* A spherular concretion of a variolite.

1890 *Q. Jrnl. Geol. Soc.* XLVI. 312 The spherulites or 'varioles' [of the variolite-diabase] are grouped or drawn out in bands parallel to the surface.

variolic (vɛərɪˈɒlɪk), *a.* *rare*$^{-1}$. [f. VARIOL-A + -IC. Cf. F. *variolique.*] Variolar, variolous.

1827 in Baron *Life Jenner* I. 335 Till I had inoculated my children again with variolic matter.

varioline (ˈvɛərɪəlɪn). *rare.* [f. as prec. + -INE.] The hypothetical infectious principle of variola.

1864 FARR *Rep. Reg. Gen.* Suppl. 34 When any zymotic matter such as varioline, scarlatinine or typhine finds its way into a village.

ˈvariolist. *rare*$^{-1}$. [f. VARIOLA + -IST.] One who prefers smallpox to vaccination.

1799 *Gentl. Mag.* Aug. 665 A consciousness of propriety, which it seems that the Variolists have not had sufficient shame to acknowledge.

variolite (ˈvɛərɪəlaɪt). *Geol.* [f. med.L. *variol-a* VARIOLA + -ITE[1] 2. Cf. F. *variolite*, G. *variolit.*] A kind of rock embedded with spherulites which give it the appearance of being pock-marked (see quots.); esp. the diabase (diorite) of Brongniart.

1796 KIRWAN *Elem. Min.* (ed. 2) I. 368 Variolites. Stones that have rounded protuberances, of a different nature from the common mass of the stone. **1811** PINKERTON *Petrol.* I. 133 When the crystals..assume an oval, but particularly a round shape, the rock may be aptly styled a variolite. *Ibid.*, The stones called variolites of Durance, being pebbles rolled down by that river in Dauphiny. **1879** RUTLEY *Stud. Rocks* xiii. 248 Variolite is an aphanitic diabase of compact texture and greenish-grey colour, in which there occur little concretions of a paler colour, ranging up to the size of small nuts.

ˌ**varioˈlitic**, *a.* *Geol.* [f. prec. + -IC.] Of the nature of, or containing, variolite; spherulitic.

1862 G. P. SCROPE *Volcanoes* 365 The clinkstone is usually variolitic. **1878** LAWRENCE tr. *Cotta's Rocks Classified* 139 Diabase..is sometimes..variolitic or amygdaloidal.

varioliti'zation. *Geol.* [f. VARIOLITE + -IZATION.] The process of becoming variolitic; change or conversion into variolite.

1890 *Q. Jrnl. Geol. Soc.* XLVI. 330 As variolitization seems to have resulted from the same causes that have built up ordinary spherulites.

variolization (vɛərɪəlɪˈzeɪʃən). *Med.* [f. VARIOL-A + -IZATION.] Variolation.

1891 in *Cent. Dict.* **1910** *Edin. Rev.* Oct. 276 Variolisation ..is said to have been known to the Chinese from the commencement of the eleventh century.

varioloid (ˈvɛərɪəlɔɪd), *a.* and *sb.* *Path.* [ad. mod.L. *varioloides*, *-odes* (Frank, *c* 1790): see VARIOLA and -OID. So F. *varioloïde*, It. *vajuoloide.*]

A. *adj.* Resembling variola or smallpox; like that of variola.

In early use 'applied to a supposed special disease spontaneously developed in our climate under certain atmospheric conditions and capable of being propagated by infection or inoculation' (Mayne *Expos. Lex.*).

1821 W. STOKER (*title*), Observations on the Varioloid Disease. **1825** GOOD *Study Med.* (ed. 2) V. 737 Varioloid eruptions, III. 88. **1851** LEADAM *Homœopathy* 354 Varioloid Diseases. This term is applied to those diseases which resemble small-pox, and are more or less dependent upon the same epidemical constitution of the atmosphere for their production. **1899** *Allbutt's Syst. Med.* VIII. 479 Sometimes it [a pathological process] is partial, and a varioloid lesion results.

B. *sb.* A modified form of variola, esp. a mild variety occurring after vaccination or in those who have previously had smallpox.

1828–32 in WEBSTER. **1843** R. J. GRAVES *Syst. Clin. Med.* xiv. 148 One of the former was attacked by varioloid just after the crisis of long-continued spotted fever. **1870** T. W. HIGGINSON *Army Life* 234 A case or two of varioloid in the regiment. **1897** *Allbutt's Syst. Med.* II. 103 A papular appearance which if the rash be scanty, may resemble the early stage of varioloid.

fig. **1860** EMERSON *Cond. Life, Culture* Wks. (Bohn) II. 364 Is egotism a metaphysical varioloid of this malady?

variolous (vəˈraɪələs), *a.* [f. med.L. *variola* VARIOLA, or a. F. *varioleux*: see -OUS.]

1. Of the nature of, resembling (that of), variola or smallpox; of or pertaining to, appearing in, characteristic of, variola.

1676 *Phil. Trans.* XI. 569 The third Epidemical Constitution..was that of the Small-pocks, and of a Variolous Feaver, resembling..the Smal-pocks. **1749** *Ibid.* XLVI. 235 From the Dissections of those who have died of the Small-Pox, we find that the Viscera are subject to the variolous Abscesses. **1780** *Ibid.* LXX. 139 She was delivered of a child, as full of variolous pustules as herself. **1802** *Med. Jrnl.* VIII. 170 [They] thought it [an eruption] had a variolous appearance. **1845** *Encycl. Metrop.* VII. 754/2 When a person has been inoculated with a mixture of the variolous and vaccine poisons. **1899** *Allbutt's Syst. Med.* VIII. 639 In these respects its evolution is not unlike that of a variolous or vaccine vesicle.

Comb. **1801** *Med. Jrnl.* V. 453 Others were distinguishable by a variolous-like aspect and circular inflammation.

b. ***variolous matter*** (***fluid*** or ***virus***), the virus of smallpox, esp. as used for purposes of inoculation.

1747 tr. *Astruc's Fevers* 278 From the first reception of the variolous matter. **1798** JENNER *Variolæ Vaccinæ* (1801) 23 Cow-pox virus..renders the constitution unsusceptible of the variolous. **1800** *Med. Jrnl.* IV. 22, I immediately inoculated the whole party with the most virulent variolous matter I could procure. **1825** GOOD *Study Med.* (ed. 2) V. 192 When vaccine or variolous fluid is properly inserted under the cuticle. **1875** RICHARDSON *Dis. Mod. Life* 83 He therefore inoculated patients with diluted solutions of variolous matter.

c. ***variolous contagion***, ***disease***, ***infection***, etc., variola, smallpox. ? *Obs.*

c **1792** *Encycl. Brit.* (ed. 3) IX. 245/2 The variolous matter only produces the variolous disease. **1799** *Med. Jrnl.* I. 318 In every instance, the patient..has completely lost the susceptibility for the variolous contagion. **1807** *Ibid.* XVII. 27 Six full days..during which they had been exposed to the variolous infection. **1827** DE QUINCEY *Last Days Kant* Wks. 1854 III. 123 He thought, that, as a guarantee against the variolous infection, it required a much longer probation.

2. Of persons: Affected with, suffering from, smallpox.

1668 SYDENHAM *Let. Boyle* B.'s Wks. 1744 V. 639/2 In visiting..many of my variolous patients. *c* **1792** *Encycl. Brit.* (ed. 3) IX. 245/2 Inoculation with the blood of variolous patients hath been tried without effect. **1804** *Med. Jrnl.* XII. 184 Variolous patients. **1897** *Allbutt's Syst. Med.* II. 207 It is..exceptional to find that the children born of variolous mothers..have had small-pox in uterus.

3. *Ent.* (See quot.)

1826 KIRBY & SP. *Entomol.* IV. xlvi. 270 *Variolous* (Variolosa), beset with many varioles.

variometer (vɛərɪˈɒmɪtə(r)). [f. VARI- + -OMETER.] **1.** An instrument for measuring variations in the intensity of the earth's magnetic field.

1889 in *Cent. Dict.* **1916** *Proc. R. Soc.* A. XCII. 321 There can be no question of the enormous simplification of the field work which such a portable variometer produces. **1972** *Nature Physical Sci.* 25 Dec. 184/2 Telluric recording equipment was operated in conjunction with a magnetic variometer array.

2. *Electr.* (*a*) An inductor (INDUCTOR 3 d) whose total inductance can be varied by altering the relative position of two coaxial coils connected in series, and can thus be used to tune a circuit. (*b*) A device achieving a similar function by means of permeability tuning.

1908 C. C. F. MONCKTON *Radio-Telegr.* xv. 255 The antenna and the receiving circuit are tuned to the incoming oscillations by means of the variometer. **1921** *Wireless World* IX. 6/1 For amateur use the variometer has the advantage that it is cheap compared with a variable condenser. **1926** 'R. KEVERNE' *Carteret's Cure* vii. 168 Mr. Pell turned to the listening set and picked up the head-phones while his fingers played deftly with the variometer. **1959** K. HENNEY *Radio Engin. Handbk.* (ed. 5) iii. 14 Another form [of variable inductor], which is rather bulky.. and now little used, is the variometer... Much more common is the variation of inductance through the variation of the permeability of the core. **1977** *Elektor* Mar. 22/1 The variometer is an updated version of the old permeability tuners.

3. An instrument for indicating the rate of climb or descent of an aircraft.

1924 *Sci. Amer.* Feb. 83/2 Air speed indicator... Turn indicator... Variometer. **1930** STARTUP & KINNEAR tr. *Stamer & Lippisch's Gliding & Sail-Planing* x. 111 An instrument called a variometer exists for the purpose of indicating ascent and descent and is much used in balloons. **1969** *Daily Tel.* (Colour Suppl.) 21 Nov. 64/2 A variometer can confuse you; you might be going down in a rising thermal, so it's no good just knowing how you are doing relative to the air you're in. **1973** *Q. Jrnl. Meteorol. Soc.* XCIX. 768 Height changes give a check on the calibration of the variometer.

variorum (vɛərɪˈɔərəm), *sb.* (*a.*) [L., gen. pl. masc. of *varius* VARIOUS *a.*, in the phrase *editio cum notis variorum* (see def.).]

1. a. An edition, esp. of the complete works of a classical author, containing the notes of various commentators or editors. Also in the full phrase ***variorum edition***.

1728 CHAMBERS *Cycl.* s.v., A set of Dutch *Variorums*. *Ibid.*, The *Variorums*, for the generality, are the best Editions. **1824** SCOTT *Let. to Constable* 6 Jan., In the shape of these inimitable Variorums, who knows what new ideas the Classics may suggest? **1826** MISS MITFORD *Village* II. (1863) 268, I should like to see a variorum edition of our Pizarro. **1870** LOWELL *Among My Bks.* Ser. I. 162 The serious notes of a *variorum* edition of Shakespeare.

b. *attrib.*, as ***variorum classic***, ***comment***, or with the name of the author.

a **1763** BYROM *Misc. Poems* (1773) II. 333 The *variorum* Comments. **1802** DIBDIN *Edit. Classics* 11 The second edition [of Claudian]..is esteemed one of the scarcest of the *Variorum* Classics. **1822** SCOTT *Nigel* Introd. Epist., The Prolegomena of the Variorum Shakspeare.

c. As *adj.* in the sense 'obtained or collected from various books or sources'. Also applied to a single reading.

1850 *N. & Q.* 19 Oct. 325 A very curious variorum reading. **1873** (*title*) Osorio. A tragedy as originally written in 1797 by Samuel Taylor Coleridge. Now first printed from a copy recently discovered by the publisher with the variorum readings of 'Remorse' and a monograph on the history of the play in its earlier and later form by the author of 'Tennysoniana'. **1883** *American* VII. 170 Outlines of the Chief Political Changes in the History of the World, Arranged by Centuries, with Variorum Illustrations. **1887** *Athenæum* 13 Aug. 210/3 In his variorum readings of the name from old records he has obviously misread t for c in several instances.

d. Used, chiefly *attrib.*, to denote an edition, usu. of an author's complete works, containing variant readings from manuscripts or earlier editions.

This use is deplored by some scholars.

1955 *Times* 11 June 9/3 How delighted he [*sc.* Johnson] would have been to have known of the Yale University project for a really complete variorum edition of his works. **1957** (*title*) The variorum edition of the poems of W. B. Yeats. **1964** *Times Lit. Suppl.* 29 Oct. 979/4 The variorum edition of Emily Dickinson..(meaning, it appears, an edition containing variant readings). The..use of the term is incorrect. **1980** *N.Y. Times* 26 July II. 22 The book, a variorum, records every usable fact and opinion about the play—every significant textual variant, every influential interpretation, [etc.]. **1983** P. G. RUGGIERS in Beadle & Griffiths *St. John's College Cambridge MS. L.1.* p. xiii, Having then presented these two essential manuscripts, consideration was given by the Variorum editors [*sc.* the editors of the Variorum Chaucer] to providing other materials essential to the understanding of an evolving Chaucer text.

2. *fig.* Variation; a varying or changing scene. *Sc.*

177. SKINNER *Tullochgorum* Wks. 1809 III. 136 Dull Italian lays,..They're dowf and dowie at the best, Wi' a' their variorum. **1785** BURNS *Jolly Beggars* 8th Air, Life is all a variorum, We regard not how it goes. **1876** J. SMITH *Archie & Bess* 95 It's a lang time since I heard ye sing't and it'll aye be a variorum. **1901** R. TROTTER *Galloway Gossip* 11 They widna let the Paraphrases be sung in the kirk, or tunes wi' variorum about them. **1930** in *Sc. Nat. Dict.* (1974) IX. 520/2 A'm guid at readin' write gin it has nane o' your variorums and whirligigs.

variotinted, *a.* [Irreg. f. L. *varius* varied.] Of various tints or colours.

1903 AGNES M. CLERKE *Probl. Astrophysics* 44 The dazzling variotinted fireworks disclosed by the prism.

various (ˈvɛərɪəs), *a.* [f. L. *vari-us* changing, different, diverse, variegated + -OUS. Cf. It., Sp., Pg. *vario*.]

I. †**1.** Of things: Undergoing, exhibiting, subject to, variation or change; variable, changeful. *Obs.*

1552 HULOET, Variouse, *uacillans,..uarius.* **1570** LEVINS *Manip.* 226 Variouse, *varius, instabilis.* **1622** J. TAYLOR (Water P.) *Sir G. Nonsence* Wks. (1630) 1/2 Most conscript Vmpire in this various Orbe. **1647** COTTERELL tr. *Davila's Hist. Fr.* I. 13 As the condition of the Court is ever various and unconstant. *a* **1676** HALE *Prim. Orig. Man.* (1677) 191 The Instances of latter Discoveries which make evident this various state of the Globe of Earth and Water. **1708** *Lond. Gaz.* No. 4463/3 The Winds were so various that we could not make to the Bay of la Hogue 'till the 11th. *a* **1763** SHENSTONE *Elegies* v. 11 Ill can I bear the various clime of Love! **1775** SHERIDAN *Rivals* Epil., The servile suitors watch her various face, She smiles preferment, or she frowns disgrace.

†**b.** Of fortune, life, etc. *Obs.*

1623 J. TAYLOR (Water P.) *Discovery by Sea* Wks. (1630) 24/1 Whilst we like various Fortunes Tennis ball, At euery stroake, were in the Hazzard all. **1644** QUARLES *Judgment & Mercy* 12 Fear not the frowns of princes, or the imperious hand of various fortune. **1703** N. ROWE *Ulysses* I. i, Ev'ry Change Of various Life. **1741–2** GRAY *Agrippina* 54 Through various life I have pursued your steps.

†**c.** Turning different ways; going in different directions. *Obs.*

1621 QUARLES *Argalus & P.* (1678) 13 There walked she; and in her various minde, Projects and casts about which way to finde The progress of the young Partheniaes heart. **1725** POPE *Odyss.* VI. 134 Forth from her snowy hand Nausicaa threw The various ball.

†**d.** Of a war: Marked by varying success. *Obs.*

1754–8 BP. NEWTON *Obs. Proph. Daniel* xii. 179 Hence arose a various war between Antiochus and Epiphanes, each of them seizing Phœnicia and Cœle-Syria by turns.

†**2.** Of persons: **a.** Changeable in character; inconstant, unstable; fickle. *Obs.*

1636 E. DACRES tr. *Machiavel's Disc. Livy* I. 231 A Prince loosen'd from the law, will be unthankfull, various, and imprudent. **1670** G. H. *Hist. Cardinals* III. IV. 328 So Cardinal Alexandrino dealt with Cardinal de S. Sisto, a various and unconstant man. **1670** MARVELL *Corr.* Wks. (Grosart) II. 330 Truly he seems to me so various and fickle in handling this businesse all along. **1719** SWIFT *Hist. Eng.* Wks. 1841 I. 544/2 Robert, who was various in his nature, and always under the power of the present persuader. **1776** GIBBON *Decl. & F.* i. (1782) I. 9 The various character of that emperor, capable, by turns, of the meanest and the most generous sentiments. **1820** E. THOMPSON *Cullen's Nosologia* (ed. 3) 227 The mind, involuntarily various and unsteady.

†**b.** Marked by change or vacillation in opinions or views. *Obs.*

1645 VISCT. FALKLAND *Infallibility* 13 Saint Austin, who is very various I confess in it. **1653** GATAKER *Vind. Annot. Jer.* i. 3 In this point he seems somewhat various. **1661** J. DAVIES *Civil Warres* 373 The officers of the army themselves began to be various and uncertain what to do.

†**c.** *poet.* Appearing in or assuming a variety of forms. *Obs.*

1725 POPE *Odyss.* IV. 524 Watch with insidious care his known abode; There fast in chains constrain the various god [*sc.* Proteus].

II. 3. Of persons: †**a.** Versatile in knowledge or acquirements; exhibiting variety in work or writings. *Obs.*

1621 BP. MOUNTAGU *Diatribæ* 1 His name was already up ..for a great scholar: a various Linguist. **1646** SIR T. BROWNE *Pseud. Ep.* I. viii. (1686) 24 A delectable Author, very various. **1657** S. PURCHAS *Pol. Flying-Ins.* I. i, What in this respect is wiser, or better instructed than the Bee? What Artificer is so various, what Painter..can imitate her works? **1681** DRYDEN *Abs. & Achit.* I. 545 A man so various, that he seem'd to be Not one, but all Mankind's Epitome.

b. Giving attention to many different subjects.

1878 R. CHOATE *Addresses* 235 It is a common belief that Mr. Webster was a various reader; and I think it is true.

4. a. Varied in colour; vari-coloured, variegated. Chiefly *poet.*

a **1618** [see VARNISH *v.* 1 b]. **1697** DRYDEN *Æneid* IX. 2 The various Iris Juno sends with haste, To find bold Turnus. **1718** PRIOR *The Garland* ii, At Morn the Nymph vouchsafd to place Upon her Brow the various Wreath. **1735** SOMERVILLE *Chase* II. 106 The rising Sun..As many Colours from their glossy Skins Beaming reflects, as paint the various Bow. **1757** W. WILKIE *Epigoniad* III. 54 A polish'd casque her lovely temples bound, With flow'rs of gold and various plumage crown'd. **1855** LONGF. *Hiawatha* xii. 186 He saw the nine fair sisters..Changed to birds of various plumage.

b. Exhibiting variety in appearance; presenting different aspects at different times or places.

1656 RIDGLEY *Pract. Physick* 288 Use these till the pain, and various colour cease. **1667** MILTON *P.L.* v. 89, I.. underneath beheld The Earth outstretcht immense, a prospect wide And various. **1694** CONGREVE *Double-Dealer* v. xvii, Ten thousand meanings lurk in every corner of that various face. **1712** ADDISON *Spectator* No. 417 ¶3 The various Scenary of a Country Life. **1725** *Portland Papers* (Hist. MSS. Comm.) VI. 98 If one gets safe to the top, he may enjoy..a very extensive and various prospect on both sides. **1796** CHARLOTTE SMITH *Marchmont* I. 118 Her road lay..through a country various and rich. **1832** LANDER *Exped. Niger* I. i. 32 They were clad in all their finery, their apparel being as gaudy as it was various. **1863** W. W. STORY *Roba di Roma* xiii, Various as the Campagna is in outline, it is quite as various in colour, reflecting every aspect of the sky and answering every touch of the seasons. **1872** BLACKIE *Lays of Highlands* Introd. 49 The various outline of the Orcadian coast..presents a fine background.

5. Characterized by variation or variety of attributes or properties; exhibiting or possessing (several) different characters or qualities; varied in nature or character.

pred. a **1633** J. AUSTIN *Medit.* (1635) 270 Let the Pleasure be full to give Content; Let it be Various to avoid Satietie. **1762** SIR W. JONES *Arcadia* Poems (1777) 109 His tune so various and uncouth he made, That not a dancer could in cadence move. **1780** *New Newgate Cal.* V. 100 After conviction their behaviour was very various. On some occasions they appeared hardened in a very high degree, and at others [etc.]. **1853** FELTON *Fam. Lett.* xliv. (1865) 324 Since our return from our journey, the weather has been very various. **1858** LARDNER *Hand-bk. Nat. Phil.* 99 The velocity of rivers is very various, the slower class moving at less than 3 feet, and the more rapid at so much as 6 feet per second. **1876** PARKER *Paraclete* I. vii. 107 The ministration of the spirit is various: by it Moses was made wise, Bezaleel was made skilful, and Samson was made strong.

attrib. **1662** STILLINGFL. *Orig. Sacræ* III. i. §14 The various motion and configuration of the particles of matter. **1670** MARVELL *Corr.* Wks. (Grosart) II. 354 We shall have much adoe to get businesse of so various nature into fashion. **1703** ROWE *Fair Penitent* I. i, The various fury of the Seasons. *a* **1720** PRIOR *Judgment of Venus* i, When Kneller's Works of various Grace, Were to fair Venus shown. **1796** BURKE *Corr.* (1844) IV. 413 We have had various health, but never any that deserved to be called good. **1807** CRABBE *Par. Reg.* III. 412 To show the various worth of Catherine Lloyd. **1844** DISRAELI *Coningsby* III. ii, Such a various prodigality of writing materials. **1868** HEAVYSEGE *Jezebel* III. 115 Then followed many years of various fate.

†**b.** Calculated to cause difference or dissimilarity. *Obs.*$^{-1}$

1667 MILTON *P.L.* XII. 53 God..in derision sets Upon thir Tongues a various Spirit,..To sow a jangling noise of words unknown.

6. a. Marked by variety of incident or action.

1634 MILTON *Comus* 379 She..lets grow her wings That in the various bussle of resort Were all to ruffl'd. **1667** —— *P.L.* VI. 242 For wide was spred That Warr and various. **1727** DYER *Grongar Hill* 97 Wave succeeding wave, they go A various journey to the deep. **1829** I. TAYLOR *Enthusiasm* (1867) 75 Pride..forbids [the heretic's] return to the truth he has..denounced from all points of his various course.

b. *poet.* Acting in many different ways.

1671 MILTON *Samson* 668 God of our Fathers, what is man! That thou towards him with hand so various.. Temperst thy providence.

7. a. Exhibiting variety of subject or topic; concerned or occupied with many different themes.

1677-8 MARVELL *Corr.* Wks. (Grosart) II. 583 The other things committed to them, being of various consideration, they will probably digest into severall Bills. **1703** POPE *Thebais* 795 Relate your fortunes, while the friendly night And silent hours to various talk invite. **1794** GODWIN *Caleb Williams* 139 Yet under this rude exterior it was easy to distinguish various knowledge, nice discrimination, and a strong and active mind. **1818** *Tuckey's Narr. Exped. R. Zaire* Introd. p. lvii, He had stored his mind with so much various knowledge..that he was considered the most eligible for the undertaking. **1852** THACKERAY *Esmond* III. v, One whose conversation was so various, easy, and delightful.

b. Exhibiting variety in the different persons or things forming a collective whole; displaying or including a variety of objects.

1769 SIR W. JONES *Palace Fortune* Poems (1777) 15 Through the four portals rush'd a various throng. **1811** SCOTT *Don Roderick* II. lvii, A various host they came, whose ranks display Each mode in which the warrior meets the fight. **1830** TENNYSON *Ode to Memory* v, Great artist Memory,..Needs must thou dearly love thy first essay, And foremost in thy various gallery Place it. **1872** BLACKIE *Lays Highl.* 163 One single law, as with a chain, Doth bind the various vast infinity.

III. 8. With pl. sb. Different from one another; of different kinds or sorts: **a.** In attrib. use.

1634 MILTON *Comus* 22 All the Sea-girt Isles That like to rich and various gemms inlay The..boosom of the Deep. **1648** CRASHAW *Delights Muses, Music's Duel* 128 The humourous strings expound his learned touch By various Glosses. **1667** MILTON *P.L.* I. 375 Then were they known to men by various Names, And various Idols through the Heathen World. **1724** WATTS *Logic* (1726) 116 As infinitely various as the Essences of Things are, their Definitions must needs have very various Forms. **1743** FRANCIS tr. *Hor., Odes* II. xviii. 39 For Earth impartial entertains Her various sons, and in her breast Princes and beggars equal rest. **1805** *Med. Jrnl.* XIV. 564 Dr. Jackson..is very careful in marking all those various effects produced from similar causes. **1857** *1st Rep. Comm. Customs* 13 To discharge the various and onerous duties of 'Shipping Masters'. **1884** tr. *Lotze's Metaph.* 196 There arises,..by help of abstraction from the content of the various impressions, the picture of empty extension.

ellipt. **1855** *Poultry Chron.* III. 415 The Various Class presented the usual number of curiosities. **1903** *Westm. Gaz.* 30 Dec. 3/1 A couple of 'cock, ground game, and such 'various' as snipe, duck, a plover or so.

b. Predicative.

1651 HOBBES *Leviath.* III. xliii. 323 The causes why men beleeve any Christian Doctrine, are various. *a* **1680** BUTLER *Rem.* (1759) I. 229 How various and innumerable Are those, who live upon the Rabble? **1721** BRADLEY *Philos. Acc. Wks. Nat.* 147 The Beetle and Water-Scorpion are little various in the outward Structure of their Bodies. **1784** COWPER *Task* I. 302 The woodland scene, Diversified with trees of ev'ry growth, Alike, yet various. **1818** SCOTT *Hrt. Midl.* xxxiv, Its springs, various in character, yet alike efficacious in virtue, are to be found in abundance. **1849** MACAULAY *Hist. Eng.* ii. I. 180 Talents great and various assisted to spread the contagion. **1851** HELPS *Comp. Solit.* xi. 213 The advantages of travel are very various and very numerous.

c. With a singular sb., and freq. preceded by *each* or *every*.

a **1721** PRIOR *Colin's Mistakes* xi, Ca'ndish-Holles-Harley stood confest, As various Hour advis'd, in various Habit drest. **1746** FRANCIS tr. *Horace, Epist.* I. xvii. 32 Yet Aristippus every Dress became: In every various Change of Life the same. **1766** [C. ANSTEY] *New Bath Guide* ix. 42, I alone his Thoughts employ Through each various Scene of Joy. **1818** SCOTT *Br. Lamm.* xxx, Sufficient care was taken that this report should find its way to Ravenswood Castle through every various channel. **1819** BYRON *Juan* I. xviii, Don José, like a lineal son of Eve, Went plucking various fruit without her leave. **1863** LONGF. *Wayside Inn* II. Prel. 63 The breakfast ended, each pursued The promptings of his various mood.

d. In the phrase ***various reading*(*s*)**. (Cf. VARIANT *a.* 4 b, *sb.* 1 b, 2 and LECTION *sb.* 1 c.)

1659 BP. WALTON *Considerator Consid.* 114 Various Readings are the difference of Copies collected and offered to the reader's judgment. **1701** *Stanley's Hist. Philos.* Introd. d b, That he might omit nothing, he has annext the various Readings,..Conjectures and Observations. **1721** BP. ATTERBURY *Let. to Pope* 27 Sept., Therefore in my Waller there is a various reading of the first of these couplets. *c* **1750** JOHNSON in *Boswell* (Oxf. ed.) II. 618 *note*, Chaucer, a new edition of him, from manuscripts and old editions, with various readings, conjectures [etc.]. **1824** J. JOHNSON *Typogr.* II. 437 An exact list of all its various readings. **1855** PALEY *Æschylus* Pref. (1861) p. x, What really is a necessary and inevitable part of an editor's duty, viz. the continual discussion of various readings. **1910** *Expositor* Apr. 352 It may rest upon a various reading in the Hebrew.

9. In weakened sense, as an enumerative term: Different, divers, several, many, more than one.

It is not always possible to distinguish absolutely between this sense and 8, as the meaning freq. merges into 'many different': cf. DIVERS *a.* 3.

1696 PRIOR *To the King at Arrival in Holland* 62 In various Tongues He hears the Captains dwell On their great Leader's Praise. **1725** N. ROBINSON *Th. Physick* 239 By this Means we shall be able to judge with the greater Exactness, of all the various Phænomena's of Nature. **1762** J. REEVE in Foley *Rec. Eng. Prov. S.J.* VII. Introd. p. xlii, From that period the College of St. Omer began to shine among the various Seminaries of piety and learning. **1848** THACKERAY *Van. Fair* lxi, But he heard of the Major's fame from various members of his society. **1879** HARLAN *Eyesight* ii. 30 The eyeball is moved in various directions by six muscles. **1897** LD. ROBERTS *41 Yrs. India* vii. (1898) 41 Various acts of incendiarism took place.

10. *Comb.* With adjs. or pa. pples., as ***various-blossomed***, ***-coloured***, ***-formed***, ***-measured***, etc.

1730-46 THOMSON *Autumn* 5 The *various-blossom'd Spring. *a* **1711** KEN *Preparatives* Poet. Wks. 1721 IV. 35 Bright *various colour'd Rays his Wings adorn. **1752** J. HILL *Hist. Anim.* 231 The various-coloured Gadus,..The Cod-fish. **1824** SCOTT *St. Ronan's* xxxi, Such triple tiaras of various-coloured gauze on her head. **1803** KENNY *Society* 54 In spite of danger *various-form'd, to wrest Nature's yet hidden secrets. **1822** *Hortus Anglicus* II. 155 *L[epidium] Perfoliatum.* *Various-leaved Pepper Wort. **1671** MILTON *P.R.* IV. 256 *Various-measur'd verse, Æolian charms and Dorian Lyric Odes. **1880** BEACONSFIELD *Endymion* lxv, The intended introduction of grain at *various-priced duties per quarter. **1727-46** THOMSON *Summer* 1110 The fiery spume Of fat Bitumen, steaming on the day, With *various-tinctur'd trains of latent flame. **1788** COLERIDGE *Sonnet to Autumnal Moon* 1 Mild Splendour of the *various-vested Night!

'variously, *adv.* [f. prec. + -LY[2].]

1. In a various manner; in various or different ways; with variation or variety; differently, diversely.

1627 MAY *Lucan* VII. 620 The war, that variously had wander'd ore The fields, there stucke, there Cæsars fortune stay'd. **1647** CLARENDON *Hist. Reb.* II. §87 This stratagem was never understood; and was then variously spoken of. **1682** J. NORRIS *Hierocles* 7 But 'twas the Law of the Creation which variously order'd things according to the dignity of their natures. **1748** HARTLEY *Observ. Man* I. iii. §6. 390 These Circumstances are variously combined in the various Kinds and Degrees of Madness. **1779** T. FORREST *Voy. New Guinea* 326 Variously do those islands groan under the tyranny of their masters. **1807** G. CHALMERS *Caledonia* I. III. vii. 406 About the lineage, and station, of this celebrated personage..writers have written variously. **1860** TYNDALL *Glac.* I. xii. 87 The sound commenced again, changing its note variously. **1880** GEIKIE *Phys. Geog.* iv. 199 A ball.. with an exterior crust which has been variously estimated at from twenty to a thousand miles in thickness.

b. With adjs.

1794 G. ADAMS *Nat. & Exper. Phil.* IV. xlix. 331 It emits the rays of light in every direction, and those rays are variously refrangible and colorific. **1849** MACAULAY *Hist. Eng.* iii. I. 398 Our prose became less majestic,..less variously musical than that of an earlier age. **1871** CARLYLE in Mrs. Carlyle *Lett.* I. 378 The consequences for the time were variously sad. **1871** TENNYSON *Last Tourn.* 226 So dame and damsel glitter'd at the feast Variously gay.

c. *U.S.* At different times. *rare.*

1892 A. E. LEE *Hist. Columbus* (Ohio) I. 756 Samuel Perkins..kept a barber shop variously under the National Hotel and the Clinton Bank.

2. *Comb.* With pa. pples., adjs., or pres. pples., as ***variously-coloured***, ***-conditioned***, ***-shaped***, ***-working***, ***-wrought***, etc.

a **1700** EVELYN *Diary* 8 Feb. 1645, The mouthes of these spiracles are bestrew'd with variously-colour'd cinders. **1768-74** TUCKER *Lt. Nat.* (1834) II. 171 A long-complicated succession of variously-working second causes. **1837** CAUNTER *Lives Moghul Emp., Baber* ix. 238 The variously-coloured page of human life. **1848** BUCKLEY *Iliad* 193 Brass, gold, and variously-wrought iron. **1855** T. JONES *Anim. Kingd.* (ed. 2) p. xvi, Variously-shaped eggs of Insects. **1868** LOCKYER *Elem. Astron.* §60 The stars shine out with variously coloured lights.

'variousness. [f. VARIOUS *a.* + -NESS.]

†1. Changeableness, inconstancy, variability. *Obs.*

1607 DANIEL *Cleopatra* Wks. (Grosart) III. 9 A Roman hath but here a Roman quayld, And onely but by Fortune's variousnes. **1647** COTTERELL tr. *Davila's Hist. Fr.* I. 22 The Prince had in the war proved the variousnesse of fortune.

†2. Difference, variance. *Obs.*

1628 T. SPENCER *Logick* 68 This space is the varietie, or variousnes that is betweene seuerall, and distinct arguments. *a* **1653** GOUGE *Comm. Heb.* xiii. 9 Here the plural number is used, which implieth a variousness and disagreement in false Doctrines.

3. Variety of character or nature; varied condition or quality.

1651 BIGGS *New Disp.* ¶98 The variousnesse..of..every single and particular form of the Individuall. **1653** BLITHE *Engl. Improver Impr.* 55 And a good experienced Millwright ..is well able to regulate them..to the incomming of the Tide, or out-going of the Floods, as the variousness of opportunities will require. **1834** WILSON in *Blackw. Mag.* XXXVI. 543 His waking thoughts had all the vividness of visions, all the variousness of dreams. **1845** BAILEY *Festus* (ed. 2) 39 Unimaginable space..Faileth to match His boundless variousness. **1865** M. ARNOLD *Ess. Crit.* IV. (1875) 163 The religious life is at bottom everywhere alike; but it is curious to note the variousness of its setting.

variphone ('vɛərɪfəʊn). *Linguistics.* [f. VARI- + PHONE *sb.*[1]] One of two or more sounds used interchangeably by the same speaker in the same phonetic context.

1932 D. JONES in E. P. Hamp et al. *Readings in Linguistics II* (1966) 32 Variphones are found in some varieties of German, where *p* and *b*, ʃ and ʒ, and other corresponding voiced and voiceless consonants are apparently used indifferently. **1934** YUEN-REN CHAO in M. Joos *Readings in Linguistics I* (1966) (ed. 4) 39/2 Bloomfield makes no explicit mention of free phonemes or variphones. *Ibid.*, Variphones are also phonemes, except that the choice of the exact shade of the sound used is determined by psychological and physiological factors other than those of phonetic environment. **1950** D. JONES *Phoneme* xxviii. 206 ŋg and ŋ form a variphone in the speech of Midland districts of England.

Variscan (və'rɪskən), *a. Geol.* [f. L. *Varisc-ī* (see quot. 1906[1]) + -AN, after G. *variscisch* (E. Suess *Antlitz der Erde* (1888) II. III. ii. 131).] Of, pertaining to, or designating a mountain system that formerly extended from southern Ireland and Britain through central France and Germany to southern Poland, or the orogeny that gave rise to it during late Palæozoic time.

1906 H. B. C. & W. J. SOLLAS tr. *Suess' Face of Earth* II. III. ii. 111 It is thus fitting that the name of this range, which includes most of the German horsts, should be borrowed from the land of the Varisci or the Vogtland; and we shall name it therefore the Variscan range, from the Latin name of Hof in Bavaria (*Curia Variscorum*). **1908** *Ibid.* III. IV. viii. 346 The Carnic mountains are a chain..and of Variscan age. **1956** W. EDWARDS in D. L. Linton *Sheffield* i. 22 Earth-movements of the Variscan orogeny were already in action during deposition of the Lower Carboniferous. **1969** BENNISON & WRIGHT *Geol. Hist. Brit. Isles* xi. 255 The building of the Variscan mountain chains profoundly affected the geography of Europe, both in the distribution of land and sea and climatically. **1974** *Encycl. Brit. Macropædia* VI. 14/1 The European geosyncline is called the Variscan.

variscite ('værɪsaɪt, 'værɪskaɪt). *Min.* [ad. G. *variscit* (A. Breithaupt 1837, in *Jrnl. f. prakt. Chem.* X. 506), f. med.L. *Varisc-ia*, name of the Vogtland district of E. Germany where the mineral was first found: see -ITE[1].] An orthorhombic hydrated aluminium phosphate, $AlPO_4.2H_2O$, which is dimorphous with metavariscite and occurs usu. as green or colourless, translucent or transparent, fine-grained masses, crusts, and nodules.

1850 D. T. ANSTED *Elem. Course Geol., Mineralogy* ix. 187 Variscite is also a phosphate of alumina, of a green colour. **1912** *Proc. U.S. Nat. Museum* XLI. 415 The variscite and variscite-matrix from this locality would yield very beautiful gems for the so-called barbaric jewelry. **1964, 1975** [see REDONDITE]. **1979** *Arizona Highways* Apr. 40/1, I did a series of shields with variscite, which is a dark stone that has some turquoise in it.

vari-sized ('vɛərɪsaɪzd), *a. rare.* [f. SIZED *ppl. a.*[1] 1 b, after *varicoloured*, etc.] Of various or different sizes.

1936 F. CLUNE *Roaming round Darling* xxi. 208 Beneath.. were nineteen dogs... All were vari-coloured, vari-bred, vari-sized and -shaped. **1940** W. FAULKNER *Hamlet* IV. i. 243 Vari-sized and -coloured tatters torn at random from large billboards.

varisoune, Sc. variant of WARISON.

varistor (vɛə'rɪstə(r)). *Electr.* [f. VAR(IABLE *a.* + RES(ISTOR.] A semiconductor diode whose resistance varies non-linearly with the applied voltage.

1937 *Bell Telephone Q.* Apr. 114 A varistor is a device, for example a copper oxide rectifier, whose resistance *varies* with the applied voltage. **1957** *Electronic Engin.* XXIX. 386/1 Varistors exhibit a practical resistance variation of several decades over their normal rated working range of current or voltage. **1978** *Sci. Amer.* Mar. 59/1 The compensation is termed equalization and is achieved by adding two varistors, or variable resistors, to the speech network.

varite, obs. Sc. form of VERITY.

Varityper ('vɛərɪtaɪpə(r)). orig. and chiefly *U.S.* Also **Vari-typer**, **varityper**. [f. VARI- + TYPER.] The proprietary name of a kind of typewriter that has interchangeable type faces. Also, a kind of type-composing machine with similar operation.

1928 *Official Gaz.* (U.S. Patent Office) 16 Oct. 494/1 *Varityper.* For typewriter machines. **1931** *Times Lit. Suppl.* 1 Oct. 760/4 Latest Hammond (Varityper) Typewriter... Turn knob and you get another type shuttle—italics, smaller letters or accented, or Greek, each with close or open spacing. **1948** *Economist* 13 Nov. 781/1 The varityper..has kept the Chicago newspapers going through a compositors' strike. **1956** *Trade Marks Jrnl.* 11 Jan. 27/1 *Vari-typer*... Type composing machines for office use and parts thereof. .. Ralph C. Coxhead Corporation,..Newark, State of New Jersey, United States of America; manufacturers. **1959** *Oxf. Univ. Gaz.* 3 Dec. 369/2 New 'Vari-typer' composition service with small-offset-litho reproduction. **1977** *San Antonio* (Texas) *Express News* 30 Oct. 5E/4 She designed the layout, type-set it at home on an old varityper and made the negatives for the printer.

Hence **'Vari-type** *v. trans.*; **'Varityping** *vbl. sb.*

1955 H. QUASTLER *Information Theory in Psychol.* p. iv, 'Information Theory in Psychology' was Vari-typed by Diane Folk, Stenographic Bureau, University of Illinois. **1960** *World's Press News* 30 Dec. 15 Varityping plus photo litho printing results in lower cost and faster delivery for brochures, handbooks, leaflets, catalogues.

‖**varix** (ˈvɛərɪks). Pl. **varices** (ˈvɛərɪsiːz). [L. (stem *varic-*). Cf. VARICE.]

1. *Path.* An abnormal dilatation or enlargement of a vein or artery, usually accompanied by a tortuous development; a varicose vein.

c **1400** *Lanfranc's Cirurg.* 178 Þe blood-letyng of þis veyne is good.. for varices & for vlcera þat ben in þe hipis ouþer in þe leggis. **1541** R. COPLAND *Galyen's Terap.* 2 C iij b, It may so be that varix, that is to say a swollen vayne that is aboue it, may be the cause. **1601** HOLLAND *Pliny* II. 279 Some writers hold, that this herb.., bound vnto the swelling veines called Varices, doth allay the paine thereof. **1668** CULPEPPER & COLE *Barthol. Anat.* 363 For that is easie to see in a Varix of the Thigh and Foot. **1767** GOOCH *Treat. Wounds* I. 188 *Varices*.. sometimes become very large and painful upon the legs, requiring opening. **1783** *Med. Comm.* I. 181 The dilatation of a vein (commonly called a *varix*) takes an oblong shape. **1835–6** *Todd's Cycl. Anat. & Phys.* I. 186/1 Pressure on the varix empties it of its contents. **1899** *Allbutt's Syst. Med.* VI. 190 In another case a similar thrombosed varix had broken from its pedicle.

b. The diseased condition characterized by this, as a specific malady.

1813 J. THOMSON *Lect. Inflamm.* 128 The dilatation of capillary vessels which occurs in some species of varix. **1876** GROSS *Dis. Bladder*, etc. 156 The veins.. have a tortuous, convoluted arrangement, similar to what occurs in varix of the leg and thigh. **1878** T. BRYANT *Pract. Surg.* I. 500 Varix is commonly an affection of the veins in the lower extremities, and mainly, of the branches of the saphena vein.

2. *Conch.* A longitudinal elevation or swelling on the surface of a shell (see quot. 1851).

1822 J. PARKINSON *Outl. Oryctol.* 201 With a marginal and sometimes a dorsal varix. **1851** G. F. RICHARDSON *Geol.* viii. 241 The *varices*.. are ribs which cross the volutions in some species of *buccinum*, *murex*, and *triton*. They are formed by the periodical growth of the shells. **1861** P. P. CARPENTER in *Rep. Smithsonian Instit. 1860*, 198 The *Struthiolariæ* have a simple varix instead of a wide lip.

vark, obs. (chiefly Sc.) f. WORK *sb.* and *v.*

varlamoffite (vɑːləˈmɒfaɪt). *Min.* [a. F. *varlomoffite* (H. Buttgenbach *Les Minéraux de Belgique et du Congo Belge* (1947) 182), f. the name of N. *Varlamoff*, mining engineer who found the mineral: see -ITE[1].] A yellowish cryptocrystalline powdery material, perhaps (Sn,Fe) $(O,OH)_2$, that is related to or perhaps identical with cassiterite.

1948 *Mineral. Abstr.* X. 354 A new mineral varlamoffite, H_2SnO_3, as yellow earthy material mixed with grains of cassiterite from Kalima, Belgian Congo, is here included for the first time. **1970** *Mineral. Mag.* XXXVII. 626 Most of the reported occurrences of varlamoffite show a strong spatial association with stannite, and most workers have concluded that it is a secondary mineral resulting from the attack of meteoric waters on stannite.

varld(ly, obs. Sc. forms of WORLD(LY.

varlet (ˈvɑːlɪt). Forms: α. 5– varlet (6 *Sc.* wARllet, 7 varlett), 5–6 varlette; 6–7 varlot (6 *Sc.* war-). β. 6 verlet (-lett, -lette), 7 verlate; 6 verlot (*Sc.* wer-), -lotte. [a. OF. *varlet* (14th c.), var. of *vaslet*, *vadlet*, *vallet* VALET. Hence also med.L. *varletus*. In mod.F. *varlet* is restricted to the historical sense 1 b.]

1. A man or lad acting as an attendant or servant; a menial, a groom. Now *arch.*

α. **1456** SIR G. HAYE *Law Arms* (S.T.S.) 240 The varlet of the labourare, that is for to say his hyre man that dryvis the pleuche. **1483** CAXTON *Gold. Leg.* 154 b/2, I haue rychesses ynough, seruantes, varlettes,.. and kynnysmen whiche serue me. *a* **1533** LD. BERNERS *Huon* lv. 187 This varlet semeth rather sone to a kyng.. then to be a varlet to a mynstrell. **1647** R. STAPYLTON *Juvenal* 94 She calls out to the varlets she doth keep,.. Braine the dog's master first, and then the cur. **1661** BLOUNT *Glossogr.* (ed. 2), *Vadelet*,.. a Benchers Clerk or Servant. The Butlers of the house corruptly call them Varlets. **1684** BURNET tr. *More's Utopia* 109 If it should so happen, that.. all this Wealth should pass from the Master to the meanest Varlet of his whole Family. **1843** CARLYLE *Past & Pr.* II. viii, Lords and varlets, where are they? **1853** JAMES *Agnes Sorel* (1860) I. 124 Acquiring very rapidly from the different varlets and pages a vast amount of information.

β. **1509** HAWES *Past. Pleas.* XXVI. (Percy Soc.) 114 Than on my jorney,.. Wyth my verlet called Attendaunce, Forthe on I rode. **1513** DOUGLAS *Æneid* XII. ii. 13 The byssy knaipis and verlettis of his stabill About thame [*sc.* the horses] stud. **1557** TUSSER *100 Points Husb.* xli, Kepe neuer such seruantes, as doth thee no good, For nestling of verlettes.. make[s] many a rich man to shet vp his doores.

b. *spec.* An attendant on a knight or other person of military importance. Now only *Hist.*

1470–85 MALORY *Arthur* X. xiv. 434 Thenne this Knyght called to hym a varlette, and badde hym ryde vntyl younder fayr manoyre. **1485** CAXTON *Paris & V.* (1868) 69 Whan Parys coude wel speke mouryske, he and his varlet took the waye toward ynde. **1523** LD. BERNERS *Froiss* I. xvi. 16 The archers who were to the nombre of iii. M. shotte faste theyr arowes, nat sparyng maisters nor varlettis. *a* **1548** HALL *Chron., Hen. V.* 50 Divers beyng wounded wer releued by theyr varlettes and conveighed out of the felde. **1590** SPENSER *F.Q.* II. iv. 37 Far away they spyde A varlet running towards hastily... Behind his backe he bore a brasen shield. **1606** SHAKS. *Tr. & Cr.* I. i. 1 Call here my Varlet, Ile vnarme againe. Why should I warre without the wals of Troy? **1825** SCOTT *Talism.* iii, Some fifty more men, archers and varlets included. **1864** BURTON *Scot. Abr.* I. iii. 123 In one month the French lost upwards of a hundred varlets. **1889** F. COWPER *Capt. of Wight* 167 Their esquires were waiting outside, and their varlets were leading their horses.. up and down.

†**c.** *varlet of the chamber*, = VALET-DE-CHAMBRE. *Obs.*

1567 THROGMORTON in Robertson *Hist. Scot.* (1851) II. 435 [She requested] to have her apothecary.. and.. to have a varlet of the chamber. **1588** *Excheq. Rolls Scot.* XXI. 403 To William Murray, varlett of his majesteis chalmer, for his pensioun. **1596** NASHE *Saffron Walden* Wks. (Grosart) III. 158 His voiage vnder Don Anthonio was nothing so great credit to him, as a French Varlet of the chamber is. [**1664** BUTLER *Hud.* II. i. 406 'Tis this that Proudest Dames enamors On Lacquies, and Varlets des-Chambres.]

†**d.** = SERGEANT *sb.* 8. *Obs.*

1598 B. JONSON *Ev. Man in Hum.* IV. ix, Why, you were best get one o' the varlets o' the citie, a serieant. **1620** MELTON *Astrolog.* 73 Those that stand before both the Compters,.. who appeare in the shapes of Sergeants, alias Varlets. **1638** SHIRLEY *Mart. Soldier* v, I was first a Varlet, then a Bum-baily, now an under Jailor.

2. A person of a low, mean, or knavish disposition; a knave, rogue, rascal.

In later use freq. without serious implication of bad qualities.

α. **1555** in COVERDALE *Lett. Martyrs* (1564) 173 Then my lord sayd, thou art a very varlet. **1584** R. SCOT *Discov. Witchcr.* XIV. iii. 297 A notable cousening varlot, who professed Alcumystrie. **1624** BP. MOUNTAGU *Immed. Addr.* 213 Is not this a varlet in graine: a fit Patron of Inuocation? **1642** D. ROGERS *Naaman* 307 All shall see that you were arrant varlots, such as Religion can receive no blemish from. **1726** SWIFT *Gulliver* II. v, A little contemptible varlet, without the least title to birth, person, wit. **1777** SHERIDAN *Trip Scarb.* v. ii, Look, if the varlet has not the effrontery to call his lordship plain Thomas. **1822** W. IRVING *Braceb. Hall* viii, A handsome boy,.. but a mischievous varlet. **1853** KANE *Grinnell Exp.* xl. (1856) 365 We are an uncouth, snobby, and withal, shabby-looking set of varlets. **1881** BESANT & RICE *Chapl. of Fleet* I. x, In the doorway were the two impudent varlets, whom he called his clerks.

β. *a* **1550** *Image Hypocr.* II. 518 in *Skelton's Wks.* (1843) II. 429/1 The helper of harlettes, And captayne of verlettes, The cloke of all vnthriftes. **1573** TUSSER *Husb.* (1878) 144 Such Lords ill example doth giue, where verlets and drabs so may liue. *a* **1604** HANMER *Chron. Irel.* (1633) 29 Now see the villany of these verlates.

b. Employed as an abusive form of address.

1566 ADLINGTON *Apuleius* 55 Thou presumest and thinkest, thou triflinge boye, thou verlette,.. that thou arte most worthy and excellent. **1608** SYLVESTER *Du Bartas* II. iv. *Schism* 116 Know you (varlets) whom you dally-with? **1676** D'URFEY *Mme. Fickle* III. i, Out of my doors thou Varlet; away. **1706** ADDISON *Rosamond* I. iii, Faithless Varlet, art thou there? **1773** GOLDSM. *Stoops to Conq.* v. ii, And is it to you, you graceless varlet, I owe all this? **1829** LYTTON *Devereux* II. iv, 'Now for thee, varlet,' cried Tarleton, brandishing his rapier. **1841** JAMES *Brigand* iii, Run, sir varlet, run.

†**c.** In the phr. *to play the..varlet*. *Obs.*

1579 TOMSON *Calvin's Serm. Tim.* 871/1 To play the verie varlets against all goodnesse:.. we see the wicked are giuen to this. **1615–20** C. MORE *Life Sir T. More* (1828) 318 He fell to scoffing,.. and played the very varlet with the king. **1651** D. CALDERWOOD *Hist. Kirk* (1843) II. 172 So faine would the comptroller have played a good varlett, and satisfeid the queene, or elles have made up his owne profite.

†**d.** *transf.* (See quot.) *Obs.*

1606 SHAKS. *Tr. & Cr.* v. i. 18 Thou are thought to be Achilles male Varlot. *Patr.* Male Varlot you Rogue: What's that? *Ther.* Why his masculine Whore.

†**3.** The knave in cards. *Obs.* [So F. *valet.*]

1508 KENNEDIE *Flyting w. Dunbar* 43 Waik walidrag, and werlot [*v.r.* verlot] of the cairtis. **1579** RICE *Invective agst. Vices* B iv, [They] are more at quiete with the Ace, Kyng, Queene, or Varlet of Spades, then thei can be with a Spade to digge.. for their liuyng. *Ibid.*, Varlette of the Hartes. **1625** B. JONSON *Staple of N.* IV. i, *Mad.* We call'd him a Coat-card O' the last order. *P. Iv.* What's that? a Knaue? *Mad.* Some readings haue it so, my manuscript Doth speake it, Varlet.

4. *attrib.* as *varlet heretic*, *page*, *rebel*.

1456 SIR G. HAYE *Bk. Knighthood* Wks. (S.T.S.) II. 15 Thai ordanyt him a squier, and a varlet page to be ever contynualy at his bidding and service. **1553** T. WILSON *Rhet.* 68 Did the maior of London thrust throughe Jacke Straw beinge but a verlet rebell, and onely disquietinge the Citye? **1563** FOXE *A. & M.* 1581/2 He is the naughtiest verlet heretique, that euer I knewe.

¶**5.** App. used for WARLOCK.

1703 BRAND *New Desc. Ork. & Zetland* viii. 110 There is a House called Kebister, where a Varlet or Wizard lived.

Hence ˈ**varletess**, a female varlet.

1748 RICHARDSON *Clarissa* I. xxxi. 196 It was more Pride than Love.. that put me upon making such a confounded rout about losing this noble varletess. *Ibid.* VI. 96 Eight o'clock at Mid-summer, and these lazy varletesses (in full health) not come down yet to breakfast!

varletry (ˈvɑːlɪtrɪ). Also 7 varlotarie. [f. VARLET + -RY.] Varlets collectively; a number or crowd of attendants or menials.

1606 SHAKS. *Ant. & Cl.* v. ii. 56 Shall they hoyst me vp, And shew me to the showting Varlotarie Of censuring Rome? **1757** DYER *Fleece* III. 461 Those Whose virtues taught the varletry of towns To useful toil to turn the pilfering hand. **1789** J. WHITE *Earl Strongbow* II. 20 The retainers.. now hurried to the barbican... I wheeled round however, and with Gridalbin made a hideous carnage of this varletry. **1840** BROWNING *Sordello* VI. 402 Gay swarms of varletry that come and go, Pages to dice with. **1891** FARRAR *Darkn. & Dawn* xlv, It was only the clientage and varletry of Octavia who had dared to assume the people's name.

‖**varletto.** *Obs.*$^{-1}$ [Italianized f. *varlet*. Cf. It. *valletto* servant, valet.] = VARLET 1 or 2 b.

1598 SHAKS. *Merry W.* IV. v. 66 *Host.* Where be my horses? Speake well of them varletto.

varlo, obs. Sc. f. WARLOCK.

varly, obs. Sc. f. WARELY *adv.*

varm, southern dial. var. FARM *v.*[1]

varme, obs. Sc. f. WARM *a.*

varment, varmint (ˈvɑːmənt), *sb.*[1] *dial.* and *U.S.* Also **varmant, -munt, verment, warment, -mint, -mit**, etc. [var. of *varmin* VERMIN, with excrescent *-t*. Rare before *c* 1825.]

1. a. *collect.* Vermin. **b.** An animal of a noxious or objectionable kind.

A large collection of American examples is given by Thornton *Amer. Gloss.* (1912) s.v.

a **1539** in Ellis *Orig. Lett.* Ser. II. II. 148 Let me not be utterly caste away here in prysson, remayening fwll of varment which cawsythe me to hawe no lyste of meytte nor dryncke. **1689** HUSNANCE *Monitor* Ep. Ded., For many who smell like a Kirkish Verment, Can now, Sir, put on a Lamb-like garment. **1823** E. MOOR *Suffolk Wds.*, *Varment*, vermin, not always confined to the verminous class of animals, but extended to any annoying or troublesome ones. **1828** J. HALL *Lett. fr. West* 297 He gave his foe [a bear-cub] a mortal shot, or to use his own language, 'I burst the varment'. **1835** W. IRVING *Tour Prairies* xxiii, 'These beavers,' said he, '.. are the knowingest varment as I know'. **1854** MISS BAKER *Northampt. Gloss.*, *Varment*, vermin.

β. **1829** *Sporting Mag.* (N.S.) XXIII. 242 Some of the followers of the gallant *varmint*. **1846** T. B. THORPE *Backwoods* 166 The idea of a 'man's keeping two varmints in a grass, when he might shoot a dozen by going a little way into the woods'. These 'varmints' were two beautiful deer. **1856** *Porter's Spirit of Times* 20 Sept. 38/2 Why, massa, dat 'tarnal varmit hab fooled me bad. **1883** PENNELL-ELMHIRST *Cream Leicestersh.* 154 Meanwhile the varmint had stolen on in his struggle for Tilton Wood and life. **1889** *Boston* (Mass.) *Jrnl.* 25 Oct. 2/3 The granger came out with his rifle and shot the varmint [a panther]. **1974** *Evening Herald* (Rock Hill, S. Carolina) 18 Apr. 13/3 She didn't care if my face was black. She didn't treat me like no varmit or nothing.

2. An objectionable or troublesome person or persons; a mischievous boy or child.

1773 GOLDSM. *Stoops to Conq.* v. 92 The poor beasts have smoaked for it: Rabbet me, but I'd rather ride forty miles after a fox, than ten with such *varment*. **1825** BROCKETT *N.C. Gloss.*, *Varment, Verment*,.. also a term of reproach, particularly to a child. **1845** C. H. J. ANDERSON *Swedish Brothers* 8 That little varmint Nettop has tickled his heels for him. **1857** HUGHES *Tom Brown* II. iv,'I've got the young varmint at last, have I,' pants the farmer. **1859** *Slang Dict.* 114 'You young varment, you!' you bad or naughty boy.

Hence ˈ**varminty** *a. colloq.*, suggestive of or resembling a varmint; sharp, cunning.

1907 A. CONAN DOYLE *Thr. Magic Door* ii. 34 Louis, thin, ascetic, varminty. **1922** R. LEIGHTON *Compl. Bk. Dog* xvii. 261 The General Appearance of the West Highland White Terrier is that of a small, game, hardy-looking terrier.. with a 'varminty' appearance. **1962** R. H. SMYTHE *Anat. Dog Breeding* 52 The 'varminty' eye of a Fox Terrier.

varment, varmint, *sb.*[2] and *a.* *slang* (now *dial.*). [Of obscure origin; there is no obvious connexion with prec.]

A. *sb.* A sporting amateur with the knowledge or skill of a professional.

1812 *Sporting Mag.* XXXIX. 9 Every professional amateur.. is denominated a Varment. **1823** BYRON *Juan* XI. xvii, Poor Tom was once a kiddy upon town, A thorough varmint, and a *real* swell, Full flash, all fancy.

B. *adj.* **1.** (See quot. 1823.) Also *Comb.*

1823 EGAN *Grose's Dict. Vulg. T.*, *Varment*, natty, dashing. He is quite varment, he is quite the go. He sports a varment hat, coat, etc., he is dressed like a gentleman Jehu. **1828** LYTTON *Pelham* II. xiv. 135 We sat down.. and looked round inquiringly at the smug and varment citizens with which the room was filled. **1859** WARBURTON *Hunting Songs* 92 A varment looking gemman on a woiry tit.

2. Knowing, clever, cunning.

1829 BROCKETT *N.C. Gloss.* 317 *Varment*.. is also a sort of cant word for knowing; as a *varment* chap, a knowing one. **1831** TRELAWNY *Adv. Younger Son* I. 179 Nevertheless there is a varment and knowing look about her [a ship] which I like. **1834** MEDWIN *Angler in Wales* II. 162 None but a very varmint dog.. will face one of these water-weazels a second time. **1890** 'R. BOLDREWOOD' *Col. Reformer* (1891) 340 He.. ran into the stockyard and caught the varmint, ambling black mare. **1891** P. H. EMERSON *East Coast Yarns* 92, I met old Jimmy Lodes, the varmintest horse-dealer about these parts.

Hence ˈ**varmentcy**; ˈ**varmentish** *a.*

1812 *Sporting Mag.* XXXIX. 9 This polite art is designated Varmentcy. *Ibid.* 10 The origin of Varmentcy, as of almost all the noble Sciences, is obscure. **1819** *Ibid.* (N.S.) V. 54 Nothing under four horses would look 'varmentish'.

varmin, obs. or dial. var. VERMIN.

varn(e, obs. ff. WARN *v.*

‖**varna** (ˈvɑːnə, ˈvʌrnə). [Skr. *varṇa*, colour, appearance.] Any one of the four early castes or social classes of Hindu society (see CASTE 2 a); the system or basis of this division.

1838 *Penny Cycl.* XII. 230/1 The division of Hindus into .. castes.. existed from the earliest times. In Sanskrit they are called *varnas*, that is 'colours'. **1876** *Encycl. Brit.* IV. 203/1 The idea of caste is expressed by the Sanskrit term *varna*, originally denoting 'colour', thereby implying differences of complexion between the several classes. **1931** [see JAT[2]]. **1959** *Times Lit. Suppl.* 1 May 262/5 Viewing the *varna* system of ancient India through rose-tinted spectacles. **1974** *Encycl. Brit. Macropædia* IX. 347/2 The traditional view that *varṇa* reflected the organization of

Indian society has recently been questioned; it has been suggested that.. the concept of *jāti* is more central to caste functioning than *varṇa*, which may be the theoretical rationalization. **1977** M. & J. STUTLEY *Dict. Hinduism* 323 *Varṇa*. The word is generally used to denote colour, but its primary meaning, derived from the root *vṛ* is 'screen, veil, covering, external appearance', and hence colour is only one of the many aspects of the term.

varnasyng, Sc. var. WARNISHING.

varngreis, obs. Sc. var. VERDIGRIS.

varnis, obs. Sc. var. WARNISH *v.*

varnish ('vɑːnɪʃ), *sb.*[1] Forms: α. 4 **vernisshe**, 4, 6 **vernysshe**, 5 **-nyshe, -nysche, -nesche**; 4 **vernisch**, 5 **vernysh (wernysch)**, 6–8 **vernish**; 4, 7 **vernich**; 6 **vernize**, *Sc.* **verneis, vernes, vernys**, 7 **vernis, -nice**. β. 6 **varnysch**, 6– **varnish** (7 **-nishe**); 6 *Sc.* **varneyis**, 7 **varnes**. [ad. OF. *vernis* (*varnis*), *verniz* (12th c.), = Prov. *vernis, -nitz*, Pg. *verniz*, It. *vernice*, Cat. *barnis*, Sp. *barniz*, of unknown origin. Cf. med.L. *vernicium* and *vernix* (*bernix*), med. Gr. βερνίκη, mod.Gr. βερνίκι. French is also the source of MHG. *firnîs*, G. *firnis(s*, Du. *vernis*, Da. *fernis*, Sw. *fernissa*.]

1. a. Resinous matter dissolved in some liquid and used for spreading over a surface in order to give this a hard, shining, transparent coat, by which it is made more durable or ornamental.

In early use, dry resinous matter for making a solution of this kind.

α. **1341–2** *Ely Sacr. Rolls* II. 121 In vj libr. de albo vernich, prec. lbr. iijd. **1358** in *Pipe Roll 32 Edw. III* m. 34/1 b, In .iij. Mill'de vernisshe; .v. lb de vermeillone. **1362** LANGL. *P. Pl.* A. v. 70 Venim or vernisch or vinegre, I trouwe, Walleþ in my wombe. **14..** in *Reliq. Ant.* I. 163 For to make wernysch.—Take a galon of good ale, and put thereto iij ounces of gumme of Arabyke [etc.]. **1466** *Mann. & Househ. Exp.* (Roxb.) 349 My mastyr receyvid of Fynches man of Colchestre a li. of vernyshe, pryse .vj.d. **1501** *Acc. Ld. High Treas. Scot.* II. 64 For iij vnce quhit vernys. **1507** *Ibid.* IV. 90 Caddes, verneis, rede lede. **1530** PALSGR. 284/2 Vernysshe, *uernys*. **1585** T. WASHINGTON tr. *Nicholay's Voy.* III. xv. 99 b, They vse by continuall artifice Terebinthe and vernish. **1598** BARRET *Theor. Warres* 135 Aqua vitæ, liquid vernize, arsenike. **1633** HART *Diet of Diseased* I. xvii. 69 The oile of walnuts is.. used.. by painters for vernice. **1638** JUNIUS *Paint. Ancients* 285 Apelles.. did by an inimitable invention anoint his finished workes with.. a thinne kinde of inke or vernish. **1658** tr. *Porta's Nat. Magic* XVI. 341 Powder Iuniper-gum, which Scriveners call Vernish, and add it to the rest. **1706** STEVENS *Span. Dict.* I, *Barniz*, Vernish.

β. **1546** *Inv. Ch. Goods Surrey* 106 Item for ij lb. of varnysch, ij s. viij d. **1620** *Shuttleworths' Acc.* (Chetham Soc.) 244 Three pound of varnishe for the caroache, xxjd. **1658** PHILLIPS, *Varnish*, is that wherewith a picture is rubbed over to make it shine and have a glosse; there is also a ground or varnish which is laid upon a plate that is to be etched. **1725** *Fam. Dict.* s.v. *Wounds*, Let him drop some Varnish with a Feather to the bottom. **1773** *Cook's Voy.* (1777) II. III. xi. 146 As we had neither pitch, tar, nor rosin, left to pay the seams, this was done with varnish of pine. **1815** J. SMITH *Panorama Sci. & Art* II. 86 As wood, and many other substances.. are porous and apt to imbibe water,.. it is proper to give them a coat of varnish. **1842** LEVER *J. Hinton* x, Like the varnish upon a picture, it brings out all the colour into strong effect. **1894** BOTTONE *Elect. Instr.* 60 When the sectors are firmly stuck down to the glass, and the varnish quite dry.

transf. **1784** COWPER *Task* I. 40 Now came the cane from India, smooth and bright With Nature's varnish.

b. With *a* and *pl.* A special preparation of this nature.

Many varieties are enumerated in special works from *Chambers' Cycl.* Suppl. (1753) onwards.

α. **1667** *Phil. Trans.* II. 417 How, in China and Japan, they make the Black-vernish. *Ibid.* 487 This Author mentions.. their [*sc.* Chinese] Vernice, of which he sets down some Receipts both for the Red and Black. **1676** *Ibid.* XI. 714 An Oyl, of which the Persians make a Vernis.

β. **1692** LUTTRELL *Brief Rel.* (1857) II. 420 A pattent is past for the invention of a varnish to preserve guns, &c. from rust. **1753** *Chambers' Cycl.* Suppl. s.v., The Varnishes used by the Chinese are two. **1774** GOLDSM. *Nat. Hist.* (1776) VIII. 24 It is only formed by a beautiful brown varnish, laid upon a white ground. **1838** T. THOMSON *Chem. Org. Bodies* 538 Dragon's blood.. is used also to give a red colour to varnishes. **1892** *Photogr. Ann.* II. 235 In using the varnishes.. care must be taken not to apply too great a quantity of them to the surface of the calico.

c. A solution of this kind spread on a surface; the coating or surface so formed.

1643 *Plain English* 13 Posts whose varnish is.. worne off. **1662** EVELYN *Chalcogr.* 9 Not much unlike to our Etching with points and Needles on the Vernish. **1726** LEONI *Alberti's Archit.* I. 33/1 Lime.. for plaistering.. gives the best varnish to the Work. **1865** DICKENS *Mut. Fr.* I. ii, All things were in a state of high varnish and polish. **1871** TYNDALL *Fragm. Sci.* ix. 240 When it was found that all chemical precipitates radiated alike, it was the radiation from a varnish common to them all which showed the observed constancy.

transf. **1715** POPE *Ep. Addison* 37 This the blue varnish, that the green endears, The sacred rust of twice ten hundred years! **1819** SCOTT *Ivanhoe* iii, By encrusting them with a black varnish of soot. **1838** EMERSON *Addr., Literary Ethics* Wks. (Bohn) II. 207 The sense of spiritual independence is like the lovely varnish of the dew.

fig. **1835** LYTTON *Rienzi* IV. iii, The varnish of power brings forth at once the defects and the beauties of the human portrait. **1860** EMERSON *Cond. Life, Behaviour* Wks. (Bohn) II. 380 They [manners] form at last a rich varnish, with which the routine of life is washed. **1884** *Pall Mall G.* 29 Feb. 1/2 There is a film of Levantine varnish around the court at Constantinople.

d. A preparation of boiled oil (or other substances) used in the making of printers' ink.

1807 T. THOMSON *Chem.* (ed. 3) II. 445 The oil is.. boiled gently till it acquires the proper consistence. In this state it is called the varnish. **1841** T. C. HANSARD *Printing & Type-f.* 106 The next.. article is nut or linseed oil boiled and burnt into a varnish.

e. A medical preparation resembling a varnish, for application to the skin.

1899 *Allbutt's Syst. Med.* VIII. 582 Both tar and pyrogallol work better as paints and varnishes than the chrysa-robin.

f. A resinous deposit formed in engines by the oxidation of fuel and lubricating oils.

1948 A. P. FRAAS *Combustion Engine* viii. 241 The resins may deposit with the sludge or may form thin adherent coatings on engine parts. In the latter case the coatings are called varnish or lacquer because of their appearance. **1967** *Boston Sunday Herald* 26 Mar. I. 1/2 Don't be fooled by slow cranking because 'varnish' on the pistons will cause so much drag that a hot engine may resist cranking until it cools. **1981** *Pop. Hot Rodding* Feb. 84/1 Oxidation produces new compounds, loosely termed sludge, varnish and acid, which are detrimental to the lubrication system.

2. *fig.* **a.** A specious gloss or outward show; a pretence.

1565 JEWEL *Reply Harding* (1611) 438 This of late yeeres was the Schoole-doctours Catholike meaning,.. which now M. Harding and his Fellowes are faine for shame, to colour ouer with some finer Vernish. **1617** HIERON *Wks.* II. 362 God will not be dallyed with; this outward varnish cannot bleare His eyes. **1647** N. BACON *Disc. Govt. Eng.* I. xliv. (1739) 71 For the better varnish, the Duke would not be his own Judge. **1765** *Priv. Lett. Ld. Malmesbury* (1870) I. 163 It is impossible to get the least certain intelligence from thence, as nothing comes out of the closet but with a double varnish. **1782** V. KNOX *Ess.* lvii. (1819) II. 1 Qualities, which, when seen in their true light, and without the varnish of deceit, are peculiarly unpleasing. **1843** PRESCOTT *Mexico* (1850) I. 285 The affectation of legal forms afforded him a thin varnish for his proceedings. **1844** MRS. CARLYLE *Lett.* I. 291 Women will.. always give a varnish of duty to their inclinations. **1895** C. GRAHAM *Notes Menteith* i. 7 Convention has lent a thin varnish of hypocrisy to manners.

b. Without article.

1743 *Lond. Mag.* 346 The authentick Gazette, which.. never once dealt in Puff or Varnish, but told the Truth. **1809** MALKIN *Gil Blas* VII. xv, From the clerk of the kitchen I required the buttery accounts without varnish or concealment. **1847** EMERSON *Repr. Men, Plato* Wks. (Bohn) I. 308 This eldest Goethe, hating varnish and falsehood, delighted in revealing the real at the base of the accidental.

3. a. A means of embellishment or adornment; a beautifying or improving quality or feature.

1591 SYLVESTER *Du Bartas* I. ii. 1150 Though.. Divinity, For only varnish, have but Verity. **1599** NASHE *Lenten Stuffe* Wks. (Grosart) V. 233, I might enamell.. this deuice more artificially and masterly, and attire it in his true orient varnish and tincture. **1605** BACON *Adv. Learn.* I. 27 My intent is without varnish or amplification, iustly to weigh the dignitie of knowledge in the ballance with other things. **1671** PANTON *Spec. Juv.* Ded., Though it have not the Romantick varnish of stile, worthy your Majestie's view and regard. **1712** STEELE *Spect.* No. 364 ¶1 This last Qualification.. serves as a Varnish to all the rest. **1727** S. SWITZER *Pract. Gard.* lxxviii. 392 Neatness and politure ought now.. to serve for a varnish to the alleys and the dress'd grounds. **1863** HAWTHORNE *Our Old Home* (1883) I. 246 A cloudy and rainy day takes the varnish off the scenery.

b. Gloss, brilliancy.

1841 T. C. HANSARD *Printing & Type-f.* 107 The turpentine is added to give greater varnish [to the ink].

4. An external appearance or display of some quality without underlying reality. (Cf. VENEER *sb.*)

1662 STILLINGFL. *Orig. Sacræ* II. ii. §8 He lived long enough to have.. judgement to distinguish a meer outside and varnish, from what was solid and substantial. **1776** GIBBON *Lett. Holroyd* 20 May, I.. laugh at her Paris varnish, and oblige her to become a simple reasonable Suissesse. **1778** MME. D'ARBLAY *Diary* 23 Aug., Such a fine varnish of low politeness!—such a struggle to appear a gentleman! **1840** THIRLWALL *Greece* lv. VII. 113 New forms.. destitute of life and reality, an empty varnish. **1853** MERIVALE *Rom. Rep.* iv. (1867) 100 But this varnish of superior culture seems to have failed in softening a rough plebeian nature. **1868** M. PATTISON *Academ. Org.* iv. 65 The youth comes up with a varnish of accomplishment beyond his real powers.

5. *attrib.* and *Comb.*, as ***varnish brush, gum, -house, -maker, pot, -remover, -sector; varnish-like*** adj.; **varnish sumach**, the Japanese tree *Rhus vernicifera* from which lacquer is obtained; **varnish-tree**, one or other of various trees yielding a resinous substance used as a varnish.

1859 F. S. COOPER *Ironmongers' Catal.* 38 *Varnish Brushes. **1892** *Daily News* 13 Feb. 7/3 Cinchona.. bark sold well, but *varnish gums generally eased off. **1839** URE *Dict. Arts* 1269 Crystal varnish may be made.. in the *varnish-house. **1916** *Nature* 25 May 269/2 Boiled linseed oil on exposure to the air is converted by oxidation into a hard *varnish-like product. **1965** FINER & SAVAGE *Sel. Lett. J. Wedgwood* 13 The ancient red-figure vases were decorated by reserving the figures on a red pottery ground, surrounding them with a black varnishlike slip. **1753** *Chambers' Cycl.* Supp., *Spike*,.. an essential oil, much used by the *varnish-makers and the painters in enamel. **1839** URE *Dict. Arts* 1267 The choice of linseed oil is of peculiar consequence to the varnish-maker. **1825** J. NICHOLSON *Operat. Mechanic* 739 Put the copal, coarsely pulverized, into a *varnish pot. **1965** P. D. SAMMAN *Nails in Disease* ix. 83 Nail varnish and *varnish removers and excess manicuring may be of some importance aetiologically. **1973** C. WILLIAMS *Man on Leash* ix. 131 That crap they shot into my arm. Battery solution or varnish remover. **1826** KIRBY & SP. *Entomol.* IV. xli. 126 *Varnish-secretor (*Colleterium*).. In the cabbage butterfly there is a pair of ovate ones [*sc.* oviduct vessels],.. filled with a yellow fluid, which Reaumur and Herold think is used for varnishing or gumming the eggs. **1822–7** GOOD *Stud. Med.* (1829) IV. 685, I mean several of the acrid poisons, as.. *rhus vernix*, *varnish sumach. **1758** *Phil. Trans.* L. 453 He says, speaking of this true *varnish-tree, that callicuts are painted with the juice of this shrub. *Ibid.* 448, I suppose he means, by this true varnish-tree, the Carolina pennated Toxicodendron. **1843** *Penny Cycl.* XXVI. 147/2 The theetsee, or varnish-tree of the Burmese, has been described and figured by Dr. Wallich, by the name of Melanorrhœa usitata. He identified it with the Kheu, or varnish-tree of Munnipore. **1866** *Treas. Bot.* 443/1 The natives speak of the tree producing this resin, *E[læagia] utilis*, as the Wax tree or Varnish tree. *Ibid.* 1204/2.

'**varnish**, *sb.*[2] Also 7 **vernish**. [f. the vb.] An act of varnishing; an application of varnish.

1601 HOLLAND *Pliny* II. 515 If you be desirous to keepe any yron-worke from rust, give it a vernish with cerusse, plastre, and tar, incorporat all together. **1755** *Dict. Arts & Sci.* s.v. *Japanning*, If it be not well done, polishing will be necessary, for which reason you must give it five or six varnishes more.

varnish ('vɑːnɪʃ), *v.* Forms: α. 4–6 **vernysshe**, 5 **vernysche (-nyschyn)**, 6 **wernysh-**, 6–8 **vernish**, 6 *Sc.* **vernes-**. β. 5 **varnesch-**, 6 *Sc.* **varneis, warnis**, 6– **varnish**. [ad. OF. *verniss(i)er, vernic(i)er* (F. *vernisser*), or *verniss-, vernir*, f. *vernis* VARNISH *sb.* Cf. med.L. and It. *verniciare*, Pg. *envernizar*, Sp. *barnizar*.]

1. a. *trans.* To paint *over*, to coat, with varnish; to overlay with a thin coating composed of varnish.

1398 TREVISA *Barth. De P.R.* XVII. xxiii. (Bodl. MS.), Bokes þat beþ yvarnesched with þe gomme þerof beþ nouȝt iȝete wiþ wormes. *c* **1440** *Promp. Parv.* 509/1 Vernyschyn, *vernicio*. **1530** PALSGR. 765/2 I vernysshe a spurre, or any yron with vernysshe, *je vernis*. Come hyther, spurryer, be my spurres well vernysshed. *a* **1548** HALL *Chron., Hen. IV*, 12 Some had their armyng sweardes freshly burnyshed and some had them conningly vernished. **1589** ALEX. HUME *Poems* (S.T.S.) 55 Corslets of pruif, and mony targe of steill, Sum varneist bright, sum dorred diuerslie. **1604** E. G[RIMSTONE] *D'Acosta's Hist. Indies* IV. xxix. 288 They bringe likewise from this Province oyle of Aspicke, which.. Painters vse much.. to vernish the pictures. **1697** J. POTTER *Antiq. Greece* III. xv. (1715) 127 Several other Colours were also made use of, nor were they barely varnish'd over with them, but very often anneal'd by Wax melted in the Fire. **1702** W. J. tr. *Bruyn's Voy. Levant* xxxvii. 147 Plaister varnish'd with a green colour. **1755** *Dict. Arts & Sci.* s.v. *Japanning*. With a pencil varnish it over with the finest white varnish. **1821** CRAIG *Lect. Drawing*, etc. ii. 112 These pictures, I am persuaded, were afterwards constantly varnished. **1861** T. A. TROLLOPE *La Beata* I. vii. 152 The copy.. was not to be sent home till it had been varnished.

absol. **1573** *Art Limming* (1588) 9 If you will vernish on silver, then take the Almon of Bengewyne. *a* **1817** JANE AUSTEN *Persuasion* (1818) III. xi. 234 He drew, he varnished, he carpentered.

b. *transf.* To invest with a bright or glossy appearance; to smear or stain with some substance similar to varnish.

c **1386** CHAUCER *Reeve's T.* 229 Wel hath the myller vernysshed his heed, Ful pale he was, for-dronken, and nat reed. *c* **1430** LYDG. *Min. Poems* (Percy Soc.) 53 Ful pale drunke, weel vernyssht of visage. *Ibid.* 54 And whan thou hast weel vernyssht thi pate, To take a sleepe in hast thou wolt the dresse. **1589** GREENE *Tullies Love* Wks. (Grosart) VII. 117, I found him in his bed chamber, his wife slaine And the blade yet varnished with bloud, grasped in his fist. *a* **1618** SYLVESTER *Spectacles* xxxiii. Wks. (Grosart) II. 300 The Leaves fresh varnisht lively green, The Blossoms various to be seen. **1664** POWER *Exp. Philos.* I. 11 Her eyes are.. of a pure golden colour, most admirable to behold, especially when varnish'd with a full light. *a* **1733** RAMSAY *Tartana* 17 You who.. Drain from the flow'rs the early dews of May, To varnish on your cheek the crimson dye. **1841** MAUNDER *Sci. & Lit. Treas.* (1848) s.v. *Scarabæus*, The colour [of the *Scarabæus auratus*] is most brilliant, highly varnished, and of a golden green. **1865** DICKENS *Mut. Fr.* I. x, Next morning, that horrible old Lady Tippins begins to be dyed and varnished for the interesting occasion.

2. To embellish or adorn; to improve, trick out, furbish *up*.

14.. *Sir Beues* (MS. C.) 3777 Blak sendel and.. rede, Vernysched wiþ rosys off syluyr bryȝt. **1580** LYLY *Euphues* (Arb.) 450 The Elizabeth of Euphues being but shadowed for others to vernish, but begun for others to ende. **1589** NASHE *Martin Marprelate* Wks. (Grosart) I. 189 All my foolerie I bequeath to my good friend Lanam;.. it.. may serue (perhappes) for yong beginners, if it be newe varnished. **1639** G. DANIEL *Vervic* 720 My Name, which stood The Boast of Fame, I varnish't with my Blood. **1699** BENTLEY *Phal.* 162 To dress up and to varnish the Story of Pausanias. *a* **1715** BURNET *Own Time* (1766) II. 154 Which were set off with all the fulsome Rhetorick that the penners could varnish them with. **1789** MRS. PIOZZI *Journ. France* II. 374 [Here is] old Franck's Seven Acts of Mercy varnished up. **1887** HUXLEY in *Life* (1900) II. 154 It will go on and be varnished into a simulacrum of success.

3. To cover or overlay with a specious or deceptive appearance; to gloss over, disguise.

1571 GOLDING *Calvin on Ps.* iv. 3 Though they be wylfully blind & vernish their unryghtuousnesse with counterfet colours. **1597** HOOKER *Eccl. Pol.* v. lxv. §15 The church of Rome hath hitherto practised and doth profess the same adoration to the sign of the cross,.. howsoeuer they varnish and qualifie their sentence. **1641** MILTON *Reform.* Wks. 1851 III. 11 But what doe wee suffer.. Prelatisme, as we do, thus to blanch and varnish her deformities with the faire colours.. of Episcopacie? **1649** DRUMM. OF HAWTH. *Skiamachia* Wks. (1711) 198 Wicked Counsels may be varnished with the shining Oil of sly Pretences. **1713** ADDISON *Cato* II. ii, Cato's voice was ne'er employed To clear the guilty, and to vernish crimes. **1783** BLAIR *Rhet.* xxv. (1812) II. 160 The art of varnishing weak arguments plausibly. **1835** *Woman* II. 241 The female character of this day is varnished, not polished. **1863** COWDEN CLARKE *Shaks. Char.* xx. 520 He does not varnish—he does not even polish vice. **1874** L. STEPHEN *Hours in Library* (1892) I. iii. 134 A corrupt heart thinly varnished by a coating of affectation.

4. With *over* (in senses 2 and 3).

1641 MILTON *Ch. Govt.* ii. Wks. 1851 III. 103 God.. never intended to leave the Government..to be patch't afterwards, and varnish't over with the devices..of mans imagination. **1643** DENHAM *Cooper's H.* 125 And yet this Act, to varnish o'r the shame Of Sacriledge, must bear Devotions Name. **1694** ADDISON *England's Greatest Poets* Misc. Wks. 1726 I. 38 Or had the Poet ne'er profan'd his pen, To vernish o'er the guilt of faithless men. **1719** YOUNG *Busiris* III. i, O, how can you abuse your sacred reason,..To varnish o'er, and paint, so black a crime! ?**1773** MACPHERSON *Ossian's Poems, Dissert. Concern. Æra of Ossian* (1785) II. 227 When they [*sc.* poets] found their themes inadequate to the warmth of their imaginations, they varnished them over with fables. **1824** SYD. SMITH *Wks.* (1867) II. 193 He may hide it by increased zeal and violence, or varnish it over by simulated gaiety. **1871** R. H. HUTTON *Theol. Ess.* iii. (1888) 49 To varnish over these distinctions.

Hence **'varnishing** *ppl. a.*

1796 *Mod. Gulliver* 203 The mischiefs flowing from my fallacious varnishing pamphlet were not thought of.

varnished ('vɑːnɪʃt), *ppl. a.* [f. prec.]

1. Coated with varnish; †painted.

1553 *Acc. Ld. H. Treas. Scot.* X. 176 Ane pair of warnist styrrep irnis. **1596** SHAKS. *Merch. V.* II. v. 33 Nor thrust your head..To gaze on Christian fooles with varnisht faces. **1599** MINSHEU *Span. Dial.* 3/2 What rapier?.. None but that varnist rapier, least it should raine. **1671** BOYLE *Usef. Exp. Nat. Philos.* II. v. 29, I am credibly inform'd, that the Art of making the like Varnish'd Wares, is now begun to be a Trade at Paris. **1755** *Dict. Arts & Sci.* s.v. *Japanning*, Laying this paper upon the table, or piece of varnished-work. **1794** R. J. SULIVAN *View Nat.* I. 247 The varnished superior surface imbibes the essential particles. **1815** SCOTT *Guy M.* xlix, Brown silk stockings, highly varnished shoes, and gold buckles.

b. *transf.* Presenting a shining or glossy appearance as if coated with varnish.

1642 H. MORE *Song of Soul* II. III. i. 25 Fresh varnish'd groves, tall hills, and gilded clouds Arching an eyelid for the glowing Morn. **1646** QUARLES *Eglogues* ix, See, how sweat imbalmes His varnisht Temples! **1733** POPE *Donne's Sat.* IV. 208 Such painted puppets! such a varnish'd race Of hollow gew-gaws, only dress and face! *c* **1820** *Dublin Hosp. Rep.* III. 23 A florid, clear, varnished tongue. **1855** MISS PRATT *Flower. Pl.* V. 83 The variety..termed the Varnished Willow, is an upright tree.

2. *fig.* **a.** Embellished; speciously tricked out.

1607 WALKINGTON *Opt. Glass* 129 A smug neate stile,.. vernished phrases. **1662** HOPKINS *Funeral Serm.* (1685) 103 Nor easily cousened by varnisht and plausible error.

b. Simulated, pretended.

1607 SHAKS. *Timon* IV. ii. 36 To haue his pompe..But onely painted like his varnisht Friends. **1685** DRYDEN *Threnodia Aug.* iv. 132 Whose noble pride Was still above Dissembled hate or varnished love.

varnisher ('vɑːnɪʃə(r)). [f. as prec.]

1. One who varnishes; *spec.* one who makes a business or trade of varnishing.

1598 FLORIO, *Inuernicatore*, a varnisher. **1669** PEPYS *Diary* 26 Apr., To Lilly's, the Varnisher, who is lately dead, and his wife and brother keep up the trade. **1706** STEVENS *Span. Dict.* I, *Barnizador*, a Vernisher. **1723** *Lond. Gaz.* No. 6224/8 William Morgan,..Varnisher. **1804** P. TINGRY (*title*), Painter and Varnisher's Guide. **1825** J. NICHOLSON *Operat. Mechanic* 745 These accidents can be repaired only by new strata of varnish, which render application to the varnisher necessary. **1864** *Daily Tel.* 7 April, Painters' and varnishers' shops.

fig. *c* **1700** POPE *Imit. Earl Rochester* 21 With thee in private modest Dulness lies, And in thy bosom lurks in Thought's disguise; Thou varnisher of Fools, and cheat of all the Wise!

2. *slang.* (See quot.)

1865 *Slang Dict.* 265 *Varnisher*, an utterer of false sovereigns.

varnishing ('vɑːnɪʃɪŋ), *vbl. sb.* [f. as prec.]

1. a. The action of applying varnish or of coating anything with varnish.

1505 *Acc. Ld. High Treas. Scot.* III. 148 For vernesing of x pair sterap irnis. **1536–7** *Durham Acc. Rolls* (Surtees) 697 Cum emendacione lez bossez, et wernysshynge. **1609** BIBLE (Douay) *Ecclus.* xxxviii. 34 He wil geve his hart to finish the vernishing thereof. **1632** SHERWOOD s.v., A kind of varnishing like to damasking. **1688** STALKER (*title*), Treatise of Japaning and Varnishing, Being a compleat Discovery of those Arts. **1753** *Chambers' Cycl.* Suppl. s.v. *Japanning*, For in this laying it on depends the principal art of varnishing. **1857** MILLER *Elem. Chem., Org.* vi. §1. 360 Linseed oil..is also largely employed..in the varnishing of oiled silk. **1885** *Athenæum* 11 July 55/2 It proves to be..untouched except for a little clumsy varnishing.

fig. **1697** COLLIER *Ess. Mor. Subj.* II. (1709) 139 Whence comes all Circumvention in Commerce, adulterating of Wares, vouching and varnishing against all good Faith and Honesty?

b. = VERNISSAGE. Cf. *varnishing day*, sense 3.

1951 N. MITFORD *Blessing* II. iv. 188, I was to go round at six, take her to a varnishing, and then dine with her. **1971** R. A. CARTER *Manhattan Primitive* vii. 63 Thatcher preferred the French word for openings; 'varnishings' were what they usually turned out to be.

2. A coating of varnish. In quot. *fig.*

1754 P. H. *Hiberniad* iii. 22 These Advantages, however shewy, are but the outward Varnishing of Man.

3. *attrib.*, as ***varnishing brush***; **varnishing day** (see quot. 1862).

c **1825** TURNER in *Westm. Gaz.* (1896) 1 May 8/3 When we have no more 'varnishing' days we shall not know one another. **1825** SIR T. LAWRENCE in D. E. Williams *Life* (1831) II. 406 Will you likewise procure a large flat varnishing brush? **1862** W. SANDBY *Hist. R. Acad. Arts* I. 274 In the year 1809..the 'varnishing days' were appointed, whereby the members of the Academy were granted the privilege of retouching and varnishing their pictures after they were hung, and prior to the opening of the exhibition. **1896** *Harper's Mag.* Apr. 680/2 Varnishing-day came at last. The portrait was received with enthusiasm and given a place of honor.

†**'varnishment.** *Obs. rare.* [f. as prec.] The act of varnishing.

1593 NASHE *Christ's T.* Wks. (Grosart) IV. 210 Thou hast ..wyth Arts-vanishing varnishment, made thy selfe a changeling from the forme I first cast thee in. **1646** JENKYN *Remora* 19 Let not humane varnishments and pretexts draw forth thy love to it.

varnys(ing, Sc. varr. WARNISH(ING.

varnysoun, Sc. var. WARNISON.

†**varon**, *a. Obs.* Also 5 **varond**, 6 **varrant**. [ad. F. *vairon.*] Wall-eyed.

1451 *Test. Ebor.* (Surtees) III. 120 De j equo trottante, vocato Varond. **1538** *Ibid.* VI. 75 To my sone..a varon meir, one blake meir with the folowers [etc.]. **1559** *Will of R. Whitehead, York* (MS.), My eldest stagg which was of my varrant meare.

varoom (və'rʊm), var. VROOM.

varp, obs. Sc. f. WARP *v.*

varra, dial. var. VERY *adv.*; Sc. f. WARRAY *v. Obs.*

varrand, obs. Sc. f. WARRANT.

varrander, obs. Sc. f. WARRENER.

varrant, variant of VARON *a. Obs.*

varrar, obs. Sc. compar. of WARE *a.*

varray, Sc. var. VERY *a.*, WARRAY *v.*

'varriated, *a. Her. rare*$^{-0}$. = VARIATED *a.*

c **1828** BERRY *Encycl. Her.* I. Gloss., *Varriated*, or *Warriated*, cut in the form of vair.

Varroa ('værəʊə). *Ent.* Also **varroa**. [mod.L., coined in Ger. (A. C. Oudemans 1904, in *Entomol. Ber.* (Amsterdam) XVIII. 161), f. the name of Marcus Terentius *Varro* (116–27 BC), Roman scholar.] A small mite, *Varroa jacobsoni*, which is a fatal parasite of the honeybee in the Far East and has spread to other parts in modern times; infection with this mite.

1974 *Jrnl. Washington Acad. Sci.* LXIV. 10/2 '*Varroa* disease' of the honey bee. **1978** *Bee World* LIX. 165 Bees imported from Japan brought *Varroa* to Paraguay. **1979** *Guardian* 26 July 1/4 The barely visible varroa began infesting Russian honey-bees in 1964 and since then it has flourished dramatically. **1984** L. A. STEPHENS-POTTER *Beekeeper's Man.* x. 111/2 In countries where varroa is present it has spread with alarming rapidity and caused enormous losses of bee colonies. **1984** *Times* 11 Oct. 3/2 At the queen examination centre..Ministry of Agriculture scientists make sure she is free of Varroa.

Varronian (væ'rəʊnɪən), *a.* [ad. L. *Varrōniān-us*, f. *Varrōn-*, *Varro*: (see def.).] Of or pertaining to the Roman author M. Terentius Varro (116–27 B.C.); admitted as genuine by Varro.

1693 DRYDEN *Disc. Satire* Ess. (Ker) II. 64 That which we call the Varronian Satire. *Ibid.* 107 The *Secchia Rapita* is an Italian poem, a satire of the Varronian kind. **1738** CHAMBERS *Cycl.* (ed. 2) s.v. *Menippean*, In imitation of him [*sc.* Menippus], Varro also wrote satyrs..: Whence this sort of composition is also denominated Varronian satyr. **1888** *Encycl. Brit.* XXIV. 93/2 The 'Varronian plays' [of Plautus] were the twenty which have come down to us, along with one which has been lost. **1911** W. W. FOWLER *Relig. Exp. Rom.* vii. 163 It can no longer be rearranged on the original Varronian plan.

varry, dial. var. FARE *sb.*[1] (pig); obs. var. VAIRY *a.*, VARY *sb.* and *v.*; dial. var. VERY *adv.*

varsal ('vɑːsəl), *a.* and *adv.* Also 7 **'varsal**. [Illiterate abbreviation of UNIVERSAL *a.* Cf. the earlier form VERSAL *a.*]

A. *adj.* **1.** Universal, whole. Only in the phr. ***in the varsal world.***

1696 VANBRUGH *Relapse* V. v, That which they call pin-money is to buy their wives everything in the 'varsal world. **1731–8** SWIFT *Polite Conv.* ii, I believe there is not such another in the varsal world. **1751** ELIZA HEYWOOD *Betsy Thoughtless* II. 203 'She must certainly be somewhat of kin to the child.'—'None in the varsal world, sir.' **1823** E. MOOR *Suffolk Wds.* s.v., I'm sewer I heent a farden i' the varsal wald. **1854** in MISS BAKER *Northampt. Gloss.*

2. Single, individual. *rare.*

1765 BICKERSTAFF *Maid of Mill* I. viii, There's nothing comes amiss to her; she's cute at every varsal kind of thing. **1818** SCOTT *Rob Roy* xiv, When every varsal soul in the family were gone to bed.

B. *adv.* Extremely, vastly. *rare*$^{-1}$.

a **1814** *Fam. Politics* III. ii. in *New Brit. Theatre* II. 220 A has now retired with his profits, and married a varsal rich woman.

varsatile, obs. variant of VERSATILE *a.*

varsity ('vɑːsɪtɪ). Also **'varsity**. [Colloquial abbreviation of UNIVERSITY. Cf. the late 17th cent. form VERSITY.]

a. University. Now (in the U.K.) somewhat *joc.* exc. in ***varsity match***, a sporting contest, esp. the annual Rugby football match between the universities of Oxford and Cambridge.

1846 in *Brasenose Ale* 84 To victory we steered, And o'er the vanquished Varsity Our flag triumphant reared. **1863** *Baily's Mag.* Jan. 360, I had conjured up all the most extravagant and erroneous ideas as to my 'Varsity career'. **1872** H. KINGSLEY *Hornby Mills*, etc. II. 66, I have such faith in the old University (never use that horrid word 'varsity, my lad; don't vulgarise the old place). **1885** A. EDWARDES *Girton Girl* III. xvi. 291, I'm darned..if it be'ant my Varsity man, after all! **1888** QUILLER-COUCH in *Echoes fr. the Oxford Mag.* (1890) 105 We'll dance at the 'Varsity Ball. **1908** E. H. W. MEYERSTEIN *Let.* 21 Oct. (1959) 33 It seems to me that the real attractions of varsity life are reserved for the sportsman and the loafer. **1921** *Granta* 30 Nov. 146/1 What would you do if in the 'Varsity match just as you were off, on a clear half-way run down the field somebody ripped your shorts off? **1927** C. CONNOLLY *Let.* 25 Jan. in *Romantic Friendship* (1975) 228 O blessed chastity (rare at the varsity). **1967** F. SARGESON *Hangover* iii. 19 And that damn cleaning man across from the varsity. **1979** *Times* 6 Dec. 4 (*heading*) The varsity match. **1982** *Guardian Weekly* 27 June 23 [He] would become the first university Blue to miss the Varsity match because he will be playing [cricket] for England. *Ibid.* 19 Dec. 23 Cambridge won 20–13, but on the next day Oxford had some revenge in winning the soccer varsity match at Wembley 4–2. **1983** *Metro* (Auckland) Feb. 13/4 Instead he went to varsity with the ambition of taking a science degree.

b. *U.S.* Applied *attrib.* to sporting events, teams, etc., at or of a university or college. Occas. *absol.*, a college team. (See also quot. 1930.)

1891 *Outing* Dec. 241/1 The 'varsity captain whistled a lively air. **1898** *Ibid.* June 305/1 The..excitement generally attendant upon..trips by 'varsity nines. **1902** L. L. BELL *Hope Loring* (1908) 79 Being on the 'Varsity football team. **1928** E. O'NEILL *Strange Interlude* VIII. 278 It's Gordon's last race, his last appearance on a 'varsity. **1930** *Amer. Speech* V. 243 *Varsity*..is applied always to a student team, as in athletics or debate, not to an institution. **1973** R. LUDLUM *Matlock Paper* iv. 32 The coach of varsity soccer. **1978** *Nature* 29 June 794/1 In the intercollegiate ('varsity') sports, which play a large role in American colleges, Conant replaced an autonomous body led by the alumni association, which is the norm in American universities and is the source of athletic scholarships, by a departmental structure administered by a faculty committee. **1978** *New Yorker* 9 Oct. 184/3 The Harvard varsity..came up a winner 10–0, against Massachusetts. **1979** *Tucson* (Arizona) *Citizen* 20 Sept. 1D/4 He went on to stardom at Niles McKinley High School... McKinley had a 21–6–1 record in Sammy's three years of varsity football. **1980** *N.Y. Times* 1 June XXIII. 12/3 Classic Yale-Harvard Regatta in New London... The four-mile varsity race..will be rowed on the Thames River.

Var'sovian, *a.* and *sb.* Also 8 **Warsovian**. [f. med.L. *Varsovia* Warsaw, or ad. F. *Varsovien.*]

A. *adj.* Belonging to Warsaw. **B.** *sb.* A native or inhabitant of Warsaw.

1764 H. GRENVILLE *Let.* 10 Mar. in *Desp. & Corr. 2nd Earl of Buckinghamshire 1762–5* (1902) II. 153 The apprehensions of your Warsovian correspondent appear but too well founded. **1902** SETON MERRIMAN *Vultures* v, There is in some Varsovian families a heritage of mourning to be worn until Poland is reinstated. **1959** *Listener* 17 Dec. 1071/2 The Palace of Culture is intensely disliked and resented by the Varsovians. **1978** M. TRIPP *Wife-Smuggler* i. 16 One of the best restaurants..where Varsovians go when they wish to treat..distinguished guests.

varsovi'ana. [var. of next, after It. or L. forms.] = next.

1860 *Cornh. Mag.* II. 332 Dances, from the dexterous hornpipe to the quiet Varsoviana. **1894** BLACK *Highl. Cousins* I. 38 Miss Jessie, do you know the Varsoviana?

‖**varsovienne.** [F., fem. of *Varsovien*, f. *Varsovie* Warsaw.] A dance, app. of French origin, resembling some of the Polish national dances.

1859 *Habits Gd. Society* v. 214 The schottische, hop-waltz, redowa, varsovienne,..and so forth, have had their day.

varstay, Sc. variant of WARESTALL *Obs.*

vartabed ('vɑːtəbɛd). Also **vardapet, vartabad, vartapet**, etc. [Armenian.] A member of an order of clergy in the Armenian church (see quot. 1847).

1718 J. OZELL tr. *Pitton de Tournefort's Voy. Levant* II. viii. 303 These Vertabiets, who make such a noise among the Armenians, are not in reality great Doctors. **1841** L. COLEMAN *Christian Antiq.* xxiii. 470 The vartabeds live not among the people, but in convents. **1847** J. WILSON *Lands Bible* II. 482 The monkish clergy are denominated Vartabeds or Doctors, and it is their peculiar office to teach and preach. **1875** *Encycl. Brit.* II. 549/2 The vartabed, or doctor of theology..has frequently charge of a diocese, with episcopal functions. **1923** *Blackw. Mag.* Aug. 252/1 The Patriarch and an Armenian *vartabed*..are pushed inside. **1957** *Oxf. Dict. Christian Church* 87/1 Bishops..are usually chosen from among the vardapets. **1964** [see RASOPHORE]. **1982** *Encycl. Brit. Macropædia* VI. 140 Another class of priests is represented by the vartabeds, or doctors, who must remain unmarried.

varth, southern dial. variant of FARTH.

'vartiwell. *dial.* Also 8 vartuale. [ad. OF. *vertevelle*: see VARDLE and VARVEL.] (See later quots.)

1763 in Peacock *N.W. Linc. Gloss.* (1889) 593 Crookes and vartuales and bands, 1 s. 8 d. **1866** BROGDEN *Linc. Gloss.*, *Vartiwells*, a part of a hinge to a gate. **1877** PEACOCK *N.W. Linc. Gloss.* 265 *Vartiwell*, the eye of a gate in which the crook works.

‖**varus**[1] ('vɛərəs). *Path.* [L. *vārus* knock-kneed.] A physical deformity in which the foot is turned inwards.

1800 *Med. Jrnl.* IV. 192 It may be granted too, that he has cured by this instrument, some deformity that he calls varus, or valgus. **1836-9** *Todd's Cycl. Anat. & Phys.* II. 349/1 The astragalus sometimes projects in front, and lower than in the varus. **1854** in T. Bryant *Pract. Surg.* (1884) II. 339 In inveterate varus the treatment might well be commenced..by ablation of the os cuboides.

‖**varus**[2] ('vɛərəs). *Path.* [L. *varus* pimple.]

a. Stone-pock. **b.** A papule (of smallpox).

1756 [see EPHELIS]. **1822-7** GOOD *Study Med.* (1829) II. 358 There is less inflammation and soreness than in the simple varus. **1845** *Encycl. Metrop.* VII. 755/1 The vaccine pustule runs a given course of varus and of vesicle, terminating by a concretion which forms the crust.

varvacite, variant of VARVICITE.

varve (vɑːv). [ad. Sw. *varv* layer, turn.] A pair of thin layers of clay and silt of contrasting colour and texture which represent the deposit of a single year (summer and winter) in still water at some time in the past (usu. in a lake formed by a retreating ice-sheet); they have been used to establish a chronology of the late glacial and post-glacial period. Also *attrib.* and *Comb.* Hence **varved** (vɑːvd) *a.*, characterized by such layers.

[**1887** *Encycl. Brit.* XXII. 740/1 The glacial clay consists generally of..darker and lighter coloured layers, which give it a striped appearance, for which reason it has often been called *hvarfvig lera* (striped clay).] **1912** G. DE GEER in *Compt. Rend. XI Session Congrès Géol. Internat.* 253 The Swedish word *varv*, subst. (old spelling: hvarf), means as well a circle as a periodical iteration of layers. An international term for the last sense being wanted it seems suitable to use the transcription *varve*, pl. *-s*, in Engl. and Fr. **1929** C. R. LONGWELL *Pirsson's Textbk. Geol.* (ed. 3) I. v. 126 Lake Deposits.—Remarkably banded clays have been formed in patches within the glaciated regions... The Swedish geologists call them varved clays. **1936** *Times Lit. Suppl.* 9 May 392/2 Varve-variation in its general features is a function of solar radiation. **1948** *Bull. Geol. Soc. Amer.* LIX. 646 In this basin (Fossil, Wyo.) hundreds of thousands of beautifully preserved fish are entombed in the varved sediments. **1953** *Antiquity* XXVII. 35 What we most need now, apart from archaeology, is a study of the post-glacial climatic fluctuations in the Tigris and Euphrates valleys. Here the techniques of Western Europe, such as pollen analysis and varve-counting, seem unlikely to be of any use. **1957** G. E. HUTCHINSON *Treat. Limnology* I. i. 8 The dating of the events, based primarily on the varve chronology, is in fair accord with the radiocarbon chronology. **1974** *Nature* 15 Nov. 182/1 The thickness of the varves..provide [*sic*] a guide to the year-by-year changes in mean climate; but that is at best a crude measure.

varvel ('vɑːvəl). Forms: α. 6 vervall, veruel, vervile, 7 (9) vervel, 7 -vell, vervail(e, vervil. β. 7 varuel(l, varvill, 8- varvel. [a. OF. *vervelle* (1350), *verviele*, *varvele*, etc. (F. *vervelle*) in the same sense (in OF. also a ring for a bolt or hinge: see VARDLE), app. a reduced form of *vertvelle*, *vertevelle* VARTIWELL, repr. a pop.Lat. derivative of L. *vertibulum* joint.] A metal ring (freq. of silver with the owner's name engraved on it) attached to the end of a hawk's jess and serving to connect this with the leash.

α. **1537** *St. Papers Hen. VIII*, VII. 674 Praying you to tell Mr. Porter his vervalles [*printed* veryalles] may be in good ordre, as also his hawkes. **1539** *Act 31 Hen. VIII*, c 12 Haukes hauinge vpon..them the marke of the kinges armes and veruels. **1575** TURBERV. *Faulconrie, Commend. Hawking* B ij b, With Belles, and Bewets, Veruels eke, to make the Falcon fine. **1615** ARMIN *Val. Welshm.* (1663) I ij, Proud Welshman, redeliver up that Bird... The Vervels that she wears belongs to Rome. **1675** *Lond. Gaz.* No. 977/4 A Soare Faulcon with the Vervailes of Sir William Godbold of Gillingham. **1697** EVELYN *Numismata* v. 186 Branded with the names..(as do now our Falkners..on the Vervils of their Hawks and Dog-Collars). [**1892** G. LAMBERT *Gold & Silversmiths Art* 49 The vervels (silver rings for the legs of hawks) on which the name of the owner was engraved.]

β. **1615** LATHAM *Falconry, Words expl.* ¶2, Iesses, are those short straps of leather,..fastned to the Hawks legs, etc. and so to the lease by varuels, anlets, or such like. **1638** SIR T. HERBERT *Trav.* (ed. 2) 233 Their Lures, Jesses, Varvills, and Hoods, are richly set with stones of great price and lustre. **1671** *Lond. Gaz.* No. 623/4 A Falcon lost..with the Kings Varvels upon her Gesses. **1833** *Blackw. Mag.* XXXIV. 943, I would give my merlin's best crimson jesses and varvels of silver to dip but my fingers' ends in that dimpling pool. **1894** *Daily News* 8 June 8/5 Hawks' varvels, lent by Lord Dillon.

Hence **'varvelled** *a.* (In later use *Her.*)

1644 T. WESTFIELD in Spurgeon *Treas. David* Ps. xxxvii. 36-7 The hawk flies high..vervelled with the gingling bells of encouragement. *c* **1828** BERRY *Encycl. Her.* I. Gloss., When the leather thongs..are borne flotant, with rings at the ends,..it is then termed jessed..and varvelled.

varvicite ('vɑːvɪsaɪt). *Min.* [f. med.L. *Varvicia* Warwickshire: see -ITE. Named by Phillips (1829).] 'An impure pyrolusite or wad, resulting from the alteration of manganite' (Chester).

1829 R. PHILLIPS in *Phil. Mag.* Ser. II. VI. 282 What you examined was principally manganite, while the mineral which I analysed was the new oxide, and which, should you agree with me as to its composition, I propose to call Varvicite. **1839** *Penny Cycl.* XIV. 381/1 Varvicite occurs massive and in pseudo-crystals. Composed of thin plates and fibres. **1868** WATTS *Dict. Chem.*, *Varvicite*, a manganese-ore from Warwickshire.

varvin, obs. form of VERVAIN.

'vary, *sb.* Also 7 varie, 8 varry. [f. VARY *v.*] A variation; †a hesitation or vacillation.

1600 E. B. in *Engl. Helicon* B iv b, When the sunshine which dissolv'd the snow Culloured the bubble with a pleasant vary. **1605** SHAKS. *Lear* II. ii. 85 (Q.[1]), And turne their halcion beakes With euery gale and varie of their maisters. **1739** ALEX. NICOL *Nat. without Art* 80 I'm at a varry Whether to keep free, or marry. **1929** R. BRIDGES *Testament of Beauty* I. 26 We should not in the field of Reason look to find less vary and veer than elsewhere in the flux of Life.

†'vary, *a. Obs.* In 4, 6 varye. [ad. L. *vari-us*: see VARIOUS *a.*] Particoloured, variegated.

1382 WYCLIF *Gen.* xxxi. 10 Y..saw3 in sleep the malis..varye, and spotti, and of dyuers colours. *Ibid.* 12. **1570** LEVINS *Manip.* 107 Varye, *varius*.

vary ('vɛərɪ), *v.* Forms: 4-7 varie, 5-6 varye (5 varyen, -yn), 5- vary (5-6 *Sc.* wary); 6 varrie, varry, varrey. [ad. OF. (also mod.F.) *varier*, or L. *variāre*, f. *vari-us* VARIOUS *a.* Cf. Sp. and Pg. *variar*, It. *variare*.]

I. *intr.* **1.** Of things: To undergo change or alteration; to pass from one condition, state, etc., to another, esp. with frequent or ready change or difference within certain limits.

c **1369** CHAUCER *Dethe Blaunche* 802 For al my werkes were flyttyng That tyme, and al my thought varyeng. **1412-20** LYDG. *Chron. Troy* IV. 1725, I not what doth enclyne 3oure worþines sodeinly to varie. *c* **1440** *Pallad. on Husb.* III. 116 For they [*sc.* the vines] from fruit to bareynesse wol vary When they be sette. **1508** DUNBAR *Poems* iv. 9 The stait of man dois change & vary, Now sound, now seik, now blyth, now sary. **1608** SHAKS. *Pericles* III. Prol. 47 Their vessel shakes On Neptune's billow;..but fortune's mood Varies again. **1617** MORYSON *Itin.* IV. v. i. (1903) 461 The first hower after the Sunne is sett, strikes one, the Noone or midday varyeth daily as the Sunne doth his setting. **1726** SHELVOCKE *Voy. round World* 436 We met with black dismal weather, with tempestuous winds, varying all around the Compass. **1791** MRS. RADCLIFFE *Rom. Forest* vi, La Motte's complexion varied to every sentence of his speech. **1828** DUPPA *Trav. Italy*, etc. 21 The view [along this road] is constantly varying. **1859** DARWIN *Orig. Spec.* i. 7 When the organisation has once begun to vary, it generally continues to vary for many generations. **1880** GEIKIE *Phys. Geog.* ii. 46 The quantity of water-vapour in the air varies from day to day, and, indeed, from hour to hour.

b. Const. *from* or *between* (specified limits).

1828 DUPPA *Trav. Italy*, etc. 128 During this week the thermometer varied only from 60° to 62° of Fahrenheit. **1843** SIR C. SCUDAMORE *Med. Visit Gräfenberg* 31 The very large number of patients on his list, varying from two to five hundred. **1852** H. ROGERS *Ecl. Faith* (1853) 380 Men's Gods have varied between the infinite Creator and a monkey.

c. To break *off* by change.

1881 TYLOR *Anthropol.* i. (1904) 10 No other explanation is possible but that an ancient parent language gave rise to them all, they having only varied off from it in different directions.

2. To differ, to exhibit or present divergence, *from* something else.

c **1400** *Rom. Rose* 6213 For varie her wordis fro her deede They thenke on gile without dreede. **1490** CAXTON *Eneydos* Prol. 2 And certaynly our langage now vsed varyeth ferre from that whiche was vsed and spoken whan I was borne. **1544** tr. *Littleton's Tenures* (1574) 56 b, An other particion may be made betweene parceners, that varieth from the particions aforesayde. **1598** GRENEWEY *Tacitus, Ann.* VI. vii. (1622) 131 That that bird [the Phœnix]..differeth in the beake, and varieth of feathers from other birds. **1600** FAIRFAX *Tasso* XIX. lxxxix, Those feigned armes he forst me to deuize, So that from yours but small or nought they varrie [*rime* carrie]. **1823** H. J. BROOKE *Introd. Crystallogr.* 189 Other oblique rhombic prisms, varying from the primary. **1842** GWILT *Archit.* §2104 Rebate planes vary from bench planes in having no tote or handle [etc.]. **1891** *Law Times* XCII. 96/1 This edition varies very little from its predecessor published in 1887.

b. Without const.

1530 PALSGR. 765/1, I dare promesse you your bookes vary nat. **1564** DAY tr. *P. Martyr's Comm. Bk. Judges* 175 Yet was not god chaunged, but the condicion of men varyed. **1597** HOOKER *Eccl. Pol.* v. lxvii. 181 Howsoeuer mens opinions doe otherwise varie, neuerthelesse touching Baptisme..we may with consent of the whole Christian world conclude [etc.]. **1611** BIBLE *1 Esdr.* v. 9 *marg.*, Nehem. 7. 9, where..looke for the true numbers:..here they vary much. **1815** STEPHENS in *Shaw's Gen. Zool.* IX. I. 17 This bird is said to vary very much, and Marcgrave mentions one which had the wing-coverts plain brown. **1854** RONALDS & RICHARDSON *Chem. Technol.* (ed. 2) I. 8 The specific gravity of wood has been observed to vary in the same variety;..it is not even the same in different parts of the same tree. **1868** LOCKYER *Elem. Astron.* §22 The first thing which strikes us when we look at the stars is, that they vary very much in brightness.

c. *ellipt.* To deviate from the true North.

1669 STURMY *Mariner's Mag.* II. vi. 67 The upper Compass doth represent the true Compass that never varieth, whereby you have a most necessary Instrument to rectifie the Compass.

3. Of persons: To differ, diverge, or depart, in respect of practice or observance (*from* some standard). Also const. †*of*.

c **1380** WYCLIF *Wks.* (1880) 301 Þe secte of macamethe takiþ meche of cristis secte, but it varieþ in som rewele & in cloþis. — *Sel. Wks.* III. 345 Þes newe ordris..varien in Goddis office fro þat þat Crist bad his preestis do. *c* **1384** CHAUCER *H. Fame* II. 299 And who so seyth of trouthe I varye Bid hym proven the contrarye. *c* **1400** MAUNDEV. (Roxb.) xiii. 60 In many poyntes þai vary fra vs and fra oure faith. *c* **1430** LYDG. *Min. Poems* (Percy Soc.) 131 Suche folke whiche..Dare to theyr wyfes be nat contrarye, Ne from theyr lustes dare not varye. **1533** J. HEYWOOD *Pardoner & Friar* A j, Knyfe nor staffe may we none cary, Except we shulde from the gospell vary. *a* **1548** HALL *Chron.*, *Hen. VIII*, 227 He was forced..to lyue in a straunge lande among people that..varyed from his maners. **1621** T. WILLIAMSON tr. *Goulart's Wise Vieillard* A 4 b, I hope I haue hit of his meaning, though I vary from his wordes, as all Translators must doe. **1680** W. ALLEN *Peace & Unity* 91 In varying from these [appointments] was the sin of those Men. **1713** M. HENRY *Ord. Serm.* Wks. 1857 II. 498/2 As God never varies from himself, so he never wavers in himself. **1723** CHAMBERS tr. *Le Clerc's Treat. Archit.* I. 9 Scamozzi is the only Author who varies from the rule. **1809** ROLAND *Fencing* 123 Many persons..are very apt, when parrying carte and tierce, to vary from the usual parades made upon this occasion.

†b. To be deprived *of* something. *Obs.*⁻¹

1387-8 T. USK *Test. Love* I. ii. (Skeat) l. 194, I shal him enfourme of al the trouthe in thy love, with thy conscience; so that of his helpe thou shalt not varye at thy nede.

†c. To depart from the truth. *Obs.*⁻¹

c **1430** LYDG. *Min. Poems* (Percy Soc.) 131 But my foode and my cherisshynge, To telle plainly and not to varye, Is of suche folke.

d. *Sc.* To wander in mind; to rave. ? *Obs.*

1500-20 DUNBAR *Poems* lxxxi. 12 This is ane felloun phary, Or ellis my witt rycht woundrouslie dois varie. **1501** DOUGLAS *Pal. Hon.* Prol. 101 My febill wit I wary, My desie heid quhome laik of brane gart vary. ? *a* **1550** *Droichis Part Play* in *Dunbar's Poems* (1893) 314 Bot 3it I trow that I vary, I am bot ane Blynd Hary, That lang hes bene with the fary. **1825** JAMIESON, *To vary, vairie*, applied to one who exhibits the first symptoms of *delirium*, as the effect of bodily disorder; as, 'I observed him vairyin' the day,' Ettr. For[est].

†4. To differ in respect of statement; to give a different or divergent account. *Obs.*

1387 TREVISA *Higden* (Rolls) V. 425 Here take heed þat auctors varieþ, for William seiþ.., but Marianus and Beda telleþ [etc.]. **1412-20** LYDG. *Chron. Troy* II. 187 Nat purposyng to moche for to varie, Nor for to be dyuerse nor contrarie Vn-to Guydo. *c* **1450** *Mirk's Festial* 207 And scho onswerd..and tolde hym all þyng, and varyet yn no poynt. *a* **1513** FABYAN *Chron.* v. (1533) 33 b, Of the firste commyng of these Saxons into great Britayn, authours in party varrey. **1529** MORE *Dyaloge* I. Wks. 175/1, I wil beleue him muche better than hym..if thei varyed in a tale and were contrary. **1607** TOPSELL *Four-f. Beasts* 477 We will..adde thereunto [the account of] Oppianus: for he doth vary in both of them.

b. Const. *from* (another or each other). In later use, to depart *from* an author by some change of statement.

a **1513** FABYAN *Chron.* II. (1811) 29 The wryters of the Story..wryten dyuersly, so that the one varyeth greatly from the other. **1577** HOLINSHED *Chron.* I. 116/2 William Malmes. wryting of this Vortimer..varyeth in a maner altogither from Geffrey of Monmouth. **1653** W. RAMESEY *Astrol. Restored* 315, I have in..other places varied somewhat from him. **1700** DRYDEN *Pref. Fables* Poet. Wks. (1910) 275, I durst not make thus bold with Ovid; lest some future Milbourn should arise, and say, I varied from my Author, because I understood him not. **1826** SOUTHEY *Vind. Eccl. Angl.* 256 Later writers, therefore, found it expedient to vary from him in describing the catastrophe.

†5. To differ in opinion, to disagree (*about*, *for*, *in*, or *of* something); to dissent *from* another. *Obs.*

? **1428** *Rec. St. Mary at Hill* (1905) 13 Yf the said parsons, wardeyns & iiij parisshens of the said Chirch..varye of their said chosyng of the same preest..& can nat accorde. *c* **1430** LYDG. *Min. Poems* (Percy Soc.) 28 Remembre wele on olde January,..and how Justyne did vary Fro placebo. **1516** *Sel. Cases Star Chamb.* (Selden) II. 108 The seid parties haue varied also in the namyng of Auditours for heryng and takyng of accomptes. **1527** GARDINER *Let. Wolsey* in Strype *Eccl. Mem.* (1721) I. App. 71 At these words the Popes Ho. casting his armes abrode, bad us put in the words we varyed for. **1579** W. WILKINSON *Confut. Fam. Love* A iiij, Where about men presently so greatly strive and varie. **1608** TOPSELL *Serpents* 68 Which sound, whether it proceedeth from the mouth, or from the motion of their winges: Aristotle and Hesychius do much vary and contend. **1657** S. PURCHAS *Pol. Flying-Ins.* 55 Give mee leave to vary from so learned an Author, and diligent observer.

†b. To disagree seriously, to discord or quarrel; to fall at variance. *Obs.*

c **1440** *Alph. Tales* 118 Þer was ij brether þat dwelte samen many yeris, & þai varid neuer nor neuer was wrothe. *c* **1500** *Communycacyon* (W. de W.) C j, And yf thou be a lytell dyspleased Thou cursed & varyest bothe nyght & daye. **1525** LD. BERNERS *Froiss.* II. CCX. [ccvi.] 650 They never varyed nor their people toguyder, therfore they reigned in great puissaunce. **1577** HANMER *Anc. Eccl. Hist.* (1619) 350 Men fell out among themselues. Wherefore, how, when, and vpon what occasion they varied, I am now about to declare.

†c. To quarrel or be at strife *with*, to contend *against*, another. *Obs.*

1496 *Cov. Leet Bk.* 581 That no maner persone..vexe, troble, assaute nor varie with eny his Neighbours. **1525** LD.

Berners *Froiss.* II. cxcv. [cxci.] 598 If euer Flaunders and Brabant shulde vary agaynst the crowne of Fraunce. *a* **1529** Skelton *Dk. Albany* 341 If our moost royall Harry Lyst with you to varry, Full soone ye should miscary. **1559** *Mirr. Mag., Jas. I. Scot.* vii, We wer driuen to the English coast, Which realme with Skotland at that time did vary.

†**d.** *spec.* In University use: (see quot. 1749).

1680 Wood *Life* (O.H.S.) II. 490 July 8, Th., Mr. [John] Conant varied. A great entertainment in the gallery. **1685** *Ibid.* 23 July, Mr. Slatter varied, being put off till that time because he had got a mischance. **1749** Pointer *Oxon. Acad.* 18 The Master-Fellows are oblig'd by their Statutes to take their turns, every Year about the Act Time, or at least before the 1st Day of August, to vary,..i.e. to perform some publick Exercise in the Common-Hall, the Variator opposing Aristotle, in three Latin Speeches.

6. †**a.** To be uncertain; to hesitate. *Obs.*⁻¹

c **1477** Caxton *Jason* (1913) 53 Thus in varyieng in this doubte she approched the loggyse.

b. To change or alter in respect of conduct. †Also with inf.

1481 Caxton *Godfrey* lxxix. (chapter heading), How the duc that was at Rages varyed for to holde this that he had promysed to Bawdwyn. **1523** Ld. Berners *Froiss.* I. ccxviii. 278 All they of his counsaile coude not make hym to vary fro that pourpose. *c* **1586** C'tess Pembroke *Ps.* lxxi. viii, As for me, resolv'd to tary In my trust, and not to vary, I will heape thy praise with praise. **1780** J. Moore *View Soc. Fr.* I. i, Our young friend seemed confirmed in his resolutions and gave me fresh assurances..that he never would vary.

c. To move in different ways or directions.

1667 Milton *P.L.* ix. 516 As when a Ship..Veres oft, as oft so steers, and shifts her Saile; So varied hee.

7. a. To be inconsistent in one's statements; to introduce a difference or discrepancy.

1557 Seager *Sch. Virtue* 526 in *Babees Bk.*, See here he [*sc.* Aristotle] doth vary. Refuse not his councell, Nor his wordes dispise. **1560** Daus tr. *Sleidane's Comm.* 139 They had alledged..that the byshop Clement varied in his sentence, and had declared to the Frenche king in priuate talke, what he thought. **1637** Prynne *Documents* (Camden) 79 For drawing wittnesses to varie from their former depositions. **1639** S. Du Verger tr. *Camus' Admir. Events* 329 She is examined hereupon, and varies in her first answer, being pressed further she acknowledgeth it in her second. **1706** Phillips (ed. Kersey), *To Vary*,..to falter in one's Answers; to disagree with, or differ from one's self.

b. *Law.* To make a departure in pleading.

1642 tr. *Perkins' Prof. Bk.* ii. §121. 54 The plaintiffe shall take nothing by his writ, because he cannot varie from the place dated in the obligation.

II. *trans.* **8.** To cause to change or alter; to introduce changes or alterations into (something); in later use freq., to adapt to certain circumstances or requirements by appropriate modifications.

1340–70 *Alex. & Dind.* 200 We han, ludus, of ȝour lif listned ful ofte, þat michil ben ȝour manerus from oþur men varied. **1382** Wyclif *Ecclus.* xxxviii. 28 Whyche grauede grauen broochis, and the bysynesse of hym varieth the peynture. **1398** Trevisa *Barth. De P.R.* iii. xxiv. (W. de W. 1495) 73 Hote ayre and colde and drye and temperate varye and chaunge the pulse. **1486** *Bk. St. Albans, Her.* (Dallaway) p. lxxxvii, The bordir of thys cros is variet as well from the coloure of the cros as fro the coloure of the felde. **1591** Spenser *M. Hubberd* 118 Shall we varie our deuice at will, Euen as new occasion appeares? **1614** Selden *Titles Honor* 252 The name of Vigniers..is the same with Vicarij, both but varying the word *Vicecomes*. **1653** W. Ramesey *Astrol. Restored* 227 Your rules being varied according to art and discretion. **1697** Dryden *Virg. Georg.* iv. 595 But thou, the more he varies Forms, beware To strain his Fetters with a stricter Care. **1725** De Foe *Voy. round World* (1840) 331 They had not varied their course in the dark. **1782** Priestley *Corrupt. Chr.* I. i. 150 Words..we can twist and vary as we please. **1802** Paley *Nat. Theol.* i. §1 (1819) 4 Nor can I perceive that it varies at all the inference. **1865** Dickens *Mut. Fr.* i. v, He had never varied his ground an inch. **1891** *Act 54 & 55 Vict.* c. 66 §16 The court, after such notice,..may vary such order in such manner..as it may think fit.

†**b.** To change the form of (a word) grammatically. *Obs.*

1648 Gage *West Ind.* 214 So likewise are varied or declined *Abix*, signifying a plantation, *Acal* earth.

c. To dispose, obtain, occupy, in a manner characterized by variety or variation.

1697 Dryden *Virg. Georg.* i. 609 The setting Sun survey, ..If dusky Spots are vary'd on his Brow [etc.]. **1748** *Anson's Voy.* i. vi. 59 We varied our depths from fifty to eighty fathom. **1758** Johnson *Idler* No. 7 ¶9 To vary a whole week with joy, anxiety, and conjecture.

†**9.** To express in different words. *Obs.*

1580 G. Harvey in *Spenser's Wks.* (1912) 626, I gaue him this Theame out of Ouid, to translate, and varie after his best fashion. **1588** Shaks. *L.L.L.* i. i. 294 *Clo.* This was no Damosell neyther sir, shee was a Virgin. *Fer.* It is so varried to, for it was proclaimed Virgin. **1599** —— *Hen. V*, iii. vii. 35 The man hath no wit, that cannot..varie deserued prayse on my Palfray. **1667** Milton *P.L.* v. 184 Let your ceasless change Varie to our great Maker still new praise. **1682** Flavel *Fear* 8 They are at their wits end,..or as it is varied in the margin all wisdom is swallowed up.

absol. **1583** Lyly in T. Watson *Poems* (Arb.) 30 In that so aptly you haue varied vppon women,..confesse I must [etc.].

†**10.** To set at variance. *Obs.*⁻¹

1795 Burke *Corr.* Wks. 1842 II. 240 When his Grace.. brought out the vapid stuff, which had varied the clubs and disgusted the courts.

vary, obs. Sc. form of wary *v.* (curse).

varying (ˈvɛərɪɪŋ), *vbl. sb.* [f. vary *v.*] The action of the verb, in various senses.

c **1380** Wyclif *Serm.* Sel. Wks. I. 141 Here telliþ Crist to his Chirche how þer wille shulde be temprid for variynge of þer heed after his resureccioun. *c* **1430** *Syr Gener.* (Roxb.) 9591 For that ye this othre day Supposed in me such variyng Whan it was told you of my wedding. *c* **1440** *Gesta Rom.* xlviii. 218 (Add. MS.), I chaunge to the tymes, to do away the variynges. **1530** Palsgr. 284/1 Varyeng, chaungyng, *muance*. **1533** J. Heywood *Johan* B j b, I gyue you good leue To chastyce her for her shreude varyeng. **1612** Brinsley *Lud. Lit.* 244 The Nowns haue so little varying or turning in them. **1628** T. Spencer *Logick* 48 Sinne (sayth the Apostle..) Is a varying from the Law. *a* **1695** Marq. of Halifax *Wks.* (1912) 211 Neither King nor People would now like just the original Constitution, without any varyings. **1771** Luckombe *Hist. Printing* 237 The varying of proper names, may be owing to the fancy of some Author ..[who] ordered them to be distinguished by different characters from the Text. **1825** Carlyle *Schiller* ii. (1845) 97 Those careless felicities, those varyings from high to low. **1829** Scott *Anne of G.* xxiv, Had my plighted vows..ever permitted me to entertain a thought of varying, or of defection. **1901** Wrench *Winchester Word-bk.*, *Varying*, a vulgus done up to books. (obs.)

varying (ˈvɛərɪɪŋ), *ppl. a.* [f. as prec.]

1. That varies, in senses of the verb; tending to vary or change. †Also const. *from.*

c **1340** Hampole *Pr. Consc.* 1413 Þe life of þis world es ful unstable, And ful variand and chaungeable. **1398** Trevisa *Barth. De P.R.* xvii. xcviii. (Bodl. MS.), Þe apple tre is rounde diuers and varying fro oþer trees of wodes. *a* **1400–50** *Alexander* 4637 Of all þe frutis on þe fold we fange at oure will, Bath venyson & volatile & variand fisches. *c* **1480** Henryson *Fables, Paddock & Mouse* x, With mynd Inconstant, fals, and wariand, Full of desait. **1500–20** Dunbar *Poems* xlviii. 1 Quhen Merche wes with variand windis past. *c* **1560** A. Scott *Poems* (S.T.S.) xxvii. 48 Gif scho steidfast stand, And be not wariand, I am at hir command. **1611** Shaks. *Wint. T.* i. ii. 170 He..with his varying child-nesse, cures in me Thoughts, that would thick my blood. *a* **1704** T. Brown *Sat. agst. Woman* Wks. 1730 I. 57, I strive in vain the varying crimes to trace, Of this salacious and destructive race. **1751** Gray *Spring* 37 In fortune's varying colours drest. **1798** S. & Ht. Lee *Canterb. T.* II. 114 With a varying complexion, and timid air, [he] enquired for her mother. **1815** Shelley *Alastor* 96 That scene of ampler majesty Than gems or gold, the varying roof of heaven. **1846** G. E. Day tr. *Simon's Anim. Chem.* II. 168 The varying amounts..excreted during equal periods by different persons. **1874** Green *Short Hist.* viii. §5. 509 The struggle..went on throughout his reign with varying success.

b. *spec.* in *Path.*

1899 *Allbutt's Syst. Med.* VII. 476 Varying squint and ptosis are very common during the irritative and pressure stages.

†**2.** Varied in colour; variegated. *Obs.*

1488 *Acc. Ld. High Treas. Scot.* I. 85 A couering of variand purpir tartar browdin with thrissillis and a vnicorne. *Ibid.* 163 Thre elne and dimid. of varyande tartar.

3. *varying hare*, a species of hare, inhabiting northern or elevated regions, the fur of which turns white in winter; the Alpine, blue, or mountain hare.

The American varying hare (*Lepus Americanus*) is a variety of the Polar hare (*L. glacialis*).

1781 Pennant *Hist. Quadrup.* II. 370 Varying Hare. **1823** Crabb *Technol. Dict.* s.v. *Hare*, The varying Hare, *Lepus variabilis*, turns white in the Winter. **1849** *Sk. Nat. Hist.*, *Mammalia* IV. 158 The Alpine or varying hare inhabits certain districts of our island, namely, the northern parts of Scotland. **1880** *Encycl. Brit.* XI. 476/2 In those parts where the common hare does not occur, its place is taken by the varying or mountain hare (*Lepus variabilis*).

Hence ˈ**varyingly** *adv.*

c **1862** Gladstone *Farew. Addr., Edinb. Univ.* 19 In modes, and in degrees, varyingly perceptible to us. **1882** F. T. Palgrave in Grosart *Spenser's Wks.* IV. p. xxxv, Spenser sees life..through more than one veil, always, though varyingly, conventional in character.

varyte, obs. form of verity.

‖**vas** (væs). Pl. **vasa** (ˈveɪsə). [L. *vās* (pl. *vāsa*), vessel.]

1. a. *Anat.* A hollow organ serving for the conveyance of a liquid in the body. Commonly in specific applications with Latin epithet, as ***vas breve*** (pl. *vasa brevia*); ***vas deferens*** (pl. *vasa deferentia*) [L. *dēferens*, pres. pple. of *dēferre* (see deferent *a.*¹ and *sb.*)], a fibromuscular tube which carries spermatozoa from the epididymis at ejaculation, in man joining the duct from the seminal vesicle at the prostate gland to form the ejaculatory duct. (Also used ellipt. for either of these.)

1578 J. Banister *Hist. Man* vi. 87 (*marginal note*) Why these ij. are called Vasa deferentia. **1651** Biggs *New Disp.* ¶174 Exhausting the stock of aliment from the *vasa* and *viscera*. **1713** W. Cheselden *Anat. of Humane Body* iv. i. 163 On the upper part of the Testicles, are hard Bodies call'd Epididymi; which are evidently the beginnings of the Vasa Deferentia. **1849–52** R. B. Todd *Cycl. Anat. & Physiol.* IV. 981/1 The vas deferens is round and indurated,—harder than any other excretory duct in the body, by which character it is easily distinguished, when handled, from the other parts constituting the spermatic cord. **1900** R. Harrison in *Lancet* 14 July 96/2, I divided both his vasa in the usual way. *Ibid.* 97/2 Vasectomy or torsion of the vas for hypertrophy. **1975** *Nature* 9 Oct. 488/1 For collection of spermatozoa, the vasa deferentia were excised aseptically from adult Wistar strain rats.

b. *Bot.* (See quots.)

Commonly with Latin epithet, as *vasa fibrosa*, etc.

1843 *Penny Cycl.* XXVI. 148/2 *Vasa* (vessels),..a term applied to several of the tissues of plants. **1866** *Treas. Bot.* 1205/1 *Vasa*, the tubes which occur in the interior of plants, and serve for the conveyance of sap or air.

†**2.** A vase. *Obs. rare.* (Cf. next.)

1698 M. Lister *Journ. Paris* (1699) 43 Brass Statues and *Vasa*, and a 100 other things relating to Antiquity. *Ibid.* 45 Urns and Funeral *Vasa* of all Materials.

†**vasa**¹. *Obs.* [Chiefly in the plural forms *vasa's*, *vasas*, f. L. *vāsa* pl. (see prec. 2); hence irregularly *vasa* as sing.] A vase.

1651 Evelyn *Char. Eng.* (1659) 36 One of their Spurs engaged in a Carpet.., drew all to the ground, break the Glass & the Vasas in pieces. **1698** M. Lister *Journ. Paris* 188 Here also were great *Vasa's* of Trelliage upon Pedestals. **1699** Evelyn *Acetaria* Pref. b 1/b, Busts, Obelisks, Columns, Inscriptions, Dials, Vasa's, Perspectives. *a* **1700** —— *Diary* 14 Nov. 1643, A vasa of onyx. *Ibid.* 29 Nov. 1644, An antiq vasa of marble neare 6 foote high.

vasa² (ˈveɪsə, ˈvɑːzə). Also **vaza.** [Malagasy *vaza.*] One or other of several Madagascar parrots belonging to the genus *Coracopsis.* Usu. *attrib.*

1811 Shaw *Gen. Zool.* VIII. 528 Vasa Parrot. *Ibid.* 529 Smaller Vasa Parrot. *Ibid.*, The Smaller Vasa measures about fourteen inches in length. **1904** *Times* 30 Jan. 10/2 The collection of foreign birds,..among others of.. macaws, a black vasa parrot, and a hoopoe.

vasal (ˈveɪsəl), *a.* [f. L. *vās* vas.] Connected with one or other of the *vasa* of the body.

1891 in *Cent. Dict.* **1899** *Allbutt's Syst. Med.* VIII. 493 Auspitz concluded that the wheal is produced by a reflex irritation from sensory to vasal nerves.

VASCAR, Vascar: see V III. 5 b.

†**vascay**, ? erron. variant of vasquine.

1609 Markham *Famous Whore* (1868) 22 Perfumed gloues, gownes, kirtles, vascaies, muffes.

vascular (ˈvæskjʊlə(r)), *a.* [ad. mod.L. *vāsculār-is*, f. L. *vāscul-um*, dim. of *vās* vas. So F. *vasculaire*, It. *vasculare*, Sp. and Pg. *vascular.*]

1. *Bot.* **a.** Of fibres, tissue, etc.: Having the form of tubular vessels; consisting of continuous tubes of simple membrane.

1672–3 Grew *Anat. Pl., Anat. Roots* (1682) 69 The Vascular Rays are not equally extended in all Roots. **1756** C. Lucas *Ess. Waters* I. 156 The solids are all vascular, and consist of elastic fibres. **1791** Hamilton *Berthollet's Dyeing* I. i. i. iii. 52 The vascular fibres of the bark. **1837** P. Keith *Bot. Lex.* 68 The membranous tissue of the plant, whether cellular or vascular, is uniformly colourless. **1847** H. Miller *Test. Rocks* (1857) 31 Its mass of soft cellular tissue is strengthened all round by internal buttresses of dense vascular fibre. **1875** Dawson *Dawn Life* ii. 32 Plants existed at that time having true woody or vascular tissues.

b. Of structure: Characterized by the prevalence of tubular vessels.

1728 Chambers *Cycl.* s.v. *Vegetable*, The vascular Structure of Vegetables, is render'd very apparent, by an Experiment of Mr. Willoughby. **1807** J. E. Smith *Phys. Bot.* 13 From preceding writers we had learned the general tubular or vascular structure of the vegetable body. **1842** Loudon *Suburban Hort.* 9 Endogens are flowering plants with a vascular structure.

c. ***vascular system***, the aggregate of tubular vessels in a plant.

1813 Sir H. Davy *Agric. Chem.* (1814) 60 The alburnum is the great vascular system of the vegetable through which the sap rises. **1832** Lindley *Introd. Bot.* 59 In both cases there is a cellular and vascular system distinct from each other. **1866** *Treas. Bot.* 1205/1 *Vascular system*, all that part of the interior structure of a plant into whose composition spiral vessels or their modifications enter.

d. Of plants: Having a vascular structure.

1830 Lindley *Nat. Syst. Bot.* Introd. p. xiv, All plants that bear flowers have spiral vessels, and are therefore Vascular. **1849** Murchison *Siluria* 287 The great mass of the plants belong to the vascular cryptogamic class. **1861** Bentley *Man. Bot.* 67 The lowest orders of Vascular Plants, like the true Mosses, are comparatively insignificant in appearance.

e. ***vascular wilt*** (***disease***): wilt disease involving the vascular system of a plant; *spec.* = *Panama disease* s.v. Panama.

1946 *Nature* 16 Nov. 712 The presence of a vascular wilt disease of the oil palm. **1951** *New Biol.* XI. 76 Vascular Wilt Disease..of bananas in the Old World made its appearance in Central America towards the end of the nineteenth century. **1972** [see *Panama disease* s.v. Panama].

2. *Anat.* or *Phys.* **a.** Having the character or properties of a conveying vessel or vessels.

1728 Chambers *Cycl.* s.v., All the Flesh in an animal Body is found to be Vascular, none of it Parenchymous. **1756** C. Lucas *Ess. Waters* I. 2 The several parts of its body being, at some time of its existence, vascular. **1802** Paley *Nat. Theol.* xi. (ed. 2) 209 It [the spleen] must be vascular, and admit of a circulation through it, in order to be kept alive, or be part of a living body. **1835** *Todd's Cycl. Anat.* I. 126/1 The vascular is another tissue extensively distributed among animals. **1880** Beale *Slight Ailments* 85 If we could see the mucous membrane in..cases of indigestion we should no doubt find it unduly vascular.

fig. **1838** Emerson *Address, Lit. Ethics* Wks. (Bohn) II. 209 An able man is nothing else than a good, free, vascular organization, whereinto the universal spirit freely flows. **1847** —— *Repr. Men, Montaigne* Ibid. I. 344 Cut these words, and they would bleed; they are vascular and alive.

b. ***vascular system***: (see quot. 1876).

1725 Robinson *Phys. & Dis.* 255 The Air..obliges the whole vascular system of the Solids to redouble their Contractions. **1800** *Med. Jrnl.* IV. 215 To restore the energy and lost tone of the vascular system. **1876** Bristowe *Th. & Pract. Med.* (1878) 485 The vascular system comprises the heart, arteries, veins, and capillaries; the lymphatic glands and vessels, together with certain ductless glands; and the blood with its tributary fluids.

c. Affecting the vascular system or tissue.

1869 SPENCER *Princ. Psychol.* II. v. (1872) I. 236 The vascular excitement, caused by emotion. **1881** *Med. Temp. Jrnl.* XLVIII. 206 The first stage of alcoholic action is vascular excitement rapidly followed by exhaustion.

vascu'larity. [f. VASCULAR *a.* + -ITY.] Vascular form or condition.

1790 *Phil. Trans.* LXXXV. 209 The great vascularity of a muscle is..for the purpose of repairing the waste in the muscular fibres, occasioned by their action. **1818–20** E. THOMPSON *Cullen's Nosologia* 321 The great vascularity and irritability of the skin at that period of life. **1861** HULME tr. *Moquin-Tandon* II. III. iv. 146 The quantity of blood a leech is capable of drawing varies..according to the vascularity of the part. **1879** *St George's Hosp. Rep.* IX. 690 In the cords some evidences of increased vascularity were visible in the grey matter.

vasculari'zation. [f. as next + -ATION.] Conversion to a vascular condition.

1818 COOPER & TRAVERS *Surg. Ess.* I. (ed. 3) 79 Several lumps of lymph effused in the anterior chamber, are undergoing vascularization. **1847–9** *Todd's Cycl. Anat.* IV. 101/1 Ascertaining the fact of vascularization of scorbutic coagula. **1896** *Allbutt's Syst. Med.* I. 195 Likewise inflammation or disease of cartilage may be followed by vascularisation and ossification.

vascularize ('væskjʊləraɪz), *v.* [f. VASCULAR *a.* + -IZE. Cf. next.] *trans.* To render vascular.

1893 A. S. ECCLES *Sciatica* 47 To increase the surface-temperature and thoroughly vascularize the skin and superficial tissues. **1898** *Allbutt's Syst. Med.* V. 3 The terminal tubes being vascularised by the pulmonary artery.

'vascularized, *ppl. a.* [Cf. prec.] Rendered vascular; converted into a vascular form.

1858 J. H. BENNET *Nutrition* i. 10 [The] mucous membrane of the stomach..becomes highly vascularized. **1874** JONES & SIEVEKING *Path. Anat.* 17 The occurrence of a vascularized coagulum in a tuberculous cavity in the lungs. **1879** *St. George's Hosp. Rep.* IX. 429 The growth consisted of small cells, and was highly vascularised.

'vascularly, *adv.* [f. VASCULAR *a.*] In a vascular manner.

1890 *Nature* 26 June 215/2 Multiple buds, one springing from another and being vascularly connected therewith. **1894** *Westm. Gaz.* 31 Aug. 3/1 When it has become vascularly attached to the tissues around the area.

'vasculated, *ppl. a.* [f. L. *vāscul-um* VASCULUM.] Provided with small vessels.

1744 *Phil. Trans.* XLIII. 187 The Wings are finely vasculated, and the Pod is lined with fine silky Down.

vasculature ('væskjʊlətjə(r)). *Anat.* [f. L. *vāscul-āris* VASCULAR *a.* + *-ature*, after *musculature*.] The vascular system and its arrangement in the body or a part.

1934 in WEBSTER. **1942** F. A. METTLER *Neuroanatomy* x. 194 Concerning the vasculature within the vertebral canal. **1962** *Lancet* 22 Dec. 1327/1 Burton has shown that a critical opening and a critical closing pressure are peculiar also to the intrarenal vasculature. **1975** *Nature* 18 Sept. 224/1 The vasculature of regenerating limbs of the newt..was investigated.

vascule, Anglicized form of VASCULUM.

1859 in MAYNE *Expos. Lex.* 1323/2

vascu'liferous, *a.* [f. L. *vāsculi-*, combining form of *vāsculum*, + -FEROUS.] (See quots.)

1704 J. HARRIS *Lex. Techn.* I, *Vasculiferous Plants*, are according to the Botanists, such as have besides the common Calyx or Flower Cup, a peculiar Vessel or Case to contain their Seed. **1731** P. MILLER *Gard. Dict.* s.v., Vasculiferous Plants are such whose Seeds are contain'd in Vessels which are sometimes divided into Cells.

'vasculiform, *a.* [f. as prec. + -FORM.] Having the shape of a small vase.

1887 W. PHILLIPS *Brit. Discomycetes* 120 Cup vasculiform, margin erect or incurved.

vasculitis (væskjʊ'laɪtɪs). *Path.* Pl. **vasculitides** (-'laɪtɪdiːz), **vasculitises.** [f. L. *vāscul-um*, dim. of *vās* VAS + -ITIS.] An inflammatory reaction in a blood vessel; any of various conditions characterized by such reactions.

1970 in DORLAND *Med. Dict.* **1945** *Jrnl. Amer. Med. Assoc.* 2 June 337/1 We believe that some of these cases could more properly be grouped with cases of nodular vasculitis. **1976** *Proc. R. Soc. Med.* LXIX. 927/1 The vasculitis and other non-articular manifestations of rheumatoid disease are distinctly uncommon in this age group. **1983** *Oxf. Textbk. Med.* II. XVI. 36/2 For clinical purposes, the vasculitides can be divided into those with skin lesions and those without.

Hence **vascu'litic** *a.*, of the nature of, or characteristic of, vasculitis.

1971 *Clin. & Exper. Immunol.* IX. 754 Endothelial changes seem to be an important component of a number of vasculitic disorders. **1980** *Jrnl. R. Soc. Med.* LXXIII. 208 His rheumatoid disease became more active and vasculitic lesions appeared once again on his fingertips. **1983** *Oxf. Textbk. Med.* II. xx. 63/2 There have been a number of more recently described vasculitic syndromes in which urticaria is the only skin manifestation.

'vasculose, *sb.* [f. VASCUL-AR *a.* + -OSE².] The principal constituent of the vascular tissue in plants.

1883 *Science* I. 80/1 Vasculose is not easily soluble in concentrated sulphuric acid. **1885** GOODALE *Physiol. Bot* (1892) 35 *note*, Vasculose increases in amount with the density of the wood. The pith contains..vasculose 25 per cent.

vascu'lose, *a. rare.* [-OSE¹.] = VASCULAR *a.*

1866 *Treas. Bot.* 1205 *Vasculose*, containing spiral vessels or their modifications.

vasculotoxic (væskjʊləʊ'tɒksɪk), *a. Physiol.* [f. as VASCULITIS + -O + TOXIC *a.*] Affecting the vessels of the body adversely. Hence ,**vasculoto'xicity.**

1957 *Dorland's Med. Dict.* (ed. 23), Vasculotoxic. **1962** *Endocrinology* LXXI. 505/1 The vasculotoxic and nephrotoxic effects of renin. **1973** *Nature* 30 Mar. 334/2 The vasculotoxicity of renin is also suggested by its presence in excessive amounts in human malignant and reno-vascular hypertension. **1977** *Lancet* 8 Jan. 83/2 There is as yet little information on the relation of blood-levels to nephrotoxic or vasculotoxic potential.

'vasculous, *a. rare*⁻¹. [f. L. *vāscul-um*: see next.] = VASCULAR *a.* 2.

1728 CHAMBERS *Cycl.* s.v. *Vesicula*, The first [membrane] whereof is Vasculous; the second Muscular; and the third Glandulous.

‖**vasculum** ('væskjʊləm). Pl. **-a, -ums.** [L., dim. of *vās* vessel.]

1. *Bot.* = ASCIDIUM 2.

1832 LINDLEY *Introd. Bot.* 96 The singular form of leaf in Sarracenia and Nepenthes, which has been called *Ascidium* or *Vasculum*. **1859** MAYNE *Expos. Lex.*, *Vasculum*,..the cup which terminates the leaves of the Nepenthes; a vascule.

2. A special kind of case used by botanists for carrying newly-collected specimens.

Usually made of tin in the form of a flattened cylinder, with a lid on one side opening lengthways.

1782 J. LIGHTFOOT *Let.* 11 July in W. H. Curtis *William Curtis* (1941) 59, I am extremely obliged to you for the contents of your Botanic *Vasculum*. **1818** G. GRAVES *Naturalist's Pocket-bk.* 295 These [specimens] must be gathered on a dry day, and placed in a common tin vasculum or pocket herborizing Box. **1839** J. D. HOOKER *Jrnl.* in L. Huxley *Life J. D. Hooker* (1918) I. 47 Two Botanising vascula. **1844** *Proc. Berw. Nat. Club* II. 82 The botanists having stored each their vasculum with specimens of the Rubi, the party again united. **1877** SIR C. W. THOMSON *Voy. Challenger* I. 14 Various implements such as.. botanical vasculums. **1887** J. BALL *Nat. in S. Amer.* 128, I shouldered my tin vasculum and went ashore.

vase (vɑːz). Also 6 **vasse**, 7 **vause, vaze.** [a. F. *vase* (= It., Sp., Pg. *vaso*), ad. L. *vās* vessel: see VAS and VASA¹.

The earlier pronunciations (veɪs) and (veɪz) are still current in America; the former of these is indicated by the rimes in the following passages. Another variant (vɔːz) has still some currency in England.

1731 SWIFT *Strephon & Chloe* 191 [*rime* face]. **1822** BYRON *Juan* VI. xcvii. [*rimes* place, grace]. **1847** EMERSON *Poems* Wks. (Bohn) I. 425 Cut a bough from my parent stem, And dip it in thy porcelain vase [*rime* grace]. **1857** WHITTIER *Skipper Ireson's Ride* 26 Girls..such as chase Bacchus round some antique vase. *c* **1860** LOWELL *Ambrose* x, The water unchanged, in every case, Shall put on the figure of the vase.]

1. *Arch.* †**a.** = BELL *sb.*¹ 6 a. *Obs.*

1563 SHUTE *Archit.* D iiij, The Abacus, the which lieth on the vasse or basket, that was founde on the maydens tombe in Corinthe. **1726** LEONI *Alberti's Archit.* II. 33/2 The bell or vase, the breadth of which at the bottom must be..that of the top of the Shaft.., and the breadth of the top of the vase must be equal to..the bottom of the shaft. **1753** *Chambers' Cycl.* Suppl. s.v. *Bell*, In this sense, *bell* is the same with what is otherwise called *vase* and *tambour*.

b. An ornament having the form of a vase (see sense 2).

1706 PHILLIPS (ed. Kersey), *Vase*,..in Architecture, an Ornament above the Cornice. **1731** BAILEY (vol. II), *Vases* ..are ornaments placed on cornices, socles, or pedestals, representing such vessels as the antients used in sacrifices, as incense-pots, &c., often inriched with Basso Relievo's.

2. a. A vessel, usually of an ornamental character, commonly of a circular section and made either of earthenware or metal, but varying greatly in actual form and use.

1629 in A. Michaelis *Anc. Marb. Gt. Brit.* (1882) 205, I desire you woulde presently..knowe what Sir Tho. Roe hath brought of antiquities, Goddes, vases, inscriptions, medalles, or such like. **1670** G. H. *Hist. Cardinals* II. II. 288 The Chamberlain..puts the names of all the Cardinals.. into a Vaze. **1703** POPE *Thebais* 207 No chargers then were wrought in burnish'd gold, Nor silver vases took the forming mold. **1781** GIBBON *Decl. & F.* xxxi. (1787) III. 240 Many a vase, in the division of the spoil, was shivered into fragments by the stroke of a battle-axe. **1832** W. IRVING *Alhambra* I. 92 A tribute of fresh-culled flowers, which are afterwards arranged in vases. **1854** *Poultry Chron.* II. 192 Seven Silver Vases, of the value of Six Guineas each, will also be awarded, instead of money prizes. **1898** G. B. SHAW *You never can tell* Plays II. 274 The vases on pillar pedestals of veined marble with bases of black polished wood.

fig. **1850** TENNYSON *In Mem.* iv, Break, thou deep vase of chilling tears, That grief hath shaken into frost!

b. (See quot.) *rare*⁻⁰.

1728 CHAMBERS *Cycl.* s.v., Goldsmiths, Pewterers, &c. also use *Vase* for the middle of a Church Candlestick; which is usually of a roundish Figure, bordering somewhat on that of a Vase. [Hence in Bailey.]

c. A calyx or other growth resembling a vase.

1728 CHAMBERS *Cycl.*, *Vase* is also sometimes used among Florists, for what they otherwise call the Calyx. [Hence in Bailey, etc.] *a* **1811** LEYDEN *On Spring* Remains (1819) 258 The tulip's vase with dew-pearl sheen And icy crystal gleams afar. **1885** C. F. HOLDER *Marvels Anim. Life* 15 Graceful stalked vases of the Campanularia appear.

3. *attrib.* and *Comb.* (in sense 2), as ***vase-carriage, -handle, -like*** adj., ***-maker, -painter, -painting, -shaped*** adj., ***-work***; **vase carpet**, an oriental (esp. Persian) carpet with a pattern incorporating a stylized vase of flowers.

1770 J. WEDGWOOD *Let.* 19 May (1965) 92 Where, amongst our potters, could I get a complete Vase-maker? **1832** LINDLEY *Introd. Bot.* 380 *Vase-shaped*,..formed like a flower-pot. **1840** *Civil Eng. & Arch. Jrnl.* III. 96/2 The two winged boys who dip into a vase-like fountain. **1843** *Penny Cycl.* XXVI. 149/2 The numerous names of vase painters. *Ibid.*, The most antient style of vase painting. **1865** LUBBOCK *Preh. Times* 48 Two curious vase-carriages, one found in Sweden and the other in Mecklenburg. **1870** G. J. CHESTER in *Recov. Jerus.* (1871) 473 Six vase-handles, found ..on a bed of rich earth. **1893** *Westm. Gaz.* 25 Feb. 5/3 The best vase-work in the period 570 to 470 B.C. **1915** *Guide to Collection of Carpets* (Victoria & Albert Mus.) i. 27 Another type of pattern, in which animal and bird life are entirely absent, has given rise in Germany to the name 'vase-carpets'. **1983** *Eastern Carpet* (Hayward Gallery Catal.) 31/2 Another group of Persian carpets with beautiful floral designs are the so-called vase carpets, believed to have been made in the Kerman area.

Hence **'vaseful, 'vaselet.**

1856 R. F. BURTON *Pilgr. El-Medinah* III. 202 A present to the Sakkas, or carriers,..who distributed a large earthen vaseful in my name to poor pilgrims. **1889** M. M. MACMILLAN *Lett.* (1893) 250, I will present the vaselet to the British Museum. **1894** *Westm. Gaz.* 14 June 3/3 A vaseful of Iceland poppies.

va'sectomized, *ppl. a.* [Cf. next.] That has had the *vas deferens* removed, or having undergone ligation of one or (usually) both *vasa deferentia*. So **va'sectomize** *v. trans.*

1900 R. HARRISON in *Lancet* 14 July 96/1 There are good reasons for believing that a vasectomised or castrated male is not liable to undergo hypertrophy of the prostate. **1923** *Physiol. Rev.* III. 342 If..the female rat undergoes a sterile coition with a vasectomized male the corpus luteum persists for a longer period. **1970** *Nature* 11 Apr. 162/2 Spontaneously ovulating females were mated with vasectomized males of strain A, whose sterility had been checked repeatedly. **1977** *Spare Rib* June 31/1 Male, 31, healthy wealthy and dull, seeks girlfriend. Vasectomised. Ideal pet for liberated woman. **1980** *Aggressive Behavior* VI. 218 All six adult males were vasectomized by double ligature of the vas deferens four months before the first copulation was seen in November. **1982** *Times* 6 Dec. 6/8 One man said the number three song on the Thai hit parade 'I'm vasectomized' had inspired him [to have a vasectomy].

va'sectomy. *Surg.* [f. L. *vās-* VAS 1 a.] Excision of the *vas deferens* or a portion of this; ligation of one or (more commonly) both *vasa deferentia*, usu. performed to render the subject infertile.

1897 *Lancet* 11 Sept. 658/1 A case of double vasectomy. **1899** R. HARRISON in *Lancet* 5 Aug. 331 Vasectomy and castration in relation to prostatic enlargement. **1900** [see VAS 1 a]. **1923** *Physiol. Rev.* III. 339 Pregnancy is prevented through coition being made sterile..by submitting the male to vasectomy. **1970** *Daily Tel.* 2 May 1/4 Vasectomy has recently become much more usual among men as a method of family planning. **1972** [see SEMEN 2]. **1979** *Toronto Star* 15 May E7/3 Commercial sperm banks in several major U.S. cities have reported growing numbers of donors, particularly..men who choose to store their sperm before undergoing vasectomies. **1985** *Times* 8 Mar. 10/7 A shipyard mechanic who had a vasectomy last autumn said yesterday he was 'lucky' after learning his wife is pregnant with sextuplets.

vased, *a. rare*⁻¹. [f. VASE.] Ornamented or provided with vases.

1806 W. TAYLOR in Robberds *Mem.* (1843) II. 144 The stately yew-hedge walks, and vased and statued terraces.

Vaseline ('væsəliːn, -ɪn), *sb.* Also **vaseline.** [Irreg. f. G. *wasser* water + Gr. ἔλ-αιον oil + -INE.] **a.** A soft, greasy substance used as an ointment or lubricant, obtained by evaporating petroleum and passing the residuum through animal charcoal. (Cf. PETROLATUM.)

A proprietary term, introduced by R. A. Chesebrough in 1872.

1874 *Eng. Mech.* 25 Sept. 36 A new petroleum product has been introduced into the trade under the name of vaseline. **1876** *Trans. Clinical Soc.* IX. 171 Applied vaseline to his head whenever the cap was off. **1884** *Pop. Sci. Monthly* XXIV. 778 Palm oil and vaseline was sold for lubricating machinery. **1897**, etc. [see *petroleum jelly*]. **1924**, etc. [see PROPRIETARY *a.* 1 a]. **1927** *Trade Marks Jrnl.* 3 Aug. 1383/2 Vaseline 479,707. Petroleum Jelly and Disinfectant Soap for Veterinary use. Chesebrough Manufacturing Company Consolidated... 11th April 1927. **1930** A. HUXLEY *Brief Candles* 13 Hearts of putty, hearts of vaseline. **1965** [see *soft ground* s.v. SOFT *a.* 29]. **1974** *Cleveland* (Ohio) *Plain Dealer* 26 Oct. 4-D/1 Walter Youngblood, one of his trainers, is smearing Vaseline on his face, torso, arms and legs. **1976** BOTHAM & DONNELLY *Valentino* xiv. 107 Vaseline, and other hair-care applications, would experience a significant sales-boost. **1978** J. IRVING *World according to Garp* xix. 410 The Vaseline made his ear slippery.

b. The greenish-yellow colour of Vaseline as used in the manufacture of glass; glasswear of this colour.

1966 J. LAVER *Victoriana* 168 The Victorians used a wide variety of colour in their glass—Bristol Blue..and the yellowy-green known as Vaseline. **1973** *Washington Post* 13 Jan. F1/7 (Advt.), Old glassware, Red Mark Prussia, Ruby, Vaseline, [etc.]. **1975** *Daily Colonist* (Victoria, B.C.) 26 Oct. 30/8 Vaseline is a greenish yellow glassware resembling its namesake. It dates from 1870 to the present day. **1980** *Times* 1 Nov. 24/7 Its shade is made of vaseline glass—a turn of the century technique which Christopher Wray has reintroduced.

Hence **'vaseline** *v. trans.*, to lubricate, rub, or anoint with Vaseline; **'vaselined** *ppl. a.*; **'vaselining** *vbl. sb.*

1891 *Bicycling News* April 117 My machine is all vaselined and put away. **1898** *Westm. Gaz.* 19 Dec. 2/1 A gentle hand had washed and vaselined and bandaged the..little heels. **1921** *Librarian* Nov. 74 The combination of vaselining and varnishing is the best thing for the text books. **1934** V. M. YEATES *Winged Victory* II. ix. 262 His neck was still sore with all yesterday's twisting to watch his tail. He ought to have vaselined it last night. **1938** F. CHESTER *Shot Full* xii. 114 A coloured man, his hair..vaselined to stick up. **1942** R. W. RAVEN *Surg. Care* xviii. 138 A piece of vaselined-gauze should be placed lightly over the colostomy. **1965** 'MALCOLM X' *Autobiogr.* iii. 55 He draped the towel around my shoulders, over my rubber apron, and began again vaselining my hair. **1977** *Rolling Stone* 16 June 39/1 Vaselined hair and a semidignified zoot suit. **1983** *Times* 21 Apr. 14/6 'Have you Vaselined your nipples?' asked a solicitor from Peckham.

vasi'factive, *a. Biol.* [f. L. *vāsi-* VAS.] Producing vessels.

1882 *Jrnl. Microsc. Sci.* Jan. 44 The spindle-shaped cells of vasifactive tissue, showed the same series of changes.

va'siferous, *a. rare*$^{-0}$. (See quot.)

1656 BLOUNT *Glossogr.*, *Vasiferous*, that carries a vessel.

vasiform ('veɪzɪfɔːm), *a.* [f. L. *vāsi-* VAS + -FORM.]

1. Having the form of a duct or similar conveying vessel; tubular.

a. *Phys.* **1835-6** *Todd's Cycl. Anat.* I. 245/2 The blood [of Cirripeds]..is propelled by a dorsal vasiform heart. **1839-47** *Ibid.* III 365/2 The systemic heart first appears in the sessile Tunicaries as a vasiform undivided ventricle. **1861** HULME tr. *Moquin-Tandon* II. v. ii. 261 The secreting glands are..vasiform tortuous tubes. **1870** ROLLESTON *Anim. Life* 98 The more elongated and vasiform heart.

b. *Bot.* **1839** LINDLEY *Introd. Bot.* (ed. 3) 21 Of Pitted Tissue, or Bothrenchyma... Vasiform Tissue, Dotted Ducts. **1866** *Treas. Bot.* 1205/1 *Vasiform tissue*, ducts, that is tubes having the appearance of spiral vessels and bothrenchyma. **1885** GOODALE *Physiol. Bot.* (1892) 87 Vasiform elements.

2. Shaped like a vase.

1846 DANA *Zooph.* (1848) 433, 1. The mode of growth:.. spreading each way from a central pedicel, and concave above (vasiform, or vase shape). **1882** *Garden* 1 Apr. 212/2 The flowers..form a vasiform tuft.

vaskene, variant of VASQUINE *Obs.*

vaso- ('veɪsəʊ), combining form, on Gr. types, of L. *vās* VAS, employed in terms of *Phys.* and *Path.* relating to the vascular system or parts of this, as ***vaso-cellular*** adj., ***-constricting*** adj., ***-constriction***, ***-constrictive*** adj., ***-constrictor***, ***-dentinal*** adj., ***-dentine***, ***-dilatation***, ***-dilating*** adj., ***-dilation***, ***-dilator***, ***-ganglion***, ***-inhibitory*** adj., ***-motive*** adj.; **vasoli'gation** *Surg.*, ligation of a vessel, esp. of the *vasa deferentia*; **'vasospasm** a sudden constriction of a blood vessel, resulting in reduced flow; hence **vaso'spastic** *a.*; **vaso'vagal** *a.*, involving the vagus nerve and the vascular system: applied to an attack (often the result of emotional stress) in which there is a slowing of the pulse and a fall in blood pressure, causing pallor, fainting, sweating, and nausea; **,vasova'sostomy** *Surg.* [-STOMY], an operation to reverse a vasectomy by rejoining the cut ends of the *vasa deferentia*.

1847 *Todd's Cycl. Anat.* III. 1026/2 *Vaso-cellular structure [of the penis]. **1925** *Proc. R. Soc.* B. XCVII. 325 The toxic and *vaso-constricting action..has not been confronted by us provided we make use of freshly defibrinated blood. **1975** *Daily Colonist* (Victoria, B.C.) 16 July 2/3 One of the vasoconstricting drugs..can be helpful. **1899** *Allbutt's Syst. Med.* VII. 249 The velocity of the blood flow is increased, whenever the arterial pressure is raised by general *vaso-constriction. **1890** W. JAMES *Princ. Psychol.* I. 97 Slowing and quickening of the heart..are independent of the *vaso-constrictive phenomenon. **1895** ROLLESTON *Dis. Liver* 271 To obtain the local vasoconstrictive effect on the bleeding vessels. **1877** M. FOSTER *Physiol.* 259 Stimulating a number of *vaso-constrictor nerves. **1896** *Allbutt's Syst. Med.* I. 112 When the vaso-constrictors alone are acting, the process is retarded. **1851** G. A. MANTELL *Petrifactions* iii. §5. 254 The softer *vaso-dentinal tract of the tooth opposed to it below. **1849-52** *Todd's Cycl. Anat.* IV. II. 878 The tubes which convey the capillary vessels through the substance of the osteo- and *vaso-dentine of the teeth of fishes. **1880** GÜNTHER *Fishes* 365 Numerous fissures radiating from the central mass of vasodentine. **1896** *Allbutt's Syst. Med.* I. 344 When one lower limb was heated, *vaso-dilatation..and sweating were observed in the other lower limb. **1956** *Nature* 18 Feb. 340/1 The well known *vasodilating effect of an increased concentration of carbon dioxide. **1962** in L. Kudrow *Cluster Headache* i. 9 Vasodilating headache: a suggestive classification. **1977** *Lancet* 30 July 231/1 A drug such as isoprenaline with a cardiac stimulant and peripheral vasodilating action can improve tissue perfusion. **1908** *Practitioner* Aug. 348 The tourniquet is then released, the affected members then become bright red, owing to a sudden *vasodilation. **1974** M. C. GERALD *Pharmacol.* vi. 111 Beta-receptor activation causes a widening of small blood vessels (vasodilation). **1881** *Nature* XXIII. 236 The nerves which act as *vaso-dilators on the mucous membrane of the buccal cavity. **1880** GÜNTHER *Fishes* 155 At the bottom of this sac there is a small *vaso-ganglion,..by which the urine is secreted. **1882** *Nature* XXVI. 411 Nerves..which, when stimulated, occasion..the dilatation of arteries—the so-called '*vaso-inhibitory' or 'vaso-dilator' nerves. **1926** W. N. BERKELEY *Princ. & Pract. Endocrine Med.* ix. 299 Vasectomy or *vasoligation in old men is said..to cause atrophy of the sperm mechanism of the testis. **1932** C. R. MOORE in E. Allen *Sex & Internal Secretions* vii. 314 There is no acceptable evidence that vasectomy or vasoligation has any rejuvenating effect. **1973** *Washington Post* 13 Jan. A-8/4 The experiments involved the use of the vasectomy technique, or a closely related one called 'vasoligation', to close off the two tiny ducts that carry the male spermatozoa. **1865** *Intell. Observ.* No. 47. 390 Excitation of *vaso-motive action. **1902** *Buck's Handbk. Med. Sci.* (rev. ed.) V. 74/1 Sedation of maniacal excitement and relaxation of *vaso-spasm in melancholic stupor are better accomplished by warm than cold baths. **1977** *Lancet* 14 May 1039/2 Workers with vibrating hand tools, such as pneumatic drills and chain saws, are at risk of episodic vasospasm, particularly when the vibration is associated with cold exposure. **1932** *Glasgow Med. Jrnl.* CXVIII. 146 Promising results have been obtained in certain cases of scleroderma in which a *vasospastic element is present. **1980** *Brit. Med. Jrnl.* 18 Oct. 1033/2 The results..indicate that prostaglandin E_1 given by central venous infusion is a safe and effective method of treating severe vasospastic disease. **1907** W. R. GOWERS *Border-Land of Epilepsy* ii. 18 When the vaso-motor spasm preponderates, the case may seem to differ from the type more than it really does. Such cases may be termed '*vaso-vagal'. **1974** R. M. KIRK et al. *Surgery* iii. 41/2 Vasovagal..shock, and fainting caused by an emotional crisis, produce marked dilation of vessels in the muscles, reducing circulatory blood volume. **1976** *Nature* 27 May 334/2 Some had a frank vasovagal reaction with yawning, bradycardia and pallor and could not continue the test procedure. **1949** *New Gould Med. Dict.* 1119/1 *Vasovasostomy. **1957** *Jrnl. Urol.* LXXVIII. 79 For this study vasovasostomy, rather than epididymovasostomy was chosen. **1982** *Jrnl. Andrology* III. 21/2 Seven patients undergoing vasovasostomy for reversal of male sterility secondary to vasectomy.

vaso'active, *a. Physiol.* [f. prec. + ACTIVE *a.*] Affecting the physiological state of blood vessels, esp. their calibre; ***vasoactive intestinal (poly)peptide***, a polypeptide 28 amino-acids long which is a neurotransmitter found esp. in the brain and gastrointestinal tract; abbrev. *VIP*.

1958 *Brit. Jrnl. Pharmacol.* XIII. 113 (*heading*) Vasoactive substances in the nasal mucosa. **1962** *Times* 17 May 14/4 New Appointments... M. R. Lee, M.A. (Oxon) ..to investigate the control of the generation of vasoactive polypeptides in the blood, at the..Radcliffe Infirmary, Oxford. **1970** *Nature* 28 Feb. 864/2 If the liver is normally the main site for inactivating this vasoactive intestinal peptide, its failure of destruction when liver function is seriously impaired..could account for..peripheral vasodilatation. **1972** [see *VIP* s.v. V 5 b]. **1976** *Nature* 22 Jan. 224/1 Release..of vasoactive lymphokines, such as prostaglandins,..might not necessarily leave a morphological trace.

Hence **vasoac'tivity**, vasoactive power.

1968 *Experientia* XXIV. 1126/1 These results have been interpreted as evidence that plasma has..intrinsic vasoactivity. **1982** *Amer. Jrnl. Path.* CVII. 289/2 When such lesions were induced in sheep and the lymph plasma draining the stimulated nodes was assayed for vasoactivity, a hyperemia-inducing activity was indeed found to be present.

vaso-motor, *a.* and *sb. Physiol.* [f. VASO-.]

A. *adj.* **1.** Acting upon the walls of the blood-vessels, so as to produce constriction or dilatation of these and thus regulate or affect the flow of blood. Chiefly with *nerve* and *centre*.

(*a*) **1868** SPENCER *Princ. Psychol.* I. vi. (1870) I. 115 The feelings that go along with discharges into the vaso-motor and sympathetic nerves, are the predominant ones. **1871** HAMMOND *Dis. Nervous Syst.* 65 Certain medicines are causes of cerebral anæmia,..by their action on the vaso-motor nerves. **1876** BRISTOWE *Th. & Pract. Med.* (1878) 41 The muscular tissue of the vascular system..is under the dominance of..the nerves of the vaso-motor system.

(*b*) **1865** *Intell. Observ.* No. 47. 390 The vaso-motor centres. **1875** H. C. WOOD *Therap.* (1879) 355 In large doses lobelia seems to paralyze the vaso-motor centres. **1897** *Allbutt's Syst. Med.* IV. 641 It also excites the vaso-motor centre, and thus leads to rise in the blood-pressure.

2. Affecting the vaso-motor nerves or centres.

1879 *St. George's Hosp. Rep.* IX. 677 The ophthalmoscope..yielded evidence of arterial relaxation, pointing to slight vaso-motor paralysis. **1881** *Trans. Obstet. Soc. Lond.* XXII. 23 Were the phenomena due to peripheral irritation reflected from the cord in the form of motor and vaso-motor disturbance? **1897** *Trans. Amer. Pediatric Soc.* IX. 195 Marked vaso-motor symptoms, and optic-nerve atrophy.

B. *sb.* A vaso-motor nerve.

1887 A. M. BROWN *Anim. Alkaloids* 47 Marked heat and injection of the ear helices from paralysis of vaso-motor. **1899** *Allbutt's Syst. Med.* VIII. 726 Hydrotherapeutic methods,..directed primarily to the cutaneous vaso-motors.

Hence **vaso-mo'torial** *a.*, **vaso-mo'torially** *adv.*, **vaso-'motory** *a.*

1877 M. FOSTER *Physiol.* 145 The vaso-motorial functions of the cervical sympathetic. **1897** *Allbutt's Syst. Med.* IV. 282 The effects of the latter experiment may be explained as a result of vaso-motorial influence. **1899** *Ibid.* VI. 28 A considerable number of instances of the purest vasomotory angina. **1901** *Lancet* 8 June 1627/1 The most efficacious way of increasing the urinary flow vaso-motorially.

vaso'pressin. *Physiol.* [f. as next + -IN[1].] A polypeptide hormone present in the neurohypophysis of mammals which controls the retention of water in the kidneys and when given in large quantities raises the blood pressure by vasoconstriction.

1928 [see OXYTOCIN]. **1951** A. GROLLMAN *Pharmacol. & Therapeutics* xxvi. 553 Vasopressin is also used in the form of a tannate... A single injection of this preparation every 24 to 48 hours may adequately control the polyuria and polydipsia of patients with diabetes insipidus. **1965** LEE & KNOWLES *Animal Hormones* ii. 29 The basic action of one of the two hormones, vasopressin or an analogous substance, is apparently the same in all terrestrial vertebrates, namely the maintenance of the osmotic tension of the extracellular fluid, and indirectly that of the intracellular fluid. **1976** SMYTHIES & CORBETT *Psychiatry* vii. 115 After surgery vasopressin secretion induced by stress makes it impossible to dilute urine. **1981** *Sci. Amer.* Oct. 114/1 Vasopressin, a peptide hormone, turns out to be also a neurotransmitter: nerve cells in the hypothalamus, a part of the brain, rely on vasopressin to signal other nerve cells in the brain.

'vasopressor, *a.* and *sb. Pharm.* [f. VASO- + PRESSOR.] **A.** *adj.* Causing the constriction of blood vessels. **B.** *sb.* A drug with this effect.

1928 *Proc. Soc. Exper. Biol. & Med.* XXVI. 243 Recently Kamm [et al.]..separated from pituitary extracts what they believe to be nearly pure vasopressor and oxytocic hormones. **1964** *Brit. Jrnl. Oral Surg.* II. 131 The conditions under which these experiments have been carried out are..far removed from clinical situations since large amounts of vasopressor were used. **1966** WRIGHT & SYMMERS *Systemic Path.* II. xxix. 1034/1 It has not yet been demonstrated that the vasopressor action of the hormone is of any importance in the normal human. **1975** *Amer. Heart Jrnl.* XC. 233/2 Vasopressors and inotropic drugs were discontinued and cardiopulmonary bypass support was ultimately discontinued. **1977** *Proc. R. Soc. Med.* LXX. 157/1 Vasopressor drugs were very seldom used and then only in an emergency.

'vasotribe. *Surg.* [f. VASO- + Gr. τρίβειν to crush.] An instrument used to arrest hæmorrhage.

1903 *Lancet* 30 May 1520/2 Even Kocher's powerful forceps..does not stop the circulation like a vasotribe.

†**vasquine.** *Sc. Obs.* Also **vaskene, waskyne, wasqwene.** [a. F. *vasquine*, obs. var. *basquine*, ad. Sp. *basquiña*. Cf. BASQUINE.] A petticoat.

1553 *Acc. Ld. High Treas. Scot.* X. 202 Item, half ane elne blak welwote to bordour ane waskyne of quhite dalmes. **1561** *Inv. R. Wardr.* (1815) 132 Of Doublettis, Vaskenis, and Skirtis. Item, ane doublett of blak velvot and the vaskene of the same. **1567** in Hay Fleming *Mary Q. of Scots* (1897) 511 Item to lyne ane vasquine of blak taffatis of the four treid v elle. [**1820** SCOTT *Abbot* xxxi, I shall endure her presence without any desire to damage either her curch or vasquine.]

vassal ('væsəl), *sb.* and *a.* Forms: 4 **vassale**, 6 **wassale**; 5-7 **vassall** (6 **phasalle**, *Sc.* **wassall**), 5- **vassal** (8 **vasal**); 5 **vayssal, vaysall**; 5 **vasseyll-**, 6-7 **vassaile**, 7 **vassail(l**; 6-7 **vassell**, *Sc.* **wassell-**. [a. OF. *vassal*, *vasal* (F. *vassal*, = It., Pg. *vassallo*, Sp. *vasallo*):—med.L. *vassall-us* man-servant, domestic, retainer, a word of Celtic origin: the simpler form *vassus* (used in the same senses) corresponds to Old Gaulish *-vassus*, *vasso-* (in personal names), OBreton *uuas* (MBret. *goas*, Bret. *goaz*), W. *gwas*, Ir. *foss* servant, serf. Cf. VAVASOUR.]

1. In the feudal system, one holding lands from a superior on conditions of homage and allegiance; a feudatory; a tenant in fee. Now *Hist.*

13.. *Coer de L.* 3365 They are doughty vassales, Kynges sones and amyrales. *c* **1489** CAXTON *Sonnes of Aymon* iii. 69 The emperour Charlemayne called to hym his goode vasseylles. **1523** [COVERDALE] *Old God & New* (1534) I, John..ye xij. pope of y[e] name..dyd prescribe an othe vnto Otho, in whiche Otho shold acknowlege him self to be y[e] popes phasalle (as we do now cal it). *a* **1578** LINDESAY (Pitscottie) *Chron. Scot.* (S.T.S.) I. 32 It becummeth ane prince to leiwe frielie..nocht subiectit to ane vassellis correctioun or chastisment. **1601** [BP. W. BARLOW] *Serm. Paules Crosse* 62 The Queene mured vp with her owne vassalles. **1665** in *Extr. S.P. rel. Friends* Ser. III. (1912) 234 The foreman and Chiefe thereof [*sc.* the jury] being all Tennants and vassalls to the Major and Aldermen. **1683** TEMPLE *Mem.* Wks. 1720 I. 453 The Emperor made an invincible Difficulty, declaring he would never treat with a Vassal of his own. *a* **1781** R. WATSON *Philip III*, IV. (1783) 293 It was enacted, that all their effects should belong to the lords whose vassals they were. **1817** BYRON *Manfred* II. i. 13 To bask by the huge hearths of those old halls, Carousing with the vassals. **1860** ADLER *Prov. Poet* 196 Princes having under them as their vassals other chiefs as renowned and valiant as themselves. **1871** FREEMAN *Norm. Conq.* (1876) IV. xvii. 29 All was trusted to the loyalty of William's new-made vassals.

b. Used in addressing persons of this class.

c **1489** CAXTON *Sonnes of Aymon* vii. 172 Tell me, vassall, knowest thou noo tidynges of Reynawde, the sone of Aymon? —— *Blanchardyn* xxviii. 104 Vassall! vassal! to whom I haue taken in hande that thynge most dere to me in this world. *a* **1533** LD. BERNERS *Huon* ix. 23 Wassale, who art thou that hath slayn my brother? **1591** SHAKS. *1 Hen. VI*, IV. i. 125 Presumptuous vassals, are you not asham'd..To trouble and disturbe the King, and Vs? **1822** BYRON *Werner* II. ii. 329 March, vassals! I'm your leader, and will bring The rear up.

c. In Scottish legal use.

1474 *Sc. Acts Parlt.* (1814) II. 107/1 Anent ourlordis þat in defraude & skaith of þair vassalis & tenentis deferris till enter to þair landis and superioriteis. **1581** *Reg. Privy Council Scot.* 407 In respect that thay nor nane of thame ar nather frehalders, vassellis, subvassellis, bot ar fewaris only.

1609 SKENE *Reg. Maj., Stat. King Robt. I*, 28 Gif it sall happen that ouer Lords poynd and distrenzie their vassellės contrare the constitution forsaid. **1689** in *Acts Parlt. Scot.* (1875) XII. 74 The forfaultors of vassells and cre[dito]rs, who shall be innocent of þair superiors or debitors crymes. **1739** *Morison's Dict. Decis.* (1806) XXXIII. 14507 The vassal is not bound to accept of a new charter, disconform to his former rights. **1765–8** ERSKINE *Inst. Law Scot.* II. iii. §13 A vassal.. may make over his property to a subvassal by a subaltern right. *Ibid.*, The vassal who thus subfeus [etc.]. **1815** R. BELL *Convey. Land* 238 The consent of both superior and vassal must be adhibited by those forms which practice has prescribed. **1853** H. BARCLAY *Digest Law Scot.* 964 Vassal is he who has the right of fee or property—*dominium utile* distinguished from the right of superiority, or *dominium directum*. **1896** W. K. MORTON *Man. Law Scot.* II. iii. 84 The law held the feu to transmit to heir of vassal, but superior could reject a stranger.

2. *transf.* One who holds, in relation to another, a position similar or comparable to that of a feudal vassal.

1563 GOLDING *Cæsar* 23 b, To bynd theyr Citye by othe, that they shoulde neyther requyre their hostages agayn,.. nor yet refuse to be their subiectes & vassales for euer. **1578** T. N. tr. *Conq. W. India* (1596) 47 The Lorde of that town and other foure Lords.. came vnto Cortez with a good trayne of their vassals and seruitours. **1732** LEDIARD *Sethos* II. VII. 51 The king of Phœnicia, whose vassal I declare myself to be. **1807** J. ROBINSON *Archæol. Græca* II. iii. 148 From the time of their [the Helots] first reduction these vassals, impatient of their servitude, often endeavoured to break their yoke. **1836** THIRLWALL *Greece* (1839) II. 173 The death of Cyrus is speedily avenged by one of his vassals, Amorges king of the Sacians. **1909** J. STUART *Burma thro. Cent.* iv. 42 The King of Bengal determined to restore the exiled King, and did so, the restored King becoming a vassal of Bengal.

b. *esp.* A humble servant or subordinate; one devoted to the service of another.

c **1500** *Melusine* xxiv. 163 Damoyselle,.. as to my part, your vassall & seruaunt shal I euer be. **1591** SPENSER *Daphnaida* 181 For rare it seemes.. That man.. Should to a beast his noble hart embase, And be the vassall of his vassalesse. **1596** J. MELVILL *Diary* (Wodrow Soc.) 370 Mr. Andro [Melvill].. calling the King bot 'God's sillie vassall'. *c* **1600** SHAKS. *Sonn.* lviii, Being your vassail bound to staie your leisure. **1651** in *Nicholas Papers* (Camden) 254 Lord Digby is a vassal of the Louvre. **1667** MILTON *P.L.* II. 90 The Vassals of his anger, when the Scourge Inexorably.. Calls us to Penance. **1757** KEENE in *10th Rep. Hist. MSS. Comm.* App. I. 220 D^n Carlos does not care to make the Figure of a Sort of Vassal. **1782** J. BROWN *View Nat. & Rev. Relig.* VI. i. 549 These donations ought to be made conscientiously under a sense of our debt to God as his vassals and tenants. **1823** SCOTT *Peveril* xxxix, Alas, for the captive princess, whose nod was to command a vassal so costly as your Grace! **1857** J. HAMILTON *Less. fr. Gt. Biogr.* 140 The man who by sin makes himself Satan's vassal may soon be his victim. **1858** LYTTON *What will He do?* VII. iv, Flora Vyvyan had still guarded.. a seat beside herself for Darrell, by lending it for the present to one of her obedient vassals.

transf. **1593** SHAKS. *Lucr.* 666 Thy thoughts, low vassals to thy state. **1692** PRIOR *Ode Imit. Horace* x, Where-e'er old Rhine his fruitful Water turns, Or fills his Vassals Tributary Urns.

c. One who is completely subject to some influence. Const. *of* or *to*.

c **1614** SIR W. MURE *Dido & Æneas* II. 780 Ȝe happy maids,.. Frie from love's plague and perillows infection, Nor wonne by men, nor vassaills to affection. **1631** R. BOLTON *Comf. Affl. Consc.* (1635) 34 These vassals of selfe-love and slaves of lust. **1676** HALE *Contempl.* II. 86 Either the Soul becomes servant and vassal to Sin, or at best it is led away Captive by it. **1732** NEAL *Hist. Purit.* I. 253 In this Bull he calls her Majesty 'an usurper and a Vassal of iniquity'. **1855** TENNYSON *Maud* II. i. ii, The feeble vassals of wine and anger and lust. **1859** —— *Merlin & V.* 341 Fame with men.. Should.. work as vassal to the larger love.

3. A base or abject person; a slave.

1589 GREENE *Menaphon* (Arb.) 37 Vassaile auant or with my wings you die, Ist fit an Eagle seate him with a Flie? **1598** R. BERNARD tr. *Terence, Heavtontim.* Prol., That I may not euer continually.. play the part of a vagabond vassaile. **1605** SHAKS. *Lear* I. i. 163 *Kent.* Now by Apollo, King, Thou swear'st thy Gods in vaine. *Lear.* O vassal! Miscreant. **1766** BLACKSTONE *Comm.* II. 53 We now use the word *vasal* opprobriously, as synonymous to slave or bondman. **1820** SCOTT *Abbot* xxvii, Thou that man!—vassal, thou liest!

4. *attrib.* or as *adj.* **a.** Having the status or character of a vassal; subject, subordinate; †servile. Chiefly *fig.*

1593 SHAKS. *Lucr.* 608 No outrageous thing From vassal actors can be wiped away. **1596** *Edw. III*, II. i, Vassell feare lies trembling at his feete. *c* **1600** SHAKS. *Sonn.* cxli, Thy proud hearts slaue and vassall wretch to be. **1616** R. C. *Times Whistle* IV. (1871) 41 Other mettals all Are but his vassaile starres. **1680** OTWAY *Orphan* I. iv, Man.. Forlorn, and silent as his Vassal-Beasts. **1718** POPE *Iliad* XV. 117 Supreme he sits: and sees.. Your vassal godheads grudgingly obey. **1735** SOMERVILLE *Chase* II. 352 When Ammon's Son With mighty Porus in dread Battle join'd, The Vassal World the Prize. **1762** FALCONER *Shipwr.* Introd. 4 Albion bids the avenging thunder roll Along her vassal deep. **1817** MOORE *Lalla Rookh* Wks. (1910) 422/1 As if the loveliest plants and trees Had vassal breezes of their own. *a* **1854** H. REED *Lect. Eng. Lit.* iii. (1855) 92 Britain was a kind of vassal nation of the Roman Empire. **1868** FREEMAN *Norm. Conq.* (1876) II. App. 686 A title most commonly given to vassal princes.

b. In predicative use. Also const. *to* or *unto*.

1592 *Nobody & Someb.* (1878) 284 Ile be no longer vassaile To such a tirannous rule. **1602** J. RHODES *Answ. Romish Rime* E, And now the other Bishops three.. Were first made vassal vnto Rome. **1671** MILTON *P.R.* IV. 133 That people victor once, now vile and base, Deservedly made vassal. **1848** W. H. KELLY tr. *L. Blanc's Hist. Ten Years* I. 325 It would have been to make Belgium vassal to the five powers. **1864** LOWELL *Fireside Trav.* 215 The eye that saw the whole earth vassal.

c. Of or pertaining to, characteristic of, a vassal.

1588 SHAKS. *L.L.L.* IV. iii. 224 Who sees the heauenly Rosaline, That.. Bowes not his vassall head. **1607** MIDDLETON *Michaelmas Term* I. i. 57 With what a vassal-appetite they gnaw On our reversions. **1898** *Atlantic Monthly* LXXXII. 562/1 The oath of vassal loyalty constraining him to stand at his post.

vassal (ˈvæsəl), *v.* Now *rare*. Also 7 vassail(e, -ayl, -all. [f. prec.]

1. *trans.* To make subject or subordinate *to* some thing or person.

1613 DRUMM. OF HAWTH. *Cypress Grove* Wks. 1913 II. 98 Celestiall thinges fauour him, earthly thinges are vassaled vnto him. **1615** G. SANDYS *Trav.* 77 Whose posterity in part remaineth to this day, though vassaled to the often changes of forraine Governours. **1628** FELTHAM *Resolves* II. lxxi. 205 It vassailes him to the world, to beasts, and men.

refl. **1622** WITHER *Philarete* (1633) H xii, Lovers.. Vassaling themselves with shame To some proud imperious Dame. **1652–62** HEYLIN *Cosmogr.* (1682) III. 209 The other nine.. have vassalled themselves to the great Mongul.

2. To reduce to the position of a vassal; to subdue or subjugate. Also *fig.*

1612 W. PARKES *Curtaine-Dr.* (1876) 17 The rules of reason, and the lawes of nature,.. vassayled, obliterate and vnregarded by him. **1621** BP. MOUNTAGU *Diatribæ* 493 For Crœsus King of Lydia.. was vanquished.. and vassalled by Cyrus of Persia. *a* **1653** G. DANIEL *Idyll* Illustr. 5 And fellow-Creatures vassail'd, tumble downe To either Face or Hand, the Axe, or Crowne.

Hence **ˈvassalled** *ppl. a.*

1606 WARNER *Alb. Eng.* XIV. lxxx, (1612) 338 And oft his vassalde English he gainst forraine Swords did bring. **1649** G. DANIEL *Trinarch., Hen. V*, cccii, The Vassail'd Earth was rent, vnder his Rule. **1815** J. C. HOBHOUSE *Substance Lett.* (1816) I. 102 To restore the kings.. of that ancient, oppressed, vassalled, decimated France. **1933** W. FAULKNER *Green Bough* 63 Thrall to the vassalled garrison that keep Thy soft unguarded breast's white citadel.

vassalage (ˈvæsəlɪdʒ), *sb.* Forms: α. 4– vassalage (7 -adge, -edge, 8 vasalage), 5–7 vassallage, 5 vassol-, 6 vassailage; 4–5, 7 vasselage (4 vassh-, 5 vess-), 4, 7 vassellage (6 vasell-), 5 vaisselage; 6 *Sc.* vaslage, -lege. β. 5 wasselage; *Sc.* 5 wassolage, waslage, 5–6 wassalage, 6 -edge, wassallage, wassilaige. [a. OF. *vassal(l)age, vas(s)elage, vessalaige*, etc. (F. *vasselage*), f. *vassal* VASSAL *sb.* So Prov. *vassal-, vasselatge*, Sp. *vasallage*, Pg. *vassallagem*, It. *vassallagio*, med.L. *vassallagium*.]

1. a. Action befitting a good vassal or a man of courage and spirit; prowess in battle, warfare, or other difficult enterprise. *Obs.* exc. *arch.*

α. **1303** R. BRUNNE *Handl. Synne* 4610 Whan he wendyþ to þe tournament She.. byt hym do for hys lemman Yn vasshelage alle þat he kan. **1338** —— *Chron.* (1810) 188 Gentille of norture, & noble of lynage, Was non þat bare armure, þat did suilk vassalage. *c* **1380** *Sir Ferumb.* 1671 Riȝt as he wil let it be do, for þat is vassalage. *c* **1400** *Laud Troy Bk.* 12873 Kyng Sarpedoun Was in his tyme a stalworth man, A noble knyȝt of vasselage. **1456** SIR G. HAYE *Law Arms* (S.T.S.) 54 To count all the vasselage that thare was done on ayther syde, it war mervaile to here. *c* **1477** CAXTON *Jason* 34 b, Our defendour.. whiche hath only in him self more of vaisselage than is in alle Esclauonye. **1508** DUNBAR *Poems* vii. 10 Welcum.. incomparable knyght, The fame of armys, and floure of vassalage. **1565** in Ellis *Orig. Lett.* Ser. I. II. 204 And maynie made knightes that never showde anye greate token of their vasellage. **1567** *Satir. Poems Reform.* iv. 141 Deianira hir husband Hercules.. Brocht to mischeif, for all his vassalage. **1825** SCOTT *Betr.* xxi, Were I to choose some knight of name,.. he would be setting about to do deeds of vassalage upon the Welsh.

ironical. *c* **1385** CHAUCER *L.G.W.* 1667 (*Hypsipyle*), And of Iason this is the vassellage That in hise dayis nas ther non i-founde So fals a louere goinge on the grounde.

β. **1375** BARBOUR *Bruce* I. 290 He had a sone.. þat wes þan bot a litill page; Bot syne he wes off gret waslage. *Ibid.* x. 268 He knew his worthy wassalage. *c* **1500** *Lancelot* 2708 Thar schew the lord sir ywan his curage, His manhed, & his noble wassolage. *c* **1550** ROLLAND *Crt. Venus* I. 171 He.. in the Net of wanhoip had bene tane, Quhilk causit him want baith welth & wassallage. *a* **1578** LINDESAY (Pitscottie) *Chron. Scot.* (S.T.S.) I. 153 He was of tender aige and could not wse no wassaledge nor feit of weiris.

†**b.** A brave or chivalrous act; a noble or gallant exploit. *Obs.*

c **1330** R. BRUNNE *Chron. Wace* (Rolls) 12331 Me þynkeþ hit were no vasselage, þre til on; hit were outrage! **1426** LYDG. *De Guil. Pilgr.* 10606 Record off folkys that be sage, Sclaundere ys no vasselage. *c* **1470** HENRY *Wallace* I. 158 Thus he conteynde in till hys tendyr age; In armys syne did mony hie waslage. *c* **1475** *Rauf Coilȝear* 887 For that war na wassalage, sum men wald say. *a* **1578** LINDESAY (Pitscottie) *Chron. Scot.* (S.T.S.) II. 118 Ane gret navie.. landit in orknay and thocht to haue done sum wassillage thair. *a* **1670** SPALDING *Troub. Chas. I* (1840) I. 23 The Erll of Morray.. rejoisit michtellie at this vassalage done be his men. *Ibid.* 182 The barronis.. left the houss, thinking it no vassalage to stay whill thay war slayne.

transf. **1570** *Satir. Poems Reform.* xiii. 132 His Fatheris murther also ȝe cleirly knew, Myschantly hangit, ane wickit vassalage.

†**c.** Pre-eminence, supremacy. *Obs.*$^{-1}$

c **1430** LYDG. *Min. Poems* (Percy Soc.) 176 Is noon so greet encress Off world tresour, as for to live in pees, Which among vertues hath the vasselage.

2. The state or condition of a vassal; subordination, homage, or allegiance characteristic of, or resembling that of, a vassal.

1594 NASHE *Terrors of Night* Wks. (Grosart) III. 266 Much more may I acknowledge all redundant prostrate vassailage to the royall descended Familie of the Careys. **1605** CAMDEN *Rem.* 4 Acknowledging no superiours, in no vassalage to Emperour or Pope. **1655** FULLER *Ch. Hist.* IV. 182 He was a worthy man in his generation, had not his vassalage to the Pope ingaged him in cruelty against the poor professors of the truth. **1667** MILTON *P.L.* II. 252 Let us not then pursue.. our state Of splendid vassalage. **1709** STEELE *Tatler* No. 46 ¶2 The only Part of Great Britain where the Tenure of Vassalage is still in being. **1756** NUGENT *Gr. Tour, Germany* II. 15 The peasants are all in a state of vassalage to the nobility. **1774** PENNANT *Tour Scot. in 1772*, 294 Tyranny more often than protection was the attendance on their vassalage. **1807** G. CHALMERS *Caledonia* I. III. iv. 347 They acknowledged their vassalage.. by receiving rulers, from the Scandian peninsula. **1844** H. H. WILSON *Brit. India* II. 461 That they had no right.. to reduce to vassalage the native Princes, who had always been treated.. as independent. **1869** FREEMAN *Norm. Conq.* (1876) III. xiii. 312 William's vassalage for England will be still more nominal than his vassalage for Normandy.

attrib. **1791** PAINE *Rights of Man* 82 Submission is wholly a vassalage term, repugnant to the dignity of Freedom.

b. In semi-personified use.

1606 SHAKS. *Tr. & Cr.* III. ii. 40 Like vassalage at vnawares encountring The eye of Maiestie. **1616** J. LANE *Contn. Sqr.'s T.* IX. 410 For trewe kinges this inscribe of soveraigntie, that vassalage backe startes at maiestie.

c. In the phrase *to hold* (lands) *in vassalage*.

1747 CARTE *Hist. Eng.* I. 195 Who being tired with beating Cerdic consented at last that he should hold a great part of the west of him in vassalage. **1761** HUME *Hist. Eng.* I. ix. 186 The prince.. offered.. to hold his kingdom in vassalage under the Crown of England. **1791** NEWTE *Tour Eng. & Scot.* 284 Several good families held their estates in vassalage of feudal Chiefs.

3. Subjection, subordination, servitude; service. Freq. const. *to*. **a.** To a person or persons.

1595 T. P. GOODWINE *Blanchardyn* II. Ded., [A] most worthy Patrone; to whose vasselage.. bountifull rewardes haue bound me during life, in all obseruancie. **1604** T. WRIGHT *Passions* v. §4. 231 Man is bound both by nature, grace, gratitude, vassaladge.. to loue, honour, and blesse thee. **1622** WITHER *Philarete* (1633) K j b, Who, beforetime held in scorne, To yeeld Vassalage, or Duty, Though unto the Queen of Beauty. **1793** BURKE *Obs. Conduct Minority* Wks. 1842 I. 626 This insolent claim of superiority on their part, and of a sort of vassalage to them on that of other members. **1849** MACAULAY *Hist. Eng.* i. I. 1 How our country, from a state of ignominious vassalage, rapidly rose to the place of umpire among European powers. **1878** *N. Amer. Rev.* CXXVII. 100 The revelation it makes of the condition of the solid South; its continued vassalage to the reckless and dangerous class.

b. To some influence, esp. of a detrimental kind.

1612 T. TAYLOR *Comm. Titus* ii. 14 It must worke in vs a.. watchfulnes against all sinn, which bringeth such vassaledge vpon vs. **1665** GLANVILL *Def. Van. Dogm.* 13 An attempt to redeem the free-born spirits of Men, from an unworthy vassallage to so stigmatiz'd an Authority. **1742** BLAIR *Grave* 598 Human Nature groans Beneath a Vassalage so vile and cruel. **1767** DR. DODD *Poems* 8 Princes.. unfortunately great, Born to the pompous vassalage of state. **1833** LYTTON *Godolphin* 24 All round bore the seal of vassalage to Time. **1849** COLERIDGE *Shaks. Notes* (1875) 126 The subservience and vassalage of strength and animal courage to intellect and policy. **1871** LOWELL *Pope* Pr. Wks. 1890 IV. 11 English literature.. showed the marks.. of an artistic vassalage to France.

4. †**a.** The authority of a superior in relation to a vassal. *Obs.*

1630 *R. Johnson's Kingd. & Commw.* 140 Lots, Sales, Homages, rights of Vassalage, Forrests, Ponds, Rivers. **1670** *Devout Commun.* (1688) 81 How many slaves under the vassallage of an enemy fare better than thou! **1681** H. NEVILE *Plato Rediv.* 37 This Vassallage over the People, which the Peers of France had, being abolisht.

b. An estate or fief held by a vassal.

1855 MILMAN *Lat. Chr.* IX. viii. IV. 190 The Countship of Foix, with six territorial vassalages.

5. A body or assemblage of vassals.

1807 WORDSW. *White Doe* II. 30 But now the inly-working North Was ripe to send its thousands forth, A potent vassalage, to fight In Percy's and in Neville's right. **1826** *Blackw. Mag.* XX. 416 The assembled vassalage were all still as death. **1849** J. GRANT *Kirkaldy* xx. 230 Kirkaldy, whose garrison was probably recruited from his own vassalage.

Hence †ˈ**vassalage** *v.*, = VASSAL *v. Obs.*

1648 *Royalist's Defence* 38 Refusing to acknowledge it His duty to bee governed by them His Subjects, and.. to vassalage unto those Rebels Himselfe, His Royall Posterity, and all the rest of the people. **1662** R. MATHEW *Unl. Alch.* 59 What man labouring to fulfil his desire, is not ten times further off by being vassalag'd more thereunto?

†ˈ**vassalate**, *v. Obs.*$^{-1}$ [f. VASSAL *sb.*] = VASSAL *v.* So †**vassaˈlation**, vassalage, subjection. *Obs. rare*$^{-1}$.

1648 W. MOUNTAGUE *Devout Ess.* I. xv. §2. 271 Thus God suffereth things which have no true goodness, to work upon our imagination;.. and this vassallation is a penalty set by the true Judge of all things, upon our attempt to design of our own heads, the forms of good and evil. **1659** GAUDEN *Tears Ch.* 496 Conventions, where either Lay-men shall over-number and over-awe the Clergy, or Clergy-men shall vassalate their consciences to gratifie any potent party.

vassaldom. *rare.* [f. VASSAL *sb.* + -DOM.] = VASSALAGE 2.

1876 BURNABY *Ride to Khiva* xxvii. 262 The khanate [of Khiva] was reduced to a state of complete vassaldom. **1965** J. A. MICHENER *Source* (1966) 224 In the end Moab had been reduced to a kind of vassaldom.

ˈvassaless. *rare.* [f. VASSAL *sb.* + -ESS.] A female vassal.

1591 [see VASSAL *sb.* 2 b]. **1842** AGNES STRICKLAND *Queens Eng.* II. 41 He could have forbidden his fair vassaless to marry the subject of King Philip.

vassalic (væˈsælɪk), *a.* [f. VASSAL *sb.*] Of or pertaining to vassals or vassalage.

1897 F. W. MAITLAND *Domesday Bk. & Beyond* 75 The very highest storeys of the feudal or vassalic edifice. **1898** —— *Townsh. & Borough* 45 There are feudal or vassalic distinctions.

ˈvassalism. [f. VASSAL *sb.*] Tendency to accept a position of vassalage.

1854 *Fraser's Mag.* L. 600 That obsequious compliance.. which indicated the shameful vassalism (if we may coin a word) of a German government.

vassalize (ˈvæsəlaɪz), *v.* [f. VASSAL *sb.*]

1. *trans.* = VASSAL *v.* 1.

1599 R. LINCHE *Anc. Fiction* C ij b, Since Asia was vassalized and subiugated to the Romanes. **1648** CROMWELL *Lett. & Sp.* 20 Nov., The former Quarrel was that Englishmen might rule over one another, this to vassalise us to a foreign nation. **1653** CHISENHALE *Cath. Hist.* 36 Their ..close practises against all that will not..vassalize themselves to their impious Lord and Master. **1670** in E. B. Jupp *Carpenters' Co.* (1887) 308 All other workemen depending on the same must lye adle [*sic*] and bee vassalized to their rudenes and exorbitances.

2. = VASSAL *v.* 2.

1641 MARCH *Act. for Slaunder* 7 He might seize all his estate..and vassalize his person at pleasure. **1654** SPITTLEHOUSE *Vind. Fifth-Mon. Men* 5 Against all arbitrary or absolute power..vassalizing the Saints and People of God in this Commonwealth. **1848** LOWELL *Fable for Critics* 1506 To vassalize old tyrant Winter.

Hence **ˈvassalized** *ppl. a.*, **ˈvassalizing** *vbl. sb.*

1647 *Maids' Petition* 3 Till then, wee'le remaine your *Vassalized Virgins. **1841** T. MACQUEEN in *Poets Ayrsh.* 216 It marked the deep bondage of vassalised man. **1607** WALKINGTON *Opt. Glass* 80 The *vassalizing of the rebellious affections. **1662** J. CHANDLER *Van Helmont's Oriat.* 215 Therefore the meat is not yet fully transchanged, unless when its own Archeus being subdued, our vital one is introduced with a full vassallizing of the former.

ˈvassalry. Also 5 vasselry, 6 vassalrie, -rey. [f. VASSAL *sb.* + -RY. Cf. med.L. *vasseleria* (1238) fief. OF. *vassellerie* warlike exploit.]

1. = VASSALAGE 5.

a **1470** HARDING *Chron.* xcix, Thei reigned vpon the vasselry That were out castes of all Britany. **1806** W. TAYLOR in *Ann. Rev.* IV. 67 Something could be done..to facilitate the acquisition of a peculium..by the negro vassalry. **1831** TYTLER *Hist. Scot.* (1864) II. 209 The Earls of Ross and Huntly, whose dominions and vassalry embraced almost the whole of the Highlands. **1882** E. ARNOLD *Pearls of Faith* xxiii. (1883) 84 Queens were his slaves, and Kings his vassalry.

2. = VASSALAGE 3.

1594 O. B. *Quest. Profit. Concern.* 13 b, The olde bondage and vassalrie men of your condition were wont to be in. *c* **1600** in *E.E. Wills* (1882) 117 This beast..disdaineth vassalrey and subjection.

Vassal's grass. (See quots.)

a **1818** M. G. LEWIS *Jrnl. W. Ind.* (1834) 251 Many years ago, a new species of grass was imported into Jamaica, by Mr. Vassal... This nuisance, which is called 'Vassal's grass',..has now completely overrun the parish of Westmoreland. **1885** LADY BRASSEY *The Trades* 262 The greater part of it was a coarse-looking but sweet herbage, called Vassal's grass.

ˈvassalship. [f. VASSAL *sb.*] Vassalage.

1578 T. N. tr. *Conq. W. India* 50 These generally gave their vassalship to the King of Spaine into the handes of Hernando Cortez. **1841** W. SPALDING *Italy & It. Isl.* I. 53 Their political rights were not affected by their vassalship.

vassand, obs. Sc. form of WEASAND.

vassayl, obs. form of WASSAIL.

vast (vɑːst, væst), *sb.* [f. the adj.]

1. A vast or immense space. Chiefly *poet.*, and freq. with adjs.

1604 E. G[RIMSTONE] *D'Acosta's Hist. Indies* I. 5 That great Chaos, and infinite Vast, which the ancient Philosophers affirmed to bee vnder the earth. **1608** SHAKS. *Per.* III. i. 1 Thou god of this great vast, rebuke these surges. **1709–11** KEN *Anodynes* Poet. Wks. 1721 III. 442, I then would higher soar, and cast My eyes o're the Ethereal Vast. **1725** POPE *Odyss.* IV. 683 By Juno's guardian aid, the wat'ry Vast Secure of storms, your Royal brother past. **1794** W. TAYLOR in Robberds *Mem.* (1843) I. 150 Our souls the bands of death shall tear, Through the whole starry vast to range. **1818** KEATS *Endym.* III. 859 Far as the mariner on highest mast Can see all round upon the calmed vast. **1850** TENNYSON *In Mem.* Concl. xxxi, A soul shall draw from out the vast And strike his being into bounds. **1898** T. HARDY *Wessex Poems* 72 And up from the vast a murmuring passed As from a wood of pines.

b. Const. *of* (heaven, sea, etc.). Also *fig.*

1610 SHAKS. *Temp.* I. ii. 326 Vrchins Shall for that vast of night that they may worke All exercise on thee. *a* **1649** DRUMM. OF HAWTH. *Poems* Wks. (1711) 34/2 Such as do Nations govern, and command Vasts of the Sea and Emperies of Land. **1667** MILTON *P.L.* VI. 203 Through the vast of Heav'n It sounded. **1795** W. BLAKE *Song Los* 42 And all the vast of Nature shrunk Before their shrunken eyes. **1838** ELIZA COOK *England* iv, I'd tread the vast of mountain range, or spot serene and flowered. **1872** GEO. ELIOT *Middlem.* xlv, Which need never stop short at the boundary of knowledge, but can draw for ever on the vasts of ignorance.

2. *dial.* A very great number or amount.

1793 *Piper of Peebles* 14 A vast o' fouk a' round about Come to the feast. *c* **1820** HOGG *Sheph. Wedding* i, They couldna get them [*sc.* leisters] sindry, else there had been a vast o bludeshed. *a* **1825–** in dialect glossaries (E. Anglia, Yks., Leic., etc.). **1853** R. S. SURTEES *Soapey Sp. Tour* (1893) 30 It takes a vast of clothes, even at Oxford prices, to come to a thousand pounds. **1888** HUXLEY in *Life* (1900) II. xii. 188, I took a vast of trouble (as the country folks say) about it.

vast (vɑːst, væst), *a.* and *adv.* [ad. L. *vastus* void, immense, extensive, etc., or F. *vaste* (1611), It., Sp., Pg. *vasto.*]

1. Of very great or large dimensions or size; huge, immense, enormous.

1575–85 ABP. SANDYS *Serm.* 360 If ye compare..one of smale stature, with a vast giant,..the combat could not choose but seeme in all pointes verie vnequall. **1603** HOLLAND *Plutarch's Mor.* 294 Unskilfull cutters..are of opinion that the enormous and huge statues, called Colosses, which they cut, will seeme more vast and mightie if they frame them stradling with their legs. **1666** BOYLE *Orig. Forms & Qual.* 171 These Bodies, that are the vastest and the most important of the Sublunary World. **1712–4** POPE *Rape Lock* V. 92 Three seal-rings, which after, melted down, Form'd a vast buckle for his widow's gown. **1762–71** H. WALPOLE *Vertue's Anecd. Paint.* (1786) I. 222 A vast ruff, a vaster fardingale..are the features by which every body knows at once the pictures of queen Elizabeth. **1860** TYNDALL *Glac.* II. xvii. 315 On the ice cascades..the river glacier has piled vast blocks on vaster pedestals. **1867** LADY HERBERT *Cradle L.* vi. 155 It is not a single building, but rather a vast collection of chambers and galleries.

absol. **1784** COWPER *Task* V. 811 A ray of heav'nly light, gilding all forms Terrestrial in the vast and the minute. **1802** FINDLATER *Agric. Surv. Peebles.* 18 The mountains,..too much upon the vast for beauty, are yet too tame for the sublime.

2. Of great or immense extent or area; extensive, far-stretching.

1590 SHAKS. *Mids. N.* V. i. 9 One sees more diuels then vaste hell can hold. **1600** J. PORY tr. *Leo's Africa* VII. 290 Betweene which two Kingdomes lieth a vast desert being much destitute of water. **1615** W. LAWSON *Country Housew. Gard.* (1626) 23 The top hath the vast aire to spread his boughs in. **1663** BUTLER *Hud.* I. i. 327 Thorough Desarts vast And Regions Desolate they past. **1697** DRYDEN *Virg. Georg.* III. 531 Such an extent of Plains, so vast a Space Of Wilds unknown..Allures their Eyes. **1722** WOLLASTON *Relig. Nat.* v. (1724) 79 What a vast field for contemplation is here opened! **1774** GOLDSM. *Nat. Hist.* (1776) I. 100 The river..overflowed the adjacent country, like a vast lake. **1816** J. WILSON *City of Plague* II. iii. 292 Another month, and I am left alone In the vast city. **1865** W. G. PALGRAVE *Arabia* I. 391 The circle of vision here embraces vaster plains and bolder mountains. **1871** FREEMAN *Norm. Conq.* (1876) IV. xvii. 70 Ruling over vast territory which had been held by the Earls.

Comb. **1861** LD. LYTTON & FANE *Tannhäuser* 85 The sun, About him drawing the vast-skirted clouds. **1888** F. HUME *Mme. Midas* I. Prol., From thence it spread inland into vast-rolling pastures.

b. Qualifying nouns of dimension.

1677 MIÉGE *Fr. Dict.* I. s.v. *Vaste*, A Country of a vast extent. **1688** PRIOR *An Ode* i, The mysterious Gulph of vast Immensity. *a* **1721** —— *To C'tess Dowager of Devonsh.* i, That Both, their Skill to this vast Height did raise, Be ours the Wonder, and be yours the Praise. **1725** DE FOE *Voy. round World* (1840) 345 A pit or hole of a vast depth. **1774** PENNANT *Tour. Scot. in 1772* 6 The church stands at a vast height above the town. **1809–14** WORDSW. *Excurs.* IV. 1161 A temple framing of dimensions vast, And yet not too enormous for the sound Of human anthems. **1865** KINGSLEY *Herew.* x, His vast breadth of shoulder.

c. In transf. or fig. uses.

1736 BUTLER *Anal.* II. ii. Wks. 1874 I. 173 The scheme of nature..is evidently vast, even beyond all possible imagination. **1738** WESLEY *Ps.* c. iv, Vast as Eternity thy Love. **1784** COWPER *Task* VI. 218 But how should matter.. satisfy a law So vast in its demands, unless impell'd [etc.]. **1806** R. CUMBERLAND *Mem.* (1807) I. 160 Time whelms us in the vast Inane. **1852** H. ROGERS *Ecl. Faith* (1853) 142 It must be accomplished in a cycle vast as those of the geological eras. **1869** KINGSLEY *Lett.* (1878) II. 292 Science is grown too vast for any one head. **1884** *Congregational Year Bk.* 56 Mightier wonders and vaster problems.

3. Of the mind, etc.: Unusually large or comprehensive in grasp or aims.

1610 HOLLAND *Camden's Brit.* 464 Cardinall Wolsey,.. whose vast minde reached alwayes at things too high. **1650** R. STAPYLTON *Strada's Low-C. Wars* II. 38 But the Prince of Orange and Count Egmont..were of vaster spirits then the rest. **1692** DRYDEN *St. Euremont's Ess.* 372 Her Spirit is extensive without being Vast, never rambling so far in general Thoughts, as not to be able to return easily to singular Considerations. **1710** STEELE *Tatler* No. 209 ⁋1 The Account we have of his vast Mind. **1743** FRANCIS tr. *Horace, Odes* I. xxxvii. 12 Vast in her Hopes, and giddy with Success. **1815** SHELLEY *Alastor* 287 With voice far sweeter than thy dying notes, Spirit more vast than thine.

4. Very great, immense, enormous, in respect of amount, quantity, or number.

1637 *Verney Mem.* (1907) I. 114 Yet what is all this but a small part of those vast treasures left him by his father. *a* **1661** FULLER *Worthies* (1840) II. 571 Sir Thomas Cooke, late lord mayor of London, one of vast wealth. **1681** FLAVEL *Meth. Grace* xix. 341 No wise man expends vast sums to bring home trifling commodities. **1730** A. GORDON *Maffei's Amphith.* 64 The vast Rain which fell at that Time. **1760** R. BROWN *Compl. Farmer* II. 62, I have known vast crops of rye upon barren lands that have been old warrens, and well dunged with rabbits. **1796** H. HUNTER tr. *St.-Pierre's Study Nat.* (1799) I. 93 The members of the vast family of Mankind. **1838** THIRLWALL *Greece* IV. 369 Carrying away vast herds of cattle. **1855** MACAULAY *Hist. Eng.* xii. III. 210 The same tyranny..had robbed his Church of vast wealth. **1872** RAYMOND *Statist. Mines & Mining* 224 The Colorado River..sends a vast body of water to the Gulf of California.

b. With nouns of quality, action, etc.

1595 SHAKS. *John* IV. iii. 152 Vast confusion waites..The iminent decay of wrested pompe. *c* **1600** *Life & Death Long Meg of Westm.* ii, On this Sir John de Castile, in a bravado, would needs make an experiment of her vast strength. **1647** *Hamilton Papers* (Camden) 148 Soe unequall..where there is so vast a disproportion in the knowledge, abilities, and interests of the persons. **1718** ROWE tr. *Lucan* I. 89 Vast are the thanks thy grateful Rome shou'd pay To wars, which usher in thy sacred sway. **1765** *Museum Rust.* IV. 166 The same vast superiority will be found in every article of employment to which these waggons can be put. **1796** BURKE *Regic. Peace* Wks. VIII. 393 Most of them engage, for a short time at a vast price, every actor or actress of name in the metropolis. **1833** HT. MARTINEAU *Fr. Wines & Pol.* i. 15 Vast labour will be required to render these lands productive once more. **1856** FROUDE *Hist. Eng.* (1858) I. ii. 174 His reading was vast, especially in theology.

c. With nouns denoting number or amount. (Passing into next.)

(*a*) **1677** MIÉGE *Fr. Dict.* II, A vast quantity, *une grande quantité.* **1716** LADY M. W. MONTAGU *Let. to C'tess of Bristol* 25 Nov., The vast number of English crowds the town so much. **1748** *Anson's Voy.* I. vii. 105 These rocks terminate in a vast number of ragged points. **1823** *Edin. Rev.* XXXIX. 49 To put vast quantities of men into prison. **1857** BUCKLE *Civiliz.* I. vii. 325 Disputes..now regarded with indifference by the vast majority of educated men. **1884** *Marshall's Tennis Cuts* 154, I saw a vast number, and examined them very carefully.

(*b*) **1718** HICKES & NELSON *J. Kettlewell* III. cxvi. 478 He took a vast deal of Pains, nicely to Examine every Thing. **1802** MAR. EDGEWORTH *Moral T.* (1816) I. v. 27 Mackenzie, with artificial admiration, said a vast deal more than he thought. **1858** DICKENS *Lett.* (1880) II. 75 We have done a vast deal here. **1872** BLACK *Adv. Phaeton* xviii. 246 He showed her a vast amount of studied respect.

5. In weakened sense as a mere intensive.

Common in fashionable use in the 18th cent.: cf. VASTLY *adv.* 3.

1696 PHILLIPS (ed. 5) s.v., Figuratively we say, such a one has a vast Fancy, a vast Wit, vast Parts, &c. **1700** S. L. tr. *Fryke's Voy. E. Ind.* 120 Every new and full Moon, the Sea drives 'em up in a vast way. *a* **1704** T. BROWN *Beauties* Wks. 1730 I. 45, I saw Armida, to my vast surprize, So rich in charms. **1764** REID *Inquiry* ii. §1 That most other bodies while exposed to the air are continually sending forth effluvia of vast subtilty. **1801** STRUTT *Sports & Past.* II. i. 61 They shot with vast precision to that distance. **1840** HAWTHORNE *Biogr. Sk., Pepperell* (1879) 186 An object of vast antipathy to many of the settled ministers. **1861** F. METCALFE *Oxonian in Iceland* iii. (1867) 33 Their wise heads go everlasting..nidding, nodding, with vast solemnity.

b. ***a vast many***, a great many. ? *Obs.*

1695 WOODWARD *Nat. Hist. Earth* I. 49 By..perpetual Circulation a vast many things in the System of Nature are transacted. **1722** DE FOE *Plague* (1754) 22 The Restoration had brought a vast many Families to London. **1771** T. HULL *Sir W. Harrington* (1797) III. 207 Jacob was sent out a vast many times. **1833** T. HOOK *Parson's Dau.* II. ii, But there are a vast many persons in the neighbourhood who would make suitable husbands for such a girl. **1853** HAWTHORNE *Tanglewood T., Pomegranate Seeds*, It troubled her with a vast many tender fears.

c. *adv.* = VASTLY *adv.* Now *dial.*

1687 MIÉGE *Gt. Fr. Dict.* II, A vast rich Town, *une Ville fort riche.* **1756** AMORY *Buncle* (1770) II. 264 Many vast high ones [*sc.* mountains] we crossed, and travelled through very wonderful glins. **1757** H. BROOKE *Female Officer* I. viii, He is vast expert at his weapon, truly! *c* **1790** 'M. P.' [DOROTHY KILNER] *Anecd. Boarding School* I. 47, I cannot say that I am vast fond of her. *Ibid.* 98 Half a dozen of them all at once calling out, O! vast fine! vast fine! **1809–** in dialect glossaries, etc.

vast, southern ME. var. FAST *sb.*, *a.*, and *adv.*; obs. Sc. f. WASTE.

†vast, *v.* *Obs.*⁻¹ [ad. L. *vast-āre.*] *trans.* To lay waste, destroy.

1434 MISYN *Mending Life* 119 For þe..fleschly sawle in-to behaldyng of þe godhede is not rauischyd bot if it be gostely, all fleschly lettyngis vastyd.

ˈvast, vast, aphetic ff. AVAST.

1841 R. H. DANA *Seaman's Man.* 133 *Avast*, or *'Vast*, an order to stop. **1894** *Outing* XXIV. 72/2 'Vast!' yells the coxswain, as the pier of the railroad bridge flies by.

†ˈvastacy. *Obs.*⁻¹ [f. VAST *a.*] Vastness.

1607 *Tiberius Claudius Nero* M 2, What Lidian desart, Indian vastacie? What wildernesse in wilde Arabia, So hatefull monster euer nourished?

†ˈvastate, *ppl. a.* *Obs.*⁻¹ [ad. L. *vastāt-us*, pa. pple. of *vastāre.*] Laid waste; devastated.

1629 T. ADAMS *Serm., Taming of Tongue* Wks. 152 The vastate ruines of ancient monuments.

ˈvastate, *v.* *rare.* [Cf. prec. and VASTATION 3.] *trans.* To render unsusceptible.

1892 *Harper's Mag.* LXXXIV. 608/1 That long passion of his early youth, which seemed to have vastated him before he came there. He was rather proud of his vastation.

vastation (væˈsteɪʃən). Also 6 **vastacion.** [ad. L. *vastātiōn-*, *vastātio*, n. of action f. *vastāre*, f. *vastus* waste. So It. *vastazione*, Pg. *vastação.*]

†1. The action of laying waste, devastating, or destroying. Also freq., an instance of this. *Obs.* (very common 1610–60).

1545 JOYE *Exp. Dan.* vii. 120 b, Howe greate vastacions and destruccions in the chirche are there prophecied! **1614** RALEIGH *Hist. World* IV. i. §1 The Greekes..doe still, as in former times, continue the inuasion and vastation of each other. *a* **1639** SPOTTISWOOD *Hist. Ch. Scot.* III. (1677) 175 Thereupon insued a pitiful vastation of Churches and Church-buildings. **1663** J. SPENCER *Prodigies* (1665) 383 No war, no sedition,..no vastation,..made so great a waste upon the religion..of that place.

†**2.** The fact or condition of being devastated or laid waste. *Obs.*

1578 BANISTER *Hist. Man* v. 64 The whole masse of man ..must needes haue runne in perpetuall ruine, and vastation. **1617** COLLINS *Def. Bp. Ely* II. x. 458 We lament their desolation and vastation. **1639** FULLER *Holy War* III. xxiv. (1840) 162 The sad spectacle of their country's vastation would disturb their minds. **1653** GAUDEN *Hierasp.* To Rdr. 24 It may be through the Lords mercy, this winters floud shall be for their mendment or fertility, and not for their utter vastation and ruine.

3. The action of purifying by the destruction of evil qualities or elements. Also *transf.*

1847 EMERSON *Repr. Men, Swedenborg* Wks. (Bohn) I. 328 He was let down through a column that seemed of brass,.. that he might descend safely among the unhappy, and witness the vastation of souls. **1888** J. ELLIS *New Christianity* xii. 290 Spirits preparing for heaven, or undergoing vastation. **1892** [see VASTATE *v.*].

†**vastative**, *a.* *Obs.*$^{-1}$ [f. L. *vast-āre*: see -ATIVE.] Devastating.

1667 WATERHOUSE *Fire London* 34 Circumstances, benign to, and corresponding with a vastative event.

†**vastator.** *Obs.*$^{-1}$ [a. L. *vastātor*, agent-n. f. *vastāre*.] Devastator.

1659 GAUDEN *Tears Ch.* 86 The cunning Adversaries and Vastators of the Church of England drive a lesser trade.

vaste, southern ME. var. FAST *a.*, *adv.*, and *v.*; obs. Sc. f. WASTE *sb.* and *v.*

vastell, obs. var. WASTEL.

vastering (obs. Sc.): see WASTERING.

va'stidity. *rare.* [Irreg. var. VASTITY.] Vastness, vastitude.

1603 SHAKS. *Meas. for M.* III. i. 68 A restraint, Though all the worlds vastiditie you had To a determin'd scope. [**1812** W. TENNANT *Anster F.* II. xvii, Their heads with curl'd vastidity of wig.] **1929** R. BRIDGES *Testament of Beauty* IV. 190 The spiritual idea of Friendship, the huge vastidity of its essence. **1931** C. WILLIAMS *Many Dimensions* xvii. 260 In the foreground of that vastidity, he saw rising the Types of the Stone. **1962** W. NOWOTTNY *Lang. Poets Use* iv. 83 The sense of vastidity of meaning in the sonnet derives from these many transformations of old into new.

'vastily, *adv.* [f. VASTY *a.*] In a vast manner.

1844 MRS. BROWNING *Drama of Exile* 972 A few Distinguishable phantasms vague and grand Which sweep out and around us vastily.

vastitude ('vɑːstɪtjuːd, 'væs-). [ad. L. *vastitūdo*, f. *vastus* VAST *a.*]

†**1.** Devastation; laying waste. *Obs.*$^{-1}$

1545 JOYE *Exp. Dan.* ix. 162 And aftir the bataill their shalbe an vtter perpetuall vastitude and destruccion of them.

2. The quality of being vast; immensity.

1623 COCKERAM I, *Vastitude*, greatness, exceeding largenesse. **1790** H. BOYD *Ruins Athens* in *Poet. Reg.* (1806-7) 75 The woodland orator,.. Mute and benumb'd, a theatre surveys Whose vastitude appalls him. **1825** T. HOOK *Sayings* Ser. II. *Passion & Princ.* i, The vastitude of the multifarious objects by which she..is environed. **1844** MRS. BROWNING *Crowned & Buried* vii, The torrid vastitude Of India felt..That name.

b. Of immaterial things.

1805 FOSTER *Ess.* I. iv, You adopted a certain vastitude of phrase, mistaking extravagance of expression for greatness of thought. **1833** *New Monthly Mag.* XXXIX. 181 The Abbey performances gave this country a character no other has ever yet achieved for vastitude, precision, and excellence in the grander demonstrations of music. **1884** *Congregational Year Bk.* 55 They could not see..the measure or the issues of their mission—or, perhaps, its very vastitude had paralysed their energies.

c. Unusual largeness.

1876 BROWNING *Shop* 12 He who owns the wealth Which blocks the window's vastitude. **1886** DOWDEN *Shelley* II. 210 If the vastitude of Mr. Gisborne's nose was, as Shelley says, Slawkenbergian.

3. A vast extent or space.

1841 HOR. SMITH *Moneyed Man* I. vi. 163 Sending up.. spires, domes, and cupolas from a superincumbent vastitude of smoke. **1854** S. NEIL *Elem. Rhet.* 71 Onward through the immense vastitudes which the Almighty hand has sprinkled with suns and world-systems. **1883** *Liverpool Courier* 25 Sept. 4/5 The enormous astral vastitudes were seen to be broken by the domain of another tenant.

vastity ('vɑːstɪtɪ, 'væs-). Now *rare.* Also 7 **vaustity.** [ad. L. *vastitās* or F. *vastité* (= It. *vastità*, Sp. *vastedad*): see VAST *a.* and -ITY.]

†**1.** The fact or quality of being desolate, waste, void, or empty. *Obs.*

1545 JOYE *Exp. Dan.* ix. 162 b, Aftir the batails were done there remayned a perpetuall vastite & desolacion. **1586** FERNE *Blaz. Gentrie* 49 Hauing warre and discorde as the causes of destruction, vastity and penurye. **1592** NASHE *P. Penilesse* Wks. (Grosart) II. 25 Finding nothing but emptines and vastitie. **1618** J. TAYLOR (Water P.) *Penniless Pilgr.* Wks. (1630) 130/2 Hee therefore did replenish the vaustity of my empty purse. **1622** PEACHAM *Compl. Gent.* 69 Earthquakes..upon the face of the Earth, raising of it in one place, leaving Gulfes and Vastitie in another. **1651** *Raleigh's Ghost* 174 The army of the Gentiles causing desolation, and vastity, shall..destroy the City.

2. The quality of being vast or immense; vastness, vastitude.

1603 FLORIO *Montaigne* II. xii. 345 In considering the clowdy vastitie and gloomie canapies of our churches. **1635** HEYWOOD *Hierarchy* I. 4 Th' unbounded Sea and Vastitie of shore, All these expresse a Godhead to adore. **1657** TOMLINSON *Renou's Disp.* 403* The Dead Sea because of its vastity..remains immovable.

transf. **1654** COKAINE *Dianea* III. 255 This [Kingdom] of Cyprus is sufficient to satiate the vastitie of these thoughts. **1859** ADOLPH *Simplicity Creation* p. xi, The fifth had read a great part of my work, admired the vastity of physical knowledge embodied therein.

3. A vast or immense space. *rare*$^{-1}$.

1652 NEEDHAM tr. *Selden's Mare Cl.* 17 Witness the manie sandie parts of Africa and the immense vastities of the new world.

vastland, obs. Sc. form of WESTLAND.

vastly ('vɑːstlɪ, 'væs-), *adv.* [f. VAST *a.* + -LY[2].]

1. In a waste or desolate manner. *rare*$^{-1}$.

1593 SHAKS. *Lucr.* 1740 Who, like a late-sackd island, vastly stood Bare and unpeopled in this fearful flood.

2. Immensely; to an extent or degree not readily grasped or estimated.

1664 POWER *Exp. Philos.* Pref. 17 Though these hopes be vastly hyperbolical. **1676** ETHEREDGE *Man of Mode* I. i, Why, first she's an Heiress vastly rich. **1708** J. CHAMBERLAYNE *St. Gt. Brit.* (1710) 7 It hath many safe and commodious Ports and Havens, as Falmouth vastly spacious. **1732** BERKELEY *Alciphr.* III. §5 This vastly great, or infinite power and wisdom. **1862** *Cornhill Mag.* Jan. 73 Popular power has increased vastly during the last half-century in our own country. **1885** *Manch. Exam.* 4 April 4/6 A policy which will add so vastly to its influence and power.

b. Freq. with words or phrases denoting comparison.

1665 GLANVILL *Def. Van. Dogm.* 25 When the Actions whereby they are produced are so vastly diverse. **1693** *Apol. Clergy Scot.* 35 In a sense vastly different from what was intended by Mr. Rule. **1710** J. CLARKE tr. *Rohault's Nat. Philos.* (1729) I. I. ii. 53 The Bullet will be carried vastly further than the small Shot. **1778** SHERIDAN *Camp* II. iii, To be sure, a circus or a crescent would have been vastly better. **1820** HAZLITT *Table-T.* Ser. II. xvi. (1869) 322 You have got on vastly beyond the point at which you have set out. **1846** GREENER *Sci. Gunnery* 229 It is of trifling consequence.. that the explosion of sporting powder is vastly more rapid and powerful. **1879** TOURGEE *Fool's Err.* xxii. 134 The Union people here are vastly in a minority.

3. In weakened sense as a mere intensive: Exceedingly, extremely, very. (Cf. VAST *a.* 5.)

Common in fashionable use in the 18th cent., chiefly with adjs. (*a*), but occasionally with vbs. (*b*) or advs. (*c*). The abuse of *vast* and *vastly* is commented on by Lord Chesterfield, *Lett.* No. 195 and 196.

(*a*) **1664** *Verney Mem.* (1907) II. 204 She putts on and assumes much, very much of the vastly extravagant humors. **1722** DE FOE *Plague* (1754) 219 The City..was vastly full of People. **1733** T. BURNET *MS. Let.* 30 Jan., Believe me most affectionately, though vastly peevish, Yours T. B. **1782** MISS BURNEY *Cecilia* VI. xi, This is all vastly true; but I have no time to hear any more of it just now. **1826** J. FOSTER in *Life & Corr.* (1846) II. 78 A vastly acute and doggedly intellectual fellow. **1850** THACKERAY *Pendennis* xxii, Mrs. Portman..was vastly bitter against Pen..since his impertinent behaviour to the Doctor. **1872** BLACK *Adv. Phaeton* vi. 68 That small person..was becoming vastly indignant.

(*b*) **1750** H. WALPOLE *Lett.* (1846) II. 358, I laughed vastly. **1766** GOLDSM. *Vicar* xii, I protest I like my Lady Blarney vastly. *c* **1850** *Arab. Nts.* (Rtldg.) 234, I should vastly like to examine this little hunchback a little more closely. **1879** MRS. MACQUOID *Berksh. Lady* 182 That will please me vastly.

(*c*) **1756** MRS. CALDERWOOD in *Coltness Collect.* (Maitland Club) 127 He..sung vastly fine. **1799** SHERIDAN *Pizarro* Prol., An't you come vastly late? **1814** JANE AUSTEN *Lady Susan* xv, She talks vastly well. **1837** LYTTON *E. Maltravers* 5 As for bed, this chair will do vastly well.

vastness ('vɑːstnɛs, 'væs-). [f. VAST *a.*]

†**1.** Desolation; waste. *Obs. rare.*

1605 BACON *Adv. Learn.* II. vii. §7 Because their excursions into the limits of physical causes hath bred a vastness and solitude in that tract. **1642** SIR E. DERING *Sp. on Relig.* 87 This Bill doth seem to me an uncouth wildernesse, a dismall vastnesse.

2. The quality of being vast; immensity.

1607 BEAUM. & FL. *Woman Hater* III. iii, Could the Sea throw up his vastness, And offer free his best inhabitants. **1667** MILTON *P.L.* VII. 472 Scarse from his mould Behemoth biggest born of Earth upheav'd His vastness. **1698** FRYER *Acc. E. India & P.* 12 The swelling Surges menace the lowering Skies, leaving a Hollow where they borrowed their Gigantine Vastness. **1794** MRS. RADCLIFFE *Myst. Udolpho* vi, Emily gazed with enthusiasm on the vastness of the sea. **1838** DE MORGAN *Ess. Probab.* 24 When we speak of the vastness, the regularity, and the permanency of the solar system. **1886** RUSKIN *Præterita* I. vi. 199 The vastness of scale in the Milanese palaces..impressed me.. at once.

fig. **1601** B. JONSON *Poetaster* v. iii, The open vastnesse of a tyrannes eare. **1873** HELPS *Anim. & Mast.* i. 8 You will be able to appreciate the vastness of this area of cruelty.

b. Of immaterial things.

1622 FLETCHER *Prophetess* II. i, You have blown his swoln pride to that vastness, As he believes the Earth is in his fathom. **1658** *Verney Mem.* (1907) II. 77 The vastnesse of my affection. **1850** TENNYSON *In Mem.* xcvii, I look'd on these and thought of thee In vastness and in mystery. **1889** RUSKIN *Præterita* III. 146 The vastness of Scott's true historical knowledge.

3. A vast or immense space.

1674 N. FAIRFAX *Bulk & Selv.* 61 The excellent Dr. Hen. More, whose soul may have roamed as far into these scopes and vastnesses as most mens in the world. **1855** LONGF. *Hiaw.* xii. 137 Then a voice was heard..Coming from the empty vastness. **1875** —— *Masque Pandora* vi, Thunder and tempest of wind Their trumpets blow in the vastness.

‖**vastrap** ('fastrap). Also †**vast-trap.** [Afrikaans, f. *vas* firm(ly), (Du. *vast*) + *trap* step, stand.] A quick South African folk dance; the music for this dance.

1913 *East London* (S. Afr.) *Dispatch* 3 Jan. 5 The *vast-trap* was performed by a number of nondescript characters who provided much amusement by their antics. **1926** O. SCHREINER *From Man to Man* 360 Then she paused and began a reel. 'This is the "vastrap",' she said... 'It's what the Hottentots dance.' **1944** M. DE B. NESBITT *Road to Avalon* xiv. 114 The band is playing a lively 'vastrap'. **1957** *Cape Times* 17 Jan. 7/1 Rock and roll has affiliations with our own vastraps and tiekiedraais to which Coloured bands used to thrum the beat. **1970** L. G. GREEN *Giant in Hiding* xi. 105 You remember the candle light, the *vastrap* music.

†**'vasture.** *Obs.*$^{-1}$ [f. VAST *a.*] = VASTNESS 3.

1596 *Edw. III*, II. i. 402 What can one drop of poyson harme the Sea, Whose hugie vastures can digest the ill And make it loose his operation?

vasty ('vɑːstɪ, 'væs-), *a.* [f. VAST *a.* + -Y.] Vast, immense. (In mod. use after Shakspere.)

1596 SHAKS. *1 Hen. IV*, III. i. 52, I can call Spirits from the vastie Deepe. **1599** —— *Hen. V*, II. iv. 105 The poore Soules, for whom this hungry Warre Opens his vastie Iawes. **1605** *Play of Stucley* K iij b, Which makes me..sorrow that thy valour should be sunke In such a vasty vnknowne sea of Armes. **1610** HOLLAND *Camden's Brit.* I. 330, I saw in a white-sandy ground divers vastie, craggie stones of strange formes.

1792 R. CUMBERLAND *Calvary* 182 Noah can tell How all the earth with violence was fill'd, Or e'er the fountains of the vasty deep Were broken up. **1845** FORD *Handbk. Sp.* I. 77 The feudal castle, the vasty Escorial, the rock-built alcazar. **1867** E. F. BULL *Ecce Coelum* i. 10 Not a whisper, not a rustle, through all the vasty dome.

fig. **1848** BAILEY *Festus* (ed. 3) 63 Yon pretty little star Shines on a vasty falsehood. **1885** PATER *Marius* II. 48 Those vasty conceptions of the later Greek philosophy.

†**'vasy**, *a.* *Obs.* Also **veasy.** [app. f. F. *vase* slime.] Slimy.

1742 *Lond. & Country Brew.* I. (ed. 4) 75 In the Marshes of Kent and Essex, the Air..is generally so infectious, by Means of those low, veasy, boggy Grounds. **1743** *Ibid.* II. (ed. 2) 143 Who sees our vasy, muddy Sediments..often increased by the Foulnesses of new Supplies, and subsided at the Bottom?

vat (væt), *sb.*[1] Forms: 3 ueat, 3-4 uet, 5- **vat**, 4, 6 vatte, 8 vatt; 4-5 vaat, 4, 6-8 vate, 6 vaette. [Southern variant of FAT *sb.*[1] The long vowel in the obs. forms *vaat*, *vate*, is derived from the OE. pl. (*fatu*, etc.) or from late forms of the gen. and dat. sing. (*fates*, *fate*).]

1. a. A cask, tun, or other vessel used for holding or storing water, beer, or other liquid; usually one of some size in which a liquor, esp. beer or cider, undergoes fermentation or is prepared; †a vessel.

a **1225** *Juliana* 31 Þe worldes wealdent þat wiste sein iuhan his ewangeliste unhurt iþe ueat of wallinde eoli. **1340** *Ayenb.* 231 Hi bereþ a wel precious tresor ine a wel fyebble uet. *c* **1380** *Sir Ferumb.* 5695 An Archebysschop..bad hym ordeyne an huge vaat, Ful of water clere. **1399** *Acc. Exch. K.R.* 473/11 m. 2 Pro xxiiij circulis ligneis emptis ad diuers[os] vattes et cowelys inde ligandis pro aqua in eisdem conseruanda. **14..** *Voc.* in Wr.-Wülcker 577 *Cuva*, a cuve or a vaat. *c* **1440** *Pallad. on Husb.* I. 465 Canels or pipis, wynes forth to lede Into the vat & tonnys, make also. **1552** HULOET, Vat, or fat, a vessell for water, ale, bere, or any licour, *labrum.* **1605** SYLVESTER *Du Bartas* II. iii. *Captaines* 745 Each grape to weep, and crimsin streams to spin Into the Vate, set to receive them in. **1662** CHARLETON *Myst. Vintners* (1675) 194 A clean and strongly-scented Cask or Vate. **1697** PRIOR *Ep. Sir F. Sheppard* 41 My Uncle..Might have..Taught me with Cyder to replenish My Vats or ebbing Tide of Rhenish. **1708** J. PHILIPS *Cyder* I. 18 Would'st thou, thy Vats with gen'rous Juice should froth? Respect thy Orchats. **1781** JOHNSON in *Boswell* 5 Apr., We are not here to sell a parcel of boilers and vats. **1830** M. DONOVAN *Dom. Econ.* I. 169 This fermenting tun is an immense circular vat or tub bound with strong iron hoops, and covered in at all parts. **1872** YEATS *Techn. Hist. Comm.* 237 For the large circular vats in which the ale was formerly fermented, slate tuns have been recently substituted.

Comb. **1611** COTGR., *Cuvelier*, a vat-maker, or tub-maker.

b. A vessel, cauldron, or cistern containing the liquid used in dyeing or some other process.

1548 ELYOT, *Ahenum*, a great vatte, wherein purple is dyed. **1632** SHERWOOD s.v., A dying Vat, *cuvier.* **1738** CHAMBERS *Cycl.* s.v. *Dying Ingredients*, Dying materials.. applied..by only dipping the stuff in the vat of dye. **1788** *Trans. Soc. Arts* VI. 165 (Papermaking), Having prepared the stuff, chest and vatt, quite clean, I chopt the clean bark or first preparation [etc.]. **1791** W. HAMILTON *Berthollet's Dyeing* I. Introd. p. ii, The Stuffs..were immersed in vats, where they received various colours. **1825** J. NICHOLSON *Operat. Mechanic* 366 The large vat or cistern [of a paper-mill], A A, is of an oblong figure on the outside. **1832** *Porcelain & Glass* 38 When the flints are thus sufficiently ground, the semi-fluid is transferred to another vat. **1873** HAMERTON *Intell. Life* XII. i. 432 Every locality is like a dyer's vat, the residents take its colour.

†**c.** = FAT *sb.*[1] 1 b. *Obs. rare.*

1507 *Pilton Churchw. Acc.* (Som. Rec. Soc.) 53 Item an oyle vatte of sylver.

†**d.** A cask or tub used as a receptacle for refuse or filth. *Obs.*

1534-5 *MS. Rawl. D.* 77 fol. 67 b, The vaettes that convayeth the Rubbysch frome the great Kechyn. **1536** *Ibid.*, Skoryng and makyng clean the Vattes of the Comen Jakes..with other vattes with in the said castell.

2. In various special uses: **a.** = CHEESE-VAT.

1669 WORLIDGE *Syst. Agric.* (1681) 334 *Vallor*, or *Vallow*, or *Vate*, a concave Mould wherein a Cheese is pressed. **1860** *All Year Round* No. 51. 19 The next step taken was to get a proper 'vat' and 'follower' made of solid mahogany.

b. *Tanning.* = TAN-VAT.

1777 *Phil. Trans.* LXVIII. 115 Until they think proper to lay it away in the Vatts. In these holes, which are the largest in the tan-yard, the leather is spread out smooth. **1875** KNIGHT *Dict. Mech.* III. 2490/1 The tan-yard contains a number of wooden-lined vats, whose tops are level with the..ground. **1885** *Harper's Mag.* Jan. 276/1 The hides are placed..in vats filled with a dissolved excrement.

c. *Cornwall.* (See quot.)

1778 PRYCE *Min. Cornub.* 225 Upon the top of the arch or back of the calciner, is made a square hollow place called a Vate or Dry, sufficient to contain a serving or hand barrow full of Tin.

d. *Mining.* (See quots.)

1802 J. MAWE *Min. Derby* Gloss., *Vat*, a wooden tub used to wash ore and mineral substances. **1872** RAYMOND *Statist. Mines & Mining* 253 Outside of the building the pulp runs first into vats, where the heavier portion settles and the rest goes into the creek. **1888** F. HUME *Mme. Midas* I. v, The wash was carried along in the trucks from the top of the shaft to the puddlers, which were large circular vats into which water was constantly gushing.

e. *Saltmaking.* A salt-pit (see quots.).

1860 MAURY *Phys. Geog.* (Low) ii. 22 There is a series of vats or pools through which the water is passed as it comes from the sea, and is reduced to the briny state. **1861** J. H. BENNET *Shores Medit.* (1875) I. v. 143 The vats or pools into which the sea-water is received for evaporation.

3. a. A cask, barrel, or other vessel for holding or storing dry goods; = FAT *sb.*[1] 3.

1766 ENTICK *London* IV. 328 Their business being to attend each ship, to top the vats, and to return an account of the coals measured. **1825** HONE *Every-day Bk.* I. 741 The arrival of a vat of Hambro' yarn. *Ibid.*, The inhabitants met the waggon,..decorated the vat with ribands,..and drew the same through the village. **1859** F. A. GRIFFITHS *Artill. Man.* (1862) 159 The horses are to be taken out; the harness ..packed in vats.

†**b.** Formerly used as a measure of capacity for coal (see quots. and FAT *sb.*[1] 4). *Obs.*

1708 *Constit. Watermen's Co.* xlii, It is agreed and order'd, that all Lightermen selling Coals, shall sell Pool-measure,.. That is to say, One and Twenty Chaldron to the Score, or otherwise to sell the same Measure each person buys, (provided the Parcel be Five Chaldron and a Vatt at the least). **1763** *Ann. Reg.* 64 Importation of coals into the port of London in the year 1762, amounting to 570,774 chaldrons and one vat. **1821** *Acc. Peculations Coal Trade* 5 The measure used in the pool is by vat; this contains nine bushels heaped.

†**c.** (See quot.) *Obs.*

1730 BAILEY (fol.), *Fat*, *Vat*, (of Merchandise) an uncertain quantity, as of yarn, from 210 to 211 bundles; of wire, from 20 to 25 pound weight, &c.

4. *Dyeing.* The liquid solution in which the material to be dyed is immersed; the dyeing liquor. Usually with defining term.

1755 *Dict. Arts & Sci.* II. 998/2 Lime is much used in working blue-vats. *Ibid.* 1000/2 The blue vats in deep blues of the fifth stall, give no considerable weight. **1765** [*indigo vat*: see INDIGO C. 1]. **1839** URE *Dict. Arts* 415 In this vat, the immediate principles..perform the dis-oxidizing function of the copperas in the cold vat. *Ibid.*, The pastel vats require most skill..in consequence of their complexity. **1868** WATTS *Dict. Chem.* III. 251 Copperas or common blue vat. *Ibid.* 252 An excess of lime yields a sharp vat;..too little lime yields a soft vat. **1900** *Jrnl. Soc. Dyers* XVI. 8 A vat prepared with caustic soda.

5. *attrib.*, as ***vat-room***; **vat colour** = *vat dye*; **vat dye, dyestuff**, a water-insoluble dye that is applied in a reducing bath that converts it to a soluble leuco-form with affinity for the fibre, the colour being obtained upon subsequent oxidation; so **vat-dyed** *a.*; **vat dyeing** *vbl. sb.*; **vat-man**, *Papermaking*, a workman who lifts the pulp from the vat and moulds the sheets of paper; a dipper or maker; **vat-net** (see quot.); **vat-press**, *Papermaking*, a press in which the sheets are placed after they leave the vat.

1912 L. A. OLNEY in A. Rogers *Industr. Chem.* xxxviii. 768 The reduction *vat colors have come into great prominence during recent years owing to their great resistance to practically all of the color destroying agencies. **1947** KIRK & OTHMER *Encycl. Chem. Technol.* I. 968 With respect to all-around tinctorial and fastness properties, vat colors have no peer in any class of dyes. **1903** C. SALTER tr. *G. von Georgievics's Chem. Dye-Stuffs* 4 *Vat Dyes..have no affinity for textile fibres, and can only be fixed thereon by reduction or subsequent oxidation. **1981** H. GUTJAHR in L. W. C. Miles *Textile Printing* v. 159 Vat dyes provide a wide range of colours of good all-round fastness properties, but great care, or specialized equipment, is required for their successful use. **1946** M. R. FOX *Vat Dyestuffs & Vat Dyeing* iv. 55 (*heading*) Fastness tests for *vat-dyed wool and silk. **1960** *Farmer & Stockbreeder* 22 Mar. (Suppl.) 11/2 These vat-dyed, colour-fast, 48in wide cotton furnishing materials, are identically patterned on both sides. **1912** L. A. OLNEY in A. Rogers *Industr. Chem.* xxxviii. 756 The alkaline bath of indigo white is commonly called an indigo vat, and this process of coloring is usually spoken of as *vat dyeing. **1946** M. R. FOX (*title*) Vat dyestuffs and vat dyeing. **1914** F. W. ATACK tr. *Wahl's Manuf. Organic Dyestuffs* xix. 220 For a long time the *vat-dyestuffs were limited to Indigo, its derivatives, and the Indophenols. **1973** *Materials & Technol.* VI. vii. 488 Nylon shows very little affinity for the vat dyestuffs. **1839** URE *Dict. Arts* 927 Meanwhile the *vat-man puts the deckel upon the other mould. **1885** *Encycl. Brit.* XVIII. 225/1 The vatman takes up enough pulp on the mould to fill the deckle. **1884** KNIGHT *Dict. Mech.* Suppl. 921/1 **Vat net*, used as a strainer over a tub or tank. **1839** URE *Dict. Arts* 931, 1 Man..in keeping in order 7 vats, *vat-presses, &c. **1840** *Penny Cycl.* XVII. 209/1 This post..is placed in the vat-press, and subjected to a strong pressure to force out the superfluous water. **1843** TIZARD *Brewing* xix. 464 Where the trade is extensive, and *vat-room is of consequent importance.

Hence **ˈvatful**.

1632 SHERWOOD, A vat-full, *cuvée*. **1862** *Sat. Rev.* XIII. 411/1 By the sudden interposition of a vat-full of pale ale details.

VAT, vat (viːeɪˈtiː, væt), *sb.*[2] Abbrev. of *value added tax* s.v. VALUE *sb.* 2 d. Cf. *TVA* s.v. T 6 a.

1966 *Economist* 29 Oct. 432/2 This may be true of the conventional VAT. **1971** *Guardian* 29 Sept. 5/3 The substitution of VAT (value added tax) for purchase tax and SET in June 1973. **1978** *Hi-Fi News* Sept. 204 (Advt.), All prices include vat at 12½%.

Hence **ˈVATable**, **ˈvat-** *a. colloq.*, liable to VAT; **ˈVATman** *colloq.*, a Customs and Excise officer who deals with VAT.

1973 *Times* 31 Oct. 14/8 A glance at how Alice is faring will show how plays themselves are affected. At present she and her like are VAT-able and non VAT-able according to circumstances. **1976** *Daily Tel.* 4 Nov. 21 The last [*sc.* higher indirect taxes] would put up the cost of living but, to a large extent, the extra cost of vatable items..is voluntary. **1977** T. HEALD *Just Desserts* ii. 30 Those absolute fiends from the Inland Revenue or..the dreaded VATmen. **1979** *Accountancy Age* 16 Feb. 7/1 (*heading*) Convincing fanciful VATmen you don't have the goods. **1984** *Listener* 11 Oct. 42/1 The income-tax inspector knows as little about it as the VAT-man.

vat (væt), *v.* [f. VAT *sb.*[1]] *trans.* **a.** To place or store in a vat.

1784 TWAMLEY *Dairying Exemplified* 48 Many people as soon as the Whey is removed immediately break the Curd small..and then put it into the Cheese Vat... I would always recommend that it rest one quarter of an Hour, before 'tis broke or vatted. **1862** *Chambers's Encycl.* IV. 727/1 The factitious compound being mixed or vatted with the wines in bond. **1880** *Act 43 & 44 Vict.* c. 24 §64 (1) The proprietor of spirits..may..vat, blend, or rack them in the warehouse.

b. To immerse in a dyeing solution or vat.

1883 R. HALDANE *Workshop Receipts* Ser. II. 210/2 The goods are next limed, vatted to shade, taken out.

vat, southern ME. and dial. var. FAT *a.*; obs. Sc. f. *wot* WIT *v.*

vatch, southern dial. var. FETCH *v.*; obs. Sc. f. WATCH.

vate, obs. Sc. f. WAIT *v.*

vater(e, obs. Sc. ff. WATER.

vaterite (ˈvɑːtəraɪt, ˈfɑː-). *Min.* [ad. G. *vaterit* (W. Meigen 1911, in *Verhandl. d. Ges. deutsch. Naturforscher und Ärzte* LXXXII. II. I. 124), f. the name of H. A. *Vater* (1859–1930), German mineralogist and geologist: see -ITE[1].] A relatively rare, metastable form of calcium carbonate, $CaCO_3$, that is polymorphous with calcite and aragonite and crystallizes in the hexagonal system.

1913 *Mineral. Mag.* XVI. 374 Vaterite... Vater's third modification of calcium carbonate prepared artificially in the form of minute spherules. **1962** *Acta Chirurg. Scand.* CXXIV. 324/1 X-ray crystallographic studies have shown that the three crystalline forms of calcium carbonate, namely vaterite, aragonite and calcite, can all occur in concretions from the pancreas, biliary- and urinary tract. **1975** *Science* 25 Apr. 363 The spicules of the common tropical ascidian, *Herdmania momus*, are mineralized with vaterite.

‖**Vaterland** (ˈfɑːtərlant). [Ger., = fatherland.] A German's fatherland.

1852 C. LEVER *Daltons* I. xxii. 184 Hansel was the kind, quaint emblem of his own dreamy 'Vaterland'. **1894** G. DU MAURIER *Trilby* I. II. 111 The buttercups and daisies of the Vaterland! **1950** *New Yorker* 26 Aug. 70/2 Germans whose every act and thought was directed..toward the enhancement of the *Vaterland*. **1977** N. FREELING *Gadget* IV. 151 A stone slab had carved upon it the..names of the village boys dead for the Vaterland in '14–'18.

‖**vates** (ˈveɪtiːz). [L. *vātēs*.]

1. A poet or bard, esp. one who is divinely inspired; a prophet-poet.

1625 PURCHAS *Pilgrims* II. IX. 1572 The people interjecting their applauses, clapping hands and running in to gratifie their Vates (Poet or Prophet) with a Present. **1687** *Acc. Author's Life* in Cleveland *Wks.* Ded. A 7, And here again he was Vates in the whole Import of the Word, both Poet and Prophet. **1855** LEWES *Goethe* I. 251 The high and priestly office which he gave the poet, as a real Vates. **1878** G. SMITH *Life John Wilson* xvii. 547 Each was the Vates of his countrymen.

2. *pl.* One of the classes of the old Gaulish druids. Cf. OVATE *sb.*

1728 CHAMBERS *Cycl.* s.v. *Druids*, The *Bardi* were the Poets; the *Vates*..were the Sacrificers, and Naturalists. **1775** L. SHAW *Hist. Moray* VI. §1. 227 Druid was the general name of the Sect or Order; and their Literati were divided into Priests, Vates, and Bards, who were their Divines. **1882–3** *Schaff's Encycl. Relig. Knowl.* I. 668 According to function they were divided into classes—bards, vates, and druids proper.

vath, dial. var. FAITH *int.*

vath(e, Sc. varr. WOTHE *sb.* (danger).

vathym, southern ME. variant of FATHOM *sb.*

vatic (ˈvætɪk), *a.* Also 7 vatick. [f. L. *vāt-ēs* a prophet, poet + -IC.] Of or pertaining to, characteristic of, a prophet or seer; prophetic, inspired.

1603 BP. HALL *King's Prophecy* xvii, My puis-nè Muse presumed to recite The vatick lines of that Cumæan Dame. **1844** MRS. BROWNING *Vis. Poets* clxxviii, If every vatic word that sweeps To change the world must pale their lips. **1868** *Good Words* 1 Jan. 53 To the sound of their vatic exordiums did Roland Laporte and Jean Cavallier march from their fastnesses. **1871** H. B. FORMAN *Our Living Poets* 291 The thought..betrays enough of the vatic exaltation of the seer.

†**ˈvatical**, *a. Obs. rare.* [f. as prec. + -AL[1].] Vatic. Hence **ˈvatically** *adv.*

1594 *Zepheria* xvi, My brow..Which whilome thou with lawrell vaticall Enobled hast, (high signall of renowne). **1634** BP. HALL *Contempl.*, *N.T.* IV. xxv. 238 Neither couldst thou have made up those vaticall predictions, without this conveyance. **1641** *Brightman's Predictions* 3 Now as Mr. Brightman vatically observeth, the Church of Thyatira [etc.].

Vatican (ˈvætɪkən). Also 6–7 Vaticane. [a. F. *Vatican* (= It., Sp., Pg. *Vaticano*), or ad. L. *Vāticān-us* (sc. *collis*, *mons*): see def.]

1. a. (Now always with *the*.) The palace of the Pope built upon the Vatican Hill in Rome.

Also, in recent use, the papal authorities or the system which they represent; the papal power; the Papacy.

1555 EDEN *Decades* (Arb.) 100 As wee are accustomed to goo on Pylgramege to Rome or Vaticane. **1607** B. BARNES *Divils Charter* II. i. E 1, Heere leaue we Charles with pompous ceremonies, Feasting within the Vaticane at Rome. **1611** BIBLE *Transl. Pref.* ¶ 3 The Latine edition.. printed in the Printing-house of Vatican. *a* **1700** EVELYN *Diary* 18 Jan. 1645, I went to see the Pope's Palace, the Vatican, where he for the most part keeps his Court. **1777** R. WATSON *Philip II*, II. (1839) 29 He expressed his dread that ere long the Vatican itself would be in the hands of the enemy. **1779** J. JAY in Sparks *Corr. Amer. Rev.* (1853) II. 284 There is as much intrigue in this State-House as in the Vatican. **1866** GLADSTONE in *Lett. Ch. & Relig.* (1911) II. 395, I repaired to the Vatican in household uniform. **1909** J. M'CABE *Decay Ch. Rome* vi. 128 England is regarded as substantially won for the Vatican.

b. Used with reference to the artistic or literary treasures preserved here; the Vatican galleries or library.

1600 HOLLAND *Livy* App. 1386 The statue of Laocoon.. now at this day..is to be seene at the Vaticane. **1610** BOLTON *Elem. Armories* 54 Such a librarie as..they had rather tosse then to bee Deipnosophists in Athenæus, or glowe-wormes in the Medicæan, or Vatican, the most renowned armaries of bookes in all the world. **1694** J. NORRIS *Curs. Refl. Locke's Hum. Underst.* 43, I..would not part with his Book for half a Vatican. **1756–7** tr. *Keysler's Trav.* (1760) IV. 34 This picture resembles that which is to be seen in the Vatican at Rome. **1796** H. HUNTER tr. *St.-Pierre's Stud. Nat.* (1799) I. 70 The man of the woods..has, certainly, a very imperfect resemblance to the Apollo of the Vatican. **1841** W. SPALDING *Italy & It. Isl.* I. 166 Of these two copies [of a statue] one..is in the Vatican.

fig. **1649** G. DANIEL *Trinarch.*, *Hen. IV*, cclxv, A Well-bought Treasure from his Vatican; Whose Volumes Numberless Nature doth Summe In one Compendious Abstract; Well-bound Man! **1854** THOREAU *Walden* iii. (1886) 102 When the vaticans shall be filled with Vedas and Zendavestas and Bibles. **1868** M. ARNOLD in *Life Ld. Coleridge* (1904) II. vi. 160 Suppose you look in your stately Vatican of a library and see if you have not half a dozen copies.

2. a. *attrib.* or as *adj.* Of or pertaining to the Vatican or its library.

Vatican Council, the council of 1869–70 which proclaimed the infallibility of the Pope; also, the Second Vatican Council (1962–5), also called Vatican II, which is noted for the introduction of the vernacular for the Mass and other reforms.

1638 R. BAKER tr. *Balzac's Lett.* (vol. III) 208 You found not these excellent qualities in the Vatican Library. *a* **1700** EVELYN *Diary* 18 Jan. 1645, By these we descended into the Vatican Gardens. **1705** ADDISON *Italy* 102 The old Vatican Terence has at the Head of every Scene the Figures of all the Persons. **1797** *Encycl. Brit.* (ed. 3) XVII. 150/2 The Vatican manuscript contained originally the whole Greek Bible. **1825** in *Ushaw Mag.* Dec. (1913) 265, I lately got a beautiful edition of the LXX,..printed from the Vatican copy. **1845** GRAVES *Roman Law* in *Encycl. Metrop.* II. 768 The Vatican fragments were taken by Mai from a manuscript of the *Collationes* of Cassianus in the Vatican Library. **1878** *N. Amer. Rev.* CXXVII. 325 The Fathers of the Vatican Council expound the doctrine of the church in these words. **1886** *Encycl. Brit.* XX. 835/2 The Vatican palace also appears to have originated in a house which existed in the time of Constantine. **1961** *Times* 12 Dec. 6/3 On Christmas Day the Pope is to issue his Bull summoning the second Vatican Council. **1963** E. SCHILLEBEECKX in *Life of Spirit* June 504 Is it possible at this stage to surmise what the outcome of Vatican II is going to be? Yes, in principle it is. The majority have expressed themselves in favour of a different approach. **1969** A. RICHARDSON *Dict. Christian Theol.* 354/2 Vatican II..teaches that bishops possess, by virtue of their consecration, 'the fullness of the priesthood', including the threefold role of sanctifying, teaching and governing. **1976** *Jrnl. R. Soc. Arts* Mar. 164/1 The Second Vatican Council may well have an understanding of the Sack of Rome and the Council of Trent which was denied to writers in the earlier part of this century. **1979** D. GAGEBY in J. J. Lee *Ireland 1945–70* 132 John Horgan, now a member of the Dáil, writing about Vatican II and the ecclesiastical changes. **1983** *Times* 16 May 12/6 The Protestant Ethic..is definitely out of fashion, theologically. Today, they all quote Temple, or Vatican II.

b. Special Combs.: **Vatican City** (or **State**), the temporal state established by the Lateran Treaty of 1929, comprising the area immediately surrounding the Vatican Palace in Rome and headed by the Pope; **Vatican roulette** *colloq.*, the rhythm method of birth control, as permitted by the Roman Catholic Church.

1929 *Times* 8 Feb. 14/1 The new Papal State, which is to be known as the 'Vatican State' or as the 'Vatican City', will be confined to a small extent of territory in the neighbourhood of the Vatican. **1974** *Encycl. Brit. Macropædia* XIX. 36/1 The Vatican City is in all ways independent from Italy. **1962** *Western Folklore* Jan. 34 Vatican roulette—the rhythm system of birth control. **1965** D. LODGE *British Museum is falling Down* 172 That's another thing against the safe method there are so many things that can affect ovulation... No wonder they called it Vatican Roulette. **1977** H. G. BURGER in B. Bernardi *Concept & Dynamics of Culture* 458 When Roman Catholicism permitted only the 'rhythm method' of birth control, sometimes satirized for its ineffectiveness as 'Vatican roulette', the Toronto archbishop authorized birth control pills.

Hence **Vati'canal**, **Vati'canic**, **Vati'canical** *adjs.*

1899 *Westm. Gaz.* 27 June 3/3 Several Catholic parishes elected priests who refused to accept the new *Vaticanal dogma. **1898** E. P. EVANS *Evol. Ethics* iv. 160 In the spirit of the *Vaticanic dictum. **1908** *Contemp. Rev.* Mar., Lit. Suppl. 10 He has announced with *Vaticanical authority that [etc.].

Vaticanism ('vætɪkənɪz(ə)m). [f. VATICAN.]

1. The tenet of absolute papal infallibility or supremacy in respect of ecclesiastical doctrine or affairs as declared by the first Vatican Council.

1875 GLADSTONE *Vaticanism* 8 The proceedings of Vaticanism threaten to be a source of some practical inconvenience. **1875** —— *Glean.* (1879) VI. 243 The antichristian action of Vaticanism on the minds and lives of men with a power and sagacity worthy of the best days of Italian thought. **1890** *Spectator* 23 Aug., But in 1870 Manning and Newman seemed to be drifting in opposite directions,—the one towards 'Vaticanism', the other towards restrictions of the Papal initiative.

2. *transf.* (See quot.)

1884 *Dublin Rev.* Jan. 187 'Vaticanism', in the sense in which we here use the term, is a word borrowed from Dr. Scrivener to express the opinion of those who think the Vatican Codex to be the truest and best text of the Greek Testament.

Vaticanist ('vætɪkənɪst), *sb.* and *a.* [f. as prec. + -IST.]

A. *sb.* An adherent or supporter of the Vatican or of Vaticanism.

1846 WORCESTER, *Vaticanist*, an adherent to the Vatican. *Ec. Rev.* **1873** *Guardian* 20 Aug. 1086/1 We are the true Catholics, we are the true members of the Church, and the Vaticanists have made a new sect. **1875** GLADSTONE *Glean.* (1879) VI. 210 The Court of Rome..filled the office with a thorough-paced Vaticanist.

B. *adj.* Of or pertaining to Vaticanism or its adherents.

1892 *Church Times* 11 Mar. 250/4 The adequate maintenance of the Vaticanist claims. **1899** *Westm. Gaz.* 17 Aug. 3/3 The fundamental question between the Vaticanist Cæsar and the English Church.

Vaticanization (,vætɪkənaɪ'zeɪʃən). [Cf. next + -ATION.] The action or fact of bringing under the authority of the Vatican or Papacy.

1873 *Contemp. Rev.* XXIII. 94 The Italianization, or rather the Vaticanization, of Latin Christendom.

'Vaticanize, *v.* [f. VATICAN + -IZE.] *trans.* To subject to the authority of the Vatican; to imbue with Vaticanism. So **'Vaticanized** *ppl. a.*

1890 *For. Ch. Chron.* March 8 Impossible for him to adopt the Vaticanised faith. **1896** BRIGHT *Rom. See in Early Ch.* 212 This bold attempt to Vaticanise antiquity.

Vaticanology (,vætɪkə'nɒlədʒɪ). *colloq.* [f. VATICAN + -OLOGY.] The study of the history, or analysis of the policies, of the Vatican. So **,Vatica'nologist**.

1975 *Guardian Weekly* 14 Dec. 27 His publishers describe him as 'a leading Vaticanologist', and he does appear to know more than most people about the Curia. **1976** *Times Lit. Suppl.* 13 Aug. 1018/4 It is..several generations since Chesterton's sallies delighted the devout, and Vaticanology has few students in non-Catholic countries. **1979** M. CRAIG *Man from Far Country* xv. 173 Father F. X. Murphy, a renowned Vaticanologist. **1982** *Times Lit. Suppl.* 12 Feb. 154/1 It is high time that Vaticanology was recognized as a serious field of historical inquiry. **1984** D. YALLOP *In God's Name* 62 If the 111 cardinals were as perplexed as the Vaticanologists then the Church was in for a long, confusing Conclave.

vaticide[1] ('vætɪsaɪd). [f. L. *vāti-*, stem of *vātēs* prophet + -CIDE 1.] One who kills a prophet. Also *fig.*

1728 POPE *Dunc.* II. 74 Then first (if Poets aught of truth declare) The caitiff Vaticide conceiv'd a prayer. **1746** SMOLLETT *Reproof* 171, I see with joy, the vaticide deplore An hell-denouncing priest and sov'reign whore. **1749** —— *Regicide* Pref. p. vii, My Patience being by this Time quite exhausted, I desired a Gentleman who interested himself in my Concerns, to go and expostulate with the Vaticide [*sc.* the Manager of Drury-lane Theatre].

'vaticide[2]. *rare.* [f. as prec. + -CIDE 2.] The killing of a prophet.

1853 LANDOR *Wks.* (1876) V. 119 Vaticide is no crime in the Statute-book.

vaticinal (və'tɪsɪnəl), *a.* [f. L. *vāticin-us* prophetic + -AL[1].] Of the nature of, characterized by, vaticination or prophecy; prophetic, vatic.

1586 J. HOOKER *Hist. Irel.* in *Holinshed* II. 1 Sylvester Giraldus Cambrensis, his vaticinall historie of the Conquest of Ireland. **1645** USSHER *Body Div.* 14 Which are the Prosaicall books? Such as are for the most part writen in prose, and foretell things to come; whence also more especially they are termed Propheticall, or vaticinall. **1652** GAULE *Magastrom.* 304 Dion..disregarded the vaticinall portent. **1775** WARTON *Hist. Eng. Poetry* (1840) I. 1 Thomas Leirmonth, or Rymer,..has left vaticinal rhymes, in which he predicted the union of Scotland with England. **1807** G. CHALMERS *Caledonia* I. II. vi. 285 He was induced.., contrary to the vaticinal warnings of Columba, to carry a mixed body of various people, into..Ireland. **1844** *Q. Rev.* LXXIV. 230 In the true vaticinal spirit of poetry and prophecy. **1897** *Advance* (Chicago) 30 Sept. 438/2 His..vaticinal conclusions have proved to be..flabby.

†**va'ticinant**, *pres. pple.* and *ppl. a. Obs. rare.* [ad. L. *vāticinant-*, *vāticinans*, pres. pple. of *vāticinārī*: see VATICINATE *v.*] **a.** Prophesying, predicting. **b.** (See quot. 1647.)

1490 CAXTON *Eneydos* vi. 29 There fonde they the preste of Iubyter, wyth his wyf and alle his meyne, vaticynaunte or prophecyeng thynges moche merueyllous. **1647** H. MORE *Song of Soul* Notes 165/1 The soul is said to be in a vaticinant, or parturient condition, when she hath some kind of sense, and hovering knowledge of a thing, but yet cannot distinctly and fully..represent it to herself.

†**vaticinar**. *Sc. Obs.*$^{-1}$ [f. L. *vāticin-*, stem of *vāticinārī* (see next) + -AR[2].] A vaticinator or prophet.

1549 *Compl. Scotl.* x. 82 The inglismen gifis ferme credit to diuerse prophane propheseis of merlyne, and til vthir ald corruppit vaticinaris.

vaticinate (və'tɪsɪneɪt), *v.* [f. L. *vāticināt-*, ppl. stem of *vāticinārī* to forebode, foretell, prophesy, f. *vātēs* VATES.]

1. *intr.* To speak as a prophet or seer; to utter vaticinations or predictions; to foretell events.

1623 COCKERAM I, *Vaticinate*, to prophesie. **1634** SIR T. HERBERT *Trav.* 220 And then goes on vaticinating,..Whiles Cambray's issue serue the Lord their Maker [etc.]. **1652** GAULE *Magastrom.* 187 Is it not by diabolical instinct that they here peremptorily vaticinate or ominate of long life, short life, marriage [etc.]? **1678** CUDWORTH *Intell. Syst.* I. iii. §29. 134 Aristotle (as it were Vaticinating concerning it) somewhere calls [the Spirit of God]..a certain Better and Diviner thing than Reason. **1744** BERKELEY *Siris* §253 All have not alike learned the connexion of natural things, or understand what they signify, or know how to vaticinate by them. **1829** GEN. P. THOMPSON *Exerc.* (1842) I. 82 What if Humphrey has vaticinated? What if he has beaten all prognosticators since Nostradamus? **1835** *Chambers's Jrnl.* Aug. 209 The plan followed by the late Mr. Coleridge in vaticinating upon the events of the last war. **1886** DOWDEN *Shelley* I. vi. 239 From a hundred platforms..gentlemen declaimed, vaticinated, and returned thanks to one another.

transf. **1642** H. MORE *Song of Soul* II. II. iii. 9 Intellection Or higher gets, or at least hath some sent Of God, vaticinates, or is parturient.

2. *trans.* To foretell, predict, prognosticate, or prophesy (a future event).

1652 GAULE *Magastrom.* 259 Chalcas did vaticinate or prognosticate the destruction of Troy. **1658** COKAINE *Obstinate Lady* II. i, He was an intricate Prognosticator of firmamental Eclipses, and vaticinated future Occurents by the mysterious influences of the sublime Stars. **1820** BYRON *Lett. to Murray* 24 April, I vaticinate a row in Italy. **1831** T. L. PEACOCK *Crotchet Castle* (1887) 178, I vaticinate what will be the upshot of all his schemes of reform. **1886** SYMONDS *Renaiss. It., Cath. React.* VII. xiv. 412 To vaticinate a reign of socialistic terror for the immediate future.

transf. **1678** CUDWORTH *Intell. Syst.* 378 My soul seemeth to vaticinate and presage its approaching dismission and freedom from this its prison. **1877** A. B. ALCOTT *Table-t.* 133 Instinct, intuition, volition, embosom and express whatsoever the Spirit vaticinates.

Hence **va'ticinating** *vbl. sb.* and *ppl. a.*

1634 SIR T. HERBERT *Trav.* 207 These vaticinating boyes who with their long-spread hair fall flat afore the Idoll. *Ibid.* (1638) 356 Virgil..from some vaticinating Notion seemes to point at it, in the 6 lib. Ænead. *a* **1693** *Urquhart's Rabelais* III. xxv. 210 The Cock Vaticinating and Alectryomantick, ate up the Pickles. **1791–1823** D'ISRAELI *Cur. Lit.* (1858) III. 278 George Withers, the vaticinating poet of our civil wars.

vaticination (vətɪsɪ'neɪʃən). [ad. L. *vāticinātiōn-*, *vāticinātio*, n. of action f. *vāticinārī*: see prec. Cf. obs. F. *vaticination* (Cotgr.).]

1. A prediction of an oracular or inspired nature; a prognostication or prophecy, a prophetic utterance or forecast.

1603 HOLLAND *Plutarch's Mor.* 1198 Sibylla, and Aristonice, or such as published their vaticinations and prophesies in verse. **1677** GALE *Crt. Gentiles* III. 63 The Law has appointed a sort of Prophets as Judges over these divine Vaticinations. **1759** STERNE *Tr. Shandy* I. xii, Yorick scarce ever heard this sad vaticination of his destiny read over to him, but..that he [etc.]. **1815** SCOTT *Guy M.* xlvii, The Dominie.. had just that moment parted from Meg Merrilies, and was too deeply wrapt up in pondering upon her vaticinations, to make any answer. **1850** MERIVALE *Rom. Emp.* iii. (1865) I. 115 The frightful vaticinations of fire and slaughter with which Cicero had kept the ears of the people tingling. **1874** H. R. REYNOLDS *John Bapt.* iv. §6. 266 The 'Sibylline Oracles'..contain many vaticinations, inextricably mingled, from Jewish, heathen, and Christian sources.

transf. **1836** EMERSON *Nature* Wks. (Bohn) II. 170 Every surmise and vaticination of the mind is entitled to a certain respect.

2. The action or fact of vaticinating; the utterance of predictions or prophecies; also, the power or gift of this.

1623 COCKERAM I, *Vaticination*, a prophesying. **1699** BENTLEY *Phal.* iv. 147 Unless we dare ascribe to the Tyrant a Spirit of Vaticination, we cannot acquit the Author of the Letters of so manifest a cheat. **1818** SCOTT *Br. Lamm.* xxiii, He despised most of the ordinary prejudices about witchcraft, omens, and vaticination. **1874** H. R. REYNOLDS *John Bapt.* iii. §3. 206 The ambiguous vaticination of the heathen oracles.

transf. **1744** BERKELEY *Siris* §252 He that foretels the motions of planets,..may be said to do it by natural vaticination.

†**b.** Divine or inspired apprehension or knowledge; intuition, insight. *Obs.*

1678 CUDWORTH *Intell. Syst.* Pref., Whether this Assurance be called a Vaticination or Divine Sagacity, (as it is by Plato and Aristotle) or Faith, as in the Scripture. *Ibid.* 409 That Vaticination, which all men have in their minds concerning the Gods.

va'ticinator. Now *rare* or *Obs.* [a. obs. F. *vaticinateur* (Cotgr.) or ad. L. *vāticinātor*, agent-noun f. *vāticinārī* to VATICINATE.] One who writes or utters vaticinations: a prognosticator or prophet.

1652 GAULE *Magastrom.* 335 Cicero derided the Bœotian vaticinators for predicting victory to the Thebanes from the crowing of cocks. *a* **1693** *Urquhart's Rabelais* III. xiii, The Owner of that Soul deserveth to be termed a Vaticinator or Prophet. **1791–1823** D'ISRAELI *Cur. Lit.* (1859) II. 483 Poetical vaticinators are prophets only while we read their verses. **1828** —— *Chas. I*, I. iv. 59 What vaticinator would have ventured to predict..that his Queen was then before him? **1841** —— *Amen. Lit.* (1867) 500 That mystical vaticinator of past events, a conjectural historian.

vaticinatory (vətɪsɪ'neɪtərɪ), *a.* [f. VATICINATE *v.*: see -ORY 2.] Vaticinal, prophetic.

1883 S. WAINWRIGHT *Sci. Sophisms* viii. 169 The vaticinatory character of these opinions is their least remarkable feature. **1895** *Starting Price* 23 Mar. 3/3 To test the vaticinatory skill of professional and amateur prophets, we offer a prize of £10 for a tipping contest. **1930** WYNDHAM LEWIS *Apes of God* XII. vii. 483 There was, as well as a great vaticinatory verve, a certain boastfulness about this Fascist. **1980** V. CUNNINGHAM *Penguin Bk. Spanish Civil War Verse* 38 Cornford is blamed for not being vaticinatory enough about these 'political surrealists' who couldn't wait for the revolution.

†**va'ticinatress**. *Obs.*$^{-1}$ [f. VATICINATOR + -ESS[1], after F. *vaticinatrice*. Cf. L. *vāticinātrix*.] A female vaticinator; a prophetess.

a **1693** *Urquhart's Rabelais* III. xvii. 137 The House of the Vaticinatress.

†**vaticinatric**, *a. Obs.*$^{-1}$ [irreg. formation on VATICINATE *v.*] Pertaining to, connected with, vaticination.

1729 *Evelyn's Sylva* III. iv. 228 As in the temple Despoene ..where they were prohibited the burning of Olive-wood, or the φυτὸν Μανικόν, the Vaticinatric Laurel, or the Thick-rind Oak [etc.].

†**vaticine**, variant of VATICINY. *Obs.*

1586 J. HOOKER *Hist. Irel.* in *Holinshed* II. 43/2 Thus (according to this vaticine) twise it was left, but the third time it shall be kept. *Ibid.* 52/2 Then was fulfilled the vaticine or prophesie of old Merlin.

†**vaticinian**, *a. Obs.*$^{-0}$ [f. L. *vāticini-us* prophetic.] Vaticinal. (Blount, 1656.)

†**vaticiny**. *Obs. rare.* [ad. L. *vāticinium*, f. *vāticinus* prophetical: cf. VATICINE.] A vatication or prophecy.

1615 R. BYFIELD *Comm. Coloss.* i. 6 The certain event of the vaticinies or prophecies. **1654** VILVAIN *Chronography* 14 Seek not to wrest a connexion of sacred Chronology from Daniels Vaticiny. **1656** in BLOUNT *Glossogr.*

Va'tinian, *a.* Now *rare.* [ad. L. *Vatīniān-us*, f. *Vatīnius* 'a Roman, whom all men hated for his odious behaviour' (Blount, 1674).] Of hatred: Bitter, intense, violent.

After L. *odium Vatinianum* (Catullus xiv. 3).

1607 WALKINGTON *Opt. Glasse* 2 The viperous and vatinian deadly hate. **1631** R. H. *Arraignm. Whole Creature* xvi. 284 King Philip of France hating King Richard the first of England: with a vatinian deadly hatred. **1654** WHITLOCK *Zootomia* 256 The Vatinian hatred of Books and Authors in Religious and Politick Differences. **1927** T. WILDER *Bridge of San Luis Rey* II. 62 The Archbishop of Lima..hated her, with what he called a Vatinian hate and counted the cessation of her visits among the compensations for dying.

vatir, obs. Sc. f. WATER.

vatje ('faci). *S. Afr.* Also **fadje**, **fagie**, **fatje**, **fikey**, **vaatje**, **vaitje**. [ad. Afrikaans *vaatjie*, dim. of *vat* water-carrier (see FAT *sb.*[1]).] A small cask or barrel for carrying water or wine; a soldier's canteen.

1850 R. G. CUMMING *Five Years Hunter's Life S. Afr.* i. 7/1 The..general stores which I carried with me were as follows:..2 large 'fagie' or water-casks, [etc.]. **1871** J. MCKAY *Reminisc. Last Kafir War* ii. 8 The soldier acts as the beast of burden, having been supplied with a large wooden vessel, by soldiers called 'fadje', or keg, capable of holding about half a gallon; and in this he had to carry with him what water he thought necessary. **1871** J. MACKENZIE

Ten Yrs. North of Orange River vii. 115 Khosimore jealously guarded his 'vatjes', or water-vessels. **1891** E. GLANVILLE *Fossicker* xix. 166 One of the three rose up .. took a final pull at the water 'fikey', and stretched himself on the bare ground. **1909** *Chambers's Jrnl.* Dec. 28/1 Some Congo brandy and a *vatje* of water. **1951** L. G. GREEN *Fully Many a Glorious Morning* xviii. 234 We gave up part of a *vaatjie* of red wine and soaked it and then roasted it in front of a huge fire. **1970** in *Voorloper* (1976) 833 The coloured people buy their wine in a vaatjie for celebrations.

VATman: see VAT *sb.*²

vatt(e, obs. ff. VAT *sb.*¹

vatte, southern ME. var. FAT *a.*, pa. t. FET *v.*

'vatted, *ppl. a.* [f. VAT *v.*] Placed or stored in a vat; said esp. of wine. Also *fig.*, mellow.

1843 TIZARD *Brewing* 463 Old and vatted Beer. **1873** *Sat. Rev.* 29 Nov. 694/1 The forged wine of Hamburg, which is variously known as Elbe sherry, vatted sherry, and Hamburg sherry. **1897** *Pall Mall Mag.* Feb. 253 A considerable company, .. most of us fine old vatted English Tories.

vatten, obs. southern var. FATTEN *v.*

vatter, -ir, -yr, obs. Sc. ff. WATER.

vattill, obs. f. WATTLE.

'vatting, *vbl. sb.* [f. VAT *v.*] The action or process of placing beer or other liquor in a vat or vats. Also *attrib.*

1843 TIZARD *Brewing* 444 Vatting of Porter. **1855** OGILVIE *Suppl.* s.v., Vatting charges at the docks. **1860** BAGEHOT *Biogr. Studies, Gladstone* (1881) 93 Let a man question the fees on vatting, or the change in the game-certificate. *c* **1886** KIPLING *Opium Factory* 93 After vatting, .. the big vats .. are probed with test rods.

vatyr, obs. Sc. form of WATER.

vau (vɔː). Also 9 **vaw**. [a. late L. *vau* (Vulgate), ad. Heb. *vāv* VAV.] The sixth letter of the Hebrew alphabet; the Hebrew particle *va-*, *ve-*, *ū-* 'and', denoted by this letter. (Cf. VAV.)

1382 WYCLIF *Ps.* cxix. 41 [*Heading*] Vau. [Also in Coverdale and later versions.] **1639** SIR W. MURE *Ps.* cxix. Wks. (S.T.S.) II. 185 He... Vau. **1643** J. CARYL *Expos. Job* I. 1586 The particle *Vau* .. usually taken as a Conjunction. *Ibid.* 1587 Thus in the Text the particle (*Vau*) is taken by some as a note of likeness. **1736** AINSWORTH *Lat. Dict.* II. s.v. *F*, Its place and analogous use favour its descent from the Hebrew *vau*. **1798** *Brit. Critic* XI. 116 There is no similarity whatever between the Syriac jod .. and vau. **1832** S. LEE *Hebr. Gram.* (ed. 2) 21 The *Vaw* .. is frequently left out. *Ibid.* 30 The *Vaw* commencing this last syllable. **1844** W. UPTON *Physioglyphics* 156 The Hebrew having no express character for *o*, the full sound of it is indicated by a *vau* with a dot above.

vauclusian (vɔːˈkluːzɪən), *a. Physical Geogr.* Also **Vauclusian**. [f. the name of the Fontaine de *Vaucluse* in S. France: see -IAN.] Applied to a type of spring, often large, occurring in karstic regions, in which the water is forced out under artesian pressure.

1937 WOOLDRIDGE & MORGAN *Physical Basis Geogr.* xix. 294 Cheddar Gorge .. and the spectacular Wookey Hole with its 'Vauclusian spring', show true karstic features. **1977** A. HALLAM *Planet Earth* 82/3 There are two main types of karst spring, one where the water issues by means of free flow, the other where the water issues under forced or artesian flow: the latter type is sometimes known as a vauclusian spring. **1980** J. C. SCHMID tr. *A. Bögli's Karst Hydrol.* ix. 124 In a genuine vauclusian spring the water course runs upwards through the rock.

vaude (vɔːd, vəʊd). *N. Amer. colloq.* Also **vaud**. [Abbrev. of VAUDEVILLE.] Vaudeville (sense 2); a vaudeville theatre. Also *attrib.*

1933 *Ladies' Home Jrnl.* Mar. 21/3 He was wearing a cap with purple and green in it and the loudest checked suit I have ever seen on anybody outside of a vaud. **1951** GREEN & LAURIE (*title*) Show biz, from vaude to video. **1975** R. DAVIES *World of Wonders* (1977) I. viii. 105 A rabble of acts .. which played for rotten pay in the worst vaude houses.

Vau'dese, variant of VAUDOIS *sb.* and *a.*

1781 *Encycl. Brit.* (ed. 2) VIII. 6179/1 The valleys between France and Italy are inhabited by the Vaudese, who are Protestants. **1882–3** *Schaff's Encycl. Relig. Knowl.* III. 2274 In Nov., 1845, the Vaudese clergy left the Established Church. *Ibid.*, The Vaudese revolution.

vaudevillain (vɔːd(ə)vɪlən, vəʊd-). *U.S. colloq.* ? *Obs.* [f. VAUDEVILLE, after VILLAIN *sb.*] = VAUDEVILLIAN *sb.*

1909 *Sat. Even. Post* 5 June 17/2 One thrifty vaudevillain made sixty-five weeks one season in this way. **1916** J. K. BANGS *From Pillar to Post* xvi. 326 The major was a great believer in the value of Author's Readings by what he used to call 'running mates'—teams, as the vaudevillains have it.

vaudeville (ˈvɔːd(ə)vɪl, ˈvəʊd-, -viːl). [F. *vaudeville*, earlier *vau* (pl. *vaux*) *de ville*, *vau de vire*, and in full *chanson du Vau de Vire* a song of the valley of Vire (in Calvados, Normandy). The name is said to have been first given to songs composed by Olivier Basselin, a fuller of Vire in the 15th c.]

1. A light popular song, commonly of a satirical or topical nature; *spec.* a song of this nature sung on the stage.

The entry in Blount *Glossogr.* (1656) is copied directly from Cotgrave (1611).

1739 H. WALPOLE *Let. to R. West* 18 June, I will send you one of the vaudevilles or ballads which they sing at the comedy after their *petites pièces*. **1818** LADY MORGAN *Autobiog.* (1859) 85 Whenever Carbonel sings his delicious vaudevilles we think of you. **1824** WATTS *Bibl. Brit.* II. 617 Simon de la Loubere .. also wrote Songs, Vaudevilles, Madrigals, Sonnets, Odes, &c.

2. A play or stage performance of a light and amusing character interspersed with songs; also without article, this species of play or comedy. Now in frequent use in the U.S. to designate variety theatre (VARIETY 9 b) or music hall.

1827 T. DIBDIN *Reminiscences* I. xii. 268, I also had the honour .. of being selected by her Royal Highness the Princess Elizabeth to write a sort of *vaudeville* farce. *c* **1831** J. H. REYNOLDS in J. R. Planché *Recollections & Reflections* (1872) I. xii. 181 And lure for you the light Vaudeville from France. **1833** LYTTON *Godolphin* ix, Fanny .. was inimitable in vaudeville, in farce, and in the lighter comedy. **1842** DICKENS *Amer. Notes* (1850) 65/2 The third, the Olympic, is a tiny show-box for vaudevilles and burlesques. **1862** MISS BRADDON *Lady Audley* xxxix, Country people always go to see tragedies. None of your flimsy vaudevilles for them! **1876** GEO. ELIOT *Dan. Der.* xx, Is this world and all the life upon it only like a farce or vaudeville, where you find no great meanings? **1891** *Times* 28 Oct. 13/4 A vaudeville entertainment, which was continued for about three months. **1899** MORROW *Bohem. Paris* 15 Paris, the great city, the vaudeville playhouse of the world. **1911** G. B. SHAW in *Daily Graphic* 2 Dec. 4/3 There are vaudeville theatres in America and variety theatres in England. **1917** *Lit. Digest* 25 Aug. 28/2 The phrase 'Jaz her up' is a common one to-day in vaudeville and on the circus lot. When a vaudeville act needs ginger the cry from the advisers in the wings is 'put in jaz'. **1940** R. CHANDLER *Farewell, my Lovely* v. 30 You would find them in tank town vaudeville acts .. in the cheap burlesque houses. **1967** *Stage* 2 Mar. 4/1 The merging of vaudeville and tombola as a major February attraction at Blackpool last week succeeded. **1976** *New Yorker* 8 Mar. 57/1 The play is a lewd, tragic vaudeville about the life of a bankrupt pursued by creditors. **1976** J. CROSBY *Nightfall* xxxii. 197 You're a fifth-rate vaudeville actor. **1982** *Verbatim* Autumn 23/2 The subject is given light-hearted treatment, as though this jargon were little more than food for variety turns (i.e., vaudeville acts).

vaudevillian (vɔːd-, vəʊd(ə)vɪlɪən), *sb.* and *a.* orig. and chiefly *U.S.* Also **-ean**. [f. VAUDEVILLE + -IAN.] **A.** *sb.* A performer in vaudeville. **B.** *adj.* Of or pertaining to vaudeville.

1913 *Technical World Mag.* Mar. 19 'That's great!' cried one of the 'vaudevillians', clapping his hands appreciatively. **1924** *Sat. Even. Post* 4 Oct. 70/2 Give them to some small-time vaudevillian to repeat. **1930** *Punch* 8 Oct. 415 The modish songs .. serve pleasantly to exercise the vaudevillean gifts of Mr. Coward and Miss Lawrence. **1961** *John o' London's* 5 Oct. 373/1 The elder Glasses were vaudevillians (music-hall artists). **1962** J. D. SALINGER *Franny & Zooey* 120 The children's father, a former international vaudevillian. **1975** *Times* 2 Aug. 12/1 (*heading*) Behind the vaudevillian smoke-screen. **1980** *Redbook* Oct. 213/3 Later, years later, he was to win an Academy award playing an old vaudevillian in *The Sunshine Boys*. **1985** *Listener* 23 May 37/1, I don't just mean old vaudevillians like George Burns.

vaudevillist (ˈvɔːd-, ˈvəʊd(ə)vɪlɪst). [ad. F. *vaudevilliste* (1735), f. *vaudeville*: see VAUDEVILLE.] A writer of vaudevilles.

1839 [see STENOGRAPHIST]. **1879** *Gentl. Mag.* Oct. 478 Whilst the writer of comedy has grown too witty, the vaudevillist too stupid. **1892** *Harper's Mag.* Sept. 502/1 The untiring inventiveness of innumerable vaudevillists.

'Vaudism. *rare*⁻¹. [Irreg. f. next.] The tenets of the Vaudois.

1855 MILMAN *Lat. Chr.* V. 17 All persons whatsoever, living or dead, .. under the suspicion of heresy or Vaudism.

‖**Vaudois** (vodwa), *sb.* and *a.* Also 6 **Valdois**. [F., repr. med.L. *Valdensis*: see WALDENSES.] **A.** *sb. pl.* Waldensians. **B.** *adj.* Waldensian.

1560 DAUS tr. *Sleidane's Comm.* 219 Ther be in the French prouince a people called Valdois. They of an auncient custome, doe not acknowledg the bishop of Rome. **1692** P. BOYER (*title*), The History of the Vaudois. **1728** CHAMBERS *Cycl.* s.v., The Vaudois had their name from this Valdo, whose Retainers they were. They were also call'd Lyonists. **1797** *Encycl. Brit.* (ed. 3) XIV. 737/1 In the valleys of Lucerne, Peyrouse, and St. Martin .. live the celebrated Waldenses or Vaudois. **1830** WHITTIER (*title*), The Vaudois teacher. *Ibid.* 27 She hath gone to the Vaudois vales. **1841** W. SPALDING *Italy & It. Isl.* III. 234 The church of Rome and its Italian princes had deeply disgraced themselves by their conduct to the unhappy Vaudois. **1896** R. PALMER *Fam. & Pers. Mem.* I. xvii. 256 He reported of the Vaudois pastors, that they were desirous of cultivating the Anglican connection.

'vaudouism. [f. next.] = VOODOOISM.

1884 *Spectator* 13 Dec. 1651/2 Vaudouism, which now rages in Hayti, is, in fact, an old African creed, and its priests hold cannibalism necessary to their rites. **1890** *U.P. Mag.* June 245 Great numbers of all ranks secretly practise vaudouism.

‖**vaudoux** (vodu). Also **vaudo**. [F.] = VOODOO *sb.* Also *attrib.*

1862 J. LE GRAND *Jrnl.* 20 Dec. (1911) 57 Heard today of the existence of a negro society here called the 'vaudo' (I believe). **1864** R. F. BURTON *Mission to Gelele* (1893) I. 62 The Vaudoux or small green snake of the Haytian negroes, so well-known by the abominable orgies enacted before the 'Vaudoux King and Queen'. **1884** in Sir S. St. John *Hayti* v. 208 The fetish sect of Vaudoux, imported into Hayti by the slaves coming from the tribes on the western coast of Africa. *Ibid.* vii. 247 A freshly built temple dedicated to the Vaudoux worship.

vaudy (ˈvɔːdɪ), *a. Sc.* Also **vady, vaudie.** [Of obscure origin.] **a.** Elated, delighted. **b.** Stout, stalwart. **c.** Gay or fine in appearance.

c **1720** W. MESTON '*How lang shall our land*' in *Jacobite Songs* (1871) 41 Then must we be sad, while the traitors are vaudie, Till we get a sight o' our ain bonnie laddie. **1793** *Piper of Peebles* 7 Cummers fled and hurl'd as weel On ice, as ony vady chiel. **1805** ANDR. SCOTT *Poems* (1808) 222 In blue worset boots that my auld mither span, I've aft been fu' vaudy [**1821** vanty] sin' I was a man. *a* **1869** CHARLES SPENCE *Poems* (1898) 72 Now I got new trews and coat, And stalked about in trappings vaudie.

vauer, obs. Sc. form of WAVER *v.*

vauessour, obs. form of VAVASOUR.

†**vaughouse.** *Obs.*⁻¹ [ad. Du. *wachthuis* or LG. *wachthûs.*] A guard-house.

1616 J. LANE *Contn. Sqr.'s T.* (Chaucer Soc.) 131 But they this leader to the vaughouse bore, wheare .. how cowardice, .. how crueltie abusd his rancke, let silence put it bye.

vaught, obs. f. VAULT *sb.*¹, *v.*¹, and *v.*²

vault (vɔːlt), *sb.*¹ Forms: α. 4–6 **voute** (5 **woute**), 4–6 (9 *Sc.*) **vout** (5 **wout**); 5–6 **vowte** (5 **wowte**), 5 (9 *Sc.*) **vowt**; 5 **voghte** (**woȝte**), 6 **vowght, vought.** β. 5 (6 *Sc.*) **woult**, 6 **voulte, voult**; 5–7 **volt** (5 *Sc.* **volut**), 5–6 **wolte**, *Sc.* **wolt.** γ. 4 **vawte**, 4–7 **vawte**, 5–6 **vaute**; 4–7 **vaut** (5 **vavtt**), **vawt**, 6 **vaught, vawght.** δ. 6 **valte, vaulte, valt**, 6– **vault.** [a. OF. *voute, voulte, volte, vaulte, vaute* (mod.F. *voûte*), = Prov. *volta, vouta, vota*, It. and Pg. *volta*:—pop.L. **volta*, ppl. sb. f. L. *volvĕre* to turn. Cf. VOLT *sb.*

It is not clear at what date the *l* finally established itself in the standard pronunciation of this word and *sb.*², together with the related verbs, etc. As in the case of *fault*, there is some tendency towards the use of a short vowel (vɒlt) in all the forms.]

1. A structure of stones or bricks so combined as to support each other over a space and serve as a roof or covering to this; an arched surface covering some space or area in the interior of a building, and usually supported by walls or pillars; an arched roof or ceiling.

The two chief varieties are the ***barrel*** or ***cylindric(al) vault*** and the ***groined vault***.

α. **1387** *Charters of Edinb.* (1871) 35 The voute abovyn Sant Stevinys auter. **1424** *E.E. Wills* (1882) 58 þe voute of Okeham stepil. *c* **1440** *Alph. Tales* 454 In a were tyme þai war sett aboue a vowte in þe kurk. **1491** *Acc. Ld. High Treas. Scot.* I. 181 To the massonis of the Palis, in drink-siluer for the pendin of three voutis, iij vnicornis. **1535** COVERDALE *2 Esdras* xvi. 59 He spredeth out the heauen like a vowte. **1539–40** in *Devon N. & Q.* (1903) Oct. 238 Hewyng of tymber for the lytell chamber vought att Powderham. **1595** DUNCAN *App. Etym.* (E.D.S.), *Camera*, a vowte. **1828** MOIR *Mansie Wauch* x. 89 Feint a hair cared he about auld kirks, or kirkyards, or vouts, or through-stanes. **1901** TROTTER *Galloway Gossip* 239 He .. cam on a vowt biggit wi' stane an lime.

β. *c* **1400** *Sc. Trojan War* II. 2434 It had vnder erd but weir Standand woltis & cavis seir. **1513** DOUGLAS *Æneid* IX. viii. 114 Sa sairly knyt that maner embuchement Semyt to be a clos volt quhar thai went. **1538** LELAND *Itin.* (1769) I. 18 The riche Cardinal of Winchester gildid all the Floures and Knottes in the Voulte of the Chirch. **1563** *Reg. Privy Council Scot.* I. 247 The wallis .. ar revin, and the volt thair-throw partit, neir hand the ane side from the uther.

γ. **13..** *K. Alis.* 7197 (Laud MS.), þe toures maken, & þe torels, Vavtes, Alures, & þe kirnels. **1387** TREVISA *Higden* (Rolls) II. 81 Vawtes of stoonwerk wonderliche i-wrouȝt. *c* **1489** CAXTON *Sonnes of Aymon* xxviii. 581 See you yonder vawte by the grete hous? **1523** SKELTON *Garl. Laurel* 476 Enuawtyd with rubies the vawte was of this place. **1585** T. WASHINGTON tr. *Nicholay's Voy.* II. xvi. 50 b, There are conduit pypes .., supported some by vautes, and othersom by .. pillars. **1609** BIBLE (Douay) *1 Kings* vii. 3 He decked the whole vaut with bordes of ceder. *c* **1640** J. SMYTH *Lives Berkeleys* (1883) II. 66 The walls, vautes, .. and windows they razed and teare a down.

δ. **1545** ELYOT, *Arcus*, .. the vault of a roufe. **1560** DAUS tr. *Sleidane's Comm.* 114 b, They set a young man .. above over the vaulte of the churche. **1585** T. WASHINGTON tr. *Nicholay's Voy.* II. xxiv. 65 The arcenal .. hath neare an hundreth arches or vaultes to builde and hale the gallies vnder couer and drye. **1604** E. G[RIMSTONE] *D'Acosta's Hist. Indies* II. xiii. 112 With a slender covering of mats or straw, they are better preserved from the heate, than in Spaine vnder a roofe of wood, or a vault of stone. **1703** MOXON *Mech. Exerc.* 271, I did intend here to have added something about the Arching of Vaults, but .. shall .. omit speaking of Vaults in this Exercise. **1750** GRAY *Elegy* 39 The long-drawn isle and fretted vault. **1790** BURKE *Fr. Rev.* Wks. V. 42 The vault of the king's own chapel at St. James. **1818** SCOTT *Br. Lamm.* xxv, The shadow of the ribbed and darksome vault, with which veneration .. had canopied its source. **1840** PARKER *Gloss. Archit.* (ed. 5) I. 506 In groined vaults the arches which cross each other do not always correspond in width.

b. *transf.* An arching roof or covering resembling a structure of this kind.

a **1470** TIPTOFT *Caesar* xii. (1530) 14, vii Legions made in a maner a vaut to hyde them. **1601** HOLLAND *Pliny* II. 405 A man shall see the drops of water become stone, as they hang to the very vaults of the rocke. **1706** ADDISON *Rosamond* II. iv, At length the bowery vaults appear! **1773** *Cook's Voy.* I. xvi. (Hawksworth) II. 172 They frequently passed under vaults, formed by fragments of the rock. **1842** LOUDON *Suburban Hort.* 557 The net is tightened .., and forms a grand vault over the whole cherry garden. **1872**

RUSKIN *Eagle's N.* §137 The coloured segments of globe out of which foam is constituted, are portions of spherical vaults constructed of fluent particles. **1877** BRYANT *Little People of Snow* 151 And now the white walls widened, and the vault Swelled upward, like some vast cathedral dome.

c. The apparent concave surface formed by the sky. Chiefly *poet.* and usually with defining terms.

a **1586** SIDNEY *Ps.* XIX. vii, His [the sun's] race is ev'n, from endes of heav'n, About that vault he goeth. **1591** SPENSER *M. Hubberd* 1229 From whence he vewes.. Whatso the heauen in his wide vawte containes. **1605** SHAKS. *Lear* V. iii. 259 Had I your tongues and eyes, Il'd vse them so, That Heauens vault should crack. **1656** COWLEY *Pindar. Odes, Nemean Ode* ii, Through earth, and ayr, and Seas, and up to th' heavenly Vault. **1737** POPE *Hor. Epist.* I. vi. 5 This Vault of Air, this congregated Ball, Self-center'd Sun, and Stars that rise and fall. **1781** COWPER *Hope* 79 When evening turns the blue vault grey. **1840** LARDNER *Geom.* 215 The intersection of the plane of the water with the hemispherical celestial vault. **1869** J. MARTINEAU *Ess.* II. 229 The vault of the nocturnal sky. **1874** SAYCE *Compar. Philol.* viii. 331 The bright vault of heaven.

d. *Anat.* One or other of certain concave structures or surfaces normally facing downwards.

1594 T. B. *La Primaud. Fr. Acad.* II. 150 Vessels and instruments, which serue the brayne,.. amongest the which there is.. another called a vault, both in respect of the fashion and of the vse. **1831** R. KNOX *Cloquet's Anat.* 95 This vault is formed by the nasal bones and the nasal processes of the maxillary bones. *Ibid.* 423 The posterior lobes and the vault of the hemispheres of the cerebrum. **1849** H. MILLER *Footpr. Creat.* iv. (1874) 45 The upper and middle portions of the cranial vault. **1875** *Encycl. Brit.* I. 812/2 He.. distinguishes the posterior pillars of the vault from the pedes hippocampi.

2. An enclosed space covered with an arched roof; *esp.* a lower or underground apartment or portion of a building constructed in this form.

a, β. **1396–7** *Durham Acc. Rolls* (Surtees) 600 Pro cariac[ione] vj^{xx} lad. petr[arum].. pro le vout. **14..** *Dorothe* 101 in Horstm. *Altengl. Leg.* (1878) 192 Sche scholde not scape so sone, he thowȝt; He put here in prison in a voghte. *c* **1440** CAPGRAVE *Life St. Kath.* IV. 1195 Alle the preson, whiche had vowtes seuene, Was light that tyme right of his presens. **1513** BRADSHAW *St. Werburge* II. 404 The buyldynge of olde antiquite In cellers and lowe voultes, and halles of realte. **1554–5** *Acc. Ld. High Treas. Scot.* X. 268 To ressave voultis fra the monkes to put in lyme. **1558** *Ibid.* 432 For carying of the foirsaid furnesing.. to ane wolt. **1616** *Extr. Aberd. Rec.* (1898) II. 339 To mack ane hewin doir in the mid wall, betuixt the northmest voult and the southermest voult.

γ. **1422** YONGE tr. *Secreta Secret.* 153 He commaundid to kepe his chylde.. and that hit were Enclosid in a vaut of stone. **1470–85** MALORY *Arthur* Pref. 2 The grete stones & meruaylous werkys of yron lyeng vnder the grounde & ryal vautes. **1503** HAWES *Examp. Virt.* xiii. 276 Than went we doune to an other vaute. **1534** in *Archæol. Cant.* VII. 286 In the Vawt where the Moncks do dyne. j olde table [etc.]. **1584** *Star Chamber Decrees Print. & Stat.* (1863) 11 That no presse be used in vaut or secret place, but such as may easily and openly be found in search. **1602** CAMPION *Bk. Airs* Wks. (Bullen) 21 That man needs neither towers.. Nor secret vauts to fly From thunder's violence.

fig. **1545** BALE *Image Both Ch.* I. xvii. R viij b, So throwing them selues into a moste confuse Chaos or vawte of double dotage.

δ. **1603** G. OWEN *Pembrokeshire* (1892) 77 These vaultes are alltogether neclected. **1687** A. LOVELL tr. *Thevenot's Trav.* II. 84 They make their little Vaults very quickly, and in building of them use Timber as with us. **1698** KEILL *Exam. Th. Earth* (1734) 117 In Vaults and Caves there is no sensible alteration of heat in Summer and Winter. **1794** MRS. RADCLIFFE *Myst. Udolpho* xxvi, From the steps they proceeded through a passage adjoining the vaults. **1836** EMERSON *Nature* Wks. (Bohn) II. 151 A paper currency is employed, when there is no bullion in the vaults. **1856** KANE *Arct. Expl.* II. xi. 113 The thermometer inside was at + 90°, and the vault [= hut] measured fifteen feet by six.

b. A place of this kind used as a cellar or storeroom for provisions or liquors.

1500 in J. Latimer *Merch. Vent. Bristol* (1903) 34 In his mansion or shop or in celers or vawts y^{t} he holdeth.. in fee. **1577** B. GOOGE *Heresbach's Husb.* (1586) 42 In our dayes we vse to keepe both Wine and Grayne in suche vaultes. **1600** NASHE *Summers Last Will* 1188 Bacchus, for thou abusest so earths fruits, Impris'ned liue in cellars and in vawtes. **1662** J. DAVIES tr. *Mandelslo's Trav.* 45 Most of them three Stories high, with very noble Lodgings, Store-Houses, Vaults and Stables belonging to them. **1699** POMFRET *Poems, The Choice*, I'd have a little Vault, but always stor'd With the best Wines each Vintage could afford. **1730** SWIFT *Panegyrick on Dean* Wks. 1751 IV. I. 136 When to the vault you walk in state, In quality of butler's mate. **1756–7** tr. *Keysler's Trav.* (1760) I. 120 Among other cellars, there is one which perhaps has not its equal... This vault communicates with another. **1880** MISS BRADDON *Just as I am* xxxvi, The wine cellar at the Homestead was not a stately vault.

fig. **1605** SHAKS. *Macb.* II. iii. 101 The Wine of Life is drawne, and the meere Lees Is left this Vault, to brag of.

3. †**a.** An arched space under the floor of a church, used for ecclesiastical purposes; a crypt.

c **1400** MAUNDEV. (Roxb.) xiv. 61 Vnder þe kirk also es a vowte, whare Cristen men dwellez. *a* **1490** BOTONER *Itin.* (1778) 176 The second way goth rygh est by the woult of Seynt Johnys chyrch. **1503–4** *Rec. St. Mary at Hill* (1905) 252 Payd for a stay bar of yerryn to stay the Nev pevys [= pews] in to þe vavtt. **1511** *Guylforde's Pilgr.* (Camden) 31 A very fayre churche,.. wherein we descendyd into a wonder fayre vaught.

b. A burial chamber (originally with arched roof), usually altogether or partly under ground.

a **1548** HALL *Chron., Edw. IV*, 223 After he was remoued to Winsore and there in a new vawte newly intumilate. **1592** SHAKS. *Rom. & Jul.* V. iii. 86 Here lies Iuliet, and her beautie makes This Vault a feasting presence full of light. **1606** BIRNIE *Kirk-Buriall* x, For some there was that to the imitation of Abraham, made vp little caues or voltes, for buriall vse. **1610** HOLLAND *Camden's Brit.* I. 379 Hee purposed.. that his bones should bee bestowed in an arched vault made under the chancell of Saint Peters Church in Oxford. **1722** *Lond. Gaz.* No. 6084/7 The Body was deposited in the Vault. **1749** in *Nairne Peerage Evidence* (1874) 81 Mrs. Jean Mercer.. lyes.. opposite to the Duke of Roxburghs vault. **1790** BURKE *Fr. Rev.* Wks. V. 172 In as few years their successors will go to the family vault of 'all the Capulets'. **1832** W. IRVING *Alhambra* I. 187 'Now,' said the priest, 'you must help me to bring forth the bodies that are to be buried in this vault'. **1843** *Penny Cycl.* XXV. 37/1 A vault cannot properly be made either in the church or churchyard, without the consent of the ordinary. *Ibid.*, A vault may be attached by prescription to a mansion. **1870** F. R. WILSON *Ch. Lindisf.* 61 The vaults beneath the Chancel, sometimes called the dead-house.

†**4. a.** A covered conduit for carrying away water or filth; a drain or sewer. *Obs.*

c **1400** *Destr. Troy* 1607 The water.. Gosshet through Godardys & other grete vautes, And clensit by course all þe clene Cite. **1533** *MS. Rawl. D.* 776 lf. 131 b, Makyng of new vawtis of bryk to Conevaye the water Commyng frome the leades of the said Castell vnder the said new wharff. **1567** in *Vicary's Anat.* (1888) App. III. ii. 154 The gouernors.. shall viewe the comen sewer or vawt at the seid house. **1596** HARINGTON *Metam. Ajax* (1814) 53 A goodly Jakes within the town with a vault to convey all filth into the Tiber. *a* **1700** EVELYN *Diary* 8 Feb. 1645, The streetes.. having many vaults and conveyances under them for the sullage.

†**b.** A cistern. *Obs.*$^{-1}$

1552 HULOET, Vault or place to receaue rayne water, *impluuium*.

†**c.** A necessary-house; a privy. *Obs.*

1617 J. TAYLOR (Water P.) *Trav. Lond. to Hamburgh* Wks. (1630) 80/2 The Hangman.. hath the emptying of all the vaults or draughts in the city. **1665** *Orders Ld. Mayor Lond.* in De Foe *Plague* (Rtldg.) 64 That no Nightman.. be suffered to empty a Vault into any Garden. *a* **1700** B. E. *Dict. Cant. Crew, Vault*, an.. House of Office.

5. A natural cavern, cave, or overarched space; †a deep hole or pit.

1535 COVERDALE *Isaiah* vii. 19 These shall come, and shal light all in the valeyes, in ye vowtes of stone. **1587** FLEMING *Contn. Holinshed* III. 1413/2 The hole or vaut being sometimes filled with water, and otherwhiles neither bottome, trees, or water maie be perceiued. **1593** NORDEN *Spec. Brit., Cornw.* (1728) 40 A holl or deepe vaute in the grounde wherinto the sea floweth at high water verie farr under the earth. **1617** MORYSON *Itin.* I. 11 This City is of a round forme, compassed of all sides with Mountaines, having many Vauts or Caves under it. **1691** RAY *Creation* I. (1692) 127 Some should digg Vaults and Holes in the Earth, as Rabbets, to secure themselves and their Young. **1796** H. HUNTER tr. *St.-Pierre's Stud. Nat.* (1799) III. 274 In the burning entrails of which.. the fire-consumed Ætnean vaults incessantly thunder. **1854** BREWSTER *More Worlds* iii. 61 It is from the deep vaults to which primæval life has been consigned that the history of the dawn of life is to be composed. **1860** TYNDALL *Glac.* I. v. 38 The vault at the end of the glacier.

transf. **1578** BANISTER *Hist. Man* I. 29 Moreouer in the interiour part of the wrest, we finde a broad, and deepe cauitie,.. through the which are concurrent, not a small number of tendons of Muscles, to be inserted to the ioyntes of the fingers. And in this vawte, or hollow, they seeme as it were included, or locked up.

†**b.** *to go to the vault*: (see quot.). *Obs.*

1576 TURBERV. *Venerie* 165, I haue seene [hares] that woulde take the ground like a Coney (whiche is called goyng to the vault) when they haue beene hunted.

6. *techn.* The inner portion of a steel furnace.

1825 J. NICHOLSON *Operat. Mechanic* 341 Inside the conical building is a smaller furnace, called the vault, built of fire-brick or stone.. D D, in the section, is the dome of the vault. **1884** W. H. GREENWOOD *Steel & Iron* 409 The temperature in each furnace is regulated by closing or opening the small flues in the arch of the vault.

7. *attrib.* and *Comb.*, as ***vault beam, -cover, door, fashion, height, -like*** adj., ***pier***, etc.

1611 BIBLE *1 Kings* vi. 9 *marg.*, [He covered] the *vault beams and the sielings with Cedar. **1875** KNIGHT *Dict. Mech.* 2694/1 A *vault-cover with glass bull's-eyes or prisms. **1553–4** *Extr. Burgh Rec. Edinb.* (1871) II. 345 Ane greit loke to the *wolt dure of Sanct Thomas ile. **1552** HULOET, Vaultyng or makyng a worke.. *vault fascion, *concameratio*. **1616** *Extr. Aberd. Rec.* (1848) II. 338 The said Thomas.. sall big the same of the breidth of the haill tolbuith quhill it be *voult hight. **1847** DICKENS *Haunted M.* i, His dwelling was so solitary and *vault-like. **1858** HAWTHORNE *Fr. & It. Note-bks.* (1872) I. 50 Whenever we emerged into the vault-like streets. **1905** F. BOND *Gothic Architecture* 58 Nowhere is the result plainer than in the construction of the Gothic *vault pier. *c* **1630** DONNE *Serm.* cli. Wks. 1839 VI. 73 These particular Spirits in their *Vault-prayers and Cellar-service shake the pillars of State and Church. **1887** BROWNING *Parleyings* Wks. 1907 XVI. 113 *Vault-roof reverberates, groans the ground! **1843** TIZARD *Brewing* 469 The brewer.. who possesses storage, cellarage, or *vault-room. **1890** C. H. MOORE *Gothic Archit.* ii. 52 Arches which.. sustain the *vault shells. **1480** CAXTON *Trevisa's Higden* I. xlviii. (1527) 47 A thre chambred hous made of *vawte stones. **1728** CHAMBERS *Cycl.* s.v., The several *Voussoirs*, or Vault-stones whereof it [an arch] consists. **1900** H. SUTCLIFFE *Shameless Wayne* ii, The.. vault-stone stared blue and cold at the cold moon. *a* **1610** G. BABINGTON *Wks.* (1622) II. 35 That late thrice-damnable Powder-Treason, or *Vault-Treason; what name might it haue answerable to the iniquitie of it? **1585** T. WASHINGTON tr. *Nicholay's Voy.* II. xxi. 58 [A] building round & strongly set vp *vawtwise in form of the Hemispherike. **1611** COTGR., *Retombe*,.. a flat vault, or a roome thats made vault-wise. **1662** J. DAVIES tr. *Olearius' Voy. Ambass.* 67 Their Cabans, or Huts, which are covered vault-wise, are built half underground. **1844** *Blackw. Mag.* LVI. 208 Every brilliant pair finished.. was briskly strung up on cobwebs, with which the cart, vaultwise, was interwoven. **1614** PURCHAS *Pilgrimage* VI. v. 584 This Temple was borne vp with *Vault-worke. **1726** LEONI *Alberti's Archit.* I. 35/2 Pit-sand.. they use.. in Vault-work, but not in plaistering.

vault (vɔːlt), *sb.*^{2} Also 6 vaute. [f. VAULT *v.*^{2}, or, in sense 2, ad. F. *volte.*]

1. An act of vaulting; a leap or spring; †*spec.* of harts (see quot. 1576).

1576 TURBERV. *Venerie* 45 It is a pleasure, to beholde them when they goe to Rutte and make their vaute. **1610** G. FLETCHER *Christ's Tri.* I. xl, So on a wither'd tree he fairly set him, And helpt him fit the rope,.. So thear he stands, readie to hell to make his vault. **1630** J. TAYLOR (Water P.) *Navy Land Ships* Wks. I. 93/1 What Necromanticke spells are Rut, Vault, Slot, Pores, and Entryes, Abatures, and Foyles. **1728** CHAMBERS *Cycl., Vault* is also used for the Manages practis'd on the wooden Horse, to learn to mount and unmount with Ease and Expedition. **1868** W. R. SMITH in *Life* (1912) iii. 94 A popular exercise is the spring vault. **1893** *Outing* XXII. 153/2 The world's record in the fence vault, and.. the pole vault. **1901** *Westm. Gaz.* 28 May 2/1 M. Brocas fell to the ground, after his vault.

†**2.** = VOLTE (in the manege). *Obs.*

1728 CHAMBERS *Cycl.* s.v., There are some Vaults wherein the Horse makes two parallel Circles.

vault (vɔːlt), *v.*^{1} Forms: *α.* 4 *Sc.*, 5 voute (4 *Sc.* wout-); 4, 6 vowte (5 vowytn), 6 vought, 7 *Sc.* wowt; 6 volt, 6, 7 *Sc.*, voult. *β.* 5–6 vawte (5 vawth-), 5–7 vaut(e, 6 vaught. *γ.* 6 vaulten, vaulte, valte, 6– vault. [ad. OF. *vouter, voulter, volter, vaulter* (mod.F. *voûter*), f. *voute*, etc., VAULT *sb.*^{1}]

1. *trans.* To construct with, to cover in with, a vault or arched roof. Also with *over*.

α. **1387** *Charters Edinb.* (1871) 35 The forsaidys.. sal mak and voute v. chapellis on the south syde of the paryce kyrc of Edynburgh. **1535** COVERDALE *Ps.* ciii. 3 Thou voltest it aboue with waters. **1616** *Extr. Aberd. Rec.* (1848) II. 338 The said Thomas.. sall voult ouer the nethermest voultis the hight of the tolbuith fluir. *a* **1656** R. GORDON *Contin. Hist. Earls Sutherl.* (1813) 509 The Earl.. finished the great tour the same yeir, wowting it to the top.

β. **1511–2** in Willis & Clark *Cambridge* (1886) I. 478 They can.. vawte the chirch.. after the fourme of a platte ther-for devised. **1577** B. GOOGE *Heresbach's Husb.* I. (1586) 42 b, They doo vaute the floore with Bryckes. **1577** HOLINSHED *Chron.* II. 1714/1 Sir William Chester.. and John Calthrop .. couered and vauted the towne ditch from Aldersgate to Newgate.

γ. **1625** K. LONG tr. *Barclay's Argenis* I. v. 12 The first builders of this house vaulted under the ground a secret way unknowne to any but my selfe. **1650** EARL MONM. tr. *Senault's Man bec. Guilty* 303 The Concavity of Trees hung in the aire, hath taught our Architects to vault buildings. **1726** LEONI *Alberti's Archit.* I. 73/2 What-ever sort of Arch you vault your Bridge with. **1829** BOWLES *Days Departed* 8 Ask of the Geologist How Nature, vaulting the rude chamber, scoop'd Its vast recesses. **1848** G. S. HILLARD in *Life Longf.* (1891) II. 111 But to combine them all, to vault them with such a sky,.. this is not easy. **1894** BARING-GOULD *Deserts S. France* II. 104 The various attempts made to vault the naves.

b. In pa. pple. used predicatively. (Cf. VAULTED *ppl. a.*)

α. **1387** *Charters Edinb.* (1871) 35 The fyfte chapel woutyt with a durre. *c* **1400** MAUNDEV. (1839) iii. 17 And undre theise Stages ben Stables wel y-vowted for the Emperours Hors. **1412–20** LYDG. *Chron. Troy* II. 689 Fresche alures with lusty hiȝe pynacles,.. Vowted aboue like reclinatories. **1511** *Guylforde's Pilgr.* (Camden) 26 There is a fayre large Chapell, well voughted and lyghted by many lampes brennynge. **1538** LELAND *Itin.* (1769) II. 53 A right fair and costely peace of Worke.. made al of Stone and curiusly voultid.

β. **1434** *Indenture Fotheringhey* in Dugdale *Monast.* (1846) VI. 1414/2 Three strong and mighty arches vawthid with stoon. **1448** HEN. VI in Willis & Clark *Cambridge* (1886) I. 356, .ij. chambres aboue, vauted. **1525** LD. BERNERS *Froiss.* II. lxxxix. 99/1 The houses within were well vawted with stone, so that the engynes nor spryngalles dyd the men but small domage. **1584** B. R. tr. *Herodotus* II. 105 b, He caused an oxe to be made of wood, inwardly vauted and hollow within. **1612** SELDEN *Illustr. Drayton's Poly-olb.* Note to iii. 238 Chedder Cleeues, rocky and vauted, by continual distilling, is the fountain of a forcible stream.

γ. **1591** SYLVESTER *Du Bartas* I. iii, Narrow Vales vaulted about with Hils. **1615** tr. *De Montfart's Surv. E. Indies* 10 The said place is all vaulted about with Porches. **1686** WOOD *Life* 10 July, Buried.. in a grave brickt and vaulted over with bricks. **1774** GOLDSM. *Nat. Hist.* (1776) IV. 165 The inside is vaulted, and is large enough for the reception of eight or ten beavers. **1815** ELPHINSTONE *Acc. Caubul* (1842) I. 19 It was rain-water, preserved in small reservoirs, vaulted over with brick and mortar. **1831** SCOTT *Cast. Dang.* viii, The study.. was vaulted with stone. **1873** TRISTRAM *Moab* v. 77 Long ranges of buildings.. most solidly vaulted.

c. Of things: To form a vault over (something); to cover like a vault; to overarch.

1667 MILTON *P.L.* VI. 214 The dismal hiss Of fiery Darts in flaming volies flew, And flying vaulted either Host with fire. **1682** WHELER *Journ. Greece* I. 70 The wall beginning to bend forward, Arch-wise, as if it were to vault a Portico. **1719** YOUNG *Busiris* IV. i, Have I not seen whole armies vaulted o'er With flying jav'lins? **1736** WESLEY *Jrnl.* 23 Jan. (1829) I. 21, I was vaulted over with water in a moment. **1777** G. FORSTER *Voy. round World* II. 187 The tufted arbours which vaulted over the paths, are hung with beautiful flowers of all kinds. **1807** J. BARLOW *Columb.* VII. 231 Blaze-trailing fuses vault the night's dim round, And shells and langrage lacerate the ground.

2. *absol.* To construct a vault or vaults. *rare*$^{-0}$.

c **1440** *Promp. Parv.* 512/1 Vowtyn, or make a vowte, *arcuo, testudino*. **1552** HULOET, Vaulten or make vaultes, or arches, *fornico*. **1570** LEVINS *Manip.* 16/40 To valte, *arcum ducere*.

3. To bend, arch, or raise (something) after the manner of a vault.

1552 HULOET, Vaulten or make bente lyke a bowe, *arcuor*. *c* 1586 C'TESS PEMBROKE *Ps.* CXXXVI. iii, Whose skillfull art did vault the skies. 1626 BACON *Sylva* §376 You must Vault the Earth, whereby it may hang over them, and not touch them. 1753 *Chambers' Cycl.* Suppl. s.v., To vault a horse-shoe, is to forge it hollow,..that the shoe, thus hollow or vaulted, may not bear upon the sole that is higher than the hoof. 1833 TENNYSON *Lotos Eaters* 85 Hateful is the dark-blue sky, Vaulted o'er the dark-blue sea. 1877 J. BRYCE *Transcauc. & Ararat* 35 Looking..across the vast expanse, with the wide blue sky vaulted over it.

†**4.** To make vaults or cavities under (something).

1599 HAKLUYT *Voy.* II. I. 77 Wee shall vault and vndermine your foundations in such maner that they shalbe torne vpside downe.

5. *intr.* To curve in the form of a vault.

1805 EUGENIA DE ACTON *Nuns of Desert* II. 166 The spangled arch, which vaulted to the footstool of the Throne of Mercy. 1807 J. BARLOW *Columb.* v. 30 A dusky deep, serene as breathless even, Seem'd vaulting downward like another heaven. 1844 EMERSON *Misc.*, *Tantalus* Wks. (Bohn) III. 323 Her mighty orbit vaults like the fresh rainbow into the deep.

vault (vɔːlt), *v.*² Forms: α. 6 **vaute**, 6–7 **vaut**; 6 **vaught**. β. 6– **vault**. [app. ad. OF. *volter* (*voulter*, etc.) to gambol, leap, assimilated in form to prec.]

1. *trans.* **a.** To mount (a horse) by leaping. *rare*⁻¹.

1538 ELYOT, *Desultor*, he that can vaute [*pr.* vaunte; 1545 vaulte] a horse, and leape frome one horsbacke vnto an other. [Cf. VAULTING *vbl. sb.*² 1, quot. 1531.]

†**b.** *fig.* (Cf. LEAP *v.* 9.) *Obs.*

1611 SHAKS. *Cymb.* I. vi. 134 Should he make me Liue like Diana's Priest, betwixt cold sheets, Whiles he is vaulting variable Rampes In your despight.

c. To get over, surmount, by vaulting.

1884 *Kendal Mercury & Times* 3 Oct. 5/1 The gate..has been locked,..so that foot passengers have to vault the gate. 1901 *Munsey's Mag.* XXIV. 550/1 Rodgers vaulted the boxwood and seated himself on her veranda.

2. a. *intr.* To spring or leap; *spec.* to leap with the assistance of the hand resting on the thing to be surmounted, or with the aid of a pole.

α. *a* 1568 ASCHAM *Scholem.* I. (Arb.) 64 To vaut lustely, to runne, to leape, to wrestle. 1591 LODGE *Hist. Dk. Normandy* G ij, He was actiue of bodie, & vaughted exceedingly well. 1599 SHAKS. *Hen. V*, v. ii. 142 If I could winne a Lady at Leape-frogge, or by vawting into my Saddle, with my Armour on my backe. 1618 BOLTON *Florus* (1636) 170 King Theutobocchus..was wont to vaut over foure or five horses set together. 1621 G. SANDYS *Ovid's Met.* II. (1626) 25 The generous and gallant Phaëton, All courage, vaut's into the blazing Throne.

β. 1609 B. JONSON *Sil. Wom.* II. i, Such a delicate steeple, i' the towne, as Bow, to vault from. 1649 JER. TAYLOR *Gt. Exemp.* II. Disc. xi. 155 When we addresse ourselves to prayer..let us..when we have done, not rise from the ground as if we vaulted, or were glad we had done. 1699 BENTLEY *Phal.* 268 In his Dances he leap'd up, and vaulted, like Phrynichus, who was celebrated for those Performances. 1734 tr. *Rollin's Anc. Hist.* (1827) I. 84 Vaulting from one to the other. 1791 COWPER *Iliad* VII. 285 In standing fight adjusting all my steps To martial measures sweet, or vaulting light Into my chariot, thence [I] can urge the foe. 1814 SCOTT *Ld. of Isles* VI. xxii, Vaulting from the ground, His saddle every horseman found. 1830 TENNYSON *Mermaid* 33, I would..lightly vault from the throne and play With the mermen in and out of the rocks. 1875 JOWETT *Plato* (ed. 2) I. 220 Can he vault among swords, and turn upon a wheel.

fig. 1809–10 COLERIDGE *Friend* (1865) 68 Ignorance seldom vaults into knowledge, but passes into it through an intermediate state of obscurity. 1836 EMERSON *Nature* viii. *Prospects* Wks. (Bohn) II. 171 As if a banished king should buy his territories inch by inch, instead of vaulting at once into his throne. 1882 J. H. BLUNT *Ref. Ch. Eng.* II. 212 *note*, He was ordained priest a day or two only before he vaulted into the Archbishopric of Canterbury.

†**b.** = LEAP *v.* 9. *Obs.*

Cf. fig. uses of VAULTER² and VAULTING *vbl. sb.*²

1576 TURBERV. *Venerie* 44 Harts do commonly beginne to Vault about the middest of September. 1725 *New Cant. Dict.*, *To Vault*, to commit Acts of Debauchery.

3. *trans.* To cause to rise *to* or *into* a considerably higher position or situation.

1976 *National Observer* (U.S.) 31 July 1/2 Nadia Comaneci's electrifying gymnastics performances vaulted her from obscurity to world-wide renown. 1977 *Detroit Free Press* 11 Dec. 2-D/2 Severiano Ballesteros of Spain shot a three-under-par 69 Saturday and vaulted his team into a three-stroke lead over Canada after 54 holes of the 25th World Cup Golf Championship Saturday.

vaultage (ˈvɔːltɪdʒ). [f. VAULT *sb.*¹] A vaulted place or area; a series of vaults.

1599 SHAKS. *Hen. V*, II. iv. 124 Hee'le call you to so hot an Answer of it, That Caues and Wombie Vaultages of France Shall chide your Trespas. 1605 HEYWOOD *If you know not me* Wks. 1874 I. 290 *D. Now.* What is this vaultage for..? *Gresh.* Stowage for merchants ware, and strangers goods. *a* 1839 GALT *Demon Destiny* II. 12 Hell rebellowing through her vaultages. 1863 K. H. DIGBY *Chapel of St. John* (ed. 2) 38 It might be well for you to cast one look back towards this sepulchral vaultage. 1863 *East London Observer* 27 June, To be let, the vaultage of a large chapel in the Commercial Road.

vaulted (ˈvɔːltɪd), *ppl. a.* [f. VAULT *sb.*¹ or *v.*¹]

1. Having the form of a vault; arched or rounded.

†**a.** Of the chin. *Obs.*⁻¹

a 1533 LD. BERNERS *Huon* cxlvi. 549 Her skynne was as whyte as yᵉ floure in the mede,..her throte smoth and clere, her chyne vauted [*printed* vaunted; Fr. *voltis*].

b. Of a roof or ceiling, etc.

1552 HULOET, Vaulted rowffe, *testudinatum tectum.* 1579–80 NORTH *Plutarch*, *Lycurgus* (1895) I. 126 The fayer embowed or vawted roofes, or..fretised seelings. 1635 SWAN *Spec. M.* iv. §1 (1643) 54 The world being mans house, the Firmament is as the vaulted roof of it. 1697 DRYDEN *Virg. Georg.* IV. 536 Now to the Court arriv'd, th' admiring Son Beholds the vaulted Roofs of Pory Stone. 1703 ROWE *Ulysses* III. i, Raging Mirth With peals of Clamour shakes the vaulted Roof. 1789 SMYTH tr. *Aldrich's Archit.* (1818) 115 Terms applied without distinction to all vaulted ceilings whatever. 1844 A. P. DE LISLE in E. Purcell *Life* (1900) I. vii. 122 It contains fine stained glass, and a vaulted ceiling painted with semi-Gothick patterns. 1879 DIXON *Windsor* III. xii. 109 A vaulted arch supported an upper chamber.

c. Of the sky. (Cf. VAULT *sb.*¹ 1 c.)

c 1590 MONTGOMERIE *Sonnets* lvi, Vnderneth the heuinly vaulted round. 1595 SPENSER *Col. Clout* 611 The fume..mounts fro thence In rolling globes vp to the vauted skies. 1611 SHAKS. *Cymb.* I. vi. 33 Hath Nature giuen them eyes To see this vaulted Arch, and the rich Crop Of Sea and Land? 1700 DRYDEN *Pal. & Arc.* III. 524 The vaulted Firmament With loud Acclaims, and vast Applause is rent. *a* 1763 SHENSTONE *Elegies* vi. 26 Pale Cynthia mounts the vaulted sky. 1804 J. GRAHAME *Sabbath* 97 A temple, one not made with hands, The vaulted firmament. 1871 B. TAYLOR *Faust* (1875) I. II. 44 Lost in the vaulted azure The lark sends down his flickering lay.

d. In miscellaneous uses.

1681 GREW *Musæum* I. VI. i. 140 The Vaulted-Limpet. *Patella concamerata.* 1793 MARTYN *Lang. Bot.* s.v., Vaulted, *fornicatus*; arched. 1796 WITHERING *Brit. Plants* (ed. 3) III. 514 Bloss[om] upper lip vaulted. 1828 STARK *Elem. Nat. Hist.* II. 47 Umbilicus large, armed with small vaulted scales. 1842 PRICHARD *Nat. Hist. Man* 47 Wild horses have larger heads than domestic horses, with more vaulted foreheads. 1858 BIRCH *Anc. Pottery* II. 75 A vase..having a vaulted cover. 1870 ROLLESTON *Anim. Life* p. lvi, The skull [in reptiles] is less vaulted and less capacious than in Aves.

2. Constructed or furnished with an arched roof; covered in or roofed by a vault.

1601 HOLLAND *Pliny* II. 243 The artificiall baines and vaulted stouves and hot houses, which then were newly come vp. 1633 P. FLETCHER *Purple Isl.* v. li, This vaulted Tower's half built of massie stone. 1687 A. LOVELL tr. *Thevenot's Trav.* II. 26 In this Court there are Lodging-rooms under a vaulted Gallery that runs all round it. 1717 BERKELEY *Jrnl. Tour Italy* Wks. 1871 IV. 520 Below stairs we saw several vaulted chambers. 1794 MRS. RADCLIFFE *Myst. Udolpho* xxxi, I have only to go..along the vaulted passage and across the great hall. 1830 WHEWELL *Archit. Notes* 5 In a vaulted church, we have in general one vault which runs longitudinally along the church. 1865 W. G. PALGRAVE *Arabia* II. 320 The heavy winter rains supply the vaulted cisterns. *a* 1878 SIR G. SCOTT *Lect. Archit.* (1879) I. 247 Viollet le Duc says, the design for a vaulted building has to be commenced at the top and worked downwards.

transf. 1730–46 THOMSON *Autumn* 78 To dig the mineral from the vaulted earth. 1820 SHELLEY *Prometh. Unb.* II. v. 104 A paradise of vaulted bowers. 1878 B. TAYLOR *Deukalion* I. i. 15 At the bases of the mountain's lofty vaulted entrances of caverns.

3. Immured as in a vault.

1863 R. S. HAWKER in *Life* xx. (1905) 450 Very few could stand this vaulted life of mine.

Hence **ˈvaultedly** *adv.*

1822 J. PARKINSON *Outl. Oryctol.* 127 The shell round it being vaultedly convex.

ˈvaulter¹. *rare*⁻⁰. [f. VAULT *v.*¹] A builder of vaults.

1648 HEXHAM II, *Een Welver*, an Archer, or a Vaulter.

vaulter² (ˈvɔːltə(r)). Also 6–7 **vauter**, **vawter**, 7 **vautor**. [f. VAULT *v.*²] One who vaults or leaps. Also *fig.* (quot. 1579).

α. 1565 COOPER *Thesaurus*, *Amphippi*,..vauters from one horse to an other. 1579 GOSSON *Sch. Abuse* (Arb.) 36 Euery Vawter in one blinde Tauerne or other is Tenant at will, to which shee tolleth resorte. 1603 HOLLAND *Plutarch's Mor.* 1278 Demetrius..was well content to heare himselfe called Jupiter Καταιβάτης, that is to say, the vawter. 1607 TOPSELL *Four-f. Beasts* (1658) 226 The Numidians,..in manner of vauters,..could leap from the weary horse to a fresh. 1647 HEXHAM I. (Of Weights), A weight of Lead that Leapers, Vaulters or Dauncers on ropes hold in their hands.

β. 1552 HULOET, Vaulter on a horse, *desultor.* 1565 COOPER *Thesaurus*, *Desultor*, a vaulter that leapeth vp and downe from a horse. 1617 MORYSON *Itin.* III. 230 He had two Tumblers or Vaulters, one an Englishman, the other an Italian. 1694 *Martens' Voy. Spitzbergen* in *Acc. Sev. Late Voy.* II. 116 They put them upwards together, as the Vaulters do when they jump over Swords. 1711 STEELE *Spect.* No. 258 ⁋3 Why should not Rope-dancers, Vaulters, Tumblers,..and Posture-makers appear again on our Stage? 1791 COWPER *Odyss.* XVIII. 317 Since fame reports the Trojans..nimble vaulters to the backs of steeds. 1848 THACKERAY *Van. Fair* lxiv, The band of renowned Bohemian vaulters and tumblers. 1884 *Harper's Mag.* Jan. 301/1 If you want..fame as..a vaulter, or a heaver of heavy weights, the Manhattan is your club.

transf. 1815 KIRBY & SP. *Entomol.* iv. (1816) I. 102 The encomium which he bestows upon these vigilant little vaulters. *a* 1825 L. HUNT *To Grasshopper & Cricket* 1 Green little vaulter in the sunny grass.

vaulting (ˈvɔːltɪŋ), *vbl. sb.*¹ and *sb.* [f. VAULT *v.*¹ and *sb.*¹]

1. a. The construction of a vault or vaults; the operation of covering or roofing with a vault.

1512 in Willis & Clark *Cambridge* (1886) I. 608 Herry Semerk shall haue duryng the tyme of the said vawtyng the vse of certeyn stuffes and necessaryes. 1552 HULOET, Vaultyng or makyng a worke wyth vaultes or vault fascion, *concameratio.* 1596 HARINGTON *Metam. Ajax* (1814) 76 Then thus it is he alloweth the vaulting or arching over of the Jakes. 1647 HEXHAM I. s.v., A vaulting or making of an arch roofe. 1663 GERBIER *Counsel* 101 The fourth for the Vaulting of Sellars or any other Offices. 1850 PARKER *Gloss. Archit.* 506 Domical..vaulting over a circular area was likewise practised by the Romans. 1875 *Encycl. Brit.* II. 465/2 Their introduction..caused an entire change in the system of vaulting.

b. The development of a vaulted space.

1897 *Allbutt's Syst. Med.* IV. 150 When the abscess comes into relation with the costal walls, more or less vaulting, with widening and effacement of the intercostal spaces, will be manifest.

2. The work or structure forming a vault.

1513 in Willis & Clark *Cambridge* (1886) I. 613 The seid John Wastell shall make and sett vpp..the vawtyng of ij porches. 1760–72 H. BROOKE *Fool of Qual.* (1809) IV. 94 A silver sconce that hung from the vaulting. 1790 PENNANT *London* (1793) 65 The vaulting of this was not finished till 1296. 1811 MILNER *Eccles. Archit. Eng.* Pref. p. xvi, The gorgeous vaulting of King's College. 1849 FREEMAN *Archit.* 401 This produces in the vaulting of St. James an effect something like a wooden roof. 1898 WATTS-DUNTON *Aylwin* IX. iv, The vaulting (supported partly on low columns..and partly on the basement wall of the church) is therefore of unusual extent.

transf. and *fig.* 1827 POLLOK *Course T.* x, Beyond the azure vaulting of the sky. 1851 MRS. BROWNING *Casa Guidi Wind.* I. 1026 His truth had barred The vaulting of his life.

b. With *a* and pl.: A species, example, or piece of such work.

1750 WREN *Parentalia* 290 The Romans used hemispherical Vaultings. 1797 S. LYSONS *Rom. Antiq. Woodchester* 17 It is probable that part of the roof was formed by diagonal vaultings, resting on the four columns. 1823 BUCKLAND *Reliq. Diluv.* 5 The natural vaultings that compose this subterraneous wonder. 1875 KNIGHT *Dict. Mech.* 2694/1 Vaultings, or arched roofs, are supported by ribs or groins, often intersecting each other.

transf. 1836 BUCKLAND *Geol. & Min.* xv. §4 (1837) I. 356 The shell..is fortified by a series of ribs and vaultings disposed in the form of arches and domes.

3. *attrib.*, as ***vaulting field***, ***pier***, ***pillar***, ***rib***, ***-span***, ***shaft***, ***-surface***.

1830 WHEWELL *Archit. Notes* 21 The vaulting pillars are half columns from the floor. *Ibid.* 44 The principal, or vaulting piers in the Romanesque style were often engaged columns. *Ibid.* 45 In sexpartite vaulting they supply vaulting shafts smaller and less important than the principal piers. 1851 RUSKIN *Stones Ven.* (1874) I. viii. 99 The entire development of this cross system in connection with the vaulting ribs. *a* 1878 SIR G. SCOTT *Lect. Archit.* (1879) II. 176 In either case..the error has to be thrown into the vaulting-surfaces. 1880 *Archaeol. Cant.* XIII. 20 The Repton crypt, with its narrow vaulting-spans. 1886 B. BROWN *Schola to Cathedral* iv. 159 Eight triangular vaulting fields corresponding to the eight sides of the drum from which it rises.

vaulting (ˈvɔːltɪŋ), *vbl. sb.*² [f. VAULT *v.*²; but in fig. uses (see 3 and 4) perh. partly suggested by the etymological sense of L. *fornicātio*.]

1. The action of leaping with a vault, esp. as a gymnastic exercise.

1531 ELYOT *Gov.* I. xvii, There is also a ryght good exercise..whiche is named the vautynge [*printed* vauntynge] of a horse: that is to lepe on him at euery side without stiroppe or other helpe, specially whiles the horse is goynge. 1545 —— *Dict.*, *Desultura*, lyghtynge vp and down, vaultyng of an horse. 1553 T. WILSON *Rhet.* (1580) 13, I maie commende hym for playing at weapons,..for vautyng, for plaiyng vpon Instrumentes. 1627 HAKEWILL *Apol.* (1630) 365 These forraine exercises of vauting and dancing the Moriske. 1663 BUTLER *Hud.* I. iii. 644 Ralpho was mounted now, and gotten O'erthwart his Beast with active vau'ting. 1700 WALLIS in *Collect* (O.H.S.) I. 318 Vaulting, leaping, and the like, are now much disused, as too violent for this softer age. 1856 'STONEHENGE' *Brit. Rur. Sports* 443/2 By vaulting a man can easily clear his own height, and often considerably more.

fig. 1598 MARSTON *Sco. Villanie* I. iii. 182 Tullus goe scotfree, though thou often bragst, That for a false French-Crowne thou vaulting hadst.

2. ***vaulting horse***: †**a.** A horse mounted by vaulting, esp. one used for the exercise of leaping into the saddle without the help of a stirrup. *Obs.*

1565 COOPER *Thesaurus*, *Desultorij equi*, vaultyng horses that light souldiours vsed in warre. 1599 B. JONSON *Ev. Man out of Hum.* III. ix, I'ld spend twentie pound my vauting-horse stood here now. 1623 HEXHAM *Tongue-combat* Ep. Ded. 3 His Puppet..ouer whom hee insults, as vpon a vaulting-horse lowe enough for his leape. 1630 B. JONSON *New Inn* I. i, Instead of backing the brave steed o' mornings, To mount the chambermaid; and for a leap Of the vaulting-horse, to ply the vaulting-house.

b. *Gymnastics.* A wooden figure of a horse employed for exercise in vaulting.

1875 KNIGHT *Dict. Mech.* 2694/1 *Vaulting horse*, a wooden horse in a gymnasium, for practice in vaulting. 1884 *Health Exhib. Catal.* 127/1 All kinds of Gymnastic Apparatus,..including..Vaulting Horses, Vaulting Bucks, Vaulting Tables. 1898 *Daily News* 23 March 6/2 The squad representing the School of Arms gave a very neat exhibition of vaulting-horse work.

†**3.** ***vaulting-house***, a brothel. Also ***vaulting-door***, the door of such a place. *Obs.*

(*a*) 1596 LODGE *Wits Miserie* I iiij, Let him but looke into a vawting house, he shall play his tricks without charges. 1606 DEKKER *Sev. Sins* IV. (Arb.) 32 Letchery is patron of al your Suburb Colledges, and sets vp Vaulting-houses, and Daunsing-Schooles. 1639 MASSINGER *Unnatural Combat* I. i, Let me but receive My pay that is behind, to set me up A tavern or a vaulting-house. While men love Or drunkenness or lechery, they'll ne'er fail me.

(*b*) 1625 MASSINGER *Parl. Love* IV. iii, No more talking, Dear keeper of the vaulting door; lead on.

†**4.** ***vaulting-school***: **a.** = prec. **b.** (See quot. *a* 1700). *Obs.*

1606 H. PARROT *Mousetrap* 93 Vnto a Garden-house, or Vaulting-schoole. **1637** NABBES *Microcosm.* II, Ayre was my father, and my mother a light-heel'd madame that kept a vaulting-schoole at the signe of Virgo. **1672** WYCHERLEY *Love in Wood* IV. v, Must my lodging be your vaulting-school still? Thou hast appointed a wench to come hither, I find. *a* **1700** B. E. *Dict. Cant. Crew, Vaulting-School,* a Bawdy-house; also an Academy where Vaulting, and other Manly Exercises are Taught. [Hence in later slang Dicts.]

5. *attrib.* in various uses, as ***vaulting bar, buck, -master, motion.***

1641 W. STOKES (*title*), The Vaulting Master; or the Art of Vaulting reduced to a Method. **1700** WALLIS in *Collect.* (O.H.S.) I. 317 Mr. Bosely (then a dancing-master and vaulting-master here). **1771** M. LORT in J. Granger *Lett.* (1805) 194 He [*sc.* William Stokes] was a noted vaulting-master and rope-dancer. **1839** 'CRAVEN' *Walker's Manly Exerc.* (ed. 6) 48 This exercise is conveniently practised on the vaulting bar, which rests upon two or three posts. **1849** *Chambers's Inform. People* II. 643/2 Exercises [in vaulting] are performed with vaulting bars. **1870** HARDY & WARE *Mod. Hoyle, Chess* 40 The Knight is the only piece that possesses what is styled the 'vaulting motion'. **1884** [see 2 b].

vaulting ('vɔːltɪŋ), *ppl. a.* [f. VAULT *v.*[2]] That vaults or leaps.

1605 SHAKS. *Macb.* I. vii. 27 Vaulting Ambition, which ore-leapes it selfe, And falles on th'other. **1637** B. JONSON *Sad Shepherd* II. i, Allbe he know her, As doth the vauting Hart his venting Hind. **1847** H. MILLER *First Impr. Eng.* xiii. (1857) 217 Such always is the vaulting liberty of a false theology. **1868** ISABELLE SAXON *Five Years Golden Gate* 52 So wild are the speculations, and so vaulting is the ambition of the majority of business men. **1887** STEVENSON *Misadv. J. Nicholson* i. 3 It could not come, without vaulting hyperbole, under the rubric of a gilded saloon.

b. ***vaulting monkey***: (see quots.).

1800 SHAW *Gen. Zool.* I. I. 51 Vaulting Monkey, *Simia Petaurista.* **1871** *Cassell's Nat. Hist.* I. 109 The White-nosed Monkey (*Ceropithecus petaurista*)... Some call it the Vaulting Monkey.

Hence '**vaultingly** *adv.*

1890 *Temple Bar* Jan. 147 The Niobe was vaultingly ambitious.

'**vaulture.** [f. VAULT *sb.*[1] Cf. obs. F. *vouture* (*voulture, volture*).] Vaulting.

1692 RAY *Three Physico-Theol. Disc.* (1713) iii. 20 The reason is the Strength and Firmness of their Vaulture and Pillars, sufficient to support the superincumbent Weight.

vaulty ('vɔːltɪ), *a.* Also 6 **vautie**, 6–7 **vaultie.** [f. VAULT *sb.*[1]] Resembling a vault; having the arching form of a vault.

1545 RAYNALD *Byrth Mankynde* H hh ij, L is ye back or bossing side of the liuer. M the holowe, caue, or vautie part of ye liuer. *a* **1586** SIDNEY *Arcadia* III. xxv. (1622) 441 Well (me thinkes) becomes this vaultie skie A stately tombe to couer him deceased. *c* **1595** J. DICKENSON *Sheph. Compl.* (1878) 8 Heau'ns light, whose vautie roofe bright orbs embosse. **1651** HOWELL *Venice* 76 Sound..which resounds in vaulty and hollow places. **1726** A. MONRO *Anat. Bones* (1741) 94 This vaulty Labyrinth. **1890** *Illustr. Lond. News* 22 Nov. 650/2 The great vaulty interior of the house.

vaumbras, obs. form of VAMBRACE.

vaumpe, obs. form of VAMP *sb.*[1]

†**vaumure,** *sb. Obs.* Forms: *α.* 5–7 (9) **vawmure** (6 **vawmeure, vawmer**), 6–7 **vaumure.** *β.* 6–7 **vamure** (6 **vamer**). *γ.* 6 **vaimure.** [Reduced form of AF. **vaunt-mur*: see VAUNTMURE and AVANTMURE.] An advanced wall or earthwork thrown out in front of the main fortifications; the outer wall or series of walls of a fortification or fortress.

α. *c* **1475** *Contin. Brut.* II. 577 The Flemmynges laid þeire gonnes to þe walles, & beete doun þe vawmures and þe walles. **1562** PHAER *Æneid* D dj, Afront the vaumures long ..the legion wayting stood. **1587** FLEMING *Contn. Holinshed* III. 1427 Gods prouidence..ouerthrew a peece of the wall and vawmure of six and twentie poles. **1609** HOLLAND *Amm. Marcell.* 179 The safe recourse they had to the wall and vaumure strengthened with turfe defended these wait-layers from all danger. *a* **1656** USSHER *Ann.* (1658) 246 [He] took the vawmure, which was of no great strength. *Ibid.* 254 The Macedons therefore not having quite battered the inner wall, but onely undermined a vaumure made of brick. [**1843** LYTTON *Last Bar.* I. i, Next, the Palace, with its bulwark and vaumure.]

β. *a* **1548** HALL *Chron., Hen. VIII,* 133 b, On the Weste side was a greate rampire or banke, very stepe without and within, and like to a vamure of a fortresse, by the vamure the diches were .xxiiii. fote depe. **1577** B. GOOGE *Heresbach's Husb.* II. (1586) 50 Wherin the vamure must be so steep, that it may not easily be climed. **1600** FAIRFAX *Tasso* XI. lxiv, A mount thereof to make, Or else some vamure fit to saue the towne. **1642** *Prince Rupert's Sp. to King* 4 Their graffes or ditches being dry and their vamures unpallisado'd.

γ. **1599** HAKLUYT *Voy.* II. 124 To make up againe their vaimures, the which were throwen downe with the fury of the artillery. *Ibid.,* He threw downe more then halfe thereof [a wall], breaking also one part of the vaimure.

Hence †**vaumure** *v. trans.,* to provide with a vaumure or advanced earthwork. †**vaumuring,** the material forming a vaumure; vaumures collectively. *Obs. rare.*

1523 SURREY in Morton *Mon. Ann. Teviotdale* (1832) 27 The said fortres was vawmeured with erthe of the beste sorte .., and had a barbican. *c* **1600** *Surv. Carlisle Castle* in Scott *Border Antiq.* (1814) I. 35 The vawmering of Calder-tower is in decay.

†**vaunce,** *v. Obs.* Also 4–6 **vaunse,** 6 **vance.** [Aphetic f. of ADVANCE *v.*] To advance, in various senses. (Common in the 16th cent.)

a. *trans.* **1303** R. BRUNNE *Handl. Synne* 5516 Þou art nat wurþy vaunsed to be. *a* **1400** LANGL. *P. Pl.* B. III. 33 (MS. Rawl. Poet. 38), Shal no lewednesse lette þe clerkes þat I louye, That he [ne] worth furst vaunsed. *a* **1450** MYRC *Par. Pr.* 1636 Ʒef hyt [*i.e.* contrition] be gret, ʒeue luyte penaunce. Ʒef hyt be luyte, þow moste hyt vaunce [*v.r.* haunce]. **1489** CAXTON *Faytes of A.* I. xviii. 54 The wyse captayne ought not to putte nor vaunce forth hym and hys men lyghtly to a bataylle. **1582** STANYHURST *Æneis* (Arb.) 85 Al thogh..winds vaunce fully thy sayls with prosperus huffing. **1594** R. CAREW *Tasso* (1881) 21 This hardie speech ..Gaue ech one care, and vaunst his courage hie. **1616** J. LANE *Contn. Sqr.'s T.* IX. 379 Which embleams hee bid vaunce, for foes to reede of mercie, iustice, death, how hee decreed.

b. *refl.* *c* **1489** CAXTON *Sonnes of Aymon* xiv. 350 He vaunced hym selfe forthe, and caught the kynge wyth bothe hys armes. —— *Blanchardyn* xxiii. 77 As blanchardyn.. perceyued p^e noble pucelle, he dyde vaunce him self toward her. *a* **1548** HALL *Chron.* (1809) 616 A picture of an armed Knight on a courser barded Vauncyng himself upon that hill. **1573** TUSSER *Husb.* (1878) 207 But marke the chance, my self to vance, By friendships lot, to Paules I got. **1587** TURBERV. *Trag. Tales* (1837) 41 They vaunst themselves, and stood mee bolt upright.

c. *intr.* **1544** BETHAM *Precepts War* I. cxcvii. I vj b, The hoste vauncyng towarde battayl, the capitayne ought to speake these wordes. **1596** SPENSER *F.Q.* IV. iv. 17 Sir Satyrane..vauncing forth from all the other band Of knights.

Hence †'**vauncing** *vbl. sb. Obs.*

c **1400** *Apol. Loll.* 56 A how bitter luf and vauncing [L. *promotio*]..þat he reys his luf at a moment a-boue a veyn þing. **1426** AUDELAY *Poems* (Percy Soc.) 33 Clerkys that han cunnyng, Schuld have monys soule in kepyng, Bot thai mai get no vaunsyng Without symony.

vaunce-roof, variant of VANCE-ROOF.

vaunchace, variant of VANCHASE *Obs.*

†**vauneant.** *Obs.*$^{-1}$ [a. older F. *vau-, vautneant,* f. *vaut* 3rd pers. sing. pres. of *valoir* to be worth + *neant* nothing.] A good-for-nothing person.

1621 T. WILLIAMSON tr. *Goulart's Wise Vieillard* 109 We can doe no other then blame these vau-neantes, vaine & vitious persons.

vaunplate, obs. form of VAMPLATE.

vaunt (vɔːnt, *U.S.* vɑːnt), *sb.*[1] Now *rhet.* or *arch.* Also 5–6 **vaunte,** 6–7 **vant.** [Aphetic f. AVAUNT *sb.*[1] Cf. VAUNT *v.*]

1. Boasting, bragging; boastful or vainglorious language or utterance; arrogant assertion or bearing.

a **1400–50** *Alexander* 1880 Bot þof þou þe victor a-vaile na vaunte sall arise. **14..** *Sir Beues* (S.) 3963 + 87 Kyng Yuor swoor with grete vaunt Be hys god Tirmegaunt. **1500–20** DUNBAR *Poems* xiv. 41 Sic vant of wostouris with hairtis in sinfull staturis. **1577** B. GOOGE *Heresbach's Husb.* I. (1586) 4 For my part (without vaunt be it spoken,) I haue seruice euery day at certaine appointed houres. **1596** SPENSER *F.Q.* VI. iv. 29 A great Gyant..Whom he did ouerthrow..And in three battailes did so deadly daunt, That he dare not returne for all his daily vaunt. **1838** PRESCOTT *Ferd. & Is.* II. i. (1846) II. 256 With all the vaunt and insolent port of a conqueror. *personified.* *a* **1510** DOUGLAS *K. Hart* II. 523 To Vant and Voky ʒe beir this rowm slef.

transf. **1553** T. WILSON *Rhet.* (1580) 14 [Certain orators] would so muche saie as their witte would giue, not weighyng the state of the cause, but mindyng the vaunt of their braine.

2. ***to make*** (***one's*** or ***a***) ***vaunt,*** to boast or brag. Also const. *of* something. Now *rare.*

(*a*) **1530** PALSGR. 619/2 He made his vaunte that he wolde beate me. **1555** EDEN *Decades* (Arb.) 147 The christians.. whom thou haste..threated to drawe by the heare of their heades to the nexte ryuer,..as thou haste often tymes made thy vaunte emonge thy naked slaues. **1573** G. HARVEY *Letter-bk.* (Camden) 5, [I] am an inch beneath him, as he ons made his vaunt.

(*b*) *a* **1533** LD. BERNERS *Huon* lii. 177 Make no vaunt of ony thynge without thou canst do it in dede, for in euery thynge I wyll proue thee. **1548** UDALL *Erasm. Par. Luke* 51 Many make vauntes and crakes of hauing visions of Aungels, whiche they yet neuer sawe. **1687** MIÈGE *Gt. Fr. Dict.* II. s.v., To make a vaunt of a Thing, to boast of it.

(*c*) **1586** G. WHITNEY *Embl.* 228 Then, let him not make vaunt of his desert. **1860** MOTLEY *Netherl.* iv. (1868) I. 114 He stoutly denied the facts of which the leaguers made vaunt.

3. A boasting assertion, speech, or statement; a boast or brag.

1597 DELONEY *Gentle Craft* Wks. (1912) 186 Tom Drums vants, and his rare intertainment at Mistris Farmers house. **1625** BACON *Ess., Vain-Glory* (Arb.) 463 They that are Glorious, must needs be Factious.. They must needs be Violent, to make good their owne Vaunts. **1667** MILTON *P.L.* IV. 84 The spirits beneath, whom I seduc'd With other promises and other vaunts Then to submit, boasting I could subdue Th' Omnipotent. **1694** DRYDEN *Love Tri.* I. i, The haughty Captive, who had made his Vaunts To lay their Dwellings level. **1716** POPE *Iliad* v. 580 Now, now thy country calls her wonted friends, And the proud vaunt in just derision ends. *a* **1735** G. GRANVILLE *Unnat. Flights Poetry* 51 Such vaunts as his who can with patience read? **1798** COLERIDGE *Fears in Solitude* 198 May the vaunts And menace of the vengeful enemy Pass like the gust. **1818** HALLAM *Mid. Ages* ix. II. (1819) III. 375 A writer of the thirteenth [century] asserts that all the world was clothed from English wool wrought in Flanders. This indeed is an exaggerated vaunt. **1855** PRESCOTT *Philip II,* I. i, Spain then first realized the magnificent vaunt,..that the sun never set within the borders of her dominions. **1882** FARRAR *Early Chr.* II. 58 For a man to boast of wisdom when his heart is full of bitter emulation and party spirit is a lying vaunt.

b. Const. *of.*

1565 JEWEL *Reply Harding* (1611) 73 But that the same humanitie of Christ is in the Sacrament, in such grosse sort, as is supposed by our Aduersaries, notwithstanding many bold vants thereof made, yet was it hitherto neuer prooued. **1589** GREENE *Menaphon* (Arb.) 73 Telling her how he was a King,..what power he had to aduance her, with many other proude vaunts of his wealth. **1593** SHAKS. *2 Hen. VI,* III. i. 50 [He] by reputing of his high discent..And such high vaunts of his Nobilitie, Did [etc.]. **1654** GATAKER *Disc. Apol.* 80 Of which his vain pretension, and his freqent vaunts thereof being by letters minded and admonished, he returns this Answer. **1778** BP. LOWTH *Transl. Isaiah* Notes (ed. 12) 217 They introduce him as uttering the most extravagant vaunts of his power and ambitious designs. **1826** SCOTT *Rev. Kemble's Life,* *Biogr.* (1849) 200 Assassins [were] approaching him..in the very midst of his triumphant vaunt of his repeated victories.

†**c.** (See quot. and cf. BRAG *sb.*[1] 6.) *Obs.*$^{-0}$

1598 FLORIO, *Chiesta,*..a vaunt or vye in gaming.

4. A cause or subject of boasting. *rare.*

1791 COWPER *Iliad* II. 188 Is it thus at last That the Achaians..Shall seek again their country, leaving here, To be the vaunt of Ilium and her King, Helen of Argos?

†**vaunt,** *sb.*[2] *Obs.* Also 7 **vant.** [Independent use of the prefix VANT-, VAUNT-. Cf. F. *avant* fore part.]

1. A front part or portion. *rare.*

In the first quot. with reference to the face.

1589 ? LYLY *Pappe w. Hatchet* C iij b, Take awaie this beard, and giue mee a pikede vaunt, Martin sweares by his ten bones. **1606** SHAKS. *Tr. & Cr.* Prol. 27 Our Play Leapes ore the vaunt and firstlings of those broyles, Beginning in the middle.

2. The van of an army.

1606 SHAKS. *Ant. & Cl.* IV. vi. 9 Go charge Agrippa, Plant those that haue reuolted in the Vant. **1623** BINGHAM *Xenophon* 59 Cherisophus led the Vaunt,..Xenophon and the Reare-Commanders brought vp the Reare. **1624** DONNE *Devot.* (ed. 2) 380 When an Army marches, the vaunt may lodge to night, where the Reare comes not till to morrow.

†**vaunt,** *sb.*[3] *Obs. rare.* [Of obscure origin.] A kind of fruit pie.

1508–13 W. DE WORDE *Bk. Keruynge* in *Babees Bk.* (1868) 270 Fruyter vaunte, with a subtylte, two potages, blaunche manger, and gelly. **1594** *Gd. Huswifes Handmaid Kitchin* 38 b, To make a Vaunt. Take marrow of Beefe [etc.]. *Ibid.* 39 Cut it in faire slices,..as long as your Vaunt is.

vaunt (vɔːnt, *U.S.* vɑːnt), *v.* Now *rhet.* or *arch.* Also 5–7 **vant,** 6 **vaunte,** 6 *Sc.* **wantt-, wanet-,** 6–7 **vante.** [a. OF. (also mod.F.) *vanter,* = It. and med.L. *vantare*:—pop.L. **vānitāre*: cf. AVAUNT *v.*[1]]

1. *intr.* To boast or brag; to use boastful, bragging, or vainglorious language.

Fairly common *c* 1600; now *rare* or *Obs.*

14.. LANGL. *P. Pl.* C. VII. 35 Me wilnynge þat men wende ich were..Riche,..Bostynge and Braggynge wyth meny bolde oþes, Auauntyng vp-on [*Ilchester MS.* Vauntyng vp] my veine glorie for eny vndernymynge. *c* **1440** *Promp. Parv.* 508/1 Vaunton, or a-vaunton or booston, *jacto, ostento.* **1515** BARCLAY *Egloges* iv. (1570) C vj/1 They laude their verses, they boast, they vaunt, they iet. **1570** LEVINS *Manip.* 25 To vaunt, *gloriari.* **1579** LYLY *Euphues* (Arb.) 198 But I will not vaunt, before the victorie. **1603** J. DAVIES (Heref.) *Microcosmos* Wks. (Grosart) I. 31/1 For Southward, men are cruell, moody, madd, Hot blacke, leane, leapers, lustfull, vsd to vant. **1630** R. *Johnson's Kingd. & Commw.* 476 All this (as the drunkard will vaunt,) for the honour of..the Prince. **1699** TEMPLE *Hist. Eng.* 583 He talk'd little, never vaunted, observ'd much, was very secret. **1700** DRYDEN *Ovid's Met.* xv. 342 In time he vaunts among his Youthful Peers, Strong-bon'd, and strung with Nerves, in pride of Years. **1791** COWPER *Iliad* XI. 462 Transported from his ambush forth he leap'd With a loud laugh, and, vaunting, thus exclaim'd: Oh shaft well shot! it galls thee. **1805** EUGENIA DE ACTON *Nuns of Desert* I. 145 Sometimes vowing never-ceasing affection, then vaunting in his power, threatening revenge for her disdainful repulsion of offers. **1826** ANDR. SCOTT *Poems* 97 He could vaunting tell, That he wad face the ghaist.

b. Const. *of* (or †*on*).

1548–77 VICARY *Anat.* (1888) i. 17 A cunning and skilful Chirurgion neede neuer vaunt of his dooings. **1584–7** GREENE *Morando* Wks. (Grosart) III. 67 They thinke no man so able to atchiue any enterprises as he, vanting of his victories. **1605** CAMDEN *Rem., Epigr.* 12 The vanitie of them which vaunt of their auncient nobility. **1634** W. TIRWHYT tr. *Balzac's Lett.* (vol. I) 394 He..blusheth not at Christian vertues, nor vanteth of moral ones. **1663** GERBIER *Counsel* 93 The Hollanders..Vant of their scarcity of theeves. **1718** POPE *Iliad* XIII. 82 Here Hector..Vaunts of his gods, and calls high Jove his sire. **1792** BOSWELL *Johnson* an. 1775, He did not vaunt of his new dignity, but I understood he was highly pleased with it. **1802** MRS. E. PARSONS *Myst. Visit* IV. 53 Who, like the proud Pharisee,..proudly vaunt on their own virtues. **1818** BYRON *Juan* I. i, Of such as these I should not care to vaunt. **1821** JOANNA BAILLIE *Metr. Leg., Wallace* v, The meanest drudge will sometimes vaunt Of independent sires.

c. With other preps.

1549 COVERDALE, etc. *Erasm. Par. 2 Peter* II. 19 They are rather filthe and spottes, who in their filthie glotonous bankettings vaunt against you, as though you were madde menne. **1591** SPENSER *Virg. Gnat* 559 And all that vaunts in worldly vanitie Shall fall through fortunes mutabilitie. *c* **1600** SHAKS. *Sonn.* xv, When I perceiue that men as plants increase, Cheared and checkt euen by the selfe-same skie: Vaunt in their youthfull sap, at height decrease. **1605** *1st Part Ieronimo* III. ii. (Stage direction), Andrea slain, and Prince Balthezer vanting on him. **1628** PRYNNE *Lovelockes* 40 Who vaunts, and triumphes, in the length and largenesse of his Locke. **1795** SOUTHEY *Joan of Arc* VII. 86 So erst from earth Antæus vaunting in his giant bulk, When graspt by force Herculean, down he fell Vanquish'd. **1805** EUGENIA DE ACTON *Nuns of Desert* II. 254 She vaunted over the 'humble and meek'.

†**d.** With *it.* Also *spec.* (see quot. 1611). *Obs.*

1611 FLORIO, *Chiestare*,..to vant it or vie it in gaming. **1614** W. BROWNE *Sheph. Pipe* I. i, Hearke, how yonder Thrustle chants it, And her mate as proudly vants it.

2. With clause as object, usu. introduced by *that.*

1523 LD. BERNERS *Froiss.* I. ccccxxxviii. 311/2 He had before sayd and vaunted, howe & the kynge came to reyse the siege before Ipre, he wolde abyde & fight with hym. **1562** WINȜET *Wks.* (S.T.S.) II. 37 Apollinaris in a manere crakis and waintis that he consentis in deid to the vnitie of the Trinitie. **1593** SHAKS. *2 Hen. VI*, I. iii. 87 She vaunted 'mongst her Minions t'other day, The very trayne of her worst wearing Gowne, Was better worth then all my Fathers Lands. **1601** HOLLAND *Pliny* I. 171 All others may vaunt verily, that they have vanquished men: but Sergius may boast, that he hath conquered..Fortune her selfe. **1653** H. COGAN tr. *Pinto's Trav.* viii. 25 Prester-John, of whose race the Abissins vaunt they are descended. **1815** W. H. IRELAND *Scribbleomania* 136 *note*, The emperor..vaunting that, with his good sword,..he could cut a man in twain. **1853** J. H. NEWMAN *Hist. Sk.* (1873) II. I. i. 33 Attila vaunted that the grass never grew again after his horse's hoof.

†**3.** *refl.* To boast, extol, glorify, or praise (oneself). Usu. const. *for*, *of*, or *in*. *Obs.*

a **1400–50** *Alexander* 2713 For vertu ne no victori ne vant noght þi-selfe. *a* **1500** in *Ratis Raving*, etc. 81 Thai rus thaim nocht of done foly,..Na wanttis thaim nocht of thar gud deid. **1624** WOTTON *Arch.* 55 Apelles [did excel] in Invention and Grace, whereof he doth himself most vaunt. **1825** SCOTT *Talism.* iii, Thou shouldst know, ere thou vauntest thyself, that one steel glove can crush a whole handful of hornets. **1876** SWINBURNE *Erechtheus* 1180 Who may vaunt him as we may in death though he die for the land?

transf. **1576** GASCOIGNE *Kenilworth Castle* Wks. 1910 II. 119 The Countrey craves consent, your vertues vaunt themselfe. *c* **1590** GREENE *Fr. Bacon* III. i, Fore the morning sun Shall vaunt him thrice ouer the loftie east.

†**b.** With infinitive or object clause. Also with *for* (= as), and double accusative. *Obs.*

1513 DOUGLAS *Æneid* I. ix. 85 Full oft him self extoll and vant he wald Of Troiane bluide to be descend of ald. **1562** WINȜET *Wks.* (S.T.S.) II. 27 Donatistis..quha craikis and wanetis thame be the auctoritie of that counsel to baptize agane. **1585** T. WASHINGTON tr. *Nicholay's Voy.* IV. xxviii. 146 b, Shooting.., whereof they do vaunt themselues to haue been the first inuentors. **1625** BACON *Ess., Friendship* (Arb.) 169 Pompey vaunted Himselfe for Sylla's Ouermatch. **1810** SCOTT *Bl. Dwarf* xvi, Thou vauntest thyself a philosopher?

†**c.** To bear (oneself) proudly or vaingloriously.

1570–6 LAMBARDE *Peramb. Kent* (1826) 236 The Church that yet vaunteth it selfe with two steeples. **1577** *Test. of 12 Patr.* (1604) 52 Ye shall be swoln with wickednesse in the priesthood,..not only vaunting and boasting your selves against men, but also being puffed and swoln up with pride against the commandments of God. **1611** BIBLE *1 Cor.* xiii. 4 Charitie enuieth not: charitie vaunteth not it selfe, is not puffed vp. **1663** S. PATRICK *Parab. Pilgr.* xi. (1687) 67 Hath he not crowned himself with greater glory in not vaunting himself in those Trophies?

†**4.** *trans.* To proclaim or display proudly. *Obs.*

1590 SPENSER *F.Q.* III. ii. 16 Tell me..What shape, what shield,..And what so else his person most may vaunt? **1592** KYD *Sp. Trag.* I. ii. 27 There met our armies in their proud aray: Both furnisht well, both full of hope and feare,..Both vaunting sundry colours of deuice.

5. To boast of (something); to commend or praise in a vainglorious manner.

a **1592** GREENE *Alphonsus* II. i, And then I meane to vaunt our victorie. *c* **1696** PRIOR *Partial Fame* 7 He vaunts His Conquest, She conceals Her Shame. **1718** *Free-thinker* No. 65. 68 A Keeper of Bears may as well vaunt his Policy, as a Ruler of Slaves. **1762–71** H. WALPOLE *Vertue's Anecd. Paint.* (1786) I. Pref. 11 This country, which does not always err in vaunting its own productions. **1821** SCOTT *Kenilw.* xxxvii, He really felt the ascendency which he vaunted. **1850** MERIVALE *Rom. Rep.* viii. (1865) I. 226 The Roman matron was taught indeed to vaunt her ignorance as a virtue. **1878** EMERSON *Misc. Papers, Sov. Ethics* Wks. (Bohn) III. 372 In ignorant ages it was common to vaunt the human superiority by underrating the instinct of other animals.

†**b.** To utter boastingly. *Obs.*$^{-1}$

1633 P. FLETCHER *Poet. Misc.* 87 They cut my heart, they vant that bitter word, Where is thy trust? where is thy hope?

†**vaunt**, *int. Obs. rare.* [Aphetic form of AVAUNT *int.*, etc.] Avaunt, away, be off!

1598 *Mucedorus* Induct. 13 Vaunt, churlish curre,..Blush, monster, blush, and post away with shame. **1608** H. CLAPHAM *Errour Right Hand* 50 Then, vaunt Dogge! damn'd of thine owne conscience.

vaunt-, *prefix*, an AF. variant of VANT-. (For examples see VAUNT-CHASE, -COURIER, etc.)

'**vauntage.** *rare*$^{-1}$. [f. VAUNT *sb.*[1]] Boasting, vaunting.

1818 MILMAN *Samor* III. 374 Frisian and Scandinavian, Cimbrian rich In ancient vauntage of his sires, who clomb The Alpine snows, and shook free Rome with dread.

vauntbrace, -bras(se, varr. and obs. forms of VANTBRACE.

†**vaunt-chase.** *Obs. rare.* [prob. ad. AF. **vauntchace*: see VAUNT-.] = VANCHASE. (See also quot. 1688.)

1576 TURBERV. *Venerie* 113 'There he goeth, thats he,..to him, to him,' naming the hound that goth away with the vautchace [*sic*] and hallowing the rest vnto him. **1688** HOLME *Armoury* III. 189/1 Vaunt-chase is the Hound that leadeth the rest in the Chase.

vaunt-courier ('vɔːnt-, 'vɑːnt,kʊərɪə(r)). Forms: α. 6 vantcorrour, -currour, -curor, 6–8 -curror, 7 -curreur, -currer; 6 vauntcurrour, 7 -curror, 6–7 vauntcurrer. β. 6 vaunte-, 6–7 vauntcurrier, 7 -currior, 6–7 vantcurrier, 7 -curier. γ. 7 vantcourier, vauntcourrier, 7, 9 vauntcourier. δ. 7 vauntcourer, vantcourrer. ε. *erron.* 7 vaunt carrier. [ad. F. *avant-coureur* AVANT-COURIER, with assimilation to forms in VANT-, VAUNT-, and to COURIER *sb.* Cf. VANCOURIER.]

†**1.** One of the advance-guard of an army or body of troops; a soldier or horseman sent out in advance of the main body. Usually in *pl.* *Obs.*

α. **1560** DAUS tr. *Sleidane's Comm.* 433 b, He by his vauntcurrers levied as muche power as he possible mighte. **1569** STOCKER tr. *Diod. Sic.* II. x. 55 The vauntcurrers of eche side gaue intelligence of the approch of one an other. **1570** R. HICHCOCK *Quintess. Wit* 68 b, In the spyes, in the guides, in the vantcorrours, in the principall officers. **1601** R. JOHNSON *Kingd. & Commw.* 184 Vpon the head of the battell ranged 200 thousande horsemen in small troupes, like our vantcurrers. **1614** RALEIGH *Hist. World* III. x. II. 114 On the sodaine one of their Vaunt-currors brought newes of the King's approch. **1650** R. STAPYLTON *Strada's Low C. Wars* IX. 50 Some Vantcurrers advancing a little before the Army.

β. **1579–80** NORTH *Plutarch, Publicola* (1895) I. 275 Lucretius..was appointed to make head against the vauntcurriers of the Sabynes. **1600** DYMMOK *Ireland* (1843) 31 The rebel..deliveringe some few shott out of the woods and ditches upon our vaunt-curriers. *a* **1642** KYNASTON *Leoline & Sydanis* 1265 How as the swift vant-curriers rode about As sentinell perdue. *a* **1670** HACKET *Abp. Williams* I. (1692) 190 Unless the leader look about him in his march and search every hedge by vant-curriers.

γ. **1609** DEKKER *Gull's Hornbk.* Wks. (Grosart) II. 219 Thou dost not only send out the lively spirits, like vauntcouriers, to fortify and make good the uttermost borders of thy body.

δ. **1604** R. CAWDREY *Table Alph.*, *Vauntcourers*, forerunners. **1614** RALEIGH *Hist. World* V. iii. II. 449 The Carthaginian Horse, and light Armature, fell vpon the Roman Vant-courrers.

ε. **1677** W. HUBBARD *Narrative* 73 A party of Indians..fired upon the front and mortally wounded two of the vaunt Carriers.

2. *transf.* One who goes or is sent out in advance in order to prepare the way or to announce the approach of another; a forerunner.

α. **1561** DAUS tr. *Bullinger on Apoc.* (1573) 177 And this latter so impugned the supremacie of the Patriarch of Constantinople, that he sticked not to call hym the vauntcurrour of Antichrist. **1567** DRANT *Horace, Ep.* iii. c v, And those that wil vauntcurrers be Not I wil draw theim backe. **1607** DEKKER *Northward Hoe* II. Wks. 1873 III. 29 Ile send my vant-currer presently. **1709** STRYPE *Ann. Ref.* I. II. xliv. 479 All such as had been vantcurrors in private colleges to enter into this apostasy.

β, γ. **1603** HARSNET *Pop. Impost.* 12 The harbinger, the host, the Steward, the Vauntcourrier. **1606** DEKKER *News from Hell* Wks. (Grosart) II. 137 To all which questions the vant curier answers briefly. **1886** R. F. BURTON *Arab. Nts.* (abr. ed.) I. 4 He despatched vaunt-couriers and messengers of glad tidings.

b. Of things.

1598 BARKCLEY *Felic. Man* v. (1603) 472 The crying and lamenting of a childe when hee first entereth into this world, doth seeme to presage his painefull life, as a vauntcurrer of his miseries to come. **1605** SHAKS. *Lear* III. ii. 5 You Sulph'rous and Thought-executing Fires, Vaunt-curriors to Oake-cleauing Thunder-bolts. **1639** CHAPMAN & SHIRLEY *Chabot* III. ii, I will relate to your honours his most cruel exactions upon the subject—the old vantcouriers of rebellions. **1821** MILMAN *Fall Jerusalem* 39 And gloom of deepest mid-night the vaunt-courier Of your dread presence. **1849** LONGF. *Kavanagh* xix, These were the vaunt-couriers and attendants of the hot August.

†**vaunt-currying**, *a. Obs.*$^{-1}$ [? f. *vaunt-currier* VAUNT-COURIER. Cf. CURRY *v.*[2]] (Meaning not clear.)

1606 *Sir G. Goosecappe* I. iii. in Bullen *Old Plays* (1884) III, *Will.* How will they digest it thinkest thou, when they shall finde our Ladies not there? *Ia.* I haue a vaunt-Curriing deuise shall make them digest it most healthfully.

'**vaunted**, *ppl. a.* Also 7 vanted. [f. VAUNT *v.*] Boasted or bragged of; highly extolled.

1635 A. STAFFORD *Fem. Glory* (1869) 123 Whose meanest Perfection so farre excels all your so long vanted masculine merits. **1667** MILTON *P.L.* III. 251 My Vanquisher, spoild of his vanted spoile. **1789** MRS. PIOZZI *Journ. France* II. 42, I have seen the vaunted present of porcelain. **1825** SCOTT *Talism.* xiii, Our cousin Edith must first learn how this vaunted wight hath conducted himself. **1838** PRESCOTT *Ferd. & Is.* (1846) II. I. xvii. 124 Their vaunted purity of blood. **1893** PEMBER *Earth's Earliest Ages* 67 How..all our vaunted wisdom in this life is said to be at best but a knowledge in part.

vauntegarde, variant of VANTGUARD *Obs.*

vaunter ('vɔːntə(r)). Now *arch.* Forms: 5–6 vantour, 6 vauntour; 6 *Sc.* vantar; 6–7 vanter, 7– vaunter. [ad. OF. *vantere*, *vanteor* (AF. *vanteour*), *vanteur* (F. *vanteur*), f. *vanter* VAUNT *v.* Cf. Prov. *vantaire*, *-ador*, It. *vantatore*.]

A boaster or braggart.

1456 SIR G. HAYE *Law Arms* (S.T.S.) 30 Thai ar..grete vantouris of litill foredede. **1484** CAXTON *Chivalry* 65 By surete ben mesprysed many cowardes, vauntours, and many vayne semblaunces. **1525** LD. BERNERS *Froiss.* II. xxxiv. 104 These frenchmen ar great vantours and hyghe mynded. **1573** TYNE in *Cath. Tract.* (S.T.S.) 29 Tratours,..vantars, luffars of thame selues mair than of God. **1588** SHAKS. *Tit. A.* V. iii. 113 Alas you know, I am no Vaunter I. *a* **1610** HEALEY *Theophrastus* (1636) 79 A vanter or forth-putter is he, that boastes upon the Exchange, that he hath store of banke mony. **1640** GENT *Knave in Gr.* II. i. E b, If it prove not correspondent to my word, thinke me an idle vanter. **1716** POPE *Iliad* V. 347 Mistaken vaunter! (Diomed replied;) Thy dart has err'd, and now my spear be tried. **1718** HEARNE *Collect.* (O.H.S.) VI. 125 A very pert, conceited Person, full of himself, and a mere Vaunter. **1831** TRELAWNY *Adv. Younger Son* III. 222 De Ruyter's curled lip indicated his contempt of the vaunter. **1848** LYTTON *Harold* VII. iii, Now thou shalt see if the Norman is the vaunter thou deemest him. **1888** DOUGHTY *Arabia Deserta* II. 146 Such is the unmasking of vaunters, who utter their wishes, as if they were already performances.

b. A boastful assertor, extoller, commender or praiser, *of* something.

1553 T. WILSON *Rhet.* 95 b, By vocation of life a souldiour is counted a great bragger, and a vaunter of hymselfe. **1623** COCKERAM II, A Vaunter of his owne vertues, *aretalogon.* **1700** DRYDEN *Homer, Iliad* I. 336 Tongue-valiant Hero, Vaunter of thy Might. **1789** MRS. PIOZZI *Journ. France* I. 222 They are really no puffers, no vaunters of that which they possess. **1856** MRS. BROWNING *Aurora Leigh* VII. 1079 The large-mouthed frogs (Those noisy vaunters of their shallow streams). **1866** *Fortn. Rev.* V. 540 The proud vaunter of universal knowledge had been transformed into the humble student of the Bible.

'**vauntery.** Now *Obs.* or *arch.* Also 5, 7 vaunterye, 6 -erie, 7 vanterie, 7–8 -ery. [a. OF. (also mod.F.) *vanterie*, f. *vanter* to vaunt (cf. AVAUNTRY), or in later use f. VAUNT *v.* + -ERY.]

1. Vaunting, boasting; boastful or vainglorious bearing or show.

1491 CAXTON *Vitas Patr.* (W. de W. 1495) II. 272 b/1 She was not so indyscrete for tenhaunce her self by ouer moche vaunterye. **1592** *Conspiracie for Pretended Reform.* 5 [He] held it vp triumphantly, and shewed it with great vaunterie and glorie. **1603** HOLLAND *Plutarch's Mor.* 303 This vanterie and glorious boasting of a mans selfe. **1636** in *4th Rep. Hist. MSS. Commiss.* 291/1 In Wentworth's Declaration..there was much smoke of the vanterie of his own service. **1755** T. H. CROKER *Orl. Fur.* XXXIII. lxxi, They gave them-selves too lofty vantery, That France no knight or Paladin could shew To stand before the weakest of them three. **1814** SOUTHEY *Roderick* XXII. 23 She had led The infatuate Moor, in dangerous vauntery, To these aspiring forms. *Ibid.* XXV. 308 The same [horse] on whom The apostate Orpas in his vauntery Wont to parade the streets of Cordoba.

†**2.** A boast, a vaunt. *Obs.*

1603 HOLLAND *Plutarch's Mor.* 476 They stood much upon promises of future prowesse or vanteries of present valour. **1605** DANIEL *Queen's Arcadia* I. iii, That Touch Of deep Dislike of both their Vaunteries. **1626** T. H[AWKINS] tr. *Caussin's Holy Court* 432 She shewed to take not much pleasure in these his vaunteryes.

'**vauntful**, *a.* (and *adv.*) Now *arch.* [f. VAUNT *sb.*[1] + -FUL.] Boastful.

1590 SPENSER *Muiopot.* 54 Yong Clarion with vauntfull lustie hed After his guize did cast abroad to fare. **1608** SYLVESTER *Du Bartas* II. iv. *Decay* 532 Rabsakeh..Thus braves the Hebrews and upbraids their Prince (Weening, them all with vaunt-full threats to snib). **1838** *Tait's Mag.* V. 707 The English King forthwith entrusted to the vauntful captain his two sons. **1850** BLACKIE *Æschylus* II. 180 His lightnings and his thunders Recking no more—so speaks the vauntful tongue—Than vulgar noonday heat. **1890** *Blackw. Mag.* CXLVIII. 513 Invincible men call her [*i.e.* the Armada]:..Well won that vauntful title by the dread, That all around is by her coming spread.

b. As *adv.* Boastfully. *rare*$^{-1}$.

a **1814** A. BECKET *Genii* i. in *New Brit. Theatre* I. 499 Albeit the agent only Of him who bears it [a name] vauntful, man's prime enemy.

vauntgard(e, -guard, varr. VANTGUARD *Obs.*

'**vauntiness.** *rare.* [f. VAUNT *a.*] Boastfulness.

1820 in JODRELL (citing Bailey, app. in error: see VAUNTINGNESS). **1851** SPURGEON *Treas. David* ii. 2 Peaceful and joyful notwithstanding the proud and boastful vauntiness of his enemies.

'**vaunting**, *vbl. sb.* Now *arch.* [f. VAUNT *v.*] The action of the vb.; boasting, bragging.

c **1340** HAMPOLE *Pr. Consc.* 1145 Honours nuryshes, als men may se, Vayn glory, vauntyng and vanite. **1586** DAY *Eng. Secretary* II. (1625) 51, I could alwaies find an Asse by his braying, and scorne a rascall though he were neuer so full of vaunting. **1601** SHAKS. *Jul. C.* IV. iii. 52 You say, you are a better Souldier: Let it appeare so; make your vaunting true. **1611** BIBLE *Wisdom* xvii. 7 As for the illusions of arte Magicke, they were put downe, and their vaunting in wisedome was reproued with disgrace. **1826** SCOTT *Woodst.* vii, Be moderate in speech, and forbear oaths or vaunting. **1849** MACAULAY *Hist. Eng.* iii. I. 349 To our generation the honest vaunting of our ancestors must appear almost ludicrous. **1864** BURTON *Scot Abroad* I. iii. 112 The Earl of Flanders..having, in his vain vaunting, defeated so important a project.

attrib. *c* **1586** C'TESS PEMBROKE *Ps.* LXIV. v, The hartes uprightly playn Shall have their vaunting scope.

b. An instance of this; a boast.

1793 LD. AUCKLAND *Corr.* (1862) III. 27 His vauntings increase with his disgraces. *a* **1800** COWPER *Iliad* (ed. 2) XXI. 550 Let me never in my father's courts Such vauntings hear of thine again. **1838** DICKENS *Lett.* (1880) I. 8 We had many delightful vauntings of the same kind. **1877** *Smith's Dict. Chr. Biog.* I. 133/2 The hypocritical vauntings of Clytemnestra.

'vaunting, *ppl. a.* [f. as prec. + -ING².]
1. That vaunts or boasts; given or addicted to boasting.
1589 NASHE *Anat. Absurditie* Wks. (Grosart) I. 51 No matter though such vanting vpstarts.. become the scoffe of a Scholler. **1596** SHAKS. *1 Hen. IV*, v. iii. 43 Many a Nobleman lies starke and stiffe Vnder the hooues of vaunting enemies. **1601** HOLLAND *Pliny* II. 231, I my selfe have seen these vaunting Mountebanks calling themselves Psylli. **1632** SHERWOOD, A vaunting woman, *ostentatrice.* **1714** GAY *Sheph. Week* i. 39 Begin thy carols, then, thou vaunting slouch. **1730** BAILEY (fol.), *Braggard*, a bragging, vaunting, vain glorious fellow. **1819** SCOTT *Ivanhoe* xxxix, Would to God, Richard, or any of his vaunting minions of England, would appear in these lists! **1853** LYNCH *Self-Improv.* ii. 45 An empty, vaunting person who has brass enough to face the world and to say there is no God in it. **1884** *Marshall's Tennis Cuts* 195 In the evenings he was vaunting, boastful, and declared he could play even Renshaw at evens.
transf. **1599** SHAKS. *Hen. V*, II. iii. 4 Nim, rowse thy vaunting Veines: Boy, brissle thy Courage vp.
2. Of a boastful nature or character; indicative of, proceeding from, boasting or vainglory.
1647 HEXHAM I. s.v., Vaunting and bragging wordes. **1748** *Anson's Voy.* II. xi. 252 The vaunting accounts given by the Spaniards of her size, her guns, and her strength. **1770** LANGHORNE *Plutarch's Lives* (1879) I. 134/1 The vaunting shouts and songs of the barbarians. **1802** *Med. Jrnl.* VIII. 66 Does not Pyrrho likewise speak in a 'vaunting manner' on several occasions? **1855** MACAULAY *Hist. Eng.* xxi. IV. 583 Over one gate had been placed a vaunting inscription which defied the allies to wrench the prize from the grasp of France. **1897** SARAH TYTLER *Lady Jean's Son* 205 Rejoicing over him in a vaunting and insolent manner.

'vauntingly, *adv.* [f. prec.] In a vaunting manner; boastfully, ostentatiously, vaingloriously.
1593 NASHE *Christ's T.* (1613) 16 Let me speake truely and not vauntingly. **1593** SHAKS. *Rich. II*, IV. i. 36, I heard thee say (and vauntingly thou spak'st it) That thou wer't cause of Noble Glousters death. **1611** COTGR., *Piaffeusement*, braggingly,.. stroutingly, vauntingly. **1636** PRYNNE *Unbish. Tim.* Ded. (1661) 1 Whether seriously or vauntingly only, let the event determine. **1689** T. PLUNKET *Char. Good Commander*, etc. 6 Who threatned vauntingly That he.. would England Invade. **1798** ELLIS in *Anti-Jacobin* 1 Jan. (1852) 28 And dare you vauntingly decide, The fortune we shall meet. **1804** EUGENIA DE ACTON *Tale without Title* II. 100 Should the scrutiny proclaim your innocence, receive not vauntingly the clearing verdict. **1836** W. IRVING *Astoria* I. 91 Upon which Mr. M'Dougal would vauntingly lay down Mr. Astor's letter,.. a document not to be disputed.

'vauntingness. *rare.* [f. VAUNTING *vbl. sb.*] Boastfulness.
1727 BAILEY (vol. II), *Ostentatiousness*, vauntingness, bragging, shewiness. **1955** E. BOWEN *World of Love* v. 83 If she chose to make history out of her vicissitudes, that was really from vauntingness—nothing beat her.

†vauntise. *Obs.*⁻¹ [ad. OF. *vantise* vaunting, vanity, pride: see -ISE².] A vaunt or boast.
c **1477** CAXTON *Jason* (1913) 22 Moche was Iason desplaysaunt whan he had vnderstande the vauntises of his mortall ennemy.

vauntlay. Now *arch.* Also 5 (9) vauntelay. [f. VAUNT- + *-lay* as in RELAY *sb.*¹ The compound may have existed in AF. Cf. VANLAY *v.*] The releasing or setting on of a relay of hounds before the other pursuing hounds have passed; the relay of hounds so released.
1486 *Bk. St. Albans* E viij b, Even at his comyng yf thow lett thy howndys goo While the oder that be behynde fer arn hym froo That is a vauntelay. **1616** BULLOKAR *Eng. Expos.*, *Vauntlay*, a terme of hunting, when they sette hounds in readynes, where they thinke a chace will passe, and cast them off before the rest of the kennell come in. [Hence in Blount (1656), Phillips, Holme, etc.] *a* **1700** B. E. *Dict. Cant. Crew*, *Vauntlay*, Hounds or Beagles set in readiness [etc.]. **1842** SIR H. TAYLOR *Edwin the Fair* I. vi, She holds them all together; Relay or vauntlay 'tis the same to her.

vauntless ('vɔːntlɪs), *a. nonce-wd.* [f. VAUNT *sb.* + -LESS.] Not bragging or boasting.
c **1879** G. M. HOPKINS *Poems* (1967) 82 Tongue true, vaunt- and tauntless.

†vauntmure. *Obs.* Also 6 vauntemure, vauntmire, vantmure. [Aphetic form of AVANTMURE: see VANT-, VAUNT-.] = VAUMURE.
1562 J. SHUTE tr. *Cambini's Turk. Wars* 16 b, Throughe their long.. neglygence of the Greekes for want of reparation, their vauntemures were utterlye decaied in many places. **1583** STOCKER *Civ. Warres Lowe C.* III. 135 b, There fell downe a pane of the wall, and vauntmire of the Towne.. sixe and twentie Poles longe. **1596** DANETT tr. *Comines* (1614) 231 Wherewith the wals, towers, and vantmures of the castell and towne were throughly battered. **1605** CAMDEN *Rem.* (1623) 206 He with another engine named the Warwolfe pierced with one stone, and cut as even as a thread, two Vauntmures.

†vauntparler. *Obs.* Also vaunt(e)perler, vauntperlor, -parler, vantperlor, -parlar. [ad. AF. *vaunt-parlour*, obs. F. *avant-parleur* 'fore-speaker'.]
1. 'One that is too forward to speak' (Cotgr.).
a **1529** SKELTON *Sp. Parrot* 427 He tryhumfythe, he trumpythe, he turnythe all vp and downe, With, skyregalyard, prowde palyard, vaunteperler, ye prate! *a* **1548** HALL *Chron., Hen. VIII*, 36 Then sodainly was ther in yᵉ counsaill, a vauntparler, a botcher which heryng this, called a great number of his affinitie and went out of the counsayll. **1577** HOLINSHED *Chron.* I. 408/1 This Prince.. followed vpon a wilfull pretence.. the councell and aduice of vauntperlors, and suche as (being aduanced from base degree vnto hygh authoritie) studyed more to keepe themselues in fauoure than [etc.].
2. One who speaks for or on behalf of others; a spokesman.
1534 *St. Papers, Hen. VIII* (1830) I. 424 It shuld be best bestowed.. upon Frire Whitford, and upon Lache, whiche bee the vauntperlers, and heddes of thair faction. **1579** FULKE *Heskins's Parl.* 66 He doeth honestly confesse, that.. Damascen [was] the first and chiefest of the lower house, he may make him Vantparlar if he will. **1586** J. HOOKER *Hist. Irel.* in *Holinshed* II. 120/1 Their vantparler was sir Christopher Barnwell knight, who being somewhat learned, his credit was so much the more, and by them thought most .. worthie to haue beene the speaker for that house.

†vauntpe. *Obs.*⁻⁰ [ad. older F. *vantpié.*] = VAMP *sb.*¹ 1.
1530 PALSGR. 284/1 Vauntpe of a hose, *uantpie.*

†vauntplate. *Obs.*⁻¹ [f. VAUNT- + PLATE *sb.*] = VAMPLATE.
1632 J. HAYWARD tr. *Biondi's Eromena* 145 He bore him a thrust under the vauntplate.

†vauntsquare, *v. Obs.*⁻¹ [f. VAUNT- + SQUARE *v.*] *intr.* To face or front squarely.
1562 PHAER *Æneid* IX. A a ij, Messapus voward helde, the rerward kept yong princes twayne Of Tirrhus, but himself king Turnus midst in battaile mayne, Vauntsquaring spreds his armes.

vauntward(e, variants of VANTWARD *Obs.*

'vaunty, *a. dial.* (chiefly *Sc.*). Also 9 *Sc.* **vanty.** [f. VAUNT *v.*] Boastful, proud, vain.
1724 RAMSAY *Tea-t. Misc.* (1733) I. 21 Altho' my father was nae laird, 'Tis daffin to be vaunty, He keepit ay a good kail-yard. **1789** BURNS *To Dr. Blacklock* i, Wow, but your letter made me vauntie! **1821** [see VAUDY *a.*]. **1842** LOUISA S. COSTELLO *Pilgr. Auvergne* II. 120 Certainly he had reason to be 'vaunty', for his grand new house was worthy of a more populous town than Thiers. **1875** PORSON *Quaint Words S. Worcs.* 19 A vaunty dame,.. proud woman.

vaupyn, obs. Sc. form of WEAPON.

†'vauqueline. *Obs.* [a. F. *vauqueline*, f. the name of the French chemist L. N. *Vauquelin* (1768–1829).]
1. *Chem.* Strychnine.
1819 J. G. CHILDREN *Chem. Anal.* 290 Vauqueline.. was discovered by M. M. Pelletier and Caventou, in the bean of St. Ignatius, and the nux vomica.
2. *Min.* Vauquelinite.
1823 in W. PHILLIPS *Min.* (ed. 3) 350.

vauquelinite ('vəʊklɪnaɪt). *Min.* [f. as prec. + -ITE. Named by Berzelius (1818).] Chromate of lead and copper, found in amorphous masses or crystalline crusts of a green colour (Chester).
1823 W. PHILLIPS *Min.* (ed. 3) 350 Vauquelinite. Chromate of Lead and Copper. **1836–41** BRANDE *Chem.* (ed. 5) 914 The mineral called Vauquelinite is a double chromate of lead and copper.

‖vaurien (vorjɛ̃). Also **vaut-rien, vaut rien.** [F. *vaurien*, f. *vaut* 3rd pers. sing. pres. of *valoir* to be worth + *rien* nothing.] A worthless, good-for-nothing fellow; a scamp.
α. **1825–9** MRS. SHERWOOD *Lady of Manor* V. xxx. 152 Then to be called an idle fellow—a *vaut rien*—a Miss Molly —it is what I cannot bear. **1880** RUSKIN *Fors Clav.* lxxxix. 142 You will have every blackguard and vaut-rien in the world claiming his share.
β. **1868** M. COLLINS *Sweet Anne Page* II. 118 Leaving her to be slowly murdered by the vaurien who possesses her. **1874** LISLE CARR *J. Gwynne* II. vii. 189 When that *vaurien* St. Clair's health broke down. **1885** *Diary Actress* 133 They are only vauriens who loaf about town.., not men of honour.

†'vausing, *vbl. sb. Obs.*⁻⁰ (See quots.)
1688 HOLME *Armoury* III. 112/2 Vausing, is to make the Jaumes or sides of Stone Windows and Doors,.. to over sail the other part of the Wall they are set in. *Ibid.* 473/2 The Vausing, is to make the Jaumes to over sale the Mullions, and that is wrought into severall kind of Mouldings.

vaustity, obs. form of VASTITY.

vaut, southern dial. var. *faut* FAULT *sb.*
1568 FULWEL *Like will to Like* A iiij b, It is a common trade... A small vaut as the world is now brought to passe.

vaut(e, obs. forms of VAULT *sb.* and *v.*

†'vauterer. *Obs. rare.* [ad. med.L. *vautrarius*, f. OF. *vautre* hunting-dog.] = FEWTERER.
1679 BLOUNT *Anc. Tenures* 35 To be the Kings Vauterer or Dog-leader in Gascoigny.

Vauxhall (vɒks'hɔːl). [The name of a locality in London on the south bank of the Thames, where Vauxhall Gardens (see def.) were situated.] **1. a.** Used *ellipt.* for Vauxhall Gardens, a popular pleasure resort from the 17th to the middle of the 19th century; a place of resort or amusement resembling or imitating this.
Evelyn records in his memoirs under the date 2 July 1661, 'I went to see the New Spring Garden at Lambeth, a pretty contriv'd plantation'. The gardens were finally closed on 25 July 1859.
1769 *Ann. Reg., Chron.* 111 Sieur Torre opened his new Vauxhall, near St. Martin's gate [in Paris], under the denomination of the Feasts of Tempe. **1815** *Ibid., Chron.* 50 Mr. Sadler appeared in Mr. Harper's gardens, or the Vauxhall of this place [*sc.* Norwich], in the evening.
attrib. **1822** *Lond. Lit. Gaz.* 61/1 But the portions [of food] are of the Vauxhall order. **1892** DOBSON *18th Cent. Vignettes* 253 The popular legend that an expert Vauxhall waiter could cover the entire garden (about eleven acres) with slices from one ham.
b. *Comb.*, as **Vauxhall lamp, light,** an ornamental glass lantern designed to hold a candle and used for outdoor illumination.
1907 *Yesterday's Shopping* (1969) 258/2 Garden or Vauxhall lamps. For illuminations, &c. Diamond moulding, size 2¼ in. by 3½ in... Wired ready for hanging. **1974** *Country Life* 17 Oct. 1075/3 A pleasure ground.. at Tollard Royal.. in late Victorian and Edwardian times... The Gardens were illuminated with thousands of Vauxhall lights.
2. Used *attrib.* and *absol.* to designate antique plate glass resembling that made at the Vauxhall Glassworks from *c* 1663 to the end of the 18th cent.
1830 W. DAWSON in W. H. Bowles *Hist. Vauxhall & Ratcliff Glass Houses* (1926) 58 Edward Dawson of the Glass House Vauxhall who died Jan. 12 1755 made some great improvements which enabled John Dawson his son to produce those brilliant glasses still distinguished as 'Vauxhall plates'. **1900** *Archit. Rev.* June p. xxii, The mirror has a flat bevel, after the manner of the old Vauxhall plates. **1926** W. H. BOWLES *Hist. Vauxhall & Ratcliff Glass Houses* iii. 19 To this day all mirrors made in this country between 1670 and 1750 are styled by dealers 'Vauxhall'. **1972** *Country Life* 27 Jan. (Suppl.) 24/1 (Advt.), Queen Anne walnut bureau-bookcase.. retaining original Vauxhall mirror door. **1975** *Oxf. Compan. Decorative Arts* 571/1 In 1663 the second Duke of Buckingham established a plate-glass manufactory at Vauxhall, of which the products have become legendary. The term 'Vauxhall glass' has for long been used to describe any old-looking mirror although no existing example can be traced with certainty to that source. **1977** *Times* 20 Aug. 8/5 English merchants began to export Vauxhall glass.. to China.
Hence **Vaux'hallian** *a.*, **Vaux'hallify** *v. trans.*
1815 SOUTHEY *Lett.* (1856) II. 429 There is an illumination to-night in the Allée Vert, or Green Walk, which is to be Vauxhallified in honour of the Emperor. **1827** *Westm. Rev.* VIII. 353 Here follows a description of a very gay festival, much more Vauxhallian than Attic.

vauxite ('vɔːksaɪt). *Min.* [f. the name of George *Vaux* (1863–1927), U.S. mineral collector + -ITE¹.] A secondary mineral that is a hydrated basic phosphate of aluminium and ferrous iron, $Fe^{2+}{}_2Al_2(PO_4)_2(OH)_2.6H_2O$, and occurs as blue, transparent triclinic crystals, usu. in association with paravauxite and wavellite.
1922, 1944 [see *paravauxite* s.v. PARA-¹ 2 c]. **1974** *Amer. Mineralogist* LIX. 843 Montgomeryite, $Ca_4Mg(H_2O)_{12}$ $[Al_4(OH)_4(PO_4)_6]$,.. possesses chains of corner-linked Al–O octahedra which are topologically and geometrically equivalent to the chains in vauxite.

vav (væv), variant of VAU. ***vav conversive***: see CONVERSIVE *a.*¹ 2 b.
1828 GIBBS *Gesenius' Hebr. Lex.* (1833) 54/1 A prefix.. usually called Vav conversive of the future. **1869** LIDDELL & SCOTT *Gr. Lex.* s.v. δίγαμμα, But the Lat. F. holds the same place in the alph[abet] with the Hebr. *vav.* **1870** J. F. SMITH *Ewald's Introd. Hebr. Gram.* 229 Then the calm regular narration may come in with the Vav of sequence.

'vavasory. Also 7 valuasserie, 9 vavassory. [ad. OF. *vavas(s)orie*, *va(u)vasserie*, or med.L. *vavasoria*, f. *vavasor*: see next.] An estate held by a vavasour.
1611 COTGR., *Vavassorie*, a Valuasserie; th'estate, land, or territorie of a Vavassor, Mesne Lord. **1656** HARRINGTON *Oceana* (1700) 65 The Middle-Thane.. was also call'd a Vavasor, and his Lands a Vavasory. *Ibid.* 67 It cannot be imagin'd, that the Vavasorys or Freeholds in the People amounted to any considerable proportion. **1728** CHAMBERS *Cycl.* s.v., There are base Vavasories, and frank, or noble Vavasories, according as it hath pleas'd the Lord to make his Vavasour. **1839** STONEHOUSE *Isle of Axholme* 124 He was enfeoffed with the vavasories of Camville and Wyville. *a* **1861** SIR F. PALGRAVE *Norm. & Eng.* III. 405 It is not practicable to ascertain the others who received their rewards by Vavassories or Sub-tenancies.

vavasour ('vævəsʊə(r)). Now *arch.* and *Hist.* Forms: α. 4 vauasour(e, 4, 7– vavasour (4 -oure), 5 favasour, *Sc.* wawasour, vauesowre, 7 vavesour; 5 vavyssoure, vauyssour, 7 vauessour, vauassour, 9 vavassour. β. 5 vauaser, 7, 9 vavasor, vavassor. γ. 6–7 valuasor, 6 8 -vasor, 7–8 valvasour, 9 valvassor. [a. OF. *vavas(s)our*, *vavas(s)or*, *vavasseur* (so mod.F.), or med.L. *vavassor*, *valvassor*, also *vasvassor*, app. f. *vassi vassorum* 'vassals of vassals'. Cf. OProv. *va(l)vasor*, It. *varvassore*, *-oro*, *barbassore*, *-oro.*] A feudal tenant ranking immediately below a baron.
α. **13..** *K. Alis.* 3300 (Laud MS.), Noot ich no tale of his squyers, Ne of vavasours, ne of Bachilers. *c* **1330** R. BRUNNE *Chron. Wace* (Rolls) 10996 He gaf giftes of honurs, & landes

& rentes, to vauasours. *c* **1380** *Sir Ferumb.* 430 Litel prowesse for me it were wiþ a vauasour for to melle. **1456** SIR G. HAYE *Bk. Knthood.* iii. (S.T.S.) 21 All kingis suld have under thame dukkis and princis, Erllis and vicountes, and vauvassouris and barouns. *a* **1500** *Lancelot* 1729 Syne to thi tennandis & to thi wawasouris, If [= give] essy haknays, palfrais, and cursouris. **1614** SELDEN *Titles Honour* II. v. §4 Now for the nature of a vavasour;..it is plain that he was ever beneath a baron. **1647** N. BACON *Disc. Govt. Eng.* I. xxxi. (1739) 47 Others served on horseback, and were called Rad-Knights,..and these I take to be the Vavasours, noted in the Conqueror's Laws. **1660** SHERINGHAM *King's Supremacy Asserted* (1682) v. 32 There are other great men under the King which are called Barons, and other which are called Vavasours, men of great dignity. **1756** *Connoisseur* No. 102 ¶1 Upon my accession..to my elder brother's estate and title of a Baronet I received a visit from Rouge Dragon..to congratulate me upon my new rank of a Vavasour. **1766** BLACKSTONE *Comm.* II. 65 William the conqueror..directing..that a certain quantity..should be paid by the earls, barons, and vavasours respectively. **1831** SCOTT *Cast. Dang.* vii, One or two Scottish retainers or vavasours..sat at the bottom of the table. **1848** LYTTON *Harold* III. ii, The..ignominious flight of the counts and vavasours of great William the Duke. **1875** STUBBS *Const. Hist.* II. xv. 207 It was ordered that the sheriff should be a vavasour of the County.

β. *c* **1386** CHAUCER *Prologue* 360 A schirreue hadde he ben and a counter, Was nowher such a worthi vauaser. **1605** CAMDEN *Rem., Surnames* (1623) 110 Baron, Knight,.. Vavasor, Squire, Castellan. **1642** BIRD *Mag. Honour* 8 There be others which are called Vavasors,..men of great dignity. **1656** HARRINGTON *Oceana* 35 The Middle-Thane was feudall, but not honorary; he was also call'd a Vavasor. **1818** HALLAM *Mid. Ages* (1872) I. 194 The vassals of this high nobility, who..were usually termed Vavassors. **1875** K. E. DIGBY *Real Prop.* (1876) 41 *note*, Similar provisions follow as to the relief to be paid by barons, vavassors, and villeins.

γ. **1577** HARRISON *England* II. v. (1877) I. 113 As for the valvasors, it was a denomination applied unto all degrees of honor under the first three. **1610** HOLLAND *Camden's Brit.* 696 The Kings Valvasors in times past they were. **1614** SELDEN *Titles Hon.* 289 For a Corollarie to this Discourse of Barons, we add..the ancient title of Vauassours or Valuasors. **1708** J. CHAMBERLAYNE *St. Gt. Brit.* I. III. iv. (1710) 186 Baronets..are constituted in the Room of the Ancient Valvasours, between the Barons of England, and the Orders of Knights. **1765** BLACKSTONE *Comm.* I. 403 The first name of dignity, next beneath a peer, was antiently that of *vidames, vice domini*, or *valvasors.* **1840** BROWNING *Sordello* I. 768 Lord, liegeman, valvassor and suzerain, Ere he could choose, surrounded him. **1854** MILMAN *Lat. Chr.* III. 57 Heribert refused to admit the valvassors of the Church of Milan to this privilege.

vavengeour (obs. Sc.): see WAVENGER.

† **vaver**, obs. southern variant of FAVOUR *sb.*
1536 *Cal. Anc. Rec. Dublin* (1889) 499 That he mythe the rather bye youre grases mene obtayne the kyng his vaverys.

vavte, obs. form of VAULT *sb.*[1]

vaward. *Obs.* exc. *arch.* Forms: α. 4- vaward (6 va-ward), 5-6 vawarde. β. *Sc.* 5 waward(e, waywarde, 5-6 wawart. γ. 5 vauwarde, fauward, 6-7 vauward; 5-6 vawe-, 6 vawwarde, 6, 8 vawward. δ. 5 wowarde, 5-6 vowarde, 6-7 voward. [Reduced form of *vaumward* VAMWARD. See VANT- *prefix.*]

1. *Mil.* = VANGUARD 1.

α. **1375** BARBOUR *Bruce* VIII. 48 Thai saw in battale cum arayit The vaward with baner displayit. *a* **1400-50** *Alexander* 3617 Þe men out of Medy he mas..To enverom alle þe vaward of all þe vile yndes. *c* **1430** *Syr Gener.* (Roxb.) 3554 Abel, his son bold and hard, Bare the baner in the vaward. *c* **1471** *Arriv. K. Edw. IV* (Camden) 29 His vawarde so sore oppressyd them, with shott of arrows, that they gave them right-a-sharpe shwre. *a* **1548** HALL *Chron., Hen. V*, 48 Beside this, he appoincted a vawarde, of the which he made capitayne Edward duke of Yorke. **1579** DIGGES *Stratiot.* 132 To give their attendance at the lodging of their Chiefes of the Armie, whether it be of the Battaile, or Vawarde. **1610** HOLLAND *Camden's Brit.* II. 178 The English were the first that entered with great vigour upon the front and vaward. **1640** HABINGTON *Edw. IV*, 81 The Vaward commanded by the Duke of Glocester, the Rere by the Lord Hastings. [**1706** PHILLIPS (ed. Kersey), *Vaward*, an obsolete Word for Van-Guard.] **1828** TYTLER *Hist. Scot.* (1864) I. 116 He intrusted the command of the vaward, or centre, to the Earl of Moray. **1846** TORRENS *Rem. Milit. Hist.* 148 The disposition of troops seems..to have been a vaward, or advance, a centre, and rear.

β. **1375** BARBOUR *Bruce* XII. 340 And thai haf tald thair reboyting, Thai of the waward. *c* **1425** WYNTOUN *Cron.* VI. xix. 2261 He askyt at þe kynge Til haf þe wawarde [*v.r.* wawart] of his batale. **1500-20** [see b].

γ. *c* **1400** *Sege Jerus.* 430 Þe fauward Titus toke,..With six þousand soudiours. *c* **1440** *Bone Florence* 604 The vawewarde and the myddyll soone, And the rere-warde owte of Rome The grete oost removyd and yode. **1529** RASTELL *Pastyme* (1811) 222 Havinge the rule of the Frenche kynges vawewarde. **1570** FOXE *A. & M.* (ed. 2) I. 127 Sebastian..was Lieue tenant general of the Vawward of Diocletian the emperour. **1603** KNOLLES *Hist. Turks* (1621) 39 The Vauward of his armie was conducted by Iohn and Andronicus. **1791** COWPER *Iliad* VIII. 119 Then, Diomede, unaided as he was, Rush'd ardent to the vaw-ward.

γ. **1430-40** LYDG. *Bochas* IX. xxviii, In his passage to gouerne the wowarde. **1432-50** tr. *Higden* (Rolls) VII. 241 In the vowarde of whom were foote men with bawes. **1526** *Pilgr. Perf.* (W. de W. 1531) 179 Whiche is more fered of the feendes than ony vowarde of a batayle. **1543** *St. Papers Hen. VIII* (1849) IX. 393 The other galees of thEmperour appoynted for the vowarde. **1577** HOLINSHED *Chron.* II. 1593/1 Forthwith the Lord Lieutenant sent to the vowarde, commaunding that they shoulde marche towarde the towne. **1631** CHAPMAN *Cæsar & Pompey* Plays 1873 III. 162 The voward of the foe Is ranged already.

b. In fig. context.
1401 *Pol. Poems* (Rolls) II. 57 It ar ȝe that stonden bifore, in Anticristis vauwarde. **1500-20** DUNBAR *Poems* xlii. 58 Than to battell thai war arreyit all, And ay the wawart kepit Thocht. **1561** T. NORTON *Calvin's Inst.* I. (1634) 10 And therefore he doubteth not to set their mouthes in the vaward, as being strongly armed to subdue their madnesse. *a* **1586** SIDNEY *Arcadia* I. VIII. (1622) 30 Her haire being laide at the full length downe her backe, bare shew as if the voward fayled, yet that would conquer.

c. *fig.* The forefront; the early part.
In later use only as an echo of Shakespeare.
1597 SHAKS. *2 Hen. IV*, I. ii. 200 We that are in the vaward of our youth. **1599** NASHE *Lenten Stuffe* 22 The vaward or subburbes of my narration. **1827** SCOTT *Jrnl.* I. 378 She is not in the vaward of youth. —— *Chron. Canongate* vi, Those who write themselves in the vaward of youth. **1884** A. BIRRELL *Obiter Dicta* Ser. I. 208 He..states that he and his accomplices..are in the vaward of their youth.

2. *attrib.* (Cf. VANWARD *a.*)
1808 SCOTT *Marm.* VI. xxiv, Myself will rule this central host,..My sons command the vaward post. *Ibid.* xxxiii, Where's now their victor vaward wing? **1814** —— *Lord of Isles* VI. xii, To centre of the vaward-line Fitz-Louis guided Amadine.

vawe, ME. var. FAIN *a.* and *adv.*, FEW *a.*

† **vawegard**, obs. variant of VANGUARD (after VAWARD).
a **1548** HALL *Chron., Hen. VI*, 176 b, The vawegard was conducted by the erle of Warwycke.

vawght, obs. form of VAULT *sb.*[1]

vawmer, -meure, -mure, varr. VAUMURE *Obs.*

vawmewarde, variant of VAMWARD *Obs.*

† **vaws-cornice.** *Obs.*$^{-0}$ (See quot.)
1688 HOLME *Armoury* III. 102/1 *Vaws-Cornice*, is any small Cornish lying under a great swelling out peece, as under a Planchier, or swelling Friese.

vawt(e, obs. ff. VAULT *sb.*[1] and *v.*[1]

vawthe, obs. f. VAULT *v.*[1]

vax, obs. Sc. f. WAX *sb.* and *v.*

vax-cayme, obs. Sc. f. WAX-COMB.

† **vay(e**, obs. southern variants of FAY *sb.*[1]
1586 FERNE *Blaz. Gentrie* 27 By my vaye, shee looketh lyke a foule Kite that haunteth our yarde at home. **1602** *Contention betw. Liberality & Prodigality* IV. iii, Come on, surrah, chill make you vast, bum vay.

vay, southern dial. var. FAY *v.*[1]; obs. Sc. f. WAY.

vayage, obs. Sc. var. VOYAGE.

vayd, obs. Sc. f. WADE *v.*

vaye, obs. Sc. f. WAY *sb.*

vayk, obs. Sc. f. WEAK *a.*

vayle, obs. f. VEIL *sb.*

vaylliaunce, obs. f. VALIANCE.

vayn, southern ME. var. FAIN *a.*; obs. Sc. f. WAIN; Sc. var. WANE *sb. Obs.*

vaynd, var. WAIND *v. Sc.*

vayndis, Sc. var. WANDIS *v.*

vayne, obs. f. VEIN *sb.*

vayowre, var. VEYOUR *Obs.*

vayr, southern ME. var. FAIR *a.*

vayrd, obs. Sc. f. WARD *v.*

vayre, southern ME. var. FAIR *a.*; obs. f. VAIR.

väyrynenite (veɪːˈriːnənaɪt). *Min.* [ad. G. *väyrynenit* (Volborth & Stradner 1954, in *Anz. Math.-Naturwiss. Kl. Österr. Akad. Wissensch.* XCI. 21), f. the name of H. *Väyrynen*, 20th-c. Finnish mineralogist: see -ITE[1].] A phosphate and fluoride of beryllium and manganese, $BeMnPO_4(OH,F)$, found as red transparent monoclinic crystals.
1954 *Chem. Abstr.* XLVIII. 4380 Optical data of väyrynenite are presented. **1977** *Mineral. Abstr.* XXVIII. 207/2 Crystals acquired in a bazaar in Chitral, Pakistan, have been identified as väyrynenite.

vch(e, ME. varr. EACH *a.*

vddir, vder, obs. Sc. ff. OTHER *a.*

VE (viːˈiː). [f. the initial letters of *V*ictory in *E*urope.] Used *attrib.* and *absol.* to denote the victory of the Allied forces over those of Germany during the second World War; esp. as ***VE-day***, designating the date of Germany's surrender, 8 May 1945.
1944 *Washington Post* 10 Sept. 3/1 James F. Byrne, director of War Mobilization, found a new designation for the two victory days... Last night he referred to the date of Germany's impending surrender as V-E (victory in Europe) Day, and the day of Japan's defeat as V-J (Victory over Japan) Day. **1945** *Daily Mirror* 8 May 1/2 Today is VE-Day—the day for which the British people have fought and endured five years, eight months and four days of war. **1956** A. H. COMPTON *Atomic Quest* iv. 273 At Yalta,..President Roosevelt endeavored..to obtain Stalin's commitment to enter the war against Japan. Eventually Stalin agreed to do so within three months after V-E day. **1974** P. LIVELY *House in Norham Gardens* x. 130 Mrs Hedges..talked about ..D-day and VE night. **1977** *Wandsworth Borough News* 16 Sept. 12/4 The jubilee street parties are reminiscent of those marvellous V.E. and V.J. celebrations, when pianos were pulled on to the streets and everyone—strangers or not—were welcomed. **1978** R. V. JONES *Most Secret War* xxxvi. 312 Some months after V-E Day he was arrested in the American Zone of Germany.

ve, obs. Sc. f. WE *pron.*, WEE *sb.*[1] and *a.*

† **vea**, *int. Naut. Obs.* (See quots.)
1626 CAPT. SMITH *Accid. Yng. Seamen* 30 To row a spell, hold-water, trim the boate, *vea, vea, vea, vea, vea.* **1627** —— *Seaman's Gram.* vi. 27 One and all, Vea, vea, vea, vea, vea, that is they pull all strongly together.

veadge, veage, obs. varr. VOYAGE *sb.*

veak, obs. Sc. form of VAKE *v.*

veal (viːl), *sb.*[1] Forms: 4 vel (5 vell), 5-7 vele; 5 veel (feel), 6 veele; 5 veylle, 6 veyle (*Sc.* veil, weill); 6-7 veale (6 ueale, feale), 6- veal (*Sc.* 7 weall, 8 veall). [a. AF. *vel*, OF. *veel* (*viel, veal, vael*, etc.; mod.F. *veau*), *vedel*, = Prov. *vedel(h*, Cat. *vedel*, It. and Pg. *vitello*:—L. *vitellus*, dim. of *vitulus* calf.]

1. The flesh of a calf as an article of diet.
c **1386** CHAUCER *Merch. T* 176 'Bet is,' quod he, 'a pyk than a pikerell, And bet than olde boef is the tendre vel'. *c* **1400** MAUNDEV. (1839) vi. 72 Thei eten but lytille or non of Flessche of Veel or of Beef. *c* **1420** *Liber Cocorum* (1862) 28 A sawce hit is For vele and venyson, iwys. *c* **1440** *Promp. Parv.* 508/2 Veel, flesche, *vitulina.* **1515** BARCLAY *Egloges* II. (1570) B iii/2 Fat porke or vele, & namely such as is bought For easier price when they be leane & nought. **1555** EDEN *Decades* (Arb.) 177 They also coompare the fleshe of these tortoyses to be equall with veale in taste. **1620** VENNER *Via Recta* iii. 51 Veale is a more odoriferous flesh then any other. **1653** H. COGAN tr. *Pinto's Trav.* xxxiv. 137 These people feed on all, as Veal, Mutton, Pork,..and finally of all other beasts whatsoever. **1706-7** FARQUHAR *Beaux' Strat.* I. i, *Aim.* Have you any Veal? *Bon.* Veal! Sir, we had a delicate Loin of Veal on Wednesday last. **1780** BECKFORD *Biog. Mem.* 125 The most perfect fillet of veal that ever made the mouth of man to water. **1846** J. BAXTER *Libr. Pract. Agric.* (ed. 4) II. 127 In the rearing of calves for veal in Holland, it is usual to confine them in..pens. **1890** *Spectator* 4 Oct., What insipid and tasteless cheer does veal afford!

2. A calf, esp. as killed for food or intended for this purpose. Now *rare.*
1422 YONGE tr. *Secreta Secret.* 244 Flesh of Velis, Vynegre, hemroll, and Potage of oot-mell. *c* **1450** *Mirour Saluacioun* (Roxb.) 71 The ydolatiers of the golden veel. **1466** *Paston Lett.* II. 269 For purveying of all the velys, lambes,..certain piggs and polaly. **1513** DOUGLAS *Æneid* XII. Prol. 185 Tydy ky lowys, veilys by thame rynnis. **1544** in *Star Chamber Cases* (Selden) II. 305 The prices of Flesh, as of Beefes, Muttons, Veales, & Porkes. **1582** *Nottingham Rec.* IV. 199, vj. fatte wethres, at viij s. viij d. a pece, and ij. veyles, at vj s. viij d. a pece. **1601** R. JOHNSON *Kingd. & Commw.* 25 The flesh..of their swine, oxen, and veales haue the best relish. **1648** HERRICK *Hesper., Paneg. Sir L. Pemberton* 63 When guests make their abode To eate thy Bullocks thighs, thy Veales, thy fat Weathers. **1688** HOLME *Armoury* III. 315/1 Upon these [drag hooks] are hung two Veals or Muttons at a time. **1737** *Ochtertyre House Bk.* (S.H.S.) 13 Killd a Veall. **1801** *Farmer's Mag.* Aug. 319 In selling veals to butchers, their haggling was extremely disagreeable. **1855** THACKERAY *Newcomes* I. 265 My mother ..would receive her prodigal and kill the fatted veal for me. **1898** WESTCOTT *David Harum* xvii, Jim brought three or four veals into town one spring to sell.
collect. **1710** ADDISON *Tatler* No. 148 ¶1 The Flesh of Lamb, Veal, Chicken, and other Animals under Age.

3. a. *attrib.*, chiefly in names of dishes, etc., made from veal, as ***veal (and ham) pie, veal broth, cutlet, gravy***, etc.
a **1625** FLETCHER *Hum. Lieut.* III. vii, Ye Porridg gutted Slaves, ye Veal broth-Boobies! **1630** J. TAYLOR (Water P.) *Gt. Eater Kent* 14 Three sixe-penny veale pyes..were presented to the scalado. **1675** E. W[ILSON] *Spadacrene Dunelmensis* 39 This [water]..helpeth all internal corrosions, if taken in Veal Broath fasting. **1725** *Fam. Dict.* s.v., Put your Veal Stakes into the Pan again, and finish the dressing with Veal Sweet-Breads. *Ibid.*, Some Veal Gravy must be pour'd upon it. **1728** E. SMITH *Compl. Housewife* (ed. 2) 41 (*heading*) To make veal cutlets. **1747** tr. *Astruc's Fevers* 340 Let the patient also drink plentifully of veal broth. **1769** MRS. RAFFALD *Eng. Housek.* (1778) 19 About a pound of beef or veal suet. **1811** JANE AUSTEN *Sense & Sens.* II. iv. 53 Preferring salmon to cod, or boiled fowls to veal cutlets. **1827** SCOTT *Surg. Dau.* ii, Lamb and spinage, and a veal Florentine. **1833** L. RITCHIE *Wand. by Loire* 182 A large baby in one arm, and a basket of..cold veal-pie in the other. **1848** DICKENS *Dombey* xviii, He treats Mrs. Perch to a veal cutlet and Scotch ale. **1848** THACKERAY *Pendennis* (1849) I. v. 49 That girl, sir, makes the best veal and ham pie in England. **1858** SIMMONDS *Dict. Trade*, *Veal-tea*, a thick gelatinous soup or broth made of the fleshy part of the fillet or knuckle of veal. **1861** MRS. BEETON *Bk. Househ. Managem.* 942 *Saturday.* 1. Rump-steaks, broiled, and oyster sauce, mashed potatoes; veal-and-ham pie. **1885** JEROME *On the Stage* 48 Property Man, behind, making a veal and ham pie, out of an old piece of canvas and a handful of shavings.

b. Special Combs.: **veal-bled** *a.*, bled to exhaustion, like a calf intended for veal; **veal-bones**, *fig.* youth, nonage; **veal calf**, (*a*) = sense 2; (*b*) a variety of leather; **veal-farmer**, one who rears calves for the butcher; **veal-like**

a., resembling (that of) veal; †**veal money** (see quot.); **veal parmigiana** [It. *parmigiano* Parmesan cheese], a dish of small escalopes of veal and cheese; **veal piccata**, a dish of small escalopes of veal; **veal-skin**, (*a*) the skin of a calf; (*b*) a skin-disease characterized by white shining spots.

1899 *Westm. Gaz.* 8 Sept. 3/1 The exhausted, and almost *veal-bled and forlorn bull. **1785** R. CUMBERLAND *Observer* No. 92, Our process seldom fails in either case, when we apply it timely, and especially to young poets in their **veal bones*, as the saying is. **1888** ADDY *Sheffield Gloss.* 272 There is a saying 'married in the veal bones always a calf'. ?**1556** *Wills & Inv. N.C.* (Surtees, 1835) 153 To Thomas morison ..for ij *veale calves. **1895** *Boston Herald* 21 March 5/6 Colored leather is firmer and selling more freely: Grain, 12 @ 14c; veal calf, 16 @ 18½c. **1946** F. H. GARNER *Brit. Dairying* xi. 228 Veal calves demand much milk when being reared. **1981** *Times* 25 July 3/2 Veal calves are penned in tight crates on liquid feeds throughout their lives. **1844** H. STEPHENS *Bk. Farm* II. 469 The *veal-farmers keep from 6 to 12 cows each. **1822–7** *Veal-like [see *veal-skin* below]. **1897** W. ANDERSON *Surg. Treat. Lupus* 7 An unwholesome, veal-like whiteness, diversified by tiny blood-vessels. **1684** MANLEY *Cowell's Interpreter* s.v., *Veale money or Veale noble money. The Tenants of one of the Tythings within the Mannor of Bradford in Wiltshire, pay a yearly Rent by this name..in lieu of veale paid formerly in kind. **1963** R. CARRIER *Gt. Dishes of World* ix. 161 *Veal parmigiana. **1972** [see LINGUINE]. **1983** C. MCCARRY *Last Supper* IV. i. 184 He ..ordered veal parmigiana..crusty veal with its rubbery slab of strange white cheese covered with tomato sauce. **1973** *Veal piccata [see PRIME *a.* 4a]. **1982** J. D. MACDONALD *Cinnamon Skin* xvii. 172 The veal piccata.. went well with the Valpolicella. **1591** *Exch. Rolls Scotl.* XXII. 171 [10*s.* of certain] barkit *weillskynnis. **1822–7** GOOD *Study Med.* (1829) V. 694 *Epichrosis Leucasmus.* Veal-Skin... This is the vitiligo or veal-skin of Willan, so called from the veal-like appearance which these spots produce on the general colour of the surface. **1858** SIMMONDS *Dict. Trade, Veal-skins*, an Irish trade-name for hides of the calf, which are dearer than other leather.

Hence **veal** *v. trans.*, to rear (calves) for use as veal; **'vealer**, a calf intended or fit for veal.

1901– in American dicts. **1931** *Daily News-Journal* (Murfreesboro, Tennessee) 17 Apr. 4/1 Better grade vealers around 50c higher. **1977** *West Briton* 25 Aug. 11/1 Calves —vealers to £26. **1984** *Grass Roots* (N.Z.) Feb. 13/1 We have been developing a thriving vealer mini project on 25 acres at Neerim South in West Gippsland, Victoria.

veal, *sb.*[2] *Sc. Mining.* (See quots.)

1883 GRESLEY *Gloss. Coal-M.* 269 *Veal*, a tank or water-barrel placed upon a cage for emptying the sump. **1886** J. BARROWMAN *Sc. Mining Terms* 69 *Veal*, or *voun*, a water box or chest, usually on wheels, for removing water.

veale, var. VELE *Obs.*; obs. Sc. f. WELL *adv.*

'vealing, *vbl. sb.*[1] [f. VEAL *sb.*[1]] **a.** *a-vealing*, procuring veal. **b.** Conversion into veal.

1664 COTTON *Scarron.* I. 47 And up he starts, to go a stealing, Either a Mutt'ning, or a Vealing. **1847** *Jrnl. R. Agric. Soc.* VIII. II. 394 It is equally suitable, whether the calf is intended for vealing or to be reared.

†**'vealing**, *vbl. sb.*[2] *Obs.* (See quot.)

1688 HOLME *Armoury* III. 86/2 Working, is to lay them on the Beam and with the Fleshing Knife and Vealing Knife, to scrape off the Lime and cleanse them from their Fleshyness.

'vealing, *vbl. sb.*[3] *Sc. Mining.* [f. VEAL *sb.*[2]]

1886 J. BARROWMAN *Sc. Mining Terms* 69 *Vealing*, or *vouning*, chesting; getting out water by means of veals.

vealinous, obs. form of VILLAINOUS *a.*

vealy ('vi:lɪ), *a.* [f. VEAL *sb.*[1]]

1. Resembling veal.

1769 MRS. RAFFALD *Eng. Housekpr.* (1778) 17 Then put in a few boiled forcemeat balls, which must be made of the veally part of your turtle. **1864** LOWELL *Fireside Trav.* 259 When we were fairly at anchor..they crawled out again,.. their vealy faces mezzotinted with soot.

2. *fig.* Imperfectly developed; immature; characterized by youthful immaturity.

1890 *Columbus* (Ohio) *Dispatch* 17 July, A vealy medical-school graduate, whose employment is an insult to intelligent people. **1907** *Outlook* 19 Jan. 80/1 The sylvan thief shared our vealy homage with moonlighters, smugglers [etc.].

Hence **'vealiness**, want of maturity.

1895 in *Funk's Stand. Dict.*

veand, obs. Sc. variant of *weighing* WEIGH *v.*

veany, variant of VENY[2] *Obs.*

vear, obs. f. VEER *v.*; obs. Sc. f. WAR *sb.*; south-w. dial. f. FEAR *v.*

veare, southern ME. variant of FARE *v.*

vearie, obs. Sc. form of VERY *adv.*

vease. Now only *south-w. dial.* Forms: 4 (9) vese (9 veze); 6–7 (9) vease, 7 veaze; 7 veeze (9 veese); 9 vaise, vaze, etc. [Southern var. of FEEZE *sb.*] A rush, impetus; a run before a leap. (Cf. FEEZE *sb.* 1 and 1 b.)

c **1386** CHAUCER *Knight's T.* 1127 And ther out cam a rage, and such a vese, That it made al the gate for to rese. **1573** TWYNE *Æneid* XII. Nn4b, This vp in hand he caught, and tremblyng at his foe did flyng, Arysing up therwith, and forth his vease he fet withall. **1614** GORGES *Lucan* I. 41 In this flitting whirle-winde vease, I passe the Mountaines Pyrinees. *Ibid.* VIII. 346 O Marriners stay not my veaze, Headlong to plunge into the seas. *a* **1618** J. DAVIES (Heref.) *Wit's Pilgrimage* Wks. (Grosart) II. 31/2 From whence Loues lightest Muses take their veeze To leape into those Seas, which cares destroy. **1646** in Dircks *Life Marq. Worcester* x. (1865) 171, I only would retire myself from further present charge, as a ram doth to take a greater vease. **1678** RAY *Prov.* 78 Every pease hath its veaze, and a bean fifteen..signifies Pease are flatulent, but Beans ten times more. **1825** JENNINGS *Dial. W. Engl.* 80 *Vaze*,..the distance employed to increase the intensity of motion or action from a given point. **1875** PORSON *Quaint Words S. Worcs.* 26 What a vese they [*sc.* the hounds] did go, surely.

vease, dial. var. FEEZE *v.*[1]

veasy, var. VASY *a. Obs.*

veatchite ('vi:tʃaɪt). *Min.* [See quot. 1938 and -ITE[1].] Any of three polymorphs of a hydrous strontium borate, $Sr_2[B_5O_8(OH)]_2.B(OH)_3.H_2O$, of which two (*veatchite* and *p-veatchite*) are monoclinic and one (*veatchite-A*) is triclinic.

1938 G. SWITZER in *Amer. Mineralogist* XXIII. 411 It seems fitting to name this new borate veatchite after Dr. John A. Veatch, who was the first to detect the presence of borates in the mineral waters of California, on January 8, 1856. **1960** *Mineral. Mag.* XXXII. 500 A mineral from the Permian lower evaporite bed of the Eskdale No. 2 boring in Yorkshire... Single-crystal X-ray work now proves that this mineral is *p*-veatchite. **1979** *Amer. Mineralogist* LXIV. 362 A third modification of veatchite occurs in Emet colemanite deposit, Kütahya, Turkey, as white cauliflower-shaped nodules associated with colemanite, hydroboracite, realgar, orpiment and montmorillonite. The new mineral is triclinic... Crystals are transparent, colorless... The new modification is named veatchite-A.

veawe, southern ME. var. FEW *a.*; obs. var. VIEW *v.*

veaze, var. VEASE.

veb, obs. form of WEB *sb.*

veber, obs. var. WEBER[1].

Veblenian (və'bli:nɪən), *a.* and *sb.* [f. the name *Veblen* + -IAN.] **A.** *adj.* Of or pertaining to the work of Thorstein Veblen (1857–1929), U.S. economist and social scientist, esp. the ideas (as of conspicuous consumption) expounded in his book *Theory of the Leisure Class* (1899). **B.** *sb.* One who supports or advocates Veblenian ideas.

1931 *Encycl. Social Sci.* V. 388/2 The Veblenian terminology of American institutionalism. **1953** D. RIESMAN *Thorstein Veblen* viii. 180 Those high-income poeple..who buy..with a Veblenian ascetic eye on their own motivations. **1968** *Internat. Encycl. Social Sci.* IV. 462/2 Economists working in the Veblenian tradition. **1973** *Hist. Political Econ.* V. 449 (*heading*) Hoxie's economics in retrospect: the making and unmaking of a Veblenian. **1982** *Jrnl. Econ. Issues* XVI. 757 The Veblenian dichotomy is the central analytical tool of institutional economists in the Veblen-Ayres tradition. **1982** J. D. MACDONALD *Cinnamon Skin* xix. 210 Veblen died in 1929 at the age of seventy-two. .. I have never been a Veblenian myself.

vecche, vechche, southern ME. varr. FETCH *v.*

‖**vecchio** ('vɛkɪəʊ). *rare.* [It.] An old man.

c **1570** *Bugbears* I. ii. 61 Yet it dothe not content our pinchefiste, the old vecchio. *Ibid.* 79 The three thousand Crownes that our vecchio dothe require. **1938** E. HEMINGWAY *Fifth Column* 273 'Three marsalas,' said the young gentleman to the girl behind the pastry counter. 'Two, you mean?' she asked. 'No,' he said, 'One for a vecchio.' **1944** G. B. SHAW *Let.* 4 Dec. in *To a Young Actress* (1960) 180, I am a vecchio, nearly eightyeight and a half.

vech(e, obs. ff. VETCH.

vecht, vechtie, obs. Sc. ff. WEIGHT *sb.*, WEIGHTY *a.*

†**vecke.** *Obs.* Also 5 **vekke, wekke.** [app. ad. It. *vecchia*, fem. of *vecchio* old.] An old woman.

As direct adoption from Italian would be remarkable in the 14th cent., it is possible that the word existed in OF. colloquial use.

1390 GOWER *Conf.* I. 98 This olde wyht him hath awaited ..: Florent his wofull heved uplefte And syh this vecke wher sche sat. *c* **1400** *Rom. Rose* 4495 A rympled vekke, ferre ronne in age, Frownyng and yelowe in hir visage. **1412–20** LYDG. *Chron. Troy* I. 2795 Sche cleped anoon vn-to hir presence An aged vekke, fer in 3eris ronne. **1426** —— *De Guil. Pilgr.* 12752 An olde wekke a-noon I mette. **1430–40** —— *Bochas* I. xx. (1554) 36 b, Whan these veckes, ferre yronne in age, Within them selfe hath vaine glory and delite For to farce and poppe their visage.

†**vecked**, *ppl. a. Obs.* = INVECKED *ppl. a.*

1562 LEGH *Armory* II. 56 b, Hee beareth Azure, a crosse formye vecked Argent.

vecord. *rare*[−1]. = next.

1788 tr. *Swedenborg's Wisdom of Angels* v. §378. 364 Hence too the Terms Concord, Discord, Vecord (malicious Madness) and other similar Expressions.

vecordy. *rare*[−0]. [ad. L. *vēcordia*, f. *vēcors* senseless, foolish.] (See quot.)

1656 BLOUNT *Glossogr.* [copying Cooper], *Vecordy*, madness, trouble of minde, folly, doting.

vecount, obs. Sc. form of VISCOUNT.

vec'tarious, *a. rare*[−0]. [f. L. *vectāri-us* (*equus*), f. *vectāre* to convey.] (See quot.)

1656 BLOUNT *Glossogr.*, *Vectarious*, belonging to a coach, waggon or any carriage. [Hence in Phillips (1658); in later edd. (1671–96) *Vectorious.*]

vectayllys, obs. variant of VICTUALS.

Vectian ('vɛktɪən), *a. Geol.* [f. L. *Vect-is*, name of the Isle of Wight + -IAN.] Of or pertaining to the Isle of Wight or the Lower Greensand strata exposed there; *spec.* (see quot. 1961).

[**1845** W. H. FITTON in *Q. Jrnl. Geol. Soc.* I. 189 If hereafter a change [from Lower Green Sand] be thought desirable, he [*sc.* the author] conceives that the new denomination should be taken from the *Isle of Wight*..; and if such a case should arise, he suggests the name of *Vectine* for the strata now called Lower Green Sand, from the ancient name of that island,—*Insula Vectis* of the Romans.] **1885** A. J. JUKES-BROWNE in *Geol. Mag.* Decade III. II. 298 The Lower Greensand can be studied so well in the Isle of Wight..that no name can be more appropriate than *Vectian*; and I regard the introduction of a new name as preferable to the adoption of the French names *Aptien* and *Urgonien*. **1922** [see SELBORNIAN *a.* 2]. **1961** *Palaeontology* III. 502 The Vectian Province comprises the Isle of Wight and a small part of the Dorset mainland where a strip of Lower Greensand extends westwards from Swanage to Lulworth Cove. **1969** BENNISON & WRIGHT *Geol. Hist. Brit. Isles* xiv. 323 In this Vectian Province the Lower Greensand becomes attenuated westwards at a more rapid rate than the Wealden (Neo-comian) Beds.

'vectible, *a. rare*[−0]. [f. L. *vect-*, ppl. stem of *vehĕre* to carry.] (See quot.)

1656 BLOUNT *Glossogr.*, *Vectible*, that is or may be carried.

vectigal (vɛk'taɪgəl), *sb.*[1] Now only *Rom. Hist.* Also 6 **vecti-**, *Sc.* **victigall.** [a. L. *vectīgal* a payment to the State, etc.] A payment of the nature of tribute, tax, or rent, made to a superior or to the State.

1535 STEWART *Cron. Scot.* II. 243 Grit tribute and victigall alsua, Ilk 3eir by 3eir to king Arthure till pa. **1538** LELAND *Itin.* (1769) IV. 111 Thereupon they give a Fee Farme or Vectigall of an 100. l. yearely. The Vectigall is as it was. **1656** BLOUNT *Glossogr.*, *Vectigal*,..used substantively for toll, impost-money or tribute it self. **1774** T. WEST *Antiq. Furness* (1805) 104 His lands and tenants were exempted from all regal exactions of talliage, toll, passage, pontage, and vectigal. **1838** ARNOLD *Hist. Rome* (1846) I. xvii. 366 The tribunes demanded..that the occupiers of the remainder should pay their vectigal regularly.

†**vectigal**, *sb.*[2] and *a. Obs. rare.* Also 6 *Sc.* **victogall.** [ad. L. *vectīgāl-is*, f. *vectīgal*: see prec.] **a.** *sb.* A collector of tribute. **b.** *adj.* (See quot. 1656.)

1535 STEWART *Cron. Scot.* I. 188 Mark Terebell..Hes constat him his victogall that tyde, For to collect his tribute and his rent. **1656** BLOUNT *Glossogr.*, *Vectigal*, that pays or pertains to paying tribute, subsidy, pension or rent.

†**vection.** *Obs. rare.* [ad. L. *vectiōn-*, *vectio*, n. of action f. *vehĕre* to carry.] The action of carrying; vectitation.

c **1610** SIR C. HEYDON *Astrol. Disc.* (1650) 42 For whatsoever moveth another, it doth it either by impulsion, attraction, volutation, or vection. **1635** SWAN *Spec. M.* (1670) 198 Albertus calls this motion a vection or a carrying. **1654** Z. COKE *Logick* 40 Local motion... Traction or drawing. Vection or carrying.

‖**vectis** ('vɛktɪs). [L. *vectis* lever, crow-bar.]

†**1.** A lever. *Obs.*

1648 WILKINS *Math. Magic* I. v. 33 Rather suppose BC, to be a Vectis or Leaver, towards the middle of which is the place of the fulciment. **1674** PETTY *Disc. Dupl. Proportion* 119 In the Fuze of a Watch, the greatest strength of the Spring is made to work upon the shortest Vectis.

2. *Surg.* **a.** An obstetrical instrument employed as a lever to free the head of the child.

1790 *Med. Comm.* II. 397 It is now near forty years since an account of the vectis or lever of Roonhuysen was published. **1822–7** GOOD *Study Med.* (1829) V. 190 If, at the same time, the head be lying clear on the perinæum, the vectis or forceps should be had recourse to. **1841** RAMSBOTHAM *Obstet. Med. & Surg.* 314 Another instrument that has been much employed with the view of extracting the child living, is the vectis or lever. **1881** *Trans. Obstet. Soc. Lond.* XXII. 78, I passed in a vectis, and by its aid as a lever..I brought down the second larger head and left arm.

b. An instrument employed in operations on the eye.

1882 *Illustr. to Maw's Price-current* 77 [Eye instruments.] Vectis, Taylor's. **1891** *Ibid.* 42 Ophthalmoscope lamp, operation scissors,..and vectis. **1895** *Arnold & Sons' Catal. Surg. Instr.* 158 Vectis (Taylor's), for Extraction of Soft Lens.

vecti'tation. *rare.* [f. L. *vectitāre* (rare), freq. of *vectāre* to carry, convey.] The action of carrying or conveying (frequently); the fact of being carried or conveyed.

1656 BLOUNT *Glossogr.*, *Vectitation*, an often carriage. **1727** POPE, etc. *Martinus Scriblerus* vi, Whilst their enervated Lords are lolling in their chariots (a species of Vectitation seldom used amongst the Ancients, except by old men). **1823** *New Monthly Mag.* VIII. 253 A method of aerial vectitation.

ˈ**vectitory**, *a. rare*$^{-1}$. [Cf. prec.] Of the nature of carrying or conveying.

1822 *Examiner* 8/1 Heaven forbid that..the bodies of Turks should be applied to vectitory purposes.

vector (ˈvɛktə(r)), *sb.* [a. L. *vector*, agent-noun f. *vehĕre* to carry. So (in sense 1) Sp. and Pg. *vector*, F. *vecteur*.]

† **1.** *Astr.* (See quot. 1704.) Also ***vector radius***, = *radius vector*, RADIUS *sb.* 3 e. *Obs.*

1704 J. HARRIS *Lex. Techn.* I. s.v., A Line supposed to be drawn from any Planet moving round a Center, or the Focus of an Ellipsis, to that Center or Focus, is by some Writers of the New Astronomy, called the Vector; because 'tis that Line by which the Planet seems to be carried round its Center. **1796** MORSE *Amer. Geog.* I. 28 If a right line, called by some the vector radius, be drawn from the sun through any planet, and supposed to revolve round the sun with the planet [etc.].

2. a. *Math.* A quantity having direction as well as magnitude, denoted by a line drawn from its original to its final position. ***axial vector*** = PSEUDOVECTOR *sb.*; ***polar vector***, a vector which changes sign when the signs of all its components are changed.

1846 W. R. HAMILTON in *Phil. Mag.* XXIX. 27 The algebraically imaginary part, being geometrically constructed by a straight line, or radius vector, which has, in general, for each determined quaternion, a determined length and determined direction in space, may be called the vector part, or simply the vector of the quaternion. *a* **1865** W. R. HAMILTON *Elem. Quaternions* I. i. 1 A right line AB, considered as having not only length, but also direction, is said to be a Vector. **1873** J. C. MAXWELL *Treat. Electr. & Magn.* I. 9 A Vector, or Directed Quantity, requires for its definition three numerical specifications, and these may most simply be understood as having reference to the directions of the coordinate axes. **1882** MINCHIN *Unipl. Kinemat.* 109 The resultant of a system of vectors whose type is *ω* . *IP dm*, if each were directed from *I* to *P*, would be a vector *ω M* . *IG* directed from *I* to *G*. **1903** *Nature* 22 Oct. 610/1 This algebra..does not discriminate between 'polar' vectors, *e.g.* forces and 'axial' vectors, *e.g.* couples. **1968** M. S. LIVINGSTON *Particle Physics* v. 101 Angular momentum is an axial vector quantity, unlike linear momentum which is a polar vector.

b. *Math.* An ordered set of two or more numbers (interpretable as the co-ordinates of a point); a matrix with one row or one column; also, any element of a vector space.

[**1873**: see prec. sense. **1881** J. W. GIBBS *Sci. Papers* (1906) II. 17 The numerical description of a vector requires three numbers.] **1922** J. B. SHAW *Vector Calculus* i. 6 A vector is usually designated by a triple as (*x*, *y*, *z*), and usually such triple is called a vector. **1938** R. A. FRAZER et al. *Elem. Matrices* i. 2 A row matrix is often called..a vector of the first kind..; while a column matrix is referred to as a vector of the second kind. **1940** D. E. LITTLEWOOD *Theory Group Characters* i. 5 A square matrix..of order n^2 may be regarded as composed of *n* column vectors. **1961** *Communications Assoc. Computing Machinery* IV. 424/2 The analysis of a program into phases and sequences is accomplished by associating with each sequence a vector of ones and zeros. **1965** PATTERSON & RUTHERFORD *Elem. Abstr. Algebra* v. 155 The polynomial ring *P*(*F*) is a vector space over the same field *F*... The polynomials are in this case the vectors of this vector space. **1976** *Biometrika* LXIII. 438 Given N_0, the vector $(n_1, \ldots, n_{X0})$ will have a multinomial distribution with N_0 trials. **1981** N. RAU *Matrices & Math. Programming* i. 16 Up to this point, vectors have been considered simply as a special case of matrices... For the rest of this book..'vector' will always be used to mean column vector.

c. *Aeronaut.* A course to be taken by an aircraft, or steered by a pilot.

1941 D. MASTERS *So Few* xxx. 333 'I've got to get a Hun tonight. I'll give you a bottle of champagne if you put me on to one.'.. 'All right,..I'll give you a vector.' **1951** O. BERTHOUD tr. *Clostermann's Big Show* 102, I am climbing flat out on vector 095. **1978** R. V. JONES *Most Secret War* xxi. 177 The ground station ordered an aircraft to steer a course of 270° (i.e. due west) presumably because it was east of the beam, and this was the vector required to bring it to the right point to start its bombing run.

d. *Computing.* A sequence of consecutive locations in memory; a series of items occupying such a sequence and identified within it by means of one subscript; *spec.* one serving as the address to which a program must jump when interrupted, and supplied by the source of the interruption.

1961 *Communications Assoc. Computing Machinery* IV. 61/1 Since it is often necessary to refer to memory addresses and the contents of memory cells in this discussion, the almost-legitimate device of the 'Memory vector' will be used. This is done by assuming the entire memory of the machine in question to constitute a single one-dimensional vector, named 'Memory'. **1962** E. W. DIJKSTRA *Primer of ALGOL 60 Programming* 37 The simplest example of such an array is a vector, i.e. a sequence of subscripted variables. **1967** D. G. HAYS *Introd. Computational Linguistics* ii. 26 When the program stops, the J-th column of the matrix F has been copied into the vector G. **1967** P. A. STARK *Digital Computer Programming* xiv. 255 After checking the transfer vector to see that the subroutine name is there, the loader goes back into the mainline program and fixes the linkage so that the mainline program jumps into the transfer vector. **1975** R. H. ECKHOUSE *Minicomputer Systems* vi. 186 The new contents of the PC [*sc.* program counter] and the PS [*sc.* processor status] are loaded from two preassigned consecutive memory locations called an interrupt vector... The contents of these vectors are determined by the programmer. **1982** *Economist* 3 Apr. 128/3 Individual units of data (ie, binary numbers) are stored in the computer's memory in long lists called vectors. **1982** R. A. SPARKES *Microcomputers in Sci. Teaching* v. 199 A test must be included into the routine to ascertain if the user wants to return to normal working. If so, the ISR [*sc.* interrupt service routine] vector is changed back to 58926 and the extra routine is by-passed. **1984** *Personal Software* Winter 89/3 During loading, a message is displayed on the screen and the keyboard and screen vectors are changed to effect automatic program execution.

3. a. *Med.* and *Biol.* A person, animal, or plant which carries a pathogenic agent and acts as a potential source of infection for members of another species. Also *transf.* Cf. CARRIER 1 l (i).

1922 [see ARTHROPODA, ARTHROPOD]. **1944** *Nature* 5 Aug. 167/2 Regular transmission of viruses by the egg of the host plant (the insect vector does not concern us unless it suffers) probably does not occur. **1963** R. CARSON *Silent Spring* xvi. 220 An even more serious problem concerns the vector of yellow fever. **1972** *Lancet* 17 June 1338/2 The stethoscope is yet another vector of pathogenic organisms. **1974** PASSMORE & ROBSON *Compan. Med. Stud.* III. xii. 64/2 The spread of each of the insect-borne diseases depends on a complicated chain of events involving..a reservoir of infection which may be either in man or in other animals,.. the insect vector and..a susceptible human population. **1976** *Dumfries & Galloway Standard* 25 Dec. 8/6 A small boy recovered after being bitten by a rabid bat, it being thought that the disease had been modified by passage through this unusual vector.

b. *Genetics.* A bacteriophage which transfers genetic material from one bacterium to another; also, a phage or plasmid used to transfer extraneous DNA into a cell.

1958 *Abstr. 7th Internat. Congr. Microbiol.* 53 The modified phage particle so produced has been identified as the transducing vector. **1968** W. HAYES *Genetics of Bacteria & their Viruses* (ed. 2) xvii. 478 Some other temperate phages..can act as vectors for the transfer, to recipient bacteria, of virtually any region of the host chromosome. **1976** *Proc. Nat. Acad. Sci.* LXXIII. 2838/1 Gene transfer between two closely related mouse cell lines has been carried out, using as the vector a cell-free preparation of metaphase chromosomes and nuclei. **1982** T. M. DEVLIN *Textbk. Biochem.* xx. 986/2 The methodology involves obtaining the DNA of the desired gene; placing the DNA into a vector or vehicle capable of transporting the gene and maintaining it inside an *E. coli* cell;..and determining whether the gene is functional in *E. coli*. **1983** *Sci. Amer.* Jan. 58/2 Plasmids are routinely used as vectors for introducing foreign DNA into bacteria. **1985** OLD & PRIMROSE *Princ. Gene Recombination* (ed. 3) 222 This may have the additional property of being a shuttle vector, capable of stable replication in *E. coli* and *A. tumefaciens*.

4. *transf.* and *fig.*

1926 *Spectator* 30 Oct. 735/1 Even if there was a listener-in within the narrow vector of the vibrations, he could not hope to receive the messages at the rate at which they will be sent. **1954** W. FAULKNER *Fable* 82 He identified himself, naming his battalion and its vector. **1957** L. DURRELL *Bitter Lemons* 37 But I was on a different vector, hunting for other qualities which might make residence tolerable, or might isolate me from my fellows. **1976** *Listener* 15 Apr. 466/1 Once, a long vector of geese flew over. **1977** A. HECHT in *Oxf. Bk. Contemp. Verse* (1980) 173 The athlete's dancing vector, the spirit's need, And muscle's cleanly diction. **1979** *UCT Studies in English* (Univ. Cape Town) Sept. 39 Antithesis is, of course, the chief trope of the rape genre, not only in respect of the obvious contrasts drawn between the heroine's purity and her shame, but also with regard to the vectors of these states—contrastive images of light and dark.

5. *attrib.* **a.** In the sense 'of the nature of a (mathematical) vector, representable by a vector'; also as *adj.*

1846 [see sense 2 a above]. **1873** J. C. MAXWELL *Treat. Electricity & Magn.* I. 9 A vector quantity has direction as well as magnitude, and is such that a reversal of its direction reverses its sign. **1880** *Nature* XXI. 256 Some vector property (such as rotation about an axis). **1881** J. W. GIBBS *Sci. Papers* (1906) II. 37 Maxwell has called $-\nabla.\nabla u$ the concentration of *u*, whether *u* is scalar or vector. **1962** CORSON & LORRAIN *Introd. Electromagnetic Fields & Waves* i. 1 Wind velocity, gravitational force, and electric field intensity are examples of..vector quantities. **1975** *Nature* 18 Sept. 191/1 *β*-decay within isospin multiplets of $J^\pi = 0^+$ is pure vector because there is no nuclear spin to flip.

b. In the sense 'involving (mathematical) vectors', as ***vector addition***, ***algebra***, ***analysis***, ***calculus***, ***method***, etc.

1873 KELLAND & TAIT *Introd. Quaternions* iii. 32 (*heading*) Vector multiplication and division. **1881** A. S. HARDY *Elem. Quaternions* i. 3 The operation of vector addition is commutative. **1881** J. W. GIBBS *Sci. Papers* (1906) II. 17 An algebra or analytical method in which a single letter or other expression is used to specify a vector may be called a vector algebra or vector analysis. **1897** CURRY *Theory Electr. & Magnetism* 361 If we replace the vector-equation by its three component-equations and the vector-integrals of the latter by the above values. **1904** *Rep. Brit. Assoc. Adv. Sci. 1903* 53, I cannot help thinking that he would have used vector methods throughout if he had found ready to hand a vector analysis instead of a theory of quaternions. **1955** A. HUXLEY *Genius & Goddess* 38 The great man would get bored and quietly fade away, leaving me to solve Timmy's problem by some method a little simpler than vector analysis. **1964** J. W. LINNETT *Electronic Struct. Molecules* i. 7 The resultant angular momentum is, therefore, by vector addition $..\sqrt{2}h/2\pi$. **1968** E. T. COPSON *Metric Spaces* ix. 138 This is ordinary vector algebra without scalar and vector products. **1969** *Jane's Freight Containers 1968–69* 147/2 It has been assumed..that the vector sum (the actual value of the lashing tension) will not exceed 30 400 kgf. **1972** M. KLINE *Math. Thought* xxxii. 786 By Maxwell's time a great deal of vector analysis was created by treating the scalar and vector parts of quaternions separately. **1973** H. M. SCHEY *Div, Grad, Curl, & All That* i. 1 Much of vector calculus was invented for use in electromagnetic theory and is ideally suited to it. **1982** *Sci. Amer.* Jan. 117/3 For any operation that can be applied to a single operand (such as the extraction of the square root) there is a corresponding vector operation that consists of applying the same operation to every element of a vector.

c. *Particle Physics.* Used to designate particles with a spin of 1; ***vector boson***, esp. any of a group of three heavy bosons (the $W^{\pm}$ and Z^0, qq.v.) thought to exist as mediators of the weak interaction. [See quot. 1976.]

1942 *Physical Rev.* LXII. 403 The *β*-matrices in the vector meson theory can be reduced to the simpler *ζ*-matrices and *S* matrices (spin matrices). **1949** *Ibid.* LXXVI. 784/1 The exchange of two charged vector mesons. **1959** *Bull. de l'Acad. Polonaise des Sci.: Série des Sci. Math.* VII. 729 Recently a hypothesis of a charged vector boson, which would mediate in weak interactions, was much discussed. **1968** M. S. LIVINGSTON *Particle Physics* xii. 218 The agency of this weak force is presumed to be a vector boson. **1975** *Nature* 3 Apr. 387/2 In a simple SU(4) scheme there is an obvious place for one *ψ* particle, in the same multiplet as the well established vector mesons *ρ*, *ω* and *ϕ*. **1976** *Sci. Amer.* Jan. 46/1 They are called vector bosons because the quantum-mechanical equation that describes particles with a spin of 1 takes the form of a four-dimensional vector. **1978** *Nature* 12 Oct. 483/1 These fermions interact through vector particles: the photon, charged and neutral massive vector bosons, and gluons, which are responsible for the electromagnetic, weak and strong interactions, respectively. **1983** *Ibid.* 27 Jan. 285 Physicists in Geneva have discovered the intermediate vector boson.

d. Special Combs.: **vector address** *Computers*, an address specified by an interrupt vector (see sense 2 d above); **vector-borne** *a.*, (of a disease or pathogen) transmitted or carried by a vector (sense 3 a above); **vector field**, a field defined at each point by a vector quantity; a map from a space to a space of two or more dimensions; **vector function**, a function whose value is a vector quantity; **vector potential**, a potential function that is a vector function (see POTENTIAL *sb.* 4 a); **vector product**, a vector function of two vectors, (a_1, a_2, a_3) of length *a* and (b_1, b_2, b_3) of length *b*, equal to $(a_2b_3-a_3b_2,\ a_3b_1-a_1b_3,\ a_1b_2-a_2b_1)$, representing a vector perpendicular to them both and of magnitude *ab* sin *θ* (where *θ* is the angle between them); **vector space**, a group whose elements can be combined with each other and with the elements of a scalar field in the way that vectors can, addition within the group being commutative and associative and multiplication by a scalar being distributive and associative; **vector triple product**, a vector function of three three-vectors equal to the vector product of one of them with the vector product of the other two, i.e. $\mathbf{a} \times (\mathbf{b} \times \mathbf{c})$.

1975 R. H. ECKHOUSE *Minicomputer Systems* vi. 189 The various vector addresses and priority levels for the teletype, high-speed reader/punch, and clock on the PDP-11 are as follows. **1982** R. A. SPARKES *Microcomputers in Sci. Teaching* v. 199 All we have to do is to change the vector address and the ISR [*sc.* interrupt service routine] will start by executing our routine instead. **1956** *Nature* 25 Feb. 367/1 With its further expansion..the designation of the East African Malaria Unit has been changed to the East African Institute of Malaria and Vector-Borne Diseases. **1963** *Lancet* 12 Jan. 109/2 This tumour..might be due to a vector-borne virus. **1971** P. C. C. GARNHAM *Progress in Parasitol.* i. 3 In order to prevent too wide a diffusion of parasitology it is useful to impose some sort of restriction, and this perhaps can best be done by adding to the classical subjects of protozoology and helminthology, only vector-borne infections of other types. **1922** J. B. SHAW *Vector Calculus* iii. 26 A vector field is a system of vectors each associated with a point of space, or a point of a surface, or a point of a line or curve. **1932** [see *scalar field* s.v. SCALAR *sb.* 2]. **1976** *Physics Bull.* Sept. 387/3 The vector fields that are particularly relevant to cosmology are those representing the motion of particles and electric charges. **1873** J. C. MAXWELL *Treat. Electr. & Magn.* I. 10 Quantities of this class require *nine* numerical specifications. They are expressed in the language of Quaternions by linear and vector functions of a vector. **1971** [see POTENTIAL *sb.* 4 a]. **1972** M. KLINE *Math. Thought* xxxii. 786 Maxwell noted.. that the curl of a gradient of a scalar function and the divergence of the curl of a vector function are always zero. **1873**, etc. Vector-potential [see POTENTIAL *sb.* 4 a]. **1881** J. C. MAXWELL *Electr. & Magn.* II. 28 The vector, whose components are F.G.H., is called the vector-potential of magnetic induction. **1962** CORSON & LORRAIN *Introd. Electromagn. Fields* v. 186 We shall now show that the magnetic induction **B** is related to a certain quantity **A** through the equation $\mathbf{B} = \nabla \times \mathbf{A}$, where the vector **A** is called..the vector potential. **1878** W. K. CLIFFORD *Dynamic* 95 We are led to two different kinds of product of two vectors,..a vector product..and a scalar product. **1901** [see *scalar triple product* s.v. SCALAR *sb.* 2]. **1965** [see *outer product* s.v. OUTER *a.* 3]. **1972** A. G. HOWSON *Handbk. Terms Algebra & Anal.* xxxiv. 169 Given two vectors **a**.., **b**..we define their vector product (cross product or outer product) denoted by $\mathbf{a} \times \mathbf{b}$ (or $\mathbf{a} \wedge \mathbf{b}$). **1937** A. A. ALBERT *Mod. Higher Algebra* 319/2 (Index), Vector space; *see* Linear set. **1965** [see sense 2 b above]. **1970** *Nature* 19 Dec. 1234/2 A vector space is built up linearly by means of 'scalar' multipliers from a number field. **1972** A. G. HOWSON *Handbk. Terms Algebra & Analysis* viii. 39 Homomorphisms of vector spaces..preserve linear combinations of the type $\lambda_1 a_1 + \lambda_2 a_2 + \ldots + \lambda_n a_n$. **1901** GIBBS & WILSON *Vector Analysis* ii. 72 The vector triple product may be used to express that component of a vector **B** which is perpendicular to a given vector **A**. **1964** Vector triple product [see *scalar triple product* s.v. SCALAR *sb.* 2].

vector (ˈvɛktə(r)), *v.* [f. the sb.] *trans.* **a.** To direct (an aircraft) on its course or towards a target.

1945 *Radar* 34 If the pilot had to ditch, the radar set spotted where he went down, vectoring out to that exact spot the air-sea rescue planes. **1958** *Daily Mail* 24 Oct. 9/2 If the pilot of a military aircraft wants to cross one of the ten-mile-wide airways radiating from the big airports..he can be 'vectored' across by R.A.F. radar. **1976** B. JACKSON *Flameout* i. 20 He'd been first officer of a DC-8 vectored over Newark when a Constellation had collided with the jet.

b. *gen.* To direct, esp. towards a destination; to change the direction of.

1966 *New Scientist* 27 Jan. 213/3 A flexible cup to hold a rocket's nozzle and so allow it to be vectored or swung for steering purposes. **1978** K. AMIS *Jake's Thing* ii. 20 This time Brenda's tone was warm but the warmth was firmly vectored on her friend. **1979** KRAFT & TOY *Mini/Microcomputer Hardware Design* viii. 391 The address found..vectors the processor to the appropriate device service routine. **1983** *Your Computer* Aug. 21/2 Version 1.2 contains several new features, such as the ability to vector output to one of a number of outputs.

Hence **ˈvectored** *ppl. a.*; ***vectored thrust***, thrust that can be varied in direction.

1960 *Aeroplane* XCVIII. 261/1 The Ryan VZ-3RY Vertiplane 'vectored-slipstream' VTOL research aircraft was destroyed early this month during a test flight. **1962** *Flight International* LXXXI. 234/1 The future will undoubtedly see larger, heavier and more complex VTOL aircraft using the principle of 'vectored thrust'. **1973** *Black World* May 6/2 Our scholars and leaders and common people must have vectored minds if we are to prevail. This means we must actively seek stabilizing forces. **1982** *Daily Tel.* 15 June 3/1 He knew of no occasion in which a Harrier had found it necessary to use the special jump-jet tactic of using vectored thrust..to hop out of the way of an attacking aircraft.

vectorˈcardiogram. *Med.* [f. VECTOR *sb.* + *cardiogram* s.v. CARDIO-.] An electrocardiogram (usu. a photograph of an oscilloscope display) that represents the directions as well as the magnitudes of electric currents in the heart.

1938 WILSON & JOHNSTON in *Amer. Heart Jrnl.* XVI. 15 In 1920 Mann..constructed a number of curves of this kind and called them monocardiograms. Granting the priority of this name, we prefer to call them vectorcardiograms in order to emphasize the true nature of the difference..between them and ordinary electrocardiographic curves, which are scalar functions of the time.

Hence ˌ**vectorcardiˈography**, the practice or technique of obtaining and interpreting vectorcardiograms.

1946 *Brit. Heart Jrnl.* VIII. 160 (*heading*) Possible application to vector-cardiography. **1976** *Lancet* 18 Dec. 1339/1 A parallel science of vectorcardiography grew up in specialist centres, in which cardiac currents were studied on oscilloscopes in more than one dimension at a time and with leads and electrodes appropriate to three orthogonal or right-angled axes.

vectored (ˈvɛktəd), *a. Computing.* [f. VECTOR *sb.* + -ED².] Of a facility for interrupting a program: supplying the address to which the program must jump when it is interrupted.

1976 M. HEALEY *Minicomputers & Microprocessors* iv. 136 The obvious advantage of vectored interrupts is the low time that exists between an interrupt being accepted and the specific service routine commencing. **1979** *Sci. Amer.* July 1/2 (Advt.), The new Series Sixteen stands out for state-of-the-art technology as well:..no fewer than 255 vectored interrupts and battery backup for memory retention during power failures. **1982** A. CLEMENTS *Microcomputer Design & Construction* vi. 170 Motorola have introduced a hardware device giving the 6800 a vectored interrupt facility.

vectorial (vɛkˈtɔərɪəl), *a.* [f. L. *vectōri-us* or directly f. VECTOR *sb.*]

†**1.** Capable of carrying or conveying. *Obs.*

1715 DERHAM *Astro-Theol.* (1726) 66 From a Vectorial Power, or Emanations from the Sun. *Ibid.* 68 If..we should imagine the Moon to be wheeled about our Earth, by the Motion and Vectorial Power of the Earth.

2. *Math.* Of or pertaining to, connected with, a vector or radius vector.

1882 MINCHIN *Unipl. Kinemat.* 84 The vectorial area of the complex path thus traced out..is the area of the roulette. **1882** C. SMITH *Conic Sect.* (1885) 10 The radius vector is considered positive if measured from O along the line bounding the vectorial angle.

3. *Path.* Of or pertaining to the ability to act as a vector of a disease.

1964 *Bull. World Health Organization* XXXI. 71 In malaria eradication the residual insecticide exerts upon the mosquito's vectorial capacity a direct insecticidal impact. **1981** *Trop. Med. & Hygiene News* Feb. 24 The vectorial capacity (i.e., the risk of transmission of the parasite) was found to be about 1000 times the critical value required for the maintenance of endemic malaria.

Hence **vecˈtorially** *adv.*, as a vector or vectors.

1895 *Phil. Trans. R. Soc.* A. CLXXXVI. 706 The integral of this rotation taken (vectorially) throughout a small volume including the initial and final positions of the electron is equal to the strength of the electron multiplied by its linear displacement. **1909** BEDELL & PIERCE *Direct & Alternating Current Man.* vi. 201 Currents,..when of different phases, are added vectorially to obtain the resultant current. **1947** *Proc. Physical Soc.* LIX. 24 If the remaining admittance is plotted vectorially, a circle of diameter $1/(S + Si)$ is obtained. **1978** *Sci. Amer.* May 126/2 The point will have two components of apparent motion... The components add vectorially, and the point appears to move diagonally rather than either horizontally or vertically.

vecˈtorian, *a. rare*⁻⁰. [Cf. prec.] (See quot.)

1656 BLOUNT *Glossogr.*, *Vectorian*, apt to carry, serving for carriage.

vectoring (ˈvɛktərɪŋ), *vbl. sb.* [f. VECTOR *sb.*, VECTOR *v.* + -ING¹.] **1.** The action of VECTOR *v.*

1956 W. A. HEFLIN *U.S. Air Force Dict.* 553/1 Vectoring is usually done from the ground, or from a mother aircraft.

2. *Computers.* The provision or use of interrupt vectors.

1977 E. E. KLINGMAN *Microprocessor Systems Design* xii. 352 These [lines] are for 'cascading' several 8214s if more than eight interrupting devices need vectoring. **1979** *Personal Computer World* Nov. 84/4 Software vectoring of interrupts to allow more than one interrupt driven peripheral at a time, and also multi-programming.

vectorscope (ˈvɛktəskəʊp). *Electronics.* [f. VECTOR *sb.* + -SCOPE.] A type of oscilloscope used to analyse colour television signals (see quot. 1957).

1957 SMITH & MATLEY in *Electronic & Radio Engineer* XXXIV. 198/1 The vectorscope..has been designed to display the chrominance component of the colour television signal as a pattern of vectors. **1979** A. A. LIFF *Colour & Black & White Television Theory & Servicing* xviii. 652 Some manufacturers recommend the vectorscope for the alignment of the bandpass amplifier tuned circuits.

†**ˈvectorship.** *Obs.* [f. L. *vector* VECTOR *sb.*] Conveying agency or activity.

1649 BULWER *Pathomyot.* I. iv. 19 This Animall Faculty.. by the vectorship of the spirit flowes from the Braines into every particle.

†**ˈvecture.** *Obs.* [ad. L. *vectūra*, f. *vect-*, *vehĕre* to carry.] Carriage, conveyance.

1625 BACON *Ess., Sed. & Troubles* (Arb.) 405 There be but three Things, which one Nation selleth vnto another; The Commoditie..; The Manufacture; and the Vecture or Carriage. *a* **1643** [see SECTURE].

ved, obs. Sc. form of WED *v.*, WEED *sb.*

‖**Veda** (ˈveɪdə). Also 8 **Beda**; **Vidam, Viedam, Vedam.** [a. Skr. *vēda* knowledge, sacred knowledge, sacred book, from the root *vid-* to know: see WIT *v.* The α-forms are from the Skr. nom. and acc. *vēdam*, perh. partly through Tamil. The Urdū form *bed* (Hindī *ved*) is also represented in older use by *Bead* (1698), *Beid* (1776), and *Bede* (1789).] One or other of the four ancient sacred books of the Hindus (called the *Rig-*, *Yajur-*, *Sāma-*, and *Atharva-vēda*); the body of sacred literature contained in these books.

α. **1734** PICART tr. *Roger's Relig. & Manners Bramins* in *Cerem. & Relig. Customs Var. Nations* III. 353 The Vedam is the Book of the Law among these People, and contains all they are to believe or practise. **1763** SCRAFTON *Indostan* (1770) 4 The Bramins say, that Brumma, their law-giver, left them a book, called the Vidam, which contains all his doctrines and institutions. **1766** J. Z. HOLWELL *Interesting Hist. Events* (ed. 2) I. 12 The great absurdities and impurities of the Viedam. **1778** ORME *Hist. Milit. Trans.* VI. II. 5 The Shaster..they assert to be the genuine scripture of Bramah, in preference to the Vidam. **1794** R. J. SULIVAN *View Nat.* IV. 295 The Vedams, or texts of scripture, were published by Brahma, together with the Shasters, or commentaries, about six hundred years afterwards.

β. **1776** JUSTAMOND tr. *Raynal's Hist. Ind.* I. 33 The Bramin..promised to pardon him on condition that he should swear never to translate the Bedas, or sacred volumes. **1788** *Asiatic Researches* I. 340 The first four [parts of knowledge] are the immortal *Véda's* evidently revealed by God. **1808** COLEBROOKE *Ibid.* VIII. 387 It may be here proper to remark, that each Véda consists of two parts, denominated the Mantras and the Bráhmanas; or prayers and precepts. **1841** ELPHINSTONE *Hist. Ind.* I. 71 The religion taught in the Institutes is derived from the Védas, to which scriptures they refer in every page. **1871** MATEER *Travancore* 35 Accordingly, as a matter of fact, the Sudras never do read the Sanscrit Vedas.

attrib. **1841** *Penny Cycl.* XX. 403/1 In like manner, the Veda-hymns..led to the consideration of the laws of metre. **1843** *Ibid.* XXVI. 171 These various schools of the Veda theology.

Hence **Veˈdaic** *a.*, = VEDIC *a.*; **ˈVedaism,** = VEDISM.

1865 BARING-GOULD *Werewolves* x. 176 In ancient Indian Vedaic mythology the upsaras were heavenly damsels who dwelt in the æther, between Earth and Sun. **1887** L. PARKS *Star in East* viii. 202 Their religion sprung from the same root as Vedaism.

vedalia (vɪˈdeɪlɪə). *Ent.* Also **Vedalia.** [mod.L. (E. Mulsant 1850, in *Ann. de la Soc. d'Agric. de Lyon* II. 901), of unkn. etym.] The ladybird *Rodolia cardinalis* (formerly included in the genus *Vedalia*), which is native to Australia but has been imported into California and elsewhere to control scale insects.

1889 *Insect Life* II. 112 The Vedolia [*sic*] has multiplied in numbers and spread. **1935** H. T. FERNALD *Applied Entomol.* (ed. 3) xxvi. 222 In Australia it [*sc.* the cottony cushion scale] had an enemy known as the Vedalia. **1964** *Discovery* Oct. 62/3 The vedalia ladybird..in less than a year had brought about the virtual elimination of the cottony cushion scale. **1973** P. A. COLINVAUX *Introd. Ecol.* xxix. 410 All stages of the vedalia beetle were carnivorous.

‖**Veˈdanta.** Also **Vedānta, Vedânta.** [Skr. *vēdānta*, f. *vēda* VEDA + *anta* end.] One of the leading systems of Hindu philosophy. Also *attrib.*

The Hindī form *Vedant* has also been occas. used.

1788 *Asiatick Researches* I. 223 The word *máyá*, or *delusion*, has a more subtile and recondite sense in the *Védánta* philosophy. **1823** COLEBROOKE *Philos. Hindus* in *Trans. Roy. Asiatic Soc.* (1827) I. 19 The latter (Uttara) commonly called Védánta, and attributed to Vyása, deduces from the text of the Indian scriptures, a refined psychology, which goes to a denial of a material world. **1849** C. S. HENRY tr. *Epit. Hist. Philos.* 28 The Vedanta philosophy is an exhibition of pantheism in its greatest metaphysical strictness. *Ibid.* 29 The Vedanta system shows us..how pantheism must logically result in scepticism. **1895** *Westm. Gaz.* 23 Oct. 1/3 The philosophy of Vedânta is the abstract science which embraces all these methods.

Hence **Veˈdantic** *a.*, **Veˈdantism, Veˈdantist.**

The Skr. *Vedantin* and Hindī *Vedanti* have also been used instead of 'Vedantist'.

1882 MAX MÜLLER *India* vii. 270 The Brahma-Samâg.. was *Vedântic in spirit. **1882** *Athenæum* 8 July 41/1 He commences his enumeration with that system which is furthest removed from Vedāntic speculation,..omitting, however, the Vedānta itself. **1849** C. S. HENRY tr. *Epit. Hist. Philos.* 29 *Vedantism embraces in its wide comprehension, a multitude of other conceptions, which are common to it and to the other philosophies of India. **1880** BIRDWOOD *Ind. Arts* I. 4 But Vedantism is really nothing else than Nihilism. **1849** C. S. HENRY tr. *Epit. Hist. Philos.* 26 Brahma alone exists; everything else is an illusion. The *Vedantists prove this capital axiom by [etc.]. *Ibid.* 29 In order to avoid misconception of the Vedantist reasoning. **1864** TREVELYAN *Compet. Wallah* (1866) 215 His sect went by the name of 'Vedantists'; in fact, the 'Evangelicals' of the East.

ˈVedda. Also 7 **Vaddah,** 9 **Veddah,** 9– **Wedda.** [Sinhalese *veddā* archer, hunter.] A member of an aboriginal people inhabiting the forest districts of Sri Lanka.

1681 R. KNOX *Hist. Ceylon* 61 In this Land are many of these wild men, they call them Vaddahs. **1851** CARPENTER *Man. Phys.* (ed. 2) 289 The Veddahs or wild hunters of Ceylon. **1875** JEVONS *Money* iv. 28 Somewhat similar pieces circulated in Abyssinia, the Soulou Archipelago.., and among the Veddahs. **1876** B. F. HARTSHORNE in *Fortn. Rev.* Mar. 406 The Weddas, or, as they are more commonly but inaccurately called, the Veddas of Ceylon. **1881** TYLOR *Anthropology* vi. (1904) 164 In the forests of Ceylon are found..the Veddas or 'hunters', shy wild men who build bough huts, and live on game and wild honey. **1900** *Contemp. Rev.* Mar. 453 Practices, which are worthy of the Weddas or the Maories.

vedde, obs. Sc. f. WITHY.

vedder, -ir, obs. Sc. f. WEATHER, WETHER.

Veddoid (ˈvɛdɔɪd), *sb.* and *a. Physical Anthrop.* [f. VEDD(A + -OID.] **A.** *adj.* Belonging or pertaining to a racial group of uncertain status typified by the Veddas of Sri Lanka, characterized by dark skins, short stature, and wavy hair, and occurring chiefly in parts of southern Asia. **B.** *sb.* A member of this group.

1948 A. L. KROEBER *Anthropology* (ed. 2) iv. 139 The Veddoids are almost invariably culturally retarded hill or jungle people who evidently represent an old stratum of population pushed back by Caucasians or Mongoloids, or almost absorbed by them. **1956** *Nature* 7 Jan. 41/2 The sickle cell trait was found to be present in a number of Veddoid communities of southern India. **1963** S. COLE *Races of Man* vii. 85 The Veddoids are short, average stature 157 c.m., skin colour is chocolate brown, hair very wavy or curly. **1974** *Encycl. Brit. Macropædia* XIX. 1081/1 Non-Mediterranean Veddoids (Australoids) are found as minorities [in Southern Yemen]. *Ibid.*, The original islanders [of Socotra in the Arabian Sea], forming about half the population, are Veddoid. **1977** G. CLARK *World Prehist.* (ed. 3) vi. 260 Low-headed people [in the Indian sub-continent] with retreating foreheads, pronounced supraorbital ridges and relatively broad noses with depressed roots appear to be related to a Veddoid-Australoid stock of indigenous character.

veddy (ˈvɛdɪ), repr. a childish, affected, or (*U.S.*) British pronunc. of *very*. Freq. *joc.*

1859 E. EDEN *Semi-Detached House* xix. 257 Charlie would gravely say, 'Yes, veddy true, pooty Rachel.' **1938** *Amer. Speech* XIII. 157/2 For jocularity, newspaper writers ..now sometimes write *veddy* for 'very'. **1960** L. KAUFFMANN *Waldo* i. 14 Elegant and veddy sophisticated and all that sort of thing. But wastrels. **1967** J. P. CARSTAIRS *No Thanks for Shroud* ii. 17 'Is that British?' '*Veddy*,' I grinned. **1975** *Publishers Weekly* 24 Feb. 114/1 Note humorous anachronism as Dylan's fish-girl pours him tea from a bone china teapot—veddy British!

vede, obs. Sc. f. WEED *sb.*

vede(n, southern ME. varr. FEED *v.*

veder, southern ME. var. FATHER, FEATHER.

‖**vedette** (vɪˈdɛt). Also 9 **vedet;** 7– **vidette.** [F., ad. It. *vedetta*, prob. f. *vedere* to see. The incorrect spelling *vidette*, now rare, was common in the first half of the 19th cent.]

1. *Mil.* A mounted sentry placed in advance of the outposts of an army to observe the movements of the enemy.

a. **1690** DAVIES *Diary* (Camden) 129 And then lay down to sleep..without posting any scouts or videttes abroad. **1778** GOUV. MORRIS in Sparks *Corr. Amer. Rev.* (1853) II. 228 A few good cavalry may be requisite for the videttes. **1812** *Examiner* 7 Sept. 561/2 He fell in with the enemy's videttes. **1843** PRESCOTT *Mexico* III. iii. (1864) 152 One of the videttes perceived..a large body of Indians moving towards the

Christian lines. **1868** *Regul. & Orders Army* §892 Instructions for the guidance of Outposts, .. videttes, and sentries. **1902** R. W. CHAMBERS *Maids of Paradise* xxii. 376 The rigid system of patrol which brought death .. to our sleet-soaked videttes.

β. **1702** *Milit. Dict.*, *Vedette*, a Sentinel of the Horse detached from the main Body of the Army [etc.]. **1746** *Rep. Cond. Sir J. Cope* 78 To post the Out-Guard, and see the Vedettes placed properly. **1786** GILLIES *Hist. Greece* iii. I. 100 The order of their guards and watches was highly judicious; they employed, for their security, out-sentries and vedettes. **1809** WELLINGTON in Gurw. *Desp.* (1836) V. 355 *note*, The vedettes of the outposts were within shot of each other. **1844** *Queen's Reg. & Ord. Army* 394 Whether they have been in the habit of placing piquets, posting vedets, conducting patrols, &c. **1879** *Blackw. Mag.* July 23 A vedette was killed to-day. Half-a-dozen Zulus rushed out on him soon after he had been posted for the day.

transf. **1807** PIKE *Sources Mississ.* (1810) 248, I made a pretext to halt—established my boy as a vedet, and sat down peacably under a bush and made my notes. **1812** COL. HAWKER *Diary* (1893) I. 53 An old cock, who was the vidette. **1878** L. W. M. LOCKHART *Mine is Thine* xxii. II. 98 The blackcock *vedette* rolled his burnished plumage leisurely against the sun.

fig. **1801** JEFFERSON *Writ.* (1859) VII. 483 Philosophical vedette at the distance of one thousand miles .. is precious to us here. **1880** *Spectator* 13 Nov. 1439 They cannot bear to see the landlords, whom they regard as their own vedettes, terrorized.

2. ***vedette boat***, a small vessel used for scouting purposes in naval warfare; hence more widely, any motor launch. Also *ellipt.*

1884 *Pall Mall G.* 6 Oct. 6/1 Building armour-clads, fast cruisers, vedette and torpedo boats. **1892** *Times* (weekly ed.) 7 Oct. 7/2 They are vedette boats and not torpedo boats in the proper sense. **1977** E. W. MIDDLETON *Lifeboats of World* v. 178, 90 fast vedettes. **1982** H. A. WILLIAMS *Some Day I'll find You* I. viii. 23 If it was low tide the passengers had to land in *vedettes*.

3. With pronunc. (və'dɛt). A stage or film star.

1963 *Listener* 28 Mar. 572/2 The 'pop' singers' predecessors were the music-hall vedettes, among them Marie Lloyd and Maurice Chevalier, who .. lit up the souls of their audiences with wit and innuendo. **1980** L. ST. CLAIR *Obsessions* viii. 150 At the sight of .. the Hollywood *vedette*, the maitre d' .. escorted his guests to the window table.

Vedic ('veɪdɪk), *a.* and *sb.* [f. VED-A + -IC.] **A.** *adj.* Of or pertaining to, contained or mentioned in, contemporary with, the Vedas. **B.** *sb.* The language of the Vedas, an early form of Sanskrit.

1848 *Rep. Brit. Assoc. Adv. Sci. 1847* 321 It may be observed that in the Vedic hymns .. some dialectic differences and many grammatical discrepancies occur. **1853** *Jrnl. Amer. Oriental Soc.* III. 297 In many of the points in which Vedic and Sanskrit disagree, the former strikingly approaches its next neighbors to the westward, the language of the Avesta [etc.]. **1859** MAX MÜLLER *Anc. Sanskrit Lit.* 10 The sacred literature of the Vedic age. *Ibid.* 11 The .. publication of all Vedic texts and commentaries. **1864** PUSEY *Lect. Daniel* ix. 558 The old Vedic worship was a libation to the god of fire. **1873** WHITNEY *Oriental & Ling. Stud.* 1 A general view of the whole body of Vedic literature. **1884** *American* VIII. 90 There are still orthodox Brahmans, who .. maintain old Vedic sacrifices. **1890** SCHRUMPF *First Aryan Reader* p. xi, Specimen B ought to have preceded specimen A, as Vedic is older than Sanskrit.

vedir, obs. Sc. f. WEATHER.

'Vedism. [f. VED-A + -ISM. Cf. VEDAISM.] The system of religious beliefs and practices contained in the Vedas.

1882 *Athenæum* 29 Apr. 542/3 In this paper he showed the relationship between the Vaishnava religion and three other forms of the Hindu religious system, viz., Vedism, Brâhmanism, and Saivism. **1895** J. KIDD *Morality & Relig.* v. 191 Vedism, then, generally speaking, was a religion of nature.

'Vedist. [f. as prec. + -IST.] A student of, or authority on, the Vedas.

1896 SEELEY *Introd. Pol. Sci.* (1902) 364 Not dealing with the new matter introduced by Egyptologists or Assyriologists or Vedists.

vedlak, obs. form of WEDLOCK.

vedo(u, obs. Sc. ff. WIDOW.

‖**vedro.** Also 8 wedro. [Russ. *vedró* pail.] A Russian liquid measure equal to 2.7 imperial gallons.

1753 HANWAY *Trav.* VI. lxxxi. (1762) I. 371, 8 Krushquas, 1 wedro—13 english quarts. **1799** W. TOOKE *View Russian Emp.* II. 523 The greater part was then already podraded (contracted) for at 148 kopecks for every vedro. **1802–3** tr. *Pallas's Trav.* (1812) I. 234 Boiled in large kettles containing from forty to forty-three Russian vedros, or eimers, of water. **1833** R. PINKERTON *Russia* 77 The .. distilleries .. issue about twenty-five millions of vedros. **1907** *Edin. Rev.* Jan. 224 The peasants of that province .. drank this year 62,924 vedros of vodka more than last.

‖**veduta** (ve'duta). Pl. vedute; vedutas. [a. It. *veduta* a view, f. *vedere* to see.] A realistic, detailed picture of a town scene with buildings of interest, esp. one belonging to the genre represented by eighteenth-century Italian artists such as Canaletto, Guardi, and Piranesi; ***veduta ideata*** (pl. *vedute ideate*), a picture in this style but showing an imaginary scene, esp. one by Pannini.

1906 *Studio* (Special Summer No.) A. p. iii, Rudolf [von Alt] was the leader of the Viennese 'Veduta' painting, the true biographer of Vienna. **1934** *Burlington Mag.* Aug. 71/2 Topographical exactitude and the precision of linear perspective—the two essential elements of an ideal *veduta*. **1944** *Ibid.* Sept. 216/2 Little *vedutas* of the Swedish countryside. **1959** *Listener* 25 June 1118/1 Such *vedute ideate* were .. a regular branch of Italian landscape painting since the latter part of the seventeenth century. **1961** *Guardian* 16 Nov. 7/7 The boom in Venetian *vedute* by Guardi in 1948. **1967** G. SIMS *Last Best Friend* xix. 180 There was an eighteenth-century Venetian Veduta painting. **1970** *Oxf. Compan. Art* 199/1 Canaletto .. enlarged his repertory to include subjects from the Venetian mainland .. and *vedute ideate* or imaginary landscapes. **1978** *New York* 3 Apr. 64/2 Instead it dwells on the fresh spring light and dank shade falling over ordinary buildings, with a sparseness, accuracy, and austere gaiety that suggest Canaletto's *vedute* of London.

Hence **vedu'tista** (pl. -i, -e), a painter of *vedute*.

1962 R. G. HAGGAR *Dict. Art Terms* 355/1 The most notable *vedutisti* .. were Pannini and Piranesi .. and Canaletto and Guardi. **1967** C. ROUGVIE *When Johnny Died* ii. 55 *Vedute* .. are .. paintings of Venice .. both Canaletto and Guardi were *vedutiste* (sic).

vee (viː). The name of the letter V, used to denote things having or arranged in this shape.

1883 GRESLEY *Gloss. Coal-M.* 269 *Vee*, the junction of two underground roadways meeting in the form of a V. **1933** *Jrnl. R. Aeronaut. Soc.* XXXVII. 845 This .. can easily be achieved by making the vee of the hull sufficiently deep. **1939** *War Illustr.* 29 Dec. 538/2 A Squadron of fighters or bombers will fly in a 'vee' with three Flights of three machines each. **1950** B. PYM *Some Tame Gazelle* i. 9, I must have something to cover up the neck of my green frock. Perhaps it would have been better if I hadn't tried to alter it to a Vee. **1965** G. MCINNES *Road to Gundagai* xiii. 222 A tall man with .. a shock of receding curly hair in a Vee. **1970** *Commercial Motor* 25 Sept. 97 The trend in diesel engine development in this country is now clearly towards vees and/or turbocharging. **1977** 'E. CRISPIN' *Glimpses of Moon* vi. 93 At some stage she stood in the vee with her back to the parapet .. and lost her balance and went headlong.

b. *attrib.* and *Comb.*, as ***vee aerial***, ***antenna***, ***belt***, ***block***, ***formation***, ***joint***, ***neck(line)***, ***thread***; ***vee-necked***, ***-shaped*** adjs.; **vee engine**, an engine with two lines of cylinders inclined so as to form a V. Cf. V 2b.

1939 *Amat. Radio Handbk.* 158/2 Such an arrangement .. is known as the RCA Vee aerial. **1950** A. L. ALBERT *Electr. Communication* (ed. 3) xii. 481 (*caption*) The non-resonant Vee antenna is composed of two wires several wavelengths long, and connected to ground through terminating resistors. **1981** R. S. ELLIOTT *Antenna Theory & Design* ix. 436 The Vee antenna .. is a simplification of the rhombic, with legs 3 and 4 removed. **1937** *Motor Catal.* (E. London Rubber Co. Ltd.) 39/2 A range of twelve Romac New-Vee Fan Belts will fit 194 popular cars. **1971** *Power Farming* Mar. 44/2 Machines .. lift the root by gripping the leafy top growth of the plant between a pair of .. rubber vee-belts. **1893** J. G. HORNER *Princ. Fitting* v. 64 The vee blocks are employed chiefly for supporting shafts and circular spindle-like work generally. **1975** BRAM & DOWNS *Manuf. Technol.* i. 27 Place the component in a suitable vee-block and slowly rotate it about the diameter to be checked. **1957** J. M. BRUCE *Brit. Aeroplanes 1914–18* 213 It was one of the first aeroplanes to have the then-new Rolls-Royce Condor twelve-cylinder vee engine. **1972** *Practical Motorist* Oct. 70/1 Vee engines have a non-return valve for the crankcase emission control system in the offside rocker cover. **1960** *Times Rev. Industry* Nov. 18/1 Cylinders in Vee formation. **1964** S. CRAWFORD *Basic Engin. Processes* iii. 93 Fig 17(a) shows the single vee-joint suitable for plates up to $\frac{5}{8}$ inch in thickness. **1970** *Islander* (Victoria, B.C.) 15 Feb. 15/4 The original interior finish has been retained. The walls of pine 'Vee' joint; pews, chancel and rails of Douglas fir have darkened and mellowed with age. **1970** *Times* 24 Mar. 9/4 They are all of the same shape, vee neck front. **1973** *Guardian* 10 Apr. 13/2 Checked vee-necked dress with contrast ribbing. **1949** *Sun* (Baltimore) 24 Mar. 8 (Advt.), Elongated vee neckline, especially becoming to the larger woman! **1959** *Listener* 31 Dec. 1157/2 Conditions began to take a happy turn .. but, very unfortunately, they never became perfectly vee-shaped. **1964** S. CRAWFORD *Basic Engin. Processes* i. 36 The vee-shaped grooves are accurately ground parallel and square with the outside faces. **1914** E. PULL *Mod. Workshop Pract.* xii. 229 (*heading*) Vee threads. **1975** BRAM & DOWNS *Manuf. Technol.* iv. 120 The buttress thread combines the anti-friction advantages of the square thread with the strength of the vee thread.

Hence **veed** *a.*, V-shaped.

1934 *Times* 23 Oct. 7/4 The radiator is in a case which has a Vee'd dummy honeycomb front. **1938** *Times* 9 Aug. 8/7 A movable section—in front of the driver—in a sloping, divided, veed screen. **1972** C. MUDIE *Motor Boats & Boating* 144 Outwardly the racing boats have developed from a heterogeneous collection towards a clean, fine lined, deep Veed fleet.

veeboer (fɪəbuːr). *S. Afr.* Also as two words and with capital initial(s). Pl. -boer, -boere, -boers. [Afrikaans, f. *vee* cattle, livestock (f. Du. *vee*: see FEE *sb.*[1]) + BOER.] A livestock farmer.

1824 *S. Afr. Jrnl.* I. 29 Poor Gert Schepers, a Vee Boer of the Cradock District, was less fortunate in an encounter with a South African lion. **1912** *Agric. Jrnl. Union of S. Afr.* July 61 These plants were known to the veeboer or schaapboer as the cause of the troubles they produce long before any scientific investigation of their properties had been made. **1944** J. MOCKFORD *Here are S. Africans* iv. 39 Here the free burghers, the vee-Boers, rapidly acquired qualities unknown to the more sedate residents of Table Valley. **1954** H. GIBBS *Background to Bitterness* I. i. 25 Most free men at the Cape wanted to become a *veeboer*, cattle-farmer. **1965** M. G. ATMORE *Cape Furniture* iii. 56 Thus arose the 'veeboere', each tenant on some 6,000 acres of cattle ranching country.

‖**veedor.** *Obs.* Also 6 veadore, viador. [a. Sp. and Pg. *veedór*, Pg. *vedor*, *veador*, *viador*, f. *ver* to see.] An official invested with inspecting or controlling power.

α. [**1555** EDEN *Decades* (Arb.) 158 One Gonzalus Fernandus Ouiedus beinge one of the maiestrates appointed in that office which the Spanyardes caule *Veedor*.] **1595** T. SCARLETT *Est. Engl. Fugitives* G, Sammariba, the Veedors chiefe officer. **1612** SHELTON *Quix.* III. viii. 192 The office of a Bawde .. should not be practised but by people well borne; and ought besides to haue a Veedor, and examinator of them.

β. **1599** HAKLUYT *Voy.* II. II. 129 We spake with his Veadore, or chiefe man, that hath the dealing with the Christians. **1625** PURCHAS *Pilgrims* II. VII. 949 (Guinea), They haue one attending on them, whom they call Viador (which word they haue learned of the Portugals); hee is the Kings Treasurer, and keepeth his Gold and other Riches.

veejay (viː'dʒeɪ). *slang* (chiefly *U.S.*). Also vee-jay, VJ. [Pronunc. of the initial letters of *video jockey*, after *D.J.* s.v. D III. 3; cf. DEE-JAY, DEEJAY.] One who presents a programme of (popular music) videos, esp. on television.

1982 *N.Y. Times* 4 July III. 17/1 The image .. flashes .. to a loft studio where a video jockey—or 'veejay', a cross between a disc jockey and a TV emcee—announces what has just been played on MTV. **1983** *Amer. Way* June 170/1 VJs, or video jockeys, at MTV's studio cue up as many as 13 videos an hour. **1984** *Sunday Tel.* (Colour Suppl.) 29 Jan. 16 (*caption*) Mike Read and colleagues—today's disc jockeys will be tomorrow's 'veejays'.

veel, southern dial. var. FEEL *v.*, FIELD *sb.*

‖**veena** ('viːnə). Also 8 vena, 8– vina. [Skr. and Hindi *vīṇā*.] An Indian musical instrument consisting of a fretted fingerboard, to which seven strings fitted with pegs are attached, with a gourd at each end; an Indian lyre. Also *attrib.* and in *Comb.*

1788 W. JONES in *Asiatick Researches* I. 265 His [*sc.* Nared's] invention of the Víná, or Indian lute, is thus described. **1796** ELIZA HAMILTON *Lett. Hindoo Rajah* (1811) I. 211 A musician softly touched the chords of a vena. **1817** MOORE *Lalla Rookh*, *Fire-worshippers* v. Introd., As the story was chiefly to be told in song, .. he borrowed the vina of Lalla Rookh's slave. **1837** [MRS. MAITLAND] *Lett. fr. Madras* (1843) 55 First .. came in an old man .. to play and sing to the vina, an instrument like a large mandoline. **1848** J. H. STOCQUELER *Oriental Interpreter* s.v., *Veena*, an instrument of the guitar kind, with seven metal strings. It is the most ancient musical instrument of the Hindoos, and in good hands is capable of yielding great melody and expression. **1891** [see TAMBOURA b]. **1896** *Ind. Mag.* Jan. 39 Instrumental music on the veena .. is also much in vogue among them. **1896** [see SURBAHAR]. **1921** H. A. POPLEY *Music of India* vii. 104 The vīṇā has seven strings, four of which pass over the frets and constitute the main playing strings. **1945** R. K. NARAYAN *Eng. Teacher* v. 109 He hardly made any special sound or noise, but it was there all the time, a permanent background against which all his speech and gestures occurred, something like the melody of a veena string from which music arises and ends. **1964** S. MARCUSE *Mus. Instruments* 564/2 *Vinā* .., stringed instr. of ancient and modern India. In modern times the word has become a generic term for chordophones in S. India. **1969** R. SHANKAR *My Music* i. 34/2 The stringed instrument par excellence .. is the *veena* (also spelled *vina*). **1972** P. HOLROYDE *Indian Mus.* 258 It has been said by Yajnavalkya, the ancient Indian writer and philosopher: 'He who knows the art of veena-playing and sruti shastra can attain God easily.'

veep (viːp). *U.S. colloq.* Also Veep. [f. the initials *V.P.* (viː'piː); cf. JEEP *sb.*] A vice-president.

1949 *News-Age-Herald* (Birmingham, Alabama) 12 June D-24 (*heading*) 'Veep' Barkley's name now often tied with some eligible widow's. **1952** *N.Y. Times* 19 June 25/1 (*heading*) Woman 'veep' urged. **1961** *Manila Times* 12 Sept. 1 (*heading*) Veep offers self as rice czar. **1977** *Time* 17 Oct. 14/1 Kremlinologists have been speculating about who might be named to the newly created post of Vice President. A Veep was needed to take over the fatiguing ceremonial functions of the presidency. **1983** *Fortune* 28 Nov. 152/3 His Makati business club constituents would be happy to nominate E.Z. for veep.

veer (vɪə(r)), *sb.* [f. VEER *v.*[2]] An act or instance of veering; a change of direction.

1611 COTGR., *Virevoulte*, a veere, whirle, .. friske, or turne. **1633** T. JAMES *Voy.* 70 Wee .. expected a lower veere of the water. **1871** TENNYSON *Last Tourn.* 231 Till the warm hour returns With veer of wind. **1890** *Daily News* 21 Aug. 5/7 This project of the Emperor William would explain the sudden veer round a short time ago against Prince Ferdinand.

veer, southern ME. var. FIR; var. VERE (spring) *Obs.*

veer (vɪə(r)), *v.*[1] *Naut.* Forms: 5–7 vere (6 *Sc.* vire); 6 vyere, 7 vier-; 6–7 veare, 7 vear; 7 veere, 7– veer. [a. MDu. *vieren* to let out, slacken, = OHG. *fieren*, *fiaran* to give direction to. Hence also G. *vieren*, *fieren*, Da. *fire*, Sw. *fira* in nautical use.]

1. *trans.* To allow (a sheet or other sail-line) to run out to some extent; to let out by releasing. Also with *out.* ? *Obs.*

So Du. and Flem. (*de*) *schoot vieren*, freq. used fig.

c **1460** *Pilgrim's Sea-Voy.* 25 Hale the bewelyne! now, vere the shete! **1522** *Lett. & Papers Hen. VIII*, III. II. 975 [The galley was next them, but if she] may vyere the shit, she will go from us all. **1530** *Hickscorner* 302 A-le the helme! a-le! vere! shot of! vere sayle! **1549** *Compl. Scot.* vi. 41 Vire the trossis, nou heise. *Ibid.*, Vire ȝour liftaris and ȝour top sail trossis. **1590** SPENSER *F.Q.* I. xii. 1 Behold I see the hauen nigh at hand,.. Vere the maine shete, and beare vp with the land. **1626** CAPT. SMITH *Accid. Yng. Seamen* 28 Loure the maine top saile, veare a fadome of your sheat. **1627** —— *Seaman's Gram.* ix. 39 Veere more sheat, or a flowne sheat, that is, when they are not haled home to the blocke. **1669** STURMY *Mariner's Mag.* I. ii. 17 Vere out some of your Fore and Main-sheets. *Ibid.* 18 Vere out the main Sheet, and fore Sheet. **1694** [see MAIN-SHEET 1].

absol. **1530** [see above]. *a* **1658** CLEVELAND *Inund. of Trent* 74 Now Bedfellows do one another greet I' th' Saylors Phrase, Vere, vere, more Sheet.

b. To let *out* (any line or rope); to allow to run *out* gradually to a desired length.

1574 W. BOURNE *Regiment for Sea* xiv. (1577) 42 They haue a pece of wood, and a line to vere out ouer borde. **1628–9** DIGBY *Voy. Medit.* (Camden) 75, I bore vp to her, and by a barrell viered her out a long hawser. **1690** LEYBOURN *Curs. Math.* 608 As you veer out the Log-Line, set the Drift of the Log with your Compass. **1721** *Phil. Trans.* XXXI. 178 [He] marches on the bottom of the Sea, vearing out the Coiles of his Pipe. **1793** SMEATON *Edystone L.* §68 They rowed it towards the rock, veering out a rope, which they had fastened to the large boat. **1839** *Civil Eng. & Arch. Jrnl.* II. 178/2 They had the appearance of a single rope capable of being coiled and veered out conveniently. **1893** W. R. MACKINTOSH *Around Orkney Peat Fires* (1905) II. 136 [He] veered out the boat's tether till he came alongside the vessel.

†**c.** Similarly without adv. *Obs. rare.*

1624 CAPT. SMITH *Virginia* VI. 219 As fast as you can hale and vere a line. **1787** BEST *Angling* (ed. 2) 169 *Veer your line*, let it off the reel after striking.

2. To allow (a boat, buoy, etc.) to drift further off by letting out a line attached to it. Usually with *away* or *out*.

1539 in R. G. Marsden *Sel. Rec. Crt. Adm.* (Selden) I. 67 The marinars of the sayd Venys shippe did vere owt there grete bote. **1824** *Mechanic's Mag.* No. 41. 215 They tried the means of veering away a buoy. **1831** TRELAWNY *Adv. Younger Son* lxxiv, We veered an empty cask astern, with a rope attached to it. **1834** MARRYAT *P. Simple* (1863) 207 They veered out a buoy with a line, which we got hold of. **1846** A. YOUNG *Naut. Dict.* 357 To veer a buoy in a ship's wake, means to slack out a rope to which the buoy has been attached, in order to let it go astern.

3. To let out or pay out (a cable).

1604 *Adm. Ct. Exam.* 21 May, The cables were not viered. **1622** R. HAWKINS *Voy. S. Sea* (1847) 203 On both sides was crying out to veere cable. *Ibid.*, Those [cables were] very short, and vered to the better end. **1627** CAPT. SMITH *Seaman's Gram.* vii. 30 Veere more Cable, is when you ride at Anchor. **1745** P. THOMAS *Jrnl. Anson's Voy.* 156 Tho' they immediately let go the Sheet-Anchor, and veer'd almost two Cables on it, yet they drove out to Sea. **1789** *Trans. Soc. Arts* VII. 211 Cables veered astern, with tackles leading from them to the ship's quarters. **1854** G. B. RICHARDSON *Univ. Code* v. (ed. 12) 1280, I cannot veer more cable. **1870** MEADE *New Zealand* 290 After veering cable we went to quarters. **1899** F. T. BULLEN *Way Navy* 41 Every anchor fell and cable was veered to five shackles.

fig. **1616** B. JONSON *Devil an Ass* v. v. 46 Traines shall seeke out Ingine,.. euery cable Is to be veer'd.

absol. **1769** FALCONER *Dict. Marine* (1780) A a a 4 b, *Ne file plus amarre!* keep fast the cable! stopper the cable! veer no more! **1775** *Phil. Trans.* LXVIII. 404 At 4 a.m. found ship drove, veered to a whole cable.

b. With *away* or *out*.

(*a*) **1697** DAMPIER *Voy.* I. 437 This obliged us to let go our Sheet Anchor, veering out a good scope of Cable. **1769** FALCONER *Dict. Marine* (1780) A a a 4 b, *Filer le cable bout par bout*,.. to veer out the cable end-for-end. **1899** F. T. BULLEN *Log Sea-waif* 74 The warships, which, with topmasts housed and cables veered out to the clinch, were all steaming full speed ahead.

(*b*) **1748** *Anson's Voy.* II. iii. 138 To veer away the cable briskly. *Ibid.* III. ii. 319 After we had veered away one whole cable. **1765** COMMODORE BYRON *Voy.* (1773) I. 79 A thick fog coming on with hard rain, we veered away the stream cable. **1846** A. YOUNG *Naut. Dict.* 357 'Veer away the cable,' that is, slack it and let it run out.

fig. **1769** M. CUMBERLAND *Brothers* in *Brit. Theat.* (1808) XVIII. 17 I'll veer away no more good advice after you.

c. To put *on* (cables) end to end. *rare*$^{-1}$.

1806 A. DUNCAN *Nelson* 86 The latter continued.. to drop to leeward, and the Theseus was obliged to veer on two cables to keep within reach of them.

4. ***to veer and haul***: (see quots.).

1769 FALCONER *Dict. Marine*, *To Veer and haul*, to pull a rope tight, by drawing it in and slackening it alternately,.. so that the rope is straitened to a greater tension. **1841** R. H. DANA *Seaman's Man.* 133 *To veer and haul*, is to haul and slack alternately on a rope, as in warping, until the vessel or boat gets headway. **1867** SMYTH *Sailor's Word-bk.*, *To veer and haul*, to gently tauten and then slacken a rope three times before giving a heavy pull, the object being to concentrate the force of several men. **1875** BEDFORD *Sailor's Pocket Bk.* viii. 282 By hauling and veering on it,.. a sufficiently uniform strain on it would be obtained.

fig. **1891** C. ROBERTS *Adrift Amer.* 251 The agents have a certain margin to veer and haul on in their commission. **1901** *Speaker* 27 April 109/2 Here is a sum on which the British Government may fairly veer and haul.

†**5.** *intr.* Of a ship: To sail with the sheet let out. *Obs.*

a **1625** *Nomenclator Navalis* (MS. Harl. 2301) s.v., When a Shipp sailes, and the Sheate is veered-out, wee saie she goes veering. **1692** *Capt. Smith's Seaman's Gram.* I. xvi. 76 The Ship goes Lasking, Quartering, Veering, or Large; are terms of the same signification, *viz.* that she neither goes by a Wind nor before the wind, but betwixt both.

veer (vɪə(r)), *v.*^{2} Forms: 6 verre (?), 7 vere, vear(e, veere, 7– veer. [ad. F. *virer* (= Sp. *virar*, *birar*, Pg. *virar*, It. *virare*), to turn, to veer; of obscure origin. See also VIRE *v.*]

1. *intr.* **a.** Of the wind: To change gradually; to pass by degrees from one point to another, *spec.* in the direction of the sun's course. Orig. *Naut.*

1582 N. LICHEFIELD tr. *Castanheda's Conq. E. Ind.* 73 And after that the winde verred [*sic*] to the Southwest they bare with the same. **1627** CAPT. SMITH *Seaman's Gram.* ix. 39 Now the wind veeres, that is, it doth shift from point to point. **1665** SIR T. HERBERT *Trav.* (1677) 6 The wind in one hours space veering about every point of the Compass. **1686** GOAD *Celest. Bodies* II. vii. 234 Their Influence may be separated so far as to suffer a cooler Wind to blow, which upon their Rising shall vere to a warmer point. **1744** J. CLARIDGE *Sheph. Banbury's Rules* 15 The wind commonly veers to the South West. **1777** *Phil. Trans.* LXVIII. 230 The wind was Easterly. At the instant of the shock it is said to have veered to the West. **1836** MARRYAT *Midsh. Easy* xxxi, The wind had veered round, and the Aurora was now able to lay up clear of the island of Maritimo. **1849** MRS. SOMERVILLE *Connex. Phys. Sci.* (ed. 8) xv. 138 When north and south winds blow alternately, the wind at any place will veer in one uniform direction through every point of the compass. **1899** F. T. BULLEN *Log Sea-waif* 317 The next night the wind veered to the eastward.

†**b.** To turn round, revolve. *Obs.*

1598 SYLVESTER *Du Bartas* II. ii. *Columnes* 459 O! thou fair Chariot,.. thou do'st alwaies veer About the North-Pole. *Ibid.* 484 As long as Heav'n's swift Orb shall veer. **1611** COTGR., *Virer*, to veere, turne round, wheele or whirle about.

2. *Naut.* Of a ship: To change course; *spec.* to turn round with the head away from the wind in order to sail on another tack.

c **1620** Z. BOYD *Zion's Flowers* (1855) 134 The other veres as slowe, Lar-board and Star-board. **1697** DRYDEN *Æneid* v. 1088 A-head of all the Master Pilot steers, And, as he leads, the following navy veers. **1761** *British Mag.* II. 497 The Packet in haste to Beaumaurice was veering, When, lo! a large ship towards our vessel was steering. **1798** COLERIDGE *Anc. Mar.* III. iii, It plunged and tacked and veered. **1848** LYTTON *Harold* III. ii, The Earl's fleet after a brief halt veered majestically round. **1878** SUSAN PHILLIPS *On Seaboard* 119 The coble tossed, and veered, and tacked, As she strove to make the shore.

3. Of things: To turn round or about; to change from one direction or course to another.

Also in fig. context (quot. 1690): cf. sense 4.

1633 T. JAMES *Voy.* 12 The water veer'd to a lower ebbe. **1690** DRYDEN *Amphitryon* v. 48 Thou Weather-cock of Government; that when the Wind..changes for the Soveraign, veers to Prerogative.

1810 SCOTT *Lady of L.* I. xiii, A narrow inlet,.. Lost for a space, through thickets veering, But broader when again appearing. **1823** BYRON *Island* I. iii, No more at thy command The obedient helm shall veer, the sail expand. **1865** SWINBURNE *Poems & Ball.*, *Rondel* 5 Grief a fixed star, and joy a vane that veers. **1878** GEO. ELIOT *Coll. Breakf. P.* 811 The shadows slowly farther crept and veered Like changing memories.

b. Of persons or animals.

1760–72 H. BROOKE *Fool of Qual.* (1809) III. 17 Susanna slipped.. from the side of her mamma, and veering toward Harry, she went on one side. **1805** WORDSW. *Prelude* IV. 20 'Twas but a short hour's walk, ere veering round I saw the snow-white church. **1825** COBBETT *Rur. Rides* 322 After passing Bullington, Sutton, and Wonston we veered away from State-Charity. **1879** TOURGEE *Fool's Err.* xxxvi. 256 The amazed horse veered quickly to one side, and stopped as if stricken to stone.

4. *fig.* To change or alter; to pass from one state, position, tendency, etc., to another; to be variable or changeable: **a.** Of persons.

1670 DRYDEN *Conq. Granada* III. i, Two Factions turn him with each Blast of Wind. But now he shall not veer. **1682** S. PORDAGE *Medal Rev.* 2 When the Tide turn'd, then strait about he veers, And for the stronger side he still appears. **1714** SWIFT *Jacks put to their Trumps* Wks. 1841 II. 852 Those few at last veer'd quite about, And join'd in my disgrace. **1734** tr. *Rollin's Anc. Hist.* VIII. §4 (1841) I. 312/1 Alcibiades was of a pliant and flexible disposition, that would take any impression which the difference of times and circumstances might require, still veering either to good or evil with the same facility and ardor. **1821** PRAED *Gog* Poems 1865 I. 95 Linda, like many a modern Miss, Began to veer around at this. **1858** H. BUSHNELL *Nat. & Supernat.* x. (1864) 308 The infirmity.. shown by human teachers, when they veer a little from their point.. to catch the assent of multitudes. **1884** F. M. CRAWFORD *Rom. Singer* I. 56 He is a man to veer about like a weather-cock.

b. Of feelings, thoughts, conditions, etc.

1669 DRYDEN *Tyrannic Love* IV. i, Like a wind it [love] in no quarter stays; But points and veers each hour a thousand ways. **1711** SHAFTESB. *Charac.* (1737) I. 296 For as these passions veer, my interest veers, my steerage varys. **1756** H. WALPOLE *Lett.* (1846) III. 198 Madame Pompadour, perceiving how much the King's disposition veered to devotion, artfully took the turn of humouring it. **1813** SCOTT *Rokeby* I. xxii, While his own troubled passions veer Through hatred, joy, regret, and fear. **1833** HT. MARTINEAU *Fr. Wines & Pol.* iii. 47 Her thoughts were ready to veer any way in hope of escape. **1878** BOSW. SMITH *Carthage* 52 Seldom has the fortune of war veered round so rapidly.

c. To diverge or differ *from* something. *rare*$^{-1}$.

1796 *Campaigns, 1793–4* I. I. iv. 25 Your opinion, dear Richard, veer'd widely from mine.

5. *absol.* To alter the course of a ship, *spec.* by causing it to swing round with the stern to windward so as to sail on another tack. Also of a ship: To admit of veering.

1625 in Foster *Eng. Factories Ind.* (1909) III. 54 [The Portuguese] payde away, vearinge to delay time for our cominge upp with them. **1627** CAPT. SMITH *Seaman's Gram.* ix. 40 Foundering is when she will neither veere nor steare, the Sea will.. ouer rake her. **1686** tr. *Chardin's Trav. Persia* 66 If the Wind be contrary, they never strive against it, but vere about. **1692** *Capt. Smith's Seaman's Gram.* I. xvi. 76 In keeping the Ship near the Wind, these terms are used, ..Veer no more, keep her to, touch the Wind. **1769** FALCONER *Dict. Marine* s.v. *Veering*, If..it is absolutely necessary to veer, in order to save the ship from destruction. **1810** J. H. MOORE *Pract. Navigator* 290 *To veer*, to change a ship's course from one tack to the other, by turning her stern to windward. **1884** PAE *Eustace* 124 My lads, lie to, then veer and sail against the wind.

b. *trans.* (with *ship* as object).

1769 FALCONER *Dict. Marine* s.v. *Veering*, When it becomes necessary to veer the ship, the sails towards the stern are either furled, or brailed up.

6. *trans.* To turn (something) from one course or direction to another. Also *fig.* (cf. 4).

(*a*) **1647** N. WARD *Simple Cobler* (1843) 30, I veer'd my tongue to this Kind of Language *de industria*. **1809** KENDALL *Trav.* III. 18 The tone of the British Cabinet is veered by every incidental change of war. **1883** MEREDITH *Poet. Wks.* (1912) 212 Cities and martial States, Whither soon the youth veered his theme.

(*b*) **1804** J. GRAHAME *Birds of Scot.* 85 Her bleeding wing she veers..; on him she springs. **1855** SINGLETON *Virgil* I. 81 A lofty beech To veer [L. *torqueat*] the bottom of the carriage [*sc.* the plough]. **1876** *Trans. Clinical Soc.* IX. 167 At each successive scarification he veers the direction of the parallel incisions.

†**7.** To turn *about* or screw in order to adjust; to cause to revolve or whirl. *Obs.*

a **1649** DRUMM. OF HAWTH. *Hist. Jas. V*, Wks. (1711) 107 In musical Instruments, if a String jar and be out of Tune, we do not frettingly break it, but leisurely veer it about to a Concord. *a* **1693** *Urquhart's Rabelais* III. xvii. 140 A pair of Yarn Windles, which she.. unintermittedly veered, and frisked about.

veer, south-western dial. variant of FEER *v.*

ˈveerable, *a.* [f. VEER *v.*^{2} 1.] †Of the wind: Tending to veer; changeable.

1670–1 NARBOROUGH *Jrnl.* in *Acc. Sev. Late Voy.* I. (1694) 56 The wind veerable round the compass. **1698** CORANT in Dampier *Voy.* (1699) II. III. 55 When we find the Winds.. veerable to S.W. and back to South, we stand off to the Westward. **1712** W. ROGERS *Voy.* (1718) 13 Yesterday the wind was very little and veerable. **1742** WOODROOFE in Hanway *Trav.* (1762) I. II. xxiii. 98 The winds being light and veerable favored us very much.

ˈveerer^{1}. *rare*$^{-0}$. [f. VEER *v.*^{2}] (See quot.)

1611 COTGR., *Vireur*, a veerer, or whirler, a round turner, or turner of things often about.

ˈveerer^{2}. *Mining.* (See quot.)

1883 GRESLEY *Gloss. Coal-M.* 269 *Veerer* (Som[erset]), an old word for Banksman.

ˈveering, *vbl. sb.*^{1} [f. VEER *v.*^{1} 3.] The action of causing or allowing to run out; *attrib.* in ***veering cable, chain.***

1867 SMYTH *Sailor's Word-Bk.* 711 *The veering cable*, that cable which is veered out in unmooring, and not unspliced or unshackled in clearing hawse. **1894** *Times* 20 Mar. 3/5 From the top of the swivel a single veering chain passed into the lightship through the hawse pipe.

ˈveering, *vbl. sb.*^{2} [f. VEER *v.*^{2}] The action or fact of changing course or direction.

a. Of the wind (or a vane), or in general use.

1611 COTGR., *Virement*, a veering, whirling, wheeling. **1696** WHISTON *Th. Earth* IV. (1722) 367 It will not now depend on the Season of the Year alone, but on the Veering of the Wind. **1809** MALKIN *Gil Blas* XI. i. (Rtldg.) 393 Scipio ..asked whether the veering of the wind in the political horizon might not blow me some good. **1853** HERSCHEL *Pop. Lect. Sci.* iv. §31 (1873) 168 Nothing apparently can be more capricious than the shifting and veering of a weather-cock on a gusty day. **1860** VAUGHAN in *Merc. Mar. Mag.* VII. 323 The direction and veering of the wind..gave him.. warning.

b. Of a ship. Also in fig. context.

1682 SIR T. BROWNE *Chr. Mor.* 2 Expect rough seas, flaws, and contrary blasts, and 'tis well if by many cross tacks and veerings you arrive at the port. **1769** FALCONER *Dict. Marine* (1780) s.v., It is evident, that veering as well as tacking is a necessary consequence of the same.. principle. **1843** *Penny Cycl.* XXVI. 177/2 The disadvantage of veering is that..the ship is sometimes carried far to leeward. **1865** W. G. PALGRAVE *Arabia* II. 301 After some tacking and veering, we worked up to the entrance.

c. In figurative uses.

1716 ADDISON *Freeholder* No. 25 ¶7 A soveraign..that is prone to fall in with all the Turns and Veerings of the People. **1780** J. BROWN *Lett. Toleration* (1803) II. 216 After much sinful veering towards the abjured abominations of Popery, they..lamented their perfidy to God. **1861** TULLOCH *Eng. Purit.* i. 147 The strange and apparently inconsistent veerings in Cromwell's own mind.

ˈveering, *vbl. sb.*^{3} *s. dial.* = FEERING *vbl. sb.*

1733 TULL *Horse-Hoeing Husb.* xi. 116 The Word Veering ..is the Plowman's Term for turning two Furrows toward each other, as they must do to begin a Ridge; and there-fore they call the Top of a Ridge, a Veering. *Ibid.*, Our Intervals wholly consist either of Veerings or Hentings. **1839** [G. C. LEWIS] *Hereford Gloss.* 115 Ploughed land is said to be laid out into broad veerings, when many furrows are turned up on each side against the same ridge. **1882–90** in Glouc. and Worc. glossaries.

ˈveering, *ppl. a.* [f. VEER *v.*^{2}]

1. Changing course or direction; †turning round, revolving.

1598 SYLVESTER *Du Bartas* II. ii. *Columnes* 635 On th' other side [of the astrolabe], under a veering sight, it Table veers. **1736** YALDEN *Poet. Wks.* (1833) 66 Nor tax me with inconstancy; we find The driving bark requires a veering wind. **1798** *Loves of Triangles* in *Anti-Jacobin* (1852) 124 The veering helm the dexterous steersman stops. **1827** KEBLE *Chr. Y., 3rd Sund. after Easter*, Like a bright veering cloud Grey blossoms twinkle there. **1873** R. W. CHURCH *Influence Christ. National Character* i. 17 Fickle as the veering wind. **1896** *Strand Mag.* XII. 250 A ringing shout of encouragement rent the veering smoke-wreaths.

2. *fig.* Vacillating, variable, changeful.

1684 ROSCOMMON *Ess. Verse* 241 But if a wild Uncertainty prevail, And turn your vearing Heart with ev'ry Gale. **1747** COLLINS *Odes, Passions*, Of diff'ring themes the veering song was mix'd. *c* **1838** MRS. BROWNING *Island* xix, Man's veering heart and careless eyes. **1853** W. JERDAN *Autobiog.* III. xvii. 262 It was thought a veering speech the Duke had just made in the House of Peers. **1875** POSTE *Gaius* I. 116 After much veering legislation.., Justinian enacted that a man or a woman who divorced without a cause should retire to a cloister.

Hence **'veeringly** *adv.*, 'changingly, shiftingly' (Webster, 1847).

veery ('vɪərɪ). *U.S.* [? Imitative.] A North American thrush (*Hylocichla fuscescens*), also called *tawny* and *Wilson's thrush*.

1838 THOREAU *Jrnl.* in *Writings* (1906) VII. 70 Sometimes I hear the veery's silver clarion. **1845** S. JUDD *Margaret* II. i, The place flows with birds, .. deep in the forest [are] olive-backs, veeries, oven-birds. **1860** WHITTIER *My Playmate* xv, There in spring the veeries sing The song of long ago. **1883** *Cent. Mag.* Sept. 685/1 Our thrushes are all frank, open-mannered birds; but the veery and the hermit build upon the ground.

† **vees**[1], Sc. variant of VIVES.

a **1585** MONTGOMERIE *Flyting* 318 The weam-eill, the wild-fire, the vomit and the vees [*v. rr.* veis, weis]. **1608** *Melrose Recs.* (S.H.S.) I. 60 [The mare] thairefter tuik ane seikness callit the veis.

vees[2]. *Mining.* (See quot.)

1883 GRESLEY *Gloss. Coal-M.* 269 *Vees, Veez*, and *Viese*, a kind of soft earth in a fissure or upon the sides of a dyke.

veeze, south. dial. variant of FEEZE *v.*[1]

veg (vɛdʒ). Pl. **veg, veges**. Colloq. abbrev. of *vegetable* (in quot. 1898, of *vegetarian* (restaurant)). Cf. VEGIE.

1898 A. BENNETT *Man from North* xi. 95 You know Miss Roberts at the veg—red-haired tart. **1918** G. FRANKAU *One of Them* xxviii. 219 Clerk of the Court, begone to veg. and joint! **1940** WODEHOUSE *Quick Service* ii. 21 Have a custard apple? It's on the house. The fruit and veg. department has just given of its plenty. **1946** KOESTLER *Thieves in Night* 115 She had come in straight from the veg-garden. **1960** A. WESKER *I'm talking about Jerusalem* I. 26 Good garden here. Grow your own veges. **1974** J. AIKEN *Midnight is a Place* v. 146 A crudely painted sign that said *Veg Soup Half-Penny Per Cup*. **1983** *Truck & Bus Transportation* June 81/3 We'll heat a can of veges. **1984** *Economist* 3 Nov. 18/1 Treasury officials paying for their meat and two veg are rightly suspicious.

‖ **vega**[1] ('veɪgə). [Sp. and Catal. *vega*, Pg. *veiga*, of obscure origin.] In Spain and Spanish America, an extensive, fertile, and grass-covered plain or tract of land.

c **1645** HOWELL *Lett.* I. i. 24, I am now in Valentia, one of the noblest Cities in all Spain, situate in a large Vega or Valley, about sixty miles compass. **1827** LONGF. *Life* (1891) I. ix. 131 We crossed the beautiful Vega—those delicious and luxuriant meadows which stretch away to the south and west of Granada. **1838** PRESCOTT *Ferd. & Is.* I. viii. (1846) I. 363 Their spacious vegas afforded an ample field for the display of their matchless horsemanship. **1850** B. TAYLOR *Eldorado* vii. (1862) 67 The grass on the vega before the house was still thick and green. **1887** F. FRANCIS *Saddle & Mocassin* 85 The horses were driven in from the vega.

b. In the West Indies, a piece of fertile meadowland used for the cultivation of sugar or tobacco; a tobacco-field.

1871 KINGSLEY *At Last* ix, The vega is usually a highly cultivated cane-piece. **1871** HAZARD *Cuba* 329 The best properties known as *vegas*, or tobacco farms, are comprised in a narrow area in the south-west part of the island.

Vega[2] ('viːgə). [a. Sp. or med.L. *Vega*, ad. Arab. *wāqiʿ* falling, in (*al nasr*) *al wāqiʿ* 'the falling (vulture)', the constellation Lyra. So F. *Wéga*.] The brightest star in the constellation Lyra; α Lyræ.

1638 CHILMEAD tr. *Hues' Treat. Globes* (1889) 53 The bright Starre in this Constellation, being the first in number, Alfonsus calleth Vega. **1839** *Penny Cycl.* XIV. 225/2 Its brightest star, α Lyræ, also called Vega, is a conspicuous object. **1889** C. R. MARKHAM tr. *Hues' Treat. Globes* 221 Vega contains hydrogen, iron, sodium, and magnesium.

vegan ('viːgən, *U.S.* 'vɛdʒən). [f. VEG(ETABLE *sb.* + -AN.]

1. A person who on principle abstains from all food of animal origin; a strict vegetarian.

1944 D. WATSON in *Vegan News* Nov. 2 'Vegetarian' and 'Fruitarian' are already associated with societies that allow the 'fruits' of cows and fowls, therefore .. we must make a new and appropriate word... I have used the title 'The Vegan News'. Should we adopt this, our diet will soon become known as the *vegan* diet, and we should aspire to the rank of *vegans*. **1945** *Ibid.* Feb. 3 Two members have asked how 'Vegan' is pronounced. Vegan, not Veejan. **1955** *Irish Press* 29 Nov. 618 A true-blue Vegan, I'm assured, .. will even exclude from his or her diet, milk and .. honey. **1965** *New Scientist* 20 May 526/3 Vitamin B_{12} .. is found almost exclusively in animal foods, so that strict vegetarians (like vegans) may go short unless they take special precautions to ensure a supply. **1977** J. F. FIXX *Compl. Bk. Running* xiv. 170 There are .. three kinds of vegetarians: the 100 percent vegetarian, sometimes called a vegan; the lacto-vegetarian ..; and the lacto-ovo-vegetarian. **1979** J. I. M. STEWART *Our England* 177 Robin had discovered the duty of being a vegetarian. Indeed, he had become a vegan, and that seemed to mean that he could eat virtually nothing at all. **1985** *Times* 1 Feb. 12/2 'Beanmilk: milk that's never even seen a cow' is to vegans, who deplore exploitation of animals and eat nothing derived from them, a highly desirable commodity.

2. *attrib.* or as *adj.*

1944 [see sense 1 above]. **1945** *Vegetarian Messenger* XLII. 163 Following the articles and correspondence regarding the use of dairy products .. in *The Vegetarian Messenger* last year, a number of our members who do not use animal products of any kind formed themselves into a group which has since adopted the title of 'The Vegan Society'. **1951** *News Chron.* 13 Dec. 3 A true vegetarian or vegan diet may not be nutritionally adequate, said Dr. Hill. **1973** *Listener* 8 Feb. 178/1 The good ecological life; no car, vegan cooking, and a mangle technology in a tumbledown cottage. **1978** *Peace News* 25 Aug. 18/3 A group of people from a 1750 acre vegan farming community in Tennessee .. are coming to visit Britain in late September or early October. **1984** *Listener* 9 Aug. 17/2 The facts that CIWF is able to marshal must drive many who read its literature to a vegan diet.

Hence **'veganism**, the beliefs or practice of vegans; abstention from all food of animal origin.

1944 *Vegan News* May 1 Veganism is the practice of living on fruits, nuts, vegetables, grains, and other wholesome non-animal products. **1972** *New Scientist* 4 May 297/2 Universal vegetarianism would .. tend to disrupt organic farming and the organic cycle—soil, plant, animal, man. It would also, if logically carried on as in Veganism, abolish milk and eggs. **1977** S. R. L. CLARK *Moral Status of Animals* ix. 185 Veganism is a better project than lacto-vegetarianism, though we may in the end be able to take *some* milk from our kin without injustice.

Veganin ('vɛdʒənɪn). *Pharm.* Also **veganin**. A proprietary preparation of aspirin, paracetamol, and codeine phosphate used as an analgesic.

1926 *Trade Marks Jrnl.* 23 June 1442 *Veganin*... Chemical substances prepared for use in medicine and pharmacy. Gödecke & Co., Chemische Fabrik Aktien Gesellschaft .. Berlin-Charlottenburg, Germany; manufacturers. **1943** S. ERTZ *Anger in Sky* iv. 98 Take an aspirin, take two, take three. Take veganin. Take anything. **1951** G. GREENE *End of Affair* III. vii. 141 'I've got a bad headache, that's all.' .. 'I'll get you some veganin.' **1979** G. WATSON *Black Jack* i. 9 There was a stock of Veganin in the house.

vegeculture ('vɛdʒɪkʌltjʊə(r)). [f. VEGE(TABLE *sb.* + CULTURE *sb.*] The cultivation of vegetables. Hence **vege'cultural** *a.*

1917 H. A. DAY (*title*) Vegeculture: how to grow vegetables, salads, and herbs. **1962** J. D. CLARK in Braidwood & Willey *Courses toward Urban Life* 23 The distribution of the bored stone in central and south-central Africa suggests that it may also sometimes accompany a vegecultural, .. even an incipient agricultural, level of economy during later stone age times. **1964** S. COLE *Prehist. E. Afr.* x. 275 Only after the introduction of ironworking do we find evidence of food production... This does not mean that some form of vegeculture did not exist—perhaps based mainly on plants with edible roots or tubers. **1977** G. CLARK *World Prehist.* (ed. 3) v. 226 It looks as if there was a greater emphasis on vegetable food and even as if some form of vegeculture may have been practised.

veget, obs. var. VEGETE *a.*

vegetability (ˌvɛdʒɪtə'bɪlɪtɪ). [ad. med.L. **vegetabilitas*, f. L. *vegetābilis* VEGETABLE *a.*: see -ITY. Cf. OF. *vegetablete* (Godef.), F. *végétabilité*, It. *vegetabilità*, Sp. *vegetabilidad*.]

† **1.** A vegetable organism. *Obs. rare*⁻¹.

c **1400** tr. *Secreta Secret., Gov. Lordsh.* 90 It shewys opynly .. þat euerylk kende of vegetabilitez haues a propre ordre, þat ys, complexioun.

2. Vegetable character, quality, or nature.

1646 SIR T. BROWNE *Pseud. Ep.* II. v. 91 [The] lapidificall juyce of the Sea, which entring the parts of that plant [*sc.* coral], overcomes its vegetability, and converts it into a lapideous substance. **1670** *Phil. Trans.* V. 2035 A description of sundry new Metals, or Semi-metals, as he calls them; together with a discourse of their Vegetability. **1686** PLOT *Staffordsh.* 189 These .. have their vegetability the same way, with the porous species of Coral. **1854** *Fraser's Mag.* L. 192 If any additional proofs of the vegetability of coral-lines were needed. **1858** T. R. JONES *Aquarian Nat.* 136 The mineralogists .. questioned the vegetability of such of these productions as were of a hard and stony nature.

vegetable ('vɛdʒɪtəb(ə)l), *sb.* Also 6 **vegitable**. [f. the adj.]

1. a. A living organism belonging to the vegetable kingdom or the lower of the two series of organic beings; a growth devoid of animal life; a plant in the widest or scientific sense (= PLANT *sb.*[1] 2).

1582 J. HESTER *Compendium Ration. Secr.* (title-p.), The Hidden Vertues of sondrie Vegitables, Animalles, and Mineralls. **1598** R. HAYDOCKE tr. *Lomazzo* II. 125 Some of them are taken from minerals .., some from the vegetables, and some from the animals. **1653** W. RAMESEY *Astrol. Restored* 12, I suppose there is none will .. deny .. the Heavens and Planets to have influence over Herbs, Corn, Plants, and all Vegetables. **1690** LOCKE *Hum. Und.* IV. vi. (1695) 337 In Vegetables, which are nourished, grow, and produce Leaves, Flowers, and Seeds, in a constant Succession. **1737** GRAY *Lett.* Poems (1775) 24 Both vale and hill are covered with most venerable beeches, and other very reverend vegetables. **1782** V. KNOX *Ess.* clii. (1819) III. 169 They [*i.e.* speeches] are like vegetables of a night, or insects of a day. **1805** R. W. DICKSON *Pract. Agric.* I. 387 After the rushes or other coarse vegetables have been cut down and carried away. **1822–7** GOOD *Study Med.* (1829) I. 265 The expressed oils of mild vegetables, as the pistachio, olive, and almond. **1858** O. W. HOLMES *Aut. Breakf.-t.* (1883) 205 Both [trees] are pleasant vegetables. **1884** *De Candolle's Orig. Cultivated Pl.* 4 The *Tetragonia*, an insignificant green vegetable.

fig. *a* **1635** NAUNTON *Fragm. Reg.* (Arb.) 44 He was a meer vegetable of the Court, that sprung up at night, and sunk again at his noon. **1709** STEELE *Tatler* No. 86 ¶3, I met him with all the respect due to so reverend a vegetable; for you are to know, that is my sense of a person who remains idle in the same place for half a century.

† **b.** *pl.* in collective sense: Vegetation. *Obs.*

c **1645** HOWELL *Lett.* (1650) II. 43, I have bin alwaies naturally affected to woods and groves, and those kind of vegetables. **1695** WOODWARD *Nat. Hist. Earth* VI. (1723) 295 June, July, and August .. exhibit a still different Shew of Vegetables, and Face of Things. **1780** A. YOUNG *Tour Irel.* I. 18 Their only way is to let it cover itself with such vegetables as may come. **1821** SCOTT *Pirate* xxv, Scrubby and stunted heath, intermixed with the long bent, or coarse grass, .. were the only vegetables that could be seen.

† **c.** Applied to the earth or to a mineral regarded as capable of growth. *Obs. rare.*

a **1676** HALE *Prim. Orig. Man.* I. iii. (1677) 96 Though the Earth be not animated with a Sensible Soul, yet it is possible that it may be a great Immortal Vegetable. **1716** CHEYNE *Philos. Princ. Nat. Relig.* I. 278 A hill is nothing but the Nest of some Mettle or Mineral, either of Stone, Iron, Tin, Copper or such like lower Vegetables.

2. A plant cultivated for food; *esp.* an edible herb or root used for human consumption and commonly eaten, either cooked or raw, with meat or other article of food.

1767 A. YOUNG *Farmer's Lett. to People* (1771) I. 461 The cultivation of the new-discovered vegetables, and all the modes of raising the old ones. **1796** MRS. INCHBALD *Nature & Art* xlvi. (1820) 158 At a stinted repast of milk and vegetables. **1840** LOUDON *Cottager's Man.* 4 in *Husb.* III. (L.U.K.), To supply the cottager's family .. with vegetables, potatoes, and faggots. **1846** SOYER *Cookery* 450 Where a dish of vegetables are required for second course. **1875** JOWETT *Plato* (ed. 2) III. 243 Cabbages or any other vegetables which are fit for boiling.

3. *fig.* A person who leads an uneventful or monotonous life, without intellectual or social activity; also, one reduced by illness to little more than a physical body. Cf. VEGETABLE *a.* 5.

1921 G. B. SHAW *Back to Methuselah* I. 26 What use is this thousand years of life to you, you old vegetable? **1933** A. HUXLEY *Let.* 9 Oct. (1969) 373, I was so glad to hear from Norah that you were going on as well as cd be expected. It will be a weary business for a bit, .. sitting still and being a vegetable. **1953** *Chicago Daily Sun-Times* 29 Dec. 40/5 It should not be inferred that Rocky is a vegetable, incapable of thinking for himself. **1961** J. DAWSON *Ha-Ha* iii. 48 I'm going to go on working... Tony says he would hate a wife who was just a vegetable. **1976** SMYTHIES & CORBETT *Psychiatry* vii. 123 Eventually they become bedridden and incontinent 'vegetables'. **1980** B. CASTLE *Castle Diaries* 242, I hope and pray she will die with dignity and not be reduced by a stroke into a vegetable.

4. *attrib.* and *Comb.* **a.** Simple attrib. in sense 2, as ***vegetable-basin, dish, food, garden, juice, -market, oil, patch, rack***, etc.

1728 CHAMBERS *Cycl.* s.v. *Vegetation*, The common Opinion .. is, that Water is the great vegetable Food. **1820** D. WORDSWORTH *Jrnl.* 20 July (1941) II. 39 A level bottomed oval vessel like the foundations of our vegetable dishes. **1825** T. HOOK *Sayings* Ser. II. III. 15 Two vegetable dishes. **1853** HICKIE *Aristoph.* (Bohn) II. 416 In the pottery-market and the vegetable-market alike. *a* **1860** ALB. SMITH *Med. Student* (1861) 17 Threading their way through the crowd of the vegetable-waggons arriving for to-morrow's market. **1887** *Outing* X. 12/1 Back of its hacienda is a fine orchard and vegetable garden. **1898** F. G. LEE *Negl. Bapt.* 11 A vegetable-basin or a soap-dish was used instead of the font. **1898** *Cent. Mag.* Jan. 337/1 May I tell him .. about your vegetable garden? **1907** *Yesterday's Shopping* (1969) p. lxi/5 (Index), Vegetable racks. **1921** *Daily Colonist* (Victoria, B.C.) 20 Mar. 17/1 The born gardener is still looking ahead in the Fall when other people store their tools and never do a hand's turn in the vegetable patch until the Spring urge comes upon them again. **1926** *Ibid.* 16 Jan. 15/3 Listed in the .. general cargo .. is a large quantity of vegetable oil in bulk. **1975** P. G. WINSLOW *Death of Angel* ii. 65 Vegetable juice and soya beans. **1977** *Times* 6 May 13/4 EEC imports of vegetable oils and oil-cakes. **1978** G. MITCHELL *Mingled with Venom* x. 102 The poison roots were never in your vegetable rack. **1979** J. D. MACDONALD *Green Ripper* (1980) i. 15 One of her vegetable juice cocktails. **1979** A. CLARKE *Poisoned Web* x. 77 She was down .. in the vegetable patch .. staring at the runner-beans.

b. Objective or obj. genitive, as ***vegetable-eater, -feeder, -seller; vegetable-eating, -feeding*** adjs.

Also with the names of instruments, as ***vegetable-chopper, -cutter, -grater, -slicer***, etc. (Knight *Dict. Mech.*)

(*a*) **1792** A. YOUNG *Trav. France* 28 There are both sorts [of bears], carnivorous and vegetable-eaters. **1851–6** S. P. WOODWARD *Mollusca* (1858) 12 All the land-snails are vegetable-feeders. **1867** M. ARNOLD *Celtic Lit.* 4 Bathing people, vegetable-sellers, and donkey boys. **1875** C. C. BLAKE *Zool.* 54 The cheiroptera are, however, vegetable-feeders.

(*b*) **1838** *Penny Cycl.* XII. 493/1 In a vegetable-feeding insect the stomach is very voluminous. **1874** J. W. LONG *Amer. Wild-fowl* xxv. 262 They are exceedingly expert divers, and can swim under water to much longer distances than any others of the vegetable-eating ducks. **1897** *Allbutt's Syst. Med.* III. 966 These stony masses are found in the intestines of many vegetable-feeding animals.

vegetable (ˈvɛdʒɪtəb(ə)l), *a.* Also 6 vegitabile, 7 -able. [a. OF. *vegetable* (mod.F. *végétable*, = It. *vegetabile*, Sp. *vegetable*, Pg. *vegetavel*), or ad. L. *vegetābilis* animating, vivifying, f. *vegetāre*: see VEGETATE *v*.

In some instances the adj. cannot be clearly distinguished from the attributive uses of the sb.]

†**1. a.** Having the vegetating property of plants; living and growing as a plant or organism endowed with the lowest form of life. (Cf. VEGETAL *a.* 1.)

c **1400** tr. *Secreta Secret., Gov. Lordsh.* 90 What þinge vegetable þat..makys fruyt, to þe sonne ys apropird. **1412–20** LYDG. *Chron. Troy* II. 674 Zephirus, þat is so comfortable For to norysche þinges vegetable. **1432–50** tr. *Higden* (Rolls) I. 73 Hit may be concludede Paradise not to be there, sythe noo thynge vegetable may haue lyfe þer. *c* **1532** DU WES *Introd. Fr.* in *Palsgr.* 1053 All thynges created of God under the moone..ben elemented vegetables and sensytyves. **1604** R. CAWDREY *Table Alph.*, *Vegetable*, springing, or growing as hearbes. **1629** H. BURTON *Truth's Tri.* 197 How far themselues differ from senslesse stockes, or come short of the vegetable trees. *a* **1676** HALE *Prim. Orig. Man.* III. iv. (1677) 206 Things vegetable, that have simply Life, with those operations incident to Life.

fig. **1641** W. CARTWRIGHT *Lady-Errant* I. ii, The other counts her apricots,..lays 'em naked And open to the sun, that it may freely Smile on her vegetable embraces. *a* **1678** MARVELL *Poems, To coy Mistress* 11 My vegetable love should grow Vaster than empires and more slow.

†**b.** Of the soul. *Obs.*

1412–20 LYDG. *Chron. Troy* III. 5686 Comparysownyd, as it were semblable, To a sowle þat were vegetable, þe whiche, with-oute sensibilite, Mynystreth lyf in herbe, flour, and tre. *c* **1532** DU WES *Introd. Fr.* in *Palsgr.* 1053 In the whiche [body] our Lorde hath planted the soule vegetable by the whiche it groweth. **1610** HEALEY *St. Aug. Citie of God* XXII. iv. (1620) 821 The earth is full of vegetable soules, strangely combined with earthly bodies. **1610** GUILLIM *Heraldry* III. vi. (1611) 101 A vegetable Soul is a facultie or power that giueth life vnto bodies.

†**c.** ***vegetable power***, the principle of simple life and growth. *Obs.*

1601 DOLMAN *La Primaud. Fr. Acad.* (1618) III. 672 The vegetable power common to men and plants. **1625** HART *Anat. Ur.* I. ii. 29 The state of the nourishing or vegetable power ouer the whole bodie.

†**d.** ***vegetable stone***, one of the three varieties of the philosophers' stone, supposed to possess health-preserving properties. *Obs.*

After med.L. *lapis vegetabilis*: cf. Gower *Conf.* II. 86.

1652 ASHMOLE *Theatr. Chem. Brit.* Proleg. 7 By the Vegetable [Stone] may be perfectly known the Nature of Man.

2. Of or pertaining to, composed or consisting of, derived or obtained from, plants or their parts; of the nature of or resembling a vegetable. Freq. as contrasted with animal or mineral products.

a. Of material substances.

1582 HESTER *Secr. Phiorav.* I. xxxiii. 39 You shall giue them ʒj of our Vegitabile Sirrup. **1594** PLAT *Jewell-ho.* I. 3 All sorts of soyle..do draw their generatiue & fructifying vertue from that vegetable salt. **1695** WOODWARD *Nat. Hist. Earth* II. (1723) 101 By Retrenching a considerable Quantity of the vegetable Matter. **1721** MORTIMER *Husbandry* II. 207 Statues are a lasting Ornament when vegetable Ornaments are out of Season. **1725** POPE *Odyss.* IV. 320 The direful bane Of vegetable venom. **1755** *Dict. Arts & Sci.* IV. 2679/1 Almost all concretes that abound either with mineral or vegetable sulphur. **1800** *Hull Advertiser* 31 May 2/2 The superiority of coal to vegetable tar. **1857** MILLER *Elem. Chem., Org.* ii. §3. 84 The insoluble pectose contained in the vegetable tissue. **1875** SCRIVENER *Lect. Greek Test.* 18 The ancient ink was purely vegetable, without any metallic base.

poet. **1667** MILTON *P.L.* IV. 220 And all amid them stood the Tree of Life, High eminent, blooming Ambrosial Fruit Of vegetable Gold. **1820** SHELLEY *Prometh. Unb.* III. iv. 110 My coursers sought their birthplace in the sun,..Pasturing flowers of vegetable fire. **1857** EMERSON *Poems* 91 The zephyr in his garden rolled From plum-trees vegetable gold.

b. Of conditions, actions, qualities, etc.

1690 LOCKE *Hum. Und.* II. xxvii. §4 The wood, bark, and leaves, &c. of an oak, in which consists the vegetable life. **1697** DRYDEN *Virg. Georg.* IV. 178 My Song to flow'ry Gardens might extend, To teach the Vegetable Arts. **1712** POPE *Vertumnus & Pomona* 4 None taught the trees a nobler race to bear, Or more improv'd the vegetable care. **1733** ARBUTHNOT *Ess. Effects Air* i. 9 The Heat arising from vegetable Perspiration is very sensible in a hot Day near a Field of Corn. **1788** GIBBON *Decl. & F.* l. V. 172 The lonesome traveller derives a sort of comfort and society from the presence of vegetable life. **1806** *Med. Jrnl.* XV. 571 The learned President begins this paper by a theory of animal and vegetable processes, deriving them..from fermentation. **1842** LOUDON *Suburban Hort.* 25 This short passage comprehends the essence of all that can be said on the subject of vegetable development. **1874** SPURGEON *Treas. David* Ps. xcii. 10 The brutish men grow with a sort of vegetable vigour of their own.

c. Of earth, mould, etc.: (see later quots.).

1774 GOLDSM. *Nat. Hist.* I. vi. (1776) I. 55 In regions which are uninhabited,..where the forests are not cut down,..the bed of vegetable earth is constantly encreasing. **1812** *New Botanic Gard.* I. 53 Beds of light vegetable earth. *Ibid.*, Good light vegetable mould. **1830** M. DONOVAN *Dom. Econ.* I. 137 What remains, when the decomposition has totally broken down the structure of the vegetable, is a black pulverulent substance... This constitutes what is called vegetable mould, and is also the chief ingredient in vegetable manure. **1855** *Orr's Circ. Sci., Inorg. Nat.* 185 Whatever rocks may be composed of, they are sure to be covered, after a time, with debris,..until at last there is a covering of vegetable soil.

3. ***vegetable creation, kingdom, world***, etc., that division of organic nature to which plants belong.

1668 COWLEY *Ess. Prose & Verse, Garden* (1906) 427 Who would not joy to see his conquering hand Ore all the Vegetable World command? **1692–** [see KINGDOM 5]. **1718** PRIOR *Solomon* I. 49 The Vegetable World, each Plant, and Tree,..I am allow'd, as Fame reports, to know. **1823** J. BADCOCK *Dom. Amusem.* 206 This extends in more or less degree to every part of vegetable creation. **1843** *Penny Cycl.* XXVI. 180/2 The distinction given between the animal and vegetable kingdoms is the possession of sensation by the former. **1878** HUXLEY *Physiogr.* 84 To supply the vegetable world with its carbon.

4. Of, composed or consisting of, made from, esculent vegetables.

1746 FRANCIS tr. *Horace, Sat.* II. v. 22 What your Garden yields,..To him be sacrific'd, and let him taste, Before your Gods, the vegetable Feast. **1789** W. BUCHAN *Dom. Med.* (1790) 449 A milk and vegetable diet..will often perform a cure. **1842** COMBE *Digestion* 305 Vegetable food and fruit might, with propriety, be used by the middle and richer classes in this country to a greater extent than it is. **1858** SIMMONDS *Dict. Trade, Vegetable-soups*, soups made with green pease, turnips, and carrots cut small, cabbages, &c.

5. Resembling that of a vegetable; *esp.* uneventful, featureless, monotonous, dull.

1854 J. S. C. ABBOTT *Napoleon* (1855) II. ii. 46 The pauper peasantry, weary of a merely vegetable life, were glad of any pretext for excitement. **1874** SAYCE *Compar. Philol.* vii. 298 They had no occasion to mark the lapse of time in their monotonous and vegetable existence.

6. *ellipt.* Living on vegetables; vegetarian.

1812 SHELLEY in Hogg *Life* (1858) II. 197, I continue vegetable; Harriet means to be slightly animal, until the arrival of spring.

7. a. Special collocations.

vegetable acid, an organic acid derived from a plant. ***vegetable alkali*** (see quots. and ALKALI 3). ***vegetable brimstone*** (see quot. and LYCOPODIUM 2). ***vegetable butter*** (see quot. and BUTTER *sb.*[1] 3). ***vegetable camel*** (see quot.). ***vegetable casein***, = LEGUMIN. ***vegetable caterpillar, egg, ethiops*** (see quots.). ***vegetable fat***, fat obtained or manufactured from plants. ***vegetable fire-cracker, flannel***, †***fly*** (see quots.). ***vegetable gelatin***: see GELATIN 1 b. ***vegetable gold***, †(*a*) saffron (Mayne, 1859); (*b*) an acid derived from the roots of the plant *Trixis Pipizahuac* (*Treas. Bot.* 1866). ***vegetable hair***, the long-beard, *Tillandsia usneiodes* (Ibid.). ***vegetable horse-hair***, the fibre of the leaves of the European palm *Chamærops humilis* (Ibid. Suppl. 1874). ***vegetable ivory*** (see IVORY 2); also *attrib.* ***vegetable jelly***, = PECTIN. †***vegetable lamb***: see LAMB *sb.* 5 c. ***vegetable lard***, a solid cooking fat prepared from vegetable products. ***vegetable leather***, the plant *Euphorbia punicea* (*Treas. Bot.* 1866). ***vegetable marrow***: see MARROW *sb.*[1] 3. ***vegetable mummy***: see MUMMY *sb.*[1] 2 c. ***vegetable oil***, oil obtained or manufactured from plants. ***vegetable oyster***: (*a*) *U.S.*, salsify; (*b*) scorzonera. ***vegetable parchment***: see PARCHMENT *sb.* 1 b. ***vegetable pear***, the chocho (see PEAR *sb.* 3). ***vegetable sheep, silk*** (see quots.). ***vegetable spaghetti***, a variety of vegetable marrow bearing fruits whose flesh resembles spaghetti in appearance; also, the fruit itself or its flesh. ***vegetable sponge*** = *dishcloth gourd* s.v. DISH-CLOTH 2. ***vegetable sulphur***, vegetable brimstone. ***vegetable tallow, vellum*** (see quots.). ***vegetable wax***, a wax or wax-like substance obtained from plants or vegetable growths. ***vegetable wool*** (see quot.).

1728 CHAMBERS *Cycl.* s.v. *Alkaly*, Since *Vegetable Acids are originally no other than Mineral ones. **1815** J. SMITH *Panorama Sci. & Art* II. 389 The acetous, and most other vegetable acids, have some action upon tin. **1892** *Photogr. Ann.* II. 684 Acids, including vegetable acids. **1778** *Encycl. Brit.* (ed. 2) III. 1809/1 The fixed kind are subdivided into ..the *vegetable, and mineral or fossile alkali. **1796** KIRWAN *Elem. Min.* (ed. 2) II. 5 Of the fixed [alkalis] there are two species, the one generally afforded by the incineration of inland vegetables, and thence called the Vegetable Alkali. **1807** T. THOMSON *Chem.* (ed. 3) II. 588 Carbonate of Potash ..was characterized by a great variety of names, according to the manner of preparing it; such as fixed nitre, salt of tartar, vegetable alkali. **1846** LINDLEY *Veget. Kingd.* 70 The powder contained in the spore-cases of Lycopodium clavatum and Selago..is employed under the name of Lycopode, or *vegetable brimstone,..in the manufacture of fireworks, and..to roll up pills. **1836** *Penny Cycl.* VI. 68/2 **Vegetable butters*, the name given to the concrete oil of certain vegetables, from its resemblance to the butter obtained from the milk of animals, and from being employed for similar purposes. The term is also occasionally, but improperly, applied to some vegetable products which are entirely of a waxy nature, such as the wax of the *Myrica cerifera*. **1845–50** MRS. LINCOLN *Lect. Bot.* vi. 40 Some of them [plants] flourish in the most dry and sandy places, exposed to a burning sun; as the *Stapelia*, sometimes called the *vegetable camel. **1841** *Vegetable caseine [see CASEIN 1]. **1889** E. WAKEFIELD *New Zealand after 50 Yrs.* 81 The aweto, or *vegetable-caterpillar, called by the naturalists *Hipialis virescens*... For some inexplicable reason, the spore of a vegetable fungus *Sphæria Robertsii*, fixes itself on its neck.., takes root and grows vigorously. **1866** *Treas. Bot.* 1018/2 *S[apota] mammosa*..yields the Marmalade fruit sometimes called the *Vegetable Egg. **1823** J. BADCOCK *Dom. Amusem.* 26 Of ivory shavings, sponge, and the *vegetable æthiops, bladerwrack, is charcoal also made. **1860** URE *Dict. Arts* (ed. 5) III. 949 *Vegetable ethiops*, a charcoal prepared by the incineration in a covered crucible of the *fucus vesiculosus*, or common sea wrack. **1884** *Vegetable fat [see VEGETABLE OIL]. **1956** [see *nordihydroguaiaretic acid* s.v. NOR-]. **1967** Vegetable fat [see VEGETABLE OIL]. **1874** *Treas. Bot.* Suppl. 1350/2 *Vegetable firecracker, *Brodiæa coccinea*. **1875** KNIGHT *Dict. Mech.* 2695/1 **Vegetable-flannel*, a fabric made of a fine fiber obtained from the leaves of the *Pinus sylvestris*. Pine-wool. **1763** *Phil. Trans.* LIII. 271 The *vegetable fly is found in the island Dominica, and (excepting that it has no wings) resembles the drone both in size and colour more than any other English insect. In the month of May it buries itself in the earth, and begins to vegetate. **1842–** *Vegetable ivory [see IVORY 2]. **1880** C. R. MARKHAM *Peruv. Bark* 219 A hut was made among vegetable-ivory palms. **1885** LADY BRASSEY *The Trades* 109 The vegetable-ivory plant (*Phytelephas macrocarpa*)..attracted a large share of attention. **1826** HENRY *Elem. Chem.* II. 194 *Vegetable jelly, unless when tinged by the fruit from which it has been obtained, is nearly colourless. **1857** MILLER *Elem. Chem., Org.* ii. §3. 83 Vegetable Jelly (formerly called *pectin*). **1894** C. R. A. WRIGHT *Animal & Vegetable Fixed Oils* xiv. 305 Amongst the Hindoos and others whose religious beliefs preclude the use of animal fats..a large sale now exists for purely vegetable fats of buttery consistence (*vegetable lard). **1918** C. A. MITCHELL *Edible Oils & Fats* iii. 33 Coconut oil is treated with alcohol and animal charcoal and the resulting product, which is practically tasteless, is sold as 'vegetable lard'. **1797** *Encycl. Brit.* XIII. 192/1 *Vegetable oils are obtained by expression, infusion, and distillation. **1884** *Ibid.* XVII. 741/1 The ordinary method for separating vegetable oils and fats from the nuts, seeds, &c., of which they form constituent parts is by pressure. **1967** *Ann. Reg. 1966* 166 The long-delayed common market regulations for sugar, vegetable fats and oils, and fruit and vegetables. **1845–50** MRS. LINCOLN *Lect. Bot.* 185 Such [compound flowers] as have ligulate florets; as the dandelion, lettuce, and *vegetable-oyster. **1859** BARTLETT *Dict. Amer.* (ed. 2) 307 *Oyster-plant*, salsify.., so called from its resemblance in taste, when cooked, to the oyster. It is also called the Vegetable Oyster. **1882** *The Garden* 11 Nov. 425/3 Salsafy and Scorzonera. Those fond of using pet names often call one or other of these the..'vegetable oyster'. **1866** *Treas. Bot.* 959/1 The name of *Vegetable Sheep (!) is given by the settlers in New Zealand to *R[aoulia] eximia*, because, from its growing in large white tufts on elevated sheep-runs, it may be readily mistaken for the sheep. **1895** in Morris *Austral Engl.* (1898) 246/2 There is in the Alpine regions of the South Island a plant popularly called the 'vegetable sheep', botanically named *Raoulia*. **1853** T. C. ARCHER *Pop. Econ. Bot.* 181 *Vegetable silk. **1866** *Treas. Bot.*, *Vegetable Silk*, a cotton-like material obtained from the seed-pods of *Chorisia speciosa*. **1973** *Times* 2 Nov. 22/8 If *vegetable spaghetti is as tasteless as marrow, which I believe it is, no self-respecting British housewife would buy it at any price. **1978** J. U. CROCKETT *Vegetables & Fruits* v. 109 There are also several unusual kinds [of marrow], including the vegetable spaghetti, with bright yellow, 20 cm (8 in.) marrows, which, when cooked, spill out their flesh like spaghetti. **1978** R. WHITLOCK *Growing Unusual Vegetables* 50/2 The vegetable spaghetti plant is of the trailing type, not bush, so allow room for it to ramble. **1889** *Cent. Dict.* s.v. *Sponge-gourd*, The netted fiber from the interior of the fruit is used for washing and other purposes, hence called *vegetable sponge. **1984** *Gardening from 'Which?'* Mar. 75/1 The loofah's other common names of vegetable sponge or dish cloth gourd give a clue to its true identity. **1855** OGILVIE *Suppl.* 402/2 **Vegetable sulphur*, a powder obtained from the theca of..common club moss [etc.]. **1846** *Foreign Q. Rev.* April 88 Among the exports of Borneo..[are] *vegetable tallow,..coffee [etc.]. **1866** *Treas. Bot.* 1206 *Vegetable tallow*, a fatty substance obtained from *Stillingia sebifera*, *Vateria indica*, and other plants. **1888** JACOBI *Printers' Vocab.* 151 **Vegetable vellum*, Japanese vellum-paper specially prepared to imitate vellum. **1815** J. SMITH *Panorama Sci. & Art* II. 495 In China and in North America, wax is obtained directly from plants, and is then called *vegetable-wax. **1843** *Penny Cycl.* XXVI. 180/1 *Myrica quercifolia*, a native of the Cape of Good Hope, is another species which yields a vegetable wax. **1853** T. C. ARCHER *Pop. Econ. Bot.* 281 Vegetable Wax (South American). *Ibid.* 282 Vegetable Wax, or Myrtle Wax (of North America). **1884** *Chambers's Jrnl.* 8 March 146/2 The prepared fibre of this plant [Neilgherry nettle] is sometimes called *Vegetable wool.

b. In the names of pigments, as ***vegetable black, blue***, etc.

1807 T. THOMSON *Chem.* (ed. 3) II. 174 This acid reddens vegetable blues, and gradually destroys the greater number of them. **1875** BEDFORD *Sailor's Pocket Bk.* x. (ed. 2) 365 *Vegetable Black.*—This is the cheapest and best black for all ordinary work.

ˈ**vegetablize**, *v. rare.* [f. VEGETABLE *sb.* or *a.* + -IZE.] *trans.* and *refl.* To render vegetable; to convert into, or cause to resemble, a vegetable substance.

a **1843** *Encycl. Metrop.* VII. 113 Having been vegetablized ..in the leaves, it [the sap] passes into vessels..in the bark. **1869** in *Cosmopolitan* 19 Aug. 314 The mineral vegetablises itself, the vegetable animalises itself. *a* **1891** O'NEILL *Dyeing & Calico Print.* 36 (Cent. Dict.), Silk is to be vegetablized.. by an immersion in a bath of cellulose dissolved in ammoniacal copper oxide.

ˈ**vegetably**, *adv. rare.* [f. as prec. + -LY².]

1. In the manner of a vegetable or plant; with vegetative properties.

1651 BIGGS *New Disp.* 39 These things happen in plants vegetably animate.

2. In respect of, by means of, vegetables; towards vegetables. Only in combs.

1827 *Examiner* 248/1 There is a bold enrichment in the vegetably-marked foreground. **1867** F. FRANCIS *Angling* i. (1880) 31 A bait for roach when they are vegetably-minded.

vegetal (ˈvɛdʒɪtəl), *a.* and *sb.* Forms: 5 vegytalle, vygital, 6–7 vegitall, 7 vegital, vegetall, 7– vegetal. [ad. med.L. **vegetālis*, f. L. *vegetāre*: see VEGETATE *v.* Cf. F. *végétal* (16th c.), Sp. and Pg. *vegetal*, It. *vegetale*.]

A. *adj.* **1. a.** Characterized by, exhibiting or producing, the phenomena of physical life and growth. (Cf. VEGETABLE *a.* 1.) Now usually in expressed or implied contrast with *animal*.

The modern use is due to Herbert Spencer (see Lewes *Physiol. Common Life* (1860) II. 430 *note*), and has largely influenced the retention or revival of the form in other senses.

c **1400** in Ashm. *Theatr. Chem. Brit.* (1652) 211 Wyth vygital moyster and of the red Grap. **1490** CAXTON *Eneydos* iv. 19 Whan..the naturel hete of blood humayn comforte my membris, & made theym vegytalle wyth sencyble moeuynges. **1611** COTGR., *Vegetal*, vegetall, hauing or giuing a (plant-like) life, increase,..or growing. **1621** BURTON *Anat. Mel.* I. i. II. v, Necessary concomitants or affections of this Vegetall facultie is life, and his privation death. **1666** BP. S. PARKER *Free & Impart. Censure* (1667) 180 They can exert no acts but of Imagination, whence spring forth the powers of the Vegetal life.

1852 SPENCER *Ess., Architect. Types* (1891) II. 377 That there is some relation between Gothic architecture and vegetal forms is generally admitted. **1861** —— *Education* 21 Phenomena of animal and vegetal life. **1879** G. ALLEN *Colour-Sense* iv, Not a trace of any vegetal organism has yet been discovered in the primary rocks to which [etc.]. **1893** J. FISKE *Man's Destiny* 27 The myriad fantastic hues of animal and vegetal life.

b. In expressed or implied contrast with *sensible* (or *sensitive*) and *rational*. *Obs.* exc. *Hist.*

1621 BURTON *Anat. Mel.* Democritus to Rdr. 16 All creatures, vegetal, sensible and rational. *Ibid.* I. i. II. v, Vegetal Plants, Sensible Beasts, Rational Men. **1664** H. MORE *Myst. Iniq.* 384 The functions and delights of the mere Vegetal and Animal nature. **1744** BERKELEY *Siris* §275 The inferior classes of life: first the rational, then the sensitive, after that the vegetal. **1871** TYLOR *Prim. Cult.* I. 393 The famous classic and mediæval theories of the vegetal, sensitive, and rational souls.

2. Of or pertaining to, derived or obtained from, plants or vegetables.

1596 J. HESTER *Experiments & Cures*, etc. (title-p.), Certaine Secrets of Isacke Hollandus concerning the Vegetall and Animall worke. **1669** W. SIMPSON *Hydrol. Chym.* 343 Scorbutick pills are so prepared with noble vegetal extractions. **1725** *Fam. Dict.* s.v. *Lye*, Take this Lye, put into it an Ounce or two of vegetal Salt. **1758** J. S. *Le Dran's Observ. Surg.* (1771) 142 Manna, Cassia, and vegetal Salt. **1850** *Fraser's Mag.* XLI. 300 Most of their vegetal riches might be matched in Covent Garden. **1859** GULLICK & TIMBS *Paint.* 143 Vegetal lakes, and the most tender colours. **1866** WATTS *Dict. Chem.* IV. 363 All vegetal tissues which contain pectose. **1879** G. ALLEN *Colour-Sense* iii, The bright hues of vegetal products like fruits and flowers.

3. = VEGETABLE *a.* 3.

1664 POWER *Exp. Philos.* I. 61 The main..Agent in all Natures three Kingdoms Mineral, Vegetal, and Animal. **1804** CHARLOTTE SMITH *Conversations*, etc. I. 71 The rose, ..Pride of the vegetal creation. **1859** *All Year Round* No. 34. 175 This advice is equally just in regard to many other members of the vegetal world. **1876** *Contemp. Rev.* Jan. 243 Many of the lowest forms of life cannot positively be assigned either to the vegetal or to the animal kingdom.

4. ***vegetal pole*** (*Embryology*), the lower pole of an ovum or a young embryo, which divides more slowly than the upper (animal) pole and in telolecithal ova contains most of the yolk. Cf. *animal pole* s.v. ANIMAL C. 1.

1914 W. E. KELLICOTT *Textbk. Gen. Embryol.* iii. 92 The vegetal pole is frequently occupied largely by the relatively inert food substance, the materials in general related with the vegetative organs of the developing embryo. **1926** JORDAN & KINDRED *Textbk. Embryol.* v. 32 When the yolk is more abundant,..it tends to segregate at one pole, thus determining a yolk-free pole, the animal pole, and a yolk-laden pole, the vegetal pole. **1947** L. B. AREY *Devel. Anat.* (ed. 5) ii. 31 At the other end of the polar axis is the vegetal pole. Its territory tends to be more sluggish and is concerned with the development of nutrient organs. Cytoplasmic components..are often disposed in a polarized or stratified way. This is well illustrated in telolecithal eggs, whose animal pole is more protoplasmic and whose vegetal pole is more yolk-laden. **1978** *Nature* 16 Mar. 255/1 (*caption*) Injection was aimed at the vegetal pole.

B. *sb.* **a.** An organic substance which is neither animal nor mineral; a plant: = VEGETABLE *sb.* 1.

Very common in the first half of the 17th c. In recent use going with the modern application of the adj. in sense 1.

1599 THYNNE *Animadv.* (1875) 15 All other armes whiche are not Anymalls and vegitalls,..as Cheuerons, pales, Bendes [etc.]. **1599** ALEX. HUME *Poems* (S.T.S.) 21 He knawes..The vertue of all kinde of fruites, and euerie vegetal. **1610** B. JONSON *Alch.* I. i, Your mineralls, vegetalls and animalls..Could not relieue your corps. *c* **1640** WALLER *For Drinking of Healths* 1 Let brutes and vegetals, that cannot think, So far as drought and nature urges, drink. **1678** BUTLER *Hud.* III. ii. 1622 All th'other Members shall.. Spring out of this, as from a Seed, All sorts of Vegetals proceed.

1864 H. SPENCER *Princ. Biol.* I. 112 The largest species of both animals and vegetals belong to the highest classes.

†**b.** *fig.* (See quot.) *Obs.*$^{-1}$

1626 T. H[AWKINS] *Caussin's Holy Crt.* 244 A great number of men are now a dayes vegetalls, that is to say, who so liue, as if they had no other soule but the vegetatiue, as plantes, and lead the very life of the mushrome.

vege'talcule. *rare*$^{-1}$. [f. prec. + -CULE, after *animalcule*.] A minute vegetable organism.

1856 GRINDON *Life* xxv. (1875) 322 Between the first animalcules and the first vegetalcules there is a seeming identity.

vege'tality. *rare.* [f. as prec. + -ITY. Cf. F. *végétalité*.] = VEGETABILITY 2.

1860 LEWES *Physiol. Common Life* II. 430 *note*, We may thus say vegetal, and vegetality, as well as animal, and animality. **1879** —— *Study Psychol.* 54 In its evolution it passes from Vegetality to Animality, and through Animality to Humanity.

vegetant ('vɛdʒɪtənt), *a.* and *sb.* [a. F. *végétant*, or ad. L. *vegetant-*, *vegetans*, pres. pple. of *vegetāre*: see VEGETATE *v.*]

A. *adj.* †**1.** Animating, vivifying, invigorating. ***vegetant stone***: see VEGETABLE *a.* 1 d. *Obs. rare.*

1576 G. BAKER tr. *Gesner's Jewell of Health* 112 The making of the vegetant stone..is borowed out of the practises of the above sayde Aucthour. **1615** CHAPMAN *Odyss.* v. 629 The sea's chill breath, And vegetant dews, I fear will be my death.

2. Vegetating; vegetable, vegetal. Now *rare.*

1610 W. FOLKINGHAM *Art of Survey* I. iii. 6 The Grouth & Repletion of productions, both Vegetant and Animall. **1654** Z. COKE *Logick* 28 Life vegetant as Trees, fruitful and unfruitful. **1675** EVELYN *Terra* (1729) 313 Vegetant and indissoluble salts. **1903** R. BRIDGES *Wintry Delights* 70 Rejoicing In vegetant or brute existence.

3. *nonce-use.* Vegetarian.

1858 HOGG *Shelley* II. 420 Tooke proposed shrimps and treacle to one of the fathers of the church vegetant here on earth.

†**B.** *sb.* = VEGETABLE *sb.* 1, VEGETAL *sb.* *Obs.*

1605 TIMME *Quersit.* I. xvi. 85 Simple vegetants, with metallick substances, doe draw those mercurialls..of a purging nature. **1610** W. FOLKINGHAM *Art of Survey* I. vi. 13 It intimates howe and wherewith the Plot is.. replenished both with Vegetants, and Animals.

vegetarian (vɛdʒɪ'tɛərɪən), *sb.* and *a.* [Irreg. f. VEGET-ABLE after sbs. and adjs. in *-arian*. Hence F. *végétarien*, G. *vegetarianer*.

The general use of the word appears to have been largely due to the formation of the Vegetarian Society at Ramsgate in 1847.]

A. *sb.* **1. a.** One who lives wholly or principally upon vegetable foods; a person who on principle abstains from any form of animal food, or at least such as is obtained by the direct destruction of life.

1839 F. A. KEMBLE *Jrnl. Residence on Georgian Plantation* (1863) 251 If I had had to be my own cook, I should inevitably become a vegetarian. **1842** *Healthian* Apr. 34 To tell a healthy vegetarian that his diet is very uncongenial with the wants of his nature. **1854** H. MILLER *Sch. & Schm.* (1858) 332 A man can scarce become a vegetarian even without also becoming in some measure intolerant of the still large..class that eat beef with their greens, and herrings with their potatoes. **1885** SALMON *Introd. N.T.* xi. 241 Even those who used animal food themselves came to think of the vegetarian as one who lived a higher life.

b. *transf.* Of animals, etc.

1854 *Poultry Chron.* I. 307 For though ours are not vegetarians, every chicken we have is a stanch teetotaler! **1861** P. P. CARPENTER in *Rep. Smithsonian Instit. 1860*, 194 It is almost certain that some tribes [of Gasteropods] which have a permanently elongated muzzle are not vegetarians.

2. A member of a fanatical Chinese sect. Also *attrib.*

1895 *Tablet* 10 Aug. 208 Some 80 men belonging to a sect known as Vegetarians stormed the station..at night. **1896** *Mission. Herald* (Boston) July 279 A large portion of the vegetarians were unwilling to even plunder the missionaries. *Ibid.*, The vegetarian leaders imagined that the missionaries were at the bottom of this activity against themselves.

B. *adj.* **1.** Of or pertaining to vegetarians or vegetarianism; practising or advocating vegetarianism.

In this group possibly attrib. uses of the sb.

1849 *Vegetarian Messenger* Introd. 1 Condensed accounts of meetings and the transactions of the Vegetarian Society. **1860** [JOHN SMITH] (*title*), The Principles and Practice of Vegetarian Cookery. **1890** J. KNIGHT *Vegetarianism in Practice* 11 The moral aspects of the Vegetarian practice. *Ibid.* 12 The Vegetarian system affords such articles as will give all requisite nourishment.

2. Of animals: Living on vegetables.

1856 T. R. JONES *Aquarian Nat.* 342 Mr. Darwin gives an interesting account of a crab..which lives on cocoa-nuts... This vegetarian crab [etc.]. **1869** R. TRIMEN in Noble *The Cape & its People* 100 An order..composed almost wholly of vegetarian insects.

3. Consisting of vegetables or plants.

1868 R. OWEN *Anat. Vertebrates* III. 293 The diprotodont [type of dentition] obtains in the majority of the Australasian marsupials, and is associated usually with vegetarian or promiscuous diet. **1911** SWANTON *Ind. Tribes Lower Mississ.* (Bureau Amer. Ethnol.) 317 The diet of the Tunica was more vegetarian than that of American tribes generally.

vegetarianism (vɛdʒɪ'tɛərɪənɪz(ə)m). [f. prec.] The doctrine or practice of vegetarians; abstention from eating meat, fish, or other animal products.

1851 DUNGLISON *Dict. Med. Sci.* (ed. 8) 896/2 *Vegetarianism*,..a modern term, employed to designate the view that man..ought to subsist on the direct productions of the vegetable kingdom and totally abstain from flesh and blood. **1852** *Punch* 7 Aug. 68/1 Vegetarianism is evidently progressing. **1861** *Q. Rev.* Oct. 324 All this was partly owing, no doubt, to mere physical illness; not improbably to vegetarianism. **1879** TYNDALL *Fragm. Sci.* (ed. 6) I. xi. 339 Is it contrary to the rules of Vegetarianism to eat eggs? **1885** SALMON *Introd. N.T.* 241 Among ourselves..vegetarianism is regarded as a harmless eccentricity.

†**'vegetary,** *a. Obs.*$^{-1}$ [f. L. *vegetāre* VEGETATE *v.* + -ARY^{1}.] Vegetable, vegetative.

a **1595** SOUTHWELL *Hundred Medit.* (1873) 178 As Thou are one in essence, so is my soul, containing all the powers, with a vegetary, sensible and reasonable life.

†**'vegetate,** *a. Obs. rare.* Also 7 vegit-. [ad. L. *vegetāt-us*, pa. pple. of *vegetāre*: see next.] Endowed with vegetable life; growing as plants.

1574 J. JONES tr. *Galen, De Elementis* Ep. Ded. p. ii, Whether they be *Inanimata*..as the Minerals; or *Animata*, with life, Vegetat, Sensit, & Rational, Growing thinges, as Hearbes. *a* **1691** BOYLE *Hist. Air* (1692) 79 This may be evidenced, by undeniable experiments, from things inanimate and vegitate.

vegetate ('vɛdʒɪteɪt), *v.* [f. L. *vegetāt-*, ppl. stem of *vegetāre* to animate, enliven, f. *vegetus* active, lively, vigorous: see VEGETE *a.*]

1. *intr.* Of plants, seeds, etc.: To exercise or exhibit vegetative faculties or functions; to grow or develop, or begin to do so.

1605 TIMME *Quersit.* I. x. 38 You might see..the manifest forme of a rose, vegetating and growing. **1707** *Curios. in Husb. & Gard.* 27 A Plant..vegetates; that is to say..it nourishes itself, shoots, increases in size, and produces Leaves, Flowers, and Seeds. **1765** A. DICKSON *Treat. Agric.* (ed. 2) 97 Seeds will not vegetate without air. **1791** W. GILPIN *Forest Scenery* II. 107 A young oak, just vegetating from the acorn. **1815** J. SMITH *Panorama Sci. & Art* II. 627 The plants being well earthed up, vegetate with increased luxuriance. **1838** T. THOMSON *Chem. Org. Bodies* 859 The leaves [of the tea-plant] are not fit to be pulled till the shrub has vegetated for three years. **1852** ROBERTSON *Serm.* Ser. III. (1857) xviii. 263 The sun in autumn may be bright and clear, but the seed which has not been sown until then will not vegetate.

transf. and *fig.* **1706-7** FARQUHAR *Beaux' Strat.* Prol., A weed that has to twenty summers ran, Shoots up in stalk, and vegetates to man. **1733** POPE *Ess. Man* III. 16 See dying vegetables life sustain, See life dissolving, vegetate again. **1792** BURKE *Corr.* (1844) III. 408 That corruption has cast deep roots in that party, and they vegetate in it..every day with greater and greater force. **1836** I. TAYLOR *Phys. The. Another Life* xiii. 173 Such dispositions..are living powers; they vegetate, and cover the entire surface of the soul.

b. *transf.* To increase as if by, to present the appearance of, vegetable growth.

1744 BERKELEY *Siris* §177 All parts of the world vegetate by a fine subtle æther. **1782** *Phil. Trans.* LXXIII. 79 They vegetate, if solutions of both metals [i.e. silver and mercury] in the same acid be mixed together. **1796** MORSE *Amer. Geog.* I. 501 Naturalists have observed that ore in swamps and pondy ground vegetates and increases. **1823** URE *Dict. Chem.* s.v. *Vegetation* (*Saline*), When salts are suffered to vegetate in this manner [etc.]. **1895** *Funk's Stand. Dict.*, *Vegetate*,..as a wart or pimple; [to] produce excrescences.

c. To produce vegetation.

1799 KIRWAN *Geol. Ess.* 105 It is well known that beds of volcanic ashes and pumice vegetate sooner than any other.

2. *fig.* Of persons: To live a merely physical life; to lead a dull, monotonous existence, devoid of intellectual activity or social intercourse; to live in dull retirement or seclusion.

1740 CIBBER *Apol.* (1756) I. 18 The man who chuses never to laugh..seems to me only in the quiet state of a green tree; he vegetates, tis true, but shall we say he lives? **1777** G. FORSTER *Voy. round World* I. 542 In short, we rather vegetated than lived. **1800** MRS. HERVEY *Mourtray Fam.* I. 25 He repaired with his family..to vegetate (as they called it) at Wilmington Park. **1860** ADLER *Prov. Poet* xvii. 380 Weary..of the obscurity in which he vegetated he resolved to apply himself to the culture of poetry. **1886** W. J. TUCKER *E. Europe* 252 The family was vegetating in dingy privacy in an Austrian provincial town on the shattered remnants of what had once been a princely fortune.

b. Of a country, nation, etc.

1796 MORSE *Amer. Geog.* II. 294 The Polish nation might, after having vegetated so long in obscurity [etc.]. **1809** W. IRVING *Knickerb.* VII. vi. (1849) 407 The vast empire of China..has vegetated through a succession of drowsy ages. **1832** tr. *Sismondi's Ital. Rep.* xv. 341 The republics of Genoa, Sienna, and Lucca had permission to vegetate under the imperial protection. **1851** KOSSUTH in *Daily News* 22 March (1894) 5/6 The House of Hapsburg, as a dynasty, exists no more. It merely vegetates at the whim of the mighty Czar.

†**3.** *trans.* To cause to grow; to stimulate growth or development in; to animate, quicken. *Obs.*

1620 T. GRANGER *Div. Logike* A 4 b, The Roote, whose sappe doth vegetate the rest. **1646** J. HALL *Horæ Vac.* 79 The continuing and placing of Ideas..doth greatly quicken and vegetate the Invention. **1678** CUDWORTH *Intell. Syst.* 347 This Sensible World, is the Receptacle of all Forms, Qualities, and Bodies, all which cannot be vegetated and quickned without God.

absol. **1671** H. M. tr. *Erasm. Colloq.* 300 Therefore in some parts it [the soul] animates only, and vegetates.

†**4.** To make strong or vigorous. *Obs.*$^{-0}$

1623 in COCKERAM.

5. To provide or supply with vegetables (see quot.). *rare*$^{-1}$.

1838 PARKER *Exploring Tour beyond Rocky Mts.* (1846) 386 Our stay at Tahiti was employed by the ship's crew..in vegetating the ship, as they phrase it; that is, in collecting oranges, bananas, sweet potatoes,..yams and squashes.

6. In *pa. pple.* Provided with vegetation or plant-life. Usually with qualifying adv.

1876 *Nature* 9 Nov. 31/1 The head of the bay, which appeared from the distance to be well vegetated. **1892** *Pall Mall G.* 25 Nov. 6/1 New Amsterdam..is densely vegetated, and consequently more valuable.

Hence **'vegetated** *ppl. a.*; **'vegetating** *vbl. sb.*

1775 ASH, *Vegetating*, the state or act of growing like plants. **1804-20** BLAKE *Jerus.* To Deists, Your Greek Philosophy, which is a remnant of Druidism, teaches that Man is righteous in his Vegetated Spectre. **1884** E. P. ROE *Nat. Ser. Story* ii, Frequent removal from one part of the country to another prevents anything like vegetating.

'vegetating, *ppl. a.* [f. prec. + -ING^{2}.]

1. Characterized by, associated with, or causing vegetation.

1704 RAY *Creation* (ed. 4) I. 95 It's not unlikely, that the Rain-water may be endued with some vegetating or prolifick Vertue. **1768** *Phil. Trans.* LVIII. 78 Seeds in a vegetating state. **1794** R. J. SULLIVAN *View Nat.* II. 48 The vegetating power which is operating during the whole year in evergreens. **1800** *Asiatic Ann. Reg.* 265/1 Root fleshy,..

soon after taken out of the earth becomes highly scented, which it retains as long as in a vegetating state.

2. Exhibiting vegetation or growth.

1783 JUSTAMOND tr. *Raynal's Hist. Indies* VI. 313 Six veins of vegetating earth, which were in process of time discovered, received sugar canes. **1796** WITHERING *Brit. Plants* (ed. 3) II. 152 Mr. Gough informs me that vegetating germs of the viviparous variety,..planted in his garden in the year 1790, still continue viviparous. **1801** *Farmer's Mag.* April 128 Sheep may occasionally be allowed to take a walk over the fallow, to pick up any vegetating weeds or grass roots that may come in their way. **1882** VINES tr. *Sachs's Bot.* 630 The Lemnaceæ consist of small branched leafless floating vegetating bodies.

vegetation (vɛdʒɪ'teɪʃən). Also 6 vegitacion, 7-8 -tion. [ad. (late and) med.L. *vegetātio*, f. *vegetāre* VEGETATE *v.* So F. *végétation*, It. *vegetazione*, Sp. *vegetacion*, Pg. *vegetação*.

The definitions 'a comforting, making strong', etc., in Cockeram (1623) and Blount (1656) are merely copied from Cooper's explanation of *vegetatio* in Apuleius.]

I. Abstract senses.

1. The action of vegetating or growing; the faculty, process, or phenomena of growth and development as possessed by certain organic substances; vegetal activity or property.

a. In general use.

1564 J. DAY tr. *Martyr's Comm. Judges* xiii. 212 To eate, is not onely to chawe the meate,..but moreouer to conuert it into the substawnce of hys bodye, by concoction thoroughe the power of vegitacion. **1594** PLAT *Jewell-ho.* II. 11 Salt..causeth the vegetation, perfection, maturitie, and the whole good that is contained in euery thing that nourisheth. **1605** TIMME *Quersit.* I. xiii. 57 A most pure and perfect body, replenished with vital spirits, and full of vegetation. **1768** PENNANT *Brit. Zool.* I. Pref. 10 Through every species of animal life,..to that point where sense is almost extinct, and vegetation commences. **1813** SIR H. DAVY *Agric. Chem.* (1814) 7 The phenomena of vegetation must be considered as an important branch of the science of organized Nature.

fig. **1755** YOUNG *Centaur* vi. Wks. 1757 IV. 281 The light of God's countenance is the sun of the human soul, whence all its vegetation of real felicity.

†**b.** Of the soul. *Obs.* (Cf. VEGETATIVE *a.* 1 a.)

1613 PURCHAS *Pilgrimage* (1614) 16 One soul hath those three essentiall faculties of Vnderstanding, Will, and Memorie, or (as others) of Vegetation, Sense, and Reason. **1620** T. GRANGER *Div. Logike* 55 Sence, and vegetation is an effect by emanation of the soule.

c. Of plants or seeds. †Also, vegetative power (quot. 1665).

1661 SIR K. DIGBY (*title*), A Discourse concerning the Vegetation of Plants. **1665** SIR T. HERBERT *Trav.* (1677) 333 The root where the sap lies constantly conveying vegetation to the tree in those warm Regions. **1707** *Curios. in Husb. & Gard.* 28 The Operations of each Plant, which are Nutrition, Augmentation and Propagation,..we..express by the single Word Vegetation, which in Effect includes them all. **1760** J. LEE *Introd. Bot.* I. vii. (1765) 14 The Seed..is a deciduous Part of the Vegetable, the Rudiment of a new one, quickened for Vegetation by the Sprinkling of the Pollen. **1789** MRS. PIOZZI *Journ. France* II. 191 In these countries vegetation is so rapid, that every thing makes haste to come and more to go. **1813** BAKEWELL *Introd. Geol.* (1815) 250 The vegetation of perennial grasses in the spring is at least a fortnight sooner on lime-stone and sandy soils..than on clayey. **1853** ROBERTSON *Serm.* Ser. III. (1872) iii. 31 Seeds and germs..incapable of vegetation in the unkindly climate of their birth. **1884** BOWER & SCOTT *De Bary's Phaner.* 561 The intercellular air-spaces of the cortical parenchyma are in open communication with the external air at the time of active vegetation.

†**d.** Of inorganic substances. *Obs.*

1676 *Phil. Trans.* XI. 739 They are prepossest with an opinion against the vegetation of all Stones. **1748** *Earthquake Peru* Pref. 11 As a Proof of the quick Vegitation of Silver. **1774** GOLDSM. *Nat. Hist.* (1824) I. 33 This is not a place for an inquiry into the seeming vegetation of those stony substances.

†**2.** An act or instance of vegetating; a stage in plant growth or development. *Obs.*

1672 GREW *Anat. Pl., Idea* (1682) 1 The Method of Nature her self, in her continued Series of Vegetations; proceeding from the Seed sown, to the formation of the Root.

†**3.** *transf.* The production of a plant-like formation. *Obs.* (Cf. 5 b.)

1707 *Curios. in Husb. & Gard.* 305 The Artificial Vegetation of Silver, commonly called Diana's Tree. **1823** URE *Dict. Chem.* s.v., The Influence of the Air and Light upon the Vegetation of Salts. **1842** FRANCIS *Dict. Arts, Vegetation of Salts*, a curious phenomena [*sic*], which takes place when strong solutions of metallic salts are left in glass, earthenware, or other vessels.

4. *fig.* Existence similar or comparable to that of a vegetable; dull, empty, or stagnant life spent in retirement or seclusion.

1760 M. W. MONTAGU *Let.* 25 Oct. (1967) III. 245, I am not surpriz'd at the long Vegetation of the D[uche]sse of Argyle. **1797** GODWIN *Enquirer* I. xiii. 114 His state is rather a state of vegetation. **1833** T. HOOK *Parson's Dau.* I. xi, In this state of vegetation he remained until about ten o'clock. **1854** J. S. C. ABBOTT *Napoleon* (1855) I. xvi. 290 Hedouville ..went to spend a life of mere vegetation in Spain. **1882** MISS BRADDON *Mt.-Royal* II. iv. 53 You can't expect to find much difference in me after three years' vegetation in Cornwall.

II. Concrete senses.

5. †**a.** A vegetable form or growth; a plant.

1683 TRYON *Way to Health* 518 At which times all Vegitations are in their flourishing state. **1691** —— *Wisd. Dictates* 110 The pleasant Ferment..of the Stomach can with much more facility..digest Vegitations, than Flesh or Fish. **1707** *Curios. in Husb. & Gard.* 29 Some Vegetations, ..as..Mushrooms and Mosses: the maritime Vegetations, ..are not properly Plants.

b. A plant-like growth or formation due to chemical action. (Cf. 3.)

1790 *Phil. Trans.* LXXX. 378 Bergman relates, that he has sometimes observed beautiful crystallizations or vegetations of metallic silver formed on pieces of iron immersed long in a solution of silver. **1796** KIRWAN *Elem. Min.* (ed. 2) II. 446 The Nickel forming greenish vegetations. **1800** tr. *Lagrange's Chem.* II. 133 At the end of some hours there will be formed, at the surface of the small mass of amalgam, a vegetation in the form of a bush. **1823** J. BADCOCK *Dom. Amusem.* 124 A beautiful white vegetation will be perceptible round the wire. **1849** J. R. JACKSON *Min.* 287 A pretty metallic vegetation in glass jars:..called the Tree of Diana.

c. *Path.* A morbid fungoid growth or excrescence occurring on some part of the body.

1835 *Cycl. Pract. Med.* IV. 419/2 Warty vegetations of the valves.—These excrescences bear a close resemblance to venereal warty vegetations. **1861** BUMSTEAD *Ven. Dis.* (1879) 242 Vegetations are papillary growths springing from the skin or mucous membrane, chiefly in the neighborhood of the genital organs. **1879** *St. George's Hosp. Rep.* IX. 327 The posterior flap at its right corner bore a large vegetation, assuming the shape of a mushroom, of about $1\frac{1}{4}$ inch in diameter.

6. a. Plants collectively; plants or vegetal growths as a product of the soil, freq. considered in respect of a certain area.

1727-46 THOMSON *Summer* 440 Deep to the root Of vegetation parch'd, the cleaving fields..an arid hue disclose. **1794** MRS. RADCLIFFE *Myst. Udolpho* xliii, The paths were rude, and frequently overgrown with vegetation. **1813** SHELLEY *Q. Mab* VIII. 170 Blue mists..Scattered the seeds of pestilence, and fed Unnatural vegetation. **1859** DARWIN *Orig. Spec.* iii. (1860) 74 When an American forest is cut down, a very different vegetation springs up. **1881** *Nature* No. 619. 448 An admirable summary of the vegetation of the different regions of the globe.

transf. **1847** LEITCH tr. *C. O. Müller's Anc. Art* §275. 265 The Corinthian places in the room of the simple bulge of the Doric order a slender body..gradually enlarging and richly clothed with vegetation.

attrib. **1878** W. R. S. RALSTON in *Contemp. Rev.* Feb. 536 A reference to vegetation-spirits and their foes.

b. (See quot.)

1870 *Eng. Mech.* 21 Jan. 448/2 In old object glasses there is occasionally an appearance which has been called 'vegetation', and which consists of a number of very thin lines disposed in an arborescent form.

c. Used *attrib.* with reference to the death and regeneration of plant life and the alternation of the seasons as symbolized or represented in religious or cultic beliefs and rituals.

1914 J. G. FRAZER *Golden Bough: Adonis Attis Osiris* (ed. 3) II. III. vii. 126 Professor Ed. Meyer also formerly regarded Osiris as a sun-god; he now interprets him as a great vegetation god. **1918** in Gray & Moore *Mythol. All Races* XI. 25 Here there seems to be indication of a vegetation cult. *Ibid.* 75 Closely connected with the earth goddesses are their children, the vegetation-deities. **1922** T. S. ELIOT *Waste Land* 53 Anyone who is acquainted with these works will immediately recognize in the poem certain references to vegetation ceremonies. **1967** *Listener* 6 Apr. 471/3 It [*sc.* the Easter holiday] should have been all outside broadcasts of drunken baroque processions.., villages abusing each other's religious banners.., vegetation ceremonies still describable in pace-egging and mummers' plays.

Hence **vege'tational** *a.*; **vege'tationless** *a.*

1855 LEWES *Goethe* I. 233 On the vegetationless surface the radiation is direct. **1926** *Spectator* 4 Sept. 354/2 The dark areas observable on the surface of Mars are vegetational regions. **1958** *New Biol.* XXVI. 32 These communities..are prevented, by haymaking and the grazing of sheep, cattle, and rabbits, from entering the normal phases of vegetational succession. **1977** J. L. HARPER *Population Biol. Plants* iv. 95 The buried seed population of mature or climax communities generally contains a living..record of the past vegetational history of the succession.

vegetative ('vɛdʒɪteɪtɪv, -tətɪv), *a.* and *sb.* Also 5 vegetatiff, -tyf(f, 6 -ife, 6-7 -iue; 6 vegitatiue, 8 -ive. [ad. med.L. *vegetāt-īvus*, f. the ppl. stem of L. *vegetāre* VEGETATE *v.*: see -IVE. So F. *végétatif* (13th c.), Sp., Pg., It. *vegetativo*.]

A. *adj.* **1.** Having the function of vegetation; endowed with the power or faculty of growth.

a. Of the soul. (Cf. SENSITIVE *a.* 1.)

1398 TREVISA *Barth. De P.R.* (W. de W. 1495) III. xiii, þe [soule] vegetatyf desyryth to be,..& the resonable soule desyreth to [be] best. **1433** LYDG. *St. Edmund* App. 334 Quyk lyk a soule moore than vegetatyff. **1531** ELYOT *Gov.* III. xxiv, The one [part of the soul], wherin is the powar or efficacie of growinge, which is also in herbes and trees.., & that parte is callen vegetatife. **1594** T. B. *La Primaud. Fr. Acad.* II. 338 That order, which God hath set betweene the vertues of the Vegetatiue soule for the nourishing of the bodie. **1609** BIBLE (Douay) *Gen.* vi. *comm.*, The powre or force to engender belongeth to the vegetative soul. **1659** *Gentl. Calling* (1696) 9 As we distinguish mens souls into the vegetative, the animal, and the rational. **1692** RAY *Creation* I. (ed. 2) 40 For my part, I should make no scruple to attribute the Formation of Plants, their growth and nutrition to the vegetative Soul in them. **1725** [see SOUL *sb.* 6 (*a*)]. **1808** BARCLAY *Muscular Motions* 262 The ancient *Δυναμεις*, the ministers of Physis, were classed by Plato under three souls, the rational, animal, and vegetative. **1879** TYNDALL *Fragm. Sci.* II. xi. 243 How..is this vegetative soul to be presented to the mind? where did it flourish before the tree grew?

b. Of material things; in later use esp. of plants or parts of these.

1477 NORTON *Ord. Alch.* i. in Ashm. (1652) 20 Also nothing multiplyed shall ye finde, But it be of Vegetative or of Sensitive kinde. **1483** CAXTON *Gold. Leg.* 357 b/1 Alle thyngys obeyed to this holy man as well thynges not sensible as vegetatyf and not resonable. **1509** HAWES *Past. Pleas.* XXII. (1555) N iv b, Herbes and fruytes..In erthe he planted for to haue their life By diuers vertues and sundry growing, So to continue and be vegitatiue. **1601** HOLLAND *Pliny* XVII. xxi, This marrow, this vegetative and vitall substance. **1613** tr. *Mexia's Treas. Aunc. & Mod. Times* 32 The vegetative Bodies; as Plants, Trees, and such like. **1670** *Moral State Eng.* 5 None but sensitive and vegetative Creatures pursue the primitive end of their institutions. **1711** STEELE *Spect.* No. 100 ⁋2 The indolent Man descends from the Dignity of his Nature, and makes that Being which was Rational merely Vegetative. **1796** BP. WATSON *Apol. Bible* 318 Somewhat after the way of your vegetative speck in the kernel of a peach. **1812** MISS L. M. HAWKINS *C'tess & Gertr.* I. 262 The vegetative adhesions [to books] of the undisturbed damp. **1853** G. JOHNSTON *Nat. Hist. E. Bord.* I. 220 A very common weed, and so vegetative and retentive of life that it requires much labour..to clear the lands infested with it. **1880** C. & F. DARWIN *Movem. Pl.* 523 When a new root-cap and vegetative point had been formed, they bent themselves perpendicularly downwards.

fig. **1782** PAINE *Let. Abbé Raynel* (1791) 40 The mind is presented with a wide extended prospect of vegetative good, and sees a thousand blessings budding into existence.

†**c.** *vegetative stone*, = VEGETABLE *a.* 1 d. *Obs.*$^{-1}$

c **1450** LYDG. & BURGH *Secrees* 531 Of stoonys, Specially of three—Oon myneral, Anothir vegetatyff, Partyd on foure to lengthe a mannys lyff.

d. *spec.* in *Physiol.* and *Bot.* Concerned with growth and development, as opposed to *reproductive*; *vegetative pole* (*Embryology*) = *vegetal pole* s.v. VEGETAL *a.* 4.

(*a*) **1857** BULLOCK tr. *Cazeaux's Midwifery* 172 One has been called the external, or serous layer, and the other is denominated the internal, mucous, or the vegetative one. **1891** W. A. JAMIESON *Dis. Skin* i. (ed. 3) 5 The deepest layer of all is the vegetative or mucous proper. **1892** E. L. MARK tr. *O. Hertwig's Text-bk. Embryol.* i. 11 The dissimilar poles are distinguished:..the under, heavier and richer in yolk, as the vegetative pole. **1909** J. W. JENKINSON *Exper. Embryol.* 245 A blastopore is in very numerous cases formed at the vegetative pole. **1946** B. M. PATTEN *Human Embryol.* iv. 60 In mammals, as is the case with surprising uniformity throughout the animal kingdom, the mitotic spindle of the first cleavage division forms at right angles to an imaginary axis passing through the ovum from animal to vegetative pole. **1958** —— *Foundations Embryol.* ii. 52 The region opposite the animal pole is called the vegetative, or vegetal, pole because while material for growth is drawn from this region, it remains itself relatively less active.

(*b*) **1875** BENNETT & DYER tr. *Sachs's Bot.* 117 A conical elongation..distinguished as the Vegetative Cone. **1882** VINES tr. *Sachs's Bot.* 246 The multiplication of individuals being effected by the separation of the ordinary vegetative cells. **1884** BOWER & SCOTT *De Bary's Phaner.* Introd. 2 Under the term vegetative organs we include all those organs of the plant which are not organs of reproduction. *Ibid.* 282 In the main vegetative axes of L[ycopodium] clavatum and L. annotinum.

e. *Biol.* Pertaining to or being a stage in the replication of a virus at which non-infective viral components are synthesized and assembled within the host cell prior to its lysis.

1953 M. DELBRÜCK in *Cold Spring Harbor Symp. Quantitative Biol.* XVIII. 1/1 One new feature is the recognition that the infecting virus undergoes an essential change before it multiplies. The multiplying form is here called the vegetative phase, in analogy to the use of the word 'vegetative' in the bacteriology of sporulating bacteria. **1967** K. M. SMITH *Insect Virol.* viii. 147 Whenever it has been shown that viruses of animals or higher plants go through cycles as described for bacteriophages, the terms provirus, vegetative virus and infective virus are appropriate for the corresponding stages. **1973** [see PROPHAGE]. **1982** FRAENKEL-CONRAT & KIMBALL *Virology* i. 11 The relative simplicity of extracellular viruses, termed the dormant phase, and the complexity of their interaction with host cell components leading to their replication, termed the vegetative phase, have placed viruses among the most useful tools in the study of all phenomena related to replication, information transfer, mutation, and many other aspects of molecular biology.

2. Of or pertaining to, concerned or connected with, characterized by, vegetation or growth.

a. Of faculty, power, principle, etc.

c **1400** tr. *Secreta Secret., Gov. Lordsh.* 96 þe wirkynge of þis last [virtue], (þat þe Auctour clepys vegetatyf, & I here strenght sustantyf). *c* **1430** LYDG. *Min. Poems* (Percy Soc.) 196 To tempre the spiritis by vertu vegetatiff.

1606 BRYSKETT *Civ. Life* 44 This power of the soule..is called vegetatiue (you must giue me leaue to vse new words of Art..) because it giueth life and increase to growing things. **1636** FEATLY *Clavis Myst.* xi. 143 The sensitive faculty includeth the vegetative. **1653** W. RAMESEY *Astrologie Restored* 215 All things decay and diminish in their vegetative vigour. **1712** HUGHES *Spect.* No. 554 ⁋12 The Soul has in this Respect a certain vegetative Power, which cannot lie wholly idle. **1791** COWPER *Yardley Oak* 34 Thou fell'st mature, and in the loamy clod Swelling with vegetative force instinct Didst burst thine egg. **1802** GOUVR. MORRIS in Sparks *Life & Writ.* (1832) III. 161 There is a vigorous vegetative principle at the root which will make our tree flourish. *a* **1871** GROTE *Eth. Fragm.* v. (1876) 178 Of the irrational soul, one branch is, the nutritive and vegetative faculty. **1874** BLACKIE *Self Cult.* 41 This growth is a constant and habitual exercise of vital or vegetative force.

b. Of life.

1567 MAPLET *Gr. Forest* 25 b, For in them is the life vegetatiue or that life which nourisheth. **1598** BARCKLEY *Felic. Man* (1631) 288 In naturall things there are three kinds of life: vegetative or increasing which is in plants; sensitive which is in beasts; rationall or reasonable which is in men. **1600** SURFLET *Countrie Farme* I. ix. 47 The Sunne ..giueth vnto earthly bodies their forme and vegetatiue life. **1678** NORRIS *Miscell.* (1699) 251 In Rationals [there is]

Vegetative Life, Sense and Reason. **1726** LEONI *Alberti's Archit.* I. 5/2 Plants, Seeds, and every thing else that has the vegetative Life. **1729** SAVAGE *Wanderer* IV. 124 Hail, glorious sun! to whose attractive fires, The waken'd, vegetative life aspires! **1835–6** *Todd's Cycl. Anat.* I. 126/2 The nerves of organic or vegetative life. **1867** J. HOGG *Microsc.* II. i. 259 The whole vegetative life is run through in the same cell. **1870** ROLLESTON *Anim. Life* 1 Common Rat, .. dissected so as to show .. portions of most of the organs of vegetative life.

c. In general use.

1594 PLAT *Jewell-ho.* II. 16 To proue that salt is no enemie, either to the vegetatiue, or sensatiue natures. **1647** H. MORE *Poems* Interpret. Gen. 432 That immense diffusion of atoms is to be referred to Psyche, as an internall vegetative act. **1683** TRYON *Way to Health* 130 [In] Winter .. the Vegitative Quality stands as it were still. **1762** J. H. STEVENSON *Crazy Tales* 7 The work of vegetative laws. **1782–3** W. F. MARTYN *Geog. Mag.* II. 147 Olives and mulberries arrive at full vegetative perfection. **1836** J. GILBERT *Chr. Atonem.* iv. (1852) 93 A survey of the minute action of vegetative energies. **1880** HAUGHTON *Phys. Geogr.* vi. 301 The Europasian Forest region is characterized by a pretty uniform temperature during the vegetative season.

3. Causing or promoting vegetation; inducing vegetable growth; productive, fertile.

1594 PLAT *Jewell-ho.* II. 3 A Philosophicall discourse .. vpon the vegetatiue and fructifying Salt of Nature. **1612** PEACHAM *Gentl. Exerc.* II. iii. (1634) 114 The vegetative humour or moisture that quickeneth and giveth life to trees, plants, herbs and flowers, whereby they grow and increase. **1675** EVELYN *Terra* (1729) 317 Composts .. are by no means fit for the Earth, .. unless .. so order'd as .. to .. communicate heat, and vegetative Spirits to what you shall apply them. **1707** MORTIMER *Husb.* (1721) I. 98 Fullers-earth is .. very full of that vegetative Salt that helps the growth of Plants. **1782** CREVECŒUR *Lett.* 50 In Europe they were as so many useless plants, wanting vegitative mould, and refreshing showers. **1834** *Brit. Husb.* I. 360 The vegetative mould which covers the earth in all situations undisturbed by the plough. **1853** KANE *Grinnell Exp.* xviii. (1856) 138 The question whether unmixed snow can act as a vegetative matrix.

†**4.** Obtained or derived from, consisting of, vegetables or plants. *Obs. rare.*

1662 R. MATHEW *Unl. Alch.* 2 This pill is a Corrector of all Vegetative poysons. **1691** TRYON *Wisd. Dictates* 110 All Vegetative Foods are not only wholsom, but easily concocted.

5. = VEGETABLE *a.* 3.

1677 PLOT *Oxfordsh.* 175 Having done with the Vegetative, I proceed to the Animal Kingdom. **1695** LD. PRESTON *Boeth.* III. 144, I, casting an Eye upon the Vegetative World, consider Herbs and Trees. **1722** WOLLASTON *Relig. Nat.* ix. 209, I think I may be sure that neither lifeless matter, nor the vegetative tribe, .. have any reflex thoughts. **1772–84** *Cook's Voy.* (1790) I. 39 In regard to the vegetative and brute creation. **1859** I. TAYLOR *Logic Theol.* 44 The living world, vegetative and animal.

6. a. *fig.* Vegetating; inactive.

1802 MRS. E. PARSONS *Myst. Visit* IV. 74 In this vegetative state of happiness you found me.

b. *Path.* Characterized by the exercise or activity of the physical functions only.

1893 *Daily News* 25 Apr. 5/4 He is in what his doctor calls a vegetative state, and incapable of connecting two ideas together. **1899** *Allbutt's Syst. Med.* VIII. 196 Idiots of vegetative grade. *Ibid.* 237 This girl led a vegetative life, but learnt to recognize those around her. **1969** *Sci. Jrnl.* Feb. 11/3 Two other patients .. had flat EEG readings for prolonged periods, but subsequently recovered, although they remained 'vegetative'. **1972** *Lancet* 1 Apr. 734/1 Patients with severe brain damage due to trauma .. may now survive indefinitely. .. Such patients are best described as in a persistent vegetative state. **1976** *National Observer* (U.S.) 19 June 2 (*caption*) Their comatose daughter .. has been in what doctors call a 'vegetative state' for 14 months. .. The Quinlans last March won court permission to turn off Karen's life-sustaining devices. **1982** *Brit. Med. Jrnl.* 20 Oct. 1022/2 The term 'persistent vegetative state' was suggested in 1972 to describe those patients with irreversible brain damage .. who on recovery from deep coma pass into a state of seeming wakefulness and reflex responsiveness but do not return to a cognitive sapient state.

B. *sb.* †**1.** Vegetative faculty or power. *rare.*

1605 TIMME *Quersit.* I. xiv. 68 In vegetables there were only those vegetatiues; which, in beastes, beside the vegetation which they retain, .. become also sensatiue.

†**2.** An organic body capable of growth and development but devoid of sensation and thought; a vegetable or plant. *Obs.*

1634 W. WOOD *New Eng. Prosp.* I. vi, Having related unto you the .. nature of the Soile, with his vegetatives, and other commodities. *a* **1668** FELTHAM *Resolves* I. xxviii. (1677) 152 Even Plants, which are but Vegetatives, will not grow in Caues, where the .. Air is barred from them. **1668** CLARENDON *Ess.* Tracts (1727) 93 We live rather the Life of Vegetatives or Sensitives .. than the lives of reasonable men. **1712** E. COOKE *Voy. S. Sea* 210 Having run over the living Creatures and Vegetatives. **1764** in *10th Rep. Hist. MSS. Comm.* App. I. 372 We are vegetatives formed by education.

Hence **'vegetatively** *adv.*, **'vegetativeness**.

1886 *Encycl. Brit.* XX. 431/2 In some instances the one generation may spring *vegetatively from the other without the intervention of a spore. **1905** *Brit. Med. Jrnl.* 25 Feb. 442 They develop into one of the three following forms all of which can reproduce themselves vegetatively. **1727** BAILEY (vol. II), **Vegetativeness*, a vegetative Quality. **1889** GEDDES & THOMSON *Evol. Sex* 48 Superior constitutional vegetativeness in the females [of Lychnis].

vegete (vɪ'dʒiːt), *a.* Now *rare.* Also 7 veget, vegit. [ad. L. *vegetus*, f. *vegēre* to be active or lively. Cf. It. and Pg. *vegeto*, obs. F. *vejete* (Cotgr.).]

1. Healthy and active; flourishing in respect of health and vigour: **a.** Of persons, the body, etc.

1639 W. CARTWRIGHT *Roy. Slave* III. i, The veget Artist and the vigorous Poet, whose braines are full and forging still. **1649** JER. TAYLOR *Gt. Exemp.* I. 22 Even her body was made aëry and vegete. **1670** MAYNWARINGE *Vita Sana* vii. 85 Active stirring people are .. more vegete and lively in spirit. *a* **1734** NORTH *Lives* (1826) III. 350 His face was always tinted with a fresh colour, and his looks vegete and sanguine. **1774** J. BRYANT *Mythol.* II. 361 That animal .. was supposed to renew its life, and to become .. vegete and fresh. **1870** LOWELL *Study Wind.* 380 If I forgot that ample and vegete countenance of Mr. R——.

b. Of age, condition, etc.

1651 JER. TAYLOR *Holy Dying* iv. §1 He had lived an healthful and vegete Age till his last sickness. **1665** NEEDHAM *Med. Medicinæ* 401 That florid Vegete vigorous condition which ought to be in the less Vegete, or the Valetudinary state of Bodies. **1684** tr. *Bonet's Merc. Compit.* VI. 230 He that is of a firm habit of body, and has a vegete heat.

c. Of the faculties, mind, etc.

1660 SOUTH *Serm.* (1727) IV. i. 21 A well radicated habit, in a lively, vegete Faculty, is like an Apple of Gold in a Picture of Silver. **1662** *Ibid.* (1697) I. 55 The understanding .. was vegete, quick, and lively. **1727** EARBERY tr. *Burnet's St. Dead* 84 Before the organical Construction of the Body is impair'd, and the Spirits are vegete and vigorous. **1769** GRANGER *Biogr. Hist. Eng.* (1804) II. 155 His body was firm and erect, and his faculties lively and vegete. **1846** J. HAMILTON *Mount Olives* v. 126 If you would possess such a mind you must keep it fresh and vegete and lifesome by secret prayer.

2. Of plants or their parts: Healthy, vigorous; growing strongly or promoting active growth.

1651 R. CHILD in *Hartlib's Legacy* (1655) 106 This be a very necessary management in taller Plants, and serves to make them much more vegete and lusty. **1670** *Phil. Trans.* V. 2069 Whether the Juyce of Trees, whil'st alive and vegete, can properly be said .. to descend. **1756** AMORY *Buncle* (1825) II. 120 Active in sending the vegete juices through the vessels of all plants. **1794–6** E. DARWIN *Zoon.* (1801) I. 137 There are many trees, whose whole internal wood is perished, and yet the branches are vegete and healthy. **1800** —— *Phytol.* 167 Because the lower leaf dies, and the sweet juice is absorbed, as the upper leaf becomes vegete.

transf. **1653** ASHWELL *Fides Apost.* 189 The Nicene Creed, .. by this meanes become vegete and growen, was afterwards used in the Greeke Church.

†**3.** Lively, bright. *Obs.*$^{-1}$

a **1643** CARTWRIGHT *Ordinary* IV. iii, In troth a stone of lustre, I assure you It darts a pretty light, a veget spark.

Hence **ve'geteness**.

1727 BAILEY (vol. II), *Vegeteness*, Liveliness, Quickness, Soundness, the Quality of having a growing Life.

†**'vegetist.** *nonce-word.* [Irreg. f. VEGET-ABLE + -IST.] One who is concerned with the growth or cultivation of vegetable products.

1778 [W. H. MARSHALL] *Minutes Agric.* 7 Sept. 1775, The Vegetist, perhaps, more than any other man, is subject to the power .. of the elements. *Ibid.*, *Digest* 25 The Vegetist ought never to lose sight of this maxim.

†**vegetity.** *Obs.*$^{-1}$ In 7 vegititie. [Irreg. f. VEGET-ATE *v.* + -ITY.] Vegetative power or quality.

But perhaps a misprint for *vegitivitie*.

1628 T. SPENCER *Logick* 43 The soule of Peter hath the same rationalitie with all other mens soules: no singular tree differs from other trees in vegititie.

vegetive ('vɛdʒɪtɪv), *a.* and *sb.* Also 6 vegeetyve, 7 vegitiue. [Reduced form of VEGETATIVE *a.*, after L. *veget-āre* or *veget-us*.]

A. *adj.* **1.** Of or pertaining to, characteristic of, vegetables or plants; = VEGETATIVE *a.* 2.

1526 *St. Papers Hen. VIII*, VI. 534 The oolde tre for lakk of vegeetyve sprytis maye nott opteeyne perfect rote fastnesse. **1573** TUSSER *Husb.* (1878) 123 Not rent off, but cut off, ripe beane with a knife, for hindering stalke of hir vegetiue life. **1605** SYLVESTER *Du Bartas* II. iii. *Vocation* 1354 The pleasant Soyl .. is all dry'd and dead; Voyd of all force, vitall, or vegetive. **1631** W. SALTONSTALL *Pict. Loquent.* F ii, His knowledge consists in the vegetive nature of Plants. **1675** J. SMITH *Chr. Relig. App.* II. 15 Man had not Power so much as over the green Herb, to deprive it of its Vegetive Life; .. but by God's Donation.

1830 COLERIDGE *Church & State* (1839) 192 Thus, without the first power, that of growth, or what Bichat and others name the vegetive life or productivity, the second power .. could not exist. **1852** BAILEY *Festus* (ed. 5) 333 What if it were that life .. through all The countless grades, vegetive, animal, Of nature should progress at last to man.

2. Endowed with the faculty of vegetation or growth; = VEGETATIVE *a.* 1 b.

1615 G. SANDYS *Trav.* 140 The Castle of Catie, about which there is nothing vegetiue, but a few solitary Palmes. **1642** H. MORE *Song Soul* II. i. xlvii, That full grasp of vast Eternitie 'Longs not to beings simply vegetive. **1657** TOMLINSON *Renou's Disp.* 41 Such as are alwayes vegetive and juicy. **1700** DRYDEN *Pal. & Arc.* III. 1076 So man, at first a Drop, dilates with Heat, .. First vegetive, then feels, and reasons last. **1700** —— *Ovid's Met.* I. 751 The Tree still panted in the unfinish'd part, Not wholly vegetive, and heav'd her Heart.

†**b.** Of the soul: = VEGETATIVE *a.* 1 a. *Obs.*

a **1623** PEMBLE *Justification* (1629) 196 The Vegetiue soule whereby Plants liue.

c. Covered with or productive of vegetation.

1855 BAILEY *Mystic* 68 Ocean and continent, sea, desert, plain Mineral and vegetive.

d. Leading a merely physical existence. Cf. VEGETATIVE *a.* 6.

1882 SYMONDS *Animi Figura* 111 Shall these arise winged by immortal mind, Who toiled on earth obscure and vegetive?

B. *sb.* = VEGETATIVE *sb.* 2, VEGETABLE *sb.* 2.

Common in the 17th c.

1602 WARNER *Alb. Eng.* XIII. lxxvi. (1612) 316 Nor lesse the only Vegitiues, as trees, fruits, herbes, and such. *a* **1640** MASSINGER *Old Law* I. i, Make us better then those vegetives Whose soules die within em. **1678** T. P[ORTER] *Fr. Conjurer* I. 8 Have you not already eat about three parts of a Pilchard, besides a dish of Vegetives? **1689** PLUNKET *Char. Good Commander*, etc. 55 The Sun to Plants more welcome is .. Thus they of Vegetives might learn some good. **1819** H. BUSK *Banquet* III. 479 In snug retreat this vegetive [i.e. a mushroom] demure, From human reach long deem'd itself secure.

vege'tivorous, *a.* [Irreg. f. the stem *veget-* after *herbivorous*, etc.] Feeding on vegetables or plants.

1859 *Todd's Cycl. Anat.* V. 304/1 The true vegetivorous genera [of marsupials] have a cæcum which is thrice as long as the body. **1881** *Nature* XXIII. 406/1 Vegetivorous snails (*Lymnaeus*) eating young newts.

'vegetizing, *ppl. a.* [f. as prec.] Vegetarian.

1857 *Tait's Mag.* XXIV. 6 Those vegetising friends, whose finer feelings are said to be distressed horribly at the smell of hot joints.

vegeto- ('vɛdʒɪtəʊ), irregular combining form of the L. stem *veget-*, used in the sense of 'vegetable and ..' or 'having a vegetable origin'. **a.** With adjs., as ***vegeto-alkaline***, ***-animal***, ***-bituminous***, ***-carbonaceous***, ***-mineral***, ***-sulphuric***, etc.

Cf. F. *végéto-animal*, *-minéral*, *-sulfurique*.

1833 *Penny Cycl.* I. 80/1 The *vegeto-alkaline acetates .. are decomposed. **1799** ANDERSON *Recreations* I. 267 Hairs, spines, feathers, &c., are all *vegeto-animal productions. **1842** LOUDON *Suburban Hort.* 65 Composts of vegetable or vegeto-animal matter and earth are of various kinds. **1876** tr. *Schützenberger's Fermentation* 34 The matter which decomposes sugar is a vegeto-animal substance. **1796** KIRWAN *Elem. Min.* (ed. 2) II. 40 By Inflammable substances I understand all those of Mineral Origin whose principal character is Inflammability. .. Of these the simplest kinds may be reduced to six Genera, namely the Aeriform, the Bituminous, Carbonaceous, *Vegeto-Carbonaceous, *Vegeto-Bituminous, and the Sulphureous. **1776** PERCIVAL *Ess.* III. 247 Each ounce, therefore, of the *vegeto-mineral water contains only four tenths of a grain of this metal. **1785** *Med. Comm.* II. 31 A poultice with Goulard's vegeto mineral extract had been .. prescribed. **1857** BULLOCK tr. *Cazeaux's Midwifery* 25 Some of the vegeto-mineral lotions are usually sufficient to cause their [i.e. carbuncles] disappearance. **1838** T. THOMSON *Chem. Org. Bodies* 654 Some *vegeto-sulphuric acid is formed at the same time.

b. With sbs., as ***vegeto-alkali***, ***-alkaloid***, ***-mineral***, ***-principle***, ***-veratrine***, etc.

1830 LINDLEY *Nat. Syst. Bot.* 205 Dr. Sertürner has obtained some other *vegeto-alkalies from Cinchona. **1844** FOWNES *Chem.* 478 The vegeto-alkalis, or alkaloids, constitute a remarkable, and at present isolated, group of bodies. *c* **1865** J. WYLDE in *Circ. Sci.* I. 416/1 An account of the vegeto-alkalies. **1887** A. M. BROWN *Anim. Alkaloids* 60 The means of distinguishing the *vegeto-alkaloid. **1839** URE *Dict. Arts* 40 The most interesting fact relative to this *vegeto-mineral is its geological position. **1830** *Amer. Jrnl. Sci.* XVII. 385 M. Dulong has obtained a particular *vegeto-principle from the roots of *Plumbago Europæa*. **1887** A. M. BROWN *Anim. Alkaloids* 59 The *vegeto-veratrine does not reduce the ferricyanide.

†**vegetous**, *a. Obs.* [f. L. *veget-us* VEGETE: see -OUS.] = VEGETE *a.*

1609 B. JONSON *Sil. Wom.* II. ii, If shee be faire, yong, and vegetous. *a* **1670** HACKET *Cent. Serm.* (1675) 422 A vegetous faith is able to say unto a mountain, Be removed into the sea. **1696** WHISTON *The. Earth* IV. (1722) 351 The Seeds of those Vegetables which God originally Created were fresh and vegetous.

veȝer, southern ME. var. FAIR *a.*

vegie ('vɛdʒɪ), Also veggie. Colloq. abbrev. of *vegetable*. Usu. *pl.* Cf. VEG.

1955 C. BROWN *Lost Girls* xii. 132, I did get a job for myself, selling vegies at a stall in the market. **1966** [see KINDY]. **1973** *Philadelphia Inquirer* (Today Suppl.) 14 Oct. 8/3 Sushi rice (rice and vegies wrapped in seaweed). **1976** *New Yorker* 8 Mar. 28/3 They wash and chop veggies and hand them out at the right time to the right people. **1983** *Chicago Sun-Times* 27 Aug. (Guide) 83 Also included, a fresh veggie and .. a carafe of one of eight wines of your choice. **1984** *Grass Roots* (N.Z.) Feb. 8/2 The vegie gardens are fenced.

vegit, obs. f. VEGETE *a.*

Vegliote (vɛl'jɒt). Also Vegliot, Veliote. [f. *Veglia* + -OTE.] An extinct dialect of Dalmatian, formerly spoken on the island of Veglia (now called Krk) off the Dalmatian coast of Yugoslavia.

1910 *Encycl. Brit.* XIV. 891/2 The Vegliote dialect is the last remnant of a language which some long time ago extended .. along the Dalmatian coast. **1933** Veliote [see DALMATIAN *sb.* and *a.* 2]. **1960** W. D. ELCOCK *Romance Lang.* i. 163 Lat. *mensa*, attested as *mesa* .. is also found in Rheto-Romance .. and in Vegliote (*maisa*). **1974** *Encycl. Brit. Macropædia* XV. 1038/1 Romanian, Vegliot, Spanish, and perhaps Rhaetian show similar developments in all accented syllables. **1984** *Trans. Philol. Soc.* 20 Vegliot is a 'dead' language once spoken on the island of Veglia (Krk) off the Jugoslav coast.

vehemence ('viːɪməns, 'viːhɪməns). Also 6 -ens. [a. late OF. *vehemence* (F. *véhémence*), or ad. L. *vehementia*: see next.

'In this and the related words the only pron. recognized by dictionaries, with the exception of the most recent, is that with ('viːh-); this is now unusual in Britain, but appears to be still the standard pron. in the United States.'—N.E.D.]

1. Intensity or strength *of* smell or colour. *rare.*

1535 COVERDALE *2 Macc.* ix. 10 Him might no man now abyde ner beare, for the vehemence of styncke. **1844** HOOD *Haunted Ho.* III. xvii, The Bloody Hand shone strangely out With vehemence of colour!

2. Impetuosity, great force or violence, of physical action or agents.

1542 BOORDE *Dyetary* xxxv. (1870) 297 The dust also that ryseth in the strete thorow the vehemens of the wynde. **1667** MILTON *P.L.* II. 954 A universal hubbub wilde Of stunning sounds and voices all confus'd..assaults his eare With loudest vehemence. **1756** BURKE *Subl. & B.* IV. iii, His eyes are dragged inwards, and rolled with great vehemence. **1794** R. J. SULIVAN *View Nat.* I. 148 The action, by which a body is deprived of phlogiston by means of pure air, with such vehemence as to generate not only heat but flame. **1857** MILLER *Elem. Chem., Org.* 49 Owing to the feebler affinities of these elements, the reactions take place with less vehemence.

3. Great or excessive ardour, eagerness, or fervour of personal feeling or action; passionate force, violence, or excitement.

1529 MORE *Dyaloge* Wks. 265/2 By waye of excesse & yperbole, to declare the vehemence of his mynde in the matter of fayth. **1600** SHAKS. *A.Y.L.* III. ii. 200 Nay, I pre'thee now, with most petitionary vehemence, tell me who it is. **1651** HOBBES *Leviath.* I. viii. 35 Sometimes the hurt.. is caused by the vehemence, or long continuance of the Passion. **1699** BURNET *39 Art.* i. 27 Passion produces a Vehemence of Action. **1748** *Anson's Voy.* III. x. 544 Hypocrisy and fraud are often not less mischievous..than impetuosity and vehemence of temper. **1769** *Junius Lett.* xxxv. (1778) 187 You measure their affections by the vehemence of their expressions. **1839** DICKENS *Nickleby* xii, With all the vehemence that his indignant and excited feelings could bring to bear upon it. **1839** FR. A. KEMBLE *Resid. in Georgia* (1863) 29 With an almost savage vehemence of gesticulation. **1874** GREEN *Short Hist.* vii. §1. 347 Cromwell..was quick to profit by the vehemence of the Catholic reaction.

b. An instance of this. *rare.*

1748 RICHARDSON *Clarissa* (1811) I. 33 Is it possible that my brother and sister could make their very failings, their vehemences, of such importance to all the family?

vehemency ('viːɪmənsɪ, 'viːhɪ-). Now *rare.* Also 6 -entie, 6–7 -encie. [ad. L. *vehementia*, f. *vehement-* VEHEMENT *a.*: see -ENCY. Cf. prec., and Sp. and Pg. *vehemencia*, It. *veemenza.*]

1. = VEHEMENCE 3 and 3 b.

1538 TONSTALL *Serm. Palm Sund.* (1823) 51 The greatness and vehemency..of his fayth. **1579** FULKE *Refut. Rastel* 735 He..excuseth them, by vehemency of desire. **1598** SHAKS. *Merry W.* II. ii. 247 Would it apply well to the vehemency of your affection that I should win what you would enioy? **1612** T. TAYLOR *Comm. Titus* iii. 8 He could not satisfie himselfe in his vehemencie against such a doctrine as this was. **1665** GLANVILL *Def. Van. Dogm.* 74 That which excites men to endless brawlings, and altercations; Schisms, Heresies, and Rebellions, by the vehemencies of Dispute. **1671** WOODHEAD *St. Teresa* II. ii. 92 The vehemency of the Spirit, if Nature be feeble, draws it inward, and masters it. **1753–4** RICHARDSON *Grandison* xxii. (1781) III. 211 Well do I know the vehemency with which you are wont to pursue a new adventure.

b. *esp.* Of utterance or expression.

1542–5 BRINKLOW *Lament.* (1874) 91 God shall rayse other that shall speake..with no lesse loue & vehemency. **1568** GRAFTON *Chron.* II. 97 Polidore..wryteth very vehemently against him in his History, which vehemency or fonde malice I thought meete..to suppresse. **1613** SHAKS. *Hen. VIII*, v. i. 148 The best perswasions to the contrary Faile not to vse, and with what vehemencie Th'occasion shall instruct you. **1679** PRANCE *Narr. Popish Plot* 28 Which he pronounced with a great deal of vehemency and earnestness. **1760–72** H. BROOKE *Fool of Qual.* (1809) III. 148 [He] exclaimed with some vehemency, Never, never did I behold such beauty. **1830** J. MILNE *Widow & Her Son* iv. (1851) 232 You'll learn henceforth to chide with far less vehemency. **1845** LD. CAMPBELL *Chancellors* xlvii. (1857) II. 314 All these speeches were spoken with great vehemency.

2. Intensity or severity: **a.** Of pain, illness, etc.

1543 TRAHERON *Vigo's Chirurg.* II. i. 13 That the payne, and the accidens encrease not, nor diminische, but contynue in great vehementie. **1558** BP. WATSON *Sev. Sacram.* xxx. 193 Doo not differre this tyl the vehemencie of your sickenes decaye your speache and memorie. **1612** WOODALL *Surg. Mate* Wks. (1653) 359 According to the strength of the sick, and vehemency of the disease. **1642** R. CARPENTER *Experience* II. vii. 173 No man ever endured such rage, and vehemencie of pain. **1656** J. SMITH *Pract. of Physick* 146 A Pestilent Feaver differs from the Plague by the vehemency of the mischief and contagion.

b. Of cold, heat, or other influences.

1594 T. B. *La Primaud. Fr. Acad.* II. 109 Humour refresheth heate, and slaketh the vehemencie thereof. **1596** DALRYMPLE tr. *Leslie's Hist. Scot.* I. 259 The Podagra or Gout, quhilk of the Vehemencie of calde he contracted. **1604** E. G[RIMSTONE] *D'Acosta's Hist. Indies* II. vii. 96 The vehemencie of the fire forceth and driveth vp an aboundance of vapours. **1651** WITTIE tr. *Primrose's Pop. Err.* 309 Which if it were Hippocrates his opinion notwithstanding the vehemency of his remedies [etc.]. **1725** *Fam. Dict.* s.v. *Flower*, On these they hang a Piece of Cloth, which.. defends 'em from the Vehemency of its [*sc.* the sun's] Rays. **1815** SCOTT *Guy M.* iv, Those farther rules by which diviners pretend to ascertain the vehemency of this evil direction.

3. = VEHEMENCE 2.

1555 EDEN *Decades* (Arb.) 120 The vehemencie of the wynde is not of poure to caste downe those houses. **1569** STOCKER tr. *Diod. Sic.* III. ix. 118 Many Barques..with the vehemencie of the wether were runne on lande. **1609** BIBLE (Douay) *Deut.* xxviii. 49 In likenes of an eagle that flieth with vehemencie. **1668** CULPEPPER & COLE *Barthol. Anat.* II. vi. 105 It is continually forced along with Celerity and Vehemency.

b. Used of sounds.

1555 EDEN *Decades* (Arb.) 84 The earth trembeled through the vehemencie of theyr owtcry. **1632** LITHGOW *Trav.* x. 439 Least the vehemency of chirking frogs vexe the wish'd-for Repose of his..body.

4. = VEHEMENCE 1. *rare*$^{-1}$.

1565 COOPER *Thesaurus*, *Vehementia odoris*, the vehemencie of, &c.

vehement (viːɪmənt), viːhɪmənt), *a.* (and *adv.*) Also 6 *Sc.* **viement.** [a. OF. *vehement* (F. *véhément*, = Sp. and Pg. *vehemente*, It. *veemente*), or ad. L. *vehement-*, *vehemens* violent, impetuous, etc., usually regarded as f. *vehe-* (= *vē-* in *vēcors*) lacking, wanting + *mens* mind.]

I. 1. Intense, severe; rising to a high degree or pitch: **a.** Of pain, illness, etc.

1485 *St. Wenefryde* (Caxton) 12 The languour and maladye was vehement and encreaced dayly. **1555** EDEN *Decades* (Arb.) 148 Vaschus..fell into a vehement feuer by reason of excesse of labour. **1563** T. GALE *Antidot.* II. 39 It doeth also cease vehement dolour and payne. **1653** W. RAMESEY *Astrol. Restored* 325 [A] Comet..signifieth.. vehement sicknesses. **1725** N. ROBINSON *Th. Physick* 268, I order'd the following Mixture to be externally apply'd to his Side..while his Pain was very vehement. **1804** ABERNETHY *Surg. Obs.* 96 Vehement erysipelatous or irritative inflammation took place.

b. Of heat or cold, etc.

1554 W. PRAT *Discript. Aphrique* C viii b, The earthe..is made hote in a lytle space by the vehemente heate of the ayre. **1576** NEWTON *Lemnie's Complex.* (1633) 62 The fire is vehementer, and the hearth is of heat sometime extreme, sometime more soft and milde. **1609** C. BUTLER *Fem. Mon.* (1623) R 3, The Snow..causeth them presently to fall, and with his vehement cold to rise no more. **1666** BOYLE *Orig. Forms & Qual.* 320 Salt of Tartar requires a vehement fire to flux it. **1796** H. HUNTER tr. *St.-Pierre's Stud. Nat.* (1799) I. 564 The action of the Sun would there have been too vehement.

2. Of natural forces: Operating with great strength or violence; *esp.* of wind, blowing very strongly or violently.

1531 ELYOT *Gov.* I. ii, The bees may issue out of theyr stalles without peryll of rayne or vehement wynde. **1563** FULKE *Meteors* (1640) 30 When the lightning is not vehement. **1579** *Reg. Privy Council Scot.* III. 242 Aganis sa suddane and viement ane storm. **1613** PURCHAS *Pilgrimage* (1614) 832 The Land..would be violently hot, if a fresh easterly breeze did not coole it with vehement breath in the heat of the day. **1625** in Ellis *Orig. Lett.* Ser. I. III. 196 The barge-windows, notwithstanding the vehement shower, were open. *a* **1701** MAUNDRELL *Journ. Jerus.* (1732) 9 The Rain was so vehement. **1728** MORGAN *Algiers* II. v. 299 The succeeding vehement Deluges of Rain rendered their Incampment superlatively comfortless. **1837** BARHAM *Ingol. Leg.* Ser. I. *Look at Clock*, Like a Weather-cock whirled by a vehement puff, David turned himself round.

b. In general use: Strong and rapid.

1732 ARBUTHNOT *Rules of Diet* in *Aliments*, etc. 317 Violent Sweats proceed from a Laxity of the Vessels and too vehement a Circulation of the Blood.

c. Of sound: Excessively loud.

1752 H. WALPOLE *Lett.* (1846) II. 415 The two Gunnings, who have made so vehement a noise.

3. Of actions: Characterized by great physical exertion; performed with unusual force or violence.

1531 ELYOT *Gov.* I. xvi, By exercise, whiche is a vehement motion,..the helthe of man is preserued, and his strength increased. **1574** NEWTON *Health Mag.* 6 Those persons.. may use vehementer exercise and stronger ambulations. *c* **1650** *Don Bellianis* 34 With such vehement vigour he assaulted his foes, that his men regained their lost advantage. **1824** W. IRVING *T. Trav.* I. 191 At the close of each stanza a hearty roar, and a vehement thrumming on the table. **1833** HT. MARTINEAU *Manch. Strike* 92 The clapping ..was twice as long and twice as vehement as usual. **1873** M. ARNOLD *Lit. & Dogma* 309 Who that observes this delighted adoption of vehement rites..can doubt, that [etc.].

transf. **1638** JUNIUS *Paint. Ancients* 12 They must secondly, consider what a vehement efficacy there is in man's wit. **1758** JOHNSON *Idler* No. 1 ⁋11 These vehement exertions of intellect cannot be frequent. **1865** TROLLOPE *Belton Est.* v. 53 The woman was making a vehement effort to speak in her natural voice.

†4. Of remedies, etc.: Having a powerful effect upon the system. *Obs.*

1541 R. COPLAND *Galyen's Terap.* 2 E iij, All the body muste be emptyed..or that any partye be take subiecte to the stronge and vehement remedyes. **1562** BULLEIN *Bulwarke, Bk. Simples* (1579) 5 b, The longe Onion is more vehementer then the rounde, and the Redde more then the white. **1607** TOPSELL *Four-f. Beasts* 691 The gall of swine is not very vehement. **1612** WOODALL *Surg. Mate* Wks. (1653) 199 In the beginning over vehement warmings are to be avoided. **1656** J. SMITH *Pract. Physick* 96 The juyce of wild Cucumber is not so vehement as they commonly report.

†b. Of taste: Strong, pungent. *Obs.*

1600 J. PORY tr. *Leo's Africa* Introd. 42 Being in shape somewhat like to the Millet of Italy, but of a most vehement and firy tast.

†c. Vivid; intensely bright. *Obs.*

1635 SWAN *Spec. M.* v. §2 (1643) 131 These colours in some rain-bows are more vehement or apparent. **1692** RAY *Creation* (ed. 2) II. 25 Preserving the Eye from being injured by too vehement and lucid an Object.

II. 5. a. Of suspicion or likelihood: Very strong. Now *arch.*

1516 *Acts Parl. Scot.* (1875) XII. 36/2 All Lawis excludis þe said governour fra administracion and governance for suspicioun vehement and violent. **1565** in Ellis *Orig. Lett.* Ser. I. II. 208 The Quenes howsbande beinge entred into a vehement suspicion of David. **1586** A. DAY *Eng. Secretary* II. (1625) 20 Notwithstanding all those vehement likelihoods, yet I will not condemne you till I see how you confute me. **1610** DONNE *Pseudo-martyr* 342 From your Syluester wee learne, That the Popes precepts binde not, where there is vehement likelyhood of trouble or scandall. **1811** SOUTHEY in *Life A. Bell* (1844) II. 644 Mrs. Trimmer's book..I much wish to see, having a vehement suspicion that some parts of it have been misrepresented.

†b. Of proof, etc.: Strong, forcible, cogent; capable of producing conviction. *Obs.*

1530 TINDALE *Wks.* (Parker Soc. 1848) 428 There is not a better, vehementer, or mightier thing to make a man understand..than an allegory. **1561** T. NORTON *Calvin's Inst.* I. 33 And these vehement demonstrations twice repeted suffer it to be drawen no other where but to Christ. **1576** FLEMING *Panopl. Epist.* 61 The valliantnesse, constancie, and sobernesse of your person, then which nothing can be more vehement and patheticall. **1731** CHANDLER tr. *Limborchi's Hist. Inquis.* II. 215 When these Proofs are vehement or sufficient for the Torture, it is left for the Judge to determine.

†c. Very close or intimate. *Obs.*$^{-1}$

1596 BACON *Max. & Use Com. Law* xiv. (1630) 59 The law is more strong in that case, because of the vehement relation which the enrolment hath to the time of the bargaine and sale.

6. Of thoughts, feelings, etc.: Extremely strong or deep; ardent, eager, passionate.

1526 *Pilgr. Perf.* (W. de W. 1531) 233 Meditacyon is a vehement or a huge goostly applicacion of the mynde. **1560** DAUS tr. *Sleidane's Comm.* 328 The Phisitions..judged by and by the disase to come of a vehement thought. **1574** tr. *Marlorat's Apocalips* 8 It is a salutation or greeting full of vehement and hartie good wil. **1604** T. WRIGHT *Passions* v. §3. 177 The vehementer passion venteth forth the liuelier action. **1651** HOBBES *Leviath.* I. vi. 27 Weeping..is caused by such accidents, as suddenly take away some vehement hope. **1711** ADDISON *Spect.* No. 73 ⁋5 The Passion for Praise, which is so very vehement in the Fair Sex. **1775** DE LOLME *Eng. Const.* Adv. (1784) p. xix, Influenced by vehement prepossessions. **1812** CARY *Dante, Parad.* v. 107 Vehement desire Possess'd me. **1846** H. ROGERS *Ess.* (1874) I. iv. 162 Leibnitz..began to tell his beads with vehement devotion. **1907** *Verney Mem.* I. 62 The Queen's vehement partisanship.

b. Of anger or similar feelings: Violent; intense.

a **1548** HALL *Chron., Edw. IV* (1550) 50 b, Ye olde rancor betwene them beyng newly reuiued (The which betwene no creatures can be more vehement then betwene bretherne). **1552** HULOET, Vehement anger, *excandescentia.* **1659** HAMMOND *On Ps.* cii. 503 By those is meant a vehement displeasure and anger.

7. Of language: Very forcibly or passionately uttered or expressed; resulting from, and indicative of, strong feeling or excitement.

1533 *Chron. Calais* (Camden) 114 The French kynges mother with very ardente and vehemente wordes sayd [etc.]. **1560** DAUS tr. *Sleidane's Comm.* 176 b, Aboute this time came forth..a boke of Martin Luthers very vehement. **1596** *Edw. III*, I. ii, Sharpely to solicit With vehement sute the king in my behalfe. **1628** DONNE *6 Serm.* 56 In that remarkable and vehement place where he expostulates with them. *a* **1700** EVELYN *Diary* 12 Feb. 1683, A vehement speech he made about the compositions. **1734** tr. *Rollin's Anc. Hist.* VIII. vii. IV. 40 That lively and vehement eloquence which like a torrent bears down all things on its way. **1836** THIRLWALL *Greece* xi. II. 80 The Corinthian deputy Sosicles, in vehement language, remonstrated with the Spartans on their inconsistency. **1848** W. H. KELLY tr. *L. Blanc's Hist. Ten Y.* II. 92 He..replies with the most vehement protestations of gratitude and fidelity.

8. Of persons, their character, etc.: Acting, or tending to act, in a manner displaying passion or excitement.

1560 DAUS tr. *Sleidane's Comm.* 29 b, I confess to have been more vehement then became me. **1575–85** ABP. SANDYS *Serm.* (1841) 194 Vehement therefore and zealous must we be for the house of God. **1602** MARSTON *Ant. & Mel.* I. Wks. 1856 I. 15 Vouchsafe me, then, your hush't observances, Vehement in pursuite of strange novelties. **1609** BIBLE (Douay) *Ezekiel* xxxviii. 15 Thou and manie peoples with thee,..a great companie, and a vehement armie. **1791** COWPER *Odyss.* xv. 254 Summon thy crew on board, Ere my arrival notice give of thine To the old King; for vehement I know His temper. **1847** JAMES *J. Marston Hall* ix, My nature was too quick and vehement to take pleasure in vice without passion. **1848** CLOUGH *Amours de Voy.* II. 293 For the woman..Ever prefers the audacious, the wilful, the vehement hero. **1876** MOZLEY *Univ. Serm.* xiii. 237 The Pharisees were scrupulous, exact, vehement, and eager, about everything connected with religion.

9. Of debate, strife, etc.: Characterized by great heat or bitterness.

1620 BEDELL *Lett.* 26, I would to Christ that of all other Controuersies this were the vehementest betweene vs. **1665** MANLEY *Grotius' Low C. Wars* 93 Nor by this was the Warre lessened, onely it was delayed, and not vehement enough for the time. **1844** THIRLWALL *Greece* VIII. 135 This..was a sufficiently difficult undertaking,..in which he had to expect powerful and vehement opposition. **1847** HARRIS *Life Ld. Hardwicke* III. xii. 44 A very vehement debate took place in the House of Lords. **1903** W. BRIGHT *Age of Fathers* I. v. 70 The dissension caused by Arianism became daily more vehement.

III. †10. *Sc.* As *adv.* = VEHEMENTLY *adv. Obs.*

1549 *Compl. Scot.* vi. 52 The tua vintirs that thai hef ar nocht verray vehement cald. *a* **1578** LINDESAY (Pitscottie) *Chron. Scot.* (S.T.S.) I. 407 He became so vehement seik that no man had hope of his lyffe. **1596** DALRYMPLE tr.

Leslie's Hist. Scot. II. 10 Althoch the king prudentlie dissemblet, thay knew him to be vehement angrie.

vehemently ('viːɪməntlɪ, 'viːhɪ-), *adv.* [f. prec.]

1. To a very great extent; in a very high degree. Now *rare*.

a **1513** Fabyan *Chron.* vii. (1811) 460 In Fraunce this yere the people dyed..so vehemently that in the cytie of Parys dyed..ouer I.M. people. **1563** T. Gale *Antidot.* ii. 18 This [unguent]..taketh awaye superfluous fleshe, and doth vehemently excicate and drie. **1586** A. Day *Eng. Secretary* i. (1625) 46 Two onely that were the conveyers of him, sickned vehemently, and one of them died. **1658** A. Fox *Würtz' Surg.* ii. iv. 56 Vomiting is not very dangerous.. unless it hold the Patient vehemently. **1695** Ld. Preston *Boeth.* iv. 172 Whom Wickedness, the most extreme Evil, doth not only affect, but even vehemently infect. **1753** *Chambers' Cycl.* Suppl. s.v. *Womb*, This tumour returned again, and..in three days it became vehemently enraged. **1858** Carlyle *Fredk. Gt.* ii. ii. (1872) I. 54 Preussen was a vehemently Heathen country.

b. Used with reference to suspicion: cf. prec. 5 a.

1533 More *Debell. Salem* Wks. 981/1 Such thinges..as maketh him not slightly but very vehemently suspected. **1588** J. Udall *Demonstr. Discipline* (Arb.) 76 One..that is vehemently suspected, to haue haynously offended. **1621** Bp. Mountagu *Diatribæ* 289 It will be very vehemently suspected that he is Antichrist indeed. **1684** *Lond. Gaz.* No. 1938/4 He is vehemently suspected to be concerned in these Robberies and Burglaries following. **1821** Southey *Lett.* (1856) III. 233 Mr. Wilson's letter..having led me vehemently to suspect that the document which impeached his character was an invention of his wife's.

2. a. With strong or violent language; in a manner showing strong feeling or excitement.

1545 Brinklow *Compl.* xx. 42 Marke what, and how vehemently the Holy Gost speakyth here in the prophete. **1568** Grafton *Chron.* II. 97 Polidore had no good opinion of king John, and therfore wryteth very vehemently against him in his History. **1612** in *10th Rep. Hist. MSS. Comm.* App. I. 610 The Deputies of the Religion have very vehemently protested against these proceedings. **1665** Glanvill *Scepsis Sci.* Addr. p. xi, Reckoning it a great instance of Piety and devout Zeal, vehemently to declaim against Reason and Philosophy. *a* **1721** Prior *Cromwell & Porter* 116 Wks. 1907 II. 265, I did actually fight in the field, Preached loudly in the Church, and talked vehemently in the Parliament. **1756** Burke *Vind. Nat. Soc.* Wks. 1808 I. 60, I could shew how vehemently they have contended for names. **1839** Fr. A. Kemble *Resid. in Georgia* (1863) 14 The slave-owners..insist vehemently upon the mental and physical inferiority of the blacks.

b. With strong or intense feeling; ardently, eagerly.

1560 Daus tr. *Sleidane's Comm.* 329 Wherewith being wehemently moued,..he began more and more to be confirmed. **1576** Fleming *Panopl. Epist.* 54 It was alwayes of me maruellous vehemently and earnestly desiered. **1642** R. Carpenter *Experience* ii. iii. 141 Doe you think his heart is not vehemently prompted to Deifie his saint? **1682** Burnet *Rights Princes* ii. 36 That they did vehemently, and out of all measure aspire to that Chair. *Ibid.* iv. 112 Against this, the Zeal of some Bishops appeared vehemently. **1753–4** Richardson *Grandison* IV. vii. 54 For a week together she was vehemently intent upon visiting England. **1817** Jas. Mill *Brit. India* II. iv. viii. 277 It requires a high degree of improbability to prevent the greater part of mankind from believing what they vehemently wish.

3. With violence or impetuosity.

1538 Elyot, *Perflo*, to blowe vehemently or strongly. *a* **1578** Lindesay (Pitscottie) *Chron. Scot.* (S.T.S.) I. 312 Ane blast of eistrene winde..raissit the flame of fyre sa wehementlie that it blew wpoun the freir that accussit him. **1611** Bible *Luke* vi. 48 When the flood arose, the streame beat vehemently vpon that house. **1666** in *Verney Mem.* (1907) II. 257 The fire broke out vehemently again last night. *a* **1796** Waterhouse in Morse *Amer. Geog.* I. 500 We see the mineral water boiling vehemently like a pot over the fire. **1821** W. Irving *Sketch Bk.* I. 57 He was observed to smoke his pipe vehemently.

'vehementness. [f. as prec.] = vehemence.

1561 T. Norton *Calvin's Inst.* iii. 280 The same ought to be asked with no lesse feruentnes and vehementnesse of desire. **1571** Golding *Calvin on Ps.* iv. 2 Both the vehementnesse of his grefe, & the earnestnesse of his praying. **1600** Surflet *Countrie Farme* iii. lxxxiv. 625 Tainted with some ill smell..gotten through the vehementnes of the fire. **1674** R. Godfrey *Inj. & Ab. Physic* 99 The blame is impos'd on the too vehementness of the Disease, when the Doctor is often more in fault.

vehicle ('viːɪk(ə)l, 'viːhɪk(ə)l), *sb.* Also 7 vehickle. [ad. F. *véhicule* (= Sp. and Pg. *vehiculo*, It. *veiculo*, *veicolo*) or L. *vehiculum*, f. *vehĕre* to carry.

On the pronunciation see the note to vehemence.]

I. 1. A substance, *esp.* a liquid, serving as a means for the readier application or use of another substance mixed with it or dissolved in it: **a.** *Med.* A medium of a suitable kind in which strong or unpalatable drugs or medicines are administered.

1612 Woodall *Surg. Mate* Wks. (1653) 303 Let all your Vehicles for your Medicines..be soft and pleasing to your Patients. **1658** A. Fox *Würtz' Surg.* iii. xix. 281 Let him have of the same pill in a convenient vehicle, of four grains. **1689** G. Harvey *Curing Dis. by Expect.* v. 34, I seldom give less than half a spoonful,..diluted with a sufficient measure of a temperate Vehicle. **1733** Cheyne *Eng. Malady* ii. iv. §4 (1734) 148 Mineral Chalybeat Waters..are the most agreeable and beneficial Vehicle for such Medicines. **1771** Percival *Ess.* (1777) I. 72 A sufficient dose of the medicine cannot be given on account of the heating nature of its vehicle. **1816** A. C. Hutchison *Pract. Obs. Surg.* (1826) 169 The Doctor..exhibited to him an ounce of castor-oil, uncovered by any vehicle. **1875** H. C. Wood *Therap.* (1879) 31 The dried petals..are almost destitute of therapeutic virtues, but their preparations are used as elegant vehicles.

fig. **1665** Boyle *Occas. Refl.* (1848) 19 Both these pleasing Vehicles, if I may so call them, and Correctives of Reproofs [etc.]. **1751** Johnson *Rambler* No. 87 ¶3 With what vehicles to disguise the catharticks of the soul. **1755** H. Walpole *Lett.* (1846) III. 181 The invasion..I really believe was dressed up for a vehicle (as the apothecaries call it) to make us swallow the treaties. **1844** Wardlaw *Prov.* (1869) II. 102 If we have a bitter..medicine to administer, we are desirous ..to convey it in a pleasant *vehicle*.

b. In general use.

1699 Evelyn *Acetaria* (1729) 149 There ought to be one of the Dishes, in which to beat and mingle the liquid Vehicles, and a second to receive the crude Herbs in. **1725** *Fam. Dict.* s.v. *Malt-Liquor*, The Substance of high dry'd Malts, which retain many fiery Particles in their Contexture, and are therefore best lost in a smooth Vehicle. **1831** J. Davies *Mat. Med.* 376 It is..soluble..in more than 2000 of cold water, and 9000 of this vehicle when boiling. **1901** *Brit. Med. Jrnl.* No. 2097. 39 When the crusts [of eczema] form, acid, salicyl., in a vehicle of olive oil, is useful.

c. *Painting.* A fluid (as water, oil, etc.) with which pigments are mixed for use.

1787 *Trans. Soc. Arts* V. 103 The well known disadvantages that Paintings in Oil lie under, have rendered the discovery of some other Vehicle an object of attentive enquiry. **1807** J. Opie in *Lect. Art* iv. (1848) 320 Colours.. little muddled by vehicles. **1859** Gullick & Timbs *Paint.* 202 The term 'vehicle', which is borrowed from pharmacy, is applied in art to the fluid employed to bring pigments into a proper working state. **1883** R. Haldane *Workshop Receipts* Ser. ii. 427/1 A perfect vehicle mixes readily with the pigment.

2. That which serves as a means of transmission, or as a material embodiment or manifestation, of something: **a.** With reference to matter or physical conditions.

1650 Bulwer *Anthropomet.* 117 Drink may not be only esteemed the Vehicle of aliment. **1683** Tryon *Way to Health* 265 To cleanse and purifie those grosser Excrements, the Vehickles (or Lodgings) of malignant Spirits. **1749** Fielding *Tom Jones* x. ii, As fa, la, la, ra, da, &c. are in music, only as the vehicles of sound, and without any fixed ideas. **1779** J. Moore *View Soc. Fr.* (1789) I. xxvii. 221 If the water be in reality the vehicle of this disease. **1813** Sir H. Davy *Agric. Chem.* (1814) 239 Water, as it is the vehicle of the nourishment of the plant, is the substance principally given off by the leaves. **1841** Myers *Cath. Th.* iii. §14. 52 There is a considerable portion of all natural food..serving rather for the vehicle than for the substance of our support. **1874** Carpenter *Ment. Phys.* i. i. (1879) 3 That more advanced Philosophy of the present day, which regards Matter merely as the vehicle of Force.

b. In other contexts.

1786 Mme. D'Arblay *Diary* 8 Aug., To receive a favour through the vehicle of insolent ostentation—no! no! **1796** Morse *Amer. Geog.* I. 297 They viewed the tea as a vehicle of an unconstitutional tax. **1870** Dale *Week-day Serm.* ii. 51 Making the very form of Christian forgiveness the vehicle of revenge. **1876** Geo. Eliot *Dan. Der.* IV. lix. 183 It is.. possible to feel gratitude even where we discern a mistake that may have been injurious, the vehicle of the mistake being an affectionate intention prosecuted through a lifetime of kindly offices.

c. A substance employed as a material in or on which some work is executed.

1837 Hallam *Hist. Lit.* i. i. §58 The more extended use of paper as the vehicle of writing instead of parchment. **1850** Mrs. Jameson *Leg. Monast. Ord.* 441 The whole [picture] has been significantly described as a 'parody of Divine love'. The vehicle, white marble,—its place in a Christian church, —enhance all its vileness.

3. a. A means or medium by which ideas or impressions are communicated or made known; a medium of expression or utterance.

a **1652** J. Smith *Sel. Disc.* iv. 123 A spiritual kind of vehicle, whereby corporeal impressions are transferred to the mind. **1709** T. Robinson *Vindic. Mosaick Syst.* Introd. 7 Philosophical Mythology..a more agreeable Vehicle, found out for the conveying to us the Truth and Reason of Things. **1762** in *10th Rep. Hist. MSS. Comm.* App. I. 347 It might not be improper to contradict it by some vehicle of the publick papers. **1836** Thirlwall *Greece* xii. II. 138 But a metrical vehicle did not so well suit Zeno's dialectic genius. **1887** Saintsbury *Hist. Elizab. Lit.* x. (1890) 378 Quarles was a kind of journalist to whom the vehicle of verse came more easily than the vehicle of prose.

b. Const. *of*.

1687 Dryden *Hind & P.* iii. 106 And alms are but the vehicles of pray'r. **1688** J. H. Stevenson *Mr. Bays* Pref. A 2, Rhyme (which he very Judiciously somewhere calls the Vehicle of Nonsense). **1751** Johnson *Rambler* No. 121 ¶14 Allegory is perhaps one of the most pleasing vehicles of instruction. **1781** Cowper *Charity* 625 Did charity prevail, the press would prove A vehicle of virtue, truth, and love. **1822** Hazlitt *Table-T.* Ser. ii. xv. (1869) 305 Music is not made the vehicle of poetry, but poetry of music. **1856** Merivale *Rom. Emp.* xxii. (1865) III. 40 In the common intercourse of life Greek became a fashionable vehicle of expression. **1885** Clodd *Myths & Dr.* i. iv. 77 The myths.. yielded themselves with ease as vehicles of new ideas.

c. Const. *to* or *for*.

1722 Wollaston *Relig. Nature* v. 123 Words seem to be as it were bodies or vehicles to the sense or meaning. **1753–4** Richardson *Grandison* I. xii. 67 You consider skill in Languages then as a Vehicle to Knowledge—Not I presume as Science itself. **1836** Thirlwall *Greece* xii. (1839) II. 141 It is extremely doubtful how far they were ever used as a vehicle for the exposition of theological doctrines differing from the popular creed. *c* **1850** Kingsley *Misc.* (1860) I. 385 Which makes it..a far better vehicle..for many forms of thought. **1877** Dowden *Shaks. Primer* iv. 45 In the same play, rhyme is often employed as a vehicle for generalising reflections.

d. In a metaphor, the literal meaning of the word or words used metaphorically, as distinct from the subject of the metaphor; the image or idea whose association with the subject constitutes the metaphor. Opp. tenor *sb.* 1 d.

1936, etc. [see tenor *sb.* 1 d]. **1957** S. Ullmann *Style in French Novel* vi. 214 It is an essential feature of a metaphor that there must be a certain distance between tenor and vehicle. Their similarity must be accompanied by a feeling of disparity. **1977** *Studies in Eng. Lit.: Eng. Number* (Tokyo) 36 In this metaphor, the tenor and vehicle are not expected to fit each other perfectly.

4. The form, the material or other shape, in which something spiritual is embodied or manifested.

Freq. *c* 1650–1700, esp. of the body in relation to the soul or spirit.

a **1652** J. Smith *Sel. Disc.* v. 176 The spiritual vehicle of the soul,..a kind of umbra or aërial mantle in which the soul wraps herself. **1670** *Moral State England* 121 When our souls are divested of their grosser vehicles. **1699** Burnet *39 Art.* i. 18 God being considered as the Supreme Light, this might lead men to worship the Sun as his chief Vehicle. **1756** T. Amory *J. Buncle* iv. (1770) 288 My friend is now present with his Saviour, beholding his glory, in a vehicle resembling the body of the Lord. **1773** *Cook's Voy.* (1784) II. iii. ix. 164 They speak of spirits being..not totally divested of those passions which actuated them when combined with material vehicles. **1836** I. Taylor *Phys. The. Another Life* i. (1847) 19 There is a spiritual body and another vehicle of human nature as well as a natural body.

II. 5. A material means, channel, or instrument, by which a substance or some property of matter (as sound or heat) is conveyed or transmitted from one point to another.

1615 H. Crooke *Body of Man* 80 The vmbilicall veine.. is the first of all the veines,..because it is the vehicle or conueigher of blood. **1660** Boyle *New Exp. Phys. Mech.* xvii. 120 If I thought your Lordship could..imagine that Light could be convey'd without..having (if I may so speak) a Body for its Vehicle. **1707** *Cur. in Husb. & Gard.* 39 He had observ'd..Pores or little Channels in..the Wood of different Trees... Some of these little Vehicles of Communication go from the bottom upwards. *Ibid.* 49 Fibres and little Vehicles that are in the Bodies of Plants. **1776** Burney *Hist. Music* (1789) I. 433 Pythagoras supposed the air to be the vehicle of sound. **1803** *Imison's Sci. & Art* (1822) I. 227 Air is the usual vehicle of Sound, but it is not absolutely essential. **1861** Buckle *Civiliz.* II. 499 The vapour..becomes another storehouse of heat, and a vehicle by which it is removed from the earth.

transf. **1783** Burke *Rep. Affairs of India* Wks. 1842 II. 18 Finding a great parliamentary corporation turned into a vehicle for remitting to England the private fortunes of those [etc.].

6. A means of conveyance provided with wheels or runners and used for the carriage of persons or goods; a carriage, cart, wagon, sledge, or similar contrivance.

1656 Blount *Glossogr.*, *Vehicle*, a Cart, Wain, Wagon, or Chariot. **1700** Collier *2nd Def. Short View* 56 You may take it in a Cart, or a Waggon, but..I think a Wheelbarrow may do; for the word Vehicle..will carry that sense. **1709** *Tatler* No. 32 ¶2 She calls her Chariot, Vehicle. **1749** Byrom *Rem.* (1857) ii. 486, I went with Mr. Freke, who had his vehicle there, to the King's Chapel. **1784** Johnson in *Boswell* 17 Nov., I staid at Oxford till Tuesday, and then came in the common vehicle easily to London. **1829** Lytton *Disowned* 28 The rumbling and jolting vehicle stopped at the door of a tavern in Holborn. **1856** Kane *Arctic Explor.* I. x. 113 The shortest, directly fastened to the sledge runner, as a means of guiding or suddenly arresting and turning the vehicle. **1872** Yeats *Techn. Hist. Comm.* 327 The direct effects of superior means of communication have been to create a better class of vehicles.

Comb. **1768** Tucker *Lt. Nat.* (1834) I. 493 Such a peculiar species of insanity as vehicle-madness must have been pointed at by everybody. **1843** *Zoologist* I. 36 Several vehicle-drivers tried to cut it down. **1890** *Daily News* 10 Dec. 3/6 The National Coach and Van Trade Union, which comprised the whole of the workers in the vehicle-building trades.

7. a. Any means of carriage, conveyance, or transport; a receptacle in which anything is placed in order to be moved.

1678 Butler *Hud.* iii. i. 1572 The Spirit hors'd him like a Sack, Upon the Vehicle, his Back. **1692** Bentley *Boyle Lect.* 220 Unless the æthereal matter be supposed to be carried about the sun like a vortex or whirlpool, as a vehicle to convey it and the rest of the planets. **1728** Morgan *Hist. Algiers* I. ii. 21 The Sunbeams are so fierce and scorching, that all the Water would, infallibly, be exhal'd thro' the Pores of those leathern Vehicles. **1774** Bryant *Mythol.* II. 407 It was a cup..in which Hercules passed the seas; and the same history is given of Helius, who was said to have traversed the ocean in the same vehicle. **1812** *Ann. Reg., Chron.* 120 The balloon descended... On a sudden, his crazy vehicle struck upon the roof of a house. **1815** *Ibid.* 4 His three sons fatally committed themselves to this treacherous vehicle [*sc.* a boat], in order to shoot wild-fowl. **1841** *Peter Parley's Ann.* II. 250 The show-woman now procured a lamp; and, fixing it in a proper vehicle, gradually lowered it to the bottom of the well. **1947** *N.Y. Times* 20 Mar. 3/1 The statement 'there is no defense against the atomic bomb'..assumes that this bomb is being carried by a vehicle at a velocity well in the supersonic range. *Ibid.*, V-2 type vehicles. **1973** *Sci. Amer.* Feb. 72/3 [They] mounted sensitive probes on a vehicle towed horizontally behind a ship. **1982** *Nature* 27 May 254/1 Vehicles carrying people, whether ships or aircraft, moving in an environment in which radar detection at long range is technically straightforward, have become exceedingly vulnerable to attack.

b. A space rocket, in relation to its (actual or intended) payload.

1959 *Daily Tel.* 13 Mar. 15/6 Black Knight is entirely a research vehicle and will never be manufactured into a weapon. **1967** *Technology Week* 20 Feb. 36/1 A satellite launched into an eight-hour orbit by an *Atlas-Agena* vehicle. **1983** *Chicago Sun-Times* 13 July 17 Last week, the Soviets proposed a sub-ceiling of 1,100 on MIRVed missiles and bombers within the over-all ceiling of 1,800 strategic nuclear delivery vehicles.

8. *fig.* A song, play, film, etc., that is intended or serves to display the actor (or performing artist) to the best advantage.

1863 *Illustrated Times* 15 Aug. 103/3 Then came.. Lady Gifford's quasi-comedy of '*Finesse*', which.. simply served as a vehicle for some of Mr. Buckstone's practical drolleries and preposterous costumes. **1868** in P. Bailey *Leisure & Class in Victorian Society* (1978) vii. 152 A good song must be written, not for its own sake, but for that of the singer... It must simply be a vehicle. **1922** *N.Y. Times* 16 Oct. 20/2 Charles Ray is back on Broadway—his vehicle being 'A Tailor Made Man', and his stopping place for a week the Strand Theatre. **1928** MRS. P. CAMPBELL *Let.* 19 Jan. in *B. Shaw & Mrs. Campbell* (1952) 264, I only saw it as a commonplace, ordinary and good sort of working vehicle, or whatever the right word or expression is for that kind of play. **1955** *Times* 16 Aug. 5/4 It might be as well to rule out at the beginning the 'vehicle' especially created to exploit the talents and personality of the individual actor. **1966** *Listener* 27 Jan. 131/1 If at the start of his career an actor can somehow gain acceptance from the critics, it is possible for him to go on and give a series of inadequate performances in low-calibre vehicles and still emerge with reputation intact. **1981** *Times* 2 July 10/6 Star names and vast budgets.. wedded to a limp vehicle, can destine a feature to oblivion.

9. *Comb.*, as ***vehicle-park***; ***vehicle-actuated*** adj.; **vehicle-mile**, a distance of one mile travelled by one vehicle, used as a statistical unit; **vehicle mine**, a land-mine designed to destroy vehicles.

1937 *Times* 13 Apr. p. viii/1 With the wide adoption of electromatic vehicle-actuated traffic lights of recent years, complaints of unnecessary delay at signal-controlled crossings have been much dispelled. **1967** *Gloss. Highway Engin. Terms (B.S.I.)* 62 *Vehicle actuated traffic signals*, traffic signalling equipment in which the duration of the red and green signals and the time of the cycle vary in relation to the traffic flow into and through the controlled area. It is actuated by the traffic. **1964** *Times Rev. Industry* Feb. 36/2 The statistics of vehicle-miles travelled.. show that usage of light vans has, in fact, been steadily increasing faster than road transport in general. **1976** *New Yorker* 16 Feb. 68/2 About eighty per cent of highway use (measured in vehicle-miles) is auto travel. *a* **1944** K. DOUGLAS *Alamein to Zem Zem* (1946) xiv. 82 The verges of gaps in the road were mined with anti-personnel and vehicle mines. **1972** *Times* 27 Dec. 6/2 There had been almost no interference with road building, apart from the odd vehicle mine. **1940** Vehicle park [see *gun-park* s.v. GUN *sb.* 16 a]. **1976** *Cumberland News* 3 Dec. 11/6 (Advt.), Training hall and use of adjacent site as vehicle park at Parkhill Road, Kingstown, Carlisle.

vehicle ('viːɪk(ə)l, 'viːhɪ-), *v.* [f. prec.] *trans.* To place or convey in a vehicle. Chiefly in pa. pple.

a **1711** KEN *Hymns Evang.* Poet. Wks. 1721 I. 28 There the Babe's Soul is vehicled, said he; God must with perfect Man united be. **1717** FENTON *Poems* (1790) 38 When vehicled in flame, thou slow didst pass Prone through the gates of night. **1732** M. GREEN *Grotto* Wks. (1790) 251 O.. guard us through polemic life; From poison vehicled in praise. **1905** SALMOND *Relig. Quest. France* iii. 33 Helping to vehicle to heaven the praises of ransomed souls.

'vehicled, *a.* [f. as prec.] Covered with, occupied by, vehicles.

1894 *Cornh. Mag.* July 67 Joe's attempt to cross a thickly vehicled road was immethodical.

vehicula, pl. of VEHICULUM.

vehicular (viː'hɪkjʊlə(r)), *a.* Also 7 **-are**. [ad. late L. *vehiculār-is*, f. *vehicul-um* VEHICLE *sb.*]

1. Of or pertaining to, associated or connected with, a (wheeled) vehicle.

1616 CHAPMAN *Homer's Hymn Venus*, Charriots and all the frames vehiculare. **1656** BLOUNT *Glossogr.*, *Vehicular*, pertaining to any instrument or engine of carriage. **1754** FIELDING *Voy. Lisbon* Wks. 1882 VII. 12 By making use of a vehicular story, to wheel in among them worse manners than their own. **1818** SCOTT *Hrt. Midl.* i, The Insides and Outsides, to use the appropriate vehicular phrases. **1847** L. HUNT *Men, Women, & B.* I. ii. 12 Coachmen and cabmen, and conductors, and horses, and all the exterior phenomena of things vehicular. **1860** G. MEREDITH *Evan Harrington* x, I heard your welcome vehicular music.

fig. **1885** *Cent. Mag.* XXIX. 510 The poet's walk, talk, bearing, and intellect, are illustrated by a series of images, and in a style so vehicular as to deserve unusual praise.

b. Made, performed, or carried on, by means of a vehicle or vehicles.

1742 FIELDING *J. Andrews* III. xii, In his heart he preferred the pedestrian even to the vehicular expedition. **1816** SCOTT *Antiq.* xxxvi, It is the vehicular, not the equestrian exercise, which he envies. **1854** LOWELL *Jrnl. Italy* Prose Wks. 1890 I. 130, I am quite sure that he believes.. the Pre-Adamites were.. incapable of any but vehicular progression. **1879** *Daily News* 26 Dec. 5/2 Vehicular traffic was almost entirely suspended.

c. Of the nature of, serving as, a vehicle.

1807 BYRON *Let. to Miss Pigot* Aug., Places inaccessible to vehicular conveyances. **1844** EMERSON *Ess., Poet,* All language is vehicular and transitive, and is good.. for conveyance, not as farms and houses are, for homestead. **1871** LYTTON *Coming Race* xiv, They prefer their wings, for travel,.. to vehicular conveyances.

†**2.** Invested with a vehicle or special form; embodied. *Obs.*

1656 S. HOLLAND *Zara* (1719) 29 That every Grove, Grot and Stream has its tutelar and vehicular Deity. *a* **1774** TUCKER *Lt. Nat.* II. xxi. 47 We may gather that the rational soul is compleatly formed.. before entrance into the human body, and that the fashion and lineaments it afterwards takes.. are not necessary for its subsistence in the vehicular state. *Ibid.* xxvi. 140 To behold the wonders of the vehicular state, and boundless glories of the mundane soul.

Hence **ve'hicularly** *adv.*

1882 SALA *Amer. Revis.* x. 130/1 Pullman the beneficent did not fail.. to be vehicularly manifest on the train which conveyed us from Washington to Philadelphia.

ve'hiculary, *a.* *rare*$^{-1}$. [ad. late L. *vehiculāri-us.*] = VEHICULAR *a.* 1 c.

1835 J. KNOWLES *Dict., Litter*, a kind of vehiculary bed.

ve'hiculate, *v.* *rare.* [f. L. *vehicul-um* VEHICLE *sb.*: see -ATE[3].] **a.** *trans.* To carry or convey in, or as in, a vehicle. In quots. *fig.* **b.** *intr.* To travel, to ride or drive, in a vehicle.

1660 WATERHOUSE *Arms & Arm.* 27 Giving.. a document to mortal menageries, which are then only vehiculated to their central point. *Ibid.* 195 For this courage which vehiculates his attempts, and occasions his glory, is God's royal donative. **1843** CARLYLE *Past & Pres.* II. i, The vehicle for truth, or fact of some sort,—which surely a man should first try various other ways of vehiculating, and conveying safe.

ve'hiculated, *ppl. a.* *rare*$^{-1}$. [Cf. prec.] Invested with form; embodied.

a **1727** J. REYNOLDS *View of Death* (1735) 89 There may be vehiculated Spirits, of very different orders.

vehicu'lation. [f. as VEHICULATE *v.*: see -ATION, and cf. med.L. *vehiculatio.*] Conveyance by means of a vehicle or vehicles; vehicular activity or traffic.

1834 GEN. P. THOMPSON *Exerc.* (1842) III. 148 By a sort of parallel to the Game Laws, certain modes of vehiculation were to be peculiar to the magnificos. **1851** CARLYLE in *New Review* Dec. (1891) 482 Boulevards very stirring, airy, locomotive to a fair degree, but the vehiculation very light. **1866** —— *E. Irving* in *Remin.* (1881) II. 212 The New Road with its lively traffic and vehiculation. **1895** *Daily Chron.* 12 Nov. 4/4 We know of nothing more handsome or inviting in the literature of vehiculation.

ve'hiculatory, *a.* [f. as prec.: see -ORY[2].] Of the nature of, pertaining or relating to, vehicles.

1851 CARLYLE *Sterling* I. viii, He would accumulate.. logical swim-bladders,.. and other precautionary and vehiculatory gear, for setting out. **1865** —— *Fredk. Gt.* XIX. v. (1872) VIII. 177 To cart from Bohemia such a cipher of human rations daily.. will surpass all the vehiculatory power of Daun.

†**vehicule.** *Obs.*$^{-1}$ [a. F. *véhicule* or ad. L. *vehiculum*: see next.] = VEHICLE *sb.* 1.

1541 COPLAND *Galyen's Terap.* 2 H ij b, Of theyr sodayne passynge as a vehicule, with yͭ there is hunny it noyeth nat the vlcere.

‖**vehiculum.** Now *rare* or *Obs.* Pl. **vehicula**; also 7 **-aes.** [L.: see VEHICLE *sb.*]

1. = VEHICLE *sb.* 1. Also *fig.* and *transf.*

1624 BEDELL *Lett.* x. 143 Here is.. some truth mingled among, to giue the better grace, and to be as it were the *Vehiculum* of a lie. **1655** CULPEPPER, etc. *Riverius* I. vii. 33 The Dose is one dram in any proper Liquor or Vehiculum to swallow it down with. **1678** CUDWORTH *Intell. Syst.* I. i. §8. 12 We doubt not but to make a Sovereign Antidote against Atheism, out of that very Philosophy, which so many have used as a *Vehiculum* to convey this Poyson of Atheism by. **1787** MATY tr. *Riesbeck's Trav. Germ.* III. 76 Burgundy is the standing vehiculum of green pease.

2. = VEHICLE *sb.* 6. In quots. *fig.*

1633 PRYNNE *1st Pt. Histrio-m.* 65 Unchast, Obscene, and Amorous wordes, are but so many vehiculaes, to carrie men on to Adulterous and Sinfull deedes. **1642** HOWELL *Instr. Forr. Trav.* (Arb.) 59 Speech is the.. Ambassador of the mind, and the Tongue the Vehiculum, the Chariot, which conveyeth.. the notions of the Mind to Reasons Palace.

3. = VEHICLE *sb.* 2.

1652 ASHMOLE *Theat. Chem.* Annot. 451 She is the Planet neerest the Earth, and appointed as it were the *Vehiculum* of all other heavenly Influences unto what is Sublunary. **1668** HOWE *Bless. Righteous* 325 Are not the exceeding great and precious promises, the Vehicula, the conveighances of the Divine Nature?

4. = VEHICLE *sb.* 4.

1656 STANLEY *Hist. Philos.* (1687) 189/1 Having imposed each one his proper Star as a vehiculum. *Ibid.* 191/1 The rest of the body they appointed as a vehiculum to serve this. **1794** R. J. SULIVAN *View Nat.* IV. 15 Plato.. supposes, that into the vehiculum of the soul.. is infused.. a particular formative virtue, distinct, according to that star.

5. = VEHICLE *sb.* 5.

1668 CULPEPPER & COLE *Barthol. Anat.* I. xvii. 44 The wheyish.. exceeds the two excrementitious Cholers, by reason of the Blood, whose vehiculum it was to be.

‖**Vehme** ('veɪmə, ‖'feːmə). *Hist.* Also **Fehm.** [a. older G. *Vehme* (now *Fehme, Feme*), MHG. *veme, veime* judgement, punishment.] = next.

1829 SCOTT *Anne of G.* xx, Go hence,.. and let the fear of the Holy Vehme never pass from before thine eyes. **1838** *Spark's Biogr., Eaton* IX. 350 Individual opinions are restrained by a tyranny as inexorable as that of the Holy Vehme, the secret tribunal of the Middle Ages. **1879** *Encycl. Brit.* IX. 63/2 It was necessary that a candidate for initiation into the Fehm.. should not be a party to any process before a Fehmic court.

‖**Vehmgericht** ('veɪm-, ‖'feːmgərɪçt). *Hist.* Also **Vehme-, Fehm-.** [a. older G. *Vehm-*, now *Fehm-, Femgericht* (pl. *-gerichte*), f. prec. + *gericht* court, tribunal.] A form of secret tribunal which exercised great power in Westphalia from the end of the 12th to the middle of the 16th century.

1829 SCOTT *Anne of G.* xx, Men initiated and intrusted with high authority by the Vehme-gericht, or tribunal of the bounds. **1839** LONGF. *Hyperion* I. vi, Two Black Knights, who pretended to be ambassadors from the Vehm-Gericht. **1879** *Encycl. Brit.* IX. 63/2 It was only with the restoration of public order.. that the influence of the Fehm-gerichte gradually waned.

transf. **1848** THACKERAY *Van. Fair* xliv, 'Was Rebecca guilty or not?' The Vehmgericht of the servants' hall had pronounced against her. **1880** *Edin. Rev.* Jan. 143 The horrors of the Karmathian, the detestable Vehmgericht of the 'Assassins',.. all owe their origin to the schism of the House of 'Ali.

Vehmic ('veɪmɪk, 'feɪmɪk), *a.* Also **Vehmique, Fehmic.** [f. VEHM-E + -IC.] Pertaining to, connected with, the Vehmgericht.

1829 SCOTT *Anne of G.* xx, Machinations for the destruction of the Vehmique institutions. *Ibid.*, In the Vehmique court all must be Vehmique. **1831** *Ibid.* Introd., The Vehmic tribunals of Westphalia, a name so awful in men's ears during many centuries. *a* **1849** H. COLERIDGE *Ess.* (1851) I. 276 Invisible as a familiar or agent of the Vehmic association. **1879** [see VEHME]. **1882–3** SCHAFF *Encycl. Relig. Knowl.* III. 2451/1 When the State became able to maintain its laws, the Vehmic Court became superfluous.

'Vehmist. [f. as prec. + -IST.] A member of the Vehmgericht.

1841 *Blackw. Mag.* XLIX. 234 [They] thus, like the Vehmists of Germany, pursued a faithless or refractory member, even on the throne, with the steel and the cord.

veht(en, southern ME. varr. FIGHT *sb.* and *v.*

Vei, var. VAI.

veiage, obs. var. VOYAGE *sb.*

veicht, obs. Sc. f. WEIGHT *sb.*

veid, obs. Sc. f. WEED *sb.*

veie, southern ME. var. FAY *a.*

veien, southern ME. var. FAY *v.*[1]

veiȝe, southern ME. var. FEY *a.*

veighor, var. VEYOUR (viewer) *Obs.*

'veigle, *v.* Now *dial.* [Aphetic f. INVEIGLE *v.*] *trans.* To inveigle. Also *absol.*

1745 *Gentl. Mag.* 161 Venus may veigle to the grove, To taste the trifling sweets of love. **1778** FOOTE *Trip Calais* II. Wks. 1799 II. 345, I asked, if they had veigled one Miss Minnikin into their clutches. **1887** T. GIBSON *Leg. & Notes Westm.* Gloss. 307 *Veigle*, to entice.

veik, obs. Sc. form of WEAK *a.*

veil (veɪl), *sb.*[1] Forms: α. 3 **ueile**, 4–5 (7) **veile**, 5 **veylle**, 5–7 **veyle**; 4–5, 7 **veyl**, 6 **veyll**, **veill** (**vell**), 3–5, 7– **veil.** β. 4 **uayle**, 4–5 **vayl**, 5–7 **vayle**, 5–8 **vaile**, **vail** (5 *Sc.* **waile**, **wail**), 6 **vayel(l)e**, 8 **vaill.** γ. 5 *Sc.* **wale**, **val**, 4, 6–7 **vale.** [a. AF. and ONF. *veile* (*veille*) or *veil* (*veyl*), = OF. *voile* (*voille*) and *voil*:—L. *vēla* (neut. pl., taken as fem. sing.) and *vēlum* sail, curtain, veil. Cf. F. *voile* m. (veil) and f. (sail), = Prov. *vel*, It. and Sp. *velo*, Pg. *veo*. See also VELE.]

I. 1. a. A piece of linen or other material forming part of the distinctive head-dress of a nun, and worn so as to fall over the head and shoulders and down each side of the face.

a **1225** *Ancr. R.* 420 Ȝif ȝe muwen beon wimpel-leas, beoð bi warme keppen and þeruppon blake ueiles. *c* **1375** *Sc. Leg. Saints* x. (*Matthew*) 422 þe apostil þane.. þai madynnis all blyssit, & gefe þam waile & pall. **1387** TREVISA *Higden* (Rolls) V. 33 He ordeynede þat a nonne.. schulde nouȝt handle þe towayles of þe awter,.. but sche schal bere a veile on hire heed. *c* **1425** WYNTOUN *Cron.* v. viii. 1563 He gaf biddynge to þaim ay þat þar wail war na tyme lewide, þan þai sulde wer it on þar hewide. *c* **1430** LYDG. *Min. Poems* (Percy Soc.) 200 Rympled liche a nunnys veylle. *c* **1515** *Cocke Lorell's B.* 14 And many whyte nonnes with whyte vayles. *c* **1530** *Crt. of Love* 1102 The nonnes, with vaile and wimple plight. **1596** DALRYMPLE tr. *Leslie's Hist. Scot.* I. 228 Eftir her consecratione, haueng put on the Vale of her Virginitie.. eftir the consuetude of the kirke. **1610** HOLLAND *Camden's Brit.* 699 Heina.. that put on the Vaile and religious habite of a Nunne. **1631** TOWNSHEND *Albion's Triumph* 17 Religion, a woman in a short Surplisse of lawne full gathered about the neck, and vnder it a garment of watchet, with a short vale of siluer. **1728** CHAMBERS *Cycl.* s.v., The Prelate before whom the Vows are made, blesses the Veil, and gives it to the Religious. **1753** *Diary Blue Nuns* in *Cath. Rec. Soc. Publ.* VIII. 126 June the 19ᵗʰ Peggy Johnson received the vail of postulante from Mother Abbess Agnes Howard. **1825** SCOTT *Talisman* iv, Six [of the females], who, from their black scapularies, and black veils over their white garments, appeared to be professed nuns of the order of Mount Carmel.

b. ***to take the veil***, to become a nun; to enter a convent or nunnery. (See also quots. *a* 1700–56.)

Originally in sense 34 of the verb TAKE, but in later use passing into sense 16 c.

c **1325** *Metr. Hom.* 78 Thir maydens ware sent thaire uayles to take Of that bisschope, of whaim I spake... Thir maydens come bifore the autere, And toke thaire uayles. *c* **1375** *Sc. Leg. Saints* xxi. (*Clement*) 661 Throw hyme þe wale has tan a cusing of domycyane. *c* **1425** WYNTOUN *Cron.*

VII. iii. 264 Hir systyr þan dame Cristyane Off religion þe wail had tane. **1526** *Pilgr. Perf.* (W. de W. 1531) 262 b, She had forsaken the worlde and taken the holy veyle and habyte of religion. **1610** HOLLAND *Camden's Brit.* 395 Taking herself the Vale for opinion of holinesse. *a* **1700** *Diary Blue Nuns* in *Cath. Rec. Soc. Publ.* VIII. 15 Margarite Pigin came from England to be a lay sister and took the litle vaile for religion. **1756** MRS. CALDERWOOD in *Coltness Collect.* (Maitland Club) 259 It was the white vaill she was to take, that is, she was to enter her noviscet, for there is here no publick ceremony in takeing the black vaill, and last vows, for that is done within the convent, after a year's wearing the white. **1791** MRS. RADCLIFFE *Rom. Forest* iii, My father intended I should take the veil. **1818** SCOTT *Hrt. Midl.* lii, She never took the veil, but lived and died in severe seclusion, and in the practice of the Roman Catholic religion. **1867** LADY HERBERT *Cradle L.* iii. 103 Then it.. became a large and flourishing Convent, the wife of Baldwin I having taken the veil there.

c. ***the veil***, the life of a nun.

1812 CARY *Dante, Parad.* IV. 95 And thou mightst after of Piccarda learn That Constance held affection to the veil. **1827** HOOD *Bianca's Dream* 202 By twenty she had quite renounced the veil. **1831** SCOTT *Cast. Dang.* xiv, One who, ..according to the laws of the Church, had a right to make a choice between the world and the veil.

2. a. An article of attire consisting of a piece of thin cloth, silk, or other light fabric, worn, especially by women, over the head or face either as a part of the ordinary head-dress, or in order to conceal or protect the face; now usually a piece of net or thin gauzy material tied to the hat and completely covering the face in order to protect it from the sun or wind. Also in fig. context (quot. 1648).

α, β. *c* **1250** *Gen. & Ex.* 3616 Ðat folc on him [Moses] ne mi3te sen But a veil wore hem bi-twen. **13..** *Gaw. & Gr. Knt.* 958 Þat oþer wyth a gorger was gered ouer þe swyre, Chymbled ouer hir blake chyn with mylk-quyte vayles. **14..** *Siege Jerus.* (E.E.T.S.) 15 3it is þe visage in þe vail, as Veronyk hym bro3t. **1513** DOUGLAS *Æneid* III. viii. 77 Our hedis befoir the altar we aray With valis brown, eftir the Troiane gise. **1555** EDEN *Decades* (Arb.) 255 His heare long downe to his shulders,..with a vaile of silke rowled abowte his head. **1564** *Brief Exam.* ****iiij b, A Byshop that suffered a wydowe to syt without a vayle in the Church among other wydowes. **1638** JUNIUS *Paint. Ancients* 250 This same wise Tragædian bringeth in Agamemnon with a vaile before his eyes. **1648** CRASHAW *Delights Muses* Poems (1904) 146 How at the sight did'st Thou draw back thine Eyes, Into thy modest veyle? **1688** HOLME *Armoury* III. 240/1 Gipsies..in the Countrey for a Vaile use some Durty Clout, having holes only for their Eyes. **1718** *Free-thinker* No. 73. 125 She wore a white, unspotted Vail. **1760–2** GOLDSM. *Cit. W.* cxviii, They were covered from head to foot with long black veils. **1774** PENNANT *Tour Scotl. in 1772*, 124 Over her face a veil, so transparent as not to conceal. **1823** F. CLISSOLD *Ascent Mt. Blanc* 17 We all put on our veils, as a protection from the heat and light. **1838** *Murray's Handbk. N. Germ.* 139 The women of the lower orders here [Antwerp] wear a veil, resembling the Spanish mantilla. **1859** W. COLLINS *Q. of Hearts* (1875) 20 A bright laughing face, prettily framed round by a black veil, passed over the head, and tied under the chin. **1900** J. G. FRAZER *Golden Bough* (ed. 2) I. 313 Amongst the Touaregs..the veil is never put off, not even in eating or sleeping.

transf. **1591** SYLVESTER *Du Bartas* I. iv. 200 A Peacock.. spreads round the rich pride of his pompous vail.

γ. **1580–3** GREENE *Mamillia* Wks. (Grosart) II. 112 Where eyther the person or place should haue neede of a vale for Sunne burning. **1621** QUARLES *Hadassa* Wks. (Grosart) II. 60/1 Haman went home and mourn'd, (His visage muffled in a mournfull vale).

†b. A loin-cloth. *Obs.*$^{-1}$

1634 SIR T. HERBERT *Trav.* 187 A small vaile ouer their priuities.

c. *Eccl.* = *humeral veil*, HUMERAL *a.* 2. (Cf. also OFFERTORY 5.)

1782 [see 4]. **1905** *Ch. Times* 3 Feb. 136 The Offertory veil is worn on the shoulders like a broad scarf, the pendant ends being gathered up in the hands for holding and covering the sacred vessels.

3. A piece of cloth or other material serving as a curtain or hanging: **a.** *Jewish Antiq.* The piece of precious cloth separating the sanctuary from the body of the Temple or the Tabernacle.

a **1300** *Cursor M.* 16762+85 Dede men risen out of þer graue, Þe temple vayl clef in twoo. **13..** *Gosp. Nicod.* 660 Þe son wex dim ful sone, þe vail rafe in þe kirk. **1382** WYCLIF *Exod.* xxvi. 33 The veyle forsothe be it sett yn bi cercles, with ynne the whiche thou shalt put the arke of testymonye. **1412–20** LYDG. *Chron. Troy* I. 1747 In þe temple þe veil was kut on two. **1528** MORE *Dyalogue* III. Wks. 246/1 Yᵉ veyle of the temple is broken asunder yᵗ diuided among yᵉ Jewes. **1535** COVERDALE *2 Chron.* iii. 14 He made a vayle also of yalow sylke, scarlet, purple and lynenworke, and made Cherubins theron. **1611** BIBLE *1 Macc.* i. 22 Antiochus.. entred proudly into the sanctuarie, and tooke away..the vaile. **1737** WHISTON tr. *Josephus, Antiq.* III. vii. §7 The vails, too, which were composed of four things, they declared the four elements. **1782** J. BROWN *Nat. & Revealed Relig.* IV. iii. 363 While he expired, an earthquake rent the rocks, and the vail of the temple. **1842** *Penny Cycl.* XXIV. 186/2 The inner sanctuary was separated from the holy place by a rich curtain or veil.

fig. **1382** WYCLIF *Heb.* x. 20 Bi a veyl, or keuering, that is to seye, his fleisch. **1526** TINDALE *Heb.* x. 20 Through the vayle, that is to saye by his flesshe. **1642** ROGERS *Naaman* Ep. Ded. a 2, We are come..even to the Holy of Holies, through his flesh that hath broken downe the vaile of seperation.

b. *Eccl.* The curtain hung between the altar and the choir, esp. during Lent. Now *Hist.*

1427–8 *Rec. St. Mary at Hill* (1905) 68 For makyng of iiij polesis of bras & iron werk and lede þat serued for þe vayl. *a* **1450** *Mirk's Festial* 126 Þe vayle þat haþe be drawen all þe Lenton bytwene þe auter and þe qwere. **1505** *Acc. Ld. High Treas. Scot.* II. 294 For xxvij elne Bertane claith, to be the vail in the chapel of Halyrudhous agane Lenterane. **1530** PALSGR. 284/2 Veyle for the church in lent, *custode*. **1556** *Chron. Gr. Friars* (Camden) 67 That day the vayelle was hongyd [up] benethe the steppes. *Ibid.* 69 The xxviij. day after was Ester evyne, and then was the tabulle remevyd, and sette benethe at the vayele northe and sowthe. **1877** J. D. CHAMBERS *Div. Worship* 94 A large Curtain or Veil should be suspended in the Presbytery between the Choir and Altar.

c. Used fig. or allusively in various prepositional phrases, as ***behind, beyond,*** or ***within the veil***, chiefly after Heb. vi. 19 in Tindale's (1526) and later versions of the Bible; now commonly with reference to the next world.

1528 TINDALE *Obed. Chr. Man* 91 b, Christe hath brought vs all in into the inner temple within the vayle or forehanginge, and vnto the mercy stole of God. **1722** WOLLASTON *Relig. Nat.* ix. 180 To participate of the mysteries of love with modesty, as within a veil or sacred inclosure, not with a canine impudence. **1850** TENNYSON *In Mem.* lvi, What hope of answer, or redress? Behind the veil, behind the veil. **1859** E. FITZGERALD *Omar* xlvii, When You and I behind the Veil are past. **1877** A. J. ROSS *Mem. Alex. Ewing* xxx. 521 In March, 1870, Thomas Erskine passed on within the veil.

†d. A curtain or awning (cf. quots.). *Obs.*

1781 GIBBON *Decl. & F.* xxi. (1787) II. 277 The master of the offices stood before the veil or curtain of the sacred apartment. **1790** *Bystander* 33 To prevent inconvenience from the heat of the sun, they extended veils..by means of cords attached to the extremity of the building.

4. A piece of silk or other material used as a covering, *spec.* (*Eccl.*) to drape a crucifix, image, picture, etc., esp. during Lent, or to cover the chalice.

(*a*) **1399** *Mem. Ripon* (Surtees) III. 129 In salario Johannis Payntour pictantis j magnum vale ad cooperiendum crucem stantem infra corpus ecclesiæ in Quadragesima. **1501** *Acc. Ld. High Treas. Scot.* II. 64 For xliiij elne lynnyn claith, that wes antependis and vales in the Kirk of Strivelin. **1570** B. GOOGE *Pop. Kingd.* I. 11 One vp a lofte the patten holdes, enclosde in silken vayle. **1728** CHAMBERS *Cycl.* s.v., In the Romish Churches, in time of Lent, they have Veils, or large Curtains over the Altar, Crucifix, Images of the Saints, &c. **1782** in J. H. Harting *Hist. Sardinian Chapel* (1905) 25 Burse and veil for the chalice, veils for Benediction and the desk. **1877** J. D. CHAMBERS *Div. Worship* 427 There was a similar veil used also for covering over the Sepulchre on Good Friday.

(*b*) **1781** GIBBON *Decl. & F.* xix. (1787) II. 151 He.. respectfully unfolded the silken veil which covered the haughty epistle of his sovereign.

5. *fig.* Something which conceals, covers, or hides; a disguising or obscuring medium or influence; a cloak or mask. (Common in the 19th c.)

a. Of immaterial things. †***under veil***, surreptitiously.

1382 WYCLIF *2 Cor.* iii. 15 But til in to this day, whanne Moyses is radd, the veyl is putt vpon her hertis. **1412–20** LYDG. *Chron. Troy* IV. 4542 Daunz Anthenor, and Pollydamas, þat han contreued amonge hem outterly, And vnder veil concelyd secrely, 3iffe [etc.]. **1597** HOOKER *Eccl. Pol.* v. lv. §8 Till that humilitie which had bene before as a vaile to hide and conceale maiestie were layd aside. **1611** BIBLE *Transl. Pref.* ¶17 Hee remoueth the scales from our eyes, the vaile from our hearts. **1619** SIR H. WOTTON in *Eng. & Germ.* (Camden) 51, I have likewise a zeale to the cause, which I hope wilbe some vaile to myne other infirmities. **1660** JER. TAYLOR *Worthy Communicant* i. iv. 90 For Christ in the Sacrament is Christ under a veil. *a* **1735** LANSDOWNE *Progr. Beauty* 242 Hide with a vail those griefs that none can paint. **1783** W. THOMSON *Watson's Philip III*, VI. (1839) 337 His indulgence to the reformed religion covered the violence of his usurpations with a specious veil. **1820** SHELLEY *Naples* 93 From Nature's inmost shrine, Strip every impious gawd, rend Error veil by veil. **1838** T. THOMSON *Chem. Org. Bodies* 1006 The thickest veil covers the whole of these processes; and so far have philosophers hitherto been from removing this veil, that they have not even been able to approach it. **1898** 'MERRIMAN' *Roden's Corner* xvii. 182 Tearing aside the veils behind which human hearts have slept through many years.

b. Const. *of* (with defining term).

1382 WYCLIF *Wisd.* xvii. 3 Bi the derc veil of for3eting thei ben scatered,..and with..myche w[o]ndring disturbid. *a* **1475** in *Contin. Brut* 601 Thou, shewyng there a face ful benygne, Vndyr a veyle of fals decepcioun. **1543–4** *Act 35 Hen. VIII*, c. 1 The vaile of darcknes of the vsurped power ..of the see and bishoppes of Rome. **1598** SHAKS. *Merry W.* III. ii. 42, I will..plucke the borrowed vaile of modestie from the so-seeming Mist. Page. *a* **1639** W. WHATELEY *Prototypes* I. xi. (1640) 90 To use the mantle or veile of love to cover a multitude of sinnes. **1681** WYNDHAM *King's Concealment* 86 Striving to cover her trouble with the vail of chearfulness. **1719** YOUNG *Busiris* II. i, That chastity of look, which seems to hang A vail of purest light o'er all her beauties. **1769** ROBERTSON *Chas. V*, VIII. III. 77 Under whatever veil of artifice or secrecy the Emperor still affected to conceal his designs. **1823** SCOTT *Quentin D.* viii, Qualities which were visible even through the veil of extreme dejection, with which his natural character was..obscured. **1844** H. H. WILSON *Brit. India* II. 150 [He] dropped the veil of Mahratta diplomacy, and gave utterance to his opinions. **1882** J. HATTON *Journalistic London* ix. 162 If the veil of anonymity were completely raised, other..names would appear in the list.

c. Of material substances, the clouds, etc. With *of* or other defining addition.

1598 FLORIO, *Velo*,..the mortal vaile, mans carkas or body. **1629** MILTON *Hymn Nativ.* ii, She woo's the..Air To hide her guilty front with innocent Snow, And on her naked shame..The Saintly Vail of Maiden white to throw. **1648** J. BEAUMONT *Psyche* x. cccxx, He who in his Bodie's vail till now The Rays of his Divinity hath hid. **1663** BP. PATRICK *Parab. Pilgr.* xvii, Between us and the invisible World there is a gross cloud and vail of flesh which interposes. *a* **1708** BEVERIDGE *Priv. Th.* I. (1730) 1, I am sure, within this Veil of Flesh there dwells a Soul. **1816** J. WILSON *City of Plague* II. iii. 45 When the veil Of mist was drawn aside, there hung the sun. *c* **1853** KINGSLEY *Misc.* (1860) I. 44 Fifty years of ruin would suffice to wrap them in a leafy veil. **1872** BLACK *Adv. Phaeton* ix. 121 A great veil of rain stretches from the sky to the earth.

d. Similarly without specific qualification.

1604 E. G[RIMSTONE] *D'Acosta's Hist. Indies* III. xxi. 188 They do vsually see as it were two heavens, one cleere and bright above, and the other obscure, and as it were a graie vaile spread vnderneath. *a* **1652** BROME *Queenes Exch.* II. i, Imagine now you see break through a Vail Amidst those Stars,..The bright Cynthia in her full of Lustre. **1784** COWPER *Task* IV. 332 The green And tender blade..Escapes unhurt beneath so warm a veil. **1813** SCOTT *Trierm.* III. xxxvii, Such soften'd shade the hill receives, Her purple veil when twilight leaves Upon its western swell. **1897** MARY KINGSLEY *W. Africa* 129 The climbing plants..form great veils and curtains between and over the trees.

e. ***to draw*** or ***throw*** (also ***cast***) ***a veil over***, to hide or conceal, to refrain from discussing or dealing with, to hush up or keep from public knowledge. Also without const.

(*a*) **1701** DE FOE *True-born Eng.* I. 90 Satyr, be kind! and draw a silent Veil! Thy native England's vices to conceal. **1744** in *10th Rep. Hist. MSS. Comm.* App. I. 211, I wished from my Soul that I could draw a Veil over Vice-Admiral Lestock's Conduct in the late Skirmish. **1808** *Med. Jrnl.* XIX. 55 As far as regards their private characters, it may.. be the duty of those who are 'liable to other imperfections', to draw a veil over them. **1858** GREENER *Gunnery* 351 There was evidence of proceedings having been enacted over which I would rather draw a veil.

(*b*) **1711** ADDISON *Spect.* No. 169 ¶12 The ill-natured Man..exposes those Failings..which the other would cast a Veil over. **1806** SURR *Winter in Lond.* II. 101 His faithful attachment to the family caused him to throw a veil over suspicions that the rest of the world will for ever indulge. **1823** LAMB *Elia* II. *Barbara S——*, I must throw a veil over some mortifying circumstances. **1864** PUSEY *Lect. Daniel* (1876) 545 It throws a veil over the grossness of its error. **1875** JOWETT *Plato* (ed. 2) III. 109 He throws a veil of mystery over the origin of the decline.

6. a. A slight tinge or colouring. *rare*$^{-1}$.

1646 SIR T. BROWNE *Pseud. Ep.* II. i. 40 As for colour, although Crystall in his pellucid body seems to have none at all, yet in its reduction into powder, it hath a vaile and shadow of blew.

b. *Mus.* A slight obscuration or want of clearness in the voice. (Cf. VEILED *ppl. a.* 3 b.)

1884 *Grove's Dict. Music* IV. 235 Let no student of singing endeavour to cultivate a veil because some great singers have had it naturally. A superinduced veil means a ruined voice.

c. *Photogr.* An obscure or veiled appearance.

1893 HODGES *Elem. Photogr.* 132 The clear portions of the negatives should remain unclouded and free from veil or fog until the last.

7. In various specific uses: A veil-like membrane, membranous appendage or part, serving as a cover or screen; a velum: (see quots.).

a. *Bot.* **1760** J. LEE *Introd. Bot.* I. ii. (1765) 4 *Calyptra*, a Veil, in Mosses. **1796** WITHERING *Brit. Plants* (ed. 3) III. 811 *Polytr[ichum] striatum*... The veils appear in winter, and the capsules in Feb. **1822–7** GOOD *Stud. Med.* (1829) I. 248 For the most part the smell of these [mushrooms] is virulent, and they are covered with a calyptre or veil. **1832** LINDLEY *Introd. Bot.* 208 The *velum*, or veil [in fungi], is a horizontal membrane, connecting the margin of the pileus with the stipes. **1887** W. PHILLIPS *Brit. Discomycetes* Gloss., *Veil*, a partial covering of the cup; a membranaceous, fibrous, or granulose coating stretching over the mouth of the cup, soon breaking up into fragments.

b. *Anat.* **1829** COOPER *Good's Stud. Med.* I. 599 Certain phenomena, which occasionally show themselves in the glottis, larynx, and even in the pendulous veil of the palate. **1854** BUSHNAN in *Orr's Circ. Sci., Org. Nat.* I. 140 This expulsion of water is produced by means of a peculiar arrangement of the veil of the palate. **1859** MAYNE *Expos. Lex.* s.v. *Velum*.

c. *Zool.* **1810** *Encycl. Brit.* (ed. 4) VIII. 190/2 When young it [the larva] is covered with a veil of black silk. **1834** MCMURTRIE *Cuvier's Anim. Kingd.* 258 A membranous veil on the mouth supplies the want of tentacula. **1861** J. R. GREENE *Man. Anim. Kingd., Cœlent.* 36 Around the margin of the nectosac, the wall of the nectocalyx is produced inwards, forming a shelf-like membrane, or 'veil'.

8. *dial.* = CAUL *sb.*[1] 5.

1857 *Quinland* I. xiii. 186 Aunt Hepsa says he was born with a veil over his face, and says he can see things that we must not inquire about. **1879–** in dial. glossaries, etc. (N. Cy., Yks., Chesh., Shrops., and U.S.).

9. ***attrib.*** and ***Comb.***, as (in senses 3 b and 4) ***veil-cloth, -rope***, (in sense 2) ***veil (head)-dress, -maker, net***; also ***veil-hid*** adj.

1424 *Mem. Ripon* (Surtees) III. 151 Pro..ij tenterapes, et j veylrape cum j corda. **1552–3** *Inv. Church Goods* in *Ann. Lichfield* (1863) IV. 24 Item,..iij clothes to hang afore thalters, ix towelles, a vell clothe. **1611** FLORIO, *Velaro*, a vaile or sipres maker. **1813** BREWER *Beauties Eng. & Wales* XII. II. ii. 146 A woman in a veil head-dress. **1826** W. ELLIOTT *The Nun* 41 A veil-hid sister beckons at the door. **1876** EDERSHEIM *Jewish Life Days Christ* xiii. 217 The veil-dress was a kind of mantilla, thrown gracefully about the whole person, and covering the head. **1888** *Daily News* 3 Dec. 2/7 Veil nets continue in steady request. **1899** *Westm. Gaz.* 26 Jan. 3/2 The milliner must watch the coiffeur, the veil-maker the milliner.

II. †10. A sail. *Obs.*$^{-1}$

c **1430** *Pilgr. Lyf Manhode* IV. xxviii. (1869) 191 Aboue was þe mast of þe ship dressed wher vpon heeng þe seyl ystreight, whiche ooþer weys is cleped veyl.

†**veil**, *sb.*^{2} *Obs.* Also 4 veille, 5 veyle. [a. OF. *veille*:—L. *vigilia* waking, watching.] A watcher or watchman.

1362 LANGL. *P. Pl.* A. v. 223 Sleuþe for serwe fel doun i-swowene Til *vigilate* þe veil fette water at his eiȝen [*Harl. MS.* Til.. *vigilate* þe wakere warned him þo]. 1480 CAXTON *Myrr.* III. viii. (1913) 147 Thus is he [i.e. the sun] the right veyle and patrone of all the other sterres.

veil (veɪl), *v.* Forms: α. 4, 7– veil, 4 veyle, veill-, 5 veyll-, weyll-, 7 veile. β. 6 *Sc.* vale, vaill, 6–7 vayle, vaile, 6–8 vail. [f. VEIL *sb.*^{1}, in early use after OF. *veler*, *voiller* (mod.F. *voiler*) or L. *vēlāre*. Cf. Sp. and Pg. *velar*, It. *velare*.]

1. *trans.* To cover (the person, etc.) with, or as with, a veil; to conceal or hide (the face, etc.) by means of a veil or other material; to enveil.

Freq. in the pa. pple., which in some contexts may be taken as the passive of sense 3.

1382 WYCLIF *Luke* xxii. 64 And thei veyliden him, or hidden, and smyten his face. 1513 DOUGLAS *Æneid* XII. xiii. 218 Thus mekill said scho; and tharwyth bad adew, Hir hed valit with a haw clayth or blew. 1601 SHAKS. *Twel. N.* I. i. 28 The Element it selfe.. Shall not behold her face at ample view: But like a Cloystresse she will vailed walke. *a* 1700 EVELYN *Diary* 23 May 1645, A Venus of marble, veiled from the middle to the feete. 1725 DE FOE *Voy. round World* (1840) 246 She was veiled till she came into the room. 1791 COWPER *Odyss.* VIII. 103 Then his robe.. with both hands o'er his head Ulysses drew, behind its ample folds Veiling his face, through fear to be observed. 1816 J. WILSON *City of Plague* II. ii. 309 We veil our eyes before thy light. 1867 LADY HERBERT *Cradle L.* v. 119 The same women closely veiled.. were toiling down the rugged and slippery street. 1885–94 R. BRIDGES *Eros & Psyche* April xxii, 'Midst them there Went Psyche, all in lily-whiteness veil'd.

refl. 1891 'ANNIE THOMAS' *That Affair* I. x. 171 Miss Polthuan hats and veils herself.

transf. and *fig.* 1614 SYLVESTER *Bethulia's Rescue* III. 315, I.. Will with my Silence vail their Countenance. 1667 MILTON *P.L.* IX. 425 Eve separate he spies, Veil'd in a Cloud of Fragrance. *a* 1699 J. BEAUMONT *Psyche* VII. lxxix, She Vail'd in the scarlat of her modest cheek, Reply'd. 1728–46 THOMSON *Spring* 3 Come, gentle Spring, And.. veil'd in a shower Of shadowing roses, on our plains descend.

b. *transf.* with a thing as object. Also, to enclose or hang with a veil or curtain (quot. 1656).

Occas. passing into sense 4, but with material object.

1582 N. LICHEFIELD tr. *Castanheda's Conq. E. Ind.* I. xvi. 42 This church.. was made all of free stone, and couered or vayled ouer with bricke. 1607 TOURNEUR *Rev. Trag.* III. v, In some fit place vaylde from the eyes a' th' Court. 1656 J. SMITH *Pract. Physick* 208 The sides of the Cradle must be vailed, that the child may look only straight forward. *a* 1700 KEN *Edmund* Poet. Wks. 1721 II. 279 Three Leagues in Compass they the Ocean vail'd, And press'd the Billows prostrate as they sail'd. 1750 GRAY *Long Story* 39 With.. aprons long they hid their armour, And veil'd their weapons bright and keen. 1837 DISRAELI *Venetia* I. ii, A group of elms, too scanty at present to veil their desolation. 1847 TENNYSON *Princ.* III. 272 She bow'd as if to veil a noble tear. 1869 J. MARTINEAU *Ess.* II. 367 She veils the solar radiance and brings on the night.

fig. 1589 *Commendatory Verses Spenser's F.Q.* S.'s Wks. (1912) 409 That faire Ilands right: Which thou doest vaile in Type of Faery land, Elyzas blessed field, that Albion hight.

c. *refl.* To hide, cover, or wreathe (oneself) *in* something. Usually *fig.*

1799 S. & HT. LEE *Canterb. T.* I. 129 [His] grieved and rankling heart.. veiled itself in smiles. 1840 DICKENS *Old C. Shop* lix, 'Done, I say,' added Sampson, rubbing his hands and veiling himself again in his usual oily manner. 1850 MCCOSH *Div. Govt.* III. i. (1874) 286 High truths, like high mountains, are apt to veil themselves in clouds.

d. *absol.* To put on or wear a veil.

1713 MRS. CENTLIVRE *Wonder* II, You must veil and follow him. 1835 BURNES *Trav. Bokhara* (ed. 2) III. 24 Their head-dress is, perhaps, a little large, but.. as they never veil, it becomes them.

2. To bestow the veil of a nun upon (a woman); to admit into monastic life as a nun.

1387 TREVISA *Higden* (Rolls) V. 305 Seint Bryde þat Patrik veillede.. overlevede him by sixty ȝere. 1390 GOWER *Conf.* III. 317 Thei.. make a worthi pourveance Ayein the day whan thei be veiled. *c* 1420 *Chron. Vilod.* 623 And other maydones mony mo also, Weron veylled þo in þat abbay. *a* 1604 HANMER *Chron. Ireland* (1633) 43 The Nunne Cecubris whom Patricke first vailed of all the women in Ireland. *a* 1661 FULLER *Worthies, Essex* (1662) 337, I.. conceive she [Matilda Fitz-Walter] had surely been Sainted if vailed. 1886 CANON MONAHAN *Rec. Ardagh & Clonmacnoise* 3 Some hold.. that St. Bridget of Kildare was veiled by St. Macchilla.

b. *refl.* To make (oneself *a nun*) by taking the veil. *rare*$^{-1}$.

1631 WEEVER *Anc. Funeral Mon.* 760 A daughter of his, vailed herselfe a Nunne.

3. To cover, enshroud, or screen as or in the manner of a veil; to serve as a veil to (something).

a. Of a garment, cloth, etc.

1513 DOUGLAS *Æneid* VIII. i. 73 A linȝe wattry garmond dyd hym vaill. 1596 SHAKS. *Merch. V.* III. ii. 99 Thus ornament is but.. The beautious scarfe Vailing an Indian beautie. 1703 POPE *Thebais* I. 432 His ample hat his beamy locks o'erspread, And veil'd the starry glories of his head! 1797 MRS. RADCLIFFE *Italian* xii, Their beauty, softened by the lawn that thinly veiled it. 1867 MORRIS *Jason* XIV. 732 Scarlet cloth, and fine silk, fit to veil The perfect limbs of dreaded Goddesses.

transf. 1842 J. WILSON *Chr. North* (1857) II. 9 Shame never veiled the light of those bold eyes.

b. Of clouds, vapour, etc.

1614 GORGES *Lucan* x. 436 Thus they the time securely spent, Till mid-night vail'd the Element. 1667 MILTON *P.L.* IX. 452 And now from end to end Nights Hemisphere had veild the Horizon round. *Ibid.* XI. 229 Yonder blazing Cloud that veils the Hill. 1779 COWPER *Olney Hymns, Submission* 23 The next cloud that vails my skies. 1794 MRS. RADCLIFFE *Myst. Udolpho* xxxv, The clouds.. veiling the sun and stretching their shadows along the distant scene. 1820 LAMB *Elia* I. *My First Play*, The green curtain that veiled a heaven to my imagination. 1836 MACGILLIVRAY *Trav. Humboldt* xiv. 178 The heat became suffocating, and a reddish vapour veiled the horizon. 1871 T. R. JONES *Anim. Kingd.* (ed. 4) 134 A cloud veiling the sun will cause their tentacles to fold, as though apprehensive of danger from the passing shadows.

4. *fig.* To conceal (some immaterial thing, condition, quality, etc.) from apprehension, knowledge, or perception; to deal with, treat, etc., so as to disguise or obscure; to hide the real nature or meaning of (something). Freq. with implication of bad motives.

1538 LATIMER *Remains* (Parker Soc.) 399 And in what case are they in, that hath veiled treason so long! 1602 MARSTON *Ant. & Mel.* I. Wks. 1856 I. 15 Weele not vaile our names. 1620–6 QUARLES *Feast for Wormes* Ded., I dedicate.. these few leaues to your truly-Noble Selfe, hoping your Lordship wil vaile my boldnes in your good acceptance. 1653 HOLCROFT *Procopius, Persian Wars* I. 30 Tribonianus.. being a faire spoken man,.. able to vail his Covetousness with abundance of Learning. 1718 *Freethinker* No. 106. 6 Popery does not appear Bare-faced in England: the Terrours of it are veiled. *a* 1770 JORTIN *Serm.* (1771) I. i. 4 *note*, Pythagoras learned to veil his precepts. 1841 D'ISRAELI *Amen. Lit.* (1867) 311 The literary delusion.. long veiled the personal history of the Earl of Surrey. 1863 KINGLAKE *Crimea* I. 209 That which had so long veiled his cleverness from the knowledge of mankind. 1869 FREEMAN *Norm. Conq.* (1875) III. xii. 145 The real names are veiled under the obsolete titles delighted in by the Latin writers.

5. To render less distinct or apparent; to reduce, soften, tone down.

1843 R. J. GRAVES *Syst. Clin. Med.* xxv. 306 The mucilage veils the astringent and irritating qualities of the metallic salt. 1878 ABNEY *Photogr.* xiv. 102 The chance of veiling the image through the reduction of the bromide unacted upon by light is increased.

6. *intr. Photogr.* To become dark or obscure; to darken.

1890 [see VEILING *vbl. sb.* 4]. 1907 HODGES *Elem. Photogr.* (ed. 6) 127 The high lights.. should be just commencing to veil.

veil, obs. f. VAIL *sb.*^{1}; var. VAIL *v.*^{2}; obs. Sc. form of WEAL *sb.*, WELL *adv.*

veild, obs. Sc. form of WIELD *v.*

veildar, obs. Sc. form of WIELDER.

veile, obs. form of VAIL; obs. Sc. f. WELL *adv.*

veiled (veɪld), *ppl. a.* [f. VEIL *v.* or *sb.*^{1}]

1. Covered with or wearing a veil; shrouded in a veil.

1593 MARLOWE tr. *Lucan* I. 597 The Nunnes And their vaild Matron, who alone might view Mineruas statue. 1607 SHAKS. *Cor.* II. i. 231 Our veyl'd Dames Commit the Warre of White and Damaske In their nicely gawded Cheekes. 1614 J. DAVIES (Heref.) *Eclogue* 33 Wks. (Grosart) II. 19/2 Than vp (sad swaine) pull fro thy vailed cheeke Hur prop, thy palme. 1815 SHELLEY *Alastor* 151 He dreamed a veiled maid Sate near him. 1820 —— *Prometh. Unb.* II. iv. 1 What veiled form sits on that ebon throne? 1851 RUSKIN in Collingwood *Life* (1900) 129 Those veiled vestals and prancing Amazons.. will all be forgotten. 1891 FARRAR *Darkn. & Dawn* iii, No one recognised the veiled figure.

b. *poet.* Of the eyes.

1817 SHELLEY *Pr. Athan.* I. 99 'Tis the shadow of a dream Which the veiled eye of Memory never saw. 1821 —— *Adonais* ii, With veiled eyes, 'Mid listening Echoes, in her Paradise She sate.

c. *Bot.* Having a velum; velate.

1793 MARTYN *Lang. Bot.* s.v. *Calyptra*, In this sense *Euonymus* is said to be calyptred, calyptrate or veiled. 1866 in *Treas. Bot.*

2. Concealed, covered, hidden, as if by a veil; obscure, unrevealed.

1612 T. TAYLOR *Comm. Titus* i. 1 The vailed knowledge of the law. 1674 BOYLE *Excell. Theol.* I. i. 49 A close and critical account of the more vailed and pregnant parts of Scripture. 1821 SHELLEY *Epipsych.* 26 Seraph of Heaven!.. Veiled Glory of this lampless Universe! 1858 HAWTHORNE *Fr. & It. Note-bks.* II. 119 Returning the inquirer's thoughts and veiled recollections to himself, as answers to his queries. 1878 J. P. HOPPS *Rel. & Moral Lect.* xiii. 42 On the one hand, all the masks will drop off; and, on the other hand, all the veiled goodness will appear.

b. *fig.* Covert, disguised; not openly declared, expressed, or stated.

1875 E. WHITE *Life in Christ* II. x. (1878) 105 There is a wide difference between a veiled promise and a veiled threatening. 1891 FARRAR *Darkn. & Dawn* v, The scarcely veiled sneer which marked his tone of voice. 1899 ALDENHAM *Colloq. Currency* (1900) 316 The Imperfect or Veiled Bimetallism such as that practised under the Bank Act of 1844.

3. †**a.** Of sight: Dim, indistinct. *Obs.*

1633 P. FLETCHER *Purple Isl.* VI. lxv, Why do we.. With curious labour, dimme and vailed sight, Prie in the nature of this King and Queen?

b. Of sound, the voice, etc.: Indistinct, muffled, obscure.

1834 J. FORBES *Laennec's Dis. Chest* (ed. 4) 35 It sometimes also presents a further modification, which I call the veiled puff (*souffle voilé*). In this case, it seems to us as if every vibration of the voice.. agitates a sort of moveable veil interposed between the excavation and the ear. 1884 *Grove's Dict. Music* IV. 235 *Veiled Voice*... A voice is said to be veiled when it is not clear, but sounding as if it passed through some interposed medium. 1897 *Daily News* 10 Dec. 7/4 Jenny Lind's Veiled Voice. 1898 *Allbutt's Syst. Med.* V. 871 The heart-sounds become veiled and impure.

c. *Photogr.* Of a negative: Lacking clearness or distinctness; dim.

1892 *Photogr. Ann.* II. 477 Isochromatic and other very sensitive plates requiring the greatest possible protection during development, to avoid veiled negatives.

Hence **'veiledly** *adv.*, **'veiledness**.

1879 C. & MARY COWDEN CLARKE *Shaks. Key* 690 In the 'Sonnets', there is the same spirit of modesty.. with the utmost veiledness of diction. 1881 E. ARNOLD *Indian Poetry* 73 Blue lotus-blooms, seen veiledly Under the wave.

veilfair, -fare, obs. Sc. forms of WELFARE.

veiling ('veɪlɪŋ), *vbl. sb.* [f. VEIL *v.* or *sb.*^{1}]

I. 1. Something serving as a veil, cover, or screen; a veil or curtain. Also *fig.*

In quot. 1748 prob. confused with VALANCE *sb.*

1398 TREVISA *Barth. De P.R.* II. viii. (1495) 36 A Seraphin louith to see god wythout ony wayllynge of fygure eyther of creature sette bytwene. *Ibid.* xviii. 43 He seeth god face to face wythout veyllynge put bytwene. 1611 FLORIO, *Velame*,.. vailings, shadowings or curteins. 1748 *Phil. Trans.* XLV. 386 The Breach on the East Side, near a Window,.. was opposite to the Vailings of the Bed, which were singed. 1842 IS. WILLIAMS *Baptistery* I. xiv. (1874) 175 Then when strongest heart is failing Death it calls in to its aid, Strips aside the fleshly veiling Round ourselves that we have made. 1900 *Daily News* 14 Feb. 7/4 Vivid flashes of lightning illuminated the whole room, piercing the veiling of the windows.

2. Material of which veils are made. Also pl.

nun's veiling: see NUN *sb.*^{1} 6c.

1882 CAULFEILD & SAWARD *Dict. Needlework* 510/1 The widths of gauze for Veiling measure from half a yard to three-quarters in width. 1894 *Times* 16 April 4/2 The sale of veilings is fairly well sustained.

attrib. 1891 *Times* 15 Oct. 9/5 A considerable business is being done in silk veiling nets.

II. 3. The action of putting on or covering with a veil. Also *attrib.* in ***veiling place***.

a 1586 SIDNEY *Ps.* XIX. vi, [The sun comes forth] like a bridegroome From out his vailing places. 1611 FLORIO, *Velatio*, a vailing. 1826 MISS MITFORD *Village* Ser. II. (1863) 277 Oh the lacing,.. the bonneting, the veiling, the gloving [etc.].

4. The action or fact of becoming blurred, dim, or indistinct; dimness or indistinctness of appearance, esp. in a photographic film or negative.

1890 *Anthony's Photogr. Bulletin* III. 57 Films which have a tendency to veiling and thinness. 1893 HODGES *Elem. Photogr.* 122 It is of the utmost importance that the high lights of a lantern slide should be transparent and free from the slightest veiling or discoloration. 1899 *Allbutt's Syst. Med.* VI. 843 A little veiling or uncertainty of the outlines of the discs.

veiling ('veɪlɪŋ), *ppl. a.* [f. VEIL *v.*] That veils, covers, or conceals.

a 1672 STERRY *Freed. Will* (1675) 128 God is seen by the Soul, but shadowed by this shadowy and vailing Image within which he resides. 1820 KEATS *Isabella* xlvii, Then 'gan she work again; nor stay'd her care, But to throw back at times her veiling hair. 1855 ROSSETTI *Poems* (1904) 183/1 Not till this veiling world shall cease And harvest yield its whole increase. 1867 JEAN INGELOW *Story of Doom* I. 278 Then she pushed Her veiling hair back from her round, soft eyes.

veill, obs. Sc. form of WEAL *sb.*, WELL *adv.*

veillane, obs. Sc. form of VILLAIN.

veilless ('veɪllɪs), *a.* [f. VEIL *sb.*^{1} + -LESS.]

1. Having no veil; unprovided with or unprotected by a veil.

1822 MILMAN *Martyr Antioch* 55 That head, whose veilless blaze Fill'd angels with amaze. 1859 TENNYSON *Geraint & Enid* 536 Half whistling and half singing a coarse song, He drove the dust against her veilless eyes. 1882 F. MYERS *Renewal Youth* 86 They scarce could bear Veilless the tingling incidence of air.

2. *transf.* Unshaded, unclouded.

1870 MISS BROUGHTON *Red as Rose* I. 117 The corn has been whitening under the sun's hard veilless stare. 1888 H. DRUMMOND *Tropical Africa* v. 109 The glittering ball, whose daily march across the burnished and veilless zenith brings him untold agony.

‖**veilleuse** (vɛjœz). [F.] A small and usually highly decorated night-light or night-lamp; also, a small, decorative, bedside food-warmer, usu. burning oil in a wick and made of pottery or porcelain so as to let out some light.

1826 H. D. BESTE *Four Yrs. France* 379 The reflection of a veilleuse, or small night lamp. 1897 *Private Life of Queen* xv. 122 The Queen betakes herself to bed... The signal comes for extinguishing all the lights but the *veilleuse*. 1955 *Apollo* LXI. 35/1 The *veilleuse* of pottery or porcelain is.. a hollow pedestal on which sits either a covered warming bowl.. or a teapot. 1961 *Times* 2 Sept. 9/6 One was the earthenware bedside food warmer. Some collectors know these companionable little sets as *veilleuses*. 1969 E. H. PINTO *Treen* 124/2 The oddest material for making *veilleuses* was probably wood and the fact that so few have survived is doubtless.. because of their inflammability. 1983 *Thames & Hudson Catal.* July-Dec. 31 The *veilleuse*, intended as a food or tea warmer for bedroom use.. consists of.. a supporting hollow pedestal, a small burner (*godet*) and a covered bowl or.. teapot.

veillfair, obs. Sc. form of WELFARE.

veil-like, *a.* [f. VEIL *sb.*[1]] Like or resembling a veil, or that of a veil; having the appearance or character of a veil.

1835 LYTTON *Rienzi* x. viii, He saw the pale and veil-like mists that succeed the sunset. **1873** LELAND *Egypt. Sketch-Bk.* 115 She had a long flowing white veil-like robe. **1887** HISSEY *Holiday on Road* 154 The air has a perceptible quality... You feel its veil-like influence pervading all.

veilme, obs. form of FILM *sb.*

veily (ˈveɪlɪ), *a.* [f. VEIL *sb.*[1] + -Y.] Veil-like; diaphanous.

1839 T. MILLER *Rural Sk.* 9, I had watched.. until the veily twilight was let down from heaven. **1843** RUSKIN *Mod. Paint.* I. II. iv. §6. 244 The.. rain-cloud, with its ragged and spray-like edge, its veily transparency [etc.].

vein (veɪn), *sb.* Forms: *α.* 3-7 **veyne** (4-5 **weyne**, 6 **ueyne**), 4, 7 **veyn**; 4-7 **veine** (4 **vene**), 7- **vein.** *β.* 4-7 **vayne** (5 **wayne**), 5 **vayn** (**wayn**), 6-7 **vain**(**e.** *γ.* 5, 6-7 *Sc.*, **vane** (5, 6 *Sc.*, **wane**). [a. OF. *veine*, *vaine* (F. *veine*):—L. *vēna* (cf. VENE), whence also Prov., Sp., It. *vena*, Pg. *veia* (†*veya*, *vea*).]

I. 1. a. One or other of the tubular vessels in which the blood is conveyed through the animal body; in later use *spec.* one of those by which the blood is carried back to the heart from the extremities (opposed to *artery*).

Many veins are distinguished by special epithets, as *alar*, *auricular*, *axillary*, *basilic*, *cardiac*, etc.: see these words.

α. **13..** *K. Alis.* 1175 (Laud MS.), þe kynges veynes wexen chelde. *Ibid.* 2414 þer was.. many veyn leten blood. **1387** TREVISA *Higden* (Rolls) I. 59 For betynge of veynes is bettre i-knowe in þe vttre parties of bodies þan ynward and in þe myddel wiþynne. **1422** YONGE tr. *Secreta Secret.* 229 Tho men whych haue the neke abowte and the temples, grete ruddy weynes, bene wrothy and hugely angry. *c* **1450** *Mirk's Festial* 291 þe prest blessuth a ring.. and duth hit on hur fyngur þat haþe a veyne to hure herte. **1526** *Pilgr. Perf.* (W. de W. 1531) 254 For yᵉ whiche his senewes and veynes brast. **1559** MORWYNG *Evonym.* 359 This oyll anoynted upon the pulsing veynes, where they appeare moste, as of the temples,.. delivereth.. from all poysons. **1592** SHAKS. *Rom. & Jul.* IV. iii. 15, I haue a faint cold feare thrills through my veines. **1631** R. BOLTON *Comf. Affl. Consc.* (1635) 199 When a veine is broken and bleeds inwardly,.. the Physition is wont to open a veine in the arme so to divert the current of the blood. *c* **1673** TRAHERNE *Poet. Wks.* (1906) 180 Veins wherein blood floweth, Refreshing all my flesh, Like rivers. **1727** DE FOE *Eng. Tradesm.* vi. (1841) I. 44 Being drawn off, like the blood let out of the veins. **1774** GOLDSM. *Nat. Hist.* (1776) VI. 388 With us and quadrupedes the blood goes from the veins to the heart. **1804** ABERNETHY *Surg. Obs.* 21 The superficial veins appear remarkably large. **1840** THIRLWALL *Greece* lvi. VII. 197 Demosthenes now felt the poison in his veins. **1871** T. R. JONES *Anim. Kingd.* (ed. 4) 227 All these veins terminate in two large venous canals.

β. *c* **1340** HAMPOLE *Pr. Consc.* 1908 [If] ilka vayne of þe mans body Had a rote festend fast þarby. *c* **1400** *Destr. Troy* 5829 The gret vayne of his gorge. **1422** YONGE tr. *Secreta Secret.* 240 The blode rynnyth into the waynys throgh al the body. **1480** CAXTON *Myrr.* II. xix. (1913) 109 Alle in lyke wyse as the blood of a man gooth and renneth by the vaynes of the body. **1523** FITZHERB. *Husb.* §50 Some men vse to let them bloudde vnder the eye in a vaine. **1582** HESTER *Secr. Phiorav.* I. xxiv. 28 When the bloud is altered of that putrefaction, it goeth to the vaines. **1603** J. DAVIES (Heref.) *Microcosmos* Wks. (Grosart) I. 67/1 Seas of Blood.. Might still haue kept the Chanells of the Vaynes. **1647** HEXHAM I, A Vaine, *een Ader*... Great Vaines or Arteres, *Groot Aderen.*

γ. *c* **1450** in *Vicary's Anat.* (1888) App. ix. 229 Thy ryght hande has I. wane, in fay, Thy litill fynger hath yt aye. **1487** *Barbour's Bruce* VII. 173 Quhen the vanys fillit ar, The body vorthis hevy euirmar. **1500-20** DUNBAR *Poems* lxxii. 35 Blude birst out at every vane. *c* **1560** A. SCOTT *Poems* (S.T.S.) ix. 34 Ane hairt of ȝouris bayth vane and nervis. **1596** DALRYMPLE tr. *Leslie's Hist. Scot.* II. 95 A vane.. cuttit in his body, al the blude of his body is lattne outbleid at the samyn. **1655** in *Verney Mem.* (1907) I. 557, I had only a vomitt.. and breathed a vane.

†b. ***lacteal***, ***lacteous***, or ***milky veins***, = LACTEAL *sb.* 1. *Obs.*

1656 J. SMITH *Pract. Physick* 4 Obstruction of the Vessels, especially of the Pancreas, and fault of the milky veins. **1664** POWER *Exp. Philos.* I. 66 The stomach and guts, and their appendent Vessels, the lacteal Veins. **1704** RAY *Creation* (ed. 4) I. 29 The Food.. is further subtiliz'd and render'd so fluid and penetrant, that the thinner and finer part of it easily finds its way in at the streight Orifices of the lacteous Veins.

c. ***fluid vein***, a separate flow of blood in a larger vein. (Cf. 6 c.)

1897 *Allbutt's Syst. Med.* IV. 659 The formation of innumerable small fluid veins. **1898** *Ibid.* V. 502 This change in the continents sets up fluid veins in the contained blood.

2. In phrases and figurative uses:

†a. ***to taste***, or ***feel***, ***one's vein***(***s***, to feel the pulse. ***to die in a vein***, to die through loss of blood. *Obs.*

13.. *Seuyn Sages* (W.) 1048 The yonge man segh the childes peyne, And tasted his senewe, and his veyne. **1390** GOWER *Conf.* III. 315 This noble clerk with alle haste Began the veines forto taste. *c* **1440** *Alph. Tales* 74 þis Joseph was passand connyng in grapyng of þer vaynys at war seke, and he come vnto hym & felid his vaynys. **1547-64** BALDWIN *Mor. Philos.* (Palfr.) 35 Seneca.. supposing that to dye in a veyne was the easiest kinde of death, desired to be let bloud in the veynes of his arme.

b. In various fig. uses.

1382 WYCLIF *Job* iv. 12 To me is seid a woord hid, and as theefli myn ere toc the veynes [L. *venas*] of his gruching. *c* **1530** TINDALE *Prophete Jonas* Prol. A ij, The fleshly minded ypocrites stoppe upp the Vaynes of life which are in yᵉ scripture. **1583** STUBBES *Anat. Abus.* II. (1882) 24 Now the cloth being thus stretched forth in euery vaine, how is it possible either to endure or hold out? **1606** J. KING *Serm.* Sept. 47 By all princely meanes to put bloud into the veines of the Church againe. **1651** in M. Sellers *Eastland Co.* (Camden) Introd. 75 In equity and reason the benefitt of trade should be equally disposed into all the vaines of the Commonwealth. **1719** W. WOOD *Surv. Trade* 73 It is a true Sign, that our foreign Traffick has since convey'd Spirits and Nourishment into each Vein of the Body Politick. **1831** CARLYLE *Sart. Res.* II. iii, Here, too, as in the Euphrates and the Ganges, is a vein or veinlet of the grand World-circulation of Waters. **1864** LOWELL *Fireside Trav.* 303 Great poets.. crowding the happy veins of language again with all the life.. that had been dribbling away. **1866** B. TAYLOR *Poet's Jrnl.* 58 As ardent veins of summer heat Throb thro' the innocence of spring.

c. In miscellaneous fig. phrases.

(*a*) *c* **1400** *Rom. Rose* 3459 If he were touchid on somme good veyne, He shuld yit rewen on thi peyne. **1589** *Pasquil's Ret.* C iij b, *Vetus Comædia* beganne to pricke him.. in the right vaine. **1677** GILPIN *Demonol.* (1867) 59 Satan.. makes it his next care.. to strike in the right vein; for he loves to have his work easy and feasible.

(*b*) **1587** STANYHURST *Descr. Ireland* 34/2 in *Holinshed*, Let him with all the veines of his heart beseech God. **1589** COOPER *Admon.* 215 There were many of them that would haue bene glad with all the veines in their heartes. **1589** R. HARVEY *Pl. Perc.* (1590) 10, I see the vaine is vp in the forhead, and Martin shall haue as good as he brings. **1662** STILLINGFL. *Orig. Sacræ* III. iv. §6 A kinde of a breaking of vein in which the salt water was conveyed up and down the body of the earth.

3. †a. A sap-vessel in plants. *Obs.*

c **1386** CHAUCER *Prol.* 3 Whan that Aprille.. hath.. bathud every veyne in swich licour, Of which vertue engendred is the flour. **1398** TREVISA *Barth. De P.R.* XVII. i. (Bodl. MS.), þei [trees] haue weyes and veynes in þe whiche kinde moisture is ikepte and passeþ þerbi fro þe erþe into alle þe parties abowte. **1513** DOUGLAS *Æneid* XII. Prol. 255 Welcum support of euery rute and vane, Welcum confort of alkynd fruyt and grane.

b. *Bot.* A slender bundle of fibrovascular tissue forming an extension of the petiole in the parenchyma of a leaf.

In early use less specific in sense. Some botanists have restricted *vein* to branches of the midrib, in contrast to *nerves* proceeding from the base of the leaf.

1513 DOUGLAS *Æneid* XII. vii. 76 The herb sweit, Of levis rank,.. With sproutis, sprangis, and vanis our allquhair. **1553** EDEN *Treat. New Ind.* (Arb.) 18 These [leaves] are somewhat grosser and fatter, with small vaynes running betwene on the contraryе side. **1731** P. MILLER *Gard. Dict.* s.v. *Leaves*, They.. consist of a very glutinous Matter, being furnished every where with Veins and Nerves. **1793** MARTYN *Lang. Bot.* s.v. *Venosum*, When it has no veins,.. it is called *Folium Avenium*, a veinless leaf. **1812** *New Botanic Gard.* I. 42 The leaves,.. with a network of veins underneath. **1832** LINDLEY *Introd. Bot.* 88 Till within a few years the distribution of veins in the leaf had not received much attention. **1866** *Treas. Bot.* 1206/2 Costal or primary veins are such as spring from the midrib; external veins are those next the edge. **1880** BESSEY *Bot.* 145 The disposition of the veins in a leaf depends largely upon its mode of growth. Usually several veins form early.

c. *Ent.* A nervure of an insect's wing.

1817 KIRBY & SP. *Entomol.* xxiii. II. 347 French naturalists use this term (*nervure*) for the veins of wings. **1834** MCMURTRIE *Cuvier's Anim. Kingd.* 326 The wings.. are traversed in various directions by more or less numerous nervures,.. now forming a net-work, and then simple veins. **1855** *Orr's Circle Sci.*, *Org. Nat.* II. 336 Each wing is found to consist of a double membrane, between which a variable number of veins, or *nervures*, ramify in different directions.

†4. *Sc.* A slender stripe of a different colour or material on a garment. (Cf. VEIN *v.* 1 a.) *Obs.*

1539 *Inv. R. Wardr.* (1815) 34 Ane coit of fresit claith of silvir vanit with ane small inset vane of gold. **1542** *Acc. Ld. High Treas. Scot.* VIII. 74 To jeit the cote witht thre vanis aboute the taill.

5. a. A marking or an appearance suggestive of a vein; *esp.* an irregular stripe or streak of a different colour in marble or other stone.

1642 FULLER *Holy & Prof. St.* III. xiv. 189 The red veins in the marble may seem to blush at the falshoods written on it. **1688** HOLME *Armoury* II. 40/1 The Absistos is.. marvellous weighty and black of colour, bestroked with red Veins. **1712** ADDISON *Spect.* No. 414 ¶2 Those accidental Landskips of Trees, Clouds and Cities, that are sometimes found in the Veins of Marble. **1799** G. SMITH *Laboratory* I. 178 When [the paint is] dry, you may with the point of a needle open fine veins or other embellishments. **1860** TYNDALL *Glac.* I. vii. 54 The blue veins of the glacier are beautifully shown. **1861** B. SILLIMAN *Physics* 378 The beautiful play of colors seen upon mother of pearl is caused by the delicate veins with which the surface is covered.

b. A streak or seam of a different material or texture from the main substance.

1663 GERBIER *Counsel* 28 The Mason must work no Stone with Sandy veines. **1815** J. SMITH *Panorama Sci. & Art* I. 7 Wrought iron may be hardened.. by ignition and plunging in water, but the effect is confined to the surface; except.. the iron contain veins of steel. **1831** BREWSTER *Optics* x. 85 The spectrum formed by a fine prism of flint glass, free of veins. **1869** SIR E. REED *Ship-build.* xviii. 384 Angle-irons have to be free from veins and cracked holes, and rivet-iron has to be free from cracks and veins when laid up and finished.

c. A fibre (in metal). *rare*$^{-1}$.

1715 LEONI *Palladio's Archit.* (1742) I. 4 It will be a sign of its Goodness, if being made into Bars, its veins are continu'd strait..; because the streightness of its veins shews the Iron to be without knots.

II. 6. a. A small natural channel or perforation within the earth through which water trickles or flows; a flow of water through such a channel. Also *transf.* (quot. 1598).

c **1290** *S. Eng. Leg.* I. 318/639 Wellene comiez of grete wateres and muche del of þe se þoruȝ veynes al vnder eorþe: .. For þare beoz ase it veynene weren onder eorþe on. **1297** R. GLOUC. (Rolls) 662 In þe veines of þe water, as þe water deþ vp walle He let closy fur in metal. **1390** GOWER *Conf.* III. 93 For riht as veines ben of blod In man, riht so the water flod Therthe of his cours makth ful of veines. **1483** CAXTON *Gold. Leg.* 382/2 Lete us al praye unto our lord that he opene to us.. here the vaynes of a fontayn or of a welle. **1594** KYD *Cornelia* II. 370 Perceiue we not a petty vaine, Cut from a spring by chaunce or arte, Engendreth fountaines. **1598** SYLVESTER *Du Bartas* II. i. *Handycrafts* 492 A burning Mountain from his fiery vain An yron River rowls along the Plain. **1601** R. JOHNSON *Kingd. & Commw.* (1603) 12 These mountaines are full of bathes and veines of warme water. **1667** MILTON *P.L.* IV. 227 The rapid current,.. through veins Of porous Earth with kindly thirst up drawn. **1789** BRAND *Newcastle* I. 442 There is an order of common-council for cutting off a vein of water which had lately been discovered and brought into the town. **1858** LARDNER *Hand-bk. Nat. Phil.* 90 A feeding reservoir placed above that from which the invariable vein flows. **1864** BRYANT *Sella* 487 She taught The skill to pierce the soil and meet the veins Of clear cold water winding underneath.

fig. **1382** WYCLIF *Jer.* xvii. 13 For thei forsoken the veyne of lyuyng watris [**1388** the Lord, a veyne of quyk watirs]. *c* **1430** LYDG. *Min. Poems* (Percy Soc.) 62 O welle of swetnes replete in every veyne, That al mankynd preserved has fro dethe. **1602** MARSTON *Antonio's Rev.* Prol., Wks. 1856 I. 71 The rawish danke of clumzie winter ramps The fluent summers vaine. **1609** BIBLE (Douay) *Jer.* xvii. 13 They have forsaken the vaine of living waters. **1640** GAUDEN *The Love of Truth*, etc. 7 Then doth the ray or veyn of truth flow aright from God to us.

†b. A streamlet or rivulet; a current. *Obs.*

1600 PORY tr. *Leo's Africa* III. 158 Through the midst of these gardens, they deriue some small vaine of the riuer. **1613** PURCHAS *Pilgrimage* (1614) 705 When hee entred into the Streits, he encountred a great veine of redde water, extending it selfe from Aden as farre as they could see from the Ships tops.

c. *Physics.* A slender body of water or other liquid. (Cf. 1 c.)

1843 *Civil Eng. & Arch. Jrnl.* VI. 39/2 The impulse of a 'vein' of fluid falling perpendicularly, is equal to the weight of a column whose base is the area of the vein.

7. *Min.* A deposit of metallic or earthy material having an extended or ramifying course under ground; a seam or lode; *spec.* a continuous crack or fissure filled with matter (esp. metallic ore) different from the containing rock.

1387 TREVISA *Higden* (Rolls) II. 15 þe water þat renneþ and passeþ by veynes of certayn metal takiþ in his cours grete hete. *c* **1460** J. METHAM *Wks.* (E.E.T.S.) 149 The fourthe day ys gode.. to seke spryngys for wellys off water, to seke also veynys off metel. **1530** PALSGR. 698/2 Al this yerth, so farre as this vayne goth, savoureth of brimstone. **1555** EDEN *Decades* (Arb.) 211 Although golde be founde in maner euery where in these regions of golden Castile.. the myne or veyne whiche owghte to be folowed, ought to bee in a place whiche may stande to saue muche of the charges of the labourers. **1596** DALRYMPLE tr. *Leslie's Hist. Scot.* II. 247 In Clidisdale war funde in Craufurd mure vndir the erd sum vanes ful of golde. **1617** MORYSON *Itin.* III. 136 The inward parts abound with a rich vaine of Mettals, where wonderfull quantitie of most pure Tinne is digged up. **1670** PETTUS *Fodinæ Reg.* 2 When the Miners by these Shafts or Adits do strike or threed a Vein of any Metal.. then the Metal which is digged from those Veins is called Oar. **1709** T. ROBINSON *Nat. Hist. Westmoreld.* 24 These Fissures, by the Miners, are called Dykes, Rakes, Riders, or Veins, according to the Nature of those Classes of Matter they pervade. **1747** HOOSON *Miner's Dict.* O 2, Ore is the very Vein itself, all other Signs of Ore or Vein are not comparable to it; yet this is allowed, that two Sides and Soil between them, formes a dead Vein. **1793** [EARL DUNDONALD] *Descr. Estate Culross* 15 At that time the vein of Roch Salt in Cheshire had not been discovered. **1813** BAKEWELL *Introd. Geol.* (1815) 274 Veins of quartz, and also of slate and granite, and various earthy minerals.. frequently intersect granitic and schistose rocks. **1836-41** BRANDE *Chem.* (ed. 5) 586 Metals are chiefly found in the earth in veins which traverse the granitic, schistose, and limestone rocks. **1875** DAWSON *Dawn Life* ii. 13 Strata often diversified with veins .. of crystalline minerals.

fig. *a* **1667** COWLEY *Death Mr. Jordan* Poems (1905) 22 Like those that work in Mines for others gain. He.. had much more to do, To search the Vein, dig, purge, and mint it too. **1875** WHITNEY *Life Lang.* ix. 171 These are telling indications of an original relationship among all the groups of languages mentioned: outcroppings, as it were, of a vein which invites further exploration.

8. †a. A strip or limited stretch of ground or soil, *esp.* one having a particular character or quality. *Obs.*

1555 WATREMAN *Fardle Facions* II. ii. 119 The whole contrie (excepte a litle vaine of sandie grauelle) is fertile. **1580** TUSSER *Husb.* (1878) 48 Each soile hath no liking of euerie graine, nor barlie and wheat is for euerie vaine. **1611** CORYAT *Crudities* 49, I saw in divers places very fat and fruitfull veines of ground as goodly meadowes, very spatious champaigne fieldes [etc.]. **1624** CAPT. SMITH *Virginia* 144 The most plantations were placed straglingly and scatteringly, as a choice veine of rich ground inuited them. **1693** EVELYN *De la Quint. Compl. Gard.* I. 19 Some Earths are much better than others in every Climate, nay even sometimes in a small Compass of Ground, vulgarly term'd Veins of Earth.

b. A channel or lane of water.

1606 S. GARDINER *Bk. Angling* 1 He prouideth himselfe a ship, keele, or cocke-boat, out of which he may lay out and take in his nets, and be in the vaine and way where the best doing is. **1673** H. STUBBE *Further Vind. Dutch War* App. 131 The King of Sweden.. hath also several districts, channels, or veins Royal in his Seas, which are appropriated to his particular use. **1820** SCORESBY *Acc. Arctic Reg.* I. 229

A lane, or vein, is a narrow channel of water in packs, or other large collections of ice. *Ibid.* 269 Whenever a vein of water appears in the required direction, it is if possible attained. **1835** [see LANE *sb.* 2]. **1867** SMYTH *Sailor's Word-bk.*, *Vein*, the clear water between the openings of floes of ice. The same as *ice-lane*.

c. A current of wind; the track in which this moves.

1792 BELKNAP *Hist. New Hampsh.* III. 24 The next day a whirlwind began..and directed its course toward the east, in a vein of near half a mile wide. **1860** MAURY *Phys. Geog.* xv. §677 Lieutenant Jansen has called my attention to a vein of wind which forms a current in the air as remarkable as that of the Gulf Stream is in the sea. **1867** SMYTH *Sailor's Word-bk.*, *Vein*,..a very limited current of wind—a cat's-paw.

d. *Whaling.* (See quot.)

1851 H. MELVILLE *Whale* II. ii. 5 When making a passage from one feeding-ground to another, the sperm whales, guided by some infallible instinct,..mostly swim in veins, as they are called, continuing their way along a given ocean-line with..undeviating exactitude.

III. *fig.* **9. a.** A strain or intermixture *of* some quality traceable in personal character or conduct, in a discourse or writing, etc.

1565 STAPLETON tr. *Staphylus' Apol.* 153 With the like vaine of euangelicall sincerite. **1587** HOLINSHED *Chron.* III. 1266/1 Bicause it is a veine of godlie deuise, and tending to a verie honorable purpose. **1680** W. ALLEN *Peace & Unity* 16 'Let all your things be done with Charity': a line and vein of this should run through all. **1690** C. NESSE *Hist. Myst. O. & N.T.* I. 117 This is a fear of faith, which hath always a vein of love running along with it. **1701** W. WOTTON *Hist. Rome* 389 A vein of Superstition ran through all his Actions. **1773** BURKE *Corr.* (1844) I. 446 There is a vein of natural good sense in him, from which a good deal might be expected. **1820** *Examiner* No. 612. 11/2 A fine vein of sentiment runs through it. **1849** MACAULAY *Hist. Eng.* vi. II. 20 An English Dominican..with some learning and a rich vein of natural humour. **1867** FREEMAN *Norm. Conq.* (1877) I. 331 There is a vein of bitter sarcasm in the way in which the tale is told.

b. A line or course *of* thought, etc.; a source *of* information.

1704 SWIFT *T. Tub* ii, I have..collected out of ancient authors this short summary of a body of philosophy and divinity, which seems to have been composed by a vein and race of thinking very different from any other systems. **1751** JOHNSON *Rambler* No. 169 ⁋12 Delay opens new veins of thought. **1824** W. IRVING *T. Trav.* I. 217 In the midst of a vein of thought or a moment of inspiration. **1875** JOWETT *Plato* (ed. 2) II. 6 He professes to open a new vein of discourse. **1887** MOLONEY *Forestry W. Africa* 32 The many gentlemen who make the Science of Botany a lifelong study, and who have so many veins of information.

†**10. a.** The tenor or general character *of* something. *Obs.*[-1]

1555 R. TAYLOR in Coverdale *Lett. Martyrs* (1564) 171, I doe beleiue that the Religion set forth in King Edwardes dayes was accordyng to the vayne of the holy Scripture.

†**b.** A kind or species. *Obs. rare.*

1568 BP. CHENY in Strype *Ann. Ref.* (1709) I. lii. 525 These young men, which are of a lower vein,..be not men perfect, as they seem. **1652–62** HEYLIN *Cosmogr.* (1673) III. 29/1 Other Commodities of this Island are..Honey as good as any the world affordeth; and a vein of most delicious vines.

11. A natural tendency towards, a special aptitude or capacity for, the production of literary or artistic work; a particular strain of talent or genius: **a.** With possessives. (The common use.)

1577 GRANGE *Golden Aphrod.* N ij b, If I had Virgilles vayne to indite, or Homers quill. **1581** SIDNEY *Apol. Poetrie* (Arb.) 21 They beeing Poets, dyd exercise their delightful vaine in those points of highest knowledge. **1624** WOTTON *Arch.* Reliq. (1672) 57 Artizans have not only their Growths and Perfections but likewise their Vains and Times. **1697** EVELYN *Numismata* viii. 286 Vittoria Colonna,..whose extraordinary Vein in Poetry was equal with Petrarchs. **1729** T. COOKE *Tales*, etc. 63 Indulge, my Friend, thy modest Vein;..Prospects, gay smiling, aid the Strain. **1762** KAMES *Elem. Crit.* (1833) 336 The fertility of Shakspeare's vein betrays him frequently [etc.]. **1837** LOCKHART *Scott* I. iv. 122 His boyish addiction to verse, and the rebuke which his vein received from the Apothecary's..wife.

b. With *a*, *that*, etc.

1580 G. HARVEY *Three Lett.* Spenser's Wks. (1912) 628 They sauour of that singular extraordinarie veine and inuention, whiche I euer fancied moste. **1599** B. JONSON *Cynthia's Rev.* III. i, You must prove the aptitude of your genius; if you find none, you must hearken out a vein, and buy. **1601** HOLLAND *Pliny* I. 72 All the fabulous veine, and learning of Greece, proceeded out of this quarter. **1656** BRAMHALL *Replic.* ii. 78, I doe not take my self to have so happy a vein, that all that I utter should be a definition. **17..** PHILIPS *Epistle* in *Steele's Poet. Misc.* (1714) 37 Why then, in making Verses should I strain For Wit, and of Apollo beg a Vein? **1732** BERKELEY *Alciphr.* III. §15 For the coffee-houses and populace, we have declaimers of a copious vein. **1820** HAZLITT *Lect. Dram. Lit.* 2 To these might be added others not less learned, nor with a scarce less happy vein.

12. A special or characteristic style of language or expression in writing or speech: **a.** With possessives.

1548 UDALL *Erasm. Par.* Pref. C j b, Though euerie translatour folowe his owne veine of turnyng the Latin into Englishe. **1579** SPENSER *Sheph. Cal.* Oct. 23 To restraine The lust of lawlesse youth with good aduice: Or pricke them forth with pleasaunce of thy vaine. **1597** *Return fr. Parnass.* IV. i. 1166 Lett mee heare Chaucer's vaine firste. I love antiquitie, if it be not harshe. **1605** BACON *Adv. Learn.* I. iv. §2 Then grew the flowing and watery vein of Osorius, the Portugal bishop, to be in price. **1641** BROME *Joviall Crew* I, What say, Sir, to our Poet Scribble here? *Spr.* I like his vain exceeding well. **1818** SCOTT *Provinc. Antiq. Scotl.* (1826) 119 After adorning it with an inscription, somewhat in the vein of Ancient Pistol. **1902** G. SAMPSON *Newman's Sel. Ess.* Introd. p. xxxvi, They [*sc.* these words] are not in Blougram's vein.

b. With *a*, *this*, etc.

1576 N. R. in *Gascoigne's Steele Glas* Wks. 1910 II. 138 Thus divers men with divers vaines did write, But Gascoigne doth in every vaine indite. **1598** BARRET *Theor. Warres* II. i. 29 To haue a sweet vaine in speech. **1620–6** QUARLES *Div. Poems, Hadassa* Pref., A Sober vaine best suits Theologie. *a* **1704** LOCKE *Cond. Underst.* Posth. Wks. (1706) 18 Many a good poetick Vein is buried under a Trade. **1746** FRANCIS tr. *Horace, Sat.* I. iv. 133 Such Rancour this, of such a poisonous Vein, As never, never, shall my Paper stain. **1850** KINGSLEY *A. Locke* ix, Is it not noteworthy also, that it is in this vein that the London poets have always been greatest? **1875** JOWETT *Plato* (ed. 2) I. 276 The answer, Meno, was in the orthodox solemn vein.

c. With *his*, etc., and qualifying term.

1865 KINGSLEY *Herew.* xii, To which Hereward answered, in his boasting vein, that he would bring home that mare. **1873** DIXON *Two Queens* xx. i. IV. 61 Writing a letter in his smoothest vein to Wolsey. **1877** 'H. A. PAGE' *De Quincey* I. xi. 213 The following shows him in his best vein.

†**13. a.** A particular course of action or conduct; a habit or practice. *Obs.*

1597 MORLEY *Introd. Mus.* 124 The composers of that age ..followed only that vaine of wresting in much matter in small boundes. **1615** *Lieut. of Tower's Sp.* in *Harl. Misc.* (Malh.) III. 319, I was much addicted to that idle Vein of Gambling. **1616** R. C. *Times' Whistle* (1871) 62 Thus he runs on his course, til 's drunken vaine Ruines his substance. *c* **1725** SWIFT *Serm.* x. Wks. 1841 II. 164/1 Hence it is become an impertinent vein among people of all sorts to hunt after what they call a good sermon.

†**b.** An inclination or desire, a tendency, towards something specified. *Obs.*

1587 HARRISON *England* II. iii. (1877) 88, I perceiue the abbeie lands haue fleshed you and set your teeth on edge, to aske also those colleges... As you loue your welfares therfore, follow no more this veine, but content your selues with that you haue alreadie. **1625** BACON *Ess.*, *Of Envy* (Arb.) 513 Adrian the Emperour, that mortally Enuied Poets, and Painters, and Artificers, in Works, wherein he had a veine to excell. **1673** TEMPLE *Ess. Ireland* Wks. 1720 I. 109, I suppose the Vein I have had of running into Speculations of this kind..have cost me this present Service.

14. a. Personal character or disposition; also, a particular element or trait in this.

1565 COOPER *Thesaurus* s.v. *Vena*, To know the naturall disposition and veyne of euery man. **1575** GASCOIGNE *Glasse Govt.* Wks. 1910 II. 6 No Terence phrase:..The verse that pleasde a Romaine rashe intent, Myght well offend the godly Preachers vayne. **1590** SHAKS. *Com. Err.* IV. iv. 83 It is no shame, the fellow finds his vaine, And yeelding to him, humors well his frensie. **1639** N. N. tr. *Du Bosq's Compl. Woman* I. 17 They have need of somewhat more than a pleasant veyne, and..at least they have as much discretion as vertue. *a* **1660** *Contemp. Hist. Irel.* (Ir. Archæol. Soc.) II. 145 The veine of those petty Bourkes..may seeme strange to any that is both well affected and fully acquainted with them. **1774** GOLDSM. *Retal.* 59 So provoking a devil was Dick, That we wished him full ten times a day at Old Nick; But, missing his mirth and agreeable vein, As often we wished to have Dick back again. **1819** SHELLEY *Cenci* I. ii. 28 You have a sly, equivocating vein. **1820** LAMB *Elia* I. *Oxford in Vacation*, When the peacock vein rises, I strut a Gentleman Commoner. **1854** KINGSLEY *Lett.* (1878) I. 433, I am afraid I have a little of the wolf-vein in me, in spite of fifteen centuries of civilization.

b. A temporary state of mind or feeling; a humour or mood.

1577–82 BRETON *Toys Idle Head* Wks. (Grosart) I. 28/2 For who continues in this vaine Of setting still,..in the ende he shall be faine To leaue it. **1588** *Marprel. Epist.* (Arb.) 34, I am hardly drawn to a merie vaine from such weightie matters. **1602** *2nd Pt. Return fr. Parnass.* II. iv. 699 Ile take the Gentleman now, he is in a good vayne, for he smiles. **1640** BROME *Sparagus Gard.* IV. vii, Could I get her In a marriage vaine, but she'll not look Upon a man not she. **1723** POPE *Lett.* Wks. 1737 VI. 146 The merry Vein you knew me in, is sunk into a Turn of Reflection. **1760–72** H. BROOKE *Fool of Qual.* (1809) IV. 113 Harry was in no manner of vein ..for entertaining. **1825** SCOTT *Talism.* vi, He knew not how to pursue the pleasing theme, so as to soothe and prolong the vein which he had excited. **1863** GEO. ELIOT *Romola* I. iv, If thou art in a classical vein, put myrtle about his curls and make him a young Bacchus.

c. *in the vein*, in a fit or suitable mood for something.

1593 SHAKS. *Rich. III*, IV. iii. 122 Thou troublest me, I am not in the vaine. **1865** M. ARNOLD *Ess. Crit.* iii. (1875) 119 To produce constantly, to produce whether in the vein or out of the vein. **1879** MEREDITH *Egoist* xxxiv, I like to hear them when I am in the vein. **1905** R. BAGOT *Passport* xix. 176 Nobody can be more amusing when she is in the vein.

†**d.** A fit *of* laughter. *Obs.*[-1]

1734 tr. *Rollin's Anc. Hist.* (1827) VII. 29 He burst into a loud vein of laughter.

IV. 15. *attrib.* and *Comb.* **a.** In sense 1, as ***vein-blood*** (also = blood-letting), ***-healing*** adj., ***-pipe***, ***-streaked*** adj., ***-work***.

c **1386** CHAUCER *Knt.'s T.* 1889 That nother veyne blod, ne ventusyng, Ne drynk of herbes may ben his helpyng. *c* **1425** *St. Christina* ix. in *Anglia* VIII. 123/16 She lete her blode ful often of mykel veyne blode. **1528** PAYNELL *Salerne's Regim.* b iiij, Hit is nat clere nor flowynge, but more lyke to veyne bludde. **1545** RAYNALD *Byrth Mankynde* 17 b, Vayne blood and artire blood. **1590** SPENSER *Muiopot.* 197 Veyne-healing Veruen, and hed-purging Dill. **1594** T. B. *La Primaud. Fr. Acad.* II. To Rdr., The coole refreshing it hath from the lungs, or the veine-pipes proceeding from the liuer. **1890** LE GALLIENNE *G. Meredith* 32 The human form disappears beneath nets of veinwork and muscle. **1894** MRS. DYAN *Man's Keeping* (1899) 118 Urquhart..saw the vein-streaked hand gripping the pipe-stem tremble.

†**b.** In sense 6 b, as ***vein-riveret***. *Obs.*[-1]

1656 HEYLIN *Surv. France* 34 A veine riveret of the Seine.

c. In sense 7, as ***vein fissure***, ***-form***, ***-formation***, ***-gallery***, ***-granite***, ***marble***, etc.; **vein-gold**, gold occurring in a vein or veins.

1855 J. R. LEIFCHILD *Cornwall* 105 The general course of the mineral *vein fissures in these localities. **1883** *Science* 9 Feb. 18/1 A *vein-form similar to the terrestrial veins commonly known as *filons en cocardes*. **1877** RAYMOND *Statist. Mines & Mining* 115 The creeks and gulches.. cutting channels through this *vein-formation. **1897** P. WARUNG *Tales Old Régime* 96 The chamber..into which the *vein-galleries..opened. **1848** W. COLTON *Jrnl.* 6 Nov. in *Three Years Calif.* (1850) xxiii. 312 *Vein-gold in these rocks is as uncertain and capricious as lightning. **1956** G. TAYLOR *Silver* i. 2 The bankets of Witwatersrand, in which vein-gold and alluvial deposits are mixed. **1979** *Econ. Geol.* LXXIV. 1420 (*heading*) Fluid inclusion and geochemical studies of vein gold deposits. **1833** LYELL *Princ. Geol.* III. 355 The *vein-granite of Cornwall very generally assumes a finer grain, and frequently undergoes a change. **1862** *Catal. Internat. Exhib., Brit.* II. No. 2430, Its great strength, ten times that of *vein marble and statuary, renders it safe from breakage. **1872** RAYMOND *Statist. Mines & Mining* 19 Quartz or quartzite predominating as *vein-matrix, and compact limestone as foot-wall. **1874** *Ibid.* 329 The *vein-matter in the westerly portion..is of quite a different nature. **1875** J. H. COLLINS *Metal Mining* 47 In *vein mining trial borings are not often made. **1877** RAYMOND *Statist. Mines & Mining* 131 The active vein-mining counties of California. *Ibid.* 213 The *vein-system consists in most part of a series of nearly parallel veins. **1778** PRYCE *Min. Cornub.* 42 Pyritæ are to be met with..*vein-wise.

d. In sense 3 b, as **vein-banding**, a symptom of some virus diseases of plants, characterized by a change of colour along the main veins of leaves; freq. *attrib.*

1930 *Bull. Kentucky Agric. Exper. Station* No. 309. 481 Veinbanding is a common disease of tobacco in locations where potatoes have been grown. **1957** *Phytopathology* XLVII. 139 (*heading*) Effects of insecticides and physical barriers on field spread of pepper veinbanding mosaic virus. **1979** *Jrnl. Horticultural Sci.* LIV. 23/1 Gooseberry vein banding virus..is aphid transmitted..and, although it is widespread in Europe.., little is known of its economic importance.

vein (veɪn), *v.* Forms: 6 **veyne**, 6–7 **veyn**, 7 **veine**, 7– **vein**; 6 *Sc.* **vane**, 6–7 **vaine** (*Sc.* **uaine**, **wayne**), 7 **vain**. [f. prec. Cf. F. *veiner* in sense 1 b.]

1. *trans.* † **a.** *Sc.* To ornament (a garment, etc.) with narrow stripes of some suitable material. *Obs.*

1502 *Acc. Ld. High Treas. Scot.* II. 200 For ij elne wellus to veyne the samyn cote, iiij li. **1505** *Ibid.* 332 For ane elne wellus to veyn the said cote. **1549** *Ibid.* IX. 351 Ane elne tannye welwote to vane the said goun. **1654** *Burgh Rec. Glasgow* (1881) II. 297 Ane covering of grein cloathe uained [*printed* named] with gallowne lace.

b. To ornament with coloured, incised, or impressed lines or streaks suggestive of veins. Also with *in*.

1686 [see VEINING *vbl. sb.* 1]. **1687** MIÉGE *Gt. Fr. Dict.* II. s.v., To vein a Mantle-piece, to paint it Marble-like with Veins. **1707** MORTIMER *Husb.* (1721) II. 25 They often vein it by Art, especially for Gun stocks and such uses, by steeping of filings of Iron in *Aqua Fortis*. **1755** JOHNSON, *To Marble*, v.a., to variegate, or vein like marble. **1858** SIMMONDS *Dict. Trade*, *Vein*, to stripe or mottle, to marble, etc. **1895** ROWE *Chip-Carving* 40 In veining in the marginal lines of a box or blotter, a ruler is often of great assistance. **1896** *Daily News* 9 June 9/6 The tinted petals are passed up to another room, where they are 'veined' by being squeezed into a sort of mould.

2. *refl.* To diffuse like a vein. *rare*[-1].

1681 T. FLATMAN *Heraclitus Ridens* No. 19 (1713) I. 129 This is *Vox Populi*, this is *Plato Redivivus*, this is Hunt-scrap Mr. Petyt,..and indeed veins it self through all the late Pamphlets and Libels.

3. *trans.* Of things: To extend over or through (something) after the manner of veins.

1807 J. BARLOW *Columb.* x. 226 Proud Mississippi.. Flings forth..Ten thousand watery glades; that, round him curl'd, Vein the broad bosom of the western world. **1844** MRS. BROWNING *Drama of Exile* 399 Yon spectacle of cloud Which seals the gate up to the final doom, Is God's seal manifest... The unmolten lightnings vein it motionless. **1847** TENNYSON *Princ.* IV. 522 All the gold That veins the world. **1889** RIDER HAGGARD *Cleopatra* II. x, Half Hercules and half a fool, with a dash of genius veining his folly through.

†**4.** *intr.* To put oneself into a particular 'vein' or mood. Also with *it*. *Obs.*

1589 WARNER *Alb. Eng.* VI. xxxi. (1612) 154 But her, not coy I found so chast, as saue a kisse or twaine, I nothing got, although in all I vained to her vaine. **1592** *Ibid.* IX. xlvi. 217 Hence Citizens with Courtiours so do vaine it for the time, That with their paper Ladders they euen stately Castels clyme.

†**5.** *refl.* To injure (oneself) in a vein. *Obs.* Cf. *self-vein'd* in Warner *Albion's Engl.* (1602) x. lix. 263.

1631 G. MARKHAM *Country Contentm.* (ed. 4) I. xix. 117 If your Cocke haue in his fight veined himselfe eyther by narrow striking, or other crosse blow, you shall find out the wound.

vein, obs. Sc. form of WEEN *v.*

ˈ**veinage.** *rare.* [f. VEIN *sb.*] The course of a vein or veins; a collection or system of veins.

1875 BLACKMORE *Alice Lorraine* xlviii, Therefore one might see the rich fruit..with russet veinage mellowing. **1881** —— *Christowell* II. ii. 24 His housekeeper, following quickly the veinage of his thoughts,..called back from the top of the back stairs. **1904** *Academy* 23 Apr. 454/2 There is a veinage of supernaturalism through the book.

'veinal, *a.* *rare*—⁰. [f. VEIN *sb.*] = VENOUS *a.*
1846 in WORCESTER (citing Boyle; but perh. a mere error for VENAL *a.*).

veined (veɪnd), *ppl. a.* [f. VEIN *sb.*]
1. Furnished or marked with veins (in various senses): **a.** In predicative use; also with adverbial qualification, as ***finely veined***.
a **1529** SKELTON *P. Sparowe* 1121 Handes soft as sylke, Whyter than the mylke, That are so quyckely vayned. **1611** COTGR., *Veiné*, veined, or full of veines. **1707** MORTIMER *Husb.* (1721) II. 15 The knot of an old Oak..is often finely veined like Walnut. **1760** J. LEE *Introd. Bot.* Explan. Terms 385 *Venosum*, veined, with Veins many Ways. **1796** WITHERING *Brit. Plants* (ed. 3) II. 313 Leafits..veined, of the appearance of those of Skirrets. **1834** McMURTRIE *Cuvier's Anim. Kingd.* 424 Males and females..furnished with long wings, less veined than those of the other Hymenoptera of this section. **1883** JEFFERIES *Story My Heart* i. 13 The million leaves, veined and edge-cut, on bush and tree. **1891** FARRAR *Darkn. & Dawn* lvii, On abaci of carved ivory stood myrrhine vases..red, veined, lustrous.
b. Used attributively.
1793 MARTYN *Lang. Bot.*, *Venosum folium*, a Veined leaf. **1802** PLAYFAIR *Illustr. Huttonian The.* 12 Where that stone is stratified and either coincides with veined granite or with gneiss. **1860** TYNDALL *Glac.* I. i. 7 The means of observing together the veined structure of the ice. **1895** ROWE *Chip-Carving* 39 A series of arcs described from point 2, where the two veined circles meet.
2. Intersected or marked *with* something (esp. a colour) suggestive of veins.
1612 DRAYTON *Poly-olb.* To Rdr., Conveying..through delicate embrodered meadowes, often veined with gentle gliding brooks. **1728** CHAMBERS *Cycl.* s.v. *Marble*, Marble of Brabançon, in Hainault, is Black, vein'd with White. **1766** ENTICK *London* IV. 59 Four Gothic demi-pillars, painted white, and veined with blue. **1769** SIR W. JONES *Palace Fortune* Poems (1777) 13 The round earth with foaming oceans vein'd. **1806** *Med. Jrnl.* XV. 266 Flowers large, white, beautifully veined with purple. **1857** DICKENS *Dorrit* II. xxv, The white marble at the bottom of the bath was veined with a dreadful red. **1882** FLOYER *Unexpl. Baluchistan* 198 Beautiful blue and purple marble veined with white.
3. *fig.* ? Fixed in the blood; ingrained.
1633 FORD *Love's Sacr.* v. i, Come, black Angel, Fair devil, in thy prayers reckon up The sum in gross, of all thy vained follies.
4. Lodged or distributed in veins.
1827–35 WILLIS *Wife's Appeal* 87 To course the veined metals of the earth.

veiner ('veɪnə(r)). [f. VEIN *sb.* or *v.*]
1. a. (See quot. 1883, and cf. VEINING *vbl. sb.* 1 b.)
1864 [F. W. ROBINSON] *Mem. Jane Cameron* I. 119 There were..menders and darners, veiners and winders,..needle-women [etc.]. **1883** SIMMONDS *Dict. Trade, Veiner*, a sewer of muslin in the neighbourhood of Belfast.
b. One who makes veins in artificial flowers.
1881 *Instr. Census Clerks* (1885) 55 [Artificial] Flower Making: Stiffener. Cutter-out. Veiner. *Ibid.*, Leaf Making: ..Cutter-out. Veiner. Shader.
2. In wood-carving, a small V-shaped tool used for making veins in leaves.
1895 ROWE *Chip-Carving* 31 If the student has not a **V** tool he can use the veiner.

'veinery. *rare*—¹. [f. VEIN *sb.*] = VEINAGE.
1826 *Blackw. Mag.* XIX. 392 That arm, through whose blue veinery flowed..blood as pure as the celestial ichor.

veing, obs. Sc. form of *weighing* WEIGH *v.*

'veinify, *v.* *rare*—¹. [f. VEIN *sb.*] *intr.* To produce or form veins.
1615 CROOKE *Body of Man* 57 True it is, that in the Bones there is, that I may so say, a power to bonify or make bones, in the veins to veinefy, so there be an apt disposition of the matter.

'veininess. [f. VEINY *a.*] The condition of being veiny.
1730 BAILEY (fol.), *Veininess*, Fulness of Veins. **1884** TROWBRIDGE *Farnell's Folly* II. l. 233 Incipient veininess of cheek and pendency of jowl were also observable.

veining ('veɪnɪŋ), *vbl. sb.* [f. VEIN *sb.* or *v.*]
1. a. The action or process of ornamenting with vein-like markings.
1686 *Lond. Gaz.* No. 2197/4 A New Art or Invention of Making, Marbling, Veining, and Finishing of Mantle-pieces for Chimneys. **1879** *Cassell's Techn. Educ.* IV. 350/1 (Jewellery), This operation of 'matting', and another which is called 'veining', and which consists in indenting fine lines on and between the work, are to the raised design what shading is to a drawing.
attrib. **1873** SPON *Workshop Rec.* Ser. I. 422/1 Removing some portions of the graining colour with a small veining fitch. **1881** YOUNG *Ev. Man his own Mechanic* §648. 297 The veining-tool..being narrow and used to engrave the veins of leaves and similar work.
b. The operation of producing vein-like patterns with the needle; the result of this work.
c **1840** [see SEEDING *vbl. sb.* 4]. **1849** CRAIG, *Veining*, a kind of needle-work, in which the veins of a piece of muslin are wrought to a pattern. **1888** *Catholic Househ.* 1 Sept. 14/1 The fine needlework on muslin which includes 'veining', 'spoking', 'pointing', and 'lace stitching'. **1900** *Westm. Gaz.* 26 July 3/2 Only very coarse twist veinings, revealing an underlay of white or any contrasting tone. **1903** *Ibid.* 5 Feb. 4/2 The veining itself is simply the common and universally known herring-bone stitch.

2. The arrangement of veins or vein-like markings on or in something; a veined appearance or structure; venation.
1826 KIRBY & SP. *Entomol.* III. xxxv. 610 The circumstance that most strikingly distinguishes *tegmina* from *elytra* is their neuration or veining. **1835** URE *Philos. Manuf.* 86 All the beautiful veining of the riband surface in these circumstances disappears. **1861** S. THOMSON *Wild Fl.* I. (ed. 4) 38 Throughout plants generally, the ribbing or veining is arranged according to two..plans. **1892** *Nation* 8 Dec. 435/1 He may also, occasionally, have deserted a statue because of veinings in the marble.
fig. **1860** O. W. HOLMES *Prof. Breakf.-t.* x, All the veinings of her nature were impressed on these pages.
3. In weaving, a stripe in the cloth formed by a vacancy in the warp. (1849 in CRAIG.)

veinless ('veɪnlɪs), *a.* [f. VEIN *sb.*] Having no veins; destitute of veins. Chiefly *Bot.*, of leaves.
1793 MARTYN *Lang. Bot.* s.v. *Venosum*, When it [a leaf] has no veins,..it is called *Folium Avenium*, a veinless leaf. **1832** LINDLEY *Introd. Bot.* 91 *Veinless*.., when no veins at all are formed, except a slight approach to a costa. **1844** *Florist's Jrnl.* (1846) V. 43 Leaves in pairs, oblong, and veinless. **1863** *Cornh. Mag.* VII. 397 Health gives the bright veinless splendour to the cornea, and lustre to the pupil.

veinlet ('veɪnlɪt). [f. VEIN *sb.* Cf. VEINULET.]
1. A small or minor vein (in various senses).
1831 CARLYLE *Sart. Res.* II. iii, Here, too,..is a vein or veinlet of the grand World-circulation of Waters. **1855** EMERSON *Misc.* viii. 63 He no longer fills the veins and veinlets. **1872** HUXLEY *Physiol.* v. 120 The blood of the capillaries of the lobule is poured into that vein by a minute veinlet.
2. a. *Bot.* A branch or subdivision of a vein or venule.
1832 LINDLEY *Introd. Bot.* 91 The area of parenchyma, lying between two or more veins or veinlets. **1849** BALFOUR *Man. Bot.* §141 There are also other veins of less extent.. given off by the midrib, and these give origin to small *veinlets*. **1857** T. MOORE *Handbk. Brit. Ferns* (ed. 3) 8 The branches of the veins are venules, and the branches of the venules are veinlets. **1877** HEATH *Fern World* 215 Along on each side of the mid veins of the lobes are alternate veinlets.
b. *Geol.* Cf. VEIN *sb.* 7.
1927 [see IANTHINITE]. **1955** [see KUTNAHORITE]. **1974** *Encycl. Brit. Micropædia* IX. 699/1 Sussexite occurs as hydrothermal fibrous veinlets in the U.S. at Franklin, N.J.

'veinling. *rare*—¹. [f. VEIN *sb.*] = prec.
a **1618** SYLVESTER *Job Triumphant* III. 273 Sure, there are mines and veinlings (under ground) Whence Silver's fetcht, and wherein Gold is found.

veinous ('veɪnəs), *a.* [f. VEIN *sb.* Cf. VENOUS *a.* and F. *veineux* (16th c.).]
1. *Phys.* **a.** Full of, traversed by, veins.
1634 T. JOHNSON *Parey's Chirurg.* XI. Wks. (1678) 277 The liver and all the veinous parts being polluted. **1719** BOYER *Dict. Royal* I, *Veineux*,..veinous, full of Veins. **1878** F. J. BELL *Gegenbaur's Comp. Anat.* 68 We find representatives of this in the parasitic Dicyemidæ, which live in the so-called veinous appendages of the Cephalopoda.
b. Occupying the veins.
1801 *Med. Jrnl.* V. 564 The black or veinous blood not sufficiently stimulating the left ventricle.
c. Consisting of veins.
1831 T. HOPE *Ess. Orig. Man* II. 85 In organized matter and bodies only pressures and counterpressures..produce all the divisions and differences of a later and more minute description, first in systems vital, aqueous and aerial,..next ..in later systems sanguineous, veinous and arterial.
2. Having large or prominent veins (also *transf.*); formed by outstanding veins.
1848 DICKENS *Dombey* xxvii, The witch..crouched on the veinous root of an old tree, pulled out a short black pipe. **1859** —— *T. Two Cities* II. viii, She clasped her veinous and knotted hands together. **1885** RIDER HAGGARD *Witch's Head* II. iv. 68 Plowden's thick lips turned quite pale, the veinous cross upon his forehead throbbed.

'vein-stone. Also veinstone. [f. VEIN *sb.*]
1. Stone or earthy matter composing a vein and containing metallic ore; gangue, matrix.
1709 T. ROBINSON *Nat. Hist. Westmoreld.* 37 The appearance of several Veins of Spar, Soil, and Vein-Stone breaking out upon the Surface. **1789** J. WILLIAMS *Min. Kingd.* I. 273 Several feet wide of ore, mixed with spar and vein-stone. *Ibid.* 284 What I call veinstone, is a compound mineral concretion, of various colours, appearances, and degrees of hardness. **1830** LYELL *Princ. Geol.* I. 423 Before sufficient time is allowed for the accretion of a large quantity of veinstone. **1869** *Eng. Mech.* 31 Dec. 380/1 Quartzose veinstone often contains iron pyrites. **1882** *U.S. Rep. Prec. Met.* 599 A simple and cheap mode of extracting the gold from low-grade vein-stone.
b. With pl.: A portion or variety of this.
a **1728** WOODWARD *Fossils* I. 163 Vein-stones, or Bodies consisting of Spar, earthy Stones, or other Matter..found lodg'd in the Veins..of the Strata along with the Ores of Metals and Minerals. **1799** KIRWAN *Geol. Ess.* 410 Of these, the most soluble were first carried off,..and being deposited on the surfaces of the rift, formed, what are called, the vein-stones. **1833–4** J. PHILLIPS *Geol.* in *Encycl. Metrop.* (1845) VI. 777/1 The veinstones are chiefly quartz. **1883** *Science* I. 130/1 All serpentines not veinstones..appear to belong to peridotite.
2. = PHLEBOLITE, -LITH.
1835 *Cycl. Pract. Med.* IV. 443/1 Of phlebolites, vein-stones, or calculi in the veins. **1849–52** *Todd's Cycl. Anat.* IV. II. 1400/2 The curious bodies called phlebolites, phlebolithes, or vein-stones,..are true vascular calculi.

'vein-stuff. [f. VEIN *sb.*] = VEIN-STONE 1.
1833–4 J. PHILLIPS *Geol.* in *Encycl. Metrop.* (1845) VI. 769/1 Metallic matter and certain nonmetallic substances usually connected therewith, and commonly called vein-stuff. **1872** SMYTH *Mining Statistics* 49 The vein-stuff got from the deepest levels is not so rich per ton as the stone obtained in the upper half of the mine. **1881** *Nature* XXV. 59 Malleable native copper..intimately mixed with siliceous vein-stuff.

'veinulet. *rare.* [f. VEIN *sb.* Cf. VENULE.] A small vein or veinlet.
Recent Dicts. also give ***veinule*** 'a minute vein, a venule', as a term of *Bot.* and *Geol.* (perh. after F. *veinule*).
1668 CULPEPPER & COLE *Barthol. Anat.* II. vi. 105 There is plenty of blood..running back from the remotest Veinulets or smallest branches of the Veins. **1846–50** A. WOOD *Class-bk. Bot.* 85 The secondary branches, or those sent off from the veinlets, are the veinulets.

veiny ('veɪnɪ), *a.* [f. VEIN *sb.*]
1. † **a.** ***veiny artery***, one or other trunk of the pulmonary vein. *Obs.*
1594 T. B. *La Primaud. Fr. Acad.* II. 227 For this cause it is called the veiny artery, because it holdeth of the nature both of an artery and of a veine. **1603** J. DAVIES (Heref.) *Microcosmos* Wks. (Grosart) I. 29/1 The Lunges through veiny-artire, aire doth shoue Vnto the hart, it to refresh againe. **1633** P. FLETCHER *Purple Isl.* IV. xxiii. *note*, The third is called the Veiny arterie, rising from the left side, which hath two folds three-forked.
b. Full of blood-veins; having prominent veins; of or pertaining to veins. Also *fig.* (quot. 1612).
1611 COTGR., *Veineux*, veinie, full of veines. **1612** DRAYTON *Poly-olb.* v. 327 So Gresholme far doth stand;.. and Gatholme, nearer land (Which with their veiny breasts intice the Gods of sea). **1681** GREW *Musæum* II. I. iv. 198 Within this Veiny-Coat, lie's a soft, white, thick and Oval Body. **1706** PHILLIPS (ed. Kersey), *Veiny*, belonging to, or full of Veins. **1789** M. MADAN tr. *Persius* (1795) 163 If you say these things among veiny centurions. **1813** SHELLEY *Q. Mab* IX. 234 A gentle start convulsed Ianthe's frame; Her veiny eyelids quietly unclosed. **1813** *Examiner* 22 Feb. 124/1 The hands..are divested of their too veiny inflation. **1888** 'L. SCOTT' (Mrs. Baxter) *Tuscan Stud.* II. iv. 223 There is a general darkness and veiny roughness about the hands of the performers.
2. a. Traversed by veins of a different (mineral) substance or structure.
1708 OZELL *Boileau's Lutrin* 46 The veiny Flint and hardy Steel ingage. **1778** PRYCE *Min. Cornub.* 96 A kind of Stone ..not at all of a veiny quality. **1783** JUSTAMOND tr. *Raynal's Hist. Indies* IV. 476 Veiny diamonds, in which these extremities are not uniform, and in the same direction. **1797** MRS. RADCLIFFE *Italian* vi, She could see the veiny precipices and tangled thickets that closely impended over the road.
b. Full of, having the nature of, veins or continuous passages.
1827 HOOD *Mids. Fairies* lx, We bear the gold and silver keys Of bubbling springs and fountains, that below Course thro' the veiny earth. **1854** H. E. J. HOWARD *Rape Proserpine* 11 Is it the wind, that works its stealthy way Where veiny clefts the secret pass betray?
3. Marked by veins of colour.
c **1711** PETIVER *Gazophyl.* Dec. VIII. Tab. 71 A hard reddish veiny Wood from the Philippine Isles. **1727–46** THOMSON *Summer* 135 Effulgent, hence the veiny marble shines. **1800** *Hull Advertiser* 11 Oct. 2/3 Six blocks of very superior veiny marble. **1816** J. SCOTT *Vis. Paris* (ed. 5) 162 The finest specimens..have been cleansed and repaired till they look like lapis lazuli jars, stained and veiny.
4. *Bot.* Of leaves: Having many veins.
c **1711** PETIVER *Gazophyl.* Dec. VI. Tab. 59 The true Ipecacuanha..a low Plant with..soft veiny Leaves. **1760** J. LEE *Introd. Bot.* III. v. (1765) 184 *Venose*, veiny. **1807** J. E. SMITH *Phys. Bot.* 166 *Venosum*, veiny, when the vessels by which the leaf is nourished are branched, subdivided, and more or less prominent. **1828** —— *Eng. Flora* II. 89 Leaflets ..ovate, veiny, deeply serrated and cut. **1849** *Florist* 232 It will give an idea of coarseness, as in a veiny Pelargonium.

veip, obs. Sc. f. WEEP *v.*

veir, southern ME. var. FAIR *a.*; obs. var. VAIR *sb.*; var. VERE (spring) *Obs.*; obs. Sc. f. *weir* WAR *sb.*, WEAR *v.*

veird, obs. Sc. form of WEIRD *sb.*

veirdit, obs. form of VERDICT.

† **veire**, *adv.* and *sb.* *Obs.* Also veyre; veir, vair. [a. ONF. *veire*, *veir*, = OF. *voire*, *voir*, adv. and sb., f. *voir*:—L. *vēr-um* true.] (*in*) *veir*(*e*, truly, in truth. (Cf. VAIRES.)
13.. *K. Alis.* 1000 (Laud MS.), [They] sworen, & seiden veire, Alisaundre was fals ayre. *Ibid.* 5660. *Ibid.* 5663 And ȝif of fele hiwe is þe eyre, So shullen þe stones ben in veyre. *c* **1330** *Arth. & Merl.* 7640 He had made him in al air To þe lond, þat of hem com veir. *Ibid.* 8613, etc.

veire, southern ME. var. FAIR *a.* and *adv.*; obs. f. VAIR.

veiring, obs. Sc. f. WEARING *vbl. sb.*

veirs, obs. Sc. f. VERSE *sb.*

veis, var. VEES[1].

veise. *Mining.* Also veize, etc. [Of obscure origin.] (See quots.)
1883 GRESLEY *Gloss. Coal-M.* 269 *Veises*, joints in the coal strata. **1886** J. BARROWMAN *Sc. Mining Terms* 69 *Veize*, *vees*, *vise*, the line of fracture of a fault or hitch.

veit, obs. Sc. f. WET *a.*, WITE *v.*

veitchberry ('viːtʃbɛrɪ). [f. *Veitch*, surname of a family of nurserymen + BERRY *sb.*[1]] A hybrid bramble produced in 1925 by crossing a raspberry and a blackberry; the fruit of this, resembling a large reddish blackberry.

1925 *Daily News* 26 Aug. 3/2 One of the novelties at the Royal Horticultural Society's Show, in Vincent-square, W., held yesterday, is the veitchberry—produced from a blackberry and a raspberry. *Ibid.* (*caption*) The veitchberry compared with the size of a halfpenny. **1956** *Good Housek. Home Encycl.* (ed. 4) 118/1 Plant..veitchberries and wineberries 6 feet apart. **1980** *Amat. Gardening* 25 Oct. 20/1 Other hybrid berries..include the boysenberry, with large fruits but darker than a Loganberry, the Veitchberry and the Youngberry.

veiunge, southern ME. var. FAYING *vbl. sb.*

veive, Sc. var. VIVE *a.*

veize, obs. dial. var. FEEZE *v.*[1]

vejour, var. VEYOR *Obs.*

vekke, var. VECKE *Obs.*

vekyt, obs. Sc. f. WICKED *a.*

vel, southern ME. var. FELL *sb.* and pa. t. of FALL *v.*; obs. Sc. f. WELL *adv.*

vela, pl. of VELUM.

velaghe, southern ME. var. FELLOW *sb.*

velam(e, obs. ff. VELLUM.

‖**velamen** (vɪ'leɪmən). Pl. **-amina**. [L. *vēlāmen*, f. *vēlāre* to cover.]

1. *Bot.* The outer envelope or covering of the aerial roots of some arums and orchids.

1882 VINES tr. *Sachs's Bot.* 690 Rain or dew which moistens the root-envelope (velamen) or wounded surfaces. **1884** BOWER & SCOTT *De Bary's Phaner.* 227 A continuous layer of air-containing tracheides covers, as a *sheath* or *velamen*, the aerial roots of epiphytic orchids.

2. *Anat.* A membranous covering or integument.

In recent Dicts., which also give *velamentum* in the same sense.

vela'mentous, *a.* [f. mod.L. *velamentum*: cf. prec. and L. *vēlāmenta* pl.] Of the nature of a membrane or membranous covering.

1891 *Cent. Dict.* s.v., The velamentous arms of the nautilus. **1902** *Brit. Med. Jrnl.* 29 March 773 Velamentous insertion of the cord.

velans, -ly, varr. VILLAINS *a.*, VILLAINSLY *adv.*, *Obs.*

velany, obs. f. VILLAINY.

velar ('viːlə(r)), *a.* (and *sb.*) Also 9 *erron.* **vellar**. [ad. It. *velare*, F. *vélaire*, or L. *vēlār-is*, f. L. *vēlum* sail, curtain, etc.: cf. VELUM.]

1. *Arch.* (See quots.)

1726 LEONI *Alberti's Archit.* I. 55/1 A Vault..which for its resemblance to a swelling Sail, we..call a Velar Cupola. **1823** P. NICHOLSON *Pract. Build.* 595 *Vellar cupola*, a cupola or dome, terminated by four or more walls. **1842** GWILT *Archit.* 1050.

2. a. *Phon.* Of sounds: Produced by means of the soft palate.

Applied specifically to one of the two sets of guttural sounds existing in the original Indo-European language.

1876 *Academy* 4 Nov. 457/1 The author begins with the now well-known distinction of the *k* sounds into two sets, which he calls velar and palatal. **1883** I. TAYLOR *Alphabet* I. 160 The Semitic alphabets..have no symbols for certain classes of sounds, such as the velar gutturals. **1888** KING & COOKSON *Sounds & Infl.* vi. 117 According to place of articulation they can be divided into labial, dental, palatal, and velar sounds.

b. As *sb.* A velar guttural.

1886 T. LE M. DOUSE *Introd. Gothic* 37 The guttural element of a velar may vanish. *Ibid.*, The velars themselves may be palatalized. **1888** KING & COOKSON *Sounds & Infl.* vi. 118 The distinction between palatals and velars is comparatively recent and of great importance in the history of modern philology.

3. *Zool.* Of or pertaining to a velum.

1878 F. J. BELL *Gegenbaur's Comp. Anat.* 328 The cilia in the velar circlet are those that are most markedly developed. **1880** *Nature* XXII. 147/2 Velar centrifugal canals..are peculiar to this genus. **1883** *Encycl. Brit.* XVI. 663/1 The post-oral hemisphere of the Trochosphere grows more rapidly than the anterior or velar area.

Hence **ve'larity**, velar quality.

1952 *Archivum Linguisticum* IV. 72 The apostrophe after *n* and *g* indicates velarity. **1964** [see *alveolarity* s.v. ALVEOLAR *a.* and *sb.*].

velaric (vɪ'lærɪk), *a.* *Phonetics.* [f. VELAR *a.* + -IC.] Produced or characterized by a velar articulation, in which there is total or partial closure between the back of the tongue and the velum.

1934 in WEBSTER. **1938** D. M. BEACH *Phonetics of Hottentot Lang.* vi. 74 A..bilabial implosive may be made by closing the lips together, raising the back of the tongue to touch the velum, and then producing a partial vacuum between the lips & the velum by lowering the front of the tongue... This bilabial implosive may be termed a bilabial velaric click. **1959** [see GLOTTALIC *a.*].

‖**velarium** (vɪ'lɛərɪəm). Pl. **velaria**. [L. *vēlārium* awning, f. *vēlum* sail, etc., VELUM.]

1. *Rom. Antiq.* A large awning used to cover a theatre or amphitheatre as a protection against sun or rain.

1834 LYTTON *Pompeii* v. ii, The obstinate refusal of one part of the velaria to ally itself with the rest. **1836** C. WORDSWORTH *Athens* xiii. (1855) 76 As if for the insertion of horizontal beams, on which, in the more effeminate times of Athens, a velarium, or awning, was perhaps extended. **1880** L. WALLACE *Ben-Hur* 267 When he sat under the purple velaria of the Circus Maximus.

transf. **1892** *Contemp. Rev.* Nov. 681 The great velarium of the pulpit, intended as a sounding board for the preacher's voice, was spread over the nave like a vast bird.

2. *Zool.* A thin marginal rim on the bell of certain hydrozoans.

1888 ROLLESTON & JACKSON *Anim. Life* 782 The bell itself is somewhat flattened... Its margin never becomes inflected inwards: when it is thin and velum-like..it is termed by Haeckel 'velarium'.

velarization (viːləraɪ'zeɪʃən). *Phonetics.* [f. VELAR *a.* + -IZATION.] A (normally secondary) articulation of a consonant, in which the back of the tongue is raised to or towards the velum; also, in some languages, applied to the articulation of some vowels.

1915 G. NOËL-ARMFIELD *Gen. Phonetics* xvii. 102 If it be found necessary to indicate velarisation in a script it may be done by placing a small ᵘ over the usual symbol. **1936** *Language* XII. 17 A further example is the velarization of the nasal consonant of Spanish *Cinco* [θiŋko], which is still felt to be a member of the *n* phoneme. **1962** A. C. GIMSON *Introd. Pronunc. Eng.* iv. 30 In the so-called 'dark' [ɫ]..there is an essential raising of the back of the tongue towards the velum (velarization). **1975** I. R. MACPHERSON *Spanish Phonology* vi. 43 When *a* precedes a velar consonant, the semivowel *w*, or a velar vowel, it is..attracted towards the point of articulation of the following sound and may become slightly velarized. The diacritical sign - can be placed under the vowel to indicate a degree of velarization. **1976** *Archivum Linguisticum* VII. 93 These [Rhenish] dialects further have velarization of final [n] in, for example, [wiŋ'] *Wein*, [bruŋ'] *braun*.

So **'velarize** *v. trans.* (*rare*), (*a*) to prescribe velarization for, (*b*) to produce by velarization; **'velarized** *ppl. a.*

1915 G. NOËL-ARMFIELD *Gen. Phonetics* xvii. 102 Similarly there are consonants, otherwise normal, in the production of which the back of the tongue is raised to the *u* position. These are known as velarised sounds. *Ibid.*, [*Note*] Confusion should not be made between velarised and velar consonants. nᵘ is quite different from ŋ. The Arabic emphatics are velarised consonants. **1939** L. H. GRAY *Found. Lang.* iii. 57 There are..many modifications of consonants, such as palatalised (e.g., Irish *te*..'hot'..); velarized or pharyngalized (e.g. the final sound of English *little, feel*). **1960** D. DE CAMP in Le Page & De Camp *Jamaican Creole* II. 137 Postvocal /l/ is so strongly velarized that such pairs as /fuul/ *fool* and /fuo/ *foe* are acoustically very similar. **1977** *Word* 1972 XXVIII. 173 The rule which velarizes an alveolar consonant must precede the one which reduces prestress syllables. **1980** A. ALPERS *Life K. Mansfield* 12 His sisters..often called him 'Bogie', or 'Bogey' (which perhaps was velarised from 'Boy').

'velary, *a.* [f. L. *vēl-um* sail: see -ARY.] Pertaining to the sails of a ship.

1891 in *Cent. Dict.*

velat, obs. form of VELVET.

velate ('viːlət), *a.* [f. L. *vēl-um* VELUM, or ad. L. *vēlāt-us*, pa. pple. of *vēlāre* to cover.] **a.** *Bot.* (See quots. 1857–66.) **b.** *Zool.* Having a velum.

1857 A. GRAY *First Less. Bot.* (1866) 236 *Velate*, furnished with a veil. **1866** *Treas. Bot.* 1206/2 *Velate*, partially concealed from view; veiled. **1880** *Nature* XXII. 147/1 It is remarkable among all Hydromedusæ (velate medusæ, that is, exclusive of Charybdæa).

†**velated**, *ppl. a.*[1] *Obs.* [f. L. *vēlāt-us*: see prec.] Covered over; veiled, hidden.

1542 BECON *Potat. Lent* iv. H vj, But what doth it mene. That the Crosse is caried forth beynge couered with a clothe..? *Phil.* The Crosse so velated & couered signifieth Christ. **1653** R. SANDERS *Physiogn.* A 4 By a sedulous search into their velated nature, and abscond disposition.

'velated, *ppl. a.*[2] *Zool.* [f. L. *vēl-um* VELUM.] Furnished with a velum or sail-like membrane.

1835–6 *Todd's Cycl. Anat.* I. 527/2 The physiologist, in contemplating the structure of the velated arms [of the octopus], is compelled to disallow them the power of being ..expanded to meet the breeze. **1895** A. H. COOKE in *Molluscs & Brachiopods* 384 The principal agents in the deposition of the shell [of young *Argonauta*] are the two velated or web-like arms.

ve'lation. *rare*⁻¹. [ad. late L. *vēlātio*, f. *vēlāre* to veil.] **a.** The action of veiling or the fact of being veiled. **b.** The formation of a velum.

1891 in *Cent. Dict.* **1922** JOYCE *Ulysses* 719 The visible signs of post-satisfaction? A silent contemplation: a tentative velation.

velau-, velaȝrede, southern ME. var. FELLOWRED *Obs.*

velawe, southern ME. var. FELLOW *sb.* and *v.*

velcom, -cum, obs. Sc. ff. WELCOME.

Velcro ('vɛlkrəʊ). Also **velcro**. [f. F. *vel(ours cro(ché* hooked velvet.] A proprietary name for a fabric made in narrow strips for use as a fastener, one strip having tiny loops and the other hooks so that they can be fastened or unfastened simply by pressing together or pulling apart.

1960 *Trade Marks Jrnl.* 30 Nov. 1521/1 *Velcro*... Narrow fabrics in imitation of velvet being textile smallwares for use as fasteners or fastenings for clothing. **1961** *Practitioner* July 113 We have been experimenting for some time with the new Bri-nylon fastener, 'velcro', using it particularly for patients who have difficulty in doing up buttons, trousers and belts. **1968** *Guardian* 9 May 9/4 False ringlets on a Velcro band. **1971** 'A. YORK' *Infiltrator* vii. 96 They had dressed him in a blue sleepcoat, which..was secured up the front by a strip of velcro. **1979** P. L. G. BATEMAN *Household Pests* II. 76 Fly screening of windows..is fairly easy with flexible plastic flyscreens which use Velcro to fasten them to the window frames. **1982** *Habitat Catal.* 1982/83 14/1 The roll overarm cushions, filled with polyester, can be held in place with velcro, if required.

Hence **'Velcroed, 'velcroed** *a.* (or pa. pple. of *Velcro* vb.), provided with Velcro; attached by Velcro.

1972 O. SELA *Bearer Plot* xxiv. 152 He..pulled the carpet. 'Note the velcroed edge... Just put it back and it sticks.' **1981** J. D. MACDONALD *Free Fall in Crimson* xviii. 204 By early June I was walking... I worked with the weight Velcroed around my ankle every evening. **1983** *Washington Post* 13 Feb. c-3/3 You put a hand out to stop yourself..and bump all those Velcroed things off the wall.

‖**veld** (vɛlt, vɛld, fɛlt). Also **veldt, velt**. [a. older Du. *veldt*, now *veld* (vɛlt): see FIELD *sb.* The spelling *veld* is now the only permissible form in S. Africa and the most usual form in other varieties of English.]

1. In South Africa, the unenclosed country or open pasture-land.

Freq. with defining terms denoting character or locality, as *bush-, grass-, high, low, sour, sweet veld.* Hence occas. in *pl.*(quot. 1876).

α. **1785**, **1801** [see next sense]. **1835** A. STEEDMAN *Wanderings S. Afr.* I. II. i. 92 Here for the first time we bivouacked in what is called the *Veld.* **1852** C. BARTER *Dorp & Veld* 43 My preference for a less confined sleeping-place on the open 'veld'. **1863** W. C. BALDWIN *Afr. Hunting* ix. 404 The velt is now full of a poisonous herb, which is certain death in a few hours to oxen. **1876** *Encycl. Brit.* V. 42/1 The pastoral lands or velds..are distinguished according to the nature of the grass or sedge which they produce as 'sweet' or 'sour'. **1892** *Tablet* 13 Aug. 260 The priest lived under a tent on the veld.

β. **1862** COLENSO *Pentateuch* I. 114 Joseph..wandering alone upon the veldt in search of his brethren. **1879** *Daily News* 28 June 5/6 In the veldt..with a saddle for one's pillow. **1888** *Times* (weekly ed.) 25 May 7/3 Streets and squares and public buildings, where a year and a half ago was nothing but the boundless veldt.

2. a. *attrib.*, as ***veld fire, knowledge, lily, side, stool***, etc.

Similar uses are common from 1900 onwards.

1785 G. FORSTER tr. *Sparrman's Voy. Cape of Good Hope* II. xiv. 144 The *land-drost* has appointed one of the farmers, with the title of *veld-corporal*, to command in these wars. **1801** J. BARROW *Trav. S. Afr.* I. 378 Louw, the Veld Commandant, readily offered his services. **1861** ANDERSSON *Okavango River* 49 The tremendous 'veldt' fires, which, ravaging the country far and wide, make it like a huge fiery furnace. **1863** W. C. BALDWIN *Afr. Hunting* i. 25 A deal table and a lot of velt stools and wagon chests the only furniture. **1895** J. G. MILLAIS *Breath fr. Veldt* (1899) 78 A faithful native, who instructed him in veldt knowledge and all the arts of spooring. **1899** *Daily News* 24 Oct. 5/4 Here the veldt lilies and creeping convolvulus are beginning to bloom. **1946** R. CAMPBELL *Talking Bronco* 66 With veld-flowers as an afterthought. **1959** *Cape Times* 18 July 2/5 The veld flowers should be excellent this year.

b. Special Comb. (chiefly with the spelling *veld*), as **veld-cornet**, = *field-cornet* FIELD *sb.* 21; **veld-craft**, skill in matters pertaining to survival on the veld; **veld fever** (see quot.); **veld-kos, -kost** [Du. *kost* food] (see quot.); **veldman, veldsman**, one skilled in living or hunting on the veldt; **veld pig**, the Ethiopian wart-hog (*Phacochœrus ethiopicus*); **veld rat**, the striped rat of S. Africa; **veld sickness** (see quot.); **veld sores**, a form of skin eruption due to living on the open veldt.

1802 G. M. THEAL *Rec. Cape Colony* (1899) IV. 324, I have the honor to add the original report of the *Veld Cornet Nicholaus Johannes Roets, sent to me with those Hottentots. **1852** J. C. BROWN *Arbousset's Narrative* xxiii. 350 He went to the drinking place of a veldcornet, a kind of country magistrate. **1899** RIDER HAGGARD *Swallow* ix, I, as Veld-Cornet of the district, have tried the case according to the law. **1905** D. BLACKBURN *R. Hartley, Prospector* 205 He associated with greedy, scheming directors, who were ignorant of *veld-craft. **1910** J. BUCHAN *Prester John* xiv. 232 The veld-craft I had mastered had taught me a few things. **1980** *Country Life* 9 Oct. 1258/1 Olive Schreiner.. possessed considerable veldt-craft and also the power of minute observation. **1899** MRS. PHILLIPS *S. Afr. Recoll.* 9 '*Veld fever' is a malady, a longing indescribable, which comes over many South Africans, who have lived much on the veld. **1834** PRINGLE *Afr. Sk.* 82 The *veld-kost we will gather. *Ibid.* 523 *Veld-kost*, literally *country-food*, is the term used for the wild roots and bulbs eaten by the Bushmen. **1948** *Cape Argus* (Mag. Section) 23 Oct. 1/7 The summer rains of 1915 had revived the fountains and veldkos was abundant. In a drought year he could not have survived. **1961** *Africa* XXXI. 231 When !U had a baby, her sister, Di!ai, gathered veldkos for her for five days. **1899** *Contemp.*

Rev. Oct. 475 Stout wardens of the marches who are known to be as good *veldmen and riflemen as any Boers in Africa. **1895** J. G. MILLAIS *Breath fr. Veldt* (1899) 286 Tace..liked to parade himself as an old Veldtsman. **1863** W. C. BALDWIN *Afr. Hunting* vi. 155 Just after sunset..a flac farc (*veldt pig) came out of a hole near me. **1905** *Rep. Brit. Assoc.* 551 The disease has been observed in *veld rats (*Arvicanthus pumilio*), cats, and in one dog. **1896** R. WALLACE *Farming Ind. Cape Colony* 82 Animals brought from sweet veld suffer from what is termed *veld sickness, which results from insufficient nutrition and the hard and irritating nature of the food consumed. **1898** RAE *Malaboch Campaign* 61 Owing to the insufficient supply of vegetables, there were several cases of *veld sores. **1901** *Brit. Med. Jrnl.* No. 2095. 486 Veld sores formed the most frequent entry in the morning company sick reports.

velde, southern ME. var. FIELD, pa. t. FEEL *v.*, FELL *v.*, FOLD *v.*; obs. Sc. f. WIELD *v.*

†**velderude.** *Obs.*$^{-0}$ [app. f. *velde* FIELD *sb.* + *rude* RUD *sb.*^{2}] = HERB JOHN 1.

c **1265** *Voc.* in Wr.-Wülcker 557 *Ypis, i.* herbe Johan, *i.* uelderude.

veldevare, -ver, dial. varr. FIELDFARE.

veld-shoe ('vɛldʃuː), **vel(d)skoen** ('fɛl(t)skʊn). orig. *S. African.* Forms: veld(t)(-)shoe; veldschoen, -schoon, -skoen (*pl.* -skoen(e), -skoens), vel(d)t-; velschoen (*pl.*), velskoen. [a. or ad. Cape Du. *veldschoen*, earlier *velschoen*, f. Du. *vel* skin, FELL *sb.*^{1} + *schoen* SHOE *sb.*; the first element has been assimilated to *veld* VELD.

The most common forms in S. Afr. English are *veldskoen* and *velskoen* (pl. *-s* or *-e*) but the anglicized form *veld-shoe* is occasionally used.]

Formerly, a light shoe made of untanned hide. Now, a heavy boot or shoe for outdoor work.

α. **1822** BURCHELL *Trav.* I. 214 The Hottentots..soon took off the hide, which they cut in small pieces, for the purpose of making *velschoen* (hide-shoes). **1883** OLIVE SCHREINER *Afr. Farm* I. ii, On their feet they wore home-made 'vel-schoen'.

β. **1834** PRINGLE *Afr. Sk.* iv. 178 A sort of sandals..are in common use, called *veld-schoenen* (country shoes). **1850** R. G. CUMMING *Hunter's Life S. Afr.* (1902) 139/1 Here I divested myself of my leather trousers, shooting belt, and veltschoens. **1885** RIDER HAGGARD *K. Solomon's Mines* (1887) 201, I discarded my trousers,..retaining only my veldt-schoons. **1892** *Journal* (Grahamstown) 11 July 3 (Advt.) Colonial-made 'Star' Standard screw veldschoens and boots. **1894** *Pall Mall Mag.* Sept. 38 A Boer veldt-schoen upon the right foot. **1919** *Manch. Guardian* 10 Dec. 4 (Advt.), I believe this is the latest development of the Lotus welted-veldtschoen. **1962** L. DEIGHTON *Ipcress File* xxxii. 207, I put on Irish tweed with Veldtshoen, cotton shirt, and wool tie. **1969** J. SELBY *Boer War* i. 34 They wore wide-brimmed felt hats and soft veldschoen on their feet. **1977** *Listener* 3 Mar. 279/4 (Advt.), Veldtschoën... Virtually waterproof... Double leather soles..£21.50.

γ. **1863** W. C. BALDWIN *Afr. Hunting* vi. 212 No heels to my veldt shoes, which were made of blesbuck skin. **1972** *Stand. Encycl. S. Afr.* XI. 545/1 By the end of the 1960s.. the veld-shoe industry..declined because antiquated machinery..proved too much of a handicap.

δ. **1939** S. CLOETE *Watch for Dawn* xxii. 312 He made a new belt, new velskoen. **1942** 'B. KNIGHT' *Sun climbs Slowly* ii. 12 The life in Pretoria is very simple..to be called 'Lotta' and wear print frocks and *veldskoen*. **1945** *Cape Times* 29 Oct. 1/3 He was wearing..grey flannel trousers, a white silk shirt and velskoene. **1974** N. GORDIMER *Conservationist* 215 Alina..finds a pair of veldskoen in the house and brings them.

veldt-marshal, variant of VELT-MARSHAL.

†**vele.** *Obs.* Also **veale.** [var. of VEIL *sb.*^{1}, after It. and Sp. *velo*, L. *vēlum.*] A veil or covering.

α. **1580** SPENSER *Three Proper Lett.* i. Wks. (1912) 611 Wote ye why his Moother with a Veale hath coouered his Face? **1591** —— *Ruines Rome* i, Thrice hauing seene vnder the heauens veale Your toombs deuoted compasse ouer all. **1593** HARVEY *Pierce's Superer.* Wks. (Grosart) II. 161 To examine matters barely, without their veales, or habiliments.

β. **1582** N. T. (Rhem.) *Heb.* ix. 3 After the second vele, the tabernacle. *Ibid.* x. 20 By the vele, that is, his flesh. **1590** SPENSER *F.Q.* I. viii. 19 In his fall his shield, that couered was, Did loose his vele by chaunce, and open flew. *Ibid.* II. xii. 77 [Acrasia] was arayd..All in a vele of silke and siluer thin. **1591** SAVILE *Tacitus, Hist.* I. lxvi. 37 They..with sacred veles and infules afore them..mollified the soldiers minds.

vele, southern ME. var. FEEL *v.*, FELE *a.*; obs. f. VEAL; obs. Sc. f. WEEL *sb.*, WELL *adv.*

†**veled**, *ppl. a. Obs.*$^{-1}$ [Cf. VELE.] Veiled.

1565 STAPLETON *Fortr. Faith* 116 They were veled, attended to singing Gods seruice, came to a common refectory.

‖**Ve'lella.** *Zool.* [mod.L. (Gmelin and Lamarck), f. L. *vēlum* sail.] A genus of siphonophorous oceanic hydrozoans; a member of this genus.

1834 MCMURTRIE *Cuvier's Anim. Kingd.* 482 The Porpita and Velella..which were formerly joined with the Medusæ. **1860** WRAXALL *Life in Sea* x. 243 The Velellæ have a very extended geographical range. **1861** P. P. CARPENTER in *Rep. Smithsonian Instit. 1860*, 240 The animals are believed to sleep by day and prey upon the Jelly Fish and Velellas by night. **1882** *Cassell's Nat. Hist.* VI. 284 The little Velella.. has been compared to a little raft with an obliquely placed upright sail.

Hence **ve'lellidous** *a.*, related to *Velella.*

1845 *Encycl. Metrop.* VII. 268/1 The Velellidous Acalephs have within their soft substance a cartilaginous or calcareous plate or disc.

velem, obs. f. VELLUM.

velen, velenie, obs. ff. VILLAIN *a.*, VILLAINY.

veleta (və'liːtə). Also **valeta.** [f. Sp. *veleta* weathervane.] A ballroom round dance for couples in triple time, originating in England in 1900.

1900 A. MORRIS (*sheet-music title*) Veleta. **1911** D. H. LAWRENCE *White Peacock* I. viii. 148 She made me take her through a valeta, a minuet, a mazurka, and she danced elegantly. **1936** 'R. HYDE' *Passport to Hell* 84 The pre-war dances—..the Maxina, the Valeta. **1966** [see *Gay Gordons* s.v. GAY *a.* 9]. **1974** D. SMITH *Look back with Love* xii. 113 Most of the evening was taken up with waltzes, barn dances and veletas. **1978** S. SHERLOCK in D. Abse *My Medical School* 105 We danced the Veleta, the Gay Gordons, the Dashing White Sergeant.

velewit, obs. f. VELVET.

velfull, obs. Sc. f. WEALFUL *a.*

velic ('viːlɪk), *sb.* and *a. Phonetics.* [f. VEL(UM + -IC.] **A.** *sb.* (See quot. 1943.) **B.** *adj.* Pertaining to or involving the velum or its movement.

1943 K. L. PIKE *Phonetics* iv. 58 The upper part of the soft palate facing the nasopharynx is the velic (so called in this discussion to distinguish it from the velum, which represents the lower side toward the mouth); the closure of the nasal passage is therefore a velic closure (in contrast to velar closure, when the tongue touches the soft palate). **1971** CHIN-WU KIM in W. O. Dingwall *Survey Linguistic Sci.* 34 At time 4, the lip rounding for [u] and [w] is super-imposed on [k]; at time 5, their velic quality underlies [l]. **1975** *Amer. Speech 1972* XLVII. 244 *Pin* and *bin* are the same at the end and in the middle and *partly* the same at the beginning: for both, the lips are closed and the velic is closed. **1981** *Canad. Jrnl. Linguistics* Spring 81 The key features involved are velic closure (for nasalization), apical closure (for stops, fricatives, liquids), and vocal cord vibration (voicing).

velicotte, obs. variant of WYLIECOAT.

veliferous (viː'lɪfərəs), *a.* [f. L. *vēlifer*, f. *vēlum* VELUM: see -FEROUS.]

†**1.** Carrying sails. *Obs.*

1656 BLOUNT *Glossogr.*, *Veliferous*, that bears saile, or is under sail, as a ship. **1674** EVELYN *Navig. & Commerce* 53 Nay, so addicted were they to Sailing, that they invented Veliferous Chariots, and to Sail upon the Land. **1697** —— *Numismata* viii. 280 Stevinus who framed the Veliferous Chariot.

2. *Zool.* Bearing a velum; membranous.

1871 T. R. JONES *Anim. Kingd.* (ed. 4) 614 With its veliferous arms thus firmly embracing its abode, the Argonaut has two modes of progression.

†**ve'lific(al**, *a. Obs.*$^{-0}$ [f. L. *vēlificus.*] (See quots.) Also †**ve'lificate** *v.* [f. L. *vēlificāre, -ārī*], **velifi'cation** [ad. L. *vēlificātio*]. *Obs.*$^{-0}$

1623 COCKERAM I, *Velificate*, to saile. *Ibid.*, *Velification*, a sailing. **1656** BLOUNT *Glossogr.*, *Velifical*, that is done with sails displayed or full spread. *Ibid.*, *Velification*, a sailing forwards, or hoysting sail; a course or voyage. **1727** BAILEY (vol. II), *Velifick*, done or performed with Sails.

'**veliform**, *a. rare*$^{-0}$. [f. L. *vēli-* VELUM.] Having the form of a velum.

1891 in *Cent. Dict.*

veliger ('viːlɪdʒə(r)). *Zool.* [f. as prec. + *-ger* bearing. Cf. L. *vēliger* sail-bearing.] A molluscan larva furnished with a velum or ciliated swimming-membrane. Also *attrib.*

1877 HUXLEY *Anat. Inv. Anim.* viii. 497 In the great majority of the *Odontophora*, the young leaves the egg as a *veliger* very similar to that of the *Lamellibranchiata.* **1878** F. J. BELL *Gegenbaur's Comp. Anat.* 319 The Veliger stage is not always developed. **1883** *Encycl. Brit.* XVI. 654/2 In development they pass through the typical trochosphere and veliger stages provided with boat-like shell.

veligerous (viː'lɪdʒərəs), *a. Zool.* [Cf. prec. and -GEROUS.] Of certain larval forms: Bearing, or furnished with, a velum.

1877 HUXLEY *Anat. Inv. Anim.* viii. 485 It is obvious that the two have, in common with..the *Annelida*, the ciliated or veligerous larval form. **1880** F. M. BALFOUR *Comp. Embryol.* I. 192 In prosobranchiate Gasteropods..the free-swimming veligerous larva may have a long existence.

Velikovskianism (vɛlɪ'kɒvskiːənɪz(ə)m). [f. the name *Velikovsky* + -IAN + -ISM.] The (controversial) theories of cosmology and history propounded by Immanuel Velikovsky (1895–1979), Russian-born psychologist, based on the hypothesis that other planets have approached close to the Earth in historical times. Also **Veli'kovskyism**, in the same sense. So **Veli'kovskian** *a.*, of or pertaining to Velikovskianism; **Veli'kovskyite**, an adherent of Velikovskianism.

1972 P. MOORE *Can you speak Venusian?* vi. 61 Therefore, say the anti-Velikovskyites, it is rather difficult to see how a comet could change into a planet. *Ibid.* 62 Neither of these gentlemen accepted Velikovskyism hook, line and sinker. **1974** *Science* 15 Mar. 1061/1 The earliest known examples of writing..contain references to regular appearances of Venus in the sky 1500 years before its Velikovskian brushes with Earth. **1978** *Ibid.* 20 Jan. 288/2 A platform to square off pro- and anti-Velikovskyites. *Ibid.*, In a succinct foreword Isaac Asimov discusses the human psychology of Velikovskianism. **1979** *N.Y. Rev. Bks.* 25 Oct. 52/2 Professor Rose, an intrepid contributor to Velikovskian publications, is right on one count. *Ibid.* 52/3, I suppose it is too much to expect the Buffalo philosopher, when he teaches his next course on Velikovskianism, to let his students know some of the overwhelming evidence against such hoary balderdash.

velim(e, obs. ff. VELLUM.

velinche(r: see VALINCH(ER.

velipend, obs. Sc. f. VILIPEND *v.*

†**velitand**, *v. Obs.*$^{-1}$ In 7 vilitande. [Irreg. f. L. *vēlit-ārī*: cf. next.] *intr.* To skirmish.

1641 SIR E. DERING *4 Sp. conc. Laud*, etc. iii. 9 [As] the Roman Velites, who did use to begin the Battaile, so shall I but vilitande, and skirmish, whilst the maine Battaile is setting forwards.

†'**velitary**, *a. Obs.* [ad. L. *vēlitāris*, f. *vēlit-, vēles*: see VELITES.] Of or pertaining to, characteristic of, light-armed troops.

1600 HOLLAND *Livy* 995 The Consull..had made provision aforehand of great store of darts, light velitarie javelines, arrowes,..and small stones. **1623** BINGHAM *Lipsius's Comparison Xenophon* 5 Surely the most of our men are vnarmed, and what else, but to be compared to velitarie bands? **1632** HOLLAND *Cyrupædia* 139 They, who at that time defaited the velitary fight and skirmish of Archers and Javeletiers. **1649** J. ROBINSON *Misc. Propositions* Pref. p. iv, My intention is..by excursions, in a velitary way, to skirmish with some, whom..I dissent from.

veli'tation. Now *rare.* Also 7 vellet-. [ad. L. *vēlitātio*, n. of action f. *vēlitārī*, f. *vēlit-, vēles*: see next.]

1. A slight or preliminary engagement with an enemy; a skirmish.

1616 BULLOKAR *Eng. Expos.*, *Velitations*, skirmishes, fightings. **1621** BURTON *Anat. Mel.* III. iv. I. iv, Let him read those Pharsalian fields fought of late in France for religion, their massacres,..and he shall find ours to be but velitations to theirs. **1692** O. WALKER *Grk. & Rom. Hist.* 160 If any one killed an Enemy in any Velitation or pickering when they fought man to man, he was rewarded with a Spear without a head, call'd Hasta pura. **1832** J. P. KENNEDY *Swallow B.* xxix. (1860) 265 In which latter species of employment it was his luck to hold frequent velitations with the enemy.

2. *fig.* A wordy skirmish or encounter; a controversy, debate, or dispute not carried to extremes. (Very common in 17th cent.)

1607 B. BARNES *Divils Charter* II. i. D 4b, Forbeare your idle velletations. **1657** W. MORICE *Coena quasi Κοινή* xxiv. 249 In all these velitations against their dear brethren..the Apologists..have not drawn much blood. **1679** JENISON *Narr. Popish Plot* Pref. 9 This Censure is but a light Velitation, if compar'd with that black charge of guilt. **1702** C. MATHER *Magn. Chr.* VII. ii. (1852) 503 All the velitations were peaceably furled up in this result. **1722** WOLLASTON *Relig. Nat.* iii. §4 That question in Plato may have place among the velitations of philosophers; but a man can scarce propose it seriously to himself. **1824** SCOTT *St. Ronan's* viii, While the ladies..were engaged in the light snappish velitation, or skirmish, which we have described. **1831** DE QUINCEY in *Blackw. Mag.* XXIX. 905 The very best of his performances being mere velitations, skirmishes, or academic exercises.

‖**velites** ('viːlɪtiːz), *sb. pl.* [L. *vēlitēs*, pl. of *vēlit-, vēles.* So F. *vélites.*] Light-armed soldiers employed as skirmishers in the Roman armies.

1600 HOLLAND *Livy* 532 The light armed darters (called Velites)..so assailed the defendants, that they [etc.]. **1641** [see VELITAND *v.*]. **1728** CHAMBERS *Cycl.*, *Velites*, in the Roman Army, a kind of antient Soldiery, who were arm'd with a Javelin, a Cask, Cuirasse, and Shield. **1845** *Encycl. Metrop.* XVI. 191 Of the *velites*, or youngest and fourth order of troops,..Polybius makes no mention in his details of Roman castrametation. **1869** BOUTELL *Arms & Armour* iv. 59 The *velites*, or light infantry, whose entire equipment was in exact conformity with their distinctive denomination. **1892** L. VILLARI *Life & Times Machiavelli* II. viii. 326 [Transl. M.'s Art of War] In order that the battalion may be protected on all sides..it is strengthened by 1500 extra foot soldiers, of whom 1000 are armed with pikes,..and 500 velites.

†**ve'livolant**, *a. Obs.*$^{-0}$ [ad. L. *vēlivolans.*] (See quot.)

1656 BLOUNT *Glossogr.*, *Velivolant*, running and (as it were) flying with full sail.

vell, *sb. dial.* Also 8–9 **velve.** [Of obscure origin; *vell* is no doubt a reduction of *velve*, and the initial *v* may stand for original *f.*] (See quots.)

1724 *Act 11 Geo. I.* c. 7 Addit. Bk. Rates, Calves Velves to make Rennet. *c* **1789** *Encycl. Brit.* (ed. 3) IV. 369/2 Let the vell, maw, rennet-bag (or by whatever name it is called), be perfectly sweet. **1812** J. SMYTH *Pract. of Customs* (1821) 58 Calves Velves, or Vells, are the Maws or Stomachs of Calves, which have fed entirely upon Milk. After being salted or kept some time, the Vells are infused in a preparation of salt and water for the making of Rennet. *c* **1830** *Glouc. Farm Rep.* 32 (L.U.K.) III, Rennet or runnet is made from the stomachs of calves, called here 'vells'. Irish vells are the best. **1861** *Jrnl. R. Agric. Soc.* XXII. I. 59 The rennet does not keep well when made in any quantity of pickled vells. **1886–93** in dial. glossaries (Glouc., Wilts., Som.).

vell, *v. s.w. dial.* Also 9 fell. [f. *vell*, southwestern dialect var. FELL *sb.*^{1}] *trans.* To strip (land) of turf by means of a skimming-plough. Also **velled** *ppl. a.*, **'velling** *vbl. sb.*

1674 RAY *S. & E.C. Words* 78 *Velling*, Plowing up the turf or upper surface of the ground, to lay on heaps to burn. West-countrey. [Hence in Phillips (1706), etc.] **1796** W. H. MARSHALL *Rur. Econ. W. Devon.* I. 143 For velling, the share is made wide, with the angle or outer point of the wing or fin turned upward, to separate the turf entirely from the soil. *Ibid., W. England* II. 8 A considerable portion of the country is now set with roof heaps of Lime, and with velled Beat, now burning. *Ibid.* 47 Grass Inclosures velled for Wheat. **1837** J. F. PALMER *Devonsh. Dial.* Gloss. 38 The balk or narrow slip which is left in velling the land. **1871** J. COUCH *Hist. Polperro* 118 If an old grass field with a thick face is to be taken into culture, the skimming plough is used, and the process is called 'felling'.

vell, obs. var. VEAL.

vellam, obs. f. VELLUM.

vellat, obs. f. VELVET.

velle, southern ME. var. FELL *sb.* and *v.*, FILL *v.*; pa. t. FALL *v.*

velleity (vɛ'liːɪtɪ). Also 7 velleitie. [ad. med.L. *velleitāt-*, *velleitās*, f. L. *velle* to will, wish: see -ITY. Cf. F. *velléité* (16th c.), It. *velleità*, Sp. *veleidad*, Pg. *velleidade*.]

1. The fact or quality of merely willing, wishing, or desiring, without any effort or advance towards action or realization.

1618 BP. HALL *Contempl., N.T.* (1634) 101 Thy word alone, thy beck alone, thy wish alone, yea, the least act of velleity from thee might have wrought this cure. **1662** BAXTER *Saints' R.* IV. To Rdr. 831 We must distinguish.. Between the simple Velleity of the Will, and the choice that followeth the Comparate act of the intellect. **1690** NORRIS *Beatitudes* (1694) 105 By impotent willing meaning that natural Inclination or Velleity we have to every Good as such. **1768** TUCKER *Lt. Nat.* (1834) I. 20 Velleity can scarce be called a power, for a power which never operates is no power at all. **1808** BENTHAM *Sc. Reform* 77 In your Lordship will is volition, clothed and armed with power—in me, it is bare inert velleity. **1838** *New Monthly Mag.* LII. 110 This singular exuberance of velleity for education must presuppose a corresponding qualification for the task. **1866** LOWELL *Study Wind.* (1870) 191 Châteaubriand..had the same harmless velleity of self-destruction. **1867** —— *Rousseau* Prose Wks. 1890 II. 250 He and all like him mistake emotion for conviction, velleity for resolve.

2. With *a* and pl. A mere wish, desire, or inclination without accompanying action or effort.

Very common in the 17th c.; now somewhat rare.

1624 F. WHITE *Repl. Fisher* 78 The antecedent will of God is only a velleitie or wishing that a thing might be. **1640** BP. REYNOLDS *Passions* xvii. 180 They are onely Velleities and not Volitions: halfe and broken wishes, not whole desires. **1692** J. NORRIS *Curs. Reflect.* 37 The same might also be illustrated from the Actions of the Will, some of which are perfect and compleat Determinations, others only Velleities or Endeavours. **1710** —— *Chr. Prud.* vi. 229 The one loves it only in some respect or degree, with an incomplete Love or Velleity as 'tis call'd. **1740** CHEYNE *Regimen* 315 We may have vehement Willings, Longings, Volitions, and Velleities. **1808** BENTHAM *Sc. Reform* 2 Preceding administrations reckoned this..in the number of their velleities: what they had been thinking of doing, your Lordship has done. **1841** CARLYLE in Froude *Life in Lond.* (1884) I. 218 He had no fixed intentions, only rebellious impulses, blind longings and velleities. **1873** BROWNING *Red Cott. Nt.-cap* IV. 415 No matter what his least velleity, I was determined he should want no wish.

b. Const. with various preps., as *after*, *against*, *for*, *of*, *towards* (something). Also with *to* and inf.

1633 AMES *Fresh Suit agst. Ceremonies* II. 20 No imperfect velleities of good are so interpreted. **1652** N. CULVERWEL *Lt. Nature* (1857) 268 Nature that has but some weak glimpses of Him, has but faint and languishing velleities after Him. **1680** H. DODWELL *Two Lett.* (1691) 7 The designing the more noble end for the less noble..implies no volition, but only a velleity, for that which is more noble. *Ibid.* 48 Terrifying men from their sins, so as not only to make them entertain some strugling velleities against them [etc.]. **1795** HUSSEY in Burke *Corr.* (1844) IV. 280 Some of her prelates have..showed a *velleity* to make a stand in the upper house. **1853** GROTE *Greece* II. lxxxiv. XI. 102 The effect was not the less produced, of disgusting Dionysius with his velleities towards political good. **1861** MILL *Repr. Govt.* 330 The executive, with their real but faint velleities of something better. **1887** *Dublin Rev.* July 194 There is no reason to suspect the slightest velleity to bring any pressure to bear on the matter.

vellem, obs. f. VELLUM.

vellenage, obs. f. VILLAINAGE.

vellet(t, obs. forms of VELVET.

velletation, obs. f. VELITATION.

'vellicate, *v.* Now *rare* or *Obs.* Also 7 vellicat. [f. L. *vellicāt-*, ppl. stem of *vellicāre*, frequentative of *vellĕre* to pull, pluck, twitch, etc. Cf. Sp. *velicar*, Pg. *vellicar*.]

1. *trans.* Of things: To act upon or affect so as to irritate; *esp.* to pluck, nip, pinch, or tear (a part of the body) by means of small or sharp points.

Chiefly in old medical use with reference to the action of medicaments, sharp or acrid substances, etc., on the tissues of the body. Freq. in the 17th and 18th centuries.

1604 F. HERING *Modest Defence* 16 They [i.e. strong medicines] doe forcibly vellicat, offend and violat her [Nature]. **1669** W. SIMPSON *Hydrol. Chym.* 27 Those corrosive fretting, pontick, and acid juyces, which vellicate and prick the nerves. **1685** BOYLE *Enq. Notion Nat.* 223 The Fibres..of the Stomach, Bowels, and other Parts, being.. Vellicated by the Plenty or Acrimony of the Peccant Matter. **1708** *Brit. Apollo* No. 113. 2/2 Some sharp Humor on that part..may vellicate and twitch it. **1783** BRYANT *Flora Diætetica* 168 A hairy, bristly substance, which..will, by pricking and vellicating the coats of stomach and bowels, many times occasion sickness. **1822-7** GOOD *Study Med.* (1829) I. 82 The same effect is produced whenever the teeth are vellicated by smooth substances, as a piece of silk or velvet.

absol. **1744** BERKELEY *Siris* §61 The æthereal oils being deprived of the acid spirit in distillation, which, vellicating and contracting as a stimulus, might have proved a counterpoise to the excessive lubricating..qualities of the oil.

b. Of persons: To tickle or titillate.

1755 *Phil. Trans.* XLIX. 242, I vellicated the pericranium with the end of a knife. *a***1778** C. DARWIN *Experiments* (1780) 94 Thus, if you vellicate the throat with a feather, nausea is produced. **1794-6** E. DARWIN *Zoon.* (1801) I. 281 So when children expect to be tickled in play..by gently vellicating the soles of their feet, laughter is most vehemently excited.

† **2.** *fig.* To carp at; to criticize adversely. *Obs.*

1633 T. ADAMS *Exp. 2 Peter* ii. 1 These are they that vellicate authority. **1662** OWEN *Animad. Fiat Lux* vi, If any one..have a mind..to vellicate commonly received maxims. **1686** H. MORE in J. Norris *Lett.* (1688) 208 Reading the confirmation of your Hypothesis, which I took the boldness a little to vellicate.

3. *intr.* To twitch; to contract or move convulsively. *rare.*

1670 MAYNWARING *Vita Sana* xiii. 120 Fast not, but satisfie the Stomach when it vellicates and calls for meat. **1864** WEBSTER, *Vellicate*, to move spasmodically; to twitch; as, a nerve vellicates.

Hence **'vellicating** *ppl. a.*

1669 *Address to Gentry Eng.* 81 Many a pregnant spirit is suffocated in the streight enclosures of a confining vellicating fortune. **1684** tr. *Bonet's Merc. Compit.* III. 67 It washes the vellicating Humours from the original of the Nerves. **1743** tr. *Heister's Surg.* 365 The increased Flux of Tears, excited by the vellicating Body. **1751** SMOLLETT *Per. Pic.* (1779) I. xiii. 112 Lubricating injections to defend the coats of the stomach..from the vellicating particles. **1768** *Elaboratory* 218 A vellicating and pungent action. **1853** MAYNE *Expos. Lex.* 48 *Amycticus*,..irritating; vellicating.

velli'cation. Now *rare* or *Obs.* [ad. L. *vellicātio*, noun of action f. *vellicāre* to VELLICATE. Cf. older F. *vellication* (Cotgr.), It. *vellicazione*, Sp. *velicacion*, Pg. *vellicação*.]

1. The action or process of pulling or twitching; irritation or stimulation by means of small or sharp points; titillation or tickling.

1623 COCKERAM I, *Vellication*, plucking. **1626** BACON *Sylva* §37 Therfore we see that almost all Purgers have a kind of Twiching and vellication. **1655** CULPEPPER, etc. *Riverius* VI. i. 130 The Nerve and Membrane in the hole of the Tooth..which doth..suffer distension and vellication. *a***1693** *Urquhart's Rabelais* III. xlv. (1694) 371 Is it not daily seen how School-masters..shake the Heads of their Disciples..that, by this Erection, Vellication, stretching and pulling their Ears..they may stir them up? **1718** QUINCY *Compl. Disp.* 177 The Vellication or Irritation of the Fibres and Membranes. **1794-6** E. DARWIN *Zoon.* (1801) I. 281 Here the pleasurable idea of playfulness coincides with the vellication. **1822-7** GOOD *Study Med.* (1829) I. 547 The vellication of a hair-brush contrived for the purpose. *Ibid.* IV. 690 The best artificial means of obtaining so salutary an action is by a free and laborious process of friction, vellication or shampooing.

2. An instance or occasion of this; also, a twitching or convulsive movement, esp. of a muscle or other part of the body.

1665 *Collection Plague Pieces* (1721) 21 There happens a Vellication of the nervous Parts. **1686** PLOT *Staffordsh.* 302 Severe vellications in the Intestines by sharp humors. **1723** STUKELEY in *Mem.* (1882) I. 69 After some vellications and preludes the Gout seiz'd upon my right foot. **1756** C. LUCAS *Ess. Waters* II. 67 Sharp uneasy vellications of the skin. **1783** JOHNSON *Lett.* (1788) II. 339 These vellications of my breast shorten my breath.

transf. **1781** JOHNSON *Prayers & Medit.* (1817) 193 At night, I had some mental vellications, or revulsions.

'vellicative, *a. rare*⁻¹. [f. as VELLICATE *v.* + -IVE.] Having the quality of vellicating; causing irritation or twitching.

1822-7 GOOD *Study Med.* (1829) I. 82 They [i.e. teeth] are colloquially said to be set on edge; and that in two ways, as follows:—..From jarring noises... From vellicative or acrid substances.

† **'vellicle**. *Obs. rare.* [ad. L. type **velliculum*, f. *vellĕre* to pluck, pull.] Something which pinches or nips so as to hold fast (see quot.).

1676 H. MORE *Rem.* 145 The Power..of the Laws of Nature, in colligating strictly Parts of the most distantial Textures and Consistencies, without the Help of Vellicles, Hooks, or Grappers. *Ibid.* 147.

velling, *vbl. sb.*: see VELL *v.*

vellom, obs. form of VELLUM.

‖ **vellon** (ve'ʎon). Also 7 vellion. [Sp. *vellon*: see BILLON.] Copper, as used in Spanish coinage. Used esp. in the denomination of certain coins, as *real (of) vellon*: see REAL *sb.*²

1676 LADY FANSHAWE *Mem.* (1830) 202 We let our dispense for 72,000 reals vellon, a year. **1681** RYCAUT tr. *Gracian's Critick* To Rdr., We were dispatched thence with ..something under the name of a Largess, to bear our Expences, paid in Vellion, or the Base Copper Money of Spain. **1728** CHAMBERS *Cycl.* s.v. *Money*, Spanish Money of Account, is the Peso, Ducat of Silver and Vellon, Rial of Vellon, and Cornados and Maravedis of Silver and Vellon. **1798** MALTHUS *Popul.* (1817) II. 489 The price of the load of four fanegas of wheat was..100 reals vellon. **1839** *Penny Cycl.* XV. 323/1 It passes in Spain for 20 reals vellon.

attrib. **1676** LADY FANSHAWE *Mem.* (1830) 196 October the 14th, the King proclaimed the lowering the vellon money to the half.

vellon, dial. form of FELON *sb.*²

velloped, error for *jelloped* JOLLOPED *a.*

1780 EDMONDSON *Heraldry* II. Gloss., *Velloped*; a cock is said to be armed, crested, and velloped, when his spurs, comb, and gills, are of a different tincture from the body.

vellot(e, obs. forms of VELVET.

† **vellous**, *sb.* and *a. Sc. Obs.* Forms: α. 5 vell-, wellowis, vellous, -us, 5-6 wellus. β. 5 veluous, -vous, -uus, welwous, 6 -uous, -uos, velvois, etc. [a. OF. *velous*, *velos*, *velwis*, *velvis*, later F. *velours* VELOURS.] = VELVET *sb.* and *a.*

α. *c***1450** *Maitl. Club Misc.* III. 196, j reid cap of vellowis. *Ibid.* 197 A blew claith wellowis. **1474** *Acc. Ld. High Treas. Scot.* I. 16, 2½ elne of vellous for a fute mantil. *Ibid.* 69, vj elne of vellus for a kirtil. **1503** *Ibid.* II. 297 For ane wellus bonet to the Erle of Murray.

β. **1473** *Acc. Ld. High Treas. Scot.* I. 73, iiij½ elne of rede crammacy veluous. **1491** *Acta Dom. Conc.* 199/1, xviij elne of Welwous. **1530** *Burgh Rec. Edinb.* (1871) II. 27 Ane schitt of grene weluos. **1561** *Inv. R. Wardr.* (1815) 124 Ane bed of blak velvois. *a***1586** SIR R. MAITLAND *Poems* (Pinkerton, 1786) 326 Thair gouns..Barrit with velvous.

vellum ('vɛləm). Forms: α. 5 velym, 5-6 velyme, 5, 7 velim, 6 velime, velem, 7 vellem. β. 5, 7 velum, 5-7 velume (7 velumne), 7- vellum. γ. 7 velom, 7-8 vellom. δ. 7 velame, 7-8 velam, vellam. [ad. OF. *velin* (*vellin*, *veelin*, etc.; mod.F. *vélin*), f. *vel* VEAL *sb.*, with change of *n* to *m* as in *pilgrim*, *venom*.]

1. A fine kind of parchment prepared from the skins of calves (lambs or kids) and used especially for writing, painting, or binding; also, any superior quality of parchment or an imitation of this.

vegetable vellum: see VEGETABLE *a.* 7.

α. *c***1440** *Promp. Parv.* 508/2 Velyme, *membrana*. *c***1449** PECOCK *Repr.* I. xv. 81 That Holi Writt mai be take for the outward lettris writun and schapun vnder dyuerse figuris in parchemyn or in velim. **1519** HORMAN *Vulg.* 80b, That stouffe that we wrytte vpon, and is made of beestis skynnes, is somtyme called parchement, somtyme velem. **1598** R. HAYDOCKE tr. *Lomazzo* II. 127 The Painters vse general groundes..; saue vpon paper, parchment or velime. **1644** *Direct. Publ. Worship* Ord. 3 A fair register book of velim.

fig. **1611** J. DAVIES (Heref.) *To Worthy Persons* Wks. (Grosart) II. 62/1 Vpon th' unspotted vellem of thy face Nature hath printed characters of grace.

β. **1474** CAXTON *Chesse* III. iii. (1883) 93 The Notayres, skynners, coryours, and cardewaners werke by skynnes and hydes, As parchemyn, velume, peltrye and cordewan. **1499** *Croscombe Church-w. Acc.* (Som. Rec. Soc.) 24 A mass boke of velum lymmyde. *a***1586** SIDNEY *Astr. & Stella* Sonn. xi, A childe..With gilded leaues or colourd velume playes. **1616** DRUMM. OF HAWTH. *Flowers of Sion, Bk. World*, But sillie wee (like foolish Children) rest Well pleas'd with colour'd Velumne. **1699** BENTLEY *Phal.* xvi. 506 And without doubt it was immortal Vellum, and stoln from the Parchmentes of Jove. **1700** CONGREVE *Way of World* V. iii, I have an old fox by my thigh that shall hack your instrument of ram vellum to shreds, sir! **1710** J. CLARKE tr. *Rohault's Nat. Philos.* (1729) I. 243 The Retina [of an artificial eye] was made of a very white thin Piece of Vellum. *a***1781** R. WATSON *Philip III*, III. (1839) 159 The deed..was written on paper, and not on vellum, as was usual in all transactions of importance. **1819** KEATS *Fall Hyperion* I. 5 Pity these have not Trac'd upon vellum or wild Indian leaf The shadows of melodious utterance. **1855** MRS. GASKELL *North & S.* iii, The Paradise of Dante in the proper old Italian binding of white vellum and gold. **1875** SCRIVENER *Lect. Gk. Test.* 16 The durable fine vellum of our oldest extant codices.

fig. **1784** COWPER *Task* I. 569 The sportive wind blows wide Their flutt'ring rags, and shows a tawny skin, The vellum of the pedigree they claim.

γ. **1601** HAKEWILL *Van. Eye* xxii. (1615) 110 [To] beholde the heavens, and in them (as in large characters drawn in faire velom) the glory of their maker. **1683** MOXON *Mech. Exerc., Printing* i, One of the first Books Printed on Paper; (that of Tully being on Vellom). **1728** CHAMBERS *Cycl.* s.v. *Parchment*, What we call Vellom is only Parchment made of the Skins of abortive Calves, or at least of sucking Calves.

δ. **1600** FAIRFAX *Tasso* XIV. lxxvi, The house is builded like a maze within,..The shape whereof plotted in velam thin I will you giue. **1617** BARBIER *Jan. Ling.* 114 He cancelled a line in the margent of the velame. **1632** QUARLES *Div. Fancies* II. xiii, Hee..Whose milk-white Vellam did incurre No least suspition of a Blurre. **1706** HEARNE *Collect.* (O.H.S.) I. 258 A MS. in velam. **1715** *Ibid.* V. 130 King Henry the VIIIth's Primer upon Vellam.

fig. **1631** MASSINGER *Emperor East* IV. iv, Can you think This master peece of heauen, this pretious vellam, Of such a puritie and virgin whitenesse, Could be design'd to haue periurie, and whoredome,..writ vpon 't?

2. A piece or sheet of this material; a manuscript or testimonial written on vellum.

c **1430** LYDG. *Min. Poems* (Percy Soc.) 204 A froward velym upon to wryt. **1687** *Death's Vision* (1713) 2 *note*, Like a Velum upon the Head of a Drum. **1878** G. VIGFUSSON *Sturlunga Saga* I. p. clx, A quarto of 200 leaves when entire (about the largest size ever reached by an Icelandic vellum). **1900** *Westm. Gaz.* 15 Oct. 6/3 He and his brother..received the vellum of the Royal Humane Society for their plucky conduct.

3. *attrib.* and *Comb.* **a.** Attrib. in the senses 'made of, resembling, of the nature of, bound in, vellum'.

1565 GOLDING *Ovid's Met.* IV. 507 With shere and velume wings. **1570** DEE *Math. Pref.* aj, All these, liuely designementes..be in velame parchement described. **1586** HOOKER *Hist. Irel.* in *Holinshed* II. 94/1 He ought rather to make sute for some good vellam parchment for the ingrossing thereof. **1636** DAVENANT *Platonick Lovers* IV. i, Not all thy Leathern, nor thy Vellum friends, those dead companions on thy Shelves shall be more faithful [etc.]. **1651** CLEVELAND *Poems* 46 Who place Religion in their Velam-ears; As in their Phylacters the Jews did theirs. **1707** HEARNE *Collect.* (O.H.S.) I. 330 A very Ancient Vellam MS^{t}. **1740** RICHARDSON *Pamela* (1824) I. 216 Mr Longman has already furnished me with a vellum-book of white paper. **1820** LAMB *Elia* I. *South-Sea House*, The costly vellum covers of some of them [*sc.* books]. **1882** MISS BRADDON *Mt. Royal* III. v. 88 A large vellum envelope.

b. *Comb.* With pa. pples., as ***vellum-bound***, ***-covered***.

1837 DICKENS *Pickw.* iv, With vellum-covered books under their arms. **1856** LEVER *Martins of Cro' M.* 605 A square vellum-bound book, with massive silver clasps. **1866** GEO. ELIOT *F. Holt* (1868) 11 Her writing-table, with vellum-covered account-books on it.

c. Special Combs.: **vellum-binder** (see quot. 1858); **vellum-binding**, the process or trade of binding account-books; also *attrib.*; **vellum cloth**, tracing-cloth; †**vellum mode** (see MODE *sb.* 11, quot. 1795); **vellum paper**, a paper made to imitate vellum; hence ***vellum-papered*** adj.; **vellum post** (see quot.); **vellum thunder** *poet.*, the noise made by the parchment of a drum.

1858 SIMMONDS *Dict. Trade*, **Vellum-binder*, a book-binder who covers books with vellum, and makes account-books. **1891** *Pall Mall G.* 20 Nov. 3/1 Three of them are concerned with the bookbinders—that is, the binders of printed books—and the fourth with the vellum-binders, the technical name for account-book binders. **1835** J. HANNETT *Bibliopegia* III. (Heading) 139 Of Stationery, or *Vellum Binding. **1891** *Pall Mall G.* 20 Nov. 3/1 As soon as it was known that the bookbinders were going to concede the eight hours, several of the best vellum-binding firms conceded it also. **1888** JACOBI *Printers' Vocab.* 151 **Vellum laid paper*, a laid writing paper with a vellum surface. *Ibid.*, *Vellum wove paper*, a wove writing paper with a vellum surface. **1858** O. W. HOLMES *Aut. Breakf.-t.* (1883) 73 Look at..the ..*vellum-papered 32 mo. **1847** WEBSTER, **Vellum-post*, a peculiar sort of superior writing-paper. **1716** GAY *Trivia* II. 18 Here Rows of Drummers stand in martial File, And with their *Vellom-Thunder shake the Pile.

Hence **'vellumy** *a.*, relating to or resembling vellum.

1846 WORCESTER, citing *Ec. Rev.* **1925** H. A. MADDOX *What Stationer & Printer ought to know about Paper* (ed. 3) i. 14 There are smooth vellums which derive their title from ..a vellumy thickness and clarity of appearance.

'vellumize, *v.* [f. VELLUM + -IZE] *trans.* To convert into vellum.

1907 C. DAVENPORT *The Book* 173 The white 'vellumized' pigskin has always been the most favourite material for the covering of German books.

vellure, obs. form of VELURE.

†**vellute.** *Obs. rare.* [ad. It. *velluto*, or var. of *vellet* VELVET *sb.* after this.] Velvet.

1561 T. HOBY tr. *Castiglione's Courtyer* I. (1577) F ij, Wyth hir shooes of vellute, and hir hose fitting cleane to hir legge. **1632** B. JONSON *Magn. Lady* v. iii, [It] will save charges Of coaches, vellute gowns, and cut-work smocks.

velly ('vɛlɪ). A representation of a Chinese pronunc. of 'very'; also used *joc.*

1898 *Applause Reciter* 16 Ole man talkee, 'No can walk, Bimeby lain come, velly dark; Have got water, velly wide!' **1937** D. & H. TEILHET *Feather Cloak Murders* ii. 48 The Chinese woman rushed to him. 'You neahlly killed... Velly neahlly killed.' **1948** L. DURRELL *Spirit of Place* (1969) 98 Shakespear him velly fine big-speak sing song man. **1970** J. LEES-MILNE *Another Self* iii. 47 Poor Janie still loves her little cousin velly, velly much. **1974** N. BENTLEY *Inside Information* xiii. 135 'Velly good, sir.' Cheng bowed.

velly, dial. var. *felly* FELLOE.

†**ve'lociman.** *Obs. rare.* [ad. F. *vélocimane*, f. *véloci-* (after VELOCIPEDE) + L. *man-us* hand.] A contrivance of the nature of a velocipede, but propelled by hand.

A ***velocimanipede*** was advertised in the *Morning Chron.* of 13 May 1819: see HOBBY *sb.*[1] 4.

[**1869** *N. & Q.* 4th Ser. IV. 240 The Swiss inventor styles his Carriage a *velocimane.*] **1882** C. L. DODGSON in Collingwood *Life* v. (1899) 219 Went out with Charsley, and did four miles on one of his velocimans, very pleasantly. **1883** SIMMONDS *Dict. Trade*, *Velociman*,..a species of tricycle.

velocimeter (vɛlə'sɪmɪtə(r)). [f. L. *vēlōci-*, *vēlox* swift + -METER.] An instrument or apparatus (variously constructed) for measuring the speed or velocity of engines, vessels, projectiles, etc.

1842 H. SPENCER in *Civil Eng. & Arch. Jrnl.* V. 231/2 The instrument represented in the annexed plate, which I have named a 'Velocimeter', is intended to supersede the long calculations, frequently necessary, in obtaining velocities in engine trials. **1853** in *Abridgm. Specif. Patents, Opt.* etc. *Instrum.* (1875) 183 An instrument for measuring the steerage-way of vessels... [The apparatus is called a] Velocimeter. **1876** *Catal. Sci. Appar. S. Kens.* 55 Patent electric Velocimeter,..arranged for water currents and ascertaining the speed of vessels.

Hence **velo'cimetry**, the measurement of speed, esp. speed of flow, by special techniques.

1969 *IEEE Trans. Aerospace & Electronic Systems* V. 687/1 (*heading*) Fundamentals of holographic velocimetry. **1978** *Sci. Amer.* Aug. 30/3 Swedish and Japanese workers have been testing laser velocimetry, a technique that utilizes the reflection of light from small particles in the flow to determine the magnitude and direction of the circulatory patterns. **1980** *Recent Adv. Surg.* X. 84 The first to apply the technique of Doppler ultrasound velocimetry to the detection of pulsatile arterial flow in the digital vessels.

ve'locious, *a. rare.* [f. L. *vēlōci-*, *vēlox* swift + -OUS.] Rapid. Also **ve'lociously** *adv.*

In quot. 1872 humorously for 'fast'.

1680 C. NESSE *Ch. Hist.* 357 Satan was seen to fall like lightning from heaven, to wit, viewably, violently, and velociously or swiftly. **1775** ROMANS *Florida* App. 62 Providing so facile a navigation for the regions of the west, by means of a velocious current. **1872** DASENT *Three to One* III. 233 They are not at all like some of the young ladies of the present day, 'velocious,' as we have heard a Yankee say.

velo'cipedal, *a. rare.* [f. next + -AL[1].] Of or relating to, depicting, a velocipede.

1868 *Pall Mall G.* No. 1022. 1908/2 The velocipedal skill of M. de Visin. **1869** *N. & Q.* 4th Ser. IV. 240 Nor have I any recollection of a velocipedal plate [= picture].

velocipede (vɪ'lɒsɪpiːd). Now *Hist.* [ad. F. *vélocipède*, f. L. *vēlōci-*, *vēlox* swift + *ped-*, *pēs* foot.]

1. a. = DANDY-HORSE, HOBBY *sb.*[1] 4, HOBBY-HORSE *sb.* 5. *Obs.* exc. *Hist.*

1818 W. SEWALL *Diary* 19 June (1930) 53/2 Then I went to the circus and rode on the velocipede, which is a new machine. **1819** *Monthly Mag.* March 156 A machine called the Velocipede, or Swift Walker. Invented by Baron Drais and patented in England by Denis Johnson, coachmaker, of Long Acre, in 1818. **1819** KEATS *Lett.* (1895) 300 The nothing of the day is a machine called the velocipede. It is a wheel carriage to ride cock-horse upon, sitting astride and pushing it along with the toes, a rudder-wheel in hand. **1823** J. BADCOCK *Dom. Amusem.* 209 He never proceeded with his machine at a greater rate than five miles an hour, and yet named it Velocipede. **1839** *Civil Eng. & Arch. Jrnl.* II. 242/1 The horse will take longer steps, and longer springs or leaps,..in the same way as a man upon a velocipede. **1850** in OGILVIE.

†**b.** A kind of roller-skate. *Obs.*

1825 *Mech. Mag.* V. 79 A Velocipede intended to be fixed on one foot;..the *velocipedestrian* pushes himself away with the other.

2. A travelling-machine having wheels turned by the pressure of the feet upon pedals; *esp.* an early form of the bicycle or tricycle, a 'bone-shaker'. Now *rare.* (Quot. 1853 may belong to sense 1.)

1849-50 WEALE *Dict. Terms* s.v. **1851** *Catal. Grt. Exhib.* v. No. 991, Velocipede, consisting of three wheels. **1853** R. S. SURTEES *Soapey Sp. Tour* (1893) 369 He is riding a miserable rat of a badly-clipped mouse-coloured pony, that looks like a velocipede under him. **1868** G. DUFF *Pol. Surv.* 126 The unprecedented reaction is moving on with the swiftness of a velocipede. **1886** *Cyclist Touring Club Gaz.* IV. 146 Bicycles, tricycles, and other velocipedes. *Ibid.* 149 Every cyclist using a velocipede.

3. *transf.* **a.** Applied to persons.

1822 *New Monthly Mag.* VI. 344 In the Ballet we have nothing new to report. M. Paul, a true velocipede, continues to electrify the astonished spectators. **1891** MEREDITH *One of our Conq.* xvi, He's a worthy little velocipede, as Fenellan calls him.

b. A swift-moving vehicle.

1838 *Blackw. Mag.* XLIII. 340 Stage-coaches..were not the velocipedes that they now are. **1842** R. FORD in Smiles *Publisher & Friends* (1891) II. 491, I read Borrow with great delight all the way down per rail, and it shortened the rapid flight of that velocipede.

4. *attrib.* and *Comb.*, as ***velocipede carriage***, ***-crank***, ***traffic***, ***velocity***, ***-wise*** adv.

1819 *Gentl. Mag.* LXXXIX. I. 423 With our heavy population, Velocipede carriages may hereafter be substituted..worked by two or more men. **1839** *Blackw. Mag.* XLVI. 39 The rush of waiters hurrying with velocipede velocity in opposite directions. **1869** H. BUSHNELL *Wom. S.* viii. 178 He sings velocipede-wise, turning the crank himself. **1870** *Belgravia* Feb. 444 A paddle-wheel..furnished with velocipede-cranks.

Hence **veloci'pedean**, **ve'locipeder**, = VELOCIPEDIST. **velocipe'destrian** *a.*, = VELOCIPEDIC *a.*; *sb.* one who uses a velocipede (see sense 1 b above); also **velocipe'destrianism**, the practice of using the velocipede. **veloci'pedian**, = VELOCIPEDIST. **veloci'pedic** *a.*, of or pertaining to velocipedes. **ve'locipeding** *vbl. sb.*, the action or practice of using a velocipede. **ve'locipedist** [ad. F. *vélocipédiste*], one who rides a velocipede.

1842 HOWITT *Vis. Remark. Places* Ser. II. 431 He was a very adroit *Velocipedean. **1869** *Daily News* 9 March, As the bicycles gained the open country the velocipedeans began to work in earnest. **1819** *Sporting Mag.* IV. 39 A *Velocipeder presented himself at a turnpike, and demanded, 'What's to pay?' **1869** *Sci. Amer.* 13 Feb. 101 The votaries of *Velocipedestrian Science. *Ibid.* 9 Jan. 25 *Velocipedestrianism, a word coined for the times, is easier to learn than skating. **1869** *Echo* 3 Dec., The invention of the crank-axled machine gave a great impulse to velocipedestrianism. **1869** *Velocipede* (N.Y.) April 20 A *velocipedian, after a fair amount of experience, finds himself..at home astride his two-wheeler. **1892** *Times* 21 April 5/5 Dr. Mussy, spokesman of the *Velocipedic Union, dwelt on the advantages of cycling to school-boys, tourists, and soldiers. **1869** *Velocipede* (N.Y.) April 21 *Velocipeding is a hopeful sign of progress. **1886** W. J. TUCKER *E. Europe* 109 Just like that velocipeding and Danube-boating at Pesth! **1820** WILLIAMS *Hist. Acc. Invent.* II. 486 The rest afforded to the *velocipedist between his steps which set the machine in motion, enables him to proceed much quicker. **1868** *Lond. Soc.* Nov. 408 The velocipedists have stolen a march on the coming flying man. **1885** *Pall Mall G.* 28 April 10/2 The 'St. Petersburg Society of Amateur Velocipedists'.

velocity (vɪ'lɒsɪtɪ). Also 6 *Sc.* **velocite**, 6-7 **velocitie.** [ad. F. *vélocité* (14th cent.; = It. *velocità*, Sp. *velocidad*, Pg. *-idade*) or L. *vēlōcitāt-*, *vēlōcitās*, f. *vēlōci-*, *vēlox* swift, rapid: see -ITY.]

1. a. Rapidity or celerity of motion; swiftness, speed.

c **1550** ROLLAND *Crt. Venus* II. 672 Thay bad him pas with all velocite To the Gracis. **1555** EDEN *Decades* (Arb.) 220 This byrde..is of such velocitie and swyftnes in flying that [etc.]. **1607** TOPSELL *Four-f. Beasts* 115 The Lybian Roes ..(saith hee) are of an admirable velocity or swiftnes. **1646** SIR T. BROWNE *Pseud. Ep.* 235 Dolphins..Being the Hyeroglyphick of celerity,..men best expressed their velocity by incurvity, and under some figure of a bowe. **1665** GLANVILL *Scepsis Sci.* xi. 61 The supposed motion will be near a thousand miles an hour under the Equinoctional line; yet it will seem to have no Velocity to the sense. **1704** FULLER *Med. Gymn.* (1711) 14 His Blood flows with its due Velocity. **1789** MRS. PIOZZI *Journ. France* II. 370 Black heaths, and wild uncultivated plains, over which the unresisted wind sweeps with a velocity I never yet was witness to. **1802** BINGLEY *Anim. Biog.* (1805) III. 74 Some of the species..are enabled to spring with great force and velocity on their prey. **1849** MACAULAY *Hist. Eng.* iii. I. 379 The flying coaches are extolled as far superior to any similar vehicles ever known in the world. Their velocity is the subject of special commendation.

b. *spec.* Relative rapidity; rate of motion.

1656 tr. *Hobbes' Elem. Philos.* (1839) 113 Motion, in as much as a certain length may in a certain time be transmitted by it, is called Velocity or swiftness: &c. **1715** tr. *Gregory's Astron.* (1726) I. 91 The Velocity in *A* is to the Velocity in *P*, as *SN* to *SH*. But as the Velocities in *A* and *P*, so are the Spaces run in the same time, by the Bodies. **1743** W. EMERSON *Fluxions* v, It is the general Practice in Mechanics, to measure the Velocity of a Body by the Space uniformly described in given Time. *c* **1790** IMISON *Sch. Arts* I. 1 Mechanics is a science which treats of the forces, motions, velocities, and in general, of the actions of bodies upon one another. **1813** BAKEWELL *Introd. Geol.* Pref. (1815) 16 In mechanics, the important question of the ratio between the velocity and momentum is still undecided. **1857** LIVINGSTONE *Trav.* xvi. 284 *note*, A declivity of three inches per mile gives a velocity in a smooth straight channel of three miles an hour. **1880** HAUGHTON *Phys. Geogr.* iii. 137 It has ..a velocity of upwards of three knots per hour.

c. In scientific use, speed together with the direction of travel, as a vector quantity.

1847 *Proc. R. Irish Acad.* III. 345 We may always imagine a succession of straight lines, or vectors, to be drawn from some one point, as from a common origin, in such a manner as to represent, by their directions and lengths, the varying directions and degrees (or quantities) of the velocity of the moving point. **1873** J. C. MAXWELL *Treat. Electr. & Magn.* I. 9 The velocity of a body, its momentum,..an electric current,..are instances of vector quantities. **1883** *Encycl. Brit.* XV. 680/1 We are concerned only with what we may call the 'speed' of the motion. (We purposely avoid the use of the term 'velocity' here, because it properly includes direction as well as speed.) **1963** A. F. ABBOTT *Ordinary Level Physics* v. 50 In ordinary conversation the word 'velocity' is often used in place of speed. In science, however, it is important to distinguish between these two terms.

2. a. Rapidity (absolute or relative) of operation or action; quickness.

a **1674** CLARENDON *Surv. Leviath.* (1676) 18 Mr. Hobbes ..was with the velocity of a thought..able to decipher that impertinent Question. **1743** W. EMERSON *Fluxions* 2 He will find some to increase faster, others slower; and consequently that there are comparative Velocities (or Fluxions) of Increase during their Generation. **1794** HUTTON *Philos. Light*, etc. 198 Neither the quantity of the fire, nor the velocity of its propagation. **1817** JAS. MILL *Brit. India* II. v. v. 479 Colonel Brathwaite was instructed to anticipate resistance by velocity of completion. **1858** FROUDE *Hist. Eng.* IV. 481 The velocity with which the English world was swept into the New Era. **1871** B. STEWART *Heat* (ed. 2) §228 The rate at which it loses temperature or the velocity of cooling.

b. *Econ.* The rate at which notes and coins change hands; the rate of spending in an economy.

1909 I. FISHER in *Jrnl. R. Statistical Soc.* LXXII. 618 When we know statistically the velocity of circulation of money we shall be in a position to study inductively the 'quality theory' of money. **1911** —— *Purchasing Power of Money* ii. 17 Velocity of circulation, or rapidity of turnover, is simply the quotient obtained by dividing the total money payments for goods in the course of a year by the average amount of money in circulation by which these payments are effected. **1930** J. M. KEYNES *Treat. Money* II. xxiv. 20 The expression 'velocity (or rapidity) of circulation' first came into use before the development of the cheque system. .. The 'velocity' measured the average frequency with which a loan (or a bank-note) changed hands. **1957** *Economist* 19 Oct. 209/1 The note issue is a good indicator because the velocity of notes, unlike that of deposits, is fairly steady. **1982** *Chase Economic Observer* Jan.–Feb. 3/1 Velocity, the rate of turnover of money, is typically measured as the ratio of GNP to the narrowly defined money stock.

3. *attrib.* and *Comb.*, as ***velocity-measurer, ratio***; **velocity head** [HEAD *sb.* 17], the velocity pressure of a fluid expressed in terms of the height from which the fluid would have to fall to attain the velocity exerting this pressure; **velocity microphone**, a microphone whose diaphragm is freely exposed to the air on both sides and so responds to the particle velocity within a sound wave rather than its pressure; **velocity potential** [tr. G. *geschwindigkeits-potential* (H. von Helmholtz 1858, in *Jrnl. für die reine u. angewandte Math.* LV. 25)], a scalar function of position such that its space derivatives at any point are the components of the fluid velocity at that point; **velocity pressure**, that part of the total pressure exerted by a fluid which is due to the velocity it possesses.

[**1881** *Encycl. Brit.* XII. 462/2, $v^2/2g$ may be termed the head due to the velocity *v*.] **1884** A. DANIELL *Text Bk. Princ. Physics* xi. 276 We may say that the velocity-head and the pressure-head are together equal to the total head. **1937** O'BRIEN & HICKOX *Appl. Fluid Mech.* ix. 271 The true velocity head to be used in Bernoulli's equation is the average kinetic energy per unit weight of water flowing. **1979** A. L. LYDERSEN *Fluid Flow & Heat Transfer* i. 5 (*caption*) Pressure head ($p/\rho g$) and velocity head ($V^2/2g$) for frictionless flow from point 1 to point 2. **1849–50** WEALE *Dict. Terms* s.v. *Velocimeter*, Such a velocity-measurer was constructed by Breguet, of Paris. **1931** H. F. OLSON in *Jrnl. Soc. Motion Picture Engineers* XVI. 695 The ribbon microphone..can therefore very appropriately be termed a 'velocity microphone'. **1951** A. SHEINGOLD *Fund. Radio Communications* xiii. 281 Velocity microphones may be designed to be unidirectional in their response. **1978** V. CAPEL *Microphones in Action* ii. 19 The polar diagram of a velocity microphone is different from anything we have discussed so far. **1867** P. G. TAIT tr. Helmholtz in *Phil. Mag.* XXXIII. 485 In integrating the hydrodynamical equations, the assumption has been made that the components of the velocity of each element of the fluid in three directions at right angles to each other are the differential coefficients, with reference to the coordinates, of a definite function which we shall call the velocity-potential. **1878** W. K. CLIFFORD *Dynamic* III. 203 The circulation along any path from *o* to *p*..is called the velocity-potential at *p*. **1882** MINCHIN *Unipl. Kinemat.* 160 If..the velocity potential has at each point of the curve an assigned value. **1907** F. W. LANCHESTER *Aerodynamics* iii. 91 Fluid in irrotational motion has a velocity potential. **1937** [see *stream function* s.v. STREAM *sb.* 9c]. **1980** BOBER & KENYON *Fluid Mech.* ix. 417 The velocity potential, Φ, or the stream function, Ψ, are often introduced into fluid-flow problems because they frequently reduce the difficulty in obtaining a solution to a particular problem. **1904** *Proc. Inst. Mech. Engin.* Feb. 298 They used dry, clean air, and therefore it was possible to keep the Pitot tube extremely small, and to measure the static pressure in the close neighbourhood of the point at which the velocity pressure was measured. **1959** N. C. HARRIS *Mod. Air Conditioning* xv. 293 Velocity pressure is best measured by a Pitot tube combined with a draft gage which reads in inches of water. **1969** *Oceanology* IX. 585 The instrument is based on the measurement of the velocity pressure created by the wind. **1887** D. A. LOW *Machine Draw.* (1892) 36 Velocity Ratio in Belt Gearing.

'velodrome. [a. F. *vélodrome*, f. *vélo* colloq. abbrev. of *vélocipède* VELOCIPEDE + *-drome* as in HIPPODROME.] A special place or building in which exhibitions of cycle-riding, cycle or motor races, etc., are held.

1902 *Times* 26 Nov. 5/6 The Alexandra Palace Velodrome. *Ibid.*, The sides slope gently from the floor to the 'hog-backs', which are placed at either end of the velodrome. **1973** *Trinidad Guardian* 1 Feb. 18/9 Neither the all-weather athletic track nor the cycling velodrome will be trampled upon at Carnival time. **1975** *Daily Colonist* (Victoria, B.C.) 22 Aug. 19/6 Taillibert designed the 70,000-seat stadium, velodrome, an underpass..and the competition swimming pool.

velodyne ('vɛləʊ-, 'viːləʊdaɪn). *Electr.* [f. L. *vēlo-x* swift + Gr. δύν-αμις force.] A device in which the output of a tachogenerator is fed back so as to keep the rotational speed of a shaft proportional to an applied voltage.

1947 CROWTHER & WHIDDINGTON *Science at War* 83 The Velodyne..is an electro-magnetic system that integrates the resultant of several motions. **1952** *Electronic Engin.* XXIV. 382 An electro-mechanical differential analyser, employing velodynes. **1972** *Internat. Jrnl. Control* XVI. 37 The amplified output is fed to the split field of the velodyne motor, the armature of which is supplied from a constant current source.

velom, obs. variant of VELLUM.

velometer (vɛ'lɒmɪtə(r)). [Irreg. f. VELO(CITY + -METER or by contraction of VELOCIMETER.]

†**1.** A kind of governor for a marine steam engine. *Obs.*

1878 *Engineer* 13 Sept. 190/1 A marine governor or antiracer... The..'Velometer'..has got into use entirely by force of its own merits.

2. An instrument for measuring the speed of air, or of an aircraft through the air.

1914 *Flight* 24 Jan. 82/2 The velometer..balances a pressure due to the speed through the air against the apparent weight of a column of liquid. **1939** *Jrnl. R. Aeronaut. Soc.* XLIII. 931 The design and application in mines of a spring-controlled vane-type air flow meter known as the Velometer. **1974** *IEEE Trans. Instrumentation & Measurement* XXIII. 203/1 A sonic velometer uses the passage of sound waves through air to determine the air velocity.

velonea, velonia, variants of VALONIA.

velonye, southern ME. variant of FELONY.

†**velope**, aphetic form of ENVELOPE *v. Obs.*⁻¹

1722 W. HAMILTON *Wallace* 93 With Darkness velop'd, soon they reach'd the Gate.

velouet, obs. form of VELVET.

‖**velours** (vəlur). Also velour, veluse. [F. *velours* (OF. *velour, velous*) velvet. Cf. VELURE.]

1. (See quots. and cf. LURE *sb.*[4])

1706 PHILLIPS (ed. Kersey), *Velours*, a Velvet-Rubber for a Hat. **1831–3** *Encycl. Metrop.* (1845) VIII. 762/2 A uniform direction is given to the nap by means of..a plush brush called a *velours*. **1851–4** *Tomlinson's Cycl. Usef. Arts* (1866) I. 837/2 The general surface of the hat is..improved by means of..a plush cushion called a *velours*, or *veluse*. **1875** KNIGHT *Dict. Mech.* 2699/1 *Velour*, a hatter's lustering and smoothing pad of silk or plush.

2. a. (See quot. 1858.)

1794 A. YOUNG *Trav. France* (ed. 2) I. xix. 550 Rouen... At present, the velours and *cotton toiles* are the most flourishing. The fabrics spread over all the country... They have also some woollens. **1805** T. FREMANTLE *Let.* 19 Nov. in *Wynne Diaries* (1940) III. vi. 234 Mistress Tittler with a black Velour pelisse. **1822** M. EDGEWORTH *Let.* 24 Feb. (1971) 357 My sage-colored French velours simulé pelisse and Fanny and Harriets purple ditto are quite the thing for carriage visits. **1858** SIMMONDS *Dict. Trade*, *Velours*, a kind of velvet or plush for furniture, carpets, etc. manufactured in Prussia, partly of linen and partly of double cotton warps with mohair yarn weft.

b. A woollen dress-stuff with a velvet pile.

1884 KNIGHT *Dict. Mech.* Suppl. 923/1 *Velours*.., a French goods, all wool. **1913** *Play Pictorial* No. 134. p. ii/3 A medium shade of striped grey velours.

‖**velouté** (vəlute). *Cookery.* [Fr., = velvety.] In full ***velouté sauce***. A white sauce made with chicken or veal stock.

1830 [see RAVIGOTE]. **1835** E. A. POE in *Southern Lit. Messenger* May 516/1 He mentioned..Muriton of red tongue and Cauliflowers with *Velouté* sauce. **1868**, etc. [see ALLEMANDE *sb.* 3]. **1936** LUCAS & HUME *Au Petit Cordon Bleu* 71 Have ready ½ pint of *velouté* sauce. **1948**, **1961** [see SUPRÊME *sb.*[2] *(a.)* 1]. **1973** *Times* 6 Dec. 9/6 The vegetable and fish chefs will have made up *velouté* sauce, lobster sauce and a little bechamel sauce.

‖**veloutine** (vəlutin). [F., f. *velouté* velvety + -INE.] (See quot. 1884.)

1884 KNIGHT *Dict. Mech.* Suppl. 923/1 *Veloutine* [printed *Velontine*].., a corded French fabric, with fancy wool warp and merino wool weft. **1890** *Daily News* 29 May 3/1 The chemisette is generally made of finely pleated silk, whether it be in the richest veloutine, bengaline, or ordinary surah.

velt, southern dial. variant of FELT *sb.*[3]

1879 JEFFERIES *Wild Life* 301 The ploughboys call the fieldfares 'velts'.

velt, var. VELD; obs. Sc. form of WELT *v.*

†**velter.** *Obs.*⁻¹ [ad. OF. *veltre* or med.L. *veltris*: see FEWTERER.] A small hunting-dog.

1598 MANWOOD *Lawes Forest* Carta de Foresta of Canutus §32 *margin*, These little Dogges called Velteres, and such as are called Ramhundt (al which Dogges are to sit in ones lap) may be kept in the Forest.

'velterer. *rare*⁻¹. [Cf. prec.] = FEWTERER.

1911 J. H. ROUND *King's Serjeants* 272 The number of greyhounds..accompanying them varied, but each velterer, normally, had charge of from four to six.

†**veltfare**, obs. dial. variant of FIELDFARE.

Cf. the mod. dial. form *veltiver*.

a **1732** SWIFT *Country Parsons Blessings* (Hoppe), Or else a veltfare or a snipe.

velth(t, obs. Sc. forms of WEALTH.

veltheimia (vɛlt'haɪmɪə). [mod.L. (J. G. Gleditsch 1769, in *Nouveaux Mém. Acad. R. Sci. Berlin* 66), f. the name of August Ferdinand, Graf von *Veltheim* (1741–1801), German patron of botany + -IA[1].] A bulbous plant of the genus of this name, belonging to the family Liliaceæ, native to South Africa, and bearing thick, oblong leaves and spikes of pink, red, or yellow flowers.

1808 *Curtis's Bot. Mag.* XXVII. 1091 (*heading*) Glaucous-leaved veltheimia. **1946** M. FREE *All about House Plants* facing p. 240 (*caption*) Veltheimia, a dependable winter-flowering bulb with glossy green foliage. **1980** *Flower & Garden Mag.* Sept. 24 The remarkable veltheimia deserves more attention as a houseplant.

velthy, obs. form of WEALTHY *a.*

†**velt-marshal.** *Obs.* Also veldt-marshal, velt-mareschal. [ad. G. *feld-marschall*, with the spelling of the first element influenced by LG. or Du.] = FIELD-MARSHAL.

1709 *Lond. Gaz.* No. 4560/2 The King of Denmark and King Augustus stood as Godfathers to a Son of the Velt-Marshal. **1737** *Gentl. Mag.* VII. 641/2 To resign the Command of the Army provisionally to Velt-Marshal Philippi. **1774** H. WALPOLE *Corr.* (1846) V. 368 You may be a veldt-marshal by this time. **1819** SCOTT *Leg. Montrose* xi, Anent whilk I have heard the great Velt-Mareschal Bannier hold a learned argument with General Tiefenbach.

‖**velum** ('viːləm). Pl. **vela** ('viːlə). [L. *vēlum* a sail, awning, curtain, covering, veil.]

1. †**a.** A screen or protection. *Obs.*

1781 PRIESTLEY in Young *Autobiogr.* (1898) v. 99 A glass velum, interposed between the retort and the recipient for the air, remains quite cool and dry.

b. A velarium.

1843 *Penny Cycl.* XXVI. 197/2 Such ceiling or vault therefore assumes somewhat the appearance of an awning or *velum* stretched immediately upon arches.

2. *Anat.* **a.** The soft palate; the membranous septum extending backwards from the hard palate.

Also more fully ***velum palati*** and ***velum pendulum***.

(*a*) **1771** *Encycl. Brit.* I. 303/1 The septum, which may likewise be termed *velum*, or *valvula palati*, terminates below by a loose floating edge. **1782** HEBERDEN *Comment.* vii. (1806) 27 The velum pendulum was putrid. **1805** *Med. Jrnl.* XIV. 179 One was removed..from behind the velum pendulum by the forceps. **1847** *Todd's Cycl. Anat.* III. 951 The velum palati is a soft moveable curtain stretching backwards and downwards into the cavity of the pharynx [etc.]. *Ibid.*, Muscles of the velum palati. **1859** SEMPLE *Diphtheria* 55 The posterior column of the velum palati.

(*b*) **1753** *Dict. Arts & Sci.* III. 2313/2 The great uses of this membrane are..for preventing by its claustrum or velum, the things to be swallowed from getting up into the nostrils. **1826** S. COOPER *First Lines Surgery* 241 The velum and uvula are occasionally destroyed. **1846** BRITTAN tr. *Malgaigne's Man. Oper. Surg.* 365 You see then the importance of passing the needles through a well determined point of the velum. **1879** *St. George's Hosp. Rep.* IX. 725 A child..was attacked by sore-throat with false membrane, which spread from the tonsils over the velum.

attrib. **1879** *St. George's Hosp. Rep.* IX. 570 Voice husky; glands of velum palate enlarged.

b. One or other of two membranes extending from the vermiform process of the brain.

1840 G. V. ELLIS *Anat.* 52 The two medullary vela are inclined obliquely towards each other. *Ibid.*, The anterior medullary velum or valve of Vieussens. **1873** MIVART *Elem. Anat.* 377 The velum consists only of the ependyma, the pia mater, and the arachnoid.

c. A triangular fold of the pia mater lying between the third ventricle and the fornix of the brain. (In full ***velum interpositum***.)

c **1845** *Todd's Cycl. Anat.* III. 635 The velum interpositum is best exposed..by removing carefully in succession the corpus callosum and the fornix. In raising the velum itself [etc.].

d. A small triangular space in the inferior region of the bladder.

1835–6 *Todd's Cycl. Anat.* I. 385/1 This membrane presents some peculiarities throughout the extent of a small region named the 'trigone' or the 'velum' of the bladder.

3. *Zool.* A membrane or membranous integument, esp. one occurring in molluscs, medusæ, or lower forms of animal life.

1826 KIRBY & SP. *Entomol.* III. 370 *Velum* (the Velum), a membrane attached to the inner side of the cubital spur in *Apis*. **1840** *Penny Cycl.* XVI. 110/1 Though the term *velum* is used, which would hardly be applicable to the palmated arms or *vela* of the other kind [of Nautilus]. **1877** HUXLEY *Anat. Inv. Anim.* iii. 129 The inner margin of the bell in these medusoids is always produced into a velum. **1887** *Encycl. Brit.* XXII. 420/1 In the majority of sponges both excurrent and incurrent canals are constricted at intervals by transverse diaphragms or *vela*, which contain myocytes concentrically and sometimes radiately arranged.

4. *Bot.* A membranous structure or covering in certain fungi.

1832 LINDLEY *Introd. Bot.* 208 The *velum*, or veil, is a horizontal membrane, connecting the margin of the pileus with the stipes. **1866** *Treas. Bot.* 1207/1 *Velum*, the annulus of certain fungals. **1882** VINES tr. *Sachs's Bot.* 337 This formation of a velum is connected with the entire growth of the whole fructification.

velum(e, velumne, obs. ff. VELLUM.

velunge, southern ME. variant of FEELING *sb.*

veluot, obs. Sc. form of VELVET.

velure (vɪ'l(j)ʊə(r)). Also 6 vellure. [ad. OF. *velour*: see VELOURS.]

†**1.** Velvet. Also *attrib. Obs.*

1587 HARRISON *Descr. Eng.* III. i. in *Holinshed* I. 221/1 But now..the same [wool] hath beene imploied vnto sundrie other vses, as mockados, baies, vellures, grogeraines, &c. **1596** SHAKS. *Tam. Shr.* III. ii. 62 One girth sixe times peec'd, and a womans Crupper of velure. **1602** MARSTON *Ant. & Mel.* v. Wks. 1856 I. 57 A yellow taffata dubblet, cut vpon carnation velure. *a* **1625** FLETCHER *Noble Gent.* v. i, Did you not walk the Town, In a long Cloak half compass? an old Hat, Lin'd with Vellure? **1640** in Entick *London* (1766) II. 179 Velures: English, the single piece. **1748** *Whitehall Evening-Post* No. 405, [He] had on when he was last seen, a light Dove-coloured Coat, black Velure Waistcoat, grey Breeches, and a light Grizzle Wig.

Comb. **1607** DEKKER *Northward Hoe* II. i, The bragging velure-canion'd hobbi-horses praunce vp and downe as if some a the Tilters had ridden them.

2. = VELOURS 1. Hence **ve'lure** *v. trans.*, to dress (a hat) by means of a velvet pad.

1880 *Encycl. Brit.* XI. 520/1 Dressing and polishing.. come next, after which the hat is 'velured' in a revolving machine by the application of haircloth and velvet velures.

ve'lutinous, *a. Ent.* and *Bot.* [f. mod.L. *velutin-us*, f. med.L. *velutum* velvet.] (See quots.)

1826 KIRBY & SP. *Entomol.* IV. xlvi. 276 *Velutinous*,.. covered with very thick-set upright short hairs or pile, resembling velvet. **1857** A. GRAY *First Less. Bot.* (1866) 236 *Velutinous*, velvety to the touch. **1866** *Treas. Bot.* 1207/1 *Velutinous*, velvety; having a hairy surface, which in texture resembles velvet, as in *Rochea coccinea*.

velvatter, obs. Sc. form of WELL-WATER.

'velveret. Now *rare*. Also -ett. [Irreg. f. VELVET *sb.* Hence F. *velverette*.] A variety of fustian with a velvet surface.

1769 *De Foe's Tour Gt. Brit.* (ed. 7) III. 268 The Cotton Trade..has been greatly improved of late..by the Invention of Velverets. **1776** [see VELVETEEN 1]. **1787** G. CANNING *Microcosm* No. 22 (1788) 258, I shall presently see landscapes beautifully diversified with..plains of Plush,.. vallies of Velveret, and meadows of Manchester. **1803** *Ann. Reg.* 828 Cotton velvets, velveteens, velverets, thicksets, cords, and other cotton piece goods. **1839** URE *Dict. Arts* 537 The cotton stuffs called corduroy, velverett, velveteen, thicksett, used for men's wearing apparel, belong to the same fabric. *Ibid.* 538 Plain Velveret..Cord and Velveret. **1882** CAULFEILD & SAWARD *Dict. Needlew.* 510/2 *Velveret*, an inferior sort of Velvet, employed for trimmings, the web of which is of cotton, and the pile of silk.

attrib. **1795** SOUTHEY *Lett. fr. Spain* (1799) 12 A soldier was the other character, in old black velveret breeches.

velvet ('vɛlvɪt), *sb.* Forms: α. 4–7 veluet, 4, 6 -ett (5 feluett), 6 -ette; 4– velvet (5 felvet, velveut, -ved, velavet), 5–7 velvett (6 -vytt), 7 villvet, 8 velvit. β. 5–6 velwet (5 felwet, 6 -weth); 5 vele-, vellewet (fellewet, felewote); velouet, -owet. γ. 5 weluette, 5– 6 -wet(t, 6 wellweut, welvet, *Sc.* wellvet, welwete. δ. *Sc.* 5 veluate, 6 -uote, -uot(t; 6 weluot, -wot(e, wellwott, wolwat. ε. 6 vellett, -at (velat), *Sc.* -ot(e, 6–7 vellet. [ad. med.L. *velvetum* (-*ettum*), also *vel(l)uetum* (-*ettum*), app. representing a Romanic type **villūtettum*, dim. of **villūtum*, whence med.L. *vel(l)utum* (*velotum*), It. *velluto*, OF. *velut*, -*ute*, Sp. and Pg. *velludo*, ultimately f. L. *vill-us* shaggy hair. Cf. VELLUTE, VELOURS, and VELURE.]

I. 1. a. A textile fabric of silk having a short, dense, and smooth piled surface; a kind or variety of this.

Also with defining terms as *cotton, Genoa, raised, stamped velvet*: see these words.

α. **1320** *Wardr. Acc. Edw. II*, 22/14, 1 couerchief de veluett. **13..** *Gaw. & Gr. Knt.* 2027 His cote, wyth þe conysaunce of þe clere werkez, Ennurned vpon veluet vertuuus stonez. **1351** *Cal. Pat. Rolls 25 Edw. III*, 137, j fanoun de murre velvet. *a* **1400** T. CHESTRE *Launfal* 950 Her sadell was semyly sett, The sambus wer grene felvet. *c* **1441** *Pol. Poems* (Rolls) II. 208 Farewelle, damask and clothes of gold; Farewelle, velvet, and clothes in grayn. **1483** in *Somerset Med. Wills* (1901) 245 To Allhalow Church of Aisheton my gown of blew feluett. **1538** STARKEY *England* I. iv. (1871) 130 Yf the nobyllys..be not appayraylyd in sylkys and veluettys, they thynke they lake much of theyr honowre. **1555** WATREMAN *Fardle Facions* I. iv. 46 Tentes and pauilions placed in good ordre, of veluet and saten. **1601** HOLLAND *Pliny* I. 124 That our ladies and wiues when they go abroad in the street may..shine again in their silks and veluets. **1694** *Marten's Voy. Spitzbergen* in *Acc. Sev. Late Voy.* II. 166 He is not as black as Velvet, as the Whale is, but like a Tench. **1735** JOHNSON *Lobo's Abyssinia, Descr.* iii. 55 They wear all sorts of Silks, and particularly the fine Velvets of Turkey. **1756–7** tr. *Keysler's Trav.* (1760) II. 376 A *suite* of seven rooms furnished with red damask and velvet. **1807–8** W. IRVING *Salmag.* (1824) 262 The lady in blue velvet, who so attentively peruses her book. **1815** ELPHINSTONE *Acc. Caubul* (1842) I. 385 Embroidered satin, velvet, and Persian brocade are, of course, confined to the great. **1879** *Cassell's Techn. Educ.* IV. 261/2 Mohair..is largely made into fabrics for ladies' wear, linings, tabinets, plushes, and velvets.

β. *a* **1400** T. CHESTRE *Launf.* 235 Har manteles wer of grene felwet, Ybordured with gold. **1423** *Rolls of Parlt.* IV. 255/1 Upon velowet, and Cloth of Gold. *c* **1430** LYDG. *Min. Poems* (Percy Soc.) 3 The noble Mayer clad in reed velewet. *Ibid.* 6 The tour arrayed withe velwettes softe. **1531** *Rec. St. Mary at Hill* (1905) 45, iij olde doblettes and Shredys of velwet. **1558** in Noake *Worcester Mon.* (1866) 172 A coope of blewe felweth with oystars fethers.

γ. **1441–2** *Durham Acc. Rolls* (Surtees) 471, j vestimentum ..de welwett. *a* **1450** *Le Morte Arth.* 2615 Hyr paraylle All of one hewe, Off a grene weluette. **1507** *Pilton Churchw. Acc.* (Som. Rec. Soc.) 52 A westement of grene wellweut. *Ibid.*, A mantell of purpull wellweut. *a* **1548** HALL *Chron.*, *Edw. IV*, 234 On hys bonet of blacke welvet a floure delyce of golde. *a* **1578** LINDESAY (Pitscottie) *Chron. Scot.* (S.T.S.) I. 174 Ane ryding pie of blak wellvet. *Ibid.* 368 Claith of gould, welwete, sataine and dameis.

δ. **1436** *Registr. Aberdon.* (Maitland Cl.) II. 142 Vnus mantellus pro nostra domina borderatus cum ly veluate. **1500–20** DUNBAR *Poems* lxxvii. 12 Four men of renoun, In gounes of veluot. **1572** *Satir. Poems Reform.* xxxiii. 254 His wyfe weiris weluot on hir Gowne and Coller. **1581** BURNE in *Cath. Tract.* (S.T.S.) 136 That the altaris vas vont to be ornit with veluot.

ε. **1546–7** in Feuillerat *Revels Edw. VI* (1914) 6 For making of one doble turff Cappe of vellett white & Grene chekyd. **1547** *Harl. MS.* 1419 B. fol. 555 b, One placarde of Murrey vellat; another of crimson vellat. *c* **1550** LYNDESAY *Tragedie* 21 [A man] In Rayment reid..Off vellot and of Saityng Crammosie. **1605** *London Prodigal* I. i. 161 My ryding breeches, Vnckle, those that you thought had bene vellet. **1668** BP. HACKET in *Surtees Misc.* (1861) Introd. p. xiv, The most curious piece that I have seen of purple vellet.

b. A piece of this material. *rare.*

c **1386** CHAUCER *Sqr.'s T.* 636 By hir beddes heed sche made a mewe, And covered it with veluettes [*v.r.* velowetys] blewe. **1848** THACKERAY *Van. Fair* xli, Ropes, palls, velvets, ostrich feathers, and other mortuary properties.

c. In various fig. or allusive uses.

a **1592** GREENE & LODGE *Looking Gl.* G.'s Wks. (Grosart) XIV. 90 If he were a king of veluet, I will talke to him. **1607** *Merry Devil Edmonton* IV. i. 37 Thou speakst as true as veluet. **1672** T. JORDAN *Lond. Triumph.* 4 My father, store of velvet wore; My grandsire, beggars' velvet! *a* **1700** B. E. *Dict. Cant. Crew*, *Velvet*, a Tongue. *Tip the Velvet*, to Tongue a Woman. [Hence in later slang Dicts.] **1814** [see GENTLEMAN 5 c]. **1821** P. EGAN *Real Life in London* I. ix. 182 And when that they had sluiced their gobs With striving to excel wit, The lads began to hang their nobs, And tip their frows the velvet. **1823** —— *Grose's Dict. Vulg. T.* s.v. *Velvet*, To the little gentleman in velvet, i.e. the mole that threw up the hill that caused Crop (King William's horse) to stumble. **1882** PIDGEON *Engineer's Holiday* (1883) 167 Whose hand of iron was never ungloved with velvet. **1898** *Westm. Gaz.* 5 Jan. 3/2 Paul Mercer is born, not indeed in the purple, but in the velvet of vast wealth.

d. *on velvet*, in a position of ease or advantage; in an advantageous or prosperous condition.

Chiefly in sporting slang (see later quots.), but formerly in more general use.

1749 J. CLELAND *Mem. Woman Pleasure* II. 114 The deceiving him became so easy, that it was perfect playing upon velvet. **1769** BURKE *Obs. Pres. St. Nat.* Wks. II. 142 Not like our author, who is always on velvet, he is aware of some difficulties. **1785** GROSE *Dict. Vulgar T.*, *To be upon velvet*, to have the best of a bet or match. **1789** ANBURY *Trav.* II. 382 Therefore, only tell General Phillips 'that on that day I fought upon velvet'. **1828** SCOTT *Jrnl.* 23 Feb., We stand on velvet as to finance. **1845** DISRAELI *Sybil* (1863) 41 Before that we were on velvet; but the instant he appeared everything was changed. **1874** *Slang Dict.* 334 Men who have succeeded in their speculations, especially on the turf, are said to stand on velvet. **1897** *Daily News* 1 June 3/5 Is that what you call being 'On velvet' when you are sure to win something?—Yes.

e. A wearer of velvet.

1782 MRS. H. COWLEY *Which is the Man* III. iii, We had all the law ladies from Lincoln's Inn, a dozen good velvets from Bishopsgate, with the wives and daughters of half the M.D.'s and LL.D.'s in town.

f. Gain, profit, winnings; *to the velvet*, to the good. *slang.*

1901 S. E. WHITE *Westerners* xxiii. 228 They's a good many ton of ore in four hundred foot of shaft.'..'Let that go for now... We can call that 'velvet'.' **1908** K. MCGAFFEY *Sorrows of Show Girl* 240 Before the whistle blew for dinner I was several hundred to the velvet. **1912** F. IRWIN *Fine Points Auction Bridge* 56 Do your doubling early in the rubber (so as to pile up 'velvet' for yourself). **1940** WODEHOUSE *Eggs, Beans & Crumpets* 138 It would be money for jam... Just so much velvet. **1942** *Amer. Speech* XVII. 93/2, I have been taking in plenty of velvet these days working the Fair. **1951** E. PAUL *Springtime in Paris* ii. 38 A good French mechanic..would have to work two and one half days to earn 2,430 francs, which on account of taxes.. would not be all velvet.

g. A velvet dress.

1851 E. RUSKIN *Let.* 6 Nov. in M. Lutyens *Effie in Venice* (1965) II. 212, I had on my black velvet because it was mourning. **1944** R. LEHMANN *Ballad & Source* V. v. 222 We stood revealed in our long-sleeved velvets—Jess's sapphire blue, mine claret-coloured. **1963** N. STREATFEILD *Vicarage Family* ii. 16 Isobel's velvet was of a pale green with a very full skirt.

2. *transf.* **a.** The soft downy skin which covers a deer's horn while in the growing stage.

c **1410** *Master of Game* (MS. Digby 182) ii, Hir hornes benn keuered with a softe heer, þat hunters call veluetz. **1576** TURBERV. *Venerie* 47 Then they discouer themselues, going vnto the trees to fray their heads, and to rub of the veluet. *Ibid.* 244 His heade when it commeth first out, hath a russet pyll upon it, the whiche is called *Veluet*. **1697** *Phil. Trans.* XIX. 492 The Surface of the Horn, and the smooth Hairy Skin that covers them whilst they are growing (which is commonly call'd the Velvet). **1859** *Todd's Cycl. Anat.* V. 518/1 In the early condition the horn is soft and yielding, and is protected only by a..delicate integument... From this circumstance the skin is here termed the 'velvet'. **1892** PIKE *Barren Ground N. Canada* 43 It was a full-grown bull in prime condition, the velvet not yet shed, but the horns quite hard underneath.

b. In the phr. *in velvet*, said of the deer.

1880 W. GILL *River Golden Sand* I. viii. 370 The deer are only hunted when in velvet, and from the horns in this state a medicine is made. **1884** JEFFERIES *Red Deer* iv. 72 While this bark or skin remains on the horn the stag is said to be *in velvet* and is not hunted.

3. a. A surface, substance, etc., comparable to velvet in respect of softness or general appearance.

1597 A. M. tr. *Guillemeau's Fr. Chirurg.* 41/2 The Potentiall Cauteryes nowe-adayes are indeede of velvet, and verye excellent. *Ibid.* 41 b/1 That is one of the best, which Mr. Paré calleth the Cauterye of Velvet. **1747** GRAY *Death Fav. Cat* 9 The velvet of her paws. **1781** COWPER *Ep. Prot. Lady* 15 Where Nature has her mossy velvet spread. **1897** 'O. RHOSCOMYL' *White Rose Arno* 267 Here is something to put velvet in the ale. **1904** R. J. FARRER *Garden Asia* 240 Every peak is clad in the velvet of wood and copse.

b. *ellipt.* A velvet cork.

1830 *Edinb. Cycl.* VII. I. 217/1 The finished corks are finally sorted by a boy into four kinds, superfine or velvets, fine, common, and coarse.

II. *attrib.* and *Comb.* **4. a.** Attrib., in the sense 'made of velvet', as ***velvet bag, band, cap, gown***, etc., or 'covered with velvet', as ***velvet cushion, furniture***.

c **1350** *Lybeaus Disc.* 838 A velvwet mantyll gay..Sche caste abowte her swyre. **1480** *Wardr. Acc. Edw. IV* (1830) 149 A longe gowne of grene velvet upon velvet tisshue cloth of gold. **1500–20** DUNBAR *Poems* lxxxviii. 36 Many a semely knyght..in velvet gownes and cheynes of gold. **1542** *Test. Ebor.* (Surtees) VI. 159 One other jackett..with velvett bandes. **1612** *Pasquil's Night-cap* (1877) 37, I thinke them in their hattes as good, As Gentle-women in their veluet-hood. **1621** SIR R. BOYLE in *Lismore Papers* (1886) II. 17 My wives Tawney vellet gown. *c* **1645** in *Verney Mem.* (1907) I. 5 The red velvet furniture. **1780** BURKE *Œcon. Reform* Wks. III. 321 Have their velvet bags, and their red boxes, been so full, that nothing more could possibly be crammed into them? **1796** WOLCOT (P. Pindar) *Satire* Wks. 1812 III. 408 Who with a velvet lash would flog a bear. **1828** LYTTON *Pelham* III. v, Beneath this was a faded velvet waistcoat. **1848** LADY LYTTELTON *Corr.* (1912) 388, I am sending some narrow velvet ribbon to trim it along the tucks.

b. Attrib., in the sense 'smooth or soft like velvet, velvety', as ***velvet down, hand, leaf***, etc.

1588 SHAKS. *L.L.L.* IV. iii. 105 Through the Veluet leaues the winde, All vnseene, can passage finde. **1598** CHAPMAN *Hero & Leander* V. 439 Come Night and lay thy veluet hand On glorious Dayes outfacing face. **1616** J. LANE *Contn. Sqr.'s T.* VI. 23 Which fertil zephirs velvet spirit bloweth. **1634** MILTON *Comus* 898 Thus I set my printless feet O're the Cowslips Velvet head. **1754** GRAY *Progr. Poesy* 27 O'er Idalia's velvet-green The rosy-crownèd Loves are seen On Cytherea's day. **1775** SHERIDAN *Duenna* II. i, Then the roses on those cheeks are shaded with a sort of velvet down. *a* **1805** H. K. WHITE *Remains* (1825) 365 Stretch'd supinely on the velvet turf. **1862** MRS. NORTON *Lady of La Garaye* Prol. 108 The soft white owl with velvet wings. **1880** MRS. FORRESTER *Roy & V.* I. 2 A tuft of dark velvet pansies on one side.

fig. **1592** *Arden of Feversham* I. i. 324 Why, what art thou now but a Veluet drudge, A cheating steward, and base minded pesant? **1597** A. M. tr. *Guillemeau's Fr. Chirurg.* 41 b/1 Receipte of the Velvet Cauterye. **1609** *Ev. Woman in Hum.* I. i. in Bullen *O. Pl.* IV, I cannot soothe the World With velvet words and oyly flatteries. **1639** FULLER *Holy War* Ep. Ded., History is a velvet study and recreation work. **1647** N. WARD *Simple Cobler* (1843) 86, I have..taken a few finish stitches, which may..please a few Velvet eares. **1818** KEATS *Endym.* IV. 297 With as sweet a softness as might be Remember'd from its velvet summer song. **1878** BROWNING *Poets Croisic* xciii, He..to such purpose intervenes That you get velvet-compliment, three-pile.

c. With names of colours, as ***velvet black, -blue, -brown, -crimson, -green, -red.***

1646 SIR T. BROWNE *Pseud. Ep.* 335 Of the suffitus of a torch, doe Painters make a velvet blacke. **1662** MERRETT tr. *Neri's Art of Glass* cii, This is a most fair Velvet Black. **1798** COLERIDGE *Anc. Mar.* IV. xiii, Blue, glossy green, and velvet black, They coiled and swam. **1809** SHAW *Gen. Zool.* VII. II. 496 Velvet-black Paradise Bird. **1811** *Ibid.* VIII. I. 292 Velvet-crimson Humming-Bird. **1924** 'J. SUTHERLAND' *Circle of Stars* iv. 26 She looked up sharply to see herself in the mirror, a rather pale face..and dusky velvet-brown eyes. *Ibid.* ix. 95 Overhead the sky is deep velvet-blue all a-fire with stars. **1952** A. G. L. HELLYER *Sanders' Encycl. Gardening* (ed. 22) 31 *Sanderianus*, large, velvet-green with copper-red veins. **1976** *Flintshire Leader* 10 Dec. 27/1 (Advt.), New Fords for immediate delivery... Granada 2000GL, Velvet Red.

5. Parasynthetic and instrumental, as ***velvet-bearded, -caped, -coated, -draped, -eared, -eyed***, etc.

1611 L. BARRY *Ram Alley* III. i, These *Veluet bearded boyes will still be doing, say what we old men can. **1593** MARLOWE *Edw. II*, II. i. 754 A *Veluet cap'de cloake, fac'st before with Serge. **1881** O. WILDE *Poems* 74 After yon *velvet-coated deer the virgin maid will ride. **1926** M. LEINSTER *Dew on Leaf* II. vi. 227 Your pretty face can charm of itself,..as a pale rose standing still lures the velvet-coated bee. **1888** MISS BRADDON *Fatal Three* I. i, The gentleman was standing with his back to the *velvet-draped mantelpiece. **1805** R. W. DICKSON *Pract. Agric.* I. 540 The *hoary white* [wheat], by some called the **velvet-eared*, is by far the most valuable. **1702** PETIVER *Gazophyl.* I. §10 The *Velvet-eyed Virginia Snap-Beetle. **1848** THACKERAY *Van. Fair* lxi, The *velvet-footed butler brought them their wine. **1691** [? J. BANCROFT] *Edw. III with Fall Mortimer* II. ii, These Peuking *velvethearted Wary Knaves that pretend to Scruples. **1876** 'OUIDA' *Winter City* vi, She let him sit by her in little sheltered *velvet-hung nooks. **1855** THACKERAY *Newcomes* xxxv, The broad-hatted,..*velvet-jacketed, jovial colony of the artists. **1859** GEO. ELIOT *A. Bede* xxxvii, There were the locket and earrings in the little *velvet-lined boxes. **1796** BURKE *Lett. to Noble Lord* Wks. (1907) VI. 71 The demure, insidious,..*velvet-pawed, green-eyed philosophers. **1854** GREENWOOD *Haps & Mishaps* 17 The *velvet-sheathed dagger of Queen Elizabeth. **1891** C. JAMES *Rom. Rigmarole* 103 The two miles home were like walking in *velvet-soled shoes. **1870** *Pouchet's Universe* 109 Certain *velvet-winged Phalenæ.

6. Objective, with agent-nouns, as ***velvet-dresser, -maker, -weaver***, etc.; also ***velvet merchant***.

1530 PALSGR. 284/2 Velvetmaker, *ueloustier*. **1653** URQUHART *Rabelais* I. lvi. 247 Velvet-weavers, Tapestriemakers and Upholsterers. **1677** MIÈGE *Fr. Dict.* I, *Veloutier*, ..a Velvet-maker. **1848** MILL *Pol. Econ.* I. v. §9 (1876) 51 This change..only transfers Employment from velvetmakers to bricklayers. **1858** SIMMONDS *Dict. Trade*, *Velvet-dresser*, a cleaner and dyer of velvet. *Ibid.*, *Velvet-manufacturer*, a weaver of velvet. **1860** RUSKIN *Unto this Last* iv. §76 *note*, He pays, probably, an intermediate shipowner, velvet merchant, and shopman.

7. a. Special Combs.: **velvet-brush** (see quot.); † **velvet-cap**, one who wears a cap of velvet; a physician or student; **velvet carpet**, a cut-pile carpet similar to Wilton; **velvet-cloth** (see quots.); † **velvet-coat**, ? a young fop; **velvet copper-ore**, cyanotrichite; **velvet-cork** (see quot. and cf. 3 b); **velvet glove**, an appearance of suavity and gentleness of manner, esp. one that masks determination or inflexibility (cf. *iron hand* s.v. IRON *a.* 3 c); also *attrib.* (with hyphen); † **velvet-guard**, a trimming of velvet; a wearer of such trimmings; † **velvet-jacket**, an attendant or retainer wearing a jacket of velvet; **velvet-loom**, a loom for weaving velvet; **velvet-painting** (see quot. 1849-50); **velvet-paper** (see quot.); **velvet-pile** *attrib.*, having a pile like that of velvet; also *absol.*, a carpet or cloth of this kind; **velvet-plain** *poet.*, a card-table; **velvet sauce** = VELOUTÉ; **velvet tip** (see sense 2; in quot. used allusively); **velvet tree, wire drawer, work** (see quots.).

1858 SIMMONDS *Dict. Trade*, **Velvet-brush*, a brush used by ladies to remove dust, &c. from garments made of velvet. **1602** *2nd Pt. Return fr. Parnass.* II. i. 554 It is requisite that the French Phisitions be learned and carefull, your English *veluet cap is malignant and enuious. **1630** RANDOLPH *Aristippus* 12 Euery Prenctice can ieere at their braue Cassockes, and laugh the Veluet Caps out of countenance. **1860** GEO. ELIOT *Mill on Floss* II. IV. iii. 188 Good society has its claret and its *velvet carpets. **1908** L. M. MONTGOMERY *Anne of Green Gables* xxix. 325 'Velvet carpet,' sighed Anne luxuriously, '*and* silk curtains!' **1979** A. S. GARSTEIN *How-To Handbk. Carpets* ii. 15 At first velvet carpets were woven of solid colors in pile heights ranging from closely woven low pile to longer 'plush' fabrics. **1882** CAULFEILD & SAWARD *Dict. Needlew.* 511/1 **Velvet cloth*, a plain cloth with a gloss, employed in Ecclesiastical Embroidery. *Ibid.*, *Velvet cloths*,.. beautifully soft and warm descriptions of cloth, suitable for ladies' jackets. **1549** LATIMER *2nd Serm. bef. Edw. VI*, Ej, Heare menes suetes your selfe I require you in goddes behalfe & put it not to the hearing of these *veluette cotes, these vp skippes. **1850** ANSTED *Elem. Geol., Min.*, etc. §504 *Velvet copper ore is probably also a silicate [of copper]. **1855** *Orr's Circ. Sci., Geol.*, etc. 542 (Sulphates) Lettsomite, Velvet Copper Ore. **1883** SIMMONDS *Dict. Trade*, **Velvet cork*, the best kind of cork bark, which is of a reddish colour. **1850**, etc. *Velvet glove [see IRON *a.* 3c]. **1946** W. S. MAUGHAM *Then & Now* xxii. 125 The velvet glove was off and the mailed fist was bared. **1969** S. HYLAND *Top Bloody Secret* II. 202 Concentrated velvet-glove charm. **1973** 'M. INNES' *Appleby's Answer* iv. 41 Blackmail.. of the very most genteel and velvet-glove sort. **1596** SHAKS. *1 Hen. IV*, III. i. 261 Sweare me, Kate,.. A good mouth-filling Oath: and leaue in sooth, And such protest of Pepper Ginger-bread, To *Veluet-Guards, and Sunday-Citizens. **1610** *Histriomastix* III. i. Ej, Out on these veluet gards, and black lac'd sleeues, These simpring fashions simply followed. **1600** HEYWOOD *1 Edw. IV*, Wks. 1874 I. 17 Spoken like a man, and true *veluet-iacket, And we will enter, or strike by the way. **1875** KNIGHT *Dict. Mech.* 2699/1 **Velvet-loom*, a pile-fabric loom. **1809** *Charges against H.R.H. Duke of York* 386/1 Did he ever instruct you in *velvet-painting? **1813** *Examiner* 10 May 298/1 A little skill in velvet painting. **1849-50** WEALE *Dict. Terms*, *Velvet painting* is the art of colouring on velvet with transparent liquid and other ready diluted colours. **1875** KNIGHT *Dict. Mech.* 2699/1 **Velvet-paper*, wall-paper printed with glue and dusted with shearings of cloth or flock. **1851** *Catal. Gt. Exhib.* II. 564/1 *Velvet-pile carpeting. *Ibid.*, Patent velvet-pile and Brussels carpets. **1862** *Catal. Internat. Exhib., Brit.* II. No. 4006, Pilots, Cheviots, velvet piles. **1780** COWPER *Progr. Error* 169 Oh the dear pleasures of the *velvet plain, The painted tablets, dealt and dealt again. **1893** T. F. GARRETT *Encycl. Pract. Cookery* II. 398/2 *Velvet sauce (Velouté). **1952** E. WHITE *Good Eng. Food* IV. i. 171 Aspic Cream. Take ½ pint of liquid aspic jelly and mix it with ¼ pint of velvet sauce.., ¼ pint thick cream and four sheets of gelatine. **1638** FORD *Fancies* III. iii, What, what, what, what! nothing but *velvet tips; you are of the first head yet. **1875** KNIGHT *Dict. Mech.* 2699/1 **Velvet-tree* (Puddling), the point where the draft from the neck of the furnace is turned upward into the stack. **1883** SIMMONDS *Dict. Trade*, **Velvet wire drawer*, a manufacturer of the metal wire used in velvet making. **1882** CAULFEILD & SAWARD *Dict. Needlew.* 511/1 *Velvet work.. is.. largely used in Church Embroideries as a background for altar cloths and hangings.

b. In names of animals (birds, insects, etc.), as **velvet ant**, (*a*) a spider-ant (*Cent. Dict.* 1891); (*b*) a parasitic wasp of the family Mutillidæ, having a velvety appearance; **velvet crab**, a species of swimming crab (*Portunus puber*); **velvet-duck**, a species of scoter (*Œdemia fusca*); **velvet fairy** (see quot.); **velvet fiddler crab**, = *velvet crab*; **velvet fish** (see quot.); † **velvet runner**, the water-rail; **velvet scoter**, = *velvet duck*; **velvet sponge** (see quots.).

1748 M. CATESBY *Nat. Hist. Carolina* App. 13 The *Velvet Ant... The whole body and head resembled crimson velvet. **1842** T. W. HARRIS *Insects Injurious to Vegetation* 14 Stinging velvet-ants.. are predaceous in their habits. **1932** E. STEP *Bees, Wasps, Ants Brit. Isles* 57 The Velvet-ants are not Ants: the name is only a courtesy title given when.. the wingless female.. was a more familiar object than the winged male. **1968** T. WOLFE *Electric Kool-Aid Acid Test* xxi. 305 He can *feel*.. every veruca fly, velvet ant, murine fleas and crabs. **1975** *Sci. Amer.* Dec. 115/1 The natural enemies of *Bembix* include mutillid wasps (sometimes called velvet ants). **1681** GREW *Musæum* I. v. iv. 120 The Claw of the Punger, or the *Velvet-Crab, called Pagurus. **1850** MISS PRATT *Comm. Things Sea-side* v. 288 Some of the most beautiful of our British crabs are those termed Velvet-crabs, on account of the velvety down with which the shell is covered. **1862** ANSTED *Channel Islands* II. ix. 232 The spider crab, and swimming or velvet crab, are also eaten. **1678** RAY *Willughby's Ornith.* 363 The feathers of the whole body are so soft and delicate as nothing more, so that it might be not undeservedly called the *Velvet-Duck. **1768** PENNANT *Brit. Zool.* II. 493 Velvet Duck;.. the plumage is of a fine black, and of the soft and delicate appearance of velvet. **1840** COL. HAWKER *Diary* (1893) II. 175, I made a capital shot at 6 black velvet ducks. **1870** GILLMORE tr. *Figuier's Reptiles & Birds* 235 The Velvet Duck (*Anas fusca*).. is the largest of the Scoters. **1881** LYELL *Fancy Pigeons* 86 The black Nürnberg swallow has most of these grease quills, and from its beautiful green lustre is called the '*velvet fairy'. **1882** *Cassell's Nat. Hist.* VI. 199 The *Velvet Fiddler Crab (*Portunus puber*) has.. its entire carapace densely covered with hairs. **1898** MORRIS *Austral Eng.* 489/1 **Velvet-fish*, [the] name given in Tasmania to the fish *Holoxenus cutaneus*. **1678** RAY *Willughby's Ornith.* 315 The *Velvet Runner. **1706** PHILLIPS (ed. Kersey), *Velvet-Runner*, a Water-Fowl, whose Feathers are black and smooth as Velvet. **1843** YARRELL *Brit. Birds* III. 215 *Oidemia fusca*, *Velvet Scoter. **1882** *Cassell's Nat. Hist.* VI. 318 The 'wool' Sponge, which appears to be one or perhaps two species of the Hippospongia, *H. gossypina*, and *H. meandriformis*, the '*velvet' Sponge. **1883** W. S. KENT in *Fisheries Bahamas* 47 The so-called Velvet, Abacco-velvet, or Boat-sponge (*S. equina*, var. *meandriniformis*), differing from the Sheep's-wool in the absence of the fleece-like tufts upon its outer surface.

c. In names of plants, as **velvet-bean**, an annual climbing-plant (*Macuna utilis*) bearing velvety pods; **velvet-bur**, a tropical plant of the vervain family; **velvet-dock**, common mullein; **velvet-ear(ed) wheat**, = *velvet wheat*; † **velvet-flower** (see quots.); **velvet flower-de-luce, -grass, -moss** (see quots.); **velvet rose**, a variety of rose with velvety petals; **velvet-seed**, a small evergreen West Indian tree; **velvet wheat**, a variety of white wheat with downy ears.

1898 *Gardener's Mag.* 3 Sept. 569/2 The accounts.. respecting the agricultural value of the Florida *velvet bean must be received with caution. **1866** *Treas. Bot.* 1207/2 *Velvet-bur, *Priva echinata*. **1863** PRIOR *Plant-n.*, *Velvet-Dock, from its soft leaves, *Verbascum Thapsus*. **1837** *Brit. Husb.* (L.U.K.) II. 138 We have.. the 'golden-ear', the '*velvet-ear', the 'egg-shell', and 'hedge-wheat'. **1862** MORTON *Farmer's Cal.* 547 Among white wheats.. the *Velvet-eared, a short-strawed sort, is of remarkable quality and productiveness. **1548** TURNER *Names Herbes* (E.D.S.) 11 The other kynde [of *Amaranthus*] is called here in Englande of some purple *veluet floure, of other flouramore. *Ibid.* 80 Viola flammea,.. in englishe veluet floure or french Marigoulde. **1573** TUSSER *Husb.* (1878) 96 Veluet flowers, or french Marigolds. **1578** LYTE *Dodoens* I. xviii. 168 These pleasant.. floures are called.. in English floure Gentill, Floramor, and Purple veluet floure. [Hence in Gerarde and Cotgr.] **1863** PRIOR *Plant-n.*, *Velvet-flower*, from its crimson velvety tassels, *Amaranthus caudatus*. **1597** GERARDE *Herbal* 94 *Iris Tuberosa*. *Veluet flower de-luce. **1856** A. GRAY *Man. Bot.* (1860) 573 *Holcus lanatus*, *Velvet-Grass. **1858** SIMMONDS *Dict. Trade*, **Velvet-moss*, a name for the *Gyrophora murina*, a lichen used in dyeing, obtained in the Dovrefeldt mountains of Norway. **1597** GERARDE *Herbal* 1085 *Rosa Holosericea*, the *veluet Rose... The flowers.. of a deepe and blacke red colour, resembling red crimson veluet, whereupon some haue called it the Veluet Rose. **1786** ABERCROMBIE *Gard. Assist.*, Arr. 33/1 Velvet rose (single). **1893** G. D. LESLIE *Lett. Marco* i. 5 A rose that is almost obsolete,.. called the velvet rose. **1866** *Treas. Bot.* 1207/2 *Velvet-seed, *Guettarda elliptica*. **1771** A. YOUNG *Farmer's Tour East Eng.* II. 485 Mr. Arbuthnot gathered six ears of this wheat,.. and carrying it to market, the farmers remarked that they knew it, but had lost the sort, and called it *velvit wheat. **1856** MORTON *Cycl. Agric.* II. 1131/1 Some Scotch wheats have become greatly mixed with velvet wheat.

'velvet, *v. rare.* [f. prec.]

1. *intr.* To imitate velvet in painting.

1612 PEACHAM *Gentl. Exerc.* 83 Take your verditure,.. it is the faintest and palest greene that is, but it is good to veluet vpon blacke in any manner of drapery.

2. *trans.* 'To make like velvet; to cover with velvet' (W.) Also *fig.*

1864 in WEBSTER. **1959** R. GRAVES *Coll. Poems* 96 We velveted our love with fantasy Down a long vista-row of Christmas trees.

'velveted, *a.* [f. VELVET *sb.*] Covered with velvet or a velvety down; dressed in velvet; having velvet trappings.

1611 COTGR., *Velouté*, Velueted, of Veluet, clad, or couered with Veluet. **1686** W. HARRIS tr. *Lemery's Course Chem.* (ed. 3) 544 Its Leaves are long, divided, and hairy, or velveted. **1737** BRACKEN *Farriery Impr.* (1757) I. 223 They .. are.. velveted on the Back like a Bat. **1850** HAWTHORNE *Scarlet L.* xx, This yellow-starched and velveted old hag. **1868** *Morning Star* 7 Jan., The miniature sleighs, each containing a fair passenger velveted and furred. **1886** *Pall Mall G.* 10 Aug. 8/2 An open hearse, heavily plumed and drawn by half a dozen horses, also velveted and plumed.

velveteen (vɛlvə'tiːn). Also 8 **velvatean**. [f. VELVET *sb.* Hence F. *velvetine*.]

1. a. A fabric having the appearance or surface of velvet, but made from cotton in place of silk.

1776 *Specif. Woolstenholme's Patent* No. 1123, For his new kind of goods called velvateans, being an improvement on velveretts. **1795** J. AIKIN *Manchester* 299 Velvets, velveteens, thicksets. **1843** LD. MELBOURNE in Benson & Esher *Lett. Q. Victoria* (1908) I. 467 George Byng came the other morning in a waistcoat of Peel's velveteen. **1860** *All Year Round* No. 53. 63 The barragons and fustians,.. dimities and velveteens, for which Bolton was famous. **1882** CAULFEILD & SAWARD *Dict. Needlew.* 511/1 *Velveteen*, a description of fustian, made of twilled cotton, and having a raised pile, and of finer cotton, and better finish than the latter.

b. *attrib.* Made of this material.

1824 MISS MITFORD *Village* Ser. I. (1863) 200 He.. generally sticks to his velveteen jacket. **1841** LYTTON *Nt. & Morn.* I. i, A man.. plainly clad in a velveteen shooting-jacket. **1860** *All Year Round* No. 57. 156 He wore a fur cap, and shorts, and was of the velveteen race, velveteeny. **1887** DOYLE *Study in Scarlet* (1892) 26 A railway porter in his velveteen uniform.

c. A dress of velveteen.

1873 *Young Englishwoman* Aug. 414/1 Would a black velveteen be suitable for the autumn? **1932** 'E. M. DELAFIELD' *Thank Heaven Fasting* II. i. 156 Run upstairs and put on the green velveteen. It suits you.

2. *pl.* **a.** Trousers or knickerbockers made of velveteen.

1863 KINGSLEY *Water-Bab.* i, He.. thought of the fine times coming, when he would be a man,.. and wear velveteens and ankle-jacks. **1865** DICKENS *Mut. Fr.* I. ii, 'The man,' Mortimer goes on,.. 'was only son of a tremendous old rascal who made his money by Dust'. 'Red velveteens and a bell?' the gloomy Eugene inquires.

b. *transf.* A gamekeeper (as commonly wearing velveteen clothes).

1857 HUGHES *Tom Brown* I. ix, What business is that of yours, old Velveteens? **1880** CARNEGIE *Pract. Trap.* 23 Be it known that Velveteens placed those 'brammels' there in order that we might move them.

Hence **velve'teened** *a.*, dressed in velveteen; also **velve'teeny** *a.* (*nonce-word*).

1860 Velveteeny [see sense 1 b above]. **1896** *Daily News* 10 Nov. 2/1 In the procession thereafter were the velveteened foresters.

† **velvet head.** *Obs.* Also 6 **vellet head**, 7 **velvet-head.** [f. VELVET *sb.* 2.]

1. The head of a deer while the horns are still covered with velvet. Also *transf.* of a kid (quot. 1579).

1576 TURBERV. *Venerie* 244 His heade is called then a veluet heade. **1579** SPENSER *Sheph. Cal.* May 185 His Vellet head began to shoote out, And his wrethed hornes gan newly sprout. **1607** TOPSELL *Hist. Four-f. Beasts* 124 Hornes.. couered with a rough skinne, which the hunters for honours sake call a Veluet head. **1626** BRETON *Fantasticks* Wks. (Grosart) II. 12/1 The veluet heads of the Forrests fall at the loose of the Crosse-bow. **1674** N. COX *Gentl. Recreat.* (1677) 65 If you geld him when he hath a Velvet-head, it will ever be so, without fraying or burnishing.

2. Applied contemptuously to a person.

1630 B. JONSON *New Inn* II. ii, What says old velvet-head?

Hence † **velvet-headed** *a.* In quots. *fig. Obs.*

1647 N. BACON *Disc. Govt. Eng.* vi. 23 Roman Prelacy in these younger times was but Velvet-headed. **1650** B. *Discolliminium* 41 You will expose your Flocks to all the new-fangled Errours.. that bud so fast, out of the Brow-antlers of our velvet-headed Brockets. **1678** MARVELL *Growth Popery* 6 He lays the same claim still,.. and though Velvet-headed hath the more itch to be pushing.

'velvetiness. [f. VELVETY *a.*] The quality of resembling velvet in smoothness, etc. Also *fig.*

1882 *Good Literature* 6 May 142 In America, where.. black women have that happy Ethiopian velvetiness of cuticle. **1889** MARY E. CARTER *Mrs. Severn* I. i. Prol. 10 The dense velvetiness of the furze. **1906** GALSWORTHY *Man of Property* II. iv. 167 The peculiar exasperation, velvetiness, and mockery, of which Bosinney's manner had been composed.

'velveting. [f. VELVET *sb.*]

† **1.** The nap or pile of velvet. *Obs.*

1728 CHAMBERS *Cycl.* s.v., The Nap or Shag, call'd also Velveting, of this Stuff.. is form'd of part of the Threads of the Warp. *Ibid.*, The threads that make the Velveting.

2. Velvet as a commercial fabric; velvet in the piece; esp. *pl.* velvet goods.

1891 in *Cent. Dict.*

velvet-leaf. [f. VELVET *sb.* 4 b.]

1. The tropical shrub *Cissampelos Pareira*, the root and bark of which are employed medicinally.

1707 SLOANE *Jamaica* I. 200 Velvet-Leaf. This has a round, whitish, wooddy stalk.. having several leaves,.. very thick set with a whitish down, or soft hair, feeling to the touch as velvet, whence its name. **1756** P. BROWNE *Jamaica* (1789) 397 The Velvet-Leaf is looked upon as an excellent diuretic. **1866** *Treas. Bot.* 288/2 The most important plant of the genus is the Velvet Leaf, *C. Pareira*, a native of the West Indies, Central America, and India. **1871** GARROD *Mat. Med.* (ed. 3) 168 Pareira Root. The dried root of *Cissampelos Pareira*, or Velvet leaf.

2. The tree-mallow, *Lavatera arborea*, or a leaf of this.

1728 E. SMITH *Compl. Housew.* (1750) 312 Take velvet-leaves, wipe them clean, chop them small,.. and boil them gently, till they are crisp. **1796** WITHERING *Brit. Plants* (ed. 3) III. 614 Tree Mallow, or Velvet-leaf. **1863** PRIOR *Plant-n.* 232.

3. (See quots.)

(*a*) **1856** A. GRAY *Man. Bot.* (1860) 68 *Abutilon Avicennæ*, Velvet-Leaf. **1866** *Treas. Bot.* 1207/2 Velvet-leaf,.. *Sida Abutilon*.

(*b*) **1891** *Cent. Dict.* s.v. *Tournefortia*, *T. Argentea* is sometimes cultivated under the name of East Indian velvet-leaf.

velvet-like, *a.* [f. VELVET *sb.*] Resembling (that of) velvet.

1677 MIÈGE *Fr. Dict.* I, *Velouté*,.. made velvet-like. **1770** PENNANT *Brit. Zool.* IV. 4 Velvet Crab with the thorax quinquedentated; body covered with short brown velvet-like pile. **1796** WITHERING *Brit. Pl.* (ed. 3) II. 134 The whole plant [is] of a velvet-like softness. **1819** STEPHENS in Shaw's *Gen. Zool.* XI. I. 173 The greater portion of the head covered by short and serrated, velvet-like feathers. **1829** LOUDON *Encycl. Plants* (1836) 615 The species are border flowers, in much esteem for their velvet-like leaves. **1845** G. DODD *Brit. Manuf.* Ser. IV. 109 The rib or raised part.. is cut.. so as to form a velvet-like pile.

velvetory. (See quot.)

1829 *Glover's Hist. Derby* I. 99 Arch-bricks, proper for the tops of reverberatory furnaces,.. vulgarly called velvetory bricks.

'velvetry. *rare*$^{-1}$. [f. VELVET *sb.*] Velvet, or material resembling this, in a collective sense.
1887 BLACKMORE *Springhaven* (ed. 4) III. v. 61 They had sleeved their bent arms with green velvetry of moss.

velvety ('velvɪtɪ), *a.* [f. VELVET *sb.*]
1. Having the smooth and soft appearance or feel of velvet.
1752 J. HILL *Hist. Anim.* 77 The oriental velvety Papilio, with short antennæ. **1796** WITHERING *Brit. Pl.* (ed. 3) III. 569 Leaves very soft, and almost velvety. **1807** VANCOUVER *Agric. Devon* (1813) 337 Skin loose, free, and velvety to the touch. **1830** LINDLEY *Nat. Syst. Bot.* 185 Their stigmas generally long and velvety externally. **1882** *Garden* 10 June 399/3 Its dark velvety and rich yellow flowers are very fine indeed.
Comb. **1846–50** A. WOOD *Class-bk. Bot.* 209 Leaves.. velvety-tomentose. **1878** MRS. F. D. BRIDGES *Jrnl. Lady's Trav. round World* i. Aug. (1883) 2 Our ship moving almost noiselessly across the velvety-looking sea.
b. Applied to colours. (Cf. VELVET *sb.* 4 c.)
1819 STEPHENS in Shaw's *Gen. Zool.* XI. I. 135 The under part of the wings are of a fine velvety black. **1876** BLACK *Madcap Violet* vii, She was calling attention..to the light velvety green. **1883** 'OUIDA' *Wanda* I. 40 A deep brown hue, like the velvety brown of a stag's throat.
2. Characteristic of velvet; similar to that of velvet.
1846 G. E. DAY tr. *Simon's Anim. Chem.* II. 397 Presenting a beautiful white velvety appearance. **1847–9** *Todd's Cycl. Anat.* IV. I. 143/2 Of velvety look and feel. **1880** *Daily Tel.* 16 Feb., The well-remembered tones had lost something of their old velvety quality. **1884** *Law Times Rep.* L. 421/1 It is the grouping and velvety effect they produce which is original.
3. *fig.* Unusually or attractively smooth, soft, or gentle.
1861 CUNNINGHAM *Wheat & Tares* 82 The other's velvety manner made him chafe and fret. **1896** *Strand Mag.* XII. 329/1 The tiny bells of the lime-blossoms..mingled their soft, velvety murmur with the other peaceful sounds of Nature.
b. Smooth and soft to the taste.
1888 *Harper's Mag.* July 216/2 The rum is velvety, sugary, with a pleasant, soothing effect. **1908** R. BAGOT *A. Cuthbert* xi. 125 Accompanied by the softest and most velvety of sauces.

velveut, -vytt, -wet, obs. ff. VELVET.

vely, southern ME. variant of *felly* FELLOE.

†**velyard.** *Obs.*$^{-1}$ [ad. F. *vieillard*, †*viellard.*] An old man.
c **1520** SKELTON *Magnyf.* 1904 Vyle velyarde, thou must not nowe my dynt withstande.

velym(e, obs. ff. VELLUM.

vem, obs. Sc. f. WEM *sb.*

vemen, southern ME. var. *feme* FOAM *v.*; obs. Sc. pl. WOMAN.

vemon, vemynous, obs. erron. varr. VENOM, VENOMOUS.

ven, southern ME. and dial. var. FEN *sb.*; obs. Sc. f. WEEN *v.*

‖**vena** ('viːnə). Pl. venæ ('viːniː). [L. *vēna.*] A vein.
Used only in conjunction with Latin adjs. or genitives; many of the specific names thus formed are recorded in special Dictionaries from the 17th cent. onwards.
c **1400** *Lanfranc's Cirurg.* 177 Summe of þese veynes comeþ fro a veyne of þe lyuer, þat is clepid vena ramosa. *a* **1425** tr. *Arderne's Treat. Fistula*, etc. 54 Agayne þe mormale be þer lesnyng of vena basilica, i. lyuer vayne. **1548** VICARY *Anat.* (1888) vii. 54 Of *vena Sephalica* springeth *vena occularis*; and of *vena Bazilica* springeth *vena Saluatella*. **1598** FLORIO, *Assellare vena*, a large vaine being a branch of Vena caua. **1626** B. JONSON *Staple of N.* IV. iv, The Doctor..tells you, Of *Vena caua*, and of *vena porta*. **1676** WISEMAN *Surg. Treat.* 343 The Bloud being prest out into the *Vena cava*. **1755** *Dict. Arts & Sci.* IV. 3148/2 Between the aorta and the vena azygos. **1793** HOLCROFT tr. *Lavater's Physiog.* vii. 47 A blue vena frontalis..in an open, smooth, well-arched forehead. **1822–7** GOOD *Study Med.* (1829) II. 8 The abdominal branches of the vena portæ. **1840** E. WILSON *Anat. Vade M.* (1842) 352 The Venæ Thebesii are numerous minute venules [etc.]. **1899** *Allbutt's Syst. Med.* VII. 245 The aortic and vena cava pressures are obtained by passing canulæ down the carotid artery and jugular vein respectively.

†**'venable,** *a. Obs.*$^{-1}$ [f. L. *vēn-um* (see VENAL *a.*^{1}) + -ABLE.] = VENDIBLE *a.*
1507 in Man *Reading* (1816) 357 Everie burgess..may.. also bye and sell all manner of merchandies and thyngs venable in feyres and markets.

venabule. *rare*$^{-0}$. [ad. L. *vēnābulum*, f. *vēnārī* to hunt.] (See quot.)
1623 COCKERAM I, *Venabule*, a hunting staffe.

venæsection, variant of VENESECTION.

venaker, obs. Sc. variant of VINEGAR.

venal ('viːnəl), *a.*^{1} Also 6 venall. [ad. L. *vēnālis*, f. *vēnum* that which is sold or for sale. So OF. *venal*, F. *vénal*, Sp. and Pg. *venal*, It. *venale.*]
1. Of things: **a.** Exposed or offered for sale, that may be bought, as an ordinary article of merchandise. Also, associated or connected with ordinary sale or purchase. Now *arch.*
1662 EVELYN *Chalcogr.* 147 Not as a Venal addition to the price of the Book..but..as a Specimen of what we have alledged. **1663** BOYLE *Usef. Exp. Nat. Philos.* II. 358 Premising..that by Sal Armoniack I here mean the Factitious and Venal. **1746** FRANCIS tr. *Horace, Epist.* II. ii. 14 He sinks in Credit, who attempts to raise His venal Wares with over-rating Praise, To put them off his Hands. **1849** CLARIDGE *Cold Water Cure* 38 Men..avoid water—perhaps because it costs nothing (for, in our artificial life, we are led to esteem things according to their venal price). **1883** *Athenæum* 3 Nov. 564/3 The book, though open for many years to the frequenters of great libraries, has not been venal on the shelves of the ordinary bookseller. **1888** *Sat. Rev.* 7 Jan. 12 The figs..might be venal at the nearest stall without our troubling the stall-keeper.
b. Of offices, privileges, etc.: Capable of being acquired by purchase, instead of being conferred on grounds of merit or regarded as above bargaining for.
1675 BROOKS *Gold. Key* Wks. 1867 V. 9 When these places of honour and trust were made venal,..and sold for ready money to such as gave most for them. **1772** in *Lett. Lit. Men* (Camden) 405 In the last Parliament, the places being quite venal, the young men, who had purchased, were the majority. **1796** H. HUNTER tr. *St.-Pierre's Stud. Nat.* (1799) III. 169 The face of affairs in France is at present greatly altered; every thing there is now become venal. **1839** J. MENDHAM (*title*), The Venal Indulgences and pardons of the Church of Rome, exemplified [etc.]. **1845** FORD *Handbk. Spain* I. 5 They see that wealth is safety and power where everything is venal. **1860** MOTLEY *Netherl.* ii. (1868) I. 41 All posts and charges were venal.
c. Of support, favour, etc.: That may be bought or obtained for a price; ready to be given in return for some reward without regard for higher principles.
1652 GAULE *Magastrom.* 196 Prophecy is not venal, or to be bought and hired with mony and preferments. **1725** POPE *Odyss.* II. 217 From him some bribe thy venal tongue requires. **1738** JOHNSON *London* 198 The Laureate Tribe in venal Verse relate, How Virtue wars with persecuting Fate. **1769** *Junius Lett.* xi. (1788) 73 You may command a venal vote. **1815** W. H. IRELAND *Scribbleomania* 26 *note*, Deigning to subsidize a venal pen in order to throw a gloss over the flagrant dereliction. **1888** BRYCE *Amer. Commw.* xliv. II. 165 As the Senate is smaller..the vote of each member is of more consequence, and fetches, when venal, a higher price.
2. Of persons: Capable of being bought over or bribed; ready to lend support or exert influence for purely mercenary considerations; of an unprincipled and hireling character.
1670 MARVELL *Corr.* Wks. (Grosart) II. 326 We are all venal cowards, except some few. **1748** *Anson's Voy.* III. x. 414 Their Magistrates are corrupt..and their tribunals crafty and venal. **1781** COWPER *Table-t.* 352 And every venal stickler for the yoke Felt himself crush'd at the first word he spoke. **1842** W. C. TAYLOR *Anc. Hist.* x. §6 (ed. 3) 284 Venal orators conducted the prosecution. **1881** FROUDE *Short Stud.* (1883) IV. II. vi. 252 Rome was as venal under the popes as Jugurtha found her under the Republic.
3. Connected or associated with sordid and unprincipled bargaining; subject to mercenary or corrupt influences.
1718 ROWE tr. *Lucan* I. 338 Hence slaughter in the venal field returns, And Rome her yearly competitions mourns. **1730–46** THOMSON *Autumn* 1067 Thy pathetic eloquence! that..Of honest Zeal th' indignant lightning throws, And shakes Corruption on her venal throne. **1796** BURKE *Regic. Peace* Wks. VIII. 194 To squander us away..for a venal enlargement of their own territories. **1838** PRESCOTT *Ferd. & Is.* (1846) III. xxiv. 371 No one has accused him of attempting to enrich his exchequer by the venal sale of office. **1885** FARGUS *Slings & Arrows* 62 The compartment of the train which was, by a venal arrangement of the guard's, reserved to ourselves.

venal ('viːnəl), *a.*^{2} Now *rare* or *Obs.* [f. L. *vēna* VEIN *sb.* + -AL^1. Cf. VENIAL *a.*^{2}]
1. Of blood: Contained in the veins.
1615 CROOKE *Body of Man* 30 So the Heart..containeth in his right ventricle venal, in his left arterial blood. **1665** NEEDHAM *Med. Medic.* 417 Bleeding drains onely the Venal Bloud. **1745** FRANKLIN *Lett.* Wks. 1887 II. 10, I cannot conceive how they are dilated. It is said, by the force of the venal blood rushing into them. **1781** P. BECKFORD *Hunting* (1802) 123 He made a strong ligature on his neck, that the venal blood might be emitted with the greater impetus. **1807** *Med. Jrnl.* XVII. 302 The blood that was discharged was evidently venal.
2. Of or pertaining to, connected with, forming, of the nature of, a vein or veins.
1661 LOVELL *Hist. Anim. & Min.* 319 The right [auricle] before the vena cava, and the left [before] the venal arterie. **1669** W. SIMPSON *Hydrol. Chym.* 70 Making it [the blood] to restagnate in some of the arterial or venal chanels. **1744** *Phil. Trans.* XLIII. 60 The Blood is stopp'd, as mentioned before, in the little venal parallel Canals. **1748** HARTLEY *Observ. Man* I. i. §1. 45 The venal Sinuses which surround the Brain and spinal Marrow. **1797** M. BAILLIE *Morb. Anat.* (1807) 107 There was no obstruction at the entrance of the thoracic duct into the venal system. **1822–7** GOOD *Study Med.* (1829) III. 479 To make the skin do the office of a valve to the venal opening.

venal(e, obs. forms of VENNEL.

vena'litious, *a. rare*$^{-0}$. [ad. L. *vēnālītius* (-*īcius*), f. *vēnālis* VENAL *a.*^{1}] (See quot.)
1656 BLOUNT *Glossogr.*, *Venalitious*, belonging to the sale of men or children, or of slaves; that is to be bought or sold.

venality (vɪ'nælɪtɪ). [ad. F. *vénalité*, or late L. *vēnālitās*, f. *vēnālis* VENAL *a.*^{1} So It. *venalità*, Sp. *venalidad*, Pg. -*idade.*]
1. The quality or fact of being for sale. *rare.*
1611 COTGR., *Venalitie*, venalitie, vendiblenesse; a being salable; a letting or setting vnto sale. [Hence in Blount (1656).] **1820** RANKEN *Hist. France* VII. I. ii. 158 They proposed..to abolish altogether the venality of offices, which would have cut off one of the principal sources of finance in the state. **1874** TYRWHITT *Sketch. Club* 168 The intense vulgarity of so much English work comes direct from its venality.
2. The quality of being venal; readiness to give support or favour in return for profit or reward; prostitution of talents or principles for mercenary considerations.
a **1683** SIDNEY *Disc. Govt.* II. xxv. (1704) 183 Such as will rise, must render themselves conformable in all corruption and venality. **1734** tr. *Rollin's Rom. Hist.* (1827) III. 288 A soul superior to venality and views of interest. **1749** BOLINGBROKE *Lett. Patriotism*, etc. 128 Want is the consequence of profusion, venality of want, and dependance of venality. **1836** THIRLWALL *Greece* xxiii. III. 309 It only proves the opinion generally entertained of Spartan venality. **1874** GREEN *Short Hist.* ix. §3. 622 His pride and venality had made him unpopular with the nation at large.

,venali'zation. *rare*$^{-1}$. [See VENAL *a.*^{1} and -IZATION.] The action or process of making venal.
1906 *Athenæum* 3 Nov. 549/2 We fear the venalization of Literature and a monopoly of its distribution.

'venally, *adv. rare*$^{-1}$. [f. VENAL *a.*^{1}] In a venal or mercenary manner.
1756 *Demi-Rep* 35 Their souls all free, not venally profuse.

'venalness. *rare*$^{-0}$. = VENALITY.
1727 BAILEY (vol. II), *Venalness*, Saleableness.

venarie, -ary, obs. varr. VENERY^1.

venatic (vɪ'nætɪk), *a.* [ad. L. *vēnātic-us*, f. *vēnārī* to hunt. So obs. F. *venatique.*] Of or pertaining to, employed in, devoted to, hunting.
1656 BLOUNT *Glossogr.*, *Venatick*, belonging to hunting or chasing. **1731** MEDLEY *Kolben's Cape G. Hope* I. 244 The Hassagaye the Hottentots look upon as the most notable martial and venatick weapon they have. **1849** *Fraser's Mag.* XL. 3 [Stories of hunting] written with ten times the.. vigour, and picturesqueness, either venatic or literary. **1865** *Daily Tel.* 4 March, Why are not other nations which have passed through the same venatic period as deeply imbued with the spirit of sport? **1889** BADEN-POWELL *Pigsticking* 19, I adore, with a sort of venatic worship, both a fox and a hound.
So **ve'natical** *a.* Hence **ve'natically** *adv.*
a **1666** HOWELL *Lett.* (1678) IV. 4 Ther be three [places] for Venery or Venatical plesure in England, viz. a Forrest, a Chase and a Park. **1887** *Field* 26 Feb. 267/1, I do not know whether that vernal saint, Valentine, was venatically-minded. **1893** *Ibid.* 11 March 345/1 Venatically workmanlike.

ve'nation^1. Now *rare* or *Obs.* Also 4 venacyon. [ad. L. *vēnātio*, f. *vēnārī* to hunt. So F. *vénation* (†*venacion*), It. *venazione.*] The action or occupation of hunting wild animals.
1386 *Almanak* 17 In December..þe son es in Capricorn, for Esau by venacyon lost hys fader benyson. **1610** GUILLIM *Heraldry* IV. xi. (1611) 217 The last of the foresaid Arts wee reckoned to bee Venation, which Plato divideth into three species, Hunting, Hawking and Fishing. **1646** SIR T. BROWNE *Pseud. Ep.* I. viii. 32 There are extant of his in Greeke, foure bookes of Cynegeticks or venation. *Ibid.* VI. vi, At one venation the King of Siam took four thousand Elephants. **1694** MOTTEUX *Rabelais* v. 249 Some in ferine Venation take delight. **1832** *Fraser's Mag.* VI. 160 What sumphs all the ancients were in venation, notwithstanding their boasted prowess!

venation^2 (vɪ'neɪʃən). [f. L. *vēna* VEIN *sb.*]
†**1.** The arrangement or structure of sap-vessels in plants. *Obs.*$^{-1}$
1646 SIR T. BROWNE *Pseud. Ep.* III. i. 106 As for the manner of their venation,..we shall find it to be otherwise then as is commonly presumed, by sawing away of trees.
2. a. *Bot.* The arrangement of the veins in the leaves of plants.
1830 LINDLEY *Nat. Syst. Bot.* Introd. p. xxii, Many other orders are distinguished without exception by modifications of venation. **1851** G. F. RICHARDSON *Geol.* vii. 170 In leaves we can rarely recognise, in a fossil state, more than their mode of venation, division, arrangement, and outline. **1890** *Science Gossip* XXVI. 181, I took a specimen..with six well-developed leaves, the venation being very distinct.
b. *Ent.* The arrangement of the veins in the wings of insects.
1861–2 LE CONTE *Classif. Coleoptera N. Amer.* I. Introd. p. xviii, The venation is subject to variation in different genera. **1891** *Science Gossip* XXVII. 53 The venation in many genera [of the Nematocera] varies in the relative lengths of some of the veins and their respective positions.
Hence **ve'national** *a.*, of or relating to venation.
1891 in *Cent. Dict.*

ve'natious, *a. rare*$^{-1}$. [f. L. *vēnāt-*, ppl. stem of *vēnārī* to hunt.] Inclined to hunting.
1660 R. COKE *Justice Vind.*, *Arts & Sci.* 22 Take a Hare, Dear, or Fox, &c. and let them be kept among Hounds in their kennel, or so that the venatious appetite of them is not excited, and they will not meddle with them.

veˈnator. *rare.* [a. L. *vēnātor*, agent-noun f. *vēnārī* to hunt.] A hunter or huntsman.

1656 BLOUNT *Glossogr.*, *Venator*, a hunter or huntsman. **1831** J. TAYLOR in Edwards *Freedom of Will* Introd. p. lxviii, It by no means appears that the little unlicensed venator invariably directs his flight towards the nearest or the best-fed gnat.

venatorial (vɛnəˈtɔərɪəl), *a.* [f. L. *vēnātōri-us* (see VENATORY *a.*) + -AL[1].]

1. Connected with hunting.

1830 *Fraser's Mag.* II. 200 What are your sylvan or venatorial exploits compared to the high games enacted in the broad prairies? **1848** *Blackw. Mag.* LXIV. 85 The most northerly tribe..surpass their southern neighbours in venatorial skill. **1872** COUES *Birds N.-W.* 365 The contrast between the physique of Rough-legged Hawks and their venatorial exploits, is striking.

2. Given to hunting; addicted to the chase.

a **1881** BLACKIE *Lay Serm.* i. 52 The migrations of a tropical bird, or the nosings of a venatorial hound. **1885** MEREDITH *Diana* i, Her main personal experience was in the social class which is primitively venatorial still, canine under its polish.

So †**venaˈtorious** *a. Obs. rare*[−0].

1656 BLOUNT *Glossogr.*, *Venatorious*, belonging to hunting and chasing, serving for that game.

venatory (ˈvɛnətərɪ), *a.* [ad. L. *vēnātōri-us*, f. *vēnāt-*, ppl. stem of *vēnārī* to hunt: see -ORY.] = VENATORIAL *a.*

1837 CARLYLE *Misc. Ess.*, *Mirabeau*, Man being a venatory creature. **1837** —— *Fr. Rev.* III. VII. v, The venatory Attorney-spirit which keeps its eye on the bond only. **1846** *Blackw. Mag.* LX. 393 Regarding deer-stalking—a branch of the art venatory which few have the opportunity to study.

vench, obs. Sc. form of WENCH *sb.*

†**vencue,** *v. Obs. rare.* In 4 venku, 5 vencu. [a. OF. *vencu*, pa. pple. of *veintre*: see VANQUISH *v.*] *trans.* To vanquish, subdue.

13.. *Seuyn Sages* (W.) 2024 He ne mighte..in batail spede, That he ne was euer more biwraid, Ouercomen, venkud, and bitraid. *c* **1400** *Laud Troy Bk.* 13240 With-oute his help & his vertu We schal these other sone vencu.

vencus(e, -cushe, etc., obs. varr. VANQUISH *v.*

vend, *sb.* [f. VEND *v.* Cf. VENT *sb.*[3]]

1. Sale; opportunity of selling.

1618 in Foster *Eng. Factories Ind.* (1906) I. 42 This place never yet..gave vend to any quantety of our commodity. **1681** R. KNOX *Hist. Ceylon* 32 Neither have they any encouragement for their industry, having no Vend by Traffic and Commerce for what they have got. **1695** KENNETT *Par. Antiq.* ix. 510 This Market is of great resort, and a good vend for all Country Commodities. **1727** A. HAMILTON *New Acc. E. Ind.* II. xlvi. 152 Pepper is planted for Export, but not above 300 Tuns in a Year, because they want Vend for more. **1748** RICHARDSON *Clarissa* (1811) IV. 165 There is a person..who is a great dealer in Indian silks, ..and has a great vend for them. **1818** COLEBROOKE *Import Colonial Corn* 60 Corn is stored..and kept for years..in expectation of a future vend and a less glutted market.

2. *spec.* Sale of coals from a colliery; the total amount sold during a certain period.

1708 J. C. *Compl. Collier* (1845) 17 This I think is shameful for Owners, who striving to get all the Trade to themselves, or to have a Major Part of Vend, will fall out among themselves. **1793** [EARL DUNDONALD] *Descr. Estate Culross* 59 Sir Archibald had better have contented himself with a more limited vend at a greater price. **1834** McCULLOCH *Dict. Commerce* (ed. 2) 289 The annual vend of coals carried coastwise from Durham and Northumberland is 3,300,000 tons. **1858** SIMMONDS *Dict. Trade*, *Vend*,..the whole quantity of coal sent from a colliery in the year. **1893** NEASHAM *North-country Sk.* 28 By agreement..they were limited to an annual vend of 12,000 chaldrons.

vend (vɛnd), *v.* [ad. F. *vendre* (= It. *vendere*, Sp. and Pg. *vender*) or L. *vendĕre* to sell; but in senses 3 and 4 app. substituted for VENT *v.*[2] 4 and 5, through association of this with VENT *v.*[3]]

1. *intr.* To be disposed of by sale; to find a market or purchaser.

1622 in Foster *Eng. Factories India* (1908) II. 46 Course and fine pursleene..which vend both slowlye and at cheape rates. **1640** in Rushw. *Hist. Coll.* III. (1692) I. 96 Whereby Wool, the great Staple of the Kingdom, is become of small value, and vends not. **1689** HICKERINGILL *Modest Inquiries* v. 32 No Books vend so nimbly, as those that are sold (by Stealth as it were) and want Imprimaturs. **1768** FRANKLIN *Ess.* Wks. 1840 II. 371 If our manufactures are too dear they will not vend abroad.

2. *trans.* To sell; to dispose of by sale; to trade in as a seller.

1651 N. BACON *Disc. Govt. Eng.* II. vii. 70 No Nation can be rich that receives more dead Commodities from abroad, then it can spend at home, or vend into Forrain parts. **1673** RAY *Journ. Low C.* 279 Formerly all the Silk made in Sicily was vended at Messina. **1727** A. HAMILTON *New Acc. E. Ind.* II. xxiii. 124 The Company vends a great Deal of Cloth and Ophium there, and brings Gold-dust in Return. **1769** ROBERTSON *Chas. V*, VI. Wks. 1851 IV. 153 They opened warehouses in different parts of Europe, in which they vended their commodities. **1807** VANCOUVER *Agric. Devon* (1813) 224 The produce of these small dairies is generally vended at Plymouth. **1840** THACKERAY *Shabby genteel Story* vii, Fishmongers who never sold a fish, mercers who vended not a yard of riband. **1879** *Echo* No. 3374. 2/5 A license or patent to sell no matter what, includes the right to vend books and newspapers.

3. *fig.* To give utterance to, to put forward, advance (an opinion, etc.).

1657 *North's Plutarch* Add. Lives (1676) 7 Doubtless many have heard some Coridons, or Mechanick fellows.. vending their judgements on him whose Effigies or Portraiture is here represented. **1673** CAVE *Prim. Chr.* III. v. 364 This uncomfortable Doctrine was if not first coined yet mainly vended by the Novatian Party. **1715** BENTLEY *Serm.* x. 369 He that zealously vends his Novelties, what is he but a Trader for the fame of Singularity? **1718** *Freethinker* No. 26, To incite the Men of Scholarship and Capacity to traffick together in Truths; and never to vend Falshoods of any kind to the Vulgar. **1799** MRS. WEST *Tale of Times* III. 387 The most fashionable, and perhaps most successful, way of vending pernicious sentiments has been through the medium of books of entertainment. **1846** G. S. FABER *Lett. Tractar. Secess.* 126 Those requisite proofs of a fact, which convict him and Mr. Ward of having..vended a double falsehood. **1907** P. T. FORSYTH *Positive Preaching* iii. 101 He is not free to vend in his pulpit the extravagances of an eccentric individualism.

†**4.** To give vent to, to direct. *Obs.*

1681 HICKERINGILL *Black Non-Conf.* v. Wks. 1716 II. 49 If they will be angry, they should vend their spleen against the said wickedness of their Under-Officers.

vend, southern ME. var. FIEND; var. WEND *sb.*; obs. f. WEND *v.*; obs. Sc. f. WIND *sb.* and *weened* WEEN *v.*

Venda (ˈvɛndə), *sb.* and *a.* [An African word; since 1973 the name of a Bantu homeland in north Transvaal.] **A.** *sb.* **a.** (A member of) a Bantu people inhabiting the north-eastern Transvaal and southern Zimbabwe. **b.** The language of this people. **B.** *adj.* Of or pertaining to this people or their language.

[**1905** *Jrnl. Anthropol. Inst.* XXXV. 365 That part of the Bantu race of which I have to treat in this paper calls itself *Bawenda*, that is to say, people of Wenda, or inhabitants of Wenda.] **1908** *Jrnl. Afr. Society* VII. 412 Venda. Spoken by the Bavenda in North Transvaal. **1912** H. A. JUNOD *Life S. Afr. Tribe* I. I. i. 18 We find colonies of emigrated Thonga in many parts of the Transvaal. The largest is in the Spelonken district... There they are called *Magwamba* by the Venda and Bvesha who possessed the country before them. *Ibid.* II. VI. i. 327 There is a third tradition relating to the first man, but it has..been borrowed from the Venda or Pedi tribes. **1921** *S. Afr. Jrnl. Sci.* Apr. 208 All these Venda clans (and the Malemba also) speak of their mountain. **1931** H. A. STAYT *BaVenda* p. xi, These boys..were familiar with the whole country and understood the different Venda dialects. **1937** [see INKOSI]. **1950** I. SCHAPERA in Radcliffe-Brown & Forde *Afr. Syst. Kinship & Marriage* 144 Paternal aunts..do not command anything like the great authority they are said to possess among the Venda. **1977** *Times* 23 Nov. 20/8 We are oppressed..not as Zulus, Xhosas, Vendas or Indians. We are oppressed because we are black. **1979** J. DRUMMOND *I saw him Die* vii. 74 She began talking in some dialect I didn't understand—Venda, perhaps. **1979** *Guardian Weekly* 12 Aug. 6/3 In last year's general election, Chief Mphephu's ruling Venda National Party was decisively defeated by the Opposition Venda Independence Party.

ˈvendable, *a.* Now *rare.* [a. OF. *vendable*, f. *vendre* to sell, or (in later use) directly f. VEND *v.* + -ABLE.] = VENDIBLE *a.*

c **1400** *Rom. Rose* 5804 But chaunged is this world unstable; For love is over alle vendable. **1474** CAXTON *Chesse* III. iv. (1883) 112 Saluste..saith that alle thynges be vendable. *c* **1580** W. SPELMAN *Dialoge* (1896) 4 He to returne to me such goodes, as I thought to be vendable in Inglond. **1662** J. BARGRAVE *Pope Alex. VII* (1867) 90 He courted a long time the Barberini..to be made clerk of the apostolick chamber, he being very rich (and that a vendable honour). **1688** HOLME *Armoury* III. 292/2 The Axe and Cleever are used to cut the quarter of Beasts into smaller and more vendable pieces. **1893** *Advance* (Chicago) 21 Sept., The vendable commodities of the United States have fallen in price in 20 years more than 45 per cent.

vendace (ˈvɛndɪs). Also 8 vangis, 9 vendis, vendise. [app. ad. OF. *vendese*, *vendoise* (mod.F. *vandoise*) dace.] **a.** A species of small freshwater fish (*Coregonus vandesius*) belonging to the same genus as the pollan and powan or gwyniad, found in the lake of Lochmaben in Scotland. **b.** A closely-allied species (*Coregonus gracilior*) found in Derwentwater, formerly identified with the preceding.

[**1684** SIBBALD *Scotia Illustrata* II. II. 26 Piscis in Lacu Mabano, Vandesius. In eodem Lacu Gevandesius.] **1769** PENNANT *Brit. Zool.* III. 268 It [the gwiniad] is the same with the Ferra of the lake of Geneva, the Schelley of Hulsewater, the Pollen of Lough Neagh, and the Vangis and Juvangis of Loch Mabon. **1777** —— in Lightfoot *Flora Scot.* (1789) I. 61 Guiniad. Found in Loch-Mabon; called in those parts the Vendace, and Juvangis; and in Loch-Lomond, where it is called the Poan. **1805** FORSYTH *Beauties Scotl.* II. 272 There is one [fish] that, from every information that can be obtained, is peculiar to that loch [Castle Loch]... It is called the Vendise or Vendace. **1820** SCOTT *Abbot* xxiv, *Herlings*, which frequent the Nith, and *vendisses*, which are only found in the Castle-Loch of Lochmaben. **1856** 'STONEHENGE' *Brit. Rur. Sports* 231/1 The Vendace (*Coregonus Albula*), found also in the Scotch lakes. **1884** BRAITHWAITE *Salmonidæ Westmld.* ii. 5 The vendace or vendis and the smelt, or sparling.

attrib. **1867** *Chambers's Encycl.* IX. 744/1 Vendace-fishing at Lochmaben takes place only on the 1st of August each year. **1883** *Fisheries Exhib. Catal.* 366 Vendace Nets, from Lake Wetter. *Ibid.* 372 Gwyniad Roe,..Vendace Roe.

†**vendage.** *Obs.* Also vind-, vyndage. [ad. OF. *vendange* (also mod.F.), *vendenge*:—L. *vindēmia.*] Vintage.

α. **1377** LANGL. *P. Pl.* B. XVIII. 367 May no drynke me moiste ne my thruste slake, Tyl þe vendage falle in þe vale of iosephath. **1388** WYCLIF *2 Esdras* x. 37 The firste fruytes.. of vendage, and of oile. **14..** *Voc.* in Wr.-Wülcker 619 *Vindemix* [sic], vendage.

β. **1382** WYCLIF *Lev.* xxv. 5 Grapes of thi first fruytis and vyndage thou shalt not gedere. *c* **1440** *Palladius on Husb.* I. 134 Kitte hem streit aftir thi good vyndage. *Ibid.* x. 114 This mone in placis warme & nygh the see, Vyndage is hugely to solempnyse.

‖**vendange** (vɑ̃dɑ̃ʒ). Also †8 vandange. [Fr.: see VENDAGE.] In France, the annual grape harvest, the vintage (sense 2).

1766 SMOLLETT *Trav.* I. viii. 133 The mountains of Burgundy are covered with vines... The *vandange* was but just begun, and the people were employed in gathering the grapes. **1852** MRS. E. TWISLETON *Let.* 9 Oct. (1928) iv. 56 The *vendange* for the year is over, but the crop is not good and..they say none of the best wines will be made from it. **1893** SOMERVILLE & 'ROSS' *In Vine Country* viii. 147 Of course we left vowing to return for the *vendange* next year. **1944** W. FORTESCUE *Mountain Madness* xi. 83 And when the *jasmin* harvest was over, there was the *vendange*, my grapes to be picked and made into wine. **1969** B. WEIL *Dossier IX* xxiii. 180 It's a good time to go south. The *vendange* is just starting. **1972** *Daily Tel.* 8 Apr. 14/7 Last year's *vendange*.

Hence **vendangeur**, a grape-picker.

1893 SOMERVILLE & 'ROSS' *In Vine Country* v. 91 We had to drive for some distance before we saw the first group of *vendangeurs*, standing waist-deep in the vines, snipping off the bunches and putting them into square wooden baskets. **1971** *Country Life* 2 Dec. 1501/3 The carver of a misericord in Ely cathedral certainly knew what was what when he displayed an Ely *vendangeur* of 1340 or thereabouts.

vende, southern ME. variant of FIEND *sb.*

Vendean (vɛnˈdiːən), *sb.* and *a.* Also Vendéan. [f. F. *Vendée*, the name of a maritime department in western France.]

A. *sb.* An inhabitant of La Vendée, esp. one who took part in the insurrection of 1793 against the Republic.

1796 *Gentl. Mag.* May 407 The Vendeans are extraordinary men. **1837** ALISON *Hist. Europe* (1847) III. 326 The Vendéans were in that stage of society when ascendancy is acquired by personal daring. **1843** *Penny Cycl.* XXVI. 201/1 The unhappy Vendeans..were defeated with fearful loss. **1903** W. BRIGHT *Age of Fathers* I. xii. 244 The experience of a fugitive Jacobite or Vendéan.

B. *adj.* Of or pertaining to La Vendée, esp. in connexion with the insurrection of 1793.

1796 *Gentl. Mag.* May 408/1 The Vendean generals. *Ibid.* 412/1 The History of the Vendean War. **1839** tr. *Lamartine's Trav.* 149/1 The west..would have been organised once more into Vendean guerillas. **1848** W. H. KELLY tr. *L. Blanc's Hist. Ten Y.* II. 86 The Vendéan insurrection had been combated by means neither suggested nor directed by the executive. **1911** *Edin. Rev.* Oct. 319 The Breton and Vendéan royalists were still formidable.

ˈvended, *ppl. a.* [f. VEND *v.*] Sold.

1812 CRABBE *Tales* xiv. 116 Suppose..your vended numbers rise The same with those which gain each real prize.

vendee (vɛnˈdiː). [f. VEND *v.* + -EE.] The person to whom a thing is sold; the purchaser.

Most frequently in immediate contrast to *vendor.*

1547 *Act 1 Edw. VI*, c. 3 §8 Such Lessee, donee, vendee, or assignee. **1594** WEST *2nd Pt. Symbol.* §59 If the writ of covenant be brought against all the vendors by all the vendees. **1631** *Star Chamber Cases* (Camden) 117 The Vendee cannott get leave to cutt these trees by any meanes, but the partie must sell the trees to him. **1670** R. COKE *Discourse Trade* 19 Vexatious Suits between Vendor and Vendee, Morgager and Morgagee. **1766** BLACKSTONE *Comm.* II. 447 If the vendor says, the price of a beast is four pounds, and the vendee says he will give four pounds, the bargain is struck. **1817** W. SELWYN *Law Nisi Prius* (ed. 4) II. 769 A few days after the sale, the vendee gave the factor, in part payment, two promissory notes. **1881** NICHOLSON *From Sword to Share* xiii, Unpaid accounts of three months standing are charged against the vendee at the rate of 12 per cent.

‖**Vendémiaire** (vɑ̃demjɛr). [Fr., f. L. *vindēmia* vintage.] The first month of the French republican calendar, introduced in 1793, extending from Sept. 22 to Oct. 21.

1799 *Times* 1 June 3/1 In the month of last Vendemiaire. **1910** B. MIALL tr. *Aulard's French Revolution* III. vi. 267 An important measure of police law..was not presented and voted until the 6th and 7th of *Vendémiaire* of the year IV. **1923** S. MATTHEWS *French Revolution* xx. 293 Bonaparte.. with the true adventurer's instinct accepted the command (Vendémiaire 13). **1981** *Encounter* Dec. 31/1 *Vendémiaire* could be joyfully evoked..by those who had not the first idea of the process of wine-making.

‖**vendemmia** (venˈdɛmmja). [It.] The Italian grape-harvest or vintage. Cf. VENDANGE, VENDIMIA.

1826 M. KELLY *Reminisc.* I. 179, I..was delighted by the appearance of the elegant villas.., belonging to noble Venetians, who, during the theatrical season, pass their vendemmias there. **1871** C. M. YONGE *Little Lucy's Wonderful Globe* iii. 21 Ah, ah! 'tis the *vendemmia*! all may eat grapes. **1926** D. H. LAWRENCE *Let.* 17 Oct. (1962) II. 942 The peasants finished the *vendemmia* two days after we got here—but the wine is still to be made. **1978** J. PEARSON *Façades* xxviii. 473 The vineyards had yielded a record crop in the *vendemmia* that year.

vender (ˈvɛndə(r)). [f. VEND *v.* + -ER[1]. Cf. VENDOR.]

1. One who sells; a seller; sometimes in restricted sense, a street-seller.

1596 BACON *Max. & Use Com. Law* ii. (1635) 62 A deed of gift of goods is..good against the executors, administrators, or vender of the party himselfe. **1681** *Sc. Acts Parlt.* (1820) VIII. 243/2 Venders & dispersers of forbidden books. **1711** ADDISON *Spect.* No. 251 ⁋5 Take care in particular, that those may not make the most Noise who have the least to sell, which is very observable in the Venders of Card-matches. **1751** JOHNSON *Rambler* No. 181 ⁋11, I inquired diligently at what office any prize had been sold, that I might purchase of a more propitious vender. **1800** COLQUHOUN *Comm. Thames* iv. 193 Small Grocers, and venders of Smuggled Goods. **1837** HALLAM *Hist. Lit.* I. iv. §57 The Swiss reformer was engaged in combating the venders of indulgences. **1866** ENGEL *Nat. Mus.* viii. 301 The melodious cries of venders in the noisy streets of large and populous towns.

fig. **1834** SOUTHEY *Doctor* vi. (1862) 17 He gathered the fruit of knowledge for himself instead of receiving it from the dirty fingers of a retail vender.

2. One who advances or advocates an opinion, etc.

1818 DWIGHT *Theol.* (1830) I. 92 Epicurus, the principal vender of this system.

Hence **ˈvenderess**, **ˈvendress**, a female seller.

1800 HURDIS *Fav. Village* 98 Vendress of ballads and the bundled match. **1863** MISS M. B. EDWARDS *John & I*, I. v. 96 A stout girl, venderess of coarse green earthenware from the town.

vendetta (vɛnˈdɛtə). [a. It. *vendetta*:—L. *vindicta* vengeance. Cf. VINDICTIVE *a.*]

1. A family blood-feud, usually of a hereditary character, as customary among the inhabitants of Corsica and parts of Italy.

1855 *Edinb. Rev.* CI. 456 Paoli..succeeded in making the vendetta disgraceful. **1860** *All Year Round* No. 63. 299/2 The deadly 'vendetta'..which has sacrificed whole families, and once depopulated an entire village for one girl. **1870** O. W. HOLMES *Old Vol. of Life* (1891) 291, I came away thinking I had discovered a new national custom, as peculiar ..as the Corsican vendetta.

2. A similar blood-feud, or prosecution of private revenge, in other communities.

1861 PEARSON *Early & Mid. Ages* vii. 66 But there are no traces [among the early Anglo-Saxons] of that *vendetta*, which was the sombre glory of the Welsh. **1891** *Spectator* 7 Mar., The Papuan..would eat everybody, but that he fears arousing endless vendettas.

attrib. **1897** *Humanitarian* X. 209 The vendetta spirit is hereditary.

Hence **venˈdettist**, one who takes part in, or carries on, a vendetta.

1904 *Times* 2 June 10/3 We..perceive that they are blood-thirsty vendettists.

‖**vendeuse** (vɑ̃døːz). [Fr.] A saleswoman; *spec.* one employed in a fashion house.

1913 E. WHARTON *Custom of Country* xiii. 181 Slender *vendeuses* floating by in a mist of opopanax. **1936** 'R. WEST' *Thinking Reed* ii. 61 This girl had been a *vendeuse* with a great French couturier. **1957** M. SHARP *Eye of Love* iii. 37 In the show-room Miss Molyneux, vendeuse and model, and Miss Harris, who fitted, were as usual discussing the private lives of film-stars. **1976** *Times Lit. Suppl.* 3 Sept. 1074/5 Went into a smart milliners and asked the *vendeuse* to 'show me a hat for an ugly middle-aged woman whose husband no longer loves her'.

vendiˈbility. [See next and -ITY.] The quality of being vendible or saleable.

1660 JER. TAYLOR *Ductor* IV. i. rule 2 §31 In Merchandise, ..in the price of market, and the vendibility of commodities. **1875** LOWER *Eng. Surnames* (ed. 4) II. App. 162 In former times, a bush or a besom affixed to any article denoted its vendibility. **1892** *Jrnl. Education* 1 Feb. 98/1 A course calculated to give their degrees all the prestige attaching to vendibility.

vendible (ˈvɛndɪb(ə)l), *a.* and *sb.* [ad. L. *vendibilis*, f. *vendĕre* to sell. So Sp. *vendible*, It. *vendibile*. Cf. VENDABLE *a.*]

A. *adj.* **1.** Capable of being vended or sold; that may be disposed of by sale; saleable, marketable.

Freq. with *more*, *most*, etc., denoting the readiness with which a thing can be sold.

1382 WYCLIF *2 Macc.* xi. 3 In to wynnynge of money,.. by eche ȝeeris prestehode vendible, or able to be soold. **1530** in W. H. Turner *Select. Rec. Oxford* (1880) 91 Wyne.. alowed by hym to be good and vendyble. **1581** W. STAFFORD *Exam. Compl.* ii. (1876) 37 They come not alwayes for our commodities, but sometimes to sell theirs heere, knowing it heere to be best vendible. **1633** PRYNNE *1st Pt. Histriom.* Ep. Ded., Play-books..being now more vendible than the choycest Sermons. *Ibid.* 905 They cannot therefore bee vendible because they are not valuable. **1679** in Gutch *Coll. Cur.* I. 275 The University of Oxford, by their printing of Bibles, and other saleable books, will be enabled to go forward with those other less vendible. **1747** HOOSON *Miner's Dict.* Kivb, This to make it vendible, is first knocked out with a Hammer, and the dead Stuff picked out as clean as may be. **1788** V. KNOX *Winter Even.* IX. iii. III. 232 They get rid of some commodity, not very vendible. **1839** URE *Dict. Arts* 980 In this way all the vendible coal becomes available. **1879** *Cassell's Techn. Educ.* IV. 90/2 A thing made which is useful for its own sake, and vendible as such.

transf. **1581** BURGHLEY in D. Digges *Compl. Ambass.* (1655) 394 He is altogether French and will seek to draw this King into France, where his life I fear will be vendible. **1596** SHAKS. *Merch. V.* I. i. 112 Silence is onely commendable In a neats tongue dri'd, and a maid not vendible.

b. = VENAL *a.*[1] 1 b and 1 c.

1579 FENTON *Guicciard.* x. (1599) 427 Fauors and voyces being made vendible and corrupted, discords..haue bin kindled amongst themselues. **1586** T. B. *La Primaud. Fr. Acad.* (1594) I. 377 So long as the places of judgement shall be vendible, and bestowed upon him that offereth most. **1624** CAPT. SMITH *Virginia* III. 76 It is not our custome, to sell our curtesies as a vendible commodity. **1665** MANLEY *Grotius' Low C. Wars* 788 In England and Germany Forces were levied and raised for both parties with a vendible faith. **1791** BURKE *Wks.* (1837) I. 566 It attached, under the royal government, to an innumerable multitude of places, real and nominal, that were vendible.

†**c.** Of persons: = VENAL *a.*[1] 2. *Obs.*

1609 HOLLAND *Amm. Marcell.* 293 Environed he was with a multitude thronged together of vendible or sale souldiors. **1637–50** ROW *Hist. Kirk* (Wodrow Soc.) 424 Those were sellable, vendible men,..to be sold for money. *a* **1668** LASSELS *Voy. Italy* (1698) Pref. p. xxiii, I would not have him learn the custom of those vendible souls there, who.. serve any prince for money.

†**2.** Offered for sale; that may be bought or purchased. *Obs.*

1552 HULOET, Vendible, or whych maye be bought, *mercalis, vendibilis.* **1605** WILLET *Hexapla Gen.* 281 Lentils ..was the vsuall food.. commonly vendible in their tabernes. **1634** SIR T. HERBERT *Trav.* 150 Houses, like our Tauernes. Where is vendible Wine. **1665** G. HAVERS *P. della Valle's Trav. E. India* 144 He, not finding any [book] vendible therein, caus'd a small one to be purposely transcrib'd for me. **1756** EARL CHESTERF. in *Connoisseur* No. 107, I am so great an admirer of the fair sex, that I never let a tittle of their vendible writings escape me.

†**3.** *fig.* Current, accepted, acceptable. *Obs.*

1642 HOWELL *For. Trav.* (Arb.) 20 Certaine vulgar Phrases, Proverbs, and Complements, which are peculiar to the English, and not vendible or used in French. **1645** MILTON *Tetrach.* Wks. 1851 IV. 234 Let the foppish canonist with his fardel of matrimonial cases goe and be vendible where men bee so unhappy as to cheap'n him. **1678** CUDWORTH *Intell. Syst.* I. iv. §16. 281 Some may still suspect all this to have been nothing else but a refinement and interpolation of Paganism,..or a kind of Mangonization of it, to render it more vendible and plausible.

B. *sb.* A thing admitting of being sold or offered for sale.

1681 WOOD *Life* (O.H.S.) II. 520 The prizes of all vendibles for the belly of man and horse were stuck up in public places. **1691** —— *Ath. Oxon.* (1721) II. 384 It appears that the said Revolutions were occasion'd by the excessive Gabells laid upon common Vendibles. **1697** J. POTTER *Antiq. Greece* I. xv. (1715) 83 In the Market, where they had the care of all Vendibles. **1821** GALT *Ann. Parish* xxix, The farmers..taking their vendibles to the neighbouring towns on the Tuesdays. **1905** HOLMAN HUNT *Pre-Raphaelism* I. 368 The gorgeous group of vendibles in the market.

Hence **ˈvendibleness**; **ˈvendibly** *adv.*

1563 HYLL *Art Garden.* (1593) 20 The greater they do then abide, the vendiblier, or readier they will be to be solde. **1611** COTGR., *Venalité*, venalitie, vendiblenesse; a being salable. *Ibid.*, *Venalement*, vendibly, salably. **1727** BAILEY (vol. II), *Vendibleness*, Saleableness.

†**ˈvendicate**, *v. Obs.* [ad. L. *vendicāt-*, ppl. stem of *vendicāre*, variant of *vindicāre* VINDICATE *v.* Cf. obs. F. *vendiquer*.]

1. *trans.* To claim for oneself.

1531 ELYOT *Gov.* III. iii, His body so pertayneth unto him, that none other without his consent may vendicate therein any proprietie. **1543–4** *Act 35 Hen. VIII*, c. 1, They..haue vsurped, and vendicated a fayned and an vnlawfull power and iurisdiction within this realme. **1560** BIBLE (Geneva) To Rdr. iiij, Not that we vendicat any thing to our selues aboue the least of our brethren. **1611** COTGR., *Vendiquer*, to vendicate; to claime, or challenge. [Hence in Blount (1656).]

2. With inf.: To assert a claim, to claim ability, *to* do something.

1557 N. T. (Geneva) *1 Cor.* ii. 2, I dyd not vendicat to my selfe to knowe any thyng among you, saue Iesus Christe. **1616** J. LANE *Contn. Sqr.'s T.* XII. 230 Wee have twoe Ladies, which, with your trim paire, dare vendicate to singe.

vendicatife, -yue, obs. varr. VINDICATIVE *a.*

†**vendication.** *Obs.*[−0] [f. VENDICATE *v.*, after the entry in Blount *Glossogr.*] (See quot.)

1658 PHILLIPS, *Vendication*, a challenging to onesself, a claiming.

vendicion, obs. form of VENDITION.

‖**vendimia** (venˈdimja). [Sp., = vintage.] The Spanish grape harvest; also, the festival celebrating the end of the vintage. Cf. VENDANGE, VENDEMMIA.

1965 *Listener* 30 Sept. 495/3 The vendimia or harvest festival at Jerez..is a time of gaiety and laughter. **1975** *Harpers & Queen* May 50/2 The well-known 'vendimias' or wine harvest cavalcades. **1978** *Times* 21 Nov. 12/2 The crowning of the queen of the *vendimia* or wine harvest. **1979** *Country Life* 25 Oct. 1392/2 (*caption*) Last month's ceremony was the 32nd Vendimia to be celebrated in Jerez de la Frontera.

ˈvending, *vbl. sb.* [f. VEND *v.*]

1. The action of selling or retailing.

1666 *Act 17 Chas. II*, c. 5 §2 Any publick Vending of the said Books. **1745** *De Foe's Eng. Tradesman* (1841) I. xxvi. 254 For the raising and vending of provisions. **1761** HUME *Hist. Eng.* I. xiii. 338 The famous mercantile society, called the Merchant Adventurers,..was instituted..for the vending of the cloth abroad. **1822** LAMB *Elia* I. *Praise Chimney-Sweepers*, [He] kept open a shop..for the vending of this 'wholesome and pleasant beverage'. **1875** HELPS *Soc. Press.* iii. 38 Now it will astonish most of my hearers that I have included the vending of oysters amongst noxious trades.

2. Special Comb.: **vending machine**, a slot machine from which comestibles or other small goods may be obtained.

1895 *Funk's Stand. Dict.*, *Vending-machine*, a machine having a mechanism, controlled by the dropping of a coin into a slot, for delivering any small article with which it has been charged, as a slot machine for selling chewing-gum. **1947** J. C. RICH *Materials & Methods of Sculpture* i. 15 A medium to low relief is used for coins, with a raised rim about the edge of the coin to protect the relief from such wearing factors as vending machines, turnstiles, and stacking. **1980** *Times* 13 Nov. 4/8 The tea trolley is being wheeled back into offices and the anonymous vending machine, the butt of many jokes..is on the way out.

vendis(e, variants of VENDACE.

Vendish, variant of WENDISH *a.*

†**ˈvenditate**, *v. Obs.* [f. L. *venditāt-*, ppl. stem of *venditāre*, frequentative of *vendĕre* to sell.] *refl.* and *trans.* To set out as if for sale; to put forward or display in a favourable light or in a specious manner; to exhibit ostentatiously. (Common *c* 1600–50.)

refl. **1600** HOLLAND *Livy* III. xxxv. 110 Using them as instruments to venditate himselfe forth to the common people. **1621** BURTON *Anat. Mel.* I. ii. I. ii, Although hee.. venditate himselfe for a God, by curing of seuerall diseases. **1629** H. BURTON *Truth's Tri.* 361 Their doctrine..wanting fit opportunity to venditate it self publickly vpon the stage. *a* **1652** J. SMITH *Sel. Disc.* i. 10 Those philosophers..which made their knowledge only matter of ostentation, to venditate and set off themselves.

trans. **1601** HOLLAND *Pliny* II. 345 Euer as any of these new commers can venditat and vaunt his owne cunning with braue words, straitwaies we put our selues into his hands. **1624** F. WHITE *Repl. Fisher* 457 The miracles which Romists venditate..are eyther Fryars fables, or reports misapplyed. **1678** MARVELL *Def. J. Howe* Wks. (Grosart) IV. 239 Let it, in the meantime, venditate all its street adages, its odd ends of Latin.

vendiˈtation. [ad. L. *venditātio*, noun of action from *venditāre*: see prec.]

†**1.** The action of putting forward or displaying in a favourable or ostentatious manner. *Obs.*

1609 SIR E. HOBY *Lett. Mr. T. H.* 74 Caluins censure of Purgatorie is held by you as a specious venditation. **1633** BP. HALL *Occas. Medit.* (ed. 3) xxx. 76 The venditation of our owne worth, or parts, or merits, argues a miserable indigence in them all. *a* **1637** B. JONSON *Discoveries* Wks. (Rtldg.) 747/2 Some [wits], by a..false venditation of their own naturals, think to divert the sagacity of their readers from themselves.

2. The action of offering for sale. *rare*[−1].

1854 *Fraser's Mag.* L. 163 The orangewomen stride over the benches with clamorous 'venditation'.

vendition (vɛnˈdɪʃən). Also 6 **vendicion**, *Sc.* **-itioune**, **wend-**, 7 *Sc.* **venditioun**. [ad. L. *venditio*, noun of action from *vendĕre* to sell. So OF. *vendicion*, obs. F. *vendition*, Sp. *vendicion*, It. *vendizione*.] The action of selling; disposal or transfer by sale.

1542 UDALL *Erasm. Apoph.* 109 b, It might more truely bee called a spuyng, then a vendicion or sale. **1559** *Abst. Protocols Town Clerks Glasgow* (1896) II. 73 The uenditioune and alienatioune maid thairof to the said Androw. **1602** FULBECKE *2nd Pt. Parallel* 29 It is of a vendition by the tenant in taile. **1659** ARROWSMITH *Chain Princ.* 490 His directing and ordering great sins to great good, as Josephs vendition to the Churches preservation. **1754** FIELDING *Voy. Lisbon* Wks. 1882 VII. 60 Several taverns are set apart solely for the vendition of this liquor. **1828** SEWELL in *Oxf. Prize Ess.* 26 The still more prevailing practice of vendition to slavery and prostitution. **1863** *Temple Bar* IX. 65 The Marché St. Honoré is the most usual place for their vendition.

†**ˈvenditive**, *a. Obs.*[−1] [f. L. *vendit-*, ppl. stem of *vendĕre* to sell.] (See quot.)

1633 T. ADAMS *Exp. 2 Peter* ii. 10 There is a service of Inferioritie; which is either: 1. Voluntary,..Or..5. Native, such as are borne servants,..Or 6. Venditive, that have sold themselves.

†**ˈvenditor.** *Obs. rare.* Also 8 *Sc.* **vanditor**. [a. L. *venditor*, agent-noun from *vendĕre* to sell, or ad. It. *venditore*.] A seller, vendor.

1698 *Money masters all things* 89 The Venditors of Oat-meal round and small, Do diligently wait on Money's Call. **1733** LADY BAILLIE *Househ. Bk.* (S.H.S.) 340 To the venditor in full for Moneths 5, £4 0 0.

†**vendonging.** *Obs.*[−1] [f. OF. *vendenger*, *-anger* (F. *vendanger*), f. *vendenge*, *-ange*: see VENDAGE.] The vintage.

1340 *Ayenb.* 36 Þe oþre beggeþ..ine herueste þet corn, ine uendonginge þet wyn.

vendor (ˈvɛndə(r)). [a. late AF. *vendor*, earlier *vendour* (F. *vendeur*), agent-noun from *vendre* VEND *v.* Cf. VENDER.] One who disposes of a thing by sale; a seller.

Orig. *Law*, and still the regular spelling in legal use.

1594 WEST *2nd Pt. Symbol.* §59 If the writ of covenant be brought against all the vendors by all the vendees. **1660** R. COKE *Power & Subj.* 131 It is true indeed..that then such vendor does equally to all sellers, and in exchanging observes arithmetical proportion. **1670** [see VENDEE]. *a* **1692** POLLEXFEN *Disc. Trade* (1697) A 6 From the first Buyer to the last Vendor. **1766** BLACKSTONE *Comm.* II. 447 Where the vendor hath in himself..the property of the thing sold. **1818**

CRUISE *Digest* (ed. 2) VI. 30 The vendor would immediately have become a trustee for the purchaser. **1862** BURTON *Bk. Hunter* (1863) 4 The vendors of quack medicines and cosmetics are aware of the power of Greek nomenclature. **1891** M. WILLIAMS *Later Leaves* v. 63 A well-known.. vendor of ladies' hats and bonnets.

transf. **1887** *Pall Mall G.* 30 March 2/2 The automatic vendor has become an institution in our midst.

attrib. **1896** *Westm. Gaz.* 9 May 6/2 The vendor company is now selling the business to a public company.

†**vendosy.** *Obs.*⁻¹ [ad. F. *vendoise*: see VENDACE.] The dace.

1528 PAYNELL *Salerne's Regim.* O iij, The perche and pike are the best, so they be fatte: and nexte are the vendosies, and than lopsters.

vendress, var. VENDERESS.

vendrosse: see REREDOS 2 (quot. 1552).

vendue (vɛn'djuː). *U.S.* and *W. Indies*. Also 7 vendu, 9 vendoo, vandew. [a. Du. *vendu*, †*vendue*, a. older F. (now dial.) *vendue* sale, f. *vendre* to sell.]

1. A public sale; an auction. Freq. in phr. *at (a) vendue, by vendue*: see first group of quots.

(*a*) **1686** *Ann. Albany* (1850) II. 93 Which said lotts of grounde ye common councill will dispose of at a publike vendu or out cry. **1748** SMOLLETT *R. Random* xxxvi. I. 324, I went ashore [at Port Royal], and having purchased a laced waistcoat..at a vendue [1760 a sale], made a swaggering figure. **1757** WOOLMAN *Jrnl.* iv. (1840) 45 When estates are sold by executors at vendue. **1776** *Pennsylv. Even. Post* 25 May 263/2 To be sold by public vendue,..a large quantity of Ship Timber. **1804** *Europ. Mag.* XLV. 20/2, I was.. knocked down at vendue to old 'Squire Kegworth. **1898** PARMENTER *Hist. Pelham, Mass.* 167 Bidding off the poor to support at the inverted vendue, or lowest bidder.

(*b*) **1759** J. ADAMS *Diary* Wks. 1850 II. 73, I am to attend a vendue this afternoon at Lambert's. **1781** MRS. ABIGAIL ADAMS in *Fam. Lett.* (1876) 402 The retailing vendues, which are tolerated here, ruin the shop-keepers. **1806** PINCKARD *Tour W. Indies* II. 325 A Dutch 'vendue' of slaves. **1836** HALIBURTON *Clockm.* Ser. I. xxvii, Is it a vandew, or a weddin,..or what is it? **1897** W. D. HOWELLS *Landlord at Lion's Head* 6 [To] have a vendue, and sell out everything before the snow flew.

2. *attrib.* and *Comb.*, as *vendue-crier, master, room, store*.

1710 *S. Carolina Stat.* (1837) II. 348 The person herein after appointed publick vendue master, or his deputy. **1761** *Descr. S. Carolina* 33 There is also..a Receiver-general of the Quit-rents, a Vendue Master, and Naval Officer. **1798** *Bay's Rep.* (1809) I. 103 The goods were in a vendue store, a common market, a public place known and established in law. **1799** *The Aurora* (Philad.) 10 Apr. (Thornton), By profession he is a vendue crier. He said he would cry the vendue in spite of the Standing Army. **1828** *Life Planter Jamaica* 180 Marly entered the vendue room. **1828-32** WEBSTER, *Vendue-master*,..an auctioneer.

†**vene.** *Obs. rare.* [ad. L. *vēna*.] A vein.

1606 J. CARPENTER *Solomon's Solace* xxxiv. 139 The Sea.. powreth foorth in venes to fill the springs and receiueth it againe from the Riuers. **1654** VILVAIN *Epit. Ess.* v. lxxv, In ech Mans Body so many Venes appeer. **1716** M. DAVIES *Athen. Brit.* III. *Diss. Physick* 5 Likewise Virsungus might treat more fully of the Pancr[e]atick Juice, as Asellius of the Lacteal Venes.

vene, obs. Sc. form of WEEN *sb.* and *v.*

†**venecreke**, variant of *fenegreke* FENUGREEK.

1486 *Bk. St. Albans* ciiij b, Take venecreke and then anoynt itt with this Oyntement afforsayde.

†**Ve'nedic**, *a. Obs.* [f. med.L. *Venedi* (pl.): see WEND *sb.*] Wendish, Vendish.

1768 T. NUGENT *Trav. Germany* II. 178 Mirow is.. supposed to have derived its name from the Slavonic, or Venedic word *mir*, signifying peace. **1790** DORNFORD *Pütter's Hist. Developm. Ger. Emp.* I. 8 Except in Bohemia and Lusatia, the Venedic language has been under the necessity of yielding to the German.

Vene'dotian, *a.* [f. med.L. *Venedotia* North Wales.] Of or pertaining to North Wales.

1841 *Anc. Laws & Inst. Wales* Pref. p. vii, The Venedotian Code, said to be the compilation of Jorwerth, son of Madog. *Ibid.* p. x, The Venedotian or North Wales Code. **1877** J. RHYS *Lect. Welsh Philol.* iv. 145 Here also may be mentioned..the Venedotian versions of the Laws of Wales, which Aneurin Owen found to be in manuscripts of the 12th century. **1887** *Edin. Rev.* Jan. 77 The last important head of law in the Venedotian code.

venee, variant of VENY² *Obs.*

veneer (vɪ'nɪə(r)), *sb.* Also 8 fanneer, vaneer, venear, 9 vineer. [ad. G. *furni(e)r, fourni(e)r*, †*fornier* in the same sense: see next and VENEERING *vbl. sb.* The loss of *r* in the unstressed first syllable also appears in Da. *finer*, Sw. *fanér*, Russ. *fanír*.]

1. One of the thin slices or slips of fine or fancy wood, or other suitable material, used in veneering.

1702 *Lond. Gaz.* No. 3806/8 A Large Parcel of French Walnutt-Tree Venears will be exposed to Sale..on Thursday. **1806** *Ann. Reg.* (1808) 960/2 A new mode of cutting veneers, or thin boards. **1823** *Macclesfield Courier* in O. W. Roberts *Voy. Centr. Amer.* (1827) 302 The largest and finest log of mahogany ever imported into this country.. sawn into vineers. **1875** BEDFORD *Sailor's Pocket Bk.* §x. 372 Put in as many veneers as the liquor will cover.

2. a. Material prepared for use in veneering, or applied to a surface by this or some similar process.

1750 W. ELLIS *Mod. Husb.* VII. II. 43 This [ash] wood and walnut-tree..makes the best of fanneer. **1778** W. PAIN *Carpenter's Repository* Pl. 56 A circular Plan..representing the Vaneer and Backing for the Stiles. **1825** J. NICHOLSON *Operat. Mechanic* 586 By gluing several thicknesses of veneer upon each other. **1845** G. DODD *Brit. Manuf.* Ser. IV. 212 The cabinet-maker buys the veneer in this rough state. *Ibid.*, He cuts a piece of veneer. **1886** W. J. TUCKER *E. Europe* 319 One of the legs [of the chair was] broken and the grand veneer knocked off the back.

b. *in veneer*, in thin plates or slips.

1855 SINGLETON *Virgil* I. 333 Presents, ponderous with gold And ivory in veneer, commands he to be borne Unto the ships.

3. *fig.* **a.** A merely outward show or appearance *of* some good quality. (Cf. VARNISH *sb.*¹ 4.)

1868 HOLME LEE *B. Godfrey* xxxii, A veneer of useful knowledge. **1874** FARRAR *Christ* I. iv. 44 A savage barbarian with a thin veneer of corrupt and superficial civilisation. **1882** W. BALLANTINE *Exper.* xv. 148 [The] heartfelt courtesy..was replaced by a superficial veneer of forced politeness.

b. Without article.

1871 *Daily News* 7 Dec., A gentleman with some polish —I was almost tempted to say with some veneer. **1883** *Harper's Mag.* July 165/2 These days of veneer and affectation in buildings and nomenclature.

4. One or other of many species of moths of the genus *Crambus* or family *Crambidæ*; a grass-moth.

1819 SAMOUELLE *Entomol. Compend.* 386 *Crambus sanguinea*. The buff-edged rosy Veneer. *Ibid.* 408 *C. arborum*. The yellow satin Veneer. **1832** RENNIE *Consp. Moths* 215-9.

5. *Dentistry*. = *veneer crown* in sense 6 below.

1930 G. M. HOLLENBACK in I. G. Nicholls *Prosthetic Dentistry* xlii. 653 It..does not provide as good retention, nor as good support for the abutment tooth as a partial veneer. **1965** L. A. WEINBERG *Atlas Crown & Bridge Prosthodontics* xii. 232/1 Plastic veneers or porcelain jacket restorations should be tried in the mouth before final finishing. **1975** D. STANANOUGHT *Laboratory Procedures Inlays, Crowns & Bridges* ii. 22 Full veneers may be constructed entirely in metal, or in a combination of metal with either acrylic resin or porcelain on the labial surface.

6. *attrib.* and *Comb.*, as *veneer-cutter, -making, merchant, -mill, -room, saw, wood*; **veneer crown** *Dentistry*, a crown in which the restoration is placed over the prepared surface of a natural crown.

Also *veneer-press*, and *veneer-bending, -cutting, -planing, -polishing, -straightening machine* (1875 Knight *Dict. Mech.* 2699-2702).

1845 G. DODD *Brit. Manuf.* IV. 148 The 'veneer-rooms' at such [pianoforte] factories are places of importance. **1852** JERDAN *Autobiog.* II. xiv. 181 He..purchased all the veneer wood which he could obtain. **1854** *Tomlinson's Cycl. Usef. Arts* (1867) II. 798/1 In all veneer saws the edge must run very true. *Ibid.*, In saw-mills where veneers are cut, the arrangement of the segment saw is called a veneer-mill. **1858** SIMMONDS *Dict. Trade*, *Veneer-cutter*, one who saws furniture wood into thin lengths, by steam-power machinery. **1888** *Encycl. Brit.* XXIV. 138/2 These methods of veneer-making. **1894** *Daily News* 8 June 8/4 Witnesses.. who deposed to knowing prisoner in the characters of a veneer merchant, a tankard maker, and an inventor. **1927** *Dental Cosmos* LXIX. 951 The next application [of porcelain to dental restoration]..was the so-called porcelain veneer crown which was the progenitor of the present highly perfected porcelain-jacket crown. **1954** J. E. EWING *Fixed Partial Prosthesis* xi. 61 The three-quarter partial veneer crown is primarily concerned with esthetics, for which function it owes its origin. **1975** D. STANANOUGHT *Laboratory Procedures Inlays, Crowns & Bridges* ii. 21 The restoration..may be a full veneer crown (shell crown) with the restoration covering the whole of the crown, or a partial veneer crown (three-quarter crown) with the labial or buccal surface of the crown excluded from the restoration.

veneer (vɪ'nɪə(r)), *v.* Also 8 vaneer, veneir. [Later form (cf. next) of FINEER *v.*, ad. G. *furni(e)ren, fourni(e)ren*, ad. F. *fournir* FURNISH *v.* Cf. Da. *finere*, Sw. *fanéra*.]

1. *trans.* To apply or fix as veneering.

1728 CHAMBERS *Cycl.* s.v. *Marquetry*, All the Pieces thus formed with the Saw,..they vaneer or fasten each in its Place on the common Ground. **1875** KNIGHT *Dict. Mech.* 2700/2 To veneer marble on zinc.

2. To cover or face with veneer.

Also occas. *transf.*, to cover with a layer or facing of some different or superior material.

1742 *Baskerville's Pat.* in *Sixth Rep. Dep. Kpr.* App. II. 156 To veneir the Frames of Printings and Pictures,..the fronts of Cabinets, Buroes, &c., now usually vineered with Ebony, Whalebone, &c. **1766** ENTICK *London* IV. 171 The pulpit is veneered, and carved with..figures. **1845** G. DODD *Brit. Manuf.* IV. 206 We suppose our table..made either of solid mahogany or veneered upon deal. **1854** *Tomlinson's Cycl. Usef. Arts* (1867) II. 797/2 Pape, of Paris, some years ago, veneered a piano-forte entirely with ivory. **1874** *Contemp. Rev.* Oct. 758 Mr. Burges' proposal to veneer the lower part..with marble is objectionable.

transf. **1857** DUFFERIN *Lett. High Lat.* (ed. 3) 316 The salt-water bay..was veneered over with a pellicle of ice one-eighth of an inch in thickness.

b. *fig.* To invest with a merely external or specious appearance of some commendable or attractive quality. Usu. const. *with*.

1847 TENNYSON *Princ.* Prol. 117 And one the Master, as a rogue in grain Veneer'd with sanctimonious theory. **1868** HOLME LEE *B. Godfrey* lxvi, Another lady of neglected education, whom..Elizabeth was veneering with thin plates of knowledge. **1872** JEAFFRESON *Brides & Bridals* I. viii. 126 Paganism thinly veneered with Christianity.

absol. **1858** O. W. HOLMES *Aut. Breakf.-t.* (1883) 123 He? *Veneers* in first-rate style. The mahogany scales off now and then.

c. To serve as a veneer to (something).

1875 M. COLLINS *Sweet & Twenty* II. II. i. 175 He returned with a vast amount of polish, which, however, veneered a good deal of conceit.

Hence **ve'neered** *ppl. a.*

1766 ENTICK *London* IV. 18 A carved pulpit, a veneered sounding-board. **1846** G. DODD *Brit. Manuf.* IV. 214 They are placed so that the veneered surface shall be grasped between the two clamps. **1875** *Carpentry & Join.* 140 The veneered furniture has ousted the more solid, trustworthy articles.

fig. **1884** *Harper's Mag.* Oct. 798/1 The thinly veneered Berserkir in the English race.

transf. **1889** *Textile News* 5 Apr. 26/2 The Hat Trade... Large quantities of coloured veneered goods are in demand from abroad.

ve'neering, *vbl. sb.* [Later form of *faneering, fineering* (cf. FINEER *v.*), ad. G. *furni(e)rung, fourni(e)rung*: see prec. and cf. Da. *finering*, Sw. *fanering*.

The form *faneering* occurs in 1670 in Evelyn *Sylva* xxiv. 121, and in 1685 in Cotton *Montaigne's Ess.* (1711) III. 247. *Fineering* is common in the 18th cent.]

1. The process of applying thin flat plates or slips of fine wood (or other suitable material, as ivory) to cabinet-work or similar articles in order to produce a more elegant or polished surface than that of the underlying material; also, the result obtained by this process.

1706 PHILLIPS (ed. Kersey), *Veneering*, a sort of in-laid Work among Joyners, Cabinet-makers &c. **1728** CHAMBERS *Cycl.* s.v. *Marquetry*, The whole is..polish'd with the Skin of the Sea-dog, Wax, and Shave-Grass, as in simple Vaneering. **1762** DERRICK *Lett.* (1767) II. 66 Their polish is high; the inlaying and veneering very beautiful. **1829** LOUDON *Encycl. Plants* (1836) 611 The old wood furnishes the cabinet-maker with a beautiful material for veneering. **1854** *Tomlinson's Cycl. Usef. Arts* (1867) II. 798/2 The operations of veneering consist in glueing the veneer to the prepared surface, and cleaning and polishing it when so fixed. **1873** SPON *Workshop Rec.* Ser. I. 411/1 In veneering with the hammer, cut the veneer a little larger than the surface to be covered.

transf. **1875** KNIGHT *Dict. Mech.* 2700 A process termed *veneering* has been adopted with some kinds of pottery where a strong but coarse and unsightly ware is dipped.. into a paste of superior color and quality.

b. *fig.* (Cf. VENEER *v.* 2 b.)

1808 SCOTT *Let.* in *Lockhart* (1837) II. vi. 208 By this sort of veneering, he converts..articles which, in their original state, might hang in the market [etc.]. **1846** FORD *Gatherings fr. Spain* (1906) 238 There is little originality in Spanish medicine. It is chiefly a veneering of other men's ideas. **1867** O. W. HOLMES *Guardian Angel* iv, He had been a good scholar in college, not so much by hard study as by skilful veneering. **1884** G. MOORE *Mummer's Wife* (1887) 126 The ..veneering of the mind with new impressions.

2. Wood or other material in the form of veneer; a facing of this.

1789 BURNS *Sketch*, Veneering oft outshines the solid wood. **1849** RUSKIN *Sev. Lamps* ii. §18. 46 A veneering of marble has been fastened on the rough brick wall. **1862** *Catal. Internat. Exhib., Brit.* II. No. 3411, The veneering being laid in cement instead of glue, will bear an immense amount of heat..before it will strip from the underwood.

transf. **1866** CARLYLE *Remin.* (1881) II. 275 Book press of rough deal, but covered with newspaper veneering where necessary.

b. *fig.* (Cf. VENEER *v.* 2 b.)

1865 *Reader* 4 Mar. 253/3 Though the great mass..have but a veneering of education and accomplishment. **1874** L. STEPHEN *Hours in Library* (1892) I. x. 372 A very thin veneering of mediævalism..covered his modern creed. **1891** C. ROBERTS *Adrift Amer.* 235 The thin veneering of civilisation gets worn off.

3. *attrib.*, as *veneering-hammer, -plane, -press*.

A *faneering-saw* is mentioned in 1688 by R. Holme *Armoury* 365/1.

1846 G. DODD *Brit. Manuf.* IV. 212 This veneering-plane is of small size, and the iron..is jagged with a number of notches. *Ibid.* 213 A piece of wood about three inches square and an inch thick has a straight strip of iron-plate fixed to one edge, and is called a veneering-hammer. **1888** *Encycl. Brit.* XXIV. 138/2 The surfaces..are..tightly pressed together in a veneering press.

†**ve'nefic**, *a.* and *sb. Obs.* In 7-8 venefick. [ad. L. *venēfic-us*, f. *venēnum* poison: see -FIC. So older F. *venefique*, It., Sp., Pg. *venefico*.]

A. *adj.* Practising, or dealing in, poisoning; acting by poison; having poisonous effects.

1646 GAULE *Cases Consc.* 27 So may it bee the Serpentine, the Venefick or Poysonous Witch. **1651** tr. *Father Paul Sarpi's Life* (1676) 92 But it appears that science hath a venefick vertue of swelling many men. **1702** C. MATHER *Magn. Chr.* II. App. (1852) 212 They gave it under their hands that if we believe no venefick witchcraft, we must renounce the Scripture.

B. *sb.* One who practises poisoning as a secret art; a sorcerer or sorceress; a wizard or witch.

So L. *venēficus* masc. and *venēfica* fem.

1652 GAULE *Magastrom.* 173 Is it a matter of much artifice for veneficks, or witches, to forespeak their own purposed and laboured malefice?

†**ve'nefical**, *a.* *Obs.* [See prec. and -AL[1].]
a. = VENEFIC *a.* Also *fig.* **b.** Practising, associated with, malignant sorcery or witchcraft.

1584 R. SCOT *Discov. Witchcr.* VI. iv. (1886) 95 *marg.*, Of a butcher a right veneficall witch. **1609** B. JONSON *Masque of Queens* Wks. (Rtldg.) 566 These witches..came forth..with spindles, timbrels, rattles, or other venefical instruments. **1652** GAULE *Magastrom.* 39 This they urge as a proof of the possibility of veneficall and metamorphosing or transforming magick. **1715** M. DAVIES *Athen. Brit.* I. Pref. 57 The loose sheets of Northern Sorceries, translated from the original Code of the venefical Text. **1716** *Ibid.* II. To Rdr. 9 The same Contagious and Venefical Distemper of Brains and Body.

Hence †**ve'nefically** *adv.* *Obs.*

1652 GAULE *Magastrom.* 280 A magician..wrought it venefically, so that the poore man fell suddenly into a strange disease.

†**'venefice.** *Obs.* [ad. L. *venēficium*, f. *venēficus* VENEFIC *a.* So OF. *venefice*, F. *vénéfice*, It., Sp., Pg. *veneficio*.] The practice of employing poison or magical potions; the exercise of sorcery by such means.

c **1380** WYCLIF *Sel. Wks.* II. 349 þe sixte werk of leccherie is venefice, þat is þanne done whan men usen experimentis to geten þis werk of leccherie. **1588** J. HARVEY *Disc. Probl.* 72 By knots,..incantations, or other impoisonings, and venefices, to harme, endamage, or hurt any other. **1626** SIR J. ELLIOTT *Def.* in Rushw. *Hist. Coll.* (1659) I. 362 Nor did he apply the Veneries and Venefices of Sejanus to the Duke. **1652** GAULE *Magastrom.* To Rdr., I..fear them not at all; not their..incantations, venefices, malefices, &c.

†**vene'ficial**, *a.* *Obs.* [f. prec.] = VENEFICAL *a.*

a **1646** J. GREGORY *Posthuma* (1650) 200 Simaetha the Witch..doth manifestly declare it, where speaking of her veneficial Philtra [etc.]. **1646** SIR T. BROWNE *Pseud. Ep.* II. vi. 99 As for the Magicall vertues in this plant, and conceived efficacie unto veneficiall intentions, it seemeth unto me a Pagan relique derived from the ancient Druides. **1658** —— *Gard. Cyrus* 199 Why the Goddesses sit commonly crosse-legged in ancient draughts, Since Juno is described in the same as a veneficial posture to hinder the birth of Hercules?

vene'ficious, *a.* Now *rare.* [f. as prec.] = VENEFICAL *a.*

1646 SIR T. BROWNE *Pseud. Ep.* 266 That it was an old veneficious practice, and Juno is made in this posture to hinder the delivery of Alcmæna. **1650** CHARLETON tr. *Van Helmont's Paradoxes* 53 In this place we have nothing to doe with Veneficious Witches, properly called Sorcerers. **1702** SHERBURNE *Seneca's Trag.* 207 *note*, The Bonds and Fetters of veneficious Incantations. **1904** LE QUEUX *Closed Book* xxxvi, The actual poison-ring of that veneficious bacchante, Lucrezia Borgia.

Hence **vene'ficiously** *adv.* Now *rare* or *Obs.*

1646 SIR T. BROWNE *Pseud. Ep.* 265 Lest witches should draw or pricke their names therein, and veneficiously mischiefe their persons.

ve'neficous, *a.* *rare.* [f. L. *venēfic-us* + -OUS.] = VENEFICAL *a.*

1657 TOMLINSON *Renou's Disp.* 593 Mercury, wherewith a veneficous Circulator at Lutetia promised the cure of all diseases. **1831** in Madden *Will. Werwolf* (Roxb. Cl.) 10 A cup of beer, prepared by one who is skilled in such veneficous arts.

†**venefy.** *Obs.*$^{-1}$ = VENEFICE.

1616 J. LANE *Contn. Sqr.'s T.* VIII. 130 *note*, Leyfurcke..vsd all violence and art, which lay in vile Videreaes venefies, to crosse and disappoint the destanies.

venegre, obs. var. VINEGAR.

veneison, obs. f. VENISON.

venel, obs. f. VENNEL.

venem(e, obs. ff. VENOM *sb.* and *v.*

venemous(e, obs. ff. VENOMOUS *a.*

venemyn, obs. f. VENOM *v.*

†**'venenate**, *a.* *Obs.* [ad. L. *venēnāt-us*, pa. pple. of *venēnāre*: see next.] Poisoned; infected or imbued with poison or poisonous properties.

1633 T. JOHNSON *Gerarde's Herbal* App. 1605 They affirme that this fruit hath a wonderfull efficacie against venenate qualities and putrefaction. **1634** —— *Parey's Chirurg.* IX. xi. 331 The wound must be dilated..that so the venenate matter may flow forth more freely. **1672** *Phil. Trans.* VII. 4029 The fermentation of the venenate humors being quelled, and the pores closed. *a* **1728** WOODWARD *Fossils* (1729) II. I. 22 They give this in Fevers after Calcination, by which means the venenate Parts are carried off.

†**'venenate**, *v.* *Obs.* [f. L. *venēnāt-*, ppl. stem of *venēnāre*, f. *venēn-um* poison.] *trans.* To poison; to render poisonous.

1623 COCKERAM II, To Poyson, *Venenate.* **1665** G. HARVEY *Adv. agst. Plague* 5 The air..must be first venenated or rendred poysonous. *Ibid.* 7 The said Miasms entring the Body are not so Energick as to venenate the intire mass of blood in an instant.

So †**'venenated** *ppl. a.* *Obs.*

1597 MIDDLETON *Wisd. Solomon* xvi. 11 When poyson'd iawes and venenated stings, Were both as opposite against content.

†**vene'nation.** *Obs.* [See prec. and -ATION.] The action of, or a means of, poisoning.

1646 SIR T. BROWNE *Pseud. Ep.* III. vii. 119 That this venenation shooteth from the eye, and that this way a Basilisk may empoyson,..it is not a thing impossible. *Ibid.* VII. xix. 385 For, surely there are subtiler venenations, such as will invisibly destroy.

ve'nene, *a.* Now *rare* or *Obs.* [Irreg. ad. L. *venēn-um* poison.] Poisonous, venomous.

1665 G. HARVEY *Adv. agst. Plague* 2 A great ebullition or fermentation ensuing between the Venene Corpuscles and the Vital Spirits. *Ibid.* 7 The more sulphurous parts..assume a venene nature, which expiring infect and venenate the air. **1694** SALMON *Bate's Dispens.* (1713) 503/1 Which drives away by sweat the malignity of Venene, Pestilential, and Venereal Diseases. **1839** J. ROGERS *Antipapopr.* vi. §2. 225 It would leave behind no poisonous or venene particle of matter.

vene'niferous, *a.* *rare*$^{-0}$. [f. L. *venēnifer* (Ovid): see -FEROUS.] (See quot.) Also **vene'nifluous** *a.*, flowing with or discharging venom.

1656 BLOUNT *Glossogr.*, *Veneniferous*, that bears poyson, venemous. **1891** *Cent. Dict.* s.v., The venenifluous fang of a rattlesnake.

ve'neno-, employed as combining form of L. *venēnum* poison, as ***veneno-'salivary*** adj.

1899 *Allbutt's Syst. Med.* VIII. 944 They finally find their way into the large grape-like cells and ducts of the three-lobed veneno-salivary gland.

venenose, *a.* Now *rare.* [ad. late L. *venēnōs-us*, f. *venēn-um* poison: see -OSE. So It., Sp., Pg. *venenoso*.] Poisonous, venomous.

1673 RAY *Journ. Low C.* 275 The venenose vapour..ascends not a foot from the ground. **1691** —— *Creation* II. (1692) 77 All..Warts, Tumors and Excrescencies, where any Insects are found, are excited or raised up..by some Venenose Liquor. **1698** —— in *Phil. Trans.* XX. 85 The venenose Quality of this Plant. **1837** MILLINGEN *Cur. Med. Exp.* (1839) 376 Many absurd ideas regarding venenose substances prevailed in ancient days as well as in modern times. **1845** T. COOPER *Purgatory of Suicides* II. xxix, The younger Hellene ceased; and..The elder..now, ebriate with rage, Dashes to earth the foul venenose draught.

†**vene'nosity.** *Obs.* [ad. med.L. *venēnōsitas*: see prec. and -OSITY. So It. *venenosità*, Sp. *venenosidad*, older F. *venenosité* (Paré).] Poisonous quality or property.

1539 ELYOT *Cast. Helthe* (1541) 56 b, Men have nede to beware, what medycines they receyve, that in them be no venenositie, malyce, or corruption. **1574** NEWTON *Health Mag.* 24 Notwithstanding this their venenositie attributed to them by Avicen,..I woulde not willinglie refuse them for sustentation. **1638** A. READ *Chirurg.* xv. 109 Poysonable spirits..may be mingled with metals, so that they may participate of their venenositie. **1665** G. HARVEY *Adv. agst. Plague* 14 We should continually fortifie our spirits with internal Antidotes, to expell those Venenosities, as fast as they croud in. *a* **1691** BOYLE *Wks.* (1772) IV. 318 The venenosity they suspect in that corrosive menstruum.

ve'nenous, *a.* Now *rare.* Also 5 *Sc.* **wenenows**, 7 **venenouse**. [ad. late L. *venēnōs-us*, or f. L. *venēn-um* + -OUS. Cf. F. *vénéneus*.]
= VENENOSE *a.*

c **1425** WYNTOUN *Cron.* VI. iv. 319 A serpent al vgly,..Fel apperande and wenenows. *Ibid.* VII. viii. 1353 His mynyster, þat made hym þan serwis, Prewaly put in his chalice Wenenows poysson. **1656** BLOUNT *Glossogr.*, *Venenous*, full of poyson or venom. **1661** LOVELL *Hist. Anim. & Min.* 328 If it exceed it's turned into the plague, which is a venenouse disease of the heart. **1682** *Lond. Gaz.* No. 1714/5 That Traiterous, Venenous, Insinuating and Trapaning Association, lately found in the Closet of the Earl of Shaftsbury.

venepuncture ('vɛnɪ-, 'viːnɪˌpʌŋktjʊə(r)). *Med.* Also **veni-**. [f. L. *vēna* VEIN *sb.* + PUNCTURE *sb.*] Puncture of a vein, esp. with a hypodermic needle to withdraw blood or for intravenous injection.

1923 *Jrnl. Biol. Chem.* LVI. 106 Blood was drawn by venepuncture from a normal man. **1935** WHITBY & BRITTON *Disorders of Blood* xxiv. 475 Blood is obtained by venipuncture without using a tourniquet. **1957** W. MARTIN in R. K. Merton *Student-Physician* 196 Being able to do a venipuncture without difficulty. **1974** F. ELLIS in R. M. Kirk et al. *Surgery* viii. 172/1 A period of six weeks is necessary before the veins are sufficiently dilated to be used for regular venepucture. **1979** *Arizona Daily Star* 5 Aug. (Advt. section) 3/4 Venipuncture hospital experience preferred.

venera'bility. [ad. med.L. *venerābilitās*: see next and -ITY. So It. *venerabilità*, Pg. *-ilidade*.]
1. The quality of being venerable.

1664 H. MORE *Antid. Idolatry* viii. 93 The Images have according to the excellency and venerability of their Prototypes, some Latria [etc.]. **1805** R. P. KNIGHT *Princ. Taste* (ed. 2) II. ii. 161 This air of venerability (which belongs to the sublime, and not to the beautiful). **1826** *Blackw. Mag.* XIX. 388 [They] have lost the loveliness of youth, without having gained the venerability of age. *a* **1849** POE *Wks.* (1864) III. 405 Far be it from us..to dwell irreverently on matters which have venerability. **1904** *Athenæum* 24 Dec. 886/1 Its conventions are..as much a part of its venerability as the trappings of the Lord Mayor's Show.

2. Employed as a form of address to an ecclesiastic. *rare*$^{-1}$.

1842 BORROW *Bible in Spain* v, I lived in the family of the Countess **, at Cintra, when your venerability was her spiritual guide.

venerable ('vɛnərəb(ə)l), *a.* and *sb.* Also 5–6 *Sc.* **venerabill** (5 **-ille**). [a. OF. *venerable* (mod.F. *vénérable*, = Sp. *venerable*, Pg. *veneravel*, It. *venerabile*) or ad. L. *venerābilis*, f. *venerārī* to venerate.]

A. *adj.* **1.** Of persons: Worthy of being venerated, revered, or highly respected and esteemed, on account of character or position: **a.** As an epithet of ecclesiastics (or ecclesiastical bodies), now *spec.* of archdeacons or, in the Roman Catholic Church, of those who have attained the first degree of canonization. (Freq. abbreviated as *Ven.*)

1432–50 tr. *Higden* (Rolls) V. 187 Venerable faders of religion were in Egipte in this tyme. **1437** *Dunfermline Reg.* (Bann. Cl.) 285 A venerabill fadir in crist Androw..Abbot of Dunfermlyn. **1455** *Reg. Aberdon.* (Maitland Cl.) I. 275 Be it kende..me Valter of Deskfurde..to be oblysit..til ane venerabille man master Johnne of Clat. **1500** *Reg. Privy Seal Scotl.* I. 69/1 Ane Letter..to ane venerable fader Henry, abbot of Cambuskynneth. *a* **1700** in *Cath. Rec. Soc. Publ.* (1911) IX. 336 Much Relishing ven^ble^ Father Bakers ..Bookes, wch she write out and faithfully practised. **1730** BOSTON *Mem.* xii. 418 Having the Dissent by me in writ, from which I read it before this Venerable Assembly [the synod]. **1756–7** tr. *Keysler's Trav.* (1760) III. 103 Here..lie together the sacred bodies of the venerable fathers Sosius and Severinus. **1834** K. H. DIGBY *Mores Cath.* v. iv. 110 In the same age, Peter the Venerable, of Cluny, was defending the use of them [organs] against the Petrobrusians. **1872** *The Month* Aug. 25 The Ven. Bartholomew Holzhauser..died in Germany in 1658. **1894** *Daily News* 29 Jan. 5 Joan of Arc has been..declared 'venerable' by the Congregation of Rites. That is..the first step to saintship.

b. In general use. *rare.*

1641 J. JACKSON *True Evang. T.* II. 131 Hee was..a man so venerable amongst both the Christians, and Heathen, that his ordinary style was, The Doctor of whole Asia. **1681** in Ingleby *Shaks. Cent. Praise* (Shaks. Soc.) 386, I can't..omit the first Famous Masters in't of our Nation, Venerable Shakespear and the great Ben Johnson. **1748** RICHARDSON *Clarissa* (1811) III. 195 We have often regretted the particular fault, which, though in venerable characters, we must have been blind not to see. **1755** W. DUNCAN *Cicero's Sel. Orat.* ix. (1816) 297 It is with justice..that Ennius bestows upon poets the epithet of *venerable*.

c. Const. *for* (something) or *to* (persons). *rare.*

1653 VAUX tr. *Godeau's St. Paul* 53 A man even to his enemies venerable for his piety. **1713** BERKELEY *Ess. Guardian* i. Wks. III. 144 Persons who have devoted themselves to the service of God are venerable to all who fear Him. **1849–50** ALISON *Hist. Europe* II. viii. §29. 256 The Archbishop of Arles, venerable for his years and his virtues.

2. Commanding veneration or respect by reason of age combined with high personal character and dignity of appearance; having an impressive appearance in virtue of years and personal qualities.

c **1480** HENRYSON *Fables, Lion & Mouse* 64, I said, Esope, my Maister Uenerabill, I ȝow beseik [etc.]. **1515** BARCLAY *Egloges* ii. (1570) B j b/2 Suche men with princes be sene more acceptable Then men of wisedome & clarkes venerable. **1545** JOYE *Exp. Dan.* vi. 86 b, Daniel was now a right venerable sage olde father more then lxxx. yeares olde. **1609** DEKKER *Gull's Horn-bk.* Proem. 4 O thou venerable father of antient (and therefore hoary) customes, Syluanus, I inuoke thy assistance. **1650** BULWER *Anthrop.* 130 Man shews more venerable, especially if by age his hairs be every where fairly superaboundantly circumfused. **1687** T. BROWN *Saints in Uproar* Wks. 1730 I. 73 A venerable old gentleman, who, they say, had been high pontiff of Rome in the days of yore. *a* **1701** MAUNDRELL *Journ. Jerus.* (1732) 87 Said to be the House of Simeon, that venerable old Prophet. **1787** BURNS *Let. J. Skinner* 25 Oct., Reverend and Venerable Sir, Accept..my most sincere thanks [etc.]. **1847** MRS. A. KERR tr. *Ranke's Hist. Servia* 303 Amongst those executed before Belgrade were venerable Senators..and aged and renowned Woiwodes. **1862** MISS BRADDON *Lady Audley* i, A white beard which made him look venerable against his will. **1873** HAMERTON *Intell. Life* IV. ii. 143 A venerable country gentleman who had seen a great deal of the world.

transf. **1878** STEVENSON *Inland Voy.* 4 Cattle and gray venerable horses came and hung their mild heads over the embankment.

b. Applied to personal features or attributes of these.

1726 POPE *Odyss.* XXIV. 325 The father, with a father's fears: (His venerable eyes bedimm'd with tears). **1738** GLOVER *Leonidas* II. 192 His slender hairs, which time had silver'd o'er, Flow'd venerable down. **1808** W. WILSON *Hist. Dissent. Ch.* II. 50 Mr. Barker was in person well made, ..and of a venerable appearance. **1816** SCOTT *Old Mort.* xxx, He wore a breast-plate, over which descended a grey beard of venerable length. **1861** PALEY *Æschylus* (ed. 2) *Supplices* 314 *note*, The king might naturally call the old man πάνσοφος from his prudence and venerable aspect.

3. Of things: **a.** Worthy of, to be regarded with, religious reverence.

1504 LADY MARGARET tr. *De Imitatione* IV. i. 261 Wherefore than shulde nat I be more inflamed in thy venerable presence? **1509** BARCLAY *Shyp of Folys* (1570) 173 Our Lordes holy woundes fiue, His handes, his feete, and his crosse venerable. **1596** BELL *Surv. Popery* III. x. 405 How wilt thou touch thy mouth with his venerable blood? **1615** CROOKE *Body of Man* 339 Among the vnequall numbers the seauenth hath the first place, whose maiesty and diuinitie is so great, that the antients tearmed it sacred and venerable. **1642** JER. TAYLOR *Episc.* (1647) 169 A Bishop hath no new power in the consecration of the Venerable Eucharist, more then a Presbyter hath. *c* **1680** BEVERIDGE *Serm.* (1729) I. 539 The day of Expiation was..much more sacred and venerable than the common sabbath. **1837** J. H. NEWMAN *Par. Serm.* I. 322 What a venerable and fearful place is a Church. **1855** BAIN *Senses & Int.* III. iii. §12 A strong natural feeling of reverence accumulates a store of ideas of things venerable. **1879** C. G. ROSSETTI *Seek & Find* 308 Awful then and by us venerable is the dignity of each Christian priest.

b. Worthy of veneration or deep respect; deserving to be revered on account of noble qualities or associations.

1601 HOLLAND *Pliny* I. 81 Ios from Naxus 24 miles, venerable for the sepulchre of Homer. **1646** SIR T. BROWNE *Pseud. Ep.* I. viii. 33 Holy Writers, and such whose names are venerable unto all posterity. **1665** GLANVILL *Def. Van. Dogm.* 77 To oppose what custom and great names have render'd venerable. **1700** ROWE *Ambit. Step-Mother* I. i, The thoughts of Princes dwell in sacred Privacy Unknown and venerable to the Vulgar. **1769** ROBERTSON *Chas. V*, x. Wks. 1813 III. 207 The ancient and venerable fabric of the German Constitution. **1830** MACKINTOSH *Eth. Philos.* Wks. 1846 I. 93 Those qualities which are naturally amiable or venerable. **1849** MACAULAY *Hist. Eng.* i. I. 74 Throughout the whole course of his reign, all the venerable associations by which the throne had long been fenced were gradually losing their strength.

c. Fitted to excite feelings of veneration; impressive, august.

1615 CROOKE *Body of Man* 70 For it is a venerable sight to see a man when he is come to the yeares fit for it, to haue his face compassed about with thicke and comely haire. **1718** LADY M. W. MONTAGU *Let. to Conti* 31 July, We saw..yet standing the vast pillars of a temple of Minerva. This venerable sight made me think..on a beautiful temple of Theseus. **1737** WHISTON *Josephus, Antiq.* XI. viii. §5 The procession was venerable, and the manner of it different from that of other nations. **1764** GOLDSM. *Trav.* 110 While oft some temple's mould'ring tops between With venerable grandeur mark the scene.

4. Worthy of veneration or respect on account of age or antiquity; rendered impressive by the appearance of age.

1610 HOLLAND *Camden's Brit.* 738 An affectionate lover of venerable Antiquity. **1653** VAUX tr. *Godeau's St. Paul* 151 Against an ancient tradition, which to many seems so venerable. **1671** PHILIPPS *Reg. Necess.* Ep. Ded., Those evidences and venerable Monuments of Time. **1770** GOLDSM. *Des. Vill.* 178 His looks adorn'd the venerable place. **1796** H. HUNTER tr. *St.-Pierre's Stud. Nat.* (1799) II. 421 Thus it is that you are clothed with majesty, venerable ruins of Greece and Rome! **1817** MOORE *Lalla Rookh* (1824) 171 That venerable tower, he told them, was the remains of an ancient Fire-temple. **1870** DICKENS *E. Drood* iii, In the midst of Cloisterham stands the nuns' house, a venerable brick edifice. **1904** J. T. FOWLER *Durham Univ.* 63 The oldest of the venerable lime-trees date from time immemorial.

absol. **1693** DRYDEN *Juvenal* (1697) p. lxxxv, Ancient Words, which, with all their Rusticity, had somewhat of Venerable in them.

b. Ancient, antique, old.

1792 S. ROGERS *Pleas. Mem.* I. 65 Those muskets cased with venerable rust. **1842** H. ROGERS *Introd. Burke's Wks.* I. 1 Thus a single generation often witnesses the complete demolition of certain venerable errors, propagated and believed through a long succession of ages. **1847** C. BRONTE *Jane Eyre* xi, Chests in oak or walnut,..rows of venerable chairs, high-backed and narrow. **1857** GRINDON *Life* iv. 35 The periodical (atomic) renewal of the body is one of the most venerable ideas in physiology.

†**5.** Giving evidence of veneration; reverent, reverential. *Obs.* (So L. *venerabilis.*)

1613 PURCHAS *Pilgrimage* (1614) 145 They speake in order, and obserue euen without the house a venerable silence. **1624** FISHER in F. White *Repl. Fisher* 224 Kissing their feet, and their sores, out of venerable affection vnto Christ. **1675** G. R. tr. *Le Grand's Man without Passion* 77 Although I have a venerable value for the favourers of this opinion. *a* **1701** MAUNDRELL *Journ. Jerus.* (1732) 7 The Venerable presents of some Itinerant Fryars. **1710** SHAFTESB. *Charact.* (1737) II. II. 269 To talk magisterially and in venerable Terms of..an Infinite Being.

6. *Comb.*, as ***venerable-like, -looking*** adjs.

1632 LITHGOW *Trav.* VI. 264 Wee found twelue Venerable like Turkes. **1766** GOLDSM. *Vicar* xiv, Was he not a venerable-looking man, with grey hair? **1854** tr. *Hettner's Athens & Peloponnese* 31 Tall, venerable-looking men, with noble features.

B. *sb.* A venerable person; an ecclesiastic having the title of 'Venerable'.

1748 RICHARDSON *Clarissa* VI. 122 Lord M. has engaged the two venerables to stay here, to attend the issue. **1826** SOUTHEY *Vind. Eccl. Angl.* 444 But can heresy have come from the Venerables and Saints of the Romish Church? **1891** MEREDITH *One of our Conq.* xxxv, He described his country's male venerables as being distinguishable from annuitant spinsters only in presenting themselves forked.

b. A venerable thing; an antique. *nonce-use.*

1803 SOUTHEY *Lett.* (1856) I. 222 My old and ugly stall-gleanings are all now turning to account... In turning over these venerables, you would be surprised to see how much I find that bears upon biography.

'venerableness. [f. prec. + -NESS.] = VENERABILITY 1.

1681 *Whole Duty Nations* 59 Things that have only the thin pretexts of Antiquity to give them some venerableness. **1710** PALMER *Proverbs* 232 As there is a native venerableness in grey hairs, so 'tis impious to make 'em the subject of a jest. **1753** RICHARDSON *Grandison* VI. xxiv. 133 Years written by venerableness, rather than by wrinkles, in her face. **1823** LAMB *Elia* II. *Tombs in Abbey*, You owe it to the venerableness of your ecclesiastical establishment. **1872** SHIPLEY *Gloss. Eccl. Terms* 346 The office..is one of extreme venerableness and antiquity.

'venerably, *adv.* [f. as prec.] In a venerable manner; so as to be venerable; †with veneration.

c **1610** *Women Saints* (1886) 180 Whose happie passage the Greeke and Latine Churche do venerablie recorde..[on] the fift of August. **1693** DRYDEN *Juvenal's Satires* VI. 31 So venerably Ancient is the Sin. **1699** GARTH *Dispens.* 8 Each Faculty in Blandishments they lull, Aspiring to be venerably dull. **1753** HANWAY *Trav.* III. xxx. (1762) I. 130 The years that had rendered his beard so venerably hoary. **1791** HUDDESFORD *Salmagundi* 135 Might I but..See thee in scarlet robe encase thy fur, And at St. Mary's venerably purr! **1818** BYRON *Ch. Har.* IV. xxxi, His mansion and his sepulchre; both plain And venerably simple. **1838** *Fraser's Mag.* XVII. 58 It [the beard] had become venerably red.

†**'veneral,** *a.*[1] *Obs.* [ad. med.L. *Venerāl-is*, f. *Vener-*, *Venus* VENUS[1].]

1. = VENEREAL *a.* 1.

1591 SPARRY tr. *Cattan's Geomancie* 105 This figure is ill, except it be for warre or actes venerall. **1624** HEYWOOD *Gunaik.* IX. 453 By their unanimous consent they vowed perpetual abstinence from all venerall actions.

2. = VENEREOUS *a.* 1 and 3.

1623 COCKERAM I, *Venerall*, giuen to fleshly wantonnesse. **1651** J. F[REAKE] *Agrippa's Occ. Philos.* 97 They that will gather a Venerall, Mercuriall, or Lunary Hearb must look toward the West.

3. = VENEREAL *a.* 2.

1651 FRENCH *Distill.* iii. 75 This Oil so purifies the bloud, ..that it cures all distempers that arise from the impurity thereof, as the venerall disease. **1698** G. THOMAS *Pensilvania* 19 Sarsaparilla, so much us'd in Diet-Drinks for the Cure of the Veneral Disease. **1803** *Med. Jrnl.* IX. 556 A more recent case of a true elephantiasis, that followed a veneral infection, is added.

†**veneral,** *a.*[2] *Obs.*[−1] [Cf. med.L. *venerālitas* venerability.] = VENERABLE *a.* 2b.

1631 MABBE *Celestina* I. 29 What a venerall and reverend countenance did hee carry!

'venerance. *rare*[−1]. [Cf. OF. *venerance*, It. *veneranza*, med.L. *venerantia.*] Venerability.

1884 J. PAYNE *Tales fr. Arabic* I. 256 There was once in a province of Persia, a King of the Kings,..endowed with majesty and venerance.

†**'venerand,** *a. Obs. rare.* [ad. L. *venerandus*, gerundive of *venerārī* to venerate. So It., Sp., Pg. *venerando.*] Entitled to veneration.

1549 CHALONER *Erasm. on Folly* K iij, These friers..upholde them in their sermons to the people callyng them worshipfull and venerande maisters. **1677** GALE *Crt. Gentiles* IV. II. iv. §3. 286 Seing we conceive of Eternitie as most venerand, there is nothing more venerand than the intelligible Divine Essence.

'venerant, *a. rare*[−1]. [ad. L. *venerant-*, *venerans*, pres. pple. of *venerārī* to venerate. So F. *vénérant*, Sp. *venerante.*] Engaged in veneration.

1846 RUSKIN *Mod. Paint.* II. III. i. §9 *note* 2, When we pronounce the name of Giotto, our venerant thoughts are at Assisi and Padua.

†**'venerate,** *a. Obs.*[−1] [ad. L. *venerāt-us*, pa. pple. of *venerārī*: see next.] = prec.

1592 R. D. *Hypnerotomachia* 53 b, They stood all waiting with such a venerate attention, that..they all at one instant time alike made their reverent courtesies.

venerate ('vɛnəreɪt), *v.* [ad. L. *venerāt-*, ppl. stem of *venerārī* (also *venerāre*) to reverence, worship, adore; whence also It. *venerare*, Sp. and Pg. *venerar*, F. *vénérer.*]

1. *trans.* To regard with feelings of respect and reverence; to look upon as something exalted, hallowed, or sacred; to reverence or revere.

1623 COCKERAM I, *Venerate*, to worship. **1656** BLOUNT *Glossogr.*, *Venerate*, to reverence, worship or honour. **1742** YOUNG *Nt. Th.* II. 355 Who venerate themselves, the world despise. **1794** R. J. SULIVAN *View Nat.* I. 481 But there was a class of Alchymists, whose genius, probity, and conduct, we have reason to venerate. **1851** D. WILSON *Preh. Ann.* IV. iv. (1863) II. 293 The ruined chapels are still venerated. **1870** J. BRUCE *Life Gideon* iv. 70 [We] have learned to venerate the Word of God.

2. To pay honour to (something) by a distinct act of reverence.

1844 LINGARD *Anglo-Sax. Ch.* (1858) I. v. 189 Thrice he venerated the sacred remains.

Hence **'venerated, 'venerating** *ppl. adjs.*

1790 BURKE *Fr. Rev.* Wks. V. 84 You would have had..a reformed and *venerated clergy. **1818** COBBETT *Pol. Reg.* XXXIII. 169 In the Reports, the Resolutions, and in the venerated Acts, of your Honourable House. **1847** PRESCOTT *Peru* (1850) II. 143 It would be easier to govern under the venerated authority to which the homage of the Indians had been so long paid. **1873** BROWNING *Red Cott. Nt.-cap* 272 Smiling and sighing had the same effect Upon the venerated image. **1663** BOYLE *Usef. Exp. Nat. Philos.* I. iii. 55 The Queen of Sheba..then brake forth into pathetic and *venerating exclamations. **1828** MISS HIGGINSON in Drummond & Upton *Life Martineau* (1902) I. iii. 50 [Her reply declines to accept from him a] venerating love. **1863** GEO. ELIOT *Romola* III. xxxiv, He..saw the faces of men and women lifted towards him in venerating love. **1888** RUSKIN *Præterita* III. 8 Without..trouble to their venerating visitors in coming so far up hill.

veneratingly, ('vɛnəreɪtɪŋlɪ), *adv. rare*[−1]. [f. VENERATING *ppl. a.* + -LY[2].] In a reverential manner.

c **1925** V. WOOLF in *Mrs Dalloway's Party* (1973) 68 She and Bertram sat down on deck chairs, she looked at the house veneratingly, enthusiastically.

veneration (vɛnə'reɪʃən). Also 5-6 **veneracion** (6 **-acyon**). [ad. L. *venerātiōn-*, *venerātio*, noun of action f. *venerārī* to venerate. So OF. *veneration* (F. *vénération*), It. *venerazione*, Sp. *veneracion*, Pg. *veneração.*]

1. A feeling of deep respect and reverence directed towards some person or thing: **a.** In the phrases ***to have***, or ***hold in veneration.***

1432-50 tr. *Higden* (Rolls) I. 389 In that londe the memory of Seynte Andrewe thapostole is haloede gretely, and hade in veneracion. *Ibid.* III. 193 That clerke Pictagoras was hade so in veneracion of his disciples, that [etc.]. **1548** UDALL *Erasm. Par. Matt.* v. 20 b, So men shall haue you in veneration. **1596** SPENSER *State Irel.* Wks. (Globe) 634/1 All those Northern nations..are wonte therfore to have the fire and the sunn in great veneration. **1629** J. MAXWELL tr. *Herodian* (1635) 391 In the Temple of Jupiter Capitolinus (which the Romans have in chief veneration). *a* **1704** T. BROWN *Praise Drunkenness* Wks. 1730 I. 38 A custom framed and cemented by nature.. ought to be..had in veneration by all succeeding ages. **1759** DILWORTH *Pope* 62 Mr. Pope held the duke's judgement in such high veneration [etc.]. **1833** CRUSE *Eusebius' Eccl. Hist.* VII. xix. (1847) 300 This See..has ever been held in veneration by the brethren, that have followed in the succession there.

b. In general use.

1647 CLARENDON *Hist. Reb.* I. §12 They would..have been of no less Esteem with the Crown, than of Veneration with the People. **1683** ROBINSON in *Ray's Corr.* (1848) 133 He speaks with great veneration of you. **1774** J. BRYANT *Mythol.* II. 372 The persons..who were stiled Baalim, had a great regard paid to their memory, which at last degenerated into a most idolatrous veneration. **1791** BURKE *App. Whigs* Wks. VI. 143 That memory will be kept alive with particular veneration by all rational and honourable whigs. **1825** in *Ushaw Mag.* Dec. (1913) 267 When I am in its company, I feel a certain awe and veneration. **1844** DICKENS *Mart. Chuz.* ix, A gentleman..whom two accomplished..females regard with veneration. **1891** NISBET *Insanity of Genius* 298 Simple piety or veneration seems to resolve itself into an absence of the identifying faculty.

c. Const. *of* or *for* (a person or thing).

(*a*) **1662** STILLINGFL. *Orig. Sacræ* III. ii. § 1 All that is left, is only a kind of Veneration of a Being more excellent than our own. **1671** F. PHILIPPS *Reg. Necess.* 409 So tender were the Judges..of the Supreme Authority they sate under,.. and had such an awe and veneration of Majesty [etc.]. **1806** SURR *Winter in Lond.* I. 243 The old domestic..had almost intoxicated him with a silly, yet enthusiastic, veneration of old times.

(*b*) **1681** in Somers *Tracts* I. 131 The greatest motive that begot in me a Veneration for the Duke. **1691** NORRIS *Pract. Disc.* (1698) IV. 13 He has a secret esteem and Veneration for him there [in his heart]. **1718** LADY M. W. MONTAGU *Let. to C'tess Bristol* 10 April, They show here the tomb of the Emperor Constantine, for which they have a great veneration. **1759** ROBERTSON *Hist. Scot.* v. Wks. 1851 II. 35 She expressed a great veneration for the liturgy of the Church of England. **1841** D'ISRAELI *Amen. Lit.* (1867) 106 It is unquestionable that the Reformation began to diminish the veneration for the Latin language. **1863** KINGLAKE *Crimea* (1877) I. 79 At this time extravagant veneration was avowed for mechanical contrivances.

2. The action or fact of showing respect and reverence; the action or practice of venerating.

1526 *Pilgr. Perf.* (W. de W. 1531) 192 b, The lower veneracyon or worshyp exhibyte & done to the sayntes of god, called in the greke dulia. *a* **1540** BARNES *Wks.* (1573) 357/2 What faith, what learning, what reason will that Images shoulde bee iudged worthy veneration? **1609** BIBLE (Douay) *Exod.* xxxix. 29 They made also the plate of sacred veneration of most pure gold. **1663** BP. PATRICK *Parab. Pilgr.* xxiii, He blushed exceedingly, and fell down in a humble veneration of her. **1741** WARBURTON *Div. Legat.* v. Note B. Wks. 1788 III. 200 Josephus..saw well the consistency between the veneration paid to Abraham's God, and the idolatry of the venerators. **1827** HALLAM *Const. Hist.* ii. (1876) I. 86 No part of exterior religion was more prominent..than the worship, or at least veneration of images. **1852** MRS. JAMESON *Leg. Madonna* Introd. (1857) 18 The veneration paid to Mary in the early Church. **1882-3** SCHAFF *Encycl. Relig. Knowl.* III. 2562/1 The veneration of martyrs was accompanied by the feeling that their intercession made prayer effective.

3. The fact or condition of being venerated.

1625 BACON *Ess.*, *Of Empire* (Arb.) 309 Princes are like to Heauenly Bodies,..which haue much Veneration, but no Rest. **1665** SIR T. HERBERT *Trav.* (1677) 116 Claudian observes there was scarce any Tree that had not its veneration. **1712** *Spect.* No. 467 §2 The various Arts.. which now give a Dignity and Veneration to the Ease he does enjoy. **1750** JOHNSON *Rambler* No. 71 ¶1 They think veneration gained by such appearances of wisdom. **1774** REID *Aristotle's Logic* i. §1. 3 That the air of mystery might procure great veneration.

†**b.** In the phrase ***to be in* (..) *veneration.*** *Obs.*

1628 LE GRYS tr. *Barclay's Argenis* 352 At that time it was in highest veneration among the Moores. **1678** HOBBES *Decam.* i. 5 The first Astronomers were also in such veneration with the People, that they were thought to have discourse with their Gods. **1736** BUTLER *Anal.* II. vii. 335 The leaders of them are in veneration with the multitude.

Hence **vene'rational** *a.*

1854 *Orr's Circ. Sci.*, *Org. Nat.* I. 310 There is little vitality in any of their venerational feelings.

'venerative, *a. rare.* [f. VENERATE *v.* + -IVE.] Of the nature of, inclined or disposed to, veneration. Also **'venerativeness**.

1829 T. HOOK *Bank to Barnes* 104 They found the Organ of Venerativeness strongly developed. **1860** COCKBURN MUIR *Pagan or Chr.?* 37 A venerative love for the teachings of the Christian Faith. **1862** *All the Year Round* 27 Sept. 61/1, I for one, when a venerative youth, have felt a thrill of joy at being kindly nodded to over a bumper by some distinguished personage.

'venerator. [a. L. *venerātor*, agent-noun f. *venerārī* to venerate. Cf. It. *veneratore*, Sp. and Pg. *venerador*, F. *vénérateur* (rare).] One who venerates; a reverencer *of* something.

1656 *Artif. Handsom.* 123 The report seems fitted to the pulse and bent of those times, which were high venerators of vowed virginity. *a* **1676** HALE *Prim. Orig. Man.* 74 Those great Priests and Venerators of Nature and its appearances. **1789** BURNEY *Hist. Mus.* (ed. 2) II. i. 29 This prelate, who was a great venerator of ancient rites. **1818** BENTHAM *Parl. Reform* 75 So many indifferent and incurious observers, if not prostrate venerators. **1847** TENNYSON *Princ.* IV. 403 Not a scorner of your sex But venerator.

venereal (vɪ'nɪərɪəl), *a.* and *sb.* Also 5 venerealle, 6–7 -all. [f. L. *venere-us*, f. *Vener-*, *Venus* VENUS[1]. Cf. VENERIAL *a.*]

1. a. Of or pertaining to, associated or connected with, sexual desire or intercourse.

1432–50 tr. *Higden* (Rolls) II. 199 The sawle of man in the vse venerealle [L. *usu venereo*] transmittethe interially formes other similitudes conceyvede exterially. **1509** BARCLAY *Shyp of Folys* (1570) ⁋⁋iv, Here are vile women, whom loue immoderate, And lust Venereall, bringeth to hurt and shame. **1610** HEALEY *St. Aug. Citie of God* XIV. xv. (1620) 490 Such is hunger and thirst, and the venereall affect, vsually called lust. **1688** NORRIS *Love* II. §ii. 95 Concerning sensual pleasure, especially that eminent species of it which we call venereal, there is more difficulty. **1727** SWIFT *Circumcision of E. Curll* Wks. 1755 III. I. 163 Those appetites are now become venal, which should be venereal. **1753** SMOLLETT *Ct. Fathom* (1784) 159/1 We have formerly descanted upon that venereal appetite which glowed in the constitution of our adventurer. **1831** J. DAVIES *Mat. Med.* 55 In the cure of..anaphrodisia or want of venereal passion.

†**b.** (See quot.) *Obs.*$^{-1}$

1658 ROWLAND tr. *Moufet's Theat. Ins.* 999 Divers Authors do speak of four other sorts of Moths, *viz.* the Venereal, bred in the genitals of men; the Bee Moth, the Cloth Moth, and the Library or Book Moth.

2. a. Resulting from, or communicated by, sexual intercourse with an infected person; symptomatic of, or associated with, a disease so caused.

1658 PHILLIPS, Venereal disease..is vulgarly called the French Pox. **1660** MILTON *Free Commw.* Wks. 1851 V. 445 These new Fanatics of..the sweating-tub, inspir'd with nothing holier than the Venereal Pox. **1667** *Phil. Trans.* II. 564 A lusty robust Souldier dangerously infected with the Venereal Disease. **1710** ADDISON *Tatler* No. 226 ⁋5 [He] was particularly famous for the Cure of Venereal Distempers. **1758** J. S. *Le Dran's Observ. Surg.* (1771) 16 He looked upon the Distemper to proceed from a Venereal Cause, therefore exhibited Antivenereals. **1805** *Med. Jrnl.* XIV. 127 Unless we suppose the pain he has in his joints to arise from latent venereal virus. **1860** TANNER *Pregnancy* v. 228 Another way in which it is highly probable that a woman may receive the venereal taint. **1878** T. BRYANT *Pract. Surg.* I. 174 Venereal warts are very abundant.

b. Of persons: Infected with, suffering from, venereal disease.

1683 SNAPE *Anat. Horse* III. v. (1686) 112 Till it have mortified and consum'd them (as happens sometimes to venereal Persons). **1843** R. J. GRAVES *Syst. Clin. Med.* xxiv. 296 A return of the venereal patients treated in the 38th Regimental Hospital.

c. *ellipt.* as *sb.* Venereal disease.

1843 R. J. GRAVES *Syst. Clin. Med.* xxv. 317 [He] does not consider it [i.e. mercury] a specific for the venereal. *Ibid.* xxix. 371 His skin became covered with an extensive papular ..eruption, which was looked upon by many as true venereal.

d. *ellipt.* as *sb.* A person with venereal disease.

1788 W. BLIGH in R. M. Bowker *Mutiny!!* (1978) vi. 266 Three Venereals in the List. **1933** *Sun* (Baltimore) 23 Feb. 8/3 A veneral draws $257.50 a month, or more than a man blinded by an enemy shell.

†**3. a.** Of persons: Under the influence of Venus; inclined to be lascivious; addicted to venery or lust. *Obs.*

1652 GAULE *Magastrom.* 188 Pronouncing the man..to be saturnine, jovial, martial, solar, venereal, mercurial, lunar? **1665** BRATHWAIT *Comment. Two Tales* (1901) 62 In Sense, she was Venereal; in Heart, Martial; Venus gave her the Gift to be lascivious; Mars to be couragious. **1728** CHAMBERS *Cycl.* s.v., A Venereal Person.

†**b.** Of animals: (see quot.). *Obs.*$^{-1}$

1661 LOVELL *Hist. Anim. & Min.* Isagoge c3, The Venereall [animals], are the delitious,..mild, kinde, pleasant, and tame; as the Calfe, cony, dog, goat, and scinck.

†**c.** (Cf. *vitriol of Venus* s.v. VENUS[1].) *Obs.*

1684–5 BOYLE *Min. Waters* 55 Common English Vitriol, as also that of Danzick which is Venereal.

†**4.** Physically beautiful or attractive. *Obs.*$^{-1}$

1598 R. HAYDOCKE tr. *Lomazzo* I. 117 Raph. Vrbine was famous for making of delicate and Venereall bodies.

venereally (vɪ'nɪərɪəlɪ), *adv.* [f. VENEREAL *a.* + -LY[2].] **a.** By sexual intercourse. **b.** With venereal disease. *rare.*

1945 [see BEJEL]. **1973** *Sci. Amer.* Apr. 119/2 His [*sc.* Linnæus's] chief practice was among the venereally ill young rakes of Stockholm. **1978** *Nature* 28 Sept. 334/2 Genital warts..are benign tumours which are mostly venereally transmitted.

†**Ve'nerean**, *a.* (and *sb.*). *Obs.* Also 6 *Sc.* venereane. [f. as VENEREAL *a.* + -AN.]

1. Connected or associated with, relating or pertaining to, Venus or her service.

c **1550** ROLLAND *Crt. Venus* I. 223 For hir sake sum sang venereane I wald thow sang. *Ibid.* III. 758 Thay thre was of the Court venereane. **1597** BP. HALL *Sat.* I. ix, His statue trimd with the venerean tree. **1653** GATAKER *Vind. Annot. Jer.* 64 Oh but when, trow we, may some loose people say, will these Halcyon, or Venerean dayes rather appeer? **1685** COTTON tr. *Montaigne* (1711) I. xx. 117 My Figures proved more Venerean than Solar.

2. Of or pertaining to sexual desire or intercourse.

c **1550** ROLLAND *Crt. Venus* III. 720 Thamar and Raab.. And Barsabe..War all of sport Ladeis venereane. **1634** WITHER *Embl.* 71 The scarres they get in their Venerean fights. *c* **1645** HOWELL *Lett.* (1650) II. 17 With the assurance of Venerean delights in a far higher degree to succeed after death. *c* **1700** *Jane Shore* in Evans *Old Ball.* (1784) I. 325 Those with Scythian lad engag'd in several fights, And in the brave Venerean wars did foil advent'rous knights.

b. = VENEREAL *a.* 2.

1612 CHAPMAN *Widowes T.* I. B iv, The Venerean disease, to which they say, he has beene long wedded.

3. Addicted to venereal pleasures. Also as *sb.*, a person of this character.

1612 CHAPMAN *Widowes T.* v. I ij b, It will be such a cooler To my Venerean Gentlemans hot liuer. **1631** MABBE *Celestina* XIV. 156 Just about this time rise..your Venereans and love-sicke soules, such as our master.

venere'ology. *Med.* [f. as next + -OLOGY.] The science or study of venereal diseases. Hence **venereo'logical** *a.*; **venere'ologist**, an expert or specialist in venereology.

1894 GOULD *Dict. Med.* 1595/2 Venereology. **1934** WEBSTER, Venereologist. **1944** *Jrnl. R. Army Med. Corps* LXXXIII. 102 Non-gonococcal urethritis..is worrying many venereologists nowadays. **1946** *Nature* 17 Aug. 242/2 (*heading*) Adviser in venereology to the War Office. **1961** *Lancet* 29 July 246/2 Their study..included others admitted to non-venereological departments. **1970** *Daily Tel.* 25 Sept. 6/8 Permissive doctors..were condemned yesterday by Dr Ambrose King, consulting venereologist to the London Hospital. **1972** *Lancet* 10 June 1295/1 He could not see why venereology should be considered a specialty in its own right. **1979** D. BARLOW *Sexually Transmitted Diseases* iii. 29 This is the only country in the EEC..that recognizes venereology as a distinct specialty. **1982** *Acta Dermato-Venereologica* LXII. 367/2 Every patient with a finding or history of Pediculosis pubis should be offered a venereological examination including test for both gonorrhea and syphilis.

†**ve'nereous**, *a. Obs.* Also 6 venereus. [f. L. *venere-us* (whence It., Sp., Pg. *venereo*) + -OUS. Cf. OF. *venereux* and VENERIOUS *a.*]

1. Of persons (or animals): Addicted to, desirous of, sexual enjoyment; libidinous, lustful.

1509 BARCLAY *Shyp of Folys* (1570) 115 Venereous people haue all their whole pleasaunce Their vice to nourishe by this unthrifty daunce. **1562** LEGH *Armory* 95 The gote, saieth Isidore, is very venereus, but fighteth not therefore. **1607** TOPSELL *Four-f. Beasts* 300 There is no kind (man only excepted) that is so venereous and nimble in generation as is a Horsse or Mare. **1662** J. DAVIES tr. *Olearius' Voy. Ambass.* 94 The Muscovites are extremely venereous. **1713** DERHAM *Phys.-Theol.* (1727) 391 The Males are less than the Females [and] are very venereous.

2. = VENEREAL *a.* I.

1542 UDALL *Erasm. Apoph.* 204 The acte of venereous copulation. **1578** LYTE *Dodoens* 182 The Conserve of the floures thereof..putteth away all venereous dreames. **1615** G. SANDYS *Trav.* IV. 307 In that heate and moisture are the parents of venereous desires. **1650** HUBBERT *Pill Formality* 138 His sinful and venereous thoughts must carry him on. **1681** H. MORE in Glanvill *Sadducismus* 36 Their having any lustful or venereous transactions with them. **1795** MACKNIGHT *Epist.* (1820) III. 297 This signifies the gratification of venereous desires.

b. = VENEREAL *a.* 2.

1661 LOVELL *Hist. Anim. & Min.* 11 The greene caustick oil of brasse, cureth venereous pushes.

3. Exciting or stimulating sexual desire.

1611 CORYAT *Crudities* 268 As for thine eyes, shut them and turne them aside from those venereous Venetian objects. **1626** BACON *Sylva* §546 Upon the same reason Mushrooms are a Venereous meat. **1694** MOTTEUX *Rabelais* v. xxix. 146 Salads, wholly made up of venereous Herbs and Fruits.

4. Dedicated to Venus. *rare*$^{-1}$.

1592 R. D. *Hypnerotom.* 79 Such hayre as Berenice did never vow to in the Venereous Temple for her Tholemæus.

Hence †**ve'nereously** *adv.*; †**ve'nereousness**.

1659 H. MORE *Immort. Soul* III. viii. 408 Theocritus merrily sets out the Venereousness of the Goatheard he describes. **1665** M. N. *Med. Medicinæ* 65 Let a man that hath the Gout be venereously infected.

'venerer. *arch.* [f. VENER-Y[2].] A huntsman.

1845 BROWNING *Flight of Duchess* x, Our Venerers, Prickers, and Verderers. **1908** H. NEWBOLT *New June* xxxii, [He] drove the point into the hart's neck, with the action of a venerer killing the real animal.

Veneres, pl. of VENUS[1].

†**ve'nerial**, *a.*[1] *Obs.* Also 6–7 -all. [f. L. *veneri-us*, f. *Vener-*, *Venus*. Cf. VENEREAL *a.*]

1. = VENEREAL *a.* I.

1531 ELYOT *Gov.* III. xviii, Thinking..to remoue him from the faythe, rather by veneriall motions, thanne by sharpenesse of tourmentes. **1552** HULOET, Veneriall pastime, *aphrodisia.* **1589** NASHE *Anat. Absurdity* Wks. (Grosart) I. 26 Craftie Cupid..meditates new shifts, which each amorous Courtier by his veneriall experience may coniecturallie conceiue. **1615** CROOKE *Body of Man* 553 Those that do too much follow venerial combats haue their eyes smal and extenuated. **1636** DAVENANT *Platonick Lovers* III, I found him..Lesse apt for our veneriall Love than Muscovites Benighted when they travell on the Ice.

2. = VENEREAL *a.* 3 a.

1577 GRANGE *Golden Aphrod.* Ep. Ded. A iij b, I (who as yet neuer receyued one poynt of discourtesie of any veneriall Dame). *Ibid.* A iv b, Veneriall dames, and ruffling Nymphes. **1630** J. TAYLOR (Water P.) *A Bawd* Wks. II. 93/2 Besides, I found a cursed Catalogue of these veneriall Caterpillers who were suppress with the Monasteries in England.

3. a. Beautiful or attractive like Venus.

1661 MORGAN *Sph. Gentry* III. iv. 38 They described him like a martial man, when they would express his heat,.. when a venerial woman, described him with a Mirtle garland on his head.

b. Associated with the planet Venus.

1683 TRYON *Way to Health* vi. (1697) 106 The cooler the Water is when you put in the Malt, the Paler or more Venerial will the Colour of your Wort be. *Ibid.* 109 The predominant Quality..in Ale is Solar and Venerial, viz. Sweet and Balsamick.

4. Employed in curing venereal disease.

17.. M. BARRETT in Morse *Amer. Geog.* (1796) I. 682 The next is the venerial root, which, under a vegetable regimen, will cure a confirmed lues.

Hence †**ve'nerialist**, a specialist in venereal diseases. *Obs.*$^{-1}$

1763 A. SUTHERLAND *Attempts Anc. Med. Doctr.* I. Introd. 21 Every disease, every member of the body, has its particular professor. The city swarms with Oculists, Aurarists, Dentists, Venerialists, Nostrumites, &c.

†**ve'nerial**, *a.*[2] *Obs.*$^{-1}$ [f. VENERY[1].] Belonging to the chase. In quot. *absol.*

1612 DRAYTON *Poly-olb.* XIII. 93 Of all the Beasts which we for our veneriall name, The Hart amongst the rest, the Hunters noblest game [etc.].

†**Ve'nerian**, *a.* (and *sb.*) *Obs.* Also 5 ueneryan. [f. L. *veneri-us*, f. *Vener-*, *Venus* VENUS[1]. Cf. VENEREAN and VENERIEN.]

1. Influenced by, subject to, Venus; inclined to wantonness.

14.. [see VENERIEN *a.*]. *c* **1590** J. STEWART *Poems* (S.T.S.) II. 78/192 Heirfoir to vichts venerian I quyt To form in verse virgilian perfyt Thair facund fassons. **1596** NASHE *Saffron Walden* Wks. (Grosart) III. 120 Pigmey Dicke aforesaid..is such another Venerian steale placard as Iohn was. **1608** TARLTON *Cobler Canterb.* (1844) 133 In every house where the venerian virgins are resident, hospitalitie is quite exiled.

b. As *sb.* A person of this character.

1601 DOLMAN *La Primaud. Fr. Acad.* III. 130 They name one man a Saturnist, another a Martialist,..or else a Mercurialist, or a Venerian.

2. = VENEREAL *a.* I.

1448 METHAM *Wks.* (E.E.T.S.) 57 Nwe radvffyid with the flame off ueneryan dysyre. **1513** DOUGLAS *Æneid* IV. Prol. 92 Be nevir ourset, myne author teichis so, With lust of wyne, nor werkis veneriane. **1598** SYLVESTER *Du Bartas* II. ii. *Ark* 419 A vast multitude Of since-born mongrels, that derive their birth From monstrous medly of Venerian mirth. **1602** DOLMAN *La Primaud. Fr. Acad.* (1618) III. 734 Euen as the aire and winde coupleth and conioineth things seuered, so doth the Venerian power.

3. = VENEREAL *a.* 2.

1617 MORYSON *Itin.* III. 59 Because the beds are suspected for filthinesse of the Venerian disease, passengers use to weare linnen breeches of their owne. **1650** BULWER *Anthropomet.* 87 The Nose that is sunk into this figure by the Venerian rot.

4. *Venerian pear*, the Venus-pear.

1601 HOLLAND *Pliny* I. 439 The Barbarian or Venerian pears, which also be called Coloured.

†**ve'neriate**, *v. Obs.* [f. L. *Veneri-* stem of *Venus* VENUS[1].] *trans.* ? = VITRIOLATE *v.*

1665 D. DUDLEY *Mettallum Martis* (1854) 31 Sulphurious veneriated redshare Iron... The Sulphurious Arceniall and Veneriating qualities, which are oftentimes in Iron stone.

venerid ('vɛnərɪd). *Zool.* [f. mod.L. *Venerid-æ*, f. *Vener-*, *Venus* VENUS[1].] A bivalve mollusc of the family *Veneridæ*, of which *Venus* is the typical genus.

1861 P. P. CARPENTER in *Rep. Smithsonian Instit. 1860*, 259 The characters of the Venerids, the Cyprinids, and the Cockles.

†**Ve'nerien**, *a.* and *sb.* Also 6 -yen. [a. OF. *venerien* (F. *vénérien*).] = VENERIAN *a.* and *sb.*

c **1386** CHAUCER *Wife's Prol.* 609 For certes I am al Venerien [*Corpus MS.* Venerian] In feelyng and myn herte is Marcian. **1390** GOWER *Conf.* III. 111 Ther mai no maner man withdrawe, The which venerien is bore Be weie of kinde. *Ibid.* 130 Canis maior..The fifte sterre is of Magique, The whos kinde is venerien. **1530** PALSGR. 327/2 Veneryen, belongyng to Venus, *Venerien.* **1567** *Gude & Godlie B.* (S.T.S.) 211 O wickit vaine Veneriens, ȝe ar not Sanctis (thocht ȝe seem hally).

venerilla. *rare*$^{-1}$. [Dim. f. L. *Vener-*, *Venus.*] A little Venus.

1621 BURTON *Anat. Mel.* III. ii. III, He admires her on the other side, she is his idol, lady, mistress, venerilla, queen, the quintessence of beauty.

†**ve'nerious**, *a. Obs.* Also 6 -yous. [f. L. *venerius*: cf. OF. *venerieux* and VENEREOUS *a.*]

1. = VENEREAL *a.* 1.

1542 BOORDE *Dyetary* xviii. (1870) 246 Beware of Veneryous actes before the fyrste slepe. **1594** PLAT *Jewell-ho.* 8 Salt..is very stirring in our bodies, and provoketh them to venerious actes. **1607** WALKINGTON *Opt. Glass* vii. 44 b, Hee that presumes with his all-daring quill to put foorth lewde pamphlets,..to set vp a venerious schoole. **1634** SIR T. HERBERT *Trav.* 195 Titulation in venerious exercises. **1650** BULWER *Anthropomet.* 242 Immoderate Venery or venerious cogitations.

b. = VENEREAL *a.* 2.

1615 CROOKE *Body of Man* 247 Their inflamation or exulceration breeds the venerious gonorrhæa or running of the reines.

2. = VENEREOUS *a.* 1.

1547 BOORDE *Brev. Health* lvi. 25 [A] man that is full of heare is euer venerious. **1562** LEGH *Armory* 138 b, This prety Ruddoke,..of nature, though he be not Venerious, yet [etc.]. **1617** MORYSON *Itin.* III. 41 Aristotle saith, that they who ride most, are most venerious. **1634** SIR T. HERBERT *Trav.* 146 [The Persians are] mirthfull and venerious.

3. = VENEREOUS *a.* 3.

1620 VENNER *Via Recta* vii. 136 They are both somewhat windie and also venerious, especially the Parsnep.

Hence †**ve'neriousness**. *Obs.*⁻¹

1547 BOORDE *Brev. Health* cccxxvii. 106 This infirmitie doth come..of to much veneriousnes, specially used after a full stomake. **1727** in BAILEY (vol. II).

†**'venerist**. *Obs. rare.* [f. L. *Vener-*, *Venus*: see -IST.] One addicted to venery or lust.

1596 FITZ-GEFFREY *Sir F. Drake* (1881) 27 Cease to eternize in your marble verse The fals of fortune-tossed Venerists. **1623** COCKERAM I, *Venerist*, a whoremonger.

venerology, var. VENEREOLOGY.

'venerous, *a.* Also 6 venerus. [f. L. *Vener-*, *Venus*: see -OUS and cf. obs. F. *venereux.*]

†**1.** = VENEREAL *a.* 1. *Obs.*

1562 BULLEYN *Bk. Simples* (1579) 10 Dandelion..with Roses and Vineger..rebateth venerous and fleshly heat. **1594** CAREW *Huarte's Exam. Wits* xv. (1596) 265 Men who desire to satisfie their venerous lusts, do yet greatly shame to confesse it. **1603** HOLLAND *Plutarch's Mor.* 655 Hee was not so forward in venerous matters, nor given much to women. **1621** BURTON *Anat. Mel.* III. ii. II. iii, For a remedy of venerous passions. **1651** H. MORE *Enthus. Tri.* (1712) 37 A measurable Abstinence..from all venerous pleasures and tactual delights of the Body.

2. = VENEREOUS *a.* 2. Now *rare.*

1597 *Legh's Armory* 54 b, The Goate, sayeth Isidore, is verie venerous. **1607** WALKINGTON *Opt. Glass* 60 She is a venerous bird. **1651** H. MORE *Enthus. Tri.* (1712) 25 For it is very hard to find an healthy body very comely and beautiful, but the same proves more than ordinarily venerous and lustful. **1968** W. D. JORDAN *White over Black* I. 33 Long before the first English contact with West Africa, the inhabitants of virtually the entire continent stood confirmed in European literature as lustful and venerous.

†**3.** = VENEREOUS *a.* 3. *Obs.*

1587 HARRISON *Descr. Brit.* II. vi. in *Holinshed* I. 167/1 The potato and such venerous roots as are brought out of Spaine, Portingale, and the Indies to furnish vp our bankets. **1620** VENNER *Via Recta* vii. 137 They..are..of a venerous windy faculty. **1651** H. MORE *Enthus. Tri.* (1712) 28 For what means this bold purpose..but that his judgment was overclouded by some venerous fumes and vapours?

venery¹ ('vɛnərɪ). Now *arch.* Forms: 4-5 **veneri, -erye**, 5-7, 9 **venerie**, 5 **wenery**, 5- **venery**; 4 **venorye**, 5 **-ur(i)e**, 7 **-arie**, 7-8 **-ary**. [a. OF. *venerie* (F. *vénerie*), f. *vener*:—L. *venārī* to hunt: see -ERY.]

1. The practice or sport of hunting beasts of game; the chase. Also *attrib.*

c **1320** *Sir Tristr.* 296 On hunting oft he ȝede, To swiche a lawe he drewe.., More he couþe of veneri þan couþe manerious. *c* **1330** R. BRUNNE *Chron. Wace* (Rolls) 856 To venerye he gaf his tent; An herde of hertes sone þey met. **1422** YONGE tr. *Secreta Secret.* 247 Delite in honeste Play, and hit beholde, as..bestis to chase in venurie. **1486** *Bk. St. Albans* e v b, That is the first worde, my sonne, of venery. **1577** HARRISON *Descr. Brit.* II. xv, They..daily ouerthrew townes, villages, and an infinite sort of families for the maintenance of their Venery. **1602** *2nd Pt. Return fr. Parnass.* II. v. 893 These are your speciall beasts for chase, or as wee Huntsmen call it, for venery. *a* **1666** [see VENATICAL *a.*]. **1719** BOYER *Dict. Royal* II, A venery Book, or Book of Venery.

1837 W. IRVING *Capt. Bonneville* III. 122 These veterans of the wilderness are exceedingly pragmatical on points of venery and woodcraft. **1883** *Standard* 4 May 2/2 Other worthy professors of venery were glad to 'coach' him. **1891** J. G. AUSTIN *Betty Alden* 110 'Tis bad venerie when you have trapped a wolf to let him go free on the chance some other man will finish your work.

b. In the phrases ***beasts, game, hounds of venery***.

c **1400** MAUNDEV. (Roxb.) xxiii. 105 All maner of wylde bestez of wenery, as hertez and hyndez. **1432-50** tr. *Higden* (Rolls) VI. 379 That place..havynge in hit diverse kyndes of bestes of venery. *c* **1450** *Pol., Rel., & L. Poems* (1903) 60 Howndes of venery coste more then they aveyle. **1539** *Act 31 Hen. VIII*, c. 5 A chace..for norisshinge, generacion, and feeding of beastes of venery and of fowles of Warren. **1563** Q. ELIZ. *Let.* in Abp. Parker *Corr.* (Parker Soc.) 175 Keeper of park-houses, warrens, or other game of venerie. **1587** HARRISON *Descr. Brit.* II. xix. in *Holinshed* 206/1 The beasts of the chase were commonlie the bucke, the roe, the fox, and the marterne. But those of venerie in old time were the hart, the hare, the bore and the woolfe. **1603** G. OWEN *Pembrokeshire* (1892) 266 These beastes of chace are not in estimacion soe royall as the former beastes of Venerye. **1760-72** tr. *Juan & Ulloa's Voy.* (ed. 3) I. 436 Many beasts of venery, which feed on the straw or rush peculiar to those parts. **1765** BLACKSTONE *Comm.* I. 289 Forests are waste grounds belonging to the king, replenished with all manner of beasts of chase or venary.

†**2.** Wild animals hunted as game. Also *fig.*

c **1350** *Will. Palerne* 1685 Hyndes & hertes,..bukkes and beris and oþer bestes wilde, of alle fair venorye þat falles to metes. *c* **1440** *Ipomydon* 415 This lady to hyr mete gan gone, And of venery had hyr fille, For they had take game at wille. **1470-85** MALORY *Arthur* X. lxxxvii. 568 In the meane whyle syr Tristram chaced and hunted at alle maner of venery. **1539** ELYOT *Cast. Helthe* 29 The hunting of them [*sc.* deer] beinge not so pleasant, as the huntynge of other venery or vermyne. **1550** J. COKE *Eng. & Fr. Heralds* §3 Parkes..full of venery, as hartes, hyndes, falow-dere, wylde bores, and wolves for noble men to course. **1590** SPENSER *F.Q.* I. vi. 22 To the wood she goes, to..seeke her spouse, that from her still does fly, And followes other game and venery. **1630** *R. Johnson's Kingd. & Commw.* 115 Woods wonderfully abounding with venerie.

transf. **1550** LATIMER *Serm.* (1562) 114 b, They must haue swyne for theyr foode to make theyr veneryes or bacon of; theyr bacon is theyr venison.

†**3.** A place where hunting-dogs are kept. *Obs.*⁻¹

1653 URQUHART *Rabelais* I. lv. 242 The Venerie, where the Beagles and Hounds were kept, was a little farther off drawing towards the Park.

venery² ('vɛnərɪ). Also 5-6 **venerie**. [f. L. *Vener-*, *Venus* VENUS¹ + -Y.]

1. The practice or pursuit of sexual pleasure; indulgence of sexual desire.

1497 *Extr. Aberd. Reg.* (1844) I. 425 It was statut..that all licht weman be chargit and ordanit to decist fra thar vicis and syne of venerie. **1535** STEWART *Cron. Scot.* II. 430 As brutell beistis takand appetyte, In venerie putting thair haill delyte. **1567** MAPLET *Gr. Forest* 34 Birdes tongue, is an Herbe whose chief working is to prouoke Uenerie. **1607** DEKKER *Northward Hoe* III, Venery is like vsery,..it may be allowed tho it be not lawfull. **1643** SIR T. BROWNE *Relig. Med.* I. §30 A body, wherein there may be action enough to content decrepit lust, or passion to satisfie more active veneries. **1698** FRYER *Acc. E. India & P.* 378 Nor does it seldom fall out, from their aptness to Venery,..that they are afflicted with terrible *Mariscæ*. **1725** N. ROBINSON *Th. Physick* 152 The Passions of the Mind have a great Influence, as also excessive Venery. **1774** GOLDSM. *Nat. Hist.* (1776) III. 197 If the tusks..be broke away, the animal abates of its fierceness and venery. **1803** *Med. Jrnl.* IX. 139 He..gave himself up to his former intemperance in spirits and in venery. **1876** GROSS *Dis. Bladder*, etc. I. i. 18 Occasionally it [i.e. acute cystitis] is traceable to the effects of excessive venery.

†**2.** *fig.* A source of great enjoyment. *Obs.*

1602 MIDDLETON *The Phœnix* III. i. F 4, 'Twas e'en Venerie to me, y'faith, the pleasantst course of life. *a* **1625** FLETCHER *Noble Gent.* IV. iv, To me The fooling of this fool is venery.

Venes, obs. variant of VENICE.

'venesect, *v.* [Back-formation from next.] *intr.* To practise venesection. Hence **'venesecting** *ppl. a.*

1833 *Fraser's Mag.* VIII. 690 He was once a great enthusiast for the venesecting art.

venesection (vɛnɪ'sɛkʃən). *Med.* Also *β.* 7-9 **venæsection**. [ad. med. or mod.L. *vēnæ sectio* cutting of a vein: see VENA and SECTION.]

1. The operation of cutting or opening a vein; phlebotomy; the practice of this as a medical remedy.

α. **1661** LOVELL *Hist. Anim. & Min.* 327 The small-pocks ..are cured by..venesection in the adult. **1669** W. SIMPSON *Hydrol. Chym.* 78 Too much blood spent in venesection. **1767** GOOCH *Treat. Wounds* I. 370 We must first endeavour to stop the flux of blood,..repeating venesection occasionally. **1791** J. TOWNSEND *Journ. Spain* (1792) II. 39 Notwithstanding this repeated venesection, his pulse was remarkably full and strong. **1834** J. FORBES *Laennec's Dis. Chest* (ed. 4) 67 Leeching has the advantages and disadvantages of venesection, only in a less degree. **1877** F. T. ROBERTS *Handbk. Med.* (ed. 3) I. 29 To diminish the quantity of the blood, either by venesection, or by local methods.

β. **1676** WISEMAN *Surg. Treat.* I. iii. 16 The Fever which attends Pain is removed by Venæsection, or by the resolution or suppuration of the Tumour. **1728** CHAMBERS *Cycl.* s.v. *Angina*, In the external Angina, before any Suppuration appears, recourse is had to repeated Venæsection in the Jugulars. **1754-64** SMELLIE *Midwifery* I. 153 In a woman of a full habit of body venæsection is necessary. **1805** *Med. Jrnl.* XIV. 307 The wishes of the medical attendant who advises venæsection. **1884** PYE *Surg. Handicraft* 70 This expedient, with the practice of venæsection in general, has been out of fashion for many years now.

2. An instance of this.

1834 J. FORBES *Laennec's Dis. Chest* (ed. 4) 233 The same scene is renewed..after as many successive venesections. **1845** G. E. DAY *Simon's Anim. Chem.* I. 248 The three following tables show the mean results of the first, second, and third venesections. **1876** tr. *Wagner's Gen. Path.* 2 Change in the fibrin after frequent venesections.

'venesector. [Cf. VENESECT *v.*] Formerly, one who practises venesection; a blood-letter. In mod. use, one who takes blood samples as a profession; a phlebotomist.

1890 *Cosmopolitan* June 139 Our barber also acts as venesector. **1976** *Nursing Times* 17 June A53/3 (Advt.), Venesector required to take blood samples from patients for Pathology Department. **1977** *Lancet* 5 Nov. 969/2 The use of a technician rather than a medically qualified venesector is economical and reduces the need to involve the family doctor in the somewhat troublesome, repetitive, and perhaps tedious routine of taking, packaging, and posting, blood-samples.

Venesion, obs. form of VENETIAN.

veneso(u)n, -sun, obs. forms of VENISON.

†**venet**, *a. Obs. rare.* [ad. L. *venet-us.*] ***venet colour***, a greyish-blue colour.

c **1425** *MS. Digby 233* fol. 224/2 Loke þat..þe mennes clothing by coloured with venet colour þat is water coloure. *a* **1661** HOLYDAY *Juvenal* 226 Vegetius..says that ships, which are sent out as spies, should have their sails of the venet colour, that they may not be discerned by the enemies.

venet, obs. form of VIGNETTE.

†**ve'netia**. *Obs.*⁻¹ = VENETIAN *sb.* 2.

1579 G. HARVEY *Letter-Bk.* (Camden) 72 Eloquence, if a man had it, were more worth then..a payer of tatterid venetias in his presse.

Venetian (vɪ'niːʃən), *sb.* and *a.* Forms: *α.* 5 **Venycyen, Venecien**, 6 **Venesien**. *β.* 5-6 **Venecian**, 6 **-ycian, -esyan, -etyan**, 7- **Venetian**; 5 **Venicyan**, 7, 9 **Venitian**. *γ.* 6 **Venytyon, Venyscyon, Venecyon, Venesion**, 8 **Venition**. [ad. med.L. *Venetiān-us*, f. *Venetia* Venice: cf. It. and Pg. *Veneziano*, Sp. *Veneciano*. In early use also a. OF. *Venicien*, *-esien*, etc. (mod.F. *Vénitien*).]

A. *sb.* **1. a.** A native or inhabitant of mediæval or modern Venice; a member of the mediæval republic of Venice; more rarely, one of the ancient Veneti inhabiting the district of Venetia.

1432 LYDG. *Minor Poems* (Percy Soc.) 4 Other alyens:.. Florentyns, and Venycyens. *c* **1436** *Libel Eng. Policy* in *Pol. Poems* (Rolls) II. 172 The commodites..of Venicyans and Florentynes. *Ibid.* 175 These seyde Veneciance. **1528** in Ellis *Orig. Lett.* (1824) I. 294 His Highnes also liketh wel the Frenche Kings Lettres to the Venecians for Ravenna and Servia. **1547** BOORDE *Introd. Knowl.* xxiiii. (1870) 181, I am a Venesien both sober and sage. *Ibid.* 185 The Venyscions hath great prouision of warre. **1621** in Foster *Eng. Factories Ind.* (1906) I. 257 Two gentlemen, Venetians, who are not unknowne to you. **1695** LUTTRELL *Brief Rel.* (1857) III. 447 The Venetians, we hear, have taken several French ships. *a* **1715** BURNET *Own Time* v. (1734) II. 129 The Venetians and the Great Duke had not thought fit to own the King till then. **1756-7** tr. *Keysler's Trav.* (1760) IV. 57 German bravery under the auspices of the Venetians. **1841** W. SPALDING *Italy & It. Isl.* II. 164 There were other slaves besides Mohammedans in the service of the rich Venetians. **1876** BANCROFT *Hist. U.S.* I. v. 129 The Venetians.. purchased alike infidels and Christians. **1880** *Encycl. Brit.* XIII. 446/1 The Gauls, the Ligurians, and the Veneti or Venetians.

b. The dialect of Italian spoken by the inhabitants of Venice.

1598 [see LOMBARD *sb.*¹ 1 c]. **1642** [see ROMAN *sb.*¹ 3 c]. **1852** E. RUSKIN *Let.* 27 June in M. Lutyens *Effie in Venice* (1965) II. 328 You may imagine how I am put to it sometimes when three or four people question me at once in Venetian. **1901** M. CARMICHAEL *In Tuscany* 99 Had Dante ..written in Venetian..there would have been two classical languages in Italy today. **1921** R. L. GALES *Old-World Essays* 140 It is strange to think of these careless people, all talking Venetian in the clear Paduan air four hundred years ago. **1980** *Listener* 23 Oct. 528/2 Catalan..is to Castilian Spanish what Venetian is to Italian.

†**2. a.** *pl.* Hose or breeches of a particular fashion originally introduced from Venice. *Obs.*

1582 in Feuillerat *Revels Q. Eliz.* (1908) 350, vi paire of venetians of Russet gold tyncell. **1586** *Fermor Acc.* in *Archæol. Jrnl.* (1851) VIII. 183 It. for an ell half of brod taffaty to make him a dublet and venytyons. **1598** FLORIO, *Brache*, all maner of breeches, slops, hosen, breekes, gascoines, venetians. **1611** COTGR., *Chausses à la gigotte*, a fashion of very close Venitians; old fashioned Venitians. *a* **1612** HARINGTON *Epigr.* (1618) I. xx, A Captaine..brought three yards of Veluet, & three quarters To make Venetians downe below the garters.

†**b.** In sing. with *the*. *Obs.*⁻¹

1592 GREENE *Def. Conny-catching* Wks. (Grosart) XI. 95 The venetian and the gallogascaine is stale, and trunke slop out of vse.

†**3.** A sequin of Venice, as current in India and adjacent countries. *Obs.*

1698 FRYER *Acc. E. India & P.* 406 The Money which passes is a Golden Venetian, equivalent to our Angel. **1752** in J. Long *Sel. Unpubl. Recs.* 32 (Yule & B.), At this juncture a gold mohur is found to be worth 14 Arcot Rupees, and a Venetian 4½ Arcot Rupees. **1835** BURNES *Trav. Bokhara* (ed. 2) I. 90 You are then to present a handsome bow, and each of you eleven gold Venetians.

4. A closely-woven cloth having a fine twilled surface, used as a suiting or dress material.

1710 *Lond. Gaz.* No. 4706/4 For Sale.., Venitions,.. Tabbies,..and other Stuffs. **1883** SIMMONDS *Dict. Trade*, *Venetian*, a fine twilled fabric of carded wool for gentlemen's suits. **1899** *Daily News* 30 Oct. 2/6 The newest designs in coloured tweeds, serges, coverts, meltons,..Venetians, beavers, and cashmeres.

5. *ellipt.* †**a.** A Venetian window. *Obs.*

1766 ENTICK *London* IV. 376 The body of the church is enlightened by two ranges of windows, with a Venetian in the center. **1779** *Mirror* No. 61, His dusky Gothic windows have been contrasted to great advantage, with their Bows and Venetians.

b. A Venetian blind.

1816 'QUIZ' *Grand Master* VII. 167 They're soon disturb'd —a sudden rap 'Gainst the Venetians spoil'd their nap. **1881** EMMA J. WORBOISE *Sissie* xvi, It was observed that no one, all through the day, proposed raising that side-venetian.

c. *pl.* (See quot.)

1882 CAULFEILD & SAWARD *Dict. Needlew.* 514/1 *Venetians*, a heavy kind of tape or braid, resembling double Londons. They are employed more especially for Venetian blinds, whence the name.

6. = DOMINO 1.

1891 *Century Mag.* June 283, I then put off my sword, and put on my Venetian or domino, and entered the bal masqué.

B. *adj.* **1. a.** Of or pertaining to Venice. Also (*rare*), of or pertaining to the ancient Veneti of Gaul or Venetia.

1554 in Feuillerat *Revels Q. Mary* (1914) 166 A maske of viij patrons of galleis like venetian Senatours. **1593** G. HARVEY *New Lett.* Wks. (Grosart) I. 264 Who honoureth not..the security of the Venetian state. **1642** HOWELL *For. Trav.* (Arb.) 53 There is in Italy the Toscan, the Roman, the Venetian, the Neapolitan [languages],..and all these have severall Dialects and Idiomes of Speech. **1648** HEXHAM II, *De Venetiaensche Zee*, the Venetian Sea, or, the Gulfe of Venice. **1756–7** tr. *Keysler's Trav.* (1760) III. 378 It is now some centuries since Padua has been brought under the Venetian yoke. **1841** W. SPALDING *Italy & It. Isl.* III. 37 The republic at first embraced..the Venetian provinces of Bergamo, Brescia, and La Polesina. **1866** W. P. DICKSON tr. *Mommsen's Hist. Rome* IV. v. vii. 252 The legions expended their time and strength in the sieges of the Venetian towns. *Ibid.* 253 Caesar caused..the people of the Venetian canton to the last man to be sold into slavery. **1893** W. G. COLLINGWOOD *Life Ruskin* I. II. iv. 147 The treatment..of Venetian matters had to be indefinitely postponed. **1897** *Archæol. Jrnl.* LIV. 393 Through the Venetian traders the beautiful southern designs..on the golden and bronze ornaments in Ireland might..have been introduced.

b. ***Venetian School***, (*a*) a school of painting, distinguished by its mastery of colouring, which originated in the 15th century and reached its climax in the 16th; (*b*) a school of Italian architecture originating in the early part of the 16th century.

(*a*) **1748** MELMOTH *Fitzosborne Lett.* lxi. (1749) II. 116 On the contrary, the Venetian school is said to have neglected design a little too much. **1859** RUSKIN *Two Paths* I. §20 The Venetian school proposed to itself the representation of the effect of colour and shade on all things.

(*b*) **1842** GWILT *Archit.* §349 The Venetian School is characterised by its lightness and elegance; by the convenient distribution it displays; and by the abundant, perhaps exuberant, use of columns, pilasters, and arcades.

2. In special collocations, denoting things characteristic of Venice, esp. articles actually produced there, or others made in imitation of these. (Cf. similar uses of VENICE.)

Venetian ball (see quots.). ***Venetian bar***, in needlework, a bar formed by means of button-hole work on a thread or threads. ***Venetian blind***, a window-blind composed of narrow horizontal slats so fixed as to admit of ready adjustment for the exclusion or admission of light and air. ***Venetian blue***, a turquoise or cobalt blue. † ***Venetian breeches***, = VENETIAN *sb.* 2. ***Venetian brown***, a variety of brown used for colouring glass. ***Venetian carpet***, a common make of carpet, usually striped, in which the warp alone is shown. ***Venetian chalk*** (see quots.). ***Venetian cloth***, = VENETIAN *sb.* 4. ***Venetian dentil*** (see quot.). ***Venetian door*** (see quot. 1842). † ***Venetian earth***, ? Venetian chalk. ***Venetian embroidery*** (see quot.). ***Venetian enamel***, a hard enamel used for the dials of clocks and watches. ***Venetian filigree***, a variety of coloured glass. ***Venetian frame***, a form of window-frame (see quot. 1833). ***Venetian glass***, Venice glass. ***Venetian-Gothic*** adj. (see quot. 1867); also *absol.* as *sb.* † ***Venetian hose***, = VENETIAN *sb.* 2. ***Venetian mast***, a tall pole ornamented with spiral bands of colour, used in the decoration of streets or open spaces on special occasions. ***Venetian pearl***, a solid artificial pearl. ***Venetian point*** (***lace***), a variety of point-lace; also ***Venetian raised point*** (***lace***), a point lace in which all outlines are in relief; = *punto a rilievo* s.v. PUNTO[1] 7; cf. *Venice point* s.v. VENICE 1. ***Venetian red***, ***satin*** (see quots.). ***Venetian shutter***, a shutter constructed on the same principle as a Venetian blind; hence ***Venetian-shuttered*** adj. ***Venetian sole***, ***stitch*** (see quots.). † ***Venetian sublimate*** (?). ***Venetian sumach***, the southern European shrub *Rhus Cotinus*. ***Venetian swell***, an organ-swell having the front constructed like a Venetian shutter. ***Venetian talc***, a hydrous silicate of magnesia. † ***Venetian thyme*** (see quot.). ***Venetian turpentine***, Venice turpentine. ***Venetian varnish*** (see quot.). ***Venetian vetch***: see VETCH. ***Venetian white*** (see quot.). ***Venetian window*** (see quot. 1842). ***Venetian window-blind***, = Venetian blind. Also ***Venetian bead***, † ***dollar***, ***lace***.

1851–4 *Tomlinson's Cycl. Usef. Arts* (1866) I. 783/2 The *Venetian ball consists of a number of pieces of filigree glass packed into a pocket of transparent colourless glass. **1875** KNIGHT *Dict. Mech.* 2702/2 *Venetian ball*, an ornamental form of glass for paper-weights, etc. **1882** CAULFEILD & SAWARD *Dict. Needlew.* 511/2 *Venetian bar..is used in modern Point Lace. **1660** F. BROOKE tr. *Le Blanc's Trav.* 195 Some bracelets made of *Venetian Beads of several colours. **1791** in *Harper's Mag.* March (1885) 535/2 Surcharge for *Venetian blinds. **1794** W. FELTON *Carriages* I. 148 The Venetian blind..[is] frequently used as a substitute for the common shutter and spring curtain. **1840** DICKENS *Old C. Shop* xiv, It was easy to hear through the Venetian blinds all that passed inside. **1882** CAULFEILD & SAWARD *Dict. Needlew.* 514/1 Another kind of braid or tape is made for Venetian blinds. *c* **1840** LADY WILTON *Art of Needlework* vii. 75 A rich robe of *Venetian blue embroidered with golden eagles. **1947** J. H. BUSTANOBY *Princ. Color* 12/2 *Cobalt blue*, similar brands: Cobalt ultramarine, Hungary blue,..Venetian blue. **1976** *Milton Keynes Express* 18 June 40/4 (Advt.), New Kitten Estate. Venetian blue. **1587** FLEMING *Contn. Holinshed* III. 1354 Walton..rent his *venecian breeches of crimsin taffata, and distributed the same peecemeale. *c* **1791** *Encycl. Brit.* (ed. 3) VII. 774/2 *Venetian brown, with gold spangles, commonly called the philosopher's stone. **1845** G. DODD *Brit. Manuf.* IV. 95 '*Venetian' carpets were never, it has been asserted, made at Venice at all. **1868** *Rep. U.S. Commissioner Agric.* (1869) 51 Carpets, treble ingrain, three-ply, and worsted chain Venetian. **1839** URE *Dict. Arts* 1271 *Venetian chalk is Steatite. **1883** SIMMONDS *Dict. Trade*, *Venetian chalk*, a white compact talc or steatite, used for marking on cloth. *c* **1790** *Encycl. Brit.* (ed. 3) VI. 404/2 A new suit of French and *Venetian cloths. **1900** *Daily News* 6 Jan. 6/6 Venetian cloth is, next to panne, still the favourite material for dresses. **1881** *Archit. Dict.*, **Venetian dentil*, a molding consisting of a fillet with its sides cut alternately into notches, which reach the middle of the face, and produce the effect of a double row of dentils. **1626** in Foster *Eng. Factories India* (1909) III. 156 The *Venetian doller will yeald 5 mahmudis if full weight. **1731** POPE *Ep. Burlington* 36 Imitating-Fools Who..[are] Proud to catch cold at a *Venetian door. *a* **1744** —— *Hor. Sat.* II. vi. 191 Palladian walls, Venetian doors, Grotesco roofs, and Stucco floors. **1842** GWILT *Archit.* 1050 *Venetian door*, a door having side lights on each side for lighting an entrance hall. **1660** J. H[ARDING] *Basil. Valent. Chariot Antimony* 123 Mix one part of this Salt with three parts of *Venetian Earth. **1882** CAULFEILD & SAWARD *Dict. Needlew.* 512/1 *Venetian embroidery..is work resembling Roman Work and Strasbourg Embroidery, but is lighter than either in effect. **1837** HEBERT *Engin. & Mech. Encycl.* I. 468 [In] hard enamelling..the *Venetian enamels are chiefly employed. **1851–4** *Tomlinson's Cycl. Usef. Arts* (1866) I. 783/2 The *Venetian filigree consists of plain and coloured enamel. **1833** LOUDON *Encycl. Archit.* §1585 Fix a large solid *Venetian frame (a frame in three divisions, the two side divisions being narrower than the centre one). **1842** GWILT *Archit.* 639 Venetian deal cased frames. **1845** *Encycl. Metrop.* Index 139/2 *Venetian Glass. **1875** KNIGHT *Dict. Mech.* 2703/1 The Venetian-glass ball [see *Venetian ball*, quot. 1851–4]. **1849** E. RUSKIN *Let.* 3 Dec. in M. Lutyens *Effie in Venice* (1965) I. 81 We..looked over several Palaces. .. The outsides are splendid *Venetian Gothic. **1867** *Chambers's Encycl.* IX. 748/1 'Venetian-Gothic' [style of architecture] indicates the peculiar phase of that style so common in Venice and the north of Italy. **1933** J. BETJEMAN *Ghastly Good Taste* vii. 116 The red brick Flemish revival of Brondesbury and the Venetian Gothic of Kew. **1980** J. LEES-MILNE *Harold Nicolson* I. ix. 170 They went up the Canal in a gondola, arguing about Venetian-Gothic. **1583** STUBBES *Anat. Abus.* E 3, The *Venetian-hosen, they reach beneath the knee to the gartering place of the Leg. **1882** CAULFEILD & SAWARD *Dict. Needlew.* 513/1 In 1654 Colbert prohibited the exportation of the *Venetian Laces into France. **1883** *Harper's Mag.* Jan. 311/2 The Strand being one blaze of colour with *Venetian masts, and streamers overhead. **1886** BESANT *Childr. Gibeon* II. xxxiii, There should have been joy-bells and..Venetian masts with streamers and flags. **1864** *Chambers's Encycl.* VI. 5/1 *Venetian-point,..Maltese-point: in all these the pattern is flatter than in the Rose-point. **1872** F. B. PALLISER *Notes Hist. Lace* 27 Finest raised Venetian point. **1877** W. S. GILBERT *Foggerty's Fairy* I, Look at the lace! It's Venetian point. **1882** CAULFIELD & SAWARD *Dict. Needlework* 513/1 The raised Venetian Points were not worked before 1600. **1883** *Mag. of Art* Dec. 66/2 Richard III wore Venetian point at his coronation. **1882** CAULFIELD & SAWARD *Dict. Needlework* 513/1 The *Venetian Raised Points are extremely rich and varied. **1960** H. HAYWARD *Antique Coll.* 295/1 *Venetian raised point lace*, needlepoint. **1974** [see PUNTO[1] 7]. **1753** *Chambers' Cycl.* Suppl., *Veneta bolus*, a fine red earth used in painting, and called in the colour-shops *Venetian red. **1823** P. NICHOLSON *Pract. Build.* 413 Venetian-Red is a native ochre, rather inclining to scarlet. **1849–50** WEALE *Dict. Terms*, *Venetian-red*:..the colours sold under this name are prepared artificially from sulphate of iron, or its residuum in the manufacturing of acids. **1867** BLOXAM *Chem.* 322 Red oxide of iron has been already.. referred to as occurring in commerce under the names of colcothar, jeweller's rouge, and Venetian red. **1786** *Sixth Rep. Dep. Kpr. Public Rec.* App. II. 175 A method..of manufacturing Silk and Mohair,..with materials which have never before been combined or manufactured together [as wood, reed, cane, straw, etc.], and which is called (by the Specifier) '*Venetian Sattin'. **1844** H. STEPHENS *Bk. Farm* I. 142 *Venetian shutters, which may be opened more or less at pleasure. **1892** *Photogr. Ann.* II. p. cxxxiii, The Plate, after exposure, goes into back chamber, a Venetian shutter being opened and closed. **1897** MARY KINGSLEY *W. Africa* 86 An infinity of flies going into the venetian shuttered window. **1803** SHAW *Gen. Zool.* IV. II. 304 *Venetian Sole, *Pleuronectes Linguatula*. **1882** CAULFEILD & SAWARD *Dict. Needlew.* 514/1 **Venetian stitch*, a term sometimes applied to close rows of Buttonholes as Fillings in Needlepoint Laces. **1725** *Fam. Dict.* s.v. *Ulcer*, A Solution of *Venetian Sublimate. **1755** *Dict. Arts & Sci.* IV. s.v. *Sumach*, *Venetian Sumach, *cotinus*, in botany. **1846** LINDLEY *Veg. Kingd.* 467 *R[hus] Cotinus*,..Venetian Sumach of the English, has wood called Young Fustick. **1882** *Garden* 19 Aug. 163/3 There are few more striking objects than a large bush of the Venetian Sumach. **1852** SEIDEL *Organ* 27 The *Venetian Swell..is the only sort used in England. **1881** C. A. EDWARDS *Organs* 121 It is to Green that we owe the Venetian swell, which took its name from the resemblance it bears to the Venetian shutter. *a* **1728** WOODWARD *Fossils* I. 62 This very much resembles what is sold in the Shops for *Venetian Talc. **1836** T. THOMSON *Min., Geol.*, etc. I. 186 This mineral..was formerly carried to Venice as an article of commerce, being employed in medicine. Hence the name Venetian talc. **1548** TURNER *Names Herbes* (E.D.S.) 78 The greate kynde of thyme, wherof Dioscorides maketh mention of in Epithymo, is called nowe *Venetian thyme. **1597** A. M. tr. *Guillemeau's Fr. Chirurg.* 42 b/2 *Venetiane Terebentine. **1857** MILLER *Elem. Chem., Org.* 505, 48 parts of shell-lac, 12 of Venetian turpentine. **1755** *Dict. Arts & Sci.* s.v. *Varnish*, White varnish, called also *venetian varnish, made of oil of turpentine, fine turpentine, and mastic. **1867** *Ure's Dict. Arts* (ed. 6) III. 984 **Venetian white*, a carefully prepared carbonate of lead. **1779** SHAW *Hist. Moray* (1882) I. 347 It is lighted, besides several windows in the side-walls, by a *Venetian window..in the western gavel. **1837** LOCKHART *Scott* IV. v. 148 A square small room... It had but a single Venetian window. **1842** FRANCIS *Dict. Arts*, *Venetian window*, a window in three separate apertures, the two side ones being narrow, and separated from the centre by timber only. **1769** *Public Advertiser* 25 May 3/2 *Venetian Window Blinds made by Edward Bevan.

Hence **Ve'netianly** *adv.*

1851 H. MELVILLE *Moby Dick* II. xii. 91 Through all the wide contrasting scenery..flows one continual stream of Venetianly corrupt and often lawless life. **1965** *Guardian* 3 Apr. 7/5 If you want to eat well and Venetianly in Venice.. go to the best restaurants.

venetianed (vɪ'ni:ʃənd), *a.* [f. VENETIAN *sb.* 5 b.] Furnished with Venetian blinds or shutters.

1839 *Fraser's Mag.* XIX. 366 Through the open Venetianed window I caught a passing glimpse. **1854** STOCQUELER *Handbk. Brit. India* 125 The airy little bauleahs, with their light venetian'd rooms. **1881** MRS. C. PRAED *Policy & P.* III. 37 Along the white road, past the row of neat venetianed houses.

Venetic (vɪ'nɛtɪk), *a.* and *sb.* [f. L. *Venet-ī* or *Venet-ia* + -IC.] **A.** *adj.* Of or pertaining to the ancient Veneti, their country, or their language, or to the modern province of Venice.

1880 *Encycl. Brit.* XIII. 494/1 The population of the Venetian cities is 'Venetian' in language, but the country districts are in various ways Venetic. **1902** *Nature* 2 Jan. 212/2 Inscriptions on the outside of their rims, said to be in Venetic or old North Etruscan alphabet. **1903** *Ibid.* 29 Oct. 635 A large admixture of Albanian, Venetic, or Slav intruders. **1922** *Jrnl. Anthropol. Inst.* XXV. 214 Indiscriminate combinations of letters from the Venetic alphabet. **1949** M. S. BEELER *Venetic Lang.* 4 That the Venetic alphabet in particular is in fact derived from the Etruscan is now certain.

B. as *sb.* The language of the ancient Veneti.

1904 [see ETEOCRETAN *a.* and *sb.*]. **1932** [see MESSAPIAN *sb.* and *a.*]. **1977** [see RHAETIC *sb.*].

venett, obs. form of VIGNETTE.

venev, venew(e, obs. forms of VENUE.

veney, variant of VENY[2] *Obs.*

veneymen, obs. form of VENOM *v.*

Venezuelan (vɛnɪz'weɪlən, -'wɪ:lən), *a.* and *sb.* [See def.] **A.** *adj.* Of or pertaining to the republic of Venezuela in the north of South America. **B.** *sb.* A native or inhabitant of Venezuela.

1820 *Ann. Reg. 1819* 242/1 On every point the efforts of the Venezuelans were crowned with success. *Ibid.* 242/2 The Venezuelan fleet. **1836** *Penny Cycl.* V. 81/2 The congress of the Venezuelan Republic..at Angostura. *Ibid.* 82/1 The Venezuelan congress. **1881** W. H. BRETT *Mission Work Guiana* vi. 109 From the Spaniards and Venezuelans they have suffered greatly. **1882** CAULFEILD & SAWARD *Dict. Needlew.* 514/1 Venezuelan drawn work..resembles the Oriental Drawn Thread Work and the Italian and Swedish Drawn Works.

veng(e, southern ME. variant pa. t. FANG *v.*

† **venge**, *sb. Obs.* [f. VENGE *v.* Cf. AVENGE *sb.*] Vengeance.

1587 T. HUGHES *Misf. Arthur* I. ii, Why shunst thou feare-full wrath? Adde coales afreshe—preserve me to this venge. **1632** CHAPMAN & SHIRLEY *Ball* II. D 2 b, You must Lay in betimes to prevent mutinie Among the small guts, which with winde of venge else Will breake your guarde of buttons.

venge (vɛndʒ), *v.* Now *arch.* Forms: 4–5 **vengyn** (5 **vengy**), 4– **venge** (4 **venie, uenge**); 4–5 **wenge**, 4, 5 *Sc.*, **weng**. [ad. OF. *vengier*, *venger* (mod.F. *venger*, = It. *vengiare*, Sp. *vengar*, Pg. *vingar*):—L. *vindicāre* VINDICATE *v.* Cf. AVENGE *v.*]

1. a. *refl.* = AVENGE *v.* 1 b.

a **1300** *Cursor M.* 5345 For þat þai na wight drightin dred, He wenged him o þam ful sare. *a* **1340** HAMPOLE *Psalter* ii. 5 When he venges him, his vengaunce is cald woednes. *c* **1386** CHAUCER *Melib.* ¶45 But lete us now putte, that ye han leve to venge yow; I say ye ben nought of might ne power as now to venge you. *c* **1430** LYDG. *Min. Poems* (Percy Soc.) 31 Be nat to hasty to venge the on thi foo. *c* **1450** *Mirour Saluacioun* (Roxb.) 72 He vengid hym on his enemys horribly. **1509** FISHER *7 Penit. Ps.* vi. Wks. (1876) 18 Grete laude and prayse is in wylde beestes lackynge reason, that they wyll forgyue and not venge themselfe vpon other weyker beestes. **1581** A. HALL *Iliad* II. 29 Til that ech one here of vs al, at wil and ease be plast With Troyan Dames.. to venge vs of Paris. **1599** SHAKS. *Hen. V*, I. ii. 292 Tel you the Dolphin, I am comming on, To venge me as I may. **1817** SCOTT *Harold* II. xv, Thou shalt know, If I can venge me on a foe. **1914** *Contemp. Rev.* April 578 To venge themselves they pursued a policy of obstruction in the Diet.

b. *trans.* = AVENGE *v.* 1.

c **1325** *Metr. Hom.* 137 Ef thou prai Godd that he Apon thi fais venge the. *c* **1340** HAMPOLE *Pr. Consc.* 5533 Haly Loverd,..How lange sal be ar þow venge our blude Of our enemys þat in erthe duelles. *c* **1440** *Gesta Rom.* x. 29 (Harl. MS.), Do vs to knowe, if þer be eny þat þretenith þe; For we ben redy to venge þe. *c* **1450** LOVELICH *Grail* lvi. 435 Thus owre lord venged kyng Lawncelot certayn. **1581** A. HALL *Iliad* I. 16, I greatly dread, hir sonne to venge, obtainde some suit she hath. **1590** GREENE *Orlando Furioso* 1093 Now let vs seeke to venge the Lampe of France That lately was eclipsed in Angelica. **1613** HEYWOOD *Braz. Age* II. ii, I sweare..to.. venge the Gods that gouerne Sea and Sunne. **1814** SCOTT *Lord of Isles* III. xxix, With this he cross'd the murderer's path, And venged young Allan well! **1887** BOWEN *Æneid* IV. 656, I have..Venged a beloved one, meted a brother measure for guilt.

c. *pass.* = AVENGE *v.* 1 c.

c **1380** WYCLIF *Wks.* (1880) 24 For to plede, for to fiȝtte and..to be vengid on men þat don aȝenst here wille, worschipe, or profit. **1390** GOWER *Conf.* I. 202 Bot I wol make this beheste, I schal be venged er I go. *c* **1400** *Pilgr. Sowle* (Caxton) II. lvii. (1859) 55, I myght haue ben fully venged vpon the. **1480** *Cov. Leet Bk.* II. 441 Be-cause þe seid Laurens..feyned maters to þentent to haue be venged for þe due punysshement yeven to hym be þe seid Maire. **1489**

CAXTON *Faytes of A.* I. i. 7 They that gretly be vengid on their enemyes. **1611** B. JONSON *Catiline* II. i, I should be right sorry To have the means so to be venged on you.

†**d.** *intr.* = AVENGE *v.* 1 d. *Obs.*

13.. *E.E. Allit. P.* B. 201 [He] Ne venged for no vilte of vice ne synne,.. Ne neuer so sodenly soȝt vnsoundely to weng. *Ibid.* 559 Felly he uenged Quen fourferde alle þe flesch þar he formed hade. *c* **1400** *Destr. Troy* 7333 Achilles ..Of þo kynges, þat were kild,.. Wold haue vengit of þe velany, & þe vile harme. **14..** in Arnolde *Chron.* (1811) 208 A priest ought to be swete and softe more rather to foryeue than to vengy. *a* **1500** *Ratis Raving* 3540 Traist nocht thine honore in a fulle, Na weng nocht quhil thi blud be cule.

2. *trans.* = AVENGE *v.* 2.

1303 R. BRUNNE *Handl. Synne* 3806 Þys yche chylde toke hym to rede For to venge hys fadrys ded. *c* **1374** CHAUCER *Troylus* I. 62 (Harl. MS.), In dyverse wise.. The ravysshyng to vengyn of Heleyn, By Paris done, they wroughten all hir peine. *a* **1450** *Mirk's Festial* 44 The thre oþer also deyden on spytues deþes, so þat, wythyn þre ȝere aftyr, Thomas deth was thus venget. *c* **1489** CAXTON *Sonnes of Aymon* ix. 244, I praye god that I maye venge your deth vpon theym or ever I deceasse. **1538** STARKEY *England* 141 That hys ennemy may not pluke hym out at hys lyberty, nor yet in such place to venge hys iniury. **1587** TURBERV. *Trag. Tales* (1837) 160 To venge which deede, and cursed cruell acte, He slue them all. **1620** PYPER tr. *Hist. Astrea* I. II. 13 Venge not my death vpon this faire Lady. **1638** SANDERSON *Serm.* (1681) II. 111 We find our selves ready to fret at any cross occurrent, to venge every injury, to rage at every light provocation. **1802** LEYDEN in *Life & Poems* (1875) 39 Thine the mighty boast ..To venge each ancient violated bust. **1851** C. L. SMITH tr. *Tasso* XXIII. xlviii, And much he hoped with such a fiery brood To venge the felling of the precious wood.

†**b.** To punish (wrongdoing). *Obs.*

a **1340** HAMPOLE *Psalter* xxix. 5 Wreth, þat is vengaunce, þat he vengid in ȝow þe first syn with ded. *c* **1375** *Sc. Leg. Saints* xxv. (*Julian*) 116 Syk wykyt wordis of dyspyt In þat dekine ware wengyt tyt. **1401** *Pol. Poems* (Rolls) II. 111 Thou seist..that charite is chacid, to vengyn oure defautis, and mende us of oure mysse.

†**3.** = AVENGE *v.* 3. *Obs.*⁻¹

a **1470** HARDING *Chron.* LXV. iii, The Scottes and Peightes he venged & ouercam.

†**4.** To execute (vengeance); to wreak (anger) by vengeance. *Obs. rare.*

1382 WYCLIF *Jer.* li. 36 Lo! Y shal deme thi cause, and venge thi vengyng. *a* **1470** H. PARKER *Dives & Pauper* (W. de W. 1496) IV. xv. 179/2 He is goddes mynystre, to venge the wrath of god in hym that dooth amys.

vengeable, *a.* and *adv. Obs.* or *dial.* Forms: 4–5 **veniable,** 5–7 **vengable, vengeable** (6 **uen-**); 5 **vengeabyl, -yll(e, -abil.** [a. AF. *vengable* (Gower), f. *venger* VENGE *v.* Cf. VENGIBLE *a.*]

1. Inclined or ready to take vengeance or inflict retaliative injury. (Cf. VENGEFUL *a.* 1.)

a. Of persons (or animals).

Very common *c* 1400–1550; in mod. dial. use = destructive.

c **1380** WYCLIF *Sel. Wks.* II. 189 For ȝif he were veniable here no man myȝte suffre his veniaunce. **1390** GOWER *Conf.* II. 119 Such a Sor is incurable, And ek the goddes ben vengable. *c* **1400** LYDG. in *Pol., Rel. & L. Poems* (1903) 48 Where god list spare, a tygre is not vengeable. **1421** HOCCLEVE *Min. Poems* 153 Al-thogh þat shee were in this cas vengeable,.. Shee was in þat in partie excusable. *c* **1450** *Mirk's Festial* 140 Forto schew you how vengabull God ys apon hom þat ben lef forto sched Cristys blod. **1529** S. FISH *Supplic. Beggers* 3 Whate tiraunt euer oppressed the people like this cruell and vengeable generacion? **1547** BOORDE *Introd. Knowl.* xvii. (1870) 167 There is a beast called a Bouy, lyke a Bugle, whyche is a vengeable beast. **1573** G. HARVEY *Letter-bk.* (Camden) 138 To be notoriously revenged on this vengeable feende. *c* **1610** SIR J. MELVIL *Mem.* (1735) 206 The Appetites of envious, vengeable and greedy Counsellors. **1640** BASTWICK *Lord Bishops* iii. C 3, Who should prove the most vengable Instruments of persecuting and oppressing Gods true children. **1866** GREGOR *Banffsh. Gloss.* 232 Rottans are vengeable craiturs on young deuks.

b. Of the mind, will, etc.

1411–12 HOCCLEVE *De Reg. Princ.* 2330 He rathir chees be disobedient To his vengeable wil,.. Than be forsworn of þat he swoor so depe. **1513** BRADSHAW *St. Werburge* I. 1041 His vengeable mynde was hymselfe to magnyfy.. Or destroye hymselfe. **1539** CROMWELL in Merriman *Life & Lett.* (1902) II. 169 His Inique covetous and vengeable disposicion. **1540** HYRDE tr. *Vives' Instr. Chr. Wom.* (1592) H iiij, To keepe her vengeable mind unto.. occasion of revengement.

c. Of weapons.

c **1400** HOCCLEVE *Compl. Virgin* 179 Wel feele I þat deeth his vengeable bowe Hath bent, & me purposith doun to throwe. **1430–40** *Wycliffite Bible, Rom.* xiii. 4 (Cardwell MS.), For not withoute cause he berith the vengeable swerd.

2. Characterized by, arising from, vengeance or revenge; cruel, dreadful.

c **1430** HOCCLEVE *Min. Poems* 71/128 Þat the feend.. Ne sese hem nat in the vengeable day! *c* **1440** CAPGRAVE *Life St. Kath.* IV. 1414 Ȝe shulde not suffren þis cristen foolk here Repreue oure goddis with swiche veniable manere. **1509** BARCLAY *Shyp of Folys* (1570) 201 For none.. This hurt outchaseth which is so vengeable. **1582** STANYHURST *Æneis* I. (Arb.) 29 Such folck as the tyrant pursude with vengeabil hatred. **1627** H. BURTON *Baiting Pope's Bull* 18 Iezabell, for all her vengeable malice and impotent fury, yet could not wreck it vpon Elias.

3. As an intensive: Very great, severe, strong, intense, etc.

1532 MORE *Confut. Tindale* Wks. 655/2 As the churche of Christe is but one, so be there of those [heretics] a vengeable maynye. **1542** UDALL *Erasm. Apoph.* 49 b, He gave a vengeable check to those persones. **1583** STOCKER *Civ. Warres Lowe C.* IV. 61 A mischeuous mistakyng of a matter ..bredde a vengeable suspition in the heddes of many. **1601** DEACON & WALKER *Spirits & Divels* To Rdr. 13 [They] will couertly flutter their wings, and keepe a vengeable coyle in Conuenticles and corners.

b. As *adv.* = VENGEABLY *adv.* 2.

1542 UDALL *Erasm. Apoph.* 7 Socrates asked wherfore he was so vengeable eagre. **1566** *Pasquine in Traunce* 48 A vengeable long leape, or a vengeable lowde lye. **1866** GREGOR *Banffsh. Gloss.* 232 He's vengeable greedy; he can hardly be honest.

4. Punishable. *rare*⁻¹.

1650 S. CLARKE *Eccl. Hist.* I. (1654) 488 [He] delivered him over to the secular power; Declaring that..it was a vengeable matter to eat or drink with him.

'vengeably, *adv.* Now *arch.* or *Obs.* Also 5 **vengably,** 6 **vengeablie, -eiably, veangeably.** [f. prec.]

1. In a revengeful manner; vindictively; cruelly, pitilessly.

1412–20 LYDG. *Chron. Troy* IV. 2775 Þis Achille of cruelte ..þe dede cors toke oute of þe taas, And vengably bond it. *a* **1450** *Knt. de la Tour* (1868) 105 Right so it plesed vnto God that he shulde deye vengeably. *c* **1489** CAXTON *Sonnes of Aymon* xx. 453 He.. smote a knyghte soo vengably that he cast hym doun deed to the erthe. **1549** LATIMER *4th Serm. bef. Edw. VI* (Arb.) 103 So that they do it charitiablye louyngelye, not of malyce, not vengeably, not couetouslye. **1586** J. HOOKER *Hist. Irel.* in *Holinshed* II. 78/1 The Irish enimie..vengeablie haue brent a great towne of mine inheritance in Meth, called Ramore.

1848 ANNE BRONTE *Agnes Grey* xiv, Miss Matilda, having ..vengeably thumped the piano for an hour, in a terrible humour both with me and it.

2. Exceedingly, greatly, very.

c **1550** BALE *Apol.* 113 But ye are lyke to come vengeably short. **1575** LANEHAM *Let.* (1871) 12 It woold haue made mee, for my part, az hardy az I am, very veangeably afeard. **1607** R. C[AREW] tr. *Estienne's World of Wond.* 291 Some [priests and monks].. haue bin so vengeably learned.

vengeance ('vɛndʒəns), *sb.*, *adv.*, and *a.* Forms: α. 4 **veniance, -iaunce, -y(e)aunce,** 4–5 **venieaunce,** 5 **veniauns, -iawnce, weniaunce;** 4 **veniounse,** 5 **venions.** β. 4 **vengaunse,** 4–6 **-aunce,** 4–5 **-ance, -ans;** 4 **vengiaunce,** 5 **-anse,** 6 **-ans;** 4 **vengeans,** 4–6 **-aunce,** 4– **vengeance** (7 **veng'ance**), 6 **vengence;** 4 **wengans, -anz, -aunce, -eans, -eance,** 4, 6 *Sc.*, **wengance,** 6 *Sc.* **wengence.** [a. AF. *veniaunce, -ance, veng(e)aunce, -ance,* = OF. and F. *vengeance* (It. *vengianza*, Sp. *venganza*, Pg. *vinganza*), f. *venger* VENGE *v.*]

1. The act of avenging oneself or another; retributive infliction of injury or punishment; hurt or harm done from vindictive motives.

a **1300** *Cursor M.* 827 Son bigan wenganz to kiþe. *Ibid.* 13184 But þis ded was sald ful dere,.. Wit a greithful soth vengeance. *c* **1315** SHOREHAM III. 248 He þat spilleþ mannes lyf, Veniounse hyt schel acwyte. *c* **1380** WYCLIF *Serm.* Sel. Wks. I. 149 Þis is noo good praier, but more axinge of Goddis venjaunce. *a* **1450** *Knt. de la Tour* (1868) 37 She tolde..that it was the uengeaunce of God that fell on her, the whiche she had welle deserued. **1474** CAXTON *Chesse* II. iv. (1883) 53 For hit is the most hyest and fayr vengeance that a man may doo. **1535** COVERDALE *Ps.* xciii. 1 Thou God to whom vengeaunce belongeth, shewe thy self. **1592** KYD *Murther I. Brewen* Wks. (1901) 287 The blood of the iust Abel cried.. for vengeance and reuenge on the murderer. **1613** PURCHAS *Pilgrimage* (1614) 156 Diuine mercie.. remoued the Christians to Pella out of the danger, that without any impediment the floud-gates of vengeance might bee set wide open for Desolations black-guard to enter. **1667** MILTON *P.L.* I. 170 But see the angry Victor hath recall'd His Ministers of vengeance and pursuit Back to the Gates of Heav'n. **1757** GRAY *Bard* 96 Stamp we our vengeance deep, and ratify his doom. **1769** *Junius Lett.* xv. (1788) 92 The injuries you have done..demand not only redress, but vengeance. **1837** W. IRVING *Capt. Bonneville* III. 67 Alarm signals, to arouse the country and collect the scattered bands for vengeance. **1891** FARRAR *Darkn. & Dawn* xxv, That in some way she regarded Britannicus..as the ultimate resource of her vengeance and despair.

b. In the phrase *to take* (also †*nim*) *vengeance*.

1297 R. GLOUC. (Rolls) 6859 Þe king..suor he nolde abide, Þat he nolde uerst nyme vengaunce in is side. *a* **1300** *Cursor M.* 6094 Þair goddes i me on wil wrake, O þam mi wengeance sal i take. *c* **1386** CHAUCER *Melib.* ¶ 49 Savinge your grace, I can nat seen that it mighte greetly harme me though I toke vengeaunce. *c* **1400** *Rom. Rose* 5780 God can wel vengeaunce therof take. *c* **1400** MAUNDEV. (Roxb.) xii. 51 In taken of þe vengeaunce þat Godd tuke on þa fyue citeez. **1460** CAPGRAVE *Chron.* (Rolls) 106 He receyved him with grete worchip, took veniauns on his enimes. *c* **1489** CAXTON *Sonnes of Aymon* ii. 59 Vengance we sholde take therof. **1526** TINDALE *Rom.* xiii. 4 To take vengeaunce on them that do evyll. **1611** SHAKS. *Cymb.* v. i. 8 Gods, if you Should haue 'tane vengeance on my faults, I neuer Had liu'd to put on this. **1727** BAILEY (vol. II), *Avenger*, one who takes Vengeance on an Offender. **1808** SCOTT *Marmion* II. xxxi, Full soon such vengeance will he take, That [etc.]. **1847** SARAH AUSTIN *Ranke's Hist. Ref.* III. 17 The strong city of Pavia, on which cruel vengeance was taken for the resistance it had made.

c. Personified or otherwise regarded as an entity.

1602 SHAKS. *Ham.* II. ii. 510 Arowsed Vengeance sets him new a-worke. **1642** D. ROGERS *Naaman* 39 Left to conflict nakedly with hell and vengeance, till it carry them away quicke. **1721** YOUNG *Revenge* II. i, Vengeance is still alive; from her dark covert.. She stalks in view. **1799** CAMPBELL *Pleas. Hope* I. 395 Where was thine arm, O Vengeance! *a* **1839** PRAED *Red Fisherman*, Look how the fearful felon gazes On the scaffold his country's vengeance raises. **1891** MARIE A. BROWN tr. *Runeberg's Nadeschda* 67 Then saw I vengeance beckon, it lit my path In years of woe.

2. With *a* and pl. An act or instance of retributive or vindictive punishment. (Also as in 1 c.)

a **1300** *Cursor M.* 1592 For-þi in forme of iugement He thoght a neu wengaunce to sent. *c* **1400** *Sowdone Bab.* 14 For the offences to God i-doon Many vengeaunces haue be-falle. *c* **1440** *Jacob's Well* 41 Foure vengaunces comyn to man here in erthe for fals tythyng. *c* **1480** HENRYSON *Fables, Wolf & Lamb* xxi, It cryis ane vengeance vnto the heuinnis hie. **1659** HAMMOND *On Ps.* cix. 6–10 Sad executions, judgments, and vengeances. *a* **1704** T. BROWN *Sat. agst. Woman* Wks. 1730 I. 56 He falls a willing pris'ner to her arms, There meets a veng'ance of ne'er-ending harms. **1718** POPE *Iliad* XIII. 832 With his full strength he bent his angry bow, And wing'd the feather'd vengeance at the foe. **1728** P. WALKER *Life Peden* (1901) I. 155 Hasty marriages are sudden vengeances. **1791** BURKE *App. Whigs* Wks. VI. 220 Taking.. a cruel vengeance on these deluded wretches. **1838** THIRLWALL *Greece* xxxi. IV. 201 Thrasybulus..animated his men by..the prospect of a just vengeance. **1873** MISS BROUGHTON *Nancy* I. 45, I am planning five distinct and lengthy vengeances against Bobby.

b. In imprecations, usually with *on.* Also rarely without article. *Obs.* or *arch.*

? *a* **1500** *Chester Pl.* XIII. 164 Must we afore the pharisies appeare? A vengeance on them, far and neere! **1562** J. HEYWOOD *Prov. & Epigr.* (1867) 178 A vengeance on that lame iade. **1591** SHAKS. *Two Gentl.* II. iii. 21 A veng'ance on't, there 'tis. **1604** [? CHETTLE] *Wit of Woman* G 4 b, A vengeance pepper such braines, as cannot beare one draught of Ipocras. **1814** SCOTT *Wav.* xxx, D'ye think the lads..will care for..yer stool o' repentance? Vengeance on the black face o't!

c. A person of a violent temper.

1711–2 SWIFT *Jrnl. to Stella* 21 Mar., The D—— he is! married to that vengeance!.. Who would have her?

3. Used to strengthen interrogations. ? *Obs.*

1598 R. BERNARD tr. *Terence* (1607) 167 *Thr.* Where are the other? *San.* What other in a vengeance. **1607** SHAKS. *Cor.* III. i. 262, I would they were in Tyber. What the vengeance, could he not speake 'em faire? **1620** *Frier Rush* 28 His wife..said vnto him: what a vengance needest thou to take a seruant? **1663** BUTLER *Hud.* I. iii. 213 But what a-vengeance makes thee fly From me too, as thine Enemy? *a* **1779** D. GRAHAM *Writings* (1883) II. 40 What the vengeance uncle, sudna fouks die when they're auld? **1828** SCOTT *F.M. Perth* vi, Art thou beside thyself, boy? or what a vengeance takes thee from the city, like the wing of the whirlwind?

4. *with a vengeance*: †**a.** With a curse or malediction. *Obs.*

1525 W. SMITH *Merry Iests Widow Edyth* (1573) D j b, In she goth,.. And came out agayne, saying wᵗ a vengeaunce: They must go by water. **1581** HANMER *Jesuites Banner* E 2 b, Let such then goe with a vengeaunce, and leaue those toyes for Poets to prate of and let them preach better stuffe vnto the people. **1598** R. BERNARD tr. *Terence, Andria* II. i, *Abi hinc in malam crucem.* Away with a vengeance: get thee hence with a mischiefe: goe hence with sorrow enough. **1635** R. N. tr. *Camden's Hist. Eliz.* IV. 493 The Queene..waxing impatient gave him [Essex] a cuffe on the eare and bade him be gone with a vengeance. **1673** *Vinegar & Mustard* (Hindley) III. 8 You are land-sick now, and not sea-sick, with a vengeance to you for me. **1836** CARLYLE in Froude *Life in London* I. 70 Why not quit literature—with a vengeance to it—and turn, were it even to sheep herding?

b. As an intensive: With great force or violence; in an extreme degree; to an unusual extent.

1568 V. SKINNER tr. *Montanus' Inquisition* 24 b, He shall come downe with a vengeaunce. **1594** GREENE & LODGE *Looking Gl.* I. ii. 236 A plaister..that mends him with a verie vengeance. **1611** MIDDLETON & DEKKER *Roaring Girle* M j, Are you too well, too happy? *Alex.* With a vengeance. **1654** H. L'ESTRANGE *Chas. I* (1655) 88 The furious multitude.. struck him down, and malled him with a vengeance. **1673** [R. LEIGH] *Transp. Reh.* 63 Accordingly he lays it on with a vengeance. **1711** 'J. DISTAFF' *Char. Don Sacheverellio* 6 This ..is proving the..Existence of Gyants..with a Vengeance. **1761** FOOTE *Liar* II. Wks. 1799 I. 293 His friends..gloss over his foible, by calling him an agreeable novelist: and so he is, with a vengeance. **1834** L. RITCHIE *Wand. by Seine* 94 Some readers will think that we are drawing our traveller's bow with a vengeance. **1867** M. ARNOLD *Celtic Lit.* 29 Here, at any rate, are materials enough with a vengeance.

†**c.** So *with the vengeance*. *Obs.*⁻¹

1693 *Humours Town* 29 This is following the Dictates of Reason with the vengeance.

†**5.** As *adv.* **a.** Extremely, intensely. *Obs.*

1548 [L. SHEPHERD] *John Bon & Mast person* (1808) 5 Is not here a mischeuous thynge? The Messe is vengaunce holye for all ther sayeinge. **1566** *Pasquine in Traunce* 41, I remember that disputation. It is vengeaunce subtile. *Ibid.* 44 They were also vengeance angry against the Pope. **1607** SHAKS. *Cor.* II. ii. 6 That's a braue fellow: but hee's vengeance prowd. *a* **1616** BEAUM. & FL. *Little Fr. Lawyer* II. i, How it grumbles! This Sword is vengeance angry. **1710–11** SWIFT *Jrnl. to Stella* 21 Jan., It has snowed terribly all night, and is vengeance cold.

†**b.** Not at all, never. *Obs.*

1556 J. HEYWOOD *Spider & Fly* xxxix. 7 Vengeance the whit I am for their woordes the nere.

†**6.** As *adj.* Very great or large. *Obs.*⁻¹

1602 FULBECKE *2nd Pt. Parall.* Introd. 4, I bought the booke..because it was in English: yet there is a vengeance deale of Latin in it.

7. *attrib.* and *Comb.*, as ***vengeance-cryer, -crying, -oath, -scathed, -sword, -taking.***

c **1386** CHAUCER *Melib.* ¶ 65 For al-be-it so that alle tarying be anoyful, algates it is nat to repreve in yevinge of Iugement, ne in vengeance-taking, whan it is suffisant and resonable. *c* **1515** *Cocke Lorell's B.* 11 Cursers, chyders, and grete vengeaunce cryers. **1608** SYLVESTER *Du Bartas* II. iv. *Schisme* 1061 Lord, sheath again thy vengeance-sword a space. **1617** A. NEWMAN *Pleas. Vis.* 15 Haples wretches, with the memory Tortur'd of woe, and vengeance-crying Sins. **1838** S. BELLAMY *Betrayal* 43 When o'erthrown In first rebellion, vengeance-scathed he fled. **1844** MRS. BROWNING *Duchess May* xxviii, Thou and I have parted troth,—yet I keep my vengeance-oath.

Hence †'**vengeancely** *adv.*; †'**vengeancer**.

c **1440** *Promp. Parv.* 508/2 Veniawncere, . . *vendicator, ultor, vindex.* **1622** FLETCHER *Prophetess* I. iii, Yet I could poyson him in a Pot of Perry, He loves that veng'ancely.

†'**vengeant**, *a. Obs.*⁻¹ In 4 vengaunt. [a. AF. *vengant* (F. *vengeant*), pres. pple. of *venger* VENGE *v.*] Avenging; executing vengeance.

a **1340** HAMPOLE *Psalter* xcviii. 9 Lord oure god þou herd þaim: god þou was til þaim merciabil, and vengaunt in all þaire fyndyngis.

vengear, obs. form of VENGER.

vengeful ('vɛndʒfəl), *a.* [f. VENGE *v.*, after *revengeful*. Cf. AVENGEFUL *a.*]

1. Harbouring revenge; seeking vengeance; prone or inclined to avenge oneself; vindictive.

a **1599** SPENSER *F.Q.* VII. vi. 48 [She] thinkes what punishment were best assign'd And thousand deathes deuiseth in her vengefull mind. **1701** F. MANNING *Poems* 77 A worse Event . . The vengeful Cupid sent. **1713** SWIFT *On Himself* Wks. 1755 IV. I. 12 The queen incens'd, his services forgot, Leaves him a victim to the vengeful Scot. *a* **1763** SHENSTONE *Inscription* vi. 24 Fair and flow'ry is the brake, Yet it hides the vengeful snake. **1812** COMBE *Syntax, Picturesque* xxv. 452 Again the vengeful foes appear'd, Again their angry standards rear'd. **1856** KANE *Arct. Expl.* I. xxx. 414 One of them, the male, is excited—the other, the female, collected and vengeful. **1873** SYMONDS *Grk. Poets* i. 9 Ulysses is . . pitiless in his hostility; subtle, vengeful, cunning.

transf. *c* **1600** SHAKS. *Sonn.* xcix, But for his theft . . A vengfull canker eate him vp to death. **1848** FABER *Spir. Confer.* (1870) 124 Wasted time is a vengeful thing. **1879** GEO. ELIOT *Theo. Such* iv. 159 An abandoned belief may be more effectively vengeful than Dido.

b. Inflicting vengeance; serving as an instrument of vengeance. Said of a weapon, the hand or arm, etc.

(*a*) *a* **1586** SIDNEY *Ps.* XXI. xii, Thou shalt . . ready make thy vengefull bow Against their guilty faces. **1593** SHAKS. *2 Hen. VI*, III. ii. 198 Here's a vengefull Sword, rusted with ease. *a* **1623** FLETCHER *Love's Cure* v. iii, I pray His vengeful sword may fall upon thy head Successfully. **1725** POPE *Odyss.* I. 154 The proud oppressors fly the vengeful sword. **1807** G. CHALMERS *Caledonia* I. II. iii. 253 The victorious career of Ida was stopt . . by the vengeful sword of the valorous Owen. **1869** GOULBOURN *Purs. Holiness* i. 1 So could he bid the vengeful fire fall from heaven.

(*b*) **1696** TATE & BRADY *Ps.* cvi. 17 Her vengeful Jaws extending wide. **1729** T. COOKE *Tales*, etc. 140 Of all who fought beneath this Chief's Command Not one escap'd the Critic's vengeful Hand. **1748** JOHNSON *Van. Hum. Wishes* 168 Rebellion's vengeful talons. *a* **1800** COWPER *Iliad* (ed. 2) XXI. 343 Allow no respite to thy vengeful arm Till ev'ry Trojan . . within Ilium's lofty walls Be fast enclosed.

2. Of actions or feelings: Characterized or prompted by revengeful motives; arising from a desire for vengeance.

1635–56 COWLEY *Davideis* III. Poems (1905) 328 Full thrice six years they felt fierce Eglons yoke, Till Ehuds sword Gods vengeful Message spoke. **1649** MILTON *Eikon.* viii. Wks. 1851 III. 392 That choleric, and vengefull act of proclaiming him Traitor. **1709** PRIOR *Carm. Sec.* xvii, With wise Silence pond'ring vengeful Wars. **1774** GOLDSM. *Nat. Hist.* VII. 193 To us who seldom feel the vengeful wound, it is merely a subject of curiosity. **1818** SCOTT *Hrt. Midl.* xxix, The fury darted her knife at him with the vengeful dexterity of a wild Indian. **1845** LD. CAMPBELL *Chancellors* liv. (1857) III. 77 In no composition that I have met with is there a greater display of vengeful malignity. **1874** GREEN *Short Hist.* viii. §7. 534 The Massacre had left them the objects of a vengeful hate.

Hence '**vengefully** *adv.*, '**vengefulness**.

1830–1 RUSKIN *Iteriad* II. 300 His dark lightning-eye made him seem . . like his own Thalaba, *vengefully fired. **1844** KINGLAKE *Eothen* iv, On he goes vengefully thirsting for the best blood of Troy. **1897** *Advance* (Chicago) 31 July 143/1 He looked at his mother vengefully. **1727** BAILEY (vol. II), *Vengefulness, vindictive or revengeful Temper or Nature. **1862** MEREDITH *Poet. Wks.* (1912) 134 He fainted on his vengefulness, and strove To ape the magnanimity of love.

†'**vengement**. *Obs.* [a. OF. *vengement*, f. *venger* VENGE *v.* Cf. AVENGEMENT.] Vengeance.

1338 R. BRUNNE *Chron.* (1810) 197, I wille of þat feloun tak vengement, þat so fordos my coroun. **1390** GOWER *Conf.* III. 282 His oghne brother therupon . . Tok of that Senne vengement. **1484** CAXTON *Curiall* 2, I telle to the that thy vengement shal engendre to the more greuous aduersytes. **1555** WATREMAN *Fardle Facions* App. 351 That thei should take vengemente vpon them, bothe by officer, and without. **1596** SPENSER *F.Q.* VI. iii. 18 Witnesse thereof he shew'd his head there left, And wretched life forlorne for vengement of his theft.

vengence, -ency, varr. VENGEANCE, -ANCY.

†'**vengeously**, *adv. Obs. rare.* [Irreg. f. VENGE *v.* Cf. VENGEAUNCEABLY.] Violently, viciously.

1599 BRETON *Miseries Manillia* Wks. (Grosart) II. 43/1 If I did but even touch her, the monkie would set out the throate, and crie so vengeouslie, that to it must the mother come. **1824** in *Spirit Pub. Jrnls.* (1825) 312 He came up to me so vengeously in the street, and I said to him, 'Can't it be done without fighting?'

venger ('vɛndʒə(r)). Forms: 4–5 veniour, -iere, vengere, 5– venger (5 wen-), 6 vengear (van-). [a. AF. or OF. *vengeour (vangeor, vencheur*, F. *vengeur*) and *vengiere*, agent-n. f. *venger* VENGE *v.*] An avenger. Now *poet.* or *rhet.*

a **1340** HAMPOLE *Psalter* viii. 3 þat þou distroy the enmy & þe vengere. *c* **1380** WYCLIF *Sel. Wks.* III. 297 He is Goddis mynystre, vengere into wraþþe to hym þat doþ evyl. **1382** —— *Hosea* v. 13 And Effraym wente to Assur, and sente to the kyng veniour. **1447** BOKENHAM *Seyntys* (Roxb.) 54 And this I wyl thou know for sekyrnesse That god is wenger of wyckydnesse. **1483** *Cath. Angl.* 400/1 A venger, *vindex, vindicator.* **1526** TINDALE *Prol. Ep. Romans* A iij, Thou woldest thatt their were no . . God, the auctor and vangear of the lawe. **1590** SPENSER *F.Q.* I. iii. 20 His bleeding hart is in the vengers hand. **1601** YARINGTON *Two Lament. Trag.* IV. viii. in Bullen *O. Pl.* IV, I, he is well, in such a vengers handes, As will not winck at your iniquitie. **1865** *Reader* 16 Sept. 399/2 Other champion of our cause shall come, . . venger of his sire. **1881** H. PHILLIPS tr. *Chamisso's Faust* 10 The Venger's Vengeance smites the guilty head.

†'**vengeress**. *Obs. rare.* [a. OF. *vengeresse*: cf. prec. and -ESS.] A female avenger.

In quot. *c* 1450 as the name of a spear.

c **1374** CHAUCER *Boeth.* III. met. xii. (1868) 107 þe þre goddess s, furijs, and vengerisse of felonies. *c* **1450** *Merlin* xiv. 229 This kynge alain was seke of the woundes of the spere vengeresse [F. *la lance vengeresse*]. **1490** CAXTON *Eneydos* xxvii. 99 O cruelle vltryces, wycked vengeresses, Furyes infernalle & Iusticers of helle. **1647** HEXHAM I, A vengeresse, *een wreeckster.*

†**vengesour**. *Obs. rare.* [f. OF. *vengeis-on* vengeance.] An avenger.

1382 WYCLIF *Lev.* xxvi. 25 And I shal brynge vpon ȝow a swerd, vengesoure [1388 vengere] of my boond of pees. —— *Numb.* xxxv. 25 The hoond of the vengesour.

†'**vengible**, *a.* and *adv. Obs.* [var. of VENGEABLE *a.*]

1. Vengeful, vindictive.

1548 COOPER *Elyot's Dict.*, *Dirus*, . . vengible, cruell, terrible. **1595** *Locrine* I. ii. 16 The desperate god Cuprit, with one of his vengible birdbolts, hath shot me vnto the heele. **1607** TOPSELL *Four-f. Beasts* 461 These also are the Epethites of the Lionesse: . . bold, stony-harted, vengible. **1609** HOLLAND *Amm. Marcell.* 321 A vengible wayt-layer, . . by bloudie grudges and displeasures doing much mischief.

b. Grievous, severe.

1601 HOLLAND *Pliny* I. 4 Impose they doe upon them hard and vengible charges to execute.

2. Remarkable, extraordinary. Also as *adv.*

1594 LYLY *Mother Bombie* III. ii, He spake nothing but sentences, but they were vengible long ones. **1602** *Contention betw. Liberality & Prodigality* IV. ii, Thornes, thistles, and nettles most horrible stingers, Rauens, grypes, and gryphons, oh vengible wringers. **1610** HOLLAND *Camden's Brit.* I. 78 Hee was a vengible fellow in linking matters together, whereupon he came to be surnamed Catena, that is, a chain.

Hence †'**vengibly** *adv. Obs.*

1580 G. HARVEY *Three Lett.* Wks. (Grosart) I. 40 Some as vengibly and frowardly bent, as for Example, Woormes, and Moules, and Cunnyes.

venging, *vbl. sb.*: see VENGE *v.* 4 (quot. 1382).

'**venging**, *ppl. a.* [f. VENGE *v.*] Avenging; executing vengeance.

c **1470** *Gol. & Gaw.* 759 Thay fechtin sa fast, With vengeand wapnis of were throu wedis thai wet. **1598** SYLVESTER *Du Bartas* II. i. *Imposture* 495 So that th' old yeers' renewed generations Cannot asswage his venging indignations. **1605** *Ibid.*, *Sonn. Late Peace* xxvi, The furie of Heav'ns venging Sword.

vengit, obs. Sc. form of WINGED *a.*

‖**vengolina**. *Obs.* [mod.L., = F. *vengoline* (Buffon), from the native name in Angola, given as *benguelinba* by Edwards.] The Angola finch (*Serinus angolensis*).

1773 *Phil. Trans.* LXIII. 254, I therefore educated a young linnet under a vengolina, which imitated its African master so exactly, . . that it was impossible to distinguish the one from the other.

veniable, obs. form of VENGEABLE *a.*

†'**veniable**, *a. Obs. rare.* [ad. late L. *veniābilis*, f. *venia*: see VENIAL *a.*¹] Venial, excusable, pardonable.

1646 SIR T. BROWNE *Pseud. Ep.* III. xxiii. 168 It is an insufferable delusion, and with more veniable deceit it might have beene practised in Harts horne. *Ibid.* VII. xix. 385 In things of this nature silence condemneth history, 'tis the veniable part of things lost.

So †'**veniably** *adv. Obs.*⁻¹

1646 SIR T. BROWNE *Pseud. Ep.* v. xxi. 268 The Pictures of the Ægyptians were more tolerable, and in their sacred letters more veniably expressed the apprehension of Divinity.

venial ('viːnɪəl), *a.*¹ and *sb.* Forms: α. 4 uenial, veniale, 4–7 veniall, 4– venial; 4–5 venyal (5 -ale), 4–6 venyall. β. 4 veniele, 4–5 veniel. [a. OF. *venial, veniel* (mod.F. *véniel*, = Sp. and Pg. *venial*, It. *veniale*), or ad. L. *veniālis* (rare), f. *venia* forgiveness, indulgence, pardon.]

A. *adj.* **1.** Worthy or admitting of pardon, forgiveness, or remission; not grave or heinous; pardonable, light: **a.** Of sin; *spec.* in *Theol.* as opposed to *deadly* or *mortal*.

a **1300** *Cursor M.* 27541 Bot þar-of es oþer sines smale, þat clerkes clepes veniale. *Ibid.* 27545 Man cals þam venial and light. *c* **1340** HAMPOLE *Pr. Consc.* 2638 þe saul þat es clensed wele Of al dedely syn and of veniele. *c* **1386** CHAUCER *Pars. T.* 287 In þis wise skippith venial in to dedly synne. *c* **1400** *26 Pol. Poems* ix. 85 In venyale synne longe to byde, Makeþ dedly synnes to growe grete. **1483** CAXTON *Gold. Leg.* 60/2 To swere lyghtly without hurte or blame is venyal synne. **1526** *Pilgr. Perf.* (W. de W. 1531) 180 Whome no synne sholde defoule, neyther originall nor actuall, mortall ne venyall. **1558** BP. WATSON *Sev. Sacram.* i. 5 If he hath lightly offended in any venyall synne, he pardoneth him. **1615** BRATHWAIT *Strappado* (1878) 83 If I but tutch, to tutch 's a veniall sin, The pretty circle of thy dimpled chin. **1682** BURNET *Rights Princes* Pref. 33 That it is only a Venial Sin in any, to lessen the great authority of another. *a* **1700** in *Cath. Rec. Soc. Publ.* IX. 360 She had rather have suffered a thousand deaths, then wittingly commite yᵉ least veniall sinne. **1737** CHALLONER *Cath. Chr. Instr.* (1753) 116 By what Rule shall a Person be able to make a Judgment whether his Sins be mortal or venial? **1830** SCOTT *Demonol.* ii. 56 The crime of the person who . . consulted the oracle of Apollo;—a capital offence in a Jew, but surely a venial sin in an ignorant and deluded pagan. **1875** JOWETT *Plato* (ed. 2) I. 408 Those who have only committed venial sins are first purified of them.

b. Of crimes, offences, etc.

1604 SHAKS. *Oth.* IV. i. 9 If they do nothing, 'tis a Veniall slip. **1622** J. TAYLOR (Water P.) *Sir Gregory Nonsence* Wks. (1630) 4/1 The man that seeketh straying minds to weane all, From veniall vices, or offences penall. **1665** BOYLE *Occas. Refl.* Pref. p. x, I hope it will be thought a venial Crime, if in some of these Meditations I have not aim'd to express Eloquence, but only to cherish Piety. **1746** FRANCIS tr. *Hor.*, *Sat.* I. iv. 174 Thus, pure from more pernicious crimes I live: Some venial frailties you may well forgive. **1796** W. H. MARSHALL *Rur. Econ.* II. 115 The practice of pruning off the side boughs of Hedgerow Elms is a venial crime. **1872** YEATS *Growth Comm.* 56 Our own laws not long ago punished forgery and even more venial crimes with death. **1876** FARRAR *Marlb. Serm.* xiv. 134 Laughter may be the right cure for venial follies.

†**c.** Of an offender: Committing a venial sin or offence. *Obs.*⁻¹

1796 MME. D'ARBLAY *Camilla* I. 225 The venial offender had been released with a gentle reprimand.

2. a. Of an error or fault: That may be excused or overlooked; of a light, unimportant, or trivial nature; excusable.

1581 PETTIE *Guazzo's Civ. Conv.* II. (1586) 66 b, Whereby we may gather, that if the fault in wordes be veniall, the fault in sentence and matter be mortall. **1639** FULLER *Holy War* v. ix. 243 In the prosecuting and managing thereof, many not only veniall errours but unexcusable faults were committed. **1699** BENTLEY *Phal.* 326 He thinks it a more venial fault to make a mistake at Second hand after others. **1735** BOLINGBROKE *On Parties* xix. 235 He, who would have been ashamed to participate in Fraud, or to yield to Corruption, may begin to think the Faults venial, when he sees Men, who were far below Him, rise above Him by Fraud and by Corruption. **1784** COWPER *Task* VI. 418 Witness at his foot, The spaniel dying, for some venial fault. **1825** SCOTT *Betrothed* Concl., This is a venial error compared to that of our ancestors. **1876** FARRAR *Marlb. Serm.* xxxvi. 362 If a boy has committed some . . quite venial fault.

b. In general use.

1806 in *Mrs. Hutchinson's Mem. of Col. H.* 304 *note*, The account here given of Col. Hutchinson's motives . . lays his conduct fairly open to the discussion . . of the reader, who . . will determine it for himself to be commendable, censurable, or venial. **1809–10** COLERIDGE *Friend* (1865) 138 This was indeed a gross delusion, but, assuredly for young men at least, a very venial one too. **1850** W. IRVING *Mahomet* xvi. (1853) 96 An act of plunder and revenge—a venial act in the eyes of the Arabs. **1880** R. G. WHITE *Every-Day Eng.* 79 Mere provincialism in pronunciation . . is venial in comparison with slovenly speech.

†**3.** Allowable, permissible; blameless. *rare.*

1597 HOOKER *Eccl. Pol.* v. lxxi. §8 The Iewes . . not doubting that bodily labours are made by necessitie veniall, though otherwise, especially on that day [i.e. the Sabbath], rest be more conuenient. **1667** MILTON *P.L.* IX. 5 Where God . . With Man . . familiar us'd To sit indulgent, . . permitting him the while Venial discourse unblam'd. **1725** POPE *Odyss.* I. 219 With venial freedom let me now demand Thy name, thy lineage, and paternal land.

B. *sb.* A venial sin or offence; a light fault or error. Now *rare.*

c **1380** WYCLIF *Sel. Wks.* III. 452 þouȝ þis be synne, ȝit it is venyal, and not dedly, and venyals ben waschen awey wiþ preieris of a Pater-noster. *a* **1395** HYLTON *Scala Perf.* I. xxxiii. (W. de W. 1494), Neuertheles yet shalt thou for this defawte & all other venyals whyche may not be eschewed in this wretchyd lyf lyft up thyn hert to god. *c* **1425** *St. Mary of Oignies* I. vi. in *Anglia* VIII. 138/47 þof she so eshewed fro smal [sins] and veniels. *c* **1540** *Schole House Women* (1572) D ij b, And were not two small veniales, The feminine might be glorifide. **1596** BELL *Surv. Popery* III. ix. 364 Howsoeuer our late papists flatter themselues in their venials. **1609** BP. HALL *Disswas. Poperie* Wks. (1627) 642 It . . gently blanches ouer the breaches of Gods law with the name of venialls, and fauourable titles of diminution. **1671** WOODHEAD *St. Teresa* I. iv. 15, I was careful not to commit any Mortal sin; . . but of Venials I made no great account. **1969** J. D. CRICHTON in J. Fitzsimons *Penance* ii. 32 One thing that the present system inhibits, with . . its neat parcels of 'mortals' and 'venials'—the sin-grid, in fact—is the expression of the diffused feeling of sinfulness.

†'**venial**, *a.*² *Obs. rare.* [Irreg. var. of VENAL *a.*²] Venous.

1574 J. JONES *Nat. Beginn. Growing & Living Things* 8 When the heart is opened, it receueth Aire by the veniall arterie. **1578** BANISTER *Hist. Man* v. 70 Galen seemeth rather willyng to call this veyne a certaine veniall passage or way.

‖**veni'alia**, *sb. pl. Obs.*⁻¹ [L. *veniālia*, neut. pl. of *veniālis*: see VENIAL *a.*¹] Venial sins or offences.

1654 GAYTON *Pleas. Notes* IV. ii. 183 The peccadillo's and venialia, which never come into the black book.

veni'ality. ? *Obs.* [f. VENIAL *a.*[1] + -ITY; cf. Sp. *venialidad*, Pg. *venialidade*.] **a.** The property or quality of being venial. **b.** A matter of favour or grace.

1628 BP. HALL *Serm. Westm.* 54 They palliate wickednesse with the faire pretence of Venialitie. **1654** H. L'ESTRANGE *Chas. I* (1655) 138 The Flemish Busses..were soon reduced..to intreat the favour of fishing by his Majesties commission: a veniality the king was most ready to indulge them.

venially ('viːnɪəlɪ), *adv.* [f. VENIAL *a.*[1] + -LY[2].] In a venial manner, esp. in the way of venial sin; pardonably, excusably.

a **1340** HAMPOLE *Psalter* xvii. 26 Na man is in erthe þat synnes noght venyally. *c* **1386** CHAUCER *Pars. T.* ¶288 þylk worldly thynges þat he loueth, þurgh which he synneth venially. *c* **1440** *Jacob's Well* 80 þerfore, takyth heed be my woordys, whanne ȝe synnen in pride venyally, & whanne dedly. **1534** MORE *Comf. agst. Trib.* II. Wks. 1183/1 Wher as els in dede he had offended but venyally. **1588** A. KING tr. *Canisius' Catech.* 227 Thay ar aduersaries to the doctrine of trew religion quha sayis that ane iust man sinnes at leist veniallie in euery guid wark. **1608** WILLET *Hexapla Exod.* 659 A iust man in his good workes doth not sinne so much as venially. **1658** SIR T. BROWNE *Hydriot.* Ded., The Antients venially delighted in flourishing Gardens. **1740** CIBBER *Apol.* (1756) I. 128 All the faults, follies, and affectation of that agreeable tyrant were venially melted down into so many charms and attractions. **1847** *Fraser's Mag.* XXXVI. 53 So it fares with genius which, when only venially erroneous, is not to be forgiven. **1878** tr. *Villari's Machiavelli* II. I. viii. 249 If he sinned again however venially, he would certainly be hung.

'venialness. *rare*[−0]. [f. as prec. + -NESS.] = VENIALITY.

1727 BAILEY (vol. II), *Venialness*, Pardonableness. **1755** JOHNSON, *Pardonableness*, venialness; susceptibility of pardon.

veniance, etc., obs. ff. VENGEANCE.

Venice ('vɛnɪs). Also 6 **Venysse, Venise, Ven(i)ys, Vennys, Venes,** 7 **Vennis, Venis.** Also VENUS[2]. [a. F. *Venise*:—L. *Venetia* (It. *Venezia*, Sp. *Venecia*, Pg. *Veneza*): see def.]

1. The name of the city (the capital of the province of the same name) in the north-east of Italy, used attrib. to designate various articles made there or having some connexion with the locality, as ***Venice lace, looking-glass, paper, point*** (lace), ***tinsel, vial, work,*** etc. (Cf. VENETIAN *a.* 2.)

† ***Venice beam***: see ROMAN *a.*[1] 15. ***Venice blue*** (see quot.). ***Venice crown***, *Her.* (see quot.). ***Venice gold, silver*** (cf. GOLD *sb.* 4, SILVER *sb.* 4). ***Venice lac*** (see LAC[1] 2, quot. 1763). ***Venice soap*** (see quots.). † ***Venice sumach***, Venetian sumach. ***Venice talc, white*** (see quots.).

1611 COTGR., *Traineau à plommée*,..a Roman, or *Venice beame, for the weighing of things. **1598** FLORIO, *Veneto*, a light or *Venice blew, a Turkie colour. *c* **1828** BERRY *Encycl. Her.* I. Gloss., **Venice Crown*, the crown, or cap of state, worn by the Doge, is made of cloth of gold,..covered with precious stones, and having two long ears, or lappets, pointed at the ends, hanging down at the sides. **1506** *Paston Lett.* III. 404 The [horse-] harnes of *Venys gold. **1520-1** *Rec. St. Mary at Hill* (1905) 310 Item, paid for a vnce of venes golde iijs viijd. **1535** *Wardr. Kath. Arragon* 26 in *Camden Misc.* III, Fringid withe grene silke and Venysse golde. **1558** in Feuillerat *Revels Q. Eliz.* (1908) 40, viii Aperns of white gowlde sarsnet edged with veniys gowlde frenge. **1821** SCOTT *Kenilw.* ii, Her hat..being of tawny taffeta, embroidered with scorpions of Venice gold. **1865** F. B. PALLISER *Hist. Lace* iv. 45 It is not, however, till the reign of Elizabeth, that Italian cutworks and *Venice lace came into general use. **1929** *Oxford Poetry* 3 Every fallen shadow weaves Venice lace for kindly aunts. **1974** *Times-Picayune* (New Orleans) 15 Aug. v. 6/1 A flounce capelet edged in venice lace. *c* **1645** HOWELL *Lett.* (1655) IV. 43 A new *Venice Looking-Glasse, wherin you may behold that admired Maiden-City in her true complexion. **1848** THACKERAY *Van. Fair* lxiv, The great Venice looking-glasses, framed in silver. *a* **1661** FULLER *Worthies, Cambridge* I. (1662) 149 To such who object that we can never equall the perfection of *Venice-paper. **1865** F. B. PALLISER *Hist. Lace* iv. 47 This is our Rose (raised) *Venice point, the Gros Point de Venise, the Punto a rilievo, so highly prized and so extensively used for albs, collerettes.. and costly decoration. **1882** CAULFEILD & SAWARD *Dict. Needlew.* 513/1 The fine Needlepoints made at Brussels.. were worn..in preference to the heavier Venice Points. **1883** *Mag. of Art* Dec. 66/2 Louis XIV. had a passion for Venice point. **1574** in Feuillerat *Revels Q. Eliz.* (1908) 234 Ritchly wroughte with *venys sylver. **1673** J. RAY *Observations Journey Low-Countries* 202 **Venice-Sope*..is very like and nothing inferiour to *Castile-Sope*. It is made of the best Oil Olive. **1792** J. WOODFORDE *Diary* 26 July (1927) III. 364 At D[itt]o. for Venice Soap 1. o. **1842** *Penny Cycl.* XXII. 171/1 White soda soap..in a less pure state..is called Alicant, Venice, or Spanish soap. **1858** SIMMONDS *Dict. Trade*, *Venice-soap*, a mottled soap made with olive-oil and soda, with a little sulphate of iron in solution, or sulphate of zinc. **1597** GERARDE *Herbal* 1293 The first is called *Coggygria* and *Coccygria*: in English *Venice Sumach, or Silken Sumach. **1728** BRADLEY *Dict. Bot.* s.v. *Rhus*, The Venice Sumach, or *Coggygria, sive Colinus Coriaria*. **1867** *Chambers's Encycl.* IX. 109/1 Steatite, or Soap-stone,..is sold..under the names of Briançon Chalk, French Chalk, and *Venice Talc. **1697** T. BROWN *Dispensary* II. Wks. 1709 III. III. 77 My cordials are all put into *Venice Vials. **1547** in Feuillerat *Revels Edw. VI* (1914) 23 Tilsent [= tinsel] whyte and *venice. **1839** URE *Dict. Arts & Manuf.* 1298 When white lead is mixed in equal quantities with ground sulphate of barytes, it is known in France and Germany by the name of *Venice white. **1860** *Chambers's Encycl.* VI. 722/1 Venice White contains 1 part of Baryta, and 1 part of White Lead. **1555** EDEN *Decades* (Arb.) 257 They esteeme nothyng more precious then drynkyng glasses of *Venice woorke.

2. a. Venice glass, (*a*) a very fine and delicate kind of glass, originally manufactured at Murano, near Venice; (*b*) an article made of this, esp. a drinking vessel or vial; (*c*) a Venetian mirror.

The extreme brittleness of vessels made of this glass is freq. alluded to in the 17th century.

(*a*) **1527** ANDREW *Brunswyke's Distyll. Waters* A ij b, They must be made of venys glasse bycause they sholde the better withstande the hete of the fyre. *a* **1583** in Halliwell *Rara Mathem.* (1841) 41 Then they must prepare very cleare and white Glasse..; as fyne and white Vennys Glasse. **1626** BACON *Sylva* §770 The Crystalline Venice Glass is reported to be a mixture, in equal portions, of Stones brought from Pavia, by the River Ticinum, and the Ashes of a Weed called by the Arabs, *Kall.* **1673** A. WALKER *Lees Lachrymans* 13 Their Venice-glass..cracks with as slight a blow as pots of courser clay.

(*b*) **1587** HARRISON *England* II. vi. in *Holinshed* I. 166/2 As for drinke it is vsuallie filled in..bols of siluer in noble mens houses, also in fine Venice glasses of all formes. **1591** SYLVESTER *Du Bartas* I. ii. 72 In a Venice Glass before our eyne, We see the Water intermix with Wine. **1620** GATAKER *Marriage Duties* 41 The more britle a Venice glasse is, the more gingerly we handle it. **1669** BOYLE *Certain Physiol. Ess.* (ed. 2) *Absol. Rest Bodies* 22 Having enquired of a famous..Maker of Telescopes..whether he did not observe that the Venice-Glasses he employed would sometimes crack of themselves whilst they were yet in Plates. **1688** *On Death* in Jane Barker *Poet. Recreations* II. 44 Life is a Bubble;..Tis far more brittle than a Venice-Glass.

(*c*) **1850** MRS. BROWNING *Sonn. fr. Portug.* ix, I will not.. breathe my poison on thy Venice-glass. **1852** THACKERAY *Esmond* I. ix, On which poor Lady Castlewood gave a rueful smile, and a look into a little Venice glass she had.

b. Venice treacle, in old pharmacy, an electuary composed of many ingredients and supposed to possess universal alexipharmic and preservative properties. Cf. TREACLE *sb.* 1 c. Now *arch.*

Also occas. called ***treacle of Venice***.

1612 WOODALL *Surg. Mate* Wks. (1653) 95 A little Venice Triacle or other Triacle. **1635** J. TAYLOR (Water P.) *Life Thomas Parr* C 3, And Garlick hee esteem'd above the rate Of Venice-Triacle, or best Mithridate. **1691** T. H[ALE] *Acc. New Invent.* p. xxv, And as well may we be afraid to take the Venice Treacle, because of its being long kept in boxes of Lead. *c* **1720** W. GIBSON *Farrier's Dispens.* III. (1721) 146 Venice Treacle. This is also called the *Theriaca*, or Treacle of Andromachus. **1753** J. BARTLET *Gentl. Farriery* xlii. (1754) 323 Internally, for bites from vipers, may be given cordial medicines, such as Venice treacle and salt of hartshorn. **1797** *Encycl. Brit.* (ed. 3) XVI. 573/2 The Muscovites at all times reject as impure..rabbit, ass's milk, mare's milk, and Venice-treacle. **1821** SCOTT *Kenilw.* xiii. *footnote*, Orvietan, or Venice treacle, as it was sometimes called, was understood to be a sovereign remedy against poison.

c. Venice turpentine (see quots. *c* 1789, 1800, and TURPENTINE *sb.* 1 b).

1577 FRAMPTON *Joyful News* 45 Adde therto three ounces of Venise Turpentine. **1736** BAILEY *Househ. Dict.* s.v. *Ague*, Mix the powder of white Hellebore roots with right Venice Turpentine. *c* **1789** *Encycl. Brit.* (ed. 3) IV. 567/1 The kind now called Venice turpentine, is no other than a mixture of eight parts of common yellow or black rosin with five parts of oil of turpentine. What was originally Venice turpentine is now unknown. **1800** E. DARWIN *Phytol.* vi. 84 Thus what is called Venice turpentine is obtained from the larch by wounding the bark about two feet from the ground, and catching it as it exsudes. **1846** J. BAXTER *Libr. Pract. Agric.* (ed. 4) II. 278 The ointment is made as follows:—Quicksilver, 1 lb.; Venice Turpentine, ½ lb. **1857** MILLER *Elem. Chem.*, *Org.* 503 The common varnish used for oil paintings and maps consists of 24 parts of mastic, 3 of Venice turpentine, and 1 of camphor.

venidium (vɛ'nɪdɪəm). [mod.L. (C. F. Lessing 1831, in *Linnæa* VI. 91), f. L. *vēna* vein, in allusion to the ribbed achenes of some species.] An annual or perennial herb of the genus *Venidium*, belonging to the family Compositæ, native to South Africa, and bearing cream or yellow flowers.

1937 R. HAY *Annuals* 230 Venidiums prefer a light soil. **1962** [see CLEOME]. **1976** *Hortus Third* (L. H. Bailey Hortorium) 1147/2 Venidiums are usually treated as annuals in the garden.

venie, var. VENY *Obs.*

venieaunce, obs. f. VENGEANCE.

venifice, var. VENEFICE *Obs.*

ve'nigenous, *a. Geol.* [f. L. type **vēnigena*.] Of rock-masses: Bearing or containing veins of metal or quartz.

1817 *Blackw. Mag.* I. 421 A series of specimens of the diamond imbedded in a venigenous mass. **1833-4** J. PHILLIPS *Geol.* in *Encycl. Metrop.* (1845) VI. 762/2 The intricate character of the venigenous masses of Mousehole.

venim(ous, obs. ff. VENOM(OUS.

†**venin**, *sb.*[1] *Obs.* In 4-5 venyn. [a. OF. *venin*:—L. *venēn-um*.] Venom, poison.

c **1330** R. BRUNNE *Chron. Wace* (Rolls) 9005 Venyn for salue wyþ hym he nam, Als a monk to court he cam. *c* **1380** WYCLIF *Three Treat.* (1851) p. xxxvi, As Crist techiþ in his gospel, hou þat men shulden..forsake her cumpenye as venyn [*v.r.* venym]. *c* **1400** *Apol. Loll.* 57 Triacle is turnid in to venyn, and þis þat was foundun to remedie, is foundun to deþ.

Hence †**venin** *v. trans.*, to poison. *Obs.*[−0]

a **1500** *Prompt. Parv.* 508/2 (MS. H.), Venynyn or venymyn, *veneno*.

'venin, *sb.*[2] *Chem.* Also **-ine, -ene.** [f. VENOM + -IN[1].] A toxic substance forming the distinctive element in snake-venom.

(In recent Dicts.)

veniour, obs. var. VENGER.

‖**venire** (vɪ'naɪəriː). *Law.* [Ellipt. for next.]

1. = next 1.

1665 EVER *Tryals per Pais* iii. 31 Therefore where the Sheriff ought not to retorn the Venire, he cannot retorn the Tales. **1676** *Office Clerk Assize* 82 In the mean time doth the Clerk of the Peace file the *Venire*, and the pannel with the Indictment. **1722** BEVERLEY *Hist. Virginia* IV. vi. 223 A Writ of *Venire* issues in such Cases, to summon six of the nearest Neighbours to the Criminal. **1771** E. LONG in Hone *Every-day Bk.* (1826) II. 200 You must have a *venire* for a jury. **1821** ARCHBOLD *Digest Law Pleading & Evidence* 415 Stating the names, &c. of the knights and recognitors, as in the *venire*. **1825** *Act 6 Geo. IV*, c. 50 §16 *marg.*, If Plaintiff sue forth a Venire, etc. in order to Trial, and proceed not, he may afterwards sue forth another Venire, etc. and try at any subsequent Assizes.

b. *venire de novo*, = next 1 b.

1797 TOMLINS *Jacob's Law Dict.* s.v. *Venire Facias de novo*, The following seem to be the cases in which a *Venire de Novo* is grantable. **1885** *Law Rep. 10 App. Cas.* 414 Without some such power [of ascertaining what the circumstances were] no judgment, except a venire de novo, could be given.

c. *venire man*, one summoned to serve on a jury under a writ of *Venire facias*, a juryman. *U.S.*

1780 *Virginia Statutes at Large* X. 489 An act for regulating tobacco fees, and fixing the allowance to sheriffs, witnesses, and venire-men. **1895** *Weekly Examiner* (San Francisco) 5 Sept. 2/1 Sheriff Whelan's deputies had apparently summoned most all of the veniremen from the foreign sections of the city.

†**2.** = next 2. *Obs.*

1763 LD. HARDWICKE in Harris *Life* (1847) III. 344, I believe he came in upon the venire or capias, & put in bail. **1769** [see VENIRE FACIAS 2].

†**3.** The place from which the jurors were to be summoned or in which the cause was to be tried; = VENUE 5. *Obs.*

1682 LUTTRELL *Brief Rel.* (1857) I. 185 Mr. Graham haveing moved once or twice the court of kings bench that the venire might be laid in another county. **1682** *Lond. Gaz.* No. 1720/7 This day the great Case between the Earl of Shaftsbury and Mr. Cradock came on in the Kings-Bench about changing the *Venire* out of London.

‖**venire facias** (vɪ'naɪəriː 'feɪʃɪæs). *Law.* [L., lit. 'that you cause to come'. Cf. prec.]

1. A former judicial writ directed to a sheriff requiring him to summon a jury to try a cause or causes at issue between parties. *Obs.* or *Hist.*

1444 *Rolls of Parlt.* V. 112/1 Thissue joyned and entred of record, and a venire fac' of ye Jure retorned. **1531** *Star Chamber Cases* (Selden) II. 189 They have pursued seuerall venire facias retornable the First day of the terme of seynt Hillary next comyng. **1543** *Ludlow Churchw. Acc.* (Camden) 14 Payde for a venire facias, xvj d. **1607** MIDDLETON *Phœnix* B 4 b, Youl get a *Venire facies* to warne your Iurie, a *Decem tales* to fill vp the number. **1665** EVER *Tryals per Pais* iii. 24 Of a *Venire facias*: To whom it shall be directed [etc.]. **1768** BLACKSTONE *Comm.* III. 352 When therefore an issue is joined,..the court awards a writ of *venire facias*. **1790** *Amer. State Papers* Misc. (1834) I. 32 (Stanf.), Juries shall be summoned by writs of *venire facias*. **1821** ARCHBOLD *Digest Law* 414 The jury process is the same as in ordinary cases, namely, a *venire facias* and a *habeas corpora juratorum*. **1825** *Act 6 Geo. IV*, c. 50 §16. 125 No former Writ of Venire Facias had been prosecuted in that Cause.

b. *venire facias de novo* (lit. 'that you cause to come anew'), an order for a new trial of a cause, upon the same record, owing to some defect or irregularity in the first trial.

1797 TOMLINS *Jacob's Law Dict.* s.v., New Trials are generally granted where a General Verdict is found; a *Venire Facias de Novo*, upon a Special Verdict.

†**2.** A writ issued against a person indicted of a misdemeanour, summoning him to appear before the court. *Obs.*

1463-4 *Plumpton Corr.* (Camden) 10, I shall send you another [capias] with the Copie of your new suites and a venire facias against the ministre. **1769** BLACKSTONE *Comm.* IV. 313 The proper process on an indictment for any petty misdemesnor, or on a penal statute, is a writ of *venire facias*, which is in the nature of a summons to cause the party to appear. And if by the return to such venire [etc.].

Venis(e, obs. forms of VENICE.

venison ('vɛnz(ə)n, 'vɛnɪz(ə)n, 'vɛnɪs(ə)n). Forms: *α.* 3-5 **venesun,** 3-6 **veneson,** 4 **veneison, ueneysun,** 4-5 **venesoun,** 5 *Sc.* **wennesone,** 6 **vennesoun,** 7 **venneson;** 4 **venisun,** 4-5 **venisoun,** 5 **venisyn,** 6 **venicen, vennisone,** 7 **venizon,** 4- **venison;** 4-5 **venysoun,** 4-6 **venyson,** 5 **venysone, -soune, -sowne, vennysoun,** *Sc.* **wenysoune, -son.** *β.* 5 **vensoun,** 6-8 **venson,** 7-8 **ven'son,** 7 (9) **venzon.** [a. AF. *veneso(u)n, veneysun, venysoun, venison*, OF. *veneson, veneisun, venison, venoison* (mod.F. *venaison*, = Pr. *venaizo, venazo*, obs.

Sp. *venacion*, Pg. *veação*, It. *venagione*):—L. *vēnātiōn-em* hunting, f. *vēnāri* to hunt.]

1. a. The flesh of an animal killed in the chase or by hunting and used as food; formerly applied to the flesh of the deer, boar, hare, rabbit, or other game animal, now almost entirely restricted to the flesh of various species of deer. Cf. b.

α. *a* **1300** *Havelok* 1726 Kranes, swannes, ueneysun, Lax, lampreys, and god sturgun. **13..** *K. Alis.* 5233 (Laud MS.), To mete was greiþed beef & motoun, Bredes, briddes, & venysoun. **1387** TREVISA *Higden* (Rolls) I. 89 þei..eteþ no flesche but venysoun. *c* **1420** *Liber Cocorum* (1862) 28 A sawce hit is For vele and venyson, iwys. *c* **1425** *Voc.* in Wr.-Wülcker 662 *Hec ferina*, wenyson. *c* **1489** CAXTON *Sonnes of Aymon* xxi. 463 Soo toke he a dysshe that was before hym, that was full of venyson, and sente it to hym by a squyre of his. *a* **1500** *Remedie of Loue* in Thynne *Chaucer* (1532) 367 b/2 Venyson stolne is aye the swetter. **1578** T. N. tr. *Conq. W. India* 200 They sel in this market venison by quarters or whole, as Does, Hares, Conies,..and many other beastes, which they bring up for the purpose, and take in hunting. **1598** MANWOOD *Lawes Forest* v. (1615) 49 Amongst the common sort of people, nothing is accompted Venison, but the flesh of Red and Fallow Deere. **1617** MORYSON *Itin.* III. 149 Hares are thought to nourish melancoly, yet they are eaten as Venison, both rosted and boyled. **1672** JOSSELYN *New Eng. Rarities* 48 Bears are very fat in the fall of the leaf, at which time they are excellent venison. **1736** SHERIDAN in Swift *Lett.* (1768) IV. 167 Our venison is plenty: our weather too hot for its carriage. **1769** GRAY *Lett.*, etc. (1775) 363 Fell mutton is..in season..; it grows fat on the mountains, and nearly resembles venison. **1818** SCOTT *Br. Lamm.* ix, The huntsman's knife, presented to her for the purpose of making the first incision in the stag's breast, and thereby discovering the quality of the venison. **1837** W. IRVING *Capt. Bonneville* III. 63 The party ..hunted for a few days, until they had laid in a supply of dried buffalo meat and venison. **1885** J. G. BERTRAM *Brit. Alm. Comp.* 70 The best venison for the table is supplied by the fallow deer raised in the home parks of England.

β. *c* **1460** J. RUSSELL *Bk. Nurture* 689 in *Babees Bk.*, Capoun, pigge, vensoun bake, leche lombard. **1502–3** *Rec. St. Mary at Hill* (1905) 248 Payd..ffor a reward for bryngyng of venson. **1598** MANWOOD *Lawes Forest* v. (1615) 50 Our eldest English writers doe call the same Venson, and not Venison: But by what reason I see not. **1697** DRYDEN *Æneid* I. 274 The jars of gen'rous wine..He set abroach, and for the feast prepar'd, In equal portions with the ven'son shar'd. **1717** PRIOR *Alma* I. 378 If You Dine with my Lord May'r, Roast-beef, and Ven'son is your Fare. **1780** COWPER *Progr. Err.* 220 Turtle and ven'son all his thoughts employ. **1784** —— *Task* IV. 612 Whoso seeks an audit here Propitious, pays his tribute, game or fish, Wild-fowl or ven'son.

b. With *of* (an animal) or defining term.

c **1290** *S. Eng. Leg.* I. 472 Huy nomen with heom into heore schip bred i-novȝ and wyn, Venesun of heort and hynd, and of wilde swyn. *a* **1400** *Sqr. lowe Degre* 324 Storkes and snytes ther were also, And venyson freshe of bucke and do. *c* **1410** *Master of Game* (MS. Digby 182) iii, þe venysoun of hem [i.e. bucks] is reght goode, and ykept and salted, as þat of þe hert. **1545** ELYOT, *Aprugna*, the venyson of a wylde boore. **1609** BIBLE (Douay) *1 Kings* iv. 23 The venison of hartes, roes, and buffles. **1648** HEXHAM II, *Het wildt-braedt van een Beer*, the Venison of a wilde Boare. **1650** FULLER *Pisgah* I. v. 12 Venison both red and fallow. **1814** SCOTT *Wav.* xii. *note*, The learned in cookery..hold roe-venison dry and indifferent food, unless [etc.]. **1852** MUNDY *Antipodes* (1857) 6 A haunch of kangaroo venison. **1885** J. G. BERTRAM *Brit. Alm. Comp.* 70 A haunch of red deer venison is not much appreciated, as it is expensive and troublesome to cook.

c. Used allusively (see quot.).

1579 NORTHBROOKE *Dicing* (1843) 22, I pray God the olde prouerbe be not found true, that gentlemen and riche men are venison in Heauen (that is), very rare and daintie to haue them there.

2. a. Any beast of chase or other wild animal killed by hunting, esp. one of the deer kind. Now *arch.*

13.. *K. Alis.* 1863 (Laud MS.), Hij charged many a selcouþe beeste..Wiþ Armure & ek vitayles; Longe Cartes wiþ pauylounes, Hors & oxen wiþ venisounes. **1338** R. BRUNNE *Chron.* (1810) 64 Whan Harald or þe kyng wild com þider eftsons In þe tyme of g[r]ese, to tak þam venysons. *c* **1400** *Sowdone Bab.* 51 To chase the Bore or the Veneson, The Wolfe, the Bere and the Bawson. **1456** SIR G. HAYE *Law Arms* (S.T.S.) 234 He sittand in a busk..bydand the venysoun come stalkand by him stillely. **1535** COVERDALE *Isaiah* li. 20 Thy sonnes lie comfortles at yᵉ heade of euery strete like a taken venyson. **1588** PARKE tr. *Mendoza's Hist. China* 9 One whole venison is bought for two rials. **1611** SHAKS. *Cymb.* III. iii. 75 He that strikes The Venison first, shall be the Lord o' th' Feast. **1651** CLEVELAND *Poems* 12 The Ven'sons now in view, our hounds spend deeper. **1727** [DORRINGTON] *Philip Quarll* 15 Ten to one but I may give you a Venison. **1854** THOREAU *Walden* (1884) 302 One [hare] sat by my door... I took a step, and..away it scud with an elastic spring,..the wild free venison, asserting its vigor. **1876** *Forest & Stream* 13 July 368/2 When you see a 'venzon', shoot him, shoot him, When you shoot a venson, send me some to cook.

b. *collect.* (See quot. 1603.) Now *arch.*

a. **1338** R. BRUNNE *Chron.* (1810) 112 þe kyng..Forsters did somoun, enquered vp & doun, Whilk men of toun had taken his venysoun. *c* **1386** CHAUCER *Doctor's T.* 83 A theof of venisoun..Can kepe a forest best of every man. *c* **1400** *Brut* 105 þe Kyng Elle was gon to þe wode him forto desporte: and of venysoun somdele he hade tak. **1464** *Rolls of Parlt.* V. 533 The surveyng aswell of the Verte as of the Venyson of oure forest. *a* **1513** FABYAN *Chron.* I. clxxii. (1516) 99/2 Yet therin is Venyson and other wylde beestes, and Fowle, and Fysshe great plente. **1550** J. COKE *Eng. & Fr. Heralds* §6 You say you have fayre forestes, chases and parkes full of venyson marvelous. **1603** G. OWEN *Pembrokeshire* (1892) 268 The fyv sortes of beastes of the Foreste..as alsoe the fyve sortes of the beastes of Chace, all which ten sortes are comprehended vnder the name of Venison. **1680** MORDEN *Geog. Rect.* (1685) 347 Their Venison is the Wild Boar, the Hart, the Stag, the Fallow Deer and Hare, which are most excellent. **1700** TYRRELL *Hist. Eng.* II. 819 The Verderers and Foresters shall meet to view the Attachments of the Forest, as well of Vert, as Venison. **1791** W. GILPIN *Forest Scenery* II. 17 Under him are two distinct appointments of officers, the one to preserve the venison of the forest; and the other to preserve its vert. **1854** THOREAU *Walden* xiii, I was interested in the preservation of the venison and the vert more than the hunters.

β. **1597** CONSTABLE *Poems* (1859) 75 Course the fearefulle Hare, Venson do not spare. *a* **1618** SYLVESTER *Little Bartas* 484 Wks. (Grosart) II. 89 For Him, the Mountains, downs, & Forrests breed Buffs, Beefs, Sheep, Venzon.

†**3.** The action or practice of hunting; venery. *Obs. rare.*

1390 GOWER *Conf.* II. 68 Ther scholde he with his Dart on honde Upon the Tigre and the Leon Pourchace and take his veneison. **1398** TREVISA *Barth. De P.R.* xv. xxxiv. (Tollem. MS.), These men..gon aboute in large wildirnesse as wylde men,..and lyuen by prayes and by venison. *c* **1520** *Adam Bell, Clim of Clough*, etc. iv, They were outlawed for venyson, These thre yemen euerechone.

4. *attrib.* and *Comb.*, as ***venison dish, plate, provider, salesman, thief***, etc.; ***venison-like*** adj.

1567 MAPLET *Gr. Forest* 74 b, His flesh is Venesonlike: for the which he is so often hunted. **1734** ARBUTHNOT in Pope *Lett.* (1735) I. 340 My Venison Stomach is gone. *a* **1743** R. SAVAGE *Progr. Divine* Wks. 1777 II. 120 Some plunder fishponds; others (ven'son thieves) The forest ravage. **1753** *Chambers' Cycl.* Suppl. s.v., Thus, in some places, the wolf and the fox are reckoned among the Venison beasts. **1854** *Poultry Chron.* II. 167 Thomas Fricker, Game, Poultry, Pork, Venison, and Egg Salesman. **1858** SIMMONDS *Dict. Trade*, *Venison-dish*, a metal dish to keep venison hot at table. *Ibid.*, *Venison-plate*, a hot plate for eating venison on. **1897** *Outing* XXIX. 437/2 A hound-master, gamekeeper, and venison provider.

b. In the sense of 'made of or with, consisting of, venison', as ***venison dinner, ham, pasty, pâté, pie, steak.***

1598 SHAKS. *Merry W.* I. i. 202 We haue a hot Venison pasty to dinner. **1665** in *Maitland Club Miscell.* (1840) II. 527 For Venusone py, 005 08 00. **1681** T. FLATMAN *Heraclitus Ridens* No. 28 (1713) I. 184 The Whigs shall not always Rule the Roast, nor the Custards and Venison-Pasties neither. **1721** AMHERST *Terræ Fil.* No. I. 4 To see the virtuous munificence of founders..tost up in fricasees and venison pasties. **1772** B. ROMANS *Jrnl.* 16 Jan. in *Nat. Hist. Florida* (1775) 331, I purchased some bear, bacon and venison hams of them. **1788** M. CUTLER *Jrnl.* 7 Sept. (1888) I. 419 Dined..on venison steak and squirrel pie; very good dinner. **1818** SCOTT *Rob Roy* vi, Thorncliffs person, stuffed as it is with beef, venison-pasty, and pudding. **1833** J. HALL *Harp's Head* 214 A little further up were venison steaks, then fried ham. **1841** THACKERAY *Gt. Hoggarty Diamond* iv, Since my venison dinner and drive with Lady Doldrum. **1860** E. J. LEWIS *Jrnl.* 26 May in *Colorado Mag.* (1937) XIV. 219 Bought some venison ham for a dollar. **1864** C. GEIKIE *Life in Woods* vi. (1874) 117 Venison pie,..for days after, furnished quite a treat in the house. **1975** *Harpers & Queen* May 68/2 The chef makes the most delicious venison paté. **1980** J. WAINWRIGHT *Man of Law* xliv. 205 Venison pâté sandwiches and watered-down whisky. **1980** C. & T. CONRAN *Cook Bk.* II. 248/1 Charcoal grilled venison. 1 venison steak from the leg or loin, weighing 2–3 lb.

Hence **'venisonized** *ppl. a.*, cooked so as to resemble venison. **veniso'nivorous** *a.*, given to eating venison. *nonce-words.*

c **1831** G. C. LEWIS *Lett.* (1870) 10 People are very venisonivorous. **1881** MRS. A. R. ELLIS *Sylvestra* II. 29 The venisonized loin of mutton.

Ve'nitary. *rare*⁻¹. [ad. med.L. *venitarium*, f. *venite*: see next.] (See quot.)

1853 ROCK *Ch. of Fathers* III. II. xii. 213 The *Venitary* was a small book, in which the 'Venite, exultemus Domino,' ..with the appropriate invitatorium,..was written out, and the notation for the chant put beneath the words.

‖**Venite** (vɪ'naɪtiː). [L.: 2nd pers. pl. imp. of *venīre* to come.] The ninety-fifth psalm (the ninety-fourth in the Vulgate, beginning *Venite, exultemus Domino*) used as a canticle at matins or morning prayer; the invitatory psalm; also, a musical setting of this.

a **1225** *Ancr. R.* 18 þus doð et euerich Gloria Patri, & et te beginnunge of þe Venite. *c* **1450** in Aungier *Syon* (1840) 364 The two sustres that be tabled to synge the versicles schal synge the *Venite* and the first verse at matens. **1657** SPARROW *Bk. Com. Prayer* 32 The Venite. O come let us sing unto the Lord. This is an Invitatory Psalm. **1713** GIBSON *Codex Juris Eccl. Angl.* 299 Invitatories, Some Text of Scripture, adapted and chosen for the Occasion of the Day, and used before the *Venite*. **1853** ROCK *Ch. of Fathers* III. II. xii. 213 On high feast days, the 'Venite' used to be sung with great solemnity, by the rulers of the choir. **1877** J. D. CHAMBERS *Div. Worship* 134 The mode of singing the 'Venite', with an Invitatory superadded. **1899** A. C. BENSON *Life Abp. Benson* I. xv. 589 He had himself ushered to his place by the verger before the Venite.

†**b.** ***Venite book***, a book containing a musical setting of the 'Venite'; a venitary. *Obs.*

1434 *Invent. St. Mary's, Scarborough* in *Archaeologia* LI. 66 Et unum librum vocatum Venite boke. **1537** in Glassock *Rec. St. Michaels* 127 Item iij pryntid masbooke and a venyte booke. **1559** *Dunmow Churchw. MS.* 43 b, A booke of parchment conteyninge in yt a Venite booke, an ymnall, and a boke for diriges and berialls.

Venitian, obs. f. VENETIAN.

Venizelist (vɛnɪ'zeɪlɪst), *a.* and *sb.* [f. the name of the Greek statesman Eleuthérios *Venizélos* (1864–1936) + -IST.] **A.** *adj.* Of, pertaining to, or supporting Venizélos or his political policies.

1915 *Times* 12 June 5/3 The Venizelist Press, in discussing the Government electoral programme, observes that the promised reforms are almost the same as those brought forward by M. Venizelos. **1916** *Morning Post* 25 Apr. 6/5 (*heading*) Repressing a Venizelist ovation. **1920** *Glasgow Herald* 4 May 7 Even the so-called Venizelist Divisions were nothing more than a collection of supers. **1931** *Times Lit. Suppl.* 19 Mar. 218/2 He confesses that..he was blown about by every wind of doctrine—now Venizelist, now Royalist. **1946** R. CAPELL *Simiomata* II. 61 There were senior officers of integrity, old Venizelist colonels like Tsamákos and Matsoukos in Thessaly. **1972** D. DAKIN *Unification of Greece* xvi. 238 The majority of the government was moderate Venizelist. **1980** J. LEES-MILNE *Harold Nicolson* I. vi. 84 Harold..was..put to work on.. the supply of stores to the Venizelist forces in Egypt.

B. *sb.* A supporter or adherent of Venizélos or his political policies.

1915 *Times* 15 June 5/3 The processions formed by the Venizelists became so numerous that several attempts were made by the cavalry to disperse them. **1920** V. J. SELIGMAN *Victory of Venizelos* 8 The views..of leading 'Venizelists' and 'Constantinians'. **1946** R. CAPELL *Simiomata* III. 127 There used to be furious feeling between Venizelists and monarchists. **1981** *Times Lit. Suppl.* 22 May 584/3 Is it not a little unfair to say that there have been no distinguished Cretans apart from King Midas and El Greco? The verdict will not please the Venizelists.

Hence **Veni'zelism.**

1931 C. MACKENZIE *First Athenian Memories* xv. 380 This result was not gained merely by abstentions in the Islands and the new territories where Venizelism was naturally predominant.

venizon, obs. f. VENISON.

venk, southern ME. pa. t. FANG *v.*¹

venkes(s, -is, -us, obs. varr. VANQUISH *v.*

†**venlin.** *Obs.* [a. obs. LG. *venlîn* (obs. G. *fenlin*, *-lein*; now *fähnlein*), dim. of *vāne* (G. *fahne*) banner. Cf. BANNER *sb.*¹ 3.] A company (of soldiers). (See also VANLIN.)

1541 *St. Papers Hen. VIII* (1849) VIII. 550 [They had set up four] venlins [or banners, each of which ought to] conteyne [500]. **1587** FLEMING *Contn. Holinshed* III. 1994/1 They prouided the best they could to repell them, appointing foure venlins or ensignes of lance knights to keepe a standing watch that night in the trenches.

ven'mowse, obs. form of VENOMOUS *a.*

venn(e, southern ME. variant of FEN *sb.*¹

Venn diagram (vɛn). [Named after its inventor, John *Venn* (1834–1923), English logician.] A group of circles that may or may not intersect according as the logical sets they represent have or have not elements in common.

[**1884** J. N. KEYNES *Stud. & Exerc. Formal Logic* III. v. 207 The application of Mr Venn's diagrammatic scheme to syllogistic reasonings. **1894** *Ibid.* (ed. 3) III. iv. 298 Syllogisms in *Barbara* and *Camestres* may be taken in order to show how Dr Venn's diagrams can be used.] **1918** C. I. LEWIS *Survey Symbolic Logic* i. 77 This method resembles nothing so much as solution by means of the Venn diagrams. **1952** W. V. QUINE *Methods of Logic* 70 Whiteness of a region in a Venn diagram means nothing but lack of information. **1970** O. DOPPING *Computers & Data Processing* i. 28 By means of Venn diagrams..set theoretic operations such as intersection can be shown in geometrical form. **1977** J. L. HARPER *Population Biol. Plants* xxiii. 725 These results are interpreted as a Venn diagram in Fig. 23/11a to show presumed niche relationships between the groups of species.

vennel ('vɛnəl). *Sc.* (*Ir.*) and *north.* Forms: 5– **vennel**, 5 **venal(e, 6 wennall, -el**, 6–9 **vennell**, 7 **venel**, 7–9 **vennal**, 8 **vennile**; 7 **vinell**, 9 **vinnel**. [a. OF. *venele*, *venelle*, *vanelle* (mod.F. *venelle*) :—Rom. type **vēnella* (med.L. *venella*), dim. of L. *vēna* vein.]

1. A narrow lane, passage, or thoroughfare in a town or city; an alley or wynd. Chiefly *Sc.*

1435 in *Laing Charters* (1899) 30 A land in the west gate lyand neste the comoune vennel. **1439** *Charters*, etc. *of Edinb.* (1871) 64 The comon venale callit Sanct Leonardis wynde. **1477** *Extr. Aberd. Rec.* (1844) I. 36 That the alderman..pass through the toune to see the venalis that are closit. **1531** *Abst. Protocols Town Clerks of Glasgow* IV. (1897) 43 The common wennel of the Gray Freris. **1562** in *Archæol. Æliana* (1856) I. 41 Two burgages or tenements lying together in Spycer Lane, abutting on a vennel called the Stonye Hyll. **1609** SKENE *Reg. Maj.* 155 Gif ther be any venels stopped, or bigged vp. **1706** in M'Naught *Kilmaurs* xix. 251 To send one man out of every house..to repair the high wayes and venniles. **1727** *Rec. Elgin* (New Spald. Cl.) I. 425 The vennell or wynd called Lossie or Carman's wynd. *a* **1774** D. GRAHAM *Writ.* (1883) I. 101 Some through Preston vennal fled. **1859** W. ANDERSON *Disc. Ser.* II. (1860) 106 When he is away to hold the prayer-meeting down the Vennel. **1879** *N. & Q.* 5th Ser. XI. 137/1 In the town of Strabane, Ireland, there are a number of narrow passages, called 'vennels', from the main street to the river shore.

2. *north.* An open drain or gutter; a sewer.

1641 in Heslop *Northumbld. Wds.* s.v., Paid Strother for making cleane the common vennell before Widdow Wilson's doore, 1s. *a* **1800** PEGGE *Suppl. Grose*, *Vennel*, a gutter, called the *kennel*..elsewhere. Northumb. **1825** BROCKETT *N.C. Gloss.*, *Vennel*, a sewer. **1881** SARGISSON *Joe Scoap* 93 (E.D.D.), Carry't t' watter off beaath ways inteh t' vennels.

venneson, -soun, obs. ff. VENISON.

venney, vennie, varr. VENY² *Obs.*

Vennis, obs. f. VENICE.

vennisone, -ysoun, obs. ff. VENISON.

venny, var. VENY² *Obs.*; dial. f. FENNY *a.*²

veno- (viːnəʊ), comb. form of L. *vēna* VEIN *sb.*, employed in terms relating to the vascular system, as **veno'clysis** [Gr. κλύσις drenching], the introduction of liquid into the circulation by an intravenous drip; **venocon'striction,** constriction of a vein; **veno-oc'clusive** *a.*, characterized by occlusion of veins: applied esp. to a tropical disease in which this is the chief pathological feature; **'venospasm,** sudden, transient contraction of a vein; **veno'stasis,** a reduction (induced or spontaneous) in the flow of venous blood from a part of the body.

[**1910** M. F. DONAHOE *Man. of Nursing* ix. 166 In preparing for a veneclysis the nurse should take as much care as for an abdominal operation.] **1926** *Texas State Jrnl. Med.* XXI. 664/2, I regard the main indications for venoclysis as being any form of grave collapse, grave toxemia, prolonged shock, or serious dehydration from any cause. **1961** *Lancet* 2 Sept. 538/2 Some such device is essential for venoclysis in infancy. **1937** K. J. FRANKLIN *Monograph on Veins* x. 127 Perfusion of the corpus striatum with hot and cold fluids resulted in superficial venodilation and venoconstriction respectively. **1977** *Proc. Soc. Med.* LXX. 691/2 Blood samples were taken without venoconstriction at 13:00 and 14:00. **1954** G. BRAS et al. in *Arch. Path.* LVII. 285 (*heading*) Veno-occlusive disease of liver with nonportal type of cirrhosis, occurring in Jamaica. **1969** EDINGTON & GILLES *Path. in Tropics* xi. 489 It is now generally accepted that veno-occlusive disease in the West Indies is due to ingestion of 'bush tea' containing the alkaloids of *C*[*rotolaria*] *fulva*. **1950** P. WOOD *Dis. Heart & Circulation* i. 13 Venospasm is avoided by proper skin anæsthesia, and by choosing a catheter that is not too large for the vein. **1977** *Lancet* 1 Jan. 29/2 The damage is caused by pulmonary venospasm (occurring as the shock is relieved). **1931** R. J. E. SCOTT *Gould's Med. Dict.* (ed. 3), Venostasis. **1965** *Thrombosis & Diathesis Hæmorrhagica* XIV. 501 Venostasis was induced by means of a sphygmomanometric cuff (systolic pressure diminished by 20 mmHg). **1976** *Lancet* 11 Dec. 1265/2 Despite the presence of venostasis in the legs, intermittent compression of the arms during and after surgery reduced the incidence of deep venous thrombosis..in the legs to half that in control patients.

venography (vəˈnɒ-, vɪˈnɒgrəfɪ). *Med.* [f. VENO- + -GRAPHY.] Radiography of a vein after injection of a contrast medium.

1935 *Arch. Surg.* XXXI. 272 Venography..showed an obstruction in the axillary vein distal to the first rib. **1980** *Brit. Med. Jrnl.* 18 Oct. 1039/1 No arteriovenous malformation was detected by venography or arteriography.

Hence **veno'graphic, -ical** *adjs.*; **veno'graphically** *adv.*; also **'venogram,** a radiogram of a vein.

1935 *Arch. Surg.* XXXI. 272 A venogram made with a stabilized solution of thorium dioxide on the third day after admission showed a point of obstruction in the axillary vein to the first rib. **1940** *Surg., Gynecol. & Obstetr.* LXXI. 701/1 Venographic studies were carried out. **1940** *Acta Chir. Scand.* Suppl. LXI. 22 The venographical method has proved to be a very valuable diagnostic aid in manifest and suspect..thrombosis. **1940** Venographically [see *thromboembolic* adj. s.v. THROMBO-]. **1972** *Science* 16 June 1236/3 A considerable advantage of these images [produced by ultrasonic Doppler technique] is that they look like present-day arteriograms and venograms. **1978** *Lancet* 12 Aug. 331/2 Limbs with chronic venous insufficiency which had no venographically detected thrombosis. **1980** *Ibid.* 16 Feb. 332/2 We found venographic evidence of compression of popliteal veins by such a cyst in only 1 case.

venom (ˈvɛnəm), *sb.* and *a.* Forms: α. 3-6 **venym,** 4 **uenym, fenym (femyn),** 4-5 **wenym, venyme;** 3 **uenim,** 3-7 **venim,** 4 **wenim,** 4-7 **venime,** 6 **venimme;** 4-5 **wenem,** 5-7 **venem(e.** β. 4-6 **venum** (6 *Sc.* **winam**); 4-7 **venome,** 7 **venombe,** 4- **venom** (4, 9 *dial.*, **vemon,** 9 *dial.* **wenom**); *Sc.* 5 **wennome,** 6 **vennom(e.** [a. AF. and OF. *venim* (*venym*), variant of *venin* (see VENIN¹):—L. *venēn-um* (whence also It., Sp., Pg. *veneno*) poison, potion, drug, dye, etc.

The change of the final *n* to *m* may have been due to dissimilation (a different effect of which appears in the OF. variant *velin* and It. *veleno*), but cf. *pilgrim*, *vellum*.]

A. *sb.* **1.** The poisonous fluid normally secreted by certain snakes and other animals and used by them in attacking other living creatures.

The venom of snakes is secreted in a poison gland communicating with the fangs, through which it is ejected in the act of striking.

α. *c* **1220** *Bestiary* 139 in *O.E. Misc.* 5 Oc he [*sc.* a serpent] speweð or al ðe uenim ðat in his brest is bred. *a* **1300** *Cursor M.* 14871 Strangli was þis folk felun,..Was nedder nan o mar wenim. *c* **1325** *Prose Psalter* xiii. 5 Venim of aspides, .i. nedders. *c* **1386** CHAUCER *Pars. T.* ¶ 195 The galle of the dragon shal been hire drynke, and the venym of the dragon hire morsels. *c* **1450** *St. Cuthbert* (Surtees) 6313 A serpent him our qweld..; Bot his venym it did na sare. **1484** CAXTON *Fables of Æsop* v. viii, The serpent came oute and slewe the child through his venym. **1555** EDEN *Decades* (Arb.) 67 *marg.*, Serpentes without venime. **1652** J. WRIGHT tr. *Camus' Nat. Paradox* III. 49 Like Spiders which make venim of Roses.

β. *a* **1300** *Cursor M.* 20959 þe nedder o venum sa strang. *a* **1340** HAMPOLE *Psalter* xiii. 5 Venome of snakis [is] vndire þe lippes of þa. *a* **1400-50** *Alexander* 4797 As gotis out of guttars in golanand wedres, So voidis doun þe vemon be vermyns schaftis. **1614** *Disc. Strange & Monstrous Serpent* B 4, [The dragon] will cast his venome about foure rodde from him. *a* **1645** MILTON *Arcades* 53 What the..hurtfull Worm with canker'd venom bites. **1727-46** THOMSON *Summer* 909 He [*sc.* a serpent].., Whose high-concocted venom thro' the veins A rapid lightning darts. **1774** GOLDSM. *Nat. Hist.* VII. ix. 195 The venom contained in this bladder is a yellowish thick tasteless liquor. **1813** BYRON *Corsair* I. xi. 28 Man spurns the worm, but pauses ere he wake The slumbering venom of the folded snake. **1821-2** SHELLEY *Chas. I*, I. 127 As adders cast their skins And keep their venom, so kings often change. **1873** MIVART *Elem. Anat.* 438 Poisonous serpents however are provided with an extra glandular structure placed beneath and behind the orbit. This gland it is which secretes the venom.

†**b.** *of venom*, = VENOMOUS *a.* 3. *Obs.*

1387 TREVISA *Higden* (Rolls) I. 311 þey3 þere be no grete bestes of venym, 3it þere beeþ venemous attercoppes.

2. Poison, esp. as administered to or drunk by a person; any poisonous or noxious substance, preparation, or property; a morbid secretion or virus. Now *rare.*

α. *c* **1290** *S. Eng. Leg.* 408/207 Venim ich habbe, strong i-nov3h, þat ho-so þarof nimeth ou3t..to deþe he worthþ i-brou3t. **1297** R. GLOUC. (Rolls) 1010 Ech gras þat þerinne wexþ, a3en venim is. *a* **1300** *Cursor M.* 21055 Venim he drank wit-outen wath. **1377** LANGL. *P. Pl.* B. XVIII. 152 For venym for-doth venym. **1380** *Lay Folks Catech.* (Lamb. MS.) 1133 Whi schuld venym or stynk lette vs to visite men in presun? *c* **1400** MAUNDEV. (Roxb.) xvii. 80 If venym or puyson be bro3t in place whare þe dyamaund es, alsone it waxez moyst. **1422** YONGE tr. *Secreta Secret.* 195 Many kingys..that myght not be ouercome with armys by wenym loste thar lywis. **1527** ANDREW *Brunswyke's Distyll. Waters* C j, Water of the same..is good to be dronke for venym and impoysonynge. **1555** EDEN *Decades* (Arb.) 108 Fogeda,.. throwgh the maliciousnes of the veneme [of a poisoned arrow], consumed and was dryed vp by lyttle and lyttle. **1593** Q. ELIZ. *Boeth.* I. pr. iii. 6 Thou haste not knowen Anaxagoras flight, nor Socrates Venim, nor Zenos torment. **1616** SURFL. & MARKH. *Countrie Farme* 179 Garlicke eaten fasting, is the Countrey mans Treacle in the time of the Plague,..as also against all manner of Venime and Poyson.

β. *a* **1340** HAMPOLE *Psalter* xxx. 5 As venome is hid vndire a swet morsell. *c* **1375** *Sc. Leg. Saints* v. (*John*) 329, I wil þat þu drinke þe venome I sal þe gyfe. *c* **1430** LYDG. *Min. Poems* (Percy Soc.) 186 Ther is no venome so parlious in sharpnes, Os when it hathe of treacle a lyknes. *c* **1480** HENRYSON *Orpheus & Eurydice* (Asloan) 106 This cruell wennome was so penitryf, As natur is of all mortall poisoun. **1584** COGAN *Haven Health* ccxliii. 265 The houses and the houshoulde stuffe, vnlesse they bee purified with fire..and such like, keepe their venom for the space of a yeare or more. **1594** SHAKS. *Rich. III*, IV. i. 62 Anoynted let me be with deadly Venome. **1651** HOBBES *Leviath.* II. xxix. 173 Till (if Nature be strong enough) it break at last the contumacy of the parts obstructed, and dissipateth the venome into sweat. **1685** TEMPLE *Ess., Gardens* Wks. 1720 I. 178 A great Preservative against the Plague, which is a sort of Venom. **1797** COLERIDGE *Rev. G. Coleridge* 29 Some [trees]..Have tempted me to slumber in their shade..; then breathing subtlest damps, Mixed their own venom with the rain from Heaven, That I woke poisoned! **1896** *Allbutt's Syst. Med.* I. 731 Infection of the deeper tissues and of the whole body is chiefly due to absorption of soluble venom from the place where the growth of microbes is proceeding. **1910** *Contemp. Rev.* Mar. 337 Fields of nightshade that are sufficient to themselves in their own foul venom.

3. *fig.* Something comparable to or having the effect of poison; any baneful, malign, or noxious influence or quality; bitter or virulent feeling, language, etc.

α. *a* **1300** *Cursor M.* 15389 Of all venim and of envi ful kindeld vp he ras. *c* **1325** *E.E. Allit. P.* B. 574 þe venym & þe vylanye & þe vycios fylþe, þat by-sulpez mannez saule in vnsounde hert. *c* **1380** WYCLIF *Wks.* (1880) 417 3if manye wolden holde togedere in þis bileue a3enus þe fend, it were a triacle a3enus venym þat emperour prelatis sowen in þe folc. *c* **1400** *Pilgr. Sowle* II. xlv. (1859) 51 They have ben wretched and irous, ful of venym, of rancour, and of hate. *c* **1450** *Myrr. our Ladye* 205 God gaue mankynde fowde of lyfe wherin the enmy spued venym by a worde of lesyng. **1509** FISHER 7 *Penit. Ps.* xxxviii. Wks. (1876) 79 They laye before a man venym pryuely hyd vnder the colour of apperynge vertue. *a* **1569** KINGESMYLL *Man's Est.* vi. (1580) 33 That venime hath infected the whole race. **1607** HIERON *Wks.* I. 361 Hauing in him the arrowes of the Almightie, the venime thereof drinking vp his spirit. *a* **1674** CLARENDON *Surv. Leviath.* (1676) 168 The veneme of this Book wrought upon the hearts of men.

β. **1508** DUNBAR *Tua Mariit Wemen* 166 To speik..I sall nought spar... I sall the venome devoid with a vent large. **1567** *Satir. Poems Reform.* iv. 152 Lat men be war, and keip thame suire Fra wemenis vennome. **1596** DALRYMPLE tr. *Leslie's Hist. Scot.* (S.T.S.) II. 215 Quha venum verie poysonable and deidlye in Germanie had souked out of Luther, and otheris Archheritikis. **1599** B. JONSON *Cynthia's Rev.* III. ii, Well, I am resolv'd what Ile doe.—What, my good spirituous sparke?—Mary, speake all the venome I can of him. **1602** SHAKS. *Ham.* II. ii. 533 Who this had seene, with tongue in Venome steep'd, 'Gainst Fortunes State would Treason haue pronounc'd. **1675** MARVELL *Corr.* Wks. (Grosart) II. 467 He was gone into the country, swoln with his new honour, and with venom against the fanatics. **1715-6** HEARNE *Collect.* (O.H.S.) V. 170 Dr. Charlett continued his venom ag[ains]t non-jurors. **1759** FRANKLIN *Ess.* Wks. 1840 III. 416 A dose of venom apparently prepared, and administered to poison the province. **1818** SCOTT *Br. Lamm.* xxxiii, The venom of your present language is sufficient to remind her, that she speaks with the mortal enemy of her father. **1860** EMERSON *Cond. Life, Fate* Wks. (Bohn) II. 321 Whilst art draws out the venom, it commonly extorts some benefit from the vanquished enemy.

b. With *of* (sin, envy, etc.).

α. *c* **1315** SHOREHAM IV. 93 þorwe þe fenym of senne þat al mankende slakþ. *c* **1386** CHAUCER *Pars. T.* ¶ 530 Certes than is love the medicine that casteth out the venime of envie fro mannes herte. **1497** BP. ALCOCK *Mons Perfect.* B iij, Yᵉ deuyl ..sessed neuer with his venym of dyscorde. **1557** *Tottel's Misc.* (Arb.) 245 Beware also the venym swete Of crafty wordes and flattery.

β. **1435** MISYN *Fire of Love* 64 If any odyr gretter, fayrar or strengar be cald in þe pepyll, onon he is heuy touchyd with venum of envy. *c* **1440** *Alph. Tales* 122 He told so mekull horrible venom of syn at þaim irkid to here hym. **1562** WIN3ET *Wks.* (S.T.S.) I. 40 The sweit venum of deuyllish eloquence of wordis. **1597** SHAKS. *2 Hen. IV*, IV. iv. 45 Mingled with Venom of Suggestion. **1643** R. BAKER *Chron., Rich. I*, 91 If it may not have the name, yet certainely it had the venome of a bitter Taxation. **1654** WHITLOCK *Zootomia* 445 It were to be wished all the Venome of Detraction were spent against it selfe. **1697** PRIOR *A Satire* 51 The Venom of a spiteful Satire.

†**c.** Used in addressing persons. *Obs. rare.*

1592 BRETON *Pilgrim. Paradise* Wks. (Grosart) I. 12/2 The pilgrime gan replie, Die ougly venum in thy villany. **1601** SHAKS. *Twel. N.* III. ii. 2 *And.* No faith, Ile not stay a iot longer: *To.* Thy reason deere venom, giue thy reason.

4. With *a* and pl. A poison; a particular kind of poison or virus.

α. **1377** LANGL. *P. Pl.* B. XVIII. 153 Of alle venymes, foulest is þe scorpioun. **1402** HOCCLEVE *Lett. Cupid* 258 With oo venym another was distroyed. **1460-70** *Bk. Quintessence* 16 þanne it schal be no nede to vse in this perilous cure venemys, as some lechis doon. *a* **1533** LD. BERNERS *Gold. Bk. M. Aurel.* (1546) U iij b, Suche herbes and venims that might poyson them in theyr meates. **1556** *Chron. Gr. Friars* (Camden) 102 One Richard Roose..dyd caste a certyne venym or poyson into a vessell replenysshed with yeste or barme. **1594** WEST *2nd Pt. Symbol., Chancerie* §29 Discerning and tempering by just proportions good venims from evil. **1604** JAS. I *Counterbl. to Tobacco* (Arb.) 100 The stinking Suffumigation whereof they yet vse against that disease, making so one canker or venime to eate out another. **1611** LOVELL *Hist. Anim. & Min.* 255 [Salamanders'] biting is deadly, having as many venims as colours.

β. **1513** DOUGLAS *Æneid* VII. iv. 88 King Picus.., Quham, revist for his lufe, throu vennomys seyr, Circes his spous smate wyth ane goldin wand. **1580** FRAMPTON tr. *Monarde's Two Med. agst. Venome* 115 These venoms partly doe kill us; partly we use them for our profite, and bodily health. **1613** PURCHAS *Pilgrimage* (1614) 480 A man, whose nature infected with a stronger venome, poysoned other venemous creatures, if any did bite him. **1859** TENNYSON *Vivien* 459 Were all as tame..as their Queen was fair? Not one to flirt a venom at her eyes, Or pinch a murderous dust into her drink? **1904** *Brit. Med. Jrnl.* 10 Sept. 571 The anti-effect of different specific antivenoms upon their venoms. *Ibid.* 574 The toxicity of the most powerful venoms.

b. *fig.* (Cf. 3.)

1523 LD. BERNERS *Froiss.* I. ccclxxxiv. 647 These people ..retourned into their owne countreis; but the great venym remayned styll behynde, for Watte Tyler, Jacke Strawe, and John ball..wolde nat departe so. *a* **1578** LINDESAY (Pitscottie) *Chron. Scot.* (S.T.S.) II. 82 Ane winam aganis the poure man. **1583** BABINGTON *Commandm.* (1590) 346 There is no speciall calling amongst men, whereunto by name this vice is not forbidden as a venome of all vertue. **1757** BURKE *Abridgm. Eng. Hist.* Wks. X. 411 Taunts and mockeries..which infused a mortal venom into the war. **1910** A. R. MACEWEN *Antoinette Bourignon* ii. 54 All the poisons and venoms with which sin has polluted God's handiwork.

†**5.** A colouring matter; a dye. *Obs. rare.*

c **1374** CHAUCER *Boeth.* ii. met. 5 (1868) 50 þei couþe nat medle the bri3te flies of þe contre of siriens wiþ þe venym of tirie. **1552** HULOET, *Venym*,..is generallye [to denote] anye thynge whych altereth coloure, or nature of that wher-with it is myxt.

6. *attrib.* and *Comb.* **a.** Comb., as ***venom-breeding, -hating, -sputtering; venom-fanged, -noyed, -spotted*** adjs.; ***venom-maker; venom-cold*** adj.

venom mouthed: see VENOMED *ppl. a.* 4.

a **1340** HAMPOLE *Psalter* lvii. 5 Crist..lufes not charmers and venym makers. **1382** WYCLIF *Ps.* lvii. 6 The vois of the enchaunteres; and of the venym makere. *c* **1400** *Laud Troy Bk.* 926 Medee..By-tau3t Iason a riche ryng, That alle venym for-dede & strued,—That he schul not be venym-noyed. **1598** MARSTON *Sco. Villanie* III. xi. 229 Avaunt lewd curre, presume not to speake, Or with thy venome-sputtering chaps to barke 'Gainst well-pend poems. **1612** DRAYTON *Poly-olb.* I. 52 Jernsey,..whose venom-hating ground The hard'ned emeril hath. **1760** FAWKES *Anacreon, Odes* xlii. 12 By rankling Malice never stung, I shun the venom-venting Tongue. **1828** *Blackw. Mag.* XXIV. 481 The venom-spotted coils and serpent eyes. *a* **1847** ELIZA COOK *There's a Hero* iv. 2 A venom-breeding Ocean. **1864** J. C. ATKINSON *Stanton Grange* 220 A venom-fanged viper. **1889** R. B. ANDERSON tr. *Rydberg's Teut. Mythol.* 92 The venom-cold Elivogs. **1904** *Brit. Med. Jrnl.* 10 Sept. 581 The treatment of venom poisoning.

b. Simple attrib., as ***venom-albumen, -flood, -globulin, -peptone, -snake,*** etc.

1845 *Zoologist* III. 1031, I found also five pairs of rudimental fangs,..apparently unattached to the venom-sac. **1847-9** *Todd's Cycl. Anat.* IV. 291/1 In the most deadly venom-snakes..the poison fangs acquire their largest size. **1855** BAILEY *Mystic* 54 Fire, ice and scalding venom-floods of hell. **1883** *Science* II. 24/1 Three distinct proteids may be isolated from the venom of the moccason and the rattle-snake. These they propose to call respectively, venom-peptone, venom-globulin, and venom-albumen. **1897** *Allbutt's Syst. Med.* II. 811 One observer classing a venom proteid with the albumins or globulins.

B. *adj.* Venomous; virulent, malignant, spiteful. *Obs.* exc. *dial.*

a **1350** *St. Laurence* 158 in Horstm. *Altengl. Leg.* (1881) 109 And seyn bete his body bare With scorpions þat uenym ware. **1398** TREVISA *Barth. De P.R.* XVIII. xi. (Bodl. MS.), The venem spiþer hatte Aranea. *a* **1425** *Cursor M.* 20959 (Trin.), þe venym nedder þat was strong. *c* **1511** *1st Eng. Bk. Amer.* (Arb.) Introd. p. xxxiv/1 Forestis full of snakes and other venym beestes. **1538** BALE *God's Promises* III. in Dodsley *Old Plays* (1780) I. 18 In my syght, he is more venym than the spyder. **1590** SHAKS. *Com. Err.* v. 69 The venome clamors of a iealous woman. **1594** NASHE *Unfort. Trav.* Wks. (Grosart) V. 116 Things like sheep-lice, which aliue haue the venomest sting that may be. **1600** BRETON *Melanch. Hum.* Wks. (Grosart) I. 13/1 Tis a subtill kinde of spirit, Of a venome kinde of nature. **1892** *E. Anglian Daily Times* (E.D.D.), A man remarked to two boys fighting, 'You-a-munshy [you amongst you] fare as wenom as harnets'.

'venom, *v.* Now *Obs.* or *arch.* Forms: α. 4–5 **venem(e, 4–6 venym(e, (4 venymp-, femyne),** 4, 6–7 **venim(e, 6 veneymen.** β. 5–7 **venome** (5 **vemon), 6– venom, 7 vennum.** [ad. OF. *venimer* to envenom, or f. VENOM *sb.* Cf. ANVENOM *v.* and ENVENOM *v.*]

1. *trans.* To injure by means of venom; to poison (a person, etc.); = ENVENOM *v.* 1.

c **1320** *Sir Tristr.* 1526 Þe tong [of þe dragon] y bar oway; Þus venimed he me þan. **1375** in Horstmann *Altengl. Leg.* (1878) 136/1 Who so were..venympd wiþ eny wikked beste. *a* **1400–50** *Alexander* 4842 A Basilisk..vemons in þe vaward valiant kniȝtis. *c* **1440** *Gesta Rom.* xviii. 332 (Harl. MS.), It befelle in shorte tyme, that dragons and venemous bestes venemed men. **1483** *Cath. Angl.* 400/1 To venome, *venenare, jntoxicare.* **1552** HULOET, Veneymen, *inficio, cis, intoxico, as, ueneno, nas.* **1579** LANGHAM *Gard. Health* 202 He that rubbeth his hands with the root [of Dragons] in May, take adders, and they shall not venim him. **1610** MARKHAM *Masterp.* II. cviii. 390 Out of the same will runne a..humor, which will venome the whole foote. **1665** BUNYAN *Holy Citie* 230 The Dragon is a venemous beast, and poisoneth all where he lieth; he beats the Earth bare, and venoms it, that it will bear no grass. **1694** *Phil. Trans.* XVIII. 280 These with many other different Herbs spreading and running upon the Trees choak and venom them.

fig. **1579** TOMSON *Calvin's Serm. Tim.* 116/2 We shall see these vermine that seeke nothing else but to rotte or venime the Church of God. **1607** TOURNEUR *Rev. Trag.* III. E4b, Since I must, Through Brothers periurie, dye, O let me venome Their soules with curses.

transf. **1679** DRYDEN & LEE *Œdipus* III. i, Oh his murd'rous Breath Venoms my airy Substance!

b. *absol.*

1563 HYLL *Arte Garden.* (1593) 111 Linnen cloathes.. laid to any place, where either Spider or waspe hath venomed, dooth quickly take away the paine thereof. **1575** TURBERV. *Venerie* 187 She venometh with hir byting when she is sault, as the Wolfe doth. **1607** TOPSELL *Four-f. Beasts* 515 A shrew, which biting horses and labouring cattell, it doth venome vntill it come vnto the hart, and then they die. **1610** MARKHAM *Masterp.* II. cxxv. 427 Looke that you touch no part of the horse therewith, saue the sorrance onely; for it will venome.

2. To put venom in or on (something); to render venomous; = ENVENOM *v.* 2.

c **1350** *Libeaus Desc.* 2050 For þoruȝ þat swordes dint..þe venim will me spille: I venimed [*v.r.* femynede] hem boþe, ..Our fomen for to fille. **1387** TREVISA *Higden* (Rolls) V. 443 A swerdman, wiþ a swerd i-venymed. *a* **1470** HARDING *Chron.* LXXII. xiii, There was a well whiche his enemyes espied,..Whiche they venomyd with poyson on a daye. **1569** J. SANFORD tr. *Agrippa's Van. Artes* 105b, They have poysoned the water, infected the corne, and venomed the victuals. *a* **1604** HANMER *Chron. Ireland* (1633) 52 He also was sore wounded with a Speare, whose head was venomed. **1612** J. DAVIES (Heref.) *Muse's Sacr.* Wks. (Grosart) II. 18/1 The Med'cine, so, thou gau'st to cure my Wounds, I venomed to make my hurt the more. **1725** POPE *Odyss.* x. 272 Venom'd was the bread, and mix'd the bowl, With drugs of force to darken all the soul. **1834** BECKFORD *Italy* II. 78 The heat seems..to have new venomed the stings of the fleas and the musquitoes.

fig. **1794** SOUTHEY *Elinor* 52 All her rankling shafts Barb'd with disgrace, and venom'd with disease. **1800** COLERIDGE *Piccolom.* v. v, Wherefore barb And venom the refusal with contempt?

b. To embitter; = ENVENOM *v.* 2b.

1621 LADY M. WROTH *Urania* 154 Loue like a serpent poysoning my ioyes, and biting my best daies, venomd all my blisse. **1819** KEATS *Vis. Hyperion* I. 175 Only the dreamer venoms all his days, Bearing more woe than all his sins deserve.

3. *fig.* To infect with moral evil; to corrupt, deprave, vitiate; = ENVENOM *v.* 3.

13.. *K. Alis.* 2860 [They] saide wel, er that tyme, Al Grece was of heom venyme [*v.r.* venymed]. *c* **1380** WYCLIF *Wks.* (1880) 286 Þes religious & seculere prestis,..bi brekynge of þis lawe, ben cursid of god & venemyn cristendome. *c* **1407** LYDG. *Reson & Sens.* 3391 And of venym..Venus pleynly took her name. For she venemyth many wyse Al that doon to hir servise. **1536** BELLENDEN *Cron. Scot.* (1821) I. 51 Sen our time is now sa venomit with uncouth and superflew metis and drinkis. **1591** R. TURNBULL *St. James* 161b, Lyes, blasphemie,..filthie talke, ..whereby the soules of men are often poysoned and venomed to death. **1616** BRETON *Invective agst. Treason* Wks. (Grosart) I. 4/2 Pride doth blinde y[e] Eie, Infects y[e] Minde, vennums y[e] harte, and gives the Sowle a sting. **1681** *Peace & Truth* 10 This was the felicity of innocent Man before his Heart was venomed with Lust and Vanity. **1906** *Westm. Gaz.* 24 Dec. 2/1 To the pyre With this fiend that venoms all our sinful veins!

'venomed, *ppl. a.* [f. VENOM *sb.* or *v.* Cf. ENVENOMED *ppl. a.*]

1. Of reptiles, insects, etc.: Endowed with venom; = VENOMOUS *a.* 3.

1382 WYCLIF *Wisdom* xvi. 10 Thi sonus forsothe, nouther the teth of dragounes, ne of venymed thingus ouercamen. **1445** in *Anglia* XXVIII. 269 She [Lechery] misshapith som bodies More cruelly than circes herbis, which venemyd be with poysoun. **1552** HULOET, Venemed, *infectus, intoxicatus.* **1587** MASCALL *Govt. Cattle, Oxen* (1627) 15 Against the venomed tongue of a beast, and also his body. **1592** BRETON *Pilgrim. Paradise* Wks. (Grosart) I. 8/2 A wood..Where Snakes, and Adders, and such venumed things, Had slaine a number, with their cruell stinges. **1607** TOPSELL *Four-f. Beasts* 26 The liver of an asse burnt, driueth away venomed things. **1697** DRYDEN *Virg. Georg.* III. 629 To drive the Viper's Brood, and all the venom'd Race. **1794** MATHIAS *Purs. Lit.* (1798) 157 And venom'd insects cluster round the tomb. *a* **1806** HORSLEY *Serm.* (1816) IV. 35 The natural advantages of man over the venom'd reptile.

2. Covered, charged, imbued, impregnated, or smeared with venom; full of venom; poisoned, poisonous; = VENOMOUS *a.* 5.

? **1402** QUIXLEY *Ball.* iii. in *Yorks. Arch. Jrnl.* (1908) XX. 44 Hercules Of a venymed schert was foul deseyue And brent hym self. **1540** HYRDE tr. *Vives' Instr. Chr. Wom.* II. iv. 69 Her husband in warre against the Syrians had catched a great wounde in his arme with a venomed sworde. **1555** EDEN *Decades* (Arb.) 116 Theyr weapons are nother bowes nor venemed arrowes. *a* **1604** HANMER *Chron. Ireland* (1809) 103 A Speare, whose head was venomed. **1631** P. FLETCHER *Piscatory Eclog.* IV. xvii, The fish their life and death together drink, And dead pollute the seas with venom'd stink. **1634** MILTON *Comus* 916 This marble venom'd seat Smear'd with gumms of glutenous heat. **1700** DRYDEN *Ovid's Met.* xv. 360 With venom'd Grinders you corrupt your Meat. **1746** FRANCIS tr. *Horace, Sat.* I. viii. 33 They, who turn poor people's brains With venom'd drugs and magic lay. **1757** W. WILKIE *Epigoniad* VII. 210 The venom'd garment hiss'd; its touch the fires Avoiding. **1824** in *Spirit Pub. Jrnls.* (1825) 308 Though he often sting me with a dart, Venomed and barbed. *a* **1839** PRAED *Poems* (1864) II. 20 Beneath their venomed breath Life wears the pallid hue of death. **1882** MISS BRADDON *Mt. Royal* II. ix. 168 He had aimed many a venomed arrow at her breast.

b. Of a wound.

1425 tr. *Arderne's Treat. Fistula,* etc. 79 Also vitriol combuste be itself or with salt combuste yputte vpon a venemyd wonde draweþ þe venym fro byneþ vnto aboue. **1597** A. M. tr. *Guillemeau's Fr. Chirurg.* 2/2 Some woundes are of a worser nature, as beinge venoumede, rebellious and entermingled with some badde accidentes. **1805** SCOTT *Last Minstrel* VI. ix, The venom'd wound..Long after rued that bodkin's point. **1870** BRYANT *Iliad* II. I. 71 A venomed wound Made by a serpent's fangs.

c. Of a bite, sting, etc. Also *fig.*

1602 MARSTON *Ant. & Mel.* IV. Wks. 1856 I. 53 We have breasts of proofe Gainst all the venom'd stings of misery. **1697** DRYDEN *Virg. Georg.* II. 522 The greedy Flocks; Their venom'd Bite, and Scars indented on the Stocks. **1765** GOLDSM. *New Simile* 48 The serpents round about it twin'd, Denote the rage with which he writes, His frothy slaver, venom'd bites. **1812** S. ROGERS *Ep. to Friend* 4 When..thy curious mind Has class'd the insect-tribes of human-kind, Each with its busy hum,..Its subtle web-work, or its venom'd sting. **1822** JODRELL *Persian Heroine* II. ii. 758 How sharp thy venom'd sting is, O Remorse! **1903** BRIDGES *Wintry Delights* 377 All the venom'd stings And dread sharpnesses of fury.

3. *fig.* Imbued with some virulent or malevolent quality; harmful or injurious in some way; noxious; = ENVENOMED *ppl. a.* 2.

c **1375** *Sc. Leg. Saints* l. (*Katherine*) 222 Gyf þou had mycht, me think þu wald with venemyt slycht, tak ws in gyrne dissatfully. **1382** WYCLIF *Josh.* Prol., To reproue with venymyd tonge. **1435** MISYN *Fire of Love* 90 So þat non erthly þinge nor odir of venemyd swetnes in qwhilk þa suld haue luste þa take. **1602** MARSTON *Ant. & Mel.* I. Wks. 1856 I. 11 Till their soules burst with venom'd arrogance. **1656** EARL MONM. tr. *Boccalini's Advts. fr. Parnass.* I. xxx. (1674) 34[They] appease the minds of incenst Princes, and the hearts of venomed people. **1718** PRIOR *Solomon* III. 206 The Venom'd Tongue injurious to his Fame. **1726** POPE *Odyss.* XIX. 115 Him, my guest, thy venom'd rage hath stung. **1821** SHELLEY *Epipsych.* 256 One, whose voice was venomed melody. **1859** TENNYSON *Merlin & V.* 170 She play'd about with slight and sprightly talk, And vivid smiles, and faintly-venom'd points Of slander. **1865** *Spectator* 14 Oct. 1133/2 The kind of scribe who speaks of Mr. Delane as having left behind him 'a venomed trail'.

4. *Comb.* in ***venomed-mouthed*** adj.

1613 SHAKS. *Hen. VIII,* I. i. 120 This Butchers Curre is venom'd-mouth'd [*Rowe* (1709) venome mouth'd; *mod. edd.* venom-mouth'd], and I Haue not the power to muzzle him.

Hence † **'venomedness.** *Obs.*[−0]

1611 COTGR., *Venenosité,* venomednesse, venomousnesse.

'venomer. *rare.* [f. VENOM *v.*] One who administers venom; a poisoner.

1647 HEXHAM I. s.v., A venomer, or poysoner. **1880** HOWELLS *Venetian Life* xii. 181 As sovereign against the arts of venomers as an exclusive diet of boiled eggs.

† **'venomful**, *a. Obs.* [f. VENOM *sb.*] Venomous, poisonous.

1544 *Exhort.* in *Priv. Prayers* (1851) 569 We must beware ..of that venomful poison of all good prayer, that is to say, when our mouth prayeth, and our hearts pray not. **1612** R. FENTON *Usury* 54 Verily they discerned some malignant and venomfull qualitie in vsurie.

'venoming, *vbl. sb.* [f. VENOM *v.*] The action of the verb; poisoning; †poison.

1382 WYCLIF *2 Kings* ix. 22 ȝit the fornycaciouns of Jezabel..and hyr many venymyngis thrijuen. *a* **1470** HARDING *Chron.* CCX. v, Some in his sherte put ofte tyme venemyng. **1610** MARKHAM *Masterp.* II. cxxi. 421 All bruisings and swellings come vnto a horse..by accident, as by some blow, rush, pinch, or outward venoming. **1657** W. COLES *Adam in Eden* xxxvi, The wreathed form of the Root is a sign that it is good for the venoming of Toads, Spiders, Adders.

venomization (ˌvɛnəmaɪˈzeɪʃən). [f. VENOM *sb.* + -IZATION.] The action or process of treating with snake venom.

1905 *Jrnl. Exper. Med.* VII. 201 The effect of washing the Corpuscles after Venomization.

† **'venomly**, *adv. Obs. rare.* In 4 **venymliche**, 6 **venumly.** [f. VENOM *sb.* + -LY[2].] Venomously; with venom.

1387 TREVISA *Higden* (Rolls) VIII. 147 Also among þe peple he blamede venymliche [*Harl. MS.* venymouslich; *Caxton* venymously]..þe outrage of riche men. **1556** J. HEYWOOD *Spider & Fly* xliii. 40 This formost spider and flie ..Frowning ech on other, this prosesse thei perst, And vengeable venumly, ech other verst.

'venomness. Now *rare.* [f. VENOM *sb.* + -NESS.] Venomousness.

1543 TRAHERON *Vigo's Chirurg.* II. iv. 21 Than stampe them togyther excepte the Psillium bycause of his venomnisse whych he hath in him. **1648** HEXHAM II, *Fenijnigheyt,* venomnesse, or poison. **1654** COKAINE *Dianea* II. 162 Perceiving the Infanta began to shew signes of the venomnesse of the poyson. **1886** B. ROOSEVELT *Copper Queen* I. ii. 30 A glittering serpent coiled in arrogant and tortuous venomness.

ˌvenomo-'salivary, *a. Zool.* [Irreg. f. VENOM *sb.* + SALIVARY *a.* Cf. VENENO-.] Of or pertaining to, secreting or conveying, venomous saliva.

1888 *Amer. Naturalist* XXII. 886 The venomo-salivary duct [of the mosquito]. *Ibid.* 888 The two efferent ducts.. carry forward..the venomo-salivary products. **1900** *Lancet* 18 Aug. 528/2 The secretion of the venimo[*sic*]-salivary glands.

venomous (ˈvɛnəməs), *a.* Forms: α. 4–5 **venymus, -ouse,** 4–6 **-ous,** 5 **-ows, venymm(o)us (vemynousse);** 4 **uenimous, venimouse,** 4, 6 **-us,** 5–7 **-ous;** 4–6 **venemouse,** 4–8 **-ous,** 5 *Sc.* **-us,** 5–6 *Sc.* **vennemous;** 5 **venamous,** *Sc.* **-us, -use,** 7 *Sc.* **ven'mowse.** β. 5– **venomous,** 5 *Sc.* **wenomose,** 6 *Sc.* **wennomus, vennomous,** 6 **venumous, venoumous.** [a. AF. *venimus, venimous,* = OF. (also mod.F.) *venimeux,* f. *venim* VENOM *sb.,* after L. *venēnōsus*: see VENENOUS *a.*]

† **1.** *fig.* Morally or spiritually hurtful or injurious; pernicious. *Obs.*

c **1290** *S. Eng. Leg.* I. 120/484 Þat word me þinchez venimous to þe pays of þe londe. *a* **1340** HAMPOLE *Psalter* cxlix. 2 To forsake þe venymous delitis of þis warld. *c* **1380** WYCLIF *Sel. Wks.* III. 20 Venemouse lustis and likingis of deedly synnes. *c* **1480** HENRYSON *Fables, Cock & Fox* 606 (Harl. MS.), Thir twa sinnis, flatterie and vane gloir, Ar vennomous. *c* **1490** CAXTON *Rule St. Benet* (E.E.T.S.) 129 Yf ony be founde gylty in this venemouse offence of properte. **1526** *Pilgr. Perf.* (W. de W. 1531) 55 The relygyous seruaunt of god..destroyeth by holy meditacyon y[e] flyes & spyders of venymous thoughtes. **1580** LYLY *Euphues* (Arb.) 414, I will at large proue that there is nothing in loue more venemous then meeting. **1610** HOLLAND *Camden's Brit.* 707 Saint German, who happily confuted that venemous Pelagian Heresie.

2. Containing, consisting or full of, infected with, venom; possessing poisonous properties or qualities; destructive of, harmful or injurious to, life on this account.

Common from *c* 1470 to *c* 1650; now *rare.*

c **1330** R. BRUNNE *Chron. Wace* (Rolls) 16594 By passagers wel herde he seye þe venimouse eyr was al a-weye. *c* **1340** HAMPOLE *Pr. Consc.* 6751 Another manere of drynk þat es ille, þat sal be bitter and venemus. *c* **1366** CHAUCER *A.B.C.* 149 With thornes venymous, O heuene queen,..I am wounded. **1474** CAXTON *Chesse* III. v. (1883) 126 That they put in theyr medicynes no thynge venemous. **1490** —— *Eneydos* xxiv. 88 Herbes..wherof the Iuse is passyng venymouse. **1555** EDEN *Decades* (Arb.) 45 Of the venemous apples wherwith the Canibales inueneme theyr arrowes. **1584** COGAN *Haven Health* ccxliii. (1636) 297 Not that the ayre is venomous of it selfe, but through corruption hath now gotten such a quality. *c* **1614** SIR W. MURE *Dido & Æneas* III. 108 Collecting als..The milkie poyson of each ven'mowse weed. **1651** HOBBES *Leviath.* II. xxix. 173 The fleshy parts being..by venomous matter obstructed. **1672** MARVELL *Reh. Transp.* I. 132 The cultivating of a Garden of venimous Plants. **1817** SHELLEY *Rev. Islam* x. xxxviii, On the heap Pour venomous gums. *a* **1839** PRAED *Red Fisherman* Poems 1864 I. 197 The trees and herbs that round it grew Were venomous and foul.

† **b.** Of a wound, etc.: Marked or characterized by the presence of poisonous matter; foul with venom; envenomed. *Obs.*

1398 TREVISA *Barth. De P.R.* XIX. lvii, Aȝens þe venemos posteme þat hatte antrax & aȝens oþer venemous postemes. **1541** R. COPLAND *Guydon's Form.* Uj, It shulde be an oyntment profitable to all sores that be venymous. *c* **1550** H. LLOYD *Treasury Health* Tv, Leuen of whete breketh the venemouse humors and apostumes. **1656** J. SMITH *Pract. Physic* 363 A wound made by bullets is not venemous, nor alwaies bruised. **1702** ECHARD *Eccl. Hist.* I. i. 36 His Distemper daily encreas'd,..and he himself labour'd under ..venomous Swellings in his Feet,..accompany'd with intolerable Smells. **1707** WATTS *Hymns* II. cliii. Poet. Wks. IV. 148 Sin like a venomous disease Infects our vital blood. **1774** GOLDSM. *Nat. Hist.* VII. ix. 196 When the serpent is irritated to give a venomous wound.

fig. **1597** HOOKER *Eccl. Pol.* v. lii. (1611) 292 A soueraigne preseruatiue..from the venemous infection of heresie.

c. Of a bite or sting.

1567 *Gude & Godlie Ball.* (S.T.S.) 81 He ouerthrew The Serpent, and his vennemous stang. **1653** WALTON *Angler* 146 The biting of a Pike is venemous and hard to be cured. **1753** J. BARTLET *Gentl. Farriery* 322 Of Venomous Bites from Vipers and Mad Dogs. **1787** BEST *Angling* (ed. 2) 48 Be careful how you take a pike out of the water, for his bite is venomous.

† **d.** Harmful or injurious *to* something. *Obs.*

1607 SHAKS. *Cor.* IV. i. 23 Thy teares are salter then a yonger mans, And venomous to thine eyes. **1691** T. H[ALE]

Acc. New Invent. 17 A Cancarous and Corroding substance, and venomous to Iron.

3. Of animals, *esp.* snakes, or their parts: Secreting venom; having the power or property of communicating venom by means of bites or stings; inflicting or capable of inflicting poisonous wounds in this way.

Formerly in general literary use, now chiefly restricted to certain species of poisonous snakes.

a. c **1375** *Sc. Leg. Saints* xxxi. (*Eugenia*) 396 Na serpent has a hed sa fel, sa venamuse, na sa cruel, as þe hed of þe colubre is. **1387** TREVISA *Higden* (Rolls) I. 51 Yuel doers, corrupte ayre, wylde bestes and venemous woneþ þerynne. *c* **1400** MAUNDEV. (1839) 199 Thanne have thei no drede of no Cocodrilles, ne of non other venymous Vermyn. *c* **1450** METHAM *Wks.* (E.E.T.S.) 46 For off summe off thise serpentys, the eyn so venymmus be That with her loke thei slee yche erthly creature. **1480** CAXTON *Myrr.* II. xiv. 97 Irland is a grett Ilonde in whiche is no serpent ne venemous beeste. **1522** MORE *De quat. Noviss.* Wks. 85/1 Like as the venemous spider bringeth forth her cobweb. **1596** SPENSER *F.Q.* VI. vi. 9 That beastes teeth, which.. Are so exceeding venemous and keene. **1600** SHAKS. *A.Y.L.* II. i. 13 Aduersitie Which like the toad, ougly and venemous, Weares yet a precious Iewell in his head. **1653** W. RAMESEY *Astrol. Restored* 229 Those places subject thereunto shall be afflicted with water, and venemous Creatures. **1748** *Anson's Voy.* III. ii. 314 We found.. scorpions, which we supposed were venemous. **1791-3** in *Spirit Public Jrnls.* (1799) I. 225 To sleep in a dungeon with venemous reptiles.

β. c **1515** *Henryson's Orpheus & Eurydice* (Asloan MS.) 105 As scho ran, all bairfut, in ane bus Scho trampit on a serpent wennomus. **1595** *Locrine* I. i. 76 Triple Cerberus with his venomous throte. **1651** WITTIE tr. *Primrose's Pop. Err.* IV. xxxviii. 271 If poyson, or some venomous creature be neare unto it, it sweats. **1671** SALMON *Syn. Med.* III. xxii. 442 It.. cures the bitings of venomous beasts. **1713** DERHAM *Phys.-Theol.* II. vi. 56 Many.. of our European venomous animals carry their Cure.. in their own Bodies. **1774** GOLDSM. *Nat. Hist.* VII. ix. 194 If it [*sc.* the serpent] has the fang teeth, it is to be placed among the venomous class. **1834** MCMURTRIE *Cuvier's Anim. King.* 182 Serpents are divided into venomous and non-venomous; and the former are sub-divided into such as are venomous with several maxillary teeth, and those which are venomous with insulated fangs. **1876** MISS BRADDON *J. Haggard's Dau.* III. 23 The serpent had lifted his venomous crest from among the flowers. *c* **1880** *Cassell's Nat. Hist.* IV. 301 The poisonous Snakes are divided into two groups—the Viperiform Snakes and the Venomous Colubrines.

b. *fig.*, chiefly with allusion to the Devil.

1340 *Ayenb.* 171 þe uenimouse eddre of helle. *c* **1450** *Mankind* 40 in *Macro Plays* 2 Yt hath dyssoluyde mankynde from þe bittur bonde Of þe mortall enmye, þat vemynousse serpente. *a* **1548** HALL *Chron., Hen. IV*, 25 The Earle of Northumberland.. bare still a venemous scorpion in his cankered heart. *Ibid., Hen. VI*, 169 That venemous worme, that dreadfull dragon, called disdain of superioritie. *a* **1578** LINDESAY (Pitscottie) *Chron. Scot.* (S.T.S.) II. 239 The Devill,.. that wicked and venimus serpent quho gois about to sie quhome he may catch.

4. *fig.* Having the virulence of venom; rancorous, spiteful, malignant, virulent; embittered, envenomed.

a **1340** HAMPOLE *Psalter* x. 2 þai haf redy in þaire hertis venymouse wordis and sharpe. *Ibid.* xxviii. 8 þaim.. þat.. puttis away venomus tongis. **1340** *Ayenb.* 27 þe venimouse herte of þe enuiouse zeneȝeþ generalliche. *c* **1400** *Rom. Rose* 5528 With tonge woundyng, as feloun, Thurgh venemous detracccioun. *a* **1450** *Knt. de la Tour* (1868) 56 It is not good to.. take sodeyne acqueintaunce that hathe the herte of faire speche, for sum tyme her speche is deseyuable and venomous. *c* **1489** CAXTON *Blanchardyn* li. 196 The venymouse malyce of the false traytoure Subyon. **1555** EDEN *Decades* (Arb.) 52 To speake venemous woordes.. ageynst the annoynted of god. **1588** SHAKS. *Titus Andron.* v. iii. 13 The Venemous Mallice of my swelling heart. **1648** HEXHAM II, *Feenijnighlick*, venommously, spightfully, or [with] a venomous envy. *a* **1721** PRIOR *Session of Poets* 36 That with very much Wit he no anger exprest Nor sharpen'd his Verse with a Venemous Jest. **1737** *Gentl. Mag.* VII. 623/2 One R. C... sent me venemous Libels against the Great Man. **1857** PALGRAVE *Hist. Normandy & Eng.* II. 18 A venomous opposition was festering against him. **1879** FROUDE *Cæsar* xii. 153 The most innocent intimacies would not have escaped misrepresentation from the venomous tongues of Roman society. **1885** *Manch. Exam.* 20 May 4/7 A venomous and scurrilous attack.

b. Of persons, their character, etc.

?*a* **1400** *Morte Arth.* 299 Of this grett velany I salle be vengede ones On ȝone venemus mene, wyth valiant knyghtes! **1567** *Satir. Poems Reform.* iv. 109 O wickit wemen, vennomus of nature! **1579** TOMSON *Calvin's Serm. Tim.* 901/2 What shall men say, when a mortall man dareth thus to become venemous against God. **1585** T. WASHINGTON tr. *Nicholay's Voy.* III. ii. 71 [Of these] christian children Mahometised, the venemous nature is so great, mischieuous and pernitious. **1607** HIERON *Wks.* I. 225 [Satan is] a venimous aduersary to empoyson our soule. **1643** SIR T. BROWNE *Relig. Med.* II. §10 There are in the most depraved and venemous dispositions, certaine pieces that remaine untoucht. **1882** J. H. BLUNT *Ref. Ch. Eng.* II. 244 His most bitter enemy, the venomous and unscrupulous Foxe. **1911** *Blackw. Mag.* Aug. 221 The doctor seemed to me a venomous little creature.

†**5.** Treated with venom or poison; envenomed, poisoned. *Obs.*

?*a* **1400** *Morte Arth.* 2570 With the venymous swerde a vayne has he towchede. *c* **1400** *Pilgr. Sowle* I. i. (1859) 1 Thenne comme cruel dethe and smote me with his venemous darte. *a* **1470** HARDING *Chron.* II. cxxxix, Kyng Rychard.. Was hurt right ther, with dartes venemous. **1555** EDEN *Decades* (Arb.) 107 These people also, vse bowes and venemous arrowes. **1578** LYTE *Dodoens* 305 It is good against.. venimous shot of dartes and arrowes. **1631** GOUGE *God's Arrowes* Ded. p. ix, How farre the venime thereof (for it is a venimous arrow) may infect, who knowes?

6. Of or pertaining to, of the nature of, venom.

c **1425** WYNTOUN *Cron.* VIII. clviii. 3135 þai thoucht to gere Him with sum venamus poisoun Be distroyit. **1604** JAS. I *Counterbl. to Tobacco* (Arb.) 103 Tobacco.. hath a certaine venemous facultie ioyned with the heate thereof. **1650** BULWER *Anthropomet.* 159 There being a venemous quality in the paint. **1675** J. OWEN *Indwelling Sin* vi. (1732) 50 It is in the Heart like Poison, that hath nothing to allay its venemous Qualities, and so infects whatever it touches. **1774** GOLDSM. *Nat. Hist.* VII. ix. 195 The glands that serve to fabricate this venomous fluid. **1826** MISS MITFORD *Village* Ser. II. (1863) 417 It has a fine venomous smell,.. and will certainly when stilled be good for something or other. **1887** A. M. BROWN *Anim. Alkaloids* 2 Gaspard and Stick.. had detected a venomous principle in cadaverous extracts.

fig. **1572** PERRY in Strype *Eccl. Mem.* (1721) III. 363 The God of Truth defend you.. from the venomous Poyson of Lyars. **1596** DALRYMPLE tr. *Leslie's Hist. Scot.* II. 41 Lyk a traytour he steilis in, that.. he may saw his venumous poyson. **1866** C. J. VAUGHAN *Plain Words* i. 10 The personal sins of each one of us.. eating like a venomous poison into his soul.

7. *Comb.* in ***venomous-hearted***, ***-looking*** adjs.

1740 RICHARDSON *Pamela* (1824) I. xv. 256 Several innocent creatures, might have been entangled.. in the ensnaring web of this venomous-hearted spider. **1899** F. T. BULLEN *Way Navy* 65 We sighted the enemy in the shape of one of those venomous-looking four-funnelled destroyers.

†**venomoushead.** *Obs.*$^{-1}$ [f. prec. + -HEAD.] Venomousness.

14.. *Langland's P. Pl.* C. XXI. 161 þenne hit destroieþ The ferst venemoste [*v.r.* venymous-heede] thorgh vertu of hymselue. [Cf. VENOMOUSTY.]

'venomously, *adv.* [f. VENOMOUS *a.* + -LY².] In a venomous manner; with venom or virulence; fiercely, malignantly, virulently. Chiefly *fig.*

c **1400** [see VENOMLY *adv.*]. *c* **1450** METHAM *Wks.* (E.E.T.S.) 47 The serpent namyd jaculus,.. Qwat that he vppon fallyth, so venymusly he doth yt smyght, That forth-with yt deyth. **1591** PERCIVALL *Sp. Dict.*, *Chinche*, a worme that in hot countries lieth about beds, and biteth venemously. *Cimex.* **1605** SHAKS. *Lear* IV. iii. 48 (Q.), These things sting his mind, So venomously that burning shame detaines him from Cordelia. **1652** GAULE *Magastrom.* 360 He.. put his hand into the hole, and had it most venomously bitten by a poysonous serpent. **1687** DRYDEN *Hind & P.* III. 1172 His praise of Foes is venomously Nice. **1868** FARRAR *Seekers* I. ii. (1875) 34 These facts are surely sufficient to refute.. those gross charges against the private character of Seneca, venomously retailed by a jealous Greekling. **1880** MRS. FORRESTER *Roy & V.* III. 134 'Oh, yes,' he cried venomously, 'you look very innocent'. **1898** J. ARCH *Story Life* xvi. 385 The Union.. was venomously assailed by men who up till then had declared they were its best friends.

'venomousness. [f. as prec. + -NESS.] The condition or quality of being venomous; †venomous matter.

c **1530** *Judic. Urines* II. xiv. 45 b, Through excesse and vyolence of hete and of venymousnes and malyce of the sekenesse. **1571** GOLDING *Calvin on Ps.* lv. 21 They wounded him with their privie venemousnes. **1597** A. M. tr. *Guillemeau's Fr. Chirurg.* 38/2 The parte is onlye soacked throughe with some certayne venoumousenes. **1599** —— tr. *Gabelhouer's Bk. Physicke* 132/2 When the people doe suddaynly dye of this disease, it is then to be feared ther was any venoumousnes annexed thervnto. **1611** COTGR., *Virulence*,.. poison, venomousnesse. **1727** BAILEY (vol. II), *Venomousness*, poisonous Nature or Quality. **1728** CHAMBERS *Cycl.*, *Viper*,.. a kind of Serpent, famed.. for the exceeding Venomousness of its Bite. **1775** in ASH; and in later Dicts.

†**'venomousty.** *Obs.*$^{-1}$ In 4 **venymo(u)ste, venemoste.** [f. VENOMOUS *a.* + -TY. Cf. OF. *venemosté, venemeuseté*, etc.] Venomousness.

1377 LANGL. *P. Pl.* B. XVIII. 156 For of alle venymes foulest is þe scorpioun, May no medcyne helpe þe place þere he styngeth, Tyl he be ded & do þer-to þe yuel he destroyeth, þe fyrst venymouste [*C. text* venemoste, venymoste, etc.] þorw venym of hym-self.

'venomsome, *a.* Now *dial.* Also 9 **vemon-.** [f. VENOM *sb.* + -SOME¹.] Venomous, spiteful.

1660 *Treasons*, etc. *W. Lilley* 2 Many hundreds such venomsome passages as these. **1876** *Whitby Gloss.* 209 *Vemonsome*, spiteful. **1895** J. PRIOR *Renie* vii. 71 Like a raivenous roaring lion or a venomsome sarpent.

†**'venomy,** *sb. Obs.*$^{-1}$ [f. VENOM *sb.* + -Y.] Venomousness.

1548 CRANMER *Catech.* 88 Yᵉ venomie of such persons, which secretly by poysened wordes or other meanes causeth his neyghboure to be suspected.

'venomy, *a. rare.* Also 5 **venemi, -y.** [f. VENOM *sb.*] Venomous, spiteful, malignant.

c **1400** *Lanfranc's Cirurg.* 80 If þe vlcus be virulent, þat is to seie venemi [*v.r.* venemy], loke if þat þe venym þat goiþ out be redisch or ȝelowisch. **1594** CAREW *Tasso* (1881) 74 Ruddy his eyes and plaguefull venomy. *a* **1849** MANGAN *Poems* (1859) 394 Except the hate that persecutes him Nothing hath crueler venomy might.

†**ve'nosal,** *a. Obs.*$^{-1}$ [f. L. *vēnōs-us*: see next.] Venose, venous.

1621 BURTON *Anat. Mel.* I. i. II. iv, His.. office is to coole the Heart, by sending aire vnto it, by the Venosall Artery.

venose (viːˈnəʊs), *a.* [ad. L. *vēnōs-us* (whence also It., Sp., Pg. *venoso*), f. *vēna* VEIN *sb.*] Venous; *spec.* in *Bot.* and *Ent.* (see quots.).

1661 LOVELL *Hist. Anim. & Min.* 321 The short vessels arteriose and venose. *Ibid.*, By this branch of the artery it passeth to the spleen..; by the venose branches to the trunk of the vas breve. **1753** CHAMBERS *Cycl. Supp.* s.v. *Leaf*, Venose Leaf, that on the surface of which there are a vast number of branched vessels, which frequently unite in an odd manner one with another. **1760** J. LEE *Introd. Bot.* III. v. (1765) 184 *Venose*, veiny; when the Vessels are branched all over the Leaves, and their Anastomose[s] or Joinings are plain to the naked Eye. **1826** KIRBY & SP. *Entomol.* IV. xlvi. 290 *Venose*,.. painted with lines that branch like veins. **1828** *Ibid.* (ed. 2) xxxix. 91 The arterial and venose currents [in insects]. **1866** *Treas. Bot.* 1208/1 Indirectly venose is when lateral veins are combined within the margin, and emit other little veins.

Hence **ve'nosely** *adv.*

1846 DANA *Zooph.* (1848) 271 The disks and ridges.. venosely furcate, or reticulate.

venosity (viːˈnɒsɪtɪ). *Path.* [ad. mod.L. *vēnōsitās*: see VENOSE *a.* and -ITY.] The state of being venous; *spec.* of the blood (see VENOUS *a.* 2 b).

1855 DUNGLISON *Med. Lex.* (ed. 12), *Venosity*, a condition in which, it has been supposed, the blood is moved slowly; is more venous; and the venous blood itself in greater quantity. **1874** JONES & SIEVEKING *Pathol. Anat.* 42 The venosity of the blood is marked. **1896** *Allbutt's Syst. Med.* I. 333 Abdominal venosity is a prominent feature of many chronic ailments.

venoso-reticulated, *a. Bot.* (See quot.)

1802 R. HALL *Elem. Bot.* 194 *Venoso-reticulated*,.. having the veins disposed so as to form a net work.

venous (ˈviːnəs), *a.* [ad. L. *vēnōs-us* (cf. VENOSE *a.*), or f. L. *vēn-a* + -OUS.]

1. Filled with, full of, or having veins; veined; veiny. ***venous leaf*** (see quot. 1832).

1626 BACON *Sylva* ¶ 839 The Consistences of Bodies are very diuers; Dense, Rare;.. Venous, and Fibrous [etc.]. **1796** WITHERING *Brit. Plants* (ed. 3) II. 250 [Root-leaves] above somewhat glossy, with scattered hairs; underneath venous and woolly. **1832** LINDLEY *Introd. Bot.* 88 If the veins diverge from the midrib towards the margin, ramifying as they proceed, such a leaf has been called a venous or reticulated leaf. **1833** LYELL *Princ. Geol.* III. 373 If the more remote beds.. are not thus affected,.. they never could have existed, or would have been all granitic and venous gneiss.

2. *Anat.* and *Phys.* Of or pertaining to, of the nature of, a blood-vein or veins; having the form or function of a vein.

†*venous artery* = *veiny artery* VEINY *a.* 1. ***venous hum*** (see quot. 1891).

1681 in *Willis's Rem. Med. Wks.* Vocab. **1694** W. WOTTON *Anc. & Mod. Learn.* (1697) p. xxx, The subtil Blood.. is.. transfused out of the Arterious Vein into the Venous Artery. **1728** CHAMBERS *Cycl.* s.v. *Circulation*, Both Venous Sinus's are fill'd, and grow turgid at the same time. **1744** ARMSTRONG *Art Preserv. Health* (1770) 8 The drunken venous tubes, that yawn In countless pores o'er all the pervious skin. **1746** R. JAMES *Moufet's Health Improv.* 10 The Blood conveyed by the Arteries, is carried to corresponding venous Canals. **1838** *Penny Cycl.* XII. 85/2 A fluctuating motion in the jugular vein, called 'venous pulse'. **1876** BRISTOWE *Th. & Pract. Med.* (1878) 562 The symptoms of venous inflammation. **1876** F. T. ROBERTS *Handbk. Med.* (ed. 2) 433 Venous hum... This is the only venous murmur.. likely to be met with. **1891** F. TAYLOR *Pract. Med.* (ed. 2) 677 If the stethoscope be placed over the lower end of the jugular vein.. a continuous humming or rushing noise will be heard, which has been called the venous hum, or *bruit de diable*.

b. Of blood: Contained in the veins; characterized by a dusky or blackish red colour due to loss or oxygen. (Opposed to *arterial*.)

1728 CHAMBERS *Cycl.* s.v. *Circulation*, The venous Blood.. continually moves out of the Sinus.. thro' the right Auricle, and right Ventricle, into the Pulmonary Artery. **1793** T. BEDDOES *On Calculus*, etc. 225 This experiment proves.. that the deep colour of the venous blood is not owing to the combination of hydrogene air. **1802** *Med. Jrnl.* VIII. 501 In the act of respiration then, the venous blood loses some combustible principles. **1834** MCMURTRIE *Cuvier's Anim. Kingd.* 29 In all the Vertebrata, the blood which furnishes the liver with the materials of the bile is venous blood. **1896** NEWTON *Dict. Birds* 1009 The venous blood is collected and conveyed to the right atrium of the heart by 3 great trunks.

c. Consisting or composed of veins. ***venous system***, the aggregate of veins by which the blood is conveyed from the various parts of the body to the heart.

1826 KIRBY & SP. *Entomol.* IV. 81 In the Arachnida and Branchiopod Crustacea the long dorsal vessel.. is connected with an arterial and venous system, which receives, distributes, and returns the blood. **1852** E. HAMILTON *Flora Homœopathica* I. 94 Berberis.. seems to act upon the venous system and mucous membranes. **1875** C. G. BLAKE *Zool.* 1 The venous portal system is entirely formed of veins derived from the spleen and other viscera.

3. Of or pertaining to, characteristic of, vein-blood.

1845 G. E. DAY tr. *Simon's Anim. Chem.* I. 192 These experiments are sufficient to prove that.. the dark venous tint [of the blood] does not arise from carbonic acid or carbon. **1846** CARPENTER *Man. Phys.* vi. 324 After passing through these, it is transmitted to the general system; and on returning thence, in a completely venous state, it is mingled with the blood which has been arterialized in the lungs.

4. *Comb.* in ***venous-arterial*** adj. In quot. *fig.*

1831 CARLYLE *Sart. Res.* III. vii, Venous-arterial circulation of Letters.

Hence **'venously** *adv.*, **'venousness.**

1727 BAILEY (vol. II), *Venousness*, fulness of or having Veins. **1890** *Lancet* 5 April 751/2 The membranes of the brain were venously congested.

†**venque**, *v.* *Obs.*$^{-1}$ [f. OF. *venq-*, stem of *veintre* VANQUISH *v.* Cf. VENCUE *v.*] *trans.* To vanquish, subdue.

?**1402** QUIXLEY *Ball.* xvi. in *Yorks. Arch. Jrnl.* (1908) XX. 48 Who þat his flessh venqueth most haue þe prys.

venqueresse: see VAINQUERESSE. *Obs.*

venques, -quis, etc., obs. ff. VANQUISH *v.*

venson, ven'son, vensoun, obs. ff. VENISON.

vent (vɛnt), *sb.*[1] Also 5 ventte, 5-6 vente. [Variant of FENT *sb.*]

1. An opening or slit in a garment, = FENT *sb.* 1; now *spec.* the slit in the back of a coat.

c **1430** *Pilgr. Lyf Manhode* IV. lviii. (1869) 203 She hadde ..drawen out hire con brest bi þe vente of hire cote. **1459**, *a* **1500** [see FENT *sb.* 1]. **1535** in *Archaeologia* IX. 244 A dublette;..the ventes lyned with sarcenette. *a* **1548** HALL *Chron., Hen. VIII*, 207 b, Twoo gounes;..the capes and ventes were of frettes of whipped gold of damaske very riche. **1587** HOLINSHED *Chron.* (ed. 2) III. 820/1 The trappers of the coursers were mantell harnesse coulpened, and in euerie vent a long bell of fine gold in bullion. **1828** CARR *Craven Gloss.*, *Vent*, the opening of the breast of a shirt, or of the sleeve, etc. **1851** MAYNE REID *Scalp-Hunters* vii. 55 Dark-velvet embroidery around the vent and along the borders. **1906** *Daily Chron.* 4 Oct. 3/4 The vent is necessary..owing to the length of the coat.

†**2.** = CRENEL 1. *Obs.*

1429 in Willis & Clark *Cambridge* (1886) II. 445 Item ventes crest xij fott et di., v[s]. *Ibid.*, Item pro xij pedibus de ventes pro enbatylment', v[s]. ij[d]. **1532** in Bayley *Hist. Tower* (1821) p. xvii, Also fynnysshed and made the vents of brycks of the White Tower. **1570-6** LAMBARDE *Peramb. Kent* (1596) 424 Kernellare..signifieth that indented forme of the top of a Wall which hathe Vent, and Creast, commonly called Embatteling. **1603** B. JONSON *K. Jas.'s Entertainm.* Wks. (1616) 843 The Scene presented it selfe in a square and flat vpright, like to the side of a Citie: the top thereof, aboue the Vent, and Crest, adorn'd with houses, towres, and steeples.

vent (vɛnt), *sb.*[2] [Partly a. F. *vent* (= It., Pg. *vento*, Sp. *viento*):—L. *vent-us* wind; partly ad. F. *évent* (OF. *esvent*), vbl. sb. from *éventer* EVENT *v.*[2]]

I. 1. a. The action of emitting or discharging; emission or discharge *of* something; utterance *of* words. *rare.*

1508 DUNBAR *Tua Mariit Wemen* 166, I sall the venome devoid with a vent large, And me assuage of the swalme, that suellit wes gret. **1592** SHAKS. *Ven. & Ad.* 334 Free vent of words love's fire doth assuage. **1626** DANIEL *Hist. Eng.* Wks. (Grosart) IV. 95 By this immoderate vent, both of the Garrisons, and the ablest people of the Land hee dis-furnisht and left it in that impotencie.

†**b.** *to make vent of*, to speak or talk of. *Obs.*$^{-1}$

1601 SHAKS. *All's Well* II. iii. 213 Thou didst make tollerable vent of thy trauell.

2. a. The action, usually on the part of something confined or pent up in a comparatively small space, of escaping, or passing out; means, power, or opportunity to do this; issue, outlet. Chiefly in phrases with verbs, as ***to find, get, have, make, take,*** or ***want vent.*** (Cf. senses 4 and 5.)

1558 WARDE tr. *Alexis' Secr.* (1568) 12 b, Stop well the said violle, that nothing maie take vent. **1594** NASHE *Unfort. Trav.* Wks. (Grosart) V. 121 Ye tail of the siluer pipe stretcht itselfe into the mouth of a great paire of belowse, where it was close soldered, and bailde about with yron, [that] it coulde not stirre or haue anie vent betwixt. **1605** SYLVESTER *Du Bartas* II. iii. *Fathers* 293 New Wine.. wanting vent, Blows up the Bung, or doth the vessell rent. **1652** FRENCH *Yorkshire Spa* ii. 18 By reason of the Suns opening the earth, and making vent. **1684** *Contempl. St. Man* ii. vi. (1699) 196 That Fire of Sulphur, being pent in without vent or respiration, shall send forth a poysonous scent. **1703** *Art & Mystery of Vintners & Wine-Coopers* 60 Beat them and put them into your Wines, so let it rest with Vent, and it will be pursued. **1802** *Med. Jrnl.* VIII. 263 They [waters] got vent chiefly in the night, when in an horizontal position. **1860** TYNDALL *Glac.* I. iii. 24 The smoke found ample vent through the holes. **1875** KNIGHT *Dict. Mech.* 1463/1 *Blow*, the forcing of displaced air through the molten metal from insufficient vent.

transf. **1798** MALTHUS *Popul.* (1817) I. 161 The enterprising spirit and overflowing numbers of the Scandinavian nations soon found vent by sea. **1854** J. S. C. ABBOTT *Napoleon* (1855) I. xxxii. 496 The inhabitants of Lombardy felt the foreign yoke only in the quickened circulation of wealth, the increased vent for industry.

b. The windage of a firearm or gun.

1644-7 N. NYE *Art of Gunnery* 46 Divide the Bore of the Piece into Twenty equal parts, and one of these parts is sufficient vent for any Piece; the rest of the nineteen parts must be the height of the shot. **1704** J. HARRIS *Lex. Techn.* I, *Vent*, in Gunnery,..the Difference between the Diameter of a Bullet, and the Diameter of the Bore of the Piece. [Hence in Phillips (1706), etc.] **1798** HUTTON *Course Math.* (1807) II. 353 The loss of the elastic fluid by the vent and windage of the gun.

c. ***full vent***, advb. phr., at full pitch; to the utmost of one's capacity.

1927 D. H. LAWRENCE *Mornings in Mexico* 11 It is so unlike him, to be whistling full vent, when any of us is around.

3. ***to give vent*** (with *to* or indirect object): **a.** To afford or provide with an outlet or means of escape; to cause or allow to issue or flow out.

After F. *donner vent*, used in the same senses.

1594 PLAT *Jewell-ho.* 68 Be carefull in the beginning to give some little vent to the hogshead while it worketh. **1661** HICKERINGILL *Jamaica* 32 A milky liquor running out, so soon as you give it vent. **1662** CHARLETON *Myst. Vintners* (1675) 181 To cure Rhenish of its Fretting..they seldom use any other art, but giving it vent, and covering the open Bung with a Tile or Slate. **1706** PHILLIPS (ed. Kersey) s.v., To give Vent to a Cask of Wine. **1725** *Fam. Dict.* s.v. *Tart*, You must..make a small Hole in the form of a Cross in the middle to give the Farce in the Crust some vent. **1830** LYELL *Princ. Geol.* I. 318 The principal region in the old World, which, from time immemorial, has been agitated by earthquakes, and has given vent at certain points to subterranean fires. **1842** LOUDON *Suburban Hort.* 289 In order to give vent to the rising sap. **1875** [see *vent-wire* in sense 17 a].

transf. **1719** BOYER *Dict. Royal* I, *Eventer une Mine* (*la rendre inutile*), to give vent to a Mine, to counter-work or countermine it.

b. *fig.* To give outlet, expression, or utterance (to an emotion, faculty, etc.); to relieve in this way.

1625 MASSINGER *Parlt. Love* III. ii, Had I not found out a friend to whom I might impart them [i.e. emotions], and so give them vent, In their abundance they would force a passage. **1677** GILPIN *Demonol.* III. ii. 10 The vent which the afflicted parties give by their bemoaning of their Estate. **1719** DE FOE *Crusoe* II. (Globe) 597, I found he wanted to give Vent to his Mind. **1781** JOHNSON *Lett.* (1788) II. 198, I have nobody whom I expect to share my uneasiness,..I give it little vent. **1823** CHALMERS *Serm.* I. 423 Oh! how I rejoice when compassion may give full vent to its tenderness. **1852** LONGF. *Emperor's Bird's-nest* iii, Thus as to and fro they went,..Giving their impatience vent. **1904** *Spectator* 20 Feb. 285/2 The voices which gave vent to any great wave of feeling.

c. To utter, burst out with (an exclamation).

1870 J. BRUCE *Life of Gideon* xi. 193 He gives vent to the exclamation 'Oh my Lord, wherewith shall *I* save Israel?'

†**4.** ***to take vent***, in various fig. or transf. senses. *Obs.* **a.** Of news, etc.: To become known, to be divulged or let out.

1611 SIR D. CARLETON in *10th Rep. Hist. MSS. Comm.* App. I. 542 Though all care haithe bene taken to carrie y[e] matter secretly,..yet hath it taken vente [etc.]. **1668** D. SMITH in *Misc. Cur.* (1708) III. 57 This presently took vent, and the Turks thought that they had got a Man among them, that could Cure all Diseases Infallibly. **1723** *Pres. St. Russia* II. 123 If Affonassief is no longer at Petersbourg, this Affair cannot take vent; for besides us two and him, no body knows of it. **1728** MORGAN *Algiers* II. iii. 253 A conspiracy was formed against him: But it took Vent; and he made cruel Examples of many of the Contrivers.

b. Of coin: To pass into circulation. *rare*$^{-1}$.

1641 *Sc. Acts, Chas. I* (1870) V. 341/2 Concerneing..the copper money allreddy coyned, how the same shall take vent and passe in payment in tyme comeing.

c. Of a mine, or powder: To explode imperfectly; to lose explosive power.

1684 J. PETER *Siege Vienna* 41 At which time they sprung two Mines..without any considerable Effect, one of them taking Vent. **1693** EVELYN *De la Quint. Compl. Gard.* I. 27 Gun-Powder, which being bad, or having taken Vent, cannot take Fire.

5. *fig.* **a.** Means of outlet afforded to or obtained by a feeling, faculty, activity, etc.; expression or utterance, or the relief afforded by these. Now chiefly in the phr. ***to find vent (in*** something).

1603 J. DAVIES (Heref.) *Microcosmos* Wks. (Grosart) I. 76/2 Griefes doe breake the heart if vent they misse. **1682** DRYDEN *Medal* 295 The swelling Poison of the sev'ral Sects, Which, wanting vent, the Nations Health infects. **1724** A. COLLINS *Gr. Chr. Relig.* Pref. p. xxviii, Enthusiasm..would spend itself by free vent and amicable collision. **1803** *Edwin* I. 206 At his words I found my angry passions heave for vent. **1838** FR. A. KEMBLE *Resid. in Georgia* (1863) 13 A malevolent feeling, which might find vent in some violent demonstration against this family. **1880** W. H. DIXON *Royal Windsor* III. xii. 113 Passion found vent in words.

†**b.** ***to get*** or ***have vent***, = sense 4 a. *Obs.*

1667 DRYDEN & DK. NEWCASTLE *Sir M. Mar-all* III. ii, This frightened him into a study how to cloak your disgrace, lest it should have vent to his lady. **1672** MARVELL *Reh. Transp.* I. 46 Should they unhappily get vent abroad,..what scandal must it raise! *a* **1715** BURNET *Own Time* (1766) II. 197 But the thing had got some vent. **1722** DE FOE *Plague* 2 As it had gotten some Vent in the Discourse of the neighbourhood, the Secretaries of State gat Knowledge of it.

6. a. With *a*: An opportunity or occasion of escaping or issuing from a receptacle; a discharge or evacuation. (Cf. 12.)

1644 Z. BOYD *Gard. Zion* in *Zion's Flowers* (1855) App. 10/1 Which by some chink, if it get not a vent, Blowes up the bung, or doth the Hodg-head rent. **1672** R. WILD *Poet. Licent.* 30 The other day into a place I went, Where Mortals use to go, that want a vent. **1719** DE FOE *Crusoe* I. (Globe) 290, I verily believe, if it had not been eas'd by a Vent given in that Manner, to the Spirits, I should have dy'd. **1725** N. ROBINSON *Th. Physick* 255 Whereupon the Fluids..run to the Bowels for a Vent.

b. *fig.* (Cf. senses 3 and 5.) Now chiefly ***to find a vent.***

(*a*) *a* **1614** D. DYKE *Myst. Self-Deceiving* (1630) 341 Tappes to giue a vent to corruption. **1669** GALE *Crt. Gentiles* I. I. ix. 49 The Egyptians..gave a great vent to Jewish Learning and Institutes. **1777** PITT in Almon *Anecd.* (1810) II. xliv. 319, I could not have slept..without giving this vent to my eternal abhorrence of such preposterous and enormous principles.

(*b*) **1697** COLLIER *Ess. Mor. Subj.* II. (1703) 64 Those who live within the communication of friendship have a vent for their misfortunes. **1814** WORDSW. *Excurs.* IX. 752 For, though in whispers speaking, the full heart Will find a vent. **1838** PRESCOTT *Ferd. & Is.* Introd. (1846) I. 60 The tumultuous spirits of the aristocracy,..instead of finding a vent..in these foreign expeditions, were turned within. **1873** BLACK *Princess Thule* (1874) 46 His distress at his own rudeness now found an easy vent.

7. Something which serves as an outlet for an emotion, energy, etc.

1667 MILTON *P.L.* XII. 374 With such joy Surcharg'd, as had like grief bin dew'd in tears, Without the vent of words. **1713** *Guardian* No. 29, Laughter is a vent of any sudden joy. **1828** SOUTHEY *Minor Poems* Poet. Wks. 1837 II. 255 This love,..and the woe Which makes thy lip now quiver with distress, Are but a vent..From the deep springs of female tenderness. **1832** LYTTON *Eugene A.* I. x, Words at best are but a poor vent for a wronged and burning heart. **1883** *19th Cent.* May 887 The French have..to find and to use such vents for their energy in undeveloped and promising regions.

II. †**8.** *Sc.* A flaw in a mould. *Obs.*$^{-1}$

Fr. *évent* is used in similar senses.

1541 *Acc. Ld. High Treas. Scot.* VIII. 125 At the quhilk melting becaus of ane vent in the cuppeling of the mulde witht the tayll, the pece felȝeit.

9. †**a.** An opening by which blood issues from the body. *Obs.*

1567 MAPLET *Gr. Forest* 7 b, Ematites..is called of some stench bloud, for that it stoppeth his vent or course of flowing. **1606** SHAKS. *Ant. & Cl.* v. ii. 353 Heere on her brest There is a vent of Bloud, and something blowne.

b. The anus, anal, or excretory opening of (†persons or) animals, esp. of certain non-mammalians, as birds, fishes, and reptiles; †the vulva of a female animal.

1587 FLEMING *Contn. Holinshed* III. 1270/2 For those that bled till they died, stroue so much with their sickenesse, that the blound issued out at their vents. **1655** MOUFET & BENNET *Health's Improv.* (1746) 241 As for their [i.e. crabs'] manner of Preparation, their Vents are first to be stopped with a Stick's end. **1675** HANNAH WOOLLEY *Gentlew. Comp.* 132 Geese Boiled... Fasten the neck and vent. *Ibid.* 146 Take a Pig, and draw out his Entrails, Liver, and Lights, draw him very clean at vent. **1697** DRYDEN *Virg. Georg.* III. 421 For when her pouting Vent declares her Pain, She [i.e. a mare] tears the Harness, and she rends the Rein. **1769** MRS. RAFFALD *Eng. Housekpr.* (1778) 21 Take a lobster, if it be alive, stick a skewer in the vent of the tail. **1774** GOLDSM. *Nat. Hist.* (1776) IV. 347 Like birds, they [i.e. sloths] have but one common vent for the purposes of propagation, excrement, and urine. **1790** BEWICK *Hist. Quadrup.* (1807) 488 As soon as the Otter has caught a fish, it..devours a part, as far as the vent. **1833** JARDINE *Humming-B.* 111 The vent and under tail-coverts are dirty white. **1874** CARPENTER *Ment. Phys.* I. ii. (1879) 68 If the vent of a Frog be irritated with a probe, the hind-legs will endeavour to push it away.

10. a. An aperture or opening occurring or made in something and serving as an outlet for air, liquid, or other matter; a passage or hole by which matter is carried off or discharged from the interior of something; a vent-hole.

1570 LEVINS *Manip.* 66 A Vent, *meatus, porus.* **1580** HARVEY *Three Lett.* Wks. (Grosart) I. 44 The poores, and ventes, and crannies of the Earth being so stopped. **1605** B. JONSON *Volpone* II. iv, Now, he flings about his burning heat, As in a furnace, some ambitious fire, Whose vent is stopt. **1648** WILKINS *Math. Magic* II. xii. 250 Others are of opinion that this may be effected in a hollow vessell, exactly luted or stopped up in all the vents of it. **1677** in *Misc. Curiosa* (1708) III. 249 They leave a small vent about two Inches from the bottom, by which it empties it self into a little Pit... The vent being stopped, they fill the Cistern they have made with Water. **1712-4** POPE *Rape Lock* IV. 92 The swelling bag he rent, And all the Furies issu'd at the vent. **1728** E. SMITH *Compl. Housew.* (1750) 3 If the knife be greatly daubed, has a rank smell, and a hoogoo issue from the vent, it is tainted. **1796** MORSE *Amer. Geogr.* I. 609 The Shenandoah having ranged along the foot of the mountain an hundred miles to seek a vent. **1831** J. HOLLAND *Manuf. Metal* II. 165 It was generally thought sufficient for the purpose..that the smoke should ascend the proper vent. **1877** in J. A. Allen *Amer. Bison* App. 459 There are old spring vents..that no longer give forth saline waters.

b. *spec.* An aperture or outlet by which volcanic matter or exhalations are emitted; the funnel or pipe of a volcano.

1604 E. G[RIMSTONE] *D'Acosta's Hist. Indies* III. xxiv. 193 Although we finde vents of fire in other places, as mount Ætna and Wesuvio. **1684-5** BOYLE *Min. Waters* 19 Any subterraneal fire, that hath manifest chimneys or vents. **1725** DE FOE *Voy. round World* (1840) 242 A volcano, or burning vent among the hills, had flamed out. **1772-84** *Cook's Voy.* (1790) IV. 1219 Another volcano, which had opened by at least thirty different vents within the compass of half a mile. **1830** LYELL *Princ. Geol.* I. 135 These igneous vents were extremely numerous. **1869** J. PHILLIPS *Vesuv.* iii. 60 A new vent was formed below the lip of the old mountain. **1882** GEIKIE *Text-bk. Geol.* 201 A 'solfatara', or vent emitting only gaseous discharges.

c. In various special uses (see quots.).

1611 COTGR., *Esvent*, the vent of a wine vessell. **1730** BAILEY (fol.), *Vents* (in Archit.), Pipes of Lead or Potters-Ware, one End of which opens into a Cell of a Necessary-House, the other reaching to the Roof of it for the Conveyance of the fetid Air; also Apertures made in those Walls that sustain Terrasses to furnish Air, and to give a Passage for the Waters. **1756** *Dict. Arts & Sci.* s.v. *Foundery of Statues*, The vents are passages at top to let the air freely out, whilst the metal runs. **1823** E. MOOR *Suffolk Wds.*, *Vent*, the hole of a cask for the reception of a vent-peg. **1875** KNIGHT *Dict. Mech.* 2703/1 *Vent*, the term employed to comprehend the channels and passages by which the air, or gases, escape from the mold.

d. *Sc.* The flue or funnel of a chimney; a chimney.

1756 MRS. CALDERWOOD in *Coltness Collect.* (Maitl. Club) 253 Neither are they [the stoves] put in the place for the chimney, but in another part of the room, and have a communication with the vent. **1798** in Gordon *Shaw's Hist. Moray* (1882) I. 322 Each vent springs lightly from the blue roof of its own separate airy column. **1815** *Ann. Register, Chron.* 43 A hole broke through into a neighbouring vent to carry off the smoke. **1842** J. Aiton *Domest. Econ.* (1857) 77 Sometimes all the purposes of a stove have been served by having a flue introduced into the kitchen vent. **1889** Barrie *Window in Thrums* 11 Ye micht gang up to the attic, Leeby, an' see if the spare bedroom vent at the manse is gaen.

e. *Mining.* (See quot.)

1886 J. Barrowman *Sc. Mining Terms* 69 *Vent*, .. a return airway.

f. = port *sb.*³ 4 d.

1940 *Electronics* Mar. 54/2 The vent should be located near the speaker... The vent areas need not necessarily be circular. **1975** G. J. King *Audio Handbk.* vi. 143 (*caption*) Inside of Rectavox Omni Mk II loudspeaker system, showing the bass and treble units, the tube extension from the vent and the frequency divider network at the bottom.

11. a. An opening, aperture, or hole; occas., one by which air, etc., enters or is admitted.

1593 Shaks. *Lucrece* 310 Through little vents and crannies of the place The wind wars with his torch to make him stay. **1597** —— *2 Hen. IV*, Induct. 2 Open your Eeres: For which of you will stop The vent of Hearing, when loud Rumor speakes? **1659** Leak *Waterwks.* 23 Pour Water into the Vessels by the hole or vent M. **1697** Dryden *Virg. Georg.* iv. 56 Th' industrious Kind..contrive To stop the Vents and Crannies of their Hive. **1728** Pope *Dunc.* ii. 80 A place there is.. Where, from Ambrosia, Jove retires for ease. There in his seat two spacious vents appear. **1730** Bailey (fol.), *Vents* (with Essayers, Glass-makers, &c.) is a Term applied to the Covers of Wind-Furnaces, by which the Air enters. **1768** White *Selborne* xiv, Deer [when drinking].. can open two vents, one at the inner corner of each eye, having a communication with the nose. **1810** *Encycl. Brit.* (ed. 4) VI. 410/2 An oblong gaping vent on the anterior slope [of the shell]. **1827** *Gentl. Mag.* XCVII. ii. 69/2 One of the numerous cracks or fissures (locally called vents) that intersect the strata at this place [near Maidstone].

†**b.** A creek or inlet. *Obs.*⁻¹

1604 E. G[rimstone] *D'Acosta's Hist. Indies* iii. xi. 155 Having discovered this vent [Sp. *abra*], they found it ranne more and more into the land.

c. An opening or aperture in a building, etc., communicating with the outside air.

1617 Moryson *Itin.* i. 223 This Church..is very darke, having no light but by one window or vent, made through the earth. **1632** Lithgow *Trav.* vii. 306 The streets are.. couered to saue them from the parching heate with open vents for light. **1675** Worlidge *Syst. Agric.* (ed. 2) 286 You may this Month stop up your Bees close, so that you leave breathing vents. **1821** Scott *Kenilw.* x, By some concealed vent the smithy communicated with the upper air.

d. The hole or channel in the breech of a cannon or firearm through which fire is communicated to the charge; the touch-hole; the adjustable part of a gun containing this, a vent-piece.

1667 Milton *P.L.* vi. 583 For sudden all at once thir Reeds Put forth, and to a narrow vent appli'd With nicest touch. **1797** *Phil. Trans.* LXXXVII. 238 The velocity of the bullet is considerably greater when the cannon is fired off with a vent tube,..than when the vent is filled with loose powder. **1802** James *Milit. Dict.* s.v., The most common method is to place the vent about a quarter of an inch from the bottom of the chamber or bore. **1828** Spearman *Brit. Gunner* (ed. 2) 412 Spare vents should be sent to replace such as might be damaged. **1859** Wraxall tr. *R. Houdin* xxi. 319 The pistols were handed to me; I called attention to the fact that the vents were clear. **1876** Voyle & Stevenson *Milit. Dict.* s.v., A vent is formed by drilling a channel, ⅜-inch in diameter, through a copper bush. *Ibid.*, There are two kinds of copper bushes used, viz. the through vent, and the cone vent.

e. *Mining.* (See vent-hole 1 b, quot. 1883.)

12. *transf.* Any outlet or place of issue; a passage, exit, or way out. Chiefly *fig.*

In some contexts not clearly separable from sense 6.

1602 Marston *Antonio's Rev.* ii. iii, Here is a vent to passe my sighes. **1629** Ford *Lover's Melancholy* v. Mj, My teares like ruffling winds lockt vp in Caues, Do bustle for a vent. **1642** Fuller *Holy & Prof. St.* i. x. 25 Such widows grief is quickly emptyed, which streameth out at so large a vent. **1711** Pope *Temple Fame* 481 When thus ripe lies are to perfection sprung,..Thro' thousand vents, impatient, forth they flow. **1794** Cowper *Needless Alarm* 86 Winds for ages pent In earth's dark womb have found at last a vent. **1860** Emerson *Cond. Life, Behaviour* Wks. (Bohn) II. 389 There is some reason to believe that, when a man does not write his poetry, it escapes by other vents through him. **1868** Bain *Ment. & Mor. Sci.* iv. iii. §2. 339 There is at the outset a struggle, but the refusal of the muscular vent seems to be the extinction of the other effects.

III. †**13. a.** The scent given off by a hunted animal; = scent *sb.* 2. *Obs. rare.*

1576 Turberv. *Venerie* 61 When my Hounde doth streyne vpon good vent. **1591** Harington *Orl. Fur.* xvii. xxiv, He hunteth like a spaniell by the vent, His sent is such as none can hope to shun him. **1719** Boyer *Dict. Royal* i. s.v., The Stag leaves a stronger wind, vent, or scent than the Hare.

†**b.** Perception by scent or smell. *Obs.*⁻¹

1576 Turberv. *Venerie* 73 These be olde hartes.., which chaunge their laire, as the wynd chaungeth, to haue perfect vent..what faulte may perhappes be in their feede.

†**14.** A wind. *Obs.*⁻¹

1580 Hudson *Du Bartas' Judith* v. (1613) 64 Let him that serues the time,..With faith vnconstant saile at euerie vent.

†**15.** A hint or whisper *of* something. *Obs.*⁻¹

1613 in *Buccleuch MSS.* (Hist. MSS. Comm.) I. 149 There is great reason you should..recommend this cause to my secresy; for if there come forth but the least vent of it, I know *actum est de me*.

16. The action on the part of an otter of coming to the surface of the water in order to breathe; an instance or occasion of this.

1653 Walton *Angler* ii. 43 The Otter, which you may now see above water at vent. **1741** *Compl. Fam.-Piece* ii. i. 306 Observe his Vents, that you may strike him with your Otter Spear. **1856** 'Stonehenge' *Brit. Rur. Sports* 144/2 Unless the hunters are in sufficient numbers to watch the stream for miles, for his 'vent', he will probably never be seen again. *a* **1862** Foster in *Whistle-Binkie* (1878) II. 262 The vents grow more frequent, the music more deep, And scarce from the surface the otter can keep.

IV. 17. *attrib.* **a.** In the sense 'used for, serving as, providing, or connected with a vent', as ***vent-pit, -shaft, -way***; in the names of things or devices, as ***vent-cock, -faucet, -pipe, -plug, -wire*** (see quots.). See also vent-peg.

1875 Knight *Dict. Mech.*, *Vent-cock, a device for admitting air to a vessel from which liquid is to be drawn, or permit the escape of gas. *Ibid.*, **Vent-faucet*, an instrument which may act as a vent-hole borer or a faucet to draw a portion of liquor from the vessel. **1843** Tizard *Brewing* 451 This plan is greatly superior to the iron *vent nail. **1858** Simmonds *Dict. Trade*, **Vent-pipe*, an air-pipe; an escape pipe for steam. **1725** J. Reynolds *View Death* (ed. 2) 22 This pit is, with us, call'd the *vent-pit or the air-shaft. **1843** Tizard *Brewing* 451 The nature of the materials employed..demands an adequate number of *vent plugs. **1875** Knight *Dict. Mech.*, **Vent-wire* (Founding), a long steel wire,..used..for giving vent to green and dry sand-molds.

b. In sense 11 d, as ***vent-astragal, -bit, -field, -piece, -plug, -server, tube***, etc. (see quots.).

Also *vent-cover, -punch, -stopper* (1875 in Knight).

1769 Falconer *Dict. Marine* (1780) s.v. *Cannon*, The first reinforce therefore includes..the vent-field; the *vent-astragal, and first reinforce-ring. **1802** James *Milit. Dict.*, *Vent-astragal*, that part of a gun or howitzer which determines the vent-field. **1846** A. Young *Naut. Dict.* 358 **Vent-bit*, a species of gimblet used for clearing the vent of a gun when choked. **1769** *Vent-field [see *vent-astragal* above]. **1802** James *Milit. Dict.*, *Vent-field*, is the part of a gun or howitz between the breech mouldings and the astragal. **1846** A. Young *Naut. Dict.* 358 *Vent-field*, a rectangular piece of the metal raised a little upon a gun; through it the vent is bored. **1859** F. A. Griffiths *Artill. Man.* (1862) 205 **Vent Piece*, a plug of steel or wrought iron, containing the vent. **1868** *Rep. Munitions War* 146 A 7-inch breech-loading polygroove rifled gun on the Armstrong ventpiece system. **1875** Knight *Dict. Mech.*, *Vent-piece*,.. the block which closes the rear of the bore in a breech-loader. **1846** A. Young *Naut. Dict.* 358 **Vent-plug*, a tight plug made of leather, plaited rope-yarn, or oakum, which one of the men thrusts into the vent of a gun. **1867** Smyth *Sailor's Word-bk.*, *Vent-plug*, a fid or stopple made of leather or oakum fitting in the vent of a piece to stop it against weather, etc. **1876** Voyle & Stevenson *Milit. Dict.* 452/1 **Vent-server*, an article used for serving the vents of M.L.R. guns, 64-prs. and upwards, in lieu of serving the vent with the thumb. **1797** *Phil. Trans.* LXXXVII. 238 The velocity of the bullet is considerably greater when the cannon is fired off with a *vent tube.

c. In sense 9 b, as ***vent-feather***, one of the feathers covering or surrounding a bird's vent.

1776 Pennant *Brit. Zool.* II. 571 The whiteness of the coverts of the tail and vent-feathers. **1797** *Encycl. Brit.* (ed. 3) XIII. 505/2 The Vent, or vent-feathers (*crissum*), which lies between the thighs and the tail. **1815** Stephens in Shaw's *Gen. Zool.* IX. i. 98 Abdomen and vent-feathers whitish. **1834** Mudie *Feathered Tribes* I. 11 The vent feathers, and under tail coverts, which cover the hinder part of the bird.

vent, *sb.*³ *Obs.* exc. *arch.* Also 6–7 vente. [In senses 1–3 a. F. *vente* (= Sp. *venta*, Prov. and Pg. *venda*, It. *vendita*):—pop.L. **vendita* sb., from L. *venditus*, pa. pple. of *vendĕre* to sell. Cf. vend *sb.* In sense 4 directly ad. Sp. *venta*.

In senses 1 and 2 the word is very common from *c* 1550 to *c* 1750, freq. with adjs. denoting the readiness or profitableness of trade.]

1. The fact, on the part of commodities, of being disposed of by sale or of finding purchasers; freq. in the phrases ***to find*** or ***have*** (..) ***vent***. **a.** With *a* (or *no*).

1545 Brinklow *Compl.* ii. (1874) 11 This being reformed, aboue all other actes shal bryng the cloth of England to a contynuall vent. *a* **1548** Hall *Chron., Edw. IV*, 236 b, The wolles at Caleis, because of the warre, could haue no vent, nor be vttred. **1655** tr. *Sorel's Com. Hist. Francion* iii. 70 Divers Authors of this our Age have more ridiculously clad their names in a Roman disguise..that their books might have a better vent. **1714** *French Bk. Rates* 242 The Merchandizes carried there from France..lie on Hand, and cannot find a Vent or Market. **1730** *Col. Rec. Pennsylv.* III. 391 Encouragement..given to raise such Commodities that might have a constant and ready vent in Britain. **1782** Pegge *Curialia Misc.* 141 One often sees them advertised for sale; and, if bought at all, they find a vent, no doubt, at Wapping.

b. Without article.

1564 in Hudson & Tingey *Rec. Norwich* (1910) II. 332 The seyde clothes which nowe were owte of estimation and vente. **1573–80** Tusser *Husb.* (1878) 45 A remedie sent, where pease lack vent. **1581** W. Stafford *Exam. Compl.* iii. (1876) 84 Whatsoeuer thing is rered vpon grasing, hath free vente both ouer this side and also beyond the sea, to be sold at the highest penny. **1617** Bacon in *Fortescue Papers* (Camden) 34 For the yearely makeinge of soe many tonnes of allome as..can possibly receave vent eyther at home or abroade. **1641** Best *Farm. Bks.* (Surtees) 112 Att these three fayres..the most timely sorte of lambes have very goode vente. **1694** J. Locke in Ld. King *Life* (1830) I. 383 For our books are so dear, and ill printed, that they have very little vent among foreigners. **1768** H. Walpole *Lett.* (1891) V. 116 Like fish that could not find vent in London. *a* **1797** —— *Geo. II* (1847) II. vii. 228 The original caricature, which had amazing vent, was of Newcastle and Fox.

2. The fact, on the part of persons, of disposing of goods by sale; opportunity for selling; market or outlet for commodities.

a **1548** Hall *Chron., Hen. VIII*, 174 We trust you will not moue vs to bye the thyng, whiche wee cannot vtter, for in all places our vent is stopped and forbidden. **1575** *Brieff Disc. Troub. Frankford* (1846) 84 Saying that he woulde stoppe all mennes vents (as he termed it) and receiptes. **1600** Holland *Livy* 1002 To the end, that..they might..be served of a mart-towne for vent, and a place of receit for all forreine merchandise. *c* **1630** T. Mun *England's Treas.* (1664) 17 So far forth as the high price cause not a less vent in the quantity. **1671** *Charente's Customs Tafiletta* 69 As for the Trade and Traffick of those parts, it is much the same, ..unless it be that the vent is better in some places than others. **1709** in Hearne *Collect.* (O.H.S.) II. 191 The Amsterdam publisher..carrying a considerable part of his impression into France, and hoping for a quick vent there. **1760–72** tr. *Juan & Ulloa's Voy.* (ed. 3) II. 398 The traders ..consign..their European goods..to their correspondents in other parts for vent. **1778** [W. H. Marshall] *Minutes Agric.* 19 May 1776, What, then, must be the fate of those who do not keep a minute account, neither of the yield nor of the vent?

b. In phrases with verbs, as ***to find*** or ***have vent***.

1557–71 A. Jenkinson *Voy. & Trav.* (Hakl. Soc.) I. 116 We be vncertaine what vent or sale you shall finde in Persia. **1601** Holland *Pliny* I. 367 They vsed in old time to gather the Incense but once a yere; as hauing little vent, and small returne, and lesse occasion to sell than now adaies. **1674** Marvell *Reh. Transp.* ii. 54 Or by only naming it hoped to procure vent or better their livelyhood. **1707** Mortimer *Husb.* (1721) II. 62 Such Uses as you design to sell your Wood for, which you must be regulated in by the vent you have.

c. Const. *of.*

a **1548** Hall *Chron., Edw. IV*, 241 Thether was one of their common trafficques and ventes of all their Merchaundice. **1577** Holinshed *Chron.* II. 951/2 By this grant it was thoughte, yᵗ the king might dispend a M. markes sterling a day, such vent of woolles had the English merchants. **1600** Hakluyt *Voy.* (1810) III. 594 Where he had peaceable traffique, and made vent of the whole number of his Negros. **1690** Child *Disc. Trade* (1698) 59 Much foreign trade will encrease the vent of our native manufactures, and much vent will make many workmen. **1700** Law *Council of Trade* (1751) 141 This demand..at home will in all probability make way for the exportation and foreign vent of at least so much more. **1778** *Eng. Gaz.* (ed. 2) s.v. *Malton*, Malton..was heretofore famous for its vent of corn, fish, and country utensils. **1812** G. Chalmers *Historical View* 46 The alien duties, which had always obstructed the vent of native manufactures.

d. Const. *for.*

1583 Stubbes *Anat. Abus.* ii. (1882) 39 To filch and steale whatsoeuer they can lay their hands vpon, seing they may haue such good vent for yᵉ same. **1591** Greene *Conny Catch.* ii. 3 Any Faire, Mart, or other place where any good vent for horses is. *a* **1661** Fuller *Worthies, Essex* i. (1662) 318, I know not whether it be better to wish them good Wares to Vent, or good Vent for their Wares. **1689** *Apol. Fail. Walker's Acc.* 23 The tenth being more than he hopes to have vent for in England. **1727** Pope, etc. *Art of Sinking* 72, I doubt not, but we shall..procure a farther vent for our own product. **1761** Hume *Hist. Engl.* II. xxvi. 118 If husbandmen understand agriculture, and have a ready vent for their commodities. **1788** Priestley *Lect. Hist.* v. lviii. 460 If..they find a vent for these goods abroad, they will have wherewith to purchase the produce of other countries. **1828** Southey in *Q. Rev.* XXXVII. 546 Yet, even then, more goods were produced than there was vent for. **1868** E. Edwards *Ralegh* I. vi. 97 The ordinary vent for timber of any sort, in Ireland, was very limited.

†**3.** A place where goods are or may be sold; a market, mart. *Obs.*⁻¹

1580 R. Hitchcock *Politic Plat* f ij, At Rone in Fraunce which is the chefest vent, be solde our Englishe wares, as Welche and Manchester Cottons.

†**4.** [After Sp. *venta*.] An inn or tavern; a baiting or posting house. *Obs.* (Cf. venta.)

1577 Hellowes *Gueuara's Chron.* 14 The seate of Ystobriga was, where nowe the ventes of Caparra, being bayting places, stand. **1612** Shelton *Don Quix.* i. ii. (1620) 10 He perceiued an Inne, neere vnto the high way;.. forthwith as soone as he espied the Vent, he fained to himselfe that it was a Castle. *a* **1625** Fletcher *Love's Pilgr.* i. i, Our house Is but a *vent* of need, that now and then Receives a guest, between the greater Towns As they come late.

vent, *sb.*⁴ Theatr. slang abbrev. of ventriloquist.

1893 R. Ganthony *Practical Ventriloquism* iii. 89 The Vent: does not suffer provided he makes capital out of unforeseen interruptions. **1945** L. Lane *How to become Comedian* xiv. 116 When an imaginary character answers from the roof the 'vent' looks upwards. **1976** *National Observer* (U.S.) 4 Sept. 6/3 We've got magicians here... We've got jugglers, mentalists, clowns, and vents.

†**vent**, app. a variant spelling of went *sb.*

1513 Douglas *Æneid* iii. iv. 40 Fro that place syne ontill ane cave we went, Vndir a hingand hewch, in a derne vent [*v.r.* went].

†**vent**, *v.*¹ *Obs. rare.* [f. vent *sb.*¹]

1. *trans.* To trim the openings or slits of (a garment). Cf. fent *v.*

1547 in Feuillerat *Revels Edw. VI* (1914) 16 Longe gownes or Cassockes for women of red Sarcenet..puffyd with whyte sarcenet & ventyd with the same. **1606** in *Lismore Papers* Ser. ii. (1887) I. 111 Fustain to ventt it [*sc.* a gown] doune before.

2. To crenellate (a wall).

1531 in Bailey *Hist. Tower* (1821) p. xi, The walls.. rounde aboute to be copyde, ventyde, lowpyde, and crestyde. *Ibid.*, The walls of the same with one turret to be ventyde.

vent (vɛnt), *v.*² Also 7 vente, ventt. [f. vent *sb.*², or ad. F. *éventer* event *v.*² Cf. also avent *v.* The senses of OF. and F. *venter* are barely represented here.]

I. *trans.* **1. a.** To provide (a liquor cask, etc.) with a vent or outlet for gas or vapour. Also, to empty (a confined space) of gas in this manner.

1398 [see VENTING *vbl. sb.*] **1495** *Trevisa's Barth. De P.R.* XVII. clxxxvi. 727 The strengthe of feruent must..brekyth ful stronge vesselles that it is put in, but thei be vented. **1570** LEVINS *Manip.* 66 To vent, *aperire, euacuare.* **1580–3** GREENE *Mamillia* Wks. (Grosart) II. 57 The wine vessel beyng ful, lets passe no wine, though neuer so wel vented. **1607** WALKINGTON *Opt. Glass* 45 The vessel beein[g] vented and broch't, tels the taste what liquor issueth from it. **1703** *Art & Myst. Vintners & Wine-Coopers* 11 They draw them forth for sale as fast as they can vent them. **1947** J. C. RICH *Materials & Methods of Sculpture* xi. 355 Molds may be vented to permit the ready escape of air from undercuts. **1969** *Times* 23 May 1/2, To close their hatch, the pressure in the tunnel had to be lowered. 'I am not able to vent the tunnel,' Commander John Young reported at 6.15 p.m... last night. **1978** *Daily Tel.* 18 Aug. 30/6 The balloon's crew were then able to..fall into the most likely airstream by..venting the balloon—letting out the helium and allowing it to drop.

fig. **1589** NASHE *Anat. Absurdity* Wks. (Grosart) I. 35 These Bussards thinke knowledge a burthen, tapping it before they haue half tunde it, venting it before they haue filled it.

b. *fig.* To relieve or unburden (one's heart or soul) in respect of feelings or emotions. Also *refl.*

c **1626** W. BOSWORTH *Arcadius & Sepha* I. 843 With these, and such like words, he vents his soul Of those..Conjectures. **1631** HEYWOOD *Engl. Elizabeth* (1641) 55 The King having something vented himselfe with laughing, replied. **1709** STEELE *Tatler* No. 22 ¶2 Without any Purpose in his Talk, but to vent an Heart overflowing with Sense of Success. **1799** WINTER *Let.* in Jay *Wks.* (1843) V. 92, I vented my soul in a line to Mr. Peronet.

2. a. To discharge, eject, cast or pour out (liquid, smoke, etc.); to carry off or away; to drain in this way. Also with advs., as *away, down, forth, out.* Freq. *pass.*

Said usually of the containing thing, but sometimes of the force or means by which outlet is given. Examples with advs. are placed under (*a*).

(*a*) **1587** HOLINSHED *Chron.* (ed. 2) III. 558/1 The infectious smother of this venemous vapor..had beene readie to choke all christendome, had not by the wisedome..of the princes there, the same the sooner beene vented away. **1602** *2nd Pt. Return fr. Parnass.* IV. iii. 1888 Those leaden spouts, That nought downe [*v.r.* doe] vent but what they do receiue. **1644** G. PLATTES in *Hartlib's Legacy* (1655) 198 The pits..will vent away the superfluous water continually, and keep the sellar alwaies dry. **1652** FRENCH *Yorkshire Spa* ii. 19 They being vented forth, the heat would..be extinguished.

(*b*) **1633** G. HERBERT *Temple, Providence* xviii, Springs vent their streams, and by expense get store. **1646** P. BULKELEY *Gospel Covt.* I. 114 Be not like dry vessels that will vent nothing. **1712** W. ROGERS *Voyage* (1718) 383 We found it [the leak] did not encrease more than one pump could vent. **1793** SMEATON *Edystone L.* §297 The copper funnels for venting the smoke from the kitchen fires. **1962** F. I. ORDWAY et al. *Basic Astronautics* v. 197 After arrival on the moon the fluid is vented. **1969** *Daily Mail* 15 Jan. 5/4 The rocket..vented quite a lot of fuel overboard and the fuel formed millions of ice particles. **1980** *Nature* 29 May 278/3 A total of 10 millicuries of krypton-85 was vented to the atmosphere during the procedure and the engineers received a whole body radiation dose of 10 to 15 mrem. **1983** *Sci. Amer.* Apr. 80/1 The pilot vented the ballast tanks, surrounding *Alvin* with a column of bubbles.

fig. **1622** BACON *Hen. VII*, 98 If there should bee any bad Bloud left in the Kingdome, an Honourable Forraine Warre will Vent it. *a* **1627** SIR J. BEAUMONT *Bosworth F.* 552 My Strength is spent, And some perhaps of Villain Blood will vent My weary Soul.

†**b.** Of persons, animals, or their organs: To cast out, expel, or discharge, esp. by natural evacuation; to evacuate (urine, etc.). *Obs.*

1607 TOPSELL *Four-f. Beasts* 249 With a medicine made of an Affrican Sparrow mixed with this, he procured one to make water, and to void a great stone which had not vented his vrine in many daies. **1611** SHAKS. *Cymb.* I. ii. 5 Where ayre comes out, ayre comes in: There's none abroad so wholesome as that you vent. **1641** MILTON *Reform.* II. Wks. 1851 III. 70 The very maw of Hell ransack't, and made to give up her conceal'd destruction, ere shee could vent it in that horrible and damned blast. **1656** J. SMITH *Pract. Physick* 94 The Chylus..cannot all be changed into water, and if it were changed, yet the Reins can vent it forth. **1738** tr. *Guazzo's Art Convers.* 74 Such as vent such pestiferous Blasts, ought to have their Wind stopt with a Halter. **1846** J. BAXTER *Libr. Pract. Agric.* (ed. 4) II. 99 Sheep that are infected with this disorder cannot vent the seed, the ova, from their liver, on the ground.

transf. *c* **1611** CHAPMAN *Iliad* XIX. 97 When Alcmena was to vent the force of Hercules.

fig. **1608** T. MORTON *Preamb. Encounter* 121 Whatsoeuer bitternesse the gall of this man could vent out.

†**c.** To shed (tears). Also with *out. Obs. rare.*

1632 J. HAYWARD tr. *Biondi's Eromena* 123 Having first suffered me to vent out my teares, for the disburdning of my heart [etc.]. **1760–72** H. BROOKE *Fool of Qual.* (1809) III. 16 He..vented the tears of..pleasure, love, and gratitude.

3. a. To give, heave, or utter (a groan, sigh, etc.). Now *rare* or *poet.*

1602 MARSTON *Antonio's Rev.* IV. iv, I..vent a heaving sigh. **1615** T. ADAMS *White Devil* 42 The poore confident plaintife goes home undone; his moanes, his groanes are vented up to heaven. **1718** POPE *Iliad* XV. 123 Behold Ascalaphus! behold him die, But dare not murmur, dare not vent a sigh. *a* **1763** SHENSTONE *Elegies* xiv. 45 Beneath her palm Idume vents her moan. **1858** H. BUSHNELL *Serm. New Life* 10 They even complain, venting heavy sighs. **1872** BLACKIE *Lays Highl.* 122 Not wise is he who vents an angry breath.

†**b.** *poet.* To pour out (one's soul) in death. *Obs.*

1718 POPE *Iliad* XVI. 387 He sinks,..And vents his soul, effused with gushing gore.

4. *fig.* **a.** To give vent to (an emotion, feeling, passion, etc.); to give free course or expression to; to express; to make manifest or known.

1596 SHAKS. *Tam. Shr.* I. ii. 179 Gremio, 'tis now no time to vent our loue. **1602** MARSTON *Antonio's Rev.* II. iv, I must vent my griefes, or heart will burst. **1641** TATHAM *Distr. State* II. i, Did you e'er Hear spleen better vented. **1676** HOBBES *Iliad* IV. 174 Would Agamemnon thus would alwaies vent His Choler. **1722** DE FOE *Plague* (1840) 74 Others, unable to contain themselves, vented their pain by incessant roarings. *a* **1781** R. WATSON *Hist. Philip III* v. (1783) 349 The resentment of Spain was farther vented in a manifesto. **1820** SCOTT *Monast.* xiv, Martin..suppressed not his indignation a moment after he could vent it with safety. **1841** DICKENS *Barn. Rudge* xxxii, He vented the lightness of his spirit in smiles and sparkling looks. **1873** SYMONDS *Grk. Poets* v. 139 Habituated to associate together in large bodies, the Dorians felt no need of venting private feeling.

transf. *a* **1716** SOUTH *Serm.* (1744) XI. 222 Things contrary will vent their contrariety in mutual strife.

b. To let loose, pour out, wreak (one's anger, spleen, etc.) *on* or *upon* a person or thing. (Cf. 5 b.)

1697 DRYDEN *Æneid* III. 703 The Winds and Waves complain, And vent their malice on the Cliffs in vain. **1710** *Tatler* No. 260 ¶3 That fatal distemper, which has always taken a particular pleasure in venting its spight upon the Nose. **1735** JOHNSON *Lobo's Abyssinia, Descr.* ix. 93 The Viceroy disappointed in this Scheme, vented all his rage upon Father James. **1750** —— *Rambler* No. 87 ¶9 The unsuccessful vent their discontent upon those that excel them. **1816** T. L. PEACOCK *Headlong Hall* xiii, To vent their spleen on the first idle coxcomb they can find. **1878** BOSW. SMITH *Carthage* 55 The Carthaginians unable to vent their anger even on the lifeless corpse of the unfortunate Hamilcar,..vented it on his innocent son.

5. *fig.* **a.** To give out or forth, publish or spread abroad, by or as by utterance; to give utterance or publicity to (a doctrine, opinion, etc.); to utter (a word, expression, etc.). †Also const. *forth* or *out.*

Very common from *c* 1600 to *c* 1750; now somewhat *rare* or *arch.*

1602 *2nd Pt. Return fr. Parnass.* II. vi. 954 What Iack, faith I cannot but vent vnto thee a most witty iest of mine. **1633** BP. HALL *Hard Texts, N.T.* 277 After that God had once vented and declared that his good purpose to mankind. **1648** GAGE *West Ind.* 102 And they will be sure to vent out some non-truth. **1712** STEELE *Spect.* No. 278 ¶1 Learning by Heart Scraps of Greek, which she vents upon all Occasions. **1764** H. WALPOLE *Lett.* (1891) IV. 279, I hate to send you every improbable tale that is vented. **1817** JAS. MILL *Brit. India* II. v. iv. 431 The Presidency vent the most bitter complaints. **1850** MERIVALE *Rom. Emp.* iii. (1865) I. 107 The noisy declamations he vented about the imaginary dangers of his new Carthage. **1871** BLACKIE *Phases of Morals* i. 48 He who in an impulse of fearless fervour vents a little too much truth [etc.].

b. With *on* or *upon.* (Cf. 4 b.)

1832 HT. MARTINEAU *Hill & Valley* vi. 85 Many a curse did the least wise..vent upon the French. **1843** GLADSTONE *Glean.* (1879) V. 65 The nameless author who has recently vented his chaff..upon the public. **1844** LEVER *T. Burke* v, The curse vented on me by one whose ruin..lay at my own father's door.

†**c.** To disclose, divulge, or let *out* (a secret, etc.). *Obs.*

1678 MARVELL *Growth Popery* Wks. (Grosart) IV. 276 This affair was carried on with all the secresie of so great statesmen, that they might not by venting it unseasonably, spoil [etc.]. **1679** EVERARD *Popish Plot* 7 When these matters were vented out of [= by] Sir Robert.

6. *refl.* Of a thing: To discharge (itself); to find issue or exit.

1650 FULLER *Pisgah* IV. v. 81 Nilus venteth itself into the Mediterranean Sea with seven mouths. **1665** SIR T. HERBERT *Trav.* (1677) 120 That very year the earth swelled with such a tympany, that in venting it self all Larr was forced to quake. **1684** J. PETER *Siege Vienna* 45 It hapned that they were all left standing, the Mine venting it self upon the Edge of the Ditch. **1726** *Nat Hist. Ireland* 193 A lake..called Loughchorib..vents it self into the sea at Galway.

b. *esp.* Of an emotion, faculty, quality, etc.: To find vent; to express or show (itself) *in* something.

(*a*) **1650** FULLER *Pisgah* IV. vii. 138 It is to be feared that this sin finding its usuall way obstructed, will watch its own advantage, to vent itself by some other conveyances. **1702** ROWE *Amb. Step-Moth.* I. i. 375 The Malice of the Faction which I hate Would vent it self even on thy Innocence. **1808** in *Knox & Jebbs' Corr.* I. 456 The fears of men..having been taught..to vent themselves, if I may so speak, through the channel of sacrifice. **1849** MACAULAY *Hist. Eng.* iii. I. 367 The coffee houses were the chief organs through which the public opinion of the metropolis vented itself. *a* **1862** BUCKLE *Civiliz.* (1869) III. iv. 193 This ill-feeling increased until, in 1580, it vented itself by the abolition of episcopacy.

(*b*) *a* **1661** FULLER *Worthies* (1840) III. 468 Able and active bodies are not to vent themselves in such vain, though gainful, ostentation. **1669** GALE *Crt. Gentiles* I. III. i. 8 Affections..delight to vent themselves in Poesie. **1763** J. BROWN *Poetry & Music* 102 When the first Fire of Enthusiasm had vented itself in the Rapture of Hymns and Odes. **1819** SCOTT *Ivanhoe* xxvii, The..decrepit hag..whose wrath must vent itself in impotent curses. *a* **1854** H. REED *Lect. Brit. Poets* xiii. (1857) II. 159 This cheerfulness has vented itself in his playful poetry.

†**7. a.** To eject or expel (people) *out of* a country. *Obs.*$^{-1}$

1609 in Gardiner *Hist. Eng.* I. 438 [A wish that as many natives as possible might be] vented out of the land.

†**b.** To rid (a kingdom) *of* people. *Obs.*$^{-1}$

1613 SIR T. STAFFORD in *Lismore Papers* Ser. II. (1887) I. 199 It will be a good meanes to vent that Kingdome..of a number of Idle men that haue nothinge to doe.

†**c.** *fig.* To spend, get rid of (a fortune). *Obs.*$^{-1}$

1610 B. JONSON *Alch.* III. iv, How doe they liue by their wits, there, that haue vented Sixe times your fortunes?

†**8. a.** To dispense, distribute. *Obs.*$^{-1}$

1616 CHAPMAN *Odyss.* XVII. 345 The Pallace royall..he enter'd..and his Trencher's fraight The Keruers gaue him, of the flesh there vented.

†**b.** To put (coins, etc.) in circulation or currency; to give in payment; to pay out. *Obs.*

1629 *Reg. Privy Counc. Scotl.* Ser. II. III. 20 That nane of thame presoome..to vent and putt amongs his Majesteis subjects anie of the saids Embden dollours. **1655** tr. *Sorel's Com. Hist. Francion* XII. 31 Valerius having filled his Purse with pieces more current than those which he ordinarily vented. **1683** *Col. Rec. Pennsylv.* I. 84 A Question put whether there be not some persons to vent such money here.

†**9.** To explode or fire (a mine). *Obs. rare.*

1687 J. RICHARDS *Siege Buda* 14 With directions that if the Miners should meet with the Turks Mine, to Vent it.

10. To supply (a gun) with a vent or vent-piece.

1828 SPEARMAN *Brit. Gunner* (ed. 2) 412 It was recommended that iron ordnance..might be vented previously to their being issued. *Ibid.*, A gun of the same description vented with pure copper. **1879** *Man. Artill. Exerc.* 201 The 80-pr. is vented in the same manner as the 64-pr. 58-cwt. gun.

II. *intr.* **11. a.** Of an exhalation, liquid, smoke, etc.: To find or make an outlet or way of escape from a confined space; to come, flow, pass, or pour *out* or *away* by a vent or opening. Also used of a force causing an outlet to be made.

(*a*) **1540–1** ELYOT *Image Gov.* (1556) 64 Corrupt exhalacions, ventynge out of mens bodyes. **1560** WHITEHORNE *Ord. Souldiours* (1588) 45 It will bee surer to let nothing vent out but the glasse it selfe. **1615** DAY *Festivals* iv. 100 They were full of new Wine, and the new Wine venting out, the Tongues of all Nations were immediately set a float. **1704** *Dict. Rust.* (1726) s.v. *Blood-Spavin*, When the Blood and Water have vented away as much as they will do.

(*b*) **1604** T. WRIGHT *Passions* IV. i. 110 New wine..by venting bursteth the bottle. **1645** RUTHERFORD *Tryal & Tri. Faith* (1845) 69 Smoke venteth at the window, when the chimney refuseth passage. **1694** CONGREVE *Double-Dealer* IV. ii, A cold deadly dew already vents through all my pores. **1886** J. BARROWMAN *Sc. Mining Terms* 69 To *Vent*, to have room to pass away. **1966** *Economist* 19 Feb. 686/3 Some of these test explosions 'vent' through the earth's surface and thus contaminate the atmosphere. **1970** *Times* 15 Apr. 1/7 The particles have diminished greatly—almost ceased now, which indicates maybe what was venting has almost stopped. **1980** *Courier-Mail* (Brisbane) 27 Nov. 31/4 Fuel was venting from the tanks. The loss was so great that it was doubted that they would make it to an airfield.

fig. **1615** BRATHWAIT *Strappado*, etc. (1878) 265 For loue enclos'd like raging elements of fire and water, though imprisoned, vents. *a* **1635** NAUNTON *Fragm. Reg.* (1641) 4 It staved off all Emulations..apt to rise and vent in obloquious acrimonie..where there is one onely admitted into high administrations.

†**b.** To become known, be divulged. *Obs.*$^{-1}$

1622 BACON *Hen. VII* (1876) 26 The earl presently communicated the matter with some of the nobles,..at the first secretly; but finding them of like affection to himself, he suffered it of purpose to vent and pass abroad.

†**12. a.** Of a bottle, confined space, etc.: To have or obtain an outlet by which the contained matter can escape. Freq. *fig.* or in fig. context. *Obs.*

1599 *Broughton's Let.* ii. 9 Like an old bottle with new wine, vnlesse you should vent, you would burst. **1614** J. COOKE *Greene's Tu Quoque* in Dodsley *O. Pl.* (1744) III. 56 My heart is swol'n so big, that it must vent, Or it will burst. **1626** B. JONSON *Staple of N.* I. ii. (1905) 13 Quiet his mouth, that Ouen will be venting else. **1655** *Nicholas Papers* (Camden) II. 324, I cannot forbeare filling vpp my paper with it, for such as we are must vent or we burst.

b. *Sc.* To let out or discharge smoke; to carry off smoke (well or ill).

1756 MRS. CALDERWOOD in *Coltness Collect.* (Maitl. Club) 225 And neither great nor small [houses] will vent, which obliges them to use stoves: nay, these stoves will not vent at the chimney, but are often let out in a hole in the outer wall. *Ibid.* 236 As you know we cannot have in any kitchin above two stoves, because they must vent up the chimney. **1816** SCOTT *Antiq.* xi, The Green Room disna vent weel in a high wind. **1825** JAMIESON *Suppl.* s.v., That lum vents very ill.

c. *U.S.* Of a brook: To flow *into* a river.

1784 J. BELKNAP *Tour to White Mts.* (1876) 7 A large brook, which vents into Pine River.

†**13.** *spec.* (See quot.) *Obs.*$^{-1}$

1721 BAILEY, To *Vent*, (among Glass Plate Workers,) is to crack in Working.

III. †**14. a.** *intr.* Of an animal: To snuff up the air, esp. in order to pick up the scent of something. *Obs.*

1538 ELYOT, *Nicto, tere*, to vent as the hound doth, whiche foloweth the dere or hare, or other game. **1552** HULOET s.v., Vent or snucke as a hound or spaniell doth, *nicto.* **1579** SPENSER *Sheph. Cal.* Feb. 75 Seest, howe brag yond Bullocke beares, So smirke, so smoothe, his pricked eares?..See howe he venteth into the wynd. **1612** DRAYTON *Polyolb.* xiv. 20 At the full-bagg'd cow, Or at the curl-fac'd bull, when venting he doth low,..He never seems to smile. **1660** R. COKE *Justice Vind.* 9 It is observed of the Fox, that whensoever hunted to ground, he never comes out, but at the mouth of the Burrow, he lies and vents a while.

†**b.** *transf.* To search or seek *for*. *Obs.*$^{-1}$

1574 HELLOWES *Gueuara's Fam. Ep.* (1577) 344, I cannot denie, but that after the manner of a drunkarde, that venteth for the best wine: so doe mine eyes stare and wander to finde out some olde Sepulture.

†**15. a.** *trans.* Of animals, hounds, etc.: To become aware of, to detect or perceive, by means of the sense of smell; = SCENT *v.* 1. *Obs.*

1576 TURBERV. *Venerie* 75 If they chaunce once to vent the huntesman or his hounde, they will straight way dislodge from thence. *Ibid.* 187 He which maketh the trayne, must rubbe the soales of his shoes with Cowes dung, least the Foxe vent his footing. **1611** *Noble Art Venerie* 96 My liege, I went this morning on my quest, My hound did sticke, and seem'd to vent some beast. **1660** R. COKE *Justice Vind.* 9 The Fox,..if he vents any thing which causes fear, returns to ground again. *Ibid.*, So Deer do naturally desire to eat Apples, but if approaching, they vent them to have been handled by man, they forsake them. **1735** SOMERVILLE *Chace* III. 544 Then as o'er the Turf he [a stag] strains, He vents the cooling Stream, and up the Breeze Urges his Course with eager Violence.

†**b.** *transf.* To discover or discern. *Obs.*$^{-0}$

1611 COTGR., *On flaire cela*,..men begin to discouer it, vent it, find it out.

16. To smell or snuff at (something). *rare.*

1634 MASSINGER *Very Woman* III. v, *Antonio (pours out some wine)*. She stirs, and vents it: Oh! how she holds her nose up! **1880** SHORTHOUSE *J. Inglesant* I. ii. 43 The hounds came trailing and chanting along by the riverside, venting every tree root.

17. a. *intr.* Of an otter, or beaver: To rise to the surface in order to breathe. Also *transf.* of a person (quot. 1600).

1590 COCKAINE *Treat. Hunting* D ij b, He [the otter] will vent so oft, and put vp ouer water... At which time some must runne vp the water, some downe, to see where he vents. **1600** FAIRFAX *Tasso* XV. lx, As when the morning starre escapt and fled, From greedie waues with dewie beames vp flies,..So vented she. **1647** HEXHAM I. s.v., To Vent or take breath as an Otter. **1733** *Phil. Trans.* XXXVIII. 180 When she [*sc.* a beaver] swam under Water, which she would do for two or three Minutes, and then come up to vent, sometimes raising her Nostrils only above Water. **1735** SOMERVILLE *Chace* IV. 433 Th' ascending Bubbles mark his [i.e. an otter's] gloomy Way. Quick fix the Nets, and cut off his Retreat Into the shelt'ring Deeps. Ah! there he vents! **1818** SCOTT *Rob Roy* xxxiii, One of the otter-hunts ..where the animal is detected by the hounds from his being necessitated to put his nose above the stream to vent or breathe. **1856** 'STONEHENGE' *Brit. Rur. Sports* 144/2 The otter..is obliged to come up and 'vent' for want of air. **1885** *Standard* 2 April 5/3 Their prey is rising to 'vent'.

†**b.** *trans.* To cause or force (an otter) to come to the surface. *Obs.*$^{-0}$

1688 HOLME *Armoury* II. 134/2 An Otter: We watch, and Vent him, when we disturb him. *a* **1700** B. E. *Dict. Cant. Crew*, *Vent the Otter*, Dislodge him.

†**18.** *trans.* To blow (a horn). *Obs.*$^{-1}$

1601 F. TATE *Househ. Ord. Edw. II*, §57 (1876) 44, j to vent the horne shal have ij[d]. a day wages.

†**19.** To supply with fresh air; to ventilate. *Obs.*

1601 HOLLAND *Pliny* I. 440 That all the Apples..be so couched as that they touch not one another, but haue spaces between to receiue equall aire for to bee vented.

†**20.** To lift *up* so as to admit air. *Obs.*$^{-1}$

1590 SPENSER *F.Q.* III. i. 42 The braue Mayd would not disarmed bee, But onely vented vp her vmbriere, And so did let her goodly visage to appere.

vent, *v.*[3] Now *dial.* Also 6 *Sc.* **went**, 7 **vente**. [f. F. *vente* VENT *sb.*[3]]

1. *trans.* To sell or vend (commodities or goods); to dispose of by sale.

Very common from *c* 1600 to *c* 1670.

1478–9 *Burgh Rec. Edin.* (1869) I. 36 It is thocht expedient that all persouns haif licence and leif to cum to the towne with victualls to..vent the samyn on Monoday, Wedinsday, and Fryday. **1542–3** *Act 34 & 35 Hen. VIII*, c. 6 Pynnes which be dailie vented, uttered, and put to Sale within this Realme. **1598** SYLVESTER *Du Bartas* II. ii. *Colonies* 665 The In-land Lands might truck and barter, And vent their Wares about to every Quarter. **1605** B. JONSON *Volpone* II. ii, They are quack-saluers, Fellowes, that liue by venting oyles, and drugs? **1661** in J. Simon *Ess. Irish Coins* (1749) 127 Several persons..took a liberty..to make a kind of brass or copper tokens,..and vented them to the people for a penny each piece. **1672** COLLINS in Rigaud *Corr. Sci. Men* (1841) I. 200 England doth not vent above twenty or thirty of any new mathematical book he brings over. **1719** W. WOOD *Survey Trade* 217 While Spain remains an independant Nation,..we may always hope to maintain..our Trade to that Kingdom, and vent our Manufactures in the Indies. **1764** BURN *Poor Laws* 153 Hemp and flax,..which now people neglect to sow, because they have no way to vent or employ it. **1790** SHIRREFS *Poems* 316 Tak ye tent, How, and to whom your bills ye vent. **1864** in O'DONOGHUE *St. Knighton* (Cornwall) *Gloss.* 301.

transf. **1652** GAULE *Magastrom.* xxvi, Hereupon the astrologers doe mart or vent the effects of the heavens and the stars.

†**b.** With various advs., as *away*, *forth*, *off*. *Obs.*

c **1550** *Disc. Common Weal Eng.* (1893) 62 As much as he should haue for the more woll vented ouer, so much should he haue for the lesse woll at a greater custome vented ouer. **1602** CAREW *Cornwall* 3 The nearenesse helpeth them..to vent forth and make return of those comodities, which their owne, or either of those countries doe afford. *c* **1630** T. MUN *England's Treas.* 79 We trade to divers places where we vent off our native commodities. **1631** HEYWOOD *Fair Maid of West* III, To vent away our bad commodities.

†**c.** To let *out* (land). *Obs.*$^{-1}$

1603 G. OWEN *Pembrokeshire* viii. (1891) 63 Some landlordes..founde it more comodiouse to keape it in their owne handes then to vente it out at xii[d] an acre which is the vsualle rent thireof.

†**2.** *intr.* Of goods: To have or find sale; to sell, go off (well or ill). *Obs.*

1622 in M. Sellers *Eastland Co.* (Camden) Introd. 54 Either over cheap pennyworths must cause our said cloths to vent there, or else they will not vent at all. **1628–9** DIGBY *Voy. Medit.* (Camden) 29 Other thinges that I had which would vent better in that place then in England. **1670** J. SMITH *Eng. Improv. Reviv'd* 202 Cherries will vent at most Markets. **1670** NARBOROUGH *Jrnl.* in *Acc. Sev. Late Voy.* I. (1694) 110 Commodities would bear a much greater price than what I mention, and there would vent greater quantities.

‖**venta** ('venta). Also 7 **vento**. [Sp. *venta* (= Pg. *venda*):—L. *vendita*: see VENT *sb.*[3]] A Spanish hostelry or wayside inn.

1610 in Birch *Crt. & Times Jas. I* (1848) I. 107 Our ventas and hostelries without victuals or lodging. **1618** R. COCKS *Diary* (1883) II. 89 As we retorned, we went into a *vento* or tavarne. **1662** J. DAVIES tr. *Olearius' Voy. Ambass.* 205 Those places..are as the *Ventas* in Spain, and serve for Inns upon the High-way. **1775** TWISS *Trav. Portug. & Sp.* 39 *note*, A *venta* is a lone house, established by public authority, for the convenience of travellers. **1792** TOWNSEND *Journ. Spain* iii. 104 The waggoners and drovers..being seated on the grass before the doors of a *venta*. **1817** KEATINGE *Trav.* I. 69 A venta is seated at the foot of this road of ascent. **1846** THACKERAY *Cornhill to Cairo* Wks. 1900 V. 609 Through the flaring lattices of the Spanish ventas comes the clatter of castanets. **1897** 'H. S. MERRIMAN' *In Kedar's Tents* v, Beguiling the journey with cigarette and song, calling at every venta on the road.

†'**ventage**[1]. *Obs.*$^{-1}$ In 6 **-adge**. [f. VENT *v.*[3] + -AGE.] The action of selling or vending; sale.

1577 in *10th Rep. Hist. MSS. Comm.* App. V. 426 The great losse they sustayned in this ventadge by meanes of those with whom they have sente..their goodes in to Spayne.

ventage[2] ('vɛntɪdʒ). Also 7–9 **ventige**. [f. VENT *sb.*[2] + -AGE.]

1. One of the series of apertures or holes in the length of a wind instrument for controlling the notes; a finger-hole.

In mod. use perh. originally from Shakespeare.

1602 SHAKS. *Ham.* III. ii. 373 (Q.[2]), Gouerne these ventages [*fol.* ventiges] with your fingers,..& it wil discourse most eloquent musique. **1776** BURNEY *Hist. Music* I. 264 It was found practicable to produce the same variety of tones with a single pipe, by means of ventiges or holes. **1794** BURNS *Let. to G. Thomson* 20 Nov., The stock has six or seven ventiges on the upper side, and one back-ventige, like the common flute. **1834** M. SCOTT *Cruise Midge* xxiii, An instrument made of some bright yellow hard wood,..the ventiges [**1842** ventages] inlaid with gold. **1876** J. WEISS *Wit, Hum. & Shaks.* v. 171 It is enough for him to finger the ventages of a recorder and invite Guildenstern to play upon it.

transf. **1612** WEBSTER *White Devil* II. i. 299 He will shoot pils into a mans guts, shall make them have more ventages than a cornet or a lamprey.

2. A comparatively small opening for the passage of air, etc.; an air-hole or vent-hole.

1623 WEBSTER *Duchess Malfi* II. v, I would have their bodies Burnt in a coal-pit with the ventage stopp'd. **1726** LEONI *Alberti's Archit.* II. 112/2 In subterraneous Conduits you shou'd open Ventiges like Wells... I have seen such Ventiges in the Country of the Marsi.

b. = VENT *sb.*[2] 11 d.

1875 KNIGHT *Dict. Mech.* 2703/1 The ventages of ordnance are bushed with copper.

3. Means for the escape of air.

1615 J. STEPHENS *Satyr. Ess.* (1857) 226 She rises with a purpose to be extreamely sober: this begets silence, which gives her a repletion of aire without ventage; and that takes away her appetite.

ventage, obs. form of VINTAGE.

ventail. Now *Hist.* Forms: α. 4–6 (9) **ventayle**, 5 **-tayll(e**, **-tayl**; 4–6 (9) **ventaile**, 5–6 **-tale**, 5 **-taill** (9 **-taile**), 4, 9 **ventail** (5 *Sc.* **wen-**). β. 5 **ventalle**, 5–6 **-tall**, 6 **-tal**. [a. OF. *ventaille*, *-taile*, *ventalle* (mod.F. *ventail* masc., = OProv. *ventalha*, It. *ventaglia*), f. *vent* wind, air. Hence also MHG. *vin-*, *finteile*, *vintale*. A purely English variant is AVENTAIL.

As the sense of 'breathing-place' appears to be inapplicable to the earliest use of the word (see sense 1) in French and English, the name may originally have been given to the piece of armour from a real or fancied resemblance to some other article so designated. Other senses of the OF. word (and of the related forms *ventele*, *ventail*, and *vental*) are fan, vane (of a windmill), sluice, shutter, leaf (of a folding door or picture). In OF. romances the *ventaille* is freq. mentioned as covering the heart or breast: cf. Chaucer *Clerk's Tale* 1148.]

†**1.** A piece of armour protecting the neck, upon which the helmet fitted; a neck-piece. *Obs.*

α. *a* **1330** *Roland & V.* 863 His ventail he gan vn-lace & smot of his heued in þe place. **13..** *Guy Warw.* (A.) 92 His helme was of so michel miȝt, Was neuer man ouer-comen in fiȝt þat hadde it on his ventayle. *a* **1400** *Sir Perc.* 1722 He hitt hym evene one the nekk-bane, Thurgh ventale and pesane. *c* **1400** *Laud Troy Bk.* 14375 Her helmes were on her ventayles sperde. *c* **1450** LOVELICH *Grail* XIV. 33 Helmes, hawberkes, & ventaylles also, Alle to the Grownde he dyde hem go.

β. *a* **1400** *Sqr. lowe Degre* 222 Your basenette shall be burnysshed bryght, Your ventall shalbe well dyght, With starres of gold it shall be set.

2. The lower movable part of the front of a helmet, as distinct from the vizor; latterly, the whole movable part including the vizor.

c **1400** *Destr. Troy* 7030 The duke with a dynt derit hym agayn, þat the viser & the ventaile voidet hym fro. *c* **1400** *Anturs of Arth.* xxxii, Then he auaylet vppe his viserne fro his ventalle. *c* **1470** *Gol. & Gaw.* 867 He braidit vp his ventaill, That closit wes clene. *a* **1533** LD. BERNERS *Huon* cxxiv. 448 Vnder the ventayle of his helme the terys of water fell downe fro his eyen. **1590** SPENSER *F.Q.* III. ii. 24 Through whose bright ventayle..His manly face..lookt foorth. **1600** FAIRFAX *Tasso* VI. xxvi, He ventall vp so hie, that he descride Her goodly visage, and her beauties pride. **1802** JAMES *Milit. Dict.*, *Ventail*, that part of a helmet which is made to lift up. **1865** KINGSTON JAMES *Tasso* XX. xii, Thro' the barred ventayle his flushed features shone. [**1869** BOUTELL *Arms & Armour* viii. 127 This piece, called the *mesail*, or *mursail*,..but more generally known in England as the *ventaile*, or visor, was pierced for both sight and breathing.] **1906** S. HEATH *Effigies in Dorset* 10 Some-times with a movable 'ventaille' or visor.

†**b.** One of the vents or air-holes of this. *Obs.*$^{-1}$

1470–85 MALORY *Arthur* X. lx. 516 The blood brast oute at the ventayls of his helme.

†**3.** Something acting as a sail or fan. *Obs.*

a **1529** SKELTON *Col. Cloute* 400 [The nuns] Must cast vp theyr blacke vayles, And set vp theyr fucke sayles, To catch wynde with their ventales.

†**ventailet.** *Obs.*$^{-1}$ In 5 **ventaylett**. [Dim. of (or error for) prec.] = prec. 2.

1459 *Paston Lett.* I. 487 Item, v. ventayletts for bassenetts.

vental ('vɛntəl), *a. rare.* [f. L. *vent-us* VENT *sb.*[2] + -AL[1].] Of or pertaining to the wind.

1887 *Field* 14 Nov. (Cassell's), The strange, vental eccentricities that had been occurring on our coasts.

‖**ventana.** Also 7 **ventanna**. [Sp., f. L. *vent-us* wind.] A window.

1670 DRYDEN *Conq. Granada* I. iii, What after pass'd—Was far from the *Ventanna* where I sate. **1851** MAYNE REID *Scalp Hunt.* ix. I. 121, I..dress myself, and sit in my 'ventana'. **1873** DIXON *Two Queens* V. iii. I. 249 She could.. breathe her evening hymn from the ventana of Zoraya.

vented ('vɛntɪd), *ppl. a.* [f. VENT *v.*[2]]

†**a.** Exploded, blown up. *Obs.* **b.** Allowed to escape; discharged.

1639 S. DU VERGER tr. *Camus' Admir. Events* 30 All the subtilties..were as so many vented mines, without any effect. **1911** *Contemp. Rev.* Oct. 522 The moral forces disengaged by the death of David Livingstone are a singular instance of this vented energy. **1977** *Sci. Amer.* Apr. 27/2 Fortunately the vented gas did not ignite.

vented ('vɛntɪd), *a.* [f. VENT *sb.*[2] + -ED[2].] Equipped with vents or apertures. Cf. PORTED *a.*[1] 2.

1940 *Electronics* Mar. 34/1 The vented speaker enclosure uses a conventional cone type dynamic speaker mounted in a box lined with sound absorbent material. **1957** *IRE Trans. on Audio* V. 38/2 The vented enclosure allows the hf speaker to be mounted with its centroid to lie on the same point as that of the lf speaker. **1975** [see PORTED *a.*[1] 2].

venteduct, obs. form of VENTIDUCT.

ventelde, misreading in the following passage for *vntelde*: see UNTELD *v.*

? *a* **1400** *Morte Arth.* 737 Qwene alle was schyppede that scholde, they schounte no lengere, Bot ventelde theme tyte, as þe tyde rynnez.

venter[1] ('vɛntə(r)). Also 6 **ventre**. [a. AF. *ventre*, *venter*, or L. *venter* (whence It., Fr., Prov., and Pg. *ventre*, Sp. *vientre*), paunch, womb, etc. In anatomical use the L. pl. *ventrēs* is occas. employed.]

I. 1. a. One or other of two or more wives who are (successively or otherwise) sources of offspring to the same person. Usually in phrases with *by*. Orig. (and in later use chiefly) *Law* (after AF. *per un*, *per autre*, *venter*).

1544 tr. *Littleton's Tenures* 2 b, Yf man haue issue .ii. sonnes by .ii. ventres. *Ibid.* 157 b, Yf a tenaunt in tayle haue issue .ii. daughters by dyuers ventres. **1628** COKE *On Litt.* I. i. §7 If a man hath issue a sonne and a daughter by one venter, and a son by another venter. **1650** WELDON *Crt. Jas. I*, 89 Mr George Villers a younger sonne by a second Venter. **1665** SIR T. HERBERT *Trav.* (1677) 60 To his Sons by another Venter..he gave Money-portions. **1677** SANDFORD *Geneal. Hist. Kings Eng.* 101 Sons of his said Father by the first Venter. **1726** AYLIFFE *Parergon* 35 A man dying left Issue by two several Venters. **1760** STERNE *Tr. Shandy* IV. xxix, His sister by the father's side (for she was born of the former venter). **1766** BLACKSTONE *Comm.* II. 227 If the father has two sons..by different venters or wives. **1818** CRUISE *Digest* (ed. 2) VI. 463 A. having two sons, B. and C., by several venters.

fig. **1651** CLEVELAND *Poems* 3 Her Speech..is a Kiss oth' second Venter. *c* **1651** —— *London Lady* 24 The small Drink Country Squires of the first venter. **1687** R. L'ESTRANGE *Ans. to Dissenter* 47 The Author Writes himself a Church-of-England-Man, but it must be by a Second Venter then; for he gives his Orthodox Mother most Bloody hard Words.

†**b.** Irregularly used of a woman's first or second marriage. *Obs.*

1707 CIBBER *Double Gallant* IV, An unlick'd thing, she call'd Son—I suppose by her first Venter. **1765** FOOTE *Commissary* I. (1782) 16 *Mrs. Lov.* Because..the more children I have by the second venter, the greater [etc.].

2. The womb as the source of one's birth or origin; hence *transf.*, a mother in relation to her children: **a.** In the phrase ***of one*** (or ***the same***) ***venter***. (After AF. *de mesme le venter*.) ? *Obs.*

1579–80 North *Plutarch* (1656) 113 Mnesiptolema..was married unto her half brother Archeptolis, for they were not both of one venter. *a* **1641** Bp. Mountagu *Acts & Mon.* (1642) 19 Of Isaac by Rebekah, twins were born,..Of one venter, though not..of one minde or disposition. **1655** Stanley *Hist. Philos.* I. 47 He allowed brothers and sisters by the same father to marry, and prohibited only brothers and sisters of the same venter. [**1865** F. M. Nichols *Britton* II. 319 The sister of the same venter as the purchasor shall be the nearest heir.]

fig. **1669** *Truth Triumphant* (title-p.), That Quaking is the Off-Spring of Popery; at the least, the Papist and Quaker are both of one Venter.

b. In phrases with *by* (passing into sense 1).

1591 Harington *Orl. Fur.* xxxi. xxvi, I am your fathers sonne, not by one venter. **1621** G. Sandys *Ovid's Met.* xiii. (1626) 258 Laertes was my Sire... By the venter I From Hermes spring. *c* **1630** Risdon *Surv. Devon* §266 (1810) 275 My Sister, by one Venter. **1756** Nugent *Montesquieu's Spirit Laws* I. v. 63 It was not permitted to marry a sister by the same venter.

†**c.** *transf.* (See quot.) *Obs.*$^{-1}$

1661 Lovell *Hist. Anim. & Min.* 138 Those egges are most wholesome that are most temperate, they being like their venters.

3. a. The womb *of* a woman. *rare.*

a **1656** Ussher *Ann.* (1658) 342 Another son of Lysimachus, but by the Venter of Odryssias, another wife of his. **1767** tr. *Voltaire's Ignorant Philos.* 169 The brother Cordeliers averred that Mary had not sinned in her mother's venter.

†**b.** A single occasion of child-bearing. *Obs.*$^{-1}$

1657 *Penit. Conf.* vii. 127 As to bring forth at one venter twins. **1728** Chambers *Cycl.* s.v., *Venter* is also used for the Children whereof a Woman is deliver'd at one pregnancy. *Ibid.*, Thus, two Twins are said to be of the same Venter.

4. *Bot.* The enlarged, basal part of an archegonium, where the egg cells develop.

1887 Balfour & Garnsey tr. *K. Goebel's Outl. Classification & Special Morphol. Plants* 175 The archegonium when fully formed consists of a thick and rather long stalk, a roundish-ovoid venter resting on the stalk, and above it a long slender neck usually twisted on its axis. **1938** G. M. Smith *Cryptogamic Bot.* II. ii. 17 The mature venter is therefore 12 to 20 cells in perimeter instead of six cells as in the neck. **1978** T. L. Hufford *Botany* vii. 177 The archegonia are frequently long stalked with an only slightly enlarged venter (egg chamber) and an elongated neck.

II. 5. a. In man, quadrupeds, etc.: One or other of the three chief cavities containing viscera, consisting of the abdomen, thorax, and head. Usu. in *pl.* or with qualifying term. ? *Obs.*

1615 Crooke *Body of Man* vii. i. (1631) 432 It is now time wee should ascend into the third venter, the seate and very residence of the Soule. **1661** Lovell *Hist. Anim. & Min.* 299 The venters are the inferiour, or abdomen; the midle, or thorax; or the supreame, which is the head. **1682** Gibson *Anat.* 2 The three venters are the cavities of the abdomen or Belly, the Chest, and Head. **1720** *Phil. Trans.* XXXI. 84 The Liver, Spleen and other parts of the lower Venter. **1758** J. S. *Le Dran's Observ. Surg.* (1771) 218 Deep Abscesses, in the Neighbourhood of one of the three Venters. **1771** *Encycl. Brit.* I. 277/1 The middle venter, or cavity of the breast.

†**b.** *spec.* The chest or thorax. *Obs.*$^{-1}$

1668 Culpepper & Cole *Barthol. Anat.* ii. Introd. 85 The middle Venter or Belly termed Thorax the Chest, and by some absolutely Venter.

6. †**a.** One of the four stomachs in ruminants.

1607 Topsell *Four-f. Beasts* 83 In the second venter of a cow there is a round black Tophus found. **1661** Lovell *Hist. Anim. & Min.* 45 They [elephants] have short joynts, 4 venters; a liver four times as bigge as an oxes. **1676** Grew *Musæum, Anat. Stomach & Guts* iv. 17 The Stomachs or Venters in a Sheep are Four. **1706** Phillips (ed. Kersey), *Venter*,..one of the four Stomachs of Beasts that chew the Cud.

transf. **1661** Lovell *Hist. Anim. & Min.* Isagoge b 8, Neere to the mouth is a venter, like the craw of birds.

b. *Anat.* The abdomen, the belly.

1706 Phillips (ed. Kersey), *Venter*, the Belly or Paunch. **1738** Chambers *Cycl.* s.v., Jonah is said..to have been three days in the whale's venter, or belly. **1847–9** *Todd's Cycl. Anat.* IV. i. 639/2 Those very structures which in the saurian venter opposite its lumbar spine..appear as the ventral ribs. *Ibid.* 654 The reptilian venter and loins. **1859** in Mayne *Expos. Lex.* s.v.

c. That part in lower forms of animal life more or less corresponding in function or position to the belly of mammals. (Sometimes distinguished from *abdomen*: see quots.)

c **1790** *Encycl. Brit.* (ed. 3) VI. 678/1 *Venter*, the Belly, is the inferior part [of the insect]. **1842** Brande *Dict. Sci.*, etc. 1288 *Venter*, in Entomology, signifies the lower part of the abdomen. **1848** *Proc. Berw. Nat. Club* II. 306 *Venter*..of a paler tint than the back. **1852** Dana *Crust.* i. 629 The animal frequently throws its abdomen forward along its venter towards its head. **1872** Coues *N. Amer. Birds* 17 Abdomen ..has been unnecessarily divided into *epigastrium*, or 'pit of the stomach', and *venter*, or 'lower belly'; but these terms are rarely used.

7. *Anat.* †**a.** (See quot. 1728.) *Obs.*

1615 Crooke *Body of Man* 759 [This muscle] was called Digastricus because it hath two Venters or Bellies. **1728** Chambers *Cycl.* s.v. *Muscle*, The Venter or Belly is the body of the Muscle, being a thick, fleshy part, into which are inserted Arteries and Nerves. *Ibid.* s.v., *Venter*, or Belly of a Muscle [etc.]. [Hence in later Dicts.]

b. The belly or hollowed surface of a bone.

1851 Ramsbotham *Obstetric Med. & Surgery* 2 The chief extent of the inner surface [of the hip bone] is concave and smooth, and is called the venter. *a* **1883** C. H. Fagge *Princ. & Pract. Med.* (1886) I. 89 A large bossy prominence projecting from both the dorsum and the venter. **1887** *Cassell's Encycl. Dict.*, *Subscapular muscle*,..a muscle arising partly by muscular..fibres from the venter of the scapula.

†**8.** *transf.* The space included within the outline of the square Hebrew characters. *Obs.*$^{-1}$

1771 Luckombe *Hist. Printing* 467 The Powers of the Hebrew Alphabet are distinguished by Points that letters have either in their venter, or over their body.

venter^{2} (ˈvɛntə(r)). [f. vent *v.*^{2} + -er.]

1. One who utters or gives vent to a statement, doctrine, etc., esp. of an erroneous, malicious, or objectionable nature.

1611 G. H. *Anti-Coton* 76 This erroneous doctrine ought to be refuted, and the venters thereof punished. **1683** Hooker *Pordage's Myst. Div.* Pref. Ep. 15 But what of.. Blasphemies stupendous; to pass by..their Utterers, the villanous Venters? **1707** Hearne *Collect.* (O.H.S.) I. 318 A Venter of Lies and false Stories. **1739** W. Wilson *Def. Ref. Ch. Scot.* ii. 79 The Venters of the said Errors. **1885** Beveridge *Culross & Tulliallan* I. ix. 243 Venters of strange oaths..are called to account and forced to do penance. **1906** Oman *Study Hist.* 4 Some earlier venter of such harangues.

†**2.** One who smells or scents out. *Obs.*$^{-1}$

1611 Cotgr., *Flaireur*,..a senter, smeller, venter.

†**3.** *Sc.* One who utters forbidden coin. *Obs.*$^{-1}$

1629 *Reg. Privy Council Scot.* Ser. ii. III. 20 Panes.. upoun persouns venters, outputters, and homebringers of forbiddin and discharged coyne.

†ˈ**venter**^{3}. *Obs. rare.* [f. vent *v.*^{3} + -er.] One who sells or offers for sale; a vendor.

1620 Shelton *Quix.* (1746) III. 188 Now let the Venter and the grand Sancho be Arbitrators and Price-Setters between your Worship and me... The Venter and Sancho both agreed. **1681** *Sc. Act* in *Lond. Gaz.* No. 1649/2 Venters and Dispersers of forbidden Books.

venter, etc., obs. or dial. varr. venture, etc.

†ˈ**venter-point.** *Obs.*$^{-1}$ (Some game.)

1600 Rowlands *Lett. Humours Blood* Sat. iv. D 8 b, At shoue-groate, venter poynt, or crosse and pile.

vent-giver. [vent *sb.*^{2}] = venter^{2} 1.

1611 Cotgr., *Esventeur*,..a venter, or vent-giuer.

vent-hole. Also **venthole, vent hole.** [f. vent *sb.*^{2} + hole *sb.*]

1. A hole or opening for the admission or passage of air, light, etc.

1577 B. Googe *Heresbach's Husb.* ii. (1586) 70 Afterward stop the vent holes that the Mole hath in euery place. **1733** Tull *Horse-Hoeing Husb.* xiv. 186 A large Basket drawn up the middle of each [rick of sainfoin], to leave a Vent-Hole there. **1756–7** tr. *Keysler's Trav.* (1760) III. 110 Two large vent-holes for light and air are made through the roof of this grotto. **1763** Mills *Pract. Husb.* III. 123 It was covered with good oak planks,..leaving only some vent-holes, with trap doors, or covers, fitted very exactly to them. **1856** Kane *Arct. Expl.* II. 113 Two huts and four families, but for these vent-holes entirely buried in the snow.

2. A hole or opening in a furnace, etc., for escape of smoke and gases or the admission of fresh air.

1612 Sturtevant *Metallica* (1854) 118 The lower vent-holes let out the smoak. **1664** Evelyn *Sylva* 101 You must make Vent-holes..through the stuff which covers your heap to the very wood. **1678** R. R[ussell] tr. *Geber* ii. i. iv. vi. 96 A Furnace with large Ventholes giveth both a clear and strong Fire. **1715** Desaguliers *Fires Impr.* 16 The Passage X of the Bellows or Vent-Hole. *Ibid.*, The Air will be made so thin over the Vent-Hole, as to press less than that which is coming from without. **1862** M. Hopkins *Hawaii* 25 The suffocating gases which escaped from the red hot ventholes of these furnaces.

b. Any hole by which an enclosed space communicates with, or discharges into, the outside air.

1750 Warburton *Julian* ii. vi, A bare and hollow rock; which would here and there afford vent-holes for such fumes as generated within to transpire. **1799** G. Smith *Laboratory* I. 43 Water-balls have a hollow-globe, turned some-what oblong, with a vent-hole. **1800** *Phil. Trans.* XC. 234 The case..was charged through its vent-hole, and introduced into a twelve-pounder carronade. **1802** *Encycl. Brit.* Suppl. II. 748/1 Vent-holes may be bored in convenient parts of the deck..from whence the state of the corn may be known by the effluvia which ascend.

c. In fig. uses.

1711 E. Ward *Vulgus Brit.* ii. 124 The Ventholes of their Passion. **1908** *Parish Councils* 22 The council serves as a vent-hole for complaints and suspicions.

3. *spec.* **a.** An air-hole in a cask; a vent.

1669 Worlidge *Syst. Agric.* 120 Turn it up into the Vessel..to ferment, allowing but a small Vent-hole, lest the spirits waste. **1707** Mortimer *Husb.* 573 Have near the Bung-hole a little Vent-hole stopp'd with a Spile. **1725** *Fam. Dict.* s.v. *Brewing*, Opening and stopping the Vent-hole on every Change of Weather.

Comb. **1875** Knight *Dict. Mech.* 2703 *Vent-faucet*, an instrument which may act as a vent-hole borer.

b. (See quots.)

1728 Chambers *Cycl.*, *Vent*, *Vent-Hole*, or *Spiracle*, a little Aperture, left in the Tubes or Pipes of Fountains, to facilitate the Wind's escape. **1883** Gresley *Gloss. Coal-M.* 269 *Vent* or *Vent Hole*, a small passage made with a needle through the tamping, which is used for admitting a squib, to enable the charge to be ignited.

ventiduct (ˈvɛntɪdʌkt). Also 7 **venteduct.** [f. L. *venti-*, *ventus* wind + *duct-us* a conducting.]

1. A pipe or passage serving to bring cool or fresh air into an apartment or place, esp. in Italy and other warm climates.

1615 G. Sandys *Trav.* 261 Cold winds..such as by venteducts from the vast caues aboue Padua they let into their roomes at their pleasure. **1660** Boyle *New Exp. Phys.-Mech.* 173, I have been informed of divers Ventiducts (as they call them) by very knowing Travellers that have observ'd them. **1685** Cotton tr. *Montaigne* III. 320, I would fain know what pain it was to the Persians..to make such ventiducts..as Xenophon reports they did. **1702** Floyer *Cold Baths* i. iv. (1709) 108 They stop their Sweats, un-seasonably by Cold Air, by Fanning, Ventiducts, or Cold Baths. **1715** Leoni *Palladio's Archit.* (1742) I. 33 From these Caves arise extreme cold Winds..through certain subterranean Vaults, named..Ventiducts: and..through all the Chambers..these Wind-Pipes, or Ventiducts, are discharg'd. [**1818** Southey in *Q. Rev.* XIX. 18 (copying Evelyn *Acetaria* ii. xi) His scheme of a Royal Garden comprehended..precipices and ventiducts.] **1884** *Health Exhib. Catal.* 106/1 Ventiduct, to bring in fresh air without dust or fog.

fig. **1652** Benlowes *Theoph.* xii. cxvii, Th' herb [*sc.* tobacco] that cramp and tooth-ache drives away,..whose pipe's both ventiduct and stove. *a* **1658** Cleveland *News from Newcastle* 52 What need we baths? What need we bower, or grove? A Coal-pit's both a Ventiduct and Stove.

b. A conduit for the passage of wind, air, or steam.

1685 *Phil. Trans.* XV. 922, I..discover'd in severall dry places of the ground thereabouts, many little Ventiducts, passages, or clefts, where the Steam issued forth. **1725** J. Reynolds *View of Death* (1735) 23 This channel is called by ..the English miners the *drift*; by Mr. Boyle, the *venti-duct*. **1843** in C. Morfit *Tanning & Currying* (1853) 177 A ventiduct, made of plank,..should extend from the centre.

transf. **1876** Mrs. Whitney *Sights & Ins.* II. xvi. 458 From these cold, dark ventiducts [i.e. thoroughfares] you may come out suddenly upon a bright warm corner of an open square.

2. *attrib.* Of a hat: = ventilatory *a.*

1862 *Catal. Internat. Exhib., Brit.* II. No. 4808, Patent corrugated ventiduct hat.

ventifact (ˈvɛntɪfækt). [f. L. *vent-us* wind *sb.*^{1} + -i- + *fact-us*, pa. pple. of *facere* to make.] A faceted stone shaped or altered by wind-blown sand.

1911 J. W. Evans in *Geol. Mag.* Decade V. VIII. 335 If a general expression be required for any wind-shaped stone, we might speak of a 'ventifact', on the analogy of artifact, sometimes spelt 'artefact',..and of 'ventiduct', which has been employed in architecture. **1935** *Times* 28 Jan. 15/4 Dr. Spencer brought back many fine examples on wind-worn rock and ventifacts for further study. **1944** [see dreikanter.] **1949** K. P. Oakley *Man the Tool-Maker* ii. 10 Stones splintered by fire, or faceted by sandstorms (ventifacts or dreikanters) are occasionally mistaken for the work of man. **1970** [see dreikanter].

†**ventil**^{1}. *Obs.*$^{-1}$ [ad. med.L. *ventile*: see next. So OF. *ventelle*, *-aille*.] A sluice.

1570 Dee *Math. Pref.* d ij, All occasions of waters possible leading. To speake of the allowance of the Fall..or of the Ventills (if the waters labour be farre, and great) I neede not.

ventil^{2} (ˈvɛntɪl). *Mus.* [a. G. *ventil*, ad. med.L. *ventile* sluice, shutter, f. L. *vent-us* wind.]

1. One or other of the valves or shutters which control the wind-supply of the various groups of stops in an organ.

1876 Hiles *Catech. Organ* vii. (1878) 50 A Ventil, or Wind-trunk valve is a valve in the wind-trunk for..stopping the wind from certain stops in the manuals or pedals, and thus making them silent. **1884** *Encycl. Brit.* XVII. 835 Practical opinion appears decidedly to condemn the use of ventils.

attrib. **1876** *Nature* XIV. 275/1 The French ventil system of shutting off or bringing on the wind to a complete..group of stops by the depression of a pedal.

2. (See quot.)

1876 Stainer & Barrett *Dict. Mus. Terms* 446/1 *Ventil*, a valve, by means of which brass tubes may be made to sound the semitones and tones between the natural open harmonics.

ˈ**ventilable,** *a.* *U.S.* [f. ventil-ate *v.* + -able.] Capable of being ventilated.

1882 *Pop. Sci. Monthly* XX. 713 Ventilable and perfectly dry floors and areas are made. **1886** *Philadelphia Times* 28 Feb. (Cent.), The sleeping room is rarely ventilable, and still more rarely ventilated.

ventilabral, *a.* *rare*$^{-1}$. [f. L. *ventilābr-um* winnowing-fan + -al^{1}.] Concerning or pertaining to a fan or fans.

1882 *World* 14 June 9 One hundred and sixty fans... Mr. Walker's collection may,..from a ventilabral point of view, [be] quite enchanting.

†**ventilary,** *a.* *Obs.*$^{-1}$ [f. L. *ventil-āre* ventilate *v.* + -ary^{1}.] Due to or caused by the wind.

1683 Pettus *Fleta Min.* ii. 15 The neighbouring Motions of the Sea (which are regular, lunary, or ventilary).

†ˈ**ventilate,** *pa. pple.* *Obs. rare.* [ad. L. *ventilāt-us*, pa. pple. of *ventilāre*: see next.] Discussed or debated; thoroughly sifted or ventilated.

1432–50 tr. *Higden* (Rolls) II. 141 A cause was ventilate and movede thro the commaundemente of the pope. *Ibid.* 299 This Foroneus ordeynede..causes to be ventilate afore a iugge. **1528** in Burnet *Hist. Ref.*, *Rec.* (Pocock) I. 126 All the matter declared and ventilate. **1532-3** *Act 24 Hen. VIII*, c. 12, Courtes..where the said mattier nowe beyng in contencion..shall happen to be ventilate, commensed, or begunne.

ventilate ('vɛntɪleɪt), *v.* Also 5 **ventilatte**, 6 **-tylate**, 7 **-tulate**, **-tillate**. [f. L. *ventilāt-*, ppl. stem of *ventilāre* to brandish, fan, winnow, agitate (whence It. *ventilare*, Prov., Sp., Pg. *ventilar*, F. *ventiler*), f. *vent-us* wind. Cf. EVENTILATE *v.*]

I. †**1.** *trans.* Of wind: To blow away (something); to scatter. *Obs.*$^{-1}$

a **1440** *Found. St. Bartholomew's* (E.E.T.S.) 8 Of .iiii. wyndys, remembrith Zacharie seiynge,..'these ben the hornnys that shall blowe and ventilatte [L. *ventilaverunt*] Iude, Israel, and Ierusalem'.

2. To fan or winnow (corn, etc.). Also in fig. context.

1609 [BP. W. BARLOW] *Answ. Nameless Cath.* 323 Yet is it not the peeuish..tongue of Father Parsons, that must Ventilate the Corne of this Floore, to trie whether I bee chaffe or wheate. **1623** in COCKERAM I. **1791** COWPER *Iliad* v. 594 As flies the chaff..O'er all the consecrated floor, what time Ripe Ceres with brisk airs her golden grain Ventilates. **1846** LANDOR *Imag. Conv.* Wks. I. 226 It is required..not merely that we place the grain in a garner, but that we ventilate and sift it; that we separate the full from the empty.

†**3.** To increase (a fire or flame) by blowing or fanning. Chiefly *fig.* or in fig. context. *Obs.*

1613 JACKSON *Creed* I. 144 They blow the fire which it had kindled, ventilating and inlarging the deuouring flame. **1648** SPARKE *Pref. Shute's Sarah & Hagar* b j b, Pouring out the water of his tears upon our common Flames, which others ventilated. **1691** NORRIS *Pract. Disc.* (1707) IV. 21 So will Devotion [languish] if it have not vent by good Discourse, which fans and ventilates its Holy Fire. **1742** YOUNG *Nt. Th.* II. 478 Speech ventilates our intellectual fire.

†**4.** To put or set (air) in motion; to move or agitate; to renew or freshen in this way. *Obs.*

1635 VALENTINE *Foure Sea-Serm.* 41 If a man have a fan in his hand he may ventilate and agitate the still ayre into a winde. **1664** POWER *Exp. Philos.* III. 180 To keep constant fires under-ground to purifie and ventilate the Ayr. **1710** J. B. *Let. Sacheverell* 4 You..seem to fight Blindfold,..and by thus ventilating and beating the Air,..expose your own Persons. **1775** SIR E. BARRY *Observ. Wines* 403 Putrid exhalations in low marshy ground..where the air is not ventilated.

5. †**a.** To expose (blood) to the chemical action of the air; to aerate, oxygenate. *Obs.*

1668 CULPEPPER & COLE *Barthol. Anat.* 377 The blood is yet more ventilated if it be speedily moved. **1706** PHILLIPS (ed. Kersey) s.v., When the Bloud is ventilated and purged from oppressing Vapours. **1891** *Cent. Dict.* s.v., Lungs ventilate the blood.

b. To expose (substances, etc.) to fresh air so as to keep in, or restore to, good condition.

1755 HALES in *Phil. Trans.* XLIX. 344, I ventilated three gallons of stinking Jessops-well purging water. **1763** MILLS *Pract. Husb.* III. 123 This corn..was not ventilated more than six days in a year. **1771** A. YOUNG *Farmer's Tour East Eng.* I. 345 The cows gave vast quantities of milk,..but it was very strong, though ventilated. **1846** LANDOR *Imag. Conv.* Wks. II. 86/1 Thy carcase did not even receive a fly-blow... Thy guardian angel..could not ventilate thee better. **1855** *Poultry Chron.* III. 449 The wheat should be kept cool, well ventilated, and frequently moved.

c. *trans.* To supply air to (the lungs); to supply air, esp. artificially, to the lungs of; also *transf.*

1919 FLACK & HILL *Textbk. Physiol.* xxxii. 288 It is only when the lungs are well ventilated that the parts most remote from these surfaces of direct expansion are brought properly into action. **1946** J. F. FULTON *Howell's Textbk. Physiol.* (ed. 15) xxxix. 871 Under normal rest conditions.. 5·6 litres of air..are available to ventilate the alveoli. **1971** *Nature* 21 May 181/1 When necessary the lungs were ventilated mechanically with a Palmer respiration pump. **1975** *Ibid.* 23 Oct. 674/1 Animals were artificially ventilated with a mixture of $N_2O-O_2-CO_2$. **1978** *Sci. Amer.* Aug. 95/2 Heating the hypothalamus caused the fish to ventilate its gills faster. **1979** *Daily Tel.* 6 Nov. 3/6 All they had in fact when the plug was pulled was a corpse being ventilated by a machine.

6. a. Of air: To blow upon, to pass over or circulate through, so as to purify or freshen.

1695 WOODWARD *Nat. Hist. Earth* IV. (1723) 229 The Air, which ventilates and cools the Mines. **1784** COWPER *Task* III. 426 That air and sun, Admitted freely, may..ventilate and warm the swelling buds. **1810** SIR A. BOSWELL *Edinburgh* in Chambers *Sc. Poems* (1862) 166 Sweeping breezes ventilate each street. **1835** MRS. SOMERVILLE *Connex. Phys. Sci.* (ed. 2) xxv. 267 Neither can the warmth of mines be attributed to the condensation of the currents of air which ventilate them. **1869** J. PHILLIPS *Vesuv.* ii. 37 Strabo describes it as ventilated by the south-west wind.

fig. **1760** GOLDSM. *Ess.* No. 15, Opposition, when restrained within due bounds, is the salubrious gale that ventilates the opinions of the people. **1795** BURKE *Let. W. Smith* Wks. 1812 IX. 403 The divisions, which formerly prevailed in the Church,..only purified and ventilated our common faith.

b. Of a fan: To cool by producing a current of air.

1805-6 CARY *Dante, Inf.* xv. 39 Whoever..One instant stops, lies then a hundred years, No fan to ventilate him, when the fire Smites sorest.

7. To supply (a room, building, mine, etc.) with fresh air in place of that which is vitiated, exhausted, or stagnant; to produce a free current of air in (some enclosed space) so as to maintain a fresh supply. Cf. VENTILATOR 1.

1758 S. HALES *Descr. Ventilators* II. 39 When the Wards of the lower Floors are to be ventilated. **1797** *Encycl. Brit.* (ed. 3) XVIII. 639/1 The order for ventilating the fleet issued by the lords of the admiralty in 1756. **1842** LOUDON *Suburban Hort.* 217 The great object in ventilating houses which are kept at a high temperature is to avoid thorough-draughts. **1854** RONALDS & RICHARDSON *Chem. Technol.* (ed. 2) I. 251 The House of Commons..has been warmed and ventilated under the superintendence..of Dr. Reid. **1888** MISS BRADDON *Fatal Three* I. v, How to ventilate and purify his cottages.

absol. **1845** *Encycl. Metrop.* XXV. 1054 About the year 1741, Dr. Hales introduced a method of ventilating by bellows. **1854** RONALDS & RICHARDSON *Chem. Technol.* (ed. 2) I. 244 A very admirable system of heating and ventilating by hot water.

8. †**a.** = BREATHE *v.* 16. *Obs.*$^{-0}$

1706 PHILLIPS (ed. Kersey) s.v., To ventilate a vein, i.e. to breath or open it.

b. To provide (a mould, etc.) with a vent or vents to allow the escape of air or gas.

1895 in *Funk's Stand. Dict.*

c. *slang.* To shoot (someone or something) with a gun, usu. to kill. Also of a bullet: to make a hole in (something).

1875 C. B. LEWIS *Quad's Odds* 473 Some of our folks cleaned up their revolvers..hoping to get a shot at McGrady and to ventilate the mule. **1917** [see COCKPIT 3 c]. **1948** 'R. MACDONALD' in H. Q. Masur *Murder Most Foul* (1973) 103 'A man was shot in one of his rooms.'.. 'Who was it got himself ventilated?' **1979** C. EGLETON *Backfire* ix. 98 You'd just better pray he doesn't kill somebody..because he's talking about ventilating people.

†**9.** *intr.* To get rid of exhalations. *Obs.*$^{-1}$

1698 FRYER *Acc. E. India & P.* 39 The Lamps always burning, are by open Funnels above suffered to ventilate.

II. 10. *trans.* To examine or investigate (a question, topic, etc.) freely or thoroughly by discussion or debate; to sift or discuss in free argument, controversy, or examination; to bring to public notice or consideration in this way.

Freq. *c* 1620–*c* 1680, and from *c* 1850.

1527 in Fiddes *Wolsey* (1726) II. 172 This cawse of matrymonie myght no where be ventylated or dyscussed. **1597** J. KING *On Jonas* (1618) 225 There was no Father in the Church who had greater reason to ventilate this argument vnto the bottome. **1622** DONNE *Serm.* Wks. 1839 VI. 213 Some Articles concerning the falling away from justifying grace..had been ventilated in Conventicles. **1657** HEYLIN *Ecclesia Vind.* 95 The point had been somewhat ventilated betwixt the honourable Remonstrant on the one part, and the Smectymnians on the other. **1674** GREW *Lect.* in *Anat. Pl.* (1682) 222 The experience of so many years, wherein it hath been ventilated by the disputes of men, proveth as much. **1726** AYLIFFE *Parergon* 151 Nor is the Right of the Party..so far perempted, but that the same may be..ventilated *de Novo.* **1759** HURD *Mor. & Pol. Dial.* (1760) 97 Questions of natural science will doubtless be effectually..ventilated in the new society. **1784** in Boswell *Johnson* 27 June, He is..not enough known: his character has been only ventilated in party pamphlets. **1846** W. H. MILL *Five Serm.* (1848) 52 We have discussed and ventilated all points. **1857** *Fraser's Mag.* LVI. 351 Politicians do not 'discuss' subjects in the year of grace 1857: they 'ventilate' them. **1868** M. PATTISON *Academ. Organ.* 2 The subject has not been sufficiently ventilated. **1870** BEACONSFIELD *Sel. Sp.* (1882) II. 325 Those friends who were, to use a barbarous expression, 'ventilating' the question.

11. To publish *abroad*; to make public. *rare.*

1530 PALSGR. 765/2 He is nat worthy to be a counsaylour that ventylateth the maters abrode. *a* **1734** NORTH *Lives* (1826) II. 65 Such a step..would have been loudly ventilated abroad as a plain declaration that popery was to govern. **1837** LANDOR *Pentameron* v. Wks. 1853 II. 346/1 Deeming it better, when irregular thoughts assailed me, to ventilate them abroad.

12. a. To utter; to give utterance or expression to (an opinion, view, etc.): to make known to others.

1637 GILLESPIE *Eng. Pop. Cerem.* II. ix. 44 Why then doeth he ventilate words for reason? **1855** F. STEPHEN in *Cambr. Ess.* 183 The habit..of using novels to ventilate opinions. **1861** HUGHES *Tom Brown at Oxf.* iv, There were already several things in his head which he was anxious to ventilate. **1872** E. W. ROBERTSON *Hist. Ess.* 219 An angry Kentish landholder..might have ventilated his grievances upon Pennenden Heath. **1883** *Jrnl. Education* XVII. 264 To rush into print and 'ventilate his views'.

transf. **1856** *Sat. Rev.* 2 Feb. 241/2 Although it is necessary for Lord Derby..to ventilate his oratory, Parliament and the country are ready for peace. **1870** W. R. GREG *Polit. Problems* 198 It reflects and ventilates the national conceptions.

b. To give vent to, provide outlet or escape for (passion, etc.).

1823 LAMB *Lett.* xiii. 128 He is welcome to them..if they can divert a spleen or ventilate a fit of sullenness.

†**13.** To carry on, take part in (a controversy).

1607 R. C[AREW] tr. *Estienne's World Wond.* 275 There was neuer yet controuersie in Christian religion so.. virulently canuased and ventilated. **1678** GALE *Crt. Gentiles* IV. Pref., Strangius..has ventilated this controversy with.. force of argument beyond his sectators.

†**14.** To estimate the value of; to appraise. *Obs.*

Directly from F. *ventiler*: cf. EVALUATE *v.* b.

1682 WARBURTON *Hist. Guernsey* (1822) 82 [To] see his goods..ventilated, i.e. appraised and sold for discharge of the debt.

Hence '**ventilating** *ppl. a.*

1817 KIRBY & SP. *Entomol.* II. 196 Approach your hand to a ventilating bee, and you will find that she causes a very perceptible motion in the air. *c* **1853-4** *Tomlinson's Cycl. Arts*, etc. (1866) II. 836/1 Throttle-valves..by which the rate of the ventilating current can be increased or diminished.

'**ventilated**, *ppl. a.* [f. prec.] Purified by or as if by ventilation; provided with means of ventilation; supplied with continual fresh air.

1743 S. HALES *Descr. Ventilators* I. 111 As ventilated Corn may lie thick without leaving any spare Room to turn it. **1758** *Ibid.* II. 110 That wet State will be more unwholsome in a close unventilated, than in a ventilated Ship. **1840** *Civil Eng. & Arch. Jrnl.* III. 363/1 The pieces of wood..so combined..[become] what the inventor terms a 'Ventilated Faggot.' **1868** *Chambers's Encycl.* X. 67/2 Close ill-ventilated apartments. **1892** *Photogr. Ann.* II. p. ccxxi, It is a Three-cornered Lamp; the back has a sliding ventilated door. **1951** D. W. RICHARDS in Cecil & Loeb *Textbk. Med.* (ed. 8) 844/1 The trapping of air in poorly ventilated air spaces, on repeated deep breathing, is shown by a step-wise rise in the spirogram. **1975** *Anaesthesia & Intensive Care* III. 237 (*heading*) A simple clinical method of quantitating the effects of chest physiotherapy in mechanically ventilated patients. **1980** *Daily Tel.* 3 Nov. 16 A substantial sample has ..accrued from the innumerable ventilated patients who have not become organ donors.

fig. **1736** THOMSON *Liberty* IV. 790 The wholesome winds Of Opposition hence began to blow... A pestilential ministry they purge, And ventilated states renew their bloom.

'**ventilating**, *vbl. sb.* [f. as prec.] The action of the verb in various senses; ventilation.

1661 J. CHILDREY *Brit. Bacon.* 86 This is a very strange thing indeed, and very well worth the Ventilating. **1743** S. HALES *Descr. Ventilators* I. 50 The thus ventilating of Ships. **1802** *Encycl. Brit.* Suppl. II. 748/1 It is the centre of the cargo which most requires ventilating. **1845** *Encycl. Metrop.* XXV. 1053 The ventilating of rooms by openings at any height above the level of the floor.

b. *attrib.*, as ***ventilating-engineer***, ***-fan***, ***tube***, etc.

A few technical combs. are recorded in Knight *Dict. Mech.* and *Suppl.*, as ***ventilating-brick***, ***heater***, ***saw***, ***-stack***, ***water-wheel***. Also ***ventilating grate***, ***jack***, ***mill-stone*** in recent Amer. Dicts.

1753 *Phil. Trans.* XLVIII. 44 This ward..had been supplied by a ventilating tube. **1845** *Encycl. Metrop.* XXV. 1054/2 The ventilating fan of Dr. Desaguliers. *Ibid.* 1055/2 A ventilating pump 3 feet square and 5 feet high. **1868** *Chambers's Encycl.* X. 68/1 Dr. Arnott's ventilating-valve. *Ibid.*, Special ventilating-flues in the walls. **1889** WELCH *Text Bk. Naval Archit.* 132 Fresh air..led into the bunkers from the ventilating shafts. *c* **1890** W. H. CASMEY *Ventilation* 1 My experience as a ventilating engineer.

ventilation (vɛntɪ'leɪʃən). Also 5 *Sc.* **ventulacioun**, 6 **ventilacyon**. [a. L. *ventilātiōn-*, *ventilātio* (Pliny), an exposing to the air, f. *ventilāre* VENTILATE *v.*; hence also It. *ventilazione*, F. *ventilation*, Sp. *-acion*, Pg. *-ação*.]

I. †**1.** A stir or motion of the air; a current of air; a breeze. *Obs.*

1456 SIR G. HAY *Gov. Princes* Wks. (S.T.S.) II. 158 The ayr passis sa throu the warlde, throu blastis of wyndis, and othir maner of ventulaciounis. **1644** HOWELL *Twelve Treat.* (1661) 9 Sometimes we have a clear azur'd skie with soft gentle ventilations. **1665** *Phil. Trans.* I. 52 'Tis affirmed that almost any Ventilation and stirring of the Air doth refrigerate. **1716** ADDISON *Freeholder* No. 40 ¶4 The Soil.. must lie fallow..till it has..again enriched itself by the Ventilations of the Air. **1743** S. HALES *Descr. Ventilators* I. 24 A like Ventilation of warm dry Air from the adjoining Stove.

fig. **1643** SIR T. BROWNE *Relig. Med.* I. §32 Whosoever feels not the warme gale and gentle ventilation of this Spirit [of God] (though I feele his pulse) I dare not say he lives. **1752** JOHNSON *Rambler* No. 205 ¶5 The mind that is to be moved by the gentle ventilations of gayety.

2. Movement or free course of the air.

1605 TIMME *Quersit.* II. vii. 138 That renuing is to be attributed to the fire,..the outward ventilation or winding comming between as the instrument. *a* **1682** SIR T. BROWNE *Tracts* (1683) 44 Upon such consideration of winds and ventilation the Ægyptian granaries were made open. **1690** T. BURNET *Theory Earth* II. 55 This present earth..is in most places capable of ventilation, pervious and passable to the winds. **1804** C. B. BROWN tr. *Volney's View Soil U.S.* 271 The mercury ranges between 84 and 88 degrees in the shade, where there is ample ventilation. **1813** J. THOMSON *Lect. Inflam.* 487 The first of these means that is usually mentioned, is a free ventilation of air. **1883** GRESLEY *Gloss. Coal-M.* 270 *Ventilation*, the atmospheric air circulating in a mine.

3. †**a.** Oxygenation of the blood, *spec.* in the act of respiration; = AERATION 3. *Obs.*

1615 CROOKE *Body of Man* 121 By ventilation to cherish, refresh and increase his naturall heate with their heat and vitall spirit. **1660** BOYLE *New Exp. Phys. Mech.* 350 Another Opinion there is touching Respiration, which makes the genuine use of it to be Ventilation..of the Blood. **1665** G. HARVEY *Disc. Plague* xiv. in *Morb. Angl.* (1673) 144 To procure the Blood and Spirits..a free Course, ventilation, and transpiration, by suitable Purges. **1822-7** GOOD *Study Med.* (1829) I. 504 The lungs,..in which the air undergoes the important process of ventilation. *Ibid.* III. 209 The new and unripe blood is hurried forward to the lungs..to be completed by the process of ventilation.

b. The supply of fresh air or oxygen to the lungs (or gills), by the process of breathing or artificially.

1891 A. D. WALLER *Introd. Human Physiol.* iv. 136 The bronchus being blocked a portion of the lung is cut off from ventilation. **1919** FLACK & HILL *Textbk. Physiol.* xxxii. 284 To facilitate gaseous interchange, the process of breathing or ventilation of the lungs takes place. **1951** E. A. STEAD in Cecil & Loeb *Textbk. Med.* (ed. 8) 1052/2 In cardiac failure the increased ventilation..is produced by the reflex stimulation of respiration from the congested lungs and great vessels. **1974** *Nature* 19 Apr. 631/1 Where the patient is being kept 'alive' artificially by ventilation the doctor..

must decide when the brain has died and when the ventilator has passed the point at which it will invoke any involuntary response in the patient. **1978** *Sci. Amer.* Aug. 95/2 The fish could .. wait until an oxygen deficit occurs and then respond by increasing its gill ventilation.

4. a. The admission of a proper supply of fresh air, esp. to a room, building, mine, or other place where the air readily becomes stagnant and vitiated; the means or method by which this is accomplished.

1664 POWER *Exp. Philos.* I. 65 We see in wet Hay, how the Spirits .. (if they be not cooled and prevented by Ventilation) .. break out into a flame also. **1743** S. HALES *Descr. Ventilators* I. 34 This Ventilation will also be of service to preserve .. the Timber and Planks of the Hold itself. **1753** *Scots Mag.* Feb. 99/2 Before ventilation, the foul air .. became infectious. **1789** W. BUCHAN *Dom. Med.* (1790) 111 When cleanliness and ventilation are neglected. **1836–41** BRANDE *Chem.* (ed. 5) 145 The rooms are close and oppressive, because due ventilation is not associated with the admission of the hot air. **1854** *Poultry Chron.* I. 32 Sufficient ventilation to prevent the house becoming too hot or close in summer .. must also receive attention. **1889** WELCH *Text Bk. Naval Archit.* 131 Pipes .. leading from above the upper deck to the compartments requiring ventilation.

fig. **1751** JOHNSON *Rambler* No. 101 ¶14 The mind stagnates without external ventilation.

b. Const. *of* (the place ventilated).

1827 *Gentl. Mag.* XCVII. 509 Attention to the construction, ventilation, and cleanliness of prisons. **1875** KNIGHT *Dict. Mech.* 307/1 The steam-jet for the ventilation of mines was used long ago, and then abandoned. **1893** HODGES *Elem. Photogr.* 36 To ensure the efficient ventilation of the dark-room.

c. *attrib.*, as ***ventilation duct, -fan, -pipe, shaft***, etc.

1823 in Hebert *Engin. & Mech. Encycl.* (1837) II. 846 The end of the ventilation-pipe. **1839** URE *Dict. Arts* 853 The ventilation shaft. **1889** WELCH *Text Bk. Naval Archit.* 133 Where .. platforms are pierced for ventilation purposes. *c* **1890** W. H. CASMEY *Ventilation* 7 We must bring the ventilation-fan to our aid. **1937** *Discovery* Nov. 345/1 The original roof of the Saxon chapel was almost certainly of wood, probably with ventilation ducts or cowls of a shape which may have suggested to the 16th century builders their idea for the dormer roof lights. **1964** *Listener* 12 Nov. 751/2 The claim to carry a ventilation duct across another's property was just as novel as the claim to protection against the weather.

II. 5. The action of fanning or blowing; †the winnowing of corn in this way.

1519 HORMAN *Vulg.* 42 It is no good phisike, that whan a man is sore chafed with heate, for to cole hym with ventilacyon of clothes. **1658** PHILLIPS, *Ventilation*, a fanning, or gathering of winde; also a winnowing of Corn. **1668** WILKINS *Real Char.* 245 Operations belonging to Agriculture, do concern .. the grane .., [as] Winnowing, fan, Ventilation. **1743** S. HALES *Descr. Ventilators* I. 97 If it [*sc.* corn] were afterwards dried by the Ventilation of these Bellows. **1755** —— in *Phil. Trans.* XLIX. 316 In several other distillations of a quart at a time, I found the quantity distilled by ventilation to be more than the double of that in the usual way. **1817** KIRBY & SP. *Entomol.* xx. II. 194 These vibrations are so rapid as to render the wings almost invisible. When they are engaged in ventilation, the bees [etc.]. *Ibid.* 199 Amongst the bees .. ventilation goes on even in the depth of winter.

6. *fig.* **a.** Free or open discussion of or debate upon a doctrine, question, or subject of public interest; the action or fact of bringing to public notice in this way.

Freq. *c* 1645–1660, and from *c* 1860.

a **1614** DONNE *Βιαθανατος* (1644) 97 The other reasons of Divine Authors .. shall have their ventilation in this Distinction. **1651** BAXTER *Inf. Bapt.* 19 If the kindled humor had not had a free ventilation in Pulpit and in Press. **1677** GALE *Crt. Gentiles* IV. 392, I shal not now enter on the solemn ventilation and debate of this Antithesis. **1850** J. H. NEWMAN *Diff. Anglicans* 177 Careful ventilation of questions. **1856** FROUDE *Hist. Eng.* (1858) I. iii. 205 That the grievances of the nation .. should be submitted to a complete ventilation. **1892** *Photogr. Ann.* II. 237 What new aspect of the subject can call for ventilation and publicity in *Photography Annual*?

†**b.** The utterance or expression *of* one's thoughts, etc. *Obs.*

1615 CROOKE *Body of Man* 300 So by the ventilation or skirmish of aduersary opinions the truth comes best to be knowne. *a* **1639** WOTTON *Buckingham* in *Reliq.* (1651) 106 Dr. Mason, whom he layed in a Pallet neer him, for naturall Ventilation of his thoughts.

†**c.** *pl.* Windy speculations; vapourings. *Obs.*$^{-1}$

1648 LIGHTFOOT *Horæ Hebr.* (1684) II. 611 It would be very tedious to quote their Ventilations about it.

ventilative (ˈvɛntɪleɪtɪv), *a.* [f. VENTILATE *v.* + -IVE.] Of or pertaining to, producing or promoting, ventilation.

1791 BENTHAM *Panopl.* I. Postscr. 199 Over these impure methods of obtaining heat, the ventilative is capable of possessing a great advantage. **1864** WEBSTER s.v., Ventilative apparatus. **1892** A. E. LEE *Hist. Columbus* II. 576 The introduction of fireplaces and other ventilative expedients.

ventilator (ˈvɛntɪleɪtə(r)). [f. VENTILATE *v.* + -OR, or a. L. *ventilātor* a winnower. Cf. F. *ventilateur*, It. *ventilatore*, Sp. and Pg. *-ador*.]

1. a. A mechanical contrivance or apparatus (such as a revolving fan or wheel fixed in a special opening) by which the vitiated or heated air is drawn or removed from a building, ship, mine, etc., and a fresh supply introduced; also freq. a simple opening, or open shaft, so placed or contrived as to facilitate renewal of the air.

1743 S. HALES (*title*), A Description of Ventilators; whereby Great Quantities of Fresh Air may with Ease be conveyed into Mines, Goals, Hospitals, Work-Houses and Ships. **1753** *Scots Mag.* Feb. 99/1 Ventilators, worked by a wind-mill, having been fixed. **1766** *Complete Farmer* 7 S 3/1 Two of the ventilators are constantly drawing in the air, and two of them .. are blowing it out at their proper valves. **1802** M. CUTLER in *Life*, etc. (1888) II. 79 Giving opportunity to workmen to fix some ventilators, which were greatly wanted in the Hall. **1836–41** BRANDE *Chem.* (ed. 5) 143 The different ventilators may terminate in tubes connected with a chimney. **1874** MICKLETHWAITE *Mod. Par. Churches* 216 The ventilators should always be above the heads of the congregation. **1889** WELCH *Text Bk. Naval Archit.* xii. 132 It is down these ventilators that air is drawn by the steam fans F to supply the boilers.

attrib. **1824** TREDGOLD *Princ. Ventilating Buildings* (ed. 2) 94 At this centre the ventilator tube T should be placed. **1884** KNIGHT *Dict. Mech.* Suppl. 924–5 Ventilator deflector, hood, shaft.

b. The former Ladies' Gallery in the House of Commons.

1822 M. EDGEWORTH *Let.* 9 Mar. (1971) 369 We went one night to the House of Commons—to the Ventilator. **1832** MACAULAY in Trevelyan *Life* (1876) I. 269 A discussion by which Nancy, if she had been in the ventilator, might have been greatly edified. **1850** CARLYLE *Latter-d. Pamph.* vi. 20 A modern honourable member, with .. his strangers' gallery, his female ventilator. **1880** DISRAELI *Endym.* lxxix, Lady Roehampton and Lady Montfort were both in the ventilator, and he knew it.

c. *Naut.* A wind-sail (see quots.).

1846 A. YOUNG *Naut. Dict.* 368 *Wind-sail*, or *Ventilator*, a sort of long canvass bag .. let down a vessel's hatchway for circulating air below. **1851** KIPPING *Sailmaking* (ed. 2) 59 The .. ventilator is made of canvas No. 5. It is employed to convey a stream of fresh air downwards into the lower apartments of a ship.

d. Applied to devices for admitting air into a head-dress, boot, etc.

1870 C. C. BLACK tr. *Demmin's Weapons of War* 255 Large tilting heaume of the fifteenth century.... It has a hinged flap or ventilator. **1875** KNIGHT *Dict. Mech.* 2706 The ventilator for hats consists of a hole in the crown, and a head-band supported at a certain distance from the sweat-lining. *Ibid.*, The ventilator for boots consists of a double upper with holes.

e. *Med.* = RESPIRATOR 3.

1961 I. W. B. GRANT in D. Dunlop et al. *Textbk. Med. Treatment* (ed. 8) 945 The patient retains fairly powerful respiratory movements and may have difficulty in synchronizing with any ventilator which is not triggered by his own inspiratory efforts. **1976** *Lancet* 13 Nov. 1069/1 It has become commonplace for hospitals to have deeply comatose and unresponsive patients with severe brain damage who are maintained on artificial respiration by means of mechanical ventilators. **1982** *Times* 10 June 7/2 Mr Argov was taken off his ventilator for two hours yesterday, although he remained unconscious.

2. One charged with ventilating a building, etc. Also *transf.*

17.. in *Tomlinson's Cycl. Arts*, etc. (1866) II. 833/1 [This wheel was] able to suck out the foul air, or throw in fresh, .. according as the Speaker is pleased to command it, whose order the ventilator waits to receive every day of the session. **1817** KIRBY & SP. *Entomol.* II. 195 A certain number of workers .. vibrating their wings before the entrance of their hive.... The station of these ventilators is upon the floor of the hive. **1860** tr. *Hartwig's Sea & Wond.* v. 55 The sun is not only the great fountain of warmth, he is also the universal ventilator.

3. One who ventilates a subject.

1891 in *Cent. Dict.*

ˈventilatory, *a.* [f. VENTILATE *v.* + -ORY.]

1. Of a hat: Provided with ventilation. *rare*$^{-1}$.

1850 in 'Bat' *Cricket Man.* 112 Light summer hats, made on a principle entirely new, and being quite permeable to air, are .. perfectly ventilatory.

2. Of, pertaining to, or serving for ventilation of the lungs.

1946 J. F. FULTON *Howell's Textbk. Physiol.* (ed. 15) xxxix. 871 The maximum voluntary ventilatory rate is a useful index of the capabilities of an individual for doing work. **1963** J. B. HICKAM in Beeson & McDermott *Cecil-Loeb Textbk. Med.* (ed. 11) 524/1 Pulmonary tests are awkward to group according to particular kinds of function because they frequently overlap categories. A common and useful procedure is to divide them into tests of ventilatory and respiratory function. 'Ventilatory function' refers to lung volumes and the process of moving gas in and out of the lungs from ambient air to alveolar wall. 'Respiratory function' refers to the transfer of gas between alveoli and blood. **1980** *Daily Tel.* 16 Oct. 20 There is a time in the management of patients with severe brain damage .. when the decision as to continue or not with ventilatory support is made.

†**ventile.** *Obs.*$^{-1}$ [f. L. *ventil-āre* VENTILATE *v.*, or ad. OF. *ventail* (F. *éventail*), *ventaille* fan. Cf. also VENTIL² and next.] A fan.

1555 WATREMAN *Fardle Facions* II. vii. 156 Making winde as it ware with a ventile, or trenchour.

†**ˈventilous,** *a. Obs.*$^{-1}$ In 5 ventillous. [ad. OF. *ventilleus, -tileux*.] Fluttering, unsteady.

1483 CAXTON *G. de la Tour* Bj b, [The eldest daughter] had her sight ventillous lyke a vane.

†**ventilow.** *Obs. rare.* [app. ad. It. *ventola*.] A fan.

1653 H. COGAN tr. *Pinto's Trav.* iii. 6 Whereupon we .. kissed the Ventilow that she held in her hand. *Ibid.* viii. 23 [He] made one of his followers to fan me with a Ventilow to refresh me.

ˈventing, *vbl. sb.*¹ [f. VENT *v.*² + -ING¹.]

I. 1. a. The free emission or passing of air, etc., from some confined space; *spec.* the emission into the atmosphere of radioactive dust and debris from an underground nuclear explosion.

1382 WYCLIF *Job* xxxii. 19 My wombe as must withoute venting, that breketh newe litle win vesselys. **1398** TREVISA *Barth. De P.R.* XI. i. (Tollem. MS.), And so eyer is element of bodies and spirites, for ventynge of eyer comynge to spirites is cause of .. clensynge and of purgacion. *Ibid.* XVII. clxxxvii. (Bodl. MS.), Bi ventinge fome & oþer vnclennes of wine is brouȝth vp to þe mouþe of þe vessel. **1600** SURFLET *Countrie Farme* VI. xiv. 754 The vessels to auoid the venting which commonly hapneth vnto wine, must haue the bunghole very well stopt. **1611** COTGR., *Halenée*, a breathing, venting, winding, exhaling.

1963 *Wall St. Jrnl.* 27 Sept. 1/1 More unsettling, however, is the possibility that ventings of underground blasts have been adding undetected amounts of radioactive iodine to milk. **1971** *Nature* 30 July 291/3 One fear .. is that if massive venting does occur .. radioactive fallout could be carried outside United States territory. **1980** *New Scientist* 3 July 4/1 The venting of radioactive krypton-85 from the crippled reactor at Three Mile Island .. began at 8 am last Saturday.

b. ***venting-hole***, a vent-hole. *rare*$^{-1}$.

1601 HOLLAND *Pliny* II. 409 If pits be subject to the rising of such vapours, cunning and expert workemen make .. tunnels, or venting-holes.

2. The action or fact of giving utterance, expression, or publicity to an opinion, etc.

1654 D. DICKSON *Expos. Ps.* lxix. 26 The very talking and venting of ill speeches .. is a high provocation of God's wrath. **1665** BOYLE *Occas. Refl.* IV. xi. (1848) 174 He .. was wont .. as much to aim at the exciting others thoughts, as the venting of his own. **1825** COLERIDGE *Aids Refl.* xxii. 12 The venting of that knowledge in speech. *a* **1854** H. REED *Lect. Brit. Poets* (1857) 403 They seem to be rather the relief of a heavy heart than the ventings of a light one.

II. †**3.** The action of snuffing or smelling. *Obs.*$^{-0}$

1611 COTGR., *Flairement*, a senting, smelling, sauoring, venting, winding.

4. The rising of an otter to the surface of water in order to breathe.

1741 *Compl. Fam.-Piece* II. i. 305 When he lifts up his Nose above Water for Air, it is termed Venting. **1856** 'STONEHENGE' *Brit. Rur. Sports* 144/1 The remainder [of the otter-hunters] must watch every intervening yard for his 'ventings'.

†**ˈventing,** *vbl. sb.*² *Obs.* [f. VENT *v.*³ + -ING¹.] The action of selling; = VENDING *vbl. sb.*

Frequent from *c* 1600 to *c* 1645.

1532–3 *Act 24 Hen. VIII*, c. 4, Straunge countreis .. by the .. makyng and ventyng therof are greately enriched. **1548** *Burgh Rec. Edinb.* (1871) II. 144 Vnder the payne of .. spayning fra the venting of wyne be the space of ane yeir thairafter. **1605** BRETON *Old Man's Lesson* Wks. (Grosart) II. 6/2 The Vinter, the Grocer, .. and the Butcher, doe by the venting of their wares, the better maintaine their trades. **1641** MILTON *Church Govt.* II. Wks. 1851 III. 139 How they may suppresse the venting of such rarities and such a cheapnes as would undoe them. **1656** EARL MONM. tr. *Boccalini's Advts. fr. Parnass.* I. x. (1674) 12 A very spruce Politician who looked to the venting of Wares.

ˈventing, *ppl. a.* [f. VENT *v.*² + -ING².]

†**1.** That snuffs or smells. *Obs.*$^{-1}$

1637 B. JONSON *Sad Shepherd* II. i, As doth the vauting Hart his venting Hind.

2. Of gas: that finds escape by the action of venting.

1974 *Physics Bull.* June 253/1 An air filter cartridge for dehydration of the venting gas.

ˈventless, *a. rare*$^{-1}$. [f. VENT *sb.*² + -LESS.] Having no vent or outlet.

1603 J. DAVIES (Heref.) *Microcosmos* Wks. (Grosart) I. 61/1 A restlesse ventlesse Flame of fire, That faine would finde the way streight to aspire.

ventle-trap, obs. variant of WENTLETRAP.

ventner, obs. form of VINTNER.

†**venˈtorious,** *a. Obs.* [Irreg. f. VENT-URE *v.*: see -ORIOUS.] Characterized by venturesomeness.

1640 R. BAILLIE *Canterb. Self-Conviction* 48 Their ventorious boldnesse seemes not more marveillous then their ingenuitie commendable. **1707** SIR W. HOPE *New Method Fencing* (1714) 105 This ventorious, uncertain, and dangerous play upon time.

‖**venˈtosa.** *Surg. Obs.* [med.L.: see VENTOSE *sb.*] = VENTOSE *sb.*

1562 BULLEIN *Bulwarke, Sick Men* 68 There are twoo kindes of the ventosas, or Boxinges.

†**venˈtosal,** *a. Obs.*$^{-1}$ [f. L. *ventōs-us* VENTOSE *a.* + -AL¹.] Performed or done by the wind.

1782 W. HOOPER *Rational Recr.* (ed. 2) II. 209 A ventosal symphony. At the top of a summer-house, or other building, freely exposed to the wind, let there be fixed [etc.].

†**ventose,** *sb.*¹ *Surg. Obs.* Also 7 *Sc.* **vantose.** [a. OF. *ventose, ventouse* (F. *ventouse*, = Prov., Sp., Pg., It. *ventosa*), ad. L. *ventōsa* (sc. *cucurbita*), fem. of *ventōsus*, f. *ventus* wind.] A species of cupping-glass. Also *attrib.*

1500 *Ortus Vocab.*, *Guna*, a ventose boxe. **1541** R. COPLAND *Guydon's Quest. Chirurg.* N iij, Ventose is an instrument made in maner of a boxe with a streyt necke and a wyde bely. **1599** A. M. tr. *Gabelhouer's Bk. Physicke* 346/1 Exhauste the bloode and froth therout with ventoses, a kinde of boxinge. **1603** HOLLAND *Plutarch's Mor.* 137 Cupping glasses, boxes, and ventoses, draw the woorst matter out of the flesh. **1656** J. SMITH *Pract. Physick* 44 Heurnius useth first Cupping-glasses and ventoses to the feet and Liver. **1704** J. HARRIS *Lex. Techn.* I, *Ventose*, a Cupping-glass... The ingenious Mr. Hawksbee hath now found a way of applying Cupping-glasses without Fire, by means of a small Air-Pump.

‖**Ventôse** (vãtoz), *sb.*[2] [Fr., ad. L. *ventōsus*: see VENTOSE *a.*] The sixth month of the French republican calendar, introduced in 1793, extending from 19 Feb. to 20 Mar.

1802 C. WILMOT *Let.* 13 Mar. in *Irish Peer* (1920) 50 (*heading*) 13 March, 1802. 22 Ventose. **1910** *Encycl. Brit.* XI. 171/1 The winter months were Nivôse, the snowy, Pluviôse, the rainy, and Ventôse, the windy month. **1943** J. M. THOMPSON *French Revolution* xxiv. 463 The attempt, shown in the *maximum* decree of February 21st [1794] and the so-called 'Laws of Ventôse'..to conciliate the working-class support. **1981** *Encounter* Dec. 41/2 The Year III... Ventôse this time witnessed a sudden and massive thaw.

ventose (vɛn'təʊs), *a. rare.* [ad. L. *ventōs-us* (It., Sp., and Pg. *ventoso*, Prov. *ventos*, obs. F. *ventous*, mod.F. *venteux*) windy, conceited, etc., f. *vent-us* wind.] Windy, flatulent.

1721 BAILEY, *Ventose*, windy, also empty, bragging, vaunting. **1867** J. BIGELOW *Bench & Bar* v. 294 (Stand.), The ventose orator was confounded, and put himself and the glass down together. **1885** HUXLEY in *Life* (1900) II. vi. 94 It is better to wind up that way than to go growling out one's existence as a ventose hypochondriac.

†**ventose**, *v. Surg. Obs.* Also 5 ventosen, -touse, -tuse. [ad. OF. *ventouser* (13th c.), *ventoser* (F. *ventouser*, = Prov. *ventozar*, It. *ventosare*), ad. med.L. *ventosāre*, f. L. *ventōsa* VENTOSE *sb.*] *trans.* To bleed (a patient) by means of a cupping-glass; to apply the cup to (a wound, etc.).

α. *c* **1400** *Lanfranc's Cirurg.* 12 Ventose him on þe two buttokkis, if þat he be feble. *c* **1410** *Master of Game* (MS. Digby 182) xii, Let þe wounde be ventosed and garsede. **1541** R. COPLAND *Guydon's Quest. Chirurg.* N iv b, Howe ought they to [be] gouerned that must be ventosed?

β. *c* **1400** *Lanfranc's Cirurg.* 13 Þe oþere..schal not be leten blood ne ventusid. *c* **1440** *Astron. Cal.* (MS. Ashm. 391), Which places been perlous to ventuse or to kutte in þ[t] tyme. *c* **1440** *MS. Linc. A.* I. 17 fol. 301 b, Or elles be ventoused on the thee with a boyste.

b. *absol.* To practise cupping.

c **1400** *Lanfranc's Cirurg.* 51 Þou schalt not lete blood, but þou maist ventosen, if þat it be nessessarie.

ventoseness. ? *Obs.* [f. L. *ventōs-us* VENTOSE *a.* + -NESS.] Windiness, flatulence, ventosity.

a **1425** tr. *Arderne's Treat. Fistula*, etc. 78 No medicyne so sone helpeþ... And it avoideþ soueranly ventosenez. **1727** BAILEY (vol. II), *Ventoseness*, windiness.

†**ventoser.** *Obs.*[−1] In 4 ventuser. [ad. AF. *venteuser* (F. *ventouseur*, = Prov. *ventozaire*), f. *vento(u)ser* VENTOSE *v.*] = CUPPER[1] 2.

c **1340** *Nominale* (Skeat) 378 The ventuser of rawe flesch.

†**ventosing,** *vbl. sb. Surg. Obs.* [f. VENTOSE *v.*] The operation of drawing blood by means of a cupping-glass; cupping. Also *attrib.*

c **1386** CHAUCER *Knt.'s T.* 1889 That neither veyne blood, ne ventusynge..may ben his helpynge. **1386** *Almanak* 52 Mynucyons to be made by blode-lattyng or ventosyng es ful profytabul. *a* **1425** tr. *Arderne's Treat. Fistula*, etc. 62 And þer be no blode-later redy, be þer made ventosyng with garsyng atuix þe buttokez. *c* **1440** *MS. Linc. A.* I. 17 fol. 299 Of bolnyng or whelynge of garsynge or ventousynge. **1483** *Cath. Angl.* 400/2 A ventisynge boxe (*A.* a ventisynge box), *guma*. **1541** R. COPLAND *Guydon's Quest. Chirurg.* N iij, What is ventosyng?.. It is the puttynge of boxes vpon any membre for to expuls the mater betwene the skynne and the flesshe.

†**ven'tositous,** *a. Obs. rare.* [f. next: cf. VENTOSE *a.* and -ITOUS.] Full of wind; windy.

1601 B. JONSON *Poetaster* v. iii. 515 *Hora.* Barmy froth, puffy, inflate, turgidous and ventositous are come vp. *Tibv.* O, terrible, windie wordes! *Ibid.* 513.

ventosity (vɛn'tɒsɪtɪ). ? *Obs.* Forms: 5 ventosytee, 6 -ytie, -yte; 4–6 -ite, 6 -itee, -itye, 7 -itie, 6– ventosity. [a. OF. (and F.) *ventosité* (= It. *ventosità*, Prov. *ventositat*, Sp. *-idad*, Pg. *idade*), ad. L. *ventōsitas* windiness, flatulency, conceit, f. *ventōs-us* VENTOSE *a.*]

1. *Path.* The state of having the stomach or other part of the alimentary canal charged with wind; flatulency.

Freq. from 1540 to 1600.

1398 TREVISA *Barth. De P.R.* v. xxxvii. (Bodl. MS.), Þat comeþ of..þikke humours oþer of grete ventosite. *a* **1400** in *Rel. Antiq.* I. 51 For wynd and ventosite, that men callis *collica passio*. *a* **1425** tr. *Arderne's Treat. Fistula*, etc. 58 If þe flowyng be olde, Anathemasis is made for aboundance of blode or for ventosite descendyng doune. *c* **1530** *Judic. Urines* III. iii. 49 It sheweth but lytell crudyte and ventosyte of the humours. **1582** HESTER *Secr. Phiorav.* III. lxv. 89 It will defende hym from all interiour passions that are caused of ventositie. **1612** WOODALL *Surg. Mate* Wks. (1639) 197 The Collick... This infirmitie is engendred of ventositie, or winde in the gut *Colon*. **1639** T. DE GRAY *Compl. Horsem.* 115 Peccant humours..being hindred by oppilations in the guts, through costivenesse and ventosity. **1684** tr. *Bonet's Merc. Compit.* I. 31 The Gout arises from..a flatulent Ventosity. **1748** tr. *Vegetius Renatus' Distempers Horses* 75 The Disease which arises from Ventosity or Constipation.

b. *pl.* Gases generated in the stomach or bowels; attacks of flatulence.

Common from *c* 1600 to *c* 1630.

1422 YONGE tr. *Secreta Secret.* 241 Goynge afor mette dryuth away the ventositeis. **1456** SIR G. HAYE *Gov. Princes* Wks. (S.T.S.) II. 140 Quhen it [*sc.* wine] is our suete it.. engenderis ventositeis. *c* **1530** *Judic. Urines* II. x. 38 And therfor are caused many fumosytes and ventosites in the body. **1545** RAYNALD *Byrth Mankynde* 77 The which do vaynqueshe and expelle ventositees and windenesse. **1602** DOLMAN *La Primaud. Fr. Acad.* (1618) III. 790 It driueth away ventosities, and flourisheth first amongst all trees. **1628** VENNER *Baths of Bathe* (1650) 355 To take cold betwixt the bathings..induceth ventosities. **1659** MACALLO *Can. Physick* 72 Belching Ventosities, or Winds,..are prognosticks that a future Crise will be by vomit.

c. The quality in things that produces flatulence.

1822–7 GOOD *Study Med.* (1829) I. 171 Many of the vegetable materials introduced into the stomach possess far more ventosity than apples.

2. A blast or puff of wind, esp. one coming from the stomach.

1513 DOUGLAS *Æneid* VII. Prol. 123 Quhais cryis bene pronosticatioun Off wyndy blastis and ventositeis. **1568** *Bk. Culture*, Belke nere no mans face;..it is a stinking ventosity. **1614** PURCHAS *Pilgrimage* IX. v. 842 This commeth of a ventositie which it voideth..or casteth..out being in danger to be taken. **1725** *Fam. Dict.*, *Belching*, a Ventosity coming out of the mouth with a disagreeable noise.

3. The state of being windy; windiness.

c **1570** *Pride & Lowl.* (1841) 30 His breeches great, full of ventositie. **1582** STANYHURST *Æneis* I. (Arb.) 35 Wee caytiefe Troians, with storms ventositye mangled. **1599** B. JONSON *Ev. Man out of Hum.* III. iv, The..ventositie of the Tropicks. *a* **1661** FULLER *Worthies*, *Essex* I. (1662) 319 The ventosity thereof [*sc.* powder] causing the violent explosion of the bullet.

4. *fig.* The state of being inflated or puffed up; pompous conceit, vanity, or bombast.

c **1550** H. RHODES *Bk. Nurture* in *Babees Bk.* (1868) 77 But turne from such occasyon, friend, hate such ventositye. **1589** NASHE *Martin Marprelate* Wks. (Grosart) I. 120 They are so full of ventositie, that I cannot come at their matter for winde and words. **1605** BACON *Adv. Learn.* I. iv. §3 Some effects of that venome which is ventositie or swelling. **1631** R. H. *Arraignm. Whole Creature* iv. 24 Vaine glory..is windy and full of ventosity, consisting of popular applause. **1710** SHAFTESBURY *Charac.* (1711) I. I. 159 Apprehensive of the Effects of this Frothiness or Ventosity in Speech. **1807** W. IRVING *Salmag.* (1811) 139 He is a man of superlative ventosity, and comparable to nothing but a huge bladder of wind. *Ibid.* (1849) 304 This general, with all his outward valour and ventosity.

b. An instance of this; an idle conceit.

1605 BACON *Adv. Learn.* II. 13 Many men..do esteeme desire of name and memory but as a vanitie and ventositie. **1657** G. STARKEY *Helmont's Vind.* 240 Whose rash ventosities and aery promises we reject. **1681** RYCAUT tr. *Gracian's Critick* 164 The Swelling Ventosities of Vanity.

†**5.** *Surg.* = VENTOSING *vbl. sb. Obs. rare*[−1].

? **1485** tr. *Bp. Knutsson's Litil Bk. Pestilence* 9 And if a swellyng appere in the sholdres lesse it with ventosite.

†**ventoso.** *Obs.*[−1] [Cf. Sp. *ventosa* vent, air-hole.] (See quot.)

1698 FRYER *Acc. E. India & P.* 222 The Structures are all plain atop, only Ventoso's, or Funnels, for to let in the Air.

†**ven'tosous,** *a. Obs. rare.* [ad. L. *ventōsus*: see VENTOSE *a.*] Windy, flatulent.

1639 T. DE GRAY *Expert Farrier* 86 Paines and gripings.. do proceed ofttimes from..the working of the spleene, which is most ventosous. **1662** J. DAVIES tr. *Olearius' Voy. Ambass.* 320 Unless the ventosous humour of it [hemp] be also expulsive.

ventour, obs. Sc. variant of VENTURE *v.*

ventousing, var. VENTOSING *vbl. sb. Obs.*

†**ventoy.** *Obs. rare.* [? ad. obs. F. *ventail* = *éventail*.] A fan.

1602 MIDDLETON *Blurt, Master-Constable* II. ii, One of you open the casements, t'other take a ventoy and gently cool my face. **1616** in BULLOKAR *Eng. Expos.* **1631** DEKKER *Match Mee* II, Lacke you no rich..Venetian ventoyes, Madam?

vent-peg. [VENT *sb.*[2]] A small peg for inserting in the vent-hole of a cask; a spile.

1707 MORTIMER *Husb.* 573 Leaving your Vent-peg always open palls it [*sc.* March-beer]. *Ibid.* 574 If once you pull out the Vent-peg, to draw a Quantity at once. **1747–96** MRS. GLASSE *Cookery* xxii. 349 Mind you have a vent-peg at the top of the vessel. **1830** M. DONOVAN *Dom. Econ.* I. 209 If on drawing out the vent-peg of the cask the liquor spurts up with force. **1844** DICKENS *Chimes* iii, Pulling out the vent-peg of the table-beer. **1875** KNIGHT *Dict. Mech.* 2703/2 The vent-peg [of the vent-cock] consists of a tubular, threaded stem, which may be screwed into a cask.

ventrad ('vɛntræd), *adv. Anat.* and *Zool.* [f. L. *ventr-*, stem of *venter* abdomen, + -AD.] Toward the ventral surface of the body.

1847–9 *Todd's Cycl. Anat.* IV. I. 639 There appears ventrad of the saurian cervix..that series of osseous pieces marked *c*, *d*. **1882** WILDER & GAGE *Anat. Technol.* 44 C may be said to lie either ventrad or laterad of B. **1895** MIVART in *Proc. Zool. Soc.* 369 The greater extension ventrad of the apex of the prosopium.

ventral ('vɛntrəl), *a.* and *sb.* [a. F. *ventral* (= Sp. and Pg. *ventral*, It. *ventrale*), or ad. L. *ventrāl-is*, f. *venter* abdomen.]

A. *adj.* **1.** Occurring or taking place in the region of the abdomen; abdominal.

a. *Path.* Of ruptures.

1739 *Phil. Trans.* XLI. 644 In some ventral Ruptures (as they are called) this also may be necessary. **1797** *Encycl. Brit.* (ed. 3) XVIII. 155/2 Ventral rupture is a protrusion of some of the bowels through the interstices of the abdominal muscles. *Ibid.* margin, Ventral hernia. **1838** *Penny Cycl.* XII. 160/1 Umbilical and ventral herniæ. **1891** MOULLIN *Surg.* 1047 *Ventral Hernia*, hernia through the linea alba (except at the umbilicus),..or some other part of the abdominal wall that is not usually weak.

b. Of laughter or breathing, or in general use.

1859 GEO. ELIOT *A. Bede* xii, He continued at intervals to ..shake luxuriously with a silent, ventral laughter. **1860** O. W. HOLMES *Elsie V.* (1891) 65 A trained rector, who read the service with such ventral depth of utterance. **1892** STEVENSON *Vailima Lett.* (1895) 197 His breathing seemed wholly ventral: the bust still, the belly moving strongly.

2. *Anat.* and *Zool.* Of, pertaining to, situated in or on, the abdomen; abdominal.

a. In *ventral fin.* (Cf. B. 1.)

1752 J. HILL *Hist. Anim.* 242 The ventral fins are connected in a remarkable manner together. **1769** PENNANT *Brit. Zool.* III. *34 The ventral fins placed behind the pectoral fins as in the minow. **1802** PALEY *Nat. Theol.* xii. §8 The pectoral, and more particularly the ventral fins, serve to raise and depress the fish. **1862** HUXLEY *Lect. Working Men* 23 [In] the Codfish.. you have the hinder limbs restored in the shape of these ventral fins.

b. In general use.

1817 KIRBY & SP. *Entomol.* xxii. II. 290 By the assistance of their mandibles,..and also of several dorsal and ventral tubercles. **1828** STARK *Elem. Nat. Hist.* I. 86 Mammæ six, two pectoral and four ventral. **1852** DANA *Crust.* I. 26 What is the proper relation of the ventral pieces of the Carapax? **1872** HUXLEY *Physiol.* i. 6 Nearer the dorsal (or back) than the ventral (or front) aspect of the body.

c. *ventral cord*: (see quots.).

1874 CARPENTER *Ment. Physiology* I. ii. 52 The longitudinal gangliated chain of Articulated animals is often distinguished as the ventral cord. **1880** BASTIAN *Brain* 91 The double ventral cord has a fibrous structure along its upper surface, whilst below there is an irregular stratum of ganglion cells.

3. *Bot.* Of or belonging to the anterior or lower surface.

1832 LINDLEY *Introd. Bot.* 144 These edges often appear in the carpellum like two sutures, of which..that which corresponds to the united margins is named the *ventral* suture. **1870** HOOKER *Stud. Flora* 114 Fragaria:..styles ventral. **1872** OLIVER *Elem. Bot.* I. vii. 89 The inner angle of each carpel..answers to the line of union of its infolded edges. This line is called the ventral suture. **1875** DARWIN *Insectiv. Pl.* xvii. 398 The lower side where the foot stalk arises is nearly straight and I have called it the ventral surface.

4. *ventral segment*, in Acoustics: (see quots.).

1830 HERSCHEL in *Encycl. Metrop.* (1845) IV. 782 Such points of rest are called nodes or nodal points, the intermediate portions [of a cord] which vibrate are termed bellies or ventral segments. **1873** W. LEES *Acoustics* I. iii. 24 The direct and reflective pulses..divide the string into a series of vibrating parts, called ventral segments.

5. quasi-*adv.* = VENTRALLY *adv.* 1.

1899 *Allbutt's Syst. Med.* VI. 807 Structures which respectively lie ventral and lateral.

B. *sb.* **1.** A ventral fin; one of the fins corresponding to the hind legs of quadrupeds.

1834 MCMURTRIE *Cuvier's Anim. Kingd.* 217 The anal.. seems to be continued forwards by the ventrals. **1854** OWEN in *Orr's Circ. Sci.*, *Org. Nat.* I. 186 The ventrals are situated near the vent. **1875** C. C. BLAKE *Zool.* 202 The pectoral fins are distant from the head, and not produced to the ventrals.

2. *Ent.* One or other of the segments of the abdomen, esp. in *Coleoptera*. (1891 in *Cent. Dict.*)

ventrally ('vɛntrəlɪ), *adv.* [f. prec. + -LY[2].]

1. In a ventral direction; on or toward the venter; with respect to the venter or abdomen.

1870 HOOKER *Stud. Flora* 368 *Actinocarpus Damasonium*: ..carpels dehiscing ventrally. **1872** HUMPHRY *Myology* 2 Ventrally, it is attached to the margin of the lower jaw. **1883** MARTIN & MOALE *Vertebr. Dissect.* 137 The anterior abdominal vein..runs ventrally and forward.

Comb. **1870** ROLLESTON *Anim. Life* 83 The various ventrally-placed appendages of the articulate Neuropods. **1904** *Brit. Med. Jrnl.* 17 Dec. 1631 The ventrally bending limb..having no mesoblastic somites dorsal to it.

2. In or from the venter or abdomen.

1889 H. J. BARKER *Orig. Eng.* i. 15, I laughed myself (ventrally, of course,) when the youngsters so innocently committed themselves.

ventralward(s, *adv.* [f. VENTRAL *a.* + -WARD(S.] To or towards the belly or ventral surface of the body.

1883 SEDGWICK & HEAPE *Embryol.* 165 This branch, starting from near the dorsal beginning of the fold, runs ventralwards and forwards. **1893** TUCKEY *Amphioxus* 156 Here the mesoblast does not grow forward so far ventralwards.

ventre, obs. f. VENTER[1], VENTURE, VINTRY.

‖**ventre à terre** (vãtr a tɛr), *adv. phr.* [Fr., lit. 'belly to the ground'.] **a.** In the posture assumed (esp. in sporting prints) by a horse at full gallop; hence at full speed, 'all out'. Also *attrib.*

1847 THACKERAY *Van. Fair* (1848) iii. 476, I instantly called for the carriage, and..drove *ventre à terre* to Nathan's. **1867** 'OUIDA' *Under Two Flags* I. xiii. 302 You know what the Arabs are... They..pick up their sabre from the ground, while their horse is galloping *ventre à terre.* **1918** G. B. SHAW in F. Harris *Oscar Wilde* II. 28 To be called on to gallop ventre à terre to Erith. **1947** J. STEVENSON-HAMILTON *Wild Life S. Afr.* xxii. 170 He [*sc.* a charging lion] goes not in a series of bounds, but at a *ventre à terre* gallop, and incredibly fast. **1974** *Country Life* 2 May 1059/1 His personal progression from the 19th-century *ventre à terre* animal motion—*à la* Herring and Pollard—to the transverse and rotatory images. **1977** 'E. CRISPIN' *Glimpses of Moon* xi. 223 Man and horse..went on to gallop almost *ventre à terre* in the direction of the hedge.

b. Lying on one's stomach, prone.

1960 *Times* 18 July 15/4 Down at the firing point they formed a line *ventre à terre.* **1968** *Economist* 27 Jan. 4/3 The Cresta, which is run by the St. Moritz Toboggan Club, on which the rider uses a skeleton, or the bob run in which the bobsleigh crew descend either *ventre à terre* or sitting up.

ventri- ('vɛntrɪ), comb. form of L. *ventri-*, *venter* VENTER[1], occurring in various terms, as **ventri'cornu** *Anat.*, the ventral extension of gray matter in the substance of the spinal cord; hence **ventri'cornual** *a.*; **ventri'cumbent** *a.*, lying on the belly; prone, prostrate; **'ventriduct** *v.*, to bring to or turn towards the belly; †**ventrifluous** *a.* [ad. L. *ventrifluus*], 'laxative, purging the belly' (1727 in BAILEY); **ventri'meson** *Anat.*, the median line on the ventral surface of the body; hence ***ventrimesal*** adj. (1891 in *Cent. Dict.*); **ven'tripetal** *a.* [after CENTRIPETAL *a.*], directed towards the belly or stomach; **ventri'pyramid** *Anat.*, = PYRAMID *sb.* 7 (*a*).

1890 *Buck's Handbk. Med. Sci.* VIII. 528 The *ventricornu (ventral or 'anterior' extension of the myelic cinerea). *Ibid.*, The myelic cornua are strictly dorsal and ventral,..permitting the adjectives dorsicornual and *ventricornual. **1882** WILDER & GAGE *Anat. Technol.* 36 The body is *ventri-cumbent, so as to expose the dorsal aspect. *Ibid.* 537 To pith [a frog] *ventriduct the head with the index, and pass the tip of the right index [etc.]. *Ibid.* 33 For convenience, the dorsal and ventral borders of this plane may be called the dorsimeson and the *ventrimeson respectively. **1819** L. HUNT *Indicator* No. 12 (1822) I. 90 Every thought of mind, and every feeling of his affection,..tends to one point, with a *ventripetal force. **1882** WILDER & GAGE *Anat. Technol.* 485 *Ventripyramid.

ventric ('vɛntrɪk), *a. rare*⁻¹. [f. L. *ventr-*, stem of *venter* VENTER[1] + -IC.] Connected with, pertaining to, the stomach.

1869 M. COLLINS in F. Collins *Lett. & Friendships* (1877) I. 63 *Magister artis..venter*, says Persius—the art of accurate time-keeping is ventric.

ventrical, prob. a misspelling and misuse of VENTRICLE.

1824 GALT *Rothelan* II. IV. iv. 125 He reached a small postern entrance, which..many years after..became celebrated as the ventrical into Moorfields.

ventricle ('vɛntrɪk(ə)l). *Anat.* and *Zool.* Also 6 **ventrikle, ventrycle,** 7 **ventrickle.** [ad. L. *ventriculus* VENTRICULUS or F. *ventricule*: see VENTRICULE.]

1. One or other of the two cavities in the heart by means of which the blood is circulated through the body; also, the cavity of the heart in certain animals and molluscs which fulfils this function.

c **1400** *Lanfranc's Cirurg.* 162 Þe herte haþ two ventriclis .i. two holowe placis wiþinne, & þat oon ventricle sittiþ in þe riȝtside of þe herte, & þat oþer in þe liftside. **1607** TOPSELL *Four-f. Beasts* 195 There is a double ventrickle and bone in the heart of an Elephant. **1660** BOYLE *New Exp. Phys. Mech.* Digress. 347 The Blood that passes out of the right Ventricle of the Heart into the Lungs. **1692** RAY *Creation* (ed. 2) I. 33 An Ebullition and sudden Expansion of the Blood in the Ventricles. **1730** CHAMBERLAYNE *Relig. Philos.* I. vi. §2 The Heart has two Cavities or Ventricles, separated from each other by a thick fleshy Wall, or Septum. **1760** H. WALPOLE *Lett. to Mann* (1846) IV. 105 The great ventricle of the heart had burst. **1828** STARK *Elem. Nat. Hist.* I. 365 The animals of this order [*sc.* Batrachia] have a heart with a single auricle and ventricle. **1876** BRISTOWE *Th. & Pract. Med.* (1878) 173 In the ventricles of the heart fibrinous clots may be discovered.

transf. **1851** S. P. WOODWARD *Mollusca* I. 63 Branchiæ two, furnished with muscular ventricles.

attrib. **1898** *Allbutt's Syst. Med.* V. 789 Cases of right ventricle failure. *Ibid.* 794 The hypertrophy was probably..due to left ventricle strain.

2. One or other of a series of cavities in the brain (normally numbering four in the adult human being) formed by enlargements of the neural canal.

pineal ventricle: see PINEAL *a.* b.

c **1400** *Lanfranc's Cirurg.* 113 Summen seien þat þer ben .iiij. ventriclis of þe brayn. *Ibid.*, Þ is ventricle is sett bitwene two addiamentis of þe brayn. **1548** VICARY *Anat.* iv. (1888) 31 From the foremost Ventrikle of the brayne springeth seuen payre of sensatiue or feeling senews. **1594** T. B. *La Primaud. Fr. Acad.* II. Ep. Rdr., Heere may you see..the seuerall ventricles of the braine, as so many sundrie chambers for the intertainment of the animal spirits. **1620** VENNER *Via Recta* ii. 35 Beere that is too bitter..causeth the head-ach, by filling the ventricles of the braine with troublesome vapors. **1655-87** H. MORE *App. Antid.* (1712) 206 Suppose Memory were thus seal'd upon the Brain, and transmitted its Image through the Animal Spirits in the ventricles. **1748** HARTLEY *Observ. Man* I. i. §1. 8 Blood, Matter, or Serum, lying upon the Brain, or in its Ventricles. **1800** *Med. Jrnl.* IV. 553 The vapour or water in the ventricles of the brain. **1840** G. V. ELLIS *Anat.* 23 The calamus scriptorius in the floor of the fourth ventricle. **1872** HUXLEY *Physiol.* vii. 158 Cilia are found..in the ventricles of the brain.

3. The stomach in man or animals. ? *Obs.*

Freq. in 17th cent. use.

1574 NEWTON *Health Mag.* 9 It is good for the Ventricle or Stomacke also. **1594** T. B. *La Primaud. Fr. Acad.* II. 343 Wee will beginne at the ventricle, commonly called the stomacke. **1620** VENNER *Via Recta* viii. 182 That no part of the meat may sticke..about the mouth of the stomacke, but may..be carried into the ventricle, which is the bottome of the stomack. *a* **1676** HALE *Prim. Orig. Man.* I. ii. (1677) 59 Whether I will or will not,..my Heart beats,..my Ventricle digest what is in it. **1710** T. FULLER *Pharm. Extemp.* 18 Purging Ale..takes off the slipperiness of the Ventricle and Intestines. **1805-6** CARY *Dante, Inf.* XXVIII. 26 Dangling his entrails hung, the midriff..and wretched ventricle, That turns the englutted aliment to dross.

b. The digestive sac or organs in birds, fishes, insects, and certain reptiles.

1575 TURBERV. *Faulconrie* 249, I have thruste my fore finger into hir gorge..and by that meanes have caused hir to fill in the ventricle sooner than otherwise she woulde have done. **1607** TOPSELL *Four-f. Beasts* 182 The powder of a Storks craw or Ventrickle. **1658** ROWLAND tr. *Moufet's Theat. Ins.* 907 It may..be termed the Chylus of the Bees, ..having its perfection and consummation from their ventricles. **1681** CHETHAM *Angler's Vade-m.* xli. §1 (1689) 307 His ventricle is large and capacious. **1704** RAY *Creation* (ed. 4) I. 30 The Meat [is]..transferr'd into the Gizzard.., where by the working of the Muscles compounding the sides of that Ventricle,..it is..ground small. **1826** KIRBY & SP. *Entomol.* xlviii. IV. 424 That the Orthoptera have a ventricle or gizzard. **1868** DUNCAN *Ins. World* Introd. 10 Two kinds of appendages belong to the chylific ventricle. **1877** HUXLEY *Anat. Inv. Anim.* 412 That part of the alimentary canal which lies in front of the chylific ventricle [in cockroaches].

†**c.** The belly. In quot. *fig. Obs.*

1588 SHAKS. *L.L.L.* IV. ii. 70 Ideas, apprehensions,..are begot in the ventricle of memorie, nourisht in the wombe of primater.

d. *attrib.* in †***ventricle unguent.***

1599 A. M. tr. *Gabelhouer's Bk. Physicke* 238/2 [A recipe for] An excellent Ventricle vnguente, which is verye commodious for the Childebedde Woemen.

4. Any small hollow or cavity in an animal body, serving as a place of organic function; in later use, the recess or space between the true and false vocal cords on each side of the larynx; a laryngeal pouch or sac.

1641 MILTON *Church Govt.* II. Wks. 1851 III. 44 All the faculties of the Soule are confin'd of old to their severall vessels, and ventricles. **1692** BENTLEY *Boyle Lect.* 109 The various ducts and ventricles of the body. **1730** BAILEY (fol.), *Ventricles*, any round Concavities in a Body. **1808** BARCLAY *Muscular Motions* 500 The lateral depressions that have been denominated the ventricles of the larynx, or the ventricles of Morgagni. **1877** M. FOSTER *Physiol.* III. vii. (1878) 532 The ventricles of Morgagni are apparently of use in giving the vocal cords sufficient room for their vibrations. **1888** *Encycl. Brit.* XXIV. 273/2 The ventricles no doubt permit a free vibration of the true vocal cords.

†**5.** In gen. use: A cavity or hollow. *Obs. rare.*

1627 DONNE *Serm.* IV. 5 In what corner, in what ventricle of the sea lies all the jelly of a body drowned in the general flood? *c* **1630** RISDON *Surv. Devon* §225 (1810) 237 The caverns and ventricles of the earth.

ventricose (vɛntrɪ'kəʊs), *a.* [ad. mod.L. *ventricōsus*, f. L. *ventr-*, *venter* belly VENTER[1]: see -IC and -OSE.]

1. Swelling out in the middle, or on one side, after the manner of an animal's belly; bellied, protuberant, strongly convex. **a.** *Bot.* (esp. of the corolla or calyx).

1756 J. HILL *Hist. Plants* 153 (Jod.), There is no pericarpium; but the calix becomes more ventricose, and contains a single seed. **1785** MARTYN *Lett. Bot.* xvi. (1794) 179 In Comfrey and Cerinthe the corolla is ventricose. **1821** W. P. C. BARTON *Flora N. Amer.* I. 13 Capsule setigerous.., included in the ventricose calix. **1841** *Florist's Jrnl.* (1846) II. 243 The flowers are white and ventricose. **1872** OLIVER *Elem. Bot.* App. 310 Outer Glumes [of wheat] nearly equal, ..ventricose.

b. *Conch.* (Usually of the body of the shell.)

1770 PENNANT *Brit. Zool.* IV. 123 *M*[*urex*] *carinatus* with five or six spires, the body ventricose. **1828** STARK *Elem. Nat. Hist.* II. 79 Shell rounded, ventricose, golden red. **1851** S. P. WOODWARD *Mollusca* I. 70 *Cranchia.* Body large, ventricose. *Ibid.* 110 Whirls ventricose. **1865** GOSSE *Land & Sea* 155 Their ventricose or parallel-sided form.

Comb. **1828** STARK *Elem. Nat. Hist.* II. 25 Shell oblong, ventricose-cylindrical.

c. *Zool.* or *Anat.*

1804 SHAW *Gen. Zool.* V. II. 394 Ventricose Sucker... Olivaceous Sucker, with ventricose abdomen. **1813** MONTAGU *Ornith. Dict.* Suppl. s.v. *Golden-eye*, The ventricose part consists of the same cartilaginous rings as the rest of the windpipe. **1835-6** *Todd's Cycl. Anat.* I. 533 The ventricose and short-bodied species of Cephalopoda. **1841** E. NEWMAN *Hist. Insects* III. iii. 185 The gullet..is ventricose or *ventricous* when it dilates into a large bag or crop before its union with the stomach.

2. Of persons: Big-bellied; having an unusually or abnormally large abdomen.

1843 F. E. PAGET *Warden Berkingholt* 266 The Reverend Rory O'Flannigan rose like the full moon..when first she peeps from behind the hill, rubicund, coppery, ventricose. **1856** KANE *Arct. Expl.* II. xxv. 248 Ending with the ventricose little Accommodah. **1876** W. ROBERTS *Urin. & Renal Dis.* III. viii. (ed. 3) 485 A little boy, who had been ventricose from birth.

Hence **ventri'coseness, ventri'cosity.**

1857 TURTON *Land & Fresh-W. Shells* 183 [The shell] varies greatly in size, ventricoseness, and colour. **1868** *Proc. Zool. Soc.* May 374 The greater ventricosity of form..of *M*[*elo*] *georginæ.* **1909** J. W. JENKINSON *Exper. Embryol.* 71 The 'ventricosity' (ratio of breadth to length) of the shell of the Periwinkle.

ventri'coso-, comb. form of prec., with the sense 'distended and ——', as ***ventricoso-globose.***

1822 J. PARKINSON *Outl. Oryctol.* 58 *Alcyonium putridosum.*—Ventricoso-globose, somewhat pear-shaped.

'ventricous, *a. rare.* [See -OUS.] = VENTRICOSE *a.*, in various senses.

1702 BAYNARD *Cold Baths* (1709) II. 341 Such Children..are usually ventricous, and not so agil and nimble as other Children. **1828-32** WEBSTER, *Ventricous*, in botany, bellied; distended; swelling out in the middle; as, a ventricous perianth. **1850** OGILVIE, *Ventricous*,..in conchology, applied to shells which are inflated, or which swell in the middle.

ventricular (vɛn'trɪkjʊlə(r)), *a.* Chiefly *Anat.* and *Path.* [f. L. *ventricul-us* (see next) + -AR, or ad. mod.L. **ventriculāris.* So F. *ventriculaire.*]

1. Of or pertaining to the stomach; abdominal, gastral, ventral.

1822-7 GOOD *Study Med.* (1829) I. 249 It is also said that the common garden rue.., when eaten to excess, is succeeded by the same symptoms of ventricular pains. **1840** *New Monthly Mag.* LIX. 164 No one..ever listens to ventricular admonitions, but 'greatly daring dines' on, in defiance of dyspepsia. **1845** *Blackw. Mag.* LVII. 610 Louis XIV actually did wear it buttoned below the ventricular curve.

b. Distended in the middle; ventriculous.

1850 in OGILVIE.

2. a. Affecting a ventricle or ventricles (of the heart, brain, etc.).

1838 *Penny Cycl.* XII. 79 Its [the heart's] point..strikes at each ventricular contraction, or *systole*, as it is called, against the wall of the chest. **1853** MARKHAM *Skoda's Auscult.* 205 The ventricular systole may also be accompanied by two distinctly different sounds. **1888** W. R. GOWERS *Man. Dis. Nerv. Syst.* II. 298 Limited ventricular meningitis occurs especially in young children.

b. Of or pertaining to, forming part of, a ventricle.

1840 E. WILSON *Anat.'s Vade M.* (1842) 338 The Deep or Ventricular veins commence within the lateral ventricles by two vessels. **1870** ROLLESTON *Anim. Life* Introd. p. lvi, A complete separation of the ventricular part of the heart into two cavities. **1875** PAYNE *Jones & Siev. Pathol. Anat.* ix. 244 The surface either of the plexus or the ventricular walls. **1896** *Allbutt's Syst. Med.* I. 109 So far as regards the heart and ventricular muscle.

3. Of the nature of a ventricle.

1841 T. R. JONES *Anim. Kingd.* xxiii. 397 A single auricle that communicates with a strong ventricular cavity. *Ibid.* xxix. 606 The heart..separated into two distinct sets of cavities, each composed of an auricle and of a strong ventricular chamber. **1877** HUXLEY *Anat. Inv. Anim.* iii. 115 In the simplest *Calcispongiæ*,..the pores open directly into the ventricular cavity.

ventricule ('vɛntrɪkjuːl). *Anat.* [a. OF. *ventricule* (14th c. in Littré; = Sp. and Pg. *ventriculo*, It. *ventricolo*), ad. L. *ventriculus* VENTRICULUS.] = VENTRICLE in various senses.

a **1425** tr. *Arderne's Treat. Fistula*, etc. 14 Þe synowez.. haþe festnyng with þe stomake and wiþ þe ventriculez of þe brayne. **1677** GALE *Crt. Gentiles* IV. 97 The Apostle addes 'Meats are for the belly', i.e. for the ventricule or stomach and intestines. **1742** *Phil. Trans.* XLII. 125 In the Right Auricle and Ventricule of his Heart was found a large tough subrubicund *Polypus.* **1880** GÜNTHER *Fishes* 152 The walls of the ventricule are robust.

ventriculite (vɛn'trɪkjʊlaɪt). [ad. mod.L. *Ventriculites*, f. L. *ventriculus* ventricle: see -ITE[1] 2.] A fossil sponge belonging to the genus *Ventriculites* or the family *Ventriculitidæ.*

1822 MANTELL *Geol. Sussex* 176 The difference in the form of this ventriculite. **1885** J. E. TAYLOR *Brit. Fossils* i. 24 In the white chalk of Sussex,..Ventriculites occur in great numbers.

Hence **ventricu'litic** *a.*, of or belonging to, containing, ventriculites.

(In recent Dicts.)

ventriculitis (vɛntrɪkjʊ'laɪtɪs). *Path.* [f. L. *ventricul-us* VENTRICLE + -ITIS.] Inflammation of the lining of the ventricles of the brain.

1926 in R. J. E. SCOTT *Gould's Med. Dict.* **1946** *Med. Jrnl. Australia* 13 Apr. 513/1 A case of staphylococcal ventriculitis. **1967** *Brit. Med. Jrnl.* 27 May 542/2 Three babies with meningitis and ventriculitis were successfully treated with gentamicin. **1977** *Proc. R. Soc. Med.* LXX. 234/1 A considerable percentage will survive ventriculitis from an infected back.

ventriculo- (vɛn'trɪkjʊləʊ), comb. form of L. *ventricul-us* VENTRICLE, occurring in various words in *Anat.*, as **ven,triculo'atrial** *a.*, involving or connecting a ventricle (usu. of the brain) and the atrium of the heart; **ven,triculoperito'neal** *a.*, involving or connecting a ventricle of the brain and the peritoneum.

1959 *Amer. Jrnl. Dis. Children* XCVIII. 467/2 (*heading*) Clinical observations on twenty hydrocephalic children subjected to ventriculoatrial shunt. **1962** *Lancet* 12 May 991/1 The experiments with the rubber slings designed to reduce ventriculoatrial reflux were not consistent. **1977** *Proc. R. Soc. Med.* LXX. 235/2 The ventriculo-atrial shunt is the most physiological, and in spite of its draw-backs I prefer it to ventriculopleural or ventriculoperitoneal drainage except in special circumstances. **1913** *Ann. Surg.* LVII. 468 Ventriculoperitoneal drainage. In 1905, Kausch performed this operation by uniting the lateral ventricle with the peritoneal cavity by means of a small rubber tube, placed subcutaneously. **1977** *Lancet* 30 Apr. 951/1 A ventriculoperitoneal shunt was inserted for relief of the hydrocephalus.

ventriculography (vɛntrɪkjʊˈlɒgrəfɪ). *Med.* [f. VENTRICULO- + -GRAPHY.] Radiography of the brain with the cerebral fluid of the ventricles replaced by air or some other contrast medium. Hence **venˌtriculoˈgraphic** *a.*; also **venˈtriculogram**, a radiogram of the ventricles of the brain.

1918 W. E. DANDY in *Ann. Surg.* LXVIII. 5 (*heading*) Ventriculography following the injection of air into the cerebral ventricles. *Ibid.* 7 Owing to the lighter weight of air, the ventriculogram represents the ventricle farthest from the X-ray plate. **1932** *Amer. Jrnl. Roentgenol.* XXVII. 660/1 The size of the lateral ventricle, and the patency of the foramen of Munro, can be determined readily during this particular part of the ventriculographic procedure. **1936** *Brit. Med. Jrnl.* 28 Mar. 661/2 The usual procedure.. was to make a ventriculogram first thing in the morning, and start operating two or three hours later. **1947** *Radiology* XLVIII. 59/1 Ventriculography..showed the posterior portions of both lateral ventricles to be dilated and revealed similar enlargement of the temporal horns. **1974** C. B. T. ADAMS in R. M. Kirk et al. *Surgery* xiv. 273/2 Often, the brain plugs the fracture and a rise of intranasal pressure by nose blowing forces the air into the brain, an aerocele, and, occasionally, into the ventricle, producing a ventriculogram on X-ray. **1978** *Science* 24 Feb. 854/1 Asymmetries in the size of the left and right lateral ventricles [of the brain] can..be demonstrated..by injecting air into the ventricles during pneumoencephalography and ventriculography.

ventricuˈlose, *a. rare*$^{-0}$. [ad. L. *ventriculōsus* pertaining to the belly, f. *ventriculus* VENTRICULUS.] **a.** 'Paunch-bellied' (1727 in BAILEY, vol. II). **b.** *Bot.* = next. (1891 in *Cent. Dict.*)

venˈtriculous, *a. rare*$^{-0}$. [Cf. prec. and -OUS.] (See quots.)

1802 R. HALL *Elem. Bot.* 194 *Ventriculous*,..somewhat ventricose. **1828–32** in WEBSTER, *Ventriculous*, somewhat distended in the middle.

‖**ventriculus** (vɛnˈtrɪkjʊləs). [L. (in senses 1 and 2), dim. of *venter* VENTER[1].]

1. *Anat.* and *Zool.* = VENTRICLE 3.

[**1693** tr. *Blancard's Phys. Dict.* (ed. 2), *Ventriculus*, the Stomach.] **1710** J. HARRIS *Lex. Techn.* II. s.v., The Stomach or *Ventriculus* is placed immediately under the Midriff. **1771** *Encycl. Brit.* I. 258/1 Ventriculus, or Stomach,..a great bag or reservoir, situated [etc.]. **1843** WILKINSON tr. *Swedenborg's Anim. Kingd.* I. iv. 109 The stomach or ventriculus is a hollow membranous viscus. **1894** *Athenæum* 21 April 514/3 The alimentary canal is more of the type of other Gamasidæ than of the Uropodinæ, the ventriculus being small and its cæca long.

b. The gizzard in birds and insects.

1891 in *Cent. Dict.* **1896** NEWTON *Dict. Birds* 916 [The] Stomach..consists of an interior portion, the *Proventriculus*,..and a posterior, the *Ventriculus* or Gizzard, which is muscular.

2. = VENTRICLE 1.

1771 *Encycl. Brit.* I. 278/2 The heart..is hollow within, and divided by a septum which runs between the edges into two cavities, called *ventriculi*.

3. The body-cavity of a sponge.

1877 HUXLEY *Anat. Inv. Anim.* iii. 115 In the simplest *Calcispongiæ*..the wall of the ventriculus is thin. *Ibid.* vii. 409 The anterior end of the ventriculus.

†**ventriloˈcution**. *Obs.*$^{-0}$ = VENTRILOQUISM.

1846 in WORCESTER (citing C. B. Brown).

ventriloqual (vɛnˈtrɪləkwəl), *a. rare.* [Cf. next and -AL[1].] = VENTRILOQUIAL *a.*

1864 *Tallis's Theatr. Newspaper* 30 July 258 The phenomenon will be attributed to some kind of ventriloqual trick. **1888** DOUGHTY *Arabia Deserta* I. 89 These Western men are distinguished by their harsh ventriloqual speech.

Hence **venˈtriloqually** *adv. rare*$^{-1}$.

1871 B. TAYLOR *Faust* (1875) II. II. 152 Proteus, speaking ventriloqually, now near, now at a distance.

ˈventriloque, *sb.* and *a. rare.* [Anglicized form of VENTRILOQUUS: cf. F. *ventriloque*.] **a.** *sb.* A ventriloquist. **b.** *adj.* Ventriloquial.

1681 GLANVILL *Evid. Witches London* II. 63 This Pythoness being a Ventriloque, that is, speaking as it were from the bottom of her Belly. **1826** HOOD *Irish Schoolm.* iii, And oft, indeed, the inward of that gate, Most ventriloque, doth utter tender squeak. **1834** MUDIE *Brit. Birds* (1841) I. 314 The voice of the birds..is also made up partly of echo-notes, in all cases where it is ventriloque, or varies in apparent place.

ventriloqui, pl. of VENTRILOQUUS.

ventriloquial (vɛntrɪˈləʊkwɪəl), *a.* [f. VENTRILOQUY + -AL[1].]

1. Of sounds: Such as are produced by ventriloquism.

1836–7 DICKENS *Sk. Boz., Char.* viii, The symphony.. was soon afterwards followed by a faint kind of ventriloquial chirping. *a* **1845** HOOD *To Kitchener* viii, Potent to hush all ventriloquial snarling. **1879** BODDAM-WHETHAM *Roraima* xiii. 152 It was very delightful to hear one of them pouring forth his rich and ventriloquial notes.

2. Of or belonging to, consisting of, ventriloquism.

1818 in A. Mathews *Mem. Charles Mathews* (1838) II. 452 So well did he by his ventriloquial power imitate the voice of a child, without any movement of the natural organs of speech. **1838** DICKENS *O. Twist* xli, 'A bad one!'.. growled Mr. Grimwig, speaking by some ventriloquial power, without moving a muscle of his face. **1865** *Pall Mall G.* 23 Oct. 11 His ventriloquial entertainment is..a clever piece of vocal imitation. **1875** FLO. MARRYAT *Open Sesame* I. x. 146 Expecting to receive another proof of her ventriloquial skill.

Hence **ventriˈloquially** *adv.*

1893 GANTHONY *Pract. Ventriloquism* 27 Should Ventriloquial practice make your throat ache,..do not use it ventriloquially for a time.

ventriloquism (vɛnˈtrɪləkwɪz(ə)m). [f. VENTRILOQU-Y + -ISM: cf. next.]

1. The art or practice of speaking or producing sounds in such a manner that the voice appears to proceed from some person or object other than the speaker, and usually at some distance from him. (The common use.)

1797 *Encycl. Brit.* (ed. 3) XVIII. 639/2 It is with no great propriety that..their art [is called] *ventriloquism*, since they appear more frequently to speak.. from the roof or distant corners of the room, than from their own mouths or their own bellies. **1826** SCOTT *Diary* 12 Jan., Mathews..confirms my idea of ventriloquism (which is an absurd word), as being merely the art of imitating sounds at a greater or a less distance. **1832** BREWSTER *Nat. Magic* vii. 167 This uncertainty with respect to the direction of sound is the foundation of the art of ventriloquism. **1856** KANE *Arct. Expl.* II. xii. 126 Their deceptions are simply vocal, a change of voice, and perhaps a limited profession of ventriloquism. *transf. c* **1819** COLERIDGE *Rem.* (1836) II. 275, I call it ventriloquism, because Sejanus is a puppet, out of which the poet [Jonson] makes his own voice appear to come. **1874** *Fortn. Rev.* Feb. 244 We consider the poem ['Maud'] about as striking an instance as could be named of what we call poetical ventriloquism.

b. An instance of this; a ventriloquial sound.

1839 T. BEALE *Nat. Hist. Sperm Whale* 302 All our talent and ingenuity in these ventriloquisms were thrown away. **1878** HARDY *Ret. Native* v. vi, Soft strange ventriloquisms came from holes in the ground, hollow stalks,..and other crannies.

2. The fact or practice of speaking or appearing to speak from the abdomen.

1818 in TODD. **1846** TRENCH *Mirac.* v. (1862) 156 *note*, The notion of a ventriloquism such as this, of a spirit having his lodging in the body of a man. **1852** CONYBEARE & HOWSON *St. Paul* I. ix. (1862) 276 It was usual for the prophetic spirit to make itself known by an internal muttering or ventriloquism.

ventriloquist (vɛnˈtrɪləkwɪst). [f. VENTRILOQU-Y + -IST.] One who practises, or is expert in, ventriloquy or ventriloquism; *spec.* in modern use, one who gives public exhibitions of his skill in this art.

With early quots. cf. prec. 2. The modern application (corresponding to VENTRILOQUISM 1) appears just before 1800.

1656 BLOUNT *Glossogr.*, *Ventriloquist*, one that hath an evil spirit speaking in his belly, or one that by use and practise can speak as it were out of his belly, not moving his lips. **1681** H. MORE in *Glanvill's Sadducismus* I. Postscr. (1726) 19 Who knows but some of his counterfeit Ventriloquists may prove true ones. **1718** BP. HUTCHINSON *Witchcraft* 11 There are also many that can form Words and Voices in their Stomach, which shall seem to come from others rather than the Person that speaks them. Such people are call'd Engastriloques, or Ventriloquists. **1749** WESLEY *Wks.* (1872) IX. 7 There was a compact..between the ventriloquist and the exorcist. **1797** *Encycl. Brit.* (ed. 3) XVIII. 639/2 As the ancient ventriloquists, when exercising their art, seemed generally to speak from their own bellies, the name..was abundantly significant. **1815** *Stage* I. 176 A ventriloquist at Paris has attracted the attention of the whole metropolis. **1840** DICKENS *Old C. Shop* xix, And pale slender women with consumptive faces lingered upon the footsteps of ventriloquists and conjurors. **1893** GANTHONY *Pract. Ventriloquism* 147 It is curious that Ventriloquists are nearly all English.

fig. c **1819** COLERIDGE *Rem.* (1836) II. 317 The scenes are mock dialogues in which the poet solus plays the ventriloquist. **1885** *Pall Mall G.* 10 Jan. 1/1 The 'Ventriloquist of Varzin', who can pull the strings of three Imperial Chancelleries.

attrib. **1850** *N. & Q.* Ser. I. II. 101 It can hardly be doubted that the Archbishop's miracle was a ventriloquist hoax.

b. Applied to birds or animals. Also *attrib.*

1802 PALEY *Nat. Theol.* x. §5 A tuneful bird is a ventriloquist. The seat of the song is in the breast. **1879** JEFFERIES *Wild Life* 218 The belief that the [corn-]crake is a ventriloquist. **1895** *Funk's Stand. Dict.*, *Onappo* (Braz[il]), a reddish-gray nyctipithecine monkey or teetee (*Callithrix discolor*). Called also *ventriloquist-monkey*.

ventriloquistic (vɛntrɪləˈkwɪstɪk), *a.* [f. prec. + -IC.]

1. Using or practising ventriloquism.

In first quot. used to translate Gr. ἐγγλωττογάστωρ, which has also been rendered by 'ventrilinguist'.

1830 tr. *Aristophanes, Birds* 1651 At Phanæ..live a villanous ventriloquistic race,..and from these same ventriloquistic Philippi in Attica the tongue is severed in twain. **1851** G. S. FABER *Many Mansions* 79 Hence the Seventy scruple not to express their sense of the hebrew Baalath Ob, by rendering it a Ventriloquistic Woman.

2. Of or pertaining to ventriloquism or ventriloquists; ventriloquial.

1853 F. O. MORRIS *Brit. Birds* III. 182 This ventriloquistic power is certainly very remarkable. **1873** B. HARTE *Fiddletown* 32 He even uttered a short ventriloquistic laugh without moving his mouth. **1885** H. O. FORBES *Nat. Wand. E. Arch.* 72 Its deep and ventriloquistic voice.

ventriloquize (vɛnˈtrɪləkwaɪz), *v.* [f. as prec. + -IZE.]

1. *intr.* To use or practise ventriloquism; to speak or produce sounds in the manner of a ventriloquist; to cast the voice.

1844 H. STEPHENS *Bk. Farm* I. 297 When the corn-crake ..ventriloquises in the corn or grass. **1846** LANDOR *Imag. Conv.* Wks. I. 148/2 The horses capered and neighed and ventriloquized right and left. **1855** KINGSLEY *Westw. Ho!* ii, Leave thy caverned grumblings,..and discourse eloquence from thy central omphalos, like Pythoness ventriloquising. **1879** JEFFERIES *Wild Life* 219 Some say in like manner that the starling ventriloquizes.

fig. **1832** COLERIDGE *Table-t.* 21 July, I have no admiration for the practice of ventriloquizing through another man's mouth. **1890** *Spectator* 1 Nov., It looks as if the new Radicalism had entered into his soul and were ventriloquising through his organisation.

2. *trans.* To utter as a ventriloquist.

1865 *Spectator* 14 Jan. 45 It is a falsehood ventriloquizing truth. **1871** FARRAR *Witn. Hist.* iv. 131 The little Temple, up which the priests..crept to ventriloquise behind the deceptive statue their lying oracles. **1900** *Daily News* 18 July 2/5 He not only mimics but ventriloquises his imitations.

Hence **venˈtriloquizing** *vbl. sb.* Also *attrib.*

1805 EUGENIA DE ACTON *Nuns of Desert* II. 52 Mrs. Mervin's ventriloquising powers, exhibited in the church.

ventriloquous (vɛnˈtrɪləkwəs), *a.* [f. L. *ventriloqu-us* (see next) + -OUS.]

1. Of persons: = VENTRILOQUISTIC *a.* 1.

1713 DERHAM *Phys.-Theol.* IV. vii. (1727) 149 *note*, In the same Tract, Chap. 6 is this Observation of Ventriloquous Persons. **1737** BYROM *Rem.* (1857) 116 There came the ventriloquous fellow, who imitated a friend's voice out of his mouth. **1775** in ASH, and in later Dicts.

2. Produced by or as by ventriloquy; ventriloquial.

1768 G. WHITE *Selborne* xvi, In breeding-time, snipes play over the moors, piping and humming... Is not their hum ventriloquous, like that of the turkey? **1844** H. STEPHENS *Bk. Farm* III. 738 The harsh ventriloquous cry of the corn-craik amongst the grass. **1880** CABLE *Grandissimes* (1898) 200 The dismal ventriloquous note of the rain-crow.

‖**venˈtriloquus**. *Obs.* Usu. in pl. **ventriloqui**. [L., f. *ventri-*, *venter* belly + *loqui* to speak, after Gr. ἐγγαστρίμυθος. Cf. VENTRILOQUE.] A ventriloquist (esp. in the original sense).

The fem. *ventriloqua* (pl. *-loquæ*) is employed by R. Scot *Discov. Witchcr.* (1584) VII. i. 126 and xiii. 150.

1644 DIGBY *Nat. Bodies* xxviii. §2. 251 They that are called ventriloqui, do persuade ignorant people that the Diuell speaketh from within them deepe in their belly. **1667** *Phil. Trans.* II. 603 How by a peculiar use of the Epiglottis, one may come to speak inwardly, as do the Ventriloqui. **1706** HEARNE *Collect.* (O.H.S.) I. 306 Two or three pretty stories..of *Ventriloqui*, or those that speak in their bellies. **1748** HARTLEY *Observ. Man* I. ii. §5. 228 We may see how *Ventriloqui*, or Persons that speak in their Throats, without moving their Lips, impose upon the Audience. **1762** *Ann. Reg.* I. 143/2 The known faculty many people called *Ventriloqui* have had of uttering strange noises [etc.].

ventriloquy (vɛnˈtrɪləkwɪ). [ad. med. or early mod.L. *ventriloqui-um* (It. *ventriloquio*, Sp., Pg. *ventriloquia*, F. *ventriloquie*), f. L. *ventriloquus*: see prec.]

1. = VENTRILOQUISM (in both senses).

1584 R. SCOT *Discov. Witchcr.* VII. i. (1886) 101 A wench, practising her diabolicall witchcraft and ventriloquie An. 1574. **1642** FULLER *Holy & Prof. St.* II. ix. 83 Some have questioned ventriloquie, when men strangely speak out of their bellies, whether it can be done lawfully or no. *a* **1680** GLANVILL *Sadducismus* II. (1684) 64 For Ventriloquy, or speaking from the bottom of the Belly, 'tis a thing..as strange..as anything in Witchcraft. **1775** in ASH. **1823** *Examiner* 338 His excellent imitations of ventriloquy. **1843** *Penny Cycl.* XXVI. 248/1 The lips and jaws being always somewhat open during ventriloquy, a slight labial movement remains unnoticed. **1889** MACCOLL *Mr. Stranger's Sealed Packet* xxx, You would have put it all down to ventriloquy and imposture.

¶**2.** (See quot.) *Obs.*$^{-0}$

1623 COCKERAM I, *Ventriloquie*, diuination by the inwards of beasts.

ˈventrine, *a. rare*$^{-1}$. [f. L. *ventr-*, *venter* belly + -INE[1].] Of or pertaining to the abdomen.

a **1859** DE QUINCEY *Posth. Wks.* (1891) I. 235 *note*, Prompted by a principle that sank him to the level of the brutes, viz., acquiescing in total ventrine improvidence.

†**ventriˈose**, *a. Obs. rare.* [ad. L. *ventriōs-us*, f. *ventri-*, *venter* belly.] **a.** *Bot.* = VENTRICOSE *a.* 1 a. **b.** 'Gorbellied' (1727 in BAILEY, vol. II).

1707 SLOANE *Jamaica* (1725) II. 60 Pods..having here and there eminences over the peas within, or being ventriose. *Ibid.* 59 Smooth ventriose pods.

ventripotent (vɛnˈtrɪpətənt), *a.* [a. F. *ventripotent* (Rabelais), f. L. *ventri-*, *venter* belly + *potent-*, *potens* powerful, etc.]

1. Having a large abdomen; big-bellied.

1611 COTGR., *Ventripotent*, ventripotent, big-paunch, bellie-able, huge-guts. [Hence in Blount.] **1892** *Harper's Mag.* Sept. 504/2 His mind is obviously not of the finest fibre, nor his massive and ventripotent person either. **1905** FITZMAURICE-KELLY *Cervantes in Eng.* 5 The short, ventripotent rustic [= Sancho Panza].

2. Having great capacity of stomach; gluttonous.

1823 *New Monthly Mag.* VII. 115 These ventripotent melodists called up from the Red Sea of my port and claret all their buried swells, shakes, and cadences. **1837** *Blackw. Mag.* XLII. 425 The ventripotent vermin [*sc.* fleas] were in the midst of their meal. **1863** LD. LENNOX *Biogr. Reminisc.* I. 303 Louis des huîtres, as the ventripotent monarch was called.

Hence **ventripoˈtential** *a. nonce-word*; **venˈtripotence** *rare*.

1824 *New Monthly Mag.* XI. 313 A ventri-potential citizen, into whose Mediterranean mouth good things are perpetually flowing; **1922** Ventripotence [see OVABLASTIC *a.*].

ventro- (ˈvɛntrəʊ), comb. form, on Gr. models, of VENTER[1], occurring in various terms (chiefly *Anat.* and *Surg.*), as **ventro-ˈaxial** *a.*, of or pertaining to the ventral and axial portions of the human trunk; **ventro-ˈdorsal** *a.*, of sections or lines of direction: extending from venter to back; hence **ventro-ˈdorsally** *adv.*; **ventro-ˈinguinal** *a.*, of or pertaining to the abdominal cavity and the inguinal canal; **ventro-ˈlateral** *a.*, of or belonging to the ventral and lateral sides of the body; hence **ventro-ˈlaterally** *adv.*; **ventroˈmedial** *a.*, both ventral and medial; situated towards the median line and the ventral or anterior surface; hence **ventroˈmedially** *adv.*, in a ventromedial direction; **ventro-ˈmesal, -ˈmesial** *adjs.*, of or pertaining to, situated at or on, the ventrimeson; **ˌventronudiˈbranchiate** *a.* [cf. NUDIBRANCHIATE *a.*], characterized by having naked gills depending from the ventral region; **venˈtropodal** *a.* [cf. PODAL *a.*], walking with the venter or breast touching the ground; **ventro-poˈsterior** *a.*, situated on, pertaining to, the under and hinder part of an organ, etc.; **venˈtrotomy**, the operation of opening the abdomen by incision; abdominal section. (Cf. VENTRI-.)

Various other terms, as *ventrocystorraphy*, *-fixation*, *-scopy*, *-suspension*, etc., appear in recent Dicts. or special works.

1902 *Encycl. Brit.* (ed. 10) XXV. 399/1 These muscles may be divided into two series—those of the trunk (*ventroaxial), and those of the limb (appendicular). **1895** *Funk's Stand. Dict.* s.v., *Ventro-dorsal. **1888** *Encycl. Brit.* XXIII. 613/1 When the heart contracts *ventro-dorsally. **1882** WILDER & GAGE *Anat. Technol.* 28 *Ventroinguinal. **1835–6** OWEN in *Todd's Cycl. Anat.* I. 522/1 *Ventro-lateral cartilages of the mantle. **1883** MARTIN & MOALE *Verteb. Dissect.* 141 The ventro-lateral aspect of the trachea. **1888** HOWES & SCOTT *Elem. Biol.* (ed. 2) 95 Slitting open the body-wall *ventro-laterally. **1908** H. E. SANTEE *Anat. Brain & Spinal Cord* vi. 340 Only the *ventro-medial group is present above the sixth cervical segment. **1942** F. A. METTLER *Neuroanatomy* x. 199 Ventromedial to these small cells and encapsulated by them, is a round collection of cells of varying size. **1974** D. & M. WEBSTER *Compar. Vertebr. Morphol.* v. 99 In Crocodilia the girdle is primarily endochondral with a large dorsal scapula and a ventromedial procoracoid. **1984** *Brit. Med. Jrnl.* 25 Aug. 455/1 Patients with hyperthalamic defects—especially in the ventromedial-arcuate region, which has been implicated in GH regulation—may show raised plasma immunoreactive GRF concentrations. **1960** J. D. BOYD in G. H. Bourne *Struct. & Function Muscle* I. iii. 68 These mesenchymal cells migrate *ventromedially round the notochord. **1978** *Nature* 31 Aug. 871/1 The bristles on the wing margin..send similar short, dense projections ventromedially. **1882** WILDER & GAGE *Anat. Technol.* 36 The line..might be called dorso-lateral instead of dorso-sinistral; or it might be called *ventro-mesal. **1872** HUMPHRY *Myology* 8 The *ventro-mesial position and relations of the pelvic bones. *a* **1843** *Encycl. Metrop.* (1845) VII. 289/2 The naked branchial fringes.. indicate the *Infero* or *Ventronudibranchiate Order [of molluscs]. **1898** SHUFELDT in *Ibis* Jan. 48 Audubon..gave them [grebes] both the erect attitudes, as well as, what may be termed, the *ventropodal ones. **1903** *Trans. Amer. Microsc. Soc.* Nov. 62 (*Cent. Suppl.*), The *ventro-posterior limit of the proton. **1887** H. A. REEVES in *Brit. Med. Jrnl.* 12 March 593 There is much need for a single and simple word to express the operation of opening the abdominal cavity, for whatever purpose... I would therefore suggest the use of an etymologically hybrid word, namely, '*ventrotomy'.

venˈtrose, *a. rare*—⁰. [ad. late L. *ventrōs-us*, f. *venter* belly.] (See quot. and VENTRICOSE *a.*)

1859 MAYNE *Expos. Lex.*, *Ventrosus*, having a belly, or swellings like the belly; ventrose.

Hence **venˈtrosity**, corpulence. (1891 in *Cent. Dict.*)

ventr(o)us, -ly, obs. ff. VENTUROUS, -LY.

†**ˈventuous**, *a. Obs.* Also 5 ventuos. [Irreg. f. L. *ventu-s* wind + -OUS.] Windy, flatulent.

Some other instances of the word in the same work (v. lx. and XVII. clxxxvi.) are due to mistranslation of the Latin text.

1398 TREVISA *Barth. De P.R.* XIX. liv. (1495) 895 Rawe hony not well clarefyed is ryght ventuous and bredyth curlynge and swellyng in the wombe.

†**ˈventurable**, *a. Obs. rare.* [f. VENTURE *v.*]

a. Adventurable, attemptable. **b.** Venturous, hazardous.

1576 FLEMING *Panopl. Epist.* 390 That whiche is harde and skarse venturable. **1597** J. PAYNE *Royal Exch.* 34 Whose value and venturable servys..deserveth the favour..of all true subiects.

venture (ˈvɛntjʊə(r), -tʃə(r)), *sb.* Also 5–6 ventur. *β.* 6–7 (9 *dial.*) venter. [Aphetic f. *aventure* ADVENTURE *sb.*: cf. It. and Pg. *ventura*. In some senses perh. from the verb.

The form is no doubt partly due to the initial *a-* of *aventure* having been taken as the indefinite article, esp. after the stressing *a'venture* had become usual. In 15th cent. texts it is probable that occasional instances of *a venture* or *a venter* should be read as one word.]

I. † **1. a.** Fortune, luck; chance. = ADVENTURE *sb.* 1.

a **1450** *Le Morte Arth.* 2811 Launcelot saw ther was no socoure, nedysse muste he hys venture abyde.

†**b.** ***a venture's stroke***, one delivered at a venture; a chance stroke. *Obs.*—¹

c **1450** in *Rel. Ant.* I. 308 Come in with a rake in every a syde, An hole rownde and an halfe, wath so hit betyde, iiij. quarters and a rownd and a ventures stroke wyth.

c. ***at a venture***, at random, by chance, without due consideration or thought; = ADVENTURE *sb.* 3 b.

1509 HAWES *Past. Pleas.* IV. vii, Howe at a venture, and by sodayne chaunce He met with Fame, by fortunes purueyaunce. *c* **1590** *Sir T. More* IV. i. 157 Then, good Inclination, beginne at a venter. **1602** FULBECKE *1st Pt. Parall.* 15 But if the things aforesaid be not..weighed or marked, but be sold at a venture. **1611** BIBLE *1 Kings* xxii. 34 A certaine man drew a bow at a venture. **1696** WHISTON *Th. Earth* II. (1722) 215 'Tis possible that I may several times by guess, or at a venture, hit upon it. **1720** DE FOE *Capt. Singleton* xv. (1840) 256 They should rather fire at a venture. **1780** COWPER *Let.* 2 June, I never in my life began a letter more at a venture than the present. **1841** LANE *Arab. Nts.* (Rtldg.) 77 As I no longer knew where I was, I continued swimming at a venture. **1886** MRS. LYNN LINTON *Paston Carew* xvi, 'And your mother was an Indian,' said Lady Jane, drawing her bow at a venture.

†**2. a.** Danger, jeopardy, hazard, or peril; the chance or risk of incurring harm or loss. *Obs.*

a. **1550** CROWLEY *Last Trumpet* 655 Thy lyfe thou must put in venture For Christes congregation. **1634** SIR T. HERBERT *Trav.* 79 [He pressed] on the Persians, that they desired to come off without more venture, and so..retired home. **1677** YARRANTON *Eng. Improv.* 156 By this way the Seed was put into the Husbandmans hand, and no venture to him. *c* **1705** POPE *Jan. & May* 182 The venture's greater, I presume to say, To give your person, than your goods away. **1823** SCOTT *Quentin D.* xxviii, 'Nevertheless,' said the King, 'it is not our pleasure so to put thee in venture'.

β. **1599** B. JONSON *Cynthia's Rev.* I. iii, One that hath now made the sixth returne upon venter. **1623** T. SCOT *Highw. God* 75 The venter and hazard is the buyers and the sellers, but the certaine gaine fals betwixt both to the usurer. **1640** HABINGTON *Edw. IV*, 90 When she perceived the Lords earnest to have the Prince present in the battle, shee violently opposed. In respect of his youth, want of experience, and the so mighty venter.

†**b.** ***to run the venture of***, to run the risk of.

1722 DE FOE *Col. Jack* (1840) 169 To run the venture of the gallows rather than the venture of starving. **1729** BUTLER *Serm.* Wks. 1874 II. 164 [He] had rather forego his known right than run the venture of doing even a hard thing.

3. a. An act or occasion of trying one's chance or fortune; a course or proceeding the outcome of which is uncertain, but which is attended by the risk of danger or loss; an enterprise, operation, or undertaking of a hazardous or risky nature.

a **1566** R. EDWARDS *Damon & Pithias* E j b, *Gronno.* Wilt thou venter thy life for a man so fondly? *Pithias.* It is no venter, my friende is iust, for whom I desire to die. *a* **1625** FLETCHER *Noble Gent.* IV. i, I'll be your scholar, I cannot lose much by the venture sure. **1665** BOYLE *Occas. Refl.* Ded. Let. A 4 Your Charity..made you so resolute and pressing to have me run a Venture, which you are pleas'd to think but a very Small One. **1686** tr. *Chardin's Trav. Persia* 181 The rest, which they durst not remove, for fear of endangering all at one venture. **1819** SHELLEY *Peter Bell 3rd* VII. xxiii, No bailiff dared..to enter; A man would bear upon his face, For fifteen months,..The yawn of such a venture. **1856** KANE *Arct. Expl.* II. v. 60, I made the desperate venture of sending off my..huntsman..to find the Esquimaux. **1868** FREEMAN *Norm. Conq.* (1877) II. 326 He deemed it better not to make his great venture till he had strengthened his force.

transf. **1871** R. H. HUTTON *Ess.* I. 7 A kind of probationary venture of the will.

†**b.** In the phrases ***to put in*** or ***to a*** (or ***the***) ***venture***, to hazard or risk. *Obs.*

1638 R. BAKER tr. *Balzac's Lett.* (vol. II) 18, I have put my selfe to the venture to goe as far as Gascogny to seek you out. **1639** S. DU VERGER tr. *Camus' Admir. Events* 101 He resolved to put all in a venture. **1642** D. ROGERS *Naaman* 146 How loath would I bee..to have the matter put to a venture. *c* **1670** M. BRUCE *Gd. News in Evil Times*, etc. (1708) 33 This Love of Christ makes us put all to the venture; what loss had thir poor Women that put their All to the venture for him? **1700** S. L. tr. *Fryke's Voy. E. Ind.* 323 As soon as they have paid their Debts, what is left they put to the venture. **1706** PHILLIPS (ed. Kersey), To *Adventure*, to venture, or put to the Venture, to hazard.

†**c.** ***to give the venture***, to make the attempt.

1599 HAKLUYT *Voy.* II. II. 58 That although the people were blacke and naked, yet they were ciuill: so that hee would needs giue the venter without the consent of the rest to go without weapon. **1601** HOLLAND *Pliny* I. 194 Then Patroclus gave the venture. **1652** HEYLIN *Cosmogr.* 28 However I will give the venture, and make as..profitable a discovery, as the times enable me, of the whole World.

d. An adventure or remarkable feat, incident, etc. *rare.*

1810 SCOTT *Lady of L.* III. i, The race of yore, Who..told our marvelling boyhood legends store, Of their strange ventures happ'd by land or sea. **1844** KINGLAKE *Eothen* vi, The ventures of the Greeks are surrounded by such a multitude of imagined dangers, that [etc.].

4. a. An enterprise of a business nature in which there is considerable risk of loss as well as chance of gain; a commercial speculation.

1584–7 GREENE *Carde of Fancie* Wks. (Grosart) IV. 145 Your venter was much, but your gaines such, as..you are like to liue by the losse. **1596** SHAKS. *Merch. V.* III. ii. 270 Hath all his ventures faild, what not one hit? **1605** B. JONSON *Volpone* I. ii, If you died to day, And gaue him all,..What large returne would come of all his venters. **1610** —— *Alch.* II. ii, But I buy it. My venter brings it me. **1660** PEPYS *Diary* 3 Oct., I heard the Duke speak of a great design that he and my Lord of Pembroke have..of sending a venture to some parts of Africa, to dig for gold ore there. **1810** CRABBE *Borough* xvii. 219 Of both he keeps his ledger:—there he reads Of gainful ventures and of godly deeds. **1867** SMILES *Huguenots Eng.* i. 5 [He] agreed to join them in their venture, and supply them with the necessary means. **1884** *Law Rep.* 29 *Chanc. Div.* 465 Inducing other people to spend their money..on such a venture as a limited company.

b. That which is ventured or risked in a commercial enterprise or speculation.

1597 SHAKS. *2 Hen. IV*, II. iv. 69 There's a whole Marchants venture of Burdeux-Stuffe in him. **1598** B. JONSON *Ev. Man out of Hum.* II. iii, He may pricke his foot with a thorne, and be as much as the whole venter is worth. *a* **1764** R. LLOYD *Temple Fav.* Poet. Wks. 1774 II. 135 The consequence has Æsop told, He lost his venture, sheep and gold. **1771** MME. D'ARBLAY *Early Diary* 3 June, As to merchandise, the few ventures he took out with him, he has brought back unchanged. **1814** CANNING in *Croker Papers* (1884) I. 57 It is the ship *Kingsmill*,..destined for the East Indies... She is a venture of 40,000*l*. **1841** STEPHEN *Comm. Laws Eng.* (1874) II. 565 The importer is now enabled to bring his goods into this country, without being obliged to pay the duties until he finds for his venture either a foreign or a home purchaser.

†**5.** Chance or risk *of* something (*Sc.*); also *ellipt.*, chance of being efficacious or beneficial. *Obs.*

1623 LODGE *Poore Mans Talent* Wks. (Hunt. Cl.) IV. 16 Dropp..two or three dropps into your eies. If you could get the liuer of a buck and mix it with these, it would be the better, and the water would haue greater venture. **1637** RUTHERFORD *Lett.* (1862) I. lxxviii. 200 Your Lordship hath now a blessed venture of winning court with the Prince of the Kings of the earth. **1671** M. BRUCE *Gd. News in Evil Times* Pref. (1708) A 2, That it is better for you to come and take your venture of suffering nor bide away.

6. The (or an) act of venturing upon something; an attempt *at* some action; also, the means or result of so venturing.

1842 LOVER *Handy Andy* Preface 6 A few short papers, under the title of this little venture, appeared at intervals in Bentley's Miscellany. **1849** RUSKIN *Sev. Lamps* iv. §3. 96 There are many forms of so called decoration in architecture, habitual, and received,..without any venture at expression of dislike. **1883** MEREDITH *Earth & Man* i, On her great venture, Man, Earth gazes.

7. = ADVENTURE *sb.* 8. *rare.*

1844 KINGLAKE *Eothen* vi, Navigating the seas of their forefathers with the same heroic..spirit of venture. **1872** BLACKIE *Lays Highl.* 26 Who..fled from pomp of Courts.. to win lost souls..with loving venture.

II. †**8.** A prostitute; = VENTURER 3. *Obs.*—¹

1611 SHAKS. *Cymb.* I. vi. 123 Diseas'd ventures That play with all Infirmities for Gold, Which rottennesse can lend Nature.

†**9.** One who or that which ventures *out*. *Obs.*—¹

1702 in *Pennsylv. Hist. Soc. Mem.* IX. 123 The cruisers.. may pick up all ventures out without hazard.

10. a. ***venture-girl, -miss***, a girl or woman who goes to India in order to get a husband (both now *Hist.*).

1825 T. HOOK *Sayings* Ser. II. *Passion & Princ.* iii. II. 287 It was a rule in the carnal bazar of Bengal for Venture-Misses to take the first man who proposed. **1836** —— *G. Gurney* III. 107 Mrs. Nubley was a venture girl from England.

b. Special Comb.: **venture capital** = *risk capital* s.v. RISK *sb.* 3; hence **venture capitalist**; **Venture Scout**, a male or (since 1976) female member of that section of the Scout Association for those between 16 and 20 years of age (cf. *rover scout* s.v. ROVER[1] 3 d); hence **Venture Scouting**.

1943 M. A. SHATTUCK in *Addresses at Membership Forum* (Nat. Assoc. Investment Companies) 22 Industry during the last decade has not only lacked venture capital for new enterprises; it has also lacked venture capital for established concerns. **1971** *Financial Mail* (Johannesburg) 26 Feb. 681/1 These are some of the..successes which have brought just about every major US institution into the venture capital arena. *Ibid.* 681/2 Some venture capitalists insist on a majority equity stake. **1981** *Sci. Digest* Aug. 118/1 Venture capital, the money that bankrolls people with an innovative product, dried up in 1969. **1966** Venture scout [see ROVER[1]

3 d]. 1978 *Broadcast* 27 Mar. 20/3 With many young men of 20 Venture Scouts..'Boy' Scout is hardly an accurate description for a large part of our membership. 1982 *Scouting* Sept. 582/1 This is the year the Venture Scout Section celebrates its fifteenth birthday. *Ibid.* 582/2 (*caption*) Female Venture Scouts have played an important part in the Section since 1976. 1967 *Venture Scouting* (Scout Assoc.) xv. 168 Venture Scouting is not always cheap; it isn't easy to get the right kind of gear. 1983 *Times* 23 Aug. 2/5 Venture Scouting has increased from a membership of 30,000 in 1979 to more than 36,000 this year... Girls..make up about 20 per cent of overall numbers.

venture ('vɛntjʊə(r), -tʃə(r)), *v.* Forms: α. 5–7 **venter** (6 **ventre**). β. 6 **ventur** (*Sc.* **ventour**), 6– **venture**. [Aphetic f. *aventure* ADVENTURE *v.* Cf. prec.]

I. 1. *trans.* To risk the loss of (something); to expose to the chance of loss or injury, esp. in the hope of obtaining some advantage or gain; to hazard, risk, or stake.

Freq. const. with preps., as *for*, *in*, *on*, or *upon*.

α. *c* 1430 LYDG. *Min. Poems* (Percy Soc.) 109 Alle ys for your love, madame, my lyfe wold I venter, So that ye wylle graunt me, I have desyryd many a wynter. 1560 DAUS tr. *Sleidane's Comm.* 260 Som of the religion and league of the Protestauntes..wil venter their lives & spend their blud in this war. 1596 SHAKS. *1 Hen. IV*, v. i. 101 And Prince of Wales, so dare we venter thee, Albeit, considerations infinite Do make against it. 1628 WITHER *Brit. Rememb.* II. 1992 There many thousands are Of Townes and Cities..Who would conceive it were unjustly done, That he should venter all their wealth in One. 1645 in Ellis *Orig. Lett.* Ser I. III. 306 Hee that venters his life for the libertye of his countrie [etc.]. 1689 POPPLE tr. *Locke's 1st Let. Toleration* L.'s Wks. 1727 II. 418 We are persuaded to venter our eternal Happiness on that Belief.

β. 1575 GASCOIGNE *Flowers* Wks. 1907 I. 77 He..lyke a venturer..Determined for to venture me and all his worldly pelfe. 1580 in Heath *Grocers' Comp.* (1869) 75 *note*, A girdle ventured by Brothers of the Company in the Lottery. 1634 W. WOOD *New Eng. Prosp.* I. i, Many of his Majesties faithfull Subjects have beene imboldned to venture persons, states, and indeavors. 1665 PEPYS *Diary* 27 Dec., I will not venture my family by encreasing it, before it is safe. 1690 LOCKE *Hum. Und.* II. xxi. §66 It is a very wrong and irrational way of proceeding, to venture a greater Good for a less. 1701 W. WOTTON *Hist. Rome* 486 Mamaea, who durst not venture her son thro her overmuch Fondness. 1779 JOHNSON *L.P.*, *Pope* Wks. IV. 46 Pope was seized with the universal passion, and ventured some of his money. 1802 MAR. EDGEWORTH *Moral T.* (1816) I. xi. 89 Few people chose to venture a hundred guineas upon the turn of a straw. *c* 1853 KINGSLEY *Misc.* (1859) I. 34 His whole fortune is ventured in an expedition over which he has no control. 1885–94 R. BRIDGES *Eros & Psyche* April xix, What hour the happy bride Ventures for love her maiden innocence.

b. Const. *to* with inf.

1583 MELBANCKE *Philotimus* O ij b, I rather would to shield mine honour, & preuent his shame,..so venter life & limme. 1584 COGAN *Haven Health* cxxvi. (1636) 137 Many men rashly will venter their credit, yea, and sometimes their lives too, to steale Venison. 1647 R. STAPYLTON *Juvenal* 76 As D. Junius Brutus ventured his [life], to free Rome of Tarquin. 1667 PEPYS *Diary* 4 April, Himself and three more would venture their carcasses upon it to pay all the King's debts in three years. 1706 STEVENS *Sp. Dict.* s.v. *Rico*, *O rico, o pinjado*, Either rich, or hang'd, when a Man ventures his Neck to get Wealth. 1748 *Anson's Voy.* I. ii. 17 The Commodore did not care to venture the ships long boats to fetch the water off. 1860 MOTLEY *Netherl.* ii. (1868) I. 59 To further this end, many leading personages in France avowed ..their determination to venture their lives and their fortunes.

c. In proverbial use, esp. in the phrase ***nought*** (or ***nothing***) ***venture, nought*** (or ***nothing***) ***have***.

1546 J. HEYWOOD *Prov.* (1867) 31 Nought venter nought have. 1553 EDEN *Treat. New Ind.* (Arb.) 42 Nought venter nought haue, is a saying of old. 1604 [? CHETTLE] *Wit of Woman* C4b, And she that will not venter her egges shall neuer haue chickens. 1668 SEDLEY *Mulberry Gard.* III. ii, Who ever caught any thing with a naked hook? Nothing venture, nothing win. 1777 BOSWELL in *Life Johnson* (1904) II. 145, I am, however, generally for trying, 'Nothing venture, nothing have'. 1885 *Cent. Mag.* XXIX. 186 'Nothing venture, nothing have,' Betty replied saucily.

†**d.** ***to venture a joint***, to take some risk. *Obs.*

1573–80 TUSSER *Husb.* (1878) 173 To trust without heede is to venter a ioint. 1590 GREENE *Never too late* (1600) 17 The poore woman..promised to venture a ioynt, but shee would further him.

2. *refl.* To risk (oneself); to dare to go. Now *arch.*

Const. with preps., as *in*, *on*, *upon*, *with*, or adverbs of place, as *abroad*, *thither*.

1572 *Satir. Poems Reform.* xxxviii. 80 For better it is to fecht it,..With speir men and weir men, and ventour our sellis. 1597 DELONEY *Gentle Craft* (1912) 169 Lo thus her selfe she ventred, And streight her streets we entred. 1642 D. ROGERS *Naaman* 21 Yet so venture thyselfe as a forlorne wretch upon the Lord. 1676 *Doctrine of Devils* 92 For who being of the Demonologists opinion..will..so much as venture himself in a sound Boat? 1705 ADDISON *Italy*, etc. 518 We were advis'd by our Merchants, by no means to venture our selves in the Duke of Bavaria's Country. 1735 JOHNSON *Lobo's Abyssinia*, *Descr.* xi. 108 When I was to Cross this River at Boad, I durst not venture myself on the Flotes. 1746 HERVEY *Medit.* (1818) 153 One so..delicate in her constitution, that she dares not venture herself abroad in the open air. 1777 SHERIDAN *Trip Scarb.* IV. i, Dare you venture yourself alone with me? 1825 SCOTT *Talism.* xxiii, Was it not through thy conversation..that I ventured me thither in disguise.

3. To take the risk of sending, or causing to go, where loss or detriment is possible. Now *rare.*

1599 SHAKS. *Hen. V*, I. ii. 192 Others like Merchants venter Trade abroad. 1611 in *10th Rep. Hist. MSS. Comm.* App. I. 552, I have thought good to venture these with yᵉ Frenche poste by yᵉ way of Lyons. 1617 MORYSON *Itin.* II. 82 The streame..he found so exceeding swift, that it was like to be dangerous to venture our horses ouer. 1686 tr. *Chardin's Trav. Persia* 173 No body would venture their Goods into Mingrelia. 1707 DOBSON in Hearne *Collect.* (O.H.S.) II. 83, I can't think any Gentlemen will venture their Sons here. 1718 LADY M. W. MONTAGU *Let. C'tess Mar* 10 Mar., Which induces me to venture this letter to your house at London. 1734 in *Swift's Lett.* (1768) IV. 77 As I would not venture my character abroad in the world without the advice of those who have succeeded in it. 1780 COWPER *Progr. Err.* 520 Like something precious ventur'd far from shore, 'Tis valued for the danger's sake the more. 1814 SCOTT *Diary* 19 Aug. in *Lockhart*, Our own log-boat being too heavy and far too valuable to be ventured upon this Cocytus.

b. To risk entrusting (a thing) *with* a person, or letting go *out of* one's hands.

1618 FLETCHER *Chances* III. i, Now could I willingly.. Venture my Body with thee. 1666 BUNYAN *Grace Abound.* §329 But yet..I must venture you all with God, though it goeth to the quick to leave you. 1726 SWIFT *Gulliver* I. ii, I apprehended they might be lost or spoiled, if I ventured them out of my possession.

II. 4. To run or take the risk of (something dangerous or harmful); to brave the dangers of (ice, water, etc.).

Passing into sense 5, and now *rare.*

1548 COOPER *Elyot's Dict.* s.v. *Coeo*, *Societatem periculi coire*, to venture the..daunger of a thing with an other. 1582 STANYHURST *Æneis* II. (Arb.) 67, I was determined fully, too ventur al hazards, Al Troy too trauerse, too suffer danger al hapning. *a* 1604 HANMER *Chron. Ireland* (1633) 156 Such as would not venter the water, were slaine by the English. 1604 SHAKS. *Oth.* IV. iii. 77 Why, who would not make her husband a Cuckold, to make him a Monarch? I should venture Purgatory for't. 1675 *Hatton Corr.* (Camden) 120 That they had rather venter hanging than starving. 1707 FREIND *Peterborow's Cond. Spain* 38 They were unwilling to venture the disorders that might have happened to their Army. 1741 LADY HARTFORD *Corr.* (1805) III. 3 Eighty-one of them ventured his resentment. *a* 1774 GOLDSM. tr. *Scarron's Com. Romance* (1775) I. 213 They could hardly believe his relation that I threw him into the water, and ventured my own drowning to procure his. 1853 KANE *Grinnell Exp.* xl. (1856) 362 The temptations of the flesh were too much for me: I ventured the ice.

b. To risk allowing (a person) *to* do something.

1710 ADDISON *Spect.* No. 21 ¶8 A Man would be well enough pleased to buy Silks of one, whom he would not venture to feel his Pulse.

c. To risk trusting or confiding in (a person).

1777 SHERIDAN *Trip Scarb.* IV. i, Well, this once I'll venture you. But if you disparage me——. 1817 JAS. MILL *Brit. India* II. IV. ii. 92 His Sepoys deserted for want of pay, and he durst not venture them in sallies.

5. To dare, or have the courage, to attempt or undertake (some action); to risk the issue or result of; to venture upon (see 9b).

1595 SHAKS. *John* IV. iii. 5 The Wall is high, and yet I will leape downe... I am afraide, and yet Ile venture it. 1598 GRENEWEY *Tacitus, Ann.* II. xv. (1622) 54 Catualda.. ventured a reuenge. 1633 T. STAFFORD *Pac. Hib.* I. viii. 62 O Conner did undertake that the Connaught men should not..take our parts, being the only encouragement of the English, to venter this Enterprize. 1650 MILTON *Eikon.* (ed. 2) Pref. A3, It shall be ventur'd yet, and the truth not smother'd, but sent abroad. 1742 C. MIDDLETON *Cicero* III. xi. 230 For we neither think it safe to venture a battel, nor [etc.]. 1774 GOLDSM. *Nat. Hist.* VII. 257 It hunts about to find out the web of another spider,..with whom it ventures a battle. 1815 SCOTT *Guy M.* l, Miss Bertram accompanied her friend..without venturing a second glance at the object of her terror. 1858 FROUDE *Hist. Eng.* IV. xviii. 71 The garrison did not wait to make closer acquaintance with men who would venture such an enterprise. 1879 —— *Cæsar* xxii. 384 No more opposition was ventured by the Greek cities.

b. To dare to give, put forth, or express (an opinion, statement, etc.); to make or utter tentatively, or with some degree of presumption.

1638 R. BAKER tr. *Balzac's Lett.* (vol. II) 101 A prudence that is so..scrupulous, that feares to venture a word for a vertuous friend. 1828 LYTTON *Pelham* II. xxvi, I..ventured a sly joke at the good effects of matrimony. 1849 EASTWICK *Dry Leaves* 64 Those who had not the shadow of a ground for venturing any statement at all. 1906 MARJ. BOWEN *Viper of Milan* viii, 'They say in Milan Lady Valentine is to marry the Duke of Orleans,' Tomaso ventured presently.

†**c.** With *abroad*: To risk publishing (an article, etc.). *Obs.*

1674 BOYLE *Excell. Theology* Pref. 3 The Philosophical papers I have hitherto ventured abroad. 1709 CHANDLER *Eff. agst. Bigotry* Ded. A2b, When I first ventur'd it abroad in the World, I expected the Fate that usually attends such as attempt to part a Fray, even to be box'd on both Ears.

III. 6. *intr.* To risk oneself; to brave the risks or chances of a journey, voyage, etc.; to dare to go or proceed. Const. with preps. and advs.

1534 in *Star Chamb. Cases* (Selden) II. 292 Your marchantes..venteryng to Iseland for Fysshe. 1550 CROWLEY *Last Trumpet* 1033 If thou venter into straunge landes, And bringe home thynges profitable. 1587 *Mirr. Mag.*, *Sabrina* xxii, For love to ayde her, venter in would I. 1624 CAPT. SMITH *Virginia* III. 66 Into the great vast deep to venter out. 1676 *Doctrine of Devils* 92 For who being of the Demonologists Opinion..will dare to venture to either of the Indies. *a* 1727 NEWTON *Chronol. Amended* (1728) 111 The first men who left the Sea-coasts, and ventured out into the deep. 1797 S. & HT. LEE *Canterb. T.* I. 328, I thought not of venturing near this spot till dark. 1823 F. CLISSOLD *Ascent Mt. Blanc* 21 It being half past six, it was considered too late now to venture to the summit. 1832 W. IRVING *Alhambra* II. 239 Venturing on, she came at last to a great hall. 1856 KANE *Arct. Expl.* II. iii. 46 With a good stock of fresh meat..I can venture away from the vessel to draw supplies from the Esquimaux.

fig. 1610 DONNE *Pseudo-Martyr* 133 Olde Monkes were vsed heretofore to be but Coasters,..further then the Contemplation of Heauen..guided them, they did not easily venter. 1633 MASSINGER *Guardian* III. i, I affect A handsome mistress..and on good terms, Will venture as far i' the fire, so she be willing To entertain me. 1877 FROUDE *Short Stud.* (1883) IV. I. ix. 104 The archbishop had not ventured so far to be frightened at the first hard word. 1898 'H. S. MERRIMAN' *Roden's Corner* xvi, She knew that in love he was the incarnation of caution, and would only venture so far as she encouraged him to come.

7. To run or take risks; to incur the chance of danger, peril, loss, disapproval, etc.

1560 DAUS tr. *Sleidane's Comm.* 64 And where as you may preuayle more by other meanes, why wyll you venter with so great daunger? 1589 GREENE *Menaphon* (Arb.) 53 It is the token of a high minde to venter for a Queene. 1621 LADY M. WROTH *Urania* 503 Three Gentle-women were then sent forth to seeke a Knight that would venter in her defence. 1657 T. JORDAN *Walks Islington* v. ii, As I live here's Sir R. Lamard that broke the prison; how the devil dares he venter? 1725 WATTS *Logic* II. v. §4 Where the improbabilities of success or advantage are greater than the probabilities, it is not prudence to act or venture. 1820 BYRON *Mar. Fal.* I. ii. 539 You have deeply ventured; But all must do so who would greatly win. 1895 H. H. FURNESS *Mids. N. Dream* Pref. p. xxi, In emending Shakespeare's text..those who know the most, venture the least.

b. To be boldly speculative. *rare*⁻¹.

1559 AYLMER *Harborowe* E4, It is a wonder, that men vnskilled in the diuersities of times, and historis, dare thus ventre in so great matters.

c. To take part in, invest in, a financial venture or speculation. *rare*⁻¹.

c 1620 in *Eng. Hist. Rev.* Jan. (1915) 20 The Lottery shall be presently removed..with speciall care of the Governors that the poor be not suffered to venture.

8. With inf.: To dare, presume, go so far as, be so bold as (*to* do something).

Common from *c* 1610; in later use frequently in weakened sense (cf. next).

1559 AYLMER *Harborowe* E4, A Quene in Illiria, who durst venture to withstand the Romains. 1589 *Pasquil's Ret.* Db, The holie Patriarche..neuer venturde to alienate the possessions of Idolatrous Priestes. 1609 ROWLEY *Search for Money* (Percy Soc.) 11 Biskets, which..nere a souldier there durst venter to breake. 1656 COWLEY *Pindar. Odes*, *New Year* iv, Upon the Brink..We should stand shivering, and but slowly venter The Fatal Flood to enter. 1699 BURNET *39 Art.* xviii. 173 Instead of stretching the severity of Justice.. we may rather venter to stretch the Mercy of God. 1725 DE FOE *Voy. round World* (1840) 252 He would at any time venture to send his two sons into the mountains. 1774 BURKE *Sp. Amer. Tax.* Wks. II. 355 Why do you venture to repeal the duties upon glass, paper, and painters colours? 1840 THIRLWALL *Greece* lv. VII. 71 Archias..did not even venture to cross over to the Arabian side of the Persian Gulph. 1849 MACAULAY *Hist. Eng.* v. I. 617 Thirty times the fugitives ventured to look through the outer hedge: but everywhere they found a sentinel on the alert. 1887 BOWEN *Virg. Ecl.* VIII. 102 Over thy shoulders fling them, nor venture behind thee to look!

b. Used with reference to the expression of opinions, etc.

1610 HOLLAND *Camden's Brit.* I. 354 Some of these..were by a new English Saxons name called Wiccij: but whereupon, I dare scarse venture to guesse. 1660 BOYLE *New Exp. Phys.-Mech.* xviii. 134, I should not undertake to answer so difficult a question, and should venter to say no more. *a* 1687 PETTY *Pol. Arith.* (1690) 95, I humbly venture to say, all these things may be done. *a* 1774 TUCKER *Lt. Nat.* IV. III. 203 If you observe those people who pretend to be fullest of doubts you will find them most fond of that positive phrase, I will venture to say. 1803 *Med. Jrnl.* X. 297, I now ventured to pronounce, that what I took for a bilious fever was in reality the influenza. 1850 GROVE *Corr. Phys. Forces* (ed. 2) 98 The view which I would venture to suggest is, that such vibrations are themselves electricity or magnetism. 1875 JOWETT *Plato* (ed. 2) V. 244 The sound of the voice which reaches and educates the soul, we have ventured to term music.

9. ***to venture on*** or ***upon***: †**a.** To make trial of (a person or animal); to dare to advance upon, approach, or attack. *Obs.*

? *c* 1520 *Everyman* 484 in Pollard *Eng. Mir. Plays* (1890) 87 Yet will I venter on her now. My Good Dedes, where be you? 1591 SYLVESTER *Du Bartas* I. vi, The sly Rhinocerot: Who..doth venter Upon his Foe. 1592 SHAKS. *Ven. & Ad.* 628 Being irefull, on the lyon, he [the boar] will venter [*rime* enter]. 1631 A. WILSON *The Swisser* II. iii, I'le venture on the Beauty. (He kisses her.)

b. To attempt or undertake (something of a dangerous or difficult nature) without assurance of success; to accept or take the risk of (an action, course, or proceeding); to dare to do, make, or take (something), realizing that a risk is being run. †Also with *of*.

1557 CHEKE *Let. to Hoby* in Hoby *Courtyer* (1561) Zzv, If the old denisoned wordes could..ease this neede we wold not boldly venture of vnknowen wordes. 1560 DAUS tr. *Sleidane's Comm.* 282 There is no daunger so great, that they wyl refuse to venter vpon for his preseruation. 1609 B. JONSON *Sil. Wom.* I. ii, Can he endure no noise and will venter on a wife? 1652 H. L'ESTRANGE *Amer. no Jewes* 7 To venter upon such another voyage as Noah's. 1711 ADDISON *Spect.* No. 121 ¶1 They never venture upon the Fruit of any Tree,..unless they observe that it is marked with the Pecking of Birds. 1755 YOUNG *Centaur* i. Wks. (1757) IV. 123, I venture on it out of what I conceive to be charity, greater still! 1781 COWPER *Charity* 6 A task I venture on, impell'd by thee. 1863 KINGLAKE *Crimea* I. 296 Not only could they have no semblance of a public meeting, but they could not even venture upon the slightest approach to.. lesser gatherings. 1876 'L. CARROLL' *Hunting Snark* II. xviii,

The third is his slowness in taking a jest, Should you happen to venture on one.

10. *to venture at*, to make a venture or attempt at; to guess at.

1613 SHAKS. *Hen. VIII*, II. i. 156 [It is] held for certaine The King will venture at it. **1653** MORE *Antid. Ath.* II. xii. §17 To view the asperities of the Moon through a Dioptrick-Glass and venture at the Proportion of her Hills by their shadows. **1671** R. BOHUN *Wind* 85 Wee might likewise venture at a better account. *c* **1710** CELIA FIENNES *Diary* (1888) 158 They cannot venture at that sort of tillage. **1736** AINSWORTH I. s.v., Mankind will venture at any thing. **1823** J. SIMPSON *Ricardo the Outlaw* I. 24 She debated for a few minutes, which door she should venture at. **1863** COWDEN CLARKE *Shaks. Char.* xx. 508 The only time he.. ventures at a reason for what he says.

Hence **'ventured** *ppl. a.*

1623 MASSINGER *Dk. Milan* II. i, Is this.. The fair return of both our ventured favours! *c* **1625** BRADFORD *Plymouth Plant.* (Massach. Hist. Soc.) III. 201 The catle were yᵉ best goods, for yᵉ other, being ventured ware, were neither at yᵉ best,.. nor at yᵉ best prises. **1892** J. B. MAYOR *Ep. James*, Author p. xxiv, His mother.. did nevertheless.. draw upon herself his reproof for ventured interference.

†**'ventureling.** *Obs.*$^{-1}$ In 6 venterlyng. [f. VENTURE *sb.* or *v.*] A young or petty adventurer.

1562 BULLEIN *Bulwarke, Dial. Sorenes & Chir.* 27 b, It is not to be marueiled, that soche venterlynges and younglinges, stomble so ofte at a strawe.

'venturer. Also 6 venterer, -our. [f. VENTURE *v.* Cf. ADVENTURER and It. *venturiere.*]

1. One who ventures, in various senses; an adventurer.

1530 PALSGR. 284/2 Venturer on the lande, *aduenturier. Ibid.*, Venturer on the see, *piratte.* **1538** TONSTALL *Serm. Palm Sund.* (1823) 67 To make this realme a praye to al venturers, al spoylers,.. all rauenours of the worlde. *a* **1560** PHAER *Æneid* x. (1562) G gij b, Fortune is frend to venturers, and cowards hateth most. *a* **1631** DONNE *Poems* (1635) 274 No family Ere rigg'd a soule.. With whom more Venturers more boldly dare Venture their states. **1654** WHITLOCK *Zootomia* Pref. a 6, Lastly for Detraction and Censure.. it is more my scorn than feare, and ought to be to any Venturer abroad into publike view. **1727** in BAILEY (vol. II). **1841** DICKENS *Barn. Rudge* xxviii, A visit to the gaming-table—not as a heated, anxious venturer, but [etc.]. **1863** KINGLAKE *Crimea* I. 447 The next night Prince Louis Bonaparte and his fellow venturers destroyed the French republic. **1872** O. W. HOLMES *Poet. Breakf.-t.* vii, No Arctic venturer on the waveless sea Feels the dread stillness [etc.].

fig. **1624** DONNE *Serm.* (1649) II. xlix. 463 Was God a venturer with me in my sinne?

transf. **1821** CLARE *Vill. Minstr.* II. 201 Airy leaves of woodbine.. Are earliest venturers to unfold their buds.

†**b.** (See quot.) *Obs.*$^{-1}$

1599 HAKLUYT *Voy.* II. I. 129 The venturers with the sword were 60. thousand in number [*marg., Gli Venturieri da spada*, are a kind of venturing souldiers, who commonly are wont to folow the army in hope of the spoile.].

2. One who undertakes or shares in a commercial or trading venture, esp. by sending goods or ships beyond seas; a merchant-venturer.

1557 RECORDE *Whetst.* a ij, The gouerners, Consulles, and the reste of the companie of venturers into Moscouia. **1593** R. HARVEY *Philad.* 3 What traffique should a venturer haue [etc.]. **1621–3** MIDDLETON & ROWLEY *Changeling* I. i, I meant to be a venturer in this voyage. **1632** MASSINGER *City Madam* I. iii, You were.. the main venturer In every ship that launched forth. **1661** WEBSTER *Cure for Cuckold* III. iii, This beginning May make us of small venturers to become Hereafter wealthy merchants. **1844** KINGLAKE *Eothen* vi. 88 The great Capitalist whose imperial sway is more withering than despotism itself, to the enterprises of humble venturers.

†**3.** A strumpet or prostitute. Cf. VENTURE *sb.* 8. *Obs.*$^{-1}$

1607 DEKKER & WEBSTER *Westw. Hoe* II. ii, *Mist. Just.* Had thy Circæan Magick me transformd.. that I were turn'd common Venturer, I could not loue this old man.

†**'ventureship.** *Obs.*$^{-1}$ In 6 venter-. [f. VENTURE *sb.*] Venturousness.

1583 GOLDING *Calvin on Deut.* cxxx. 801 For there must bee no ventershippe in this behalf.

'venturesome, *a.* Also 7, 9 *dial.*, venter-. [f. VENTURE *sb.* or *v.* + -SOME.]

1. Of persons: Disposed or ready to venture or take risks; bold, daring; = VENTUROUS *a.* 1.

1677 GILPIN *Demonol.* I. xviii. 155 Even as courage whetted on and enraged, makes a Man ventersome beyond the due bounds of prudence, or safety. **1698** HEARNE *Duct. Hist.* (1714) I. 134 Does he not make his Hero more Rash than Wise, and more Venturesome than Ambitious? **1798** EDGEWORTH *Pract. Educ.* (1811) II. 395 We should even in trifles avoid every circumstance which can tend to make girls venturesome. **1863** KINGLAKE *Crimea* I. 214 He was most venturesome in his schemes for action. **1886** C. E. PASCOE *Lond. of To-day* xxix. (ed. 3) 262 Some persons.. are sufficiently venturesome to visit Billingsgate when at the high-tide of business.

2. Of the nature of, characterized by, or involving risk; hazardous, risky.

1661 in *Phœnix* (1721) I. 84 These two last Opinions of the Father, which seem the most bold and venturesome of all the rest. **1721** STRYPE *Eccl. Mem.* I. iii. 391 It must ever redound unto the honour of his memory, that bold and venturesome act of his. **1755** JOHNSON, *Hazardable*, venturesome; liable to chance. **1849** DANA *Geol.* ix. (1850) 451 From the sunny plain above, the streamlet made the venturesome descent. **1885** *Public Opin.* 9 Jan. 28/2 General Stewart has returned safely from his venturesome ride across the desert.

Hence **'venturesomely** *adv.*, **'venturesomeness.**

1727 BAILEY (vol. II), **Venturesomly*, daringly. **1882** *Sat. Rev.* LIV. 597 To a butterfly also, may we venturesomely compare this strange.. tome of weird verse. **1883** *Evang. Mag.* Aug. 343 The rocks toasted almost enough to blister the hand that should venturesomely touch them. **1727** BAILEY (vol. II), *Fool Hardiness*, Rashness, Temerity, a Thoughtless *Venturesomness. **1740** RICHARDSON *Pamela* I. 236 She seem'd full of Wonder at my Resolution and Venturesomeness. **1869** *Routledge's Ev. Boy's Ann.* 16 Did ever one hear of such venturesomeness? **1876** GEO. ELIOT *Dan. Der.* III. xxiv, A handsome girl, whose lively venturesomeness of talk has the effect of wit.

Venturi (vɛn'tjʊərɪ). Also **venturi**. The name of G. B. *Venturi* (1746–1822), Italian physicist, used: **a.** *attrib.* to designate a short constriction in a tube between two longer tapered portions that are usu. of unequal length but terminate with the same diameter, so that there is a drop in pressure in a fluid flowing through the constriction which may be used to determine the rate of flow or used as a source of suction; also devices having this form and the effect involved.

1887 C. HERSCHEL in *Trans. Amer. Soc. Civil Engineers* XVII. 231 Bourdon's anemometer is founded upon the property of a Venturi tube to exercise a sucking action. *Ibid.* 232 Then came the Bourdon anemometer.. and now the instrument herein described, the Venturi Water Meter. *Ibid.* 239 The actual operations of the Venturi meter as applied to a water-pipe in ordinary service. **1894** W. K. BURTON *Water Supply of Towns* 285 The 'Venturi tube', which has long been used as a means of roughly estimating the velocity of air-currents, has recently been used as a water-meter. **1917** *Jrnl. Agric. Res.* IX. 115 Preliminary experiments on a new type of device, called the 'Venturi flume', for measuring water in open channels. **1930** *Engineering* 24 Jan. 97/1 Each branch has a Venturi section for measurement of flow. **1931** *Handbk. Aeronautics* (R. Aeronaut. Soc.) viii. 515 Venturi anemometer heads use a venturi for producing a suction in order to increase the pressure difference obtainable with a pitot static tube. **1937** *Times* 4 Oct. 23/4 Provision against freezing and against blocking by ice and snow must be made in carburettors, venturi tubes, and the vents of fuel and oil tanks in new passenger aircaft. **1951** *Industr. & Engin. Chem.* June 1325/1 Deposition of a spray on the walls must be considered in the design and operation of several types of industrial equipment, including Venturi scrubbers and atomizers, combustion chambers in which liquid fuels are burned, and spray dryers. **1971** J. W. IRELAND *Mechanics of Fluids* ix. 340 A venturi-flume is to be installed in a channel conveying water with the object of raising the level of the water upstream. **1973** *Times* 12 Feb. (Anchor Project Suppl.) p. ii/6 Collection of exhaust gases from the BOS vessels will be by the OG suppressed combustion system, and their cleaning by a two-stage venturi scrubber system. **1974** *Sci. Amer.* Feb. 100/3 The venturi effect in the narrow spaces between buildings can increase the velocity of the wind. **1977** *Lancet* 24 Sept. 641/1 We describe a method of pooling the contents of several packs by means of a simple vacuum box worked from an ordinary water tap and a Venturi pump.

b. *absol.*

1887 C. HERSCHEL in *Trans. Amer. Soc. Civil Engineers* XVII. 239 The water was passing through the Venturi with similar velocities. **1921** *Sci. Amer.* 15 Oct. 275/1 An idea of the shape of the venturi becomes obvious by comparing it with an old-fashioned blunderbuss. **1942** G. CASEY in Murdoch & Drake-Brockman *Austral. Short Stories* (1951) 361 Venturis down below [in a mine] and water everywhere to keep the dust down. **1952** *Archit. Rev.* CXI. 138/2 A drip-proof high efficiency burner with fixed venturi, providing flame stability at low consumptions. **1976** K. THACKERAY *Crownbird* ii. 36 The wind played strange tricks, the entrance acting as a venturi with gusts swirling in great spirals.

†**venturine.** *Obs.* [ad. It., Sp., or Pg. *venturina*, = F. *aventurine* AVENTURINE.]

1. (See quots.)

The sense is not recorded for the Continental word, and may be due to some misunderstanding.

1704 *Dict. Rust.* (1726) s.v. *Japan*, That it [*sc.* varnish] may not dry before the Venturine or Gold-Wire reduced to powder is sifted on it. *Ibid.*, *Venturine* or *Aventurine*, is the most delicate and slender sort of Gold-wire, us'd by Embroiderers, &c. **1799** G. SMITH *Laboratory* II. 441 As for the black and venturine, you must first lay a coat of varnish on the wood [etc.].

2. *venturine-stone*: (see quot. and cf. AVENTURINE 1).

1775 ASH, *Venturinestone*, a kind of transparent stone brought from Italy powdered with a kind of gold dust.

'venturing, *vbl. sb.* [f. VENTURE *v.*]

1. The action of the vb.; *spec.* engagement or participation in a commercial venture or enterprise.

1548 *Admiralty Crt.* 17 Dec. Exam. 35 Having the licence of the Lorde Protectors Grace to goe a venturing [*i.e.* having a letter of marque]. **1562** J. HEYWOOD *Prov. & Epigr.* (1867) 139 Ventryng of much, May haue a lyttle. **1595** [? J. C.] *Alcilia* xlviii. (Grosart) 27 Much good successe men misse for lack of ventring. **1631** in *10th Rep. Hist. MSS. Comm.* App. V. 476 Theire daylie losses sustained in the ventring of theire goods by sea. *a* **1695** MARQ. OF HALIFAX *Wks.* (1912) 245 Wise Venturing is the most commendable Part of human Prudence. **1706** STEPHENS *Sp. Dict.* I, *Arriesgamiento*, hazarding or venturing.

†**2.** *venturing pin*, a disposition to use, or the habit of employing, the phrase 'I venture to say'. (Cf. PIN *sb.*[1] 15.) *Obs.*

1671 EACHARD *Obs. Answ. Cont. Clergy* 23 Thus far I durst venture to say, (seeing that we are yet upon the Venturing-Pin) that [etc.]. **1680** *Refl. Late Libel Curse-ye-Meroz* 5, I know him by the same old, insipid, phlegmatic-style, the same old Supposals, Dilemma's, and venturing-pins.

'venturing, *ppl. a.* Now *rare.* [f. as prec.] Of a person: That ventures; engaged or engaging in a venture; venturous.

15.. *Vox populi vox Dei* 288 in *E.P.P.* (Hazlitt) III. 278 For of one C ye have not ten, That now be marchantes ventring men. **1599** [see VENTURER 1 b]. **1616** J. LANE *Contn. Sqr.'s T.* VII. 536 Enginers, stronge laborers and ventringe pioners. **1747** HOOSON *Miner's Dict.* S iv b, In the High and Low Peaks, where ventureing Miners get but small Quantitys of Booss.

†**b.** Of an expression: Bold, daring. *Obs.*$^{-1}$

1652 N. CULVERWEL *Lt. Nature* xi. (1661) 79 The Stoicks.. have indeed some doting, and venturing Expressions.

Hence **'venturingly** *adv.*

1884 FAWCETT *Rutherford* i, 'They were very nice people..', Rutherford proceeded, somewhat venturingly. **1893** *Sunday Mag.* July 465/1 He bent down and touched the child's cheeks venturingly with a hard, horny finger-tip.

venturous ('vɛntjʊərəs, 'vɛntʃərəs), *a.* Also *β.* 6–7 venterous. *γ.* 6 ventrus, 6–7 ventrous, 6–8 vent'rous. [Aphetic f. of ADVENTUROUS *a.* after VENTURE *sb.* and *v.*]

1. Of persons, etc.: Disposed to venture upon or undertake something of a dangerous or risky nature; willing to take risks or incur danger; bold, daring, or enterprising in action or opinion; adventurous, venturesome. Also const. *at*, *in*, *of*, or with *to* and inf.

α. **1576** FLEMING *Panopl. Epist.* ¶ iii b, I waxed venturous, and like a confident fellowe amended my pase. **1581** PETTIE tr. *Guazzo's Civ. Conv.* II. (1586) 63 b, I count those, which wil vndertake to speake of euerie matter, rather venturous than learned. **1675** tr. *Camden's Hist. Eliz.* III. (ed. 3) 328 Skenk a Frieslander and Sir Roger Williams a Welshman, two venturous men. **1694** KETTLEWELL *Comp. Penitent* 21 A most presumptuously venturous and daring Sinner. **1719** DE FOE *Crusoe* I. (Globe) 110 But I had no need to be venturous; for I had no Want of Food. **1800** WORDSW. *Brothers* 275 Every corner Among these rocks, and every hollow place That venturous foot could reach. **1831** SCOTT *Ct. Rob.* ii, I know I am but too apt to be venturous in action. **1853** C. BRONTE *Villette* xi, The directress was very prudent, but she could also be very venturous.

β. **1578** T. N. tr. *Conq. W. India* Pref. p. ii, It is nowe approoved by the venterous travellour.. Martin Frobisher. **1579** LYLY *Euphues* (Arb.) 94 Thou art not.. more venterous to challenge the combatte, then I valiant to aunswere the quarrell. **1601** HOLLAND *Pliny* II. 156 Some bold and venterous Empiricke, who made great boast of his deepe skill. **1629** H. BURTON *Truth's Tri.* 101 Taking vpon him (as he is very venterous) to answer an argument. *a* **1660** *Contemp. Hist. Irel.* (Ir. Archæol. Soc.) I. 256 The noble and venterous sparke, Phelim mc Tuhill Oneylle.

γ. **1596** NASHE *Saffron Walden* 71 His ventrous manhood and valure. **1601** WEEVER *Mirr. Mart.* C v b, All the Armie, ventrous, valorous, bold. **1642** D. ROGERS *Naaman* 249 Let a besieger of a City be too ventrous, and what perill ensueth. **1667** MILTON *P.L.* II. 205 Those who at the Spear are bold And vent'rous. **1725** POPE *Odyss.* III. 89 Savage Pirates seek thro' seas unknown The lives of others, vent'rous of their own. **1747** FRANCIS tr. *Horace, Odes* (ed. 2) I. xxxi. 16 The golden Goblet let Him drain, Who vent'rous plows th' Atlantic Main.

b. *absol.* with *the.*

1583 MELBANCKE *Philotimus* Ff ij, And nowe shalt thou trie it, that fortune most vsually fauoures the venterous. **1589** NASHE *Anat. Absurd.* Wks. (Grosart) I. 35 The acts of the ventrous, and the praise of the vertuous.

c. Of things.

1565 COOPER *Thesaurus*, *Abies audax*, a venterous shippe. **1598** SYLVESTER *Du Bartas* II. i. Eden 27 But (sacred Pilot) thou canst safely steer My vent'rous Pinnasse to her wished Peer. **1634** BP. REYNOLDS *Shieldes of Earth* (1636) 41 Remember a Shield is a venturous weapon, a kind of suretie, which.. receives the injuries which were intended to another. **1676** SHADWELL *Virtuoso* I. i, Those venturous blossoms, whose over-hasty obedience to the early spring does anticipate the proper season. **1705** WATTS in *Sotheby's Sale Cat.* 30 July (1902) 49 Accept of this first labor of the press, this ventrous Essay of Poesie in so Nice and censorious an Age. **1764** GOLDSM. *Trav.* 187 He.. drives his venturous plough-share to the steep. **1804** CHARLOTTE SMITH *Conversations*, etc. I. 151 The first bud whose venturous head The Winter's lingering tempest braves. **1862** CALVERLEY *Verses & Transl.* (ed. 2) 28 He who erst with venturous thumb Drew from its pie-y lair the solitary plum.

2. Of the nature of a venture; marked or characterized by, attended with, involving, hazard or risk; hazardous, risky.

1570 FOXE *A. & M.* (ed. 2) I. 114/1 Desperation,.. which is wont in ventrous affaires to do much. **1598** BARRET *Theor. Warres* III. ii. 75 It is venturous to set ones fortune vpon the brunt of one sole battell. **1670** EACHARD *Cont. Clergy* 22 The meer venturous and inconsiderate determining of youths to the profession of learning. **1709** PRIOR *Carm. Sec.* 75 Bloody Wreaths in vent'rous Battels won. **1783** CRABBE *Village* I. 117 The tost vessel.. Which to their coast directs its vent'rous way. **1840** F. D. BENNETT *Whaling Voy.* II. 186 Now but few seas are entirely free from the visits of ships occupied in this venturous service. **1862** *Jrnl. R. Agric. Soc.* XXIII. 277 Twenty years ago the manufacture and sale of artificial manures partook more of the character of a venturous speculation.

b. Marked by, full of, adventures.

1813 SCOTT *Rokeby* III. ii, And well his venturous life had proved The lessons that his childhood loved.

3. Arising from, indicative of, a readiness to encounter hazard or risk; bold, daring.

1584 *Mirr. Mag.* Epist., If their forfeats were wel knowen, I fere, thei do acts as ventrus. **1587** Turberv. *Trag. Tales* 74 b, I thinke him such a one as dares Such ventrous parts to play. **1622** Bacon *Henry VII*, 51 Meane men, who would make it their Master-piece of Credite and Fauour, to giue Venturous Counsels. *a* **1661** Fuller *Worthies* iii. (1662) 43 He was..knighted by the King for his venturous Activity. **1711** Shaftesb. *Charac.* (1737) II. iii. 346 Bear with my ventrous and bold Approach. **1818** Scott *Hrt. Midl.* xxvii, There was something of romance in Jeanie's venturous resolution. **1856** Mrs. Browning *Aur. Leigh* viii. 349, I scarce marvel much you took it for a venturous piece of spite. **1877** Bryant *Sella* 21 Her clear, calm eye Was bright with venturous spirit.

b. Of opinions, etc.: Daringly bold or original; going further than the evidence or facts appear to warrant.

1608 Willet *Hexapla Exod.* 571 Contrarie then to this orthodoxall doctrine of the Fathers..are these ventrous and bold positions. **1644** Milton *Areop.* (Arb.) 57 One sentence of a ventrous edge, utter'd in the height of zeal. **1681** Baxter *Apol. Nonconf. Min.* 5 Men's uncertain and venturous reports. **1830** W. Taylor *Hist. Surv. Germ. Poetry* I. 333 Lessing..was distinguished by the venturous originality of his opinions. **1837** J. H. Newman *Proph. Office Church, &c.* 138 Nothing is gained to the intellect; rather, something is lost by this venturous claim.

'venturously, *adv.* Also 6 venter-, 6–7 ventrously, 8 vent'rously. [f. prec. + -ly².] In a venturous manner; boldly, daringly.

α. *a* **1533** Ld. Berners *Huon* xvi. 42 Than venturously they releuyd them. **1591** Horsey *Trav.* (Hakluyt Soc.) 199, I stode emonge the rest venturously. **1603** Holland *Plutarch's Mor.* 476 To make shifts and expose themselves venturously into any danger. **1651** Fuller *Perkins* in *Abel Redivivus* 435 A difficult taske no lesse valiantly performed than venturously undertaken. **1701** Norris *Ideal World* i. v. 324 They..determine venturously upon the first views. **1814** Scott *Wav.* i, I have venturously essayed to read a chapter to the public.

Comb. **1629** Hobbes *Thucydides* 104 You ought not to bee lesse venturously minded against the enemie.

β, γ. *c* **1555** Harpsfield *Divorce Hen. VIII* (Camden) 150 He sticketh not venterously to avouch that it was not lawful. **1573** Twyne *Æneid* Ded. A ij, I haue enterprised more ventrously then wisely..to end that which he left vnperfect. **1650** Bulwer *Anthropomet.* 170 This agitation of mind..makes the Soule more boldly and ventrously to reflect upon it self. *a* **1656** Hales *Gold. Rem.* (1673) i. 85, I have often wondred with my self, how men durst die so ventrously, except they were sure they died well. *a* **1701** Sedley *Ven. & Ad.* Wks. (1766) 251 He vent'rously again the chace pursues.

'venturousness. [f. as prec.] The character or state of being venturous; boldness, daring, venturesomeness.

1583 Golding *Calvin on Deut.* cxxxvii. 842 Although men ..through their venturousenesse and their rashnes, make a confusion of all thinges, and enterprise whatsoeuer their lust fancieth. **1642** D. Rogers *Naaman* 40 Checking and taming them from old ventrousnesse, and saucinesse against God. **1663** Boyle *Usef. Exp. Nat. Philos.* ii. i. 11 Though his relation may be credited, his venturousness ought not to be imitated. **1727** Bailey (vol. II), *Venturousness*,..Boldness, Daringness, Hardiness. **1828** Webster s.v., The event made them repent of their venturousness. **1902** A. T. Innes in A. B. Davidson *Called of God* 46 The faith which they demand always goes out..with an objective venturousness or heroism.

ventuse, variant of ventose *v. Obs.*

venue ('vɛnjuː). Forms: 4 venov, venev, veneu, 5 venyw, 6–8 venew, 6–7 venewe; 6 venu, fenue, 6– venue. See also veny². [a. OF. *venue* coming, vbl. sb. from *venir* to come.]

I. †1. A coming on, in order to strike; an assault or attack. *Obs. rare.*

a **1330** *Roland & V.* 845 And at anoþer venov, Roland smot vernagu, þat he fel doun to grounde. **13..** *Sir Beues* (A.) 811 Beues in þat ilche venev,..Wiþ is swerd out a slinte Twei toskes at þe ferste dent. **13..** *Coer de L.* 1074 The lyon made a gret venu, And wolde have him al to-rent.

†2. a. A thrust or hit in fencing; a stroke or wound with a weapon. *Obs.* Cf. veny² 1.

1591 Percivall *Sp. Dict.*, *Treta*, a fenue at defence, *tactus*. **1600** Holland *Livy* 513 Divers of the guard let flie at Indigemines, who by this time was readie to oppose himselfe, and to ward all venues. *c* **1605** Harington in *Month. Rev.* (1770) 53 Like a perfect fencer that will tell aforehand in which button he will give the venew. **1652–62** Heylin *Cosmogr.* iii. (1682) 146 He valiantly charged upon the Rebel, and at the second venew slew him.

b. *fig.* and in fig. context.

1588 Shaks. *L.L.L.* v. i. 62 A sweet tutch, a quicke venewe of wit, snip, snap, quick & home. **1590** Nashe *Pasquil's Apol.* i. C ij, The second venue the Welch-man hath bestowed vpon vs, is a wipe ouer the shinnes of the Non Residents. **1622** Mabbe tr. *Aleman's Guzman d'Alf.* ii. 195 Shee had no more any Nunnerie to shelter, but lay open to the venues of Fortune. *a* **1640** Massinger, etc. *Old Law* iii. ii, I've breath enough at all times, Lucifer's musk-cod, To give your perfumed worship three venues.

†3. A bout or turn of fencing. Also *fig. Obs.*

1598 B. Jonson *Ev. Man in Hum.* i. v, *Mat.* But one venue, sir. *Bob.* Venue! Fie: Most grosse denomination, as euer I heard. **1615** Heywood *Foure Prentises* i. ii, Into the Fencing-schoole, To play a venew with some friend. **1640** Shirley *Love's Cruelty* ii. i, Faces about, good Master Fencer!..You and I will try a venue below. **1659** Fuller *App. Injured Innoc.* (1840) 357 If the Animadvertor hath a mind to..have a venue with him to try whose skill is most and weapon best. [**1820** Scott *Monast.* xxi, Let us pause for the space of one venue, until I give you my opinion on this dependence.]

II. †4. a. The action of coming; arrival. *Obs.*⁻¹

? *a* **1400** *Arthur* 307 Eche of þese vyve at her venyw Brouȝt zyx þousand at har retenyw.

†b. *concr.* That which has come; an importation *of* something. *Obs.*⁻¹

a **1483** *Liber Niger* in *Househ. Ord.* (1790) 74 To kepe the first venues of wynes in vesselles or shippes..from any sale.

5. a. *Law.* The county, district, or locality where an action is laid; the place where a jury is summoned to come for the trial of a case. Freq. in the phrase ***to lay*** (also ***fix*** or ***place***) ***the venue***.

1531 *Star Chamb. Cases* (Selden) II. 190 The venewe most nedes be of Stevenage aforsed. *Ibid.* 194 The layng of the venew or issue at Stevenege..to have an indefferent Jury. **1543–4** *Act 35 Hen. VIII*, c. 6 §3 Within the saide hundred where the venewe lieth. **1641** *Termes de la Ley* 260 *Venew* or *Visne* is a terme used..often in our bookes, and signifies a place next to that where any thing that comes to be tryed is supposed to bee done. And therefore..some of the Jury must be of the same hundred, or sometimes of the same parish in which the thing is supposed to be done. **1664–5** *Act 16–17 Charles II*, c. 8 §1 The Plaintiffe might have demurred and shewen the same for Cause, nor for want of the Averment..or for that there is noe right Venue. **1728** Chambers *Cycl.* s.v., Thus we say, Twelve of the Assize ought to be of the same Venew where the Demand is made. **1796** J. Anstey *Pleader's Guide* i. i. (1826) 5 For Bards and Lawyers, both, with ease, May place the *Venue* where they please. **1826** Syd. Smith *Lett. Electors Cath. Quest.* Wks. 1859 II. 227/1 The *venue* of several crimes imputed to the prisoner is laid in countries to which the jurisdiction of this court does not extend. **1838** Meeson & Welsby *Reports* II. 23 The Attorney-General may lay the venue where he pleases. **1883** S. C. Hall *Retrospect* I. 350 The plaintiff laid the venue in Warwickshire.

b. In the phrases ***to change the venue*** or (*a*) ***change of venue***.

1768 Blackstone *Comm.* III. 294 If the defendant will make affidavit, that the cause of action, if any, arose not in that but another county, the court will direct a change of the *venue*, or *visne*. **1796** J. Anstey *Pleader's Guide* To Rdr., Partly owing to..the changing of the Venue in the Trial. **1817** W. Selwyn *Law Nisi Prius* (ed. 4) II. 984 Where the writing and publication are confined to the same county.. the venue may be changed into such county. **1881** *Macm. Mag.* XLIV. 134 If we often change a venue because a fair jury cannot be had, why should we not go further to insure justice? **1893** *Times* 3 June 13/4 The dropping of such obvious and effective weapons as secret inquiry and change of venue.

c. The scene of a real or supposed action or event; also *fig.*, a position taken up by a disputant.

a **1843** Southey *Doctor* clxxxviii. (1848) 496 When I was young there was no tradition of any such thing in the town where the venue of the action is laid. **1845** Ford *Handbk. Spain* i. 46 Sterne would have done better to have laid the venue of his sentimentalities over a dead ass in Spain rather than in France. **1861** Sala *Dutch Pict.* 269 A something far more..vexatious..changes the *venue* to a kingdom of realities. **1873** Spencer *Stud. Sociol.* ii. 38 Here Mr. Froude changes the venue and joins issue on the old battle ground.

d. An appointed place of meeting, esp. for a match or competition.

1857 G. Lawrence *Guy Liv.* iv, A steeple-chase in which both Universities were to take part... The venue was fixed at B. **1884** *Truth* 13 March 369/2 It showed a great want of judgment..to select the former town as the venue for the semi-final tie. **1901** *Scotsman* 12 March 5/4 The question of the venue of the annual meeting: at present this was held on one of four greens.

e. *Theatr.* The site of a theatrical performance, *spec.* one used by touring companies.

1967 *Stage* 2 Mar. 21/4 (Advt.), Clubland Promotions urgently require first-class artists..for venues in South and West Wales. **1980** *Times* 25 Nov. 6/4 Cologne Opera and San Francisco Ballet have both inspected the theatre and are considering it as a venue. **1984** *Times* 8 Mar. 4/2 The largest computerized box office system in Britain, which will link every main venue in the city. Instant ticket printing means that venues can put on performances at short notice.

venued, obs. variant of vinowed *ppl. a.*

venuing, obs. form of vinowing *vbl. sb.*

'venular, *a. rare*⁻¹. [f. next + -ar.] Marked with veins; veined.

1811 Pinkerton *Petral.* I. 387 The marble statues.. present the following colours; milk-white, the same with venular silver-white mica,..and yellowish white.

venule ('vɛnjuːl). [ad. L. *vēnula*, dim. of *vēna* vein *sb.* Cf. F. *veinule* and veinulet.] A small or minor vein.

a. *Bot.* **1850** Ogilvie, *Venules*,..the name given to the last ramifications of the veins of a leaf, which intermingle frequently, and form the skeleton. **1857** T. Moore *Handbk. Brit. Ferns* (ed. 3) 8 The branches of the veins are *venules*, and the branches of the venules are *veinlets*. **1866** J. Smith *Ferns Brit. & For.* (1879) 101 Venules arcuately or angularly anastomosing, producing two or more excurrent free veinlets.

b. *Anat.* *a* **1852** Macgillivray *Nat. Hist. Dee Side* (1855) 171 The minute glandular bodies are all situated on the venules, and are of a circular form. **1876** *Trans. Clinical Soc.* IX. 91 The white cells accumulate in the small venules in surprising numbers. **1899** *Allbutt's Syst. Med.* VIII. 826 The venules on the skin of the nose and cheeks of old people.

'venulite. *rare*⁻⁰. [Irreg. f. Venu-s¹ + -lite.] (See quot. and Venus¹ 10.)

1828–32 Webster, *Venulite*, a petrified shell of the genus Venus.

venu'lose, *a. Bot.* [f. venule + -ose.] (See quot.)

1857 A. Gray *First Less. Bot.* (1866) 236 *Venulose*, furnished with veinlets.

venum(ous, obs. forms of venom(ous.

†venundate, *v. Obs.*⁻⁰ [f. L. *vēnun-dat-*, ppl. stem of *vēnun-dare*, var. (by assimilation) of *vēnum-dare* to sell, vend.] (See quots.) Hence **†venundation.** *Obs.*⁻⁰

1623 Cockeram i, *Venundate*, to sell. *Venundation*, a selling and buying. [Also in Phillips (1658).] **1656** Blount *Glossogr.*, *Venundate*, to buy and sell.

Venus¹ ('viːnəs). Pl. Venuses (7, 9 Veneres). Also 5–6 *Sc.* **Wenus.** [L. *Venus* (gen. *Veneris*).]

I. 1. a. *Mythol.* The ancient Roman goddess of beauty and love (esp. sensual love), or the corresponding Greek goddess Aphrodite.

a **1000** *Sal. & Sat.* (Kemble) 124 Ðone syxtan dæȝ hi ȝesetton ðære sceamleasan gydenan Uenus ȝehaten, and Frycg on Denisc. **1297** R. Glouc. *Chron.* (Rolls) 2433 After him [Jupiter] we honoureþ venus mest, þat frie ycluped is. *c* **1330** R. Brunne *Chron. Wace* (Rolls) 604 So faire ladies ar none lyuand; Bot me þynkes of ȝow þre Dame Venus semes fairest to be. **1390** Gower *Conf.* II. 84 The Coper set is to Venus, And to his part Mercurius. **1412–20** Lydg. *Chron. Troy* ii. 3443 In honour only of Venus, þe goddes, Whom þe Grekis with al her besynes Honoured most of euery maner age. **1490** Caxton *Eneydos* xiv. 50 Certes, Venus, thou and thy sone Cupydo are gretely to be praysed. **1508** Dunbar *Gold. Targe* 21 The birdis sang..With curiouse note, as Venus chapell clerkis. **1590** Marlowe *2nd Pt. Tamburl.* iv. ii, Thou shalt..Sit like to Venus in her chaire of state, Commanding all thy princely eie desires. **1687** Dryden *Hind & P.* iii. 1064 As if this troublesome intruding Guest Would drive the Birds of Venus [= doves] from their Nest. **1781** Cowper *Conversat.* 824 Certain feasts..Where Venus hears the lover's tender vow. **1835** Thirlwall *Greece* I. 141 The temple of Venus at Eryx, which was most probably founded by Phœnicians. **1875** *Encycl. Brit.* II. 172/2 The native Roman goddess Venus, as distinguished from the Venus who through contact with the Greeks was afterwards identified with Aphrodite.

b. In allusive use: (cf. sense 2).

c **1412** Hoccleve *De Reg. Princ.* 3890 Þere wole he outen his langage, And do to Bachus and Venus homage. *c* **1508** *C. Blowbol's Test.* 62 in Hazlitt *E.P.P.* I. 94 He gaf me many a good certacion..That he had laboured in Venus secret celle. **1693** tr. *Blancard's Phys. Dict.* (ed. 2) s.v. *Maslach*, Sometimes they take Three Drams, without any prejudice, especially when they are about to Fight the Battels of Mars or Venus. *a* **1796** Burns *Lines Windows Globe Tavern, Dumfries*, In wars at hame I'll spend my blood, Life-giving wars of Venus. **1809** Malkin *Gil Blas* iv. vii. ¶8 He could not stomach those beauties who call a spade a spade. Such were not for his market; the rites of Venus must be consummated in the temple of Vesta.

c. A representation, esp. a statue or image, of Venus.

a **1568** Ascham *Scholem.* ii. Wks. (1904) 301 Cæsar..is like the halfe face of a Venus, the other part of the head beyng hidden, the bodie and the rest of the members vnbegon. **1601** Holland *Pliny* II. 566 But of all the images that ever were made,..his [*sc.* Praxiteles] Venus passeth, which hee wrought for them of Gnidos. *a* **1700** Evelyn *Diary* 23 May 1645, 'Twixt the pictures two *naked Venus's* by Titian. *Ibid.*, A Venus of marble, veiled from the middle to the feete. **1722** Richardson *Statues etc. in Italy* 134 There is a Venus which stands just by This which is Irreproachable. **1834** *Penny Cycl.* II. 157/2 Many representations of the goddess [Aphrodite]..are extant: among these, the celebrated statue, called the Venus de' Medici, is that with which we are most familiarized. **1850** Thackeray *Pendennis* lii, The wig-box beside the Venus upon the middle shelf of the book-case.

d. A local or other distinct conception of the goddess; also *transf.*, a goddess in other mythologies corresponding to Venus.

1770 Percy tr. *Mallet's Northern Antiq.* I. 94 This Frea became in the sequel..the Venus of the north, doubtless because she passed for the principle of all fecundity. **1828** Duppa *Trav. Italy*, etc. 136 He also shewed us a little bronze statue of a Venus. **1877** W. R. Cooper *Egypt. Obelisks* vii. (1878) 30 Under the special protection of Hathor, the Egyptian Venus.

e. *Archæol.* A palæolithic female figurine distinguished by exaggerated breasts, belly, and buttocks. Cf. steatopyga.

1912 R. Munro *Palæolithic Man* x. 239 Laugerie Basse has supplied a fragment of bone with a pregnant woman and reindeer engraved on it..; the Venus..a headless statuette carved in ivory. **1920** H. C. Bailey *Call Mr. Fortune* 191 'My new palæolithic Venus.' 'You left her in the library... There are not many men..who have a Hottentot Venus to lose.' **1937** Auden & MacNeice *Lett. from Iceland* xvii. 245 We leave to that poor soul A. M. Ludovici the Venus of Willendorf. **1958** *Times Lit. Suppl.* 11 Apr. 198/4 One archaeologist's interpretation of palaeolithic figurines or 'Venuses' as 'the characteristic products of unregenerated male imagination'. **1979** Mills & Mansfield *Genuine Article* ii. 34 The Venus figurine[s]..date from around 25,000 to 22,000 B.C.... One of the most celebrated is the 'Venus of Willendorf' from Austria.

†2. The desire for sexual intercourse; indulgence of sexual desire; lust, venery. *Obs.*

1513 Douglas *Æneid* iv. Prol. 97 Childir to engener ois Venus, and nocht in vane. **1573** L. Lloyd *Marrow of Hist.* (1653) 253 Sardanapalus..was alwaies werid but never satisfied with Venus. **1620** Venner *Via Recta* iii. 61 It yeeldeth very good nourishment, which..encreaseth seede, and exciteth Venus. **1697** Dryden *Virg. Georg.* iv. 289 What's more strange, their modest Appetites, Averse from Venus, fly the Nuptial Rites. **1746** Francis tr. *Horace, Epist.* i. xviii. 43 If Venus be his darling Vice. **1746** —— *Sat.* i. iv. 148 An honest Venus will indulge your Flame.

†**3. a.** A quality or characteristic that excites love; a charm, grace, or attractive feature. *Obs.*

1540 PALSGR. *Acolastus* L iv b, Here dwell Venusis and graces of al kynd. **1607** MIDDLETON *Five Gallants* I. i, A pretie, fat eyde wench, with a Venus in her cheeke. **1621** BURTON *Anat. Mel.* I. ii. IV. vi, All the Graces, Veneres, pleasures, elegances attend him. **1647** R. STAPYLTON *Juvenal* 236 Know'st not how many Venuses appear In others gold? **1711** SHAFTESB. *Charac.* (1737) I. 138 Every-one is a virtuoso, of a higher or lower degree: every-one pursues a Grace, and courts a Venus of one kind or another. *Ibid.* 337 If he knows not this Venus, these Graces [etc.].

†**b.** Beauty; charm. *Obs. rare.*

1657 G. THORNLEY *Daphnis & Chloe* 181 The Garden;.. the place now made a waste;.. all the Venus of the place was gone. **1711** SHAFTESB. *Charac.* (1737) I. 337 To discover, amidst the many false manners and ill stiles, the true and natural one, which represents the real beauty and Venus of the kind. *Ibid.*, 'Tis the like moral Grace, and Venus, which ..is copy'd by the writing artist.

4. A beautiful or attractive woman.

a **1579** T. HACKET tr. *Amadis of Fr.* VIII. 188 (Stf.), One day ye reputed me for a Venus, that rested .. in your heart. **1675** J. SMITH *Chr. Relig. App.* III. 8 The great Beauty of the Land, an Helen, a Venus. **1706–7** FARQUHAR *Beaux Strat.* IV. ii, Had my Spark call'd me a Venus directly, I shou'd have believ'd him a Footman in good earnest. *a* **1814** *Woman's Will* II. i. in *New Brit. Theatre* IV. 62 Witness the Hottentot Venus before she has strung on her beads. **1816** TUCKEY *Narr. Exped. R. Zaire* i. (1818) 18 The dreams they had indulged in of the sable Venuses which they were to find on the banks of the Congo. *a* **1841** T. HOOK *Ned Musgrave* i, The evening on which he first saw this Venus of the village.

II. 5. *Astr.* The second planet in order of distance from the sun, revolving in an orbit between those of Mercury and the earth; the morning or evening star.

c **1290** *S. Eng. Leg.* I. 311 Sethþe þe sonne is, Venus sethþe, þe clere steorre. **1297** R. GLOUC. *Chron.* (Rolls) 4704 To tueye sterren, þat me sucþ ylome, Venus & Mercurius, hii wenep þat hii bicome. *c* **1374** CHAUCER *Troylus* v. 1016 The bryght venus folwede and ay taughte The wey, ther brode Phebus down alighte. *c* **1400** *Treat. Astron.* 8 b (MS. Bodl. B. 17), The secunde owre of þe same day is the owre of þe planet Venus. *c* **1480** HENRYSON *Test. Cres.* 11 Fair Venus, the bewtie of the nicht, Uprais. **1590** SHAKS. *Mids. N.* III. ii. 107 Let her shine as gloriously As the Venus of the sky. **1664** BUTLER *Hud.* II. iii. 530 Venus you retriv'd, In opposition with Mars, And no benigne friendly Stars T' allay th' effect. **1727–46** THOMSON *Summer* 1695 Sudden to heaven Thence weary vision turns; where .. with purestray Sweet Venus shines. **1771** *Encycl. Brit.* I. 436/2 When Venus appears west of the sun, she rises before him in the morning, and is called the morning-star; when she appears east of the sun, she shines in the evening after he sets, and is then called the evening-star. **1842** FRANCIS *Dict. Arts* s.v., Venus changes her phases like those of the moon, according to her position, relative to the earth and sun. **1868** LOCKYER *Guillemin's Heavens* (ed. 3) 81 Thus the solid ground of Venus is uneven, like that of Mercury and the Earth.

†**6.** *Alch.* Copper. (In quot. 1797 allusively.)

c **1386** CHAUCER *Can. Yeom. Prol. & T.* 276 Sol gold is,.. and Jubiter is tyn, And Venus coper, by my fader kyn. **1594** PLAT *Jewell-ho.* I. 20 The Alcumists giue a blauncher vnto Venus with the salt of Tartar. **1610** B. JONSON *Alch.* II. i, The great med'cine! Of which one part proiected on a hundred Of Mercurie, or Venus, or the Moone, Shall turne it to as many of the Sunne. **1728** CHAMBERS *Cycl.* s.v. *Copper*, The Chymists call it *Venus*; as supposing it to have some more immediate Relation to that Planet. **1758** [see JUPITER 2 b]. **1797** W. JOHNSTON tr. *Beckmann's Invent.* I. 398 One may justly doubt whether, at present, Mars, Venus, or Saturn, is most destructive to the human race.

†**b.** So in ***crystals, saffron, salt, vinegar, vitriol of Venus*** (see quots.). *Obs.*

1693 *Phil. Trans.* XVII. 901 This very elaborate method of procuring the Salt of Venus. **1704** J. HARRIS *Lex. Techn.* I, *Vitriol of Copper* or *Venus* is Blue Chrystals made by a Solution of Copper in Spirit of Nitre, Evaporation, and Chrystallization in a cool place. **1728** CHAMBERS *Cycl.* s.v. *Copper*, The Calx of Brass, called .. sometimes .. Saffron of Venus, is nothing but Copper calcin'd in a violent Fire. **1797** *Encycl. Brit.* (ed. 3) XVI. 623 The acetous salt of copper, called crystals of Venus, or of verdigris, by the chemists. **1807** T. THOMSON *Chem.* (ed. 3) II. 259 When acetate of copper, reduced to powder, is put into a retort and distilled, there comes over a liquid .. and afterwards a highly concentrated acid... The acid .. was formerly distinguished by the names of radical vinegar and vinegar of Venus.

†**7.** *Her.* A name for the tincture green or vert when the names of planets are used in blazonry.

[**1562** LEGH *Armory* 16, I pray you what planet belongeth to this colour [*sc.* vert]? Venus.] **1572** BOSSEWELL *Armorie* II. 78 b, The fielde is parted per Fesse Dented, Venus, and Saturne, five brasauntes. **1680** SIR G. MACKENZIE *Her.* 18–19. **1704** J. HARRIS *Lex. Techn.* I, *Vert*, the Heralds Word for a Green Colour;.. in Coats of Nobles, 'tis called Emerauld; and in those of Kings 'tis called Venus.

8. The highest or most favourable cast or throw in playing with huckle-bones.

1611 COTGR. s.v., The play at huckle-bones, wherein he that turnes vp Venus (figured on one side of the bone) doth winne; whereas he that turnes vp the dog, doth lose. *c* **1650** in *MS. Ashmole 788* fol. 162 The game of Astragalls... When all yᵉ fower boanes shal shew seuerall sides this is the most fortunate cast & is called Midas or Venus take all Cock-all. **1737** OZELL *Rabelais* III. p. xvi, Venus was the best Cast, three Sices. [**1876** BROWNING *At the 'Mermaid'* xv, Well may you blaspheme at fortune! I 'threw Venus' (Ben, expound!).]

9. ***girdle, mound, mount, ring of Venus***, in palmistry (see quots.); also ***mount of Venus***, in anatomy (see quot. 1728).

Cf. *Venus girdle* (1653) in 12 below.

1695 CONGREVE *Love for L.* II. iii, She has .. a moist Palm, and an open Liberality on the Mount of Venus. **1728** CHAMBERS *Cycl.* s.v., Mount of Venus, *Mons Veneris*, among Anatomists, is a little hairy Protuberance, in the middle of the *Pubes* of Women. *Ibid.*, Among Chiromancers, the Mount of Venus is a little Eminence in the Palm of the Hand, at the Root of one of the Fingers. **1865** BEAMISH *Psychon. Hand* 31 The line of Saturn, the ring of Venus, and the line of Apollo. **1894** PAUL BELLO *Palmistry* 21 The Girdle of Venus is a line describing a semicircle, extending from between the Mounts of Jupiter and Saturn to the Mount of Mercury. This girdle is generally absent. **1900** INA OXENFORD *Mod. Palmistry* 22 The Mount of Venus encircles the root of the thumb, and is bounded more or less by the Life-line.

10. *Zool.* A genus of bivalve molluscs typically representing the family *Veneridæ*; a member of this genus or family; a venerid. Cf. CLAM *sb.*² 1 d.

1770 PENNANT *Brit. Zool.* (1777) IV. [p. xiv], Commercial Venus [and various other species]. *Ibid.* 93. **1802–3** tr. *Pallas's Trav.* (1812) II. 293 A ribbed Venus, rounded at one extremity. **1857** GOSSE *Omphalos* viii. 228 That lilac-tinted Prickly Venus (*Dione Veneris*). **1880** BASTIAN *Brain* 75 The Razor-fish, Cockle, Venus, and other bivalves possessing .. 'siphon-tubes'.

β. pl. **1770** PENNANT *Brit. Zool.* (1777) IV. 89 *Tellina rugosa*... Dredged up at Weymouth. Misplaced among the Venuses. **1822** J. PARKINSON *Outl. Oryctol.* 257 That these supposed fresh-water shells are sometimes found scattered among a multitude of acknowledged sea shells, as, Oysters, Venus's, &c. **1843** *Penny Cycl.* XXVI. 209/2 In the Veneres the animal, furnished with longer siphons, is provided with a retractor muscle.

III. *attrib.* and *Comb.*

11. a. Simple attrib. (also possessive without *'s*), as ***Venus bower, court, knot***, † ***mole***, † ***star, throw***, etc.

c **1550** ROLLAND *Crt. Venus* I. 90 In *Venus Bowr to eik baith game and glew. **1513** DOUGLAS *Æneid* IV. Prol. 159 Lat ws in riot leif, in sport and gam, In *Venus court. **1579** LYLY *Euphues* (Arb.) 108 If [she is] one of Venus court, they haue vowed dishonestye. **1590** SHAKS. *Mids. N.* I. i. 171, I sweare to thee,.. By the simplicitie of *Venus Doues. **1876** T. HARDY *Ethelberta* (1877) 35 Her hair fastened in a sort of *Venus knot behind. **1620** *Swetnam Arraigned* (1880) 45 By Art they know .. how to adde A *Venus mole on euery wanton cheeke. **1596** SHAKS. *Merch. V.* II. vi. 5 O ten times faster *Venus Pidgions flye To steale loues bonds new made. **1902** *Edinb. Rev.* Oct. 321 Helen, by reason of the *Venus-spell,.. loves Paris. **1591** SPENSER *Daphn.* 483 And night without a *Venus starre is found. **1611** FLORIO, *Venere*,.. the day or morning star, called Lucifer or Venus star. *a* **1593** MARLOWE & NASHE *Dido* 39 *Venus swannes shall shed their siluer downe, To sweeten out the slumbers of thy bed. **1879** LEWIS & SHORT *Lat. Dict.*, *Venereus*, the *Venus-throw at dice.

b. In sense 2, as ***Venus act, exercise, life, play, work***, etc.

c **1400** *Destr. Troy* 753 Þai solast hom samyn .. With venus werkes, þat hom well pleasid. **1508** DUNBAR *Tua Mariit Wemen* 399 He that wantes riches, And valȝeandnes in Venus play, is ful vile haldin. **1513** DOUGLAS *Æneid* IV. Prol. 187 With Venus henvifis quhat wyse may I flite? *a* **1578** LINDESAY (Pitscottie) *Chron. Scot.* (S.T.S.) I. 158 That licherie and wenus lyfe hes oft tymes a euill end. **1611** FLORIO, *Venereo*,.. given to Venus-sports, or letchery. **1617** MORYSON *Itin.* II. 166 Most of them when they were stripped, were seene to have scarres of Venus warfare. **1623** COCKERAM I, *Venus-escuage*, wanton fleshlinesse. *Ibid.* III, *Barnacle*, a kinde of Sea Gull, it growes not by Venus act, but as Dubartas writes [etc.]. **1634** SIR T. HERBERT *Trav.* 151 Opium .. makes them strong and long in Venus exercises. **1658** ROWLAND tr. *Moufet's Theat. Ins.* 1004 Unless there had been plenty of milk at hand, this Venus bird had died and suffered deservedly for his Lechery. **1786** BURNS *A Dream* xiii, A glorious Galley,.. Weel rigg'd for Venus barter. **1821** LIDDLE *Poems* 26 Your venus jobs now's a' kend thro' The Loudins braid.

c. In sense 10.

1816 TUCKEY *Narr. Exped. R. Zaire* ii. (1818) 58 Fragments of shells of the cockle and venus genera. **1861** P. P. CARPENTER in *Rep. Smithsonian Instit. 1860*, 256 The Venus-tribe may be regarded as the types of the Lamellibranchs.

12. a. Special combs. (of the possessive, with or without *'s*): **Venus †gem, †girdle, †hair, Venus's hair-stone, pencil** (see quots.).

1601 HOLLAND *Pliny* II. 621 Such Amethysts as these..; many give them the name of Venus gems, for the great grace that they have .. both in fashion and colour. *Ibid.* 629 The stone called Venus haire, is exceeding blacke and shining; howbeit it maketh a shew of red haires sprinckled among. **1653** R. SANDERS *Physiogn.* 49 Venus Girdle is a Semicircle that begins between the fore-finger and the middle finger, and ends between the fourth finger and the little one. **1884** *Imp. Dict.* IV, *Venus's hair-stones*, *Venus's pencils*, fanciful names applied to rock crystals inclosing slender hair-like or needle-like crystals of horn-blende, asbestos, oxide of iron, rutile, oxide of manganese, &c.

b. *Bot.* **Venus's basin, bath**, the wild teasel, *Dipsacus sylvestris*; **Venus's comb**, the shepherd's needle, *Scandix Pecten-Veneris*; **Venus's cup**, Venus's basin; **Venus's flytrap**, the North American marsh-plant *Dionæa muscipula*; † **Venus' garden**, = *Venus's navelwort* (*a*); † **Venus' glass**, Venus's looking-glass; **Venus golden apple** (see quot.); **Venus' hair**, the maiden-hair, *Adiantum Capillus-Veneris* (see also quot. *c* 1711); † **Venus' laver**, Venus's basin; **Venus('s) looking-glass**, one or other of certain plants belonging to the genus *Specularia*, esp. *S.* (or *Campanula*) *Speculum* (†*Speculum Veneris*); **Venus' navel**, = next (*a*); **Venus's navelwort**, (*a*) the pennywort, *Cotyledon Umbilicus*; (*b*) one or other species of annual plants belonging to the genus *Omphalodes*, esp. *O. linifolia*; † **Venus needle**, Venus's comb; **Venus-pear**, a variety of pear mentioned by Pliny and Columella; **Venus's pride**, *U.S.* (see quot.); **Venus's slipper**, the lady's slipper, *Cypripedium Calceolus*.

1551 TURNER *Herbal* I. O iv b, Dipsacus, called in latin labrum veneris: that is *venus basin, because it holdeth alwayes water. **1578** [see below]. **1597** GERARDE *Herbal* II. ccccIxxi. 1006 Teasell is called .. Carde Teasell, and Venus Bason. **1671** SKINNER, Venus-bason, *Dipsacus vulgaris*. **1763** STUKELEY *Palæogr. Sacra* 25 Ladys fingers, ladys traces, ladys linnen, Venus glass, Venus bason,.. etc. **1863** PRIOR *Plant-n.*, Venus Bason, *Veneris labrum*, so named .. from the hollows formed by the united bases of the leaves being usually filled with water, that was used .. to remove warts and freckles. **1578** LYTE *Dodoens* 522 Called in .. Englishe, Fullers Teasel, Carde Thistell, and *Venus bath or Bason. **1855** MISS PRATT *Flower. Pl.* III. 169 Wild Teazel .. is still often called Venus's Bath. **1866** *Treas. Bot.* 1208/1 Venus' bath, *Dipsacus sylvestris*: so named from water collecting in the connate bases of the opposite leaves. **1597** GERARDE *Herbal* II. cccc. 884 *Pecten Veneris, siue Scandix*, Shepheards Needle, or *Venus combe. **1671** SKINNER, Venus-Comb. **1753** *Chambers' Cycl.* Suppl., *Scandyx*, venus comb... The flower is of the rosaceous kind, consisting of several petals, which are arranged in a circular order on a cup. **1785** MARTYN *Lett. Bot.* xvii. (1794) 238 Venus's-comb is remarkable for long processes or beaks terminating the seeds. **1863** PRIOR *Plant-n.*, Venus' Comb, from the slender tapering beaks of the seed-vessels being set together like the teeth of a comb. **1855** MISS PRATT *Flower. Pl.* III. 69 Wild Teazel .. is still often called .. *Venus's Cup. **1775** *Ann. Reg.* II. 93 A Description of a newly discovered Sensitive Plant, called *Dionæa Muscipula*, or *Venus's Fly-trap. **1857** A. GRAY *First Less. Bot.* (1866) 171 The Venus's Fly-trap .. growing where it is always sure of all the food a plant can need. **1867** H. MACMILLAN *Bible Teach.* vii. (1870) 148 The leaf of the Venus' fly-trap of North America, closing together on its prey by turning on its mid-rib as on a hinge. **1597** GERARDE *Herbal* II. cxliii. 424 Nauelwort is called .. of some *Hortus Veneris*, or *Venus garden. **1611** COTGR., *Nombril de Venus*,.. Wall Penniwort, Venus garden, Hipwort. **1728** BRADLEY *Dict. Bot.* II. s.v., *Venus Glass,.. *Speculum veneris sive Viola Pentagona.* **1763** [see *Venus basin*]. **1888** *Nicholson's Dict. Gard.* IV, *Venus' Golden Apple, a common name for *Atalantia monophylla*. **1548** TURNER *Names Herbes* (E.D.S.) 9 *Venus heir is in a meane tempre betwene hote & colde. **1578** LYTE *Dodoens* 409 Venus heare groweth in walles, and in stony shadowy places. **1661** LOVELL *Hist. Anim. & Min.* 450 Leaves, of venus-haire, and lungwort. *c* **1711** PETIVER *Gazophyl.* VI. liv, Round leaved Malabar Venus-hair... Its large notch'd Leaves on single Stalks, distinguish it from others. **1858** SIMMONDS *Dict. Trade* s.v., Venus'-hair, the *Adiantum capillus-Veneris*, given as an expectorant, and forming the basis of the celebrated syrup of capillaire. **1601** HOLLAND *Pliny* II. 376 The little grub or worme which is found in the hearbe Tazill, called *Venus Laver. **1597** GERARDE *Herbal* II. civ. 356 *Speculum Veneris*, *Venus Looking glasse .. groweth in ploughed fields among the corne. **1681** GREW *Musæum* II. iii. iii. 234 The Seed of Venus Looking-Glass. *a* **1689** MRS. BEHN tr. *Cowley's Plants* C.'s Wks. 1711 III. 372 But say Corn-Violet, why thou dost claim Of Venus Looking-Glass the pompous Name. **1785** MARTYN *Lett. Bot.* xvi. (1794) 189 Venus's Looking-glass is a Campanula, with a weak, low, and very branching stalk. **1863** PRIOR *Plant-n.*, Venus' Looking-Glass, from the resemblance of its flowers set upon their cylindrical ovary to an ancient round mirror at the end of a straight handle. **1592** R. D. *Hypnerotomachia* 24 b, With other murall and wall weeds comming out of the chinkes as .. *Venus Navill. **1625** B. JONSON *Pan's Annivers.* Wks. (Rtldg.) 643/1 Bring .. Bright crown imperial, kingspear, holyhocks, Sweet Venus-navel. **1678** PHILLIPS (ed. 4), **Venus Navelwort*,.. a Plant of Venus, esteemed of great use;.. otherwise called Wall Penywort, and Kidneywort. **1731** MILLER *Gard. Dict.* s.v. *Omphalodes*, Low Vernal Venus Navel-wort, with a Comfry-leaf, or Lesser Borage. **1767** ABERCROMBIE *Ev. Man his own Gardener* (1803) 104 Hardy Annual Flower-seeds:.. Lobel's catch-fly, Venus' navel-wort, dwarf poppy. **1866** *Treas. Bot.* 812/1 *Omphalodes*;.. several species are grown in English gardens, under the name of Venus's Navelwort. **1882** *Garden* 10 June 411/3 Small bouquets of pink Brier Roses with Venus's Navelwort. **1597** GERARDE *Herbal* II. cccc. 884 *Scandix*,.. Venus Coombe, or *Venus Needle. **1648** HEXHAM II. App., *Venus-peere*, a *Venus-peere. **1879** LEWIS & SHORT *Lat. Dict.*, *Venerea pira*, a kind of pear, Venus-pear. **1845–50** MRS. LINCOLN *Lect. Bot.* 143 The *Houstonia cærulea* .. is known by different common names; as Innocence, *Venus's Pride, and Blue Houstonia. **1785** MARTYN *Lett. Bot.* xxvii. (1794) 423 It has more resemblance to a wooden shoe in form, and therefore is unworthy the title of *Venus's Slipper, which Linnæus has bestowed upon it.

c. *Zool.* **Venus-basket**, Venus's flower-basket; **Venus('s) comb, Venus's cup** (see quots.); **Venus's ear**, a sea-ear or ear-shell; **Venus's fan**, a sea-fan, esp. *Rhipodogorgia* (*Gorgonia*) *flabellum*; **Venus's flower-basket**, a glass-sponge of the genus *Euplectella*, esp. *E. aspergillum*; **Venus's girdle** (see quots.); † **Venus purr** (see quot. and PURR *sb.*²); **Venus' purse**, Venus's flower-basket (*Funk's Stand. Dict.* 1895); **Venus-shell**, a bivalve mollusc belonging to the family *Veneridæ* or related species; a venus, murex, or cowry; **Venus's slipper** (see quot.); † **Venus-winkle** (see quots. and cf. PORCELAIN 3).

1882 *Cassell's Nat. Hist.* VI. 318 In some the form is constant and characteristic, as in the fairy-like *Venus-basket (*Euplectella*). **1842** *Penny Cycl.* XXII. 54/2 *Murex Tribulus*, Linn... This is the *Venus's Comb of collectors, and when perfect is a most delicate and striking shell. **1864** *Chambers's Encycl.* VI. 616/2 The Venus Comb of the Indian seas is .. a very .. beautiful shell, with many long thin spines. **1885** LADY BRASSEY *The Trades* 312 There were .. grey sponges, sometimes called *Venus's cups,—in shape not unlike coral Neptune's cups. **1859** H. KINGSLEY *G. Hamlyn* xxxiv, They fell to gathering shells..like children, ..Trochuses,..and '*Venus-ears', scarlet outside. **1880** MISS BIRD *Japan* II. 87 One urn and a large covered bowl are beautifully inlaid with Venus' ear. **1855** KINGSLEY *Glaucus* 33 The great stony *Venus's fan which hangs in seamen's cottages, brought home from the West Indies. **1860** WORCESTER (citing Baird), *Venus's Fan*,..the common name of much branched and reticulated polypes of the family *Gorgoniæ*. **1872** *Good Words* 703 One of the most beautiful of all natural productions, the *Euplectella*, or '*Venus's Flower-basket'. **1896** tr. *Boas' Text Bk. Zool.* 121 The beautiful Philippine Venus's Flower-Basket (*Euplectella aspergillum*), which like several of its allies, lives at considerable depths. **1870** NICHOLSON *Man. Zool.* xvi. I. 114 In *Cestum*, or *Venus' Girdle, 'elongation takes place to an extraordinary extent'. **1896** tr. *Boas' Text Bk. Zool.* 118 *Cestus veneris* (Venus's girdle), with body much compressed and elongated to a ligamentous form. **1713** PETIVER *Aquat. Anim. Amboinæ* Tab. 18/12 *Purra Venerea*,..White *Venus Pur. **1589** RIDER *Bibl. Schol.* 1723 A sea snaile, or *Venus shell, *cochlea Veneris*. **1615** tr. *De Montfart's Surv. E. Indies* 31 Their Venus-shells consist of certaine kind of earth or clay which hath remaind a 100 yeares in one place. **1666** J. DAVIES tr. *Rochefort's Caribby Isles* 121 The Venus-shells may justly be numbred among the rarest productions of the Sea. **1681** GREW *Musæum* I. vi. i. 137 Venus-Shell. *Concha Veneris*. Because beautiful. **1872** A. DOMETT *Ranolf* VI. ii. 112 Exact as roseate streak for streak Some opened Venus-shell displays. **1836** *Penny Cycl.* VI. 294/1 The shells of this genus [sc. *Carinaria*] were formerly known to collectors under the name of '*Venus's Slipper' and 'Glass Nautilus'. **1601** HOLLAND *Pliny* I. 253 The Porcellanes or *Venus Winkles swimme above the water, and with their concavitie and hollow part which they set into the weather, helpe themselves in stead of sailes. **1611** FLORIO, *Veneria*, a Scallop called a Purcelane or Venus-winkle.

'Venus², error for VENICE, by association with prec.

1629 in Foster *Eng. Factories India* (1909) III. 349 Cordage, wheat, Venus cloth. **1841** *Penny Cycl.* XIX. 485/1 *Rhus Cotinus*, Venus Sumach, or Wild Olive. **1866** *Treas. Bot.* 980/1 *R. Cotinus*, another South European species, called the Venus or Venetian Sumach, yields the yellow dye-wood called Young Fustic.

Venusberg ('viːnəsbɜːg, ‖'veːnəsbɛrk). [Ger., lit. 'mountain of Venus'.] The court of Venus, in German legend and esp. in Wagner's *Tristan* found in a grotto on the Hörselberg mountain; hence in *transf.* use, any environment whose primary characteristic is sensual pleasure.

1855 [see SAGA¹ 2]. **1890** G. B. SHAW *How to become Mus. Critic* (1960) 192 Not even a visit from the ghost of Sterndale Bennett could have waved him back from the Venusberg then. **1925** H. CRANE *Let.* 28 Feb. (1965) 199 A perfect Venusberg of flowers and shrubbery. **1934** H. G. WELLS *Exper. Autobiogr.* I. iii. 107 Bowkett had his own secret incidental twilight Venusberg. **1962** *Guardian* 15 Nov. 9/3 We had wonderful plans for Windsor. It was to have been an expense account Venusberg. **1981** M. J. BENKOVITZ *Aubrey Beardsley* iv. 110 Beardsley depicted..[a] more violent encounter between satyrs and the residents of the Venusberg.

Hence **Venus'bergian** *a.*

1896 G. B. SHAW *Let.* 19 Feb. (1965) I. 602 A Venusbergian Asta is too much. **1977** *Gramophone* Dec. 1087/1 Those whining Wagnerian tubas in 'Mars' are matched by the almost Venusbergian sensuousness of 'Venus' here.

Venusian (vɪ'njuːsɪən), *a.*¹ *rare.* [f. L. *Venusia* (see below) + -AN.] Of or pertaining to Venusia, an ancient town in southern Italy, and birthplace of the poet Horace; hence used allusively.

1616 B. JONSON *Poetaster* in *Workes* 310 And to his steps my Genius inclines, Lucanian, or Apulian, I not whether; For the Venusian colonie plowes either. **1875** F. ARNOLD *Our Bishops & Deans* I. v. 289 But the Venusian adage is true how the generous wine evermore retains the early flavour which was accidentally imparted to it.

Venusian (vɪ'njuːsɪən), *sb.* and *a.*² [f. VENUS¹ II + -IAN.] **A.** *sb.* **1.** *Science Fiction.* A supposed inhabitant of the planet Venus; also, the language spoken by such a being.

1874 A. BLAIR *Ann. 29th Cent.* III. iii. 56, I suspected from the circumstances the frames of the Venusians were so constituted that sustenance was superfluous. **1897** J. MUNRO *Trip to Venus* ix. 173 'The good of it?' rejoined the Venusian; 'it is beautiful, and gives us pleasure.' **1927** *Spectator* 24 Dec. 1127/1 It is the Venusians who record the Last Judgment. **1955** W. GIRVAN *Flying Saucers & Common Sense* i. 15, I do not think it is because of a desire that I should be visited by Martians or Venusians. **1972** P. MOORE *Can You Speak Venusian?* xvi. 167 He is fluent in Venusian, Plutonian and Krügerian. **1977** *N.Y. Rev. Bks.* 12 May 36/4 There are several stories which insist on the..general nastiness of human beings, who thus take on the..role which used to be assigned to Martians and Venusians and the like in Fifties science fiction.

2. *Astrol.* A person born under the sign of Venus and thus supposedly subject to the influence of the planet. *rare.*

a **1963** L. MACNEICE *Astrol.* (1964) ii. 55 But the sensuality of the *Kalendar* Venusians is not of the violent 'dark god' type.

B. *adj.* **1.** Of, pertaining to, or characteristic of the planet Venus or its supposed inhabitants.

1874 A. BLAIR *Ann. 29th Cent.* III. iii. 58 At the first glimpse I received of Venusian waters, my admiration was taken by storm. *Ibid.*, I now commenced the acquisition of the Venusian language. **1934** *Jrnl. Brit. Interplanetary Soc.* II. 4 It cannot be over-emphasised that Venusian life cannot be other *than* Venusian. **1956** C. SIMAK *Time & Again* ix. 42 Earth news..was followed by Martian news, by Venusian news, by the column from the asteroids. **1968** *Times* 12 Oct. 18/6 Further reason for doubting the radius of Venus..has emerged from a computer simulation of the Venusian atmosphere. **1982** *Austin* (Texas) *Amer.-Statesman* 28 Feb. A-17/1 The first [space probe]..is expected to drop through thick Venusian clouds.

2. *Astrol.* Designating or pertaining to the movement or influence of the planet Venus. *rare.*

1913 'SEPHARIAL' *Kabala of Numbers* II. xii. 189 Suppose .. that a child is born when the influence of Venus is predominant, and the local mode of etheric vibration is what may be termed Venusian. **1924** C. E. O. CARTER *Conc. Encycl. Psychol. Astrol.* 30 Attractiveness is an essentially Venusian quality. *Ibid.* 81 In the horoscopes of poets and painters we see the faculty of artistic imagination denoted by the mixture of Lunar, Mercurial, and Venusian action.

† **venust**, *a.* *Obs.* [ad. L. *venust-us*, f. *Venus* VENUS¹. Cf. It. and Pg. *venusto*.] Handsome, beautiful; elegant, graceful; comely in appearance.

1513 DOUGLAS *Æneid* XII. Prol. 87 The variant vestur of the venust vaill. *a* **1568** in *Bannatyne MS.* (Hunterian Cl.) 672 My bird, my bony ane, my tendir bab venust. **1604** R. CAWDREY *Table Alph.*, *Venuste*, faire, beautifull. **1657** TOMLINSON *Renou's Disp.* 673 Amber is a..Rosine flowing from the incisures of a..Venust tree. **1663** WATERHOUSE *Fort.* 187 As the Infancy of Rome was venust, so was its Manhood notably strenuous. **1698** FRYER *Acc. E. India & P.* 270 Nor could [they] have ever thought it [*supra* so Magnificent a Pile] venust enough, whilst they abounded with Pious Benefactors.

Hence † **venustity**, † **venustness**. *Obs.*$^{-0}$

1727 BAILEY (vol. II), *Venustness*, *Venustity*, beautifulness.

† **venustate**, *v.* *Obs.*$^{-0}$ [f. L. *venustāt-*, ppl. stem of *venustāre*, f. *venust-us*: see prec.] (See quot.) Hence † **venustation**. *Obs.*$^{-0}$

1656 BLOUNT *Glossogr.*, *Venustate*, to make beautiful, fair or sightly. **1658** PHILLIPS, *Venustation*, a making handsome or beautiful.

† **venusty**. *Obs.*$^{-1}$ [ad. L. *venustas*, f. *venustus* (see VENUST *a.*), or a. obs. F. *vénusté*. Cf. It. *venustà*.] Elegance of form; beauty.

1559 BERCHER *Nobylytye Wymen* (Roxb. 1904) 105 Nature hathe geven hym [*sc.* man] a bewtye—it is called maiestye, or venustie,.. —which passethe all other bewtye.

venville ('vɛnvɪl). *local.* Forms: 4 **wenge-**, **vengefeild**, **vennefeld**, 6 **vyndefelde**, 7 **fen(g)field**, **venvill**, 8- **venville**. [Of obscure origin; the suggestion made in quot. 1829 does not account for the earliest forms of the word.]

1. A special form of tenure obtaining in parishes adjoining Dartmoor, by which the tenants enjoy certain privileges in the use of the forest. Usually in the phrase ***in venville***.

?**13..** in *Trans. Devonsh. Assoc.* (1876) VIII. 408 M[emorandu]m quod Tenent[es] d[omi]ni princip[is in] Wengefeild al[ia]s Vennefeld clamant..habere eos articulos et libertates subscript. infra forestam de Dartmoore. *Ibid.*, Et eorum Tenentes iacent in vengefeild [etc.]. **1609** in S. Rowe *Peramb. Dartmoor* (1848) 279 Blacktorrebeare (which is part in the Forest of Dartmoore and part in Venvill). **1794** R. FRASER *Gen. View Devon* 49 It is customary..to take from those not in venville one shilling. **1829** T. MOORE *Hist. Devon* IV. i. I. 473 Many of them belonged to parishes lying in what is called venville, which paid annually for the cattle, when trespassing within the forest bounds, certain compensations, entitled 'fines villarum', thence corrupted into 'fin vil' and 'venville'. **1837** *Penny Cycl.* VIII. 450/2 Part of the waste [of Dartmoor] is appropriated by the surrounding parishes, the freeholders of which possess the right of common, or as it is termed the right of *venville*, on these appropriated parts. **1887** W. F. COLLIER in *Trans. Devonsh. Assoc.* XIX. 378 The tenants in venville are said to have the right to take anything off Dartmoor..except green oak and venison.

2. *attrib.*, as ***venville farm***, ***man***, ***money***, ***rent***, ***rights***, ***tenant***, etc.

a **1600** in S. A. Moore *Rep. Dartmoor Preserv. Assoc.* (1890) 48 The vyndefelde men of Chagford and Mannaton. **1609** in S. Rowe *Peramb. Dartmoor* (1848) 279 Payinge for the same their Venvill rents and other dues as hath bene tyme out of mynde accustomed. *c* **1630** [see FENFIELD]. **1676** in *Trans. Devonsh. Assoc.* (1899) XXXI. 142 Paid.. Phillip Andrew for Venvill rent,..[4s. 1 d.]. **1796** W. H. MARSHALL *W. England* II. 26 Many of those lands have a prescriptive right, on the forest, by paying an inconsiderable sum.. annually, under the name of Venville money, to the Duchy. *Ibid.* 28 The good estimation in which Venville farms are held. **1829** T. MOORE *Hist. Devon* IV. i. I. 473 The names of the venville parishes are Sheepstor, Walkhampton, Sampford Spiney [etc.]. **1848** S. ROWE (*title*), A Perambulation of the antient and royal Forest of Dartmoor, and the Venville Precincts. **1887** W. F. COLLIER in *Trans. Devonsh. Assoc.* XIX. 377-85 Venville Rights on Dartmoor.

† **veny**¹. *Obs.* Also 3 **uenie**, 5 *pl.* **venyse**, **veneis**. [a. AF. *venie* (= OF. *veine* VEYNE), ad. L. *venia* indulgence, pardon, remission.] Pardon or forgiveness; a request for this; the gesture of kneeling or prostrating oneself as an indication of penitence and desire for pardon.

a **1225** *Ancr. R.* 46 ʒif ʒe þurh ʒemeleaste gluffeð of wordes ..nimeð ower uenie dun et ter eorðe mid te honden one. *Ibid.* 426 Ase ofte ase heo hit doð..makien hore uenie akneon adun to þer eorðe biuoren hire, & sigge 'Mea culpa'. *c* **1400** *Rule St. Benet* (Prose) 141 When sho comes whare the cuuent takis þare venyse, þan sall sho prostrate downe. **14..** in Maskell *Mon. Rit.* II. 279 All other observance of the order as..Inclinacyons, veneis and prostracyons. **1482** *Monk of Evesham* (Arb.) 33 And thanne y came and lay prostrate before hym, askyng my *veny* and rehersyd ageyne my *Confiteor*, etc.

veny². *Obs.* exc. *dial.* Forms: 6-7 **veny**, **veney**, **venie**, 7 **venee**, **veany**; 6-7 **vennie**, **venney**, **venny**; 8 *dial.* **vinny**, 9 **finney**. [Alteration of VENUE, with the terminal vowel weakened through loss of stress. Freq. *c* 1580-*c* 1640.]

1. A hit or thrust in fencing; a wound or blow; = VENUE 2.

1578 H. WOTTON *Courtlie Controuersie* 27 In daunger to receiue a venny at my hande. **1591** SYLVESTER *Du Bartas* I. i. 813 A sacred Fencer..Whose two-hand Sword, at every veny,..keenly slyces through whole Troops at once. **1635** *Long Meg of Westminster* vii. (1816) 14 Or else take that staffe and haue a bout with me for thy brakefast, hee that giues the first three Venies scape free. **1652** URQUHART *Jewel* Wks. (1834) 223 The three aforesaid gentlemen, who were wounded in the very same parts of their bodies by other such three venees as these.

b. *fig.* and in fig. context; *esp.* a sharp retort, a pungent remark.

1586 BRIGHT *Melanch.* xxxvi. 224 Accompt not these small venies of Sathan for deadly woundes. **1592** GREENE *Def. Conny-Catching* To Rdr., I meane..to giue him such a veny, that he shalbe afrayd heereafter to disparage that mysticall science of Conny-catching. **1606** HEYWOOD *2nd Pt. If you know not me* (1609) F 4 b, *Iohn.* Name the weapon. *Courtez.* Nothing but kisses, and enticing lookes. *Iohn.* Then ward your lips well, or youle ha the first venney. **1643** SIR T. BROWNE *Relig. Med.* I. §55 That whilst we lye at close ward against one vice we lye [not] open to the vennie of another. **1685** *Life William Bedell* 302 As for these vain flourishes of mine, if he had not taken a veny in them, and found it smart, he had not strook again so churlishly.

c. ***veny for veny***, tit for tat.

1611 CHAPMAN *Widow's T.* Wks. 1873 III. 20 So, there's venie for venie, I haue giuen't him 'ith speeding place for all his confidence.

2. A bout or turn of fencing; = VENUE 3.

1594 GREENE *Fr. Bacon & Fr. Bungay* 1944 Why standst thou Serlsbie? doubtst thou of thy life? A venie man: faire Margret craues so much. **1598** SHAKS. *Merry W.* I. i. 296, I bruiz'd my shin..with playing at Sword and Dagger with a Master of Fence (three veneys for a dish of stew'd Prunes). **1615** HEYWOOD *Foure Prentises* I. i, I am no sooner got into the fencing-school To play a venie with some friend [etc.]. **1673** *Jackson's Wks.* III. 134, I had a Venie or 'Bout for it, and the Intent, though not the Hap, to kill him.

fig. **1606** DEKKER *Seven Sins* III. (Arb.) 28 One Vennie more with thee, and then I haue done. **1618** MYNSHUL *Ess. & Charac. Prison*, *Jailers* 34 One Venny more, and if that hit, so, if not..I will lay downe the Bucklers. **1644** SIR E. DERING *Prop. Sacr.* Pref. c, And now, my sacrificing Jesuite, stand forth and let us occasionally here try a veny.

3. *south. dial.* (See quots.)

1746 *Exmoor Scolding* (E.D.S.) 139 Dist hire ma, Dem? Chell ha tether Vinny wi' tha. *Ibid.* Gloss., *Vinny*,..a scolding Bout. **1881** *Isle of Wight Gloss.* 11 *Finney*, a frolic; to have to do with. 'I'll hey a bit of a finney at that'; I'll have something to do with that.

venyed, obs. var. VINNIED *ppl. a.*

venym(e, obs. ff. VENOM *sb.* and *v.*

venymous(e, **-ows**, **-us**, etc., obs. ff. VENOMOUS *a.*

venyng, obs. Sc. f. WEENING *vbl. sb.*

venyson(e, **-oune**, **-owne**, **venzon**, obs. ff. VENISON.

Venyss(e, obs. ff. VENICE.

venyw, obs. f. VENUE.

veo, southern ME. var. FEE *sb.*¹; south-west dial. var. FEW *a.*

veolar, obs. Sc. f. VIOLER.

veolau, southern ME. var. FELLOW.

veolaureden, southern ME. variant of FELLOWRED *Obs.*

veole, ME. var. FELE *a.* *Obs.*

veol(l), southern ME. pa. t. FALL *v.*

veolthe, **veond**, **veor**, **veorlich(e**, southern ME. varr. FILTH *sb.*, FIEND, FAR *adv.*, FERLY *a.* and *adv.*

veorme, var. FARM *sb.*¹ *Obs.*

veorne, **veorðe**, **veotere**, southern ME. varr. FERN *a.* *Obs.*, FOURTH *a.*, FETTER *v.*

vepe, obs. Sc. f. WEEP *v.*

vepen, ME. var. WEAPON.

veper, obs. Sc. f. VIPER.

vepre'cose, *a.* *Obs.*$^{-0}$ [ad. med. or early mod.L. *veprecōs-us*, f. L. *vepres* (*vepris*) brier-bush, bramble-bush.] (See quot.)

1721 BAILEY, *Veprecose*, full of Brambles.

† **vepri'cosous**, *a.* *Obs.*$^{-0}$ (See prec. and quot.)

1656 BLOUNT, *Vepricosous*, full of briars or brambles.

Vepsian ('vɛpsɪən). Also Veps, Vepsic, Vesp, Wepsian, etc. [f. Russ. *Vépsi* + -AN, -IAN.]

a. (A member of) a Finnish people dwelling in the region of Lake Onega, now in the north-west of the U.S.S.R. **b.** The Finno Ugric language spoken by this people. Also *attrib.* or as *adj.*

1859 R. G. LATHAM *Descr. Ethnol.* I. xix. 409 *Tshud*..is a word which the Slavonians of Novgorod applied to the Non-slavonic populations with which they came in contact. We shall see it import more clearly after a notice of the Vod, and the Vesp. **1863** —— *Nationalities of Europe* I. xvi. 162 Of the Vesp dialect, *eo nomine*, I have seen no specimens. **1877** A. H. KEANE tr. *Hovelacque's Sci. of Lang.* iv. 91 With the Suomi are grouped..the *Chudic* [language], situated in a very scattered district south of Lake Onega; the *Wepsic*, which is northern Chudic, [etc.]. **1878** *Encycl. Brit.* VIII. 700/1 Finnic or Ugrian represented by..Finnish proper.. Karelian..Tchudic..Vepsic. **1879** *Ibid.* IX. 219 The Chudic, a Slav term..now restricted to the Veps or northern Chud and the Votic or southern Chud, dwelling.. round the shores of Lake Onega. **1921** [see LUDIAN]. **1933** L. BLOOMFIELD *Language* iv. 68 The other languages of the Baltic branch [of the Finnish-Lapponic languages], Carelian, Olonetsian, Ludian, Vepsian, Livonian, Ingrian, and Votian, are far smaller, and some of them are near extinction. **1933** *Amer. Anthropologist* XXXV. 309 The Leningrad section studied the Finnish tribes, the Vesps, the Izhors, and some purely Russian peoples. **1955**, etc. [see LUDIAN]. **1964** *Language* XL. 98 The Veps, Votic, and Estonian cognates. **1977** *Ibid.* LIII. 477 Since the boundaries of the European continent make up the geographical frame-work of H's analysis, he includes such little-known languages as Votyak, Cheremis, and Vepsian (Uralic), and Bashkir, Karaim, and Kalmyk (Altaic).

† **ver**, *sb.*[1] *Obs.* Also *Sc.* 5–6 **wer**, 6 **uer**. [a. L. *vēr* or OF. *ver*. In ME. a variant of VERE.] The season of spring; springtime.

1382 WYCLIF *Ecclus.* l. 8 He shyneth..as the flour of roses in the daȝes of ver. *c* **1407** LYDG. *Reson & Sens.* 91 Whan the clere sonne aroos In grene ver, ful of delyt. *c* **1450** *Harl. Contin. Higden* (Rolls) VIII. 435 In whiche yere in the tyme of ver [etc.]. **1450–80** tr. *Secreta Secret.* 27 Ver bigynneth whan þe sonne entrith into the signe of þe Ram. **1535** STEWART *Cron. Scot.* II. 226 Syne into ver, quhen that the da grew lang, This king..tuke the feild. **1581** T. HOWELL *Deuises* (1879) 197 The more to mourne Our Ladie lost in source of sorrowes shaken Which loe in Ver to heauen hath tane the waye. **1600** *Eng. Helicon* (1887) 253 Ver hath made the pleasant field Many several odours yield.

b. In more or less personified use.

1390 GOWER *Conf.* III. 118 Whan Ver his Seson hath begonne. *c* **1400** *Destr. Troy* 4037 Ver entrid full euyn, eger with all. **1430–40** LYDG. *Bochas* v. xv. (1554) 132 Ver came in with hys newe grene. *a* **1547** SURREY in *Tottel's Misc.* (Arb.) 8 There might I se how Ver had euery blossom hent. **1568** T. HOWELL *Arb. Amitie* (1879) 24 Now Lady Ver in liuely greene doth showe her grace in fielde. **1577** GRANGE *Golden Aphrod.* etc. P iv b, When Ver is in hyr pryme. **1630** DRAYTON *Muses Eliz.* Nymphal iii. 179 Whilst fresh Ver is flinging Her Bounties abroad.

† **ver**, *sb.*[2] *Obs.*$^{-1}$ (Meaning obscure.)

13.. *Gaw. & Gr. Knt.* 866 Þe ver by his uisage verayly hit semed Wel neȝ to vche haþel alle on hwes.

† **ver**, *v.*[1] *Obs.*$^{-1}$ [Of obscure origin.] *trans.* ? To spot or bespatter *with* something.

? *a* **1400** *Morte Arth.* 2573 The vesere, the aventaile, his vesturis ryche, With the valyant blode was verrede alle ouer!

† **ver**, *v.*[2] *Obs.*$^{-1}$ [Aphetic f. AVER *v.*] *trans.* To aver, declare.

c **1400** *Destr. Troy* 49 Ouyd and othir þat onest were ay, Virgill þe virtuus, verrit for nobill.

ver, southern ME. var. FAR *a.* and *adv.*, FIR, FIRE *sb.*, FOR *prep.*

ver, obs. Sc. f. *were*, pa. t. of BE *v.*; obs. Sc. f. WAR *sb.* and *a.*, WERE *sb.* (doubt).

ver-, southern ME. var. FOR- *pref.*[1]

† **vera.** *Naut. Obs.* [App. f. VEER *v.*[1]] ? A command to let out more of the sheet.

c **1530** *Hickscorner* 302 A-le the helme! a-le! vere! shot of! vere sayle! vera!

vera, obs. or dial. f. VERY *a.*

‖ **vera causa** ('vɛərə 'kaʊzə). *Philos.* [L., lit. 'real cause'.] A true cause which brings about an effect as a minimum independent agency.

[**1687** I. NEWTON *Philosophiae Naturalis Princ. Math.* III. 402 Causas rerum naturalium non plures admitti debere, quam quæ & vera [*sic*] sint & earum Phænomenis explicandis sufficiunt.] **1831** J. F. W. HERSCHEL *Prelim. Discourse* II. vi. 144 To such causes Newton has applied the term *veræ causæ*; that is, causes recognized as having a real existence in nature, and not being mere hypotheses or figments of the mind. **1865** MILL *Exam. Hamilton's Philos.* xxiv. 469 By *verae causae* Newton meant agencies the existence of which was otherwise authenticated. **1890** W. JAMES *Princ. Psychol.* I. ii. 67 Inhibition is a *vera causa*, of that there can be no doubt. **1927** B. RUSSELL *Analysis of Matter* ii. 19 In Newton, 'force' plays a great part, and there seems no doubt that he regarded it as a *vera causa*. **1942** R. G. COLLINGWOOD *New Leviathan* xxxiii. 279 Stupidity, I reply, is not a *vera causa*. If he thought that, I want to know why; and to say 'because he was stupid' is not an answer. **1977** *Brit. Jrnl. Hist. Sci.* X. 238 Darwin's commitment to the *vera causa*—or 'true cause'—principle.

veracious (və'reɪʃəs), *a.* [f. L. *vērāc-*, *vērax* according to truth, that speaks the truth + -IOUS. Cf. next.]

1. Habitually speaking or disposed to speak the truth; observant of the truth; truthful.

a **1677** BARROW *Serm.* (1686) II. 63 That God is good, veracious, and faithfull. **1778** JOHNSON *L. P., Swift* (1781) III. 409 The credit of the writers, both undoubtedly veracious. **1820** SHELLEY *Hymn Merc.* lxii, I am a most veracious person, and Totally unacquainted with untruth. **1839** DICKENS *Nickleby* xxviii, The testimony of the two veracious and competent witnesses. **1864** BOWEN *Logic* xiii. 431 A witness is presumed to be veracious in this case, in proportion as his love of truth is already established from others.

2. Characterized by veracity, truthfulness, or honesty; conforming to truth; true, accurate.

1777 JOHNSON *Let. to Mrs. Thrale* 27 Oct., Is not my soul laid open in these veracious pages? **1802–12** BENTHAM *Ration. Judic. Evid.* (1827) V. 718 The testimony which has served as the instrument of the mischief, has been.. veracious. **1868** W. R. GREG *Lit. & Soc. Judgm.* 400 He.. showed His back but not His face to Moses; and dictated the veracious narrative of Balaam and his ass. *a* **1871** DE MORGAN *Budget Parad.* (1872) 250 That it was the most veracious of books written by the most honest of men.

3. That estimates or judges truly or correctly.

1851 CARLYLE *Sterling* I. v, The young ardent soul that enters on this world..with veracious insight,..will find this world a very mad one.

Hence **ve'raciously** *adv.*, **ve'raciousness**.

1807 G. CHALMERS *Caledonia* I. III. vii. 405 In Shakspeare, it was fiction, to lay the murder of Duncan, at a place different from Bothgowanan, where the Chronicle has veraciously fixed it. **1860** I. TAYLOR *Sp. Hebr. Poetry* (1873) 63 The veraciousness of the record. **1879** MORLEY *Burke* v. 97 Burke's habitual veraciousness. **1905** *Athenæum* 25 Nov. 719/1 How diplomatists plot..is veraciously related.

veracity (və'ræsɪtɪ). Also 7 **veracitie**. [ad. F. *véracité* (= It. *veracità*, Sp. *veracidad*, Pg. *veracidade*), or med.L. *vērācitāt-*, *vērācitās*, f. L. *vērāci-*, *vērax*, f. *vēr-us* real, true.]

1. The quality or character in persons of speaking or stating the truth; habitual observance of the truth; truthfulness, veraciousness.

1623 in COCKERAM I. **1624** H. MASON *New Art Lying* v. 95 Truth morally taken, which hee calleth veracitie. **1678** NORRIS *Coll. Misc.* (1699) 154 A due conformity between the Words and the Understanding, when I speak as I think; which is moral Truth or Veracity. **1714** R. FIDDES *Pract. Disc.* II. 87 Veracity..is a moral virtue, and consists in a due conformity of our words, or declarations, with our thoughts. **1775** JOHNSON *Tax. no Tyr.* 57 To send deputies to the Congress of Philadelphia, to that seat of Virtue and Veracity. **1809** COLERIDGE *Friend* (1865) 23 Veracity, therefore, not mere accuracy; to convey truth, not merely to say it, is the point of duty in dispute. **1860** EMERSON *Cond. Life, Illusions* Wks. (Bohn) II. 447, I look upon the simple and childish virtues of veracity and honesty as the root of all that is sublime in character. **1900** L. HUXLEY *Life & Lett. T. H. Huxley* II. 427 Huxley's passion for veracity was perhaps his strongest characteristic.

b. *of veracity*, trustworthy, veracious, truthful. (Also with qualifying adjectives.)

1671 J. WEBSTER *Metallogr.* i. 8 Authors..of the greatest authority and veracity. **1700** ASTRY tr. *Saavedra-Faxardo* I. 88 Speaking of a Man of Veracity, we say he carries his Heart in his Hands. **1704** in *Pennsylv. Hist. Soc. Mem.* IX. 331 Those in this place, of unblemished credit and undoubted veracity, who were witnesses. **1737** *Gentl. Mag.* VII. 11 The same Author of veracity attests, that [etc.]. **1780** HARRIS *Philol. Enq.* Wks. (1841) 494 Philosophers, men of veracity, studied the heavenly bodies. **1839** JAMES *Louis XIV*, III. 31 A few instances..from one author alone, of undoubted veracity.

c. This quality as manifested in individuals. Const. *of* (a person) or with possessive.

1669 W. SIMPSON *Hydrol. Chym.* 114, I..doubt not of the veracity of that noble philosopher. **1687** T. BROWN *Saints in Uproar* Wks. 1730 I. 81 Authors of that undoubted credit, that no body..will call their veracity in question. **1726** SWIFT *Gulliver* I. viii, Which, after great astonishment, clearly convinced him of my veracity. **1785** PALEY *Mor. Philos.* III. I. xv, All the benefit of conversation, depends upon our opinion of the speaker's veracity. **1840** HOOD *Up Rhine* 2 But for the preparations..going on before my eyes, I should have..doubts of my own veracity. **1870** J. H. NEWMAN *Gram. Assent* I. ii. 14 The child assents..to the veracity of his mother in her assertion of the inapprehensible.

2. Agreement of statement or report with the actual fact or facts; accordance with truth; correctness, accuracy.

1736 BUTLER *Anal.* II. vii. 369 Mere genealogies..perhaps do carry some presumption of veracity. **1750** JOHNSON *Rambler* No. 4 ¶ 19 In narratives where historical veracity has no place. **1825** COLERIDGE in *Lit. Rem.* (1839) IV. 275 The character of veracity and simplicity on the very countenance, as it were, of the Gospel. **1860** EMERSON *Cond. Life, Fate* Wks. (Bohn) II. 316 No picture of life can have any veracity that does not admit the odious facts.

b. Const. *of* or with possessive.

1664 H. MORE *Myst. Iniq.* 101 The veracity of the voice of Christ sounding in the Scriptures. **1684** T. GODDARD *Plato's Demon* 100 For Testimony concerning the Veracity of his History, we find even [etc.]. *a* **1706** EVELYN *Hist. Relig.* (1850) I. 386 Were the tradition of the Scriptures' antiquity and veracity not enough. **1755** LLOYD in *Connoisseur* No. 73. 434 The veracity of these posthumous encomiums may, indeed, be fairly suspected. **1803** *Edwin* I. vi. 89 The band of warriors no longer doubting the veracity of his words. **1843** G. S. FABER *Eight Dissert.* (1845) I. 151 Such, at least, is the ancient narrative:..and..I see no reason to disbelieve its general veracity. **1902** HICHENS *Londoners* 42 Finding the veracity of his paragraph thus impugned.

3. Correspondence with external facts; exactness in the indication of these.

1666 BP. S. PARKER *Free & Impart. Censure* (1667) 59 Suppose that we were born with these congenite Anticipations,..how can I be certaine of their Truth and Veracity? **1837** DICKENS *Pickw.* ii, He was under the painful necessity of admitting the veracity of his optics. **1869** F. W. NEWMAN *Misc.* 53 Every Specific Informant [*i.e.* scientific instrument] needs to have its veracity put to the test.

4. That which is true; a truthful statement; a truth.

1852 F. W. ROBERTSON *Serm.* Ser. III. xvi. (1857) 204 It is possible for a man to utter veracities and yet to be false to himself and to his God. **1867** STUBBS *Study Med. & Mod. Hist.* (1886) 18 A world whose falsehoods and veracities are separated by so very thin a barrier.

5. *Comb.*, as ***veracity-assuring***, ***-serving***.

1802–12 BENTHAM *Ration. Judic. Evid.* (1827) I. 194 According as..the force of..the veracity-insuring.. motives is the strongest. *Ibid.* 282 Veracity-serving information, information considered as a source of truth.

‖ **vera copula** ('vɛərə 'kɒpjʊlə). *Law.* [L., lit. 'true union'.] Sexual intercourse; coitus requiring erection and penetration.

1845 J. E. P. ROBERTSON *Rep. Cases Argued & Determined in Ecclesiastical Courts at Doctors' Commons* I. I. 299 If there be a reasonable probability that the lady can be made capable of a *vera copula*—of the natural sort of coitus, though without power of conception, I cannot pronounce this marriage void. **1945** *Times Law Rep.* LXI. 526/2 It is well established that there must be what Dr. Lushington referred to as *vera copula*. **1961** *Times* 30 June 5/4 The question was whether the fact that the wife would have an artificial vagina would prevent sexual intercourse achieved by such means from constituting, in law, *vera copula*. **1971** *Rayden on Divorce* (ed. 11) I. vi. 156 Sexual intercourse or consummation is sometimes referred to as *vera copula*.

verade, variant of FERRED *Obs.*

verai, obs. form of VERY *a.*

† **'verament**, *adv. Obs.* Forms: α. 4 **vere-**, 4–6 **verrement** (4 **verree-**). β. 4–6 **vera-**, 4–5 **verra-**, 5 *Sc.* **werrament**. [ad. AF. *veirement* (cf. mod. Walloon *vèrement*), = OF. *voirement* (still in dial. use), f. *veir*, *voir*:—L. *vērus* true. The β-forms may be partly due to the influence of *verraiment* VERIMENT.] Really, truly; = VERIMENT *adv.*

Freq. *c* 1330–*c* 1560, esp. in β-form, often as a mere tag or rime-word.

α. **1303** R. BRUNNE *Handl. Synne* 651 Ȝyf þou wene þat verement, Hyt ys aȝens þys comaundement. *c* **1325** *Spec. Gy Warw.* 877 Þu shalt fonge verreement þare þi rihte iugement. *c* **1400** T. CHESTRE *Launfal* 485 Many a knyght, verement, To ground was ibore. *a* **1450** MYRC *Par. Pr.* 390 These þre poyntes verement Nowþer schale do, bot boþe assent. **15..** W. BROUN in *Bannatyne MS.* (Hunt. Cl.) 138/6 With havy hairt and mekle dreid I red the scriptour verement.

β. *c* **1325** *Lai le Freine* 255 He..bad his man sigge, verrament, He schuld toward a turnament. *c* **1386** CHAUCER *Sir Thopas* 2 Listeneth, lordings, in good entent, And I wol tell you verament Of mirth and of solas. **1426** AUDELAY *Poems* 6 Fore thou art bounden, go were thou goo,..Ther is no mon may hit undoo Bot he be cursid verament. *c* **1460** *Towneley Myst.* iii. 6 The son, the moyne, verament, Thou maide. *a* **1510** DOUGLAS *K. Hart* II. 470 Go send for Deid, thus said he verament. **1561** *Queen Esther* A iij b, In their mynde they thyncke verament That either for riches & honour Iustis will doe. **1606** N. BAXTER *Sidney's Ourania* D 4 b, Yet not in any sort colour verament For no colours hath the starrie firmament. **1611** in *Coryat's Crudities* Panegyr. Verses, He did his homage verament And salued them each one.

b. Quasi-*sb.* ***in verament***, = prec.

c **1450** *Songs, Carols*, etc. (1907) I. xi. 3 In this tyme God hath sent Hys own Son..To dwell with vs in verament. *c* **1470** HENRY *Wallace* IX. 1208 It is for gud at he is fra us went; It sall ye se, trast weill, in werrament. *c* **1550** ROLLAND *Crt. Venus* I. 763 [They] deput ane to gif diffinitiue Answer agane..Quhilk Lady hecht Themis in verament. **1599** NASHE *Lenten Stuff* Wks. (Grosart) V. 247 In verament and sincerity, I neuer crouded through this confluent herring faire.

veranda, verandah (və'rændə). Forms: α. 8– **veranda** (8 **-do**, **-der**). β. 8– **verandah**. γ. 8–9 **viranda**, **-dah** (8 **-do**, **-der**). δ. 8 **feranda**, **feerandah**, **verunda**, **voranda**, 8–9 **varanda**, 9 **varhandah**. [Originally introduced from India, where the word is found in several of the native languages, as Hindi *varandā*, Bengali *bārāndā*, mod.Skr. *baranda*, but appears to be merely an adoption of Pg. and older Sp. *varanda* (*baranda*) railing, balustrade, balcony. F. *véranda* appears to have been adopted from English.

The evidence for the origin of the word is fully presented in Yule and Burnell's *Hobson-Jobson*. The supposition that it was native to India accounts for some of the spellings placed under δ.]

1. a. An open portico or light roofed gallery extending along the front (and occas. other sides) of a dwelling or other building, freq. having a front of lattice-work, and erected chiefly as a protection or shelter from the sun or rain.

α. **1711** C. Lockyer *Acc. Trade India* 20 The Building is very ancient, two Story high, and has..two large Verandas or Piazzas. **1757** J. H. Grose *Voy. E. Indies* 84 A pent-house or shed, that forms what is called in the Portugueze Lingua-franca *Verandas*, either round, or on particular sides of the house. **1793** Hodges *Trav. India* 39 These boats..are, however, extremely commodious, having in the center a small verander, or open portico. **1866** Lowell *Biglow P.* Introd., Poems (1890) II. 201 The Captain was walking up and down the veranda of a country tavern in Massachusetts while the coach changed horses. **1884** J. Gilmour *Mongols* xxvii. 325 A crowd of women..take their stand in the veranda of a temple.

β. **1800** *Asiat. Ann. Reg.* 314/1 All around is a wide verandah, containing ranges of cells. **1808** Eleanor Sleath *Bristol Heiress* V. 208 Emma..advanced to meet Lady Castelton as she quitted her chair at the verandah. **1859** L. Oliphant *China & Japan* II. ix. 198 The building itself was in the form of a shed, with very deep verandahs. **1879** R. H. Elliot *Written on Foreheads* II. 2 After dinner we will sit in the verandah.

γ. **1751** 'Philalethes' *Jrnl. Boscawen's Voy. Bombay* (ed. 2) 45 When we got to the Prince's, he was sitting in a miserable little Virando or Piazza. **1765** *Phil. Trans.* LVII. 219 Hence people get out into the virando's and elsewhere for breath. **1793** Hodges *Trav. India* vii. 146 The space between the angle rooms are viranders, or open porticoes, to sit in during the evenings. **1818** Lady Morgan *France* (ed. 3) II. 5 The pretty *grisettes*..were..not unconscious..of the glasses pointed from the virandas of Tortoni's or Hardy's cafés. **1833** N. Arnott *Physics* (ed. 5) II. 184 When a slightly projecting roof, or a viranda, shadows..the whole front of a house. **1844** Dickens *Pictures from Italy* (1846) 174 There are virandas and balconies..to almost every house.

δ. **1754–73** E. Ives *Voy. India* I. iii. 45 Near each of the *vorandas*, there is a square room with a pillar in the middle. **1784** in *Archaeologia* VII. 287 A feerandah, or piazza, which extends from east to west sixty feet. **1786** *Ibid.* VIII. 254 The other gate leads to what in this country [India] is called a *veranda* or *feranda*, which is a kind of piazza, or landing place. **1800** *Asiat. Ann. Reg.* 128/2 His Lordship is supposed to be seated in the east verunda of the government-house. **1836** T. Hook *G. Gurney* I. 46 Vestibules, varhandahs,..palanquins and punkahs.

†**b.** Without article. *Obs.*

1776 *Trial Nundocomar* 33/2 He was not in the room I saw him in yesterday; but in a little room of Veranda.

c. *Austral.* and *N.Z.* A roof-like structure built along the side of a building, esp. one built over the pavement outside business premises.

1873 Trollope *Australia* I. 418 The verandah is a kind of open exchange,—some place on the street pavement apparently selected by chance, on which the dealers in mining shares do congregate. **1898** Morris *Austral Eng.* 489/1 Verandahs..are an architectural feature..of most City shops, where they render the broad side-walks an almost continuous arcade. 'Under the Verandah' has acquired the meaning, 'where city men most do congregate'. **1940** F. Sargeson *Man & Wife* (1944) 45 The house is a very old house. Once it was a grocer's shop..but..the old man couldn't get another shopkeeper to take it. So he had the verandah roof pulled down, and the front altered. **1959** M. Shadbolt *New Zealanders* 80 An untidy collection of bicycles and boys in the shade of a shop verandah.

2. *attrib.* and *Comb.*, as ***veranda-chair***, ***pillar***, ***-post***, etc.; ***veranda-builder***, ***-like*** adj.

1852 *Life in Bombay* 17 A support to a light verandah-like roof. **1858** Simmonds *Dict. Trade*, *Verandah-builder*, a maker of wire or wood lattice-work. **1868** *Rep. U.S. Commissioner Agric.* (1869) 204 There is no..climbing plant that can excel this as a covering for veranda pillars. *c* **1890** A. Murdoch *Yoshiwara Episode* 73 She clasped the verandah post..to keep her from falling in a swoon. **1897** Kipling *Capt. Cour.* 196 Cheyne, in a verandah-room,..toiled along wearily from day to day. **1902** *Chambers's Jrnl.* 14 June 437/2 Miss Tresscott..sought to show her disapproval..by turning her veranda-chair with its back to the gay scene. **1973** *Advocate-News* (Barbados) 17 Feb. 12/6 (Advt.), Household furniture... It includes:—Verandah chairs.

ve'randa(h)ed, *a.* Also 9 virandoed. [f. prec.]

1. Provided with a veranda; furnished with verandas.

α. **1823** L. Hunt *Poems* (1860) 272 Nor would I have Veranda'd windows to forestall my grave; Veranda'd truly from the northern heat! **1885** Howells *Silas Lapham* (1891) I. 144 The stretch of verandaed hotels and restaurants..along the shore.

β. **1825** Heber *Jrnl.* 14 Sept., Three good-sized rooms, verandahd all round. **1865** E. Lott *Governess in Egypt* 107 The lower basin was surrounded by a marble-paved verandahed walk or terrace. **1885** R. L. & F. Stevenson *Dynamiter* 145 A large verandahed court.

γ. *transf. a* **1818** M. G. Lewis *Jrnl. W. Ind.* (1834) 84 The whole house is virandoed with shifting Venetian blinds to admit air.

2. Abounding in verandas.

1893 *The Critic* (U.S.) 16 Nov. 316/2 The verandahed South is the home of the open-air *trouvère*.

†**verangene.** *Obs.*[−1] [ad. Sp. *berengena*.] = brinjal.

1587 Harrison *Descr. Eng.* II. xx. in *Holinshed* I. 208/2 The nobilitie..adventure further upon such fruits as are verie dangerous and hurtfull, as the verangenes, mushrooms.

verapamil (və'ræpəmɪl). *Pharm.* [f. v(al)er(onitr)il(e with inserted *-apam-* (of unkn. origin).] A drug, $C_{27}H_{38}N_2O_4$, that is given orally and intravenously (usu. as the hydrochloride) in the treatment of angina pectoris and cardiac arrhythmias.

1967 *Lancet* 5 Aug. 310/2 The effect of verapamil..on tachycardia was studied in 6 healthy male volunteers. **1983** R. Balcon in *Oxf. Textbk. Med.* II. xiii. 171/1 Nifedipine and verapamil are the two calcium antagonistic agents..widely used in the treatment of angina pectoris.

ver-arnd, var. *vor-arnd*: see for- *pref.*[1] 6 b.

veratr-, combining form or stem of veratrum, occurring in chemical terms, as **veratralbia**, **-albine** (see quots.); **veratrate**, a salt of veratric acid (1884 *Imp. Dict.*); **veratric** *a.*, derived from or contained in species of *Veratrum*; **ve'ratridine** [-idine], an alkaloid ester, $C_{36}H_{51}NO_{11}$, present in veratrum and sabadilla and having anti-hypertensive properties, but now used chiefly for experimental purposes; **veratroidea (-oidia)**, = veratrine; **veratroidine** (see quot.); **veratrol**, a colourless aromatic oil obtained by distilling veratric acid with excess of baryta.

1876 H. C. Wood *Therap.* (ed. 2) 156 Chas. L. Mitchell..finds two alkaloids in the rhizome [of *Veratrum album*], one of which he denominates jervia, the other *veratralbia. **1891** *Cent. Dict.*, **Veratralbine*, an alkaloid obtained from *Veratrum album*. **1843** *Penny Cycl.* XXVI. 251 **Veratric acid*, the acid with which veratria exists combined in Cevadilla. **1866** *Chambers's Encycl.* VIII. 395/2 Two special organic acids, to which the names Cevadic and Veratric acids have been given. **1877** Watts *Fownes' Chem.* II. 542 Dimethyl-protocatechuic or Veratric acid..is contained in sabadilla seeds (from *Veratrum Sabadilla*). **1907** *Brit. Pharmaceut. Codex* 242 Cevadine is accompanied in cevadilla seeds by the alkaloids *veratridine..and sabatrine. **1935** *Jrnl. Chem. Soc.* 123 On hydrolysis, veratridine gave veratric acid and..cevine. **1954** O. Krayer in V. A. Drill *Pharmacol. in Med.* xxxiii. 8/2 The monoester veratridine is of no clinical use because it has an inadequate therapeutic range and its duration of action is too short. **1976** *Nature* 25 Mar. 337/2 The effects of veratridine, an alkaloid well known for its ability to increase Na^+ permeability in nerve cells, were examined. **1976** Veratridine [see sabadine]. **1874** Garrod & Baxter *Mat. Med.* 382 This rhizome is stated to contain two alkaloids, *Viridia* and **Veratroidea*;..the latter is insoluble in ether. **1879** H. C. Wood *Therap.* 156 Recently Prof. Wormley has arrived at the conclusion that veratroidia is identical with veratria. **1891** *Cent. Dict.*, **Veratroidine*, an alkaloid, supposed to be identical with rubijervine, obtained from *Veratrum viride*. **1868** Watts *Dict. Chem.* V. 997 *Veratrol does not appear to unite with alkaline bisulphites.

veratria (və'reɪtrɪə). *Chem.* [f. veratr-um + -ia[1].] = veratrine.

1821 Ure *Dict. Chem.*, *Veratria*, a new vegetable alkali, discovered lately [in July, 1819] by MM. Pelletier and Caventou, in the..cevadilla, the..white hellebore, and the..meadow saffron. **1843** *Penny Cycl.* XXVI. 251/1 Veratria is a white or greenish-white powder, which has a silky and crystalline appearance under the microscope. **1865** *Daily Tel.* 20 Oct. 2/2 An alkaloid known as veratria or white hellebore. **1876** Harley *Royle's Mat. Med.* 388 It..does not excite sneezing like the closely allied substance veratria.

veratrin ('vɛrətrɪn). *Chem.* [f. as next + -in[1]. Cf. F. *vératrin*.] **a.** = veratrine. **b.** Veratrum-resin (Watts, 1868).

1830 Lindley *Nat. Syst. Bot.* 272 The medicinal properties of the root of Veratrum are owing to a peculiar alkaline principle, called Veratrin. **1866** Aitken *Pract. Med.* II. 730 Of all remedies, digitalis, aconite, and veratrin are the most useful in tranquilizing the action of the heart. **1899** *Allbutt's Syst. Med.* VIII. 726 Ergot, aconite, veratrin,..and many others have been prescribed.

veratrine ('vɛrətraɪn). *Chem.* [a. F. *vératrine*, f. veratr-um + -ine[5]. The mod.L. form *veratrina* has also been employed.] A poisonous vegetable alkaloid or mixture of alkaloids, obtained esp. from various species of *Veratrum* (as the seeds of *V. Sabadilla* and the root of *V. album*), and used medicinally as an ointment for the relief of neuralgia, rheumatism, etc.; veratria.

1822 A. T. Thomson *Lond. Disp.* (ed. 3) 257 Its [*sc.* Colchicum] acrimony resides in a peculiar alkali, which can be separated from the other principles, and has been named *veratrine* by M. M. Pelletier and Caventou, who discovered it. **1852** W. Gregory *Handbk. Org. Chem.* (ed. 3) 362 Veratrine, in the form of tincture, and still more in that of ointment,..is now much used. **1883** R. Haldane *Workshop Receipts* Ser. II. 27/1 Veratrine is easily exhausted from the seeds of *Veratrum Sabadilla*.

attrib. **1865** Mrs. Carlyle *Lett.* III. 259, I got the thing he mentioned, Veratrine liniment. **1868** Watts *Dict. Chem.* V. 997 A solution of a veratrine-salt, mixed with tartaric acid.

'veratrize, *v. rare.* [f. veratr-ine + -ize.] *trans.* To drug, poison, or treat with veratrine. Hence **'veratrized** *ppl. a.*

1874 H. C. Wood *Therap.* 143 These facts, however, do not prove that the convulsions in the veratrized frog are not spinal. **1891** in *Cent. Dict.*

‖**veratrum** (və'reɪtrəm). *Bot.* [L. *vērātrum* hellebore.]

1. A perennial genus typical of the family *Veratreæ* of liliaceous plants; a plant belonging to this genus, esp. the white hellebore (*V. album*); also, the rhizome of this.

[**1398** Trevisa *Barth. De P.R.* xvii. lv. (Bodl. MS.), Eloborus;..þe Romayns clepeþ þis herbe Veratrum,..and þerof is twei manere of kinde, white & blacke. **1548** Turner *Names Herbes* (E.D.S.) 79 Veratrum..maye be called in englishe Nesewurte.] **1577** B. Googe *Heresbach's Husb.* II. (1586) 69 Veratrum, there are two kindes of it, the blacke and the white. **1601** Holland *Pliny* II. 232 The root of Veratrum or Ellebore..maketh a most excellent medicine to rid it [dandruff] away. **1693** tr. *Blancard's Phys. Dict.* (ed. 2), *Veratrum*, the same with *Helleborus*. **1753** *Chambers's Cycl.* Suppl. s.v., The species of white Hellebore, enumerated by Mr. Tournefort, are these: 1. The greenish-flowered *Veratrum*. And 2. The early-flowering *Veratrum*, with blackish purple flowers. **1797** *Encycl. Brit.* (ed. 3) XVIII. 642/1 Veratrum has likewise been found useful in epilepsy, and other convulsive complaints. **1823** Crabb *Technol. Dict.* s.v., White-flowered Veratrum, or White Hellebore. **1836** *Penny Cycl.* VI. 448/1 We strongly suspect that all these supposed Veratrums really belong rather to the genus Helonias [etc.]. **1871** Garrod *Mat. Med.* (ed. 3) 345 Therapeutics [of Veratria]. As veratrum, but much more powerful.

2. *attrib.* and *Comb.*, as ***veratrum family***, ***-leaved*** adj.; **veratrum-resin** (see quots.).

1836 J. M. Gully *Magendie's Formul.* (ed. 2) 69 That all the individuals of the *veratrum* family possessed a very acrid taste. **1843** *Florist's Jrnl.* (1846) IV. 156 *Calanthe veratrifolia*. (Derived from veratrum-leaved.) **1853** Royle *Mat. Med.* (ed. 2) 664 Veratrum Wine. **1868** Watts *Dict. Chem.* V. 997 *Veratrum-resin*,..a constituent of sabadilla-seeds. **1888** *Cassell's Encycl. Dict.*, *Veratrum-resin*,..a brownish resin, extracted from sabadilla seeds.

veray, obs. form of very *a.* and *adv.*

verayly, obs. f. verily *adv.*

verb (vɜːb). Also 4–7 **verbe**. [a. OF. (also mod.F.) *verbe* or ad. L. *verbum* word, verb (whence also It., Sp., Pg. *verbo*).]

1. *Gram.* **a.** That part of speech by which an assertion is made, or which serves to connect a subject with a predicate.

For the numerous kinds of verbs distinguished by special epithets see the adjs. *active*, *auxiliary*, *deponent*, *desiderative*, *frequentative*, etc.

1388 *Wycliffite Bible* Prol. xv. (1850) I. 57 Sumtyme it mai wel be resoluid into a verbe of the same tens. **1483** *Cath. Angl.* 400/2 A verbe, *verbum*. **1530** Palsgr. Introd. p. xxx, Of verbes in the frenche tong be two dyvers sortes. **1542** Udall *Erasm. Apoph.* 120 b, The greke verbe ἐκπίπτειν souneth in latin *excidere*. **1544** tr. *Littleton's Tenures* (1574) 107 b, In some case these verbes *dedi & concessi* have the same effect in substaunce. **1655** S. Ashe *Fun. Serm. Gataker* 6 There is no verb to limit it unto any term of time, either past, present, or to come. **1668** Wilkins *Real Char.* III. i. §8. 303 That part of speech, which by our Common Grammarians is stiled a *Verb*,..ought to have no distinct place amongst Integrals in a Philosophical Grammar. **1725** Watts *Logic* I. iv. §6 There are also verbs, or words of action, which are equivocal as well as nouns or names. **1784** Cowper *Tiroc.* 619 No nourishment to feed his growing mind, But conjugated verbs and nouns declin'd? **1835** T. Mitchell *Acharn. of Aristoph.* 241 *note*, The four forms of future verbs with a passive signification, which occur in Greek writers. **1904** *Verney Mem.* I. 42 The inversion of the sentences, the verb coming at the end, is curiously like the German construction.

fig. **1730** Fielding *Rape upon Rape* II. v, I will be a verb active, and you shall be a verb passive.

b. *attrib.* and *Comb.*, as ***verb-complement***, ***-form***, ***-formation***, ***-grinder***, ***-phrase***, ***-root***, ***-stem***, ***-tense***; ***verb-centered***, ***-like*** adjs.; also in combinations (freq. *attrib.*) with the sense 'verb and —', as ***verb-adverb***, ***object***.

1809 Malkin *Gil Blas* v. i. ¶3 The verb-grinder engendered in his noddle a most ingenious device. **1865** Tylor *Early Hist. Man.* iv. 63 The reference of substantives to a verb-root in the Aryan languages. **1884** *Philol. Soc. Trans.* 557 A more systematic consideration of the verb-formations. **1887** Southworth & Goddard *Our Lang.* II. iv. 35 A verb-phrase is a group of words used as a single word. **1888** B. H. Kennedy *Rev. Lat. Primer* 94 Verbs..in which the Verb-Stem was formed by a so-called Thematic vowel added to the root. **1904** Bradley *Making English* 124 Prefixing an adverb to a verb-stem, such as 'outbreak, outfit'. **1912** A. D. Sheffield *Gram. & Thinking* vi. 92 These classes we can then subdivide, thus... Auxiliaries, forming 'verb phrases' (*is white, may go*) [etc.]. **1924** H. E. Palmer *Gram. Spoken Eng.* 121 The Anomalous Finites are the only verb-forms which may be shifted to front-position. **1933** *Amer. Speech* VIII. iv. 7/1 The verb-adverb combination *make up* was capable of expressing at least fourteen different meanings. **1935** Verb-like [see *noun-like* adj. s.v. noun 1 c]. **1935** T. Hudson-Williams *Short Introd. Stud. Compar. Gram.* 6 The personal endings of a verb-tense or the case-endings of a noun serve all practical purposes. **1957** *Publ. Amer. Dial. Soc.* xxviii. 132 If the IW appears with no accompanying verb-complement..the contrast..is suspended. **1962** C. L. Barber in F. Behre *Contrib. Eng. Syntax* 21, I shall use traditional terminology ..in the discussion of verb-tenses and of subordinate clauses. **1963** F. T. Visser *Hist. Syntax* iv. 356 The verb-object relation..is always easily recognisable when the complement is in an unequivocal genitive case. **1964** R. H. Robins *Gen. Linguistics* 331 Abaza, a Caucasian language, has been cited as an extreme case of a verb-centred language. **1965** N. Chomsky *Aspects of Theory of Syntax* ii. 64 The grammatical relation Verb-Object holds of the pair (*frighten, the boy*). *Ibid.* 105 'Unspecified—subject is working at this job quite seriously', where 'at this job' is a Verb-Complement. **1965** *English Studies* XLVI. 76 The statements about the correlations between verb-forms and contextual factors. **1966** *Ibid.* XLVII. 56 The problem of the verb-adverb combination (e.g. he *takes off* his hat). **1974** *Amer. Speech 1970* XLV. 266 Not only does he place himself in the mainstream of..the verb-centred approach..but he also clearly anticipates the drift towards..the verb-centered generative semantics of..Chafe. **1977** *Dædalus* Fall 118 It might have a rule that rewrites sentence as Noun Phrase followed by Verb Phrase. **1978** *Language* LIV. 118 When we consider the range of verb-like elements, the explanation in terms of proximity becomes more interesting.

†**2.** ***principal verb***, the chief or most important thing. *Obs.*

1616 J. Lane *Contn. Sqr.'s T.* vii. 582 'Sirrah,' Cambuscan lowrd, 'all yee haue loste Your principale verbe (credite) which yee boste'. **1642** *Remonstr. Lords & Comm. in Parl.* 26 May 20 That therefore which is the principle Verbe in this Statute, is the serving of the King for the time being. **1670** in C. N. Robinson *Brit. Fleet* (1894) 122 The Quality of the Commodity is not considered, but the gratuity to the officer is the principal Verb. **1728** North *Mem. Music* (1846) 80 The violin was scarce knowne tho' now the principall verb.

†**3.** A word. *Obs. rare.*

a **1716** South *Serm.* (1744) IX. 125 That so it might appear, that the assistance of the spirit promised to the church was not a vain thing, or a mere verb.

verbage, variant of verbiage. *rare*$^{-1}$.

1787 Polwhele *Engl. Orator* iii. 770 As the flippant Phrase Glides from his hollow Tongue, tho' oft debas'd By low commercial Verbage.

verbal ('vɜːbəl), *a.* and *sb.* Also 6–7 **verbale, -all(e.** [a. OF. (also mod.F.) *verbal* (= Sp. and Pg. *verbal*, It. *verbale*), or ad. L. *verbālis* consisting of words, pertaining to verbs, f. *verbum* word, verb.]

A. *adj.* **1.** Of persons: **a.** Dealing in or with words, esp. with mere words in contrast to things or realities.

1484 Caxton *Curiall* 4 We be verbal or ful of wordes and desyre more the wordes than the thynges. **1613** Purchas *Pilgrimage* (1614) 38 Henoch himselfe is made, not a verball but a reall Preacher. **1648** Milton *Ten. Kings* (1650) 58 While they are onely verbal against the punishing of Tyrants, all the Scripture they bring is direct to inferr it altogether lawful. **1677** in Hubbard *Indian Wars* (1865) II. 275, I am perswaded if Mars and Minerva go Hand in Hand, they will effect more Good in an Hour than those verbal Mercurians in their Lives. **1770** Beattie *Ess. on Truth* Introd. (1776) 4 A verbal disputant! what claim can he have to the title of Philosopher?

b. Using many words; talkative, verbose; ready to use words; articulate. Now *rare*.

1611 Shaks. *Cymb.* ii. iii. 111, I am much sorry (Sir) You put me to forget a Ladies manners By being so verball. **1620** Middleton *Chaste Maid* i. i, He's growne too verball, this Learning is a great Witch. **1647** Lilly *Chr. Astrol.* i. xiii. 78 A meer verball fellow, frothy,.. constant in nothing but idle words and bragging. **1976** *National Observer* (U.S.) 12 June 15/2 It's made a difference... She's more confident and verbal.

c. Interested in, attending to, the mere words of a literary composition.

1709 Pope *Ess. Crit.* 264 Neglect the rules each verbal critic lays, For not to know some trifles, is a praise. **1782** V. Knox *Ess.* xxxiii. (1819) I. 180 It is from the labours of verbal critics, that our language will receive the only excellencies it wanted. **1855** Paley *Æschylus* Pref. (1861) p. xxviii, Hermann, the leader of the verbal-critics.

2. a. Consisting or composed of words; also, of or pertaining to, manifested in, words.

verbal inspiration: see inspiration 3 a.

1530 Palsgr. 327/2 Verball, full of wordes, *verbal, verballe.* **1589** Cooper *Admon.* 60 As he and other of his crewe babbling in their verbale sermons vse to doe. **1592** Shaks. *Ven. & Ad.* 831 All the neighbour caves, as seeming troubled, Make verbal repetition of her moans. **1620** W. Folkingham *Brachigraphy* i, Short-writing is either of the bare Letter, or of Words composed of Letters. That I call Literall or Elementall, this Dictionall or Verball. **1662** Hibbert *Body Divinity* i. 253 There is a threefold lie... 1. Verbal, when a man tells a false tale. **1677** *Govt. Venice* 163 The Council of Ten having stretched their Law against Treason, to Verbal Expressions. **1722** Wollaston *Relig. Nat.* i. 9 Now.. what has a meaning, may be either true or false; which is as much as can be said of any verbal sentence. **1751** Johnson *Rambler* No. 140 ⁋11 Samson's complaint of the inconveniences of imprisonment is not wholly without verbal quaintness. **1791** *Gentl. Mag.* 26/2 Several pages of his sermons consisting of a series of verbal quibbles and jingles. **1820** Hazlitt *Table-T.* Ser. ii. iii. (1869) 72 We cannot by a little verbal sophistry confound the qualities of different minds. **1868** Peard *Water-farm.* vi. 67 Instead of a verbal description, we will give a rough sketch of the nursery. **1874** Green *Short Hist.* vii. §7. 424 The young playwright quizzes the verbal wit and high-flown extravagance of thought and phrase which Euphues had made fashionable.

b. Of the nature of, or denoting, a word.

1605 *Tryall Chev.* iii. iii, Bourbon! who names him? that same verball sound Is like a thunderclap to Philips eares. **1690** Locke *Hum. Und.* ii. xi. §8 These verbal signs they [*sc.* children] sometimes borrow from others, and sometimes make themselves. **1701** Grew *Cosmol. Sacra* ii. vi. 68 Observing by degrees, that all Words consist of a certain Number of Simple Sounds; they.. brought them [*sc.* marks], from many Thousands of Verbal Marks, to Two or Four and twenty Literal ones.

†**c.** ***verbal process*** (also ***process verbal***), a detailed account or report. [After F. *procès-verbal*.]

1682 Burnet *Rights Princes* viii. 263 In the Process Verbal of the Assembly General of the Clergy of France. **1688** *Lond. Gaz.* No. 2330/2 But the Nuncio and Clergy.. have drawn up a Verbal Process of all that passed, which they have transmitted to Rome. **1749** Smollett *Gil Blas* vii. xv, I took an inventory of the particulars, of which I formed in my pocket-book a small verbal process. **1756–9** A. Butler *Lives of Saints, St. Jane Frances*, He left an authentic verbal process of this vision, but as of a third person. **1762** *Ann. Reg.* i. 129 The next day, what is called the verbal process, was taken at the town-house... This verbal process is somewhat like our coroner's inquest.

d. ***verbal note***, in diplomacy, an unsigned note or memorandum sent as a mere reminder of some matter not of immediate importance.

1860 Wharton *Law-Lex.* (ed. 2).

e. ***verbal diarrhœa*** (*colloq.*), a tendency to talk too much; extreme verbosity. Cf. diarrhœa 2.

1823 *London Mag.* Sept. 281/1 All our modern tragedists indulge in.. the talking-principle... A verbal diarrhoea is the epidemic disease which afflicts the whole tribe. **1938** N. Marsh *Death in White Tie* xiii. 146 Her chief complaint is.. acute verbal diarrhoea. **1981** N. J. Crisp *Festival* vi. 142 This fathead suffers from verbal diarrhoea.

f. ***verbal conditioning*** (*Psychol.*), the reinforcing of certain verbal responses with the object of establishing the use of particular words or ways of speaking.

1954 *Jrnl. Exper. Psychol.* XLVIII. 355 (*title*) Influence of awareness of reinforcement on verbal conditioning. **1967** M. Argyle *Psychol. Interpersonal Behaviour* vii. 131 People may embark on all kinds of self-improvement,.. including the modification of styles of interaction as in operant verbal conditioning. **1971** *Jrnl. Gen. Psychol.* Apr. 267 Verb impression value.. was an important variable influencing response tendencies in verbal-conditioning and sentence-making tasks. **1979** J. P. Houston et al. *Invitation to Psychol.* v. 177 Verbal conditioning is another example of reward training in which a particular response is rewarded if it occurs.

3. a. Concerned with, affecting or involving, words only, without touching things or realities.

1605 Bacon *Adv. Learn.* ii. 36 Socrates.. separated Philosophy and Rhetoricke, whereupon Rhetorick became an emptie and verball Art. **1611** Bible *Transl. Pref.* ⁋16 Wee might iustly feare hard censure, if generally wee should make verball and vnnecessary changings. **1690** Locke *Hum. Und.* iii. xi. §7 Whether the greatest part of the Disputes in the World, are not meerly Verbal, and about the Signification of Words. *a* **1761** Law *Comf. Weary Pilgr.* (1809) 122 Men fallen from the.. truth of the Christian life under the power of natural reason, and verbal learning. **1785** T. Reid *Powers Hum. Mind* iv. 369 If all the general words of a language had a precise meaning,.. all verbal disputes would be at an end. **1807** *Knox & Jebb's Corr.* I. 372 If our liturgy.. had been cast.. in a vulgar mould; subsequent alterations, not only verbal but radical, would have been indispensable. *c* **1820** Whately *Logic* in *Encycl. Metrop.* (1845) I. 224/1 A definition of the term..; viz. a verbal, not necessarily a real definition. **1875** Jowett *Plato* (ed. 2) V. 121 The opposition between these two modes of speaking is rather verbal than real.

b. Finding expression in words only, without being manifested in action.

1622 Rowlands *Good Newes & B.* 32 Telling him that her selfe, and her estate Is not to be obtain'd with verball prate Of loue, and fancie. **1639** Massinger *Unnat. Combat* iv. i, Nor shall you find A verbal friendship in me, but an active. **1690** C. Nesse *Hist. & Myst. O. & N.T.* I. 68 They put not God off with empty complements, and verbal acknowledgments. *a* **1718** Prior *Knowledge* 706 My Prophets, and my Sophists finish'd here Their Civil Efforts of the Verbal War. **1741** Butler *Serm.* Wks. 1874 II. 256 These merely verbal professions.. were thought the proper language for the public ear. **1838** Thirlwall *Greece* xli. V. 173 Some solid and extraordinary benefit, something.. beyond a mere verbal recognition of its independence.

c. Consisting merely in words or speech.

1618 Bolton *Florus* (1636) 301 How true is that speech.. That vertue was only a verbal thing, and not a real. **1633** P. Fletcher *Purple Isl.* vii. v, Of these great monarchies.. Onely a fading verball memorie, And empty name in writ is left behinde. **1653** Milton *Hirelings* Wks. 1851 V. 349 But our Ministers.. for the verbal labor of a seventh days Preachment.. exact as due the tenth.. of our.. Labors.

4. a. Expressed or conveyed by speech instead of writing; stated or delivered by word of mouth; oral.

1591 Horsey *Trav.* (Hakluyt Soc.) 241 His Majestys verball answer to those two points conteyned within her Majestys letters. **1617** Moryson *Itin.* i. 193 The Chamber of the Pallace where verbal appeales are decided, is called, the Golden Chamber. **1646** *Hamilton Papers* (Camden) 131 The gentleman.. carried nothing from hence in writing; but I belieue he had a verbal commission. **1667** Pepys *Diary* 14 June, He did it by verbal order from Sir W. Coventry. **1727** Swift *Poisoning of E. Curll* Wks. 1755 III. i. 150 Mr. Curll .. immediately proceeded to make a verbal will. **1728** Chambers *Cycl.* s.v., A Verbal Contract, is that made merely by Word of Mouth; in opposition to that made in Writing. **1776** *Trial Nundocomar* 61/2 Did you send a verbal or a written message? **1807** Landseer *Lect. Engraving* Pref. 8 The verbal communications of Sir Henry Englefield, and Mr. Douce; the printed researches of Raspe, Hayley,.. and various other authors. **1834** Marryat *P. Simple* xiv, Sending a polite verbal refusal to the commissioner, upon the plea of there being no paper or pens on board. **1877** Froude *Short Stud.* (1883) IV. i. iii. 37 The archbishop believed that a verbal agreement was all which would be demanded of him.

b. Of persons: Using uttered words.

1822 Scott *Nigel* i, The verbal proclaimers of the excellence of their commodities, had this advantage over those who.. use the public papers for the same purpose.

5. a. Corresponding word for word; = verbatim *a.*

1612 Brinsley *Lud. Lit.* 238, I take the very same help of translations, either Verball or Grammaticall, to be the most speedy furtherances. **1656** Cowley *Pindar. Odes* Pref., When he that understands not the Original [of Pindar] reads the verbal Traduction of him into Latin Prose. **1712** Addison *Spect.* No. 464 ⁋1 Of this kind is a beautiful saying in Theognis;.. to give it in the Verbal Translation, *Among Men* [etc.]. **1786** Jefferson *Writ.* (1859) II. 46 You will perceive that it is almost a verbal Copy. **1909** R. Law *Tests of Life* ii. 29 We have what may be supposed to be almost verbal quotations of current forms of Gnostic profession.

b. In respect of each single word.

1790 Paley *Horæ Paul.* i. 4 In close and verbal conformity with the account.. preserved by St. Luke. **1882** Farrar *Early Chr.* I. 443 *note*, The sacred writers never aim at verbal accuracy in their quotations.

6. Of, pertaining to, or derived from a verb.

1530 Palsgr. 37 They come of latyn nownes verballes endyng in *tio. Ibid.* 154 All nownes verballes endyng in *eur* be of the masculyne gendre. **1636** B. Jonson *Eng. Gram.* xvi. Wks. (Rtldg.) 780/1 A person is the special difference of a verbal number, whereof the present, and the time past, have in every number three. **1648** Hexham ii. Gramm. (1658) V u 4 b/2 All Substantives derived from Verbals are called Verball words. **1706** Phillips (ed. Kersey), *Verbals* or *Verbal Nouns*, those Nouns that are derived from Verbs; as *Considerable*,.. from the Verb, To consider. **1755** Johnson, *Abandoning.* (A verbal noun from *abandon*.) *c* **1818** *Encycl. Metrop.* (1845) I. 54/2 Verbal adjectives (commonly so called), which express the conception in the form of an attribute, as the Latin verbals in *bilis*, &c. **1843** *Proc. Philol. Soc.* I. 31 The Grammar proceeds to describe other verbal derivatives. **1875** Whitney *Life Lang.* iii. 38 The plural verbal inflection.

7. Forming compound adjs. with the sense 'verbal and —', as ***verbal-acoustic, -metrical, -visual***, etc.

1901 E. B. Titchener *Exper. Psychol.* I. xii. 393 The verbal-motor type stands, in the author's experience, next in order of frequency to the visual. **1911** S. S. Colvin *Learning Processes* vii. 107 If I recall the name as written or printed on a page, I have a verbal-visual image; if I recall the name as spoken by some one, I have a verbal-acoustic image; if I recall the name in terms of the movements of my throat in speaking, I have a verbal-motor image. **1948** L. Spitzer *Linguistics & Lit. Hist.* 201 The verbal-metrical scheme of the strophe. **1972** R. E. Ornstein *Psychol. of Consciousness* ii. 39 The scientist, the writer, the mathematician are examples of the culturally 'dominant' verbal-rational mode. *Ibid.* x. 225 Modern Science is primarily verbal-logical.

B. *sb.* **1.** *Gram.* A noun, or other part of speech, derived from a verb.

1530 Palsgr. 154 *Broderésse*, a woman brodurar, ..*tenceresse*, a woman chyder; and so of all other verballes. **1570** Levins *Manip.* 89 Some verbals in *bilis.* **1591** Percivall *Sp. Dict.* B 4 b, Verbals in *or*, are of the masculine gender. *c* **1620** A. Hume *Brit. Tongue* (1865) 19 [Words] that we derive from latin verbales in tio, sould also be wrytten with t. **1665** R. Johnson *Scholars Guide* 6 The Latine tongue loves Verbals, Participials, Gerundives, and Participles of the future in *rus.* **1726** S. Lowe *Lat. Gram.* 12 Verbals are wanting, for the most part in Impersonals. ? *a* **1800** *Lett. on Eng. & Fr. Nation* I. 293 (Jod.), The rules of etymology and formation of Greek verbals evince that it must be so. **1836** J. R. Major *Guide Grk. Trag.* 105 A is long before *μα* in verbals derived from the first person of the preterite passive. **1882** F. W. Newman *Libyan Vocab.* 38 Kabail Verbs and Verbals, including Adjectives.

†**2.** [After med.L. *verbale*.] A collection of words; a vocabulary or dictionary. *Obs. rare.*

1599 *Bk. Preserv. K. Hen. VII*, i, Untill I have set forth a Verball or little Dictionarie. **1623** T. Spicer in Cockeram *Eng. Dict.* A vij b, To the Reader on this Verball of his esteemed friend, Master Henry Cockeram of Exeter.

3. *Gram.* A word or group of words performing the function of a verb.

1935 [see particle *sb.* 3]. **1965** *Amer. Speech* XL. 206 Adverbials which serve purely as modifiers of sentences and verbals. **1978** *Language* LIV. 88 Some support for the status of the items listed as verbals is that they are considered predicates in generative-semantic treatments of syntax.

4. *colloq.* A verbal statement, *spec.* a damaging admission, alleged to have been made by a suspected criminal and offered in evidence against him at a trial. Freq. *pl.*

1963 *Times* 22 Feb. 6/5 Who will believe you after I said I wasn't going to make a verbal? **1974** 'M. Underwood' *Pinch of Snuff* xxi. 171 'Have a look through the police evidence.'.. 'At least, they haven't put in any verbals.' **1980** *Daily Mirror* 24 June 19 Opponents of 'verbals' (alleged admissions of arrested persons to police which are not signed but are admitted in evidence) could see the meeting as a chance to further their campaign.

5. *slang.* Insult or abuse. Esp. in phr. ***to give*** (someone) ***the verbal*** and varr.

1973 *Time Out* 2–8 Mar. 13/2 We faced them, and gave them a load of verbal across the street. **1977** *Times Educ. Suppl.* 21 Oct. 43/2 Insulting and humiliating rivals—'giving them the verbal'. **1982** *Observer* 10 Oct. 40/7 Each 'ball' consisted of a distinctly lethargic head-high bouncer .., followed by a rousing collection of verbals (money will be paid to lip-reading viewers for translation).

'verbal, *v. colloq.* [f. verbal *sb.* 4.] *trans.* To attribute a damaging statement to (an accused or suspected person). Also const. *up*.

1963 *Times* 22 Feb. 6/5 Those chaps were about and they won't be able to verbal me. **1970** P. Laurie *Scotland Yard* vi. 146 The aggravation of it. He verbals up my villain and then says he'll let him off. **1973** *Courier-Mail* (Brisbane) 17 Oct. 10/4 Finch has claimed that detectives 'verballed' him—fabricated a confession to arrest him. **1981** C. Ross *Scaffold* 145 'He's made no statement yet either.' 'But you verballed him?'.. The police officer said nothing.

Hence **'verballing** *vbl. sb.*

1973 *Observer* 11 Nov. 15/2 'Verballing'—putting damaging remarks or 'verbals' into suspects' mouths—has existed as long as detectives have been dealing with criminals. **1977** 'C. Aird' *Parting Breath* iv. 47 It wasn't, the policeman consoled himself, really and truly verballing. Verballing was putting words into a man's mouth—and statement.

verbalism ('vɜːbəlɪz(ə)m). [f. verbal *a.* + -ism.]

1. A verbal expression; a word or vocable.

1787 Anna Seward *Lett.* (1811) I. 372, I always write in too much haste to pause for best-possible verbalisms. **1799** *Ibid.* V. 207 This propensity has probably left several erroneous verbalisms in myself-revised sheets. **1837** Whittock *Compl. Bk. Trades* 390 With those instructions, and other verbalisms, that he acquires daily,.. the apprentice may acquire a taste for the art. **1881** J. Russell *Haigs* xi. 308 Its quaint orthography and archaic verbalisms.

b. *collect.* Words, phrasing.
1800 ANNA SEWARD *Lett.* (1811) V. 285 It is not amongst our modern songs that the musical composer is to look for his happiest verbalism.

2. Predominance of what is merely verbal over reality or real significance.
1871 A. C. FRASER *Life Berkeley* ii. 28 His abhorrence of scholastic verbalism and empty abstractions. **1879** H. N. HUDSON *Hamlet* Pref. p. xv, Our children must be continually drilled in a sort of microscopic verbalism. **1889** J. M. ROBERTSON *Christ & Krishna* xii. 65 The rest is modern Talmudism—the ancient 'demoniacal possession' of verbalism over again.

verbalist ('vɜːbəlɪst). [f. as prec. + -IST.]
1. One who deals in, or directs his attention to, words only, apart from reality or meaning.
c **1609** F. GREVILLE *Hum. Learn.* xxxi. (1894) 209 Yet not ashamed these Verbalists still are.. To engage the Grammar rules in civil war For some small sentence which they patronize. **1629** GAULE *Holy Madn.* 100 Vaine Verbalists! whose words are but wind. **1660** GAUDEN *Brounrig* 171 Not that he was such a Formalist, Verbalist, and Sententiolist, as could not endure any alteration of words, or phrases, or method. *a* **1750** A. HILL *Wks.* (1753) II. 236 God grant now, that he mayn't think, I have piddled out this little heedlessness, with purpose to be even with him, in behalf of the poor verbalists. **1797** *Monthly Mag.* III. 509 That this circumstance should have escaped the notice of mere verbalists, is not surprising. **1864** *Reader* No. 99. 638/2 The extreme conclusions of the Verbalists. **1883** J. PARKER *Apost. Life* II. 15 The mere verbalist; yes, and even the mocker, may find his way into the church.
b. *attrib.* or as *adj.*
1889 J. M. ROBERTSON *Ess. Crit. Meth.* 130 The verbalist and confused pantheism of last century. **1891** —— *Mod. Humanists* 43 He himself became viciously verbalist.
2. One who is skilled in the use or knowledge of words.
1794 T. TAYLOR *Pausanias's Descr. Greece* I. Pref. p. viii, His meaning is, frequently, on this account, inaccessible to the most consummate verbalists. **1822** —— *Apuleius* 351 This blunder of the editor, who was otherwise a good verbalist, is a deplorable specimen of ignorance in things of the greatest importance. **1860–1** *Philol. Soc. Trans.* 164 The opinion of the best English verbalist I ever knew.

verbalistic (vɜːbə'lɪstɪk), *a.* [f. VERBALIST + -IC.] Of, pertaining to, or characterized by verbalism.
1934 *Mind* XLIII. 409 (*title*) Verbalistic tendencies. **1953** H. H. PRICE *Thinking & Exper.* viii. 237 It is no sillier than the purely Verbalistic theory which is at present fashionable. **1975** *Amer. Speech 1969* XLIV. 128 We live in a highly verbalistic culture.
Hence **verba'listically** *adv.*
1934 *Mind* XLIII. 411 To do full justice to a speaker's intended meaning.. instead of verbalistically insisting that he 'must' mean exactly what he *says.* **1940** *Theology* XL. 426 Pose the question thus verbalistically, and at once one suggests the method of lexicographical analysis.

verbality (vɜː'bælɪtɪ). [f. as VERBAL *a.* + -ITY.]
1. The quality of being (merely) verbal; that which consists of mere words or verbiage.
1645 BP. HALL *Peace-Maker* 23 That it may appeare, this controversie hath in it more verbality then matter. **1646** SIR T. BROWNE *Pseud. Ep.* I. x. 42 He will seem to be charmed with words of holy Scripture, and to flye from the letter and dead verbality. **1661** FELTHAM *Resolves* I. iii. 181 Let men be never so specious in the formall profession and Verbalities of Religion. **1721** BAILEY, *Verbality,* a being Verbal. **1816** J. GILCHRIST *Philos. Etym.* 251 Verbality is the covering which such quack philosophers as Kant and Stewart put over their poor, naked, false theories. **1826** —— *Lecture* 45 *note,* I know of nothing so much calculated to reduce it [*sc.* Scripture] to a mere mass of verbality. **1877** W. R. ALGER *Life Edwin Forrest* II. xxii. 767 He was no starveling fed on verbality and ceremony, no pigmy imitator or empty conformist.
2. *pl.* Verbal expressions or phrases.
1840 *New Monthly Mag.* LX. 316, I recollect.. the glorious emanations.. of my author—but I cannot remember the intoxicating verbalities wherein he clothes them. **1899** W. JAMES *Talks to Teachers* 257 We are stuffed with abstract conceptions, and glib with verbalities and verbosities. **1935** B. MALINOWSKI *Coral Gardens & their Magic* II. VI. vi. 246 The fact that the community are aware of the spell and know its wording is the most important clue to the appreciation of the verbalities of magic.
3. The quality appropriate to a verb.
1884 tr. *Lotze's Logic* 26 The forms of substantivity, adjectivity, and verbality.

verbalizable (ˌvɜːbə'laɪzəb(ə)l), *a.* [f. VERBALIZ(E *v.* + -ABLE.] Capable of being expressed in words; able to be verbalized. Hence **ˌverbaliza'bility.**
1951 C. KLUCKHOHN et al. in Parsons & Shils *Toward Gen. Theory of Action* IV. ii. 397 'Verbalizable' is not to be equated with 'clearly and habitually verbalized'. The actor's values are often.. incompletely.. verbalized by him. But implicit values remain 'conceptions'.. which can be put into words by the observer... Verbalizability is a necessary test of value. **1981** *N.Y. Times Mag.* 24 May 10/4 The path was cleared for the substitution of the verbalizable 'or' by the unspeakable '/' in the legalistic term 'and/or'.

ˌverbali'zation. [f. next + -ATION. Cf. F. *verbalisation.*] **1.** The action of verbalizing or the fact of being verbalized.
1846 WORCESTER (citing Palmer). **1860** G. P. MARSH *Lect. Eng. Lang.* xiv, The verbalization, if I may so express it, of a noun, is now a difficult matter. *a* **1901** F. W. MYERS *Hum. Personal.* (1903) I. 27 Each of the four forms of communication, of verbalisation, with which human life is familiar.
2. A verbal expression or statement.
1951 C. KLUCKHOHN et al. in Parsons & Shils *Toward Gen. Theory of Action* IV. ii. 398 Implicit values will be manifested only in behavior and through verbalizations that do not directly state the pertinent values. **1965** *Times Lit. Suppl.* 16 Sept. 812/1 Many of these potential multiple nouns will founder because.. a more efficient verbalization is to hand. **1976** *Howard Jrnl.* XV. I. 17 The practitioner 'sees through' the client's verbalizations to a reality that lies behind them.

verbalize ('vɜːbəlaɪz), *v.* [a. F. *verbaliser* (16th c.; = Pg. *verbalizar*), or f. VERBAL *a.* + -IZE.]
1. *intr.* To use many words; to talk diffusely; to be verbose.
1609 [BP. W. BARLOW] *Answ. Nameless Cath.* Ded. p. vii, Verbalize he can, dispute he cannot. **1648** HEXHAM II. App., *Verbaliseren,* to Verbalize, or make a speech. **1721** BAILEY, *Verbalize,* to be tedious in Discourse, to make many Words. **1889** J. M. ROBERTSON *Ess. Crit. Meth.* 130 Mr. Lowell verbalizes as to Duty being an eternal harmony.
2. *trans.* To make into a verb.
1659 O. WALKER *Instr. Oratory* 31 So nouns.. are sometimes verbalized; as, to complete, to contrary, to experience. **1818** *Q. Rev.* XIX. 207 To supply the place of the nouns thus verbalized Mr. Keats, with great fecundity, spawns new ones. **1860** G. P. MARSH *Lect. Eng. Lang.* viii, English no longer exercises.. the protean gift of transformation, which could at pleasure verbalize a noun.
3. To express in words.
1875 DORA GREENWELL *Liber Humanitatis* 42 The man of the world, whose creed has been thus.. verbalized, 'There's nothing new, and nothing true, and it's no matter'. **1886** GURNEY, etc. *Phantasms of Living* II. 23 It is more natural.. to visualise it,.. than to verbalise it in some imagined or remembered phrase.
Hence **'verbalizing** *vbl. sb.* and *ppl. a.*
1824 J. GILCHRIST *Etym. Interpr.* 90 What that something more or verbalizing property is, he either could not or would not inform the world. **1869** W. G. T. SHEDD *Homiletics* vi. 133 If the formation of the plan is merely a verbalizing process. **1880** MEREDITH *Tragic Com.* iv. (1892) 48 A burst unnoticed in the incessantly verbalizing buzz of a continental supper-table.

verbalizer ('vɜːbəlaɪzə(r)). [f. VERBALIZE *v.* + -ER[1].] One who registers stimuli or thoughts mentally in verbal terms rather than in visual images (cf. VISUALIZER); one who verbalizes.
1937 *Brit. Jrnl. Psychol.* Jan. 278 The meaning of many a word may be more clear-cut to a visualizer, because accompanied by a visual image, than to a verbalizer. **1952** *Ibid.* May 122 It would.. be expected that the better verbalizers would be the better learners. **1975** C. L. BURT *ESP & Psychol.* 7 A verbalizer who (like myself) may be almost devoid of visual or other kinaesthetic imagery, tends rather to think in terms of abstractions and for him material and mechanical structures lose much of their theoretical importance. **1980** *Times Lit. Suppl.* 15 Feb. 173/2 In Ireland what a man said was deemed more important than what he did. The tradition of verbalizer is old and deep.. and sprang from the imperative to keep the old cultural matrix alive.

verbally ('vɜːbəlɪ), *adv.* [f. VERBAL *a.* + -LY[2].]
1. Word for word; in respect of each word.
1588 LAMBARD *Eiren.* IV. v. 502 It is not of necessitie, that the Statute be verbally rehearsed, but only that the offence against the Statute be sufficiently and with full words described. **1680** DRYDEN *Pref. Ovid's Ep.* Ess. (Ker) I. 238 'Tis almost impossible to translate verbally, and well, at the same time. **1841** MYERS *Cath. Th.* III. §8. 29 To make them .. such a record of Divine utterances as to be throughout verbally and literally true. **1864** FROUDE *Short Stud.* (1867) I. 245 If all three agreed verbally, we should feel certain it was more than accident. **1883** A. ROBERTS *O.T. Revision* ix. 198 They could not but verbally agree in the reports which they furnished of His addresses.
2. In or with (mere) words, without accompanying action or reality.
1610 HEALEY *St. Aug. Citie of God* 573 This passion of Christ, the reprobate preach verballie onely. **1640** BP. HALL *Episc.* III. §8. 257 Would God I might not say, even the Lords Anointed, whom they verbally professe to honour. **1678** CUDWORTH *Intell. Syst.* 55 Some of the Pagans.., though they Verbally acknowledged a Deity, yet supposed a certain Fate superiour to it.
b. So far as words (only) are concerned.
1855–6 T. T. LYNCH *Lett. Scattered* (1872) 572 It is vain to be verbally right, if we are not livingly real. **1862** SPENCER *First Princ.* I. ii. §11 (1875) 35 Thus these three different suppositions.., verbally intelligible though they are,.. turn out.. to be literally unthinkable. **1908** W. M. RAMSAY *Luke Physician* viii. 251 You can with sufficient ingenuity always explain—verbally—any thing out of anything.
3. In actual words; by means of words or speech.
1646 JENKYN *Remora* 12 They said not so verbally, but mentally and practically. **1650** BP. HALL *Cases Consc.* (ed. 2) Addit. 402 Justly supposing, there may be as strong a prohibition in a sense implyed, as verbally expressed. *a* **1691** BOYLE *Hist. Air* (1692) 55 Nature.. has furnished men with sensories capable of distinctly perceiving a far greater variety of objects, than they are able verbally to express. **1796** MME. D'ARBLAY *Camilla* II. 395 But, till then, here he will stay.. till you have deigned to pronounce verbally his doom. **1840** DICKENS *Old C. Shop* xxxi, She verbally fell upon and maltreated her.
b. In speech, as contrasted with writing.
1637–50 ROW *Hist. Kirk* (Wodrow Soc.) 503 Then, after long reasoning and protesting,.. the King's Commissioner arose, dischargeing the Assemblie verballie. **1673** *Essex Papers* (Camden) I. 70 My humble advice.. is to content your selfe with what his Ma[jes]ty has verbally been pleased to declare in this matter. **1761** HUME *Hist. Eng.* II. xxxvi. 292 It was universally said that the Emperor.. would verbally agree to any terms. **1782** MISS BURNEY *Cecilia* VII. vii, Give me but the commission, either verbally or in writing. **1817** W. SELWYN *Law Nisi Prius* (ed. 4) II. 793 It was verbally agreed between plaintiff, defendant, and J. S. that the defendant.. should pay the amount. **1864** LINCOLN in E. McPherson *Hist. U.S. Rebell.* (1864) 336 You ask me to put in writing the substance of what I verbally said the other day in your presence. **1878** S. WALPOLE *Hist. Eng.* II. 675 The King was verbally assured.. that at least fifty fresh peerages would be required.
4. With the function of a verb.
1875 WHITNEY *Life Lang.* xii. 233 The verbally used [Scythian] forms are, rather, but one step removed from nouns used predicatively.

ver'barian, *a.* and *sb.* [f. L. *verb-um* word, after forms in *-arian.*] **a.** *adj.* Having to do with words. **b.** *sb.* An inventor or coiner of words.
1830 COLERIDGE *Church & State* (1839) 25 *note,* A verbarian Attorney-General, authorized to bring information.. against the writer or editor of any work.. who .. should persevere in misusing a word. **1873** F. HALL *Mod. Eng.* 21 In *The Doctor,* Southey gives himself free scope as a verbarian.

verbarnd, southern var. pa. t. FORBURN *v. Obs.*

‖**verbascum** (vɜː'bæskəm). [L. (Pliny), whence also It., Sp., Pg. *verbasco.*] A widely distributed genus of herbaceous plants, = MULLEIN; one or other species of this.
1562 TURNER *Herbal* II. 161 The whyte Verbascum is called commonly in English mollen or hickis taper, and.. longwurt. **1601** HOLLAND *Pliny* II. 264 That kind of Verbascum or Mullen, the flower whereof resembleth gold. **1741** *Compl. Fam.-Piece* II. iii. 367 Venetian Vetch, Borrage-leav'd Verbascum. **1765** *Phil. Trans.* LVI. 234 Phlomis, verbascum, stœchas, sage, thyme. **1843** *Penny Cycl.* XXVI. 254/1 All the species of verbascum are tall, robust, handsome plants, and may be cultivated in gardens and shrubberies. **1857** HENFREY *Bot.* §528 *Verbascum,* having 5 stamens, is sometimes referred to Solanaceæ.

†**verbate,** *v. Obs.*$^{-1}$ [f. L. *verb-um* word, perh. after *verbatim.*] *trans.* To reproduce word for word.
1512 *Helyas* in Thoms *Prose Rom.* (1828) III. 2, I have al onely verbated and folowed mine auctour as nighe as I could with the profoundite of good herte.

†**ver'batical,** *a. Obs.*$^{-1}$ [Irreg. f. L. *verb-um* word: see -ATIC and -AL[1].] Verbal.
1612 T. WILSON *Chr. Dict.* Pref., His is Axiomaticall, of simple propositions; mine is partly Verbaticall and Rematicall,.. of Wordes with their significations [etc.].

verbatim (vɜː'beɪtɪm), *adv., a.,* and *sb.* [a. med.L. *verbātim,* f. L. *verb-um* word: cf. LITERATIM.]
A. *adv.* **1.** Word for word; in the exact words:
a. With reference to a copy of a document or passage in a book, or to the report of a speech, etc.
1481 *Cov. Leet Bk.* 477 Stodealf.. brought like writyng as is before wreton verbatim direct to þe Maire. ? **1503** in *9th Rep. Hist. MSS. Comm.* App. 263/2 The said patent.. which is now verbatim copied in this boke in the xlviii. lef. **1557** *Order of Hospitalls* F vij, And.. make for him a treue and iust.. Coppie thereof verbatim. **1579** W. WILKINSON *Confut. Fam. Love* 9 b, Although the place.. be verbatim and word for word as I alledged it, yet will he not be satisfied. **1602** WILLIS *Stenographie* A ij b, He that is well practized in this Art, may write *Verbatim,* as fast as a man can treateably speake. **1653** W. RAMESEY *Astrol. Res.* 155 A Volume five times as large as is this, is not able to contain them all *verbatim.* **1709** STEELE *Tatler* No. 11 ¶4, I shall give you my Cousin's Letter Verbatim, without altering a Syllable. **1771** *Encycl. Brit.* I. 620/2 Merchants are provided with a large book, in *folio,* into which is copied *verbatim* every letter of business before it be sent off. **1826** F. REYNOLDS *Life & Times* II. 184 It was, according to the previous directions of the great critic and editor, inserted verbatim. **1893** FORBES-MITCHELL *Great Mutiny* 274 The following is the English version, verbatim,.. word for word, and point for point, italics and all.
b. With reference to a translation.
1583 FULKE *Def. Tr. Script.* i. 69 The Scriptures translated verbatim, exactly, and according to the proper vse and signification of the wordes. **1612** BRINSLEY *Lud. Lit.* xxi. (1627) 251 The Hebrew, in most places translated *verbatim,* doth keepe a perfect sense. **1668** DRYDEN *Even. Love* Pref., Witness the speeches in the first act, translated *verbatim* out of Ovid. **1687** A. LOVELL tr. *Thevenot's Trav.* I. C ij, The Translator could do no less than *Verbatim* to English the aforesaid letter from the Original. **1786** tr. *Beckford's Vathek* (1883) 28 The venerable personage read the characters with facility, and explained them verbatim as follows. **1815** W. H. IRELAND *Scribbleomania* 124 *note,* A translation verbatim from the french.
c. In the phrase ***verbatim et literatim.***
1742 FIELDING *J. Andrews* IV. v, We have.. procured an authentick Copy; and here it follows *verbatim et literatim.* **1787** HAWKINS *Johnson* 94 *note,* Mr. Newsham printed and dispersed some thousand copies verbatim et literatim of this letter. **1828** *Congress. Debates* IV. 276 (Stf.), It was, *verbatim et literatim,* a copy of the log-book of the brig. **1900** *Jrnl. Sch. Geog.* (U.S.) Jan. 7 The following story is copied.. from his note-book *verbatim et literatim.*
†**2.** In so many words; exactly, precisely. *Obs.*
1501 *Plumpton Corr.* (Camden) 151 That your sayd counsell may have all the estayts.. wrytten *verbatim* in paper. **1564** *Brief Exam.* ****ij, Did he not appoynt temperall rites.., which he had not *Verbatim* expressely at his masters hands? *a* **1638** MEDE *Wks.* (1672) 666 That which the Spirit speaks in the Written Word, that it speaks ῥητῶς, verbatim, expresly.
†**b.** In exact accordance with the words. *Obs.*
1575 in W. H. Turner *Select. Rec. Oxford* (1880) 368 Ye said Citie could not.. performe ye same verbatim.
†**3.** ? By word of mouth; verbally. *Obs.*$^{-1}$

1591 SHAKS. *1 Hen. VI*, III. i. 13 Thinke not..That therefore I haue forg'd, or am not able *Verbatim* to rehearse the Methode of my Penne.

B. *adj.* **1.** Corresponding with, or following, an original word for word.

1737 *Gentl. Mag.* VII. 14/1 Which grammatically represented in a *verbatim* Translation of the Verse into English, will run thus. **1834** *Tait's Mag.* I. 732/1 A mere simple *verbatim* repetition..of the romances and scandalous anecdotes. **1878** HUXLEY *Physiogr.* Pref. p. viii, Verbatim reports were taken on the former occasion. **1880** *Print. Trades Jrnl.* XXXI. 6 A machine for *verbatim* reporting, which will print phonetically.

2. *transf.* **a.** Able to take down a speech word for word (in shorthand).

1882 *Daily News* 24 May 8/5 Thoroughly experienced and efficient verbatim reporter. **1897** *Westm. Gaz.* 9 April 7/2 The Major spoke so rapidly that the fastest 'verbatim' hands seemed to be embarrassed.

b. Of a speaker: Usually reported, or worth reporting, word for word.

1892 *Pall Mall G.* 7 April 1/3 The verbatim men, the column men,..and the paragraph men. *Ibid.* 14 May 1/2 So much has Lord Rosebery slipped out from the front rank of 'verbatim' politicians.

C. *sb.* A full or word-for-word report of a speech.

1898 *Daily News* 14 April 10/4 Crisp writer wanted, who can also do a verbatim. **1899** *Ibid.* 6 March 8/5 Verbatims of Mr. Morley were at a discount even before he quitted the Irish Office.

Hence † **ver'batimly** *adv. Obs.*$^{-1}$ = prec. A. 1.

1597 E. TILNEY in Feuillerat *Revels Q. Eliz.* (1908) 417 A Composition layd uppon me..rated verbatimly by certain orders sett doun by my Lord Treasorer.

verbena (vɜːˈbiːnə). [a. L. *verbēna* (usually in pl. *verbēnæ*) in sense 1, med. and mod.L. *verbēna* (= L. *verbēnāca*) in sense 2; hence also It., Sp., Pg. *verbena*, and F. *verveine* VERVAIN.]

1. *Roman Antiq.* In *pl.*, the leaves or twigs of certain plants or shrubs (as olive, myrtle, laurel, etc.) having a sacred character and employed in religious ceremonies.

1600 HOLLAND *Livy* App. 1359 There was an hallowed place likewise upon the Capitoll, from whence they gathered Verbenæ, or sacred hearbs. **1685** TEMPLE *Ess.*, *Gardens* Wks. 1720 I. 178 *Verbenas*, which signifies all Kinds of Sweet or Sacred Plants that were used for adorning the Altars; as Bays, Olive, Rosemary, Myrtle. **1856** R. A. VAUGHAN *Mystics* (1860) I. 98 Passages were culled..with as much care and reverence as the sacred *verbenæ* that grew within the enclosure of the Capitolini.

2. The plant VERVAIN; also, one or other plant of the genus *Verbena* or the order *Verbenaceæ*.

1562 TURNER *Herbal* II. 161 b, And Pliny maketh two kindes of Verbena, or Verbenaca. **1706** PHILLIPS (ed. Kersey), *Verbena*, the Herb Vervain, much us'd by the ancient Heathens in their Sacrifices. **1731** MILLER *Gard. Dict.*, *Verbena*, Vervain. **1827–44** WILLIS *Declaration* 4 A scent Of orange leaves and sweet verbena. **1842** LOUDON *Suburban Hort.* 261 Cuttings of hardy or half-hardy herbaceous plants, such as pinks,..petunias, verbenas, rockets. **1891** HALL CAINE *Scapegoat* ix, The country of the verbena and the musk that lies outside the walls of Fez.

attrib. **1855** MISS PRATT *Flower. Pl.* IV. 207 *Verbenaceæ*. The Verbena Tribe.

b. With distinguishing terms.

1847 DARLINGTON *Amer. Weeds* (1860) 228 Nettle-leaved Verbena. Common Vervain. **1852** G. W. JOHNSON *Cottage Gard. Dict.* 27/1 *Aloysia*, sweet-scented Verbena. **1866** *Treas. Bot.* 1210/1 The *Aloysia citriodora* is the Lemon-scented Verbena of the gardens. **1888** *Encycl. Brit.* XXIV. 163/2 The garden verbenas, once so popular for bedding out, are derivatives from various South-American species.

3. A perfume obtained from the leaves of vervain. ***oil of verbena*** (see quots.).

1858 SIMMONDS *Dict. Trade*, *Verbena*, an otto, one of the finest perfumes, obtained by distillation from the citron-scented leaves of *Aloysia citriodora*. Owing to its high price it is..imitated..by mixing the otto of lemon grass with rectified spirits, and this passes as oil of verbena. **1866** *Treas. Bot.* 1210/1 The lemon-grass, *Andropogon Schœnanthus* or *A. citratum*, from which the 'oil of verbena' is extracted.

verbenaceous (vɜːbiːˈneɪʃəs), *a. Bot.* [See prec. and -ACEOUS.] Of or pertaining to the *Verbenaceæ*, an extensive order of monopetalous (chiefly tropical) plants.

1883 *Encycl. Brit.* XV. 481/2 The 'white mangrove' *Avicennia*, a verbenaceous plant.

'verbenate, *v. rare*$^{-0}$. [f. VERBENA.] *trans.* To strew with vervain. (Webster, 1847, citing Drake.)

ver'bene. *rare*. [Anglicized f. VERBENA.]

† **1.** (See VERBENA 1.) *Obs.*

1533 BELLENDEN *Livy* (S.T.S.) I. 54 'Deliuer to me,' said þe ffeciall, 'the herbe namyt verbene'. *Ibid.* 55 This fecial..twichit baith his hede and his hare with þe herbe verbene.

2. A plant of the order *Verbenaceæ*.

1846 LINDLEY *Veg. Kingd.* 663 The properties of Verbenes are much the same as those of Labiates. *Ibid.* 664 By far the most interesting plant..belonging to the Order of Verbenes is the Teak. **1879** *Cassell's Encycl. Dict.*, *Aloysia*, ..a genus of plants belonging to the..Verbenes.

† **'verberable**, *a. Obs.*$^{-0}$ [ad. L. *verberābilis* (Plautus).] (See quot.)

1656 BLOUNT *Glossogr.* (copying Cooper), *Verberable*, that may be, or is worthy to be beaten.

verberant (ˈvɜːbərənt), *a.* [ad. L. *verberant-*, *verberans*, pres. pple. of *verberāre*: see next.] Reverberant.

1890 *Advance* (Chicago) 23 Jan., He was grateful then, that he had escaped before the streets became verberant with such shrill echoes. **1891** MEREDITH *One of our Conq.* I. xiii. 251 Like the verberant twang of a musical instrument that has had a smart blow.

verberate (ˈvɜːbəreɪt), *v.* [f. L. *verberāt-*, ppl. stem of *verberāre* to beat, flog, f. *verber* a lash, scourge, blow. Cf. It. *verberare*, Sp. and Pg. *verberar*, obs. F. *verberer*.]

1. *trans.* **a.** To strike so as to produce a sound. *rare*.

1587 *Mirr. Mag.*, *Albanact* lxxv, The sounde that both by sea and land out flies, Reboundes agaime, and verberates the skies. **1656** STANLEY *Hist. Philos.* I. VIII. 114 Hearing is made when the aire betwixt the speaker and hearer is verberated in a circulation.

b. To beat or strike so as to cause pain, esp. by way of punishment.

1625 SHIRLEY *Love Tricks* III. v, You shall be verberated, and reverberated, my exact piece of stolidity. **1656** BLOUNT *Glossogr.*, *Verberate*, to beat, punish or strike. **1657** ABP. SANCROFT *Mod. Pol.* (ed. 7) B 7, He feels sometimes, those Bosome-quarrels that verberate and wound his Soul. **1873** LELAND *Egypt. Sketch-Bk.* 201 So the native verberated him till he reverberated. **1880** *Daily Tel.* 14 Oct. 5 It was proved ..that he had been verberated to this extent while with his regiment.

† **c.** To beat or whip up (a substance). *Obs.*$^{-1}$

1657 TOMLINSON *Renou's Disp.* 648 Oyl is assumed, verberated, and washed in Fountain-water.

2. *intr.* To vibrate or quiver.

1755 T. H. CROKER *Orl. Fur.* XXXIV. l, A fragrant breeze.. Made the air trem'lous verberate [It. *tremolar*] around.

Hence **'verberating** *ppl. a.*

1867 J. B. ROSE tr. *Virgil's Æneid* 338 Crooked beak and verberating wings.

verberation (vɜːbəˈreɪʃən). [ad. L. *verberātio*, noun of action from *verberāre*: see prec. So F. *verbération* (13–14th cent.), Sp. *verberacion*, Pg. *verberação*.]

1. The action of beating or striking, or the fact of being struck, so as to produce sound; percussion.

1610 HEALEY *St. Aug. Citie of God* XVI. vi. (1620) 547 Not admitting sound or verberation of aire. **1696** PHILLIPS s.v., The cause of sounds that proceed from the Verberation of the Air. **1728** CHAMBERS *Cycl.* s.v., Sound..arises from a Verberation of the Air. **1865** SALA *Diary Amer.* II. 131 Canada has often been declared..to be 'knocking at the door of the Union';..if Canada ever resorts to that method of verberation [etc.].

b. Reverberation of sound.

1855 SINGLETON *Virgil* I. 186 Where The vaulted rocks with verberation ring.

† **2.** (See quot.) *Obs.*$^{-0}$

1688 HOLME *Armoury* II. 387/2 A Verberation, or Verberous feeling; a smarting pain, as when we are beaten with rods, whips, or scourges.

3. The action of beating or striking so as to cause pain or hurt; *esp.* flogging or scourging; also, a blow or stroke.

c **1730** ARBUTHNOT (J.), Redness and inflammation; all the effects of a soft press or verberation. **1768** BLACKSTONE *Comm.* III. 120 The Cornelian law..prohibited pulsation as well as verberation; distinguishing verberation, which was accompanied with pain, from pulsation which was attended with none. **1774** GOLDSM. *Nat. Hist.* (1862) II. 427 It is by the strong folds of the body, by the fierce verberations of the tail, that the enemy is destroyed. **1860** THACKERAY *Round. Papers*, *Lazy little Boy*, The anger, or..the verberations of his schoolmaster. **1879** *Daily Tel.* 21 July, The beadle, alas! was armed with a different instrument of verberation. **1895** *Class. Rev.* April 146/1 It is idle to translate 'go on striking', for the word is found repeatedly when the verberation had not yet started.

'verberative, *a.* [f. VERBERATE *v.*: see -ATIVE.] Addicted to the practice of flogging.

1866 *Pall Mall G.* 1 Aug. 9 Her mother was a strict disciplinarian of the verberative school.

verbere, southern ME. var. FORBEAR *v.*

† **'verberous**, *a. Obs.*$^{-0}$ [f. L. *verber* a blow.]

1688 [see VERBERATION 2].

verbiage (ˈvɜːbiɪdʒ). [a. F. *verbiage* (17th c.), irreg. f. L. *verb-um* word: see -AGE. So Pg. *verbiagem*.]

1. Wording of a superabundant or superfluous character, abundance of words without necessity or without much meaning; excessive wordiness.

a **1721** PRIOR *Dial. Locke & Montaigne* 275 Without.. being guided by any sort of Verbiage like this. **1738** WARBURTON *Div. Legat.* I. 69 The Matter, when..cleared from the Perplexity of his abounding Verbiage, lies open to this easy Answer. **1787** CHARLOTTE SMITH *Rom. Real Life* I. 167 The repetitions and verbiage of the pleadings [have been] reduced. **1858** SEARS *Athan.* I. iii. 20 In vain you take refuge in abstractions and verbiage. **1880** L. STEPHEN *Pope* iii. 73 The Homeric phrase is thus often muffled and deadened by Pope's verbiage.

2. Diction, wording, verbal expression.

1804 WELLINGTON in Gurw. *Desp.* (1835) III. 193 All that is nothing; the previous verbiage [of the treaty] is thought sufficient to bind us. **1814** *New Brit. Theatre* III. 286 The language of the dialogue is as familiar as the verbiage of the parlour fireside. **1882** FARRAR *Early Chr.* I. 186 Independently of this distinctiveness of verbiage there is a wide difference between the two Epistles in the general form of thought.

Hence [or f. F. *verbiager* vb.] **verbi'agerie**.

1817 *Blackw. Mag.* I. 469 Her obscurity,—her high-sounding phrases,—..and all the imposing apparatus of verbiagerie, are not unsparingly employed.

verbicide[1] (ˈvɜːbɪsaɪd). [f. L. *verbi-*, *verbum* word + -CIDE 1.] One who mutilates or destroys a word.

1867 *Independent* (N.Y.) 2 May (Cent.), These clownish verbicides have carried their antics to the point of disgust. **1894** *Let.* in *Melbourne Argus* 10 Jan., It is this laziness in speaking which makes them [the Australians] grow up habitual verbicides.

'verbicide[2]. [f. as prec. + -CIDE 2.] The act of destroying the sense or value of a word; the perversion of a word from its proper meaning.

1858 O. W. HOLMES *Aut. Breakf.-t.* i. (1859) 10 Homicide and *verbicide*—that is, violent treatment of a word with fatal results to its legitimate meaning..—are alike forbidden. **1886** *Q. Rev.* Jan. 177 It is 'verbicide' in a higher sense than that in which Oliver Wendell Holmes applied the term to punning.

Hence **'verbicidal** *a.*, tending or liable to destroy the sense or value of a word.

1978 *Forum on Med.* Apr. 85/1 Other verbicidal entertainers who were school dropouts have also received 'honorary' degrees. **1985** *Times* 27 Mar. 12/8 The verbicidal impulses of Pentagonese.

verbid (ˈvɜːbɪd). [f. VERB + -ID[1].] *Gram.* A word, as an infinitive, gerund or participle, which has some verbal characteristics but lacks the power of forming sentences. Also *attrib.* and in *Comb.*

1914 O. JESPERSEN *Mod. Eng. Gram.* II. 7 We shall.. restrict the name of verb to those forms that have the eminently verbal power of forming sentences, and..apply the name of verbid to participles and infinitives. **1940** BRYANT & AIKEN *Psychol. of Eng.* 23 Such a unit [*sc.* John having called the dog] is called a verbid clause, because *having called* is not a full verb. **1966** R. L. ALLEN *Verb System Present-Day Amer. Eng.* 136 Of the 4800 verb and verbid-clusters included in the corpus, 1191..are clusters with some form of BE as the verb.

verbification (vɜːbɪfɪˈkeɪʃən). [See next and -FICATION.] The action of converting a substantive into a verb.

1871 EARLE *Philol. Eng. Tongue* vi. 259 Reason will be given..for supposing that it had its beginning in the verbification of a French substantive. **1884** *Trans. Amer. Philol. Assoc.* XV. p. xxxii, The languages of Maskoki affinity..have the power of expressing accidental and real existence by a verbification of the noun.

verbify (ˈvɜːbɪfaɪ), *v.* [f. VERB 1 + -(I)FY.] *trans.* To convert (a noun, etc.) into a verb. Also *absol.*

a **1813** [see *ppl. a.*]. **1871** EARLE *Philol. Eng. Tongue* 183 Not only does the language avail itself of this facility of verbifying a noun, but even [etc.]. **1884** *Trans. Amer. Philol. Assoc.* XV. p. xxvii, Nouns become verbified by the appending of inflectional affixes, generally suffixes, and are inflected like verbs. *Ibid.* p. xxxii, Hitchiti verbifies in the same manner.

So **'verbified**, **'verbifying** *ppl. adjs.*

a **1813** MURRAY *Hist. Europ. Lang.* (1823) II. 265 A consonant or long vowel may intervene, which vowel or consonant may be justly called the verbifying consignificative. **1884** *Trans. Amer. Philol. Assoc.* XV. p. xxxii, An instance of a verbified substantive, miki, 'chief', was presented above.

verbigerate (vəˈbɪdʒəreɪt), *v.* [f. ppl. stem of L. *verbigerāre* to talk, chat, f. *verbi-*, *verbum* word + *gerĕre* to conduct, carry on.]

† **1.** *intr.* (See quot.) *Obs.*$^{-0}$

1656 BLOUNT *Glossogr.*, *Verbigerate*, to speak, to talk, to noise abroad.

2. *Path.* To go on repeating the same word or phrase in a meaningless fashion, as a symptom of mental disease.

1892 TUKE *Dict. Psychol. Med.* II. 1355/1 The patient repeats in a verbigerating monotone the sentence, 'Please, do give me the keys'.

Hence **verbige'ration**. *Path.*

1886 *Jrnl. Nerv. Dis.* XIII. 699 Some emotion, at variance with his 'verbigeration'. **1892** TUKE *Dict. Psychol. Med.* II. 1355/1 Verbigeration is an abnormal and unnecessary repetition of words. *Ibid.* 1355/2 Verbigeration as a symptom, is not rare. **1899** *Allbutt's Syst. Med.* VIII. 345 Verbigeration has been noticed in some during the post-paroxysmal automatism.

verbill, obs. Sc. f. WARBLE.

'verbing, *vbl. sb.* [f. VERB 1.] The using of words as verbs.

1757 MRS. GRIFFITH *Lett. Henry & Frances* (1767) IV. 60 As to the Nouning and Verbing, which he so heavily charged you with, I told him..that you never confounded Grammar.

verbless (ˈvɜːblɪs), *a.* [f. VERB + -LESS.] Having no verb.

a **1849** H. COLERIDGE *Ess.* (1851) I. 75 What is called a fluent man,..in whose discourse are no verbless nominative cases. **1858** J. ROBERTSON *Poems* 80 The nounless, verbless tongue. **1908** *Daily Chron.* 27 Jan. 4/7 After searching through a solid page of verbless matter.

verbo- (ˈvɜːbəʊ), irreg. comb. form of L. *verbum* word, employed in a few nonce-words, as ***verbo'mania*** (also ***-'maniac***), ***verbo'tomical***, ***ver'botomist***, ***ver'botomy***.

1802 (*title*), Hints to Legislators, by W. P. Russel, Verbotomist. **1804** W. P. RUSSEL (*title*), Verbotomical Spelling-book. **1805** —— (*title*), Verbotomy, or a classical improved vocabulary..of the English language. **1923** OGDEN & RICHARDS *Meaning of Meaning* ii. 89 A veritable orgy of verbomania. **1977** J. GARVIN in D. Ó Muirithe *Eng. Lang. in Ireland* 112 *Finnegans Wake* abounds in Anglo-Irish idiom..but it is subsumed into..'slanguage' which leaves the book adrift in a polyglottic sea of verbomania.

† **verboci'nation.** *Obs. rare.* [a. F. *verbocination* (Rabelais), f. L. *verb-um*, after *ratiocination*.] Expression of ideas by means of words.

1653 URQUHART *Rabelais* II. vi. 31 We despumate the Latial verbocination. **1694** MOTTEUX *Rabelais* v. 252 Where Rules to polish Loquels are prescrib'd, and Doct Verbocination is imbib'd.

verbose (vəˈbəʊs), *a.* [ad. L. *verbōs-us*, f. *verbum* word. Cf. It., Sp., Pg. *verboso*, OF. *verbos*, mod.F. (from 17th c.) *verbeux*.]

1. Expressed in an unnecessary number of words; prolix, wordy.

1672 PENN *Spir. Truth Vind.* 8 Which I am assur'd is quite another thing, from what is Verbose, Abusive Cavelling, Airy, and meerly Notional. **1681** H. NEVILE *Plato Rediv.* 159 For there was no need to make Acts verbose, when the great Persons could presently force the Execution of them. **1721** STRYPE *Eccl. Mem.* I. xlviii. 357 [They] foresaw, that in these conferences..there would happen nothing but verbose janglings and endless disceptations. **1756–7** tr. *Keysler's Trav.* (1760) I. 170 A verbose, but not a very elegant inscription. **1781** GIBBON *Decl. & F.* xxviii. (1787) III. 75 *note*, Few facts, and few sentiments, can be extracted from his verbose correspondence. **1826** F. REYNOLDS *Life & Times* II. 97 Wilkes,..instead of attempting to gain silence, by any verbose circumlocutory appeal, proceeded at once to the point. **1841** W. SPALDING *Italy & It. Isl.* II. 392 His style..is not only inartificially complex, but verbose to the very brink of tediousness. **1870** BURTON *Hist. Scot.* lxix. (1873) VI. 164 Countless papers, expressed in..verbose and tedious tenor.

2. Using an excessive number of words; writing or speaking at excessive length; long-winded.

1692 WASHINGTON *Milton's Def. People Eng.* M.'s Wks. 1851 VIII. Pref. 1, I fear, lest..I might seem to deserve justly to be accounted a verbose and silly Defender. **1726** AYLIFFE *Parergon* 56 They ought to be brief, and not too verbose in their way of speaking. **1776** ADAM SMITH *W.N.* II. iv. (1869) I. 358 The conveyances of a verbose attorney. **1820** SCOTT *Monast.* x, Undergoing the legends of the dull and verbose Father Nicolas. **1874** GREEN *Short Hist.* ii. §3. 67 Dudo of S. Quentin, a verbose and confused writer, has preserved the earliest Norman traditions.

b. quasi-*adv.* In a verbose manner.

1791 COWPER *Odyss.* XVII. 474 Peace! answer not verbose a man like him.

verbosely (vəˈbəʊslɪ), *adv.* [f. prec. + -LY².] In a verbose manner; wordily.

1775 in ASH. **1784** COWPER *Ep. J. Hill* 44, I hate long arguments, verbosely spun. **1794** W. TAYLOR in *Monthly Rev.* XIII. 45 Passages may be found which will seem to have been rendered indolently or verbosely. **1902** *Sat. Rev.* 29 Nov. 682/2 Miss Taylor..tells the story effectively if a little verbosely.

verboseness (vəˈbəʊsnɪs). [f. as prec. + -NESS.] The character or quality of being verbose; verbosity.

1727 BAILEY (vol. II), *Verbosness*, the using many Words, Fulness of Words, Prolixity in Discourse. **1748** RICHARDSON *Clarissa* (1811) III. 73, I don't often gratify him.. with giving him the praise for his verboseness. *a* **1797** H. WALPOLE *George II* (1847) II. xi. 378 When his verboseness did not persuade, he quickened it with impertinence. **1843** *Fraser's Mag.* XXVIII. 73 He has been mesmerised into a mystical verboseness without positive thought.

† **verbosious**, *a.* *Obs.*⁻¹ = VERBOSE *a.* 2.

1676 J. SMITH *Old Age* (ed. 2) 258 Among all the Verbosious Græcians there is not one compleat Tract upon this Subject only.

verbosity (vəˈbɒsɪtɪ). Also 6 verbositee, 6–7 -tie. [a. F. *verbosité* (16th cent.), or ad. L. (post-classical) *verbōsitas*, f. *verbōsus* VERBOSE *a.* Cf. It. *verbosità*, Sp. *verbosidad*, Pg. *-idade*.] The state or quality of being verbose; superfluity of words; wordiness, prolixity.

1542 UDALL *Erasm. Apoph.* 74 b, Diogenes noted Plato of unmesurable verbositee. **1588** SHAKS. *L.L.L.* v. i. 18 He draweth out the thred of his verbositie, finer then the staple of his argument. *a* **1610** HEALEY *Theophrastus* (1636) 29 Seeking the like occasions of pratling and verbosity. **1649** MILTON *Eikon.* ix. Wks. 1851 III. 397 It were an endless work to walk side by side with the Verbosity of this Chapter. *a* **1680** BUTLER *Rem.* (1759) I. 373 But O! the Verbosity of thy Writings! **1781** MME. D'ARBLAY *Diary* May, He gave his opinion..with an emptiness and verbosity, that rendered the whole dispute..ridiculous. **1837** HALLAM *Hist. Lit.* I. ii. §31 Vitello, avoiding the tediousness of Arabian verbosity, is far more readable than Alhazen. **1898** BODLEY *France* II. III. iv. 197 A high standard of style is a check on rash verbosity.

b. With pl. An instance of this.

1665 GLANVILL *Scepsis Sci.* 116 These Verbosities emasculate the understanding, and render it slight and frivolous.

‖**verboten** (fɛrˈboːtən), *a.* [Ger.] Forbidden; not allowed.

1912 R. BROOKE *Old Vicarage, Grantchester* (1916) 8 Meads towards Haslingfield and Coton Where *das Betreten*'s not *verboten*. **1916** J. BUCHAN *Greenmantle* v. 63, I got very bored, for I had nothing to read and my pipe was *verboten*. **1949** E. BENN *Happier Days* xviii. 217 The unfortunate German, bred and trained from childhood to understand that everything is *verboten* unless specifically permitted. **1968** FINCH & CAIN in J. Marmor *Mod. Psychoanal.* xvii. 446 The obviously important but almost verboten subject of the implicit structure of rewards. **1979** R. MUTCH *Gemstone* viii. 94 She was *verboten*, strictly off limits.

† **'verbous**, *a.* *Obs. rare.* = VERBOSE *a.*

1657 G. STARKEY *Helmont's Vind.* 46 Which Art..hath been opposed, slandered, reproached, reviled and gainsaid by the verbous, railing Galenists. **1659** O. WALKER *Oratory* A 4 b, To be Concise for the Pen;..Yet more circumlocutory and verbous for extempore-speech.

verbroyde, var. pa. pple. FORBRAID *v.* *Obs.*

‖**verbum sap.** [A shortening of L. *verbum sapienti sat est* 'a word is sufficient to a wise person'.] A phrase used in place of making a full statement or explanation, implying that an intelligent person may easily infer what is left unsaid, or understand the reasons for reticence. Also freq. further abbreviated to **verb sap.**

Examples of the full phrase, and of the shortened forms *verbum sapienti (sat)*, occur in English works from at least 1602 onwards. The wording appears to be a combination of *verbum sat est* (see next) and *dictum sapienti sat est*, both of which are used by Plautus, the latter also by Terence.

1818 T. MOORE *Fudge Fam. in Paris* vi. 6 But never fear —I know my chap, And he knows *me*, too—*verbum sap.* **1828** LYTTON *Pelham* xxiv, I am very sorry I could not see you to breakfast—a particular engagement prevented me—*verbum sap.* **1841** E. BRONTË in *Brontës: Lives, Friendships & Corr.* (1932) I. x. 238, I have just made a new regularity paper! and I mean *verb sap* to do great things. **1862** W. COLLINS *No Name* III. 12, I say no more. *Verbum sap.* **1889** E. DOWSON *Let.* 9 Nov. (1967) 115 Mark that horse & when he runs next plump on him with all your available capital. Verb Sap. This tip I may add doesn't come from Museum Mansions but from a man who spotted Primrose Day for the C'wtch. **1976** J. I. M. STEWART *Young Pattullo* ii. 40 Mind your Ps and Qs, if I were you. *Verb. sap.*—eh?

‖**verbum sat.** Also **sat verbum.** [See note to prec.] A phrase used to conclude a statement, implying that further explanation or comment is unnecessary or unadvisable.

In the first quot. perhaps equivalent to prec.

1649 EVELYN *Corr.* (1850) III. 49 Against which [conquest] I find most men inclined to oppose, by a juncture with the new Commonwealth. Verbum sat—. **1668** in *Extr. St. P. rel. Friends* III. (1912) 277 Ile say they are not of yᵉ brood of yᵉ old Presbyterian. verbum sat. **1838** THACKERAY *Misc. Ess.* (1885) 129 *Verbum sat*—this naughty 'Somnolency' ought to go to sleep in her night-gown. **1856** KANE *Arct. Expl.* II. xix. 195 The thing can be done, and we did it: *sat verbum*.

verby (ˈvɜːbɪ), *a.* *rare*⁻¹. [f. VERB + -Y.] Abounding in verbs.

a **1845** HOOD *Sir John Bowring* 10 No grammar too abstruse he meets However dark and verby.

vercifier, obs. f. VERSIFIER.

verclef, southern ME. pa. t. of *forcleave* FOR-*pref.*¹ 5 b.

verd, *sb.* [a. obs. F. *verd* (= Cat. *verd*, Sp., Pg., It. *verde*):—L. *virid-em*, *viridis*: cf. VERT *sb.*¹]

1. † **a.** *Her.* The tincture green or vert. *Obs.*

c **1450** J. METHAM *Wks.* (E.E.T.S.) 36 For Arge, [w]hos kyng a lebard passaund Off syluer in uerd bare, he vsyd greuys that with grene were dyght.

b. *poet.* The colour green. *rare.*

1915 G. C. M. BIRDWOOD *Sva* 59 The whole paradisaical scene shining in the setting sun with the transcendent resplendence of its various verds and shimmering gold. **1929** S. LESLIE *Anglo-Catholic* ix. 110 The pavement was tesselated purple and verd. Great tapestries hung between pillars.

† **2.** *transf.* Verdancy, freshness. *Obs.*

1603 HARSNET *Pop. Impost.* 121 For Reliques..worke like an Apothecaries potion or new Ale: they have best strength and verd at the first.

† **3.** Forest-verdure; = VERT *sb.*¹ 1. *Obs.*

1641 *Termes de la Ley* 261 b (*heading*), Verde or Vert. **1664** in *Spelman's Gloss.*

† **4.** *Geol.* ? = GREEN-STONE 1. *Obs.*

1799 W. TOOKE *View Russian Emp.* I. 142 There are likewise..mica spathosa, verd, serpentine,..and marlstone.

verd, southern ME. var. pa. t. of FERE *v.*¹ *Obs.*

† **verd**, *v.* *Obs.*⁻¹ [Back-formation from next.] *trans.* To sow for verdage. In quot. *absol.*

1778 [W. H. MARSHALL] *Minutes Agric., Digest* 60 If Verdage and Pasturage be wanted, verd with Spring-Corn and Ley-Grasses.

† **'verdage**, *sb.* *Obs.* [f. *verd-* (as in *verdure*) + -AGE; introduced by Marshall. Cf. F. *verdage* young grain ploughed in as manure.] 'Green herbage, cut and given to cattle green' (Marshall).

1778 [W. H. MARSHALL] *Minutes Agric.* 9 June 1775, The weeds are now tender and full of sap, and make very good verdage. *Ibid., Digest* 74 Lucerne is an excellent Spring-verdage. *Ibid.* 84 Clover and Tare verdage.

Hence † **'verdage** *v.* *trans.*, to cut or use as verdage. Also with *off*.

1778 [W. H. MARSHALL] *Minutes Agric., Digest* 62 Plow-in or Verdage-off a foul Crop. *Ibid.* 71 Verdaging the Corn encourages the young Grasses. *Ibid.* 72 Verdage weedy margins early in Summer.

verdancy (ˈvɜːdənsɪ). [See VERDANT *a.* and -ANCY.]

1. The quality, condition, or character of being verdant; greenness.

1631 MAY tr. *Barclay's Mirr. Mindes* I. 39 But the greatest delight is, that soe faire a verdancy is almost distinguished into diuerse colours. *Ibid.* 100 England abounding in rich pastures..doth euery where delight the eyes of the beholders with a most beautifull verdancy. **1882** *Gd. Words* 608 Yellow freckles in some leaves may bestrew a surface of unfaded verdancy. **1888** *Harper's Mag.* July 220 We see.. the same wonderful varieties of verdancy.

† **b.** *transf.* Freshness of appearance. *Obs.*⁻¹

1678 NORRIS *Coll. Misc.* (1699) 368 Had not the Youth and Verdancy of her Face contradicted the ripeness of her Discoursings, you would have thought her well in years.

2. *fig.* Innocence, inexperience; rawness, simplicity.

1849 W. S. MAYO *Kaloolah* xxxvii, True, in the verdancy of youthful sentiment, many a one has shrunk from the profane association of ruby lips with the processes of mastication and deglutition. **1863** *Baily's Mag.* Jan. 358 Alas for my verdancy!

verdant (ˈvɜːdənt), *a.* Also 7 **verdent**. [f. *verd-* (as in *verdure*) + -ANT, perhaps partly after L. *viridant-*, *viridans*, pres. pple. of *viridāre*, f. *viridis* green. Cf. also OF. *verdeant* (*virdeant*), *verdoiant* (F. *verdoyant*).]

1. Of a green hue or colour; green: **a.** Of vegetation.

1581 A. HALL *Iliad* I. 1 Chryses..With verdant crown, wherewith Apoll his seemely head had clad. **1590** SPENSER *F.Q.* I. ix. 13 The verdant gras my couch did goodly dight. **1633** COWLEY *Constantia* 114 Th' verdant grasse was dew'd with many a teare. **1662** J. DAVIES tr. *Mandelslo's Trav.* 267 Fruit-trees,..which keep on their verdant Liveries all the year long. **1698** FRYER *Acc. E. India & P.* 64 The Walks which before were covered with Nature's verdent awning.. are now open to the Sun. **1764** R. LLOYD *Capricious Lovers* v. ii, When eve embrowns the verdant grove. **1796** H. HUNTER tr. *St.-Pierre's Stud. Nat.* (1799) III. 334 We soon discovered the profound and verdant forests which cover Celtic Gaul. **1842** LOUDON *Suburban Hort.* 337 Where ornamental hedges and other verdant architectural structures are to be grown. **1853** KANE *Grinnell Exp.* l. (1856) 474 Crowned each with its little verdant tuft,—ten radishes!

b. In other applications. *rare.*

1649 LOVELACE *Grasshopper* Poems 35 Poore verdant foole [*sc.* a grasshopper], and now green Ice! **1667** MILTON *P.L.* IX. 501 [The] Serpent..With burnisht Neck of verdant Gold, erect Amidst his circling Spires. **1738** GRAY *Tasso* 67 Here the soft emerald smiles of verdant hue.

2. Green with vegetation; characterized by abundance of verdure.

1590 SPENSER *F.Q.* I. ii. 17 Streames of purple bloud new dies the verdant fields. **1647** OGILBY *Virg. Georg.* IV. 322 Gliding Streams..Which border nigh the Quiver'd Persian Land, And verdant Egypt Marl with fruitful Sand. **1667** MILTON *P.L.* VIII. 631 The parting Sun Beyond the Earths green Cape and verdant Isles Hesperian sets. **1738** WESLEY *Ps.* XXIII. ii, Where peaceful Rivers soft and slow Amid the verdant Landskip flow. **1784** COWPER *Task* VI. 70 As I tread The walk, still verdant, under oaks and elms. **1815** ELPHINSTONE *Acc. Caubul* (1842) I. 381 In the midst of a verdant and pleasing country, which enjoys a temperate climate. **1817** MOORE *Lalla R., Fire-Worshippers* iv. 90 Like those verdant spots that bloom Around the crater's burning lips. **1868** MISS BRADDON *Dead Sea F.* ii, The verdant avenues and placid water.

3. *fig.* Of persons: Green, inexperienced, gullible.

1824 BYRON *Juan* XV. xciii, Because my business is to *dress* society, And stuff with *sage* that very verdant goose. **1854** *Poultry Chron.* I. 269/2, I spoke of simple facts in my own experience, and with the..object of warning 'verdant' purchasers. **1869** *Punch* 14 Aug. 57/1 Flush of his money and just as refreshingly verdant.

Hence **'verdantness**, verdancy. *rare*⁻⁰.

1727 BAILEY (vol. II), *Verdantness*, a flourishing, bright, or lively Greenness.

‖**verd-antique, verd antique** (ˌvɜːd ænˈtiːk). Also 9 verde-. [Older F. (now *vert antique*), 'antique green'. Cf. VERDE ANTICO.]

1. An ornamental variety of marble, consisting chiefly of serpentine mixed with calcite and dolomite.

1745 POCOCKE *Descr. East* II. I. 193 The hills of Antioch are part of them of a crumbling stone, like verd antique. **1755** *Phil. Trans.* XLIX. 109 Columns of verd' antique and oriental alabaster. **1806** J. PINKERTON *Recollect. Paris* II. 139 Egyptian breccia..has been mistaken for the serpentine-marble, called verd antique. **1838** MACAULAY in Trevelyan *Life* vii. (1876) II. 32, I should like to see the walls of St. Paul's incrusted with porphyry and verde antique. **1884** *Mag. Art* Apr. 226/1 Its design must have been made entirely to suit the twelve columns of verd-antique which surround its walls.

attrib. **1828** *Lights & Shades* II. 282 A verd-antique pitcher with an ear. **1857** DANA *Min.* (1862) 147 Serpentine forms a handsome marble when polished, especially when mixed with limestone, constituting *verd-antique* marble.

b. ***oriental verd-antique***, green porphyry. Occasionally without adj. Also *attrib.*

1852 E. BARBER *Painters'* (etc.) *Assist.* 75 To imitate Oriental Verdantique Marble. **1857** DANA *Min.* (1862) 356 Green porphyry is the *oriental verd antique* of the ancients, and was held in high esteem. **1879** RUTLEY *Stud. Rocks* xii. 240 The verde-antique porphyry is one of the diabase-porphyrites.

2. A green incrustation on brass or copper; verdigris.

a **1835** MRS. HEMANS *Last Wasp Scot.* Poems (1849) 523 Never may housemaid wipe the verd antique From coin of thine. **1851** D. WILSON *Preh. Ann.* III. v. 447 Another example.., covered with verd antique, is a light beautiful bracelet.

verdantly ('vɜːdəntlɪ), *adv.* [f. VERDANT *a.* + -LY[2].] In a green or verdant manner; freshly, flourishingly.

1828 MOORE *Believe me, if all those endearing young charms* i, Around the dear ruin each wish of my heart Would entwine itself verdantly still. **1847** in WEBSTER. **1889** GRETTON *Memory's Harkb.* 257 The special song of Madame A. was 'With verdure clad'... Madame B. elected to be 'verdantly' clothed.

b. In a raw or inexperienced manner; greenly.

1864 R. KIMBALL *Was he successful?* I. xiii. 151 Perhaps to give the young fellow who was so verdantly staring at him a start.

†**verdate.** *Chem. Obs.* [f. VERD-IC *a.* + -ATE[1] 1 c.] (See quot. 1859.)

1843 *Penny Cycl.* XXVI. 256/1 The earthy or metallic *verdites* are yellow, while the *verdates* of the same bases are green. **1859** MAYNE *Expos. Lex.*, *Verdate*,.. a combination of verdic acid with a salifiable base.

verd-azure, *a. rare*$^{-1}$. [ad. It. *verdazzurro* sea-green: see VERD *sb.* and AZURE *a.* Cf. obs. F. *verd d'azur* (Cotgr.), used by Holland *Pliny* (1601) II. 528.] Of a bluish-green colour; sea-green.

1876 WHITNEY *Sights & Ins.* xxxiii. II. 147 The gold-green water that, out from the mountain shadows, grew verd-azure in the sun.

†**verdazurine,** *a. Obs.*$^{-1}$ [See prec. and -INE[2].] Bluish-green; sea-green.

1681 GREW *Musæum* III. iii. 349 A Verdazurine Bole. So I call it, for that it is on the out-side of a blewish-green, like Verdegriese.

verde, southern ME. var. FERD *sb.*[1] and pa. t. FERE *v.*[1] *Obs.*

†**verdé.** *Obs. rare.* Also verdi(e. [ad. It. *verdèa* or F. *verdée.*] = next.

c **1645** HOWELL *Lett.* (1650) II. 74 Nor is ther in Italy any wine transported to England but in bottles, as *Verdé* and others. *Ibid.* (1655) IV. 16 They must not be us'd like Saffron bags, or *Verdé* bottles which are thrown into som by-corner when the wine and spice are taken out of them. **1656** BLOUNT *Glossogr.*, *Verdi*, a kind of white Muscadine wine.

ver'dea. Also 8 verd(e)dea. [a. It. *verdèa* (whence F. *verdée*, Pg. *verdea*), f. *verde* green.] A wine made of a white grape grown in the neighbourhood of Arcetri near Florence. Also *attrib.*

a **1625** FLETCHER & MASS. *Elder Bro.* II. i, Say it had been at Rome, and seen the Reliques, drunk your Verdea Wine, and rid at Naples. **1656** BLOUNT *Glossogr.*, *Verdea*, a kind of white Muscadine wine, made in Toscany, which is sometimes brought into England in bottles. **1719** BOYER *Dict. Royal* I, *Verdée*,.. Verd-dea, White-Florentine Wine. **1760** BARETTI *Ital. Dict.*, *Verdea*, a kind of white grapes called Verdedea, of which is made a kind of wine, called also Verdedea. **1833** C. REDDING *Hist. Mod. Wines* (1851) 278 The celebrated Verdea is a white wine, having a bright green tinge, grown at Arcetri; it was formerly held in high esteem. **1845** *Encycl. Metrop.* XXV. 1285/1.

b. *transf.* (See quot.)

1858 SIMMONDS *Dict. Trade*, *Verdea*, a white Tunisian wine.

‖**verde antico.** [It.] = VERD-ANTIQUE 1.

1753 *Chambers' Cycl.* Suppl. s.v. *Marble*, Carystium Marmor..; the Italian antiquaries particularly mean this, by a name also in use among us, and prostituted to every other species of green marble, the *verde antiquo.* **1765** SMOLLETT *Trav. Italy* xxviii. Wks. (1841) 756/2 The great profusion of granite, prophyry, jasper, verde antico, lapis-lazuli, and other precious stones. **1839** *Penny Cycl.* XIV. 409/1 Some Verde Antico, as that dug near Susa in Piedmont. **1883** MISS BRADDON *Gold. Calf* II. vi. 185 Placid gods and goddesses smirking at vacancy, on pedestals of verde antico. **1883** *Encycl. Brit.* XV. 529/1 The famous *verde antico* is a rock of this character [i.e. serpentinous limestone].

verdegreace, -gres(e, etc., obs. ff. VERDIGRIS.

‖**verdelho** (və'dɛʎuː). [Pg.] A prolific vine yielding a white grape orig. grown in Madeira and now found in Portugal, Sicily, Australia, and South Africa; also, a medium white Madeira wine made from this grape.

1824 A. HENDERSON *Hist. Anc. & Mod. Wines* viii. 249 Among the various species of grapes cultivated, those called *verdelho, negra*..and *sercial*, yield the best wines. **1883** *Encycl. Brit.* XV. 178/1 The wine usually termed Madeira.. is made from a mixture of black and white grapes, which are also made separately into wines called Tinto and Verdelho. **1926** P. M. SHAND *Bk. Wine* iii. 41 Two thirds of the vines grown on the island are of the celebrated Verdelho species. **1935** A. L. SIMON *Dict. Wine* 249 *Verdelho*, one of the white fortified wines of Madeira, which used to be made with the Verdelho grape, now all but extinct. **1959** W. JAMES *Word-bk. Wine* 195 *Verdelho*, a white grape which gives its name to a sweet dessert type of madeira, though the vine is not grown on the island to any great extent. **1980** *Times* 27 Nov. 20/4 The two drier styles of wine, Sercial and Verdelho.

verdeour, variant of VERDOUR[1] *Obs.*

†**'verder**[1]. *Obs.* Also 6 vardar. [var. of VERDOUR[1], with weakened ending on the analogy of agent-nouns in *-our*, *-er*, *-ar*.]

1. = VERDOUR[1] 2, VERDURE 3: **a.** In plural.

1500 *Inv.* in *Ann. Reg.* (1768) II. 134 One dozen of cushions of verders stuffed with feathers. **1542** in Harrison *Ann. Old Manor Ho.* (1893) 207, vij peces of smale verders storyed with bests & ffowles; iiij peces of verders paued with redd and white. **1547** in Kempe *Losely MSS.* (1836) 152 Sixe longe carpytts of grene vardars, with flowers lyned with canvys. **1660** in *Statutes of Realm* (1819) V. 198/1 Verders of Tapistry with haire. **1662** in *Stat. at Large, Ireland* (1765) II. 417 Verders Tapistry, containing eight or ten ells with hair.

b. In singular.

1522-3 *Inv.* in *Archaeol.* (1860) XXXVIII. 364 A counter-paynt of verder and a pleyn cubborde. *Ibid.*, ij° gret cownterpoyntes of verder. **1535-6** in Dugdale *Monast. Angl.* (1823) IV. 542 One chare of lether frynged with one cuysshon of verder. **1594** *Inv.* in *Archaeol.* (1884) XLVIII. 126 Item two wollen blancketes and a coveringe of verdere xl*s*.

2. = VERDURE 4. *rare*$^{-1}$.

1532 MORE *Confut. Tindale* Wks. 357/1 That the olde holsome wine..offend their dronken taste, because it is not so walowe swete but drinketh more of the verder.

†**verder**[2]. *Obs. rare.* [a. AF. *verder* (13-14th c.) = OF. and F. *verdier* VERDIER. See also VERDOUR[2].] = VERDERER[2] 1.

a **1625** SIR H. FINCH *Law* (1636) 497 *De exonerando viridario forestæ*, to discharge a verder of the forest in like sort. **1717** *Hist. Reg., Chronol. Reg.* 41 Thomas Gage, Esq., elected Verder of the Forest of Dean.

†**verder**[3], ? mispr. for VERGER[3].

a **1548** HALL *Chron., Hen. VIII*, 214 [The] high Constable of England bearyng the verder of siluer appertainyng to y[e] office of Constableship.

†**'verderer**[1]. *Obs.*$^{-1}$ [Extended form of VERDER[1]: cf. next.] = VERDURE 3.

c **1550** *Disc. Common Weal Eng.* (1893) 85 The arrisses, verderers, and tapstrie worke, wheare with they be hanged.

verderer[2] ('vɜːdərə(r)). Forms: α. 6-7 verderour, 7-9 -or. β. 7- verderer. γ. 8- verdurer. [a. AF. *verderer* (1278), extended form of *verder* VERDER[2], f. OF. *verd* (var. of *vert*: see VERD *sb.* and VERT *sb.*[1]):—L. *viridis* green. In med.L. rendered by *viridarius*.]

1. 'A judicial officer of the King's forest.. sworn to maintain and keep the assises of the forest, and also to view, receive, and enroll the attachments and presentments of all manner of trespasses of the forest, of vert and venison' (Manwood).

In later use chiefly surviving in connexion with New, Epping, and Dean Forests. Otherwise only *arch.* or *Hist.*

α. **1541-2** *Act 33 Hen. VIII*, c. 38 §5 Surveiyng of Woodes ..in any of y[e] said Parkes, Forrestes or chases,..and the namynge, rulinge and orderinge of the verderours thereof. **1614** SELDEN *Titles Hon.* 269 These..foure seem to haue been as those which later time haue stiled Verderors of the Forest. **1644** *Coke's Inst.* IV. c. 73 *Courts of Forests* (1797) 289 It was presented by the foresters, verderors, and agisters that the plaintiff has chased and taken deer within the forest. **1667-8** [see REGARDER 1]. **1747** CARTE *Hist. Eng.* I. 709 He.. appointed likewise in each [part] two gentlemen of his household, as verderors to take care of the vert and venison. **1765** BLACKSTONE *Comm.* I. 343 He is likewise to decide the elections of knights of the shire,..of coroners, and of verderors. **1791** GILPIN *Forest Scenery* II. 20 Besides these officers..there are four others, called verderors. *Ibid.* 21 The verderor is an ancient forest-officer. **1866** *Chamb. Jrnl.* Apr. 261/1 Under the Norman *régime*, the officers of the Forest were Verderors, Regarders, and Foresters (besides others). *Ibid.* 261/2 The verderor, to look after the vert.

β. **1611** COTGR., *Segrayer*, a Verderer, or such a like Officer of some authoritie, in forrests. *c* **1645** HOWELL *Lett.* (1655) II. IV. xvi. 39 A Forest hath Lawes of her own, to take cognisance of all trespasses; she hath also her peculiar Officers, as Foresters, Verderers, Regarders, Agisters, &c. **1664** EVELYN *Sylva* 114 The amplitude of the distance.. resign'd to the care of the Verderer. *c* **1710** CELIA FIENNES *Diary* (1888) 39 There are severall Rangers of y[e] forest, and 6 verderers y[t] are their justices or judges of all matters relateing to ye forest. **1812** W. TAYLOR in *Monthly Mag.* XXXIV. 210 A forest has laws and officers of its own, as foresters, verderers, &c. **1840** *Penny Cycl.* XVI. 175/1 The verderers and regarders [of the New Forest] are chosen by the free-holders of Hampshire. *Ibid.*, The verderers have no salary, emolument, or perquisite, besides a fee buck and a fee doe yearly. **1892** *Times* 16 July 11/2 Hampshire..has completed its roll of Unionist county members, the New Forest Division..returning the son of the Verderer, Lord Montagu.

γ. **1734** *Sir R. Atkins' Parl. & Pol. Tracts* 62 As Coroners and Verdurers [1689 Verderers]..are chosen by Writ at the County-Court to this day. **1763** MARTIN *Nat. Hist. Eng.* II. 221 The..Forest of Sherwood..has..a Ranger, 4 Verdurers, 12 Regarders. **1826** SCOTT *Woodst.* xxxii, [The] hut..of old Martin the verdurer. **1884** TENNYSON *Becket* I. iv, The King's verdurer caught him a-hunting in the forest, and cut off his paws.

†**2.** *local.* A petty constable having supervision of a city ward. *Obs.*$^{-1}$

1791 [see VERDERY].

'verderership. Also 8 verdurer-. [f. VERDERER[2] + -SHIP.] The office of a verderer.

1611 COTGR., *Segrarie*, a Verderership; or such a like Office of account in forrests. **1762** tr. *Busching's Syst. Geog.* VI. 296 The verderership over Osterforest. **1863** *Guardian* 14 Jan. 25/1 The election of proper persons to fill the vacancies in the verderership of the Forest. **1901** *Blackw. Mag.* Nov. 660/2 Why should not the author of 'The Forest Lovers'..be offered a verderership?

†**'verdery.** *local. Obs.* [a. OF. *verderie* (14th c. in Godef.), f. *verder* VERDER[2].] (See quots.)

1791 T. COLLINSON *Hist. Somerset* III. 375 The city of Wells..is divided into four verderies in the manner of wards, and thus denominated:—High Street Verdery,..and South over Verdery. *Ibid.*, These verderies, each of which is superintended by two verderers, or petty constables (an office originating from the Viridarii of the Bishop's Forest of Mendip). **1839** PHELPS *Somersetsh.* II. 11 These Verderys [in Wells] are named Chamberlain-street Verdery [etc.].

verdet ('vɜːdɛt). [a. OF. *verdet* (16th c., = Prov. and Cat. *verdet*, Sp. and Pg. *verdete*, It. *verdetto*), dim. of *verd* VERD *sb.*]

1. *Chem.* An acetate of copper (see quots.).

1558 WARDE tr. *Alexis' Secr.* 118 Take verdet, or Verdegrise, Vitriol of Almain, and salt Armoniacke. **1559** *Ibid.* III. I. 53 Take Spanishe greene called Verdet,.. Vitrioll, and Alome of eche equally. **1673** RAY *Journ. Low C.* 454 At Montpellier the best Verdet or Verdegreece is made, ..which is..nothing but the rust or scurf of copper calcined by the vapour of wine. **1863** WATTS *Dict. Chem.* I. 14 Acetates of Copper... The normal salt ($C^2H^3O^2$)^{2}Cu'', called also Crystallised Verdigris, Verdet,..is produced by dissolving cupric oxide or common verdigris in acetic acid. **1896** LODEMAN *Spraying Plants* 44 Verdet is an acetate of copper. There are many such combinations, all being known under the general name of verdet, or verdigris.

2. A fungus which grows upon maize.

1897 *Allbutt's Syst. Med.* II. 801 There seems therefore to be some quality in the maize itself, which when acted upon by the 'verdet' as the fungus is called, produces a specific poison.

verdeter, var. VERDITER.

‖**verdetto.** *rare.* [It.] = VERDET 1.

1598 R. HAYDOCKE tr. *Lomazzo* III. 99 They which make Greenes, are greene bize, Verdigrease, *verdetto* called holy, inclining towards a yeallow. **1835** G. FIELD *Chromatography* 129 The greens called Verona green, and Verdetto, or holy green, are similar native pigments [to terre-verte].

verdeur, var. VERDOUR *Obs.*; obs. f. VERDURE.

verdges, obs. f. VERJUICE.

Verdian ('vɛːdɪən), *a.* and *sb.* [f. the name of Giuseppe *Verdi* (1813-1901), Italian composer + -AN.] **A.** *adj.* Of, pertaining to, or characteristic of Verdi or his music. **B.** *sb.* An admirer of Verdi; a (skilled) exponent of his music.

1947 A. EINSTEIN *Mus. Romantic Era* xvi. 284 One should not think that *Otello*..became..a drama with music. It remained Italian opera, Verdian opera, which preserves almost completely its connection with the composer's earlier work. **1962** *Listener* 21 June 1091/2 An opera in a broad Verdian style brought up to date. **1976** *Gramophone* Aug. 334/1 Bergonzi is much the more stylistically correct Verdian. **1977** *Times* 20 Dec. 10/5 The Verdians cannot get out of it by saying that Beethoven was the greater genius. Of course he was. **1978** *Times* 10 Oct. 9/4 A noted Verdian and a remarkable Violetta..Miss Sass was perhaps ill-advised to begin her first London recital with Schumann. **1980** *Daily Tel.* 4 June 15/2 [Its] moral and imaginative qualities..have always endeared it to dedicated Verdians. *Ibid.* 15/4 His direction growing in authentically Verdian conviction.

†**'verdic,** *a. Chem. Obs.* [ad. mod.L. *verdicus* or F. *verdique*, f. F. *verdir* to become green. Cf. VERDOUS *a.*] (See quots.)

1836-41 BRANDE *Man. Chem.* (ed. 5) 1198 Verdic Acid. —This acid was extracted by Runge from several of the *Umbelliferæ* and *Plantagineæ*, &c., but chiefly from the root of the *Scabiosa succisa*. **1843** *Penny Cycl.* XXVI. 256/1 Runge states that he found by analysis that verdic acid contains one equivalent of oxygen more than the verdous acid.

‖**Verdicchio** (vɛ'dɪkɪəʊ). [It.] A white grape grown in the Marche region of Italy; also, the dry white wine made from this grape.

1940 H. J. GROSSMAN *Guide to Wines* vi. 80 Not many great wines are grown in this region, but two demand attention: a fine white, light wine—the Verdicchio di Jesi [etc.]. **1954** E. DAVID *Italian Food* 310 The white wines of the Castelli di Iesi, in the Marche, produced from Verdicchio grapes, and called usually by that name, are pleasant and refreshing to drink on the spot. **1967** F. SCHOONMAKER *Encycl. Wine* 305 *Verdicchio*, superior Italian white wine grape; also its wine. **1978** 'A. STUART' *Vicious Circles* 109, I ordered an ice-cold bottle of Verdicchio.

verdict ('vɜːdɪkt), *sb.* Forms: α. 3-7, 9 *dial.*, verdit, 4-7 -dite, 6-7 -ditt, 3-6 verdyt, -dyte, 5 -dytt, -dyth(e; 4 veirdit, 5 veredit, -dyte; 4-5 voirdit. β. 5 wardytte, 6 varditt, -dytt, 6, 9 *dial.*, vardit, 9 *dial.* vardite. Also VARDY. γ. 5 verdoit, 6 verduytt, 7 verduit, -duict. δ. 6-7 veredict, 6- verdict, 6 -dicte. [a. AF. *verdit* (= OF. *voirdit*), f. *ver*, *veir* true + *dit*, pa. pple. of *dire* to say, speak. Hence med.L. *verdictum* (*veredictum*), to which the mod. spelling and pronunciation are due. The mod.F. *verdict*, Pg. *verdict*, Sp. *verdicto*, are from Eng.]

1. *Law.* **a.** The decision of a jury in a civil or criminal cause upon an issue which has been submitted to their judgement.

α. **1297** R. GLOUC. (Rolls) 2980 He stod vp & sede þe verdit vor al oþere þat þere were. *a* **1325** *MS. Rawl. B.* 520 fol. 60b, ȝif..þe Juree segge in his veirdit þat te askare is bastard. *c* **1340** HAMPOLE *Pr. Consc.* 2952 Until þai have gyven þair verdite, And outher þar-of made hym qwyte Als þe laghe walde, or made hym gilty. *c* **1440** *Promp. Parv.* 508/2 Verdyte, *veridicum.* **1472** *Paston Lett.* III. 40, I took syche a wey with hym that the qwest gave no verdyt. **1544** tr. *Littleton's Tenures* (1574) 78 The verdyte of twelve men taken at large in Assise of disseysine. **1559** *Mirr. Mag.* (1563) K v, I gyltles was condempned: Such verdits passe where iustyce is contemned. **1591** Q. ELIZABETH in *Lismore Papers* Ser. II. (1887) I. 3 To order the landes to our pattentes as shalbe found due, vpon the saide Verdyte. **1614–5** BOYS *Exp. Fest. Epist. & Gosp.* Wks. (1630) 750 When any suite concerning the Clergie shall be tried by your verdite. **1621** QUARLES *Hadassa* Wks. (Grosart) II. 44/2 At last..they put their choyce Vpon the verdit of a Iurie's voyce.

β, γ. **1479** *Presentm. Juries in Surtees Misc.* (1890) 28 Thys is the wardytte of xxij men & the constabylls. **1531** *Star Chamb. Cases* (Selden) II. 193 To wryte any such presentment or vardytt. *Ibid.* 196 The same homage deed pleynly shewe..the same to be their trewe verduytt.

δ. **1533** MORE *Debell. Salem* Wks. 996/1 Whose verdicte the iudge taketh for a sure sentence..without ani examinacion of the circumstances, wherby they know.. their verdicte to be true. **1559** AYLMER *Harborowe* L j b, Our lawe committeth it to the veredict of .12. men. **1613** SHAKS. *Hen. VIII*, v. i. 131 Not euer The Iustice and the Truth o' th' question carries The dew o' th' Verdict with it. **1657** in *Verney Mem.* (1907) II. 121 A house and lande, which hee had recovered by law, and by a second verdict lost the same again. **1674** WOOD *Life* (O.H.S.) II. 281 The jury were about to pass their verdict. **1726** *Life Penn* P.'s Wks. I. 15 The Agreement of Twelve Men is a Verdict in Law. **1781** COWPER *Truth* 448 The jury meet, the coroner is short, And lunacy the verdict of the court. **1818** CRUISE *Digest* (ed. 2) II. 519 On the trial the Judge directed the jury to find a verdict for the plaintiff. **1885** *Public Opinion* 9 Jan. 36/2 An advocate who wins an unjust verdict has contributed to bring about a miscarriage of justice.

Comb. **1892** *Daily News* 10 May 2 Though Mr. Bramwell had a good practice, he was never a great verdict-getter.

b. Without article.

1437 *Rolls of Parlt.* IV. 509/2 Founde gilty be verdite of xii notable men. *a* **1500** in *Archaeol.* (1904) LIX. 10 By the comyn lawe..ther lith non atteynt upon untrewe verdit gyffyn in London. **1535** WRIOTHESLEY *Chron.* (Camden) I. 27 A jurie..incontinent gave verditt of them beinge guiltie of the same treason. **1577** HARRISON *England* II. ix. (1877) I. 202 Our trials and recoueries are either by verdict and demourre, confession or default. **1589** ? LYLY *Pappe w. Hatchet* (1844) 25 The Iurie gaue verdit and said guiltie. **1712** PRIDEAUX *Direct. Ch.-wardens* (ed. 4) 22 In case any should..obtain Verdict on their side. **1797** TOMLINS *Jacob's Law Dict.* s.v., Another rule at Common law is, that surplusage will not vitiate after Verdict.

c. With particularizing addition; esp. as ***open verdict***, a verdict of a coroner's jury affirming the commission of a crime (but not specifying the criminal), or the occurrence of a suspicious but unexplained death.

1607 COWELL *Interpr.* s.v., This verdict is two-fold: either generall or especiall... A general verdict is that, which is giuen or brought into the Court, in like generall termes to the generall issue. *Ibid.*, This speciall verdict, if it containe any ample declaration of the cause, from the beginning to the end, is also called a verdict at large. **1628** COKE *On Litt.* I. 226b, There be two kindes of verdicts; viz. one generall, and another at large or especiall. *Ibid.*, It is therefore called a speciall Verdict or a Verdict at large, because they finde the speciall matter at large, and leaue the iudgement of law thereupon to the Court. **1628** [see PRIVY a. 8]. **1665** [see SPECIAL a. 7]. **1768** BLACKSTONE *Comm.* III. 377 The only effectual and legal verdict is the public verdict; in which they openly declare to have found the issue for the plaintiff, or for the defendant. **1769** *Ibid.* IV. 354 The jury..cannot, in a criminal case, give a privy verdict. But an open verdict may be either general, guilty, or not guilty. **1835** TOMLINS *Law Dict.* s.v., Where a verdict is given by thirteen jurors, it is said to be a void verdict; because no attaint would lie. **1864** DICKENS *Mut. Fr.* (1865) I. I. iii. 18 In quest to-morrow, and no doubt open verdict. **1854, 1884** [see PERVERSE a. 1 c]. **1894** [see SEALED *ppl. a.* 2]. **1977** 'M. INNES' *Honeybath's Haven* xiii. 123 His jury..will bring in what is called an open verdict.

2. *transf.* and *fig.* A judgement given by some body or authority acting as, or likened to, a jury.

c **1381** CHAUCER *Parlt. Foules* 525, I iuge on euery folk men shul on calle To seyn the verdit for yow foulys alle. **1579** W. WILKINSON *Confut. Familye of Love* 63b, The euidence..whereby..that verdict should be gathered, which shall passe agaynst vs. **1589** WARNER *Alb. Eng.* Prose Add. (1612) 338 The Iurour could not but giue Verdict for Elisa, and the Iudge sentence against Æneas. **1611** SPEED *Hist. Gt. Brit.* IX. ii. §8 They are here presently to abide the verdite of battaile. **1671** MILTON *Samson* 324 Though Reason here aver That moral verdit quits her of unclean. **1684** T. BURNET *Th. Earth* I. 295 Ought we not in this, as well as in other things, to..bring in an honest verdict for nature as well as art? **1860** HAWTHORNE *Marb. Faun* (Tauchn.) II. xvi. 177 Might we not render some such verdict as this?—'Worthy of Death but not unworthy of Love'. **1867** FREEMAN *Norm. Conq.* (1877) I. vi. 501 The great Earl is at least entitled to a verdict of Not Proven, if not of Not Guilty.

3. *transf.* A decision or opinion pronounced or expressed upon some matter or subject; a finding, conclusion, or judgement.

α. *c* **1386** CHAUCER *Prol.* 787 (Petworth), Vs þouȝt it was not worþe to make to wis..And bad him seie his veredit [*v.rr.* verdit(e, voirdit, verdoit] as him lest. *c* **1430** LYDG. *Min. Poems* (Percy Soc.) 23 Clatering pyes, whan tha come in presence, Most malapert there verdit to purpose. **1545** ASCHAM *Toxoph.* (Arb.) 73 When the messenger was gone, euery man began to say his verdite. **1585** DANIEL *Paul. Iouius* Pref., Neither must wee depend vpon the verdite of some conceled Philosophers. **1627** BP. HALL *Epist.* II. v. 302 There is none of all my labours..whereof I would so willingly heare the verdit of the wise and iudicious. **1671** MILTON *Samson* 1228 Cam'st thou for this, vain boaster, to survey me, To descant on my strength, and give thy verdit? **1825** JENNINGS *Observ. Dial. W. Eng.* 80 *Verdi, Verdit*, opinion. **1873** WILLIAMS & JONES *Somerset Gloss.* 40 That's my verdit, therefore I zay't.

β. **1565** STAPLETON tr. *Staphylus' Apol.* 161b, For they pardie by the vardit of Luther, are all damned, if they thought, as they taught. **1577** *Misogonus* IV. ii. 97 To take thy neighboures varditt in such a case thou must not sticke. **1828** CARR *Craven Gloss.*, *Vardite*, verdict, opinion. **1877** PEACOCK *N.W. Linc. Gloss.* 265, I think we shall hev snaw; what's your vardit? *Ibid.*, Thoo's alus pokin' in thy vardit.

γ. **14..** Verdoit [see α]. **1642** D. ROGERS *Naaman* 197 No one mystery, administration, worke or ordinance of his can passe her fingers, without some verduit or other of her owne. *Ibid.* 345 The ten spies bringing a verduict of sense to their brethren.

δ. **1585** GREENE *Planetomachia, Saturnes Trag.* Wks. (Grosart) V. 111 Psamnetichus..thought it a longe time to yeelde so small a verdict. **1632** LITHGOW *Trav.* I. 43, I end with this verdict, the Iew and the Iesuite, is a Pultrone and a Parasite. **1683** D. A. *Art Converse* Pref., It..shall stand or fall by your Verdict. **1791** BURKE *App. Whigs* Wks. VI. 76 This representation is authenticated by the verdict of his country. **1819** KEATS *Otho* v. v, Those tears will wash away a just resolve, A verdict ten times sworn! **1857** W. COLLINS *Dead Secret* III. i, The verdict of humanity is always against any individual member of the species who presumes to differ from the rest. **1882** C. PEBODY *Eng. Journalism* xvii. 127 No controversy is supposed to be closed till the *Times* has given its verdict.

b. Without article.

1537 [? TINDALE] *Exp. St. John* 93 Of such he geueth verdyte contynently. *Ibid.* 100 The Apostle Jhon..gaue such verdyte. **1566** DRANT *Horace, Sat.* x. E vj b, In learnyng rype, in vertue juste, in verdite sharpe and sage. **1596** SPENSER *F.Q.* VII. vii. 27 Iudge thy selfe, by verdit of thine eye, Whether to me they are not subiect all.

†**4.** A vote or suffrage. *Obs.*⁻¹

1580 in *10th Rep. Hist. MSS. Comm.* App. V. 431 Neither the Mayor,..nor any Mayors peare, shall have either at the tyme of ellection or for any other cause but the verdicte of one man.

'verdict, *v. rare.* [f. prec.]

1. *trans.* To pass judgement upon, to give decision or pronounce an opinion concerning (some person or thing).

1594 Q. ELIZABETH in Tytler *Hist. Scot.* (1864) IV. 349 We princes are set upon highest stage, where looks of all beholders verdict our works. **1634** RAINBOW *Labour* (1635) 16 Must a Iury of Trades be busied to verdict him readie?

2. *intr.* To pronounce a verdict or sentence *against* something.

1898 *Literature* 12 Nov. 439 Lawful men of the neighbourhood..verdict entirely against their own temporal interest.

verdictive ('vɜːdɪktɪv). *rare.* [f. VERDICT *sb.* + -IVE.] An utterance which consists in the delivering of a verdict. Also *attrib.* or as *adj.*

1955 J. L. AUSTIN *How to do Things with Words* (1962) xii. 150, I call these classes of utterance..by the following more-or-less rebarbative names:..Verdictives..Exercitives [etc.]. *Ibid.* 152 A verdictive is a judicial as distinct from legislative or executive acts... Verdictives have obvious connexions with truth and falsity. *Ibid.* 160 We may dispute as to whether these [expositives] are not verdictive, exercitive, behabitive, or commissive acts as well. **1975** *Language* LI. 106 Examples of performatives assuming the agent-authority are verdictives..such as *acquit, convict, find* etc. (mostly judicial).

†**verdier.** *Obs.*⁻⁰ = VERDER².

1611 COTGR., *Verdier*, a Verdier, or ouerseer of a forest; a Iudge or Officer..who commaunds all the Raungers, Woodwards, Foresters, &c.

verdigris ('vɜːdɪgrɪs). Forms: α. 4 verdegrez, 4–6 -gres(e, 5 -greys, 7 -gresse, -griese, 7–8 -grease; 5–6 verdegrece, 6–7 -greace, 7–8 -greece; 6–9 verdigrease, 6 -grese, 6–8 -greese (7 verdie-), 6 verdigrece, 7 -greace, -greece; 6 verdygresse, -grace, 7 virdigreace, -greese. β. 4 vertegrez, 5–6 -grece (5 vertagrece, 6 verthigreace), 5 vertgrez, -grees, 6 -grese, -gresse, 7 -greece. γ. 5 vert de grece, 7 vertdegrease. δ. 6, 8–9 verdegris (6 verddegris), 7–9 verdigrise, 8– verdigris. ε. 6 vargrasse, vergres(se (wer-), vergrys, *Sc.* vern-, varngris. [a. AF. and OF. *vert de Grece* (*c* 1170), OF. *verte grez* (13th c.), *vert de grice* (1314), *vert-de-gris* (15th c.; also mod.F.), lit. 'green of Greece': see VERT *sb.*¹ Cf. med.L. *viride grecum* (14–15th c.). The terminal syllable at an early date was no longer understood and hence underwent various corruptions of spelling and pronunciation.]

1. A green or greenish blue substance obtained artificially by the action of dilute acetic acid on thin plates of copper (or a green rust naturally forming on copper and brass), and much used as a pigment, in dyeing, the arts, and medicine; basic acetate of copper.

α. **1336–7** *Ely Sacr. Rolls* (1907) II. 92 In ij libris dim. de verdegrez empt., ijs. vd. *c* **1386** CHAUCER *Chanon Yeom. Prol. & T.* 791 (Corpus), ȝit wol I telle hem,..As boole armonyak, Verdegres, Boras. **1417** in *For. Acc. 8 Hen. V*, D j/2 Vermelone, Coperos, Verdegres, Vernysshe. **14..** *Voc.* in Wr.-Wülcker 619 *Viride grecum*, verdegrece. **1495** *Trevisa's Barth. De P.R.* XIX. xxxviii. 879 In the same wyse as Cerusa is verdegreys made,..and comyth of vapour of stronge vyneygre shed vpon plates of brasse. **1532** in E. Law *Hampton Crt. Pal.* (1885) 363, 3 sackes of verdygrace conteynyng 23 lb. **1582** BATMAN *Trevisa's Barth. De P.R.* Add. 259 Verdigrese, which as it is a colour for Painters, so it is a fretting poison. **1626** BACON *Sylva* §291 Metalls give Orient and Fine Colours..in their Putrefactions or Rusts; as Vermilion, Verdegrease, Bise. **1681** GREW *Musæum* III. iii. i. 341 A sort of Native Verdegriese, from the Copper-Mines of Herngrundt. **1691** *Patent Specif.* No. 270, Verdigrease being a commodity of great vse in this our realme, especially for painting and dying, and never hitherto made here. *c* **1720** W. GIBSON *Farrier's Dispens.* II. iii. (1734) 97 The Verdigrease which is made by the pressings of the Wine put upon plates of Copper. **1758** *Ann. Reg.* 292 That their process in salt-making would dissolve the surface of the copper, into verdigreese. **1807** G. CHALMERS *Caledonia* I. I. iii. 107 The head of a Roman spear..of brass..and.. encrusted with verdigrease.

β. **1300–1** *Durham Acc. Rolls* (Surtees) 502 In vertegrez, melle, atramento. *c* **1386** CHAUCER *Can. Yeom. Prol. & T.* 791 (Ellesm.), Boole armonyak, vertgrees, Boras. *a* **1425** tr. *Arderne's Treat. Fistula*, etc. 82 Wax and oile..dulle þe scharpnez of vertgrese, and vertgrese repressep þeir putrefaccion and humeccacion. **1487–8** in Willis & Clark *Cambridge* (1886) I. 412 Pro xj li. de colore viridi, anglice, vertagrece, xs. xd. **1562** TURNER *Herbal* II. 151 [Turpentine] is good for lepres, wyth vert gresse. **1573** *Art of Limming* 6 To temper Vertgrese, called Spanishe greene. **1612** PEACHAM *Gentl. Exerc.* 82 Vert-greece is nothing else but the rust of brasse. **1656** BLOUNT *Glossogr.*, *Verd-grease* or *vert-greece.*

γ. *c* **1400** *Lanfranc's Cirurg.* 257 Take hony..& þan do þerto ʒ .ij. of vert de grece. **1674** Vertdegrease [see 2].

δ. **1565** COOPER *Thesaurus, Aerugo*,..verd degris: the rust of brasse either artificiall or naturall. **1578** LYTE *Dodoens* 196 Gladyn pounde with a little Verdegris..draweth forth al kindes of thornes. **1601** HOLLAND *Pliny* II. 471 This is altogither artificiall, and is made of Cyprian verdegris or rust of brasse. **1681** CHETHAM *Angler's Vade-m.* ii. §4 (1689) 9 Half a Pound of green Copperas, [and] as much Verdigrise. **1757** DYER *Fleece* I. 279 Corrosive drugs..Dry allum, verdigrise, or vitriole keen. **1789** MRS. PIOZZI *Journ. France* I. 378 Here is a brassy scent in the air as of verdigris. **1819** SHELLEY *Œdipus* II. i. 76 Scorpions are green, and water-snakes, and efts, And verdigris. **1839** URE *Dict. Arts* 1273 Verdigris is a mixture of the crystallized acetate of copper and the sub-acetate, in varying proportions. **1853** ROYLE *Mat. Med.* (ed. 2) 172 Ærugo or Verdigris must have been early known, from the employment of Copper vessels.

ε. **1505–6** *Acc. Ld. High Treas. Scot.* III. 187 For tua pund verngreis to him, xij s. **1506** *Ibid.* 193, vj pund varngreis. **1531–2** in Willis & Clark *Cambridge* (1886) II. 65 Pro duabus libris ly wergresse, ijs. **1595** *Shuttleworths' Acc.* (Chetham Soc.) 103 For vargrasse to dresse the oxe feete.

b. *transf.* (See quots.) *rare.*

1608 TOPSELL *Serpents* 186 There is no part of the Frog so medicinable as is the bloud... The same also being made into a Verdigreace, & drunke [etc.]. [**1844** HOOD *The Turtles* 116 He mention'd Aldermen deceased,..And speculated on that *verdigrease* That isn't poison.]

c. With qualifying adjs. (see quots.).

1747 WESLEY *Prim. Physick* (1762) 91 One or two Drams of distill'd Verdigrease. **1755** *Dict. Arts & Sci.* s.v., These are the crystals of verdegrease, improperly called distilled verdegrease. **1800** tr. *Lagrange's Chem.* II. 339 Crystallized verdigrise or acetite of copper. **1855** J. SCOFFERN *Elem. Chem.* 490 Neutral acetate of copper is known popularly by the absurd term distilled verdigris. **1863** WATTS *Dict. Chem.* I. 14 The bibasic salt or blue verdigris is prepared at Montpellier. *Ibid.* 15 Green Verdigris.

2. *attrib.*, as ***verdigris blue, colour, water***; **verdigris green**, a green of a bright, bluish hue; æruginous green.

1668 CULPEPPER & COLE *Barthol. Anat.* III. i. 129 His skin became of a Verdigrease or yellow-green colour. **1674** W. LEYBOURNE *Compl. Surveyor* 311 Vertdegrease water and yellow berry water make a transparent Green. **1758** in Dodsley *Fug. Pieces* (1761) II. 84 The Unwholesomeness of the Rust and Verdegrease Suffusions. **1796** KIRWAN *Elem. Min.* (ed. 2) I. 28 Verdigris green—that [colour] in which no shade of yellow is perceptible, rather bluish. **1805–17** R. JAMESON *Char. Min.* (ed. 3) 67 Verdigris-green is emerald-green mixed with much Berlin-blue, and a little white. **1832** T. BROWN *Bk. Butterflies & M.* (1834) I. 213 A rich verdigris blue, of fine satiny lustre. **1896** GEORGIANA M. STISTED *True Life Sir R. F. Burton* ii. 31 That leek-like verdigris green which one associates only with early spring in the temperate zone.

Hence **'verdigrisy** *a.*, of the colour of verdigris.

1897 C. MORLEY *Stud. Board Schools* 193 Can that bit of verdigrisy green be dried salt?

'verdigrised, *ppl. a.* [f. prec. + -ED.] Coated or tainted with verdigris.

1831 TRELAWNY *Adv. Younger Son* I. 218 We hoisted up four verdigrised brass nine-pounders. **1853–8** HAWTHORNE *Eng. Note-Bks.* (1879) I. 63 An old verdigrised brass bugle.

verdin ('vɜːdɪn). Also Verdin. [a. F. *verdin* yellow-hammer.] A small grey tit with a yellow head, *Auriparus flaviceps*, found in south-western North America.

1881 *Amer. Naturalist* XV. 217 Another minute species of the titmouse family, the verdin or yellow-headed titmouse. **1903** *Atlantic Monthly* July 103 The same fretful verdin was talking about something with the old emphatic monotony. **1939** G. B. PICKWELL *Deserts* 139/2 This is the voice of the Verdin, a true bird of the desert. **1974** L. GOMBRICH tr. *von Frisch's Animal Archit.* (1975) 211 The verdin barricades its nest with thorns.

verdingal(e, variants of VARDINGALE *Obs.*

verdit(e, obs. forms of VERDICT.

† **ˈverdite**[1]. *Chem. Obs.* [f. VERD-OUS *a.* + -ITE[1] 4 b.] A salt produced by the action of verdous acid on a base.

1838 T. THOMSON *Chem. Org. Bodies* 159 The precipitate consists of verdite of lead. **1843** *Penny Cycl.* XXVI. 256/1 The earthy or metallic *verdites* are yellow, while the *verdates* of the same bases are green.

verdite[2] (ˈvɜːdaɪt). [f. *verd-* (as in VERDURE) + -ITE[1].] A green ornamental rock from South Africa.

1908 *Mineral Industry* XVI. 810 During 1907 there was found on the south bank of the North Kaap river, in South Africa,..another..stone that has the deep green color of..chromiferous syenite... It has a hardness of about three, and is susceptible of a high polish; the color is a rich chrome green and the stone contains a chrome-muscovite and some argillaceous material... The stone is obtained in blocks weighing one ton or more... The name verdite has been suggested for it. **1916** *Chambers's Jrnl.* Apr. 272/2 Articles of jewellery and ornaments are made of verdite. **1935** *Archit. Rev.* LXXVIII. 104/1 In the Midland Headquarters in the City, it is said that each of the Verdite pilasters..cost a Thousand pounds, and there are a considerable number of them. **1979** HURLBUT & SWITZER *Gemology* xiii. 143/1 Verdite is a green rock consisting of fuchsite (a chrome mica), and clayey mica.

† **verditel.** *Obs.*[−1] = next 1.

1778 PRYCE *Min. Cornub.* 250 By gradually adding the powder, in some time, on the ceasing of the violence of effervescence, the Copper will precipitate in a green powder, called Verditel.

verditer (ˈvɜːdɪtə(r)). Forms: α. 6- verditer, 6 viriditer, 8 verdeter. β. 6 verdytor, 7 verditor. γ. 7-9 verditure, 7 virditur. [a. OF. *verd de terre* (later F. *vert de terre*), lit. 'green of earth': see VERD *sb.* Holland *Pliny* (1601) II. 528 employs the OF. form.]

1. A kind of pigment of a green, bluish green, or (more freq.) light blue colour, usu. prepared by adding chalk or whiting to a solution of nitrate of copper, and much used in making crayons and as a water-colour.

α. **1505-6** *Acc. Ld. High Treas. Scot.* III. 184, iij di. pund verditer; ilk pund vjs. **1558** in Feuillerat *Revels Q. Eliz.* (1908) 94 Rosset j lb. viij[d]; verditer xiij[d]. **1662** in *Statutes at Large, Ireland* (1765) II. 417 Verditer, the hundred weight, ..£1 6s. 8d. **1674** W. LEYBOURNE *Compl. Surveyor* 310 Verditer, washed and tempered with Gum-water, is a good Blew. **1738** CHAMBERS *Cycl.* s.v. *Dyeing*, Bright green is first dyed blue, then back-boiled with braziletto, and verdeter. **1783** PRIESTLEY in *Phil. Trans.* LXXIII. 406 An ounce of copper from verditer absorbed 403 ounce measures. **1839** URE *Dict. Arts* 150 Bremen blue, or verditer, a greenish blue colour obtained from copper mixed with chalk or lime. *Ibid.* 1275 Verditer, or Bremen Green..is a light powder, like magnesia, having a blue or bluish green colour. **1873** *Beeton's Dict. Comm., Sealing-Wax*..is a composition of gum-lac, melted and incorporated with resin, and afterwards coloured with some pigment, as vermilion, verditer.

β. **1532** in E. Law *Hampton Crt. Pal.* (1885) 363, 2 lb. of verdytor, at 16*d.* the lb. **1660** *Act 12 Chas. II*, c. 4 (1786) III. 157/2 Verditor, the hundred weight,..j li. vj[s] viij[d].

γ. **1606** PEACHAM *Art Drawing* 54 Take your Verditure, and grind it with a weak Gum Arabick Water, it is the faintest and palest green that is. **1674** W. LEYBOURNE *Compl. Surveyor* 310 Verditure washed and tempered with Gum water, makes a Green not transparent.

b. With particularizing terms, as ***blue, green, refined blue, refiners' verditer.***

1683 MOXON *Mech. Exerc., Printing* xxiv. ¶17 Virdigreace, and Green Virditur, for Greens... But all must be ground with soft Varnish. **1732** J. PEELE *Water-Colours* 62 Blue Verditer is a very bright, pleasant blue. **1799** G. SMITH *Laboratory* (ed. 6) I. 184 Blue verditer or smalt, mixed with enamel, will make a good blue paint. **1837** *Penny Cycl.* VII. 504/2 It [blue carbonate of copper] is of a fine light blue colour, and known by the name of refiners' verditer. **1858** SIMMONDS *Dict. Trade* s.v., There are refined blue, and green verditers. **1867** BLOXAM *Chem.* 345 The paint known as blue verditer is hydrated oxide of copper obtained by decomposing nitrate of copper with hydrate of lime.

c. Hence occas. in pl.

1665 HOOKE *Microgr.* 72 For Smalts and verditures, I have been able with a microscope to perceive their particles very many of them transparent. **1835** G. FIELD *Chromatography* 113 These blues..as pigments are precisely of the character of verditers.

2. The blue or green colour characteristic of verditer.

1819 H. BUSK *Vestriad* v. 422 The sacred hill..Clad in bright verditure and Prussian blue. **1858** *Sat. Rev.* 20 Nov. 507/2 Flies..done in the brightest of verditer and ultramarine. **1877** MISS A. B. EDWARDS *Up Nile* vii. 185 The prevailing colours..are verditer and chocolate.

3. *attrib.* **a.** With names of colours, esp. ***verditer blue.***

1551-2 in Feuillerat *Revels Edw. VI* (1914) 71 Grownde white leade, viijd. Verditer grene, ixd. **1683** MOXON *Mech. Exerc., Printing* xxiv. ¶17 Virditur Indico and Bice for Blews. *Ibid.*, Virditur Indico..and Green Virditur. **1732** J. PEELE *Water-Colours* 62 Verditer-Green is a light Green. **1857** *Fraser's Mag.* LVI. 571 Greenish blue approaching in richness to verditer blue. **1864-5** WOOD *Homes without H.* xiii. (1868) 239 A large patch of feathers on the top of the head glows and flashes with metallic splendour, and is of a vivid verditer blue. **1891** G. E. SHELLEY *Catal. Birds Brit. Mus.* XIX. 95 Throat verditer-blue, with paler blue central lines. **1901** *Q. Rev.* July 18 The magnificent verditer-blue giant plantain-eater.

b. In the sense 'of the colour of verditer'.

1857 *Fraser's Mag.* LVI. 571 A grayish white chin is followed by a verditer throat. **1893** SYMONDS *In Key of Blue* 11 Verditer hues of water-snakes.

verdius, verdjuice, obs. ff. VERJUICE.

† **verdoire.** *Obs.*[−1] [Irreg. var. *verdor* VERDOUR[1].] = VERDURE 2 c.

1586 FERNE *Blaz. Gentrie* 142 The Smaragd (commonly called the Emeraud)..exceedeth the cullors of all herbs or Verdoires.

verdoit, obs. variant of VERDICT *sb.*

‖ **verdomde** (fərˈdɔmdə), *a. S. Afr. slang.* Also verdoemde, verdomd. [Afrikaans, ad. Du. *verdoemd.*] Damned, infernal.

1850 R. G. CUMMING *Five Years Hunter's Life S. Afr.* ix. 53/1, I overheard him remark to three other gruff-looking Boers who stood beside him that I was 'a verdomd Englishman'. **1878** T. J. LUCAS *Camp Life & Sport S. Afr.* 232 Ah, you verdomde beast! **1909** R. DEHAN *Dop Doctor* 90 He was no Baas of mine the verdoemde rooinek! **1913** D. FAIRBRIDGE *That which hath Been* 125 This verdoemde Governor is obstinate on this point. **1926** E. LEWIS *Mantis* I. iv. 80 Why, even with Government helping you not to make a goat of yourself farming's a *verdomde* lottery, believe me. **1964** A. TREW *Smoke Island* vi. 106 Pride wouldn't allow him to claim that achievement for his people now, and this *verdomde* native knew it.

‖ **verdona.** [Sp., f. *verde* green.] A variety of wine (see quots.).

1703 DAMPIER *Voy.* III. I. 10 Verdona is green strong-bodied Wine, harsher and sharper than Canary. **1833** C. REDDING *Hist. Mod. Wines* (1851) 210 Verdona, a green wine, of good body,..formerly grown on the western side of that island, and shipped at Santa Cruz for the West Indian market, little or none coming to Europe.

† **verdour**[1]. *Obs.* Forms: α. 5 verdeur, 5-7 verdour (6 *Sc.* wer-), 6 veerdour, *Sc.* verdeour; 5 *Sc.* wardur, 6 vardour, *Sc.* wardour(e. β. 5 *Sc.* wardor, 6-7 verdor, 7 verdore. [a. OF. *verdour, verdor* (13th c.; = Prov., Sp., Pg. *verdor*, It. *verdore*), later *verdeur* (mod.F. dial. *vardeur*), f. *verd* green: see -OR 1 and cf. VERDER[1] and VERDURE.]

1. Fresh greenness (of vegetation); *fig.* fresh or flourishing condition.

1447 BOKENHAM *Seyntys* (Roxb.) 213 The verdour or grennesse & the redolence Of good fame. **1483** CAXTON *Gold. Leg.* 156 b/2 The blessyd George was hygh in despysyng lowe thynges and therfore he had verdeur in hym self. **1610** GUILLIM *Heraldry* III. vii. (1611) 106 He beareth Argent, three sterued branches,..this being mortified and vnuested of the verdour which sometime it had. **1646** QUARLES *Judgem. & Mercy* Wks. (Grosart) I. 87/1 (*heading*), The worldly man's Verdour. Contrasting the prosperous condition of the worldly..man [etc.].

b. Taste, *esp.* fresh or pleasant taste; = VERDURE 4. Also *fig.*

1526 *Pilgr. Perf.* (W. de W. 1531) 154 And the vyne answered sayenge, I may not leaue my swetnes and pleasaunt verdour, whiche so delyteth..bothe god & man. **1549** COVERDALE, etc., *Erasm. Par. Jas.* II. 35 But every frute is lyke unto hys owne tree, and hathe the verdour of the juyce of hys owne rote. **1570-6** LAMBARDE *Peramb. Kent* (1826) 223 Those plantes which our auncestors had brought hither out of Normandie had lost their native verdour, whether you did eate their substance, or drink their iuice, which we call Cyder. **1605** BACON *Adv. Learn.* I. viii. §5 We see in all other pleasures [than learning] there is sacietie; and after they be used, their verdour departeth.

2. = VERDURE 3.

1480 *Wardr. Acc. Edw. IV* (1830) 118 Oon other [counterpoint] of greene verdours with trees; oon other of white verdour with a scripture. **1493** *Halyburton's Ledger* (1867) 10 A cuvaryng of wardur, cost 12s. **1531-2** *Rutland MSS.* (Hist. MSS. Comm.) IV. 271 For iiij peces of verdours for hanginges, vj*li.* xiij*s.* iiij*d.* *a* **1548** HALL *Chron., Hen. VIII*, 165 b, The newe banket chamber..was hanged with a costly verdor all new, the ground therof was all gold and the flowers were all of Sattyn silver. **1574** *Burgh Rec. Glasgow* (1876) I. 32 Ane lettgant bed furneist witht Flandreis werdour, blancattis, scheittis, and coddis.

attrib. **1488** *Acc. Ld. High Treas. Scot.* I. 157 A verdour bed to the Duk. **1501** *Ibid.* II. 31, vj elne cammas deliverit to Jame Dog to mend the verdeour clathis in Strivelin. **1532** *N. Country Wills* (Surtees) 133 A covering of a bedde of verdour werke lyned with canvas.

3. = VERDURE 2.

1508 DUNBAR *Tua Mariit Wemen* 30 As new spynist rose, Arrayit ryallie about with mony rich wardour. **1587** HOLINSHED *Chron.* (ed. 2) III. 857/1 Vnder it antike images of gold inuironed with verdor of olifs cast in compassе. **1605** BACON *Adv. Learn.* I. vi. §11. 30 Salomon became inabled..to compile a naturall Historie of all Verdor, from the Cedar upon the Mountaine, to the mosse vppon the wall.

4. = VERDURE 1 b. *rare*[−1].

1555 EDEN *Decades* (Arb.) 266 There appeareth to the eye a certeyne verdour shynynge lyke the beames of the soonne.

† **verdour**[2]. *Obs. rare.* Also 6 vierdour, 6-7 verdor. [a. AF. *verdour* (1327), var. of *verder* VERDER[2].] = VERDERER[2] 1.

1502 ARNOLDE *Chron.* p. lxxx/1 And to this Swanmot..shall com to gedurs foresturs and vierdours and non other be distraint. **1594** CROMPTON *Jurisd.* 169 If a man be indited of Trespasse done in the forrest before verdors, regardors, agistors, and other Ministers of the Forrest [etc.]. **1607** COWELL *Interpr., Verdour*,..a Iudiciall Officer of the Kings forest, chosen by the King, in the full county of the same shire, within the forest, where he doth dwell. *Ibid.*, The verdour is made by the Kings writ,..which is directed to the shyreeue for the choice of him in a full Countie. **1656** BLOUNT *Glossogr.* (after Cowell), *Verderer* or *Verdor*, a Judicial Officer of the Kings Forrest. **1812** W. TAYLOR in *Monthly Mag.* XXXIV. 210 A forest has laws and officers of its own, as foresters, verdours, rangers, and agisters.

‖ **ˈverdous,** *a. Chem. Obs.* [See VERDIC *a.* and -OUS.] *verdous acid*: (see quots.).

1836-41 BRANDE *Chem.* (ed. 5) 1198 On evaporation [of an extract from the root of *Scabiosa succisa*] a yellow acid product is obtained: in this state Berzelius proposes to call it *verdous acid*. **1843** *Penny Cycl.* XXVI. 256/1 Berzelius..proposes to call the colourless the *verdous* and the coloured the *verdic* acid.

verdoy, *sb.* and *a.* [ad. F. *verdoyé*, pa. pple. of *verdoyer*: see next.]

† **A.** *sb.* = VERDURE 3. *Obs.*[−1]

1542 *Test. Ebor.* (Surtees) VI. 166 Item v peces of verdoyes for hanginges.

B. *adj. Her.* Of a bordure: (see quots. 1562 and 1610).

1562 LEIGH *Armorie* 190 b, The sixte [emborduring] is called Verdoye, as when it is occupied with frewtes, leaues, or slippes. **1610** GUILLIM *Heraldry* I. v. (1611) 20 This terme Verdoy is appropriated to all bordures charged with leaues, flowers, fruits, and other the like vegetables. [Hence in Phillips (1658), and in later Dicts.] **1661** MORGAN *Sph. Gentry* II. vi. 62 Sable, a bordure or, charged with Verdoy of Trefoiles sliped to the number of eight. **1725** *Fam. Dict.* s.v. *Bordure*, If a Bordure be charg'd with any Parts of Plants or Flowers, they say *Verdoy* of *Trefoils*, or whatever Flower it be. **1882** CUSSANS *Her.* (1893) 68.

† **verdoy,** *v. Obs.*[−1] [ad. OF. *verdoier* (12th c.), *verdoyer*, f. *verd* VERD *sb.*] *intr.* To become green.

1480 CAXTON *Ovid's Met.* x. i, A grene medowe full of herbes verdoying or wexyng grene.

† **verd-sauce,** variant of VERT SAUCE. *Obs.*

1499 *Promp. Parv.* (P.), Verd sawce, *viride salsamentum*.

† **verdue,** irreg. variant of VERDURE.

In the earliest instance app. a simple misprint, but perh. accepted by later writers.

1641 *Sylvester's Du Bartas* II. i. *Handycrafts* 334 A Grove Upon the verdue [edd. 1605, 1621 verdure] of whose Virgin-boughs Bird had not percht. **1650** EARL MONM. tr. *Senault's Man. bec. Guilty* 176 'Twill make snow black, to make a womans face seem fair, tarnish the verdue of the rose, to exalt the freshnesse of her Complexion. *a* **1670** HACKET *Abp. Williams* I. (1692) 124 The month of May coming in with its verdue.

‖ **ˈverdugal.** *Obs.* Also 6 vardygall, 7 vertugal, vertigal. [OF. *verdugale, vertugale*: see VARDINGALE.] A farthingale.

1558-9 SIR R. CLOUGH in Burgon *Gresham* (1839) I. iv. 251 After that, came 1 other horse coveryd with cloth of golde to the grownde, which stoode lyke unto the gentyllwomen's vardygalls. **1584** HUDSON *Du Bartas' Judith* v. 215 Amongst his vertugals for ayde he drew From his Lieutenant. **1611** *Coryat's Crudities* Panegyr. Verses, The Gallery of 'Donna Amorosa'..in Arabia Deserta which is a meere Magazin of verdugals.

‖ **verdugo.** *Obs. rare.* [Sp. (also Pg.) *verdugo* hangman, lash, rod, shoot, = It. *verduco* narrow-bladed sword.] A hangman or executioner. Also employed as a term of abuse.

a **1616** BEAUM. & FL. *Scornf. Lady* II. i, *Wel.* Where are my slippers Sir? *Ser*[*vant*]. Here Sir. *Wel.* Where Sir? have you got the pot Verdugo? have you seen the Horses Sir? *a* **1625** FLETCHER *Woman's Prize* IV. i, Contrive your beard o'th top cut like Verdugoes.

Hence † **verdugoship**, the personality of a verdugo or executioner. *Obs.*[−1]

1610 B. JONSON *Alch.* III. iii, His great Verdugo-ship [= a Spaniard] has not a iot of language; So much the easier to be cossin'd, my Dolly.

verduict, -duit, obs. variants of VERDICT.

† **verdurant,** *a. Obs.*[−1] [f. next + -ANT[1].] Green, verdant.

1583 MELBANCKE *Philotimus* N iv b, As she walked one daye in her verdurant garden alone.

verdure (ˈvɜːdjʊə(r)). Also 5 uerdure, 6 verdur, 7 verdeur, 8 verduer. [a. OF. *verdure* (12th c.; = It., Sp., Pg. *verdura*), f. *verd* green + -URE. Cf. VERDOUR[1].]

I. 1. a. The fresh green colour characteristic of flourishing vegetation; greenness, viridity.

13.. *Gaw. & Gr. Knt.* 161 Alle his vesture uerayly was clene verdure. **1413** *Pilgr. Sowle* (Caxton, 1483) IV. i. 58 This appel was..borne fro the grene tree and put vpon the drye tre for to restoren this drye tree to verdure and to fresshenes. *c* **1430** LYDG. *Min. Poems* (Percy Soc.) 212 The large feeldys shulde be bareyn, No corn up growe nor greyn in his verdure. **1610** SHAKS. *Temp.* I. ii. 87 He was The Iuy which had hid my princely Trunck, And suckt my verdure out on't. **1639** N. N. tr. *Du Bosq's Compl. Woman* II. 67 We see the Ivy full of Verdure, on the most withered tree. **1675** TRAHERNE *Chr. Ethics* 404 Ingratitude..cuts off the soul like a branch from the root that gave it life and verdure. **1700** PRIOR *Carmen Seculare* xli, Let twisted Olive bind those Laurels fast, Whose Verdure must for ever last. **1765** *Museum Rust.* IV. 229 When the snow lay very thick upon the burnet, that part of it which was above the snow had all the verdure of spring. **1838** *Murray's Hand Bk. N. Germ.* 165/2 Another valley..clothed with meadows of the brightest verdure. **1910** *19th Cent.* Feb. 285 The perennial verdure of cypress and pine, ilex and box was invaluable.

fig. **1675** TRAHERNE *Chr. Ethics* 390 A spark of fire,..if it falls..into green wood or watery places,..does no harm. Penitent tears, and the verdure of humility prevent such flames and extinguish the quarrel.

b. With *a* and *pl.* A shade or tint of green.

1523 SKELTON *Garl. Laurel* 776 A cronell of lawrell with verduris light and darke I haue deuysyd for Skelton. **1610** GUILLIM *Heraldry* (1611) 10 Most vegitables, so long as they flourish, are beautified with this verdure: and is a colour most wholsome and pleasant to the eie. **1796** H. HUNTER tr. *St.-Pierre's Stud. Nat.* (1799) I. p. xxv, The fir..clothed with leaves stiff, filiform, and of a dark verdure.

2. a. Green vegetation; plants or trees, or parts of these, in a green and flourishing state.

a **1400-50** *Alexander* 4979 A ferly faire tre..void of all hire verdure & vacant of leues. *c* **1477** CAXTON *Jason* 104 Some ran for to gadre of the grene herbes and verdure for to caste a long on the waye. *a* **1513** FABYAN *Chron.* VII. 431 The tyme of wynter which trees doth deface And causyth all verdure to a voyde quyte. **1667** MILTON *P.L.* XI. 828 Then shall this Mount..by might of Waves be moovd Out of his place,..With all his verdure spoil'd. **1729** T. COOKE *Tales, Proposals*, etc. 115 To him who longest shall maintain the Field This blooming Verdure on my Brows I yield. **1775** JOHNSON *Lett.* (1788) I. 288, I can look into Lucy's garden. ..I believe she has hardly any fruit but gooseberries; but so much verdure looks pretty in a town. **1822** SHELLEY tr. *Calderon's Mag. Prodig.* III. 59 Voluptuous Vine,..To the trunk thou interlacest [thou] Art the verdure which embracest. **1832** HT. MARTINEAU *Homes Abroad* i. 2 Flourishing young plantations put forth their early verdure. **1886** SHELDON tr. *Flaubert's Salammbô* 14 The fire spread from tree to tree, until the tall mass of verdure resembled a volcano beginning to smoke.

fig. **1818** KEATS *Endym.* III. 187 At this a surpris'd start Frosted the springing verdure of his heart.

Comb. **1912** *Blackw. Mag.* Sept. 316/1 Around us were the precipitous verdure-clad cliffs.

b. *esp.* Green grass or herbage.

1447 BOKENHAM *Seyntys* Introd. (Roxb.) 3 In may was neuer no medews sene Motleyd with flours on hys verdure grene. **1515** BARCLAY *Egloges* v. (1570) D ij/1 What time the verdure of ground & euery tre, By frost and stormes is priuate of beautee. **1638** COWLEY *Love's Riddle* IV, [Thoughts] and the pleasant verdure of the fields Made me forget the way. **1690** LOCKE *Hum. Und.* IV. xiii. §2 The earth will not appear painted with flowers, nor the fields covered with verdure, whenever he has a mind to it. **1794** MRS. RADCLIFFE *Myst. Udolpho* iii, Along the bottom of this valley the most vivid verdure was spread. **1846** MCCULLOCH *Acc. Brit. Empire* (1854) I. 143 The Cheviot hills are.. distinguished by their fine green verdure. **1878** BROWNING *La Saisiaz* 52 Praising still That soft tread on velvet verdure, as it wound through hill and hill.

†**c.** *pl.* Green plants or herbs. *Obs.*

c **1475** *Partenay* 3824 She lepte the fenestre vppon, Aboue beheld she uerdures floureesshing. *c* **1481** CAXTON *Dialogues* 13/22 In wodes ben the verdures, Brembles, bremble beries. **1631** G. TOWNSHEND *Tempe Restor'd* 4 All this second story seem'd of Silver worke mixt with fresh Verdures. **1693** EVELYN *De la Quint. Compl. Gard.* II. 199 Parsley..is comprehended under the Title of Verdures or green Potherbs. **1719** LONDON & WISE *Compl. Gard.* IX. 282 May. It is now the time of the flourishing reign of all Verdures and green things. **1722** WOLLASTON *Relig. Nat.* ix. 206 He might perhaps now and then meet with a little smooth way,..or be flattered with some verdures and the smiles of a few daisies on the banks of the road.

3. A rich tapestry ornamented with representations of trees or other vegetation. Now *Hist.*

Common *c* 1525–*c* 1550 after French usage: see also VERDER[1] 1, VERDOUR[1] 2.

1513 *MS. Papers 5 Hen. VIII*, No. 4101 (Publ. Rec. Office), A Counterpoynt of paly verdure,..an old counterpoint of Redde verdures. *c* **1550** *Dice-Play* (Percy) 9 Divers well trimmed chambers, the worst of them apparelled with verdures. **1586** *Rates of Custome* E viij, Tappistry with wul or Verdure the flemish elle, xii. d. **1934** *Burlington Mag.* Feb. 65/2 The work of the oldest tapestry factory in England... A 'verdure', a type very popular with Worcestershire weavers. **1977** *Anc. Tapestries from Belgium* (Nat. Arts Centre, Ottawa) 77 Oudenarde was famous for its 'verdures' (tapestries representing trees or foliage).

II. †**4. a.** Freshness or agreeable briskness of taste in fruits or liquors; also simply, taste, savour.

1513 BRADSHAW *St. Werburge* I. 614 A swete tree bryngeth forth..Swete fruyte and delycyous in tast and verdure. *c* **1540** tr. *Pol. Verg. Eng. Hist.* (Camden) I. 216 Being parched and brent..it engendereth the verdure and taste of salte. **1574** R. SCOT *Hop Gard.* (1578) 6 That Ale.. boroweth the Hoppe, as without the which it wanteth his chiefe grace and best verdure. **1601** HOLLAND *Pliny* I. 424 Upon such a chaunce and unhappie accident it [new wine] looseth the verdure and quicke tast. **1611** SPEED *Theat. Gt. Brit.* xxiv. (1614) 47/1 The very wines made thereof..being little inferior in sweet verdure to the French wines.

fig. **1630** DONNE *Serm.* (1640) 133 Every word in them [the Scriptures] hath his waight and value, his taste and verdure.

†**b.** Sharpness, tartness, or unpleasantness of taste. *Obs.*

In last quot. perh. only a contextual application of the general sense of 'taste': see prec.

1508 STANBRIDGE *Vulgaria* (W. de W.) B v b, This wyne is of verdure. *Hoc vinum est acre.* **1601** HOLLAND *Pliny* II. 152 The wines which by age and long keeping, lay downe their verdure and become sweet. **1626** BP. HALL *Contempl., O.T.* XXI. vi. 512 Something they must haue to complaine of, that shall giue an vnsauory verdure to their sweetest morsels.

†**5.** Smell; odour. Also *fig. Obs.*

1520 WHITINTON *Vulg.* (1527) 15 This wyne drynketh of a good verdure (*delicati odoris*). **1589** GREENE *Tullies Loue* Wks. (Grosart) VII. 165 Let lillies wither on the stalke, and weare violets in thy hand, the one faire and vnsauorie, the other blacke but of sweete verdure. **1594** R. C[AREW] *Huarte's Exam. Wits* (1616) 309 What is the cause, that the excrements of brute beasts haue not so vnpleasant a verdure, as those of mankind? **1601** HOLLAND *Pliny* I. 377 The good Baulme..in smell..should have an harsh verdeur. *Ibid.* 429 The Oile-oliue..hath of all other the best verdure, and in tast excelleth the rest. **1716** M. DAVIES *Athen. Brit.* II. 351 The powerful Verdures of the foresaid Allium, Cepa, &c.

6. *fig.* Fresh or flourishing condition.

c **1586** C'TESS PEMBROKE *Psalms* LXXI. v, Do not then, now age assaileth, Courage, verdure, vertue faileth, Do not leave me cast away. **1591** SHAKS. *Two Gent.* I. i. 49 Euen so by Loue, the yong and tender wit Is turn'd to folly, blasting in the Bud, Loosing his verdure, euen in the prime. **1619** DONNE *Lett.* (1651) 222 Whatsoever I should write now, of any passages of these days, would lose their verdure before the letter came to you. *a* **1664** KATH. PHILIPS *Poems* (1667) 44 In Youth she did attract (for she The Verdure had without the Vanity). **1670** CLARENDON *Contempl. on Psalms* Tracts (1727) 653 If he discontinues to give, all his former bounties have lost their verdure, and wither away. **1726** POPE *Odyss.* XIX. 149 My lord's protecting hand alone would raise My drooping verdure, and extend my praise. **1754** H. WALPOLE *Lett.* (1846) III. 67, I am in no fear of not finding you in perfect verdure. **1829** LYTTON *Disowned* x, Those years make the prime and verdure of our lives.

7. *fig.* Signs of gullibility; = GREEN *sb.* 2 c.

1861 H. C. PENNELL *Puck on Pegasus* 75 Perceiv'st thou verdure in my eye?

verdured ('vɜːdjʊəd), *ppl. a.* [f. prec. + -ED.]

†**1.** Of wine: Having a (specified) taste. *Obs.*

1533 ELYOT *Cast. Helthe* III. xviii. (1541) 69 Moderate vse of small wynes, clere and well verdured, is herein very commendable. **1548** UDALL *Erasmus Par. Luke* vi. 73 The sower verdured wyne of the olde supersticion.

2. Clad with verdure or vegetation; covered with grass.

a **1718** T. PARNELL *Gift of Poetry* (1894) 193 Lonely pleasure leads To verdur'd banks, to paths adorn'd with flowers. **1798** W. MAVOR *Brit. Tourists* V. 71 The terrific ascent of St. Catherine's..is well verdured. **1839** ARNOLD in *Life & Corr.* (1844) II. App. 398 There are two houses just built by the roadside, and opposite to them a little patch of ground just verdured. **1893** *Scribner's Mag.* June 734/2 A peculiar valley..made up of palisades and verdured plateaus.

verdureless ('vɜːdjʊəlɪs), *a.* [f. VERDURE + -LESS.] Destitute of verdure; lacking vegetation; bare, bleak. (Freq. from *c* 1850.)

1824 MOIR in *Blackw. Mag.* XVI. 394 The bright-feather'd tribes of the sea..bask on the verdureless brow of the deep. **1831** JAMES *Phil. Augustus* xiv, My heart is like a branch long broken from its stem, withered and verdureless. **1877** DAWSON *Orig. World* viii. 181 It was a world of bare, rocky peaks, and verdureless valleys.

verdurer, variant of VERDERER[2].

verdurous ('vɜːdjʊərəs), *a.* Also 7–9 *poet.* verd'rous. [f. VERDURE + -OUS.]

1. Of vegetation: Rich or abounding in verdure; flourishing thick and green.

1604 DRAYTON *Moyses* II. 51 The loathsome Hemlock as the verdurous Rose, These filthy Locusts equally deuowre. **1612** —— *Poly-olb.* xv. 196 The sent-full Camomill, the verdurous Costmary. **1708** J. PHILIPS *Cyder* I. 35 Where the lowing Herd Chews verd'rous Pasture. *c* **1750** SHENSTONE *Economy* I. 129 Lovely as when th' Hesperian fruitage smil'd Amid the verd'rous grove! **1812** CARY *Dante, Purg.* XXIX. 89 Four animals, each crown'd with verdurous leaf. **1835** J. P. KENNEDY *Horse Shoe R.* xii, The rich, verdurous and lively forest that encompassed this blighted spot. **1837** HOWITT *Rur. Life* II. i. (1862) 89 Green fields and verdurous trees or deep woodlands lying all round. **1885** *Athenæum* 23 May 669/1 Verdurous masses of foliage and sward disposed with great simplicity and breadth.

fig. and *transf.* **1857** WILLMOTT *Pleas. Lit.* xxiii. 148 Of these, Philosophy is one of the most verdurous and throws the broadest shadow. **1876** BLACKIE *Songs Relig. & Life* 197 With banners of gold and of silver,..And verdurous power in his path When he comes in the pride of the May.

b. Of places, etc.: Covered or clothed with verdure; displaying a rich (green) vegetation.

1717 E. FENTON *Poems* 93 There the Flocks And Herds of Phœbus o'er the verd'rous Lawn Browze fatt'ning pasture. **1772** SIR W. JONES *Seven Fount.* Poems (1777) 37 Green hillocks,..And verdurous plains with winding streams bedew'd. **1796** COLERIDGE *To Chas. Lloyd* 51 That verdurous hill with many a resting-place. *c* **1818** KEATS *Ep. J. H. Reynolds* 58 The verd'rous bosoms of those isles. **1856** R. A. VAUGHAN *Mystics* (1860) II. 80 Spots like those in the lowlands of Northern Germany, verdurous and seemingly solid. **1892** MRS. H. WARD *David Grieve* II. 302 A playing wind sprang up,..freshening the verdurous ways through which they passed.

2. Consisting or composed of verdure.

1667 MILTON *P.L.* IV. 143 Yet higher then thir tops The verdurous wall of Paradise up sprung. **1772** NUGENT tr. *Hist. Fr. Gerund* I. 533 Why did not the Earth protend her verdurous offerings. **1817** SHELLEY *Rev. Islam* VI. xxvii, Clasping its gray rents with a verdurous woof, A hanging dome of leaves. **1818** KEATS *Endym.* III. 420 Just when the light of morn..Stole through its verdurous matting of fresh trees. **1860** MOTLEY *Netherl.* (1868) I. v. 259 The soldiers themselves, attired in verdurous garments of foliage and flower-work,..paraded the bridge.

3. Of or pertaining to, characteristic of, verdure.

1820 KEATS *Ode to Nightingale* iv, Through verdurous glooms and winding mossy ways. **1851** MEREDITH *London by Lamplight* xxiv, This night of deep solemnity, And verdurous serenity. **1859** NEALE *Disciples at Emmaus* in *Seatonian P.* (1864) 187 Every tinted leaf Opes its young channel to the verdurous sap. **1883** *Harper's Mag.* July 166/1 Its verdurous hue is more noticeable than its elevation.

Hence '**verdurousness**.

1856 LYNCH *Lett. to Scattered* (1872) 557 Many of them [*sc.* sermons] have an invigorating verdurousness, and are like the wide green fields.

verd(u)ytt, obs. variants of VERDICT.

verdynggale, variant of VARDINGALE *Obs.*

†**vere**, *sb. Obs.* Forms: α. 4–5 veir, 5 veyr, *Sc.* weyr, 6 *Sc.* weir. β. 4 veer(e, 5 weere, 6 vear. γ. 4–6 vere, 5 *Sc.* were. See also VER *sb.*[1] [a. OF. *ver* masc. or *vere* fem.:—L. *vēr* VER *sb.*[1]] The season of spring; spring-time.

α. *c* **1325** *Prose Psalter* lxxiii. 18 Þou madest alle þe cuntres of þerþe; somer and veir, þou formedest þo þynges. *c* **1400** tr. *Secreta Secret., Gov. Lordsh.* 72 Veir bigynnes whenne þe sonne entres yn to þe toknynge of þe sheepe. *c* **1470** HENRY *Wallace* VIII. 1697 Gud Wallace..Erest in weyr to Sanct Jhonstoun couth fair. **1513** DOUGLAS *Æneid* III. i. 17 Scant begunnin was the fresch weir, Quhen that Anchises..Bad ws mak sail. *Ibid.* x. Prol. 11 Fresche veir to burgioun herbis and sweit flouris.

β. *c* **1374** CHAUCER *Troylus* I. 157 Þe tyme Of Aperil, when clothed is þe mede, With newe grene, of lusty veer the prime. **1388** WYCLIF *Ecclus.* l. 8 As a flour of rosis in the daies of veer. **1422** YONGE tr. *Secreta Secret.* 243 The tyme of weere is hote and moisti. **1483** CAXTON *Gold. Leg.* 244 b/2 Some say that the transfyguracion was made in veer. **1583** MELBANCKE *Philotimus* H iv, In vear, the husbandmen lop their trees, to the intent that afterward they may growe the better.

γ. **1387-8** T. USK *Test. Love* II. ix. (Skeat) l. 133 The same yere maketh springes and jolite in Vere..to renovel with peinted coloures. *c* **1400** *Sowdone Bab.* 965 In the prymsauns of grene vere. **1471** RIPLEY *Comp. Alch.* II. xii. in Ashm. *Theat. Chem. Brit.* (1652) 138 And then be Wynter and Vere nygh over-gon To the Est. **1509** *Payne Evyll Marr.* (Percy) 25 In tyme of vere when lovers lusty be. *a* **1529** SKELTON *On Time* Wks. 1843 I. 138 The rotys take theyr sap in tyme of vere. **1563** *Jack Juggler* (E.E.D.S.) 36, I never use to run away in winter or in vere.

Hence †**vere-time**, spring-time. *Obs.*

1382 WYCLIF *Gen.* xxxv. 16 He goon out thens, com in veer tyme to the loond that ledith to Effratam. **1388** —— *Ps.* lxxiii. 17 Thou maddist alle the endis of erthe; somer and veer tyme, thou fourmedist tho. **1483** CAXTON *Gold. Leg.* 48 b/1 He wente thens and cam in veer tyme unto the londe that goth to effratam.

†**vere**, *v. Obs.*[−1] [Of obscure origin.] *trans.* To raise *up*; to uplift.

13.. *E.E. Allit. P.* A. 254 That Iuel þenne in gemmyz gente, Vered vp her vyse with yȝen graye.

vere, ME. var. FERE *sb.*, FIRE *sb.*; obs. f. VERY *a.*; obs. Sc. var. WAR *sb.*; obs. f. WEAR *v.*; Sc. f. WERE (doubt) *Obs.*

verecund ('vɛrɪkʌnd), *a.* [ad. L. *verēcund-us* (whence obs. F. *verecond* (Cotgr.), It. *verecondo*, Pg. *verecundo*), f. *verērī* to reverence, fear.] Modest, bashful; shy, coy.

c **1550** ROLLAND *Crt. Venus* III. 325 Than said Venus vith vult verecund, Say quhat ȝe will and keip ȝow within bound. **1656** BLOUNT *Glossogr.* (following Cotgrave), *Verecund*, modest, shamefac'd, demure, bashfull. [Hence in later Dicts.] **1872** 'ALIPH CHEEM' (Yeldham) *Lays of Ind* (1876) 2 One day this said verecund Mr. McPherson He chanced at a nautch to be present in person. **1873** RUSKIN *Fors Clav.* xxvii. 12 And verecund Mr. McCosh,..has he no suggestion to offer?

Hence vere'cundity, 'verecundness. *rare*[−0].

1721 BAILEY, *Verecundity*, Modesty, Bashfulness. **1727** *Ibid.* (vol. II), *Verecundness*, Modesty,..Verecundity.

†**vere'cundious**, *a. Obs.*[−1] [f. prec. + -IOUS.] Characterized or accompanied by modesty.

a **1639** WOTTON in *Reliq.* (1651) 160 Your brow proclameth much fidelity, a certain verecundious generosity graceth your eyes.

So †**verecundous** *a.* [-OUS.] *Obs.*[−0]

1656 BLOUNT, *Verecundous*, modest, shamefac'd, demure.

†**verefiance.** *Obs.*[−1] [f. *verefy* VERIFY *v.* + -ANCE.] Verification, confirmation.

c **1450** LOVELICH *Grail* xliv. 113 To morwen schole ȝe hem alle se To londe aryven,..Whiche to ȝow schal ben gret verefiaunce And gret fulfillenge to ȝoure creaunce.

verefie, -fy, obs. ff. VERIFY.

verejouse, obs. f. VERJUICE.

Verel ('vɪərəl). orig. *U.S.* The proprietary name of a synthetic acrylic fibre.

1956 *Official Gaz.* (U.S. Patent Office) 2 Oct. TM3 *Verel*, for synthetic staple fiber. **1956** *Trade Marks Jrnl.* 24 Oct. 1050/2 Verel B755,848. Raw or partly prepared synthetic textile fibres. Eastman Kodak Company..343, State Street, Rochester, State of New York, United States.. Manufacturers. **1956** *America's Textile Reporter* 22 Mar. 13/2 Processing and ironing temperatures should be held to a maximum 300 degrees Fahrenheit when 100 per cent 'Verel' fabrics are being handled. **1959** A. J. HALL *Stand. Handbk. Textiles* (ed. 5) i. 73 Verel fibres are more hydrophile than usual for synthetic fibres. **1963** —— *Textile Sci.* ii. 87 This [acrylic] group includes all those fibres made from polymers consisting wholly or partly of acrylonitrile, and important members are..Courtelle, Verel, Zefran, etc. **1978** P. G. TORTORA *Understanding Textiles* ix. 134 For many years only two modacrylic fibers were made commercially: Dynel..and Verel.

verelaie, obs. f. VIRELAY.

vereli, -liche, -ly(e, -lyche, obs. ff. VERILY *adv.*

†**verement.** *Obs.*−⁰ (See quot.)
c **1440** *Promp. Parv.* 56/2 Buschement, or verement, *cuneus.* [Also 508/2.]

veren, obs. pl. f. *were*, pa. t. of BE *v.*

veresimilous, var. VERISIMILOUS *a. Obs.*

veretie, obs. Sc. form of VERITY.

vere'tilliform, *a. Zool.* [f. mod.L. *Veretillum* + -(I)FORM.] Having the form of a member of *Veretillum*, the typical genus of *Veretillidæ*, a family of pennatuloid polyps.
1838 *Penny Cycl.* XII. 270/2 The ordinary or Veretilliform *Holothuriæ.* **1891** in *Cent. Dict.*

verey(e, -liche, obs. ff. VERY, VERILY.

‖**Verfremdungseffekt** (fɛr'frɛmdʊŋsɛ,fɛkt). [Ger.: see ALIENATION 1 d.] = *alienation effect* s.v. ALIENATION 1 d. Similarly **Ver'fremdung**, distancing, alienation (occas. in sense of ALIENATION 1 c).
1945 *Kenyon Rev.* VII. 470 The distancing ('Verfremdung') which Brecht desires is complemented by his concreteness which makes any escape from the reality demonstrated upon the stage impossible. **1951** *World Rev.* Jan. 67/2 Brecht generally sticks closely and with success to his technique of alienation (*Verfremdungseffekt*, he calls it). **1959** *New Statesman* 28 Mar. 442/2 His famous principle of *Verfremdung*, for example: of the distancing of the actor from his part, of breaking that theatrical illusion which mesmerises the audience into a witless passivity. **1960** J. BAYLEY *Characters of Love* iii. 145 We are to feel nothing but alienation, a Brechtian *Verfremdungseffekt.* **1980** *Times Lit. Suppl.* 17 Oct. 1172/5 Rylance Waters..provides a brilliant *Verfremdungseffekt.* **1981** F. INGLIS *Promise of Happiness* iii. 86 If, with Marx, we are to speak of *Verfremdung*, estrangement or alienation, as the most destructive and wounding experience of labour under capitalism.

vergaloo. *U.S.* Also vergaleu, virgaloo, -ieu. [var. of VIRGOULEUSE, prob. taken as a pl.] The white doyenné or Warwickshire bergamot.
1828–32 WEBSTER, *Vergouleuse*, a species of pear; contracted to *vergaloo.* **1840** J. BUEL *Farmer's Comp.* 269 It is as easy to cultivate the vergaleu as it is the choke pear. **1845** A. J. DOWNING *Fruits & Fruit-trees Amer.* 378 Virgalieu, of New York... Virgaloo, Bergaloo, of some American gardens... It is an old French variety, but with us, is in the most perfect health.

†**'vergantine.** *Obs. rare.* [a. older Sp. *vergantin* (Sp. *bergantin*, Pg. *bergantim*) BRIGANTINE.] = BRIGANTINE 1.
1578 T. N[ICHOLAS] tr. *Conq. W. India* 18 Hee then bought a Carvell and Vergantine. **1648** GAGE *West Ind.* 38 Hernando Cortez went..from Ihaxcallan to Mexico, to besiege it by land and by water, with Vergantines which for that purpose he had caused to be made.

verge (vɜːdʒ), *sb.*¹ Also 6–7 verdge, vierge, 7 varge. [a. OF. (also mod.F.) *verge* (= It. *verga*):—L. *virga* rod, etc.: cf. VIRGE.]

I. 1. a. The male organ; the penis. *rare.*
a **1400** *Stockh. Med. MS.* i. 343 in *Anglia* XVIII. 303 ȝif þe verge be brente, As man of woman may so be schente. **1887** [see FELLATIO].

b. *Zool.* [After mod.F. use.] The male organ of a mollusc, crustacean, or other invertebrate.
1774 GOLDSM. *Nat. Hist.* (1824) III. 114 All [sea-snails].. that have this orifice, or verge, as some call it, on the right side. **1852** DANA *Crust.* I. 242 The male verges are similar in position. **1861** HULME tr. *Moquin-Tandon* II. VII. 333 In these animals the sexes may be separated or united. The males are generally provided with a verge or spiculum.

†**2.** *Arch.* 'The shaft of a column, or a small ornamental shaft in Gothic architecture' (Parker). *Obs.*−¹
1412–20 LYDG. *Chron. Troy* II. 653 If I schulde rehersen by and by þe korve knottes by crafte of masounry, þe fresche enbowyng, with vergis riȝt as linys [etc.].

†**3.** A species of torch or candle. *Obs. rare.*
1494–5 *Durham Acc. Rolls* (Surtees) 653 Pro factura viij torchez, xij torchettes, cum iiij vergez pro capella d'ni Prioris. **1500–1** *Ibid.* 656, ij torches, iij torchetez, ij verges.

4. a. A rod or wand carried as an emblem of authority or symbol of office; a staff of office; a warder, †sceptre, mace. † ***sergeant of the verge***, = SERGEANT *sb.* 8 b.
1494 *Househ. Ord.* (1790) 124 The abbott to take to her her scepter and her verge to her hand. **1514** in Ellis *Orig. Lett.* Ser. II. I. 251 The said Cardinall..delivered her the Scepter in her right hande, and the vierge of the hand of Justice in her lyfte hand. **1566** ADLINGTON *Apuleius* 11, I pray you tell me what meaneth these servitours that follow you and these roddes or verges which they beare? **1602** SEGAR *Hon., Mil. & Civ.* IV. viii. §4. 218 To this degree of Archduke belongeth a Surcoat;..hee also beareth a Verge or rod of gold. **1609** HOLLAND *Amm. Marcell.* d iv b, He used to go before the Emperour with a golden Verge or Warder. **1679** BLOUNT *Anc. Tenures* 22 To support his [the King's] right Arm..whilst he held the Regal Verge or Scepter. **1688** HOLME *Armoury* IV. xii. (Roxb.) 506/1 Then marched the sergeants of the Verge of the Guildhall in Paris. **1708** J. CHAMBERLAYNE *St. Gt. Brit.* I. II. vi. (1710) 62 Putting into his Hand a Verge of Gold. **1791** BURKE *App. Whigs* Wks. 1842 I. 530 His mind will be heated as much by the sight of a sceptre, a mace, or a verge. **1867** *1st Rep. Commissioners Publ. Worship* 38/1 Have you any cross or other emblem carried in procession in your church?—Only a verge. **1894** C. N. ROBINSON *Brit. Fleet* 151 The verge formerly borne in state before a newly-appointed member of the Board.

†**b.** A rod or wand put in a person's hand when taking the oath of fealty to the lord on being admitted as a tenant, and delivered back on the giving up of the tenancy. Also in phr. ***tenant by the verge.*** *Obs.*
1607 J. NORDEN *Surv. Dial.* III. 101 Tenants of Base tenure, are they that hold by verge at the will of the Lord. **1628** COKE *On Litt.* 61 Tenant[s] by the Verge are in the same nature as tenants by copy of Court roll. **1651** tr. *Kitchin's Courts Leet* (1675) 161 Plow-holders of base tenure are those which hold by Verge at the Will of the Lord.

5. †**a.** A chariot-pole. *Obs.*−¹
1611 SPEED *Hist. Gt. Brit.* V. iv. §13. 25 They will..run vpon the vergies [L. *per temonem*], and stand stedfastly vpon the beames [L. *in jugo*], and quickly recouer themselues backe againe into the waggons.

b. A rod, wand, or stick. *rare.*
1897 *Church Q. Rev.* 5 The Pope's pastoral staff gradually swallowed up the sceptres of kings, as Aaron's verge devoured the other rods.

†**6.** An accent-mark. *Obs.*−¹
1555 EDEN *Decades* III. vii. (Arb.) 166 The names..are pronounced with thaccent, as yowe may know by the verge sette ouer the heddes of the vowels.

7. *Watchmaking.* **a.** The spindle or arbor of the balance in the old vertical escapement.
1704 in J. HARRIS *Lex. Techn.* I. **1757** *Phil. Trans.* L. 201 In the..clock..the verge, that carries the pallets, was bent downwards. **1825** J. NICHOLSON *Operat. Mechanic* 521 The socket..is turned pretty small on the outside, in order to allow the arbors of the detents to be laid as close to the verge as may be. **1876** *Clin. Soc. Trans.* IX. 145 He..contrived to break the verge of one watch and the cylinder of another. **1884** F. J. BRITTEN *Watch & Clockm.* 279 The Verge..has no pretensions to accuracy in presence of such escapements as the Lever and Chronometer.

b. *ellipt.* A verge watch (see next).
1871 'M. LEGRAND' *Cambr. Freshm.* iii, Mr. Samuel had previously worn an antiquated verge, once the property of the worthy Captain. **1904** *Times* 11 July 2/6 The watch was simply described as a gold verge with seal.

c. *attrib.* and *Comb.*, as ***verge escapement, -file, hole, -maker, -pivot, spring, watch.***
1792 *Trans. Soc. Arts* X. 217 Common verge watches have no oil upon the pallets. **1825** J. NICHOLSON *Operat. Mechanic* 508 The verge-pivots of a good sized pocket-watch. **1841** *Civil Eng. & Arch. Jrnl.* IV. 29/1 The end of the screw is attached to a strong verge spring. **1858** SIMMONDS *Dict. Trade, Verge-maker*, a maker of pallets; a branch of the watch-movement trade. **1875** KNIGHT *Dict. Mech.* 2707/1 *Verge-file*, a fine file with one safe side, formerly used in working on the verge of the old vertical escapement. *Ibid.* 2708/1 The vertical or verge escapement is old-fashioned. **1884** F. J. BRITTEN *Watch & Clockm.* 128 In good clocks the pallets and verge holes are jewelled. **1963** *Times* 6 Feb. 12/4 An anonymous purchaser gave 290gns. for a seventeenth-century verge watch by John Drake. **1977** *Cleethorpes News* 6 May 22/4 (Advt.), Clocks, silver watches, verge watches.

8. a. A part of a stocking-frame (see quot.).
1851–4 *Tomlinson's Cycl. Usef. Arts* (1867) II. 877/1 In front of the needle-bar is a small piece of iron, called the *verge*, to regulate the position of the needles.

b. *U.S.* That part of a linotype machine which carries the pawls by which the matrices are released; an escapement pawl link.
In recent use.

II. †**9. a.** A measure of length or superficies for carpentry work. *Obs.*−⁰
c **1440** *Promp. Parv.* 508/2 Verge, yn a wrytys werke, *virgata.*

†**b.** ***verge of land*** [tr. OF. *verge de terre*, med.L. *virga terræ*], = VIRGATE. *Obs. rare.*
1467–8 *Rolls of Parlt.* V. 609/1 A mese, iii verge of Land, ..iii Acres of Medowe. **1651** tr. *Kitchin's Courts Leet* (1675) 152 Upon two Verges of Land are built houses. **1672** *Cowell's Interpr., Yardland*..is a quantity of Land various, according to the place... It is called a Verge of Land, *anno* 28 E. 1, Statute of Wards.

III. 10. a. ***within the verge***, within an area subject to the jurisdiction of the Lord High Steward, defined as extending to a distance of twelve miles round the King's court. Also with *in*, and freq. const. *of* (the court, etc.). *Obs.* exc. *Hist.*
The phrase is a rendering of AF. *dedeinz la verge* (in Anglo-L. *infra virgam*), in which *verge* originally referred to the Steward's rod of office (see sense 4 a); in early use the full expression *verge de noster hostel* (L. *virga hospitii nostri*) is employed. In the 18th century commonly denoting the precincts of Whitehall as a place of sanctuary.
1509–10 *Act 1 Hen. VIII*, c. 14 §1 The Lorde Stuarde of the Kynges House..wythin the Verge and Justices of Assize, and Justices of the Peace,..have also power to inqwere..of every Defaulte. **1529** in Fiddes *Wolsey* II. (1726) 177 According to the ancient custom us'd within your verge. **1591** LAMBARDE *Archeion* (1635) 38 That the Marshall of the Kings House have the place of the King, to heare and determine Pleas of the Crowne within the Verge. **1604** *Proclam. Prices Victuals* 10 July, The Clarkes of the market of our Houshold within the Verge of our Court. **1643** in Clarendon *Hist. Reb.* VI. §231 That both He, and the Lord Herbert,..may likewise be restrain'd from coming within the Verge of the Court. **1669** E. CHAMBERLAYNE *Pres. St. Eng.* 244 Murders..committed in the Court or within the Verge, which is every way within 12 miles of the chief Tunnel of the Court. **1711** ADDISON *Spect.* No. 101 ¶7 Men and Women were allowed to meet at Midnight in Masques within the Verge of the Court. **1764** in *10th Rep. Hist. MSS. Comm.* App. I. 375 M. D'Eon who was to have receiv'd his sentence on fryday last..chose rather to take post in the neighbourhood of Whitehall, in the Verge of the Court. **1839** *Penny Cycl.* XIV. 448/1 The original court of the marshalsea is a court of record, to hear and determine causes between the servants of the king's household and others within the verge.
transf. **1606** BP. ANDREWES *Serm.* (1841) II. 202 We were not only within the dominion, but within the verge, nay even within the very gates of death.

b. Hence ***the verge (of the court)***, employed with other prepositions or in other constructions to designate this area or jurisdiction.
1529 in Fiddes *Wolsey* II. (1726) 177 All manner of victuals within the precinct of the verge. **1614** *Nottingham Rec.* IV. 319 Ye Clarke of the Markett for the verge. **1641** *Termes de la Ley* 261 The Coroner of the Kings house.. cannot intermeddle within the County forth of the Verge, because that his office extendeth not thereunto. **1748** SMOLLETT *Rod. Rand.* (1812) I. 431, I got safe into the verge of the court, where I kept snug. **1768** BLACKSTONE *Comm.* III. 76 By the statute of 13 Ric. II. st. 1. c. 3..the verge of the court in this respect extends for twelve miles round the king's place of residence. **1813** H. & J. SMITH *Horace in Lond.* 75 Place me beyond the verge afar, Where alleys blind the light debar. **1865** NICHOLS *Britton* I. p. xxxiv, This officer [of measures] appears to have been styled Clerk, or Keeper, of the Market; and his duties were generally united with those of the Coroner of the Verge.
attrib. **1708** J. CHAMBERLAYNE *Pres. St. Gt. Brit.* (1710) 538 [Officers of the Hall... Marshalsea... Verge.] *Ibid.* Index, Verge Officers, [p.] 538.

c. ***Court of (the) Verge***: (see quot. 1730).
1647 N. BACON *Disc. Govt. Eng.* I. lxviii. 285 All cases.. of trespassis *vi et armis*, where one [party]..was of the houshold, were handled in the court of the Verge, or the Marshals court. **1682** LUTTRELL *Brief Rel.* (1857) I. 159 Sir Phillip Lloyd..haveing been tried at the court of verge for killing one Mr. Holborne. **1730** BAILEY (fol.), *Court of Verge*, is a Court or Tribunal in the Manner of a King's Bench, which takes Cognisance of all Crimes and Misdemeanours committed within the Verge of the King's Court. **1904** MARY BATESON in *Scottish Hist. Soc. Misc.* II. 11 A well-developed Court of the Verge, presided over by the Constable, is here revealed in the Scotland of 1305.

11. a. The bounds, limits, or precincts *of* a particular place. Chiefly after the preps. *within, in, out of.*
The examples placed under (*a*) keep closer to the original use (see sense 10) than those under (*b*).
(*a*) **1641** in Rushw. *Hist. Coll.* III. (1692) I. 411 The English and Dutch Merchants within the Verge of the Castle [of Dublin]. *a* **1668** DAVENANT *Poems* (1673) 219 Th' Aldermen by Charter, title lay ('Cause writ 'ith City's Verge) to my new play. **1693** SOUTHERNE *Maid's last Prayer* IV. i, I wou'd not be known by any good will out of the verge of Whitehall. **1761** HUME *Hist. Eng.* II. xxxvi. 294 She should be beheaded within the verge of the Tower. **1778** *Eng. Gazetteer* (ed. 2) s.v. *Lidford*, The parish [of Lidford] may..compare with any in the kingdom, the whole forest of Dartmore being in the verge of it.
(*b*) **1650** FULLER *Pisgah* 394 Probably there were some wells within the verge of the Temple. **1703** DAMPIER *Voy.* III. I. 13 The Canary Islands are..within the usual Verge of the True or General Trade-Wind. **1727** A. HAMILTON *New Acc. E. Ind.* II. xlvii. 165 Whatever Animal comes within the Verge of a Temple, it is secured from Pursuit or Violence. **1772–84** *Cook's 3rd Voy.* I. iii. I. 31 This shews that the Cape de Verde Islands are either extensive enough to break the current of the trade-wind, or that they are situated just beyond its verge. **1860** HAWTHORNE *Marb. Faun* xxxviii, All splendour was included within its [*sc.* the cathedral's] verge.
fig. **1742** YOUNG *Nt. Th.* II. 633 The chamber..Is privileg'd beyond the common walk Of virtuous life, quite in the verge of heav'n.

†**b.** In *pl.* in the same sense. *Obs. rare.*
1680 H. MORE *Apocal. Apoc.* 46 The Circle of the Throne ..is thus conceived to be drawn about it, but so near that the Beasts..will have the same faces appear within the verges of the Throne that appeared without. **1690** C. NESSE *O. & N. Test.* I. 324 This only of all Jacob's children was born within the verges of the land of Canaan.

†**12.** In phrases (as prec.). **a.** The range, sphere, or scope *of* something; all that is naturally included or comprehended under a particular concept, category, etc. *Obs.* (common in 17th c.).
1599 NASHE *Lenten Stuffe* Wks. (Grosart) V. 219 Voide ground in the towne from the walls to the houses..is not within the verge of my Geometry. **1633** P. FLETCHER *Purp. Isl.* I. xlvi, He..gave it..a perfect motion, To move it self whither it self would have it, And know what falls within the verge of notion. **1664** OWEN *Vind. Animad. Fiat Lux* Wks. 1855 XIV. 294 These things are without the verge of Christian religion,—chimeras, towers and palaces in the air. **1679** C. NESSE *Antichrist* 188 They fall within the verge of that dispensation. **1717** *Col. Rec. Pennsylv.* III. 35 Made without the Verge of the ancient Laws of that Kingdom. **1734** *Treat. Orig. & Progr. Fees* 34 They do not fall within the Verge of my Undertaking in the present.
transf. **1607** TOURNEUR *Rev. Trag.* I. iii, Nay, brother, you reach out o' th Verge now.

†**b.** The pale or limit *of* a class or community.
1602 MARSTON *Antonio's Rev* V. vi, We will live inclos'd In holy verge of some religious order. **1649** JER. TAYLOR *Gt. Exemp.* I. 57 As he was included in the vierge of Abrahams posterity. **1699** SHAFTESB. *Charac.* II. I. I. §1 'Tis as hard to persuade..the other [sort] that there is any Virtue out of the Verge of their particular Community. **1768** STERNE *Sent. Journ., Dwarf* (1778) I. 188 Driven out of their own proper class into the very verge of another.

†**c.** The power, control, or jurisdiction of a person or persons. *Obs.*
1648 MILTON *Observ. Art. Peace* Wks. 1851 IV. 573 For the Conscience, we must have patience till it be within our verge. **1653–4** WHITELOCKE *Jrnl. Swed. Emb.* (1772) I. 227 The master of the ceremonies (as in his own verge) imperiously urged Whitelocke to pledge the health. **1676** MARVELL *Gen. Councils* Wks. 1875 IV. 143 The dextrous bishops..hooked within their verge, all the business and power that could be catch'd. **1704** SWIFT *Mech. Operat.*

Spirit (1711) 291 Engag'd in wise Dispute about certain Walks and Purlieus, whether they are in the Verge of God or the Devil.

IV. 13. a. The edge, rim, border, or margin *of* some object of limited size or extent. Now *rare.*

1459 *Paston Lett.* I. 468, ij. galon pottes of silver wrethyn, the verges gilt. *Ibid.*, ij. flagons of silver, with gilt verges. **1482** *Ibid.* III. 282 A scochen..with a scripture wretyn in the verges therof rehersyng thise wordes, 'Here lieth Margret Paston [etc.]'. **1587** FLEMING *Contn. Holinshed* III. 1337/1 About the verges [of the coins] was written; Francis of France duke of Brabant. **1616** B. JONSON *Masques, Hymenæi* 926 A transparent veile..whose verge, returning up, was fastened [etc.]. **1633** G. HERBERT *Temple, Love Unknown* 25 A boyling caldron, round about whose verge Was in great letters set Affliction. **1673-4** GREW *Anat. Trunks* I. i. §14 On the inner Verge of the Barque, stands another Sort of Sap-Vessels, in one slender and entire Ring. **1716** HEARNE *Collect.* (O.H.S.) V. 256 A Gravestone, round the verges of which [etc.]. **1747** GRAY *Death Fav. Cat* 29 Again she bent, Nor knew the gulf between... The slipp'ry verge her feet beguil'd, She tumbled headlong in. **1864** BOUTELL *Hist. & Pop. Her.* xix. §5 (ed. 3) 310 The Verge of the Escutcheon charged with 4 half Fleurs de lys or. **1865** DICKENS *Mut. Fr.* III. i, He stood on the verge of the rug.

†b. With *a* and *pl.*, etc.: A brim or rim; a circle of metal, etc. *Obs.*

1561 J. DAUS tr. *Bullinger on Apoc.* (1573) 64 b, A raine-bow lyke an Emeraud compasseth or incloseth it as a verdge. **1594** SHAKS. *Rich. III*, IV. i. 59 The inclusiue Verge Of Golden Mettall, that must round my Brow. **1621** AINSWORTH *Annot. Pentat.* (1639) 102 These Cups..had verges at the bottome, that they might rest upon the table. **1649** MARKHAM *Eng. Housew.* II. ii. 116 Then having rold the coffin flat, and raised up a small verdge of an inch, or more high. *c* **1710** CELIA FIENNES *Diary* (1888) 129 There is another [statue]..whose garments and all are marble..and a verge all down before and round ye neck with ye figures of the Apostles done in Embroydery as it were.

†c. *Bot.* (See quots.) *Obs.*

1704 *Dict. Rust.* (1726), *Verge*,..among Florists,..is taken for the edge or outside of a Leaf; as *A dented Verge.* **1728** CHAMBERS *Cycl.* s.v., Among Florists, a dented Verge, is a jagged edge or outside of a Leaf.

d. *Arch.* (See quots.) Cf. VERGE-BOARD.

1833 LOUDON *Encycl. Archit.* §83 To give a slight inclination to the verge or border-slates, where they butt against brick-work. *Ibid.* §849 The verges are the external edge of the tiling in gables, which are covered with lime and hair, or Roman cement. **1875** *Encycl. Brit.* II. 475/2 *Verge*, the edge of the tiling projecting over the gable of a roof.

14. a. The extreme edge, margin, or bound *of* a surface of an extensive nature, but regarded as having definite limits. Also occas. without const.

1593 SHAKS. *Rich. II*, I. i. 93 The furthest Verge That euer was suruey'd by English eye. **1602** MARSTON *Ant. & Mel.* III. Wks. 1856 I. 30 The shuddering morne that flakes, With silver tinctur, the east vierge of heaven. **1628** WITHER *Brit. Rememb.* I. 73 The spacious verge of that well peopled Towne. **1667** MILTON *P.L.* II. 1038 Here Nature first begins Her fardest verge, and Chaos to retire. **1698** FRYER *Acc. E. India & P.* 16 To return to Johanna; the innermost part we suppose to be fruitful, by what the Verge of it declares. **1727-46** THOMSON *Summer* 944 Sad..he sits, And views the main that ever toils below, Still fondly forming in the farthest verge. **1735** SOMERVILLE *Chase* III. 549 Close to the Verge Of a small Island. **1774** GOLDSM. *Nat. Hist.* (1776) III. 337 The jackall..pursues even to the verge of the city, and often along the streets. **1791** MRS. RADCLIFFE *Rom. Forest* ii, The first tender tints of morning now appeared on the verge of the horizon. **1829** SCOTT *Rob Roy* Introd. ¶2 He owed his fame in a great measure to his residing on the very verge of the Highlands. **1849** MACAULAY *Hist. Eng.* iii. I. 342 About a day's journey south of Leeds, on the verge of a wild moorland tract, lay an ancient manor. **1876** PAGE *Adv. Text-bk. Geol.* iii. 53 On the western verge of Egypt.

b. *fig.* The end *of* life.

1750 JOHNSON *Rambler* No. 71 ¶11 The computer..believes that he is marked out to reach the utmost verge of human existence. **1864** PUSEY *Lect. Daniel* (1876) 503 The utmost verge of this life. **1874** HOLLAND *Mistr. Manse* xxvii, It had the power to stay his feet Yet longer on the verge of life. **1884** W. C. SMITH *Kildrostan* 55 The mind was wandering, as it often does On the dim verge of life.

c. The utmost limit to which a thing or matter extends; the distinctive line of separation between one subject and another.

1796 MME. D'ARBLAY *Camilla* V. 406 Having lived up to the very verge of his yearly income. **1818** SCOTT *Hrt. Midl.* x, He carried his dislike to youthful amusements beyond the verge that religion and reason demanded. **1820** HAZLITT *Lect. Dram. Lit.* 173 Sforza's resolution..is..out of the verge of nature and probability. **1870** EMERSON *Soc. & Solit., Work & Days* Wks. (Bohn) III. 70 The verge or confines of matter and spirit. **1874** L. STEPHEN *Hours in Libr.* (1892) I. v. 180 The very outside verge of the province permitted to the romancer.

15. a. The extreme edge of a cliff or abrupt descent. Used *absol.* or with *of.*

(*a*) **1605** J. ROSIER in Capt. Smith *Virginia* (1624) 19 The rocky clifts..are all overgrown with Firre,..and Oke, as the Verge is with Gousberries [etc.]. **1728** ELIZA HEYWOOD tr. *Mme. de Gomez' Belle A.* (1732) II. 61 He fell off the Verge he had been so bold to climb, dying the Sea with his Blood. **1784** COWPER *Task* VI. 519 His steed.., wheeling swiftly round, Or e'er his hoof had press'd the crumbling verge, Baffled his rider, sav'd against his will! **1813** BYRON *Corsair* I. xvi, The verge where ends the cliff, begins the beach. **1832** W. IRVING *Alhambra* II. 234 In the centre of this basin yawned the mouth of the pit. Sanchica ventured to the verge and peeped in.

(*b*) **1677** GILPIN *Demonol.* (1867) 320 Like a man that walks upon the utmost verge of a river's brink. **1817** MOORE *Lalla R., Fire-Worshippers* iv. 128 The mighty Ruins..Upon the mount's high, rocky verge. **1823** F. CLISSOLD *Ascent Mt. Blanc* 23 This rock is seated upon the verge of a precipitous eminence. **1863** BARING-GOULD *Iceland* 257 Thorbjorn shouted and brought Grettir and his brother to the verge of the cliff.

fig. **1742** YOUNG *Nt. Th.* I. 62 My hopes and fears..o'er life's narrow verge Look down—on what? a fathomless abyss. **1760** GRAY *Let. to Wharton* 22 June, You see him [i.e. Sterne] often tottering on the verge of laughter. **1817** JAS. MILL *Brit. India* II. IV. viii. 276 The fortunes of Hyder tottered on the verge of a precipice. **1849** SIR J. GRAHAM in Parker *Life & Lett.* (1907) II. iv. 86 He is now tottering on the verge of the grave. **1861** SIR G. TREVELYAN *Horace at Athens* iii. (1862) 39 We still consume..Veal that is tottering on the verge of beef.

b. The margin *of* a river or the sea. Also without const.

1606 SYLVESTER *Du Bartas* II. iv. *Tropheis* 1157 The flowry Verge that longst all Jordan lies. **1614** GORGES *Lucan* I. 26 Where the Tarbellians bound at large A calmed sea, with crooked varge. **1624** CAPT. SMITH *Virginia* IV. 111 Vpon the verge of the Riuer there are fiue houses. **1814** SCOTT *Ld. of Isles* v. vii, The leaders urge Their followers to the ocean verge. **1855** MACAULAY *Hist. Eng.* xii. III. 163 There, at length, on the verge of the ocean,..the imperial race turned desperately to bay. **1878** SUSAN PHILLIPS *On Seaboard* 81 What do they [*sc.* ships] bring to us? who..Sport by the verge and gather rosy shells.

fig. **1843** NEALE *Hymns for Sick* 23 And when I tread the utmost verge Do Thou divide the flood.

c. *poet.* The horizon.

1822 BYRON *Heav. & Earth* I. iii, Their brazen-colour'd edges streak The verge where brighter morns were wont to break. **1847** TENNYSON *Princ.* VII. 23 She..sees a great black cloud..Blot out the slope of sea from verge to shore.

16. a. With *a* and *pl.* A limit or bound; a limiting or bounding belt or strip. Somewhat *rare.*

1660 H. MORE *Myst. Godl.* I. 16 Within the narrow verges of this mortal life. **1667** MILTON *P.L.* XI. 877 Serve they as a flourie verge to binde The fluid skirts of that same watrie Cloud? **1790** *Trans. Soc. Arts* VIII. 6 A verge, six yards broad, on two sides, is filled with a variety of Forest-trees. **1851** MEREDITH *Death of Winter* 19 He melts between the border sheen And leaps the flowery verges. **1852** WIGGINS *Embanking* 136 Such pasturable verges or grassy fringes as have already been subject to acts of ownership.

b. *spec.* A narrow grass edging separating a flower border, etc., from a gravel walk. Hence also, an unpaved strip of land, usu. planted with grass, separating a pedestrian pavement from a road; a (grass-covered) edging to a road. Cf. *grass verge* s.v. GRASS *sb.*[1] 14.

1728 CHAMBERS *Cycl.* s.v. *Grass-plot*, The Quarters, or Verges, are to be prepared with..Earth to lay the Turf on. **1731** MILLER *Gard. Dict.*, *Verge*..in Gardening..is generally understood to be a Slip of Grass which joyns to Gravel Walks, and divides them from the Borders in the Parterre Garden. **1858** GLENNY *Gard. Every-day Bk.* 71/1 The verges of green turf, so apt to encroach upon the gravel-walks and inwardly upon the beds. **1953** H. E. BATES *Nature of Love* 16 She had just time to pull the pram into the verge before Parker went past her and the Ford, bouncing, hit the snake fence thirty yards beyond. **1955** *Times* 9 July 7/5 If there were three lanes the slow traffic would be far more inclined to keep within their lane nearer the verge and allow faster vehicles to pass. **1972** *Human World* Nov. 29 The other passengers..crowded towards the windows. The excitement was caused by a small tribe of gypsies encamped on the verge. **1979** J. GRIMOND *Memoirs* vii. 108 Before the stupid and expensive cutting of the verges the roadsides were thick with clover and cow-parsley.

attrib. and *Comb.* **1822** LOUDON *Encycl. Gard.* §617 Verge-Shears..are a smaller variety, in which the blades are joined to the handles by kneed shanks, to lessen stooping in the operator. They are chiefly used for trimming the sides of box-edgings [*ed.* 1824 *adds* and grass-verges]. **1882** *Garden* 28 Jan. 65/1 Verge cutting and levelling of turf.

17. a. The brink or border *of* something towards which there is progress or tendency (from without); the point at which something begins. Usually in the phrases *on* or *to the verge of.*

Various types of context are illustrated by the different groups of quotations.

(*a*) **1602** MARSTON *Ant. & Mel.* Induct., I will..ding his spirit to the verge of hell. **1718** POPE *Iliad* XV. 14 His senses wandering to the verge of death. **1749** SMOLLETT *Regic.* IV. ii, But let us seize him on the verge of bliss. **1791** COWPER *Iliad* v. 787 Sheer into his bone He pierced him, but..Jove Him rescued even on the verge of fate. **1820** SCOTT *Abbot* xiii, Her maternal fondness for her grandson..carried almost to the verge of dotage. **1842** J. PEDDIE *Exp. Jonah* v. 88 He seems to have been driven to the very verge of despair. *a* **1859** MACAULAY *Hist. Eng.* xxiii. (1861) V. 5 Spencer..was more than once brought to the verge of ruin by his violent temper. **1884** *L'pool Mercury* 22 Oct. 5/4 He was jealous and volatile to the verge of insanity.

(*b*) **1754** JOHNSON *Let. to Chesterfield* 7 Feb., I have been pushing on my work..and have brought it, at last, to the verge of publication. **1772** SHRUBSOLE & DENNE *Hist. Rochester* 35 The nation seemed on the verge of a civil war. **1848** W. H. KELLY tr. *L. Blanc's Hist. Ten Y.* I. 599 A generous city..driven to the verge of revolt. **1851** ROBERTSON *Serm.* Ser. II. xi. (1864) 145 Such men tread..on the very verge of a confession. **1866** G. MACDONALD *Ann. Q. Neighb.* xxiv, I had driven Catherine Weir to the verge of suicide.

(*c*) **1793** SMEATON *Edystone L.* §121, I was now upon the verge of the proper season for action. **1876** MOZLEY *Univ. Serm.* v. (ed. 2) 107 Just before death..his expressions and signs upon the verge of that moment awaken our curiosity.

(*d*) **1837** WHEWELL *Hist. Induct. Sci.* (1857) I. 173 [This] brings us to the verge of modern astronomy. **1862** SIR B. BRODIE *Psychol. Inq.* II. iv. 138 We are here on the verge of an inquiry which has perplexed the greatest philosophers.

ellipt. **1859** MEREDITH *R. Feverel* xxxviii, She touched on delicate verges to the baronet, and he understood her well enough.

b. With vbl. sbs. *on the verge of*, on the very point of (doing something).

1858 FROUDE *Hist. Eng.* III. xiii. 123 He..reached the town to find..the commons and the gentlemen on the verge of fighting. **1858** DICKENS *Lett.* (1880) II. 42 We were on the very verge of granting an..annuity. **1887** [? MISS INGHAM] *Poor Nellie* (1888) 91 Twice she was on the verge of telling all.

18. a. The space within a boundary; room, scope. Also const. *to* or *for.*

Chiefly in echoes of quot. 1757.

1690 DRYDEN *Don Sebastian* I. i, Let fortune empty her whole quiver on me, I have a Soul, that like an ample Shield Can take in all; and verge enough for more. **1757** GRAY *Bard* 51 Give ample room, and verge enough The characters of hell to trace. **1837** LOCKHART *Scott* II. i. 8 The bard..had ample room and verge enough..for every variety of field sport. **1860** HAWTHORNE *Marb. Faun* xxiv, In this vast house..a great-grandsire and all his descendants might find ample verge. **1877** 'H. A. PAGE' *De Quincey* I. xiii. 283 When numbers of freebooters found ample verge for their predatory propensities.

b. *fig.* and in fig. context.

1836 SIR W. HAMILTON *Discuss.* (1852) 338 In no other country was there so little verge, far less encouragement, allowed to theological speculation. **1863** D. G. MITCHELL *My Farm of Edgewood* 263 Here is verge, surely, for a man's cultivation. **1879** M. PATTISON *Milton* 178 Not giving verge enough for the sweep of his soaring conception.

†verge, *sb.*[2] *Obs. rare.* [f. VERGE *v.*[2]] The act of verging or inclining *to* or *towards* some object, etc.

1661 GLANVILL *Van. Dogm.* 223 If by this verge to the other extream, I can bring the opinionative Confident but half the way. **1662** —— *Lux Orient.* xiv. 119 Though they have had..their Verges towards the body and its joys, as well as their Aspires to nobler..objects.

verge (vɜːdʒ), *v.*[1] Also 7 verdge. [f. VERGE *sb.*[1]]

†1. *trans.* **a.** To provide *with* a specified kind of verge or border; to edge. Chiefly in passive. Also with *about. Obs.*

1605 J. ROSIER in Capt. Smith *Virginia* (1624) I. 20 An equall plaine..verged with a greene border of grasse. **1621** MARKHAM *Prev. Hunger* 13 This Net shall be verdgd on each side with very strong Corde. [Hence in later works.] **1625** —— *Bk. Hon.* II. x. §10 Long Mantles..verdged about with a small fringe of siluer. **1708** *New View of London* I. 101/1 The Figures of a Man and a Woman in Brass, and the Stone verged with Plates of the same.

b. To bound or limit *by* something. *rare*[−1].

1759 MILLS tr. *Duhamel's Husb.* I. viii. 20 Sending..for horse-dung, to manure those very lands which never fail of being verg'd, or bottom'd, by a substance..more proper for the end they aim at.

c. To form the verge or limit of.

1817 CHALMERS *Astron. Disc.* iv. (1830) 132 How to draw the vigorous land-mark which verges the field of legitimate discovery.

d. To pass along the verge or edge of; to skirt.

1890 F. BARRETT *Betw. Life & Death* II. xxviii. 179 The chariot can verge the daïs all the way.

2. *intr.* **a.** To be contiguous or adjacent to; to lie on the verge of. Const. *on* or *upon, along.*

1787 G. WHITE *Selborne* vii, Forests and wastes..are of considerable service to neighbourhoods that verge upon them. **1821** CLARE *Vill. Minstr.* II. 37 The air was still; The blue mist, thinly scatter'd round, Verg'd along the distant hill. **1858** HAWTHORNE *Fr. & It. Note-Bks.* (1872) I. 11 The Place de la Concorde.., verging on which is the Champs Elysées.

b. To border *on* or *upon* some state, condition, etc. (Cf. VERGE *v.*[2] 3.)

1825 [see VERGENCY[1]]. **1827** FARADAY *Chem. Manip.* vii. (1842) 197 Mercury or zinc require one [*sc.* a temperature] verging upon, or even surpassing, a red heat. **1853** C. BRONTE *Villette* xviii, Your generosity must have verged on extravagance. **1874** H. R. REYNOLDS *John Bapt.* v. §3. 352 Philo, however, verges on allowing the λόγος to be the centre of the personality of God.

fig. **1842** TENNYSON *Gardener's Dau.* 71 Vague desires..made..all kinds of thought, That verged upon them, sweeter than the dream [etc.].

3. To rise *up* so as to show the edge. *rare*[−1].

1726-46 THOMSON *Winter* 868 Wish'd Spring returns; and..The welcome sun, just verging up at first, By small degrees extends the swelling curve!

Hence **'verging** *ppl. a.*

1796 W. H. MARSHALL *W. England* I. 165 Wild Deer..were found very injurious to the verging crops.

verge (vɜːdʒ), *v.*[2] [ad. L. *vergĕre* to bend, incline, turn. Cf. CONVERGE *v.*, DIVERGE *v.*]

1. *intr.* Of the sun: To descend toward the horizon; to sink, or begin to do so. Also *transf.*

1610 G. FLETCHER *Christ's Tr.* II. xxv, Yet when he [the sun] verges, or is hardly ris, She [the moon] the vive image of her absent brother is. **1825** SCOTT *Talism.* iii, The light was now verging low, yet served the knight still to discern that they two were no longer alone in the forest. **1890** R. BRIDGES *Indolence* Poems (1912) 270 The summer day Had verged already on its hot decline.

2. To move in a certain direction (esp. downwards); also, to extend or stretch.

a **1661** FULLER *Worthies, Somerset* (1662) 32 Henceforward the Sun of the Kings cause declined, verging more and more Westward, till at last it set in Cornwal. **1732** POPE *Ess. Man* I. 59 So Man..Touches some wheel, or verges to some goal. **1775** S. J. PRATT *Liberal Opin.* cv. (1783) IV. 6 A tear..still upon the back of my hand, verging to the very finger that [etc.]. *Ibid.* cxxvi. 149 The higher we climb..the nearer to the gods..: as we verge towards earth..we convolve with the dirt. **1797** *Monthly Mag.* III. 513/1 Verge not downwards, a precipice lies under the earth. **1822**

'B. CORNWALL' *Misc. Poems, Hall of Eblis,* The pillars.. verged away In long innumerable avenues. **1886** MRS. HUNGERFORD *Lady Branksmere* i, Towards this rather dilapidated apartment they always verge when perplexed. *fig.* **1780** COWPER *Progr. Err.* 430 Learning, once the man's exclusive pride, Seems verging fast towards the female side.

b. To diverge or deflect; to run or trickle *off*.
1692 BENTLEY *Boyle Lect.* 215 The Epicurean theory, of atoms descending down an infinite space.. and verging from the perpendicular no body knows why. **1780** S. J. PRATT *Emma Corbett* (ed. 4) II. 74 The tear had verged off, possibly while he was bowing.

3. To incline or tend, to approach or draw near, *towards* or *to* some state or condition. Also with advb. complement. (Cf. VERGE *v.*^{1} 2 b.)
(*a*) **1664** H. MORE *Myst. Iniq., Apol.* 514 Presbytery.. that verges nearer toward Populacy or Democracy. **1837** CARLYLE *Fr. Rev.* I. II. iv, A man of light wit, verging towards fourscore. **1840** THIRLWALL *Greece* VII. lvi. 135 At a time when the people is supposed to have been verging toward utter degeneracy. **1856** DOVE *Logic Chr. Faith* Introd. §5. 19 The more human knowledge progresses, the more does man.. verge towards the infinite.
(*b*) *a* **1677** BARROW *Serm.* xvii. Wks. 1686 III. 195 The farther we go on, especially in a bad course, the nearer we verge to the dregs of our life. **1732** ARBUTHNOT *Rules of Diet* 256 Where the Blood verges to the contrary State. **1737** POPE *Let. to Swift* 23 Mar., The nearer I find myself verging to that period of life which is to be labour and sorrow. **1762–71** H. WALPOLE *Vertue's Anecd. Paint.* (1786) IV. Advt. 6 As refinement generally verges to extreme contrarieties. **1823** SCOTT *Quentin D.* Introd., A man whose credit was actually verging to decay. **1844** THIRLWALL *Greece* VIII. lxi. 125 When the reign of Demetrius was verging to its close. **1851** TRENCH *Poems* 14 When I began First to verge upward to a man. **1865** PARKMAN *France in Amer.* ii. (1876) 16 Yet, verging to decay, she [Spain] had an ominous and appalling strength.
(*c*) **1776** BENTHAM *Fragm. Govt.* iv. Wks. 1843 I. 288/2 It is not that,.. or any discourse verging that way, that can tend to give him the smallest satisfaction. **1837** CARLYLE *Fr. Rev.* I. I. ii, In such a decadent age, or one fast verging that way.

b. Const. *to* with inf. *rare*$^{-1}$.
1818 COLEBROOKE *Import Colonial Corn* 45 A country in which capital has accumulated, population become dense,.. is necessarily a manufacturing one, or verging to become so.

c. To approximate in shade or tint *to* a specified colour.
1815 STEPHENS in Shaw's *Gen. Zool.* IX. I. 87 Plumage nearly black, with a green gloss, which, in some parts, verges to a violet. **1835–6** *Todd's Cycl. Anat.* I. 462/2 When large, its colour is dark red, verging to purple.

d. To pass or undergo gradual transition *into* something else.
1756 BURKE *Subl. & B.* Wks. 1842 I. 57 It is not to make a strong deviation from the line of the neighbouring parts; nor to verge into any exact geometrical figure. **1854** *Poultry Chron.* I. 282/1 The 'Poultry Chronicle' is fast verging into a state of monomania. **1858** MRS. C. GORE *Heckington* II. xiii. 267 The close and trimly shrubbery verged, after a few hundred yards, into a beautiful copse.

4. To have a particular direction; to lie or extend towards a specified point.
1726 LEONI *Alberti's Archit.* II. 74/2 A large semi-circular area verging to the South. **1796** MORSE *Amer. Geog.* I. 557 The flat [boat] always being put in an oblique direction, with its foremost end verging towards the line described by the rope. **1813** SHELLEY *Q. Mab* IX. 7 Whose rays.. Verge to one point and blend for ever there. **1822–7** GOOD *Study Med.* (1829) I. 469 Indurated tumour in the left hypochondrium, verging towards the spine. **1828–32** WEBSTER s.v., A hill verges to the north.

Hence **ˈverging** *ppl. a.*, approaching, converging.
1741 H. BROOKE *Constantia* Poems (1810) 397/1 Through his foe's shield the verging weapon press'd, And raz'd the plume that wanton'd on his crest. **1910** *Contemp. Rev.* Mar. 339 My sleek limbs cramp in this verging gloom.

verge, *v.*^{3} [Back-formation f. VERGER^{2} I.] *intr.* To act as a verger; to be a verger. Hence **ˈverging** *vbl. sb.*
1900 W. HOW *Lighter Moments* 54 He werges up one side of the church and I werges up the other. **1926** *Punch* 13 Oct. 400/2, I verges up the centre aisle; he verges up the sides. **1927** H. V. MORTON *In Search of England* i. 14 The profession of verging appears to induce mousey manners. **1976** *Church Times* 29 Oct. 18/4 (Advt.), A Christian couple required by St. Paul's Church, Slough. Lady to do cleaning, gent for verging at weekends.

verge-board. *Arch.* Also *dial.* varge-. [f. VERGE *sb.*^{1} 13 d.] = BARGE-BOARD.
1827 T. F. HUNT *Designs for Parsonage Houses* 5 Ornamental barge-boards... [*Note*] By some called *verge*-boards. **1833** LOUDON *Encycl. Archit.* §470 Sixty-six feet lineal one and a half inch verge board to gables. **1835** F. GOODWIN *Rural Archit.* Add. 2 The Verge Boards to be cut out of 2½ inch Timber plank, well spiked to the rafter-ends of the Roof and Purlins. **1861** B. POSTE in *Archæol. Cantiana* IV. 116 There are mouldings on the verge-boards of the pediment. **1910** *Athenæum* 3 Sept. 272/2 The.. church of Witley has good fourteenth-century verge-boards attached to the gable of its stone porch.

Hence **verge-boarding.** *rare*$^{-1}$.
1835 F. GOODWIN *Rural Archit.* Add. 2 The Gables and Verge Boarding.

vergée (ˈvɛːrʒeɪ). [Anglo-Norman, f. F. *terre vergée* measured land.] In the Channel Islands, a superficial measure of land, varying between Jersey and Guernsey (see quot. 1971).
In quot. 1915, in Flanders.
1834 H. D. INGLIS *Channel Islands* I. ix. 180 Rent in the neighbourhood of St. Helier is as high as from £3 to £4 per vergée... Two vergées and one quarter, make an English acre. **1858** F. F. DALLY *Channel Islands* v. iv. 235 The Guernsey vergée is forty perches, and two vergées and a half are rather more than the English acre. **1915** *Contemp. Rev.* July 107, 400 *vergées* (about one acre and a half), were kept under cultivation. **1971** *Nat. Geogr. Mag.* May 722/2, I do 50 *vergées* of potatoes a year... The vergée, an old Norman measure, is still the legal land unit of the Channel Islands. On Jersey, two-and-a-quarter vergées make one English acre, but Guernsey disagrees, and counts two-and-a-half to the acre. **1977** *Jersey Even. Post* 26 July 11/2 The IDC would like to transfer 1¾ vergées of land at the corner of Rouge Bouillon and Roussel Street.

verge-line. *rare.* [f. VERGE *sb.*^{1}] (See quot.)
1712 J. JAMES tr. *Le Blond's Gardening* 119 The Verge-Line, in the Business of Terrasses, is the Place where the Corner of a Wall, or the Bank of a Terrass, comes to terminate. *Ibid.* 121 The Verge-Line of the Terrasses.

vergelt, obs. Sc. form of WERGELD.

vergence (ˈvɜːdʒəns). [f. VERGE *v.*^{2} + -ENCE.]
1. *Ophthalm.* The simultaneous movement of both eyes towards or away from one another, as when they focus on a point that is nearer or farther away.
1902 E. C. ELLETT in *Jrnl. Amer. Med. Assoc.* 18 Oct. 969/2, I would suggest as a temporary table at least, a sort of composite arrangement, as follows: Movements of the visual axis... Associated disjunctive movements (vergences).. convergence.. supervergence. **1940** F. B. CHAVASSE in Ridley & Sorsby *Mod. Trends Ophthalmol.* xxvi. 280 By growth, extension, and refinement of this reflex is developed the proper vergence (notably convergence) of the eyes upon (say) the prey. **1979** *Sci. Amer.* Jan. 88/1 Abrupt target jumps generate two types of eye movements: slow, smooth vergence eye movements.. and sharp, rapid saccadic eye movements.

2. *Geol.* [ad. G. *vergenz* (H. Stille 1930, in *Nachrichten von d. Ges. d. Wissensch. zu Göttingen, Math.-Physik. Klasse* III. 380).] The direction in which a fold is inclined or overturned.
1960 *Trans. Edin. Geol. Soc.* XVIII. 51 Isoclinal recumbent folds with an average trend ENE-WSW; vergence SSE to NNW. [*Note*] The authors use the term 'vergence'.. to indicate the direction of overturning of folds. **1978** *Nature* 7 Dec. 604/1 At the northern apex of the Tyrrhenian Sea, two mountain chains face each other displaying opposite vergence: the Corsican alpine chain and the Northern Apennines.

ˈvergency^{1}. [f. VERGE *v.*^{1}: cf. next.] The fact of bordering *on* something.
1825 LD. COCKBURN *Mem.* iii. (1856) 179 [He] said of himself, 'I often verge so nearly on absurdity' [etc.]... This was quite true; especially the vergency on absurdity.

vergency^{2} (ˈvɜːdʒənsɪ). [f. VERGE *v.*^{2} + -ENCY.]
†**1.** The act or fact of verging or inclining towards some condition, etc.; tendency, leaning; an instance of this. Also const. *to, toward. Obs.*
a **1665** J. GOODWIN *Filled with the Spirit* (1867) 486 The general vergency and leaning of the Scriptures on that hand we speak of. **1668** H. MORE *Div. Dial.* II. 451 The visible vergency of the World to another Degeneracy or Apostasie from the Kingdome of Christ. **1680** —— *Apocal. Apoc.* 27 Which is a sign you are in a state of languishment and vergency towards death. **1702** C. MATHER *Magn. Chr.* III. II. xxix. 164/1 Scarce a Minute [would] pass him without a Turn of his Eye towards Heaven, whereto his heaven-touch'd Heart was carrying of him, with its continual Vergencies.
†**b.** Bent or inclination. *Obs.*
1649 J. H. *Motion to Parl. Adv. Learn.* 33 It were but justice to him that the naturall vergency of his Genius should be found out.
2. The fact or condition of being inclined toward some object or in some direction.
1668 WILKINS *Real Char.* II. vii. §3 That respect of the imaginary face of a thing towards some other thing or place, called vergency, tending, leaning, inclining. *a* **1696** SCARBURGH *Euclid* (1705) 13 First, there must be.. an Inclination, Vergency,.. or Tendency, of Two lines one to the other.
b. *Optics.* (See quots.)
1832 SIR W. R. HAMILTON in *Trans. R. Irish Acad.* (1837) XVII. 80 We may therefore call the curvatures of these two diametral sections the two vergencies of the final ray-lines. **1860** WORCESTER (citing Lloyd), *Vergency,*.. the reciprocal of the focal distance, being the measure of the degree of divergence or convergence of a pencil of rays.

ˈVergent, *a. Geol.* [ad. L. *vergent-, vergens,* pr. pple. of *vergĕre* to VERGE.] Constituting, or belonging to, a series of Appalachian strata corresponding in age to the middle Devonian strata of British geologists.
1858 H. D. ROGERS *Geol. Pennsylv.* I. 108 Vergent Flags (Portage Flags of New York). *Ibid.*, Vergent Shales (Chemung Group of New York). *Ibid.* II. 732 The Cadent and Vergent rocks contain important bands of iron ore.

vergeous, obs. form of VERJUICE.

†**ˈverger**^{1}. *Obs.* Also 5 vergere, vergier, *Sc.* virger. [a. OF. *verger* (11th c.; so in mod.F.), *vergier* (12th c.; = Pr. *vergier*):—L. *virdiārium, viridiārium* (also *viridārium*), f. *viridis* green.] A garden or orchard; a pleasure-garden.
13.. *Seuyn Sag.* 167 Thai wolde make a riche halle, Withouten Rome, in on verger.. bi o riuer. *c* **1400** *Rom. Rose* 3831 Why hast thou ben so necligent, To kepen.. This verger heere left in thi warde? *c* **1450** *Merlin* xix. 310 Merlin lete rere a vergier, where-ynne was all maner of fruyt and alle maner of flowres. **1480** CAXTON *Ovid's Met.* XIV. xii, To wede and pyk oute alle the evyl herbes and wedes out of her verger or gardyn. **1501** DOUGLAS *Pal. Hon.* I. Prol. 44 The greshoppers amangis the vergers gnappit.

verger^{2} (ˈvɜːdʒə(r)). Also 7 vierger. [prob. a. AF. *verger, f. verge VERGE *sb.*^{1} Cf. OF. *vergiere* (*vergeur*) gauger, *vergier* maker of rings, obs. F. *verger* verger (Cotgr.); also med.L. *virgārius,* and VIRGER.]
1. An official who carries a rod or similar symbol of office before the dignitaries of a cathedral, church, or university (†or before justices).
c **1402** in *Peterborough Registry* (MS.), fol. 457, Officium hostiarii, alias dictum verger, in eodem [collegio de Wyndesore] vacans. **1472–3** *Rolls of Parlt.* VI. 48/1 Howe that Henr' late Duke of Lancastr'.. founded.. a Churche.. of a Deane,.. vi Choresters, and a Verger perpetuell. **1530** PALSGR. 284/2 Verger that bereth a rodde in the churche, *sergent de lesglise. c* **1549** in Swayne *Sarum Churchw. Acc.* (1896) 75 To Thomas Johnson yᵉ verger at owr ladye churche. **1607** COWELL *Interpr., Vergers*.. be such as cary white wands before the Iustices of either banke, &c...; otherwise called Porters of the verge. **1616** B. JONSON *Devil an Ass* IV. iv, I must walk With the French sticke, like an old Vierger, for you. **1688** R. HOLME *Armoury* III. 197/1 The Verger [of the Cathedral Church] is a Man in a Gown.. whose Office it is to conduct the Reader to his place [etc.]. **1818** BYRON *Ch. Har.* IV. Notes 117 The Emperor,.. taking a wand in his hand, officiated as *verger*,.. preceding the pontiff to the altar. **1846** HOOK *Ch. Dict.* (ed. 5) 900 *Verger*, ..he who carries the mace before the dean in a cathedral or collegiate church. **1854** *Ibid.* (ed. 7) 782 *Verger.* An officer with a similar title precedes the vice-chancellor in the English universities. **1867** TROLLOPE *Chron. Barset* II. xlix. 59 For nearly a week.. he had been unable to face the minor canons and vergers.
attrib. c **1530** in Gutch *Coll. Cur.* II. 340 Item oone Verger Rodde of silvar parcel gilte. **1546** *Inv. Ch. Goods* (Surtees) 137 Two verger rodys of sylver.
transf. **1615** CHAPMAN *Odyss.* XII. 555 This by Calypso, I was told, and she Inform'd it, from the verger Mercurie.
b. One whose duty it is to take care of the interior of a church, and to act as attendant.
1707 FARQUHAR *Beaux' Strat.* II. ii, Then I, Sir, tips me the Verger with half a Crown. **1784** *Gentl. Mag.* May 349/1, I felt a secret satisfaction on visiting.. the tombs in Westminster Abbey, that the verger no longer amuses the gaping vulgar [etc.]. **1824** W. IRVING *T. Trav.* I. 258 The parish clerk bowed low before him [*sc.* the squire] and the vergers humbled themselves unto the dust in his presence. **1861** *Sat. Rev.* 30 Nov. 568 How splendid an opportunity for architectural study is afforded by the Abbey, if only the vergers would allow any one to enjoy it. **1881** BESANT & RICE *Chapl. of Fleet* I. 182 The beadles and vergers curtsied to the quality and remained behind for doles.
†**2.** (See quot.) *Obs.*$^{-1}$
1469 *Liber Niger* in *Househ. Ord.* (1790) 48 Mynstrelles, xiii, whereof one is verger that directeth them all in festivall dayes to theyre stations, to bloweings, pipynges [etc.].
Hence **ˈvergerless** *a.*, unaccompanied by a verger; **ˈvergership,** the office of a verger.
1485 *Rolls of Parlt.* VI. 383/2 The Office of our Sergeauntship at Armes, and.. the Office of Vergership of Wyndesore. **1871** *Daily News* 12 Aug., The Vergership in St. Paul's Cathedral, vacant by the death of Mr. Cummings. **1886** HISSEY *On Box Seat fr. Lond. to Land's End* 167 The cathedral, over which we were considerately allowed to ramble vergerless, much to our enjoyment.

†**verger**^{3}. *Obs.*$^{-1}$ [? a. AF. *vergiere* (Gower).] A rod carried as a symbol of office; = VERGE *sb.*^{1} 4 a.
1547 in Strype *Eccl. Mem.* (1721) II. App. A. 10 Then came the sergeant of the vestry with his verger, and after him the cros, with the children [etc.]. **1647** HEXHAM I, A Verger, *een roedeken.*

†**ˈvergerer.** *Obs.* Also 5 vergerar-. [Extended f. VERGER^{2} I: see -ER^{1} 3.] = VERGER^{2} I. Hence †**vergerership.** *Obs.*
1485 *Rolls of Parlt.* VI. 347/2 The Office of Vergerarshipp of Wyndesore. **1566** tr. *Beza's Admon. to Parlt.* Dj, Cathedrall churches, where master Deane,.. pentioners, readers, vergerirs, &c. liue in great idlenesse. **1617** MINSHEU *Ductor* s.v., Vergerers.. be such, as carry *Virgas*, i. roddes before the Iustices of either banck, &c. **1676** WOOD *Life* (O.H.S.) II. 362 His father was vergerer of Westminster.

vergeress (ˈvɜːdʒərɪs). [f. VERGER^{2} + -ESS.] A female verger or caretaker of a church.
1889 *Daily News* 13 Nov. 3/3, I wonder some old vergeress did not come forward to claim the purse. **1902** *Westm. Gaz.* 4 Jan. 3/1 The vergeress who sweeps the floor.

ˈvergerism. *rare*$^{-1}$. [f. as prec. + -ISM.] Action, etc., characteristic of a verger.
1857 RUSKIN *Elem. Drawing* ii. 155 There is always some discordant civility, or jarring vergerism about them [*sc.* English cathedrals].

vergery (ˈvɜːdʒərɪ). *rare*$^{-1}$. [f. as prec. + -Y.] A sacristy.
1882 M'CLINTOCK & STRONG *Cycl. Bib. Lit.* VIII. 515 (Cassell's Suppl.), The consecrated priests repair to the vergery, and put down the missal garments.

verges, obs. form of VERJUICE.

†**verge-salt.** *Obs.*$^{-1}$ (Meaning obscure.)
1656 S. H. *Golden Law* To Rdr., All which.. are immaterial to Matter, and but ceremonies to substance, as Rose-leaves and Verge-salt are to a sound and wholsome dish of meat.

†**verge-sauce.** *Obs. rare.* = VERD-SAUCE.
c **1440** *Promp. Parv.* 509/1 Vergesawce,..*viride salsamentum.* *c* **1450** *Two Cookery Bks.* 102 þe sauce is verge sauce.

vergesse, -geus, etc., obs. ff. VERJUICE.

verȝete, southern ME. var. FORGET *v.*

vergier, variant of VERGER[1] *Obs.*

vergiform ('vɜːdʒɪfɔːm), *a. Zool.* [f. VERGE *sb.*[1] + -(I)FORM.] Of the feet of certain crustaceans: Resembling a rod; rod-like.
1837 *Penny Cycl.* VIII. 197/2 Podophthalmia..; feet or extremities vergiform, partly prehensile, partly ambulatory. **1852** DANA *Crust.* I. 433 There are a few in which these feet are vergiform.

Vergilian, var. VIRGILIAN.

vergine, obs. f. VIRGIN.

vergious, -is, -ius, obs. ff. VERJUICE.

verglas ('vɛəglɑː). Also (formerly) **ver-glas, ver glas.** [Fr., f. *verre* VERRE + *glas* (mod.F. *glace*) ice: see GLACE *sb.*[1]] = *silver thaw* s.v. SILVER *sb.* and *a.* 21.
1808 H. GRAY *Lett. from Canada* (1809) 301 During the thaw, a very extraordinary effect is produced, sometimes, on the trees. The Canadians call it a *ver-glas.* **1863** E. H. WALSHE *Cedar Creek* 310 Perhaps you could tell me the cause of the *ver glas*? What makes that thin incrustation of ice over the trunk and every twig? **1886** G. MEREDITH *Let.* 26 Dec. (1970) II. 844, I dread the many possible things from verglas to bronchitis. **1925** N. E. ODELL in E. F. Norton *Fight for Everest: 1924* III. iii. 310 A considerable snowfall will in spring and summer have evaporated into thin air in a few hours without any visible melting. Consequently, and fortunately, 'verglas' does not exist. **1950** tr. *Mountaineering Handbk.* (Assoc. Brit. Members Swiss Alpine Club) vi. 69 Verglas, which is the result of a frozen trickle of water or rainwater, and which covers the rocks like a sheet of glass, is no less dangerous. **1972** D. HASTON *In High Places* i. 12 Verglas can also be very difficult. This is a thin veneer that forms on rock, caused by the thawing and re-freezing of running water or drips.

vergobret ('vɜːgəbrɛt). [ad. L. *vergobretus,* of Gaulish origin. So obs. F. *vergobert.*] The chief magistrate among the ancient Ædui of Gaul. Also *transf.*
1563 GOLDING *Cæsar* I. 12 The principall office, which they call Vergobret,..is an offyce that lasteth but from yere to yere, and for the tyme hath absolute power of life and deathe. **1656** in BLOUNT *Glossogr.* **1839** KEIGHTLEY *Hist. Eng.* I. 3 The power of the Vergobret, or Prince of each tribe, was absolute. **1892** FREEMAN *Hist. Ess.* Ser. IV. v. 107 The present literary *vergobret* of the Æduan state..refused all help.

vergon, southern ME. variant of FORGO *v.*

†**vergoyne.** *Obs.* [ad. OF. (also mod.F.) *vergogne* (= It. *vergogna,* Pg. *vergonha*):—L. *verēcundia,* f. *verēcundus* VERECUND *a.*] Shame.
1484 CAXTON *Fables of Æsop* II. xv, Hast thow no shame ne vergoyne to come in oure companye. *c* **1500** *Melusine* xxxvi. 285, I shuld haue grete vergoyne yf I smote the behynd.

†**vergoynous,** *a. Obs.* [ad. OF. *vergoignos* (12th c., later F. *vergogneux,* = It. *vergognoso,* Pg. *vergonhoso*), f. *vergogne*: see prec.] Ashamed.
1483 CAXTON *G. de la Tour* cxxxiv. 190 Wherof he was moche vergoynous and shamefull. *c* **1500** *Melusine* iv. 21 Whan Raymondyn herde thus spek hys vncle, he was in hymself vergoynouse.

vergres(se, obs. ff. VERDIGRIS.

vergus, -uys, -ws, etc., obs. ff. VERJUICE.

vergyn(e, obs. ff. VIRGIN.

verhede, southern ME. var. *ferhede* FERRED *Obs.*

veri, obs. f. VERY.

veridian, var. VIRIDIAN *sb.* and *a.*

veridical (vɪ'rɪdɪkəl), *a.* [f. L. *vēridic-us* (whence F. *véridique,* It., Sp., Pg. *veridico*), f. *vērum* truth, and *dīc-* stem of *dīcĕre* to speak.]
1. Speaking, telling, or relating the truth; truthful, veracious.
1653 URQUHART *Rabelais* II. xxviii. 185 Who shall read this so veridical history. *a* **1693** *Ibid.* III. xlvi. 375 The veridical Triboulet did therein hint at what I liked well. **1784** S. HENLEY *Beckford's Vathek* Note (1868) 147 Notwithstanding the reference of Ariosto to the veridical archbishop. **1816** KEATINGE *Trav.* I. 321 The veridical Gulliver. **1847** MEDWIN *Life Shelley* I. 359 That very veridical review which assumes to be the oracle..of literature. **1861** A. HAYWARD *Sel. Ess.* (1878) II. 105 Mr. Gladstone's argument for converting Homer into a veridical historian.
2. *spec.* in *Psychol.* Of hallucinations, phantasms, etc.: Coincident with, corresponding to, or representing real events or persons.
1884 F. W. H. MYERS in *Proc. Soc. Psychical Research* Apr. 48 The truth-telling, or, as we may call them, *veridical* hallucinations which do, in fact, coincide with some crisis in the life of the person whose image is seen. **1898** *Athenæum* 25 June 824/1 The vision of the lady..is certainly spoken of ..as if it had been 'veridical'.
Hence **veridi'cality, ve'ridically** *adv.,* †**ve'ridicalness.**
1727 BAILEY (vol. II), *Veridicalness,* Truth-speaking, or the Quality or Faculty of speaking Truth. **1832** F. BURNEY *Mem. Dr. Burney* II. 179 Next to Shakespeare himself, Pope draws human characters the most veridically, perhaps, of any poetic delineator. *a* **1901** F. W. H. MYERS *Hum. Personality* (1903) I. p. xliii, The only valid evidence..for veridicality depends on a coincidence with some external event.

veri'dicity. [f. VERI(DICAL *a.* + -ICITY.] Veridicality.
1937 *Theology* XXXIV. 284 The veridicity of psychic phenomena. **1942** *Mind* LI. 67 The Pragmatist holds that what works is true. If the arguments of this paper were wrong, that would probably be about the best status one could find for the veridicity of memory. **1977** *N.Y. Rev. Bks.* 29 Sept. 21/3 There are various reasons, particular and general, why this example of tampering with what Mr. Stewart likes to call 'veridicity' is important.

ve'ridicous, *a.* [f. L. *vēridic-us* (see VERIDICAL *a.*) + -OUS.] Veridical, veracious.
App. used by Peacock only.
1817 T. L. PEACOCK *Melincourt* xix, Our Thalia is too veridicous to permit this detortion of facts. **1831** —— *Crotchet Castle* xvii, This veridicous history began in May.

verie, obs. form of VERY *a.* and *adv.*

verie(n, southern ME. varr. FERRY *v.*

verielie, obs. form of VERILY *adv.*

verier, veriest, compar. and superl. VERY *a.*

verifiability (ˌvɛrɪfaɪə'bɪlɪtɪ). [f. next + -ITY.]
a. The fact of being verifiable.
a **1881** A. BARRATT *Physical Metempiric* (1883) p. xxv, I cannot believe that the test of sensible verifiability will ever satisfy the higher longings..of humanity. **1893** F. ADAMS *New Egypt* 234 Doubts..as to the verifiability of that conception.
b. *Philos.* The fact of being capable of verification (sense 3 c). Freq. *attrib.*
1936 A. J. AYER *Lang., Truth & Logic* i. 31 Every empirical hypothesis must be relevant to some actual, or possible, experience, so that a statement which is not relevant to any experience is not an empirical hypothesis, and accordingly has no factual content. But this is precisely what the principle of verifiability asserts. **1936** M. SCHLICK *Gesammelte Aufsätze* (1938) xiv. 348 When we speak of verifiability we mean logical possibility of verification. **1939** I. BERLIN in *Proc. Aristotelian Soc.* XXXIX. 225 The thesis which I shall try to establish is that the principle of verifiability or verification after playing a decisive rôle in the history of modern philosophy..leads to wholly untenable consequences. **1951** H. REICHENBACH in Feigl & Brodbeck *Readings Philos. of Sci.* (1953) 93 The verifiability theory of meaning lays down rules for the construction of meaningful expressions. **1967** *Encycl. Philos.* VIII. 241/1 We shall understand the verifiability principle as claiming that the cognitive meaning..of a sentence is to be determined by reference to the verifiability..of the statement expressed by the sentence.

verifiable ('vɛrɪfaɪəb(ə)l), *a.* Also 7 **verefiable.** [f. VERIFY *v.* + -ABLE.] That can be verified or proved to be true, authentic, accurate, or real; capable, admitting, or susceptible of verification.
Common in the 17th cent., and freq. from *c* 1865.
1593 G. HARVEY *Pierce's Super.* Wks. (Grosart) II. 116, I could peradeunture arread him his fortune in a fatall booke, as verifiable, as peremptorie. **1593** R. HARVEY *Philad.* 9 Why should not..Geffrey be as plaine and verifiable as Buchanan? *a* **1638** MEDE *Wks.* (1672) 789 It is commended for a modest, discreet, learned, regular, and of all in that list most verifiable, discovery. **1661** GLANVILL *Van. Dogm.* 199 If this notion be strictly verifiable. **1677** CARY *Chronol.* II. i. I. iv. 102 That of the Foundation of the City..is verifiable by the like Authorities. **1843** RUSKIN *Mod. Paint.* I. II. v. i. §4 A few only of the broadest laws verifiable by the reader's immediate observation. **1846** GROTE *Greece* II. xix. (1862) II. 76 Neither Homer nor Hesiod mentioned any verifiable present persons or circumstances. **1885** CLODD *Myths & Dr.* II. xii. 227 The authority..will rest on the accredited, because verifiable, experience of man.
Hence **'verifiableness, verifiability.**
1881 A. BRUCE *Chief End Revelation* i. 42 While the abstract possibility of a revelation is admitted, its verifiableness is in effect denied. **1886** —— *Mirac. Element Gospels* 294 They satisfy the modern requirements of verifiableness.

†**ve'rifical,** *a. Obs.*$^{-1}$ [f. med.L. *vērific-us* (Diefenbach), true, truthful + -AL[1].] True, veridical.
a **1660** *Contemp. Hist. Irel.* (Ir. Archæol. Soc.) I. 157 This proposition transposed unto its verificall sense.

†**ve'rificate,** *v. Obs.*$^{-0}$ [f. med.L. *vērificāt-,* ppl. stem of *vērificāre*: see next.] (See quot.)
1721 BAILEY, *To Verificate,* to prove a thing true.

verification (ˌvɛrɪfɪ'keɪʃən). Also 6 **verificatioun, -acioun, veryfycacyon.** [a. OF. *verificacion* (mod.F. *vérification,* = It. *verificazione,* Sp. *verificacion,* Pg. *verificação*), f. *verifier,* or ad. med.L. **vērificātiōn-, vērificātio,* f. *vērificāre*: see VERIFY *v.* and -ATION.]
1. The action of demonstrating or proving to be true or legitimate by means of evidence or testimony; formal assertion of truth. Now *rare.*
1523 *Reg. Aberdon.* (Maitl. Cl.) I. 388 For þe verificatioun and prewyng of his indorsyng and execution of my lordis precept. **1533** BELLENDEN *Livy* I. xix. (S.T.S.) I. 110 In verificacioun hereof [i.e. an intended act of treason] þe said turnus did maist cruelie inway aganis him. **1599** SKENE *De Verb. Sign.* (ed. 2) Q 3 b, The Schireffe..suld summond certaine persons..& suld be present in proper persone.. with the verification of the saidis summoundes. **1634** W. TIRWHYT tr. *Balzac's Lett.* 19, I say nothing (my Lord) I am not ready to sweare in verification of my belief. **1660** JER. TAYLOR *Ductor* II. i. rule 7 §2 If she be a woman, if she can be a wife, and can be his, there is no more requir'd to a verification of the contract in the law of nature. **1911** A. G. HOGG *Christ's Message Kingd.* III. xi. 140 To use an oath even for the purpose of verification, is to make a convenience of God.
2. Demonstration of truth or correctness by facts or circumstances.
1541 R. COPLAND *Guydon's Quest. Chirurg.* B j b, Thus than appereth the veryfycacyon of the fyrste condycyon that a Cyrurgyen ought to haue, for he ought to be lettred and learned. **1651** HOBBES *Leviath.* II. xxvi. 142 The Sentence of the Judge..is a sufficient Verification of the Law of Nature in that individuall case. **175.** WARBURTON *Disc., Rise Antichrist* Wks. 1788 V. 443 It hath..only the traditional verification of the Evidence of a past Fact. **1782** J. BROWN *View Nat. & Rev. Relig.* II. i. 139 All the dispositions and actions of mankind are a plain verification of the leading truths of his word. **1802** PLAYFAIR *Illustr. Hutton. Th.* 507 A very unexpected verification of some of the conclusions deduced above. **1830** HERSCHEL *Stud. Nat. Phil.* 12 They afford the readiest and completest verifications of his theories. **1882** *U.S. Rep. Prec. Met.* 613 Let us await the verification of time.
3. a. The action of establishing or testing the truth or correctness of a fact, theory, statement, etc., by means of special investigation or comparison of data.
1603 FLORIO *Montaigne* III. v. 521 You waste away and die in pursuite of so concealed a misterie of so obscure a verification. **1635** JACKSON *Creed* VIII. x. §3 Fitter occasion ..could not be offered for the exquisite verification or exact fulfilling of this prophecy. **1677** PLOT *Oxfordsh.* 222 The latter wrote a verification of all the fix'd stars, as to their longitude and latitude, for the year 1440. **1837** WHEWELL *Hist. Induct. Sci.* I. III. iv. §1. 190 Periods of verification, as well as epochs of induction, deserve to be attended to. **1855** MAURY *Phys. Geog. Sea* v. §294 This estimate..is not capable of verification by any more than the rudest approximations. **1885** *Manch. Exam.* 12 May 5/3 Nearly a month will be swallowed up in the verification of the returns.
b. The action of verifying or testing the accuracy of an instrument, or the quality of goods. Also *attrib.*
1832 BABBAGE *Econ. Manuf.* xiv. 103 In the Irish flax trade, a similar example of the high price paid for verification occurs. **1888** *Pall Mall G.* 6 Dec. 5/2 The total number of instruments rejected as unfit for a verification certificate owing to excess of error or to other causes was only 346.
c. *Philos.* The action or process of verifying a proposition or sentence through empirical experience (associated esp. with logical positivism). Freq. *attrib.,* esp. as ***verification principle.***
1932 M. SCHLICK *Gesammelte Aufsätze* (1938) viii. 181 The meaning of a proposition is the method of its verification. **1934** C. I. LEWIS in *Philos. Rev.* XLIII. 131 Suppose it maintained that no issue is meaningful unless it can be put to the test of decisive verification. **1936** A. J. AYER *Lang., Truth & Logic* 12, I adopt what may be called a modified verification principle. **1937** *Mind* XLVI. 348, I should have thought the first duty of any advocate of a verification theory of meaning would be to inquire how his theory itself was to be verified. **1956** J. O. URMSON *Philos. Anal.* vii. 107 The verification principle is not essentially a very novel or obscure doctrine except in its traditional formulation. This formulation is that the meaning of a statement is the method of its verification. **1963** W. H. WALSH *Metaphysics* i. 15 Logical Positivists..sought to fashion, in their celebrated Verification Principle of Meaning, a weapon which would destroy metaphysics once and for all. **1977** A. GIDDENS *Stud. in Social & Polit. Theory* i. 45 What came to be called the 'Verification Principle' went through numerous versions, as the inadequacy of Schlick's original formulation..became very rapidly apparent.
d. *spec.* (see quot. 1972).
1953 *Ann. Reg. 1952* 145 This plan provides for the discussion of the regulation of all armaments..and of their disclosure and verification by two committees. **1962** *Listener* 1 Nov. 720/1 Mr Khruschev says he agrees to order dismantling of missile sites in Cuba under U.N. verification. **1972** *Dict. Milit. Terms* (U.S. Dept. Defense) 316/1 *Verification*.., in arms control, any action, including inspection, detection, and identification, taken to ascertain compliance with agreed measures.
4. [After French usage.] Ratification.
1789 A. YOUNG *Jrnl.* 8 June in *Trav. France* (1792) I. 103 If..by the verification of their powers in one chamber, they shall once come together, the popular party hope that there will remain, no power afterwards to separate. **1845** S. AUSTIN *Ranke's Hist. Ref.* III. v. iv. 141 When the verification of it was laid before the parliament, the procureur général..solemnly protested against it. **1865** M. ARNOLD *Ess. Crit.* ii. (1875) 50 By the old constitution of France, these letters patent required the verification of the Parliament. **1902** W. L. MATHIESON *Pol. & Rel. Scotl.* I. i. 49 The Parliament of Paris in their act of verification adopted a very superior tone.

verifi'cationism. [f. VERIFICATION + -ISM.] The philosophical doctrine or principles associated with verification (sense 3 c).

1939 I. BERLIN in *Proc. Aristotelian Soc.* XXXIX. 226 It will tend to show that historical connexion between phenomenalism and 'verificationism' is not a logical one, and that the failure of the latter does not necessarily invalidate the former. **1943** *Mind* LII. 98 Full-blooded verificationism..has now commonly been abandoned in favour of what might be called methodological verificationism. **1965** [see OPERATIONALISM].

verifi'cationist, *a.* and *sb.* [f. VERIFICATION + -IST.] **A.** *adj.* Of, pertaining to, or supporting verificationism. **B.** *sb.* An adherent or supporter of verificationism.

1940 *Mind* XLIX. 456 He [*sc.* Eddington] is as empirically 'verificationist' as any Logical Positivist. **1941** *Mind* L. 163 Most verificationists contend that realism is meaningless. **1952** R. M. HARE *Lang. Morals* i. 8 The so-called 'verificationist' theory of meaning. **1956** J. O. URMSON *Philos. Anal.* xi. 169 If..the verificationist takes the line that the verification principle is a rule of language for the use of the word 'meaningful'..it is a hard saying. **1980** *Times Lit. Suppl.* 17 Oct. 1181/5 How far such verificationist arguments are sound..depends on questions of meaning.

'verificative, *a. rare.* [f. L. *vērificāt-*, ppl. stem of *vērificāre*: see VERIFY *v.* and -ATIVE. Cf. OF. *verificatif*, obs. F. *vérificatif*, Sp., Pg., It. *verificativo*.] Verificatory.

1860 in WORCESTER (citing *N. Amer. Rev.*). Hence in recent Dicts.

verificatory ('vɛrɪfɪˌkeɪtərɪ), *a.* [f. as prec. + -ORY².] That verifies; having the property of verifying; of the nature of, serving as, a verification.

1834 *Fraser's Mag.* X. 362 There is nothing new under the sun—an observation which is indeed verificatory of itself. **1870** J. H. NEWMAN *Gram. Assent* II. viii. 297 Syllogism has no part, even verificatory, in the action of my mind. **1875** W. JACKSON *Bampton Lect.* 156 The evidence becomes accumulative, or, if you please, verificatory.

verified ('vɛrɪfaɪd), *ppl. a.* [f. as next + -ED¹.] Proved to be true by verification.

1594 CAREW *Huarte's Exam. Wits* Proem to Rdr. ii, By this example of our first parents..it is a verifyed conclusion, that he infused the lesser portion [of wisdom] into her. **1911** *Edin. Rev.* Oct. 281 To lay down principles..as a basis or verified induction.

verifier ('vɛrɪfaɪə(r)). [f. VERIFY *v.* + -ER.]

1. a. One who verifies, in various senses.

In quot. 1718 a translation of the Arabic title of *Abubekir*.

1648 HEXHAM II, *Een waer-maker*, a Verifier, or a Maker good. **1718** OCKLEY *Saracens* II. 355 Then the Verifier succeeded him with the good liking of the Muslemans. **1736** AINSWORTH I, A verifier, *confirmator*, *assertor*. **1865** *Reader* No. 141. 283/2 Valued by some verifier of the past. **1885** MRS. LYNN LINTON *Chris. Kirkland* II. vii. 223 Who will keep the keeper? and who will verify the verifier?

b. That which verifies.

1845 J. S. MILL in *Edin. Rev.* LXXXII. 384 In the philosophy of society,..we look upon history as an indispensable test and verifier of all doctrines and creeds. **1944** *Mind* LIII. 341 If I say 'you are hot', this sentence expresses my belief.., and if you are hot, it indicates your state... Your hotness can be called the 'verifier' of my sentence. **1959** B. RUSSELL *My Philos. Devel.* xv. 185, I call the fact which makes the statement true its 'verifier'.

2. *techn.* **a.** In the names of tools or devices (see quots.).

1881 RAYMOND *Mining Gloss.*, *Verifier*, a tool used in deep boring for detaching and bringing to the surface portions of the wall of the bore-hole at any desired depth. **1884** KNIGHT *Dict. Mech.* Suppl. 394 *Gas verifier*, an apparatus intended to verify whether the gas comes up to a given standard.

b. A keyboard device for checking whether a card or paper tape is correctly punched by indicating any discrepancy when it is inserted and the data on it keyed a second time.

1940 W. J. ECKERT *Punched Card Methods* 9 The mechanical verifier is used to check the punching of the initial data on the cards. **1949** [see INTERPRETER 5 a]. **1956** G. A. MONTGOMERIE *Digital Calculating Machines* viii. 154 More complicated electrically driven verifiers are available and in some makes they resemble the electrically driven punches. **1978** J. KELLOCK *Elements of Accounting* xii. 214 After the information has been punched on to the cards, the cards are verified on a machine known as a verifier.

verify ('vɛrɪfaɪ), *v.* Forms: 4–6 veryfy, 5 -fye, *Sc.* weryfy, 6 veryfie; 4–7 verifie (5, 7 verrifie), 6 verifye, 5– verify (4 ferify); 4–6 verefy (5 -effy, 6 *Sc.* vare-, warefy), verefye (6 *Sc.* werafye), 5–6 verefie. [ad. OF. *verifier* (1348; = mod.F. *vérifier*, Sp., Pg., Pr. *verificar*, It. *verificare*), ad. med.L. *vērificāre*, f. L. *vērus* true.]

1. *trans. Law.* To prove by good evidence or valid testimony; to testify or affirm formally or upon oath. Also const. *that*, and *to* with inf.

a **1325** [see VERIFYING *vbl. sb.*]. *c* **1450** *Godstow Reg.* 638 [The abbess appeared, denying] þat she leuied or causid ony noiinge or turnid ony course of watur as hit was presentid afore, & þat she is a-redi to verifie. *c* **1482** in *Cal. Proc. Chanc. Q. Eliz.* (1830) II. Pref. 65 Alle whiche maters the seid Richard is redy to verifie and prove, as this court woll awarde. **1533–4** *Act 25 Hen. VIII*, c. 12 ¶1 To the intent to maynteyne, upholde, and veryfie suche reporte as he had made. **1561** in *Maitl. Club Misc.* III. 289 The saidis George and Wiliam diaconis warefyis That thai lawfullie chergit ye said Mr. Thomas Meffen..to compeyr. **1579** W. WILKINSON *Confut. Fam. Love* Brief Descr. iij b, Iohn Careles in his examination by Doctor Martin verifieth that to be true, whiche..those two were burdened withall by Steuen Norish. **1632–3** *Canterb. Marriage Licences* (MS.), Catherine Whitfield..is expressly consenting to this intended marriage, as is verified by Thomas Hatcher. **1689** *Acta Parlt. Scotl.* (1875) XII. 66/1 The Heraulds who denunced the viscount of Dundee at the mercat cross..did verefie þeir executiones upon oath. [**1768** BLACKSTONE *Comm.* III. 312 In any stage of the pleadings, when either side advances or affirms any new matter, he usually..avers it to be true; 'and this he is ready to verify'.] **1786** BURKE *W. Hastings* Wks. XII. 192 The said charge to be verified by the oath of the said Frazer. **1838** W. BELL *Dict. Law Scot.* 1028 He must be prepared with a cautioner..at giving in his defences, unless he instantly verify a defence excluding the action. **1884** *Law Times Rep.* 10 May 320 The Court..ordered that the receiver should withdraw and verify his accounts by affidavit.

b. In general use: To testify to, to assert, to affirm or confirm, as true or certain. Now *rare.*

1525 LD. BERNERS *Froiss.* II. cc. 252 b/2 The landes, seignories, lordshippes, and baronyes in Acquytayne, whiche they verifyed to pertaygne to the kynge and realme of Englande. **1586** DAY *Eng. Secretary* II. (1625) 20 Him, whose approued fidelity for that it remaineth of no small record to my certaine knowledge, I will presume to verifie. **1600** HOLLAND *Livy* XXXIX. xlix. 1054 At first the tidings seemed so incredible, that the formost messenger was held ..for a vaine lyar..: but after that there came one after another, and all with one voice verefied and affirmed the same. **1608** TOPSELL *Serpents* 19 So that it may as truly be verified of the Serpent as it was of Esau, that the hands of all men and beastes are against them. **1617** MORYSON *Itin.* I. 239 This Novice at his confession made this knowne and after verified as much to the Guardian and chiefe Friars. **1866** MEREDITH *Vittoria* xxxix, 'Does Major Weissspriess know it to be true?' The question came from Anna. Weissspriess coolly verified it, on the faith of a common servant's communication.

c. To support or back up by testimony.

1607 SHAKS. *Cor.* v. ii. 17, I haue euer verified my Friends ..with all the size that verity would without lapsing suffer.

2. To show to be true by demonstration or evidence; to confirm the truth or authenticity of; to substantiate: **a.** Of persons. Now *rare.*

c **1386** CHAUCER *Can. Yeom. Prol. & T.* 515 As witnessen thise olde wyse; And that ful soone I wol it verifie In this Chanon. **1406** HOCCLEVE *La Male Regle* 35 'Prosperitee is blynd':..And verifie I can wel it is so. *c* **1425** AUDELAY *XI Pains Hell* 211 in *O.E. Misc.* 217 In erþ, þe fyndis þem verefyd, [The soul] Dispisid godis laus euerechon. *c* **1500** *Melusine* i. 16 Be nat you displesed yf I haue recounted vnto you this auenture, For it is for to adiouste more of feyth, & for to veryfy thistory. **1535** STEWART *Cron. Scot.* (Rolls) II. 250 This suith example..I verifie ma richt weill be the Britis. **1582** BENTLEY *Mon. Matrones* III. 286 Verifie Lord the words on me, drawe me after thee. **1595** SHAKS. *John* II. i. 277, I bring you Witnesses Twice fifteene thousand hearts of Englands breed,..To verifie our title with their liues. **1627** *Lisander & Cal.* v. 87 [He] only desired to cleer so dangerous a suspicion, and never to speake of it but when he could verifie it. **1671** MILTON *P.R.* I. 133 Gabriel this day by proof thou shalt behold..how I begin To verifie that solemn message late, On which I sent thee. **1782** J. BROWN *View Nat. & Rev. Relig.* v. ii. 430 The covenant-form of this law is not changed; and God hath verified it in the..dreadful sufferings of his only begotten Son. **1828** WEBSTER s.v., The first act of the house of representatives is to verify the powers, by exhibiting their credentials to a committee of the house, or other proper authority.

b. Of things, or in passive.

c **1449** PECOCK *Repr.* I. x. 53 Therfore neuer neither of tho ij. textis..serueth neither forto grounde neither forto verrifie the seid firste opinioun. *c* **1475** *Mankind* 9 in *Macro Plays* 1 þat may be seyde & veryfyede: mankynde was dere bought. **1508** KENNEDIE *Flyting w. Dunbar* 354 In to thy mowis and mokis It may be verifeit that thy wit is thin. **1560** DAUS tr. *Sleidane's Comm.* 150 If this myght be verefied of us in dede, it were..detestable to be heard of. **1583** STOCKER *Civ. Warres Lowe C.* II. 63 The prince greatly marueileth that such great learned men..would set downe and propound such matters, as neuer can nor shalbe any way verified. **1651** HOBBES *Leviath.* II. xxvi. 142 The knowledge of the publique Registers, publique Counsels, publique Ministers, and publique Seales; by which all Lawes are sufficiently verified. **1756** MITCHELL in Ellis *Orig. Lett.* Ser. II. IV. 376 All which has been verified by the examination of the persons in whose company he was. **1849** MACAULAY *Hist. Eng.* v. I. 629 The strongest evidence by which the fact of a death was ever verified. **1876** MOZLEY *Univ. Serm.* iii. (1877) 55 The same scene of action which brought the rational expectation brings also the event which tests and verifies the correctness of it.

3. In passive: To be proved true or correct by the result or event, or by some confirming fact or circumstance; to be fulfilled or accomplished in this way.

1387 TREVISA *Higden* (Rolls) I. 213 So þat now beeþ ferified þe vers þat Hildebertus..made. *c* **1400** MAUNDEV. (Roxb.) xxxiv. 154 þus es þe prophecy verified. **1456** SIR G. HAYE *Law Arms* (S.T.S.) 10 That is ane office of ane angel, to..bring the hye new tydingis, the quhilk is verifyit be the haly writt. **1462–3** *Pol. Poems* (Rolls) II. 268 Scripture saithe heritage holdyn wrongfully Schal never cheve..As hathe be verified late ful playne. **1527** *Prose Life St. Brandan* (Percy) 49 Than the sayenge of Saynt Brandon was veryfyed. **1567** MAPLET *Gr. Forest* 38 The old Prouerbe is herein verified: the ill weede ouercroppeth the good corne. **1631** GOUGE *God's Arrows* III. §6. 192 The like hath been verified time after time. **1667** MILTON *P.L.* x. 182 So spake this Oracle, then verifi'd When Jesus..Saw Satan fall like Lightning down from Heav'n. **1736** BUTLER *Anal.* I. vi. Wks. 1874 I. 123 This reasoning from fact is confirmed, and ..verified, by other facts. **1799** HT. LEE *Canterb. T., Frenchm. T.* (ed. 2) I. 221 Of these doubts one only was verified. **1812** H. & J. SMITH *Rej. Addr.* x, Professions lavishly effused and parsimoniously verified are.. inconsistent. **1852** MISS YONGE *Cameos* I. xxxiv. 286 The Pope's suspicions were verified. **1875** JOWETT *Plato* (ed. 2) IV. 226 The picture..is verified in the course of the dialogue.

b. Const. *in*, *of*, *on*, or *upon*.

1387–8 T. USK *Test. Love* I. i. (Skeat) l. 71 God graunt that proposicion to be verifyed in me. *a* **1400** *Apol. Loll.* (Camden) 8 And þe pope is Petir's vicar, þerfor it be howfiþ to trowe þat þis feiþ is verifiȝed of him. **1456** SIR G. HAYE *Law Arms* (S.T.S.) 4 The prophecyes..be verifyit in ȝour maist noble and worthy princehede. **1530** RASTELL *Bk. Purgat.* I. vii, Everythynge in the world is verefyed upon one of them. **1577** NORTHBROOKE *Dicing* (1843) 153 And as this was spoken of the Phariseys, I feare me it may be likewise verified in vs. **1597** HOOKER *Eccl. Pol.* v. lxix. §2 That which is vttered of the time, is not verified of time it selfe, but agreeth vnto those things which are in time. *c* **1645** HOWELL *Lett.* (1650) I. 242 If he doth, I fear it will be verified in him, that a 'fool and his money is soon parted'. **1719** DE FOE *Crusoe* II. (Globe) 387 It is true, they..made Fences; but Solomon's Words were never better verified than in them. **1768** STERNE *Sent. Journ., Dwarf* I. 191, I..content myself with the truth only of the remark, which is verified in every lane and by-lane of Paris.

c. Used actively of the circumstances, person, etc., serving as proof or confirmation.

c **1430** *Hymns Virg.* 127 For soth then y sobbed Veryfyyng thys wordys. *c* **1450** *Mirk's Festial* 152 The fyrst [cause] ys, forto verefy þe fayþ of his resurreccyon. **1530** PALSGR. 765/2 He hath nowe verifyed my sayenges. **1598** BARCKLEY *Felic. Man* II. (1603) 72 The Temple fell downe and verified the answere of the oracle. **1631** GOUGE *God's Arrows* I. §25. 37 The issue verifieth thus much. **1659** MILTON *Touching Hirelings* 9 A voice [was] heard from heaven..crying aloud, This day is poison pourd into the church. Which the event soon after verifi'd. **1671** —— *P.R.* III. 177 So shall thou best fullfil, best verifie The Prophets old, who sung thy endless raign. **1785** TRUSLER *Mod. Times* III. 47 The case of Wheble, the bookseller, verifies this assertion. **1860** TYNDALL *Glac.* II. xv. 308 The measurements of Agassiz.. completely verify the anticipations of Rendu. **1870** J. BRUCE *Life Gideon* xiii. 229 The people themselves did verify this pregnant saying of the Lord by their own immediate conduct.

†**d.** *refl.* To demonstrate or prove (oneself) to be of a certain character. *Obs.*

c **1586** C'TESS PEMBROKE *Ps.* LXXVI. v, And so him self [the Lord] most terrible doth verify, In terrifying kings. **1596** DRAYTON *Leg., Dk. Normandie* cxxxiv, Fortune..Turned her selfe, as shee away would flie,..As what she was, her selfe to verifie.

4. To ascertain or test the accuracy or correctness of (something), esp. by examination or by comparison with known data, an original, or some standard; to check or correct in this way.

1527 R. THORNE in Hakluyt *Voy.* (1589) 254 For this cause can be no certaine situation of that coast and Islands, till this difference betwixt them be verified. **1559** W. CUNNINGHAM *Cosmogr. Glasse* 162 When you will verifie your nedle..you shall use the healpe of the Sunne. **1774** M. MACKENZIE *Maritime Surv.* II. i. 67 To verify these protracted Distances, go to any of the Objects, as D, take the Bearing of X and Y, to find if they agree with the Protraction. **1796** H. HUNTER tr. *St.-Pierre's Stud. Nat.* (1799) III. 18 Let us now proceed to verify the elongation of the Poles. **1802** MAR. EDGEWORTH *Moral T., Forester, A Clerk*, Hours..spent in casting up and verifying accounts. **1834** HT. MARTINEAU *Demerara* iii. 43, I have seen a calculation and I mean to verify it. **1848** H. H. WILSON *Brit. India* III. 237 Capt. Dillon was..sent back..to verify the reported existence of some of the survivors of the wreck. **1875** *Chambers's Jrnl.* No. 133. 7 A set of instruments which have been properly verified at Kew Observatory.

b. To establish by investigation.

1801 *Med. Jrnl.* V. 386 A medical committee was appointed to verify the phænomena which precede, accompany, and follow the Vaccine Inoculation. **1854** BADHAM *Halieut.* 537 In reading over various poetic bills of fare preserved by Athenæus, we have verified twenty-six species in one Attic supper. **1880** BARWELL *Aneurism* 52 If ..the disease [be] verified as seated on the second or third part of the subclavian vessel.

5. To give the appearance of truth to; to cause to appear true or authentic. *rare.*

1581 [see VERIFYING *vbl. sb.*]. **1768** H. WALPOLE *Hist. Doubts* 99 All Henry's art and power could never verify the cheat of Perkin. **1815** SCOTT *Guy M.* xl, He assumed the name and profession of his friend Dudley, having command enough of the pencil to verify his pretended character to his host of Allonby.

Hence **'verifying** *ppl. a.*

1634 WOOD *New Eng. Prosp.* (1865) 61 A false asseveration usually winneth more beleefe than two verifying negatives can resettle. **1870** J. BRUCE *Life Gideon* xxiii. 412 An appendix..of verifying deeds and documents. **1884** R. BURN in *Athenæum* 15 Nov. 630/3 Its [i.e. archæology's] verifying and corrective spirit in historical investigations.

'verifying, *vbl. sb.* [f. VERIFY *v.* + -ING¹.] The action of the vb. in various senses; the proving *of* something; verification. Cf. VERIFIER 2 b.

a **1325** *MS. Rawl. B.* 520 fol. 47 b, Wan ha beȝ icleped to uerefihinge, þoru þat þulke i-voched weren in present. *c* **1450** *Mirk's Festial* 23 In verefiyng of thys thyng þe fyrst masse..begynnyth thus. **1561–2** *Reg. Privy Council Scot.* I. 196 Sik richtis..and documentis as thai will use for verefying of thair content. **1581** SIDNEY *Apol. Poetrie* (Arb.) 37 Zopirus..fayned himselfe in extreame disgrace of his King: for verifying of which, he caused his own nose and eares to be cut off. **1598** FLORIO, *Verificatione*, a verifying, an approouing, an auerring. **1632** LE GRYS tr. *Velleius Paterc.* 168 Catullus second to none in verifying of the worke which he tooke in hand. *a* **1653** BINNING *Serm.* (1845) 480 For verifying whereof, We appeal to the Knowledge of some Noblemen and Ministers. **1670** MILTON *Hist. Eng.* II. 79 The verifying of that true sentence, the first shall be last. **1706** PHILLIPS (ed. Kersey), *Verification*, a verifying, or proving. **1932** *Monthly Notices R. Astron. Soc.* XCII. 700 In commercial practice punching is usually verified by a special verifying punch. **1954, 1965** [see *keypunching* vbl. sb. sv. KEYPUNCH *v.*]. **1968** *Brit. Med. Bull.* XXIV. 207/1 Four-fifths of the costs of linking a record by computer arise in preparation of the data—i.e., abstraction, classification and coding, card or tape punching and verifying. **1973** F. R. CRAWFORD *Business Systems with Punched Card Data Processing* v. 89 Proper design of documents and card forms is essential for accurate, efficient card punching and verifying.

† **'verifyment.** *Obs.*⁻¹ In 4 uerefiement. [a. OF. *verifiement*: see VERIFY *v.* and -MENT.] Verification.

a **1325** *MS. Rawl. B.* 520 fol. 47 ȝif þilke þat is i-voched.. wolle waranti þe tenaunt þe foreseidc uerefiement to þe askare ne costumez noȝt.

'verigreen. *U.S. slang.* [f. VERY *a.* + GREEN *a.*] A very simple or gullible person.

1854 in M. Johnson *W. L. Garrison & Times* (1880) 269 That man must be a veritable verigreen who dreams of pleasing slaveholders.. by any method but that of letting slavery alone.

verilay, obs. form of VIRELAY.

† **ve'riloquous,** *a. Obs.*⁻¹ [f. L. *vēriloquus.*] Speaking the truth; truthful, veracious.

Cf. *Veriloquent* (Blount, 1656), *Veriloquious* (Bailey, 1727), and *Veriloquy* (Blount).

1672 G. THOMSON *Let. to H. Stubbe* 14 Those.. Galenists ..contrived therefore a scurrilous Pamphlet against a veriloquous Treatise of mine.

verily ('vɛrɪlɪ), *adv.* (and *a.*). Now *arch.* or *rhet.* Forms: α. 4 verrailiche, verrayle, 4-5 verrayly (4 varrayly), verraily, 4-6 verayly, 5 veraily; 4 verei-, ver(r)eyliche, verreyly, -li, verreili, 4-5 -ly, 5 vereilly. β. 4 verali, 4-6 veraly, 4-5 verraly, 5 verralye, 5-6 -ie, 6 veralie, 5 *Sc.* wer(r)aly, weralie. γ. 5 verelyche, -liche, 4-5 verrely, 5 vereli, 5-6 verelye, 5-7 verely, 6 verelie, verrelle, *Sc.* werelie. δ. 4 verilyche, verrylyk, verrili, 4-5 verry-, verrily (5 varily), 5-8 veryly, 6 verilye, *Sc.* verie-, weri(e)-, verrilie, 5- verily. [f. VERY *a.* + -LY². Cf. next and VERAMENT *adv.*]

A. *adv.* In truth or verity; as a matter of truth or fact; in deed, fact, or reality; really, truly.

Freq., latterly almost entirely, used as an emphatic affirmation of the truth of a statement, esp. with verbs of believing, thinking, etc. In ME. and older Sc. poetry often used as a mere rime-tag.

α. *a* **1300** *Cursor M.* 17288 + 422 þai.. told þam [*sc.* the apostles] openly, How þai saȝe crist & with him spake, on-liue ful verraily. *c* **1340** HAMPOLE *Pr. Consc.* 9239 þe nerrer þat þai sal hym be, þe verreylyer þai sal hym se. **1387** TREVISA *Higden* (Rolls) I. 177 So þat þe raþer welles beeþ now but lakes, oþer more vereyliche dreye chanels wiþ oute watir. *c* **1400** MAUNDEV. (Roxb.) xv. 70 þe whilk.. descryued me þe maners of oþer cuntrees.. als graythely and als verraily as þai had bene euer ȝit dwelland in þam. *c* **1430** *Pilgr. Lyf Manhode* I. lxxxvii. (1869) 49 With inne this bred al the souereyn good is put,.. presentliche and verreyliche. *c* **1450** *Mir. Saluacioun* (Roxb.) 44 This prophecie was fullfillid in dede fulle verrayly. **1485** CAXTON *Paris & V.* (1868) 33 Knowe ye verayly that it is not longe sythen, that the sayd Iewels were.. gyuen to me.

β. *a* **1340** HAMPOLE *Psalter* cxviii. 175 My saule sall verraly & perfitly loue þe in new sange. *c* **1350** *Will. Palerne* 5197, I schal hastili me hiȝe.. to venge þe verali for ouȝt þat bi-tideþ. **1422** YONGE tr. *Secreta Secret.* 135 Who so weraly desyryth good rennoune he shall be renounet and preysid. *c* **1475** *Golagros & Gaw.* 1036 Me think farar to dee, Than schamyt be, verralie, Ane sclander to byde. **1508** DUNBAR *Poems* iv. 90 Gud Maister Walter Kennedy, In poynt of dede lyis veraly. **1562** WINȜET *Wks.* (S.T.S.) I. 87 Gif ȝe beleue that our Saluiour did thir thingis veralie and indeid.

γ. *c* **1374** CHAUCER *Boeth.* IV. pr. iv. (1868) 127 Whan I considre þi resouns, quod I, I ne trowe nat þat men seyn any þing more verrely. *c* **1380** WYCLIF *Sel. Wks.* III. 399 Lazar and oþer weren verely deede, and verely reysid by Crist to lyve. **14..** *Sir Beues* (O.) 2577, I thanke you, sayde Beuys, verely. *c* **1460** FORTESCUE *Abs. & Lim. Mon.* (1885) 153 Wich materes thrugly considered, it semyth verely good, þat [etc.]. *a* **1513** FABYAN *Chron.* (1516) 27/1 Whenne he had reygned or more verely vsurped by the terme of .iiii. yeres. **1568** GRAFTON *Chron.* II. 295, I think verely by his valyantnesse that he will not flie. **1594** PLAT *Jewell-ho.* II. 7, I doo verely beleeue yᵗ the spirit of God.. did make them to be of that nature. *a* **1647** HABINGTON *Surv. Worcs.* (Worc. Hist. Soc.) II. 301 The father, I verely thincke, of Sir Walter Skule.

δ. **1303** R. BRUNNE *Handl. Synne* 10045 Whan þe vble was on þe auter leyd,.. Alle þre þoȝt þan verrylyk, Before þe prest, þat a chyld lay quyk. *c* **1380** WYCLIF *Serm.* Sel. Wks. I. 374 þei knowen verrili how þat Crist is Goddis Sone. *c* **1410** *Sir Cleges* 305 The vsscher lyfte vp the lede smartly, And sawe the cheryse verily. **1451** *Paston Lett.* I. 215 If he wold make yow promys that ye myght veryly trust upon hym. **1483** *Cath. Angl.* 399/2 Varily,.. *vere.* *a* **1533** LD. BERNERS *Huon* lxxxii. 255, I beleue veryly that thou dydyst dye on the holy crosse to redeme vs all. **1552** HULOET, Verilye so manye, *totidem.* **1604** E. G[RIMSTONE] *D'Acosta's Hist. Indies* III. ix. 147 Some in the passage demaunded confession, thinking verily to die. **1610** HOLLAND *Camden's Brit.* 207, I am therefore verily perswaded, that the name of Hercules even to this place came either [etc.]. **1682-3** *Pennsylv. Arch.* I. 55 Though I could veryly hope my enemy were reconciled. **1708** SWIFT *Sacram. Test* Wks. 1755 II. I. 127 We are verily persuaded, the consequence will be an entire alteration of religion among us. **1771** *Junius' Lett.* liv. (1788) 293 He.. verily believes him an honest man. **1802** MAR. EDGEWORTH *Moral T., Forester, A Clerk,* A person whom he now verily believed to be, as he had originally suspected, insane. **1839** CARLYLE *Chartism* i. (1858) 3 The time is verily come for acting in it. **1851** MRS. BROWNING *Casa Guidi Wind.* I. 122 Thou couldst.. laugh the laugh back, I think verily.

Comb. **1586** DAY *Eng. Secretary* II. (1625) 4 The first.. appeareth to be Accusatorie, which.. either simply by coniectures or by matter of knowne, or verily supported truth,.. may bee conueyed.

b. Placed in front of a sentence or statement as an emphatic asseveration of its truth or accuracy; freq. connoting the truth of a preceding statement.

In versions of the N.T. regularly used to render L. *amen*, G. ἀμήν, which are freq. strengthened by repetition.

1303 R. BRUNNE *Handl. Synne* 10068 þys y beleue, and euer y shal; For verryly we se hyt alle. **1382** WYCLIF *Gen.* xx. 12 Forsothe and verreili my sister she is. *c* **1440** *Gesta Rom.* xlvi. 194 (Harl. MS.), þerefor he that hathe þe Ringe of Feithe, vereliche he shalle have al thinges to his likinge. *c* **1460** FORTESCUE *Abs. & Lim. Mon.* (1885) 114 But verely thai liven in the most extreme pouertie and miserie. **1500-20** DUNBAR *Poems* l. 52 Verralie, that war gryt rycht. **1535** COVERDALE *John* iii. 3 Verely verely I saye vnto the [etc.]. *Ibid.* 11 Verely I saye vnto yᵉ [etc.]. **1548** HALL *Chron., Edw. IV*, 44 b, Verely the kyng of England had so great trust.. in the honor.. of the French kyng. **1610** HOLLAND *Camden's Brit.* (1637) 268 And verily there remaineth yet a great Castle. **1632** SANDERSON *Serm.* 11 As if despising were an especiall.. kind of offending, or scandalizing. And verely so it is, especially to the Weake. **1711** STEELE *Spect.* No. 43 ⁋4 Verily, Mr. Spectator, we are much offended at the Act for Importing French Wines. **1849** LYTTON *Caxtons* 37 Verily at times he looked on him as a book. **1871** B. TAYLOR *Faust* (1875) II. II. iii. 127 Verily, we sit securely! **1879** BUTCHER & LANG *Odyssey* 158 For verily the might of the sun was sore upon him.

c. Used to emphasize a negative or affirmative particle.

c **1489** CAXTON *Sonnes of Aymon* ix. 224 Dyde ever ony man so grete a trayson as I have doon, nay vereli. **1509** FISHER *Fun. Serm. C'tess Richm.* Wks. (1876) 307 Were not she an vnkinde & vngentyl moder? Yes verayly. **1549** CHALONER *Erasm. on Folly* F iij, Naie, verilier, that is it to be a man. **1559** W. CUNNINGHAM *Cosmogr. Glasse* 138 You saye I shall take the Angles of sight of euerye place that I can see. .. Yea verelye. **1597** MORLEY *Introd. Mus.* Annot., Should they then becom perfect chords? No verily. **1611** BIBLE *Acts* xvi. 37 Nay verily, but let them come themselues, and fetch vs out. **1647** HEXHAM, Yea verily, *ia trouwens, ofte ja voorwaer.* [**1865** DICKENS *Mut. Fr.* III. viii, Yes, verily, my lords and gentlemen,.. so you must.]

† **B.** *adj.* True, very. *Obs. rare.*

a **1340** HAMPOLE *Psalter* cxxxix. 8 Lord, verralyest lord, noght as men ere lordis. *c* **1425** LYDG. *Assembly of Gods* 1285 Morpheus, That hym before warnyd of the verryly tyde.

† **'veriment,** *adv., sb.,* and *a. Obs.* Forms: 4 verrei-, verrey-, 4-5 verray-, 6 *Sc.* verrie-, 6 veriment. [a. OF. *veraie-, verrai-, vraiement,* etc. (mod.F. *vraiment*) truly, f. *verai* true: see VERY *a.* and -MENT and cf. VERAMENT *adv.*]

A. *adv.* In truth or verity; truly, verily.

13.. *K. Alis.* 717 (Laud MS.), By sterren & by þe firmament He hym tauȝtte verrayment. *c* **1325** *Chron. Eng.* 617 in Ritson *Metr. Rom.* II. 296 From him verreiment He brohte a riche present. **1370-80** *Visions of St. Paul* 235 in *O.E. Misc.* 229 þo Fendes seiden verreyment—He haþ seȝen his Iuggement. *c* **1400** *Ywaine & Gaw.* 1491 The lady said, Sir, verrayment, I wil do al yowr cumandment.

B. *sb.* Truth; verity.

1528 LYNDESAY *Dreme* 801 Efter my sempyll intandiment, .. I sall declare the suith and verrayment As I best can. **1535** STEWART *Cron. Scot.* (Rolls) II. 27 Gif that he traistit nocht To that tha said wes suith and verriement [etc.]. **1570** LEVINS *Manip.* 68 Veriment, *veritas.*

C. *adj.* Veritable, correct.

c **1590** GREENE *Fr. Bacon* 940 To speake like a proctor, And tell vnto you, what is veriment and true.

† **Verinas.** *Obs. rare.* Also 7 Verrinus. [var. of VARINAS. Cf. Sp. *verina* and F. *vérine* (1675).] A superior quality of roll tobacco (see VARINAS).

1618 in Capt. Smith *Wks.* (Arb.) 541 There are so many sofisticating Tobaco-mungers in England, were it neuer so bad, they would sell it for Verinas, and the trash that remaineth should be Virginia. **1670** *Merry Drollery* I. 10 But all the day long you do us the wrong; When for Verrinus you bring us Mundungus.

† **'veriness.** *Obs.*⁻¹ In 6 verynesse. [f. VERY *a.*] Actuality, reality, truth.

1574 tr. *Marlorat's Apocalips* 21 He is sayde to be lyke the sonne of man, to betoken the truenesse or verynesse of humane nature in him, with the same fygure of speeche that Paule vsed.

veriour, obs. Sc. form of WARRIOR.

verious, -iowce, -ioyce, obs. ff. VERJUICE.

verisimilar (vɛrɪ'sɪmɪlə(r)), *a.* Also 7 very-, 9 veri-similar. [f. L. *vērisimilis, vērī similis* (see VERISIMILITUDE), after SIMILAR *a.* Cf. It. *verisimile*, Sp. *verosimil*, Pg. *veri-, verosimil.*] Having the appearance or semblance of truth or reality; appearing true or real; probable.

In early use *rare.* Frequent from *c* 1845, app. after Carlyle, who used it freely.

1681 *Ess. Peace & Truth Ch.* 2 As the Opposition to Truth is either from a downright Lie; or a verisimilar Semblance. **1682** DRYDEN *Dk. Guise* Dram. Wks. 1725 V. 334 Now I am to perform all this it seems, without making any Thing verisimilar or agreeable. **1683** T. HUNT *Def. Charter Lond.* 29 Our Poet hath not so much art left him as to frame any thing agreeable or very-similar to amuse the People or wherewith to deceive them. **1727** BAILEY (vol. II).

1827 CARLYLE *Misc.* (1857) I. 39 Are these dramas of his not verisimilar only but true? **1846** G. S. FABER *Lett. Tractar. Secess.* 3 Since I judge the doctrines of Rome to be more rational and verisimilar than any other doctrines whatever. **1887** LOWELL *Democracy*, etc. 165 But 'Don Quixote', if less verisimilar as a narrative,.. appeals to far higher qualities of the mind.

Hence **veri'similarly** *adv.*

1833 CARLYLE in Froude *Life* (1882) II. xiv. 338 Wordsworth.. [was] represented verisimilarly enough as a man full of English prejudices, idle [etc.].

† **veri'similary,** *a. Obs.*⁻¹ [Cf. prec. and SIMILARY *a.*] Verisimilar.

1653 URQUHART *Rabelais* II. vi. 31 Like verisimilarie [F. *verisimiles*] amorabons, we captat the benevolence of the.. fæminine sexe.

† **veri'simile.** *Obs.*⁻¹ In 7 very simile. [See VERISIMILAR *a.* and SIMILE *sb.*] A plausible semblance or appearance *of* something.

1652 CULPEPPER *Eng. Physic.* (1656) 300 Almost al Astrologo-Physitians hold this to be an Herb of Mars, and they give a very simile of a truth for it too, viz. Because it cures diseases of the Head.

verisimilitude (vɛrɪsɪ'mɪlɪtju:d). Also 8-9 veri-similitude. [a. obs. F. *verisimilitude* (1549), or ad. L. *vērī similitūdo, vērisimilitūdo,* f. *vērī similis, vērisimilis,* f. *vērī*, gen. of *vērum* truth, and *similis* like. Cf. Sp. *verisimilitud*, Pg. *verisimilitude*, It. *verisimilitudine.*]

1. The fact or quality of being verisimilar; the appearance of being true or real; likeness or resemblance to truth, reality, or fact; probability.

In very frequent use from *c* 1850.

1603 HOLLAND *Plutarch's Mor.* 1031 If we wil use the rule of probability and verisimilitude. **1654** FLECKNOE *Ten Years Trav.* 30 Truth has no greater Enemy than verisimilitude and likelihood. **1661** GLANVILL *Van. Dogm.* 64 Verisimilitude and Opinion are an easie purchase; and these counterfeits are all the Vulgars treasure. **1727** WARBURTON *Tracts* (1789) 83 Was it but Falshood's Mask of Veri-similitude that we doated after. **1764** REID *Inquiry* vi. §19 His conjectures have more verisimilitude than dogmatic theories. **1826** MISS MITFORD *Village* Ser. II. (1863) 289 A depth of tenderness in her large black eyes.. gave a great verisimilitude to her representation of the lovelorn damsel. **1870** J. H. NEWMAN *Gram. Assent* II. vii. 221 They are nothing more to me than.. judgments on the verisimilitude of intellectual views, not the possession and enjoyment of truths. **1892** STEVENSON & OSBOURNE *Wrecker* i, To add a spice of verisimilitude 'college paper' had an actual marketable value.

b. *esp.* Of statements, narrative, etc.

1671 MILTON *Samson, Of Tragedy*, The Plot,.. which is nothing indeed but such œconomy, or disposition of the fable as may stand best with verisimilitude and decorum. **1733** G. CHEYNE *Eng. Malady* I. vi. §1 (1734) 48 If what I have advanc'd.. have any Truth or Verisimilitude. **1777** ROBERTSON *Hist. Amer.* II. v. 60 They would appear.. so extravagant, as to go far beyond the bounds of that veri-similitude which must be preserved even in fictitious narration. **1817** COLERIDGE *Biog. Lit.* xvii. (1882) 165 The characters.. have all the verisimilitude and representative quality that the purposes of poetry can require. **1858** MERIVALE *Rom. Emp.* lv. (1865) VII. 2 We must accept in the main the verisimilitude of the picture they have left us of this arch-tyrant. **1875** JOWETT *Plato* (ed. 2) I. 422 The traditional form was required in order to give verisimilitude to the myth.

2. A statement, etc., which has the mere appearance or show of being true or in accordance with fact; an apparent truth.

1783 HAILES *Antiq. Chr. Ch.* iv. 141 Perhaps, the author had no farther view, than to state the Academical verisimilitudes on each side of the controversy. **1797** J. LAWRENCE in *Monthly Mag.* (1819) XLVIII. 112/1 The advantages of sophistry are infinitely beyond those of real truth; because a fortunate and well-sounding verisimilitude is so adapted to the comprehension of nine-tenths of mankind. **1821** LAMB *Elia* I. *Old Benchers Inner T.*, Henceforth let no one receive the narratives of Elia for true records! They are, in truth, but shadows of fact—verisimilitudes, not verities. **1850** L. HUNT *Autobiog.* vii. (1860) 128, I felt.. that there was more truth in the verisimilitudes of fiction than in the assumptions of history.

† **verisimili'tudinary,** *a. Obs.*⁻¹ [Cf. prec. and SIMILITUDINARY *a.*] Of persons: Having a show of being correct in opinion or judgement.

1675 E. W[ILSON] *Spadacrene Dunelm.* 4 Those that hold the materiality of the Air to be from water, are not in opinion altogether paradoxical, but verisimilitudinary.

† **verisi'mility.** *Obs.* Also 7 veri-simility. [f. L. type **vērisimilitās*, f. *vērisimilis* (*vērī similis*): see VERISIMILITUDE.] Verisimilitude.

1646 SIR T. BROWN *Pseud. Ep.* III. xxi. 157 Touching the verisimility or probable truth of this relation. *Ibid.* VII. xviii. 382 Assuredly it was a noble Nation.. upon whom, if not such verities, at least such verisimilities of fortitude were placed. **1668** DRYDEN *Dram. Poesy* Ess. (Ker) I. 59 The spirit of man cannot be satisfied but with truth, or at least verisimility. **1706** tr. *De Piles' Art Painting* 71 The third [copy], which is Faithful and Easy,.. puzzles the greatest Criticks, and often hazards their Pronouncing against the Truth, tho' it may be agreeable to Verisimility.

veri'similous, *a.* Now *rare.* Also 7 veresimilous. [Irreg. f. L. *vērī similis, vērisimilis*: see VERISIMILITUDE.] Verisimilar.

1635 F. WHITE *Sabbath* 16 Many erronious doctrines of Pontificians, are in our dayes wholly supported by verisimilous and probable reasons. **1642** GAUDEN *Three Serm.* 62 A Judge.. needs bee a Critick,.. to discerne betweene man and man, cause and cause, just and unjust, true and veresimilous. **1675** E. W[ILSON] *Spadacrene Dunelm.* 33 Any verisimilous conjecture concerning the causation of Springs. **1958** *New Scientist* 23 Oct. 1119/2 Narratives which, although verisimilous to a degree, are shot through and through with the credulous and superstitious outlook of the seventeenth century.

verism ('vɪərɪz(ə)m). [f. as VERIST + -ISM. Cf. VERITISM.] The literary or artistic style practised or advocated by the verists.

1892 *Illustr. Lond. News* 24 Sept. 407/1 This triumph of realism, verism, naturalism, or whatever sort of 'ism' it may be called.

‖**verismo** (vɛ'riːzməʊ). [It.] Realism or naturalism in the arts; esp. with reference to Italian opera of the late 19th century. Freq. *attrib.* Cf. VERISM.

1908 R. DUNSTAN *Cyclopædic Dict. Music* 435/1 *Verismo*, truth, naturalism. **1919** G. KOBBÉ *Compl. Opera Bk.* 91 What is true of 'Aida', is equally applicable to the whole School of Italian *versimo* [sic] that came after Verdi—Mascagni, Leoncavallo, Puccini. **1940** *Scrutiny* IX. 51 If the opera is too realistic it may be boring... The *verismo* of the latterday Wagnerians cannot escape this charge. **1954** *N.Y. Times* 28 Dec. (Late City Ed.) 21/1 Gian-Carlo Menotti's 'The Saint of Bleecker Street'..is Italian 'verismo' opera. **1970** R. LOWELL *Notebk.* 224 *Verismo* is no *vehicle* for Death. **1976** *Times* 23 Jan. 14/8 The movement towards *verismo* in film and theatre. **1978** LD. DROGHEDA *Double Harness* xxi. 289 Unfortunately Colin Anderson himself took against what he dimissed somewhat derisorily as Franco's *verismo* method. **1983** *Observer* 29 May 33/2 Kiri Te Kanawa, happily back on Mozartian territory after her unhappy excursion into *verismo*.

verist ('vɪərɪst). [f. L. *vēr-um* (neut.) or It. *ver-o* true + -IST. Cf. VERITIST.] One who believes in or practises the rigid representation of the truth or reality in literature or art. Also *attrib.*

1884 *Contemp. Rev.* Mar. 395 This observation..would lead us to a controversy with the verists, realists, naturalists, or whatever their name. **1899** *Academy* 18 Feb. 213/2 These provoked the Verist reaction which followed.

Hence **ve'ristic** *a.*

1884 *Contemp. Rev.* Sept. 450 The veristic school does indeed go too far in holding up the things of sense as exclusively true and real. **1891** *Blackw. Mag.* CL. 869/1 The keynote of George Eliot's art Signor Negri qualifies as essentially realistic, or, as he puts it, veristic.

verita'bility. *rare*$^{-1}$. [f. next.] A truth or verity.

1864 A. LEIGHTON *Myst. Leg. Edinb.* (1886) 119 It even happens often that many veritabilities pass through the mind without leaving any traces.

veritable ('vɛrɪtəb(ə)l), *a.* (and *adv.*) Also 5 **veritabill**, 6 **verytable**. [a. OF. and AF. *veritable* (mod.F. *véritable*, = It. *veritevole*), f. *verite* VERITY: see -ABLE.

App. the word had become obsolete by the middle of the 17th century, and was revived early in the 19th. Webster (1828–32) notes it as 'little used'.]

1. Of a statement, etc.: That is in accordance or conformity with the truth or verity; true. ? *Obs.*

1474 CAXTON *Chesse* II. i. (1883) 21 Therfore hym ought to saye no thynge but yf hit were veritable and stable. *c* **1485** *Digby Myst.* (1882) IV. 1068 We shall here tidinges.. shortlye; For that is suth veritabill. **1514** BARCLAY *Cyt. & Uplondyshm.* (Percy) 20 In good fayth..thy tale is verytable, Grounded in lernynge, and gretly commendable. **1604** SHAKS. *Oth.* III. iv. 76 *Des.* Indeed! is't true? *Oth.* Most veritable, therefore looke too 't well. **1649** EVELYN *Liberty Servitude* iv. Misc. Writ. (1825) 21 It was not lesse lawfull to men who comprehended thoughts worthy and veritable, such as we might have of things divine, to possesse an heart elevated and a courage invincible.

†**b.** Of persons: Speaking the truth; truthful, veracious. *Obs.*

1489 CAXTON *Faytes of A.* I. vii. 11 The maners and condicions whiche belongen to a good conestable ben these, that he be not testyf..ne angry, But amesured and attemporat,..verytable in worde and promesse hardy. *a* **1533** LD. BERNERS *Gold. Bk. M. Aurel.* (1546) E vij b, The greatest faute..is to spare the trouthe and not to be verytable. **1594** R. ASHLEY tr. *Loys le Roy* 46 The second warned him to bee all his life true, and veritable.

2. Genuine, real, true; not counterfeit, false, or spurious; correctly or properly so called.

1483 CAXTON *Gold. Leg.* 19/1 And to thende to preve that his deth was veritable he wold lye therin thre dayes. **1646** SIR T. BROWNE *Pseud. Ep.* v. xix. 262 But where the real works of Nature, or veritable acts of story are to be described, digressions are aberrations.

1830 J. G. STRUTT *Sylva Brit.* 24 Few persons..form anything like just estimates of the veritable size of trees. **1855** MISS COBBE *Intuit. Mor.* I. 73 Then Intuition must be given its natural position as the basis of the only veritable System of Ethics. **1872** MORLEY *Voltaire* (1886) 8 A moral relish for veritable proofs of honesty.

b. Of things or persons.

1649 EARL MONM. tr. *Senault's Use Passions* 9 The same Philosophers..imagined it [the soul] had parts as well as the body, and though they were more subtle, they were not less veritable. **1833** LAMB *Elia* II. *Imaginative Faculty in Productions Mod. Art*, He had painted a laudable orchard, with fitting seclusion, and a veritable dragon. **1852** MISS YONGE *Cameos* II. xxiii. 249 A veritable personage was Whittington. **1881** *Lit. World* 21 Jan. 37/1 Nelson, we all know, was a veritable sea king.

c. With *the*, in emphatic use.

1831 MISS MITFORD in L'Estrange *Life* (1870) II. xiv. 320 A cast of the skull of Raphael—the veritable skull dug up at Rome. **1856** KANE *Arct. Expl.* II. ix. 94 Next, sugar; what complex memories the word brings back!—the veritable sugar has been long ago defunct. **1871** BLACKIE *Four Phases* i. 150, I who am now talking..am the veritable Socrates.

3. In extended use, denoting possession of all the distinctive qualities of the person or thing specified.

1862 C. STRETTON *Chequered Life* I. 24, I tell you that Charley is a veritable eel. **1869** A. HARWOOD tr. *De Pressensé's Early Years Chr.* III. i. 360 They had a succession of governors who were veritable brigands. **1897** *Standard* 2 Feb. 7/5 At Rochefort there was..a veritable hail of tiles, slates, etc. blown off the roofs.

†**4.** As *adv.* Veritably, truly. *Obs.*$^{-1}$

1490 CAXTON *Eneydos* xxvi. 93, I beleue veritable that it is for to take vengeaunce of the feyth & of the grete othe.. whiche I haue violated falsly.

Hence **'veritableness**, truth, veracity.

1664 J. NEWBURGH in Evelyn *Pomona*, etc. 44, I am so well assured of the veritableness of my neighbours relation, that I dare not question it. **1890** W. JAMES *Princ. Psychol.* I. vii. 189 But the psychologist must not only *have* his mental states in their absolute veritableness, he must report them and write about them. **1926** R. CLEMENTS *Stately Southerner* 142 Whatsoever shape the apparition may have taken, a belief in its veritableness has persisted from of old.

veritably ('vɛrɪtəblɪ), *adv.* [f. VERITABLE *a.* + -LY².] In a veritable manner; with truth or verity; truly, truthfully; genuinely, really.

1481 CAXTON *Godfrey* cxliii. 214 The nombre of them that were slayn was neuer verytably knowen. *a* **1513** FABYAN *Chron.* I. xxiii. 18 Kymarchus yᵉ sone of Secilius, as some wryters haue, but more veritably as sayth yᵉ olde Cronycle, the brother of Iago was made ruler of Brytayne. *c* **1532** DU WES *Introd. Fr.* in *Palsgr.* 927 Veritably, *veritablement.* **1567** MAPLET *Gr. Forest* 25 b, They esteeme many things by figure and fanticie, but few veritably and vprightly.

1804 ANNA SEWARD *Lett.* (1811) VI. 143 All possible hazard may be precluded, by observing more veritably to the youthful reader, that [etc.]. **1875** POSTE *Gaius* II. (ed. 2) 237 Veritably afterborn, that is to say born after their father has made his will.

‖**vérité** (verite). [Fr., = truth.] Realism or naturalism, esp. in cinema, radio, and television; documentary method. Also *attrib.* and in *Comb.* Cf. CINÉMA-VÉRITÉ; VERISM.

1966 *Listener* 15 Dec. 880/2 There is an advanced cinema, a cinema of *vérité* which is rightly admired by intellectuals. **1976** *Ibid.* 23 & 30 Dec. 841/1 Jack Gold's early vérité-style account of an industrial dispute. **1978** *Broadcast's Programme Edin. TV Festival* 10/2 The film was heavily criticised..[as] impressionistic, partial..an indication of the problematic nature of verite's claim to be..untainted evidence. *Ibid.*, Verite film brings to the screen the pathetic death of a drowned boy. **1979** *Daily Tel.* 7 Dec. 17/3 The method of 'radio vérité' reporting, with victims telling their own emotional stories and the guilty parties often getting quite annoyed, make [*sic*] compulsive listening. **1984** *Listener* 1 Mar. 32/1 What is over-the-top in a vérité film may be just what is required in sit-com.

'veritism. [f. VERIT-Y + -ISM.] = VERISM. So **'veritist, veri'tistic** *a.* = VERIST, VERISTIC *a.*

Originally and chiefly *U.S.*

1894 *Nation* (N.Y.) 19 July 53/2 Veritism is the name by which devils are to be cast out, and the artist himself is to be a veritist. **1894** H. GARLAND in *Forum* (N.Y.) Aug. 690 My own conception is that realism (or veritism) is the truthful statement of an individual impression corrected by reference to the fact. *Ibid.*, The veritist chooses for his subject not the impossible, not even the possible, but always the probable. *Ibid.* 693 The critic cannot distinguish between the entirely fictitious characters of the veritistic novel and the characters drawn from life.

verity ('vɛrɪtɪ). Forms: 5 **varyte**, *Sc.* **weryte**, 5–6 **verite**, *Sc.* **veryte**, 6 **veritee**, *Sc.* **varite**; 5–6 *Sc.* **veretie**, 6 **veritye**, **verytie**, **ueritie**, *Sc.* **werietie**, **weratie**, 6–7 **veritie**, *Sc.* **verritie**, 7– **verity**. [a. AF. and OF. *verite*, *veritet* (mod.F. *vérité*, = It. *verità*, Prov. *veritat*, *vertat*, *verdad*, Sp. *verdad*, Pg. *verdade*):—L. *vēritāt-*, *vēritās*, f. *vēr-us* true, VERY *a.*: see -ITY.

App. not in common use in the 18th cent., but revived in the 19th.]

1. Without article. Truth, either in general or with reference to a particular fact; conformity to fact or reality. Also *personif.*

c **1375** *Sc. Leg. Saints* i. (*Peter*) 254 Bot-gyf þat pece be and concorde, to fynd veryte In-to na thing may be profyte. **1422** YONGE tr. *Secreta Secret.* 161 Verite getyth hatredyn. *Ibid.*, Verite [is] caste doune, whan any vnryghtly thynge is preferrid to trouthe. *c* **1470** HENRY *Wallace* VIII. 1406 And verite war seyn, That ye me luffyt, I awcht yow luff agayn. **1540–1** ELYOT *Image Gov.* 87 Than demaunded he of hym, what thyng he professed. He aunswered: Veritee. **1579** W. FULKE *Confut. Sanders* 575 Betweene veritie & falsitie there is no meane. **1642** H. MORE *Song of Soul* II. III. iii. 58 Mirth, and Free-mindednesse, Simplicitie,..These be the lovely play-mates of pure veritie. **1653** GATAKER *Vind. Annot. Jer.* 66 Historical verity, saith he, shews the sepulkers of their false Gods here on earth. **1698** G. THOMAS *Pensilvania* 30, I..have all along, and shall still declare nothing but Verity. **1816** SCOTT *Old Mort.* xxxiii, He is a prelatist.., and all, and more than all, that has been said of him must needs be verity. **1851** CARLYLE *Sterling* II. vi. (1872) 137 A little verdant flowery island of poetic intellect, of melodious human verity. **1874** H. R. REYNOLDS *John Bapt.* v. §2. 325 The hypothesis of Catholic verity does not attempt to solve the problem.

Comb. **1802–12** BENTHAM *Ration. Judic. Evid.* (1827) I. 191 A motive of any description may be termed a veracity or verity-promoting, or mendacity-restraining, motive.

b. In various prepositional phrases and constructions used adverbially, freq. with emphatic force, as *in* (†*of*) *verity*.

14.. *Sir Beues* (S.) 4313 + 127 Foure þousand men, pur varyte, þey brouȝten with hem to Lundone cyte. **1533** GAU *Richt Vay* 39 Thir cleyne virginite wes [w]vnderlie and in verite prouine be the prophetis. *a* **1557** *Diurn. Occurr.* (Bann. Cl.) 14 The quhilk Johne Scott fastit without meit or drink of veritie xxxij dayes. **1597** HOOKER *Eccl. Pol.* v. lvii. §5 For we take not baptism nor the eucharist for bare resemblances.., but (as they are indeed and in verity) for means effectual. **1849** JAMES *Woodman* xxxiv, It is somewhat sudden in verity and truth; but he must depart for Dorset by daybreak to-morrow. **1875** RUSKIN *Fors Clav.* lvi. 231 In verity it was not I who fed my nurse, but my nurse me.

†**c.** *of verity* (used predicatively): True. *Sc. Obs.* (Cf. 3 b.)

1549 *Compl. Scot.* v. 35 Bot admittand..that Socrates opinione var of verite, ȝit [etc.]. *a* **1578** LINDESAY (Pitscottie) *Chron. Scot.* (S.T.S.) II. 134 The provist ansuerit and said, 'that is of truth and weratie, and gif' [etc.]. *c* **1593** in *Spalding Club Misc.* I. 5 Gif this be of veritie I remit me to the Erlle of Angus declaratioun. **1658** in *Hawick Archæol. Soc. Trans.* (1868) 30/2 The which the said David Baddie hes maid faith before the baillies that it was of verritie.

2. With article or pronoun. The truth; the true or real facts or circumstances.

Freq. in the 16th c. in reference to religious belief, sometimes taking the sense of 'the true religion or faith'.

1422 YONGE tr. *Secreta Secret.* 161, I sey that ham lackyth men that sholde say to ham the Verite, or the trouthe. *c* **1450** *Merlin* xxi. 372 Telle me what ye be, and of youre felowes telle me the verite. *c* **1480** HENRYSON *Fables, Sheep & Dog* x, Seikand full mony Decreitis of the Law, And Glosis als, the veritie to knaw. **1535** COVERDALE *1 John* iii. 19 Hereby knowe we, that we are of the verite. **1582** STANYHURST *Æneis* II. (Arb.) 46 King: my faith I plight heere, to relate thee veritye soothlye. **1607** J. CARPENTER *Plaine Mans Plough* 22 Therefore Lactantius approacheth neerer to the veritie. **1613** PURCHAS *Pilgrimage* (1614) 73 The Apostles preached here the Christian veritie. **1696** in *Aubrey's Misc.* (1721) 212, I have set it down fully,..being curious for nothing but the Verity. **1754** in *Nairne Peerage Evidence* (1874) 55 [To] grant commission for taking his oath on the verity.

b. Const. *of* (something).

1509 HAWES *Past. Pleas.* xi. (Percy) 39 The comon wyt.. Maye well ajudge the perfyt veritie Of theyr sentence. **1535** in *Lett. Suppress. Monasteries* (Camden) 80 Howbeit no farder than the verity of Scripture will justifie my cause. **1604** T. WRIGHT *Passions* I. x. 43 By which auncient Proverbes may be collected the verity of the assertion set downe. **1651** HOBBES *Leviath.* III. xl. 250 The verity of his Miracles. **1679** PENN *Addr. Prot.* II. iii. (1692) 79 We cannot ..allow That a meer Belief of the Verity and Authority of the History and Doctrine of Scripture is..Faith. **1727** SWIFT *Further Acc. E. Curll* Wks. 1755 III. I. 154 The verity of this hypothesis is justified by the symptoms. **1788** FRANKLIN *Autobiog.* Wks. 1840 I. 210 He wrote a volume denying the verity of my experiments. **1830** GEN. P. THOMPSON *Exerc.* (1842) I. 238 The most powerful proof of the verity of the rule. **1860** TYNDALL *Glac.* I. x. 66, I felt in all its force the brave verity of the remark of Mirabeau. **1888** *Sat. Rev.* 21 Jan. 83 It is a pity Mr. Ashton should not have clearly distinguished..between the veracity of the author and the verity of his book.

c. Said of God or of Christ. Usu. with defining adj. preceding.

1535 JOYE *Apol. Tindale* (Arb.) 6 The verite hath sayd it and wryten it. **1559** *Homilies* I. *Of Faith* II. G iij b, Chryst hymself: the eternal and infallible veritie. **1563** *Ibid.*, *Of the Resurrection* G ggg ij b, O man, cal to thy minde, that therefore hast thou receyued into thyne owne possession the euerlasting veritie, our Sauiour Jesus Christ. **1645** VANE *Lost Sheepe* 41 God being the Prime Verity. **1870** J. H. NEWMAN *Gram. Assent* I. v. 126 We have no experiences in our memory which we can..transmute into an Image of the Ineffable Verity.

†**d.** The exact wording and meaning of the original Hebrew or Greek text of the Bible. *Obs.*

1535 JOYE *Apol. Tindale* (Arb.) 45 But yet let Tindale loke ouer his Testament once agene and conferre yt a lytle beter withe the verite and greke to [= too]. **1539** BIBLE (Great) *title*, The Byble in Englyshe, truly translated after the veryte of the Hebrue and Greke textes. **1627** W. BEDELL in *Lett. Lit. Men* (Camden) 136 For the translation sake (being not in the Vulgar, but according to the Hebrew verity). **1659** BP. WALTON *Consid. Considered* 91 The greatest assertors of the Hebrew verity. **1771** LUCKOMBE *Hist. Print.* Pref. B 2 b, When they quote the Scripture wrong.., the authority of the Greek and Hebrew verity should be cast in their teeth.

e. The actuality or reality *of* something.

a **1633** AUSTIN *Medit.* (1635) 176 He [Christ] offered also his Hands, to the other Disciples,..to proove..the veritie of his humane Body. **1686** W. HOPKINS *Ratramnus' Body & Bl.* Dissert. v. (1688) 75 Concerning the Verity of Christ's Body and Blood in the Eucharist. **1913** *Act 3 & 4 Geo. V*, c. 20 §21 Such oath..shall be taken by him to the verity of the debt.

3. With *a* and pl. A true statement, doctrine, or opinion; an established fact, a reality; a truth.

1533 FRITH *Answ. More* (1548) 42 There are many verities, which yet may be no such artycles of our faithe. **1577** HARRISON *England* II. vii. in *Holinshed* I. 80/2 Sith coniectures are no veritics & mine opinion is but one mans iudgement. **1605** CAMDEN *Rem.* (1623) 221 Magicke, in the time of Nero, was discouered to be but a vanity, in the declining state of the Roman Empire, accounted by the Gentiles a verity. **1649** BULWER *Pathomyot.* II. i. 60 A great Anatomist, whom I find running away with an errour instead of a conceited verity. **1690** LOCKE *Hum. Und.* IV. vii. §11 Which [propositions] being settled in the minds of their scholars, as unquestionable verities. **1765** STERNE *Tr. Shandy* VII. xxxiv, But it is an indubitable verity, continued I, addressing myself to the commissary. **1845** BAILEY *Festus* (ed. 2) 122 Thus dreams are verities. **1867** FREEMAN *Norm. Conq.* (1877) I. App. 643 The quarrel and the reconciliation are unquestionable verities. **1878** TAIT & STEWART *Unseen Univ.* vii. §203. 202 Our strength lies in keeping up a communication with those verities which we all acknowledge.

b. ***of a verity*** (chiefly in parenthetic use): Truly, assuredly, in truth, indeed. (Cf. 1 b.) *rhet.*

1850 W. IRVING *Mahomet* vi. (1853) 33 Oh Mahomet, of a verity, thou are the prophet of God! **1856** KANE *Arct. Expl.* II. i. 15 The liver of a walrus eaten with little slices of his fat; ..of a verity it is a delicious morsel. **1860** SALA *Baddington Peerage* I. xv. 271 Down she came, in about ten minutes, looking of a verity, radiant.

4. Truthfulness, veracity, sincerity. ? *Obs.*

c **1555** HARPSFIELD *Divorce Hen. VIII* (1878) 51 Justice, verity, holiness, fear of God. **1565** T. STAPLETON *Fortr. Faith* 14 b, Thou hast sworen to Dauid in thy verite. **1605** SHAKS. *Macb.* IV. iii. 92 The King-becoming Graces, As Iustice, Verity, Temp'rance, Stablenesse. **1606** BRYSKETT *Civ. Life* 242 Veritie is the vertue..by which a man in all his conuersation, in all his actions, and in al his words sheweth himselfe sincere and ful of truth. **1808** E. S. BARRETT *Miss-led General* 47 If my verity is called in question, I will state in what manner, and by what means it was paid. **1848** *Scottish Jrnl. Topog.*, etc. II. 167/1 Scoto-Gallicisms... On my veritie, [from French] vérité. My certie, [from French] certes.

verjuice (ˈvɜːdʒuːs), *sb.* Forms: α. 4–5 verious, 5 veryous, -yose, -ius(e, -iuys, -jusse, -iowce (vere jouse), 6 werius, verioyce, -juce (verdjuice), 6–7 veriuice, -iuce, -iuyce, 7 veriuyce, -juce, -jus, 7– verjuice. β. 4 vergws, 5 wergoys, 6 vergus, -uys; 4 vergieux, 4–6 -eous, 6 -ews, -eus, 5 vergyous, 6 -ious, -yus, -ius (4 verdius, 5 vertious). γ. 5 vergys, 5–7 vergis, 6–7 verges, 6 werges, vergesse, -i(e)sse, 7 verdges; 6 warges, 6–7, 9 *dial.* varges, 7, 9 *dial.* vargis. [a. OF. *vertjus*, *verjus*, *vergus*, etc. (mod.F. *verjus*), f. *vert* green, unripe + *jus* JUICE.]

1. The acid juice of green or unripe grapes, crab-apples, or other sour fruit, expressed and formed into a liquor; formerly much used in cooking, as a condiment, or for medicinal purposes. Also in comparisons as, ***as sour*** (***bitter, tart***, etc.) ***as verjuice***.

α. **1302–3** *Ely Sacr. Rolls* (1907) II. 18 Pro j barillo ad verious. **14..** *Voc.* in Wr.-Wülcker 619 *Viridis succus*, veriuys. *c* **1440** *Promp. Parv.* 508/2 Veriowce, sawce, *agresta*. **1450–80** tr. *Secreta Secret.* 33 Make him drynke of verious and watir. *c* **1460** *Towneley Myst.* XII. 236 A calf lyuer skorde with the veryose; Good sawse. This is a restorete To make a good appete. **1534** in Peacock *Eng. Ch. Furniture* (1866) 187 A brake to make verioyce with. **1544** PHAER *Regim. Lyfe* (1560) B iv b, The juce of Purcelane, of Plantaine, and verjuce of grape, or crabbes. **1594** PLAT *Jewell-ho.* III. 71 Crabs after the veriuice is expressed from them. **1626** MIDDLETON *Women Beware Wom.* III. iii, Having a crabbed face of her own, she'll eat the less verjuice with her mutton. **1657** TRAPP *Comm. Ezra* vi. 13 II. 22 Their obedience was wrung out of them, as verjuice is out of a crab. **1748** HARTLEY *Observ. Man* I. ii. 124 The good Effects of Vinegar, Verjuice, Spirits of Wine, in Sprains. **1799** G. SMITH *Laboratory* (ed. 6) I. 343 Beat pumice stones to an impalpable powder, and mix up with verjuice. **1853** ROYLE *Mat. Med.* (ed. 2) 358 When unripe the fruit is remarkable for the harsh acidity of its juice, which is then called verjuice. **1881** *Harper's Mag.* LXIII. 266 To distort the face as if one were quaffing verjuice.

fig. **1616** R. C. *Times' Whistle* (1871) 80 They must have veriuice that will squeese such crabbes. **1624** MIDDLETON *Game at Chess* v. iii, 'S foot this Fat Bishop hath..so squelch'd and squeez'd me, I've no verjuice left in me. **1662** HIBBERT *Body Div.* I. 269 Take heed of matching with one of the daughters of Heth; he that graffs into a crab-stock, is like never to want verjuice.

β. **1349–50** *Durham Acc. Rolls* (Surtees) 551 In xvj lag. de vergeous. **1392** *Earl Derby's Exped.* (Camden) 155 Et pro viij galonibus vergws. *a* **1400** *Leg. Holy Rood* viii. 175 3it Moyses in Rule haþ rad, We schulde ete vr lomb in sour vergeous. *c* **1430** *Pilgr. Lyf Manhode* II. cxlvii. (1869) 134, I serue of vinegre and of vergeous, and of greynes þat ben soure. *c* **1440** *Douce MS.* 55 fol. 7 Then take..a quantite of vertious & saffron & salte & cast ther to. **1463** *Bury Wills* (Camden) 23 A barell with wergoys, and a botel for wynne. **1513** W. DE WORDE *Bk. Keruynge* in *Babees Bk.* 278 It ought for to be eten with grene garlyke, or with sorell, or tender vynes, or vergyus in somer season. **1558** WARDE tr. *Alexis' Secr.* (1568) 65 b, Boile it in iii glasses full of good vergeous or whyte wyne. **1577** B. GOOGE *Heresbach's Husb.* II. (1586) 57 Some adde thereunto Vergius, or the iuyce of soure Grapes, to make the taste more tarte.

γ. **1412–3** *Abingdon Acc.* (Camden) 75 De vuis..pro vergis inde fact'. *c* **1518** SKELTON *Magnyf.* 1779 Somtyme, parde, I must vse largesse. Ye, mary, somtyme in a messe of vergesse. **1527** *Luton Trin. Guild* (1906) 186 Payd..for j galone of wargis. **1557** *Lanc. & Chesh. Wills* (Chetham Soc. 1884) 64, ij barrells to keepe varges in. **1573** TUSSER *Husb.* (1878) 53 Be sure of vergis..so good for the kitchen. **1610** MARKHAM *Masterp.* I. lxxi. 148 You shall then every day giue a pint of strong verdges to drinke. **1630** J. TAYLOR (Water P.) *Begger* Wks. I. 97/2 And for a Sauce he seldom is at Charges, For euery Crabtree, doth affoord him Vergis. **1639** O. WOOD *Alph. Bk. Secrets* 102 Make a posset of Varges or Vinigar and Milke, bath the joynt very hot therewith. **1837** HOOD *Ode to Dr. Hahnemann* 38 A drop of 'varges'. **1854** MISS BAKER *Northampt. Gloss.* 375 As sour as vargis. **1904** E. STEP *Wayside & Woodland Trees* 103 Cyder is made from the rotting Crabs; also a kind of vinegar called verjuice or vargis.

†**b.** In fig. phrases ***to crowd, crush, squeeze to verjuice***. *Obs.*

1605 *Tryall Chev.* II. i. in Bullen *Old Pl.* (1884) III. 289 And that sowre crab do but leere at thee I shall squeeze him to Vargis. **1621** FLETCHER *Isl. Princess* III. i, They love a man that crushes 'em to verjuce. *a* **1625** —— *Wife for Month* II. i, They have crowded me to Vergis, I sweat like a butter-box.

2. In fig. use, with reference to the characteristic acidity or sourness of verjuice.

1598 E. GUILPIN *Skial.* (1878) 39 Oh how the varges from his blacke pen wrung, Would sauce the Idiome of the English tongue. *Ibid.* 65 To mittigate The sharp tart veriuice of his snap-haunce hate. **1626** B. JONSON *Staple of N.* v. i, Hang him, an austere grape, That has no iuice, but what is veriuice in him. **1685** CROWNE *Sir C. Nice* I, The Devil of Envy suck'd it all out, and left verjuice in the roome. **1759** MRS. DELANY in *Life & Corr.* (1862) 543 To be sure there must be an infinite deal of verjuice in her composition! **1791** J. WOLCOT (P. Pindar) *Rights of Kings* xviii. Wks. 1816 II. 209 The heart should be a medlar, not a crab; Milk, and not Verjuice, from its fount should flow. **1825** SCOTT *Betrothed* xxii, Raoul, glancing towards her a look of verjuice [etc.]. **1833** T. HOOK *Parson's Dau.* II. xi, Miss Budd, although she said nothing, looked vinegar and verjuice. **1873** SYMONDS *Grk. Poets* iv. 101 The temper of his proposed son-in-law was a mixture of gall, wormwood, vinegar, verjuice, vitriol and nitric acid.

3. *attrib.* or as *adj.* **a.** Simple attrib., as ***verjuice barrel, bottle, brake, house, sauce, tub, vessel***.

1432 *E.E. Wills* (1882) 91 A vergyous barell. *c* **1450** *Two Cookery Bks.* 103 The sauce is vergyus sauce or sauce ginger. **1516–7** *Durham Acc. Rolls* (Surtees) 106 Pro ostiis le Weriushouse. **1551–60** in Hall *Eliz. Soc.* (1887) 150 A verguys tubbe. **1578** *Knaresb. Wills* (Surtees) I. 134 In the buttrie..a kitt, a vergious brake. **1588** *Lanc. & Chesh. Wills* (Chetham Soc. 1893) 150, ij kneadinge tubes, iij cheises, ij verges barrells. **1629** *Inv. Househ. Goods* in *Trans. Essex Archæol. Soc.* III. II. 161 In the West Larder..8 vergis vessells.

b. Passing into adj. in the sense of 'bitter, sour, sour-looking', as ***verjuice countenance, face, wit***.

1598 MARSTON *Sco. Villanie* To Iudiciall Perusers, I dare defend my plainenesse against the veriuice-face of the Crabbedst Satyrist that euer stuttered. **1613** HEYWOOD *Brazen Age* II. iii, She scarce will let me kisse her, But shee makes vergisse faces. **1632** BROME *Court Beggar* II. i, Thou hast a verjuice wit. **1823** SCOTT *Peveril* vii, A verjuice countenance..is no such temptation. **1853** HICKIE tr. *Aristoph.* (1887) I. 12 You bear the basket prettily, with a verjuice face.

†**c.** ***verjuice grape***, one or other variety of grape suitable for the making of verjuice (cf. quot. 1725 and F. *verjus* a sour or green grape). *Obs.*

1648 HEXHAM II, *Verjuys-besien*, Verjus or Sowre grapes. **1653** URQUHART *Rabelais* I. xxv, The great red grapes, the muscadine, the verjuice grape. **1664** EVELYN *Kal. Hort.* Sept. 74 The Verjuyce-grape excellent for sauce, &c. **1706** LONDON & WISE *Retir'd Gard.* I. xi. 52 Having planted your Trees, you ought..to set some Chasselas, or Verjuice Grapes, about your Squares. **1725** *Fam. Dict.* s.v., There are three sorts of Grapes to which they properly give the Name of Verjuice, *viz.* the Gouais, Farineus, and Bourdelas, otherwise le Grey; and 'tis from these three that they commonly press Verjuice.

Hence **ˈverjuice** *v. trans.*, to embitter, make sour; **ˈverjuiced** *ppl. a.*

1836 W. H. MAXWELL *Capt. Blake* xv, The maid was a verjuiced spinster. **1848** LOWELL *Fable for Critics* (1865) 217 His sermons with satire are plenteously verjuiced. **1892** W. G. THORPE *Still Life Mid. Temple* 3 Sir John Key, where the inherent rhyme to 'donkey' verjuiced the baronetcy.

verk(e, obs. Sc. forms of WORK *sb.*

†**verken**, obs. form of FIRKIN.

1485 *Cely Papers* (Camden) 184 P[d] per me for an verken of gonpouder, viij d.

verkramp (fɛrˈkramp), *predic. a. S. Afr.* Also **verkrampte** (-ˈkramptə) when used *attrib.* [a. Afrikaans, lit. 'narrow, cramped'.] Narrow or reactionary in political, religious, social, etc., matters.

1968 *Green Bay Tree* 29 June p. xlv, The most *verkrampte* Nationalist politicians are frightened of liberal foreign propaganda appearing on their screens. **1969** *Sunday Times* (Johannesburg) 24 Aug., On a very strict, narrow interpretation, my guess is that most Nationalists are verkramp. **1971** *Ibid.* 11 Apr. 3 Mr. —— is verkramp. He can make what threats he likes, I'll keep on wearing split skirts. **1973** *Deb. Senate S. Afr.* 17 May 2790 A Sunday paper fairly recently referred to certain members of the United Party as a 'verkrampte mafia'. This was not defamatory. **1974** *Argus* (Cape Town) 2 Aug. 3/2 It is believed that conservative resistance to more enlightened policies has been significantly reduced and that verkrampte views will in future meet with little sympathy. **1974** *Rand Daily Mail* 30 Nov. 1/1 This reasoning has now become an excellent excuse for talking verligi and acting verkramp. **1977** *Time* 31 Oct. 19/3 The Cabinet was clearly aware of charges by the *verkrampte* (conservative) wing of the Nationalist Party that the government's power and authority were eroding in the face of protests by urban blacks. **1981** *Observer* 5 Apr. 11/7 Like most black African Muslims, Edvis favours a liberal interpretation of the Koran, being *verligte* rather than *verkrampte* in that regard. Very wisely he likes to drink Pinot Noir from California.

Hence (the *attrib.* form **verkrampte**) as *sb.* A person with rigidly traditional views, esp. as regards apartheid and the preservation of white supremacy. Cf. VERLIG *a.*

At first applied only to politicians but now extended to any person holding narrow-minded or ultra-conservative views on social, religious, etc., matters.

1967 *Race Relations News* Sept. 7/4 The verligtes-verkramptes controversy must have raised in many minds the hope of a change of outlook in influential South African circles. **1968** *Economist* 17 Aug. 32/2 The real object was to strengthen Mr Vorster in the ideological dispute that has arisen within his party in recent months between the *verligte* ('enlightened') wing and the *verkramptes* (that is, literally, the cramped ones). **1969** *Times* 18 Sept. 9/1 The Army and its political directors have come in for much criticism..from Unionist *verkramptes*, for apparent irresolution in bringing down the barricades. **1971** *Leader* (Durban) 7 May 6/5 With a so-called outward-looking policy, the Government is beginning to see things in better light. It has shaken itself of some of the old die-hard Calvinistic verkramptes and is able to look at the world at large a little verlig. **1979** *Economist* 8 Sept. 59/3 Now Transvaal *verkramptes* (Conservatives) are saying he exploited Muldergate to destroy their leaders.

Verlainesque (vɛəleɪˈnɛsk), *a.* [f. the name *Verlaine* (see below) + -ESQUE.] Of, pertaining to, or characteristic of the French poet Paul Verlaine (1844–96), or his works.

1891 E. DOWSON *Let.* 20 Mar. (1967) 189 Its an attempt at mere sound verse..a vague, Verlainesque emotion. **1915** WYNDHAM LEWIS *Lett.* (1963) 68 He told me he had written a lot of filthy sexual verse... He described it as Verlainesque, damn his shifty little eyes.

verlay, verlet(te, obs. ff. VIRELAY, VARLET.

verlich(e, ME. varr. FERLY *a.* and *adv. Obs.*

verlig (fɛrˈlɪx), *predic. a. S. Afr.* Also **verligte** (-ˈlɪxtə) when used *attrib.* [a. Afrikaans, = enlightened.] Regarded as progressive or enlightened, in political, religious, social, etc., matters. Cf. VERKRAMP *a.*

1968 [see VERKRAMPTE *sb.*]. **1969** *Sunday Times* (Johannesburg) 24 Aug. 25 The odd thing about the whole affair is that the word 'verlig' should become an embarrassment to the Nationalists... There must be few countries where it is an insult to be called 'enlightened'. **1969** *Rand Daily Mail* 25 Sept. 17/3 Verlig long before it was comparatively easy to be so, he condemned arrogant racialism or nationalism wherever he found it. **1970** *Times* 19 Aug. 8/4 It is not just non-aligned countries such as Tanzania, Zambia or Yugoslavia, which are benefiting from the new spirit of goodwill emanating from Peking. China's *verligte* policies have even percolated as far as London. **1971** [see VERKRAMPTE *sb.*]. **1974** *Argus* (Cape Town) 2 Aug. 3/2 The United Party is believed to have irrevocably committed itself to a more boldly verligte political stance. **1974** [see VERKRAMP *a.*] **1977** *Cape Times* 10 Oct. 3/4 The vast majority of Nationalist voters are a lot more verlig than they think and support the need for change in South Africa. **1981** *Guardian* 14 Dec. 6/5 The Verligte or enlightened faction of his party.

Hence (the *attrib.* form **verligte**) as *sb.* A person regarded as progressive or enlightened in politics, esp. with regard to the future of apartheid. In extended use, one who is enlightened or broadminded in other matters.

1967 [see VERKRAMPTE *sb.*]. **1969** *Guardian Weekly* 24 July 14 If the *verkramptes* of Louis Stoffberg and Dr Herzog win the day, against Mr Vorster's *verligtes* and their good neighbour policy towards black Africa, it will be a useful gain for Peking. **1970** *News/Check* 29 May 9 People who later on were to become known as verligtes sided with Silbersteins; the verkramptes summed up the book as sinful. **1976** *Times* 26 June 5/4 The increasingly vocal Verligtes in the universities. **1980** *Economist* 21 June (S. Afr. Suppl.) 6/1 To the more radical verligtes who make up his praetorian guard, a sort of strategy is clear.

†**verling-line.** *Naut. Obs.* (Origin and meaning obscure.)

1420 in *For. Acc. 3 Hen. VI*, ij. haunsers pro verlyng-lynes ponderis cx. lb.

verlore, var. f. pa. t. and pa. pple. FORLESE *v. Obs.*

verlot(te, obs. ff. VARLET.

verm, southern dial. var. FARM *sb.*; obs. Sc. var. WORM *sb.*

vermayn(e, obs. ff. VERMIN *sb.*

†**verme.** *Her. Obs.* [ad. L. *vermis* worm (Honorius of Autun *De Imag. Mundi* I. xiii), incorrectly taken as the name of a fish.] An alleged fish of the Ganges, able to seize and destroy elephants.

Bossewell elsewhere (II. 66) has the form *vermante*, prob. an error for *verme hariante* by accidental omission of letters.

1572 BOSSEWELL *Armorie* III. 25 b, H. hathe to hys Creste, a Verme hariante propre, subsigned aboute the tayle with a scrowe.

ˈvermean, *a. rare*[−1]. [f. VERME-S + -AN.] = VERMIAN *a.* 1.

1905 *Q. Rev.* Apr. 493 Parasites, both external and internal, both protozoan and vermean, were met with.

vermechulli, obs. f. VERMICELLI.

vermeil, vermil (ˈvɜːmɪl), *a.* and *sb.* Forms: α. 5 vermaile, -mayle, -meyle, 6 vermayll, 7 -meyl; 6 vermeill, 8–9 -meille, 6– vermeil. β. 6 vermell, 7 vermel; 6–7 vermile, 7 -myle; 8–9 vermil. [a. AF. and OF. *vermail*, *vermeil* adj. and sb. (11th c., mod.F. *vermeil*, = Prov. *vermelh*, *vermel*):—acc. sing. of L. *vermiculus*, dim. of *vermis* worm: see VERMICLE, and cf. VERMILION *sb.* and VERMILY.]

A. *adj.* Of a bright scarlet or red colour; vermilion. Chiefly *poet.*

a. *c* **1400** *Rom. Rose* 3645 Ful fayre it [*sc.* the rose] spradde the god of blesse For suche another as I gesse Aforne ne was ne more vermayle. *c* **1420** LYDG. *Ballad at Reverence Our Lady* 45 (Skeat), Benigne braunchelet of the pyne-tree, Vyneyerd vermayle. **1509** BARCLAY *Shyp of Folys* (1570) 74 Take not colde water in stede of vermayll wine. **1549** *Compl.*

Scot. vi. 37 The pretty fische..vitht there rede vermeil fynnis. **1596** SPENSER *Prothal.* ii, With store of vermeil Roses, To decke their Bridegromes posies. **1802** *Sporting Mag.* XII. 359 Nature's vermeil robe and lilied vest. **1807** WORDSW. *White Doe* II. 12 This Maid, who wrought..In vermeil colours and in gold An unblest work. **1812** S. ROGERS *Columbus* Poems (1839) 42 Tinging with vermeil light the billows blue. **1898** MÉNIE M. DOWIE *Crook of Bough* 165 The vermeil flood mounted in her cheeks, but she met his glance fully.

β. **1592** WYRLEY *Armorie, Ld. Chandos* i, A vermile crosse the Cyprian king still wore. **1637** MILTON *Lycidas* (MS. draft), That sad Floure that strove To write his own Woes on the vermel Graine. **1692** J. SALTER *Triumphs Jesus* 17 A Face with Vermile Paint still over-laid. **1791** E. DARWIN *Bot. Gard.* I. I. 4 In noon's bright blaze thy vermil vest unfold. **1800** MOORE *Anacreon* lvi, The ripe and vermil wine, Sweet infant of the pregnant vine.

b. Freq. of the countenance, lips, etc.

c **1614** SIR W. MURE *Dido & Æneas* I. 626 The dimples of a vermile cheek. **1754** GRAY *Pleasure fr. Vicissitude* 3 With vermeil cheek and whisper soft She [*sc.* the morn] woo's the tardy spring. **1780** S. J. PRATT *Emma Corbett* (ed. 4) II. 176 The invisible sigh steals through its vermeil passages. **1820** C. R. MATURIN *Melmoth* (1892) III. xxx. 198 A lip as vermeil as her own. **1864** MUSGRAVE *Ten Days in Fr. Parsonage* I. i. 29 The vermeil cheeks..faded away into creamy hues.

transf. **1759** MALLET *Fragment* Wks. I. 50 The vivid pulse, the vermil grace,..Youth, beauty, pleasure, all are thine! **1800** MOORE *Anacreon* xiv. *note* 3 So many vermil, honeyed kisses, Envy can never count our blisses.

c. With names of colours; esp. ***vermeil red.***

1590 SPENSER *F.Q.* II. iii. 22 In her cheekes the vermeill red did shew. **1791** HUDDESFORD *Salmag.* 121 Thy vermeil red and living green In mimic folds thou shalt display. **1859** TENNYSON *Enid* 364 Like a blossom vermeil-white, That lightly breaks a faded flower-sheath. **1906** C. M. DOUGHTY *Dawn in Britain* I. 68 Her rud as apple blossoms, vermeil-white, Her locks..Like sunny rays.

B. *sb.* **1.** Vermilion hue or colour.

1590 SPENSER *F.Q.* II. xii. 45 The snowy substaunce [*ante* frothy billowes] sprent With vermell, like the boyes bloud therein shed. **1633** P. FLETCHER *Purple Isl.* x. xli, So when cleare ivorie vermeil fitly blots, By stains it fairer grows. **1728** FIELDING *Love in Sev. Masques* I. v, It has exagitated my complexion to that exorbitancy of vermeille. *c* **1750** SHENSTONE *Ruined Abbey* 180 The vivid vermeil fled his fady cheek. **1848** LYTTON *Harold* III. iv, The orb was sinking red and lurid, amidst long cloud-wracks of vermeil and purple. **1892** 'M. FIELD' *Sight & Song* 1 A cloak Of vermeil and of blue.

†**b.** *transf.* Blood. *Obs. rare.*

1590 SPENSER *F.Q.* II. x. 24 How oft that day did sad Brunchildis see The greene shield dyde in dolorous vermell? **1594** GREENE *Selimus* 670 Ile follow Mars,..And die my shield in dolorous vermeil. **1812** CARY *Dante, Parad.* XVI. 151 With these [I] saw her so glorious and so just, that ne'er The lily from the lance had hung reverse, Or through division been with vermeil dyed.

†**2.** = VERMILION *sb.* 1 a. *Obs. rare*$^{-1}$.

1610 G. FLETCHER *Christ's Vict.* II. xxxii, A painted face, belied with vermeyl store.

3. (See quots.)

1796 KIRWAN *Elem. Min.* (ed. 2) I. 250 Oriental Ruby. Its colour is carmine red,..sometimes red and white, or red and blue, and thence called sapphire ruby, or orange red, by some called vermeille or rubicelle. **1884** *Imp. Dict., Vermeil,* a jeweller's name for a crimson-red garnet inclining slightly to orange.

4. *Gilding.* (See quot.) Also *attrib.*

Directly from mod.F. *vermeil*; the quotation is part of a description of the French method of gilding.

1839 URE *Dict. Arts* 613 The *vermeil* coat. Vermeil is a liquid which gives lustre and fire to the gold, and makes it resemble *or moulu.* [Hence in later Dicts.]

b. Silver-gilt; gilt bronze.

1858 SIMMONDS *Dict. Trade, Vermeil* (French), silver gilt, or gilt bronze. [Hence in later Dicts.] **1889** *Harper's Mag.* Aug. 334/2 The iconostase or screen is a high wall of burnished vermeil. **1911** *19th Cent.* May 841 Golden pheasants sat..on platters of embossed vermeille.

C. *Comb.* (chiefly parasynthetic), as ***vermeil-cheeked, -dyed, -rimmed, -tinctured, -tinted, -veined.***

1634 MILTON *Comus* 752 What need a vermeil-tinctured lip for that? **1777** POTTER *Æschylus, Furies* 451 Let th' Athenian train...now advance, Array'd in richest vesture darting round Its vermeil-tinctur'd radiance. **1810** SHELLEY *Hope* iv. Orig. Poetry (1898) 25 The vermeil [*sic*] tinted flowers. **1818** KEATS *Endymion* I. 50 Before the daisies, vermeil rimm'd and white, Hide in deep herbage. **1820** —— *St. Agnes* xxxviii, Thy beauty's shield, heart-shap'd and vermeil dyed. **1821** L. HUNT *Indicator* No. 67 (1822) II. 117 The bearded and the vermeil-cheeked. **1905** HOLMAN-HUNT *Pre-Raphaelitism* i. 4 Cheeks vermeil-veined by the pencilling of nature.

vermeil, vermil ('vɜːmɪl), *v.* Chiefly *poet.* [f. prec. Cf. the earlier ENVERMEIL *v.*] *trans.* To colour or suffuse, to stain *over,* with or as with vermilion or bright red. Also *transf.*

1596 DANETT tr. *Comines* (1614) 278 The presses painted & vermiled with golde. **1609** HEYWOOD *Brit. Troy* XIII. lxxxix, Euen till his armes with blood were vermeil'd o're. **1616** J. LANE *Contn. Sqr.'s T.* XI. 164 Their bewties, all sophisticate to viewe (Vulgarlie vermilld to pretende as trewe). **1785** J. STERLING *Cambuscan* cclii, Abundant roses vermil o'er the plain. **1832** J. BREE *St. Herbert's Isle,* etc. 171 'Twas vermilled o'er with sweetest dye That nature's pencil ever spread.

Hence '**vermeiled, 'vermiled** *ppl. a.*

1616 J. LANE *Contn. Sqr.'s T.* IX. 17 Her painted truith, her vermild modestie.

vermeillone, -meleon, obs. ff. VERMILION.

†**vermelet.** *Obs.*$^{-1}$ [ad. OF. *vermellet, vermeillet,* dim. of *vermeil* VERMEIL *a.*] Vermilion.

c **1530** *Crt. of Love* 141 O bright Regina, who made thee so fair? Who made thy colour vermelet and white?

vermelon(e, -oun, etc., obs. ff. VERMILION.

vermen, obs. form of VERMIN.

†'**verment.** *Obs.*$^{-1}$ Aphetic f. AVERMENT.

1472 *Rolls of Parlt.* VI. 64/1 By his Othe,..withouten any issue, triall or verrement to be takyn bitwene you and hym theruppon.

verme'ologist. [f. VERME-S + -OLOGIST.] One who treats of worms; a helminthologist.

1828-32 WEBSTER.

So **verme'ology,** = HELMINTHOLOGY. (*Ibid.*)

vermeon, variant of VERMION *Obs.*

‖**vermes** ('vɜːmiːz). [L., pl. of *vermis* worm.]

1. *Path.* (See quot. 1728.)

[**1693** tr. *Blancard's Phys. Dict.* (ed. 2), *Vermes,* see *Lumbrici.*] **1728** CHAMBERS *Cycl., Vermes,* in Medicine, a Disease popularly call'd *Worms*; arising from some of those Reptiles being generated, and growing in the Body. **1800** *Med. Jrnl.* IV. 203 Observations on Diseases in London... Vermes,..Epistaxis,..Epilepsia.

2. *Zool.* (With capital initial.) One or other of the primary divisions, sub-kingdoms, or groups of the animal kingdom proposed or adopted at various times by certain classifiers, comprehending worms and allied forms, but differing widely as to the nature and number of the classes or families included.

The term was introduced by Linnæus in his *Systema Naturæ* (1766).

1771 *Encycl. Brit.* III. 362/2 Linnæus divides the whole animal kingdom into 6 classes... Class VI. Vermes, or Worms. **1796** MORSE *Amer. Geog.* I. 225 The following catalogues of insects and vermes. **1828** STARK *Elem. Nat. Hist.* II. 418 Linnæus..arranged the whole in his class Vermes. **1878** BELL *Gegenbaur's Comp. Anat.* 125, I arrange the various divisions of the *Vermes* in the following order..I. Platyhelminthes..II. Nemathelminthes [etc.]. **1888** *Encycl. Brit.* XXIV. 677/2 The group *Vermes* as used..by Claus includes several distinct phyla, viz., Nematoidea [etc.]. **1888** ROLLESTON & JACKSON *Anim. Life* 579 Other Vermes are certainly unisegmental.

vermeselly, obs. f. VERMICELLI.

'**vermetid.** *Zool.* [ad. mod.L. *Vermetid-æ,* f. L. *vermes* VERMES.] An individual of the family *Vermetidæ* of holostomatous gasteropods.

1860 P. P. CARPENTER in *Rep. Smithsonian Instit. 1859* 205 [The Vermetidæ (worm shells). *Ibid.*] Some of the Vermetids assume a looseness of growth as great as that of the worm.

vermi- ('vɜːmɪ), comb. form of L. *vermi-s* (cf. VERMES), used in various words, as VERMICIDE, VERMIFORM *a.*, VERMIFUGE, VERMIPAROUS *a.*, etc.; also as a base in a few other terms, as **ver'miceous** *a.*, of or pertaining to worms; wormy (Webster, 1847); **ver'micious** *a.*, = prec. (Craig, 1849); '**vermidom** [cf. L. *dom-us* house] *Zool.* (see quots.); **ver'miferous** *a.* [-FEROUS], producing worms; **ver'migerous** *a.* [-GEROUS], infested with intestinal worms.

1877 HUXLEY *Anat. Inv. Anim.* v. 242 The ova undergo their development..in masses of gelatinous matter which adhere to the tubes of the *vermidom in *Protula.* **1894** *Jrnl. Marine Zool.* May 57 The examples..were not all from the same cluster of tubes or vermidom. **1854** H. MILLER *Sch. & Schm.* x. (1857) 206 Many a half-hour have I spent beside it, ..watching its numerous inhabitants,—insect, reptilian, and *vermiferous. **1853** G. JOHNSTON *Nat. Hist. E. Bord.* I. 129 The inexperienced mother is recommended to give..cakes and puddings tainted with Tansy to her *vermigerous child. **1860** *Encycl. Brit.* (ed. 8) XXI. 974/1 It must not..be concluded, that..every individual [animal] is vermigerous.

vermian ('vɜːmɪən), *a.* [f. VERM-ES + -IAN; see VERMI- and -AN.]

1. Of or pertaining to *Vermes*; characteristic of worms; worm-like.

1878 BELL *Gegenbaur's Comp. Anat.* 307 In this point also we can make out an affinity with Vermian larvæ (Actinotrocha). **1888** ROLLESTON & JACKSON *Anim. Life* 578 The types of structure seen in most Vermian classes are very distinct from one another. **1905** *Outlook* 28 Oct. 589/2 Human nature is not the same in all ages;..it was once simian nature, once vermian, once lower still.

2. *Anat.* Pertaining or belonging to the vermis of the cerebellum. (In recent Dicts.)

†**vermicell.** *Sc. Obs.*$^{-1}$ [a. F. *vermicel, -celle,* ad. It. *vermicelli*: see next.] ***soup-vermicell,*** = next 2.

1724 RAMSAY *Health* 63 Soup-vermicell, sous'd turbot, cray, and soles.

vermicelli (vɜːmɪ'sɛlɪ, vɜːmɪ'tʃɛlɪ). Also 7 vermechulli, virmizzelli, 8 vermigelly; 8 vermicelly (-cella), vermeselly. [a. It. *vermicelli,* pl. of *vermicello,* dim. of *verme*:—L. *vermem,* acc. sing. of *vermis* worm. Cf. prec.]

1. A kind of pasta made in the form of long, slender, hard threads, and used as an article of diet. Cf. MACARONI 1.

1669 DAVENANT *Man's the Master* I. i, Vermechulli shall my Palat please, Serv'd in with Bisques, Ragous, and Intermets. **1674** BOYLE *Excell. Theol.* I. i. 54 Vermicelli, wafers, and pie-crust, are all of them diversified meal. **1709** PRIOR *Paulo Purganti* 65 With Oysters, Eggs, and Vermicelli, She let Him almost burst his Belly. **1747** MRS. GLASSE *Cookery* xix. 155 It will run up like little Worms, as Vermicella does. **1767** *Ann. Reg.* I. 92 The free importation of rice, sago dust, and vermicelli..from the American colonies. **1819** BYRON *Juan* II. clxx, Ceres presents a plate of vermicelli. **1839** URE *Dict. Arts* 1276 The macaroni requires to be made of a less compact dough than the vermicelli. **1887** L. OLIPHANT *Episodes* (1888) 153 A soup in which was floating what appeared to be pieces of vermicelli.

b. *attrib.*, chiefly in the sense 'made of vermicelli', as ***vermicelli pudding, soup***; also 'resembling or suggestive of vermicelli', as ***vermicelli braid, braiding.***

1769 MRS. RAFFALD *Eng. Housekpr.* (1778) 1 When you make any kind of soups, particularly portable, vermicelli, or brown gravy soup. *Ibid.* 175 A Vermicelli Pudding. Boil four ounces of vermicelli in a pint of new milk till it is soft [etc.]. **1806** A. HUNTER *Culina* (ed. 3) 207 White Vermicelli Soup. **1884** *Illustr. Lond. News* 20 Sept. 267/2 We had vermicelli soup (flavoured with grated parmesan cheese). **1904** *Daily Chron.* 23 Aug. 8/1 Quite the newest of these embroideries are the so-called vermicelli braids, narrow crinkled cords formed into whirligig devices of no decidedly definite pattern. **1907** *Ibid.* 1 Oct. 8 Sleeveless coats in fine cloth, covered entirely with vermicelli braiding.

2. *ellipt.* Vermicelli soup.

1771 SMOLLETT *Humph. Cl.* 26 April, We..commonly stop at Mr. Gill's, the pastry-cook, to take a jelly, a tart, or a small basin of vermicelli. **1850** MAYNE REID *Rifle Rangers* xiv, 'Perhaps you would prefer Julienne or vermicelli, gentlemen?' inquired the Don.

'**vermicidal,** *a.* [f. next + -AL[1].] Of the nature of a vermicide; destructive to worms; anthelmintic. (In recent Dicts.)

vermicide ('vɜːmɪsaɪd). *Med.* [f. VERMI- + -CIDE 1.] A medicine for killing intestinal worms; an anthelmintic, a vermifuge.

1849 tr. *Pereira's Mat. Med. & Therap.* (ed. 3) 230 Anthelmintics are of two kinds:—Some act obnoxiously on intestinal worms—destroying or injuring them... These are ..the vermicides of some authors. **1876** BARTHOLOW *Mat. Med.* (1879) 490 Vermicides are remedies which kill as well as expel worms. **1899** CAGNEY *Jaksch's Clin. Diagn.* vi. (ed. 4) 228 Sandwith finds thymol by far the most efficient vermicide in cases of anchylostomiasis.

vermicle ('vɜːmɪk(ə)l). Also 4 **vermycle.** [ad. L. *vermiculus* little worm; also (late L.) scarlet colour. Cf. VERMICULE and VERMEIL.]

†**1.** = VERMILION *sb.* 3 a. *Obs. rare.*

1382 WYCLIF *Exod.* xxxviii. 23 A worcher with nedlis, of iacynct, and purpur, reed clooth [*altered from* vermycle], and bijs. *Ibid.* xxxix. 1.

2. *Biol.* A small worm or grub; a vermicule.

1657 TOMLINSON *Renou's Disp.* 392 A certain insect, or fly or vermicle. **1667** *Phil. Trans.* II. 426 A little Vermicle, as small as a Mite. **1746** *Ibid.* XLIV. 353 The Vermicles [of Ants]..in a few Days infold themselves in a soft silken kind of Tissue. **1747** GOULD *Eng. Ants* 76 The next..Exercise belonging to the working Ants, is feeding the Maggots or Vermicles. **1822-7** GOOD *Study Med.* (1829) III. 366 Vermicles or the larvæ of insects have at times been found in the open ulcer of a cancer. *Ibid.* V. 661 An egg, which gives rise to a minute vermicle or larve. **1880** *Nature* XXI. 453 The bodies thus evolved simulate worms so closely..that Gaule styles them 'Würmchen', which may be translated vermicles.

†**ver'miculant,** *a. Physiol. Obs.*$^{-1}$ [a. med.L. *vermiculant-, vermiculans* (*pulsus*), pres. pple. of L. *vermiculārī*: see VERMICULATE *v.*, and cf. F. *vermiculant,* Pg. *-ante.*] Of the pulse: = VERMICULAR *a.* 1 b.

1707 FLOYER *Physic. Pulse-Watch* 33 The Pulse before a Syncope is very quick, then small, languid,..obscure, vermiculant, formicant.

vermicular (və'mɪkjʊlə(r)), *a.* and *sb.* [ad. med.L. *vermiculāris,* f. L. *vermiculus*: see VERMICULE. So F. *vermiculaire* (Paré), Sp., Pg. *vermicular,* It. *vermicolare.*]

A. *adj.* **1.** *Physiol.* †**a.** ? Full of vermicules. *Obs. rare*$^{-1}$.

1655 CULPEPPER & COLE tr. *Riverius* VII. iii. 159 Somtimes it [the blood] is intermitting, watery, vermicular, when the Lungs are rotten by too much moisture.

b. = PERISTALTIC *a.*

Freq. from *c* 1835.

1672 *Phil. Trans.* VII. 5137 We instance the Vermicular motion of the veins [of plants] when exposed to the air. **1713** CHESELDEN *Anat.* III. xii. (1726) 236 After this it [the food] is continually moved by the..vermicular motion of the guts. **1791** E. DARWIN *Bot. Gard.* I. Notes 99 In such a structure it is easy to conceive how a vermicular or peristaltic motion of the vessel..must forcibly push forward its contents. **1834** *Good's Study Med.* (ed. 4) I. 9 Its [the stomach's] muscular fibres are calculated to produce a constant undulatory vermicular movement. **1835-6** *Todd's Cycl. Anat.* I. 668/1 On the supposition that the arteries undergo an undulatory or vermicular contraction. **1881** MIVART *Cat* 181 This form of movement is also spoken of as the vermicular motion of the intestine.

transf. **1899** *Allbutt's Syst. Med.* VIII. 201 Sometimes these muscles are seen working under the skin in vermicular fashion.

2. Having the sinuous shape or form characteristic of a worm; consisting of, characterized by, tortuous outlines or markings; sinuous, wavy.

1712 tr. *Pomet's Hist. Drugs* I. 180 The Vermicular, or Worm-like Gum, is one of the Arabian or Senega Gums. **1753** *Phil. Trans.* XLVIII. 87 This second furrow was.. not in a strait line, but in a vermicular direction. **1784** COWPER *Task* I. 30 A generation more refin'd.. made three legs four, Gave them a twisted form vermicular. **1815** KIRBY & SP. *Entomol.* xiv. (1816) I. 438 The vermicular shape.. of the masses with which the [larval] cases are surrounded. **1860** HOOK *Lives Abps.* I. i. 33 His mantle.. ornamented with stripes or vermicular figures. **1875** FORTNUM *Maiolica* ii. 16 Pottery of Moresque character and ornamentation with vermicular pattern in copper lustre.

b. *Bot.* (See quot. 1866.)

1766 *Compl. Farmer* s.v. *Madder*, The [madder] plants which are raised from layers.. produce very few of those vermicular roots, which are the only valuable ones. **1849** BALFOUR *Man. Bot.* Gloss. 641/1. **1866** *Treas. Bot.* 1210/2 *Vermicular*, worm-shaped; thick, and almost cylindrical, but bent in different places.

c. *Anat.* = VERMIFORM *a.* 3, 3 b.

1843 J. G. WILKINSON *Swedenborg's Anim. Kingd.* I. v. 148 The vermicular appendage is seen on one side of the fundus of the cœcum, resembling a miniature intestine. **1891** *Cent. Dict.* s.v., Vermicular appendix or process.

3. Of or pertaining to, characteristic of, a worm or worms; resembling or like a worm.

1713 DERHAM *Phys.-Theol.* (1716) 385 In its Vermicular State it is a red Maggot. **1720** S. PARKER *Bibliotheca Bibl.* I. 152 Without the Taint of the polluted Vermicular Life. **1752** *Phil. Trans.* XLVII. 449 Several species of vermicular tubes found in the sea. **1802** BINGLEY *Anim. Biog.* (1813) III. 7 Across the body there are several annular divisions, or rather rugæ of the skin, from which the fish should seem to partake of a vermicular nature. **1804** J. GRAHAME *Sabbath* (1839) 16/1 We may compare the erect spirit of a British legislature with the vermicular servility of.. the senate of France. **1892** *Scottish Leader* 24 May 4 Vermicular patience, however, has its limits.

b. Accomplished or made by worms; performed by means of worms. Also *fig.*

1715 tr. *Pancirollus' Rerum Mem.* II. i. 266 From thence came also Indian Figs, Nuts and Canes, and a vermicular kind of Web made of Silk. **1822** *Blackw. Mag.* XII. 153 The party, which the work stood pledged to oppose through all its vermicular attacks on the glorious fabric of British Institutions. **1887** C. HAZARD *Mem. J. L. Diman* xv. 338 The trout here disdain flies. As Lewis phrases it, vermicular fishing is what succeeds.

c. ***vermicular work***: (see quot. and VERMICULATED *ppl. a.* 1 c).

1728 CHAMBERS *Cycl.*, *Vermicular Work*,.. in Sculpture, a sort of Ornaments used in Rustick Work; consisting of Frets, or Knobs, cut with Points, representing, in some sort, the Tracks made by Worms.

4. Of the nature of a worm. ***vermicular ascaris***, the threadworm, *Oxyurus* (*Ascaris*) *vermicularis*.

1784 COWPER *Let.* 13 Dec., No animal of the vermicular or serpentine kind is crested but the most formidable of all. **1802** BINGLEY *Anim. Biog.* (1813) III. 395 The Vermicular Ascarides are very common in the intestines of children. **1822-7** GOOD *Study Med.* (1829) I. 365 For the cure of vermicular ascarides, or maw-worms and bots, these oils have been used in the form of injections.

fig. and *transf.* **1825** *Examiner* 307/2 Fawcett.. wanted a little more personal flexibility..; he cannot, at his time of life, be sufficiently vermicular. **1854** LOWELL *Cambridge 30 Y. Ago* Prose Wks. 1890 I. 89 Refusing to molest the canker-worms.. because we were all vermicular alike. **1872** RUSKIN *Arrows of Chace* (1880) II. 189 Criminals.. are partly men, partly vermin; what is human in them you must punish—what is vermicular, abolish.

b. Comprising or consisting of worms.

1886 H. F. LESTER *Under two Fig Trees* viii. 117 Their [*sc.* worms'] minds, like their bodies, must be glutinous; hence they stick to the thin-end theory... There is no sect of 'bigendians' in the vermicular fold.

5. *Path.* Of diseases: Due to, caused by, intestinal worms.

1794 R. J. SULIVAN *View Nat.* I. 237 Hence the probable utility of fixed air in vermicular diseases. *a* **1822** SHELLEY *Devil* Pr. Wks. 1880 II. 400 Persons subject to vermicular and animalcular diseases.

†**B.** *sb.* = VERMICULE. *Obs. rare.*

1690 R. CLARK *Vermiculars Destroyed* 9 A sort of invisible Worms or Vermiculars. *Ibid.* 11 The Putrefaction.. is degenerated into innumerable Vermiculars.

Hence **ver'micularly** *adv.*

1812 *New Bot. Gard.* I. 84 The seeds.. vermicularly wrinkled.

vermiculate (və'mɪkjʊlət), *a.* [ad. L. *vermiculāt-us*, pa. pple. of *vermiculārī*: see next. Several other senses given in various Dicts. are merely inferences from senses of the ppl. adj.]

Vermiculated; vermicular; sinuous. Chiefly *fig.*

1605 BACON *Adv. Learn.* I. iv. §5 It is the propertie of good and sound knowledge to putrifie and dissolve into a number of subtile, idle, vnholesome, and (as I may tearme them) vermiculate questions. **1658** PHILLIPS, *Vermiculate*, worm-eaten. *a* **1864** R. CHOATE (Webster), Vermiculate logic. **1872** G. MACDONALD *Wilf. Cumb.* III. xvi. 214 My life seemed only a vermiculate one, a crawling about of half-thoughts-half-feelings through the corpse of a decaying existence. **1891** *Cent. Dict.* s.v., Vermiculate color-markings.

b. *spec.* in *Ent.* (See quot.)

1826 KIRBY & SP. *Entomol.* IV. xlvi. 271 *Vermiculate*,.. having tortuous excavations as if eaten by worms.

†**ver'miculate**, *v. Obs.* [f. L. *vermiculāt-*, ppl. stem of *vermiculārī* (Pliny), f. *vermiculus*, dim. of *vermis* worm.

Other senses which appear in various Dicts. are merely assumed from the ppl. adj.]

1. *intr.* To become worm-eaten. *rare*⁻¹.

c **1631** *Elegy on Donne* D.'s Poems (1654) B b iv b, Speake, Doth his body there vermiculate, Crumble to dust, and feele the lawes of Fate?

2. To beat with peristaltic motion. *rare*⁻¹.

1706 HEARNE *Collect.* (O.H.S.) I. 183 Her pulse indeed vermiculates, Her Breath is short & little.

ver'miculated, *ppl. a.* [See prec. and -ED[1].]

1. Worm-eaten; covered or ornamented with markings resembling those made by the gnawing of worms.

1623 COCKERAM I, *Vermiculated*, worme-eaten. [Hence in Blount.] **1707** SLOANE *Jamaica* I. 78 The pinnæ set in the middle are largest,.. having on the backside several vermiculated, ferrugineous lines, in which is the seed. **1886** C. D. WARNER *Their Pilgrimage* vi. (1888) 157 The worms worked underneath.. until the bark came off and exposed the stems most beautifully vermiculated. **1914** H. L. JOLY *Catal. Behrens Coll.* IV. 24 Bronze Koro, vermiculated design charged with dragons.

†**b.** *Bot.* Of plants or leaves: ? Presenting a worm-eaten appearance. *Obs.*

1731 MILLER *Gard. Dict.*, *Santolina*, *vermiculata*, *Cretica*, Tourn[efort]. Vermiculated Lavender Cotton of Candy. **1746** ROBT. JAMES *Introd. Moufet's Health's Improv.* 17 Those Vegetables also which contain an aromatic alcaline Oil.. [include] Savory. Acrid vermiculated Houseleek. Mustard. **1753** *Chambers' Cycl.* Suppl. s.v. *Santolina*, The species.. enumerated by Mr. Tournefort, are these. 1. The common santolina with cylindric vermiculated leaves... And 14. The Cretic santolina with vermiculated leaves.

c. *Arch.* Of stone-work or other surfaces so carved or moulded as to present the appearance of worm-tracks.

1788 *Encycl. Brit.* (ed. 3) II. 242/1 The rustics may either be plain, hatched, or vermiculated. **1823** P. NICHOLSON *Pract. Build.* 482 In different parts of the Louvre, wormy or vermiculated rustics are to be found. **1833** LOUDON *Encycl. Archit.* §1926 The rocky surface,.. the vermiculated, and the punctured, are among the kinds used by the Italians. **1881** YOUNG *Ev. Man his own Mech.* §1173 The caps and key-stone are frequently of stone, the latter being 'vermiculated', as it is called, or indented with irregular hollows.

2. Of mosaic work: Wrought, ornamented, or inlaid so as to resemble the sinuous movements or tracks of worms.

After L. (*opus*) *vermiculatum*.

1656 BLOUNT *Glossogr.*, *Vermiculated*,.. embroidered, wrought with checquer work, or with small pieces of divers colours, representing sundry pictures, as we see in Tables and Counters. **1712** HEARNE *Collect.* (O.H.S.) III. 311 So livelily were their Countenances describ'd in this vermiculated work. **1883** *Encycl. Brit.* XVI. 850/2 For Walls and Vaults:—Fictile or vermiculated; pieces of opaque glass, in small cubes, arranged so as to form complicated pictures.

3. Ornamented *with* sinuous or wavy lines or markings of a specified colour.

1872 COUES *N. Amer. Birds* 124 Our species are.. white more or less evidently vermiculated with black below.

vermiculation (vəmɪkjʊ'leɪʃən). [ad. L. *vermiculātiōn-*, *vermiculātio* (Pliny), noun of action f. *vermiculārī*: see VERMICULATE *v.*]

1. The fact or condition of being infested with or eaten by worms; conversion into small worms.

1611 FLORIO, *Vermiculatione*, a vermiculation, a breeding or crauling of vermine or grubs. **1630** DONNE *Last Serm.* Wks. 1839 VI. 285 Putrefaction and Vermiculation and Incineration and Dispersion in.. the Grave. **1640** HOWELL *Dodona's Gr.* 70 This huge Olive which flourishd so long.. fell, as they say, of vermiculation, being all worme-eaten within. **1658** J. ROWLAND *Moufet's Theat. Ins.* 933 A certain kinde of Flies which are begotten in the bark of the Elm,.. and so perchance in other herbs and plants, without any preceding vermiculation, or being turned into little worms first. **1704** J. HARRIS *Lex. Techn.* I, *Vermiculation*, is an Infection of Plants by Worms. **1706** PHILLIPS (ed. Kersey), *Vermiculation*,.. the breeding of Worms in Trees, Herbs, or Fruits.

fig. **1907** *Daily Chron.* 3 Apr. 3/1 The decay and vermiculation of faith has already brought European theology to the verge of collapse.

†**2.** *Path.* Vermicular or peristaltic movement of the intestines, etc.; peristalsis. Also *transf.*

1652 SPARKE *Prim. Devot.* (1663) 117 [There is] a vermiculation in his muscles. Convulsions seize on his whole body. **1671** [R. MACWARD] *True Nonconf.* 44 This is the vermiculation of your pulse. *a* **1676** HALE *Prim. Orig. Man.* I. i. (1677) 31 My Heart moves.. by the motion of Palpitation, my Blood by the motion of Circulation,.. my Guts by the motion of Vermiculation. **1710** T. FULLER *Pharm. Extemp.* 192 Hypochondriac.. Affections, such as Vermiculations, Flushings.

†**b.** (See quot.) *Obs.*⁻⁰

1706 PHILLIPS (ed. Kersey), *Vermiculation*,.. the griping of the Guts, a Disease.

3. With pl. A tortuous boring or marking made by, or resembling the track of, a worm.

1670 EVELYN *Sylva* (ed. 2) xxv. 123 The wood of the Enzina,.. when old, is curiously chambletted, and embroidered with Natural vermiculations. **1874** T. HARDY *Far fr. Madding Crowd* ix, The face of the boards is shown to be eaten into innumerable vermiculations. **1891** G. E. SHELLEY *Catal. Birds Brit. Mus.* XIX. 24 The under surface of the body pale sulphur-yellow, more or less mottled.. with dull ashy vermiculations.

b. (See quot.) *rare*⁻⁰.

1828-32 WEBSTER, *Vermiculation*, the act of forming so as to resemble the motion of a worm.

c. Without article. Vermicular marking or ornamentation.

1866 *Daily Tel.* 17 Feb. 5/3 This enigma of honeycombing and vermiculation. **1872** COUES *N. Amer. Birds* 21 *note*, Cross-wise streaking is called barring, and always runs transverse to the axis of a bird; if the lines are straight, it is banding..; if very fine and irregular, it is vermiculation.

vermicule ('vɜːmɪkjʊl). *Biol.* [ad. L. *vermicul-us*, dim. of *vermis* worm. Cf. VERMICLE.] A small worm or worm-like creature; a maggot or grub. Also *attrib.*

1713 DERHAM *Phys.-Theol.* VIII. vi. (1716) 391 We see many Vermicules towards the outside of many of the oak-apples. **1778** [W. H. MARSHALL] *Minutes Agric.* 24 Jan. 1775, Perhaps, from insects or vermicules, or both, comes smut. **1822-7** GOOD *Study Med.* (1829) IV. 392 A transfer of vermicules from one individual to another. **1898** P. MANSON *Trop. Diseases* i. 18 The halteridium.. slowly changes form, becoming elongated into a pigmented spindle-shaped body or vermicule. **1899** *Allbutt's Syst. Med.* VIII. 943 In the former.. there is a corresponding or travelling vermicule stage.

Hence †**ver'miculist**, a supporter of the view that generation is due to vermicules.

1784 tr. *Spallanzani's Diss. Nat. Hist.* II. 249 The three principal systems respecting the generation of animals, the system of the ovarists, that of the vermiculists, and that founded upon the two liquors.

vermiculite (və'mɪkjʊlaɪt). [f. L. *vermicul-ārī* (see VERMICULATE *v.*) + -ITE[1].]

1. *Min.* **a.** 'Hydrous silicate of aluminium, iron, and magnesium, occurring in small foliated scales' (Chester).

1824 T. H. WEBB in *Amer. Jrnl. Sci. & Arts* VII. 55 If subjected to the flame of a blowpipe,.. it expands and shoots out into a variety of fanciful forms, resembling most generally small *worms*... If this proves to be a new variety.. I term it Vermiculite (worm breeder). **1862** DANA *Man. Min.* 149 Vermiculite.. looks and feels like steatite; but when heated before the blowpipe, worm-like projections shoot out, owing to a separation of the thin leaves composing the grains. **1888** RUTLEY *Rock-forming Min.* 199 Vermiculite and Jeffreysite are considered to be altered varieties of phlogopite.

b. *pl.* (See quot.)

1875 *Ure's Dict. Arts* (ed. 7) III. 1074 *Vermiculites*, a group of minerals resembling the chlorites, remarkable for their exfoliation before the blowpipe.

c. Flakes of this mineral used as a moisture-holding medium for plant growth or as a protective covering for the storage of bulbs or tubers.

1950 *Los Angeles Times Home Mag.* 12 Feb. 38/3 Vermiculite is one of the finest storage materials for bulbs, tubers and corms as it insulates them from sudden temperature changes. **1981** *Farmstead Mag.* Winter 71/1 All that is necessary for this March project is a few water-proof trays, fiber or wooden slats, vermiculite for seed germination, and soilless mix such as 'Promix' for filling the flats. **1983** *Which?* Sept. 398/3 Wash off as much soil as possible, then stand the tubers, stem-down, in a dry, frost-free place.. before.. storing in boxes of dry peat or vermiculite.

2. *Geol.* 'A short worm-track seen on the surface of many flagstones' (1884 *Imp. Dict.*).

vermicu'lose, *a. rare.* [ad. late L. *vermiculōs-us* (Palladius), f. *vermiculus* VERMICULE. Cf. It. *vermicoloso* and next.]

†**1.** Of the pulse: = VERMICULAR *a.* 1 b. *Obs.*⁻¹

1707 FLOYER *Physic. Pulse-Watch* 124 The Pulse is languid, slow, vermiculose if without a Fever.

2. Infested with worms; worm-like. *rare*⁻⁰.

1727 BAILEY (vol. II), *Vermiculose*, full of worms. **1847** WEBSTER, *Vermiculose*, 1. full of worms or grubs. 2. resembling worms. [Hence in later Dicts.]

Hence **vermicu'losity**. *rare*⁻⁰.

1727 BAILEY (vol. II), *Vermiculosity*, Abundance or Fulness of Worms.

vermiculous (və'mɪkjʊləs), *a.* [See prec. and -OUS. Cf. F. *vermiculeux*.]

1. Full of worms. *rare*⁻¹.

1690 R. CLARK *Vermiculars Destroyed* 14 Slime and vermiculous matter.

2. Of or pertaining to worms.

1813 T. BUSBY *Lucretius* I. III. Comm. p. xxv, Otherwise, the vermiculous souls will be portions of human souls. **1819** H. BUSK *Banquet* III. 462 The race vermiculous.

3. Having a wormy appearance.

1818 TODD, *Vermiculous*,.. resembling grubs. **1839** *New Monthly Mag.* LVII. 406 The more prominent part of the [man's] nose, on whose vermiculous top, the Prussian blue mostly prevailed.

4. *Path.* Of strangury: Accompanied or marked by the discharge of worms or helminths.

1822-7 GOOD *Study Med.* (1829) V. 469 They lay a foundation for the following varieties:.. Spasmodic strangury... Scalding strangury... Vermiculous strangury.

†**ver'miculus.** *Obs.* Pl. vermiculi. [L., dim. of *vermis* worm. Cf. VERMICULE.]

1. A small worm or grub; a vermicule.

1694 W. SALMON *Bate's Dispens.* (1713) 12 All the *Vermiculi*, or *Miasmata*, which are the Progenerators of the

Plague, or Pestilence. **1728** CHAMBERS *Cycl.* s.v. *Vermes*, Some Authors assert,..that this *Spolium* is not animated, but receives its Sense and Motion from *Verminculi*, or *Cucurbitini* inclosed in it. *Ibid.* s.v. *Vermicular*.

2. A species of marine annelid; a sea-worm.

a **1728** WOODWARD *Fossils* (1729) I. II. 22 A Vermiculus growing to a Piece of a *Pinna Marina*. **1753** *Chambers' Cycl. Suppl.* s.v., These shells are called *vermiculi*,..from the fish contained in them, which is always a sort of worm. **1776** DA COSTA *Elem. Conchol.* 284 A chambered Vermiculus, taken from Davila's Catalogue.

† **ˈvermified,** *pa. pple. Obs.*$^{-1}$ [See VERMI- and -FY.] Troubled with, infested by, intestinal worms.

1666 G. HARVEY *Morbus Angl.* xvii. (1672) 36 Persons thus vermifyed, seldom go to stool without avoiding a great quantity of those verminous seeds.

vermiform (ˈvɜːmɪfɔːm), *a.* [ad. med.L. *vermiform-is* (whence F., It., Sp., and Pg. *vermiforme*), f. L. *vermis* worm: see -FORM. Cf. VERMES and VERMIS.

Vermiformal is used by Urquhart *Rabelais* (1653) II. xiii, translating F. *vermiforme*.]

1. *Zool.* Having the form of a worm; resembling a worm in appearance or shape; long, thin, and more or less cylindrical.

1730 BAILEY (fol.), *Vermiform*,..shaped like a Worm. **1816** KIRBY & SP. *Entomol.* I. 437 A covering of vermiform masses, apparently composed of honey and pollen. **1828** STARK *Elem. Nat. Hist.* II. 211 Body elongated, but not vermiform or linear. **1857** *Fraser's Mag.* LVI. 641 [It] feeds on the insects with its protruded vermiform tongue. **1881** DARWIN *Veg. Mould* iv. (1882) 186 Five or six vermiform castings had been thrown up.

b. Of animals.

1826 KIRBY & SP. *Entomol.* IV. xlvii. 374 One species, which much resembles the vermiform larvæ of *Hymenoptera*. **1846** PATTERSON *Zool.* 57 The Leeches and Worms present very much the same aspect as the vermiform or worm-shaped Echinodermata. **1846** CARPENTER *Man. Phys.* 505 In some of the lowest Vermiform (worm-like) Fishes, such as the Lamprey. **1883** *Fisheries Exhib. Catal.* 283 These young vermiform and semi-transparent eels.

c. *spec.* (see quot.)

1877 COUES *Fur Anim.* iv. 116 In general form, the Stoat typifies a group of carnivorous Mammals aptly called 'vermiform', in consideration of the extreme length, tenuity and mobility of the trunk, and shortness of the limbs.

2. Of or pertaining to, characteristic of, a worm; like or resembling that of a worm; vermicular.

1835–6 *Todd's Cycl. Anat.* I. 327/2 The Spleen..in Birds ..sometimes presents an elongated and vermiform shape. **1859** DARWIN *Orig. Spec.* (1860) xiii. 442 If we look to the admirable drawings..of the development of this insect, we see no trace of the vermiform stage. **1878** BELL *Gegenbaur's Comp. Anat.* 118 In the Discophora they form tufts of filaments,..and execute vermiform movements.

3. *Anat.* **a.** ***vermiform appendix*** or ***appendage***, a small, worm-like process or diverticulum extending from the cæcum in man and a few other mammals.

(*a*) **1778** *Encycl. Brit.* (ed. 2) I. 368/2 Of the little vermiform appendix of the cæcum, it will be sufficient to say that its uses have never yet been ascertained. **1872** HUXLEY *Phys.* vi. 150 An elongated, blind process..which from its shape is called the vermiform appendix of the cæcum. **1888** ROLLESTON & JACKSON *Anim. Life* 28 Caecum with vermiform appendix..of rabbit.

(*b*) **1841** T. R. JONES *Anim. Kingd.* 680 In Man, the Orangs,..and the Wombat,..both cæcum and vermiform appendage are met with. **1876** BRISTOWE *The. & Pract. Med.* (1878) 674 Concretions are mostly found in the vermiform appendage and are the usual causes of perforative ulceration of this part.

b. ***vermiform process***, the median lobe of the cerebellum, the upper and lower laminæ of which are distinguished as the ***superior*** and ***inferior vermiform processes***.

Also, = prec. (In some recent Dicts.)

1836 *Penny Cycl.* V. 332/1 The cerebellum... In the centre of its upper surface there is a distinct prominence termed the vermiform process. **1840** E. WILSON *Anat. Vade M.* (1842) 383 The cerebellum is divided into two lateral hemispheres or lobes, two minor lobes called superior and inferior vermiform processes, and some small lobules. **1899** *Allbutt's Syst. Med.* VII. 497 A very little lymph on the superior vermiform process of the cerebellum.

Hence **vermiformous** *a.*, 'shaped like a worm' (Bailey, 1727, vol. II).

vermifugal (vəˈmɪfjʊgəl), *a. Med.* [f. next + -AL[1].] = VERMIFUGE *a.*

1830 LINDLEY *Nat. Syst. Bot.* 8 The seeds of Delphinium Staphisagria are vermifugal and caustic. **1875** H. C. WOOD *Therap.* (1879) 447 Especially in the case of the seat-worm the vermifugal enemata should be medicated.

vermifuge (ˈvɜːmɪfjuːdʒ), *a.* and *sb. Med.* [a. F. *vermifuge* (= It., Sp., Pg. *vermifugo*), or ad. mod.L. type **vermifugus*, f. L. *vermi-s* worm: see -FUGE.]

A. *adj.* Causing or promoting the evacuation or expulsion of worms or other animal parasites from the intestines; anthelmintic.

In some instances perh. an attributive use of the sb.

1697 in *Mem. Rokeby* (Surtees) 58 Vermifuge pills, a box 3s. 4d. **1769** E. BANCROFT *Guiana* 54 Their vermifuge quality..justly intitles them to particular attention. **1803** *Med. Jrnl.* IX. 468 The physician had suspected the presence of worms, and prescribed vermifuge medicines accordingly. **1858** SIMMONDS *Dict. Trade, Sindhooka, Sinduya*, vernacular names in India for the *Vitex Negundo*, the fruit of which is considered vermifuge. **1876** BRISTOWE *The. & Pract. Med.* (1878) 711 The administration of vermifuge drugs.

B. *sb.* A medicament or substance having the power or property of expelling worms from the intestines; an anthelmintic.

1718 QUINCY *Compl. Disp.* (1719) 110 It is used hardly in any other Intention in Medicine, than as a Vermifuge. **1763** *Phil. Trans.* LIII. 14 Vermifuges of the most celebrated kind,..and such other medicines as tend..to carry off or destroy the worms, were assiduously administered. **1822–7** GOOD *Study Med.* (1829) I. 364 In the former [class of anthelmintics] we may rank..all the oleaginous vermifuges, as oil of olives, beech-nuts, castor, and turpentine [etc.]. **1843** YOUATT *Horse* xiii. (1847) 292 Arsenic was once in great repute as a tonic and vermifuge. **1871** GARROD *Mat. Med.* (ed. 3) 404 Anthelmintics are employed for the following purposes:—..2. The indirect, or vermifuges, to expel any worms, living or dead.

† **verˈmifugous,** *a. Obs. rare.* [f. as prec. + -OUS.] Vermifugal, vermifuge.

1726 C. D'ANVERS *Craftsman* xxxix. (1727) 374 If my ingenious friend can by any vermifugous preparation bring away or destroy this pernicious Animalcule.

vermigelly, obs. form of VERMICELLI.

† **vermiglion,** obs. var. VERMILION *sb.* (perh. after It. *vermiglione*).

1592 GREENE *Conny-Catch.* III. Wks. (Grosart) X. 234 Paynters coulde not..make away theyr Vermiglion, if tallow faced whoores vsde it not for their cheekes.

vermigrade (ˈvɜːmɪgreɪd), *a. rare*$^{-1}$. [f. VERMI- + -GRADE.] Proceeding in a worm-like manner. (In context *fig.*)

1938 S. BECKETT *Murphy* viii. 134 Celia was in a state indeed, trembling and ashen. The footsteps overhead had become part and parcel of her afternoon, with the rocking-chair and the vermigrade wane of light. An Ægean night-fall suddenly in Brewery Road could not have upset her more than this failure of the steps.

vermil(e, obs. or var. ff. VERMEIL *a.*, *sb.*, and *v.*

vermilion (vəˈmɪljən), *sb.* and *a.* Forms: *α.* 3 vermelyon, 6 -eleon, -eleoun; 4–5 vermilyon, 5 -ylyoun, 5–6 -ylyon(e, 6 -ylion; 4–5 vermilioun, 5– vermilion (6–7 -milian, 7 virmilion). *β.* 4 vermeillone, 5 -elone, 5–7 -elon, 6 *Sc.* -eloun; 4–5 vermylone, 4 fer-, 5 vermyloun, 5–6 vermylon; 4–5 vermulon, 4–5 vermilon(e, -ioun; also 6 vermelonde, *Sc.* wermeling, -myling. *γ.* 6–9 vermillion, 7 virmillion. [a. AF. and OF. *vermeillon*, *vermillon*, *vermilo(u)n*, etc. (mod.F. *vermillon*, = Prov. *vermeillon*, *vermillon*, *vermelho*, Cat. *bermello*, Sp. *bermellon*, *bermillon*, *vermellon*, Pg. *vermelhaõ*, It. *vermiglione*), f. *vermeil* VERMEIL *a.* Hence also Du. *vermiljoen*, Da. and Sw. *vermilion*.]

A. *sb.* **1.** Cinnabar or red crystalline mercuric sulphide, esp. in later use that obtained artificially, much valued on account of its brilliant scarlet colour, and largely used as a pigment or in the manufacture of red sealing-wax; also, any red earth resembling this and similarly used as a pigment.

In early use rendering L. *minium* and occas. confused with 'red lead' (as in quot. 1546 in *β*): see MINIUM.

α. **1296** *Acc. Exch. K.R.* 5/20 m. 4 In duabus libris de Vermelyon emptis. **1336–7** *Ely Sacr. Rolls* (1907) II. 83 In ij libris de vermilioun empt. *c* **1440** *Promp. Parv.* 508 Vermylyone, *minium*. **1471** RIPLEY *Comp. Alch.* Adm. i. in Ashm. *Theat. Chem. Brit.* (1652) 189 Many Experyments I have had in hond;..Which I wyll tell the rehersyng sone: Begynnyng wyth Vermylion. *a* **1533** LD. BERNERS *Gold. Bk. M. Aurel.* (1546) Kkj, All the Decade was written with blacke ynke, and these wordes with redde vermylyon. **1555** EDEN *Decades* (Arb.) 384 Cinoper or vermilion which the paynters vse in certeyne coloures. **1626** BACON *Sylva* §291 Metals give Orient and fine Colours..in their Putrefactions or Rusts, as Vermilion, Verde-grease [etc.]. **1669** STURMY *Mariner's Mag.* II. 119 This will be..as ready to you, as if these Letters were painted out for you in Vermilion. **1758** REID tr. *Macquer's Chym.* I. 82 Cinabar finely levigated acquires a much brighter red colour, and is known to painters by the name of Vermilion. **1841** THACKERAY *Gt. Hoggarty Diam.* xii, All this while Mary was anxiously looking in his face,..as pale as death; while Gus..was as red as vermilion. **1871** GARROD *Mat. Med.* (ed. 3) 103 Dark scarlet shining crystalline masses, forming, when powdered, a beautiful scarlet colour, known by the name of vermilion.

β. **1300–1** *Durham Acc. Rolls* (Surtees) 503 In tribus libr. Gummi, di. li. de vermiloun, iij s. **1356** *Pipe Roll* 32 *Edw. III*, m. 33/2 b, In..ij. clench' hamers, iiij. boltes ferri,.. xxxj. lb. de vermeillone. **1387** TREVISA *Higden* (Rolls) I. 63 Of the..strondes of þe Reed See is i-gadered vermylon. *Ibid.* II. 331 And þere is i-founde scharpe fermyloun [L. *minium*]. *c* **1400** *Pety Job* 580 in 26 *Pol. Poems* 139 Ynke blak or rede, Made with gumme and vermylone. **1412–20** LYDG. *Chron. Troy* II. 4717 We may al day oure colour grynde & bete, Tempre our azour and vermyloun. **1480** *Robt. Devyll* 21 Robertes clothes were readde as vermulon. **1505–6** *Acc. Ld. High Treas. Scot.* III. 184 For iij di. pund vermeloun to him, xiiij s. **1546** LANGLEY *Pol. Verg. de Invent.* II. xiv. 59 b, Vermilon or redde lead was founde in Ephesus by Gallius an Athenien. **1567** MAPLET *Gr. Forest* 98 The Parret..about hir necke..hath a Collar or Chaine naturally wrought like to Sinople or Vermelon. **1609** BIBLE (Douay) *Isa.* i. 18 If they be red as vermelon, they shal be white as wooll.

γ. **1591** SYLVESTER *Du Bartas* I. iii. 901 I'le onely now emboss my Book with Brass, Dye't with Vermillion, deck't with Coperass. **1594** PLAT *Jewell-ho.* III. 46 Mingle.. Vermillion with Masticke for a red colour. **1604** E. G[RIMSTONE] *D'Acosta's Hist. Indies* IV. xi. 237 Quicke-silver is found in a kinde of stone, which dooth likewise yeelde Vermillion. **1698** T. FROGER *Voy.* 112 Calicœs..made of Gold, Vermillion, and silver. **1762–71** H. WALPOLE *Vertue's Anecd. Paint.* (1786) IV. 8 New cloathing them in vermillion and ultramarine. **1796** WITHERING *Brit. Pl.* (ed. 3) IV. 397 Dust the colour of vermillion. **1839** URE *Dict. Arts* 1278 The vermillion of commerce is often adulterated with red lead, brickdust, dragon's blood, and realgar. **1865** WATTS *Dict. Chem.* III. 912 Mercuric Sulphide,..in the latter [crystallised state],..has a fine red colour and constitutes the well-known pigment called cinnabar or vermillion.

b. Used as a cosmetic or for painting the body.

In later use chiefly with reference to the 'war-paint' of the American Indians.

1600 J. PORY tr. *Leo's Africa* III. 144 The morrow after a companie of women goe to dresse the bride, to combe her locks, and to paint her cheekes with vermillion. **16..** MIDDLETON *Old Law* III. i, The old wrinkles are well filled up, but the vermillion is seen too thick. **1635** SWAN *Spec. M.* vi. (1643) 294 Camillus, when he triumphed in Rome, was painted with this Vermilion. **1788** *Encycl. Brit.* (ed. 3) I. 542/2 A thick coat of vermilion commonly distinguishes the [Red Indian's] cheeks. **1809** A. HENRY *Trav.* 247 The men were almost entirely naked, and their bodies painted with a red ochre, procured in the mountains, and often called vermilion. **1836** W. IRVING *Astoria* II. 71 Happy was he who could render himself hideous with vermilion. **1843** MARRYAT *M. Violet* xxiii, When does a Comanche turn his back on receiving the vermilion from his chief? Never!

2. The colour of this pigment; a bright red or scarlet.

a **1400–50** *Alexander* 4336 Nouthire to toly ne to taunde transmitte we na vebbis, To vermylion ne violett ne variant littis. **1430–40** LYDG. *Bochas* II. xiii. (1554) 51 b, Fenix as Clerkes eke endite Found fyrst the colour of vermilion. **1530** PALSGR. 284/2 Vermylon, reed colour, *uermillon*. **1587** A. DAY *Daphnis & Chloe* (1890) 51 A vermillion more perfect, thair rested in the freshe springing rose. **1590** SPENSER *F.Q.* I. v. 9 Streames of bloud..With which the armes, that earst so bright did show, Into a pure vermillion now are dyde. **1638** *Guillim's Her.* (ed. 3) I. ii. 19 Amongst Colours..this Colour Vermilion, or Red, hath the prime place. **1646** J. HALL *Poems* 52 A Rose can more Vermilion speake, Then any cheeke. **1681** DRYDEN *Abs. & Achit.* I. 649 His long Chin prov'd his Wit; his Saint-like Grace A Church Vermilion, and a Moses's Face. **1708** OZELL tr. *Boileau's Lutrin* 30 Streight the Vermillion vanish'd from her Face. **1793** BEDDOES *Calculus* 230 The blood became of a brighter vermilion. **1822** [M. A. KELTY] *Osmond* I. 274 The soft vermillion..of her complexion. **1838** THIRLWALL *Greece* II. xv. 255 The negroes of Nubia—with their bodies painted half white, half vermilion. **1882** *Garden* 23 Dec. 548/1 The colour is a vivid vermilion.

† **b.** A blush. *Obs.*$^{-1}$

1787 *Minor* III. ix. 183 Miss Charlotte..never beheld me without the vermilions increasing in her cheeks.

† **3. a.** (Rendering L. *vermiculum*.) Wool or yarn of a red or scarlet colour. *Obs.*

1388 WYCLIF *Exod.* xxxv. 25 Tho thingis, whiche thei hadden spunne, iacynt, purpur, and vermyloun, and bijs. —— *Lev.* xiv. 4 He schal comaunde to the man which is clensid, that he offre for hymsilf..a tree of cedre, and vermyloun, and isope.

† **b.** A fabric dyed with vermilion. *Obs.*$^{-1}$

1641 L. ROBERTS *Treas. Traffick* 33 They buy Cotton wooll, in London,..and perfit it into Fustians, Vermilions, Dymities, and other such Stuffes.

† **4.** A red or reddish coloured variety of pear.

1699 EVELYN *Kal. Hort.* (ed. 9) 169 Pears:..Ambrosia, Vermilian, Lunsac.

† **5.** (Also ***vermilion-stone***.) A particular gem or precious stone. Cf. VERMEIL *sb.* 3. *Obs.*

1703–4 in Ashton *Soc. Life Reign Q. Anne* (1882) I. xiv. 181 Several Gold Rings set with Turky and Vermillions. *a* **1728** WOODWARD *Fossils* (1729) I. I. 191 The Common Crystal..appears to be the Basis..of the Opal,..the Jacinth, the Vermilion. **1747** *Phil. Trans.* XLIV. 504 The Vermilion-Stone is more tawny than the Jacinth.

6. a. *Comb.*, as ***vermilion-dyed***, ***-like*** adjs.; † ***vermilion-writer***, a scribe or illuminator using vermilion.

c **1470** *Cath. Angl.* 400 A vermylon wrytter, *minographus*. **1581** G. PETTIE tr. *Guazzo's Civ. Conv.* III. (1586) 125 b, Those dawbed, pargetted, vermilion died faces. **1647** HEXHAM I, Vermillion like, *roodtachtigh*.

b. *attrib.* with *colour*, etc. (passing into next); hence in combs., as ***vermilion-coloured***.

1594 T. B. *La Primaud. Fr. Acad.* II. 327 The face is painted with a vermilion colour. **1655** tr. *Sorel's Com. Hist. Francion* I. iii. 56 It was of a vermilian colour like blood. **1675** TRAHERNE *Chr. Ethics* 465 Modesty..is a tincture of humility, visible in a vermilion and deeper die. **1687** MIÉGE *Gt. Fr. Dict.* II. s.v., A vermilion Tincture, *couleur vermeille*. **1697** DRYDEN *Virg., Past.* x. 40 Great Pan arrived;..His cheeks and temples of vermilion hue. **1706** PHILLIPS (ed. Kersey), *Vermillion-Tincture*, a Natural red Die upon the Face; a Cherry-red. **1728** CHAMBERS *Cycl.* s.v. *Kermes*, Unless, perhaps, it be so call'd from its beautiful Vermillion Colour. **1796** H. HUNTER tr. *St.-Pierre's Stud. Nat.* (1799) III. 381 Of a vermilion hue. **1835** *Todd's Cycl. Anat.* I. 414 If vermilion-coloured blood be subjected to the action of carbonic acid. **1856** HENSLOW *Dict. Bot. Terms* 107 *Miniatus* (of a vermillion colour).

B. *adj.* Having the colour of vermilion; of a bright red or scarlet colour.

1589 GREENE *Menaphon* (Arb.) 45 Shee..died her cheekes with such a vermillion blush. **1612** DRAYTON *Poly-olb.* x. 153 The pure vermillion blood, that issu'd from her vaines. **1639** G. DANIEL *Vervic.* 442 Let, let, that fatall Day record my Name, In bright vermilion Letters. **1675** HOBBES *Odyssey* 101 For the good ship with the vermilion cheeks The Cyclopses have not. *a* **1721** PRIOR *Vicar of Bray & Sir*

T. Moor ₱64 A lusty young Fellow with large white Teeth, and a Vermillion countenance. **1788** GIBBON *Decl. & F.* lxvii. VI. 462 The Greek monarch..with his own hand impressed three vermillion crosses on the golden bull. **1853** C. BRONTE *Villette* xvi, How warm [the room] in its amber lamp-light, and vermilion fire-flush! **1878** H. M. STANLEY *Dark Cont.* II. vi. 167 The handiwork of their artisans in copper and iron and wood, the vermilion camwood.

Comb. **1818** KEATS *Endymion* II. 111 All my clear-eyed fish, Golden, or rainbow-sided, or purplish, Vermilion-tail'd.

†**b.** Painted with vermilion; rouged. *Obs.*

1632 LITHGOW *Trav.* I. 27 These vermillion Nymphs, to let me vnderstand they trauelled with a chearefull stomacke, would oft runne races.

c. With names of colours, as ***vermilion-crimson, -red, -scarlet, -tawny***, etc.

1815 J. SMITH *Panorama Sci. & Art* II. 411 With mercury, a vermilion red; with silver, a carmine red. **1828** STARK *Elem. Nat. Hist.* I. 246 Rump and upper coverts vermilion-red. **1882** *Garden* 15 July 57/3 Well formed flowers of a brilliant vermilion-crimson. *Ibid.* 14 Oct. 347/2 The colour being a vivid vermilion-scarlet. **1887** W. PHILLIPS *Brit. Discomycetes* 85 *Peziza asperior*... Scattered, vermilion-tawny, applanate.

ver'milion, *v.* Also 7–9 vermillion, 7 virmilion. [f. the sb. Cf. OF. *vermeilloner*, later and mod.F. *vermillonner*.]

1. *trans.* To colour or paint with, or as with, vermilion; to give the colour of vermilion to (the face, etc.).

1606 WARNER *Alb. Eng.* XVI. ci. 400 Nay, why should faces faire indeed bo-peepe behinde a Fanne, Or be conceild in Satten, now Vermiliond, now drugd wanne. **1740** tr. *De Mouhy's Fort. Country-Maid* (1741) II. 85, I disapprov'd of the Red with which their Faces were vermillion'd. **1756** TOLDERVY *Hist. 2 Orphans* IV. 215 Lusty lovely health vermillions the honest cheek. **1771–2** *Ess. fr. Batchelor* (1773) I. 93 When a blush vermilions the face of a well-bred woman. **1812** G. COLMAN *Br. Grins, Lady of Wreck* II. viii, A transient hectic spread, Vermilioning health's softer red. *a* **1849** MANGAN *Sel. Poems* (1897) 105 The pall of the sunset fell, Vermilioning earth and water.

fig. **1667** DENHAM *Direct. Paint.* IV. viii, Vermilion this mans guilt, ceruse his fears. *a* **1849** MANGAN *Poems* (1859) 154 By thee [*sc.* Hope] are his visions vermillioned.

b. Const. *over* (*o'er*).

1656 S. HOLLAND *Zara* (1719) 32 That lip..was not Vermillion'd over for any to kiss. **1697** CONGREVE *Mourn. Bride* II. iii, I..chaf'd Thy temples, 'till reviving blood arose, And, like the morn, vermillion'd o'er thy face. **1769** W. JACKSON in *Monthly Rev.* XLII. 171 The choicest fruits ..vermillioned over with maiden blushes.

c. *slang.* To cover or besmear with blood.

1817 *Sporting Mag.* L. 53 Holt's face was completely vermillioned.

2. *intr.* To blush. *rare*$^{-0}$.

1719 BOYER *Dict. Royal* II. s.v.

Hence **ver'milioned** *ppl. a.*

1615 R. NICCOLS *Marriage & Wiving* vii. 21 To what end is the laying out of the embrodred haire, embared breasts, virmilioned cheekes, alluring lookes [etc.]. **1725** *Fam. Dict.* s.v. *Verjuice*, The Secret how to keep Verjuice Grapes, as vermillion'd and as fresh as if they were growing. **1773** J. ROSS *Fratricide* v. 697 (MS.), Those once-vermillion'd lips now pale with death! **1836–48** B. D. WALSH *Aristoph., Acharnians* I. i, The citizens are..running up and down, To get away from the vermilion'd rope. **1867** AUGUSTA WILSON *Vashti* xxv, Then, pink flesh, hazel eyes, vermilioned lips, and glossy hair had preferred incontestable claims to beauty.

vermilio'nette. [f. VERMILION *sb.* + -ETTE.] A substitute for or imitation of the pigment vermilion, the chief constituent of which is eosin or similar dye.

1897 *Allbutt's Syst. Med.* II. 989 Several of the bright red colours used as pigments..contain arsenic; for example cochineal red, Persian red, vermilionette, and rosaniline. **1900** *Daily News* 3 Aug. 7/5 [He] said defendants had been making vermillionette, without providing a bath.

ver'milionize, *v. rare.* [f. as prec. + -IZE.] *trans.* To vermilion. Also *fig.*

1854 *Blackw. Mag.* LXXVI. 325 The genius of Mr. Owen Jones, which, plunging into colouring matter, would vermilionise the palest face of Death. **1924** W. J. LOCKE *Coming of Amos* iv. 43 If I had found myself at five-and-twenty with fifty thousand pounds lying at the bank, verily, I should have vermilionized the cosmos.

†**'vermily.** *Obs.*$^{-1}$ [Irreg. f. *vermile* VERMEIL *sb.*] Vermilion.

1590 SPENSER *F.Q.* III. viii. 6 The same she tempred with fine Mercury, And virgin wex,..And mingled them with perfect vermily.

vermin ('vɜːmɪn), *sb.* (and *a.*) Forms: α. 4–6 **vermyn**, 4–7 **vermyne**, 6 **vermynne**, *Sc.* **verming**, 6–8 **vermine**, 6– **vermin**; 7, 9 *dial.*, **varmin**, 7, 9 *U.S.*, **virmin**. β. 5–7 **vermen**, 6 **varmen**. γ. 5 **vermayn**, 6 **vermayne**. See also VARMENT[1]. [a. AF. and OF. *vermin* masc., *vermine* fem. (mod.F. *vermine*, Pg. *vermena*, It. *vermine*) :—pop.L. **verminum*, *-ina*, f. *vermi-s* worm. The rare γ-form is prob. directly from the OF. variant *vermain* (cf. mod.Burg. *vermaigne*, Picard. *vermeinn*).]

1. *collect.* Animals of a noxious or objectionable kind: **a.** Orig. applied to reptiles, stealthy or slinking animals, and various wild beasts; now, except in *U.S.* and *Austr.* (see sense b), almost entirely restricted to those animals or birds which prey upon preserved game, crops, etc. †Also in phr. ***beast of vermin***.

α. (*a*) **13..** *K. Alis.* 6112 (Linc. Inn MS.), Euetis & snakes and paddokes brode, þat heom þouȝte mete gode, Al vermyn þey etep. *a* **1400–50** *Alexander* 5422 A vale full of vermyn & all of vile neddirs. **1406** *Patent Roll 7 Hen. IV*, II. m. 28 Feras et alia animalia vermyne nuncupata. **1439** *Rolls of Parlt.* V. 24/1 Chese and Buttur is a Merchaundise that.. wil take grete empayryng by bestes of Vermyn and Wormes. **1523** FITZHERB. *Husb.* §146 Whan they haue broughte forthe theyr byrdes, to see that they be well kepte from the gleyd, crowes, fullymartes, and other vermynne. **1576** FLEMING *Panopl. Epist.* 355 The Catt frayeth away rattes, myce, and noysome vermine. **1577** B. GOOGE *Heresbach's Husb.* 40 When the Corne is ripe..it is to be cut downe out of hande ..because that birdes and other vermine wyll devoure it. **1603** G. OWEN *Pembrokeshire* (1892) 268 The rest..are rather vermyne than beastes of game; such is the wild Catte, the Brocke and such like. *a* **1631** DRAYTON *David & Goliah* 38 His father's flock..he From ravenous vermin hourly us'd to free, His only arms his sling and sheep-hook were. **1642** D. ROGERS *Naaman* 23 We are still at Gods advantage in all, by wet, by drought, by fire, and vermine. **1684** *Contempl. St. Man* II. vi. (1699) 193 A hole..filled with Snakes, Lizards, and other poisonous Virmin. **1719** DE FOE *Crusoe* I. 120 From these three Cats, I afterwards came to be so pester'd with Cats, that I was forc'd to kill them like Vermin, or wild Beasts. **1825** HONE *Every-day Bk.* I. 991 The other dogs were good-looking savage vermin, averaging about 40 lbs. weight. **1859** DARWIN *Orig. Spec.* iii. (1860) 68 That the stock of partridges, grouse, and hares on any large estate depends chiefly on the destruction of vermin. **1900** *Westm. Gaz.* 29 Dec. 10/1 The fox..is..regarded in the Highlands by farmers and game-preservers as one of the worst species of vermin.

(*b*) **1832** KENNEDY *Swallow Barn* xvi, The finest place to catch *vermin*, as they call the three latter species of animals [racoons, opossums, and rabbits]. **1872** DE VERE *Americanisms* 564 *Varmin*, as all wild animals are called in hunter's phrase, whether they are hunted for sport, for profit, or for extermination. **1891** E. JENKS *Govt. Victoria* xxxi. 291 *note*, 'Vermin' includes kangaroos, wallabies, dingoes, stray dogs, foxes, and rabbits, and any other animal or bird proclaimed by the Governor in Council.

β. *c* **1400** *Pilgr. Sowle* (Caxton, 1483) III. x. 56 There also sawe I a wondre grete pytte ful of vermen. **1526** TINDALE *Acts* x. 12 A certayne vessell..where in wer all maner of iiij. foted beastes of the erth and vermen and wormes. —— *Rev.* vi. 8 Power was geven vnto them..to kyll with swearde, and with honger, and with deeth that cometh of vermen of the erth. **1592** WARNER *Alb. Engl.* VII. xxxvii. (1612) 178 The Weasell, Prince of Vermen.

γ. *a* **1513** FABYAN *Chron.* ccxix. 140b/1 Of the Famyne.., wonders are reported that they shuld ete all maner of Vermayne, as Cattes, rattes, dogges, & other.

b. Applied to creeping or wingless insects (and other minute animals) of a loathsome or offensive appearance or character, esp. those which infest or are parasitic on living beings and plants; also occas. applied to winged insects of a troublesome nature.

a. *c* **1340** HAMPOLE *Pr. Consc.* 916 Aftir man,..vermyn es, And aftir vermyn stynkand uglynes. *c* **1400** MAUNDEV. (Roxb.) viii. 31 In þat abbay commes neuer fleess, ne flyes, ne nan oþer swilk vermyn of corrupcioun. **1484** CAXTON *Curial* 6 We after ouermoche drynkyng of wynes and grete paynes lye doun ofte in beddes ful of vermyne. **1486** *Bk. St. Albans* c v b, A medecyne for vermyn. **1552** HULOET s.v., Vermyn, as flees, lyse, wormes, etc. **1591** NASHE *Prognostication* Wks. (Grosart) II. 165 Beggers on Sunne shine dayes..commit great murthers vpon their rebellious vermine. **1608** TOPSELL *Serpents* 103 Some of them..are transformed very strangely into a kind of vermin or wormes, who beeing couered with a hard crust or shell, lye as it were dead all the winter. **1665** SIR T. HERBERT *Trav.* (1677) 314 In Summer, their Slaves attend about them..to scare away the Gnats and such like buzzing vermine. **1671** MILTON *Samson* 574 Here rather let me drudge and earn my bread, Till vermin or the draff of servil food Consume me. **1722** DE FOE *Plague* (Rtldg.) 278 Hot Weather fills the Air with Vermine. **1748** *Anson's Voy.* I. v. 42 These operations were extremely necessary for correcting the noisome stench on board, and destroying the vermin. **1819** KEATS *Otho* IV. ii, No wrinkles where all vices nestle in Like crannied vermin. **1846** J. BAXTER *Libr. Pract. Agric.* (ed. 4) II. 374 Vermin of the Insect kind. The insects which infest plants, orchard trees, &c., are almost as numerous as the plants or trees themselves. **1875** H. C. WOOD *Therap.* (1879) 364 For this reason tobacco ought never to be employed, as it formerly was, to kill vermin on the person.

transf. and *fig.* **1592** LODGE *Euphues Shadow* (Hunter. Club) 10 Many there were that carryed vermine in theyr toongues to open secrecie. *c* **1621** DONNE *Serm.* lviii. (1640) 585 To the Consideration of those Vermin of the Soule, lesser and Unconsidered Sins.

β. **1553** EDEN *Treat. New Ind.* (Arb.) 16 When any flyes or other creping vermen are entered into the sayde riftes of theyr skinnes. **1599** DALLAM in *Early Voy. Levant* (Hakl. Soc.) 54 Thare we saw diverse sortes of varmen, which we have not the like in Inglande.

2. With *a*, *that*, *this*, etc. **a.** In generic or collective sense: A kind or class of obnoxious animals.

c **1386** CHAUCER *Clerk's T.* 1039 Youre woful moder wende stedefastly, That cruel houndes or som foul vermyne Had eten yow. *a* **1400–50** *Alexander* 3948 Quen he had voidid þis vermyn & vencust þat of ynde. **1548** COOPER *Elyot's Dict.*, *Volucra*, a vermine, whiche eateth the tender vines. **1553** EDEN *Treat. New Ind.* (Arb.) 16 Euen this greate beaste [i.e. the elephant] also..is troubled with this lyttle vermyne [i.e. flies]. **1599** DALLAM in *Early Voy. Levant* (Hakl. Soc.) 54 We..weare sodonly wonderfully tormented with a varmen that was in our pillowes, the which did bite farr worss than fleaes. **1609** HOLLAND *Amm. Marcell.* 212 This Crocodile is..a dangerous vermine used to both elements. **1634** WITHER *Embl.* 215 Though the mice a harmfull vermine be. **1725** T. THOMAS in *Portland Papers* (Hist. MSS. Comm.) VI. 110 A fox just suspended on a pole,..the shepherds..being much infested by this vermin all hereabouts. *a* **1774** TUCKER *Lt. Nat.* (1834) II. 44 Diseases..proceeding from an imperceptible vermin swarming within us.

†**b.** A single animal or insect of this kind.

c **1460** J. METHAM *Wks.* (E.E.T.S.) 62/1668 As at the sege off Thebes Ampyorax..Fyl in-to helle alle qwyk, ryght so this foule best an vermyne Myght falle thorw the erth to helle pyne. **1484** CAXTON *Fables of Æsop* v. viii, Ha cursed & euylle serpent, vermyn and fals traytour, thow hast deceyued me. **1526** TINDALE *Acts* xxviii. 5 He shuke of the vermen [L. *vipera*] into the fyre. **1590** SPENSER *World's Vanitie* 77 The subtill vermin [*sc.* a spider] creeping closely neare, Did in his drinke shed poyson priuilie. **1604** BRETON *Passionate Sheph.* Wks. (Grosart) I. 10/1 If I see the Wolfe, the Brocke, the Foxe, Or any varmin stealing downe a furrowe. **1613** CHAPMAN *Rev. Bussy D'Ambois* K j b, Storme not, nor beate your selfe thus gainst the dores, Like to a sauage vermine in a trap. **1678** BUTLER *Hud.* III. ii. 1030 'Tis true, a Scorpion's Oyl is said To cure the Wounds the Vermine made. **1809** SCOTT *Poacher* 11 Thine eye, applausive, each sly vermin sees, That baulks the snare, yet battens on the cheese.

†**c.** In *pl.* in preceding senses. *Obs.*

1470–85 MALORY *Arthur* VIII. iii. 277 Of beestes of venery and beestes of chace, and alle manere of vermayns. *Ibid.* x. lii. 500 Whiche were beestes of chace and beestes of venery, and whiche were vermyns. **1563** *Homilies* II. *Agst. Idolatry* III. Nn iij, We haue not folowed the Gentyles in makyng of images of beastes, fyshes, and vermins also. **1585** PARSONS *Chr. Exerc.* I. viii. 86 It must be cast out to serue for the food of vermines. **1601** HOLLAND *Pliny* II. 145 There doe engender in pulse, certain little venomous Vermins. **1648** HEXHAM II. s.v. *Vermeluwen*, To be full of Maggots, Vermins, or Wormes.

3. *fig.* Applied to persons of a noxious, vile, objectionable, or offensive character or type.

Freq. used as a term of abuse or opprobrium; in mod. dial. sometimes without serious implication of bad qualities.

a. In collective use.

1562 WINȜET *Wks.* (S.T.S.) II. 31 On the wthir syde, contrare cryis certane padokis, filthy verming, and fleis.., of the quhilk sort are the Pelagianis. **1577** *F. de L'isle's Legendarie* M iv b, We may then vtterly roote out this vermine (for so did the Cardinal call the Protestantes). **1586** T. B. *La Primaud. Fr. Acad.* I. (1594) 148 Dancers, minstrels, bands, and such like vermin, whereof commonly there is no want about great personages. **1610** HOLLAND *Camden's Brit.* (1637) 107 Whole swarmes of duskish vermin, to wit, a number of hideous highland Scots and Picts. **1690** T. BURNET *Theory Earth* II. 214 No knaves, cheats, hypocrites; the vermin of this earth, that swarm every where. **1710** PALMER *Proverbs* 81 He that falls once into the company of such vermin has a misfortune. **1767** [A. YOUNG] *Farmer's Lett. to People* 243 These vermin, who are generally labourers, swarm in every village round me. **1820** MACAULAY in Trevelyan *Life* (1876) I. ii. 98 A coronation all unknown To Europe's royal vermin. **1859** TENNYSON *Geraint* 217, I will avenge this insult,..And I will track this vermin to their earths. **1876** G. MEREDITH *Beauch. Career* I. ii. 29 The poacher was another kind of vermin than the stupid tenant.

b. A single person or individual of this type.

1581 J. BELL *Haddon's Answ. Osor.* 76 b, O monstruous vermine: did I ever speake or thinke any such matter? **1627** J. TAYLOR *Navy of Land Ships* C viij, As a Horse being dead in the feilds and stripd, is a banquet for Dogs,..so is a Surety to those Vermins, who..prey vpon his estate. *a* **1656** ROLLE *Abridgm. Lit. Action sur Case* (1668) 57 He is a corrupt man, he is a Vermine in the Commonwealth. **1682** DRYDEN *Medal* 31 A Vermin wriggling in th' Usurper's ear, Bart'ring his venal wit for sums of gold. **1720** *Humourist* 192 Human Society is not infested with a more dangerous Vermin than a Flatterer. **1796** SOUTHEY *Lett. fr. Spain* (1799) 373 Here I was shown a den in which a Hermit lived twelve years; a small hole for so large a vermin. **1842** J. WILSON *Chr. North* (1857) I. 137 The accursed vermin died somewhere in the Cottage. **1881** LD. SALISBURY in *Daily Tel.* 14 Nov. 2/5 The landlord is an outcast, and a vermin so horrible [etc.].

4. ***to stand true vermin***, to show pluck and persistency. *rare*$^{-1}$.

1834 COL. HAWKER *Diary* (1893) II. 67 My horse shied.. and down we both came... But I stood true vermin, and tried the islands afterwards for snipe.

5. *attrib.* and *Comb.* **a.** Simple attrib., as ***vermin head, -trap***, etc. **b.** Objective and obj. genitive, as ***vermin-catcher, -destroyer, -killer***; ***vermin-destroying, -killing***; ***vermin-proof*** adj. **c.** Instrumental or similative, as ***vermin-covered, -eaten, -footed, -haunted, -ridden, -tenanted*** adjs.; ***vermin-like*** adj.; also **vermin puddle** (see quot.).

It is not clear whether *wermine brome*, glossing L. *murica* in Wr.-Wülcker 644, is an attrib. use of this word.

1811 *Sporting Mag.* XXXVIII. 221 Were they associated as a body of *vermin-catchers? *Ibid.* 222 They were a club of *vermin-destroyers. ? **188.** *Dogs* (Brit. Stand. Handbks.) iv. 18 Any of the *vermin-destroying powders. **1837** DICKENS *Let.* 7 Sept. (1965) I. 304 If the *Pickwick* has been the means of putting a few shillings in the *vermin-eaten pockets of so miserable a creature, [etc.]. **1931** R. CAMPBELL *Georgiad* i. 16 So many poets..sigh to share their [*sc.* gypsies'] vermin-eaten ways. **1865** E. BURRITT *Walk Land's End* 182 There were scarcely any daisies or buttercups, or even the *vermin-footed charlock. **1831** GEN. P. THOMPSON *Exerc.* (1842) I. 417 To throw it off like a *vermin-haunted garment. **1861** NEALE *Notes Dalmatia* 97 A tolerable inn, not more dirty nor vermin-haunted than usual. **1799** *Addingham* (Cumberld.) *Par. Bk.* (MS.), 8 *Vermin Heads, 2 : 8. **1680** W. W. (*title*), The *Vermin Killer, being a very necessary Family-Book, containing Exact Rules and Directions for the Artificial Killing and Destroying of all manner of Vermin, etc. **1772** T. SIMPSON (*title*), The Complete Vermin-killer. **1889** *Daily News* 21 June 7/1 Two packets of vermin killer containing about six grains of strychnine. **1893** W. H. HUDSON *Idle Days Patagonia* v. 59 The common dog of the country is..a good watch-dog and vermin-killer. **1772** *Ann. Reg.* I. 129 He acquired 2000*l*. by *vermin-killing. **1829** Scott *Guy M.* Note B, The race of Pepper and Mustard are in the highest estimation at this day, not only for vermin-killing, but for intelligence and fidelity. **1863** Atkinson *Stanton Grange* (1864) 67 Vermin-killing was well carried out there. **1685** *Roxb. Ballads* (1884) V. 214 His..disagreeable *Vermin-like Face. **1914** Joyce *Dubliners* 86 A horde of grimy children populated the street... He picked his way deftly through all that minute vermin-like life. **1937** *Discovery* Dec. 388/1 *Vermin-, rot- and fire-proof. **1982** M. Young *Elmhirsts of Dartington* iv. 81 A vermin-proof rice store. **1850** Ogilvie, **Vermin Puddle*, puddle formed of stiff clay and small stones or gravel beaten together until it forms a mass like pudding stone. It is used in the embankments of reservoirs, to prevent..the inroads of water rats and other vermin. **1861** Neale *Notes Dalmatia* 104 The *vermin-tenanted houses are washed by the pure green waves of the lovely bay. **1664** Evelyn *Kal. Hort.* 61 February... Continue *Vermine Trapps, &c. **1862** *Catal. Internat. Exhib., Brit.* II. No. 6133, Every description of wild beast, game, and vermin traps. **1859** Tennyson *Elaine* 139 The *vermin voices here May buzz so loud—we scorn them, but they sting.

†**6.** As *adj.* Verminous. *Obs.*⁻¹

1602 *2nd Pt. Return fr. Parnass.* I. iv. 443 See how a little vermine pouerty altereth a whole milkie disposition.

†**'vermin**, *v. Obs.*⁻¹ [f. the sb.] *trans.* To clear of vermin.

1573-80 Tusser *Husb.* (1878) 72 Get warrener bound to vermin thy ground.

†**vermi'naille.** *Obs.*⁻¹ [f. vermin *sb.*, after *canaille*, etc.] = vermin *sb.* 3 a.

1600 O. E. (M. Sutcliffe) *Repl. Libel* I. v. 129 The Parliament of Paris..did banish the whole society or rather verminaille of Jesuites out of France.

verminate ('vɜːmɪneɪt), *v. rare.* [f. L. *vermināt-* ppl. stem of *vermināre* to have worms or griping pains, f. *vermis* worm. Cf. L. *vermina* griping pains caused by worms, stomach-ache.]

1. *intr.* To breed or produce parasitic vermin.

1693 Sir T. P. Blount *Nat. Hist.* 263 He having taken extraordinary care and pains to observe, that always on the Flesh, before it did Verminate, there sate Flies of the self same kind with those that were afterwards produc'd thence. **1721** Bailey, *To Verminate*, to breed Worms. **1912** D. Crawford *Thinking Black* xxii. 441 Here, then, we see them [*sc.* people] crowding and verminating in their filth.

†**2.** *Path.* (See quot.) *Obs.*⁻⁰

1721 Bailey, *To Verminate* (among Physicians), to have a griping or wringing in the Belly; to..void Worms.

Hence **'verminating** *vbl. sb.* (used *attrib.*) and *ppl. a.*

1720 S. Parker *Bibliotheca Biblia* I. 152 The Seed of the Serpent, and its Verminating Principle. **1856** Boker *Leonor de Guzman* I. i, Out, thou flea-bitten, verminating rogue! **1912** D. Crawford *Thinking Black* vi. 97 Their average beehive hut is a verminating hole, a den of disease.

vermination (vɜːmɪ'neɪʃən). [ad. L. *verminātiōn-*, *verminātio*, n. of action f. *vermināre*: see prec. Cf. obs. F. *vermination.*]

†**1.** The fact or condition of being gnawed by worms; vermiculation. *Obs. rare.*

1628 Donne *Serm.* liv. (1640) 542 Against this vermination, (as the originall denotes) against this gnawing of the worme, that may bore through and sink the strongest vessell that sailes in the sea of this world, there is no other varnish.

2. The breeding, growth, or production of vermin, esp. parasitic vermin. Also *fig.* ? *Obs.*

1628 Feltham *Resolves* II. lxxxiv. 241 A Mouth, nasty with offensive fumes, till it sicken the Braine with giddy verminations. **1665** Needham *Med. Medicinæ* 203 This.. may serve to give some light, how much Diseases are altered from their old state in reference to Vermination. **1699** R. Burthogge *Soul of World* 37 The Vermination in Human (as well as other Animal) Bodies, of which there are innumerable Instances in Medical Writers. **1713** Derham *Phys.-Theol.* VIII. vi. 414 Seigneur Redi..tryed more Experiments relating to the Vermination of Serpents, Flesh, Fish, putrified Vegetables,..than any one hath done since.

†**3.** (See quot.) *Obs.*⁻⁰

1656 Blount *Glossogr.* (copying Cooper), *Vermination*,.. a disease with worms, properly in Cattle, a vehement ache by the wringing of the Guts, as if they were gnawn with worms.

4. The fact of being infested with parasitic vermin; esp. *Med.*, the morbid condition due to this.

1818-20 E. Thompson *Cullen's Nosol. Method.* (ed. 3) 318, 76 *Parasitismus*... Vermination. **1822-7** Good *Study Med.* (1829) V. 656 Cutaneous Vermination. *Ibid.* 657 Generally speaking, vermination is a proof of weakness, whether in animals or in plants. **1836** J. M. Gully *Magendie's Formul.* (ed. 2) 91 His success was particularly great in the vermination of children.

'vermine, *a. Zool. rare.* [ad. mod.L. *vermineus.*] = vermineous *a.*

1839-47 *Todd's Cycl. Anat.* III. 237 The smaller ones with a long slender body, and short extremities, as the Weasel or Vermine tribe. *Ibid.*, The canine and vermine genera.

'vermined, *ppl. a.* [f. vermin *sb.*] Infested with vermin.

1852 *Meanderings of Mem.* I. 210 Yon vermined Sarcophage. **1859** Gen. P. Thompson *Audi Alt.* II. lxxxvi. 55 Why not..bring back the Stuarts, or install Saint Thomas of the vermin'd shirt at Canterbury?

†**ver'mineous,** *a. Zool. Obs.*⁻¹ [f. mod.L. *vermine-us* (Ray): see -eous.] Belonging to the animals classed as vermin.

1693 *Phil. Trans.* XVII. 851 The Wolf, Fox, Badger,.. which from their long slender Bodies, like to the Weasel, we call the Vermineous or Weezel-kind.

'verminer. *rare.* Also 7 **varminer.** [f. vermin *sb.* + -er¹.] A destroyer of vermin.

1615 Markham *Country Contentm.* I. i. 5 The grissell.. shag-haird [hounds] are the best varminers, and therefore are chosen to hunt the Fox, Badger, or any other hot sent. **1848** Ainsworth *Lancs. Witches* III. i. (1878) 421 The lurchers, and, lastly, the verminers, or, as we should call them, the terriers.

†**ver'minian,** *a. Obs.*⁻¹ [f. vermin *sb.* + -ian.] Consisting or composed of vermin.

1640 Balfour in Maidment *Scottish Ball.* (1868) I. 334 God, Whose heavie hand with his verminian hoast Hath quell'd our courage and laid all our boast.

verminicide (və'mɪnɪsaɪd). [f. vermin *sb.* + -cide¹.] A preparation for killing vermin.

1925 *Blackw. Mag.* Sept. 313/2 During the summer verminicide became a necessary item in the 'bazar'. **1965** N. H. Johnson *Compl. Bk. Dogs* (1968) xii. 387 Detergents and verminicides, as well as sleeping and reducing pills, are equally dangerous.

vermi'niferous, *a. rare.* [f. vermin *sb.* + -(i)ferous.] Breeding or producing vermin. Also *fig.*

1895 Farrar in *Clarion* 9 Nov. 1/2 Places horrible to live in,..foul with..gin, and verminiferous dirt. **1898** —— *One Flock, Many Folds* 53, I usually commit these verminiferous fragments [R.C. newspaper cuttings] to the purging flame unread.

†**'verminly,** *a. Obs. rare.* [f. as prec. + -ly¹.] Of the nature of vermin; like (that of) vermin.

1653 Gauden *Hierasp.* Pref. 37 A verminly generation (ever destroyed, yet ever breeding) who owe their best education to their bellies. *Ibid.* 379 They have nothing in them but a verminly nimbleness and subtlety.

vermi'nology. *rare*⁻¹. [f. as prec. + -ology.] The science of vermin.

1830 Kitto in Eadie *Life* vi. (1857) 184 On removing some clothes..one day, I found one [scorpion],..and not being sufficiently acquainted with verminology to recognise it, I felt no alarm.

†**vermi'nose,** *a. Obs.*⁻¹ [ad. L. *verminōs-us*: see next and -ose.] = verminous *a.* 4.

1747 tr. *Astruc's Fevers* 9 In like manner the verminose fevers are so called from their cause, viz. worms.

verminous ('vɜːmɪnəs), *a.* [f. vermin *sb.* + -ous, or ad. L. *verminōs-us* (whence OF. *verminous, vermenous, -eux*, etc., = mod.F. *vermineux, -euse*, It., Sp., Pg. *verminoso*, Prov. *vermenos*):—*vermis* worm.]

1. Of the nature of, consisting of, vermin; like or resembling vermin in character; noxious, objectionable, offensive: **a.** Of animals or persons.

1621-3 Middleton & Rowley *Changeling* III. iv, Do you place me in the rank of verminous fellows, To destroy things for wages? **1624** —— *Game at Chess* IV. iv, Like that verminous labourer [*sc.* the mole], which thou imitat'st In hills of pride and malice. **1691** Ray *Coll. Words* (ed. 2) 128 A Fowmart, a Polecat, is a noted Beast of this verminous kind. **1795-6** Wordsw. *Borderers* II. 587 That soft class of devotees who..spare The verminous brood, and cherish what they spare While feeding on their bodies. **1830** Southey *Lett.* (1856) IV. 177 Both in Russia and Poland I believe they [i.e. Jews] are a verminous population, preying upon others. **1887** Swinburne *Stud. Prose & Poetry* (1894) 140 He has exactly as much claim to a place beside Dante as any..other murderous and verminous muckworm.

b. Of things.

c **1616** Chapman *Batrachom.* Ded., If yet the vile soul of the verminous time Love more the sale-muse and the squirrels chime. **1846** Landor *Imag. Conv.* Wks. I. 201/2 The smoky, verminous, unconcocted doctrine of passive obedience. **1884** Browning *Ferishtah, Sun* 14 Fancies verminous Breed in the clots there.

2. Infested with, full of, vermin, esp. parasitic vermin; foul or offensive on this account.

1632 Brome *Crt. Beggar* I. i, Note the necessity, that they [perruques] be well made Of..No verminous or sluttish locks or combings, But [etc.]. **1641** Milton *Prel. Episc.* 11 Searching among the verminous and polluted rags dropt overworn from the toyling shoulders of Time. *a* **1691** Boyle *Hist. Air* (1692) 230 He..found that divers drugs, salves, and..especially ointments, were verminous. **1774** Goldsm. *Nat. Hist.* (1862) I. xix. 110 In these tropical climates also, ..drugs and plasters lose their virtue, and become verminous. **1819** *Metropolis* III. 128 The lively companions of a verminous bed. **1865** *Pall Mall G.* No. 211. 1/2 A verminous, over-crowded vagrant ward. **1899** *Allbutt's Syst. Med.* VIII. 866 In 'verminous persons' the hair is sometimes matted together by pus, nits, scales and scabs.

transf. **1861** Dickens *Tom Tiddler's Ground* i, How long he had held verminous occupation of his blanket and skewer.

3. Tending to breed vermin. *rare*⁻¹.

1666 G. Harvey *Morb. Angl.* (1672) 39 A wasting of their [*sc.* children's] flesh..must depend upon some obstruction of the Entrails, or Verminous disposition of body.

4. a. Of diseases, or morbid conditions, etc.: Caused by, due to, characterized by the presence of, parasitic vermin or intestinal worms.

1666 G. Harvey *Morb. Angl.* (1672) 35 Of a Verminous Consumption. **1684** tr. *Bonet's Merc. Compit.* x. 366/2 Their hypothesis is sufficiently known, concerning verminous putrefaction. **1733** tr. *Bellosté's Hosp. Surg.* II. 71 Pestilence, Small-pox and all Verminous diseases. **1748** *Phil. Trans.* L. 837 The lead..might, by its weight, assist in removing the verminous filth, especially as the bowels were made slippery by the oil. **1756** P. Browne *Jamaica* 25 You may frequently observe..ladies poisoned with bark in verminous inflammations. **1832** Barker *Lempriere's Class. Dict.* (ed. 2) s.v. *Æthiopia*, Almost all these people die of verminous diseases produced by this food. **1861** Hulme tr. *Moquin-Tandon* II. vii. 332 Some families appear to be more predisposed to verminous affections than others. **1897** *Allbutt's Syst. Med.* II. 1033 There have been many instances of verminous abscess recorded.

b. Of persons: Subject to vermin or intestinal worms.

1860 *Encycl. Brit.* (ed. 8) XXI. 974/2 Females may be more verminous than males.

c. ***verminous bronchitis*** = hoose, hooze *sb.*

1925 [see parasitic *a.* 5]. **1970** W. H. Parker *Health & Dis. in Farm Animals* xx. 268 This is the first sign of the disease known as Husk, or Verminous Bronchitis.

Hence **'verminously** *adv.*, **'verminousness.**

1727 Bailey (vol. II), *Verminousness*, Fulness of Worms, Worm-eatenness. **1860** Worcester (citing *Ec. Rev.*), Verminously. **1891** *Cent. Dict.* s.v., Verminously unclean.

†**ver'minulous,** *a. Obs.*⁻¹ [f. vermin *sb.*] Made by vermin.

1665-6 *Phil. Trans.* I. 205 In the shaking he saw all the Communications of these little Verminulous holes, like to the hole of the Worms in Wood.

'verminy, *a. rare.* [f. vermin *sb.* + -y.] Infested with vermin; verminous.

1859 *All Year Round* No. 36. 219, I avoid his verminy robes and his flowing rags.

vermion, -eon, obs. varr. vermilion *sb.*

Cf. med.L. *vermeum*, var. of *vermellum*, etc.

1399 *Mem. Ripon* (Surtees) III. 129 In j lib. de vermion emp. pro prædicto vale [= veil], 22*d*. *a* **1400-50** *Alexander* 3945 Þan come a fliȝtir in of fowls as fast as it dawid, To vise on as vowtres, as vermeon hewid. **14..** *MS. Harl.* 2257, *Miniographus*, a writer with vermion. *Minium est genus coloris rubei*,..*anglice* vermion.

ver'miparous, *a. rare.* [f. vermi- + -parous. Cf. Sp. and Pg. *vermiparo.*]

1. Producing young, or produced as young, in the form of small worms or maggots.

1646 Sir T. Browne *Pseud. Ep.* 135 We deny not that many animals are vermiparous, begetting themselves at a distance. *Ibid.* 297 In creatures oviparous, as birds and fishes; in vermiparous, as Flies, Locusts, and Gnats; in animals also viviparous, as Swine and Conies. **1650** *Ibid.* (ed. 2) v. v. 203 The same..may be also true in some verminparous exclusions. **1765** *Treatise on Dom. Pigeons* 14 All animals are distinguished into three sorts: oviparous,.. viviparous,..and vermiparous, or such as are formed from a worm. **1910** D'A. W. Thompson tr. *Aristotle's Hist. Anim.* 538 In oviparous and vermiparous creatures..the female is larger than the male.

2. Producing verminous parasites.

1860 *Encycl. Brit.* (ed. 8) XXI. 974/2 Very few avertebrated animals are vermiparous, while there is probably no species of vertebrate that is exempted from parasites.

Hence †**ver'miparousness**, 'worm-breeding quality' (Bailey, 1727, vol. II). *Obs.*⁻⁰

‖**vermis** ('vɜːmɪs). *Anat.* [L. *vermis* worm.] The vermiform process of the cerebellum.

1890 *Cent. Dict.*, *Postvermis*, the vermis inferior of the cerebellum. *Ibid.*, *Prevermis*, the anterior and prominent part of the vermis of the cerebellum. **1899** *Allbutt's Syst. Med.* VII. 365 In one [case of cerebellar atrophy]..the vermis was less affected by atrophy than the hemispheres.

vermivorous (və'mɪvərəs), *a.* [f. mod.L. *vermivor-us* worm-eating + -ous. Cf. F. *vermivore*, Sp. and Pg. *vermivoro.*] Feeding on worms, grubs, or insect vermin; said esp. of certain birds.

1704 J. Harris *Lex. Techn.* I, *Vermivorous*, are such Animals, as Feed upon Worms. **1828-32** Webster s.v., Vermivorous birds are very useful to the farmer. **1861** H. Macmillan *Footnotes fr. Page Nat.* 172 Guano, the product of those vermivorous shore-birds which inhabit the desolate islands of the South Seas. **1870** Gillmore tr. *Figuier's Rept. & Birds* 344 They [*sc.* the Pressirostres] are mostly vermivorous; some, however, are granivorous or herbivorous.

Hence **ver'mivorousness**, 'a worm-devouring nature' (Bailey, 1730).

Vermont (vɜː'mɒnt). The name of one of the north-eastern states of the United States of America, used *attrib.* in ***Vermont merino***, a sheep belonging to a breed developed there.

1891 R. Wallace *Rural Econ. Austral. & N.Z.* xxvii. 359 The Vermont Merino..is one of the most perfect as regards good covering and density of fleece. **1957** *New Biol.* XXII. 92 Vermont merinos were imported into Australia from the United States in the 1880s. These sheep had wrinkly skins, and many that crossed the Pacific by 1890 presented a concertina-like appearance.

†**Vermonteer.** *Obs.* [f. prec. + -eer.] = next.

1778 *15th Rep. R. Comm. Hist. MSS.* App. 396 in *Parl. Papers 1897* (C. 8551) LI. 1 We may hence learn that we are not to flatter ourselves with the hope of winning over the Vermonteers to the Crown side. **1801** *Hist. Rev. &*

Directory N. Amer. II. 346 Great numbers of the Vermonteers bring their produce here.

Vermonter (vɜːˈmɒntə(r)). [f. as prec. + -ER[1].] A native or inhabitant of the State of Vermont.

1787 A. HAMILTON *Works* (1886) VII. 6 The peace found the Vermonters in a state of actual independence. **1851** H. MELVILLE *Moby Dick* I. vi. 51 There weekly arrive in this town [*sc.* New Bedford] scores of green Vermonters. **1961** W. VAUGHAN-THOMAS *Anzio* v. 67 Its tough, stocky commander, General Ernie Harmon, was a Vermonter. **1979** *United States 1980/81* (Penguin Travel Guides) 662 For Vermonters maple sugaring time is a celebration of spring. **1984** *Sci. Amer.* May 22/3 [So] wrote Vermonter Zerah Colburn in 1833.

Vermontese (vɜːmɒnˈtiːz), *sb.* and *a.* Also †Vermonteze. [f. as prec. + -ESE.] **A.** *sb.* = prec. Also *collect.* **B.** *adj.* Of or belonging to Vermont.

1783 *Polite Traveller* 100 The persons, manners, and customs, of the Vermontese, are nearly the same with those provinces from whom they emigrated. **1798** I. ALLEN *Nat. & Pol. Hist. Vermont* 280 Our Vermontese house-wives are not a little vain of their knowledge in making home-made wines. **1804** T. G. FESSENDEN *Orig. Poems* 123 Hamilton was an impudent Vermonteze. **1845** *Knickerbocker* XXVI. 583 We should be pleased to hear these lines applauded by the Vermontese. **1851** *San Francisco Picayune* 20 Sept. 2/4 On a late visit to an ancient Vermontese lady, he was asked, 'Did you see Professor Webster hung?'

Vermoral (ˈvɜːmɒrəl). Also -el. [Said to be the name of V. *Vermorel*, French manufacturer.] A type of sprayer used in the war of 1914–18 to produce a fine spray of water that would absorb residual poison gas.

1916 'H. RAE' *Maple Leaves* 264 'A vermoral sprayer is a new form of frightfulness for spraying the front-line trench.' 'What with? Liquid fire?'.. 'No, liquid water.' 'For the flies?' 'No, for the gas.' **1929** R. GRAVES *Good-Bye to all That* xv. 204 Vermorel-sprayers had cleared out most of the gas, but we still had to wear our masks. **1930** BLUNDEN *De Bello Germanico* iii. 30 A 'Vermoral Sprayer' for nullifying gas.

vermouth (ˈvɜːmuːt, ˈvɜːmuːθ, ˈvɜːməθ). Also vermuth. [a. F. *vermout* (vɛrmut), ad. G. *wermuth* wormwood, WERMOD.] **a.** An alcoholic cordial or liqueur consisting of white wine flavoured with wormwood or other aromatic herbs and taken in order to stimulate the appetite. Also *attrib.*

1806 J. PINKERTON *Recollect. Paris* II. xv. 208 A decanter of Jamaica rum, Wormwood wine, or that of Vermouth. **1837** LYTTON *E. Maltrav.* VII. i, Thinking that you soften the hearts of your friends by soups *à la bisque*, and *Vermuth* wine at a guinea a bottle! **1870** *Pall Mall G.* 5 Nov. 12 Absinthe and vermouth began to be sold in them. **1884** J. COLBORNE *Hicks Pasha* 83 There is one Italian firm importing good vermouth.

b. A glass or drink of this.

1899 J. CONRAD in *Blackw. Mag.* Feb. 201/1 As we sat over our vermuths he glorified the Company's business. **1903** 'MARJORIBANKS' *Fluff-Hunters* 151 He felt discomfited, and ordered a Vermouth to gain time for reflection.

vermulon, -ylone, -yl(y)oun, etc., obs. ff. VERMILION.

vern, southern dial. var. FERN *sb.*[1]

vernaccia (vəˈnætʃə). [It.: see VERNAGE.] A wine (usu. white) produced in the San Gimignano area of Italy and in Sardinia; also, the grape from which it is made.

1824 A. HENDERSON *Hist. Anc. & Mod. Wines* II. vi. 237 Another source of error arises from the circumstance of several of the best Tuscan wines receiving their appellations from the grapes which yield them, as, for example,.. the *Vernaccia*, &c.; and as these names are not confined to Tuscany, but are common to the growths of other parts of Italy, the difficulty of distinguishing them is.. further increased. **1833** C. REDDING *Hist. Mod. Wines* ix. 241 Their sweet wines the Italians call *Abbocati*... Of the former kind are the Moscatello, Aleatico, and Vernaccia, a white wine, of considerable note among the writers of Italy. **1929** P. M. SHAND *Bk. of Other Wines* 85 The vines grown are—*red*: Chiavennasca.., Vernaccia, [etc.]. **1966** C. RAY *Wines of Italy* ix. 95 Vernaccia di Serrapetrona, sweetish sparkling red wine made from the Vernaccia Rossa grape, and interesting to those who are interested in sparkling sweet red wines. **1973** *Times* 31 Jan. (Mediterranean Suppl.) p. ii/4 Pecorino sheep cheese and vernaccia wine have enjoyed steady, if limited, markets outside the island. **1975** *Times* 14 Apr. (Ital. Wines Suppl.) p. iii/4 A.. dry golden vernaccia, from.. San Gimignano (not to be confused with that potent vernaccia in Sardinia).. is dry enough to accompany fish.

vernacle, var. VERNICLE.

†**vernacly,** *adv. Obs.*$^{-1}$ [Irreg. f. L. *vernāculus*: see below.] = VERNACULARLY *adv.*

1673 HICKERINGILL *Greg. F. Greyb.* 284 By Hebrew Jews you mean Jews that vernacly speak Hebrew.

vernacul, obs. f. VERNICLE.

vernacular (vəˈnækjʊlə(r)), *a.* and *sb.* Also 7 vernaculer. [f. L. *vernācul-us* domestic, native, indigenous (hence It. *vernacolo*, Pg. *vernaculo*), f. *verna* a home-born slave, a native.

The Latin adj. occurs in a large variety of applications; the restricted use common in English is represented by *vernacula vocabula* in Varro.]

A. *adj.* **1.** That writes, uses, or speaks the native or indigenous language of a country or district.

1601 BP. W. BARLOW *Defence* 2 A vernaculer pen-man.. hauing translated them into English. **1715** M. DAVIES *Athen. Brit.* I. 77 The Office of the Virgin Mary.. is Translated also in most Languages for the Use of the Vernacular Romanists. **1716** *Ibid.* III. 38 The Learned vernacular Editor of Hippocrates's Works in French, Mr. Dacier. **1819** W. TAYLOR in *Monthly Mag.* XLVII. 30 The vernacular public remained unmoved, and gazed at the labours of authorship, as Londoners at the opera. **1869** FREEMAN *Norm. Conq.* (1875) III. xii. 145 The vernacular poet more kindly helps us to the real names.

2. a. Of a language or dialect: That is naturally spoken by the people of a particular country or district; native, indigenous.

Usu. applied to the native speech of a populace, in contrast to another or others acquired for commercial, social, or educative purposes; now freq. employed with reference to that of the working classes or the peasantry.

c **1645** HOWELL *Lett.* II. lvi. 78 The Welsh.. is one of the fourteen vernacular and independent tongues of Europ. **1697** BENTLEY *Phalaris* (1699) 316 Being Dorians born, [they] repudiated their vernacular Idiom for that of the Athenians. **1715** M. DAVIES *Athen. Brit.* I. Pref. 35 They don't understand their Breviaries and Mass-Books, not.. when translated and expounded in their respective vernacular Tongues. **1832** G. DOWNES *Cont. Countries* I. 197 The congregation here being chiefly peasants, and artisans, a sermon was delivered in the vernacular dialect. **1858** GLADSTONE *Homer* II. ii. 50 When the Chaldee tongue became the vernacular, and the old Hebrew disappeared from common use. **1874** H. R. REYNOLDS *John Bapt.* v. §3. 338 There were 'voices'.. which expressed in some vernacular idiom of Hebrew or Greek the thoughts of the Almighty.

transf. **1778** WARTON *Hist. Eng. Poetry* II. 50 They much improved the vernacular style by the use of this exotic phraseology. **1785** *European Mag.* VIII. 467 Several passages are modulations on the vernacular airs of Otaheite. **1850** *Ecclesiologist* XI. 176 Even Rome, then, cannot consistently blame words to the vernacular Gregorian melodies.

b. In predicative use. Also with preps.

1808 SYD. SMITH *Wks.* (1859) I. 103/2 The Scriptures translated into the Tamulic language, which is vernacular in the southern parts of the peninsula. **1835** MACAULAY in Trevelyan *Compet. Wallah* (1866) 321 The intellectual improvement of those classes.. can at present be effected only by means of some language not vernacular amongst them. **1856** MRS. STOWE *Dred* II. xxxii. 323 He commenced a speech in that peculiar slang dialect which was vernacular with them. **1870** ANDERSON *Missions Amer. Bd.* III. iv. 52 The Arab-speaking race.. must receive the gospel mainly from those to whom the language is vernacular.

c. Coupled with the name of the language.

1775 WARTON *Hist. Eng. Poetry* (1870) 61 The vernacular English, as I have.. remarked, was rough and unpolished. **1840** BARHAM *Ingol. Leg.* Ser. II. *Lay St. Aloys*, The 'Requiem' was sung; Not vernacular French, but a classical tongue. **1864** DASENT *Jest & Earnest* (1873) II. 10 The vernacular Anglo-Saxon before the Conquest was undergoing that change which all languages suffer. **1883** FROUDE in *Contemp. Rev.* XLIV. 18 He [Luther] began to translate the Bible into clear vernacular German.

3. a. Of literary works, etc.: Written or spoken in, translated into, the native language of a particular country or people.

1661 GLANVILL *Van. Dogm.* 156 Though, in Greek or Latine, they amuse us, yet a vernacular translation unmasks them. **1716** M. DAVIES *Athen. Brit.* III. 20 Dr. Harvey's Family-Physician, and most of Will. Salmon's Books, with other such like Vernacular Pharmacy. **1788** WARBURTON *Tracts* (1789) 170 Long vernacular Sermons from Dr. Parr. **1841** D'ISRAELI *Amen. Lit.* Pref. (1859) p. iii, A history of our vernacular literature has occupied my studies for many years. **1868** J. H. BLUNT *Ref. Ch. Eng.* I. 495 Vernacular prayer-books had, indeed, been long known in England. **1874** GREEN *Short Hist.* i. §5. (1876) 49 The Chronicle remains the first vernacular history of any Teutonic people.

b. Performed in the native language.

1874 A. SOMERVILLE *Lect. Missions* xiii. 243 A paper which he read on Vernacular Preaching at the Ootacamund Missionary Conference.

4. a. Of words, etc.: Of or pertaining to, forming part of, the native language.

1716 M. DAVIES *Athen. Brit.* II. 174 This Ralph is call'd also Roger, the Latin name, Ranulphus, being possibly capable of both those Vernacular Appropriations. **1728** POPE *Dunc.* I. *Notes*, Which being a French and foreign termination, is no way proper to a word entirely English and vernacular. **1788** V. KNOX *Winter Even.* xxii. (1790) I. 193 Brown.. preferred polysyllabic expressions derived from the language of ancient Rome, to his vernacular vocabulary. **1816** SCOTT *Old Mort.* Peroration, O, ignorance! as if the vernacular article of our mother English were capable of declension! **1848** GALLENGA *Italy* I. ii. 146 Low-born vernacular idioms were handed down to posterity as the poet's creation. **1864** BRYCE *Holy Rom. Emp.* xv. (1875) 257 Whose official style of Augustus, as well as the vernacular name of 'Kaiser' [etc.].

b. Native or natural *to* a particular language.

1844 *Proc. Philol. Soc.* I. 176 The finding an isolated term in an Anglo-Saxon or German vocabulary by no means proves it to be vernacular to that language.

5. Connected or concerned with the native language.

1845 STOCQUELER *Handbk. Brit. India* (1854) 234 The southern side of the building is appropriated to the vernacular department, and the northern to the English. **1883** R. B. SMITH *Life Ld. Lawrence* II. 535 Efforts were made to extend vernacular education.

6. Of arts, or features of these: Native or peculiar to a particular country or locality. *spec.* in ***vernacular architecture***, architecture concerned with ordinary domestic and functional buildings rather than the essentially monumental.

1857 G. G. SCOTT *Remarks Secular & Domestic Archit.* p. ix, I want to call attention to the meanness of our vernacular architecture, and to the very partial success which has hitherto attended the attempts at its improvement. *Ibid.* 6 Look at the vernacular cottage-building of the day. *a* **1878** —— *Lect. Archit.* (1879) II. 315 The revived knowledge of the architecture of Greece rudely disturbed the vernacular style derived from Rome. **1893** *Harper's Weekly* 21 Oct. 1011/2 The theatre is a big, rather bare room, apparently of vernacular Javanese construction. **1939** *Country Life* 11 Feb. 154/2 It is as delightful an example as one could find of Georgian vernacular architecture. **1976** [see SPINNING *vbl. sb.* 7c]. **1977** *Dædalus* Summer 3 The studies of so-called vernacular architecture (like barns) no longer seem eccentric in an atmosphere in which architecture can be defined not in terms of monuments but as any changes at all that man makes in his environment.

†**7.** Of diseases: Characteristic of, occurring in, a particular country or district; endemic. *Obs.*

1666 G. HARVEY *Morb. Angl.* i. (1672) 2 Which instances do evidently bring a Consumption under the notion of a Pandemick, or Endemick, or rather a Vernacular Disease to England. **1728** CHAMBERS *Cycl.* s.v., Diseases which reign most in any particular Nation, Province, or District, are called Vernacular Diseases.

8. Of a slave: That is born on his master's estate; home-born. *rare*$^{-1}$.

1804 W. TAYLOR in *Ann. Rev.* II. 326 A disposition to use kindly, and to emancipate frequently, the vernacular slave.

9. Personal, private.

1840 G. S. FABER *Regen.* 38, I was favouring my evil propensities, as if they were specially my own vernacular property.

B. *sb.* **1. a.** The native speech or language of a particular country or district (see A. 2); also, the informal, colloquial, or distinctive speech of a people or a group. Cf. sense 1 b below.

a **1706** EVELYN *Hist. Relig.* (1850) I. 427 It is written in the Chaldaeo-Syriac, which was.. the vernacular of our Lord. **1840** BARHAM *Ingol. Leg.* Pref., Mr. Maguire,.. in his account of the late Coronation, retains his own rich vernacular. **1864** BURTON *Scot Abr.* II. i. 94 Even within the native stronghold of the Dutch vernacular. **1874** SAYCE *Compar. Philol.* v. 179 A child can learn as readily the vernacular of Canton as the language of London. **1925** F. N. SCOTT in *McNaught's Monthly Mag.* May 144 (*heading*) English and American vernacular. **1930** G. B. SHAW *Admirable Bashville* 89 With the advent of compulsory education sixty years ago,.. newspapers and plays alike soon came to be written by illiterate masters of the vernacular. **1984** *Gainesville* (Florida) *Sun* 28 Mar. 7B/2 Observe feminist vernacular: Call it a 'personhole cover'.

transf. **1807** W. TAYLOR in *Ann. Rev.* V. 575 By neglecting the vernacular in idea, he has missed in part the advantage of home praise and hereditary sympathy.

b. Freq. in phr. ***in the vernacular***. Cf. sense 1 a above.

1815 J. C. HOBHOUSE *Substance Lett.* (1816) I. 176 The court confessor in his sermon at St. Denis.. took the opportunity of what is called in the vernacular preaching *at* the Duke of Orleans. **1856** DASENT *Jest & Earnest* (1873) I. 337 The performance of the services of religion in Latin, and no longer as of old in the vernacular. **1889** JESSOPP *Coming of Friars* i. 37 Of the five.. no one of them was qualified as yet to preach in the vernacular. **1975** L. GILLEN *Return to Deepwater* iv. 62 In the vernacular,.. I couldn't care less what you do.

c. Without article. (Cf. next.)

1857 HUGHES *Tom Brown* I. i, Repeating in true sing-song vernacular the legend of St. George and his fight. **1882** B. D. W. RAMSAY *Recoll. Mil. Serv.* I. i. 25 The fair songstress opened upon me such a volley of choice Tuscan vernacular, that I fairly fled.

2. With *a* and pl. A native or indigenous language.

1715 M. DAVIES *Athen. Brit.* I. 325 Charles the Fifth, King of France, order'd the Bible to be translated.. in the Picardian and Norman Vernaculars. *a* **1734** NORTH *Lives* (1826) III. 322 Latin, and the vernaculars westward,.. carry nearly the same idiom. **1850** S. DOBELL *Roman* vii, The wayfarer Of many lands is not responsible For each vernacular. **1882** *Athenæum* 4 Mar. 280 Some of the peoples and tribes whose vernaculars that class comprises. **1892** *Times* 24 Dec. 3/1 Spain, destined to be for long the most active enemy of the circulation of the Scriptures in modern vernaculars.

3. *transf.* The phraseology or idiom *of* a particular profession, trade, etc.

1876 TAIT *Rec. Adv. Phys. Science* vi. 151 To use the vernacular of engineers. **1891** *Century Mag.* May 128/2 On the bar we found friends that we had made in Panama, who had preceded us a few days, long enough to speak the vernacular of mining.

4. A vernacular style of building. Cf. sense A. 6 above.

1910 *Encycl. Brit.* II. 436/1 The culture of the 'Queen Anne' type of architecture.. presented a simple vernacular of construction and detail. **1967** *Listener* 7 Sept. 292/3 What was normally North American about these houses.. was their general internal planning.. an open-plan vernacular that still works well today. **1977** M. GIROUARD *Sweetness & Light* ii. 25 They came back to London to design buildings in which Gothic merged into farmhouse vernacular.

Hence **verˈnacularness.** *rare*$^{-0}$.

1727 BAILEY (vol. II), *Vernacularness*, Properness, or Peculiarness to one's own Country.

vernacularism (vəˈnækjʊlərɪz(ə)m). [-ISM.]

1. A vernacular word, idiom, or mode of expression.

1846 WORCESTER (citing *Q. Rev.*). 1863 NEALE *Ess. Liturgiol.* 527 Wherever the Church..was not established till a late period, there such vernacularisms are scarcely, or not at all, perceptible. 1873 F. HALL *Mod. Eng.* 307 *note*, The more of such vernacularisms [as 'belongings'] we call up from the past, the better.

2. The use of the native language.

1850 *Ecclesiologist* XI. 176 If Rome not merely allows, but authorises such vernacularism, who can forbid us to employ our own Ecclesiastical English?

ver'nacularist. [f. VERNACULAR *a.* and *sb.* + -IST.] 1. An advocate of the use of a regional mode of speech; a speaker or writer in a regional or demotic idiom.

1867 [see ANGLICIST 1]. 1926 *Glasgow Herald* 27 July 10 There was ample material..in the industrial struggle with which Clydeside was so familiar, which in the hands of a Vernacularist of genius could produce a play so striking as 'Strife'. 1974 *Sat. Rev. World* (U.S.) 4 Dec. 46/2 Creosote bush, which the Spaniards called *hedonillo* but the American vernacularists termed 'little stinker'.

2. *R.C. Ch.* An advocate of the use of the vernacular in the liturgy. Also *attrib.* or as *adj.*

1956 *Catholic Herald* 9 Mar. 2/4 Was St. Thomas a Vernacularist? 1982 *Observer* 25 Apr. 30/3 Mr St John-Stevas's Latin is not good.., but that is a venial sin in these vernacularist days.

vernacularity (vəˌnækjʊˈlærɪtɪ). [-ITY.]

1. The fact of belonging or adhering to the vernacular or native language.

[1842 SIR W. HAMILTON in *Reid's Wks.* I. 100/2 *note*, As the expressions are scientific, it is perhaps no loss that their technical precision is guarded by their non-vernacularity.] 1847 DE QUINCEY in *Tait's Mag.* XIV. 579 The merit, which justly you ascribe to Swift, is vernacularity; he never forgets his mother-tongue in exotic forms. 1904 'O. HENRY' in *N.Y. World Mag.* 25 Dec. 2/6 Remsen touched his cap.. and took refuge in vernacularity. 1943 ENTWISTLE & GILLET *Lit. of Eng.* iv. 41 He [*sc.* John Lyly] cultivated..unexpected vernacularity amid refined 'conceits'.

2. A vernacularism.

1867 CARLYLE *E. Irving* in *Remin.* (1881) I. 335 Rustic Annandale begins it, with its homely honesties, rough vernacularities, safe, innocently kind.

verˌnaculariˈzation. [f. next + -ATION.] The action of making, or fact of being made, vernacular or native to a language.

1873 F. HALL *Mod. Eng.* 105 Thousands of words,..on their first appearance, or revival, as candidates for vernacularization, must have met with repugnance.

vernacularize (vəˈnækjʊləraɪz), *v.* [f. VERNACULAR *a.* + -IZE.] *trans.* To render or translate into the native speech of a people; to make vernacular.

1821 W. TAYLOR in *Monthly Rev.* XCIV. 384 The Stephens, or Stephenses, as their names have..been vernacularized among us. 1830 —— *Hist. Surv. Germ. Poetry* III. 450 Godfred of Strasburg, who vernacularized *Trystan & Essylda*. 1866 *Songs & Ball. Cumberld.* 397 Prince Louis Lucien Buonaparte employed him to vernacularise the Song of Solomon.

Hence **ver'nacularized** *ppl. a.*

a 1874 in A. Somerville *Lect. Missions* xiii. 243 His sanctified and vernacularized intellect lives in the numerous Tamil works.

vernacularly (vəˈnækjʊləlɪ), *adv.* [f. as prec. + -LY^2.]

1. In conformity with the vernacular manner; in the native or mother tongue.

1808 SCOTT *Let.* 23 Feb. in *Lockhart*, To expound more vernacularly, I wrote you..a swinging epistle of and concerning German Romances. 1822 *New Monthly Mag.* VI. 298 He sang..very vernacularly. 1840 *Fraser's Mag.* XXI. 23 A wonder that he, a Spaniard, could write English so vernacularly. 1878 MACLEAR *Celts* viii. (1879) 123 The family, vernacularly called '*muintir*', consisted of 'brethren'.

2. With or among the people of a particular country.

1839 MAGINN in *Fraser's Mag.* XX. 263 An author so vernacularly popular as their familiar and national dramatist.

†**ver'naculary,** *a.* *Obs.*$^{-1}$ [Irreg. f. VERNACULAR *a.* + -Y.] = VERNACULAR *a.* 2.

1652 URQUHART *Jewel* Wks. (1834) 202 After the manner of our English and other vernaculary tongues.

ver'naculate, *v.* *U.S.* [Irreg. f. VERNACULAR *a.* + -ATE^3.]

1. *trans.* To call or term in the vernacular.

1887 *Semi-weekly Tribune* (N.Y.) 15 July (Cent.), Very large Antwerp 'patches', as they are vernaculated by the average fruit-grower.

2. *intr.* To use vernacular language.

1895 in *Funk's Stand. Dict.*

vernacule, obs. form of VERNICLE.

†**vernacule,** *a.* *Obs. rare.* [ad. L. *vernāculus*: see VERNACULAR *a.*] = VERNACULAR *a.* 2.

1669 GALE *Crt. Gentiles* I. I. 71 The Syriac Tongue is now no where vernacule, save in some few towns about Libanus. *Ibid.* 76 Mariana Victorius makes three Dialects of the Ethiopic Tongue, the Vernacule, the Babylonic, the Sacred.

†**ver'naculize,** *v.* *Obs.*$^{-1}$ [See prec. and -IZE.] *trans.* = VERNACULARIZE *v.*

a 1802 A. GEDDES *Notes Ps.* cvii. 42 (1807) 205 *Tongue-tied*, lit. *mouth-shut*: which, perhaps, might be not improperly vernaculized.

†**ver'naculous,** *a.* *Obs.* [f. L. *vernācul-us*: see -OUS.]

1. a. Low-bred, scurrilous.

1605 B. JONSON *Volpone* Ded., When a Name, so ful of authority,..is..become the lowest scorne of the age: and those men..subject to the petulancy of euery vernaculous Orator, that were wont to bee the care of Kings.

b. (See quot.)

1623 COCKERAM I, *Vernaculous*, a yong or green wit.

c. (See quot.)

1656 BLOUNT *Glossogr.* (following Cooper), *Vernaculous*, that is born and brought up in our own house.

2. Of products: Indigenous, native.

1606 BIRNIE *Kirk-Buriall* (1833) 11 Where gold is vernaculous and plentifull. 1657 TOMLINSON *Renou's Disp.* 388 Some of them are exoticall, not easily cicurable in our soyle, as the Cedar of Palestina and Lebanon: others are indeed Ve[r]naculous, but altogether, wild and Sylvestrian.

3. = VERNACULAR *a.* 1 and 2.

1658 PHILLIPS *Dict.* Ded., I have..rendred it..worthy of the greatest masteries of Rhetoricians and the tongues of our Vernaculous Oratours. *a* 1682 SIR T. BROWNE *Tracts* viii. (1683) 130 The common Language, which besides their vernaculous and Mother Tongues, may serve for commerce between them.

†**'vernage.** *Obs.* [a. OF. *vernage, vernace, vernache*, ad. It. *vernaccia* 'a kind of strong wine like malmesie or muskadine, or bastard wine' (Florio, 1598). Cf. med.L. *vernagium, vernacium, vernachia.*] A strong and sweet kind of white Italian wine.

c 1386 CHAUCER *Merch. T.* 563 He drinkith ypocras, clarre, and vernage Of spices hote, to encrese his corrage. 1390 GOWER *Conf.* III. 8 In stede of drinke I underfonge A thoght so swete in mi corage, That nevere Pyment ne vernage Was half so swete forto drinke. *c* 1430 *Two Cookery-bks.* 22 Take vernage, oper strong wyne of þe beste þat a man may fynde [etc.]. *c* 1460 *Play Sacram.* 428 They faryd as dronk men of pymente or vernage. *c* 1500 *Colin Blowbol's Test.* 339 Malmasyes, Tires, and Rumneys,..Vernage, Cute, and Raspays also.

attrib. *a* 1400 *Sqr. lowe Degre* 754 Ye shall have rumney and malmesyne, Both ypocrasse, and vernage wyne.

So †**vernagelle**, a variety of vernage. *Obs.*$^{-1}$

c 1460 J. RUSSELL *Bk. Nurture* 118 The namys of swete wynes y wold þat ye them knewe: Vernage, vernagelle, wyne Cute, pyment.

vernage, Sc. form of WARNAGE *Obs.*

vernakill, -ylle, obs. forms of VERNICLE.

vernal (ˈvɜːnəl), *a.* (and *sb.*). Also 6–7 vernall. [ad. L. *vernāl-is* (rare), f. *vernus* pertaining to spring, f. *vēr* spring, VER *sb.*^{1} So OF. and F., Prov., Sp., Pg. *vernal*, It. *vernale.*]

1. Coming, appearing, happening, occurring, etc., in spring. a. *vernal equinox* (or †*equinoctial*): see EQUINOX 1 and 2.

1534 MORE *Treat. Passion* Wks. 1308/1 The xiiii. daye after theyr vernall Equinoctiall in the euenynge. 1594 BLUNDEVIL *Exerc.* I. xvi. (1597) 151 The beginning of Aries, which is called the vernal Equinoxe. 1607 TOPSELL *Hist. Four-f. Beasts* 299 From the vernall æquinoctiall to the summer solstice. 1696 WHISTON *The. Earth* I. (1722) 39 At this time, the Vernal Equinox is on the 9th of March. 1715 tr. *Gregory's Astron.* (1726) I. 316 You will have the Longitude sought from the Vernal Equinox. 1796 H. HUNTER *St.-Pierre's Stud. Nat.* (1799) I. 155 The tides at our vernal Equinox, in March, rise higher than those of September. 1837 BREWSTER *Magnet.* 216 During the three months between the vernal equinox and the summer solstice. 1868 LOCKYER *Elem. Astron.* §171 The days and nights are equal all over the world on the 22d of March and the 22d of September, which dates are called the vernal and autumnal equinoxes.

b. In general use.

1634 SIR T. HERBERT *Trav.* 4 Such time as the Sunne is vernall, [the Island of Ferro] becomes exceeding hot and scalding. 1660 SHARROCK *Vegetables* 52 Which are generall rules for vernall and autumnall settings. 1709 T. ROBINSON *Vind. Mosaick Syst.* 69 These Worms are..ordained for the Food of the Vernal Birds, such as the Cuckow. 1769 GRAY *Installation Ode* 61 Sweet is the breath of vernal shower. 1787 WINTER *Syst. Husb.* 54 The vernal heat of the sun. 1820 COMBE *Syntax, Consol.* I. (Chandos Cl.) 139 'Twas as a vernal evening clos'd. 1842 J. WILSON *Chr. North* I. 244 The whole building is..as fresh as if just washed by a vernal shower. 1872 YEATS *Growth Comm.* 24 The Babylonian plain was subject to vernal floods.

c. *Med.* Of affections or diseases.

1822–7 GOOD *Stud. Med.* (1829) II. 134 The vernal agues generally disappear with the advance of summer. 1843 SIR T. WATSON *Lect. Princ. & Pract. Physic* I. xl. 710 You will hear and read a good deal of vernal intermittents, and autumnal intermittents.

2. Of, pertaining or belonging to, the springtime; appropriate to the spring; spring-like: a. Of weather, scenery, etc.

1611 BEAUM. & FL. *Maid's Trag.* I. ii, We must have none here But vernal blasts, and gentle winds appear. 1634 T. JOHNSON tr. *Parey's Chirurg.* I. xiii. (1678) 18 Such an Air, ..if it have a vernal temper, is good against all diseases. 1646 CRASHAW *Sosp. d'Herode* xiv, He saw a vernall smile sweetly disfigure Winters sad face. 1720 PRIOR *Truth & Falsehood* 8 The purling stream, the margin green, With flowers bedeck'd, a vernal scene. 1778 WARTON *Hist. Eng. Poetry* II. 51 We fondly anticipate a long continuance of gentle gales and vernal serenity. But winter returns with redoubled horrors. 1822 W. IRVING *Braceb. Hall* xix, It was a beautiful morning, of that soft vernal temperature, that seems to thaw all the frost out of one's blood. 1847 L. HUNT *Jar Honey* ii. (1848) 23 Both heaven and hell are in it—the freshest vernal airs, with the depths of Tartarus. 1871 B. TAYLOR *Faust* (1875) II. I. i. 6 The Alpine meadows sloping, vernal, A newer beam descends.

transf. 1869 LOWELL *Under the Willows* 39 By vernal Chaucer, whose fresh woods Throb thick with merle and mavis all the year.

b. *vernal season*, the season of spring.

1644 MILTON *Educat.* 7 In these vernal seasons of the yeer, when the air is calm and pleasant. 1687 MIÈGE *Gt. Fr. Dict.* II, The Vernal Season, or the Spring, *le Printems.* 1806 *Med. Jrnl.* XV. 120 In the vernal season. 1864 A. MCKAY *Hist. Kilmarnock* 296 In the vernal season of the year.

c. In miscellaneous uses.

1725 *Fam. Dict.* s.v. *Sallet*, They also make an excellent Vernal Pottage. 1764 GOLDSM. *Trav.* 118 Whatever sweets salute the northern sky With vernal lives, that blossom but to die. 1817 WORDSW. (*title*), Vernal Ode. Beneath the concave of an April sky [etc.]. 1838 J. L. STEPHENS *Trav. Russia* 67/1 Moscow seemed basking in the mild climate of Southern Asia, rioting in its brief period of vernal existence. 1885 PATER *Marius* I. vi. 112 A kind of mystic hymn to the vernal principle of life in things.

d. *fig.* Suggestive of spring; having the mildness or freshness of spring; early, youthful.

1790 COLERIDGE *Monody Death Chatterton* viii, Ah! where are fled the charms of vernal grace, And joy's wild gleams, light-flashing o'er thy face? 1805 FOSTER *Ess.* I. i. 11 What is become of all those vernal fancies, which had so much power to touch the heart? 1827 SOUTHEY *Funeral Song Princess Charlotte* 17 Late in beauty's vernal bloom. 1844 MRS. BROWNING *Catarina to Camoens* ii, When I heard you sing that burden In my vernal days and bowers. 1898 T. HARDY *Wessex Poems* 100 Captain and Colonel, Sere Generals, Ensigns vernal, Were there.

3. Of flowers, plants, etc.: Appearing, coming up, or blooming in spring-time.

1695 LD. PRESTON *Boeth.* III. 121 Fading sooner than a vernal Flower! 1728 POPE *Dunc.* III. 33 As thick as bees o'er vernal blossoms fly. 1742 COLLINS *Ode to Liberty* 4 The youths,..Like vernal hyacinths in sullen hue, At once the breath of fear and virtue shedding. 1799 *Med. Jrnl.* II. 491 A Journal kept in Spring 1798, to record the time of flowering of several vernal plants. 1812 H. & J. SMITH *Horace in Lond.* 65 The wood nymphs crown'd with vernal flow'rs.

b. In specific or popular names of flowers, plants, or grasses, as ***vernal crocus, cyclamen, gentian, sandwort, sedge, squill***, etc. (see quots. and cf. SPRING *sb.*^{1} 7 c (*a*)).

1778 *Encycl. Brit.* (ed. 2) III. 2311 The varieties of the *vernal crocus are, the small and large [etc.]. 1882 *Garden* 18 Mar. 188/3 The common Vernal Crocus..is so predominant among spring flowers. 1725 *Fam. Dict.* s.v. *Cyclamen*, Our Botanists reckon upon several Sorts of this Plant..as the *Vernal one;..another white Vernal single, and the small Purple Cyclamen. 1728 R. BRADLEY *Dict. Bot., Gentianella minor Verna*, the smaller *Vernal Gentian. 1796 WITHERING *Brit. Plants* (ed. 3) II. 282, I thought it possible that the vernal dwarf Gentian..might be our plant. 1882 *Garden* 18 Nov. 442/3 The lovely Vernal Gentian. 1753 *Chambers' Cycl.* Suppl. s.v. *Orobus*, The *vernal, wood *orobus*, with a pale red flower. 1731 MILLER *Gard. Dict.* s.v. *Orobus*, *Vernal Purple-Wood Bitter-Vetch. 1848 JOHNS *Week at Lizard* 303 *Arenaria verna*, variety *Gerardi*, *Vernal Sandwort, is a small plant with numerous needle-like leaves, and star-like flowers of the most dazzling white. 1859 MISS PRATT *Brit. Grasses* 39 Order. Cyperaceæ... *Vernal Sedge. .. A humble plant from 3–8 inches high. 1796 WITHERING *Brit. Plants* (ed. 3) II. 13 *Veronica verna*... *Vernal Speedwell. 1855 MISS PRATT *Flower. Pl.* IV. 102 Vernal Speedwell... This very rare Speedwell..has..pale blue flowers. 1796 WITHERING *Brit. Pl.* II. 338 *Scilla verna*... *Vernal Squill. [Grows in] meadows and pastures. 1832 JOHNSTON in *Proc. Berw. Nat. Club* I. 10 It was..believed that the vernal squill was peculiar to the western coasts of England. 1796 WITHERING *Brit. Pl.* II. 5 *Callitriche verna*. .. *Vernal Stargrass. Water Starwort. Water Fennel. 1855 MISS PRATT *Flower. Pl.* II. 296 *Callitriche verna*. *Vernal Water Starwort.

c. ***vernal grass***, one of the grasses commonly cultivated for hay.

1762 B. STILLINGFLEET *Misc. Tracts* (1791) 382, I saw this spring a meadow not far from Hampstead..with some of the vernal grass and the corn brome grass. 1765 *Museum Rust.* IV. 428 The vernal, or spring grass, we find in the class *Diandria Digynia*. 1799 J. ROBERTSON *Agric. Perth* 208 The meadow fescue..and the sweet scented vernal grass (anthoxanthum odoratum). 1802 *Med. Jrnl.* VIII. 477 The vernal grass (*Anthoxanthum odoratum*, L.) which is frequently met with in hay. 1857 MILLER *Elem. Chem., Org.* 489 This substance [i.e. coumarin] is found..in the sweet scented vernal grass, to which much of the fragrance of hay is owing.

d. Sown in the spring.

1792 A. YOUNG *Trav. France* 331 They sow here a vernal rye, which is a true spring corn, that will not succeed if sown in autumn.

4. *Comb.*, as ***vernal-bearded, -seeming, -tinctured*** adjs.

1744 AKENSIDE *Pleas. Imag.* II. 104 The melting rainbow's vernal-tinctured hues. 1857 WHITTIER *Last Walk Autumn* iv, And that the vernal-seeming breeze Mocked faded grass and leafless trees. 1874 L. MORRIS *Old Maytide* iii, Here be stalwart youths and lissome, honest-eyed and vernal bearded.

5. *ellipt.* or as *sb.* †a. The vernal season; the spring. *Obs.*$^{-1}$.

1654 E. JOHNSON *Wonder-work. Provid.* 106 The vernall of the yeare 1637. being now in his prime.

b. = *vernal grass* (see 3 c above).

1771 YOUNG *Farmer's Tour East Eng.* II. 256 The grass has consisted chiefly of the holchus,..a little meadow fox tail, and great poa:..it is remarkable that no vernal has appeared. 1834 *Brit. Husb.* I. 514 *Anthoxanthum odoratum*, or sweet-scented vernal, is one of the earliest of our grasses. 1908 *Animal Managem.* 114 The aroma of good hay is due to the aromatic grasses contained in it, Sweet Vernal being the variety which is mainly responsible.

c. *pl.* Seeds of vernal grass. *rare*$^{-1}$.

1784 *Trans. Soc. Arts* II. 60 Mix the Vernals and Hay seeds together.

Hence **ˈvernally** *adv. rare.*

1727 Bailey (vol. II), *Vernally*, according to or in the Spring of the Year. **1888** Ainger *Let.* in Sichel *Life* (1906) xiii. 235 He thinks the Tweens are also vernally cleaning themselves.

verˈnality. *rare.* [f. vernal *a.* + -ity.]

† **1.** The 'spring-time' *of* something. *Obs.*

1639 Wotton in *Reliq.* (1672) 477, I was then surprized with an advertisement from Court, of the death of.. my dear nephew, in the vernality (as I may term it) of his employments and fortunes.

2. (See quot.)

1896 *Agric. Gaz.* 18 May 470/1 Vernality expresses that property of rich and shaded pasture land which makes them a lovely green, with tender and close clustering spring shoots.

vernalization (ˌvɜːnəlaɪˈzeɪʃən). [f. vernal *a.* + -ization, as tr. Russ. *yarovizátsiya.*] The technique of exposing seeds, young plants, etc., to low temperatures in order to hasten subsequent flowering; also, the natural process induced by cold weather which this technique imitates. Also *transf.* and *fig.*

1933, 1934 [see jarovization]. **1957** V. Nabokov *Pnin* ii. 47 The vernalization of the visas, and the preparations [for going to America]. **1971** E. O. Wilson *Insect Societies* viii. 154/1 The vernalization (chilling) effect that renders *Myrmica* and *Formica* brood queen-potent can be interpreted as a token stimulus. **1974** A. J. Huxley *Plant & Planet* x. 100 In beet.. the rosette normally made in the first year.. requires winter chilling for flowering the following summer. This winter chilling is called vernalization. *Ibid.* xxvii. 315 Vernalization consists.. in giving the seed to be sown in spring a cold period.. with a small amount of water.

Hence (by back-formation) **ˈvernalize** *v. trans.*, to treat or affect (seeds, etc.) in this way; **ˈvernalized** *ppl. a.* (in quots. *transf.*), **ˈvernalizing** *vbl. sb.*

1933 Whyte & Hudson in *Bull. Imperial Bureau Plant Genetics* No. 9. 8 (*heading*) Technique for vernalizing long-day plants. **1946** *Nature* 5 Oct. 485/2 The time taken for development to have begun in all the vernalized [sponge] gemmules.. is less than in December. **1947** *Ibid.* 4 Jan. 32/1 This [*sc.* premature flowering] may be due.. to a vernalizing effect on the.. germinated seed.. of naturally experienced low soil.. temperatures in early spring. **1971** E. O. Wilson *Insect Societies* viii. 150/1 It is from some of these vernalized larvae that the yearly crop of queens is matured in the spring. **1976** *Sci. Amer.* Sept. 99/3 The crop flowers and produces grain in the spring after being vernalized, or induced to flower, by the low temperatures in winter.

ˈvernalize, *v. rare.* [f. as vernal *a.* + -ize.] *trans.* To render vernal or spring-like.

1830 *Fraser's Mag.* I. 500 By the amenity of their smile and their dallying jocundity, irradiating and vernalising whatever that smile and jocundity consecrate by tipping and touching. **1898** W. Watson *Poems, Lines Richmond Park* 165 The stored sunlight in your hair and eyes Would vernalise November, and renew the aged year.

† **ˈvernancy.** *Obs.*$^{-1}$ [See next and -ancy.] The condition or quality of being vernant.

1669 *Addr. hopeful yng. Gentry of Eng.* 6 He that expects after a deluge the same vernancy, disposition and order, the soil was before adorn'd with.

ˈvernant, *a.* Now *rare* or *Obs.* Also 5 vernand, 6 vernaunte, varnaunt. [a. OF. *vernant* vernal, ad. L. *vernant-*, *vernans*, pres. pple. of *vernāre* to flourish, be verdant.]

1. Flourishing or growing in, or as in, spring.

c **1440** *York Myst.* xxv. 498 Hayll! vyolett vernand with swete odoure. **1513** Bradshaw *St. Werburge* i. 606 A.. plante, Whiche dayly encreased by sufferaunce deuyne, Merueylously growynge in her, fresshe and varnaunt. *Ibid.* 2808 Whiche tree to this day, endurynge all the yere, By myracle is vernaunte, fresshe, green, and clere. **1526** *Pilgr. Perf.* (W. de W. 1531) 83 A floure, whan it is fresshe, vernant & newe,.. is moche delectable & swete. **1567** Turbervile *Poems* 110 Vernant flowers that appeere To clad the soile with mantell newe. **1615** Brathwait *Strappado*, etc. (1878) 316 The tree sent out her Branches, which did couer their corps with vernant blossoms. **1667** Milton *P.L.* x. 679 Else had the Spring Perpetual smil'd on Earth with vernant Flours. **1728–30** Thomson *Spring* 81 The penetrative Sun ..sets the steaming Power At large, to wander o'er the vernant Earth. **1842** *Fraser's Mag.* XXVI. 80 The vernant branches feel the breeze. *Ibid.* 82 The cool delicious shade Of vernant oak.

transf. and *fig.* **1607** Brewer *Lingua* i. i. A iiij b, Oft haue I.. embelisht my entreatiue phrase With smelling flowres of vernant Rhetorique. **1615** Brathwait *Strappado*, etc. (1878) 317 Let not your vernant bosome so retaine, all comfort from the oat-pipe of a Swaine. **1661** Bp. Rust *Origen & his Opinions* 89 The excellencie of the vernant youth and spring of the renewed world.

b. Freshly green; verdant.

1594 Willobie *Avisa* (1880) 97 The flowring hearbes, the pleasant spring, That deckes the fieldes with vernant hew. **1621** Brathwait *Nat. Embassie* 3 Should I not.. garnish her with Flora's vernant hue?

2. Pertaining to the spring; vernal.

1654 Gayton *Pleas. Notes* iv. 211 The Trees.. were so closely interwoven, that the vernant and æstivall Sunne beames could not pierce their rare imbroydery.

3. Of or forming the 'spring-time' of life.

1794 W. Roberts *Looker-on* III. 381 The green platform of our vernant years.

† **ˈvernate,** *v. Obs.*$^{-0}$ [f. L. *vernāt-*, ppl. stem of *vernāre* (see prec.).] *intr.* (See quot.)

1623 Cockeram i, *Vernate*, to wax young againe.

vernation (vəˈneɪʃən). [In sense 1 ad. mod.L. *vernātiō* (Linnæus), f. L. *vernāre*: see vernant *a.* (So F. *vernation.*) In sense 2 directly f. L. *vernāt-*, ppl. stem of *vernāre.*]

1. *Bot.* The arrangement or formation of the leaves of plants or fronds of ferns in the bud; the manner in which the rudimentary or unexpanded leaves are disposed; prefoliation.

1793 Martyn *Lang. Bot.*, *Foliatio*, foliation, vernation, or leafing. **1829** Lindley *Syn. Brit. Flora* 88 *Prunus*, vernation convolute. *Ibid.*, *Cerasus*, vernation conduplicate. **1830** —— *Nat. Syst. Bot.* 157 The vernation of both the calyx and petals. **1857** P. H. Gosse *Omphalos* 131 The green and leafy arches were once coiled up in a circinate vernation. **1882** Vines *Sachs' Bot.* 428 The leaves of Ferns are usually characterised by a circinate vernation.

2. Vegetable growth or development, as characteristic of the spring. Now *Obs.* or *rare.*

1827 Steuart *Planter's G.* (1828) 320 The season of vernation erelong will come on, the leaves will be enlarged, and assume a far deeper and more lively green. **1867** A. L. Adams *Wand. Nat. India* 68 From the earliest appearance of Vernation in March up to the end of May. **1929** S. Leslie *Anglo-Catholic* x. 121 In the vernation of the year Edward felt the old desire for the earth, a renewed longing to labour and drive the plough.

Verné (ˈvɛrneɪ). Also Verneh. [Origin unknown.] **a.** A Caucasian pileless rug or kilim. **b.** An Anatolian brocaded rug. In full ***Verné kilim, rug***, etc.

1922 Kendrick & Tattersall *Hand-Woven Carpets* I. iv. 165 Thin and soft Kilims made in the neighborhood of Shusha are known in the trade by the name of *Verné. Ibid.* II. Pl. 143 (*caption*) Verné Kilim carpet. **1931** A. U. Dilley *Oriental Rugs & Carpets* Pl. 53 (*caption*) Verné animal and bird khilim. **1973** *Country Life* 29 Nov. 1823 Verné rug 7′ 1″ × 5′ 6″.. Armenia circa 1900. **1975** *Times* 13 June 3/1 An unusual feature of the sale was the presence of two antique Verneh rugs. **1981** I. Bennett *Oriental Rugs* I. 364/2 There are several varieties of so-called bird verneh rugs.

verne, obs. var. fern *sb.*^{3} (windlass).

† **verne,** obs. var. *urne* run *v.*

a **1325** *MS. Rawl. B. 520* fol. 32 Þat alle ben certein in eueriche contreie þat te foreseide peine sal verne [F. *curra*] grefliche.

Vernean (ˈvɜːnɪən), *a.* Also Vernian. [f. the name of Jules *Verne* (1828–1905), French author: see -an, -ian.] Of, pertaining to, or characteristic of the science fiction of Jules Verne. Also **Jules Vernean.**

1960 K. Amis *New Maps of Hell* (1961) i. 37 The book closes with a straightforward Vernean sermon on the dangers of scientific progress considered as an embodiment of human arrogance. **1964** *Listener* 12 Nov. 743/2 The conquest of space no longer strikes us as Wellsian or Jules Vernian. **1980** *Time* 1 Dec. 60/2 Visionaries like Jules Verne were suggesting a better way. A bullet-shaped vehicle.. could be propelled far faster by using powerful electromagnetic fields. Now, as a result of lab work in the U.S. and abroad, the Vernean scheme shows promise of becoming a practical reality.

Verner's law: see law *sb.*^{1} 17 c.

Verneuil (vɛrnœj). The name of A. V. L. *Verneuil* (1856–1913), French chemist, used *attrib.* with reference to a technique invented by him for producing artificial rubies.

1912 *Chem. Abstr.* VI. 55 A description of the Verneuil method of preparing artificial rubies. **1951** Kirk & Othmer *Encycl. Chem. Technol.* VII. 163 A typical Verneuil crystal-growth apparatus is shown schematically in Figure 2. **1979** Mills & Mansfield *Genuine Article* vii. 116 The little bubble which you often see in a Verneuil synthetic.

verneuk (vərˈnuk), *v. S. African slang.* Also vinook. [ad. Cape Du. *verneuken* (also in W. Flem., with variant *vernukken*).] *trans.* To cheat, humbug, swindle.

1871 *Cape Monthly Mag.* III. 46 (Pettman), How Hendrick enjoyed verneuking the Boer. **1905** D. Blackburn *R. Hartley, Prospector* xiii, So you have verneuked me? **1909** R. Cullum *Compact* xviii. 213 He has vinooked the Kaffir chiefs into granting large concessions.

Hence **verˈneuker.** Also **verˈneukering** *vbl. sb.*, **verˈneukery** [a. Cape Du. *verneukerie.*]

1896 in *Westm. Gaz.* 4 July 8/1 But we women of South Africa despise such maudlin *verneukery.* **1900** Sir J. Robinson *Life Time S. Africa* vii. 185 Hence arose the practice of 'verneukering'—by which buyer and seller each sought to get the better of the other. **1905** D. Blackburn *R. Hartley* xiii, Do you take me for a Boer verneuker?

vernice, obs. form of varnish *sb.*^{1}

vernicle (ˈvɜːnɪk(ə)l). Forms: α. 4, 8–9 vernicle, 4 fernycle, 4–6 vernycle. β. 5 vernacul(l, -cule, vernakill, -kylle, 5–9 vernacle, 6 varnacle. [a. AF. and OF. *vernicle*, = OF. *veron(n)icle*, varr. of *veronique*, ad. med.L. *veronica* the sudarium of St. Veronica: see veronica^{2} and cf. veronicle, veronique. On the change of *-ique* to *-icle* see the note to chronicle *sb.*]

1. The picture or representation of the face of Christ said to be impressed upon the handkerchief or sudarium of St. Veronica (see 2); any similar picture of Christ's face, esp. one engraved, painted, or worked upon a vessel, garment, ornament, etc., used for religious or devotional purposes; an ornament or token bearing this as worn by pilgrims.

α. **1362** Langl. *P. Pl.* A. vi. 14 Moni Cros on his cloke and keiȝes of Rome, And þe vernicle [*C.* fernycle] bi-fore for men schulde him knowe. *c* **1386** Chaucer *Prol.* 685 Swiche glarynge eyen hadde he as an hare, A vernycle hadde he sowed vp on his cappe. **1467** *Paston Lett.* Suppl. 111 My master gaff her a great sygnnet of goolde with the vernycle. **1726** Bailey (ed. 3). **1825** Fosbroke *Encycl. Antiq.* (1843) II. 805 The Vernicle, or Veronique,.. or face of Christ, miraculously impressed upon a handkerchief. **1853** Rock *Ch. of Fathers* III. x. 438 A medal stamped with the vernicle showed the pilgrim had visited Rome. **1901** *Athenæum* 27 July 131/3 The vernicle, or face of our Lord, appears in the centre of the paten.

β. *a* **1400** *Leg. Rood* (1871) 170 O vernacule [*v.r.* vernacul], i honoure him and the, þat þe made þorow his preuite. *c* **1450** in *Maitl. Club Misc.* III. 204 Item a tabill of the vernakill in the vestre. **1473** *Will of Belasice* (Somerset Ho.), My newe chalice with a patent of siluer, the crucifix in the foote of the same chalice gilt and the vernacle upon the same patent gilt. **1516** *Will of Grene* (ibid.), Lytle masser of syluer and gylt with the vernacles hed in the bothom. **1536** in E. Ledwich *Antiq. Sarisb.* (1771) 202 A cope of Green cloth of gold, with a goodly Orphery, having in the Morse a Vernacle. **1534** in Peacock *Eng. Ch. Furniture* (1866) 196 Item a Masar with a sengle band with a prynt of the vernacle in the bothom. **1721** Bailey. **1849** Rock *Ch. of Fathers* i. iii. I. 293 A large convex piece of fine crystal, showing beneath it the vernacle or face of our divine Redeemer. **1901** E. Hoskins *Horæ B. Mariæ Virg.* 125 (tr. text of 1510), The pope John the xxii.. hath granted unto all them that devoutly say this prayer beholding the glorious visage or vernacle of our Lord v thousand days of pardon. *Ibid.* 127 A devout orison to the blessed vernacle of our Lord.

2. The cloth or kerchief, alleged to have belonged to St. Veronica, with which, according to legend, the face of Christ was wiped on the way to Calvary, and upon which His features were miraculously impressed.

This cloth is preserved at St. Peter's, Rome, and is venerated as a relic.

a **1400** *Stac. Rome* 59 Whon þe vernicle schewed is, Gret pardoun forsoþe þer is. **1517** Torkington *Pilgr.* (1884) 33 We cam to the howse of Veronica,.. wher as our blyssyd Savyor impressyd the ymage of hys Face in hyr wymple whiche ys at Rome. And it ys callyd ther the Vernacle. **1526** *Pilgr. Perf.* (W. de W. 1531) 304 Yᵉ blessed relyke the Vernacle, whiche is the very similitude & imprynte of thy blessed & gloryous vysage. **1581** J. Bell *Haddon's Answ. Osor.* 460 The Vernycle wherewith Christes face was wyped is shewed in S. Peters Church at Rome. *a* **1648** Ld. Herbert *Hen. VIII* (1683) 625 He would ask leave to see the Vernacle; which he said, was the picture of Christ given to Women by himself as he went to death. **1677** W. Hughes *Man of Sin* ii. iii. 51 A large Handkerchief, or Towel,.. whereunto, with many others, they put up this devout Orizon: namely, to the Holy Vernacle, as they christen it. *Ibid.* 52 The most holy Face.. Imprinted on a Snow-white Cloth by th' Power above, And on the Vernacle bestow'd, as Pledge of Love. **1845** J. Saunders *Cabinet Pict. Eng. Life, Chaucer* 14 Thus originated the Sudarium or holy kerchief —the Veronica—and, by corruption, the vernicle.

verniˈcose, *a. Bot. rare*$^{-0}$. [ad. mod.L. *vernicōs-us*, f. med.L. *vernic-ium* varnish *sb.*^{1}] 'Covered with a natural varnish' (*Treas. Bot.*, 1866).

vernier (ˈvɜːnɪə(r)). [From the name of the inventor, Paul *Vernier* (1580–1637), a French mathematician, who described the device in a tract on the *Quadrant Nouveau de Mathématiques* published in 1631.]

1. a. A device, consisting of a short movable scale, by which more minute measurements may be readily obtained from the divisions of the graduated scale of astronomical, surveying, or other mathematical instruments to which it is attached.

Sometimes erroneously called a *nonius* (q.v.).

1766 *Instruct. for Hadley's Quadrant* 17 A scale of divisions graduated on the chamfered edge or sloped side of the index, which scale is called the vernier. **1774** M. Mackenzie *Maritime Surv.* 28 It would likewise be an Advantage if the Vernier was made to give every Minute of a Degree, in place of four or five, as in most Theodolites. **1798** *Phil. Trans.* LXXXVIII. 473 Another small slip of ivory is placed at each end of the arm, serving as a vernier, and subdividing these divisions into five parts. **1815** J. Smith *Panorama Sci. & Art* II. 26 The scale of variation is furnished with an instrument called a vernier or nonius. **1856** Kane *Arct. Explor.* I. xiii. 144 Though I had much clear weather we barely succeeded by magnifiers in reading the verniers. **1888** Rutley *Rock-Forming Min.* 18 For very exact work, the circle may be divided to half degrees, and a vernier may be employed.

b. *attrib.* and *Comb.*, as ***vernier circle, division, piece, plate, scale***, etc.

Also with the names of instruments or tools having a vernier scale or attachment, as ***vernier caliper, compass, transit*** (Knight *Dict. Mech.*).

1788 *Encycl. Brit.* (ed. 3) II. 587/2 The first division of the vernier piece marked 15. **1797** *Ibid.* XVIII. 644/1 *Vernier scale*, a scale excellently adapted for the graduation of mathematical instruments. **1843** *Penny Cycl.* XXVI. 267/1

In order to read off the hundredths of an inch which the vernier zero advances beyond any tenth in the scale, we have merely to see what vernier division comes nearest to a division of the scale. **1862** *Catal. Internat. Exhib., Brit.* II. No. 2947, The vernier plate is carried on four arms, and a diagonal brace. *Ibid.*, The horizontal limb, vernier circle, &c. **1884** KNIGHT *Dict. Mech.* Suppl. 925/2 *Vernier Scale sight* (*Rifle*), a hind sight with a vernier scale for accurate adjustment. **1884** F. J. BRITTEN *Watch & Clockm.* 148 To the bottom of the stock of a Vernier slide guage he attaches a spring.

2. *Astronautics.* Used *attrib.* and *absol.* to designate a small auxiliary rocket engine for effecting minor changes in the velocity or attitude of a spacecraft.

1958 *Observer* 12 Oct. 1/2 Eight small 'vernier', or guidance rockets,.. had been fitted to Pioneer. Any or all of these could be fired from the earth to make any necessary correction in the final phase of the flight. **1960** *Aeroplane* XCVIII. 562/1 In its nose would be a third stage employing low-thrust 'vernier' rocket motors. **1968** A. C. CLARKE *2001* xxxv. 184 The main thrust died and only the verniers continued to nudge *Discovery* gently into orbit. **1968** *Sci. Jrnl.* Nov. 76/2 The rocket..had no fewer than 20 main thrust chambers and 12 swivelling verniers—small motors for fine control of speed and direction. **1979** J. W. CORNELISSE *Rocket Propulsion & Spaceflight Dynamics* x. 212 A third method to ensure ignition after coasting is the use of small (Vernier) rockets, which give the vehicle a sufficiently large acceleration to position the propellant at the sump.

† **'vernile,** *a. Obs. rare.* Also 7 vernill. [ad. L. *vernīlis*, f. *verna* a home-born slave.] Servile, slavish.

1623 COCKERAM I, *Vernill*, slauish. **1727** BAILEY. **1843** DE QUINCEY in *Blackw. Mag.* LIV. 60 This scandal of Roman society was not..a pure product, from the vernile scurrility of which we hear so much in Roman writers.

† **ver'nility.** *Obs.* [ad. L. *vernīlitās*, f. *vernīlis*: see prec. and -ITY.] Servility, slavishness.

1623 COCKERAM I, *Vernilitie*, slauery. **1656** BLOUNT *Glossogr.*, *Vernility*, flattering, servile or slavish behavior. **1665** EVELYN *Let. to Sir P. Wyche* 20 June, I conceive the reason both of additions to and the corruption of the English language..has proceeded from..affectation of travellers,.. vernility & mincing of citizens, pulpits, political remonstrances,..&c. **1788** H. CLARKE *Sch. Candidates* (1877) 9 Oh, the stupidity and vernility of mankind, that there should be permitted such an abuse of power in the world, as either a public or domestic Gynecocracy!

vernish, obs. form of VARNISH *sb.*[1] and *v.*

vernis martin (vɛrni martɛ̃). Also vernis Martin, Vernis Martin, and hyphenated. [Fr., f. *vernis* varnish + *Martin* (see below).] A lacquer or varnish used in the eighteenth century by the French brothers Étienne, Guillaume, Julien, and Robert Martin and their contemporaries on a range of furniture, ornaments, etc., to imitate oriental lacquer. Also *fig.*

1877 C. SCHREIBER *Jrnl.* (1911) II. 18 Some curious boards for the game of Loto [*sic*], done in Vernis Martin. **1883** J. W. MOLLETT *Illustr. Dict. Art & Archæol.* 337/1 *Vernis-Martin work*, a Japanese style of painting and enamelling on furniture, carriages, and small objects. **1899** R. WHITEING *No. 5 John St.* xvi. 163 That polish of the world which is not exactly vernis-Martin for transparency. **1911** LOUISA OF TUSCANY *My Own Story* vi. 87 It was a magnificent historical vehicle painted in vernis Martin. **1942** *Burlington Mag.* Apr. 104/2 A fine collection of small boxes—vernis martin, ivory, etc.,..will be sold in May. **1963** *Times Lit. Suppl.* 15 Mar. 192/4 A fine example of a 'Vernis Martin' binding of *c.* 1800. **1978** *Country Life* 8 June (Suppl.) 97/3 French vernis martin snuff-box, c. 1780.

‖ **vernissage** (vɛrnisaʒ). Also Vernissage. [Fr.] A day before the exhibition of paintings on which exhibitors may retouch and varnish their pictures already hung. Now usu. denoting a private view of paintings before public exhibition. Cf. VARNISHING *vbl. sb.* 1 b.

1912 *Queen* 20 Apr. 643/2 The Salon Nationale des Beaux Arts. The vernissage was on Saturday, and was marked by the usual miscellaneous crowd of French people and foreigners. **1920** R. FRY *Let.* 28 Sept. (1972) II. 491 My landscape is accepted all right at the Autumn Salon... I went to..give it some *vernis à retoucher* at the *Vernissage*. **1930** *Observer* 26 Jan. 10 The Indépendants have once more occupied the Grand Palais... The crowd at the vernissage did not seem to be moving so fast. **1958** *Spectator* 11 July 56/2 Artists were excluded from the *vernissage* of the twenty-ninth *Biennale* at Venice. **1961** *Times* 18 Mar. 3/7 At the height of the season art critics in Paris receive an average of 20 vernissage invitations each week. **1967** *Times* 3 May 9/7, I found myself completely at sea at the 'vernissage' of an exhibition of paintings..at one of London's..art galleries. **1979** M. SOAMES *Clementine Churchill* ii. 23 Mlle Henri had procured tickets for a *Vernissage*.

‖ **vernix** ('vɜːnɪks). [med.L.: see VARNISH *sb.*[1]]

1. Varnish. *Obs. rare.*

1573 *Art of Limming* 9 To make a kynde of colouring called Vernix wherewith you may vernishe golde, siluer, or any other colour or payntinges.

2. *Med.* In full, ***vernix caseosa*** [mod.L. *caseōsus*, f. L. *caseus* cheese]. A greasy deposit covering the skin of a baby at birth.

1846 DUNGLISON *Dict. Med. Sci.* (ed. 6) 785/1 Vernix caseosa. **1882** W. T. LUSK *Sci. & Art of Midwifery* iii. 75 In the fifth month the surface of the fetal body is covered by the *vernix caseosa*, a whitish substance composed of..surface epithelium, down, and the products of the sebacious glands. **1956** *Nature* 18 Feb. 330/1 The specimens [of amniotic fluid] were centrifuged and the vernix and supernatant fluid removed. **1978** *Jrnl. R. Soc. Med.* LXXI. 212 Copious vernix caseosa is often present. **1980** *Brit. Med. Jrnl.* 25 Oct. 1138/1 With difficulty but determination she gave birth to an enormous child coated in so much vernix that it seemed to wear a cream cheese pack.

† **vernon,** error for VERNAL *a. Obs.*

1658 R. FRANCK *North. Mem.* (1694) 1 The Vernon Ingress smil'd a Blessing, when she sent the melodious Harmony of Birds to melt the Air. *Ibid.* 127 The Race of Salmon, especially the Female in the Vernon Æquinox, is for the most part..casting against the rapid Streams.

vernysoun, Sc. form of WARNISON *Obs.*

† **'verol.** *Obs. rare.* Also 7 veroll. [a. F. *vérole*, doublet of *variole* VARIOLA.]

1. French pox; syphilis.

1596 HARINGTON *Metam. Ajax* Prol. B j, He met a french Surgeon..yᵗ cured him both of that and the Verol, yᵗ he had before in his priorums.

2. (See quot.) *rare*—⁰.

1688 R. HOLME *Armoury* II. 238/1 The Veroll, the Web, are two Diseases in the eyes of Hawks, some call them the Pynne; they do proceed from Rume.

So † **ve'rola** [cf. Cat. *verola*]. = prec. 1. *Obs.*—¹

1600 BRETON *Pasquil's Passe & Passeth Not* Wks. (Grosart) I. 9/1 From..The French Verola, and the English feuer,..The blessed Lord of heau'n deliuer me.

Verona (vɪ'rəʊnə). [a. It. *Verona*: see def.]

1. The name of a city in northern Italy used attrib. to designate articles found or produced in, or associated with, the locality, as ***Verona brown, earth, green, serge***, etc. (see quots.).

1726 *Dict. Rust.* (ed. 3) s.v. *Peach*, Verona [peach]. **1835** G. FIELD *Chromatography* 129 The greens called Verona green, and Verdetto,..are similar native pigments of a warmer colour. **1839** URE *Dict. Arts* 619 Verona green is merely a variety of the mineral called green earth. **1850** ANSTED *Elem. Geol., Min.*, etc. §435 Hisingerite,.. Verona earth, Nontronite,..are also impure silicates of [iron]. **1858** SIMMONDS *Dict. Trade*, *Verona-serge*, a thin worsted and cotton fabric. It is also made of mohair and cotton, and of various colours. **1889** *Cent. Dict.* s.v. *Brown*, *Verona brown*, a pigment used by artists in oil-painting. It is a calcined ferruginous earth, of a reddish-brown tone.

2. *ellipt.* (See quot.)

1904 *Tailor & Cutter* 4 Aug. 480/2 *Verona*, a thin make of woollen material with a cotton warp, having a bright twill; used for linings.

veronal ('vɛrənəl). *Chem.* [a. G. *veronal.*] Diethyl-malonyl-urea, a white crystalline substance used as a hypnotic. Also *attrib.*

1903 *Merck's Ann. Rep.* XVII. 183 Veronal has been thoroughly tested in a large number of noted public and private hospitals. **1904** *Lancet* 23 Jan. 223/2 A box of veronal cachets, each containing eight grains.

Vero'nese, *sb.* and *a.* [a. It. *Veronese*: see VERONA and -ESE.]

A. *sb.* **1.** The natives or inhabitants of Verona. Also as *sing.*

1673 J. RAY *Observations Journey Low-Countries* 220 The Antiquities of Verona written by Torellus Saraina a Veronese. **1757** tr. *Keysler's Trav.* III. 176 The Veronese might justly erect statues to other illustrious persons. **1843** *Penny Cycl.* XXVI. 243/1 The revolutionists..threatened the other provinces which remained in obedience to the senate, and especially the Veronese. **1873** 'OUIDA' *Pascarel* I. 56 The Veronese used to call me L'Uccello. **1967** *Guardian* 10 May 7/2 A Veronese himself, Professor Forlati came to Venice in 1912.

2. The form of Italian spoken in Verona.

1872 RUSKIN *Fors Clav.* II. xix. 11 Some talk followed, of cold and heat, and anything else one knew the Italian for, or could understand the Veronese for (Veronese being more like Spanish than Italian).

B. *adj.* Of or belonging to, made in or obtained from, Verona in the north of Italy.

1757 tr. *Keysler's Trav.* III. 181 Four hundred and fifty Veronese feet. **1776** in *Encycl. Brit.* (1780) VI. 4124/2 The Vicentine and Veronese lavas and volcanic ashes. **1833** C. REDDING *Hist. Mod. Wines* (1851) 278 Even a wretched Veronese wine..is called 'vino santo'. **1885** *Encycl. Brit.* XIX. 88/1 Veronese earth or terra verde, a form of ochre. **1888** *Ibid.* XXIV. 171/2 Many good pictures of the Veronese school. **1890** *Cent. Dict.* s.v. *Green*, *Veronese green*, a pigment consisting of hydrated chromium sesquioxid... Also called *viridian.*

‖ **veronica**[1] (vɪ'rɒnɪkə). [med.L. *veronica* (whence also Sp. and Pg. *veronica*, F. *véronique*), app. from the name of St. Veronica.]

1. *Bot.* (With capital initial.) A large genus of scrophulariaceous plants (herbs or shrubs) having leafy stems and blue (rarely white or pink) flowers borne in racemes or spikes.

Many species are indigenous to the British Isles and are commonly called Speedwell. Others are cultivated in gardens for their foliage and flowers.

1527 ANDREW tr. *Brunswyke's Distyll. Waters* II. lxxix. F ij/2 A dragma of pouder of ye same herbe Veronica. **1578** LYTE *Dodoens* 27 The Female Veronica is..much weaker, and not so good as the Male. **1657** S. PURCHAS *Pol. Flying Ins.* I. xv. 92 Ordinarily they gather not of many little or small flowers, as..Veronica. **1664** EVELYN *Kal. Hort.* 67 May. Flowers in Prime... Valerian, Veronica double and single. **1706** PHILLIPS (ed. Kersey), *Veronica*, the Herb Fluellin, or Speed-well, good for Wounds and to provoke Sweat. **1753** *Chambers's Cycl.* Suppl. s.v., The common small procumbent Veronica, called male Speedwell. **1796** WITHERING *Brit. Pl.* (ed. 3) II. 15 Brooklime,..and some other species of Veronica, afford nourishment to the Papilio cinxia. **1833** B'NESS BUNSEN in Hare *Life* (1879) I. ix. 377 For the first time in Italy I found my mother's favorite veronica. **1834** MRS. SOMERVILLE *Connex. Phys. Sci.* 275 The primrose, the lily of the valley, or the veronica which adorn our meadows.

attrib. **1868** J. T. BURGESS *Eng. Wild Fl.* 42 One distinguishing feature of the Veronica tribe.

b. With distinguishing epithets, as ***earth-oak, field, foreign veronica.*** Cf. SPEEDWELL b.

1846–50 A. WOOD *Class-bk. Bot.* 406 *Veronica arvensis.* Field Veronica. Corn Speedwell. **1847** DARLINGTON *Amer. Weeds*, etc. (1860) 227 *V. peregrina*... Foreign Veronica. Purslane Speedwell. Neckweed. **1856** DELAMER *Fl. Gard.* (1861) 105 *Veronica Chamædrys*, or Earth-Oak Veronica (from the shape of its leaves).

2. a. With *a* and pl. A plant or species of the genus Veronica.

1855 *Poultry Chron.* III. 38/1 To make the garden gay, the following roots may be planted out either in beds or patches: American cowslips,..veronicas, wall-flowers. **1882** *Garden* 6 May 317/3 Tall Veronicas will now need tying up. **1899** R. BRIDGES *Idle Flowers* Poems (1912) 353 Blue-eyed Veronicas And grey-faced Scabious.

b. In pl. with *the.* The various species which compose this genus.

1856 DELAMER *Fl. Gard.* (1861) 105 The Veronicas [have] ..something graceful, feminine, and fragile in their aspect.

Ve'ronica[2]. [The name of St. *Veronica*: see also VERNICLE.] **1.** = VERNICLE 1 and 2.

In quot. 1812 stressed *Vero'nica.*

a **1700** EVELYN *Diary* 15 Jan. 1645, The Zitelle..walked in procession to St. Peter's, where the Veronica was shew'd. **1728** CHAMBERS *Cycl.* s.v., Veronica's are Imitations of that celebrated Original one, preserv'd with great Veneration at St. Peter's in Rome. **1788** GIBBON *Decl. & Fall.* xlix. V. 94 The *veronica* of Rome, or Spain, or Jerusalem, which Christ in his agony and bloody sweat applied to his face. **1812** CARY *Dante, Parad.* XXXI. 95 Like a wight, Who haply from Croatia wends to see Our Veronica. **1855** MILMAN *Lat. Chr.* IX. viii. IV. 214 The Pope..showed him the Veronica, and allowed him to touch the holy face of the Lord.

transf. **1788** *Encycl. Brit.* (ed. 3) I. 24 It is disputed whether the Veronica of Montreuil, or the granite obelisk mentioned by Gori, be *Abraxases.*

2. (With lower case initial.) [Sp.: see quot. 1957.] In *Bullfighting*, a movement typical of the first tercio in which the matador swings the cape in a slow circle round himself in order to persuade the charging bull to follow the movement of the cape. Also *fig.*

1926 E. HEMINGWAY *Sun also Rises* xviii. 217 The bull wanted it again, and Romero's cape filled again... He made four veronicas like that, and finished with a half veronica that turned his back on the bull. **1936** R. CAMPBELL *Mithraic Emblems* 18 Enemy of my inward night..whose arm against the Bull designs The red veronicas of light. **1957** A. MACNAB *Bulls of Iberia* vi. 57 In two-handed passes, the cape is held on either side of the collar. The fundamental pass is the *verónica*... The name *verónica* is derived from the attitude of the man holding the cape out in his two hands, which resembles that in which St. Veronica is depicted holding out the towel to Our Lord on the way to Calvary. **1976** *Listener* 29 Apr. 541/1 The oldest of old-time waltzes, the couples dancing a mile apart, the women—executing neat veronicas with the men in swallow-tails—got up like Christmas paper bells.

† **veronicle.** *Obs. rare.* [a. OF. *veron(n)icle*: see VERNICLE.] = VERNICLE.

14.. *Leg. Rood* (1871) 170 O vernacule [*Addit. MS.* veronicle], i honoure him and the, þat þe made þorow his preuite. *c* **1450** *MS. Harl.* 149 fol. 276 Here aftyr foloweth a story of þe veronycle.

veronique. Also 7 veronicke, 20 Véronique.

† **I.** [a. OF. and later F. *veronique* VERONICA[2].]

1. = VERNICLE 1. Also *fig. Obs. rare.*

1624 GATAKER *Transubst.* 95 The veronicke or the print of Christs face in a towel. *a* **1711** KEN *Psyche* Poet. Wks. 1721 IV. 222 My soul, Lord, thy Veronique make, That I may thy Resemblance take. **1825** [see VERNICLE 1 *a*].

‖ **II.** (verɔnik.) [F. *veronique* VERONICA[2].]

2. *Cookery.* (Usu. in form *Véronique.*) Applied to dishes (esp. of fish or chicken) prepared or garnished with grapes.

1907 G. A. ESCOFFIER *Guide Mod. Cookery* 302 *Filets de soles Véronique.* Raise the fillets of a fine sole. **1940** A. L. SIMON *Conc. Encycl. Gastron.* II. 103/2 *Véronique*, stuffed fillets of sole, rolled and poached, garnished with one muscat grape upon each fillet and muscat grapes round the dish. **1958** B. PYM *Glass of Blessings* iii. 38 He was even now preparing them a delicious sole véronique. **1960**, etc. [see SOLE *sb.*[2] 1 c]. **1963** A. SIMON *Guide Good Food & Wines* 379 Véronique, stuffed fillets of sole, rolled and poached, garnished with one muscat grape upon each fillet and muscat grapes round the dish. **1979** *United States 1980/81* (Penguin Travel Guides) 298 The menu is imaginative,.. —trout Véronique (poached and topped with green grapes and hollandaise sauce).

3. = VERONICA[2] 2.

1931 R. CAMPBELL *Georgiad* II. 32 My passes brought the colour to his cheeks, The loudest he to cheer my veroniques. **1932** —— *Taurine Provence* iii. 72 A heroic series of repeated veroniques against a bull of *grande vaillance.*

† **'verony.** *Obs.*—¹ Also weroni, veroni. [a. AF. or OF. **veronie*:—med.L. *veronica.*] = prec.

a **1300** *Cursor M.* 18859 O suilk a moder, wel slik a child, Wit fair wisage and modes mild, It es sene be þe weroni [*v.rr.* veroni, verony].

†**ver'port.** *Obs.* [f. the Du. personal name *Verpoort* or *Verport*.] A class of tulips (see quots.).

1796 C. MARSHALL *Garden.* xix. (1813) 380 The plain tulips..are called whole blowers, or breeders; and accordingly as they break into other colours, stripes and variegations,..are denominated and classed into *baguettes, bybloemens, verports*, and *bizarres*. **1824** LOUDON *Encycl. Gard.* (ed. 2) 832 The Dutch florists class their late-blowing tulips as under:..Prime baguets,..Baguets Rigaut's,..Incomparable Verports.

†**verquere.** *Obs.* [Ultimately (prob. through an obs. F. **verquere*) ad. Du. *verkeer* (in the comb. *verkeer-bord*, †*-berd*) backgammon, f. *verkeeren* to turn round, to play at backgammon (Kilian).] An old form of backgammon.

a **1700** *Games most in Use* 50 The Famous Game, call'd Verquere, came originally..from Holland, and is said to be the only noted Game, upon the Tables, that they practise and are good at. **1714** T. LUCAS *Mem. Gamesters* (ed. 2) 67 He was very dextrous also at Verquere, Tick-tack, Grand Trick-track, Irish, and Back-Gammon. **1721** T. AITKEN *Compl. Gamester* (title-p.), The Famous Game of Verquere, Tick-Tack, Irish, Back-Gammon.

verra, southern dial. var. FARROW *a.*; Sc. and northern dial. f. VERY.

verrai(e, obs. ff. VERY.

verrailiche, -ly, obs. ff. VERILY *adv.*

verrament, var. VERAMENT *adv. Obs.*

verray, obs. f. VERY; obs. Sc. f. WORRY *v.*

verrayle, -ly, obs. ff. VERILY *adv.*

verrayment, var. VERIMENT *adv. Obs.*

†**verre.** *Obs.* Also 4 verr, 5 ver, virre. [a. OF. (also mod.F.) *verre*:—L. *vitrum* glass.]

1. Glass.

c **1374** CHAUCER *Troylus* II. 867 And forthi, who that hath an hede of verre Fro caste of stonys ware hym in the werre. *a* **1400-50** *Alexander* 4351 Make we na vessall of virre ne of na clere siluir. **14..** LYDG. *Life Virgin* (MS. Antiq. Soc. 134) fol. 14 (Halliw.), In alle the erthe y-halowid and y-holde, In a closet more clere than verre or glas. *c* **1440** *Promp. Parv.* 508/2 Verre, glasse, *vitrum*.

2. A vessel made of glass, esp. a drinking-vessel; a glass.

1382 WYCLIF *Prov.* xxiii. 31 Ne beholde thou the win, whan it floureth, whan shal shine in the verr the colour of it [**1388** the colour therof schyneth in a ver]. *c* **1400** MAUNDEV. (1839) iv. 32 It is alle fulle of Gravelle,..of the which Men maken fair Verres and clere. *c* **1410** *Master of Game* (MS. Digby 182) xii, Putte it in þe houndes þrote þe mountance of a verre full. *a* **1450** *Knt. de la Tour* 27 She..lepte upon the borde,..and brake the verres, and spilt all that there was on the borde. **1532** *Acc. Ld. High Treas. Scotl.* (1905) VI. 75 For iiij verris with thair caceis,..price of the pece vj. s.

verre, ME. var. FAR *a.* and *adv.*; obs. f. VERY.

‖**verre églomisé** (vɛr eglɔmize). [Fr., f. *verre* (see VERRE) + EGLOMISÉ *a.* and *sb.*] Glass decorated with a layer of engraved gold (see quots. 1971, 1977).

1907 E. DILLON *Glass* viii. 140 The variety of painted glass known in later times as *verre églomisé*. **1933** *Connoisseur* XCII. 372/2 The term '*verre églomisé*'..has for long been applied to this work, in common with the art of painting under glass. **1941** *Burlington Mag.* Feb. 59/1 The cabinet illustrated..and a pair of looking-glasses, with glass borders ornamented with *verre églomisé* decoration in scarlet and gold..were brought from Spain five or six years ago. **1967** [see ÉGLOMISÉ]. **1971** *Country Life* 15 July 150/2 He was a native of Amsterdam and worked in *verre églomisé*—that is gold and silver leaf laid under glass and engraved with a pointed tool. It is a very ancient technique going back to Roman times, but its customary name is derived from that of a well-known 18th-century picture-frame maker named Glomy who employed the method extensively. **1977** FLEMING & HONOUR *Penguin Dict. Decorative Arts* 826/2 *Verre églomisé*, glass decorated on the back by unfired painting or, usually, by gilding... The painting or gilding is protected by another sheet of glass or by a coat of varnish or a layer of metal foil.

verrei(lly, etc., obs. ff. VERY, VERILY *adv.*

'**verrel**, *sb. Obs.* exc. *dial.* Forms: 5 **verelle**, 7 verrill, 8 verril, 8-9 **verrel**, 9 verel, verrell. [ad. OF. *virelle, virol* (mod.F. *virole*): see FERRULE *sb.* and VIRL *sb.*] A ferrule.

1483 *Cath. Angl.* 400/2 A verelle of a knyffe, *spirula*. **1611** COTGR., *Frete*, a Verrill; th' yron band or hoope that keeps a wooden tool from riuing. *Ibid.*, *Tourillon*, an inner Verrill; the round plate of yron whereby a peece of wood, often turned on, is preserued from wearing. **1706** PHILLIPS (ed. Kersey), *Verrel* or *Verril*, a little Brass or Iron-ring, at the small end of a Cane, or Handle of a Tool, &c. **1773** *Phil. Trans.* LXIII. 418, I cover this part of the tube with a brass verrel. **1807** VANCOUVER *Agric. Devon* (1813) 129 On the upper end of this spar is fixed a stout ring or verrell. **1828** CARR *Craven Gloss.*, *Verel*,..a small iron hoop.

†'**verrel**, *v. Obs.*$^{-1}$ In 5 virell, vyrell. [ad. OF. *vireler, viroler.*] *trans.* To furnish with a ferrule; = FERRULE *v.*

a **1450** *Fishing w. Angle* (1883) 8 Þen virell [*v.r.* vyrell] þe staff wel at bothe endys with hopy[s] of yren.

verrelay, obs. f. VIRELAY.

verrelle, -ly, obs. ff. VERILY.

verrement, var. VERAMENT *adv.*

verren, ME. var. FERREN *adv.* and *a.*

†'**verrer.** *Obs.*$^{-1}$ In 5 verrour. [ad. AF. *verrer* (1300), = OF. (and mod.F.) *verrier* (1265 in Godef.), f. *verre* VERRE.] A worker in glass; a glazier.

1415 in *York Myst.* p. xxvi, Sellers, Verrours, Fuystours.

verret, dial. f. FERRET *sb.*[1]

verrey, obs. f. VERY; obs. Sc. f. WORRY *v.*

verreyli, -liche, -ly, obs. ff. VERILY *adv.*

verreyment, var. VERIMENT *Obs.*

verri, southern ME. var. FAR *v.*; obs. f. VERY *a.* and *adv.*

†**ve'rricular**, *a. Obs.*$^{-0}$ [ad. mod.L. *verriculāris*, f. L. *verriculum* VERRICULE.] Resembling a net in form or construction (see quot.).

1706 PHILLIPS (ed. Kersey), *Verricular Tunick* (in Anat.), a Coat of the Eye, the same with *Amphiblestroides*. [After *Blancard's Phys. Dict.* (1693).]

ve'rriculate, *a. Ent.* [ad. mod.L. *verriculātus*, f. L. *verriculum*: see next.] (See quot.)

1826 KIRBY & SP. *Entomol.* IV. xlvi. 277 Verriculate,..having one or more verricules.

'**verricule.** *Ent.* [ad. L. *verricul-um* a dragnet, seine, f. *verrĕre* to sweep, etc.] (See quot.)

1826 KIRBY & SP. *Entomol.* IV. xlvi. 277 *Verricule*,..a thick-set tuft of parallel hairs.

verrie, obs. form of VERY.

†**verril**, obs. variant of *vervil* VARVEL.

c **1665** *God Speed the Plow* 23 in *Roxb. Ball.* (1889) VI. 524 When the Hauk on his fist doth stand, His hood and his verril's brave, and other things we have, Which yeelds joy to a Serving-man.

verrili, -ly, obs. ff. VERILY *adv.*

Verrinus, var. VERINAS *Obs.*

verritie, obs. Sc. f. VERITY.

Verrocchiesque (vɛrɒkɪ'ɛsk), *a.* [f. the name of Andrea del *Verrocchio*, a Florentine painter and sculptor (1435–88) + -ESQUE.] Suggestive of or resembling in subject or style the works of Verrocchio. Also **Ve'rrocchian** *a.* [-IAN].

1902 R. FRY *Let.* 23 Jan. (1972) I. 188 He went on to Verrochian and Botticellian ideas as the *Archangel and Virgin Enthroned* suggest. **1933** *Burlington Mag.* Mar. 140/1 The whole technique is closest to the most Verrocchiesque of all Leonardo's drawings. **1942** *Ibid.* Oct. 243/2 This panel has been attributed to Verrocchio; and..we must expect to find in it pronouncedly Verrocchiesque features.

verrore, southern ME. var. *farrer* FAR *a.*

verrour, var. VERRER *Obs.*; var. *werrour* WARRER.

‖**verruca** (vɛ'ruːkə). Pl. **verrucæ** (vɛ'ruːsiː). [L. *verrūca* wart, excrescence on precious stones. Cf. It. *verruca*, Prov. *veruca*.] **a.** A wart. **b.** *Bot.*, *Conch.*, *Ent.* A wart-like formation, growth, or prominence.

The pl. appears as *veruce* in Lanfranc's *Cirurg.* (E.E.T.S.) 296-7.

a. 1565 J. HALL *Lanfrank's Cirurg.* Table 41 Galen (rekening it with *Veruca*,..and other lyke affectes of the skinne,) teacheth how with a holowe quille to plucke it out. [**1671** SALMON *Syn. Med.* I. xlviii. 115 *Verruca*, a Wart, is a little tubercle on the Skin. **1693** tr. *Blancard's Phys. Dict.* (ed. 2), *Verrucæ*, Warts, a sort of *Tubercula*.] **1770** PENNANT *Zool.* IV. 85 On the chin [of the Noctule bat is] a little verruca. **1876** DUHRING *Dis. Skin* 349 *Verruca* is a hard or soft, rounded, flat, or acuminated, circumscribed, papillary formation. *a* **1883** FAGGE *Princ. & Pract. Med.* (1886) II. 718 Warts.—*Verrucæ, papillomata*.—These are small cutaneous tumours consisting in overgrowth of the papillæ of the cutis.

b. 1822 J. PARKINSON *Outl. Oryctol.* 118 The upper parts of all the areas [of *Echinus pentagonus*] are remarkably bare; but, about the rounded margin, the verrucæ..become frequent. **1826** KIRBY & SP. *Entomol.* IV. xlvi. 273 *Verruca*, a small flattish wart-like prominence. **1861** BENTLEY *Man. Bot.* i. 51 When sessile glands consist of cells containing solid secretions so that they form hardened spherical or other appendages upon the surface of the epidermis, they are termed *verrucæ* or *warts*.

'**verrucated**, *a. Conch.* Also 8 veruccated. [f. mod.L. *verrūcāt-us*, f. L. *verrūca* VERRUCA + -ED[1].] Having or covered with verrucæ or warty growths.

a **1728** WOODWARD *Fossils* (1729) I. II. 33 This small Shell has Stripes of brown, very thick, running parallel with the Volutæ... Two veruccated. **1819** SAMOUELLE *Entomol. Compend.* 88 Verrucated shell [of a crab].

ve'rruci-, combining form, on L. models, of L. *verrūca* VERRUCA, occurring in a few terms in *Biol.* and *Bot.*, as **verru'ciferous** *a.*, of a zoophyte: bearing verrucæ; **ve'rruciform** *a.*, wart-shaped.

verrucæform adj. (= prec.) occurs in Henslow *Dict. Bot. Terms* (1856) s.v.

1833 HOOKER in Smith *Eng. Flora* V. I. 132 *Apothecia* verruciform. **1846** DANA *Zooph.* (1848) 506 Corallum with deep immersed cells, interstices verruciferous, verrucæ convex. *Ibid.* 525 Summit branchlets verruciform.

verrucose (vɛruː'kəʊs), *a.* [ad. L. *verrūcōsus*, f. *verrūca* VERRUCA.]

1. Covered or furnished with, full of, verrucæ or wart-like excrescences or growths. Now *Nat. Hist.* and *Path.*

1686 PLOT *Staffordsh.* 181 A verrucose stone found near a petrifying Spring. **1721** BAILEY, *Verrucose*, Full of Warts. **1826** KIRBY & SP. *Entomol.* IV. xlvi. 273 *Verrucose*,..having several verrucæ. **1828** STARK *Elem. Nat. Hist.* II. 68 *Tritonia Hombergii*... Body oblong, subtetragonous, verrucose above. **1846** DANA *Zooph.* (1848) 527 Branches rather stout,..verrucose. **1883** LE CONTE & G. H. HORN *Classif. Coleoptera N. Amer.* 242 Head roughly granulate, or verrucose. **1899** *Allbutt's Syst. Med.* VIII. 816 The skin is covered by epidermis, in some parts thin and delicate, in others thick, horny, and verrucose.

fig. **1823** *Blackw. Mag.* XIV. 311 What designation could be more apt to mark the scurvy, verrucose, uneven,..and repulsive style of this man?

2. *Bot.* Studded with small warty swellings or protuberances; tubercular.

1802 R. HALL *Dict. Bot. Terms* 194 Verrucose,..warty. **1821** W. P. C. BARTON *Flora N. Amer.* I. 79 Seeds numerous, small, oval, verrucose, yellowish. **1874** COOKE *Fungi* 77 The sporidia in many cases are large, reticulated, echinulate or verrucose, and mostly somewhat globose. **1887** W. PHILLIPS *Brit. Discomycetes* 292 The verrucose epispore distinguishes this from its congeners.

Hence **verru'coseness**, 'fulness of warts'.

1727 BAILEY (vol. II).

verrucous (vɛ'ruːkəs), *a.* [ad. L. *verrūcōs-us*, f. *verrūca* VERRUCA: cf. prec. So OF. *verrucueux, veruqueux*, mod.F. *verruqueux, -euse*.]

1. = VERRUCOSE *a.* 1 and 2. *rare.*

1656 BLOUNT *Glossogr.* (following Cooper), *Verrucous*, full of warts, hillocks or knaps. **1658** PHILLIPS, *Verrucous*, full of warts or little excrescences of the flesh. [Similarly in CHAMBERS *Cycl.* (1728).] **1828-32** WEBSTER s.v., A verrucous capsule.

2. *Path.* Of the nature of a wart or warts; characterized by the formation of warts.

1728 CHAMBERS *Cycl.* s.v. *Verruca*, *Verrucous* is applied to any Excrescencies which have a resemblance to Warts. **1849-52** *Todd's Cycl. Anat.* IV. II. 1262/2 The urethra is sometimes occupied by verrucous vegetations, the result of gonorrhœa. **1876** DUHRING *Dis. Skin* 165 In thickened,..localized patches of eczema a peculiar warty, verrucous condition at times shows itself. **1900** *Hutchinson's Arch. Surg.* XI. 223 They are of the kind known as the Verrucous nævus.

verruculose (vɛruːkjʊ'ləʊs), *a.* [ad. mod.L. *verrūculōs-us*, f. L. *verrūcula*, dim. of *verrūca* VERRUCA.] Covered with small verrucæ or warts.

1846 DANA *Zooph.* (1848) 656 A series of granules..range along each side of the medial space, as if the surface were minutely verruculose. **1866** *Treas. Bot.* 1211/2.

verruga (vɛ'ruːgə). *Path.* [a. Sp. (also Pg. and Prov.) *verruga* wart:—L. *verrūca* VERRUCA.] The second, chronic stage of an infection by the bacterium *Bartonella bacilliformis*, characterized by wart-like skin lesions: see OROYA FEVER; formerly also called *Peruvian wart*. Also ***verruga peruana, peruviana*** [Sp. *peruana* Peruvian; *peruviana*, mod.L. rendering of this], and in pl. ***verrugas***.

[**1825** W. B. STEVENSON *Hist. & Descr. Narr. Twenty Years' Residence in S. Amer.* I. xiv. 347 *Berrugas*, warts of a peculiar kind, are common in some of the valleys of the coast [of Peru].] **1873** T. J. HUTCHINSON *Two Years in Peru* II. xx. 58 He was getting through an attack of that dreadful disease, the verrugas, and appeared but the shadow of a man. **1897** *Allbutt's Syst. Med.* II. 499 Patients suffering from verruga ..do not communicate the contagion to others. **1949**, etc. [see OROYA FEVER]. **1961** R. D. BAKER *Essent. Path.* ix. 190 Bartonellosis is a peculiar disease which occurs in Peru and is characterized by Oroya fever and verruga peruviana.

attrib. **1897** *Allbutt's Syst. Med.* II. 498 Verruga cases do better in warm places. *Ibid.* 499 The inhabitants of these verruga districts. **1968** T. WOLFE *Electric Kool-Aid Acid Test* xxi. 305 He can *feel*..every verruga fly, velvet ant, murine fleas and crabs.

†'**verry**, *a.* (and *sb.*). *Obs.* Forms: 6 verrye, verrie, 6-9 verrey, 6-8 verry. [var. of *varry* VAIRY *a.*]

1. *Her.* = VAIRY *a.* 1.

a **1550** LELAND *Itin.* II. 93, I marked yn the Wyndowes 3 sortes of Armes, one al verry of blew and white. **1562** LEGH *Armorie* 131 b, The seuenth doubling, is properly called Verrey, and is on this fashion, Argent, and Azure, or els Azure and Argent. **1572** BOSSEWELL *Armorie* II. 31 b, Some are borne Barrie vndee, barrye verrye, or enuecked. **1610** GUILLIM *Her.* (1611) I. iv. 15 Hee beareth Verry, Or and Azure by the name of Claude de Rochford. **1655** M. CARTE *Hon. Reviv.* (1660) 99 The next is called Vayre or Verry, this being of Argent and Azure, is termed Vaire onely; but if any other Colours, then must it be blazoned Verry of such Colours. **1656** BLOUNT *Glossogr.* [Hence in Phillips, Harris, Kersey, etc.] **1780** EDMONSTON *Heraldry* II, *Verrey*, or *Varry*, are names given to..fur..called *Vair*, if it is composed of..any other tincture than argent and azure.

¶**2.** Used as *sb.*, as if the name of a material or colour. Cf. VAIRY 2.

Drayton's use may be due to confusion with VAIR *sb.* 1. **1603** DRAYTON *Bar. Wars* II. xxii, A Ladies sleeue hie-spirited Hastings wore, Ferrer his Taberd with rich verry spred. **1812** CARY *Dante, Par.* XVI. 100 The column, clothed with verrey [It. *vajo*], still was seen Unshaken.

verry, southern ME. var. FAR *v.*; obs. f. VERY.

vers, southern ME. var. FRESH *a.*; abbreviation of VERSIN.

† **versa'bility.** *Obs.* [See next and -ITY.] **a.** = VERSATILITY 2. **b.** Aptness or readiness to be changed or turned (round).

1673 O. WALKER *Educ.* xi. 122 Wit..consists (saith Thesauro) in 1. perspicacity, which is the consideration of all..circumstances: and 2. versability, or speedy comparing them together. **1721** BAILEY, *Versability*, an aptness to be turn'd, chang'd or wound any way. **1762** STERNE *Tr. Shandy* v. xlii, By the versability of this great engine, round which they are twisted, to open new tracts of enquiry.

'versable, *a. Obs.*—⁰ [ad. L. *versābilis*, f. *versāre*: see VERSE *v.*²] (See quots.)

1623 COCKERAM I, *Versable*, which may be turned. **1656** BLOUNT *Glossogr.*, *Versable*, that turns, or may be turned; turned or wounden one about another. **1721** BAILEY; and in later Dicts.

Hence † **'versableness.** *Obs.*

1727 BAILEY (vol. II), *Versableness*, Aptness to be turned, or wound any way. [Hence in later Dicts.]

versail, var. VERSLE *v. Obs.*

Versailles (vɛə'saɪ). The name of a hunting lodge to the south-west of Paris built by Louis XIII and enlarged into a palace by Louis XIV in the 17th century, used to denote: **1.** *transf.* A building of similar style or splendour. Also *fig.*

1749 J. CLELAND *Mem. Woman Pleasure* I. 134 But had it been a dungeon..his presence would have made it a little Versailles. **1899** KIPLING *From Sea to Sea* I. xvii. 159 Jeypore Palace may be called the Versailles of India. **1959** M. CROSLAND tr. *J. Rovan's Germany* 140 Potsdam, the Prussian Versailles. **1968** *N.Y. City* (Michelin Tire Corp.) 47 The Hotel Pierre..a sort of '40-story Versailles'. **1977** 'R. PLAYER' *Month of Mangled Models* vii. 125 It was Jules Goncourt who had called the whole house the Versailles of Whoredom.

2. The site of the peace conference held there at the conclusion of the 1914–18 war which gave its name to the treaty signed there in 1919. Also *transf.*

1928 J. BUCHAN *Runagates Club* x. 273 The soldiers..would have made a cleaner and fairer job of it than the kind of circus that appeared at Versailles. **1936** G. B. SHAW *Millionairess* 117 There remained the clauses of the Versailles Treaty by which Germany was to be kept in a condition of permanent, decisive, and humiliating military inferiority to the other Powers. **1967** *Sat. Rev.* (U.S.) 8 Apr. 16/3 Most German politicians..ominously refer to this treaty as another 'Versailles'. **1971** *Guardian* 5 Aug. 10/4 In 1936..the Guardian was busily condemning the Versailles terms. **1981** J. WAINWRIGHT *Urge of Justice* I. ix. 59 Versailles is being repaid... Hitler..is putting greatness back into Germany.

'versal, *sb.* (and *a.*¹) [f. L. *vers-*, ppl. stem of *vertĕre* to turn (cf. *reversal*), associated with VERSE *sb.*] † **1.** = VERSIFICATION 3. *Obs. rare.*

1657 BAMPFIELD in *Burton's Diary* (1828) II. 222 Such..as they shall think fit to advise with, concerning the best versal of the Psalms. *Ibid.*, The amendment of Mr. Sternhold and Mr. Hopkins's Versal of the Psalms.

2. A special style of ornate capital letter used at the beginning of a verse or paragraph, etc., esp. in an illuminated manuscript; in modern calligraphy applied to capitals built up by inking between pen strokes and having serifs in the form of long, thin, straight lines. Freq. *attrib.* as *adj.*

1895 E. F. STRANGE *Alphabets* ix. 257 (*caption*) Versal letters. *Ibid.* 258 The versal is [a letter]..at the beginning of a chapter or section thereof. **1906** E. JOHNSTON *Writing & Illuminating* vii. 114 The earlier Versals had very simple and beautiful pen shapes... After the fourteenth century they were often..overdone with ornament. *Ibid.* xii. 205 In twelfth-century MSS. long delicate flourishes are commonly found, in red, blue, or green—matching the colours of the Versals. **1912** A. W. POLLARD *Fine Books* vi. 84 The small red letters at the beginning of each verse of a psalm, sometimes called versals. **1979** T. GOURDIE *Calligraphic Styles* 53 Versal Capitals are a pen-built form of the 'Trajan Roman' and are normally used to begin verses and chapters but may also be used to make impressive panels of lettering. **1981** D. MAHONEY *Craft of Calligraphy* 90 A versal letter is built up with a definite number of pen strokes. *Ibid.* 93 The stem width is the same in Versals of varying height.

versal ('vɜːsəl), *a.*² ? *Obs.* Also 8 'versal. [Illiterate or colloq. abbrev. of UNIVERSAL *a.* Cf. the later VARSAL *a.*]

1. Universal; whole. Usu. coupled with *world.*

1592 SHAKS. *Rom. & Jul.* II. iv. 219 Shee lookes as pale as any clout in the versall world. **1664** BUTLER *Hud.* II. iii. 930 Some, for brevity, Have cast the Versal World's Nativity. **1777** SHERIDAN *Trip to Scarborough* IV. i, That which they call pin-money, is to buy everything in the 'versal world.

2. Single; individual.

1709 MRS. MANLEY *Secret Mem.* I. 151 She..had provided no versal Thing for the Child. **1717** SUSANNA WESLEY in Southey *Wesley* (1820) I. 444 We are secluded from sight, or hearing, of any versal thing except Jeffrey.

versalie, pres. subj. of VERSLE *v. Obs.*

versant ('vɜːsənt), *sb.* [a. F. *versant* (15th c. in Littré), f. *verser*: see VERSE *v.*²]

1. The slope, side, or descent of a mountain or mountain-chain; the area or region covered by this. (Usu. with specifying epithet.)

1851 *Catal. Gt. Exhib.* IV. 1341/2 The species of oak which produces the cork vegetates..over the versants or faces of the Pyrenees. **1883** *Encycl. Amer.* I. 477/2 The best part of the United States for bee-farming is considered to be the Pacific versant. **1901** *Q. Rev.* July 18 The conifer forests..which clothe the eastern versant of the Victoria Nyanza.

2. Tendency to slope or descend; declination.

1859 R. F. BURTON *Centr. Afr.* in *Jrnl. Geog. Soc.* XXIX. 30 Thus the oriental half of the African continent has a compound versant, eastward with southing, and westward with southing.

versant ('vɜːsənt), *a.* [f. L. *versant-*, *versans*, pres. pple. of L. *versāre*, *versārī*: see VERSE *v.*² Cf. CONVERSANT *a.*]

1. Concerned, anxious, or busy *about*, occupied or engaged *in* or *with*, something.

1645 *Arraignm. of Persecution* 15 [His] nature hath ever been and is always versant in such cruelties. **1681** FLAVEL *Method of Grace* xxv. 432 His fears were once versant about noxious creatures, now God is the object of the fear of reverence. **1682** BOYLE *Cont. New Exp. Phys.-Mech.* II. Pref., The other [matter] was [for me] to be versant about those trials, which were not to be made..with natural air..but factitious air. **1861** *Temple Bar Mag.* III. 409 The literary question of the age was versant almost exclusively with verbal accuracy.

2. Of persons: **a.** Skilled, versed, or experienced *in* a subject, practice, etc., as the result of having been occupied with it.

In frequent use from *c* 1790 to *c* 1860. Now *rare.*

1766 W. GORDON *Gen. Counting-ho.* 3 It may be known..by any person versant in accounts, what sums are due. **1777** BOSWELL in *Johnson* 18 Sept., That is owing to his being so much versant in old English poetry. **1789** *Phil. Trans.* LXXIX. 107 Who is perfectly versant in the method of breeding the insect. **1805** T. HARRAL *Scenes of Life* II. 113 This gentleman..was completely versant in the grammatical niceties..of the language. **1842** SYD. SMITH *Wks.* (1850) 669 These excellent directors, versant in wood and metal. **1870** BURTON *Hist. Scot.* lxxii. (1873) VI. 312 Persons versant in the history of Scotland.

b. Conversant, familiar, or intimately acquainted *with* a subject or person.

1787 J. HOWIE in *Reformation Princ. Re-exhib.*, etc. 151 The Author,..being mostly versant with country-people, labours to speak and write in the vulgar dialect. **1822** SYD. SMITH *Wks.* (1850) 351 A man not versant with courts of justice will not believe it. **1836** *Fraser's Mag.* XIII. 289 Mr. Puff..had become versant with all the private affairs of all the boroughs. **1877** 'H. A. PAGE' *De Quincey* II. xvi. 30 A shepherd..who was versant with all the approaching changes of the weather.

3. *Conch.* Turning or curling over.

1839 *Penny Cycl.* XIV. 321/1 Family Columellidæ... Shell without a canal, but having the base of its aperture notched or versant, and the whorls of the spire large.

4. *Her.* (See quot.) *rare*—⁰.

c **1828** BERRY *Encycl. Her.* I. Gloss., *Versant*, the same as *reclivant*, called also *sursuant*; and implies erected, or elevated.

'versate, *v. rare*—¹. [f. L. *versāt-*, ppl. stem of *versāre*: see VERSE *v.*²] *trans.* To turn about.

1887 *Sat. Rev.* 17 Sept. 405 An edition which we can really versate in the..hand without causing the said hand to droop and ache.

versatile ('vɜːsətaɪl, 'vɜːsətɪl), *a.* Also 7 versatle, versatil, varsatile. [a. F. *versatile* (16th c., = It. *versatile*, Sp., Pg. *versatil*), or ad. L. *versātilis*, f. *versāre*: see VERSE *v.*²]

I. 1. a. Marked or characterized by changeability or inconstancy; subject to change or fluctuation; variable, changeable.

1605 BACON *Adv. Learn.* I. iii. §6. 15 It is rather the reuerence which many times both aduerse parts doe giue to honestie, than any versatile aduantage of their owne carriage. **1659** *Quæries on Proposalls of Officers of Armie to Parlt.* 4 To mold the versatle hypocrisy of his depraved mind. **1665** GLANVILL *Scepsis Sci.* xxvi. 161 Those versatile representations in the neck of a Dove. **1682** BURNET *Rights of Princes* Pref. 36 He also observes the Varsatile Temper of the Jesuits. **1791** BURKE *Let. to Member of Nat. Assemb.* Wks. 1842 I. 482 The versatile tenderness which marks the irregular and capricious feelings of the populace. **1798** GRANT *Surv. Prov. Moray* 279 The number of scholars vibrates from 20 to 90; but from the versatile state of the establishment, it is not possible that [etc.]. **1801** *Farmer's Mag.* Jan. 67 Our author..is of such a versatile disposition, that..he states [etc.]. **1853** KANE *Grinnell Exp.* ix. (1856) 67 The things were there half an hour ago. I saw them, capricious, versatile, full of forms, but bright and definite as the phases of sober life.

Comb. **1850** THACKERAY *Pendennis* lxiii, For at one instant to hate and defy a man,..and at the next to be..friendly with him, was not an unusual process with our versatile-minded Baronet.

b. Of persons: Fickle, inconstant. *rare.*

1682 BURNET *Rights Princes* viii. 293 Thomas Becket..was a proud varsatile and factious Man. **1697** EVELYN *Numism.* ix. 315 The French, Versatile, Unconstant. **1855** MILMAN *Lat. Chr.* VII. iv. (1864) IV. 148 The versatile people rose on his side [and] drove out the troops. **1882** MISS BRADDON *Mt.-Royal* iii, He is too versatile, too soft-hearted and impressionable.

c. Both heterosexual and homosexual. *slang.*

1959 [see BENT *ppl. a.* 5 c]. **1960** M. SPARK *Ballad Peckham Rye* iii. 32 Dougal was probably pansy. 'I don't think so... He's got a girl somewhere.' 'Might be versatile.'

2. Characterized by readiness or facility in turning from one subject, pursuit, or task to another; marked by many-sidedness or variety of talent.

In early use somewhat rare; freq. from *c* 1795.

1656 STANLEY *Hist. Philos.* (1687) 151/1 He was of a versatile wit, and in composure of his speech a difficult adversary. **1667** SPRAT *Hist. Royal Soc.* 18 Disputing is a very good instrument, to sharpen mens wits, and to make them versatil. **1791** COWPER *Odyssey* I. 2 Make the man thy theme, for shrewdness famed And genius versatile. **1796** H. HUNTER tr. *St.-Pierre's Stud. Nat.* (1799) II. 290 What then is that versatile faculty, called *reason?* *a* **1828** H. NEELE *Lit. Rem.* 19 Chaucer's genius was vast, versatile and original. **1856** FROUDE *Hist. Eng.* I. 158 A multitude of other subjects, with which his versatile ability made him conversant. **1874** GREEN *Short Hist.* i. §6 (1876) 52 His nature was sunny, versatile, artistic.

transf. **1791** NEWTE *Tour Eng. & Scot.* 171 The physical as well as the moral nature of man is extremely versatile, and accommodating to circumstances. **1801** *Lusignan* IV. 152 Absorbed in meditations and versatile reflections, he wandered, unconscious of the progress of time.

3. a. Of persons: Turning easily or readily from one subject or occupation to another; having an aptitude or faculty for fresh pursuits or tasks; showing facility in varied subjects; many-sided.

1762–71 H. WALPOLE *Vertue's Anecd. Paint.* (1786) II. 95 In 1665 the versatile Gerbier published a piece he called Subsidium Peregrinantibus. **1815** W. H. IRELAND *Scribbleomania* 213 Of this versatile writer, ah! what should be said. **1841** MACAULAY *Ess., W. Hastings* (1851) 634 The able and versatile Henry Dundas. **1851** THACKERAY *Eng. Hum.* vi. (1858) 327 The vivid and versatile genius who has touched on almost every subject of literature. **1874** STUBBS *Const. Hist.* I. xii. 460 He was an able man of business, versatile, politic.

b. Const. *in.*

1807 D'ISRAELI *Cur. Lit.* (ed. 5) I. 22 An individual, however versatile and extensive in his genius, would soon be exhausted. **1842** MISS MITFORD in L'Estrange *Life* (1870) III. ix. 144 O'Connell is versatile in his words and ways, and the Repeal seems to me incomprehensible. **1872** MINTO *Eng. Prose Lit.* I. i. 58 He is more versatile in the 'pitch' of his style.

II. 4. a. Capable of being turned round on, or as on, a pivot or hinge; that may be turned different ways. In later use *spec.* in *Ent.* and *Ornith.*

1658 PHILLIPS, *Versatile*, apt to be wound or turned any way. **1671** R. BOHUN *Wind* 72 A feather, or other versatil body. **1678** *Phil. Trans.* XII. 930 The Eyes resemble a Lens or Convex Glass set in a Versatile globular Socket. **1826** KIRBY & SP. *Entomol.* IV. xliii. 172 Some muscle of this kind must be in *Gryllotalpa*, and in those that have a versatile head. *Ibid.* 175 The Head..is sometimes versatile. **1840** *Penny Cycl.* XVIII. 306/1 Tarsus [in barbets is] shorter than the versatile toe. **1872** COUES *N. Amer. Birds* 200 Hallux of average length,..outer toe more or less perfectly versatile (but never permanently reversed).

b. *Bot.* Of an anther: Swinging or turning about freely on a filament to which it is attached.

1760 J. LEE *Introd. Bot.* III. xxii. (1765) 228 The Anthera is versatile and incumbent, when it is fastened on at its Side. **1787** *Families of Plants* I. 254 Anthers oblong, versatile. **1830** LINDLEY *Nat. Syst. Bot.* 47 Their small round and versatile anthers. **1861** S. THOMSON *Wild Fl.* I. (ed. 4) 65 The filament..may..be so attached to some point of the anther as to allow it to swing loosely, when a *versatile* anther is constituted. **1870** HOOKER *Stud. Flora* 182 Dipsaceæ,..anthers versatile.

c. Of a leaf: turning either way. *rare*—¹.

1870 HOOKER *Stud. Flora* 335 Populas tremula... Leaves 1–4 in., versatile.

Hence **'versatilely** *adv.*, **'versatileness.**

1646 GAULE *Cases Consc.* 130 [A witch] that works not only darkly and closely, but variously and versatilly, as God will permit [etc.]. **1654** R. CODRINGTON tr. *Iustine* viii. 129 According to the versatilness of his wit. **1727** BAILEY (vol. II), *Versatileness*, aptness to be turned or wound any way. **1791** J. LEARMONT *Poems, Mutability of Man* 20 Versatileness attends him still; A deep inwoven art Conceals..the guile And rancour of his heart. **1872** M. COLLINS *Two Plunges for Pearl* iv, An intellect so different from his own—so versatilely fluent, yet passionately obstinate.

versatility (vɜːsə'tɪlɪtɪ). [a. F. *versatilité* (= It. *versatilità*, Sp. *versatilidad*, Pg. *-idade*), or directly f. prec. + -ITY.]

1. The condition or quality in persons, their conduct, etc., of being changeable, fickle, or inconstant; tendency or liability to vary in opinion or action; variableness, inconstancy.

1755 JOHNSON, *Versatility*, the quality of being versatile. **1782** V. KNOX *Ess.* xii. (1819) I. 71 This versatility and duplicity of the *grande monde.* **1783** W. THOMSON *Watson's Philip III*, v. 324 To his holiness, whom they suspected of a versatility of character, which might soon lead him to relapse:..they answered [etc.]. **1814** D'ISRAELI *Quar. Auth.* (1867) 346 We are apt to condemn their versatility of principles as arising from dishonest motives. **1849** MACAULAY *Hist. Engl.* ii. I. 213 Ashley's versatility was the effect, not of levity, but of deliberate selfishness. **1855** MILMAN *Lat. Chr.* VII. ii. III. 168 He might indeed dread the versatility of Henry's character, and his ready assent to the advice of flattering..counsellors.

2. The faculty or character of turning or being able to turn readily to a new subject or occupation, esp. of an intellectual nature;

facility in taking up varied pursuits or tasks with some success or distinction; many-sidedness.

1798 BISSET *Life Burke* 210 Wedderburne [was] eminent for acuteness, versatility, and ingenuity. 1827 SCOTT *Surg. Dau.* x, His intelligence, his learning, above all, his versatility and freedom from prejudices of every kind. 1874 GREEN *Short Hist.* vi. §6 (1876) 325 It was with Italian versatility that he turned from the camp to the counting house. 1882 J. SULLY in *Mind* No. 27. 366 In the scientific treatment of the subject..we shall make versatility synonymous with width of faculty, or diversity of capability in all its measures.

b. Const. *of* (wit, character, etc.).

a 1773 CHESTERF. *Charac. Pitt* (1777) 46 He..had such a versatility of wit, that he would adopt it to all sorts of conversation. *a* 1842 ARNOLD *Hist. Rome* II. 495 Cineas.. was in the versatility and range of his talents worthy of the best ages of Greece. 1853 J. H. NEWMAN *Hist. Sk.* (1873) II. I. ii. 70 Not often indeed do the Oriental nations present us with an example of versatility of character. 1866 FELTON *Anc. & Mod. Gr.* I. xii. 231 [Aristophanes] reminds us.. still oftener of the splendid versatility of poetical genius.. displayed by Goethe.

c. *pl.* Features or traits of versatile intellect.

1841 D'ISRAELI *Amen. Lit.* (1859) II. 123 A voluminous commentary expounded the morality of the ravishing versatilities of Ariosto.

3. Diversity of nature or character; variety of application, etc.

1802 PLAYFAIR *Illustr. Hutton. The.* 339 The Huttonian system cannot boast of theories of equal versatility. 1822–7 GOOD *Study Med.* (1829) II. 419 The symptoms, that principally mark the progress of this disease in all their versatility;..it is this versatility that has produced the chief differences of opinion, entertained concerning it. 1871 EARLE *Philol. Eng. Tongue* 458 The Book of Proverbs abounds in examples of the versatility of the Hebrew *and.* 1879 CHURCH *Spenser* 35 The inexhaustible versatility of the English tongue.

4. Capability of turning about as on a pivot.

1884 COUES *Key N. Amer. Birds* 126 We have no case of true versatility of the hind toe among North American birds.

† **ver'satilous**, *a. Obs. rare.* [f. L. *versātil-is* VERSATILE *a.* + -OUS.] Marked or characterized by versatility or variableness; versatile.

1629 H. BURTON *Truth's Triumph* 347 He can finde no certaine demonstration..but that he can stoppe with his versatilous wit. 1650 ELDERFIELD *Civ. Right Tythes* 135 Whose versatilous shifts are hard to be avoided.

Hence † **ver'satilousness**. *Obs.*$^{-1}$

1640 BP. REYNOLDS *Passions* xxvi. 269 Another cause of Boldnesse, is Immunity from Danger, or at least a Versatilousnesse and Dexterity of wit to evade it.

† **ver'sation.** *Obs.* [ad. L. *versātiōn-*, *versātio*, noun of action f. *versāre*: see VERSE *v.*^{2}] A turning over or backwards and forwards. Also *attrib.*

1656 BLOUNT *Glossogr.* (following Cooper), *Versation*, a turning or winding. 1673 OLEY *Pref. to Jackson's Wks.* I. p. xxx, Reader, if thou wilt believe thirty or forty years experience, or versation of this author, thou wilt find at every return new matter both of observation and delight in him. 1716 M. DAVIES *Athen. Brit.* III. 8 Any other of the Rough Versation-Orders of our Dissenting Separatists. 1837 *Fraser's Mag.* XV. 717 Requiring such perpetual versation of the pages backwards and forwards to connect one section with another.

'**versative**, *a. rare*$^{-1}$. [f. L. *versāt-*, ppl. stem of *versāre* VERSE *v.*^{2}] Marked by adaptability or variety.

1846 *Blackw. Mag.* LIX. 416 Homer possibly had no choice; but in the hexameter there is the greatest versative power.

versche, southern ME. variant of FRESH *a.*

‖ **vers de société** (vɛr də sɔsjete). [Fr., lit. 'verse of society'.] Verse that treats of topics provided by polite society in a light, often witty style.

1796 I. D'ISRAELI *Miscellanies* 149 This species of poetry can only exist in an age where refinement is introduced into literature, as well as into everything else. We must, therefore, look for it..among a people the most refined among it's [*sic*] neighbours... It has been significantly called '*Vers de Societé*'. 1817 G. CRABBE *Jrnl.* 11 July in *Poet Wks.* (1834) I. 248 His poetry [is] far beyond that implied in the character of *Vers de Société*. 1867 F. LOCKER-LAMPSON *Lyra Elegantiarum* 9 Smoothly written *vers de société*, where a boudoir decorum is, or ought always to be, preserved; where sentiment never surges into passion, and where humour never overflows into boisterous merriment. 1934 T. S. ELIOT *Elizabethan Ess.* 35, I am used to..being informed that something which I meant seriously is *vers de société*. 1976 *Times* 26 Jan. 7/5 Quirky *vers de société*..by Ogden Nash.

‖ **vers d'occasion** (vɛr dɔkazjɔ̃). [Fr.] Light verse written for a special occasion (see OCCASIONAL *a.* 2b).

1867 F. LOCKER-LAMPSON *Lyra Elegantiarum* 11 *Vers de société* and *vers d'occasion* should be short, elegant, refined, and fanciful. 1933 *N. & Q.* 26 Aug. 143/1 Many of his pieces are somewhat unskilful *vers d'occasion*. 1946 R. LEHMANN *Gipsy's Baby* 71 She was a great one for *vers d'occasion*. Upon my birthday..I received..a pale pink scalloped gilt-edged card inscribed..in a frame of hand-painted roses. 1960 *20th Cent.* Sept. 276 The *vers d'occasion* includes some limericks and clerihews. 1982 B. ASKWITH *Piety & Wit* vii. 112 The bons mots, the puns, the vers d'occasion, travel badly in time.

verse (vɜːs), *sb.* Forms: 1, 4 **fers** (1 **færs, fyrs**), 3 *Orm.* **ferrs**; 1–4 **uers**, 1, 3–4, 5–6 *Sc.*, **vers**, 4–5 **wers**; 4– **verse**, 5, 6 *Sc.*, **werse**; 5 **veerse, veerce**, 6 **vearse**, 5–6 *Sc.* **veirs**, 6 *Sc.* **veirse**. [OE. *fers*, corresponding to OFris. *fers* (WFris. *fêrs*, NFris. *fês*, etc.), MDu. (Du.) and MLG. *vers*, OHG., MHG. *vers*, *fers* (G. *vers*), ON. (Da., Sw.) *vers*, ad. L. *versus* a line or row, spec. a line of writing (so named from turning to begin another line), verse, f. *vertĕre* to turn; in ME. reinforced by or newly a. AF. and OF. (also mod.F.) *vers* (= Pr. *vers*, It., Sp, Pg. *verso*) from the same source.

In OE. (the word being neuter), and to a certain extent in ME., the pl. was the same as the sing.]

1. a. A succession of words arranged according to natural or recognized rules of prosody and forming a complete metrical line; one of the lines of a poem or piece of versification.

c 900 tr. *Baeda's Hist.* IV. xxiv. (1890) 344 Þa ongon he sona singan in herenesse Godes Scyppendes þa fers [*v.r.* uers] & þa word þe he næfre ȝehyrde. *c* 1000 ÆLFRIC *Gram.* xxxvii. (Z.) 218 *Uersificor*, ic fersiȝe oððe ic wyrce fers. *c* 1050 *Byrhtferth's Handboc* in *Anglia* (1885) VIII. 313 Þæt pentimemeris byð þe todælð þæt vers on þam oðrum fet. *c* 1200 ORMIN Ded. 59 And icc ne mihhte nohht min ferrs Aȝȝ wiþþ Goddspelless wordess Wel fillenn all. 13.. *Cato* 633 in *Minor P. Vernon MS.* 609 Þe [= thee] merueyles of þise nakede vers [that] Beoþ maked bi two and two. *c* 1369 CHAUCER *Dethe Blanche* I. 463 He made of ryme ten verses [*v.r.* vers] or twelue Of a complaynt. *c* 1380 WYCLIF *Last Age Ch.* (1840) 33 Sibille acordiþ herto þat suche tribulacioun is nyȝe in þes verse. *c* 1400 MAUNDEV. (Roxb.) ii. 5 As it es contende in þis werse, whilk es here writen. 1479 *Paston Lett.* III. 242 Thes too verse afore seyde be of myn own makyng. 1483 CAXTON *Cato* 9, I haue made this lytel book in double verses the whiche conteynen two shorte and utyle sentences for the symple folke. *a* 1513 FABYAN *Chron.* (1516) 200 And for this Scisme thus graciously was endyd, a Vercifier made this verse folowynge: Lux fulsit mundo cessit Felix Nicholao. 1567 in *Gude & Godlie B.* (S.T.S.) [p. cxxxiv], Sing thir four veirs efter euerie Psalme as followis. 1597–8 BACON *Ess., Ceremonies* (Arb.) 26 Some mens behauiour is like a verse wherein euery sillable is measured. 1642 FULLER *Holy & Prof. St.* IV. xv. 316 When..the Spanish Embassadour..had summed up the effect thereof in a Tetrastich, she instantly in one verse rejoined her answer. 1664 BUTLER *Hud.* II. i. 28 But those that write in Rhime, still make The one Verse for the others sake. 1709 HEARNE in *Chron. R. Gloucester* (1724) App. 601 There are eight Verses in the Tale it self, which are not in the common Editions. *a* 1771 GRAY *Observ. Eng. Metre* Wks. 1843 V. 260 The verse of fourteen [syllables]..and verse of six. 1822 S. TILLBROOK in *Southey's Poet. Wks.* (1853) p. xx/2, Eight verses of hexametrical dimensions. 1842 *Penny Cycl.* XXII. 370/1 An hexameter verse which has a spondee in the fifth place, is called a spondaic verse. 1895 A. W. WARD *Pope's Wks.* p. li, The ordinary rule as to the position of the *cæsura* in the verse.

(*b*) *spec.* with historical reference to Old English poetry.

1715 E. ELSTOB *Rudiments Gram. Eng.-Saxon Tongue* 68 The Saxon Verses consist of three, four, five, six, seven, eight, or more syllables. 1883 H. M. KENNEDY tr. *Ten Brink's Hist. Eng. Lit.* I. 22 The sentence rarely closes with the ending of the verse. 1938 A. CAMPBELL *Battle of Brunanburh* 16 Sievers showed once and for all the combinations of accentual elements, which might be used to build a verse. 1958 A. J. BLISS *Metre of Beowulf* 1 The term 'verse' is here used instead of the more cumbrous 'half-line' or 'hemistich'.

b. In the pl. occas. merging into sense 5.

1477 EARL RIVERS (Caxton) *Dictes* 14 He hadde many verses techyng folkis to eschewe their propre willes. 1500–20 DUNBAR *Poems* lix. 16 He hes indorsit myn indytting With versis off his awin hand vrytting. 1579 SPENSER *Sheph. Cal., June* 42 Tho couth I sing of loue, and tune my pype Vnto my plaintiue pleas in verses made. 1601 SHAKS. *Jul. C.* III. iii. 34 *Cinna.* I am Cinna the Poet...4[*th Cit.*] Teare him for his bad verses. *a* 1643 W. CARTWRIGHT *Love's Convert* IV. v, They do swarm hither with their Verses, Like Town-poets on some Lord's Son's Wedding-day. 1714 (*title*), Rymer's Translations from Greek, Latin and Italian Poets; with other Verses and Songs. 1779 JOHNSON *L.P., Lyttelton* ¶1 The verses cant of shepherds and flocks, and crooks dressed with flowers. 1805 H. K. WHITE *Let. to B. Maddock* 18 Oct., I have this week written some very elaborate verses for a college prize.

c. With distinguishing terms. (Cf. 6c.)

1546 LANGLEY tr. *Pol. Verg. De Invent.* I. viii. 16 A songe of Exameter Verses. 1576 FLEMING *Panopl. Epist.* 377 To write in heroicall Verses. 1603 HOLLAND *Plutarch's Mor.* 1246 A chronicler penning the historie of these affaires in elegiack verses. 1605, 1656 [see SERPENTINE *a.* 1b]. 1658 [see LEONINE *a.* 2]. 1728 CHAMBERS *Cycl.* s.v. *Hexameter*, Epic Poems, as the Iliad, Odyssee, Æneid, &c. consist of Hexameter Verses alone. *Ibid.*, *Serpentine Verses*, are such as begin and end with the same Word. 1756 J. WARTON *Ess. Pope* x. (1782) II. 211 Like Ovid's Fasti, in hexameter and pentameter verses. 1774 WARTON *Hist. Eng. Poetry* (1870) 30 The verses which we call Alexandrine. 1815 [see FESCENNINE *a.*]. 1818 J. C. HOBHOUSE *Hist. Illust.* (ed. 2) 442 [Italian] heroic verses have not the advantage of the hexametral length.

2. *Liturg.* = VERSICLE 1. Now *rare.*

c 960 *Rule St. Benet* ix. (1885) 33 Cweþe ærest þis fers: Deus in adiutorium meum intende. *Ibid.* xi. 35 Singe man ærest six sealmas and þonne on ende fers. *c* 1030 *Ibid.* (Logeman) 41 Æfter þisum rædingum fylian..syx sealmas mid antiphonam, swa swa þa æreran & mid ferse. *a* 1400 *Prymer* (1891) 88 R'. Delyuere me lord. With these thre ueers. V'. Now cryst. V'. Brennynge soules wepiþ [etc.]. V'. Schappere of alle þynges. *c* 1450 *Myrr. Our Ladye* 114 What is vnderstonded by the thre lessons wyth the Responces & verses folowynge. *a* 1500 *Chaucer's Dreme* 1806 Many orisones and verses, Withoute note full softely Said were and that full heartily. 1548–9 (Mar.) *Bk. Com. Prayer* Pref., Respondes, Verses, vaine repeticions. 1627 *Cosin's Corr.* (Surtees) I. 111 Doth he begin with the Lord's Prayer; orderly proceeding with the Verses and Responds. 1657 SPARROW *Rationale* 29 Then follow the Verses, 'O Lord open Thou our Lips, And our mouth shall shew forth thy praise'. 1762 *Evening-Office of Church* (ed. 2) Direct. 3 Then is sung the Hymn with its Verse and Responsory. 1763 BURN *Eccl. Law* I. 38 The invitatories, responsories, verses, collects, and whatever is said or sung in the quire. 1877 J. D. CHAMBERS *Div. Worship* 91 The Gradual, Alleluya, and Responsory and Verses.

† **3.** A clause, sentence, or the like; an article of the Creed. *Obs.*

c 1000 ÆLFRIC *Gram.* l. (Z.) 291 Se þridda hatte *distinctio* oððe *periodos*, se belycð þaet fers [*v.rr.* færs, fyrs]. *c* 1000 —— *Pref. Genesis* (Grein) 23 Eft stynt on þære bec on þam forman ferse: *Et spiritus dei ferebatur super aquas.* *c* 1175 *Lamb. Hom.* 75 Þet rihte ileue setten þe twelue apostles on write,..& ec of heom wrat ther of his uers, & sancte peter wrat þet ereste. *Ibid.* 77 We habbeð bigunnen ou to seggen on englisch hwat biqueþ þe crede, & habbeð ou iseið twa uers. *c* 1425 WYNTOUN *Cron.* v. xi. 3495 Sancte Ierome wrat til hym..*Gloria Patri* in til twa werse. 1535 COVERDALE *Deut.* iv. 13 He declared vnto you his couenaunt, which he commaunded you to do, namely, the ten verses. 1560 *Proude Wyves Pater Noster* 116 in Hazl. *E.P.P.* IV. 157, I pray you, gossyp dere, vnderstand well this verse.

4. a. One of the sections of a psalm or canticle corresponding to the compound unit (usually a couplet) of Hebrew poetry. (Now merged in next.)

c 1200 ORMIN 11943 Forr þær iss sett an oþerr ferrs þatt spekeþþ off þe deofell. *a* 1225 *Ancr. R.* 36 Þe vorme psalm is 'Iubilate'.., þe vifte, 'Laudate Dominum in sanctis ejus'; and in euerichon beoð vif vers. *c* 1290 *S. Eng. Leg.* I. 34 [He] seide þeos two vers of þe sauter. *Ibid.* 225 Þe foweles sunge ek here matyns,..& of þe sauter seide þe uers. *c* 1325 *Spec. Gy Warw.* 460 Sein Daui seiþ, if þu wolt loke In a vers of þe sauter boke [etc.]. 1377 LANGL. *P. Pl.* B. XII. 290 Þe glose graunteth vpon þat vers [Ps. xxiii. 4] a gret mede to treuthe. *c* 1425 WYNTOUN *Cron.* v. xi. 3508 Of þe psalmys distyntly Þe ta syde sulde þe fyrst werse say, Þe toþir þe next werse ay Sulde begyn. *c* 1450 *Rewle Sustris Menouresses* (1915) 103 Þan þe quere on þat one syde schal take his verse, & þe Quere on þat oþer syde schal take anoþer verse [of Ps. li]. 1508 FISHER *7 Penit. Ps.* cxxx. Wks. (1876) 208 It is also profytable for good & ryghtwyse people ofte to reherse this verse [Ps. cxxx. 1] wherby they may auoyde the grete perylles of this wretched worlde. 1526 *Pilgr. Perf.* (W. de W. 1531) 163b, Yf..for ony necessite, a psalme scape ony persone, or a lesson, or else y^t they omyt one verse or twayne.

b. One of the sections into which a chapter of the Bible is divided. Freq. abbreviated as *v.* ***chapter and verse***: see CHAPTER *sb.* 10b.

The practice of dividing the chapters of the Bible into verses, introduced by Stephanus in 1551, was adopted by Whittingham in his New Testament (1557) and followed in the Geneva Bible (1560).

1560 BIBLE (Geneva) To Rdr., The argumentes bothe for the booke and for the chapters with the nombre of the verse are added. 1643 CARYL *Expos. Job* 178 Verse 2 [of ch. iii]... This verse is only a transition into the matter of the next. 1678 BUTLER *Hud.* III. ii. 1170 One single Red-Coat Sentinel ..could disperse Whole Troops, with Chapter rais'd, and Verse. 1685 BAXTER *Paraphr. N.T.* John viii. 3 The last Verse of the foregoing Chapter and the eleven first Verses of this Chapter. 1729 LAW *Serious C.* i. 8 That Religion..is to be found in almost every verse of Scripture. 1818 HORNE *Introd. Script.* (1834) II. 75 The verses into which the New Testament is now divided. 1847 *Kitto's Cycl. Bibl. Lit.* II. 909 *note*, The twentieth verse of the tenth chapter of Matthew. 1888 E. ABBOT *Crit. Ess.* xx. 465 The first edition of the New Testament divided into our present verses was printed by Robert Stephens at Geneva in 1551.

Comb. 1855 I. TAYLOR *Restor. Belief* (1856) 186 A verse-by-verse commentary.

5. a. A small number of metrical lines so connected by form or meaning as to constitute either a whole in themselves or a unit in longer composition; a stanza.

In quots. *c* 1340 and 1387 applied to elegiac and hexameter couplets. In later use the pl. is sometimes not clearly distinct from 1b.

c 1308 *Sat. Kildare* i. in *E.E.P.* (1862) 153 Þis uers is ful well iwroȝt, hit is of wel furre y-broȝt. *Ibid.* iii, Þis uers is imakid wel of consonans and wowel. *c* 1340 HAMPOLE *Pr. Consc.* 246 Of þis Saynt Bernard witnes bers And er þa four wryten in þis vers. 1387 TREVISA *Higden* (Rolls) II. 83 So hit semeþ þat þis vers wolde mene þat þese feyned goddes regneþ..in Chestre. 1502 DOUGLAS *Pal. Hon.* III. xcii, In laude of honour I wrait thir versis thre. 1573–80 BARET *Alvearie* s.v., A verse: a charme: a prophesie, *carmen.* 1598 GRENEWEY *Tacitus, Ann.* III. xiii. (1622) 83 The Smyrnæans alleaged an oracle of Apollo,..the Tenians a verse [L. *carmen*] of the same Apollo, commanding them to offer an image and Temple to Neptune. 1601 SHAKS. *Twel. N.* II. iv. 7 Now good Cesario, but that peece of song, That old and Anticke song we heard last night;..Come, but one verse. 1711 ADDISON *Spect.* No. 74 ¶5 The Country of the Scotch Warriors, described in these two last Verses [of 'Chevy Chase']. 1793 BURNS *Let. to G. Thomson* 7 April, I remember the two last lines of a verse in some of the old songs of 'Logan Water',..which I think pretty. 1801 BUSBY *Dict. Mus.* s.v., In secular music, as a song or ballad, each stanza of the words is a verse. 1838 DICKENS *O. Twist* xxvi, A young lady proceeded to entertain the company with a ballad in four verses. 1860 TYNDALL *Glac.* I. xxiii. 167 It was at once proposed to sing a verse from Schiller's play.

b. *Mus.* (See quot.)

1801 BUSBY *Dict. Mus.*, *Verse*, the appellation given to those portions of an anthem meant to be performed by a single voice to each part.

c. That part of a modern popular song which leads into the chorus, or separates one chorus from another. Cf. CHORUS *sb.* 6c.

1927 *Melody Maker* Aug. 782/2 The verse is then taken 'hot' by the trumpet, who gives a fine example of what modern 'hot' playing..should be. 1929, 1935 [see CHORUS *sb.* 6c]. 1966 *Melody Maker* 7 May 13/1 Wonder charges through the verse and builds up into the repetitious chorus.

6. a. Without article: Metrical composition, form, or structure; language or literary work written or spoken in metre; poetry, esp. with reference to metrical form. Opposed to *prose*.

a **1300** *Cursor M.* 22227 We wat bath thoru stori and wers, þat þe kingrikes o grece and pers War hefd kingrikes in form tide. **14..** *Chaucer's Sompn. T.* 297 (Harl. MS.), Schortly may no man, by rym and vers, Tellen her thoughtes, thay ben so dyvers. *c* **1425** WYNTOUN *Cron.* v. xi. 3492 This Damasyus.. Couth mak rycht weill in metyre vers. *a* **1586** SIDNEY *Apol. Poetrie* (Arb.) 50 That Verse farre exceedeth Prose in the knitting vp of the memory, the reason is manifest. **1651** HOBBES *Leviath.* II. xxvi. 141 In antient time, before letters were in common use, the Lawes were many times put into verse. **1696** PRIOR *Secretary* 16 Athens.., Where people knew love, and were partial to verse. **1728** CHAMBERS *Cycl.* s.v. *Stanza*, For though we speak Verse on the Stage, 'tis still presumed we are speaking Prose. **1779** JOHNSON *L.P.*, *Dryden* (1868) 186 To write verse, is to dispose syllables and sounds harmonically by some known and settled rule. **1827** POLLOK *Course T.* III, He searched again.. For theme deserving of immortal verse. **1883** R. NOEL in *Contemp. Rev.* Nov. 709 *note*, We find.. much nakedly argumentative ratiocinative verse, but that is not, strictly speaking, poetry at all.

personif. **1580** SPENSER *Let. to Harvey* Wks. (1912) 636 Unhappy Verse,.. Make thy selfe fluttring wings of thy fast flying Thought. *c* **1645** MILTON *Sonn. to Lawes* 9 Thou honour'st Verse, and Verse must lend her wing To honour thee.

b. Freq. ***in verse***, in metrical form. Also *fig.* (quot. 1390).

c **1315** SHOREHAM VII. 191 O god hyt hys, and stent in uers Ine þulke song [= Athanasian Creed]. **1340** *Ayenb.* 128 He wenþ libbe yet uourti yer, ase zayþ elyuans ine uers of þe dyaþe. **1390** GOWER *Conf.* III. 3 For Dronkeschipe is so divers, It may no whyle stonde in vers. *c* **1425** WYNTOUN *Cron.* VI. x. 859 His epitaphi þan in werse Wryttyn þus men may rahers. **1483** CAXTON *Cato* 3 Two partyes—the fyrst is in prose and the second in verse. **1500–20** DUNBAR *Poems* xxxii. 43, I will no lesingis put in vers. **1557** *Tottel's Misc.* To Rdr., That to haue wel written in verse.. deserueth great praise [etc.]. **1586** W. WEBBE *Eng. Poet.* (Arb.) 30 Thinking nothing to be learnedly written in verse, which fell not out in ryme. **1643** CARYL *Expos. Job* 178 Job breaths out his passion in verse, and in verse receives his answer. **1689** PRIOR *Ep. to Fleetwood Shephard* 97 In Verse or Prose, We write or chat. **1762–71** H. WALPOLE *Vertue's Anecd. Paint.* (1786) I. 132 The Introduction to knowledge, partly in verse and partly in prose. **1838** THIRLWALL *Greece* II. 124 In Crete and at Sparta.. the maxims of the constitution were delivered in verse. **1841** W. SPALDING *Italy & It. Isl.* III. 272 The Romans choose this form.. for conveying their feelings in verse.

c. With distinguishing terms. (Cf. 1 c.)

Adonic, Alexandrine, blank, elegiac, heroic(al, hexameter, Leonine, Saturnian verse, etc.: see those words.

1552 HULOET s.v., Verse heroicall, or of sixe feete, *versus heroicus*. **1585** JAS. VI *Ess. Poesie* (Arb.) 68 For flyting, or Inuectiues, vse.. Rouncefallis, or Tumbling verse. **1685** DRYDEN (*title*), The twenty-ninth Ode of the third Book of Horace; paraphrased in Pindarick Verse. **1711** ADDISON *Spect.* No. 39 ¶5 Aristotle observes, that the Iambick Verse in the Greek Tongue was the most proper for Tragedy. **1855** MILMAN *Lat. Chr.* XIV. iv. VI. 488 An interminable length of harsh hexameter, or of elegiac verse.

7. a. The metrical or poetical compositions of a particular author, etc.; a certain amount of metrical work or poetry considered as a whole.

1586 W. WEBBE *Eng. Poetrie* (Arb.) 32 Lydgate.., surely for good proportion of his verse.. comparable with Chawcer. **1611** SHAKS. *Wint. T.* V. i. 101 Thus your Verse Flow'd with her Beautie once. *c* **1715** POPE *Ep. Jervas* 1 This Verse be thine, my friend, nor thou refuse This, from no venal or ungrateful Muse. **1810** SCOTT *Lady of L.* I. xxxii, Till to her lips in measured frame The minstrel verse spontaneous came. **1849** MACAULAY *Hist. Eng.* iii. I. 401 The verse of Waller still breathed the sentiments which had animated a more chivalrous generation. **1906** *Lit. World* 15 Nov. 487/2 Some of the poems are spoiled by.. hate of England... Had it been omitted the verse would have been improved.

†**b.** A particular style of metre or versification.

1586 W. WEBBE *Eng. Poetrie* (Arb.) 30 A singuler gyft in a sweete Heroicall verse. *Ibid.* 34 Master D. Phaer.. had the best peece of Poetry whereon to sette a most gallant verse.

8. *attrib.*, as ***verse-beat, -book, -craft, -cup, -end, -form, -line, -pair, -rhythm, -shot, -unit, -wit***, etc.; †**verse-fellow**, a fellow or companion verse-maker; **verse anthem** (see quots.); **verse-service** (see quots.).

1801 BUSBY *Dict. Mus.*, **Verse*,.. the epithet applied to an anthem beginning with verse. **1876** STAINER & BARRETT *Dict. Mus. Terms* 446/1 A verse anthem is one which begins with soli portions as opposed to a full anthem, which commences with a chorus. **1943** E. SITWELL *Poet's Notebk.* xxviii. 134 The *verse-beat is *not* very strong in this passage. **1849** LYTTON *Caxtons* 22 Rude songs, modelled from such *verse-books as fell into my hands. **1894** *Daily News* 20 Oct. 6/1 Her own skill in *versecraft gives her unusual felicity of insight. **1885** S. COX *Expositions* xxii. 290 We have kept the best wine in this little *Verse-cup until now. **1930** T. SASAKI *On Lang. R. Bridges' Poetry* I. v. 24 The fully strong stress at the *verse-end. **1592** NASHE *Four Lett. Confuted* Wks. (Grosart) II. 235 To beare his old *verse-fellow noble M. Valanger company. **1887** G. M. HOPKINS *Let.* 20 Oct. (1956) 381 The style of prose is a positive thing and not the absence of *verse-forms. **1906** G. P. KRAPP *Andreas* p. xlvi, The distinctively epic verse-form. **1966** *English Studies* XLVII. 97 In a difficult and restrictive verse-form, one might expect the poet to resort to the use of convenient whole-line units more.. often. **1927** D. H. LAWRENCE *Mornings in Mexico* 66 He had written the thing [*sc.* a love-poem] straight ahead, without *verse-lines or capitals. **1953** *Speculum* XXVIII. 449 The recurrence of verses and *verse-pairs in Anglo-Saxon poetry. **1930** T. SASAKI *On Lang. R. Bridges' Poetry* I. v. 21 Lines in verse.. form units of *verse-rhythm intermediate between a 'foot' and a 'stanza'. **1942** J. C. POPE *Rhythm of Beowulf* 22 In no case is it necessary to pass beyond the limits of accentual adjustment that verse-rhythm everywhere allows. **1851** J. S. ADAMS *5000 Mus. Terms* 105 **Verse service*, a service in which verses are introduced. **1889** *Grove's Dict. Music* (1902) IV. 257 A verse-service or verse-anthem sometimes includes portions set for a voice *solo*. **1794** MATHIAS *Purs. Lit.* (1797) II. 13 *note*, Before they were half finished,.. as many of the others as were within hearing or **verse-shot*.. were all found fast asleep!!! **1948** *Mod. Philology* XLVI. 77 When the character of the dipody, or *verse unit, is examined, the first impression is one of extreme variation. **1966** *English Studies* XLVII. 96 The verse-unit, the half-line, was quite short. **1668** DRYDEN *Evening's Love* III. i, The prose-wits playing and the *verse-wits rooking.

b. In the sense 'composed or written in, consisting of, verse', as ***verse drama, epistle, epitaph, -exercise, letter, miscellany, narrative, -part, play, -tale, -text, translation***, etc.

1685 DRYDEN *Sylvæ* Pref. ¶1 The hot [prose], which succeeded them, in this volume of Verse Miscellanies. **1687** NORRIS *Coll. Misc.* Pref. (1699) 4 Thus much for the Verse-part. **1817** COLERIDGE *Biog. Lit.* 23 In verse or prose, or in verse-text aided by prose-comment. **1881** *Encycl. Brit.* XII. 19/1 Verse narrative, even when it deals with true events,.. is either more or less than history. **1896** R. PALMER *Mem.* I. I. viii. 122 He.. gained both the University prizes for verse-exercises. **1925** R. GRAVES *Welchman's Hose* 31 Then the first draft of a verse-epitaph. **1931** *Times Lit. Suppl.* 5 Nov. 850/2 It might be inferred certainly from the verse-epistles [of Burns] alone: not quite so certainly from the prose letters alone. **1952** T. S. ELIOT *Film of 'Murder in the Cathedral'* 7 *Murder in the Cathedral* is, I believe, the first contemporary verse play to be adapted to the screen. **1962** *Times* 14 Aug. 11/1 Jean Cocteau's verse-drama *Renaud et Armide*. **1963** M. H. ABRAMS in N. Frye *Romanticism Reconsidered* 37 In a verse-letter of 1800 Blane identified the crucial influences in his spiritual history as a series beginning with Milton.

c. *Comb.* Objective or obj. genitive, as ***verse-gracer, -merchant, -reciter, -smith, -wright, -writer***; ***verse-making, -painting, -reading, -speaking, -writing***; ***verse-repeating, -speaking*** adjs.; instrumental, as ***verse-commemorated*** adj. Also ***verseward*** adv.

1842 S. C. HALL *Ireland* II. 339 The long celebrated and *verse-commemorated month of August. **1881** W. WILKINS *Songs of Study* 127 *Verse-gracer! deign to grace mine With lucky chosen words. **1811** ANDW. SCOTT *Poems* p. x, My attachment to *verse-making. **1873** SYMONDS *Grk. Poets* v. 147 A father taught the trade of flute-playing and chorus-leading and verse-making to his son. **1845** BROWNING *Lett.* (1899) I. 18 The Rialto where *verse-merchants most do congregate. **1942** BLUNDEN *Romantic Poetry & Fine Arts* 19 A single touch of his originality in the 'Ancient Mariner' holds the secret of his *verse-painting. **1585** JAS. I *Ess. Poesie* (Arb.) 31 Ye procure By your lasciuious speache, that fathers sage Defends *verse reading, to their yonger age. **1938** L. MACNEICE *Mod. Poetry* ii. 41 This [*sc.* the *Golden Treasury*] was my chief verse-reading for two years. **1822** SHELLEY *To Jane, The Invitation* 36 You, tiresome *verse-reciter, Care. *a* **1704** T. BROWN *Dial. Dead* Wks. 1711 IV. 75 The *Verse-repeating Beaux of Will's Coffee-House. **1820** T. MITCHELL *Aristoph.* I. 205 Ye *verse-smiths and bard-mechanicians! **1887** SAINTSBURY *Hist. Elizab. Lit.* i. (1890) 8 The supposed editor.. is but a journeyman verse-smith. **1933** *Amer. Speech* VIII. IV. 39/2 Outside of the school there may be a place for *verse-speaking choirs. **1980** *Times* 5 Sept. 11/7 His verse-speaking consists of a heavy lurch from beat to beat. **1810** MISS MITFORD *Let.* 3 Apr. in L'Estrange *Life* (1870) I. 99 That feeble *verse-spinner Bloomfield. **1809** BYRON *Bards & Rev.* 230 But if, in spite of all the world can say, Thou still wilt *verseward plod thy weary way. **1729** SAVAGE *Wanderer* I. 335 These scorn (said I) the *verse-wright of their age. **1840** PIERPONT *Airs Palestine* p. v, The pieces that make up this volume will be seen.. to be .. the wares of a verse-wright, made 'to order'. **1726** SWIFT (*title*), Advice to the Grub-street *Verse-Writers. **1885** PATER *Marius* I. vii. 121 A familiar playfulness of the Latin verse-writer in dealing with mythology. **1755** M. BARBER in Colman & Thornton *Poems by Eminent Ladies* I. 23 There's nothing I dread, like a *verse-writing wife. **1850** THACKERAY *Pendennis* ii, If he was distinguished for anything it was for verse-writing. **1884** TENNYSON *Becket* II. ii, So if the city be sick.. your lordship would suspend me from verse-writing?

†**verse**, *a. Obs. rare.* [ad. L. *vers-us*, pa. pple. of *vertĕre* to turn, change, vary.] ***verse-sine***, = versed sine: see VERSED *a.*

1772 *Phil. Trans.* LXII. 102 An arch equal to the verse-sine of the deviation.

verse (vɜːs), *v.*[1] Also 1 fyrsian, fersian, uersian, 4 uersie. [f. VERSE *sb.*, prob. formed afresh at different times.]

1. *intr.* To compose or make verses; to versify. Also with *it*.

c **1000** ÆLFRIC *Gram.* xxxvii. (Z.) 218 *Uersificor*, ic fersige [*v.rr.* uersige, fyrsige] oððe ic wyrce fers. **1393** LANGL. *P. Pl.* C. XVIII. 109 For þer is nouthe non who so nymeþ hede, That can uersie [*v.r.* versifie] fayre, oþer formeliche endite. **1606** CHAPMAN *Mons. D'Ol.* IV. i. F iij b, Prettie little Witt, y' faith; Can he verse?.. I meane, has he a vaine Naturall? **1647** WARD *Simp. Cobler* 87 You verse it simply, what need have we of your thin Poetry. **1688** W. SCOT *Hist. Scots* II. (1776) 73 Come on as many as you will, And for a wager, I'l verse with them still. **1787** in Currie *Burns' Wks.* (1800) II. 105 It sets na ony lawland cheel Like you to verse or rhyme. **1812** COMBE *Syntax, Picturesque* I. 129 I'll prose it here, I'll verse it there, And picturesque it everywhere. **1856** MEREDITH *Shav. Shagpat* (1909) 66 He began to verse extemporaneously in her ear.

2. *trans.* To tell in verse; to turn into verse; to write, recount, or celebrate in verse.

1446 LYDG. *Two Nightingale Poems* i. 108 This brid, of whom y haue to you rehersed, Whych in her song expired thus ande deyede, In latyn fonde y in a boke well versed. **1590** SHAKS. *Mids. N.* II. i. 67 When thou.. sate all day, Playing on pipes of Corne, and versing loue To amorous Phillida. *c* **1712** PRIOR *'Full oft doth Mat'* 4 But Topaz his own Werke rehearseth; And Mat. mote praise what Topaz verseth. **1869** F. HALLECK *Connecticut* xxxiv, He.. versed the Psalms of David to the air Of Yankee-Doodle, for Thanksgiving Days. **1892** STOPFORD BROOKE *Early Eng. Lit.* I. 12 The wanderer.. sang his stave of thanks, or versed for the chief in the high seat, who he was.

†**3.** To accompany or bring with verses. *Obs.*[−1]

1602 MARSTON *Ant. & Mel.* V. If that thou canst not give, goe hang thy selfe: Ile time thee dead, or verse thee to the rope.

Hence '**versing** *ppl. a.*

1630 J. TAYLOR (Water P.) *Pennilesse Pilgr.* Wks. I. 125/1 My versing Muse craues some repose, And whilst she sleeps Ile spowt a little prose. **1665** J. SPENCER *Vulg. Proph.* 55, I should.. throw out the vast rabble of rhyming, clinching, versing Prophets, as persons that tell the worst lies in the best maner.

verse (vɜːs), *v.*[2] [a. F. *verser* (12th c.; = Pr. and Pg. *versar, vessar*, Sp. *versar*, It. *versare*), or ad. L. *versāre*, freq. of *vertĕre* to turn, etc. In mod. use, in sense 4, app. a back-formation from VERSED *ppl. a.*[1]]

†**1.** *trans.* To pour *out* (the voice). *Obs.*[−1]

c **1530** LD. BERNERS *Arth. Lyt. Bryt.* (1814) 453 Than she [*sc.* a nightingale].. fylled her throte full of wynde, the more shryller to verse out her swete voyce.

†**2.** To overthrow, overturn, or upset. *Obs.*[−1]

1556 J. HEYWOOD *Spider & F.* xliii. 40 This formost spider and flie, in furius fret,.. this prosesse thei perst. And vengeable venumly, ech other verst.

†**3.** To turn over (a book) in study or investigation. *Obs.*

1606 BIRNIE *Kirk-Buriall* (1833) 6 By versing and searching the Scriptures. *a* **1656** HALES *Gold. Rem.* I. (1673) 271 If you be versing the Ancient Histories, then provide you Ptolomy's Maps.

†**b.** To revolve or turn over (something) *in* the mind. *Obs.*

1614 T. ADAMS *Sinners Passing Bell* Wks. (1629) 260 Who versing in his minde this thought, can keepe his cheekes dry?

4. To instruct, to make (one) conversant or experienced, *in* something. Now *refl.* Cf. VERSED *ppl. a.*[1] 1.

1673 O. WALKER *Educ.* 132 For reading: verse him well in inventive Authors. **1677** W. COMBE *Diaboliad* (1777) 43 Having vers'd them in each common evil, [you] Lead them to Masques to personate the Devil. **1786** MRS. A. M. BENNETT *Juvenile Indiscr.* V. 164 The intrigues of state affairs had thoroughly versed him in chicanery and dissimulation. **1895** G. ALEXANDER in *Daily News* 4 Oct. 2/2 If students while versing themselves in the classics were [etc.]. **1898** R. F. HORTON *Commandm. Jesus* xx. 362 This is my own feeling—a feeling which grows and intensifies the more I verse myself in His commandments.

†**verse**, *v.*[3] *Cant. Obs.* [Of uncertain origin; perh. a special sense of VERSE *v.*[2] Cf. VERSER[2].]

1. *intr.* To practise fraud or imposition. Also with *it*.

1591 ? GREENE *Def. Conny-catch.* (1859) 4, I had consorts that could verse, nippe, and foyst. **1591** GREENE *Discov. Cosenage* 10 b, If the poore Farmar be bashfull, and passeth by one of these shameles strumpets, then wil she verse it with him, and claime acquaintance of him. *c* **1592** —— *Theeues Falling out* (1615) A iv, We goe so neate in apparell ..that wee are hardly smoakt; versing vpon all men with kinde courtesies and faire wordes.

2. *trans.* To impose upon; to cozen, cheat, defraud. Also const. *to*.

1591 GREENE *Discov. Cosenage* 10 b, Till shee and her crosse-biters haue verst him to the beggers estate. *Ibid.* 11 b, Heere is a Simpler, quoth shee, Ile Verse him or hang me.

Hence †**versing** *vbl. sb. Cant. Obs.*

1591 GREENE *Discov. Cosenage* 7 Versing Law, coosenage by false gold.

verse, obs. form of VERST.

†**verse-coloured**, obs. var. VERSICOLOURED *a.*

1607 TOPSELL *Four-f. Beasts* 57 The Chamæleon and Polypus-fish, are pilled or bare without haire, and therefore may more easily be verse-coloured.

versed (vɜːst), *a.* [f. mod.L. *vers-us* (sc. *sinus*), pa. pple. of L. *vertĕre* to turn.]

1. ***versed sine***. **a.** *Trig.* Originally, the segment of the diameter intercepted between the foot of the sine and the extremity of the arc; in mod. use, the ratio of this line to the radius, or (equivalently, as a function of an angle) the quantity obtained by subtracting the cosine from unity.

In mod. use also in the contracted form VERSIN.

1596 W. B[URROUGH] *Variation of Compasse* B 5 b, The versed signe of the semidiurnall arke. *a* **1652** S. FOSTER *Descr. Ruler*, A large Scale of Versed-Sines. **1690** LEYBOURN *Curs. Math.* 397 The Line VS.. is the Line of Versed Sines. **1732** HADLEY in *Phil. Trans.* XXXVII. 353 Draw *b* D the Sine, and *b r* the Sine complement of the Arch B *b*: BD is the versed Sine of the same. **1763** EMERSON *Meth. Increments* 91 Hence we have the following series of versed sines. **1828** J. M. SPEARMAN *Brit. Gunner* (ed. 2) 319 The arcs being similar, the versed sines are proportional to the arcs or to their radii. **1853** SIR H. DOUGLAS *Milit. Bridges* (ed. 3) 43 A segment of a sphere whose radius is *r*, the sagitta, or versed sine, being *d*.

b. *Bridge-building.* The rise of an arch.

1838 *Civil Eng. & Arch. Jrnl.* I. 127/1 The Dover road is carried over the railway by a flat segmental arch, 30 feet span, the rise or versed sine [*printed* line] is only two feet. **1839** *Ibid.* II. 191/2 Span of the arch.. 58 feet—the rise or versed sine being ten feet. **1879** *Cassell's Techn. Educ.* IV. 384/1 It forms the strongest arch;..but in consequence of the height of the versed sine..it becomes necessary..to limit the span.

†**2.** ***versed scale***, a scale of versed sines. *Obs.*

a **1652** S. FOSTER *Descr. Ruler* viii. 31 The Versed Scale is in length four times the same Radius. *Ibid.* 32 Let the Tangents..be measured out of the Versed Scale.

versed (vɜːst), *ppl. a.*[1] Also 7 verst. [ad. L. *versātus*, pa. pple. of *versārī* to occupy oneself, be busied or engaged (in something). So F. *versé*, It. *versato*, Sp. and Pg. *versado*.]

1. Of persons: Experienced, practised, or skilled *in* a subject, matter, art, etc.; conversant with, having an intimate knowledge of, something; expert, skilful; = VERSANT *a.* 2 a.

Very frequent from *c* 1630 in this and sense 1 b.

1622 BACON *Hen. VII*, 16 [The bishops of Ely and Exeter] had beene both versed in his Affaires, before hee came to the Crowne. **1663** GERBIER *Counsel* 24 A Clarke of the works must be verst in the prises of Materials. **1686** tr. *Chardin's Trav. Persia* 34 Levant Merchants, and others that were verst in the Affairs of Turkey. **1712** HEARNE *Collect.* (O.H.S.) III. 361 Neither of us being vers'd in Latin. **1769** *Junius Lett.* xii. (1788) 80, I am not versed in the politics of the north. **1822** W. IRVING *Braceb. Hall* xviii, The servants are all versed in the common modes of trying luck. **1843** MILL *Logic* I. i. §1 A mind not previously versed in the meaning and right use of the various kinds of words. **1880** L. STEPHEN *Pope* vi. 137 Curll was..versed in every dirty trick of the Grub-street trade.

b. With defining or limiting adverbs, esp. *well* (*better, best*) *versed*.

(*a*) *a* **1610** HEALEY *Theophrastus* To Rdr. (1616) I 3 b, Such as are well verst in Antiquitie. **1653** W. RAMESEY *Astrol. Restored* 160 A Physician..must be better versed in his Art before he can do any thing. **1655** *Nicholas Papers* (Camden) II. 176 He is certainly best versed in all his Majesty's present affairs. **1711** ADDISON *Spect.* No. 108 ⁋3 He is extreamly well versed in all the little Handicrafts of an idle Man. **1791** BURKE *App. Whigs* Wks. 1808 VI. 18 Men [*sc.* Jews] well versed in swearing. **1825** COBBETT *Rur. Rides* 279 He was very well versed in his prayer-book. **1841** BORROW *Zincali* II. xi. III. 56 Reverend gentlemen..much better versed in the points of a horse than in points of theology. **1874** BURNAND *My time* xxix. 277 Our tutor was sufficiently well versed in his subjects.

(*b*) **1634** W. TIRWHYT tr. *Balzac's Lett.* A iv, A man no less versed in the art of well-speaking then himself. **1641** *Vind. Smectymnuus* x. 107 He that is but meanly versed in Cyprian. **1662** STILLINGFL. *Orig. Sacr.* III. iv. §10 Those who profess themselves most versed in their own Antiquities. *a* **1721** PRIOR *Ess. Learning* ⁋3 Other parts of general Learning in which they may not be so perfectly versed. **1747** tr. *Astruc's Fevers* 106 He was ill-versed in anatomy, botany and chemistry. **1780** J. PICKERING in Jesse *Selwyn & Contemp.* (1844) IV. 356, I wish I was sufficiently versed in politics [etc.]. **1815** W. H. IRELAND *Scribbleomania* 190, I am not much versed in Egyptian hieroglyphics. **1836** H. COLERIDGE *North. Worthies* Introd. (1852) p. xxiv, Men long versed in public affairs. **1888** BURGON *Lives 12 Gd. Men* I. iii. 346 He..delivered his opinion..like one thoroughly versed in the law of farms.

c. Without const. *rare.*

1734 tr. *Rollin's Anc. Hist.* XVIII. iii. (1841) II. 214/1 A general..prudent, able, versed by long experience. **1888** *Pall Mall G.* 23 Feb. 6/1 Observing that Lord Randolph Churchill used to keep the Premier and Foreign Secretary combined in order, which at present there was no one in the Cabinet versed enough or bold enough to do.

†**2.** Employed or exercised *about* something; = VERSANT *a.* 1. *Obs.*[−1]

1654 VILVAIN *Theol. Treat.* ii. 80 Hope is properly versed about some good to be attained by industry.

versed (vɜːst), *ppl. a.*[2] [f. VERSE *v.*[1]] Composed or written in verse; turned into verse.

1890 *Athenæum* 27 Dec. 896/2 *Monsieur Pouf*, the versed biography of a dog. **1901** *Dublin Rev.* Apr. 413 Versed commonplaces set to florid music.

'verseless, *a.* [f. VERSE *sb.*] Lacking verse or poetry; unable to compose verses.

1738 *Gentl. Mag.* VIII. 655 Verseless myself, I conn'd not blithsom song; Nor lute had I, nor harp, nor tuneful lyre. *c* **1873** G. M. HOPKINS *Note-bks. & Papers* (1937) 221 Where verse ends and prose (or verseless composition) begins. **1975** *Gramophone* May 2020/3 The rapid succession of verseless office antiphons..gave me a slight feeling of dizziness because of their varying pitches.

'verselet. [f. VERSE *sb.* + -LET.] A little verse; a small poem.

1836 B. D. WALSH *Aristophanes, Acharnians* II. iii. 43 His mind, which is collecting Small verselets out of doors, is not at home. **1865** *Reader* No. 151. 567/2 Each page containing a verselet. **1880** WARREN *Book-plates* i. 8 Mottoes, texts, and verselets directed against borrowers.

'versemaker. Also verse-maker, verse maker. [f. VERSE *sb.* + MAKER *sb.* Cf. Du. *verzenmaker*, G. *versmacher*, Da. *versemager*.] One who makes or writes verses; a poet or versifier.

1647 HEXHAM I. s.v., A verse maker, or a Poet,..*een Poët.* **1728** YOUNG *Love Fame* 191 All other trades demand, verse-makers beg. **1791** BOSWELL *Johnson* (1904) II. 124 A mere verse-maker, in whose numbers..there is no poetry. **1836** SOUTHEY in *Life & Corr.* VI. 302 The versemaker gets the habit of weighing the meanings and qualities of words. **1871** TYLOR *Prim. Cult.* I. 269 What we call poetry was to them real life, not as to the modern versemaker a masquerade of gods and heroes.

verseman ('vɜːsmən). Also verse man, verse-man. [f. as prec. + MAN *sb.*] A man who writes verse; a versemaker; a poet, esp. (in recent use) a minor poet or versifier.

1652 GAULE *Magastrom.* 235 To conclude, all the antient verse men consent in this. **1718** PRIOR *Better Answer* v, The God of us Verse-men (you know Child) the Sun. **1733** [see PROSEMAN]. **1779** JOHNSON *L.P., Prior* ⁋13 When the battle of Blenheim called forth all the versemen. **1847** L. HUNT *Men, Women, & B.* I. xv. 300 Even miserly Pulteney was a verseman. **1883** *Pall Mall G.* 30 Oct. 5/1 Almost alone among recent English versemen, he preserves..a fine-gentlemanly air of urbanity. **1892** A. DOBSON *18th Cent. Vignettes* 171 Madrigalists and minor versemen.

Hence **'versemanship**, verse-making. *rare*[−1].

1762 J. WILKES *N. Briton* No. 22, The dull mechanical part of versemanship indeed is found, but the spirit of true poetry is wanting.

versemonger ('vɜːsmʌŋgə(r)). Also verse-monger. [f. as prec. + MONGER.] A versifier, esp. one who writes poor or indifferent verse; a poetaster.

1634 BP. HALL *Contempl., N.T.* IV. xii, Which of those verse-mongers ever durst write a ballad, without imploring of some deity? **1768** BARETTI *Acc. Mann. & Cust. Italy* I. 254 Some few verse-mongers of Rome. **1866** BLACKIE *Homer & Iliad* I. 120 A set of inferior versemongers. **1902** W. L. MATHIESON *Pol. & Relig. Scotl.* I. x. 338 His virtues ..were cordially recognised even by the scurrilous verse-mongers of the day.

Hence **'versemongering** *vbl. sb.*, **'verse-mongery.**

1836 *Fraser's Mag.* XIV. 488 Earning his bread by scribblement and verse-mongery. **1875** LOWELL *Spenser* Prose Wks. 1890 IV. 268 There is little to distinguish it from the contemporary verse-mongering south of the Tweed.

Versene ('vɜːsiːn). Also versene. A proprietary name for a preparation containing ethylenediamine tetra-acetic acid (q.v. s.v. ETHYLENE 2) or a similar chelating agent.

1944 *Official Gaz.* (U.S. Patent Office) 29 Aug. 734/2 The Martin-Dennis Company, Newark, N.J... *Versene* for water softening agents in powdered and liquid form with or without detergents. **1951** *Trade Marks Jrnl.* 14 Nov. 1040/2 *Versene*... Chemical products used in industry. Bersworth Chemical Company,..Framingham,..Massachusetts, United States of America; manufacturers. **1952** *Nature* 19 July 119/2 Although versene protects the enzyme systems from the inactivation caused by the incubation, it does not reverse such inactivation. **1980** *Bull. Environmental Contamination & Toxicol.* XXIV. 543 (*heading*) Acute fish toxicity of the Versene family of chelating agents.

verser[1] ('vɜːsə(r)). [f. VERSE *v.*[1] + -ER[1]. Cf. *versyowre* s.v. VERSIFIER 1 *a*, quot. *c* 1440.] A writer of verse; a verseman, versifier.

c **1611** CHAPMAN *Iliad* XIII. Comm., Such as abuse the name of Critics as many versers do of poets. **1619** DRUMM. OF HAWTH. *Conv. w. Ben Jonson* Wks. (1711) 225 He thought not Bartas a poet, but a verser; because he wrote not fiction. **1644–58** CLEVELAND *Gen. Poems* (1677) 63 O That I could but vote my self a Poet,..Or like the Doctors Militant could get Dubb'd at adventure Verser Banneret. **1854** MRS. OLIPHANT *Magd. Hepburn* I. 9 The archer Simon,..a verser as much as a bowman. **1907** *Westm. Gaz.* 21 Aug. 4/1 The invidious task of separating the poets from the versers.

†**'verser**[2]. *Cant.* [Cf. VERSE *v.*[3]] One of a gang of cozeners or swindlers (see quots.).

c **1550** *Dice-Play* (Percy Soc.) 38 He lightly hath in his company a man of more worship than himself, that hath the countenance of a possessioner of land, and he is called the verser. **1591** GREENE *Discov. Cosenage* 1 There bee requisite effectually to act the Art of Conny-catching, three seuerall parties: The Setter, the Verser, and the Barnackle. *Ibid.* 3 Imagine the Connie is in the Tauerne, then sits down the Verser, and saith to the Setter, what sirha, wilt thou giue mee a quart of wine, or shall I giue thee one? [etc.]. **1606** CHAPMAN *Mons. D'Ol.* IV. i. F iij b, *D'Ol.* Can he verse? *Pac.* I, and sett too, my Lord; Hee's both a Setter and a Verser.

verset ('vɜːsɪt). Also 5 werset. [a. OF. (also mod.F.) *verset* (= Pr. *verset*, Pg. *verseto*, It. *versetto*), dim. of *vers* VERSE *sb.*]

1. = VERSE *sb.* 2, VERSICLE 1. Now *Hist.*

a **1225** *Ancr. R.* 16 Siggeð so al ðe imne vt mid te uerset 'Emitte Spiritum tuum'. *Ibid.* 42 Her siggeð fifti auez.., alast þet uerset, 'Ecce ancilla Domini' [etc.]. **1377** LANGL. *P. Pl.* B. XII. 189 *Dominus pars hereditatis mee* is a meri verset. *c* **1400** *Rule St. Benet* (Prose) 16 Wen þai [i.e. psalms] ere said and te verset, þabbasse saie þe benecun. *Ibid.*, And efter [sing] oþir sexe salmis wid þe antefens,..wid þe werset. **1641** MILTON *Animadv.* Wks. 1851 III. 209 They beare an equall part with the Priest in many places, and have their cues and versets as well as he. **1844** LINGARD *Anglo-Sax. Ch.* (1858) I. App. M. 378 The manuscript, both here and in several other places, interposes two versets with their responses.

2. A little or short verse, esp. one of the Bible or similar book; a short piece of verse.

1625 LISLE *Du Bartas, Noe* Pref. 1 Among the sundrie versets or prosets which besides this I have or shall set out. **1861** I. TAYLOR *Spir. Hebr. Poetry* 335 The metrical Scriptures—infixed as they were in the memory by the very means of these artificial devices of versets,..became food to the mind. **1888** DOUGHTY *Arabia Deserta* I. 143 A Koran verset is often written above.

versical ('vɜːsɪkəl), *a. rare.* [f. VERSE *sb.* + -ICAL, after *poetical, metrical.*] Of or pertaining to, of the nature of, composed or written in, verse.

1854 *Tait's Mag.* XXI. 257 He already made some versical efforts in the literary periodicals of Vienna. **1886** R. F. BURTON *Arab. Nts.* (Abr. ed.) I. Forew. p. xiv, When treating the versical portion,..I have not always bound myself by the metrical bonds of the Arabic.

versicle ('vɜːsɪk(ə)l), *sb.* Also 5 *Sc.* wersikill, 5–6 versycle, 6 versickil. [ad. L. *versicul-us* VERSICULUS. Cf. VERSICULE.]

1. *Liturg.* One of a series of short sentences, usually taken from the Psalms and of a precatory nature, said or sung antiphonally in divine service; *spec.* one said by the officiant and followed by the response of the congregation or people; often *collect. pl.*, a set of these with their accompanying responses.

a **1380** *St. Paula* 191 in Horstm. *Altengl. Leg.* (1878) 7 Þeos versicles heo seide and bad. **1425** in Entick *London* (1766) IV. 354 This psalm, *de profundis*, with the versicles and *Orissons* that longeth thereto. **1486** *Rec. St. Mary at Hill* (1905) 16 To go on procession..syngyng a Respond..; that done, a versicle with the colet of S3 Stephen. **1579** W. FULKE *Ref. Rastel* 743 The very sound and sense of the.. Respondes, and Versicles, declare whence they proceeded. **1625** *Gonsalvio's Sp. Inquis.* 97 The Psalme being ended.., the chiefe Inquisitour singeth a sort of Versicles: and the whole Quier answereth them with their Responses. **1631** BRATHWAITE *Whimzies, Zealous Brother* 120 Anthems and versicles he holds papisticall. **1710** WHEATLY *Bk. Com. Prayer* ii. §21. 50 Of the Versicles before the Lord's Prayer. **1721** in *Cath. Rec. Soc. Publ.* VIII. 295 The Ordinary Discipline is to last the time of a *Miserere*, with the Versicle *Christus factus est*, and the prayer *Respice quæsumus.* **1795** MASON *Ch. Mus.* II. 154 The unaccompanied Chaunt, used in the versicles and responses. **1832** W. PALMER *Orig. Liturg.* I. 219 From this it appears, that these versicles were not, perhaps, originally repeated in church, but at home, as a preparation for divine service. **1893** W. WALKER *Three Churchmen* 175 When he repeated the versicle 'Lord save this woman, Thy servant!' the clerk responded [etc.].

b. The sign (*V*, *V'*, ℣, or *V̸*) with which these are noted or indicated in prayer-books, etc.

1888 JACOBI *Printers' Voc.* 151.

2. A little verse, in various senses of that term:

†**a.** A short clause or sentence; = VERSE *sb.*[1] 3.

1483 CAXTON *Gold. Leg.* 231/1 A boke..in whiche was wreton thys versycle In euerlastyng memorye shal be my rightful hoostesse. **1613** PURCHAS *Pilgrimage* (1614) 198 Proceed in like manner, with the titles, attributes, and workes of God. Doe it for thy name, Doe it for thy goodnesse,..&c. in seuerall versicles. **1668** HALE *Rolle's Abridgm.* Pref. 5 In Justinians time there were an incredible number of Versicles and Volumes of their Laws. *c* **1710** BURNET *Autobiog.* II. (1902) 507 The condemnatory versicles in Athanasius' Creed. **1721** R. KEITH tr. *T. à Kempis, Vall. Lilies* vi. 13 Expound me this Word which thou spakest, open the Sense of this Versicle for the Comfort of thy Servant.

b. †A verse of the Psalms or the Bible (*obs.*); now *spec.*, one of the subdivisions of a Hebrew verse.

1624 BP. HALL *Art Medit.* (1627) 36 Wee shall lift vp our heart and voice to God in singing some versicle of Dauids diuine psalmes. **1641** J. JACKSON *True Evang. T.* I. 82 That versicle of Psal. 119, 'Righteous art thou, O Lord, and right are thy Judgements'. **1721** STRYPE *Eccl. Mem.* (1822) II. I. 204 The psalms were in number fifteen,..made in imitation of David's Psalms; being digested into versicles. **1737** CHALLONER *Cath. Chr. Instructed* (1753) 100 Then wiping the Chalice,..he goes to the Book, and reads a Versicle of the holy Scripture, called the Communion. **1783** BLAIR *Lect.* xli. II. 389 When..one band began the Hymn thus: 'The Lord reigneth, let the earth rejoice', the chorus..took up the corresponding versicle. **1873** *Speaker's Commentary* IV. 483/2 The second clause of the first versicle of this verse.

c. A short or single metrical line; a little verse.

1573 G. HARVEY *Letter-bk.* (Camden) 128 On[e] pore simple versicle Had bene too mutch for such an article. **1589** PUTTENHAM *Eng. Poesie* I. v. (Arb.) 26 The American..and the very Canniball, do sing and also say, their highest and holiest matters in certaine riming versicles and not in prose. **1620** VENNER *Via Recta* v. 89 It behoueth him..to be mindfull of that prouerbiall versicle: *Caseus est sanus, quem dat auara manus.* **1637** GILLESPIE *Eng. Pop. Cerem.* IV. iii. 7 The principall circumstances..are comprehended in this versicle: *Quis, Quid, Vbi, Quibus auxiliis, Cur, Quomodo, Quando.* **1652** NEEDHAM *Selden's Mare Cl.* Ep. Ded. 8 According to that old Versicle *Frangit & attollit vires in Milite causa.* **1817** BYRON *Let. to Moore* 25 Mar., Here are some versicles. **1849** THACKERAY *Pendennis* (1850) II. 257 To these pretty little compositions Mr. Pen replied..with points of wit, nay, with pretty little verses very likely, in reply to the versicles of the Muse of 'Mes Larmes'. **1893** MCCARTHY *Red Diamonds* III. 143 She was fond of writing versicles and setting them to music.

†**d.** Without article. *Obs.*[−1]

1589 PUTTENHAM *Eng. Poesie* I. v. (Arb.) 26 How the wilde and sauage people vsed a naturall Poesie in versicle and rime as our vulgar is.

Hence †**'versicle** *v. intr.* (with *it*), to sing versicles. *Obs.*[−1]

1550 BALE *Apol.* 131 b, I knowe theyr progresse was great, as ye were wont to versycle it on theyr daies.

'versicler. *rare.* [f. VERSICLE *sb.*] A writer of versicles or short verses; a versifier.

1860 G. MEREDITH *Let.* ? Aug. (1970) I. 61 But do, pray, exclude some of your present versiclers. **1885** —— *Diana* xxx, I'll read your versicler tomorrow morning early.

versicolorate, *a. Ent.* [-ATE[2].] = VERSICOLOURED *a.*

1826 KIRBY & SP. *Entomol.* IV. xlvi. 292 *Versicolorate*,.. when a surface changes its colour as the light varies.

versico'lorous, *a.* *rare*⁻¹. [f. late L. *versicolōrus*: cf. VERSICOLOUR *a.*] = prec.
1847 HARDY in *Proc. Berw. Nat. Club.* II. 242 Abdomen shining, versicolorous.

†**'versicolour**, *sb. Obs.* ⁰ (See quot. and next.)
1775 ASH, *Versicolour*, a variegated or changeable colour.

'versicolour, *a. rare.* Also 7, 9 -color. [ad. L. *versicolor*, f. *vers-*, ppl. stem of *vertĕre* to turn, change, VERSE *v.*² + *color* COLOUR *sb.* So F. *versicolore*.] = next.
1628 BURTON *Anat. Mel.* (ed. 3) 264 Neate gardens full of exotick, versicoloure, diuersly varied, sweete smelling flowers. **1632** *Ibid.* (ed. 4) 478 Why doe they..decke themselues with..chaines, girdles, rings,..versicolor ribbands? [**1828–32** WEBSTER, *Versicolor*,..having various colors; changeable in color.]

versicoloured ('vɜːsɪˌkʌləd), *a.* [f. as prec. + COLOURED *ppl. a.* Cf. the earlier VERSE-COLOURED.] Changing or varying in colour; iridescent; also, of various colours, variegated.
1721 BAILEY, *Versicoloured*, changing Colour, of sundry and changeable Colours. **1822–7** GOOD *Study Med.* (1829) I. 421 Under these circumstances, the bile has at different times..been found..whitish, black, green, eruginous, and versicoloured. **1846** LANDOR *Imag. Conv.* Wks. I. 467/1 If thou hadst enveloped him in thy versicoloured and cloud-like vestiary. **1873** M. COLLINS *Squire Silchester* III. xxii. 246 A rocket..drops its versicoloured shower.
fig. **1867** VISCT. STRANGFORD *Selection* (1869) I. 135 Such views..on the subject of the versicoloured policy of France in the East.

Hence **versicolouredness**, 'the being of changeable Colours' (Bailey, 1727, vol. II).

†**ver'sicular**, *sb. Obs.*⁻¹ [ad. med.L. *versiculārius*, f. L. *versiculus* VERSICULUS: see -AR².] One whose office it was to say or sing the versicles.
c **1450** in Aungier *Syon* (1840) 364 Of the versiculars for the wyke. The two sustres that be tabled to synge the versicles schal synge the *Venite*.

versicular (vəˈsɪkjʊlə(r)), *a.* [f. L. *versiculus* VERSICLE *sb.* + -AR¹.] Of or pertaining to, characterized by, consisting of, versicles or verses, esp. Biblical verses.
1812 J. JEBB *Corr.* (1834) II. 72 The theological uses of the hebraic versicular system. **1840** G. S. FABER *Christ's Disc. Capernaum* 20 That the sort of unconscious delusion, produced by the versicular figures, may be dissipated, I have ..omitted those figures altogether. **1882–3** *Schaff's Encycl. Relig. Knowl.* III. 2242 It was in this edition that the versicular division of the New Testament was..introduced.

versicu'lation. *rare.* [f. L. *versicul-us* or VERSICULE.] The action or practice of making versicules; the result of this.
1893 *Edin. Rev.* Oct. 484 But here we will escape from the polyglot versiculations of Sir Edwin Arnold.

versicule ('vɜːsɪkjuːl). *rare.* [a. OF. (also mod.F.) *versicule* (14th c.; = It., Sp., Pg. *versiculo*), or ad. L. *versiculus*: see next and VERSICLE *sb.*] A versicle; a short verse or poem.
1491 *Cartul. St. Nicholai Aberdon.* (New Spald. Cl.) I. 256 Gif he be ane chorister and playne Sangster þat can singe Anthoms, Responseris and Versiculis. **1517** in *Archaeol.* LXI. 84 A booke with the Invitatorys and the versiculis noted. *a* **1550** *Wyntoun's Cron.* (Wemyss MS.) v. xi. 3625 Versiculis thare to he can write, And ympnis alsua maid in dite. **1861** W. H. RUSSELL in *Times* 14 May, A variety of versicules, songs, and rhetorical exercitations.

‖**versiculus** (vəˈsɪkjʊləs). Pl. -culi. [L., dim. of *versus* VERSE *sb.* Cf. prec. and VERSICLE *sb.*] A versicle. Chiefly in pl.
1755 *Gentl. Mag.* XXV. 93 The late bishop Hare..began his enquiry by attempting to discover the length of the versiculi or lines. **1820** *Blackw. Mag.* June 323 A sentence of panegyric on my own *versiculi*. **1820** BYRON *Lett. & Jrnls.* (1900) IV. 395 Pray let not these versiculi go forth with *my* name, except among the initiated.

versie: see VERSY *a. Obs.*

versifiable ('vɜːsɪfaɪəb(ə)l), *a.* *rare*⁻¹. [f. VERSIFY *v.* + -ABLE. Cf. OF. *versifiable*.] That can be versified or put into verse.
1828 SOUTHEY *Lett.* (1856) IV. 107 Names and dates, &c., will precede it [i.e. the epitaph] in the usual form, telling all that is not versifiable.

†**ver'sifical**, *a. Obs.*⁻¹ In 6 versyfycall. [f. late L. *versific-us* (cf. L. *versificāre* to versify) + -AL¹.] Of or pertaining to the making of verse.
1545–7 in *Archaeol.* XXXIV. 40 They have the versyfycall rulys of Sulpice gevyn in the mornyng of one of the vjᵗʰ forme.

†**'versificate**, *v. Obs.*⁻⁰ [f. L. *versificāt-*, ppl. stem of *versificāre* to versify.] *intr.* 'To make verses' (Bailey, 1721).

versification (vɜːsɪfɪˈkeɪʃən). [ad. L. *versificātiōn-*, *versificātio*, noun of action f. *versificāre* to versify. So F. *versification* (1680), Sp. *versificacion*, Pg. *-ação*, It. *-azione*.]
1. The action of composing verse; the art or practice of versifying.
In Rolland *Crt. Venus* (*c* 1550) II. 176 'Versification, meter' should perhaps be read for 'Versificat in meter' of the text.
1603 HOLLAND *Plutarch's Mor.* 1198 The order of writing an historie..came downe as one would say from the stately chariot of versification, to prose, and went a foot. **1658** PHILLIPS, *Versification*, a making of Verses. **1706** POPE *Lett.* Wks. 1736 V. 53 The thoughts I have already sent you on the subject of English Versification. **1774** WARTON *Hist. Eng. Poetry* I. II. 27 Camden affirms, that Aldhelm..taught his countrymen the art of Latin versification. **1790** COWPER *Lett.* 13 Sept., After perpetual versification during five years I find myself..reduced to read for my amusement. **1824** COLERIDGE *Table-t.* 7 June, How lamentably the art of versification is neglected by most of the poets of the present day! **1861** WRIGHT *Ess. Archæol.* II. xx. 153 The southern ecclesiastics..adopted this new style of versification for their chant music. **1875** OUSELEY *Mus. Form* ii. 3 You may teach a man the rules of versification or of melody.
2. The form or style in which the words in a poetical composition are arranged; the structure of poetry or verse; measure, metre.
1693 DRYDEN *Juvenal* Ded. p. v, Donn alone, of all our Country-men, had your Talent; but was not happy enough to arrive at your Versification. **1720** J. WELWOOD *Pref. to Rowe's Lucan* p. xliii, As to the Translation it self,..the Language is pure, and the Versification both musical and adapted to the subject. **1729** T. COOKE *Tales*, etc. 137 His Versyfcation is mostly as faulty as his Sentiment. **1759** JOHNSON *Idler* No. 60 ¶7 The versification of Rowe he thought too melodious for the stage. **1813** BYRON *Corsair* Ded., I shall..take my chance, with that versification in which I have hitherto published nothing. **1841** W. SPALDING *Italy & It. Isl.* I. 139 Virgil was the great model, and his picturesque groups and flowing versification were imitated by many men of letters. **1880** L. STEPHEN *Pope* iii. 75 To make the versification as smooth and the sense as transparent as possible.
3. A poetical or metrical version *of* something.
1821 *Q. Rev.* XXV. 36 Of this song we have been favoured with the following beautiful versification. **1858** DORAN *Crt. Fools* 154 Many of his epigrams..are said to have been versifications of his own jokes.

versificator ('vɜːsɪfɪkeɪtə(r)). [a. L. *versificātor* (whence also It. *versificatore*, Sp., Pg. *versificador*, F. *versificateur*), f. *versificāre* to versify.] One who writes verse; a poet, versifier.
1611 COTGR., *Versificateur*, a versificator, versifier, maker of verses. **1682** SHADWELL *Medal* Ep. A j b, His Fort is, that he is an indifferent good Versificator. **1693** DRYDEN *Juvenal* Ded. p. xi, Statius, the best Versificator next to Virgil. **1746** W. HORSLEY *Fool* (1748) I. 15 The Sons of Imagination, whether Lovers or..Prose-Writers, or Versificators. **1760** JORTIN *Erasm.* II. 105 Erasmus was very far from being as mean a poet as this versificator. **1805** *Edin. Rev.* VI. 291 The system, upon which a certain sect of versificators have lately proceeded. **1841** D'ISRAELI *Amen. Lit.* (1867) 477 Alliterations and epithets..with mechanical versificators are a mere artifice.

versificatory, *a. rare.* [f. VERSIFICATE *v.*] 'Belonging to versifying' (Bailey).
1727 in BAILEY II. **1963** V. NABOKOV *Gift* iii. 146 It was then also that my versificatory illness began.

versifi'catrix. [a. L. type **versificātrix*, fem. of *versificātor* VERSIFICATOR.] A female versifier; a poetess.
1784 BEATTIE in Forbes *Life* (1806) II. 147 Johnson told me, with great solemnity, that she [Hannah More] was 'the most powerful versificatrix' in the English language.

versified ('vɜːsɪfaɪd), *ppl. a.* [f. VERSIFY *v.* + -ED.] Written or composed in verse.
1841 W. SPALDING *Italy & It. Isl.* III. 205 His versified epistles are greatly prized..for their taste and feeling. **1874** L. STEPHEN *Hours in Libr.* (1892) II. vii. 210 His poems were versified sermons.

versifier ('vɜːsɪfaɪə(r)). Forms: α. 4–5 versifiour, 5 -fyowre; 5 versefiour, -fyour. β. 5 versyfyer, -fyar, 6 vercyfyer, 5 vercifier, 5– versifier, 6 -fiar, 6, 8 -fyer; 5 versefier, 5–6 -fyer. [a. AF. *versifiur* (13th c.), *versifiour*, OF. *versefiere*, *-fierre* (13th c.), *versifieur* (14th c.), f. *versifier*: see VERSIFY *v.* and -ER.]
1. One who versifies or composes verses; a verser or verse-maker; a poet.
α. *c* **1340** HAMPOLE *Pr. Consc.* 897 He suld fynd ful litel matere To mak ioy whilles he here duelles, Als a versifiour in metre þus telles. **1382** WYCLIF *Job* Pref., The whiche thing versifioures more than a symple redere vnderstonden. **1398** TREVISA *Barth. De P.R.* XVII. xci. (Bodl. MS.), It is seide þᵗ versifiours likned þe lelye to mannes inwitte. *a* **1425** tr. *Arderne's Treat. Fistula*, etc. 4 Wherfore seiþ a versifiour, ..'lat werke ouercome thi worde, for boste lesseneþ gode lose'. *c* **1440** *Promp. Parv.* 508/2 Versifyowre (*H.* versyowre), *versificator*.
β. **14..** *Voc.* in Wr.-Wülcker 681 *Hic versificator*, a versyfyer. *a* **1450** *Mankind* 746 in *Macro Plays* 27 As a nobyll versyfyer makyth mencyon in þis verse. **1477** EARL RIVERS (Caxton) *Dictes* 13 Omer was an auncient vercifier in Grece. *a* **1513** FABYAN *Chron.* VII. 405 Of this noble prynce a vercyfyer made these .ii. verses folowynge. **1567** DRANT *Horace, Ep.* II. ii. H iv, Euil versefyers mocked be, yet haue they to theire ioy. **1603** DANIEL *Def. Rhime* Wks. (1717) 32 This Self-Love, whereunto we Versifiers are ever noted to be especially subject. **1670** MILTON *Hist. Eng.* v. Wks. 1851 V. 227 Other pretious things,..describ'd in Malmsbury, tak'n..out of an old versifier, some of whose verses he recites. **1741** WATTS *Improv. Mind* I. xvi. §1 More elevated language than the fondest critics have ever found in any of the Heathen versifiers either of Greece or Rome. **1789** BELSHAM *Ess.* I. xii. 232 Pope has often been stiled the best versifier in the English language. **1828** *Harrovian* 46 He was a good classic, and an excellent versifier. **1873** SYMONDS *Grk. Poets* x. 333 Those purely rustic poems which..have..been imitated by versifiers emulous of his gracefulness.
2. With depreciative force: A mere or poor writer of verse(s); a rimester, a poetaster.
1531 ELYOT *Gov.* I. xiii, Semblably they that make verses, expressynge therby none other lernynge but the craft of versifyeng, be..of auncient writers..onely called versifyers. **1581** SIDNEY *Apol. Poetrie* (Arb.) 28 Now swarme many versifiers that neede neuer aunswere to the name of Poets. **1589** PUTTENHAM *Eng. Poesie* I. i. (Arb.) 19 The translator, who..may well be sayd a versifier, but not a Poet. **1642** MILTON *Apol. Smect.* Wks. 1851 III. 262 Rather nice and humerous in what was tolerable, then patient to read every drawling versifier. **1652–62** HEYLYN *Cosmogr.* IV. (1682) 85 Philip whom the Versifier (I do not say the Poet) called Philippus Hispanus. **1696** PHILLIPS (ed. 5), *Versifier*, a maker of Verses, generally taken in an ill sense. **1781** SIR J. REYNOLDS *Journ. Flanders* Wks. 1797 II. 112 The modern versifiers,..carrying no weight of thought, easily fall into that false gallop of verse. **1821** BYRON *Diary* Wks. (1846) 531/2 As different from an orator as an improvisatore or a versifier from a poet. **1880** MISS BRADDON *Just as I am* xi, She thought Byron an ephemeral versifier.

'versiform, *a. rare*⁻⁰. [ad. L. *versiformis* (post-class.): see -FORM.] (See quots.)
1727 BAILEY (vol. II), *Versiform*, that changes its Shape. **1884** *Imp. Dict.*, *Versiform*, varied in form; changing form: used in botany.

versify ('vɜːsɪfaɪ), *v.* Also 4–7 versifye, -fie (5 uersefiȝe, versfy), 5 versyfyyn, wersyfy, 5–6 versyfy. [ad. OF. *vercifier*, *versifier* (13th c. in Godef. *Compl.*, = Pr. *versifiar*), ad. L. *versificāre* (whence It. *versificare*, Sp., Pg. *versificar*), f. *versus* VERSE *sb.* + *facĕre* to make.]
1. *intr.* To make or compose verses; to write poetry; = VERSE *v.*¹ 1. Also const. *upon* (or †*of*) a theme.
1377 LANGL. *P. Pl.* B. xv. 367 For is none of þis newe clerkes..þat can versifye faire ne formalich enditen. *c* **1440** *Promp. Parv.* 508/2 Versyfyyn, *versificor*. **1483** *Cath. Angl.* 401/1 To versifye, *versificare*, *versiculare*. *c* **1520** SKELTON *Magnyf.* 1162 Yes, in faythe; I can versyfy. **1579** LODGE *Def. Poetry*, etc. (Hunt. Club) 15 Tully atributeth it for prais to Archias yᵗ vpon any theame he cold versify extempory. **1612** BRINSLEY *Lud. Lit.* viii. (1627) 121 To learne to versifie, *ex tempore*, of any ordinary Theame. **1656** H. MORE *Enthus. Tri.* (1712) 8 Maracus a Poet of Syracuse, who never versified so well as when he was in his distracted fits. **1693** DRYDEN *Juvenal* I. 24 Since the World with Writing is Possest, I'll versifie in spite. **1718** *Free-thinker* No. 136. 236 The Subject..promises no small Glory to the Genius who shall versify upon it. **1798** LADY BEDINGFIELD in *Betham Lett.* (1905) 51 Cannot you versify as you walk? **1824** BYRON *Juan* XV. xix, Speculating..On what may suit..my story, And never straining hard to versify. **1841** D'ISRAELI *Amen. Lit.* (1867) 394 A few scholars..had the intrepidity to versify in French with the ancient metres. **1897** *Pop. Sci. Monthly* L. 391 The true poet does not versify because he would, but because he must.
2. *trans.* To narrate or recount in verse; to treat as the subject of verse.
c **1386** CHAUCER *Monk's Prol.* 90 They [tragedies] ben versified communely Of vj. feet which men clepen Exametron. **1596** DANIEL *Civ. Wars* I. vi, I versify the truth, not poetize. **1766** GOLDSM. *Vic. W.* xvii, The silly poet runs home to versify the disaster. **1868** FREEMAN *Norm. Conq.* II. App. 533 The story is versified at great length in the French Life. **1871** LOWELL *Study Wind.*, *Pope* 315 His more ambitious works may be defined as careless thinking carefully versified.
3. To turn or convert (a literary piece) into verse; to change from prose into verse; to translate or rewrite in verse-form.
1735 POPE (*title*), The Satires of Dr. John Donne,.. Versified. **1756** J. WARTON *Ess. Pope* I. 11 The exalted prophesy of Isaiah, which Pope has so successfully versified. **1789** BURNEY *Hist. Mus.* III. 35 *note*, The 30th. Psalm was the first which Luther versified. **1814** D'ISRAELI *Quarrels Auth.* (1867) 256 Bolingbroke really wrote the 'Essay on Man', which Pope versified. **1837** LOCKHART *Scott* I. viii. 247 These are all in prose like their originals; but he also versified..some lyrical fragments of Goethe.

versifying ('vɜːsɪfaɪɪŋ), *vbl. sb.* [f. prec. + -ING¹.] The act or practice of making verses; an instance of this; the art of composing verse; versification.
c **1450** *Cov. Myst.* (Shaks. Soc.) 189 No clerke abyl to bere oure book Of versyfyeng, nor of other scyens. **1479** *Paston Lett.* III. 241, I lake no thynge but wersyfyynge, whyche I troste to have with a lytyll contynuance. *a* **1568** ASCHAM *Scholem.* II. (Arb.) 147 Yet neither of them hath fullie hite perfite and trew versifying. **1580** SPENSER *Let. to Harvey* Wks. (1912) 636, I perceiue you other whiles continue your old exercise of Versifying in English. *a* **1653** GOUGE *Comm. Hebr.* v. 14 A scholar exercised in versifying will readily distinguish between a true and false verse. **1677** J. PETER (*title*), Artificial Versifying; a New Way to make Latin Verses. **1740** J. CLARKE *Educ. Youth* (ed. 3) 61 Of what Use Versifying is,..I do not understand. **1830** SOUTHEY *Bunyan* p. xlix, In versifying he was attempting an art which he had never learnt, and for which he had no aptitude. **1892** *Athenæum* 6 Aug. 190/1 What really genuine poetic inspiration he showed is lost in the commonplace of too idle versifyings.
b. *attrib.*, as *versifying dialogue*, etc.
1686 in *Verney Mem.* (1907) II. 424 As to y[ou]r Versifying Dialogue with Him, I like it very well. **1725** WATTS *Logic* III. ii. §3, I confess some of these logical Subtilties have much more Use than those versifying Tables. **1737** *Gentl. Mag.* VII. 148/1, I shall exemplify by a Text, where a Singing, or mere Versifying Repetition, is literally express'd. **1787** SKINNER *Let.* in *Wks. Burns* (1800) II. 127, I know a classical education will not create a versifying taste. **1811** BYRON *Hints fr. Hor.* 839 If free, all fly

his versifying fit. **1885** *Athenæum* 11 July 50/1 Godwin desired Wordsworth to undertake the versifying part of the business.

'versifying, *ppl. a.* [f. as prec. + -ING².] That versifies or writes verses.

1580 *2nd & 3rd Blast Plays & Theatres* 110 These versifieng Plaie-makers. **1750** GRAY *Long Story* 18 Shame of the versifying tribe! **1893** WALKER *Three Churchmen* 134 The reviewers he looks upon as 'gamekeepers', doing invaluable service to literature by keeping the versifying 'poachers' off Parnassus.

†ver'siloquy. *Obs.*⁻⁰ [Cf. late L. *versiloquus* that speaks in verse.] (See quot.)

1727 BAILEY (vol. II), *Versiloquy*, speaking in Verse.

versin, contracted f. *versed sine* (VERSED *a.*).

1827 AIRY in *Encycl. Metrop.* (1845) I. 685 Versin $c = 1 - \cos c$. *Ibid.*, Versin c = versin $a - b$ [etc.]. **1859** PARKINSON *Optics* (1866) 254 The quantity of light received by the disc is $2\pi^2a^2B$ versin a.

versine ('vɜːsaɪn). [Expansion of prec. after SINE².] = *versed sine* a s.v. VERSED *a.* 1 a.

1943 R. A. HAMNETT *Brit. Railway Track* ix. 273 To obtain the versine of a turnout curve on a chord joining the switch heel and the intersection point of the crossing, (G—H) must be substituted for 'G'. **1958** CLARK & CLENDINNING *Plane & Geodetic Surveying* (ed. 5) I. 634 (*heading*) 'Versine' method of establishing intermediate points on the Euler spiral transition curve. **1976** J. B. GARNER et al. *Surveying* 278 Versines are used to compute slope corrections.

versine, variant of VERZINE *Obs.*

versing ('vɜːsɪŋ), *vbl. sb.* [f. VERSE *v.*¹ + -ING¹.] The action or practice of writing verse; an instance of this; the art or science of verse-making.

1581 SIDNEY *Apol. Poetrie* (Arb.) 49 That which gyueth greatest scope.., is ryming and versing. **1613** W. BROWNE *Brit. Past.* II. i. (1616) 9 For well it seemes in versing he hath skill. **1633** G. HERBERT *Temple, Flower* vi, I once more smell the dew and rain, And relish versing. **1644** BULWER *Chirol.* A iij b, Physick and Versing in his flaming Chaire Plac'd Phoebus, and bestow'd that blazing Haire. **1856** ANNE MANNING *Tasso & Leonora* 46 Charmed with his smooth versings. **1874** M. COLLINS *Transmigr.* II. ix. 162 The man who can..relish versing has nothing much the matter with his..psychical health. **1892** STOPFORD BROOKE *Early Eng. Lit.* I. vii. 146 He had before him some ancient versings of the fight.

attrib. **1645** G. DANIEL *Poems* Wks. (Grosart) II. 51 What mad men are wee of the versing trade!

†versing box. *Obs.*⁻¹ (Of obscure meaning; perh. connected with VERSE *v.*³ and VERSER².)

a **1529** SKELTON *Bouge of Court* 232 As I stode musynge in my mynde, Haruy Hafter came lepynge, lyghte as lynde. Vpon his breste he bare a versynge boxe.

version ('vɜːʃən, 'vɜʒən), *sb.* [a. F. *version* (= It. *versione*, Sp. *version*, Pg. *versão*), or ad. L. *versiōn-*, *versio*, noun of action from *vertĕre* to turn.]

1. a. A rendering of some text or work, or of a single word, passage, etc., from one language into another; a translation; also (rarely), the action or process of translating.

Freq. with adjs. denoting the language into which the translation is made.

1582 N.T. (Rhemish) Pref. b ij, Trusting that it may giue occasion to you..to lay away at lest such their impure versions as hitherto you haue ben forced to occupie. **1607** TOPSELL *Four-f. Beasts* 435, I vtterly seclude al their opinions, which translate this word Arabian wolues, for the Hæbrew notes cannot admit such a version or exposition. *c* **1645** HOWELL *Lett.* (1650) II. 61 Things translated into another tongue lose of their primitive vigor and strength, unless a paraphrasticall version be permitted. **1682** GREW *Anat. Plants* Pref., The Second Lecture..is also translated into French, by Mons. Mesmin,..whose Version is very well approved by those who are competent Judges. **1718** PRIOR *Poems Several Occas.* Pref., His excellent Version of the *Carmen Seculare*. **1794** BURKE *Pref. to Brissot's Addr. Constit.* Wks. VII. 327 The translator has only to say for himself, that he has found some difficulty in this version. *c* **1806** H. K. WHITE *Rem. Eng. Poets* Remains (1825) 156 None of our better versions have been able to preserve the original graces of these verses [of Ps. xviii]. **1841** ELPHINSTONE *Hist. India* I. III. vi. 293 Such of those literal versions as we possess in English (which are mostly from the 'Rámáyana'). **1874** GREEN *Short Hist.* viii. §1. 448 The English version of the Bible remains the noblest example of the English tongue.

b. *Sc.* A translation from English into Latin prose done as a school or university exercise; a piece of English prose set for translation into Latin.

1711 *Burgh Rec. Aberdeen* (1872) II. 345 Ther proficiency in themms, versions, poeticall composurs, and orations. *c* **1850** HURRY in Walker *Bards Bon-Accord* (1886) 629 When we our versions wrote, nae Lexicon had we To help us.

2. a. The particular form of a statement, account, report, etc., given by one person or party; an account resting upon limited authority or embodying a particular point of view.

1788 in *Ld. Auckland's Corr.* (1861) II. 93 The version which we received here respecting the famous Scarborough cruise. **1855** MACAULAY *Hist. Eng.* xviii. IV. 214 The Whig version of the story was that the old robber Mac Ian had laid an ambuscade for the soldiers... The Jacobite version.. appeared in the Paris Gazette of the seventh of April. **1879** FROUDE *Cæsar* xi. 140 The version generally received of what he actually did say. **1907** *Verney Mem.* II. 154 Sir Roger sends his version of the reconciliation between Monk and the City.

b. A special form or variant of something.

1835 I. TAYLOR *Spir. Despot.* viii. 345 To see Christianity freed from the bonds of every peculiar version. **1858** MASSON *Milton* (1859) I. 679 In the cause of true religion, or of the Scottish version of it. **1908** SIR H. MAXWELL *Guide Holyrood* 20 This painting is a larger version of one at Windsor Castle.

†3. a. A turning about; a change of direction. *Obs.*

1625 BACON *Ess., Viciss. of Things* (Arb.) 571 What Kinde of Comet, for Magnitude, Colour, Version of the Beames,.. or Lasting, produceth what Kinde of Effects. **1706** CONGREVE *Disc. Pindaric Ode* A j b, The first was call'd the Strophé, from the Version or circular Motion of the Singers in that Stanza from the Right Hand to the Left.

b. *Obstet.* The operation of manually turning the child so as to facilitate delivery.

1853 J. Y. SIMPSON *Obstet. Path. & Pract.* 17, I now found an obstruction to the complete version of the infant. **1889** *Buck's Handbk. Med. Sci.* VII. 628/2 The term version is applied to all operations by which the long axis of the child is changed in its relation to the long axis of the uterus.

†4. Conversion, transformation. *Obs.*

1626 BACON *Sylva* §27 Springs, which the Ancients thought..to be made by the Version of Aire into Water. **1626** —— *New Atl., Magn. Nat.* g iij, Version of bodies into other Bodies. **1666** BOYLE *Orig. Forms & Qual.* 407 As to the version of Water into Earth, by a seemingly slight Operation.

Hence **'version** *v. trans.*, to translate. **'versional** *a.*, pertaining to a version or translation. **'versioner, 'versionist,** one who produces a version; a translator. **'versionize** *v. trans.*, to render into another tongue, to translate.

1716 M. DAVIES *Athen. Brit.* III. *Arianism* 19 Biddle's brief Scripture-Catechism was caus'd to be *version'd into Latin. **1884** *Advance* (Chicago) 3 Jan., At the time the Scriptures had been versioned into the King James version. **1871** *Independent* (N.Y.) 23 Mar. (Cent.), All the suggestions for emendations [of the Bible], whether textual or *versional. **1910** *Expositor* Nov. 409 The versional variants rest on divergent Hebrew texts. *c* **1806** in *H. K. White's Rem.* (1825) 159 Our *versioner, by adding an *s* to it, has rendered them both plurals. **1782** ELPHINSTONE tr. *Martial* Pref. p. iv, His [*sc.* Martial's] Editor and *Versionist. **1811** R. DIXON *Interpr. Sixty-eighth Ps.* 46 *note*, All the ancient versionists seem to have thought, that the valley in this verse received its name [etc.]. **1861** I. TAYLOR *Spir. Hebr. Poetry* 338 Serviceable as Jewish versionists..are, it was not their function to concern themselves with the soul..of the national literature. **1874** H. COPPÉE *Eng. Lit.* (ed. 3) 52 Wace's poem..was soon again..to be *versionized into English.

†versipellous, *a. Obs.*⁻¹ [f. L. *versipell-is*, f. *vers-*, *vertĕre* to turn + *pellis* skin.] Having the faculty of changing the skin. In quot. *fig.*

1650 B. *Discolliminium* 28, I could demonstrate it to be Heterogeneous, Heterodoxous, Incongrous,.. Versipellous.

†'versity. *Obs.* [Abbrev. of UNIVERSITY.] = VARSITY.

c **1680** HICKERINGILL *Hist. Whiggism* I. Wks. 1716 I. 37 M. Tantivee is a Graduate, and no small Fool, I assure you, he has been at the —— Versity. **1691** MRS. D'ANVERS *Academia* 8 When e're he's sent to th' Versity.

†'versle, *v. Obs. rare.* Also 3 **uerslen, uersalien,** 4 **versail.** [ad. OF. *verseiller*, *-sailler*, *-seller*, etc.:—L. type **versiculāre*, f. L. *versiculus* VERSICLE *sb.*] *intr.* To say or sing versicles or verses of the Psalms, esp. during Divine Office. Also *trans.*

a **1225** *Ancr. R.* 44 Mid him ne schule ȝe nouðer uerslen ne singen þet he hit muwe iheren. *Ibid.* 120 þauh heo uersalie, & sigge hire vres, & hire Pater nosters. *a* **1325** *Prose Psalter* c. 1 Lord, y shal synge mercy and iugement to þe; y shal versail and vnderstonde in wai unfiled. *c* **1330** R. BRUNNE *Chron. Wace* (Rolls) 16472 þys salme þey songe, & versled hit al wyþ o tonge.

Hence **†'versling** *vbl. sb. Obs.*

a **1225** *Ancr. R.* 44 Verslunge of hire sautere; redinge of Englichs, oðer of Freinchs; holi meditaciuns.

‖vers libre (vɛr libr). Pl. **vers libres.** [Fr., free verse.] Poetic writing in which the traditional rules of prosody, esp. those of metre and rhyme, are disregarded in favour of variable rhythms and line lengths; a composition in this style; = *free verse* s.v. FREE *a.* D. 2.

1902 *Encycl. Brit.* XXVIII. 497/2 M. Viele-Griffin..and M. Gustave Kahn..gave us *vers libres* which, but for their typographical arrangement, are indistinguishable from prose. **1912** *Poetry* I. II. 65 Mr. Richard Aldington is a young English poet, one of the 'Imagistes', a group of ardent Hellenists who are pursuing interesting experiments in *vers libre*. **1920** *Glasgow Herald* 8 July 4/2 Mr. Bunker..is most interesting in his vers-libres; unfortunately they are not poetry, though happily free of the pretentiousness of most vers-librists. **1928** T. S. ELIOT in E. Pound *Sel. Poems* p. viii, I remarked some years ago, in speaking of *vers libre*, that 'no *vers* is *libre* for the man who wants to do a good job'. The term, which fifty years ago had an exact meaning, in relation to the French alexandrine, now means too much to mean anything at all. **1937** W. INGE *Modernism in Lit.* 13, I have no doubt that cubism and futurism and most of *vers libre* will soon pass into limbo. **1955** C. CARRINGTON *Rudyard Kipling* xiv. 352 Kipling..experimented in almost every conventional verse-form, and wrote remarkably successful *vers libres*. **1978** *Times Lit. Suppl.* 1 Dec. 1406/3 His was.. a phrased rather than a cadenced poetry. His rhythmic strategy meant that he retained the option of vers libre, the thematic resources of dream, and the technical resources of modernism.

Hence **vers-'librist(e** (also **-libre-ist** and as one word without hyphen), a writer of *vers libre*.

1916 *Independent* LXXXVIII. 104/3 If the public can be convinced that the vers libristes have something to say worth attention, it will have more sympathy. **1926** *British Weekly* 21 Jan. 395/2 Vers-libre-ists are in poetry very much what the futurists were in art, rebels against the established order. **1957** *Archivum Linguisticum* IX. 142 Certain *vers-libristes* of the Symbolist movement. **1969** J. GROSS *Rise & Fall Man of Lett.* viii. 229 By 1911 Ezra Pound was a regular contributor, the verslibrists were arguing their case, Imagism was already in the air. **1981** *N. & Q.* Dec. 571/2 Whether one should see in the experiments of modern vers-libristes a fusion of the two systems..must remain a matter for individual response.

‖verso ('vɜːsəʊ). [L. *verso* (sc. *folio* leaf), abl. sing. neut. of *versus*, pa. pple. of *vertĕre* to turn. So F. and Pg. *verso*.]

1. The back of a leaf in a manuscript or printed book; the side presented to the eye when the leaf has been turned over. Also abbrev. *v.*, *v°*.

The left-hand page of a book is the verso of that leaf, and faces the RECTO of the next.

1839 HALLIWELL *Maundevile* Introd. p. xiii, See f. 2, v°. **1850** FORSHALL & MADDEN *Wycliffite Bible* I. p. lxi, The verso commences with the eleventh chapter of the Epistle to the Romans. **1873** *Rep. Brit. Assoc.* I. 43 Sines, cosines, and secants are given on the versos of the pages in columns. **1898** *Athenaeum* 12 Nov. 676 The text begins on the verso of the title-page.

fig. **1873** J. HENRY *Aeneidea* I. Pref. 77 It was not long before I had the verso of this agreeable recto of one leaf of my library life.

2. The reverse of a coin, medal, or the like.

1891 *Cent. Dict.* **1914** P. E. NEWBERRY in *Anc. Egypt* 6 On the verso of the same palette there is a scene [etc.].

‖Versöhnung (fɛr'zøːnʊŋ). [Ger., conciliation, propitiation.] A reconciliation of opposites.

1867 J. A. SYMONDS *Let.* 22 Aug. (1967) I. 750 The truest *Versöhnung* in art I know is to be found in Beethoven's C Minor Symphony. There he first posits all the contradiction of passions, aspirations, and sorrows, then combines them.. so transfiguring them that the termination is triumph; the victory and majesty of the soul are wrought out of its defeats and humiliations. **1976** G. TALBOT *Permission to Speak* viii. 106 It was a jarring note in an evening of festive international *versöhnung*.

versoke, southern ME. pa. t. FORSAKE *v.*

†versor¹. *Obs.* In 5 **versour(e.** [a. AF. **versour* (F. *verseur*), f. *verser* to pour, VERSE *v.*²] (See quots.)

a **1483** *Liber Niger* in *Househ. Ord.* (1790) 77 One chief sobyr yeoman versoure, to resceyve all the ale or beere that shall be pourveyede. *Ibid.*, Othyr twoe groomes versours in this office to helpe to lodge theyre ale, to helpe drawe it [etc.].

versor² ('vɜːsə(r)). [a. L. type **versor*, f. *vers-*, *vertĕre* to turn.]

†1. The needle of a compass. *Obs. rare.*

1640 G. WATTS tr. *Bacon's Adv. Learn.* v. ii. 229 So the versor of a Mariners needle applies it selfe to the Poles of the world.

2. *Math.* In quaternions, an operator which changes the direction of a vector without altering its length.

a **1865** SIR W. R. HAMILTON *Elem. Quaternions* II. i. (1866) 133 We shall now say that every Radial Quotient is a Versor. A Versor has thus, in general, a plane, an axis, and an angle. **1886** W. S. ALDIS *Solid Geom.* (ed. 4) xiv. 235 If the two vectors OA and OB be of equal length the change of one into the other is merely an operation of rotation. In this case the quaternion is called a versor.

verss(e, southern ME. varr. FRESH *a.*

verst (vɜːst). Forms: α. 6–8 **werste,** 6, 8–9 **werst,** 7 **worst,** 7–8 **wurste.** β. 6– **verst,** 6–8 **verste,** 7 **vorst;** 6 **verse** (*pl.* **versse**), 7 **ferse.** [ad. Russ. *verstá*, partly through G. *werst* and F. *verste*.] A Russian measure of length equal to 3500 English feet or about two-thirds of an English mile.

α. **1555** EDEN *Decades* (Arb.) 322 From Moscouia to the citie of Vuolochda, are numbered [500] Werstes, one Werst conteynynge almoste the space of an Italyan myle. **1662** J. DAVIES tr. *Olearius' Voy. Ambass.* 27 We left Novogorod and got forwards 36. Werstes, or seven Leagues. **1715** *Lond. Gaz.* No. 5293/2 He was not gone above 12 Wurstes or Russian Miles. **1774** *Ann. Reg.* II. 151 Having approached this island within almost three wersts, or two English miles, their vessel was suddenly surrounded by ice. **1818** BYRON *Mazeppa* xvii, Many a werst, Panting as if his heart would burst, The weary brute still stagger'd on. **1841** MOTLEY *Corr.* (1889) I. iv. 73 The road from Tauroggen to Petersburg is 14 wersts.

β. **1557** JENKINSON in Hakluyt *Voy.* (1886) III. 198 Vologhda and Mosco..are accompted 500 verstes asunder. *c* **1571** J. STOW *Voy. & Trav.* (Hakl. Soc.) II. 339 The ryuer oca, which is 20 versse distant from ye moscow; a verse is iii quarters of an yngleshe myle. **1591** G. FLETCHER *Russe Commw.* (Hakl. Soc.) 7 A little isthmus or narrow slippe of lande, a fewe versts ouerthwart. **1617** MORYSON *Itin.* I. 295 In Russia among the Moscovites confining upon Poland, a mile is called a ferse. **1635** PAGITT *Christianogr.* 23 From the furthest part westward..to Siberia Eastward, is 4400. verst or thereabouts. *a* **1670** [S. COLLINS] *Pres. St. Russia* (1671) 83 Some ran away ten Versts before they could be overtaken. **1760** *Phil. Trans.* LI. 490 It runs from a great lake, which lies a verste and a half from its mouth. **1775** WRAXALL *Tour*

North. Europe 218 Muscovite lords commonly go fifty and sixty versts..to make visits to each other. **1808** R. K. PORTER *Trav. Sk. Russ. & Swed.* (1813) I. iv. 27 Seventy or eighty versts above St. Petersburgh. **1864** BURTON *Scot Abr.* II. ii. 204 A country house of the Tzaar's seven versts from Moscow. **1879** BROWNING *Ivàn Ivànovitch* 194 No strength, old crone,—not she!—to crawl forth half a verst!

verst(e, southern ME. varr. FIRST *a.* and *adv.*; obs. Sc. ff. WORST *a.*

‖**Verstandesmensch** (fɛr'ʃtandəsmɛnʃ). Pl. -menschen. [Ger.] A matter-of-fact person; a realist.

1879 W. JAMES *Coll. Ess. & Rev.* (1920) 133 Such also is the attitude of all hard-minded analysts and *Verstandesmenschen.* **1938** *Mind* XLVII. 528 He rejects as an unhistorical caricature the view of Kant as a cold *Verstandesmensch.*

‖**Verstehen** (fɛr'ʃteːən). *Social Sci.* Also ver-. [Ger., comprehension.] The use of empathy to understand human action and behaviour, as a method of interpreting historical and sociological phenomena. Also **ver'stehende** (fem. pres. pple. of *verstehen* comprehend) *a.*, employing *Verstehen.*

1933 *Economica* XIII. 31 In this sense *verstehende* sociology is rationalistic. **1934** *Psychol. Bull.* XXXI. 298 Ch. Bühler makes use of *Verstehen* as well as statistics in her analysis of life histories. **1937** T. PARSONS *Structure Social Action* xvi. 583 This is the first appearance in Weber's methodology of the fundamentally important concept of *Verstehen.* **1948** T. ABEL in Feigl & Brodbeck *Readings in Philos. of Sci.* (1953) 682 The characteristic feature of the operation of *Verstehen* is the postulation of an intervening process 'located' inside the human organism, by means of which we recognize an observed..connection as relevant. **1974** R. D. JESSOP *Traditionalism, Conservatism & Brit. Political Culture* i. 18 A pure *verstehende* technique which treats action as the logical concomitant of the actor's ideas, motives, reasons, and beliefs. **1979** *Internat. Jrnl. Sociol. of Law* VII. 327 Problems of *verstehen* sociology—that the analysis should have some regard to the meanings that the actors give to their actions.

versuore, southern ME. var. *forswore* FORSWORN.

‖**versus** ('vɜːsəs), *prep.* [L.] Against; employed in *Law* to denote an action by one party against another. Also *transf.* Freq. abbrev. *v.* (also *ver.*, *vs.*).

1447–8 SHILLINGFORD *Lett.* (Camden) 53 Also the jugement by twene..John Husset *versus* John Notte. **1451** *Paston Lett.* I. 221, I send yow the *scire facias* for Osbern and Foke *versus* Heydon and Wyndam. **1621** *Debates Ho. Lords* (Camden) 26 Suyt per Fowles in the Starr-chamber *versus* Lake and others. **1744** J. COMYNS *Reports of Cases* 634 Wallis *ver.* Pain and Underhill. **1774** J. ADAMS in *Fam. Lett.* (1876) 19, I am engaged in a famous case,—the cause of King, of Scarborough, *versus* the mob that broke into his house. **1822** SCOTT *Peveril* Pref. Ep., She may sue me for damages, as in the case Dido *versus* Virgil. **1839** DE QUINCEY *Casuistry Rom. Meals* Wks. 1890 VII. 22 Generally such a person is 'rather yellow, rather yellow' (to quote Canning *versus* Lord Durham). **1873** H. SPENCER *Stud. Sociol.* ii. 38 The old battle-ground of free will *versus* necessity. **1894** *Outing* Feb. 397/2 The Rambler *vs.* the Lumberman; an indictment for the larceny of a path.

versute (və'sjuːt, 'vɜːsjuːt), *a.* [ad. L. *versūtus*, f. *vers-*, *vertĕre* to turn.] Cunning, crafty, wily.

1616 J. LANE *Contn. Sqr.'s T.* IX. 15 Her artishe liers, wittie versute theeves. *Ibid.* 73 Ne bee out reachd at versute pollecie, or once out runn at hardie chivalrie. **1659** GAUDEN *Tears Ch.* I. xiv. 132 A person of very supercilious gravity, also of versute and vertigenous policy. **1790** PALEY *Horæ Paul.* i. 6 The second, which is a more versute and specious forgery.

Hence **versutely** *adv.*; **versuteness**.

Also ***versutiloquent***, 'a crafty talker, one using words craftily' (Blount *Glossogr.*, 1656), and ***versutiloquous***, 'talking cunningly or craftily' (Bailey, vol. II, 1727): both after L. *versūtiloquus.*

1616 J. LANE *Contn. Sqr.'s T.* x. 128 Now guiltie Horbell, Leifurcke, Gnartolite, castinge on chaunge, the lipp versutlie bite. **1685** H. MORE *Cursory Refl. Baxter* 29 That he may become really sensible and ashamed of his present Crooked Versuteness and Hypocrisie. **1710** R. WARD *Life H. More* 81 Some Neatness of Stile, Versuteness of Temper, and Hypocrisie in Religion. **1857** MAURICE *Mor. & Met. Philos.* IV. vi. §89. 286 An ingenious explanation of astuteness and versuteness.

†**versutious**, *a. Obs.*⁻¹ [f. L. *versūt-us.*] = prec.

1660 *3rd Conf. betw. Cromwell & H. Peters* 7 What do I not ow thee for thy versutious Complements to my Lady Lambert.

†'**versy**, *a. Obs.*⁻¹ *Her.* In 6 versie. [a. F. *versé*, pa. pple. of *verser*: see VERSE *v.*² F. *versé* has been used in some mod. heraldic books.] Renversé, reversed.

1572 BOSSEWELL *Armorie* II. 36b, He beareth d'Or, a Cheuron Versie d'Azure.

versycle, obs. form of VERSICLE *sb.*

versyowre: see VERSER¹.

vert (vɜːt), *sb.*¹ (and *a.*¹) Also 5 veert, 5–7 verte. [a. AF. and OF. *vert* (so mod.F.; formerly also *verd* VERD *sb.*), = Pr. *vert*, Cat. *verd*, Sp., Pg., and It. *verde*:—L. *virid-em*, *viridis* green, VIRID *a.*]

1. Green vegetation growing in a wood or forest and capable of serving as cover for deer.

14.. *Forest Laws* (MS. Douce 335) fol. 73 As touching the kinges veert, that is to say, the kinges wodes; if ther be ony mann, that hath felled ony grete okes [etc.]. **1577** HARRISON *England* II. xv. in *Holinshed* I. 89b/1 The better preseruation of such venery and vert of all sortes as were nourished in the same. **1598** MANWOOD *Lawes Forest* vi. §1. 33b. [Hence in later Dicts., etc.] **1702** *Phil. Trans.* XXIII. 1073 While this Country was a Chace, and while the Vert was preserv'd. **1768** BLACKSTONE *Comm.* III. 71 The punishment of all injuries done to the king's deer or *venison*, to the *vert* or greenswerd. **1818** CRUISE *Digest* (ed. 2) III. 143 Destruction of vert is destruction of venison. **1839** STONEHOUSE *Axholme* 62 A royal demesne..covered with vert, and well stocked with deer. **1871** *Daily News* 18 Sept., The Lord of the Manor..had..enclosed four hundred acres of waste land, and had destroyed the vert on parts thereof.

transf. **1635** A. STAFFORD *Fem. Glory* c vij b, The fourth is humble Ivy, intersert, But lowlie laid,..Preserved, in her antique bed of Vert, No faith's more firme,..then where't doth creep.

b. Coupled with *venison*. (The common use.) Freq. without article.

1455 *Rolls of Parlt.* V. 319/2 The oversight of verte and venyson, in all the Parkes. **1577** HOLINSHED *Chron.* II. 459/2 The k[ing]..appointed foure iustices..to be as surueyers aboue all other Foresters of vert & venison. **1598** MANWOOD *Lawes Forest* xvii. 102b, That which tendeth to the hurt and annoyance of the Vert and the Venison. **1612** SIR J. DAVIES *Why Ireland*, etc. (1747) 164 The great plenty both of Vert and Venison within this land. **1700** TYRRELL *Hist. Eng.* II. 820 Every Forester in Fee shall..Attach Pleas of the Forest, as well concerning Vert as Venison. **1772** *Junius Lett.* lxviii. (1788) 347 If a man was taken with vert, or venison, it was declared to be equivalent to indictment. **1835** J. P. KENNEDY *Horse Shoe R.* xxxvii, He gave much of his time to the concerns of vert and venison. **1840** *Penny Cycl.* XVI. 175/1 The master-keepers' and groom-keepers' duty is to preserve the vert and venison in their respective bailiwicks and walks.

†**c.** ***nether, over, special vert***: (see quots.). *Obs.*

1598 MANWOOD *Lawes Forest* vi. §2. 34 There are two sorts of Vert in euery Forrest, that is to say, Ouer vert, and, Neather vert: Ouer vert is that, which the Lawiers do call Hault Boys, and Neather vert is that, which the Lawiers do call South Boys, and in the Forrest lawes, Ouer vert is all manner of Hault Boys, or great wood, aswel such as beareth fruit, as such as beareth none. *Ibid.* 35 Speciall vert, which is euery tree and bush within the Forrest, that doth beare fruite to feed the Deere withall, as Peare trees, Crabtrees, Hawthornes,..and such like. [Hence in later Law Dicts., etc.] **1727** NELSON *Laws conc. Game* 231 *Special-vert*, which may be either over or nether-vert, or both if it bears fruit, for nothing is accounted special-vert but such which beareth fruit to feed the deer.

2. *ellipt.* The right to cut green trees or shrubs in a forest. Now *arch.*

1639 in Maitland *Hist. Edinburgh* (1753) II. 151/1 All their antient Rights,..with Pit and Gallows, Sack and Soke, Thole, Theam, Vert, Wrack, Waifs [etc.]. **1707** in *State, Fraser of Fraserfield* 310 (Jam.), Cum furca, fossa,..vert, veth, venison,..pit et gallows. **1819** SCOTT *Ivanhoe* xl, The Holy Clerk shall have a grant of vert and venison in my woods of Warncliffe. **1843** JAMES *Forest Days* vii, His rights of vert and venison, extended over a wide distance around. **1864** KINGSLEY *Rom. & Teut.* 257 The nobles about gave up to him their rights of venison, and vert, and pasture, and pannage of swine.

†**3.** A green plant or shrub. *Obs.*⁻¹

1648 J. RAYMOND *Il Merc. Ital.* 129 Bayes, Locusts, Pomegrannets, and such like Verts, that grow wild in the Hedges.

†**4.** A green colour or pigment. *Obs.*

1481–90 *Howard Househ. Bks.* (Roxb.) 339 Item,..for iiij. dos. of golde paper, and silver rowche clere and verte, viij. s. **1572** in Feuillerat *Revels Q. Eliz.* (1908) 178 Vert,..Sapp, ..Crymsen,..White,..Broune. **1582** *Ibid.* 359 Paste bord, paper, and paste, white, sise, verte, Syneper.

5. *spec.* in *Her.* The tincture green. Also as *adj.*

c **1507** *Justes Moneths May & June* 28 in Hazl. *E.P.P.* II. 114 For a cognysaunce Of Mayes month they bare a souenaunce, Of a verte cocle was the resemblaunce, Tatched ryght fast. **1562** LEIGH *Armorie* 15b, That is greene, & blased Vert. *Ibid.*, And nowe we to the fourth colour, Vert. *a* **1586** SIDNEY *Astr. & Stella* xiii, In vert field Mars bare a golden speare. **1622** PEACHAM *Compl. Gentl.* xv. (1906) 194 A plaine crosse Vert, by the name of Hussey. **1646** G. DANIEL *Poems* Wks. (Grosart) I. 44 [To] tell you how they beare Gules, or, vert, azure,—heathen words for Red, Yellow, green, blue. **1655** FULLER *Antheologia* (1867) 278 The whole field was vert or green. **1656** BLOUNT *Glossogr.* [Hence in Phillips, etc.] **1727** BAILEY (vol. II), *Vert* (in Heraldry) signifies Green, and in Graving, is expressed by Diagonal Lines, drawn from the Dexter Chief Corner, to the Sinister Base. **1815** KIRBY & SP. *Entomol.* i. (1816) I. 10 Some [insects] she [*sc.* Nature] blazons with heraldic insignia, giving them to bear in fields..vert—gules—argent and or, fesses—bars..and even animals. *c* **1828** BERRY *Encycl. Her.* I. Gloss., *Vert*, the common French term for green, and the proper heraldic term for that colour.

vert (vɜːt), *sb.*² Also 'vert. [Shortened f. CONVERT *sb.*, PERVERT *sb.*] One who converts from one religion to another, esp. to the Roman Catholic faith.

1864 *Union Rev.* May 277 Old friends call me a pervert: new acquaintances a convert: the other day I was addressed as a 'vert... This term "vert" I have every reason to believe has been only just coined. **1886** *Pall Mall G.* 25 May 4/2 Cardinal Manning stands alone.., and as he is an Anglican 'vert he does not count.

transf. **1886** *North Star* 5 May, Your 'vert [to Home Rule] is ever vigorous.

vert *a.*¹: see VERT *sb.*¹

vert (vɜːt), *a.*² *poet. nonce-wd.* [Cf. VERT *v.*¹] Turning.

1947 AUDEN *Age of Anxiety* (1948) ii. 49 O Primal Age When we danced deisal, our dream-wishes Vert and volant.

vert, *v.*¹ [ad. L. *vertĕre* to turn, overturn, etc.]

†**1.** *trans.* To turn up, root up (the ground).

1578 *Burgh Rec. Aberdeen* (1848) II. 32 It sall be lesum to quhatsumewir personne apprehendand the said swyne.. vertand the ertht, to distroy the samen.

2. To turn in a particular direction; to turn or twist out of the normal position. Now *spec.* in *Path.* or *Anat.* Hence '**verting** *ppl. a.*

c **1590** J. STEWART *Poems* (S.T.S.) II. 47 His sourd..did clinck and clak, Quhair euir he verts his force And awfull face. **1659** FULLER *App. Inj. Innoc.* III. 21 When a Writer's words are madly vetted, inverted, perverted, against his true intent, and their Grammaticall sense.

1883 DUNCAN *Clin. Lect. Dis. Wom.* (ed. 2) viii. 59 A lady had ulceration of the interior of the body of the uterus, which was not flexed or verted. **1903** *Med. Record* 7 Feb. 210 All of the muscles of the eyes may be relatively weak. The ducting or verting power is not as great as it should be.

3. *intr.* To change direction; to dart about.

1859 MEREDITH *R. Feveril* II. x. 198 He flew about in the very skies, verting like any blithe creature of the season.

vert, *v.*² Also 'vert. [f. VERT *sb.*²] *intr.* To become a convert from one religion to another, esp. to Roman Catholicism.

1888 *Echo* 17 Mar. (Cassell's), As a man he is welcome to vert and re-vert as often as he pleases. **1891** *Hist. Sk. Par. St. Martin, Colchester* 7 William Murray..'verted to the Roman Church after J. H. Newman.

'**vertant**, *a. Her.* [a. F. *vertant*, = L. *vertent-*, *vertens*, pres. pple. of *vertĕre*: see VERT *v.*¹] Bending, curving.

1688 R. HOLME *Armoury* II. 473/1 He beareth Argent, eight Leaves, the Stalks conjoyned and contrary bowed... But the most compendious, is to blazon them conjoyn'd dorse endorse: though good Artists will say, conjoyned and vertant to the Dextre and Sinister. *c* **1828** BERRY *Encycl. Her.* I. Gloss., *Vertant* and *Revertant*, or *Verted* and *Reverted*, the same as *flexed* and *reflexed*, or *bowed embowed*, that is formed like the letter S reverted. [Hence in later Dicts.]

vertdegrease, vert de grece, obs. forms of VERDIGRIS.

verte, southern ME. var. FART *v.*

verteber, var. VERTEBRE.

vertebra ('vɜːtɪbrə). Pl. **vertebræ** ('vɜːtɪbriː); also 7–8 **vertebras**. [a. L. *vertebra* joint, joint of the spine, f. *vertĕre* to turn. Hence It., Sp., Pg. *vertebra*, F. *vertèbre*: cf. VERTEBRE.]

1. *Anat.* and *Zool.* One or other of the joints composing the spinal column in man or other vertebrate animals; any segment of the backbone.

α. **1615** CROOKE *Body of Man* (1631) 930 The vertebra in the middest receiueth that spondell which is aboue it. **1634** A. READ *Descr. Body Man* C vj/1 The transvers processe of the first vertebra. *a* **1728** WOODWARD *Fossils* (1729) I. II. 82 A large Vertebra of a Fish. **1767** GOOCH *Treat. Wounds* I. 367 The Thoracic Duct or canal runs..as far as the fifth vertebra of the back. **1788** *Encycl. Brit.* (ed. 3) I. 726 The œsophagus..terminates in the stomach about the eleventh or twelfth vertebra of the back. **1840** E. WILSON *Anat. Vade M.* (1842) 7 A Vertebra consists of a body, two laminæ, a spinous process, two transverse processes, and four articular processes. **1881** MIVART *Cat* 35 Each of these small bones is called a vertebra.

Comb. **1839** G. ROBERTS *Dict. Geol.* 180 *Vertebralis*,.. vertebra-like.

β. **1664** POWER *Exp. Philos.* I. 42 The Lamprey..hath a Cartilaginous flexible Tube or Channel, without any Vertebræ or Spondyls in it. **1666** J. DAVIES *Hist. Caribby Isles* 132 Having no vertebræ in the back-bone,..he [*sc.* the crocodile] goes straight forwards, not being able to turn. **1732** ARBUTHNOT *Rules of Diet* 362 For there be some with fewer Vertebræ in their Necks than others. **1774** GOLDSM. *Nat. Hist.* (1824) II. 140 The vertebræ of the neck [of the ourang-outang] also were shorter. **1851** S. P. WOODWARD *Mollusca* I. i. 3 A backbone, composed of numerous joints, or vertebræ. **1867** F. FRANCIS *Angling* iii. 73 The angler should..sever the vertebræ at the back of the neck.

transf. **1864** LOWELL *Fireside Trav.* 233 The shattered vertebræ of the [Roman] aqueducts.

γ. **1661** LOVELL *Hist. Anim. & Min.* Isagoge b 8b, Their vertebra's are cartilagineous and flexile. **1667** *Phil. Trans.* II. 461 The Vertebra's descending from the Back. **1706** PHILLIPS (ed. Kersey), *Cyphoma*,..a bending backwards of the *Vertebra's*, or Turning-joynts of the Back. **1770** *Phil. Trans.* LXI. 134 It..extended..to the right ovarium, and vertebras of her back.

b. With particularizing terms.

1726 MONRO *Anat. Bones* 178 The Spine is commonly divided into true and false Vertebræ. **1771** *Encycl. Brit.* I. 169 The lumbar vertebræ, as they descend, have their oblique processes at a greater distance from each other. **1847–9** *Todd's Cycl. Anat.* IV. I. 624 The cervical vertebra ..differs in this respect from the dorsal vertebra; this from the lumbar vertebra; this from the sacral vertebra; and this from the coccygeal vertebra. **1854** OWEN in *Orr's Circ. Sci., Org. Nat.* I. 193 This unusually developed spine of the mesencephalic vertebra. *Ibid.* 236 In the odd-toed.. ungulates, the dorso-lumbar vertebræ differ in different species. **1866** HUXLEY *Preh. Rem. Caithn.* 109 A horse's skull with its upper cervical vertebræ. **1872** —— *Phys.* vii. 171 The odontoid peg of the axis vertebra.

2. *pl.* (with *the*). The vertebral column; the spine or backbone.

a **1627** MIDDLETON *Anything for Quiet Life* III. i, I will finde where his Disease of Cozenage lay, whether in the Vertebræ, or in Oscox-Index [= Os Coxendix]. *a* **1700** EVELYN *Diary* 2 May 1644, They show also the ribs and vertebræ of the same beast. **1728** CHAMBERS *Cycl.* s.v., A Weakness of the Ligaments and Muscles fasten'd to the backside of the *Vertebræ*. **1759** STERNE *Tr. Shandy* II. ix, Dr. Slop's figure, coming..waddling thro' the dirt upon the vertebræ of a little diminutive pony. **1834** McMURTRIE *Cuvier's Anim. Kingd.* 27 They are articulated at one extremity with the vertebræ. **1856** KANE *Arct. Expl.* II. xv. 160 The vertebræ of a whale similar to that at the igloë of Anoatok. **1872** HUXLEY *Phys.* i. 6 The bones thus cut through are called the bodies of the vertebræ.

fig. **1768** TUCKER *Lt. Nat.* (1834) I. 429, I should have known you for a true Search by the pliableness of your neck: the Knowals have a wonderful stiffness in the vertebræ.

b. Without article.

1849 MURCHISON *Siluria* xx. 478 Large fossil fishes with vertebræ sometimes ossified. **1861** MUSGRAVE *By-roads* 314 He had made the tour of all Europe without once leaning back in his carriage! This indicated matchless rigidity of fibre and strength of vertebræ.

3. In sing. = sense 2. *rare*$^{-1}$.

1791 WALKER *Pron. Dict.* s.v. **1876** J. G. WOOD *Nat. Hist.* 501 We now enter upon another vast division in which there is no true brain and no vertebra.

4. *Zool.* (See quots.)

1704 RAY *Disc.* II. iv. (1713) 182 Great Stones, and even broken Pieces of Lime-stone Rocks,..almost wholly compos'd of those *Vertebræ*, or broken Pieces of the *Radii* of Sea-Stars, which are commonly call'd Fairy-Stones. **1891** *Cent. Dict.*, *Vertebra*, in echinoderms, any one of the numerous axial ossicles of the arms of starfishes.

vertebral ('vɜːtɪbrəl), *a.* and *sb.* [ad. med. or mod.L. *vertebrālis* (= F. *vertébral*, Sp., Pg. *vertebral*, It. *vertebrale*), or f. prec. + -AL[1].]

A. *adj.* **1.** Of or pertaining to, situated on or near, the vertebræ; spinal.

1681 tr. *Willis' Rem. Med. Wks.* Vocab., *Vertebral*, belonging to the joynts of the back-bone. **1704** RAY *Creation* II. (ed. 4) 319 The carotid, vertebral and splenick Arteries are..variously contorted. **1737** BRACKEN *Farriery Impr.* (1756) I. 83 The Carotidal and the Vertebral Arteries. **1771** *Encycl. Brit.* I. 218 Of the Vertebral Muscles. **1831** R. KNOX *Cloquet's Anat.* 27 Vertebral Canal..extends along the whole length of the spine, following its various curvatures. **1840** E. WILSON *Anat. Vade M.* (1842) 342 The Vertebral vein descends by the side of the vertebral artery. **1854** OWEN in *Orr's Circ. Sci., Org. Nat.* I. 197 The pleurapophyses or vertebral ribs in serpents. **1887** *Encycl. Brit.* XXII. 111/2 A sort of bony canal in which runs the vertebral artery.

transf. **1824** GALT *Rothelan* I. i, The acts of..the Black Prince constitute the vertebral portion of his history.

b. *Ent.* 'Situated on or noting the median line of the upper surface' (*Cent. Dict.* 1891).

2. Composed of vertebræ; spinal. Freq. in ***vertebral column***.

1822 J. FLINT *Lett. Amer.* 234 The vertebral column was completely pliant, her body..bent in every direction successively. **1847–9** *Todd's Cycl. Anat.* IV. I. 632/1 Every lesser unit of the vertebral chain. **1877** J. A. ALLEN *Amer. Bison* 449 The smaller size of the posterior part of the vertebral column in the American bison.

3. Of the nature of a vertebra.

1847–9 *Todd's Cycl. Anat.* IV. I. 648 The vertebral pieces hold their own serial order, and thus we know them. *Ibid.* 670 These two iliac bones (*c, c*) are homologous..to the two vertebral laminæ of A.

b. *Zool.* (See quots.)

1877 HUXLEY *Anat. Inv. Anim.* 563 [In] the Ophiuridea, ..each of these [quadrate axial] ossicles (which are sometimes termed *vertebral*) is surrounded by four plates. **1877** F. BUTLER in *Encycl. Brit.* VII. 633 The deep ambulacral grooves which occupy the middle of the lower face of each ray [in star-fishes] are formed each by a series of plates, the *vertebral ossicles*.

4. Of animals: Having a spinal column; = VERTEBRATE *a.* 1.

1816 J. SCOTT *Vis. Paris* (ed. 5) 299 Cuvier, who was the first to divide animals into vertebral and invertebral. **1822–7** GOOD *Study Med.* (1829) IV. 16 All the classes of vertebral animals possess the same number of senses as man. **1854** H. MILLER *Sch. & Schm.* xxi. (1860) 229/1 Under what peculiarities of form..vertebral life existed in the earlier ages of the world.

B. *sb.* **1.** A vertebral artery or vein.

1718 J. CHAMBERLAYNE *Relig. Philos.* (1730) I. iii. §3 We here see the Jugular Veins, and the Vertebrals. **1755** *Dict. Arts & Sci.* s.v. *Medulla*, The arteries and veins of the spinal marrow..are derived from the vertebrals of the neck, the intercostals, and the lumbar. **1880** BARWELL *Aneurism* 53 If we ligature the first part of the subclavian, ought we also to occlude the vertebral? **1899** *Allbutt's Syst. Med.* VII. 390 The arteries of the medulla oblongata..arise from the vertebrals.

2. A vertebrate animal. *rare*$^{-0}$.

1828–32 WEBSTER, *Vertebral*, n., an animal of the class which have a back-bone.

3. One of the unpaired dorsal plates in the carapace of a turtle.

1883 *Encycl. Brit.* XXIII. 456 Dermal Scutes [of *Testudo pardalis*]:—*co*, costals; *v*, vertebrals; *m*, marginals.

Hence **'vertebrally** *adv.*

1891 *Cent. Dict.* s.v., Segmented vertebrally; vertebrally articulated ribs.

vertebrar'terial, *a.* *Anat.* and *Zool.* [f. VERTEBR-A + ARTERIAL *a.*] Of or belonging to a vertebra and an artery; vertebro-arterial.

1884 COUES *N. Amer. Birds* 139 The series of these foramina is called the vertebrarterial canal. **1902** *Cunningham's Text-bk. Anat.* (1906) 75 The vertebrarterial foramen..is traversed by the vertebral artery and vein in the upper six vertebræ.

‖**Vertebrata** (vɜːtɪ'breɪtə). *Zool.* [mod.L. (Cuvier), a. L. *vertebrāta* (sc. *animālia*), neut. pl. of *vertebrātus* VERTEBRATE *a.*]

1. With *the*. A division of the animal kingdom including all animals which have a backbone or its equivalent.

1826 KIRBY & SP. *Entomol.* xxviii. III. 44 The difference here between Insects and the Vertebrata seems very wide. **1834** McMURTRIE *Cuvier's Anim. Kingd.* 232 The blood of the Mollusca..appears to contain a smaller proportionate quantity of fibrine than that of the Vertebrata. **1843** *Penny Cycl.* XXVI. 277/2 In the *Vertebrata* the brain and principal trunk or chord of the nervous system is enclosed in a bony or gristly case composed of the skull and the vertebræ. **1877** HUXLEY *Anat. Inv. Anim.* 49 Even the hiatus between the *Vertebrata* and the *Invertebrata*, is partly, if not wholly, bridged over.

2. A group or class of these; a number of vertebrate animals.

1851 D. WILSON *Preh. Ann.* IV. vii. 644 The geologist, without seeking to reanimate these extinct vertebrata, learns much regarding the past from..their colossal remains. **1855** H. SPENCER *Princ. Psychol.* (1872) I. I. i. 4 Between the water-breathing vertebrata and..air-breathing vertebrata there is an equally conspicuous unlikeness in energy. **1870** ROLLESTON *Anim. Life* 5 In every Mammalian skeleton.. the vertebrae in the trunk always differ from those of the different lower vertebrata in..the following points.

vertebrate ('vɜːtɪbrət), *a.* and *sb.* [ad. L. *vertebrāt-us* (Pliny), jointed, articulated, f. *vertebra* VERTEBRA. Cf. prec. and INVERTEBRATE.]

A. *adj.* **1.** *Zool.* Of or belonging to the Vertebrata; characterized by having a backbone or spinal column. Freq. in ***vertebrate animal***.

1826 KIRBY & SP. *Entomol.* xxviii. III. 42 Size forms a pretty accurate distinction between insects and the great bulk of vertebrate animals. *a* **1843** *Encycl. Metrop.* (1845) VII. 292 The passive motive Organs or Skeleton of the Vertebrate Series of Animals. **1870** GILLMORE tr. *Figuier's Rept. & Birds* Introd. 4 A bountiful Creator appears to have adopted one general plan in the organization of all the vertebrate creation. **1881** MIVART in *Nature* No. 615. 337 The highest of them, called the vertebrate sub-kingdom.. comprises ourselves, with all beasts, birds, reptiles, efts, frogs and toads, and fishes.

Comb. **1863** DANA *Man. Geol.* 276 In most of these vertebrate-tailed species the vertebral column extends into the upper lobe of the tail.

b. *Bot.* (See quot.)

1832 LINDLEY *Introd. Bot.* 390 *Vertebrate*,..when the leaf is contracted at intervals, there being an articulation at each contraction; as in Cussonia spicata.

2. Of or pertaining to, characteristic of, found in, a vertebrated animal or animals.

1848 OWEN (*title*), On the Archetype and Homologies of the Vertebrate Skeleton. **1854** H. MILLER *Sch. & Schm.* xxi. (1860) 229/1 The second age of vertebrate existence on our planet. **1857** H. SPENCER in *Westm. Rev.* Apr. 450 The earliest known vertebrate remains are those of Fishes. **1883** *Encycl. Brit.* XVI. 663/2 In the vertebrate eye, the filaments of the optic nerve penetrate the retina.

fig. **1872** MINTO *Eng. Prose Lit.* I. iii. 201 A vertebrate skeleton of the work.

3. *fig.* **a.** Of persons: Having connective mental powers.

1879 O. W. HOLMES *Motley* xix. 146 The archivists and annalists will pile up facts..until the vertebrate historian comes with his generalizing ideas.

b. Of writings, etc.: Connectedly put together; characterized by strength or consistency.

1882 GOSSE in Grosart *Spenser* III. p. xlvi, Ramsay's *Gentle Shepherd*..remains the most vertebrate and interesting bucolic drama produced in Great Britain. **1884** *Athenæum* 15 Nov. 635/2 The new comedy..is more than a little lachrymose and is scarcely vertebrate. **1900** *Sat. Rev.* 24 Mar. 367 We have the right..to expect something more vertebrate, if he is to take place in literature.

B. *sb.* A member of the Vertebrata; a vertebrate animal.

1826 KIRBY & SP. *Entomol.* xlv. IV. 240 The antennæ of insects are analogous to ears in Vertebrates. **1840** *Cuvier's Anim. Kingd.* 33 The general plan of their organization is not so uniform..as that of the vertebrates. **1870** F. BOWEN *Logic* vi. 155 Some wingless animals are not vertebrates.

'vertebrate, *v.* [f. prec.] *trans.* To connect or join after the manner of vertebræ.

1891 in *Cent. Dict.* **1894** BLACKMORE *Perlycross* 129 As like each other as three peas vertebrated in one pod. **1910** *Q. Rev.* Jan. 69 They [*sc.* satires] were written in rough dialect and vertebrated with peasant phrases and peasant wit.

vertebrated ('vɜːtɪbreɪtɪd), *ppl. a.* [f. VERTEBRATE *a.* + -ED.]

1. = VERTEBRATE *a.* 1. Freq. in ***vertebrated animal(s)***.

1828 STARK *Elem. Nat. Hist.* I. 371 Vertebrated animals with cold red blood, respiring by gills or branchiæ. **1835** J. DUNCAN *Beetles* (Nat. Lib.) 74 Certain relations of analogy which some of the species are thought to bear to the vertebrated tribes. **1849** SAXE *Poems* (1873) 120 One of those vertebrated vermin That lie in the grass so prettily curled. **1874** CARPENTER *Ment. Phys.* I. ii. §57 (1879) 57 The Vertebrated series, of which Man is the highest representative.

2. Consisting of, provided with, vertebræ.

1863 DANA *Man. Geol.* 276 All these ancient fishes [Ganoids] have vertebrated tails. **1864** BOWEN *Logic* x. 323 Among inorganic bodies,..the metallic property is an instance of the former class; among animals, the possession of a vertebrated column or backbone.

3. *transf.* Constructed in a manner suggestive of vertebræ.

1840 *Civil Eng. & Arch. Jrnl.* III. 56/2 A vertebrated carriage..left the station at Euston Square with one of the trains for Birmingham. *Ibid.*, The vertebrated carriage.. adapted itself to all curves with the greatest facility.

vertebration (vɜːtɪ'breɪʃən). [f. VERTEBRA.]

1. Vertebral formation; division into segments like those of the spinal column. Also in fig. context.

1888 *Encycl. Brit.* XXIV. 179/2 Some writers have maintained that the vertebration of the *Vertebrata* may be understood as having reference to the segmentation of the muscles of the body-wall. **1889** *Theol. Monthly* Jan. 48 His style rather resembles a cellular tissue..which may advance by growth on many sides, rather than a..compact logical vertebration.

2. *fig.* 'Backbone'; strength or firmness.

1884 W. G. WILLS in *Pall Mall G.* 28 July 4/2 Poetry and rhetoric,..which have not the heart, life, and vertebration behind, are an impertinence and intrusion. **1892** W. S. LILLY *Gt. Enigma* 313 Doctrine is the vertebration of religion.

'vertebratist. *rare*$^{-1}$. [f. VERTEBRATE *sb.* + -IST.] An authority upon the spine or backbone.

1866 *Reader* 31 Mar. 331 (Theory of the skeleton), The 'orthodox' ideas of ordinary vertebratists.

'vertebre. *Anat.* and *Zool.* ? *Obs.* Also 7, 9 verteber. [a. F. *vertèbre*: see VERTEBRA. In sense 1 ad. L. *vertebrum*.]

†**1.** The rounded top of the thigh-bone. *Obs.*$^{-1}$

1541 R. COPLAND *Guydon's Quest. Chirurg.* I v, The endes of the bones of the thyghes, called vertebres.

2. = VERTEBRA 1.

α. **1578** BANISTER *Hist. Man* I. 19 b, The first Vertebre.. of the necke is more solid,..then all the bones els of the backe. **1650** BULWER *Anthropomet.* 9 That part of the neck which is next to the Atlantick Vertebre. **1692** RAY *Disc.* 109 The Vertebres of Thornbacks and other Cartilagineous Fishes. **1738** *Phil. Trans.* XL. 37 The upper extremity of the *medulla spinalis*, in the first vertebre of the neck. **1769** *Ibid.* LX. 32 A kitten..had its head cut off betwixt the first and second vertebre of the neck. **1834** CAUNTER *Orient Ann.* viii. 107 A morah, or footstool, formed of a vertebre of some huge creature. *Ibid.* 108 The attendants brought away the jaw and half a dozen of the vertebres.

β. **1828–32** WEBSTER, *Verteber*. *a* **1843** *Encycl. Metrop.* (1845) VII. 292/2 The spine consists of a set of consecutive, cartilaginous, horny pieces,..called Vertebers.

†**3.** The spine; = VERTEBRA 2. *Obs.*$^{-0}$

1623 COCKERAM I, *Verteber*, the chine or backe bone.

†**b.** *pl.* = prec. *Obs.*$^{-0}$

1696 PHILLIPS (ed. 5), *Vertebers*, the whole Ridge of the Back-Bone.

vertebriform, *a.* *rare.* [f. VERTEBR-A + -(I)FORM.] Having the form of a vertebra.

1847–9 *Todd's Cycl. Anat.* IV. I. 672/2 The mode in which the vertebriform scapulæ contract a connection with the costiform clavicles and coracoid bones. *Ibid.*

vertebro- ('vɜːtɪbrəʊ), comb. form, on Greek models, of VERTEBRA, occurring in various terms of *Anat.*, as ***vertebro-arterial, -basilar, -chondral, -costal, -femoral, -iliac, -sacral, -sternal***.

In recent medical and other Dicts.

'verted, *ppl. a.* *Her.* *rare*$^{-0}$. [f. VERT *v.*[1]] (See quot. *c* 1828 s.v. VERTANT *a.*)

verte(e)go, obs. ff. VERTIGO.

†**vertely,** *adv.* *Obs.*$^{-1}$ [After OF. *vertement*, *verdement* (15th c.) in the same sense, f. *verte* green, youthful, energetic, etc.] With activity or readiness; quickly, readily.

? *a* **1400** *Morte Arth.* 3168 Vertely the avawmwarde voydez theire horsez, In the Vertennone vale, the vines i-mangez.

†**'vertent,** *a.* *Obs. rare.* [ad. L. *vertent-*, *vertens*, pres. pple. of *vertĕre* to turn, etc.] ***vertent year***, a cycle of the celestial bodies, containing 15,000 solar years.

After L. *annus vertens* (Cicero *Rep.* vi. 22, 24).

1635 HEYWOOD *Hierarch.* III. 147 This great and vertent yeare is, when we see All stars and planets brought to their first station After their much and long Peregrination. **1636** —— *Love's Mistress* 2nd Prol., Who so un-read, doth not of Plato heare, His Annus Magnus, and his Vertent yeare?

verteous, -ly, obs. forms of VIRTUOUS, -LY.

vertew, obs. form of VIRTUE.

vertex ('vɜːtɛks). Pl. **vertices** ('vɜːtɪsiːz); also **vertexes**. [a. L. *vertex* whirl, whirlpool, VORTEX; crown of the head, highest point, summit, etc., f. *vertĕre* to turn. Cf. VERTICE.]

1. a. *Geom.* The point opposite to the base of a (plane or solid) figure; the point in a curve or surface at which the axis meets it; an angular point, as of a triangle or polygon.

1570 DEE *Math. Pref.* C ij, From the vertex, to the Circumference of the base of the Cone. **1571** DIGGES

Pantom. IV. xxv. Hh ij, A transfigured Icosaedron may be resolued into 12 Pentagonal and 20 hexagonal Pyramides, concurring with their toppes or vertices all in the centers of this transformed body. *a* **1608** DEE *Relat. Spir.* I. (1659) 355, 4 Triangles or rather Cones, of water, whose vertices rest cut off (as it were) by the middle stream of water. **1672** BOYLE *Virtues Gems* 12 So as to make six triangles, that terminated like those of a Pyramid in a Vertex. **1715** DESAGULIERS *Fires Impr.* 13 Two half Parabolas's whose Vertex's are C c. **1743** EMERSON *Fluxions* 150 In the vertices of Curves, where they cut the Abscissa at right angles. **1840** LARDNER *Geom.* ii. 17 These lines are called the sides of the angle, and the point C where the sides unite, is called its vertex. **1860** TYNDALL *Glac.* I. vii. 54 Along the two sides of a triangle, the vertex of which was near the centre of the glacier. **1882** MINCHIN *Unipl. Kinemat.* 12 The parallelogram must now be jointed at its four vertices.

b. *Optics.* (See quots.)

1704 J. HARRIS *Lex. Techn.* I, *Vertex of a Glass* (in Opticks) is the same with its Pole. **1797** *Encycl. Brit.* (ed. 3) XIII. 288 Draw the ray RC through the centre, cutting the [spherical] surface in the point V, which we shall denominate the *vertex*, while RC is called the *axis*. **1803** IMISON *Sci. & Art* I. 348 To find the vertex or centre of a lens. **1867** J. HOGG *Microsc.* I. ii. 18 The point where the axis cuts the surface is called the vertex of the lens.

c. *Astr.* (See quot.)

1876 G. F. CHAMBERS *Astron.* 922 *Vertex*.., a term used to designate that point in the limb of the Sun, the Moon, or of a planet, intersected by a circle passing through the zenith and the centre of the body.

d. *Math.* A junction of two or more lines in a network or graph (GRAPH *sb.*[1] 1); = NODE *sb.* 7 b.

1931 *Proc. Nat. Acad. Sci.* XVII. 125 A graph *G* is composed of two sets of symbols: vertices, *a*, *b*, ..., *f*, and arcs, α(*ab*).., β(*ac*), ..., δ(*ef*). **1942** G. T. WHYBURN *Analytic Topol.* x. 182 Such a decomposition of a graph *A* into vertices and edges is called a subdivision of *A*. **1975** I. STEWART *Concepts Mod. Math.* xi. 160 A network has two main parts: (i) a set *N*, whose elements are called nodes or vertices, (ii) a way of specifying when two vertices are joined together. **1979** *Sci. Amer.* May 98/3 Alpha-actinin was localized primarily at the vertexes of the network and tropomyosin was localized along the short fibers connecting the vertexes.

2. The point in the heavens vertically overhead, or directly above a given place; the zenith. ***latitude*** or ***meridian of vertex*** (see quot. *c* 1850).

1646 SIR T. BROWNE *Pseud. Ep.* II. ii. 62 The true meridian is a major circle passing through the poles of the world, and the Zenith or Vertex of any place. **1665** SIR T. HERBERT *Trav.* (1677) 5 These sorts of people freeze within the polar circles,..the Pole being their vertex, and the Æquator..their direct Horizon. *Ibid.* 39 The heat..when the Sun comes to the Vertex, is much more intense..than it is about the Polar Circles. **1715** tr. *Gregory's Astron.* (1726) I. 346 When the Phænomenon..is in *XDZ* the common Azimuth..of the two places on the Earth pitch'd upon for this purpose, whose Vertices are *X* and *Z*. **1748** *Anson's Voy.* II. v. 182 The Sun was within about three degrees of the vertex. *c* **1850** *Rudim. Navig.* (Weale) 54 Either of these points is called the *vertex* of the great circle to which it belongs; the arc intercepted between the vertex and the equator is the *latitude of vertex*; the meridian that passes through the vertex is the *meridian of vertex*. **1867** SMYTH *Sailor's Word-bk.*, *Vertex*, the zenith, the point overhead.

3. a. *Anat.* (and *Zool.*). The crown or top of the head; *esp.* in man, the part lying between the occiput and the sinciput. ***vertex presentation***, a presentation (PRESENTATION 8 b) in which the vertex of the fœtus lies nearest to the cervix as labour begins.

[**1615** CROOKE *Body Man* VII. ii. (1631) 434 The middle part of the scalpe..is gibbous or round;..the Latins call it *Vertex*, because in that place the haires runne round in a ring as waters doe in a whirle-poole.] **1638** A. READ *Man. Anat.* III. i. 389 *Vertex*, the crown, that which is betweene the former two, somewhat arched. **1680** S. HAWORTH *Disc. Conc. Man* 115 The middle Part between these which is Gibbose is called Vertex. **1754–64** SMELLIE *Midwif.* I. 86 [In child-birth] the crown or vertex is the first part that is pressed down, because..the bones at that part of the skull make the least resistance. **1771** *Encycl. Brit.* II. 226/2 The [Columba] turbita, with..a short bill, and a plain vertex. **1840** E. WILSON *Anat. Vade M.* (1842) 43 The skull..is divisible into four regions,—a superior region or vertex, a lateral region, an inferior, and an interior region. **1841** F. H. RAMSBOTHAM *Princ. & Pract. Obstetr. Med.* 135 (*heading*) Comparative frequency of the various modes of vertex presentation. **1873** COUES *Birds N.W.* (1874) 281 The young males have more or less of the vertex red or yellow, instead of an occipital crescent of scarlet. **1888** P. L. SCLATER *Argentine Ornith.* I. 137 Vertex more or less tinged with rufous. **1899** *Allbutt's Syst. Med.* VII. 482 In these vertex cases [of tuberculous meningitis]. *Ibid.* VIII. 8 The forceps was employed fifteen times in vertex presentations. **1974** *Encycl. Brit. Micropædia* VIII. 195/2 In vertex presentations the head of the fetus most commonly faces to the right and slightly to the rear. This position is said to be the most usual one, because the fetus is thus best accommodated to the shape of the uterus.

b. *Ent.* (See quots.)

1826 KIRBY & SP. *Entomol.* III. 365 *Vertex*, the horizontal part of the *Facies*, next the front, that lies behind the eyes and between the temples. *Ibid.* 487 In *Blatta* and some other *Orthoptera* the posterior angle of the head is the vertex. **1861–2** LE CONTE *Classif. Coleoptera N. Amer.* I. Introd. p. x, The upper surface is divided into regions, the back part being called the *occiput*, the middle the *vertex*, and the anterior the *front*. **1897** W. F. KIRBY in Mary Kingsley *W. Africa* 719 *Trichomera insignata*... Face nearly smooth, shining black below the vertex.

4. The top, summit, or highest point of something, esp. a hill or structure; the crown of an arch. †Also, a high piece of land, an eminence (*obs.*).

1641 R. BROOKE *Eng. Episc.* 21, I am neere the Apex of this question, which yet (Pernassus-like) hath a double Vertex, a twofold toppe. **1691** RAY *Creation* I. (1692) 203 The great diversity of Soyls that are found there, every Vertex, or Eminency, almost affording new kinds. **1762** FALCONER *Shipwr.* III. 243 Its [an altar's] vertex thirty cubits from the ground. **1770** PENNANT *Brit. Zool.* (1777) IV. 142 *Patella vulgata*... Vertex pretty near the centre. **1811** PINKERTON *Petralogy* II. 338, I was not more than a hundred and fifty paces distant from the vertex of the cone. **1827** *Gentl. Mag.* XCVII. II. 9 A conical dome, on the vertex of which is a gilt cross. **1879** *Cassell's Techn. Educ.* I. 197/1 The highest point in the intrados is called the vertex or crown.

fig. **1865** MOZLEY *Mirac.* vi. 130 The question whether man is or is not the vertex of nature.

vertgrees, -gres(s)e, etc., obs. ff. VERDIGRIS.

verþe, verþing, verþore, verþuorþ, southern ME. variants of FOURTH, FARTHING, FARTHER, FAR-FORTH.

†verti'bility. *Obs.* Also 5 vertybylyte, 6 vertibilite. [ad. med.L. *vertibilitāt-*, *vertibilitās*: see next and -ITY. Cf. Sp. *vertibilidad*.] Capacity for turning or changing; changeableness, inconstancy, mutability.

1447 BOKENHAM *Seyntys* (Roxb.) 255 Whom fro servyl condycyoun fortune up hente Of hyr whele by vertybylyte And put hym in the state of hy degre. *a* **1529** SKELTON *Agst. Venemous Tongues* Wks. I. 134 Ye are so full of vertibilite, And of frenetyke folabilite. *a* **1617** P. BAYNE *On Eph.* i. 11 (1618) 268 God may..will that his creature shall sinne, being suffered to it selfe, by accident of it own liberty and vertibilitie. **1675** H. MORE in R. Ward *Life* (1710) 296 In this capacity of being United with the Matter, consists the Liberty and Vertibility of the Soul.

†'vertible, *a.* *Obs.* Also 5 vertybyl. [a. OF. *vertible*, or ad. med.L. *vertibilis*, f. L. *vert-*, stem of *vertĕre* to turn: see -IBLE.] Capable of turning or being turned; changing, inconstant, mutable.

1447 BOKENHAM *Seyntys* (Roxb.) 272 By the vertybyl cours of fatal deth. **1657** J. SERGEANT *Schism Dispach't* 134 A parallel of your vertible and Wind-mill uncertainty. **1667** H. MORE *Div. Dial.* II. xx. (1713) 151 But were it not better that God Almighty should annihilate the Individuals of this middle vertible Order, as you call it, as soon as they lapse into Sin?

Hence **†'vertibleness**, 'aptness or easiness to turn' (Bailey, vol. II. 1727). *Obs.*—0

'vertic, *a.* *poet.* Also 7 vertick. [Irregular shortening of next, after *tropic*, etc.] Vertical, esp. of the sun.

1607 BARKSTED *Mirrha* (1876) 51 Thus much the Goddesse of the floods doth deign to change thy shape, into a vertick flower. **1762** FALCONER *Shipwr.* I. 745 While Phœbus down the vertic-circle glides. *a* **1769** —— *Occ. Elegy* ix, Unfelt by you the vertic sun may glow. **1800** T. SANDERSON *Orig. Poems* 9 Where vertic suns, that torrid fervour pour, Check the grove's music and the vernal flow'r. **1876** J. ELLIS *Cæsar in Egypt* 79 Their sacred Well, One day illumined by the vertic Sun.

vertical ('vɜːtɪkəl), *a.* and *sb.* Also 6–7 verticall. [a. F. *vertical* (1545, = Sp., Pg. *vertical*, It. *verticale*), or ad. late L. *verticālis* (Quicherat), f. *vertic-*, stem of *vertex* VERTEX.]

A. *adj.* **1.** Of or pertaining to, placed or situated at, passing through, the vertex or zenith; occupying a position in the heavens directly overhead or above a given place or point.

†a. ***vertical point***, = VERTEX 2. Also *fig.*, the culminating or highest point, the point of greatest development or perfection (freq. in the 17th c.). *Obs.*

1559 W. CUNNINGHAM *Cosmogr. Glasse* 16 Leuell with th' earth, and his verticall point, in the forsaid Æquinoctial. **1622** PEACHAM *Compl. Gentl.* ix. (1906) 61 Latitude is the distance of the Meridian, betweene the verticall point (or pole of the Horizon) and the Æquinoctiall. **1653** W. RAMESEY *Astrol. Restored* I. viii. 15 Those that live further North are of stronger body,..because their vertigal [*sic*] point being far removed from the Suns course, they more abound in cold and moisture. **1715** tr. *Gregory's Astron.* (1726) I. 368 Let XBL be a Vertical Circle, X the Zenith, (for the Vertical point may be consider'd as mov'd in regard of the Ecliptic unmov'd). **1728** CHAMBERS *Cycl.* s.v. *Point*, The Zenith and Nadir are the Vertical Points.

fig. **1611** SPEED *Hist. Gt. Brit.* IX. xii. 103 Such successe, as well declared it was Gods will..., that the English name should now be brought to the verticall poynt thereof without any thing being able to resist it. **1626** T. H. *Caussin's Holy Court* 363 Saint Ireneus..calleth Charity..the top, and verticall point of all vertues, guifts, and fauours of God. *a* **1649** DRUMM. OF HAWTH. *Hist. Jas. III*, Wks. (1711) 43 This family seemed now in the zenith and vertical point of its greatness. *a* **1671** LD. FAIRFAX *Mem.* (1699) 103 Here was the vertical point on which the army's honour and reputation turned into reproach and scandal. **1698** FRYER *Acc. E. India & P.* 284 Both Christianity and their Country are past their Vertical Point, and are upon their Declension.

b. ***vertical circle***, an azimuth-circle (see AZIMUTH 1).

1559 W. CUNNINGHAM *Cosmogr. Glass* 22 Here you se A.E.C. represent the verticall point, B.D. the poles of the world, by which and A. (being the vertical circle) is the meridian circle A.B.C.D. delineated. **1594** BLUNDEVIL *Exerc.* III. I. xix. (1597) 154 b, Ther is another great circle called the circle Verticall, which passeth right over our heades through our Zenith. **1594** J. DAVIS *Seamen's Secr.* II. (1607) 8 Circles of Azumuths, or verticall circles, are quarters of great circles, concurring together in the Zenith. **1669** STURMY *Mariner's Mag.* VI. iii. 112 Measure the extent CM on the Vertical-Circle, and apply it to the Line of Signs. **1704** J. HARRIS *Lex. Techn.* I, *Azimuths* or *Vertical Circles*, are great Circles intersecting each other in the Zenith and Nadir,..and cutting the Horizon at Right Angles. **1715** tr. *Gregory's Astron.* (1726) I. 348 Let ZBL be a Vertical Circle, in which Z is the Zenith. **1846** A. YOUNG *Naut. Dict.* 24 The vertical circle which passes through the east and west points of the horizon is termed the Prime Vertical. **1860** OLMSTEAD *Mech. Heavens* 23 But if the point is *above* the horizon, then its azimuth is estimated by passing a vertical circle through it [etc.].

c. Of the sun, stars, etc., or in general use.

1594 BLUNDEVIL *Exerc.* IV. xxvi. (1597) 228 As many stars as passe right vnder your Zenith are said to bee verticall. **1625** N. CARPENTER *Geog. Del.* I. x. (1635) 220 To them the Sunne is twice in the yeere verticall, that is directly ouer their heads. **1665** SIR T. HERBERT *Trav.* (1677) 43 The extream heat of the Sun, which when vertical usually raises vapors in abundance. **1679** MOXON *Math. Dict.* s.v. *Vertex*, The Equator is said to be *Vertical* to them who have a continual Equinox; because, it constantly passes by the Vertex of the Place. **1715** tr. *Gregory's Astron.* (1726) I. 271 The Globe must be turn'd about till the first of the two Places becomes Vertical, (which it will be, when it arrives at the Meridian of the Globe). **1796** MORSE *Amer. Geog.* I. 21 He knew that the sun, at the summer solstice, was vertical to the inhabitants of Syene. **1815** J. SMITH *Panorama Sci. & Art* II. 53 We find the services of the winds almost equally important in meliorating the fervour of a vertical sun. **1844** KINGLAKE *Eothen* xvii, Becalmed under a vertical sun in the midst of the wide ocean. **1880** GEIKIE *Phys. Geog.* I. ii. 16 At each equinox the sun appears vertical over the equator.

fig. **1593** HARVEY *Pierce's Super.* Wks. (Grosart) II. 266 Come all the daintiest dainties of this toungue, and doe homage to your Verticall Starre. *a* **1734** NORTH *Exam.* I. ii. §96 (1740) 82 It fell out in a Conjuncture so vertical, that without it both Nations might have plunged into a mischievous Condition of Civil War. **1844** KINGLAKE *Eothen* iv, The strong vertical light of Homer's poetry is blazing so full upon the people and things of the Iliad.

†d. *fig.* Pertaining to, characteristic of, or denoting the period or position of greatest eminence or perfection; at one's highest point or position. Cf. *vertical point* (a. *fig.* above). *Obs.*

1641 LD. J. DIGBY *Sp. in Ho. Com.* 19 Jan. 25 In voting this bill, we shall contribute..to the perpetuating our Sun, our Soveraigne, in his vesticall [*sic*], in his noone-day lustre. **1655** FULLER *Ch. Hist.* IV. 175 But now in the time of the aforesaid William Heyworth, the Cathedral of Litchfield was in the verticall height thereof. **1655** —— *Hist. Camb.* (1840) 186 As Cambridge was his vertical place, wherein he was in height of honour. **1673** HICKERINGILL *Greg. F. Greyb.* 38 Though Greg. and his virtuoso's seem to themselves to be vertical and cock-a-hoop.

2. ***vertical angle***: **a.** An opposite angle (see OPPOSITE *a.* 1 and quot. 1704). **b.** The angle opposite the base of a triangle or polygon.

1571 DIGGES *Pantom.* I. vi. C iij, Two right lines crossing one another, make the contrary or verticall angles equall. **1660** BARROW *Euclid* I. xv. Schol., The vertical (or opposite) angles. **1704** J. HARRIS *Lex. Techn.* I. s.v. *Angles*, Opposite or vertical Angles, as, I. Those that are made by two Right Lines crossing each other, and which touch only in their Angular Point. **1771** *Encycl. Brit.* III. 910/2 The tangent of half the vertical angle. *Ibid.*, The line CF bisecting the vertical angle. **1798** HUTTON *Course Math.* (1806) I. 368 In a Triangle, having given the two Sides about the Vertical Angle. **1862** TODHUNTER *Euclid* I. 15 If two straight lines cut one another, the vertical or opposite angles shall be equal.

3. Placed or extending at right angles to the plane of the horizon; perpendicular; upright.

a. *Geom.* Of a straight line or plane surface.

1704 J. HARRIS *Lex. Techn.* I, *Line Vertical*, in Perspective, is the common Section of the Vertical Plane and of the Draught. *Ibid.* s.v. *Plane*, *Vertical Plane*, in Opticks and Perspective, is a Plain Surface which passeth along the Principal Ray, and consequently thro' the Eye, and is perpendicular to the Geometrical Plane. **1715** tr. *Gregory's Astron.* (1726) I. 436 Therefore there is given the Angle *Llλ* the Difference or Sum of them, and *Flf* Vertical to it. **1812–6** PLAYFAIR *Nat. Phil.* (1819) I. 11 A plane at any place perpendicular to the line in which bodies gravitate, is called a horizontal plane; and any plane passing through that line is called a vertical plane. **1851** S. P. WOODWARD *Mollusca* I. 62 Their shell is usually straight, or coiled in a vertical plane. **1871** TYNDALL *Fragm. Sci.* (1879) I. iv. 111 When the short diagonal of the prism was vertical.

b. In general use.

1725 *Fam. Dict.* s.v. *Windmil*, That is reputed the best made with vertical Sails, like the ordinary Windmils. **1756** tr. *Keysler's Trav.* (1760) I. 10 Vertical rainbows in the sky are not uncommon, whereas the horizontal are very extraordinary. **1813** BAKEWELL *Introd. Geol.* (1815) 187 In some coal fields one part of a stratum is inclined, and the other part vertical. **1831** BREWSTER *Optics* xxxi. 260 Some phenomena both of vertical and lateral mirage. **1855** MAURY *Phys. Geog. Sea* vi. 326 Under the vertical rays of the never clouded sun. **1882** VINES *Sachs' Bot.* 940 The adaptation of the Virginian Creeper to climbing up vertical walls.

Comb. **1857** T. MOORE *Handbk. Brit. Ferns* (ed. 3) 10 The vertical-ringed spore-cases, when mature, split suddenly with a transverse fissure.

c. With abstract nouns, esp. of movement or direction.

1794 [see VERTICITY 1]. **1802** PALEY *Nat. Theol.* ix. §6 The compound motion of the lower jaw, half lateral, and half vertical. **1813** BAKEWELL *Introd. Geol.* (1815) 31 Plates of rock, separated by seams which have generally a vertical direction. **1830** LYELL *Princ. Geol.* I. 410 Four-fifths of the town of Cumana was shaken down by a vertical shock. **1859** J. R. GREENE *Man. Anim. Kingd.* I. *Protozoa* Introd. p. xxix, The relations of animals to the elements in which they live... Their vertical (bathymetrical) distribution. **1872** DARWIN *Emotions* xi. 273 We give a vertical nod of approval ..when we approve of their conduct.

Comb. **1850** DENISON *Clock & Watch-m.* 48 It would fail for a balance or vertical-force-magnetometer.

d. Of mechanical appliances or structures. Also in technical use applied to machines which operate vertically.

Numerous other examples are given in Knight *Dict. Mech.* (1875 and 1884).

1825 J. NICHOLSON *Operat. Mechanic* 141 The comparative power of horizontal and vertical windmills. **1859** *Handbk. Turning* 79 The vertical, or universal cutter. **1875** KNIGHT *Dict. Mech.* 2708/1 *Vertical Boring-machine*, a drill or boring-machine having a vertical spindle. *Ibid.*, Vertical Planing-machine. **1888** JACOBI *Printers' Voc.* 151 *Vertical engine*, an upright engine, as distinct from a 'horizontal one'.

e. *Mus.* Involving, pertaining to, or directed at the relationship between notes sounded simultaneously, rather than the pattern of successive notes; harmonic or chordal rather than melodic.

1889 *Cent. Dict.*, *Vertical composition*, musical composition in which the chief attention is put on the harmonic structure of the successive chords. **1928** *Grove's Dict. Mus.* (ed. 3) V. 164/1 Later events have made it almost superfluous to discuss..his [*sc.* R. Strauss's] theories of 'vertical hearing'. **1942**, etc. [see HORIZONTAL *a.* (*sb.*) 4]. **1946** A. BLISS in A. L. Bacharach *Brit. Mus. of our Time* xi. 156 As in all his music, one must concentrate on horizontal as well as vertical listening so as to savour the beauty and interest of the inner parts.

f. Special collocations, as ***vertical bond***, ***care-grinder***, ***dial*** (cf. B. 3), ***escapement***, ***file***, ***filing***, ***fire***, ***watch***, etc. ***vertical breeze*** = BREEZE *sb.*² 3 b; ***vertical cut***, motion of a recording stylus up and down, rather than from side to side; also *attrib.*; cf. *hill and dale* s.v. HILL *sb.* 1 b; opp. *lateral cut* s.v. LATERAL *a.* 4 j; ***vertical gust*** = *vertical breeze* above; ***vertical interval***, the vertical distance between the heights represented by adjacent contours on a map; ***vertical man***, a living man, one standing upright (as opposed to a recumbent or dead one); ***vertical recording***, magnetic recording in which the direction of magnetization is at right angles to the plane of the recording medium. Also in collocations often used *attrib.*, as ***vertical-shaft***, ***-spindle***, ***-take-off***.

A number of other scientific or special terms are defined in encyclopædic Dicts.

1833 LOUDON *Encycl. Archit.* 1131 *Vertical bond is a course of bricks, stone, or other materials, tending to support or strengthen the building vertically. **1925** FRASER & GIBBONS *Soldier & Sailor Words* 296 *To suffer from a *vertical breeze* (also *vertical gust*), to be nervous. **1934** D. L. SAYERS *Nine Tailors* III. 279 He got a vertical breeze up. **1965** J. R. HETHERINGTON *Selina's Aunt* 59 The term 'vertical breeze' was co-temporary [with 'wind up'], and may have been either the originating phrase or a further refinement. **1859** *Slang Dict.* 114 **Vertical care-grinder*, the treadmill. **1935** J. MILLS *Fugue in Cycles & Bels* (1936) xi. 145 *Vertical-cut phonograph discs of the most recent type can record from 40 to 9000 cycles. **1975** [see LATERAL *a.* 4 j]. **1977** *Gramophone* Apr. 1522/1 Every one of these hill-and-dale vertical-cut labels had given place to lateral-cut issues under the same mark by that year [*sc.* 1920]. **1669** STURMY *Mariner's Mag.* VII. vi. 11 The *Vertical Dial, when whose Plane lieth in the Horizon, for which cause many call it the Horizontal Dial. **1728** [see B. 3 a]. **1877** *Encycl. Brit.* VII. 155/1 *Vertical dials*, when on a vertical plane facing one of the cardinal points. **1850** DENISON *Treatise Clock & Watch-making* 33 The escapement was exactly the same as that of a bottle-jack, or the commonest kind of watch, and is called a *vertical escapement. **1884** F. J. BRITTEN *Watch & Clockm.* 248 Vertical Escapement..[is] an escapement in which the pallet axis or the balance staff is set at right angles to the axis of the escape wheel. **1906** *Library Jrnl.* XXXI. 13 A newspaper man..goes to the *vertical file, picks out a handful of articles on the subject. **1909** *Independent* (N.Y.) 18 Nov. 1126/1 An assistant..deposits the article in an oblong *vertical filing-envelope, ten by eleven inches. **1842** BURN *Nav. & Mil. Techn. Dict.* I. s.v. *Feu*, *Feu courbe ou vertical*, curved or *vertical fire, generally from mortars laid at an angle of not less than 15°. **1867** SMYTH *Sailor's Word-bk.* 712 *Vertical fire*, in artillery, that directed upward at such an angle as that it will fall vertically, or nearly so, to its destination. **1917** *Daily Mail* 19 July 4/5 Stalled his 'bus and pancaked thirty feet...crashed completely...put a *vertical gust up me. **1925** Vertical gust [see *vertical breeze* above]. **1885** G. W. USILL in H. S. Marrett *Pract. Treat. Land & Engin. Surveying* (ed. 4) 320 In this way a table may be calculated showing the horizontal equivalents for the required *vertical interval at each degree of slope up to about 30°. **1969** G. C. DICKINSON *Maps & Air Photographs* iv. 62 Although contours are widely understood several aspects of their significance are not always fully appreciated. For example their effectiveness in representing terrain is closely controlled by the vertical interval. **1930** AUDEN *Poems* 2 Let us honour if we can The *vertical man Though we value none But the horizontal one. **1961** *Guardian* 16 Feb. 10/5 He was..a 'vertical man', and that in an age when intellectuals have been found flat on their faces. **1975** G. HOWELL *In Vogue* 61 T. S. Eliot was one vertical man who was honoured..by contemporary writers. **1982** *Sci. Amer.* July 71/3 A number of companies in the U.S., Europe and Japan are working on high-density memory systems based on *vertical recording. **1983** *Austral. Microcomputer Mag.* Aug. 67/1 It has announced prototypes of vertical-recording technology disk drives. **1940** *Chambers's Techn. Dict.* 891/2 *Vertical shaft alternator. **1967** Vertical-shaft [see PLANETARY *a.* 1 f]. **1935** *Discovery* May 143/1 *Vertical spindle pump. **1964** S. CRAWFORD *Basic Engin. Processes* vii. 190 Vertical-spindle machine employing the face of a cup or segmental wheel. **1935** *Jrnl. R. Aeronaut. Soc.* XXXIX. 1137 So that probably on any day one could actually hover in an autogiro; and they knew also that with the machine which had been illustrated they could achieve *vertical take-off as well. **1960** *Daily Tel.* 26 Apr. 1 Britain, France and West Germany are to co-operate in developing a supersonic, vertical-take-off military aircraft. **1972** *Guardian* 28 June 1/2 The fourth of the RAF's vertical take-off Harriers to crash in the past few weeks came down yesterday at Düsseldorf. **1838** *Penny Cycl.* XII. 302/2 We shall now give a description of a common *vertical watch. **1850** DENISON *Clock & Watch-m.* 145 The old vertical watch, so called because the scape-wheel stands vertically when the other wheels are horizontal.

4. Having a position at right angles to the plane of the axis, body, or supporting surface; pointing or situated directly upwards or downwards.

a. *Bot.* Of a leaf or other part.

Martyn *Lang. Bot.* (1793) also gives ~~*vertical leaf*~~ (after Linnæus's *folium verticale*) as = *obverse leaf*, but objects to the use of the term.

1776 J. LEE *Introd. Bot.* Explan. Terms 382 *Vertical*, Leaves so situated that the Base is perpendicular to the Apex. **1866** *Treas. Bot.* 1212 I. **1879** A. GRAY *Struct. Bot.* iii. §4 (ed. 6) 108 *Vertical leaves*, those with blades of the ordinary kind, but presenting their edges instead of their faces to the earth and sky, or when erect with one edge directed to the stem and the other away from it.

b. *Zool.*, esp. of certain fins of fishes.

1834 McMURTRIE *Cuvier's Anim. Kingd.* 203 A vertical caudal, as in Gymnetrus, but shorter. **1880** GÜNTHER *Fishes* 40 The vertical fins are situated in the median dorsal line, from the head to the extremity of the tail.

5. *Zool.*, *Anat.*, etc. Of or pertaining to, situated on, affecting, the vertex of the head.

1826 KIRBY & SP. *Entomol.* IV. 315 Stemmata: *Vertical*, when they are placed in the Vertex. **1891** *Cent. Dict.* s.v., Vertical eyes of a fish. *Ibid.*, The vertical crest of some birds is horizontal when not erected. **1899** *Allbutt's Syst. Med.* VII. 546 Meningitis, whether vertical or posterior-basic, is caused by an invasion of micro-organisms.

†**6.** Belonging to giddiness. *Obs.*$^{-0}$

1623 COCKERAM.

7. Of or pertaining to the different levels of a hierarchy or progression. **a.** Extending over or involving successive stages in the production of a particular class of goods. Opp. HORIZONTAL *a.* (*sb.*) 3 b.

1920 *Westm. Gaz.* 2 Dec. 6/1 The vertical Trusts constructed by Stumm, Thyssen and the other raw-material magnates. **1927** *Daily Tel.* 11 Oct. 15/4 He had created what is technically called a vertical combination, embracing every stage of the soap industry. **1959** *Listener* 5 Nov. 768/2 The existing vertical firms have been operating in a market dominated by the factors created by horizontal trading and few indeed have controlled their price policies by vertical statistics and vertical objectives. **1960** [see AGRIBUSINESS]. **1962** R. B. FULLER *Epic Poem on Industrialization* 27 A corporation gun nuzzling trick;..precipitating vertical merger. **1967**, **1968** [see HORIZONTAL *a.* (*sb.*) 3 b]. **1975** *N.Y. Times Mag.* 3 Oct. 15 Proponents of the effort call it vertical divestiture, by which they mean forcing the largest oil companies to pick one activity—production or refining or transportation/marketing—and sell off the other parts of the action. **1975** J. DE BRES tr. *Mandel's Late Capitalism* xii. 384 The process of centralization can only find expression in a growing centralization of capital, among other things, in the form of vertical integration of big companies.

b. Involving differences or changes of level as in social class, income group, or the like.

1927 P. A. SOROKIN *Social Mobility* vii. 133 There are two principal types of social mobility, horizontal and vertical. **1931**, etc. [see HORIZONTAL *a.* (*sb.*) 3 c]. **1976** F. ZWEIG *New Acquisitive Society* I. v. 52 The shedding of middle-class values and style of life in the younger generation..is of much deeper significance, transcending the confines of vertical mobility.

c. ***vertical union***, a trade union which draws its members from a particular industry without regard to their individual crafts; ***vertical market***, one comprising all the potential purchasers in a particular occupation or industry.

1933 *Sun* (Baltimore) 1 Sept. 2/1 This means a vertical union in each industry, free of domination or control either by employers or outside labor leaders. **1937**, **1950** Vertical union [see HORIZONTAL *a.* (*sb.*) 3 d]. **1978** *Business Week* (Industr. Ed.) 17 July 36G H-P's role has been primarily as a systems company emphasizing vertical markets needing a wide variety of supporting electronics. **1983** *Austral. Microcomputer Mag.* Aug. 16/3 HiSoft believes there is a big need for vertical market software, in which a common shell is modified to suit individual needs. **1984** *Sydney Morning Herald* 10 Nov. 6/1 (Advt.), They are presently expanding into a new and highly promising vertical market and offer a Sales Management Opportunity. **1985** *Which Computer?* Apr. 45/1 This means that BOS is one of the richest potential sources of vertical market software written in the UK for the UK market.

d. ***vertical proliferation*** (see quots.).

1966 *Economist* 22 Oct. 350/2 Like other near-nuclear nations, they are unwilling to promise to stay out of the club unless its members will promise to halt what Canada's foreign minister has called their 'vertical proliferation'; that is, promise to stop testing, producing and piling up nuclear arms. **1980** *Sci. Amer.* July 31/2 In the circumstances what can be done to curb both 'vertical' proliferation (the increase in the numbers and kinds of nuclear weapons in the hands of the nuclear-weapons states) and 'horizontal' proliferation (the further spread of nuclear weapons to nations that do not already have them)?

e. ***vertical thinking***, deductive reasoning; opp. *lateral thinking* s.v. LATERAL *a.* 1 b.

1966, **1967** [see LATERAL *a.* 1 b]. **1970** G. GREER *Female Eunuch* 108 The take-over by computers of much vertical thinking has placed more and more emphasis on the creative propensities of human thought.

8. Pertaining to or being an aerial photograph taken looking vertically downwards.

1925 JONES & GRIFFITHS *Aerial Surveying by Rapid Methods* ii. 8 Such a procedure will..be necessary when mapping any large area, whether the work be done by 'vertical' or 'oblique' photographs. **1932** *Jrnl. R. Aeronaut. Soc.* XXXVI. 503 The first field operation is the vertical photography along strips about thirty miles apart. *Ibid.*, As soon as each vertical flight was completed the films were developed. **1974** P. R. WOLF *Elem. Photogrammetry* vi. 117 Relief displacement often causes straight roads, fence lines, etc., on rolling ground to appear crooked on a vertical photograph. **1983** J. C. MCCORMACK *Surveying Fund.* xxii. 404 The oblique view is more easily understood by the public than is the plan view contained in vertical aerial photographs.

B. *sb.* [Ellipt. use of the *adj.*]

†**1.** The vertical point; the vertex or zenith. In quots. *fig. Obs.*

1611 SPEED *Hist. Gt. Brit.* IX. xv. §119 King Henries glory thus ascended to the highest verticall in France. *a* **1652** J. SMITH *Sel. Disc.* IV. vi. (1821) 104 A naked intuition of eternal truth which is always the same, which never rises nor sets, but always stands still in its vertical, and fills the whole horizon of the soul with a mild and gentle light. **1655** FULLER *Ch. Hist.* IX. 100 Now she was in the Verticall of her favour, wherein hence-forward she began to decline.

2. a. A vertical circle, line, or plane.

prime vertical: see PRIME *a.* 9 b.

1669 STURMY *Mariner's Mag.* VII. x. 15 If you have not time until the Sun cometh unto the Azimuth of the Wall, or the Vertical of it, which cutteth the Pole thereof. *Ibid.*, The Sun is neerer to the Meridian, than to the Vertical of the Plane. **1674** MOXON *Tutor Astron.* v. Prob. iv. (ed. 3) 154 You may reduce all Verticals into Horizontals [in dialling]. **1774** M. MACKENZIE *Maritime Surv.* 52 This Angle PZs..is therefore equal to the horizontal Distance of the Vertical of the two Stars from the Meridian. **1834** MRS. SOMERVILLE *Connex. Phys. Sci.* vii. 55 The difference of the latitudes being the angle contained between the verticals at the extremities of the arc. **1868** LOCKYER *Guillemin's Heavens* (ed. 3) 449 Every portion of matter left to itself..falls in the direction of the vertical of the place on which it falls. **1882** GEIKIE *Text-bk. Geol.* IV. VI. 526 In an inclined fault the level of the selected stratum is protracted across the fissure until a vertical from it will reach the level of the same bed.

b. *Math.* A vertical angle (see A. 2).

1728 CHAMBERS *Cycl.* s.v. *Angle*, The Measure of an Angle without the Centre, is half of the Arches HI and LM, where-on it and its Vertical K do stand.

c. ***the vertical***, the vertical line or position; the perpendicular.

1834 MRS. SOMERVILLE *Connex. Phys. Sci.* vii. 56 Local attractions, which cause the plumb-line to deviate from the vertical. **1840** *Ibid.* xxix. (ed. 5) 335 The dip [of the needle] was 89° 59′, which was within one minute of the vertical. **1882** VINES *Sachs' Bot.* 849 A line drawn tangentially to the apical portion will very nearly coincide with the vertical. *Ibid.* In consequence of the continuing curvature..the now erect apical portion becomes bent over out of the vertical.

d. *Austral. Opal-Mining.* (See quots.)

1934 *Geol. Survey, Mineral Resources* (New South Wales Dept. Mines) No. 36. 116 The mineral is found also in vertical or sub-vertical joints and cracks..known locally as 'verticals'. **1967** I. L. IDRIESS *Opals & Sapphires* 48 A vertical seam cuts in: that is, a seam running downward from the roof..which in general we used to call a 'vertical'.

3. A vertical dial (see A. 3 f).

In contrast to later use, Sturmy gives the name of *vertical* to the horizontal dial.

1669 STURMY *Mariner's Mag.* Aaaa 2, I will name the Dials,..viz. Eight Verticals and Decliners. **1728** CHAMBERS *Cycl.*, *Vertical Dial*, is a Sun-Dial, drawn on the Plane of a Vertical Circle; or perpendicular to the Horizon... These are particularly call'd..East,..West,..South, and..North Verticals, when opposed to one, or other of these Cardinal Points of the Horizon.

4. (See quot.)

1902 CORNISH *Naturalist Thames* 180 In the slang of the rock garden the plants living..on upright rocks are called 'verticals'.

5. A vertical aerial photograph (see sense A. 8 above).

1925 JONES & GRIFFITHS *Aerial Surveying by Rapid Methods* vi. 69 These [oblique photographs] provide valuable information about the nature of the ground which eventually is to be mapped by verticals. **1954** W. D. THORNBURY *Princ. Geomorphol.* xxi. 535 Verticals are more widely used than obliques in geologic field work. **1976** J. B. GARNER et al. *Surveying* xiii. 233 If it is required to photograph a long strip of land, many photographs will be required. Each photograph should be a good vertical.

Hence **'verticalness.** *rare*$^{-0}$.

1727 BAILEY (vol. II), *Verticalness*, the being right over one's Head. [Hence in later Dicts.]

'verticalism. *rare*$^{-1}$. [-ISM.] = next 2 b.

1860 COCKBURN MUIR *Pagan or Christian?* xii. 88 The spirituality of Verticalism is so positive and manifest, that it is hard to believe that the pious Architects..had not these things ever in their mind.

verticality (vɜːtɪ'kælɪtɪ). [f. VERTICAL *a.* + -ITY. Cf. F. *verticalité*, It. *verticalità*.]

1. The fact on the part of the sun or other celestial body of being at the vertex or zenith.

1570 J. DEE *Math. Pref.* 23 To consider..Sterres in their Longitudes, Latitudes, Declinations, and Verticalitie. **1646** SIR T. BROWNE *Pseud. Ep.* VI. xi. 284 For unto them the Sunne is verticall twice a year, making two distinct Summers in the different points of verticality. **1656** W. D. tr. *Comenius's Gate Lang. Unl.* §557 In the Torrid [Zone], by reason of the perpetual verticality of the Sun, there are most vehement heats. **1867** E. B. DENISON *Astronomy without Mathematics* i. 37 The heat received anywhere depends on the directness of the sun's rays, or its apparent verticality overhead.

2. The condition or quality of being vertical or perpendicular; vertical position; perpendicularity.

1799 KIRWAN *Geol. Ess.* 283 Their [i.e. argillites] verticality arising only from the drain of water. **1833** LYELL *Princ. Geol.* III. 318 The verticality of the strata in the Isles of Wight and Purbeck. **1856** RUSKIN *Mod. Paint.* IV. v. xvi. §6 Precipices which produce on the imagination the effect of verticality. **1884** G. M. DAWSON in *Handbk. Dom. Canada* 325 Good sections of..Cretaceous rocks..become folded together and lie at all angles up to verticality.

b. Of buildings, or architecture.

1843 *Civil Eng. & Arch. Jrnl.* VI. 99/1 The verticality which is designed and usually conveyed by the orders he communicated to his buildings by rustic quoins. **1860** COCKBURN MUIR *Pagan or Christian?* 61 The first and most striking feature [of the architecture of the 12th and 13th c.] is the Verticality of composition, as directly opposed to the Horizontality of all anterior structural modes. *a* **1890** LIGHTFOOT *Hist. Ess.* iii. (1895) 146 The leading conception of Gothic architecture,..I mean its verticality, as contrasted with the horizontal lines of the Greek.

c. In weakened sense: Erectness, uprightness.

1838 *Fraser's Mag.* XVII. 687 She walked..in unswerving verticality.

'verticalize, *v.* [f. VERTICAL *a.* + -IZE.] *trans.* and *absol.* To render vertical, in any sense. Hence **'verticalized, 'verticalizing** *ppl. adjs.*

1959 *Times Rev. Industry* Dec. 6/3 The..Fair..was one of the first..trade fairs to verticalize by organising..specialised events during..a year, rather than staging one general fair. **1964** M. CRITCHLEY *Developmental Dyslexia* ix. 59 There is a tendency for the child to convert figures, especially those that are verticalised and closed, into a man by drawing a face within the enclosure. **1965** *Economist* 2 Jan. 54/2 The three or four main 'verticalising' companies will have less to feed their appetites and more time to digest what they have. **1982** *Christian Sci. Monitor* 21 Sept. B2/2 As a matter of corporate policy, Hewlett-Packard divisions are 'verticalized', each one functioning as a small company on its own.

Also **,verticali'zation,** the action or result of verticalizing.

1962 G. PERLE *Serial Composition & Atonality* iii. 42 Verticalization..represents a fundamental concept of atonal composition—that any group of notes which is statable in horizontal succession is also statable as a simultaneity.., a concept sometimes designated by the rather questionable term, 'vertical melody'. **1964** M. CRITCHLEY *Developmental Dyslexia* ix. 59 There is some disorientation of the background, usually by rotation of mobile figures, or by 'verticalisation'. **1965** *Economist* 19 June 1439/3 Courtaulds being particularly weak in weaving so that effective verticalisation ends at the yarn stage. **1970** *Daily Tel.* 10 Jan. 7/7 He does renounce..that festering sore of serialism, the automatic verticalisation of melodies. **1979** *Nature* 15 Mar. 226/1 The late alkaline rocks in the ring-complexes may be related to verticalisation of the Benioff plane accompanied by a diapiric rise of mantle material. **1984** *Christian Sci. Monitor* 7 Feb. 39/2, I praised Masotti's movement of his necktie from his stomach to his pocket and its slight verticalization.

'vertically, *adv.* [f. VERTICAL *a.* + -LY².]

1. a. In a vertical manner, direction, or position; so as to be vertical to the plane of the horizon, the earth's surface, or some other horizontal line or plane; perpendicularly, or approximately so; directly overhead or down below.

1646 SIR T. BROWNE *Pseud. Ep.* VI. x. 326 The Dogstarre, ..although it be not verticall unto any part of Asia,..yet is it so unto America, and vertically passeth over the habitations of Peru and Brasilia. **1677** GREW *Anat. Fruits* v. §17 The Seed-Case of Anagallis..opens not by its Meridian or Vertically,..but by its Horizon. **1679** MOXON *Math. Dict.* s.v. *Vertex*, A Star is said to be *Vertical*, that.. Vertically hangs over any place. **1686** PLOT *Staffordsh.* 17 If Lightening causes these Circles, it must also be allowed that it descends vertically. **1794** G. ADAMS *Nat. & Exp. Philos.* II. xvii. 261 *note*, The pupil in animals of the cat kind..is oblong vertically. **1796** WITHERING *Brit. Plants* (ed. 3) III. 763 Capsules opening vertically. **1828** STARK *Elem. Nat. Hist.* II. 221 Some [insects], as the butterflies, raise their wings vertically in repose. **1842** LOUDON *Suburban Hort.* 615 Some modification of lateral training will, in almost every case, be found preferable to training vertically. **1880** HAUGHTON *Phys. Geog.* ii. 21 An earthquake occurred, vertically under the town of Arica.

Comb. **1793** MARTYN *Lang. Bot.* s.v. *Verticale*, A vertically ovate leaf is the same with an obversely-ovate or obovate leaf; and a vertically cordate leaf is the same with an obversely cordate or obcordate leaf. **1878** ABNEY *Treat. Photogr.* xxxiii. 268 A fair general focus can..be obtained by using with the camera a vertically-pivoted swing-back.

b. *Math.* (Cf. VERTICAL *a.* 2.)

1660 BARROW *Euclid* I. xv. Schol., If four right lines, proceeding from one point, make the angles vertically opposite equal. **1840** LARDNER *Geom.* 24 When two straight lines cross each other,..the angle BAD is said to be vertically opposite to the angle EAC.

c. *Mus.* Harmonically rather than melodically. (Cf. VERTICAL *a.* 3 e).

1934 *Hound & Horn* July–Sept. 596 He..feels that he is tired of exploiting the folk tune, horizontally, vertically, atonally, seriously, or comically. **1954** *Grove's Dict. Mus.* (ed. 5) VIII. 126/2 Pre-war controversy as to the justification of programme music and 'hearing vertically' began to have no more than antiquarian interest. **1969** *Listener* 26 June 905/1 Strauss's counterpoint tends to be the result of thinking 'vertically', against strongly defined chord-progressions.

2. Throughout the different levels of a hierarchical system.

1933 *Sun* (Baltimore) 2 Sept. 2/1 With an industry organized vertically, the logical labor organization is vertical. **1958** *Listener* 9 Oct. 547/2 Differences throughout the Arab sectors run both vertically and horizontally: between religious sects, social strata, settlers and nomads. **1962** *Economist* 27 Oct. 393/1 The industry should..be concentrated into fewer, vertically-integrated firms. **1974** J. WHITE tr. *Poulantzas's Fascism & Dictatorship* III. ii. 95 The big stores competed for growth as they were vertically integrated into the industrial trusts.

†**'vertice.** *Obs.*⁻¹ [a. F. *vertice* (= Sp., Pg., and It. *vertice*), ad. L. *vertic-em, vertex* VERTEX.] The vertex or zenith.

1665 SIR T. HERBERT *Trav.* (1677) 5 But the *Periscii* have their shadow circulating, their meridional shadow having no existence from the vertice, but oblique and extended to the plain of the terrestrial Horizon.

verticil ('vɜːtɪsɪl). Also 8–9 verticel. [ad. L. *verticill-us* VERTICILLUS. Cf. F. *verticille* in sense 2 (also, in earlier use, a whorl).]

†**1.** (See quot.). *Obs.*⁻¹

1703 A. DE LA PRIME *Let. to Sir H. Sloan* (Sloan MSS. 4056) fol. 33 Verticels or glass Beads formed on purpose to wind thread on.

2. *Bot.* A number or set of organs or parts arranged, disposed, or produced in a circle round an axis (see quot. 1882); a whorl. *false* or *spurious verticil*, a verticillaster.

Also similarly in *Zool.* (in recent Dicts.).

α. **1793** MARTYN *Dict. Bot.* s.v., A Verticil or Whirl may be 1. Sessile or peduncled. 2. Naked... 3. Crowded. **1806** J. GALPINE *Brit. Bot.* §258 *Ajuga*... Hairy: verticils crowded into a pyramidal form, many-flowered. **1826–34** *Encycl. Metrop.* (1845) VII. 43/2 The stamens in the same verticil are sometimes joined together, and sometimes with the neighbouring verticils. **1882** VINES *Sachs' Bot.* 170 An axial structure may produce either several equivalent lateral members at the same level, or only one; in the second case the members formed in succession are termed solitary, in the first case a Whorl or Verticil.

β. **1856** HENSLOW *Dict. Bot. Terms* 214 Verticel, *Verticillus*,..a whorl. **1872** NICHOLSON *Palæont.* 483 The joints of the stems give off verticels of leaves. **1881** SPENCER in *Science Gossip* No. 202. 229 It is generally supposed that the branches were arranged in verticels.

†**verticillary,** *a. Obs. rare.* [f. L. *verticillus* VERTICILLUS: see -ARY.] Of motion: Rotatory, whirling, vertiginous.

1757 E. DARWIN in *Phil. Trans.* L. 247 The verticillary motion given to charcoal-dust thrown on nitre in fusion. **1794–6** —— *Zoon.* (1801) III. 145 When the legs are straight, as in standing erect, there is no verticillary motion in the knee-joint.

verticillaster (,vɜːtɪsɪ'læstə(r)). *Bot.* [mod.L., f. L. *verticill-us* VERTICILLUS + -ASTER.] A form of inflorescence occurring in certain labiate plants (see quots.); a false whorl.

1832 LINDLEY *Introd. Bot.* 112 If the cyme is reduced to a very few flowers, and those few become corymbose, such a disposition has been called a *verticillaster* by Hoffmansegg. **1861** BENTLEY *Man. Bot.* 213 The Verticillaster.—This kind of cyme is seen in the White Dead-nettle. **1872** OLIVER *Elem. Bot.* II. 217 A coarse perennial herb, with..axillary cymes (forming verticillasters) of bilabiate white flowers.

verticillate (vətɪ'sɪlət, və'tɪsɪlət), *a.* Also 9 verticellate. [ad. mod.L. *verticillāt-us*, f. L. *verticillus* VERTICILLUS: see -ATE² 2. So It. *verticillato*, Sp. *verticilado*, Pg. *verticillado*, F. *verticillé* (1694).]

1. a. *Bot.* Of plants: Having leaves, flowers; branches, etc., arranged or produced in circles or whorls around the stem. Now *rare* or *Obs.*

1668 WILKINS *Real Char.* II. iv. §4. 81 Herbs considered according to their flower..may be distinguished into ..*Verticillate*; by which those kinds of Plants are meant, whose flowers grow in rundles or whirles about the stalk. **1686** *Phil. Trans.* XVI. 286 The Verticillate Herbs, so called from the Flowers embracing the stalk like a whirl, or wherle. *c* **1711** PETIVER *Gazophyl.* x. 94 A Verticillate Water Herb, whose Husks stick to Cloaths like Burrs or Clivers. **1720** P. BLAIR *Bot. Ess.* iii. 135 The Verticillate Kind are for the most part Irregular. **1796** C. MARSHALL *Garden.* xix. (1813) 357 Coreopsis, verticillate, yellow. **1822–7** GOOD *Study Med.* (1829) I. 174 The verticillate order affords an abundant stock, from which we may select [carminatives] at pleasure. *Ibid.* IV. 568 Many of the warmer sedatives and antispasmodics, as assafœtida, camphor, most of the verticillate plants, and cajeput.

b. *Ent.*, etc. (See quots.)

1826 KIRBY & SP. *Entomol.* IV. xlvi. 324 *Verticillate*.., antennæ beset with hair in whorls. **1883** LE CONTE & HORN *Classif. Coleoptera N. Amer.* Introd. p. xv, In this form the joints are frequently surrounded at tip with a circle of longer hairs, in which case the antennæ are said to be verticellate.

2. a. *Bot.* Of leaves, flowers, branches, etc.: Disposed in, or forming, verticils or whorls.

1793 MARTYN *Dict. Bot.* s.v., Verticillate flowers; or flowers growing in a Whirl; or round the stem in rings one above another at each joint. **1830** LINDLEY *Nat. Syst. Bot.* 202 Square stems and verticillate leaves [of the Madder tribe]. **1851** MANTELL *Petrifactions* i. §2. 26 Specimens of a common..tribe of coal-plants.., whose verticillate foliage is too remarkable to escape notice. **1882** VINES *Sachs' Bot.* 396 The branches and roots spring exclusively from within the base of the leaf-sheath; and as this forms a whorl, the branches and roots are also verticillate.

b. Similarly in *Zool.*, *Ent.*, etc.

1828 STARK *Elem. Nat. Hist.* II. 378 Antennæ filiform, long, of from fifteen to sixteen globular joints, furnished with verticillate hairs. **1846** DANA *Zooph.* (1848) 675 Verrucæ ascending,..verticillate. **1871** DUNCAN *Transform. Insects* 111 Each tubercle carries several verticillate hairs.

3. Marked or characterized by verticillation.

1832 LINDLEY *Introd. Bot.* 113 The most exterior verticillate series of the integuments of the flower within the bracteæ. **1836–9** *Todd's Cycl. Anat.* II. 414/1 Simple tubes, divided in a verticillate manner. **1877** COUES & ALLEN *N. Amer. Rod.* 475 The verticillate whorls of scales between which the short hairs spring. **1882** VINES *Sachs' Bot.* 464 The phyllotaxis is sometimes verticillate, sometimes spiral.

ver'ticillated, *a.* Now *rare.* [Cf. prec.]

1. = prec. 1 and 1 b.

1698 J. PETIVER in *Phil. Trans.* XX. 315 Like the Whorles on a Verticillated Plant. **1752** J. HILL *Hist. Anim.* 110 The Lacerta, with the tail verticillated with denticulated scales. **1822–7** GOOD *Study Med.* (1829) IV. 531 The verticillated stimulant plants have, in many instances, also, been found serviceable. **1882** *Gard. Chron.* XVIII. 70 To make trial of seeds of any verticillated plants.

2. = prec. 2, 2 b, and 3.

1718 CHAMBERLAYNE *Relig. Philos.* I. x. §17. 184 Tho' the Calculation had been made from a greater Number of the Fibres of a verticillated Body. *c* **1789** *Encycl. Brit.* (ed. 3) III. 440/2 Different species of stellated or verticillated leaves. **1828** STARK *Elem. Nat. Hist.* II. 377 Antennæ.. furnished with verticillated hairs, or simply pubescent. **1844** *Florist's Jrnl.* (1846) V. 84 Flowers produced from the base of the bulb on a long drooping raceme, verticillated along the raceme. **1857** H. MILLER *Test. Rocks* i. 20 Its fluted stem and verticillated series of linear branches.

verticillation (vɜːtɪsɪ'leɪʃən). [f. VERTICILLATE *a.*: see -ATION.] The formation of verticils; a verticillate form or structure, a verticil.

1830 LINDLEY *Nat. Syst. Bot.* 297 The degree of verticillation requisite to constitute a calyx. **1843** *Penny Cycl.* XXVI. 131/2 The tail is rounded..; its verticillations are composed, above, of large tubercles, and below, of flat, quadrangular scales. **1888** *Riverside Nat. Hist.* I. 167 In the *Diadematidæ* the spines are hollow, long, and set with rings or verticillations.

verticillato-, combining form, on Greek models, of mod.L. *verticillātus* VERTICILLATE *a.*, as *verticillato-pinnate* (see quot.).

1829 T. CASTLE *Introd. Bot.* 71 Verticillato-pinnate—when the leaflets, instead of being arranged in the same plane on each side of the common leaf-stalk, are placed around it.

verticillium (vɜːtɪ'sɪlɪəm). *Bot.* [mod.L. (C. G. Nees von Esenbeck *Das System der Pilze und Schwämme* (1816) 56), f. VERTICILL(US + -IUM.] A hyphomycete fungus of the genus of this name, some species of which cause plant disease; *verticillium wilt*, wilt caused by this fungus, affecting many flowers, vegetables, and fruit bushes.

1916 *Sci. Proc. R. Dublin Soc.* XV. 63 (*heading*) The Verticillium wilt of the potato. **1931**, etc. [see *hadromycosis* s.v. HADROME]. **1951** *Sci. News* XXI. 110 Verticillium wilt of hops..has been a serious disease in Great Britain since 1932. **1971** *Country Life* 18 Feb. 381/1 So serious have they [*sc.* chrysanthemum diseases] become (two caused by viruses and one by a verticillium, in particular) that the future popularity of this florist's flower is said to be in danger. **1978** *Sci. Amer.* Aug. 68/3 In California..plantings [of tomato] are mainly limited to cultivators that resist the wilt caused by fusarium and verticillium fungi.

‖**verticillus** (vɜːtɪ'sɪləs). *Bot.* Pl. **verticilli** (-'sɪlaɪ). [L. *verticillus* (Pliny) whorl (sc. of a spindle), dim. of *vertex* VERTEX. Cf. VERTICIL.] A verticil or whorl.

1760 J. LEE *Introd. Bot.* III. iv. (1765) 174 *Verticillus*, a *Whorl*, expresses a Number of Flowers that are subsessile, and are produced in Rings round the Stems. **1783** *Encycl. Brit.* (ed. 2) X. 8570/2 The..smaller creeping germander, hath..reddish flowers, growing almost in a verticillus, or whorls, round the stalk. **1829** T. CASTLE *Introd. Bot.* 94 In the verticillus or whorl, the flowers surround the stem in a sort of ring. **1830** LINDLEY *Nat. Syst. Bot.* Introd. p. xxv, In most orders the sepals occupy one series or verticillus only. **1870** tr. *Pouchet's Universe* 388 When the floral apparatus is complete it is formed of four rosettes, or verticilli, of depressed concentrated leaves.

verticity (və'tɪsɪtɪ). Now *rare.* [ad. mod.L. *verticitās*, f. L. *vertic-*, stem of *vertex* VERTEX. So F. *verticité*, Sp. *verticidad*, Pg. *verticidade*.]

I. 1. The faculty of turning, or tendency to turn, towards a vertex or pole, esp. as exhibited in the loadstone or magnetic needle.

Very common in the 17th c.; now *rare* or *Obs.*

1625 N. CARPENTER *Geog. Del.* I. iv. (1635) 72 The Verticity is that whereby the Poles of the Earthly Spheare, conforme and settle themselues vnto the Poles of the Heauen. **1661** GLANVILL *Van. Dogm.* 140 We believe the verticity of the Needle, without a Certificate from the dayes of old. **1705** DERHAM in *Phil. Trans.* XXV. 2136 And having again straitened it, I was surprized to find it had quite lost its Verticity. **1794** G. ADAMS *Nat. & Exp. Philos.* (1806) IV. l. 393 His poker and tongs were natural magnets, and had their verticity fixed by being heated and cooled in a vertical position. **1837** BREWSTER *Magnet.* 169 The little magnet or needle turned itself briskly,..shewing great verticity. **1867** SMYTH *Sailor's Word-bk.* 712.

fig. **1687** NORRIS *Coll. Misc.* 184 The Soul will then point to the center of Happiness with her full bent and verticity. **1691** —— *Pract. Disc.* 170 His Will has lost much of its Verticity or Magnetick Inclination towards the chief Good.

b. With *a* and pl.

1646 SIR T. BROWNE *Pseud. Ep.* 68 A Loadstone fired.. according to the position in cooling contracts a new verticity. **1658** —— *Gard. Cyrus* v. 72 If any shall further quæry why magneticall Philosophy excludeth decussations, and needles transversly placed do naturally distract their verticities. **1705** C. PURSHALL *Mech. Macrocosm* 265 If you heat an Iron Red, and let it cool perpendicular to the Earth, ..its lowest end will gain a Verticity towards the North Pole. **1728** CHAMBERS *Cycl.* s.v. *Magnet*, A Bar of Iron that has gain'd a Verticity by being heated red-hot and cool'd again. *fig.* **1661** GLANVILL *Van. Dogm.* 244 Though the body by a kind of Magnetism be drawn down..; yet the thus impregnate spirit contracts a Verticity to objects above the Pole.

2. The power of turning or revolving; rotation, revolution. ? *Obs.*

1672 HOOKER in Rigaud *Corr. Sci. Men* (1841) I. 181 The verticity of Jupiter and Mars on their axes. **1690** LOCKE *Hum. Und.* IV. ii. §11 (1695) 307 A certain number of Globules,..having a verticity about their own Centres. **1819** H. BUSK *Banquet* III. 241 Hence on all subjects sparks of light you throw..: Blaze with the comet in his swift verticity, Or rouse us with a flash of electricity.

II. †**3.** The vertex or top of something. *Obs.*$^{-0}$

1656 BLOUNT *Glossogr.*

†**4.** Vertical position in the heavens. *Obs. rare.*

1646 J. GREGORY *Notes & Obs.* (1650) 151 The verticity of any of those [stars] could not haue come and 'stood over the place where the young child was'. **1686** GOAD *Celest. Bodies* II. xiii. 333 The Æstival Part of Heaven does more invigorate those Planets which attend the ⊙, not only by their higher Exaltation or Approches to Verticity, but [etc.].

5. *pole of verticity* (see quot.).

1886 CUMMING *Electricity* 54 There are two points, one in the northern hemisphere and one in the southern, at which the dip is 90°, or the magnetic force is vertical. These points are called the Magnetic Poles of the earth... The term *Pole of Verticity* is sometimes applied to them.

† **'verticle**, erron. f. VERTICAL *a.* and *sb. Obs.*

1611 COTGR., *Azimuth*, an Azimuth, or Verticle circle, which discends from the Zenith. **1653** WATERHOUSE *Apol. Learning* 51 Now grows Our Nation to its Zenith: Fame is no friend to Continuance; the Verticle is near, when Admiration from abroad, and Luxury at home, threaten our Change.

† **'verticle.** *Obs. rare.* [ad. L. *verticula, -us, -um* joint, vertebra, dim. of *vertex* VERTEX, or OF. *verticule* (rare) vertebra.] A vertebra.

1658 A. FOX *Würtz' Surg.* v. 363 Some Childrens back bone have I seen crackt in two, and the verticles thereof were disjoyned.

† **verti'cordious**, *a. Obs.*$^{-1}$ [f. L. *verticordia* turner of hearts (an epithet of Venus), f. *vertĕre* to turn + *cord-*, *cor* heart: see -OUS.] That turns the heart (from evil); regenerative.

1702 C. MATHER *Magn. Chr.* III. II. xxvi. 149/1 The Regenerating and Verticordious Grace of Heaven, took advantage from his Religious Education..to steal into the Heart of this young Disciple.

† **ver'ticularly**, *adv. Obs.*$^{-1}$ [f. L. *verticula*, etc., VERTICLE.] In a whorled or verticillate manner.

1657 TOMLINSON *Renou's Disp.* 610 Spinous cups do verticularly circumvest its Caulicles.

† **ver'tiginal**, *a. Obs.*$^{-1}$ [f. L. *vertīgin-*, *vertīgo* VERTIGO.] = VERTIGINOUS *a.* 2.

1612 *Benvenuto's Passenger* I. ii. 177 For vertiginall dizzines.

ver'tiginate, *a. rare*$^{-0}$. [Cf. next.] 'Turned round, giddy' (Webster, 1864).

vertiginate (vəˈtɪdʒɪneɪt), *v. rare.* [f. L. *vertīgin-*, *vertīgo* VERTIGO.] *intr.* To turn round, spin, or rush dizzily.

[**1767** A. CAMPBELL *Lexiph.* (ed. 2) 23 My steed..with an incredible acceleration of velocity, vertiginated along the arable. *Ibid.* 52 Brine, that once vertiginated in the pacifick ocean.] *a* **1814** *Last Act* I. iii. in *New Brit. Theatre* II. 372, I, your great Chiron, was your instructor; and thitherward my glory vertiginates. *a* **1834** COLERIDGE in *Lit. Rem.* (1839) IV. 212 Surely never did argument vertiginate more!

vertigine, -inie: see VERTIGINY.

vertigi'nosity. *rare.* [ad. F. *vertiginosité* (16th c.). Cf. next.] (See quot.)

1656 BLOUNT *Glossogr.* (copying Cotgr.), *Vertiginosity*, a giddiness, dizziness, swimming of the head or brain.

vertiginous (vəˈtɪdʒɪnəs), *a.* Also 7 virt-. [ad. L. *vertīginōsus* one suffering from giddiness, f. *vertīgin-*, *vertīgo* VERTIGO. So F. *vertigineux*, Sp., Pg., It. *vertiginoso*.]

1. Of persons, the head, etc.: Affected with, suffering from, vertigo or giddiness; giddy, dizzy.

1621 BURTON *Anat. Mel.* I. iii. I. i, Many phantasticall visions about their eyes, vertiginous, apt to tremble. **1653** JER. TAYLOR *Serm. for Year* I. xix. 233 They grew vertiginous and fell from the battlements of heaven. **1695** WOODWARD *Nat. Hist. Earth* IV. 206 The former of these [damps]..makes the Workmen faint, and vertiginous. **1707** *Reflex. upon Ridicule* 136 The Head turns and grows vertiginous. **1787** BEST *Angling* (ed. 2) 69 By these balls fishes are rendered vertiginous, and as it were intoxicated. **1808** *Med. Jrnl.* XIX. 299 The ocular spectra of objects.. augment the disturbance of the eyes, and thereby add to the confusion of the vertiginous person. **1822–7** GOOD *Study Med.* (1829) I. 170, I have never been able to raise it [the drug] above seven grains without making the head stupid and vertiginous. **1906** G. TYRRELL in *Life* (1912) II. xi. 260 At first I was very vertiginous, but am slowly getting my nerves in hand.

fig. **1624** [SCOTT] *Vox Regis* 41 The heighth of prosperitie so amazeth the eyes of men, as it makes them vertiginous. **1687** NORRIS *Misc., Disc. Rom.* xii. 3 §19 If they can stand there without growing vertiginous,..they are still within the Region of Humility.

b. *fig.* Giddy-minded; unstable or unsettled in opinions, etc.; inconstant; apt to change quickly; marked by inconstancy, instability, or rapid change.

Frequent in the 17th century.

1609 BP. W. BARLOW *Answ. Nameless Cath.* 209 This vertiginous Vertumnus, whom Plato observed for an in-artificiall disputant. **1632** BURTON *Anat. Mel.* (ed. 4) I. iii. I. ii. 185 Inconstant they are in all their actions, vertiginous, restlesse, vnapt to resolue of any businesse. **1681** MANTON *Serm. Ps. cxix.* 20 Wks. 1872 VI. 190 Therefore take heed of being given up to this vertiginous spirit, to be turned and 'tossed up and down with every wind of doctrine'. **1789** GOUV. MORRIS in Sparks *Life & Writ.* (1832) II. 66 As all men and things are in the same vertiginous condition. **1841** DISRAELI *Amen. Lit.* (1859) II. 378 The sphere of publication widened, in this vertiginous era. **1898** BODLEY *France* III. v. 271 When one thinks of the vicissitudes of those vertiginous days, it is not surprising that..sons of the Revolution [etc.].

2. Of the nature of, characterized by, vertigo.

1608 TOPSELL *Serpents* 76 Sluggish dulness, a giddy and vertiginous pace,..are sure arguments that Bees are not in good health. **1620** VENNER *Via Recta* vii. 134 Fisticke Nuts ..distemper the bloud, and being much eaten, often-times procure the vertiginous euill. **1699** EVELYN *Acetaria* (1729) 133 Mustard..strengthening the Memory, expelling Heaviness, preventing the Vertiginous Palsey. **1733** CHEYNE *Eng. Malady* III. iv. (1734) 327, I was suddenly seiz'd with a vertiginous Paroxysm. **1822–7** GOOD *Study Med.* (1829) I. 460 That staggering or vertiginous disease which is provincially known by the name of *Dunt.* **1854** GILFILLAN *Beattie* p. xvii, Beattie was troubled with a vertiginous complaint. **1876** *Clin. Soc. Trans.* IX. 183 He found that if he closed his eyes the vertiginous feeling was mitigated. **1901** *Brit. Med. Jrnl.* No. 2092. Epit. Anc. Lit. 18 Vertiginous attacks became troublesome at times.

fig. **1626** AILESBURY *Passion Serm.* 13 Their theory was vertiginous, swom in the braine, there floating without anchor, and was of no credit with the will. **1642** H. MORE *Song of Soul* II. III. iii. 22 My strong-winged Muse feeble to slide Into false thoughts and dreams vertiginous.

3. Liable to cause vertigo or dizziness; inducing giddiness. Also *fig.*

1649 JER. TAYLOR *Gt. Exemp.* I. ix. 143 There..the station is least firm, the posture most uneasie, the prospect vertiginous. **1665** SIR T. HERBERT *Trav.* (1677) 326 The Dervis and other Santoons..express their zeal by turning round,..and others I have seen in this vertiginous exercise at the Cavalcades. *a* **1701** MAUNDRELL *Journ. Jerus.* (1721) 95 After they had by these vertiginous circulations and clamours turn'd their heads. **1865** W. KAY *Crisis Hupfeldiana* 78 If any one chooses to look further into this vertiginous subject, he may examine [etc.]. **1874** STEVENSON *Ess. Trav., Unpleasant Places* (1905) 242 There is nothing more vertiginous than a wind like this among the woods, with all its sights and noises. **1899** *Allbutt's Syst. Med.* vii. 796 It is generally necessary to avoid crowded rooms and the vertiginous influence of the dance.

4. Of motion: Having the character of rotation or revolution; rotatory.

In some cases prob. implying the preceding sense.

1663 BAXTER *Div. Life* 215 The thoughts of earthly fleshly things have power to delude men, and mislead them, and hurry them about in a vertiginous motion. **1690** LEYBOURN *Curs. Math.* 449 It is found to have a Vertiginous Motion about its own Axis. **1712** BLACKMORE *Creation* 251 So give the air impression from above, It in a whirl vertiginous would move. **1751** JOHNSON *Rambler* No. 117 ⁋10 That vertiginous motion, with which we are carried round by the diurnal revolution of the earth. **1766** G. CANNING *Anti-Lucretius* IV. 323 We see, with whirl vertiginous, the Sun From west to east around his axis run. **1832** *Nat. Philos., Electro-Magn.* xii. §257. 80 (L.U.K.), The peculiar kind of movement..which Dr. Wollaston attributed to the electro-magnetic agent, and which he termed its *vertiginous motion.* **1837** CARLYLE *Fr. Rev.* I. III. vii, It is the centre whereon infinite contentions unite and clash. What new universal vertiginous movement is this? **1883** SALMON in *Contemp. Rev.* Oct. 512 All the souls in hell and purgatory..who, in the earth's vertiginous double motion, must roll about like grains of coffee in a grocer's mill.

b. Of an axis: Revolving, rotating.

1680 *Counterplots* 6 Whirl'd about with perpetual agitations upon the Vertiginous Axis of that Globe.

Hence **ver'tiginously** *adv.*, giddily, dizzily.

1766 G. CANNING *Anti-Lucretius* v. 368 Which..to the centre of the cloud repair, And there..With furious rage vertiginously roll. **1868** BROWNING *Ring & Bk.* XI. 2365 The smoothest safest of you all..Will rock vertiginously in turn, and reel, And, emulative, rush to death like me. **1886** SYMONDS *Renaiss. It., Cath. React.* (1898) VII. ix. 45 A new philosophy occupied his brain, vertiginously big with incoherent births of modern thought.

verti'ginousness. [f. prec. + -NESS.] The condition or state of being vertiginous; dizziness, giddiness. Also *fig.*

1599 A. M. tr. *Gabelhouer's Bk. Physicke* 12/1 Applye it on his Forehead and on the Temples of the heade,..as long as the vertiginousnes dureth and continueth. *c* **1628** DONNE *Serm.* 658 It was a staggering, a vertiginousnesse, an ignorance. **1653** JER. TAYLOR *Serm.* I. xxi. 282 He that commits sacriledge, is marked for a vertiginousnesse and changeable fortune. *a* **1677** BARROW *Serm.* (1810) II. 416 We would all climb into high places, not considering the precipices on which they stand, nor the vertiginousness of our own brains. **1727** BAILEY (vol. II), *Giddiness*,.. Vertiginousness. **1846** BROWNING *Lett.* (1899) II. 528, I got up with the old vertiginousness, or a little worse.

† **ver'tiginy.** *Obs.* Also 5, 7 vertigine, 6–7 -inie. [a. L. *vertīgine*, abl. sing. of *vertīgo*.] = VERTIGO.

c **1400** *Lanfranc's Cirurg.* 310 [It] is good for þe brayn wiþinneforþ as for scotomia & vertigine. **1583** STUBBES *Anat. Abus.* E vj b, Yͤ vertiginie, & instability of their more than fantastical brains. **1605** B. JONSON *Volpone* II. ii, For the Vertigine, in the head,..a most soueraigne, and approoued remedy. **1608** TOPSELL *Serpents* 32 It induceth a kinde of heauines or drunkennesse in their head, with a vertiginie [1658 vertiginy] or giddines.

† **ver'tigious**, *a. Obs. rare.* = VERTIGINOUS *a.*

1623 COCKERAM, *Vertigious*, belonging to giddinesse. **1653** E. CHISENHALE *Cath. Hist.* xv. 461 The nauseating juyce..hath intoxicated them, making their Vertigious heads turn after the Laterane Weather-cock. **1656** BLOUNT.

‖ **vertigo** (ˈvɜːtɪgəʊ, vəˈtaɪgəʊ, vəˈtiːgəʊ). Also 7 vertego, -teego, virtigo. [L. *vertigo* a turning or whirling round, giddiness, etc., f. *vertĕre* to turn. Cf. F. and Sp. *vertigo*; also F. *vertige*, Pg. *vertigem*, It. *vertigine*.

The various modes of pronouncing this word form the subject of an elaborate note by Walker (1797), arguing in favour of that with the stress on the first syllable. The fashionable pronunciation, however, appears to have been (vəˈtiːgəʊ), and this alone is given by Smart (1836–40) as really current, in spite of its divergence from English analogy.]

1. *Path.* A disordered condition in which the person affected has a sensation of whirling, either of external objects or of himself, and tends to lose equilibrium and consciousness; swimming in the head; giddiness, dizziness:

a. Without article.

Sometimes applied to the staggers in horses or the sturdy in sheep, and in quot. 1619 to a disease of hawks.

1528 PAYNELL *Salerne's Regim.* C iij b, The heed ache called vertigo: whiche maketh a man to wene that the world turneth. **1558** BULLEIN *Govt. Health* A v, Apoplexia and Vertigo will neuer fro the[e] starte, Untill the vitall blode be killed in the harte. **1619** E. BERT *Hawkes & Hawking* III. v. 85 A disease..of some called *Vertego*, it is a swimming of the braine. **1681** tr. *Willis' Rem. Med. Wks.* Vocab., *Vertigo.* **1766** BEATTIE *Let.* in *Life & Writ.* (1806) I. 93 Have I not headachs, like Pope? vertigo, like Swift? **1799** *Med. Jrnl.* II. 119 The most common effects observed from full doses, are vertigo, pain, or throbbing of the forehead. **1803** *Ibid.* X. 396 The general symptoms were pain across the forehead with vertigo. **1840** THACKERAY *Paris Sk. Bk.* (1872) 185 He felt as if attacked by vertigo, and his thoughts whirled in his brain. **1875** RICHARDSON *Dis. Mod. Life* 72 In those who have irregular circulation through the brain, the tendency to giddiness and vertigo is more easily developed.

b. With *the.*

1605 B. JONSON *Volpone* III. vii, Our drinke..we will take, vntill my roofe whirle round With the vertigo. **1631** BRATHWAIT *Eng. Gentlew.* (1641) 316 What a circular gesture wee shall observe some use in their pace as if they were troubled with the vertigo. **1725** *Fam. Dict.* s.v., The Vertigo will sometimes seize upon those who look down from an high Place. **1794** E. DARWIN *Zoon.* (1801) I. 335 Thus on turning round on one foot, the vertigo continues for some seconds of time after the person is fallen on the ground. **1827** SCOTT *Let.* in *Lockhart* (1838) VII. 29 Your letter has given me the vertigo—my head turns round like a chariot-wheel. *a* **1883** FAGGE *Princ. & Pract. Med.* (1886) I. 702 The vertigo caused by derangement of the liver.

c. With *a*, etc., and pl.

c **1620** FLETCHER & MASSINGER *Trag. Barnavelt* v. ii, Here's a Sword..cures all rhumes, all Catharres, megroomes, verteegoes. **1641** R. BROOKE *Eng. Episc.* 5 Your Faulkners seele a Pigeons eye..to prevent a Vertigo. **1698** FRYER *Acc. E. India & P.* 129 The Mountains fenced with horrible Gulphs, till strange Vertigoes prejudicate Fancy. **1731** SWIFT *On his Death* Wks. 1755 III. II. 242 That old vertigo in his head Will never leave him, till he's dead. **1789** W. BUCHAN *Dom. Med.* (1790) 39 These..occasion palsies, vertigoes, and other nervous affections, which often prove fatal. **1830** GALT *Life Byron* xlvii. 310 He complained of frequent vertigos, which made him feel as though he were intoxicated. **1895** ZANGWILL *Master* III. ii. 302 The fumes of expensive wines and cigars gave him a momentary vertigo.

2. *fig.* A disordered state of mind, or of things, comparable to giddiness.

1634 WITHER *Embl.* 231 Those uselesse and vaine temp'rall things..which if thereupon our hearts we set Make men and women the vertigo get. **1661** BAGSHAW in Baxter *Acc. to Inhabitants Kidderminster* 43 For him now to be suddenly advanced so much beyond his Art, will run the poor man into a dangerous Vertigo. **1702** STEELE *Funeral* I. ii, How dizzy a Place is this World you live in! All Human Life's a mere Vertigo! **1709** —— *Tatler* No. 29 ⁋7 Absolute Power is only a Vertigo in the Brain of Princes. **1810** BENTHAM *Packing* (1821) 187 The British Themis seems little..in danger of being healed of her habitual vertigo by this one hand. **1831** CARLYLE *Sart. Res.* II. v, There was a certain delirious vertigo in the thought. **1875** JEVONS *Money* (1878) 217 That dangerous kind of intellectual vertigo which often attacks writers on the currency.

3. The act of whirling round and round.

1853 DE QUINCEY *Autobiog. Sk.* Wks. I. 44 It was not a humming-top that was required, but a peg-top. Now, this, in order to keep up the vertigo at full stretch,..needed to be whipped incessantly.

† **'vertilage.** *Obs.* [Irreg. f. L. *vert-ĕre* to turn.] (See quots.)

1610 W. FOLKINGHAM *Art of Survey* I. vii. 14 Tillage generally taken may comprehend all maner of husbandings of grounds, but it is heere limited to Vertilage and Fertilage. Vertilage consists in Deluage and Fictilage. **1688** R. HOLME *Armoury* III. 333/2 Vertillage, is a preparing of Ground to receive its Seed by stirring, tossing or turning the same.

† **vertingale**, obs. var. FARTHIN-, VARDINGALE.

1552 HULOET, Vertingale for a gentilwoman, *limus.* **1869** MRS. PALLISER *Lace* vi. 79 Under the vertingale of black taffety they wear a dozen or more petticoats.

vertious, obs. form of VERJUICE.

vertisol (ˈvɜːtɪsɒl). *Soil Sci.* Also Vertisol. [f. VERTI(CAL *a.* + -SOL.] A clayey soil with little organic matter found in regions having distinct wet and dry seasons, characterized by deep, wide cracks when dry and an uneven surface owing to the swelling and shrinking of the clay.

1960 *Soil Classification: 7th Approximation* (U.S. Dept. Agric.) ix. 124/1 The central concept of Vertisols is one of soils that crack widely, and that often remoisten from water that runs into the cracks rather than from water that percolates through the soil. **1970** *Nature* 2 May 429/1 Dark, cracking tropical clays, that is, vertisols, are characteristic of .. the restricted clay plugs and back-swamps of the Omo Floodplain [in Ethiopia]. **1981** *Jrnl. Soil Sci. Soc. Amer.* XLV. 668/1 In Vertisols, because of swelling and shrinking, bulk density of the soil is dependent on moisture content.

†**vertoll**, obs. var. VARDLE, VARTIWELL.

1552 HULOET, Vertoll of a dore, *vertebra, vertibulum.*

vertousnes, obs. f. VIRTUOUSNESS.

vertouyse, obs. Sc. f. VIRTUOUS *a.*

vertre, southern ME. var. FIR-TREE.

†**vert-sauce**. *Obs. rare.* [ad. OF. (also mod.F.) *sauce verte* green sauce.] A sauce made principally with green herbs. Cf. GREEN SAUCE.

c **1440** *Anc. Cookery* in *Househ. Ord.* (1790) 441 Vert Sause. Take parsel, and myntes, and peletur [etc.]. *c* **1440** *Promp. Parv.* 509/1 Vertesawce, or vergesawce, .. *viride salsamentum.* *c* **1450** *Two Cookery Bks.* 104 And sauce is vergesauce [*Douce MS.* vert sauce]. **1483** *Cath. Angl.* 401/1 Vert sawse, *viridis salsa.*

vertu, vertú, varr. VIRTU.

vertual, obs. f. VIRTUAL *a.*

vertue(less, obs. ff. VIRTUE(LESS.

vertuest, obs. superl. of VIRTUOUS *a.*

vertueux, obs. var. VIRTUOUS *a.*

vertugal, var. VERDUGAL *Obs.*

vertuise, obs. Sc. f. VIRTUOUS *a.*

vertules(se, obs. ff. VIRTUELESS.

†**verˈtumnal**, *a. Obs. rare.* [f. L. *Vertumnus* (see next); by Adams falsely associated with *vēr* spring, VER *sb.*[1]] **a.** Vernal. **b.** Of or pertaining to Vertumnus.

1622 T. ADAMS *Eirenopolis* 182 Her smiles are more reuiuing then the Vertumnall Sunneshine. **1633** —— *Exp. 2 Peter* iii. 8 We cannot .. keep back the cowslip to August, nor the vertumnal flowers to autumn. **1705** N. TATE tr. *Cowley's Plants* C.'s Wks. 1711 III. 405 The Goddess her Vertumnal Rites prepares.

†**verˈtumnals**, *sb. pl. Obs.*$^{-0}$ [ad. L. *Vertumnāl-ia* sb. pl., the festival of Vertumnus, f. *Vertumn-us* god of the changing year.] (See quot.)

1656 BLOUNT *Glossogr.* (citing Broughton), *Vertumnals*, Feasts dedicated to, or Books treated [1674 treating] of the god Vertumnus.

vertuose, obs. f. VIRTUOUS.

vertuositie, obs. f. VIRTUOSITY.

vertuoso, obs. f. VIRTUOSO.

vertuous(ness, obs. forms of VIRTUOUS(NESS.

vertuse, -tuyse, obs. Sc. ff. VIRTUOUS *a.*

vertw, obs. Sc. f. VIRTUE.

†**vertwell**. *Obs.*$^{-1}$ [ad. OF. *vertevelle*: see VARTIWELL.] = VARVEL.

13.. *Parl. Three Ages* 238 He .. henntis thaym [*sc.* the hawks] one honde .., Lowppes in thaire lesses thorowe vertwells of siluere.

ˈverty, *a. Sc.* Also 5 **werty**, 9 **vertie, vairtie.** [Aphetic f. AVERTY *a.*] Attentive to business; prudent, cautious, wide-awake, early, etc. In early use coupled with *wise.*

1375 BARBOUR *Bruce* XVIII. 439 King Robert .. was Wis in his deid and ek verty. *c* **1425** WYNTOUN *Cron.* VIII. 3121 He wes wys and rycht werty. **1456** SIR G. HAYE *Law Arms* (S.T.S.) 115 It efferis wele to a constable to be wys and verty, and wele avisit in all his dedis. **1804** TARRAS *Poems* 2 Archie, fu' vertie, owre the moorlan' spangs Ilk strype and stank; nae doubt he itchin langs To crack wi' San'. **1825** JAMIESON *Suppl.*, *Vairtie*, early. Buchan.

Hence **ˈvertyness**. *rare*$^{-1}$.

1456 SIR G. HAYE *Bk. Knighthood* Wks. (S.T.S.) II. 54 A man can .. mend ane evill fortune apperand be vertynasse.

veruel, obs. var. VARVEL.

Veruˈlamian, *a. rare.* [f. L. *Verulami-um* St. Albans.] Performed by, emanating from, Francis Bacon, Lord Verulam.

1671 R. BOHUN *Wind* 13 From another of the Verulamian experiments. **1849** MACAULAY *Hist. Eng.* iii. I. 406 The discipline .. had brought the public to a temper well fitted for the reception of the Verulamian doctrine.

†**verule**, obs. f. FERRULE *sb.* and *v.*

c **1828** BERRY *Encycl. Her.* I. Gloss., *Verules*, or *Ferrils*, several rings, one within another, which have the same centre. *Ibid.*, *Veruled*, or *Ferriled*, .. are terms used in heraldry to express the ornamental rings round hunting-horns, &c.

‖**verumonˈtanum**. *Anat.* [f. L. *verū* spit + *montānum*, neut. of *montānus* hilly.] (See quots. 1728 and 1831.)

1728 CHAMBERS *Cycl.*, *Veru-montanum*, in Anatomy, .. a kind of little Valve, in the Place where the Ejaculatory Ducts enter the Urethra... Its use is, to prevent the Urine, in passing the Urethra, from getting in at those Ducts. **1771** *Encycl. Brit.* I. 273/1 A small oblong oval eminence .. terminating forward in a point, called *caruncula* or *verumontanum.* **1831** R. KNOX *Cloquet's Anat.* 817 The inferior median line ends posteriorly at an oblong, rounded prominence, about an inch long, called the *Verumontanum* (*Caput Gallinaginis*). This prominence is formed by the mucous membrane... Anteriorly, it becomes thin and ends in a point. **1860** SIR H. THOMPSON *Dis. of Prostate* (1868) 16 Some minute vessels, chiefly venous, .. on either side of the verumontanum. **1876** GROSS *Dis. Bladder*, etc. 557 The sinus in front of the verumontanum.

verunda, obs. form of VERANDA.

veruorþ, southern ME. var. FAR-FORTH *adv.*

vervail(e, obs. ff. VARVEL.

vervain (ˈvɜːveɪn). *Bot.* Forms: α. 4–6 **verueyn(e, -veyn(e**, 5, 7 **-ueine**, 4, 7 **verveine**, 4, 7–9 **vervein.** β. 5, 7 **vervaine**, 5 **-wayne (warwayn)**, 6–7 **-uaine**, 7– **vervain.** γ. 5–6 **veruen(e**, 6–7 **-ven.** δ. 6 **veruyne**, 6–7 **veruine**, 6–8 **-vine**; 6 **veruin, -uyn**, 6–7 **vervin, -vyn** (7 **varvin**). [a. AF. and OF. *verveine* (13th c.; OF. also *vervainne*, mod.F. *verveine*, = Prov., It. *vervena*), ad. L. *verbēna* VERBENA.]

1. The common European and British herbaceous plant, *Verbena officinalis*, formerly much valued for its reputed medicinal properties. Also rarely, some other species of the genus *Verbena*, or the genus itself. Cf. VERBENA 2.

α. **1390** GOWER *Conf.* II. 262 Tok sche fieldwode and verveyne, Of herbes ben noght betre tueine. *c* **1400** *Lanfranc's Cirurg.* 243 A ȝelke of an eij, & as miche of oile of rosis, & as miche of iuys of verueine. *a* **1425** tr. *Arderne's Treat. Fistula*, etc. 64 Vitriol .. made with Iuyse of moleyn, or of plantayne, or verueyn. **1611** COTGR., *Verveine*, Verueine, Holie hearbe, Iunoes teares. **1706** STEVENS *Sp. Dict.* I, *Verbena*, the Herb Vervein. **1866** *Treas. Bot.* 1210/1 The common name of *Verbena officinalis*, .. Vervein, our only native species. **1874** O'SHAUGHNESSY *Music & Moonlight* 161 Between the pathway and the wood She seemed to make a softer clime For vervein, violet, and thyme. **1887** MOLONEY *Forestry W. Afr.* 401 Vervein (*Verbena officinalis*, L.).—Herbaceous plant.

β. *a* **1400** *Stockholm Med. MS.* ii. 315 in *Anglia* XVIII. 315 A lytyll wyl I tellyn of verwayne, Herbe þat meche is of mayne. *c* **1425** *Voc.* in Wr.-Wülcker 645 *Hec ueruena*, warwayn. **1477** NORTON *Ord. Alch.* iii. in Ashm. (1652) 39 Vervaine, Lunara, and Martagon. **1597** GERARDE *Herbal* II. ccxxxv. 580 There be two kindes of Veruaine as Pliny saith, the male, and the female; or as others affirme, vpright, and creeping. **1612** DRAYTON *Poly-olb.* xiii. 218 And hard by them againe he holy Vervaine finds. **1671** SALMON *Syn. Med.* III. xxii. 439 Vervain .. is good against Tertian and Quartan Agues. **1718** QUINCY *Compl. Disp.* 132 Vervain flowers in June and July. **1757** BURKE *Abridgm. Eng. Hist.* Wks. X. 196 The Druids also looked upon vervain, and some other plants, as holy. **1782** J. SCOTT *Poet. Wks.* 97 Vervain blue for magic rites renown'd. **1816** SCOTT *Antiquary* xxiii, You have used neither charm, .. magic mirror, nor geomantic figure. Where be .. your May-fern, your vervain? **1830** LINDLEY *Nat. Syst. Bot.* 239 The properties formerly ascribed to the Vervain appear to have been imaginary. **1873** 'OUIDA' *Pascarel* III. vi. II. 90 About the feet of the Tower of Galileo, ivy and vervain, and the Madonna's herb, grew among the grasses.

γ. *a* **1425** tr. *Arderne's Treat. Fistula*, etc. 63 Mirabolan ow to be dissolued in gote mylk, .. or in rayne water or rose water, or of veruene, or of anoþer stiptike herbe. **1545** ELYOT, *Hierobotane*, the herbe called Veruen. **1567** MAPLET *Gr. Forest* 64 Veruen, of some after their language is called Holy Herbe. **1591** LODGE *Hist. Dk. Normandy* B ij b, Thou art like the veruen, .. poyson one wayes, and pleasure an other.

δ. **1530** PALSGR. 284/2 Vervyn an herbe, *uerueyne.* **1533** ELYOT *Cast. Helthe* (1541) 9 b, Thynges good for the eyes: Eyebryght: Fenell: Vervyn. **1562** TURNER *Herbal* II. 162 The second kinde of Veruine... The leaues of thys .. are good agaynst .. serpentes. **1596** COGAN *Haven Health* xxi. 41 Also one olde saying I haue heard of this herbe, That whosoeuer weareth Veruin and Dill, May be bold to sleepe on euery hill. **1610** FLETCHER *Faithf. Sheph.* II. i, And thou light Varvin too, thou must go after, Provoking easie souls to mirth and laughter. **1638** RAWLEY tr. *Bacon's Life & Death* (1650) 32 These yield a Robust heat, especially Elecampane, Garlick, .. Vervin, Valerian. *a* **1802** in Leyden *Cout of Keeldar* xxiv. *note*, Gin ye wish to be leman mine, Lay off the St. John's wort and the vervine.

b. With distinguishing terms, denoting varieties of this or other species of the genus *Verbena.* Also applied to various species of plants resembling or allied to (and sometimes formerly classed with) the vervains.

1578 LYTE *Dodoens* 125 *Verbena recta*, .. Upright or straight Veruayne. *Ibid.*, *Verbena supina*, .. Low and base Veruayne. **1601** CHESTER *Love's Mart.* xlii, Base or flat Veruine, and the wholesome Tansie. **1611** COTGR., *Verveine basse*, Holie Verueine, creeping Verueine. *Ibid.*, *Verveine femelle*, Female Verueine. *Ibid.*, *Verveine masle*, Male Verueine, straight or vpright Verueine, common Verueine. *c* **1711** PETIVER *Gazophyl.* x. 93 Luzone Vervain with Mint like Leaves. **1731** MILLER *Gard. Dict.* s.v. *Verbena*, Taller broad-leav'd Portugal Vervain. *Ibid.*, Canada Nettle-leav'd Vervain. *Ibid.*, American Vervain with many Spikes. **1753** *Chambers' Cycl.* Suppl. s.v., The fine leaved Vervain... The narrow-leav'd nettle Vervain of America. **1842** *Penny Cycl.* XXII. 403/2 *Stachytarpha Jamaicensis*, Jamaica Bastard Vervain. **1843** *Ibid.* XXVI. 254/2 *Verbena Aubletia*, Rose-coloured Vervain... *V.* [now *Lippia*] *triphylla*, Lemon-scented Vervain. **1846–50** A. WOOD *Class-bk. Bot.* 412 *Verbena Spuria*, Spurious or Jagged-leaved Vervain. *V. Angustifolia*, .. Narrow-leaved Vervain. **1856** A. GRAY *Man. Bot.* (1860) 298 *Verbena hastata*, Blue Vervain... *V. stricta*, Hoary Vervain. **1868** —— *Less. Bot.* (1874) 340 *Verbena officinalis*, European Vervain. **1891** *Cent. Dict.* s.v. *Stink*, *Stinking vervain*, the guinea-hen weed.

c. With *a* and pl. A single species or plant of the genus *Verbena.*

1597 GERARDE *Herbal* II. ccxlvi. 718 The Veruaines floure in July and August. **1842** *Penny Cycl.* XXII. 403/2 Many of them [species of *Stachytarpha*] have been described as Vervains, but they are distinct from that genus. **1891** F. TENNYSON *Psyche* i, Garden sweets, Jasmin and vervains, and old lavender.

2. Incorrectly used to render (or represent) L. *verbena*: see VERBENA 1.

1548 COOPER *Elyot's Dict.*, *Verbenarius*, was one of the ambassadours sent from the Romaines vnto their ennemies, which ware on his heade a garlande of Veruen. **1567** GOLDING *Ovid's Met.* VII. (1593) 159 Altars twaine of turffe she builded: .. Both the which as soone as she had dight With vervine [etc.]. **1600** HOLLAND *Livy* XXX. xliii. 771 They should carrie with them every one by himselfe, certaine flint stones of their owne, and likewise Verven. **1603** B. JONSON *Sejanus* v. iv, Bestow your garlands: and, with reverence, place The vervin on the altar. **1697** DRYDEN *Virg. Past.* VIII. 90 Bind those Altars round With Fillets; and with Vervain strow the Ground. **1720** OZELL *Vertot's Rom. Rep.* I. v. 276 Shall we .. say to the Æqui and Sabines, take Branches of Vervain, and return and sue to us humbly for Peace? **1759** W. MASON *Caractacus* Poems 1830 II. 77 Lift your boughs of vervain blue, Dipt in cold September dew. **1855** SINGLETON *Virgil* I. 55 Festoon these altars and fat vervains burn. **1863** CONINGTON *Odes Hor.* IV. xi. 7 The altar, strew'd With vervain, hungers for the flow Of lambkin's blood.

3. *attrib.* and *Comb.*, as ***vervain family, order, root, tree***, etc.; ***vervain-like*** adj.; **vervain humming-bird**, the small Jamaican species, *Mellisuga minima*; **vervain-sage** *U.S.* (see quot.).

c **1580** G. HARVEY *Marginalia, Hopperus* (1913) 182 Redd Roses, Verueyn rootes, .. Good for the sight. **1712** tr. *Pomet's Hist. Drugs* I. 144 Which signifies the *Ricinus*, or a kind of Vervain Tree. **1753** *Chambers' Cycl.* Suppl. s.v. *Veronica*, American shrubby Speedwell, with vervain-like leaves. **1849** BALFOUR *Man. Bot.* §968 Verbenaceæ, the Vervain Family. **1861** BENTLEY *Man. Bot.* 611 The Vervain Order.—Herbs, shrubs, or trees. **1865** WOOD *Homes without H.* xxviii. 560 This is the Vervain Humming Bird, .. one of the minutest of the feathered race. Its popular name is derived from its fondness for the West Indian vervain. **1888** *Encycl. Brit.* XXIV. 163/2 The vervain genus gives its name to the natural order (*Verbenaceæ*) of which it is a member. **1895** *Funk's Stand. Dict.*, *Vervain-sage*, a European species of sage (*Salvia Verbenaca*) with small bluish flowers, sparingly naturalized in the United States.

b. vervain mallow, a species of mallow, *Malva alcea.*

1548 TURNER *Names Herbes* (E.D.S.) 10 Alcea .. in englishe .. may be named Veruen mallowe, or cut mallowe. **1611** COTGR., *Guimauves sauvages*, the wild Mallowes called, Veruine Mallowes, cut Mallowes, and Simons Mallowes. **1681** GREW *Musæum* II. iii. iii. 235 The Seed of the Vervaine Mallow of Japan. *c* **1710** PETIVER *Cat. Ray's Eng. Herbal* Tab. xxxix. **1753** *Chambers' Cycl.* Suppl. s.v. *Alcea*, The common larger vervain mallow with red flowers. **1785** MARTYN *Lett. Bot.* xxiv. (1794) 342 Vervain Mallow has an erect stem, .. the flowers large, and light purple. **1822** *Hortus Angl.* II. 204 Vervain Mallow. Stem erect; lower leaves angular.

vervall, obs. variant of VARVEL.

verve (vɜːv). [a. F. *verve*, of obscure origin; in OF. (from 12th cent.) the sense is 'caprice, fancy'.]

1. Special bent, vein, or talent in writing. Now *rare* or *Obs.*

1697 DRYDEN *Æneid* Ded., Ess. (Ker) II. 216 If he be above Virgil, and is resolved to follow his own *verve*, (as the French call it,) the proverb will fall heavily upon him: Who teaches himself, has a fool for his master. **1756** GRAY in W. Mason *Mem.* (1807) II. 119 You will not expect therefore I should give you any account of my *Verve* which is at best .. of so delicate a constitution. **1783** H. WALPOLE *Let. to W. Mason* 8 Nov., One of my most fervent wishes has long been that you would exercise more frequently the *verve* that is so eminently marked as your characteristic talent. **1878** SMILES *Robt. Dick* 412 He had a strong poetic verve.

2. Intellectual vigour, energy, or 'go', esp. as manifested in literary productions; great vivacity of ideas and expression. (Common from *c* 1870.)

1803 BEDDOES *Hygeia* x. 35 Many such processes .. are carried on with as high a *verve* or as true fervour as ever accompanied poetic fiction. **1818** LADY MORGAN *Autobiog.* (1859) 233 There is Madame de Genlis, .. approaching her eightieth year, full of *verve*, and announcing her 'Mémoires de Dangeau'. **1872** MORLEY *Voltaire* 327 He .. launched forth during the rest of the meal with his usual verve and fanciful extravagance of imagination. **1879** M. PATTISON *Milton* 172 That thorough enjoyment of the labour, which is necessary to give life and verve to any creation, whether of the poet or the orator. **1894** A. BIRRELL *Ess.* v. 56

Cumberland tells the story with the irresistible verve of falsehood.

3. In general use: Energy, vigour, spirit.

1863 'Ouida' *Held in Bondage* iv. I. 87 There isn't one half the *verve* among you new people there was in my young time. **1885** Miss Braddon *Wyllard's Weird* I. 250 Such a man, not too young nor yet too old,..full of verve and enjoyment of life. **1893** Vizetelly *Glances back* II. xxiv. 48 Thackeray's 'Mahogany Tree', which..[Mayhew] gave in his deep bass voice with uncommon verve.

†**vervecean**, *a.* *Obs.*$^{-0}$ [See next and -EAN.] (See quot.)

1656 Blount *Glossogr.*, *Vervecean*, *Vervecine*, of or belonging to a Weather or Sheep; like a Weather.

'**vervecine**, *a.* *rare.* [a. F. *vervecine* (Rabelais), or ad. L. *vervēcīn-us*, f. *vervēc-is*, *vervex* wether: see -INE¹.] Of or belonging to a sheep.

The first quot. merely follows the burlesque diction of the original text.

1653 Urquhart *Rabelais* II. vi, Goodly vervecine spatules perforaminated with petrosile. **1656** [see prec.]. **1835** Kirby *Hab. & Inst. Anim.* I. xi. 330 The vervecine and ovine hydatids, which penetrate into their [*sc.* sheep's] lungs and liver and occasion the rot.

vervel(l, variants of VARVEL.

†**verven**, obs. variant of FERVENT *a.* 2.

Attributed to a rustic speaker.

1633 B. Jonson *Tale Tub* III. ix, To mark the verven Heart of a Beast.

verven, etc., obs. ff. VERVAIN.

vervens, **vervente**, obs. varr. FERVENCE, FERVENT.

vervet ('vɜːvɪt). *Zool.* [a. F. *vervet* (Cuvier), of obscure origin.] A species of monkey (*Cercopithecus pygerythrus* or *C. lalandii*), native to various parts of Africa. Also *attrib.*

1884 *Imp. Dict.* **1893** Lydekker *Roy. Nat. Hist.* I. 97 Still better known than the malbrouck is the South African vervet monkey. *Ibid.*, The fur of the vervet is of a greyish-green colour. **1897** H. O. Forbes *Hand-bk. Primates* II. 60 The Vervet Guenon..[is] very nearly allied to the Grivet,..the Malbrouck, and..the Green Guenon.

vervil(e, obs. variants of VARVEL.

†**vervise.** *Obs.*$^{-1}$ (See quot. and PLUNKET *sb.*)

1483 *Act 1 Rich. III*, c. 8 §18 Eny Clothe called Vervise, otherwise called Plounkettes, Turkyns, or Celestrines with broode listes.

verwound, southern ME. var. FORWOUND *v.*

very ('vɛrɪ), *a.*, *adv.*, and *sb.*¹ Forms: α. 3-5 (6 *Sc.*) verray (4 verrai, -aie, 6 *Sc.* varray), 4-6 werray (4 werrai, warrai, 6 *Sc.* warray), veray (5-6 veraye, weray), verai; 4-6 verrey (4 verrei, ferrey, 5 werrey), verey (5 uerey, vereye, 7 *Sc.* werey). β. 4-5 verra, 6 *Sc.* vera, werra; 8-9 *Sc.* vera, 9 *Sc.* and *north.* verra; 6-7 (9 *north.*) vara, 9 *Sc.* varra. γ. 4-5 verre (5 vere), 5-6 werre (6 were). δ. 4-5 verri, verry (5, 9 *dial.* werry), 6-7 *Sc.* verrie (6 werrie), 9 *dial.* varry, vurry; 4-6 veri, 5- very (5 vary, 5, 7 *Sc.*, wery), 5-6 verye, 5-7 verie (6 werie, *Sc.* vearie). [a. AF. *verrai*, *verrey*, *verai*, *veray*, OF. *verai*, *varai*, *vrai* (mod.F. *vrai*, Pr. *verai*), f. the stem of L. *vērus* true.]

A. *adj.* **I. 1.** Really or truly entitled to the name or designation; possessing the true character of the person or thing named; properly so called or designated; = TRUE *a.* 5.

Very common from *c* 1300 to *c* 1600; now *rare* except as an echo of Biblical usage.

a. Of persons, or the Deity.

α, β. *c* **1250** *Kent. Serm.* in *O.E. Misc.* 27 Be þet hi offrede gold..seawede þet he was sothfast kink, and be þet hi offrede Stor..seawede þet he was verray prest. *a* **1300** *Cursor M.* 22729 A clude..bar him vp, wonder bright; Warrai man and godd warrai. **13..** *Guy Warw.* 3568 Wele haþ Gij don þat day, As gode kniȝt & verray. *a* **1380** in Horstm. *Altengl. Leg.* (1878) 32/1 A mayden, forsoþe, wente her in, But now forsoþe, as i seo con, Ȝonde sitteþ a verrei mon. *a* **1400-50** *Alexander* 389 A verra victor a-vansid with all þe vayne werde. *c* **1400** Maundev. (Roxb.) xv. 66 He..es a haly prophete and a verray in worde and in dede. **1413** *Pilgr. Sowle* I. xv. (Caxton, 1483) 14 Ihesu,..that were of Mary veray mayd bore in veray flesshe and bloode. *c* **1470** *Gol. & Gaw.* 957 Grant me confort this day, As thow art God verray! **1509** Fisher *Funeral Serm. C'tess Richmond* Wks. (1876) 301 All the lerned men of Englonde to whome she was a veray patronesse. **1521** —— *Serm. agst. Luther* i. Ibid. 313 To be vnto her in all suche stormes a veray comforter. **1533** Gau *Richt Vay* 37 Be this word..he is veray God.

γ, δ. *c* **1380** Wyclif *Sel. Wks.* III. 310 Siþ Crist, verrest bischop of alle, cursede not for his tiþes. *c* **1403** Lydg. *Temple Glas* 571 Nou am I cauȝt vnder subiecciou̅n, Forto be a verre homagere, To god of loue. *c* **1450** *Myrroure our Ladye* 323 Thow arte the certayne hope of wretches, very mother of motherlesse. *c* **1460** *Wisdom* 15 in *Macro Plays* 36 Þe belowyde sone.., Spows of þe chyrche, & wery patrone. **1526** Tindale *Mark* xi. 32 All men counted Ihon, that he was a veri prophett. *a* **1548** Hall *Chron., Hen. VI*, 150 b, She had one poynt of a very woman,..she was..mutable, and turnyng. **1549** *Bk. Com. Prayer, Comm. Creed*, Very God of very God. **1574** tr. *Marlorat's Apocalips* 21 In respect wherof he is called the sonne of man, that is too say, verie man. **1615** Bedwell *Moham. Imp.* II. §53 God is a very spirit. *a* **1680** Butler *Rem.* (1759) I. 102 Th' are very Men, not Things That move by Puppet-work. **1801** Mar. Edgeworth *Moral T., Mlle. Panache* (1832) 252, 'I confess, I am a very woman,' said Lady Augusta, with a sigh. **1854** Trench *Synonyms* §8 (ed. 2) 30 But he is ἀληθινός,..*very* God, as distinguished from idols and all other false gods. **1857** Hawthorne *Eng. Note-Bks.* (1870) II. 329 Thence we went into Queen Mary's room, and saw that beautiful portrait—that very queen and very woman.

b. Of abstract things, conditions, or qualities.

α. *a* **1300** *Cursor M.* 26103 And þan we sal þe pointes rede þat warrai scrifte al of has nede. **13..** *E.E. Allit. P.* A. 1184 So was hit me dere þat þou con deme, In þys veray avysyoun. *c* **1380** Wyclif *Sel. Wks.* I. 15 For riȝt-wisnesse generaly is fulfillinge of lawe, and so fulfillinge of Goddis lawe is verrei riȝt-wisnesse. *c* **1412** Hoccleve *De Reg. Princ.* 3313 Mercy..Of herte is a verray compassioun Of othir menys harm. *c* **1440** *Pallad. on Husb.* IX. 91 The fertilitee Of withi, reede, aller, yvy, or vyne That ther is water nygh is verrey signe. *c* **1470** Henry *Wallace* I. 3 Our antecessowris..We lat ourslide, throw werray sleuthfulnes. **1539** Cromwell in Merriman *Life & Lett.* (1902) II. 202 Under the colour of a veray peax, whiche is neuertheles but a cloked and furred peax. **1562** Winȝet *Cert. Tractatis* i. Wks. (S.T.S.) I. 12 Thre of the gretast ydolis,..verray ydolis in deid.

β, δ. **1303** R. Brunne *Handl. Synne* 1659 Þere was verry matrymony, with oute fleshly dede of any. *c* **1380** Wyclif *Sel. Wks.* I. 315 Crist axiþ here mekenes and poverte, wiþ verri pees. **1422** Yonge tr. *Secreta Secret., Priv. Priv.* 146 This goodis of Fortune or of kynde..be not werry goodys, for now thay byth, and now thay bythagone. *c* **1450** *Merlin* i. 11 Thou..haste very repentaunce of herte. *Ibid.* 13, I haue very trust on god, that [etc.]. **1486** *Bk. St. Albans* a ij, Therfore thys book fowlowyng in a dew forme shewys veri knawlege of suche plesure. **1526** *Pilgr. Perf.* (W. de W. 1531) 24 A generall syght of yᵉ principles & processe of very religyon. **1540-1** Elyot *Image Gov.* 7 The moste precioust garment of verie nobilitee. **1572** J. Jones *Bathes Buckstone* 5 Which wee abusively call worldely wealth, when as very wealth, is health. **1651** Hobbes *Leviath.* II. xxvi. 147 Also, Unwritten Customes..by the tacite consent of the Emperour..are very Lawes. *a* **1679** —— *Rhet.* xvi. (1681) 39 The written Law is but seeming justice; the Law of Nature very justice. **1868** Morris *Earthly Par.* I. 58 Half dead with very death still drawing nigh.

c. Of material things.

a **1330** *Roland & V.* 129 For to wite þe soþe þere, Ȝif þe relikes verray were. *c* **1375** *Sc. Leg. Saints* xvii. (*Martha*) 188 Scho..bad þame hyre in askis lay, & schaw til hyre a croice verra. *c* **1449** Pecock *Repr.* II. ix. 193 Ech lyuyng man is verier..ymage of Crist..than is eny vnquyk stok. **1495** *Trevisa's Barth. De P.R.* XVI. xlvii. 569 It is harde..to knowe betwene the very precyous stones and fals. **1555** Eden *Decades* (Arb.) 356 Many bouwes and branches,..muche like vnto verye trees that are in owlde woddes. **1581** Pettie *Guazzo's Civ. Conv.* I. (1586) 23 The other parts which we call compound, or instrumentall, which are the verie members of the bodie. **1592** Timme *Ten Eng. Lepers* K j b, They which are out of their wittes do not see the verie things, but the fantasies of their passion. **1678** Hobbes *Decam.* ix. 106 Such Iron were indeed a very and vigorous Loadstone.

†**d.** Full, thorough, unqualified. *Obs.*

1446 in Willis & Clark *Cambridge* (1886) I. 339 The said maister..shal do his verray diligence to pourvey..a place as gode. **1496** *Rolls of Parlt.* VI. 512/1 The said Quene is of verrey will and mynde, that the same Erle shall be truly and fully contented.

†**e.** *spec.* in *Law.* (See quot. 1607.) *Obs.*

1544 tr. *Littleton's Tenures* (1574) 96 b, But if it be verye lord and verye tenaunt, and the tenaunte maketh a feoffement in fee. [So Coke *On Litt.* (1628) 269.] **1607** Cowell *Interpr.* s.v., Very Lord, and very Tenent,..are they that be immediate Lord & Tenent one to the other.

2. With limitation (usually expressed by *the* or a possessive) to particular instances: The true or real; that is truly or properly entitled to the name. Now *arch.* **a.** Of material things or places.

c **1375** *Sc. Leg. Saints* xix. (*Christopher*) 61 Þe king can ma þe takine of þe croice verra on hyme. **1387** Trevisa *Higden* (Rolls) I. 255 Ysidre seiþ þat verray [L. *proprie dicta*] Germania haþ in þe est side þe mouth of þe ryuer Danubius. **1414** *Lay Folks Mass Bk.* App. ii. 120 The materyall bred that was before is turnyd into Chrystys verray body. *c* **1450** *Merlin* xx. 329 Than he made vpon hym the signe of the very crosse. **1526** *Pilgr. Perf.* (W. de W. 1531) 4 Theyr iourney..signifyeth the iourney to yᵉ very Jerusalem. **1535** Coverdale *John* vi. 55 For my flesh is yᵉ very meate, and my bloude is yᵉ very drynke. **1567** *Gude & Godlie B.* (S.T.S.) 61 He is the way, trothe, lyfe, and lycht, The varray [*v.r.* verray, verie] port, till heaven full rycht. **1651** Hobbes *Leviath.* I. i. 4 Though..the reall, and very object seem invested with the fancy it begets in us. **1849** Neale *Hymns for Sick* (1906) 26 Thy very Flesh and Blood.

b. Of abstract things, conditions, etc.

c **1374** Chaucer *Boeth.* III. pr. iii. (1868) 69 And by a maner þouȝt..ȝe looken from a fer til þilk verray fyn of blisfulnesse. *c* **1400** Maundev. (1839) xii. 139 Thei that scholden ben converted to Crist..ben thorghe oure Wykkednesse..fer fro us and straungeres fro the holy and verry Beleeve. *c* **1449** Pecock *Repr.* I. xii. 65 But the trewe and verry vndirstonding ther of is this. *c* **1465** *Pol., Rel., & L. Poems* (1903) 3 Þe welfare of Edward Rex moste riall, That is þe verie purpos that we labure fore. *c* **1470** *Gol. & Gaw.* 161 The verray cause of his come I knew noght the cace. **1526** *Pilgr. Perf.* (W. de W. 1531) 1 b, Euery religious persone sholde intende the perfeccyon of his soule, whiche is the very peace of the spiryte. **1538** Starkey *England* I. i. 10 Thys ys the veray true and cyuyle lyfe. **1577** *St. Aug. Manual* (Longman) 106 The very wisedome of God shall shew himselfe to them. **1647** Saltmarsh *Sparkles Glory* (1847) 80 Pastors,..who cannot now minister as the oracles of God, nor according to the very gifts of the Holy Ghost then. **1859** Gen. P. Thompson *Audi Alt. Part.* II. lxxxvii. 57 The vulgar animosity against a skin,—the stamp of lowly-mindedness, and very indication of cart blood.

c. Of persons or the Deity.

c **1450** *Mirour Saluacioun* 3 Xrist, goddes verray son and wysdame. **1456** Sir G. Haye *Law Arms* (S.T.S.) 24 The verray pape sanct Innocent had bene put out [by a false pope]. **1523** [Coverdale] *Old God & New* (1534) B j, After yᵗ yᵉ eternall & the verye god had shewed hym selfe vnto Adam. **1548-9** (Mar.) *Bk. Com. Prayer, Comm., Pref. Easter* 126 He is the very Pascall Lambe. **1567** *Gude & Godlie Ball.* (S.T.S.) 184 The Priestis..ar the verray Antichristis. **1600** Shaks. *A.Y.L.* IV. i. 71 What would you say to me now, and I were your verie, verie Rosalind? **1613** Purchas *Pilgrimage* (1614) 21 His minde was enlightened to know the onely very God.

†**d.** Proper, correct. *Obs.*$^{-1}$

c **1410** *Master of Game* (MS. Digby 182) xv, Þough þer be alauntes of alle hewese, þe verrey hewe of þe good alauntes..shuld be white with a blake spotte aboute þe eres.

3. In emphatic use, denoting that the person or thing may be so named in the fullest sense of the term, or possesses all the essential qualities of the thing specified. Cf. VERITABLE *a.* 3.

Common from *c* 1550 to *c* 1700; now chiefly in the superlative, freq. qualifying something bad, objectionable, or undesirable. Occasionally repeated in order to give additional emphasis.

a. With *a* or *the* preceding (or rarely without article), or with pl. sb.

(*a*) **1384** Chaucer *L.G.W.* 259 (*Prol.*), Thow thynkist in thyn wit..That he nys but a verray propre fole. **1484** Caxton *Fables of Auian* vi, He..is a very fole. **1535** Coverdale *2 Kings* xxii. 19 They shall become a very desolacion and curse. **1545** Brinklow *Compl.* xxv. 75 Euery one of them is become a very Nero. **1576** Gascoigne *Kenelworth Castle* Wks. 1910 II. 122 Heaven was not heaven, it was rather a verye Hell. **1609** Holland *Amm. Marcell.* F j b, When he was dead, Valentinian his sonne a very childe, was by the army stiled Augustus. **1662** Petty *Taxes* 83 Not to rate..wool until it be cloth, or rather until it be a very garment. **1693** Dryden *Juvenal* vi. 592 When Poor, she's scarce a tollerable Evil; But Rich, and Fine, a Wife's a very Devil. **1711** Steele *Spect.* No. 157 ¶1 Marius was then a very Boy. **1771** Franklin *Autobiog.* Wks. 1840 I. 55 The attorney was a very knave. **1826** Disraeli *Viv. Grey* III. vi, Yes, it is madness; very, very madness. **1829** Scott *Anne of G.* xxi, Sigismund Biederman will aid him willingly, and he is a very horse at labour. **1888** J. Inglis *Tent Life in Tigerland* 1 North Bhangulpore..is admittedly even for India a very sportman's paradise.

(*b*) **1593** Hooker *Eccl. Pol.* II. vii. §6 Which insolency must be repressed, or it will be the very bane of Christian religion. **1648** *Art. Peace* in *Milton's Wks.* (1851) IV. 546 The intermedling of Governours and Parties in this Kingdom, with Sidings and Parties in England, have been the very betraying of this Kingdom to the Irish. **1712** Addison *Spect.* No. 393 ¶2 A Region, which is the very Reverse of Paradise. **1729** Law *Serious C.* xiv. 234 Mortification, of all kinds, is the very life and soul of piety. **1779** Warner in Jesse *Selwyn & Contemp.* (1844) IV. 308 And then for owls, it is their very kingdom. **1872** Morley *Voltaire* 5 Voltaire was the very eye of modern illumination. **1883** *Manch. Exam.* 29 Nov. 5/4 The atmosphere of most of the courts..is the very reverse of healthy.

b. With *a* inserted between the adj. and the sb. qualified, esp. *as* or *so very a.* Cf. SO *adv.* 14 d. Now *rare* or *Obs.*

1560 Daus tr. *Sleidane's Comm.* 405 There can no man be imagined so very a coward or so barbarouse. **1565** Cooper *Thesaurus*, *Adæque miser*, euen as very a wretch. **1573-80** Tusser *Husb.* (1878) 69 For oftentimes seene, no more verie a knaue than he that doth counterfait most to be graue. **1634** W. Tirwhyt tr. *Balzac's Lett.* (vol. I) 352, I will onely content myself to protest that you were never so very a poet, as when you spake of me. **1667** Pepys *Diary* 29 July, He is as very a wencher as can be. **1704** J. Trapp *Abra-Mulé* III. i. 1047 Thou cam'st to find as very a Madman As ever rav'd in Chains. **1739** A. Hill in *Richardson's Corr.* (1804) I. 36, I was so very a boy when I suffered that light piece of work to be published, that [etc.]. **1747-8** Richardson *Ibid.* I. 182 A thing..so very a nothing in itself. **1804** H. Martin *Helen of Glenross* IV. 118 So very a soldier. **1828** Scott *Tapestr. Chamb.* ¶47, I sank back in a swoon, as very a victim to panic terror as ever was a village girl. **1844** C. Macfarlane *Camp of Refuge* v. (1897) 77 Without knowing..how very a prisoner she is in her own manor-house.

c. In the comp. verier and (in later use more commonly) the superl. veriest.

(*a*) **1548** Cooper *Elyot's Dict.* s.v. *Certus*, There is no veryer knaue. **1579** Tomson *Calvin's Serm. Tim.* 767/1 The Lord will..suffer vs to come home verier fooles and doltes then wee went. **1648** *Hunting of Fox* 40 Your selves, veryer beasts then the hogs you lost. **1681** Flavel *Meth. Grace* vii. 145 To represent it as a verier trifle, and needless thing than these his agents have done. *a* **1701** Maundrell *Journ. Jerus.* (1732) 94 Where the stump of the Tree stood it meets with not a few Visitants so much veryer stocks than it self, as to fall down and worship it. **1735** Pope *Donne's Sat.* iv. 28 A verier monster than on Africk's shore, The Sun e'er got, or slimy Nilus bore. **1814** Southey '*Who counsels peace?*' iv, All too long in blood had he been nurst, And ne'er was earth with verier tyrant curst. **1840** Clough *Dipsychus* II. vi. 111 A verier Mercury, express come down To do the world with swift arithmetic. **1856** Aytoun *Bothwell* (1857) 8 A verier knave ne'er stepped the earth.

(*b*) **1530** Palsgr. 327/2 [The] Veryest foole, *le plus fol.* **1571** Digges *Pantom.* I. xxx. K j b, He hath erred euen in the principall, and as I might tearme them the veriest trifles. **1581** Pettie *Guazzo's Civ. Conv.* III. (1586) 126, I know not which of these two sortes are the veriest fooles. **1630** Prynne *Anti-Armin.* 155 He is no more..for the Elect, than hee is for the veriest Reprobate. **1695** Congreve *Love for L.* III. vi, I swear Mr. Benjamin is the verriest Wag in nature; an absolute Sea-wit. **1709** Steele *Tatler* No. 11 ¶5 His Sons and his Sons Sons, have all of 'em been the veriest Rogues living. **1742** Blair *Grave* 642 The veryest Gluttons do not always cram. **1780** *Mirror* No. 104, From the same causes, the veriest trifle..had become to him an object of importance. **1833** Chalmers *Const. Man* (1835) I. ii. 129 There is no enjoyment whatever in the veriest hell of assembled outcasts. **1859** Kingsley *Misc.* (1860) I. 227 Poetry, which read by the veriest schoolboy makes music of itself. **1878** Huxley *Physiogr.* 200 Even the deep sinking at the Rosebridge Colliery is but the veriest dent in the earth's surface.

4. †**a.** Truthful, true; sure, reliable. *Obs.*

a **1300** *Cursor M.* 3473 Oure lauerd..Had don hir in to sikernes, Thoru his werrai prophecie, Quat suld be þaa childer vie. **1303** R. BRUNNE *Handl. Synne* 9965 þese wurdes are verry and clere; Dauyd hem seyth yn þe sautere. **1375** BARBOUR *Bruce* II. 87 Sekyrly I hop that Thomas prophecy Off Hersildoune sall verray be. In him. *c* **1450** *Mirour Saluacioun* 34 Come lord yt thi prophets be fonden lele and verray. *c* **1450** *Harl. Contin. Higden* (Rolls) VIII. 516 A verey prove cowthe not be hade in that mater, wherefore the kynge grawntede to þeim bothe theire lyves. *a* **1505** *Chron. Lond.* (Kingsford) 222 This yere..came veray tydynges vnto the kyng.. that the frensh kyng was dede.

b. Of truth: Exact, simple, real, actual.

c **1386** CHAUCER *Sqr.'s T.* 158 This is a verray sooth with outen glose. *c* **1400** *Laud Troy Bk.* 66 Herkenes now, and ȝe may here The werre sothe alle plenere. *c* **1425** LYDG. *Assembly of Gods* 1226 And I shall yow tell the verrey sothe of all. **1483** CAXTON *G. de la Tour* e vij b, And alle this is very trouthe. **1534** MORE *Comf. agst. Trib.* II. Wks. 1193/2 If he..can by no meane be shogged oute of his deadde slepe, but wil nedes take hys dreame for a verye trouth. **1597** SHAKS. *2 Hen. IV*, III. ii. 237 In very truth, sir, I had as lief be hang'd sir, as goe. **1611** FLORIO, *Verità*, truth, veritie, verie-sooth. **1668** CULPEPPER & COLE *Barthol. Anat.* I. v. 8 To speak the very truth. **1850** HAWTHORNE *Scarlet L.* xi. (1852) 133 He had spoken the very truth, and transformed it into the veriest falsehood. **1882** MYERS *Teneriffe* vii, And is the World's in very truth An impercipient Soul?

†**c.** Of decisions, etc.: Just, true. *Obs.*

c **1440** *Gesta Rom.* I. xlvii. 202 (Addit. MS.), Therfore we are turned agayn, to here a verry dome, what is for to done of this thynge. **1483** CAXTON *Gold. Leg.* 86 b/1 Alle they meruaylled and said that thys was a veray and ryght good answere of the question.

†**d.** ***of very*** (***due***) ***right***, justly, properly, rightly, truly. *Obs.*

?*a* **1366** CHAUCER *Rom. Rose* 1627 This welle is clepid, as welle is knowen, The welle of Love, of verray right. *c* **1430** LYDG. *Min. Poems* (Percy Soc.) 7 Fortune gaff him eke prosperite, and richesse, Withe scripture appering in ther sighte, To him applyed of verray dew righte. *c* **1440** —— *Hors, Shepe & G.* 57 Eques, ab 'equo' is seid of verray riht And cheualere is saide of cheualrye. **1470–85** MALORY *Arthur* x. lxxxvi. 565, I and ony knyght..oughte of veray ryght socoure and rescowe soo noble a knyghte as ye are. **1526** *Pilgr. Perf.* (W. de W. 1531) 117 He that of very ryght owed ye cappe.

e. ***in*** (or †***of***) ***very deed***: see DEED *sb.* 5 c.

†**5. a.** Exact or precise, as opposed to *approximate*; = TRUE *a.* 4. *Obs.*

1338 R. BRUNNE *Chron.* (1810) 83 How mykelle lond & rent holy kirke had to a prowe, Alle þei did enditte to witte þe verrey valowe. **1382** WYCLIF *Deut.* xxv. 15 Weiȝt thow shalt haue iust and verrey, and euen busshel and verrey shal be to thee. *c* **1391** CHAUCER *Astrol.* I. §17 Euermo this cercle equinoxial turnyth Iustly fro verrey est to verrey west. **1463** *Bury Wills* (Camden) 40 The seid places with the portenances [to] be soold to the verrey valew. **1485** *10th Rep. Hist. MSS. Comm.* App. V. 318 The veray value of the same. **1577** B. GOOGE *Heresbach's Husb.* II. (1586) 53 The verie time, as Theophrastus writeth, is at the spring. **1594** WEST *Symbol.* II. *Chancerie* §95 Gently requiring him..to deliver..such and so many of the said sheepe,..or the verie value thereof. **1652** NEEDHAM tr. *Selden's Mare Cl.* 33 They are not well agreed about the very particular place. **1657** TRAPP *Comm. Job* xxxix. 25 Horses will perceive aforehand the very time of the fight.

b. Of a copy, writing, etc. *Obs.* (Cf. 10 c.)

1470–85 MALORY *Arthur* XIX. xiii. 796 And by cause I haue lost the very mater of la cheualer du charyot I departe from the tale of sir Launcelot. *a* **1548** HALL *Chron., Hen. VII*, 49 b, His awne confession written with hys awne hande, the very copy wherof hereafter ensueth.

†**6.** Of a friend, servant, etc.: True, faithful, sincere, staunch; = TRUE *a.* 1. *Obs.*

Very common in the 16th c. In later use perh. merely intensive.

c **1385** CHAUCER *L.G.W.* 1686 *Lucretia*, To..drawe to memorye The verry wif, the verry trewe Lucresse. *c* **1386** —— *Wife's T.* 348 Pouerte a spectakele is, as thynkyth me, Thorw whech he may his veray frend i-see. *a* **1475** G. ASHBY *Dicta Philos.* 245 Who that cannat disseure wise from bad Shal haue no verrey freendes þat be sad. *c* **1487–1500** in Willis & Clark *Cambridge* (1886) I. 474 Your verrey bedeman the provost of the kynges College. **1532** CROMWELL in Merriman *Life & Lett.* (1902) I. 347 My veraye Frend and Felow Mr. John Welsborne. **1584** B. R. tr. *Herodotus* To Rdr., I ende. Your very friende. B. R. **1607** R. C[AREW] tr. *Estienne's World of Wonders* 283 A gentlewoman of Lorraine, my very friend. **1608** ROWLANDS *Humors Looking Gl.* 14 A Gentleman a verie friend of mine. **1676** WYCHERLEY *Pl. Dealer* III. i, Sir, Sir, your very Servant; I was afraid you had forgotten me.

†**7. a.** Of persons: Truly or rightfully standing in a certain position or relationship; rightful, lawful, legitimate. *Obs.*

?**1461** *Paston Lett.* II. 68, I am very heyre, by the disceas of my fader, to a place called Keswyk. **1495** *Act 11 Hen. VII*, c. 56 Preamble, Landes..to the whiche the vere owners be now restored by dyvers actes. **1513** *Test. Ebor.* (Surtees) V. 51, I do give my full power..unto my saide suster Lucie, and I do charge hir, as she is very mother of my saide nece [etc.]. **1545** *Charters rel. Glasgow* (1906) II. 509 His varray lawful cessionaris, donatouris and assignais. **1568** GRAFTON *Chron.* (1809) II. 105 Neither King Edward himselfe nor the Duke of Clarence were lawfully begotten, nor were they very children of the Duke of Yorke. **1606** *Munim. Melros* (Bann. Cl.) 657 We..constitutis..Oure verrie lauchfull vndoubtit and irreuocabill Procuratouris, actoris, factoris [etc.].

transf. **1570–6** LAMBARDE *Peramb. Kent* (1826) 203 In the yeere, 1146, was founded Boxley in Kent, the verie daughter of Clarevalle.

b. Legally valid or established. *Obs.*

1475 *Bk. Noblesse* (Roxb.) 24 To be put in rememoraunce of youre auncien enheritaunce, verray right and title in youre duchies of Gascoigne and Guien. **1487** *Munim. Melros* (Bann. Cl.) 618 þe Abbot..hes verray richt to þe erde siluer of þe quer of þe said Kirk.

II. 8. a. Used as an intensive, either to denote the inclusion of something regarded as extreme or exceptional, or to emphasize the exceptional prominence of some ordinary thing or feature.

In very common use from the 16th cent. With slight change of syntax the sense may commonly be expressed by the advs. 'even' or 'actually'. Various types of context (with *the*, possessives, etc.) are illustrated in the several groups of quotations; the use in (*d*) is now obsolete, and that in (*c*) a rare archaism.

(*a*) *c* **1386** CHAUCER *Nun's Pr. T.* 565 Ran cow and calf, and eek the verray hogges Sore fered were for berkyng of dogges. **1526** TINDALE *Luke* ii. 35 The swearde shall pearce the very hert off the. **1535** COVERDALE *Ps.* xcvi. 6 The very heauens declare his rightuousnes, & all people se his glory. **1590** SIR J. SMYTH *Disc. Weapons* Ded. 8 b, All Coronells and Captaines of footmen, yea euen the verie Lieutenants generalls. **1632** J. HAYWARD tr. *Biondi's Eromena* 180 Sore was she troubled with vomiting, so as having nothing in her stomack, she cast up the very pure bloud. **1655** FULLER *Ch. Hist.* IV. 184 The Provost..being provided for in all particulars, to the very points of his hose. **1712** STEELE *Spect.* No. 306 ¶1 It goes to the very Soul of me to speak what I really think of my Face. **1728** POPE *Dunc.* III. Notes (1736) 223 All tastes and degrees of men, from those of the highest quality to the very rabble. **1782** MISS BURNEY *Cecilia* VII. ix, The very air was rent with cries. **1823** SCOTT *Quentin D.* xxxiii, He flew like the very wind. **1832** WARREN *Diary Late Physic.* II. iii. 122 The room was crammed to the very door. **1874** GREEN *Short Hist.* iii. §5 (1882) 140 The very retainers of the royal household turned robbers. **1891** 'J. S. WINTER' *Lumley* xv, It's absurd on the very face of it.

(*b*) **1535** COVERDALE *Hab.* iii. 2 In thy very wrath thou thinkest vpon mercy. **1563** *Homilies* II. *Rogation Week* iv. ¶2 To striue for our very rightes and dueties, with the breche of loue & charitie,..is vtterly forbydden. **1595** *Locrine* I. i. 68 A greater care torments my verie bones. **1600** in Morris *Troubles Cath. Foref.* (1872) I. iv. 194 Oftentimes their very beds they lie upon..are sold before their faces. **1620** T. GRANGER *Div. Logike* 100 Yet in their verie mutuall relation there is also force of arguing to explicate a sentence. **1681** DRYDEN *Abs. & Archit.* To Rdr., The Chyrurgeon's work of an *Ense rescindendum*, which I wish not to my very Enemies. **1705** tr. *Bosman's Guinea* 27 You may imagine what Case we were in when one of them began to hack our very doors with an Ax. **1768** GOLDSM. *Good-n. Man* I. i, His very mirth is an antidote to all gaiety. **1807** CRABBE *Par. Reg.* I. 725 His very soul was not his own. **1831** CARLYLE *Sart. Res.* I. i, That we do not..see what is passing under our very eyes. **1836** J. H. NEWMAN *Par. Serm.* (1837) III. vi. 86 The plain and solemn sense which they bear on their very front. **1880** MCCARTHY *Own Times* III. xlvii. 433 His very defects were a main cause of his popularity.

(*c*) **1548** UDALL, etc. *Erasm. Par. John* 118 b, So nowe they sawe certainly at very hande the thing to be true. **1561** T. HOBY tr. *Castiglione's Courtyer* II. (1577) K iij, There needeth no art, bicause very nature hir selfe createth and shapeth men apt to expresse pleasantly. **1571** DIGGES *Pantom.* I. xvii. E iij b, And yet in conueying of waters any great distance, very experience wil bewray an error. **1609** BIBLE (Douay) *Numb.* xiv. *comm.*, It is so absolutely necessarie in everie communitie to have one Superior of al, that verie mutiners themselves do ever choose such a one. **1617** MORYSON *Itin.* I. 233 They keepe the Roman Lent, but more strictly, abstaining from Fish, and very Oyle (which they use for butter). **1649** EARL MONM. tr. *Senault's Use Passions* (1671) 81 The noise of Trumpets puts them in good humor, and..very hurts do animate their courage. **1657** CROMWELL in *Burton's Diary* (1828) II. 329 Their greatest persecution hath been of the people of God,..as I think very experiences will sufficiently demonstrate. **1851** KEBLE *Occas. Papers & Rev.* (1877) 240 By the way in which things are managed all Apostolic authority is denied in the Church, and very unbelievers may settle what we are to believe.

(*d*) **1616** in J. Russell *Haigs* (1881) vii. 158 For fear that his very being my brother left..some impression of the truth of his accusations. **1665** BOYLE *Occas. Refl.* v. x. (1675) 335 Those Beams, which derive a new Glory from their very being broken.

b. Emphasizing sbs. which denote extremity of degree or extent.

c **1391** CHAUCER *Astrol.* II. §1 Ley thi reule vp that same day, & thanne wol the verray point of thy rewle sitten in the bordure, vp-on the degree of thy sonne. **1530** PALSGR. 806/1 At the very dawnyng of the daye. *Ibid.* 820/1 In the very myddes..of a thyng. **1560** BIBLE (Geneva) *John* viii. 4 The Scribes..said,..Master, this woman was taken in adulterie, in the verie act. **1565** ALLEN *Def. Purgat.* (1886) 3 That matter which..I perceived of all other causes in the world, most to touch the very core of heresy. **1590** SWINBURNE *Testaments* 61 He that is at the very pointe of death. **1605** CAMDEN *Rem.* 1 It cannot be impertinent, at the verie enterance, to say somewhat of Britaine. **1609** HOLLAND *Amm. Marcell.* 116 From the very brims of Tigris banke, as farre as to Euphrates, there was no greene thing left. **1771** LUCKOMBE *Hist. Printing* 401 He..then draws the lower part of that noose close up to the very corner of it. **1851** GALLENGA *Italy* 359 The Milan government, we are informed, was a bankrupt from the very outset. **1872** *Routledge's Ev. Boy's Ann.* 347/1 Reduce this movement to the very minimum. **1878** BROWNING *La Saisiaz* 18 Quiet slow sure money-making proves the matter's very root.

†**c.** Qualifying pronouns in order to give emphasis. Sometimes emphasizing identity (cf. sense 10 b). *Obs.*

1542 UDALL *Erasm. Apoph.* 281, I wys even veray I myself am ye manne. **1548** —— *Erasm. Par. Luke* i. 17 And verai he shal be the expectacion of all nacions. **1561** T. HOBY tr. *Castiglione's Courtyer* I. (1577) E v, For very such make the greatnesse and gorgeousnesse of an Oration. **1624** QUARLES *Job* xv. 26 I'm turn'd a laughing-stock To boyes, & those, that su'd to tend my Flock,..these (euen very these) Flout at my sorrowes. **1632** HOLLAND *Cyrupædia* 200 And this is even very she, whom you..were wont to sport with. *a* **1701** SEDLEY *Venus & Ad.* Wks. (1766) 56, I am ty'd to very thee By ev'ry thought I have.

d. Coupled with *own*.

1863 KINGLAKE *Crimea* (1877) I. vi. 89 A prince who wielded with his own very hand the power of All the Russias. **1884** MRS. EWING *Mary's Meadow* (1886) 72, I had to have it, for my very own.

9. a. Neither more nor less than (that expressed by the sb. qualified); exactly that specified without qualification; = SHEER *a.* 8.

Qualifying abstract nouns, esp. those denoting emotions or conditions, and usually following a prep., esp. *for*.

c **1386** CHAUCER *Frankl. T.* 132 For verray feere so wolde hir herte quake. *a* **1440** *Partonope* 849 She gynneth to wepe For verray joye. **1456** SIR G. HAYE *Law Arms* (S.T.S.) 69 [He] throu verray fors was the first lord of that realme. **1463** *Bury Wills* (Camden) 37, I yeve..to my neve..my best purs ..and xxli. to put ther inne,.. and wil he be servyd apart with the fyrst, of verray love. **1535** COVERDALE *Zech.* viii. 4 Soch as go with staues in their hondes for very age. **1568** GRAFTON *Chron.* II. 168 The Sommer was so hote that men dyed with very heat. **1577** HOLINSHED *Hist. Scot.* in *Chron.* I. 157/1 Through verie dipleasure of suche iniuries as shee daylye susteyned at the handes of his concubines, shee founde meanes to strangle him. **1671** MILTON *P.R.* IV. 12 As a man who..for very spight Still will be tempting him who foyls him still.

1812 CRABBE *Tales* xviii. 73 Fondly she pleaded and would gently sigh, For very pity, or she knew not why. **1849** MACAULAY *Hist. Eng.* ii. I. 191 The sailors mutinied from very hunger. **1878** *Masque Poets* 31 For veriest joy her red mouth laughs.

b. With a limiting or restrictive force: That alone to the exclusion of any thing else; = MERE *a.*[2] 5.

1546 *Yorks. Chantry Surv.* (Surtees) 495 Having no other promocions but theyre verye stipende or wages. **1574** BOURNE *Regiment for Sea* xix. (1577) 50 b, Then haue they no other helpe but onely the very account of the shippes way. **1611** SHAKS. *Cymb.* II. iv. 9 Your very goodnesse, and your company, Ore-payes all I can do. **1618** in Gutch *Coll. Cur.* II. 424 There be..17,000 Sheets of paper in that Book, which, upon ordinary account, cometh to eight hundred and fifty pound, the very writing. **1657** CROMWELL *Speech* 23 Jan. (*Carlyle*), So give me leaue, in a very word or two, to congratulate with you. **1703** ROWE *Fair Penit.* I. i, At thy very Name My eager Heart springs up. *Ibid.*, Sure 'tis the very Error of my Eyes. **1817** JAS. MILL *Brit. India* II. v. vii. 595 The Governor-General treated the very request as a high offence. **1843** A. W. PUGIN *Apol. Reviv. Chr. Archit.* 40 The very weight and massiveness of the work causing it frequently to settle and give. **1894** P. H. HUNTER *Jas. Inwick* xii. 153 The verra mention o' Tod-Lowrie's name was eneuch.

10. Used (after *the*, *this*, *that*, etc.) to denote or emphasize complete or exact identity: **a.** Of points of time.

1582 N. T. (Rhem.) *Luke* x. 20 In that very houre he reioyced in spirit, and said [etc.]. **1610** DAY *Festivals* i. (1615) 20 Even in this nicke of time, this very, very instant. **1617** MORYSON *Itin.* I. 193 The bell of that Church was sounded upon the verie day of Saint Bartholmew. **1683** *Brit. Spec.* Pref. p. ii, To which..this our Island has been so fortunate as to have been subjected from its very first being inhabited to this very Day. *a* **1721** PRIOR *Down-Hall* xxviii, Come this very instant. **1738** SWIFT *Pol. Conversat.* 141 She died just this very Day Seven Years. **1796** STEDMAN *Surinam* I. i. 29 On the very day of our debarkation. **1818** CRUISE *Digest* (ed. 2) II. 268 It is a rule of law..that a remainder must vest, either during the continuance of the preceding estate, or at the very instant of its determination. **1820** KEATS *St. Agnes* xiv, My lady fair the conjuror plays This very night. **1849** MACAULAY *Hist. Eng.* v. I. 643 Jeffreys gave directions that Alice Lisle should be burned alive that very afternoon.

b. In general use.

In quots. under (*b*) corresponding to a defining clause which follows the sb.

1598 SHAKS. *Merry W.* II. i. 84 Why this is..the very hand: the very words. **1605** —— *Macb.* I. vii. 76 When we haue mark'd with blood those sleepie two.., and vs'd their very Daggers. **1611** BIBLE *Ps.* xxxv. 8 Into that very destruction let him fall. **1657** SPARROW *Bk. Com. Prayer* 22 We are taught to pray, 'And lead us not into temptation',.. which very method holy church here wisely imitates. **1661** *Act 13 Chas. II*, c. 9 §6 All the Papers..shall bee duely preserved and..the very Originals sent up intirely and without fraud to the Court of Admiralty. **1712** ARBUTHNOT *John Bull* III. i, Timothy Trim; whom they did, in their conscience, believe to be the very prisoner. **1771** LUCKOMBE *Hist. Print.* 390 We put neither folio nor any thing else over the very Dedication. **1818** SCOTT *Hrt. Midl.* xxxv, 'Young woman,' said he, 'your sister's case must certainly be termed a hard one'. 'God bless you, sir, for that very word!' said Jeanie. **1836** J. GILBERT *Chr. Atonem.* vii. (1852) 201 It must be made apparent, that what was demanded of human nature was the perfection of that very human nature. **1875** JOWETT *Plato* (ed. 2) I. 394 First of all answer this very question.

(*b*) **1641** J. SHUTE *Sarah & Hagar* (1649) 151 We have but little reason to expect, that God should gratifie us in the very individual thing that we desire. **1681** DRYDEN *Abs. & Achit.* I. 61 Those very Jews who at their very best Their Humour more than Loyalty exprest Now wondred. **1705** STANHOPE *Paraphr.* III. 566 Each are continually intent upon that very thing, to which Each are respectively appointed. **1780** *Mirror* No. 99, The supposition, that this is the very character which Shakespeare meant to allot him. **1796** JANE AUSTEN *Pride & Prej.* x, Seeking the acquaintance of some of those very people, against whom his pride had revolted. **1857** BUCKLE *Hist. Civiliz.* I. i. 6 They..take for granted the very question at issue. **1891** *Law Times* XC. 463/1 The contents of the deed were falsely stated by the very person who ought to have advised her on such legal matters.

c. Of words: Exactly corresponding to those of an original or previous statement.

1598 [see b]. **1778** JEFFERSON *Autobiog.* App., Wks. 1859 I. 146 Preserving, however, the very words of the established law. **1838–9** HALLAM *Hist. Lit.* II. II. i. §57. 51 He has neglected to quote the very words of his authorities. **1865** KINGSLEY *Herew.* xv, I said it, I said it. Those were my very words!

d. ***the very thing***, the thing exactly suitable or requisite.

1768 STERNE *Sent. Journ., Montreuil* (1778) I. 90 It occurr'd to me that *that* was the very thing. **1802** MRS. J. WEST *Infidel Father* II. 123 This behaviour was certainly the very thing. **1868** NEWMAN *Let.* in *The Month* July (1909) 66, I am both surprised and glad at your news... I think it is the very thing for you.

B. *adv.* †**1. a.** Truly, really, genuinely; in or with truth or reality; truthfully. *Obs.*

13.. *E.E. Allit. P.* C. 333, I dewoutly awowe, þat verray bes halden, Soberly to do þe sacrafyse when I schal saue worþe. *c* **1375** *Cursor M.* 22973 (Fairf.), Bot mani man þat wele can rede vnderstandis noȝt al verray quat þe vale of Iosaphat is to say. *c* **1384** CHAUCER *H. Fame* II. 571 It..hath so very hys lykenes That spack the word. *c* **1440** *Bone Florence* 1928 The abbas, and odur nonnes by, Tolde hyt full openlye, That hyt was so verraye. *c* **1485** *Digby Myst.* (1882) II. 357 The compyler here-of shuld translat veray so holy a story.

b. Qualifying an adj. or pa. pple. *Obs.*

Not always clearly distinguishable from next.

1387 TREVISA *Higden* (Rolls) V. 329 But for he was verray repentaunt he was exciled for þe fey. **1423** JAS. I *Kingis Q.* clxix, O! verray sely wrech, I se wele by thy dedely coloure pale, Thou art to feble of thy-self to streche Vpon my quhele. *c* **1450** in Aungier *Syon* (1840) 335 None schal be ouer skypped in any wyse for any suche chaunge, withe oute a very resonable cause. *c* **1489** CAXTON *Sonnes of Aymon* viii. 191 Two thousand knyghtes.., all yonge men of pryme berde, whiche were very frenshe. **1529** MORE *Dyaloge* III. Wks. 244/1 Both those tonges [i.e. Greek and Latin] wer as verye vulgare as ours. *c* **1593** in *Spalding Club Misc.* I. 5 Your Maiestie and the consell hes to Judg gif thay be lauchful, and uerray qualifiit.

2. In a high degree or measure; to a great extent; exceedingly, extremely, greatly.

Sometimes emphasized in speaking, and italicized in printing, to give additional force. (Cf. 4.)

a. Qualifying positive adjs. (and ppl. adjs.) used predicatively, attributively, or absolutely. ***very high*** and ***low frequency*** (*Telecommunications*): see *VHF, VLF* s.v. V 5 b; freq. *attrib.*

a. *c* **1470** HENRY *Wallace* I. 86 Erle Patrik than till Berweik couth persewy; Ressawide he was and trastyt werray trew. **1542** UDALL *Erasm. Apoph.* 328 In the latine it hath a veray good grace. **1554-5** in Feuillerat *Revels Q. Mary* (1914) 173 Of verey fayer quaint & strange attier. **1560** DAUS tr. *Sleidane's Comm.* 255 Machlin (a veraye fayre Towne..in Brabant). *a* **1578** LINDESAY (Pitscottie) *Chron. Scot.* (S.T.S.) I. 4 To pray me think it is verray necessarie.

δ. *a* **1500-34** *Cov. Corp. Christi Pl.* II. 513 Those fowlys the ar full far fro me And werie yvill for me to fynde. **1530** PALSGR. 327/2 Very good, *fort bon. Ibid.* 828/1 Very farre, very hye, very lowe, etc. *a* **1578** LINDESAY (Pitscottie) *Chron. Scot.* (S.T.S.) II. 317 The said pest come in the towne of kirkcaldie that thair deit verrie mony. **1588** *Knaresborough Wills* (Surtees) I. 169 My father..ys a verye old man. **1600** J. PORY tr. *Leo's Africa* 56 This isle is very scarce of oile and of corne. *Ibid.* IV. 224 Batha, whereof now there remaine but very few ruines. **1661** PR. RUPERT in *11th Rep. Hist. MSS. Comm.* App. V. 8 Tell him that [I] am very glad to heere of his recouvry. **1676-7** MARVELL *Corr.* Wks. (Grosart) II. 530 A Bill for exporting Coals free, or at a very easy custome. **1709** STEELE *Tatler* No. 44 ¶6, I have, I fear, huddled up my Discourse, having been very busy. **1774** GOLDSM. *Nat. Hist.* (1776) V. 56 They lay very large eggs, some of them being above five inches in diameter. **1799** E. DU BOIS *Piece Family Biog.* III. 175 You say this to relieve me, and 'tis very kind of you. **1803** *Med. Jrnl.* X. 304 An intermittent tendency was also *very* observable in some instances. **1838** T. THOMSON *Chem. Org. Bodies* 580 A soft mass,..very soluble in alcohol. **1856** LD. GRANVILLE in *Life* (1905) I. 211 Very few of our Embassy were invited [to the party]. **1880** DISRAELI *Endym.* lxvii, Cards of invitation to banquets and balls and concerts, and 'very earlies'. **1920** *Radio Rev.* Sept. 579 (*heading*) Circuit for producing very high frequencies. **1938**, etc. [see *VLF* s.v. V 5 b]. **1958** *Economist* 26 July 271 With very high frequency radio broadcasting..providing almost perfect reception, the collector of classical music.. can make high fidelity recordings..on a £2 tape. **1967** *Electronics* 6 Mar. 68/2 Navy project officers expect a go-ahead..on construction of a worldwide very-low-frequency Omega navigation system. **1972** *McGraw-Hill Yearbk. Sci. & Technol.* 229/2 Some of the techniques developed for determining the geodetic coordinates for land use..can be applied at sea... In addition, the very-long-baseline interferometry (VLBI) technique is potentially applicable. **1974** *Encycl. Brit. Macropædia* XV. 425/1 The variation of carrier frequency is known as the frequency deviation, and for very-high-frequency broadcasting it can reach ±75 kilohertz. **1976** *Time* 24 May 64/3 The Japanese government..has declared the development of Very Large Scale Integrations—the technical heart of the next generation of computers—a 'national project'. **1978** PASACHOFF & KUTNER *University Astron.* xxvi. 667 With this ability, astronomers can make up an interferometer of two or more dishes very far apart, even thousands of kilometers. This technique is called very-long-baseline interferometry. **1982** *Times* 14 Jan. (Information Technol. Suppl.) p. v/4 Very large-scale integration (VLSI)... VLSI puts as many as 100,000 components on a chip.

(*b*) *Mountaineering.* ***very difficult, severe***: two of the categories used in classifying rock climbs; also *absol.*

1951, etc. [see SEVERE *a.* 9 b]. **1969** 'A. GARVE' *Ascent of D. 13* ii. 35 I've been climbing ever since I was a kid... I've done more Very Severes than I can remember.

b. Qualifying another adverb.

1448 *Paston Lett.* I. 76 Vere hartely your, Molyns. **1530** PALSGR. 814/1 Very erly in the mornyng, *au plus matyn. Ibid.* 843/2 Very gladly, *moult voulentiers.* Very hardly, *a paynes.* .. Very seldome, *peu souuent.* *a* **1553** UDALL *Royster D.* IV. vi. (Arb.) 70 But very well I wist he here did all in scorne. *a* **1578** LINDESAY (Pitscottie) *Chron. Scot.* (S.T.S.) I. 22 The gouernour hard thir vordis verrey plesandlie. **1630** B. JONSON *New Inn* Dram. Pers., Sir Glorious Tipto..talks gloriously of any thing, but very seldom is in the right. **1664** JER. TAYLOR *Dissuas. Popery* ii. §8. 118 For if it were [necessary], very extremely few would do their duty. **1691** tr. *Emilianne's Frauds Rom. Monks* (ed. 3) 130 The next day we set out very betimes in the Morning towards Mount Alverne. **1711** ADDISON *Spect.* No. 58 ¶4 Several Pieces which have lived very near as long as the Iliad it self. **1795** *Gentl. Mag.* 543/1 Nonjuring clergymen and their families partook very largely of his benevolence. **1818** CRUISE *Digest* (ed. 2) III. 510 Courts of equity would do very ill by not adopting that rule. **1835** URE *Philos. Manuf.* 158 The spindles should revolve very quickly in the spinning frame. **1867** DRANE *Chr. Schools* II. iii. 129 The school at Sempringham very soon became famous.

c. Qualifying past pples. used predicatively or attributively: = Very much. (See MUCH *adv.* 1 c.) Also exceptionally with *like* vb.

The correctness of this usage, which has been prevalent from the middle of the 17th cent., depends on the extent to which the participle has acquired a purely adjectival sense.

1641 in Nicolas *Priv. Mem. Digby* (1827) Introd. p. lix, At which the good Knight seemed very discontented. **1664** *Extr. St. P. rel. Friends* III. (1912) 215 Faber, A Jerman,.. being a very suspected person, reather of crafty principalls. **1702** ADDISON *Dial. Medals* ii. (1726) 35 Many very valued pieces of French, Italian, and English appear in the same dress [i.e. dialogue]. **1782** R. CUMBERLAND *Anecd. Painters* (1787) II. 90, I was a very interested and anxious spectator. **1792** W. ROBERTS *Looker-on* No. 14 (1794) I. 179 Betty.. looked very pleased at several passages. **1804** SYD. SMITH *Mor. Philos.* (1850) 54 A very over-rated man. **1842** GEO. ELIOT *Life in Lett. & Jrnls.* (1885) I. 112, I am becoming very hurried. **1874** DASENT *Half a Life* III. 60, I should so very like to know who this Mr. Ball and his daughter are. *Ibid.* 177 Her foot is very swollen. **1876-7** GLADSTONE *Glean.* (1879) I. 79 In this rather confused and very disappointed letter.

d. With a negative, freq. denoting 'only moderately', 'rather un——'.

1710 SWIFT *Jrnl. to Stella* 31 Oct., Then it went off, leaving me sickish, but not very. **1758** J. S. *Le Dran's Observ. Surg.* (1771) 269 It was not very adherent to any other Place than the Coccyx. *a* **1871** GROTE *Eth. Fragm.* i. (1876) 24 They leave them unnoticed, and are not very willing to admit them in their full extent at all.

e. Qualifying a sb. or proper name used adjectively (for emphasis).

1937 [see PREDICATIVAL *a.*]. **1968** *Listener* 21 Mar. 389/3 The total effect is very Kirov: it has more in common with the Leningrad *Cinderella*..than with ours. **1978** *Hot Car* July 87/5 *Scallops*, a very fifties paint idea, consisting of a long U-shaped design, the ends of which taper off to points.

3. In purely intensive use. **a.** Emphasizing superlatives, esp. *best, last, next.*

†Also with virtual superlatives, as *principal.*

1567 DRANT *Horace, Ep.* vii. D iij, He will see the..wyth the swallowe verye firste that cummes into that place. **1654** GATAKER *Disc. Apol.* 17 This fel out to be the verie next day after Qeen Elizabeths decease. **1664** *Extr. St. P. rel. Friends* II. (1911) 188 A greater meeting..at her house then ever, the very next Sunday after the Sessions. **1684** *Scanderbeg Rediv.* vi. 142 The City was now reduc'd to the very last Extremity. **1717** ATTERBURY *Serm., 1 Pet. ii 21* (1734) I. vi. 163 How then should the very Best of us..expect..to be free from them? **1753** MISS COLLIER *Art Torment., Gen. Rules* (1811) 199 If you know yourself to be of some consequence, although not the very principal person of the party. **1767** STERNE *Tr. Shandy* IX. xxx, In the very next page. **1849** MACAULAY *Hist. Eng.* iii. I. 308 Three of the very richest subjects in England. **1865** BARING-GOULD *Werewolves* v. 53 Whenever they stray in the very least. **1892** E. REEVES *Homeward Bound* 143 You have missed *the very* best thing in Kandy.

b. Denoting and emphasizing absolute identity or difference, esp. with *same* or *opposite.*

? *a* **1500** *Chester Pl.* (Shaks. Soc.) 215 It is the vereye same [blind man]. **1542** UDALL *Erasm. Apoph.* I. *Socrates* §86 e iij, Plato,..whiche in rebukyng hym [Socrates] did committe the veraye selfe same faulte, that he rebuked. **1601** SHAKS. *All's W.* II. iii. 29 That's it, I would haue said, the verie same. **1662** J. DAVIES tr. *Olearius' Voy. Ambass.* 182 That which happen'd on the very same day the year before. **1711** ADDISON *Spect.* No. 44 ¶6 Whose Murther he would revenge in the very same Place where it was committed. **1781** [see SELFSAME *a.* 1]. **1833** I. TAYLOR *Fanat.* i. 7 The very same spirit of kindness which should rule us in the performance of a task such as the one now in hand. **1835** T. MITCHELL *Acharn. of Aristoph.* 690 *note*, The very opposite word was of course expected.

†**c.** With advs. of time, place, or manner: Exactly, precisely, just; = EVEN *adv.* 6. *Obs.*

(*a*) **1530** PALSGR. 808/1 Evyn very now, *tout fyn mayntenant.* *a* **1553** UDALL *Roister D.* IV. vi. (Arb.) 70 *T. Trusty.* But when gost thou for him? *M. Mery.* That do I very nowe. *a* **1555** PHILPOT *Exam. & Writ.* (Parker Soc.) 334 It is possible some part of the Church for a time to be deceived when..they have a zeal of the truth,..yea, very then when they err, and plunge into any vice or sin. **1644** MAXWELL *Prerog. Chr. Kings* 74 If we alleadge Ignatius, it is to be feared he'l fare no better, for a great Scholar..hath very now rejected all we have of him. **1645** QUARLES *Sol. Recant.* VIII. 41 Did not that voice, that voted Wisdome vain But very now, now cry it up again?

(*b*) **1530** PALSGR. 823/2 Very here, very ther, *droit cy, droit la.* **1612** *Two Noble K.* V. iv. 115 In this place first you fought: ev'n very here I sundred you.

(*c*) *a* **1592** GREENE *Alphonsus* II. ii, What newes is this? and is it very so? Is our Alphonsus yet in humane state? **1632** SANDERSON *Serm.* 98 Very so ought we to conceiue the meaning of the vniversall particle 'Every man'.

4. Repeated in order to convey greater emphasis. Also *veryvery* (as one word).

1649 *Nicholas Papers* (Camden) 128, I have a verry verry great jealousy Lord Digby will be left in the lurch. **1653** WALTON *Angler* 137 He [the salmon] is very, very seldom observed to bite at a Minnow..and not oft at a Fly. **1722** DE FOE *Plague* (1896) 46 It was indeed very, very, very dreadful. **1807** SIR R. WILSON *Priv. Diary* 13 July (1862) II. 317 The retribution may be just but it is very very severe. **1825** T. HOOK *Sayings* Ser. II. *Man of Many Fr.* I. 306, 'I think him pleasant, and handsome, and—.' 'Oh! very, very,' said George. **1837** DICKENS *Pickw.* iii, Oh! I see..; negus too strong here—liberal landlord—very foolish—very. **1969** A. LURIE *Real People* 16 Croquet's become veryvery intense this year. **1977** *Transatlantic Rev.* LX. 68 You have a very nice face... And were veryvery nice to me.

C. *sb.* †**a.** Truth, verity. *Obs.*⁻¹

1382 WYCLIF *Rom.* Prol., Thes reuokith the apostle to the verrey [1388 treuthe] and the gospels bileue.

†**b.** *for, in,* or *into very*, = Truly, verily. *Obs.*

15.. *Smyth & his Dame* 52 in Hazl. *E.P.P.* III. 203, I am mayster of all, That smyteth with hamer or mall, And so may thov me call, I tell the for ueray. *c* **1550** ROLLAND *Crt. Venus* II. 96 Terpsichore [the] fift is callit in verray. *Ibid.* 772 Ane messinger said scho, into verray Thair erandis gais, baith nicht and als be day.

Very *sb.*² ('vɛrɪ, 'vɪərɪ). Also (*erron.*) **Verey, Vérey.** The name of Edward W. *Very* (1847–1910), U.S. naval officer, used *attrib.* with reference to a coloured pyrotechnic flare projected from a special pistol for signalling or temporarily illuminating an area; as ***Very light, pistol***, etc.

1907 *Jrnl. Mil. Service Inst. U.S.* XLI. 368 In connection with night signaling it may be well here to mention the Very system,..found serviceable in sea-coast signaling. **1915** D. O. BARNETT *Let.* 17 Mar. 95 When the 'Very' pistol came, I fired a rocket. **1917** R. NICHOLS in E. B. Osborn *Nurse in Arms* 49 Before he was aware The 'Verey' light had risen.. on the air It hung glistering. **1920** *Blackw. Mag.* June 747/2 Very flares were continually being fired into the air to light up dark corners. **1928** BLUNDEN *Undertones of War* ii. 16 Another officer..showed me..how to fire a flare... He had with him a cumbrous brass gun, called a duck-gun; from this he fired a Vérey cartridge. **1930** C. R. SAMSON *Fights & Flights* 177 My sole equipment consisted of an electric torch ..and a Verey-light pistol. **1959** *Chambers's Encycl.* XI. 390/1 The Very pistol, a short-barrelled smooth-bore weapon of 1-in. or 1½ in. calibre, firing a cartridge which is in effect a short roman candle throwing up a single star, is the most generally used pyrotechnic signal. **1976** 'A. YORK' *Dark Passage* xiii. 162 He..found a Very pistol..and fired. The glowing orange ball arced over his head, and then hung, perhaps a hundred feet above the yacht. **1981** J. B. HILTON *Playground of Death* ii. 15 What we were really playing at was War... A Roman candle..was a Very light.

†**very(e).** *Obs.*⁻¹ (Meaning obscure; occurring only as part of a charm.)

c **1386** CHAUCER *Miller's T.* 299 Ihesu Crist and seint Benedight Blesse this hous from euery wikked wight For nyghtes uerye [*v.rr.* very(e, verie, verray] the white pater noster.

very(e), obs. Sc. ff. WARY *v.*, WEARY *a.*, WORRY *v.*

veryen, southern ME. var. FERRY *v.*

veryly, obs. form of VERILY *adv.*

veryn, obs. variant of FERN *sb.*³

verynes, obs. Sc. f. WEARINESS.

verynesse: see VERINESS.

very-similar, obs. f. VERISIMILAR *a.*

†**verzine.** *Obs. rare.* Also **versine.** = next.

1558 WARDE tr. *Alexis' Secr.* 90 A pounde of Verzine or Brasyl cutte in pieces. **1599** HAKLUYT *Voy.* II. I. 218 Sandols, Marsine, Versine, Porcelane of China.

‖**verzino.** *Obs. rare.* Also **verzina.** [It.] Brazil-wood.

[**1555** EDEN *Decades* (Arb.) 80 None other trees then brasile, whiche the Italians caule *Verzino.*] **1588** T. HICKOCK tr. *C. Frederick's Voy.* 23 b, In whose harbour euerie yere there ladeth some Shippes with Verzina, Nypa, and Beniamin. **1599** HAKLUYT *Voy.* II. I. 229 There goeth another ship for the said Captaine of Malacca to Sion, to lade Verzino.

ves, obs. Sc. form of *was*: see BE *v.*

vesage, obs. Sc. form of VISAGE.

Vesak ('vɛsɑːk). Also **Wesak; Vai-, Ve-, Visākha.** [Skr. *vaiśākhá*, name of a month, f. *vi-sākhā* branched, (also) the name of a constellation, f. *ví* apart + *śākhā* branch.] An important Buddhist festival commemorating the birth, enlightenment, and death of the Buddha, observed on the day of the full moon in the month Visākha (April–May).

1927 E. J. THOMAS *Life of Buddha* iii. 34 In 1922 the Feast of Wesak (Visākha) in Ceylon was at full moon on May 10. **1961** R. A. GARD *Buddhism* iv. 156 Doctrinally speaking, there is the practice of venerating the Buddha..especially the Vesākha/Vaiśākha-puja (often called 'Wesak' in South and Southeast Asia). **1965** *Festival Malaysia 1965: Calendar of Events* 9/3 May 15—Wesak Day: Celebration of Lord Buddha's Birthday. **1971** *Carry Singapore in your Pocket* (Singapore Tourist Promotion Board) (ed. 3) 38 May 9. Vesak Day. Celebration of Lord Buddha's birth, death and enlightenment. **1978** C. HUMPHREYS *Both Sides of Circle* x. 109 The Buddhist Society too carried on. *Wesak*, the annual equivalent of Christmas Day, was held in May as usual. **1978** *Oxford Diocesan Mag.* Aug. 20/3 It is instructive to know what our Jewish neighbours are doing and why at, for example, Yom Kippur, or our Buddhist friends at Vesakha or the Moslems at Meelad al Nabi.

Vesalian (vɪˈseɪlɪən), *a.* [f. the name of the Belgian anatomist Andreas *Vesalius* (1514–64).]

1. Connected with anatomical researches.

In quot. with reference to body-snatching.

1870 H. LONSDALE *Life R. Knox* 65 The students..set out on Vesalian crusades, and succeeded beyond expectation.

2. *Vesalian foramen, vein*: (see quots.).

1891 *Cent. Dict.* s.v., The Vesalian foramen (foramen Vesalii) of the sphenoid bone (a small venous opening). **1902** *Hughes' Man. Pract. Anat.* III. 188 The Vesalian, an emissary vein from the cavernous sinus, which, however, is only occasionally present. **1913** *Dorland's Med. Dict.* 1040/2 *Vesalian vein*, a vessel which connects the pterygoid plexus with the cavernous sinus.

‖**vesania** (vɪˈseɪnɪə). *Path.* [L. *vēsānia*, f. *vēsānus* mad, f. *vē-* not + *sānus* sane.] Mental derangement, esp. of a particular type (see quot. 1857).

[**1693** tr. *Blancard's Phys. Dict.* (ed. 2), *Vesania*, Madness from Love. *c* **1793** *Encycl. Brit.* (ed. 3) XI. 282 Order IV. Vesaniæ.] **1800** tr. *Cullen's Nosology* 130 *note*, For who would consider..any other Hallucinatio or Morositas, which do not depend on the judgment, as a Vesania? **1820** GOOD *Nosology* 278 Parr..makes Vesania the genus, and arranges melancholia, mania, and even oneirodynia as separate species under it. **1857** DUNGLISON *Dict. Med. Sci.* 964/2 *Vesania*, madness; derangement of the intellectual and moral faculties, without coma or fever.

veˈsanic, *a. Path.* [f. L. *vēsān-us* insane + -IC.] Of or pertaining to, of the nature of, vesania.

1899 *Allbutt's Syst. Med.* VIII. 196 This includes eight types [of mental disease], namely i. vesanic type.

†**veˈsanous,** *a.* [ad. L. *vēsānus*.] (See quot.)

1656 BLOUNT *Glossogr.* (following Cooper), *Vesanous*, mad, wood, furious, out of his wit, cruel, outragious.

vesar, obs. f. VISOR.

vesatour, obs. Sc. var. VISITOR.

vescel, veschale, -all, -el, obs. ff. VESSEL *sb.*[1]

vesch(e, obs. Sc. varr. WASH *v.*

†**ˈvesculent,** *a. Obs.*$^{-0}$ [ad. med.L. *vesculent-us* (full of dainties, f. L. *vescus* small, dainty), associated with L. *vescī* to feed.] (See quots.)

1656 BLOUNT *Glossogr.*, *Vesculent*, apt to eat or feed. **1658** PHILLIPS, *Vesculent*, to be eaten, fit for food.

vese, ME. var. VEASE *Obs.* and FEEZE *v.*[1]; obs. var. VIZY *v. Sc.*

veseal, obs. f. VESSEL *sb.*[1]

veseir, obs. Sc. f. VISOR.

vesen, southern ME. var. FEEZE *v.*[1]

veshel(l, obs. Sc. ff. VESSEL *sb.*[1]

†**vesiar.** *Sc. Obs.* [f. *vesy* VIZY *v.*] An inspector. So †**vesiater.** *Obs.*

? *a* **1500** *Aberdeen Reg.* (Jam.), Cerciouris, vesiaris. **1517** *Burgh Rec. Edin.* (1869) I. 167 Vesiater and serchare of the skynnis..within the said burgh.

‖**vesica** (vɪˈsaɪkə). [L. *vēsīca*, a bladder, blister.]

1. *Anat.* A bladder.

Rarely used exc. with defining term, esp. *v. natatoria* or *v. urinaria*.

[**1693** tr. *Blancard's Phys. Dict.* (ed. 2), *Vesica*, the Bladder, an hollow membranaceous Part, wherein any Liquor that is to be excerned, is contained.] **1706** PHILLIPS (ed. Kersey), *Vesica*, a Bladder. [Hence in Bailey, etc.] **1859** MAYNE *Expos. Lex.*

†**2.** A copper vessel used in distilling. *Obs.*

1683 SALMON *Doron Medicum* I. 21 Put a quarter of the infusion..into a vesica and powre on more rain or river water. **1694** —— *Bate's Dispens.* (1713) 12/2 You may either distil in a Copper Vesica,..or.. in a Glass Body. **1704** J. HARRIS *Lex. Techn.* I, *Vesica*,..the large Copper Body Tinned within-side, which is commonly used in Distillation of Ardent Spirits. **1712** tr. *Pomet's Hist. Drugs* I. 126 Put all the Matter into a Copper Vesica, tinn'd within. **1728** CHAMBERS *Cycl.* s.v. *Distillation*, Odoriferous Plants..are distill'd by the Cucurbite, or *Vesica*.

3. *vesica piscis* (also *piscium*), a pointed oval figure, the sides of which are properly parts of two equal circles passing through each other at their centres, freq. employed as an architectural feature and by early artists as an aureole enclosing figures of Christ, the Virgin, etc.

The reason for the name (fish's or fishes' bladder) is disputed: see quot. 1813.

1809 T. KERRICH in *Archaeol.* (1812) XVI. 313 [A figure] formed by two equal circles, cutting each other in their centers... We are told that it was called Vesica Piscis. **1813** J. S. HAWKINS *Gothic Archit.* 244 Vesica piscium cannot, therefore, signify a fish's bladder, but a bladder, which when filled with wind, would be in the form of a fish. **1820** T. KERRICH in *Archaeol.* XIX. 353 Observations on the Use of the mysterious Figure, called Vesica Piscis, in the Architecture of the Middle Ages, and in Gothic Architecture. **1845** PARKER *Gloss. Archit.* (ed. 4) I. 399 *Vesica piscis*, a name applied by Albert Durer to a pointed oval figure [etc.]. *a* **1878** SIR G. SCOTT *Lect. Archit.* I. v. 189 Their heads [*sc.* of the two portals of Ely] were formerly filled with the Vesica Piscis.

attrib. **1884** *Imp. Dict.* s.v., Vesica piscis Seal, Wimborne Minster. **1901** *Athenæum* 16 Nov. 667/2 A Vesica Piscis window of unusual character at Millom Church, Cumberland.

b. *ellipt.* in this sense. Also *attrib.* and *Comb.*

1820 T. KERRICH in *Archaeol.* XIX. 361 The precise form of the Vesica which was used. **1848** RICKMAN *Styles Archit.* App. p. xxxvi, A figure standing in a shallow niche, holding a vesica, probably intended to represent the Trinity. **1878** MCVITTIE *Christ Ch. Cathedr.* 68 The figures are combined in vesica-shaped medallions. **1907** *Times* Lit. Suppl. 25 Jan. 30/2 The very beautiful vesica form..adopted in consequence of the prevailing taste for the pointed arch, and the fashion for the vesica in architecture.

vesical (ˈvɛsɪkəl), *a.* [ad. mod.L. *vesical-is*, f. L. *vēsīca*: see prec. and -AL[1]. So F. *vésical* (16th cent.), Pg. *vesical*, It. *vessicale*.]

1. Of or pertaining to, formed in, the urinary bladder.

1797 *Phil. Trans.* LXXXVIII. 45 The specimen.., which was said to be a vesical calculus of a horse. **1857** MILLER *Elem. Chem.*, *Org.* 711 Urine..always contains a little vesical mucus, together with some other ill-defined azotised principles.

b. *spec.* in *Anat.* of various appendages of the bladder (see quots.).

1831 R. KNOX *Cloquet's Anat.* 511 Vesical Nerves. These nerves vary in number, and are irregularly interlaced. **1835–6** *Todd's Cycl. Anat.* I. 388/2 The pelvic and vesical fasciæ. **1840** E. WILSON *Anat. Vade M.* (1842) 348 The vesical and prostatic plexus is an important plexus of veins which surrounds the neck and base of the bladder and prostate gland. **1881** MIVART *Cat* 213 Amongst them we have the superior vesical [branch], which goes to the side of the bladder.

c. *Path.* Affecting or occurring in the urinary bladder.

1846 G. E. DAY tr. *Simon's Anim. Chem.* II. 183 When mucus is separated in large quantity (as in vesical catarrh). **1859** R. F. BURTON *Centr. Afr.* in *Jrnl. Geog. Soc.* XXIX. 61 A violent cough and vesical irritation. **1876** GROSS *Dis. Bladder*, etc. 82 Of the causes of vesical neuralgia very little is known. **1888** DOUGHTY *Arabia Deserta* I. 527, I found the women lying on the ground far gone in a vesical disease.

2. Having the form of a vesica; pointedly oval.

1865 *Reader* No. 121. 462/2 Seals..of vesical shape. **1880** *Archæol. Cant.* XIII. 72 The circular boss or knob, and the elliptical or vesical shape, are seen upon the jewels in the cover of the celebrated Durham Gospels of St. Cuthbert.

vesicant (ˈvɛsɪkənt), *sb.* and *a. Med.* [ad. mod.L. *vesicant-*, *vesicans*, pres. pple. of *vesicare*: see next and -ANT. So F. *vésicant*, Pg. *vesicante*, It. *vessicante*.]

A. *sb.* An application employed to raise blisters; a vesicatory. Also in mod. use, a vesicant substance for use in warfare.

1661 LOVELL *Hist. Anim. & Min.* 459 Vesicants. Simple. Roots, of thapsia, and pellitory of Spaine. Seeds, of mustard. **1836** *Penny Cycl.* VI. 249/1 The terebinthinate solution may be used as a most efficacious vesicant. **1871** GARROD *Mat. Med.* (ed. 3) 417 The pustulants induce a still deeper action, and are sometimes of greater value than vesicants. **1923** *Biochem. Jrnl.* XVII. 275 We are trying to find what common factor..underlies the effect of the mustard gas group of vesicants. **1936** A. HUXLEY *Olive Tree* 87 To go and throw thermite, high explosives and vesicants upon the inhabitants of neighbouring countries. **1936** [see *blister gas* s.v. BLISTER *sb.* 6]. **1944**, **1964** [see *B.A.L.* s.v. B III]. **1974** M. C. GERALD *Pharmacol.* vii. 137 Lewisite is an arsenic-containing vesicant capable of producing immediate pain.

B. *adj.* Causing, efficacious in producing, blisters; vesicatory.

1826 KIRBY & SP. *Entomol.* IV. xlviii. 468 There appears no particular affinity between the Predaceous and Vesicant beetles. **1857** HENFREY *Elem. Bot.* §531 *Polygonum Hydropiper*, a common native weed, is very acrid, even vesicant when fresh. **1864** GARROD *Mat. Med.* (ed. 2) 54 It is astringent, irritant, vesicant, or even escharotic, according to the mode of its application.

vesicate (ˈvɛsɪkeɪt), *v.* Chiefly *Med.* [f. ppl. stem of mod.L. *vesicare*: see VESICA and -ATE.]

1. *trans.* To cause to rise in a blister or blisters; to raise blisters on (the skin, etc.).

1657 G. STARKEY *Helmont's Vind.* 173 He will perhaps apply pigeons or the like to the feet or vesicate the external members for revulsion sake. **1676** WISEMAN *Surg. Treat.* VI. viii. 435 Celsus proposes, that..the externall Parts be vesicated, to make more powerfull Revulsion from within. **1720** QUINCY tr. *Hodges' Loimologia* 189 The Parts thus vesicated were never suffered to heal till the Malignity of the Disease was spent. **1753** *Phil. Trans.* XLVIII. 149 If..this bark is stripped off with their teeth, it inflames and vesicates their lips and gums.

b. In *pa. pple.* Covered with, converted into, blisters.

1676 WISEMAN *Surg. Treat.* I. vi. 38, I saw [the arm] swelled, the *Cuticula* vesicated, and shining with a burning heat of a citron colour. **1802** JENNER *Instr. Vaccine Inoculation* (1884) 59 A little red spot will appear on the third day..which..becomes perceptibly vesicated. **1899** *Allbutt's Syst. Med.* VIII. 482 Outbursts of persistent wheal-like formations, sometimes vesicated.

2. *absol.* To produce blisters.

1809 *Phil. Trans.* XCIX. 343 The fluid effused by vesicating with cantharides. **1816** KIRBY & SP. *Entomol.* (ed. 2) I. 315 In America the *Lytta cinerea* and *vittata*..are said to vesicate more speedily and with less pain. **1843** R. J. GRAVES *Syst. Clin. Med.* xii. 133 Blisters [applied] would be doubtful, and the probability was that the patient would sink before they vesicated. **1864** GARROD *Mat. Med.* (ed. 2) 41 Liquor ammoniæ fortior..will vesicate rapidly, if evaporation is prevented.

3. *intr.* To become blistered.

1899 *J. Hutchinson's Arch. Surg.* X. 120 It [i.e. an eruption] consists of erythematous patches which vesicate at their borders and spread.

Hence **ˈvesicated** *ppl. a.*, **ˈvesicating** *vbl. sb.* (also *attrib.*) and *ppl. a.*

In quot. 1703 app. meaning 'having large air-cells': cf. VESICULATED *a.*

1703 *Phil. Trans.* XXIII. 1393 The Lungs of these Water Lizards being *vesicated, and not vesiculated. **1806** *Med. Jrnl.* XV. 44 Blistering plasters were applied, and the vesicated parts treated as above. **1843** R. J. GRAVES *Syst. Clin. Med.* ix. 102 *note*, Dressing the vesicated surface with the French blistering paper. **1663** BOYLE *Usef. Exp. Nat. Philos.* II. ii. 61 The Chirurgion, unknown to me, made use of Cantharides, among other ingredients of his *vesicating plaister. **1771** T. PERCIVAL *Ess.* (1777) I. 196 Neither mustard,..nor any other vesicating stimulus but cantharides, excite this complaint. **1836** *Penny Cycl.* VI. 249/1 A yellow viscid matter..which has no vesicating power. **1872** T. G. THOMAS *Dis. Women* 297 There are two preparations of vesicating collodion.

vesication (vɛsɪˈkeɪʃən). *Med.* [ad. mod.L. *vesicatio*, noun of action from *vesicare*: see prec. So F. *vésication* (16th cent.), Pg. *vesicação*, Sp. *vejigacion*. Cf. VESICULATION.]

1. The result of blistering or of rising in blisters; a blister or group of these.

1543 TRAHERON *Vigo's Chirurg.* II. xi. 25 This.. appayseth the paine, and purgeth the vesication or bladerynge and inflation. **1676** WISEMAN *Surg. Treat.* I. iii. 23, I applied a Pledgit of basilicon upon it, and dressed the Vesications with *unguent. tutiæ*. **1720** QUINCY tr. *Hodges' Loimologia* 110 Those poisonous Vesications called Blains. **1769** E. BANCROFT *Guiana* 105 These leaves are also applied to vesications, to promote a copious discharge. **1785** C. KITE in *Med. Commun.* II. 47 A small vesication appeared on the navel. **1813** J. THOMSON *Lect. Inflam.* 595 The early opening of the vesications will..not occasion pain. **1861** HULME tr. *Moquin-Tandon* II. IV. i. 236 The stinging apparatus of the Medusæ..may even give rise to vesications. **1899** *Allbutt's Syst. Med.* VIII. 466 In exceptional cases vesications are produced.

2. The formation or development of blisters; the action or fact of blistering.

1753 *Phil. Trans.* XLVIII. 325 An enlargement of the eyelids, and vesication of the *tunica conjunctiva*. **1807** *Med. Jrnl.* XVII. 320 A complete vesication had taken place over the whole extent of the metatarsal bones. **1843** R. J. GRAVES *Syst. Clin. Med.* vii. 85 They have no hesitation in applying a large blister, leaving it on until it produces full vesication. **1864** GARROD *Mat. Med.* (ed. 2) 335 Vesication is also made use of on account of its revulsive action in internal congestions, as of the head, &c.

vesicatory (ˈvɛsɪkeɪtərɪ, vɛˈsɪkətərɪ), *sb.* and *a. Med.* [ad. med. or early mod.L. *vesicatorius*, *-orium* (whence F. *vésicatoire*, It. *vessicatorio*, Pg. *vesicatorio*, Sp. *vejigatorio*), f. L. *vēsīca*: see VESICATE *v.* and -ORY.]

A. *sb.* A sharp irritating ointment, plaster, or other application for causing the formation of a blister or blisters on the skin; = BLISTER *sb.* 3.

Very frequent from *c* 1650 to *c* 1780; now somewhat *rare*.

1604 F. HERING *Mod. Defence* 18 Vesicatorys to be applied neere vnto the most principall Part. **1655** CULPEPPER, etc. *Riverius* I. vii. 32 You must apply a Vesicatory to the fore part of the head. **1676** T. DE GARENCIERES *Coral* 58 Carrying in his pocket a vesicatory made of cantharides. **1704** F. FULLER *Med. Gymn.* (1711) 38 It can't be done by Vesicatories without some Pain. **1752** *Phil. Trans.* XLVII. 504 These were blistered slightly, by means of a small vesicatory. **1803** *Med. Jrnl.* X. 310 A vesicatory applied to the affected part, constantly relieved the pain, and produced the desired effect. **1830** LINDLEY *Nat. Syst. Bot.* 7 The leaves of Knowltonia vesicatoria are used as vesicatories in Southern Africa. **1875** H. C. WOOD *Therap.* (1879) 561 Epispastics, vesicatories, or, more colloquially, blisters.

B. *adj.* Of the nature of a vesicant; capable of, characterized by, raising blisters.

1612 WOODALL *Surg. Mate* Wks. (1653) 173 The use of Vesicatory medicines; namely, Cantharides in painfull swolne limbs. **1663** BOYLE *Usef. Exp. Nat. Philos.* II. ii. 43 If you duly perpend what I lately mentioned, of the transmutation of water into hot and vesicatory substances. **1817** KIRBY & SP. *Entomol.* II. 227 The vesicatory beetles.. are not improbably defended from their assailants by the remarkable quality..that distinguishes them. **1822–7** GOOD *Study Med.* (1829) I. 59 The *cerambyx moschatus*, which possesses a vesicatory power nearly equal to that of the lytta. **1868** *Rep. U.S. Commissioner Agric.* (1869) 102 Many of these beetles [*sc. Meloidæ*] possess strong vesicatory powers.

vesicle (ˈvɛsɪk(ə)l). Also 6, 8 vessicle. [ad. F. *vésicule*, or L. *vēsīcula* VESICULA.]

1. a. *Anat.* and *Zool.* A small bladder-like vessel in an animal body; a cavity or cell with a membranous integument; a small sac or cyst.

Freq. with defining terms, as *blood-*, *food-*, *germinal*, *seminal*, *umbilical vesicles*; see also GRAAFIAN, PURKINJEAN.

1578 BANISTER *Hist. Man* v. 64 The intrels, which receiue the dryer excrement, as the Vessicle of Choler. **1607** WALKINGTON *Opt. Glass* ix. 103 Those men which want the vesicle of cholor, are both strong and couragious. **1664** POWER *Exp. Philos.* I. 4 If you divide the Bee near the neck, you shall see the heart beat most lively, which is a white pulsing vesicle. **1691** RAY *Creation* II. (1692) 63 That the Lungs should be made up of such innumerable Air-pipes and Vesicles interwoven with Blood Vessels in order to purifie, ferment, or supply the sanguineous Mass with Nitro-aerial Particles. **1713** CHESELDEN *Anat.* I. i. (1726) 12 The marrow in the larger cells is also contained in their membranous vesicles. **1774** GOLDSM. *Nat. Hist.* (1862) I. ii. 156 The vesicles, that go to form the brain. **1797** M. BAILLIE *Morb. Anat.* (1807) 390 The small vesicles which make a part of the natural structure of the ovaria. **1843** R. J. GRAVES

Syst. Clin. Med. xxii. 260 These cells may be represented as so many minute vesicles. **1870** ROLLESTON *Anim. Life* Introd. p. xxxvi, The brain [of Amphioxus] consists of three primary vesicles.

Comb. **1870** ROLLESTON *Anim. Life* 155 Contractile Polian vesicle-like sacs are developed.

b. Similarly in *Bot.*

1670 *Phil Trans.* V. 1176 There are found many leaves of other trees, on which grow Vesicles, or small baggs. **1673** GREW *Anat. Trunks* I. i. §3 A simple, white, and close Parenchyma or Barque; made up of Vesicles.. hardly visible without a Glass. **1760** J. LEE *Introd. Bot.* III. v. (1765) 183 *Pappillose*, nipply; when it is covered with Vesicles, little Bladders. **1766** *Compl. Farmer* s.v. *Vegetation*, All the roots becoming longer, put forth new branches out of their sides, the second leaf withers, and its vesicles are emptied. **1832** LINDLEY *Introd. Bot.* 158 This third envelope always begins by being a mass of cellular tissue,.. and generally finishes by becoming a vesicle. **1882** VINES *Sachs' Bot.* 59 The older hypothesis of a deposition of new layers from within presupposes that the starch-grains were at first hollow vesicles.

c. *Physics.* A minute bubble or spherule of liquid or vapour, esp. one of those composing a cloud or fog.

1731 MILLER *Gard. Dict.* s.v. *Dew*, The thin Vesicles of which Vapours consist. *Ibid.*, The Warmth.. forms those Vesicles that are specifically lighter than the Air. **1794** G. ADAMS *Nat. & Exp. Philos.* IV. lii. 446 Clouds are composed of a mass of vesicles like soap-bubbles. **1854** BREWSTER *More Worlds* iii. 61 The aqueous vapour which it [*sc.* the atmosphere] contains, whether it exist in minute vesicles, or in masses of clouds. **1869** PHIPSON tr. *Guillemin's Sun* (1870) 42 When the vesicles which constitute clouds are cooled they unite to form drops. **1884** J. TAIT *Mind in Matter* (1892) 87 The salt is brought by the travelling clouds, each vesicle charged with a precious burden.

d. *Geol.* A small spherical or oval cavity produced by the presence of bubbles of gas or vapour in volcanic rocks.

1811 PINKERTON *Petralogy* II. 328 The vesicles are sometimes of an oblong form, but often spherical. **1849** DANA *Geol.* vi. (1850) 346 Occasionally we see fragments in which the vesicles are thickly disseminated. **1879** RUTLEY *Stud. Rocks* xi. 191 In some of the obsidians of Hawaii the vesicles are quite spherical.

2. A hollow swelling. *rare*$^{-1}$. (Cf. next.)

1672 MARVELL *Reh. Transp.* II. 11 He demonstrates at large how impossible it was.. for Mankind to be produced at first from certain Vesicles or Pimples of the Earth.

3. *Path.* A small, generally round, elevation of the cuticle containing fluid matter.

1799 JENNER *Further Obs. Variolæ Vaccinæ* (1801) 33 The patient felt no general indisposition, although there was so great a number of vessicles. **1801** *Med. Jrnl.* V. 338 He has twice scratched off the surface of the rising vesicle. **1847** YOUATT *Horse* viii. 204 Vesicles will sometimes appear along the under side of the tongue. **1867** BAKER *Nile Tribut.* viii. (1872) 107 Small vesicles rose above the skin. **1876** BRISTOWE *Th. & Pract. Med.* (1878) 295 The amount of fluid relatively to the solid constituents of vesicles varies very much.

b. Without article.

1845 *Encycl. Metrop.* VII. 755/1 The vaccine pustule runs a given course of varus and of vesicle.

vesico- (ˈvɛsɪkəʊ), combining form, on Greek models, of VESICA, occurring in various terms referring to the bladder in connexion with some other part of the body denoted by the second element (so F. *vésico-*); also occas. used for VESICULO-; so ***vesico-cervical***, ***-intestinal***, ***-prostatic***, ***-rectal***, etc.; ˌ**vesicoˈpustular** *a.* = *vesiculo-pustular* adj. s.v. VESICULO-; ˌ**vesico-uˈreteral**, **-ureˈteric** *adjs.*, of or pertaining to the bladder and the ureters; *spec.* applied to a flow of urine from the former back into the latter.

Various other terms, as *vesicocele*, *vesicoclysis*; ***vesico-abdominal***, ***-pubic***, ***-spinal***, etc., appear in Dicts.

1889 *Buck's Handbk. Med. Sci.* VIII. 581/2 The tear, beginning in a rigid os, extends.. up the cervix to the *vesico-cervical junction. **1835-6** *Todd's Cycl. Anat.* I. 400 *Vesico-intestinal fistulæ sometimes establish a communication between the bladder and the ileum or colon. **1878** T. BRYANT *Pract. Surg.* (1879) II. 64 Vesico-intestinal Fistula is sometimes met with. **1839-47** *Todd's Cycl. Anat.* III. 933/2 The veins in the neighbourhood of the prostate gland and of the neck of the bladder.. are called the *vesico-prostatic plexus. **1876** GROSS *Dis. Bladder*, etc. 156 Varicose enlargement of the vesico-prostatic plexus of veins was described. **1902** H. W. STELWAGON *Treat. Dis. Skin* 63 The lesions often do not become strictly purulent, but are of a seropurulent character, forming vesicopustules, and when such a feature is a predominant one, the eruption is usually designated *vesicopustular. **1951** WHITBY & HYNES *Med. Bacteriol.* (ed. 5) xxiv. 393 The viruses of this group.. characteristically produce a vesico-pustular eruption. **1876** GROSS *Dis. Bladder*, etc. 339 *Vesico-Rectal Fistule is between the bladder and rectum, and between the latter tube and the urethra. **1835-6** *Todd's Cycl. Anat.* I. 400/2 When the disease is a *vesico-umbilical fistula, the communication is with the summit of the bladder. **1906** DORLAND *Med. Dict.* (ed. 4) 815/1 *Vesico-ureteral. **1951** M. CAMPBELL *Clin. Pediatric Urol.* i. 67 Vesico-ureteral reflux also results from obstructions of the lower urinary tract. **1982** *Jrnl. Urol.* CXXVIII. 774/1 Vesicoureteral reflux is a common abnormality occurring in children and a major cause of renal failure in early adult life. **1965** *Brit. Jrnl. Urol.* XXXVII. 531 *Vesico-ureteric reflux may follow operations on the vesico-ureteric junction. **1977** *Proc. R. Soc. Med.* LXX. 149/2 This finding is not necessarily applicable to children with symptomless infection even though infection in these children is accompanied by vesicoureteric reflux in 23% of cases. **1885** *Buck's Handbk. Med. Sci.* I. 526/2 *Vesico-urethral fissure.. is a crack or fissure between the folds of the mucosa, at the point of junction of the urethra and bladder. **1839-47** *Todd's Cycl. Anat.* III. 943/1 There are a pair of recto-uterine peritoneal folds in the female and a pair of *vesico-uterine folds. **1889** *Buck's Handbk. Med. Sci.* VIII. 581/2 All the tissues below may heal, leaving an opening at the upper angle of the tear —a vesico-uterine fistula. **1835-6** *Todd's Cycl. Anat.* I. 400/2 *Vesico-vaginal fistulæ are sometimes.. the result of the progress of a uterine cancer. **1876** GROSS *Dis. Bladder*, etc. 326 Vesico-vaginal fistule is an opening between the bladder and vagina. **1889** *Buck's Handbk. Med. Sci.* VIII. 580/2 The tear reaches up to, or dissects off the vesico-vaginal tissue from the uterus.

‖**vesicula** (vɪˈsɪkjʊlə). Pl. **vesiculæ** (-juliː). [L. *vēsīcula* a little blister, a vesicle, dim. of *vēsīca* VESICA.]

1. = VESICLE 1. Usually in pl.

In *Anat.* also with defining terms, as *vesiculæ seminales*.

a. *Anat.* **1715** CHEYNE *Princ. Relig.* I. iii. §12 (ed. 2) 134 Spiral Threads, which divide these hollow Fibrils into so many elastick Cystes and Vesiculæ. **1728** CHAMBERS *Cycl.* s.v. *Lungs*, A Stone-Cutter, the Vesiculæ of whose Lungs were.. stuffed with Dust. **1771** *Encycl. Brit.* I. 282/2 The thoracic duct.. terminates in some subjects by a kind of vesicula. **1835-6** *Todd's Cycl. Anat.* I. 380/2 (Bladder), Towards the vesiculæ it [the cellular coat] is dense and white, and supports a number of veins. **1849-52** *Ibid.* IV. II. 1431/1 The difficulty of proving the identity of sacs called vesiculæ in other animals.

b. *Bot.* **1728** CHAMBERS *Cycl.* s.v. *Vegetation*, These Seed-Leaves consist of a great Number of little Vesiculæ, or Bladders. **1832** LINDLEY *Introd. Bot.* 207 *Vesiculæ*, inflations of the thallus, filled with air, by means of which the plants are enabled to float.

c. *Physics.* **1713** DERHAM *Phys.-Theol.* I. iii. 22 *note*, Vapours being.. no other than inflated Vesiculæ of Water.

2. *Path.* = VESICLE 3.

1876 DUHRING *Dis. Skin* 43 Vesiculæ are circumscribed, rounded elevations of the epidermis. varying in size from a pin-point to a split-pea, containing a clear serous fluid.

vesicular (vɪˈsɪkjʊlə(r)), *a.* [ad. early mod.L. *vesicular-is* (whence F. *vésiculaire*, Pg. *vesicular*, It. *vescicolare*), f. L. *vēsīcula*: see prec.]

1. Having the form or structure of a vesicle; bladder-like.

a. *Anat.* *c* **1720** GIBSON *Farrier's Guide* I. App. (1722) 101 These receive the Chyle.. into the vesicular Kernels of the Mesentery. **1725** *Fam. Dict.* s.v. *Lungs*, Its inner Laminæ fill up the Interstices, which are below the Bunches of the small Lobes [in the lungs], with little vesicular Cells. **1822-7** GOOD *Study Med.* (1829) V. 10 There are no organs of generation that differ so much.. as these vesicular bags. **1873** MIVART *Elem. Anat.* x. 416 A simple vesicular heart may be continued on forwards into a median artery. **1888** ROLLESTON & JACKSON *Anim. Life* 859 The nucleus is single; it is large when full grown, vesicular, with chromatin globules or ribbons.

b. *Bot.* **1848** LINDLEY *Introd. Bot.* (ed. 4) I. 147 A vesicular organ, which he terms *Cistome*. **1867** J. HOGG *Microsc.* II. i. 303 The spores are developed freely in the vesicular cells destined to produce them. **1882** VINES *Sachs' Bot.* 514 Their capacity for transport is increased by the vesicular hollow protrusions of the extine.

c. *Physics.* **1860** A. GREELY *Amer. Weather* vii. (1888) 60 It was formerly advanced that these minute drops of rain or fog were vesicular—that is, hollow spheres! **1863** TYNDALL *Heat* vi. §224 (1870) 176 If the particles of water be sufficiently small they will float.. without being vesicular.

2. Characterized by the presence of vesicles; composed of parts having the form of vesicles.

a. *Anat.* **1715** CHEYNE *Princ. Relig.* I. vi. §37 (ed. 2) 312 A Muscle is a bundle of Vesicular Threads, or of solid Filaments, involved in one common Membrane. **1833** SIR C. BELL *Hand* (1834) 69 Cold-blooded animals.. respire less frequently than other creatures,.. hence their vesicular lungs. **1848** CARPENTER *Anim. Phys.* i. (1872) 76 We find a form of nervous tissue,.. generally known as the vesicular. **1855** BAIN *Senses & Int.* I. ii. §16 These central masses all contain grey substance, the cellular or vesicular matter. **1860** GOSSE *Rom. Nat. Hist.* 364 A true serpent, with large vesicular lungs.

b. *Bot.* **1793** MARTYN *Lang. Bot.*, *Vesicularis*.. *scabrities*, vesicular or bladdery ruggedness. **1802** R. HALL *Elem. Bot.* 195 *Vesicular*,.. having small bodies like bladders on the surface.

c. *Physics.* **1794** SULIVAN *View Nat.* I. 357 He calls them vesicular vapour, whose particles may be distinguished by the eye. **1832** MACGILLIVRAY *Trav. Humboldt* xvi. 204 In the beginning of March the accumulation of vesicular vapours became visible. **1834** MRS. SOMERVILLE *Connex. Phys. Sci.* xxviii. 296 The vesicular state constituting a cloud. **1880** *Times* 25 Dec. 5 The silicate of soda was left in the state of a highly vesicular mass.

d. *Geol.* **1811** PINKERTON *Petralogy* II. 328 (*heading*), Vesicular Lava. **1813** BAKEWELL *Introd. Geol.* (1815) 330 The cavities in vesicular lava vary in size from that of a pea to a small nut. **1843** PORTLOCK *Geol.* 106 The whiter grits are also sometimes vesicular from the local removal of the calcareous paste. **1882** GEIKIE *Text-bk. Geol.* II. II. iii. 89 When this cellular structure is marked by comparatively few and small holes, it may be called vesicular.

3. *Zool.* Of worms: (see quot. 1861).

1830 R. KNOX *Béclard's Anat.* 378 The cysts which contain vesicular worms. **1861** HULME tr. *Moquin-Tandon* II. VII. xiii. 391 Under the name of Vesicular or Cystic Helmintha are included those entozoa which terminate in a vesicle, are contained in a cyst, or are composed of the latter only. **1876** tr. *Wagner's Gen. Pathol.* (ed. 6) 115 Vesicular Tape-worms are of considerable size.

4. *Path.* **a.** Characterized by the formation or presence of vesicles on the skin.

1818-20 E. THOMPSON *Cullen's Nosol. Method.* (ed. 3) 328 Pemphigus; Vesicular Fever. **1843** R. J. GRAVES *Syst. Clin. Med.* xxv. 318 The vesicular and scaly eruptions occurred in delicate persons. **1876** DUHRING *Dis. Skin* 78 Vesicular eczema exhibits the lesion in its most perfect state. **1886** *Buck's Handbk. Med. Sci.* II. 632/1 Vesicular eczema may occur in very small patches or in quite extensive areas.

b. Affecting or connected with the vesicles or air-cells of the lungs.

1829 COOPER *Goods Study Med.* (ed. 3) I. 622 These organs [the lungs] are in a state of vesicular or pulmonary emphysema. **1853** MARKHAM *Skoda's Auscult.* 101 By vesicular breathing, I understand that murmur only which is heard during inspiration. **1866** A. FLINT *Princ. Med.* (1880) 244 Vesicular emphysema.. consists in an abnormal accumulation of air within the air-cells, whereby they become distended and their walls often atrophied. *a* **1883** FAGGE *Princ. & Pract. Med.* (1886) I. 853 It is commonly called the 'vesicular murmur', having been so named when the idea that it arose in the air-cells of the lung was accepted without question.

So **veˈsiculary** *a. rare*$^{-1}$.

1754 *Phil. Trans.* XLVIII. 632 We found, that the animals in the vesicles were dead; but.. we had an opportunity of discovering the vesiculary polypes alive, in another coralline.

vesicularity (vɪsɪkjʊˈlærɪtɪ). [f. VESICULAR *a.* + -ITY.] Vesicular condition.

1908 *Mineral. Mag.* XV. 129 The first results.. were usually increased vesicularity in the quartz and assumption by much of it of the idiomorphic condition. **1978** *Nature* 20 July 218/1 Vesicularity of seafloor basalt, when plotted against depth of eruption, defines a family of three curves.

vesiculate (vɪˈsɪkjʊlət), *a.* [ad. mod.L. *vesiculat-us*, f. L. *vēsīcula* VESICULA.] = VESICULATED *a.*

1828-32 WEBSTER s.v., *Vesiculate a.*, bladdery; full of bladders. **1866** *Treas. Bot.* 1212/2 *Vesiculate*, inflated, bladdery. **1874** COOKE *Fungi* 55 Innumerable protuberances, which.. soon become round vesiculate cells. **1881** *Encycl. Brit.* XII. 551/2 One of the vesiculate medusæ.

veˈsiculate, *v.* [Back-formation from next.]

1. *trans.* To make vesicular or full of air-cells.

1865 *Pall Mall G.* 18 Oct. 10 He tells us that bread is 'vesiculated' by the carbonic acid gas forced into the dough.

2. *intr.* To become vesicular; to develop vesicles.

1891 in *Cent. Dict.* **1966** *Earth-Sci. Rev.* I. 158 A gas-charged lava flow.. might vesiculate so violently at and near its surface that it would form glass and pumice fragments. **1971** *Nature* 31 Dec. 539/1 Pulsations of ejected molten lava vesiculated and disintegrated passing immediately into the grey ash cloud. **1978** *Jrnl. Histochem. & Cytochem.* XXVI. 1 When a semisynthetic diet containing 1% orotic acid.. is fed to rats, the endoplasmic reticulum.. of hepatocytes vesiculates and lipoprotein.. droplets accumulate within the vesicles.

Hence **veˈsiculating** *ppl. a.*

1966 *Earth-Sci. Rev.* I. 158, 10 years later Iddings (1909) .. omitted the vesiculating flow idea. **1971** *Nature* 31 Dec. 538/2 Blobs and droplets of expanded, molten, vesiculating magma are carried aloft with an expanding vapour. **1979** *Biochim. & Biophys. Acta* DL. 222 Electron microscopy of vesiculating cells shows physical continuity between cell plasma membrane and vesicle membrane. **1983** *Sci. Amer.* Nov. 148/3 Both pumice and ash are frothy glassy materials created by the chilling of vesiculating magma.

veˈsiculated, *a.* [f. as VESICULATE *a.* + -ED.]

1. Having or full of small cavities or air-cells.

1703 *Phil. Trans.* XXIII. 1390 Frogs, Toads, Snakes,.. that have their Lungs Vesicated, as well as Vesiculated. **1774** *Ibid.* LXIV. 213 Any air, which gets beyond the vesiculated lungs themselves. **1886** A. H. CHURCH *Food Grains Ind.* 33 Its [*sc.* wheat's] admirable appropriateness for the making of a light vesiculated bread.

2. Of the nature of a vesicle or vesicula.

1898 P. MANSON *Trop. Diseases* xxxvii. 565 A threatening boil may often be aborted by touching the little initial itching or vesiculated papule with some penetrating antiseptic.

3. *Path.* Covered with vesicles.

a **1858** BRIGHT *Abdominal Tumours* (1860) 210 They both presented most extreme specimens of the vesiculated kidney.

vesiculation (vɪsɪkjʊˈleɪʃən). *Path.* and *Geol.* [f. VESICULA + -ATION. Cf. VESICATION.] The formation of vesicles, esp. on the skin; a vesicular condition or pustule.

1876 DUHRING *Dis. Skin* 67 Typical fluid exudation is observed in vesiculation, in the vesicles of eczema and herpes. **1897** *Allbutt's Syst. Med.* II. 138 In some cases.. the minute papules which characterize the scarlatinal eruption actually proceed to vesiculation. **1898** P. MANSON *Trop. Diseases* xxxv. 546 There may be evidence in the shape of vesiculations and thickening of the mucosa of a greater or less degree of catarrh. **1914** R. A. DALY *Igneous Rocks & their Origin* xiii. 264 The basal assumption, that vesiculation occurs at great depth in a volcanic conduit, is.. difficult to test. **1971** *Nature* 31 Dec. 538/2 Both articles describe the vesiculation of a magma in terms of the formation, motion and coalescence of bubbles.

vesiculi- (vɪˈsɪkjʊlɪ), combining form of VESICULA, occurring in a few terms, as **vesicuˈliferous** *a.*, bearing vesicles; **veˈsiculiform** *a.*, resembling a vesicle; **vesicuˈligerous** *a.*, vesiculiferous.

1846 DANA *Zooph.* 125 The inner tentacles clavate and vesiculigerous. **1859** MAYNE *Expos. Lex.* 1330 Vesiculiferous. **1891** *Cent. Dict.* s.v., Vesiculiform.

‖**vesiculitis** (vɪsɪkjʊˈlaɪtɪs). *Path.* [f. VESICULA + -ITIS.] Inflammation of a vesicle, esp. of the seminal vesicles.

1861 BUMSTEAD *Ven. Dis.* (1879) 183 A case in which vesiculitis terminated in an abscess. **1895** *Buck's Handbk. Med. Sci.* IX. 380/2 In chronic vesiculitis local measures are of little value.

vesiculo- (vɪˈsɪkjʊləʊ), combining form, on Greek models, of VESICULA, occurring in a few terms referring to vesicles in connexion with some part or thing denoted by the second element, as ***vesiculo-bronchial***, ***-spinal***, ***-tympanitic***; **veˌsiculo-ˈbullous** *a.*, characterized by or involving both vesicles and bullæ; **veˌsiculo-ˈpustular** *a.*, characterized by or involving both vesicles and pustules.

1898 *Allbutt's Syst. Med.* V. 98 Mingled with this diminished dulness and with the 'vesiculo-bronchial' breathing,..may be heard an adventitious murmur. **1923** R. W. MACKENNA *Dis. Skin* xii. 250 In every well-marked case of Dermatitis herpetiformis it is the vesiculo-bullous lesion which predominates. **1980** *Brit. Med. Jrnl.* 18 Oct. 1041/2 Herpes gestationis (HG) is a severely itching, vesiculobullous skin affection. **1911** STEDMAN *Med. Dict.* 959/1 Vesiculopustular. **1946** *Nature* 27 July 119/1 A fully developed vesiculopustular reaction developed at the site of inoculation. **1973** *Ibid.* 16 Feb. 425/3 There was a prodromal illness of a few days' duration followed by a vesiculopustular rash which was peripheral in distribution. **1885** *Encycl. Brit.* XIX. 35/2 Ano-spinal and vesiculo-spinal centres. **1886** *Buck's Handbk. Med. Sci.* II. 82/1 In emphysema a characteristic sound, somewhat less resonant, is heard, which is called vesiculo-tympanitic.

vesiculose (vɪsɪkjʊˈləʊs), *a.* [ad. L. *vēsīculōs-us* full of blisters: see VESICULA + -OSE.] Full of vesicles; vesicular.

1817 KIRBY & SP. *Entomol.* II. 223 The elytra.., shrowding its vesiculose abdomen, gave it much the appearance of a fine flower. **1856** W. CLARK *Van der Hoeven's Zool.* I. 332 Abdomen inflated, vesiculose. **1861** HAGEN *Synopsis Neuroptera N. Amer.* 171 Abdomen compressed at base, vesiculose, triquetral.

Hence **vesicuˈloso-**, employed as a combining form, as ***vesiculoso-cellular*** adj.

1826 KIRBY & SP. *Entomol.* IV. xxxviii. 69 In *Sphinx Ligustri* the *bronchiæ* terminate in oblong vesiculoso-cellular bodies, almost like lungs.

† **veˈsiculous**, *a. Obs.* [f. VESICUL-A + -OUS. So F. *vésiculeux*.] = VESICULOSE *a.*

1698 *Phil. Trans.* XX. 119 The vesiculous Parts of the Body; which, according to my Notion, are part Muscles, part Glands. **1712** tr. *Pomet's Hist. Drugs* I. 150 This Rind covers a Vesiculous Substance.

vesigh, obs. form of VIZY *sb. Sc.*

† **ˈvesike**. *Obs.* Also 6 **vesyke**, **visyke**. [ad. L. *vēsīca* VESICA.] **a.** The bladder. **b.** A bladder-like vessel or formation; a vesicle.

1540 R. JONAS *Birth Man.* I. 14 b, Sometyme the vesyke or bladder..be also apostumat & blystered. **1545** RAYNALD *Byrth Mankynde* p. i, Yf..the visyke or bladder be swollen or encombred with the stone. **1548-77** VICARY *Anat.* viii. (1888) 71 The chest of the Gal..is as a purse or a pannicular vesike in the holownesse of the Lyuer.

vesir, obs. form of VIZIER.

Vespa (ˈvɛspə). Also **vespa**. Pl. **Vespas**, ‖ **Vespe** (ˈvespe). [It., lit. 'wasp, hornet'.] A proprietary name for an Italian make of motor scooter.

1950 *Trade Marks Jrnl.* 22 Mar. 270/2 *Vespa*... Motor Cycles. Piaggio & C. Societa Perazioni,..Genova, Italy: manufacturers. **1956** A. THORNE *Baby & Battleship* I. 28 Those eternal bantam motor-bicycles, the little *Vespe* that the Italians love. **1958** J. CANNAN *And be a Villain* vii. 164 It was one of the first of the motor scooters—before the Vespas. **1960** AUDEN *Homage to Clio* 80 This could be a reason why they take the silencers off their Vespas. **1965** D. DU MAURIER *Flight of Falcon* v. 56 The young were everywhere, pouring out of lecture rooms, laughing, talking, getting on to vespas. **1983** 'D. RUTHERFORD' *Stop at Nothing* iv. 76 A three-wheeler Vespa with a miniature van on the back.

vespasian (vɛˈspeɪʒən). [Anglicized form of next.] = next.

1938 I. GOLDBERG *Wonder of Words* 139 Vespasian. **1980** *Times* 27 Feb. 6/8 The City of Paris has decided to erect.. three space age vespasians..new 'chalets of necessity'—as they are called.

‖ **vespasienne** (vɛspazjɛn). [Fr. (19th cent.), shortening of *colonne vespasienne* Vespasian column, f. the name of Titus Flavius *Vespasianus*, Roman Emperor, 69–79, who introduced a tax on public lavatories.] A public lavatory in France.

1922 E. E. CUMMINGS *Enormous Room* iii. 44 My first request was permission to visit the *vespasienne*. **1962** P. BRICKHILL *Deadline* x. 130 A pissoir, or, to give it its polite name, a vespasienne, after the emperor who was so solicitous of man's frailty. **1975** *Times* 4 Mar. 6/1 The vicissitudes of a village *vespasienne*.

vesper (ˈvɛspə(r)). Also 7 *pl.* **vespres**. [Partly a. L. *vesper* masc. (hence OF. *vespre*, older F. *vêpre*, Pr. *vespre*, Sp. *vespero*, Pg. *vespera*, It. *vespero*, *vespro*), evening star, evening, cognate with Gr. ἕσπερος HESPERUS. Partly ad. older F. *vespres* (mod.F. *vêpres*), vespers, evensong, ad. L. *vesperas* (nom. *vesperæ*), acc. pl. of *vespera* fem.; hence also Pr. *vespras*, Sp. *visperas*, Pg. *vesperas*. For the use of the plural form cf. *matins*, *nones*.]

I. In the singular form.

1. *poet.* (or *rhet.*). With capital. The evening star; Hesper, Hesperus.

1390 GOWER *Conf.* II. 109 Whan that thi liht is faded And Vesper scheweth him alofte. **1508** DUNBAR *Gold. Targe* 2 Ryght as the stern of day begouth to schyne, Quhen gone to bed war Vesper and Lucyne, I raise. **1577** GRANGE *Golden Aphrod.*, etc. Riij b, Phebus..His course was done, & Vesper she with Luna playde their partes. **1593** G. PEELE *Hon. Order Garter* B j, About the time when Vesper in the West Gan set the euening watch. **1633** P. FLETCHER *Purple Isl.* v. lxx, Vesper fair Cynthia ushers, and her train, See, th' apish earth hath lighted many a starre. **1697** DRYDEN *Virg. Georg.* I. 343 Red Vesper kindles there the tapers of the night. **1762** FALCONER *Shipwr.* I. 657 While glowing Vesper leads the starry train. **1820** KEATS *Ode to Psyche* 27 Fairer than Phœbe's sapphire-region'd star, Or Vesper, amorous glow-worm of the sky.

transf. **1815** SHELLEY *Adonais* xlvi, Assume thy winged throne, thou Vesper of our throng!

2. Evening, eventide; an evening. Also *personif.* Now *rare* or *Obs.*

1606 SHAKS. *Ant. & Cl.* IV. xiv. 8 Thou hast seene these Signes, They are blacke Vespers Pageants. **1613** PURCHAS *Pilgrimage* (1614) 123 From which ninth houre the Iewes began their Vespera or Euening... In these Vespers, as also on the Euen of euery Feast and Sabbath, after the euening sacrifice, they which doe any worke..shall neuer see good signe of a blessing. **1712** BUDGELL *Spect.* No. 425 ¶3 The one [companion] was Aurora..: The other was Vesper in a Robe of Azure beset with Drops of Gold. **1798** COLERIDGE *Anc. Mar.* 76 In mist or cloud, on mast or shroud, It perched for vespers nine. **1849** THOREAU *Week Concord Riv.* 26 From highest noon till the red vesper sinks into the west. *fig.* **1701** NORRIS *Ideal World* I. iii. 160 There cannot be any vespers in the great sun of truth.

3. Vespers, evensong. (See 6.) Also *transf.* †In early use with *a* or *the*.

1636 MASSINGER *Bashf. Lover* I. i, If you miss him when She goes to the vesper or the matins, hang me! **1657** THORNLEY tr. *Longus' Daphnis & Chloe* A iij b, I will tell you a storie, one I had at a Tavern vesper. **1737** *Ozell's Rabelais* I. xl. 315 A Mass, a Matine, a Vesper well sung is half said. **1815** SHELLEY *Alastor* 694 Mighty Earth From sea and mountain, city and wilderness, In vesper low or joyous orison, Lifts still its solemn voice. **1844** *Mem. Babylonian Princess* II. 309, I knew that many of those with whom I was acquainted attended mass and vesper at this chapel.

4. *ellipt.* The vesper-bell.

1808 SCOTT *Marmion* II. xxxiii, Even in the vesper's heavenly tone, They seem'd to hear a dying groan. **1817** MOORE *Lalla R.*, *Paradise & P.* 440 But, hark! the vesper calls to pray'r. **1874** O. W. HOLMES *Poetical Wks.* (1892) I. 352 How blest to the toiler his hour of release When the vesper is heard With its whisper of peace! **1927** A. CLARKE *Son of Learning* 18 *Brother*: I must ring the Vesper.

II. In collective pl. **vespers**.

†**5. a.** In Univ. use: The public disputations and accompanying ceremonies which immediately preceded the inception or commencement of a Bachelor of Arts; esp. in later use at Oxford, the day on which these were held, the eve *of* the Act. Cf. VESPERY. *Obs.*

1574 M. STOKYS in Peacock *Stat. Cambr.* (1841) App. A. p. xxii, The Bedyll shall bryng the Inceptours in Arte to the Place where the commensement shall be kepte, and so shall begynn the Vespers in Arte and in Civill. *Ibid.* p. xxiv, The Father in Arte in the Ve[s]pers shall sytt in the West ende off the Chyrche. **1657** OWEN *Vind. Treat. Schism* i. Wks. 1855 XIII. 217 A learned gentleman, whom I had prevailed withal to answer in the Vespers of our Act, sent me his questions. **1681** GREW *Musæum* IV. ii. 361, I read two Publique Lectures at Oxford, on the Vespers of the Publique Act. **1715** HEARNE *Collect.* (O.H.S.) V. 93 Lectures in the Vespers. The Vespers on Saturday.

†**b.** The eve *of* a festival, or *of* the Passion.

1629 DONNE *Serm.* 73 What a dimme Vespers of a glorious festivall. **1660** JER. TAYLOR *Worthy Commun.* i. §3. 49 The Sacrament of the Lords Supper..being instituted in the vespers of the passion. **1663** —— *Serm. 1 Cor. xv. 23*, 33 And as the Apostles in the vespers of Christs passion, so he in the Eves of his own dissolution was..heavie unto death. **1697** BURGHOPE *Disc. Relig. Assemb.* 132 Our blessed Lord in the vespers of his death.

6. *Eccl.* **a.** The sixth of the Canonical Hours of the breviary, said or celebrated towards evening; = EVENSONG 1; also, the time of this office.

Usually without article, but occas. with *the*, and sometimes with a sing. verb.

1611 CORYAT *Crudities* 14, I came into their Church at the time of prayers in the afternoone, the Nunnes being then at their Vespers. **1644** in *Eng. Hist. Rev.* Apr. (1913) 341 The parish Church in Ruell where the King and Queene were at Vespres. **1702** in *Cath. Rec. Soc. Publ.* VII. 127 Afternoon we went to Vespers to ye Abbay of St Floraux, a Benedictine Order. *c* **1731** *Diary Blue Nuns* Ibid. VIII. 92 About three a clock in the afternoon whilst we were at vespers. **1756** tr. *Keysler's Trav.* (1760) IV. 19 On Ascension-eve, vespers are performed with great pomp and splendor. **1832** G. DOWNES *Lett. Cont. Countries* I. 34, I stopped to attend vespers at the Cathedral of St. Denis. **1871** MISS MULOCK *Fair France* iv. 142 Vespers is, I conclude, a litany rather than a mass. **1884** F. M. CRAWFORD *Rom. Singer* I. 24 Then we went into the Capella del Coro to wait for the vespers.

†**b.** Applied to the Evening Prayer or Evensong of the Church of England. *Obs. rare.*

1660 PEPYS *Diary* 2 Oct., At Will's I met with Mr. Spicer, and with him to the Abbey to see them at vespers.

c. With distinguishing terms denoting special forms of this office.

Sicilian vespers: see SICILIAN *a.* 2 a.

a **1700** in *Cath. Rec. Soc. Publ.* IX. 368 At ye first vespers of ye Assomption of or Blessed Lady. **1762** *Evening-Office of Church* (ed. 2) 300 In the second Vespers, is a commemoration of S. Paul. *Ibid.* 363 After *Benedicamus Domino*, the Vespers of the Dead are said. **1908** *Ch. Times* 13 Mar. 347/2 Vespers for the Dead, in the form sanctioned by Bishop Creighton, was sung.

d. *poet.* Evening prayers or devotions.

1814 SHELLEY in Dowden *Life* (1887) I. 496 Adieu; remember love at vespers before sleep, I do not omit my prayers. **1820** KEATS *Eve St. Agnes* xxvi, Her vespers done, Of all its wreathed pearls her hair she frees.

7. *transf.* The evening song of a bird. Cf. EVENSONG 2. Chiefly *poet.*

1678 H. VAUGHAN *Pious Th.* 225, I heard last May..The pleasant Philomel her vespers sing. **1795-1814** WORDSW. *Excurs.* IV. 1169 If the solemn nightingale be mute, And the soft woodlark here did never chant Her vespers. **1813** SCOTT *Rokeby* v. ii, Hoarse into middle air arose The vespers of the roosting crows. **1854** THOREAU *Walden* iv. (1884) 135 The whippoorwills chanted their vespers for half an hour.

III. 8. *attrib.* **a.** In the sense 'of or belonging to, used at or for, vespers or evensong', as ***vesper-bell***, ***-carol***, ***-chime***, ***-hymn***, ***light***, ***psalm***, ***-song***, etc.; **vesper-book** (also † **vespers book**), a vesperal; **vesper music** (see quot.); **vesper service**, vespers, evensong.

In general use freq. passing into next.

1794 MRS. RADCLIFFE *Myst. Udolpho* xxxvi, The monastery, whose *vesper-bell she had heard on the preceding evening. **1844** DICKENS *Pictures from Italy* (Collins) 244 To the ringing of vesper-bells, darkness sets in. **1864** SKEAT *Uhland's Poems* 223 The sun sinks down, the vesper-bell bids men to rest and pray. **1772** in *Catholic Records Soc. Publ.* I. 138, 4 Vols: of Mass Books, ..*Vesperse Book. **1850** (*title*), Vesper-Book; containing the complete Order for Vespers for the entire Year, according to the Roman Breviary. **1865** *Pall Mall G.* No. 140. 3/1 The vesper-book used by Roman Catholics. **1818** KEATS *Endym.* IV. 834 Therefore for her these *vesper-carols are. *a* **1835** MRS. HEMANS *My own Portrait* Poems (1875) 487 Even as a sound of *vesper-chimes Can wake departed things. **1808** SKURRAY *Bidcombe Hill* 7 The blackbird from the ivied temple chants His *vesper-hymn. **1866** ENGEL *Nat. Music* viii. 281 The Roman Catholics.. have their Vesper Hymns, and the singing of these appears to be customary in most countries where the Roman Catholic faith prevails. **1892** *Ch. Times* 4 Nov. 1094/2 An oaken altar..with *vesper lights. **1888** JACOBI *Printers' Voc.* 151 **Vesper music*, plain chant or Gregorian music is thus designated. **1823** MRS. HEMANS *Vespers of Palermo* III. iii, Here..meet me, when the bell Doth sound for *vesper-prayer! **1896** SWETE *Ch. Serv.* 62 The *vesper Psalms were five in number, recited as at Mattins in regular course. **1797** MRS. RADCLIFFE *Italian* vi, The *vesper-service of the monks. **1844** DICKENS *Mart. Chuz.* v, The old cathedral bell began to ring for vesper service. **1904** WORDSW. & LITTLEHALES *Old Service Bks.* 79 The Evensong or vesper service of Sunday and other days of the week. **1810** SCOTT *Lady of Lake* III. xxiii, To-morrow eve..My *vesper song [may be] thy wail, sweet maid! **1871** LONGF. *Wayside Inn* II. *Baron St. Castine* 169 No day is so long But it comes at last to vesper-song. **1813** SCOTT *Trierm.* I. i, Holy as hermit's *vesper strain. **1866** NEALE *Sequences & Hymns* 81 It shall blend its *vesper summons With the day's departing smile. **1808** SCOTT *Marmion* v. vi, There must the Baron rest, Till past the hour of *vesper tide. *a* **1849** MANGAN *Poems* (1859) 49 From streaky gleam of morning's light Until the *vesper-toll. **1845** R. S. HAWKER *Ball. Cornw.*, etc. (1869) 45 Teach me, Father John, to say *Vesper-verse and matin-lay.

b. In the sense 'of or belonging to, characteristic of, occurring in, the evening; vespertinal'.

1791 E. DARWIN *Bot. Gard.* I. 63 Soft fell the vesper-drops, condensed below, Or bent in air the rain-refracted bow. **1794** *Sporting Mag.* IV. 58 A vesper-blue curricle. **1810** *Associate Minstrels* 6 Fair shines the vesper-star. **1832** G. DOWNES *Lett. Cont. Countries* I. 63 To preside over bread and butter at the vesper tea-table. **1839** DE QUINCEY *Recoll. Lakes* Wks. 1862 II. 134 Yet in these eyes of vesper gentleness, there was a considerable obliquity of vision. **1887** J. ASHBY STERRY *Lazy Minstrel* (1892) 208 When rooms with the vesper tobacco are clouded. **1890** *Sat. Rev.* 23 Aug. 225/1 Rich in every imaginable tint of vesper beauty. **1928** BLUNDEN *Retreat* 50 O vesper-born, Stiff-necked I stand like that hewn knotty tree, As if heaven were my halo.

c. (Chiefly *U.S.*) In the names of animals, birds, or insects, as **vesper-beauty**, **vesper-bird** or **-sparrow** (see quots.); **vesper mouse**, a mouse of the genus *Hesperomys* or *Vesperimus* or related genera; a white-footed mouse.

1832 J. RENNIE *Consp. Butterfl. & M.* 115 The Vesper Beauty (*Epione vespertaria*) appears the middle of July. **1859** S. F. BAIRD *Mammals N. Amer.* 455 A striking feature of the North American vesper mice, to anglicize Wagner's name, is their diminutive size compared with the South American. **1869** J. BURROUGHS in *Galaxy Mag.* Aug., They [*i.e.* grass-finches] sing much after sundown, hence the aptness of the name vesper-sparrow, which a recent writer, Wilson Flagg, has bestowed upon them. **1884** COUES *N. Amer. Birds* 364 *Passerculus gramineus*,..Grass Finch. Bay-winged Bunting. Vesper Bird. **1893** *Scribner's Mag.* June 764/1 Our little vesper sparrow is said to have had the same end in view when he made his soft sweet carol the vesper-song of the uplands.

†**d.** In sense 5 a, as ***vesper disputations***. *Obs.*

1715 HEARNE *Collect.* (O.H.S.) V. 93 Vesper Disputations in Philosophy. Vesper Disputations in Law.

vesperal (ˈvɛspərəl), *a.* and *sb.* [ad. late L. *vesperāl-is*, f. L. *vespera*: see prec. Cf. F. *vesperal* sb.]

A. *adj.* **a.** Vespertinal, vespertine. **b.** Pertaining to vespers or the vesper-bell. *rare.*

1623 COCKERAM I, Vesperall, of or belonging to the euening. [Hence in Blount.] **1827** CARLYLE *Germ. Rom.* III. 135 Amid the vesperal melodies of the steeple sounding-holes. **1887** L. JOHNSON *Incense in Ireland* (1897) 60 Pensive and solitary old age finds Calm in the vesperal, mild air. **1951** V. NABOKOV *Speak, Memory* iv. 47 The day would take hours to fade, and everything..would be kept in a state of infinite vesperal suspense.

B. *sb.* **1.** *Eccl.* An office-book containing the psalms, canticles, anthems, etc., with their musical settings, used at vespers; an antiphonary containing the vesper-chants.

1869 *Life Marg. M. Hallahan* (1870) 431 They were presented with a Vesperal and Processional. **1884** *Grove's Dict. Music* IV. 257 The most correct Vesperals now in print are those published at Mechlin in 1870, and at Ratisbon in 1875.

2. An evening song.

In quot. as the title of a poem.

1896 E. Dowson *Verses* 39 Vesperal. 'Strange grows the river on the sunless evenings!'

†**'vesperate,** *v. Obs.*⁻⁰ [f. ppl. stem of med.L. *vesperāre* to become evening, f. L. *vesper* VESPER.] 'To wax night' (Cockeram 1, 1623).

ve'sperian, *a. rare*⁻¹. [f. VESPER + -IAN.] Vespertine.

1777 Toplady *Solar System* Wks. 1794 IV. 271 [Venus] enters on her short vesperian regency, and shines by the name of Hesperus, or the evening-star.

'vespering, *ppl. a. rare*⁻¹. [f. VESPER + -ING².] Flying westwards (towards sunset).

1914 Hardy *Year's Awakening* in *New Weekly* 21 Mar. 9 O vespering bird, how do you know?

vesper'tilian, *a.* [See next and -AN.] Bat-like. Also *fig.*

1874 Ruskin *Proserpina* I. iv. §22 Mr. Darwin..in his vespertilian treatise on the ocelli of the Argus pheasant. **1911** W. J. Locke *Glory of Clementina Wing* xxii. 277 As the studio was rigorously closed to him during the daylight hours his visits were vespertilian. **1955** R. Graves *Crowning Privilege* 222 The fiend..Flaunts vespertilian wing and cloven hoof.

‖**vesper'tilio.** *rare*⁻¹. [L. *vespertīlio* bat, f. *vesper* VESPER.] A bat.

In modern Zoology *Vespertilio* (pl. *-iones*) is one of the many genera of Cheiroptera: cf. next.

1665 Sir T. Herbert *Trav.* (1677) 385 These vespertilios ..hang in swarms upon the boughs of Trees.

vesper'tilionid, *a.* (and *sb.*) *Zool.* [ad. mod.L. *Vespertilionid-æ* (see def.).] Of or belonging to the *Vespertilionidæ*, a large family of insectivorous bats, including the common British species. Also as *sb.*, a bat of this family.

1875 Dallas in *Cassell's Nat. Hist.* I. 332 The tail traverses the interfemoral membrane in the fashion of that of a Vespertilionid Bat. **1965** B. E. Freeman tr. *Vandel's Biospeleology* xxvii. 454 The ears of vespertilionids are immobile. **1976** *Nature* 15 Apr. 628/1 Within our sample alone, species are represented whose primary foods are.. insects (the mormoopids, natalids, vespertilionids and molossids).

vesper'tilionine, *a.* (*sb.*). *Zool.* [f. L. *vespertīliōn-*, *vespertīlio* bat + -INE.] **a.** *adj.* Of or belonging to, comprising or consisting of, a large distinct group of insectivorous bats included in the sub-order *Microchiroptera.*

1875 G. E. Dobson in *Ann. Nat. Hist.* XVI. 350 The families of Microchiroptera..form two natural alliances, which may be called the Vespertilionine and Emballonurine alliances respectively.

b. *sb.* A bat belonging to this group.

1891 *Cent. Dict.*

vesper'tilionize, *v. nonce-word.* [f. as prec. + -IZE.] *trans.* To convert or turn *into* a bat.

1854 Badham *Halieut.* 451 Others..have vespertilionized this skate into the Sea-bat.

vespertinal (vɛspə'taɪnəl), *a.* [ad. late L. *vespertīnāl-is*, f. L. *vespertīnus*: see next and -AL¹. Cf. obs. F. *vespertinal, -el.*] = next.

1839 *Fraser's Mag.* XIX. 469 All my troubles, cares, anxieties, perplexities—matutinal, meridional, and vespertinal. **1849** Thoreau *Week Concord Riv.* 119 The vespertinal pout had already begun to flit on leathern fin. **1854** Lowell *Cambridge 30 Yrs. Ago* Prose Wks. 1890 I. 90 F. became purely vespertinal, never stirring abroad till after dark. **1901** *Athenæum* 28 Dec. 876/3 Vespertinal events.. might be dated in Saxon times in four different ways.

vespertine ('vɛspətaɪn, -ɪn), *a.* (and *sb.*). [ad. L. *vespertīn-us* (hence also OF. *vespertin*, It., Sp., Pg. *vespertino*), f. *vesper* VESPER: see -INE¹.]

1. Of or pertaining to the evening; coming, occurring, or taking place in the evening; *spec.* in *Astrol.* (cf. 2).

1502 Arnolde *Chron.* 168 Yf thou wil kepe late set plantis, kepe hem from vespertyn reynes. *c* **1550** Rolland *Crt. Venus* II. 695 Fra Phebus rais to the hour vespertine. *c* **1610** Sir C. Heydon *Astrol. Disc.* (1650) 60 The second is..the Vespertine oriental Apparition, which he calleth the last rising. **1634** Sir T. Herbert *Trav.* (1638) 217 The starres; their heliacall, acronicall, matutine, and vespertine motions. **1716** M. Davies *Athen. Brit.* I. 33 The Morning and Vespertin Service in that Church. **1812** Cary *Dante, Purg.* xv. 140 Far onward as our eyes..could stretch against the bright Vespertine ray. **1851** Glenny *Handbk. Fl. Gard.* 68 It is desirable on account of its powerful vespertine fragrance. **1901** *Athenæum* 28 Dec. 877 The vespertine portion of the ecclesiastical day.

b. Of animals, birds, etc.: Appearing or especially active in the evening.

In quot. 1607 after L. *lupus vespertinus*, the Vulgate rendering of Heb. *z'ēb ʿereb* in Hab. i. 8.

1607 Topsell *Four-f. Beasts* 435 This first and vulgar kinde of Hyæna is bred in Affricke and Arabia... God himselfe in holy scripture calleth it by the name of a Vespertine Wolfe. **1802** Shaw *Gen. Zool.* III. I. 114 Vespertine Frog... Native of Siberia. **1891** *Cent. Dict.* s.v., The vespertine or evening grosbeak, *Hesperiphona vespertina.*

†**c.** Dim, imperfect. *Obs.*⁻¹

1623 Bp. Hall *Best Bargaine* Wks. (1625) 518 If ye had already that vespertine knowledge of the Saints which ye shall once haue in heauen.

2. *Astr.* and *Astrol.* Of a star, planet, etc.: Setting at or just after sunset.

1601 Holland *Pliny* II. xvi. I. 11 These stars or planets in their evening setting, are neerest to the earth:..and then they be called Occidentall Vespertine, i. when the sun toward the evening covereth them with his raies. **1647** Lilly *Chr. Astrol.* cxxvii. 577 An Infortune in the Nativity, ..if Vespertine, [shows] long Diseases. **1679** Moxon *Math. Dict., Vespertine*, when a Planet sets after the Sun. [Hence in Harris, Kersey, etc.] **1690** Leybourn *Curs. Math.* 449 She [i.e. Venus] is..sometimes almost Full, at other times Gibbous,..as well when she is Vespertine as Matutine. **1819** J. Wilson *Dict. Astrol.* 288 Vespertine planets, viz. those between the 10th and 7th, or on the cusp of the 4th or near it, or ☿ and ♀ rising vespertine by day.

3. *Geol.* Used to designate the lowest carboniferous formation of the Pennsylvanian coal-measures.

1858 H. D. Rogers *Geol. Pennsylv.* II. 735 The..horizon which separates the Umbral red shale from the underlying Vespertine conglomerate. *Ibid.* 756 The Vespertine, or Lower Carboniferous series. **1888** *Encycl. Brit.* XXIV. 258/1 In its Vespertine areas are numerous patches of anthracite and semi-anthracite coals.

†**4.** As *sb.* Vespers, evensong. In quot. *fig. Obs.*

a **1635** Randolph *Hey for Honesty* v. Wks. (1875) 489 Their breakfasts are their matins holy zelibus, Their vespertines are eating beef and velibus.

‖**Vesperugo.** *Obs. rare.* [L.] Evening, or the evening star. (Cf. VESPER 1 and 2.)

In mod. *Zool.* used as the name of a genus of bats belonging to the group *Vespertiliones.*

1600 Tourneur *Trans. Metam.* vii, The skie..Is cloath'd with moorie Vespervgoe's coate. **1679** Moxon *Math. Dict., Vesperugo*, the Evening-Star, Venus, when she shines after Sun-Set. [Hence in Kersey, Bailey, etc.]

'vespery. Now *Hist.* [a. F. *vespérie* (16th c.), or ad. med.L. *vesperia*, f. L. *vesper* VESPER.] *pl.* = *vespers*, VESPER 5 a.

[**1656** Blount *Glossogr.* (copying Cotgr.), *Vesperies*, Evening Exercises or Disputations (among the Sorbonists). **1706** Phillips (ed. Kersey), *Vesperies*, the last Act, or Exercise for taking the Degree of Doctor, among the Sorbonists in France.] **1886** Lyte *Hist. Univ. Oxford* 213 The vesperies of the Faculty of Arts might be held..on any day that was available for lectures. The exercise consisted of a disputation between the inceptor and some Masters of Arts on certain questions propounded in Latin verse by the presiding Master.

vespiary ('vɛspɪərɪ). [Irreg. f. L. *vesp-a* wasp, after *apiary*. Cf. med.L. *vesparium.*] A wasps' nest.

1817 Kirby & Sp. *Entomol.* II. 108 The number of females in a populous vespiary is considerable. **1830** *Insect Architecture* (L.E.K.) 71 We have never met with a single vespiary in any situation likely to have been frequented by moles. **1890** *Science-Gossip* XXVI. 122/1 Wasps clothe their vespiary with ten or twelve layers of paper.

'vespidous, *a. Ent. rare.* [f. med.L. *Vespid-æ* (see def.) + -OUS.] Of or belonging to the *Vespidæ*, an extensive family of wasps, including the social wasps and hornets; vespoid.

1848 Maunder *Treas. Nat. Hist.* 724 A Vespidous insect having the first joint of the abdomen elongated into a pedicel.

'vespiform, *a. Ent.* Also 8 vespæ-. [f. L. *vesp-a*, *-æ*, wasp + -(I)FORM.] Having the form or appearance of a wasp; wasp-like.

1752 J. Hill *Hist. Anim.* 31 The vespæform Asilus, with the antennæ longer than the head. **1817** Kirby & Sp. *Entomol.* II. 263, I once found one of the vespiform bees (*Apis Goodeniana*..) hanging by its mandibles from the edge of a hazel-leaf.

†**vespillo(n.** *Obs. rare.* Also vespilone. [a. L. *vespillōn-*, *vespillo* (also *vespa*), acc. to Festus f. *vesper* evening. So obs. F. *vespillon.*] (See quot. 1656.)

1631 Weever *Anc. Funeral Mon.* iii. 11 Such as..were of high parentage..were buried in the euening by certaine men who had that charge, who were called Vespillons. *Ibid.* iv. 12 Such..were buried in the night time, by the Vespillons clothed all in white. **1643** Sir T. Browne *Relig. Med.* I. §38 By raking into the bowells of the deceased, continuall sight of Anatomies, Skeletons, or Cadaverous reliques, like Vespilloes, or Grave-makers. **1656** Blount *Glossogr., Vespilone*, he that carries forth dead bodies in the night to be buried, as they use in time of plague and great sickness.

vespine ('vɛspaɪn), *a.* [f. *vesp-a* wasp + -INE¹.] Of or pertaining to a wasp or wasps; consisting of wasps.

1843 *Penny Cycl.* XXVII. 105/1 The neuters are the.. busiest class of the vespine community. **1863** Miss Yonge *Wars Wapsburg* 25 Vespine laws of fortification could not be more perfectly observed. **1884** *Cornh. Mag.* Oct. 400 To meet this abnormal fancy of the vespine intellect, the fig-wort makes its sensitive surface mature first.

'vespoid, *a. Ent.* [f. L. *vesp-a* wasp + -OID.] Resembling a wasp; wasp-like; *spec.* of or belonging to the *Vespoidea*, a super-family of *Hymenoptera* containing the typical wasps.

1815 Kirby & Sp. *Entomol.* iv. (1816) I. 122 *Pompilus viaticus*, a vespoid insect that deposits its eggs in spiders. **1859** Mayne *Expos. Lex.* s.v. *Vespoides.*

vessche, obs. form of VETCH.

†**vesse.** *Obs.* [Of unknown origin.] A kind of worsted fabric formerly made in Suffolk. Only in pl.

1483 *Act 1 Rich. III*, c. 8 §18 The makyng of any Clothes called Vessees, Cogware, or Worstedes. **1511–2** *Act 3 Hen. VIII*, c. 7 The drapyng and makyng of such clothes, called vesses, rayes, saylynge clothes, and other clothes. **1523** *Act 14 & 15 Hen. VIII*, c. 11 That Vesses otherwyse called Set Clothes of dyvers Colours be made in your said Countie of Suffolk, which be made to be worne in far Countries and nat in Englond.

vesse, var. VESSEY *Obs.*

vessel ('vɛsəl), *sb.*¹ Forms: α. 4, 6 **vessele** (4 **wessele**), 4–5 **vesselle** (5 **wess-**), **vessale**; 4 **vescel**, **vessil**, 4– **vessel** (4–5 **wessel**, **uessel**, 4, 6 **fessel**), 5–7 **vessell** (**wessell**, 5 **fessell**); 4 **vesseal**, 5 **veseal**, **vessall**. β. *Sc.* 5 **vyscele**, **weschele**, 5–6 **wesch-**, **veschale**, 5 **wes(s)chael(le**; 5 **wischeall**, 5–6 **veschall** (5 **wesch-**, **vessche-**), 6 **weschail**; 5–6 **wesch-**, 5–7 **veschell** (6 **vessch-**), 6 **veshel**, 7–8 **veshell**. γ. 4–5, 7 **vessayle**, 5 **veassayle**, **vessaile**. δ. 5 **vayssel**, **vaissel**. [a. (1) AF. and OF. *vessel*, OF. *vesseal*, *vaissel*, *vaisseau*, etc. (mod.F. *vaisseau*) masc., = Pr. *vaisel*, Sp. *vasillo*, It. *vascello*:—L. *vascellum* small vase or urn, ship, etc., dim. of *vās* VAS; (2) AF. and OF. *vessele*, *veselle*, OF. *vasselle*, *wasselle*, *vaisselle*, etc. (mod.F. *vaisselle*) fem., repr. the L. pl. *vascella* and used in a collective sense.]

1. †**a.** In collective singular: Vessels or utensils for the table or for use in the household, esp. those made of gold or silver; = PLATE *sb.* 16. *Obs.*

Freq. from *c* 1300 to *c* 1600.

α. *a* **1300** *Cursor M.* 6145 Fra þis folk..þe folk of israel to boru Asked silueren vessel [*v.r.* wessel] sere. **13..** *Coer de L.* 1488 Now, styward, I warne the, Bye us vessel gret plente, Dysschys, cuppys, and sawsers, Bolles, treyes, and platers. *c* **1400** Maundev. (1839) xx. 220 Alle the Vesselle, that men ben served with, in the Halle or in Chambres, ben of precious Stones. **1420** *E.E. Wills* (1882) 46 A dosen of peutre vessell. **1424** *Ibid.* 56 All my seluere vessell. **1477** *Rolls of Parlt.* VI. 184/2 That Sterlyng Halpeny nor Ferthyng, shuld not be molten for Vessell. **1523** Ld. Berners *Froiss.* I. xx. 29 All his Vessell was of golde and siluer, pottis, basons, ewers, dysshes, flagons, barels, cuppes, and all other thyngis. **1587** Harrison *England* III. xi. in *Holinshed* I. 237/2 Such furniture of houshold of this mettall [*sc.* pewter], as we commonlie call by the name of vessell, is sold vsuallie by the garnish. **1609** Holland *Amm. Marcell.* 192 They shamed now to drinke out of earthen vessell. **1613–8** Daniel *Coll. Hist. Eng.* (1826) 107 He.. made restitution of much Church vessell, that had beene taken and sold for ransome. **1664** Marvell *Corr.* Wks. (Grosart) II. 148 Have I..layd them in mine own beds, mine own hangings, and treated them continually in mine own vessel?

β. **1375** Barbour *Bruce* XI. 117 All thai..that chargit war Of palȝeonys and veschall vith-all. *c* **1375** *Sc. Leg. Saints* xviii. (*Mary Egypt*) 1094 þan godis blud & his body put in to weschale, þare-to worthy. *c* **1425** Wyntoun *Cron.* II. xii. 1073 Golde, siluir and wesschaelle, Cleynly made of gud metaille. **1490** *Acc. Ld. High Treas. Scot.* I. 132 For the caryage of the siluer vesscheall to Lythgow again Payce. **1513** Douglas *Æneid* I. ix. 109 Siluer plait..was brocht To set on buirdis; and weschail forgit of gold. **1549** *Compl. Scotl.* xvii. 145 Coppir, bras, and yrn and vthir mettellis var meltit to mak vtensel veschel necessair to serue ane houshald. *a* **1578** Lindesay (Pitscottie) *Chron. Scot.* (S.T.S.) I. 337 Costlie beding, weschell and naiperie according for ane king. **1627** [see sense 7].

γ, δ. **1474** Caxton *Chesse* II. v. (1883) 69 He sayde that hit was better and more noble thynge to shyne in good maners than in vayssel. **1605** *Tryall Chevalr.* IV. i, And so, sir, you that walk in pewter vessayle, like one of the worthyes, will you be rul'd by me? [**1820** Scott *Monast.* xvi, Every bit of vassail and silver work have we been spoiled of since Pinkie Cleuch.]

b. *dial.* (See quots.)

1854 Miss Baker *Northampt. Gloss.* 375 *Vessel*,..all the plates, dishes, and culinary utensils which are put into requisition during a meal. 'Wash the vessel up.' Never applied to a tea-service or to glasses. **1893** *Wilts. Gloss.* 176 To wash up the vessel is to wash up plates, dishes, &c.

2. a. Any article designed to serve as a receptacle for a liquid or other substance, usually one of circular section and made of some durable material; *esp.* a utensil of this nature in domestic use, employed in connexion with the preparation or serving of food or drink, and usually of a size suitable for carrying by hand.

Often with defining term preceding (sometimes hyphened), indicating its special use, as *dairy, drinking, kitchen, milk-, wine-vessel.* See also AIR-, STEAM-VESSEL 1.

α. *a* **1300** *Cursor M.* 13395 Iesus badd þam þan o-nan Fil þair gret wessels [*Fairf.* vessels] o stan O water clere. **1340** *Ayenb.* 235 þe þinges þet byeþ y-halȝed, ase þe uesseles y-blissed, þe chalis, þe copereaus. *c* **1386** Chaucer *Monk's T.*

204 Goth, bringeth forth the vessealx.. The which my fader in his prosperite Out of the temple of Jerusalem byraft. **c 1400** MAUNDEV. (Roxb.) xi. 43 A vessell of gold full of manna. *c* **1450** *MS. Douce* 55 fol. 11 Steep hem with sugre water..in to a feyre fessell. *c* **1471** FORTESCUE *Wks.* (1869) 458 Oftyntyms his Highnesse must and will bye.. Wessels, Westments, and other Ornaments for his Chapel. **1526** TINDALE *Luke* v. 37 Also no man poureth newe wyne into olde vessels. **1550** *N.C. Wills* (Surtees, 1908) 208 Such vessels, barkes, and other thinges as belonges to the tanners craft. **1577** HARRISON *England* in *Holinshed* I. 110/1 Afterward putting it [*sc.* brawn] into close vessels, they poure..good small ale..thereto tyll it be couered. **1610** HOLLAND *Camden's Brit.* 650 An earthen vessel in which was hourded a mighty deale of Romaine coine. **1658** J. HARRINGTON *Prerog. Pop. Govt.* II. ii. 11 His Enemies breaking down his Statues,..made homely Vessels of them. **1719** DE FOE *Crusoe* I. 121 To my great Misfortune, I had no Vessel to boil or stew any Thing. **1791** COWPER *Odyss.* II. 381 Join thou the suitors, and provide, In separate vessels stow'd, all needful stores. **1831** BREWSTER *Optics* iii. 23 Let the board with its pedestal be placed..in a glass vessel of water. **1855** DICKENS *Dorrit* II. ix, Bending over a steaming vessel of tea. **1907** *Verney Mem.* I. 8 Queer tin vessels of many shapes.

Prov. phr. **1599** SHAKS. *Hen. V*, IV. iv. 71 But the saying is true, The empty vessel makes the greatest sound.

transf. **1645** USSHER *Body Div.* (1647) 100 The third night (as it seemeth) God caused the Waters to retire into their Vessels.

β. *c* **1425** WYNTOUN *Cron.* v. 1458 Þat..his blude In til a weschael tycht and gude Sulde be put. *a* **1500** *Ratis Raving*, etc. 101 As lekand weschell haldis no thinge, Sa opin tung has na traistinge. **1561** WINȜET *Wks.* (S.T.S.) I. 94 The weschelis and ornamentis appropriat to the seruice of God. **1596** DALRYMPLE tr. *Leslie's Hist. Scot.* II. 120 In dischis of daintie, in veschelis of al sortis. **1756** MRS. CALDERWOOD *Jrnl.* (1884) 84 They immediatly put those veshells into cold water.

γ. **13..** *E.E. Allit. P.* B. 1713 Þou..has hofen þy hert agaynes þe hyȝe dryȝtyn,..& now his vessayles [are] avyled in vanyte vnclene. *c* **1420** *Liber Cocorum* (1862) Lay pigges in a vessayle, with bothe hande.

b. In various fig. applications. (Cf. 3.)

1303 R. BRUNNE *Handl. Synne* 7859 Þe Iew þey called 'a voyde vessel', And forsoþe, so hyt fel. *c* **1315** SHOREHAM I. 1548 Þer-fore ech man..wessche and greydy hys fessel, And do trewlyche hys charge. **1587** HOLINSHED *Chron.* (ed. 2) III. 832/1 The vessell of amitie betweene the king of Enggland & the French being first broched by this popes letters. **1599** SHAKS. *Hen. V*, IV. Chorus 3 Of a time, When creeping Murmure.. Fills the wide Vessell of the Vniuerse. **1605** —— *Macb.* III. i. 67 For them, the gracious Duncan haue I murther'd; Put Rancours in the Vessell of my Peace Onely for them. *a* **1650** MAY *Old Couple* v, Gently, my joys distil Lest you do break the vessel you should fill. **1667** MILTON *P.L.* XII. 559, Greatly instructed I shall hence depart..and have my fill Of knowledge, what this vessel can containe. **1883** H. DRUMMOND *Nat. Law in Spir. W.* (1884) 270 Who will not willingly exchange his shallow vessel for Christ's well of living water?

c. The contents of a vessel; a vesselful. *rare.*

1526 *Pilgr. Perf.* (W. de W. 1531) 25 b, The vyntenar gyueth frely..a taste of his wyne though he gyue not the hole vessell at ones. **1609** SKENE *Reg. Maj., Stat. K. William* 3 Ane free man..sall gif for multure the aucht part of ane sextene veshell.

†**d.** *Arch.* (See quot. and VASE 1 b.) *Obs.*—0

1704 J. HARRIS *Lex. Techn.* I, *Vessels*, in Architecture, are certain Ornaments, usually set over the Cornices, and so named, because they represent divers sorts of Vessels, which were in use among the Ancients.

†**e.** *slang.* The nose. *Obs.*

1813 *Sporting Mag.* XLI. 170 There d——n your eyes, I've tapped your vessel.

3. *fig.* (chiefly in or after Biblical use). **a.** Said of a person regarded as having the containing capacity or function of a vessel. Freq. const. *of* (a condition, quality, etc.). Now *arch.*

For the phr. *the weaker vessel*, see WEAK *a.*

a **1300** *Cursor M.* 19674 Þou ga til him [*sc.* Paul], he es me lele, And o mi chesing he es wessele. **1382** WYCLIF *2 Tim* ii. 21 He schal be a vessel halwid into honour, and profytable to the Lord. **1388** —— *Gen.* xlix. 5 Symeon and Leuy,..fiȝtynge vessils of wickidnesse. *a* **1400** *N.T.* (Paues) Acts ix. 15 For he es maked vnto me a vessel of choos forto bere my name bifore kenges ande folke. **1451** CAPGRAVE *Life St. Gilbert* xxxvii. 115 [They] came on-to þe graue wher.. Gilbertes body was hid, and..þei lifte up þat holy uessel of God. **1526** *Pilgr. Perf.* (W. de W. 1531) 19 Therfore let vs apply our wylles at all tymes to be vesselles of grace. **1552** LYNDESAY *Dreme* 254 The cursit Empriour Nero, Off euerilk vice the horrabyll weschell. **1597** HOOKER *Eccl. Pol.* v. xlix. § 1 We know there are vessels of wrath. *a* **1629** HINDE *J. Bruen* ii. (1641) 6 If he [God] had a purpose to reserve him as a vessell of honor, and for his own house. **1667** MILTON *P.L.* IX. 89 Him after long debate..his final sentence chose Fit Vessel, fittest Imp of fraud, in whom To enter. **1738** WESLEY *Psalms* LVI. v, And cast into the burning Lake The Vessels of thine Ire. **1773** MRS. CHAPONE *Improv. Mind* (1774) I. 93 We know not whether..they might not prove.. chosen vessels to promote the honour of God. **1819** SCOTT *Ivanhoe* xxxviii, Nature..grieves that so goodly a form should be a vessel of perdition. **1837** DICKENS *Pickw.* lii, It makes a vessel's heart bleed! **1905** A. INNES SHAND *Days of Past* vii. 129 As for the archbishop, he was a seasoned vessel.

†**b.** Said of the body, esp. as the receptacle of the soul. *Obs.*

c **1360** *Know Thyself* 4 in *E.E.P.* (1862) 130 Vche cristen creature knowen hym self ouht His oune vessel. **1382** WYCLIF *1 Thess.* iv. 4 That ech of ȝou kunne welde his vessel in..hoolynesse and honour. —— *1 Pet.* iii. 7 Ȝeuynge honour to the wommans vessel, or body. **1532** DU WES *Introd. Fr.* in *Palsgr.* 1061 The body..is the vessell of the soule. **1535** COVERDALE *2 Esdras* iv. 11 How shulde thy vessel then be able to comprehende the waye of the Hyest? **1610** HEALEY *St. Aug. Citie of God* 526 The seede of generation should have been sowne in the vessell, as corne is now in the fielde. *a* **1629** HINDE *J. Bruen* vii. (1641) 28 They possessed their vessels in holinesse, and in honour. **1704** SWIFT *Mech. Operat. Spirit* (1711) 299 The Saint felt his Vessel full extended in every Part.

†**c.** In other Biblical uses (see quots.). *Obs.*

1340 HAMPOLE *Psalter* vii. 14 And þare in he has redid vessels of ded [L. *vasa mortis*]; his aruys till brennand he made. [So in Wyclif (1382).] **1382** WYCLIF *1 Macc.* xiv. 10 The citees he..ordeynyde..that thei weren vessels of strengthing. **1545** ASCHAM *Toxoph.* I. (Arb.) 71 Dauid in the Psalmes calleth bowes the vessels of death. **1609** BIBLE (Douay) *1 Macc.* xiv. 10 He gave victuals to the citie, and he appointed them that they should be vessels of munition.

4. a. Any structure designed to float upon and traverse the water for the carriage of persons or goods; a craft or ship of any kind, now usually one larger than a rowing-boat and often restricted to sea-going craft or those plying upon the larger rivers or lakes.

Freq. with distinguishing terms, as *bomb-*, *fishing*, *gun-*, *machine-*, *sailing-*, *steam-*, *trading-*, *transport-*, *war-vessel*, etc.

α. *a* **1300** *Cursor M.* 1662 Bot ar i wil mi wengeaunce tak I wil þat þou a wessel mak... A schippe be-houes þe to dight. **1390** GOWER *Conf.* I. 197 Hire Schip goth in among hem alle,..And hath the vessell undergete, Which Maister was of al the Flete. **1452** *Wars Eng. in France* (Rolls) II. 477 Ordeyne as meny shippes and vessels of thoo that bylonge to oure port of A. as ye shal mowe. *a* **1489** CAXTON *Blanchardyn* xxxv. 131 Blanchardyn drew hymsylf aside wyth-in his vessell. *a* **1533** LD. BERNERS *Huon* xxxv. 110 Sum maner of shyppe or wessell to passe ouer yᵉ see. **1590** SIR J. SMYTH *Disc. Weapons* 12 All the long boates and vessells of oares for the landing of men. **1625** BP. HALL *Wks.* 59 A little saile to a large vessell, rids no way. **1683** *Col. Rec. Pennsylv.* I. 69 All Ships and Vessells vnder 10 Tunns..to pay no fees. **1736** GRAY *Statius* II. 21 Where..parting surges round the vessel roar. **1769** FALCONER *Dict. Marine*, *Vessel*, a general name given to the different sorts of ships... It is, however, more particularly applied to those of the smaller kind, furnished with one or two masts. **1836** MARRYAT *Midsh. Easy* xix. 67 All the varieties of vessels which float upon the wave. **1844** KINGLAKE *Eöthen* vi, I knew enough of Greek navigation to be sure that our vessel would cling to earth. **1889** WELCH *Naval Archit.* 13 For ships of ordinary form (including probably the great majority of vessels).

fig. **1611** SHAKS. *Cymb.* IV. ii. 319 Damn'd Pisanio Hath with his forged Letters..From this most brauest vessell of the world Strooke the maine top! Oh Posthumus, alas, Where is thy head? **1781** COWPER *Hope* 168 Hope, as an anchor..., holds fast The Christian vessel, and defies the blast. **1876** TREVELYAN *Macaulay* I. v. 250 In 1832 the vessel of Reform was still labouring heavily.

transf. **1882** F. M. CRAWFORD *Mr. Isaacs* i. 6 And every variety of horseflesh may be seen,..from Lord Stephen Kildare's thoroughbreds to the broad-sterned equestrian vessel of Mr. Currie Ghyrkins.

β. *c* **1375** *Sc. Leg. Saints* xvii. (*Martha*) 106 Bot for na vyscele wes þane nere, he enterit in riuere faste, & swemand ay. *c* **1470** HENRY *Wallace* XI. 326 He A weschell gat, and maid him to the se. *a* **1568** SEMPILL in *Satir. Poems Reform.* xlvi. 25 A fair vesschell abone þe watter. **1609** *Reg. Mag. Sig. Scot.* 71/1 The dewtie of coqueitis, entres of shipis, barkis, crearis and wtheris veshellis.

γ. *c* **1460** FORTESCUE *Abs. & Lim. Mon.* vi. (1885) 123 To borde with carrikkes and oþer grete vessailes. **1470–85** MALORY *Arthur* VIII. vi. 282 He commaunded his seruaunt Gouernayle to goo to his vessaile ageyne. **1497** *Naval Acc. Hen. VII* (1896) 250 The seid veassayle fyrst freight at London with cordage.

δ. *c* **1477** CAXTON *Jason* 76 And the sayd vaissels and ships were blowen unto the perrillous yle of Colchos.

†**b.** In collective singular. *Obs.*

c **1400** *Destr. Troy* 13996 Whan Eneas was exiled, euyn were his shippes Two hundreth full hole, all of hede vessell. **1436** *Libel Eng. Policy* in *Pol. Poems* (Rolls) II. 166 The haven of Sluse,..Where many wessell and fayre arne abydynge. *c* **1470** HENRY *Wallace* IX. 749 Sum fled to Tay, and in small weschell ȝeid.

c. An airship or hovercraft.

1915 *Sphere* 3 Apr. 22/1 The long covering of the balloon seemed to have been broken. Some people were running beside the vessel. **1916** *Ibid.* 18 Mar. 293/1 As an airship rises it encounters air which has less supporting power, and ultimately..the vessel floats in equilibrium. **1957** I. ASIMOV *Naked Sun* ix. 93 Baley was in an air-borne vessel again, as he had been on that trip from New York to Washington. **1972** *Daily Tel.* 25 Apr. 1/4 British Rail's hovercraft Princess Anne made an emergency landing on a sandbank yesterday... The vessel was beached at Andressells, eight miles north of Boulogne.

5. a. *Anat.* and *Zool.* One of the membranous canals, ducts, or tubes in which the fluids of the body are contained and by means of which they are circulated; freq., a blood-vessel.

Often with distinguishing term, as *blood-*, *iliac*, *lymphatic*, *pulmonary*, etc.

1398 TREVISA *Barth. De P.R.* IV. vii. (1495) 90 Veynes ben the vessels of blode. **1548–77** VICARY *Anat.* (1888) 21 There is no more difference betweene these two vessels of blood, but that the Artere is a vessel of blood spiritual or vytal. **1615** CROOKE *Body of Man* 113 The double membrane of this mesenterie doth inclose and sustaine the vessels which runne through it. **1635–56** COWLEY *Davideis* IV. Poems (1905) 389 A nimble thrust his active En'emy made,..And opened wide those secret vessels where Life's Light goes out, when first they let in aire. **1691** RAY *Creation* II. (1692) 65 All the Bones, and all the Muscles, and all the Vessels of the Body. **1732** ARBUTHNOT *Rules of Diet* 279 In short whatever relaxeth the too strict vessels, or straitens the too lax,..is a Cordial. **1793** HOLCROFT *Lavater's Physiog.* xii. 65 Vessels everywhere penetrate the bones, supplying them with juices and marrow. **1831** R. KNOX *Cloquet's Anat.* 5 The Vessels..are canals which divide and subdivide into branches, are more or less elastic, and are formed by the superposition of different membranes. They are distinguished according to their uses and general disposition into Arteries, Veins, and Lymphatic Vessels. **1871** T. H. GREEN *Introd. Pathol.* 286 Portions of new growths,..which having perforated the vessels, have been carried away by the current. **1893** W. R. GOWERS *Man. Dis. Nerv. Syst.* (ed. 2) II. 422 If a clot forms in an artery it may be detached..and may obstruct the vessel further on.

b. *Bot.* One of the cellular or tubular structures composing the vascular system of plants and having the function of containing or carrying sap or other secretion; a duct.

1671 GREW *Anat. Plants* I. iii. § 30 Of the Lignous Body it is so apparent by its Pores, or rather by its Vessels, that we need no farther Evidence. For to what end are Vessels, but for the conveyance of Liquor? **1731** MILLER *Gard. Dict.* s.v. *Vegetable*, Bulk for Bulk, the Plant imbibes into its Vessels 17 times more Fluid than the Quantity of the Chyle which enters into a Man's Vessels. **1787** WINTER *Syst. Husb.* 93 Air ..passes..into the absorbent vessels of the root. **1796** WITHERING *Brit. Plants* (ed. 3) I. 368 The leaf has no rib, but seems composed of vessels equally dispersed. **1842** LOUDON *Suburban Hort.* 40 Whenever the sap in the vessels of a plant freezes, they become ruptured and the plant dies. **1875** DARWIN *Insectiv. Pl.* xii. 285 Some of the vessels are barred and punctured instead of being spiral.

6. *Bot.* = PERICARP. *rare.*

Common in the comb. *seed-vessel*: see SEED *sb.* 9.

1691 RAY *Creation* I. (1692) 100 Such Mosses as grow upon Walls,..and other high Places, have Seeds so excessively small, that when shaken out of their Vessels they appear like Vapor. [**1704** J. HARRIS *Lex. Techn.* I, *Vasculiferous Plants*, are..such as have besides the common Calyx or Flower Cup, a peculiar Vessel or Case to contain their Seed.]

7. *attrib.* and *Comb.* **a.** In senses 1 and 2, as ***vessel ambry***, ***-cleaner***, ***cloth***, ***house***, ***maker***, ***-man***, ***stuff***. Chiefly *Sc.*

vessel-bearing, defining *vasiferous* (q.v.), is given by Coles (1676) and Bailey (1721).

c **1450** *Bk. Curtasye* 367 in *Babees Bk.*, For wesselle clothes,..þe porter hase þat warde in holde. **1488** *Acta Dom. Conc.* (1839) 98/2 A weschale almery, a cop almery. **1532** *Acc. Ld. High Treas. Scotl.* VI. 39 To the court weschellmen. **1590–1** *Exch. Rolls Scotl.* XXII. 121 To.. William Murra, aid in the vessel hous. **1598** FLORIO, *Vascellaro*, a potter, or vessell maker. **1627** *Reg. Decreets Sc. Admiralty Ct.* I. 93 Clapeburde, pype stalves, veschell and veschell stuff, pitche, tar, rosin, etc. **1886** *Cheshire Gloss.* 377 *Vessel-cleaner*, an under dairymaid, whose business it is to clean the cheese tub, cans, and dairy apparatus.

b. In sense 5, as ***vessel-dilator***, ***-sheath***, ***-wall***.

1879 *St. George's Hosp. Rep.* IX. 428 In the right lateral sinus, where the clot was adherent to the vessel-wall. **1896** *Allbutt's Syst. Med.* I. 234 Vessel dilators are of special use. **1899** *Ibid.* VIII. 609 A proliferative inflammation of the vessel-sheaths.

c. In sense 4, as ***vessel-load***, ***man***, etc.

1894 *Pop. Sci. Monthly* XLIV. 483 The first Russian crew which 'rescued' a vessel-load of Circassians on their way to Turkey. **1898** *Daily Tel.* 6 Jan. 10/7 Other couriers were despatched to see the railroads and the vessel men.

ˈvessel, *sb.*² [Of uncertain origin: connexion with prec. is not clear.] ***vessel of paper*** (see quots.).

1790 GROSE *Prov. Gloss.*, *Vessel of paper*, half a quarter of a sheet. *a* **1825** FORBY *Voc. E. Anglia.* **1840** SPURDENS *Suppl. Forby*, *Vessel*,..was used for theme-papers formerly at Bury School, and perhaps at others. **1860** *Guide to Eton* Gloss., *Vessel*, the eighth of a sheet of foolscap, on which derivations are written. **1891** WRENCH *Winchester Word-Bk.* 51 *Vessel*, a half quarter of Long-paper. **1910** *Sat. Rev.* 10 Dec. 751/1 Acton..made copious extracts,..written on vessels of paper specially made for him.

ˈvessel, *v.* Now *rare* or *Obs.* [f. VESSEL *sb.*¹]

1. *trans.* To put or enclose (a liquid, etc.) in a vessel. Also with *up*.

1577 HARRISON *England* III. vi. (1878) II. 37 Our honie.. is harder, better wrought, and clenlier vesselled up, than that which commeth from beyond the sea. **1626** BACON *Sylva* § 529 The Fourth Rule shall be, to mark what Herbs some Earths doe put forth of themselves; And to take that Earth, and to Pot it, or to Vessell it. **1640** HARVEY *Synagogue* (1647) C vij b, I would have this bread, This wine, Vessel'd in what the Sun might blush to shed His shine, When he should see. **1670** W. SIMPSON *Hydrol. Ess.* 129 In vesselling up and stopping in the Tunbridg-waters.

transf. **1650** T. VAUGHAN *Anthroposophia* 2 Man had at the First, and so have all Souls before their Entrance to the Body, an explicit methodicall Knowledge, but they are noe sooner Vessel'd but that Liberty is lost.

2. To take or lift *out* by means of a vessel.

1673 *Phil. Trans.* VIII. 6022 When they pour this solution into the Vessel, they use a stick,..whereby they agitate and beat the Wine in the Vessel, and then they vessel it out into other vessels.

vessel-cup, north. dial. var. WASSAIL-CUP.

ˈvesselful. [f. VESSEL *sb.*¹] As much or as many as a vessel will hold.

1860 WORCESTER.

ˈvesselled, *ppl. a.* [f. VESSEL *v.* or *sb.*¹]

1. Enclosed in a vessel. Now *rare* or *Obs.*

1660 BOYLE *New Exp. Phys. Mech.* iii. 42 The Vessel'd Mercury. **1664** POWER *Exp. Philos.* II. 91 You may with great facility move the Tube to and fro in the vessel'd Quicksilver. **1670** BOYLE in *Phil. Trans.* V. 2037 That 4 parts of 5, or rather 5 of 6 of the vessel'd Air (if I may so call that which was shut up in the Receiver) had been pump'd out. **1708** R. NEVE *Baroscop.* 10 Upon opening of the inverted Tube into the vessel'd Mercury.

2. *Bot.* Having or provided with vessels or ducts.

1895 *Pop. Sci. Monthly* Feb. 499 The vesseled thorns.. are disposed in a fixed and regular manner.

† **'vesselling.** *Obs. rare.* [f. VESSEL *sb.*[1] + -ING[1].] Vessels collectively. (Cf. next.)

c **1440** *Pallad. on Husb.* IV. 410 When they beth cold, in picched vessellynge And cleyed, close hem vp. *Ibid.* XI. 110 The chanels of this oil & vesselynge.

† **'vesselment.** *Obs.* [a. AF. *vessellment*, OF. *vesselement*, *vaissellement*, etc., f. *vaisselle* VESSEL *sb.*[1]: see -MENT.] Vessels collectively, esp. church vessels or plate.

1303 R. BRUNNE *Handl. Synne* 9338 Curteynes, or ouþer vestyment, Or any oþer vesselement þat falleþ to holy cherches seruyse. *Ibid.* 9480 For sacrylage, alle þys ys tolde, þat vesselment of cherche ys wyþholde. **13..** *E.E. Allit. P.* B. 1280 Dere disches of golde & dubleres fayre, þe vyoles & þe vesselment of vertuous stones. *Ibid.* 1288.

† **vessey.** *Obs. rare.* Also 6 vesse (9 vesey). [Of uncertain origin. Cf. FESSE[2].] ***vessey colour***, a light-blue or sky-blue colour.

1562 LEIGH *Armorie* (1597) 116 b, Fishes, or something.. appertaining to them, Whereof the maisterie must bee of colour vesse, that is, the colour of the Turcas. *c* **1573** in Nichols *Progr. Q. Elizab.* (1823) I. 413 He hath twoe clokes, th' one of Vessey Collor garded with..black Clothe and twisted lace. [Hence **1826** HOR. SMITH *Tor Hill* I. 186 A vesey-coloured cloak, guarded with black cloth, and twisted lace of carnation.]

vessicle, obs. f. VESICLE.

vest (vɛst), *sb.* Also 8 *dial.* west. [a. F. *veste*, a. It. *veste* (also *vesta*) robe, gown:—L. *vest-em*, *vestis* garment, attire, clothing, cognate with Gr. ἐσθής, Skr. *vastra.* Cf. Sp. *veste* garment, † *vesta* vest, Pg. *veste* garment, *vestia* vest.]

1. a. A loose outer garment worn by men in Eastern countries or in ancient times; a robe or gown.

1613 SHERLEY *Trav. Persia* 20 We were forced to send his maister three verstes [*sic*] of cloth of gold, for beholding his person. **1634** SIR T. HERBERT *Trav.* 146 Their [Persians'] out Garment or Vest is commonly of Callico quilted with Cotton. **1665** *Ibid.* (1677) 131 Artaxerxes the Great gave Mithridates..a Gown or Vest of gold which he wore during a Royal banquet. **1725** DE FOE *Voy. round World* (1840) 85 The Persians make their long vests of such cloths. **1746** FRANCIS tr. *Horace, Epist.* I. vi. 63 Lucullus..being ask'd to furnish for a Play An hundred martial Vests. **1791** COWPER *Odyss.* I. 555 Putting off his vest Of softest texture. **1817** SHELLEY *Rev. Islam* XI. xiv, A hermit's vest Concealed his face. **1838** ARNOLD *Hist. Rome* I. 215 Kaeso then put on his vest, such as the Roman generals were used to wear in battle. **1842** BARHAM *Ingol. Leg.* Ser. II. *Fragment*, The slanting ray of the evening sun shone..With fitful light on regal vest, and warrior's sculptured mail.

transf. **1643** DAVENANT *Unfort. Lovers* I. i, Not in his Perfume and Silks; but in his Iron Vest. **1671** GREW *Anat. Plants* i. §3 If then we take a Bean and dissect it, we shall find it cloathed with a doubled Vest or Coat.

b. A similar garment worn by women. Chiefly *poet.*

1700 DRYDEN *Pal. & Arc.* III. 193 Attended by her Maiden Train, Who bore the Vests that Holy Rites require. **1717** LADY M. W. MONTAGU *Let. to C'tess of Mar* 18 April, I found the lady sitting on her sofa, in a sable vest. **1759** JOHNSON *Rasselas* xxxvii, When my upper vest was taken off, they were apparently struck with the splendour of my clothes. **1797** SOUTHEY *Triumph Woman* 30 Thy daughters ..for this high feast Weave the loose robe, and paint the flowery vest. **1801** SCOTT *Glenfinlas* xli, O gentle huntsman, hast thou seen..A lovely maid in vest of green? **1810** —— *Lady of Lake* IV. xii.

c. A garment, in various fig. uses.

1655 H. VAUGHAN *Silex Scint.* 118 The fair woods.. flourished in that youthful vest With which their great Creator had them drest. **1678** CUDWORTH *Intell. Syst.* I. v. 790 The Ancient Asserters of the Souls Immortality, supposing it to have besides this Terrestrial Body another Spirituous or Airy Body..as its Interiour Vest or Tunicle. **1746** COLLINS *Ode Poet. Charac.* 45 Truth, in sunny vest array'd. **1781** COWPER *Charity* 262 When ev'ning in her sober vest Drew the grey curtain of the fading west. **1820** SHELLEY *Witch Atl.* Ded. v, Light the vest of flowing metre She wears.

†**d.** Without article. Clothing, attire. *rare*[−1].

1694 MOTTEUX *Rabelais* v. 252 Our Means of Life are Pote, and Cibe, and Vest.

2. An ecclesiastical vestment. *rare.*

1663 PEPYS *Diary* 16 Feb., A priest was taken in his vests officiating somewhere in Holborne the other day. *a* **1700** EVELYN *Diary* 17 Nov. 1644, The precious vessels of gold, silver, and gems, with the vests and services to be seene in the Sacristy. **1732** LEDIARD *Sethos* II. VIII. 222 The initiate's vest..hung out under my cuirass. **1829** CASSAN *Bps. Bath & Wells* 162 He gave also many splendid vests to the Churches of Bath and Wells.

3. a. A sleeveless garment of some length worn by men beneath the coat. (Introduced by Charles II: see first quot.) Now *Hist.* **b.** A short garment worn beneath the coat or jacket as a usual part of male attire; a waistcoat. Now *N. Amer.*

1666 PEPYS *Diary* 8 Oct., The King hath yesterday, in Council, declared his resolution of setting a fashion for clothes... It will be a vest, I know not well how; but it is to teach the nobility thrift. *Ibid.* 15 Oct., This day the King begins to put on his vest;..being a long cassocke close to the body, of black cloth, and pinked with white silk under it, and a coat over it, and the legs ruffled with black riband like a pigeon's leg. **1667** in *Verney Mem.* (1907) II. 300, I doubt the old fellow must have a new vest and tunick. **1668** ETHEREDGE *She would if she could* III. iii, You are not To learn..how absolutely necessary A rich Vest and a Perruque are to a man that aims At their favours. **1712** *Overseers' Acc. Holy Cross, Canterb.*, Payd for mackin a west and briches for gouddins child, [£]o. 1. 6. **1818** SCOTT *Rob Roy* v, She wore ..a coat, vest, and hat, resembling those of a man. **1848** THACKERAY *Van. Fair* lix, Provided with some of the most splendid vests that Calcutta could furnish. **1907** *Daily News* 3 Sept. 3/2 Lightish striped cashmere trousers would not be correct..if worn with a dark blue coat and vest. **1925** F. SCOTT FITZGERALD *Great Gatsby* ix. 202 While he took off his coat and vest I told him all arrangements had been deferred. **1937** H. G. WELLS *Brynhild* vii. 103 He was sitting without jacket or vest, looking neat and healthy in his shirt and black tie. **1968** *Globe & Mail* (Toronto) 17 Feb. 7/3 Hooking his thumbs in his vest, he answered questions in a calm, almost offhand manner. **1978** J. IRVING *World according to Garp* ii. 37 Bodger..tucked in his shirt, which was escaping..from under his tight vest.

transf. **1830** WHITTIER *Mogg Megone* 1237 The rivets of the vest Which girds in steel his ample breast. **1863** BATES *Nat. Amazon* viii. (1864) 220 A bird resembling our starling in size..and not unlike it in colour with the exception of the rich rosy vest. **1876** HOLLAND *Sev. Oaks* i, Among the charms that dangled from this liquid chain—depending from the vest of a landscape, which ended in a ruffle of woods.

c. A knitted or woven undergarment for the upper part of the body, worn next to the skin.

1851 *Catal. Gt. Exhib.* III. 583/1 Cotton,..spun silk, merino and Cashmere gentlemen's and ladies' vests. **1883** 'SYLVIA' *Lady's Guide to Home Dressm. & Millinery* xiii. 107 [List of under-linen], 4 merino vests, [£]o 5 9.

d. Part of a woman's dress bodice, consisting of a collar and front, usually of lace, net, silk, or other soft material.

1887 *Lady's World* June 256/1 Vests of spotted kerseymere..are made with military collars and two pockets. **1913** *Daily Graphic* 26 Mar. 12/4 The bodices having vests and collars of écru lace. **1913** *Play Pictorial* No. 134 p. ii/1 It [a 'waistcoat blouse'] has a soft net vest that ends in short sharp points.

e. A short, sleeveless jacket for a woman. *U.S.*

1909 in WEBSTER. **1974** *Times-Picayune* (New Orleans) 14 Aug. III. 1 (Advt.), Plaid vest, 18.00. **1978** *Detroit Free Press* 5 Mar. (Spring Fashion Suppl.) 11/1 Vests have never looked quite so fresh and right as they do this spring. They can be the perfect sleeveless jacket, topping all the softness.

f. A singlet denoting membership of a representative athletics team.

1971 N. STACEY *Who Cares?* ii. 25 It was harder to get a Blue than an international vest.

g. *attrib.* and *Comb.*, as ***vest-maker***, etc.; **vest-pocket**, a pocket in a vest (sense 3 b); also *attrib.* as *adj.*: small enough to fit into a vest pocket, very small of its kind; also *fig.*; **vest-pocket voter** *U.S.* (see quot. 1883); **vest-slip** = sense 3 b.

1879 G. W. CABLE *Grandissimes* xliii, I could be a confectioner, a milliner, a dressmaker, a vest-maker. **1828** WEBSTER, *Vesting*, cloth for vests; vest patterns. **1823** *Mass. Spy* 3 Dec. (Thornton), He found him asleep, took from his vest pocket the key [etc.]. **1848** *Sporting Life* 29 July 274/1 This vest pocket companion for cricketers. **1883** in Bryce *Amer. Commw.* (1888) III. v. lxxxix. 217 The class of 'vest-pocket voters'—men who come to the polls with their tickets made up, to the confusion of 'the boys.' **1897** 'MARK TWAIN' *Following Equator* 629 Toy peaks, and a dainty little vest-pocket Matterhorn. **1912** *Brit. Jrnl. Photogr.* 5 July 525 The vest-pocket 'Tenax' camera. **1931** *Times* 16 Mar. 1/3 (Advt.), Unique vest-pocket treatment for catarrh. **1947** *Horizon* Apr. 152 Our provincial hotels with their vest-pocket electric fires. **1983** *Chicago Sun-Times* 9 July 15 Vest-pocket garden-parks provide relaxed places for people to interact with one another. **1984** *Newslet. Amer. Dial. Soc.* Sept. 23/1 He was responsible for..a series of popular vest-pocket dictionaries and reference books. **1920** *Punch* 9 June 456/2 My top-hat was on my head and my vest-slip was all right. **1922** Vest-slip [see OXFORD 1 b].

vest (vɛst), *v.* Also 5 *Sc.* west. [ad. OF. *vestir* (mod.F. *vêtir*, = Sp. and Pg. *vestir*, It. *vestire*):—L. *vestīre* to clothe, f. *vestis* clothing: see prec.]

I. 1. *trans.* To place, settle, or secure (something) in the possession of a person or persons; = INVEST *v.* 6. Chiefly in passive, and usually const. *in* (rarely *upon* or *with*). **a.** With reference to estates, rights, titles, etc.

c **1425** WYNTOUN *Cron.* VIII. xl. 7089 Al Gascon wiþe þe portynance To be insesit and westit He and al his ayris qwhit. **1475** *Rolls of Parlt.* VI. 147/1 That all such astate, title, right,..and possession..in the same persone and persones and their heires be vested. **1503–4** *Act 19 Hen. VII*, c. 34 §7 The seid Castels..[shall] in the same persone or persones and their heires be vested and they therin be intiteled. **1585** HOLINSHED *Hist. Scot.* in *Chron.* II. 244/2 The right of which countie king Dauid affirmed to be iustlie in him..as truelie vested in his possession by the forfeiture. **1650** *Vind. Hammond's Addr.* §60. 24 What is vested in me, I may give or derive to another; what is intrusted onely, I cannot. **1651** N. BACON *Disc. Govt. Eng.* II. viii. (1739) 52 No Legiance is due to him, before the Crown is vested upon him. **1702** *Lond. Gaz.* No. 3830/4 Until all the said Estates and Interests vested in them are disposed of. **1758** in *Nairne Peerage Evid.* (1874) 68 The late act of parliament vesting the estates of certain traitors in his majesty. **1818** CRUISE *Digest* (ed. 2) II. 22 There were no words to vest the portions in the daughters till a marriage with consent. **1847** BRIGHT *Sp., Ireland* 13 Dec. (1876) 155 A bill with this title to vest the ownership of the land with the present occupiers. **1858** LD. ST. LEONARDS *Handy Bk. Prop. Law* xvi. 107 The Court may direct the parts so laid out to remain vested in the trustees.

b. With reference to power or authority.

1659 HAMMOND *On Ps.* lxxx. 17 By which the power is vested on him. **1672** MARVELL *Reh. Transp.* I. 98 The Government of Religion was vested in Princes by an antecedent right to Christ. **1691** T. H[ALE] *Acc. New Invent.* p. lxxxvii, That power of abating Nusances..is vested in both of their Offices, both by Grant and Prescription. **1756** C. LUCAS *Ess. Waters* III. 244 There is a particular jurisdiction vested in the officers. **1774** PENNANT *Tour Scotl. in 1772*, 45 The right of voting is vested by burgess tenure in certain houses. **1801** WELLESLEY in Owen *Desp.* (1877) 210 It is my intention to proceed immediately to vest the administration of the ceded districts in the hands of the Company's civil servants. **1841** ELPHINSTONE *Hist. India* I. 37 The government of the society thus constituted was vested in an absolute monarch. **1867** FREEMAN *Norm. Conq.* I. 533 That vague power of recommending a successor which the Law vested in him.

c. *transf.*

1849 RUSKIN *Sev. Lamps* v. §21. 157 If completeness is thought to be vested in polish, and to be attainable by help of sand paper. **1852** THACKERAY *Esmond* I. iii, Proud of this confidence and secret vested in him.

2. a. To put, place, or establish (a person) in full or legal possession or occupation of something; = INVEST *v.* 5. Chiefly in passive, and usually const. *in* (or †*of*).

In early use only *Sc.* in the phrase ***vested*** (also ***vest***) ***and seized.***

1464 in *Acc. Fam. Innes* (1864) 78 The said schir Robert deyt last ves[t]it and sesit as of fee. **1488** *Acta Dom. Audit.* (1839) 123/2 It beis prefit þat Williame þe barde deit last westit and Sesit in þe said landis. **1557** *Rec. Inverness* (New Spald. Cl.) I. 6 For sesing takyn of all landis Wilyam Paterson his fadyr deit last vestit and sesit conforme to his serwing. **1597** *Burgh Rec. Glasgow* (1876) I. 186 All landis, rowmes, heretageis,..quhairin he deitt last vest and seasit. **1672** PETTY *Pol. Anat.* (1691) 329 Of which the Irish that are vested by restoration, seem rather to take part with the divested. **1749** FIELDING *Tom Jones* IX. iv, The sergeant presently inquired for the principal magistrate of the town, and was informed by my landlord that he himself was vested in that office. *a* **1774** GOLDSM. *Hist. Greece* I. 108 Miltiades thus vested in the supreme command [etc.]. **1905** *Times* 8 June 6/4 The Government proposed that the Free Church should be vested in the property to be allocated to her.

fig. **1654** H. L'ESTRANGE *Chas. I* (1655) 126 Not all his most gracious and debonair mine towards them could vest him in that Nations affections. *c* **1680** BEVERIDGE *Serm.* (1729) I. 29 In order to their being actually vested in that salvation. **1705** STANHOPE *Paraphr.* II. 442 All, who partake of this Nature, are not only certain of, but may in some sense be said already vested in, the Happiness, which [etc.].

b. To invest (a person) ***with*** some quality, esp. power, authority, etc. Chiefly in passive.

1674 OWEN *Holy Spirit* (1693) 126 It is his Person as vested with all his Offices, that is the immediate Fountain of all Grace unto us. **1699** BURNET *39 Art.* iv. (1700) 67 He is vested with an unconceivable high degree of Glory. **1719** DE FOE *Crusoe* II. (Globe) 574 God's most glorious and best Creature,..vested with a reasonable Soul. **1727** —— *Hist. Appar.* iv. (1840) 32 They may be reasonably supposed to be vested with the same powers. **1771** GOLDSM. *Hist. Eng.* IV. 13 [He was] created a peer, and was soon after vested with the dignity of chancellor. **1797** HT. LEE *Canterb. T., Old Woman's T.* (1799) I. 361 [Thou] art vested with the mission of thy..king. **1803** in Gurwood *Wellington's Desp.* (1837) II. 50 *note*, I further vest you with full powers to decide any question which may arise. **1817** JAS. MILL *Brit. India* II. IV. ix. 288 To vest the officers of the Crown in India with powers independent of the Company. **1844** H. H. WILSON *Brit. India* I. 227 The Indian Government was vested with the power of sovereignty within its own limits.

c. To endow formally or legally ***with*** some possession or property.

1756 *Anson's Voyages* (ed. 8) I. v. 70 This company, in consideration of a sum paid to the king, is vested with the property of all diamonds found in Brazil. **1858** in J. B. Norton *Topics* 246 We propose..that every ryot should be vested with the freehold of his farm.

3. *intr.* To become vested (*in* a person); to pass into possession; to descend or devolve *upon* one as possessor.

1592 WEST *1st Pt. Symbol.* §44 Euerie estate either executed maintenant, or executorie by limitation of use, which vesteth in possession by vertue of the Statute of 27 H. 8. **1647** N. BACON *Disc. Govt. Eng.* I. xli. (1739) 66 In those days the title vested not unless the Child opened his eyes. *a* **1715** BURNET *Own Time* (1766) II. 137 If the Duke came to be King, the prerogative would by that vest in him. **1765** BLACKSTONE *Comm.* I. 196 For the right of the crown vests ..upon his heir. **1818** CRUISE *Digest* (ed. 2) VI. 500 The Court held..that the whole estate vested in L. his executors and administrators. **1827** JARMAN *Powell's Devises* II. 223 The principle..does not apply, if there be an express declaration that the land shall vest at twenty-one. **1865** LOWELL *Reconstruct.* Prose Wks. 1890 V. 227 In all cases of land granted to freedmen no title should vest till a fair price had been paid. **1885** SIR R. BAGGALLAY in *Law Times' Rep.* LII. 671/2 The property vests in the official receiver *qua* trustee.

II. 4. a. *trans.* In pa. pple.: Dressed, clothed, robed *in* some garment. Also without const. (*spec.* with reference to ecclesiastical vestments).

1513 DOUGLAS *Æneid* VII. ii. 3 And heich abuf..cleirlie schane Aurora vestit into broun sanguane. *Ibid.* xi. 29 In rob ryall vestit,..And ryche purpour. **1582** N. T. (Rhem.) *Rev.* i. 13 One like to the Sonne of man, vested in a priestly garment to the foote. **1622** I. W. *Oudin's Sp. Gram.* 297 He ..saies that a Frier stayes for you readie vested at the Altar. *c* **1655** MILTON *Sonn.* xxiii, My late espoused Saint..Came vested all in white, pure as her mind. *a* **1668** DAVENANT *Fair Favorite* Wks. (1673) 97 Your Brother (Madam) and he brings A Lady with him, vested like a Nun. **1718** OZELL tr. *Tournefort's Voy.* I. 92 The Priest being vested, sets about the Preparation of the Bread and Wine at the little Altar. **1761** *Brit. Mag.* II. 362 On the dexter side, a pilgrim or friar, vested in russet. **1849** ROCK *Ch. of Fathers* I. v. (1903) I. 328 The thurifers and taper-bearers, in our large collegiate and cathedral churches, were vested in tunicles. **1859** JEPHSON *Brittany* vi. 76 A priest, vested in surplice and stole.

b. *transf.* and *fig.* Also const. *with.*

1679 DRYDEN *Troil. & Cress.* Pref., Ess. (Ker) I. 219 Spirits, according to Plato, are vested with a subtle body. *a* **1706** EVELYN *Hist. Relig.* (1850) I. 81 We see other living creatures come vested, armed, able immediately to find their pasture. *a* **1721** PRIOR *Dial. betw. Charles & Clenard* ¶18 Hast thou not seen me..vested in all the Types and Ornaments that Human Greatness is capable of receiving. **1805** D. JOHNSTON *Serm. for Blind* 44 The brightest ornaments with which our natures can be vested. **1865** NEALE *Hymns Paradise* 8 The Saints, in beauty vested.

5. Of a garment: To clothe or cover (a person). Also *fig.* Cf. INVEST *v.* 1 b.

1582 STANYHURST *Æneis* I. (Arb.) 38 Which plad vested Helen, from Greece when to Troy she flitted. **1812** CARY *Dante, Parad.* XXI. 59 The light that vests me.

6. a. To dress (a person) in a robe or garment, esp. as a formal act or ceremony. Cf. INVEST *v.* 1.

In the 17th cent. chiefly with reference to Oriental usage.

1648 W. L. *Newes fr. Turkie* 7 My Lord was privatly informed he intended an affront by not Vesting him. **1670** CLARENDON *Hist. Reb.* XV. §47 The Speaker..vested him with a rich purple Velvet Robe lined with Ermines. **1695** *Voy. Eng. Merch. to Tadmor* in *Misc. Cur.* (1708) III. 130 To draw him near the City, he vested and caressed some of his Followers. **1840** H. JOLLY *Sunday Services* 219 The words formerly pronounced at vesting the baptized with their white garments, were very solemnly expressive. **1868** GLADSTONE *Juv. Mundi* viii. 292 The Charites receive her on her return from the scene of the Net to Cyprus, where they bathe, anoint, and vest her.

fig. **1639** G. DANIEL *Ecclus.* ii. 71 Prepare their hearts, and in Humilitye New vest their Soules.

b. *Eccl.* To drape or cover (an altar).

1848 C. H. HARTSHORNE *Eng. Medieval Embroidery* 130 The sides [of the altar] must be covered or vested... Where the table stands away from the wall, the back must be vested likewise. **1867** *Portuary Calendar* p. v, Our right..to vest the Altar in colours..is grounded on the old law of the English church. **1874** MICKLETHWAITE *Mod. Par. Churches* 305 It is best for the ends as well as the front of an altar to be vested. **1875** *Encycl. Brit.* I. 641/2 Altars are 'vested' during service; that is, covered with cloths of various kinds.

7. a. *refl.* To apparel or robe (oneself), esp. in ecclesiastical vestments. Also *fig.*

a **1668** LASSELS *Voy. Italy* (1698) I. 41 Thinking it had been a priest putting on the amice and vesting himself to say Mass. **1727** DE FOE *Hist. Appar.* iv. (1840) 30 If we grant that spirit..may vest itself so with flesh and blood. **1748** RICHARDSON *Clarissa* (1811) VIII. 63, I shall vest myself, as I may say, in classical armour. *c* **1771** in E. H. Burton *Life Bp. Challoner* (1909) I. ix. 140 Just before the Bishop vested himself to say Mass. **1892** C. E. NORTON *Dante's Parad.* iii. 17 There are who vest and veil themselves. **1905** R. BAGOT *Passport* xvii. 159 Don Agostino disappeared into the sacristy to vest himself.

b. *absol.* in the same sense.

1882 MASKELL *Anc. Liturgy Ch. Eng.* (ed. 3) 219 A common custom..that the priest (whether or not he vested before the altar) should vest in the sanctuary. **1892** in A. E. Lee *Hist. Columbus* (Ohio) II. 657 The imposing procession ..moved..up the main aisle to the sanctuary where the celebrant vested.

III. 8. *trans.* = INVEST *v.* 9. Now *rare* or *Obs.*

1719 DE FOE *Crusoe* I. (Globe) 36 The Merchant..vesting this Hundred Pounds in English Goods. **1771** H. WALPOLE *Vertue's Anecd. Paint.* (1786) IV. 139 He was then in good circumstances, and it was said came to vest his money in our stocks. **1794** BURKE *Corr.* (1844) IV. 247 He vested in some kind of property..all, or almost all, that he had brought out of France. **1804** EARL LAUDERD. *Publ. Wealth* (1819) 178 He vests his capital either in seed..or in a stock of cattle. **1845** MCCULLOCH *Taxation Introd.* (1852) 11 Her capitalists were tempted to vest very large sums in foreign countries. **1863** [see VESTED *ppl. a.* 3].

vest, southern ME. var. FAST *a.*; obs. Sc. f. WEST.

‖**Vesta** ('vɛstə). Also 4 Veste. [L. *Vesta*, the goddess of that name (see sense 1) answering to the Gr. Ἑστία, identical with ἑστία hearth, house, household.]

1. *Mythol.* A Roman female divinity, the daughter of Saturn, goddess of the hearth and household.

1387 TREVISA *Higden* (Rolls) III. 73 He ȝaf a temple..wiþ fyre to þe goddes Vesta and here maydenes to be worschipped. **1390** GOWER *Conf.* II. 157 Sche which was the Prioresse In Vestes temple the goddesse. **1513** DOUGLAS *Æneid* II. v. 91 The..garlandis Of Vesta, godes of the erd and fyre. **1589** GREENE *Roundelay* Poems (1876) 102 Vesta's virgins with their holy fires Do cleanse the thoughts that fancy hath defiled. **1600** HOLLAND *Livy* XXVIII. xi. 676 The minds of men were put in feare, for the going out of the fire in the chappell of Vesta. **1632** MILTON *Penseroso* 23 Yet thou art higher far descended, Thee bright-hair'd Vesta..To solitary Saturn bore. **1697** DRYDEN *Æneid* II. 395 He said, and brought me..The venerable statues of the gods, With ancient Vesta from the sacred choir. **1728** CHAMBERS *Cycl.* s.v. *Vestals*, The Romans were not the only People who kept the perpetual Fire of Vesta, in imitation of the celestial Fires. **1820** SHELLEY *Witch Atl.* xxxiv, Couched..as on Vesta's sceptre a swift flame. **1843** *Penny Cycl.* XXVI. 285/1 Vesta was regarded as the goddess of domestic union and happiness. **1888** *Encycl. Brit.* XXIV. 193/1 If ever the sacred fire of Vesta did go out, the negligent vestal was to be punished by scourging.

attrib. **1888** *Encycl. Brit.* XXIV. 193/1 Fire was solemnly sent from the prytaneum or Vesta temple of the mother colony.

2. *Astr.* One of the minor planets, revolving in an orbit between Mars and Jupiter.

1807 *Phil. Trans.* XCVII. 245 Observations and Measurements of the Planet Vesta. **1843** *Penny Cycl.* XXVI. 285/2 Vesta performs its revolution in about 1326 mean solar days. **1868** LOCKYER *Guillemin's Heavens* (ed. 3) 214 The distance, and other elements of the orbit of Vesta, presented serious differences both with this theory and Bode's law.

3. Used as the distinctive name of a special make of household stove.

1843 *Penny Cycl.* XXVII. 68/2 In..the 'Vesta stove',.. the ashes can be raked from the grate..without any dust rising into the room. **1843** *Civil Eng. & Arch. Jrnl.* VI. 422/2 The various stoves, Vesta, Chunk, &c.,..are all founded on the Arnott Stove.

4. A kind of wax match. Orig. *attrib.*

1839 CATH. SINCLAIR *Holiday House* ii. 25 Laura afterwards singed a hole in her muslin frock, while lighting one of the Vesta matches to seal these numerous notes. **1857** *Act 20 & 21 Vict.* c. 62 §2 The following Duties of Customs shall be charged:..Lucifers, Vesta, of Wax, the 1,000 Matches, 0. 0. 0½. **1859** CORNWALLIS *Panorama New World* I. 326 Wax vestas, pipes, maccaroni, and candles. **1863** ABEL in *Lond.* (etc.) *Phil. Mag.* Nov. 356 Varieties of wax or Vesta matches. **1864** STRAUSS, etc. *Eng. Workshops* 233 The vesta boxes are put in parcels of half-a-dozen and one dozen. **1886** D. C. MURRAY *First Person Singular* xix, Frost's trembling fingers had to strike one or two vestas. **1899** T. M. ELLIS *Three Cat's-eye Rings* 68 The major pulled a vesta-case from his pocket.

vestal ('vɛstəl), *a.* and *sb.* [ad. L. *vestālis*, f. *Vesta* VESTA. So Sp. and Pg. *vestal*, It. and F. *vestale*.]

A. *adj.* **1.** *vestal virgin*, one of the priestesses (originally four, subsequently six in number) who had charge of the sacred fire in the temple of Vesta at Rome.

1432–50 tr. *Higden* (Rolls) IV. 473 Cornelia, the most noble of virgynes vestalle,..was put in to therthe on lyve. **1533** BELLENDEN *Livy* II. xix. (S.T.S.) I. 202 Þai condampnit Oppia þe virgine vestal for hir Incest. **1600** HOLLAND *Livy* I. xx. 14 Numa..instituted also a Nunnerie as it were, of religious vestall virgines. *Ibid.* XXVIII. xi. 676 The Vestall virgin who had the charge that night..was.. throughly skourged. **1692** tr. *Sallust* 20 Cataline had.. Debauch'd a Lady of Noble Extraction, and a Vestal Virgin. **1710** W. KING *Heathen Gods & Heroes* ix. (1722) 26 The Vestal Virgin Claudia, whose..freedom of Behaviour had made her Modesty suspected. **1770** LANGHORNE *Plutarch* (1851) II. 882/2 What is there in Rome so sacred and venerable as the vestal virgins who keep the perpetual fire? **1865** LECKY *Ration.* (1878) I. 23 The miracles which clustered so thickly around the vestal virgins. **1891** FARRAR *Darkn. & Dawn* xlix, In defiance of every law..he had recently seized Rubria, one of the Vestal Virgins.

2. Of fire, etc.: Of or pertaining to Vesta.

1599 *Broughton's Let.* xii. 40 They counted it vnlawfull to refresh the Vestall fire. **1627** DRAYTON *Sheph. Sirena* 53 My coate with light should shine, Purer then the Vestall fire. **1697** DRYDEN *Virg. Georg.* IV. 553 She sprinkl'd thrice, with Wine, the Vestal Fire. **1782** V. KNOX *Ess.* cxiv. (1819) II. 287 Those institutions..have still kept the light burning like the vestal fire. **1792** S. ROGERS *Pleas. Mem.* Poems (1839) 4 Oblivion steals upon her vestal-lamp. **1853** KANE *Grinnell Exp.* xxxiv. (1856) 301 Three stoves and a cooking-galley, four Argand and three bear-fat lamps, burn with the constancy of a vestal shrine.

fig. **1752** YOUNG *Brothers* I. i, Thou in whose eye, so modest, and so bright, Love ever wakes, and keeps a vestal fire. **1817** SHELLEY *Rev. Islam* Ded. xi, Through thine eyes, even in thy soul I see A lamp of vestal fire burning internally. **1853** *Chr. Remembrancer* Jan. 70 Then it was that the Jeromes and the Eustochiums retired..from a world whose light seemed on the eve of extinction, to nurse the vestal fire which was never to be really put out.

3. Resembling a priestess of Vesta in respect of chastity; chaste, pure, virgin.

1595 *Locrine* V. iv. 54 Beleeue me, Locrine, but the girle is wise, And well would seeme to make a vestall Nunne. **1705** POPE *Jan. & May* 202 Demure and chaste as any vestal Nun. **1749** FIELDING *Tom Jones* XV. ix, Jones had no reason to imagine the lady to have been of the vestal kind. **1821** SHELLEY *Epipsych.* 390 The day is come, and thou wilt fly with me. To whatsoe'er of dull mortality Is mine, remain a vestal sister still. **1822** W. IRVING *Braceb. Hall* xviii, Mrs Hannah, the vestal gentlewoman of my Lady Lillycraft, has had long walks and talks with Phœbe.

transf. **1806** MOORE *Dream Antiq.* i, Upon the bank awhile I stood, And saw the vestal planet weep Her tears of light on Ariel's flood. **1818** KEATS *Endym.* I. 874 Oft have I brought thee flowers, on their stalks set Like vestal primroses.

4. Pertaining to, characteristic of, a vestal virgin or virgins; marked by chastity or purity.

1592 SHAKS. *Rom. & Jul.* II. ii. 8 Her Vestal liuery is but sicke and greene. **1594** DRAYTON *Min. Poems* (1907) 4 Since holy Vestall lawes haue been neglected. **1612** *Two Noble K.* V. i. 156 This is my last Of vestall office; I am bride habited, But mayden harted. **1729** T. COOKE *Tales*, etc. 18 Young Men, and Virgins,..Attend a Song fit for a vestal Ear. **1813** SHELLEY *Q. Mab* III. 68 O dear and blessed peace! Why dost thou shroud thy vestal purity In penury and dungeons? **1825** SCOTT *Betrothed* xvii, Necessarily introducing many male guests within those vestal precincts. **1847** TENNYSON *Princ.* II. 204 Love whispers may not breathe Within this vestal limit.

B. *sb.* **1.** A vestal virgin.

1579–80 NORTH *Plutarch's Lives, Numa* (1612) 68 He also hath the keeping of the holy virgines which they call Vestales. *Ibid.* 69 [He] taketh out..the condemned Vestall, muffled vp close. **1616** BULLOKAR *Eng. Exp.* s.v., These Vestals were first instituted by Numa Pompilius, or as some write, by Romulus. **1671** PHILLIPS (ed. 3) s.v. *Vesta*, Certain Virgins called Vestalls, who were to take care of the Vestal fire. **1722** J. RICHARDSON *Acc. Statues*, etc. *Italy*, etc. 135 The Head of the young Vestal was the most engaging thing I had seen in Italy. **1740** J. DUPRÉ *Conform. Anc. & Mod. Cerem.* 47 The Chief of the Vestals was called Maxima. **1774** GOLDSM. *Nat. Hist.* (1776) II. 265 A..face formed exactly like the Venus of Medicis, or the sleeping vestal. **1843** *Penny Cycl.* XXVI. 286/1 The habits which the vestals had acquired during their priesthood. **1869** LECKY *Europ. Mor.* I. iii. 433 *note*, The vestal Urbinia was buried alive on account of a plague.

fig. and *transf.* **1594** DRAYTON *Min. Poems* (1907) 4 Here Chastity that Vestall most diuine, Attends that Lampe with eye which neuer sleepeth. **1767** STERNE *Tr. Shandy* IX. xvii, I keep neither man or boy,..or any thing that can eat or drink, except a thin, poor piece of a Vestal (to keep my fire in). **1828** HAWTHORNE *Fanshawe* iv, A flame..which Hugh was so far a vestal as to supply with its necessary fuel at all seasons of the year.

2. A virgin; a chaste woman; a nun.

1590 SHAKS. *Mids. N.* II. i. 158 A certaine aime he tooke At a faire Vestall, throned by the West. **1593** NASHE *Christ's T.* 80 A grosse-pencild Painter, who..vnder colour of drawing of pictures, drawes more to his shady Pauilion, then depart thence pure Vestals. **1608** SHAKS. *Per.* IV. v. 7 Shall's go hear the vestals sing? **1717** POPE *Eloisa to Abelard* 207 How happy is the blameless vestal's lot! The world forgetting, by the world forgot. **1784** COWPER *Task* IV. 554 The stain Appears a spot upon a vestal's robe, The worse for what it soils. **1848** THACKERAY *Van. Fair* x, She was the most hospitable and jovial of old vestals, and had been a beauty in her day. **1879** GLADSTONE *Glean.* II. i. 10 He states that he never knew souls more polluted than those of some of the professed vestals of the Church.

Hence '**vestalship**, the state or condition of being a vestal or virgin.

1893 F. THOMPSON *Poems* 42 A mouth too red for the moon to buss it, But her cheek unvow its vestalship.

† **vestament**, erroneous var. of VESTIMENT or VESTMENT.

1632 MASSINGER & FIELD *Fatal Dowry* IV. i. Hjb, His vestaments sit, as if they grew vpon him.

veste, southern ME. var. FAST *v.* and *adv.*, FIST *sb.*[1]

vested ('vɛstɪd), *ppl. a.* [f. VEST *v.* + -ED.]

1. a. Clothed, robed, dressed, *spec.* in ecclesiastical vestments. Also *fig.*

1671 MILTON *P.R.* I. 257 Just Simeon and Prophetic Anna..spake Before the Altar and the vested Priest. **1769** GOLDSM. *Des. Vill.* 360 The cooling brook, the grassy vested green. **1841** CHALMERS in Hanna *Mem.* (1852) IV. 256 Why do I not go forth as a forgiven and vested creature. **1842** WORDSW. *Eccles. Sonn.* III. xxvi, The Vested Priest before the Altar stands.

b. *Her.* (See quot.)

c **1828** BERRY *Encycl. Her.* I. Gloss., *Vested*, habited, or clothed, as a cubit arm, &c. vested *az.* or the like.

2. a. Established, secured, or settled in the hands of, or definitely assigned to, a certain possessor.

1766 BLACKSTONE *Comm.* II. 168 *Vested* remainders..are where the estate is invariably fixed, to remain to a determinate person, after the particular estate is spent. *Ibid.* 513 A legacy to one, to be paid when he attains the age of twenty-one years, is a *vested* legacy. **1818** CRUISE *Digest* (ed. 2) VI. 185 He held it to be a vested estate in fee in the son. **1832** LEWIS *Use & Ab. Pol. Terms* iii. 25 In its legal sense, vested is opposed to contingent. **1845** WILLIAMS *Real Prop.* 241 The alienation of an executory interest, before its becoming an actually vested estate. **1868** E. EDWARDS *Ralegh* I. Introd. p. xlv, After..months of struggle with the vested privileges of record-keepers.

b. *esp.* with *right* or *interest*. Also *fig.*

(*a*) *a* **1797** J. P. ANDREWS *Man. Constit.* 211 (Thornton), Violative of a vested legal right. **1832** AUSTIN *Jurispr.* App. p. xxxiv, Vested rights essentially differ..from rights which are contingent. **1848** MILL *Pol. Econ.* I. ix. §3 (1876) 89 The vested right which Parliament has allowed to be acquired by the existing companies. **1858** J. MARTINEAU *Stud. Chr.* 285 Let its vested right, of paying out the truth, be flung into the free air of history. **1876** DIGBY *Real Prop.* v. §3. 233 It is not such a right as the law regards as vested, that is, as completely created.

(*b*) **1818** CRUISE *Digest* (ed. 2) V. 481 The limitation..gave him an immediate vested interest in the surplus of the estate. **1842** ABDY *Water Cure* (1843) 154 Finding that new truths have not as many vested interests to recommend them as old fallacies. **1859** MILL *Liberty* iv. (1865) 53/1 The doctrine ascribes to all mankind a vested interest in each other's moral, intellectual, and even physical perfection. **1889** W. DONISTHORPE *Individualism* iv. 122 Vested interests may perhaps be defined as rights based not upon contract but upon custom.

3. Invested.

1863 P. BARRY *Dockyard Econ.* 20 The returns for vested capital and the comfort of the working classes both [being] considered.

'**vested** *a.* Chiefly *N. Amer.* [f. VEST *sb.* + -ED[2].] Of a suit: three-piece, having a waistcoat.

1976 *Daily Colonist* (Victoria, B.C.) 6 Oct. 5/8 (Advt.), Save a great deal on a Tip Top vested suit. **1982** 'W. R. DUNCAN' *Queen's Messenger* viii. 74 Ross..nattily dressed as usual in his vested dark suit.

ve'stee[1]. *Law.* [f. VEST *v.* + -EE[1].] One who is vested with a right, property, etc. Also *transf. rare.*

1879 *Austin's Jurispr.* II. lii. 883 Subject to a series of vested rights (descendible perhaps from present vestees). **1937** *Virginia Q. Rev.* XIII. 591 In a department of English, as in any other going business, the proprietary interest becomes vested, and in old and reputable departments the vestees have uniformly been gentlemen who have gone through the historical mill.

ve'stee[2]. Chiefly *N. Amer.* [f. VEST *sb.* + -EE[2].] A vest (sense 3 a or 3 d) or dickey (sense 6).

1904 *T. Eaton & Co. Catal.* Spring & Summer 87/3 Boys' Vestee Suits, three-piece style, with single-breasted vest. **1916** *Daily Colonist* (Victoria, B.C.) 7 July 14/5 (Advt.), Silk Crepe de Chine Waists..featuring the small button front and vestee effect outlined by French Veining. **1928** *Daily Express* 17 Aug. 4 (*heading*) Vestee and cuff set. **1943** *Sun*

(Baltimore) 4 Feb. 17/2 The Chicago Cubs..have worn sleeveless baseball shirts, or vestees, for the last three years. **1963** J. Mitford *Amer. Way of Death* iv. 56 The women's lingerie department of Practical Burial Footwear supplies a de-luxe package..of 'pantee, vestee' and nylon hose.

vesten, southern ME. variant of FAST *v.*

'vester. *rare.* [f. VEST *v.* 8.] One who invests money; an investor.

1829 Southey *Lett.* (1856) IV. 146 They declare that their vesters aim at..a community in land and in goods.

†**vesterer.** *Obs. rare.* In 4 **westerer.** [f. *vester-ie* VESTRY, or OF. *vestier* vestiary.] A person having charge of vestments.

1388 in *Archaeol.* LII. 213 Fyrste the westerer shall lay the abbotes cope lowest opon the awter wᵗin the sayd westre.

vesterie, obs. form of VESTRY¹.

†**vesteye**, *v. Obs. rare.* Also **vestoy-**. [app. ad. an unrecorded AF. **vesteier*, OF. **vestoier*, of obscure origin.] *trans.* To inspect, examine. Hence †**vesteying** *vbl. sb.*

c **1410** *Master of Game* (MS. Digby 182) xxv, It is to weten þat ofte tyme a deere is herbored with vestoynge of mannys eye. *Ibid.* xxx, If his lymer be dislaue, late him vesteye it with his eye. *Ibid.* xxxiii, And if þe lymer ouershete, or kan not put it forth, euery hunter þat þere is, ought to go somedele a broode forto se yf þei myn fynde þe reghtes with vesteynge of eye.

vestiarian (vɛstɪ'ɛərɪən), *a.* [f. VESTIAR-Y + -IAN.]

1. Of or relating to, concerned with, ecclesiastical vestments or their use.

1850 Marsden *Early Purit.* (1853) 19 The question of the habits, or as it has since been termed the vestiarian controversy. **1866** *Contemp. Rev.* II. 557 The ecclesiastical Adria, agitated by ritualistic and vestiarian gales, has thrown up a great heap of pamphlets. **1881** *Guardian* 16 Feb. 232/3 We should have been well pleased had these vestiarian differences never found place amongst us.

2. Of, belonging or peculiar to, clothing or dress; vestiary. *rare*⁻¹.

1854 R. H. Patterson *Ess. Hist. & Art* (1862) 34 Whitening of the seams—a disagreeable vestiarian phenomenon produced by the surface, or best-coloured portion, of the cloth being rubbed off.

†**vestiarier.** *Obs. rare*⁻⁰. Also **vestyaryer(e.** [f. med.L. *vestiārius* sb. Cf. OF. *vestiarieur* (Godef.).] = VESTERER.

c **1440** *Promp. Parv.* 509/1 Vestyaryer [*printed* -ce] (*K.* vestiariere [*Winch. MS.* vestyaryere], *P.* vestyar), *vestiarius.*

‖**vesti'arium.** *rare.* [L. *vestiārium*, f. *vesti-s* clothes, clothing: see -ARIUM.] A vestiary, vestry.

1855 Thackeray *Newcomes* xliv, The chapel by the little door near to the Vestiarium. **1875** *Encycl. Brit.* I. 13/1 The upper story of the refectory [in a Benedictine abbey] is the 'vestiarium', where the ordinary clothes of the brethren were kept.

vestiary ('vɛstɪərɪ), *sb.* Forms: 3-6 **vestiarie**, 4 **vestiare**, 5 **vestyarye**, **-iarye**, 5- **vestiary**. [a. OF. *vestiarie*, *vestiaire*, *vestyaire*, etc. (mod.F. *vestiaire*, = Pr. *vestiari*, Pg. and It. *vestiario*), or ad. L. *vestiārium* clothes-chest, wardrobe, neut. sing. of *vestiārius* adj., f. *vesti-s* clothing, vesture. Cf. VESTUARY.]

I. 1. A vestry of a church. Now *rare* or *Obs.*

c **1290** *S. Eng. Leg.* I. 455 A lodlich cloth he bouȝhte for fif panes; to þe bischope he gan it bringue. Þe bischop eode into þe vestiarie; is Cope he gan of strepe. **1427-8** *Rec. St. Mary at Hill* (1905) 69 For a plomer on þe vestyarye. **1448** Hen. VI *Will* in Willis & Clark *Cambridge* (1886) I. 354 The vestiarie to be sette oon the north syde of the saide Quere. **1503** in Blyth *Hist. Notices & Rec. Fincham* (1863) 57 My bodye to be beryed in the vestiary of Sent Martyns Chirche. **1551** T. Wilson *Logike* (1580) 57b, The Church, the pulpite, the vestiarie, the chauncell. **1668** T. Smith in *Phil. Trans.* (1697) XIX. 604 Toward one end of the English Church, just by the Vestiary. **1727** Bailey (vol. II), *Vestiary*, a Vestry or Dressing-Room. **1819** W. Tennant *Papistry Storm'd* (1827) 212 And monie ane that day did herrie Braw spulyie frae the vestiary. **1841** Gresley *For. Arden* (1842) 61 The service being at length finished,..he returned to the Vestiary. **1866** Mrs. R. T. Ritchie *Village on Cliff* xvii, The curé..walked through his wild overgrown wilderness to the vestiary.

b. A room or building, esp. one in a monastery or other large establishment, in which clothes are kept. Also, a cloak-room (quot. 1893).

c **1450** Capgrave *Life St. Aug.* 45, I haue do mad ȝou clothis & hosyn and schon..whech I wil þat þei be kept in a comon vestiarie, þat euery man may haue part as him nedith. **1467-8** *Rolls of Parlt.* V. 596/2 Davy Chirke, Yoman of oure Vestiarye of oure Houshold. **1706** Phillips (ed. Kersey), *Vestiary*, a place in a Monastery, where the Monks Cloaths are laid up; the Friers Wardrobe. **1860** Ainsworth *Ovingdean Grange* 157 The room..being used, at the present day, as a vestiary. **1862** Sir H. Taylor *St. Clement's Eve* II. i, Go to the vestiary, wherein thou'lt find Provision of all garbs for the masqued ball. **1893** McCarthy *Red Diamonds* II. 161 'All right,' said Granton,..turning to the vestiary for his light overcoat.

†**c.** (See quot.) *Obs.*⁻⁰

1656 Blount *Glossogr.* (copying Cooper), *Vestiary*,..a Wardrobe, Press, or Chest, where apparel is laid. [Hence in Phillips, and recent Dicts.]

†**2.** = VESTIBULE 1. Cf. VESTRY 1 b. *Obs. rare.*

1382 Wyclif *Exod.* xxxv. 17 The tentis in the ȝatis of the vestiarie [L. *in foribus vestibuli*]. **1382** —— *2 Sam.* xvii. 18 Thei wenten in a swift paase in the hows of a maner man in Bahurym, that hadde a pit in his vestiarye.

II. 3. Clothes, dress, garments. *rare*⁻¹.

1846 Landor *Imag. Conv.* Wks. I. 467/1 Thy versicoloured and cloudlike vestiary, puffed and effuse, rustling and rolling.

vestiary ('vɛstɪərɪ), *a.* [ad. L. *vestiāri-us*: see prec. and -ARY¹. Cf. obs. F. *vestiaire* (Littré).] Of, pertaining or relating to, clothes or dress.

1622 E. Misselden *Free Trade* (ed. 2) 109 The Superfluity of other Commodities may bee restrained by lawes Vestiary and Sumptuary. **1648** Bp. Hall *Select Th.* §93. 271 Some are for manuary trades,..another for Vestiary services. **1829** *Blackw. Mag.* XXV. 346 The soul may remain the same, but a new body is actually given to it by the interposition of vestiary talent. **1866** R. Chambers *Ess.* Ser. II. 113 A collection of vestiary curiosities. **1870** W. R. Greg *Polit. Problems* 167 Some vestiary materials have become more abundant and lower in price. **1891** Han. Lynch *G. Meredith* 78 We learn of vestiary elegances, and temper.

vestible, obs. form of VESTIBULE.

vestibular (vɛ'stɪbjʊlə(r)), *a.* [f. next + -AR¹. Cf. obs. F. *vestibulaire.*] Of or pertaining to, of the nature of, resembling or serving as, a vestibule: **a.** *Anat.* (Cf. VESTIBULE *sb.* 2); *spec.* of or pertaining to the vestibule of the ear or its function as an organ of equilibrium.

1836-9 *Todd's Cycl. Anat.* II. 537/1 The vestibular part of the membraneous labyrinth..is all that is really fundamental in the structure of an organ of hearing. **1851** Woodward *Mollusca* I. (1856) 23 As in the vestibular cavities of fishes. **1872** Huxley *Phys.* viii. 211 The vestibular nerve tells us that sounds are weak or loud, but gives no impression of tone or melody or harmony. **1899** *Allbutt's Syst. Med.* VII. 580 The vestibular termination of the auditory nerve. **1902** D. J. Cunningham *Text-bk. Anat.* 482 Its fibres..end in the nucleus of Deiters, the chief vestibular nucleus. **1923** *Physiol. Rev.* III. 209 (*heading*) The function of the vestibular apparatus. **1948** A. Brodal *Neurol. Anat.* vii. 213 The parts of the labyrinth generally assumed to be concerned with vestibular function..are..the saccule and the utricle, and the three semicircular canals. **1956** A. C. Guyton *Textbk. Med. Physiol.* xlvi. 575/1 Equilibrium is controlled especially by the vestibular apparatus. **1962** V. Grissom in *Into Orbit* 80 The doctors call this sensation 'vestibular nystagmus', and it is an uncontrollable movement of the eyeballs which occurs when the balance mechanism in your body gets all messed up from the twisting and tumbling. **1983** *Oxf. Textbk. Med.* II. xxv. 29/2 Either the cochlear or the vestibular fibres of the eighth nerve may be damaged within the brainstem, although vestibular symptoms are appreciably more common from this cause.

b. In general use.

1861 Beresf. Hope *Eng. Cathedr. 19th C.* 158 The outer world was fenced off by the interposed atrium or vestibular cloister.

c. *Zool.* (See quot.)

1887 Sollas in *Encycl. Brit.* XXII. 416/1 This pseudostomosis is due to a folding of the entire sponge, so as to produce secondary canals or cavities, which may be incurrent (vestibular) or excurrent (cloacal).

So **ve'stibulary** *a. rare.*

1843 in F. H. Ramadge *Curab. Consumption* (1850) 37 The ..morbid conditions of this vestibulary portion of the respiratory apparatus.

vestibule ('vɛstɪbju:l), *sb.* Also α. 7-8 **vestible.** [ad. L. *vestibulum* (hence F. *vestibule*, OF. *vestible*, It., Sp. and Pg. *vestibulo*), entrance-court, fore-court, entrance. The origin of the L. word is uncertain.]

1. In reference to ancient times: The enclosed or partially enclosed space in front of the main entrance of a Roman or Greek house or building; an entrance-court or fore-court.

In some instances approximating to next.

α. **1623** Cockeram I, *Vestible*, the porch of a dore. **1656** Blount *Glossogr.*, *Vestible*,..a void place without the door, a Porch, an Entry. **1753** *Chambers' Cycl.* Suppl. s.v. *Atrium*, Some have mistakenly confounded the *Atrium* with the porch or vestible, from which it was distinct. **1796** Burney *Mem. Metastasio* II. 163 Porticos, vestibles of temples, and other public buildings.

β. *a* **1751** Bolingbroke *Study Hist.* ii. (1752) I. 19 The citizens of Rome placed the images of their ancestors in the vestibules of their houses. **1770** Langhorne *Plutarch* (1851) II. 1081/1 This tyrant..would not suffer his guards to do duty in the palace, but only in the vestibule and porticos about it. **1791** Cowper *Iliad* XI. 942 While ye on preparation of the feast Attended both, Ulysses and myself Stood in the vestibule. **1819** Keats *Lamia* II. 163 He met within the murmurous vestibule His young disciple. **1819** Shelley *Cyclops* 219 [To] Throw you as ballast into the ship's hold, And then deliver you, a slave, to move Enormous rocks, or found a vestibule. **1891** Farrar *Darkn. & Dawn* i, In its vestibule was a bronze statue, fifty feet high.

b. In modern usage: A chamber or hall immediately between the entrance-door and the interior of a building or house (usually one of some size), to which it gives admittance; an ante-chamber, entrance-hall, or lobby.

α. **1730** Bailey (fol.), A *Vestible* is also used for a Kind of little Anti-Chamber before the Entrance of an ordinary Apartment. **1747** in *Nairne Peerage Evidence* (1874) 80 In the low vestible ane old clock.

β. **1756** Mrs. Delany in *Autobiog. & Corr.* (1861) III. 437 Her apartment is the prettiest thing I ever saw, consisting of a skylight antechamber or vestibule, adorned in the Gothic way. **1797** Mrs. Radcliffe *Italian* i, He was soon admitted to a small vestibule, where he found Bianchi winding balls of silk. **1828** *Ann. Reg.* 76/1 A scene almost of butchery took place in the staircases and vestibules. **1862** Miss Braddon *Lady Audley* xxxvi, The clock in the vestibule struck nine as Robert opened the library-door. **1881** Owen in *Nature* No. 618. 425 The impressive and rather gloomy vestibule which leads to the great hall.

Comb. **1887** *Pall Mall G.* 11 Nov. 2/2 This room opens into a long and lofty vestibule-like chamber.

c. *transf.* and *fig.*

Freq. from *c* 1800; usu. const. *of*, as in the first group.

(*a*) **1755** Young *Centaur* ii. Wks. 1757 IV. 141 The dark, solemn approaches to, or dismal vestibules of, the grave. **1785** Burns *Common-pl. Bk.* Oct., If ever any young man, in the vestibule of the world, chance to throw his eye over these pages [etc.]. **1800** *Med. Jrnl.* III. 254 There can be no very great deviation, while we remain at the vestibule of useful inquiry. **1833** H. Coleridge *Lives Northerns* 3 A single copy of verses [by Marvell]..keeping its station in the vestibule of Paradise Lost. **1861** J. G. Holland *Less. Life* iii. 48 To-day we stand in life's vestibule. **1875** Grindon *Life* i. 4 True figurative language is..the vestibule of philosophy.

(*b*) **1781** Harris *Philol. Eng.* II. iv. 106 Looking upon Knowledge..to pass into the Mansions of the Mind thro' Language, they were careful..not to offend in the Vestibule. *a* **1848** R. W. Hamilton *Rew. & Punishm.* viii. (1853) 379 The present is the vestibule to a boundless existence. **1850** Maurice *Mor. & Met. Philos.* (ed. 2) 131 One large class of the Platonic Dialogues, which are the induction or vestibule to the rest. **1873** Symonds *Grk. Poets* i. 3 Language and Mythology form the vestibules and outer courts to Homer, Pheidias, Lycurgus.

d. An enclosed and covered-in portion at either end of a railway carriage, serving as a means of passage from one carriage to another. Also *attrib.* in ***vestibule train*** (see VESTIBULED *a.*). Orig. *U.S.*

1889 *Daily News* 7 May 7/3 Communication was then established by throwing a board across, and privacy secured by stretching a piece of canvas above to connect the two roofs. It was the vestibule train principle established unexpectedly in a new quarter. **1890** T. M. Cooley, etc. *Railways Amer.* 246 A perfectly enclosed vestibule of handsome architectural appearance between the cars. **1896** *Daily News* 14 July 9/7 The new vestibule East Coast train.

2. *Anat.* (and *Zool.*). One or other of various cavities or hollows regarded as forming an approach or entrance to another, usually a larger or more important, part.

A number of these, as ***vestibule of the aorta***, ***larynx***, ***mouth***, ***pharynx***, are specified in recent encyclopædic and medical Dicts.

a. The osseous cavity which forms the central portion of the labyrinth of the ear and is situated between the tympanum and the internal auditory canal, immediately behind the cochlea.

1728 Chambers *Cycl.* s.v. *Ear*, The Labyrinth..is divided into three Parts; the first called the Vestibule. **1782** A. Monro *Anat.* 72 The other [hole] ends in several very small canals that allow a passage to the branches of the *portio mollis*..into the vestibule and cochlea. **1836-9** *Todd's Cycl. Anat.* II. 530/1 Of the compartments of the osseous labyrinth, the vestibule lies in the middle, the semi-circular canals behind it, and the cochlea in front. **1856** Todd & Bowman *Phys. Anat.* II. 96 The essential part of the organ of hearing is the vestibule. **1884** Coues *N. Amer. Birds* 188 The bony labyrinth consists of an irregular central cavity, the vestibule.

b. (See quot. 1857.)

1841 Ramsbotham *Obstetr. Medicine* 55 The *Meatus Urinarius*,..which is the canal leading to the bladder, is situated at the further extremity of the vestibule. **1857** Bullock *Cazeaux' Midwif.* 43 The vestibule is a small triangular space placed at the upper part of the vulva. **1883** Duncan *Clin. Lect. Dis. Wom.* (ed. 2) xvii. 167, I call them inflammations of the pudendum; but they are often called inflammations of the vulva, and sometimes of the vestibule.

c. ***membranous vestibule***, the membranous sacs contained within the osseous vestibule of the ear.

1857 Dunglison *Med. Lex.* s.v., There is also another membrane, constituting the membranous vestibule, but it is not an exact imitation of the osseous cavity.

d. *Zool.* = VESTIBULUM 2 b. *rare.*

1875 Huxley & Martin *Elem. Biol.* 87 When fæcal matters are discharged, they make their way out by an aperture which is temporarily formed in the floor of this vestibule.

'vestibule, *v.* [Back-formation from next.] *trans.* To provide or supply (a railway carriage) with vestibules; to unite by means of vestibules.

1891 in *Cent. Dict.* **1896** *Westm. Gaz.* 20 Apr. 2/1 The two cars..are 'vestibuled' together by a central lobby. **1904** *N. & Q.* 10th Ser. I. 346/2 Through carriages on a certain train between London and Hull will henceforward be 'vestibuled through' to an express.

'vestibuled, *a.* [f. VESTIBULE *sb.*] Of a train: Provided with vestibules. Orig. *U.S.*

1890 T. M. Cooley, etc. *Railways Amer.* 249 The first of the vestibuled trains went into service on the Pennsylvania Railroad in June, 1886. **1898** *Westm. Gaz.* 26 Apr. 6/4 The vestibuled corridor dining-car trains on the East and West Coast routes to Scotland.

vestibu'litis. *Path.* [f. VESTIBULE *sb.* + -ITIS.] Inflammation of the vestibule of the vulva.

1889 Duncan *Clin. Lect. Dis. Wom.* (ed. 4) xi. 65 When they do so women suffer..from slight superficial inflammation—vestibulitis.

vestibulo- (vɛ'stɪbjʊləʊ), comb. form of L. *vestibul-um* VESTIBULE *sb.*, used chiefly with reference to the vestibule of the ear, as **veˌstibulo-ˈauditory** *a.*, involving the vestibules and hearing; **veˌstibulocereˈbellar** *a.*, applied to nerves running from the vestibular nucleus of the brain to the cerebellum; **veˌstibulocoˈchlear** *a.*, designating or pertaining to the vestibular and cochlear nerves jointly; **veˌstibulo-ˈocular** *a.*, involving both the vestibular and the oculomotor nerves; **veˌstibuloˈspinal** *a.*, applied to a tract of nerves in the spinal cord that originate in the vestibular nucleus of the brain. Also VESTIBULOTOMY.

1945 *Arch. Ophthalmol.* XXXIII. 149/1 The vestibulo-auditory symptoms began abruptly with vertigo, tinnitus and deafness. **1980** *Medicine* (Baltimore) LIX. 426/1 Cogan syndrome..is a disease of young adults and consists of acute interstitial keratitis..with vestibuloauditory dysfunction. **1932** *Jrnl. Compar. Neurol.* LIV. 150 Vestibulocerebellar fibers. **1974** D. & M. WEBSTER *Compar. Vertebr. Morphol.* xii. 292 The vestibulocerebellar tract runs from the vestibular nuclei in the brainstem through the restiform body to terminate in the cerebellar cortex. **1962** *Gray's Anat.* (ed. 33) 1141 The vestibulo-cochlear nerve appears in the groove between the pons and the medulla oblongata. **1974** *Encycl. Brit. Micropædia* III. 413/1 In nerve deafness, some defect in the sensory cells of the inner ear..or in the vestibulocochlear nerve prevents transmission of sound impulses from the inner ear to the auditory centre in the brain. **1982** *Audiology* XXI. 172 Streptomycin..passes into the fetus..producing vestibulocochlear neural abnormalities. **1921** TILNEY & RILEY *Form & Function Central Nervous System* xxx. 532 Vestibulo-ocular associated reflex. This reflex is elicited by electrical, thermal and mechanical stimulation of the receptors in the vestibule of the internal ear. **1963** *Jrnl. Theoret. Biol.* IV. 215 The simplest description of this vestibulo-ocular reflex is to say that, if the head is rotated in one direction, the eyes tend to rotate, with respect to the head, in the opposite direction, and then come back to their undeviated position. **1979** *Sci. Amer.* Jan. 88/1 The two other major types of eye movements—the vestibulo-ocular movements, which maintain visual stability during head movements, and the smooth-pursuit eye movements, which follow a moving object such as a flying bird—do not appear..since neither of these types of movements is elicited by target jumps. **1899** L. F. BARKER *Nervous System* lviii. 960 It would seem that this uncrossed descending vestibulo-spinal neurone system has been described by various authors under different names. **1948** A. BRODAL *Neurological Anat.* v. 118 The most important descending connexion appears to be the vestibulo-spinal tract. **1983** *Brain Res.* CCLIX. 217/1 The vestibulospinal system has a complex organization both in aspects of its afferent connection and of its spinal projection.

vestibuˈlotomy. *Surg.* [f. VESTIBULO- + -TOMY.] The operation of cutting or opening the vestibule of the ear.

1908 *Lancet* 9 May 1341/2 We have come to regard inferior vestibulotomy as a good and adequate means of draining the vestibule in cases of infection... Double vestibulotomy was performed with partial removal of the cochlea.

‖**vestibulum** (vɛˈstɪbjʊləm). [L.: see VESTIBULE *sb.*]

1. = VESTIBULE *sb.* 1.

1662 J. DAVIES tr. *Olearius' Voy. Ambass.* 286 In the midst of the *Vestibulum*, there was a great Fountain. **1664** EVELYN tr. *Freart's Archit.* 132 In those large *Xystas, Porticos, Atrias* and *Vestibula* of the Greeks and Romans. **1699** HOWE *Redeemer's Dominion* Wks. 1724 II. 64 Having the Keys of the Celestial House of God,..he should also have the Keys of the Terrestrial Bethel; which is but a sort of Portal or Vestibulum to the other. **1718** OZELL tr. *Tournefort's Voy.* II. v. 176 In the Vestibulum of a Convent of Greek Nuns, there is a Christ very ill painted. **1834** LYTTON *Pompeii* I. iii, You enter..by a small entrance-passage (called *vestibulum*) into a hall.

2. *Anat.* and *Zool.* **a.** = VESTIBULE *sb.* 2.

1704 J. HARRIS *Lex. Techn.* I, *Vestibulum*, is a Cavity in the *Os Petrosum*, behind the *Finestra Ovalis*. **1726** A. MONRO *Anat.* 101 Canals, that allow a Passage to the Branches of the *Portio mollis* of the seventh Pair of Nerves, into the *Vestibulum* and *Cochlea*. **1797** M. BAILLIE *Morb. Anat.* (1807) 420 The external parts, particularly the inside of the nymphæ and the vestibulum, are subject to inflammation. **1800** *Phil. Trans.* XC. 9 The vestibulum..is completely separated from the tympanum. **1880** GÜNTHER *Fishes* 116 The membranous vestibulum is continued by a canal to a single opening in the roof of the skull.

b. *Zool.* The cavity or chamber in certain infusorians into which the œsophagus and anus open.

1859 J. R. GREENE *Man. Anim. Kingd., Protozoa* 56 In addition to the oral orifice, the vestibulum is provided with a lateral aperture which would appear to discharge the function of an anus. **1875** HUXLEY & MARTIN *Elem. Biol.* 87 A groove [in the bell-animalcule], which, at one point, deepens and passes into a wide depression, the *vestibulum*.

†**ˈvestigate**, *v. Obs. rare.* [f. L. *vestīgāt-*, ppl. stem of *vestīgāre* to track, trace out, investigate.] *intr.* and *trans.* To investigate, in various senses.

a **1562** G. CAVENDISH *Wolsey*, etc. (1825) II. 4 Wherefore Dame Reason did me persuade, and move To be content with my small estate, And in this matter no more to vestigate. **1623** COCKERAM I, *Vestigate*, to tracke, or trace. **1656** BLOUNT *Glossogr.* (following Cooper), *Vestigate*, to seek out, to seek by the print of the foot, to trace, to search, diligently, to hunt after. **1780** J. T. DILLON *Trav. Spain* (1781) 28 To vestigate their mode of propagation.

Hence †**ˈvestigating** (*vbl.*) *sb.*, a footprint. (Cf. VESTIGIATING.) †**vestiˈgation** (see quot. and INVESTIGATION). *Obs. rare.*

1634 SIR T. HERBERT *Trav.* 189 [The Cingalese hold] that Adam was their Created and liued there; they beleeue it rather in regard his vestigatings are yet imprinted in the earth. **1658** PHILLIPS, *Vestigation*, a seeking any one by the print of their foot, a searching diligently.

vestige (ˈvɛstɪdʒ). [a. F. *vestige*, ad. L. *vestīgium* footstep, footprint, trace, mark, etc. Cf. the earlier VESTIGY.]

I. 1. A mark, trace, or visible sign *of* something, esp. a building or other material structure, which no longer exists or is present; a piece of material evidence of this nature; something which remains after the destruction or disappearance of the main portion.

In the singular freq. in negative phrases.

pl. **1602** J. COLVILLE *Paræenese* u ij, Not..farder..nor vnto ye vall of Septimius Seuerus..vharof the vestiges yit remane. *a* **1700** EVELYN *Diary* 20 Nov. 1644, Descending the Mons Cælius we come against the vestiges of the Palazzo Maggiore. **1730** A. GORDON *Maffei's Amphith.* 297 We see the beginning of a Vault..with the Vestiges of the Stair upon it. **1791** W. GILPIN *Forest Scenery* II. 136 The vestiges of different buildings, and the walls of a small chapel, still remain. **1816** SIR H. DAVY in *Faraday's Exp. Res.* (1859) 4 Vestiges of extinct volcanoes exist in all the low countries on the western side of the Appennines. **1847** PRESCOTT *Peru* III. viii. I. 459 They had not been molested by enemies. But more than once they had seen vestiges of them in smoking hamlets and ruined bridges. **1864** D. G. MITCHELL *Sev. Stor.* 243 Others wandered thither, seeking vestiges of old inheritance.

sing. **1730** A. GORDON *Maffei's Amphith.* 240 Of these there is not the least Vestige remaining. **1743** KAMES *Decis. Crt. Sess. 1730–52* (1799) 63 There was no remaining vestige of any moveable effects. **1756** C. LUCAS *Ess. Waters* III. 370 No..vestige of the inflammable principle [will] appear. **1806** *Med. Jrnl.* XV. 98 Not the least vestige of a slough could be perceived. **1839** YEOWELL *Anc. Brit. Ch.* xii. 140 A vestige of some ancient fabric may be seen..near the church. **1886** RUSKIN *Præterita* I. 280 There is now scarce vestige left of any building prior to the fifteenth century.

b. A surviving memorial or trace *of* some condition, quality, practice, etc., serving as an indication of its former existence. Usu. in pl.

a **1700** EVELYN *Diary* 29 Jan. 1645, The once mighty Capua..shewing some vestige of its former magnificence in pieces of temples, arches [etc.]. **1792** BURKE *Corr.* (1844) III. 378 That line of policy which government has pursued: ..that, I mean, of wearing out the vestiges of conquest. **1805** FOSTER *Ess.* I. iii. I. 35 The vestiges of the first indelible impression. *a* **1850** CALHOUN *Wks.* (1874) III. 282 These consolidation doctrines sweep away at a blow every vestige of State Rights. **1872** YEATS *Growth Comm.* 197 A toll.. drove away the last vestige of lawful traffic. **1875** JOWETT *Plato* (ed. 2) V. 71 Modern enquirers..have also detected.. the vestiges of a patriarchal state still surviving.

c. Without *of*, in prec. senses.

1735 THOMSON *Liberty* II. 404 Scarce any trace remaining, vestige grey, Or nodding column..To point where Corinth, or where Athens stood. **1789** MRS. PIOZZI *Journ. France* I. 127 A mode..that I think will..leave no vestiges behind. **1789** J. WILLIAMS *Min. Kingd.* I. 32 A solid body of stone.. which exhibits no manner of vestige or leader whatever to point out which way the coal is gone. **1814** SCOTT *Border Antiq.* I. 1 This ancient baronial edifice is now in ruins,.. and nothing scarcely remains but a few melancholy vestiges, which [etc.]. **1830** G. A. COOKE *Topogr. Descr. Surrey* 68 Not a vestige is now standing, but the coloured bricks, stones, etc...prove that the materials have not been entirely destroyed.

d. A very small or slight trace, indication, or amount (*of* something); a particle, a scrap.

1756 C. LUCAS *Ess. Waters* I. 111 If it contains the least vestige, the slightest taint,..precipitation follows. **1781** COWPER *Conversat.* 219 On all the vestiges of truth attend, And let them guide you to a decent end. **1802** PLAYFAIR *Illustr. Huttonian Theory* 334 The mountain..appeared to me to be without any vestige of stratification. **1834** PRINGLE *Afr. Sk.* ix. 298 Not a vestige of green pasturage was to be descried. **1884** *Chr. Commonwealth* 12 June 824/1 The general ruck and run of our politicians have scarcely a vestige of lofty motive or noble principle.

2. *Biol.* A surviving trace *of* some part formerly existing in the species; a vestigial organ or structure (see quot. 1886).

1859 DARWIN *Orig. Species* xiii. (1860) 454 Rudimentary organs,..as..the vestige of an ear in earless breeds. **1868** LYELL *Princ. Geol.* (ed. 10) III. xxxv. II. 274 The aquatic reptile called *Proteus anguinus*,..which retains only the vestiges or rudiments of eyes. **1886** J. A. RYDER in *Proc. U.S. Nat. Mus.* 80 On investigating the condition of the vestiges of these limbs we find that the skeletal parts have actually been arrested. *Ibid.* note, Structures which are disappearing should be called vestiges.

II. 3. A mark or trace left on the ground by the foot; a footprint; a track. *rare.*

1656 BLOUNT *Glossogr.* (following Cooper), *Vestige*, the print of a mans foot, a footstep, a trace, or track, or mark of any thing. **1719** BOYER *Dict. Royal* I, *Vestige*, step, footstep, vestige. **1820** SHELLEY *Hymn Merc.* xxxvii, Who with unwearied feet could e'er impress The sand with such enormous vestiges? **1841** ELPHINSTONE *Hist. India* I. 363 In a dry country a bare foot leaves little print to common eyes; but one of these people..will pursue a robber by these vestiges for a distance that seems incredible.

fig. **1824** LANDOR *Imag. Conv.* I. 8 A country where prophet comes after prophet, and each treads out the last vestige from the sand.

b. *transf.* An impression made upon the brain by an image. *rare.*

1885 J. MARTINEAU *Types Eth. The.* I. ii. §2 Through the senses, external objects act upon the brain,..leaving a durable vestige there. *Ibid.* I. ii. §8 An image of sense or fancy, persistent in proportion to the depth of the cerebral vestige.

†**vestigia**, error for VESTIGIUM.

1789 J. WILLIAMS *Min. Kingd.* I. 28 Every slip of the coal metals has a vise, or vestigia, which points out to a skilful eye which way the metals are thrown out of their former course.

vestigial (vɛˈstɪdʒɪəl), *a.* [f. L. *vestīgi-um* (see VESTIGE) + -AL[1].] **1.** Of the nature of a vestige; remaining or surviving in a degenerate, atrophied, or imperfect condition or form:

a. *spec.* in *Biol.* of certain organs or structures.

1877 *Gray's Anat.* (ed. 8) p. cxlvi, The only remains of the Wolffian body in the complete condition of the female organs are two rudimentary or vestigial structures. **1884** COUES *N. Amer. Birds* 215 The transitory wolffian bodies and ducts..ultimately disappear from the female,..leaving only a trace of their former existence in certain vestigial structures. **1892** *Month* Jan. 16 The existence of what are called 'rudimentary' or 'vestigial' organs. **1898** *Allbutt's Syst. Med.* V. 727 A triangular fold—the 'vestigial fold' of Marshall—formed by a duplicature of the serous layer,.. passes between the left pulmonary artery and the subjacent pulmonary veins.

b. In general use.

1892 *19th Cent.* Jan. 37 They are only the stunted remnants, the vestigial and atrophied traces indicating the later stages of ages of [mental] development. *a* **1901** F. W. MYERS *Hum. Personality* (1903) II. 308 Vestigial beliefs which still encumbered the spirit have had time to atrophy.

2. *Telecommunications.* ***vestigial side band***, a side band which is partially attenuated (usu. at the higher frequencies) before transmission; freq. *attrib.*, with reference to a system in which one full side band and one vestigial side band are transmitted (with or without the carrier), esp. to improve the transmission of low-frequency components of the signal.

1940 D. G. FINK *Princ. Television Engin.* vii. 288 At the transmitter, the principal problem of vestigial side-band transmission (as the above-described system is called) is the design of a filter having the pass characteristics shown in Fig. 162. **1966** *McGraw-Hill Encycl. Sci. & Technol.* I. 352/1 In standard television broadcasting in the continental United States..the vestigial sideband has a bandwidth one-sixth that of a full sideband. **1979** A. A. LIFF *Colour & Black & White Television Theory & Servicing* ii. 55 The FCC standards require that the lower sideband be transmitted in vestigial sideband form and that the upper sideband be transmitted in its entirety.

Hence **veˈstigially** *adv.*

1902 *Amer. Anthropologist* IV. 33 This conception persists up through barbarism, albeit vestigially, into civilization.

veˈstigian, *a.* and *sb. rare.* [f. VESTIGE + -IAN.] **a.** *adj.* Of or pertaining to, or designating, the theory of evolution propounded by R. Chambers in his *Vestiges of the Natural History of Creation* (1844). **b.** *sb.* One who agrees with or supports this work or theory.

1860 DARWIN in *Life & Lett.* (1887) II. 295 The case would be a decided difficulty on the Lamarckian or Vestigian doctrine of necessary progression. **1891** *Tablet* 12 Sept. 414 Men who had never been known to read a scientific book in their lives, were found poring over it, and taking sides as Vestigians and anti-Vestigians.

†**veˈstigiary.** *Obs.*[−1] [f. L. *vestīgi-um* + -ARY[1].] A vestige or trace.

1651 BIGGS *New Disp.* §238 The adored Fontanell.. helpes nothing, before the crustous eschar be taken away; and the vestigiaries of heat and drynesse be first removed.

†**veˈstigiating.** *Obs.*[−1] [f. L. *vestīgi-um*: cf. VESTIGATING.] Footprints, tracks.

1638 SIR T. HERBERT *Trav.* (ed. 2) 307 Upon Colombo's high peake..is also shew'd and seene..the vestigiating or footsteps of old Adam.

‖**veˈstigium.** Pl. vestigia (also 7 vestigia's). Now *rare.* [L.: see VESTIGE.] **a.** A vestige or trace; a mark or indication left by something destroyed, lost, or no longer present.

1637 NABBES *Microcosm.* v. in Dodsley *O. Pl.* (1744) V. 355 Repentance stays as the vestigium, Or mark impress'd, by which the past disease Is found to have been. **1644** DIGBY *Nat. Bodies* vii. §7. 50 Experience assureth vs, that after it [*sc.* light] is extinguished, it leaueth not the least vestigium behind it of hauing beene there. **1665** SIR T. HERBERT *Trav.* (1677) 353 Upon better view I may discover his [Jerah's] Vestigia near Malacca amongst his other Brethren. **1749** *Phil. Trans.* XLVI. 197 Ruinous Heaps and Vestigia nearly effaced by Length of Time.

b. Const. *of.*

1644 [H. PARKER] *Jus Populi* 54 Neither Nature nor History afford us any Vestigia of it. **1664** EVELYN tr. *Freart's Archit.* ii. 9 Of which there is to this day some Vestigia's remaining. **1722** WOLLASTON *Relig. Nat.* v. 92 So universally and utterly abolishd, that no part, no vestigium of them should remain. **1769** E. BANCROFT *Guiana* 42 It is covered with bark of a light brown colour, variegated by the vestigia of the fallen off stamina of the leaves. **1771** *Ann. Reg.* II. 200/1 The vestigia of antiquity in a vicinage ought always to have great weight in determinations of this kind. **1970** H. BRAUN *Parish Churches* ix. 124 These [arches] are not, as might have been supposed, the remains of an earlier clearstory, but simply vestigia of the original windows of a pre-medieval nave.

†**c.** *spec.* (See quot. 1704.) *Obs.*

1695 WOODWARD *Nat. Hist. Earth* 22 The same Vestigia of Tendons..in each [fossil shell]. **1704** J. HARRIS *Lex. Techn.* I. s.v., Vestigia of Tendons, are the little Hollows in the Shells of Fishes, which are formed on purpose for the fastening or rooting of the Tendons of their Muscles.

†**'vestigy.** *Obs.* [a. older F. *vestigie*, or ad. L. *vestigium* VESTIGE: see -Y.] A vestige or trace.

1545 JOYE *Exp. Dan.* i. 13b, In that cite yet..there remaineth the temple of Iupiters image,..or els is there no nother memoriall or skant any vestigie thereof. *Ibid.* x. 169b, It behowued not one stone vpon another nor vestigie of the temple to stand and remaine. **1637** GILLESPIE *Eng. Pop. Cerem.* III. viii. 192 The Canon Law it self hath some vestigies of the auncient order. **1644** DIGBY *Nat. Bodies* xxxvi. §13. 317 We see how the doubting, the resoluing,.. and the like, which we experience in beasts, may by the vestigies we haue traced out, be followed vnto their roote.

†**'vestiment.** *Obs.* Forms: 3-4 **uestiment**, 4-6 **vestyment** (5 **-mente**), 4-7, 9 **vestiment** (5 *Sc.* **westiment**); also *pl.* 3 **-menz**, 4 **-mens**, 4-5 **-mentz**. [a. OF. *vestiment* (= Pr. *vestimen*, Sp. and It. *vestimento*, Pg. *vestimenta*), or ad. L. *vestīmentum* clothes, a garment, etc., f. *vestīre* to clothe, VEST *v.* Cf. VESTMENT *sb.*]

1. A vestment, esp. one worn by an ecclesiastic.

Common from *c* 1380 to *c* 1600, freq. in pl.

a **1225** *Ancr. R.* 418 Ne wite 3e nout in oure huse of oðer monnes þinges.., ne nout ne underuo 3e þe chirche uestimenz. *c* **1290** *S. Eng. Leg.* I. 133 Þo seint thomas hadde is masse i-songue his chesible he gan of weue, Alle is oþur uestimenz on him he let bi-leue. **1303** R. BRUNNE *Handl. Synne* 9337 Curteynes, or ouþer vestyment, Or any oþer vesselement þat falleþ to holy cherches seruyse. **1387** TREVISA *Higden* (Rolls) V. 87 He ordeyned þat mynystres of holy cherche schulde nou3t were holy vestymentis in þe comyn use of every day. *c* **1400** *Plowman's Tale* in *Pol. Poems* (Rolls) I. 332 Now been pristes pokes so wide, That men must enlarge the vestiment. *c* **1450** *Merlin* vi. 107 And therwith thei risen vp, and toke hym by-twene their armes, and ledde hym to the vestymentz rioall. **1523** [COVERDALE] *Old God & New* (1534) Lj, This day the preest hath a redde vestiment.., and when he syngeth masse of requiem, he hath on a blacke vestiment. **1551** ROBINSON tr. *More's Utopia* II. (1895) 287 Thies priestes,..whiles the armes be fighting together,..knele vpon their knees in their hallowed vestimentes. **1596** NASHE *Saffron Walden* Wks. (Grosart) III. 108 Hee creditted Newgate with the same metamorphized costly vestiment. **1605** BACON *Adv. Learn.* II. §5. 9 Socrates answereth: you haue reason, and it becomes you well, beeing a man so trimme in your vestiments. **1661** MORGAN *Sph. Gentry* II. ii. 27 The High Priests Vestiments was linnen Breeches next his flesh. **1850** BROWNING *Christmas Eve* II. 74 Mine's the same right with your poorest and sickliest, Supposing I don the marriage-vestiment [*rime* Testament].

Comb. **1479-81** *Rec. St. Mary at Hill* (1905) 101 The Vestyment makere. *c* **1515** *Cocke Lorell's B.* 10 Stacyoners, vestyment sewers, and ymagers.

transf. and *fig.* **1590** SPENSER *F.Q.* III. xii. 29 All that day she outwore in wandering,..Till that againe the second euening Her couered with her sable vestiment. **1620** E. BLOUNT *Horæ Subs.* 30 Howsoeuer a man may appeare to himselfe more complete, and full, in the vestiments of Vertue. **1655** T. VAUGHAN *Euphrates* 91 With the fire he attracts the Air which is the vestiment or body of the fire. **1656** HEYLIN *Surv. France* 51 There we beheld nature in her richest vestiments.

2. *collect.* Clothing, garb, vesture. *rare.*

1637 G. DANIEL *Genius of Isle* 25 The Naiades in Azure vestiment, With Hairs vnbound, the willing Sand shall print.

vesti'mental, *a. rare.* [f. as prec. + -AL[1].] = next.

1849 ROCK *Ch. of Fathers* I. v. 495 John of Salisbury, in one of his letters to Alexander III, reminds that Pontiff of a belt,—very likely one of these vestimental ones, which he had deigned to bestow upon him. **1908** *Times* 25 Nov. 4/2 If they were going into vestimental matters, it would take too long.

vestimentary (vɛstɪ'mɛntərɪ), *a.* [f. as prec. + -ARY[1].] Of or pertaining to, in respect of, clothes or dress; vestiary.

Freq. in journalistic use.

1803 in *Spirit Pub. Jrnls.* VII. 15 What has been the effect of all the sermons, dissertations, essays, and paragraphs that have been written against vestimentary errors and offences? **1863** *Sat. Rev.* XV. 174/2 Such vestimentary sufferings as he has been exposed to in the changing course of fashion. **1890** *Spectator* 10 Mar., An American dentist's wife was not quite the person to inaugurate a vestimentary revolution.

vestin, obs. Sc. form of WESTEN *a.*

'vesting, *sb.* [f. VEST *sb.* 3b.] Cloth or material for making vests or waistcoats. Usually in pl.

1813 *Weekly Reg.* IV. 295/1 For the best and handsomest fancy vesting, of cotton..a premium..of..forty dollars. **1828** WEBSTER, *Vesting*, cloth for vests; vest patterns. *United States.* **1851** *Catal. Gt. Exhib.* III. 495/1 Chinese prints for vestings. *Ibid.*, Angora velvet plushes for vestings. **1889** *Textile News* 20 Sept., Advt., Damasks, Vestings, Piques, Twills. **1892** *Daily News* 5 Dec. 2/4 The Berlin vesting is still much liked, as it is produced in such pleasing combinations of colour.

'vesting, *vbl. sb.* [f. VEST *v.* + -ING[1].]

1. The action or fact of investing, confirming, or establishing, esp. by legal process.

1596 BACON *Max. Com. Law* ix. (1630) 42 But that holdeth place onely upon the first vesting of the vse. **1611** COTGR., *Vesture*,..a vesting, inuesting, or putting into possession of. **1678** CUDWORTH *Intell. Syst.* 798 This Christian Resurrection of Life, is the Vesting and Setling of the Souls of Good men, in their..Immortal Bodies. **1729** JACOB *Law Dict.* s.v. *Remainder*, The Vesting of the Estate in the Crown, during the Life of the Father. **1826** G. BELL *Comm. Laws Scot.* (ed. 5) II. 609 Of some Points in the Vesting of Estates in Trust, Judicial or Voluntary. **1827** JARMAN *Devises* II. 217 The Court held..that the adverbs of time, *when*, &c. do not make any thing necessary to precede the settling (*i.e.* the vesting) of the remainder. **1880** MUIRHEAD *Ulpian* xxiv. §23 It is requisite that, when the time of vesting arrives, the legatee shall be no longer in the heir's *potestas.*

attrib. **1700** LUTTRELL *Brief Rel.* (1857) IV. 631 Yesterday the lords..went thro most part of the land tax and Irish forfeiture bill; postponed the first clause, called the vesting clause. **1922** *Act 12 & 13 Geo. V* §188. 238 In relation to settled land, 'vesting deed' or 'vesting order' means the instrument whereby the land is conveyed or vested; 'vesting assent' means the instrument whereby a personal representative, after the death of a tenant for life..vests the land in the successor in title..; 'vesting instrument' means a vesting deed, assent or order. **1948** *Secretary* July 180 (*heading*) Vesting day, 1st April, 1948. **1950** *Engineering* 24 Mar. 318/3 It is difficult to forecast whether or not the iron and steel industry will..pass into State ownership on the vesting date, January 1, 1951. **1964** *Financial Times* 23 Mar. (Defence Suppl.) 14/5 With 'vesting day' only a few days off, staffs are still settling down. **1967** *Economist* 1 Apr. 21/2 For compulsory purchase, the commission may use a procedure called the 'vesting declaration' which virtually cuts out conveyancing, while granting a firm title. **1977** *Belfast Tel.* 19 Jan. 7/2 A vesting order for the land was signed on February 12 last. **1982** *Equity & Law Life Ann. Rep. 1981* 16 Vesting bonus of 30% of the total pension will be allotted to personal pension deferred annuities.

2. The action or process of putting on, or investing with, vestments. Also *attrib.*

1648 W. L. *Newes fr. Turkie* 9 To hinder his Lordships Vesting. *c* **1660** JER. TAYLOR *Serm.* Wks. 1831 IV. 144 That observation of St. Jerome made concerning the vesting of the priests in the Levitical ministrations. **1879** SIMMONS *Lay-Folks Mass-bk.* 164 The subsequent directions prove that this vesting was not at the altar. **1905** *Times* 27 Sept. 4/2 Liturgical vestments are worn..and the vesting prayers used in the Church of Rome.

Vestinian (vɛ'stɪnɪən), *sb.* and *a.* [f. L. *Vestīni* + -AN.] **A.** *sb.* **a.** A member of an ancient Oscan people who lived in the Gran Sasso d'Italia area of Italy. **b.** The language of this people. **B.** *adj.* Of or pertaining to this people or their language.

1578, etc. [see MARRUCINIAN *sb.* and *a.*]. **1933**, **1939** [see MARSIAN *sb.* and *a.*]. **1966** M. S. BEELER in Birnbaum & Puhvel *Anc. Indo-European Dial.* 53 So far as I know no voice has..ever been raised to question the propriety of regarding these languages (and the minor dialects of the Paelignians, Marrucinians, Vestinians, and Volscians) as differentiated forms of a single common ancestor..here termed Oscan-Umbrian.

†**'vestite,** *v. Obs. rare.* [f. L. *vestīt-*, ppl. stem of *vestīre* to VEST.] *trans.* To cover or clothe as with a garment.

1597 A. M. *Guillemeau's Fr. Chirurg.* 42b/1 [To] vestite the edges of the vlcerationes with plasters. **1657** TOMLINSON *Renou's Disp.* 372 Citrons..vestited with a thin cortex.

vestiture ('vɛstɪtjʊə(r)). [ad. med.L. *vestitura*, f. L. *vestīre* to VEST. Cf. INVESTITURE.]

1. Investiture of a person in an office or *with* power, etc.; = INVESTITURE 2 and 3. *rare.*

1387 TREVISA *Higden* (Rolls) VII. 419 He resigned to God and to seint Peter þe vestiture of prelates þat was i-doo by seculer hondes. **1861** J. A. ALEXANDER *Gosp. Jesus Christ* xxxix. 521 A proof of man's original formation in God's image, and his original vestiture with delegated power as God's vicegerent.

2. *concr.* That which clothes or covers: †**a.** = VESTURE *sb.* 2. *Obs. rare.*

In quots. translating L. *vestitura* in documents of the second half of the 13th c.

c **1460** *Oseney Reg.* (1913) 152 Þe saide Abbot and oþer lordes aforenamed..haue i-suffrid þat þe saide John the vestiture (or grasse) of þe same telthe þe which abode..in þis 3ere alone may gadur & haue. *Ibid.* 156 Þe vestiture of þe saide In-hoke.

b. Clothes, clothing, vesture. Also *transf.* and *fig.*

The first quotation is the source of the inexact definition given by Worcester (1846) and some later Dictionaries.

1842 R. PARK *Pantology* (1847) 472 Under the head of Vestiture, we include all those arts which relate immediately to the manufacture of cloth, and preparation of clothing. **1853** KANE *Grinnell Exp.* xl. (1856) 366, I claim to be the first who has reduced all vestiture to a primitive form. **1856** — *Arct. Expl.* II. i. 23 A pair of bear-skin breeches,..the characteristic and national vestiture of this strange people. **1877** *Tinsley's Mag.* XX. 512/1 It is night in the streets of a fair Italian city, and the lonely queen of light is..arraying in snowy vestiture the tall shafts and broad walls of marble that rise here and there. **1879** J. HAWTHORNE *Sebast. Strome* II. xi. 175 Mary..felt herself pointedly unequal to introducing her ungainly news under a graceful vestiture of words.

Hence †**'vestitured** *a. Obs.*[−0]

1623 COCKERAM I, *Vestitured* [printed *-uted*], apparelled.

'vestless, *a.* [f. VEST *sb.*] Having no vest; lacking a vest.

1888 *Daily News* 28 Sept. 5/3 The plucky clergyman pursued the vestless burglar. **1891** *Ibid.* 29 April 7/1 Bodices are often vestless now.

'vestlet. *Zool.* [f. VEST *v.*] A sea-anemone of the genus *Cerianthus*, which is invested with a tube-like stem.

1860 GOSSE *Actinologia Brit.* 268 The Vestlet, *Cerianthus Lloydii. Ibid.* 272 The Vestlet feeds freely in captivity.

vestment[1] ('vɛstmənt). Forms: α. 4 **uestement**, 4-6 **westement(e**, 4-6 **vestement** (6 **festement**). β. 5-6 **westment**, 5 **vestmente**, 5- **vestment** (7 **vest'ment**). [a. AF. and OF. *vestement* (mod.F. *vêtement*), ad. L. *vestīmentum*: see VESTIMENT.]

1. A garment or article of clothing, esp. one of the nature of a robe or gown; freq. an outer garment of this kind worn by a king or official either ordinarily or upon some ceremonial occasion. Also *collect.*, clothing, dress, vesture.

Now somewhat *rare* or *rhet.*

a **1300** *Cursor M.* 3701 Þe odor o þi uestement It smelles als o piement. *c* **1386** CHAUCER *Sqr.'s T.* 51 This Kambynskan..In riall vestement syt on hys deys. **1474** CAXTON *Chesse* IV. v. (1883) 176 He is bounden to deffende and kepe them that make his vestementis & couertours necessarye vnto his body. **1489** — *Faytes of A.* IV. xvii. 280 The scripture saith that the vestement of Ih[es]u Crist dide seme to his apostles white as snowe. *a* **1578** LINDESAY (Pitscottie) *Chron. Scot.* (S.T.S.) I. 374 The herauldis with thair awfull westmentis. **1590** SHAKS. *Com. Err.* II. i. 94 Doe their gay vestments his affections baite? **1662** J. DAVIES tr. *Olearius' Voy. Ambass.* 288 The five principal Persons of the Retinue had each of them a satin Vestment, and another of Taffata. **1718** PRIOR *Solomon* I. 99 A fairer Red stands blushing in the Rose, Than that which on the Bridegroom's Vestment flows. **1764** HARMER *Observ.* vi. §23. 280 Presents of vestments..are frequently made in these countries to the great and those that are in public stations. **1771** H. WALPOLE *Vertue's Anecd. Paint.* IV. 2 The slightness of their vestment and the lankness of their hair. **1790** COWPER *Odyss.* VI. 313 Her charge Of folded vestments neat the Princess placed Within the royal wain. **1826** LAMB *Elia* II. *Wedding*, She stood at the altar in vestments white and candid as her thoughts. **1856** KANE *Arct. Expl.* I. xxix. 381 Their clothes saturated with the freezing water of the floes, these iron men ..did not strip themselves naked..and hang up their vestments in the air to dry. **1899** *Allbutt's Syst. Med.* VIII. 497 Remembering to warn [the patient] against heated rooms,..stewing in bed, and any possible irritation by vestments.

2. A garment worn by a priest or ecclesiastic on the occasion of some service or ceremony; a priestly robe. †In early use also *collect.*, a set of these.

13.. *K. Alis.* 1560 (Laud MS.), Þe Bisshop..dude hym on a vestement, And made..To jubiter sacrifise. *c* **1425** WYNTOUN *Cron.* v. 1898 Hee [a priest of Jupiter] tuggit wiþe his teythe in taggis His westment rewyn al in raggis. *c* **1485** *Digby Myst.* (1882) III. 1183 To my awter I wyll me dresse; On xall my westment and myn aray. **1560** BIBLE (Genev.) *2 Kings* x. 22 Bring forthe vestements for all the seruants of Baal. And he broght them out vestements. **1598** J. HOWSON *Serm. 21 May* 35 Thimelicus, a dauncer, had bought by chaunce some holy vestement, and abused it publickly in the open theater. **1651** HOBBES *Leviath.* III. xxxvi. 228 The High Priests..put on the holy vestments, and enquired of the Lord [etc.]. **1737** WHISTON tr. *Josephus, Antiq.* III. vii. §2 Over this he [the priest] wore a linen vestment, made of fine flax doubled. *Ibid.*, This vestment reaches down to the feet, and sits close to the body. **1796** MORSE *Amer. Geog.* II. 659 The surplice, a vestment of the Pagan Priests, introduced into churches. **1843** PRESCOTT *Mexico* VI. v. (1864) 371 A few priests, clad in their usual wild and blood-stained vestments, were to be seen. **1868** MARRIOTT *Vest. Chr.* Introd. p. v, The attempt..to trace out in detail a correspondence between the 'eight vestments' of the Jewish high-priest, and those of Christian ministry.

b. An article of attire worn by the clergy of various branches of the Christian church, or by certain of their assistants, during divine service or on some special occasion; *spec.* one or other of those worn by the priest or priests at the celebration of the Eucharist; esp. the chasuble.

In early use perh. sometimes (like med.L. *vestimentum*) employed in the collective sense of 'a set of vestments'.

α. **1303** R. BRUNNE *Handl. Synne* 4675 3yf prest or clerk lene vestement þat halwed ys þurgh sacrament. **1340** *Ayenb.* 41 Þe crouchen, þe calices, þe creyme, þe corporeaus, þe yblissede uestemens. *c* **1400** *Plowman's Tale* xxix. in *Pol. Poems* (Rolls) I. 311 They halow no thing but for hire, Church, ne font, ne vestement. *c* **1450** *Mirk's Festial* 140 Thys was þe fyrst man þat euer song masse yn vestementys, as prestes now doþe. **1493-4** *Rec. St. Mary at Hill* (1905) 199 Payd to mastyr parson for halowyng of the westementes, xij d. **1549** *Bk. Com. Prayer, Holy Commun.*, The Priest.. shall put upon hym..a white Albe plain, with a vestement or Cope. **1566** in Peacock *Eng. Ch. Furniture* (1866) 35 Item iij vestements—sold to Christopher Baudwine in anno 1565 who hathe put them to prophane vse.

β. *c* **1440** *Promp. Parv.* 509/1 Vestment.., *vestimentum*. *c* **1460** FORTESCUE *Abs. & Lim. Mon.* vii. (1885) 125 Often tymes he [the king] woll bie riche hangynges and other apparell for his howses; vessaill, vestmentes, and oþer ornamentes for his chapell. **1509** *Will* in *Archaeologia* LXVI. 312 A payre of Vestmentes of Whit clothe of gold of Tissue. **1531** *Test. Ebor.* (Surtees) VI. 23, Item, I will that a vestment be maide..of my damaske gowne. **1580** PARSONS in *Relig. Pamphlets* (1898) 166 For this Sacrifice was Preistes apparell made: Vestments, Sensors, Frankensence, and the lyke. **1600** FAIRFAX *Tasso* XI. xiv, In costly vestments sacred William dight, With fear and trembling to the altar went. **1687** A. LOVELL tr. *Thevenot's Trav.* I. 82, I shall not here spend time in describing their way of celebrating Mass,.. nor shall I speak of their Sacerdotal Vestments. **1782** in J. H. Harting *Hist. Sardin. Chapel* (1905) 25 Priest's vestment, two dalmatics to correspond, with maniples and stoles [etc.]. **1797** MRS. RADCLIFFE *Italian* xvi, Your years, old man, and those sacred vestments protect you. **1816** SCOTT *Antiq.* xxv, Another churchman in his vestments bore a holy-water sprinkler. **1867** TROLLOPE *Chron. Barset* II. xlix. 59 He had kept his surplice in his own room, and had gone down in his vestment. **1881** A. O'SHAUGHNESSY *Christ will Return, Songs of Worker* 10 And where, 'mid all the glory Of vestments rich, are Joseph's working coat And Mary's rags?

3. *transf.* and *fig.* Something which covers as a garment; a covering.

1483 CAXTON *Gold. Leg.* 118/2 Ryght so the majeste of god hydde the lyght of hys dyuynyte by a carnal vestement whyche he toke of our nature humayne. **1620** QUARLES

Jonah 1300 Their nakednesse with sackcloth let them hide, And mue the vest'ments of their silken pride. **1660** SHARROCK *Vegetables* 40 The verdure..that is generally the beauteous vestment of all vegetables. **1669** W. SIMPSON *Hydrol. Chym.* 146 This hidden spirit..putting on new shapes according to the mineral vestment wherewith he is cloathed. **1753** HOGARTH *Anal. Beauty* xi. 84 Green,..which colour nature hath chosen for the vestment of the earth. **1836** EMERSON *Nature, Lang.* Wks. (Bohn) II. 152 A material image..arises in his mind, contemporaneous with every thought, which furnishes the vestment of the thought. **1842** W. A. BUTLER *Serm.* Ser. I. x. (1849) 172 His perpetuated humanity is, then, in heaven,..the vestment of the divine priesthood.

4. *Comb.* in **vestment-maker**.

Freq. in 15th and early 16th c. accounts.

1405 *Close Roll, 6 Hen. IV*, b, Johannes Est, vestment makere. **1477-9** *Rec. St. Mary at Hill* (1905) 80 Item, paid to a vestment-maker for the mendyng of the Blak Copes. **1530** PALSGR. 284/2 Vestmentmaker, *chasublier*. **1537-8** *Rec. St. Mary at Hill* (1905) 378 Paid to a vestment maker for xxvij dayes labour.

'vestment². *rare*⁻¹. [f. VEST *v.* Cf. INVESTMENT.] A right or privilege with which a person or body is invested or endowed.

1795 J. PHILLIPS *Hist. Inland Navig.* Add. 149 It is enacted, that they be one body politic and corporate, by the name of 'The Company of Proprietors of the Mersey and Irwell Navigation', with all customary powers, vestments, &c.

'vestmental, *a. rare.* [f. VESTMENT¹ + -AL¹. Cf. VESTIMENTAL *a.*] Vestimentary.

1849 ROCK *Ch. of Fathers* II. vi. 249 Amongst the few episcopal ornaments still to be found in England..is one of the 'caligae', or vestmental stockings of Bishop Waneflete's. **1978** *New York* 3 Apr. 92/1 Hermitage prospers now on the commerce of those who pursue chic and never catch it... They occupy every table, tailored flannels and sharkskins seated beside superb little Bendel numbers—vestmental perfections without a stitch of art.

'vestmented, *a.* [f. as prec.] **a.** Of persons: Dressed or robed in vestments. **b.** Of a service: Celebrated or conducted in vestments.

1859 SALA *Tw. round Clock* (1861) 338 The black-vestmented groom of the chambers. **1867** *1st Rep. Commissioners Publ. Worship* 52/1 From your changing the service from the high choral to the vestmented service. **1871** MISS MULOCK *Fair France* 142 There came filing in a line of priests richly vestmented.

vestni, southern ME. var. FASTEN *v.*

vestock ('vɛstɒk). [Blend of VEST *sb.* and STOCK *sb.*¹] A clerical stock that extends to the waist.

1975 *Rep. Patent Cases* 473 The..vestock..can be described as a sort of black bib, with a hard upstanding collar round at the front. **1981** *Oxf. Diocesan Mag.* May 24 (Advt.), Fine bespoke tailors and hosiers. Now stock clerical shirts, collars, stocks, vestocks, etc.

vestorie, obs. f. VESTRY¹.

vestour, var. VOUSTER, boaster. *Sc.*

vestoure, obs. form of VESTURE.

vestoy, var. VESTEYE *v. Obs.*

vestral, vestrical, vestrification, etc.: see after VESTRY¹.

vestry¹ ('vɛstrɪ). Forms: 4, 6 **westre**, 6 **vestre**; 5 **vestri**, 5-6 **vestrye**, 6-7 **vestrie** (6 **vestorie**, 7 **vesterie**), 5- **vestry**. [Prob. a. AF. **vest(e)rie*, f. VEST *v.* + -(E)RY, substituted for OF. *vestiarie*, *vestiaire*: see VESTIARY. Cf. REVESTRY.]

1. a. A room or part of a church, usually situated in close proximity to the chancel or choir, in which the vestments, vessels, records, etc., are kept, and in which the clergy and choir robe for divine service; a room used for similar purposes in connexion with any church, chapel, or place of worship.

The vestry of parish churches is also used as a place of meeting for the transaction of certain parochial business (see 2).

1388 in *Archaeologia* LII. 213 The awter wᵗ in the sayd westre. **14..** in Wr.-Wülcker 619 *Vestibulum*, a vestrye. *c* **1440** *Promp. Parv.* 509/2 Vestrye, *vestiarium*. **1496-7** *Rec. St. Mary at Hill* (1905) 225 For colys to brenne in the vestrye. **1506-7** *Ibid.* 261 Payd for makyng of ij keyes for the tresory chest in the vestry, vi d. **1540-1** in *Archaeologia* XIX. 272 On the South Syde of the same Churche ys the Vestrye well covered with lead. **1593** *Rites of Durham* (Surtees, 1903) 8 When the monkes went to say or singe the high masse they put on theire vestments..in the Vestrye. **1617** MORYSON *Itin.* I. 110 In the Vesterie lie the bodies of nine kings in coffins of wood. **1682** N. O. *Boileau's Lutrin* III. 25 With equal pace the Temples Nave they measure! Into the Vestry came: Here lies the Treasure! **1698** T. FROGER *Voy.* 111 The Jesuits are very potent there... Their Vestry is one of the most magnificent that ever was seen. **1756-7** *Keysler's Trav.* (1760) III. 73 Formerly, in the Tribuna hung a large picture of St. Joseph;..but this is removed into the vestry. **1796** MME. D'ARBLAY *Camilla* I. 303 They sauntered about the church while the Doctor retired to the vestry to take off his gown. **1798** SOUTHEY *Surgeon's Warning* xxiii, Three men in the vestry watch To save him if they can. **1837** DICKENS *Pickw.* xxviii, The ceremony was performed..in the parish church,..and Mr. Pickwick's name is attached to the register, still preserved in the vestry thereof. **1864** A. MCKAY *Hist. Kilmarnock* 225 The church consists of a nave with an organ-gallery, a chancel, and a vestry. **1873** HALE *In His Name* viii. 73 Candles which furnished the light to the dim vestry.

fig. **1648** MILTON *Observ. Art. Peace* Wks. 1851 IV. 572 So that this rough Garment to deceive, we bring ye once again, Grave Sirs, into your own Vestry. **1847** EMERSON *Repr. Men, Swedenborg* Wks. (Bohn) I. 324 The worshipper, escaping from the vestry of verbs and texts, is surprised to find himself a party to the whole of his religion.

b. A similar room or part in a temple or other non-Christian place of worship.

1535 COVERDALE *2 Kings* x. 22 Then sayde he vnto him that had the rule of the vestrye: Brynge forth rayment for all Baals mynisters. **1584** B. R. tr. *Herodotus* I. 57 In this sacred house or vestry no image is erected. **1609** BIBLE (Douay) *Ezek.* xliv. 19 They shal put of from them their vestiments ..and shal lay them up in the vesterie of the sanctuarie. **1641** MILTON *Reform.* I. Wks. 1851 III. 2 In Palls and Miters, gold and guegaw's fetcht from Arons old wardrope, or the Flamins vestry.

c. A place or room where clothes (†or valuables) are kept; a robing room, cloak-room; †a treasure house or chamber. Now *rare*.

1574 HELLOWES *Gueuara's Fam. Ep.* (1577) 263 Also they make report of your Ladyship here, that you entred the vestorie or treasure house of Toledo, to fetche the plate that was there. **1600** HOLLAND *Livy* XXIX. xxi. 725 For all the holy money which they found..they bestowed againe in the privie vestries where the treasure was kept. **1613** T. GODWIN *Rom. Antiq.* (1625) 109 By the Scene in this place, I vnderstand the partition betweene the players vestry, and the stage or scaffold. **1684** BUNYAN *Pilgr.* II. (1900) 192 Then said the Interpreter again to the Damsel that waited upon these Women, Go into the Vestry and fetch out Garments for these People. **1891** G. GISSING *New Grub Street* I. 198 Where are your out-of-door things? I think there is a ladies' vestry somewhere isn't there?

2. a. In English parishes: An assembly or meeting of the parishioners or a certain number of these, held originally in the vestry of the parish church, for the purpose of deliberating or legislating upon the affairs of the parish or upon certain temporal matters connected with the church (see next).

Also without article (*b*).

(*a*) **1589** R. HARVEY *Pl. Perc.* (1590) 24 This worke being finished and red ouer and ouer by the head of the parish, they called a Vestry, wherin they concluded [etc.]. **1596** in W. H. Hale *Prec. Causes Office* (1841) 87 That they cause a vestrye to be warned on Sondaye next..to mete at the evening the same daye. **1640** *Minutes Archdeaconry of Essex* (MS.) fol. 195 William Petchie..notatur for keeping a private vestry in Rookitt's hall on Easter Munday in tyme of divine service. **1642** SIR E. DERING *Sp. on Relig.* 90 The Parish Minister to hold weekly Vestries. *a* **1700** EVELYN *Diary* 6 Nov. 1692, There was a Vestry call'd about repairing or new building of the Church. **1762** FOOTE *Orator* I. Wks. 1799 I. 194, I did speechify once at a vestry. **1885** *Encycl. Brit.* XVIII. 296/2 Common vestries are meetings of all the ratepayers, assembled on a three days' notice.

(*b*) **1764** in W. Wing *Ann. Steeple Aston* (1875) 63 It was agreed at vestry to sow Sandhill *turnoops* this next year. **1845** STEPHEN *Comm. Laws Eng.* (1874) I. 120 The affairs of a parish..are regulated in vestry, which is, properly speaking, an assembly of the minister, churchwardens and parishioners. **1857** HUGHES *Tom Brown* I. iii, He himself had ..gone birds'-nesting with the farmers whom he met at vestry.

b. The body of parishioners meeting in this way and constituting a parochial board or council of management; ***select vestry*** (*Obs.* exc. *Hist.*) (see quots. 1845, 1906).

This body had formerly the administration and management of the whole of the business affairs of the parish; but its authority was later restricted to certain temporal matters connected with the parish church, its former powers being invested in the Parish or District Council. In England the sole remaining power of the vestry is the election of churchwardens, its other ecclesiastical powers having been transferred to the parochial church council and the annual parochial church meeting.

a **1672** M. WREN in Gutch *Coll. Cur.* I. 229 It was very difficult to find a man, who..followed the persuasion of Calvin, who had not also strong propensions to the Eldership and Vestry. **1698** *MSS. House of Lords* (1905) III. 261 Dec. 9. Poor Relief (Select Vestries) Bill.—Draft of an Act for preventing the Poor's being cheated. *a* **1700** EVELYN *Diary* 6 Apr. 1662, Being of the Vestry,..we order'd that the Communion Table should be set as usual altar-wise. **1708** SWIFT *Reply to Bickerstaff detected* S.'s Wks. 1755 II. I. 167 If I had not used my utmost interest with the vestry. **1766** ENTICK *London* IV. 45 The vestry is select, pursuant to the will of William Tudman, who, hoping thereby to prevent the inconveniences which usually arise from a general vestry [etc.]. **1792** YOUNG *Trav. France* 549 The first attempt towards a democracy in England would be the common people demanding an admission and voice in the vestries. **1820** SOUTHEY *Wesley* II. 402 As the vestry would not be persuaded to erect a gallery, he built one at his own expense. **1845** *Encycl. Metrop.* XXIII. 486/2 In other Parishes,..the rate-payers place the powers intrusted to them in the hands of a small Body, chosen by them from their own number, called sometimes the Select Vestry, and sometimes the Guardians of the Poor. **1882** BESANT *Revolt of Man* iv. (1883) 78 The Lower House..had degenerated into something noisier than a vestry. **1882** *Encycl. Brit.* XIV. 820/1 The vestries and district boards are entrusted with the management of local sewers, the lighting, paving, and cleaning of their own thoroughfares, and the removal of nuisances. **1906** S. & B. WEBB *Parish & County* I. v. 173 The Close or..Select Vestry...consisted of a body of one or two dozen persons, or occasionally more, serving for life and filling vacancies among themselves by co-option. **1921** *Parochial Church Councils (Powers) Measure* 4 From the commencement of this Measure there shall be transferred to the Council of every parish—(i) All powers, duties and liabilities of the Vestry of such parish relating to the affairs of the Church, except as regard the election of churchwardens and sidesmen and as regards the administration of ecclesiastical charities. **1959** JOWITT *Dict. Eng. Law* II. 1610/1 The Select Vestries Bill is the title of a Bill always formally read a first time in the House of Lords at the beginning of a new session before the House proceeds to debate the king's or queen's speech, as an assertion of its independence.

c. Any similar body elected by members of the congregation of a church and invested with the conduct of its business affairs; a meeting of such body.

1891 *Cent. Dict.*

†**3.** Clothing or vesture. Also *fig. Obs. rare.*

1606 J. WELSH in *Sel. Biog.* (Wodrow Soc.) I. 22 She shall be arrayed with the golden vestry, and needlework of his manifold graces. **1616** B. JONSON *Masques, Love freed fr. Ignorance*, One o' the Black-guard had his hand in my vestrie.

4. *attrib.* and *Comb.* **a.** In sense 1, as ***vestry door, fire, -keeper, window***, etc.

1477-9 *Rec. St. Mary at Hill* (1905) 81 A key to the vestry dore beneth. **1510** in Willis & Clark *Cambridge* (1886) II. 200 The largienge of the vestrie dore. **1611** COTGR., *Sacristain*, a Sexton, or Vestrie-keeper, in a Church. **1670** G. H. *Hist. Cardinals* I. III. 75 They are oblig'd..to give to the Popes Vestry-keeper..five and twenty Ducats. **1706** PHILLIPS (ed. Kersey), *Vestry-Keeper*, a Sexton, whose Business is to look after the Vestry. **1772** tr. *Life Lady Guion* II. 5, I had taken the office of Sacristan (or Vestry Nun) and the care of waking the Sisters at the hour they were to rise. **1844** DICKENS *Mart. Chuz.* xxxi, I have left the vestry window unfastened. **1855** —— *Dorrit* xiv, Having stirred the Vestry fire, he looked round the shelves of registers.

b. In sense 2, as ***vestry assessment, -brother, -business, -consult*** (= consultation), ***meeting***, etc.

1631 T. POWELL *Tom All Trades* (1876) 139 Like a Reuerend Vestry wit. **1682** N. O. *Boileau's Lutrin* I. 224 Him time preferr'd..From poor Church-warden to a Vestry-brother. *a* **1683** OLDHAM *Satyrs* Wks. (1686) 194 At Vestry-Consults when he does appear For choosing of some Parish Officer. **1731** *Gentl. Mag.* I. 159 In the Parish where I serve, the Vestry is compos'd of thirty select Members, besides the Rector, and two Vestry Justices of the Peace. *a* **1734** NORTH *Exam.* II. v. §94 (1740) 374 No more of Plot than a Vestry Meeting to settle their Rates. **1808** *Edin. Rev.* XII. 509 An imperial sovereign summoned to settle a petty vestry-squabble! **1833** *Act 3 & 4 Will. IV*, c. 37 §63 Such Expences..as have been heretofore defrayed by Vestry Assessment in Ireland. **1888** W. MORRIS in Mackail *Life* (1899) II. 206, I don't see why they should not keep out of the vestry-business.

c. Special Combs.: **vestry-book**, (*a*) a book in which the proceedings of a parochial vestry are recorded; (*b*) a book kept in a vestry in which the births, marriages, and deaths of the parishioners are registered; **vestry cess**, in Ireland, a church rate or tax levied by a vestry; **vestry-clerk**, the clerk of a parochial vestry; **vestry-tax**, = *vestry-cess*.

1773-4 *Ir. Acts 13 & 14 Geo. III*, c. 10 §4 The said election or nomination shall be entered in the *vestry book of every parish, union, or chapelry. **1789** SIR W. SCOTT in J. Haggard *Rep. Consist. Crt. London* (1822) I. 13 As..no poll appears for Anthony, and the vestry book, which must be taken to be the authentic book, makes no mention of him, I cannot look on him as elected. **1856** LEVER *Martins of Cro' M.* lxv, I was sent for to the Castle to give a private baptism ..., and requesting that I would bring the vestry-book along with me for the registration. **1912** A. GORDON in *Jrnl. Friends' Hist. Soc.* IX. 202 A modern forgery, entered in the church-wardens' vestry-book at Cheltenham. **1864** *Act 27 & 28 Vict.* c. 17 §1 It is expedient to abolish *Vestry Cess in Ireland. **1706** PHILLIPS (ed. Kersey), **Vestry-Clerk*, a Scrivener that keeps the Parish Accounts. **1763** BURN *Eccl. Law* II. 478 The vestry clerk is chosen by the vestry. **1836** DICKENS *Sk. Boz, Our Parish* ii, The vestry-clerk..is an attorney, and generally in a bustle. **1807-8** SYD. SMITH *Plymley's Lett.* Wks. 1859 II. 170/1, I request to know if the *vestry taxes in Ireland are a mere matter of romantic feeling?

Hence in various terms, chiefly in nonce-use, with reference to sense 2: **'vestral** *a.*, of or pertaining to a vestry or vestries. **ˌvestraliˈzation**, administration by means of vestries. **'vestrical** *a.*, = *vestral*. **ˌvestrifiˈcation**, the action of vestrifying. **'vestrified** (*ppl.*) *a.*, governed by a vestry. **'vestrify** *v. trans.*, to transform into, cause to resemble, a vestry in character or function. **'vestrydom**, the system of local government by a vestry or vestries; parochial vestries collectively; hence, the parochial narrowmindedness or selfish spirit regarded as characteristic of vestries. **'vestryhood**, = prec. **'vestryish** *a.*, affected with or characterized by the spirit of vestrydom. **'vestryism**, vestrydom. **'vestryize** *v. trans.*, = *vestrify*.

1884 *Contemp. Rev.* June 802 The fire-brigade as administered by the *vestral authorities. *Ibid.* 805 The disadvantages of disunity under the vestral administration. **1886** *Times* 13 Mar. 5/1 The wastefulness of *vestralization. **1881** *Daily News* 31 Jan. 5 The magistrate..discovered on Saturday an instance of *vestrical sapience which [etc.]. **1884** *Ibid.* 31 Dec. 5/4 The *vestrification of Parliament. **1865** *Sat. Rev.* 4 Feb. 144/1 We can hardly expect an ordinary *vestrified general-reading Englishman to understand..the intensity of passion [etc.]. **1884** CHAPLIN in *Daily News* 5 Dec. 3/1 If he might coin a phrase, its general effect would be to *vestrify the House of Commons. **1860** *Temple Bar Mag.* I. 80 It was the defeat of beadledom and *vestrydom. **1884** *Christian World* 22 May 409/1 The opposition raised by a stolid vestrydom to a more rational system of local self-government. **1871** *Contemp. Rev.* XVI. 374 *Vestryhood had for generations flourished as a calling. **1882** *Society* 16 Dec. 10/2 The public instinct recognises something petty and *vestryish about the Board. **1861** *Illustr. Lond. News* 23 Feb. 168/1 The House displayed a greater tendency to what may be called '*vestryism' than ever. **1870** W. R. GREG *Polit. Problems* 226 To deal systematically and thoroughly with the giant evil of pauperism,.. would bring those who undertook it face to face with the vast opposing army of vestryism. **1869** *Contemp. Rev.* XI. 235 How many disappointed competitors for that honour.. will submit to be *vestryized.

vestry². *Mining.* [Of uncertain origin.] The refuse or rubbish of a mine.

1784 (MS.), Rubbish and vestry from a lead mine. **1830** *Eng. & For. Mining Gloss.* (Newcastle), *Vestry*, refuse.

'vestryman. Also vestry-man, vestry man. [f. VESTRY¹ 2.] A member of a parochial vestry. Also *fig.*

1614 in W. H. Hale *Prec. Causes Office* (1841) 39 So many of the vestrie men as shall.. meet there for the makeing of a rate. **1641** 'SMECTYMNUUS' *Vind. Answ.* Pref. a iij b, Indeede hee saith, that these were but as our Church-wardens, or Vestry men. **1651** CLEVELAND *Poems* 26 These Linsie-Woolsie Vestry-men. **1701** *Maryland Laws* (1723) 15 Two New Vestrymen shall be annually chosen in the Places of Two others. *a* **1721** PRIOR *True Statesmen* 35 If thou ever has't a voice Tho it be only in the Choice Of Vestry Men or grey-Coat-Boys. **1847** C. G. ADDISON *Law of Contracts* xv. §3. 391 Vestrymen, in vestry assembled, may, like any other persons, exceed their duties as vestrymen. **1873** B. HARTE *Fiddletown* 37 She was roused by a formal visit from a vestryman. **1910** *Blackw. Mag.* Apr. 585/1 Mr. Shaw is the vestry-man of dramatists. His work savours horribly of St. Pancras.

Hence **'vestrymanly** *a.*, befitting a vestryman; **'vestrymanship**, the position of a vestryman.

1885 *Pall Mall G.* 12 Jan. 4/1 That may be *vestrymanly, but it is hardly gentlemanly. **1879** ESCOTT *England* I. 123 The mere fact of a parochial office being the coveted prize of a political competition raises its duties above the level of *vestrymanship.

vestry-room. Also vestry room. [f. VESTRY¹.] The vestry of a church; the room in which a parochial vestry assembles.

1710 *Lond. Gaz.* No. 4721/4 The Vestry-Room of the Parish Church of Lambeth was broke open. **1745** VINER *Abridgm. Law & Equity* XXI. 549 His proper Remedy for the Injury done by the Defendant, by hindring him to come into the Vestry-room. **1810** W. WILSON *Hist. Dissent. Ch.* III. 224 He opened a day-school, in the vestry-room of his meeting. **1842** *Penny Cycl.* XXII. 227/1 It comprehends a nave,.. and a chantry, now used as a vestry-room. **1891** 'S. MOSTYN' *Curatica* 136, I thought I should have seen you in the vestry-room.

attrib. **1838** DICKENS *O. Twist* v, The clerk, who was sitting by the vestry-room fire.

vestschipe: see FASTSHIP *Obs.*

'vestuary. Now *arch.* [ad. OF. *vestuaire* (= Pr. and Cat. *vestuari*, Sp. and Pg. *vestuario*), or med.L. *vestuarium*, f. *vestura* VESTURE *sb.* Cf. VESTIARY *sb.*] A vestiary or vestry; a wardrobe. Also *transf.*

c **1490** CAXTON *Rule St. Benet* 136 Whan in þe chirche he shall doo of his seculer arraye and be cladde with the habite of the place; those [clothes] that he puttyth off shall be kept in the vestuary. **1610** HOLLAND *Camden's Brit.* 449 Some.. small bones wrapped up in fine silke of fresh colour, which the Abbot tooke for the reliques of some Saints, and laied uppe in his Vestuary. **1860** TRENCH *Serm. Westm. Abb.* xxxii. 368 The trappings of men's outward existence.. must be laid aside in the vestuary of the grave.

†'vesturage. *Obs.*⁻¹ [f. VESTURE *sb.* + -AGE.] An allowance for vesture or clothing.

1679 E. CHAMBERLAYNE *Pres. St. Eng.* II. (ed. 12) 262 Note that out of the Sergeants afore-mentioned, the King by Writ, usually calls some to be of his Council at Law, allowing each one Wadage, Feodage, Vesturage, and Regardage.

vestural ('vɛstjʊərəl), *a.* [f. as prec. + -AL¹.] Of or pertaining to vesture or clothing; vestiary.

1831 CARLYLE *Sart. Res.* I. i, How, then, comes it.. that the grand Tissue of all Tissues.. should have been quite overlooked by Science,—the vestural Tissue, namely, of woollen or other cloth? **1883** *Times* 13 Nov. 9/3 Vestural adornments less suited to military purposes than to a masquerade. **1891** MISS DOWIE *Girl in Karp.* ii. 17 His vestural advantages.. are what I grudge a man sole possession of.

vesture ('vɛstjʊə(r)), *sb.* Also 5 vestoure, wester (9 *dial.* vester), 6–7 vestur. [a. AF. and OF. *vesture* (mod.F. *vêture*), f. *vestir* VEST *v.* Cf. med.L. and It. *vestura*.]

I. 1. That with which a person is clothed or dressed: **a.** With *a* or pl. An article of apparel or clothing; a garment or vestment.

13.. *E.E. Allit. P.* B. 1288 Wyth alle þe coyntyse þat he [i.e. Solomon] cowþe clene to wyrke Deuised he þe vesselment, þe vestures clene. *c* **1384** CHAUCER *H. Fame* III. 235 Alle and euery man Of hem.. Had on him throwen a vesture, Whiche that men clepen a cote armure. *a* **1400–50** *Alexander* 1539 (Ashm.), And sithen he castis on a Cape of kastand hewes,.. A vestoure to vise on of violet floures. *a* **1513** FABYAN *Chron.* VII. 558 Fyre was put to the vesturis of the disguysers. *c* **1550** *Disc. Common Weal Eng.* ii. (1893) 75, I haue hearde vestures weare made only of gold then. **1555** EDEN *Decades* (Arb.) 113 A certeyne Kynge made towarde theym appareled with vestures of gossampine cotton. **1611** BIBLE *Gen.* xli. 42 Pharaoh.. arayed him in vestures of fine linnen. **1643** BURROUGHES *Exp. Hosea* xi. (1652) 344 It anathematizes all those that shall judge one vesture, one garment more holy then another. **1827** G. HIGGINS *Celtic Druids* 214 Clothed with never-fading vestures. **1856** MRS. BROWNING *Aur. Leigh* v. 322 The whirling white Of choral vestures. **1871** LONGF. *Wayside Inn* II. *Leg. Beautiful* 17 And he saw the Blessed Vision Of our Lord, with light Elysian Like a vesture wrapped about him.

b. *collect.* Apparel, clothing, garb, raiment.

c **1385** CHAUCER *L.G.W.* 2691 (*Hypermnestra*), I am a mayde,.. And be my semblant, and by my vesture, Myn handes ben nat shapen for a knyfe. **1393** LANGL. *P. Pl.* C. II. 23 Aren non nudful bote þo þre [things]... The ferst of þo ys fode, and vesture þe secounde. **1432–50** tr. *Higden* (Rolls) V. 347 A knyȝhte.. clothede also with regalle vesture, as if he hade bene the kynge. *a* **1475** ASHBY *Active Policy* 535 Lete nat the pouer Comyns be dysguised Nee haue precious clothe in theire Vesture. **1523** LD. BERNERS *Froiss.* I. ccxx. 283 The kyng of Cypre holpe them to complayne the dethe of the kyng,.. and.. clothed hymselfe with the vesture of doloure. **1535** COVERDALE *Ps.* xxi. 18 They haue parted my garmentes amonge them, and cast lottes vpon my vesture. *a* **1548** HALL *Chron., Hen. IV*, 13 They adorned Magdalene .. in roiall and princely vesture. **1601** SHAKS. *Jul. C.* III. ii. 200 Kinde Soules, what weepe you, when you but behold Our Cæsars Vesture wounded? **1670** MILTON *Hist. Eng.* III. Wks. 1851 V. 132 The Abbots Coap, which he had thrown over them, thinking by the reverence of his vesture to have withheld the murderer. **1790** COWPER *Receipt Mother's Pict.* 75 Could time.. restore the hours, When, playing with thy vesture's tissued flowers,.. I prick'd them into paper with a pin. **1813** SCOTT *Trierm.* III. xxxv, Her graceful vesture swept the ground. **1855** MACAULAY *Hist. Eng.* xiii. III. 305 Seers wrapped themselves up in bulls' hides, and awaited, in that vesture, the inspiration which was to reveal the future. **1856** MRS. BROWNING *Aur. Leigh* I. 887 The rustling of your vesture through my dreams.

attrib. *a* **1743** SAVAGE *Progr. Divine* Wks. 1775 II. 119 To tear off rings,.. To part 'em, for the vesture-shroud cast lots.

c. *transf.* and *fig.* (Freq. in the 19th c.)

1526 *Pilgr. Perf.* (W. de W. 1531) 8 For there all shall be clothed with the vesture of immortalite & garment of glory. **1575–85** ABP. SANDYS *Serm.* (Parker Soc.) 208 To clothe ourselves with the comely vesture of innocency. **1602** MARSTON *Ant. & Mel.* II. Wks. 1856 I. 26 Would'st thou have us sluts, and never shift the vestur of our thoughts? **1653** J. HALL *Paradoxes* 76 The strongest and most handsome Animalls are satisfied in their owne naturall Vestures. **1727** DYER *Grongar Hill* 99 Thus is nature's vesture wrought. **1738** GLOVER *Leonidas* I. 271 The moon through all the dreary vapour spreads The radiant vesture of her silver light. **1768** JOHNSON in *Johnsoniana* (1836) 438 When a nation.. acquires new ideas, it must necessarily have a suitable vesture for them. **1862** STANLEY *Jew. Ch.* I. xii. (1877) 223 The golden clusters of the Syrian vine,.. so beautiful a vesture of the bare hills of Palestine. **1867** H. MACMILLAN *Bible Teach.* iii. (1870) 45 Nature as a whole was meant to be for man the vesture of the spiritual world.

d. *Conch.* (See quot.) *rare*⁻⁰.

1755 *Gentl. Mag.* XXV. 32 *Vesture*, the inner covering of a shell that first appears upon removing the epidermis.

2. *Law.* All that grows upon or covers the land, with the exception of trees; one or other of the products of land, such as grass or corn.

1455 *Rolls of Parlt.* V. 305/1, xl acres of Wode, and the Vesture of the same, in our Forest. **1467–8** *Ibid.* V. 575/2 The vesture of Grasse and Cornes therof. **1523** FITZHERBERT *Surv.* v, It is to be enquered of parkes.. howe many acres ar conteyned in them, and for how moche the vesture of euery acre may be sold. **1622** CALLIS *Stat. Sewers* (1647) 105 He which hath the Vesture or Herbage of grounds.. may be charged to the repairs. **1630** CAPT. SMITH *Advt. Planters* 25 The best [ground] is ever knowne by the greatnesse of the trees and the vesture it beareth. **1768** BLACKSTONE *Comm.* III. 210 It is requisite that the party have a lease and possession of the vesture and herbage of the land. **1817** W. SELWYN *Law Nisi Prius* (ed. 4) II. 1217 Where plaintiff is intitled to the vesture of land, that is, corn, grass, underwood, and the like. **1869** *Austin's Jurispr.* (ed. 3) II. 881 In English Law it has been held that one person may have a freehold in the soil and another in the vesture. **1885** *Law Times Rep.* LII. 572/2 Certain hay, straw, and other vestures which have arisen on the said farm.

II. †3. The investiture of a person as a novice in a religious order. *Obs.*⁻¹

1639 S. DU VERGER tr. *Camus' Admir. Events* 184 The two youngest, designated to the monastery, were yet farr from the age not only of profession but of vesture.

†4. *Law.* (See quot. and INVESTURE.) *Obs.*⁻⁰

1607 COWELL *Interpr.*, *Vesture*,.. in the vse of our common lawe, [is] turned metaphorically to betoken a possession, or an admittance to a possession.

Hence **'vesture** *v. trans.*, to array in a vesture or vestments. *rare.*

1555 EDEN *Decades* (Arb.) 309 That he shuld bee honorably receaued and vestured with silke.

'vestured, *ppl. a.* [f. prec.] Clothed or dressed in vesture; wearing vesture. Also *transf.* Chiefly in predicative use and const. *with* or *in.*

1523 LD. BERNERS *Froiss.* I. ccclxxxi. 640 They ar clothed in veluet.. and we be vestured with pore clothe. *c* **1530** —— *Arth. Lyt. Bryt.* (1814) 156 She was vestured wyth a samyte of grene. *a* **1814** *Apostate* II. iv. in *New Brit. Theatre* III. 319 When I contrast my naked ignorance, With that rich-crown'd, that flowing vestured knowledge. **1882** *Nature* XXVI. 61 Cables have.. been lifted richly vestured with the spoils of the bottom. **1893** R. H. CHARLES *Bk. Enoch* 129 They will be vestured with life.

'vesturer. [f. VESTURE *sb.* + -ER. Cf. VESTERER.] (See quot. 1877.)

1779 G. KEATE *Sketches fr. Nat.* (ed. 2) I. 20 The vesturer conducted us thro' this great repository of the dead. **1877** F. G. LEE *Gloss. Eccl. & Liturg. Terms* 437 *Vesturer.* 1. A sacristan. 2. A sexton. 3. A keeper of the vestments. 4. A sub-treasurer of a collegiate church or cathedral. **1898** *Guardian* 31 Aug. 1313 The site [of the depository of the Easter sepulchre] has recently been localized by.. the worthy hon. vesturer.

vestynge, obs. form of FASTING *vbl. sb.*

Vesuvian (vɪ's(j)uːvɪən), *a.* and *sb.* [f. VESUVIUS; cf. G. *vesuvian*, F. *vésuvien*.]

A. *adj.* Of or pertaining to Vesuvius; esp. (*a*) like or resembling Vesuvius, or that of Vesuvius, in volcanic violence or power.

(*a*) **1673** R. HEAD *Canting Acad.* 11 The fury of this smoaking rage being.. abated, and having pretty well drench'd their Vesuvian throats. **1809** CAMPBELL *Gert. Wyom.* III. xx, Then looked they to the hills, where fire o'erhung The bandit groups in one Vesuvian glare. **1831** CARLYLE *Sart. Res.* II. v, Such a fire.. did actually burst-forth, with explosions more or less Vesuvian, in the inner man of Herr Diogenes. **1878** HUXLEY in L. Huxley *Life* (1900) II. xxv. 432 The inflammation of the pudding was highly successful—in fact Vesuvian not to say Ætnaic.

(*b*) **1833** LYELL *Princ. Geol.* III. 125 There is a tendency in almost all the Vesuvian dikes to divide into horizontal prisms. **1886** A. WINCHELL *Walks Geol. Field* 87 History records a large number of Vesuvian eruptions. **1897** GEIKIE *Anc. Volcanoes Brit.* li. II. 471 The three modern types of Vesuvian cones.

†b. ***Vesuvian salt***, aphthitalite. *Obs.*

1813 SMITHSON in *Phil. Trans.* CIII. 262 This Vesuvian salt.. has presented no less than nine distinct species of matters.

B. *sb.* **1.** *Min.* A silicate of aluminium, lime, and iron, or other base, occurring massive but more freq. in square crystals of various colours, found originally in the ancient Vesuvian lavas; idocrase.

Named by Werner, the German mineralogist, in 1795.

1796 KIRWAN *Elem. Min.* (ed. 2) I. 285 *Vesuvian*, or white Garnet of Vesuvius. Found principally in the lava of Vesuvius. **1815** AIKIN *Min.* (ed. 2) 224 Vesuvian occurs crystallized in groups, or lining cavities, or massive. **1859** R. HUNT *Guide Mus. Pract. Geol.* (ed. 2) 255 *Idocrase* was first observed in the ancient Vesuvian lavas, and thence it is called sometimes *Vesuvian*. It is a compound of silica, alumina, lime, and iron. **1879** RUTLEY *Study Rocks* x. 142 Idocrase or Vesuvian is in its chemical composition closely allied to the lime-alumina garnets.

2. A kind of match or fusee, burning with a sputtering flame, used especially for lighting cigars or tobacco-pipes in the open air.

1853 *Pract. Mechanics Jrnl.* VI. 147 One of Palmer's Vesuvians is a still more sure.. way of igniting the fuze. **1862** WHYTE-MELVILLE *Inside Bar* 348 Striving by the aid of a 'Vesuvian' to relight my cigar. **1886** R. C. LESLIE *Sea-Painter's Log* 103 Beyond a few vesuvians, they had nothing among them that would burn.

attrib. **1879** *Man. Artillery Exerc.* 175 A vesuvian matchbox. **1904** 'E. NESBIT' *Phœnix & Carpet* i. 4 They tried to light it with Vesuvian fusees.

ve'suvianite. *Min.* [f. prec. + -ITE¹.] = VESUVIAN *sb.* 1.

1888 *Cassell's Encycl. Dict.* **1892** E. S. DANA *Min.* 480 Vesuvianite was first found among the ancient ejections of Vesuvius and the dolomitic blocks of Monte Somma.

ve'suviate, *v. nonce-wd.* [f. VESUVI-US.] *intr.* Of weather: To be very hot.

a **1876** M. COLLINS *Th. in Gard.* (1880) I. 166 It vesuviates. This sudden heat in the atmosphere has something to do with the eruption of the mountain which killed Pliny the Elder.

vesuvin (vɪ'suːvɪn). *Chem.* [a. G. *vesuvin*, f. VESUV-IUS, from its explosive property: see -IN¹.] Phenyl-brown, used esp. as a staining matter for histological preparations.

1885 KLEIN *Micro-Organisms* 84 Stained with methylene blue and vesuvin. **1886** *Buck's Handbk. Med. Sci.* III. 678/1 Bismarck Brown, Vesuvin. The chloride of triamidoazobenzol. **1897** *Allbutt's Syst. Med.* II. 4 Bismarck brown, eosin, or vesuvin may be used as a counter stain.

Vesuvius (vɪ'sjuːvɪəs, vɪ'suː-). [The name of an active volcano on the Bay of Naples in Italy.] A great explosion of emotion; something or someone liable to sudden outbursts.

1845 POE in *Broadway Jrnl.* 6 Sept. 136/2 The poetical and critical world of England were, about six years ago, violently agitated (in spots) by the eruption of 'Festus', a vesuvius-cone at least—if not an.. Ætna. **1886** G. MEREDITH *Let.* 9 June (1970) II. 815, I confess that a faint form of decent excuse for your conduct.. would have partly appeased my natural indignation. I put it by among other things for the Day of my Vesuvius. **1929** D. H. LAWRENCE *Pansies* 130 The women are like little volcanoes... It is rather agitating, sleeping with a little Vesuvius.

vesy, obs. form of VIZY *v.* *Sc.*

vesyke, variant of VESIKE *Obs.*

†vesyness. *Sc.* *Obs.*⁻¹ [f. *vesy, aphetic f. ADVISY *a.* + -NESS.] Caution, foresight, prudence.

c **1425** WYNTOUN *Cron.* VIII. 6555 Wiþ wit.. And vesynes, throu quham þai wan This batall.

vesyte, obs. form of VISIT *v.*

veszelyite ('vɛsəljaɪt, -lɪaɪt). *Min.* [ad. G. *veszelyit* (A. Schrauf 1874, in *Anzeiger d. Akad. d. Wissensch., Wien* XI. 136), f. the name of A. *Veszely*, Hungarian mining engineer: see -ITE¹.]

A hydrated basic phosphate of copper and zinc, $(Cu,Zn)_3(PO_4)(OH)_3.2H_2O$, occurring as aggregates of bluish monoclinic crystals.

1875 E. S. DANA *Dana's Syst. Min.* (ed. 5) App. II. 59 Veszelyite... In crystalline crusts on garnet-rock. **1920** *Nature* 1 July 569/2 Rare zinc-copper minerals from.. Northern Rhodesia... Still rarer are the copper-zinc minerals aurichalcite and veszelyite; the latter forms minute sky-blue monoclinic crystals.., and differs from the original material from Hungary in its colour and in containing little or no arsenic. **1977** *Mineral. Abstr.* XXVIII. 207/2 The veszelyite appears to have been formed in an oxidation zone by low-*T* hydrothermal processes.

vet (vɛt), *sb.*[1] [Contraction of VETERINARIAN or VETERINARY.] **1.** A veterinary surgeon. *colloq.*

1862 H. MARRYAT *Year in Sweden* III. 328 A lieutenant, accompanied by the vet, did the honours of the stables. **1876** BURNABY *Ride to Khiva* xv. (ed. 3) 136 The Kirghiz themselves have but little faith in doctors or vets. **1883** E. PENNELL-ELMHIRST *Cream Leicestersh.* 223 A battered stud was left in the hands of the groom and the vet.

2. A doctor of medicine. *slang.*

1925 FRASER & GIBBONS *Soldier & Sailor Words* 296 *Vet, the*, medical officer. **1938** [see *pill shooter* s.v. PILL *sb.*[2] 5]. **1965** M. SPARK *Mandelbaum Gate* v. 119 'The vet gone?' Gardnor said... 'You might have a relapse.' **1975** A. POWELL *Hearing Distant Harmonies* ii. 83 Saw my vet last week. Said he'd never inspected a fitter man of my age.

vet, *sb.*[2] N. Amer. abbrev. of VETERAN *sb.*

1848 *Sporting Life* 17 June 190/2 The same remark may be applied to a much younger man than the above 'vets', whose Spring-like qualities seem to defy old winter. **1866** *Pictorial Bk.* 452/2 Colonel A.. took it upon himself to chide the exasperated and unfortunate 'vet' for using such unchristianlike language. **1926** *Amer. Speech* I. 369/1 The [baseball] players are, as in the army, 'vets' or 'rookies' according to the length of time they have served. **1936** *Esquire* Sept. 159/2 'Jesse Laskey's Broadway Booneing' means that the vet producer is scouting plays and talent in N.Y. **1951** M. MCLUHAN *Mech. Bride* (1967) 144/2 The *Fortune* survey editors.. were surprised to find nearly all the vets in favor of getting inside a *big* business. **1968** *Listener* 27 June 841/1 The scene is New York,.. the academic 'host' is Columbia University, where a number of young Second World War vets.. are making gestures at working for degrees. **1979** *Tucson* (Arizona) *Citizen* 20 Sept. 8c/1 When he talked to vets in other service organizations, he found a lot of them felt they owed something to the Veterans Administration too.

vet, *v.* [f. VET *sb.*[1]]

1. *trans.* To submit (an animal) to examination or treatment by a veterinary surgeon.

1891 'ANNIE THOMAS' *That Affair* II. i. 11 Beau is shaky in his fore legs. I shall have him vetted before the races. **1904** *Times* 9 Mar. 8/1 Of the 73 stallions.. only 39 came back for a second inspection after they had been 'vetted'.

2. To examine or treat (a person) medically.

1898 MRS. CROKER *Peggy of the Bartons* xiv, You will have them [*sc.* friends] round to 'vet' you. **1900** *Westm. Gaz.* 14 Apr. 2/1 'Where are you going this afternoon?'.. 'Going to be vetted,' he grunted.

3. To examine carefully and critically for deficiencies or errors; *spec.* to investigate the suitability of (a person) for a post that requires loyalty and trustworthiness.

1904 KIPLING *Traffics & Discoveries* 270 These are our crowd... They've been vetted, an' we're putting 'em through their paces. **1924** H. A. VACHELL *Quinney's Adventures* 267 Shelagh 'vetted' Dolan's brogue, and passed it as sound enough for an Irish-American. **1925** E. F. NORTON *Fight for Everest: 1924* III. vi. 338 He should have all equipment.. completely ready three or four months before shipment—only thus can everything be properly 'vetted' and criticized. **1938** G. ARTHUR *Not Worth Reading* viii. 110 The official in Pall Mall.. who 'vetted' us.. swallowed without a gulp some rather mendacious replies as to one's technical knowledge of the various parts of a Canadian boat. **1947** E. WAUGH *Let.* 29 May (1980) 251 The romantic castle was condemned by the architect I sent to vet it, as moribund. **1959** DUKE OF BEDFORD *Silver-Plated Spoon* vi. 128 We went through an awful period while Brownie was 'vetted' at a series of interviews with relations, each more embarrassing than the last. **1978** G. GREENE *Human Factor* II. i. 63 HQ had her vetted.

vet, southern ME. var. FAT *a.*, *feet* FOOT *sb.*; southern dial. var. FET *v.*; obs. Sc. f. WET *v.*, WIT *v.*

vetail(l)e, obs. ff. VICTUAL *sb.* and *v.*

†**ve'tation.** *Obs.*[−0] [f. L. *vetā-re* to forbid.] 'A forbidding to do a thing.'

1623 COCKERAM I. [Hence in Blount and Phillips.]

vetayll, obs. form of VICTUAL *sb.*

vetch (vɛtʃ). Forms: α. 4-5 fecch(e, 5 fechche, fehche, fech, 5-6 fecche, 4-7 fetche, 4-8, 9 *dial.* fetch. β. 5 vache, 5, 9 *s.w. dial.*, vatch; 5-7 veche (5 vessche), vech (5 wech), 4-6 vetche, 6- vetch (9 veitch). See also FATCH and FITCH *sb.*[1] [a. ONF. *veche, vecche, veiche, vesche*, = OF. *vecce, vece, vesse* (mod.F. *vesce*):—L. *vicia*, whence also It. *veccia*.]

1. The bean-like fruit of various species of the leguminous plant *Vicia*.

Also with defining terms, as *gore-vetch*: see 3 b.

Occas. used as a type of something of little or no value (see quots. *c* 1374, 1632).

α. *c* **1374** CHAUCER *Troylus* III. 936 (Harl. MS.), This seid is by hem that be not worth two fecchis. *c* **1400** *Lanfranc's Cirurg.* 209 Oon [cancer] comeþ of malancolie rotid, & bigynneþ for to wexe in þe mychilnes of a fecche or of a pese. *a* **1513** FABYAN *Chron.* VII. 612 For this scarcyte of whete in Englande, in many places the people made them brede of fetches, pesyn, and benys. **1533** in *Archaeologia* XXV. 519 Fetchys bought for sede.. ij combe of fetchys. **1552** COOPER *Elyot's Dict.*, *Eruum*.. is greater and bitterour then a fech. **1615** LATHAM *Falconry* (1633) 95 Take of alloes the quantity of a Fetch unwashed. **1632** ROWLEY *Woman never vext* II. 26 You may Imagine it to be Twelfe-day at night, and the Beane found in the corner of your Cake, but 'Tis not worth a fetch I'l assure you. **1661** *Petit. for Peace* 11 The Fetches are beaten out with a staff.

β. **1388** WYCLIF *Ezek.* iv. 9 Take thou.. beenys, and tillis, and mylie, and vetchis [1382 vetche]. **1398** TREVISA *Barth. De P.R.* XVII. xcv. (Bodl. MS.), Amonge codware,.. tilles & vacches beþ smalleste in quantite. *c* **1483** CAXTON *Dial.* 22 Otes, vessches, Benes, pesen. **1539** ELYOT *Cast. Helthe* 84 b, Some is lyke lyttelle redde vetches. **1578** LYTE *Dodoens* 482 Afterward there come vp long flat coddes, wherein are Vetches. **1617** MORYSON *Itin.* III. 112 English Merchants bring into Italy.. Conny skins, Veches, Kersies, and sometimes English Corne. **1711** ADDISON *Spect.* No. 59 ¶4 Cicero.. was marked on the Nose with a little Wen like a Vetch. **1756** J. KENNEDY *Curios. Wilton House* (1786) 65 The Busts of Cicero,.. with the Mark of the *Cicer* or Vetch on his Face. **1790** COWPER *Iliad* XIII. 715 As vetches or as swarthy beans Leap from the van and fly athwart the floor, By sharp winds driven. **1866** C. C. FELTON *Anc. & Mod. Gr.* I. vi. 406 Beans, lupines, radishes, Vetches, wild pears, when we can, And a locust now and then. **1870** BRYANT *Iliad* XIII. II. 32 The swarthy beans Or vetches bound before the whistling wind. **1901** *Daily News* 12 Mar. 8/6 Some large Swedish gore-vetches are now offering at attractively low rates.

†**b.** = FITCH *sb.*[1] 2 (q.v.). *Obs.*

2. *pl.* Plants belonging to the genus *Vicia*, esp. to the species *Vicia sativa*, the common tare.

Frequently with special reference to the produce.

α. *a* **1387** *Sinon. Barthol.* (Anecd. Oxon.) 43 *Vesces*, i. fecches *vel* mous pese. **1388** WYCLIF *Isaiah* xxviii. 25 He schal not sette wheete bi ordre, and barli.. and fetchis in his coostis. *c* **1440** *Pallad. on Husb.* I. 237 Lupyne and fetches sleyn, and on thaire roote Up dried, are as dounging landes boote. **1610** SHAKS. *Temp.* IV. i. 61 Rich Leas Of Wheate, Rye, Barley, Fetches, Oates and Pease. *c* **1640** J. SMYTH *Lives Berkeleys* (1883) I. 303 From hence also came their great proportions of wheat, rye, barly,.. and ffetches, apples and pears. *a* **1661** FULLER *Worthies*, *Leicester* II. (1662) 126 Whereas lean land will serve for puling peas and faint fetches. **1879** MISS JACKSON *Shropsh. Word-bk.* 145.

β. **1552** HULOET, Tares or vetches, a kinde of pulse or grayne, *eruila, eruum, orobum*. **1575** in Phillipps *Wills* (*c* 1830) 457 Corne in the felde... Item, 9 acres of peaze... Item, 12 acres vetches. **1576** FLEMING *Panopl. Epist.* 352 With Wheate,.. with Vetchesse, with Millette, & all other kinde of pulse. **1601** HOLLAND *Pliny* I. 572 Vetches also doe manure and fat the ground where they be sowed. **1688** R. HOLME *Armoury* II. 97/2 Vetches, Lentils, Tares, have leaves like Pease. **1697** DRYDEN *Virg. Georg.* I. 110 Where Vetches, Pulse, and Tares have stood, And Stalks of Lupines grew. **1765** *Museum Rust.* IV. 386 Beans, Peas, and Tares or Vetches. **1792** A. YOUNG *Trav. France* 7 A piece of wheat; a scrap of lucerne; a patch of clover or vetches. **1846** J. BAXTER *Libr. Pract. Agric.* (ed. 4) I. 28 The vetches attained by the 4th of July a height of ten inches. **1882** 'OUIDA' *Maremma* I. 188 Amidst the maiden-hair and the vetches about the orifice of the warrior's tomb.

3. In generic use as a plant-name (or, in early use, as that of a grain), usually without article or with *the*; also occas., with *a* and pl., one or other species of the genus *Vicia*.

1382 WYCLIF *Ezek.* iv. 9 Take thou.. bene, and lent, and mylie, and vetche. **14..** *Voc.* in Wr.-Wülcker 619 *Vicia*, a wech. *Ibid.* 625 *Uicia*, vache. *c* **1440** *Promp. Parv.* 153/1 Fetche, corne, or tare,.. *vicia*. *c* **1532** DU WES *Introd. Fr.* in *Palsgr.* 915 Fetche, *uesche*. **1552** HULOET, Vetche, fetche, or tare, *passilus*. **1578** LYTE *Dodoens* 482 The Vetche hath stalkes of a sufficient thicknesse. **1649** J. OGILBY *Virg. Georg.* I. 241 Wouldst thou the Ground should Vetch and Fasels bear. **1707** MORTIMER *Husb.* (1721) I. 139 The Chich, Fetch or Vetch are of several sorts, but the most known are the Winter and the Summer Vetch. **1750** SHENSTONE *Rural Elegance* 204 The tangled vetch's purple bloom. **1797** WASHINGTON *Writ.* (1892) XIII. 407 The Vetch of Europe has not succeeded with me. **1821** CLARE *Vill. Minstr.* II. 144 Heath's creeping vetch, and glaring yellow brooms. **1866** *Treas. Bot.* 662/2 The true *Lathyri*.. are herbs.. with fewer and larger leaflets than in the vetches. **1867** BAKER *Nile Tribut.* viii. (1872) 125 A peculiar species, that resembles a vetch, bears a circular pod as large as a horse-bean. **1890** D. DAVIDSON *Mem. Long Life* viii. 211 In a field of toor (a kind of vetch), we saw a fine buck antelope lying pretty well concealed.

b. With distinguishing names, denoting various species of *Vicia*.

a **1722** LISLE *Observ. Husb.* (1757) 125 The pebble-vetch is a summer-vetch, different from the goar-vetch and not so big; they call it also the rath-ripe vetch. **1725** *Fam. Dict.* s.v., The most known [sorts] are the Winter and Summer Vetch. **1731** MILLER *Gard. Dict.* s.v. *Vicia*, Common Vetch or Tare... White Vetch... Many-flower'd Vetch. **1753** *Chambers' Cycl.* Suppl. s.v. *Vicia*, The species of Vetch, enumerated by Mr. Tournefort are these: 1. The common cultivated Vetch... 4. The great wild bush Vetch... 12. The white-flowered hairy wild Vetch [etc.]. **1777** JACOB *Catal. Plants* 122 *Vicia sativa*, Common Vetch... *Vicia sepium*, Bush Vetch. *Vicia lathyroides*,.. Wild Vetch. **1777** LIGHTFOOT *Flora Scot.* (1789) I. 394 *Vicia cracca*. Tufted Vetch. **1796** WITHERING *Brit. Pl.* (ed. 3) III. 638 *Vicia lathyroides*. Strangle Vetch. *Ibid.* 639 *V. lutea*. Yellow Vetch... *V. hybrida*. Bastard Vetch... *V. bithynica*. Rough Vetch. **1805** [see TUFTED *a.* 3]. **1813** [see TARE *sb.*[1] 4]. **1829** LOUDON *Encycl. Pl.* (1836) 622 [Many species]. **1843** *Penny Cycl.* XXVI. 296 [Biennial, Pea-like, Bush, Rough-podded Yellow and Purple Vetch, etc.]. **1846-50** A. WOOD *Class-bk. Bot.* 220 *Vicia Americana*. American Vetch... *V. Caroliniana*. Carolinian Vetch... *V. tetrasperma*. Slender Vetch. **1850** MISS PRATT *Comm. Things Sea-side* 78 The rough-podded Yellow Vetch (*Vicia lutea*). *Ibid.* 79 The smooth-podded Vetch (*Vicia lævigata*)... The rare rough-podded purple Vetch (*Vicia Bithynica*).

4. Applied, with distinguishing terms, to plants of various genera more or less resembling vetches.

See also *milk vetch* MILK *sb.* 10 b, *wood-vetch*.

[**1562-1727** (see AX-FITCH).] **1753** *Chambers' Cycl.* Suppl. *App.*, *Ax-vetch, in botany, the English name of a genus of plants, called by authors *securidaca*. **1760** J. LEE *Introd. Bot.* App. 330 Ax Vetch: see Hatchet Vetch. **1829** LOUDON *Encycl. Pl.* (1836) 636 *Phaca*. *Bastard Vetch. **1753** *Chambers' Cycl.* Suppl. s.v. *Aphaca*, There is only one known species of *Aphaca*, which is the yellow vetchling, called by some the *bind-weed-leaved vetch. **1578** LYTE *Dodoens* 482 Of the *bitter Veche called in Greeke *Orobus*, and in latine *Eruum*. **1597** GERARDE *Herbal* 1051 Cich, or true Orobus..: in English it is called bitter Vetch. **1661** LOVELL *Hist. Anim. & Min.* 44 Betony,.. bitter vetch with Wine. **1728** BRADLEY *Dict. Bot.*, *Ervum* of Columella.. is the Orobus or Bitter Vetch. **1760** J. LEE *Introd. Bot.* App. 330 Jointed Podded Bitter Vetch, *Ervum*. **1866** *Treas. Bot.* 1212/2 *Bladder Vetch, *Phaca*. **1731** MILLER *Gard. Dict.*, *Lathyrus*, *Chichling Vetch. **1756-1861** [see CHICKLING[2] b]. **1887** *Amer. Naturalist* XXI. 710 Chickling Vetch. *Lathyrus sativus* L. **1846-50** A. WOOD *Class-bk. Bot.* 221 *Ervum hirsutum*. Hairy or *Creeping Vetch. **1671** PHILLIPS s.v., The crimson *grasse Vetch [is called] Cantananee. **1731** MILLER *Gard. Dict.*, *Nissolia*, Crimson Grass-Vetch. **1760** J. LEE *Introd. Bot.* App. 331 Crimson Grass Vetch, *Lathyrus*. **1822** *Hortus Anglicus* II. 243 *Lathyrus Nissolia*. Crimson Lathyrus, or Grass Vetch. **1846-50** *Hairy Vetch [see *Creeping vetch*]. **1597** GERARDE *Herbal* 1055 The first kinde of *hatchet Fetch, hath many small branches trailing.. vpon the ground. **1706** PHILLIPS (ed. Kersey), *Pelecinus* or *Pelecinum*.., Hatchet-vetch, a Weed that grows amidst Corn. **1728** BRADLEY *Dict. Bot.*, *Hedysarum*,.. in English, Hatchet Vetch, or Sickle-wort. **1760** J. LEE *Introd. Bot.* App. 331 Hatchet Vetch, *Coronilla*. *Ibid.*, Clusius's foreign Hatchet Vetch, *Biserrula*. **1829** LOUDON *Encycl. Pl.* (1836) 628 *Coronilla Securidaca*. Hatchet-Vetch. *Ibid.* 638 *Biserrula Pelecinus*. Bastard Hatchet Vetch. **1640** PARKINSON *Theat. Bot.* 1091 The greater *Horse shoe Vetch. *Ibid.*, Many codded Horse shoe Vetch. **1671** SKINNER *Etymol. Ling. Angl.* L lll, Horshoe Vetch, *Ferrum Equinum*. **1760** J. LEE *Introd. Bot.* App. 331 Horse-shoe Vetch, *Hippocrepis*. **1640** PARKINSON *Theat. Bot.* 417 *Galega*... Some with us call it *Italian Vetch, but most commonly Goates Rue. **1728** BRADLEY *Dict. Bot.* s.v., Italian Vetch, or Goats-Rue, in Latin, Galega. **1597** GERARDE *Herbal* 1060 *Kidney Vetch hath a stalke of the height of a cubite. *Ibid.*, The Starrie Kidney Vetch, called *Stella leguminosa*. **1640** PARKINSON *Theat. Bot.* 1094 Bladder Pease or Kidney Vetch of Spaine. *Ibid.*, Crooked Kidney Vetch of Candy. **1753** *Chambers' Cycl.* Suppl. s.v. *Vulneraria*, The common yellow-flowered *Vulneraria*, called kidney-vetch, and ladies finger. **1760** J. LEE *Introd. Bot.* App. 331 Kidney Vetch, *Anthyllis*. **1865** GOSSE *Land & Sea* (1874) 7 The kidney vetch or lady's finger. **1640** PARKINSON *Theat. Bot.* 1098 The most common *Licoris Vetch. **1731** MILLER *Gard. Dict.*, *Apios*, the knobbed rooted Virginian Liquorice-Vetch. *Ibid.*, *Astragalus*, Wild Liquorice, or Liquorice Vetch. **1753** *Chambers' Cycl.* Suppl. *App.* s.v., *Liquorice-Vetch*, the English name of a genus of plants, known among botanists by that of *glycine*. **1882** [see LIQUORICE 4]. **1597** GERARDE *Herbal* 1064 *Onobrychis montana*... Mountain *Medick Fetch. **1753** *Chambers' Cycl.* Suppl. *App.* s.v., *Medic-Vetch*, the name by which many call the *onobrychis*. **1760** J. LEE *Introd. Bot.* App. 331 Medic Vetch, *Hedysarum*. **1731** MILLER *Gard. Dict.* s.v. *Orobus*, Broad-leav'd Creeping Orobus, with a small Pod, commonly call'd, *Venetian Vetch. **1741** *Compl. Fam.-Piece* II. iii. 367 Persian Lilly, Lichnis, Venetian Vetch. **1578** LYTE *Dodoens* 485 The *wilde Vetche [*Galega altera*].. serueth onely but for pasture, and feeding for cattell. **1597** GERARDE *Herbal* 1053 Of the yellow wilde Fetch, or Tare euerlasting. **1640** PARKINSON *Theat. Bot.* 1067 *Aphaca*. The yellow wilde Vetch. **1725** *Fam. Dict.* s.v., The Seed of the Wild Vetch is bitter.

5. *attrib.* and *Comb.*, as ***vetch flower***, ***-grass***, ***-leaf***, ***seed***; ***vetch-leaved***, ***-like*** adjs.

1725 *Fam. Dict.* s.v., Vetch Flower mixt with Honey.. will take away Freckles. **1731** MILLER *Gard. Dict.* s.v. *Orobus*, Wood Orobus, with Vetch-Leaves. **1753** *Chambers' Cycl.* Suppl. s.v. *Onobrychis*, The great, vetch-leaved *onobrychis*. *Ibid.*, The stone *onobrychis*, with long, and narrow, vetch-like leaves. *Ibid.*, *App.* s.v. *Grass*, *Vetch-grass*, the English name of a distinct genus of plants called by authors *nissolia*. **1831** J. F. SOUTH tr. *Otto's Path. Anat.* 455 One [knot] as large as a date seed.. and a third of the size of a vetch seed. **1845-50** MRS. LINCOLN *Lect. Bot.* 184 *Vicia sativa*. Common vetch-tare. **1852** MUNDY *Antipodes* (1857) 14 The Kennedya, with a purple vetch-like blossom.

vetch, southern dial. variant of FETCH *v.*

vetchling ('vɛtʃlɪŋ). *Bot.* Also 6 vitchelinge, 7 fetchling. [f. VETCH + -LING.]

1. A plant or species of the genus *Lathyrus* (†also *Hedysarum*); the genus itself.

1578 LYTE *Dodoens* 485 *Galega altera*.. may also be wel called.. in English Small wilde Vetches or Vitchelinges. **1640** [see *buckler vetchling* in 2]. **1753** *Chambers' Cycl.* Suppl. *App.*, *Vetchling*, the English name of a distinct genus of plants, known among botanists by that of *aphaca*. **1760** J. LEE *Introd. Bot.* App. 331 Vetchling, *Hedysarum*. **1822** *Hortus Anglicus* II. 243 *Lathyrus Aphaca*. Yellow Lathyrus, or Vetchling. **1842** C. W. JOHNSON *Farmer's Encycl.* 1216/2 There are seven indigenous species of vetchling, or everlasting pea. **1861** S. THOMSON *Wild Fl.* (ed. 4) III. 200 We have a good many.. vetches and vetchlings. **1894** *Daily News* 5 June 6/5 Mineral manures, including potash, give a great development of clover, vetchlings, &c.

2. With distinguishing terms.

1777 JACOB *Catal. Plants* 57 *Lathyrus pratensis*, Tare everlasting, or common yellow *bastard Vetchling. **1640** PARKINSON *Theat. Bot.* 1082 *Onobrychis clypeata aspera minor*. The lesser *buckler Fetchling. **1842** HOOKER *Brit. Flora* I. 90 L. *Nissolia*,.. *crimson Vetchling, or Grass Vetch. **1796** WITHERING *Brit. Pl.* (ed. 3) III. 635 *Lathyrus palustris*. Chickling Vetch. *Marsh Vetchling. *Ibid.* 634

Lathyrus pratensis. Common Yellow, or *Meadow Vetchling. **1834** *Brit. Husb.* I. 511 *Lathyrus pratensis*, or meadow vetchling, furnishes a copious, succulent and tender herbage. **1902** CORNISH *Naturalist Thames* 174 Meadow vetchling and the tall meadow crowfoot. **1578** LYTE *Dodoens* 484 *Saint Foin.* *Medick Vetcheling. **1731** MILLER *Gard. Dict.* s.v. *Onobrychis*, Smaller Cock's-head, with rough Fruit or Medick Vetchling. **1760** J. LEE *Introd. Bot.* App. 331 Medic Vetchling, *Hedysarum.* **1842** HOOKER *Brit. Flora* 89 *Lathyrus hirsutus*, L., *rough-podded Vetchling. **1753** *Chambers' Cycl.* Suppl., *Aphaca*,..the *yellow vetchling. **1775** *Essays Agric.* 426 The common yellow vetchling, *Lathyrus pratensis*, or everlasting tare. **1863** GOSSE in *Intell. Observer* III. 318 The hedgerows are still gay with flowers; the abundant yellow vetchling, two species of St. John's wort, the toad-flax..and hawkweeds supply the golden colours. **1880** JEFFERIES *Gt. Estate* 138 The yellow vetchling had climbed up from the ditch.

vetchy ('vɛtʃɪ), *a. rare.* [f. VETCH + -Y.] Composed of, abounding in, vetches.

1579 SPENSER *Sheph. Cal.* Sept. 256 If to my cotage thou wilt resort,..There mayst thou ligge in a vetchy bed. **1806** J. GRAHAME *Birds of Scot.* 26 The blooming, vetchy ridge.

vete, obs. Sc. form of WET *v.*, WIT *v.*

veteran ('vɛtərən), *sb.* and *a.* Also 6-7 **veterane**, 7 **-ant**, **veterean**. [a. older F. *veteran* (F. *vétéran*, = It., Sp., Pg. *veterano*), or ad. L. *veterān-us*, f. *veter-*, *vetus* old.]

A. *sb.* **1. a.** One who has had long experience in military service; an old soldier.

1509 HAWES *Past. Pleas.* xxvii. (Percy Soc.) 132 The sturdy knight well named Fortitude, With the noble veterane syr Consuetude. **1681** tr. *Willis' Rem. Med. Wks.* Vocab., *Veterans*, old soldiers. **1700** ASTRY tr. *Saavedra-Faxardo* II. 248 Even Veterans, who had never kept Guard. **1758** JOHNSON *Idler* No. 8 ¶9 A sound that will force the bravest veteran to drop his weapon, and desert his rank. **1769** *Junius Lett.* xxxiv. (1788) 170 Military governments, which were intended for the support of worn-out veterans. **1814** SCOTT *Ld. of Isles* IV. xix, Veterans of early fields were there, Whose helmets press'd their hoary hair. **1843** PRESCOTT *Mexico* III. ix. (1864) 190 Then came the Spanish infantry, who in a summer's campaign had acquired the discipline and the weather-beaten aspect of veterans. **1882** RHYS *Celtic Brit.* iii. 80 Ostorius establishes a strong colony of veterans at Camulodunon.

b. Any ex-serviceman. Chiefly *N. Amer.*

Not always distinguishable from sense 1 a.

1798 W. DUNLAP *André* p. iv, The Author has gone near to offend the veterans of the American army who were present on the first night. **1838** *Southern Lit. Messenger* IV. 796 When the revolutionary pension-law was enacted, a majority of the war-worn veterans had travelled..beyond the reach of human reward. **1912** I. S. COBB *Back Home* 38 Saturday..was also Veterans' Day, when the old soldiers were the guests of honor of the management. **1931** *U.S. Laws & Statutes* XLVI. I. 1016 The President is authorized ..to consolidate and coordinate any hospitals and executive and administrative bureaus..into an establishment to be known as the Veterans' Administration. **1946** *Sun* (Baltimore) 7 Oct. 2/5 The War Assets Administration ordered its surplus building materials pushed into the veterans housing program within 60 days. **1954** *Birmingham* (Alabama) *News* 11 Nov. 41/1 The Sheppard murder trial jury took a Veterans Day holiday today. **1974** C. RYAN *Bridge too Far* IV. x. 348 'It was the heaviest volume of fire I ever encountered,' recalls Sergeant Spencer Wurst, a 19-year-old veteran who had been with the 82nd since North Africa. **1979** G. F. NEWMAN *List* viii. 67 He was planning for Veteran's Day weekend. November 11 fell on a Monday this year. **1982** *Times* 13 Dec. 3/6 (*heading*) Falklands veteran killed at 22.

2. One who has seen long service in any office or position; an experienced or aged person.

1597 HOOKER *Eccl. Pol.* v. xlii. §5 The Arrians for the credit of their faction take the eldest, the best experienced, the most wary and the longest practised Veterans they had amongst them. **1722** WOLLASTON *Relig. Nat.* ii. 34 A sturdy veteran in roguery. **1782** MISS BURNEY *Cecilia* II. ii. 152 The servants were all veterans, gorgeous in their liveries. **1857** DICKENS *Dorrit* II. vi, Miss Fanny..said the usual nothings with the skill of a veteran.

transf. **1774** GOLDSM. *Nat. Hist.* (1776) III. 22 The new backely [South African ox] is then joined with one of the veterans of his own kind, from whom he learns his art. **1837** WHEWELL *Hist. Induct. Sci.* I. 422 Sending into the field a reserve of new physical reasonings on the rout and dispersion of the veterans.

Comb. **1850** R. G. CUMMING *Hunter's Life S. Afr.* (1902) 95/1 Several of the adjacent veteran-looking trees.

3. A veteran car.

1965 *Guardian* 6 Nov. 3/8 A 'Veteran' is any car made before December 31, 1904. **1968** [see EDWARDIAN *a.* 3].

B. *adj.* **1.** Of soldiers: Having much experience in warfare or military matters; long practised or exercised in war.

1611 SPEED *Hist. Gt. Brit.* IX. xvi. 2 Veterant Souldiers, most of which were of skill sufficient to be Commanders themselues. **1652** EARL MONM. tr. *Bentivoglio's Hist. Relat.* 170 The Veteran Souldiery of the United Provinces. **1686** tr. *Chardin's Trav. Persia* 55 The veterane Janizaries were all either slain or dead. **1759** in *10th Rep. Hist. MSS. Comm.* App. I. 316 So much has the present War drain'd them of their Veteran Troops. **1781** GIBBON *Decl. & F.* xviii. (1787) II. 121 The loss of a veteran army, sufficient to defend the frontiers. **1829** SCOTT *Anne of G.* xxxiii, Here report said, that Adrian de Bubenberg, a veteran knight of Berne, commanded. **1849** MACAULAY *Hist. Eng.* iv. I. 460 His professional skill commanded the respect of veteran officers. **1870** EMERSON *Soc. & Solit.*, *Courage* Wks. (Bohn) III. 108 It is the veteran soldier, who, seeing the flash of the cannon, can step aside from the path of the ball.

2. Of persons in general: Grown old in service; experienced by long usage or practice.

1728 CHAMBERS *Cycl.* s.v., A Veteran Counsellor has a Voice and Seat at Audiences. **1789** BELSHAM *Ess.* II. xl. 502 Did it never occur to this veteran politician that there are degrees of misconduct? **1824** DIBDIN *Libr. Comp.* 528 The veteran English author was not slow to reply. **1849** MACAULAY *Hist. Eng.* ii. I. 255 Godolphin had..early acquired all the flexibility and the self-possession of a veteran courtier. **1883** B. SMITH *Life Ld. Lawrence* II. xxviii. 532 The veteran Viceroy walked round to the sacred spot.

transf. **1847** STODDART *Angler's Comp.* 250 Give me..the rush of some veteran water-monarch, or the gambol..of a plump new-run grilse.

3. a. Of things: Old; long-continued. *rare.*

1653 GAUDEN *Hierasp.* 44 Our old bottels and veterane Wines..are sound, sweet, well-refined, and full of spirits. **1710** PRIDEAUX *Orig. Tithes* iv. 208 The payment of Tithes was grown to be a Veteran and thorough settled Constitution of this Kingdom. **1832** LONGF. *Coplas de Manrique* lxvi, By great And veteran service to the state,.. He stood..The proudest knight of chivalry.

b. Applied to cars made before a certain stipulated date (normally a vehicle not less than fifty years old). Also *transf.* (often coupled with *vintage*).

1933 A. G. MACDONELL *England, their England* xiii. 222 A three-mile clatter in the veteran car—'never can get the new car,' explained Mr. Fielding. **1958** M. KELLY *Christmas Egg* III. 107 An apartment..was devoted to the needs of those who..wished to play vintage and veteran records. **1959** *Listener* 29 Jan. 201/2 A veteran car is generally considered to be a pre-1917 model though a few extremely exclusive owners recognise only pre-1905 cars as qualifying for the title. **1961** J. SHELDON (*title*) Veteran and vintage motor cycles. **1965** L. HUNT (*title*) Veteran and vintage aircraft. **1980** *Times* 1 Nov. 14/2 Nineteen-thirty had seen the foundation of the Veteran Car Club of Great Britain.

Hence **'veterancy**, the state or condition of being a veteran. **'veteraness**, a female veteran. **'veteranize** *v. U.S.*, (*a*) *trans.* to render a veteran; (*b*) *intr.* to re-enlist as a soldier.

1902 *Daily Chron.* 23 July 5/3 This cricketer..is now, in his *veterancy, both batting and bowling better than ever before. **1880** *Sat. Rev.* 8 May 588 On the platform..many heroines gathered, some of them *veteranesses in this war and others recruits to the cause. **1884** *A. J. Johnson's Univ. Cycl.* (1893) I. 355/2 The proportion was at first a little over three pieces for 1,000 infantry, but as the latter became more *veteranized this was reduced to about two pieces. **1891** *Columbus* (Ohio) *Dispatch* 7 Oct., They were the first to veteranize, and this signified a great deal at that time.

†**vete'rascent**, *a. Obs.*⁻¹ [ad. pres. pple. of L. *veterascĕre* to grow old.] Growing old.

1642 GAUDEN *Three Serm.* 136 The clothing of our soules, is daily veterascent and mouldring away.

†**'veterate**, *a. Obs. rare.* [ad. L. *veterāt-us*, f. *veter-*, *vetus* old.]

1. Of long standing; inveterate.

1541 R. COPLAND *Galyen's Terap.* 2 G iij b, Seing yᵗ he made no mention of veterate vlceres. **1562** BULLEIN *Bulwarke* 49 b, My sicknesse is so veterate and olde, that the aire was unsufficient to bee my helpe.

2. Having the authority of age or antiquity.

1565 J. HALLE *Hist. Expost.* 31, I have thought good to gather the councels, and good documentes of dyvers good and veterate authores.

So †**'veterated** *a. Obs.* (Cf. next.)

1547 BOORDE *Brev. Health* cviii. 41 They may be holpen so be it that the infirmitie or the impediment be not veterated or of a longe continuance.

†**'veterate**, *v. Obs.*⁻⁰ [f. late L. *veterāre.*] *intr.* 'To wax old' (Cockeram, 1623).

†**vetera'torian**, *a. Obs.*⁻⁰ [f. L. *veterātōri-us*, f. *veterātor* an old hand.] (See quot.)

1656 BLOUNT *Glossogr.* (copying Cooper), *Veteratorian*, crafty, subtil, gotten by long use.

vetere, southern ME. variant of FETTER *sb.*

veterean, obs. form of VETERAN.

veterinarian (ˌvɛtərɪ'nɛərɪən), *sb.* and *a.* [f. L. *veterīnāri-us* (see next) + -AN.]

A. *sb.* **1.** One who is skilled in, or professionally occupied with, the medical and surgical treatment of cattle and domestic animals; a veterinary surgeon.

1646 SIR T. BROWNE *Pseud. Ep.* 107 The second Assertion, that an Horse hath no gall, is very generall, nor onely swallowed by the people, and common Farriers, but also received by good Veterinarians. **1677** PLOT *Oxfordsh.* 179 Thus the subtile Veterinarians procure white stars, or other desired marks in the fore-heads of their horses. **1716** M. DAVIES *Athen. Brit.* III. 12 Such were call'd at first.. Unguentarians, Emplastrists, Veterinarians, Hippo-Jatrists. **1802** *Med. Jrnl.* VIII. 271 Mr. Barrier, veterinarian, is said to have observed a disease in dogs, perfectly similar to the small-pox in men. **1844** H. STEPHENS *Bk. Farm* II. 81 It is..not desirable that you should consider yourself a veterinarian. **1886** E. R. LANKESTER *Advancem. Sci.* iii. (1890) 124 Rabies in a dog is recognised without difficulty by the skilled veterinarian.

†**2.** (See quot.) *Obs.*⁻⁰

1656 BLOUNT *Glossogr.* (after Cooper), *Veterinarian*, he that lets Horses or Mules to hire, a Muletor, a Horse-courser, a Hackney-man.

B. *adj.* = VETERINARY *a.*

1656 BLOUNT *Glossogr.*, *Veterinarian*..is also used adjectively. **1716** M. DAVIES *Athen. Brit.* III. 43 Neither is the Collection of the Veterinarian Greek Physicians much less representative of the Series of the old Minor Physical Prophets of Medicinal Greece. **1789** *Trans. Soc. Arts* VII. 75 A few remarks on the necessity of..a Veterinarian School. **1861** *Times* 11 July, This may be a reason why some very eminent veterinarian authority should occupy a place on the bench.

Hence **veteri'narianism**.

1816 L. TOWNE *Farmer & Grazier's Guide* 10 Analogy will often hold good..between the human [maladies], and those which come under the Head of Veterinarianism.

veterinary ('vɛtərɪnərɪ), *a.* and *sb.* [ad. L. *veterīnāri-us*, f. *veterīn-us* belonging or pertaining to cattle (*veterīnæ* fem. pl., *veterīna* neut. pl., cattle). So F. *vétérinaire* (16th cent.), It., Sp., Pg. *veterinario*.]

A. *adj.* Of or pertaining to, connected or concerned with, the medical or surgical treatment of cattle and domestic animals.

1791 *Gentl. Mag.* II. 1016/1 Veterinary College, London. Established April 8, 1791. For the..Improvement of Farriery, and the Treatment of Cattle. **1799** *Med. Jrnl.* I. 182 Experiments made at the Veterinary School have confirmed this hypothesis. **1832-3** (*title*), The Veterinary Examiner; or Monthly Record of Physiology, Pathology and Natural History. **1835** H. HAREWOOD *Dict. Sports* s.v. *Clystering*, They may be purchased at any of the veterinary instrument makers in London. **1865** *Daily Tel.* 16 Oct. 4/6 Medical or veterinary problems are regarded by some as absolutely incapable of definite solution. **1888** *Field* 21 Jan. 92/3 It is curious to notice the entire absence of any idea of specific infection among the older veterinary writers.

b. ***veterinary art***, ***science***, etc.

1790 *Gentl. Mag.* I. 298/2 The veterinary art is a practical application of sure and scientific principles to the preservation of health in animals. *Ibid.* 496/1 The important subject of Veterinary Medicine. **1799** *Med. Jrnl.* I. 412 The Veterinary Art. **1804** *Ibid.* XII. 278 Hence they were led to bring the therapeutics..of the human body to veterinary science. **1825** BENTHAM *Ration. Reward* 218 The veterinary art, or the art of healing as applied to animals, has only within these few years been separately studied in England. **1884** *American* VII. 343 Medicine, veterinary.

c. ***veterinary surgeon***, = VETERINARIAN *sb.* 1. Frequently abbreviated as VET (*sb.*¹).

1802 JAMES *Milit. Dict.* **1809** *European Mag.* LV. 22 The ancient farriers of our metropolis have conferred on themselves a title highly pre-eminent, that of veterinary surgeon. **1854** *Poultry Chron.* I. 393/2 If an experimental hospital could..be established under the care of a veterinary surgeon.

B. *sb.* = VETERINARIAN *sb.* 1.

1861 S. LYSONS *Claudia & P.* 18, I must have an especial portion set off as a forge, for the armourers and veterinaries. **1881** S. R. MACPHAIL *Relig. House of Pluscardyn* ii. 51 Sometimes, indeed, a man was veterinary and a member of the fraternity too.

†**veterine**, *a. Obs. rare.* [ad. L. *veterīn-us*: see prec.] (See quot. 1656.)

1656 BLOUNT *Glossogr.* (after Cooper), *Veterine*, that bears burdens; used in carriage. **1661** LOVELL *Hist. Anim. & Min.* Isagoge b j b, The hoofes are solid in those [animals] that are not cornigerous:..and they are renewed only in the veterine... The taile is..setose in the veterine.

veterlok, southern ME. var. FETTERLOCK.

veth, dial. var. FAITH *int.*; Sc. var. WAITH *Obs.*

vethym, southern ME. variant of FATHOM *sb.*

†**vetite**, *ppl. a. Obs.*⁻¹ [ad. L. *vetit-us*, pa. pple. of *vetāre* to forbid.] Forbidden.

? *a* **1500** in *Bannatyne MS.* (Hunterian Cl.) 768 Grit was the lust that thow had for to fang The fruct vetite.

vetitive ('vɛtɪtɪv), *a. rare*⁻¹. [f. L. *vetit-*, ppl. stem of *vetāre* (see prec.) + -IVE.] Amounting to a veto.

1853 F. LIEBER *Civil Liberty* xvii. 164 The only case in which our executives have a real vetitive power, is the case of pardon.

vetiver ('vɛtɪvə(r)). Also **-veyr**, **-vert**, **vitivert**. [ad. F. *vétyver*, ad. Tamil *veṭṭivēru* (f. *vēr* root).] = CUSCUS².

[**1846** LINDLEY *Veget. Kingd.* 113 The Anatherum muricatum, called Vetiver by the French, and Khus in India.] **1858** SIMMONDS *Dict. Trade*, *Vetiveyr*, a name for the Khuskus grass; a scent or perfume so named. **1883** *Ibid.*, *Vetivert*, a perfumer's name for kuskus root. **1886** *Buck's Handbk. Med. Sci.* II. 308/1 Aromatic substances, such as vanilla, tonba bean, orris, and vetiver root. **1899** M. THORNHILL *Haunts Indian Official* 18, I saw some [roots of Khus-khus] once years ago in a shop in Bond Street. It was there known under the name of 'vitivert'.

vetles, southern ME. variant of FETLES *Obs.*

veto ('viːtəʊ), *sb.* [a. L. *veto* I forbid (1st pers. sing. pres. ind. of *vetāre*), the word by which the Roman tribunes of the people opposed measures of the Senate or actions of the magistrates. Hence also F., Sp., Pg., It. *veto*.]

1. A prohibition having for its object or result the prevention of a proposed or intended act; the power of thus preventing or checking action by prohibition. Freq. in phr. ***to put*** (also ***place***, ***set***) ***a veto on*** or ***upon*** (something).

1629 SIR W. MURE *True Crucifix* 1108 Hee who doth exalt Himselfe to raigne,..Dare gainst this Law most impudently stand, And God's great Veto boldly counter-mand. **1654** TRAPP *Comm.*, *Zach.* ii. 13 God..refraineth the remainder of mans wrath... If he do but..interpose his *Veto.* **1788** H. WALPOLE *Remin.* in *Lett.* (1857) I. p. cxviii, They persuaded her to demand of the new King an earl's coronet for Lord

Bathurst. She did—the Queen put in her veto, and Swift.. returned to Ireland [etc.]. **1794** U. PRICE *Ess. Picturesque* I. 43 *note*, Had I not advanced too far to think of retreating, I might possibly have been deterred by so absolute a veto from such authority. **1809** SYD. SMITH *Wks.* (1859) I. 139/1 It is not the practice with destroyers of vermin to allow the little victims a veto upon the weapons used against them. **1837** LOCKHART *Scott* III. x. 323 Upon this ingenious proposition Scott at once set his *veto*. **1866** GEO. ELIOT *F. Holt* xxiv, The Rector had beforehand put a veto on any Dissenting chairman. **1867** BAKER *Nile Tribut.* xv. (1872) 255 They were much displeased at my immediately placing a veto upon their bloody intentions.

transf. **1865** MOZLEY *Mirac.* iii. 73 Confounding the resistance of impression to a miracle with the veto of reason.

2. *spec.* The act, on the part of a competent person or body, of preventing or checking legislative or other political action by the exercise of a prohibitory power; the right or power to interpose prohibition against the passing, or putting in force, of an enactment or measure. ***liberum veto*** [L. *liber* free], a power of veto possessed by every member of a legislative body, *spec.* that which existed under the later Polish monarchy. Also *transf.*

[**1759** E. W. MONTAGU *Anc. Republics* 372 The Carthaginian constitution, where the single, *Veto*, of one discontented senator, referr'd the decision of the most important affair to a wrong-headed, ungovernable populace.] **1792** A. YOUNG *Trav. France* 127, I was.. answered, that the King of France must have no *veto* on the will of the nation. **1792** W. COXE *Trav. Poland* I. I. v. 96 In all state-matters of the highest importance no resolution of the diet is valid, unless ratified by the unanimous assent of every nuntio; each of whom is able to suspend all proceedings by his exertion of the *Liberum Veto*. **1806** *Gazetteer Scot.* (ed. 2) p. xxviii, In fact, though the king possessed no *veto*, yet..nothing could come before parliament which could require his negative. **1831** J. FLETCHER *Hist. Poland* iii. 89 It was in this King's reign [*sc.* 1648–68] that the *liberum veto*, or privilege of the deputies to stop all proceedings in the diet, by a simple dissent, first assumed the form of a legal custom. **1841** W. SPALDING *Italy & It. Isl.* I. 87 He deprived the plebeian tribunes of every prerogative except the veto, which he restricted to certain cases. **1860** MOTLEY *Netherl.* (1868) II. xii. 112 It could neither enact its own decrees nor interpose a veto on the decrees of the Governor. **1888** BRYCE *Amer. Commw.* I. xvi. 232 The President's veto kills off some vicious measures. **1931** E. HOWELL *Mizh* (1979) x. 96 What he had in mind was the *liberum veto* which any young hot head could exercise by the use of his rifle. **1938** H. V. HODSON *Slump & Recovery* viii. 245 Her [*sc.* Bolivia's] *liberum veto* thus stood in the way of any increase of quota allowances. **1952–4** *Proc. Brit. Acad.* XXXVIII. 217 In Jan. 1831 the opposition of a single Cabinet Minister to the proposed grant to Queen Adelaide for an outfit, compelled the Cabinet to abandon it: an example of the *liberum veto*.

b. Without article.

1837 CARLYLE *Fr. Rev.* I. VII. i, Journalism is busy, France rings with Veto. **1879** M. ARNOLD *Mixed Ess., Irish Cathol.* 124 The bishops claimed..the right of veto on the appointment of professors.

3. *attrib.*, as ***veto power***, ***proposition***, etc.; ***veto-free***, ***-proof*** adjs.

Veto Act, an act of the General Assembly of the Church of Scotland, passed in 1834, providing that no minister should be presented to a parish against the wish of the congregation.

1838 *Edinb. Christian Instructor* Jan. 47 Cases of Tain and Strathbogie.—Veto Act. **1840** in *Acts Gen. Assembly* (1843) 1103 The act anent calls, called the Veto Act. **1861** W. J. FITZ-PATRICK *Life Doyle* (1880) I. 163 The friends of the Catholic claims had abandoned the old veto propositions. **1883** *Harper's Mag.* Nov. 941/2 While it did not give them actual control, [it] allowed the exercise of a veto power somewhat akin to it. **1959** *Daily Tel.* 27 Apr. 10 The Prime Minister..proposed breaking the existing deadlock over a control system by a 'quota' plan limiting the number of veto-free inspections per year. **1972** *National Observer* (U.S.) 16 Sept. 2/5 The debt-limit extension, veto-proof because of its importance, could become a Christmas tree of Democratic proposals. **1973** *San Francisco Examiner* 20 Sept. 9/2 The American Federation of Teachers..reacted to the vote by calling for the election of a 'veto-proof Congress'..no longer intimidated by the big stick of a Nixon veto'.

veto ('viːtəʊ), *v.* [f. prec.]

1. *trans.* To put a veto on, to refuse consent to; to stop or block by this means: **a.** With reference to legislative measures or similar matters.

1706 HEARNE *Collect.* 1 Apr. (O.H.S.) I. 213 Letters for degrees..vetoed by the Proctors. **1837** HT. MARTINEAU *Soc. Amer.* II. 210 Mr. Monroe vetoed the bill authorising the collection of tolls for the repair of the Cumberland road. **1861** MAY *Const. Hist.* (1863) III. xvii. 572 Measures passed by the assembly were refused by the council, or vetoed by the governor. **1888** BRYCE *Amer. Commw.* I. I. vi. 74 Washington vetoed (to use the popular expression) two bills only. *Ibid.* App. 563 The President is permitted to veto any particular item.

b. In general use.

1879 E. K. BATES *Egypt. Bonds* I. vii. 146 Fred's common sense vetoes this suggestion at once. **1886** H. F. LESTER *Under Two Fig Trees* 7 The area garden plan was unanimously vetoed. **1902** BUCHAN *Watcher by Threshold* 182, I proposed shooting, which he promptly vetoed.

transf. **1871** E. F. BURR *Ad Fidem* iv. 66 [God] will be hampered by no necessity of general laws. The nature of free moral agents will not veto His activity.

2. To refuse to admit or accept (a person).

1885 *Graphic* 24 Jan. 74/2 The right of vetoing persons whom they deemed ineligible. **1891** *Spectator* 21 Mar., The power of choosing their own Prime Minister, and..the power of immediately vetoing and removing him.

Hence **'vetoed** *ppl. a.*; **'vetoing** *vbl. sb.* and *ppl. a.* Also **'vetoer**, one who vetoes.

1893 SIR A. GORDON *Earl of Aberdeen* vi. 144 Another *vetoed minister..applied to the Court of Session to issue a similar decree..on his behalf. **1888** *New York Weekly Tribune* 24 Oct. 1 (Cent.), *Vetoer. **1892** *Columbus* (Ohio) *Dispatch* 27 Sept., Cleveland's record as a vetoer of pension bills. **1867** LATHAM *Black & White* 72 The President..used his pardoning and his *vetoing powers. **1890** *Daily News* 12 July 3/3 A total of 433 Presidential vetoings in the century 1789–1889. **1892** *Pall Mall G.* 18 Feb. 2/2 The committee suggested the establishment of a controlling and vetoing body.

'vetoism. *rare.* [f. VETO *sb.* + -ISM.] Exercise or advocacy of the power of veto.

1815 D. O'CONNELL *Let.* 13 June (1972) II. 47 A priest suspected of Vetoism loses all his respect. **1897** *Westm. Gaz.* 17 Dec. (Cassell's Suppl.), Vetoism has nothing to say against the immense amount spent in that way.

vetoist ('viːtəʊɪst). [f. VETO *sb.* + -IST.] One who exercises the right, or supports the use, of the veto; one who advocates the possession of a power of veto, esp. for some particular purpose.

The term has been specifically applied to supporters of (*a*) a veto on the appointment of Roman Catholic bishops in Ireland, (*b*) the Veto Act of the Church of Scotland, (*c*) local veto on the sale of liquor.

1815 *Dublin Evening Post* 19 Jan. 2 The Vetoists..have been routed. **1822** *New Monthly Mag.* V. 484 A little further on you will come upon another, a group of learned vetoists and anti-vetoists. **1832** *Blackw. Mag.* XXXI. 355 The vetoists..intimate their disapprobation by hissing the unfortunate performer. **1840** GLADSTONE *Ch. Princ.* 489 The principle for which the Vetoists contend I believe is.. really this [etc.]. **1863** A. H. CHARTERIS *Life J. Robertson* iv. 68 If..the vetoists desired to give effect to the people's conscientious objections. **1896** *Westm. Gaz.* 25 Nov. 5/2 He considers that unless the Liberal Party is dissociated from the Temperance reformers and Vetoists..its future will be disastrous.

Hence **veto'istic**, **veto'istical** *adjs.*

1815 D. O'CONNELL in W. J. Amherst *Hist. Cath. Emancip.* (1886) II. 183 He came into Ireland on a vetoistical mission. **1861** W. J. FITZ-PATRICK *Life Doyle* (1880) I. 163 Dr. Milner branded Mr. Plunket's bills as vetoistic. **1862** F. C. HUSENBETH *Life Bp. Milner* 155 His subsequent uniform opposition to every form of Vetoistical arrangement.

†**veton(y.** *Obs.* Also 5 **vetoyne**, 6 *Sc.* **vetoun**, **veyton**, 7 **vett'ny**. [a. AF. **vetonie*, OF. *vetoine*, var. (after L. *vettonica*) of *betoine* BETONY.] The plant betony.

a **1400** *Stockholm Med. MS.* ii. 99 in *Anglia* XVIII. 310 Betoyne is þe erbis name, And vetonye eke in same. *c* **1440** in *Thornton Romances* p. xxxvi, Take vervayne, or vetoyne, or filles of wormod, and make lee therof. **1549** *Compl. Scot.* vi. 67, I sau veyton, the decoctione of it is remeid for ane sair hede. **1568** SKEYNE *The Pest* (1860) 25 Of herbis... Pimpinell, Vetoun, Finkill. *a* **1689** MRS. BEHN tr. *Cowley's Plants* C.'s Wks. 1711 III. 295 From Spanish Woods the wholsom Vett'ny came, The only Glory of the Vettons Name.

vette, southern ME. var. FAT *v.*, FET *v.*

vettell, obs. form of VICTUAL *sb.*

vetter ('vɛtə(r)). [f. VET *v.* 3 + -ER[1].] One who vets people or things.

1972 *Daily Tel.* (Colour Suppl.) 9 June 7/3 One should be able to assume..that for the BBC's announcers and commentators, as well as for the authors, vetters and readers of scripts, literacy and oral propriety are automatic conditions of employment. **1982** *Listener* 16 Dec. 3/3 The Americans..are privately scathing about the failure of positive vetters to pick up an obvious security risk. **1984** *Daily Tel.* 1 Nov. 2/7 This follows recommendations by the Security Commission into the case of Geoffrey Prime, the spy, whose psychological flaws went undiscovered by security vetters.

'vetting, *vbl. sb.* [f. VET *v.* 3 + -ING[1].] The action or process of vetting a person or thing; *esp.* the investigation of a person's background and credentials to determine his loyalty or trustworthiness; ***positive vetting***, vetting which includes a search for weaknesses of character or anything else that could render the subject vulnerable to exploitation.

1918 H. A. VACHELL *Some Happenings* iv. 42 Doctors were so ridiculously cocksure! All the same, he felt mildly interested in the vetting... Constitutionally he was as sound as a bell. **1927** *Observer* 17 July 13/1 The 'vetting' of applicants for loans would involve the State in an expenditure on itinerant investigators and inspectors. **1955** H. MACMILLAN in *Hansard Commons* 7 Nov. 1499 At the beginning of 1952, a regular system of positive vetting was introduced. This procedure entails detailed research into the whole background of the officer concerned. **1970** *Canadian Antiques Collector* July–Aug. 5/2, I was pleased to see that the vetting committee had done their work well. **1978** G. GREENE *Human Factor* I. iii. 38 Of course, he belongs to the slack vetting days, but I'd say he was clear. **1982** *Daily Tel.* 20 July 3/1 There are some 68,000 government posts currently requiring positive vetting. Civil servants of Under Secretary rank and above are automatic candidates.

‖**vettura** (vet'tura). [It.:—L. *vectūra*, conveyance, carriage, f. *vect-*, *vehĕre* to convey.] A four-wheeled carriage used in Italy.

1792 [see next 1]. **1851** J. GIBSON in Lady Eastlake *Life* iii. (1870) 45, I proceeded on my way in the vettura. **1883** C. E. NORTON *Lett.* (1913) II. x. 152 We took a little one horse vettura and drove..to Ponte Grande.

‖**vetturino** (vettu'rino). Pl. **-ini**. Also 7 **-ine**. [It., f. *vettura*: see prec.]

1. In Italy: One who lets out carriages or horses on hire; also, a driver of a vettura.

In early use, one who provided horses and made other arrangements for the convenience of travellers whom he accompanied on a journey.

1617 MORYSON *Itin.* I. 99 We agreed with a Vetturine or letter of horses, that each of us paying him fiftie five Poli, hee should finde us horses, and horsemeate, and our owne diet to Rome. *a* **1668** LASSELS *Voy. Italy* (1670) II. 258 Others take with them a *Vetturino*, that lets them have horses, and dyets them to. **1756** tr. *Keysler's Trav.* xxxv. I. 301, I made a little excursion into the Milanese, in which I found that the best way of performing it is with the *vetturini*. **1792** A. YOUNG *Trav. France* 209 Yesterday I agreed with a *vetturino*, to take me this morning at six o'clock, to Brescia; but..I insisted that he should not come for me without his *vettura*. *c* **1820** S. ROGERS *Italy, Harper* (1838) 232 *note*, Within a crazed and tattered vehicle,..Then degraded, and belonging to a Vetturino. **1883** W. H. RUSSELL in *19th Cent.* Sept. 483 Asserting my right of way notwithstanding the fierce opposition of many of the local *vetturini*, I toiled up the steep ascent for the hotel. **1905** R. BAGOT *Passport* xi. 104, I must drive back to Genzano. I told the *vetturino* to wait.

2. = VETTURA.

1789 A. YOUNG *Autobiog.* (1898) viii. 176, I went by a *vetturino* to Turin. **1857** LADY MORGAN *Autobiog.* iii. (1862) I. 16 A lumbering post-coach, the Irish *vetturino*, the 'leathern convenience' of that time (like those of Italy of the present day). **1881** *Blackw. Mag.* July 122/1 The lumbering *vetturino*..was packed with the jolly party of bachelors!

3. *attrib.*, as ***vetturino-carriage***, ***-fashion***, etc.

1838 *Murray's Hand-Bk. N. Germ.* 193 In vetturino travelling, he must expect to start at break of day, in all weathers. **1851** HELPS *Comp. Solit.* vi. 82 It was necessary to stay some time (for we travelled vetturino-fashion) at the little post-house. **1859** LEVER *Dav. Dunn* lxx, A miserable-looking vetturino carriage stood at the inn door.

ve'tust, *a. rare.* [ad. L. *vetustus*, related to *vetus* old.] Old, ancient.

1623 COCKERAM I. **1637** BASTWICK *Answ. Inform. Sir J. Banks* 11 Neither novell nor hereticall but according to both the Divine Scriptures and all Antient trueth, and the vetustest Bishops, and by the whole clergy of England in King Henry the eights dayes. **1847** *Blackw. Mag.* LXI. 748 This is something too vetust to abide the shock of any agitation.

Hence **ve'tustness**, 'ancientness, antiquity'.

1727 BAILEY (vol. II).

'vetusty. *rare*$^{-1}$. [ad. L. *vetustas*, f. *vetustus*: see prec.] Antiquity.

1861 J. H. BENNET *Winter Medit.* III. xv. (1875) 499 Some had on two or even three of these bournous,..in various degrees of vetusty and dilapidation.

†**veuterer.** *Obs.* Also **veutrer.** [ad. AF. *veutrier*: see FEWTERER, and cf. VAUTERER.] As an epithet of a hound: Employed for hunting.

c **1410** *Master of Game* (MS. Digby 182) xv, Oþer þer be þat men clepeth alauntes veutreres. *Ibid.*, þat other nature of alauntes is ycleped veutereres.

‖**veuve** (vœv). [Fr.] **1.** A widow; also prefixed as a title to the name.

1793 F. BURNEY *Jrnl.* 13 Apr. (1972) II. 77, I told him I should have the pleasure to present him to another sister —*la veuve!* **1868** C. M. YONGE *Chaplet of Pearls* I. xix. 258 He found her..with her hands in Veuve Laurent's flour. **1894** M. M. VERNEY *Mem. Verney Family* III. ix. 330 We hope Mrs. Aris *veuve* was treated to some of those lovely phrases for home consumption. **1922** E. E. CUMMINGS *Enormous Room* iii. 42 She must have been very pretty before she put on the black. Her friend is also a *veuve*. **1953** D. PARRY *Going up—going Down* v. viii. 252 It's quite a popular sport now, to drop in and cheer the Veuve Tyndale. **1977** T. HEALD *Just Desserts* viii. 190 In the hall were two men unmistakably French..policemen..arguing..with la Veuve.

2. Veuve Clicquot (kliko), *erron.* **Cliquot**, the shortened form of a proprietary name for champagne produced by the firm of Veuve Clicquot-Ponsardin in Reims.

1898 W. J. LOCKE *Idols* xx. 278, I am glad that you prefer champagne *extra sec*... So many women go for Veuve Cliquot, when they can. **1906** GALSWORTHY *Man of Property* I. ii. 33 His pint of champagne was dry and bitter stuff, not like the Veuve Clicquots of old days. [**1926** *Trade Marks Jrnl.* 9 June 1355 Veuve Clicquot-Ponsardin... Champagne wines. Bertrand de Mun & Cie., successeurs de Veuve Clicquot-Ponsardin.., Reims, France; wine merchants.] **1964** [see TAITTINGER]. **1968** *Guardian* 20 Sept. 11/4 A fine pink Veuve Clicquot, say, still remains a fine wine. **1979** P. ALEXANDER *Show me a Hero* xvi. 171 He came in from the other reception room with a bottle of Veuve Cliquot and two glasses on a tray.

veveres, obs. Sc. form of VIVERS, provisions.

veveri, erron. obs. form of IVORY.

vew (vjuː). *north. dial.* Also 6 **veiwe**, 7–9 **view**, 7 **vewe**, **vue**. [Prob. an alteration of YEW.] A yew-tree, or the wood of this.

16.. in Weber *Floddon Field* (1808) 383 A Scottishe Mynstrell..broughte a bowe of vewe to drawe. **1699** M. LISTER *Journ. Paris* 215 Here are several Acres of young Pines, Cypresses, Vues, &c. **1796** PEGGE *Derbicisms* Ser. I. (E.D.S.) 79 *Vew* or *View*,..the yew tree. **1828–** in northern dial. glossaries (Yks., Lancs., Chesh., Derby).

attrib. *a* **1600** *Robin Hood & Guy of Gisborne* xv, Iohn bent vp a good veiwe bow, And fetteled him to shoote. *c* **1675** O. HEYWOOD *Diary*, etc. (1883) III. 213, 4 view trees set about my house Sept. 1. 1674. **1790** GROSE *Prov. Gloss., View-tree,* yew-tree.

vew, southern dial. var. FEW *a.*

vewar, obs. Sc. f. VIVER, a fishpond.

vewe, southern ME. var. FEW *a.*; obs. f. VIEW.

vewlie, obs. f. VIEWLY.

vewter (in hunting): see FEWTERER, and cf. VAUTERER and VEUTERER.

vex, *sb.* [f. the vb.]

1. *Sc.* A cause (or state) of vexation or grief.
1815 SCOTT *Guy M.* xxxvi, It was a sair vex and grief to a' her kith and kin. **1824** —— *St. Ronan's* ii, That is another vex to auld folk such as me. **1877** G. MACDONALD *Marquis of Lossie* iii, Her man's in a sair vex. **1882** —— *Castle Warlock* xlix, A sair vex it wad be to mony a puir body like mysel' to lowse the richt o' 't.

2. Distressing or vexing commotion.
1862 R. S. HAWKER in *Life* (1905) xvii. 393 The Vex of the coming Confirmation is now great. **1866** ALGER *Solit. Nat. & Man* IV. 412 Let trust sink in peace beneath the struggling vex of mortality.

vex (vɛks), *v.* Also 5–7 vexe, wex (5 uex, wix). [a. OF. (also mod.F.) *vexer*, ad. L. *vexāre* to shake, agitate, disturb, etc., whence also It. *vessare*, Pg. *vexar*, Sp. *vejar*.]

I. 1. *trans.* To trouble, afflict, or harass (a person, etc.) by aggression, encroachment, or other interference with peace and quiet.
1426 *Paston Lett.* I. 26, I have nought trespassed ageyn noon of these iij,..and yet I am foule and noysyngly vexed with hem, to my gret unease. *c* **1440** *Alphabet of Tales* 333 So on a day hym happend to com vnto a place þer a damysell was vexid with a fend. **1487** *Munim. de Melros* (Bann. Cl.) 618, I sall neuer inquiet, vex, nor distrubil þe said Abbot and conuent. **1535** COVERDALE *2 Macc.* viii. 32 They slewe Philarches that wicked personne, which was with Timotheus, and had vexed many Iewes. **1560** DAUS tr. *Sleidane's Comm.* 184 b, He,..to thend he might vex the Turkes in an other quarter, was fully resolved to go foreward. **1576** FLEMING *Panopl. Epist.* 383 By whose meanes I am so molested, vexed, & disquieted. **1617** MORYSON *Itin.* II. 95 His Lordship hereupon had called the Counsellors to Tredagh,..to deliberate how the Army might be imployed most to vex Tyrone. **1651** HOBBES *Leviathan* II. xxvi. 142 He does unjustly, and bewrayeth a disposition rather to vex other men, than to demand his own right. **1738** WESLEY *Psalms* II. v, Then shall He in his Wrath address, And vex his baffled Enemies. **1821** SHELLEY *Adonais* xxxv, Let me not vex, with inharmonious sighs, The silence of that heart's accepted sacrifice. **1845** POLSON in *Encycl. Metrop.* II. 723/1 When intestine divisions vex a state. **1850** TENNYSON *In Mem.* xxix, With such compelling cause to grieve As daily vexes household peace. **1887** BOWEN *Æneid* VI. 111 A thousand arrows, that vexed our flight as we came, Safe from the ranks of the foemen.

b. Const. *with* (some action, etc.).
a **1540** BARNES *Wks.* (1573) 246/1, I wyll bryng you S. Augustines wordes, the which was vexed of the Donatistes wyth thys same reason. *a* **1548** HALL *Chron., Hen. IV,* 16 b, It was not sufficient.., this realme to be..vexed with the craftie practices and invencions of the Frenche men. **1610** HOLLAND *Camden's Brit.* (1637) 126 They never ceased to vexe the Britans with skirmishes and in-roades. **1641** J. JACKSON *True Evang. T.* I. 40 So did hee vexe the Church with various and interchangeable pomp of sufferances. **1667** MILTON *P.L.* II. 801 These yelling Monsters..bursting forth Afresh with conscious terrours vex me round. **1827** POLLOCK *Course of Time* III. (1869) 62 Whom she praised to-day, Vexing his ear with acclamations loud.

c. To worry (one) *out of* something. *rare*⁻¹.
1878 *Prodigal Son* III. 103 Such openhanded fellows are not often to be found. So we must fasten on him, till we have stolen and vexed him out of all he has.

2. Of diseases, etc.: To afflict or distress physically; to affect with pain or suffering. Now *poet.*
1489 CAXTON *Faytes of A.* III. xxi. 219 To putte in pryson a man that is vexed with suche a maladie what a valyauntnes were it. **1509** FISHER *Funeral Serm. C'tess Richmond* Wks. (1876) 300 To endure the moost paynful crampes soo greuously vexynge her. *a* **1548** HALL *Chron., Hen. VIII,* 179 b, He was so sore vexed with the gout that he refused all suche solempnities. **1596** MASCALL *Cattle* 208 Although they [*sc.* sheep] are housed, they are oftentimes vexed with cold. *a* **1614** DONNE *Βιαθανατος* (1644) 147 After the persecutors had beat out her teeth, and vexed her with many other tortures. **1746** FRANCIS tr. *Horace, Epist.* I. vi. 42 Would You not wish to cure th' acuter Pains, That rack thy tortur'd Side, or vex thy Reins? **1784** COWPER *Task* I. 582 Feigning sickness oft, They swathe the forehead, drag the limping limb, And vex their flesh with artificial sores. **1817** KEATS *On the Sea* 9 Oh ye! who have your eye-balls vex'd and tir'd, Feast them upon the wideness of the Sea.
transf. **1601** R. JOHNSON *Kingd. & Commw.* (1603) 22 It is most certaine, that Flaunders and Brabant are more vexed with colde and yce then England. **1718** POPE *Iliad* III. 5 When inclement winters vex the plain With piercing frosts, or thick-descending rain. **1820** SHELLEY *Prometh. Unb.* I. 169 Lightning and Inundation vexed the plains.
absol. *a* **1641** D. DYKE *Myst. Self-deceiving* 42 The stone.. so bedded in the bladder, that it cannot greatly vexe.

3. To afflict with mental agitation or trouble; to make anxious or depressed; to distress deeply or seriously; to worry with anxiety or thought.
1423 JAS. I *Kingis Q.* clxxiv, Though that my spirit vexit was tofore In sueuenyng, alssone as euer I woke, By twenty fold it was in trouble more. **1500–20** DUNBAR *Poems* lxix. 12, I walk, I turne, sleip may I nocht, I vexit am with havy thocht. **1535** COVERDALE *Dan.* v. 9 Then was the kynge sore afrayed,..and his lordes were sore vexed. **1596** SPENSER *F.Q.* VI. v. 6 She..day and night did vexe her carefull thought, And euer more and more her owne affliction wrought. **1605** SHAKS. *Lear* V. iii. 313 Vex not his ghost, O let him passe. **1651** C. CARTWRIGHT *Cert. Relig.* I. 83 Thus doe we see Christ to be on all sides so vexed, as being overwhelmed with desperation. **1806** WORDSW. *Horn Egremont Castle* 55 It was a pang that vexed him then; And oft returned, again, and yet again. **1847** HELPS *Friends in C.* I. viii. 154 Most of us know what it is to vex our minds because we cannot recall some name, or trivial thing, which has escaped our memory for the moment. **1880** WATSON *Prince's Quest* (1892) 15 There fell a sadness on him, thus to be Vext with desire of her he might not see, Yet could not choose but long for.

b. *refl.* (In later use passing into sense 4.)
c **1440** *Alphabet of Tales* 128 þis preste gretlie blamyd hym for his syn,..& þis man wexid hym [= himself] gretlie and slew hym. **1526** TINDALE *John* xi. 33 He groned in his spret and vexed hym silfe and sayde: Where have ye layed hym? **1579** LYLY *Euphues* (Arb.) 148 Not to eate our heartes: that is, that wee shoulde not vexe our selues with thoughts. **1611** BIBLE *2 Sam.* xii. 18 How will he then vexe himselfe, if we tell him that the childe is dead? *a* **1653** BINNING *Serm.* (1845) 123 Ye toil and vex yourselves and spend your time about that body and life. **1832** J. J. BLUNT *Sk. Reform. Eng.* ii. 35 He vexes himself because he cannot make a hundred watches go by his own. **1873** 'OUIDA' *Pascarel* I. 41 Why will you vex yourself about your father?

c. To trouble, exercise, or embarrass in respect of a solution.
1612 BREREWOOD *Lang. & Relig.* 68, I could produce other forceable reasons, such as might..vex the best wit in the world to give them just solution. **1871** MARKBY *Elem. Law* §531 No subject has vexed English judges more than the question, what remedy a debtor has for a wrongful..sale by a creditor of property which he holds as security.

4. To affect with a feeling of dissatisfaction, annoyance, or irritation; to cause (one) to fret, grieve, or feel unhappy.
a **1450** *Mirk's Festial* 57 þe forme woman Eue vexude God more þen dyd man. *a* **1578** LINDESAY (Pitscottie) *Chron. Scot.* (S.T.S.) I. 33 This wexit him mair nor all the troubillis that he had of befoir, and [he] was the mair crabbit with him sellffe [etc.]. **1591** SHAKS. *Two Gent.* IV. iv. 66 Away, I say: stayest thou to vexe me here? **1613** —— *Hen. VIII,* II. iv. 130 They vexe me past my patience. **1662** in *Verney Mem.* (1907) II. 182 It vexes my very soul to heare how the base bumpkins triumph. **1676** HOBBES *Iliad* I. 312 Which, angry as he is, will vexe him worse. **1710** SWIFT *Lett.* (1767) III. 37 The bishop..complains of my not writing; and what vexes me, says he knows you have long letters from me every week. **1714** LADY M. W. MONTAGU *Let. to W. Montagu* (1887) I. 95 Your letter very much vexed me. **1809** MALKIN *Gil Blas* x. viii. (Rtldg.) 358 Nothing vexes me, but that Antonia has not a thumping fortune to bring with her. **1835** *Politeness & Gd.-breeding* 28 This boy or girl..who never sneers at or jeers you, or tries to vex your feelings. **1892** *Law Rep., Weekly Notes* 188/1 The defendant had been maliciously making noises for the mere purpose of vexing and annoying the plaintiffs.

b. In pa. pple., freq. const. *at* or *with*.
c **1460** *Towneley Myst.* xxi. 187 Sir, ye ar vexed at all, And perauentur he shall here after pleas you. **1555** PHAER *Æneid* II. 31 For amends to Pallas wrath, so vext with sore offence. **1611** COTGR., *Se Marrir*, to grieue, or sorrow for,..to be sad, or vexed at. **1664** in *Verney Mem.* (1907) II. 204 I am slepy and vexet, and now I fear I have vexed you. **1711** ADDISON *Spect.* No. 165 ¶6 The Curate.., upon the reading of it, being vexed to see any thing he could not understand. **1736** BUTLER *Anal.* I. iii. Wks. 1874 I. 55 That inward feeling, which,..in familiar speech, we call being vexed with oneself. **1783** JOHNSON in Boswell *Life* 15 May, I would have knocked the factious dogs on the head, to be sure; but I was not *vexed*. **1833** HT. MARTINEAU *Briery Creek* ii. 26 He was amused at some of his foibles, vexed at others. **1865** DICKENS *Mut. Fr.* III. v, A little vexed that she had spoken precipitately. **1885** 'MRS. ALEXANDER' *At Bay* i, I am always vexed with people who don't care what they eat.

c. To irritate or tease (an animal).
a **1700** EVELYN *Diary* 19 Sept. 1657, 2 Virginian rattlesnakes,..when vexed, swiftly vibrating and shaking their tailes. **1770** LANGHORNE *Plutarch* (1851) II. 1002/2 She vexed and pricked it [an asp] with a golden spindle till it seized her arm. **1835** LYTTON *Rienzi* I. iv, Vex not too far the lion, chained though he be.

5. *intr.* To be distressed in mind; to feel unhappy or dissatisfied; to fret or grieve. Also const. *at*.
Common in the 17th cent.; now *rare* or *Obs.*
1592 GREENE *Groat's W. Wit* Wks. (Grosart) XII. 122 A yong Gentleman,..vexing that the sonne of a farmer should be so preferred, cast in his minde by what meanes..he might steale away the Bride. **1598** MARSTON *Scourge of Villanie* III. viii. (1599) 214, I doe sadly grieue, and inly vexe, To viewe the base dishonour of our sexe. **1621** LADY M. WROTH *Urania* 346 If..we should faile, I should hate my selfe, and vexe incessantly at my fortune. **1663** BP. PATRICK *Parab. Pilgr.* xxxiii. (1687) 412 It makes us vex if we be crossed in the least of our desires. *a* **1672** WILKINS *Nat. Relig.* 257 Men usually vex and repine at that which is extraordinary and unusual. **1770** MRS. THRALE *Lett. to Johnson* (1788) I. 31 Mr. Thrale particularly vexes lest you should not see Matlock on a moon-light night. **1804** CHARLOTTE SMITH *Conversations*, etc. I. 137 But since it is so,..I must not vex about it.

II. 6. *trans.* To disturb by causing physical movement, commotion, or alteration; to agitate, toss about, work, belabour or tear up, etc.
1627 HAKEWILL *Apol.* (1630) 151 Even there where they [the minerals] are most vexed and wrought upon, yet are they not worne out. **1666** DRYDEN *Ann. Mirab.* ccvii, Some English wool, vex'd in a Belgian Loom, And into Cloth of spungy softness made. **1697** —— *Virg. Past.* IV. 40 And sharpen'd Shares shall vex the fruitful ground. **1759** MILLS tr. *Duhamel's Husb.* I. viii. 20 Clay... In these cases laxatives are to be prescribed,..and continually vexing it with the spade or plow. **1775** BURKE *Sp. Concil. Amer.* Wks. 1842 I. 186 No sea but what is vexed by their fisheries. **1817** SHELLEY *Rev. Islam* VII. vii, Some calm wave Vexed into whirlpools by the chasms beneath. **1861** T. A. TROLLOPE *La Beata* II. xviii. 213 Well sheltered from the blasts that even in summer vex the upper Apennine. **1879** J. D. LONG *Æneid* VII. 905 His followers they, who vex The Massic glebe, so fruitful of the vine.

b. To disturb by handling; to twist. *rare.*
1673 [R. LEIGH] *Transp. Reh.* 35 He exalts his superciliums and vexes his formal beard.

c. *fig.* To press, strain, or urge.
1678 MARVELL *Def. J. Howe* Wks. (Grosart) IV. 191, I would not too much vex the similitude. *a* **1680** BUTLER *Rem.* (1759) I. 218 Distinctions,..By b'ing too nicely overstrain'd and vext, Have made the Comment harder than the Text.

7. To subject (a matter) to prolonged or severe examination or discussion; to debate at excessive length.
a **1614** DONNE *Βιαθανατος* (1644) 20 The best way to finde the truth in this matter, was to debate and vexe it. *a* **1648** LD. HERBERT *Hen. VIII* (1683) 243, I shall now come to the business of the Divorce; so much vexed by our Writers. **1869** BLACKMORE *Lorna D.* xli, Be that as it may; and not vexing a question (settled for ever without our votes), let us own that he was, at least, a..gentleman. **1877** R. F. BURTON in *Athenæum* 3 Nov. 569/1 Upon this point I must join issue with him, with Stanley, and with others who have vexed the subject.

vex, obs. form of WAX *v.*

vexable ('vɛksəb(ə)l), *a. rare.* [ad. L. *vexābilis*, or f. VEX *v.* + -ABLE.]

†**1.** Troublesome, oppressive. *Obs.*
1502 in *Antiq. Rep.* (1808) II. *320 Without distrobill, ensyrchyng, or any other vexable demaunds of his liage people.

2. Capable of being vexed.
1810 SOUTHEY *Lett.* (1856) II. 191 The printers use me ill, but they do not vex me, because I am not vexable by such things.

‖**vexata quæstio** (vɛk'sɑːtə 'kwiːstɪɒ). [L.] = *vexed question* s.v. VEXED *ppl. a.* 4.
1813 *Edin. Rev.* Oct. 143 We do not mean to enter upon the *vexata quæstio* of the tones and delivery. **1838** J. S. MILL in *Westm. Rev.* XXXI. 393 The *vexata quaestio* of codification..has now passed into one of Practice. **1889** G. N. CURZON *Russia in Central Asia* ix. 368 This has long been a *vexata quæstio* of Central Asian politics. **1978** *Language* LIV. 425 For the vexata quaestio of the 'gorgia toscana', cf. most recently Izzo 1972.

vexation (vɛk'seɪʃən). Forms: 5–6 **vexacione, -acyon** (5 **vexacion**), 6 **vexatyon**, 6– **vexation**; 5 **wex-, vexacioun**, 6 **vexatioun**. [a. OF. (also mod.F.) *vexation*, or ad. L. *vexātiōn-*, *vexātio*, n. of action f. *vexāre* VEX *v.* Cf. Pg. *vexação*, Sp. *vejacion*, It. *vessazione*.]

1. The action of troubling or harassing by aggression or interference (sometimes *spec.* by unjustifiable claims or legal action); the fact of being troubled or harassed in this way.
Common in the 16th cent.; now *rare*.
c **1400** *Beryn* 3842 Yee shulle fynde..amendis for to make For our vndewe vexacioun. **14..** *Cal. Anc. Rec. Dublin* (1889) 324 Such persones as will cum to the citte..be fre withoute eny wexacion, cumyng, goyng and abydyng a day befor and a day after. **1481** *Coventry Leet Bk.* 494 Be his longe defferynges, cautels, vexacions & troubles, he wold neuer haue conclucion, but fynde measne of trouble & vexacion to hurt & disheryte the pore comiens here of their rightfull comen, which he wolde do. **1523** *Act 13 & 14 Hen. VIII*, c. iii. §9 The said maire..may have and use all.. powers and auctorities..without trouble, lette, or vexacion of any of the Inhabitauntes. **1560** DAUS tr. *Sleidane's Comm.* 144 b, They loved rather the vexation of the common wealth, than peace and quietnes. **1621** SIR T. COVENTRY in *Fortescue Papers* (Camden) 156 The vexacions of informers and other new devised straynes I shall endeavour to represse. **1647** N. BACON *Disc. Govt. Eng.* I. lxvii. (1739) 161 Therefore the Law provided a Writ of remedy against unjust vexation. **1654** tr. *Martini's Conq. China* 191 Finally ..came out an Edict, which forbad all further vexation, after they had killed a hundred thousand men. **1770** GOLDSM. *Des. Vill.* 95, I still had hopes, my long vexations past, Here to return. **1788** COWPER *Negro's Compl.* 37 He, foreseeing what vexations Afric's sons should undergo. **1852** SIR W. HAMILTON *Discuss.* 232 He was constrained by their vexations to abandon that University.

†**b.** Strict examination or calling to account. *Obs.*⁻¹
a **1505** *Chron. Lond.* (Kingsford, 1905) 262 This yere was Sir William Capell ayein put in vexacion,..for thinges doon by hym in the tyme of his mairaltie.

†**2.** The action of troubling, disturbing, or irritating by physical means; the fact or state of being so troubled or distressed. *Obs.*
14.. HOCCLEVE *Minor Poems* (1892) 220 The vexacioun Of deeth so haastid him, þat his spiryt Anoon forsooke his habitacioun. *c* **1440** *Gesta Rom.* lxvi. 298 Abowte cockis crowe þe mayde, for gret vexacion þat she hadde with þe tempest, fell on slepe. **1493** *Petronylla* 18 (Pynson), Though she had of brennynge greate feruence Twene colde and hote vexacion inportable There was no grutchinge. **1515** BARCLAY *Egloges* ii. (1570) B iv/1 In all that thy sight hath delectation, Thy greedy tasting hath great vexation. *a* **1548** HALL *Chron., Hen. VII,* 3 b, By the tormentyng and vexacion of which sicknes,..they cast away the shetes & all the clothes liyng on the bed. **1577** HANMER *Anc. Eccles. Hist.* (1619) 148 Maiming, racking, and scourging, and thousands of other vexations. **1590** SHAKS. *Mids. N.* IV. i. 74 That he ..May..thinke no more of this nights accidents, But as the fierce vexation of a dreame. **1610** B. JONSON *Catiline* III. ii, No noise, no pulling, no vexation wakes thee, Thy lethargie is such. **1704** J. HARRIS *Lex. Techn.* s.v. *Assodes febris*, The Distemper usually arises from the Vexation of the Stomach by sharp and cholerick Humours.

3. The state or fact of being mentally troubled or distressed, in later use esp. by something causing annoyance, irritation, dissatisfaction, or disappointment.

c **1465** *Pol., Rel., & L. Poems* (1903) 2 Raynyng with Rewles resenable and Rightfull, The whiche for oure sake hathe sofferde grete vexacion. *c* **1471** in *Pol. Poems* (Rolls) II. 279 What vexacioun was then To the quene and the lordis... Then aftur kynge Edwarde thay cryed and did wepe. **1500–20** DUNBAR *Poems* xxv. 41 Tak consolatioun in ȝour pane, In tribulatioun tak consolatioun, Out of vexatioun cum hame agane. **1555** EDEN *Decades* (Arb.) 71 Contente onely to satisfie nature, without further vexation for knowelege of thinges to come. **1590** SHAKS. *Mids. N.* I. i. 22 Full of vexation, come I, with complaint Against my childe, my daughter Hermia. **1683** *Brit. Spec.* 101 Those Britains .. did .. so infest the Roman Province, that the very Vexation of it cost Ostorius his Life. **1725** DE FOE *Voy. round World* (1840) 344 They let it [a canoe] go to the first cataract,.. and had the vexation of seeing it dashed all to pieces. **1782** MISS BURNEY *Cecilia* III. viii, [She] very openly expressed her vexation and displeasure. **1828** SCOTT *F.M. Perth* xx, The King .. heard of this new trouble with much vexation. **1854** *Poultry Chron.* II. 122/2 The vexation of the poultry owner when he sees his favourites fall under the ravages of disease. **1887** RUSKIN *Præterita* II. 19, I spoke of the constant vexation I suffered because I could not draw better.

b. In the phr. *vexation of mind, spirit.*

1535 COVERDALE *Isaiah* lxv. 14 Ye shal crie for sorow of hert, and complayne for vexacion of mynde. **1540–54** CROKE *1st Chap. Eccles.* (Percy Soc.) 49 Nought fynde I but vexacion Of spryte and mynde. **1560** BIBLE (Genev.) *Eccl.* ii. 17 All is vanitie, & vexacion of the spirit. **1588** FRAUNCE *Lawiers Logike* Ded. ¶2b, The perpetuall vexation of Spirite, and continuall consumption of body, incident to every scholler. **1611** COTGR., *Marrison*,.. chafing, fuming, vexation of mind. **1621** BURTON *Anat. Mel.* II. iii. VII. 422 Many men spend themselues .. vpon small quarrels,.. with much vexation of spirit and anguish of minde. **1828** SCOTT *F.M. Perth* xiv, She found her reward in vanity and vexation of spirit.

4. A source or cause of mental trouble or distress; a grief or affliction. Chiefly with *a*.

1594 SHAKS. *Rich. III*, IV. iv. 305 Your Children were vexation to your youth, But mine shall be a comfort to your Age. **1612** BRINSLEY *Lud. Lit.* iii. (1627) 13 It is an extreme vexation, that we must be toiled amongst such little petties. **1638** R. BAKER tr. *Balzac's Lett.* (vol. III) 165 Sir, I am your vexation in ordinary. **1765** COWPER *Let. to Lady Hesketh* 1 Aug., It is a mark of their great charity for one who has been a disappointment and a vexation to them. **1833** HT. MARTINEAU *Loom & Lugger* II. v. 94 It may be a vexation and disadvantage to us. **1879** FROUDE *Cæsar* xx. 344 My own vexation is, that I must pay Cæsar my debt.

†**5.** The action of subjecting to violence or force; the fact of being so treated. *Obs.*

1603 B. JONSON *Sejanus* IV. ii, As the wind doth try strong trees, Who by vexation grow more sound and firm. **1610** —— *Alch.* II. v, Name the vexations, and the martyrizations Of mettalls, in the worke. **1692** L'ESTRANGE *Josephus, Antiq.* IV. viii. (1733) 94 The Earth hath enough to do .. without the superfluous Vexations of the Plow over and above.

vexatious (vɛk'seɪʃəs), *a.* Also 6 vexacyus. [f. prec.: see -IOUS.]

1. Causing, tending or disposed to cause, vexation (in later use in sense 3): **a.** Of persons, their disposition, etc.

1534 *Star Chamber Cases* (Selden) II. 319 Henry .. of his vexacyus mynde purchased a writte of monstrauerunt in the Comen place ageynst the seid defendaunt. **1651** G. W. tr. *Cowel's Inst.* 246 They might meerly through envy, and the pleasure they took in being vexatious, take men upon Writs. **1676** WYCHERLEY *Pl. Dealer* I. i, She is as vexatious as her Father was, the great Attorney. **1715** *Lond. Gaz.* No. 5343/2 The Townsmen .. are .. turbulent and vexatious to the Regiment. **1738** WESLEY *Psalms* CXVIII. iv, Begirt with Hosts of Enemies Vexatious as thick-swarming Bees. **1853** DICKENS *Bleak Ho.* xxiv, The Lord Chancellor described him, in open court, as a vexatious and capricious infant.

b. Of things.

1664 POWER *Exp. Philos.* III. 184 If he could but stiffly wrangle out a vexatious dispute of some odd Peripatetick qualities. *a* **1680** BUTLER *Rem.* (1759) II. 38 Flies and Gnats are more vexatious in hot Climates, than Creatures that are able to do greater Mischiefs. **1705–6** PENN in *Pennsylv. Hist. Soc. Mem.* X. 108 The business of Beaumont proves very vexatious to me here. **1751** JOHNSON *Rambler* No. 176 ¶1 There are many vexatious accidents and uneasy situations which raise little compassion for the sufferer. **1804** ABERNETHY *Surg. Obs.* 101 The opening of the cyst generally leaves a vexatious and intractable sore. **1842** LOUDON *Suburban Hort.* 709 It is most vexatious to find a fruit tree has been planted untrue to name. **1869** FREEMAN *Norm. Conq.* (1875) III. xii. 75 It is somewhat vexatious that we have to trust almost wholly to authorities on one side.

c. *spec.* Of legal actions: Instituted without sufficient grounds for the purpose of causing trouble or annoyance to the defendant.

1677 YARRANTON *Eng. Improv.* 9 It is a Sin, that a Gentleman .. should be the occasion of ruining so many Families .. by putting them to such vexatious Suits for their Moneys lent. **1696–7** *Act 8–9 William III*, c. 11 Diverse evil disposed Persons are incouraged to bring frivolous and vexatious Actions. **1746** FRANCIS tr. *Hor., Sat.* I. vi. 6 Persius had wealth by foreign traffic gain'd, And a vexatious suit with King maintain'd. **1856** FROUDE *Hist. Eng.* (1858) II. vi. 72 Their courts were unceasingly occupied with vexatious suits.

transf. **1909** H. M. GWATKIN *Early Ch. Hist.* I. viii. 142 If the charge turns out vexatious (*calumniæ gratia*) the accuser shall be severely punished.

†**2.** Full of trouble or uneasiness. *Obs.*

1644 DIGBY *Two Treat.* Ded. aiij b, He leadeth a vexatious life, that in his noblest actions is so gored with scruples, that he dareth not make a steppe, without the authority of an other to warrant him. **1671** H. M. tr. *Erasm. Colloq.* 529 Riches and honours which bring not a pleasant, but rather a careful and vexatious life.

†**3.** Vexed, annoyed. *Obs.*[−1]

1756 TOLDERVY *Hist. 2 Orphans* IV. 106 Heartley grew vexatious with himself for having parted with the watch.

vexatiously (vɛk'seɪʃəslɪ), *adv.* [f. prec. + -LY².] In a vexatious manner; so as to cause annoyance or irritation.

1653 R. SANDERS *Physiogn.* 140 Thy soul is vexatiously perturbated. **1709** SWIFT & ADDISON *Tatler* No. 43 ¶2, The rugged Cares and Disturbance that Publick Affairs brings with it, which does so vexatiously affect the Heads of other great Men. **1748** *Anson's Voy.* II. ix. 227 We were most strangely and vexatiously disappointed, by finding that the light .. was only a fire on the shore. **1788** MME. D'ARBLAY *Diary* 2 Aug., Very vexatiously, however, my message arrived .. late. **1847** S. AUSTIN *Ranke's Hist. Ref.* III. 531 At the same time difficulties were vexatiously thrown in the way of the protestant procurator. **1879** S. C. BARTLETT *Egypt to Pal.* xi. 242 We paused here and interrogated our Arabs, but, vexatiously enough, we could extract from them no such tradition.

b. *spec.* in *Law.* (See VEXATIOUS *a.* 1 c.)

1880 MUIRHEAD *Gaius* IV. §172 The praetor allows an oath to be exacted from him 'that he is not vexatiously denying his liability'. **1883** *Law Times* 20 Oct. 412/1 The bankrupt .. must not have vexatiously defended any action.

vexatiousness (vɛk'seɪʃəsnɪs). [f. as prec. + -NESS.] The character of being vexatious.

1668 BP. HOPKINS *Sermons, Vanity* (1685) 39 There is a fourfold vexatiousness in all worldly things. **1727** BAILEY (vol. II). *c* **1825** LD. COCKBURN *Mem.* (1856) 300 Amidst the vexatiousness of the most complicated case,.. Monypenny sat .. serenely. *a* **1859** DE QUINCEY in 'H. A. PAGE' *Life* (1877) II. xvii. 54 The vexatiousness of writing letters.

'vexatory, *a.* [f. L. *vexāt-*, ppl. stem of *vexāre* VEX *v.*: see -ORY.] = VEXATIOUS *a.* 1.

1900 *Speaker* 8 Sept. 622/1 The objection that they are not Englishmen may be brushed aside as futile and vexatory. **1902** *Fortn. Rev.* Oct. 585 The only people who would gain by these vexatory measures would be the lawyers.

†**vexed**, variant of FAXED *a. Obs.*

a **1259** [see FAXED *a.*]. *a* **1661** FULLER *Worthies, Yorks.* III. (1662) 200 Hence Mathew Westminster calleth a Comet .. a Vexed Star.

vexed ('vɛkst), *ppl. a.* Also 7 vex't, vext, 7–9 vex'd. [f. VEX *v.*]

1. Troubled, harassed; kept in a disturbed or unquiet state.

c **1440** *Promp. Parv.* 509/2 Vexid, *vexatus*. **1583** MELBANCKE *Philotimus* T j b, If you will .. kepe me still aliue in vexed plighte, for some offence I haue committed, then shew [etc.]. **1592** KYD *Sp. Trag.* III. ii. 13 The night .. With direfull visions wake my vexed soule. *c* **1670** WOOD *Life* 6 Sept. 1645, Col. Legge charged them so gallantly, that the rebels ran back... Yet farr had they not gone, before these vexed rebels came on againe. **1816** SHELLEY *Sunset* 43 The tomb of thy dead self Which one vexed ghost inhabits. **1870** BURTON *Hist. Scot.* (1873) VI. lxx. 189 He thus was chosen to settle the vexed affairs of Scotland.

2. Distressed, grieved; affected with vexation; annoyed, irritated.

1602 *2nd Pt. Return fr. Parnass.* II. i. 564 O how it greeues my vexed soule to see Each painted asse in chayre of dignitye. **1652** CRASHAW *Carmen Deo Nostro, Epiphanie* Wks. (1904) 211 [The sun] hiding his vex't cheeks in a hir'd mist. **1798** S. & HT. LEE *Canterb. T.* II. 96 The vexed father now sighed to himself. **1810** SCOTT *Lady of Lake* II. v, While her vex'd spaniel from the beach Bay'd at the prize beyond his reach. **1846** MRS. A. MARSH *Father Darcy* II. iv. 95 The priest looked vexed and perplexed. **1894** MRS. DYAN *Man's Keeping* (1899) 247 'You think I look it?' he said, with a vexed little laugh.

absol. **1824** CAMPBELL *Theodoric* 193 Hers was the brow .. That cheered the sad, and tranquillized the vexed.

3. Subjected to physical force or strain; tossed about, agitated, belaboured, etc.

1610 SHAKS. *Temp.* I. ii. 229 Where once Thou calldst me vp .. to fetch dewe From the still-vext Bermoothes. **1667** MILTON *P.L.* II. 660 Vex'd Scylla bathing in the Sea that parts Calabria from the hoarce Trinacrian shore. *Ibid.* x. 314 A ridge of pendent Rock Over the vext Abyss. **1718** POPE *Iliad* XVIII. 549 The ponderous hammer loads his better hand, His left with tongs turns the vexed metal round. **1817** SHELLEY *Rev. Islam* I. i, The peak of an aereal promontory, Whose caverned base with the vexed surge was hoary. **1850** BLACKIE *Æschylus* I. 21 What time the Chalcian strand Saw the vexed Argive masts In Aulis tides. **1852** G. W. CURTIS *Lotus-Eating* viii. 117 The vexed river rages and tumbles among channeled rocks.

4. *vexed question*, a much debated or contested question.

1657 HEYLIN *Ecclesia Vind.* 215 Nor do I mean to meddle in so vexed a question. **1848** MILL *Pol. Econ.* I. v. §8 (1876) 48 This leads to the vexed question to which Dr. Chalmers has very particularly adverted. **1860** RUSKIN *Unto this Last* iii. §54 The vexed question of the destinies of the unemployed workmen. **1874** MAHAFFY *Soc. Life Greece* ii. 9 The great vexed question of the origin and composition of the Homeric poems.

Hence **'vexedness**. *rare.*

1754 RICHARDSON *Grandison* V. xx. 90 My teazing uncle broke out into a loud laugh, which .. had more of vexedness than mirth in it. **1909** W. J. LOCKE *Septimus* xi. 160 Zora, regarding the egoist with mingled admiration and vexedness, could only say, 'Oh!'

vexedly ('vɛksɪdlɪ), *adv.* [f. prec. + -LY.] In a vexed manner; with vexation.

1748 RICHARDSON *Clarissa* (1811) II. xxiv. 165 My heart is vexedly easy, if I may so describe it. Vexedly—because of the apprehended interview with Solmes. **1796** ANNA SEWARD *Lett.* (1811) IV. 241, I am in a society which makes me vexedly feel the rapid flight of those weeks, whose period must close an intellectual intercourse very gratifying. **1856** *Household Words* XIII. 300/1 Then he turned round, neither vexedly nor impatiently. **1865** DICKENS *Mut. Fr.* II. xvi, Eugene answers, and answers hastily and vexedly: 'No, no, no; he doesn't mean that'. **1901** CLIVE HOLLAND *Mousmé* 223 'Some one else come and have her,' she remarked vexedly.

vexer ('vɛksə(r)). Also 6 vexar, -or. [f. VEX *v.*] One who or that which vexes or annoys.

1530 PALSGR. 284/2 Vexar, a grevar, *turbateur*. **1552** HULOET, Vexor, *animaduersor*. *c* **1586** C'TESS PEMBROKE *Psalms* LXXXIX. viii, I will quaile his vexers in his sight. **1608** TOPSELL *Serpents* 93 Hornets .. are great vexers and troublers. **1620** ROWLANDS *Night Raven* 34 Pray speake, had you this vexer and abuser, And were thus plagu'd as I, how would you vse her? **1691** WOOD *Ath. Oxon.* II. 235 He was .. a vexer of two Parishes with continual suits of Law. *a* **1716** BLACKALL *Wks.* (1723) I. 45 They can't be blessed because they are their own Vexers and Tormentors. **1788** BURKE *Impeachm. W. Hastings* Wks. XIII. 59 The disgracers of government, the vexers and afflicters of mankind.

†**'vexful**, *a. Obs. rare.* [f. VEX *v.* + -FUL 1.] = VEXATIOUS *a.*

1598 FLORIO, *Essoso*, vexfull, cruell, exacting. **1603** —— *Montaigne* II. xi. 243 Maintaining for his exercise the peevish frowardnes of his wife, then which no essay can be more vex-full.

'vexil. Anglicized f. VEXILLUM 2 (Webster, 1828–32). The stem of *vexillum* is also the base of the following formations given in Dicts. without evidence of their currency: **'vexillar** *a.*, of or pertaining to a vexillum, spec. in *Bot.* and *Ornith.* **vexi'llarious** *a.*, = VEXILLARY *a.* 2. **'vexillate** *a.*, having a vexillum or vexilla (*Bot.* and *Ornith.*).

vexillary ('vɛksɪlərɪ), *sb.* and *a.* Also 7 vexiliarie. [ad. L. *vexillāri-us* standard-bearer, etc., f. *vexillum* standard, VEXILLUM.]

A. *sb.* **a.** One of the oldest class of veterans in the Roman army, serving under a special standard. **b.** A Roman standard-bearer.

1591 SAVILE *Tacitus, Hist.* II. xviii. 63 Three Prætorian cohortes, and a thousand Vexillaries. *Ibid.* c. 111 With the Vexillaries of the three British Legions. **1611** SPEED *Hist. Gt. Brit.* VI. xi. §7. 84 The Vexillaries of three British Legions followed Vitellius in his Expedition against the Illyrian Army. **1656** BLOUNT *Glossogr.* **1793** A. MURPHY *Tacitus* (1805) V. 220 In the left wing were placed the vexillaries of the thirteenth legion. **1872** TENNYSON *Gareth & Lynette* 1172 In letters like to those the vexillary Hath left crag-carven o'er the streaming Gelt.

B. *adj.* †**1.** *vexillary soldier*, = prec. a. *Obs.*[−1]

1598 GRENEWEY *Tacitus, Ann.* I. ix. (1622) 16 Certaine vexiliarie souldiers which continued vnder ensignes, and were placed for a guard to the countrey.

2. *Bot.* Of estivation: (see quot.).

1832 LINDLEY *Introd. Bot.* 411 *Vexillary*, when one piece is much larger than the others, and is folded over them, they being arranged face to face.

vexillation (vɛksɪ'leɪʃən). [ad. L. *vexillātio*, f. *vexillum* standard, VEXILLUM.] A company of veteran soldiers (see prec. A. a) or of soldiers grouped under one standard.

1656 BLOUNT *Glossogr.*, *Vexillation*, a company of men of arms under one Standard. **1732** *Hist. Litteraria* III. 507 The quantity of Work perform'd by the Vexillations, appears to have nearly equalled that of the whole Legions. **1851** D. WILSON *Preh. Ann.* (1863) II. III. ii. 44 The vexillation of the twentieth Legion dedicated four thousand paces of their wall to the Emperor whose name it bore. **1876** SKENE *Celtic Scot.* I. ii. I. 78 The vallum .. had been constructed by the second .. and twentieth legions, or rather by their vexillations.

vexillator ('vɛksɪleɪtə(r)). [a. med.L. *vexillātor*, f. *vexillum*: see VEXILLUM.] A banner-bearer in a mystery or a miracle play.

1801 STRUTT *Sports & Past.* III. ii. 137 The prologue to this curious drama is delivered by three persons, who speak alternately, and are called vexillators. **1831** COLLIER *Hist. Dram. Poetry* II. 155 The Chester Whitsun-plays are preceded by a kind of proclamation .. made by certain Vexillators in various parts of the city.

vexillology (vɛksɪ'lɒlədʒɪ). [f. L. *vexill-um* flag + -OLOGY.] The study of flags.

1959 *Arab World* (N.Y.) Oct. 13/1 One of the most interesting phases of vexillology—the study of flags—is the important contribution to our heritage of flags by the Arab World. **1961** *Flag Bull.* Fall 7/2 Editors Grahl and Smith use 'vexillology' and its cognates, vexillologist, vexillological. **1966** *Occasional Newslet. to Librarians* Jan. 4 This unknown specialist has demonstrated his great knowledge of heraldry and vexillology. **1970** W. SMITH *Flag Bk. U.S.* i. 3 In 1965 the first International Congress of Vexillology was held in the Netherlands.

Hence **vexillo'logical** *a.*; **vexi'llologist**.

1961 [see above]. **1963** *Recall* (Boston) Oct. 4 (*heading*) Travel notes and vexillological addendum. **1965** W. SMITH *Bibliogr. Flags of Foreign Nations* p. v, Its three principal activities have been the encouragement of contacts and exchanges of information between vexillologists around the world, the coordination of research efforts, and the building up of a library of books and other flag materials. **1971** *Daily Tel.* 19 Nov. 13/7 Between 60 and 70 .. historians, antiquaries, designers and students of heraldry are expected at an international vexillological congress. **1973** *Smithsonian*

Dec. 50/2 Redividing the states would mean redesigning the flag. In vexillologist Whitney Smith's scheme, he retains the symbolism of 13. **1983** *Christian Science Monitor* 8 Apr. 20/1 Father Young is the official community vexillological custodian.

‖**vexillum** (vɛk'sɪləm). [L. (in sense 1), f. the stem of *vehĕre* to carry.]

1. a. A flag or banner carried by Roman troops; a body of men grouped under one banner.

1726 GORDON *Itin. Sept.* 79 The Figures of two winged Victories, supporting the Roman Vexillum. **1805** JAMES *Mil. Dict.* (ed. 2), *Vexillum*, the standard which was carried by the Roman horse. **1891** *Cent. Dict.* s.v., These vexilla averaged from 500 to 600 in strength.

b. *Eccl.* A small piece of linen or silk attached to the upper part of a crozier.

1877 F. G. LEE *Gloss. Eccl. & Liturg. Terms* 438 Many examples of the vexillum are represented in illuminated MSS. **1905** *Ch. Times* 3 Feb. 136/3 The vexillum sometimes attached to a pastoral staff was a 'sudarium' or handkerchief, in all probability.

2. *Bot.* The large external petal of a papilionaceous flower.

1727 BAILEY (vol. II), *Vexillum*, the Banner of the broad Single Leaf, which stands upright. **1760** J. LEE *Introd. Bot.* II. xx. (1765) 116 *Vexillum*, the Standard, a Petal covering the rest. *c* **1789** *Encycl. Brit.* (ed. 3) III. 446/2 The superior [petal] ascending, (called the *vexillum* or flag). **1821** W. P. C. BARTON *Flora N. Amer.* I. 11 Corolla with a long sabre-shaped vexillum of a deep carmine-red colour. **1872** OLIVER *Elem. Bot.* App. 304 Corolla [of garden pea] papilionaceous, white; vexillum large.

3. *Ornith.* The vane or web of a feather.

1867 P. L. SCLATER tr. *Nitzsch's Pterylography* 10 The Barbs..form, with the parts seated upon them, the so-called Vane (*vexillum*). **1872** COUES *N. Amer. Birds* 2 The rhachis ..alone bears vexilla. *Ibid.* 34 Except in the case of a few of the innermost remiges, their outer vexillum..is always narrower than the inner.

vexing ('vɛksɪŋ), *vbl. sb.* [f. VEX *v.* + -ING[1].] The action of the verb in various senses.

a **1450** *Mirk's Festial* 281 þat is of no wexyng of þe fend, but of grace of God. **1530** PALSGR. 284/2 Vexyng or troublyng, *conturbation*. **1611** COTGR., *Inquietation*, a disquieting,..vexing, molesting, troubling. **1617** HIERON *Wks.* II. 263 It is a kind of vexing to him, that he cannot master it. **1660** JER. TAYLOR *Ductor* I. i. §2 The first is that which Nazianzen calls..accusations and vexings of a man when he is in misery.

'**vexing**, *ppl. a.* [f. VEX *v.* + -ING[2].] That vexes; causing vexation.

a **1586** SIDNEY *Psalms* VI. vi, The while a swarm of foes with vexing feates My life besitteth. **1599** DAVIES *Immort. Soul* XXII. vi. (1714) 79 Trembling Fear, and vexing Griefs annoy. **1654** WHITLOCK *Zootomia* 28 Reckoning Impossibles not to concerne our Desires; nor Unavoydables our Feares; nor things past our Remedy, our vexing sorrow. **1684** LEIGHTON *Comm. 1 Peter* v. 8–9 The burden of vexing carefulness. **1727** BAILEY (vol. II), *Vexatiousness*, troublesome, perplexing, vexing Quality. **1762** KAMES *Elem. Crit.* xviii. (1833) 286 From this vexing dilemma I am happily relieved. **1815** SCOTT *Guy M.* xlv, I am glad to see that this vexing job hasna taen awa your appetite, Captain. **1910** *19th Cent.* Feb. 279 Let others seek..the games and pleasures which bring with them a thousand vexing cares.

Hence '**vexingly** *adv.*

1635–56 COWLEY *Davideis* IV. 81 At Courts, and Seats of Justice to complain, Was to be robb'd more vexingly again. **1643** J. CARYL *Expos. Job* I. 868 This they did so vexingly, that they are said to wrest his words. **1710** STEELE *Tatler* No. 269 ¶5 It is the same poverty which makes men speak or write smuttily, that forces them to talk vexingly.

vexor, obs. form of VEXER.

†**vey**, *v.* *Obs.*[−1] [ad. OF. *veier*: cf. SURVEY *v.* and VEYOR.] *trans.* To inspect, examine.

1512 *Act 4 Hen. VIII*, c. 18 §3 Accomptes..to be taken, veyed, surveyede, & comtrolled.

vey, southern ME. var. FEY *a.*; obs. f. WEIGH *v.*

veyage, obs. Sc. f. VOYAGE.

veycht, obs. Sc. f. WEIGHT.

veye, obs. f. WAY *sb.*; obs. Sc. f. WEIGH *v.*

veyȝe, southern ME. var. FEY *a.*

veyle, obs. f. VAIL *sb.*[1]; obs. Sc. f. WELL *adv.*

veyllard, obs. f. VIEILLARD.

veyn, obs. f. VAIN, VEIN, WEEN.

veynde, obs. Sc. f. WIND *v.*

veyne, southern ME. var. FEIGN *v.*; obs. f. VAIN, VEIN.

†**veyne.** *Obs.* Also veine. [a. OF. *veine*, ad. L. *venia* pardon.] = VENY[1].

c **1400** *Rule St. Benet* xliv. 31 When þai say 'Kirieleison', sal sho take hir veine by-fore þe auter at te grece. *c* **1450** in Aungier *Hist. Syon* (1840) 250 Any brother that hathe be seek..schal first ryse and take his veyne for hys defawtes and omissyons in tyme of hys sekenes. *Ibid.* 328 Than..the sustres may take ther veynes, and proclame ther defautes.

†**veyor.** *Obs.* Also 5 veyour, vayowr, 7 veiour (7–8 vejour), veighor. [a. OF. *veiour* (also *veier*, *vaier*, *voier*, etc.), f. *veier* (*voier*): see VEY *v.*] One appointed to view or inspect a thing.

1470 *Little Red Bk. Bristol* (1900) II. 132 Veyours sworne before John Shipward, Meire, to make vewe and put in sight of a grond and tenement. **1493** *Ibid.* 134 The vew of the partable wall,..the namysse of the sayd vayowres and ther verdyt. **1607** COWELL *Interpr.*, *Veiours*,..signifieth in our common lawe those, that are sent by the court to take view of any place in question, for the better descision of the right. *a* **1625** SIR H. FINCH *Law* (1636) 305 An action of deceit.. must be brought during the life of the Sommoners, but not when all the Sommoners and veighors be dead. *Ibid.* 344 To take the land into the Kings hands by the view of lawfull men, called thereupon Veyors.

veyr, southern ME. var. FAIR *a.*; obs. f. VAIR; var. VERE, spring; obs. Sc. f. WAR *sb.*, WEAR *v.*

†**veyra.** *Sc. Obs.* [? Cf. VERA.] (See quot.)

1549 *Compl. Scotl.* vi. 40 Than the marynalis began to veynd the cabil, vitht mony loud cry... And as it aperit to me, thai cryit thir vordis as efter follouis, veyra veyra, veyra veyra, gentil gallandis [etc.].

veyre, obs. southern var. FIRE; obs. f. VAIR.

veyton, var. VETON *Obs.*

vezar, obs. f. VISOR.

veze, obs. var. FEEZE *sb.* and *v.*[1]; var. VEASE *Obs.*

vezir, var. VIZIER.

†**vezon.** *Obs.*[−1] (Meaning obscure.)

1706 E. WARD *Hud. Rediv.* (1707) II. IV. 4 Look, look, Joan, how the Vezons fight. Who'd think they were so full of Spite?

vh-, obs. Sc. variant of WH-.

vi-, *pref.*, reduced form of *vis-* VICE-. (See VICURATE, -POLITIC, -PRESIDENT, -QUEEN.)

‖**via** ('vaɪə, 'viːə), *sb.* [L. *via* a road or way.]

Several senses of the word (by itself or with Latin adjs.), which are recorded in earlier and copied in later Dictionaries, appear to have had no real currency in English.

1. *Via Lactea*, the Milky Way.

1615 [see MILKY WAY 1]. *a* **1635** SIBBES *Breathing after God* (1639) 144 As we say of the *Via lactea*, or Milky way in the heavens,..it is nothing but a deale of light from a company of little starres, that makes a glorious lustre. **1704** J. HARRIS *Lex. Techn.* I, *Milky-way* or *Via Lactea*, the Galaxy, is a broad white Path or Track, encompassing the whole Heavens. **1786** M. CUTLER in *Life*, etc. (1888) II. 238 In the *via lactea* he found the whitish appearance completely resolved into a glorious multitude of stars of all possible sizes. **1797** *Encycl. Brit.* (ed. 3) XIII. 267 He found that the *via lactea* and *nebulæ* consisted of a collection of fixed stars. **1802** O. GREGORY *Treat. Astron.* 42 The *Via Lactea*, Galaxy, or Milky Way, may also be reckoned under the head of constellations. **1840** T. DICK *Sidereal Heavens* 185 This mighty zone..is sometimes termed..the *Via Lactea*, but more frequently..the Milky Way, from its resemblance to the whiteness of milk.

transf. a **1661** FULLER *Worthies, London* II. (1662) 208 Sir Thomas More was..born in Milkstreet, London (the brightest Star that ever shined in that *Via lactea*).

2. a. A way or road; a highway; *esp.* one in Italy or one of the great Roman roads; cf. WAY *sb.*[1] 1 c. Also *fig.*

1673 J. RAY *Observations Journey Low-Countries* 369 We departed from Rome and began our journey to Venice; riding along the Via Flaminia..which reaches as far as Rimini. **1787** J. WILLIAMS (A. Pasquin) *Childr. Thespis* II. (1792) 157 'Tis but few little years since the charms of his voice Made..thousands rejoice;..And by walking approv'd thro the Thespian *via*, Tho' a slave to the tribes, prov'd the Drama's Messiah. **1822** M. WILMOT *Jrnl.* 21–25 May in *More Lett.* (1935) 166 Cecilia Metella's Tomb..so well preserved amidst the many ruined tombs with which the old Via Appia abounds. **1851** E. B. BROWNING *Casa Guidi Windows* I. iv. 8 That winter-hour, in Via Larga, when Thou wert commanded to build up in snow Some marvel of thine art. **1909** W. J. DON in A. Reid *Regality of Kirriemuir* xxiii. 301 It was no mere track, but a substantial *via*, 20 feet wide. **1929** KIPLING *Limits & Renewals* (1932) 99 What was your best day's march on the Via Sebaste? **1973** G. SIMS *Hunters Point* xix. 177 The frontier town of Menton..where the French Route Nationale joins the Italian Via Aurelia. **1984** A. ELLIOT *On Appian Way* 6 This poem represents a journey from Rome to Brindisi, more or less following the Via Appia.

b. *Via Crucis* ('kruːtʃɪs) = *Way of the Cross* s.v. WAY *sb.*[1] 4 g; also *fig.*, an extremely painful experience that has to be borne with fortitude; *Via Dolorosa* (dɒlə'rəʊzə) [L. *dolōrōsus* DOLOROUS *a.*], the route in Jerusalem that Christ is believed to have followed from Pilate's judgement-hall to Calvary; also *fig.*, = fig. sense of prec.

1844 *Orthodox Jrnl.* 10 Aug. 100 Thirteen small altar pieces surround the arena [of the Colosseum], and Benedict XIV. introduced here the *Via Crucis*, or devotion to the passion, performed by a brotherhood of monks every Friday afternoon. **1878** R. L. STEVENSON *Inland Voyage* 186 Fitly enough may the potentate bestride his charger, like a centurion in an old German print of the *Via Dolorosa*; but the toys should be put away in a box among some cotton, until..the children are abroad again. **1901** M. CARMICHAEL *In Tuscany* 236 The loggia is 250 feet in length, on one side of it is a *Via Crucis* in bas-relief, on the other frescoes representing scenes from the life of the Saint. **1904** H. O. STURGIS *Belchamber* ii. 23 Each step in the *via dolorosa* of his existence was fated to be more awful than the last. **1910** C. E. MONTAGUE *Hind let Loose* xv. 290 Fay, with his feeble pity for all souls in trouble, winced to see this one..sneaking ..down the same *via dolorosa*. **1923** G. M. TREVELYAN *Manin & Venetian Revolution* iv. 68 Silvio Pellico, whose narrative of his own martyrdom was the guide-book of Italian patriots on their *via crucis*. **1944** *Horizon* July 71 Every human being makes the *via crucis* from innocence to experience. **1972** *Guardian* 30 Nov. 14/5 'Via Galactica' [*sc.* a play] turns out to be Peter Hall's Via Dolorosa. **1980** O. MANNING *Sum of Things* xix. 154 In the Via Dolorosa a procession was advancing slowly over the spacious, creamy flagstones. **1982** 'M. HEBDEN' *Pel & Staghound* xvii. 191 The Lord never intended the Via Crucis to be travelled with ease, child. **1984** *Observer* 25 Nov. 9/2 Whatever might have happened to other 'wets' on their *via dolorosa* between 1979 and 1983, it was..hardly on the cards that Mrs Thatcher would simply drop Peter Walker.

3. a. *via media*, a middle way; an intermediate course or state. Hence **via-medialism** (see quot. 1881).

1834 J. H. NEWMAN *Via Media* (Tracts for the Times No. 38) sig. A3[v], The glory of the English Church is, that it has taken the Via Media... It lies *between* the (so called) Reformers and the Romanists. **1845** FORD *Handbk. Spain* I. 168 The whole nation..is divided into two classes—bigoted Romanists or Infidels; there is no *via media*. **1866** GEO. ELIOT *F. Holt* Introd. I. 5 They were kept safely in the *via media* of indifference. **1881** *Church Times* XIX. 128 Via-medialism, then, signifies a scheme whereof one party is asked to believe a little more, and the other a little less, than what they conceive to be true. **1886** MRS. LYNN LINTON *Paston Carew* xxxiv, There was no via media, seeing that money was not to be found. **1936** E. UNDERHILL *Worship* xv. 324 The *Via Media* eludes not only the extremes of Catholic and Protestant cultus, but also the heights and deeps of the spiritual life. **1978** *Christian* IV. 355 What the Chalcedonian definition attempted was a compromise, a *via media*, between conflicting interpretations of the union of the human and divine natures of Christ.

b. *Theol.* ***via negativa***, the approach to God in which his nature is held so to transcend man's understanding that no positive statements can be made about it; the way to union with God in which the soul leaves behind the perceptions of the senses and the reasoning of the intellect; also *transf.*, a way of denial; so ***via affirmativa***, the approach to God through positive statements about his nature.

1856 R. A. VAUGHAN *Hours with Mystics* I. IV. ii. 124 These two paths, the *Via Negativa* (or Apophatica) and the *Via Affirmativa* (or Cataphatica) constitute the foundation of his [*sc.* Dionysius's] mysticism. **1899** W. R. INGE *Christian Mysticism* iii. 114 When Luther had the courage to break with ecclesiastical tradition, the *via negativa* rapidly disappeared within the sphere of his influence. **1942** [see ISNESS]. **1956** G. MACLEOD *Only One Way Left* viii. 152 The Via Negativa: the way of interior denial. Unfortunately the Via Negativa cuts dead across the Emmaus Road. **1963** J. A. T. ROBINSON *Honest to God* v. 95 The *via negativa* underlay the whole medieval 'way of perfection'. **1974** *Encycl. Brit. Macropædia* IV. 549/2 He [*sc.* the pseudo-Dionysius] recognizes the partial validity of the positive approach (*via affirmativa*). **1977** *Times Lit. Suppl.* 21 Jan. 88/5 As regards the Revolution, M Meyer's work is an exercise in the *via negativa*.

‖**via** ('vaɪə), *int.* *Obs.* exc. *arch.* Also 6 fia. [It. *via* (special use of *via* way: see prec.) 'an aduerbe of encouraging, much vsed by riders to their horses, and by commanders' (Florio, 1598).]

1. As an exclamation encouraging, inciting, or preparatory to movement or action, = Onward, come on, come along, etc.

1596 *Edward III*, II. ii. 12 Then *via* for the spatious bounds of Fraunce. **1596** SHAKS. *3 Hen. VI*, II. i. 182 Why Via, to London will we march. **1602** MIDDLETON *Blurt, Master Constable* II. B iv b, *Via* for fate, Fortune, loe this is all, At griefes rebound Ile mount, although I fall. **1619** FLETCHER *Mons. Thomas* II. ii, *Tho.* Away then, find this Fidler, and do not miss me By nine a Clock. *La[ncelot]*. Via. **1623** MARKHAM *Cheap & Good Husb.* I. ii. (ed. 3) 15 First the voice, which sounding sharply and cheerefully,.. crying, *Via, how, hey*, and such like, adde a spirit and liuelinesse to the horse. **1820** SCOTT *Monast.* xxi, He exclaimed, 'Thy death-hour has struck—betake thee to thy sword—Via!'

2. As an exhortation or command to depart, = Away, be off, begone.

1596 SHAKS. *Merch. V.* II. ii. 9 The..fiend bids me packe, *fia* saies the fiend, away saies the fiend. **1611** CHAPMAN *May Day* IV. i. 56 Your reward now shall be that I will not cut your strings nor breake your fidles, *via*, away. **1616** B. JONSON *Devil an Ass* II. i, *Via pecunia*! when she's runne and gone, And fled and dead; then will I fetch her, againe. **1818** SCOTT *Rob Roy* vii, Horsewhip the rascal to purpose—via —fly away, and about it.

b. Used to check argument or reply, or to dismiss a subject.

1598 SHAKS. *Merry W.* II. ii. 159 Ah ha, Mistresse Ford and Mistresse Page, haue I encompass'd you? goe to, *via*. **1821** SCOTT *Kenilw.* vii, And what was Ralph Sadler but the clerk of Cromwell,..*via*! I know my steerage as well as they. *Ibid.* xxix, Why, via, let that pass too.

‖**via** ('vaɪə), *prep.* Also viâ. [L. *viā*, abl. sing. of *via* way, VIA *sb.*] **1.** By way of; by the route which passes through or over (a specified place).

1779 J. LOVELL *Let. to Adams* 13 June, A.'s Wks. 1854 IX. 483 This night is the fourteenth since we first had the news of his victory, *via* New Providence. **1813** SIR R. WILSON *Priv. Diary* (1862) II. 139, I would sweep through Berlin, revictual the fortresses, and return *via* Magdeburg. **1833** T. HOOK *Parson's Dau.* III. x, Lord Weybridge..is on his way to London *viâ* Paris. **1856** C. M. YONGE *Daisy Chain* II. xxii. 589 Ethel's misanthropy was happily conducted off *via* the Cocksmoor children. **1882** DE WINDT *Equator* 127, I arranged to proceed through Spain and *viâ* Paris, home. **1899** KIPLING *Stalky & Co.* 56 Beetle..overturned a student's lamp, which dripped, *via* King's papers..on to a Persian rug. **1931** R. FRY *Let.* 3 Mar. (1972) II. 654, I was ever so glad to hear, via Helen, of you. **1958** A. SILLITOE *Saturday Night & Sunday Morning* iv. 60 Arthur and his father walked via the scullery into the living-room. **1959** M. GILBERT *Blood & Judgement* xiii. 138 More..had come to the Police via the Lower Deck of the Royal Navy. **1981** G. HOUSEHOLD *Summon Bright Water* iii. 149 He led me to talk of my interest in ancient economies and thus, via agriculture in the Forest of Dean, eased the way to my impressions of Broom Lodge.

2. By means of, with the aid of.

1930 in *Amer. Speech* VI. 122 Eastbay youth admits thefts via fish pole. **1972** M. KAYE *Lively Game of Death* (1974) vii. 41 Any deal..would have to be..concluded via contracts, attorneys, the whole *schmeer*. **1977** *Rep. Comm. Future of Broadcasting* iv. 30 It would in theory be possible to provide five more services with national coverage via satellite.

viability[1] (vaɪə'bɪlɪtɪ). [ad. F. *viabilité* (1812), or f. VIABLE *a.*[1]: see -ITY.] The quality or state of being viable; capacity for living; the ability to live under certain conditions. Also *transf.*: now *esp.* feasibility; ability to continue or be continued; the state of being financially sustainable.

In common use from *c* 1860.

1843 BOUVIER *Law Dict. U.S.*, *Viability*, med. jur., an aptitude to live after birth; extra uterine life. **1853** SIMPSON *Obstet. Path. & Pract.* 21, I have repeatedly been astonished at the viability of the infant after traction had been applied to it. **1870** MAUDSLEY *Body & Mind* 44 The general and ultimate result of breeding in and in is to produce barrenness and sterility, children of a low degree of viability and of imperfect mental and physical development. **1883** *Cent. Mag.* Sept. 727/1 An animal or plant which is only partly adapted to its conditions of existence is ugly in exact proportion to its lack of viability. **1893** C. B. UPTON *Bases Relig. Belief* 157 It means spiritual viability or immortality. **1955** *Bull. Atomic Sci.* Mar. 81/1 Considerations of defense, in addition to mobilizing offensive strength, do not in the least imply softness or lack of viability. **1962** *Listener* 11 Oct. 549/1 They are a main factor in giving it [*sc.* the country] such economic viability as it possesses. **1971** *Nature* 19 Feb. 518/2 Mr Stein's apparently innocent bill to limit noise at New York airports..could be..a serious threat to the viability of Concorde. **1977** K. M. E. MURRAY *Caught in Web of Words* viii. 150 He also had some doubts about the viability of the work financially.

via'bility[2]. [ad. F. *viabilité* (1878), or f. VIABLE *a.*[2]] The condition of being traversable.

1882 W. CORY *Guide Mod. Eng. Hist.* II. 470 The quality which convicts gave it [Tasmania], can be expressed by one word 'viability': they made some roads.

viable ('vaɪəb(ə)l), *a.*[1] [a. F. *viable* (1539), f. *vie* life: see -ABLE.] Capable of living; able to maintain a separate existence.

a. Of children at (normal or premature) birth.

1828-32 WEBSTER, *Viable*, capable of living, as a new-born infant or premature child. **1859** *Todd's Cycl. Anat.* V. 200/1 The delivery of a fœtus of viable or full-grown size. **1881** *Trans. Obstet. Soc. Lond.* XXII. 276 Such narrowing or deformity of the female pelvis..as will absolutely preclude the birth of a viable child.

b. In other physical applications.

1885 GOODALE *Physiol. Bot.* (1892) 446 Polyembryony [is] the production of two or more viable embryos in a seed. *c* **1890** STEVENSON *In South Seas* I. iv. (1900) 26 To judge by the eye, there is no race more viable; and yet death reaps them with both hands.

c. *fig.* Of immaterial things or concepts. In recent use *esp.* workable, practicable, esp. economically or financially.

1848 *Tait's Mag.* XV. 702 The rest are waiting for the proper medium, the viable medium, the medium of harmony. **1883** G. P. LATHROP *Hawthorne's Wks.* XI. 435 What we have here is a romance in embryo; one, moreover, that never attained to a viable stature and constitution. **1955** *Scottish Jrnl. Theol.* VIII. 93 A viable faith in the twentieth century must be able to take into itself a certain scepticism and relativism with regard to all rational systems. **1958** 'A. BURGESS' *Enemy in Blanket* xv. 174 It was time he..planted the seeds of a viable relationship between his wife and himself. **1958** *Economist* 8 Nov. 485/2 The plans must..be such as to make the farm 'viable or more viable'—i.e. capable..of yielding its occupier at least the income of a skilled agricultural worker. **1962** *Listener* 5 Apr. 605/2 The Russian nuclear capacity appears..to be..not capable of destroying anything like enough of the American potential for a Russian first strike to be a viable proposition. **1962** P. GRADON in Davis & Wrenn *Eng. & Medieval Stud.* 66 This simple explanation..is not viable for another group of texts to which I now wish to turn. **1971** H. MACMILLAN *Riding the Storm* iv. 146 It [*sc.* Jordon] was not in economic terms a viable state without British support. **1977** M. WILES in J. Hick *Myth of God Incarnate* i. 3 They do not of themselves prove that the concept of a 'Christianity without incarnation' is a viable concept.

'viable, *a.*[2] [f. L. *via* way: cf. VIABILITY[2].] Traversable.

1856 *Sat. Rev.* II. 151/2 If the building..has the advantage of standing at the end of a vista, it is but mocking the needs of the many not to make the vista viable.

†**viadant.** *Obs. rare.* [Irreg. ad. Sp., Pg., It. *viandante*, f. *via* way + *andar(e* to go.] A wayfarer, traveller.

1632 LITHGOW *Trav.* III. 129 They are but poorely cled, yet wonderfull kinde to all Viadants. *Ibid.* VIII. 353 The voluntary exposement of many vnnecessary Viadants.

viadge, obs. form of VOYAGE *sb.*

viador, variant of VEEDOR.

viaduct ('vaɪədʌkt). [f. L. *via* way, after AQUEDUCT. So F. *viaduc.*] An elevated structure, consisting of a series of arches or spans, by means of which a railway or road is carried over a valley, road, river, or marshy low-lying ground.

1816 REPTON *Fragm. Landscape Gard.* 161, I have ventured to suggest a hint for such a structure as may support the road.., rather calling it a Via-duct than a Bridge. **1837** *Civil Eng. & Arch. Jrnl.* I. 57 Great Viaduct now erecting over the River Wear, near Sunderland. This viaduct consists of four large and six small arches. **1869** *Times* 15 Oct. 7/5 New bridges and viaducts and new streets can do much in enabling Londoners to pass more quickly to their places of business. **1869** FREEMAN *Norm. Conq.* (1875) III. xii. 240 The modern viaduct, a work worthy of old Roman days.

attrib. **1831** T. GRAHAME *Lett. N. Wood* 23 The Sankey viaduct bridge..consists of nine arches of fifty feet span. **1897** *Daily News* 11 Feb. 6/4 The viaduct ganger, who would be responsible for the erection of timbers.

viaducted ('vaɪədʌktɪd), *a.* [f. VIADUCT + -ED[2].] Provided with a viaduct.

Quot. 1963 is pa. pple. of a finite verb *viaduct.*

1963 *Engineering* 18 Jan. 80 The dual carriageway will be viaducted to link up with existing roads. **1981** J. PEARSON *Kindness of Dr. Avicenna* xviii. 171 The *auto-strada*..a marvel of tunnelled mountains, viaducted gorges.

viage, obs. var. VOYAGE *sb.*

viaggiatory, *a. nonce-wd.* [f. It. *viaggiare* to travel.] Given to travelling about.

1847 MEDWIN *Life Shelley* II. 54 The viaggiatory English old maids, who scorn the continent.

vial ('vaɪəl), *sb.* Forms: α. 4-6 vyol(e, 4-8 viol(e, 4, 6-7 violl(e, 5-6 vyoll(e. β. 5-7 vyal(l, 6 voyalle, vialle, 6-7 viall, 7- vial. [var. *fyole, fiol, fiall*, etc., PHIAL *sb.* See the note on the letter V.] A vessel of a small or moderate size used for holding liquids; in later use *spec.*, a small glass bottle, a phial.

α. **13..** *E.E. Allit. P.* B. 1280 Dere disches of golde & dubleres fayre, þe vyoles & þe vesselment of vertuous stones. *c* **1386** CHAUCER *Can. Yeom. Prol. & T.* 240 Sondry vessels maad of erthe and glas,..Violes, crosletz, and sublymatories, Cucurbites and alembikes. *c* **1400** *Lanfranc's Cirurg.* 185 Sette þe viol vpon soft colis & lete hem boile. **1412-20** LYDG. *Chron. Troy* I. 3052 After þat, for his chefe socour, Sche toke to hym a viol with licour. **1470-85** MALORY *Arthur* v. x. 178 Pryamus toke fro his page a vyolle ful of the four waters that came oute of paradys. **1530** PALSGR. 285/1 Vyole, a glasse, *fiolle, uiole.* *c* **1550** H. LLOYD *Treas. Health* E vj, Mengle them togither and put them in a vyol of glasse, and stop the mouth thereof close. **1609** DEKKER *Ravens Alm.* Wks. (Grosart) IV. 238 The Iewe..spyed the Cioll that the poore man held in his hand vnder his cloak. **1660** BOYLE *New Exp. Phys. Mech.* vi. 53 The Air in the little Viol began to dilate it self. **1705** ADDISON *Italy* 232, I plac'd a thin Viol, well stopp'd up with Wax, within the Smoak of the Vapour.

β. *a* **1450** *Mirk's Festial* 146 He toke vyals of cristall and of lambur and of glas, and put þys blod yn hom. **1530** PALSGR. 284/2 Vyall, a glasse, *fiolle.* **1576** in Feuillerat *Revels Q. Eliz.* (1908) 275 Two glasse voyalles for the Lord Howardes servauntes. **1585** T. WASHINGTON tr. *Nicholay's Voy.* III. ix. 84 b, A cruese or viall ful of sweete and smelling water. **1610** HOLLAND *Camden's Brit.* (1637) 433 Glass vials also and sundry small earthen vessels. **1683** W. HEDGES *Diary* (Hakl. Soc.) I. 86, I gave him a small Vyall of Balme of Gilead. **1747** WESLEY *Prim. Physick* (1762) 67 Put a spoonful of this Water in a Vial. **1756** NUGENT *Gr. Tour, France* IV. 298 The holy vial, containing the oil used at the coronation of their kings. **1820** SHELLEY *Witch Atlas* xvii, Liquors clear and sweet..She in her crystal vials did closely keep. **1842** A. COMBE *Physiol. Digestion* (ed. 4) 114 [He] placed the vial in a basin of water on a sand-bath. **1871** R. H. HUTTON *Ess.* I. 296 France would not be what she is if men had not believed for a thousand years in the holy vial of Rheims.

attrib. and *Comb.* **1647** HEXHAM I, A viall-maker, *een..Fiolen-maker.* **1825** T. HOOK *Sayings* Ser. II. *Man of Many Friends* I. 321 There were two little vial-bottles and a box of corn-plaster in the drawer of the basin-stand. **1880** MRS. CAMERON *Three Flower-Pots* 25 He saw upon the table a large vial bottle with something very black in it.

b. In allegorical or purely figurative use.

Freq. in allusion to Rev. xv. 7, etc. (see first quots.).

1382 WYCLIF *Rev.* xv. 7 Seuen golden violes, ful of the wrathe of God. *Ibid.* xvi. 1 Go ȝe, and schede ȝe out the seuen violes of Goddis wrath in to erthe. *c* **1420** LYDG. *Ballad Commend. Our Lady* 113 O glorious viole, O vitre inviolate! **1603** DRAYTON *Bar. Wars* II. vi, And with a vial fild with baneful wrath,..Which in her blacke hand readily she hath, And drops the poison vpon euery wight. **1611** SHAKS. *Wint. T.* v. iii. 122 You Gods looke downe, And from your sacred Viols poure your graces Vpon my daughters head. **1656** BLOUNT *Glossogr.* s.v., Vials of wrath, mentioned in the Apocalipse, signifie Gods readiness to be fully revenged on sinners. *c* **1680** BEVERIDGE *Serm.* (1729) II. 5 To behold the almighty Creator..pouring out the utmost viols of his wrath..upon them. **1718** PRIOR *Solomon* III. 386 The frighted Angels..o'er the Earth from wrathful Viols pour'd Tempests and Storm. **1780** BURKE *Œcon. Reform* Wks. 1842 I. 239 You have tuns of ancient pomp in a vial of modern luxury. **1820** BYRON *Mar. Fal.* IV. ii. 134 Now the destroying angel hovers o'er Venice, and pauses ere he pours the vial. **1853** KINGSLEY *Hypatia* xvii, Everywhere sensuality, division, hatred, treachery, cruelty, uncertainty, terror; the vials of God's wrath poured out. **1880** W. G. BLAIKIE *Livingstone* vii. 135 For one so patient and good, he had a very large vial of indignation, and on occasion poured it out right heartily over all injustice.

Hence **'vial** *v. trans.*, to put into a vial; also *fig.* **'vialled** *a.*, kept or stored in a vial. **'vialful,** as much as can be contained in a vial.

1634 MILTON *Comus* 847 Helping all urchin blasts, and ill luck signes..Which she with pretious viold liquors heals. **1805** W. TAYLOR in *Ann. Rev.* III. 46 The distilled perfume of the bookmaker's style..is here not sprinkled over every page, and vialled in every sentence. **1886** RUSKIN *Præterita* xii. 404, I had, in my little clay pitcher, vialfuls, as it were, of Wordsworth's reverence [etc.]. **1906** HARDY *Dynasts* II. v. i. 188 The riskful blood of my previsioned line..To linger vialled in my veins alone.

'vial, *a. rare*$^{-1}$. [f. L. *via* way, or ad. L. *viālis.*] Serving for a way or road.

1813 J. FORSYTH *Rem. Excurs. Italy* 353 The arch of Augustus, being a vial one, was necessarily much wider than the triumphal arches, which succeeded.

vial(l, vialle, obs. forms of VIOL *sb.*

‖**viale** ('vjale). Pl. viali. [It.] A broad street in an Italian city.

1969 M. GILBERT *Etruscan Net* I. vii. 88 Broke..drove up the Viale, using dipped headlights. **1979** G. WATSON *Black Jack* xxviii. 236, I..walked over to the window looking on the broad *viale* below. **1982** J. O'FAOLAIN *Obedient Wife* ii. 39 They'd hang around the warm squares and *viali* in groups.

viallin, obs. form of VIOLIN.

vi'ameter. *rare.* [f. L. *via* way + -METER.] A device for recording the number of miles traversed by a wheeled vehicle; a hodometer or cyclometer.

1831-3 *Encycl. Metrop.* (1845) VIII. 311/1 *marg.*, Counting Machines for road carriages, or viameter. **1858** MRS. SINNETT tr. *B. Möllhausen's Diary* I. vi. 75 The viameter gave an accurate measurement of the number of miles passed, by counting the revolutions of the waggon wheel. **1860** WORCESTER. [Hence in later Dicts.]

†**viance.** *Obs.*$^{-1}$ [Alteration of *viandes* (see next) after forms in *-ance*: cf. GARDEVIANCE.] Food, sustenance.

a **1400-50** *Alexander* 4121 He..at þam enquires, Quat was þaire viaunce in þa vales. 'ser, venyson,' þai said.

viand[1] ('vaɪənd). Forms: 4-5 vyaunde, 5 viaunde; 4, 6 vyand(e, 5-8 viande, 6- viand (7 viond). [a. AF. *viaunde, viande*, OF. *viande* (= Sp. and Pg. *vianda*, It. *vivanda*):—pop.L. **vivanda*, for *vivenda*, neut. pl. gerundive of L. *vīvĕre* to live.]

1. *pl.* Articles of food; provisions, victuals.

c **1400** MAUNDEV. (1839) xxiii. 253 Flesche and dyverse vyaundes. *a* **1548** HALL *Chron., Hen. VIII*, 80 b, Then spices, fruites, ielies, and banket viandes were brought. **1597** A. M. tr. *Guillemeau's Fr. Chirurg.* 48 b/2 His viandes, or meate and drincke, must only be Diureticke. **1615** H. CROOKE *Body of Man* 629 Whilst wee chew our meate the Tongue rowleth it selfe on euerie side of the mouth and applyeth it selfe to the Viands to take a say or Taste of them. **1646** J. HALL *Horæ Vac.* 92 A good and strong stomack will convert course viands into good nourishment. **1691** RAY *Creation* I. (1692) 116 Neither of which Viands [honey and bee-bread] is any where to be found amass'd by Nature. **1735** SOMERVILLE *Chase* I. 154 Soon as the growling Pack, with eager Joy, Have lapp'd their smoking Viands. **1805** *Med. Jrnl.* XIV. 555 The means of inducing the invalid or convalescent to derive every benefit that arises from delicacy and variety of viands. **1854** MILMAN *Lat. Chr.* IV. v. (1864) II. 290 He dashed the wine on the earth and scattered about the other viands. **1886** C. BIGG *Chr. Platonists of Alexandria* iii. 104 Viands of every kind..were provided by the liberality of the wealthier brethren.

fig. **1826** LAMB *Elia* II, *Sanity of True Genius*, Lane's novels,..those scanty intellectual viands of the whole female reading public.

transf. **1870** EMERSON *Soc. & Solit., Farming* Wks. (Bohn) III. 61 He will pamper his peaches and grapes on the viands they like best.

†**b.** Applied to a viaticum. *Obs.*$^{-1}$

Compare sense 2 b, quot. 1555.

1607 HIERON *Bapt. Eunuch* (1613) 7 To passe ouer the Sacrament of the supper, to some old people..who must take it (as was said in the daies of superstition) for their viands, being neerer (in opinion and possibility) to their last passage.

2. *sing.* **a.** *collect.* Food, sustenance.

c **1450** LOVELICH *Grail* xvi. 563 Othir viaunde hadde he non verament, But everiday swich as God him sente. *a* **1483** *Liber Niger* in *Househ. Ord.* (1790) 17 His dayly dyet was not muche in sotyle and delicate vyaunde. *c* **1515** *Interl. Four Elem.* 465, I..oft refresshe nature agayne With delycate vyand. *a* **1548** HALL *Chron., Hen. IV*, 7 b, The same treasure [he] spent in folie, not paiyng pore men for their vitail and viande. *Ibid., Edw. IV*, 233 Euery table was abundantly furnished with all sortes of delicate viand. **1607** SHAKS. *Cor.* I. i. 103 The Belly..I' th' midd'st a th' body, idle and vnactiue, Still cubbording the Viand. **1643** PRYNNE *Sov. Power Parl.* I. (ed. 2) 95 All things necessary both for viande and apparell. **1847** TENNYSON *Princ.* IV. 17 Before us glow'd Fruit, blossom, viand, amber wine, and gold. **1862** CALVERLEY *Verses & Transl.* (ed. 2) 46 Say I grow hourly thinner,..Tho' I do try and absorb some viand Each day.

b. With *a*, etc. An article or kind of food. (Cf. 1.)

1527 in Ellis *Orig. Lett.* Ser. III. II. 128 Two small barrylls of a viande vsyd among the lordes here. **1555** W. WATREMAN *Fardle Facions* II. xii. 287 That euery christian manne, when he stode in any daungier of death,..should receiue it [the Sacrament] as a waifaring viande. **1658** R. WHITE tr. *Digby's Powd. Symp.* 36 By this thin viand [the air], they came in lesse than a year to a foot long. **1704** W. KING *Mully of Mountoun* 20 Thy White-wine, Sugar, Milk, together club, To make that gentle viand Syllabub. **1829** LYTTON *Disowned* 7 Not a viand they had fed on but had its appropriate legend. **1849** W. IRVING *Astoria* 320 Having made a 'famous repast', where this viand happened to be unusually plenty. **1865** DICKENS *Mut. Fr.* I. iv, After some discussion..a decision was pronounced in favour of veal-cutlet... R. W. himself went out to purchase the viand.

†**c.** ***viand rial***, as the name of a dish, *spec.* one composed of paste, eggs, sugar, wine, etc., and ornamented with gold and silver foil.

c **1400** MAUNDEV. (1839) xviii. 193 Of theise Snayles.. men maken Vyaunde Rialle, for the Kyng and for other grete Lordes. **14..** *Anc. Cookery* in *Househ. Ord.* (1790) 455 Viande Riall for xl. Mess. [Recipe follows.] *c* **1500** in *Babees Bk.* (1868) 376 Veneson in broth, viaunde Ryalle, veneson rosted.

†**viand²**. *Obs.*⁻¹ [ad. Du. *vijand*: see FIEND.] An enemy.

1616 J. LANE *Contn. Sqr.'s T.* VII. 87 Arme, arme, the viand comes!

†'**viander¹**. *Obs.* Forms: *α.* 4 **vyaundour, viandoure,** 5 *Sc.* **vyanddour, wyandoure.** *β.* 5 **vyander** (?), 6 **vyandre,** 6–7 **viander.** [a. AF. *via(u)ndour, viandere,* OF. *viandiere, viandier,* f. *viande* VIAND¹.]

1. One who provides viands or good cheer for his household or guests; a (liberal) host or entertainer. Usually with adjs., esp. *good.*

c **1330** R. BRUNNE *Chron. Wace* (Rolls) 4076 Knyght was he fol god in stour, & lyberal man, & vyaundour [*v.r.* & metegift man viandoure]. **14..** *Forme of Cury* in Warner *Antiq. Culin.* (1791) 1 Kyng Richard the Secunde kyng of Inglond,..the which was accounted the best and ryallest vyand[er] of alle cristen kynges. *c* **1425** WYNTOUN *Cron.* IX. x. 1130 This Kyng wes wys and debonare; Gud vyanddour, and fed hym fare. **1519** HORMAN *Vulg.* 152 b, Placis to kepe all maner of foulle be requyred in a good vianders house [L. *in domo dapsili*]. **1534** WHITINTON *Tullyes Offices* II. (1540) 101 One called Cimo in Athenes was also a lyberall vyandre to his frendes. **1577** STANYHURST *Descr. Irel.* iv. 18/1 in *Holinshed*, Wherein she fareth lyke one, that, to purchase yᵉ name of a sumptuous francklene or a good viander, woulde bidde diuers guestes to a costly and daintie dinner [etc.].

2. One who provides himself with good cheer; one who is fond of good living.

1539 CRANMER *Let.* in *Misc. Writ.* (Parker Soc.) II. 396 How..prebendaries have..spent..their substance in superfluous belly cheer... Commonly a prebendary is neither a learner, nor teacher, but a good viander. **1780** PEGGE *Pref. to Forme of Cury* p. v, It is certain that Hardicnut stands on record as an egregious glutton, but he is not particularly famous for being a curious Viander.

3. A supplier or seller of provisions.

1598 BARRET *Theor. Warres* v. ii. 151 These vianders, and marchants, doth the Lord Marshall assure and guard. **1622** F. MARKHAM *Bk. War* III. iv. 94 The Armie shall euer haue great resort of Victuallers, Vianders, Sutlers and all occupations to relieve euery want.

4. (See quot. 1778.)

1761 *London Gaz.* 17–21 Jan. 2/1 The Vyanders and Principal Inhabitants of the Borough of Newport. **1778** *Eng. Gazetteer* (ed. 2), *Newport, Cornw[all]*,..has sent members to parliament ever since the 6th of Edward VI, who are returned by two officers, called vianders.

†'**viander²**. *Obs.* Also 6 **viandre,** 7 **-dour.** [ad. OF. *viandier,* f. as prec.] Viands, victuals, food.

a **1548** HALL *Chron., Hen. VI,* 142 b, The Englishemen.. prohibited the Gascoynes to minister to his armie, viandre and sustenaunce. *Ibid.* 148 b, The sumptuous feast..the delicate viander. **1567** MAPLET *Gr. Forest* 105 She..goeth another way to the Viander and vittailes, and there eateth hir fyll. **1625** J. ROBINSON *Ess.* xxxi. (1851) I. 134 Though it seem unreasonable that the less way men have to go, they should be careful for the more viandour and provision for their journey.

†'**viandry.** *Obs.* In 6 **viandrye, -rie, viaundrie.** [f. VIAND¹ + -RY.] = prec.

1542 UDALL *Erasm. Apoph.* 55 They had bounteous stewardes and proctours for all their necessarie store of foode and viandrie. **1543** GRAFTON *Contn. Hardyng* 574 When they had as well sufficiente viandrye as all other thynges ready, they tooke theyr iourney to Welles. **1548** UDALL, etc. *Erasm. Par. Luke* ix. 96 The Apostles had provision of viaundrie.

†'**viary,** *a. Obs. rare.* [ad. L. *viāri-us,* f. *via* way.] Relating to, occurring on, a road or way.

1628 FELTHAM *Resolves* II. xcvi. 282 So in Beasts, in Birds, in Dreames, and all viary Omens, they are onely the guessiue interpretations of dim-ey'd Man: full of doubt, full of deceit. **1656** BLOUNT *Glossogr.*

via'tecture. *rare*⁻⁰. [Irreg. f. L. *via* way, after *architecture.*] (See quot.)

1842 R. PARK *Pantology* (1847) 447 We propose the term Viatecture, as nearly synonymous with Civil Engineering, to include the construction of roads and bridges, railroads, and canals, and water works; and the improvement of rivers and harbors. [Hence in Worcester (1846), etc.]

†**vi'atic,** *sb. Obs.* In 7 **viaticke.** = VIATICUM.

1641 *Impeachm. Father Phillips* x. A iij b, After a Viaticke, hee was dispatched againe for England, with some few small Gifts.

vi'atic, *a. Obs. rare* exc. for revived *nonce-uses.* [ad. L. *viātic-us* (rare), f. *via* way.] (See quot. 1656.)

1656 BLOUNT *Glossogr., Viatick,* pertaining to a journey, or travelling by the way. [Hence in Phillips, Bailey, and later Dicts.] **1974** V. NABOKOV *Look at Harlequins* (1975) IV. i. 156 Look at that strange fever rash of viatic tabulation in which I persevered. **1976** —— *Details of Sunset* 74, I love the process of settling into viatic quarters—the cool linen of the berth, the slow passage of the station's departing lights.

viatical (vaɪ'ætɪkəl), *a.* and *sb.* [f. L. *viātic-us* or *-um*: see prec. and VIATICUM.] **a.** *adj.* Of or pertaining to a way or road; relating to a journey. Chiefly *Bot.* **b.** *sb. pl.* Articles for use on a journey.

1847 H. C. WATSON *Cybele Britannica* I. 66 Viatical. Plants of road-sides, rubbish heaps, and frequented places. **1855** LANDOR *Imag. Conv.* Wks. 1876 II. 450 His back would have been bent..under the weight of armour and viaticals which Titus [Livius] carried with him easily and far. **1863** J. G. BAKER *N. Yorks. Stud. Bot.,* etc. 188 Such stations as are denominated by the terms paludal, viatical, agrestal, sylvestral, and septal exist no longer. **1932** G. C. DRUCE *Comital Flora Brit. Isles* 349 *A[grostis] verticillata*... Viatical. Germanic, Waysides, waste places.

vi'aticated, *a. rare*⁻⁰. [f. L. *viāticāt-us* (Plautus), f. *viātic-um*: see next.] (See quot.)

1727 BAILEY (vol. II), *Viaticated,* furnished with Things necessary for a Journey.

‖**viaticum** (vaɪ'ætɪkəm). Pl. **viatica.** [L. *viāticum* travelling-money, provision for a journey, neut. sing. of *viāticus* (rare), f. *via* way. Hence Sp., Pg., It. *viatico,* F. *viatique.*]

1. *Eccl.* The Eucharist, as administered to or received by one who is dying or in danger of death.

1562 in Cooper *Answ. Priv. Masse* (Parker Soc.) 11 Divers Christians..would..be always sure to have their *viaticum,* as it is termed in the old canons, that is to say, their voyage-provision. **1565** T. STAPLETON *Fortr. Faith* 126 Whiche the auncient fathers called *Viaticum,* the viage provision of Christen men departing oute off this world. *c* **1610** *Women Saints* 78 After that she had receiued her holie *Viaticum* or voiage foode..she departed this life. **1667** in *Cath. Rec. Soc. Publ.* III. 63 Wee durst not giue him the holy viaticum, he being so farre spent. **1685** EVELYN *Mrs. Godolphin* 151 As if presageing what was att hand, she..furnish'd herselfe with the heavenly Viaticum. **1744** in J. O. Payne *Old Eng. Cath. Missions* (1889) 28, I administered the viaticum to Will. Slie at E. Witton, he dyed Sep. 3. **1774** *Ann. Reg.* 151 Many people were dangerously wounded, 18 of whom had the viaticum administered. **1839** [WISEMAN] *Lives St. Alph. Liguori,* etc. 225 Her mother fell so dangerously ill, that the Viaticum was brought to her. **1855** KINGSLEY *Westw. Ho!* xxvi, No absolution, no viaticum, nor anything! I die like a dog! **1894** J. T. FOWLER *Adamnan* Introd. p. liv, Having received the holy viaticum at the hands of St. Kevin, he passed away in peace.

attrib. **1686** tr. *Chardin's Trav. Persia* 101 They make their *Viaticum* Bread once a year; that is to say, upon Holy Thursday.

2. A supply of money or other necessaries for a journey; a sum given or taken to cover travelling expenses.

1582–8 *Hist. James VI* (1804) 100 This was very acceptabill to the Duke, and thairfoir he gaue him a reasonabill viaticum for performance of this fact. **1594** in *Cath. Rec. Soc. Publ.* V. 243 He was sent by his superior into Scotland, and had fiftee[n] crownes for his viaticum. **1621** FLETCHER *Pilgrim* I. ii, A poor viaticum; very good gold, Sir; But holy men affect a better treasure. **1637–50** ROW *Hist. Kirk* (Wodrow Soc.) 423 The Earle of Dumbar dealt many angells of gold pretended for a viaticum, but indeed for voteing. **1649** JER. TAYLOR *Gt. Exemp.* I. vi. 102 The smallnesse of their viaticum and accommodation for their voyage..were so many circumstances of poverty. **1721** WODROW *Corr.* (1843) II. 587 There is L.120 of debt on the Church, and the viaticums are stopped. **1752** in *Scots Mag.* (1753) 512 This pannel caused to be sent him his baggage, and a *viaticum* of money. **1822** T. TAYLOR *Apuleius* XI. 285 When a few days had elapsed, I rapidly collected together my viatica in bundles. **1899** B. CAMM *Brave Days of Old* 85 This money had been given to him by the most munificent Pope Gregory XIII, for his viaticum or travelling expenses the year before.

b. Without article.

1655 FULLER *Ch. Hist.* III. 88 He allowed them only bare *viaticum* to bear their charges. **1883** *Law Rep.* 9 *Probate Div.* 41 *The Gustaf* is an authority in favour of the seamen's claim for viaticum, and it is always the practice to give subsistence money.

c. Provisions taken for use on a journey. Also *transf.* (quot. 1862).

1663 PATRICK *Parab. Pilgr.* xviii, It will be a very good *Viaticum* for you, and in the strength of this Food you may travel many days. **1666** J. DAVIES *Hist. Caribby Isles* 239 Afterwards sitting down on the grass, every one fell to what he had brought along with him for his *Viaticum.* **1701** WOLLEY *Jrnl. New York* (1860) 36 This Indian Corn is their constant Viaticum in their travels and War. **1791** W. BARTRAM *Carolina* 344, I..comforted myself with a frugal repast of biscuit and dried beef, which was all the food my viaticum afforded me by this time. **1862** RAWLINSON *Anc. Mon., Chaldæa* I. 135 In the Chaldæan sepulchres a number of dishes are always ranged round the skeleton, containing the *viaticum* of the deceased person. **1880** W. G. BLAIKIE *Livingstone* v. 89 Purchasing a loaf and a piece of cheese as *viaticum,* he started for a college at Oberlin.

3. *transf.* and *fig.* (from senses 1 and 2).

a **1618** DAVIES *Wittes Pilgr.* Wks. (Grosart) II. 46/1 And sith thy Pilgrimage is almost past Thou needst the lesse *Viaticum* for it. **1640** FLECKNOE *Trav.* xxxiii. (1667) 103 Tis to..travel without *viaticum* for any to..undertake a voyage without the Language of the Country, where he goes. **1649** JER. TAYLOR *Gt. Exemp.* II. §12. 96 The grace of God is our viaticum and entertains us by the way. **1676** HALE *Contempl.* II. (1677) 186 He..hath a great freedom from fear of Death, and no small *viaticum* to attain Tranquillity of mind in his life. **1741** WARBURTON *Div. Legat.* VI. §6 The doctrine of a future state..was their constant viaticum through life. **1775** J. JEKYLL *Corr.* (1894) i. 20 Bunbury's etchings and Sterne's journey are almost as good viaticums in France as the post book. **1853** C. D. YONGE tr. *Laertius* v. 189 Another of his sayings was, that education was the best viaticum for old age. **1891** FARRAR *Soc. & Present Day Quest.* 211 There is all Biography..to nourish you with the viaticum of good examples.

viator (vaɪ'eɪtə(r)). Also 6 **vyatour.** [a. L. *viātor,* f. *via* way. Cf. obs. F. *viateur,* It. *viatore,* Sp. *viador.*] A traveller, a wayfarer.

The ancient Roman sense of 'court-officer, apparitor' is given in various Dicts. from Chambers (1728) onwards.

1504 C'TESS RICHMOND tr. *De Imitatione* IV. i. (1893) 262 He is our helth and redempcyon, and the consolacion of vyatours, and the eternall fruycyon of payntes. **1655** CAPEL *Tentations* 12 Because the sight of God is not a duty of ours whilest we are viators here. **1660** T. WATSON in Spurgeon *Treas. Dav.* Ps. iii. 8 The saints are not only blessed when they are comprehensors, but while they are viators. *a* **1704** T. BROWN *Comm.-pl. Bk.* Wks. 1709 III. II. 128 We find the Inscriptions address'd to the Viator, or Passenger. **1875** RUSKIN *Fors Clav.* liv. 157 Concealed by the fine trees,..so ..that the passing viator remains unappalled by them.

via'torial, *a. rare.* [f. L. *viātōri-us,* f. *viātor*: see prec. and -ORIAL.] Of or pertaining to travelling.

[**1767** A. CAMPBELL *Lexiph.* (1774) 54 We continued our viatorial progression through the royal perambulations.] **1816** KEATINGE *Trav.* I. 5 As to France and Flanders, if ever a subject were exhausted of viatorial novelty, this is the case with regard to these countries.

Hence **via'torially** *adv.*

1880 *Daily Tel.* 22 Nov., The Americans, viatorially considered, are the most patient and long-suffering people in the whole world.

†**via'torian,** *a. Obs.*⁻⁰ [Cf. prec.] (See quot.) Also †**via'torious** *a. Obs.*⁻⁰

1656 BLOUNT *Glossogr., Viatorian,* belonging to the way, travelling or journeying, or serving to way-faring-men. **1727** BAILEY (vol. II), *Viatorious,* belonging to the Way.

†'**viatory,** *a. Obs. rare.* [ad. L. *viātōri-us.*] Of the nature of wayfaring.

1629 DONNE *Serm.* Wks. 1839 V. 251 In a word, this is our viatory, our preparatory, our initiatory, and inchoative blessedness. **1667** WATERHOUSE *Fire Lond.* 86 A Militant condition and a viatory state.

vibe (vaɪb), *sb.* **1.** *pl.* Abbrev. of VIBRAPHONE. *colloq.*

1940 *Swing* July 17 Lastly, some too-formal ensemble riffing with vibes. **1957** L. FEATHER *Bk. Jazz* xvi. 134 Adrian Rollini, known earlier as a bass saxophonist, had been concentrating on vibes since the early 1930s. **1962** J. WAIN *Strike Father Dead* v. 211 He could play just as well with a group led by an alto and including vibes, clarinet..or even flute. **1977** *Rolling Stone* 24 Mar., He fell back on his musical training to support the family, playing trumpet and vibes in a succession of third-rate cabaret bands.

2. Abbrev. of VIBRATION 3 d. Usu. *pl. slang.*

1967 *Sunday Times* 1 Oct. 10 We're not getting the right vibes. **1970** J. LENNON in J. Wenner *Lennon Remembers* (1973) 67 'You give off bad vibes.' That's what George said to her [*sc.* Yoko Ono] and we both sat through it, and I didn't hit him, I don't know why. **1972** *Daily Tel.* (Colour Suppl.) 1 Dec. 56/1 As I arrive they have finished rehearsing *Hair* in the lobby [of the Chateau Marmont, Los Angeles]. .. Will this diminish the place's vibes? **1976** *New Mus. Express* 31 July 16/1, I remember when I first saw The Grateful Dead... I didn't like them much but I felt that same vibe—something is happening. **1981** P. CAREY *Bliss* iv. 151 Always give out a good vibe, never let them think you hate them. **1983** E. ROSSITER *Lemon Garden* vi. 96 The damned thing's got bad vibes... Throw it in the lake.

Hence '**vibist,** a player on the vibraphone.

1955 *Jazzbook 1955* 20 The musicianly sounds produced by vibist Milt Jackson and pianist Thelonius Mark. **1962** *Melody Maker* 21 July 7/1 The vibist's phrasing shows his early Gospel penchant. **1977** *Listener* 23 June 829/2 Drummer/vibist Cal Tjader.

‖**vibex** ('vaɪbɛks). *Path.* Pl. **vibices** (vaɪ-, vɪ'baɪsiːz). [L. *vībex, vībix* mark of a blow or stripe, a weal.] A long and narrow mark or patch in the skin caused by the subcutaneous extravasation of blood, occurring esp. in some fevers. Usually in pl.

[**1693** in *Blancard's Phys. Dict.* (ed. 2). **1706** PHILLIPS (ed. Kersey), *Vibex,*..a black and blew Spot occasioned by a Flux of Blood.] **1771** *Encycl. Brit.* III. 68/2 The *vibices,* or large livid or dark greenish marks, seldom appear till very near the fatal period. **1793** BEDDOES *Consump.* 115 Dark coloured spots, vibices, or any other scorbutic symptoms. **1822–7** GOOD *Study Med.* (1829) II. 164 Petechial spots, vibices, and hemorrhages from different parts. **1876** BRISTOWE *Th. & Pract. Med.* 208 In malignant cases [of diphtheria]..petechiæ and vibices appear..beneath the skin.

†'**vibrable,** *a. Obs.*⁻⁰ [ad. L. *vibrābilis,* f. *vibrāre* to brandish, shake.] 'That may be shaken or brandished' (Bailey, 1727, vol. II).

vi'bracular, *a. Zool.* [f. VIBRACUL-UM + -AR.] Of or pertaining to, of the nature of, vibracula; furnished with vibracula.

1891 *Cent. Dict.* **1896** HARMER *Polyzoa* xvii. (Camb. Nat. Hist. II.) 486 The large vibracular zoœcia occupy nearly the whole of the surface.

vi'braculoid, *a. Zool.* [f. next + -OID.] Resembling (that of) a vibraculum or vibracula.

1896 HARMER *Polyzoa* xvii. (Camb. Nat. Hist. II.) 484 Avicularium with vibraculoid mandible. *Ibid.* 485 In *Microporella ciliata*..the avicularia are very variable, and in some cases take on a 'vibraculoid' character.

‖**vibraculum** (vaɪ'brækjʊləm). *Zool.* Pl. **-cula.** [mod.L., f. L. *vibrāre* to shake.] One of the long whip-like movable processes or organs possessed by certain polyzoans; now regarded as a modified zooid.

1854 S. P. WOODWARD *Mollusca* 165 Eye tentacles deflected at the tips, beyond the eyes; vibracula much shorter, also deflected. **1865** GOSSE *Land & Sea* (1874) 225 But..there are some special organs of defence which were wanting in the Canda. One of these is called the vibraculum, or the whiplash. **1877** HUXLEY *Anat. Inv. Anim.* viii. 457 The dilated bases of the vibracula contain muscles by the contraction of which the flagelliform appendage is moved.

vibraharp ('vaɪbrəhɑːp). [f. HARP *sb.*[1], after VIBRAPHONE.] A vibraphone; orig., a proprietary name for a particular U.S. make of vibraphone.

1930 *Official Gaz.* (U.S. Patent Office) 15 Apr. 545/1 J. C. Deagan, Inc., Chicago, Ill. Filed Jan. 22, 1930. *Vibra-harp.* .. Claims use since Aug. 1, 1928. **1949** L. FEATHER *Inside Be-Bop* III. 88 Milton Jackson, vibraharp; b. Detroit, 1923. **1959** [see *electric guitar* s.v. ELECTRIC *a.* 2 b]. **1968** *Jazz Monthly* Jan. 25/2 The programme too is attractively old-fashioned..and the accompaniment, on most tracks by guitar, clarinet, vibraharp, organ and drums, discreet and musicianly. **1977** *Melody Maker* 26 Mar. 34/1 The history of the vibraphone (or vibraharp, as it's sometimes called) in jazz has been strictly delineated by its most famous exponents.

Hence **'vibraharpist**, a player on the vibraharp.

1943 *Metronome* Oct. 32/1 Darned if I can remember hearing ten vibraharpists in my life! **1966** *Melody Maker* 29 Jan. 8/6 Ayers is a vibraharpist. **1978** *Country Life* 5 Oct. 1003/3 Milt Jackson..the great vibraharpist.

Vibram ('vaɪbrəm). Also **vibram**. The proprietary name of a kind of moulded rubber sole used on climbing boots; also applied to a boot having this sole; so **Vibram-soled** *a.* Also *absol.*

1950 tr. *Mountaineering Handbk.* (Assoc. Brit. Members Swiss Alpine Club) ii. 22 Later experience shows that boots with moulded rubber soles—'Vibrams'—are an advantage on rock climbs but are dangerous on greasy or iced rock. **1957** CLARK & PYATT *Mountaineering in Britain* xvi. 237 Vibrams, boots whose soles consisted of rubber moulded into the shape of conventional nails, were just becoming available in Britain when war broke out. **1963** 'G. CARR' *Lewker in Norway* iv. 76 The climbing breeches, thick stockings, and Vibram-soled boots he would wear. **1976** *Trade Marks Jrnl.* 24 Nov. 2470/1 *Vibram*... Soles, heels, heel-tips, cork-soles and intersoles for shoes. Vibram S.p.A. .., Albizzate, Italy; manufacturers and merchants. **1979** C. MCNEISH *Youth Hostelling* ii. 15 I'm sure you can visualise the effect a hundred pairs of vibram-soles a day can have on a lino floor.

vibrancy ('vaɪbrənsɪ). [f. next: see -CY.] The condition or quality of being vibrant.

1895 *Funk's Stand. Dict.* **1906** *Sat. Rev.* 8 Dec. 703/1 With a vibrancy of tone that seemed to bring her voice quite close to him.

vibrant ('vaɪbrənt), *ppl. a.* [ad. L. *vibrant-*, *vibrans*, pres. pple. of *vibrāre* to VIBRATE. Cf. F. *vibrant*, Sp., Pg., and It. *vibrante*.]

†**1. a.** Agitated with anger or emotion. *Obs.*$^{-1}$

c **1550** ROLLAND *Crt. Venus* I. 735 This is the case I haif to ȝow to mene, Quhilk in ane part to ȝow als dois pertene, As to my self, thocht I be mair vibrant.

†**b.** Moving or acting with rapidity or energy; stirring. *Obs.*$^{-1}$

1616 LANE *Contn. Sqr.'s T.* XI. 295 Next came a stowt couragious vibrant knight, larglie proportiond, and as large of might.

†**2.** *Her.* Brandishing, flourishing. *Obs.*$^{-1}$

1572 BOSSEWELL *Armorie* II. 97 b, P. beareth Gules and Sable,..a Lyon rampaunt d'Or, vibrante a sworde d'Argente.

3. a. Moving or quivering rapidly; vibrating.

1616 LANE *Contn. Sqr.'s T.* VI. 273 Theare, theare, three squares of vibrant pikes out glides. *Ibid.* VIII. 222 Till pikes, and pikes,..sidewise, and foreright, vibrant thrustes in strikes. **1762** FALCONER *Shipwr.* I. 239 While Phœbus down the vertic' circle glides: He, o'er th' horizon, vibrant seems to swim, And, tangent, sweeps it with his nether limb. **1817** W. TAYLOR in *Monthly Mag.* XLIII. 236 His voice of song ..Thro' their crystalline caves the vibrant billows bear. **1860** O. W. HOLMES *Elsie V.* (1861) 136 She danced with a kind of passionate fierceness,..her round arms wreathing and unwinding, alive and vibrant to the tips of the slender fingers. **1876** DOWDEN *Poems* 22 A vibrant tongue Had in a moment pricked upon my brow The mystic mark.

transf. **1858** W. CORY *Ionica* 87 That vibrant hearts of ours repeat What they with him were wont to feel.

b. Vibrating or thrilling *with* something.

1867 BAILEY *Universal Hymn* 8 Ye orbs,..Even the nebulous star,..with fearful joy Vibrant, conclude God is. **1883** *Cent. Mag.* Oct. 828/2 The greatest of commercial communities,..so stirring and vibrant with commerce and speculation. **1895** ZANGWILL *Master* II. vii. 213 The wonderful city..vibrant with the swirl of perpetual currents of traffic.

4. Of sound: Characterized by, exhibiting, vibration; resonant.

1848 BAILEY *Festus* (ed. 3) 204 While yet these words were vibrant on my tongue. **1874** HOWELLS *Foregone Concl.* viii, The vibrant accents of Chiozza. **1892** ZANGWILL *Bow Mystery* 117 The speaker paused a moment, his low vibrant tones faltering into silence.

Hence **'vibrantly** *adv.*

1926 *Record Home & Mission Wk. United Free Church of Scotland* July 316/1 The Christian Church should make its protest vibrantly felt. **1976** *Gramophone* Mar. 1481/1 The warm, vibrantly sympathetic recording acoustic makes no little contribution.

vibraphone ('vaɪbrəfəʊn). *Mus.* [f. VIBRA(TION, VIBRA(TO, etc. + -PHONE I.] A percussion instrument consisting of a series of metal bars, arranged as in a xylophone, and characterized by the vibrato that can be given to the notes, an effect produced either by electrically rotated vanes in the tube resonators under the bars or electronically.

1926 [see MARIMBAPHONE]. **1929** *Melody Maker* Apr. 359/1 Lester takes a Vibraphone solo. **1934** S. R. NELSON *All about Jazz* ii. 51 The leading drummers..are expert on the xylophone and vibraphone. **1957** L. FEATHER *Bk. Jazz* xvi. 134 The vibraphone, like the xylophone, was an instrument long associated with novelty music. **1966** *Listener* 10 Mar. 364 The programme was completed by Stockhausen's *Refrain*, for piano, celesta, and vibraphone. **1978** P. GRIFFITHS *Conc. Hist. Mod. Music* ix. 137 The vibraphone is used as a substitute for the gamelan while xylorimba and percussion suggest the influence of black African music.

Hence **'vibraphonist**, a player on the vibraphone.

1929 *Melody Maker* Dec. 1119/1 Amateur vibraphonists are requested not to attempt to copy it! **1978** *Detroit Free Press* 16 Apr. (Detroit Suppl.) 29/2 How else could he have known that Milt Jackson would become one of the world's greatest vibraphonists.

'vibrate, *pa. pple.* and *ppl. a. rare.* [ad. L. *vibrāt-us*, pa. pple. of *vibrāre*: see next.]

†**a.** *pa. pple.* Vibrated (cf. VIBRATE *v.* 7 b.).

c **1420** LYDG. *Ballad Commend. Our Lady* 115 O fyry Tytan, persing with thy bemes, Whos vertuous bryghtnesse was in thi brest vibrat.

b. *ppl. a.* Vibrating *with* something. *rare*$^{-1}$.

1849 *Tait's Mag.* XVI. 9 The sightless belfry clock..had ..rung, vibrate with triumph.

vibrate (vaɪ'breɪt, older 'vaɪbreɪt), *v.* [f. L. *vibrāt-*, ppl. stem of *vibrāre* to move rapidly to and fro, to brandish, shake, etc. So F. *vibrer*, Sp. and Pg. *vibrar*, It. *vibrare*.]

I. †**1.** *intr.* Of persons: To move to and fro in a fight or struggle. *Obs.*$^{-1}$

1616 LANE *Contn. Sqr.'s T.* IX. 177 Pusshinge, repusshinge, vibratinge agen, as valient mortal and immortal men.

2. Of a pendulum, etc.: To swing to and fro; to oscillate.

1667 *Phil. Trans.* II. 440 A Pendulum..three foot, three inches..between the middle of the Bullet and the upper end of the Thread, where it is fastned..when it vibrates. **1698** KEILL *Exam. Th. Earth* (1734) 265 At Cayenne in America, ..it is observ'd, that a Pendulum Vibrating in a second is shorter [etc.]. *Ibid.* 279 The Gravity where the swiftest Pendulum Vibrates. **1704** S. CLARKE *Attributes* iii. (1738) 26 Pendulums, which (being of equal Lengths and unequal Gravities) vibrate in equal Times. **1827** N. ARNOTT *Physics* I. 96 Long pendulums vibrate more slowly than short ones. **1827** FARADAY *Chem. Manip.* ii. (1842) 33 To ascertain that they [i.e. balances] really are in adjustment; and that, after vibrating freely, they take a horizontal position. **1883** *Encycl. Brit.* XV. 718/1 The double complex pendulum, when it vibrates in one plane.

3. a. Of sounds: To strike *on*, sound *in*, the ear, etc., with an effect like that of a vibrating chord; to resound; to continue to be heard. Chiefly *poet.*

1735 POPE *Prol. Sat.* 357 The whisper, that to greatness still too near, Perhaps, yet vibrates on his Sov'reign's ear. **1742** YOUNG *Nt. Th.* III. 91 Her song still vibrates in my ravisht ear. **1797** MRS. RADCLIFFE *Italian* i, The touching accents of her voice still vibrating on his heart. **1813** BYRON *Corsair* I. xvi, He hears The clang of tumult vibrate on his ears. **1821** SHELLEY '*Music, when* [etc.]' 2 Music, when soft voices die, Vibrates in the memory. **1910** MACINTOSH *Poets Ayrshire* 46 The sound of the anvil had ceased to vibrate in the streets.

b. To circulate *about*, move or pass *through*, pierce or penetrate *to*, by or as by vibration.

1756 W. TOLDERVY *Hist. 2 Orphans* IV. 167 This strange news had vibrated about the town. **1764** GOLDSM. *Trav.* 220 Those powers that..Catch every nerve, and vibrate through the frame. **1836** *Johnsoniana* 323 Surely the finest sensibilities must vibrate through his frame, since they breathe so sweetly through his song! **1844** H. H. WILSON *Brit. India* I. 211 The consequences of the ambition of the French Emperor thus vibrated to the heart of Asia. **1863** GEO. ELIOT *Romola* xl, The voice..had vibrated through her more than once before. **1875** B. TAYLOR *Faust* I. Notes 230 The puppet-play echoed and vibrated in many tones through my mind.

4. To move or swing backwards and forwards, or upwards and downwards, with some degree of rapidity; to quiver, shake, or tremble.

1756 BURKE *Subl. & B.* Wks. I. 267 The whole capacity of the eye, vibrating in all its parts, must approach near to the nature of what causes pain. **1802** *Med. Jrnl.* VIII. 345 The heart continued the whole time to vibrate..about thirty times in a minute. **1816** TUCKEY *Narr. Exped. R. Zaire* iii. (1818) 91 A variety of palm trees vibrating in the breeze. **1853** KANE *Grinnell Exp.* xxix. (1856) 250 The timbers.. vibrated so as to communicate to you the peculiar tremor of a cotton-factory. **1897** MARY KINGSLEY *W. Africa* 358 The burning heat..making the whole desolate, hideous scene vibrate before your eyes as you can see things vibrating through the hot air over a line of gas jets.

b. *spec.* in *Physics* (see VIBRATION 3).

1774 GOLDSM. *Nat. Hist.* (1776) II. 163 If we strike a bell, or a stretched string, for instance,..a single blow produces a sound..which is multiplied as often as it happens to undulate, or vibrate. **1812-6** PLAYFAIR *Nat. Phil.* (1819) I. 287 A musical string may vibrate, but if it is touched by a bit of cloth, or any soft body, no sound is heard. **1832** BREWSTER *Nat. Magic* viii. 180 If this string is taken by the middle and pulled aside, or if it is suddenly struck, it will vibrate between its two fixed points. **1871** TYNDALL *Fragm. Sci.* (1879) I. xiv. 384 When a hammer strikes a bell, the latter vibrates. **1875** MANNING *Mission H. Ghost* i. 25 You know that if you strike a note of music, all the octave notes will vibrate.

c. *transf.* and *fig.*

1813 SHELLEY *Q. Mab.* III. 186 When Nero..felt A new-created sense within his soul Thrill to the sight, and vibrate to the sound. **1852** MRS. STOWE *Uncle Tom's C.* xl, Nerve and bone of that poor man's body vibrated to those words. **1862** BURTON *Bk. Hunter* I. 46 A hidden pang or gust of wrath has vibrated behind that placid countenance. **1898** 'MERRIMAN' *Roden's Corner* xxix. 306 The sight of him, the sound of his voice, stirred something within her that vibrated for hours.

5. *fig.* To move or oscillate *between* (or *betwixt*) two extreme conditions, opinions, etc.; to fluctuate or vary *from* one extreme *to* another. Also without const.: To vacillate in opinion.

1782 PRIESTLEY *Inst. Relig.* (ed. 2) II. 107 A person who is less conversant in these things would feel his mind, as it were, vibrate between both [gains and losses]. **1798** *Survey Province of Moray* iii. 279 The number of scholars vibrates from 20 to 90. **1818** RANKEN *Hist. France* V. v. 403 The marc of silver..vibrated betwixt 5 livres and 20 or 30 livres. **1857** MAURICE *Mor. & Met. Philos.* IV. viii. §33. 466 The third method is to vibrate between these two opposite statements. **1874** GREEN *Short Hist.* ix. §1. 589 The life of a man of fashion vibrated between frivolity and excess. **1875** MERIVALE *Gen. Hist. Rome* lxxi. 582 While his susceptible imagination was in this state of fusion, his rival..was vibrating furiously from one side to the other.

II. †**6.** *trans.* To brandish or flourish (a sword). *Obs. rare.* (Cf. VIBRANT *ppl. a.* 2.)

1634 SIR T. HERBERT *Trav.* 188 They..shake and vibrate their Swords vpon their Shields. *Ibid.* 207 In this their Extasie..the boyes..vibrate a readie sword against the beholders.

7. To throw with vibratory motion; to launch or hurl (a thunderbolt, sentence, etc.). Now *Obs.* or *arch.*

1641 'SMECTYMNUUS' *Answ.* ix. (1653) 39 Excommunication..was never vibrated but by the hand of those that laboured in the Word and Doctrine. **1660** H. MORE *Myst. Godl.* To Rdr. p. xxi, Such a Bishop as I have hitherto described.., that..vibrates that sacred thunder and lightning, the truely-dreadfull sentence of Excommunication. **1664** —— *Myst. Iniq.*, *Apol.* 555 Though I must confess that this is very stoutly and smartly vibrated, as a dart from a strong and agil arm. **1840-1** DE QUINCEY *Style* III. in *Lett. Self-Educ.*, etc. (1860) 272 That orator [i.e. Pericles] of whom (amongst so many that vibrated thunderbolts) it was said peculiarly that he thundered and lightened. **1846** LANDOR *Imag. Conv.* II. 44/2 Many vibrate sharp comminations from the embrasures of portentously slit sleeves.

b. To emit, give forth, send out (light, sound, etc.) by, or as by, vibration or vibratory motion.

c **1643** LD. HERBERT *Autobiog.* (1824) 59 A Foil..whereby it [i.e. a diamond] may the better transmit and vibrate its native Lustre and Rays. **1665** HOOKE *Microgr.* 218, I have seen the Dog-starr to vibrate so strong and bright a radiation of light. **1788** *Encycl. Brit.* (ed. 3) I. 81/2 As to the frequency with which they [*sc.* chords] vibrate the deepest tones. **1810** W. TAYLOR in *Monthly Mag.* XXIX. 418 O chear, Editha, and allow thy bosom To vibrate sympathy. **1864** TENNYSON *Aylmer's F.* 578 Star to star vibrates light. **1874** *Contemp. Rev.* XXIV. 421 Any number of strings that are in unison will vibrate an answer to one of themselves when struck.

8. Of a pendulum, etc.: To measure (seconds) by vibration; also, to swing (so many times).

1667 *Phil. Trans.* II. 440 A Pendulum, vibrating Seconds, ..must be three foot, three inches, and one fifth of an inch long. *Ibid.* 441 A Pendulum, held in the hand, vibrating 58 single strokes in a Minute. **1704** W. DERHAM *Ibid.* XXV. 1785 The Movements..were an Eight day Clock vibrating seconds, and an Half-seconds Movement of mine. **1760** in *Sixth Rep. Dep. Kpr.* App. II. 130 A pendulum..which.. will vibrate seconds in a true and regular manner. **1803** J. WOOD *Princ. Mech.* viii. 173 A pendulum which vibrates seconds in very small arcs. **1871** C. DAVIES *Metr. Syst.* II. 22 The length of a pendulum which should vibrate seconds at a given point on the earth's surface.

9. To give a vibratory motion to (something); to cause to move to and fro or up and down, esp. with a quick motion; to put in vibration.

a **1700** EVELYN *Diary* 19 Sept. 1657, 2 Virginian rattlesnakes..swiftly vibrating and shaking their tailes. **1728** YOUNG *Love Fame* VI. 107 With skill she vibrates her eternal tongue, For ever most divinely in the wrong. **1796** MORSE *Amer. Geog.* I. 221 Their tails terminate with a hard horny spur, which they vibrate very quick when disturbed. **1822** T. TAYLOR *Apuleius* VII. 145 Though I vibrated my pendulous lips with excessive rotundity. **1879** G. PRESCOTT *Sp. Telephone* 115 Bars, which, when to be vibrated by the action of heat, are made of brass. *a* **1887** C. C. ABBOTT *Naturalist's Rambles* 303 The last spotted adder..vibrated the tail in a very marked manner.

b. *fig.* or in fig. context.

1815 KEATS *Ode to Apollo* v, Each vibrates the string That with its tyrant temper best accords. **1875** LOWELL *Wordsworth* Pr. Wks. 1890 IV. 365 He saw man such as he can only be when he is vibrated by the orgasm of a national emotion. **1876** —— *Among my Bks.* Ser. II. 165 The 'Muiopotmos' pleases us all the more that it vibrates in us a string of classical association.

c. *refl.* To bring *into* a certain state by or after vibration. *rare*$^{-1}$.

a **1849** POE *Tales, Monos & Una* (ad fin.), That feeble thrill had vibrated itself into quiescence.

Hence **vibrating** *vbl. sb.*

1743 EMERSON *Fluxions* 303 To find the Time of a Pendulum's vibrating in the Arch of a Cycloid. **1882** BAIN *Mill* iii. 133 There was a clear walk, which was his principal place for 'vibrating', as he [Bentham] called his indoor exercise.

vibrated (see the vb.), *ppl. a.* [f. prec. + -ED[1].] That has been vibrated; *spec.* designating or pertaining to concrete which is being or has been compacted with a vibrator (VIBRATOR 1 b(*a*)).

1669 *Addr. Young Gentry Eng.* 58 The pale face, vibrated eies, inequal pulse.. shew this to be under an acute feaver. **1930** *Concrete & Constructional Engin.* XXV. 686/1 The vibrated concrete acts like a liquid and the vibrator rises automatically. **1948** *Archit. Rev.* CIII. 148 The roof-covering is of pre-cast vibrated concrete slabs. **1976** *Derbyshire Times* (Peak ed.) 3 Sept. 10/6 (Advt.), Paving slabs... Remanufactured top quality vibrated plain and coloured paving in a range of sizes.

vibratile ('vaɪbrətɪl, -aɪl), *a.* [ad. mod.L. **vibratilis*: see VIBRATE *v.* + -ILE. Cf. F. *vibratile.*]

1. Of the nature of vibration; marked or characterized by vibration; vibratory.

1826 KIRBY & SP. *Entomol.* IV. xlvi. 301 Motion: ..*Vibratile*,..when there is a constant oscillation of any part. **1857** *Edin. Rev.* July 36 The effect is produced..by the propagation of alternating atomic polarisations in a vibratile way. **1862** H. W. FULLER *Dis. Lungs* 36 A body not possessed of much molecular elasticity or vibratile power. **1881** MIVART *Cat* 245 The vibratile, lashing action of the spermatozoon.

2. Of cilia, etc.: Endowed with the power of vibration; having a rapid and constant oscillatory movement.

1835-6 *Todd's Cycl. Anat.* I. 108/2 *Polygastrica*,..aquatic animals,..with a circular exsertile dental apparatus around the mouth, and with vibratile cilia for respiration and progressive motion. **1874** LUBBOCK *Orig. & Met. Ins.* iii. 55 This larva swims by means of minute vibratile hairs or ciliae. **1888** ROLLESTON & JACKSON *Anim. Life* 861 The longer process is vibratile and breaks away; the other becomes vibratile as soon as it has absorbed the remaining protoplasm.

b. *transf.* Of persons, or parts of the body.

1858 O. W. HOLMES *Aut. Breakf.-t.* viii. (1883) 158 She [a woman] is vibratile and resonant all over. **1898** H. G. WELLS *Personal Matters* 135 One has to resort to the extended arm and fingers vibratile.

vibra'tility. *rare*$^{-1}$. [Cf. prec.] The quality of being vibratile; vibratory power.

1747 tr. *Astruc's Fevers* 183 The different degrees of the spissitude and excication [*sic*] of the fluids, and vibratility of the solids. **1828-32** WEBSTER (citing Rush), *Vibratility*, disposition to preternatural vibration or motion.

vibrating (see the vb.), *ppl. a.* [f. VIBRATE *v.*]

1. Of, or characterized by, vibration; causing vibration; vibratory.

1685 BOYLE *Effects Motion* ix. 108 That a vibrating motion is thereby produced, may be argued by the dancing of the water. **1710** J. HARRIS *Lex. Techn.* II, *Vibrating-Motion*, is a very quick and short Motion of the solid Parts of Bodies, caused by the Pulse or Stroke of some Body upon them. **1765** *Phil. Trans.* LV. 105 This weight supported him in a vibrating state. **1782** A. MONRO *Compar. Anat.* (ed. 3) 252 The vibrating force of arteries. **1828** J. M. SPEARMAN *Brit. Gunner* (ed. 2) 313 The angular velocities of the vibrating system.

2. That vibrates; having a vibratory motion; oscillating.

17.. RAMSAY *Ep. to Friend at Florence* 33 The vib'rating harmonious strings, And breathing tubes, which the soft eunuch sings. **1743** EMERSON *Fluxions* 230 The Center of Oscillation is the Point in the Axis of a vibrating Body [etc.]. **1834** MRS. SOMERVILLE *Connex. Phys. Sci.* xviii. 154 Suppose a vibrating string to give the lowest C of the pianoforte. **1860** TYNDALL *Glac.* II. i. 225 The little songster's organ of voice..is a vibrating instrument, resembling..the reed of a clarionet. **1879** STAINER *Music of Bible* 149 A sistrum, either with three rings on each bar, or with three vibrating bars.

b. Of machines or their parts, implements, etc.

1831-3 *Encycl. Metrop.* (1845) VIII. 188/1 Vibrating engine... It may be worked either by high or low pressure steam, or by means of a vacuum. **1837** HEBERT *Engin. & Mech. Encycl.* II. 711 The vibrating lever, called the tumbling-bob. **1842** FRANCIS *Dict. Arts* s.v., [In the] Vibrating Steam Engine,..the steam cylinder vibrates upon two hollow gudgeons. **1875** KNIGHT *Dict. Mech.* 2709/2 Vibrating-propeller... Vibrating-roller. **1878** PRESCOTT *Sp. Telephone* (1879) 36 In the latest form of transmitter..the vibrating diaphragm is done away with altogether.

c. Of insects, etc.: Having vibratile antennæ or cilia. *rare.*

1870 tr. *Pouchet's Universe* III. iii. 163 Some ichneumons, or *vibrating flies*, are much more rapacious and bold.

3. Of sound: Vibrant.

1849 JAMES *Woodman* ix, The swinging of the great bell, as it continued to pour forth its loud vibrating call for assistance. **1898** *Allbutt's Syst. Med.* V. 754 In different cases it [i.e. a pericardial friction-fremitus] is described as harsh and grating, rasping, vibrating, or creaking.

Hence **vi'bratingly** *adv.*

1835 *New Monthly Mag.* XLIV. 280 A note to which all the tender sympathies of Miss Fanny vibratingly responded.

vibration (vaɪ'breɪʃən). [ad. L. *vibrātiōn-*, *vibrātio*, n. of action f. *vibrāre* to VIBRATE. So F. *vibration*, It. *vibrazione*, Sp. *vibracion*, Pg. *vibração.*]

†**1.** (See quots. and cf. VIBRATE *v.* 6.) *Obs.*$^{-0}$

1656 BLOUNT *Glossogr.*, *Vibration*, a brandishing, shaking, or wagging, as men do drawn swords, when they threaten others.

2. a. The action on the part of a pendulum or similarly suspended body of moving or swinging to and fro; oscillation.

1668 WILKINS *Real Char.* 191 The most probable way for the effecting of this, is that which was first suggested by Doctor Christopher Wren, namely, by Vibration of a Pendulum. **1700** MOXON *Math. Dict.*, *Vibration*, the Motion of a Pendulum in a Clock, which moves in the long sort a Secant in Time backward and forward. **1704** J. HARRIS *Lex. Techn.* I, *Vibration*, is the Swing or Motion of a Pendulum; or of a Weight hung by a String on a Pin. **1797** *Encycl. Brit.* (ed. 3) XIV. 119/2 Whence the lengths of pendulums are as the forces and the squares of the times of vibration. **1822** WEBSTER *Imison's Sci. & Art* I. 80 The vibration of bodies when suspended must have been long observed. **1830** KATER & LARDNER *Mech.* x. 129 When the alternation [of motion] is constant and regular, it is called oscillation or vibration, as in pendulums and balance-wheels. **1877** *Encycl. Brit.* VI. 14/2 The time of vibration depends entirely on the length of the pendulum.

b. A single instance of this.

1667 *Phil. Trans.* II. 442 The Pendulum was this Day adjusted,..there having been but 58 vibrations in a Minute, the other Day. **1668** WILKINS *Real Char.* 191 Let this Ball be suspended by this String, being extended to such a length, that the space of every Vibration may be equal to a second Minute of time. **1704** J. HARRIS *Lex. Techn.* I. s.v., The Proportions of the Vibrations of Pendulums. **1797** *Encycl. Brit.* (ed. 3) XIV. 118/1 The point or axis of suspension of a pendulum is that point about which it performs its vibrations. **1803** J. IMISON *Sci. & Art* I. 124 Each swing that it [i.e. a pendulum] makes, is called a vibration, or oscillation. **1812-6** PLAYFAIR *Nat. Phil.* (1819) I. 129 The time of one vibration of the pendulum in seconds. *Ibid.*, The times of the vibrations of pendulums are as the square roots of their lengths. **1895** R. H. PINKERTON *Theoretical Mechanics* (ed. 5) 103 The acceleration of gravity is proportional to the square of the number of vibrations of the same pendulum in a given time.

3. a. *Physics.* The rapid alternating or reciprocating motion to and fro, or up and down, produced in the particles of an elastic body by the disturbance of equilibrium; the motion in the particles of a sonorous body by which sound is produced.

1656 tr. *Hobbes' Elem. Philos.* (1839) 527 When the string of a lute or viol is stricken, the vibration, that is, the reciprocal motion of that string in the same strait line, causeth like vibration in another string which hath like tension. *a* **1721** PRIOR *Dial. betw. Locke & Montaigne* Wks. 1907 II. 243 The vibration of the Air and its Undulation. **1794** SULIVAN *View Nat.* I. 168 An æther,..rendered luminous, by a vibration occasioned by the planetary motion. **1802** PALEY *Nat. Theol.* iii, The office of the drum of the ear is to spread out an extended surface, capable of receiving the impressions of sound, and of being put by them into a state of vibration. **1869** TYNDALL in *Fortn. Rev.* 1 Feb. 247 The plane of vibration of the polarized light turns suddenly through an angle of 90°. **1875** *Encycl. Brit.* I. 100 Its amplitude of vibration or distance between its extreme positions.

attrib. **1801** *Encycl. Brit.* Suppl. II. 751/1 Vibration Figures, are certain figures, formed by sand or very dry saw-dust, on a vibrating surface, which is connected with the sensation of sound in our organs of hearing.

b. A single movement of this kind.

1666 PEPYS *Diary* 8 Aug., A certain number of vibrations proper to make any tone. **1731** S. HALES *Stat. Ess.* I. 143 Which perspiration is effected by the brisk rarifying vibrations of warmth. **1748** THOMSON *Cast. Indol.* I. xx, But still their trembling ears retain'd The deep vibrations of his witching song. **1808** *Med. Jrnl.* XIX. 406 The height of the longitudinal vibrations is..inversely as the length of the sonorous body. **1834** MRS. SOMERVILLE *Connex. Phys. Sci.* xviii. 153 When the particles of elastic bodies are suddenly disturbed by an impulse, they return to their natural position by a series of isochronous vibrations. **1871** TYNDALL *Fragm. Sci.* (1879) II. xi. 244 Each vibration asserts its individual rights; and all are at last shaken forth into the air by a second sound-board.

fig. **1847** EMERSON *Repr. Men, Shaks.* Wks. (Bohn) I. 358 Ben Jonson..had no suspicion of the elastic fame whose first vibrations he was attempting. **1863** GEO. ELIOT *Romola* xxxviii, The words arose within him, and stirred innumerable vibrations of memory. **1866** —— *F. Holt* (1888) 8 Vibrations that make human agonies are often a mere whisper in the roar of hurrying existence.

c. *spec.* A supposed movement of this kind in the nerves, regarded as the means by which external impressions are conveyed to the mind. *Obs.* exc. *Hist.*

1728 CHAMBERS *Cycl.* s.v. *Madness*, Confused Vibrations of the Nerves, and a remarkable Energy of Imagination. **1748** HARTLEY *Observ. Man* I. i. 11 External Objects impressed upon the Senses occasion, first in the Nerves,.. and then in the Brain, Vibrations of the small..medullary Particles. **1753** HOGARTH *Anal. Beauty* xii. 95 Those more or less pleasing vibrations of the optic nerves, which serve to inform the mind. **1777** PRIESTLEY *Matt. & Spir.* (1782) I. x. 120 The vibrations of the brain are [not] themselves the perceptions. **1801** BELSHAM *Philosphy of Mind* §4. 38 The theory of vibrations suggested by Sir Isaac Newton, [and] adopted and amplified by Dr. Hartley,..assumes that the nerves are continuations of the medullary substance of the brain, that impressions made upon the organs of sense produce vibrations in the minute particles of the nerves. **1829** CARLYLE *Misc.* (1857) II. 104 Hartley's vibrations and vibratiuncles. **1857** [see VIBRATIUNCLE].

d. *transf.* An intuitive signal about a person or thing; (*pl.*) atmosphere. Usu. *pl.* (Now somewhat *colloq.*)

In some instances more or less identical with the *fig.* use of sense 3 b.

1899 O. WILDE *Importance of being Earnest* I. 28 There is very little music in the name Jack, if any at all, indeed. It does not thrill. It produces absolutely no vibrations. **1901** *Chambers's Jrnl.* Apr. 263/1 There is a man in Denver, Thomas J. Shelton who is said to be making his £10,000 a year by selling what he calls 'vibrations'... Mr Shelton's 'vibrations'..he himself explains as being a special force of his inner consciousness, which can be sent through space to purchasers by his mere act of will; and claims for the 'vibrations' so sent a subtle power capable of influencing a man in any direction that may be desired. **1919** CONRAD *Arrow of Gold* IV. ii. 157 The Blunt atmosphere, the reinforced Blunt vibration stealing through the walls... Nothing to me, of course—the movements of Mme. Blunt, *mère*. *Ibid.* 164, I listened deferentially to the end yet with every nerve in my body tingling in hostile response to the Blunt vibration, which seemed to have got into my very hair. **1922** JOYCE *Ulysses* 497 You can rub shoulders with a Jesus, a Gautama, an Ingersoll. Are you all in this vibration? **1934** M. ALLINGHAM *Death of Ghost* i. 23 Other people's pictures in *his* studio—it's sacrilege, isn't it? The vibrations won't be right. **1956** R. M. LESTER *Towards Hereafter* ii. 36 When I had a sitting with a medium who was obviously on the same vibration as myself the results were first-class. **1957** J. KEROUAC *On Road* II. vi. 146 Something curiously unsympathetic and cold between them was really a form of humor by which they communicated their own set of subtle vibrations. **1968** T. WOLFE *Electric Kool-Aid Acid Test* ii. 20 Something's getting up tight, there's bad vibrations. **1971** J. MANDELKAU *Buttons* v. 62 William showed me upstairs to what was going to be my 'home' for the next few weeks and let me wander around the house bumping into people and picking up on the vibrations. **1977** MILLER & SWIFT *Words & Women* i. 4 Names do seem to give off vibrations of a sort. **1979** N. MAILER *Executioner's Song* II. ii. 525 Stupor on top of old woe was the sad vibration Dennis was getting from Maximum.

4. a. In wider sense: Movement to and fro or up and down, esp. when quick and more or less continuous; a quivering, swaying, or tremulous motion of any kind.

1681 tr. *Willis' Rem. Med. Wks.* Vocab., *Vibration*, a shaking, striking or quavering. **1725** N. ROBINSON *The. Physick* 83 An increas'd Motion of the Blood, arising from a Vibration of the Vessels. **1822** SHELLEY *Lines Bay of Lerici* 16 Feeling ever—oh! too much!—The soft vibration of her touch. **1853** KANE *Grinnell Exp.* xxix. (1856) 251 Our brig had just mounted the floe, and as we stood on the ice watching her vibration, it seemed so certain that she must come over on her beam-ends. **1870** DICKENS *E. Drood* x, There was a vibration in the old lady's cap. **1901** D. B. HALL & LD. A. OSBORNE *Sunshine & Surf* ii. 17 The vibration and smells of the modern steamer.

attrib. **1897** *Allbutt's Syst. Med.* IV. 678 Massage, vibration-massage, electrolysis and the constant current are said to give excellent results in suitable cases.

b. An instance of this; a quiver or tremor.

1655 VAUGHAN *Silex Scint.*, *Midnight* (1858) 54 What Emanations, Quick Vibrations, And bright Stirs are there! **1676** GLANVILL *Ess.* III. 27 He will perceive the Quick-silver to descend from the Tube into the subjacent Vessell, till it comes to 29 Digits or thereabouts; there, after some Vibrations, it ordinarily rests. **1811** SHELLEY *St. Irvyne, Sister Rosa* xviii, In long vibrations shuddered the ground. **1849** LYELL *2nd Visit U.S.* II. 298 The vibrations and noise [are] much less than in other boats on the same high-pressure principle. **1869** PHILLIPS *Vesuv.* ix. 254 Accompanied by tremors or vibrations in the rocks.

5. a. The action or fact of vacillating or varying in respect of conduct or opinion; an instance of this; a changing or swinging round.

1785 JEFFERSON *Corr.* (1829) I. 300 The late proceedings seem to be producing a decisive vibration in our favor. **1791** BOSWELL *Johnson* (1904) II. 301 This was a fair exhibition of that vibration between pious resolutions and indolence. **1848** GALLENGA *Italy* (1851) 171 It is of little importance.. to talk about the perpetual vibrations of Charles Albert's weak mind at this period. **1864** BURTON *Scot Abr.* I. iv. 170 There was the same restlessness and fickleness.., the same vibration between anarchy and abject submission. **1882** BANCROFT *Hist. Const. U.S.A.* II. 354 In Virginia there had been a great vibration of opinion.

b. Variation in extent, etc.

1860 MAURY *Phys. Geog. Sea* vi. §329 The breadth of the calms of Cancer is also variable... The extreme vibration of this zone is between the parallels of 17° and 38° north.

6. *Electr.* (See quot.)

1842 FRANCIS *Dict. Arts*, *Vibration*, in electricity, is known as a quantity of the fluid intermediate between a spark and a shock.

7. Comb. ***vibration-proof*** adj.; **vibration damper** = DAMPER 4 c; *spec.* a device for counteracting torsional vibration in a crank-shaft.

1932 *Motoring Encycl.* 183/1 Special forms of frictional clutch on the front end of the crankshaft to reduce engine vibration are dealt with under the heading Vibration Damper. **1936** *Gloss. Terms Electr. Engin.* (*B.S.I.*) 87 *Vibration-damper*, of an overhead line. A device attached to a conductor, and designed to suppress vibrations caused by the action of wind. **1952** *Chambers's Jrnl.* Jan. 64/1 Most of the risk of deterioration can be eliminated by using vibration-dampers under machinery. **1961** [see DAMPER 4 c]. **1968** R. H. BACON *Car* v. 66 (*caption*) Crankshaft tors

vi'brational, *a.* [f. prec. + -AL[1].] **a.** Of or pertaining to vibration; vibratory.

1878 PRESCOTT *Sp. Telephone* 249 The number of vibrational forms which may arise from the composition of simple forms are mathematically infinite. **1884** H. R. HAWEIS *My Musical Life* iii. 86 The very appearance of the wood would guide him to its probable vibrational powers. **1888** *Encycl. Brit.* XXIV. 242 In order that the vibrational impulse may be given as nearly as possible at the centre of the mass of air in the resonant box.

b. ***vibrational number*** (see quot. 1881).

1879 C. Parry in Grove *Dict. Mus.* I. 670 As far as the ratios of the vibrational numbers of the limiting sounds are concerned. **1881** Broadhouse *Mus. Acoustics* 48 We are accustomed to take a second of time as the unit, and consequently mean by vibrational number the number of vibrations which the particles of a sounding body perform in one second of time.

c. *Physics.* Involving or resulting from particular modes of vibration or oscillation of the atoms in a molecule.

1923 [see *isotope effect* s.v. isotope 2]. **1946** *Nature* 26 Oct. 593/2 From an analysis of a suitable vibrational spectrum, it is usually possible to trace the vibrational-levels in the ground-state from $V = 0$ to $V = c.$ 20. **1970** I. E. McCarthy *Nuclear Reactions* I. v. 109 The nuclear probability amplitude for the excitation of vibrational states is obtained from the quantum theory of harmonic vibrations. **1973** C. Sagan *Cosmic Connection* iv. 27 There are vibrational transitions that occur when two atoms in a given molecule oscillate with respect to each other.

vi'brationally, *adv.* [f. vibrational *a.* + -ly[2].] By vibration; as regards vibrational motion.

1961 *New Scientist* 16 Mar. 687/1 Vibrationally assisted forming results in more uniform deformation [of metals]. **1964** [see *de-excite* vb. s.v. de-excitation]. **1974** *Nature* 30 Aug. 714/1 The object may be a very massive star..which is vibrationally unstable. **1979** *Sci. Amer.* May 104/2 The advent of the laser would seem to be a chemist's dream come true, enabling him in principle to selectively excite reactants—electronically, vibrationally or rotationally, as he wishes.

vi'brationless, *a.* [f. as vibrational *a.*] Free from vibration.

1896 *Prospectus Lond. Electrical Cab Company*, We are of opinion that they [*sc.* motor cabs] are thoroughly adapted to meet these requirements, being practically noiseless and vibrationless. **1925** *Motor* 15 Dec. (Advt. Suppl.) 44, Ansaldo. The beautiful Italian car... Vibrationless. Silent. Fast. **1964** W. L. Goodman *Hist. Woodworking Tools* 157 To make for quicker and vibrationless cutting, the flat gullets vary in size in groups of three or four. **1982** *Sci. Amer.* Nov. 9 (Advt.), The instrument must be of rugged construction and vibrationless, without the aggravating oscillations of long-tubed conventional telescopes.

vibratiuncle (vaɪbreɪʃɪ'ʌŋk(ə)l). [ad. mod.L. *vibratiuncula*, dim. of L. *vibrātio* vibration.] A minute or slight vibration. Cf. vibration 3 c.

1748 Hartley *Observ. Man* I. i. §2. 58 Diminutive Vibrations, which may also be called Vibratiuncles and Miniatures. *Ibid.* 101 Concerning the Derivation of ideal Vibratiuncles from sensory Vibrations. **1764** Reid *Inquiry* ii. §3 Our sensations arise from vibrations and our ideas from vibratiuncles or miniature vibrations. **1794** R. J. Sulivan *View Nat.* IV. 156 Do you take the soul to be an Eolus's harp, and all the fine things in it, to be vibratiuncles? **1826** Kirby & Sp. *Entomol.* IV. 244 Their hearing or analogous sense is much nicer than ours, collecting the slightest vibratiuncle imparted by other insects, &c. to the air. **1857** Maurice *Mor. & Met. Philos.* IV. viii. §43. 478 Through what vibrations or vibratiuncles that conviction came to him we do not care to enquire.

So **vi,bratiuncu'lation**, a vibratiuncle.

1855 Coues *Dæmon of Darwin* 58 (Cent.).

vibrative ('vaɪbrətɪv), *a.* Now *rare.* [f. L. *vibrāt-*, ppl. stem of *vibrāre*: see vibrate *v.* and -ative.] Vibrating, vibratory.

1667 Sprat *Hist. R. Soc.* 254 The variation of the vibrative motion of Pendulums. **1675** J. S[mith] *Horolog. Dial.* 28 The vibrative traine of the Pendulum or Ballance. **1747** *Gentl. Mag.* 225/2 The sun, by which the ethereal medium is always kept in a vibrative motion. **1844** Mrs. Browning *Drama of Exile* 804 It throbs in on us like a plaintive heart, Pressing, with slow pulsations, vibrative, Its gradual sweetness through the yielding air.

‖**vibrato** (vi'brato), *adv.* and *sb.* *Mus.* [It.:—L. *vibrāt-us*, pa. pple. of *vibrāre* to vibrate.]

A. *adv.* With much vibration of tone.

1861 J. S. Adams *5000 Mus. Terms* 106.

B. *sb.* (See first quot.)

1876 Stainer & Barrett *Dict. Mus. Terms* 446/1 *Vibrato*, a tremulous quality of tone, as opposed to a pure equal production. **1901** *Daily News* 5 Jan. 3/2 Dr. Stanford characterised the vibrato as the most detestable of devices except when used in the proper places.

vi'bratoless, *a.* [-less.] Without vibrato.

1975 *Daily Tel.* 12 Aug. 9/7 The pure vibrato-less style of Munrow's singers took on a piercing beauty. **1983** *N.Y. Times* 19 Dec. C13/1 The soloists for the Bach..sang in an even-toned, vibratoless style.

vibrator (vaɪ'breɪtə(r), older 'vaɪ-). [Agent-noun, on L. models, f. vibrate *v.* + -or. Cf. It. *vibratore.*]

1. That which vibrates, or causes vibration.

a. One of the vibrating reeds of an organ, harmonium, etc., by which the sound is produced.

1862 *Catal. Internat. Exhib., Brit.* II. No. 3391, Notes or vibrators, keys, pipes, stops, &c., for harmonium making or organ building. **1873** *Routledge's Yng. Gentl. Mag.* Feb. 167/1 This vibrator is the origin of our reed instruments. **1885** C. G. W. Lock *Workshop Receipts* Ser. IV. 293/1 There can be no escape of wind from the wind-chest, except through the vibrators and pallet-holes.

b. One or other of various appliances, instruments, or parts, which have or cause a vibratory motion or action. *spec.* (*a*) A device for compacting concrete by vibration before it has set. (*b*) A small electrically operated device for producing sexual stimulation. Also *attrib.*

A number of others are specified in recent American Dicts.

1888 *Encycl. Brit.* XXIII. 706/1 A composition roller, called a *vibrator*. **1888** Jacobi *Printers' Voc.* 152 *Vibrator rollers*, those rollers on a machine which have a vibrating motion, and convey the ink to the slab for distribution. **1906** *Daily Chron.* 6 Apr. 9/5 There are also beauty rollers and massage vibrators.

(*a*) **1930** [see vibrated *ppl. a.*]. **1950** *Archit. Rev.* CVII. 331/3 When vibration was first introduced the lack of proper equipment prevented its use except on very large contracts, but many types of vibrator are now on the market. **1981** Mindess & Young *Concrete* x. 289 External vibrators can be clamped to formwork, when the proper use of internal vibrators is not possible.

(*b*) **1953** A. C. Kinsey et al. *Sexual Behaviour in Human Female* v. 163 Douches, streams of running water, vibrators, ..and still other methods were occasionally employed [in masturbation]. **1970** in G. Greer *Female Eunuch* 217 As vibrators have been mentioned, may I add that it need not be the penis-shaped battery model. **1979** *Brit. Med. Jrnl.* 13 Oct. 883/2 In a study in which patients used a vibrator to achieve orgasm, all the major tranquillisers were said to interfere with ejaculation. **1983** Cauthery & Stanway *Compl. Bk. Love & Sex* xxxii. 386 The biggest-selling sex aid by far is the vibrator.

2. *Math.* (See quot.)

1879 Thomson & Tait *Nat. Phil.* I. I. §345 The reciprocal of this time we shall call..the rapidity of the system, for convenience of comparison with the frequency of a vibrator or of a rotator, which is the name commonly given to the reciprocal of its period.

vibratory ('vaɪbrətərɪ), *a.* [f. vibrate *v.* + -ory[2]. Cf. F. *vibratoire*, Sp. and Pg. *vibratorio.*]

1. Of the nature of vibration; characterized by or consisting of vibration.

1728 Chambers *Cycl.* s.v. *Vibration*, Sensation is supposed to be perform'd by means of the vibratory Motion of the Nerves. *a* **1734** North *Lives* (1826) I. 247 When the vibratory pulses are so slow as may be distinguished, sound vanisheth. **1788** Gibbon *Decl. & F.* xliii. IV. 326 An impulsive or vibratory motion was felt [in the earth]. **1801** Belsham *Philosophy of Mind* §4. 41 Impressions made upon the principal organs of sensations, are vibratory; the vibratory agitations of light and of air. **1822–7** Good *Study Med.* (1829) IV. 449 The vibratory and irregular action, which we denominate palpitation of the heart. **1878** Prescott *Sp. Telephone* (1879) 7 The tone or pitch,..which depends upon the rapidity of the vibratory movement.

2. Causing or producing vibration.

1756 Burke *Subl. & B.* IV. §21 The smoothness of the oil, and the vibratory power of the salt, cause the sense we call sweetness. **1793** Smeaton *Edystone L.* §323 So many vibratory strokes, can do it no service. **1812** *Religionism* 44 Vibration lends its aid; for human throats Have vibratory powers, that swell our notes. **1899** R. W. Trine *In Tune w. Infinite* vi. (1900) 128 Don't be afraid to voice your desires. In this way you set into operation vibratory forces which go out and..make their impress felt somewhere.

3. Of or pertaining to, connected or associated with, vibration.

1831 Blakey *Free Will* 170 The vibratory, or automatic system of Dr. Hartley. **1834** Mrs. Somerville *Connex. Phys. Sci.* xvii. 140 All the particles of an undulating fluid which are at once in a vibratory state. **1838** *Penny Cycl.* XII. 85/2 Producing a peculiar vibratory sensation. **1889** *Science-Gossip* XXV. 43/1 This is explained by the vibratory theory of light.

4. Capable of vibrating; readily admitting of vibration.

1839 Darwin *Voy. Nat.* i. 17 The animals move with the narrow apex forwards, by the aid of their vibratory ciliæ. **1862** R. H. Patterson *Ess. Hist. & Art* 13 The vibratory rays of the spectrum. **1878** Prescott *Sp. Telephone* (1879) 23 It being necessary to keep the vibratory bells at each station in circuits, in order that calls may be heard.

b. Of the voice: Vibrant. Also const. *with.*

1890 'R. Boldrewood' *Miner's Right* (1899) 95 He..commenced in a resonant vibratory voice. **1891** Clark Russell *Marriage at Sea* vii, A voice vibratory with excitement.

‖**vibrio** ('vaɪbrɪəʊ, 'vɪbrɪəʊ). Pl. vibriones (-'əʊni:z) and vibrios. [mod.L., f. L. *vibrāre* vibrate *v.*]

†**1.** A genus of minute nematode worms; an anguillule. *Obs.*

1835 Kirby *Hab. & Inst. Anim.* I. iv. 150 The species of *Vibrio* found in diseased wheat by M. Bauer is oviparous. **1836–9** *Todd's Cycl. Anat.* II. 113/2 The higher organized *Vibriones* have distinct generative organs, and are ovo-viviparous.

2. A group or genus of bacterioid or schizomycetous organisms characterized by vibratory motion; a member of this genus; *spec.* in *Bacteriol.*, a form of bacterium having vibratile cilia and closely resembling spirilla.

1850 *Proc. Acad. Nat. Sci. Philadelphia* IV. 228 With them were also found two species of Vibrio. *Ibid.*, Much higher confervæ..are endowed with inherent power of movement, not very unlike that of the Vibrio. **1870** H. A. Nicholson *Man. Zool.* 33 The bacteria and the vibrios now exhibit a vibratile or serpentine movement through the surrounding fluid. **1875** Payne *Jones & Siev. Pathol. Anat.* (ed. 2) 98 This has been shown to depend upon the presence of a peculiar vibrio which lives on the surfaces of wounds and the bandages. **1879** *Encycl. Brit.* IX. 95/1 Processes of putrefaction having long been known to be invariably accompanied by the formation of vibriones and other microscopic organisms endowed with voluntary motion.

Comb. **1871** Tyndall *Fragm. Sci.* (1879) I. v. 190 In examining the secretion I regularly found..certain vibrio-like bodies in it. **1898** P. Manson *Trop. Diseases* xvii. 281 If the cholera vibrio be the germ of cholera, then such healthy, vibrio-bearing individuals may well suffice to start an epidemic.

vibriocidal (vɪbrɪəʊ'saɪdəl), *a.* *Med.* [f. vibrio + -cide + -al[1].] Destructive to vibrios.

1962 *Jrnl. Immunol.* LXXXIX. 265/1 Complement is required for the vibriocidal effect. **1978** *Nature* 14 Dec. 709/1 Table 1 indicates a good correlation between protection to challenge and vibriocidal antibodies in the serum.

'vibrioid, *a.* *rare.* [f. vibrio: see -oid.] Of or belonging to, allied to, the group *Vibrio.*

Also in recent Dicts. as a *sb.*

1864 *Intell. Observ.* VI. 70 Parasitic vibrioid worms.

'vibrion. [ad. mod.L. *vibriōn-* vibrio. Cf. F. *vibrion.*]

1. A vibratile filament or appendage.

1853 Kane *Grinnell Exp.* xlvii. (1857) 433 Clios..were flashing colored light in shady places from their ciliary vibrions.

2. *Bacteriol.* A vibrio or vibrioid bacterium.

1882 *Pop. Sci. Monthly* XX. 801 Studies on butyric fermentation and the vibrion which is characteristic of it. **1889** *Nature* 7 Nov. 3 'Vibrions' or 'microbes' and the so-called bacteriology.

vibrionic (vaɪ-, vɪbrɪ'ɒnɪk), *a.* [f. as prec. + -ic.] Of or pertaining to, caused by, vibrios.

1850 *Proc. Acad. Nat. Sci. Philadelphia* IV. 235 All the innumerable objects of living nature..from the vibrionic filament to the noble oak..are the result of a force in connection with an amorphous vesicle, the organic cell-wall, with the contained nucleus. **1875** H. C. Wood *Therap.* (1879) 637 It was found that the proto-sulphate of iron completely prevented the development of either protoplasmic or vibrionic life. **1896** *Allbutt's Syst. Med.* I. 883 A firm believer in the vibrionic unity of cholera.

vibriosis (vɪbrɪ'əʊsɪs). *Vet. Sci.* [f. vibrio + -osis.] Infection with, or a disease caused by, vibrios.

1951 W. N. Plastridge in *Univ. Pennsylvania Veterinary Extension Q.* 3 Apr. 62 Improved methods of diagnosis and the increase of brucellosis-free herds account for the present increase in the interest in vibriosis. **1951** —— et al. in *Jrnl. Amer. Veterinary Med. Assoc.* June 367 In consideration of the several clinical manifestations of *V. fetus* infection and the probable existence of infection..in some animals in the absence of clinical evidence, the term 'vibriosis' is proposed to indicate *V. fetus* infection. **1960** R. A. Runnells et al. *Princ. Veterinary Path.* xix. 560/2 In Western Australia vibriosis is reported to be the immediate cause of at least 75 per cent of the infertility in dairy cows. **1980** *Nature* 10 Apr. 566/2 Epizootics of the widespread fish disease vibriosis.

‖**vibrissæ** (vaɪ'brɪsi:), *sb. pl.* [L. (Festus), f. *vibrāre* to vibrate. Cf. next.]

1. *Anat.* (See quots.)

1693 tr. *Blancard's Phys. Dict.* (ed. 2), *Vibressæ*, the Hairs in the Nose. **1704** J. Harris *Lex. Techn.* I, *Vibrissæ*, are the Hairs which grow in the Nostrils: They, with the Mucus, which the Glands separate, stop any Filth from ascending too high up into the Nostrils. **1839–47** *Todd's Cycl. Anat.* III. 730/1 Those hairs.. which converge from the inner circumference towards the centre of the nostril... These hairs are of the kind named *vibrissæ*. **1875** *Encycl. Brit.* I. 885/1 The *vestibule* or entrance to the nasal chamber..is studded with numerous short hairs or *vibrissæ*.

2. *Zool.* Stiff or bristly hairs, esp. those growing about the mouth or other parts of the face in certain animals.

1839 *Proc. Berw. Nat. Club* I. 202 These vibrissæ [of an aquatic larva]..possess no vibratory motion, nor do they appear to be furnished with ciliæ. **1871** Darwin *Desc. Man* I. i. 25 These hairs apparently represent the vibrissæ, which are used as organs of touch by many of the lower animals. **1877** Coues *Fur Anim.* ix. 265 The vibrissae are sparse and short, the longest scarcely or not attaining the eye. **1899** *Allbutt's Syst. Med.* VI. 490 They strongly suggest the function of vibrissæ.

b. *Ornith.* The coarse hairs or bristles growing about the rictus of certain birds, esp. of insectivorous species.

1874 J. G. Wood *Nat. Hist.* 287 The beak of this species [of goat-sucker] is not so powerful as in many of its relatives, but the vibrissæ are long and well-developed.

vi'brissant, *a.* *rare*[−1]. [ad. pres. pple. of L. *vibrissāre* (Festus), f. *vibrāre* vibrate *v.*] Vibrant.

1664 Power *Exp. Philos.* I A greenish glistering circle, which is the Iris (as vibrissant and glorious as a cats eye).

vibri'ssation. *rare*[−0]. [f. L. *vibrissāre*: cf. prec. and -ation.] (See quot.)

1656 Blount *Glossogr.*, *Vibrissation*, a quavering or warbling in singing, a shaking a thing.

vibro- ('vaɪbrəʊ), irregular combining form of L. *vibrāre* to vibrate, used in some recent technical and scientific terms, as **vi'brometer**, **vibro'motor**, **'vibrophone**, **'vibroscope** (hence ***vibro'scopic*** adj.), etc.; also **'vibro-massage**, massage with a special vibrator; **vibro'tactile** *a.*, of, pertaining to, or involving the perception of vibration through touch.

1923 *Daily Mail* 10 Aug. 5/2 The owner-experts get their features in knots..and may be seen going off for *vibro-massages in the evening. **1968** *Listener* 11 July 45/3 People who see nothing either comic or disturbing about our export eastwards of..vibro-massage, canned TV, [etc.]. **1887** *Pall Mall G.* 24 May 4/2 An ingenious instrument termed a *vibrometer..accurately records the vibration, and by its means every boat is tested before it leaves the builder's hands. **1894** *Standard* 8 Feb., By Mr. Beaumont's method the cause of vibration..is converted into a *vibromotor. **1875** KNIGHT *Dict. Mech.* 2709/2 **Vibroscope*,..an instrument invented by Duhamel for counting the vibrations of a tuning-fork. **1881** BROADHOUSE *Mus. Acoustics* 101 Another method of measuring pitch is the vibroscope, which as its name implies, is a method of making vibrations visible. [**1934** tr. R. H. Gault in *L'Année Psychologique* XXXIV. 2 Le sens tactile (ou comme je préfère..dire, les 'sens vibro-tactiles').] **1934** R. H. GAULT in *Jrnl. Acoustical Soc. Amer.* V. 253/2 We may legitmately describe the results of our *vibro-tactile experiments as evidences of hearing, even though we are assured that the ear is not involved. **1980** *Pflügers Arch. European Jrnl. Physiol.* CCCLXXXIV. 170/1 Vibrotactile stimuli above the tuning threshold of the nerve fibers can elicit a continuous afferent impulse volley without adaptation during some seconds.

vibrograph ('vaɪbrəʊgrɑf). [f. VIBRO- + -GRAPH.] **a.** = PHONAUTOGRAPH. **b.** An instrument for measuring or recording mechanical vibrations.

1875 *Encycl. Brit.* I. 110/1 Greater accuracy [in studying the relation between pitch and vibration] may be attained with the so-called *Vibrograph* or *Phonautograph*. **1904** *Nature* 25 Feb. Suppl. p. iii, Vibrograph, or instrument for recording photographically vibrations of a building or of the ground. **1946** [see ACCELEROMETER]. **1965** *Economist* 25 Dec. 1434/1 It took them some time to work out the best way of getting the job done without causing too much damaging vibration in the [Abu Simbel] temples— vibrographs were installed to check that the danger level was not exceeded. **1970** *Soviet Jrnl. Optical Technol.* XXXVII. 456 A method is given..for the calculation of the amplitude-frequency and phase-frequency characteristics of a vibrograph for recording small angular vibrations.

Hence **'vibrogram**, a record produced by a vibrograph.

1932 *Jrnl. R. Aeronaut. Soc.* XXXVI. 209 Vibrograms were obtained showing the vibration of different parts of the fuselage at various frequencies. **1950** *Engineering* 21 Apr. 431/2 The principal parameters of a vibrogram from which its effect on a building can be estimated are the maximum amplitude and the average frequency of the vibration. **1975** *Soviet Appl. Mech.* XI. 445 (*heading*) Damping determination according to vibrograms of random oscillations in linear systems.

vibronic (vaɪ'brɒnɪk), *a. Physics.* [f. VIBR(ATIONAL *a.* + ELECTR)ONIC *a.*] Of or pertaining to electronic energy levels or transitions associated with the vibration of the constituent atoms of a molecule.

1941 R. S. MULLIKEN in *Physical Rev.* LIX. 880/2 The vibronic wave function ψev is a function of the electronic and vibrational coordinates. **1966** G. HERZBERG *Molecular Spectra & Molecular Structure* i. 22 For half-integral spin we have two-valued vibronic species. **1976** *Nature* 22 Apr. 675/1 No vibronic structure has been detected in the absorption spectrum of the chromophore of the rhodopsin.

Hence **vi'bronically** *adv.*

1966 D. H. WHIFFEN *Spectroscopy* xii. 160 Transitions which are permitted solely on this account are called vibronic transitions or may be said to be vibronically allowed. **1978** *Nature* 19 Jan. 236/2 The results indicate that the afterglow is due to an emission to S_0 of the monomer or to a vibronically similar ground state.

‖**viburnum** (vaɪ'bɜːnəm). [L. *vīburnum* the wayfaring-tree.] An extensive genus of shrubs, natives of Europe, Asia, and N. America, to which the guelder-rose and laurustine belong; a species or plant of this genus.

1731 MILLER *Gard. Dict.* s.v. *Acacia*, The third Sort.. will..stand in a common Stove amongst Guava's, Viburnums, &c. *Ibid.* s.v., The common Viburnum, or Pliant Mealy Tree. **1760** J. LEE *Introd. Bot.* App. 331 Viburnum, American, *Lantana*. **1782** J. SCOTT *Poet. Wks.* 267 And white viburnum o'er the border strays. **1842** BRYANT *Fountain* ii, The viburnum there, Paler of foliage, to the sun holds up Her circlet of green berries. **1867** A. L. ADAMS *Wand. Nat. India* 204 A viburnum, differing in several respects from the English Guelder rose, bloomed sweetly by the sides of streams. **1884** *Athenæum* 20 Dec. 808/1 The remaining third include rhododendrons, rues,.. viburnums.

attrib. **1753** *Chambers' Cycl.* Suppl., *Viburnum Galls*,..a species of galls, or small protuberances, frequently found on the leaves of the *Viburnum*.

Hence **vi'burnian**, a moth of the genus *Lozotænia*; **vi'burnic** *a.*, derived from *Viburnum*; **vi'burnin**, a substance found in viburnum-bark.

1832 J. RENNIE *Consp. Butterfl. & M.* 157 The Viburnian (*Lozotænia Viburnana*). **1868** WATTS *Dict. Chem.* V. 998 The bark and berries of the guelder-rose..contain valeric acid (viburnic acid). **1886** *Buck's Handbk. Med. Sci.* III. 509/2 The bark [of *Viburnum prunifolium*] is said to contain viburnin, valerianic, oxalic, citric, and malic acids, besides other ingredients.

Vic¹ (vɪk), colloq. abbrev. of VICTORIA², used to denote the Royal Victoria Theatre, London (popularly known as the ***Old Vic***).

1858 G. A. SALA *Twice round Clock* (1859) 269 There is a transpontine theatre, situated laterally towards the Waterloo Road... This is the Royal Victoria Theatre... It is popularly termed the 'Vic'. **1888** KIPLING *Soldiers Three* (1890) 55 'Ave you ever bin in the Pit hentrance o' the Vic. on a thick night? **1915** *Times* 3 Oct. 11/5 At the Royal Victoria Hall ('the Old Vic')..a Shakespearian season opened last night. **1951** *Oxf. Compan. Theatre* 582/1 In 1833 it [*sc.* the Coburg Theatre] was renamed the Victoria, from the fact that Princess (later Queen) Victoria visited it once. It soon became affectionately known as the Old Vic. **1972** W. GARNER *Ditto, Brother Rat!* iv. 32 The Vic bars get pretty hectic, especially with only one interval. **1976** *Vogue* 15 Mar. 15/3 So goodbye Old Vic, tiptoeing off into the wings of theatrical history.

vic² (vɪk). Used for *v* in telephone communications and in the oral transliteration of code messages. Hence also in *Mil.* use, a V-formation of aircraft.

1913 [see PIP *sb.*⁴]. **1927** W. E. COLLINSON *Contemp. Eng.* 98 Other artillery terms which spread were..vick for V, also ack emma for a.m. [etc.]. **1940** *Flight* 28 Mar. 295 Spitfires staged some plain and fancy beat-ups..in formation (excellent vic and echelon). **1942** I. GLEED *Arise to Conquer* 12 We flew back as a squadron, four sections in vic. **1952** M. TRIPP *Faith is Windsock* iv. 61 The Squadron was leading today's raid, and E-Easy..led the Squadron. To port and slightly behind Easy's vic was C-Charlie, also with a vic.

vi'cambulate, *v. nonce-wd.* [f. L. *vīcus* street + *ambulāre* to walk.] *intr.* To walk about in the streets.

1873 M. COLLINS *Squire Silchester* II. xiii. 159 Many strangers were there among them, as Musical Willie, who vicambulated greatly, soon perceived.

So **vi'cambulist.** *rare*⁻¹.

1822 *Etonian* I. 5 'To see and to be seen,' is the professed object of these unwearied vicambulists.

vicar ('vɪkə(r)). Forms: α. 4 vikere, 4–6 vykere, vyker (5 vykeyr), viker; 4 veker, 6 -ere; 4, 6 vicker (6 ficker, fycker, vyckyr). β. 4–6 vicare (4 wic-, 6 vycare), 4– vicar (5–6 vycar, 6 *Sc.* wicar; 5 vikar, 6 vykar), 6 *Sc.*, 7 viccar (6 *Sc.* vyccar, wickar); 5 vicour. γ. 4, 7 vicaire, 5 vic-, vycayre; 4, 7 vicair, 5 vicayr, 6 vycayr. [a. AF. *vikere, vicare, vicaire* (OF. and F. *vicaire*), ad. L. *vicārius* substitute (VICARY *sb.*¹), f. *vic-is* change, occasion, place (of another), etc. Cf. It. and Sp. *vicario*, Pg. *vigario*.] One who takes the place of, or acts instead of, another; a substitute, representative, or proxy. Chiefly *Eccl.*

1. a. Applied to persons, etc., as earthly representatives of God or Christ; also to Christ or the Holy Ghost as representing the Father.

The second line of the first quot. is partly corrupt.

a **1300** *Cursor M.* 27106 Noght anes to preist his sinnes [to] scriue, Bot elles to godd bot was wicare In mans scappe he sittes þare. *c* **1366** CHAUCER *A.B.C.* 140 God..hath þee maked vicair & maistresse Of al þe world. *c* **1380** WYCLIF *Wks.* (1880) 30 Siþ prelatis ben vikeris of crist. *c* **1400** LOVE *Bonavent. Mirr.* (1908) 122 The preostes that he hath specially ordeyned in his stede as his vikeres. **1546** *Supplic. Poore Commons* (E.E.T.S.) 73 These hierlinges intend..to be taken for Goddes vicars upon earthe. **1548** UDALL, etc. *Erasm. Par. St. John* xviii. 102 b, If thou [*sc.* Peter] wylt succede me as my vicar, thou must fight with no other swerde than of Gods woorde. **1621** BURTON *Anat. Mel.* II. i. i. 290 He calls a Magician Gods Minister and his Vicar. **1651** C. CARTWRIGHT *Cert. Relig.* II. 32 Christ sitting at the right hand of his Father, holds but a second degree with him in honour, and rule, and is but his Vicar. **1678** R. BARCLAY *Apol. Quakers* ii. §2. 21 Knowledge might be..brought to perfection by the holy Spirit, that Vicar of the Lord. **1829** I. TAYLOR *Enthus.* vii. 161 Though the vicar of Christ [*sc.* every true Christian minister] be not unconditionally responsible for the happy result of his labours. **1848** LOWELL *Biglow P.* Ser. I. viii. Introd., By and by comes along the State, God's vicar. *c* **1850** *Arab. Nts.* (Rtldg.) 496, I tell you again I am Commander of the Faithful, and vicar upon earth of the Lord of both worlds.

b. *spec.* Applied to the Pope (†or the Patriarch of Jerusalem); also to St. Peter in a similiar sense (cf. quot. 1548 above).

1340 HAMPOLE *Pr. Consc.* 3837 Þat falles hym of office to halde, For he es in erthe, Godes vicar calde. ? **1370** *Robt. Cisyle* 50 Hys oon brodur in ȝovthe the Godes generalle vykere, Pope of Rome, as ye may here. *c* **1440** *Gesta Rom.* xix. 66 (Harl. MS.) 'How of the Pope?' 'For god is oon,' seid he, 'and þerfore he hath made a vyker'. **1481** CAXTON *Godfrey* ccv. 301 The duc godeffroy and the prynce buymont,.. whiche had gyuen to hym this honour as for to be the vycayre of Ihesu Criste in that londe,..assygned rentes to the newe Patriark. **1526** *Pilgr. Perf.* (W. de W. 1531) 203 Heare deuoute chrystyan what saynt Peter the apostle and hye viccar of Chrystes chirche sayth. **1570** JEWEL *Sedit. Bull* (1609) 17 Would the Vicar of Christ give this counsell? **1638** *Penit. Conf.* vii. (1657) 132 God and the Pope..are not alwayes of one mind; and if Christ confirm not in heaven the sentence of his Vicar on earth, we [etc.]. **1728** CHAMBERS *Cycl.* s.v., The Pope pretends to be Vicar of Jesus Christ on Earth. **1756–7** tr. *Keysler's Trav.* (1760) III. 244 The victory gained by the Most Christian King, Lewis XII. when he made war upon the Vicar of Christ. **1847** S. AUSTIN *Ranke's Hist. Ref.* III. 311 The divine right of the catholic church, and the character of its head as Vicar of Christ. **1864** BRYCE *Holy Rom. Emp.* x. (1875) 160 Proclaiming that to the Pope, as God's vicar, all mankind are subject, and all rulers responsible.

c. *nonce-use.* (See quot.)

1641 MILTON *Animadv.* Wks. 1851 III. 198 For Anti-christ wee know is but the Devils Vicar, and therefore please him with your Liturgie, and you please his maister.

2. a. In early use, a person acting as priest in a parish in place of the real parson or rector, or as the representative of a religious community to which the tithes had been appropriated; hence, in later use in the Church of England, the incumbent of a parish of which the tithes were impropriated or appropriated, in contrast to a RECTOR. Now also a priest who is a member (team vicar) of a team ministry (TEAM *sb.* 11) under the leadership of a team rector.

α. *c* **1325** *Metr. Hom.* 87 Erles, knihtes, and baronnes, Prestes, vikers, and parsonnes. *c* **1380** WYCLIF *Wks.* (1880) 76 Þei..don neiþer office of prelatis,..nei er þe office of parsones ne vekeris to here parischenes. *Ibid.* 424 Þe fend haþ founden cautels to bringe in vikeris in persouns stede. **1425** *Rolls of Parlt.* IV. 290/2 All maner of Persones, and Vykeyrs, and Hospitilers. *c* **1456** PECOCK *Bk. of Faith* (1909) 224 A greet famed kunnyng mayster of divinite is curat, and parsoun and viker. **1533** in *Archaeologia* XXV. 523 To the vykers woman of Dokkynge. *Ibid.*, The vykere of Snettysham servante. **1556** *Chron. Gr. Friars* (Camden) 49 A gret generalle processione of alle parsons, vekeres, curattes, with alle other prestes. **1588** J. UDALL *Diotrephes* (Arb.) 28 How shall we doe for the parsons and vickers?

β. ? **1388** in *Wyclif's Sel. Wks.* III. 493 Þat no persone ne vicare ne prelate is excusud fro personele residense..in þer beneficys. **1402** *J. Upland* 279 Sith persounes and vicares alone,..with bishops above hem, were y-nough to..do prestes office. **1439** *Rolls of Parlt.* V. 15 She..openly seide unto yᵉ seide Vicar, that she wold never..have hym to hur Husbond. **1482** —— VI. 210 Upon the same apropriation, ther shuld be a vicour endowed sufficiently. **1521** *Lincoln Wills* (1914) I. 90 Sir Thomas Markby vykar off the sayd church. **1531** *Test. Ebor.* (Surtees) VI. 24 The vicare to have iiijd. and the clerke ijd. **1560–** [see PARSON 1]. **1598** SHAKS. *Merry W.* IV. vi. 52 Ile to the Vicar, Bring you the Maid, you shall not lacke a Priest. **1609** DEKKER *Guls Horn-bk.* Wks. (Grosart) II. 206 Like some pedantical Vicar stammering out a most false and crackt latine oration. **1647** CLARENDON *Hist. Reb.* I. §185 He was preferred..to the Bishoprick of Coventry and Litchfield..before he had been..Vicar or Curate of any Parish Church in England. *a* **1700** EVELYN *Diary* 2 Mar. 1682, Our Viccar preached on Proverbs. **1765** BLACKSTONE *Comm.* I. i. xi. 301 A vicar has generally an appropriator over him. **1796** H. HUNTER *St.-Pierre's Stud. Nat.* (1799) III. 482 Not a simple village Vicar ought to be without the actual necessaries of life. **1818** CRUISE *Digest* (ed. 2) III. 59 Where the vicar produces an endowment, then the situation of the parties is reversed. **1870** F. R. WILSON *Ch. Lindisf.* 99 The present vicar..speedily brought about a different aspect. **1972** *Daily Tel.* 7 Aug. 10/5 Only the leader of the team, usually called 'Rector', is the beneficed freeholder incumbent inducted by the bishop. His colleagues ('vicars') are licensed by the bishop as members of the team. **1977** [see RECTOR 3 a]. **1984** *Church Times* 27 Jan. 17/1 (Advt.), Vicar required... N. Birmingham Team Ministry, modern vicarage.

γ. *c* **1395** *Plowman's Tale* 830 (Skeat), Pope, bishoppes, and cardinals, Chanons, persons, and vicaire, In goddes service. **1520** *Caxton's Chron. Eng.* VII. 90/1 There was decreed yᵗ all persones & vycayres sholde be called prestes.

b. *fig.* or *transf.*

1563 *Homilies* II. *Perils Idolatry* III. Yy iij b, We nede not to complayne of the lacke of one dombe person, hauyng so manye dombe deuyllyshe vycars (I meane these ydolles and paynted puppettes) to teache in theyr steade. **1588** *Marprel. Epist.* (Arb.) 38, I doubt not..to get a hundreth of these stratagemes, especially if I trauell neere where any of the vickers of hell are. **1602** *2nd Pt. Return fr. Parnass.* IV. ii. 1722 And you Maister Amoretto, that art the chiefe Carpenter of Sonets, a priuileged Vicar for the lawlesse marriage of Inke and Paper. **1660** TATHAM *Rump* V. i, Sure the vicar of fools was his ghostly father.

c. ***Vicar of Bray***, one who readily changes his principles to suit the times or circumstances.

Bray is the village of that name near Maidenhead in Berkshire. According to Fuller (see ref. below) the 'vivacious vicar' held the benefice from the reign of Henry VIII to that of Elizabeth, and was twice a Catholic and twice a Protestant. In the later song, to which the currency of the phrase is mainly due, the sovereigns under whom the vicar successively changes his religion and politics are those from Charles II to George I.

[*a* **1661** FULLER *Worthies* I. *Berks.* (1662) 82 But first we will dispatch that sole Proverb of this County, viz. The Vicar of Bray, will be Vicar of Bray still. *c* **1720** *Song, Vicar of Bray* (Chorus), This is the law, I will maintain, Until my dying day, Sir, That whatsoever King may reign, Still I'll be the Vicar of Bray, Sir. **1735** BROME in *Lett. by Eminent Persons* (1813) II. 100, I have had a long chase after the Vicar of Bray, on whom the proverb... I am informed it is Simon Aleyn or Allen, who was Vicar of Bray about 1540, and died 1588.]

1725 LD. HARLEY in *Dk. Portland's MSS.* (Hist. MSS. Comm.) VI. 116 His chief crime is having been once Episcopal, and playing the Vicar of Bray upon them, and keeping his living, when the rest of his Episcopal brethren were ejected. **1785** GROSE *Dict. Vulg. T.* s.v. *Bray, A vicar of Bray*, one who frequently changes his principles, always siding with the strongest party. **1828** P. CUNNINGHAM *N.S. Wales* (ed. 3) II. 248 The regularly educated thieves..are *Vicars of Bray* to every man whom it is their interest to humour,—blaspheming with the blasphemer and praying with the saint.

transf. **1895** *Daily News* 12 June 5/4 A habit which the Iguana shares with many lizards..is the habit of changing its colour; most lizards are Vicars of Bray to this extent.

†**d.** ***temporal vicar*** (see quot.). *Obs.*

1726 AYLIFFE *Parergon* 509 Temporal vicars..are much the same with our Curates as we now call them; and these are constituted for some particular Acts and Seasons.

3. a. = VICAR CHORAL.

1387 TREVISA *Higden* (Rolls) VI. 465 For clerkes fliȝ þe travayle of þe queere,..and dede vikers in here stede þat hadde ful litel for to lyve by. **1531** *Protocols Town Clerks Glasgow* (1897) IV. 33 To the wiccaris of the qweyr; with the borrow maell. **1641** BAKER *Chron., Eliz.* 116 This Queene.. ordained a Dean,..forty Schollars, Vicars, Singing-men, &c. **1700** J. BROME *Trav. Eng.* 248 A Collegiate Church, consisting of a Dean, four Prebendaries, five Singing-Men, three Vicars, and four Deacons. **1878** *Grove's Dict. Mus.* I. 52 His choir was well appointed, and every vicar, clerical as well as lay, gave his daily and efficient aid in it.

b. ***lay vicar***, = prec. (Also ***priest-vicar***: see PRIEST *sb.* 10.)

1837 *Penny Cycl.* VII. 110 The Choir is also the term by which the lay-vicars, or lay-clerks, and choristers, *i.e.* the singers, of a cathedral, are collectively designated. **1843** JEBB

Choral Service xii. 108 The Lay Vicars of the old Cathedrals ..are sometimes members of the inferior Colleges, sometimes merely part of the foundation at large. **1877** LEE *Gloss. Litur g. & Eccl. Terms* 184 *Lay vicar*, a term used in the statutes of some of our cathedrals to designate the superior grade of singing men.

4. a. One who takes the place of, or acts as the representative of, another (esp. the Pope or other high dignitary) in the performance of ecclesiastical or religious functions; *spec.* in the Roman Catholic Church, a bishop's deputy.

c **1380** WYCLIF *Serm.* Sel. Wks. I. 18 ȝif þe Pope and his vikeris wolden studie wel þis mater. **1426** LYDG. *De Guil. Pilgr.* 1393 And sempte that he sholde be Lyk a vyker douteles Off Aaron & of Moyses. **1576** W. LAMBARDE *Peramb. Kent* 130 This Prelate [the Bishop of Ely], hauing nowe by the Kings commission the power of a Viceroy, and besides by the Popes gifte the authoritie of a Legate and Vicar. **1586** in *Cath. Rec. Soc. Publ.* V. 129 Directed to the Archbishopp of Cant: or to his vicar or Commissary generale. **1611** SIR D. CARLETON *Let.* in *10th Rep. Hist. MSS. Comm.* App. I. 546 Upon yᵉ late remove of our patriarch's vicar there hath fallen vacant a benefice annexed to yᵉ vicariat. **1642** JER. TAYLOR *Episc.* l. 372 When S. Paul sent for Timothy from Ephesus, he sent Tychicus to be his Vicar. *a* **1677** BARROW *Pope's Supremacy* vi. Wks. 1687 I. 261 The Popes..began to practise a fine trick,..which was to confer on certain Bishops..the title of their Vicar or Lieutenant; thereby pretending to impart Authority to them. **1782** PRIESTLEY *Corrupt. Chr.* II. x. i. 238 They [the patriarchs] appointed vicars, or deputies, to act for them in the remoter provinces. **1820** MILNER *Suppl. Mem. Eng. Cath.* 108 The late B. Berington's Vicar, Dr. Bew. **1898** W. BRIGHT *Some Aspects Prim. Ch. Life* ii. §6. 83 This 'high and Divine power', which Cyprian claimed as inherent in the episcopate, was larger than that which St. Paul had entrusted to his own 'vicars'.

b. With defining term preceding, as ***grand, papal, Pope's vicar***.

1662 in *Cath. Rec. Soc. Publ.* VIII. 236 Mʳ Hoden *Grand Vicair of Paris being Superior. **1688** [see GRAND *a.* 2]. **1696** PHILLIPS s.v., The Pope's Grand Vicar, who is a Cardinal, has a Jurisdiction..over all Secular and Regular Priests [etc.]. **1756–7** tr. *Keysler's Trav.* (1760) I. 249 Some days since,..the king unexpectedly nominated him grand vicar to the archbishop. **1796** HELEN M. WILLIAMS *Lett. France* IV. 102 (Jod.), One of my college companions had become grand-vicar and first confidant to the archbishop of my diocese. **1843** *Penny Cycl.* XXVII. 827/2 Faber, grand-vicar of the bishop of Constance. **1844** LINGARD *Anglo-Sax. Ch.* (1858) I. App. E. 341 The bishop of Arles the *papal vicar in Gaul, in place of the pope, whose representative he was. **1902** J. K. MANN *Hist. Popes* I. I. 22 He came to Thessalonica;..its metropolitan..was a papal vicar. **1670** G. H. *Hist. Cardinals* I. III. 84 And first I shall begin with the *Popes Vicar, which office is the most antient of all, and was for a long time executed by Bishops, and other Prelates. **1902** J. K. MANN *Hist. Popes* I. I. 159 Augustine..was consecrated bishop by Virgilius of Arles, the Pope's vicar in Gaul.

c. With defining term appended, as ***vicar apostolic, apostolical, capitular, episcopal, foran(e)*** or ***foreign, provincial***.

See also VICAR-GENERAL.

1766 in E. H. Burton *Life Challoner* (1909) II. xxvii. 83 After all, by the terms of the circular letter, the Vicars *Apostolic have, in case of necessity, a power to dispense. **1799** C. BUTLER *Life A. Butler* vii, The vicar-apostolic of the middle district claimed him as belonging to that district, and appointed him to a mission in Staffordshire. **1836** *Penny Cycl.* VI. 373/1 Where the succession of the Catholic hierarchy has been interrupted, as in England,..the bishops who superintend the Catholic church and represent the papal authority, are known by the name of vicars apostolic. **1851** BRIGHT *Sp., Eccles. Titles Bill* 12 May (1876) 518 The changing of vicars-apostolic to bishops in ordinary. **1731** in O. Blundell *Catholic Highlands Scotland* (1917) II. 99 His Holiness..appoints him also Vicar *Apostolical with singular powers. **1847** J. A. MANNING *Pius XI* I. 168 Differences broke out between the Vicar Apostolical and the Chilian government. **1849** STOVEL *Canne's Necess.* p. xxxv, Wolsey, to carry on the policy of his church, obtained his own appointment as vicar-apostolical of England. **1846** MCCULLOCH *Acc. Brit. Empire* (1854) II. 305 On the death of a bishop, the clergy of the diocese elect a vicar *capitular, who exercises spiritual jurisdiction during the vacancy. **1903** *Westm. Gaz.* 7 Sept. 10/2 A special meeting..for the purpose of electing a Vicar-Capitular to administer the See of Southwark during the vacancy. **1877** LEE *Gloss. Eccl. Terms* 439 *Vicar *Episcopal*, an office corresponding in some particulars to the English archdeacon, as well as to the Greek 'Chorepiscopus'. **1825** DOYLE in Fitzpatrick *Life* xi. (1861) I. 282 Whenever a priest falls into any dangerous illness, the Vicar-*Foreign within whose deanery he lives shall visit him. **1888** *Cassell's Encycl. Dict.* s.v., *Vicar-forane*, Roman Church, a dignitary or parish priest appointed by a bishop to exercise a limited jurisdiction in a particular town or district of his diocese. **1896** *Tablet* 18 Apr. 619 The *curé* and vicar-foran at Castries..receives £200 a year. **1856** VAUGHAN *Mystics* (1860) II. 134 Vicar-*provincial of Andalusia, he plies his task anew.

5. a. In general use: One acting, or appointed to act, in place of another, esp. in administrative functions; a vicegerent.

c **1375** *Sc. Leg. Saints* xli. (*Agnes*) 250 [The prefect] deput in his sted þare, þe law to hald þaim, a vicare, & sorouful went away. *c* **1400** tr. *Secreta Secret., Gov. Lordsh.* 109 Folwe þanne vche commandour tene vicaires, & vche vicaire tene lederes. **1430–40** LYDG. *Bochas* VIII. viii. (1558) 6 In his empyre he set two vicars, Gaue them power in euery region [etc.]. **1483** CAXTON *Gold. Leg.* 169/2 Gordyan that was vicayr unto Julyan themperour. **1533** BELLENDEN *Livy* v. vii. (S.T.S.) II. 170, I wil mak him (for he is weil institute in chevelrie) vicare and lieutenent for me. **1596** DALRYMPLE tr. *Leslie's Hist. Scot.* (S.T.S.) II. 278 He commandes that women, barnes, and citisenis all to him cum and craue mercie as to the Kingis vicare. **1602** T. FITZHERBERT *Apol.* 38 To assemble his friends, and witnesses of his wil, and those whome he meant to make his heyres, his vicars, and substituts. **1655** FULLER *Ch. Hist.* xxv. 207 Lord Cromwell ..sate in state above all the Bishops, as the King's Vicar, or Vicegerent-Generall in all spirituall matters. **1702** *Lond. Gaz.* No. 3814/3 It is said, the King of Spain has made the Duke of Burgundy Vicar of the Spanish Low-Countries, which Title gives him a Power over those Provinces, equal to that which the King would have if he were there in Person. **1753** *Scots Mag.* XV. 27/1 During a vacancy of the Imperial throne, the government of the empire devolves upon the two vicars. **1781** GIBBON *Decl. & F.* xvii. (1787) II. 37 The eleven remaining dioceses [= provinces]..were governed by twelve vicars, or vice-præfects, whose name sufficiently explains the nature and dependence of their office. **1835** LYTTON *Rienzi* III. iii, He was chosen afterwards vicar (or vice-gerent) of Louis in Aversa. **1870** LOWELL *Among my Bks.* Ser. I. (1873) 169 We may be very sure that Heminge and Condell did not, as vicars, take upon themselves a disagreeable task.

transf. **1474** CAXTON *Chesse* 45 The rookes ben vycayrs and legates of the kynge. **1541** R. COPLAND *Guydon's Quest. Chirurg.* C iv b, All the synewes of the body brede and come out of the brayne by it selfe, or of the noddle that is his vycare.

b. A thing substituted for another. *rare.*

1675 EVELYN *Terra* (1676) 16 All dungings and other sordid temperings, being but the vicars succedaneous to this improvement. **1846** THACKERAY *Cornhill to Cairo* xiii, Abraham caught the Ram, which was to serve as the vicar of Isaac.

vicarage (ˈvɪkərɪdʒ). Forms: 5 viker(i)age, vicerege; 5– vicarage, 6 viccar-, vyc(c)ar-, *Sc.* wicar-, vicrage, 7 vicaradge; 5 vycary-, 5–6 vicariage; 5–7 vicarege, 6–7 -edge, -ige, 6–8 -idge, 7 viccari(d)ge. [f. VICAR + -AGE.]

1. a. The benefice or living of a vicar.

1425 *Rolls of Parlt.* IV. 290/2 That they holde residence opon thaire Parsonages, Vikerages, and Hospitalites, opon payn of lesyng the valeu of thaire Benefice. *c* **1438** LD. CLIFFORD in *Finchale Priory* (Surtees) 71 There is a vicerege in Craven..of the which the presentacion longith to you. **1459** *Rolls of Parlt.* V. 365 The advouson of the Vicariage of the same. **1536** *Protocols Town Clerks Glasgow* (1897) IV. 98 Factouris as thai allegit to the vyccarage of Mwnkland. **1589** COOPER *Admon.* 47 That of Euans concerning the Vicarage of Warwike, is maliciously reported. **1631** *High Commission Cases* (Camden) 246 He was charged with the simonaicall resignation and bestowing of his viccaridge of Castor upon a young man, a minister. **1660** R. COKE *Power & Subj.* 206 Tythes appertaining to Parish-Churches, Prebends, Hospitals, Vicaredges. **1695** KENNETT *Par. Antiq.* ix. 91 We meet with no such early records that make them distinct and proper Vicariges. **1729** SWIFT *Libel on Dr. Delany* 132 The offals of a church distrest; A hungry vicarage at best. **1749** POTE *Hist. & Antiq. Windsor* 12 It is a Vicaridge in the Deanery of Reading and Diocess of Salisbury. **1815** JANE AUSTEN *Emma* iv, Though the vicarage of Highbury was not large, he was known to have some independent property. **1863** H. COX *Instit.* III. vii. 700 The hereditaments of the Crown (except advowsons and vicarages). **1884** *Manch. Exam.* 14 May 5/3 The plaintiff, a clergyman, who at one time had a vicarage at Bow.

transf. **1587** HOLINSHED *Chron.* (ed. 2) III. 558/1 The three peruerse prelats..stroue togither for the sacred see of papasie Gods vicarage. **1653** H. WHISTLER *Upshot Inf. Baptisme* 2 Whether they were redeemed by the Vicarage of a Levite, or by a ransome.

†**b.** A benefice attached to a parsonage. *Obs.*⁻¹

1501 *Reg. Privy Seal Scotl.* I. 98 The parsonage of Sanct Colinez Kirk..with the annexis and vicaragis thairof, that is to say, Kilmolowok in Rasay and Kilmory in Walternes.

†**2.** A college of vicars. *Obs.*

1485 in *Ripon Chapter Acts* (Surtees) 277, I will that my messebuke be gyffyn to the vicarage in Rypon. **1505** *Ibid.* 304 The said mese..goo to the vicarege of Ripon, they doynge therfor a yerely obbett.

3. The house or residence of a vicar; also, those who live in this.

1530 PALSGR. 285/1 Vycrage a preestes house, *presbytoire*. **1611** COTGR., *Presbitere*, a Parsonage, Vicarage, or Priests house. **1612** PEACHAM *Gentl. Exerc.* III. 157 The ancient coate of Bassingborne, which by chance I found in a window at the Vicaredge in Fulham. **1820** PRAED *Poems* (1864) II. 136 The traveller was to blame And not the Vicarage or the Vicar. **1891** 'S. MOSTYN' *Curatica* 150, I had bidden the Vicarage farewell the night before.

†**4.** *Sc.* A (or the) payment due to a vicar; vicarial tithes or other dues. *Obs.*

1579 *Munim. de Melros* (Bann. Cl.) 653 þe teind schevis.. with small teindis and Viccaragis pertenand to þe saming Kirk. **1595** in *Maitland Club Misc.* I. 73 The amount and quantitie of the vicarages of the said benefices, with the glebbis and mansis. **1684** *Rec. Baron Crt. Stitchill* (S.H.S.) 95 For not paying of Vicaradge at Mertimas, which..the Judge decerns them to pay punctually. **1762** in *Nairne Peerage Evidence* (1874) 92 The town and lands of Kinnaird and the lands of Tullybeagles with the tiends parsonage and vicarage of the saids haill lands. **1775** L. SHAW *Hist. Moray* 353 The Stipend is 80 Bolls of Victual, and about L. 50 of Vicarage. **1818** SCOTT *Hrt. Midl.* viii, What have I been paying stipend and teind, parsonage and vicarage, for?

†**5.** The position, office, or duties of a vicar or representative. *Obs. rare.*

1622 DONNE *Serm. John xi.* 35 My vicarage is to speak of his [Christ's] compassion and his tears. **1642** JER. TAYLOR *Episc.* §37. 264 This whole discourse showes..that they [the Bishops] have sole jurisdiction, and the Presbyters only in substitution and vicaridge. **1734** BP. PETRE in E. H. Burton *Life Challoner* (1909) I. 93 He gave up his pious spirit..in the ninety second year of his age and forty sixth of his episcopate and Apostolic Vicarage.

6. *attrib.* and *Comb.*, as ***vicarage church***, †***duty, house, stipend, teind***; **vicarage tea-party**, used as the type of something mild, innocuous, and uneventful.

1731 *Gentl. Mag.* I. 118 From hence the Writer takes occasion to consider the State of *Vicarage Churches. **1597** *Reg. Mag. Sig. Scot.* 303/2, 50 pundis money as for the personage dewtie and 10 merkis for the *vicarage dewtie foir-said. *a* **1550** LELAND *Itin.* (1769) IV. 118 From the which Water is conveyed to the Prebendaries Houses, to the *Vicarage Houses, and the Choristers. **1569** BP. PARKHURST *Injunctions* A iv, Whether..your Parsonage and Vicaredge house be well..maintained. **1638** H. SPELMAN in *Lett. Lit. Men* (Camden) 156 There is a reasonable Vicarage house upon it. *a* **1704** T. BROWN *Two Oxford Scholars* Wks. 1730 I. 10 An old rotten Parsonage or Vicarage-house. **1785** J. WESLEY *Serm.* lvii. Wks. 1811 IX. 25 He removed into the Vicarage-House. **1837** LOCKHART *Scott* II. xii. 378 An ornamental cottage in the style of the old English vicarage-house. **1867** J. CAMPBELL *Balmerino & Abbey* III. ii. 170 He was also minister of Logie..and drew its *vicarage stipend. **1973** *Times* 11 Apr. 1/2 Mr Heath's appearances in the Commons are never *vicarage tea parties. **1984** *Daily Tel.* 31 Jan. 12/5 He surveyed the smoking ruins of..a fine old Elizabethan rectory,..and said: 'It makes the Dissolution of the Monasteries look like a vicarage tea-party.' **1984** *Guardian* 6 June 10 Politicians..who fear that events are about to take a nasty turn, frequently say that what they are predicting will make D-Day (or the ravages of Genghis Khan..—every speaker will have his own comparison) look like a vicarage tea party. **1610** in *T. Pont's Topogr. Acc. Cunningham* (Maitl. Cl.) 185 To Mr. Williame Birsbane, of *vicarege teynd the said yeir, aucht pund. **1640–1** *Kircudbr. War-Comm. Min. Bk.* (1855) 163 The halfe of the said gleib and vicarege teindes.

vicarate (ˈvɪkərət). [f. VICAR + -ATE. Cf. VICARIATE.] A parish, district, etc., under the jurisdiction of a vicar; a vicariate.

1883 *American* V. 319 Retaining the administration of the vicarate of North Carolina. **1910** *Q. Reg. Presbyt. Ch.* Aug. 337 In the diocese of Albi,..a number of vicarates have been suppressed.

vicar choral. Also vicar-choral. [VICAR 3.] (See quot. 1854, and cf. CHORAL *a.*¹ 1 b.)

The pl. occurs in various forms, as *vicars choral*, †*vicars chorals*, and, rarely, *vicar chorals*.

1530–1 *Act 22 Hen. VIII*, c. 15 All other..canons, pety canons, vicars chorall, & clerkes. **1546** *Yorks. Chantry Surv.* (Surtees) 348 The same prebendaries have..vicars..under them..called vicars choralles, which..are bound to discharge the said prebendaryes of all their cures and service in the sayd church. *a* **1661** FULLER *Worthies, Wilts.* III. (1662) 157 William Lawes, son of Thomas Lawes, a Vicar Choral of the Church of Salisbury. **1704** *Acc. Innov. Abp. Dublin* 3 He calls..the Vicar-Chorals, and orders them to answer, notwithstanding [etc.]. **1770** in *Mem. Rev. W. Richardson* (1822) 14 You seem to have been much taken with York Minster and Cathedral Service, would you like to be one of the Vicars Choral? **1837–8** *Act 1 & 2 Vict.* c. 106 §39 Any Spiritual Person, being Prebendary, Canon, Priest Vicar, Vicar Choral, or Minor Canon. **1854** HOOK *Church Dict.* (ed. 7) 791/1 *Vicars choral* [are] the assistants or deputies of the canons or prebendaries of collegiate churches,..especially, though not exclusively, in the duties of the choir or chancel, as distinguished from those belonging to the altar and pulpit. **1873** PHILLIMORE *Eccl. Law Ch. Eng.* 161 The two classes of petty or minor canons and vicars-choral. *Ibid.*, A vicar-choral of the cathedral church of Wells.

Hence **vicar-'choralship**, the office of a vicar-choral.

1868 *Ecclesiologist* XXIX. 171 The endowments..of vicars-choralships. **1891** *Star* 1 Nov. 1/7 The vicar-choralship of St. Paul's is by no means a poor appointment.

vicaress (ˈvɪkərɪs). Also 7 viccaris. [f. VICAR + -ESS¹.]

1. The sister ranking immediately beneath the Abbess or Mother Superior in a nunnery or convent.

c **1613** in *Cath. Rec. Soc. Publ.* (1914) XIV. 34, 2 years before her death [she] was chosen first Vicaress of yˢ Monastery. *a* **1700** *Diary Blue Nuns* Ibid. VIII. 11 Sister Margarite Bruno alias Floyd was again chosen Viccaris. **1721** *Ibid.* 291 The Office of Vicaresse is nearest the Abbesse in Authority... The Vicaresse represents in every place, the Abbesse when she is absent. **1804** in *Archaeologia* (1840) XXVIII. 198 Mother Austin was afterwards Vicaress [of the Blue Nuns' convent] several years. **1857** G. OLIVER *Coll. Cath. Relig. Cornwall*, etc. 136 The vicaress, the Rev. Mother Eyston, was sent to Bruges. **1892** J. M. STONE *Faithful unto Death* 244 To govern the new community as abbess and vicaress respectively.

2. A (female) representative. In quot. *fig.*

1662 J. CHANDLER *Van Helmont's Oriat.* 125 The sensitive Soul, the vicaresse of the minde, doth surely rejoyce in a greater liberty than the souls of bruit Beasts.

3. The wife of the vicar of a parish.

1770 W. HUDDESFORD in J. Granger *Lett.* (1805) 146, I am under the greatest obligation to the vicaress, for her forgiveness of my impertinence. **1849** LD. COLERIDGE in *Life & Corr.* (1904) I. viii. 190 Nothing could be kinder than the Vicar and Vicaress. **1862** MRS. HOUSTOUN *Recommended to Mercy* xii, The encroachments of the Vicaress in the government of the parish.

'vicar 'general. Also vicar-general. [VICAR 4 c, after med.L. *vicarius generalis*, F. *vicaire général*.]

The pl. occurs variously as *vicars general(s*, *vicar generals*.

†**1.** The title assumed by or bestowed upon the Pope, as head of the Church under Christ. *Obs.*

1390 GOWER *Conf.* I. 253 At Rome..The vicair general of alle Of hem that lieven Cristes feith. **1456** SIR G. HAYE *Law Arms* (S.T.S.) 104 God.., and next him his vicare generale the pape. **1539** TONSTALL *Serm. Palm Sund.* (1823) 46 All power is gyuen to me that Christe had: and I am his vicar general, as Peter was here in erthe ouer all. **1581** ALLEN *Apol.* 17 Whither should we rather flee for releefe either of body or soul, then to..the Vicar general of Christ? **1651** HOBBES *Leviath.* IV. xliv. 335 Consequent to this claim of the Pope to Vicar Generall of Christ in the present Church,..is the Doctrine, that it is necessary for a Christian King, to receive his Crown by a Bishop.

transf. *c* **1386** CHAUCER *Doctor's T.* 20 Lo, I, Nature, Thus can I forme and peynte a creature... For He that is the Former principal, Hath maad me his viker general [etc.].

2. *R.C. Ch.* An ecclesiastical officer, usually a cleric, appointed by a bishop as his representative in matters of jurisdiction or administration.

c **1450** *St. Cuthbert* (Surtees) 8023 Before his pepill ordande he þe prior archedekyn forto be, And his generall vicare. **1498** *Reg. Privy Seal Scotl.* I. 36/1 A presentation.. Direct to the vicare general of Sanctandris, the sege thairof vacand. **1509** *Plumpton Lett.* (1839) 205 Master Plompton, ..at his departing out of England, comaunded to me John Carvar, his Vicker generall,..to wryte unto you. *a* **1578** LINDESAY (Pitscottie) *Chron. Scot.* (S.T.S.) I. 286 Pryor Johnne Hepburne was at that time wicar generall of the bischoperick of Sanctandrois. *c* **1628** in Foley *Rec. Eng. Prov. S.J.* I. I. 137 His inferior officers, dispersed throughout all the Countyes of this realme, with titles, powers, and formalities belonging to any Catholique Bishops wheresoever, as Vicaires Generalls. **1672** in *Cath. Rec. Soc. Publ.* III. 100 Mr George Richardson..was ordained in Ireland by ye Ch^{rs} dimissoryes given him by ye Vicar Gen[era]ll. **1706** PHILLIPS (ed. Kersey), *Vice-Dominus Episcopi*, the Official, Commissary, or Vicar-general of a Bishop. **1767** *Phil. Trans.* LVII. 461 The vicar-general of this diocese. **1797** MRS. RADCLIFFE *Italian* xxvi, While Vivaldi spoke the vicar-general listened with attention. **1799** C. BUTLER *Life A. Butler* xiii, He was immediately appointed vicar-general to the bishops of Arras, St. Omer's, Ipres, and Boulogne. **1847** S. AUSTIN *Ranke's Hist. Ref.* III. 81 The bishop..sent some delegates, under his vicar-general Faber. **1885** LADY HERBERT tr. *Lagrange's Life Dupanloup* I. 358 The Abbé Valgalier,..and the Abbé Desnoyers, were made titular vicar generals.

b. Similarly in the Church of England; *spec.* a permanent lay official serving as a deputy or assistant to a bishop, or to the Archbishop of Canterbury or York, in certain ecclesiastical causes.

1536 *Act 28 Hen. VIII*, c. 10 §4 All and every Archebisshoppes, Bisshippes and Archedeacons,..their Commissaries, Vicars generall, and other their Mynisters.. shall make diligente inserch [etc.]. **1588** *Marprel. Epist.* (Arb.) 3 To the right puisante, and terrible Priests, my cleargie masters of the Confocation-house, whether fickers generall,..or any other of the holy league of subscription. *a* **1700** EVELYN *Diary* 31 Aug. 1663, After which the Vicar-general went to the vestry, and brought his Grace into the Chapell [at Lambeth]. **1726** AYLIFFE *Parergon* 161 According to the common way of Speech, a Chancellor is a Vicar General to the Bishop to all Intents and Purposes of Law. **1836** *Penny Cycl.* VI. 481/2 The Chancellor of a Church or of a Bishop is Vicar-general to the bishop, holds his courts [etc.]. **1854** HOOK *Church Dict.* (ed. 7) 792/1 The Vicar-General, an ecclesiastical officer who assists the bishop in the discharge of his office, as in causes and visitations. **1887** *Pall Mall G.* 23 June 2/2 The Vicar-General [in the Isle of Man] is a man of many callings, holding, in addition to the Vicar-Generalship, the positions of secretary to the bishop, keeper of the records, coroner, and magistrate. **1907** *Who's Who* 413 Cripps, C. A... Vicar-General of Canterbury; Chancellor and Vicar-Gen. of York since 1900.

3. *Hist.* The title given to Thomas Cromwell in 1535 as representative of the King in ecclesiastical affairs. (Cf. VICEGERENT *sb.* 1, quots. 1536-38.)

1679 BURNET *Hist. Ref.* I. III. 181 The first act of the Kings Supremacy was, his naming Cromwell Vicar-General, and General Visitor of all the Monasteries and other Priviledged places. **1706** tr. *Dupin's Eccl. Hist. 16th C.* II. IV. vii. 419 *note*, The name of Vicar-General, as appointed by the Prince, had been odious ever since Cromwell's management of that office in Henry VIII's time; and was never, for that reason, taken up afterwards. **1714** JER. COLLIER *Eccl. Hist. Gt. Brit.* II. II. 104/1 It appears that Cromwell by being made Vicar General had an entire Delegation of the King's Supremacy.

†**4.** (See quot.) *Obs.*

1568 GRAFTON *Chron.* II. 235 The King was made Vicare generall, and Lieutenant for the Emperour.

Hence **vicar-ˈgeneralship**, the office of a vicar-general.

a **1578** LINDESAY (Pitscottie) *Chron. Scot.* (S.T.S.) I. 287 The bischope..be the consall of wyse men gaif to this pryour the wickar generallschip. **1714** JER. COLLIER *Eccl. Hist. Gt. Brit.* II. II. 104/1 A Mistake in confounding this Vicar Generalship with his following Dignity of Lord Vice gerent in Ecclesiastical Matters. **1850** GLADSTONE *Glean.* (1879) V. 193 The Vicar-generalship of Cromwell and..the episcopal Commissions of both these reigns. **1892** *Pall Mall G.* 4 Feb. 7/1 Twenty-five years of Vicar-Generalship under Manning..ought to weigh in the balance even against aristocratic descent and Court favour.

vicariad (vɪˈkɛərɪæd). *Ecol.* [f. as VICARIANT *sb.* and *a.* + -AD.] = VICARIANT *sb.*

1944 S. A. CAIN *Found. Plant Geogr.* xviii. 266 Most of the studies of vicariads have referred to species. **1960** N. POLUNIN *Introd. Plant Geogr.* vii. 202 True vicariads (which have arisen from a common stock) should be distinguished from false ones which have not this close genetic relationship... True vicariads..may be classified according to the manner of their separation from one another into (1) horizontal (geographical), (2) altitudinal (physiographic), (3) habitat (ecological), and (4) seasonal (..closely related forms differing in their times of development). **1972** D. M. MOORE in D. H. Valentine *Taxonomy, Phytogeogr. & Evolution* viii. 119 The aquatic *Littorella*, absent from North America, is effectively an amphitropical vicariad and certainly results from a much more recent migration.

vicariage, obs. form of VICARAGE.

vicarial (vaɪ-, vɪˈkɛərɪəl), *a.* [ad. L. type **vicāriāl-is*, f. *vicārius* VICAR. So F. and Sp. *vicarial.*]

1. Delegated, deputed; vicarious.

1617 SLINGSBY *Diary* (1836) 297 Our Lord communicated his power to preistis and his ministires and vicars, and so thar power is ministeriall and vicariall as they call it. *a* **1734** NORTH *Lives* (1826) I. 392 By these vicarial offices in the house his lordship was educated to the employ there. **1747** WEST *Resurrection* (ed. 2) 275 God..promised to continue that delegated vicarial Sceptre of Righteousness in his [David's] Posterity for ever. **1803** *Edin. Rev.* I. 390 The contest for vicarial and deputed power..is more prudent than the struggle for that which is original and supreme. **1850** CDL. WISEMAN *Pastoral* 7 Oct., The silver links of that chain which has connected their country with the See of Peter in its Vicarial Government. **1868** LIGHTFOOT *Philip.* (1885) 267 His office is representative, and not vicarial.

2. Of or belonging to a vicar or vicars.

1744 J. COMYNS *Reports of Cases* 634 Wallis ver. Pain and Underhill... Mr. Underhill the Vicar insisted upon the Tithe of Clover Seed as a Vicarial or small Tithe. **1765** BLACKSTONE *Comm.* I. 376 Hence many things, as wood in particular, is in some countries a predial, and in some a vicarial tithe. **1825** R. CHURTON in R. Chandler *Trav. Asia M.* I. Introd. p. viii, He fitted up the vicarial house. **1840** *John Bull* 7 Nov. 540/2 A question relative to the liability of vicarial lands to Church rates was mooted before the bench. **1865** M. E. C. WALCOTT *Cathedralia* 165 The vicarial stalls of Gaia major and Sandiacre have been also restored.

3. Consisting of vicars.

1771 in *Mem. Rev. W. Richardson* (1821) 13 In May, the death of poor Frank, by a consumption, made a vacancy in the vicarial body.

4. Holding the office of a vicar.

1806 V. KNOX *Serm. Isa. xxviii. 16* Wks. 1824 VI. 377 But the great proprietors of land soon..obtained for each a resident pastor, either rectorial or vicarial, either an incumbent or a substitute.

vicarian (vaɪ-, vɪˈkɛərɪən), *sb.* and *a.* [ad. late L. *vicāriān-us*, f. L. *vicārius* VICAR, or independently f. *vicāri-us* + -AN.]

A. *sb.* †**1.** A substitute or deputy holding some office. *Obs.*$^{-1}$

1598 MARSTON *Sco. Villanie* I. iii. (1599) 183 Shall Balbus, the demure Athenian, Dreame of the death of next Vicarian? Cast his natiuitie?

2. One who accepts the view of religious vicariousness.

1851 RUSKIN *Sheepfolds* 37 Ecclesiastical tyranny has, for the most part, founded itself on the idea of Vicarianism, one of the most pestilent of the Romanist theories... Of this I have a word or two to say to the modern 'Vicarian'.

B. *adj.* Of or pertaining to, governed by, a deputy ruler.

1643 USSHER *Disquis. Asia* 16 The greater part of the inland Lydia was brought under this Vicarian regiment. **1654** VILVAIN *Theol. Treat.* vi. 156 The Dragon..covertly erected a Vicarian Kingdom.

Hence **viˈcarianism** (see A. 2 above).

vicariant (vɪˈkɛərɪənt), *sb.* and *a.* *Ecol.* [f. L. *vicāri-us* substitute (see VICAR) + -ANT^1, tr. G. *vic-*, *vikarirend*, pres. pple. of *vikarieren* (now *vikariieren*) †to substitute for: cf. *vic-*, *vikarirend spezies* in F. Unger *Ueber den Einfluss des Bodens auf die Vertheilung der Gewächse* (1836) III. 92; M. Wagner *Die Darwin'sche Theorie* (1868) in *Die Entstehung der Arten durch räumliche Sonderung* (1889) 56.] **A.** *sb.* A vicariant form of a plant or animal.

1952 L. CROIZAT *Man. Phytogeogr.* iv. 224 Cruciferae and Capparidaceae..could bear being characterized as vicariants. **1957** P. DANSEREAU *Biogeogr.* ii. 104 On the Nimba mountains of West Africa, Schell..has cited many mountain vicariants in genera of both rain-forest..and savana. **1979** CARDONA & CONTANDRIOPOULOS in D. Bramwell *Plants & Islands* viii. 155 In the *Genista acanthoclada* DC. group..the following subspecies are vicariants: *G. acanthoclada* ssp. *acanthoclada* (Greece and Aegean Islands), ssp. *echinus* (Spach) Vals. (S. Anatolia), [etc.].

B. *adj.* Being or involving varieties, species, communities, or the like that have evolved out of effective contact with one another from a common ancestral stock, esp. in habitats that are similar though separated.

1952 L. CROIZAT *Man. Phytogeogr.* vi. 355 This form in the end will split up into..vicariant species. **1957** P. DANSEREAU *Biogeogr.* i. 22 Vicariant varieties, subspecies, species, and genera may differ not only in leaf shape..but also in habitat requirements. **1957** A. MACFADYEN *Animal Ecol.* i. 8 The practical advantages include the possibility of using certain 'vicariant' species as 'indicator organisms'.. for the detection..of certain types of habitat. **1972** D. BRAMWELL in D. H. Valentine *Taxonomy, Phytogeogr. & Evolution* ix. 153 A high degree of vicariant evolution is to be expected in an archipelago such as the Canaries where..sets of ecological conditions are replicated from east to west on a series of islands with similar vegetation zones. **1982** *Sci. Amer.* July 33/2 Whether they are vicariant species, with common parents but evolved in place, or whether they first became distinct and then spread is unclear.

Hence **viˈcariance**, the existence of vicariant forms; the separation or subdivision of a population by the appearance of a geographical barrier and subsequent differentiation.

1957 A. MACFADYEN *Animal Ecol.* xv. 223 It is also possible to use other criteria..such as frequency, dominance or even 'vicariance'. **1972** D. BRAMWELL in D. H. Valentine *Taxonomy, Phytogeogr. & Evolution* ix. 151 Adaptive radiation..is a positive process where genetical response to the stimulus of the environment is the main factor; but vicariance, that is divergent evolution in which geographical isolation has been a very important factor, is perhaps a more passive process where the inter-action of genetic drift and weak selection result in the establishment of distinctive characters in populations which occupy essentially similar ecological habitats to their parents. **1979** *Nature* 15 Feb. 562/1 It is possible that the presence of hadrosaurs in Laurasia and Gondwanaland represents vicariance rather than dispersal; if so, hadrosaurs would be expected to occur on most continents. **1981** NELSON & PLATNICK *Systematics & Biogeogr.* i. 45 Speciation, at least in animals, usually involves a process of geographic isolation .., and occurs when a formerly continuous population is divided by the appearance of a barrier (a process called vicariance).

vicariate (vaɪ-, vɪˈkɛərɪət), *sb.* Also 7 **vicariot**, 7-9 **vicariat**. [ad. med.L. *vicāriāt-us*, f. L. *vicāri-us* VICAR. Cf. OF. and F. *vicariat*, It., Sp., Pg. *vicariato.*]

1. The office or authority of a vicar in a religious or ecclesiastical sense: **a.** Of persons acting as earthly representatives of God or Christ.

1610 DONNE *Pseudo-martyr* 247 [To make] Kings, which before had their Lieutenancie and Vicariate from God, but Magistrates..to his Vicar. ? **1614** —— *Elegy to Ld. Harrington* Poems (1669) 249 To deliver up to God that state Of which he gave thee the Vicariate. *a* **1676** HALE *True Relig.* II. (1684) 28 Hold what you will, if you hold not the Supremacy and Vicariot of the Pope, all the rest of your Religion is not worth a rush. **1882-3** *Schaff's Encycl. Relig. Knowl.* III. 2456/1 Through St. Peter the vicariate was forever conferred on the bishop of Rome.

b. Of the deputy of a bishop, etc.

1611 SIR D. CARLETON *Let.* in *10th Rep. Hist. MSS. Comm.* App. I. 546 Upon ye late remove of our patriarch's vicar there hath fallen vacant a benefice annexed to ye vicariat. **1725** tr. *Dupin's Eccl. Hist. 17th C.* I. v. 110 Vigilius gave his Vicariate to this Arch-Bishop in the Provinces. *a* **1773** A. BUTLER *Lives Saints* (1845) XI. 103 St. Charles established a vicariat, that things might be done with deliberation and counsel, which many other bishops imitated.

c. Of a vicar in the Church of England. Also *freq.*, the period of a vicar's ministry.

1857 J. JORDAN *Paroch. Hist. Enstone* iv. 191 The Rev. J. Beckingham was at some period of his vicariat ejected. **1887** *Pall Mall G.* 24 Jan. 10/1 He..pointed to the record of his fifteen years' vicariate, during which he had taken none of the parish income.

2. A political office held by a person as deputy for another; deputed exercise of authority by a person or governing body.

1619 F. COTTINGTON *Let.* in *Eng. & Germ.* (Camden) 33 If he should chance to fayle, the vicariate of Upper Germany must neades fall upon the Palatin. **1711** *Lond. Gaz.* No. 4844/2 He has accepted and taken upon him..his part of the Vicariate of the Empire during the present Vacancy. **1769** ROBERTSON *Chas. V*, II. Wks. 1813 V. 249 The vicariat of that part of Germany which is governed by the Saxon laws, devolved to the elector of Saxony. **1844** DISRAELI *Coningsby* v. viii. 220 An educated nation recoils from the imperfect vicariate of what is called a representative government. **1898** DILL *Rom. Soc. Last Cent. Western Empire* 16 Flavianus received the vicariate of Africa.

attrib. **1762** tr. *Busching's Syst. Geog.* IV. 38 They may hold vicariate aulic courts.

3. a. A district under the rule of a deputy governor.

1755 SMOLLETT *Quix.* (1803) IV. 204 Donna Guiomar de Quinones, wife to the regent of the vicariate of Naples. **1840** *Penny Cycl.* XVIII. 404/2 The provinces which constituted, under the Christian emperors, successors of Constantine, the vicariate of Rome. [*Ibid.*, These provinces were under the lay jurisdiction of an imperial vicar.]

b. *R.C. Ch.* A district under the charge of a vicar apostolic; the see of a vicar apostolic.

1818 HALLAM *Mid. Ages* (1819) II. 226 By the constitution of the church..every province ought to have its metropolitan, and every vicariate its ecclesiastical exarch or primate. **1857** G. OLIVER *Coll. Hist. Cath. Relig. Cornwall*, etc. 425 This western vicariate becoming vacant by the death of Bishop Baggs. **1890** T. COOPER in *Dict. Nat. Biog.* XXI. 374/1 He was selected by the propaganda to preside as bishop over the vicariate of the West Indies.

c. A church ministered to by a vicar.

1762 tr. *Busching's Syst. Geog.* IV. 335 In it is one collegiate and seven other churches, which are vicariates to the former.

4. Vicariousness. *rare*$^{-1}$.

1877 A. CAVE *Script. Doctr. Sacr.* I. I. ii. 52 They knew that the lives of innocent..animals were taken in lieu of their own..; what did they regard as the reason of this singular vicariate?

Hence **viˈcariateship**. *rare*$^{-1}$.

1753 *Scots Mag.* XV. 27/1 There is a dispute..between the Elector Palatine, and the Elector of Bavaria, about one of these Vicariatships.

viˈcariate, *a. rare.* Also 7 **vicariat**. [f. L. *vicāri-us* + -ATE^2, or attrib. use of prec.] Pertaining to, characteristic of, a deputy or representative; delegated.

1619 NAUNTON in *Eng. & Germ.* (Camden) 33 Such strength and forces as may..enable him to maintaine the vicariat dignitie when it shall fall uppon him. *a* **1677** BARROW *Pope's Suprem.* vi. Wks. 1687 I. 261 We thought it convenient that you should be held up by the vicariat authority of our See. **1849** ROCK *Ch. of Fathers* II. vi. 137 To the Bishops of Arles had the Holy See deputed a vicariate power there.

vi'cariate, *v. rare.* [f. VICARIATE *sb.*] *intr.* To act as a deputy or substitute.
1827 Carlyle *Germ. Rom.* III. 139 Her he edified by his Literary History, as relating to himself and the Subrector; how, for instance, he was at present vicariating in the Second Form [etc.].

†vicaried. *Obs.*⁻¹ In 4 vikeried. (App. a mistranslation of med.L. *vicariātus* VICARIATE *sb.*)
1388 Wyclif *Ecclus.* xxxiii. 6 *note*, Netheles he [an evil prelate] scorneth God, and takith the office of his vikeried, and chargith not of his onour.

vicariism (vɪˈkɛərɪɪz(ə)m). *Ecol.* Also **vicarism**. [f. as VICARIANT *sb.* and *a.* + -ISM, or ad. G. *vikarismus.*] = *vicariance* s.v. VICARIANT *sb.* and *a.*
1939 *Bull. Misc. Information* (R. Botanic Gardens, Kew) v. 229 Vicarious species are particularly instructive to study. These are species inhabiting contiguous but not (or scarcely) overlapping areas. Vicarism may be altitudinal or geographical. **1944** S. A. Cain *Found. Plant Geogr.* xviii. 265 The concept of vicariism is equally applicable to other than the specific category, i.e., to subspecies, sections, etc., and to communities. **1953** R. Good *Geogr. Flowering Plants* (ed. 2) xi. 212 Another particular kind of vicariism, which may be described as climatic, is illustrated..by the two littoral species *Ipomoea pes-caprae* and *Calystegia soldanella*. The former is almost or quite pan-tropical, but the latter is more or less pan-temperate and the two meet at the Kermadecs and elsewhere in similar latitudes. **1969** M. D. F. Udvardy *Dynamic Zoogeogr.* iv. 192 The concept of vicarism is used widely..when comparing certain types of distributional areas. **1974** *Boissiera* XXIII. 296 The distribution patterns of the different chromosome races agree with certain main types of false vicariism.

vicarious (vaɪ-, vɪˈkɛərɪəs), *a.* [f. L. *vicāri-us* adj. and sb., f. *vic-is* change, turn, stead, office, etc.: see -ARIOUS.]

1. a. That takes or supplies the place of another thing or person; substituted instead of the proper thing or person.
1637 Gillespie *Eng. Pop. Cerem.* III. iv. 56 If I.. religiously adore before the Pastor, as the Vicarious Signe of Christ himself. **1664** H. More *Myst. Iniq.* 319 The Interreges are necessarily reducible to the Regal Power, being but a vicarious Appendage thereto. **1688** Boyle *Final Causes Nat. Things* II. 70 Gravel and little stones..are often found..in their stomachs, where they prove a vicarious kind of teeth. **1709** T. Robinson *Vind. Mosaick Syst.* 29 God.. made it [*sc.* the moon] a vicarious Light to the Sun, to supply its absence in this lower World. **1785** Burke *Sp. Nabob Arcot's Debts* Wks. 1842 I. 320 These modern flagellants are sure..to whip their own enormities on the vicarious back of every small offender. **1829** I. Taylor *Enthus.* vii. 161 Every right-minded and heaven-commissioned minister of religion is..in..a real sense..a vicarious person. **1850** Blackie *Æschylus* II. 68 This, And worse expect, unless some god endure Vicarious thy tortures. **1853** Abp. Thomson *Laws Th.* §30 (ed. 3) 59 The cry or exclamation.. would be consciously reproduced to represent or recal the feeling on another occasion; and it then became a word, or vicarious sign.

b. Const. *of* (something). *rare.*
1831 Sir W. Hamilton *Discuss.* (1852) 404 The Univeristy and Colleges are thus neither identical, nor vicarious of each other. **1836–7** —— *Metaph.* viii. (1870) 131 If the science be able to possess no single name vicarious of its definition.

2. Of punishment, etc.: Endured or suffered by one person in place of another; accomplished or attained by the substitution of some other person, etc., for the actual offender. Freq. in *Theol.* with reference to the suffering and death of Christ.
1692 Bentley *Boyle Lect.* ix. 319 Some means of Reconciliation must be contrived; some vicarious satisfaction to Justice. **1698** Norris *Pract. Disc.* (1707) IV. 137 But as Precious as it was, it was not the very thing that the Law required, but a Vicarious Punishment. **1736** Butler *Anal. Relig.* II. v. 211 Vicarious Punishments may be..absolutely necessary. **1781** Johnson in *Boswell* 3 June, Whatever difficulty there may be in the conception of vicarious punishments. **1836** J. Gilbert *Chr. Atonem.* iii. (1852) 80 The Christian doctrine of vicarious expiation. **1850** Blackie *Æschylus* II. 319 The idea of vicarious sacrifice, or punishment by substitution,..does not seem to have been very familiar to the Greek mind. **1860** Pusey *Min. Proph.* 12 The manifold harvest, which He..should bring forth..by His vicarious Death. **1883** Gilmour *Mongols* xvii. 202 Vicarious suffering too seems strange to them, their own system teaching that for his sin a man must suffer, and there is no escape.

3. Of power, authority, etc.: Exercised by one person, or body of persons, as the representative or deputy of another.
1706 Phillips (ed. Kersey), *Vicarious*, belonging to a Vicar, subordinate; as A Vicarious Power. **1777** Johnson in *Boswell* (1904) I. 126, I shall be considered as exercising a kind of vicarious jurisdiction. **1807** J. Barlow *Columb.* I. 5 Who sway'd a moment, with vicarious power, Iberia's sceptre. **1844** H. H. Wilson *Brit. India* III. 285 Such vicarious powers were conferred upon His Majesty's Courts at all the Indian Presidencies. **1855** Macaulay *Hist. Eng.* III. 487 He had..held, during some months, a vicarious primacy.
transf. **1835–6** *Todd's Cycl. Anat.* I. 322/1 Redi's opinion, that the pebbles [swallowed by birds] perform the vicarious office of teeth.

4. a. Performed or achieved by means of another, or by one person, etc., on behalf of another.
1806 Fellowes tr. *Milton's 2nd Defence* Wks. VI. 377 He had not the courage..to prefix a dedication to Charles without the vicarious aid of Flaccus. **1822** Lamb *Elia* I. *Bachelor's Complaint*, I must protest against the vicarious gluttony of Cerasia, who..sent away a dish of Morellas..to her husband at the other end of the table. **1846** *Edin. Rev.* LXXXIV. 68 The increasing laxity of the Mussulman world, and the practice of vicarious pilgrimage, have greatly diminished the numbers of the sacred caravans. **1877** Gladstone *Glean.* (1879) IV. 347 May we never be subjected to the humiliation of dependence upon vicarious labour. **1894** H. Drummond *Ascent Man* 301 Unconscious of their vicarious service, the butterfly and the bee..carry the fertilizing dust to the waiting stigma.

b. Of qualities, etc.: Possessed by one person but reckoned to the credit of another.
1842 Pusey *Crisis Eng. Ch.* 136 To confound..individual duties with vicarious merits. **1856** Froude *Hist. Eng.* (1858) II. vi. 36 A system..where sin was expiated by the vicarious virtues of other men.

c. Of methods, principles, etc.: Based upon the substitution of one person for another.
1857 Hughes *Tom Brown* II. iii, It may be called the vicarious method; it obtained amongst big fellows of lazy or bullying habits, and consisted simply in making clever boys ..do their whole vulgus for them. **1870** J. H. Newman *Gram. Assent* II. x. 400 On this vicarious principle, by which we appropriate to ourselves what others do for us, the whole structure of society is raised.

d. Experienced imaginatively through another person or agency.
1929 R. S. & H. M. Lynd *Middletown* xvii. 237 To Middletown adults, reading a book means overwhelmingly what story-telling means to primitive man—the vicarious entry into other, imagined kinds of living. **1948** E. Waugh *Loved One* 31 He had lived his twenty-eight years at arm's length from violence, but he came of a generation which enjoys a vicarious intimacy with death. **1976** A. Powell *Infants of Spring* ix. 146 My father, between spasms of grumbling about school bills, and occasional resistance to attitudes of mind inevitably acquired at Eton, had taken a fair amount of vicarious pleasure in my being there.

5. *Physiol.* Denoting the performance by or through one organ of functions normally discharged by another; substitutive.
1780 *Encycl. Brit.* VI. 4747 The Vicarious Hæmoptysis. **1822–7** Good *Study Med.* (1829) I. 650 With a view of exciting a vicarious action, I opened an issue in one of the arms. *Ibid.* 668 Where the complaint is strictly idiopathic and uncombined, it has often been found to give way to some local irritation or vicarious drain. **1846** Day tr. *Simon's Anim. Chem.* II. 170 The vicarious action of the skin and lungs. **1877** Foster *Physiol.* (1878) 477 Vicarious reflex movements may also be witnessed in mammals.

6. *Ecol.* Of two or more species, etc.: similar to one another and occurring without the other(s) in different areas; usu., = VICARIANT *a.*
1932 Fuller & Conard tr. *Braun-Blanquet's Plant Sociol.* vi. 160 Closely related species found upon lime and clay slates he [*sc.* Unger] called substitute or vicarious species. **1937** R. Hesse et al. *Ecol. Animal Geogr.* vi. 77 Transitional variation may be wanting at the boundary between the ranges of vicarious forms which are then considered specifically distinct. **1960** N. Polunin *Introd. Plant Geogr.* vii. 201 With higher groupings—and even families and whole communities may in a sense be vicarious—there is less reason to suppose that their mutual exclusiveness is due to competition. **1981** P. Stott *Hist. Plant Geogr.* viii. 115 Vicarious evolution has been invoked..to explain the distribution [in the Canaries] of endemic species in *Centaurea* sect. *Cheirolophus* subsect. *Flaviflorae.*

vicariously (vaɪ-, vɪˈkɛərɪəslɪ), *adv.* [f. prec. + -LY².]

1. By substitution of one thing or person for another; by means of a substitute.
1796 Burke *Regic. Peace* ii. Wks. 1808 VIII. 237 Not being able to revenge themselves on God, they have a delight in vicariously defacing..his image in man. **1828** Scott *F.M. Perth* xvii, Some one must drink it for him, he shall be cured vicariously. **1835–6** *Todd's Cycl. Anat.* I. 133/1 Respiration is also carried on vicariously in a very large proportion of animals. **1861** J. G. Sheppard *Fall Rome* vii. 397 His campaigns were..vicariously carried on by a general whom common report designated as the Achilles of the Vandals. **1883** 'Ouida' *Wanda* I. 60 She never did anything vicariously which concerned those dependent upon her.

2. As a substitute for another.
1868 Garrod *Mat. Med.* (ed. 3) 410 To cause the skin to act vicariously when the action of other secreting organs is excessive. **1886** J. Morley *Crit. Misc.* I. 298 He suspected the practice by which one man offered up prayer vicariously and collectively for the assembled congregation.

3. At second hand, at one remove. Cf. VICARIOUS *a.* 4 d.
1925 F. Scott Fitzgerald *Gt. Gatsby* vii. 157 Jordan and I tried to go, but Tom and Gatsby insisted..that we remain —as though..it would be a privilege to partake vicariously of their emotions. **1957** L. Durrell *Justine* II. 127 Those interminable monologues about a life which has long since receded, lost its vital momentum, only to live on vicariously in the labyrinths of memory. **1984** *N.Y. Times* 13 May. VI. 70/2, I think the greatest moral pitfall is not that we witness too much bang bang, but that, for the most part, we perceive it vicariously.

vi'cariousness. [f. as prec. + -NESS.] The quality or condition of being vicarious.
1727 Bailey (vol. II). **1858** J. Martineau *Stud. Chr.* 188 If the vicariousness be not this mere pretence, it describes an outrage upon the first principles of rectitude. **1874** H. R. Reynolds *John Bapt.* v. §2. 328 The vicariousness of the sacrifice makes a more severe demand upon our conscience and intelligence. **1889** *Lancet* 27 July 175/1 Another favourite assertion of the opponents of vaccination—the vicariousness of zymotic mortality.

'vicarish, *a.* [f. VICAR + -ISH¹.] Suitable for or characteristic of a vicar.
1938 *Times Lit. Suppl.* 26 Oct. 734/2 Two maids..an amiable vicar and his very vicarish wife and a certain Captain Carling complete the party. **1976** *New Society* 29 Jan. 206/3, I was also subject to frequent visits by vicars, who popped their heads round my door in a vicarish manner every so often. **1979** K. M. Peyton *Marion's Angels* i. 2 'It doesn't *belong* to her,' they said. 'It belongs to God, and so does Marion.' A typical, vicarish remark, they said.

†vicariship. *Obs. rare*⁻¹. [f. VICARY *sb.*¹] = VICARSHIP.
c **1430** *Pilgr. Lyf Manhode* I. xv. (1869) 11 Thow shuldest also not foryete of whom thow doost the vicarishipe.

†'vicarly, *a. Obs.*⁻¹ [f. VICAR 2.] Holding the position of a vicar.
1596 Nashe *Saffron Walden* Ep. Ded., A deuine vicarly brother of his, called Astrologicall Richard.

'vicarship. Also 6 -shyp, vycarship(pe. [f. VICAR + -SHIP.] The office or position of a vicar, in various senses of the word.
1534 Henry VIII in *Liber Regis* p. viii, Every other person that hath any dignitie, prebend, vycarship,..or other office. **1546** Bale *Eng. Votaries* I. (1560) 49 The general commission, whiche he had of Sathan his great mastre, in that vycarship of his. **1579** Fulke *Confut. Sanders* 540 Yᵉ Bishop of Ierusalem should more reasonably claime this supremacie & vicarship vnto Christ. **1611** Speed *Hist. Gt. Brit.* IX. xii. §66 Lewis of Bauar the Emperour sodainely.. re-called his Vicar-ship or delegation, which hee had made to Edward, to exercise imperiall power in lower Germany. **1653** H. Cogan tr. *Scarlet Gown* 66 After his arrival at Rome, Cardinal Capucino paid him all the profits accruing of his Vicarship by him administred in his absence. **1677** W. Hughes *Man of Sin* III. iv. 139 If St. Peters, and so his Holiness universal Vicarship follow hence. **1739** Swift *Let. to Pope* 10 May, There is a man in my choir, one Mr. Lamb; he has at present but half a vicarship. **1762** tr. *Busching's Syst. Geog.* III. 130 The crown of Spain held the vicarship of Siena as a fief of the Empire. **1839** I. Taylor *Ancient Chr.* I. 96 The universal vicarship of the bishop of Rome. **1867** R. Palmer *P. Howard* 71 He was recommended to the master-general by Cardinal Pole for the vicarship of the province. **1896** *Oxford Chron.* 25 July 5/4 The Bishop of Oxford has lost no time in filling up the Vicarship of Abingdon.

†'vicary, *sb.*¹ *Obs.* Forms: α. 4–5 **vicarie** (4 **vik-**), **-arye**, 4–6 **vycary** (4 **-arye**), 4–7 **vicary** (5 **-ari**), 6 **vykary**. β. 4–5 **vicori(e, viccorie**; 4 **vycory**, 4–5 **vicory, vecory**, 5 **vicorye**. γ. 4 **vi(c)kery**, 5 **vekery**. [ad. L. *vicāri-us* VICAR.]

1. = VICAR 1 and 1 b.
1303 R. Brunne *Handl. Synne* 11789 Þe prest ys crystys vycarye. **1338** —— *Chron.* (1810) 283 No man has powere þer of to deme no wirke, Withoute þe pape of Rome, Gode's vicarie. *c* **1381** Chaucer *Parl. Foules* 379 Nature, vicarye o the almyghty lord. **1393** Langl. *P. Pl.* C. xv. 70 Cleregie is cristes vikery to conforte and to curen. **1502** Arnolde *Chron.* (1811) 159 Unto the most holyest and fauorablist Prince in erthe, Vicary and Lieftenaunt of Cryst. **1529** More *Dyaloge* II. Wks. 179/2 The Pope which is vnder Christ vycary & the head of our churche.

2. = VICAR 2.
α. **1303** R. Brunne *Handl. Synne* 11607 Alle prestes haue nat powere..to assoyle þe..But hyt be þy parysshe preste .., Or at þy parsone or vycary. *c* **1330** —— *Chron. Wace* (Rolls) 5775 To parsones & to vicaries Was graunted grete seignuryes. *c* **1386** Chaucer *Parson's Prol.* 22 (Corpus), Sire Preest, quod he, art þou a vicary Or art þou a person? say soþ, by þy fey. **1417** *E.E. Wills* (1882) 28 Sir Iohn Dey, parsone of Bageworthe,..sir Edward Osbourne, vicary of Thornecombe. **1463** in *Somerset Medieval Wills* (1901) 200 The same writinges I send you nowe by the vicarye of Porestoke. *c* **1502** *Joseph Arim.* 253 The vykary of welles, that thyder had sought,..Released he was of part of his infyrmyte. *a* **1529** Skelton *Col. Cloute* 572 Of persons and vycaryes They make many outcryes. **1538** *North Country Wills* (Surtees, 1908) 158 To the vicarye of Willoby a mortuary.
β, γ. **1377** Langl. *P. Pl.* B. XIX. 407 Thanne is many man ylost, quod a lewed vycory. **1406** *E.E. Wills* (1882) 12 Y wyt to the vekery of the same Kyrke xij d. **1426** Audelay *Poems* 16 Alas he ner a parsun or a vecory. *c* **1450** *Chron. London* (Kingsford, 1905) 134 Ther was a prest of thaksted, that whas vicory some tyme, whas brent in Smythfelde. **1479** in *Eng. Gilds* (1870) 421 The Maire..and the Vicorye and the Propters [*sic*] with them.

3. = VICAR 3.
1432–50 tr. *Higden* (Rolls) VI. 465 For those men fleynge the laboure of the qwere..ordeynede vicaryes to occupye theire places. **1505** *Will R. Gybbys* 26 March (Prerog. Crt. Canterb.), Alsoe to Owen Parsons my rose cuppe..; but if he shold dye, thenne to my brethren the Vicaries of the Quere.

4. = VICAR 4.
1387 Trevisa *Higden* (Rolls) VI. 243 He ȝaf to þe pope, Peter his vicary, a rente by þe ȝere of everich hous of þe kyngdom. *c* **1430** *Pilgr. Lyf Manhode* I. xiii. (1869) 8 A maister j sigh fasteby that seemede to be a vicarie of aaron or of moyses.

5. = VICAR 5.
?**14..** *S. Eng. Legendary* (MS. Bodl. 779) in Herrig's *Archiv* LXXXII. 383/57 To myssian þe vecory þey were betake anon, þat he hem cholde make here sacrefise to don. **1422** Yonge tr. *Secreta Secret.* 214 Whan thou haste mestere to the Service of ten thousand men, thou cal a gouernoure, and hym shal Serve ten vicaries, and wyth euery vicarie shall cvm ten leders. **1491** Caxton *Vitas Patr.* I. clviii. (1495) 166/2 One of the sayd chyldren was made Senatour of Rome; the other Consul of Cartage, and thother vycarye in Affryque. **1648** *Hunting of Fox* (1649) 8 Yet this [council of state] is not our new intended King;..this is but his vicary.

†'vicary, *sb.*² *Obs.* Also 5 **wycari**, 6 **vicarye**. [a. AF. and OF. *vicarie* (*vikarie*), or ad. med.L.

vicāria, f. L. *vicārius* VICAR.] The office or position of a vicar; a benefice held by a vicar.

c **1420** in *Test. Ebor.* (Surtees) II. 119 *note*, Forasmuch as I am enfourmed that there is a vicary voide wᵗin your College of Hemmynburgh.. I pray yow wᵗ all myn hert that ye will graunte hym the seid vicary. *c* **1450** *Godstow Reg.* 437 The lond of the vicary of seynt Gyle.. without the north gate of Oxenford. *Ibid.* 580 Longyng.. to the said chirch of Seynt Petir by the reson of the vicary. **1483** *Cath. Angl.* 401/2 A wycari,.. *vicaria.* **1563** BECON *Reliques of Rome* 254 Houses of holy church, graunges, personages, or vicaries, or any maneries of men of holy church. **1598** MARSTON *Sco. Villanie* I. iii. (1599) 185 By chance.. [he] Hath got the farme of some gelt vicary. **1612** R. SHELDON *Serm. St. Martins* 4 The ambitious Bishop and Monarch of Rome.. in his pretended Vicary for the Messias. **1712** *Lond. Gaz.* No. 5079/3 The Vicary, part of Killcrusaper Tythes.

†'vicary, *a. Obs. rare.* [ad. L. *vicāri-us.*] Vicarious; delegated.

c **1400** *Apol. Loll.* 85 If ymagis be worschipid, not bi vicary worschip, but by þe same worschip of God, doutles it is idolatrie. **1660** J. LLOYD *Prim. Episc.* 25 Putting the hand and seal of his highest Vicary authority, as God's Vicegerent, to the resolves of the subordinate Vicary authority of the Vicegerents of our blessed Mediator.. Jesus Christ.

Vicat ('viːkɑː). *Engin.* The name of L. J. *Vicat* (1786–1861), French engineer, used *attrib.* with reference to an apparatus for measuring the consistency and setting time of Portland cement and other materials.

1904 C. F. MARSH *Reinforced Concrete* iii. 125 For this test the Vicat needle apparatus may be employed. **1910** *Brit. Standard Spec. for Portland Cement* (Engin. Standards Comm.) 10 The mixture shall be plastic when filled into the Vicat mould. **1956** J. N. ANDERSON *Appl. Dental Materials* xviii. 211 An alternative method of testing for initial set [of plaster] is to use the Vicat needle. **1979** I. SOROKA *Portland Cement Paste & Concrete* ii. 29 (*caption*) Vicat apparatus for determining the standard consistence and setting times of Portland cement.

vicayr(e, obs. forms of VICAR.

vice (vaɪs), *sb.*[1] Forms: 3- vice (5-6 *Sc.* wice), 4-6 vyce (5-6 *Sc.* wyce); 5 vise, wise, wisse; 5 vys, vijs (vyhs, *Sc.* vis), 6 vyss, *Sc.* wys. [a. AF. and OF. *vice* mod.F. *vice*, = Pr. *vici*, Sp. and Pg. *vicio*, It. *vizio*), ad. L. *vitium* fault, defect, failing, etc.]

1. a. Depravity or corruption of morals; evil, immoral, or wicked habits or conduct; indulgence in degrading pleasures or practices.

1297 R. GLOUC. (Rolls) 4025 Hit is ney vif ȝer þat we abbeþ yliued in such vice, Vor we nadde noȝt to done, & in such delice. *a* **1300** *Cursor M.* 24701 (Edinb.), If ani man in vice be cast He mai him draw fra þat last And be þat he was are. *c* **1340** HAMPOLE *Pr. Consc.* 4116 In wham al þe tresor of malice Sal be hidde with alle maner of vice. **1390** GOWER *Conf.* I. 7 Tho was the vertu sett above And vice was put under fote. *c* **1400** *Pilgr. Sowle* (Caxton, 1483) IV. xxiv. 70 Vyce destroyeth the myght and the rygour of the sowle. **1447** BOKENHAM *Seyntys* (Roxb.) 18 God.. heryth alle men gladly Wych to hym preye, puryd from vyhs. *a* **1500** *Ratis Raving*, etc. 3662 Quhen thai tak it our mesour, Thai turne in wys and in arroure. **1509** HAWES *Past. Pleas.* XI. (Percy Soc.) 46 Fy upon slouth, the nourysher of vyce, Whych unto youth doth often prejudice. **1560** DAUS tr. *Sleidane's Comm.* 119 b, That churche.. is replenyshed with theftes, robberies, and all other kynd of vice. **1620** T. GRANGER *Div. Logike* 123 As, vertue is to be insued: *Ergo*, vice is to be eschewed. **1644** MILTON *Educ.* 5 Instructing them more amply in the knowledge of virtue, and the hatred of vice. **1687** A. LOVELL tr. *Thevenot's Trav.* I. 104 It is impossible but that Vice must reign, where People are so ignorant of the commands of God. **1729** BUTLER *Serm.* Wks. 1874 II. 109 Vice is vice to him who is guilty of it. **1769** ROBERTSON *Chas. V*, IV. Wks. 1813 V. 395 In order to avoid vice (says he), men must practise perpetual mortification. **1821** BYRON *Mar. Fal.* II. i, Vice cannot fix, and virtue cannot change,.. For vice must have variety. **1835** URE *Philos. Manuf.* 406 To exist by beggary or plunder, in idleness and vice. **1873** 'OUIDA' *Pascarel* I. 6 You, who blush for your mirth because your mirth is vice.

b. Personified.

c **1420** LYDG. *Assembly of Gods* 602 A son of myn bastard, Whos name ys Vyce—he kepeth my vaward. **1602** SHAKS. *Ham.* III. iv. 154 Vertue it selfe, of Vice must pardon begge. **1634** MILTON *Comus* 760, I hate when vice can bolt her arguments, And vertue has no tongue to check her pride. **1739** R. BULL tr. *Dedekindus' Grobianus* 78 Oft in the mingled Scene, I've chanc'd to see A rev'rend Vice, a grey Iniquity. **1754** GRAY *Progr. Poesy* 80 Alike they scorn the pomp of tyrant-Power, And coward Vice, that revels in her chains. **1784** COWPER *Task* III. 106 Vice has such allowance, that her shifts And specious semblances have lost their use. **1813** SHELLEY *Falsehood & Vice* 11 Where.. War's mad fiends the scene environ,.. There Vice and Falsehood took their stand.

c. *ellipt.* for *vice squad*, sense 8 b below. *slang.*

1967 C. DRUMMOND *Death at Furlong Post* iv. 42 From his days on Vice Reed remembered the large free-spenders. **1976** *New Society* 4 Mar. 481/2 A woman they know is a junkie... She proceeds to tell them how she got picked up by the 'vice' the night before.

2. a. A habit or practice of an immoral, degrading, or wicked nature.

a **1300** *Cursor M.* 23286 Þai.. Ne wald noght here bot þair delices, Þat drogh þam vntil oþer vices. **1340** *Ayenb.* 17 Vor prede makeþ of elmesse zenne, and of uirtues vices. **1377** LANGL. *P. Pl.* B. XIX. 308 Þat loue myȝte wexe Amonge þe foure vertues and vices destroye. **1422** YONGE tr. *Secreta Secret.* 205 Als often [as] he is touchid wyth any wyce. *Ibid.*, Ofte Prayer quynchyth the Pryckynges of vices. **1474** CAXTON *Chesse* I. i. (1883) 9 Whan he reccheth not ner taketh hede unto them that repreue hym and his vices. **1545** BRINKLOW *Lament.* 79 They sett vp and mayntayne idolatrye, and other innumerable vices and wickedness. **1560** DAUS tr. *Sleidane's Comm.* 452 Such unaccustomed vices.. semed not so muche to be forboden, as shewed. **1605** SHAKS. *Lear* V. iii. 170 The Gods are iust, and of our pleasant vices Make instruments to plague vs. **1647** CLARENDON *Hist. Reb.* I. §3 Nor [to] speak of Persons otherwise, than as the mention of their Virtues or Vices is essential to the work in hand. **1729** LAW *Serious C.* ii. (1732) 16 How it comes to pass that Swearing is so common a Vice amongst Christians. **1771** *Junius Lett.* xlv. (1788) 257 There are degrees in all the private vices. **1818** MISS MITFORD in L'Estrange *Life* (1870) II. ii. 46 An Englishman's worst vice is more human than a Roman's best virtue. **1841** EMERSON *Ess.* I. x. (1905) 180 The virtues of society are vices of the saint. **1878** J. C. MORISON *Gibbon* 160 Madame de Maintenon,.. a woman, cold as ice and pure as snow, was freely charged with the most abhorrent vices.

b. Const. *of* (the vice in question).

1303 R. BRUNNE *Handl. Synne* 5967 Þou art falle þan yn þe vyce Of coueytyse, þeft, and auaryce. *c* **1375** *Sc. Leg. Saints* Prol. 7 Thru þe vicis of ydilnes, gret foly.., & vantones. *a* **1450** *Mirk's Festial* 118 Þer may no man fynde a payne, forto poynych dewly þe vyce of vnkyndnes. **1500–20** DUNBAR *Poems* xlix. 1 In vice most vicius he excellis, That with the vice of tressone mellis. **1597** SHAKS. *2 Hen. IV*, III. ii. 325 How subiect wee old men are to this vice of Lying. *a* **1637** B. JONSON *Underwoods* lv. *Ep. to Friend* 8 Not like their country neighbours that commit Their vice of loving for a Christmas-fit. **1754** J. EDWARDS *Freed. Will* III. v. 171 The Vertue of Temperance is regarded.. as a necessary Means of gratifying the Vice of Covetousness. **1859** TENNYSON *Geraint* 195 The dwarf.. doubling all his master's vice of pride, Made answer sharply that she should not know.

c. In horses: A bad habit or trick. Also without article (cf. sense 1).

1726 *Dict. Rust.* (ed. 3) s.v., Bad Horsemen occasion most of these Vices, by correcting unduely or out of time. **1753** *Chambers' Cycl.* Suppl. s.v., The rider is first cautiously to find whether this Vice proceeds from real stubbornness, or from faintness. **1810** *Sporting Mag.* XXXVI. 154 The horse was warranted sound, free from vice, and not more than three years old. **1847** T. BROWN *Mod. Farriery* 377 Of all the vices incidental to the horse, shying is one of the worst. *a* **1901** F. W. H. MYERS *Hum. Personality* (1903) I. 200 Those defects of stability which in a horse we call vice.

3. A character in a morality play representing one or other vice; hence, a stage jester or buffoon.

Very common *c* 1560–1630; now only *Hist.*

1551–2 in Feuillerat *Revels Edw. VI* (1914) 73 One vyces dagger & a ladle with a bable pendante.. deliverid to the Lorde of mysrules foole. **1553** *Respublica* (1905) 1 Avarice. .. The vice of the plaie. **1573** TUSSER *Husb.* (1878) 147 His face made of brasse, like a vice in a game, His iesture like Dauus, whom Terence doth name. **1600** W. WATSON *Decacordon* (1602) 156 He stands at their deuotion, and is but like an Ape, a Parrot, or a Vice in a play, to prate what is prompted or suggested vnto him. **1627** HAKEWILL *Apol.* (1630) 162 Luceia a common vice in playes followed the stage and acted thereon an hundred yeares. **1645** MILTON *Colast.* Wks. 1851 IV. 377 For I had rather.. not to have to doe with Clowns and Vices. **1767** S. PATERSON *Another Trav.* I. 113 Tom was the vice of every comedy, and the punch of every puppet-shew of his time. **1801** STRUTT *Sports & Past.* III. ii. 140 *note*, I remember to have seen a stage direction for the vice, to lay about him lustily with a great pole. **1886** A. W. WARD *Old Eng. Drama* (1901) 297 A favourite piece of horse-play in the old miracles and morals, when the Vice belabours the Devil.

transf. **1565** CALFHILL *Answ. Treat. Crosse* (1846) 210 When the Vice is come from the Altar, and the people shall have no more sport [etc.].

4. Moral fault or defect (without implication of serious wrongdoing); a flaw in character or conduct.

1338 R. BRUNNE *Chron.* (1810) 106 Sir Henry mad þe fyne, & mad þe mariage. Þe may withouten vice, his weddyng was wele dight. **1375** BARBOUR *Bruce* VI. 355 For hardyment vith foly is vis; Bot hardyment, that mellit is Vith vit, is vorschip ay. **1599** SHAKS. *Hen. V*, III. vi. 161 Ye forgiue me God, That I doe bragge thus; this your ayre of France Hath blowne that vice in me. **1638** JUNIUS *Paint. Ancients* 229 Whilest they thinke it enough to be without vice, they fall into that same maine vice to lacke vertues. **1794** PALEY *Evid.* III. iv. (1817) 319 Contempt, prior to examination, is an intellectual vice. **1827** MACAULAY *Ess.*, *Machiavelli* (1897) 44 Ferocity and insolence were not among the vices of the national character.

5. a. A fault, defect, blemish or imperfection, in action or procedure or in the constitution of a thing.

c **1386** CHAUCER *Sqr.'s T.* 93 He with a manly voys seith this message,.. Withouten vice of silable or of lettre. *a* **1400** *Bk. Curtasye* 131 in *Babees Bk.*, In salt saler yf þat þou pit Oþer fisshe or flesshe þat men may wyt, Þat is a vyce, as men me telles. *? a* **1400** *Morte Arth.* 911 The vesare, the aventaile,.. Voyde with-owttyne vice, with wyndowes of syluer. *c* **1440** *Pallad. on Husb.* I. 100 The londis fatte, or lene, or thicke, or rare, Or drie, or moyst, and not withouten vice. **1548** COOPER *Elyot's Dict.*, *Anacoluthos*, a vice in writyng or speakynge, whan the wordes aunswere not the one to the other. **1589** PUTTENHAM *Eng. Poesie* III. xxii. (Arb.) 257 The foulest vice in language is to speake barbarously. **1604** E. G[RIMSTONE] *D'Acosta's Hist. Indies* III. xxii. 188 There growes neither bread nor wine in these Ilands, for that the too great fertilitie and the vice of the soile suffers them not to seede. **1700** ROWE *Ambitious Step-Mother* Ded., I will engage not to be guilty of the common Vice of Dedications. **1729** SHELVOCKE *Artillery* III. 166 The first and most remarkable Vice in Rockets. **1781** J. MOORE *View Soc. Italy* (1790) I. xxxvii. 405 In edifices.. capable of sublimity from their bulk the vice of diminishing is not compensated by harmony. **1810** SOUTHEY in C. C. Southey *Life* (1849) III. 274 The vice of the Friend is its roundaboutness. **1854** A. W. FONBLANQUE in *Life & Labours* (1874) 513 Tenacity to fopperies and neglect of essentials is the vice of our Service. **1881** ARMSTRONG in *Nature* XXIV. 451 The vice of the steam-engine lies in its inability to utilise heat of comparatively low grade.

b. A physical defect or blemish; a deformity; a taint, imperfection, or weakness in some part of the system.

c **1386** CHAUCER *Wife's T.* 99 Myda hadde vnder his longe heres Growynge vpon his heed two asses eres; The which vice he hydde, as he best myghte. *c* **1400** *Lanfranc's Cirurg.* 181 If it so be þat allopucia comeþ of vijs of humouris, .. þanne vlcera wole be in þe skyn. *a* **1425** tr. *Arderne's Treat. Fistula*, etc. 81 Iuyse of caprifoile þat is called licium availeþ bi itself to al þe vicez of þe mouþe. *c* **1440** *Alph. Tales* 218 Demostenes.. laburd so agayn a vice & ane impediment in his mouthe, þat no man myght speke fayrer. **1541** R. COPLAND *Galyen's Terap.* 2 F j, Nat that the dyuturnyte indyketh the curacyon, but the vyce of the blode. **1552** HULOET, Vice of a shorte breath, or winde, *apnæa.* **1643** SIR T. BROWNE *Relig. Med.* I. §41, I perceive I doe anticipate the vices of age. **1697** DRYDEN *Virg. Georg.* III. 693 Launce the Sore, and cut the Head; for 'till the Core be found, The secret Vice is fed, and gathers Ground. **1743** tr. *Heister's Surg.* 303 Physicians.. attribute most Disorders of the Body to some Vice in the Blood. **1830** R. KNOX *Béclard's Anat.* 65 The numerous vices which consist in a disunion or separation in the median line. *Ibid.* 104 Vices of conformation are observed in some of these membranes. **1850** TENNYSON *In Mem.* iii, Shall I take a thing so blind, Embrace her as my natural good; Or crush her, like a vice of blood?

†c. A spoiled or vitiated condition. *Obs.*

1398 TREVISA *Barth. De P.R.* XVI. vi. (Bodl. MS.), Mete and wyne ikept in suche a vessel takeþ an horrible sauoure and smelle of þe vice of bras.

6. Viciousness, harmfulness.

1837 [MISS MAITLAND] *Lett. fr. Madras* (1843) 162 The poison.. will dry up,.. but.. will not lose its virtue, or rather its vice. **1857** HUGHES *Tom Brown* II. v, In fact, half the vice of the Slogger's hitting is neutralized, for he daren't lunge out freely.

7. *Comb.* **a.** With pa. pples., as ***vice-bitten***, ***-corrupted***, ***-created***, ***-haunted***, ***-polluted***, ***-worn***; also ***vice-sick*** adj.

1603 HARSNET *Pop. Impost.* 115 For a Devil to be so Vice-haunted as that he should roare at the picture of a Vice burnt in a pece of paper.. is a passion exceeding all apprehension. **1614** GORGES *Lucan* II. 56 These our vice-corrupted times. **1735** THOMSON *Liberty* II. 496 Independence stoops the head, To Vice enslav'd, and Vice-created Wants. **1754** RICHARDSON *Grandison* V. xxx. 186 What a paltry creature is a man vice-bitten, and sensible of detected folly. **1777** POTTER *Æschylus*, *Choephoræ* 337 Rouse, sting, and drive the vice-polluted wretch With brazen scourges tortur'd thro' the city. *a* **1849** H. COLERIDGE *Ess.* (1851) II. 223 He has converted.. the over-grown coxcomb boy, into the vice-sick, dispirited debauchee. **1884** 'EDNA LYALL' *We Two* iv, The usual careworn or viceworn faces. **1890** E. JOHNSON *Rise Christendom* 104 Many a vice-haunted monk must have gone mad but for this resource.

b. With pres. pples., as ***vice-loathing***, ***-punishing***, ***-rebuking***, ***-taming***, ***-upbraiding***.

1598 SYLVESTER *Du Bartas* II. i. *Imposture* 506 Vice-loathing Lord, pure Justice, Patron strong, Law's life, Right's rule; will he do any wrong? *Ibid.* ii. *Babylon* 35 Such vice-upbraiding objects Who.. Spares neither mother, brother, kiff, nor kin. **1611** COTGR., *Satyre*, a Satyre; an Inuectiue, or vice-rebuking Poeme. **1619** A. NEWMAN *Pleas. Vision* (1840) 5 And still, vice-punishing Authority, He (outlaw-like) would slight. **1642** H. MORE *Song of Soul* III. III. v, Religious Plato, and vice-taming Orpheus.

8. a. *attrib.*, as ***vice-complexion***; also *spec.* (orig. *U.S.*) with reference to certain crimes, esp. organized prostitution, as ***vice den***, ***racket***, ***trade***, etc.

1635 QUARLES *Embl.* II. x. 4 A Hagg, repair'd with vice-complexion, paint, A quest-house of complaint. **1903** *McClure's Mag.* Nov. 89 In New York, Croker has failed signally to maintain vice-bosses whom he appointed. **1915** *Sci. Amer.* 30 Jan. 98/3 The Puritan conception of life, like that of vice-crusaders, suffragettes, and most crusaders, scorns all trifling with its weighty realities. **1937** Vice society [see *strip-teasing* vbl. sb. s.v. STRIP-TEASE]. **1938** F. D. SHARPE *Sharpe of Flying Squad* vii. 78 Lots of the other men in the vice racket.. were pulled in and interviewed. **1952** *Manch. Guardian Weekly* 8 May 3 The relations of one of these with a Chicago vice-syndicate may be merely an unfair reflection on Governor Warren. **1962** *Spectator* 6 July 12/2 The vicelands of Notting Hill. **1971** *It* 2–16 June 1/1 (*heading*) Vice girls of Princedale Road—the shocking truth! **1975** J. GORES *Hammett* (1976) v. 37 In a vice raid.. police .. trailed a group of three boys.. to the house of prostitution .. and jailed the inmates of the.. vice-den. **1976** *Billings* (Montana) *Gaz.* 30 June 4-A/1 Suppose that you.. prevented vice officers from arresting a drug suspect. **1981** P. O'DONNELL *Xanadu Talisman* v. 100 His wife was.. sold into the vice trade.

b. Special Comb.: **vice ring**, a group of people criminally involved in organized prostitution; **vice squad** [SQUAD *sb.*[1] 4 c] orig. *U.S.*, a police unit concerned with the enforcement of laws relating to prostitution, drug abuse, illegal gambling, etc.

1938 F. D. SHARPE *Sharpe of Flying Squad* xi. 125, I don't think.. they were.. connected with any vice ring. **1981** C. SCOTT *Heavenly Witch* vi. 80 Men in charge of vice rings spread rumours that the converts were paid to testify. **1905** *N.Y. Times* 22 June 8/6 Six of Capt. Cottrell's Tenderloin detectives will report to Capt. Egger this noon for duty on the Vice Squad. **1939** *Daily Tel.* 18 Dec. 8/4 Scotland Yard's vice squad.. has been instructed to give special attention to small clubs opened in Soho since the outbreak of war. **1978** L. HEREN *Growing up on The Times* v. 167 The vice squad might have had a beady eye on me, but I was glad to hold his hand.

vice (vaɪs), *sb.*² Forms: (4 viz, vicz), 4–6 vys (5 vijs, 6 *Sc.* wys), vyse, 5–6 *Sc.* wise, 6– vise; 4–6 (9) vyce (6 fyce), 4– vice. [a. OF. *vis* (also mod.F.), *viz, vitz*, etc.:—L. *vītis* vine, with reference to the spiral growth of the tendrils. So Pr. *vitz*, It. *vite* screw.]

1. A winding or spiral staircase. *Obs.* exc. *arch.*

[**1334–5** *Ely Sacr. Rolls* (1907) II. 73 In j serrura empt. pro hostio in le Viz in novo Campanile, ij d.] **1382** WYCLIF *1 Kings* vi. 8 Bi a vyce [L. *cochlea*] thei stieden vp into the mydil sowpynge place, and fro the mydil into the thridde. **1387** TREVISA *Higden* (Rolls) III. 87 He ordeyned games and plaies, and made walles and vices, and oþere strong places. **1435** *Contract for Fotheringhay Ch.* (1841) 28 In the said stepill shall be a Vice towrnyng, servyng till the said Body, Isles and Qwere. *c* **1450** *Contin. Brut* 347 An aungell come doun fro þe stage on high, by a vice, and sette a croune of golde & precious stonez & perles apon þe Kingez hed. **1525** *Bury Wills* (Camden) 244 The byldyng and fynysshynge of the vise of Seynt James's Chirche. **1543** *Dunmow Churchw. MS.* fol. 36, vi. days warke and a half abowt the sowth ile and the vyse off the stepull. **1648** HEXHAM II. s.v. *Spille*, A Vice to gett up on, or a Winding-stares.

1886 WILLIS & CLARK *Cambridge* I. 16 A handsome stone vice or spiral staircase. **1900** HOPE in *Yorks. Archaeol. Jrnl.* XV. 334 In the north-east corner is a vice, partly built of glazed bricks.

†**b.** The case or shaft of a spiral stair. *rare.*

1466 in Willis & Clark *Cambridge* (1886) III. 93 Thei shal make..the Roofe of the vice of the staire. And..shal..fynde alle the bord and tymbre..for the Roof of the vice aforsaid. *a* **1500** *Chaucer's Dreme* 1312, I rise and walkt..Till I a winding staire found, And held the vice aye in my hond, And upward softly so gan creepe.

†**2.** A device of the nature of a screw or winch for bending a crossbow or catapult. Hence *bow* (etc.) *of vice*. *Obs.*

13.. *Coer de L.* 3970 Richard bent an arweblast off vys, And schotte it to a tour. [**1371–3** *Acc. Exch. K.R.* 397/10 m. 3, ij. vicz ad tendendum balistas.] ? *a* **1400** *Morte Arth.* 2424 Thane they beneyde [*read* bendyde] in burghe bowes of vyse. *c* **1425** WYNTOUN *Cron.* VIII. 4227 Awblasteris, and bowis of wise, And al thynge þat mycht mak serwice.

†**b.** A mechanical contrivance or device by which some piece of apparatus, etc., is worked. *Obs.* (common in the 16th c.).

Orig. no doubt implying some application of a screw, but in later use employed more loosely and perhaps associated with DEVICE 7 (cf. VICE *sb.*⁵).

a **1400** *R. Glouc. Chron.* (Rolls) II. 780 Man mai..þinche muche wonder hou hij were arerd For nis þer noþer gyn ne vys þat hit myȝte do. **1509** HAWES *Past. Pleas.* iii. (Percy Soc.) 15 The little turrets with ymages of golde About was set, whiche with the wynde aye moved, Wyth propre vices. *a* **1513** FABYAN *Chron.* VI. clvi. 145 Imagys on horse backe aperyd out of sondrye placis, and after departyd agayne by meane of sertayne vyces. **1547** WRIOTHESLEY *Chron.* (Camden) II. 1 He shewed a picture of the resurrection of our Lord made with vices, which putt out his legges of sepulchree..and turned his heade. **1597** A. M. tr. *Guillemeau's Fr. Chirurg.* p. xiii b/1 The vice, or meanes, wherby this Instrumente is opened and shutte agayne. *a* **1614** OVERBURY *A Wife*, etc. (1638) 169 His whole body goes all upon skrewes, and his face is the vice that moves them. **1621** T. WILLIAMSON tr. *Goulart's Wise Vieillard* 49 Idolles, and Statues, which artificially are moued by vises & gynnes. **1650** R. STAPYLTON *Strada's Low C. Warres* VIII. 20 All the power was in the Burgesses, at whose pleasure they were nominated and moved, like wooden Puppets with a Vice.

†**c.** A clasp or fastening for a hood. *Obs.*—⁰

c **1440** *Promp. Parv.* 510/1 Vice, hood sperynge, *spira*.

†**3.** A screw. *Obs.*

Not always clearly distinguishable from sense 2 b.

1412–20 LYDG. *Chron. Troy* IV. 6282 Many vys and many sotyl pyn In þe stede he made aboute goon, þe crafty lokkes vndoynge euerychon. *c* **1430** *Pilgr. Lyf Manhode* IV. xvii. (1869) 184 þe anguishe þat so harde presseth troubel herte, þat it thinketh it is streyned in a pressour shet with a vys. **1450** *Fysshynge w. Angle* (1883) 8 [A staff] with a pyke yn þe neþer ende fastnyed with a remevyng vise. **1527** *Inv. Goods Dk. Richmond* 18 in *Camden Misc.* III, A Bedstede of waynscote..well kerved, with vices and garthes to the same. **1551** SIR J. WILLIAMS *Accompte* (Abbotsford Cl.) 73 Paid for viij paier of vices of iron made for the saied seven images. *Ibid.* 76 An other paier of candellstickes..lackinge a vice. **1571** DIGGES *Pantom.* I. xxvii. H iij b, In his backe prepare a vice or scrue to be fastned in the top of some staffe. **1601** HOLLAND *Pliny* II. 484 A broad goblet or standing peece there was..with a devise appendant to it, for to be set too and taken off by a vice. **1605** STOW *Ann.* 1281 A Pinnace was made by an house Carpenter;..this was made to be taken asunder, and set togither with vices. **1611** CORYAT *Crudities* 134 He is pourtrayed in white stone,..his deske with a vice turning in it, and his bookes vnder it.

b. A screw-press. *rare.*

1633 G. HERBERT *Temple, Agony* ii, Sinne is that presse and vice, which forceth pain To hunt his cruell food through ev'ry vein. [**1866** ROGERS *Agric. & Prices* I. xxi. 548 Apples were pressed in a mill with a screw or vice.]

c. *spec.* (See quot.)

1875 KNIGHT *Dict. Mech.* 2716/2 *Vyce* (Coopering), a gimlet-pointed hand-screw employed to hold up the head while the staves are closed around it.

†**4.** A tap of a vessel; a screw-stopper. *Obs.*

1530 PALSGR. 158 *Vne vis*,..a vice of a cuppe, or suche lyke. *Ibid.* 284/2 Vyce to putte in a vessell of wyne to drawe the wyne out at, *chantepleure*. **1564** *Richmond Wills* (Surtees) 174 One vice of gold enameled, one sylver spone doble gilt. **1591** HARINGTON *Orl. Fur.* XLII. lxxv, This took the water from the azure skie From whence, with turning of some cock or vice, Great store of water would mount up on high. **1612** in *Halyburton's Ledger* (1867) 305 Flagones of glase with vices covered with leather, the dozen, xii li. **1653** URQUHART *Rabelais* I. v. (1664) 26 The bottle is stopped and shut up with a stoppel, but the flaggon with a vice.

5. A tool composed of two jaws, opened and closed by means of a screw, which firmly grip and hold a piece of work in position while it is being filed, sawn, or otherwise operated upon; used especially by workers in metal or carpenters. Cf. HAND-VICE.

The spelling *vise* is now usual only in U.S.

1500 *Nottingham Rec.* III. 72 Unum vise et diversa files. **1584** *Knaresb. Wills* (Surtees) I. 145 All my stiddes,..one vice, all my naile tooles and all my hammers. **1677** MOXON *Mech. Exerc.* i. 5 The wider the two ends of the Spring stand asunder, the wider it throws the Chaps of the Vice open. **1688** R. HOLME *Armoury* III. 321/2 The Vice, called the Bench Vice,..holdeth all sorts of Iron work that requires Fileing. **1745** ELIZA HEYWOOD *Female Spect.* No. 10 (1748) II. 201 There is no doubt but a pair of globes will make a better figure in their anti-chambers than the vice and wheel. **1797** *Phil. Trans.* LXXXVII. 258 In this machine the body to be pulled asunder is held fast by two strong vices. **1827** N. ARNOTT *Physics* I. 177 It is a screw which draws together the iron jaws of a smith's vice. **1857** DICKENS *Dorrit* xxiii, A long low workshop, fitted with benches, and vices, and tools, and straps, and wheels. **1867** F. FRANCIS *Angling* xiii. (1880) 464 The vice for trout flies is a small brass table vice. **1884** F. J. BRITTEN *Watch & Clockm.* 284 For nearly all operations connected with watchmaking either the work or the tool is gripped in the vice.

fig. **1597** SHAKS. *2 Hen. IV*, II. i. 24 If I can close with him, I care not for his thrust... If I but fist him once: if he come but within my Vice. **1866** B. TAYLOR *Poems, The Waves*, Bound in the vice Of the Arctic ice. **1901** *Munsey's Mag.* XXIV. 803/1 The doctor's hands, picking at the iron vise at his windpipe, grew feebler.

b. Used in similes or comparisons.

1828 SCOTT *F.M. Perth* ii, To secure him with a grasp like that of his own iron vice, was, for the powerful Smith, the work of a single moment. **1846** MRS. A. MARSH *Father Darcy* II. v. 110 Catesby stretched out his hand across the table; took hold of that of his friend, and held it with a grasp as of an iron vice. **1871** TYNDALL *Fragm. Sci.* (1879) I. xii. 363 The jaws of a gigantic vice appear to have closed upon them. **1885** *Harper's Mag.* Dec. 90/1 The other hand..was crossed upon my breast, and held there as if in a vise.

6. A tool used for drawing lead into grooved rods for lattice windows.

1706 PHILLIPS (ed. Kersey), *Vice*,..an Instrument with two Wheels made use of to draw the Lead in Glazing-work. **1728** CHAMBERS *Cycl.* s.v., There are some of these Vices double, and that will draw two Leads at once. **1825** J. NICHOLSON *Operat. Mechanic* 638 A vice, with different cheeks and cutters, to turn out the different kinds of lead as the magnitude of the window or the squares may require.

7. *attrib.* and *Comb.*, as (sense 1) †*vice-door*, *-foot*; (sense 3) †*vice-candlestick*, *-hasp*, *-nail*, *-pin*, *-turcas*; (sense 5) *vice-bench*, *-block*, *-board*, *-end*, *-jaw*, *-leg*, *-maker*, *-pin*, *-post*, *-screw*, etc.; †**vice-arch** (see quot.); **vice-hand** (see quot.; in mod. use = next); **vice-man**, a workman who manipulates a vice (cf. quots.). Also VICE-LIKE *a.*²

Also *vice-cap*, *-clamp*, *-press* (Knight, 1875–84).

1387 TREVISA *Higden* (Rolls) II. 71 þere were somtyme buldes wiþ *vice arches and fontes [*v.r.* voutes] in þe manere of Rome [L. *Romano more cocleata*]. **1850** WEALE *Dict. Terms*, **Vice-bench*, the bench to which a vice is fixed. **1895** *Model Steam Engine* 94 *Vice Blocks.—Of various sizes, shapes, and patterns, used as supports upon which to bend tubes. **1808** A. SCOTT *Poems* 140 An' Vulcan loud, wi' squeakin clang, Was at the *vice-board rispin Fu' soon that day. **1572** in Feuillerat *Revels Q. Eliz.* (1908) 176 *Vice candlesticks xii, xii s. **1576–7** *Ibid.* 263, vj vice-candlestickes at xijᵈ the peece, vjˢ. **1687** MIÈGE *Gt. Fr. Dict.* I, *Mâchoires d'Etau*,..*Vice-chops, or the Chops of a Vice. **1354** *Mem. Ripon* (Surtees) III. 91 In mercede..reparantis serur. et claves del *Vicedores in ecclesia. **1463** *Bury Wills* (Camden) 29 Seynt Marie preest to haue a keye of my cost of the vys dore goyng vp to the candilbem. **1501** *Yatton Churchw. Acc.* (Som. Rec. Soc.) 125 A Key..for yᵉ fyce door. **1512–3** *Rec. St. Mary at Hill* (1905) 281 Nayles for þe garnettes on the vyse dore in the steple. **1875** *Carpentry & Join.* 35 At the left hand or *vice-end of the bench. **1533** in E. Law *Hampton Crt. Pal.* (1885) 348 The dore at the *vyce fote goyng up to the bartyllmentes of the haull. **1644** BULWER *Chiron.* 76 The *Vice-hand or Thumb, extended out with the Eare-Finger. **1612** in *Halyburton's Ledger* (1867) 332 *Vice haspes the dozen, xii s. **1793–4** *Matthews's Bristol Directory*, Austin, Aaron, Clock and *Vice-maker, Old-market. **1858** SIMMONDS *Dict. Trade*, *Vice-maker*, a manufacturer of iron vices. **1837** W. B. ADAMS *Carriages* 179 The business of the *vice-man is to file and smooth the work from the rough marks of the hammer, to fit joints, and finish screw-bolts and nuts. **1858** SIMMONDS *Dict. Trade*, *Vice-men*, smiths whose work is at the vice instead of the anvil. **1488–92** *Acc. Ld. High Treas. Scot.* I. 85 A grete *vice nail maid of siluer. **1501** *Ibid.* II. 26 For mending of ane vice nale of the Kingis cowp that was brokin. **1622** F. MARKHAM *Bk. War* I. ix. 34 His screwes, with which he shall unloose euery *vice-pinne or engine about the musquet. *a* **1642** SIR W. MONSON *Naval Tracts* III. (1704) 353/2 They neither want Vice-Pins nor Scourers. **1694** MOTTEUX *Rabelais* v. vii. 28 The Hole for the Vice-pin. **1833** J. HOLLAND *Manuf. Metal* II. 145 The vice-pin intended to be screwed..is placed in the stock. *Ibid.* 146 A very simple machine used for cutting *vice-screws. **1549–50** *Burgh Rec. Stirling* (1887) 58 The gret scheris, ane taingis, ane *vice turkes.

†**vice**, *sb.*³ *Obs.* Also 4 viis, vijs, wijs, 4–5 viys (4 uiys, 5 vyys); 4 vis, vys(e; 5 vyce. [a. OF. *vis*:—L. *vīs-um*, *visus* face.] Face, visage.

Common in the first half of the 14th century.

a **1300** *Cursor M.* 18841 His vice [*v. rr.* vijs, viys] sumdel wit rede was blend; On nese and muth was noght at mend. *a* **1325** in Horstm. *Altengl. Leg.* (1878) 144 As we..went toward paradys; þus he bot him in þe viis. **1338** R. BRUNNE *Chron.* (1810) 104 Vnto þe se side chaced þei Sir Lowys, He durst not abide, no turne Thebald his vis. ? *c* **1400** *Emare* 742 Leue we at þe lady, clere of vyce. *c* **1400** *Laud Troy Bk.* 7733 His vice was red as any fir.

vice, *sb.*⁴ *Obs.* exc. *dial.* Also 4 vyse, 6 vise, *Sc.* wice, vyce, 9 *dial.* vize. [Aphetic f. *avise*, *avyse*, etc., ADVICE.] Counsel; advice.

1387–8 T. USK *Test. Love* I. ii. (Skeat) l. 60 Now thou comest goodly by thyn owne vyse, to comforte me with wordes. *a* **1500** *Lancelot* 1909 Mot euery king have this wice in mynd In tyme. *c* **1560** A. SCOTT *Poems* (S.T.S.) v. 23 Sic senȝeoris tymis our weill this sessone; Vpoun thair vyce war lang to waik.

a **1847** *Isle of Wight Gloss.* (E.D.S.) 40 *Vice*, or *Vize*, advice.

†**vice**, *sb.*⁵ *Obs.* Also 5 vyce, 6 vyse. [Aphetic f. DEVICE.] Design, figure, device.

a **1400–50** *Alexander* 1539 (D.), A vesture of vyce of vyolet flourez. **1509** HAWES *Past. Pleas.* (Percy Soc.) 180 On the fourth head, on the helmet crest There was a stremer ryght white,..Wheron was written with vyse of the best, My name is Variaunce. *a* **1650** *Sir Lambewell* 116 in Furniv. *Percy Folio* I. 148 In that pauillion was a bed of price that was couered ore with goodlie vice.

vice (vaɪs), *sb.*⁶ Chiefly *Sc.* [a. L. *vice*, abl. of *vicis* (gen. sing.), change, turn, stead, place, etc.]

1. Stead or place (of another). Now *rare.*

1598 FLORIO, *Vece*, stead, place, liew, vice, standing for another. **1607** HUME *Admonit.* (Bannatyne Cl.) 13 If suche a man, indewed with so gryte giftis, did so, Who ar ye litle ones to succede wittinglie in his vice? **1672** *Burgh Rec. Aberdeen* (1872) 283 Nominating and setleing ane postmaster..in the deceist John Wells his vice. **1681** STAIR *Instit.* I. xix. §55. 397 Succeeding in the vice is a kind of intrusion, whereby after warning any person comes in possession, by consent of the parties warned. **1838** W. BELL *Dict. Law Scot.* 1027 The person succeeding in the vice..will be subjected as an intruder, unless he have a colourable title of possession to protect him. **1868** *Act 31 & 32 Vic.* c. 101 §105 The mediate over superior, as acting in the vice of such superior.

†**2.** Turn (of sequence or alternation). *Obs.*

1637–50 ROW *Hist. Kirk* (Wodrow Soc.) 356 It was Mr Thomas Sydserf his *vice* to have sermon that day in the Grayfrier kirk. **1672** *Burgh Rec. Aberdeen* (1872) 279 Ane..watch of the inhabitants [to] be setled,..and no person to be absent in their vice without sicknes..or vther lawfull excuse. **1711** *Ibid.* 344 That the saids elementarians..be taught for this vice be Mr. William Mestone. **1775** L. SHAW *Hist. Moray* 357 After this, the Family of Seafort claimed a Vice [of nomination]. **1793** *Statist. Acc. Scot.* VII. 34 Messrs. Alexander Hamilton..and Cunningham of Seabank are vice-patrons [of the parish]. The former has the next vice.

vice (vaɪs), *sb.*⁷ Also 6 vise. [Absolute use of VICE- *prefix*.] One who acts in the place of another; a substitute or deputy. Also prefixed by *Mr.* as a form of address to a vice-chairman or vice-president.

In mod. use the second element is usually implied or expressed in the context, as in quot. 1852.

1597 HARVEY *Trimming T. Nashe* Wks. (Grosart) III. 17 The Barbers were serued and they cut them, and were as Ioues Vises to make them fit for warre. **1728** CHAMBERS *Cycl., Deputy*, is..frequently used among us, for an Office, or Employ, not a Dignity; and stands indifferently for a Vice, or Lieutenant. **1811** *Ora & Juliet* II. 180 Lord Berlington offered himself as Henry's Vice, to conduct the other end of the table. **1820** BYRON *Mar. Fal.* v. iii. 66 The few..shall fawn Round a barbarian Vice of Kings' Vicegerent. **1852** DICKENS *Bleak Ho.* x, He solaces his imagination, too, by thinking of the many Chancellors and Vices, and Masters of the Rolls, who are deceased. **1889** GRETTON *Memory's Harkb.* 140 It was indirectly a proof of the estimation in which the Vice [= Vice-Chancellor] was held. **1894** G. DU MAURIER *Trilby* II. 102 A table..at one end of which sits Mr. Chairman..and at the other 'Mr. Vice'. **1916** M. DIVER *Desmond's Daughter* II. iii. 61 The President at the far end of the table had lifted his glass. 'Mr Vice—the Queen,' said he. **1976** T. JEAL *Until Colours Fade* xxxvii. 325 The president of the mess rose..and brought down his silver mallet. 'Mr Vice, the Queen,' that officer said, addressing the vice-president at the opposite end of the table.

vice, obs. Sc. form of WISE *sb.* (manner).

vice (vaɪs), *v.*¹ [f. VICE *sb.*²]

†**1.** *trans.* To fix *on* with a screw. *Obs.*—¹

1542 in *Archæol. Jrnl.* XVIII. 144 Item oone Cuppe of glasse with a cover, the fote being of silver and gilt and viced on.

2. To force, strain, or press hard as by the use of a vice; to fix, jam, or squeeze tightly.

In early use only in highly figurative context.

1602 MARSTON *Antonio's Rev.* II. ii. D j, I see false suspect Is vicde; wrung hardly in a vertuous heart. **1611** SHAKS. *Wint. T.* I. ii. 416 He sweares, As he had seen't, or beene an Instrument To vice you to't, that you haue toucht his Queene Forbiddenly. **1637** N. WHITING *Albino & Bellama* 12 Who viceth honour, lyes. **1806** J. BERESFORD *Miseries Hum. Life* VI. iv, You find yourself suddenly viced in, from the shoulder to the hip. **1849** DE QUINCEY in *Blackw. Mag.* LXVI. 748 The coachman's hand was viced between his upper and lower thigh. *a* **1859** —— *Aelius Lamia* Wks. X. 306 The glory may envelop one in a voluminous robe,..or may pinch and vice one's arms into that succinct garment [a spencer].

3. *intr.* To employ or apply a vice. *rare*—¹.

1612 STURTEVANT *Metallica* (1854) 99 Pressing or impressioning of things is performed..secondely by screwing or viceing.

Hence '**vicing** *vbl. sb.*

1648 HEXHAM II, *Een vijsinge*, a Vicing, or a Screwing.

†**vice**, *v.*[2] *Sc. Obs.* Also wyce. [app. ad. OF. *vicier*, med.L. *viciāre*, L. *vitiāre* to spoil, vitiate, but with change of meaning.] *trans.* To treat arrogantly or oppressively.

For the explanation of *walentyne* see VOLENTINE.

c **1450** HOLLAND *Howlat* 918 Thus wycit [*v.r.* viciit] he the walentyne thraly and thrawin, That all the fowlis..plenȝeit to Natur.

‖**vice** (ˈvaɪsiː, vaɪs), *prep.* [L. *vice*: see VICE *sb.*[6]] In place of; in succession to.

1770 *Scots Mag.* Jan. 55/1, 6th reg. of foot: Capt. Mathew Derenzy to be Major, vice John Forrest; by purchase. **1787** *Gentl. Mag.* Nov. 1015/1 The Lieutenant-Governor has appointed..James Miller..Lieutenant of the said fort, vice Frederic Gottsched, who is gone to Hallifax. **1806** BERESFORD *Miseries Hum. Life* III. ix, A jarring bat;—a right-hand bat for a left-handed player;—a hat, *vice* stumps. **1849** THACKERAY *Pendennis* xxii, He was gardener and out-door man, vice Upton, resigned. **1886** C. E. PASCOE *London of To-day* xi. (ed. 3) 111 It was..soon afterwards reorganized, with Mr. Randegger, *vice* Mr. Leslie, as conductor.

vice- (vaɪs), *prefix*, representing L. *vice* in place of: see prec. Originally this governed a following word in the genitive, but in late L. the tendency to use the phrase as a compound noun appears in *vicequæstor* (equivalent to *prōquæstor* of analogous origin). In med.L. such formations became common, as *vicecomes*, *-consul*, *-decanus*, *-dominus*, *-princeps*, *-rector*, *-rex*, etc. From the 13th cent. onwards a number of these appear in OF., at first usually with the prefix in the form of *vis-*, *vi-*, but latterly assimilated as a rule to the Latin original. Similar compounds with *vice-* are also employed in It., Sp., and Pg. The older examples in English, having been taken immediately from French, also present the prefix in the reduced forms *vis-* (*vys*, *viz-*) and *vi-* (*vy-*), subsequently replaced by *vice-* (also in early use *vize-*) except in VISCOUNT. The more important compounds are given below as main words; the following are illustrations of less usual or more recent terms.

a. With personal designations, especially titles of office, indicating that the person so called acts temporarily or regularly in place of, in the absence of, or as assistant to, another who properly holds the office or bears the title or name, as *vice-abbot*, *-agent*, *-Apollo*, *-apostle*, *-architect*, etc. Also occas. *transf.*, as *vice-nature*.

In the dictionaries of Florio and Miége many examples of similar forms are employed to render the Italian and French equivalents, e.g. *vice-captain*, *-cardinal*, *-censor*, *-commissary*, etc.

a **1661** FULLER *Worthies* II. (1662) 50 Gregory of Huntington..was bred a Benedictine Monke in Ramsey, where he became Prior, or *Vice-Abbot. **1597** HOOKER *Eccl. Pol.* v. xli. §1 A vassal whom Satan hath made his *Vice-agent. **1648** CRASHAW *Poems* (1904) 138 Him the Muses love to follow, Him they call their *vice-Apollo. **1641** 'SMECTYMNUUS' *Vind. Answ.* xiii. 114 They were *Comites*, and *Vicarii Apostolorum*, *Vice-Apostles. **1779** *Phil. Trans.* LXIX. 598 M. Forfait.., *vice-architect of the French navy. **1690** *Lond. Gaz.* No. 2617/2 The Troops there under the Command of the Ban and *Vice-Ban, were obliged by the bad weather to separate. **1686** *Ibid.* No. 2201/2 He who formerly commanded that Garison was *Vice-Bassa. **1778** STILES *Diary* (1901) II. 288 The Diploma Examinatorium ..was delivered to the President, who gave it to the *Vice Bedellus, directing him to read it. **1671** F. PHILIPPS *Reg. Necess.* 433 The Baron of Limpurgh *Vice-Butler to the King of Bohemia. **1600** J. PORY tr. *Leo's Africa* I. 10 Hauing first put to flight the *vice-Califa of Aegypt. **1860** *All Year Round* No. 46. 475 The unmanageable 'Arry, who was a species of *vice-chair, and was also provided with a hammer. **1882** J. HARDY in *Proc. Ber. Nat. Club.* IX. 440 Mr. Charles Watson..discharged the duties of the vice-chair. **1858** SIMMONDS *Dict. Trade*, **Vice-chairman*, a person who presides at the lower end of a table, supporting and aiding the chairman or president; the deputy-chairman of a board of officers. **1943** W. S. CHURCHILL *End of Beginning* 69 The Chiefs of Staff Committee are assisted by a *Vice-Chiefs of Staff Committee. **1978** R. V. JONES *Most Secret War* xlv. 458 The Vice-Chiefs of Staff..advised that the threat was over. **1659** BAXTER *Key Cath.* xlii. 300 Prove that Christ hath commissioned a *Vice-Christ. **1691** —— *Nat. Churches* x. 42 Being an Usurpation of Christ's Office, and making a Vice-Christ, which is an Antichrist. **1712** [see VICE-GOD]. **1497** in Ellis *Orig. Lett.* Ser. I. I. 58 It is thought expedient that the Popes Holynesse comaund the said aide..to be publisshed by his *vicecollectour. **1858** SIMMONDS *Dict. Trade*, **Vice-commodore*, a deputy commander of a naval squadron. **1631** WEEVER *Anc. Funeral Mon.* 541 Edward the third..did substitute Edward Bohun, the Earles younger brother, *Vice-Constable vnder him. **1878** J. GAIRDNER *Hist. Rich. III*, iv. 175 Sir Ralph Ashton was..appointed Vice-Constable..to exercise all the powers of the Lord High Constable for the particular emergency. **1566** tr. *Beza's Admon. Parlt.* D j, Cathedrall churches,..where master Deane, master *Vicedeane,..readers, vergerirs, &c. liue in great idlenesse. **1637** GILLESPIE *Eng. Pop. Cerem.* III. viii. 161 Deanes, Vice-Deans,..Subdeacons. **1697** *Lond. Gaz.* No. 3341/1 The Vice-Dean with the Clergy, made a Congratulatory Speech. **1875** W. H. JONES *Fasti Eccl. Sarisb.* 265 There is always a distinction to be observed between a 'Vice-Dean' or a 'Locum Tenens', and the 'Sub-Dean'. **1647** R. STAPYLTON *Juvenal* 153 He made choice of his..master or generall of the horse, or *vice-dictatour. **1882** *Macm. Mag.* XLVI. 249 A *vice-director of the military college. **1976** *National Observer* (U.S.) 12 June 22/2 A fellow with the title of *vice editor. **1818** SHELLEY *Eug. Hills* 244 But Death promised..That he would petition for Her to be made *Vice-Emperor. **1844** THIRLWALL *Greece* VIII. lxvi. 451 Before Diæus came to Corinth, a council was held there by the *vice-general Sosicrates. **1711** HICKES *Two Treat. Chr. Priesth.* (1847) II. 188 Would he not have been a *vice-high-priest as well as a viceroy? **1749** FIELDING *Tom Jones* XI. x, As the law hath foolishly omitted this office of *vice-husband, or guardian to an eloped lady. **1817** BYRON *Beppo* xxix, And so she thought it prudent to connect her With a vice-husband, chiefly to protect her. **1609** J. DAVIES *Hum. Heaven* II. cvi, My *vice Ioues quoth he are ne'r afraid. **1555** EDEN *Decades* (Arb.) 112 Lupus Olanus the conductor of one of the shippes of Nicuesa, and nowe also *vice Leauetenaunt in his steede. **1963** *Times* 4 June 13/5 His native county of Lincolnshire, of which he was Vice-Lieutenant for many years. **1690** *Lond. Gaz.* No. 2527/3 And after them Count Popenheim, *Vice-Marshal of the Empire, carried the Sword of State naked before the Emperor. **1593** G. HARVEY *Pierce's Super.* Wks. (Grosart) II. 212 He hath not played the *Vicemaster of Poules, and the Foolemaster of the Theater for naughtes. **1618** *Barnevelt's Apol.* G j, The Vice-maisters place of the fees hath not allowed one halfe penny for stipend. **1690** C. NESSE *O. & N. Test.* I. 370 Potiphar..made him his vice-master. **1886** ABP. BENSON in A. C. Benson *Life* (1899) II. 122, I sate ..next to the Vice-Master. **1909** E. M. SATOW in *Cambr. Mod. Hist.* XI. xxviii. 865 Ōki of Hizen, and Itō, Inouyé and Yamagata of Chōshiu were retained as *vice-Ministers. **1976** *Eastern Daily Press* (Norwich) 19 Nov. 1/5 The agreement was signed by Iran's vice-minister of war. *a* **1631** DONNE *Love's Deity* i, Since this god produc'd a Destiny, And that *vice-nature, custome, lets it bee. **1707** *Lond. Gaz.* No. 4395/2 Advices from Hungary say, That Prince Ragotzki had declared Count Berezini *Vice-Palatine of that Kingdom. **1775** L. SHAW *Hist. Moray* 357 Fraser of Strichen, who, as *Vice-Patron, presented Mr. John Anand in 1640. **1793** [see VICE *sb.*[6] 2]. **1643** PRYNNE *Popish R. Favourite* 69 And therefore the Popes Holinesse hath given these his *Vice-popes instructions, Commissions thus to do. **1705** HICKERINGILL *Priest-cr.* I. (1721) 54 As the Pope keeps the Keys, they say, of Heaven Gates, being *Vice-porter under St. Peter. **1781** GIBBON *Decl. & F.* xvii. (1787) II. 37 The eleven remaining dioceses..were governed by twelve vicars, or *vice-præfects, whose name..explains the nature ..of their office. **1877** J. MORRIS *Troub. Cath. Forefathers* Ser. III. 116 During this time he was Socius to Father Henry Garret, Vice-Prefect of the English Mission. **1600** HOLLAND *Livy* XXVI. i. 582 Those legions which were commaunded by P. Cornelius the *Viz-pretour in Sicilie. **1802–12** BENTHAM *Ration. Judic. Evid.* (1827) V. 161 The celebration of the ceremony..proved by the habitual operator, the *vice-priest, a tobacconist. **1810** *Oxford Univ. Cal.* 129 Edmund Hall... Principal, George Thompson, D.D... *Vice-Principal, Daniel Wilson, M.A. **1864** J. H. NEWMAN *Apol.* i. (1904) 7/2, I became very intimate with him [Whately] in 1825, when I was his Vice-Principal at St. Alban Hall. **1857** G. OLIVER *Coll. Hist. Cath. Relig. Cornwall*, etc. 486 Adeodatus l'Angevin, elected *vice-prior at the fourth general chapter. **1602** *Archpriest Controv.* (Camden) II. 2 To present ourselves first to the Protector and *Vice-protector. *c* **1890** STEVENSON *In South Seas* I. xiv. (1900) 122 The sergeant of gendarmerie enjoys the style of the *vice-resident. **1878** STUBBS *Const. Hist.* xx. III. 421 The undue return made by the *vice-sheriff, who had substituted another name. **1704** *Lond. Gaz.* No. 4015/2 Baron Taston is made *Vice-Stadholder, and as such will preside over the Regency at Amberg. **1710** *Ibid.* No. 4664/2 Lieutenant-General Weebe, Vice-Stadtholder of Norway, is lately dead. **1835** *App. Munic. Corp. Rep.* IV. 2345 (Lincoln), A Deputy Recorder, *Vice Steward, Gaol Chaplain [etc.]. **1894** *19th Cent.* XXXVI. 425 The *vice-sultan of Haura received us right well. **1631** BRATHWAIT *Whimzies, Zealous Brother* 119 Hee was once in election to have been a *vice-verger in Amsterdam, but he wanted an audible voice. **1848** CURZON *Monast. Levant* I. iii. (1897) 22 The great man, who was **vice*-viceroy on this occasion.

b. With nouns or adjs. derived from personal designations, as *vice-apostolical*, *-cancellarian*, *-deity*, *-duchy*, etc., or associated in some way with the holding of office, as *vice-chair*, *-government*, *-throne*.

This type is represented in late L. *vice-quæstura*, med.L. *vice-comitalis*, *-comitatus*, *-dominium*, etc., and occurs freely in French and the other Romanic languages.

1641 'SMECTYMNUUS' *Vind. Answ.* xiii. 119 He bids him goe on with speed to execute his *Vice-Apostolicall office. **1843** WHEWELL in *Life* (1881) 285 Much too should I like to see you in your *Vice-Cancellarian chair. **1839** DICKENS *Nickelby* xlviii. 475 A farewell-supper..at which Mr. Snittle Timberry would preside, while the honours of the *vice chair would be sustained by the African [Sword-]Swallower. **1850** THACKERAY *Pendennis* lxxvi, The chair was taken by Sir Francis Clavering,..the vice-chair being ably filled by —— Barker, Esq. **1884** *Cyclists' Tour. Club Gaz.* Mar. 82/1 Messrs. W. B. Tanner and A. R. Sheppee occupied the vice-chairs. **1826** SOUTHEY *Vind. Eccl. Angl.* 394 You have to reconcile the pretensions of the Popes with their practices,..their *vice-deity with their crimes. **1611** FLORIO, *Vicedominanza*, a *vice-gouernment. **1876** BANCROFT *Hist. U.S.* IV. xxxvi. 113 The offer of a baronetcy and the vice-government of Virginia. **1856** MERIVALE *Hist. Rom. Emp.* l. (1865) VI. 188 In the mean time he was deputed to hold pro-consular, or *vice-imperial, power beyond the city. **1880** SWINBURNE *Stud. Shaks.* 240 His poor little vice-regal or vice-imperial parasite. *a* **1617** BAYNE *On Coloss. i. & ii.* (1634) 97 We must not supply Him with *vice-ministeriall heads. **1574** *Life 70th Abp. Canterb.* Pref. C vij, The same Austen hauinge thus gotten by conquest this uniuersall *vicepapaci ouer England. **1775** L. SHAW *Hist. Moray* 343 How far the King may claim a *Vice-Patronage, I shall not determine. **1677** MIÉGE *Fr. Dict.* I, *Vice-rectorat*, a *Vice-principalship. **1870** *Routledge's Every Boy's Ann.* Apr. 211 Fortunate enough to obtain the vice-principalship of the college. **1868** *Daily News* 23 Oct., The *Vice-Provostship of Eton College. *c* **1890** STEVENSON *In South Seas* I. xiv. (1900) 125 He was being haled to the *vice-residency, uncertain whether to be punished or rewarded. **1884** A. FORBES *Chinese Gordon* iii. 114 A royal salute was fired, and then Gordon had to make his speech from the *vice-throne.

c. With verbs, as *vice-preside* (after VICE-PRESIDENT), *-reign* (after VICEROY).

1889 *Sat. Rev.* 1 June 653/2 If it were not for the Civil Service, the Viceroy simply could not vice-reign. **1889** G. B. SHAW *London Music in 1888–89* (1937) 94 You are patronized by the Lord Mayor, presided over by the Duke of Westminster, and vice-presided over and councilled by nearly five dozen illustrious persons.

vice-ˈadmiral. Also 6 *Sc.* **wice admerall, weis admirall, 6 vize-, 7 vizadmirall, -erall.** [a. AF. *visadmirail* (OF. *visamiral*, F. *viceamiral*): see VICE- and ADMIRAL. So It. *viceammiraglio*, Sp. and Pg. *vicealmirante*.]

1. A naval officer ranking next to an admiral.

1520 in Ellis *Orig. Lett.* Ser. I. I. 165 Your Grace hath deputed the Master of the Rolles and the Vice Admirall to examyn the Inglysh marchaunts robbed and spoyled in September. **1562** *Act 5 Eliz.* c. 5 §33 The Lorde Admirall of Englande..or..any his Viceadmiralles. **1589** BIGGES *Summarie Drake's W. Ind. Voy.* 21 The Lieutenant generall, the Vizeadmirall, and all the rest of the Captaines. **1604** E. G[RIMSTONE] *D'Acosta's Hist. Indies* III. xi. 156 Returning now to the Viceadmiralles shippe,..they tooke the sea. **1620** R. COCKS *Diary* (Hakl. Soc.) II. 121 The admerall and vizadmerall gave hym to understand shipps were ready to departe. **1670** COVEL in *Early Voy. Levant* (Hakl. Soc.) 102 Capt. Robinson in the Greenwich, as Admiral,..and Capt. Wild, in the Assurance, as Vice-Admiral. **1726** SWIFT *Gulliver, Lilliput* viii, I..desired his Imperial Majesty to lend me..three thousand seamen under the command of his vice-admiral. **1777** R. WATSON *Philip II*, II. 259 Philip.. giving him Martinez de Recaldo, a seaman of great experience, for his vice-admiral. **1833** *Penny Cycl.* I. 126/2 There are also vice-admirals and rear-admirals of each flag, the former ranking with lieutenant generals..in the army. **1858** SIMMONDS *Dict. Trade* s.v., There are vice-admirals of three grades, who hoist respectively a red, white, or blue flag.

b. (See quot. 1769.)

a **1618** RALEIGH *Royal Navy* (1650) 37 If the Vice-Admirall of the Shire where men are mustered..had directions given, to joyn with the Mustermasters. **1710** J. CHAMBERLAYNE *State Gt. Brit.* (ed. 2) 581 A List of the Vice-Admirals. Sir John Molesworth, Bar., North parts of Cornwall. Earl Rivers, County of Essex [etc.]. **1769** FALCONER *Dict. Marine* (1780) s.v. *Admiral*, Vice-Admiral is also a civil officer appointed by the lords-commissioners of the admiralty. There are several of these officers established in different parts of Great-Britain, with judges and marshals under them, for executing jurisdiction within their respective districts. **1875** *Encycl. Brit.* I. 159/2.

c. (See ADMIRAL *sb.* 4.)

1698 *Act 10 Will. III*, c. 14 §4 That the Master of every such Second Fishing Ship as shall enter any such Harbour or Creeke [in Newfoundland] shall be Vice-Admirall of such ..during that Fishing Season. **1708** [see ADMIRAL *sb.* 4].

†**2.** A vessel commanded by a vice-admiral. *Obs.*

c **1595** CAPT. WYATT *Dudley's Voy.* (Hakl. Soc.) 3 Our Generall concluded that the vice-admerall with her pinness should sett saile and make for Plimworth before. **1598** W. PHILLIP tr. *Linschoten* 4/1 Their names were the Admirall S. Phillip, the vize Admiral S. Jacob. These were two new ships. **1629** WADSWORTH *Pilgr.* iv. 34 The Captaine of the Vice-Admirall..began to encourage his Marriners. **1660** INGELO *Bentiv. & Ur.* II. (1682) 180 Lysander commanded the Vice-Admiral. **1693** LUTTRELL *Brief Rel.* (1857) III. 9 Another Tripoline, their vice admiral, was the next day taken by the Malta gallies.

attrib. **1706** STEVENS *Span. Dict.* I, *Almiranta*, the Vice Admiral Ship of a Fleet.

3. *Conch.* A variety of shell of the genus *Conus*.

1819 [see ADMIRAL *sb.* 7].

Hence **vice-ˈadmiralship**.

1677 SIR C. WYCHE in *Essex Papers* (Camden) II. 118 That some man of integrity should succeed him in ye vice Admiralship of Munster.

vice-ˈadmiralty. [f. prec. + -TY. Cf. F. *vice-admirauté*.] The office or jurisdiction of a vice-admiral (in sense 1 b); an area under the jurisdiction of a vice-admiral. *court of vice-admiralty*, = vice-admiralty court.

1602 CAREW *Cornwall* I. 87 b, The Vice-admiralty is exercised by Mr. Charles Treuanion. **1679–88** *Secr. Serv. Money Chas. & Jas.* (Camden) 29 Daniel Gyles, Marshall of the Vice Admiralty of Southampton and the Isle of Wight. **1702** *Proclam.* in *Lond. Gaz.* No. 3872/2 All Vice-Admirals, and Judges of the Vice-Admiralties are also to do the same. **1706** *Act 6 Anne* c. 11 §19, That the Heretable Rights of Admiralty and Vice Admiralties in Scotland be reserved to the respective Proprietors as Rights of Property. **1773** *Gentl. Mag.* XLIII. 402 The extending the power of the courts of vice-admiralty to so enormous a degree, as deprives the people in the colonies..of their inestimable right to trials by juries. [**1876** BANCROFT *Hist. U.S.* II. xxxi. 283 The crown lawyers overruled all objections..and the king set up his courts of vice-admiralty in America.]

b. *vice-admiralty court* (see quot. 1867).

1761 *Ann. Reg.* I. 127/2 Their lordships reversed the sentence of the vice-admiralty court, and ordered restitution of ships and cargoes. **1768** BLACKSTONE *Comm.* III. 69 Appeals from the vice-admiralty courts in America..may be brought before the courts of admiralty in England. **1829** MARRYAT *F. Mildmay* xxi, The True-blooded Yankee was libelled in the Vice-Admiralty Court at Cape Town. **1863** H. COX *Instit.* I. v. 28 The Queen..may regulate the practice of her Vice-Admiralty Courts abroad. **1867** SMYTH *Sailor's Word-bk.*, *Vice-admiralty courts*, branches of the High Court of Admiralty, instituted for carrying on the like duties in several of our colonies, prize-courts, &c.

‖**vice anglais** (vis ɑ̃glɛ). [Fr., lit. 'English vice' (VICE *sb.*[1]).] The vice to which the English are said to be particularly prone (esp. with reference to corporal punishment).

1942 [see SELF-MEDICATION]. **1947** *Horizon* Nov. 269 No novelist in the last decade of the century could create a character who practised *le vice anglais* without attributing to him some of Swinburne's physical characteristics. **1950** E. H. W. MEYERSTEIN *Let.* 6 Jan. (1959) 369 You must remember that it is much more important socially for a boy to play for his public school in cricket.. than to win a prize. .. It is a very queer trait and a modern psychologist might quite possibly link it up with sadism ('le vice Anglais'), success consisting in *hitting* something, though that 'something' be no more than a ball. **1962** *Times* 21 July 4/5 *Whack-O!*—a programme whose long life testifies, if nothing else, to the continued popularity of *le vice anglais*. **1976** F. MUIR *Frank Muir Book* 73 Flogging in public schools.. has been given as the reason for so many.. English gentlemen enjoying a little corporal punishment later in life, 'le vice Anglais'. **1983** *Daily Tel.* 5 Aug. 12/1 The true *vice anglais* is the hatred felt by a sub-section of the middle class for their own country and their desire to humiliate her.

vice-'chamberlain. [VICE-.] A subordinate or deputy chamberlain; *spec.* an officer of the Royal Household under the Lord Chamberlain.

1545 in Rymer *Fœdera* (1713) XV. 81/1 Our Vice-chamberlane, Our two Principall Secretaries for the tyme being. **1589** COOPER *Admon.* 56 Master Vicechamberlaine at her Maiesties.. tolde the Bishop that her Maiestie misliked nothing. **1614** SELDEN *Titles of Honor* 358 Vpon knowledge thereof giuen to the Lord Chamberlaine of the Houshold or Vicechamberlaine for the time being. **1645** *Doc. Lett. Pat. at Oxf.* (1837) 403 Bills.. subscribed and allowed by the Chamberlaine, Vicechamberlaine, or Principal Secretary of his Maiestie. **1695** LD. LONSDALE in *Eng. Hist. Rev.* Jan. (1915) 93 The Prince had reserved for me the Vice Chamberlain's place. **1702** *Lond. Gaz.* No. 3840/1 The Rt. Hon. Peregrine Bertie Esq., Vice-Chamberlain to Her Majesty. **1780** BURKE *Œcon. Reform* Wks. III. 287 He has an honourable appointment;.. and he has the vice chamberlain to assist him. **1835** *App. Munic. Corp. Rep.* I. 154 The Chamberlains [at Worcester] are annually elected... Their business, which is performed by a deputy called a Vice-chamberlain, is to receive the rents and keep all the accounts of the corporation.

'vice-champion. [f. VICE- + CHAMPION *sb.*[1] 4.] The runner-up in a sporting contest.

1981 *N.Y. Times* 5 July v. 7/1 Only 251 fans showed up.. to see Sao Paulo, the vice champion of Brazilian professional teams, play in that city of eight million people. **1984** *Soviet Union* IX. 53 The men's team, vice-champion of Europe, has twice beaten the world champion Pakistan team.

vice-'chancellor. Forms: 5 **vichaunceller,** 6 **vychancellour, vyschancelar;** 6 **vice-chauncelour, -ellor, -chancelor,** 6– **vice-chancellor** (7 **-our**); *Sc.* 6 **vicechancellair,** 7 **-ellar, -eler.** [a. OF. *vi(s)chancelier* (F. *vice-chancelier*), or ad. med.L. *vicecancellarius*: see VICE- and CHANCELLOR *sb.* So It. *vicecancelliere*, Sp. *vicecanciller*, Pg. *vicechanceller*.]

1. The deputy or substitute of an ecclesiastical chancellor; *spec.* the cardinal at the head of the Papal Chancery.

1432–50 tr. *Higden* (Rolls) VII. 297 This bischop induede the prior of Dirhem firste with his honoure that he is decan in that bischopryche and as vichaunceller. **1670** G. H. *Hist. Cardinals* I. III. 85 Six of the Abbreviators places are in the Gift of the Cardinal Vice-Chancellor. *a* **1700** EVELYN *Diary* 18 Feb. 1645, Belonging to Cardinal Francesco Barberini as Vice-chancelor of the Church of Rome. **1845** SARAH AUSTIN *Ranke's Hist. Ref.* v. v, We have already alluded to the proceedings of his vice-chancellor, Waldkirch. **1884** *Cath. Dict.* (1897) 263 The more pressing, weighty, public, and solemn affairs of the Apostolic See.. pass through the hands of the Vice-Chancellor.

2. The acting representative of the Chancellor of a university, usually the head of a college specially appointed to the office for a limited time, or the principal of the university.

1530 *Act 22 Hen. VIII*, c. 12 Scolers of the Universites of Oxford & Cambrydge that goo aboute beggyng, not beyng aucthorysed.. by the Commyssary, Chauncelloure, or vichauncelloure of the same. *a* **1540** BARNES *Wks.* (1573) 222/2 Because I had once submitted my selfe to the Vice-chauncelour, and I was thereby circunuented. **1577** HARRISON *England* II. iii. (1877) I. 82 Ouer each vniuersitie also there is a seuerall chancelor, whose offices are perpetuall, howbeit their substitutes, whom we call vicechancelors, are changed euerie yeare. **1629** WADSWORTH *Pilgr.* Ded. A iij, The Reuerend Vice-Chancellor, Doctors, Procters, Gouernors of Colledges and Hals. **1681** *Lond. Gaz.* No. 1656/3 Afterwards several of the Nobility were admitted Doctors of Law, His Majesty allowing the Vice-Chancellor to be Covered in His Presence, while the Orator presented them. **1705** *Ibid.* No. 4114/1 Mr. Vice-Chancellor, and the other Members of the University, waited.. upon the Prince. **1763–5** CHURCHILL *Author* Poems 1767 II. 128 Vice Chancellors, whose knowledge is but small,.. Ill-brook'd the gen'rous Spirit, in those days When Learning was the certain road to praise. **1836** *Penny Cycl.* VI. 482/1 In both the English Universities the duties of the Chancellor are in nearly all cases discharged by a Vice-Chancellor. **1864** J. H. NEWMAN *Apol.* 235 The late Vice-Chancellor threatens to take his own children away from the church.

3. A deputy or subordinate of one or other state official bearing the title of Chancellor.

1587 *Reg. Privy Council Scot.* IV. 167 Schir Johnne Maitland of Thirlstane, knycht, his Majesteis secretare and vice-chancellair. **1612** *Maitland Club Misc.* III. 113 Appoynting him [*sc.* the archbishop] to be Vicechanceler in the Parlement, if my Lord Chancelar thoght not the Chancelarie and Commissionarie compatible. *c* **1653** BAILLIE in Z. Boyd *Zion's Flowers* (1855) Introd. 53 The Vice-Chancellar was dead. **1694** LUTTRELL *Brief Rel.* (1857) III. 272 Mr. Hambden, vicechancellor of the exchequer, has laid down that place. **1728** CHAMBERS *Cycl.* s.v. *Chancellor*, Sometimes the Lord Chancellor [of England] had a Vice-Chancellor, who was Keeper of the Seal. **1777** R. WATSON *Philip II*, II. 217 She was offended at their artifice, and immediately despatched her vice-chancellor to complain of their conduct. **1876** BANCROFT *Hist. U.S.* V. l. 94 The vice-chancellor [at Moscow], therefore, calmly explained the impossibility of conceding the request for troops. **1889** *Dict. Nat. Biog.* XVIII. 49 Eustace (*d.* 1215), bishop of Ely,.. became vice-chancellor and keeper of the royal seal, and ultimately chancellor.

b. *spec.* One of the higher judges in the former Court of Chancery.

1813 *Act 53 Geo. III*, c. 24 To nominate and appoint from time to time.. a fit Person,.. to be an additional Judge Assistant to the Lord High Chancellor,.. and to be called Vice Chancellor of England. **1823** EGAN *Grose's Dict. Vulg. T.*, *Vice Chancellor's court*, creditor's last shift. **1835** TOMLINS *Law-Dict.* I. s.v. *Chancellor*, In his judicial capacity, he hath divers assistants and officers, *viz.* the Vice-Chancellor of England,.. the Masters in Chancery, &c. **1876** *Encycl. Brit.* V. 390/1 Previous to being merged in the New Supreme Court of Judicature, the Court of Chancery consisted of the Lord Chancellor,.. and three Vice-Chancellors.

Hence **vice-'chancellorship,** the office or dignity of a vice-chancellor; the period during which this is held.

1579 FENTON *Guicciard.* I. 4 He made the Pope promise him.. the office of vicechancellorshippe (the principallest place in the Court of Rome). **1589** [? NASHE] *Almond for Parrat* 29 T. C. in Cambridge first inuented this violent innouation, when as his mounting ambition went through euery kinde of Ambitus, to compasse the Office of the Vice-chauncelour-ship. **1655** T. BAILY *Life Bp. Fisher* 10 But now Vicechancellour-ship, Mastership and all must be laid downe. **1691** WOOD *Ath. Oxon.* I. 593 He did undergo with great honor the Vicechancellourship of this University. **1761** T. WARTON *Life Bathurst* 94 The spirited orations which he spoke in his Vice-chancellorship. **1813** SIR S. ROMILLY *Parl. Deb.* 15 Feb., The Vice-Chancellorship might in a short time become a sinecure. **1889** W. WILSON *State* §426 (1893) 266 [The German chancellor] is.. ultimately responsible in every case—even for the non-exercise of his office. The vice-chancellorship is only a convenience.

vice-'comital, *a.* [Cf. VICE-COUNTY 2 and COMITAL *a.*] Belonging to a vice-county (sense 2).

1859 H. C. WATSON *Cybele Brit.* IV. 275 The comital and vice-comital floras are yet incompletely ascertained.

vice-'consul. [VICE-. So med.L., F., Sp., Pg. *vice-consul*, It. *viceconsolo*.]

†**1.** A Roman proconsul. *Obs.*

1559 BP. SCOT in Strype *Ann. Ref.* (1709) I. App. x. 33 Certeyn wycked persons.. brought hym before their vice-consul, called Gallio. **1579–80** NORTH *Plutarch* (1595) 346 The author of this epigramme reckoneth the two times of his being viceconsull, for two whole Consulshippes. **1601** HOLLAND *Pliny* II. 526 Aterius Labeo, a noble man of Rome,.. who otherwise had been vice-Consull in Gallia Narbonensis.

2. An assistant or deputy of a consul.

1601 W. PARRY *Trav. Sir A. Sherley* 10 The English consulls and vice consulls. **1702** W. J. *Bruyn's Voy. Levant* xxxii. 121 The next Morning we waited upon the Vice-Consul. *c* **1744** in Hanway *Trav.* (1762) I. v. lxxi. 327 Which oath or affirmation, the said embassador, agent, resident, consul or vice-consul respectively, is hereby authorized to administer. **1788** JEFFERSON *Writ.* (1859) II. 495 The consul's presence in his port should suspend, for the time, the functions of the vice-consul. **1867** SMYTH *Sailor's Word-bk.* 713 If there be a resident consul, the vice-consul is appointed and paid by him. **1882** LD. ACTON *Let. to Mary Gladstone* 9 Mar. (1904) 128 The Vice-Consul is a singularly intelligent and practical man.

Hence **vice-'consular** *a.*, **vice-'consulate, vice-'consulship.**

1587 GOLDING *De Mornay* xxiii. (1592) 344 In Afrik they sacrifized men, vntill in the Viceconsulship of Tyberius. **1819** BYRON *Let. to Murray* 29 Oct., You say nothing of the vice-consulate for the Ravenna patrician. **1836** MARRYAT *Midsh. Easy* (1863) 164 They found Mr. Hicks looking very red and vice-consular indeed. **1844** KINGLAKE *Eothen* vii, The only anomaly which had been detected by the vice-consular wisdom. **1885** *Manch. Exam.* 12 Jan. 5/1 We should re-establish our two vice-consulates in the interior of Macedonia.

†**vice-count.** *Obs.* [VICE-, after med.L. *vicecomes*.] A viscount.

1461 *Rolls of Parlt.* V. 477 Henry late Erle of Northumberlond, William Vicecount Beaumont [etc.]. **1633** T. STAFFORD *Pac. Hib.* III. xvii. (1821) 658 John Barry, brother to the Vicecount. **1655** DIGGES *Compl. Ambass.* 367 The Vice-Count of Turayne, a Gentleman very dear unto Monsieur. **1673** *Phil. Trans.* VIII. Ded., To the Right Honourable Richard Lord Vice-Count Ranalaugh.

So †**vice-countess,** a viscountess; hence †**vice-countess-ship.** †**vice-countile** *a.*, viscountile.

c **1624** J. WILLIAMS *Let.* in *Cabala* (1654) 79 A strange Creation passed of late, of a Vice-Counteship of Maidenhead, passed to the Heires Males, who must be called hereafter *Vice-Countesse Fynch. **1685** *Broadside, Coronat. James II* (T. Newcomb), Vice-Countesses, Four a-Breast. *c* **1630** RISDON *Surv. Devon* (1810) 13 The *vicecountile jurisdiction was hereditary.

vice-'county. [In sense 1 ad. OF. *viconté, -ei, -ey*, etc. (mod.F. *vicomté*) VISCOUNTY, or med.L. *vicecomitātus*, f. *vicecomes*: see prec. In sense 2, f. VICE- + COUNTY[1] 2.]

†**1.** A viscounty. *Obs.*[−1]

1639 FULLER *Holy War* III. xxii. 147 And for a breakfast to begin with, he [Simon de Montfort] was seised of the Vicecounty of Besiers. **1706** STEVENS *Sp. Dict.* I, *Villa-Nueva de Cardenas*, a Town in.. Andaluzia,.. made a Vice County by King Philip the 4th.

2. A division of a large county, treated as a county-area with regard to the distribution of species of plants, etc.

1859 H. C. WATSON *Cybele Brit.* IV. 130 Smaller and more numerous sections could be formed by dividing the great counties into vice-counties. **1873–4** —— *Topographical Bot.* (title-p.), The 112 Counties and Vice-counties of England, Wales, and Scotland. **1890** *Science-Gossip* XXVI. 110/1 Not more than ten out of the 112 counties and vice-counties into which Great Britain is divided.

vice'gerence. Now *rare.* [Cf. next and -ENCE. So older F. *vicegerence* (mod.F. *-gérance*).] = next.

1527 ANDREW *Brunswyke's Distyll. Waters* P iij, Also yf oyle be made of the same floures it hathe the offyce of bawme and vycegerence of his vertues. **1660** MILTON *Free Commw.* Wks. 1851 V. 432 Christ.. hath not left the least shadow of a command for any such Vicegerence from him in the State. **1679** C. NESSE *Antichrist* 38 His title.. signifies substitution and vice-gerence. **1681** FLAVEL *Meth. Grace* xix. 336 In which words.. the vice-gerence of his death is plainly expressed. **1814** MRS. J. WEST *Alicia de Lacy* IV. 202 He could have endured the consciousness of.. his rights invaded, from the hope that the vice-gerence of truth and retribution would return. **1835** *Penny Cycl.* III. 173 (Avignon), The Court of Vicegerence was for all cases in which the military and religious orders were concerned. **1902** R. BAGOT *Donna Diana* xiv. 156 The Papal Court.. is no freer from petty jealousies.. than the Court of any ruler in no wise claiming Divine vicegerence.

vicegerency (vaɪsˈdʒɪərənsɪ). [See next and -ENCY. So mod.L. *vicegerentia* (1601 in Du Cange), It. *vicegerenza*.]

1. The office, dignity, or rule of a vicegerent; the fact of ruling or administering as representative of another.

1596 DRAYTON *Legends* iv. 511 But to the great Vice-gerencie I grew, Being a Title as Supreme as new. **1600** W. WATSON *Decacordon* (1602) 119 If euery Priest shold take place agreeing to their Vice-gerencie vnder Christ, there could be no order kept. **1641** MILTON *Prel. Episc.* Wks. 1851 III. 73 Timothy, and Titus,.. had rather the vicegerency of an Apostleship committed to them, then the ordinary charge of a Bishoprick. *a* **1668** DAVENANT *Law agst. Lovers* Wks. (1673) 323 The Duke,.. During the time of your Vicegerency, Remain'd here in disguise. **1702** SACHEVERELL *Serm. Univ. Oxford* (1710) 9 The highest indignity.. to any crown'd head is.. denying its vice-gerency. **1761** HUME *Hist. Eng.* III. App. 75 James was vaunting his divine vicegerency. **1845** R. W. HAMILTON *Pop. Educ.* ix. 224 To gain a just conception of civil government... If it be that Divine vicegerency which many have described [etc.]. **1891** *Daily News* 29 Dec. 6/1 He has.. put to death more than forty persons who have dared to question his authority or argued against his vicegerency.

transf. **1711** G. HICKES *Two Treat. Chr. Priesth.* I. ii. 16 This Vicegerency, or mediatory Office to transact and minister in sacred Matters betwixt God and Man.

b. A district or province ruled by a vicegerent.

1865 W. G. PALGRAVE *Arabia* I. vi. 244 History and tradition record no rebellious outbreak of any importance during their sway among the numerous vicegerencies of Arabia.

†**2.** Vicarious nature or character. *Obs.*

1671 FLAVEL *Fount Life* vii. 18 His sanctifying himself for us plainly speaks the Vicegerency of his Death. **1679** C. NESSE *Antichrist* 24 Antichrist.. signifies substitution and vice-gerency.

vicegerent (vaɪsˈdʒɪərənt), *sb.* and *a.* Also 6 **vitz-,** 7 **vize-gerent.** [ad. med.L. *vicegerent-*, *vicegerens*, f. L. *vicem* (acc.) stead, place, office, etc., and *gerens*, pres. pple. of *gerĕre* to carry, hold. So F. *vicégérent* (also *-gérant*), It., Sp., Pg. *vicegerente*. The hyphen, formerly not uncommon, is now rarely used in this and the preceding words.]

A. *sb.* **1.** A person appointed by a king or other ruler to act in his place or exercise certain of his administrative functions.

1536 CROMWELL in Merriman *Life & Lett.* (1902) II. 26 Thomas Crumwell.. keper of the privey Seale of our said soueraigne Lorde the king and vitzgerent to the same for.. all his Jurisdiction ecclesiasticall within this Realme. **1538** *Ibid.* 151, I Thomas lorde Crumwell,.. Vice-gerent to the kynges said highnes. **1545** *Act 37 Hen. VIII*, c. 17 Censures ecclesiasticall made by your Highnes and your Vicegerent, officialls, commissaries, and Judges and visitators. **1593** R. HARVEY *Philad.* 1 Mordred Arthurs kinsman being appointed Vicegerent in his royalty, gaue great giftes.. to Cerdrick a Saxon. **1606** G. W[OODCOCKE] *Hist. Ivstine* VI. 30 Lysander whome Agesilaus appointed his Vize-gerent the time of his absence. **1651** N. BACON *Disc. Govt. Eng.* II. xv. (1739) 79 It hath therefore been the ancient course of Kings of this Nation, to constitute Vice-gerents in their absence. **1733** SWIFT *On Poetry* Wks. 1755 IV. I. 198 Now sing the minister of state,.. Thou great vicegerent of the king [etc.]. **1788** GIBBON *Decl. & F.* lvii. V. 671 He was trusted by the sultan as the faithful vice-gerent of his power. **1838** THIRLWALL *Greece* II. xiv. 194 His vicegerent was at first willing to resign his authority. **1878** STUBBS *Const. Hist.* III. xviii. 95 He intended.. Gloucester to act as his vicegerent in England.

b. In general sense: One who takes the place of another in the discharge of some office or duties.

1549 Coverdale, etc. *Erasm. Par. Tim.* i. 3 b, I left the there euen as my selfe, to haue the autoritie as a notable vicegerent in so excellent and so paynefull an office. **1641** Baker *Chron., Eliz.* 24 The Governours of Ireland.. were at first called Iustices,.. afterwards, Lievtenants, and their Vice-gerents were called Deputies. **1683** *Brit. Spec.* 114 [His] Vice-gerent was the Vicar General of Britain, honored with the Title *Spectabilis.* **1773** *Observ. State Poor* 47 The humanity and generosity of some of these parochial vicegerents, the farmers or managers of workhouses. **1781** Gibbon *Decl. & F.* xvii. (1787) II. 38 These prerogatives were reserved to the præfects..: their vicegerents were confined to the trifling weight of a few ounces. **1851** Hussey *Papal Power* iii. 130 For what respect will be thought due to the vicegerents of the holy apostle St. Peter if what they ordain.. be undone. **1868** M. Pattison *Academ. Org.* iv. 109 There is in all cases, a vice-gerent, who in the absence of the head exercises his powers.

c. A ruler or commander *of* a country, etc., in virtue of deputed power.

1577 Holinshed *Chron.* II. 482/1 Herewith he [Richard I] dothe commaunde them also to obey Robert Earle of Leycester, whome he appointed.. as his Lieutenant or vicegerent of those parties during his absence. **1589** Greene *Tullies Love* Wks. (Grosart) VII. 117 The Romanes had made mee Vicegerente of their forces. *c* **1610** *Women Saints* 151 Aspasius the vicegerent of Rome. **1786** Burke *Art. agst. W. Hastings* Wks. 1842 II. 208 The said Mogul has been obliged to declare the head of the Mahratta state to be vicegerent of the Mogul empire.

2. Applied to rulers and magistrates as representatives of the Deity.

Frequent in the 17th century.

1547–64 Baldwin *Mor. Philos.* (Palfr.) 74 Princes, being by God put in authority, are His vice-gerents, and should therefore require obedience. **1561** T. Norton *Calvin's Inst.* iv. xx. (1634) 735 If they [the Magistrates] remember that they bee the vicegerents of God. **1595** W. C[lerke] *Polimanteia* C iv b, This likewise is the cause why the Prince is tearmed Gods Vicegerent vpon earth. **1641** Milton *Ch. Govt.* v. Wks. 1851 III. 114 We acknowledge that the civill magistrate weares an autority of Gods giving, and ought to be obey'd as his vicegerent. **1681** Dryden *Abs. & Achit.* To Rdr., God is infinitely merciful; and his Vicegerent is only not so, because he is not Infinite. **1700** Astry tr. *Saavedra-Faxardo* I. 230 The same has place in Princes, who are God's Vicegerents in Temporals. **1710** Prideaux *Orig. Tithes* ii. 120 All Governours of Nations being Gods Vicegerents, they are bound in all things to order their Government so as will best agree with the will of him. **1840** Thackeray *Paris Sk.-Bk.* (ed. 2) II. 274 'Dieu seul est grand,' said courtly Massillon; but next to him, as the prelate thought, was certainly Louis, his vicegerent here upon earth.

b. Applied to priests, and *spec.* to the Pope, as representatives of God or Christ.

1572 R. T. *Discourse* 49 Hee onely is Antichrist that fayneth himself to do all that Christ can doo, to bee his vicegerent in earth, to sit in his place. **1593** in J. Morris *Troub. Cath. Forefathers* Ser. iii. (1877) 130 Unto all which things the jurisdiction and authority of the Pope, Christ's Vicar and Vicegerent, did extend. **1660** Milton *Free Commw.* Wks. 1851 V. 432 All Protestants hold that Christ in his Church hath left no Vicegerent of his Power. **1678** Marvell *Growth Popery* Wks. 1875 IV. 255 The Pope.. does persecute those to the death who dare worship the Author of their Religion instead of his pretended Vicegerent. **1737** Challoner *Cath. Chr. Instr.* (1753) 81 The Priest that officiates in the Mass officiates as Christ's Vicegerent. **1841** Cdl. Wiseman in E. Purcell *Life A. P. de Lisle* (1900) I. xiii. 285 Let me know that the Vicegerent of Xt. approves of my course,.. and I shall not care for all the world. **1873** H. Rogers *Orig. Bible* ii. (1875) 78 Moses.. did not affect to be, like.. the Pope, the visible representative and vicegerent of God.

transf. **1624** Gataker *Transubst.* 96 They say it to Christ, whose deputie and vicegerent the Image there is.

c. Similarly applied to man in general or in some special respect; also (*b*) to nature, the sun, conscience, etc.

(*a*) **1601** Sir W. Cornwallis *Disc. Seneca* (1631) Mm viij, That this confusion is incident to our liues, is our owne fault, since the disorders of a state belongeth to.. the Gouernors of a state; so this to man who is Vicegerent of the earth. **1626** Jackson *Creed* viii. x. 93 Our first parents being Gods vicegerents here on earth, Lords of all his visible creatures. **1654** Whitlock *Zootomia* 344 Indifferently bent to the Continuance of it, or change; as God, and his Vice-gerents, her Parents shall think fit. **1845** *Encycl. Metrop.* II. 561 [A Deity who] communicates to men a knowledge.. of his purposes that they may be his vicegerents in executing them. **1861** J. A. Alexander *Gosp. Jesus Christ* xxxix. 521 A proof of man's original formation in God's image, and his original vestiture with delegated power as God's vicegerent.

(*b*) **1646** H. P. *Medit. Seige* 76 Nature (God's great vicegerent). **1676** Sir M. Hale *Contempl.* ii. 82 God Almighty hath substituted the Soul of Man, as his Deputy or Vicegerent in that Province which is committed to him. **1681** Flavel *Meth. Grace* xxxiii. 556 Conscience,.. that noble power, God's vicegerent in the soul. **1794** G. Adams *Nat. & Exp. Philos.* (1806) II. xxi. 415 When the sun is said to rule the day,.. what else can be understood but that he acts as a vicegerent. **1821** Shelley *Hellas* Prol. 142 Thou Destiny;.. Go, thou Vicegerent of my will, no less Than of the Father's. **1835** Miss Sedgwick *Linwoods* iv, Let man beware how he wilfully or carelessly perverts and blinds God's vicegerent, conscience. **1860** Pusey *Min. Proph.* 192 They dethroned righteousness, the representative and vice-gerent of God, and made it rest on the ground. **1881** C. A. Young *Sun* i. (1882) 12 It has been reserved for more modern times.. to show clearly just how.. the sun himself [is] the symbol and vicegerent of the Deity.

d. Applied to persons as representing some other supernatural or spiritual power.

1588 Shaks. *L.L.L.* i. i. 222 Great Deputie, the Welkins Vicegerent, and sole dominator of Nauar. **1615** Heywood *Foure Prentises* i. xviii, Joves great Vice-gerent over all the world. **1701** De Foe *Trueborn Eng.* i. 17 The List of his [the Devil's] Vice-gerents and Commanders Outdoes your Cæsars or your Alexanders. **1725** Pope *Odyss.* xi. 310 Now in the time's full process forth she brings Jove's dread vicegerents, in two future kings. **1763** J. Brown *Poetry & Music* v. 61 Apollo, the God of Music, was their Author [of oracles]; The Pythia or Priestess was his Vice-gerent. **1786** tr. *Beckford's Vathek* (1868) 104 Merciful Prophet! stretch forth thy propitious arms towards thy Vicegerent!

3. A thing which takes the place of another.

1583 Melbancke *Philotimus* Cc ij, If my lasie leggs.. should deny to make this voiage, my hearte would.. substitute my handes to be their vicegerentes. **1871** Earle *Philol. Eng. Tongue* 390 The pronouns are, as their name signifies, words which are the vicegerents of nouns.

4. A vicarious bearer *of* sorrow. *rare*$^{-1}$.

1594 Southwell *M. Magd. Funeral Teares* (1823) 73 All creatures.. leaving me as the vicegerent of all their sorrow.

B. *adj.* (or *attrib.*). **1.** Taking the place, or performing the functions, of another.

1577 tr. *Bullinger's Decades* (1592) 853 The Scripture teacheth that Christ ascended into heauen, and hath established a vicegerent power, to wit, the holie Ghost. **1667** Milton *P.L.* x. 56 But whom send I to judge them? whom but thee Vicegerent Son. **1712** Blackmore *Creation* 355 Next Man arose at thy creating word, Of thy terrestrial realms Vicegerent Lord. **1749** *Deity* 17 But Conscience, fair vicegerent light within, Asserts its author.

2. Characterized by deputed or vicarious power.

1667 Milton *P.L.* v. 609 Under his great Vice-gerent Reign abide [ye],.. For ever happie. **1847** H. Bushnell *Chr. Nurt.* ii. v. (1861) 208 The vicegerent office to be maintained, and the gracious ends to be secured, make it indispensable that parents should themselves be living in the Spirit.

Hence **vice'gerentship.**

1600 O. E. (M. Sutcliffe) *Repl. Libel* i. vi. 157 Let this Noddy.. shew foorth the popes commission eyther for his vicegerentship, or for his pretended apostolicke office. **1646** Gillespie *Malè Audis* 10 The capacity of a Vicegerent, which he hath by his Vicegerentship. *Ibid.* 35 The two fold Vicegerentship of God and of Christ.

vice-god. [Vice-.] One who (on earth) takes the place, or exercises the power, of God.

Freq. in the 17th cent. as a hostile designation of the Pope.

1600 Darrell *Detect. Harsnet* 204 Our Vice Godes which are here on earth in Gods steade will take vengeance of those traitors. **1624** Bp. Mountagu *Gagg* 63 There is an headship which will not reach that illimited power giuen to the Pope, Our Lord, Vice-God vpon earth. **1664** Owen *Vind. Animad. Fiat Lux* xvi. Wks. 1855 XIV. 392 The consequences so startled the wise state of Venice that you know they disputed it to the utmost with your vice-god Paul V. **1712** M. Henry *Popery Spir. Tyranny* Wks. 1853 II. 342 To call them Anti-gods, and Anti-christs, how-ever they pretend to be Vice-christs and Vice-gods. **1724** R. Welton *Chr. Faith & Pract.* 434 Man is a vice God in the world. **1830** Bentham *Constit. Code* Wks. 1843 IX. 38 On neither side has any vice-god been seen or fancied. **1873** L. Stephen *Freethinking* ix. 347 Man.. is hopelessly ignorant, but set on a throne and properly manipulated he becomes an infallible vice-God.

Hence **vice-godhead.**

1659 Baxter *Key Cath.* xx. 84 Not only the Romish Universal Monarchy and Vice-godhead, but even its Patriarchal Primacy was no Apostolical Tradition.

vice-'governor. [Vice-.] An official acting under, or in place of, a governor; a deputy-governor. Hence **vice-'governorship.**

1598 Florio, *Vicegouernatore*, a vicegouernour, a deputie-gouernour. **1742** Woodroofe in Hanway *Trav.* (1762) I. ii. xvii. 77 The governor, vice-governor, and commander of the garrison, came on board. **1760** *Ann. Reg.* 73 He has for some time resided as vice-governor under the King of Prussia. **1842** J. F. Cooper *Jack o' Lantern* I. 159 Vito Viti had long before gone up the street to see the vice-governor. **1876** Bancroft *Hist. U.S.* VI. 500 [Francis Bernard] thankfully accepts baronetcy and vice-governorship of Virginia. **1897** Mary Kingsley *W. Africa* 393 Spanish possessions, under a Vice-Governor to the Governor of Fernando Po. *Ibid.*, The Vice-Governorship of Eloby.

vice-king. [Vice-.] One who rules as the representative of a king; a viceroy. Also *attrib.*

1579 in Hakluyt *Voy.* (1600) III. 739 In coasting along the Island of Mutyr, belonging to the King of Ternate, his Deputie or Vice-king.. came with his Canoa to vs. **1622** Mabbe tr. *Aleman's Guzman d'Alf.* ii. 132 Vnder his protection we went vp and downe the Citie, as if we had beene so many Vice Kings of the Country. **1659** Baxter *Key Cath.* xlii. 300 A Deputy, or Vice-King in Ireland. **1681** —— *Acc. Sherlocke* vi. 210 There is no need of a Vice King to make this a Kingdom. **1681–6** J. Scott *Chr. Life* (1747) III. 562 So that now he is subject to the Father in the Capacity of a Vice-King to a supreme Sovereign. **1800** *Hist. Ind.* in *Asiat. Ann. Reg.* 24/2 He appointed Don Francis D'Almeyda, Governor-general, with the pompous title of Vice King of the Indies. **1848** Lytton *Harold* iii. iii. 99 Farther still down the hall are the great civil lords and vice-king vassals of the 'Lord Paramount'. **1876** Tennyson *Harold* ii. ii, Thou shalt be verily king—all but the name—For I shall most sojourn in Normandy; And thou be my vice-king in England.

vice-'legate. [Vice-, after F. *vice-légat* or It. *vicelegato* (Sp. and Pg. *vicelegado*).] One who acts as the representative or deputy of a (Papal) legate.

1549 Sir T. Hoby *Trav.* 17 in *Camden Misc.* (1902), The Pope is lord of yt. Vicelegate there for him was Annibale Borio. **1670** G. H. *Hist. Cardinals* i. iii. 83 To meet the eldest son of any Prince, or the Ambassadors of the Dukes of Savoy,.. the Cardinals.. send their Vice-Legats with some small number of Coaches. **1683** *Apol. Prot. France* iv. 31 The conference the Queen had, as she passed by Avignon with the Vice-Legat, which gave him wonderful satisfaction, pleased them not so well. **1708** *Lond. Gaz.* No. 4497/1 The Legat and Vice-Legat are excluded from having any part in the new State. **1765** *Ann. Reg.* 143 At Avignon.. the vice legate.. dispatched couriers to the neighbouring cities. **1835** *Penny Cycl.* III. 173/1 The popes governed the city [of Avignon].. by a cardinal-legate, or rather, as the legate was always non-resident, by a vice-legate.

Hence **vice-'legateship.**

1691 *Lond. Gaz.* No. 2685/1 The Vice-Legatship of Avignon is given to the Bishop of Fieschi. **1818** *Gentl. Mag.* Aug. 127/1 In the exercise of the several governments,.. he has.. acquired great praise, as likewise in the Vice-legateship of Bolonia.

viceless ('vaɪslɪs), *a.* [f. Vice *sb.*[1] 1.] Free from vice.

1560 Rolland *Seven Sages* 5 To that effect, that he may viceless be, Of all vices, and sic thing as gais wrang. **1591** Savile *Tacitus, Hist.* i. xlix. 27 Galba.. rather vicelesse than greatly vertuous. **1665** Boyle *Occas. Refl.* v. ii. (1675) 301 Errours about Religion,.. maintain'd by Men that are resolute, and viceless. **1671–4** Lady Warwick *Autobiog.* (Percy Soc.) 164 Mr. Henry St. John was very good natured and viceless. *Ibid.*, The young men were not viceless. **1847** J. Halliday *Rustic Bard* 321 Viceless virtue, undecaying, Shed her lustre on our name. **1890** *Sat. Rev.* 22 Nov. 575/1 Those who are themselves sinless and viceless.

vice-like, *a.*[1] *rare*$^{-1}$. [f. Vice *sb.*[1] 1.] Partaking of the nature of vice.

1590 Nashe *Martin Marprelate* Wks. (Grosart) I. 184 Beeing once entered into the vicelike vaine of foolerie,.. I was caried most wickedlie.. in a scorne against the Saincts of God.

vice-like, *a.*[2] Also *U.S.* vise-like. [f. Vice *sb.*[2] 5.] Resembling (that of) a vice; firmly tenacious or compressive.

1835 E. A. Poe in *Southern Lit. Messenger* June 570/1 Clutching with a vice-like grip the long-desired rim. **1845** Bailey *Festus* (ed. 2) 127 Traitors! that vice-like fang the hand ye lick. **1856** Emerson *Eng. Traits, Lit.* Wks. (Bohn) II. 104 What he relishes in Dante is the vice-like tenacity with which he holds a mental image before the eyes. **1890** D. Davidson *Mem. Long Life* x. 258 [He] seized my hand in his vice-like fist.

vicelinge, ME. var. *fikeling* Fickling *vbl. sb.*

vice'narious, *a. rare*$^{-0}$. [See next and -ious.] 'Of or belonging to the twentieth' (Blount, 1656).

vicenary ('vɪsənərɪ, 'vaɪ-), *sb.* and *a.* [ad. L. *vicēnāri-us*, f. *vīcēnī*, distrib. f. *vīgintī* twenty.]

†**a.** *sb.* One who has command over twenty persons. *Obs.*

1603 Harsnet *Pop. Impost.* 49 Delicat, another Captaine, or vicenarie in Sara, hauing vnder him twenty assistants.

b. *adj.* 'Belonging to twenty' (Bailey, 1727); based on the number twenty. Cf. Vigenary *a.*

1826 Peacock in *Encycl. Metrop.* (1845) I. 371/1 Such a practice would naturally lead to the formation of a vicenary scale of numeration. **1834** *Penny Cycl.* II. 337/2 In France the scale from 60 to 100 is strictly vicenary (by twenties).

vi'cennals. *rare*$^{-0}$. [ad. L. *vīcennālia.*]

1656 Blount *Glossogr., Vicennals*, solemn games and vows for twenty.. years.

vi'cennial, *a. Sc. Law.* [f. L. *vīcenni-um*: see next. Cf. L. *vīcennālis*, F. *vicennal.*] Extending to twenty years.

1737 Kames *Decis. Crt. Sess. 1730–52* (1799) 19 What use would there be for the vicennial prescription of retours, if a purchase [etc.]. **1785** Arnot *Trials* (1812) 261 Lord Fountainhall laid down this doctrine, that the vicennial prescription of Crimes had no place with us. **1826** G. J. Bell *Comment. Laws Scot.* (ed. 5) I, Vicennial Prescription of Holograph Obligations. **1838** W. Bell *Dict. Law Scot.* 770 By the act 1617, c. 13, a vicennial prescription of retours was introduced.

‖**vi'cennium.** *rare*$^{-1}$. [L., f. *vīc-*, stem of *vīcies* twenty times, etc., + *annus* year.] A period of twenty years.

1846 McCulloch *Acc. Brit. Empire* (1854) II. 623 The danger of dying of consumption.. is greater in this than in the preceding vicennium.

vice-'president. [Vice-. So F. *vice-président*, It., Sp., and Pg. *vicepresidente.*] One who acts as the representative or deputy of a president (in various senses); an official ranking immediately below a president.

1574 tr. *Marlorat's Apocalips* 66 Under Sergius the Vice-president of Asia.. ther arose a great strife.. about the keeping of the Easter. **1586** in J. Morris *Troub. Cath. Forefathers* (1877) 84 The Lord Evers sitting as vice-president with Meares, Hurlstone, Cheeke, and the rest. **1629** Wadsworth *Pilgr.* vii. 64 This North was created D.D. in Paris, and was sometimes Vice-President of the College of Doway. **1660** R. Coke *Power & Subj.* 235 The President, or Vice-president of the Queens Councell established in the North. **1771** Goldsm. *Hist. Eng.* (1789) IV. 18 The college [Magdalen, Oxford] was filled with catholics; and Charnock.. was made vice-president. **1796** T. Twining *Trav. India*, etc. (1893) 54 The Vice-President always breakfasted in his own room. **1800** *St. Papers* in *Asiat. Ann. Reg.* 6/2 That nothing.. shall prevent such Governor, when absent, from nominating a Vice-President and Deputy-Governor of Fort William. **1841** W. Spalding *Italy & It. Isl.* III. 57 Melzi d'Eril was vice-president: and in the Council of State were found Serbelloni [etc.]. **1855** *Poultry Chron.* III. 411/1 The society consists of a president, vice-president, committee, secretary, and members. **1874** BANCROFT *Footpr. Time* ii. 234 The Vice-President becomes an officer of much power or dignity.

Hence **vice-presi'dential** *a.*; **vice-'presidentship**. Also **vice-'presidency**.

1690 *Lond. Gaz.* No. 2600/1 The Vice-Presidentship of the Council of Arragon. **1804** *Guardian of Freedom* (Frankfort, Kentucky) 28 July 2/3 He is charged with having been long intriguing for the vice presidency. **1804** G. ROSE *Diaries* (1860) II. 132, I would accept the Vice-Presidentship of the Board of Trade. **1833** STORY *Comm. Constit. U.S.* III. 336 Suppose there should be three candidates for the presidency, and two for the vice-presidency. **1854** T. H. BENTON *30 Years' View* I. 45/1 Mr. Calhoun was the only substantive vice-presidential candidate before the people. **1884** G. W. CABLE *Dr. Sevier* xlvi. 341 With a presidential candidate on one side and his vice-presidential man Friday on the other. **1889** W. WILSON *State* §1099 (1893) 562 Each party..nominates the candidates of its choice for the presidency and vice-presidency. **1904** *Daily Chron.* 20 June 5/6 There has never before been so pronounced a reluctance to accept the vice-presidential nomination.

vice-queen. [VICE-.] **a.** A woman ruling as the representative of a queen. **b.** The wife of a viceroy. (Cf. VICEREINE.)

1578 T. N. tr. *Conq. W. India* (1596) 7 His mother and three sisters..came to the Iland of Santo Domingo, with that vicequeene the Lady Mary of Toledo. **1628–9** DIGBY *Voy. Medit.* (Camden) 77, I..sent some letters to the Vice-queene of Sardinia. **1667** *Lond. Gaz.* No. 221/3 Naples, Dec. 13... The next day the Vice-Roy went *incognito* to visit him, which was the day after returned him by the Cardinal: who paid also his complements to the Vice Queen. **1749** SMOLLETT *Gil Blas* III. ix, Heavens! what luxury and magnificence! I believed myself in the palace of a vice-queen. **1796** NELSON 28 Sept. in Nicolas *Disp.* (1845) II. 284 If the Enemy land near Bastia, the Vice-Queen's Yatch may be useful. **1842** MISS MITFORD in L'Estrange *Life* (1870) III. ix. 139 Think of..the vice-queen of Portugal labouring as a bookseller's drudge. **1894** *Dublin Rev.* Oct. 463 A great Roman lady, who played the part of a vice-queen in Judea.

vice-'rector. [VICE-. Cf. F. *vice-recteur*, It. *vicerettore*, Sp. *vicerector*, Pg. *-reitor*.] A deputy rector (of a theological college).

1629 WADSWORTH *Pilgr.* iii. 12 Entire obseruance and duty to bee performed to the Rector.., next to the Vice-Rector as his minister. **1824** in *Ushaw Mag.* Dec. (1913) 259 Your late worthy Vice Rector has been at Ushaw some days. **1890** J. MORRIS in *Month* Apr. 491 With Dr. Ferdinand English, then Vice-Rector of the English College at Rome, ..I left England.

Hence **vice-'rectorship**.

1856 J. MORRIS in J. H. Pollen *Life* (1896) vii. 165 When the Vice-Rectorship of the English College was offered me, I did not hesitate to accept it.

vice'regal, *a.* [VICE- + REGAL *a.*, after VICEROY *sb.*] Of or pertaining to, associated with, a viceroy.

1836 DISRAELI *Lett. of Runnymede* x. 86 Ascending at last even to the Viceregal throne of India. **1839** LEVER *H. Lorrequer* ix, One of my fellow-passengers was a gentleman holding a high official appointment in the viceregal court. **1859** LANG *Wand. India* 325 He found a carriage ready to convey him to the vice-regal dwelling. **1874** STUBBS *Const. Hist.* I. xiii. 563 The viceregal character, which the justiciar certainly possessed.

Hence **vice-'regalize** *v. trans.*, to convert into a viceroyalty; **vice-'regally** *adv.*, as a viceroy.

1847 MRS. GORE *Castles in Air* xxviii, In many things, our poor vice-regalized kingdom only too strongly resembles Ireland. **1881** *Academy* April 271 The people whom he had ruled vice-regally.

vice-'regent. [VICE-. Cf. It. *vicereggente*.] One who acts in place of a regent.

In some early instances perh. an error for *vice-gerent*.

1556 *Acc. Ld. High Treas. Scot.* X. 315 To ane boy rynnand..to Dunkell witht clois writtingis of the viceregentis. **1581** MARBECK *Bk. Notes* 842 Who doubteth then, but if the Pope bee Vicar to the Prince of this world, he is Viceregent to the Diuell. **1669** DRYDEN *Tyrannic Love* III. i, But Monarchs are the Gods Viceregents here. **1827** SCOTT *Surg. Dau.* xii, The Nawaub has placed his young son, Tippoo, as Vice-Regent of his newly-conquered territory of Bangalore. **1889** W. WILSON *State* §104 (1893) 67 The five Ephors..were originally mere deputies of the kings, appointed..to act as vice-regents in the absence of their royal principals.

transf. **1660** MARQ. WORCESTER *Water-Comm. Engine* (1663) 15 A Viceregent or Countervail supplying the place and performing the full force of a Man, Wind, Beast or Mill.

Hence **vice-'regency**.

1930 BELLOC *Wolsey* ix. 243 He drafted a form of Vice-regency, a delegation of Papal power to himself.

‖**vicereine** ('vaɪsreɪn, ‖visrɛn). Also vice-reine. [a. F. *vicereine*, f. *vice-* VICE- + *reine* queen.] The wife of a viceroy; also (less usually), = VICE-QUEEN **a.**

Common from *c* 1885.

1823 MRS. A. JUDSON *Amer. Bapt. Miss. Burman Emp.* Contents, Letter v. Visit of the Vice-reine. [Cf. p. 63 Her highness, the viceroy's wife, visited us.] **1833** LADY BEDINGFELD in *Jerningham Lett.* (1896) II. 391 Residing 3 years at Brussels..at the time that it belonged to Austria and had..the Arch D. Mary Christine for Vice-Reine. **1882** *Times* 27 July 5/1 Those..who have expressed to her Highness the Vicereine and [the Khedive] himself their sympathy. **1896** *Pall Mall Mag.* Jan. 105 The Viceroy and the Vicereine stand before Tippoo's throne, supported..by the leading officials.

viceroy ('vaɪsrɔɪ), *sb.* Also 6–7 viceroye, 6 wize roy, vizeroye (7 -roy), 6–7 vizroy; 6–7 *pl.* -roies. [a. older F. *vice-roy*, *visroy* (F. *vice-roi*), f. *vice-* VICE- + *roi* king. So It. *viceré*, Pg. *vicerei*, Sp. *virey*.

Formerly freq. written or printed with hyphen and occas. as two words.]

1. One who acts as the governor of a country, province, etc., in the name and by the authority of the supreme ruler; a vice-king.

α. **1524** *Chron. Calais* (Camden) 34 The xxiiij. of February Fraunces the Frenche kynge was taken prisoner..by the vice-roy of Naples. **1555** EDEN *Decades* (Arb.) 103 Inacus Iopez Mendocius,..viceroye of Granata. **1598** BARCKLEY *Felic. Man* III. (1603) 241 The part rather of a tyrant then of a vice-roy. *a* **1641** BP. MOUNTAGU *Acts & Mon.* (1642) 135 The custome being in Persia, that in the necessary absence of the Prince in State, the Heire apparent was Vice-roy. **1698** J. FRYER *Acc. E. India & P.* 151 A long Gallery, hung round with the Pictures at length of all the Vice-Roys that had been in East India down to the present Vice-Roy. **1737** *Gentl. Mag.* VII. 685/2 His Catholick Majesty's.. dispatching all the necessary Orders to his Vice-Roys, Governors, and other Officers. **1787** A. HAMILTON *Wks.* (1886) VII. 15 The government lately established in Canada—the splendid title of Viceroy—seems to look beyond the dreary regions of Canada and Nova Scotia. **1808** PIKE *Sources Mississ.* III. App. 4 The whole political government of the vice-roy of Mexico. **1877** W. R. COOPER *Egypt. Obelisks* xi. (1878) 61 This obelisk..was presented to the late Duke of Northumberland..by the Viceroy of Egypt. **1880** *Encycl. Brit.* XII. 768/1 The supreme authority over all British India..is vested..in the viceroy or governor-general-in-Council.

β. **1582** N. LICHEFIELD tr. *Castanheda's Conq. E. Ind.* I. lxxvi. 156 b, And so they remained untill the comming of the Vizeroye Don Francisco de Almeda. **1590** WEBBE *Trav.* (Arb.) 24 These 60 Kings are all his Wize Royes in seuerall places. **1601** R. JOHNSON *Kingd. & Commw.* (1603) 236 The vizeroies of that huge tract do acknowledge him for their soueraigne and supreme gouernour. **1620** DEKKER *His Dream* Wks. (Grosart) III. 20 About him, round (Like petty Viz-royes), Spirits (me thought) all-Crownde.

2. *transf.* One having authority or rank comparable to that of a viceroy.

c **1590** GREENE *Friar Bacon* 178 Now Maisters of our Academicke State, That rule in Oxford, Vizroies in your place. **1591** LAMBARDE *Archeion* (1635) 97 The King..is within his owne Kingdome the Vice-roy of God. *a* **1631** DONNE *Serm.* i. (1634) 21 God creates man whom He constitutes His Vice-roy in the world. **1644** [H. PARKER] *Jus Populi* 45 The Judges were Gods Vice-Roys, in regard they did transact affairs by direction from Gods own mouth. **1676** GREW *Anat. Pl., Exper. Luct.* 238 For what Dominion a Prince hath over the Moral, that a Physician hath, as one of God Almighty's Vice-Roys, over the Corporeal World. **1818** LADY MORGAN *Autobiog.* (1859) 279 When Barras reigned, and the beautiful Madame Tallien reigned viceroy over him. **1827** SCOTT *Chron. Canongate* iii, Christie Steele was my mother's body servant, her very right hand, and.. something like a viceroy over her.

attrib. **1656** COWLEY *Chronicle* Wks. (1905) 41 But in her place I then obey'd Black-ey'd Bess, her Viceroy-Maid; To whom ensu'd a Vacancy.

3. *Ent.* An American species of butterfly, *Basilarchia Archippus*, distinguished by handsome red and black colouring.

1881 S. H. SCUDDER *Butterflies* vii. 103 The caterpillar of the Viceroy signifies its displeasure at any disturbance by tossing the head upward.

Hence **'viceroy** *v.* (with *it*), to rule as or like a viceroy.

1821 *Examiner* 596/1 They, forsooth, may viceroy it over authority with propriety.

viceroyal, *a.* [f. prec. + -AL[1]. Cf. VICEREGAL *a.*] Of or pertaining to a viceroy.

c **1728** SWIFT *Two Lett. Improv. Ireland* Wks. 1841 II. 91 Burnet..has not hitherto been able to persuade his vassals ..to settle a revenue on his viceroyal person. **1868** MRS. HORACE MANN *Life in Argentine Republic* 122 A viceroyal government was expressly created for it [*sc.* Buenos Ayres in 1777].

viceroyalty. [ad. F. *vice-royauté*: see VICE- and ROYALTY. Stressed either on the first or second syllable.]

1. The office, rank, or authority of a viceroy.

1703 *Lond. Gaz.* No. 3883/1 The Ambassador is not contented.., having entertained great hopes of being advanced to the Viceroyalty of Naples. **1749** SMOLLETT *Gil Blas* VIII. ii, Here I saw commanders and knights of Calatrava and St. Iago, solliciting for governments and viceroyalties. **1800** *Hist. Ind.* in *Asiat. Ann. Reg.* 29/2 Pedro Malcarenhas, on whom the viceroyalty devolved on the decease of Meneses. **1849** MACAULAY *Hist. Eng.* vi. II. 156 Sunderland..offered to procure for Tyrconnel supreme military command, enormous appointments, anything but the vice-royalty. **1867** FREEMAN *Norm. Conq.* I. vi. 475 This fact, coupled with Thurkill's similar viceroyalty in Denmark, shows that Cnut [etc.].

b. In quasi-concrete use: A viceroy or viceregal household.

1842 LOVER *Handy Andy* ix, Fancy might suggest that the house rejoiced, as it were, in its honoured position,.. because it was under the nose of viceroyalty. **1909** *Westm. Gaz.* 16 Sept. 4/2 This property..was bought by the Government in 1864 as a dwelling for Viceroyalty.

2. A province or dependency commonly administered by a viceroy.

1715 *Lond. Gaz.* No. 5323/2 The..Ship..which is to carry the Prince to his Viceroyalty of Peru. **1777** ROBERTSON *Hist. Amer.* VII. (1778) II. 332 Costa Rica and Veragua.. belong to the vice-royalty of New Spain. **1816** TUCKEY *Narr. Exped. R. Zaire* iv. (1818) 159 The opposite sides of the river form two vice royalties. **1844** *Regul. & Ord. Army* 37 The Lord-Lieutenant of Ireland shall be entitled to receive from the forts and batteries within His Vice-Royalty a Royal Salute. **1876** BANCROFT *Hist. U.S.* VI. lvi. 441 The seeds of rebellion were already [in 1782] sown in the vice-royalties of Buenos Ayres and Peru.

3. The period during which a particular viceroy holds office.

1849 HT. MARTINEAU *Hist. Peace* v. ii. (1877) III. 207 Ireland had never been so well governed as during the vice-royalty of Lord Mulgrave. **1865** MAFFEI *Brigand Life* II. 21 During the vice-royalty of the Count of Castrillo. **1883** B. SMITH *Life Ld. Lawrence* xxviii. II. 534 There had been a deficit in more than one year of his Viceroyalty.

viceroydom. *rare*$^{-1}$. [f. VICEROY *sb.* + -DOM.] = prec. 1.

1711 in *10th Rep. Hist. MSS. Comm.* App. V. 125 To putt allwayes the Viceroydom into the hands of an Irish Catholick.

viceroyed, *a.* *rare*$^{-1}$. [f. as prec.] Committed to a viceroy.

1839 BAILEY *Festus* 347 His is the sway of social sovereign peace:..His is the vice-royed, vouched-safe, sway of God.

'viceroyship. [f. VICEROY + -SHIP.]

1. = VICEROYALTY 1.

1639 FULLER *Holy War* II. xxxv. 89 The Saracen Caliph commanded in Egypt; under whom, two great Lords..fell out about the Sultanie or Vice-royship of that land. **1686** *Lond. Gaz.* No. 2156/2 The Viceroyship of Sardinia, vacant by the removal of the Count de Fuensalichi to the Government of Milan, is not yet disposed of. **1721** *Ibid.* No. 5953/1 The Prince..took Possession of the Viceroyship of this Kingdom. **1794** NELSON 24 Oct. in Nicolas *Disp.* (1845) I. 498 Since your Excellency has taken upon you the Viceroyship of Corsica. **1893** SIR H. W. NORMAN in *Mem.* (1908) 297, I cannot face the Viceroyship [of India]... I feel I am not really equal to five years of arduous work.

2. = VICEROYALTY 2.

1609 ROWLEY *Search for Money* (Percy Soc.) 24 These gardners, or guardians, of this their little viceroyship, were now approached us. **1703** J. SAVAGE *Lett. Antients* lxxxii. 225 The Dominion and Viceroyship of the Triballians. **1766** J. Z. HOLWELL *Orig. Princ. Anc. Bramins* II. iv. (1779) 20 Thus the empire was divided into as many kingdoms, as there had been Vice-royships and Governments. **1827** SCOTT *Napoleon* xlvii, I will..divide it [*sc.* Spain] into five.. vice-royships.

3. = VICEROYALTY 3.

1709 E. WARD tr. *Cervantes* 200 The Viceroy..resolv'd to be more favourable to Don Vincent, in case he should be found in Valencia, before his Viceroyship was expir'd. **1822** *New Monthly Mag.* VI. 51 His viceroyship will never be forgotten. **1889** SIR S. WALPOLE *Life Ld. J. Russell* I. xvii. 460 During the first few months of his Viceroyship.

vicesimal (vaɪ'sɛsɪməl), *a. rare.* [f. L. *vīcēsim-us* twentieth, f. *vīcēnī*: see VICENARY.] = VIGESIMAL *a.* Also †**vi'cesim.** *Obs.*$^{-0}$

1656 BLOUNT *Glossogr.*, *Vicesimal*, *Vicesim*, the same with Vicenarious. **1902** *Daily Chron.* 11 Jan. 5/2 Our system has inherent advantages for conversion over the former vicesimal and duodecimal system of France.

†**vi'cesime.** *Obs.*$^{-1}$ [ad. L. *vīcēsima* (sc. *pars*): see prec.] A twentieth part.

1600 HOLLAND *Livy* VII. xvi. 260 He proposed a law.. concerning a twentith part or vicesime, to be levied of their goods that were made free.

vice-'treasurer. [VICE-.] One who acts as the deputy or representative of a treasurer; *spec. Hist.*, an official acting in this capacity in the government of Ireland.

1541–2 in R. Bolton *Stat. Irel.* (1621) 231 Which shall be proued by writing..before the two chiefe Iustices, the chiefe Baron and the Vicethesaurer. **1547** *Privy Council Acts* (1890) II. 135 The Vicethresaurier of the Mynt at Bristowe. **1551** SIR J. WILLIAMS *Accompte* (Abbotsford) 79 Roberte Fowler, vice-treasourer, and Thomas Fowler, receivor. **1633** T. STAFFORD *Pac. Hib.* i. (1821) 31 The Vice-treasurer and generall Receiver of the Queenes Majesties revenewes of this Realme. **1676** EARL ESSEX in *Essex Papers* (Camden) II. 57 All the projects..w[hi]ch arise from our Vice Treasurer, do still tend to this not to have any money left here in the Treasury. **1710** *Lond. Gaz.* No. 4699/3 Mr. Pratt, Deputy-Vice-Treasurer, delivered..several Papers relating to the Receipts and Payments of the Vice-Treasurer. *a* **1797** in *3rd Rep. Hist. MSS. Comm.* 434/1 Mr. Flood & Mr. Hussey Burgh, the two best popular speakers, were very much softened, & Flood made Vice-Treasurer. **1860** L. HARCOURT *Diaries G. Rose* I. 71 The office of Vice-Treasurer of Ireland.

Hence **vice-'treasurership**.

1671 MARVELL *Corr.* Wks. (Grosart) II. 396 My Lord Angier, who bought..the Vicetreasurership of Ireland,..is, betwixt knavery and foolery, turned out. **1765** LD. HOLLAND in Jesse *Selwyn & Contemp.* (1843) I. 394 Will he have a Vice-Treasurership of Ireland? **1840** *Penny Cycl.* XVI. 296/2 Lord Rockingham had..offered him the chancellorship of the exchequer, and the vice-treasurership of Ireland.

†**vicety.** *Obs.*$^{-1}$ (App. f. VICE *sb.*[1] + -TY, for the sake of rime.)

1633 B. JONSON *Love's Welcome* Wks. (1641) 278 *Acci.* Here is to the fruit of Pem. *Fitz.* Grafted upon Stub his Stem. *Acci.* With the Peakish Nicetie. *Fitz.* And old Sherewood's Vicetie.

‖**vice versa** ('vaɪsi: 'vɜ:sə), *adv. phr.* Also vice versâ. [L. (also *versā vice*), from *vice*, abl. sing. of *vicis* turn, place, position, etc., and *versā*, abl. sing. fem. of *versus*, pa. pple. of *vertĕre* to turn. So F. *vice versâ*, Sp., Pg., It. *vice versa*, *viceversa*.] With a reversal or transposition of the main items in the statement just made; contrariwise, conversely.

1601 A. COPLEY *Answ. Let. Jesuited Gent.* 23 They are like to bee put to such a penance and the Arch-Priests *vice-versa* to be suspended and attained as Schismaticall. **1665** SIR T. HERBERT *Trav.* (1677) 335 When it rains and blows.. all along the Coast of Malabar.. no Sun appears: contrarily.. those Countreys on that side Bellagate have then clear Sunshine weather... And *vice versa*, the season varies. **1689** PRIOR *Epist. to F. Shephard* 60 The Thesis, *vice-versá* put, Should Hebrew-wise be understood. **1710** PALMER *Proverbs* 78 Nor can we ask his favour upon occasion, and so *vice versa* he can make no use of us. **1772** *Regul. H.M. Service at Sea* 21 The Number of the first Entry is to be noted against the Number of the Re-entry, and *vice versa*, the Number of the Re-entry against the Number of the first Entry. **1803** *Med. Jrnl.* X. 524 It may probably happen that those who have the disorder mildly are considered only to have a common cold; and, vice versa, a heavy accidental catarrh may rank as influenza. **1830** R. KNOX *Béclard's Anat.* 315 So that each portion of muscle is single at one extremity, and at the other is continuous with two portions; and *vice versa*, each of the latter is connected with a double portion of the opposite extremity.

b. Freq. in ***and*** (†*so*) ***vice versa***, or ***vice versa***, used to imply the complementary statement without expressing it in words.

1642 HOWELL *For. Trav.* ix. (Arb.) 47 The yeaue of the Conquering of France [by Spain], is the morning of the Conquest of England (and *vice versa*). **1677** PLOT *Oxfordsh.* 246 For Clay ground they have their seed from Red-land or Chalk, & *vice versa*. **1688** BOYLE *Final Causes Nat. Things* IV. 227 Not Anatomical but Chymical, or Vice Versa. **1761** STILES in *Phil. Trans.* LV. 255 These separated parts.. stretching or contracting themselves from round to oval and cylindrical, and *vice versa*. **1787** BEST *Angling* (ed. 2) 42 The larger he [the pike] is, the coarser the food, and so *vice versa*. **1835** W. R. HAMILTON tr. *Süvern's Ess. Birds of Aristoph.* 101 Flying is compared to rowing and sailing, and vice versa. **1854** *Poultry Chron.* I. 313/2 The young birds are sent packed in the old class hamper, or, *vice versâ*. **1885** LEUDESDORF *Cremona's Proj. Geom.* 122 Consequently the tangents at four harmonic points are harmonic, and *vice versa*.

vice-warden. [VICE-.] A deputy warden (esp. of the Stannaries or the Borders). Hence **vice-ˈwardenry, -ship.**

1536 in *Priory of Hexham* (Surtees) App. p. cxxxv, The lord Ogle beyng admytted as vice-warden. *Ibid.* p. cxxxvi, Sir Ingram Percy beyng dischargid of the vice-wardenry. *a***1548** HALL *Chron., Hen. IV*, 17b, In the returne he was encountered with therle of Northumberlandes vicewarden, and other gentilmen of the borders. **1640** *Act 16 Chas. I*, c. 15 The Warden, Vice Warden, or Steward of the said Stanaries. **1703** LD. GRANVILLE in *Lond. Gaz.* No. 3951/2, I refer to my Vice-Warden to lay before you the present State of the Stannaries. *c***1790** *Encycl. Brit.* (ed. 3) V. 462/1 (Cornwall), The lord-warden appoints a vice-warden to determine all stannery disputes every month. **1836** *Act 6–7 William IV*, c. 106 §1 The Court of Equity of the Vice Warden.. of the said Stannaries. **1863** *Rules for Appeals to Lord Warden of Stannaries* i, Any person desiring to appeal to the Lord Warden of the Stannaries from a.. decision of the Vice-Warden. **1901** *Westm. Gaz.* 13 Dec. 2/3 Ejected from the Vice-wardenship of the Stannaries, he was again returned to the House of Commons.

vicey-versey, vicy-versy, (ˈvaɪsɪ ˈvɜːsɪ), repr. colloq. or joc. pronunc. of VICE-VERSA *adv. phr.*

1858 J. R. LOWELL in *Atlantic Monthly* Aug. 371 How far from these unhappy days When all is vicy-versy! **1979** K. O'HARA *Searchers of Dead* ix. 102 Actors work on directors as well as vicey-versey.

vich, ME. var. EACH *a.*; obs. Sc. f. WHICH.

vichaunceller, obs. f. VICE-CHANCELLOR.

vichcraft, obs. Sc. form of WITCHCRAFT.

vicht, obs. Sc. var. WIGHT *sb.* and *a.*

‖**Vichy** (viʃi, anglicized ˈviːʃiː). [See def.]

1. The name of a town in the department of Allier in Central France, used *attrib.* and *ellipt.* to designate a mineral water obtained from springs there.

1858 SIMMONDS *Dict. Trade* s.v., Vichy-water. **1876** *Nature* XIV. 320/2 Vichy waters, from a physiological and hygienic point of view. **1882** *Harvard Lampoon* 26 Jan. 87/2 Vichy and Seltzer possessed of limpidity. **1903** *Smart Set* IX. 16 He.. mixed the contents of the phial in a glass half-filled with vichy.

2. Used to denote the government of France which operated from Vichy (1940–44) in collaboration with the Germans; freq. *attrib.* and in *Comb.* Also *transf.* and *fig.*

1941 [see COLLABORATION 2]. **1942** 'G. ORWELL' in *Partisan Rev.* Mar.–Apr. 159 Both Vichy and the Germans have found it quite easy to keep a façade of 'French culture' in existence. **1942** 'M. HOME' *House of Shade* vi. 96 Vichy French territory had been entered at Bardai. **1949** KOESTLER *Promise & Fulfilment* I. vii. 76 When, in 1941, British troops invaded Vichy-held Syria, they needed a vanguard of Commandos. **1965** B. SWEET-ESCOTT *Baker Street Irregular* ii. 54 Efforts to start something in Morocco, then occupied by the Vichy French, had been a failure. **1966** G. GREENE *Comedians* I. iii. 69 During the war.. I served in the Political Intelligence Department of the Foreign Office, supervising the style of our propaganda to Vichy territory. **1970** R. WINGATE *Lord Ismay* iv. 59 The German ability to use Vichy-controlled Syria as a route for her aircraft. **1979** P. WAY *Sunrise* xiv. 146 The jail.. had been convent no. 787 of the Poor Clares under West Africa's Vichy régime. **1980** *Times* 27 May 4/2 He went on to claim there was a 'Vichy mentality' in parts of the Foreign Office. The Home Office was 'stuffed with reactionaries'. **1981** M. WARNER *Joan of Arc* xiii. 263 Maurras's adherence to both Vichy and Joan of Arc.

Hence **ˈVichyist,** a supporter of the Vichy government.

1943 *Rev. Foreign Press* (Foreign Office Research Dept.) 23 Aug. 105/1 (*heading*) 'Combat' and 'Liberté' demand severe measures against all Vichyists. **1958** *Times* 3 Dec. 8/5 M. Soustelle was in charge of intelligence and espionage, first against occupying Germans and then against Vichyists and Communists.

Vichyite (ˈviːʃɪaɪt), *sb.* and *a.* [f. VICHY + -ITE¹.] **A.** *sb.* = *Vichyist* s.v. VICHY. **B.** *adj.* Supporting the Vichy government (see VICHY 2). Also *fig.*

1943 *Ann. Reg. 1942* 287 Yesterday a 'Vichy-ite', collaborating with the Nazis.. today a French patriot. **1945** *Times* 30 Oct. 3/4 Vichyite officials in Indo-China. **1968** [see COLLABORATEUR 2]. **1978** *Times* 9 Jan. 8/5 Each school of thought has its own pet profile of 'Treasury Man', whether it be the Institute of Economic Affairs seeing in him the symptoms of chronic Keynesianism or the Tribune Group of left wing Labour MPs sniffing for 'Vichyite' collaborators with the International Monetary Fund. **1979** *N.Y. Rev. Bks.* 8 Feb. 14/4 A *collabo*, someone who picked the wrong side, a Theban Vichyite?

vichyssoise (viːʃiːˈswɑːz). Also with capital initial and ¶**vichycoise, vichysoisse.** [a. Fr., in full *crême vichyssoise glacée* iced cream (soup) of Vichy.] A soup made with potatoes, leeks, and cream, usu. served chilled; a bowl of this soup.

1939 *Vogue's Cookery Bk.* 7 Creme Vichycoise. This is a special favourite in iced soups. **1941** A. ESCOFFIER *Escoffier Cook Bk.* 262 Vichysoisse, now called Crême Gauloise, is made by adding cream and chilling. **1943** I. S. ROMBAUER *Joy of Cooking* (ed. 3) 63/1 Vichyssoise (French potato soup)... Now called 'de Gaullesoise' in a New York restaurant. **1950** M. MILLER *Sure Thing* 35 Tetrazzini.. and two Vichyssoise to start out, large coffees, later. **1959** *News Chron.* 30 Oct. 3/4 It happened.. at the Savoy Hotel. The diner tasted his chilled Vichyssoise soup. **1969** *New Yorker* 20 Sept. 163/1 Vichysoisse.. is usually served very cold. **1982** J. AIKEN *Whisper in Night* 100 The night had grown stiflingly oppressive and humid. 'The air is like Vichyssoise,' said my uncle.

Vici (ˈvaɪsaɪ). *N. Amer.* Also **vici.** [perh. a. L. *vīcī*, pa. t. of *vincere* to conquer.] The name of a chrome-tanned kid leather used for shoes and boots. Freq. *attrib.*, esp. as ***Vici kid.***

Formerly a proprietary name in the U.S.

1888 *Shoe & Leather Reporter* 19 July 133/3 Robert H. Foerderer courts the smiles of fortune with a horseshoe enclosing the word 'vici'. **1891** *Official Gaz.* (U.S. Patent Office) 13 Oct. 128/2 Kid, goat, and similar light weight leathers... The word 'Vici'. **1904** 'O. HENRY' in *Everybody's Mag.* Feb. 187/1 He was the color of vici kid, and his whiskers was like excelsior made out of mahogany wood. **1906** *Daily Colonist* (Victoria, B.C.) 6 Jan. 12/7 (Advt.), Men's Vici Kid Shoes. **1937** H. H. KROLL *I was Sharecropper* x. 193, I had a pair of vici kid shoes for two dollars and a half. **1946** *Harper's Mag.* Oct. 311/1 There.. would be Pa in his Sunday clothes and vici shoes. **1946** H. R. QUIMBY *Pacemakers of Progress* vi. 115 Dressing high boots were often made with tops of silk or thin kid..; the lower parts were of patent leather or vici kid in black, bronze, white, or a color.

viciat(e, obs. ff. VITIATE.

vicinage (ˈvɪsɪnɪdʒ). Also 4 **vesinage,** 7 **vicenage, visinage.** [ad. OF. *visenage* (*visnage*), *vicenage*, or *voisinage* (see VOISINAGE), with assimilation of the stem to the original L. *vīcīn-us*: cf. VICINITY.]

1. A number of places lying near to each other taken collectively; an area extending to a limited distance round a particular spot; a neighbourhood.

Usu. with *the*, *this*, or similar word, but occasionally with *a* or in pl.

*a***1325** *MS. Rawl. B. 520* fol. 55 Somune þoru gode somunse xii fre men ant trewe of vesinage of N. **1552** HULOET, Vicinage, *vicinia, uicinetum*. **1655** FULLER *Ch. Hist.* II. 136 King Ethelred.. began the tryal of Causes by a Jury of twelve men to be chosen out of the Vicenage. **1685** in *Verney Mem.* (1907) II. 376 All our most able and Eminent Doctors of this Vicinage. *c***1700** POMFRET *Poet. Wks.* (1833) 37 Adam by an injured Maker driven From Eden's groves, the vicinage of Heaven. **1777** W. DALRYMPLE *Trav. Sp. & Port.* cxx, The regiments are.. recruited from the vicinage. **1791** BURKE *App. Whigs* Wks. VI. 122 The Metropolis and its Vicinage. **1813** C. VANCOUVER *Agriculture of Devon* 216 All such other parts of the district as at this time are.. open to all the inhabitants of the vicinage. *a***1853** W. JAY *Autobiog.* (1854) iv. 37 So it was with the vicinages all around Marlborough. **1868** LOSSING *Hudson* 1 The agricultural and mineral treasures of its vicinage.

b. Freq. in the phrase ***in the*** (also, ***this***, ***our***, etc.) ***vicinage.***

1638 BAKER tr. *Balzac's Lett.* (vol. II) 182, I am afraid of a Potgun or a Squib; far from running upon Muskets and Swordpoints as they say in our Vicinage. *a***1661** FULLER *Worthies* (1840) III. 394 No less than twenty thousand pounds worth of this coarse commodity [lime] is yearly made, and vended in the vicinage. **1676** *Doctrine of Devils* 92 Until he have gotten the favour and blessing of all the Witches in the Vicinage, yea in the Hemisphere. **1748** RICHARDSON *Clarissa* (1811) I. xxxiv. 255 She is the only flower of fragrance, that has blown in this vicinage for ten years past. **1791** H. WALPOLE *Let. to Misses Berry* 11 Sept. (1840) VI. 455 The French ladies in my vicinage. **1814** SCOTT *Wav.* x, He had lived in retirement, conversing almost entirely with those of his own principles in the vicinage. **1861** BERESF. HOPE *Eng. Cathedr. 19th C.* viii. 274 The.. recommendation of a sufficient population in the vicinage. **1883** *Manch. Exam.* 3 Oct. 5/4 People in the vicinage.. were not in a mood to regard it as a gratuitous picturesque display.

fig. **1649** JER. TAYLOR *Gt. Exemp.* Disc. v. §24 That soul that.. invites an enemy to view its possessions and live in the vicinage, loves the sin itself.

c. *transf.* The people living in a certain district or neighbourhood.

1647 N. BACON *Disc. Govt. Eng.* I. lxvii. 262 Barrons shall be amerced by their Peeres, others by the vicinage. **1672** [H. STUBBE] *Rosemary & Bayes* 17, I could wish they would not disturb the visinage with declamations against Mr. Calvin. **1796** BURKE *Regic. Peace* i. Wks. VIII. 187 Where there is no constituted judge,.. the vicinage itself is the natural judge. **1821** COBBETT *Rur. Rides* (1885) I. 46 Relying, for influence, not on the good will of the vicinage, but upon the dread of their power. **1836** LD. COCKBURN *Jrnl.* (1874) I. 122 Towns and their rustic vicinages are agitating against this measure. **1862** J. THRUPP *Anglo-Sax. Home* 269 The vicinage applied.. to the bishop for leave to dig up the body and burn it.

2. The fact of being or living close to another or others; nearness, proximity: **a.** Of persons; *spec.* in *Law* as entitling to certain rights of common.

1598 MARSTON *Sco. Villanie* I. iii. 182 Ile winke at Robrus, that for vicinage Enters common, on his next neighbors stage. **1602** FULBECKE *1st Pt. Parall.* 14 If I prescribe to haue common because of vicinage in such a village. **1626** DANIEL *Hist. Eng.* Wks. (Grosart) IV. 101 By reason of the vicinage, and innumerous populacie of that Nation. **1679** J. GOODMAN *Penit. Pard.* I. ii. (1713) 30 As if his father's presence or vicinage would put too great a restraint upon him. **1766** BLACKSTONE *Comm.* II. 33 Common because of vicinage, or neighbourhood, is where the inhabitants of two townships, which lie contiguous to each other, have usually intercommoned with one another. **1823** COBBETT *Rur. Rides* (1830) 203 The tarred, trowsered, and blue-and-buff crew whose very vicinage I always detest. **1830** MACKINTOSH *Partition of Poland* Wks. 1846 II. 338 In a declaration delivered at Warsaw, Catherine declared, that she did nothing but in virtue of the right of vicinage, acknowledged by all nations. **1891** J. WINSOR *Columbus* xvi. 357 St. Augustine, St. Basil, and St. Ambrose had placed the Garden of Eden far in the Old World's east, apart from the common vicinage of men.

b. Of things or places.

1686 GOAD *Celest. Bodies* I. ix. 34, I began to guess the Reason of its Activity, as borrowed from the vicinage of the warmer Corpuscles. **1696** WHISTON *The. Earth* IV. (1722) 356 The particular Prerogatives.. do not entirely depend on.. the Vicinage of the Central Heat. **1826** COBBETT *Poor Man's Friend* ii, Are they, now, to complain, if the vicinage of these same works causes a charge of rates there? **1844** DISRAELI *Coningsby* VI. ii, The common white pottery.. will not bear vicinage to a brisk kitchen fire for half-an-hour. **1880** *Scribner's Mag.* Mar. 660/2 The vicinage of the traveling studio was an occasion and a pretext for unprecedented larks.

3. ***in the vicinage of***, near or contiguous to, in the neighbourhood of. Cf. VICINITY 4.

1782 MRS. H. COWLEY *Bold Stroke for Husb.* v. ii, In the vicinage of Rosalvo, bounded on the west by the river. **1789** *Trans. Soc. Arts* I. 151 If I had had any in the vicinage of my plantation. **1812** J. HENRY *Camp. agst. Quebec* 99 The Canadians in the vicinage of Quebec lived as comfortably. **1830** CROLY *George IV*, 412 The length of canal navigation in the vicinage of London. **1852** H. ROGERS *Ecl. Faith* (1853) 151 They had become a centre and a source.. of moral pestilence, in the vicinage of which it was unsafe for men to dwell.

vicinal (ˈvɪsɪnəl, vɪˈsaɪnəl), *a.* [ad. L. *vīcīnāl-is*, f. *vīcīn-us* neighbour. So OF. and F. *vicinal.*]

1. 'Belonging to neighbours or neighbourhood.'

1623 COCKERAM I. **1656** BLOUNT *Glossogr.* **1727** BAILEY (vol. II).

2. ***vicinal way*** or ***road***, a local common way as distinguished from a highway; a by-road or crossroad.

1677 PLOT *Oxfordsh.* 314 Of these [public ways] amongst the Romans some were called publick κατ' ἐξοχήν, and others Vicinal. **1727** *Magna Brit. & Hib.* IV. 210/2 Among the Vicinal Ways, or *Chemini minores*, there is also one in this County. **1790** PENNANT *London* (1813) 13 A vicinal way went under Aldgate.. towards Oldford. **1791** NEWTE *Tour Eng. & Scot.* 259 From this permanent station, a vicinal or cross road is carried through Glenartney. **1807** G. CHALMERS *Caledonia* I. I. iv. 135 From this place.. there probably went off a vicinal way to the Roman stations in Tweedale. **1812** J. BIGLAND *Beauties Eng. & Wales* XVI. 15 This.. appears to have been only a vicinal road of the Romans. **1878** HARDY *Ret. Native* I. i, In many portions of its course it overlaid an old vicinal way, which branched from the great Western road of the Romans.

b. Similarly with other sbs.

1799 R. WARNER *Walk thro' W. Counties* (1800) 8 The operations of husbandry have depressed, and indeed obliterated in many places, this grand vicinal Dorsum. **1851** D. WILSON *Preh. Ann.* II. III. ii. 73 A small vicinal camp on the banks of the Kirble. **1901** *Speaker* 31 Aug. 618 He saw a good-looking curé smoking in a vicinal railway.

3. Neighbouring, adjacent, near.

1739 MAITLAND *Hist. London* I. ii. 10/1 The noisom Vapours incessantly emitted from that and the vicinal Marshes. **1790** *Phil. Trans.* LXXX. 232 In vicinal situations, the next best mode to angular measurement is no doubt that of marking, by means of well-regulated clocks,.. the repeated.. explosion of light. **1842** *Proc. Lond. Electr. Soc.* (1843) 355 Sparks will pass from such a wire, and, therefore, from a lightning-rod, to vicinal conducting bodies.

b. *Math.* and *Min.* Nearly coincident with a given surface or plane.

1895 CAYLEY *Math. Papers* VIII. 302, I investigate the values of a, b,.. for the point P′ on the vicinal surface. *Ibid.*

309 The lines which..correspond to the principal tangents of the vicinal surface must be the principal tangents of the given surface.

c. *Org. Chem.* Of substituted groups or atoms: Lying in consecutive order; adjacent to each other.

1898 J. Wade *Introd. Org. Chem.* 288 With regard to the higher substitution products..there should be three classes of tri-derivatives, and only three.., all conceivable arrangements being reducible to the positions 1:2:3, or vicinal, 1:2:4, or unsymmetrical, and 1:3:5, or symmetrical. **1900** E. F. Smith tr. *Richter's Org. Chem.* II. 39 We call them adjacent..or..vicinal.

4. Connected with the relations between a person and his neighbours.

1855 *Jrnl. R. Agric. Soc.* XVI. ii. 570 No harm, agricultural or fiscal, vicinal or political, shall betide the giver of such..assistance.

†**'vicinate,** *v. Obs. rare.* [ad. L. *vīcīnāt-*, ppl. stem of *vīcīnārī*, f. *vīcīnus*: see next.] *trans.* To lie near to, to adjoin.

1638 Sir T. Herbert *Trav.* (ed. 2) 23 The Land..seated so advantagiously for traffique,..and vicinating those golden countries of Mozambiq', Guiloa [etc.]. *Ibid.* 114 Iasques and Kostack in Margastan vicinating them.

'vicine, *a.* Now *rare.* Also 6 vycyne, 7 vicin. [ad. L. *vīcīn-us* neighbouring, near.] = vicinal *a.* 3.

a **1513** Fabyan *Chron.* vii. 312 These men..subdued yᵉ Partyes, and many other vycyne countreys. *a* **1550** Leland *Itin.* (1769) V. 2, A ii Myles a this side Montgomerie..is a River cumming owt of the vicine Hilles. **1553** in Hakluyt *Voy.* (1599) I. 229 God, vnder whose merciful hand nauigants aboue all other creatures naturally bee most nigh, and vicine. **1605** L. Hutten *Aunswere* 28 With..due regarde alwaies had, to the easines and familiarity of the Ceremonie, that it be vicine, hard at hand, and obvious, not far fetcht. **1661** Glanvill *Van. Dogm.* iv. 35 The opening of other vicine passages might quickly obliterate any tracks of these. **1676** Jas. Cooke *Marrow Chirurg.* iv. ii. i. 715 In Ustion take heed of Vicin parts, and apply Cauteries through a Pipe. **1824** *Guide to Aberystwyth* 31 The visitor of Aberystwyth..parading the Terrace Castle Ruins or the vicine hills..gives the subject but an ordinary thought.

vicinism ('vɪsɪnɪz(ə)m). *Biol.* [f. L. *vīcīn-us* (see vicine *a.*) + -ism.] (See quots. 1905, 1959.) Hence **'vicinist,** a form produced by vicinism.

1905 H. De Vries *Species & Varieties* 188 For this purpose I propose the word vicinism..as indicating the sporting of a variety under the influence of others in its vicinity. *Ibid.* 201 Of two hundred seeds one became a blue atavist, or rather vicinist, while all others remained true to the white type. **1929** *Hereditas* XIII. 188 The percentage of vicinism has been exactly determined for one *Tetrahit* line. .. The flower colour of this line..is recessive to the red flower colour of the line T-G. **1959** *N.Z. Timber Jrnl.* Feb. 58/2 Vicinism... The tendency to variation caused by natural crossing with related forms growing nearby.

vicinity (vɪ'sɪnɪtɪ). [ad. L. *vīcīnitās*, f. *vīcīn-us*: see vicine *a.* and -ity. So It. *vicinità*, Sp. *vecindad.*]

1. The state, character, or quality of being near in space; propinquity, proximity.

1560 Daus tr. *Sleidane's Comm.* 12 b, For the Frenchmen come of the same offspringe that we do..: and for the vicinitie therof are very necessary for the Italians and us. **1604** T. Wright *Passions* v. §4. 275 The vicinitie also of the evill moveth much, for dangers afarre off we little esteeme. **1641** J. Jackson *True Evang. T.* iii. 169 The third is 'to feed, and eate together'. Another degree of vicinity, and neerenesse. **1698** Fryer *Acc. E. India & P.* 226 The most unhealthy of these [winds] are the South-East, for that then the Air is thicker, by reason of the Seas Vicinity. **1727** Swift *St. Irel.* Wks. 1755 V. ii. 166 The abundance and vicinity of country seats. *a* **1774** Goldsm. *Hist. Greece* I. 105 But the Athenians were not to be intimidated by any vicinity of danger. **1825** Scott *Betrothed* xix, The Constable alleged the vicinity of the Welsh, as what might possibly again render the abode of his betrothed bride..perilous. **1849** Macaulay *Hist. Eng.* vi. II. 102 He had forgotten that vicinity operates in more ways than one. **1892** *Photogr. Ann.* II. 247 Under these conditions all vicinity of watercourses, unless bridged, should be avoided.

b. Const. *to, with.*

1651 Baxter *Lett. to Church at Bewdley* 10 That we may enjoy the comfort of unity..according to our vicinity with you on Earth. **1681** Rycaut tr. *Gracian's Critick* 23 All those Epithets of changeable, defective,..and the like, are.. derived from her too near vicinity with the Earth. **1781** Cowper *Heroism* 52 Ill-fated race! how deeply must they rue Their only crime, vicinity to you! **1836–7** Dickens *Sk. Boz, Scenes* xxv, How much more awful is it to reflect on this near vicinity to the dying! **1858** J. Martineau *Stud. Chr.* 206 This vicinity to the great capital drew him, however, into a wider circle of duties.

†**2.** Nearness in degree or quality; close relationship or connexion; resemblance, likeness. *Obs.*

1594 West *2nd Pt. Symbol., Chancerie* §145 Unto whom your said Oratrices husband, for the vicinity of bloud, and abilitie of substance, was bolder to make his mone for helpe. **1599** *Broughton's Lett.* xii. 42 Speeches farre more differing from any vicinitie to prophanenes then this of yours. **1614** W. B. *Philosopher's Banquet* (ed. 2) 51 The vicinity with mans nature it hath. **1642** Jer. Taylor *Episc.* (1647) 281 An honorary, and extraordinary priviledge indulged to them for their vicinity and relation to our Blessed Lord the fountaine of all benison to us. *a* **1676** Hale *Prim. Orig. Man.* i. iii. (1677) 83 There is a vicinity between Agents and Patients.

3. = vicinage 1.

1781 Jefferson *Corr.* Wks. 1859 I. 293 Lord Cornwallis had advanced to the vicinities of the Moravian towns. **1789** *Ibid.* III. 26 The progress of light..has equalled expectation in Paris only and its vicinities. **1835** I. Taylor *Spir. Despot.* iv. 173 That..tendency of things, which places the clergy of a vicinity in opposition the one to the other. **1843** Lytton *Last Bar.* i. viii, It commanded a full view of the vicinity without. **1860** Tyndall *Glac.* i. xi. 75 We were glad..to escape the vicinity of that ugly crevasse. **1875** Helps *Soc. Press.* iii. 41 That might gradually have the effect of removing all noxious trades from London and its vicinity.

4. *in the vicinity* (*of*), in the neighbourhood (of), near or close (to). (Cf. vicinage 1 b and 3.)

(*a*) **1796** H. Hunter tr. *St.-Pierre's Stud. Nat.* (1799) II. 229 It would most probably have in it's vicinity, the tree which Nature designed should contrast with it in the same site. **1820** W. Irving *Sketch Bk.* I. 121 The merchant has his snug retreat in the vicinity of the metropolis. **1840** Hood *Up Rhine* 161 The extraordinary transparency of the atmosphere in the vicinity of the Rhine. **1864** Trevelyan *Compet. Wallah* (1866) 185 Amidst the park-like undulating scenery in the vicinity of the town. **1891** *Science-Gossip* XXVII. 14/1 During a severe storm in that year the Port Glasgow ship 'Marseilles' capsized in the vicinity of Portpatrick.

(*b*) **1827** Faraday *Chem. Manip.* xviii. (1842) 479 The minute hole..may be obliterated by a little pressure towards it upon the lute in the immediate vicinity. **1843** Lytton *Last Bar.* iii. v, A young man of low stature..slowly approaching towards the arch, and every cap in the vicinity was off, and every knee bowed.

b. With similar sense in other constructions. Also *transf.*, something near to (a specified amount, etc.).

1817 Jas. Mill *Brit. India* II. iv. iv. 145 A detachment of grenadiers were very expeditiously quitting the vicinity of danger. **1901** *Proc. New-Eng. Hist. Geneal. Soc.* 9 Jan. p. xvi, Raising the extra cost of that number of the Annual Proceedings to the vicinity of one hundred dollars.

vicinous, *a. rare*⁻¹. [f. L. *vīcīn-us*: see vicine *a.* and -ous.] Extending to immediately adjacent parts.

1822–7 Good *Study Med.* (1829) V. 621 Local tetter. Limited to particular organs; stationary, or vicinous.

viciosity, variant of vitiosity.

vicious ('vɪʃəs), *a.* Forms: *α.* 4- vicious (5–6 -ouse, 6 *Sc.* -us), 4 vecyous, 6 vicyous, *Sc.* wicious; 5–6 vycious(e, vycyous (5 -owse, 6 -ouse), 5 vysyous; 4–5 viciose (4 vycios). *β.* 5–6 vitius, 6–8 (9) vitious (6 -ouse). [a. AF. *vicious*, OF. *vicious* (*vitious*), *vicieus* (F. *vicieux*, = Sp. and Pg. *vicioso*, It. *vizioso*), or ad. L. *vitiōsus* (med.L. also *viciōsus*), f. *vitium* fault, vice *sb.*¹]

I. 1. Of habits, practices, etc.: Of the nature of vice; contrary to moral principles; depraved, immoral, bad.

α. *c* **1340** Hampole *Prose Tr.* 15 Righte als before þe lykynges in þe sensualite ware fleschely, vayne, and vecyous .., righte so now þay ere made gastely, and clene. *c* **1380** Wyclif *Sel. Wks.* III. 430 Þe mor part of men, bi her vicious lijf, ben combred in þis heresye. **1390** Gower *Conf.* III. 111 He is so ferforth Amourous, He not what thing is vicious Touchende love. *c* **1420** Lydg. *Assembly of Gods* 2097 From hys gloryous syght thus he vs estraungeth, For our vycyous lyuyng, thorough owre owne foly. *c* **1430** —— *Min. Poems* (Percy Soc.) 70 O loode-sterre of al goode governaunce! Alle vicious lustes by wisdom to represse. **1535–6** *Act 27 Hen. VIII*, c. 28 §1 Ther [*sc.* monks'] vycyous lyvyng shamelesly encreasseth & augmentith. **1555** Eden *Decades* (Arb.) 53 Dissolute lyuynge, licentious talke, and suche other vicious behauoures. **1613** Purchas *Pilgrimage* iv. ix. (1614) 391 Richard Iohnson caused the English, by his vicious liuing, to bee worse accounted of then the Russes. **1690** Locke *Hum. Und.* ii. xxi. §45 He..who prefers the short pleasures of a vicious Life upon any consideration. **1736** Butler *Anal.* i. iii. Wks. 1874 I. 54 Vicious actions, considered as mischievous to society, should be punished. **1791** Mrs. Radcliffe *Rom. Forest* viii, The Marquis pursuing her with insult and vicious passion. **1838** Thirlwall *Greece* V. xliii. 249 Interpreted by his enemies as a proof of unmanly luxury and vicious habits. **1875** Jowett *Plato* (ed. 2) IV. 13 Plato attempts to identify vicious pleasures with some form of error.

β. **1535** Stewart *Cron. Scot.* (Rolls) II. 426 How Donaldus..wes crownit King of Scottis, and of his vitius Lyfe. **1585** T. Washington tr. *Nicholay's Voy.* i. xviii. 21 [He] changed his good maners and vertues into most vitious tyrannies. **1621** Burton *Anat. Mel.* i. i. ii. xi. 45 Thence come..many times vitious Habits, customes, ferall Diseases. *c* **1670** Hobbes *Dial. Com. Laws* (1681) 7 How can a man be indicted of Avarice, Envy, Hypocrisie or any other vitious Habit till it be declared? **1700** Prior *Carmen Seculare* xxxiv, Some [Societies] that to Morals shall recal the Age, And purge from vitious Dross the sinking Stage. *a* **1763** Shenstone *Elegies* xv. 54 To fire with vitious hopes a modest heir. **1791** Burke *Let. to Memb. Nat. Assembly* 32 Though his practical and speculative morals were vitious in the extreme. **1817** Jas. Mill *Brit. India* II. v. ii. 370 His conduct was vitious and weak.

2. a. Of persons: Addicted to vice or immorality; of depraved habits; profligate, wicked.

α. *c* **1386** Chaucer *Monk's T.* 473 Alþouhe Nero were as vicious As fende þat liþe ful lowe adoune. *c* **1400** *Pilgr. Sowle* (Caxton, 1483) iv. xxxv. 83 Vpon theues and morderers,.. mysprowde men and vicious they shalle be fyers in jugement. *c* **1450** *Mirk's Festial* 253 For yche good man ys loþe forto be yn company wyth a vycyous man. **1483** *Rolls of Parlt.* VI. 240/2 Personnes insolent, vicious, and of inordinate avarice. *a* **1548** Hall *Chron., Hen. V*, 33 b, A vicious prince doth muche more hurte with his pernicious example to other then to hymself by his peculier offence. **1598** Barckley *Felic. Man* v. 518 Such as he found rich & vicious, he would depriue them from the Senate. **1613** Purchas *Pilgrimage* viii. iv. 629 He saith, that the Armouchiquois are a great people, but haue no adoration. They are vicious and bloudie. **1652** Loveday tr. *Calprenede's Cassandra* iii. 161, I have known indeed many of the viciousest persons lead a long life with sweetnesse and contentment. **1729** Butler *Serm.* Wks. 1874 II. 22 Mankind is in this sense naturally vicious, or vicious by nature. **1766** Fordyce *Serm. to Yng. Wm.* (1767) I. i. 10 There are foolish and vicious women. **1793** Holcroft tr. *Lavater's Physiog.* xxxi. 164 Vicious men resemble valuable paintings which have been destroyed by varnish. **1813** Shelley *Q. Mab* vii. 124 Every soul on this ungrateful earth, Virtuous or vicious,.. Shall perish. **1862** Thackeray *Philip* v, I know his haunts, but I don't know his friends, Pendennis... I don't think they are vicious, so much as low. **1874** Green *Short Hist.* ix. §1. 589 Vicious as the stage was, it only reflected the general vice of the time.

β. *c* **1400** *Destr. Troy* 527 Voidis me noght of vitius,..Ne deme no dishonesty in your derfe hert. **1562** Winȝet *Wks.* (S.T.S.) I. 44 He causis sumtyme vitious or tyrane princes ..to haue dominioun aboue vs. **1596** Dalrymple tr. *Leslie's Hist. Scot.* I. 161 Jn the beginning of his regyne a gude Prince, eftirwarde vitious. **1628** Burton *Anat. Mel.* (ed. 3) ii. iii. vii. 330 Themistocles..was a most deboshed and vitious youth. **1660** Milton *Free Commw.* Wks. 1851 V. 451 Monarchs..whose Aim is to make the People wealthy,..but otherwise softest, basest, vitiousest, servilest. **1678** L'Estrange *Seneca's Mor.* (1702) 178 Drunkenness..does not make Men Vitious but it shews them to be so. **1755** Young *Centaur* iv. Wks. 1757 IV. 200 My less vitious companions fell frequent around me; and dismal was their fall.

†**b.** Const. *of. Obs.*

c **1374** Chaucer *Boeth.* ii. pr. v. 47 Þe whiche seruauntes yif þei ben vicious of condicions it is a greet charge and a destruccioun to þe house. **1453** *Coventry Leet Bk.* 278 Yf eny officers fro this tyme forward be founde vicious of his body, that then he be put oute of his office in eny wise. **1460** Capgrave *Chron.* 116 He was vicious of lyvyng, a hunter outeragious. **1530** Palsgr. 328 Vyciouse of conversacyon. **1557** North *Gueuara's Diall Pr.* Prol. A j b, The man that is vitious of his personne..deserveth to be banished. **1577** Holinshed *Chron.* II. 1556/1 Some Princes basterd,..high minded, full of reuenge, vitious of his body.

c. *absol.* with *the.*

1390 Gower *Conf.* III. 226 He putte awey the vicious And tok to him the vertuous. **1536** G. Wishart in *Misc. Wodrow Soc.* 18 And by all meanes compell and reproue the faultie and vicious. *a* **1581** Campion *Hist. Irel.* v. (1633) 13 In which vertue..how far the best excell, so farre in gluttonie and other hatefull crimes the vitious..are worse then too badde. **1673** O. Walker *Educ.* (1677) 220 Most men have greater averseness to the incompliant than the vitious. **1711** Addison *Spect.* No. 16 ¶3 If I attack the Vicious, I shall only set upon them in a Body. **1782** V. Knox *Ess.* xii. (1819) I. 71 With the vicious you must be vicious. *a* **1805** H. K. White *Mel. Hours* ix, She..has found, by bitter experience, that the vicious..are devoid of all feeling but that of self-gratification. **1863** *Biogr. Sk. E. Fry* 72 Her example of devotedness, in the care of the wretched and vicious, was emulated with blessed effect.

d. *the vicious one*, ? the Evil One. *rare*⁻¹.

1713 Shaftesb. *Judgm. Hercules* i. §2 He is wrought, agitated, and torn by contrary Passions. 'Tis the last Effort of the vitious-one, striving for possession over him.

3. a. Falling short of, or varying from, what is morally or practically commendable; reprehensible, blameworthy, mischievous.

c **1386** Chaucer *Melib.* ¶18 He that is irous and wroth.. may not speke but blameful thinges, and with his vicious wordes he stireth other folk to anger and to ire. **1500–20** Dunbar *Poems* xviii. 38 Thair vicious wordis and vanitie, Thair tratling tungis. **1531** Elyot *Gov.* iii. xxii. (1880) II. 346 All thoughe I dispraysed nygarshippe and vicious scarcitie,..I desyre nat to haue..meates for any occasion to moche sumptuous. **1575** Gascoigne *Glasse of Govt.* Wks. 1910 II. 45 To bee opinionate of him selfe is vitious. *a* **1578** Lindesay (Pitscottie) *Chron. Scot.* (S.T.S.) I. 47 James.. thinkand it was vicious to denude the auld herietaig of ane house [etc.]. **1611** Shaks. *Cymb.* v. v. 65 It had beene vicious To haue mistrusted her. **1648** Milton *Tenure Kings* (1651) 1 Being slaves within doors, no wonder they strive to have the State govern'd conformably to the inward vitious rule, by which they govern themselves. **1692** Prior *Ode Imit. Horace* ii, See the Repenting Isle Awakes, Her Vicious Chains the generous Goddess breaks. **1751** Johnson *Rambler* No. 159 ¶7 A timidity which he himself knows to be vicious. **1780** Cowper *Let.* 18 March, The love of power seems as natural to kings as the desire of liberty is to their subjects, the excess of either is vicious and tends to the ruin of both. **1825** Jefferson *Autob.* Wks. 1859 I. 36 Our legislation, under the regal government, had many very vicious points. **1845** McCulloch *Taxation* i. iv. 115 We look upon every system of taxation as radically vicious that sets the interest and the duty of individuals at variance. **1879** Harlan *Eyesight* viii. 107 Young people often acquire the vicious habit of reading with the book held close to the eyes.

†**b.** Of a person: Holding faulty or wrong opinions. *Obs.*

1657 Trapp *Comm. Ps.* v. 26 Pope John 22 held the morality of the soule, and was otherwise erroneous and vitious.

4. a. Of animals (*esp.* horses): Inclined to be savage or dangerous, or to show bad temper; not submitting to be thoroughly tamed or broken-in.

In quot. 1720 in fig. context, referring to persons.

1711 Shaftesb. *Charac.* II. 30 Tho we may vulgarly call an ill Horse *vitious*; yet we never say of a good-one,..that he is *worthy* or *virtuous*. **1720** Swift *Fates Clergymen* ¶9 People in power may..drive them through the hardest and deepest roads..and will be sure to find them neither resty nor vicious. **1774** Goldsm. *Nat. Hist.* (1776) II. 363 Those [horses] naturally belonging to the country, are very small and vicious. *Ibid.* IV. 319 Although in its native wildness, it is said to be fierce and vicious, this [nylghau] seemed pleased with every kind of familiarity. **1818** Ranken *Hist. France* IV. iv. iii. 267 A vicious animal, having injured any person, was forfeited. **1865** M. Arnold *Ess. Crit.* vi. 195 Look at that bay horse rearing bolt upright; what a vicious one! **1892** J. A. Henderson *Annals Lower Deeside* 156 Philip, being flung by a vicious horse, likewise succumbed.

transf. **1814** LD. J. RUSSELL in Sir S. Walpole *Life* (1889) I. iii. 75 He [Napoleon] has a dusky grey eye, which would be called vicious in a horse.

b. Full of malice or spite; malignantly bitter or severe.

1825 JENNINGS *Dial. W. Eng.*, *Vitious*, spiteful, revengeful. **1859** TENNYSON *Marriage of Geraint* 194 The dwarf,..being vicious, old and irritable,..Made answer sharply that she should not know. **1908** G. TYRRELL in Petre *Life* (1912) II. xvii. 348 Three nasty vicious letters against the poor Baron in the *Tablet*.

c. *transf.* Of weather: Severe, inclement.

1882 *Jamieson's Sc. Dict.* IV. 695/2 Vitious weather. **1902** J. BUCHAN *Watcher by Threshold* 81 The weather seemed more vicious than ever.

II. 5. a. *Law.* Marred, or rendered void, by some inherent fault or defect; not satisfying legal requirements or conditions; unlawful, illegal.

1393 in *Collect. Topographica* (1836) III. 257 To ensele the same forsaid vicious fenyd chartre. *c* **1555** HARPSFIELD *Divorce Hen. VIII* (1878) 44 The act being vicious and nought at the beginning, cannot be by tract of time confirmed. **1561** *Reg. Privy Council Scot.* I. 174, I ressavit the gudis libellit immediatlie fra the saidis Cantis eftir the spoliatioun thairof, knawing the same to be spulyeit and vicious. **1765** H. WALPOLE *Otranto* iii, I have consented to put my title to the issue of the sword—does that imply a vitious title? **1880** MUIRHEAD *Gaius* IV. §151 Nor can there be any accession in favour of a party whose own possession is vitious, *i.e.* acquired from his opponent violently, clandestinely, or in defiance of the recal of a grant during pleasure. *Ibid.* 513 In the ordinary case it was lawful to use force to eject a vitious possessor.

b. ***vicious intromission, intromitter*** (see quot. 1838 and INTROMISSION 2). *Scots Law.*

1678 SIR G. MACKENZIE *Crim. Laws Scot.* I. xix. §12 (1699) 102 If it be proved that he was actually denuded, that will liberat him from vitious intromission. **1696** [see INTROMITTER]. **1747** in *Nairne Peerage Evid.* (1874) 149 Universal and vitious intromitters with his goods and gear. **1765–8** ERSKINE *Inst. Law Scot.* III. ix. §49 Though vitious intromission be a delict, it may be referred to oath. *Ibid.* §52 Before he be cited by any creditor as a vitious intromitter. **1838** W. BELL *Dict. Law Scot.* 529 The term vitious intromission is applied exclusively to the heir's unwarrantable intromission with the moveable estate of the ancestor. *a* **1856** G. OUTRAM *Lyrics* (1887) 95 (E.D.D.), I then attempted Vitious Intromission, And was immediately conveyed to prison. *Ibid.* 216 Vitious Intromitter.

6. Impaired or spoiled by some fault, flaw, blemish, or defect; faulty, defective, imperfect, bad; corrupt, impure, debased: **a.** Of language, style, spelling, etc. Also *transf.* of writers.

1589 PUTTENHAM *Eng. Poesie* III. xxi. (Arb.) 256 It hath bene said before how..a good figure may become a vice, and ..a vicious speach go for a vertue in the Poeticall science. **1638** BAKER tr. *Balzac's Lett.* (vol. II) 208 He shall have the honour to purge his country of a vitious phrase. **1655** VAUGHAN *Silex Scint.* I. Pref., The complaint against vitious verse..is of some antiquity in this Kingdom. **1695** H. WHARTON in *Laud's Wks.* (1853) V. 371 Although the orthography be vicious (a matter common to many learned men of that time). **1711** SHAFTESB. *Charac.* I. 145 Whatever Quarter we may give to our vicious Poets, or other Composers of irregular and short-liv'd Works. **1841** W. SPALDING *Italy & It. Isl.* I. 141 His mode of writing was vicious, rhetorical, antithetical, and forced. **1883** D. H. WHEELER *By-Ways Lit.* 100 It is believed that the Welsh-Keltic manuscripts are unusually vicious in the texts.

b. *Logic.* Of arguments, etc.

1605 BACON *Adv. Learn.* II. xiii. §3. 50 The Induction which the Logitians speake of;..their fourme of induction I say is vtterly vitious and incompetent. **1646** SIR T. BROWNE *Pseud. Ep.* I. iv. 16 If this fallacy be largely taken, it is committed in any vitious illation, offending the rules of good consequence. **1697** tr. *Burgersdicius his Logic* II. viii. 40 If from true premisses follows what is false, it is a sign that the form of the syllogism is vitious. **1774** REID *Aristotle's Logic* v. §1. 219 The form [of syllogisms] lies in the necessary connection between the premises and the conclusion; and where such a connection is wanting, they are said to be informal, or vicious in point of form. **1856** P. E. DOVE *Logic Christian Faith* V. i. 290 We have..departed from the region of mind and spirit and introduced the natural method where the natural method is utterly vicious and illegitimate. **1864** BOWEN *Logic* vii. 189 It is not difficult to prove..that arguments are vicious only when they fail to observe this method, and are always good when it is observed.

c. In general use.

1638 JUNIUS *Paint. Ancients* 228 The uttermost on either side is vicious. **1650** BULWER *Anthropomet.* 4 A vitious figure of the head is known by sight. **1726** LEONI *Alberti's Archit.* II. 90 b, Rightly supposing that the truth must lie in some medium between these two vitious extremes. **1746** FRANCIS tr. *Hor., Sat.* II. iii. 35 Here the rude chizzel's rougher strokes I trac'd; In flowing brass a vicious hardness found. **1846** *Art-Union Jrnl.* Oct. 285 The foundations of the bridge were originally vicious. **1855** MACAULAY *Hist. Eng.* xxi. IV. 611 A wooden model of that edifice, the finest specimen of a vicious style, was sent to Kensington for his inspection. **1880** *Fraser's Mag.* May 672 Thus the country's money becomes thoroughly vicious: it breaks down in its most essential quality.

†**d.** Of a person: Wrong, mistaken. *Obs.*

1604 SHAKS. *Oth.* III. iii. 145 Though I perchance am vicious in my guesse.

7. a. Foul, impure, noxious, morbid. ? *Obs.*

1597 GERARDE *Herbal* III. xxxv. 1168 Berries..full of clammie or vicious moisture. **1608** TOPSELL *Serpents* 188 Theyr liuer is very vitious, and causeth the whole body to be of ill temperament. **1641** MILTON *Reform.* 55 Thou..that art but a bottle of vitious and harden'd excrements. **1656** J. SMITH *Pract. Physick* 49 The vicious matter must be evacuated. **1697** DRYDEN *Virg. Georg.* III. 721 Here from the vicious Air, and sickly Skies, A Plague did on the dumb Creation rise. **1831** SOUTH *Otto's Path. Anat.* 73 The last object of pathological anatomy is the consideration of vicious contents..which have no organic connexion with the animal body.

†**b.** Harmful, noxious. *Obs.*⁻¹

1656 EARL MONM. tr. *Boccalini's Advts. fr. Parnass.* I. x. (1674) 12 Those Shops wherein vitious things are sold.

†**8.** Of a part or a function of the body: Morbid, diseased; irregular. *Obs.*

1615 CROOKE *Body of Man* 304 Who euer saw a conception, although it were vitious and illegitimate, which was not couered with a Filme as it were with a Garment? **1646** SIR T. BROWNE *Pseud. Ep.* VII. ii. 342 The vicious excesse in the number of fingers and toes. **1707** FLOYER *Physic. Pulse-Watch* 373 The five Members and their Intestines being changed twice five times by five vitious Pulses. **1733** CHEYNE *Eng. Malady* II. vii. §2 (1734) 185 A vitious Liver seems to be one of the primary..Causes of Nervous Distempers.

9. ***vicious circle.*** **a.** *Logic.* (See sense 6 b and CIRCLE *sb.* 19.)

c **1792** *Encycl. Brit.* (ed. 3) X. 69/1 He runs into what is termed by logicians a *vicious circle*. **1812** WOODHOUSE *Astron.* viii. 52 This seems to be something like arguing in a vicious circle. **1830** HERSCHEL *Study Nat. Phil.* 209 It may seem to be arguing in a vicious circle to have recourse to observation for any part of those..conclusions. **1865** MOZLEY *Mirac.* iv. 76 The whole evidence of revelation becomes a vicious circle. **1876** [see CIRCLE *sb.* 19].

b. *Path.* A morbid process consisting in the reciprocal continuation and aggravation of one disorder by another.

1883 DUNCAN *Clin. Lect. Dis. Women* (ed. 2) x. 78 There is, in this disease, what is sometimes called a vicious circle, and I shall have, in the course of this lecture, to point out to you several instances of this vicious circle.

c. *gen.* A situation in which action and reaction intensify each other; a self-perpetuating process of aggravation. Similarly ***vicious spiral***, in which the ill-effects are cumulative. Cf. SPIRAL *sb.* 2 d.

1839 SIR H. HOLLAND *Med. Notes & Refl.* 100 Thus the practice proceeds, in a vicious circle of habit, from which the patient is rarely extricated without..injury to his future health. **1892** H. JAMES *Notebks.* (1947) 130 The whole situation works in a kind of inevitable rotary way—in what would be called a vicious circle. **1929** [see DOSTO(Y)EVSKIAN *a.*]. **1940** M. NICHOLSON *How Britain's Resources are Mobilized* (Oxf. Pamphlets on World Affairs No. 30) 24 The result, when supplies of goods are short, is to bid up prices, thus raising the cost of living, inspiring demands for increased wages and starting the 'vicious spiral' of inflation. **1958** *Spectator* 11 July 60/2 All stress disorder is subject to this vicious-spiral rule. **1965** *Listener* 11 Nov. 741/2 It is sometimes necessary to enact laws against racism as a first step towards breaking a vicious circle. **1975** *Times* 23 Aug. 1/5 This is a vicious spiral of..mounting prices and declining traffic volume. **1982** *Times* 26 Aug. 3/8 It is a vicious circle. The boats cannot be sure of selling their fish until the processors invest in the new plant to handle it, and the processors cannot risk their money until they are sure that the fleet has guaranteed fishing areas and catch quotas.

10. ***vicious abstraction*** (Philos.), the abstraction of one quality or term from a thing or concept at the expense of other qualities or terms of which it is also composed; hence ***vicious abstractionism.***

1883 F. H. BRADLEY *Princ. Logic* 511 If we recognize these elements our unit is not solitary; if we ignore them we fall into vicious abstraction. **1909** W. JAMES *Meaning of Truth* xiii. 249 Let me give the name of 'vicious abstractionism' to a way of using concepts which may be thus described. **1932** H. H. PRICE *Perception* vii. 173 To use the language of the Idealist tradition, they only seem to be mere acceptances through a 'vicious abstraction'.

11. *Comb.*, as ***vicious-looking.***

1871 'M. LEGRAND' *Camb. Freshm.* 247 The gray mare expressed her denial..by giving one or two slight but uncommonly vicious-looking kicks. **1894** MRS. DYAN *Man's Keeping* (1899) 60 Those vicious-looking knives looked as if they could do such work well.

viciously (ˈvɪʃəslɪ), *adv.* Also 4 uiciouseliche, 5 vicously; 6–8 (9) vitiously. [f. prec. + -LY².] In a vicious manner.

1. With addiction or inclination to vice; immorally, dissolutely.

a **1325** *Prose Psalter* xlviii. 13 Þys her way his sclaunder to hem; and efter hij shul plesen uiciouseliche in her mouþe. *c* **1400** *Apol. Loll.* 41 Sum are gostly pore, and sum bodily; sum vertuously, and sum vicously, or synfully; and sum peynfully. **1415** HOCCLEVE *Addr. to Sir J. Oldcastle* 130, I putte cas, a prelat or a preest Him viciously gouerne in his lyuynge. **1446** LYDG. *Nightingale Poems* i. 285 Moch peple viciously Were in this age dampnably demeyned. **1509** BARCLAY *Shyp of Folys* (1570) 57 He was..Viciously liuing in couetise and gyle. **1560** DAUS tr. *Sleidane's Comm.* 41 b, They live dissolutely and vitiously at Rome. **1611** COTGR., *Vicieusement*, viciously, lewdly, corruptly, faultily. **1682** SIR T. BROWNE *Chr. Mor.* I. §17 (1716) 17 Perversity of Will, immoral and sinfull enormities..pursue us unto Judgment, and leave us viciously miserable. **1780** COWPER *Progr. Err.* 432 By nature weak, or viciously inclin'd.

b. In weaker sense: In an improper manner or to an improper extent; reprehensibly. Also *spec.*, illegally (quot. 1880).

1617 MORYSON *Itin.* III. 17 Many..are vitiously proud, that their neighbours should see strangers thus visit them. *Ibid.* 35 The Italian being a great and somewhat viciously curious observer of ceremonious complements. **1620** VENNER *Via Recta* (1650) 297 They that against Nature viciously use the night for the day. **1824** SOUTHEY *Sir T. More* (1831) II. 200 A practice virtually or rather viciously the same has been imputed to the Venetian aristocracy. **1880** MUIRHEAD *Gaius* Dig. 512 He eventually prevailed who proved that he was actually in possession..and had not taken it vitiously from his adversary, *i.e.* either forcibly, stealthily, or by refusal.

c. Spitefully, ill-naturedly, savagely; with (or as with) animosity or intent to injure.

1841 DICKENS *Barn. Rudge* ix, 'I wouldn't,' said Miggs viciously, 'no, not for five-and-forty pound!' **1852** MRS. STOWE *Uncle Tom's C.* xxxii, The mill, from which he had viciously driven two or three tired women, who were waiting to grind their corn. **1872** *Routledge's Ev. Boy's Ann.* 114/2 One of the sharp little telegraphic bels rang viciously.

2. Faultily, badly, incorrectly; corruptly.

1635–56 COWLEY *Davideis* III. Note §8 Which Lucan (methinks) avoids viciously by an excess the other way. **1679** DRYDEN *Pref. to Tr. & Cres.* Ess. (ed. Ker) I. 226 The thoughts are such as arise from the matter, the expression of 'em not viciously figurative. **1680** BURNET *Trav.* (1686) 266 They have the Gospels in Greek Capitals, but they are vitiously writ in many places. **1706** PHILLIPS (ed. Kersey), *Viciously*,..corruptly, falsely, as *Viciously writ.* **1790** BURKE *Fr. Rev.* Wks. V. 91 An assembly..viciously or feebly composed in a very great part of it.

viciousness (ˈvɪʃəsnɪs). Also 5 vycyows-, 6 vycyous-, vyciousness(e, 6–8 (9) vitiousness, etc. [f. VICIOUS *a.* + -NESS.] The character or quality of being vicious.

1. Inclination or addiction to vice or immorality; depravity of life or conduct.

1440 J. SHIRLEY *Dethe K. James* (1818) 5 He wexe full of viciousness yn his lyvyng. *c* **1440** *Promp. Parv.* 510/1 .Vycyowsnesse, *viciositas.* **1509** BARCLAY *Shyp of Folys* Prol. a vij b, Whan this Socrates perceyued the mindes of men to be prone & extremely inclyned to viciousnes, he had gret affeccion to subdue suche maners. **1561** T. NORTON *Calvin's Inst.* II. 72 We bring with vs from the womb of our mother a vitiousnesse planted in our begetting. **1598** MARSTON *Sco. Villanie* II. vii. 203 Marke those: for naught, but such lewd viciousnes, Ere graced him. **1615** G. SANDYS *Trav.* 218 Venus,..their goddesse of viciousnesse. **1655** FULLER *Ch. Hist.* II. 99 Now began the Saxons to be infected with an universall Vitiousnesse. **1736** BUTLER *Anal.* I. iii. 72 The.. advantage..is gained by the action itself, not by the morality, the virtuousness or viciousness of it. **1796** BP. WATSON *Apol. Bible* 379 Some men have been warped to infidelity by viciousness of life. **1838** DICKENS *Nich. Nick.* xliv, I never will supply that man's extravagances and viciousness. **1892** TENNYSON *Foresters* III. i, These be the lies the people tell of us, Because we seek to curb their viciousness.

transf. **1583** MELBANCKE *Philotimus* K iv b, Hatefull viciousnes in wordes, and hurtfull loosenes in life.

b. Tendency, on the part of animals, to be savage or refractory.

1774 GOLDSM. *Nat. Hist.* (1824) I. 383 In..this country.. they [*sc.* stags] are become less common than formerly; its excessive viciousness during the rutting season..inducing most people to part with the species. **1775** ADAIR *Amer. Indians* 427 The young ambitious heroes ascribed the whole disaster to the viciousness of my horse, saying 'he was mad'. **1818** RANKEN *Hist. France* IV. IV. iii. §2. 267 If the owner of it [*sc.* an animal] swore falsely..that he was ignorant of its viciousness. **1847** T. BROWN *Mod. Farriery* 372 It is not an unfrequent occurrence for horses in harness to back instead of drawing when first started, and some add to this considerable viciousness. **1908** *Animal Managem.* 81 A playful habit of snatching at the man whilst being groomed which some horses display, may not come under the head of viciousness.

c. Maliciousness, spitefulness.

1879 HUXLEY *Hume* II. viii. 159 One feels ashamed of having suspected many excellent persons of being moved by mere malice and viciousness of temper to call other folks atheists.

2. The quality of being faulty or defective.

1601 DEACON & WALKER *Spirits & Divels* 90 The absence, the vitiousnesse, the depriuation or fault of some other thing. **1642** FULLER *Holy & Prof. St.* II. xvii. 114 Then the low value shews the viciousnesse of it. **1687** M. CLIFFORD *Notes on Dryden's Poems* iv. 13, I intended to have made no more Animadversions upon the viciousness of your Style. **1752** CARTE *Hist. Eng.* (1755) III. 763 The arret above mentioned being repealed, these conservators were to judge of the goodness or viciousness of cloths.

†**b.** Faultiness or badness in respect of physical constitution. *Obs.*

1669 STURMY *Mariner's Mag.* V. xii. 67 The Brimstone will burn up the gross victiousness [*sic*] of the Salt-peter. **1706** STEVENS *Span. Dict.* I, *Vicio*,..Rankness, Viciousness in Land, or the like.

3. Improper or illegal procedure.

1802–12 BENTHAM *Ration. Judic. Evid.* (1827) II. 458 In the cases above brought to view, as cases of unfairness or vitiousness.

viˈcissitous, *a.* *U.S.* = VICISSITUDINOUS *a.*

1865 E. BURRITT *Walk to Land's End* 165 A city set upon such a hill could not have been hidden in the vicissitous experiences of a nation. **1892** *Columbus* (Ohio) *Dispatch* 9 June, About all of them reach their affluence..along the same vicissitous road.

†**viˈcissitudal**, *a.* *Obs. rare.* [f. next.] = VICISSITUDINAL *a.* Hence †**viˈcissitudally** *adv.*

1598 J. KEEPER tr. *A. Romei's Academi* i. 7 The sensible world hath two parts, one subiect to vicissitudal generation and corruption;..the other is the celestiall world. **1612** *Benvenuto's Passenger* I. iv. 322 The which sport they continuing, for foure times vicessitudally [*sic*] euery day [etc.].

vicissitude (vɪˈsɪsɪtjuːd). [a. OF. and F. *vicissitude* (14th c.), or ad. L. *vicissitūdo*, f. *vicis* turn, change: see VICE *sb.*⁶ and *prefix*. So Sp. *vicisitud*, Pg. *vicissitude*, It. *vicissitudine*.]

1. The fact of change or mutation taking place in a particular thing or within a certain sphere;

the uncertain changing or mutability *of* something.

1570–6 Lambarde *Peramb. Kent* 105 Richeborowe.. came to ruine, by the alteration and vicissitude of the Sea. **1625** Bacon *Ess., Vicissitude of Things* (Arb.) 570 The Vicissitude or Mutations, in the Superiour Globe, are no fit Matter, for this present Argument. **1640** G. Sandys *Christ's Passion* III. 268 O dire Vicissitude of Things! **1654** Bramhall *Just Vind.* vi. (1661) 115 According to the Vicissitude and conversion of humane affairs, and the change of Monarchies. **1690** Locke *Hum. Und.* II. xxvi. 153 The notice, that our Senses take of the constant Vicissitude of Things. **1720** Welton *Suffer. Son of God* II. xxv. 659 Take Compassion of the Fleeting Inconstancy and Vicissitude of the Dangers with which we, poor Mortals, are surrounded. **1773** Cook *Voy.* III. vii. III. 606 And now, such is the vicissitude of life, we thought ourselves happy in having regained a situation, which but two days before it was the utmost object of our hope to quit. **1864** Pusey *Lect. Daniel* ii. 61 It is remarkable that this vicissitude of human things, this marked outline of the succession of Empires till our Lord should come, is laid open.. to the Heathen Monarch.

b. With *a*, in the same sense.

1631 Weever *Anc. Fun. Mon.* 3 Of all things else there is a vicissitude, a change both of cities and nations. **1643** Sir T. Browne *Relig. Med.* I. §17 Because the glory of one State depends upon the ruine of another, there is a revolution and vicissitude of their greatnesse. **1753** Johnson *Adventurer* No. 95 ¶5 There is likewise in composition, as in other things, a perpetual vicissitude of fashion. **1772** *Birmingham Counterfeit* II. viii. 106 Her history.. abounds with such an amazing vicissitude of incidents.

2. Without article: Change, mutation, mutability, as a natural process or tendency in things or in life generally; successive substitution of one thing or condition for another, taking place from natural causes.

1596 Drayton *Legends* iv. 757 Vicissitude impartially will'd The goodlyest things be subject to annoy. **1603** Holland *Plutarch's Mor.* 1310 He endeavoreth by vicissitude of mutations, and by periodicall passion, to continue alwaies yoong, as if he should never die and perish. **1654** Whitlock *Zootomia* 32 The Sisters Web of our lives is checkered with Vicissitude, The whole peece proving but a medley of Light and Shadow. *a* **1664** Kath. Philips *Submission* Poems (1667) 108 Where were our Springs, our Harvests pleasent use, Unless Vicissitude did them produce. **1758** Johnson *Idler* No. 4 ¶11 Whatever is left in the hands of chance must be subject to vicissitude. **1781** Cowper *Hope* 17 Vicissitude wheels round the motley crowd, The rich grow poor, the poor become purse-proud. **1833–5** J. H. Newman *Hist. Sk.* Ser. III. (1873) i. 1 This is a world of conflict, and of vicissitude amid the conflict. **1869** J. Phillips *Vesuvius* vii. 197 On such a fault-line atmospheric vicissitude has been effective.

3. A change or alteration in condition or fortune; an instance of mutability in human affairs.

1616 B. Jonson *Devil an Ass* II. iv. 38 Nature hath these vicissitudes. Shee makes No man a state of perpetuety, Sir. **1665** Manley *Grotius' Low C. Wars* 429 That the vicissitudes of War should be brought to a stay, if equall Counsels should be found on both sides. **1681** J. Flavel *Right. Man's Ref.* 220 His people may find.. rest and comfort amidst the vicissitudes of this unstable world. **1709** Steele *Tatler* No. 41 ¶4 A deplorable instance of the Fortune of War, and Vicissitudes of humane Affairs. **1794** Godwin *Caleb Williams* 314 Mr. Collins promised, as far as he was able, to have an eye upon my vicissitudes. **1832** Lyell *Princ. Geol.* II. 1 We shall treat first of the vicissitudes to which *species* are subject. **1856** Kane *Arct. Expl.* II. xxviii. 281 My sturdy second officer,.. long accustomed to the vicissitudes of whaling life, shed tears at the prospect. **1879** Church *Spenser* 31 For fifty years the English people had had before its eyes the great vicissitudes which make tragedy.

4. Alternation, mutual or reciprocal succession, of things or conditions; *esp.* alternating succession of opposite or contrasted things.

1624 Burton *Anat. Mel.* (ed. 2) II. ii. III. 211 At Berna.. a shippe was digged out of a mountaine... Came this from Earth-quakes,.. or is there a vicissitude of Sea and Land, as Anaximenes held of old? **1646** Sir T. Browne *Pseud. Ep.* 105 Reason cannot conceive that an animall.. should live in a continuall motion, without that alternity and vicissitude of rest whereby all others continue. **1667** Milton *P.L.* vi. 8 Which makes through Heav'n Grateful vicissitude, like Day and Night. **1689** tr. *Locke's Let. Toleration* 26 How the Church was under the Vicissitude of Orthodox and Arrian Emperors is very well known. **1711** Steele *Spect.* No. 143 ¶1 This Vicissitude of Motion and Rest, which we call Life. **1740** Cibber *Apol.* (1756) I. 323 When I consider that various vicissitude of hopes and fears we had for twenty years struggled with. **1773** Monboddo *Language* (1774) I. I. ix. 111 Corporeal forms which are.. in a constant vicissitude of generation and corruption. **1835** Thirlwall *Greece* I. vi. 219 The succession of light and darkness,.. the vicissitude of the seasons. **1854** Mrs. Oliphant *Magd. Hepburn* II. 21 Her girlish shyness.. made the colour come and go in rapid vicissitude upon her cheek.

5. An instance of alternation or succession; a change from one physical state to another, esp. as one of a constant series.

1648 Wilkins *Math. Magic* II. v. 183 How those vicissitudes of rarefaction and condensation may be maintained. **1692** Bentley *Boyle Lect.* vi. 180 The periodical and constant Vicissitudes of Day and Night. **1718** Prior *Solomon* II. 832 What Pangs, what Fires, what Racks didst Thou sustain? What sad Vicissitudes of smarting Pain? **1747** T. Story *Life*, etc. 86, I kept close to Meetings, and to Business, in their proper Vicissitudes. **1781** Gibbon *Decl. & F.* xvii. (1787) II. 6 The vicissitudes of tides are scarcely felt in those seas. **1822–7** Good *Study Med.* (1829) III. 352 Extreme heat and cold.. are far more injurious when flowing in irregular vicissitudes, than when in an uniform tenour. **1853** Phillips *Rivers Yorksh.* iii. 90 The surface influence of descending rains, and all the agency of atmospheric vicissitudes. **1893** Ball *Story of Sun* 319 There must have been remarkable climatic vicissitudes during past ages.

†**6.** Reciprocation, return. *Obs.*$^{-1}$

1565 *Testimonial to R. Campbell* in *Wodrow Soc. Misc.* (1844) 288 In doing whairof.. so shall you bynd ws to the lik vicissitude.

†**7.** A turn or occasion of action. *Obs.*$^{-1}$

1605 Bacon *Adv. Learn.* I. vi. §13. 30 In the next vicissitude or succession, he did send his diuine truth into the world.

†**b.** *by vicissitudes*, by turns. *Obs.*

1749 Lavington *Enthus. Meth. & Papists* II. (1754) 47 The Moravian Mystics are the Persons, whom Mr. Wesley represents by Vicissitudes as the best, and as the worst, of Men.

†**vicissi'tudinal**, *a. Obs.*$^{-1}$ [See next and -al[1].] Vicissitudinous. Also †**vicissitudi'narian** *a.*, **-'narious** *a.*, **-'nariously** *adv.*

1588 J. Harvey *Disc. Probl.* 23 A *vicissitudinall conuersion, or temporall transformation of the elementarie or terrestriall globe of this world. *c* **1729** W. Stukeley *Mem.* (Surtees) I. 210 Here we measure not time, nor have we need of your *vicissitudinarian planet called the sun. **1667** Waterhouse *Fire of Lond.* 2 God,.. by whom only they [*sc.* dreadful effects] can be transformed into comforts (which as elementary and *vicissitudinarious, they can in no true sense be). **1715** *Meteorological Essays* II. 191 *Vicissitudinariously.

†**vicissi'tudinary**, *a. Obs.* [f. L. *vicissitūdin-*, stem of *vicissitūdo*: see -ary.]

1. Marked by alternation; coming alternately or by turns.

1624 Donne *Devotions*, etc. (ed. 2) 296 Wee say.. the dayes of man [are] vicissitudinary, as though he had as many good days, as ill. **1640** Bp. Hall *Episc.* II. xvii. 180 This presidence.. is not perpetuall, but only for the time and vicissitudinary. **1650** *Descr. Future Hist. Europe* 6 A vicissitudinary time of Affliction and Ease, Persecution and rest, pure Doctrine and Heresies, is signified.

2. Reciprocal, responsive. *rare*$^{-1}$.

1629 Maxwell tr. *Herodian* (1635) 92 When a mans Friend hath (first) obliged him by Signall Offices; if hee shew not all vicissitudinary Expressions of a thankefull Heart [etc.].

vicissi'tudinous, *a.* [f. as prec. + -ous.]

1. Marked by vicissitudes; subject to various or frequent changes of fortune.

1846 Worcester (citing *Q. Rev.*). **1853** J. Stevenson in *Trans. Ch. Historians Eng.* II. 227 In this mode was the king's administration conducted during the whole of his vicissitudinous life. **1865** *Reader* 23 Sept. 335/1 His career has been vicissitudinous in the highest degree. **1891** *Sat. Rev.* 4 July 2/1 A second Oxford innings, which, though 'vicissitudinous', almost equalled the first Cambridge total.

2. Of a person: That has experienced changes of fortune or circumstances.

1856 Hawthorne *Eng. Note-Bks.* (1870) II. 189 An Englishman.. who suggests himself as a kind of contrast to this warlike and vicissitudinous backwoodsman.

†**vi'cissity.** *Obs.*$^{-0}$ [ad. L. *vicissitas* (rare) change, alteration.] (See quot.)

1721 Bailey, *Vicissity*, a changing or succeeding by Course; an interchangeable Course.

vicker(y, obs. forms of vicar, vicary.

Vickers ('vɪkəz). The name of a manufacturing company, orig. *Vickers*, Ltd., used: **1. a.** *attrib.* With reference to any of a variety of products of the firm, esp. armaments, aircraft, etc. Occas. also in the possessive.

1913 *303-Inch Machine Guns* (Ordnance College: Field Artillery & Small Arms Branch) 62 (*heading*) Gun, Vickers', ·303-in., Light. **1917** A. G. Empey *Over Top* 313 Vickers gun. **1919** *Vickers News* 15 Oct. 7/2 Vickers engines are occasionally tested on some such oil as Texas. *Ibid.* 1 Nov. 25 (*caption*) A Vickers airship is also seen leaving Barrow with letters for Sheffield. *a* **1944** K. Douglas *Alamein to Zem Zem* (1946) xiii. 79 Our supporting infantry manned their Vickers M.G.s on the flanks. **1945** *Penguin New Writing* XXIV. 31 In front of me the man carrying the Vickers ammunition. ? **1949** B. W. A. Dixon *Aircraft* i. 14/1 The Vickers 'Vimy', a twin-engined bomber designed originally for the long-distance bombing of Berlin. **1953** C. A. Lindbergh *Spirit of St. Louis* II. vi. 295 Alcock and Brown ..got across the ocean in their twin-engined Vickers bomber. **1974** *Encycl. Brit. Macropædia* XIX. 688/2 The Maxim machine guns, later often known as Vickers weapons, were used throughout the world well into the 1960s.

b. *absol.* One of a series of machine-guns manufactured by the company and used in both World Wars, esp. the ·303 or Vickers Maxim.

1917 G. Frankau *City of Fear* 18 You know what it's like in a listening-post, The Very candles aflare, Their bullets smacking the sand-bags, our Vickers combing your hair. **1918** T. E. Lawrence *Lett.* (1938) 243 A frontal attack of eighteen men, two Vickers, and two large Hotchkiss. **1942** E. Waugh *Put out More Flags* iii. 195 Nigel was full of questions;.. what was the difference between a Bren and a Vickers. **1946** R. Capell *Simiomata* I. 36 The caiques scattered with Brens and Vickers raking them.

2. *attrib.* With reference to a method of testing the hardness of a material (esp. metal) by measuring the indentation produced when a small diamond pyramid is applied to the surface under a specified load.

1926 *Automobile Engineer* XVI. 105/1 In designing the Vickers machine.. an impression having a diameter equal to three-eighths that of the ball has been taken as ideal. **1930** *Engineering* 12 Sept. 318/2 The hardness of hardened steel was further raised from Vickers number 950 to 1,100 by this treatment. **1973** J. G. Tweeddale *Materials Technol.* I. iv. 77 The most standard form of test is the Vickers hardness system performed by pushing a standard square pyramid diamond indenter.. into the surface of the material.

vickid, -it, obs. forms of wicked *a.*

‖**vicomte** (vikɔ̃t). [Fr.] A viscount. Similarly **vicomtesse** (vikɔ̃tɛs), a viscountess.

c **1786** T. Blaikie *Diary of Scotch Gardener* (1931) 204 The Vicomtesse de Pons.. had a Park to Make. **1847** C. Brontë *Jane Eyre* I. xv. 286, I knew him for a young roué of a vicomte—a brainless and vicious youth. **1889** C. M. Yonge *Reputed Changeling* II. xxi. 71 The mother.. was too proud of him to miss any opportunity of exhibiting him to an experienced mother and grandmother like the vicomtesse. **1928** C. A. Nicholson *Hell & Duchess* v. 94 You can scarcely blame the vicomte for suggesting a change. **1968** R. Amberley *Incitement to Murder* iii. 77 His uncle and aunt will be staying in the vicomte's house. **1980** C. Watson *Bishop in Back Seat* (1981) xxviii. 157 There was a sometime film producer,.. a French count,.. a vicomtesse who wrote best-sellers.

Viconian (vɪ'kəʊnɪən), *a.* [f. the name of Giovanni Battista *Vico* (1668–1744), Neapolitan philosopher + -ian.] Designating the theories or doctrines of Vico, esp. those concerned with the historical development of culture and its cyclical or repetitive character.

1957 N. Frye *Anat. Crit.* i. 62 Joyce and his Viconian theory of history. **1967** *Listener* 23 Mar. 391/3 Implying that the work should properly be.. bound in such a way as to have no first or last page, a very embodiment of Viconian circularity. **1976** T. Eagleton *Crit. & Ideology* iv. 157 Human societies are specific sectors of that cosmic process, determined by its unalterable laws, moving inexorably through their Viconian cycles.

vicont, obs. form of viscount.

†**vi'contiel**, *sb.* and *a. Obs.* Also 7 **vicondell**, 7–9 **viscontiel.** *β.* 6–7 **vicountiell**, 7–9 **-iel.** See also vicountile. [a. AF. *vicontiel*, f. *viconte* viscount. Cf. OF. *vicontal*, F. *vicomtal*.]

A. *sb. pl.* Certain sums regularly payable to the Crown by a sheriff and charged against him in the Exchequer accounts.

1548 *Act 2 & 3 Edw. VI*, c. 4 §3 [To] be discharged of all suche Fermes and Sommes of money.. excepte onlie of the Vicountielles of their Shires wherewithe they shalbe chardged. **1607** Cowell *Interpr.* s.v., There are also certaine fermes called Vicountiels, which the Shyreeue for his time payeth a certaine rent for to the King, and maketh what profit he can of them. **1642** C. Vernon *Consid. Exch.* 11 The.. Sheriffe.. to deliver a book written in parchment, declaring of whom and where he receiveth the vicondells, and other the Rents and Farmes written unto him in the Summons of the Pipe. **1738** *Hist. Crt. Excheq.* v. 89 This sum was an Item placed after his Vicontiels. [**1819** *Statutes of Realm* IV. 43 *marg.*, Allowance to all Sheriffs for Vicountiels out of lands coming into the King's Hands.]

B. *adj.* **1.** Of or pertaining to a sheriff.

a. **1614** Selden *Titles Honor* 253 Our officiarie *Vicecomites* or Shirifes, which haue diuers Actions Viscontiel, and inquirie of criminall causes. **1622** Callis *Stat. Sewers* (1824) 230 The highest authority that he [the sheriff] hath is but vicontiel. **1647** N. Bacon *Disc. Govt.* I. lxi. 191 Other Courts also were in the countrey, and were Vicontiel or Courts of Sheriffs and Lords of Hundreds and corporations. **1670** *Act 22 Chas. II*, c. 6 §1 Guild Rents, Pensions, Vicontiel Rents, Assart-Rents [etc.]. **1798** *Gentl. Mag.* Oct. 850/1 Not far from the church of Bromham lies.. the chantry-house, to which appertained certain annual vicontiel or fee farm rents. **1798** *Rep. Comm. Ho. Comm.* (1803) XIII. 107 The Rents whereof (called Viscontiel Rents) are in the Collection of the Sheriffs of the several Counties, Cities, and Towns in England. **1863** H. Cox *Instit.* III. vii. 684 The second consisting of certain rents called viscontiel rents, or rents for which the sheriffs were accountable.

β. **1630** Doddridge *Hist. Wales* 40 For all the ordinary Ministers and executioners of the processe of the Lawes of England, or which haue Vicountiell iurisdiction, are the Officers of particular Shires. [**1819** *Statutes of Realm* IV. 43 *marg.*, Sheriffs taking Tallies shall be chargeable for Vicountiel Farms, &c.]

2. Of writs: (see quots.).

1607 Cowell *Interpr.* s.v. *Vicountie*, Writs vicountiel are such writs as are triable in the countie or Shyreeues court. *a* **1683** Scroggs *Courts-Leet* (1714) 84 This Writ is a Vicountiel, and in the Nature of a Justicies in which the Sheriff shall hold Plea. **1768** Blackstone *Comm.* III. 238 This writ of admeasurement.. is one of those writs, that are called *vicontiel*, being directed to the sheriff,.. and not to be returned to any superior court, till finally executed by him.

vicori(e, etc., variants of vicary *sb.*[1] *Obs.*

vicount, obs. variant of viscount.

†**vicountile**, *sb.* and *a. Obs.* = vicontiel.

1542–3 *Act 34 & 35 Hen. VIII*, c. 16 §2 Where divers.. soomes of money been respected to.. Shirieffes.. upon theyre accomptes.. of the foresaide fermes and other vicountyles. **1593** Norden *Spec. Brit., Essex* 12 Hertfordshire, in the time of Edw. III, was annexed vnto this shire, as towching vicountile iurisdiction. **1664** *Spelman's Gloss.* 555/1 *Vice-comitalia*, vicountiles.

vicour, obs. form of vicar.

vicst, southern ME. f. *fightest*, fight *v.*

†**vict**[1]. *Obs.*$^{-1}$ [ad. L. *vict-us*, pa. pple. of *vincĕre* to overcome.] One who is vanquished.
c 1400 *Destr. Troy* 2145 Ofte sith hit is sene.. That a victor of a victe is vile ouercomyn.

†**vict**[2]. *Obs.*$^{-1}$ App. an abbrev. of VICTIM *sb.*
1639 G. DANIEL *Ecclus.* xlvii. 3 As the Fatt is disparted from the Vict, Soe David from the People, by the strict Survey of Heaven.

victail, -ale, obs. forms of VICTUAL *sb.*

victim ('vɪktɪm), *sb.* Also 5 **vyctym**, 6–7 **victime**. [ad. L. *victima* (in senses 1, 2). So F. *victime* (16th c.), Sp. and Pg. *victima*, It. *vittima*. The Rhemish translators of the Bible were the first to make free use of the word as English, and its general currency dates only from the latter part of the 17th century.]

1. a. A living creature killed and offered as a sacrifice to some deity or supernatural power.
1497 BP. ALCOCK *Mons Perfect.* C iij/2 Obedyence excellith al vyctyms [*printed* vyayms] and holocaustis in the whiche was sacrefyced yᵉ flesshe of other creatures. **1582** N. T. (Rhem.) *Mark* ix. 49 Euery victime shal be salted with salt. *Ibid., Acts* vii. 42 Did you offer victims and hostes vnto me? **1609** BIBLE (Douay) *Lev.* i. 2, etc. **1613** PURCHAS *Pilgrimage* I. vi. 33 Of sacrificing there were from the beginning two kinds, the one called Gifts or oblations of things without life: the other Victims (so our Rhemists have taught us to English the word *Victima*) slaine sacrifices of birds and beasts. **1616** BULLOKAR *Eng. Expos., Victime*, a sacrifice, a beast offered in sacrifice. [Also in Cockeram, Blount, etc.] **1697** DRYDEN *Virg. Georg.* IV. 784 Select four Brawny Bulls for Sacrifice,.. From the slain Victims pour the streaming Blood. **1705** ADDISON *Italy* 3 Ulysses here the Blood of Victims shed, And rais'd the pale Assembly of the Dead. **1728** CHAMBERS *Cycl.* s.v. *Sacrifice*, The Priest.. then took Wine in a Vessel.. and.. poured it between the Horns of the Victim. **1772** PRIESTLEY *Inst. Relig.* (1782) I. 202 The Mexicans used human victims. **1840** THIRLWALL *Greece* VII. lv. 105 He had inquired of Peithagoras as to the nature of the tokens which he had seen in the victims. **1867** TENNYSON *Victim* v, But the Priest was happy, His victim won. *Ibid.* vi, The rites prepared, the victim bared.
fig. **1646** CRASHAW *Carmen Deo Nostro, Hymn*, Thou art love's victime, & must dy A death more mysticall & high. **1656** COWLEY *Pindar. Odes, Isaiah xxxiv.* ii, The Altar all the Land, and all Men in't the Victims are. **1732** LEDIARD *Sethos* II. x. 374 These 20,000 men were a victim to save the rest of their nation. **1772** *Junius Lett.* lxix. (1788) 367, I have bound the victim, and dragged him to the altar. **1818** SHELLEY *Julian* 376 The red scaffold.. May ask some willing victim. **1847** TENNYSON *Princ.* IV. 112 Knaves are men, That.. dress the victim to the offering up. **1855** KINGSLEY *Heroes* IV. (1868) 50, I am accursed, devoted as a victim to the sea-gods.

b. Applied to Christ as an offering for mankind.
1736 BUTLER *Analogy* II. v. ¶6 [Jesus Christ] is described .. in the Old Testament, under the same characters of a priest, and an expiatory victim. **1745** W. ROBERTSON in *Transl. & Paraphr.* (Sc. Ch.) vi. 8 All Heaven's Wrath tho' due to us On him, our Victim, lay. *a* **1833** J. DICK *Lect. Theol.* (1834) III. lviii. 119 In the other [case], it was a man, the Son of the living God, who was the victim. *c* **1865** W. C. DIX *Hymn, 'Alleluia, sing to Jesus,'* Thou on earth both Priest and Victim. **1870** H. MARTIN *Atonement* iv. 74 They evidently concentrate attention.. on that aspect in which Christ appears as the piacular victim, or the Lamb of Sacrifice.

2. a. A person who is put to death or subjected to torture by another; one who suffers severely in body or property through cruel or oppressive treatment.
1660 R. COKE *Justice Vind.* Ep. Ded. 5, I designe no more than to demonstrate, that it was.. the iniquity of the times which made him [Charles I] a victim, and your sacred Self an Exile. **1691** tr. *Emiliane's Frauds Rom. Monks* (ed. 3) 61 The great Provost.. was one of the number of these unhappy Victims. **1783** CRABBE *Village* I. 283 A potent quack, long versed in human ills, Who first insults the victim whom he kills. **1785** BURKE *Sp. Nawab Arcot's Debts* Wks. 1882 I. 331 Among the victims to this magnificent plan of universal plunder.. you have all heard.. of an Indian Chief called Hyder Ali Khan. **1839** KEIGHTLEY *Hist. Eng.* II. 32 If he had not died the victim of a tyrant. **1854** CDL. WISEMAN *Fabiola* II. xxii. 263 The hostile passions of heathen Rome.. excited by the coming slaughter of so many christian victims. **1871** FREEMAN *Norm. Conq.* (1876) IV. xviii. 169 The list of his possessions, lands of Earl Harold, of the Sheriff Mœrleswegen, and of a crowd of smaller victims, is simply endless.

b. One who is reduced or destined to suffer under some oppressive or destructive agency.
1718 PRIOR *Solomon* III. 170 Behold where Age's wretched Victim lies: See his Head trembling, and his half-clos'd Eyes. **1742** GRAY *Prosp. Eton Coll.* 52 Alas! regardless of their doom The little victims play! **1799** *Monthly Rev.* XXX. 539 This new poet.. is M. Esmenard,.. at present a victim of the persecution which has followed that event. **1827** SCOTT *Highl. Widow* v, About the centre of the procession.. came the unfortunate victim of military law. **1865** VISCT. MILTON & W. B. CHEADLE *N.-W. Passage* viii. (1867) 124 We.. even went to the length of fixing upon one useless, toothless old fellow [*sc.* a dog] as a victim to our appetites, in case of extremity. **1890** C. B. PITMAN tr. *Boscowitz's Earthquakes* 211 The houses which had only partially fallen in continued to collapse and make fresh victims.

c. One who perishes or suffers in health, etc., from some enterprise or pursuit voluntarily undertaken.
1726–46 THOMSON *Winter* 487 The last of old Lycurgus' sons, The generous victim to that vain attempt To save a rotten state. **1832** G. R. PORTER *Porcelain & Gl.* 259 Frauenhofer died.. at an early age; a victim, it is said, to unremitting attention bestowed upon an unhealthy employment. **1847** EMERSON *Repr. Men, Montaigne* Wks. (Bohn) I. 338 The studious class are their own victims. **1852** MISS YONGE *Cameos* I. xxxi. 271 While here he narrowly escaped becoming a seventh royal victim to the Crusade.

d. In weaker sense: One who suffers some injury, hardship, or loss, is badly treated or taken advantage of, etc.
1781 GIBBON *Decl. & F.* xxvii. (1787) III. 23 Gregory soon became the victim of malice and envy. **1796** H. HUNTER tr. *St.-Pierre's Stud. Nat.* (1799) I. 342 That spirit of intolerance.. of which they are the victims. **1835** URE *Phil. Manuf.* 42 Several individuals.. are to a very great extent the victims at least, if not the dupes, of scheming managers. **1844** DICKENS *Mart. Chuz.* xx, He went off.. without further ceremony, and left his respected victim to settle the bill. **1875** ABP. BENSON in A. C. Benson *Life* (1899) I. xi. 393, I am that miserable man the Victim in Residence, and there is a Cathedral Festival to-day.

3. In the phrase *to fall a victim to* (some thing or person), in preceding senses.
1764 H. WALPOLE *Otranto* i, Manfred will suspect you,.. and you will fall a victim to his resentment. **1769** ROBERTSON *Chas. V*, IV. Wks. 1813 V. 411 Some officers, who rashly attempted to restrain them, fell victims to their fury. **1803** ELLICOTT *Jrnl.* 13 Many of the inhabitants that season fell victims to the yellow fever. **1861** M. PATTISON *Ess.* (1889) I. 46 The Flemish and other foreign residents fell helpless victims to the rage of the populace. **1884** *Times* (weekly ed.) 5 Sept. 17/2 It appeared as if he had fallen a victim to an assassin. *Ibid.* 19 Sept. 6/4 He fell a victim to goodness of heart and to the interest he felt in his people.

4. *attrib.* (chiefly appositive) and *Comb.*, as ***victim beast, carrion, -flock, -hero, horde, -lamb, ox; victim-laden*** adj.; **victim-ship**, a ship carrying victims.
1697 DRYDEN *Virg. Georg.* III. 733 The Victim Ox, that was for Altars prest,.. Sunk of Himself. **1697** —— *Æneid* IV. 293 Blood of victim beasts enriched the ground. **1725** POPE *Odyss.* XIII. 27 A victim Ox beneath the sacred hand Of great Alcinous falls. **1812** BYRON *Ch. Har.* II. lxxxix, The Battle-field, where Persia's victim horde First bow'd beneath the brunt of Hellas' sword. **1835** THIRLWALL *Greece* I. v. 133 Deceived by the black sail of the victim-ship, which Theseus had forgotten to exchange. **1843** CDL. WISEMAN *Ess., Minor Rites* (1853) I. 491 There is one altar.. on which the same Victim-Lamb reposes. *a* **1847** ELIZA COOK *Thanksgiving* iv, I could not sue for mercy at a victim-laden shrine. **1851** MRS. BROWNING *Casa Guidi Wind.* II. 660 The tyrant should take heed to what he doth, Since every victim-carrion turns to use. **1868** J. H. NEWMAN *Verses Var. Occasions* 171, I cleanse Thy victim-flock, and bring them near In holiest wise. **1962** *John o' London's* 1 Mar. 211/3 Young Cordier.. isn't the perfect victim-hero. **1975** P. FUSSELL *Gt. War & Mod. Memory* i. 8 Air bombardment, which was supposed to shorten the war, prolonged it by inviting those who were its targets to cast themselves in the role of victim-heroes and thus stiffen their resolve. *Ibid.* vi. 220 Guy Crouchback, Waugh's victim-hero.

Hence '**victim** *v. trans.*, to slay in sacrifice.
1671 CROWNE *Juliana* I. 11 Barbarous Idol, not content with blood, But must have kingdoms victim'd at thy altars! **1694** —— *Married Beau* IV. 54 I'll rather victim A hecatomb of such as thou to her.

†'**victimary.** *Obs.* [ad. L. *victimāri-us*, f. *victima* VICTIM *sb.* So F. *victimaire.*] A slayer of sacrificial victims.
1652 GALE *Magastrom.* 373 So they were burned by the victimaries or sacrificers themselves, in the sight of all the people. **1669** —— *Crt. Gentiles* I. II. ix. 261 Amongst the Romans, the Priest did not kil the Victime, but the Popa or Victimarie, at the beck of the Priest. **1778** APTHORP *Preval. Chr.* 298 Who had the same office as the latin papæ and victimaries, that of killing the victims.

†**victimate**, *sb. Obs. rare.* [ad. L. *victimāt-us*, pa. pple. of *victimāre*: see next.] = VICTIM *sb.* 1.
1583 STUBBES *Anat. Abuses* Ep. Ded., Sacrifices, Victimates & Holocaustes offred. *Ibid.* O ij b, Hauing offred vp their sacrifices, victimats and holocaustes to their false Gods.

†'**victimate**, *v. Obs.*$^{-0}$ [f. L. *victimāt-*, ppl. stem of *victimāre*, f. *victima* VICTIM *sb.*] (See quots.)
1616 BULLOKAR *Eng. Expos., Victimate*, to offer in sacrifice, to kill and sacrifice. **1656** BLOUNT *Glossogr., Victimate*, to Sacrifice, to make an Oblation.

'**victimhood.** [f. VICTIM *sb.*] The state of being a victim.
1862 MRS. CARLYLE *Lett.* (1883) III. 138 Wearing a sullen look of victimhood.

victi'mizable, *a.* [f. VICTIMIZE *v.*] Capable of being victimized.
1842 EMERSON *Ess.* II. iii. (1901) 273 Have you been victimised in being brought hither?—or, prior to that, answer me this, 'Are you victimisable?'

victimi'zation. [f. next.] **a.** The action of victimizing, or fact of being victimized, in various senses.
1840 *New Monthly Mag.* LIX. 397 The man who does not grow savage at victimization is an inert, unsentient booby. **1860** A. L. WINDSOR *Ethica* v. 278 On Pope's complete victimization, perhaps, less stress is to be laid. **1885** L. OLIPHANT *Sympneumata* 57 But the victimisation of the infant terrestrial man was not to be so fully consummated. **1900** *Pilot* 30 June 544/1 The Companies Bill and the Money-Lending Bill.. had the common object of putting down fraud and victimisation.

b. *spec.* in *Theol.* (See quot.)
1893 *Month* April 485 Christ's Body in its Eucharistic state, which Theologians, when they explain the sacrificial character of the Mass, call a state of victimization.

c. *spec.* With reference to the imposition of penalties on trade union members who go on strike.
1923 *Westm. Gaz.* 23 Apr., The expression 'no victimisation' implied that a striker's place was not to be filled by an outsider. **1925** S. O'CASEY *Juno & Paycock* I, in *Two Plays* 8 Why did they sack her? It was a clear case of victimization. **1957** *Listener* 26 Dec. 1057/1 Victimisation, that 'doubletalk' word of today, was then a vivid and frequent reality. **1961** *Daily Tel.* 16 Dec. 7/1 They will receive severance pay from the company and a share of a 'victimisation fund' to tide them over until they find other jobs. **1966** [see NEWSPEAK]. **1974** *Socialist Worker* 23 Nov. 1/3 From the miners' ballot to the strikes of bakers and journalists, to the victimisation strike at Intex in Manchester, the will to fight is there.

victimize ('vɪktɪmaɪz), *v.* [f. VICTIM *sb.*]
1. *trans.* To make a victim of; to cause to suffer inconvenience, discomfort, annoyance, etc., either deliberately or by misdirected attentions.
1830 LYTTON *Let.* Sept., in *M. Napier's Corr.* (1879) 87 Your contributors are at full liberty to ridicule, abuse, and (allow the author of Paul Clifford to employ a slang word) victimize me. **1839** COL. HAWKER *Diary* (1893) II. 166, I had the honour of being kindly victimised on the occasion by our hospitable host, as the leader of the shooting world. **1848** THACKERAY *Van. Fair* xli, Becky.. described the occurrence, and how she had been victimised by Lady Southdown.

b. To cheat, swindle, or defraud.
1839 [see *victimizing* ppl. a.]. **1848** THACKERAY *Bk. Snobs* xxxix, In a turf transaction, either Spavin or Cockspur would try to get the better of his father, and, to gain a point in the odds, victimise his best friends. **1859** J. LANG *Wand. India* 20 After several officers have been victimized at play, their friends are apt to talk about the matter in an unpleasant manner. **1883** GREENWOOD *Odd People* 96 In what way has the rascal victimised his customer?

2. To put to death as, or in the manner of, a sacrificial victim; to slaughter.
1853 *Tait's Mag.* XX. 487 Fifty thousand Gentoos were victimized by the scimitar. **1855** SINGLETON *Virgil* II. 541 By this wound 'Tis Pallas, Pallas, victimiseth thee, And taketh vengeance on thy cursed blood. **1899** *19th Cent.* Nov. 816 *note*, The sacrifice used to be human, and virgins were victimised on the hill at Kandy.
transf. **1880** MCCARTHY *Own Times* liii. IV. 148 The prisoners.. must have shared the fate of those who were victimised outside [by an explosion].

b. To destroy or spoil (plants) completely.
1849 *Jrnl. R. Agric. Soc.* X. I. 96 The wireworm had been at work to so fearful an extent, that in ten days the whole crop seemed victimised. **1882** HARDY in *Proc. Berw. Nat. Club* IX. 463 Some shrubs had been victimised by the winter.

Hence '**victimized** *ppl. a.*; '**victimizing** *vbl. sb.* and *ppl. a.*
1849 SOYER *Mod. Housew.* 242 *Victimised Cutlets. **1850** THACKERAY *Pendennis* lxiii, [He] had pledged his word.. to be content with the allowance which his victimized wife still awarded him. **1855** SMEDLEY *H. Coverdale* iv, A.. system of reprisals which those victimised individuals appeared.. inclined to resent. **1859** *Habits of Gd. Society* xv. 372 The.. broken sentences of the victimized bridegroom. **1834** *Tait's Mag.* I. 392/2 The Jews were to have his money any way. If not for their conversion, then for his own *victimizing. **1850** THACKERAY *Pendennis* lv, There was no such thing: there was no victimizing. **1839** *Morning Herald* 2 Sept., The defrauded victims of.. a *victimising artist.

'**victimizer.** [f. prec.] One who victimizes another or others.
1831 *Fraser's Mag.* IV. 578 A gambling house, in which the cards are played for the victim by the victimiser. **1837** THACKERAY *Ravenswing* ii, He.. felt the presence of a victimiser as a hare does of a greyhound. **1863** BATES *Nat. Amazon* II. 46 The dress of the victimisers is arranged with especial reference to their prey. **1879** 'E. GARRETT' *House by Works* II. 137 Rather partners in fall and loss, than victimiser and victim.

'**victimless**, *a.* orig. and chiefly *U.S.* [f. VICTIM *sb.* + -LESS.] Applied to a crime in which there is no injured party. Hence occas. *transf.* of the offender.
1965 E. M. SCHOR *Crimes without Victims* 171 A comparison of the three situations analyzed in this book may provide some hints as to the factors determining the expansion of deviance in the victimless crime sphere. **1971** *Wall St. Jrnl.* 29 Mar. 1/1 We have to find ways to clear the courts of the endless stream of 'victimless crimes'... There are more important matters.. than minor traffic offenses, loitering and drunkenness. **1976** *Australasian Express* 1 Oct. 4/3 Prostitutes are to be given a say in possible changes to laws covering victimless crimes in N.S.W. **1982** *Times* 1 Sept. 3/2 A large amount of victimless, but technical crime. **1983** *Sunday Tel.* 3 July 10/3 If we sent fewer trivial victimless offenders to prison, the numbers in custody could very easily be halved without detriment to public safety.

victi'mology. [ad. F. *victimologie* (B. Mendelsohn 1956, in *Rev. Internat. de Criminol. et de Police Technique* Apr.–June 97/1), f. *victime* VICTIM *sb.*: see -LOGY.] The study of the victims of crime, esp. of the psychological effects on them of their experience. Hence **victi'mologist**.
1958 *New Statesman* 5 July 6/1 We ought to establish a new science of victimology with chairs at the universities, field workers studying the effects rather than the causes of crime, and a special department assessing the impact of sex-crime on women. **1964** *Economist* 1 Feb. 417/1 'Victimology', an unusual aspect of the sociology of murder.

1971 *Time* 5 July 46 Some victimologists contend that rape victims invite attack. **1978** *Practitioner* Feb. 301/1 Any one of these fields of study—stress, coping, captivity, victimology—is a springboard for analysing the particular plight of the victim of terrorism.

† **victi'tation.** *Obs. rare.* [f. L. *victitāre* to subsist (on something), f. *victus* food, sustenance.] The taking of food or nourishment.

1597 A. M. tr. *Guillemeau's Fr. Chirurg.* 51/2 In eatinge and drinckinge, without observinge anye rule of victitation. **1599** —— tr. *Gabelhouer's Bk. Physicke* 155/2 He must observe a good dyet in al his victitations.

vict'lar, obs. form of VICTUALLER.

† **'victless**, *a.* *Obs.*$^{-1}$ [f. L. *vict-us* food: cf. VICTITATION.] Lacking food; hungry, starved.

1615 CHAPMAN *Odyss.* XVII. 285 Why thou vnenuied Swaine, Whither dost thou leade this same victles Leager? This bane of banquets; this most nasty begger?

victor ('vɪktə(r)), *sb.*[1] Forms: *α.* 4- victor, 5 victore, uyctor, 6 *Sc.* wictor. *β.* 4–7 victour (6 *Sc.* wictour), 5 victur, -oure, vyctour(e, -owre. [a. AF. *victor*, *victour* (OF. *victeur*), or L. *victor*, agent-noun f. *vict-*, ppl. stem of *vincĕre* to overcome, conquer.]

1. One who overcomes or vanquishes an adversary; the leader of an army which wins a battle or war. Sometimes *collect.*, the winning army or nation. Also const. *of*.

α. *a* **1340** HAMPOLE *Psalter* xxiii. 1 A bedel þat eftere þe victory cries þat all þe land is þe victors. **1387** TREVISA *Higden* (Rolls) II. 99 Þe Saxons were victors, and eueriche prouince, as he was strengere, made hem kynges. *c* **1400** *Destr. Troy* 2145 Ofte sith hit is sene.. That a victor of a victe is vile ouercomyn. **1448–9** J. METHAM *Wks.* (E.E.T.S.) 52/1403 Yowre welffare and prosperyte Is in my uyage, yff I may uyctor be. **1570** LEVINS *Manip.* 171 A victor, *victor.* **1592** WYRLEY *Armorie, Capitall de Buz* i, Assailant conqueror, this braue English king Triumphant victors his noble offspring. **1606** SHAKS. *Tr. & Cr.* IV. v. 67 What shalbe done To him that victory commands? or doe you purpose, A victor shall be knowne. **1665** MANLEY *Grotius' Low-C. Warres* 235 His Body, when found by the Victors,.. was exposed to publike shame and laughter. **1697** DRYDEN *Æneid* XII. 497 In vain the vanquish'd fly; the victor sends The dead men's weapons at their living friends. **1762** HUME *Hist. Eng.* I. 6 Boadicea herself, rather than fall into the hands of the enraged victor, put an end to her own life by poison. **1781** GIBBON *Decl. & F.* xxx. (1787) III. 161 The Huns.. soon withdrew from the presence of an insulting victor. **1821** SCOTT *Kenilw.* xxxvii, The light yet strong buckler, and the short two-edged sword, the use of which had made them victors of the world. **1841** ELPHINSTONE *Hist. Ind.* II. 567 Two of the surviving brothers soon after came to an open conflict, and the third attacked the victor on the morning after the battle. **1871** R. ELLIS *Catullus* lxiv. 112 Thence in safety, a victor, in height of glory returned.

β. **1387** TREVISA *Higden* (Rolls) I. 87 Þan afterward þey serued þe Macedonyes, when þe Macedoynes were victours in þe est londes. *a* **1400–50** *Alexander* 186 Þan sall þat victoure ȝow venge on ȝour vile fais. **1412–20** LYDG. *Chron. Troy* I. 4321 Þe feld þei han, and ben þat day victours. *c* **1440** *Promp. Parv.* 510/1 Vyctowre, *victor, triumphator.* **1508** DUNBAR *Poems* vii. 20 Welcum invincible victour moste wourthy. **1581** A. HALL *Iliad* v. 78 Thinking that victour now he stoode, thus Pandarus doth braue At the stoute Greeke. **1658** PHILLIPS, *Victour*, an overcomer or Conquerour.

b. *transf.* and *fig.* One who overcomes in any contest or struggle.

a **1400** *Minor Poems fr. Vernon MS.* xxiii. 132 Com to vs wiþ-outen wene, Victor of olde Enemys. *c* **1430** LYDG. *Min. Poems* (Percy Soc.) 97 Verray victor withe his woundes fyve. **1447** BOKENHAM *Seyntys* (Roxb.) 90 Help lady that he.. Of his goostly enmyse may victour be. *c* **1450** CAPGRAVE *Life St. Gilbert* 81 These same maydenes, desyring to be victouris of her kynde & eke of þe world. **1508** DUNBAR *Tua Mariit Wemen* 326, I crew abone that craudone, as cok that wer wictour. **1567** *Gude & Godlie B.* (S.T.S.) 23 Christ,.. Victour of deid and hell. **1638** JUNIUS *Paint. Ancients* 345 Now having obtained the chase, the victor calleth for a knife to take essay. **1687** BOYLE *Martyrd. Theodora* vii. (1703) 104 O admirable contest! where the noble antagonists did not strive for victory, but death,.. that the victor might perish for the vanquished. **1732** POPE *Ep. Bathurst* 313 There, Victor of his health, of fortune, friends, And fame, this lord of useless thousands ends. **1811** SHELLEY *Love* 7 Since withering pain no power possessed,.. Nor time's dread victor, death, confessed. **1865** *Daily Tel.* 31 Oct. 6/5 The silent Victor that meets us all, sooner or later.

†**c.** *Sc.* The dux of a school. *Obs.*

1651 *Caldwell Papers* (Maitl. Cl.) I. 105 To yᵉ shoillmaster and doctor in Glasgow for Wᵐ Mure his candilmas offering, he being victor that year, 20. 0. 0. **1724** R. WODROW *Life J. Wodrow* (1828) 78 The Archbishop Paterson's second son was then in it [the school], and was what we then called victor.

2. *attrib.* (chiefly appositive), passing into *adj.* (cf. VICTORIOUS *a.*). **a.** Of weapons, etc., as ***victor arms, arrow, -banner, -spear, sword.***

1590 SPENSER *F.Q.* II. x. 23 He with his victour sword first opened The bowels of wide Fraunce. **1605** SHAKS. *Lear* V. iii. 132, I protest,.. Despite thy victor-Sword,.. thou art a Traitor. **1726** POPE *Odyss.* XIX. 477 My victor arms Have awed the realms around with dire alarms. *Ibid.* XXIV. 202 Thro' ev'ry ring the victor arrow went. **1776** MICKLE tr. *Camoens' Lusiad* 168 O'er the wild waves the victor-banners flow'd. *Ibid.* 229 The victor-spear One hand employed. **1817** SHELLEY *Rev. Islam* IV. xxv, Why pause the victor swords to seal his overthrow?

b. Of persons, animals, etc., as ***victor brethren, eagle, god, -hand, -head, -hero,*** etc.

c **1640** SHIRLEY *Cont. Ajax & Ulysses* (1659) 128 Upon Deaths purple Altar now, See where the Victor-victim bleeds. **1697** DRYDEN *Virg. Georg.* III. 747 The Victor Horse, forgetful of his Food, The Palm renounces, and abhors the Flood. **1703** POPE *Thebais* 668 To Argos' realms the victor god resorts. *c* **1716** SOMERVILLE *To Addison, Estate Warwicks.*, The victor-host amaz'd, with horror view'd Th' assembling troops. **1717** POPE *Iliad* XII. 257 The victor eagle, whose sinister flight Retards our host. **1730** THOMSON *Sophonisba* II. ii. 7 If she may touch Thy knee, thy purple, and thy victor-hand. **1776** MICKLE tr. *Camoens' Lusiad* 96 On Jordan's bank the victor-hero strode. *Ibid.* 328 The victor-youth the Lusian flag displays. **1814** SCOTT *Lord of Isles* IV. xxx, O Scotland! shall it e'er be mine.. To raise my victor-head, and see Thy hills, thy dales, thy people free? **1845** BAILEY *Festus* (ed. 2) 388, I, it seems, am first Of all my victor brethren to declare The triumph past and coming.

c. Miscellaneous, as ***victor-deed, -pæan, -palm, -pomp, shore, -shout.***

c **1381** CHAUCER *Parl. Foules* 182 The olyue of pes, & ek the dronke vyne, The victor palm, the laurer to deuyne. **1776** MICKLE tr. *Camoens' Lusiad* 171 'Twas his in victor-pomp to bear away The golden apples from Hesperia's shore. **1803** LEYDEN *Scenes Infancy* IV. xviii, The groans of wounded on the blood-red plain, And victor-shouts exulting o'er the slain. **1808** SCOTT *Marmion* III. xxiv, Shouting crews her navy bore, Triumphant, to the victor shore. **1814** —— *Lord of Isles* V. xxxii, Then long and loud the victor-shout From turret and from tower rung out. **1819** KEATS *Otho* I. ii, I wonder not this stranger's victor-deeds So hang upon your spirit. **1885** J. H. DELL *Dawning Grey, Prefatory*, For the leader that shall bring To the field the mightiest forces, shall the victor-pæan ring.

†**3.** ***victor penny***, a fee paid to the schoolmaster by the scholar owning the victorious cock. *Obs.*

1525 *Foundation Stat. Manchester Gram. School* 15 April, [The Schoolmaster shall teach the children] with-oute any money or other reward taking therefor as cokke peny, victor peny, potacion peny or any other except his said stipend.

† **victor**, *sb.*[2] *Obs.* Chiefly *Sc.* Forms: *α.* 4–5 victor, 5 *Sc.* victour, wictour(e, 6 *Sc.* wict-, victore. *β.* 4 victoire, 5 victoyre. [a. OF. *victore* and *victoire*: see VICTORY *sb.*] Victory.

α. **1375** BARBOUR *Bruce* IV. 277 Scho.. bad him till the battale spede, For he suld victor haf but drede. *Ibid.* VIII. 255 .Gif that we may.. Haf victour of our fayis heir. *c* **1375** *Sc. Leg. Saints* XI. (*Simon & Jude*) 176 To knaw hyme & his helpe crafe, be quham þu mycht þe wictoure hafe. *a* **1400–50** *Alexander* 2096 Alexander þe athill.. A-vanced with þe victore & vengid on his faes. **1413** *26 Pol. Poems* xii. 131 Þat haþ victor, wole be euel payed, So many good men ben lest. *c* **1470** HENRY *Wallace* VII. 148 The gold takynnis.. Wictour in armys, that thou sall haiff be grace. **1533** GAU *Richt Vay* 45 Deid is swolit throw wictore. **1549** *Compl. Scot.* Ep. 4, I suld nocht forȝet the tryumphant victore,.. conqueist be the vailȝeant.. kyng of secilie.

β. **1390** GOWER *Conf.* I. 37 Fulofte is sene.. The fieble hath wonne the victoire. *Ibid.* 125 To kepe and drawe into memoire Of his bataille the victoire. **1474** CAXTON *Chesse* II. iv. (1883) 52 Scylla that was Duc of the Romayns wyth oute had many fayr victoyres agaynst the Romayns wyth Inne.

† **'victor**, *v.* *Obs.* [f. VICTOR *sb.*[1]] *trans.* To overcome, vanquish. Chiefly in pa. pple. and ppl. a. **'victored**. Hence † **'victoring** *ppl. a.*

1576 BEDINGFIELD tr. *Cardanus' Comf.* 38 For that neither in victory or victored he would hinder the common wealth. **1594** —— tr. *Machiavelli's Florentine Hist.* (1595) 12 It was condescended among them, to diuide the places victored, by foure parts. **1602** SEGAR *Hon. Mil. & Civ.* III. xii. 124 Whosoeuer is defender.. ought to be reputed victorious if hee be not victored. **1624** A. HOLLAND *Inquis. agst. Paper Persecutors* 3 All the Pamphlets and the Toyes Which I haue seene in hands of Victoring Boyes. **1683** GADBURY in *Wharton's Wks.* Pref., Where the Noble and Valiant Sir Jacob Ashley was unfortunately victor'd, and taken Prisoner.

† **'victorage.** *Sc. Obs.*$^{-1}$ In 5 wictorag. [f. as prec. + -AGE.] Victory.

c **1375** *Sc. Leg. Saints* xxii. (*Laurence*) 138 Fere mare Ioyful wictorag þu sal resawe syne to þi wag.

Victor Charlie ('vɪktə 'tʃɑːlɪ). *U.S. Services' slang.* [f. the communications code-names for the initial letters of *Viet Cong*; cf. *VC* s.v. V 5 b.] = CHARLEY, CHARLIE 8.

1966 *New Yorker* 18 June 135/2 He.. was told about being shot out of a helicopter by Victor Charlie. **1968** *Saturday Night* (Toronto) Aug. 15 [Westmoreland's] men say they have to get them one 'Victor Charlie'. **1982** T. BARLING *Terminate with Prejudice* II. i. 48 Casualties.. was inordinately high. Victor Charlie had too much bushcraft and too much jungle to hide in.

† **'victordom.** *Obs. rare.* [f. as VICTORAGE + -DOM.] The condition of being a victor; victory.

1526 *Pilgr. Perf.* (W. de W. 1531) 135 Innumerable martyrs by the lyght & strengthe of this gyfte had the triumphe & victordome of paynes vnspekable. *a* **1540** BARNES *Wks.* (1573) 278/1 Then will I stand by, and looke on, and see what victordome thou shalt get.

† **'victorer.** *Obs.* Also 6 victorour, victourer. [Extended form of VICTOR *sb.*[1], in common use *c* 1560–1610.] A victor or vanquisher.

1553 BRENDE *Q. Curtius* IV. 57 He that is so juste an enemy, and so merciful a victorour. **1555** EDEN *Decades* (Arb.) 50 Greater commoditie hath therof ensewed to the vanquisshed then the victourers. **1577** B. GOOGE *Heresbach's Husb.* I. (1586) 5 b, The Earth in the meane time reioysing to be torne with a Victorers shaare. **1601** HOLLAND *Pliny* II. 300 The manner was to hang this ridiculous puppet under the chariots of noble victorers riding in triumph. **1631** GOUGE *God's Arrows* III. §71. 314 Like victorers they continued to hold up their banners.

† **'victoress.** *Obs.* [f. VICTOR *sb.*[1] + -ESS. Cf. VICTRESS.] A female victor.

1586 WARNER *Alb. Eng.* II. xi. (1589) 44, I am his Victor, but thy selfe art Victoresse of me. **1590** SPENSER *F.Q.* III. xii. 44 But when the victoresse arriued there,.. Neither of them she found where she them lore. **1624** HEYWOOD *Gunaik.* v. 237 Oh Elphlede mightie both in strength and mind, The dread of men and victoresse of thy kind. **1634** [see VICTRESS, quot. 1601].

‖**victoria**[1] (vɪk'tɔːrɪə). [L. *victōria* (or Sp. and Pg. *victoria*): see VICTORY *sb.*]

1. The word employed as a shout of triumph.

1638 FORD *Lady's Trial* II. i, Steal her away and to her Cast caps and cry *victoria*! **1672** DRYDEN *Assignation* IV. iv, *Victoria, Victoria*! he loves you, madam. **1691** WOOD *Ath. Oxon.* II. 284 The judicious reader.. may easily rout those Troops, which began too soon to cry *victoria*, and thought.. but of dividing the spoil. **1855** KINGSLEY *Westw. Ho!* xxxi, 'There go the rest of them! Victoria!' shouted Cary, as.. every Spaniard set all the sail he could. **1861** GEN. P. THOMPSON *Audi Alt. Part.* III. clxi. 175 The opposite party at the same time made simpletons of themselves by throwing up their caps and crying 'victoria'.

transf. **1863** *Bradford Advertiser* 18 July 5/2, If you conquered, all the post-horns in Europe were set to sound 'Victoria!'

2. A figure of the goddess Victory. *rare*$^{-1}$.

a **1700** EVELYN *Diary* 6 May 1645, The stamp of the Roman *Denarius* varied;.. if with a Victoria, so nam'd.

Victoria[2] (vɪk'tɔːrɪə). [The name of the Queen of Great Britain and Ireland, etc., from 1837 to 1901, employed attributively or by itself as a designation of various things.]

1. A light, low, four-wheeled carriage having a collapsible hood, with seats (usually) for two persons and an elevated seat in front for the driver.

[**1844** *Art Union Jrnl.* VI. 238 A calèche.. which the French have named after Queen Victoria.] **1870** *Pall Mall G.* 24 Aug. 11, I have taken a victoria and driven to the Porte Maillot to watch the engineers fell the trees in the Bois de Boulogne. **1876** MARY M. GRANT *Sun-Maid* xi, A victoria is the prettiest carriage a lady can possible drive in. **1886** *Pall Mall G.* 10 May 3/2 We are threatened with an inundation of new cabs and victorias for the coming season.

attrib. **1903** *Motor. Ann.* 258 The motor-car best suited to India would be that.. with a canopy—or, better still, a victoria top.

b. A sovereign minted in the reign of Queen Victoria.

1870 E. G. E. WARD *Jrnl.* 9 Nov. in D. P. Carew *Many Years, Many Girls* (1967) i. 35 Let a packet of the bright, solid, sell-milled 'Victorias' reach you, and see if you do not deem them 'golden angels'! **1958** [see PECORINO].

2. *Bot.* A gigantic species of water-lily, *Victoria regia*, indigenous to South America.

1846 LINDLEY *Veg. Kingd.* 411 Floating plants.. on the continent of South America.. are represented by Victoria... Victoria, the most gigantic and beautiful of water plants, is.. called Water Maize in South America. **1852** *Phil. Trans.* CXLII. 289 The specimen of Victoria which flowered in the Gardens of the Royal Botanic Society. **1866** *Treas. Bot.* 1215 The *Victoria*.. has delighted.. thousands, by the size of its leaves and the beauty and fragrance of its flowers.

attrib. **1861** BENTLEY *Man. Bot.* 445 The plant is commonly known in this country as the Victoria Water-lily. **1880** BESSEY *Botany* 558 *Victoria regia*, the Victoria Lily of the Amazon Valley in South America.

3. *Astr.* One of the minor planets, discovered by Hind in 1850.

1851 J. R. HIND *Solar System* 91 The name selected for the twelfth member [of the extra-zodiacal group] is Victoria. *Ibid.* 92 The discovery of Victoria.. was quickly followed by that of another small planetary body. **1868** LOCKYER *Elem. Astron.* 328.

4. A variety of domestic pigeon.

1879 L. WRIGHT *Pigeon Keeper* 208 Victorias are simply Hyacinths of a lighter shade. **1881** LYELL *Fancy Pigeons* 97 These varieties.. have been promiscuously named Hyacinths, Victorias and Porcelains in our pigeon literature.

b. ***Victoria crown(ed) pigeon***, a queen's pigeon (QUEEN *sb.* 15 b).

c **1882** *Cassell's Nat. Hist.* IV. 127.

5. A variety of plum characterized by its luscious flavour and rich red colour. Also *attrib.*

1860 R. HOGG *Fruit Manual* 256 Denyer's Victoria... Skin bright red on the side next the sun, but pale red on the shaded side. **1883** H. DRUMMOND *Nat. Law in Spir. W.* (1884) 364 He arranges his.. plums in his shop window. He may tell me a magnum bonum from a Victoria. **1883** *19th Cent.* Nov. 870 Some sixteen years ago.. I planted two Victoria plums. *Ibid.*, A Victoria plum tree.

6. A kind of woollen dress material.

1891 *Times* 26 Oct. 4/2 The parcels of miscellaneous goods.. have consisted of blue victorias, meltons in all colours, brown venetians.

7. *attrib.* **a.** ***Victoria Cross***, a British military and naval decoration bestowed for conspicuous bravery in battle. (Abbreviated V.C.) ***Victoria Day***, the anniversary of the birthday of Queen Victoria, May 24. (Also called *Empire Day.*) ***Victoria sandwich***, a sponge cake consisting of two layers of sponge sandwiched together with a jam filling; also ***Victoria sponge*** (***sandwich***). (The ingredients and style of presentation have not always been the same since the mid-19th century.)

1856 *Royal Warrant* in *Lond. Gaz.* 5 Feb. 410/2 The distinction shall be styled and designated 'The Victoria Cross', and shall consist of a Maltese Cross of Bronze, with

Our Royal Crest in the centre, and underneath which an escroll bearing this inscription 'For Valour'. **1863** CHAMBERS *Bk. Days* I. 319/1 The 1st of March, 1857, is one among many days associated with the bestowal of the Victoria Cross upon heroic soldiers and sailors. **1901** *Scotsman* 28 Feb. 7/4 A bill was introduced in the Canadian parliament to make Victoria day—May 24th— a permanent public holiday throughout Canada. **1861** MRS. BEETON *Bk. Househ. Managem.* 751 Victoria sandwiches... Spread one half of the cake with a layer of nice preserve, place over it the other half. **1902** *Little Folks* LV. 448/2 Auntie Kate told her cook to make some cakes,..some little cakes,..and some Victoria sandwich. **1976** *Burnham-on-Sea Gaz.* 20 Apr., Victoria sandwich. **1934** *Woman's Jrnl. Home Cookery* 150 (*heading*) Victoria sponge with grated pineapple. **1951** *Good Housek. Home Encycl.* 701/2 *Victoria sponge sandwich*, a sponge made with fat, which enables it to keep moist longer than the fatless type. **1980** D. CLARK *Poacher's Bag* v. 121 He..was..handing round wedges of Victoria sponge.

b. Misc., as ***Victoria black, blue, Court, crape, frilling, green, lawn*** (see quots.).

1888 JACOBI *Printers' Voc.* 152 **Victoria black*, a fancy black-letter character. **1891** *Cent. Dict.*, *Victoria blue. **1895** *Buck's Handbk. Med. Sci.* IX. 429 *Victoria Blue*..is a brilliant and useful nuclear stain. **1899** CAGNEY *Jaksch's Clin. Diagnosis* x. 437 Staining with alcoholic solution of Victoria-blue. **1847** MCCULLOCH *Brit. Emp.* (ed. 3) II. 220 The principal sheriff..visiting the county..for the purpose of holding statutory, registration, and small debt, commonly called **Victoria* Courts. **1877** *Encycl. Brit.* VI. 553/1 A very successful imitation of real crape is made in Manchester of cotton yarn, and sold under the name of *Victoria crape. **1882** CAULFEILD & SAWARD *Dict. Needlew.* 515/1 **Victoria frilling*,..a description of cotton cambric Frilling. **1890** WEBSTER, *Victoria green. **1934** H. HILER *Notes Technique Painting* ii. 117 *Victoria green*, a potter's pigment, introduced by William Burton, but unfortunately not current, though it is absolutely permanent. *a* **1977** *Harrison Mayer Ltd. Catal.* 38/1 Body slip and glaze stains..colour.. Victoria Green. **1882** CAULFEILD & SAWARD *Dict. Needlew.* 515/1 **Victoria lawn*,..a description of muslin..employed as a lining for skirts of dresses. **1851** *Catal. Gt. Exhib.* 495 Cloakings:—Frazer tartan,..*Victoria [tartan], Royal Stewart, Forbes, and Gordon. *Ibid.* 491/1 Silk and worsted and cotton and worsted *Victoria velvet damasks.

† **vic'torial**, *a.* and *sb. Obs.* [a. OF. *victorial* or ad. late L. *victōriāl-is*, f. L. *victōria* VICTORY *sb.* So It. *vittoriale.*]

A. *adj.* Of or belonging to victory; victorious.

c **1460** *Wisdom* 1119 in *Macro Plays* 72 Now ye haue receyuyde þe crownnys victoryall To regne in blys withowtyn ende! **1501** in *Dunbar's Poems* lxxxviii. 38 London,.. thy Tour founded of old May be the hous of Mars victoryall. **1513** BRADSHAW *St. Werburge* II. 298 They kneled all downe with mycle reuerence, Salutynge the shryne with honour victoriall. **1611** COTGR., *Victorial*, Victoriall, of or belonging to victorie. **1649** ROBERTS *Clavis Bibl.* 114 This Song is a Triumphant Victorial Song, or Song for Victory that Israel had over Sisera's Host. **1653** URQUHART *Rabelais* II. xxvii. (1694) 163 Pantagruel for an eternal Memorial wrote this victorial ditton.

B. *sb. pl.* Games in honour of victory.

1657 THORNLEY tr. *Longus' Daphnis & Chloe* 83 They carows'd, and danc'd, and celebrated victorials.

Vic'torian, *a.*[1] [f. the name of *Victorius*, an ecclesiastic of the 5th century.] ***Victorian cycle, period*** (see quot. 1728 and DIONYSIAN *a.* 3).

1728 CHAMBERS *Cycl.* s.v. *Period*, *Victorian Period*, an Interval of 532 Julian Years, which elaps'd, the new and full Moons return on the same Day of the Julian Year. **1905** J. B. BURY *St. Patrick* App. 372 The Celtic Church in Britain and Ireland never adopted the Victorian cycle.

Victorian (vɪk'tɔərɪən), *a.*[2] and *sb.*[1] [f. VICTORIA[2].]

A. *adj.* **1.** Of or belonging to, designating, or typical of the reign of Queen Victoria (1837–1901).

1839 *Athenæum* 2 Nov. 825/1 Perhaps the Annean authors, though inferior to the Elizabethans, are, on a general summation of merits, no less superior to the latter-Georgian and Victorian. **1850** E. P. HOOD *Age & its Architects* ii. 71 The Victorian Commonwealth is the most wonderful picture on the face of the earth. **1875** STEDMAN *Vict. Poets* i. 6 The significant likeness between the Alexandrian and Victorian eras. **1880** C. H. PEARSON in *Victorian Rev.* I. 544 The changes..were more radical than any programme of Victorian Liberalism suggests. **1897** MARY KINGSLEY *W. Africa* 591 An old-fashioned petticoat such as an early Victorian-age lady would have worn. **1907** MISS F. F. MONTRÉSOR *Burning Torch* 426 The furniture.. was adorned in a heavy Early Victorian style.

2. *fig.* Resembling or typified by the attitudes supposedly characteristic of the Victorian era; prudish, strict; old-fashioned, out-dated.

1934 in WEBSTER. **1950** G. B. SHAW *Farfetched Fables* 72 He was helping the movement against Victorian prudery in a very practical way as a nudist. **1965** M. SPARK *Mandelbaum Gate* vi. 157 In an emergency, one can't be Victorian about things, you know. **1977** P. G. WINSLOW *Witch Hill Murder* II. xvi. 217 He was becoming rather heavily paternal to Linda. A Victorian parent. **1977** *Time Out* 17–23 June 5/2 Elsewhere in the files is an even worse example of what workers described as 'Victorian industrial relations'.

3. Special collocations: ***Victorian Gothic*** adj., designating the style of architecture typical of the Gothic Revival (see GOTHIC *a.* 1 d); freq. *absol.* as *sb.*; ***Victorian-Italianate*** adj., designating a style of architecture revived in the nineteenth century in imitation of that of the Italian Renaissance.

1910 H. G. WELLS *New Machiavelli* (1911) I. iii. 59 A new church in the Victorian Gothic. **1934** T. E. TALLMADGE *Story Eng. Archit.* (1935) viii. 256 This structure [*sc.* the Albert Memorial] typifies to the last degree the Victorian Gothic style. **1961** *Times* 18 May 16/6 This small jewel of Victorian-Gothic architecture. **1980** 'L. BLACK' *Eve of Wedding* ii. 14 A huge red-brick mansion on three floors, heavy Victorian Gothic, a massive door in the centre of the front façade, leaded windows. **1963** A. LUBBOCK *Austral. Roundabout* 97 The public buildings are mostly in Victorian-Italianate style, pillared and porticoed; painted white, or in Edinburgh-rock colours. **1982** S. RADLEY *Talent for Destruction* vi. 40 The Victorian Italianate tower of the town hall.

B. *sb.* **1.** A person, esp. an author, who lived in the reign of Queen Victoria.

1876 *N. Amer. Rev.* CXXIII. 219 We can scarcely avoid calling him [Browning] the strongest, truest poet of the Victorians. **1886** F. HARRISON *Choice Bks.* iii. 61 He [Tennyson], alone of the Victorians, has definitely entered the immortal group of our English poets.

2. a. An article of furniture from the time of Queen Victoria.

1905 ELIN. GLYN *Viciss. Evangeline* 189, I shall have the suite..done up with pale green, and burn all the Early Victorians.

b. *U.S.* A house built during the reign of Queen Victoria.

1959 *House Beautiful* June 100 (*heading*) The virtues of a Victorian. **1978** J. GORES *Gone, no Forwarding* (1979) ix. 56 The house was an old Victorian, a Queen Anne which had been converted into rental units.

Hence **Vic'torianist**; **Vic'torianize** *v.*; **Vic'torianized** *ppl. a.*

1905 *Speaker* 8 April 32/2 They Victorianise his [Bunyan's] spelling and parade his Calvinism on shiny paper. **1940** *Burlington Mag.* Apr. 127/2 The church had been so thoroughly 'Victorianised' that the discovery was all the more unexpected. **1946** J. W. DAY *Harvest Adventure* ii. 27 The gatehouse of Butley..owes its renaissance from a Victorianized ruin to a lovely house, full of medieval grace, to Dr Montague Rendall. **1970** *Guardian* 1 Oct. 11/8 Gillian Avery is an eminent Victorianist. She has written..neo-Victorian children's books..; she has edited a series of Victorian revivals. **1974** *Times* 22 Apr. 14/3, I amused myself by guessing which fellow-passengers were members of the Victorian Society. The man opposite..did not quite fit my vision of a Victorianist. **1976** I. MURDOCH *Henry & Cato* I. 47 The tall Victorianized sash windows, which also served as doors, reached down to the ground. **1979** *Guardian* 3 Sept. 2/5 The building is unusually well preserved because it was never Victorianised or modernised. **1982** *UCT Studies in English* (Univ. Cape Town) Oct. 68 Writing as a Classicist and Victorianist, Jenkyns shows the enormous extent to which Hellenism influenced the generations of Victorians between about 1832 and the First World War.

Vic'torian, *a.*[3] and *sb.*[2] [See def.] **A.** *adj.* Of or belonging to, native to, the state (formerly colony) of Victoria in Australia (named in 1851 after Queen Victoria).

In recent use occurring in a number of plant-names, as ***Victorian dogwood, laurel, lilac, parsnip.***

1857–65 (*title*), The Victorian Hansard; containing the debates..of the Legislative Council and Assembly of the Colony of Victoria. **1867** *Chambers's Encycl.* IX. 787/1 The Victorian samples [of wheat] at the last Great Exhibition ranked amongst the very best. **1889** MAIDEN *Useful Pl.* 449 *Eucalyptus globulus*... [Called] 'Tasmanian' or 'Victorian Blue Gum' from the colour of its foliage.

B. *sb.* A native or inhabitant of Victoria.

1862 *Temple Bar* Sept. 286 The Victorians went pluckily in for their second innings. **1901** A. W. JOSE *Australasia* x. 152 They are men of Melbourne, Brisbane, or Adelaide rather than Victorians or Queenslanders. **1943** K. TENNANT *Ride on Stranger* v. 47 All in the carriage were staunch Victorians, and his scathing references to the climate of Sydney were greeted with approval. **1973** *Sun-Herald* (Sydney) 26 Aug. 28/2 It's 41 years since Phar Lap died, but he lives on with a new generation of Victorians.

Victoriana (vɪktɔərɪ'ɑːnə). [f. VICTORIAN *a.*[2]: see -IANA.] **1.** Matters relating to the Victorian period; attitudes characteristic of that time.

1918 E. POUND in *Future* Oct. 265/1 For most of us, the odour of defunct Victoriana is so unpleasant..that we are content to leave the past where we find it. **1931** *Times Lit. Suppl.* 23 Apr. 326/2 This book—Victoriana. A symposium of Victorian Wisdom. **1960** *Time* 8 Jan. 13/5, I think Shakespearian production is bogged down in a mire of Victoriana in this country. **1961** *Guardian* 21 Apr. 6/3 She provides many interesting domestic details for students of Victoriana. **1977** *S. Wales Echo* 18 Jan., Mr. Litterick added: 'He was talking straight Victoriana. That statement is straight out of Queen Victoria's age—it is arrogance.'

2. Objects, as furniture, ornaments, etc., made in the Victorian period; also, buildings or architecture of that era.

1940 *Illustr. London News* 11 May 640 (*caption*) The latest vogue in 'Victoriana'. Glass paper-weights to be sold at Sotheby's. **1947** N. MARSH *Final Curtain* xiii. 197 The terrifying Victoriana within. **1958** *Listener* 12 June 973/1 Victoriana is now the fashion in furniture and house decoration. **1958, 1959** [see BETJEMAN]. **1968** *Canad. Antiques Collector* July 20/1 Whether the taste be for pine, Sheraton mahogany, or Victoriana, a lovely bouquet can be arranged to enhance antiques. **1978** *Lancashire Life* Mar. 71/1 There was one notable omission—namely, that of the dear old Princes Theatre. This was, prior to modernisation in 1932, a perfect specimen of Victoriana.

Victorianism (vɪk'tɔərɪənɪz(ə)m). [f. VICTORIAN *a.*[2] and *sb.*[1] + -ISM.] Victorian attitudes or style; (an example of) that which is characteristic of the Victorian era.

1905 *Westm. Gaz.* 2 Feb. 4/2 The turban..is, of course, an early Victorianism. **1913** CHESTERTON *Victorian Age in Lit.* iii. 196 The real revolts that broke up Victorianism at last. **1913** MRS. H. WARD *Coryston Family* xi. 216 A heavy gold setting, whereof the Early Victorianism cried aloud. **1942** J. LEES-MILNE *Jrnl.* 5 Feb. in *Ancestral Voices* (1975) 16 Others took the absurd view that this important house is once again pure Jacobean since the Victorianisms have been purged by the fire, which was the best thing that could have happened. **1974** M. TIPPETT *Moving into Aquarius* 37 The two ways forward out of Victorianism seem to be equally dispiriting. **1978** *Dædalus* Fall 72 He jettisoned much of what we think of as Victorianism, but not on the whole, the values of his family, school, and university.

Vic'torianly, *adv.* [f. VICTORIAN *a.*[2] + -LY[2].] In a Victorian manner or style; also, prudishly, formally.

1917 *Duke of Norfolk Notebk.* 112 In conventional rooms, furnished Victorianly. **1933** C. WILLIAMS *Shadows of Ecstasy* i. 22 The clothes were late Victorian; the whole picture was Victorianly idyllic. **1940** E. F. BENSON *Final Edition* xii. 249 No doubt this boom in promiscuity was partly due to reaction, for an undue reticence had been Victorianly observed about sexual instincts. **1967** A. WILSON *No Laughing Matter* III. 250 This..conventionally, almost Victorianly clad huge body.

† **vic'toriat(e.** *Obs. rare.* [ad. L. *victōriāt-us*, f. *victōria* VICTORY *sb.*] A Roman silver coin stamped with the image of Victory, equal in value to half a denarius. Also *attrib.*

1601 HOLLAND *Pliny* II. 182 If this hearbe be taken in wine to the weight of a victoriat peece of silver, *i.* halfe a Romane denier, it..stoppeth the course of a new cough. **1657** W. RAND tr. *Gassendi's Life Peiresc* VI. 205 They make so frequent mention of Coines and Weights, as Talents, Sicles,..Victoriates, Sesterces. **1771** *Phil. Trans.* LXI. 490 What is now called the Victoriat, was coined by the Clodian Law.

victorine ('vɪktəriːn), *sb.*[1] [? f. VICTOR-IA[2] + -INE[4].] A kind of fur tippet worn by ladies, fastened in front of the neck and having two loose ends hanging down.

1848 GEO. ELIOT *Let.* 31 May (1954) I. 263 We do not find it too warm, however, for I have even felt the want of my Victorine. **1849** *Ann. Reg.* 111 The several articles now produced, a bonnet, a fur victorine, &c. **1862** *Catal. Internat. Exhib., Brit.* II. No. 4502, Manufacturer of self-fasteners for victorines and mantles. **1881** MISS C. M. YONGE *Lads & Lasses Langley* i. 47 The first prize was a lovely fur victorine. **1902** *Delineator* Dec. 614/1 The Victorine and collarette are again promised favour.

victorine ('vɪktəriːn), *sb.*[2] and *a.* [ad. F. *Victorin*, f. the name of the monastery of St. *Victor* near Paris.] **a.** *sb.* One or other of the founders or adherents of the type of mysticism developed at St. Victor in the 12th and 13th centuries. **b.** *adj.* Of or pertaining to the mysticism of St. Victor.

1881 *Encycl. Brit.* XII. 583/2 The art of the Victorine school was carried to its greatest perfection by Adam of St. Victor. **1882–3** *Schaff's Encycl. Relig. Knowl.* II. 1603 There is a palpable connection..between the pseudo-Dionysian writings and the Victorines. **1886** C. BIGG *Christian Platonists of Alexandria* v. 189 Thus Origen..became also the spiritual ancestor of Bernard, the Victorines, and the author of the *De Imitatione*.

victorious (vɪk'tɔərɪəs), *a.* Also 5–6 victoriouse, -yous, -ius (6 -yus); 5–6 vyctoryous(e, 6 -ious. [a. AF. *victorious* (= OF. and F. *victorieux*) or ad. L. (ante- and post-class.) *victōriōs-us*, f. *victōria* VICTORY *sb.* So Sp. and Pg. *victorioso*, It. *vittorioso*.]

1. Having gained victory or obtained supremacy as victor; triumphant over adversaries or rivals; successful in any contest or struggle: **a.** Of persons or an army. Also const. *over*.

c **1400** *Destr. Troy* 1101 Hit was neuer herd..In any coste where ye come, but ye were clene victorius. **1432–50** tr. *Higden* (Rolls) IV. 171 This Mitridates apperede ever moore ..victoryous after that þe noble consulles of the Romanes.. hade victory of hym. **1474** CAXTON *Chesse* II. iv. (1883) 53 Be mercyfull to them wyth whom we haue ben victorious. **1535** COVERDALE *Eccl*us. xviii. 1 God onely is righteous, & remayneth a victorious kynge for euer. **1546** in *Eng. Gilds* (1870) 197 The most valiant and victorius kinge,..kinge Edward. **1596** NASHE *Saffron-Walden* Wks. (Grosart) III. 183 The victorioust Captaines and Warriours, the inuinciblest Cæsars and Conquerors. **1617** MORYSON *Itin.* I. 39 With much wonder that shee..was so victorious against the Spaniards. **1667** MILTON *P.L.* II. 997 Heav'n Gates Pourd out by millions her victorious Bands Pursuing. *a* **1727** NEWTON *Chronol. Amended* iv. (1728) 299 They led their victorious armies against the King of Egypt. **1757** tr. *Keysler's Trav.* III. 309 Giacomo da Pesaro,..victorious over the Turks in war, and over himself in peace. **1781** COWPER *Table-t.* 473 Vengeance at last pours down upon their coast, A long despis'd, but now victorious, host. **1837** J. STERLING *Ess.*, etc. (1848) I. 176 Montaigne..yet had honesty and warmth of soul to see in Socrates a victorious witness for the..lastingness of truth. **1840** KEIGHTLEY *Rom. Empire* II. vi. 246 Victorious over all his rivals,..Aurelian celebrated a triumph with unusual magnificence. **1864** PUSEY *Lect. Daniel* ii. 60 The young monarch..had already shown himself..energetic and victorious.

b. *transf.* Of things.

c **1386** CHAUCER *Man of Law's T.* 358 Victorious tre, proteccioun of trewe, That oonly were worthy for to bere The kyng of heven. *a* **1586** SIDNEY *Arcadia* III. xxii. (1904) 485 Love, be ashamed to be called Love: cruell Hate..is victorious over thee. **1667** MILTON *P.L.* II. 142 Th' Ethereal mould Incapable of stain would soon..purge off the baser fire Victorious. **1697** DRYDEN *Virg. Georg.* II. 420 The smouldering flame the trunk receives; Ascending thence, it ..At length victorious to the top aspires. **1781** COWPER *Conversat.* 320 Now the distemper, spite of draught or pill, Victorious seem'd. **1889** J. B. BURY *Hist. Later Rom. Emp.* II. ix. I. 185 Julian's championship of the dying cause furthered the victorious creed.

2. Of, belonging to, or characterized by victory; producing victory; emblematic of victory.

1490 CAXTON *Eneydos* xvi. 62 He shulde be dygne..to obteyne by bataylles the conqueste vyctoryouse of the.. empyre of Ytalye. *a* **1513** FABYAN *Chron.* cxlvii. (1533) 78 For the whyche vyctoryous acte, the sayde Charlys obteynyd a surname, and was called..Carolus Martellus. **1596** SPENSER *F.Q.* VI. iv. 36 As their victorious deedes haue often showen, Being with fame through many Nations blowen. **1606** SHAKS. *Ant. & Cl.* IV. ii. 43, I hope well of to morrow, and will leade you, Where rather Ile expect victorious life, Then death, and Honor. *c* **1630** MILTON *At a Solemn Musick* 14 The Cherubick host..With those just Spirits that wear victorious Palms. **1712–4** POPE *Rape Lock* III. 104 Sudden, these honours shall be snatch'd away, And curs'd for ever this victorious day. **1791** COWPER *Iliad* VIII. 331 And I will give to thy victorious hand, After my own, the noblest recompense. **1829** SCOTT *Guy M.* Introd., He had not power to explain the assurance of pardon which he continued to assert, or to name the victorious name on which he trusted. **1831** —— *Ct. Rob.* iv, It now became a serious and doubtful question whether our victorious eagles might be able to penetrate any farther into the country of the enemy. **1847** MRS. A. KERR *Ranke's Hist. Servia* 95 They who had borne victorious arms against the Turks.

victoriously (vɪk'təʊrɪəslɪ), *adv.* [f. prec. + -LY².] In a victorious manner; triumphantly.

1502 *Ord. Crysten Men* (W. de W. 1506) v. vi. N N ij b, Of as moche that they ben escaped the more vyctoryously. *a* **1513** FABYAN *Chron.* VI. clxxvii. 175 He..bare hym so victoryously agayne the Danys that he forced theym to obey to all theyr former promyse and condycions. **1534** *Act 26 Hen. VIII*, c. 3 §1 His majestie hathe moste victoriously.. defendyd and governyd this his Realme. **1626** GOUGE *Serm. Dignity Chivalry* §6 [They] waged many battels valiantly and victoriously. **1655** FULLER *Ch. Hist.* II. viii. §7 All whom he is said victoriously to have vanquished. **1718** POPE *Iliad* XII. Argt., Hector..enters at the Head of his Troops, who victoriously pursue the Grecians even to their Ships. **1755** JOHNSON, *Triumphantly*,..victoriously; with success. **1827** DE QUINCEY *Last Days Kant* Wks. III. 105 Over all which the benignity and nobility of his nature mount.. victoriously to the last. **1884** *Manch. Exam.* 8 April 5/1 The Bill..in due course..will be sent victoriously to the House of Lords.

victoriousness (vɪk'təʊrɪəsnɪs). [f. as prec. + -NESS.] The state or quality of being victorious.

1705 tr. *Bosman's Guinea* 4 Several Authors have represented Guinea as a Mighty Kingdom, whose Prince by his Victoriousness had subdued numerous Countries. **1805** A. KNOX *Rem.* (1834) I. 38, I will add another instance of Christian victoriousness. **1851** J. H. NEWMAN *Cath. in Eng.* 369, I have an intense feeling in me about the power and victoriousness of truth. **1876** M. ARNOLD *Last Ess. Ch.* (1877) 144 No one has spoken more truly..of the natural victoriousness of virtue.

† **'victorize,** *v. Obs. rare.* [f. VICTOR *sb.*¹ + -IZE.] **a.** *trans.* To make victorious. **b.** *intr.* To win the victory *for* one.

1614 SYLVESTER *Bethulia's Rescue* VI. 189 Most of all did Ammon's Prince admire God's dreadfull Judgement: and to scape his ire, Who Israel thus, of vanquisht, victoriz'd. **1641** J. JACKSON *True Evang. T.* II. 106 Christ Jesus..was a Lyon, but it was to victorize for us, not to prey upon us.

victor ludorum ('vɪktər luː'dɔːrəm). [L., = victor of the games.] The overall champion in a sports contest (usu. at a school or college); the championship itself. Also *transf.* and *fig.*

1901 J. H. GRAY in W. B. Thomas *Athletics* v. 103 The sack race was no longer a consolation race, for Mr. Thornton the *victor ludorum* is returned as the winner. **1926** H. M. ABRAHAMS *Athletics* xiii. 114 There is far too much of this *victor ludorum* and champion athlete business at all schools. **1950** [see RUNNING *vbl. sb.* 2 e (*b*)]. **1963** A. HOWARD in Sissons & French *Age of Austerity* i. 30 Labour, as the electoral *victor ludorum*, was collecting its long-coveted trophies. **1966** *Listener* 28 July 144/1 Last week's *victor ludorum* was undoubtedly 'Rendezvous with Death'..the story of the sinking of the Lusitania. *Ibid.* 27 Oct. 617/1 Ian outshone..generations of Etonians..being Victor Ludorum two years running, the only boy in living memory to win that honour. **1980** 'T. HINDE' *Sir Henry & Sons* xiii. 104 The school honour-board inscribed with the names of the winners of the Victor Ludorum.

† **'victorship.** *Obs. rare.* [f. VICTOR *sb.*¹] The position of a victor; the chief place.

1612 BRINSLEY *Lud. Lit.* 281 To haue a disputation for the victorship once euery quarter of the yeare. *Ibid.*, To incourage them, and all the rest of them by their ensample to striue at length to come vnto the Victorshippe.

victory ('vɪktərɪ), *sb.* Forms: 4–7 victorie (4 uict-, 4–5 vittorie, 6 *Sc.* wictorie, -orrie), victorye, 4– victory (5 *Sc.* wictory); 4–6 vyktorye (4 fyctorye), vyctory (6 vyctorie); 4–5 vict-, 4 wict-, vikt-, 5 vittori. [a. AF. and OF. *victorie* (var. of OF. and F. *victoire*), ad. L. *victōria*, f. *victor* VICTOR *sb.*¹ Cf. Sp. and Pg. *victoria*, It. *vittoria*.]

1. The position or state of having overcome an enemy or adversary in combat, battle, or war; supremacy or superiority achieved as the result of armed conflict.

a. With *the*, as in the phr. *to have* (*get, win*) *the victory*. Also const. *of* (an enemy, etc.).

13.. *K. Alis.* 7663 (Laud MS.), Of troye was þerinne al þe story, Hou Gregeis hadden þe victory. *c* **1330** *Arth. & Merl.* 3370 (Kölbing), He þonked þe king of glorie, þat him hadde ȝouen þe victorie, To ouercomen his fomen. **1387** TREVISA *Higden* (Rolls) II. 167 Þese men..beeþ i-woned to haue the victorie and þe maistrie in euerich fiȝt. *c* **1400** *Destr. Troy* 6134 Our goddis the gouerne, & soche grace lene, þat þou the victorie wyn, thi worship to saue. *c* **1400** MAUNDEV. (Roxb.) ii. 5 When any man had þe victory of his enmy. *c* **1420** LYDG. *Assembly of Gods* 1011 To wete whyche of hem shuld haue the victory. *Ibid.* 1790 Thus they contynu fyght for the victory. *c* **1440** *Gesta Rom.* iv. 9 (Harl. MS.), So þis yong knyȝt..fought with the enemeys, and wan þe victorie. **1509** HAWES *Past. Pleas.* xxxvi. (Percy Soc.) 190, I..for her sake shalbe invincible Of this great monster to have the victory. **1535** COVERDALE *Dan.* vii. 21, I behelde, and the same horne made battail agaynst the sayntes, yee and gat the victory off them. **1592** KYD *Span. Trag.* I. ii. 64 In all this turmoyle, three long houres and more, The victory to neither part inclinde. **1611** BIBLE *2 Macc.* xii. 11 Whereupon there was a very sore battell; but Iudas side.. got the victory. **1647** HEXHAM I. s.v., To carrie away the victorie. **1666** PEPYS *Diary* 29 July, A letter from Sir W. Coventry tells me that we have the victory. **1737** L. CLARKE *Hist. Bible* (1740) I. IX. 580 For Lathyrus having gotten the Victory, pursued it to the utmost. **1777** BRAND *Pop. Antiq.* 374 This so encouraged the Grecians, that they fought strenuously, and obtained the Victory over the Persians. **1811** G. BRUCE *Poems & Songs* 19 To him..Wha..can the victory bestow On those, who to his precepts bow.

b. Without article.

1375 BARBOUR *Bruce* I. 473 With few folk thai had wictory Off mychty kingis. *Ibid.* III. 224 Scipio..has off the templis tane The armys..In name off wictory offerryt thar. **1398** TREVISA *Barth. De P.R.* v. xxiii. (Bodl. MS.), Þe cok crowiþ after bataile & victorie. **1412–20** LYDG. *Chron. Troy* I. 3868 Nor in armys conquest nor victorie Ben not assured vp-on multitude. **1457** HARDYNG *Chron.* in *Eng. Hist. Rev.* Oct. (1912) 748 Of his fose he had ay vyctory. **1526** *Pilgr. Perf.* (W. de W. 1531) 15 By the whiche they crucifye the worlde, and hath victory of it. **1535** COVERDALE *Ps.* lxxxviii. 43 Thou hast taken awaye the strength of his swerde, and geuest him not victory in the battayll. **1593** SHAKS. *3 Hen. VI*, IV. i. 147 Why so: then am I sure of Victorie. Now therefore let vs hence. **1654–66** EARL ORRERY *Parthen.* (1676) 515 Surena covered with Blood and Victory came to my Chamber. **1788** GIBBON *Decl. & F.* xliii. IV. 282 Victory is the fruit of moral as well as military virtue. **1791** COWPER *Iliad* XVII. 681 For him Jove leads to victory. **1839** JAMES *Louis XIV*, I. 144 In following up the flying squadrons of Grammont and Chabot, [he] suffered victory to escape from his hands. **1847** GROTE *Greece* II. xxxi. IV. 229 Victory still continued on the side of Athens. **1881** F. W. H. MYERS *Wordsworth* 80 When in victory..Nelson passed away.

c. *personif.*

1563 B. GOOGE *Eglogs*, etc. (Arb.) 124 In fyne lo Victorye at hande.., Bent for to spoyle our Foes of Fame. **1594** SHAKS. *Rich. III*, v. iii. 79 Fortune, and Victory sit on thy Helme. **1667** MILTON *P.L.* VI. 762 At his right hand Victorie Sate Eagle-wing'd. **1783** CRABBE *Village* II. 152 Victory seems to die now thou art dead. **1820** KEATS *Hyperion* II. 342 That was before we knew the winged thing, Victory, might be lost, or might be won. **1885** *Harper's Mag.* April 819/2 He..has now fallen in the arms of victory.

d. Used interjectionally as an expression of triumph or encouragement. (Cf. VICTORIA¹ I.)

1591 SHAKS. *1 Hen. VI*, IV. vi. 1 Saint George, and Victory; fight Souldiers, fight. **1593** —— *3 Hen. VI*, v. i. 113 Lords to the field: Saint George, and Victorie. **1681** FLAVEL *Meth. Grace* xxviii. 479 The day of a believer's death is better than the day of his birth. Never till then, do we put off our armour, sheath our sword, and cry victory, victory. **1817** SHELLEY *Rev. Islam* v. Song vi, Victory, Victory to the prostrate nations! **1821** —— *Hellas* 948 Victory! Victory! Russia's famished eagles Dare not to prey beneath the crescent's light.

2. An instance or occasion of overcoming an adversary in battle, etc.; a triumph gained by force of arms.

Cadmean, Pyrrhic victory: see those words. *moral victory*: see MORAL *a.* 7 c.

13.. *Sir Beues* (A.) 2500 Ofte he þankede þe king in glori Of is grace & is viktori. *a* **1340** HAMPOLE *Psalter* xxiii. 1 A bedel, þat eftere þe victory cries þat al þe land is þe victors. *c* **1385** CHAUCER *L.G.W.* Prol. 22 These olde aprouede storyis Of holynesse, of regnys, of victoryis, Of loue, of hate [etc.]. *c* **1430** LYDG. *Min. Poems* (Percy Soc.) 3 Lyke for Davyd aftyr his victory Reyjoyssed whas alle Jerusalem. **1460** CAPGRAVE *Chron.* 33 The ix. [labour of Hercules] is the gret victorie of the beste Achildes, that blewe out fyre at his mowth. **1508** DUNBAR *Poems* vii. 66 At parlament thow suld be hye renownit, That did so mony victoryse opteyn. **1584** POWEL *Lloyd's Cambria* 11 Let vs..choose vnto vs a head, to leade, direct, and gouerne vs,..sith without a head, there is no victorie to be looked for. **1601** CHESTER *Love's Mart.* 33 This Brytish King in warres a Conqueror, And wondrous happie in his Victories. **1659** B. HARRIS *Parival's Iron Age* 53 Where, after they have been repulsed or routed, they have rallyed, and carried away many glorious victories. **1769** ROBERTSON *Chas. V*, III. ¶25 The victory at Villalar proved as decisive as it was complete. **1815** *Morning Chron.* 22 June, We stop the press to announce the most brilliant and complete Victory ever obtained by the Duke of Wellington. **1856** FROUDE *Hist. Eng.* (1858) I. ii. 90 The victory was great; but, like many victories it was fatal to the conquerors.

3. Supremacy or superiority, triumph or ultimate success, in any contest, struggle, or enterprise.

a. With *the*, or in pl., etc.

13.. *Leg. Rood* (1871) 88 Mak þis in þine armes forþi, þan sall þou haue þe victori. *a* **1340** HAMPOLE *Psalter* xxvi. 6, I hope þe victory thoro his help. **1377** LANGL. *P. Pl.* B. III. 331 Se what Salamon seith in Sapience bokes, That hij þat ȝiueth ȝiftes þe victorie wynneth. **14..** *Tundale's Vis.* 88 Whom [*sc.* martyrs] Cryst Jesu eternally in glory Ordeyned hath a palme of his victory. **1526** TINDALE *1 John* v. 4 This is the victory that ouer commeth the worlde, euen oure fayth. **1573–80** HARVEY *Lett.* Wks. (Grosart) I. 136 From my chamber the daye after mye victorye. **1597** HOOKER *Eccl. Pol.* v. lxxi. §7 Such is euer-more the finall victorie of all truth. ? **1639** J. TAYLOR (Water P.) *Part Summers Travels* 33 (Hindley, III), The cooks hath laid small Isles of mutton, which you may invade With stomach, knife and spoon... With these, the victory you cannot fail. **1683** NORRIS *Passion of Saviour* 130 This little Victory He won, Shew'd what He could have done. **1697** DRYDEN *Virg. Georg.* III. 164 Observe, if he disdains to yield the Prize; Of Loss impatient, proud of Victories. **1719** DE FOE *Crusoe* II. (Globe) 598 But I hope I have got the Victory over my self. **1779** BURKE *Corr.* (1844) II. 273 We have obtained two victories,..victories, not over our adversaries, but over our own passions and prejudices. **1849** MACAULAY *Hist. Eng.* vi. II. 74 The victory of the cabal of evil counsellors was there-fore complete. **1876** MOZLEY *Univ. Serm.* v. (ed. 2) 189 The victory over the terror of death, in self-devotion produces the highest state of mind.

b. Without article.

c **1315** SHOREHAM VII. 407 Hyȝt moste neades for þe glorye, Elles hedde y-faylled fyctorye. **1340** *Ayenb.* 167 Wyþ-oute pacience non ne heþ uictorie. **1382** WYCLIF *Prov.* xxii. 9 Victorie and worshipe shal [he] purchace, that ȝeueth ȝiftis. *a* **1450** *Knt. de la Tour* vii. (1868) 10 And that fast is to make you haue victori ayenst youre flesshe. **1500–20** DUNBAR *Poems* xxxvii. 27 All honour we this Lord with.. glory,..That wan on tre trevmphe of he victory. **1592** SHAKS. *Rom. & Jul.* IV. i. 30 The teares haue got small victorie by that: For it was bad inough before their spight. **1605** BACON *Adv. Learn.* I. v. §11 Men have entered into a desire of learning..sometimes to enable them to victory of wit and contradiction. **1667** MILTON *P.L.* XII. 570 That suffering for Truths sake Is fortitude to highest victorie. **1792** GOUV. MORRIS in Sparks *Life & Writ.* (1832) II. 261 He has gained no victory but over his own conscience. **1828** SCOTT *F.M. Perth* xxxii, 'There is neither victory nor defeat in the case,' returned the Prince, drily. 'The girl loves me not'. **1835** T. MITCHELL *Acharn. of Aristoph.* 430 *note*, The daughter of Antæus is placed at the goal, as the prize of victory.

4. The Roman goddess representing or typifying victory; a figure or statue of this.

1569 SPENSER *Sonn.*, '*I saw raisde vp on pillers*', On eche side portraide was a victorie, With golden wings. **1585** T. WASHINGTON tr. *Nicholay's Voy.* I. xxi. 26 b, Within it [the chariot] was Victory sitting with two wings. **1610** HOLLAND *Camden's Brit.* 99 Indeed by this very same portrature..I have seen..the goddesse Victorie expressed. **1704** HEARNE *Duct. Hist.* (1714) I. 437 The Sepulchral Monument of one Tatius..at Sipylus; whose Tomb was adorned with Wreaths of Plenty, held up by Victories. **1788** GIBBON *Decl. & F.* xlv. IV. 419 Crowned with a winged figure of Victory. **1820** SHELLEY *Naples* 60 Bright Altar of the bloodless sacrifice, Which armed Victory offers up unstained To Love, the flower-enchained! **1841** THACKERAY *Sec. Fun. Nap.* iii. 63 Statues of plaster representing..victories, and other female personages painted in oil so as to represent marble. **1864** TENNYSON *Boadicea* 30 Suddenly giddily tottering,..down their statue of Victory fell. **1872** HEAD *Sel. Grk. Coins in Electrotype Brit. Mus.* 6 Above is a flying Victory, crowning the bull with a wreath.

5. *attrib.* and *Comb.*, as ***victory-anthem***, ***ball***, ***celebration***, ***dance***, ***-flashing*** adj., ***match***, ***night***, ***parade***, ***-worthy*** adj. **victory bond**, a bond issued by the Canadian and British governments during or immediately after the war of 1914–18; **victory garden**, a vegetable garden maintained to provide food in wartime (*spec.* in the war of 1939–45); **victory point** *Bridge*, a point scored in a championship representing a number of international match points in accordance with an agreed scale; **victory roll**, a rotational manœuvre about a longitudinal axis performed by an aircraft as a sign of triumph (cf. ROLL *sb.*² 1 d); also *fig.*; **victory sign**, a signal made by holding up the hand with the palm outwards and the first two fingers spread apart to represent the letter V (for *victory*) to indicate triumph (cf. V-SIGN 2 a); also = V-SIGN 1 b.

1869 W. P. MACKAY *Grace & Truth* (1875) 122 After we have joyfully sung the victory-anthem recorded in Romans viii. **1945** AUDEN *Coll. Poetry* 117 We were To go to a great banquet and a Victory Ball. **1952** M. LASKI *Village* ii. 42 To bedeck the village hall on the night of the Victory Ball. **1917** *Canad. Year Bk. 1916–17* 693 On November 12, 1917, preparations were completed for the issue of a fourth Canadian War Loan in the form of five, ten and twenty year 'Victory Bonds' in denominations as low as $50. **1919** *Times* 14 June 19/1 The provision for Victory Bonds being accepted at their face value as cash for payment of death duties. **1977** JOHNS & GREENFIELD *Dymond's Capital Transfer Tax* xvii. 346 Victory bonds were accepted only for tax chargeable on death. **1945** J. REITH *Diary* 4 May (1975) vii. 347, I am dreading the victory celebrations and have no sort of heart for them. **1978** CADOGAN & CRAIG *Women & Children First* vi. 131 When the war ends [Susan]..is.. caught up in the spurious gaiety of the victory celebrations. **1921** A. NOYES *Sel. Verse* iii. 5 (*title*) A victory dance. **1976** *Billings* (Montana) *Sunday Gaz.* 27 June 1-D/1 The Sioux and the Arapaho have come to share in this victory dance with us. **1820** SHELLEY *Liberty* xv, Lift the victory-flashing sword. **1942** WYNDHAM LEWIS *Let.* 10 Sept. (1963) 336 Why doesn't she lie low..and work in her victory-garden? **1978** H. WOUK *War & Remembrance* i. 13 She had started a victory garden and seemed the merrier for it. **1709** *The Post-Boy* 1–3 Dec., The Victory Handkerchief, which gives account of..five most Glorious Victories..over the French. **1769** in Waghorn *Cricket Scores* 70 A cricket-match was played at Swaffham (being the victory match). **1952** M. LASKI *Village* ii. 41 The coloured electric lights that Mr. Waters had dug out for Victory night. **1977** *Time* 26 Sept. 17/2 The victory-night hoopla of Norway's Laborites was, however, a bit premature. **1931** F. L. ALLEN *Only Yesterday* i. 10 Every other city has its victory parade. **1982** WARNER & SANDILANDS *Women beyond Wire* xi. 179 The war in Europe became progressively less of an Axis victory parade.

1962 *Listener* 8 Nov. 786/3 In the second half Britain went further ahead and won the match 6-0 in victory points. **1972** *Daily Tel.* 21 June 14/5 Britain scored 42 victory points out of 60 during Monday's play in the World Bridge Olympiad. **1942** *Tee Emm* (Air Ministry) II. 58 On returning to his aerodrome he began a victory roll, got into a spin and failed to recover. **1971** A. PRICE *Alamut Ambush* vi. 73 There was no point in doing a victory roll, however. It might even be premature if he failed to handle Havergal with compassion. **1981** T. BARLING *Bikini Red North* xi. 241 The F15 Eagle.. passed overhead, turning in a victory roll. **1942** M. DICKENS *One Pair of Feet* vii. 132 Her bell rang, not once, but as if she were giving the Victory sign in Morse. **1959** M. STEEN *Woman in Back Seat* II. viii. 310 One gave the 'victory' sign. 'We've beaten 'em.' **1978** L. THOMAS *Ormerod's Landing* v. 100 They went quickly, only the idiotic boy turning around and giving the victory sign. **1552** HULOET, Victory worthy, *palmarius*.

†**victory**, *v. Obs. rare.* [ad. OF. *victorier* or med.L. *victōriāre* (It. *vittoriare*), f. L. *victōria*: see prec.] *trans.* To overcome, vanquish.

a **1470** HARDING *Chron.* CLXXXVII. ix, Greate syckenesse so had hym victoried, And droue hym out from all his region. **1576** BEDINGFIELD tr. *Cardanus' Comf.* 45 b, If he had beene victoryed, hee coulde not haue left to Alexander meane and power of happy procedinge.

'**victoryless**, *a.* [-LESS.] Lacking victory.

1892 BROOKE *Early Eng. Lit.* II. xvii. 102 Hell is then described, the abyss of pain, swart, victoryless, deep-daled. **1914** *Times* 14 Nov. 10/1 A protracted, victoryless affair of mere give and take on three or four vast firing-lines.

victress ('vɪktrɪs). [f. L. *victr-* + -ESS. Cf. next and VICTRIX.] A female victor or vanquisher.

1601 HOLLAND *Pliny* I. 452 Posthumius Tubertus.. rode triumphant in this manner, to wit, crowned with a chaplet of Myrtle, dedicated to Venus Victresse [**1634** Victoresse]. **1606** —— *Sueton.* 243 When the one of them was foyled and overcome, a third [eagle] came at the very instant from the sunne rising and chased the victresse away. **1637** HEYWOOD *Dial.* xviii. 244 She that's crownd Victresse by the Trojan Boy, For meed this golden Apple shall enioy. **1658** W. BURTON *Itin. Anton.* 44 She as a Mother not a Victresse calls. **1741** SHENSTONE *Judgment Hercules* 514 Not such the victress, Virtue's constant queen, Endur'd the test of truth. *c* **1780** M. MONSEY in Jeaffreson *Bk. about Doctors* (1860) II. 84 O Venus, send dire ruin on her head; Strike the destroyer, lay the victress dead. **1850** W. P. SCARGILL *Eng. Sketch-Bk.* 21 Peggy Mumps, his sister, was victress in a chemise race. **1867** HOWELLS *Ital. Journ.* 101 The painter has done his best for the victress in this rivalry. **1888** MRS. H. WARD *R. Elsmere* xlv, 'I wouldn't have given it him,'.. the supposed victress was saying to herself.

†**victrice**. *Obs.* Also 5 victrych, 6 -yce, victris. [a. OF. *victrice* or L. *victrīc-*, *victrix*: see next.] = prec.

1387 TREVISA *Higden* (Rolls) VI. 421 O Elflede myȝti, O mayde mennene drede; victrice of kynd, wel worþy þy name. **1447** BOKENHAM *Seyntys* (Roxb.) 85 He wyl now defendyn me, And of al thi serpentys me victrych make. **1500-20** DUNBAR *Poems* lxxxv. 63 Empryce of pryss,.. Victryce of wyce, hie genetrice Of Jhesu. **1533** *Anne Boleyn's Coronat.* in Furniv. *Ballads fr. MSS.* (1868) I. 399 He knewe, certes, that you, victrice, of all ladies Should haue the price of worthynes. **1567** DRANT *Horace, Ep.* x. D viij, The victris hath a swifte recourse by stealth unto her place. ? **1633** B. JONSON *Underwoods, Lady V. Digby* ix. 96 And, in her hand With boughs of Palme, [to have] a crowned Victrice stand.

‖**victrix** ('vɪktrɪks). [L., fem. of *victor* VICTOR.] A female victor; a victress.

1651 BIGGS *New Disp.* ¶113 Before Nature is victrix in diseases. **1672** [TUKE] (*title*), Souls Warfare, Comically digested into Scenes Acted between the Soul and her Enemies, Wherein she cometh off Victrix. **1716-20** *Lett. fr. Mist's Jrnl.* (1722) I. 174 Carried away by the triumphant Victrix, who will be proud of the Conquest. **1779** G. KEATE *Sketches fr. Nat.* (ed. 2) II. 9 The victrix has it [a smock] slipped over her running dress, and marches off triumphant. **1853** C. BRONTE *Villette* xxxii, In his victrix he required all that was here visible. **1895** E. J. DILLON in *Contemp. Rev.* Nov. 620 A war which, if Russia prove the victrix, will deliver Constantinople and the Balkan Peninsula into her hands.

Victrola (vɪk'trəʊlə). Also victrola. [f. the name of the *Victor* Talking Machine Co. + -OLA.] The proprietary name of a kind of gramophone.

1905 E. JOHNSON *Let.* 9 June in *Amer. Speech* (1961) XXXVI. 116 The word Victrola is similar to nothing I have ever heard of and seems to me to have a sound suggestive of music, and would in all probability be the best word to use. **1906** *Official Gaz.* (U.S. Patent Office) 9 Jan. 644/2 Victor Talking Machine Company... Filed Dec. 1, 1905. Victrola. **1906** *Trade Marks Jrnl.* 9 May 628 Victrola 279,292. Philosophical instruments, scientific instruments, and apparatus for useful purposes. **1916** 'J. WEBSTER' *Dear Enemy* 318 The children.. had a lot of new records for the victrola. **1937** N. COWARD *Present Indicative* VI. 259 A tall Renaissance chair with a red velvet cushion under which lived an electric victrola. **1952** J. STEINBECK *East of Eden* 374 He bought a Victor victrola.. and he went regularly to see what new records had come in. **1979** P. THEROUX *Old Patagonian Express* xvii. 259, I found an old phonograph. It was literally a Victrola, a 1904 Victor.

victual ('vɪt(ə)l), *sb.* Forms: α. 4-6 **vitaile** (4 **-aille**), **vitayle** (5 **-aylle**), 5 **vitayll**, 5-6 **-ail(l**; 4-6 **vytayle** (5-6 **-aylle**, 5 *Sc.* **wytaylle**), 5-6 **vytaile** (5 **-aille**), 5 **-ayl(l**; 4-5 **vetaille** (4 **-aile**), 5 **vetayle**, 6 **-ayll**; 5 *Sc.* **wittail(e**, **-aill**, **wytaill**, 6 **vittayle**, **-aile**, 6-7 **vittail**; 5 *Sc.* **wictaill**, 6 **-ayll**, **-ayle**, **vectayll**, 6-7 **victail**. β. (Chiefly *Sc.*) 5 **vitt-**, **vet-**, 6 **vict-**, 5-6 **vyt-**, **vitale**; 5 **wit(t)-**, **wyt-**, **wet-**, **wictale**. γ. 5-6 **vitall** (6 **-al**, **witall**), 5 **vytall**, 6 **-al**; 5-6 **vitell** (5 **vet-**, **wetell**), **vitel**, 5 **fyt-**, 6 **vytel(l**; 5 **wetyl**; 6 **vitoll**. δ. 5 **vittale**, 5-6 **vittall**, 5 (9) **vittal**; 5-6 **vittell** (5 **wytt-**, 6 **wett-**, **vyttell**), 6, 8, 9 *dial.*, **vittel**, 6-7, 8-9 *dial.* **vittle** (7 **victle**), 9 *dial.* **fittle**, **wittle**. ε. 6 **wyttuel**, **wittual**, 7 **vittual**, 8 **vitual**; 6 **victuayle**, *Sc.* **wictuale**, **victuale**, **-wale**, **-uel(l**, 5-7 **victuall** (6 **wictuall**, **-wall**), 6 **vyctual**, 6- **victual**. [a. AF. and OF. *vitaile*, *-aille* (OF. also *vitale*, *-alle*, *vittalle*, *victaille*) fem.:—late L. *victuālia*, neut. pl. of post-classical L. *victuālis*, f. *victus* food, sustenance: cf. Prov. *vit(o)alha*, Sp. *vitualla*, Pg. *vitualha*, It. *vettovaglia*. The variant OF. and mod.F. form *victuaille* has been assimilated to the L. original, and a similar change in spelling has been made in English, while the pronunciation still represents the forms *vittel*, *vittle*. (See also VITALY.)]

1. *collect.* Whatever is normally required, or may naturally be used, for consumption in order to support life; food or provisions of any kind.

Occasionally applied to food for animals, but more commonly restricted to that of persons.

α. **1303** R. BRUNNE *Handl. Synne* 10555 Y was wunt to lede vytayle To knyȝtes þat were yn batayle. **13..** *Sir Beues* (A.) 3025 Al þus þemperur haþ him diȝt... þar to schipes wiþ gode vitaile. *c* **1385** CHAUCER *L.G.W.* 1488 *Hypsipyle*, Askynge hem a-noon If they were broken or woo begoon Or hade nede of lodesmen or vitayle. **1399** LANGL. *Rich. Redeles* III. 371 Devourours of vetaile þat fouȝten er þei paide. *a* **1417** *York Memor. Bk.* (Surtees) I. 222 Fysshe and other vitaill ar ofte tymes conceled.. in this citee. *c* **1450** *Mirk's Festial* 98 He schuld haue vii ȝere plenteþ e of corne and all oþer vytayle. *a* **1500** in C. Trice-Martin *Chanc. Proc. 15th C.* (1904) 4 Yf the dette be surmysed to growe by the bying or sellyng of any maner of vetayll. *a* **1533** LD. BERNERS *Huon* xlvi. 156 He shall departe in this lytell shyppe.. and take vytayle in to it for there prouysyon. *a* **1548** HALL *Chron.*, *Hen. VI*, 105 By that waie neither man nor vitaill could passe or come. **1548** PATTEN *Exped. Scotl.* Pref. a viij b, The time and place whan and whither they shall cum, and with how much prouision of vitail. **1592** KYD *Sol. & Pers.* III. i. 50 Footemen.. well exercised in war; And, as it seemes, they want no needful vittaile.

β. **1375** BARBOUR *Bruce* IX. 168 Quhar thai mycht get Till thame and thairis vittale and met. *c* **1375** *Sc. Leg. Saints* xxx. (*Theodera*) 425 þai ordenyt hyr þare out-rydere, þar witale to þe house to by. *c* **1400** *Ywaine & Gaw.* 1873 Syr Alers,.. with swith grete vetale, Come that kastel to asayle. **1487** *Act 3 Hen. VII*, c. ix. §3 That every freman.. may lede, carie, and goo, with his or their Vetale, Ware or merchaundise. *a* **1500** *Bernard, de cura rei fam.* (E.E.T.S.) 110 Geff thow.. hase to sel wetale in gret substance, Se be na way na derth þat thou desyre.

γ. *c* **1400** *Destr. Troy* 5176 In þat prouyns is plenty all of prise vitell, Of corne, & of catell. **1472** *Presentmts. of Juries* in *Surtees Misc.* (1890) 23 We say yt yer have boght of late .. unsesanabyll wetyl, yt is to say, feche & herrynge, bothe Thom Smythe & John Clyffe. *Ibid.* 27 For brynghyng in of wetell for the welfare of comhons. *c* **1475** HENRYSON *Fables, Twa Mice* 102 (Bann. MS.), Thair harbery wes tane In till a spens with vitall of grit plentie. **1513-4** *Act 5 Hen. VIII*, c. 6 The great scarcyte of grayne and vytell at this present tyme. **1531** in J. Bulloch *Pynours* (1887) 61 The berne of salt ..and all wther witall.. borne be the Pynouris. **1538** STARKEY *England* I. iii. 74 In so much that vytel and nuryschment suffycyent for them can skant here be found. **1570** LEVINS *Manip.* 13 Vitall, *penu*, *victus*.

δ. *c* **1480** *Wyntoun's Cron.* I. 564 (MS. E.), Within þat ile ar citeis ten Stuffit with wittall gud and men. **1482** *Cely Papers* (Camden) 108 They schall lacke no men nor vettell. **1494** *Acc. Ld. High Treas. Scot.* I. 247 For a bayte that careit the wrychtis and thar wyttell to the loche, v s. **1573-80** TUSSER *Husb.* (1878) 41 Twise a day giue him fresh vittle and drinke. **1599** DALLAM in *Early Voy. Levant* (Hakl. Soc.) 88 The iland Zante hathe all theire provition of vittell from thence. *a* **1618** SYLVESTER *Maiden's Blush* 355 Th' Heav'nly Herald.. sees there the Brethren lying Along the Grasse, and busie at their Vittle. **1663** BUTLER *Hud.* I. I. 316 For, as we said, he always chose To carry Vittle in his Hose. **1723** SWIFT *Stella at Woodpark* Wks. 1755 IV. I. 40, I must confess, your wine and vittle I was too hard upon a little. **1748** MARY LEAPOR *Poems Sev. Occasions* 124 When you gather Strength a little, Can walk abroad and eat your Vittle. **1789** BURNS *Robin shure in Hairst* iv, Robin promised me A' my winter vittle. **1847-** in dial. glossaries, etc. (Worc., Hereford, Shropsh., Warw., Gloc., Dorset) in the form *fittle*. **1881** *Gd. Words* 846/1 It's a pity as you've no stomach to yer vittle.

ε. **1523** CROMWELL in Merriman *Life & Lett.* (1902) I. 39 The Frenche men.. lye yn wayte.. to destroye the Conductours of our victuayle. **1559-66** in *Wodrow Soc. Misc.* (1844) 71 To hinder the victuall from comeing to Edinburgh. **1570-6** W. LAMBARDE *Peramb. Kent* 130 Deuouring and consuming.. the victuall of the countrey. **1603** KNOLLES *Hist. Turks* (1621) 1247 Germenchius hath put in three moneths victuall into Hust in Transylvania. **1627** BACON *Sylva* §649 The Making of Things Inalimental, to become Alimental, may be an Experiment of great Profit, for Making new Victual. **1681** H. NEVILE *Plato Rediv.* 92 The cheapness of Victual, and the want of Labourers. **1765** BLACKSTONE *Comm.* I. 60 It might seem to prohibit the buying of grain and other victual. **1817** BYRON *Beppo* xxix, And Laura waited long, and wept a little,.. She almost lost all appetite for victual. **1856** HAWTHORNE *Eng. Note-Bks.* (1870) I. 111 A refreshment-room, with drinks and cakes and pastry, but.. no substantial victual. **1859** TENNYSON *Geraint & Enid* 201 A fair-hair'd youth, that in his hand Bare victual for the mowers.

†**b.** Produce of the ground capable of being used as food. *Obs.*

white victual (quot. 1799), = next.

c **1374** CHAUCER *Former Age* 36 Ther as vitayle is ek so skars and thinne þat nat but mast or apples is ther inne. *c* **1386** —— *Clerk's T.* 3 Ther is at the West side of Ytaille.. A lusty playne, habundant of vitaille. **1625** BACON *Ess.*, *Plantation* (Arb.) 531 Then consider, what Victuall or Esculent Things there are, which grow speedily, and within the yeere. **1627** MAY *Lucan* IV. 99 Nor can the souldiers goe To forrage: the drown'd fields no vittaile leaue. **1798** MALTHUS *Popul.* (1878) 228 This may be justly attributed to the effects of the scarcity and bad victual in the year 1783. **1799** J. ROBERTSON *Agric. Perth* 147 The land is pulverized and better made for the succeeding crop of white victual.

c. *Sc.* Grain, corn. ? *Obs.*

1473 *Rental Bk. Cupar-Angus* (1879) I. 171 Alsua tha sal haue the tend vitale for ijch of bere and mele. **1557** *Rec. Inverness* (New Spald. Cl.) I. 7 To.. pay Isbell Damster the hyest price of ane boll wyttuell and thre pects to entres. **1585** *Reg. Mag. Sig. Scot.* 292/1 For payment.. of aucht chalderis 3 bollis wictuall, thairof 45 bollis beir and the remanent meill. **1609** SKENE *Reg. Maj.*, *Stat. Robert I*, 36 It is statute be the king, that all they quha buyes victuall.. fra burgessis at their granares, they.. may carie that victuall quhere they please. **1678** SIR G. MACKENZIE *Crim. Laws Scot.* I. xxiv. §1 (1699) 119 Usury is that Crime.. committed in Bargains of Victual, or Tacks. *Ibid.* II. xiv. §1. 211 A landed man, whose Rent exceeds a thousand Merks, or ten Chalders of Victual. **1726** P. WALKER *Life A. Peden* in *Biog. Presbyt.* (1827) I. 53 He enquired at Mrs. Steil, if she wanted a Servant for threshing Victual? **1785** BURNS *3rd Epist. to Lapraik* vii, [Till] a' the vittle [be] in the yard, An' theekit right. **1799** J. ROBERTSON *Agric. Perth* 99 In drying on the iron floor, the victual must be constantly turned. **1812** G. CHALMERS *Dom. Econ. Gt. Brit.* 262 Though neither the nominal, nor the real, prices of victual were equal to those of the times of queen Anne. **1822** GALT *Sir A. Wylie* xlii, He has been very kind to the poor, having divided five load of victual among all the needful in the parish. **1843** *Report Jedburgh Thirlage Trial* 8 A portion of that corn or victual, ground at the mills, which is kept by the miller.

†**d.** (See quot.) *Obs.*—0

1688 R. HOLME *Armoury* II. 241/1 Vitell, or *Viandes*, the term for Hawks meat.

2. *pl.* Articles of food; supplies, or various kinds, of provisions; in later use *esp.* articles of ordinary diet prepared for use.

α. **13..** *K. Alis.* 855 (Laud MS.), And Olyfauntz & ek Camayles, Boþe hij charged wiþ vitailes. *a* **1350** *Will. Palerne* 1121 Wel þei were warnestured of vitayles i-now, plentiuosly for al peple. **1387** TREVISA *Higden* (Rolls) II. 55 Whanne derþe of vitailles is in al Engelond aboute, þere is þe lasse i-solde. *c* **1444** LYDG. in *Pol. Poems* (Rolls) II. 220 To chese suych vitaylles ther braynes wer to woode. **1489** CAXTON *Faytes of A.* II. xxx. 142 Cartes shal folowe for to bryng and arriue the vitailles fro the shippes. *a* **1533** LD. BERNERS *Huon* lxi. 213 They bare all in to ye shyp, & vytaylles suffycyent. **1555** EDEN *Decades* (Arb.) 77 The vytayles (especially the byskette breade) corrupted by takynge water. **1596** BP. W. BARLOW *Three Serm.* ii. 47 Among all other, Famine and Dearth of vittails is not the least. **1607** DEKKER & WEBSTER *Sir T. Wyatt* Wks. 1873 III. 103 Good victailes makes good blood. **1616** R. C. *Times' Whistle* (1871) 85 Which I paide.., Because they should not think I came to sharke Only for vittailes.

β. **1375** BARBOUR *Bruce* XV. 92 Schir Eduard gert men gang and se All the vitalis of that cite. *c* **1425** WYNTOUN *Cron.* VIII. 5027 [He] Saw his wictalis war nere gane, And hop of reskew had he nane. **1453-4** *Cal. Anc. Rec. Dublin* (1889) I. 280 That al maner of viteiloures.. shulde have bene arrested by har bodys.. that byinn of them any vittalis. **1535** COVERDALE *Ps.* cxxxi. 15, I will blesse hir vytales with increase, & wil satisfie hir poore with bred. **1547** BOORDE *Introd. Knowl.* ii. (1870) 127 In the whych is vsed good fashion and good vytales. **1575** G. HARVEY *Letter-bk.* (Camden) 97 Mye miserable Mistrisse.. is oftentymes driven very harde.. for her vittales and lodginge.

γ. *c* **1400** *Melayne* 1195 He garte dele his vetells then Firste amanges oure wonded men. **1401** in Ellis *Orig. Lett.* Ser. II. I. 15 We faylyth vitels and men. *Ibid.* 16 They mowe have godes and fytelles plente. *c* **1482** J. KAY tr. *Caoursin's Siege of Rhodes* ¶3 Also they lakked vytalles. **1510** *Sel. Cases Crt. Star Chamber* (Selden) 205 So he toke fro many pore men their vitals to ther grete hurte. **1545** BRINKLOW *Compl.* ii. 13 In London and other placys ther be many offended with the great price of vitells. **1599** DALLAM in *Early Voy. Levant* (Hakl. Soc.) 83 We could not gitt any vitels. *Ibid.* 86 We ever had vitals reddie dreste for 3 dayes.

δ. **1554-9** *Songs & Ball. Phil. & Mary* (Roxb.) 12 And dear cheape of vittels withe the thowe hast brought To the towne. **1556** *Chron. Gr. Friars* (Camden) 46 With plate, monny, harnes, horse, & wettelles. **1573-80** TUSSER *Husb.* (1878) 98 To thy sheepe go and looke, for dogs will haue vittles. **1606** *Sir G. Goosecappe* i, Good companions yfaith; I see you come not for vittles. **1621** in Foster *Eng. Factories Ind.* (1906) I. 271 Wee had great store of fresh victles. *c* **1645** T. TULLY *Siege of Carlisle* (1840) 27 One John Head.. who pretended to fetch vittells out of the Country. **1696** *Monthly Mercury* VII. 87 We saw.. vast Provision of Vittles and Ammunition. **1731-8** SWIFT *Pol. Conversat.* 112, I would rather want Vittles than Elbow-Room. **1838** JAS. GRANT *Sk. Lond.* 171 You knows that no one can hact well without vittals, and I have not had a mouthful since yesterday. **1844** DICKENS *Mart. Chuz.* ix, Dinner was announced by Bailey junior in these terms,—'The wittles is up!' **1892** 'Q' (QUILLER-COUCH) *I saw Three Ships* vi. 106 And so say I, wi' all these vittles cryin' out to be ate.

ε. **1523** CROMWELL in Merriman *Life & Lett.* (1902) I. 39 As for victuaylys in our waye we shuld be sure none to fynde. **1560** DAUS tr. *Sleidane's Comm.* 452 b, The Frenchemen, to the intent they might have victualles in a readines [etc.]. **1596** *Edward III*, IV. ii. 4 That neither victuals nor supply of men May come to succour this accursed towne. **1610** HOLLAND *Camden's Brit.* (1637) 422 Great store of victuals and all things necessary. **1618** in Foster *Eng. Factories Ind.* (1906) I. 45 When the Bannyans sayle by it they heave victuals overboard.. as a sacrifice. *a* **1687** PETTY *Pol. Arith.* (1690) 101 The Wages of a.. Labourer.. is 4s. per week without Victuals. **1727** SWIFT *Gulliver* I. vi, I had three hundred cooks to dress my victuals. **1774** GOLDSM. *Nat. Hist.* (1776) III. 299 The young animals.. began to dispute about their victuals, although they were given more than they could use. **1798** CHARLOTTE SMITH *Yng. Philos.* I. 56 She once lost a salt spoon by one of them, whom Master George thought proper to bring to her door for cold victuals. **1840** HOOD *Up Rhine* 218 It seems to me a very odd proceeding for.. a town to lay a tax on the persons who bring it victuals. **1865** KINGSLEY *Herew.* xv, There was.. decking of the hall in the best hangings..; cooking of victuals, broaching of casks.

†**b.** ***clerk of the victuals***, = the victualler of Calais (see VICTUALLER 2 a *note*). *Obs.*

c **1570** R. TURPYN in *Chron. Calais* (Camden) Introd. 18 Havinge ther another offyce of the Quenes Majesty called by the name of Clarke of the Victuals.

†**c.** ***at victuals***, engaged in eating. *Obs.*

1681 H. FOULIS *Hist. Romish Treasons* 40 Books read to him whilst he was at Victuals.

†**3.** *pl.* **a.** Animals serving for food. *Obs.*

c **1550** *Disc. Common Weal Eng.* ii. (1893) 60 The more husbandrie is occupied, the more vniversall brede should be of all victualles, as of neate, shepe, swyne, gese, eges, butter, and chese. **1641** *More's Edw. V*, 104 The Pageants were amaking day and night at Westminster, and vitailes killed which afterwards was cast away.

†**b.** Military stores; munitions of war. *Obs.*

1653 H. COGAN tr. *Pinto's Trav.* iv. 10 Moreover he added, that they had great abundance of Victuals, amongst the which there were 12 Basilisks.

4. An article of food. *rare.*

1558 BP. WATSON *Sev. Sacram.* ix. 50 This heauenly foode is..a strong vitale, making vs able to endure the painful iorney to the kingdome of heauen. **1829** CARLYLE *Misc., German Playwrights* (1840) II. 50 The Germans, who instead of a measurable and sufferable spicing of theatric matter,..have in fact nothing else to live on but that highly unnutritive victual.

5. *attrib.* and *Comb.* (chiefly *Sc.*), as ***victual-dealer***, ***-house***, ***land-male***, ***-merchant***, ***office***, ***-rent***, ***-scanting*** adj., ***silver***, ***stipend***, ***wain***.

1496 *Acc. Ld. High Treas. Scot.* I. 310 Giffin to the skippar of the schip..for ȝonk Gherardis mennis fraucht and wittalis siluir, vij *li.* **1567** MAPLET *Gr. Forest* 105 The Female..espying hir time, when and how she may come to the Lawder or Vittailehouse. **1592** in *Reg. Mag. Sig. Scot.* (1892) 90/2 The victuall land maillis of Clestrane benorthe the burne. **1593** NASHE *Christ's T.* Wks. (Grosart) IV. 95 If there were any, that had repining victuall-scanting Maisters tyrannizing neuerthelesse for their work. **1600** *Reg. Mag. Sig. Scot.* (1890) 354/2 Pro preservatione navium contra tempestates et *lie victuell-housis.* **1668** in *Extr. St. P. rel. Friends* III. (1912) 278 Of late since his Ma[jes]ties imployment has slackn'd at the Victuall Office. **1765-8** ERSKINE *Inst. Law Scot.* II. vi. §40 If the landlord refuse to receive his victual-rent when offered to him in due time. **1801** *Farmer's Mag.* Jan. 28 The farmer or victual-merchant. *Ibid.*, The profession of the farmer or the victual-dealer. **1818** SCOTT *Hrt. Midl.* xlv, There was no knowing how long he might be in paying the next term's victual stipend. **1891** DOYLE *White Company* xix, The rogue got between me and the nearest French victual wain.

Hence **victual-less** *a.*, destitute of victuals.

1831 CARLYLE in Froude *First 40 Years* (1882) II. 165, I arrived at Liverpool..quite sleepless, and but for your dinner,..quite victual-less.

victual ('vɪt(ə)l), *v.* Forms: α. 4–5 vitaile (5 -aille), 4–6 vitayle, -aylle, 6 vitaill; 4–5 vetayle, 5 -aille; 4 vytaile (5 -aille), 4–6 vytaylle, 5 -ayle; 4–7 vittaile (6 *Sc.* victaile), 6 vytteyle, vittaill- (*Sc.* wictaill). β. 5 *Sc.* vitt-, wittale, 5–6 vitale (5 vytale). γ. 4 vitele, 5–6 vitel; 5 vetele, 5–6 vitell-; 5 vytel, 6 -ell; 5 vitule, 6 -alle. δ. 5 vittall, 6 vitt-, vyttell; 5 *Sc.* wittule, 6 *Sc.* wittall, wictill; 6 vitle, 6–7 vittle (7 wictle). ε. 6–7 victuaile (6 *Sc.* wictuale), 6–8 victuall (6 *Sc.* wictwall), 6- victual (7 victu'l). [ad. AF. and OF. *vitailler* (also OF. *vit-*, *victuailler*), f. *vitaille* VICTUAL *sb.* Cf. Sp. *vitualIar*, Pg. *vitualhar*, It. *vettovagliare.*]

1. *trans.* To supply or furnish (a ship, castle, garrison, body of troops, etc.) with victuals, esp. with a store to last for some time.

α. **13..** *Coer de L.* 1382 Two hundred sehyppys ben wel vytailid, With force hawberks, swerdes and knyvys. **1375** BARBOUR *Bruce* III. 339 For thaim thocht thai mycht sekyrly Duell thar, quhill thai war wictaillit weile. **1390** GOWER *Conf.* I. 194, I charge you and bidde this, That ye the same Schip vitaile. *c* **1450** *Brut* II. 428 That Towne and the Castelle weren welle vitailid and eke mannyd. **1472** *Paston Lett.* Suppl. 143 Thei stuffe and vetayll sore the place. **1485** in *10th Rep. Hist. MSS. Comm.* App. V. 318 That no..man victaile, nor make to be victailed, none of the saide men of warre. **1523-4** R. GRUFFITHE in Ellis *Orig. Lett.* Ser. I. I. 193 They have ayded and vittailed the Kyng's enymyes. **1553** BRENDE *Q. Curtius* D vij, So great an army as he had..could not be vitailed in a desolate countrey.

β. **1375** BARBOUR *Bruce* IV. 63 The castell weill vittalit thai With met, and fwaill can purvay. **1473** WARKW. *Chron.* (Camden) 2 Certeyne castelles..whiche they hade vytaled. *c* **1520** M. NISBET *Acts* xii. 20 Thai askit pece, for alsmekile that thare cuntreis war vitalit of him.

γ. *c* **1380** WYCLIF *Sel. Wks.* III. 274 He were..ȝit more traitour, ȝif he lettide oþere knyȝttis..to vitele þes men asegid. *c* **1400** *Destr. Troy* 4710 At this tenydon truly was a tried castell,..Wele viteld, I-wisse, for winturs ynoghe. *c* **1450** *Mirk's Festial* 205 When he had vyteld his schippis, and made hym redy. **1482** *Cely Papers* (Camden) 109 Thaye hawe vetellyd and mannyd the town of Ary. *a* **1533** LD. BERNERS *Huon* lix. 203 It was impreyngnable so it were well vytellyd. **1534** in *Star Chamb. Cases* (Selden) II. 290 They may always vitalle theire townes, castelles and fortresses with suche playntie of vitalles. **1550** J. COKE *Eng. & Fr. Heralds* §75 Richard..distroyed th' oost of the Egiptians comminge to vytell the Soldane in Jerusalem.

δ. *c* **1425** WYNTOUN *Cron.* II. 1580 (Cott. MS.), Eneas gert twa schippis be Wittulyt and laid to þe se. **1490** *Acc. Ld. High Treas. Scot.* I. 129 Eftir at the Kingis schip wes chaysit in Dumbertane,..send with Johne of Haw to vittall hir,.. xviij li. **1555** BRADFORTH in Strype *Eccl. Mem.* (1721) III. App. xlv. 129 For, saye they, yf we have the sea to vyttell us, we shall have powre to rule Ingland. **1587** HARRISON *England* II. i. (1877) I. 6 The king..commanded the Londoners not to aid nor vittell them. **1611** J. DAVIES (Heref.) in Coryat *Crudities* i. 3 He his Gorge with Grapes did vittle. **1670** MILTON *Hist. Eng.* VI. Wks. 1851 V. 248 New Ships in every Port were builded, vittl'd,..and appointed to meet all at Sandwich.

ε. **1558** BP. WATSON *Sev. Sacram.* Ser. I. 3 The fift thing ..is when his armye is..well victualled,..then to merche forward. **1583** STOCKER *Civ. Warres Lowe C.* III. 97 b, Letters from the Prince, aduertising them, that hee meant the night following to victuall them. **1598** BACON *Sacr. Medit., Miracles* Ess. (Arb.) 103 He [Christ] multiplyed the scarsitie of a few loues and fishes to a sufficiency to victuaile an host of people. **1640** GENT *Knave in Gr.* I. i. B ij, A Leaguer cannot be planted, mann'd, victuall'd, and munition'd, with a small magazine. **1670** R. COKE *Disc. Trade* 34 Before the Act we could Victual Ships with good and substantial Food cheaper than the Dutch. **1709** STEELE *Tatler* No. 28 ¶5 These dangerous Captains who could victual an Army as well as lead it. **1765** *Museum Rust.* IV. 196 The very large extent of foreign trade, which requires a great many more ships to be victualled out now than formerly. **1777** ROBERTSON *Hist. Amer.* II. (1783) I. 100 This squadron..was victualed for twelve months. **1800** WELLINGTON in Gurw. *Desp.* (1837) I. 265, I have also written..requiring the reason for which he did not victual this corps..as I ordered. **1836** MARRYAT *Midsh. Easy* xvi, Jack..pushed his way through the prisoners, who were being mustered to be victualled. **1865** H. PHILLIPS *Amer. Paper Curr.* II. 84 By unscrupulous foraging the troops were victualed from day to day.

fig. **1648** BEAUMONT *Psyche* XII. 189 They who with all riotous Dainties strive To fortify the Belly, but can finde No time to victuall and enforce [1702 recruit] the Minde!

b. *refl.* To provide or stock (oneself) with victuals.

1555 EDEN *Decades* (Arb.) 375 They vyttayled them selues with fresshe meate. **1572** in Feuillerat *Revels Q. Eliz.* (1908) 163 Expences in vittelling him selfe and iii of his fellows. **1612** SELDEN *Illustr. Drayton's Poly-olb.* ix. 326 Lhewelin.. compeld the English campe to victuall them-selves with horse-flesh. **1719** DE FOE *Crusoe* II. (Globe) 335 If they could get Provisions to victual themselves with. **1768** in Kitson *Life Jas. Cook* vi. (1907) 90, £120 a year for victualling himself. **1819** SCOTT *Leg. Montrose* v, He will.. do wisely to victual himself for at least three days. **1887** *Field* 24 Dec. 973/1 To see that the crew properly victual themselves.

2. *intr.* **a.** To partake of victuals; to eat. Also of animals, to feed or pasture.

1577 TUSSER *Husb.* (1878) 187 At meales my friend who vitleth here,.. Shall both be sure of better chere, and scape with lesser cost. **1587** TURBERV. *Trag. T.* 55 b, When.. euery man at boorde Had vittled well, and all was whiste. **1622** MABBE tr. *Aleman's Guzman d'Alf.* I. 38 In houses, where men vittaile vpon the way, a man shall meete many times with a bare couple of Hens. **1822** BYRON *Juan* VII. xlviii, As a..bell-wether [will] form the flock's connection By tinkling sounds, when they go forth to victual. **1869** BLACKMORE *Lorna D.* iii, Soon we found Peggy and Smiler [the horses] in company,..victualling where the grass was good.

b. To lay in or obtain a supply of victuals.

1615 CHAPMAN *Odyss.* III. 418 When he (there victling well, and store of gold Aboard his ships brought) his wild way did hold. **1655** *Nicholas Papers* (Camden) II. 322 Others [say] that he hath only victualed or taken in fresh water in those partes and is gone southward. *a* **1687** PETTY *Pol. Arith.* iii. (1691) 61 Because the French cannot Victual so cheap as the English, and Dutch, nor Sail with so few Hands. **1709** *Lond. Gaz.* No. 4582/3 Men belonging to Ships which are..Cleaning, Refitting, or Victualling at the Ports. **1725** DE FOE *Voy. round World* (1840) 46 Which was a voyage of such a length, that no ship could victual for.

Hence **'victualled** *ppl. a.*

1855 KINGSLEY *Westw. Ho!* xxxii, Some five and twenty of the soundest and best victualled ships.

'victualage. *rare.* [f. VICTUAL *sb.*] Victualling; victuals.

1622 MABBE tr. *Aleman's Guzman d'Alf.* II. 343, I imployed all that little money that I had, in matters of victuallage. **1847** C. BRONTË *J. Eyre* xvii, I could not proceed to the schoolroom without..running the risk of being surprised with my cargo of victualage.

victualler ('vɪt(ə)lə(r)). Forms: α. 4 vit-, 4, 6 vittailler, 5–6 vitailer (6 vict-), 6 vi(t)tayler (vict-); 4 vytail(l)er, 5–6 vytayler (6 -ayller); 6 viteilour, vitaylour, vittaillor. β. 4, 6 viteler, 5–6 viteller, 5 vital(l)er, vitalar, -eer, vituller; 5 veteler, 6 -eller, -uler; 5 vytalere, 6 vytiller. γ. 5 vittaler, 6 -alar, victaller; 5 vittelour, 5–6 vitteller (6 -eler, wytteller); 5–7 vitler, 6 vittler. δ. 5- victualler (7 -ailler), 6–7 (9) victualer, 6 victuelar, 7 vict'lar. [a. AF. and OF. *vitaill(i)er*, *vitaillour* (OF. also *vitailleur*, *vit-*, *victuailleur*), f. *vitaille* VICTUAL *sb.*]

1. A purveyor of victuals or provisions; *spec.* one who makes a business of providing food and drink for payment; a keeper of an eating-house, inn, or tavern; a licensed victualler (cf. b).

Also *spec.* (in local Irish use), a butcher.

α. **1377** LANGL. *P. Pl.* B. II. 60 Forgoeres and vitaillers and vokates of þe arches. **1386** *Rolls of Parlt.* III. 226/1 While vittaillers, bi suffraunce, presumen thilke states upon hem. **1453-4** *Cal. Anc. Rec. Dublin* (1889) 279 Al maner of viteiloures, as wel deynsynes as foreynes. **1530-1** *Act 22 Hen. VIII*, c. 13 Bere bruers and bakers whiche bene comon vitaylers. **1550** J. COKE *Eng. & Fr. Heralds* §133 To robbe the marchauntes of Englande,..lykewyse pore vytaylers and fysshermen of all nacions. **1565** COOPER *Thesaurus*, *Caupo*, a hucster; a tauerner; a victayler.

β. *c* **1380** WYCLIF *Sel. Wks.* III. 153 Bot men of lawe and marchauntis, and chapmen, and viteleres, synnen more in avarice þen done pore laboreres. **1421** *Coventry Leet Bk.* 25 We commaund þat no vitaler..passe out of the Cite of Couentre for to by fische, ne non othur vitayle comyng toward the Cite. *c* **1440** *Promp. Parv.* 511/1 Vytalere, *victuarius.* **1477** *Rolls of Parlt.* VI. 186/1 Every Merchaunt Alien, and every other Vitaler, and other Straunger. **1519** *Presentmts. of Juries* in *Surtees Misc.* (1890) 32 That no veteller, nor other man, herber no begers nor vacabundys. **1530-1** *Act 22 Hen. VIII*, c. 13 (1551) C v, Bere bruers and bakers, whiche bene common vitellers. **1556** *Chron. Gr. Friars* (Camden) 72 Every viteler to selle as they wolde and had done before.

transf. ? *c* **1430** LYDG. *St. Giles* 109 [The hind] Of god provided to be thy vitaleer, With a repaast of hyr mylk moost soote.

γ. **1467** in *Eng. Gilds* (1870) 408 That no maner vitteller pay eny thynge for the occupacion of the kynges Borde. **1523** in *10th Rep. Hist. MSS. Comm.* App. V. 400 Common vittlers and hostlers. **1530** in W. H. Turner *Select. Rec. Oxford* (1880) 87 Other vitlers and artyficers yn Oxford. **1573** in Feuillerat *Revels Q. Eliz.* (1908) 227 The vitteller at Reading for the dyet of sundry persons. **1599** BRETON *Miseries Manillia* Wks. (Grosart) II. 37/2, I had sent away this olde vitler with more crownes then shee was mistresse of many a day before. **1600-12** ROWLANDS *Four Knaves* (Percy Soc.) 45 The vitlers poasts all chalk'd with scores.

δ. **1568** GRAFTON *Chron.* II. 123 The bakers, Brewers, and other victuallers of the City. **1592** GREENE *Groat's W. Wit* (1617) 34 Let not Tauerners and Victualers bee thy Executors. **1614** J. TAYLOR (Water P.) *Nipping Abuses* D iij b, The vintner and the vict'lar get most gaines From dayly drunkards, and distempered braines. **1642** *Ord. & Declar. Both Houses: Lords Day* 6 Any other Tipler or Victualler whatsoever within your Ward. **1699** *Poor Man's Plea* 19 We have as firm Laws in England as need be to compel the Victualler to sell a certain Measure of Drink, mentioning what Pots and what Price. **1742** *Lond. & Country Brewer* I. (ed. 4) 29 This may be a benefit to a Victualler that brews to sell again, and cannot vent his small Beer. **1765** BLACKSTONE *Comm.* I. 414 The several inn-keepers and victuallers throughout the kingdom. **1835** WILLIS *Pencillings* I. ii. 20 A commissary from Villa Franca, who is to be our victualler during the quarantine. **1844** LD. BROUGHAM *Brit. Const.* xv. (1862) 221 Making victuallers pay for a license to retail wines.

b. ***licensed victualler***, one who has a licence to sell food or drink, but esp. the latter, to be consumed on the premises; a publican.

1824 (*title*), The Licensed Victualler's Almanack and Tablet of General Information for..1825. **1841** DICKENS *Barn. Rudge* xiii, Believing..that the publicans coupled with sinners in Holy Writ were veritable licensed victuallers. **1878** E. JENKINS *Haverholme* 26 They are hardly governed by the abstract principle that a Licensed Victualler is a..healthy institution, I suppose.

2. *spec.* **a.** One who supplies, or undertakes to supply, an army or armed force with necessary provisions; †*pl.* those engaged in bringing up victuals to an armed force.

Applied both to purveyors on a large scale, and to mere sutlers. †*victualler of Calais* occurs as a special designation in the 15th century.

α. *c* **1380** *Sir Ferumb.* 3144 þe vytailers þay alto-hewe, & þe vytailles with hymen þai ladde. **1447** *Ordinance of Exchequer* 35. c. 62 (6) A v, Item for the tresourer of Caleis, xl.s. Item for the vytayler of Caleis, xxxiii.s. iiii.d. **1489** CAXTON *Faytes of A.* I. xiii. 35 Dyspensatours and vitaillers of the oost. *a* **1513** FABYAN *Chron.* VII. 459 The kynges boost..was plenteously vytaylled by yᵉ Flemynges and by other vytayllers. *a* **1548** HALL *Chron., Hen. VIII*, 24 b, The duke of Vandosme..toke his aduantage and set on the victailers. **1591** SAVILE *Tacitus, Hist.* II. lxxxvii. 104 With infinite vittailers and followers of the campe.

β, γ. **1375** BARBOUR *Bruce* XIV. 407 Thai raid till meit the vittelleris, That with ther wittale..Com, haldand to the host the way. *Ibid.* 429 Sum of thair mekill host has seyne Thair come, and wende weill thai had beyne Thair vittelouris. **1456** SIR G. HAYE *Law Arms* (S.T.S.) 116 Playntis of his men as to merchandis and vitalaris of the ost and otheris. **1487** *Rolls of Parlt.* VI. 407/1 William Rosse Esquier, Vittaler of the Towne of Caleis and Marches of the same. **1587** HOLINSHED *Chron.* (ed. 2) III. 823/1 At last they met with a vitteler comming from the campe, which was their guide and brought them thither.

δ. **1591** SAVILE *Tacitus, Hist.* IV. xv. 179 The victuallers and marchants [were] cut of. **1601** LD. MOUNTJOY in Moryson *Itin.* (1617) II. 200 The Victualer issues..but one pounde and a halfe of beefe *per diem*, to a souldier. **1633** T. STAFFORD *Pac. Hib.* II. ii. (1821) 235 Although it seemeth to us by the Certificate of the Victualler, that you were better stored at your writing, then you knew for. **1681** *Moores Baffled* 4 Which careful foresight nothing could hinder from being effectual, but the negligence of the Victuallers. **1709** STEELE *Tatler* No. 39 ¶4 Charles II. victual'd his Navy, with the Bread which one of his Dogs chose.., rather than trust to the Asseverations of the Victuallers. **1802** JAMES *Milit. Dict.*, Sutler and Victualler may be considered as synonimous terms as far as they relate to military matters.

attrib. **1688** R. HOLME *Armoury* III. xvi. (Roxb.) 103/2 Things necessary for Armyes... Victualler sutlers.

b. One who furnishes a ship or navy with provisions. Also ***agent-victualler*** (see quot. 1769).

In early use, one who undertook to provision a trading vessel in return for a share in the profits.

1432-50 in *Cal. Proc. Chanc. Q. Eliz.* I. Pref. 38 On balynger cleped the Cristofre,..and therof Wolfe maister, and Sir Ramfray Arundell and Sir John Trerys Knyghtes owners and vitallers. **1623** WHITBOURNE *Newfoundland* 26 Those men are yeerely hired by the Owners, and Victuallers foorth of ships in those voyages. **1626** CAPT. SMITH *Accid. Yng. Seamen* 35 The Ship hath one third part; the Victualler the other third; the other third is for the Company. **1647** HAWARD *Crown Rev.* 20 Victualer of the Navy: Fee, [£]58. o. o. **1757** W. THOMPSON *R.N. Advoc.* 18 The Victuallers and their Officers Report..being of equal Account, it will be needless to animadvert thereon. **1769** FALCONER *Dict. Marine* (1780), *Agent-Victualler*,..an officer stationed at a royal port, to regulate the victualing of the king's ships, under the direction of the commissioners for victualing the navy. **1796** NELSON in Nicolas *Disp.* (1845) II. 248 Mr. Heatly, the great victualler, writes me that the supply he is now procuring, will be the first and last, for the Port of

Genoa will be shut. **1809** R. LANGFORD *Introd. Trade* 101 Beg your victualler to get the beef properly salted. **1834** *Encycl. Metrop.* (1845) VI. 341/1 To the Victualling establishment..[at Malta] there is attached an agent victualler and clerks.

3. A ship employed to carry provisions for a fleet or squadron (or for troops over-seas); a victualling ship.

a **1572** KNOX *Hist. Ref.* Wks. 1846 I. 216 Besydis the galayis, being twenty twa then in nomber, thei had threscoir great schippis, besydis vittallaris. **1588** *Losses and Distresses of the Spanish Navy* A iij b, They were in all, at their coming forth, a hundred xxxv. sayle, whereof foure were Galliasses, foure gallies, and ix. of them were victallers. **1625** in Birch *Crt. & Times Chas. I* (1848) I. 63 To your last of the fleet, you must add five victuallers, and as many horse-ships, having only seamen in them. **1668** *Lond. Gaz.* No. 238/3 All these Men of War are to be attended by a proportionable number of Galliots, Advice Boats, and Victuallers. **1712** E. COOKE *Voy. S. Sea* 454 A Dutch Squadron of about 13 Sail of Men of War and Victuallers. **1748** *Anson's Voy.* II. ii. 131 We never were joined by any other of our ships, except our Victualler, the Anna Pink. **1780** *Ann. Reg.* 204* Some men of war, which he had sent with a convoy of store-ships and victuallers to the island of Minorca. **1813** SOUTHEY *Nelson* I. 145 There were now above 100 sail of victuallers, gun-boats, and ships of war.

4. *Sc.* 'One who deals in grain; a corn-factor.'

1808 JAMIESON.

Hence **'victuallership.**

1450 *Rolls of Parlt.* V. 196/1 As in the vitelership of the Castell. **1487** *Ibid.* VI. 407/1 The Office of Vitellershipp of the forsaid Towne [Calais].

victualling ('vɪt(ə)lɪŋ), *vbl. sb.* Forms: (see VICTUAL *v.*). [f. VICTUAL *v.*]

1. The action of providing or storing a ship, town, army, etc. (now esp. the Navy) with victuals.

α. **1462** *Cal. Anc. Rec. Dublin* (1889) 313 For the vitalyng of the sayd citte. **1462** *Paston Lett.* II. 102 My Lord Tresorer had put hym to a gret charge for the vetelyng of *Mary Talbot.* **1496** *Naval Acc. Hen. VII* (1896) 165 Certeyn vitayle & fewell bought for vitaylyng of the seid Ship. **1544** *Star Chamb. Cases* (Selden) II. 281 His highnes proclamacion for the vittalyng of his highnes Toune of Callis. **1570** B. GOOGE *Pop. Kingd.* I. E iij b, They looke to vittayling of Campes, when bloudie warres doe raigne. **1606** J. CLAPHAM *Hist. Gt. Brit.* II. I. ii. 179 By attaching some of the Roman ships..they became first acquainted with their manner of vittailing.

β. **1509–10** *Act 1 Hen. VIII*, c. 20 §1 Victuale goyng oute of this your saide Realme for the victualyng of your Towne of Calice. **1551** SIR J. WILLIAMS *Accompte* (Abbotsf. Cl.) 88 Towardes the victuellinge of his maiesties armyes then at Portesmouth. **1603** KNOLLES *Hist. Turks* (1621) 250 He commanded also the Prince..to make prouision for the victualing of his campe. **1650** *Nicholas Papers* (Camden) 168 It was become necessary for the victualling and seting forth your fleete. **1705** *Lond. Gaz.* No. 4091/3 His Royal Highness has..appointed..Captain Thomas Harlow to be a Commissioner of the Victualling. **1755** MAGENS *Ess. Insurances* I. 165 The dear Victualling of the Ship in America. **1834** *Encycl. Metrop.* (1845) VI. 339/1 A Comptroller of the Victualling of the Navy and of the Transport Service. **1849** MACAULAY *Hist. Eng.* iii. I. 390 There men might learn..how grossly the Navy Board had cheated the crown in the victualling of the fleet. **1901** *Whitaker's Alm.* 154 Admiralty... Director of Victualling.

b. The business of supplying food and drink for payment; supply of food for this purpose.

1534 in Gross *Gild Merch.* (1890) II. 192 It ys enacted.. that no person ne persons shall..exercise eny vytelyng, bying or sellyng..wythyn the seyd Town. **1552** in *10th Rep. Hist. MSS. Comm.* App. V. 390 A comon housse or ynne for victuallinge and lodginge of..strangers. **1580** LYLY *Euphues* (Arb.) 252, I keepe no victualling, yet is my house an Inne. **1891** *Anthony's Photogr. Bull.* IV. 309 The average return saloon fare is £6 including very liberal victualling.

2. A supply of food for personal use.

1532 *Acc. Ld. High Treas. Scotl.* VI. 119 To be in Edinburgh the v day of Januar with xxx dais wittaling. **1539** CROMWELL in Merriman *Life & Lett.* (1902) II. 234, I haue ..delyuered vnto him money for two monethis wagies vitailling and al other thinges for that tyme necessary. *a* **1618** SYLVESTER *Letanie 4*, v, They from thee prepared had Each one his sev'rall victualling, After his kind, herb, fruit and seed. **1792** N. CHIPMAN *Rep.* (1871) 27 The prisoner should pay to the gaoler one shilling and sixpence per day for his victualing. **1819** R. ANDERSON *Cumbld. Ball.* 112 Teyme whispert, 'twad be best, For vittelin heame to run.

3. *attrib.*, as ***victualling-bill, -board, -book,*** † ***booth,*** † ***cart,*** † ***cook, department*** (also *transf.*), ***dry store, establishment, -note, place, provisions, service, -ship, -society, -yard.***

1745 *De Foe's Eng. Tradesm.* vi. (1841) I. 41 From whence proceeded that black trade of buying and selling navy and *victualling-bills, and transport-debts. **1809** R. LANGFORD *Introd. Trade* 130 *Bills victualling*, bills issued by the Victualling board, bearing interest till due and paid. **1846** A. YOUNG *Naut. Dict.* 72 The master of any vessel outward-bound has to apply to the searcher for a victualling-bill, which is a warrant for the shipment of such stores as he may require. **1867** SMYTH *Sailor's Word-bk.*, *Victualling-bill*, a custom-house document, warranting the shipment of such bonded stores as the master of an outward-bound merchantman may require for his intended voyage. **1757** W. THOMPSON *R.N. Advoc.* 13 Half an Hour after the *Victualling-Board broke up, I was sent for. **1834–6** *Encycl. Metrop.* (1845) VIII. 380/1 The Victualling Board.. consumes many hundred tons [of old hoops] annually for the service of the navy. **1867** SMYTH *Sailor's Word-bk.*, **Victualling-book*, a counterpart of the ship's open list, which is kept by the purser, to enable him to make the necessary entries in it. **1588** *Roxb. Ball.* (1887) VI. 394 And *vittaling boothes in plentie were, Where they sold meate, bread, cheese, and beere. **1578** *Knaresb. Wills* (Surtees) I. 134 One *victualling carte, a bord and a carte in the haie laith. **1568** WITHALS *Dict.* 41 b/1 A *vittayling cooke. **1839** *Penny Cycl.* XIV. 343/2 To the eastward of Valletta..are.. spacious stores for the *victualling department. **1878** *Athletic World* 31 May 99/2 Francis..led off with a clever double on the..chin. Bassano then retaliated on the victualling department [= stomach]. **1757** W. THOMPSON *R.N. Advoc.* 52 He was..appointed to inspect all the King's *Victualling Dry Stores. **1834** *Victualling establishment [see VICTUALLING 2 b]. **1858** SIMMONDS *Dict. Trade*, **Victualling-note*, an order given to a seaman in the Royal navy by the paymaster, when he joins a ship, which is handed to the ship's steward as his authority for victualling the man. **1667** PEPYS *Diary* 2 Aug., Though I lay down my *victualling place, yet, as long as he continues victualler, I shall be the better by him. **1770** LANGHORNE *Plutarch* (1851) II. 837/2 He..furnished himself also with cattle and other *victualling provisions. **1757** W. THOMPSON *R.N. Advoc.* 20 One..had been in the *Victualling Service from a Boy. **1665** PEPYS *Diary* 28 April, Down the River to visit the *victualling-ships. **1711** *Broadside, Sailors Danger & Hardship at Sea* (title-p.), The loss of Seven large Transports and a Victualing Ship. **1858** SIMMONDS *Dict. Trade*, **Victualling-society*, a union or association of operatives, &c. to supply themselves with meat and bread, &c. at the lowest prices. **1757** W. THOMPSON *R.N. Advoc.* 48 The Timber..sent into Portsmouth *Victualling-yard was ..complained of. **1846** A. YOUNG *Naut. Dict.* 105 The Victualling Yards for the Royal Navy, where provisions and similar stores are deposited.

'victualling-house. [f. prec.] A house where victuals are supplied or sold; an eating-house, inn, or tavern.

α. **1540–1** ELYOT *Image Gov.* 57 To see that no vitailyng house..shoulde haue their doores open..either before the soonne risen, or after the soone set. **1555** EDEN *Decades* (Arb.) 148 They..determyned to buylde townes,..that they myght bee baytinge places and vytailynge houses for suche as shulde iorney towarde the southe. **1568** WITHALS *Dict.* 41 b/1 A vittellynge house, where meate is to be solde. **1617** MORYSON *Itin.* I. 122, I..tooke a chamber in a vitling house, in the Market-place.

β. **1571** in *13th Rep. Hist. MSS. Comm.* App. IV. 2 Licenced to keep a victualinge house within the towne of Ry. **1600–9** ROWLANDS *Knaue of Clubbes* 16 T'will be my castle for some three monethes space, while they search Tauerne, rifle victualing-house. **1662** in *Extr. St. P. rel. Friends* II. (1911) 146 To keepe an Alehouse or Victualling-house within your precincts. **1712** THORESBY *Diary* (1830) II. 151 After dinner at a victualling-house, I walked to Mr. Dawson's. **1737** *Gentl. Mag.* VII. 371/1 No License shall be granted to sell it by retail but to Publick Victualling-Houses, Inns, Coffee Houses or Alehouses. **1842** *Act 5–6 Vict.* c. 44 §1 Any Act or Acts in force touching the Regulation..of.. Victualling Houses. **1885** *Law Times* 28 Mar. 389/2 A refreshment and victualling house..on the Steep Holms, a rocky island in the Bristol Channel.

'victualling-'office. [f. as prec.] An office concerned with the victualling of ships, esp. of ships of the Royal Navy.

1668 *Extr. St. P. rel. Friends* III. (1912) 278 The Place was originally called Maison de diew, but now his Ma[jes]tis victualing office in this Port is seated there. **1710** C. SHADWELL *Fair Quaker Deal* I. i. 9 We..pry into the Rogueries of the Victualling-Office. **1757** W. THOMPSON *R.N. Advoc.* 48 The Labourers of Portsmouth Victualling Office are..employed in extra Hours. **1751** *England's Gazetteer* s.v. *Dover*, The courts of chancery, admiralty, &c. relating to them all, are kept in St. James's Ch., and here are a custom-house and victualling-office. **1827** SCOTT *Chron. Canongate* iii, Now, my wife had keepit a victualling office. **1834** *Encycl. Metrop.* (1845) VI. 350 The Victualling Office at Plymouth..is now brought almost into juxta-position with it [*sc.* the Dockyard].

b. *Boxing slang.* The stomach.

1751 SMOLLETT *Per. Pic.* c, He..found it impracticable to smite his antagonist upon the victualling office. **1785** GROSE *Dict. Vulg. Tongue* s.v. **1820** *Sporting Mag.* VI. 80 Spring put in a heavy claim on his opponent's victualling office.

‖**vicuña** (vi'kuɲa), **vicuna** (vɪ'k(j)uːnə). Forms: α. 7 becunia, 7– vicuna, 8–9 vicunna, 9 va-, vecuna, vicugna, vicugnia, 9– vicuña. β. 7 vicugne, 9 vicune. [a. Sp. *vicuña* (Pg. *vicunha*), the Quichuan name of the animal. See also VIGOGNE, VIGONE, and VIGONIA.]

1. A South American animal (*Auchenia vicunna*), closely related to the llama and alpaca, inhabiting the higher portions of the northern Andes and yielding a fine silky wool used for textile fabrics.

α. **1622** R. HAWKINS *Voy. S. Sea* 47 It may be surmised, that it is as that of the Becunia, and other Beasts, which breed the Beazer stone. **1661** LOVELL *Hist. Anim. & Min.* 28 The beast is about the bignesse and likeness of a Stagg. Their hair..is said also to help the gout: *sc.* Of that called Vicunas. **1704** *Collect. Voy.* (Churchill) III. 11/2 The Wild Goats are numerous; they are call'd Vicunna's. **1748** *Anson's Voy.* I. vi. 68 There are in all parts of this country a good number of Vicunnas or Peruvian sheep. **1771** tr. *Pernety's Voy. Malouine Isl.* (1773) 289 Several of our people went a shooting..and saw some carcases of vicunas. **1805** LUCCOCK *Nat. Wool* 14 We allude particularly to..the camel, and the dromedary, in the East, and the vicuna in South America. **1847** PRESCOTT *Peru* (1850) II. 100 His dress..was composed of the wool of the vicuña wrought into mantles, so fine that it had the appearance of silk. **1875** *Encycl. Brit.* I. 598/1 The vicugna is a much rarer animal than the alpaca. **1894** LYDEKKER *Roy. Nat. Hist.* II. 413 During the wet season of the year the vicunias seek the highest ridges of the Cordillera.

β. **1604** E. G[RIMSTONE] *D'Acosta's Hist. Indies* IV. xl. 316 Amongst the most remarkable things at the Indies of Peru, be the Vicugnes, and sheep of the countrie, as they call them. **1613** PURCHAS *Pilgrimage* (1614) 732 The Vicugne somewhat resembleth a Goat, but is greater. *c* **1806** *Acc. Viceroyalty Buenos Ayres* 21 *note*, There is also a wild species of the pacos, called vicunes.

2. *ellipt.* Vicuña cloth; also, a garment made of this.

1851 *Catal. Gt. Exhib.* 491/1 Ponchos:—Plain and brocade, striped; aravenas, Vicunas. **1853** *Household Words* 24 Sept. 76/1 The verbiage by which coats are transformed into..alpacas, vicunas, ponchos,..and siphonias. **1883** *Daily News* 22 Sept. 3/3 A dress of cigar-brown vicugna. **1887** *Standard* 15 Sept. 2/1 A thick diagonal vicuna has been introduced as a jacket cloth.

3. *attrib.* and *Comb.*, as ***vicuña-fur, -hunter, -skin***; **vicuña-cloth**, cloth made of vicuña-wool (hence ellipt. ***vicuña-costume***); **vicuña-wool**, (*a*) wool or fur of the vicuña; (*b*) a mixture of fine wool and cotton.

1851 *Catal. Gt. Exhib.* 490/2 Union cloth... *Vicuna cloth. **1882** CAULFEILD & SAWARD *Dict. Needlew.* 515/1 Vicuna cloth..is employed as a dress material, and is very soft in texture. **1889** *Daily News* 22 Oct. 6/1 Vicuna cloth is much in favour for dresses just now. **1884** *Cassell's Fam. Mag.* Oct. 697/2 The standing figure wears a pale brown *vicuna costume. **1851** *Catal. Gt. Exhib.* 487/1 *Vicuna fur, with woollen back. **1880** C. R. MARKHAM *Peruv. Bark* 125 This led us down into a valley, where I parted with my young *vicuña-hunter. **1840** *Penny Cycl.* XVIII. 228/2 The finest [ponchos] are made of *vicuña skins. **1804** *Gentl. Mag.* Nov. 1059 On board..were 20 sacks of *Vicuna [*mispr.* Vienna] wool. **1818** *Amer. St. Papers, For. Relat.* (1834) IV. 327 The imports..consisted of..771 arrobas of vacuna wool. **1862** *Catal. Internat. Exhib., Brit.* II. No. 4073 Tweeds..made from Vicugna wool. **1880** C. R. MARKHAM *Peruv. Bark* 135 The exquisite fabrics they weave from vicuña-wool.

†**vi-curate.** *Obs.*[−1] [See VICE- *prefix.*] A substitute in ecclesiastical functions.

a **1617** HIERON *Aarons Bells* (1623) 20 Their unlearned and for the most part ungodly Vi-Curates.

vicy-versy: see VICEY-VERSEY, VICY-VERSY.

vid.[1], abbrev. of VIDE *v.*

1609 SKENE *Reg. Maj.* Table 94 The father by reason of poverty may revoke the gift or donation made to his sonne. *vid. father. Ibid.* 95 Querrell (complaint, pley). *Vid. Pleyes.* **1706** STEVENS *Span. Dict.* I, *Enxaguaduras*, vid. *Enjuagaduras.* **1736** AINSWORTH *Eng.-Lat. Dict.* I. Index Geogr., Atrecht. *Vid.* Arras. **1788** LEMPRIÈRE *Class. Dict.*, *Iphimedusa*, one of the daughters of Danaus... *Vid.* Danaides. **1803** LEYDEN *Scenes Infancy* I. xxii. *note*, Vid. 'Minstrelsy of the Scottish Border'. **1836–9** *Todd's Cycl. Anat.* II. 626/2 Vid. the diagram *fig.* 283.

†**vid.**[2], abbrev. of VIDELICET. *Obs.*

1676 W. HARBORD in *Essex Papers* (Camden) 61 He was.. found guilty of manslaughter by 6, vid: Ld. Trea[sur]er, Ld. Privy Seale [etc.].

‖**vidame** ('viːdɑːm). Also 6 vydam(e, visdamme, 7 vidam. [a. F. *vidame*, OF. *visdame*, ad. med.L. *vicedominus*, f. *vice-* VICE- + *dominus* lord.] Formerly in France, one who held lands from a bishop as his representative and defender in temporal matters.

1523 LD. BERNERS *Froiss.* I. xlv. 25 b/2 The Vydame of Calons dyd marueyles. **1550** *Acts Privy Council* III. 121 Ordre..for the sending of..oone of the Gromes of the Chambre, to be furrer or harbenger to the saide Visdamme. **1614** SELDEN *Titles Honor* 252 Neither is there in France any Vidame which holds not of some Bishoprik, vnlesse that of Beauuais,..and from the chief Town of the Bishoprique are the Vidames denominated. **1635** R. N. tr. *Camden's Hist. Eliz.* I. 47 The French Embassadour in England solicited her that the Vidame of Chartres..might be delivered to the King. **1680** MACKENZIE *Sci. Her.* 87 To Counts, Vidames, and Viscounts [they allow] a direct standing Helmet, with 9 Barrs. **1725** tr. *Dupin's Eccl. Hist. 17th C.* I. v. 179 The Advocates and Vidames succeeded the Defenders, and by little and little these last Offices were abolish'd. **1801** RANKEN *Hist. France* I. 334 They employed a vidame, vice-dominus or commissary. **1802** *Ibid.* II. 259 They commissioned generally their avoués, or vidames, or some superior vassal, to levy and head the troops of their barony. **1852** SIR J. STEPHEN *Lect. Hist. France* I. 131 The advocate or vidame of an ecclesiastical corporation was usually some powerful count.

transf. **1622** in Birch *Crt. & Times Jas. I* (1849) II. 346 Here is a speech of a new dignity of vidams to be created, which should wedge in 'twixt knights and baronets.

Hence †**vidameship.** *Obs.*

a **1641** SPELMAN *Ant. Deeds* Eng. Wks. (1723) II. 242 These Officers obteyned likewise of their Lords the Bishops to have the Office of Vidameship in Fee.

viddeful, obs. Sc. form of WIDDIFUL *a.*

viddie, obs. Sc. form of WIDDY *sb.*

vide (vaɪd), *v.*[1] [Aphetic form of DIVIDE *v.*]

1. = DIVIDE *v.* 1. Now only in U.S. Blacks' use.

c **1400** *Destr. Troy* 1249 The bourder of his basnet [he] brestes in sonder, And videt the viser with a vile dynt. **1935** Z. N. HURSTON *Mules & Men* 20 'Way after while when He ketch dat Jew, He's goin' to 'vide things up more ekal'.

2. as *int.* A set parliamentary cry for the division of the house into two groups voting on each side of a question for the purpose of counting. Cf. DIVIDE *v.* 10.

1893 *Harper's Mag.* Dec. 39/2 This is usually done by shouting 'Divide! divide!' or, as the word is generally pronounced, "Vide! 'vide!" **1908** H. W. LUCY *Mem. Eight Parliaments* vi. 242 Opposite and around him was a crowd of hilarious gentlemen shouting "Vide! 'vide! 'vide!" **1951** J. BIGGS-DAVISON *George Wyndham* xiv. 206 From the Conservative Back Benches came a shout of "Vide! 'Vide!'

‖**vide** (ˈvaɪdɪ, ˈvɪdeɪ, ˈviːdeɪ), *v.*[2] *imp.* [L. *vidē*, imp. sing. of *vidēre* to see.] 'See, refer to, consult'; a direction to the reader to refer to some other heading, passage, or work (or to a table, diagram, etc.) for fuller or further information.

Freq. abbreviated as *vid.*: see VID.[1]; also occas. as *v.* V 5.

1565 COOPER *Thesaurus* App., *Pysades*, the sonne of Strophius:..Vide *Pisades.* **1626** BACON *Sylva* §59 For which I haue compounded an Ointment of Excellent Odour, which I call Roman Ointment, *vide* the *Receit.* **1699** EVELYN *Acetaria* 51 The Limon is somewhat more acute, cooling and extinguishing Thirst... *Vide* Limon. **1713** SWIFT *Cadenus & Vanessa* 111 She then referr'd them to a place In Virgil, *vide* Dido's case. **1823** J. BADCOCK *Dom. Amusem.* 33 *Vide* Rollin *passim.* **1837** WILKINSON *Mann. & Cust. Anc. Egypt* ii. (1841) I. 66 *note*, *Vide* my Egypt and Thebes, p. 194 note. **1857** GOSSE *Omphalos* xii. 354 *note*, I have already proved that blood must have been in..the newly-created Man (*vide* p. 276, *supra*).

†**videl.**, abbreviated f. next.

1589 PUTTENHAM *Eng. Poesie* (Arb.) 82 But the three is made of one number, videl. of two and an vnitie. **1615** W. BEDWELL *Moham. Impost.* II. 59 Therefore there remaineth yet another great difficultie, *videl.* How this law should be vniuersall.

‖**videlicet** (vɪˈdɛlɪsɛt, vaɪ-), *adv.* and *sb.* Also 7 videllicet. [L. *vidēlicet*, f. *vidē-*, stem of *vidēre* to see + *licet* it is permissible. Cf. SCILICET.

The pron. (vɪ-, vaɪˈdiːlɪsɪt) is also to some extent in use.]

A. *adv.* That is to say; namely; to wit: used to introduce an amplification, or more precise or explicit explanation, of a previous statement or word. (Cf. the abbreviated forms VID.[2], VIDEL., VIDZ(T., and VIZ.)

1464 *Mann. & Househ. Exp.* (Roxb.) 452 Alle odre percellis that are enteryd and engrosyd in my lordis book: videlicet: Ferst [etc.]. **1492** in Rymer *Fœdera* (1711) XII. 480/1 To serve him in his Werres,..*videlicet*, himself, having his Custrell and Page. **1509** *Will* in *Archaeologia* LXVI. 310 Massez of Requiem to be saide and song for my Soule by Preestes in maner and forme folowing videlicet Euery Freer [etc.]. **1563** FOXE *A. & M.* 796/1 Sundry clauses, pointes, matters..: Videlicet, amonges other thinges, where the bishop offred to make particuler aunswere [etc.]. **1579** FULKE *Heskins' Parl.* 131 We doe not take one thing: videlicet bread. **1602** T. FITZHERBERT *Apol.* 27 The words of our sauiour following the former in S. Mathew videlicet: I wil geeue thee the keyes of the kingdome of heauen. **1665** in *Parish Bks. St. Julian's, Salop* I. 125 (MS.), Due to Nath: Clemson for work done to the Clock Videlicet for a new Spring,..for wyer and oyle, 5[*s*]. **1727** SWIFT *Circumcision E. Curll* Wks. 1755 III. I. 165 The wisest man that ever was, and inasmuch the richest, beyond all peradventure was a Jew, videlicet, Solomon. **1769** *Phil. Trans.* LIX. 452 To confirm farther what I say, videlicet, that the water, the more glutinous it is, the more it is disposed to become luminous. **1829** SCOTT *Rob Roy* Introd., One of Rob's original profession, *videlicet* a drover. **1840** BARHAM *Ingol. Leg.* Ser. I. *St. Odille*, Then let's act like Count Otto, and while one survives, Succumb to *our* She-Saints—videlicet wives!

B. *sb.* The word itself as used to introduce an explanation or amplification, esp. in legal documents.

a **1658** CLEVELAND *Wks.* (1687) 100 You shall never take a Pamphleteer, one of these Haberdashers of small Wares, without his *Videlicets*, or his *Vtpotes*. *Ibid.*, A *Videlicet* is an *Hic Canis*, it argues a Bungling Writer, as that a Painter. **1774** LD. MANSFIELD in Cowper *Rep.* (1783) 170 He has stated it to be in Minorca; with a *videlicet*. **1805** EAST *Reports* V. 252 In *Stukely* v. *Butler* (Hob. 172) Lord C. J. Hobart speaking of the use of a videlicet, says [etc.]. **1824** STEPHEN *Princ. Pleading* 313 And here, as in the case of a local fact, the insertion of a videlicet will give no help.

‖**viˈdenda**, *sb. pl. rare.* [L., pl. of *videndum*, f. *vidēre* to see.] Things worth seeing or which ought to be seen.

1760 STERNE *Tr. Shandy* VII. xxxi, In my list, therefore, of Videnda at Lyons, this, tho' last,—was not, you see, least. **1771** M. TYSON *Let.* in Nichols *Lit. Anecd.* (1814) VIII. 571 Gray's notes..contain the Videnda in all parts of Great Britain, as Houses, Antiquities, Views, &c. **1790** J. BYNG *Torrington Diaries* (1954) 312 Thus is one often humbug'd by printed accounts of visionary videnda! **1964** AUDEN in *Listener* 1 Oct. 525/1 Windows averted from plausible videnda but admitting a light one could mend a watch by.

†ˈ**vident.** *Obs. rare.* [ad. L. *vident-*, *videns*, pres. pple. of *vidēre* to see.] (See quot.)

1588 J. HARVEY *Disc. Probl.* 40 The holy prophets..were properly called Vidents, or Seers.

video (ˈvɪdɪəʊ), *sb.* [f. L. *vidē-re* to see + -O, after AUDIO-.] Absol. use of VIDEO-.

1. That which is displayed or to be displayed on a television screen or other cathode-ray tube; the signal corresponding to this.

1937 *Printers' Ink Monthly* May 45/2 *Video*, the sight channel in television, as opposed to audio, the sound channel. **1940** *Broadcasting* 1 June 32 Video seen 230 miles at sea. Clear steady images picked up during test. **1946** [see DISPLAY *sb.* 1 c]. **1949** *Hollywood Q.* Winter 157 And pipe the finished output of these segments, both video and audio, instantaneously and simultaneously to the kinescope recorders. **1951** *Proc. IRE* XXXIX. 8/1 One cycle of video during active horizontal scanning represents one dark and one light picture element on a particular scanning line. **1960** J. L. BERNSTEIN *Video Tape Recording* p. vii, Directors, editors, cameramen, and others..would benefit if they could learn the processes involved in recording video on tape. **1964** *Times* 7 Feb. p. iv/3 Except for its width..video tape looks exactly like sound recording tape. But it records not only sound but a continuous picture—video—as well! **1976** *Aviation Week* 10 May 131/1 An IBM scan converter transforms radar video into a format suitable for presentation on the TV monitors. **1977** *Gramophone* Aug. 361/2, I see it as the precursor of the all-purpose high quality cassette recorder that will record both video and audio. **1979** W. C. BRANDENBURG *Introd. Television Servicing* ii. 4/2 Both the audio and video can be broadcasted from the same antenna. **1982** G. WHITE *Video Techniques* vi. 134 Sound is as important as the video and often more difficult to edit.

2. Television as a broadcasting medium. *U.S. colloq.*

1941 *Amer. Mercury* Nov. 581/2 *Vidio*,..television. **1946** *Time* 25 Feb. 72 NBC published a 55-page booklet, listing words & phrases commonly used in video. **1954** *Billboard* 13 Nov. 21 Most of the big name spinners have taken a fling in video during the last five years, but their survival-average has been low. **1979** *Boston Globe* 10 Apr. 32 Their play was flashed by video to an adjoining room where experts commented on it before a throng.

3. A video recorder; also, a VDU.

1958 *Observer* 26 Jan. 14/6 The Video is like a combined tape-recorder and cinema camera. It records your television appearance complete with sound track and can be played back at the touch of a switch. **1979** *Television & Home Video* Mar. 7/2 There's not a lot of point in owning a home video and using it to record the rubbish you might otherwise have missed. **1982** *Times* 7 May 17/5 Last year over 900,000 videos were rented or sold in Britain. **1983** *What's New in Computing* Jan. 5/1 The rest of the machine, the discs, the power supplies and the videos are all retained or upgraded and existing software can be run side by side with new software. **1984** S. TOWNSEND *Growing Pains A. Mole* 190 We are the only family in our street who haven't got a video.

4. A video recording; videotape as a recording medium.

1968 *Observer* 14 Jan. 28/4 The days of the disc, in the pop world at least, are numbered. For soon will come the video. We will have the top 20 videos which you plug into your home video-machine. **1978** *Radio Times* 4–10 Mar. 4/2 We've got some video of a man he has already made contact with... We'll just have to cut in with that if necessary. **1981** *Church Times* 7 Aug. 5/3 They..went down to BBC television... Later he popped round to the school and showed them a video of themselves. **1983** *New Scientist* 3 Mar. 569/1 The BBC recognised early on that there was money to be made from selling archive programmes on video. **1984** *Melody Maker* 6 Oct. 3/1 Spandau Ballet have just returned from Hong Kong where they filmed the video for 'Highly Strung'.

5. The production or use of video recordings.

1970 *It* 9–24 Apr. 7 There are also groups of people exploiting video in any way they can think of. **1977** *N.Y. Rev. Bks.* 23 June 25/4 Made images move (cinema) and achieved their simultaneous recording and transmission (video). **1980** *Times* 31 Mar. 24/6 There are enough able practitioners around to demonstrate how effectively video, like any other artistic tool, can be used. **1980** C. MACCABE *Godard* 26 You envisaged a different kind of distribution: film and video as a handcraft industry. **1982** *Listener* 11 Feb. 34/3 The good news is that things in video could be worse. The bad news is that things in video will get worse.

video (ˈvɪdɪəʊ), *v.* [f. the sb.]

1. *trans.* To make a video recording of.

1971 *Jrnl. Soc. Motion Picture Engineers & Television Engineers* LXXX. 414 *Video*, to dub by rerecording the video signal recovered from the tape being copied. **1984** *What Video?* Aug. 4/2 My work..is videoing anything to do with the emergency services (road accidents, fires etc.).

2. *U.S.* To televise. *rare.*

1973 E. BULLINS *Theme is Blackness* 5 Colored people knew they were black, unique, separate and had a future. For paeans of Blackness were videoed throughout Black America.

video- (ˈvɪdɪəʊ), VIDEO *sb.* used as a formative element and also as an attributive use of the simple term. (Collocations are variously hyphened or written as one or two words, and it is therefore difficult to distinguish between formative and attributive origin: the forms below offer some guide to their most common style.) **video amplifier**, an amplifier able to amplify the wide range of frequencies present in video signals and suited to delivering a signal to the picture tube of a television set; **video art**, art in which a video recording is the medium; so **video artist**; **video camera**, a camera for producing an electrical signal corresponding to a changing scene, suitable for feeding to a video recorder; **videocaˈssette**, a cassette of videotape; freq. *attrib.*; ˈ**video-ˌconference**, an arrangement in which television sets linked by telephone lines or the like are used to enable a group of people in different places to see and hear whichever of them is speaking at the time; hence **video-ˈconferencing** *vbl. sb.*, telecommunication in the form of a videoconference; ˈ**video-disc**, a disc on which (moving or static) visual images have been recorded in non-representational form for subsequent reproduction on a television screen or the like; **video display terminal** or **unit** = *visual display unit* s.v. VISUAL *a.* 6 e; abbrev. VDU s.v. V 5 b; **video film**, orig., a cinematographic film of a television broadcast; now, a recording on a videocassette; **video frequency**, a frequency in the range employed for the video signal in television (viz. a few hertz to several million hertz), *esp.* one in the higher part of this range; freq. *attrib.*; **video game**, a game played by electronically manipulating images displayed on a television screen; **video map**, a map produced electronically on a radar screen to assist in navigation; so **video mapping**; **video nasty** *colloq.*, a horror video film; ˈ**videophone**, a telephone incorporating a television screen on which the other person may be seen speaking; also as *v. trans.*; **video piracy**, the illegal production and sale of copies of commercial video films; so **video pirate**; **video-player**, a machine used in conjunction with a television for playing videocassettes; ˈ**videoporn** *colloq.*, pornography on videotape; **video signal**, a signal that contains all the information required for producing the picture in television broadcasting; **video-ˈtelephone** = *videophone* above; **video terminal** = *video display unit* above.

1937 *Electronics* Aug. 22/1 A video amplifier is one that is responsive to picture signals, and therefore, is an extremely good audio as well as a very wide band radio frequency amplifier. **1975** D. G. FINK *Electronics Engineers' Handbk.* xx. 55 Finally the video amplifier raises the signal to from 50 to 100 V to drive the picture tube. **1972** *Harper's Mag.* June 92 Few of these programs are going to win awards as video art. *Ibid.* 90 Russ Connor is now in charge of granting money through the New York State Council to independent video artists. **1975** *N.Y. Times* 14 Apr. 33 Mr. Gillette..is one of a growing breed of video artists, for whom the TV screen has become an esthetic medium... They produce video-tapes that take ingenious advantage of the technology. **1975** *New Yorker* 5 May 44/1 The video-art movement, which has been in high gear for more than three years now, can have come as a surprise to practically no one. **1978** *Chicago* June 14/4 Channel 11 producer Tom Weinburg [is] a video artist and part-owner of the White Sox. **1978** *Tucson Mag.* Dec. 28/1 Videocameras for home productions range from $300 to $1500. **1983** *New Scientist* 24 Mar. 793/1 It is neither easy nor ethical to perch with notebook or video camera over spontaneous scenes of human mating or aggression. **1970** *Times* 26 Sept. 12/1 The video-cassette comprises a pre-recorded, pre-packaged programme of pictures and sound, designed to be 'played' on a television set with a converter. **1976** *Broadcast* 23 Aug. 8/1 The videocassette editor..is a small desk-top box..controlling two Sony video-cassette recorders. **1978** *Lancashire Life* Nov. 112/1 (Advt.), The Philips N1700 uses a 2½ hour video cassette no larger than the average paperback, and like an audio cassette the video cassette recordings can be played back whenever you like and as often as you like. **1982** M. BABSON *Death beside Seaside* xv. 132 That's a video cassette recorder! Where did he get that? We couldn't afford that. **1977** *Communications: Technol. for Better Tomorrow* (Proc. 13th Ann. Internat. Conf. Communications) III. 75/1 An experimental videoconference link has been installed in France. **1983** *Times* 25 June 8/5 Whether a face-to-face meeting is in any sense 'better' than a videoconference is a different question. **1977** *Communications: Technol. for Better Tomorrow* (Proc. 13th Ann. Internat. Conf. Communications) III. 75/1 Characteristics concerning typical pictures in video-conferencing. **1983** *New Scientist* 7 Apr. 7/3 British Telecom has been running video conferencing studios for the past 12 years. **1967** *Ibid.* 2 Feb. 285/3 We shall soon have on the market the video-disc, about the size of a gramophone record and costing about 22 shillings. **1975** *Broadcast* 28 July 11/2 Consider the mind-boggling experience of a visit to your local bookstore to purchase a videodisc with perhaps 150 books on it—or maybe 54,000 slides of paintings. **1982** *New Scientist* 21 Oct. 150/1 Video discs are the video equivalent of the long-playing record. **1982** *Jrnl. R. Soc. Arts* Nov. 781/1 The floppy disc can hold the equivalent of 40 pages of the *Concise Oxford Dictionary*, but the video disc the whole of the *Encyclopaedia Britannica*. **1976** *New Yorker* 1 Mar. 23/2 A V.D.T.; or Video Display Terminal, is a machine that combines a television screen with a typewriter keyboard and is connected to 'a gigantic network of computers'. **1983** *Boston Globe* 12 July 3/5 Video display terminals, or VDTs, have become commonplace in many offices. **1968** Video display unit [see VDU s.v. V 5 b]. **1969** *Jane's Freight Containers 1968–69* 114/3 New video display units provide instantaneous information to answer inquiries from customers concerning the location of cars. **1983** *Engin. & Mining Jrnl.* May 99/1 Engineers have at their disposal newly developed hardware and soft-ware, with modern distributed control systems using computer interface and video display units. **1944** R. E. LEE *Television* ix. 182 Even with the financial savings of videofilm, television is the most expensive way of selling things that man has ever concocted. **1955** *Amer. Cinematographer* XXXVI. 365/1 Within a matter of minutes, this video film recording can be quick-processed and screened. **1978** *Washington Post* 29 Mar. D-2/5 The flight scheduled to carry the video film of Sunday's game 'did not take off' Monday night. **1983** *Daily Tel.* 10 June 2/3 Management brought in video films which were shown in updated form every few months to enable employees to know how the company was functioning. **1937** *Electronics* Aug. 23/2 There are several ways of designing an amplifier to give satisfactory response for video frequencies. **1956** AMOS & BIRKINSHAW *Television Engin.* II. i. 28 The video-frequency signal generated by scanning such a scene has a uniform level which is interrupted by the sync signals. **1982** *Electronics* 6 Oct. 63 In development,..is a..generator for cathode-ray-tube applications offering an 80-MHz video frequency. **1973** *Business Week* 10 Nov. 212/1 The astonishing ability of the video game to lure quarters from the public and the electronic techniques used in its design are forcing major changes on the coin-operated game business. **1983** *Wall St. Jrnl.* 5 Jan. 1/2 Coleco's 1982 earnings 'appear to be well in excess of five times 1981 levels of $7.7 million,' the third-largest maker of video games said. **1961** *Aeroplane* CI. 74/2 All displays are capable of accepting video map information. **1982** *Radar-82* (IEE Conf. No. 216) 307/1 Producing a video map very much more accurate than the radar data is unnecessarily costly. **1954** *Sun* (Baltimore) 18 Mar. (B ed.) 20/4 Another of the new developments, 'video mapping', electronically reproduces an area map on the radar scope—showing terrain hazards, airport runways and radio flight paths. 1962 *Flight Internat.* LXXXI. 283/2 The range of synthetic displays to be added to the raw radar..will include video mapping. 1983 *Listener* 10 Feb. 4/1 The same children are sometimes known to see video 'nasties' or horror films screened later on. 1984 *Ibid.* 14 June 3/2 Unless one has seen a video nasty ..it is difficult to imagine the depths of degradation to which certain producers are willing to sink. 1955 C. L. MOORE in 'E. Crispin' *Best SF* 129 He..called Maltzer's apartment by videophone. *Ibid.* 131 Maltzer videophoned him. 1971 *New Scientist* 1 July 14/2 The West Germans have recently begun operating a 240-mile experimental videophone link. 1976 *TV Guide* (U.S.) 1 May, To reach other videophone outlets, the user merely dials the telephone. 1980 *Times* 2 Aug. 2/4 Audio and video piracy..usually involve the copying of a legitimate product such as video-taped film. 1983 *Daily Tel.* 20 June 17/2 Customs and Excise is claiming the right to see documents seized under a court order by a firm of London solicitors acting for the British Videogram Association in a video piracy case. 1982 *Ibid.* 17 Nov. 2/3 A video pirate was fined £500 yesterday by magistrates in Chepstow, Gwent, in a test case which could start a new clampdown on the illegal copies. 1983 *New Scientist* 3 Mar. 569/1 The deal is a blow to the video-pirates, who have cashed in by selling illegal copies. 1970 *Sci. Amer.* Dec. 37/1 (Advt.), The little cartridge simply drops into the videoplayer you will have attached to your set. 1972 *Listener* 8 June 775/3, I would guess that in about fifteen years most people would have a video-player of one sort or another in their homes. 1983 *N.Y. Times* 23 Apr. 48/4 The man.. slipped a cassette into his video player... A comedian.. popped into view on the television screen. 1979 *Daily Tel.* 15 Dec. 15/5 The programme claimed that a 'video-porn' cassette of Linda Lovelace's 'Deep Throat'..was made in America with Mafia money. 1982 *Punch* 13 Jan. 83/2 Before videoporn and clockwork dildo moved inexorably in. 1937 J. C. WILSON *Television Engin.* ix. 346 Fig. 210..shows a triode valve having its grid biased approximately at zero volts, so that on receipt of positive video signals it runs into grid current and the video-signal voltage is dropped across the series grid resistance. 1937 [see FADE *v.*[1] 9 b]. 1957 AMOS & BIRKINSHAW *Television Engin.* I. i. 17 The composite signal obtained by combining a picture with a synchronising signal is known as a video signal. 1976 A. DAVIS *Television* ii. 28 The main problem was the high speed at which the tape needed to run in order to accommodate the wider range of frequencies of video signals compared with audio signals. 1964 M. MCLUHAN *Understanding Media* xxii. 233 The possibility of shopping by two-way TV, or video-telephone. 1978 *Jrnl. R. Soc. Arts* CXXVI. 270/2 The interview will remain the mainstay of any selection procedure: even if it is transferred to the video telephone. 1970 *Computer Management* Nov. 52/2 The key point in all video terminal applications, present or future, is the ease of handling and understanding information presented in a familiar form. 1983 *N.Y. Times* 28 Jan. 18/2 I.R.S. operators will still do the talking, but the computers will catalogue and display on video terminals all the taxpayers' facts, figures and prior promises.

II. Independent use of VIDEO as a quasi-sb. used *attrib.*: **1.** Of or pertaining to (*a*) television, or (*b*) the visual element of television broadcasts or the signals representing it.

1935 [see AUDIO- II]. 1937 *RCA Rev.* July 17 Another important consideration has to do with the difficulty of feeding and switching video circuits. 1944 *Jrnl. Television Soc.* IV. 69/2 Trap circuits are commonly used..to keep the sound carrier out of the video channel. 1945 J. BARZUN *Teacher in Amer.* xix. 280 The copywriter..must be the same who was impelled to call television 'the video art'. 1949 *Proc. IRE* XXXVII. 289/2 Video Techniques. Notable progress was made in the comparatively new field of television recording on film. 1951 KOESTLER *Age of Longing* 194 An American video commentator. 1959 N. MAILER *Advts. for Myself* (1961) 157 A hippopotamus of a television-radio-and-phonograph cabinet with the blind monstrous snout of the video tube. 1967 *Boston Herald* 1 Apr. 1/1 News commentator Chet Huntley claimed Friday he had the support of his video partner, David Brinkley, and all but three of 40 NBC newscasters in his bid. 1979 *Daily Tel.* 17 Dec. 12/6 Such moments..were rare in Alick Rowe's *Two People* (ITV)... Video-drama remains uncertain about the love story.

2. Of or pertaining to video recording.

1955, etc. [see *video film*, etc. above]. 1973 *Art Internat.* Mar. 42/2 The video sculpture *De La*, which utilizes the machine constructed for shooting *La Région Centrale*, carries on a discourse on perception at the same time that it exists as a fascinating mechanical object. 1976 *Broadcast* Dec. 20/1 In a video world he has still a film-stock contribution to make to the overall impression of the whole. 1977 C. MCFADDEN *Serial* (1978) iv. 14/2 He said he'd had amazing results just acting out his anger with his patients. He was also big on video feedback.., role-playing..and Japanese hot tubs. 1979 *Daily Tel.* 15 Dec. 15/5 Home video equipment is giving the Mafia a foothold in Britain, with illegal distribution of pornography and pirated films... 'Videocrime' is growing so fast that it will be the Crime of the '80s. 1980 *Times* 25 Jan. (Audio Visual Rep.) p. ii/5 Video programmes are being used by the National Bus Company for training drivers. 1982 *Listener* 23 & 30 Dec. 10/3 If you don't like what broadcast television offers, then you can supplement the diet from the video shop. 1984 *What Video?* Aug. 6/2 The VR-3995 has four video heads for noise-free still frame and slow motion.

videogram (ˈvɪdiːəʊɡræm). [f. VIDEO- + -GRAM.]

1. An apparatus for making or reproducing video recordings. *rare.*

1963 *Times* 17 Aug. 4/2 A young Wolverhampton design consultant said today that he had invented a record player which reproduced vision as well as sound..Mr. Mason's videogram—as he has named it—could be on sale soon. 1972 *Guardian* 11 Apr. 15/2 They have ordered 60 cassette recorders—videograms is the coming word.

2. A prerecorded video recording; a commercial video film or disc.

1972 *Publishers Weekly* 10 Apr. 27/2 Mr. Geranton insisting on the distinction between a video copy of a previous work (say a film) and an original 'videogram'. 1976 [see PHONOGRAM 2]. 1980 *Daily Tel.* 15 Oct. 18 The newly formed British Videogram Association..will put an end to people taping a film on one television channel while they watch football..on the other. 1982 R. DEAN *Home Video* vi. 71 Videogram sales and rentals are now dominated by features, with 'adult' subjects..running close behind. 1983 *Times* 29 Jan. 4/2 Owners and distributors of videograms (pre-recorded video cassettes and discs) are to be asked..to approve cinema-type certifications.

So **vide'ographer**, one who makes videograms; **vide'ography**, the process or activity of making a video recording using a video camera; the use of such a camera.

1976 (*title of periodical*) Videography. 1980 *Daily Tel.* 18 June 17/2 Videography is what they are calling it and it will revolutionise home movies. Following hard on the sales of video recorders..comes the video camera. 1983 *N.Y. Times* 24 July II. 30/6 One more advantage that the cinematographer has over the videographer is in the amount of lighting required. Video requires a lot of light to get a good result. 1984 *What Video?* Aug. 40/1 Colour settings are especially important with underwater videography. 1985 *Audio Visual* Feb. 54/3 Although obviously intended for a primary audience of stills photographers, David Kilpatrick's..volume could just as easily serve as a guide to in-house videographers.

videophile (ˈvɪdɪəʊfaɪl), *sb.* orig. *U.S.* [f. VIDEO- + -PHILE.] One who is very keen on watching television or video recordings.

1978 *Washington Post* 2 July M-4/2 In time there will be a videophile subculture: it is evolving now, as members of the baby-boom generation come to realize that television has played the cultural role in their lives that the movies and radio played in their parents' lives. 1980 *Business Week* 7 July 77/1 Pioneer Electronic Corp...is betting that it can turn its large base of audiophiles into videophiles. It.. recently set up a new subsidiary..to produce music for videodiscs. 1984 *New Yorker* 20 Feb. 42/1 Kodak's new system had a maximum recording time of ninety minutes —not enough for a football game. The product, he said, would have 'some appeal to the upscale videophile'.

video recording, *vbl. sb.* Also with hyphen and as one word. [f. VIDEO *sb.* + RECORDING *vbl. sb.*]

1. a. The process of making a cinematographic film of what appears on a television screen. **b.** The process of recording on videotape; videotaping.

1949 *Tele-Tech* May 31/3 The most obvious problem in designing a suitable photographic camera for video recording is that of reconciling the 30 frames per second rate of American television with the 24 frame per second rate which is standard in motion pictures. 1953 *Proc. IRE* XLI. 466/1 Work on video recording has not been restricted to film. Advances were made in the experimental recording of video information on tape. 1962 R. BRETZ *Techniques Television Production* (ed. 2) xxiii. 495 A standard sound-record head contacts the tape a half-second after the video recording has been done. 1983 *Nature* 23 June 651/3 These ..combine the recovery of [sea-] bed samples with the photography and video-recording of marine life.

2. a. A film of a television broadcast. **b.** A recording on videotape.

1950 *Tele-Tech* Nov. 32 (*heading*) Video recordings improved by the use of continuous moving film. 1968 A. WHITNEY *Every Man has his Price* vii. 59 She nearly died when we showed that videorecording to her! 1978 P. MARSH et al. *Rules of Disorder* iv. 112 Oxford fans were shown..a video-recording which was made..during their game with Plymouth Argyle. 1984 *Guardian* 5 Oct. 2/3 The court heard a video recording of an interview given by Mr. Scargill to Channel 4.

So **'videorecord** *v. trans.*, to make a video recording of; **'videorecorded** *ppl. a.*; **video recorder**, an apparatus for making video recordings; *spec.* a form of tape recorder for recording television programmes from the broadcast signal.

1951 *Jrnl. Soc. Motion Picture & Television Engineers* LVI. 222 (*caption*) Video recorder. 1954 *Tele-Tech* May 129 To be..acceptable to television stations, the magnetic video recorder must be capable of handling color signals with similar fidelity. 1960 J. L. BERNSTEIN *Video Tape Recording* i. 1 The video recorder is able to provide immediate playback after a scene has been shot. 1961 *Britannica Bk. of Year* 537/1 Science also provided a term for a relatively new process with *video-record*, to record..in pictures rather than sound. 1972 *Daily Tel.* 22 Jan. 2/5 The disadvantages of having all schools broadcasts from ITV in the mornings (.. many teachers may now videorecord them if they have the equipment). 1975 *Language for Life* (Dept. Educ. & Sci.) xxii. 322 Such activities would involve the play-back in school hours of video-recorded evening programmes. 1978 *Lancashire Life* Sept. 131/1 Now the video-recorder has arrived in the home. 1979 *Jrnl. R. Soc. Arts* Apr. 265/2 This teaching sequence is video-recorded by the use of a simple CCTV system. 1979 *Financial Rev.* (Sydney) 5 Oct. 23/1 A US District Court judge has ruled that the non-commercial use of home video recorders to record television broadcasts is lawful. 1983 L. DEIGHTON *Berlin Game* vi. 65 You should have heard George when the au pair dropped his wretched video recorder.

videotape (ˈvɪdɪəʊteɪp), *sb.* Also as two words or hyphenated. [f. VIDEO- + TAPE *sb.*[1]]

1. a. Magnetic tape on which can be recorded moving visual images such as television programmes (as well as sound).

1953 *Wall St. Jrnl.* 2 Dec. 1/4 With further development of video tape techniques, numerous possibilities will open up. Small portable television cameras are already in wide use in industry, in stores, banks and schools. 1965 *Listener* 10 June 857/2 A course of television mathematics lectures is now being recorded. Where these are transmitted from videotape the lecturer will be in the room with the students. 1973 C. BONINGTON *Next Horizon* viii. 117 We'll record the climb on video-tape the day before it actually goes out on the air. 1980 B. W. ALDISS *Life in West* i. 15 Standing by the bookstall was a white board announcing that the television series had been captured on videotape and would be shown in its entirety over the four evenings of the conference. 1985 *Listener* 24 Jan. 37/1 Videotape soon became a vehicle for prerecorded films and music programmes.

b. A length of videotape, or the recording it carries.

1960 *Guardian* 7 May 1 Video-tapes and film versions of the ceremony were being flown all over the world. 1967 *New Scientist* 2 Feb. 285/3 Americans have been at great pains to discover whether students learn as much from televised lectures and video-tapes as they do from 'live' lectures. *a* 1974 R. CROSSMAN *Diaries* (1976) II. 135 They wanted a video-tape to be made of every word said in the House of Commons and the House of Lords. 1977 *Language* LIII. 883 Videotapes of the lectures have been broadcast nationally. 1984 *What Video?* Aug. 14/1 (Advt.), You can easily view a negative or positive film image on a TV screen and also record it on a video tape.

2. *attrib.*

1958 *Times* 24 July 5/2 The BBC's VERA which tape-records complete television shows, picture and sound combined, and the AMPEX and R.C.A. videotape machines which do the same job for the independent television contractors, will greatly facilitate the provision of such Press shows. 1963 J. N. HARRIS *Weird World Wes Beattie* (1964) viii. 90 Sometimes she was in New York, holding a can of toilet-bowl cleanser in front of a videotape camera. 1976 B. JACKSON *Flameout* iii. 40 A man hefting a videotape camera on his shoulder brushed past, focusing his camera for another long shot. 1977 *Times of Swaziland* 11 Feb. 5 (Advt.), Kosie Smith v's Victor Galindez—light heavy weight title fight—in our Video-Tape Shows starting 8.30 every night. 1978 *Broadcast* 13 Nov. 23/1 The Circle is presently involved in forming..a video tape library. 1979 *Globe & Mail* (Toronto) 5 May 48/2 The [tennis] club has 24 courts,..videotape play-back, ball machines and individual stroke analysis.

b. videotape recorder, a tape recorder that will record and replay videotape recordings; **videotape recording**, a recording on videotape; also, the making of such a recording.

1954 *Proc IRE* XLII. 731/2 Video tape recorders were demonstrated. *Ibid.* 756/2 Experimental video tape recording systems were demonstrated. 1959 *Daily Tel.* 9 Mar. 13/2 Television has entered an era of video tape recording that will profoundly influence future development. 1959 *Listener* 19 Mar. 499/2 Some executives think that video-tape recordings will help them to beat the film menace. 1963 *Guardian* 11 Sept. 7/6 Increasingly the television camera and videotape recorder, an unwieldy picture development of the ordinary tape-recorder, are being used where once the cine camera stood alone. 1971 *New Scientist* 16 Sept. 633/1 Videotape recording (VTR) offers them a freedom which is impossible with film. 1978 *Tucson Mag.* Dec. 28/1 Since videotape recorders hit the scene, television addicts don't have to choose between two conflicting programs. 1980 *Brit. Med. Jrnl.* 29 Mar. 889/1 Before and during stimulation the patients were examined clinically; videotape recordings made of their movements; [etc.]. 1984 *Listener* 19 July 34/2 There is..an enormous park of video-tape-recorders in Britain.

Hence **'videotape** *v. trans.*, to record on videotape; **'videotaped** *ppl. a.*, **'videotaping** *vbl. sb.*

1964 *Times* 7 Feb. (Advt. Suppl.) p. iv/3 Even an expert cannot tell the difference between live and video-taped programmes. 1970 R. PARKES *Death-Mask* xv. 186 An agonising interview had been video-taped at the television studios. 1977 J. D. DOUGLAS in Douglas & Johnson *Existential Sociol.* i. 10 This form of linguistic ethnomethodology imposed the further constraint that only those accounts that could be tape-recorded or video-taped could be studied. 1977 *Times* 29 June 7/6 The FBI had set up an antique shop..fitted with wiretaps and hidden videotaping equipment. 1979 *Time* 30 July 12 After the lesson Carter ran through the speech and watched a videotaped replay, then practiced again, until he and Rafshoon were satisfied. 1980 B. W. ALDISS *Life in West* i. 28, I see..that some ingenious person..has videotaped my television series.

videotex (ˈvɪdɪəʊtɛks). Chiefly *U.S.* [f. VIDEO- + TEX(T *sb.*[1]] = next.

1978 *Globe & Mail* (Toronto) 16 Aug. B2/2 The Federal Department of Communications has developed a two-way television system called Videotex that it claims is superior to rival British and French systems. 1980 R. WOOLFE *Videotex* i. 4 This book is about two-way, inter-active videotex... One-way videotex..is referred to as teletext. Two-way videotex is called plain videotex. 1980 *Economist* 9 Aug. 71/1 America is proceeding equally slowly with a cousin of teletext, known as viewdata or videotex. 1981 *Sci. Amer.* Oct. E5/1 (Advt.), The Prestel videotex service has been operating for two years and is the largest information retrieval network in the world. 1983 *Amer. Banker* 8 June 8/1 The role banks will play in the emerging videotex field —a technology which permits consumers to access a variety of data bases and transaction services with a home terminal —has been much debated.

videotext (ˈvɪdɪəʊtɛkst). [f. VIDEO- + TEXT *sb.*] Any information system in which a television is used to display alphanumeric information selected by the user; viewdata or teletext, esp. the former.

1980 *Times* 25 Jan. (Audio Visual Rep.) p. i/6 There is evidence of companies in Britain becoming increasingly aware of the importance of video communications through the viewdata services such as the Prestel system of the Post Office, and a wide variety of other forms of computer-generated videotexts. 1980 *New Scientist* 3 July 49/4 The

British pioneered viewdata (now known as videotext according to international standards) with Prestel, but the Gallic Teletel is running hard to catch up. **1981** *Ibid.* 10 Dec. 721/1 The first big order for a public videotext system—in West Germany—has gone to IBM, not to British Telecom's Prestel. **1983** *Christian Sci. Monitor* 15 Apr. B-12/2 Cable television is just one of several emerging video technologies, which include videodisc, teletext, and videotext.

vide-ruff: see VIED *ppl. a.*

vidette, variant of VEDETTE.

Vidian (ˈvɪdɪən), *a. Anat.* [f. Vidus *Vidius*, Latinized form of the name of Guido Guidi, an Italian anatomist (died 1569).] The special designation of certain anatomical features of the head, as ***Vidian artery, canal, nerve.***

1831 R. KNOX *Cloquet's Anat.* 39 The posterior orifice of the vidian canal. *Ibid.* 473 The superficial petrous filaments of the vidian nerve. *Ibid.* 663 The Vidian or Pterygoid Artery. **1840** E. WILSON *Anat. Vade M.* (1842) 279 The Vidian branch passes backwards along the pterygoid canal. **1875** TURNER in *Encycl. Brit.* I. 824/1 At the root of the pterygoid processes is the vidian canal, for the transmission of a nerve of the same name. **1886** *Buck's Handbk. Med. Sci.* II. 328/2 A small nerve..goes to the spheno-palatine ganglion, and, after being joined by a branch from the carotid plexus, is known as the Vidian nerve.

vidicon (ˈvɪdɪkɒn). [f. VID(EO- + ICON(O-SCOPE.] A kind of small television camera tube in which the image is formed on a transparent electrode coated with photoconductive material, the video signal being obtained from the variation in the current flowing to or from this as it is scanned by a beam of (usu. low-speed) electrons.

1950 P. K. WEIMER et al. in *Electronics* May 72/1 The name 'vidicon' has been coined to distinguish these tubes from the photoemissive tubes. **1961** *Listener* 2 Nov. 726/3 A vidicon tube is also used in a small lightweight 'radio camera'. **1966** *McGraw-Hill Encycl. Sci. & Technol.* XIII. 465/2 Nearly all closed-circuit television cameras utilize a vidicon. **1978** *Nature* 5 Oct. 414/1 The UV vidicons, when properly erased and prepared for use, can be exposed for several hours on very weak planetary emissions. **1981** 'A. HALL' *Pekin Target* xvi. 158 These are hard copies of some stuff we took from high altitude with vidicon cameras.

‖**vidimus** (ˈvaɪdɪməs). [L. *vīdimus* 'we have seen', 1st pers. pl. perf. of *vidēre* to see. So F. *vidimus* (from 14th c.).]

1. A copy of a document bearing an attestation that it is authentic or accurate. Also *attrib.*

1436 *Rolls of Parlt.* IV. 500/2 Credence shuld be yeven to the copie named Vidimus sealed under the autentyke seales, and approved as to ye Originall. **1502** ARNOLDE *Chron.* (1811) 230 We will the vidimus or copy auctentike take effect and strenght as this present saufconduyt after ten monethis past. *a* **1560** ROLLAND *Crt. Venus* IV. 310 The prothogoll heirof I wald haif drawin In writ, for cost to be my Vidimus. **1670** BLOUNT *Law Dict.* s.v. *Innotescimus*, An *Innotescimus* and *Vidimus* are all one. [Hence in Chambers *Cycl.* (1728) s.v.] **1853** F. S. THOMAS *Handbk. Publ. Rec.* 93 A Vidimus is similar to a Notarial Certificate, in which the tenor of Royal charters..and other writings is copied and attested. *Ibid.*, Each of these persons was supplied with a vidimus copy of such letters, properly sealed and authenticated. **1899** J. H. ROUND *Cal. Doc. France* I. p. xxviii, He claims that the transcripts are most carefully made from charters, cartularies, 'vidimus', or other authentic sources.

†**b.** Without article: Confirmation of authenticity or correctness. *Obs.*⁻¹

1513 in *Trans. Roy. Hist. Soc.* VI. 362 The said Schir William is oblist to gif vidimus tharapone.

c. (See quot. 1850.)

1850 OGILVIE, *Vidimus*, an examination or inspection; as, a vidimus of accounts or documents. **1880** BLACK *White Wings* xxi, He told us that the last vidimus of the affairs of the Burgh of Strathgovan was most satisfactory.

†**2.** *Arch.* A design for a painted or stained-glass window. *Obs.*

1526–7 in H. Walpole *Vertue's Anecd. Paint.* (1765) I. App. Dddj, Good and true patrons, otherwyse called a vidimus, for to fourme glasse and make by other four wyndowes of the seid churche. **1762** H. WALPOLE *Ibid.* 108 What a rarity in a collection of drawings would be one of their vidimus's!

†**3.** The fact or reality *of* something. *Obs.*⁻¹

1610 B. RICH *Descr. Irel.* xvi. 64 The *vidimus* of the matter is, our Londoners are neither vowed nor sworne to the Pope.

4. (See quot.)

1884 *Imp. Dict.*, *Vidimus*,..an abstract or syllabus of the contents of a document, book, and the like.

‖**Vidonia** (vɪˈdəʊnɪə). [Of doubtful origin: (see quot. 1833).] A dry white wine made in the Canary Islands. Also *attrib.*

1723 *Lond. Gaz.* No. 6173/3, 31 Pipes..of..White Vidonia Madera Wine. **1816** ACCUM *Chem. Tests* (1818) 191 Various wines or spirituous liquors:..Vidonia. **1833** C. REDDING *Hist. Mod. Wines* (1851) 210 What is called Vidonia is properly the dry Canary wine, of a good body... Perhaps it was so called because it is derived from the *vidogna* grape, or is a corruption of Verdona. *Ibid.* 211 At Canary both Malmsey and Vidonia are grown. **1876** *Encycl. Brit.* IV. 797/1 (Canary Islands), None, however, is considered as good as the wine of Madeira. The most esteemed kind is sent to England under the name of Vidonia.

vidou, vidoy, obs. forms of WIDOW.

viduage (ˈvɪdjuːɪdʒ). [f. L. *vidua* widow: cf. next and -AGE.] The condition of widowhood, viduity; widows collectively.

1832 LAMB *Lett.* xviii. (1865) 174 What can twenty votes do for one hundred and two widows? I cast my eyes hopeless among the viduage. **1894** *Story of My Two Wives* 67 One of the last acts of her viduage.

vidual (ˈvɪdjuːəl), *a.* Also 6 **widual.** [ad. late L. *viduāl-is*, f. *vidua* widow. So OF. *vidual*, Sp. *vidual*, It. *viduale.*] Of or belonging to, befitting, a widow or widowhood; widowed.

1550 BALE *Apol.* 37 The estate of widual clennesse is than most fytt, whan [etc.]. **1598** FLORIO, *Vedouile*, viduall, widow-like. **1624** HEYWOOD *Gunaik.* VI. 282 Others there bee that have kept a viduall chastitie even in wedlocke. **1647** TRAPP *Comm. 1 Tim.* v. 12 'Cast off their first faith': Not that of their baptisme.. but their viduall promised chastity and service to the Saints. **1710** NORRIS *Chr. Prud.* iii. 106 One may as well say, Virginal, or Conjugal, or Vidual Prudence as any of these. **1752** RICHARDSON *Let.* in Mrs. Barbauld *Life* (1804) III. 192 Shall we show Harriet, after a departure glorious to the hero, in her vidual glory? **1876** *World* V. 12 She too retains still a deeply vidual costume. **1897** F. THOMPSON *New Poems* 34 She..Who in most dusk and vidual curch, Her Lord being hence, Keeps her cold sorrows by thy hearse. *Ibid.* 44 No more shall you sit sole and vidual.

Hence **ˈvidually** *adv.*

1818 J. BROWN *Psyche* 93 If marriage solace she prefers Before a solitary pillow, Or wearing vidually the willow.

†**ˈviduate**, *a. Obs. rare.* [ad. L. *viduāt-us*, pa. pple. of *viduāre*, f. *viduus* destitute.]

1. Destitute *of* something.

1692 PLUKENETT *Let. to Ray* 17 July (1718) 249 Its Stalks really viduate of Leaves.

2. Widowed.

c **1780** *Mock Ode* in Boswell *Johnson* (1904) II. 623 Cervisial coctor's viduate dame.

†**ˈviduated**, *pa. pple.* and *ppl. a. Obs.* [f. L. *viduāt-*, ppl. stem of *viduāre*: see prec.] Left widowed, desolate, or destitute.

1660 WATERHOUSE *Arms & Arm.* 175 St. Pauls, thy viduated Mother Church. **1687** WOOD *Life* (O.H.S.) III. 218 In the beginning of this month came up at Oxon 'a health to the Church dowager', i.e. distressed or viduated Church of England. *c* **1718** *Life R. Frampton* (1876) 202 To intercede with them at helm, that the Church might not be viduated. **1727** BAILEY (vol. II).

†**viduˈation.** *Obs. rare.* [f. L. *viduāre*: cf. prec. and -ATION.] The state of being widowed or bereaved.

1653 WATERHOUSE *Apol. Learn.* 149 (T.), Their triumphs rise from the church's viduation, from her learning's contempt and prosternation. [**1656** BLOUNT *Glossogr.*, *Viduation*, a dividing, a leaving alone, a depriving, a making widow.]

vidue, obs. Sc. form of WIDOW.

†**viduˈifical**, *a. Obs.*⁻¹ [f. L. *vidua* widow: see -FIC and -AL¹.] (See quot.)

1657 TOMLINSON *Renou's Disp.* 267 Mezereon is as much as viduifical, or widow-making plant.

ˈviduine, *a. Ornith.* [f. mod.L. *vidua* widow-bird: see -INE¹.] Belonging to the *Viduinæ* or widow-birds.

1896 G. E. SHELLEY *For. Finches* 294 By scientists the Viduine Weavers are placed among the Ornamental Finches.

viduity (vɪˈdjuːɪtɪ). Also 5 *Sc.*, 6 **viduite**, 6–7 **-tie.** [a. OF. *viduite* (AF. *veduete*; F. *viduité* = It. *viduità*), or ad. L. *viduitās*, f. *vidua* widow: see -ITY.] The state of being or remaining a widow; the time during which a woman is a widow; widowhood.

1420 *Indenture* in J. Campbell *Balmerino* IV. i. (1867) 258 The said Sir Williame is oblist that he sal nocht trete the forsaid [Alesoun ?] of Murray..noither in virginite na viduite, til [alienate ?] ony parte of hir heritage fra the richtwiss airis. **1574** *Waterford Archives* in *10th Rep. Hist. MSS. Comm.* App. V. 334 Every widowe shoulde have like benefitt..during her viduite... Aldermen's widowes shall have but a balives shift during their viduite. **1575** in Agnew *Sheriffs Galloway* (1893) I. 404 Patrick McKie..shall infeft ..Katheren Agnew..in her viduity in all and haill the lands of Larg. **1620** BP. HALL *Honour Marr. Clergy* I. vi, As for that other which hee imagines, a vow of continued viduitie, it was neither 'faith' nor 'first'. **1647** TRAPP *Comm. Corinthians* 79 Yet doth not the apostle simply prefer virginity or viduity before marriage as better. *a* **1726** GILBERT *Law Evidence* (1791) 497 If a Woman, who has an Estate during Viduity, makes a Lease for Years [etc.]. **1729** *Macfarlane's Geneal. Coll.* (S.H.S.) II. 101 Indenture betwixt Marion Oliphant in her Viduity on the One Part and Pat. Gray of Broxmouth on the other Part. *a* **1856** G. OUTRAM *Annuity*, *Lyrics* (1874) 27 There I met a waesome wife Lamenting her viduity. **1896** *Abst. Protocols Town Clerks of Glasgow* (1896) III. 9 *note*, Widows of rentallers in the barony were entitled to enjoy their husbands' lands during viduity.

viduous (ˈvɪdjuːəs), *a. rare*⁻¹. [f. L. *vidu-us* or *vidu-a* + -OUS.] Empty, unoccupied.

1855 THACKERAY *Newcomes* lxvi, She gone, and her viduous mansion your heart to let, her successor, the new occupant,..finds her miniature..hidden away somewhere.

†**vidz(t.**, obs. variants of VIZ. = VIDELICET.

1589 PUTTENHAM *Eng. Poesie* II. iv. (Arb.) 85 Both verses be of egall quantitie, vidz. seauen sillables a peece. **1616** in *Eastland Co.* (Camden) 158 That the same [allowance] be raysed vidzt to twenty nobles apeece. **1669** MRS. A. THORNTON *Autobiog.* (Surtees) 80 The articles of agreement ..vidz., that all his estate should be passed by fine and recovery.

vie (viː), *sb.*¹ Also vye, uye, uie, vi. [a. OF. (also mod.F.) *vie*:—L. *vīta* life.]

†**1.** An account of the life of a saint. *Obs.*

a **1200** *St. Marher.* 34 Here i mai tellen ou..The vie of one meidan, was hoten Maregrete. *a* **1225** *Juliana* 2 Her cumseð þe uie of seinte iuliane, ant telleð of liflade hire. *a* **1300** *Marina* 227 in Horstm. *Altengl. Leg.* (1878) 173 He þat made & wrot þis vie, & hyre haþ in memorie, From shome Crist him shilde.

†**2.** Way of, or lot in, life. *Obs.*

a **1300** *Cursor M.* 3474 Oure lauerd..Had don hir in to sikernes,..Quat suld be þaa childer vie, O þair weird and o þair lijf. *Ibid.* 21740 þe croice..es..Fondement of ur clergi, Reule it es of hali vi. **1377** LANGL. *P. Pl.* B. XIV. 122 Angeles þat in helle now ben, hadden ioye some tyme, And diues in deyntees lyued, and in douce vye.

‖**3.** (vi) Used in a number of mod.Fr. phrases, as **vie de Bohème** (də bɔɛm), a Bohemian way of life; also *attrib.*; **vie de château** (də ʃato), the way of life of a large country house; aristocratic social life; **vie de luxe** (də lyks), a life of luxury; **vie d'intérieur** (dɛ̃terjœr), private or domestic life; **vie en rose** (ɑ̃ roz) [app. from a French song by Edith Piaf containing the line '*je vois la vie en rose*'], a life seen through rose-coloured spectacles; **(la) vie intérieure** (ɛ̃terjœr), one's inner life, the life of the spirit; **(la) vie intime** (ɛ̃tim), the intimate personal life of a person; **Vie Parisienne** (parizjɛn), Parisian life, the name of a popular French magazine; used *attrib.* to denote a characteristic quality of voluptuous appeal; **vie romancée** (rɔmɑ̃se) [see ROMANCÉ *ppl. a.*], a fictionalized biography.

1888 MRS. H. WARD *Robert Elsmere* I. I. vii. 174 That golden *vie de Bohème* which she alone apparently of all artists was destined never to know. **1957** 'P. QUENTIN' *Suspicious Circumstances* i. 5 Two days later I was installed in a suitably Vie de Bohème apartment looking out on the Luxembourg gardens. **1980** S. T. HAYMON *Death & Pregnant Virgin* ii. 12 Who could have prophesied that Paul Falkener, that personification of the *vie de Bohème*, would fall so completely under her spell? **1924** A. D. SEDGWICK *Little French Girl* I. vii. 61 Is there a *vie de château* in the neighbourhood? **1979** A. BUCHAN *Scrap Screen* i. 4 The denigrated sentiment of nostalgia..feeds on reconstructions of the *vie de château*. **1920** 'K. MANSFIELD' *Let.* Nov. (1928) II. 81 You realize the vie de luxe they are living—the very table— sweets, liqueurs, lilies, pearls. **1929** O. SEAMAN *Interludes of Editor* 81 And, when in Town you take your meed, I'll mark the *vie de luxe* you lead. **1889** M. H. VAN DE VELDE *Cosmopolitan Recoll.* I. vii. 235 Under the roof that shelters them it appears to her [*sc.* the Queen of Italy] that there is no room for that happy *vie d'interieur* of which she is so honestly fond. **1933** G. ARTHUR *Septuagenarian's Scrap Bk.* 201 The *vie d'intérieur* makes far less appeal. Take a look at the English drawing-room..conspiring to give a delicious sense of the room being lived in, a sense which is wholly foreign to the French *salon.* **1957** O. NASH *You can't get there from Here* 45 He was wafted into a glamorous *vie en rose* of amorous ruses. **1974** M. CECIL *Heroines in Love* vi. 157 So many hopes had tumbled that magazine writers were reluctant to present an unending *vie en rose.* **1912** C. MACKENZIE *Carnival* xxvii. 299 Suffragism viewed in retrospect was shoddy embroidery for the *vie intérieure* of Jenny. **1977** A. FRASER in A. Thwaite *My Oxford* 175 If caught, alone and inexplicably loitering, it was conventional to snatch up a book of poetry (Donne was rather smart) and indicate sudden world-weariness, a preference for *la vie intérieure.* **1984** *Listener* 5 Apr. 23/1 A work in which the *vie intime* of the American and European bourgeoisie is brought out into the daylight. **1891** S. WEBB *Let.* 23 May (1978) I. 272 *La vie intime*—I want to talk to you about very frankly. **1939** *Times Lit. Suppl.* 7 Jan. 4/4 A novel with real characters, who, however, are not likely on that account to prosecute him for libel, despite his plain-spoken exposure of their *vie intime.* **1979** L. LERNER *Love & Marriage* p. x, Those social historians who believe that *la vie intime* has a history which can be studied. **1890** KIPLING *Abaft the Funnel* (1909) 287, I replied that all my French was confined to the Vie Parisienne [*sc.* the French weekly *La Vie Parisienne*] and translations of Zola's novels with illustrations. **1936** C. CONNOLLY *Rock Pool* iii. 57 She.. gave him long, soft Vie Parisienne glances. **1983** L. MACDONALD *Somme* viii. 78 The saucy *Vie Parisienne*, whose cut-out pictures enlivened the decor of almost every dugout on the Western Front. **1941** *New Yorker* 13 Dec. 34/1 'The Beloved Returns', last year's full-length *vie romancée* about Goethe, started as a short sketch. **1976** *Times Lit. Suppl.* 9 Jan. 39/5 In biographical matters we have *vie romancée*: 'if the question flashed through Schiller's mind, he must have dismissed it'.

†**vie**, *sb.*² *Obs. rare.* Also vye. [Aphetic f. *envie* ENVY *sb.*] Envy.

13.. *Seuyn Sages* (W.) 1028 Tho Ypocras wel he fond, Bi craft of the childes hond, That he couthe al his mastrie, And brast negh forth [*read* for] onde and vie. *a* **1450** MYRC 435 Ihesu cryst..þat..vnder pounce pylate Was I-take for vye and hate, And soffrede peyne and passyone.

†**vie**, *sb.*³ *Obs.* Also 6–7 vy(e. [Aphetic ad. F. *envi* increase of stake (in OF., challenge, provocation), vbl. sb. from *envier* to increase the stake (in OF., to challenge, provoke, invite):—L. *invitāre*: see ENVY *v.*² So Sp. and Pg.

envite (Sp. †*embite*), It. *invito*. The adv. AVIE is found slightly earlier (1509–). See also REVIE *sb.*]

1. In card-playing: A challenge, venture, or bid; a sum ventured or staked on one's cards. Also in fig. context. (Common *c* 1590–1650).

1533 MORE *Debell. Salem* Wks. 955/2 He fareth..as though we sate together playing at poste. For first he casteth my contradiction as a vye, to witte whether I woulde geue it ouer with a face. **1591** GREENE *Conny Catch.* (1859) 27 The Conny upon thys, knowing hys Card is the third or fourth Carde,..pawnes his rings if he hath any, hys sworde, his cloake, or els what hee hath about him to maintaine the vie. **1592** WOTTON *Lett.* (1907) I. 273 Not unlike a bad game at Mawe, wherein the first vye being seene, the cards are given before the second. *a* **1618** J. DAVIES (Heref.) *Wittes Pilgr.* Wks. (Grosart) II. 32/1 Both which an end do make Of all Love's Games saue when the Vies are paid. **1648** GAGE *West Ind.* ix. 26 So the cards were handsomely shuffled, the vies and revies were doubled. **1680** COTTON *Compl. Gamester* xxii. (ed. 2) 106 The Vye is what you please to adventure upon the goodness of your own hand.

b. In the phr. *to drop vie(s*, in fig. use.

1599 NASHE *Lenten Stuffe* Wks. (Grosart) V. 227 But Parish for Parish.., both for numbers in grosse of honest housholders,..and substantiall graue Burgers, Yarmouth shall droppe vie with them to the last Edward groate they are worth. **1636** B. JONSON in *Ann. Dubrensia* (1877) 23, I cannot bring my Muse to dropp Vies Twixt Cotswold, and the Olimpicke exercise.

2. A challenge to contest or rivalry; a display of rivalry or emulation; a contest or competition. Occas. const. *of*. (Very common in 17th c.)

1568 T. HOWELL *Arb. Amitie* (1879) 64 O Gratious Golde, Whose glittring vie Doth cheere and holde Eche gazing eie. **1605** SYLVESTER *Du Bartas* II. iii. *Captaines* 10 Samuel succeds: Jews crave a King: a vie Of People-Sway: States-Rule: and Monarchy. **1611** SPEED *Hist. Gt. Brit.* IX. xxiv. 876/1 They..beganne a vie, who should be first in shewing their alteration. **1662** OWEN *Animad. Fiat Lux* xxi. Wks. 1855 XIV. 169 Let him begin the vie when he pleaseth; if I live and God will, I will try this matter with him before competent judges. **1674** *Govt. Tongue* vi. 109 The King of Ethiopia in a vie of Wit with the King of Egypt, propos'd it as a Problem to him, to drink up the Sea.

b. In prepositional phrases, as *at (a) vie, at the vies, in vie (of), on vie.* Cf. AVIE *adv.*

1591 HARINGTON *Orl. Fur.* XXXIX. xiv, They wast the fields, and seeme on vye to runne, By which of them most damage may be donne. **1603** FLORIO *Montaigne* I. xxxix, Philip having heard his sonne great Alexander sing at a feast in vie of the best musitians. **1626** DANIEL *Hist. Eng.* Wks. (Grosart) IV. 231 The Empresse at the Vies with her Councell, resolues to send ouer her brother into Normandie. **1653** H. COGAN tr. *Pinto's Trav.* xlv. 264 It was worth him above ten thousand Duckats, wherewith the Lords rewarded him as it were in vye of one another in recompence of the good service he did. **1674** *Govt. of Tongue* vi. §12. 127 However as to this particular of defaming, both the sexes seem to be at a vie. *a* **1700** B. E. *Dict. Cant. Crew* s.v. *Taudry*, They..Bedeckt the Shrines and Altars of the Saints, as being at vye with each other upon that occasion.

3. A challenge as to the accuracy of something; an objection or difficulty. *rare.*

1591 HORSEY *Trav.* (Hakl. Soc.) App. 340 [He] hindred al the procedings I had begone, standinge uppon termes and vyes, saeing they were not the Quens letters I brought, nether her hand and sealle. **1603** HOLLAND *Plutarch's Mor.* 1197 Then came in Theon also with his vie, adding moreover & saying, that it could not be denied, but that in truth herein there haue bene great changes & mutations. **1640** SANDERSON *Serm.* (1681) II. 177 For private men to put in their vie, and..to call in question the decency or expediency of the things so established,..is it self indeed the most indecent and inexpedient thing.

4. *attrib.*, as *vie crown, stabs.*

The meaning of *three* [? read *thee*] *a vies wits* in quot. 1589 is not clear.

1570 FOXE *A. & M.* (ed. 2) III. 2292/2 The Lord of Tame, with an other Gentleman beyng at Tables, playing, and dropping vye crownes, yᵉ Lady Elizabeth passing by, sayd: she would see the game out. **1589** [? LYLY] *Pappe w. Hatchet* B ij, Thinkst thou thou hast so good a wit, as none can outwrangle thee? Yes Martin, wee will play three a vies wits. *Ibid.*, Art thou so backt that none dare blade it with thee? Yes Martin, we will drop vie stabbes. **1593** HARVEY *Pierce's Superer.* Wks. (Grosart) II. 128 Vie stabbes, good Ecclesiasticall learning in his Apologie; and good Christian Charitie in his Homilie.

vie (vaɪ), *v.* Also 4, 6–9 **vye**, 7 **vy**. [f. prec. or ad. F. *envier*: see prec. Sp. and Pg. *envidar* (Sp. †*embidar*), It. *invitare* are used in sense 1.

For an isolated earlier instance of the form see the note to sense 7.]

†**1.** *intr.* In card-playing: To make a 'vie'; to hazard a certain sum on the strength of one's hand.

The use of the word by Singer *Hist. Playing Cards* (1816) 245 is merely an echo of *invitasi* in the Italian original (1526) of the passage.

1565 JEWEL *Replie Hardings Answer* iv. 302 He commeth in onely with ioyly bragges, and great vauntes, as if he were plaieinge at poste, and shoulde winne al by vieinge. **1591** GREENE *Conny Catch.* Wks. (Grosart) X. 27 They vie and reuie till some ten shillings bee on the stake. *Ibid.* 95 The next game they vied, and laid some fiue pound by on the belt. **1594** CAREW *Huarte's Exam. Wits* viii. (1596) 112 To play well at Primero, and to face and vie,..and by coniectures to know his aduersaries game,..are all workes of the imagination. *a* **1618–1640** [see REVIE *v.* 4].

†**b.** In fig. context. *Obs.*

1622 MABBE tr. *Aleman's Guzman d' Alf.* II. To Rdr., He hath made a second part out of my first; and I onely imitated his second. And shall doe the like in the third, if being elder hand, he shall vye vpon me. **1646** QUARLES *Judgem. & Mercy* Wks. (Grosart) I. 83/1 As for thee, thy Cards are good, and having skill enough to play thy hopefull Game, vie boldly, conquer and triumph. **1654** [see REVIE *v.* 4].

†**2.** *trans.* To hazard, stake, or venture (a certain sum, etc.) on a hand of cards. Freq. in fig. context. *Obs.*

1577 GRANGE *Golden Aphrod.*, etc. Pj, Then will they vaunt, and graunt, and for affinitie, At cardes they will vye and reuye, each their virginitie. **1591** GREENE *Conny Catch.* Wks. (Grosart) X. 28 At last the barnacle plies it so, that perhaps he vies more mony then the cony hath in his purse. **1613** PURCHAS *Pilgrimage* I. xvi. 84 The worlds false-hood, that playeth with Scepters, and vieth Diademes, vsing men like Counters. **1640** QUARLES *Enchirid.* I. c. Giv, You,.. Princes of this lower World, who..vye Kingdomes, and winne Crownes. *c* **1645** HOWELL *Lett.* II. xv, I find that you have a very hazardous game in hand, therfore give it up, and do not vie a farthing upon't. **1658–9** *Burton's Diary* (1828) III. 35 *note*, The Commonwealth party and the Protector's or Court party, began to vie stakes, and pecked at one another in their light skirmishes.

†**b.** To venture (money) in other ways. *Obs.*

1599 HALL *Sat.* IV. ii. 93 More than who vies his pence to view some tricke Of strange Moroccoes dumb arithmeticke.

†**3.** To back (cards) for a certain sum; to declare oneself able to win (a game, etc.). *Obs.*

In first quot. in fig. context: for the use of *pair* cf. quot. *a* 1618 in 3 b.

1583 MELBANCKE *Philotimus* E e iij, So that hee which hath my misaduentures, and is enthralled with thy presente state, maye vie the paire for sorrowe, whatsoeuer the stake be. **1591** GREENE *Conny Catch.* (1592) 7 Ile vie and reuie euerie card at my pleasure, til either yours or mine come out. **1598** B. JONSON *Ev. Man in Hum.* IV. ii, *Wel.* S'light, here's a trick vyed, and reuyed! **1655** J. COTGRAVE *Wit's Interpr.* (1662) 366 The first, or eldest, 'tis possible, sayes, Ile vye the Ruff; the next says, Ile see it.

†**b.** In the phr. *to vie it*; also in fig. context.

1591 FLORIO *2nd Fruites* 69 *S.* Let vs plaie at primero... *A.* What shall we plaie for? *S.* One shilling stake, and three rest... I vye it, will you hould it? *A.* Yea Sir, I hold it, and reuie it. **1608** CHAPMAN *Byron's Trag.* Plays 1873 II. 285 *Qu.* Passe. *Byr.* I vy 't. *a* **1618** J. DAVIES (Heref.) *Wittes Pilgr.* Wks. (Grosart) II. 38/1 One, vies it, beeing but a Knaue, perchance, Against a King, or Queene, or Paires of both. **1654** GAYTON *Pleas. Notes* IV. ix. 235 All this time the Knights play'd it at Dutch Gleek, and had so vied it, and revied it, that they were all Honours in their faces. **1688** R. HOLME *Armoury* III. xvi. (Roxb.) 73/1 The eldest hand may pass and com in againe, if any of the gamsters vye it, else the dealer may play it out, or double it.

†**c.** In fig. use. *Obs.*

1604 MIDDLETON *Father Hubburd's T.* in Bullen *O. Pl.* VIII. 95 One..likened me to a sea-crab,..another fellow vied it, and said I looked like a rabbit. **1641** H. L'ESTRANGE *God's Sabbath* 31 As for the Protestant writers,..we dare vie it with the Anticiparians, and give them oddes, two for one at least. **1654** GATAKER *Disc. Apol.* 3 He makes grievous complaint elswhere of scurrilous Mercuries, that vie it with his scurrilous Merlins. **1673** [R. LEIGH] *Transp. Reh.* 100 To vye him, and see him, and re-vye him in contradictions. This figure now is lost to any man that is not a gamester.

4. To display, advance, practise, etc., in competition or rivalry *with* another person or thing; to contend or strive *with* in respect of (something). *Obs.* or *arch.* (Very common in 17th c.)

c **1570** *Bugbears* II. iv. 39 in R. W. Bond *Early Plays from Italian* (1911) 106, I will vye slepes with him that lookes oute of a hood. **1605** B. JONSON *Volpone* IV. vi, Out, thou Chameleon harlot; now, thine eyes Vie teares with the Hyæna. **1642** FULLER *Holy & Prof. St.* IV. vi. 267 The Queen, vying gold and silver with the King of Spain, had money or credit, when the other had neither. **1660** INGELO *Bentiv. & Ur.* I. (1682) 102 One eye vied drops with the other. **1692** R. L'ESTRANGE *Fables* ccclxxx. (1694) 401 Nothing else will serve him..but to vye Exellencies with those that took him out of the Dirt. **1702** S. PARKER tr. *Cicero's De Finibus* II. 126 The Mortal might vie Pleasures and *Summum Bonum* with the Eternal Being. **1720** MRS. MANLEY *Power of Love* (1741) 11 So beautiful, that thou may'st vie Advantages with the East and West. **1822** LAMB *Elia* I. *Some old Actors*, I have seen some..very sensible actresses..who..have seemed to set their wits at the jester, and to vie conceits with him in downright emulation.

†**b.** Similarly without const. *Obs.*

1597 J. KING *On Jonas* (1618) 282 An auncient historie of vowes vied and reuied between the citizens of Croto. **1598** E. GUILPIN *Skial.* (1878) 60 By and by Thei'le be by the ears, vie stabs, exchange disgraces. **1641** J. JACKSON *True Evang. T.* I. 40 They vyed cruelties, and strove who should overcome each other therein. **1650** WELDON *Crt. Jas. I*, 7 Had you seen how the Lords did vye courtesies to this poor Gentleman,..you could not but have condemned them of much basenesse. **1694** ATTERBURY *Serm.* (1723) I. 79, I think it by no means a fit and decent thing to vie Charities, and to erect the reputation of one upon the ruins of another.

†**c.** To rival (a thing). *Obs. rare.*

1607 *Schol. Disc. agst. Antichr.* I. ii. 72 He did it to vie that triple crowne which the Emperour had. **1691** J. WILSON *Belphegor* III. i, Bating that Palace, there's not a House in Genoa better furnish'd;—and for Picture—I dare almost vie Italy.

5. To match (one thing) *with* another by way of return, rivalry, or comparison. Now *arch.*

1583 MELBANCKE *Philotimus* T iij b, Though I enuie thee now, thou shouldest not vye it with malice. **1633** G. HERBERT *Temple, Sacrifice* xxii, The Jews..vying malice with my gentlenesse, Pick quarrels with their onely happinesse. **1664** J. WILSON *A. Commenius* II. ii, I'll vie his Autumn, with the pride of springs. **1685** LADY R. RUSSELL *Lett.* I. xxvii. 73, I will take your advice, and vie my state with others. **1718** *Entertainer* No. 19. 124 People would never be so vilely corrupted, as to vie Shade with Substance, and prefer Trash..to intrinsick Worth. **1877** TENNYSON *Har.* v. i. 86–7 *Leofwin.* And someone saw thy willy-nilly nun Vying a tress against our golden fern. *Harold.* Vying a tear with our cold dews, a sigh With these low-moaning heavens.

†**6.** To increase in number by addition or repetition. *Obs.*

1596 SHAKS. *Tam. Shr.* II. i. 311 Shee hung about my necke, and kisse on kisse Shee vi'd so fast..That in a twinkle she won me to her loue. **1598** SYLVESTER *Du Bartas* II. i. III. *Furies* 664 Sorrow..Creeping in corners, where she sits and vies Sighs from her heart, tears from her blubbered eyes. **1630** BRATHWAIT *Eng. Gentlem.* (1641) 24 Lest shee be forced to vie sighes for their sinnes. **1633** G. HERBERT *Temple, Easter* iii, Since all musick is but three parts vied And multiplied.

†**b.** To add on; to give or take by way of addition. *Obs.*

a **1635** RANDOLPH *Amyntas* II. iv. 161 Minds in love, Doe count their daies by minutes, measure howres,..And for each vie a teare. **1635** QUARLES *Emblems* I. viii. Wks. (Grosart) III. 57/2 One dotes; the other loathes: One frisks and sings, and vies a flagon more To drench dry cares.

7. *intr.* To enter into, or carry on, rivalry; to be rivals or competitors; to contend or compete for superiority in some respect. Also const. *for* or *in* (the object or matter of rivalry).

In Chaucer's *Dethe of Blaunche* 173 the Tanner MS. (15th c.) has *vie*, and Thynne (1532) *vye*, for *envye* of the Fairfax MS., which is prob. the correct reading.

1615 BRATHWAIT *Strappado* (1878) 146 Her teares by his finde their renew'd Supplies, Both vie as for a wager, which to winne, The more she wept, the more she forced him. **1648** GAGE *West Ind.* 209 In Rome Sir William Hamilton..vied much for the said Cardinals Cap. *a* **1700** EVELYN *Diary* 6 June 1687, The Commanders profusely vying in the expence and magnificence of tents. **1718** PRIOR *Protogenes & Apelles* 86 Howe'er Protogenes and I May in our Rival Talents vie. **1736** THOMSON *Liberty* IV. 291 Not unworthy, she [*sc.* Genoa] Vy'd for the trident of the narrow seas. **1785** WOLCOT (P. Pindar) *Lyric Odes, To P. Pindar* i, They show'd their gold-lac'd clothes with pride, In harmless sallies frequent vied. **1806** MISS MITFORD in L'Estrange *Life* (1870) I. xi. 54 They all vied in paying me every attention. **1814** SCOTT *Ld. of Isles* I. v, As vainly had her maidens vied In skill to deck the princely bride. **1860** MAURY *Phys. Geog. Sea* (Low) iii. §168 The China seas and the North Pacific may vie in the fury of their gales.

b. Const. *with*; also †*against*, †*on*, †*upon.*

1602 [see REVIE *v.* 4 b]. **1614** W. BROWNE *Sheph. Pipe* v. E 3, Who 'gainst the Sun (though weakned by the morne) Would vie with lookes, needeth an Eagles eye. *a* **1650** MONTROSE in Watson *Sc. Poems* (1711) III. 108 If..in the Empire of thy Heart, Where I should solely be, Another do pretend a Part, And dare to Vie with me. **1683** KENNETT tr. *Erasm. on Folly* (1709) 128 How the tawdry butterflies vie upon one another. **1692** WASHINGTON tr. *Milton's Def. Pop.* vii. Wks. 1851 VIII. 183 Many other things I omit, for..my design is not to vie with you in Impertinence. **1731–8** SWIFT *Polite Conv.* Introd. 81 One Isaac Newton..might possibly pretend to vye with me for Fame in future times. **1777** ROBERTSON *Hist. Amer.* IV. (1778) I. 359 They vie with one another in refinements of torture. **1832** R. & J. LANDER *Exped. Niger* I. i. 1 In fact they all vied with each other in making themselves agreeable. **1840** MACAULAY *Ess., Clive* (1897) 531 The wealth of Clive was such as enabled him to vie with the first grandees of England. **1871** FREEMAN *Norm. Conq.* (1875) III. xii. 79 Distant Kings would have vied with one another in offering their daughters to such a bridegroom.

c. *transf.* Of things.

1615 BRATHWAIT *Strappado* (1878) 173 For know (though my ability be poore) My good-will vie's with any Emperour. **1698** FRYER *Acc. E. India & P.* 184 We beheld Lamps at Night striving to vie with the Stars for Number and Lustre. **1702** POPE *Dryope* 23 Fruits that vie In glowing colours with the Tyrian dye. **1747** GRAY *Death Fav. Cat* 10 Her coat, that with the tortoise vies. **1773** JOHNSON *Let. to Mrs. Thrale* 25 Aug., A library that for luminousness and elegance may vie at least with the new edifice at Streatham. **1823** F. CLISSOLD *Ascent Mt. Blanc* 23 The glassy pinnacles of the..Alps,.. vying with the brightness of the western horizon. **1849** MACAULAY *Hist. Eng.* x. II. 617 The wealthiest merchant of London,..whose banquets vied with those of kings. **1872** JENKINSON *Guide Eng. Lakes* (1879) 224 The view from the summit will vie with that from any one of the Lake mountains.

†**8.** To contend in debate. *Obs.*

a **1610**–*a* **1734** [see REVIE *v.* 4 c].

Hence †**vied** *ppl. a.*; **'vieing** *vbl. sb.* and *ppl. a.*; **'vieingly** *adv.*

1605 ARMIN *Foole upon F.* (1880) 5 Iack Oates..was dealing to himselfe at *vide-ruffe (for that was the game he ioyed in). **1607** HEYWOOD *Wom. Killed w. Kindn.* 128 Gentlemen, what shall our game be?.. Faith, let it be vide-ruff, and let's make honours. **1610** R. COCKS *Diary* (1901) 114 Dec. 12, Loste at vyed ruffe ij s vj d. **1612** BACON *Charge touching Duels* Wks. 1879 I. 681/1 A difference..made in case of killing and destroying man, upon a fore-thought purpose, between foul and fair, and as it were between single murder and vied murder. **1620** SHELTON *Quix.* (1746) III. 245 My Sport shall be vy'd Trump at Christmas. **1591** PERCIVALL *Sp. Dict.*, *Embite*, *vieng at any game, *Iteratio.* **1689** *Tryal Bps.* 6 The King's Counsel have answered your Objections, and we must not permit Vying and Re-vying upon one another. *a* **1660** *Contemp. Hist. Irel.* (Ir. Archæol. Soc.) II. 43 Colonell Jones, governor of Dublin, the other *veyinge gamster, played his parte very well hitherto. **1832** *Examiner* 691/1 People would have to be careful how they.. exaggerate their afflictions, as they are apt *vyingly with each other to do.

vie, southern ME. variant of FAY *v.*[1]

viealde, southern ME. variant of *falde* FOLD *v.*

†**vieillard.** *Obs.* Also 5 **viellars** (*pl.*), **veyllard**, 6 **villard, vylarde**. [a. F. *vieillard* (OF. also *viellard, -art, villard*, etc.), f. *vieil* old: see -ARD.] An old man.

1475 *Bk. Noblesse* (Roxb.) 64 That noble duke Agamemnon required of the goddis six suche wise viellars as was Nestor. **1485** CAXTON *Chas. Gt.* 117 Of whens art thou, veyllard? ?*a* **1500** *Chester Pl.* I. 156 That oulde vylarde Jacobe, doted for age. *c* **1590** J. STEWART *Poems* (S.T.S.) II. 38 This vitius vieillard now mycht tak Of hir his plesour. **1621** T. WILLIAMSON (*title*), The Wise Vieillard or Old Man. Translated out of French into English.

vi'eirin(e. *Med.* Also vierin(e. [app. f. the Portuguese surname *Vieira.*] (See quot.)

1893 *Dunglison's Dict. Med. Sci.*, *Vieirin*, bitter principle from bark of Remijia Vellozi of Brazil, where it is used as an antiperiodic and tonic, like quinine.

‖**vielle** (vɪ'ɛl). [F. *vielle*, OF. *viele*, of doubtful origin.] A musical instrument with four strings played by means of a small wheel; a hurdy-gurdy. Also *Comb.*

1768 STERNE *Sent. Journ.*, *Grace*, The old man had..been no mean performer upon the vielle. **1782** *Ann. Reg.* II. 11 Few songs, guittars, vielles, or organs enliven the evenings. **1807** [see HURDY-GURDY 1]. **1880** SHORTHOUSE *J. Inglesant* II. ii, He played upon a small and curiously shaped instrument called a vielle,..with four strings, and a kind of small wheel instead of a bow. **1905** *Edin. Rev.* July 129 The vielle-player's story, and the Papal election, and much of the talk about music and the drama!

Vienna (vɪ'ɛnə). [The name of the capital of Austria.] **1. a.** In various collocations, as **Vienna blue**, cobalt blue; **Vienna caustic**, = *Vienna paste*; **Vienna Circle** [tr. G. *Wiener Kreis*], the name given to a group of empiricist philosophers, scientists, and mathematicians active in Vienna from the 1920s to 1938 who were chiefly concerned with methods of verifying statements, the formalization of language, the unification of science, and the elimination of metaphysics (cf. *logical positivism* s.v. LOGICAL *a.* 7); **Vienna coup** *Bridge*, the playing of the highest ranking card of a suit as a preparation for eventually forcing an opponent to discard winning cards; **Vienna cross**, a stitch used in fancy embroideries; **Vienna green** (see quot. 1852); **Vienna paste**, a paste made up of equal parts of caustic potash and quicklime; **Vienna sausage**, a small frankfurter made of pork, beef, or veal (cf. *wienerwurst* s.v. WIENER *a.* 2); **Vienna Secession** = SECESSION 3 d; **Vienna steak**, a flat rissole made of minced beef; **Vienna white** (see quot. 1861).

1835 G. FIELD *Chromatography* 111 [Cobalt blue] has been called *Vienna blue, Paris blue, azure, and, very improperly, ultramarine. **1865** G. B. WOOD & BACHE *Dispensat. U.S. Amer.* (ed. 12) 1279 This preparation is a grayish-white powder, sometimes called **Vienna caustic.* **1934** *Philos. Rev.* XLIII. 125 Last..one would mention the logical positivism of the *Vienna Circle. **1956** J. O. URMSON *Philos. Anal.* vi. 100 The main attack on metaphysics as such came from philosophers whom we have not previously discussed, the Vienna Circle and their associates. **1973** B. MAGEE *Popper* i. 11 The fashion prevailing..for his generation there and then was the logical positivism of the Vienna Circle. **1933** *Sunday Times* 5 Feb. 5/1 The coup formerly only known as the '*Vienna Coup', but now, more appropriately, also termed the 'Squeeze'. **1959** REESE & DORMER *Bridge Player's Dict.* 248 In technical terms, the Vienna Coup consists of the play of the top-ranking card of a suit so that a card of lower rank will be correctly positioned as a one-card threat in an automatic squeeze. **1974** *Country Life* 5 Dec. 1811/3 This is the Vienna Coup, essential if a squeeze on East is planned. **1881** C. C. HARRISON *Woman's Handiwork* I. 23 *Vienna cross stitch..consists of two stitches crossing each other..exactly alike on both sides of the material. **1882** CAULFEILD & SAWARD *Dict. Needlew.* 188/1 *Persian Cross stitch*, a stitch..also called Vienna Cross. **1842** FRANCIS *Dict. Arts*, **Vienna Green*, the same as Schweinford green; it is an arseniate of copper. **1852** W. GREGORY *Handbk. Org. Chem.* (ed. 3) 214 Schweinfurt or Vienna Green is a double salt, formed of acetate and arsenite of copper. **1867** BERKELEY HILL *Essentials of Bandaging* 148 *Vienna paste, that is, equal parts of potassa fusa and quick lime worked into a paste with spirits of wine. **1886** *Buck's Handbk. Med. Sci.* II. 5/2 To prevent its diffusion it is usually mixed with quicklime in what is known as Vienna Paste, or Potassa cum Calce. **1958** *Catal. County Stores, Taunton* June 4 *Vienna Sausages—a tin 4/-. **1977** *New Yorker* 27 June 64/3 A modest but welcome food cache—cornmeal, canned vegetables, Vienna sausage. **1964** LAKE & MAILLARD *Dict. Mod. Painting* (ed. 3) 182/2 Between 1898 and 1903, he [*sc.* Klimt] was president of the *Vienna Secession. **1971** *Guardian* 19 Jan. 8/2 There stands in angular rectitude at the Vienna Secession Exhibition at the Royal Academy—a clock..by Adolf Loos. **1900** A. N. WHYBROW *Day-by-Day Cookery Bk.* 97 *Vienna steaks... Take 1½lbs. each of rather lean beef or veal, trim.., chop very finely, add..onion or shallot,..and 2 well beaten eggs. .. Form into steaks and fry in butter. **1951** G. GREENE *End of Affair* II. iii. 71 Henry chose a Vienna steak... He..expected something like a Wiener Schnitzel. **1854** *Vienna white [see KREMS]. **1861** *Chambers's Encycl.* II. 744 The Vienna white of artists is simply purified chalk.

b. The distinctive name of a grade of wheat-flour, and of certain forms of plain or fancy bread.

1845 E. ACTON *Mod. Cookery* xx. 545 This dish is sometimes called in England a Vienna cake; and..also..a *Gateaux de Bordeaux*. **1879** *Warne's Model Cookery* 603/2 Vienna Cake... Take a large round spongecake and cut it very carefully into thin slices [etc.]. **1889** R. WELLS *Pastrycook & Confect. Guide* 12 Vienna Bread. Take 12 lbs. of Vienna flour [etc.]. **1893** —— *Mod. Pract. Bread Baker* 50 Vienna Bread. This I claim to be our highest grade of white bread. *Ibid.* 52 Common Vienna Loaves. **1906** *365 Breads & Biscuits* 61 Vienna Rolls..may stand half an hour before baking if desired.

c. Used *attrib.* and *absol.* to designate (items made of) a hard-paste porcelain, often richly decorated, manufactured at Vienna from 1719 to 1864.

1784 H. WALPOLE *Descr. Strawberry-Hill* 9 A tea-pot and bason, six handle cups and saucers, with bottles in black, of Vienna china. **1875** C. SCHREIBER *Jrnl* 13 Feb. (1911) I. 352 A most interesting Vienna tea service. **1885** *Encycl. Brit.* XIX. 640/1 Vienna porcelain..is greyish in tint; its paintings are very poor, and it depends for its effect chiefly on gilt-moulded scroll-work. **1900** F. LITCHFIELD *Pott. & Porc.* vii. 307 A..more tawdry description of Vienna china has been placed on the market... This would seem to have damaged the sale of the better class of modern Vienna. **1976** *Times* 30 Mar. 19/3 £3,850..for a Vienna teabowl and saucer decorated in schwarzlot and gold. **1980** *Radio Times* 27 Sept. 14 (Advt.), Pair of Vienna porcelain vases and covers... Dark blue and cream.

2. as *sb.* A Vienna sausage.

1963 M. LEVINSON *Taxi!* xi. 132 The modern Jewish taxi-driver..doesn't mind..a plate of ham with his viennas, the traditional Jewish 'hot dog'. **1971** *Sunday Times* (Colour Suppl.) 27 June 50/2 *Frankfurters and Viennas* are the world's best-known boiling sausages. Made from a mixture of pork and veal and well smoked. Reheat for 10 minutes.

Viennese (viːɛ'niːz, vɪə-), *sb.* and *a.* [f. VIENN-A + -ESE.]

A. *sb.* **a.** A native or an inhabitant of Vienna; also in collective sense. **b.** The variety of German spoken in Vienna.

1839 J. PAGETT *Hungary & Transylv.* I. 2 The foolish tales the good Viennese told us. **1849** E. RUSKIN *Let.* 22 Dec. in M. Lutyens *Effie in Venice* (1965) I. 94 Hanoverian German I understand pretty well, but Viennese, which these officers speak, is very different. **1860** *Chambers's Encycl.* I. 575/1 In order to prevent the Hungarians coming to the aid of the Viennese [in Oct. 1848]. **1894** PARRY *Stud. Gt. Composers, Beethoven* 166 His behaviour was not of the kind affected by polite Viennese. **1981** LD. HAREWOOD *Tongs & Bones* vi. 108 Marion..talked fluent German (or rather Viennese),..rattling the guttural Viennese 'r' round her throat.

B. *adj.* **a.** Of or belonging to Vienna; originating in Vienna.

1839 J. PAGETT *Hungary & Transylv.* I. 1 Viennese Reports of Hungary. **1888** *Encycl. Brit.* XXIV. 221/2 The Viennese school of painting is of modern origin. **1889** R. WELLS *Pastrycook & Confect. Guide* 10 Viennese Rolls. Take 8 lbs. of Vienna Flour [etc.].

b. Special collocations: **Viennese Secession** = SECESSION 3 d; **Viennese waltz**, (a piece of music for) the form of waltz originating in Vienna, characterized by a romantic, nostalgic quality (see quots. 1980, 1983).

1906 *Studio* (Special No.) p. A. iv, When, on the 3rd of April, 1897, nineteen young artists came together, to found the Viennese 'Secession', they chose as their leader Rudolf von Alt. **1960** *Burlington Mag.* CII. 395/1 The Viennese Secession movement (of which Klimt was co-founder and..first president). **1915** GIBSON & MILES tr. *Gayda's Mod. Austria* xxxi. 293 These worthy citizens..give a light,..almost healthy tone to the urban life of the Empire—like the melodies of Strauss's Viennese waltzes. **1920** G. GROSSMITH in A. M. Cree *Handbk. Ball-Room Dancing* 12 Later came tight skirts and slow 'Bostons'. Then divided skirts, the 'Viennese Waltz', 'Two-Step',..'Turkey-Trot' [etc.]. **1979** *Listener* 19 July 71/1 'Musique-Dance', the latter..segueing from Viennese waltzes..to 'oom-pah' drinking-songs. **1980** *New Grove Dict. Mus.* xx. 206/1 The Viennese Waltz compositions of the second half of the 19th century, especially when played with the slight anticipation of the second beat of a bar and the subtle use of rubato which are charateristics of the traditional Viennese performance, remain a popular feature of concerts. **1983** *New Oxf. Compan. Mus.* II. 1966/2 The Viennese waltz developed the characteristic of a slight anticipation of the second beat of the bar,..which gives a delightful and distinctive lilt to the playing.

vier ('vaɪə(r)). *rare.* [f. VIE *v.*] One who or that which vies with another.

c **1700** W. HAMILTON in Watson *Sc. Poems* (1706) I. 68 They'll witness that I was the Vier Of all the Dogs within the Shire, I'd run all Day, and never tyre. **1902** *Academy* 18 Oct. 411/2 We have flocks of poets who are word-painters and nothing more, mere viers with painting.

vier, southern dial. var. FIRE; dial. var. VAIR *sb.*; obs. f. VEER *v.*[1]; var. VIRE *sb.*

vierdour, variant of VERDOUR[2] *Obs.*

Vierendeel ('viːrəndeəl). *Engin.* The name of A. *Vierendeel*, Belgian engineer and architect, used *attrib.* with reference to a type of girder introduced by him in 1896 in which there are no diagonal members, overall rigidity of the structure being maintained by rigidity at the joints of the vertical and horizontal members.

1930 *Engineering* 20 June 790/1 The types of steel coaches usually dealt with..could be reduced to two, in one of which the sides of the body were used as girders of the Vierendeel type. **1947** *Archit. Rev.* CI. 84/1 A special system was employed, using two contiguous spaces together with the columns and beams of the two upper floors, the whole forming a Vierendeel frame. **1970** *Internat. Jrnl. Solids & Structures* VI. 353 (*heading*) The minimum weight design of Vierendeel frames.

†**vierge.** *Obs.*[−1] [a. OF. (also mod.F.) *vierge*:—L. *virgin-em* VIRGIN *sb.*] The Virgin.

1462 *Pol. Poems* (Rolls) II. 270 Now blyssed saint George, pray the vierge immaculat To be good mediatrix.

vierge, var. VERGE *sb.*[1]

Vierkleur ('fɪərklœr). [Afrikaans, f. Du. *vier* four + *kleur* colour.] The flag of the nineteenth-century Transvaal Republic (1857–77 and 1881–1900), distinguished by three horizontal stripes of red, white, and blue, and one vertical green stripe on the left-hand side. Also *attrib.*

1900 W. S. CHURCHILL in *Morning Post* 17 July 8/1 Someone..produced a Union Jack (made during imprisonment out of a Vierkleur). **1911** H. H. FYFE *S. Afr. To-day* 106 Yet in Cape Town shop-windows are exhibited cards lamenting the 'Vierkleur', the four-coloured flag of the Transvaal. **1929** D. REITZ *Commando* iii. 20 On the left of the track stood a large marquee over which floated the vierkleur flag of the Transvaal, indicating General Joubert's headquarters.

vies, var. VIVES.

viese, var. VEES[2].

viesly, obs. f. WISELY.

Viet ('viːɛt), *sb.* and *a.* Abbrev. of VIETNAMESE *a.* and *sb.*

1958 J. BUTTINGER *Smaller Dragon* i. 29 These Viets were probably moving into southeast China and toward the Indochinese peninsula at some time between 500 and 300 B.C. **1967** *Freedomways* VII. 128 Viet brothers come give us a hand We fight for freedom We fight for land. **1979** *Daily Tel.* 19 Jan. 4/6 (*heading*) Five Khmer areas fight Viet troops. **1979** *Tucson* (Arizona) *Citizen* 20 Sept. 1E/1 (*heading*) Viets say Nixon plots with China.

‖**vi et armis** (viː ɛt 'ɑːmiːs), *adv. phr.* [L., lit. 'with force and arms'.] Violently, forcibly, by compulsion; *spec.* in *Law*, causing direct damage to person or property; also *attrib.* Cf. FORCE *sb.*[1] 5 c.

1618 W. FULBECKE *Parallel of Civil & Common Laws* I. 80 a This Writ will not lye, for it is *vi et armis*. **1703** in *Eng. Rep. King's Bench* (1909) XCII. 137 So a man shall have an action against another for riding over his ground, though it do him no damage; for it is an invasion of his property, and the other has no right to come there. And in these cases the action is brought vi et armis. **1762** SMOLLETT *Launcelot Greaves* I. IV. 101 He compelled, *vi & armis*, a rich farmer's son to marry the daughter of a cottager. **1819** KEATS *Let.* 31 July (1958) II. 134 If I had not put pen to paper since I saw you this would be to me a vi et armis taking up before the Judge. *a* **1846** B. R. HAYDON *Autobiogr.* (1927) III. xvii. 338, I looked astounded, but casting a glance round the table easily saw..I was to be set at that evening *vi et armis*. **1873** C. M. YONGE *Pillars of House* II. xix. 181 It was current in the nursery that he was a black man who expelled us *vi et armis*. **1941** W. A. PERCY *Lanterns on Levee* xv. 179 The squad kept marching; it marched now like Beatrice Lillie, *vi et armis*, clear through an unyielding detachment planted in front of it. **1957** R. F. V. HEUSTON *Salmond's Law of Torts* (ed. 12) i. 5 To walk peacefully across another man's land is a forcible injury and a trespass, no less than to break into his house *vi et armis*.

Viet Cong (,viːɛt 'kɒŋ), *sb.* and *a.* Also Vietcong. [Vietnamese, lit. = Vietnamese Communist.] **A.** *sb.* (A member of) the Communist guerilla force(s) active in Vietnam between 1954 and 1976. **B.** *adj.* Of or pertaining to (the members of) this movement.

1957 *Ann. Reg. 1956* 321 Though small groups of dissidents remained in the jungles they ceased to be a danger, and the Communist dissidents known as the Viet Cong were equally ineffective. **1961** *Times* 27 Sept. 13/7 At the base of the Vietcong hierarchy is the village 'cell'. **1964** *Asia Mag.* 7 June 6 The war prevails, and it will, until the Viet Cong is wiped out. **1967** *Observer* 30 Apr. 12 The little cream schoolhouse is essential to the American dream of what we are doing in Vietnam, and it is essential for the soldiers to believe that in *Vietcong* hamlets no schooling is permitted. **1981** B. GRANGER *Schism* (1982) viii. 78 The village headman was a Viet Cong.

Viet Minh (,viːɛt 'mɪn). Also Vietminh. [f. *Việt*-Nam *Dôc-Lập Dông-Minh*, Vietnamese Independence League.] A nationalist independence movement (1941–50) in French Indo-China; *loosely*, the movement succeeding this; a member of one of these movements. Also *attrib.*

1945 *Times* 14 Sept. 3/6 There seem to be only two parties of any significance at the moment—the Viet-min and the Communists. **1945** *Times* 16 Nov. 3/3 It is believed some effort may be made to come to a compromise with the Viet Minh 'Government' in Hanoi. **1962** E. SNOW *Other Side of River* (1963) lxxxv. 684 The free Vietnamese armed forces..were guerrilla groups led largely by the Vietnamese Independence League—Viet Minh, for short. **1968** R. WEST *Sk. from Vietnam* I. 21 The Vietminh, precursors of the Vietcong, employed assassination and terror. **1975** *New Yorker* 21 Apr. 133/1 The structure of the three basic committees is reminiscent of the old Vietminh organizations established in the South between 1946 and 1954.

Vietnamese (viːɛtnə'miːz), *a.* and *sb.* Also Viet Namese. [f. *Vietnam* (see below) + -ESE.] **A.** *adj.* Of or pertaining to the S.E. Asian country of Vietnam (formed in 1945 by the union of the former French colonial provinces of Annam, Tongking, and Cochin-China, and between 1954 and 1976 divided into North and South Vietnam), its inhabitants, or their language.

1947 *Facts on File* Apr. 129 Yesterday French troops claimed that 3 Japanese officers were killed near Hanoi while leading Viet Namese troops. **1951** M. B. EMENEAU (*title*)

Studies in Vietnamese (Annamese) grammar. **1951** *Vietnam: Old Nation—Young State* (U.N.), As a result the Vietnamese language developed considerably and was able to free itself entirely from Chinese influence. **1962** E. SNOW *Other Side of River* (1963) lxxxv. 685 Gracey refused to see Vietnamese leaders who wished to negotiate terms of cooperation for disarming the Japanese. **1969** *Listener* 12 June 814/3 Whenever I see the members of the village council, I say to them: 'I'm not here to teach you what to do. I'm not Vietnamese. I don't look like you. I don't even speak your own language. You've got to make your own decisions.' **1977** *Early Music* July 365/2 *(caption)* Trân Van Khe playing the Vietnamese fiddle. **1983** P. NIESEWAND *Scimitar* xi. 247 It was an excellent meal, starting with.. Vietnamese spring rolls..and finally squirrel fish, a whole baked fish.

B. *sb.* **a.** A native, *collect.* the natives, of Vietnam. **b.** The language of this people, considered by some philologists to belong to the Mon-Khmer family.

1947 H. R. ISAACS *New Cycle in Asia* viii. 157 Matters came to a head in Hanoi on December 19, 1946, when clashes in that city resulted in generalized warfare... The French charged that the Vietnamese were the instigators of the outbreak. **1950** *Times* 25 Apr. 7/2 The new State of Viet Nam has to rely so much on foreign support that many patriotic Vietnamese hold back or join with the Communists. **1953** W. W. GAGE *(title)* Verb constructions in Vietnamese. **1965** *New Statesman* 30 Apr. 680/2 As a Vietnamese, I feel I have the right to express my resentment at the US air raids on Vietnam. **1972** M. SHEPPARD *Taman Indera* 3 The people whom we now know as Chinese, Thais, Khmers, Vietnamese and Malays. **1978** E. TIDYMAN *Table Stakes* II. i. 141 He..shouted a string of orders in Vietnamese.

Vietnamize ('viːɛtnəmaɪz), *v.* [f. *Vietnam* (see prec.) + -IZE.] *trans.* To give a Vietnamese character to; to make Vietnamese; to transfer to Vietnamese (esp. as opposed to American) influence or control. (This now *Hist.* only.)

1957 *Holiday* Aug. 119/1 Cholon's Chinese ebullience has definitely quieted down as a result of Diem's drive to 'Vietnamize' the Chinese. **1969** *Daily Tel.* 25 Oct. 5/3 It was learned..that America had handed over another base to South Vietnam. Two of the United States major port facilities, including the one in Saigon, were next on the list to be 'Vietnamised'. **1972** *Nature* 22 Sept. 185/2 Last week's statement..criticizes the policy of the United States in 'Vietnamizing' the war.

Hence ˌ**Vietnami'zation**; '**Vietnamizing** *vbl. sb.*

1957 *Holiday* Aug. 119/3 When the new idea of 'Vietnamization' is being fostered in the country..it is not surprising the Vietnamese prefer to approach..foreigners with care and reticence. **1969** *Daily Tel.* 11 Oct. 18/1 The Vietnamisation of the war continued with the transfer of 80 United States Navy river patrol boats to the South Vietnamese Navy. *Ibid.* 18 Nov. 14/4 The price for 'Vietnamising' the war..is clearly a Vietnamising of the country's politics as well. **1972** F. FITZGERALD *Fire in Lake* xvi. 404 'Vietnamization', the ironic name for the slow withdrawal of American ground troops and the buildup of Vietnamese armed forces to fight an American-directed war in their stead. **1980** *Word 1979* XXX. 125 The Committee also identified such new problems as..the Vietnamization of foreign terms.

Vietnik ('viːɛtnɪk). orig. *U.S.* [f. *Viet(nam* + -NIK after *beatnik*.] (A usu. pejorative term applied to) an active opponent of American military involvement in the war between North and South Vietnam. Also *attrib.* Cf. PEACENIK.

1965 *Time* 22 Oct. 25A/1 A ragtag collection of unshaven and unscrubbed—they could be called Vietniks—turned out last weekend to promote the most popular new anti-cause. *Ibid.*, The Vietnik rallies—which also attracted some tweedy faculty members..—seemed to bear out a Senate Internal Security report issued last week. **1966** *Wall St. Jrnl.* 31 Mar. 18/2 If the Communists believe that draft-card-burners and other Vietniks represent majority American opinion, they are simply misinformed. **1969** *T.V. Times* (Brisbane) 4 June 6/1, I am opposed to the Vietniks who want us to get out... I saw too many twisted bodies of women and children, mutilated by the Vietcong. **1977** *Time* 18 Apr. 47/2 Sometimes the argument has sounded like a replay of old Vietnik protests.

‖**vieux** (vjø), *a.* The Fr. word for 'old', used in various idiomatic phrases, as ***vieux jeu*** (ʒø) [lit. 'old game'], (something or someone) old-fashioned, hackneyed, outmoded, 'old hat'; ***vieux marcheur*** (marʃœr) ['old campaigner', f. *Le Vieux Marcheur* (1909), a play by Henri Lavedon], an elderly womanizer; also *transf.*; ***vieux port*** (pɔr) ['old port'], the old harbour area of a modern French seaport; ***vieux rose*** (roz) ['old rose'] = OLD ROSE b.

[**1888** H. JAMES *Reverberator* II. iii. 57 His father..didn't think it well painted... 'Poor dear papa, he only understands *le vieux jeu!*' **1891** M. S. VAN DE VELDE *French Fiction of Today* I. i. 7 Their contempt for what they call vieux jeu.] **1896** MRS. H. WARD *Sir George Tressady* II. xvi. 361 'Did you see the new piece at the Français?' He made a face. 'Not I! One couldn't be caught by such *vieux jeu* as that!' **1900** G. MURRAY *Let.* 30 July in G. B. Shaw *Coll. Lett.* (1972) II. 181 Cæsar..did not invent the sarcasm of calling the soldiers 'Citizens'. It was vieux jeu. **1918** R. FRY *Let.* 14 Oct. (1972) II. 435 We are *vieux jeu* and incorrigibly nineteenth century. **1955** *Times* 30 June 15/1 Are not dilatory bus drivers and conductors by now somewhat *vieux jeu?* **1972** M. GLENNY tr. *Solzhenitsyn's August 1914* lxii. 600 To indulge in arguments with hostile, half-baked youth struck him as *vieux jeu* and boring. **1975** *Harper's & Queen* June 128/3 Henri's parents are very French *vieux jeu*... My mother-in-law talks about Louis XV as though she *knew* him. **1920** G. B. SHAW *Shaw on Theatre* (1958) 133 All the young men are cads and cowards, all the old men *vieux marcheurs.* **1937** *Times Lit. Suppl.* 16 Jan. 39/1 Of all the vieux marcheurs in nature, the cock pheasant has almost the worst reputation. **1940** G. ARTHUR *Concerning Winston Spencer Churchill* 108 The immortal hero of Khartum—so ran an odious whisper—was addicted to the brandy bottle; Mr. Gladstone, so it was vulgarly suggested, pursued paths associated with a *vieux marcheur.* **1945** E. WAUGH *Brideshead Revisited* I. ii. 44 Those leprous façades in the vieux port at Marseille. **1957** 'P. QUENTIN' *Suspicious Circumstances* xvii. 198 The lights on all the boats moved in the Vieux Port. **1981** 'D. RUTHERFORD' *Porcupine Basin* i. 11 Be at the Café des Voyageurs in the *vieux port*... Take a table on the *terrasse.* **1890** *Girl's Own Paper* 11 Oct. 31/2, I should get your village dressmaker..to make you a *vieux rose* zephyr dress. **1916** *Daily Colonist* (Victoria, B.C.) 1 July 12/3 The colors include white..old rose, gold..vieux rose, mid-brown, [etc.]. **1941** E. BOWEN *Look at Roses* 55 Light blared on the *vieux rose* curtains.

view (vjuː), *sb.* Forms: 4–6 vewe, 5–7 vew, 6 veu(e, vue; 5, 7 vywe, 5–7 viewe (6 veiwe), 5–8 vieu (6 vieue, 8 viue), 5– view. [a. AF. *vewe, veue, vue, vieue, view,* = OF. *veue* (F. *vue*), ppl. sb. from *veoir* (F. *voir*) to see. The OF. *veüe* corresponds exactly to It. *veduta* in the same sense.]

I. 1. a. A formal inspection or survey of lands, tenements, or ground, for some special purpose. Now *rare* or *Obs.*

1415–6 in Madox *Form. Ang.* (1702) 16 Wee [masons and carpenters], beyng Vewers for the tyme of the seid Cite, have to these Vewes afore writton, putte our sealles. *c* **1450** *Oseney Register* 123 We schall ȝeve to them sufficient Eschaunge, by the vewe of lawfull men, in my othir londes to a conuenient valewe. **1509** *Sel. Cases Star Chamber* (Selden) II. 7 As it apperith by the viewe and ouerseyng [of the fields] takyn by maister Brudenell one of the kynges Justeses. **1523** FITZHERB. *Surv.* 35 b, The vieu of the maner of Dale taken the tenth day of May, the .xiiii. yere of the raygne of kyng Henry the .viii. **1607** J. NORDEN *Surv. Dial.* I. 21 It is true that you say, such a view was taken at the time, that euery Tribe might haue his portion of inheritance. **1622** CALLIS *Stat. Sewers* (1647) 80 There is a diversity between a view and a survey, for by the view one is to take notice only by the eye, but to survey is..by using other ceremonies and circumstances. **1834** LINCOLN, etc., in Nicolay & Hay *Life* (1890) I. 119 *note,* We..respectfully report that we have performed the duties of said view and location [of a road], as required by law, and that we have made the location on good ground.

†**b.** A formal examination or inspection of something, made by a properly appointed or qualified person; the charge or office of inspecting something. *Obs.*

In early quots. denoting the submitting of accounts to inspection. The sense in quot. 1654 is not quite clear. ***view of frank-pledge***: see FRANK-PLEDGE 1 b.

1454 *Rolls of Parlt.* V. 273/1 That the Collectours..paye the money..in youre seid Reseit, and make the views of their accomptz. **1472** *Paston Lett.* III. 49 And on Saturday next comyng he shall send me a vewe of hys acompte. **1497** *Naval Acc. Hen. VII* (1896) 83 It semeth necessarie that another viewe be taken of all the Kynges said ordenaunces within his said Tour of London. **1520** *Coventry Leet Bk.* 674 A veu was takon by the said Maier and his brethern what stores of all Maner of Corne, and what nombre of people was then whithin the said Cite. **1538** *Cartular. Abb. de Rievalle* (Surtees) 353 The office of the ferme gathering in Swawdall, and the oversight of the woddes and vue of ther grownde. **1558** in Feuillerat *Revels Q. Eliz.* (1908) Table i, The Master and officers..shall..peruse the remaines of the whole stuffe and other stoare lefte at the laste vewe. **1647** N. BACON *Disc. Govt. Eng.* I. xxxviii. 92 The Coroner..even in those old daies had the view of bloodshed. **1654** G. GODDARD in *Burton's Diary* (1828) I. Introd. 188 That the excise of all tobacco of the English plantations, be reduced from 3*d.* to 1*d.* the pound; and that thereupon, no view or allowance be made for, or in respect of the said tobacco. **1700** J. TYRRELL *Hist. Eng.* II. 819 Our Regarders or Viewers shall go through the Forests to make a View or Regard. **1802** JAMES *Milit. Dict.* s.v., The view of a place is said to be taken when the general, accompanied by an engineer, reconnoitres it. **1812** J. SMYTH *Pract. of Customs* (1821) 329 Bill of View or Sight. **1827** HALLAM *Const. Hist.* ix. (1876) II. 132 A view of this armour was to be taken twice in the year by constables chosen in every hundred.

†**c.** A review (of troops, etc.). *Obs.*

1565 COOPER *Thesaurus* s.v. *Condo, Lustrum condere,* to apoynt a muster or view. **1681** W. ROBERTSON *Phraseol. Gen.* (1693) 1269 A View of souldiers at a Muster, *armilustrium.* **1693** LUTTRELL *Brief Relat.* (1857) III. 15 The duke of Ormond took a view yesterday of his troop, and ordered all that had bay or grey horses to change them for black. **1721** DE FOE *Mem. Cavalier* (1840) 56 The view being over, and the troops returned to their camps.

d. *Law.* (See quots.) ? *Obs.*

1567 *Expos. Termes of Law* (1579), *Viewe* is when anye actyon real is brought and the tenaunt knoweth not well what lande it is, that the demaundaunt asketh, then the tenant shal praye the viewe. **1607** COWELL *Interpr., Veiours* ..signifieth in our common lawe those, that are sent by the court to take view of any place in question, for the better descision of the right. *a* **1625** SIR H. FINCH *Law* (1636) 366 View is in reall actions of the thing demanded,..when it is so necessarie as without view the defendant cannot well answer. **1768** BLACKSTONE *Comm.* III. 298 He may, in real actions, demand a *view* of the thing in question, in order to ascertain it's identity and other circumstances.

†**e.** ***by view of,*** under the inspection of. *Obs.*⁻¹

1700 TYRRELL *Hist. Eng.* II. 820 Every..Earl, or Baron, coming to us at our Command, and passing through our Forest, may Lawfully take one or two Deer by view of the Forester if present.

2. In general use: An examination, inspection, or survey. (Cf. 18.)

1568 GRAFTON *Chron.* II. 277 They roade in the fieldes all that daye, and made a diligent vewe. **1592** STOW *Ann.* 518 The which volume was since againe,..by viewe of diuers written copies, corrected by my self. **1622** BACON *Hen. VII* (1876) 29 Edward Plantagenet..having passed the view of the streets, was conducted to Paul's church. **1668** DENHAM *Poems* Ep. Ded. A iij b, Neither have I any need of such shifts, for most of the parts of this body have already had Your Majesties view. **1697** DRYDEN *Virg. Georg.* III. 450 We too far the pleasing Path pursue; Surveying Nature with too nice a view.

†**3.** An interview or meeting. *Obs. rare.*

1520 SIR R. WINGFIELD in Ellis *Orig. Lett.* Ser. I. I. 170 Suche personnaiges as shall attende apon hym at the Veue. *Ibid.* 173 The noble personnaiges of thys Realme..be asmoche affectionatt to this Veue as could be wysshyd.

4. The exercise of the faculty of sight; the faculty or power of vision; the possibility or opportunity of seeing something: **a.** Without article.

field of view: see FIELD *sb.* 16 b.

1573 TUSSER *Husb.* (1878) 211 At length by vew, to shore I drew. **1577** HOLINSHED *Chron.* I. 35/1 Thinking it good to vnderstand all things by view that might appertaine to the vse of that warre. *c* **1600** SHAKS. *Sonn.* cxli, 'Tis my heart.. Who in dispight of view is pleasd to dote. **1634** SIR T. HERBERT *Trav.* 193 Hoise him vp to his greater height of view. **1671** MILTON *Samson* 723 And now at nearer view, [it is] no other..Than Dalila thy wife. **1697** DRYDEN *Æneid* XII. 1333 The hero measur'd first, with narrow view, The destin'd mark. **1727–** [see POINT *sb.*¹ D. 12]. **1864** *Ecclesiologist* XXV. 274 The steeple..may..be taken into view with the loftier saddleback of S. Alban's. **1876–7** in Abney *Photogr.* (1878) 207 The diminution of light from the centre towards the margins of the pictures from both these causes increases rapidly with any increase of angle of view beyond 40°.

b. In the phr. ***to view,*** chiefly after vbs.

a **1593** MARLOWE & NASHE *Dido* I. i, Whose lookes set forth no mortall forme to view. **1695** WOODWARD *Nat. Hist. Earth* (1723) 24 Their Parts when dissolved have the same Appearance to View. **1746** FRANCIS tr. *Horace, Art of Poetry* 5 If he gave to View a beauteous Maid. **1757** W. WILKIE *Epigoniad* IX. 270 Towards the Cadmean gate; where full to view Expos'd, the armies and the camp she knew. **1817** JAS. MILL *Brit. India* II. v. vi. 586 One of the most important features of the case was then held up to view. **1852** MRS. STOWE *Uncle Tom's C.* xl, Tom was already lost to view among the distant swamps of the Red River. **1860** TYNDALL *Glac.* I. iii. 28 The snow-floor had, in fact, given way, and exposed to view a clear green lake.

c. Similarly with *the.* (Cf. 14.)

1585 T. WASHINGTON tr. *Nicholay's Voy.* II. ix. 42 b, Where he sayth the second to lye on the North part, he may by the view & eisight onely be reproued. **1603** G. OWEN *Pembrokeshire* i. (1892) 3 That euerye shere is of biggnes as the same appeareth to the vywe. **1664** POWER *Exp. Philos.* Pref. 15 The Knowledge of Man (saith the learn'd Verulam) hath hitherto been determin'd by the View or Sight. **1721** RAMSAY *Tartana* 148 These give not half that pleasure to the view. **1791** MRS. RADCLIFFE *Rom. Forest* ii, It seemed as if heaven was opening to the view. **1820** SHELLEY *Skylark* 50 Like a glow-worm..Among the flowers and grass, which screen it from the view! **1842** TENNYSON *Vision of Sin* 23 [They] Caught each other with wild grimaces, Half-invisible to the view.

d. With limiting terms (possessives, etc.).

1587 FLEMING *Contn. Holinshed* III. 1357/2 He hath set downe to the vew of all men these necessarie notes following. **1592** SHAKS. *Rom. & Jul.* I. i. 177 Alas that loue, whose view is muffled still, Should without eyes, see path-wayes to his will. **1614** LATHAM *Falconry* (1633) 73 For your flight to the Hearne, it is wrought, flown, and maintained by the eie and view of the Hawke. **1640** BP. REYNOLDS *Passions* Ded., This treatise hath had the marvellous felicity to light on the view ..of a very gracious Princess. *a* **1668** LASSELS *Voy. Italy* (1698) II. 118 None are suffered..to do or speak anything scandalously that may shock civility or publick view. **1711** POPE *Temple Fame* 420 Before my view appear'd a structure fair. **1812** CARY *Dante, Parad.* XXII. 19 Elsewhere now I bid thee turn thy view. **1833** TENNYSON *Lady Clara Vere de Vere* 34 When thus he met his mother's view,..She spake some certain truths of you. **1903** MORLEY *Gladstone* I. Pref. *note,* Between two and three thousand papers of one sort or another must have passed under my view.

fig. **1590** SPENSER *F.Q.* III. xi. 11 My Lady and my loue is cruelly pend In dolefull darkenesse from the vew of day.

e. Range of sight or vision.

1591 SAVILE *Tacitus, Agricola* (1622) 184 Lest any sparkle of honesty should by mischance remaine within view. **1722** WOLLASTON *Relig. Nat.* i. 29 No one can tell, in strict speaking, where another is, if he is not within his view. *a* **1732** T. BOSTON *Crook in Lot* (1805) 11 Providing that the crook in his lot should not be set afresh in his view. **1850** TENNYSON *In Mem.* lxxv, Somewhere, out of human view, Whate'er thy hands are set to do Is wrought. **1855** —— *Maud* I. xx, Was it gentle to reprove her For stealing out of view From a little lazy lover?

5. a. An act of looking or beholding; a sight, look, or glance.

1581 W. S. *Compend.* 21 b, The first view would displease many. **1590** SHAKS. *Mids. N.* III. i. 144 Mine eare is much enamored of thy note; On the first view to say,..I loue thee. **1611** SIR W. MURE *Misc. Poems* I. 50 Seik no to subdue And kill ane hert, bot for a vieu. **1667** MILTON *P.L.* II. 190 Who [can] deceive his mind, whose eye Views all things at one view? **1697** DRYDEN *Virg. Past.* VIII. 53, I view'd thee first; how fatal was the View! **1704** J. HARRIS *Lex. Techn.* I. s.v. *Measures,* To see in one View an Account of the Ancient and Present Measures of several Parts of the World. **1746** FRANCIS tr. *Horace, Art of Poetry* 495 That gives us Pleasure for a single View; And this, ten Times repeated, still is new. **1813** SHELLEY *Q. Mab* II. 100 The thronging thousands, to a passing view, Seemed like an ant-hill's citizens. **1886** *Cornh. Mag.* Aug. 224 For an hour at each view will this monstrous eye..gaze analysingly on many hundreds of stars at once.

b. *ellipt.* A view-halloo.

1903 *Longm. Mag.* Jan. 244 There is, however, in my humble opinion, no great harm in a view when the hare is first found.

6. The sight or vision *of* something. Also with possessives.

1588 SHAKS. *Titus A.* III. ii. 55 Out on the murderour: thou kil'st my hart, Mine eyes cloi'd with view of Tirranie. **1600** FAIRFAX *Tasso* XIV. xiv, Thy weak armies..Shall take new strength, new courage at his view. **1632** *Guillim's Heraldry* (ed. 3) III. ii. 113 Thus should their view put us euer more in minde, to raise our thoughts to Godward. **1634** SIR T. HERBERT *Trav.* 23 Towards night [we] got view of Ioanna Ile. *a***1771** GRAY *Dante* 29 Pisa's Mount, that intercepts the view Of Lucca. **1794** GODWIN *Caleb Williams* 247 The view of his figure immediately introduced a train of ideas into my mind. **1820** W. IRVING *Sketch Bk.* (1821) II. 29 We had now come in full view of the old family mansion. **1837** LOCKHART *Scott* IV. viii. 263 He proceeded to thread his way westwards, across moor and bog, until we lost view of him.

transf. **1815** J. SMITH *Panorama Sci. & Art* II. 191 Hitherto the distinction..appears to have been scarcely thought of. The distinct view of it was accidentally obtained by Stephen Grey, in the year 1729.

7. a. Visual appearance or aspect.

1551 RECORDE *Cast. Knowl.* (1556) 152 If the earthe were of anye bygnes in comparison to the worlde, then should his semidiameter beare some vewe of byggenesse to the semidiameter of the skie. **1570–6** LAMBARDE *Peramb. Kent* (1826) 102 The same man also, persuaded partly by the viewe of the place itselfe,..supposeth, that Richborow was of auncient time a citie of some price. **1592** SHAKS. *Rom. & Jul.* I. i. 175 Alas that loue so gentle in his view, Should be so tyrannous and rough in proofe. **1603** G. OWEN *Pembrokeshire* i. (1892) 2 It most Consequentelye followe that the shere must be but little, much lesse then other sheres which seem lesse in vywe. **1667** MILTON *P.L.* IV. 142 A Silvan Scene,..a woodie Theatre Of stateliest view. *Ibid.* 247 A happy rural seat of various view. **1713** *Guardian* No. 1 ⁋1 His Countenance is communicated to the Publick in several Views and Aspects. **1718** POPE *Iliad* XVI. 203 Like furious, rush'd the Myrmidonian crew, Such their dread strength, and such their dreadful view. **1812** CRABBE *Tales* xviii. 9 As certain ores in outward view the same.

fig. **1581** PETTIE *Guazzo's Civ. Conv.* III. (1586) 123 To maintaine himselfe in that view which belongeth to his calling.

b. Aspect as affected by position.

1847 LEITCH tr. *C. O. Müller's Anc. Art* 450 The coins exhibit his head generally in front view.

8. †**a.** *Hunting.* The footprints of a buck or fallow-deer. *Obs.*

Common in 17th c. works of reference, but merely as an echo of Turbervile.

1576 TURBERV. *Venerie* xxxvi. 97 Then if she aske, what Slot or view I found, I say, the Slot, or view, was long on ground. *Ibid.* 239 The footyng or printe of an Hartes foote is called the Slot. Of a Bucke and all other Fallow Deare, it is to be called the View. **1611** COTGR., *Foulée*, the Slot of a Stag, the Fuse of a Bucke (the view, or footing of either) vpon hard ground, grasse, leaues, or dust. **1679** LOVELL *Indic. Univ.* 26 The strain, view, slot or footing of a deer are the marks he makes in soiling.

b. A sight or prospect of some landscape or extended scene; an extent or area covered by the eye from one point.

1606 BRYSKETT *Civ. Life* 93 Hauing the prospect not onely of the citie, but also of the sea and hauen,..and some commending the ayre, some the delightfulnesse of the view. **1634** SIR T. HERBERT *Trav.* 14, I neuer saw ground more pleasant for view. **1667** MILTON *P.L.* II. 890 Before thir eyes in sudden view appear The secrets of the hoarie deep. **1718** PRIOR *Solomon* II. 22 Fish-ponds were made, where former Forrests grew; And Hills were levell'd to extend the View. **1756** MRS. CALDERWOOD in *Coltness Collect.* (Maitl. Cl.) 192 It is the finest viue ever I saw; the ground lies about it, you would think, in a circle. **1766** [ANSTEY] *Bath Guide* vii. 4 Fine Walks, and fine Views, and a Thousand fine Things. **1808** PIKE *Sources Mississ.* II. 220 From the flat roof of the church we had a delightful view of the village. **1847** TENNYSON *Princess* Prol. 68 Here were telescopes For azure views; and there a group of girls In circle waited. **1883** *Manch. Exam.* 30 Oct. 8/4 A local resident..whose house..has a beautiful view down the valley.

c. A drawing, painting, print, etc., representing a landscape or other prospect.

*a***1700** EVELYN *Diary* 18 Jan. 1645, We were then conducted into a new Gallery, whose sides were painted with views of the most famous places, towns, and territories in Italy. **1709** (*title*), Britannia Illustrata; or, Views..of the Principal Seats of the Nobility and Gentry of Great Britain. **1791** ROBERTSON *Hist. India* App., Wks. 1851 VI. 510 Mr. Hodges has published views of three of these [fortresses]. *c***1811** FUSELI in *Lect. Paint.* iv. (1848) 449 That kind of landscape which is entirely occupied with the tame delineation of a given spot,..what is commonly called 'views'. **1853** MRS. CARLYLE *Lett.* (1883) II. 220 The little view at the top of this sheet is where I live in London. **1854** HAWTHORNE *Eng. Note-Bks.* (1883) I. 527 A photographist preparing to take a view of the castle. **1898** BINNS *Story of the Potter* 222 Portraits, views, and fancy scenes were produced in different self-colours.

II. 9. a. Mental contemplation or vision (alone or combined with ocular inspection); observation, notice.

point of view: see POINT *sb.*[1] D. 12.

*c***1440** *Alph. Tales* 530 þer is no thyng bod som peple will giff þer vew and þer fantasye þer-vnto. **1593** NORDEN (*title*), Speculum Britanniæ. By the travaile and vew of John Norden. **1612** in *Eng. Hist. Rev.* April (1914) 249, I will be bold out of my zeale and duty to present yt [a proposition] unto his Magesties vieu. **1642** in *Verney Mem.* (1907) I. 243 But I hate to have my secrets laid open to everybodie's view. **1746** FRANCIS tr. *Horace, Epist.* I. ii. 26 The Poet sets Ulysses in our View. **1762** KAMES *Elem. Crit.* i. (1833) 20 The mind extends its view to a son more readily than to a servant. **1846** WHATELY *Rhetoric* (ed. 7) Introd. vi. 34 Such a habit..also, in a rhetorical point of view, if I may so speak, often proves hurtful. **1850** HAWTHORNE *Scarlet Letter* Introd., One..who appeared to have been rather a noteworthy personage in the view of our ancestors. **1911** J. H. ROUND *King's Serjeants* 254 After this, the scalding serjeanty..fades from view.

b. A single act of contemplation or attention to a subject.

1570 LEVINS *Manip.* 94 A view of things, *æstimatio.* **1676** DRYDEN *Aureng-zebe* Ded., The hasty Critick, who judges on a view, is as liable to be deceived. **1776** ADAM SMITH *W.N.* I. i. (1869) I. 10 The advantage..is much greater than we should at first view be apt to imagine it.

10. a. A particular manner or way of considering or regarding a matter or question; a conception, opinion, or theory formed by reflection or study. Freq. const. *of.*

1573 G. HARVEY *Letter-bk.* (Camden) 1 Uppon a reasnable vew of the matter. **1679** PENN *Addr. Prot.* II. ii. (1692) 60 Let us take the most impartial View we can. **1736** BUTLER *Anal.* I. iii. 50 Good Actions are never punished, considered as beneficial to Society, nor ill Actions rewarded, under the view of their being hurtful to it. **1780** *Mirror* No. 100 ⁋1 The view of Hamlet's character, exhibited in my last Number. **1800** TREVELYAN in G. O. Trevelyan *Macaulay* (1876) I. i. 22 Miss Hannah took a more unselfish view of the subject. **1836** J. GILBERT *Chr. Atonem.* ix. (1852) 281 Atonement presents to us this view of God. **1855** BAIN *Senses & Int.* I. ii. §8 The application of this view of the plan of structure of the brain will appear in the sequel. **1884** SIR W. B. BRETT in *Law Rep. 14 Q.B.D.* 798 That was the view which the judgment of the Court below upholds.

b. An aspect or light in which something is regarded or considered. (Cf. 7.)

1713 *Guardian* No. 5 ⁋3 The Widow of Sir Marmaduke is to be considered in a very different View. **1729** LAW *Serious C.* x. 145 If we consider mankind in a farther view, as a redeemed order of fallen spirits. **1794** PALEY *Evid.* III. iv. ⁋22 We are well warranted in calling the view, under which the learned men of that age beheld Christianity, an obscure and distant view.

c. *pl.* Opinions, ideas, or theories, of an individual or speculative character, held or advanced with regard to some subject.

1769 ROBERTSON *Chas. V*, III. ⁋33 Nor did his political views and maxims seem less strange. **1792** J. BARLOW *Conspir. Kings* 86 Gallia's sons..Make patriot views and moral views the same. **1818** COBBETT *Pol. Reg.* XXXIII. 106 Reformers, not so well able to express as to think, would have had an answer to all questions relating to their views. **1841** ARNOLD in *Life & Corr.* (1844) II. ix. 270 Of course, he who believes his own views to be true, must believe the opposite views to be error. **1870** JEVONS *Elem. Logic* ii. 11 It does not seem that the views of the logicians named are irreconcileable. **1883** *Law Times* 20 Oct. 408 The time must come when the views of our committee will prevail.

d. Without article: Comprehensive survey.

1821–30 LD. COCKBURN *Mem.* (1856) 177 Allen's single lecture contained as much truth and view as could be extracted from all the books in Europe on the subject.

11. A survey, a general or summary account, *of* something.

1604 DALLINGTON (*title*), The View of Fraunce. **1623** COCKERAM II, The full View of a thing, *synopsie.* **1647** MAY *Hist. Parl.* Title-p., A short and necessary view of some precedent yeares. **1729** BUTLER *Serm.* Wks. 1874 II. Pref. 14 It may not be amiss to give the reader the whole argument here in one view. **1779** *Mirror* No. 31, An author who draws characters in the other manner..gives a view of the particulars themselves. **1800** *Asiat. Ann. Reg.* II. 44/1, I proceed finally to offer a combined view of the whole. **1815** J. SMITH *Panorama Sci. & Art.* II. 157 With the record of a late excursion of his we shall close this view of the practice of aërostation.

12. a. An aim or intention; a design or plan; an object or purpose.

1634 SIR T. HERBERT *Trav.* 83 [Nicanor slew Antiochus], because interposing the view of his ambition. **1711** MARLBOROUGH in *10th Rep. Hist. MSS. Comm.* App. I. 144, I haue no other views then what tend to the firmest vnion with his Lordship. **1759** FRANKLIN *Ess.* Wks. 1840 III. 483 Whatever view the governor had to serve by his opposition, he neither did himself or views any service by it. **1771** WESLEY *Wks.* (1872) V. 20 It is necessarily implied, that a man have a sincere view of pleasing God in all things. **1815** SCOTT *Guy M.* xxii, Part of Brown's view in choosing that unusual tract..had been a desire to view the remains of the celebrated Roman Wall. **1831** *Society* I. 295, I have told you my views for Jemima. **1849** GROTE *Greece* II. xlvii. (1862) IV. 160 Such were the views of Pericles in regard to his country.

b. Regard or reference *to* a person or thing (*rare*). † *out of a view to*, with an eye to.

1718 M. TOMKINS in W. Wilson *Dissenting Ch.* (1808) II. 540 He assured me he had no particular view *to me*, or suspicion of me, when he brought down that sermon among others to Newington. **1728** CHAMBERS *Cycl.* s.v. *Choir*, But the antient Ballustrades have been since restor'd; out of a View to the Beauty of the Architecture. **1736** L. WELSTED *Wks.* (1787) 486 In view to the second [commandment], this necessity was greater.

13. A prospect, anticipation, expectation, or outlook.

1719 W. WOOD *Surv. Trade* 17 That we were brought in View of a truly safe, honourable, and advantagious Peace. **1726** SHELVOCKE *Voy. round World* 210 We could have no better views at present than of falling into their hands sooner or later. **1755** SMOLLETT *Quix.* (1803) II. 50 He that hath good in his view, and yet will not evil eschew, his folly deserveth to rue. **1758** S. HAYWARD *Serm.* xiv. 408 It gives the christian..the sweetest composure in the views of death. **1813** SHELLEY *Q. Mab* IV. 253 Are not thy views of unregretted death Drear, comfortless, and horrible? **1827** D. JOHNSON *Ind. Field Sports* Pref. p. x, I entertain no view of any emolument whatever from the present publication.

III. In various phrases.

†**14.** *at* or *to the view* (in hawking and hunting): By sight. Also in fig. context. *Obs.*

1486 *Bk. St. Albans* d j, An hawke flieth to the vew, to the Beke, or to the Toll. **1607** CHAPMAN *Bussy D'Ambois* II. Wks. (1895) 148 Both fell as their spirits flew Upwards; and still hunt honour at the view. **1628** BP. H. KING *Exp. Lord's Prayer* 144 'Tis dangerous to hunt such abstruse mysteries at the view, or looke too neere. **1657** —— *Poems* (1843) 17 Teach me to hunt that kingdom at the view Where true joyes reign.

15. in (..) view. a. *in (the) view of*, in the sight of, so as to be seen by; also, within sight of, near enough to see.

*a***1548** HALL *Chron., Hen. VI*, 174 These armies thus liyng, the one in the conspect and vewe of the other, studied all meanes and pollecies, how to take aduauntage eche of other. **1594** *Sec. Pt. Contention* (1843) 122 Richard The second in the view of manie Lords Resignde the Crowne to Henrie the fourth. **1634** SIR T. HERBERT *Trav.* 22 An Iland called Mæottey scituate in view of some three other. **1667** MILTON *P.L.* II. 394 Neerer our ancient Seat; perhaps in view Of those bright confines. **1719** DE FOE *Crusoe* I. (Globe) 22 While I was in View of the Moor that was swimming, I stood out directly to sea with the Boat. **1728** WATTS *Let.* 20 July in *Pearson's Catal.* No. 76 (1894) 64 Are not my sermons in your view and within your reach? *a***1774** GOLDSM. *Hist. Greece* II. 101 Here he chose his station, in view of a temple dedicated to Hercules. **1814** WORDSW. *Excursion* IX. 706 For sacrifice performed Exultingly, in view of open day. **1848** THACKERAY *Van. Fair* li, Shaking hands with them and smiling in the view of all persons.

b. *in view*, in sight, in such a place or position as to be seen; also (*b*) in contemplation or notice, under attention; (*c*) as an end or object aimed at.

In the latter uses chiefly after *have* or *keep.*

1605 SHAKS. *Lear* V. i. 51 The Enemy's in view. **1667** MILTON *P.L.* I. 563 And now Advanc't in view they stand, a horrid Front Of dreadful length. **1731** W. HALFPENNY *Perspective* 4 Here inserted more plainly to discover what part of the Cube is in View. **1769** ROBERTSON *Chas. V*, IV. Wks. 1813 V. 415 His soldiers, now that they had their prey full in view, complained neither of fatigue nor famine. **1780** COWPER *Progr. Error* 570 None sends his arrow to the mark in view, Whose hand is feeble, or his aim untrue. **1812** *Sporting Mag.* XXXIX. 88 The hounds..were running a hare hard in view. **1856** KANE *Arct. Expl.* II. xxvi. 262 There was nothing in view except Dalrymple Rock.

fig. **1757** FOOTE *Author* II. Wks. 1799 I. 149, I shall never be able to hold out long; I had rather be taken in view.

(*b*) **1667** MILTON *P.L.* X. 1030 Then let us seek Som safer resolution, which methinks I have in view. **1690** LOCKE *Hum. Und.* II. x. §1 By keeping the idea..for some time actually in view, which is called contemplation. **1779** *Mirror* No. 66, It is necessary that we keep in view the character of Lady Anne. **1793** SMEATON *Edystone L.* Introd. 2 It is probable the resemblance Josephus had in view, was chiefly that of the outward form. **1840** *Jrnl. R. Agric. Soc.* I. IV. 455 This should always be kept in view. **1891** 'L. MALET' *Wages of Sin* II. 38, I have a quantity of work in view.

(*c*) **1720** RAMSAY *Prosp. Plenty* 165 This, this our faithfu' trustees have in view, And honourably will the task pursue. **1771** *Junius Lett.* lviii. (1788) 312 Liberty..we all profess to have in view. ?**1782** A. SHIRREFS *Poems* (1790) 278 So fiercely they fought, having honour in view, Ten hours quite elaps'd. **1853** BROWNING *In a Balcony* Wks. 1907 VII. 30 Who keeps one end in view makes all things serve. **1878** STUBBS *Const. Hist.* (1896) III. 453 It may be questioned whether the advisers of Henry VI..had any deep political object in view. **1908** *Animal Managem.* 291 And with this in view, the saddles are very generally left on.

c. *in that (this, etc.) view*, on that account, for that reason or consideration. ? *Obs.*

1734 tr. *Rollin's Anc. Hist.* (1827) I. 108 It is in that view that Socrates..set so high a value upon Euripides. **1788** PRIESTLEY *Lect. Hist.* v. lii. 401 How vastly profitable these our plantations are to us in every view. **1827** in Scott *Chron. Canongate* Introd. *App.*, It was in that view that he proposed to drink to the memory of his late Royal Highness the Duke of York.

d. *in view of*, (*a*) in prospect or anticipation of, with a view to; (*b*) in consideration or regard of, on account of.

(*a*) **1709** MRS. MANLEY *Secret Mem.* (1736) III. 16 Let us with a chearfull Boldness loose the Reins, in View of attaining the Latter. *Ibid.* 277 In view of marrying Ethelinda. **1859** S. WILBERFORCE *Sp. Missions* (1874) 182 He writes to this lady, in a letter with which she has entrusted me, in view of this meeting. **1867** C. S. PARKER in *Quest Reformed Parl.* 197 An unreformed Parliament, which ..has never been more disposed to bestir itself for good than now in view of approaching dissolution. **1878** R. SIMPSON *Sch. Shaks.* I. 26 Musters were being taken through England in view of wars with Scotland and France.

(*b*) **1819** T. HOPE *Anastasius* II. 160 In view of the readiness she showed to second my search, all was, or appeared to be, forgiven. **1831** —— *Ess. Origin Man* III. 113 In view of the excellencies of the works embodied in it, [the language] continued to be occasionally used. **1874** MORLEY *Compromise* 54 Error, therefore, in view of such considerations may surely be allowed to have at least a provisional utility. **1885** L. OLIPHANT *Sympneumata* 212 In view of this aspect of the class of phenomena in question, we regard with leniency their presence in the human nature of the past.

16. a. *on* or *upon (the) view of*, on ocular inspection or perception of, *spec.* by way of inquest.

1488 *Rolls of Parlt.* VI. 414/1 All Enditements..taken afore any of your Corowners.., upon the viewe of the Body of the said Thomas Portyngton. **1512** *Act 4 Hen. VIII*, c. 20 Preamble, [They] caused a Crouner to sit and inquere on the vieu of the Bodies of the said John Cristofore, Gerard, and Genet. **1541** *Act 33 Hen. VIII*, c. 12 §1, All inquisicions upon the viewe of persons slayne..within any the Kinges saide pallaces or houses. **1600** E. BLOUNT tr. *Conestaggio* 228 Yet vpon view of the horse, they mette them with the keies of the citie. **1661** W. LOWTHER in *Extr. St. P. rel. Friends* II. (1911) 118 His Maiestyes Justices of the peace, vpon viewe or haueing Informacion of such persons soe offending. **1779** *Mirror* No. 66, The feelings that arise on the view of ability, self-possession, knowledge of character. **1815** *Ann. Reg., Chron.* 47 An inquest was held..on view of the body. **1841** *L'pool Mercury* 2/5 An inquest was held before Mr. Curry, on view of the body of Wm. Clare, aged 21.

b. ***on the view***, by simple inspection.

1823 J. BADCOCK *Dom. Amusem.* 31 Making an estimate of the original purity of the material..may be accomplished, first on the view; second by heat. **1855** MACAULAY *Hist. Eng.* xxi. IV. 615 The High Bailiff then walked round the three companies of horsemen, and pronounced, on the view, that Montague and Fox were duly elected.

c. ***on view***, on exhibition; open to general or public inspection.

1850 *Punch* 19 Oct. 164/1 The South Western Railway.. keeps a quantity of hissing, smoking, screaming engines always 'on view'. **1882** MISS BRADDON *Mt. Royal* III. vi. 104 He shall be on view in the drawing-room before dinner.

17. a. ***with the*** (or ***a***) ***view of***, with the object or design of (doing something).

1723 *Pres. St. Russia* II. 112 You acted only with a view of deceiving me. **1754** SHERLOCK *Disc.* (1759) I. i. 18 Religion must be formed with a View of securing a future Happiness. **1802** O. GREGORY *Treat. Astron.* 257 With a view of ascertaining more accurately the nature of the sun. **1827** FARADAY *Chem. Manip.* xxiv. 590 With the view..of expediting the acquirement of the necessary habits. **1884** in A. Cawston *Street Improv. London* (1893) 106 Power of taking possession..with the view of carrying out the necessary work.

b. ***with a view to***, with the aim or object of attaining, effecting, or accomplishing something; const. (*a*) with nouns or pronouns, or (*b*) with verbs. Also (*c*), with regard to; (*d*) in view of.

(*a*) **1728** CHAMBERS *Cycl.* s.v. *Hair*, It was with a View to this, that such..procured their Hair to be shaven off. **1767** COWPER *Let.* 20 Oct., I am willing to suspect that you make this inquiry with a view to an interview when time shall serve. **1833** HT. MARTINEAU *Vanderput & S.* i. 20 [He] allowed that such an indulgence might,—especially with a view to increased knowledge,—be extended to a sufferer like Christian. **1866** R. CHAMBERS *Ess.* Ser. II. 89 Providence has constituted us with a view to activity. **1875** HELPS *Soc. Press.* iii. 49 The tendency is more and more to promote individual effort with a view to individual comfort. **1891** *Law Times* XC. 373/1 The Belgian Government desired his extradition with a view to his trial in Belgium.

(*b*) **1723** *Present St. Russia* I. 160 With a View to secure the Cuban-Tartars to the Russian Interest. **1765-8** ERSKINE *Inst. Law Scot.* IV. iv. §55 The forcible..abduction of the woman's person, with a view to violate it. **1800** *Asiat. Ann. Reg., Charac.* 54/2 The troops had been embarked with a view to retake the island of Grenada. **1842** LOUDON *Suburban Hort.* 53 They might..be advantageously introduced with a view to watering summer crops. **1891** *Law Times* XCII. 105/2 The lady had contracted specifically with a view to bind definite separate estate.

(*c*) **1785** PALEY *Mor. Philos.* VI. xii, War may be considered with a view to its causes and its conduct.

(*d*) **1808** ELEANOR SLEATH *Bristol Heiress* V. 329 With a view to his approaching nuptials, Lord Castleton presented him with a handsome service of plate.

c. ***with this*** (or ***that***) ***view***, with this intention or aim, for this purpose.

1765 H. WALPOLE *Vertue's Anecd. Paint.* (ed. 2) III. 159 Preudhomme went to Wilton with that view. **1769** ROBERTSON *Chas. V*, IV. Wks. 1813 V. 413 With this view he dispatched a courier to Bourbon. **1815** J. SMITH *Panorama Sci. & Art* II. 191 With this view he fixed a cord to a nail which was in one of the beams of the ceiling. **1857** BUCKLE *Civiliz.* I. ix. 573 With this view, the people, even in their ordinary amusements, are watched and carefully superintended. **1893** LIDDON *Life Pusey* II. xxv. 164 With this view the writer reviews fourteen of the Articles.

18. a. ***to take a view of***, to take a look at, to make an inspection, examination, or survey of. †Also with *the* or without article.

1476 *Paston Lett.* III. 162, I suppose that my lorde wille take the vywe off alle hys retynywe heer. **1526** *Pilgr. Perf.* (W. de W. 1531) 17 [They] had sente theyr spyes to take the vewe of the countre. **1557** *Order of Hospitalls* F v, When Veiwe is taken, whether the same Childe be living..in the Howse or at Nurse. **1578** in Feuillerat *Revels Q. Eliz.* (1908) 298 When my Lord Chamberleyne toke a viewe of the stuffe at mr Brydemans. **1631** WEEVER *Anc. Funeral Mon.* To Rdr., I likewise tooke view of many ancient Monuments not inscribed. **1658** WOOD *Life* (O.H.S.) I. 236 He had taken a view of the monuments. *a* **1774** GOLDSM. *Hist. Greece* II. 233 The next day he took a view of all Darius's money and moveables. **1780** *Newgate Cal.* V. 30 No sooner had he taken a view of it, than he declared, that..he had made the paper. **1815** J. SMITH *Panorama Sci. & Art* II. 305 In order to take a view of the means employed, to lessen, increase, or otherwise modify the affinities of bodies.

b. ***to take the long view***, to have regard for more than the present; to provide for the future.

1924 *Times Trade & Engin. Suppl.* 29 Nov. 247/2 Those who took the long view and ordered more than just to meet current needs are now reaping the benefit of such a policy.

c. ***to take a poor view***: see POOR *a.* (*sb.*) 5 f. Also (in same sense) ***to take a dim view***.

1941 *Newsweek* 7 July 27/2 Take a dim view—disapprove. **1947** H. GRIEVE *Something in Country Air* 13 Mr Everard took a dim view of his youngest niece. **1977** *Daily News* (Perth, Austral.) 19 Jan. 6/3 Bukovsky said he took a dim view of the way the West was pursuing detente.

IV. 19. ***attrib.*** and ***Comb.*** **a.** In senses 1 and 4, as ***view-day***, ***-making***, ***-worthy*** adj.

1589 GREENE *Ciceronis Amor* Epistle Ded., Thinking nothing rare, nor view-worthy, sufficiently-patronized, vnlesse shrowded vnder the protection of so honorable a Mæcenas. **1600** *Maldon* (Essex) *Documents* (Bundle 162) II, xxiiid for fire, and bredd, and beare spent in the Moote-halle on the pettie vew daye. **1607** in W. H. Hale *Prec. in Causes of Office* (1841) 10 They shall certify..of the vew making by the workmen..and likewise how farr they have proceeded in the repayer of the church. **1850** *Art Jrnl.* July 224 The rooms were crowded during the 'view' days with visitors.

b. In senses 8 b and 8 c, as ***view-hunter***, ***-hunting***, ***-lens***, ***-painter***, ***-painting***, ***-station***, ***-taking***, etc.; **view card**, a picture postcard showing a view; **view-finder**, an attachment to a camera by which it is more readily adjusted to take a particular view; **view-phone**, a (proposed) device for enabling telephone users to see each other during a call; **viewsite**, a site (for a house or other building) with a view (sense 8 b).

1938 BLUNDEN *On Several Occasions*, Buying a view-card and a book. **1973** *Express* (Trinidad & Tobago) 17 Mar. 14/2 Hobbies—art, stamps and collecting viewcards. **1889** View-finder [see FINDER 3 d]. **1891** *Anthony's Photogr. Bull.* IV. 426 A revolving view-finder, flash-lamp, dark slide covers. **1837** J. E. MURRAY *Summer in Pyrenees* II. 65 The most greedy view-hunters of them all will leave it [Canigoû] satisfied with the beauty and magnificence of the prospect. **1831** CARLYLE *Sart. Res.* II. vi, I mean the epidemic, now endemical, of View-hunting. **1889** *Anthony's Photogr. Bull.* II. 38 When the ordinary view lens, giving barrel distortion, is used. **1968** *Listener* 20 June 796/1 Flocks of academic view painters.. used to set up their easels round the picturesque little harbour at St. Ives. **1971** *Country Life* 2 Sept. 536/3 Worcester's view-painters may fairly be compared with such fellow professionals. *Ibid.*, Topographical view-painting was not confined to fortunate Worcester, of course. **1982** *Nat. Gallery News* Feb. 1 Tourists visited Venice, wanting to take away reminders of the city they might not see again. The growing market must have encouraged both Canaletto and Guardi to turn to view painting. **1964** F. POHL *Alternating Currents* (1966) 38, I turned off the viewphone, got up and walked out. **1966** *New Scientist* 24 Nov. 440/3 A 'viewphone' service (which could enable telephone users, to see each other during a call). **1978** *Times* 3 Nov. 27/4 The Post Office itself has listed the main telecommunications services..envisaged for the years 1985 and 2000... By 1985 there will be..radiopaging, confravision.., viewphone. **1971** *Sunday Express* (Johannesburg) 28 Mar. 20/2 (Advt.), Each stand a spectacular viewsite! **1977** *Chicago Tribune* 2 Oct. (TV Week Suppl.) 4/1 (Advt.), This economical two-story home turns its back to the street (or takes beautiful advantage of a viewsite) to create an uncommon sense of privacy even in a busy urban setting. **1886** *Pall Mall G.* 11 Sept. 4/2 It was his delight to make..good roads to all the best view stations on his estate. **1889** *Anthony's Photogr. Bull.* II. 339 If they are view-taking in a region of streams and woods.

view, var. VEW (yew-tree). *dial.*

view (vjuː), *v.* Forms: 6-7 veue (6 vue), vewe (6 veawe), viewe (6 vieue); 6 vieu, veu, vew, 6- view (6 veiw, *Sc.* wew). [f. the sb. Cf. AVIEW *v.*]

1. a. *trans.* To inspect or examine in a formal or official manner; to survey carefully or professionally; †to review (troops).

1523 LD. BERNERS *Froiss.* I. cccxcvii. 278 b/2 Whan they were nombred and viewed, they thought themselfe able to fight with the greatest prince in all the worlde. **1539** CROMWELL in Merriman *Life & Lett.* (1902) II. 237 Furthermore his Maieste woolde that you shulde cause the stretes and Lanes there to be vieued for the pavementes. **1560** DAUS tr. *Sleidane's Comm.* 258 Captaynes were sente oute to view the situation of theyr ennemies Campe. **1617** MORYSON *Itin.* II. 251 In Christmas holidayes his Lordship viewed the toune of Galloway, and judging it a place of great importance [etc.]. **1623** GOUGE *Serm. Extent God's Provid.* §15 The Coroner and his Inquest comming to view the bodies, found remaining but 63. **1697** J. LEWIS *Mem. Dk. Glocester* (1789) 21 About this time, there came Scotch regiments of dragoons to be viewed by the King in Hyde Park. **1714** *Fr. Bk. of Rates* 419 Offices..in which all Goods coming from Foreign Parts, or going to Foreign Parts, shall be declared, viewed, visited, and discharged. **1749** FIELDING *Tom Jones* VII. xii, The Surgeon,..having viewed the wound,..ordered his Patient instantly to bed. **1793** SMEATON *Edystone L.* §227 We..took the opportunity of viewing the progress of our moorstone works at Lanlivery. **1819** SHELLEY *Cenci* I. i. 17, I once heard the nephew of the Pope Had sent his architect to view the ground, Meaning to build a villa. **1852** DICKENS *Bleak Ho.* xi, 'Well, gentlemen!' resumes the Coroner,..'the first thing to be done is to view the body'.

†**b.** *spec.* To inspect or examine (records, accounts, etc.) by way of check or control. *Obs.*

1534 HENRY VIII in J. Bacon *Liber Regis* (1786) p. vi, [They shall] also se and veu such regesters, boks of accompt, Ester boks, and all other writings. *c* **1545** in J. S. Leadam *Sel. Cas. Crt. Requests* (1898) 88 A commaundement..to vue, serche, & ouersee certayn Courte Rollis. **1554-5** in Feuillerat *Revels Q. Mary* (1914) 178 Comissyoners specially appoynted and auctorised to vewe and take the accompte state and remayne of and within that offyce. **1647** in *10th Rep. Hist. MSS. Comm.* App. V. 495 The said twelve men..shall view the late booke of Excise.

†**c.** To survey or explore (a country, coast, etc.). *Obs.*

1551 BIBLE *Josh.* vii. 2 Then Josua sent men from Jericho to Ai.., saying, get you vp, and vewe the countre. **1607** J. NORDEN *Surv. Dial.* I. 21 Joshua commaunded..that euery tribe should choose out three men, that he might send them thorow the land of Canaan, to view, suruey, and to describe it. **1652** NEEDHAM tr. *Selden's Mare Cl.* 189 They permitted none besides Merchants to sail unto the Island without their leav, nor any man at all to view or sound the Ports and Sea Coast. **1745** P. THOMAS *Jrnl. Anson's Voy.* 32 The Commodore sent the Trial Sloop to view the Island. **1796** MORSE *Amer. Geog.* I. 143 John Davis..viewed that and the more northern coasts.

d. *absol.* To look over a property to assess its suitability for purchase or rent.

1914 'E. BRAMAH' *Max Carrados* 79 The place is to be let. ..We will go on to the agents and get a card to view. **1967** N. MARSH *Death at Dolphin* i. 9 We hold the keys. Were you wanting to view? **1971** G. SIMS *Deadhand* II. iii. 92 Is it the house? No good—you can't view without a docket.

2. a. To look at (something) more or less attentively; to scrutinize; to observe closely.

Cf. examples of *view and re-view* s.v. REVIEW *v.* 2.

1548 UDALL, etc. *Erasm. Par. Luke* xxiv. 199 Vieu and beholde you my handes. **1563** B. GOOGE *Eglogs*, etc. (Arb.) 115 When I had vewd these wrytten lines and markde the Storye well, I ioyed muche. **1577** —— *Heresbach's Husb.* I. (1586) 7 b, Let vs walke aboute, that I may viewe your house tyll dinner be redy. *a* **1593** MARLOWE & NASHE *Dido* II. i. 73 *Illio.* Looke where she comes: Æneas, viewe her well. *Æn.* Well may I view her, but she sees not me. **1632** LITHGOW *Trav.* IX. 390 [He] sent a Guide with me..to view the Mountayne more strictly... Hauing viewed and reuiewed this [etc.]. **1673** RAY *Journ. Low C.* 27 A Museum well stored with natural and artificial Rarities, which we viewed. **1697** DRYDEN *Virg. Georg.* III. 36, I, to the Temple will conduct the Crew: The Sacrifice and Sacrificers view. **1718** LADY M. W. MONTAGU *Let. to Abbé Conti* 31 July, The women flocked in to see me, and we were equally entertained with viewing one another. **1748** *Anson's Voy.* III. x. 405 The Chinese contented themselves with viewing it [the conflagration]. **1791** MRS. RADCLIFFE *Rom. Forest* ii, She stood for some time viewing the shadowy scene. **1835** T. MITCHELL *Acharn. of Aristoph.* 428 *note*, The writings of one who had viewed the manners of Greece with no incurious eye. **1892** *Photogr. Ann.* II. 875 They..give no false impression when viewed in the developing tray.

absol. **1818** SHELLEY *Hymn Minerva* 18 Pallas from her immortal shoulders threw The arms divine; wise Jove rejoiced to view. **1827** POLLOK *Course T.* I. vi, Thus viewing, one they saw, on hasty wing, Directing towards heaven his course.

b. To see or behold; to catch sight of.

c **1586** C'TESS PEMBROKE *Psalms* CXIX. G ii, I quake to view how people vile Doe from thy doctryne swerve. **1634** SIR T. HERBERT *Trav.* 51 Where a little from us, wee viewed a Blacke Tent, and going thither found three old Arabians. **1660** F. BROOKE tr. *Le Blanc's Trav.* 331 One plainly views the Isle, and go to the place you find nothing. **1706** ESTCOURT *Fair Example* V. i, *Whims.* Look up and view me then. *Sym.* That's a Jest indeed, when 'tis so dark I can't see my own Hand. **1773** *Life N. Frowde* 27, I..was not a little surprized to view such an extent of Sky and Water. **1810** *Sporting Mag.* XXXV. 152 The fox was viewed several times by the horsemen. **1848** THACKERAY *Van. Fair* lxiv, The alternations of splendour and misery which these people undergo are very queer to view. **1887** *Field* 31 Dec. 981/3 Mr. Godson viewed our hunted fox sneaking away.

†**c.** To admit to an interview. *Obs.*

1676 DRYDEN *Aurengz.* III. i. 1435 I'll view this Captive Queen; to let her see, Pray'rs and Complaints are lost on such as me.

d. *Hunting.* With *away*: To see (a fox) break cover; to give notice of (the fox as doing so) by hallooing.

1853 WHYTE MELVILLE *D. Grand* x, Excitement..not diminished by me 'viewing away' a magnificent old fox. **1856** 'STONEHENGE' *Brit. Rural Sports* 127/2 The first whip is sent on to the point where the fox is most likely to break, in order to view him away, and save time by hallooing.

e. To watch (television); to watch on television. Also *absol.*

1935 *Discovery* Sept. 277/2 The comfort and interest with which the [television] pictures may be viewed in a semi-darkened room. **1936** *Times* 3 Nov. 9/2, I should be unwilling to lay heavy odds against a resident in Hindhead viewing the Coronation procession. **1948** *Something Done* 15 A number of people might now be viewing without having bothered about taking out a licence. **1956** *B.B.C. Handbk.* *1957* 104 Asking them what broadcasts they listened to or viewed 'yesterday'. **1958** *Listener* 25 Dec. 1090/1 They view on average for thirteen hours a week. **1966** C. MACKENZIE *Paper Lives* x. 145, I was anxious for Humphrey Mowart to explain to me the operation of the various knobs..of a television set so that I shall be in control of the machine when we are what they call viewing.

3. a. To survey mentally; to pass under mental review or examination; to consider.

1591 SAVILE *Tacitus, Agricola* 255 When I view and consider the cause of this warre, and our present necessity. **1634** SIR T. HERBERT *Trav.* 33 Hee had well viewed her seuerall forces. **1657** SPARROW *Bk. Com. Prayer* (1661) 50 These..have been viewed and allowed by the..Church for many ages past. **1679** PENN *Addr. Prot.* II. ii. 65 If we will yet rise higher in our enquiry and view the Mischiefs of Earlier Times. *a* **1704** T. BROWN *Satire Antients* Wks. 1730 I. 22 When we view him to the bottom, we find in him all the Gods together. *a* **1768** SECKER *Serm. 1 Thess.* v. *21-2* (1770) I. 16 Viewing Things on every Side..is grievous Labour to Indolence and Impatience. **1845** M. PATTISON *Ess.* (1889) I. 13 Bede viewed the world only from the retirement of his cell. **1875** JOWETT *Plato* (ed. 2) IV. 12 All knowledge may be viewed either abstracted from the mind, or in relation to the mind. **1875** HELPS *Soc. Press.* v. 65 He..has viewed the matter in hand more gravely.

b. Const. *with* (pleasure, etc.).

1746 FRANCIS tr. *Horace, Epist.* I. viii. 14 Whate'er may hurt me, I with Joy pursue; Whate'er may do me good, with Horror view. **1758** S. HAYWARD *Serm.* xvii. 509 The soul.. views his various perfections..with pleasure. **1769** ROBERTSON *Chas. V*, III. ¶38 To view all the constable's actions with a mean and unbecoming jealousy.

c. To regard or consider in a certain light.

1765 *Museum Rust.* IV. 110 If you, gentlemen, view this matter in that important light I do. **1779** *Mirror* No. 28, He seems to have viewed the unhappy people of that country merely as the instruments..to furnish himself and his countrymen with..wealth. **1832** LEWIS *Use & Ab. Pol. Terms* x. 84 A third manner of viewing mixed governments. **1861** PALEY *Aeschylus* (ed. 2), *Agam.* 1548 *note*, So far from regarding the murder of her husband as a crime, she views it simply as a just retaliation. **1875** JOWETT *Plato* (ed. 2) I. 32 Wisdom, viewed in this new light merely as a knowledge of knowledge and ignorance.

4. *intr.* To look or see *into* something. *rare*⁻¹.

1711 SWIFT *Exam.* No. 27 ¶11 Mr. Harley [is] sagacious to view into the remotest consequences of things.

Hence **viewed** (vjuːd), **viewing**, *ppl. adjs.*

1577 GRANGE *Golden Aphrod.* F ij b, For my vewyng eyes haue seene your paynting penne. **1882** *Society* 4 Nov. 5/1 The hounds ran on the line of a viewed fox. **1958** *Spectator* 6 June 730/3 It was a great deal better than half a dozen others which the viewing public has taken to its heart. **1975** *Listener* 18 Sept. 368/1 NHK..will continue..to give Japan's viewing public all of what it wants.

'viewable, *a.* [f. VIEW *v.* + -ABLE.]

1. That may be viewed, inspected, or looked over.

1909 in WEBSTER. **1924** E. POUND *Lett.* (1971) 189 No. The Studio is not viewable till I get back. **1959** *Historic Houses & Castles in Gt. Britain & Northern Ireland* 51 Adm. 2/-, Chd. 1/-. Gardens not viewable. **1976** *New Yorker* 1 Mar. 64/3 He said that three planeloads of bodies had arrived in Oakland—one, on Monday, of 'viewable' bodies and two, on Tuesday, of 'non-viewable' bodies.

2. *spec.* Of a television programme: capable of being viewed with pleasure or interest, worth watching.

1957 *Observer* 22 Dec. 8/6 B.B.C.'s Friday night documentary... This piece, though viewable, was often wildly unconvincing. **1971** *Daily Tel.* 21 Aug. 7 The secret of the endlessly viewable National Film Theatre series on television..seems to lie quite simply in its subjects. **1979** *Now!* 21–27 Sept. 90/2 To make it viewable, they'd have had to make it easier.

Hence **viewa'bility**.

1958 *Observer* 5 Oct. 19/4 You could argue hard about the precise degree of depth and reality in Granada's *The Liberty Man*, but there was no doubt about its viewability. **1966** *Listener* 2 June 813/1 This fascinating teaser, which I would match against any recent television drama for sheer viewability. **1977** *New Yorker* 16 May 114/1 Nicklaus.. carefully molded his holes for exceptional viewability.

'viewably, *adv. rare*⁻¹. [f. VIEW *v.*] Visibly.

1680 C. NESSE *Church Hist.* 357 Satan was seen to fall like lightning from heaven, to wit, viewably, violently, and velociously or swiftly.

viewdata ('vjuːdeɪtə). orig. also **Viewdata**. [f. VIEW *v.* + *data*, pl. of DATUM.] A system enabling a user's television set to show alphanumeric information selected from a computer database, with a telephone line providing two-way communication with the computer.

1975 S. FEDIDA in *Communications Networks* 275 An experimental study of a computer-based information distribution and retrieval interactive medium, called VIEWDATA, has been carried out. **1975** *Times* 24 Sept. 2/8 The telephone and television set could be linked to provide a significant new type of home information service... Known as Viewdata, the proposed new service was demonstrated publicly for the first time yesterday. **1976** *Nat. Electronics Rev.* Jan.–Feb. 11/1 Unlike these specialist orientated services, Viewdata has been developed as an interactive information service for use by the general public. **1979** *Guardian* 24 Sept. 20/6 The Post Office tried to register the name Viewdata for its product but this was refused on the ground that it was too all-embracing a title. Then it chose Prestel—and led a campaign to get viewdata accepted internationally as the generic term for computerised public information systems. **1979** *Austral. Financial Rev.* 21 Dec. 19/3 A meeting of a viewdata technical standards group in the Netherlands..has provided a draft standard which includes both Prestel and the French Teletel system. **1981** [see TELETEXT]. **1983** *Computerworld* 23 May ID-14/1 Telematics regards its entry as timely because of..the rise in such dissemination systems as viewdata and teletext. **1984** *N.Z. Farmer* 23 Feb. 16/1 Two Viewdata pilot trials are to be started in the North Island this year.

viewed, *a. rare*⁻¹. [f. VIEW *sb.*] Inclined or given to views or theories.

a **1635** NAUNTON *Fragm. Reg.* (1641) 33 It is a certaine note of the times, that the Queene in her choyce, never tooke in her favor a meere vew'd man, or a Mechanicke.

viewer ('vjuːə(r)). Also 5 vywer, vyewer, 5–6 vewer, 6 vewar. [f. VIEW *v.* + -ER.]

1. a. A person appointed to examine or inspect something, either on a special occasion or permanently; in later use *esp.* an inspector or examiner of goods supplied by contract; †*spec.* in *Law*, one appointed by a court to inspect a place, property, etc., and report upon it.

Formerly the designation of certain officials in the town of St. Albans: see A. E. Gibbs *Corpor. Rec. St. Albans* (1890) 11.

1415–6 [see VIEW *sb.* 1]. **1447** *Scriptores Tres* (Surtees) App. p. ccccxiii, The said..Alexander [etc.]..sall werkmanlike wirke the said myne..be the sight of certeyn vewers tharto assigned. **1479–81** *Rec. St. Mary at Hill* (1905) 111 Item, payd to the vywers for to ouerse the howse þat dyghton dwellith in. *Ibid.*, Payd for the vywers labour and attendaunce at diuerse tymez. *a* **1548** HALL *Chron.*, *Hen. VIII*, 103 For the capitaine of the horsemen was appointed sir Edward Gyldford, by whom the currers and vewers of the countrey were appointed. **1601** J. KEYMOR *Dutch Fishing* (1664) 7 She [the herring-buss] imployeth..at Land ..Viewers, Packers, Tellers, Dressers, Couchers to make the Herrings lawfull Merchandizes. **1651** G. W. tr. *Cowel's Inst.* 252 The Judg commands the Sheriffe, That at a day assigned, he cause a view to be taken by such Viewers or Surveyers, as may certifie the Court [etc.]. **1700** TYRRELL *Hist. Eng.* II. 819 Our Regarders or Viewers shall go through the Forests to make a View or Regard. **1708** J. CHAMBERLAYNE *St. Gt. Brit.* (1710) 490 Viewer and Examiner of Tobacco [at the Port of London]. **1714** in *Hist. Northfield, Mass.* (1875) 134 One-half of said fence to be accounted as Public Fence, and the whole to be under the viewers for the security of the Great Meadow. **1828** WEBSTER, *Viewer*,..in New England, a town officer whose duty is to inspect something; as, a viewer of fences, who inspects them to determine whether they are sufficient in law. **1834** in Nicolay & Hay *A. Lincoln* I. 119 *note*, To appoint viewers to view and locate a road from Musick's ferry on Salt Creek. **1863** *Cornh. Mag.* VII. 323 The very viewers who first examine the stores, and on the nature of whose report so much depends. **1886** *Pall Mall G.* 6 Mar. 4/2 A large number of viewers, male and female, are kept, whose sole duty it is to see that everything is faultless and in good order.

transf. c **1540** J. HEYWOOD *Witty & Witless* (Percy Soc.) 1 And that experyens may schowe the trewer, Accept we reson to be owr vewer. **1574** HELLOWES tr. *Gueuara's Fam. Ep.* (1577) 225 For if I will bee a Judge of your goodes, for the same you will be a viewer of my life.

b. An overseer, manager, or superintendent of a coal-mine or colliery.

1708 J. C. *Compleat Collier* (1845) 31 And now I must leave you to your Viewer, or Head Under-over Man, who is to take charge of a regular working of the colliery. **1761** *Brit. Mag.* II. 668 Mr. Curry, a viewer, and three others were burnt at Hartley Colliery, near Newcastle upon Tyne, by an explosion of foul air. **1797** CURR *Coal Viewer* 8 The viewers or superintendents of collieries. **1813** *Ann. Reg.*, *Chron.* 49 Among the sufferers..[was] one of the Viewers. **1839** URE *Dict. Arts* 964 Coal viewers or engineers regard the dislocations now described as being subject in one respect to a general law. **1867** W. W. SMYTHE *Coal & Coal-mining* 175 Many of the most experienced colliery viewers..hold to the opinion that they substitute one danger for another. **1883** GRESLEY *Gloss. Coal-M.* 273.

2. a. One who views anything closely or attentively; one who looks at a thing with attention or interest.

1565 COOPER *Thesaurus*, *Speculator*,..a beholder: a viewer. **1572** J. JONES *Bathes of Bath* I. 8 b, The Phisicyon is a viewer and sercher out of Nature. **1579** W. FULKE *Confut. Sanders* 692 You are such a narrowe vewer of such idle pictures. **1611** BIBLE *Isaiah* xlvii. 13 The astrologers (*marg.* viewers of the heauens), the starre-gazers. **1729** G. ADAMS tr. *Sophocl.*, *Oedip.-Colon.* I. iii. II. 87 Be silent, for hither come some ancient Men as Viewers of your Seat. **1857** DICKENS *Dorrit* II. xv, [The bride's outfit] was exhibited to select companies of female viewers. **1892** *Daily News* 25 May 6/8 There will probably be amongst viewers of the collection more than one..who will covet [etc.].

b. One who watches television. Cf. TELEVIEWER. Also *attrib.*

1935 *Times* 16 May 9/3 When television sets are as numerous as broadcast receivers it is possible that there may be a demand for some form of record..with which the viewer would be independent of wireless broadcasts. **1936** *Times* 3 Nov. 9/1 At Alexandra Palace yesterday, when the new television service of the B.B.C. was officially opened, the Postmaster-General and others had to address themselves not only to listeners, but to 'viewers'. Within a radius of some 25 miles, 'viewers' saw and heard a ceremony which the speakers rightly described as historic. *Ibid.*, There was a speech by Mr. R. C. Norman, chairman of the B.B.C. who was the first to use the word 'viewers' in its new meaning. **1946** *Electronic Engin.* XVIII. 276 The poor light at Wimbledon did not entirely account for television's failure to convey to viewers, comfortably seated at home, the breathless thrill [etc.]. **1955** *Britannica Bk. of Year* 489/2 *Viewer-Research* (an investigation into the relative popularity of programmes shown). **1957** *Listener* 5 Dec. 956/2 In football and boxing the viewer has an immense advantage over the spectator on the spot. **1961** A. WILSON *Old Men at Zoo* iii. 125 The viewer response so far is jolly encouraging. **1966** G. N. LEECH *Eng. in Advertising* v. 50 The [television advertising] copy-writer..does not despise the triviality of real-life conversation. In fact by deviating from it he stands to lose credibility and viewer-involvement. **1971** G. CHARLES *Destiny Waltz* i. 11 'You're probably familiar with some of our feature programmes if you watch a lot.' 'Yes, I'm a viewer all right,' said Jimmy. 'I've no false snobbery about TV.' **1977** *Rep. Comm. Future of Broadcasting* i. 3 The first decision we took was to ask individual viewers and listeners for their opinions. **1985** *Broadcast* 11 Jan. 21/3 Failure to cover such events, it is felt, would reflect badly on broadcasters in the minds of viewers.

3. One who sees or looks at anything; a beholder, observer, spectator.

1576 FLEMING *Panopl. Epist.* 143 The Prouince where you are..hath..many viewers of a yong Gentleman right nobly disposed. **1593** Q. ELIZ. *Boeth.* 56 Not thy nature but weaknes of vewars sight makes the seeme fayre. **1599** GREENE *Alphonsus* IV. ii. 16 A canapie was set..all beset with heads of conquered kings,..which..strooke a terror to the viewers harts. *a* **1625** FLETCHER & MASSINGER *Cust. Country* III. ii, Can it be possible this frame should suffer, And built on slight affections, fright the viewer? **1652** BENLOWES *Theoph.* III. xxix, Her eyes amaze the Viewers, and inspire To hearts a warm yet chast desire. **1810** CRABBE *Borough* xvii. 33 'Tis summer now; all objects gay and new; Smiling alike the viewer and the view. **1880** L. WALLACE *Ben-Hur* VII. v, The features..were ruled by a certain expression which, as the viewer chose, might [etc.]. **1885** MEREDITH *Diana* xxvi, Teaching gloom to rouse a songful nest in the bosom of the viewer.

4. An optical device for looking at film transparencies or the like.

1936 [see *microfilm viewer* s.v. MICROFILM *sb.* 2]. **1940** A. L. M. SOWERBY *Wall's Dict. Photogr.* (ed. 15) 19 The principle involved is exactly that of the 'viewers' now sold for looking at prints or small transparencies. **1958** *Woman's Own* 8 Oct. 58/3 The X-ray on the viewer. **1972** *Sci. Amer.* Jan. 65/1 When viewed through a stereoscopic viewer, the resulting image is truly three-dimensional. **1972** M. J. BOSSE *Incident at Naha* ii. 67, I wondered what Virgil would learn from the microfilm. He had taken it to the university library where he could use the viewers.

Hence **'viewership**, the viewers of a television programme collectively; the number of such viewers.

1954 *Sun* (Baltimore) 30 Apr. 16/3 The extent of viewership of the subcommittee hearings was far from excessive. **1957** *Economist* 24 Aug. 637/2 More reliable estimates of 'viewership'. **1964** D. SUSSKIND *Let.* 26 Mar. in G. Marx *Groucho Lett.* (1967) 223 Please keep watching 'Open End'. .. We need viewership very urgently. **1979** *Arizona Daily Star* 1 Apr. (Tucson T.V. Suppl.) 12/3 CBS..restored 'The White Shadow' to its former Monday night time period, where it once again is drawing a big viewership.

view-halloo (vjuːhəˈluː). Also 9 -holloo. β. -hollo(w. γ. -holla. δ. -hallo(a, -holloa, -hilloh, -hullow. [f. VIEW *sb.* + HALLOO, HOLLO(W, HOLLA, HALLO(A, and HILLO(A.

The earliest form recorded is *view-hollow* (see β), and early examples of *view-halloo* have the stress on the penultimate as in the first quot. The various forms are freq. written or printed as two words without hyphen.]

The shout given by a huntsman on seeing a fox break cover. Also *fig.*

α. **1792** S. ROGERS *Pleas. Mem.* II. 298 He scour'd the county in his elbow-chair; And, with view-halloo, rous'd the dreaming hound. **1798** *Sporting Mag.* XI. 3 At the very moment of 'Who! Whoop!' a view halloo was given by a third. **1858** TROLLOPE *Dr. Thorne* I. i. 21 He..had a fine voice for a view halloo. **1859** *Art of Taming Horses*, etc. xii. 202 When a huntsman carries the pack forward..to a view halloo. **1873** BLACK *Pr. Thule* xxv, Lavender in the distance heard a long view-halloo.

β. **1761** G. COLMAN *Jealous Wife* II. iii, What is become of the Lady all this while?.. You told me she was not here, and .. I was just drawing off another Way, if I had not heard the View-Hollow. **1806** COL. HAWKER *Diary* (1893) I. 4 A dragoon..gave a view hollow. **1833** in R. E. Warburton *Hunt Songs* (1883) ii. 8 Once more a view hollo from old Oulton Lowe! **1846** R. BELL *Canning* vii. 198 Lord Melville ..was no sooner condemned, than..Sir Thomas Mostyn is said to have given a view hollo!

γ. **1816** T. L. PEACOCK *Headlong Hall* viii, Their landing was hailed with a view-holla from the delighted Squire. **1858** GEN. P. THOMPSON *Audi Alt.* I. lxv. 250 The dogs that answered to the view-holla that chased them to their end. **1861** *Ibid.* III. clxii. 179 It is therefore 'Hark Forward' again, and the View Holla is not far off.

δ. **1840** J. T. J. HEWLETT *P. Priggins* v, Mr. Scrape gave a loud view hilloh! and galloped after me. **1853** LYTTON *My Novel* I. ii, The Squire..bellowed out with all the force of lungs accustomed to give a View-hallo! **1886** STEVENSON *Dr. Jekyll* 6, I gave a view halloa, took to my heels, collared my gentleman.

viewiness ('vjuːɪnɪs). [f. VIEWY *a.*] The state or quality of being viewy; tendency to speculative or unpractical views.

1852 J. H. NEWMAN *Scope Univ. Educ.* Pref. (1859) p. xxi, That spurious philosophism, which shows itself in what, for want of a word, I may call 'viewiness'. **1860** *Guardian* 23 May 473/1 It exhibits the broad views of the writer, of course, and is written with characteristic tendency to overgeneralisation and viewiness. **1880** *Athenæum* 2 Oct. 429/1 Viewiness is bad, no doubt, but it is still worse to be without views.

viewing ('vjuːɪŋ), *vbl. sb.* [f. VIEW *v.*] The action of beholding or observing; examination or inspection; *spec.* (*a*) (*U.S.*) The action of taking a last look at the body of a dead person before the funeral; a time during which visitors may so view a body; (*b*) the activity of watching television; an instance or period of this.

1548 COOPER *Elyot's Dict.*, *Inspectio*,..a viewynge. **1561** T. NORTON *Calvin's Inst.* I. xv. (1634) 79 The Understanding minde, which with..quiet viewing beholdeth all those things that Reason is wont to discourse upon. **1582** STANYHURST *Æneis* III. (Arb.) 79 Thee mount Leucates..Vp peaks to the viewing. **1593** *Galway Arch.* in *10th Rep. Hist. MSS. Comm.* App. V. 453 A gennerall Assembly houlden..for vewinge of the waste plott of grounde. **1613** in *Scott. Hist. Rev.* Oct. (1910) 12 Denton had the veweing and marshalling of all his evidences and was trusted to have access unto them at his pleasure. **1633** EARL MANCH. *Al Mondo* (1636) 139 Often viewing will make familiar, and free it from distaste. **1672** PENN in *Life* Wks. 1726 I. 45 Such as foolishly think thy Dreams and Impostures worth a viewing. **1785** BURNS *To W. Simpson* Postscr. iii, They thought the Moon..Woor by degrees, till her last roon Gaed past their viewin. **1838** J. P. KENNEDY *Rob of Bowl* xiv, People are quick to censure, especially such as look to the tobacco viewing.

(*a*) **1944** *Casket & Sunnyside* Dec. 31/3 At least during the trying hours of the viewings we had individualized the setting. **1955** HABENSTEIN & LAMERS *Hist. Amer. Funeral Directing* xiii. 571 The viewing is controlled in some parts of the country by the funeral director to the extent that certain visiting hours are established. **1956** *Washington Post* 10 Feb. 33/7 In addition to the viewing the mass also will be open to all who choose to attend. **1963** J. MITFORD *Amer. Way of Death* vi. 95 Demonstrably flimsy and ridiculous as the justifications for universal embalming and 'viewing' may be, they have nonetheless proved very effective and so far have been safe from authoritative contradiction. **1968** H. WAUGH *'30' Manhattan East* (1969) 182 The funeral home in which Monica Glazzard's mortal remains were to be displayed was on Lexington Avenue..and the viewing was..Friday night from 8 P.M.

(*b*) **1959** *20th Cent.* Nov. 335 After a year's viewing the newcomer to television does view rather less than at first. **1960** *Guardian* 22 July 4/6 Much of the output..[is] unsuitable for 'family viewing'. **1974** *Times* 28 Feb. 16/8 The material is largely composed of old favourites, but that is an irony of television..a second, even third, viewing is welcome.

attrib. **1571** DIGGES *Pantom.* I. xxi. G j, If it be lower at the glasse than at the viewing station. **1897** *Pop. Sci. Monthly* Nov. 138 The viewing differ from the taking screens. **1935** *Times* 15 May 13/2 A few weeks ago a similar viewing post was opened in Berlin. **1940** *Chambers's Techn. Dict.* 893/1 *Viewing room*, a small projection theatre in a studio, for viewing rushes and completed films during the process of editing. **1949** *Radio Times* 15 July 43/1 Automatically raised to viewing position by press button control. **1955** 'J. CHRISTOPHER' *Year of Comet* i. 5 He knew her viewing habits... She alternated between three channels. **1956** *B.B.C. Handbk.* 1957 104 It is of obvious interest and importance to the BBC to know how those of the television public who have a choice of programmes, divide their viewing time. **1959** *20th Cent.* Nov. 335 American viewing figures.. are slightly higher than ours. **1961** G. MILLERSON *Telev. Production* iii. 32 Clearly, if we use any camera lens-angle other than the audience's viewing angle (around 12° to 20°), distortion will occur. **1969** J. ELLIOT *Duel* I. ii. 36 Cutting rooms and a tiny viewing theatre. **1972** 'H. CALVIN' *Take Two Popes* iii. 23 Ramon could see himself herded into the viewing area. **1973** *Listener* 23 Aug. 261/3 There's a BBC view that if we have a spare viewing-room ready for researchers, we are bad housekeepers. **1975** *Broadcast* 14 July 6/2 BBC viewing hours have also gone up.. but the profile proportion has decreased. **1975** *Language for Life* (Dept. Educ. & Sci.) ii. 14 Nothing this Committee can say in isolation will change the viewing pattern of those evening hours which children spend in front of a set. **1975** M. KEYNON *Mr Big* xx. 188 At the terminal he watched from the viewing platform but.. was not even certain he was looking at the correct aircraft.

viewless ('vjuːlɪs), *a.* [f. VIEW *sb.* or *v.*]
1. That cannot be perceived by the eye; incapable of being seen; invisible. (Cf. SIGHTLESS *a.* 2.)
Originally and chiefly *poet.*; in the 19th cent. not unusual in prose, but frequently as a direct echo of quot. 1603.
1603 SHAKS. *Meas. for M.* III. i. 124 To be imprison'd in the viewlesse windes. **1634** MILTON *Comus* 92 But I hear the tread Of hatefull steps, I must be viewles now. **1651** DAVENANT *Gondibert* I. ii. 56 That viewless thing call'd Life. **1718** POPE *Odyss.* VI. 25 Light as the viewless air, the warrior maid Glides through the valves. **1762** SIR W. JONES *Arcadia* (1777) 105 This pipe, on which the god of shepherds play'd When love inflam'd him, and the viewless maid, Receive. **1794** MRS. PIOZZI *Synon.* II. 328 Whence is heard the heavy roar of waters dashing through a bottom almost viewless. *c* **1810** WORDSW. *Poems Nat. Indep. & Liberty* II. xxx, Gone are they, viewless as the buried dead. **1821** SCOTT *Pirate* vi, The air of majesty with which.. she addressed the viewless spirit of the tempest. **1849** C. BRONTE *Shirley* xxiii, The speed of the current in her veins was just then as swift as it was viewless. **1873** M. ARNOLD *Lit. & Dogma* (1876) 389 We shall find ourselves more and more, as by irresistible viewless hands, caught and drawn towards the Christian revelation.
absol. **1831** CAMPBELL *View from St. Leonards* 88 The imaginative power That links the viewless with the visible.
2. Devoid of a view or prospect.
1840 R. BREMNER *Excurs. Denmark*, etc. II. 350 Long and viewless, but with lofty, handsome houses on each side.
3. Having no views or opinions.
1885 AGNES CLERKE *Pop. Hist. Astron.* 72 The turbid sense of groping and viewless ignorance. **1892** *Pall Mall G.* 4 May 1/3 The passion-less, conscience-less, viewless creature of the *Chronicle's* fancy portrait.
Hence **'viewlessly** *adv.*, invisibly.
1828 MRS. HEMANS *Spanish Chapel* vi, For something viewlessly around Of solemn influence dwelt. **1842** *Tait's Mag.* IX. 21 They rose higher and viewlessly in distance on either side. **1890** *Lippincott's Mag.* May 668 Viewlessly your whole being has become slowly interorbed with hers.

viewly ('vjuːlɪ), *a.* Now only *dial.* [f. VIEW *sb.* + -LY[1].] Of good or attractive appearance.
c **1536** *Mem. Dk. Richmond* in *Camden Misc.* III. p. lxxiii, To knowe whether the kinges highnes will take a sertyne of my lordes servauntes suche as be veiwly men, and men of good honesty. **1638** BRATHWAIT *Barnabees Jrnl.* III. (1818) 137 A captain's wife most vewlie. **1825** BROCKETT *N.C. Gloss.*, *Viewly*, pleasant to the sight, striking to the eye, handsome. **1828-** in northern dial. glossaries. **1907** M. C. F. MORRIS *Nunburnholme* 233 The more 'viewly' appearance of the country-side.

'view-point. Also viewpoint. [f. VIEW *sb.*] A point of view: **a.** A mental position or attitude from which subjects or questions are considered.
1856 W. L. LINDSAY *Pop. Hist. Brit. Lichens* 13 To paint Nature from a higher and holier view-point. **1887** FOX BOURNE *Eng. Newspapers* I. vi. 156 Wilkes's private life was at no stage blameless from a modern viewpoint. **1892** M. W. STRYKER *Dies Irae* 13 Writing from the Roman Catholic viewpoint.
b. In literal sense.
1858 W. ARNOT *Laws fr. Heaven* Ser. II. xxv. 200 Change the view-point, and the scene will change. **1875** W. MCILWRAITH *Guide Wigtownshire* 75 Mochrum Loch is of striking beauty from this view-point. **1880** MISS BIRD *Japan* I. 127 A zigzag path on the face of the precipice tends to a view-point 200 feet below.

'viewport. [f. VIEW *sb.* + PORT *sb.*[3]]
1. A window in a spacecraft or in the conning tower of an oil rig.
1957 T. STURGEON *Thunder & Roses* 174 You just don't look through viewports very often. **1976** *Offshore Engineer* Apr. 61/1 The forward 'sphere'.. has eight round view-ports: two above, one forward, two each side and below and forward.
2. *Computers.* A defined part of a VDU display, such as may be allocated to a particular category of information.
1973 NEWMAN & SPROULL *Princ. Interactive Computer Graphics* vii. 126 It is possible to clip several different pictures to different viewports and display them simultaneously on the screen. **1982** J. E. SCOTT *Introd. Interactive Computer Graphics* ix. 183 The graphics package provides a full range of two- and three-dimensional viewing transformations, including window selection, viewport assignment, and clipping.

viewy ('vjuːɪ), *a.* [f. VIEW *sb.*]
1. Of persons: Given to adopting speculative views on particular subjects; inclined to be unpractical or visionary.
1848 J. H. NEWMAN *Loss & Gain* I. iii. 20 Sheffield.. was .. fonder of hunting for views, and more in danger of taking up false ones. That is, he was 'viewy', in a bad sense. **1865** *Pall Mall G.* I. 805/2 He there tempts viewy and inexperienced witnesses into a frank confession of their weaknesses. **1885** *Spectator* 3 Oct. 1281/2 Lord Shaftesbury .. was no viewy or screaming philanthropist;.. he was a man of hard sense.
b. Similarly of writings, theories, etc.
1883 BLACK *Shandon Bells* ix, I doubt whether the public care much about viewy books. **1885** PATER *Marius the Epicurean* II. 145 Some fine speech you were pondering, some knotty question or viewy doctrine. **1889** *Spectator* 9 Nov. 642/1 [Her] explanation of the French elections is viewy perhaps, but there is a thought in it which deserves attention.
2. *slang.* Attractive in appearance; showy.
1851 MAYHEW *Lond. Labour* I. 178/2 Then there's a sort of meal, now and then, off the odds and ends of the ham, such as isn't quite viewy enough for the public. **1851-61** *Ibid.* III. 230/2 The slaughterers cared only to have them [*sc.* chests of drawers] viewy and cheap.

vif, southern ME. var. FIVE; obs. Sc. f. WIFE.

vifda, var. VIVDA *Sc.*

vifelie, var. VIVELY *adv. Obs.*

viff (vɪf), *sb.* and *v. colloq.* Also vif and in capitals. [f. initial letters of *vector(ing) in forward flight.*] **A.** *sb.* 'Viffing'; the ability to 'viff'.
1972 *Flight* 28 Dec. 946 The one distinct and inherent advantage possessed by the Hawker Siddeley aeroplane.. is the ability to vector its thrust. The possibilities of VIFF (vectoring in forward flight) have been under examination for some time. **1981** F. K. MASON *Harrier* viii. 118 Initial investigations demonstrated that VIFF considerably enhanced the aircraft's potential in air combat.
B. *v. intr.* Of an aircraft: to change direction abruptly as a result of a change in the direction of thrust of its engine(s). So **'viffing** *vbl. sb.* and *ppl. a.*
1981 B. GUNSTON *Harrier* vi. 78 No matter how inferior the starting position, the viffing Harrier invariably won the engagement. **1982** *Times* 3 May 3/7 With the exception of the Russian Yakovlev Yak 36MP, it is the only high-speed aircraft in the world which can take off without the advantage of an airfield, fly backwards, and 'viff' (vector in forward flight)—that is 'stop' in mid-air and swerve acutely sideways. *Ibid.* 15 June 4/2 There had been few dogfights in the air and thus few opportunities for the Harriers to demonstrate their unique ability to vector-in-flight or 'vif', outmaneuvring the enemy planes. **1982** *New Scientist* 27 May 557/3 US Marine Corps pilots developed a technique known as 'viffing' with their Harriers. **1983** *Times Lit. Suppl.* 14 Oct. 1109/2 The VSTOL Harrier with its swivelable jets and ability to 'viff'.

vifte, -tene, -teþe, southern ME. varr. FIVE, FIFTEEN(TH.

vig, southern dial. var. FIG *sb.* and *v.*[1]

†**vige**, *v. Obs.*[−1] [f. L. *vigēre* to be lively, to flourish.] *trans.* To invigorate.
c **1540** tr. *Pol. Verg. Eng. Hist.* (Camden) I. 209 Rollo betooke himselfe to reste and sleape (as it is a thinge which moste of all vigethe the weried persons).

vi'genary, *a. rare*[−1]. [f. L. *vīgēnī*, var. of *vīcēnī*: see VICENARY *a.*] Of or relating to the number twenty.
1837 WHEWELL *Hist. Induct. Sci.* (1857) I. 93 A method of designating the successive numbers.. by means of names framed according to the decimal, quinary, or vigenary scale.

Vigenere, Vigenère (viʒənɛr). The name of Blaise de *Vigenère* (1523–96), French scholar and student of ciphers, used *absol.* and *attrib.* with reference to a polyalphabetic cipher described by him (*Traité des Chiffres*, 1586).
1916 P. HITT *Man. Solution Mil. Ciphers* vii. 51 The cipher disk method is practically the Vigenere cipher with reversed alphabets. **1943** [see MODULARLY *adv.*]. **1944** H. MCCLOY *Panic* 73 He tapped the cipher message.. 'This is obviously a Vigenère, and all Vigenères can be broken.' **1957** *Encycl. Brit.* V. 929/2 The Confederate army used the Vigenère cipher—which the Federal army cryptanalysts are said to have solved every time a message in it was intercepted. **1961** SHULMAN & WEINTRAUB *Gloss. Cryptogr.*, *Vigenere cipher*, a periodic substitution cipher originally employed with a 26 × 26 tableau and later converted into a slide with a normal clear alphabet over a normal cipher alphabet. **1963** H. S. M. COXETER *W. W. R. Ball's Math. Recreations & Ess.* (rev. ed.) xiv. 400 If the different alphabets are related as in a Vigenère square, certain properties of symmetry can be used to advantage.

vigent ('vaɪdʒənt), *a. rare.* [ad. L. *vigent-*, *vigens*, pres. pple. of *vigēre* to thrive.] Flourishing; vigorous; prosperous.
1590 W. CLEVER *Flower of Physicke* 4 Forthwith after these painefull defatigations, let naturall sweate and quiet sleepe, consolidat and refresh the body, to become more vigent, and the stomacke more sharpe. **1930** J. WALL *Durham Cathedral* iv. 183 Durham College.. after several changes of fortune is now vigent as Trinity College.

viger(ous, obs. ff. VIGOUR, VIGOROUS.

vigesimal (vaɪ-, vɪ'dʒɛsɪməl), *a.* [f. L. *vīgēsimus*, var. of *vīcēsim-us*: see VICESIMAL *a.*] Of or pertaining to twenty; based on the number twenty.
1656 BLOUNT *Glossogr.*, *Vigesimal*, pertaining to the twentieth in number. **1727** BAILEY (vol. II). **1827** F. A. WALTER tr. *Niebuhr's Rem. Hist.* I. 215 The ancient Azteks .. calculated a great year of one hundred and four solar years. This they divided according to the Quinal and Vigesimal scale. **1871** DARWIN *Desc. Man* I. v. 182 When we speak of three score and ten, we are counting by the vigesimal system. **1881** TYLOR *Anthropol.* xiii. (1904) 312 The vigesimal counting (by twenties) which is the regular mode in many languages.

†**vigesi'mation.** *Obs.*[−0] [ad. L. *vīg-*, *vīcēsimātio*: cf. prec. and DECIMATION.] (See quot.)
1727 BAILEY (vol. II), *Vigesimation*, a putting to Death every twentieth Man.

vi'gesimo-'quarto. = TWENTYFOURMO.
1864 WEBSTER. **1888** JACOBI *Printers' Voc.* 152.

vigeur, obs. form of VIGOUR *sb.*

viggerish, var. VIGORISH.

vight, obs. Sc. form of WIGHT.

viȝt(e, ME. variants of FIGHT *sb.* and *v.*

‖**vigia** ('vɪdʒɪə). [Sp. or Pg. *vigia* a look-out, etc.:—L. *vigilia* (see next). Hence also F. *vigie*.] A warning on a sea chart to denote some hidden danger.
1867 SMYTH *Sailor's Word-bk.*, *Vigia*, a hydrographical warning on a chart to denote that the pinnacle of a rock, or a shoal, may exist thereabout. **1875** BEDFORD *Sailor's Pocket Bk.* v. (ed. 2) 147 *Vigias.*—Numerous imaginary dangers are traditionally inserted in all Ocean Charts. **1899** M. ROBERTS in *Brit. Soldiers* (1900) 228 'There's a vigia marked on the chart for hereabouts,' said Captain Spiller.

†**vi'gidity.** *Obs.*[−1] [Irreg. f. L. *vig-ēre* to flourish.] Vegetation, growth.
1628 T. SPENCER *Logick* 46 Wee haue an example of this, in the rationalitie of man, and vigiditie of plants.

vigil ('vɪdʒɪl), *sb.*[1] Forms: 3 uigile, 4–6 vigile, 5–6 vygyle; 4–7 vigille (5 vygylle), vigill (6 vygill), 5 vigell, vygell, wygell, 6 *Sc.* wigel, 5–6 vygyl, 6 vigyl, 6– vigil. [a. AF. and OF. (also mod.F.) *vigile*, = Sp. and It. *vigilia*:—L. *vigilia* watch, watchfulness, wakefulness, f. *vigil* awake, alert. Cf. VIGILY.]
1. *Eccl.* The eve of (i.e. preceding) a festival or holy day, as an occasion of devotional watching or religious observance.
a **1225** *Ancr. R.* 412 Ȝe schulen eten.. eueriche deie twie, bute uridawes and umbridawes and ȝoing dawes, and uigiles. **1393** LANGL. *P. Pl.* C. x. 232 Eche halyday to huyre hollyche þe seruice, Vigiles and fastyngdayes forthere-more to knowe. **1417** *E.E. Wills* (1882) 28 þe date of þis my testament.. on Setrysday in þe vygyle of þe Holy Trynyte. **1432-50** tr. *Higden* (Rolls) VII. 91 Whiche takynge hym in the vigille of Ester, ȝafe choyce to hym [etc.]. **1470-85** MALORY *Arthur* XIII. i. 612 The vygyl of Pentecost whan alle the felauship of the round table were comen vnto Camelot. **1523** LD. BERNERS *Froiss.* I. ccxiii. 108b/1 And yᵉ next mornyng, yᵉ whiche was in the vigill of saynt Symonde and Iude, the Frenche kynge departed out of Calais. **1555** EDEN *Decades* (Arb.) 73 The thyrde day before the calendes of Aprell: which was that yeare the vigile of the Resurrection of owre Lorde. **1599** SHAKS. *Hen. V*, IV. iii. 45 He that shall see this day, and liue old age, Will yeerely on the Vigil feast his neighbours, And say, to morrow is Saint Crispian. **1649** JER. TAYLOR *Gt. Exemp.* III. xiv. 43 The dayes from henceforward to the death of Jesus we must reckon to be like the Vigils or Eves of his Passion. **1704** NELSON *Fest. & Fasts* ix. (1739) 566 If any of these Feasts fall upon a Monday, then the Vigil or Fast-Day shall be kept upon the Saturday. **1808** SCOTT *Marmion* I. xxi, Since, on the vigil of St. Bede, In evil hour, he cross'd the Tweed. **1834** K. H. DIGBY *Mores Cath.* v. viii. 233 By the rules of fraternities of workmen, playing cards on the vigil of Christmas subjected offenders to be banished from the society. **1884** ADDIS & ARNOLD *Cath. Dict.* 843 He even contends that the law of fasting binds on the vigil of the Epiphany.
transf. and *fig.* *a* **1533** LD. BERNERS *Gold. Bk. M. Aurel.* (1546) Ff iv, The calme seson moste sure, is the vigile of the more vnfortune. **1637** T. JACKSON *Wks.* (1844) VI. 188 The very time itself.. being the vigils of that great anniversary, November 5. **1796** BURKE *Regic. Peace* i. (1902) 42 This manifesto.. is dated.. on the vigil of the festive day of cordial unanimity so happily celebrated by all parties in the British Parliament.
b. A devotional watching, *esp.* the watch kept on the eve of a festival or holy day; a nocturnal service or devotional exercise. Chiefly in pl.
14.. *Chaucer's Prol.* 377 (Lansd.), It is ful faire to be cleped *ma dame* And gone to vigiles al to-fore. *c* **1484** *E.E. Misc.* (Warton Cl.) 24 When thy concianse wold the have mad chastessed, With wygellus, fastynge or with allmysdede. **1504** C'TESS RICHMOND tr. *De Imitatione* IV. vii. (1893) 269 Wepe and haue sorowe that thou art yet.. so slepy to holy vygylys. **1552** HULOET s.v., Vigill, or saynctes euen beynge fasted, *peruigilium*. **1591** G. FLETCHER *Russe Commonw.* (Hakl. Soc.) 138 They have also three vigils or wakes in their great Lent.. and the last Friday, their great vigil, as they cal it. **1603** DRAYTON *Odes* ii. 13 Thy ancient Vigils yeerely, I have observed cleerely. **1649** JER. TAYLOR *Gt. Exemp.* III. xvi. 54 There are some things.. voluntary, such as are.. prostration, long prayers, vigils. *a* **1681** WHARTON *Fasts & Fest.* Wks. (1683) 31 At length the Vigils themselves were inhibited; and these Fasts.. instituted in

their stead. **1781** GIBBON *Decl. & F.* xxvii. (1787) III. 34 As the patience of the multitude might have been exhausted by the length and uniformity of nocturnal vigils. **1836** J. H. NEWMAN *Par. Serm.* III. xxi. (ed. 2) 338 These holy days.. were commonly ushered in by a Vigil or religious watching. **1840** MACAULAY *Ess., Ranke's Hist.* ¶22 Thence he wandered back to the farthest West, and astonished..the schools of France by his penances and vigils. **1896** SWETE *Ch. Services* 29 The solemnity of the Easter vigil was deepened by a tradition that the Second Coming of the Lord would surprise the world on some Easter Eve.

transf. **1390** GOWER *Conf.* II. 110 Ek to thee, Diane, I preie,..With al myn herte I wolde serve Be nyhte, and thi vigile observe.

c. In the phr. ***to keep (a) vigil*** or ***vigils***. Also *transf.* (Cf. 4 b.)

1555 W. WATREMAN *Fardle Facions* II. xii. 296 The night afore euery ordenary holidaie or feastefull daie, the whole clergie, and the people, ware bounde to kiepe Vigill in euery churche. **1616** in *Cath. Rec. Soc. Publ.* III. 40 They.. expose the Blessed Sacrament, institute supplications & keep a vigil throughout the whole night in prayer before the same. **1695** PRIOR *Ode to King* i, At Mary's Tomb, (sad, sacred Place!) The Virtues shall their Vigils keep. **1714** POPE *Wife of Bath* 285 Visits to ev'ry Church we daily paid,..The Stations duly, and the Vigils kept. **1717** —— *Eloisa* 21 Shrines! where their vigils pale-ey'd virgins keep. **1803** HEBER *Palestine* 251 Ye faithful few,..Who round the Saviour's cross your sorrows shed, Not for his sake your tearful vigils keep. **1820** W. IRVING *Sketch Bk.* I. 89 The first discoverer of the river and country, kept a kind of vigil there. **1884** ADDIS & ARNOLD *Cath. Dict.* 843 St. Charles forbade the keeping of any vigil except that before Christmas.

d. *pl.* Prayers said or sung at a nocturnal service, *spec.* for the dead.

Sometimes applied to the Office for the Dead: cf. F. *vigiles des morts*, and med.L. *vigiliæ*.

1483 CAXTON *G. de la Tour* A iv, And she sayd vygylles for the dede men. **1671** MILTON *P.R.* I. 182 They in Heav'n their Odes and Vigils tun'd. **1679** *Hist. Jetzer* 5 If they would yet further sing four Vigils for his Soul. **1834** K. H. DIGBY *Mores Cath.* v. iii. 84, I have seen the sublime Cathedral of Amiens on the night of All-hallows, when the vigils of the dead were sung there.

†**2.** A wake. *Obs.*

c **1374** CHAUCER *Troylus* v. 305 Of the fyr and flaumbe funeral..And of the feste and pleyes palestral At my vigile, I pray thee take good hede That al be wel. **1606** HOLLAND *Sueton.* 234 Upon the top of the Apennine Hill, hee celebrated a sacrifice, with a Vigil [*marg.* Or wake] all night long.

†**3. a.** One or other of the four watches into which the Romans divided the night. *Obs.*

c **1380** WYCLIF *Sel. Wks.* II. 44 Aboute þe fourþe vigile of þe nyȝt cam Crist to hem, walking on þe water. **1533** BELLENDEN *Livy* (S.T.S.) II. 65 At þe fourte vigill he rasit his baner. **1536** —— *Cron. Scot.* (1821) I. 259 The Romanis ..at the third vigill maid thaim reddy to battall. **1656** BLOUNT *Glossogr.* s.v., The first Vigil began at six of the clock in the Evening, and continued till nine.

†**b.** A place from which watch was kept. *Obs.*

1533 BELLENDEN *Livy* (S.T.S.) I. 284 The romanis..be wilfull eruptiouns fra þare statiouns and vigilis [*v.r.* wigelis], effrayit þe equis.

†**c.** *Bot.* (See quot.) *Obs.*

1783 *Encycl. Brit.* (ed. 2) X. 8716/1 *Vigils of Plants*,..the precise time of the day in which the flowers of different plants open, expand, and shut. **1802** R. HALL *Elem. Bot.* 196.

4. An occasion or period of keeping awake for some special reason or purpose; a watch kept during the natural time for sleep.

1711 POPE *Temp. Fame* 301 With studies pale, with midnight vigils blind. **1713** ADDISON *Guardian* No. 120 ¶7 There is nothing that wears out a fine Face like the Vigils of the Card-Table. **1781** COWPER *Retirem.* 260 Soft airs, nocturnal vigils, and day dreams..Conspire against thy peace. **1817** BYRON *Manfred* III. iii. 2 He hath pursued long vigils in this tower. **1818** —— *Mazeppa* x, The patient search and vigil long Of him who treasures up a wrong. **1855** MACAULAY *Hist. Eng.* xxiv. V. 139 His delicate frame worn out by the labours and vigils of many months. **1879** BEERBOHM *Patagonia* 23, I confess I should have liked some companion to enliven my weary vigil.

transf. **1817** BRYON *Manfred* I. i. 6 In my heart There is a vigil, and these eyes but close To look within. **1843** J. MARTINEAU *Chr. Life* (1867) 166 The vigils of eternal Providence.

b. In the phr. ***to keep a vigil*** or ***vigils***. (Cf. 1 c.)

c **1695** KEN *Hymn, 'All praise to Thee'* x, O may my Guardian, while I sleep, Close to my bed his vigils keep. **1728** POPE *Dunc.* I. 93 While pensive Poets painful vigils keep, Sleepless themselves, to give their readers sleep. **1748** GRAY *Alliance* 42 There industry and gain their vigils keep. **1845** HIRST *Com. Mammoth*, etc. 98 Lies some quaintly sculptured God, O'er the scene no vigil keeping. **1850** S. DOBELL *Roman* i. Poet. Wks. 1875 I. 4, I steal forth to keep my twilight vigil. **1856** HARRIETT PARR *'Hear my prayer, O heavenly Father'* i, Bid Thy angels..Round my bed their vigil keep.

c. Without article: Watching, watch.

1816 BYRON *Siege of Corinth* xiii, While he alone, where thousands pass'd A night of sleep,..In sickly vigil wander'd on. **1853** KANE *Grinnell Exp.* xxiv. (1856) 195 Many miles to the south, Captain Back passed a memorable term of vigil and exposure. **1856** MERIVALE *Hist. Rom. Emp.* xli. (1871) V. 96 The abiding sense of moral obligation, which should hold sleepless vigil round the desk of the historian. **1892** C. TAYLOR *Hermas & Gospels* 35 Hermas and the twelve virgins keep vigil by the tower.

5. A wakefulness, or period of this, due to inability to sleep. Somewhat *rare*.

1747 BERKELEY *Tar-water in Plague* Wks. 1871 III. 481 In the plague are observed..drowsiness, anxiety, vigils, sinking of spirits. **1802** COLERIDGE *Dejection* xviii, 'Tis midnight, but small thoughts have I of sleep: Full seldom may my friend such vigils keep! **1822** SHELLEY *Fragm. Unfinished Drama* 74 On a wintry bough the widowed bird..Renewed the vigils of a sleepless sorrow.

6. *attrib.* and *Comb.*, as ***vigil-keeping***, ***-rage***, ***service***, ***-wasted*** adj.

1819 SHELLEY *Peter Bell 3rd* VII. xv, To wakeful frenzy's vigil-rages, As opiates, were the same [pages] applied. **1846** KEBLE *Lyra Innoc.* (ed. 3) 240 But who is this that comes with mantle rude And vigil-wasted air? **1896** SWETE *Ch. Services* 29 Every Saturday night was marked by a vigil service. **1897** R. KEARTON *Nature & Camera* 330 The terrible loneliness of his vigil-keeping.

†**'vigil**, *sb.*[2] *Obs.*$^{-1}$ [a. L. *vigil*: see prec.] A watchman, custodian.

1648 HERRICK *Hesper.*, *Panegyric to Sir L. Pemberton* 13 For no black-bearded Vigil from thy doore Beats with a button'd-staffe the poore.

†**'vigil**, *a. Obs.*$^{-1}$ [a. L. *vigil*.] Vigilant.

1576 *Common Conditions* Prol. 3 What openly by Actours deeds in place shall straight appeare Beefore your vigill wakefull eyes.

vigil ('vɪdʒɪl), *v. rare.* [f. VIGIL *sb.*[1]] *intr.* To keep a vigil or vigils.

1898 T. HARDY *Wessex Poems* 110 So I've claim to ask By what right you task My patience by vigiling here? **1915** G. FRANKAU *Tid'apa* vii. 40 Two days and two nights has he vigiled—the doctor dozes and blinks. **1975** J. MONTAGUE *Slav Dance* 57 We vigil by the dying fire, talk stilled for once.

vigilance ('vɪdʒɪləns). Also 7 **-ence**. [a. F. *vigilance* (= Sp. and Pg. *vigilancia*, It. *vigilanza*), or ad. L. *vigilantia*: see next and -ANCE.]

1. a. The quality or character of being vigilant; watchfulness against danger or any action on the part of others; alertness or closeness of observation. ***committee of vigilance*** (U.S.) = ***vigilance committee***.

1570 LEVINS *Manip.* 22 Vigilance, *vigilantia*. **1603** HOLLAND *Plutarch's Mor.* 14 In regard of which enormities, it behooved parents to represse and bridle their wilde and untamed affections with great care and vigilance. **1610** SHAKS. *Temp.* III. iii. 15 For now they are oppress'd with trauaile, they Will not, nor cannot vse such vigilance As when they are fresh. **1656** in *Nicholas Papers* (Camden) III. 261 Yᵉ discouery and preuention of his designes is attributed to yᵉ vigilance of Monke. **1713** STEELE *Guardian* No. 18 ¶3 A Soldier's [profession]..should put him upon this religious Vigilance. **1748** *Anson's Voy.* II. xi. 253 Thus we kept up our hopes, and did not abate of our vigilance. **1781** JEFFERSON *Corr.* Wks. 1859 I. 284 His vigilance has.. supplied the want of force in preventing the enemy from crossing the river. **1837** H. MARTINEAU *Society in Amer.* II. 139 He was brought to trial by the Committee of Vigilance; seven elders of the presbyterian church of Nashville being among his judges. **1841** ELPHINSTONE *Hist. Ind.* I. 45 The King is to provide for his safety by vigilance, and a state of preparation. **1857** J. W. GIHON *Geary & Kansas* 35 A committee of vigilance..was appointed, whose duty it was to observe and report all such persons [i.e. abolitionists]. **1875** HELPS *Soc. Press.* iii. 40 Does not this one fact show what constant vigilance it requires to preserve the public health in a large city.

†**b.** A guard or watch. *Obs.*$^{-1}$

1667 MILTON *P.L.* IV. 580 In at this Gate none pass The vigilance here plac't.

2. The state of being awake; *spec.* in *Path.*, abnormal wakefulness, inability to sleep, insomnia.

1748 HARTLEY *Observ. Man* I. i. §3. 92 That moderate Degree of Contraction..which is observable in all the Muscles..during Vigilance. **1777** PRIESTLEY *Matt. & Spir.* I. iv. 36 That imperfect manner [of thinking] which we call dreaming, and which is nothing more than an approach to a state of vigilance. **1858** MAYNE *Expos. Lex.*, *Pervigilium*,.. disinclination to sleep; watching; vigilance. **1897** *Allbutt's Syst. Med.* III. 25 The probability of its occurrence is still further increased if, in addition to a continuously high temperature, unusual restlessness or vigilance be present.

3. *attrib.*, as **vigilance committee** (*U.S.*), a self-appointed committee for the maintenance of justice and order in an imperfectly organized community; hence, ***vigilance man***, ***work***.

1858 *New York Tribune* 30 Sept. (Bartlett), As gross a violation of justice as vigilance committee or lynching mob was ever guilty of. **1871** MORLEY *Crit. Misc.* I. 357 Whether the resource of the strongest be the thunders of Sinai or the rope of the Vigilance Committee. **1885** W. A. COOTE in *Life J. B. Paton* (1914) xii. 211 The ordinary phases of vigilance work had failed to arouse their enthusiasm. **1892** GUNTER *Miss Dividends* (1893) 84 They..had organized a Vigilance Committee before they built the town of Hamilton. *Ibid.* 85 The best citizens of these regions were Vigilance men.

†**'vigilancy.** *Obs.* Also 6 vigilancye, 6–7 -ancie, 7 vigillancy; 7–8 vigilency. [ad. L. *vigilantia*, f. *vigilant-*, *vigilans*: see next and -ANCY.]

1. = VIGILANCE 1. (Very common *c* 1550–1700.)

1537 CROMWELL in Merriman *Life & Lett.* (1902) II. 97 For your vigilancy..touching the investigacion of th'occurrantes there. **1559** W. CUNNINGHAM *Cosmogr. Glasse* 3 If we..should by our vigilancie, fynde out suche misteries. **1594** T. B. *La Primaud. Fr. Acad.* II. 382 Wee must labour..to quench such inclinations, as much as wee can, through sobrietie, vigilancie, and continuall practise to the contrary. **1624** CAPT. SMITH *Virginia* VI. 237 Our vigilencies..preuented the aduantage they expected. **1650** WELDON *Crt. Jas. I*, 29 Endearing himself to the King by shewing his diligence and vigilancy for his safety. **1686** F. SPENCE tr. *Varilla's Ho. Medicis* 65 While he was.. labouring at this with that indefatigable vigilancy that made him subdue so many places. **1707** *Col. Rec. Pennsylv.* II. 367 The Consideration of the Vigilancy of his Enemies. **1767** ELIZ. CARTER *Lett.* (1808) 152 My material constitution cannot possibly subsist in a state of perpetual vigilancy.

2. = VIGILANCE 2. *rare*$^{-1}$.

1657 TOMLINSON *Renou's Disp.* 620 This Antidote..takes away too much vigilancy, and restrains fury.

vigilant ('vɪdʒɪlənt), *a.* and *sb.* Also 6 **-aunt**, 7 **-ent**. [a. F. *vigilant* (= Sp., Pg., It. *vigilante*), or ad. L. *vigilant-*, *vigilans*, pres. pple. of *vigilāre* to keep awake, f. *vigil* awake.]

A. *adj.* **1.** Wakeful and watchful; keeping steadily on the alert; attentively or closely observant.

c **1480** HENRYSON *Fables, Paddock & Mouse* xxiv, Be vigilant, thairfoir, and ay reddie, For mannis lyfe is brukill, and ay mortall. **1538** TONSTALL *Serm. Palm Sund.* (1823) 97 Saint Paule sayth..Gyue you to prayer, beinge vigilant in it. **1560** DAUS tr. *Sleidane's Comm.* 120 Would to God you were as diligent in avancing his glory, as they are vigilante and circumspect in handlyng of their matters. **1611** BIBLE *1 Pet.* v. 8 Be sober, be vigilant. **1640** QUARLES *Enchirid.* IV. xcix, Be very vigilent over thy Childe in the April of his understanding. **1660** in *Verney Mem.* (1907) I. 561, I am forced to be vigilant least I should be by him insnared. **1709** STEELE *Tatler* No. 65 ¶4 You are so little vigilant, as to let the Dogs run from their Kennels to this Place. **1781** GIBBON *Decl. & F.* xviii. (1787) II. 109 The vigilant citizens improved the opportunity of the night. **1821** BYRON *Mar. Fal.* III. ii, Disperse then to your posts: be firm and vigilant. **1849** MACAULAY *Hist. Eng.* ii. I. 274 A vigilant observer of all those minute circumstances which throw light on the dispositions of men. **1855** PRESCOTT *Philip II*, II. iii. I. 171 He evaded the vigilance of the custom-house officers and the more vigilant spies of the Inquisition.

absol. **1848** WHARTON *Law Lex.* 691/1 Laws come to the assistance of the vigilant, not to the sleepy.

†**b.** Const. *of*. *Obs. rare.*

1654–66 EARL ORRERY *Parthen.* (1676) 166 Blacius is so vigilant of his Daughter, that your Rival can derive no advantage by his freedom. **1739** SWIFT *Let. to Ld. Arran* Wks. 1841 II. 819/2 Your lordship's present agent being extremely vigilant of all your lordship's interests, has lately renewed the claim of the Ormond family to those tithes.

c. *Her.* Of animals: (see quots.).

c **1828** BERRY *Encycl. Her.* I. Gloss., *Vigilant*. This term is applicable to the cat, when borne in a position as if upon the watch for prey. **1863** BOUTELL *Her. Hist. & Pop.* (ed. 2) 57 The Lion..may be Vigilant or Vorant—watching for his prey, or devouring it.

d. ***vigilant men***, members of a vigilance committee (see VIGILANCE 3). *U.S.*

1824 *Missouri Intelligencer* 12 Feb. (Thornton), We hate what are called vigilant men; they are a set of suspicious, mean spirited mortals, that dislike fun.

2. Of attention, etc.: Characterized by vigilance.

1531 ELYOT *Governour* I. xiii. (1880) I. 131 To the augmentation of understandyng..is required to be moche redyng and vigilaunt studie in euery science. **1570–6** LAMBARDE *Peramb. Kent* (1826) 145 He tooke order with one Clere..that he shoulde have a vigilant eie to his arrivall. **1597** HOOKER *Eccl. Pol.* v. xxxiii. §1 That vigilant and erect attention of mind, which in prayer is verie necessarie. **1642** J. TAYLOR (Water P.) *Life Walker the Ironmonger* A ij b, In which businesse there was used such vigilant care, that they were both taken that very day. **1750** JOHNSON *Rambler* No. 12 ¶2 A long week, I lived with my cousin, before the most vigilant inquiry could procure us the least hopes of a place. **1784** COWPER *Task* III. 340 She has lost Much of her vigilant instinctive dread, Not needful here. **1836** W. IRVING *Astoria* III. 64 They kept a vigilant eye..upon every height where a scout might be posted. **1844** H. H. WILSON *Brit. India* I. 400 It was impossible for him to exercise a vigilant personal supervision over the officers of the police.

†**3.** Wakeful; sleepless. *Obs. rare.*

1620 VENNER *Via Recta* vii. 131 It is a drinke very profitable..for students, for them that are too vigilant. **1632** LITHGOW *Trav.* x. 439 Least the vehemency of chirking frogs vexe the wish'd-for Repose,..and cast him in a vigilant perplexity.

B. *sb.* **1.** A guardian or keeper. *rare.*

1822 *Repository* No. 80. 110 Persian women of rank.. hardly move but on horseback, and escorted always by trains of eunuchs and other trusty vigilants.

2. One who is wakeful or watchful.

1822 T. G. WAINEWRIGHT *Ess. & Crit.* (1880) 267 Nina no doubt shrank within her shadowy bower..from the hazy vision of these vigilants.

Hence †**'vigilantness**, vigilance. *Obs. rare.*

a **1598** ROLLOCK *Passion* xi. (1616) 97 Pilate had a great vigilantnesse in his conscience. **1727** BAILEY (vol. II), *Vigilantness*, Watchfulness.

vigilante (vɪdʒɪ'læntɪ, vɪdʒɪ'lɑːnteɪ). [a. Sp. *vigilante* VIGILANT *a.*]

1. orig. *U.S.* A member of a vigilance committee. Also *transf.* and *attrib.*

1856 C. NORDHOFF *Man-of-War Life* xv. 255 The second day after the expiration of their liberty, notice was given the *vigilantes*, ashore, that five dollars reward would be paid for every man of the crew rendered on board. **1865** A. D. RICHARDSON *Beyond Mississippi* (1867) 487 The power [in Montana] is vested in the 'Vigilantes', a secret tribunal of citizens, organized before civil laws were framed. **1883** *Cent. Mag.* XXIX. 194/2 An old-time Virginia City vigilante. **1888** *Pall Mall G.* 4 Sept. 7/2 Forty well-armed vigilantes surrounded the camp and sent in a committee..to demand the surrender of the thieves. **1890** N. P. LANGFORD *Vigilante Days* I. xiv. 181 In the name of Vigilante justice [some men] committed crimes which..were wholly indefensible. **1918** G. FRANKAU *One of Them* xxiv. 185 Shall Muses condescend to gutter-trilling; Or Pegasus, whose tail the strap-hitched star tickles, Feed like a cow-hocked yellow Rosinante In Grecian mangers of a Vigilante? **1939** JOYCE *Finnegans Wake* 78 What vigilantes and ridings then. **1948** *Daily Tel.* 22 May 3/6 The Advertising Association is asking 24 advertising clubs..to form a 'vigilantes' committee to report cases of advertising . . of a doubtful . . nature. 1959 *Times* 22 Oct. 8/2 An appeal by Nottingham 'vigilantes'—a group of businessmen—for an inquiry into the city's Labour-controlled administration has been rejected. 1980 *Sunday Times* 24 Aug. 2/3 But the critical officers say that if normal police cover is continually reduced . . there is a danger . . that could lead to highly undesirable vigilante activity. 1984 S. TOWNSEND *Growing Pains A. Mole* 42, I offered to set up a vigilante group but my father said that anyone who has carried an old mattress 300 yards in the dark is not going to be put off dumping it by a gaggle of spotty schoolboys.

2. A night-watchman.

1899 F. T. BULLEN *Log Sea-waif* 78 We . . found a big jug of water, which Zeke carefully poured upon the head of the muttering vigilante.

Hence **vigi'lantism** (orig. *U.S.*), the principles or activities of vigilantes or vigilance committees.

1937 *Sun* (Baltimore) 27 Sept. 2/7 A public investigation of 'vigilantism' in strike areas was announced today through the American League Against War and Fascism. 1942 W. STEGNER *Mormon Country* 96 Perhaps even those incidents were purely unofficial and spontaneous acts of devout Mormons, the Mormon equivalent of lynch law and vigilantism. 1953 *Economist* 19 Sept. 775/3 In the United States, neither private vigilantism nor the government seems prepared to treat a favourable verdict as final. 1979 *Times* 6 Dec. 3/1 Africa was confronted, he said, with a choice between a system of collective security and a system of international vigilantism. 1985 *Listener* 10 Jan. 9/1 The one genuine, spontaneous popular institution in the West was vigilantism.

vigilantly ('vɪdʒɪləntlɪ), *adv.* [f. VIGILANT *a.* + -LY².] In a vigilant manner; watchfully, alertly.

1531 ELYOT *Gov.* II. xiv. (1880) II. 185 To the intent to persuade the reders to enserche therfore vigilauntly. 1587 in *10th Rep. Hist. MSS. Comm.* App. V. 445 To serve him truly, humbly, diligently, vigilantly and faithfully. 1617 COLLINS *Def. Bp. Ely* II. ix. 361 Then more vigilantly, more accurately, and more circumspectly, he denies it vtterly. 1688 R. HOLME *Armoury* III. 115/1 The Corrector in his first reading of the Printed Coppy ought to be very carefull and vigilantly examine the proofe. 1732 BERKELEY *Alciphr.* VI. §21 How vigilantly you guard against imposture. 1788 GIBBON *Decl. & F.* lxiv. VI. 311 These passes had been vigilantly guarded. 1835 J. B. WILLIAMS *Life Hale* Pref. p. ix, Such a misuse . . is to be vigilantly avoided. 1884 CHURCH *Bacon* ix. 217 There is a group of them . . which show how vigilantly . . he had watched the . . intriguers of Elizabeth's and James's Courts.

† **'vigilate**, *v. Obs. rare.* [f. L. *vigilāt-*, ppl. stem of *vigilāre* to remain awake.] *intr.* To be wakeful or sleepless. Hence † **'vigilating** *ppl. a.*

1758 *Phil. Trans.* L. 517 The flowers are in their expanded or vigilating state from five or six in the morning till about ten. 1774 *Westm. Mag.* II. 184 If the same quantity be given to a person . . who is heated with exercise, instead of producing sleep it will cause him to vigilate.

† **vigi'lation**. *Obs. rare.* Also 7 vigill-. [ad. L. *vigilātio* (rare), noun of action f. *vigilāre*: see prec.] Wakefulness; watching.

1597 A. M. tr. *Guillemeau's Fr. Chirurg.* 28/1 The patient might be debilitated [by] great abstinence, continualle vigilatione. 1623 COCKERAM II, A Watching, *vigilation.* 1655 tr. *Sorel's Com. Hist. Francion* x. 22 He believed that his elaborate Vigillations were not well recompenced.

‖ **vi'gilia**. *Obs.*⁻¹ [L. *vigilia*: see VIGIL *sb.*¹] = VIGIL *sb.*¹ 5.

1728 CHAMBERS *Cycl.* s.v. *Poison*, A good Anodyne, useful in Vigilia's, Rheumatisms, Hysteric Cases, &c.

vigilous ('vɪdʒɪləs), *a. rare*⁻¹. [f. L. *vigil* wakeful, watchful + -OUS.] Of or pertaining to watching.

1853 G. J. CAYLEY *Las Alforjas* II. 1, I believe *vela* means both, acquiring its metaphorical sense from the vigilous uses of a rushlight.

† **vigily**. *Obs.* Also 5 vigilie, vigylye. [ad. L. *vigilia*: see VIGIL *sb.*¹]

1. = VIGIL *sb.*¹ 1.

1377 LANGL. *P. Pl.* B. v. 416 Vigilies and fastyng dayes, Alle þise late I passe. 1388 WYCLIF *John* xix. 42 Therfor there thei putten Jhesu, for the vigilie of Jewis feeste. 1447 BOKENHAM *Seyntys* Introd. (Roxb.) 6 In the vigylye of the natyvyte. *c* 1465 *Eng. Chron.* (Camden) 40 The king sailled forth in to Normandie . . and landid at Kitcaux, in the vigily of Assumpcion of our Lady. 1588 in *Cath. Tract.* (S.T.S.) 210 Obserue the fastes commandit . . in the euinnes or vigilies of certane solemne daies.

2. = VIGIL *sb.*¹ 5.

1665 G. HARVEY *Advice agst. Plague* 3 Continual vigilies, or a perpetual restlesness, with anguishing jactitations, or throwing ones self from one part of the bed to the other. 1694 *Phil. Trans.* XVIII. 25 A confused . . expansion of the Optick Nerve, attended with . . continual Vigilies.

vigintennial (vaɪdʒɪn'tɛnɪəl), *a. rare.* [f. VIGINTI-, after BIENNIAL *a.* and *sb.*, TRIENNIAL, *a.* and *sb.*, etc.] Occurring once in twenty years.

1921 *Glasgow Herald* 29 Jan. 13/3 Their [*sc.* the planets'] vigintennial conjunction is due a few months hence.

viginti- (vaɪ'dʒɪntaɪ). [a. L. *vīgintī* twenty], a first element employed in a few combs. in the sense 'having or consisting of twenty (things)', as **viginti'angular** *a.* [L. *viginti-angulus*], having twenty angles. Also † **vigintiquintuple** *Math.*, the result of multiplying by twenty-five.

1690 LEYBOURN *Curs. Math.* 349 If any Root be multiplied by . . 5 the Product shall be the Root of the . . Vigintiquintuple . . of the Squares of the Multipliers. 1822 T. TAYLOR *Apuleius* 329 He calls . . the other [body] vigintiangular.

† **vigintile**, *a. Astr. Obs.* [ad. med. or mod.L. *vīgintīlis*, f. L. *vīgintī* twenty: see -ILE.] *vigintile aspect*, the aspect of two planets when distant from each other a twentieth of a circle or 18°. Also *absol.*

1674 JEAKE *Arith.* (1696) 10 Aspects... Vigintil [etc.]. 1686 GOAD *Celest. Bodies* I. xi. 39 Sometimes the Quintile makes a shew, and if That have ought in it, the Biquintile will look for some Respect; and if so, then the Vigintile, and Quindecile, and Decile, &c. will also look to be courted. 1819 J. WILSON *Dict. Astrol.* 99 To these [aspects of Ptolemy] Kepler added eleven more, viz. the Vigintile, . . the quindecile, . . the semisextile [etc.].

vigintivirate (vaɪ'dʒɪntɪ,vaɪrət). *Rom. Hist.* [ad. L. *vīgintī-virāt-us*, f. *vīgintī-virī* a board of twenty men.] The office or position of the *vigintiviri*, a body of twenty men charged with certain administrative functions; this body itself.

1598 GRENEWEY *Tacitus, Ann.* III. vi. 72 He [Tiberius] recomended Nero, one of Germanicus children, . . to the Lords of the Senat: and requested that he might be dispensed with for the office of Vigintiuirat. 1656 BLOUNT *Glossogr.*, *Vigintivirate*, the Office of the *Vigintiviri*, or of twenty men in like authority. 1793 MURPHY *Tacitus, Ann.* III. xxix. 196 That the young prince might be excused from serving the office of the vigintivirate. 1904 TYRRELL & PURSER *Corr. Cicero* (ed. 3) I. 319/2 Cicero . . represents Caesar as having been offended at his refusal to become a member of the vigintivirate. 1976 *Classical Q.* XXVI. 312 He was born in about A.D. 55, and . . we might assign the *latus clavus* and a post in the vigintivirate to this reign.

vigner, variant of VINER, vineyard. *Obs.*

‖ **vigneron** (viɲərɔ̃). Also 5 vigneroun, 7 vineron. [F. *vigneron*, f. *vigne* VINE *sb.*] One who cultivates grape-vines; a wine grower.

a. 1456 SIR G. HAY *Bk. Knighthood* Wks. (S.T.S.) II. 60 The vignerounis labouraris had wroucht all the day, fra the morne early till nycht. 1480 CAXTON *Ovid's Met.* XIV. xii, Lyke a vigneron beryng a sarpe or croked knyf to cut vygnes. 1585 JAS. I *Ess. Poesie* (Arb.) 15 Let Readers also surely think and trow, They see the painfull *Vigneron* pull the grapes. 1604 E. G[RIMSTONE] *D'Acosta's Hist. Indies* IV. xxxii. 296 They are become with time and practise more expert vignerons. 1658 EVELYN *Fr. Gard.* (1675) 273 Because it is a plant which is to be governed like the other vines I refer it to my vignerons. *a* 1680 BUTLER *Rem.* (1759) II. 117 [He] prunes The End of's Life, as Vignerons Cut short the Branches of a Vine. 1731 P. MILLER *Gard. Dict.* s.v. *Vitis*, But as to this, you need not consult either the Merchants or the *Vignerons.* 1787 JEFFERSON *Writ.* (1859) II. 294, I . . can procure for you the best crops from the vigneron himself. 1801 CHARLOTTE SMITH *Lett. Solit. Wand.* II. 123 Assisting the vignerons in their now commencing labours of the vintage. 1834 MISS BERRY *Jrnl.* (1865) III. 424 To make some new wine, to give the vignerons when getting in the general crop. 1884 *Blackw. Mag.* Dec. 769/2 The *vignerons* of South Australia . . succeeded in producing a vinous liquid that [etc.].

β. 1683 PENN *Wks.* (1782) IV. 317, I would advise you to send for some thousands of plants out of France, with some able vinerons, and people of the other vocation. 1698 G. THOMAS *Pensilvania* 16 [These lands] have produc'd Choice Wine, being daily cultivated by skilful Vinerons.

vignette (vɪ'njɛt, vɪ'nɛt), *sb.* [a. F. *vignette*: see VINET.]

1. a. An ornamental or decorative design on a blank space in a book or among printed matter, esp. at the beginning or end of a chapter or other division, usually one of small size or occupying a small proportion of the space; *spec.* any embellishment, illustration, or picture uninclosed in a border, or having the edges shading off into the surrounding paper; a head-piece or tail-piece. Cf. VINET 2.

1751 H. WALPOLE *Let. to G. Montagu* 13 June, He is drawing vignettes for his [Gray's] Odes. 1802 DIBDIN *Introd. Classics* 33 *note*, The engravings have a spirit and brilliance equal to the best finished French vignettes. 1820 T. HODGSON *Ess. Stereotype Printing* 132 In the American bank notes, the vignette, words, and writing, usual in such notes, are surrounded by a curiously engraved border. 1866 GEO. ELIOT *F. Holt* iii, An excellent guide-book and descriptive cards, surmounted by vignettes, were printed. 1880 *Print. Trades Jrnl.* xxx. 5 Charming vignettes, and head and tail pieces for bookwork.

b. An ornamental design, drawing, or picture in a manuscript or written document.

1830 B'NESS BUNSEN in Hare *Life* (1879) I. ix. 347 How many vignettes did I make in my idea for my intended letter to my mother! 1860 ADLER *Prov. Poet.* xvi. 352 On the vignettes of the old manuscripts he is represented in the costume of a traveller. 1875 H. JAMES *Transatlantic Sk.* 213 Assisi, in the January twilight, looked like a vignette out of some brown old missal.

2. a. A photographic portrait, showing only the head or the head and shoulders, with the edges of the print shading off into the background.

1862 *Catal. Internat. Exhib., Brit.* II. No. 3182, Untouched and coloured photographic portraits, vignettes, cartes de visite. 1869 *Eng. Mech.* 17 Dec. 328/2 Our present style of vignettes, and the former style of cartes-de-visite, are . . very pretty. 1877 MRS. FORRESTER *Mignon* I. 296 He found a coloured vignette of her that pleased him.

b. A brief verbal description of a person, place, etc.; a short descriptive or evocative episode in a play, etc.

1880 E. SIMCOX *Diary* 28 Mar. in K. A. McKenzie *Edith Simcox & George Eliot* (1961) iii. 61, I have thought . . of writing a little book of 'Vignettes'. 1901 [see THUMB-NAIL 2]. 1934 *Punch* 19 Dec. 698/1 Its writer gets and provides what entertainment she can from them—witness her amusing vignette of the unfortunate *Habibullah.* 1957 *Practical Wireless* XXXIII. 558/1 The play was supposed to evoke the Edwardian era in a series of tiny vignettes interspersed with 'instrumental effects'. 1958 *Times* 12 Aug. 10/3 Miss Maria Lapinska, as his [dancing] partner came nearest to touching the heart in a wartime *vignette* entitled *1940.* 1980 *Jrnl. R. Soc. Arts* Mar. 226/1 Let me quote one vignette.

† **3.** (See quot.) *Obs.*⁻¹

1790 BRUCE *Trav.* I. Introd. p. ix, Vignettes, or little ornamental shrubs, which generally hang from and adorn the projections and edges of the several members [of ruined architecture], are finely expressed.

4. *attrib.* in various senses, as ***vignette head***, ***moulding***, ***view***, etc.

1790 *Loiterer* 2 Jan. 5 Three . . volumes in duodecimo; which, with . . a handsome vignette frontispiece, will cut a respectable figure. 1842 FRANCIS *Dict. Arts*, *Vignette moulding*, a moulding ornamented or enriched with vine leaves, grapes, or tendrils. 1869 TOZER *Highl. Turkey* I. 129 The prettiest effects were produced by the vignette views, seen through the depressions. 1872 RUSKIN *Fors Clav.* xviii. ¶ 12, I can get a pretty little long vignette view of the roof of the Pantheon . . through a chink between the veneering and the freestone. 1892 *Photogr. Ann.* II. 501 Placing eight ¾-lengths, eight vignette heads and so on together.

vignette (vɪ'njɛt, vɪ'nɛt), *v.* [f. prec.]

1. a. *trans.* To make a vignette of; *spec.* in *Photogr.*, to produce (a picture or portrait) in the style of a vignette by softening away or shading off the edges, leaving only the central portion.

1853 DE MORGAN in Graves *Life Hamilton* (1889) III. 478, I shall remember to have an Hippopotamus neatly vignetted for the title-page. 1878 ABNEY *Photogr.* 246 For outdoor portraiture an angle of a wall facing the north with a background formed by a blanket is suitable for producing pictures that can be vignetted. 1885 C. G. W. LOCK *Workshop Receipts* Ser. IV. 401/2 A very good enlargement is made by vignetting the picture with the opal.

transf. and *fig.* 1883 SAINTSBURY in *Academy* 5 May 307/2 Forgetting that its chief function is to finish off and vignette isolated sketches of manner, character, and thought with more precision . . than is possible or suitable in prose. 1895 *Athenæum* 5 Oct. 451/1 How happily is autumn vignetted here and there!

b. To take *in* or introduce as a vignette.

1892 *Photogr. Ann.* II. 54 Keep moving the mask so as to vignette in the clouds.

2. *Optics.* To modify so as to give rise to vignetting of an image.

1945 *Jrnl. Optical Soc. Amer.* XXXV. 499/1 Otherwise, light rays coming from those points of the light source farthest from the optical axis will not spread out over the entire striation field but will be vignetted by the condenser aperture. 1961 *Jrnl. Sci. Instruments* XXXVIII. 93/1 At the edge of the field of ±3½°, the meridial section of the aperture is vignetted to about 80% of its axial value. Over the vignetted aperture, both the meridian plane and secondary plane sections of the emergent wave front lie [etc.]. 1973 *Optical Engin.* XII. 20/2 A 1 mm diameter pinhole in 1·5 mm lead severely vignettes the field off-axis.

Hence **vi'gnetted** *ppl. a.*

1867 *Routledge's Ev. Boy's Ann.* March 169 An album of 'vignetted' heads of all my bird friends. 1886 *Athenæum* 18 Dec. 831/3 *The Wrath of the Fay*, . . with vignetted designs in outline. 1961 [see VIGNETTE *v.* 2].

vi'gnetter. [f. VIGNETTE *sb.* + -ER¹.] A device for producing photographic vignettes, usually consisting of a mask or screen with a central hole or of graduated opacity from the centre outwards.

1875 KNIGHT *Dict. Mech.* 2710/1 *Vignetter*.., the photographer's instrument for giving a vignette appearance to a portrait or print, the edges fading away insensibly into the background. 1889 *Anthony's Photogr. Bull.* II. 23 A head rest, vignetter and other accessories.

vi'gnetting, *vbl. sb.* [f. VIGNETTE *v.*]

1. a. The action or process of producing vignettes, esp. in photography.

1842 E. A. POE in *Graham's Mag.* Apr. 201/1 The peculiarities of the design, of the *vignetting* and of the frame. 1885 *Pall Mall G.* 7 May 11/2 The vignetting is, without doubt, the most difficult form of printing. 1889 *Anthony's Photogr. Bull.* II. 227 Generally, unless vignetting is desired, the background may be made of hangings of some rough material, absorbent of light.

b. *attrib.*, as ***vignetting glass***, ***mask***, ***table***, etc.

1889 *Anthony's Photogr. Bull.* II. 261 For quarter-plates and half-plates, the vignetting mask should be about three-quarters of an inch from the negative. 1892 *Photogr. Ann.* II. p. clxxix, Vignetting Glasses. *Ibid.* 486 Revolving Vignetting Table.

2. *Optics.* A dimming or disappearance of an image at its edge as a result of the blocking of some off-axis rays during their passage through the optical system.

1930 L. B. W. JOLLEY et al. *Theory & Design Illuminating Engin. Equipment* xxix. 449 This vignetting effect may result in a reduction in the illumination towards the edges of the image even in the most carefully designed lenses. 1959 BORN & WOLF *Princ. Optics* iv. 187 Designers sometimes rely on vignetting to obliterate undesirable off-axis aberrations. 1973 *Optical Engin.* XII. 20/2 A 1 mm diameter pinhole in 1·5 mm lead severely vignettes the field off-axis. 1974 *Sci. Amer.* Mar. 112/1 The diameter of the mirrors . . must be at least as large as the ruled area of the gratings to prevent vignetting..and the scattering of stray light into the image. **1978** *SLR Camera* Aug. 64/1 The negative had good contrast and no discernible vignetting.

vignettist (vɪˈnjɛtɪst, vɪˈnɛtɪst). [f. VIGNETTE *sb.* + -IST.] An artist or engraver who produces vignettes.

1884 F. WEDMORE in *Fortn. Rev.* Jan. 67 Voltaire wrote to congratulate Eisen, the vignettist. **1892** *Athenæum* 7 May 597/1 This library is rich in the work of the vignettists.

vignite (ˈviːnjaɪt, ˈvɪgnaɪt). *Min.* [ad. G. *vignit* (see def.): named by Karsten (1828).] A variety of magnetic iron ore found near Vignes in the department of the Moselle, France.

1846 WORCESTER (citing Dana). **1868** WATTS *Dict. Chem.* V. 999; and in recent Dicts.

ˈvignoble. Also 5 vygnoble. [a. F. *vignoble*:—pop.L. *vineobulum, f. L. *vinea* vine-plantation, vineyard.] A vineyard.

1480 CAXTON *Ovid's Met.* XI. ii, He [Bacchus]..lefte this contre and translated hym unto vygnobles of Thymolon. *a* **1700** EVELYN *Diary* 13 July 1683, This gentleman was owner of that excellent vignoble of Pontaq and Obrien. **1928** JOYCE *Let.* 27 May (1966) III. 178, I found that the oldest vignoble in all Provence is the Clos S. Patrice. **1978** *Country Life* 16 Nov. 1618/1 Jurançon was almost wiped out by the phylloxera... The *vignoble*..was in danger of complete disappearance.

vignour, variant of VINER² *Obs.*

‖**vigogne** (vigɔɲ). Also 7 vicogne. [F., ad. Sp. *vicuña* VICUÑA.]

1. = VICUÑA 1.

1660 F. BROOKE tr. *Le Blanc's Trav.* 381 Vicognes are like Deer without hornes. **1774** GOLDSM. *Nat. Hist.* (1862) I. xiv. 234 The Sheep, the Goat, the Lama, the Vigogne, the Gazella.

2. A textile fabric made from the wool of the vicuña, used as a dress material; vicuña-cloth.

1873 *Young Englishwoman* Feb. 75/1 Polonaise..of deep marine blue vigogne, a black silk tunic, trimmed with black Llama lace. **1876** *Echo* 30 Aug. (Stanf.). **1882** CAULFEILD & SAWARD *Dict. Needlew.* 515/1 *Vigogne*, a delicate all wool textile, twilled, and produced in neutral colours. **1887** *Pall Mall G.* 19 Feb. 8/2 The bride's going-away dress was composed of chocolate brown vigogne.

3. ***vigogne yarn***, a mixture of the wool of the vicuña, or other fine wool, and cotton.

1884 W. S. B. MᶜLAREN *Spinning* 47 In making vigogne or angola yarns, which are mixtures of cotton and wool. *Ibid.* 185 For mixing wool and cotton together for Vigogne yarn.

†**vigone.** *Obs.* [ad. F. *vigogne*: see prec.] (See quots.)

1656 BLOUNT *Glossogr.* To Rdr., The Haberdasher is ready to furnish you with a Vigone, Codebec, or Castor, &c. *Ibid.*, *Vigone*, a kind of Demicaster, or Hat, of late so called, from the fine Wool, which for the most part they are made of, borne by a kinde of sheep of Spain of that name. **1706** PHILLIPS (ed. Kersey), *Vigone*,..a sort of Spanish Wooll; or a Hat made of that Wooll. **1714** *Fr. Bk. of Rates* 379 Hats of Vigone.

vigonia (vɪˈgəʊnɪə). Also vigo(g)na, vegonia. [App. a Latinization of F. *vigogne* VIGOGNE.]

1. a. ***vigonia wool***, vicuña-wool.

1763 *Ann. Reg., Chron.* 163, 8 bales Vigonia, and 1 ditto Alpaca wool. **1804** *Gentl. Mag.* Nov. 1069 Vigona wool.

b. ***vigonia cloth***, vicuña-cloth. Also *ellipt.*, = VIGOGNE 2.

1803 T. JEFFERSON *Let.* 23 Apr. in R. G. Thwaites *Orig. Jrnls. Lewis & Clark Exped.* (1904) VII. 217, I saw a robe of what they called the Peruvian sheep, and I took to be of the Lama or Vigogna. **1818** M. EDGEWORTH *Let.* 29 Oct. (1971) 130 There is no black *Vigonia*—the Vigonia wool will not take black dye. Tell me which you prefer the Merino or the Queens cloth. **1852** *Rep. Juries, Exhibition 1851*, 375/1 [Brown & Foster's] waistcoatings of plush vegonia will be found remarkable for novelty and excellence. **1857** J. JAMES *Worsted Manuf.* 438 Vigonia cloth, merino robe cloth,.. shags, vigogna shags.

2. = VICUÑA 1. *rare.*

1834 *Nat. Philos.* III. *Phys. Geog.* 55/2 The paco, which in its domestic state is called bicunia or vigonia. **1839** *Penny Cycl.* XIV. 73 A herd of 36, including the kinds called Llamas, Alpacas, and Vicunas or Vigonias.

†**ˈvigorate,** *v. Obs.* [f. L. *vigorāt-*, ppl. stem of *vigorāre* to animate, invigorate, f. *vigor* VIGOUR *sb.*: see -ATE³.] *trans.* To invigorate or strengthen.

1613 M. RIDLEY *Magn. Bodies* 63 They will be much refreshed, vigorated and animated with the polar and directory vertue. *a* **1652** J. SMITH *Sel. Disc.* vi. 207 All this foreign force that is upon them, serves only to vigorate and impregnate their fancies and imaginations. **1670** MAYNWARING *Physycian's Repos.* 21 This Medicine vigorates and cherisheth that part. **1782** PAINE *Let. Abbé Raynel* (1791) Introd., To call three powers of the mind into action at once, in a manner..that each shall aid and vigorate the other.

Hence †**ˈvigorating** *vbl. sb. Obs.*

1670 H. STUBBE *Plus Ultra* 8 The Mercurial Cylinder riseth and falls in the Magdeburgical Air-Pump, according to the lessening or vigorating of the Spring of the Air.

†**viˈgorious,** *a. Obs. rare.* Also vigeryouse, vygoryous, -ious. [Erron. var. of VIGOROUS *a.*] = VIGOROUS *a.* 1.

1502 *Ord. Crysten Men* (W. de W.) v. vi. OO ij, By hym the whiche..is so vygoryous in all his puyssaunces. **1641** *Vox Borealis* C j b, Man by the contrary being too vigorious, looseth God his Image in his priviledge.

So †**viˈgoriously** *adv. Obs.*

c **1450** LOVELICH *Grail* xii. 413 More vigeryousely neuere reden men Into non place thanne they diden then. *c* **1489** CAXTON *Sonnes of Aymon* x. 263 Reynawd had medled hymself vygoriously among the frensshemen. **1602** WARNER *Alb. Eng.* Epitome 367 [The Danes] whom, albeit the King vigoriously withstood, yet they..forceably helde themselues..in the Land.

vigorish (ˈvɪgərɪʃ). *U.S. slang.* Also viggerish, etc. [prob. f. Yiddish, ad. Russ. *vȳigrȳsh* gain, winnings.] The percentage deducted by the organizers of a game from the winnings of a gambler. Also, the rate of interest upon a usurious loan. Also *transf.* and *fig.*

1912 A. H. LEWIS *Apaches of N. York* 51 Stuss licks up.. a round full fifth of all the East side earns, and to viggresh should be given the black glory thereof. **1943** *N.Y. Times Mag.* 31 Oct. 2/4, I have heard the word 'viggerish' used for the cut the house takes in dice games. **1959** R. CONDON *Manchurian Candidate* xv. 201 Eugénie Rose Cheyney.. loved Marco. That fact gave Marco a large edge, tantamount to wiping out the house percentage in banker's craps. No matter what the action, that is a lot of vigorish to have going for anybody. **1959** L. KATCHER *Big Bankroll* iv. 51 Today,..with pari-mutuel betting..the various states, the race tracks, the local communities, all scoop their percentage off the top of each bet. The state practices a new, and highly profitable, type of 'vigorish'. **1964** 'E. MCBAIN' *Ax* vi. 119 'Was he taking a house vigorish?' 'Nope.' 'What do you mean? He wasn't taking a cut?.. Then why'd he risk having the game in his basement?' **1966** 'E. V. CUNNINGHAM' *Helen* viii. 98 Being a widower who lived alone in the Cattleman's Club, he also bore a reputation for having no use for the vigorish. He was honest when he wanted to be honest, and he was afraid of no one. **1968** *National Observer* (U.S.) 12 Feb., Mr. and Mrs. K were paying interest rates—called 'vigorish' in the loan-shark business—of 25 per cent a week. **1978** *Film Rev. 1978–9* 13/1 The companies are not in any way stealing from the picture-makers. They have to have built-in vigorishes—or else they'd go broke. Who pays for the 21 million dollars lost on *The Sorcerer*? The Studio!

vigorist (ˈvɪgərɪst). *rare.* [f. L. *vigor* VIGOUR *sb.* + -IST.] One who acts with vigour or energy, or who advocates vigorous action.

1807 SYD. SMITH *Lett. Catholics* viii, An addition of polemics..which must highly gratify the vigorists, and give them an ample opportunity of displaying that foolish energy upon which their claims to distinction are founded. **1901** *Daily News* 2 Mar. 6/1 A repulsive study of the younger vigorist who replaces the old Abbé.

vigorite (ˈvɪgəraɪt). [f. as prec. + -ITE¹ 4.] A nitro-glycerine explosive used in blasting.

1879 WEBSTER *Suppl.* **1884** KNIGHT *Dict. Mech.* Suppl. 928/1 Bjorkmann..gives the following recipe for the manufacture of the new explosive, vigorite.

†**ˈvigorize,** *v. Obs.*⁻¹ [f. L. *vigor* VIGOUR *sb.* + -IZE.] *trans.* To invigorate.

1603 J. DAVIES (Heref.) *Microcosmos* Wks. (Grosart) I. 29/1 And, for the Veines and Artires neede each other,.. They meete, and..goe togither, Thereby to vigorize the vitall Band Which the Hart's vertue wholy doth command.

vigorous (ˈvɪgərəs), *a.* Forms: 4, 7 vigrous, 5 vygerous, 5–6 vigerous-, 7–9 *poet.* vigˈrous; 5–6 vygorous (5 vygorowse, 6 -ouse; 5 *Sc.* wygorous-), 4– vigorous (5 vigorows-, *Sc.* wigorus-); 4, 6–7 vigourous. [a. AF. *vigrus, vigerous, vigourouse*, OF. *vigorous, vigourous, vigoros*, etc. (mod.F. *vigoureux*), = Pr. *vigoros*, Sp., Pg., It. *vigoroso*, med.L. *vigorōsus* (Diefenbach): see VIGOUR *sb.* and -OUS.]

1. Of persons or animals: Strong and active in body; endowed with or possessed of physical strength and energy; robust in health or constitution; hardy, lusty, strong.

App. not in common use during the 15th and 16th cent.

13.. *K. Alis.* 6923 (Laud MS.), We habbeþ many pryuee foo, þat..willen fonde to greuen vs, Bot þou þee make vigourous! *c* **1330** *Arth. & Merl.* 9060 (Kölbing), Herui, þat was vigrous & liȝt, On þe scheld him hit a dint hard. *c* **1400** tr. *Secreta Secret., Gov. Lordsh.* 57 Euer ordeyn þi þoughtes in goodnesse; ȝeld þy seluyn glorious & vygerous. *c* **1400** *Promp. Parv.* 510/1 Vygerowse, *vigorosus, ferox.* **1530** PALSGR. 328/1 Vygorouse, *vigoreux, vigoreuse.* **1611** COTGR., *Vigoureux*, vigorous, lustie, liuely, strong. **1658** PHILLIPS, *Vigorous*, full of vigour, *i.* strength, courage, lustinesse. *a* **1687** WALLER *Presage Ruin Turkish Emp.* 20 Bred in the camp, fam'd for his valor young; At sea successful, vigorous, and strong. *a* **1721** PRIOR *Dial. Locke & Montaigne* Wks. 1907 II. 238 We commend a Horse for being Vigorous and Handsom. **1780** HARRIS *Philol. Enq.* Wks. (1841) 450, I have seen great geniuses miserably err..and, like vigorous travellers who lose their way, only wander the wider on account of their own strength. **1797** S. & HT. LEE *Canterb. T.* (1799) I. 350 Vigorous in health and youth, to him the water had long been an element almost as familiar and as natural as air. **1844** EMERSON *Lect. New Eng. Ref.* Wks. (Bohn) I. 268 Men are Conservatives when they are least vigorous, or when they are most luxurious. They are Conservatives after dinner, or before taking their rest; when they are sick, or aged. **1874** GREEN *Short Hist.* vii. §7. 428 At forty-five he was so vigorous that he made his way to Scotland on foot. **1892** MIVART *Ess. & Crit.* I. 161 The life of every healthy and vigorous animal consists mainly in the repetition of actions which have become habitual.

b. So of the body or its parts, health, etc.

1618 J. TAYLOR (Water P.) *Penniless Pilgr.* A iii j b, Mithridate, that vigrous health preserues. **1652** —— *Journ. Wales* (1859) 8 He was more then 80 yeares of age, yet of a very able body, and vigorous constitution. **1683** BURNET tr. *More's Utopia* (1684) 131 Their Bodies are vigorous and lively. **1708** *Lond. Gaz.* No. 4469/4 Thomas Scott,..round fac'd, little vigorous Eyes. **1784** COWPER *Task* IV. 363 The learned finger never need explore Thy vig'rous pulse. **1813** SHELLEY *Q. Mab* IX. 65 How vigorous then the athletic form of age! **1841** A. COMBE *Physiol. Digestion* (ed. 3) 294 In twenty five days the dog..was in the enjoyment of vigorous health and strength. **1870** MACDUFF *Mem. Patmos* xiv, The strong frame, the vigorous pulse, and undimmed eye.

c. Of plants, etc.: Growing strongly and freely. Also of growth or vegetation.

1706 LONDON & WISE *Retir'd Gard.* I. 109 Some Trees are weak, others strong and vigorous. **1748** *Anson's Voy.* I. v. 45 The vigorous vegetation which constantly takes place there. **1783** CRABBE *Village* II. 119 The tall oak, whose vigorous branches form An ample shade. **1800** *Med. Jrnl.* IV. 237 My strongest and most vigorous plants grow in a bed or bank sloping to the south. **1842** LOUDON *Suburban Hort.* 37 In general..the seeds produced by them [are] the largest and most vigorous of growth. **1881** T. MOORE in *Encycl. Brit.* XII. 242/1 Near the base of the stem are two prominent buds, which would produce two vigorous shoots.

d. Marked or characterized by, requiring or involving, physical strength or activity.

1697 WALSH *Life Virgil* ¶8 in Dryden *Virgil*, Which work took up seven of the most vigorous years of his life. **1711** STEELE *Spect.* No. 260 ¶1 The Time of Youth and vigorous Manhood. **1746** FRANCIS tr. *Horace, Epist.* I. xviii. 79 While He the vigorous Chace pursues. **1797** BURKE *Regic. Peace* iii. (1892) 215, I mean..plentiful nourishment to vigorous labour. **1836** J. H. NEWMAN in *Lyra Apost.* (1849) 237 The keenness of youth's vigorous day Thrills in each nerve and limb. **1837** LOCKHART *Scott* I. ii. 77 His professional visits to Roxburghshire and Ettrick Forest were, in his vigorous life, very frequent. **1856** KANE *Arct. Expl.* I. xxxi. 433 It requires the most vigorous efforts..to tear from the oak ribs ..a single day's firewood.

2. Full of, exhibiting, characterized by, vigour or active force; powerful, strong.

a. Of natural agencies or phenomena, substances, etc. Now somewhat *rare.*

(*a*) *a* **1548** HALL *Chron., Hen. VII*, 57 b, He had sayled no great waye before that a vygorous tempest by reason of contrarietie of wyndes sodeynly arose. **1632** LITHGOW *Trav.* VI. 295 [They] tumbled downe..starke dead, being suffocated with the vigorous Sunne. **1660** BOYLE *New Exp. Phys. Mech.* xvi. 105 We apply'd a Load-stone moderately vigorous to the out-side of the Glass. **1770** LANGHORNE *Plutarch* (1879) II. 792/1 The air was dark and heavy, for want of that vigorous heat which clears and rarefies it. **1794** SULIVAN *View Nat.* I. 209 At first they [*sc.* monsoons] are feeble, they afterwards become vigorous. **1909** A. REID *Regality of Kirriemuir* xxiv. 315 Granted a more vigorous flow of water, the Northmuir need fear no local rival.

(*b*) *a* **1661** FULLER *Worthies* (1840) III. 2 The fat of venison is conceived to be..of all flesh the most vigourous nourishment. **1691** RAY *Coll. Words, Making Salt* 209 A Rock of Natural Salt from which issues a vigorous sharp Brine. **1697** DRYDEN *Virg. Georg.* III. 764 The too vig'rous Dose too fiercely wrought; And added Fury to the Strength it brought. **1728** CHAMBERS *Cycl., Elaterium* is a vigorous Purge, and is used in Lethargies. **1759** B. MARTIN *Nat. Hist.* I. 23 Of a more vigorous and high Spirit than the Hereford Cyder. **1802** MAR. EDGEWORTH *Mor. T., Forester, a Printer*, The fresh seeds,..scattered upon the vigorous soil, took root, and flourished. **1826** DISRAELI *Viv. Grey* VI. i, A pint of most vigorous and powerful wine.

b. Of the soul, mind, etc.

1640 WALTON *Life Donne* in *D.'s Serm.* C j, His mind was liberall, and unwearied in the search of knowledge, with which his vigorous soule is now satisfied. **1797** MRS. RADCLIFFE *Italian* xvii, His soul became stern and vigorous in despair. *a* **1800** in Southey *Comm.-Pl. Bk.* (1849) II. 41/1 Whilst they lay apparently senseless,..their minds were more vigorous..than they had ever been before. **1849** MACAULAY *Hist. Eng.* vii. II. 226 His [Bunyan's] vigorous understanding and his stout English heart.

c. Of immaterial things, qualities, etc.

1634 MILTON *Comus* 628 He..Would..shew me simples of a thousand names, Telling their strange and vigorous faculties. **1662** H. HIBBERT *Body Divinity* II. 105 All the ceremonies, services and sacrifices at that time..through Christ..were vigorous, and for his sake acceptable to God. **1675** J. OWEN *Indwelling Sin* x. (1732) 121 Suggestions of the Law of Sin,..advantaged by any suitable or vigorous Temptation. **1709** BERKELEY *Th. Vision* §3 At a near distance I have experienced [an object] to make a vigorous and large appearance. **1758** S. HAYWARD *Serm.* xvii. 518 Grace may not be always in the same lively exercise; sometimes it appears cool and indifferent, at other times vigorous and lively. **1791** MRS. RADCLIFFE *Rom. Forest* ii, Whose hopes are, therefore, vigorous. **1837** LOCKHART *Scott* I. x. 347 In her case sound sense as well as vigorous ability had unfortunately condescended to an absurd disguise. **1849** MACAULAY *Hist. Eng.* iii. I. 330 Where the opportunities of vigorous intellectual exercise were frequent. **1872** MORLEY *Voltaire* (1886) 6 So vigorous and minutely penetrative was the quality of his understanding.

d. Of language, etc.: Energetic, forcible, powerful.

1821 SCOTT *Kenilw.* xxxvi, Doth your new spirit of chivalry supply no more vigorous ejaculation, when a noble struggle is impending? **1837** LOCKHART *Scott* IV. ii. 40 It contains many vigorous pictures, and splendid verses. **1864** TREVELYAN *Compet. Wallah* (1866) 156 A copious fount of vigorous English. **1873** C. M. DAVIES *Unorth. Lond.* (1876) 43 A vigorous hymn was being sung.

3. Of actions, measures, etc.: Characterized by, attended, carried out, or enforced with, vigour or energy.

Freq. connoting some degree of boldness or severity.

1599 HAKLUYT *Voy.* II. 81 They had so sharpe and vigorous answere, that there was not one mantellet that abode whole an houre. **1647** CLARENDON *Hist. Reb.* I. §146 No Man could expect that the vigorous designs and enterprizes undertaken by the Duke, would be pursued with equal resolution and courage. **1679** EVERARD *Prot. Princes*

Europe 12 [He] did also by his most vigorous Representations..cause his Imperial Majesty..to resolve to arm vigorously. **1702** in *10th Rep. Hist. MSS. Comm.* App. I. 81 The allies made a vigorous attaque on the counterscarpe of Keiserswart. **1769** BURKE *Corr.* (1844) I. 182 Various matters have so dissipated me, as to hinder me from a vigorous pursuit of this object. **1777** WATSON *Philip II*, XIII. (1812) II. 171 This measure..shewed how firmly determined the citizens were to make a vigorous defence. **1844** H. H. WILSON *Brit. India* I. 33 The Nizam's troops being either unable or unwilling to suppress the insurrection, it became necessary to adopt more vigorous measures. **1899** *Allbutt's Syst. Med.* VII. 556 If in a severe case [of simple meningitis] vigorous treatment is adopted at an early stage of the disease, recovery is by no means hopeless.

b. Of persons, etc.: Acting, or prepared to act, with vigour.

1638 BAKER tr. *Balzac's Lett.* (vol. II) 115 Having you on my side, and knowing you to be as vigorous a friend of mine, as I am [of you]. **1701** PENN in *Pennsylv. Hist. Soc. Mem.* IX. 44 Be vigorous about my property matters. **1796** BURKE *Let. Noble Lord* Wks. 1842 II. 258 To be commended by an able, vigorous, and well informed statesman. **1856** FROUDE *Hist. Eng.* (1858) II. ix. 323 A vigorous government placed in circumstances of extreme peril.

4. *Comb.*, as ***vigorous-growing***, ***-looking*** adjs.

1842 LOUDON *Suburban Hort.* 37 When it is wished to have plants of a vigorous-growing species. **1890** 'R. BOLDREWOOD' *Col. Reformer* (1891) 269 A frank, stout, gray-haired, but vigorous-looking man.

'vigorously, *adv.* Forms: (see prec.). [f. prec. + -LY[2].] In a vigorous manner; with vigour or energy; by means of vigorous action, measures, etc.; actively and strongly.

1375 BARBOUR *Bruce* III. 142 Then the king..Strak at the tothir wigorusly,..That at the fyrst strak he him slew. *c* **1440** LOVELICH *Merlin* 11378 He..forth wente thorwh the pres vigerously fyhtyng, with-owten les. *c* **1450** *Merlin* x. 155 Thei smyten in a-monge hem so vigorously that oon myght here the crassinge of speres half a myle longe. **1481** CAXTON *Godfrey* xvi. 44 The peple of the Royame of Fraunce,..aftir they herde this prechyng, entreprysed so vygorously the werke of our lord,..as ye shal here. **1518** H. WATSON *Hist. Oliver of Castile* (Roxb.) M j, They that were within the castell defended them vygorously. **1564** *Reg. Privy Council Scot.* I. 306 The Quenis Majestie will sa vigorouslie puneis him..that the West Marchis sall tak exempill thairof. **1647** CLARENDON *Hist. Reb.* I. §69 The Duke [of Buckingham]..being resolv'd to make Peace with Spain, to the end he might more vigorously pursue the War with France. **1685** PETTY *Last Will* p. iv, Having vigorously followed my studies..at Utrecht, Leyden, Amsterdam, and Paris. **1709** STEELE *Tatler* No. 4 ¶6 Except more effectual Measures were taken for acting vigorously against the Enemy. **1782** A. MONRO *Compar. Anat.* (ed. 3) 304 Pronation is performing vigorously. **1813** SIR H. DAVY *Agric. Chem.* (1814) 67 At the time the leaves are most vigorously performing their functions. **1860** TYNDALL *Glac.* I. xxv. 190, I saw Balmat..thrust his hands into the snow, and commence rubbing them vigorously. **1877** LADY BRASSEY *Voy. Sunbeam* ix. (1878) 148 Cheery looking little dogs, barking vigorously.

b. Intensely, prominently.

1638 JUNIUS *Paint. Ancients* 279 One or other inlightned part of the picture becommeth more vigorously bright.

c. *Comb.*, as ***vigorously-correct***, ***disciplined***, ***-phrased*** adjs.

1824 J. FOSTER in *Life & Corr.* (1846) II. 60 There is no one thing more urgently wanted..than a class of vigorously disciplined young scholars. **1867** F. H. LUDLOW *Fleeing to Tarshish* 132 A young man of such vigorously-correct habits. **1897** *Daily News* 31 March 8/3 The Lady Mayoress ..made a short but vigorously-phrased plea.

'vigorousness. [f. as prec. + NESS.] The quality or state of being vigorous; vigorous condition; vigour.

c **1440** *Promp. Parv.* 510/1 Vigorowsnesse, *vigorositas, ferocitas.* **1530** PALSGR. 285/1 Vygorousnesse, *uigeur*. **1648** BEAUMONT *Psyche* IX. 158 Perpetuall sparks of Vigorousnesse they shot From the two founts of their prospective fire. **1655** FULLER *Ch. Hist.* IX. xvi. 67 Her coming to the Crown inspirited the weakest and oldest with vigorousnesse and vivacity for a time. **1709** BERKELEY *Th. Vision* §56 The vigorousness or faintness of the aforesaid visible appearance. **1727** BAILEY (vol. II), *Sprightliness*, Fulness of Spirit, Liveliness, Vigorousness. **1860** PUSEY *Min. Proph.* 619 The fulness of health, that is, the vigorousness of incorruption.

vigour ('vɪgə(r)), *sb.* Forms: 4- vigour, 4-5 vigoure, 4-6 vygour, 6 vygure, vygueur, vigeur, 7 viger; 5 vigore, 6 vygor, 4-8, 9- *U.S.* vigor. [a. AF. *vigur*, *vigour*, OF. *vigor* (*vigheur*, etc.; later and mod.F. *vigueur*, = Pr., Sp., Pg. *vigor*, It. *vigore*), ad. L. *vigōr-*, *vigor* liveliness, activity, force, f. *vigēre* to be lively, to thrive, flourish, etc. In some instances directly ad. L. *vigor*.]

1. Active physical strength as an attribute or quality of living things; active force or power; activity or energy of body or constitution.

a. In persons, animals, or their limbs.

13.. *E.E. Allit. P.* A. 971 Inwyth not a fote, To strech in þe strete þou has no vygour, Bot þou wer clene withouten mote. *c* **1386** CHAUCER *Man of Law's T.* 845, I seye this entente That right as god spirit of vigour sente To hem, and saued hem out of meschance, So sente he myght and vigour to Custance. *c* **1400** *Sowdone Bab.* 2738 There was no man durst hem assayle, For drede of here vigour. **1484** CAXTON *Fables of Æsop* v. xii, Thenne the dogge toke strengthe and vygour ageyne. **1526** *Pilgr. Perf.* (W. de W. 1531) 256 b, Bycause [he] wolde shewe hym selfe more than man, he wolde, after that all his blode was shed, reserue in hym vygour and vertue of lyfe. **1588** SHAKS. *L.L.L.* IV. iii. 308 As motion and long during action tyres The sinnowy vigour of the trauailer. **1608** WILLET *Hexapla Exod.* 259 His naturall strength or vigor was not abated. **1667** MILTON *P.L.* VI. 436 Now we find this our Empyreal forme..Inperishable, and though peirc'd with wound, Soon closing, and by native vigour heal'd. **1680-90** TEMPLE *Ess., Health & Long Life* Wks. 1720 I. 278 That the Natives and Inhabitants of hilly and barren Countries have not only more Health in general, but also more Vigour than those of the Plains. **1717** PRIOR *Alma* II. 128 Thus He who runs or dances, begs The equal Vigor of Two Legs. **1775** HARRIS *Philos. Arrangem.* (1841) 289 Health and sickness, vigour and decay, are all to be found..in each individual of the human race. **1783** CRABBE *Village* II. 132 When Honour lov'd and gave thee every charm, Fire to thy eye and vigour to thy arm. **1832** TENNYSON *Œnone* 158 So that my vigour, wedded to thy blood, Shall strike within thy pulses. **1841** LANE *Arab. Nts.* I. 113 And this is the cause that prevents the return of vigour to my body. **1888** GOODE *Amer. Fishes* 276 The Muskellunge, *Esox nobilior*, is the rival of the Pike in size and vigor.

transf. **1501** in *Dunbar's Poems* (S.T.S.) lxxxviii. 19 London, thou art the flour of Cities all;..Strong Troy in vigour and in strenuytie.

†**b.** Freq. in ME. verse in the adverbial phrase ***with* (..) *vigour***. Also in pl. *Obs.*

13.. *K. Alis.* 1431 (Linc.), Boþe wiþ coyntise, and wiþ vigour, He wan of þat lond þe honour. **13..** *Coer de L.* 1936 And ever men bare them up with levours, And slew them with great vigours. *c* **1380** *Sir Ferumb.* 2322 Now habbeþ þes frensche lordes stoute conquered þe stronge tour, And habbeþ a-slawe & dryuen oute þe Sarsynz with vygour. *c* **1400** *Laud Troy Bk.* 13330 The vanwardis met with gret hidoure, Thei rod to-gedur with gret vigoure.

c. In plants or vegetable growths.

1604 E. G[RIMSTONE] *D'Acosta's Hist. Indies* IV. iii. 209 Nature is contented to give them vigour to bring forth fruites. **1664** EVELYN *Sylva* xxix. 90 It should be in this status, vigour and perfection of Trees, that a Felling should be celebrated. **1706** LONDON & WISE *Retir'd Gard.* I. 181 That the Branches for Wood may not shoot out with so much Vigour. **1731** P. MILLER *Gard. Dict.* s.v. *Vitis*, The Vines..must be annually dress'd, according to the Vigour of the Plant. **1807** J. E. SMITH *Phys. Bot.* 33 The more vigour there is in a tree,..the sooner is its alburnum made perfect wood. **1842** LOUDON *Suburban Hort.* 470 In order..to equalise the production of fruit, and maintain a sufficient degree of vigour in the vines. **1856** STANLEY *Sinai & Pal.* vii. (ed. 3) 286 The tropical temperature, calling out into almost unnatural vigour whatever vegetation receives the life-giving touch of its waters.

d. Const. *of* (life, etc.). Sometimes with implication of next. Also *fig.*

1602 MARSTON *Antonio's Rev.* III. i, Before I touch The banks of rest, my ghost shall visite her. Thou vigor of my youth, iuyce of my loue, Seize on reuenge. **1736** BUTLER *Anal.* I. i. Wks. 1874 I. 29 These surely prove even greater vigour of life than bodily strength does. **1874** GREEN *Short Hist.* v. §1. 212 The vigour of English life showed itself socially in the wide extension of commerce.

2. Mental or moral strength, force, or energy; activity, animation, or liveliness of the mind or the faculties.

1587 W. FOWLER *Wks.* (S.T.S.) I. 22 In his youthe at that tyme when the senses hes most force and vigour. **1617** MORYSON *Itin.* I. 197, I considered, that those kindes of gaining onely required strength of body, whereas this and the like required also vigor of minde. **1677** TEMPLE *Ess., Gout* Wks. 1720 I. 135 The vigour of the Mind decays with that of the Body. **1748** GRAY *Alliance* 11 Those kindly cares, That health and vigour to the soul impart. **1777** ROBERTSON *Hist. Amer.* VI. Wks. 1851 V. 584 A race of men..in their bodily constitution, as well as vigour of spirit, nearly resembling the warlike tribes in North America. **1823** J. GILLIES tr. *Aristotle's Rhet.* II. xiv. 308 The mind retains its utmost vigour to forty-nine. **1840** DICKENS *Barn. Rudge* ii, Leaving their hearts and spirits young and in full vigour. **1856** SIR B. BRODIE *Psychol. Inq.* I. i. 6 He had lost none of his intellectual vigour.

3. Active force or strength as an attribute of things, natural agencies, conditions, or qualities; intensity of effect or operation.

? *a* **1445** GASCOIGN *Life St. Bridget* in *Kal. Leg. England* (Pynson) 125 Nat dredying the vigour of the colde nor the impedyment of the great hete. **1534-5** MORE *Treat. Sacrament* (1576) 61 Although we beleeue it, yet is that beliefe in many of vs very faint & farre fro the point of suche vigour and strength, as would God it had. **1554** W. PRAT *Africa* C viij b, Moystnes shed by nyght and by the vygueur of the sonne. **1590** SHAKS. *Com. Err.* IV. iv. 81 My bones beares witnesse, That since haue felt the vigor of his rage. **1632** LITHGOW *Trav.* VI. 293 The vigour of the day gone, and the cooling night come, we aduanced. **1638** BP. WILKINS *New World* XIV. (1707) 119 The Loadstone does cast forth its own Vigour round about its Body. **1653** W. RAMESEY *Astrologie Restored* 72 Moreover a Planet that is hot and dry, is lessened of his vigour in a term that is cold and moyst. **1789** W. BUCHAN *Dom. Med.* (1790) 243 If at the turn of the disease the fever assumes new vigour,..the patient must be bled. **1798** FERRIAR *Illustr. Sterne* i. 12 They had seen absurdity in its full vigour. **1863** GEO. ELIOT *Romola* xliv, Her enthusiasm was continually stirred to fresh vigour by the influence of Savonarola. **1880** RUSKIN *Arrows of Chace* I. xii, The crystalline vigour of a truth.

b. Of drugs, medicaments, wine, etc.

1542 BOORDE *Dyetary* xx. (1870) 280 Borage..doth set a man in temporaunce. And so doth buglosse, for he is taken of more vygor, & strength, & effycacye. **1599** A. M. tr. *Gabelhouer's Bk. Physicke* 43/1 This salve must be præpared before you annoynct your heade, and it continueth in his vigor two yeares after other. **1602** SHAKS. *Ham.* I. v. 68 And with a sodaine vigour it doth posset And curd..The thin and wholsome blood. **1664** EVELYN *Pomona* xxix, It is a laudable way of trying the vigour of Cider by its promptness to burn.

c. Of words, arguments, etc.

1532 MORE *Confut. Tindale* Wks. 813/2 Some thinges yet shal I shew you..in thys laste booke besyde, that shal haue such vygour and strength therin, that [etc.]. **1581** PETTIE *Guazzo's Civ. Conv.* II. (1586) 57 It is certaine that a sentence hath so much the more or lesse force and vigor, according to the difference of persons from whom it commeth, and of the words by which it is uttered. **1596** *Edward III*, I. i. 44 The fiery vigor of thy words.

d. As an artistic or literary quality.

1774 MITFORD *Ess. Harmony Lang.* 135 Vigor is added by the rapid flow of the short syllables. **1849** RUSKIN *Sev. Lamps* iii. §23. 91 The relative majesty of buildings depends more on the weight and vigour of their masses, than on any other attribute of their design. **1873** E. SPON *Workshop Receipts* Ser. I. 255/1 If..the whole picture is wanting in vigour and contrast, it is caused by over-exposure. **1896** H. HOLIDAY *Stained Glass* i. 24 The painter has..to repeat the two matt processes till he has obtained the necessary vigour and depth in his work.

4. Legal or binding force; validity. ***in vigour***, in force or operation.

1425 *Rolls of Parlt.* IV. 277/1 But þat neverþeles þappointement stand in al thyngs unhirte, and in his vigor and strengthe. **1455** *Ibid.* 329/2 That the saide Lettres Patentes be..in alsuch force, vigore and effect. **1644** MILTON *Judgm. Bucer* xxii. 6 Neither did she know the vigor of the Gospel, wherin all cause of marying is debarr'd from women, while their husbands live. **1654** BRAMHALL *Just Vind.* i. (1661) 4 Secondly,..in abandoning the Court of Rome they make not any new Law, but onely declare and restore the old Law of the Land to its former Vigour. **1678** SIR G. MACKENZIE *Crim. Laws Scot.* I. xxiv. §2 (1699) 120 Then the former Act..was in vigour, and so the Lords could not restrict the annualrents to six [per cent], against an expresse Law. **1849** MACAULAY *Hist. Eng.* vii. II. 201 The Five Mile Act and the Conventicle Act were in full vigour.

5. Strong or energetic action, esp. in administration or government; the power, exercise, or use of this, esp. as possessed by or as an attribute of a ruler or governor.

Freq. implying some degree of severity or rigour.

c **1618** MORYSON *Itin.* IV. III. iii. 279 The Cantons of Sweitzerland,..by inviolable observation of theire leagues, constantly governed theire Commonwealth in the old viger. **1712** *Spect.* No. 467 ¶9 Never failing to exert himself with Vigour and Resolution in the Service of his Prince. **1741** C. MIDDLETON *Cicero* I. iv. 234 The vigor of his Consulship had raised such a zeal and union of all the honest in the defense of the laws. *a* **1781** R. WATSON *Philip III*, II. (1783) 143 When they reflected on the vigour and great abilities he had exerted during this campaign. **1830** D'ISRAELI *Chas. I*, III. v. 64 The Star Chamber..was invested with a vigour beyond the laws. **1844** KINGLAKE *Eothen* xiii, The slaying of the guide was of course easy enough, and would look like an act of what politicians call 'vigour'. **1874** GREEN *Short Hist.* vii. §4. 375 The issue of the Scotch war revealed suddenly to Europe the vigour of Elizabeth.

b. In wider use: Force, heartiness, energy.

1908 [MISS E. FOWLER] *Betw. Trent & Ancholme* 365 It was sung..with much vigour by the congregation.

6. The condition or state of greatest strength or activity, esp. in the life of a man; *spec.* in *Med.*, the height or acme of a disease.

1563 T. GALE *Enchirid.* 35 b (Stanf.), There is another excellent plaster which Galene vseth in the Vigour of an inflammation. **1588** KYD *Househ. Philos.* Wks. (1901) 244 They are in the vigor of their yeeres when the youth of their sonnes begin to flourish. **1656** J. SMITH *Pract. Phys.* 153[As a remedy for thirst, take] the decoction of the Roots of Sorrel, which will look like red Wine; Give drink in the vigour. **1697** BENTLEY *Phal.* (1699) 78 He was then in the Vigour of his years. **1771** *Encycl. Brit.* III. 66/2 When this disease is at its state, or vigor, all the symptoms are worse. **1798** FERRIAR *Illustr. Sterne* ii. 52 A work produced in the vigour of his fancy. **1822** LAMB *Elia* I. *Distant Correspondents*, Your puns and small jests are..extremely circumscribed in their sphere of action... Their vigour is as the instant of their birth. **1841** D'ISRAELI *Amen. Lit.* (1867) 544 Shakespeare, in the vigour of life, withdrew from the theatre and the metropolis. **1855** BREWSTER *Newton* II. xxvii. 399 The flower of his youth, and the vigour of his manhood, were entirely devoted to science.

†**7.** ***by*** or ***in vigour of***, by force of, in virtue of. *Obs. rare.*

1636 BRATHWAIT *Rom. Emp.* 383 Who..refused to performe homage in vigour of a cession made by Albertus the Arch-Duke. **1641** HEYLIN *Hist. Episc.* II. (1657) 366 By vigour of his Episcopall function and the Authority of his Chaire, he had power enough, to be straightway avenged of him for the same.

vigour, southern ME. variant of FIGURE *sb.*

†**'vigour**, *v. Obs.*[−1] In 7 vigor. [f. VIGOUR *sb.*] *trans.* To invigorate; to inspire with vigour.

1636 FELTHAM in *Ann. Dubrensia* D iij b, Nor does Apolloes harpe ere sound more high, Then when 'tis vigor'd from a Ladies eye.

'vigourless, *a.* Also vigorless. [f. VIGOUR *sb.* + -LESS.] Destitute of or lacking vigour.

1758 *Phil. Trans.* L. 756 Indeed one can scarce call it living, merely to breathe, and trail about a vigorless body. **1888** *Outlook* (N.Y.) Apr. 483 The marked contrast between the vigorless conscience of Continental Europe, and the vigorous conscience of the Puritans. **1902** *Westm. Gaz.* 20 Jan. 4/2 In those vigourless days of Whig ascendency.

vigourous(ly, obs. forms of VIGOROUS(LY.

†**vigoursly**, *adv.* In 5 vygour(e)sly. [var. of VIGOROUSLY: cf. *villainsly*, etc.] Vigorously.

c **1400** MAUNDEV. (1839) xiv. 155 Thei [*sc.* Amazons] gon often tyme in sowd..: and thei meyntenen hem self right vygouresly. *c* **1450** LOVELICH *Merlin* 14192 Merveilleng sore what these knyhtes were, That so Vygoursly fowhten there.

vigrous, vig'rous, obs. and poet. ff. VIGOROUS *a.*

‖**viguier** (vigje). [S. Fr. var. of *vicaire*: see VICAR.] **a.** *Hist.* A magistrate in pre-Revolutionary southern France. **b.** Each of two government officials in Andorra (see quot. 1983).

1744 M. W. MONTAGU *Let.* 12 June (1966) II. 331 We have a new Vice Legate... The Magistrate next to him in place is call'd the Viguier, who is chose every year by the Hotel de ville. **1898** H. L. SMITH in H. Spender *Through High Pyrenees* III. iii. 291 The President of the French Republic nominates a viguier with an unlimited tenure of office, and the Bishop of Urgel nominates another, who must be an Andorran, and who holds office for three years. **1922** *Glasgow Herald* 24 July 5 The chief of these is the supreme judicial authority, though the Viguiers—in theory at least—are also the heads of the militia. **1983** *Whitaker's Almanack 1984* 793/1 The sovereignty of Andorra is vested in two 'Co-Princes', the President of the French Republic and the Spanish Bishop of Urgel... They are represented by Permanent Delegates of whom one is the French Prefect of the Pyrenees Orientales Department at Perpignan and the other is the Spanish Vicar-General of the Diocese of Urgel. They are in turn represented in Andorra la Vella by two resident 'Viguiers'.., who have joint responsibility for law and order and overall administration policy, together with judicial powers as members of the Supreme Court.

vigure, southern ME. var. FIGURE *sb.*

vihara (vi'hɑːrə). Also †**vihar**, **vihare**. [Skr.] In Sri Lanka and (*Hist.*) India, a Buddhist temple or monastery.

1681 R. KNOX *Ceylon* III. iii. 74 Their Temples are styled Vehars... Many of the Vehars are endowed and have Farms belonging to them. **1875** [see CHAITYA]. **1901** KIPLING *Kim* i. 8 There were..fragments of statues and slabs crowded with figures that had encrusted the brick walls of the Buddhist *stupas* and *viharas* of the North Country. **1913** L. WOOLF *Village in Jungle* i. 12 Years ago..he had gone on a pilgrimage to the vihare at Medamahanuwara. **1930** J. STILL *Jungle Tide* ix. 220 In the *vihara*, every Buddhist monk is a member of an order, a celibate by profession. **1956** R. PIERIS *Sinhalese Social Organization* I. iv. 24 The *vihāra*..villages ..were exempt from their jurisdiction. **1978** C. HUMPHREYS *Both Sides Circle* v. 56 In 1928 three monks were sent from Ceylon by the Anagarika to found the first Western *vihara* or monastery.

vihte(n, southern ME. var. FIGHT *sb.* and *v.*

‖**vihuela** (vi'wela). [Sp.] An early Spanish stringed musical instrument; *spec.* one of two early types of guitar (more fully ***vihuela de mano***) or viol (more fully ***vihuela de arco***).

1832 *Amer. Railroad Jrnl.* I. 15/1 The music..consisted of several vihuèlas (a small kind of guitar). **1870** C. ENGEL *Descr. Catal. Musical Instruments S. Kensington Museum* 46 The *guitar* is evidently an importation from the East..In Spain it had formerly also the name of *vihuela*..and in England, at the time of Henry VIII. we find it occasionally called 'the Spanish viol'. **1910** *Encycl. Brit.* VII. 514/1 Spanish..vihuela de arco. Guitarra Latina or vihuela de mano. **1961** T. DART in A. Baines *Musical Instruments* 184 One hybrid..made a great contribution to the development of European music. Its origins lie in Spain, home of the flat-backed *vihuela de mano*, the five- or later six-stringed guitar. This instrument was held and played much like the plectrum guitar of the present day; the cross-fertilization consisted in applying to it a playing technique..associated with..the fiddles... The result was the *vihuela de arco* ('bowed' vihuela), which was to become known..as the *viol*. **1968** *New Oxf. Hist. Music* IV. xi. 560 Ortiz deals with the viol (*vihuela*), for which he describes three kinds of playing. **1975** *Gramophone* Dec. 1002/1 An attractive collection of Spanish Renaissance *vihuela* music..excellently played (on the lute) by Konrad Ragnossnig, would prove enjoyable.

Hence **vihue'lista**, a player of the vihuela.

1925 J. B. TREND (*title*) Luis Milan and the vihuelistas. **1978** *Early Music* Oct. 623/1 It is the largest book of the vihuelistas and is..the most complete and representative collection drawn from the rich and varied musical repertoire of mid-16th-century Spain.

vijs, obs. f. VICE *sb.*; obs. Sc. f. WISE *sb.*

viked, ME. var. WICKED *a.*

vikel(i, southern ME. varr. FICKLE *a.* and *v.*[1]

viker(y, etc., obs. ff. VICAR(Y, etc.

Viking ('vaɪkɪŋ). *Hist.* Also **vikingr**, **-er**, **-ir**; **wiking**, **wicking**. [ad. ON. and Icel. *víking-r* (whence also Norw., Sw., Da. *viking*, G. *wiking*), = OE. *wícing*, OFris. *witsing*, *wising*. Cf. also ON. and Icel. *víking* fem., the practice of marauding or piracy.

The ON. word is commonly regarded as f. *vík* creek, inlet, bay, + *-ingr* -ING[3], a viking thus being one who came out from, or frequented, inlets of the sea. The name, however, was evidently current in Anglo-Frisian from a date so early as to make its Scandinavian origin doubtful; *wícingsceaða* is found in Anglo-Saxon glossaries dating from the 8th century, and *sǽ-wícingas* occurs in the early poem of Exodus, whereas evidence for *víkingr* in ON. and Icel. is doubtful before the latter part of the 10th cent. It is therefore possible that the word really originated in the Anglo-Frisian area, and was only at a later date accepted by the Scandinavian peoples; in that case it was probably formed from OE. *wíc* camp, the formation of temporary encampments being a prominent feature of viking raids.]

1. One of those Scandinavian adventurers who practised piracy at sea, and committed depredations on land, in northern and western Europe from the eighth to the eleventh century; sometimes in general use, a warlike pirate or sea-rover.

α. **1807** G. CHALMERS *Caledonia* I. III. iii. 341 At the age of fourteen, Torfin commenced his career, as a vikingr. *c* **1827** W. MOTHERWELL *Poet. Wks.* (1847) 13 It is a Vikingir Who kisses thy hand. **1838** CRICHTON *Scandinavia* I. 176 Hákon commanded the intrepid Vikingr to be put to death. **1864** [H. W. WHEELWRIGHT] *Spring & Summer in Lapland* i. 8 When the 'Viking' or pirate vessel..bore the 'Vikinger' or dreaded sea pirate to the opposite shores of Britain.

β. **1840** LONGF. *Skeleton in Armour* iii, I was a Viking old! **1848** LYTTON *Harold* VI. v, A fleet of vikings from Norway ravaged the western coasts. **1877** BLACK *Green Past.* xxviii, I am already convinced that my ancestors were vikings.

γ. **1867** FREEMAN *Norm. Conq.* (1877) I. iv. 165 He [Rolf] is described as having been engaged in the calling of a wiking. **1868** *Ibid.* II. vii. 96 The wikings harried far and wide. **1883** VIGFUSSON & POWELL *Corpus Poet. Bor.* II. 139 The warden of the land had the heads of many Wickings (pirates) cut short with keen weapons. **1904** E. RICKERT *Reaper* 53 Beyond that, we were Wickings, back to the time of Odin.

2. *attrib.*, as ***viking age***, ***expedition***, ***invader***, ***line***, ***ship***, ***vessel***.

1847 I. A. BLACKWELL *Mallet's Northern Antiq.* 86 Halfdan enriched himself by successful Viking expeditions. **1864** [see 1 a]. **1866** G. STEPHENS *Runic Mon.* I. 226 The lower compartment is a noble Wiking-ship. **1867** FREEMAN *Norm. Conq.* (1877) I. App. 665 He may have joined the Danes or have done anything else in the wiking line. **1881** *Daily News* 3 Sept. 2/2 This Viking ship, with its sepulchre chamber, in which the Viking had been buried. **1883** VIGFUSSON & POWELL *Corpus Poet. Bor.* I. 259 The Northmen confederates of the Wicking invaders. **1889** DU CHAILLU *Viking Age* I. iii. 26 We must come to the conclusion that the 'Viking Age' lasted from about the second century of our era to about the middle of the twelfth.

Hence **'Vikingism**, **'Vikingship**, the practices or spirit of vikings.

1880 STUBBS *Lect. Stud. Hist.* (1886) 222 The conquest of Palestine was to Robert of Normandy..a sanctified experiment of *vikingism. **1899** SOMERVILLE & ROSS *Irish R.M.* 239, I prefer their total lack of interest in seafaring matters to the blatant Vikingism of the average male. **1883** G. STEPHENS *Bugge's Stud. Northern Mythol. Exam.* 15 *Wikingship began to be felt..as an unbearable curse.

vikit, **vikkid**, **-it**, obs. Sc. ff. WICKED *a.*

vil, obs. f. VILE *a.*, obs. Sc. f. WILL *sb.* and *v.*

‖**vila** ('vila). Pl. **vilas**, **vile**. [Serbo-Croat and Slovenian.] In Slavonic mythology: a fairy, a nymph, a spirit. Cf. WILI, WILLI.

1827 J. BOWRING *Servian Pop. Poetry* p. xxxvii, An omnipresent spirit—airy and fanciful—making its dwelling in solitudes..a being called the *Vila*. **1887** *Folk-Lore Jrnl.* V. 347 Whosoever has compared the northern elves with the Slavonic vilas..will see that they are of modern origin. **1911** *Encycl. Brit.* XXIV. 689/2 The [Serbian] peasants believe in charms and omens, in..ghosts, the evil eye and *vile* or white-robed spirits of the earth, air, stream and mountain, with hoofs like a goat and henna-dyed nails and hair. **1922** D. H. LOW *Kraljević's Ballads* iv. 21 In Serbian song Vilas are represented as jealous and capricious beings but on the whole not unfriendly to mankind. **1974** *Encycl. Brit. Macropædia* XVI. 876/1 Particularly feared are maidens who died before marriage and are believed to be addicted to the kidnapping of bridegrooms and babies... They are called..*vile*..in Serbo-Croatia and Bulgaria.

vilain(e, etc., obs. ff. VILLAIN, etc.

vilains(ly, var. VILLAINS(LY *Obs.*

vilanie, **-ye**, obs. f. VILLAINY.

vilans, var. VILLAINS *a. Obs.*

‖**vilayet** (vɪ'lɑːjɛt). Also **wilayet**. [Turkish, ad. Ar. *welāyeh*, *-yet* district, dominion.] A province of Turkey (formerly of the Turkish empire) ruled by a vali, or governor-general.

1869 *Times* 15 Oct., Those Ottoman subjects who have passed an examination..will be admitted for three years as boarders to the Lyceum in each chief town of a vilayet. **1880** *Fortn. Rev.* Feb. 174 An honest man is sent to introduce reforms into some vilayet. **1884** *Pall Mall G.* 5 April 3/1 Everything seems to be going as well in the late Vilayet of the Danube as it is going ill in the Pashalik of the Nile.

vilayn, obs. form of VILLAIN.

†**vild**, *sb. Obs.*^−1 (Cf. next, but perh. an error.)

1605 *London Prodigal* v. i. 265 My daughter is missing; hath been looked for; cannot be found. A vild upon thee!

vild (vaɪld), *a. Obs.* exc. *arch.* or *dial.* Also 6–7 **vylde**, 6–7 (9) **vilde**; 6 *Sc.* **vyild**, 6–7 (9) **vyld**, 7 **vil'd**. [Variant of VILE *a.*, with excrescent *-d*. The earliest instances are Scottish (cf. *tylde* for TILE *sb.*[1]), but the form is extremely common from *c* 1580 to 1650.] = VILE *a.*, in various senses: **a.** Of actions, things, etc.

1560 ROLLAND *Seven Sages* 48 The morne he sall go to the deid maist vylde, Howbeit he be my onlie gottin Chylde. **1568** T. HOWELL *Arb. Amitie* (1879) 35 Shall I be prest in simpler sort and vylder case then hee. **1597** J. PAYNE *Royal Exch.* 24 Since whose vilde death manie a good Christian have bene no less vmbraded and reproched. **1598–9** E. FORDE *Parismus* I. (1661) 49 With great patience he endured the imprisonment, continuing in that most vilde place. *a* **1613** OVERBURY *A Wife*, etc. (1638) 38 Her breath should be as horrible and vild, As ev'rie word thou speake is sweet and mild. **1650** BULWER *Anthropomet.* 158 A vild thing, thus to force and wrong Nature. **1713** CROXALL *Orig. Canto Spenser* xiv. (1714) 14 With Witch-craft vild he then enwrapt her round. **1748** THOMSON *Cast. Indol.* II. xxvi, O hide thy head, abominable war!.. From Heaven this life ysprung, from hell thy glories vild! **1767** MICKLE *Concub.* I. xx, Loud and angrie then Gan she of shame and haviour vild complain. **1805** SCOTT *Last Minstrel* III. xiii, Could he have had his pleasure vilde, He had crippled the joints of the noble child. **1853** *N. & Q.* 1st Ser. VII. 234/1 (N. Cy. sayings), Looks as vild (worthless) as a pair of Yorkshire sleeves in a goldsmith's shop. **1866** EDMONDSTON *Gloss. Shetland*, *Vyld*, dirty, filthy, vile.

b. Of persons.

1567 *Gude & Godlie B.* (S.T.S.) 122 Quhen I was impotent, Fragile, vaine, vylde, and pure. **1581** RICH *Farew.* (1846) 116 The desolate damsell..ceased not to rebuke the vilde caitive. **1588** BABINGTON *Prof. Exp. Lord's Pr.* (1596) 235 The good Prophet had a bad seruant, a vilde Gehezi. **1608** TARLTON *Cobler Canterb.* (1844) 118 Vilde strumpet as thou art. **1628** GAULE *Pract. The.* (1629) 11 Lo how the vildest Earth-Worme now turnes against thee! **1656** HEYLIN *Surv. France* 324 That vilde Butcher [Herod] caus'd to cut in sunder Every Male childe of two years old and under. **1767** MICKLE *Concub.* I. xxii, She..clept her Lemman and vild Slutt aloud. **1865** GIDLEY *Aletes* 145 Their influence mild Withdraw from presence of those monsters base and vild, Intolerance and Injustice.

absol. **1597** SHAKS. *2 Hen. IV*, III. i. 15 O thou dull God, why lyest thou with the vilde, In loathsome Beds? **1607** —— *Timon* I. i. 15 When we for recompence haue prais'd the vild.

vild, obs. Sc. form of WILD *a.*

vilderbeeste, var. WILDEBEESTE (gnu).

†**vilderoy**. *Obs.*^−1 The name of some fabric.

1769 *Lloyd's Even. Post* 30 Oct.–1 Nov. 420/3 Damasks, Vilderoys, Paolis, corded Tabbies.

vildever, dial. variant of FIELDFARE.

vildirnes, obs. Sc. form of WILDERNESS.

'vildly, *adv.* Now *rare* or *Obs.* [f. VILD *a.* Common *c* 1590–1650.] = VILELY *adv.*

1575 CHURCHYARD *Chippes* (1817) 127 So vildly agaynst my honour and trueth. **1588** BABINGTON *Prof. Exp. Lord's Pr.* (1596) 234 To haue true good will..so vnkindely, yea so vildly requited. **1602** MIDDLETON *Phœnix* II. ii. 328 Captain? off with that noble title! thou becomest it vildly. **1655** *Theophania* 162 If Parmenio had sense of honor, he could not thus vildly blemish the vertue of Artemia. **1681** HICKERINGILL *Black Non-Conf.* ii. Wks. 1716 II. 20 They are vildly loth to lose their domineering, insulting Kingdom of Darkness. **1748** MENDEZ *Sqr. Dames* II. xxix. in Dodsley *Coll. Poems* (1755) IV. 150 Have I not cause to weep from rising morn..To see my dearling's fame thus vildly torn?

'vildness. *Obs.* exc. *arch.* or *dial.* [f. as prec.] = VILENESS.

1597 J. PAYNE *Royal Exch.* 35 What vyldnes and wyckednes is not fownd in many of you? **1600** DYMMOK *Ireland* (1843) 46 Enraged with a consideration of the vildenes of his men,..[he] brake from them in a fury. **1607** MARKHAM *Caval.* I. (1617) 22 His inward parts may retaine a secret vildnes of disposition, which may be insufferable. **1654** E. CALAMY *Serm. 19 Oct.* (1655) 2 The body of vildnesse shall then be a body of glory. **1866** EDMONDSTON *Gloss. Shetland* 140 *Vyldness*, dirt, filth.

vildyveer, dial. variant of FIELDFARE.

vile (vaɪl), *a.*, *adv.*, and *sb.* Forms: 3–4 vil (3 uil, 4 wil), 3–5 vyl (5 wyl), 5–6 vyll; 3–7 vyle (4 uyle, 5–6 *Sc.* wyle), 3– vile (3–4 file, 4–5 wile, 5 *Sc.* wille). [a. AF. and OF. (also mod.F.) *vil* masc., *vile* fem. (= Pr., Sp., Pg. *vil*, It. *vile*):—L. *vilem*, *vīlis* of low value or price, cheap, common, mean, base.]

A. *adj.* **1.** Of actions, conduct, character, etc.: Despicable on moral grounds; deserving to be regarded with abhorrence or disgust; characterized by baseness or depravity.

c **1290** *S. Eng. Leg.* I. 192/4 Þare ne scholde vil dede ne word neuere fram hire wende. **1297** R. GLOUC. (Rolls) 4504 Modred..huld hire in spousbruche, in vyl flesses dede. *Ibid.* 10003 He suor he wolde awreke be of þis vil trespas. **1303** R. BRUNNE *Handl. Synne* 1586 Here wurdys were al vyle & waste. **1377** LANGL. *P. Pl.* B. XIV. 79 So vengeaunce fel vpon hem, for her vyle synnes. **1393** *Ibid.* C. XXI. 97 Thenne gan faith foully þe false Iewes to despisen, And calde hem 'caytifs a-corsed', for þis was a vil vilanye. *c* **1450** HOLLAND *Howlat* 226 The Sparrowe Wenus he wesit for his vyle deidis, Lyand in lichory, laith, vnloveable. **1477** CAXTON *Dictes* 67 Summe thinges that ye loue & preyse ar euil and vyle. **1560** DAUS tr. *Sleidane's Comm.* 65 These wycked theues..cloke al this abomination..with the couer of Christianitie, which is the vylest and moste vnworthiest thing, that can be imagined. *a* **1586** SIDNEY *Psalms* V. iv, Let their vile thoughts the thinckers ruine be. **1625** BACON *Ess.*, *Envy* (Arb.) 517 It is also the vilest Affection, and the most depraued. **1651** HOBBES *Leviath.* II. xviii. 89 Not onely an act of an unjust, but also of a vile, and unmanly disposition. **1671** MILTON *Samson* 376 If aught seem vile, As vile hath been my folly, who have profan'd The mystery of God. **1727** DE FOE *Hist. Appar.* iii. (1840) 22 Turning the whole frame of nature upside down by his vile doings there. **1784** COWPER *Tiroc.* 761 Within some pious pastor's humble cot, Where vile example..May never more be stamp'd upon his breast. **1838** LYTTON *Alice* 82, I see already that from the world, vile as it is, you have nothing of contagion to fear. **1848** THACKERAY *Van. Fair* xxxiii, That abandoned wretch, ..of whose vile arts he became a victim. **1849** MACAULAY *Hist. Eng.* V. I. 555 The Earl's past life had been stained by what they regarded as the vilest apostasy.

b. Used to qualify nouns denoting faults of mind or character. *rare.*

a **1340** HAMPOLE *Psalter* ix. 1 A vile errour it is þat sum men says that god does vnrightwisly. *Ibid.* xv. 1 Here is þe vile pride of men confoundid. **1567** *Satir. Poems Reform.* iv. 91 Quhat sall I wryte of ȝoure wyle vanitie?

c. Of names, etc.: Implying (moral) baseness or depravity.

1560 DAUS tr. *Sleidane's Comm.* 383 This greved the moste, yᵗ their religion was described by so vile & contemptuouse a name. **1590** SHAKS. *Mids. N.* II. ii. 107 Where is Demetrius? oh how fit a word Is that vile name, to perish on my sword! **1743** BULKELEY & CUMMINS *Voy. S. Seas* Pref. p. xvi, The Gentleman..represented us to the English Merchants in a very vile Light. ? *a* **1800** A. YOUNG in Baxter *Libr. Pract. Agric.* (1846) II. p. xxiv, I am disgusted with such vile assertions. **1868** FREEMAN *Norm. Conq.* (1877) II. vii. 104 This was the vilest epithet in the English language.

2. Of persons: Of a low, base, or despicable character; morally depraved or degraded; capable of the basest conduct.

a **1300** *Cursor M.* 1153 Wit all þou sal bi halden vile, Quarsa þou wendes in exile. **1303** R. BRUNNE *Handl. Synne* 2597 ȝyf an okerer myȝt founde be, þey helde hym vyler þan a Iew. *c* **1330** *Arth. & Merl.* 8738 (Kölbing), Leggeþ on þe traitours vile, Spareþ nouȝt, ac sle doun riȝt. *a* **1400–50** *Alexander* 186 þan sall þat victoure ȝow venge on ȝour vile fais. *c* **1425** WYNTOUN *Cron.* II. 731 Repruffand thaim as sottis wille..For to lieff it fayntly, And leif lowndeраris caytefly. **1500–20** DUNBAR *Poems* xx. 14 In cumpany cheiss honorable feiris, And fra vyle folkis draw the far on syd. **1535** COVERDALE *Job* xv. 16 An abhominable and vyle man, which dryncketh wickednesse like water. **1560** DAUS tr. *Sleidane's Comm.* 237 b, Freers vile in lyfe and learnyng. **1603** DEKKER *Batchelars Banquet* Wks. (Grosart) I. 156, I pray thee wife tell me, where lies thy griefe?..wherevpon the vile woman fetching a deepe sigh, makes this answere. **1677** EARL ESSEX in *Essex Papers* (Camden) II. 133 There is a vile woman who has bin guilty of severall wicked practices here. **1708** PRIOR *Turtle & Sparrow* 429 Notions like these, from Men are giv'n, Those vilest Creatures under Heav'n. *a* **1715** BURNET *Own Time* (1766) II. 47, I was against the making use of so vile a man. **1807** CRABBE *Par. Reg.* III. 578 A victim to the snare, That vile attorneys for the weak prepare. **1849** MACAULAY *Hist. Eng.* v. I. 591 In every age the vilest specimens of human nature are to be found among demagogues. **1883** STEVENSON *Silverado Sq.* (1886) 37 With that vile lad to head them off,..they would have..stumbled through the woods.

absol. **1817** MOORE *Lalla R., Fire-Worshippers* ii. 278 Bondage grows Too vile for ev'n the vile to bear!

b. Applied to animals, esp. of a destructive or dangerous nature.

13.. *Sir Beues* (A.) 2624 þar-fore hii deide in dedli sinne. .. After in a lite while þai be-come dragouns vile. **1393** LANGL. *P. Pl.* C. XXI. 158 Of alle fretynge venymes þe vilest is þe scorpion. *c* **1450** HOLLAND *Howlat* 88 The Howlet wylest in wyce, Raikit vnder the rys. *c* **1470** HENRY *Wallace* XI. 287 Lordis, behald, inwy the wyle dragoun, In cruell fyr he byrnys this regioun.

3. Physically repulsive, esp. through filth or corruption; horrid, disgusting.

Also depreciatingly applied to the body.

a **1300** *Sarmun* iii. in *E.E.P.* (1862) 1 To be-hend if we wold loke, wel file hit is þat of us come. *Ibid.* iv, Hit is wel vile þat commiþ vte. **13..** *Seuen Sages* (W.) 1353 Was nowt the boi of wit bereued, Whan he tok his fader heued, In a vil gonge slong hit inne? *c* **1340** HAMPOLE *Pr. Consc.* 610 Ilk man..Suld thynk of þe wrechednes of his kynde, þat es foul, and vile, and wlatsom. *c* **1375** *Sc. Leg. Saints* ii. (*Paul*) 773 At his mastere askit he, quhar-for his birth [*sc.* a frog] wes sa wile, sa foule, and sa horribyle. *c* **1425** WYNTOUN *Cron.* II. 576 In þar bledderis bolnyt bilis And alkyn bruk and skab þat wile is. **1535** COVERDALE *Phil.* iii. 21 Which shal chaunge oure vyle body, yᵗ it maye be like fashioned vnto his glorious body. **1553** EDEN *Treat. New Ind.* (Arb.) 17 The Image..is surely a thing most vyle to beholde, and no lesse terrible. **1560** BIBLE (Genev.) *Wisd.* xi. 13 They..worshiped serpents, that had not the vse of reason, & vile beastes. **16..** SIR W. MURE *Sonn.* xi. 2 Name spotted, fame defyld,..Too long in such a carioun vyle inclois'd. **1637** PRYNNE *Will* in *Documents agst. P.* (Camden) 96 My vile body I bequeath to the dust. *c* **1738** *Wesley's Hymns* (1744) 129 Array'd in glorious Grace Shall these vile Bodies shine. **1746** FRANCIS tr. *Horace, Epist.* II. ii. 106 Hence runs a madding Dog..: Thence a vile Pig polluted with the Mire.

b. Of clothes, etc.: Mean, wretched.

1526 TINDALE *Jas.* ii. 2 A man..in goodly apparell and..a poore man in vyle rayment. **1560** DAUS tr. *Sleidane's Comm.* 465 b, They put upon him a most vile garment. **1591** SPENSER *M. Hubberd* 465 Farre vnfit it is, that person bace Should with vile cloaths approach Gods maiestie. **1783** CRABBE *Village* I. 204 Such is that room..Where the vile bands that bind the thatch are seen, And lath and mud are all that lie between. **1819** SHELLEY *Cenci* v. i. 85, I will pass, wrapped in a vile disguise; Rags on my back.

4. Of conditions, situations, treatment, etc.: Base or degrading in character or effect; ignominious. ***durance vile***: see DURANCE 5.

1297 R. GLOUC. (Rolls) 4374 Wanne hii wolde..noblemen, as ȝe beþ, bringe in so vil seruage. **1340** *Ayenb.* 181 Huo þet him let ouercome be his ulesse, he is ine a wel zorȝuol þreldome and wel vil. *c* **1400** *Destr. Troy* 2140 Hit sittis vs all, For to proffer our persons & our pure goodes, To venge of our velany and our vile harme. *c* **1460** *Towneley Myst.* i. 146 Thou has vs doyn a vyle dispyte, and broght thi self to sorow and sitt. **1560** DAUS tr. *Sleidane's Comm.* 83 Many thousandes of men..lead away in so miserable & vyle captivitie. **1653** R. SANDERS *Moles* xlviii. 15 A Mole appearing on the lower part, or tip of the right Ear... To a Woman it predicts..she is desperately forlorn, and of most vile conditions. **1718** PRIOR *Henry & Emma* 616 Rescue my poor Remains from vile Neglect. **1749** FIELDING *Tom Jones* II. ii, Such base-born children..ought to be brought up to the lowest and vilest offices of the Commonwealth. **1770–94** [see DURANCE 5]. **1784** COWPER *Tiroc.* 456 To work at a vile trade For wages so unlikely to be paid. **1879** FARRAR *St. Paul* (1883) 689 He had been a slave, in the vilest of all positions.

5. Of things: Of little worth or account; mean or paltry in respect of value; held in no esteem or regard. Also *absol.*

c **1320** *Cast. Love* 1112 Woldestou þi finger ȝeue,..So vnworþ and so vyl chaffare to bugge? **1340** *Ayenb.* 82 Hi ne conne..deme..betuene precious an vil. **1390** GOWER *Conf.* Prol. I. 33 This world..That whilom was so magnefied, And now is old and fieble and vil. **1426** LYDG. *De Guil. Pilgr.* 21132 A thyng of no valu, And..Most wyl off reputacioun. **1526** *Pilgr. Perf.* (W. de W. 1531) 6 b, The transytory honours of this worlde sholde appere to vs vyle and nought. **1560** DAUS tr. *Sleidane's Comm.* 233 b, That doctryne began to waxe vyle to him every day more and more. **1670** *Moral State Eng.* 24 Who contemneth Religion as a vile thing? who never nameth God but in his Oaths or Burlesque? *a* **1677** BARROW *Exp. Creed* (1697) 23 The vilest and commonest stones. **1678** R. BARCLAY *Apol. Quakers* v. §23. 171 That it may cut off Iniquity from him, and separate betwixt the Precious and the Vile. **1700** ROWE *Amb. Step-Moth.* I. i. 261 All returns are vile, but Words the poorest. *Ibid.* 424 Everlasting Fame Grows vile in sight of thee. **1784** COWPER *Task* v. 589 That low And sordid gravitation of his pow'rs To a vile clod. **1818** SHELLEY *Rosal. & Helen* 667 All that others seek He casts away, like a vile weed Which the sea casts unreturningly. **1867** MORRIS *Jason* VI. 388 And all the feasts that thou hast shared erewhile With other kings, to mine shall be but vile. **1878** BROWNING *La Saisiaz* 75 Thou sea, wherein he counts Not one inch of vile dominion.

b. Similarly of persons (or animals).

1340 *Ayenb.* 132 þe zoþe milde wyle by hyalde uor vyl, naȝt ase milde y-praysed. **1390** GOWER *Conf.* Prol. I. 112 To so vil a povere wrecche Him deigneth schewe such simplesce. **1398** TREVISA *Barth. De P.R.* VI. xiv. (Bodl. MS.), Soche children for trespas be made vile pore seruauntes. *c* **1480** HENRYSON *Fables, Lion & Mouse* 10 Thow catyve wreche, and wyle vnworthy thing. **1540–1** ELYOT *Image Gov.* 8 His bondemen and moste vile servauntes. **1548** LATIMER *Ploughers* (Arb.) 27 Appoynte them Judges that are moost abiecte and vyle in the congregation. **1579** SPENSER *Sheph. Cal.* Oct. 37 Abandon then the base and viler clowne, Lyft vp thy selfe out of the lowly dust. **1653** W. RAMESEY *Astrol. Restored* 245 They shall be indigent, poor and vile. **1674** *Govt. Tongue* iii. 20 Tis God only that hath power of annihilation, and we (vile worms) seek here to steal that incommunicable right. **1718** POPE *Iliad* II. 235 But if a clamorous vile plebeian rose, Him with reproof he check'd, or tamed with blows.

†c. Cheap, low (in price). *Obs.*

? **1490** *Rule St. Benet* (Caxton) 134 To bye suche cloth that is made in that countre or prouynce, of the vilest and lyghtest pryce. **1551** CROWLEY *Pleas. & Pain* 185 In euery place Ye made my bloude vylar then golde. **1598** GRENEWEY *Tacitus, Ann.* VI. iv. (1622) 127 The value of lands was rated at a very low and vile price. **1601** B. JONSON *Ev. Man in his Hum.* I. i. 61 For he thats so respectlesse in his course Oft sels his reputation vile and cheape.

6. Of poor or bad quality; wretchedly bad or inferior.

Now freq. used as an intensive to express strong disapproval or disgust.

a **1300** *Leg. Rood* (1871) 34 þe tre was vil and old. **13..** *K. Alis.* 5953 (Laud MS.), þorouȝ goddes wrethe [they] shoten away, In to þat vile contreye. *c* **1400** *Laud Troy Bk.* 7274, I-wis thei hadde a vile nyȝt; It myȝt haue ben no worse wedur, Off heuene & erthe hadde gon to-gedur. *c* **1400** *Rule of St. Benet* 2020 Schos þai sall haue... Of þe farest þai sal not by, Bot þe vilist. **1521** *Bradshaw's St. Werburge* Prol. 20 [He] toke the payne and laboure Thy legende to translate..Out of latine in Englisshe rude and vyle. **1551** TURNER *Herbal* 115 Cistus..that cummeth out of arabia..is viler then the other be. **1700** PRIOR *Carm. Sec.* iv, With the Blood of Jove there always ran Some viler Part, some Tincture of the Man. **1746** FRANCIS tr. *Hor., Sat.* II. v. 121 Writes he vile Verses in a frantic Vein? **1756** C. LUCAS *Ess. Waters* III. 259 This vile structure was, this year, removed. **1818** SCOTT *Br. Lamm.* xvii, This appearance of Craigengelt..is a most vile augury for his future respectability. **1841** BARHAM *Ingol. Leg.* Ser. II. *Auto-da-fé*, A Vile compound..called Olla podrida. **1851** RUSKIN *Stones Ven.* (1874) I. viii. 91 The vile cathedral of Orleans. **1903** *Times* 10 Jan. 6/6 It is scarcely possible to conceive a viler day than..this.

b. Used as an intensive emphasizing some bad quality or condition; †also, heavy, severe.

a **1400–50** *Alexander* 4164 þan fandis he furth,..Come to a velans vale þare was a vile cheele. *c* **1400** *Destr. Troy* 1249 The bourder of his basnet [he] brestes in sonder, And videt the viser with a vile dynt. **1601** SHAKS. *Jul. C.* II. i. 265 Will he steale out of his wholsome bed To dare the vile contagion of the Night? **1615** *Work for Cutlers* 9, I think that Powder is a vile bragger, he doth nothing but cracke. **1712** STEELE *Spect.* No. 474 ¶ 1 To be obliged to receive and return Visits..is a vile Loss of Time. **1798** FERRIAR *Illustr. of Sterne* ii. 54 The brightest wit is confounded with the vilest absurdity.

7. *Comb.*, as ***vile-born, -hearted, -natured***, etc.

a **1548** HALL *Chron., Hen. VII*, 7 Such a dongehyll knaue and vile borne villeyne. **1591** SPENSER *M. Hubberd* 986 Be therefore counselled herein by me, And shake off this vile harted cowardree. **1607** TOURNEUR *Rev. Trag.* I. i, I wonder how ill-featur'd, vile-proportion'd That one should be [etc.]. **1660** JER. TAYLOR *Ductor* I. v. rule 8 §6 The necessities of women married to..morose vile-natur'd husbands. **1888** DOUGHTY *Arabia Deserta* II. 30 The Hâyil princes..are perhaps mostly like vile-spirited in their youth.

B. *adv.* = VILELY *adv.* Now only in combs.

a **1300** *Cursor M.* 16461 Iudas stode..for to be-hald and se Hu vile þat þai wit him delt. *c* **1400** *Destr. Troy* 2145 Ofte sith hit is sene..That a victor of a victe is vile ouercomyn. **1590** SPENSER *F.Q.* II. x. 18 The noble daughter of Corineus Would not endure to be so vile disdaind. **1595** SHAKS. *John* II. i. 586 A most base and vile-concluded peace. **1602** MARSTON *Antonio's Rev.* IV. v, No, no song; twill be vile out of tune. *a* **1734** NORTH *Lives, Guilford* (1890) I. 288 Roe was a close servant of Monmouth's: which comes vile near siding against his master and benefactor the Duke of York. **1905** *Westm. Gaz.* 16 Feb. 1/3 The vile-smelling tramp on which we had taken passage.

†C. *sb.* A base or despicable person. *Obs.*

c **1400** *Laud Troy Bk.* 818 Sche wolde be more certayn That he schulde here no-wayes be-gile Ne holde here afftir for no vile. *c* **1400** *Song of Roland* 76 They synnyd so sore in þat ylk while that many men wept and cursid þat vile. **1530** PALSGR. 285/1 Vyle, a noughty person, *loricart.*

† vile, *v. Obs.* Also 4, 6 vyle, 4 vili. [ad. AF. and OF. *viler* to blame, revile, or aphetic for AVILE *v.*]

1. *trans.* To bring to a vile or low condition; to abase or degrade. Also *refl.*

1297 R. GLOUC. (Rolls) 802 þus he bigan is mone; Alas, alas, þou luþer wate [= Fortune], þat vilest me þus one, þat þus clene bringst me adoun. *a* **1300** *Leg. Rood* (1871) 34 þe tre was vil and old; and to vili our lord also..ȝut hem þoȝte þat tre to vair þat he were þeron ido. **13..** *E.E. Allit. P.* B. 863 Avoy! hit is your vylaynye, ȝe vylen your seluen. **1526** *Pilgr. Perf.* (W. de W. 1531) 288 That the hye god omnipotent wolde vouchesafe to vyle hymself so lowe. **1530** PALSGR. 765/2 Thou oughtest to be a shamed to vyle thy selfe with thyn yvell tonge.

2. To revile.

a **1300** *Cursor M.* 25509 Suet lauerd!..þaa felun juus dai and night, vild [*Fairf.* reuiled] þe wit al þair might.

3. To defile.

c **1400** tr. *Higden* (Rolls) VII. 147 In þe nyȝt byfore he viled hym self [L. *se fœdasset*] with a comoun womman.

vile, southern ME. var. FILE *sb.*¹, *v.*¹, and *v.*²

vile, obs. var. VILLE³.

vile cotte, obs. form of WYLIECOAT.

vilefy, obs. form of VILIFY *v.*

† vilehead. *Obs.*⁻¹ [f. VILE *a.*] Vileness.

1340 *Ayenb.* 130 Huanne þe man..knauþ his pourehede, þe vilhede, þe brotelhede of his beringe.

vilein, vilein-: see VILLAIN, VILLEIN, etc.

vileins, variant of VILLAINS *Obs.*

† vilely, *a. Obs.*⁻¹ In 5 villiche, filich. [f. VILE *a.* Cf. next.] Vile in appearance.

1398 TREVISA *Barth. De P.R.* x. vii. (Tollem. MS.), The fayrer it was by his firste onynge to þe fyre, þe more unsemely and þe more villiche [*Bodl. MS.* filich; L. *vilior*] in quenchynge of þe fyre.

vilely ('vaɪllɪ), *adv.* Forms: α. 3–4 villiche (4–5 filliche), 4 vylliche, vyllyche. β. 3–5 viliche (4 vileche), 5 vilich; 4 vilike, wilik; 4, 6 vyly, 6–7 vylie; 4, 6–7 vily (4–5 vili), 6 vilie, vilye. γ. 4–5 vileliche (5 villiliche), 4 vilelik, 4, 6– vilely (6 vylely). [f. VILE *a.* + -LY², after AF. and OF. *vilement.*] In a vile manner (in various senses of the adj.).

α. *c* **1290** *S. Eng. Leg.* I. 296/82 Huy nomen and drowen þis holie man villiche þoruȝ þe strete, Forto huy comen with-oute toun. *c* **1300** *St. Margarete* 123 Hire suete tendre flesch so filliche to-drawe was so; Allas, hou miȝte eni man for reuþe such dede do. **13..** *Seuyn Sages* (W.) 1433 And than before the folk him bring, And thourgh the toun him villiche driue. **1340** *Ayenb.* 133 þet is wylny..to by y-hyealde vyl and villiche to by y-draȝe.

β. *a* **1300** *Cursor M.* 15833 þai huited on him viliker þan he had ben a hund. **1303** R. BRUNNE *Handl. Synne* 2609 No man was so hardy To bryng hym þyng opunly, þat he ne shulde vyly be shent. *a* **1340** HAMPOLE *Psalter* i. 6 Hathen men sal viliere be dampned. **1388** WYCLIF *Lev.* xviii. 28 Be ȝe war, lest it caste out viliche also ȝou in lijk manere. *c* **1400** *Destr. Troy* 6912 Vlixes, his aune cosyn,..To venge of þat vilany vili dissirit. *c* **1425** *Eng. Conq. Ireland* 4 Of the schame þat hyme was done, & of þat þat he was so vilich out of hys kynd lond I-dryue. **1553** T. WILSON *Rhet.* 56 b, We shall sone make our aduersaries to be lothed, if we..declare how cruelly, how vilie, and how maliciously thei haue vsed other men heretofore. **1568** GRAFTON *Chron.* II. 62, I will neyther cowardlye shrinke, nor vilye forsake my flocke committed to my charge. **1616** CHAMPNEY *Voc. Bps.* 119 For which reason doubtles do our English Puritans esteeme so vily of ordinations made by Bishops. **1677** GALE *Crt. Gentiles* IV. I. iv. §6. 132 It is..a vile thing, vily to obey any vile thing, such as sin is.

γ. **13..** *Cursor M.* 16951 (Gött.), He þat neuer no sin did, vr sinnes all he bare, And vilelik for vs was ledd. **13..** *K. Alis.* 3968 (Laud MS.), Ne had myne hauberk ben þe strongere þou haddest me vilely yslawe. *c* **1430** *Pilgr. Lyf Manhode* IV. ii. (1869) 175 þilke beste was disgised so vileliche, and so foule figured þat [etc.]. **1555** EDEN *Decades* (Arb.) 86 Declaringe howe vylely, vylaynously, and violently he had byn vsed of owre men. **1581** MULCASTER *Positions* xxxvii. (1887) 161 So vilely to abuse, where they ought to honour. **1611** BIBLE *2 Sam.* i. 21 The shield of the mightie is vilely cast away. **1694** WOOD *Life* (O.H.S.) III. 462 The commons [were] enraged at it and spoke vilely of the Earl of Abendon and his son—calld them Jacobites. **1745** P. THOMAS *Jrnl. Anson's Voy.* 144 This so generally received, tho' vilely mistaken Opinion, has caused many poor Sufferers to Endure more..than from the Distemper itself. **1766** GOLDSM. *Vic. W.* xxxi, How is it, sir, that..his daughter [is] vilely seduced as a recompence for his hospitality? **1815** SCOTT *Guy M.* xxi, Some drawings I have attempted, but I succeed vilely. **1856** MRS. BROWNING *Aur. Leigh* IX. 619 A woman proud As I am, and I'm very vilely proud. **1894** GLADSTONE *Horace* III. v. 20 Swords, that Roman once had seen, From unresisting legions vilely ta'en.

vilenage, obs. form of VILLEINAGE.

Vilene ('vaɪliːn). Also vilene. A proprietary name for backing or an interlining for clothing material, etc.

1954 *Trade Marks Jrnl.* 9 Feb. 159/2 *Vilene*... Lining and stiffening materials for clothing, all being textile piece goods;..The Viledon Company Limited, 15, New Street, Bishopsgate, London E.C.1.; merchants. **1960** *News Chron.* 10 Oct. 8/4 This [dress] is made in fine black wool, with a vilene-backed skirt. **1961** *Guardian* 24 Mar. 12/4 Putting a very fine netting of 'Vilene' between two layers of paper, and the resulting material handles like cloth. **1976** *Woman's*

Weekly 6 Nov. 44/2 Cut hymn book from Vilene interlining and sew to right hand.

vileness ('vaɪlnɪs). Also 5-6 vylenes(se, 6-7 vilenes(se, 6 vylynesse. [f. VILE *a.* + -NESS.]

†**1.** Foulness, filthiness, foul matter. *Obs.*

1495 *Trevisa's Barth. De P.R.* VIII. xxviii. (Caxton) 341 Though it passe by vylenesse and fylthe, it is not defoylled. **1509** BARCLAY *Shyp of Folys* (1570) 229 By suche vilenes disfigure they nature, Their chekes dirtie, their teeth by rustines Blacke, foule and rotten, expresseth their vilenes. **1530** PALSGR. 285/1 Vylenesse, nothyng clenly, *fetardise.* **1552** HULOET, Vilenes, fylth, or ordure, *sordes.*

2. The quality or character of being morally vile; moral depravity; baseness of character.

1526 *Pilgr. Perf.* (W. de W. 1531) 169 b, Secondaryly [are to be considered] the vylenesse, vnkyndnesse, & vnworthynesse of man to that loue. **1555** BRADFORTH in Strype *Eccl. Mem.* (1721) III. App. XLV. 128 The natural disposition of the Spaniards whose vylenes doubtles I cannot showe. **1588** *Marprel. Epist.* (Arb.) 32, I will so lay open your vilenes yat I wil make the very stoones in Kingstone streets shall smell of your knaueries. **1635** *Life Long Meg of Westm.* xviii. 46 (Hindley), I do enjoin you that ..you come into the church, and there..declare to the people the vileness of your life. *a* **1677** BARROW *Wks.* (1687) I. vii. 85 God being most holy and pure,..we, sensible of our corruption and vileness, may be fearfull and shy of coming near unto him. **1693** CREECH in *Dryden's Juvenal* xiii. (1697) 318 He expatiates on the Vileness of the Times. **1740-2** RICHARDSON *Pamela* (1785) III. x. 45 Her Vileness could hardly be equalled by the worst Actions of the most abandoned Procuress. **1769** *Lett. Junius* i. (1788) 37 Judges are superior to the vileness of pecuniary corruption. **1850** TENNYSON *In Mem.* li. 4 Is there no baseness we would hide? No inner vileness that we dread? **1868** E. EDWARDS *Ralegh* I. i. 8 One of the very few worthies who had redeemed the vileness of a reign. **1880** E. WHITE *Cert. Relig.* 95 The vileness of the temper which affronts the Eternal Mercy by the response of a scoffing criticism.

b. An instance of this.

1863 PUSEY in *Oxf. Lent. Serm.* 14 When years of life have been spent in such preference of self, self-will, ambition, vilenesses to God. **1872** RUSKIN *Eagle's N.* §79 Ghastly convulsions in thought, and vilenesses in action.

3. Low or mean condition.

1549 COVERDALE, etc. *Erasm. Par. Rom.* xv. 41 He therfore submitted hym self to our vilenes, to thend he would by lytle and lytle exalt vs to a hygher state.

4. Extreme badness or worthlessness.

1723 T. THOMAS in *Portland Papers* (Hist. MSS. Comm.) VI. 74 One [picture] which, upon account of the vileness of the artist, ought not to have been placed there. **1807** ANNA M. PORTER *Hungar. Bro.* iv. (1832) 40 While she plied the modelling-sticks, or the chisel, with equal vileness.

vilens(ly, varr. VILLAINS(LY. *Obs.*

vilentyne: see VOLENTINE.

†**vilesse.** *Obs. rare.* [a. OF. *villesse* (-*esce*), var. *viellesce*, etc. (mod.F. *vieillesse*), f. *vieil* old.] Old age.

c **1430** LYDG. *Min. Poems* (Percy Soc.) 32 Thouhe she be yong, yet wol she..take a buffard riche of gret vilesse. *c* **1430** *Pilgr. Lyf Manhode* IV. ix. (1869) 181 þou shalt, quod she, wite whan þou hast seyn vilesse, and þat she shal bicomen in þee. And where is vilesse, quod j, and where dwelleth she, and what thing is it? [In ch. lv, p. 202, of this work the reading *viletee* is prob. an error for *vilece.*]

vilet, vi'let, obs. forms of VIOLET.

†'**vilety.** *Obs.* Forms: α. 3-5 vilte (uilte, 4 filte), 4-5 vylte, 6 vilty. β. 4-5 vilete, 5-6 vylete(e, 6 vilety, 6-7 viletie. [a. AF. and OF. *vilte* (= It. *viltà*, Pr. *viltat*), f. *vil* VILE *a.* Cf. VILITY.] Vileness, in various senses; a vile action.

α. *a* **1225** *Ancr. R.* 380, I hwuche uilte, i hwuche wo, he ledde his lif on eorðe. **1297** R. GLOUC. (Rolls) 1081 Gret vilte þou askest ous, wanne we of one kunde Beþ icome. **1303** R. BRUNNE *Handl. Synne* 5206 He þat was hanged on a tre Bysyde Ihesu for vylte. *a* **1340** HAMPOLE *Psalter* xlix. 22 þat þou wit þat þou ill did and see þi vilte. **13..** *E.E. Allit. P.* B. 199 Neuer ȝet in no boke breued I herde þat euer he wrek so wyþerly on werk þat he made, Ne venged for no vilte of vice ne synne. *c* **1400** *Rule St. Benet* lviii. (Prose) 38 Alle þe uiltez þat man wille put hir to. **14..** *S.E. Leg.* (MS. Bodl. 779) in Herrig's *Archiv* LXXXII. 352/84 Forȝeue hem þis gult þat doþ me soch filte. **1483** CAXTON *Gold. Leg.* 290/1 After the passion the Crosse was moche enhaunced for the vylte was transported in to preciousyte. **1598** BARRET *Theor. Warres* v. i. 148 Whosoeuer shall..loose the same [ground] through vilty or negligence.

β. *a* **1300** *Cursor M.* 20340 þar-for þaron hei [*v.r.* haue] þou þe thoght,..þat tai do me na vilete. *c* **1450** tr. *De Imitatione* III. xxiii. 93 Having euer in mynde his oune wickednes & his vilete. **1485** CAXTON *Chas. Gt.* viii. 74 For yf..it happed that..[I] put the to deth it shold to me be vylete and reproche. **1504** ATKYNSON tr. *De Imitatione* III. xxiv. 217 If man consyder well his vylete, pouerte & great indygence. **1576** BEDINGFIELD tr. *Cardanus' Comf.* 57 b, And misery, vilety, shame,..are al more euil then death. **1602** SEGAR *Hon. Mil. & Civ.* III. v. 118 Better it is therefore to iustifie honour by Armes, then incurre suspition of viletie.

vileyn(e, obs. ff. VILLAIN *a.*, VILLEIN.

vileyne, etc., obs. ff. VILLAINY.

vileyns, var. VILLAINS *a. Obs.*

vilful(ly, obs. Sc. ff. WILFUL(LY.

vili, obs. f. VILELY *adv.*

†**viliaco.** *Obs.* Also villiaco, vill-, viliago. [ad. It. *vigliacco* (= Pg. *velhaco*, Sp. *bellaco*, obs. F. *viliaque, vieillaque*):—pop.L. **viliaccum*, -*us*, f. L. *vīlis* vile.] A vile or contemptible person; a villain, scoundrel.

α. **1599** B. JONSON *Ev. Man out of Hum.* v. iii, Now out, base viliaco! Thou my resolution! **1602** DEKKER *Satirom.* Wks. 1873 I. 187 Before they came near the great hall, the faint-hearted villiacoes sounded at least thrice. **1630** J. TAYLOR (Water P.) *Jacke-a-Lent* Wks. I. 115/2 Panders are plagued, and the chiefe Commanders of these valorous villiacoes..purchase the inheritance of a Jayle.

β. **1593** SHAKS. *2 Hen. VI*, IV. viii. 48 Me thinkes alreadie in this ciuill broyle I see them Lording it in London streets, Crying *Villiago* vnto all they meete. **1607** DEKKER & WEBSTER *Sir T. Wyatt* E ij b, A Dondego is a desperate Viliago, a very Castilian, God blesse vs. **1651** *Randolph's Hey for Honesty* II. i. 10 Why you Villiago's, my master has brought home an old lame..Dotard.

viliage, obs. form of VILLAGE.

†**vilicate**, *v. Obs.*[−1] [Perhaps a misprint for *vilificate.*] *trans.* To vilify.

1646 R. JUNIUS *Cure of Misprision* §54. 113 Basenesse, what it cannot attaine to, it will vilicate and deprave.

viliche, vilie, obs. forms of VILELY *adv.*

†**vi'lificate**, *pa. pple. Obs.*[−1] [ad. late L. *vīlificāt-us*, pa. pple. of *vīlificāre* VILIFY *v.*] Rendered vile.

a **1440** *Found. St. Bartholomew's* (E.E.T.S.) 48 This suttell serpent, transformyng hym-self yn-to the lyknes of a fair yonge man,..more vylyfycat with precyous ornamentis, than I-bewtified for shynyng of his bewte.

vilification (ˌvɪlɪfɪ'keɪʃən). [ad. L. type **vīlificātio*: see VILIFY *v.* and -FICATION. So OF. *vilification* (15th cent.).]

1. The action of rendering vile in worth or estate; degradation. *rare*[−1].

1630 DONNE *Deaths Duell* (1632) 22 That..the priuat and retir'd man..must [in his dust]..bee mingled with the dust of euery high way... This is the most inglorious and contemptible vilification.

2. The action of vilifying by means of abusive language; reviling; an instance of this.

1653 H. MORE *Def. Cabbala* Pref. 83, I will not deny, but they have mingled their own fooleries with it..: Such as.. reproaches against the Pleasures of the Body; Vilification of Marriage, and the like. **1660** *Trial Regic.* (1679) 203 Then you spake in vilification of Monarchical Government. **1664** H. MORE *Myst. Iniq.* 230 Either way is declared that which is a contumely and vilification of God. **1780** BENTHAM *Princ. Legisl.* xviii. §34 Thus we have two genera or kinds of offences against reputation merely; to wit, 1. Defamation and 2. Vilification or Revilement. **1859** BOYD *Recreat. Country Parson* iii. 83 If you try..to live an honest, christian life, it will go hard, but you will live down such malicious vilification. *a* **1884** M. PATTISON *Mem.* (1885) 322 The whole literary effort of the Catholic reaction..had been directed to beating down his fame by an organised system of detraction and vilification.

b. An abusive remark or speech. *rare.*

1709 STRYPE *Ann. Ref.* I. xxxii. 324 This epistle was made up of falsehoods, misrepresentations and vilifications. *a* **1734** NORTH *Lives* (1826) II. 164 In the mean time vilifications plenty there were at their tongues' end.

3. The action of bringing into disrepute.

1652 EARL MONM. tr. *Bentivoglio's Hist. Relat.* 134 The losse of reputation (the soul of Empire) to the Crown of Spain; the Truce being made to the so much vilification thereof.

vilifier ('vɪlɪfaɪə(r)). [f. next.] One who vilifies; a defamer or abuser.

1611 FLORIO, *Vilificatore*, a vilifier, a debaser. **1691** WOOD *Ath. Oxon.* I. 103 He [T. Robertson] was a great Oppugner and Vilifier of the Questionists in the University. **1707** HEARNE *Collect.* 6 June (O.H.S) II. 18 A Vilifier of the Common-Prayer. *a* **1718** PENN *Tracts* Wks. 1726 I. 713 Those that are Disturbers and Vilifiers of them that believe in Him. **1876** BANCROFT *Hist. U.S.* IV. li. 288 Meantime, the modern Prometheus..stood conspicuously erect, confronting his vilifier and the privy council. **1885** *Manch. Exam.* 28 Mar. 5/4 The apology extracted from his vilifier is the smallest retribution which can be exacted.

vilify ('vɪlɪfaɪ), *v.* Also 5-8 vilifie, 7 villifie, 8 -fy; 6 vilefy, 7 villefie. [ad. late L. *vīlificāre* (Jerome), f. *vīlis* VILE *a.*: see -(I)FY. Hence also It. *vilificare*, Pr., Pg. *vilificar.*]

1. *trans.* To lower or lessen in worth or value; to reduce to a lower standing or level; to make of little (or less) account or estimation. Also *refl.*

Freq. in the 17th c.; now *rare* or *Obs.*

(*a*) *c* **1450** tr. *De Imitatione* III. ix. 76 If..I vilifie myself & bringe me to nouȝt,..& make me dust as I am, þi grace shal be merciful to me. **1617** MORYSON *Itin.* III. 85 He who vilifies himselfe, doth not thereby save one penny. **1630** BRATHWAIT *Eng. Gentlem.* (1641) 21 Who humbled himself in the forme of man..: vilifying himself to make man like himself. **1653** H. COGAN tr. *Pinto's Trav.* lxii. 253 The recompenses which God hath promised to those that vilify themselves to serve him. *a* **1684** LEIGHTON *Comm., 1 Peter* i. 23 (1850) 212 Are you not born to a better inheritance?.. Why then do you vilify yourselves?

(*b*) **1604** T. WRIGHT *Passions* v. §4. 251 Long delayes and many suites vilifie the giftes;..for..it is bought dearely, which is purchased with long prayers. **1645** MILTON *Tetrach.* Wks. 1851 IV. 157 Such a mariage, wherin the minde is so disgrac't and vilify'd below the bodies interest, ..is not of Gods institution. **1654** WHITLOCK *Zootomia* 448 Though seeming Commendations,..yet..enough to vilifie, and cheapen the Noblest Merit. **1677** *Govt. Venice* 129 The Republick of Venice not only detains their Dukes Prisoners in their Palace,..but it daily retrenches their Priviledges, to vilifie them the more. **1768-74** TUCKER *Lt. Nat.* (1834) II. 29 It would vilify, and, I may say, vulgarize the Almighty, to imagine him resident among ourselves. **1790** BURKE *Fr. Rev.* 147 The wealth and pride of individuals..makes the man of humble rank and fortune sensible of his inferiority, and degrades and vilifies his condition. **1835** I. TAYLOR *Spir. Despot.* v. 207 When [a hierarchy's] distinctions of rank are of such vast compass as to vilify the humbler clerical orders.

†**b.** To make morally vile; to degrade; also, to defile or dirty. *Obs.*

1615 J. TAYLOR (Water P.) *Taylor's Rev.* Wks. (1630) II. 146/1 Such Motley, Medley, Linsey-Woolsey speeches Would sure haue made thee vilifie thy breeches. **1619** H. HUTTON *Follie's Anat.* (Percy Soc.) 19 You vilifie your selfe with endlesse shame, Imposing scandall to each poet's name. **1667** MILTON *P.L.* XI. 513 Thir Makers Image..then Forsook them, when themselves they villifi'd To serve ungovern'd appetite. **1684** *Contempl. St. Man* I. iv. (1699) 38 Altho' the Soul be of it self of a most Noble Substance, yet his Vices do so much vilifie it, that he makes it more abominable than the Body. **1781** [see VILIFYING *ppl. a.*].

absol. **1749** CHESTERF. *Lett.* (1774) I. 440 Nothing vilifies and degrades more than pride.

†**c.** To bring disgrace or dishonour upon. *Obs.*

1651 BAXTER *Inf. Bapt.* 139 The Anabaptists..resisting the most painfull godly Ministers, and reproaching and vilifying them, by their wicked lives. **1656** EARL MONM. tr. *Boccalini's Advts. fr. Parnass.* I. lxxxvii. (1674) 117 [They] blush to think that their Ancestors have so shamefully vilified their house. **1674** tr. *Scheffer's Lapland* ix. 34 Their Priests, who either take no care of instructing the people, or vilify their doctrine by the sordidness of their lives. **1749** SMOLLETT *Regicide* II. x, Heav'n shall not see A deed so abject vilify my name.

2. †**a.** To depreciate or disparage in discourse; to talk slightingly or contemptuously of. *Obs.* (passing into next).

1586 DAY *Eng. Secretary* I. (1595) 77 Your Vncles care, was by vilefying his wealth vnto you..to purchase for you the endowment of a farre more greater and assured treasure. **1629** H. BURTON *Truth's Triumph* 288 The Pontifician so much depressing and vilifying his owne indisposition. **1645** PAGITT *Heresiogr.* (ed. 2) 71 As these Sectaries villefie others, so they magnifie themselves. **1667** ANNE WYNDHAM *King's Concealm.* (1681) 53 Some envious persons have sought to diminish and vilifie the faithful services which the Colonel..performed. **1691** RAY *Creation* I. (1692) 162 To disparage, deride, and vilifie those Studies which themselves skill not of. **1736** BUTLER *Anal.* II. iii. Wks. 1874 I. 180, I express myself with caution, lest I should be mistaken to vilify reason. **1751** JOHNSON *Rambler* No. 117 ¶1 The disposition of vulgar minds to ridicule and vilify what they cannot comprehend.

b. To depreciate with abusive or slanderous language; to defame or traduce; to speak evil of.

1598 MARSTON *Sco. Villanie* Prol. (1599) 168 When I once hear..some span-new come fry Of Innes a-court striuing to vilefy My dark reproofes. **1624** GATAKER *Transubst.* 51 After he hath thus spent some part of his railing Rhetorick in traducing and vilifying this Protestantical Divine his Adversary. **1659** T. PECKE *Parnass. Puerp.* 175 Mother-in-Lawes, Poets much Vilifie. **1670** BAXTER *Cure Ch. Div.* Concl. Pref. §5 Not..to hate and flye from one another; nor to vilifie and backbite one another. **1713** STEELE *Englishman* No. 13. 83, I have really taken a secret Pleasure in seeing him employed in villifying me. *a* **1720** SEWEL *Hist. Quakers* (1795) I. IV. 348 One of those persons whom even his enemies could not vilify without praising him. **1764** T. HUTCHINSON *Hist. Mass.* iii. (1765) 351 Randolph, in return, vilified Dudley, in a great number of letters. **1842** BORROW *Bible in Spain* xxxviii, The priestly party..spared no effort to vilify me. **1850** MRS. JAMIESON *Leg. Monast. Ord.* (1863) 115 He was slandered and vilified by the corrupt monks. **1889** G. C. BRODRICK in *Oxf. Chron.* 11 May 7/7 Those who had devoted their whole influence to vilifying such a remedial policy.

absol. a **1854** H. REED *Lect. Eng. Lit.* iv. (1855) 439 So artfully does he misrepresent them, so vehemently does he vilify.

†**3.** To regard as worthless or of little value; to contemn or despise. *Obs.* (Common in 17th c.)

1598 MARSTON *Sco. Villanie* III. x. (1599) 223 Opinion mounts this froth vnto the skies, Whom iudgemente reason iustly vilifies. **1641** BAKER *Chron., Hen. I*, 60 A private man, vilified, and thought to have but little in him. **1652-62** HEYLYN *Cosmogr.* IV. (1682) 64 Gold here so vilified that they exchange it gladly for Brass. **1671** TRENCHFIELD *Cap Gray Hairs* (1688) 40 For no man but vilifies that person in his own estimate, who is loose bodied upon that account.

†**4.** *intr.* To become common or worthless; to lose value. *Obs.*[−1]

a **1654** BINNING *Sinners Sanctuary* x. Wks. (1735) 210/1 It is Ignorance that magnifies other Mysteries, which vilify through Knowledge.

Hence '**vilified** *ppl. a.*; '**vilifying** *vbl. sb.* and *ppl. a.*; '**vilifyingly** *adv.*

1828 SCOTT *F.M. Perth* xiv, He knows how willingly Clement Blair will lay down a *vilified life upon earth. **1611** BIBLE *Transl. Pref.* ¶12 Their second defence of their *vilifying and abusing of the English Bibles. **1643** CHAS. I *Proclam.* Wks. 1662 II. 345 To countenance the vilifying of the Book of Common Prayer. **1676** HALE *Contempl.* II. 183 In the midst of all the..Vilifyings that the World heaps upon me. **1663** PATRICK *Parab. Pilgr.* xv, I will not recite all the *vilifying language..which he was affronted with. **1705** STANHOPE *Paraphr.* I. 81 That vilifying Malice and Contempt, which Proud and Profligate People..let fly at Them and their Office. **1781** J. MOORE *View Soc. It.* (1790) II. l. 68 Free from all the villifying effects of dirt. **1682** BUNYAN *Holy War* 203 Thou didst also teach the Town of Mansoul to speak contemptuously, and *vilifyingly of their great King Shaddai.

vilike, obs. f. VILELY *adv.*

† **'viliorate**, *v. Obs.*⁻¹ [f. L. *vilior*, compar. of *vilis* VILE *a.*, after *meliorate*.] *trans.* To make less good; to worsen.

a **1722** LISLE *Husb.* (1757) 303 There is a medium in the watery temperature of the earth, either extream of which viliorates the juice.

† **vili'ority.** *Obs.*⁻¹ [f. as prec.] The fact of being cheaper or of less value.

1703 [R. NEVE] *City & C. Purchaser* 281 Mr. Wing's Prices are much cheaper than those about London;..which ..proceeds from the Viliority of Commodities in his Countrey.

vilipend ('vɪlɪpɛnd), *v.* Also 5-6 **vylypende** (5 **philipend**), 6 **vilypend**, 7 **villipende**, 8 **-pend**; 6 **velipend**, *Sc.* **weliepend**; 6-7 **vilepend**(e. [a. OF. (also mod.F.) *vilipender*, or ad. L. *vilipendĕre*, f. *vilis* vile, worthless + *pendĕre* to consider, esteem. Cf. It. *vilipendere*, Sp. and Pg. *vilipendiar*.]

1. *trans.* To rate or regard as being of little value or consequence; to contemn or despise; to treat contemptuously or slightingly.

Very common *c* 1500-1660, in some cases not clearly distinguishable from sense 2.

c **1470** G. ASHBY *Active Policy* 105 For youre birthe of theim discended, In whome al vices ben vilipended. *c* **1480** HENRYSON *Fables, Lion & Mouse* 135, For thy trespas thow can mak na defens, my noble persoun thus to vilipend. **1491** CAXTON *Vitas Patr.* (W. de W. 1495) I. xxxvi. 41 b/1 The chyrches were pylled; and the sacred vesselis vylypended or dyspysed. **1502** ATKYNSON tr. *De Imitatione* III. xlvii. (1893) 234 The more profoundly..he descendeth in humble consyderacion of hym selfe and vylypendynge hym selfe. **1573** L. LLOYD *Marrow of Hist.* (1653) 157 Phidias..was threatned with death, to vilipend so great a Goddess and to make her in Ivory, which was wont to be honoured in Marble. **1606** HOLLAND *Sueton.* Annot. 25 Whom they did vilipend and despise, they were wont to cast stones at their Images and Statues. **1635** SWAN *Spec. M.* vii. §3 (1643) 331 The terrible accidents that succeed eclipses may not be forgotten nor vilipended. **1694** MOTTEUX *Rabelais* v. 251 Since, thanks to Jove's Benignity you're valid, Choose not a frigid State, while yours is calid, Unless Salubrity you vilipend. **1771** SMOLLETT *Humph. Cl.* 4 Aug., I would not willingly villipend any Christian, if peradventure he deserveth that epithet. **1814** SCOTT *Wav.* xiii, A youth devoid of that petulant volatility, which is impatient of, or vilipends, the conversation and advice of his seniors. **1856** FROUDE *Hist. Eng.* I. 182 One Richard Hunt was summoned ..for vilipending his lordship's jurisdiction. **1879** FARRAR *St. Paul* II. 213 This then is the proof that the doctrine of Justification is not contrary to Scripture, and does not vilipend, but really establish the Law.

2. To speak of with disparagement or contempt; to represent as contemptible or worthless; to abuse or vilify. (Common in 19th c.)

a **1529** SKELTON *Bk. 3 Foles* Wks. 1843 I. 202 If that I am exalted vnto honoure..thou wylt vilepende me with thy wordes. *a* **1548** HALL *Chron., Hen. VIII*, 246 b, Vilipendyng all holy Religion, affirmyng it to bee an abusion of the people. **1584** *Leycesters Commw.* (1641) 90 Hee..did diminish, vilipend, and debase among his friends, the inestimable benefites hee hath received from her Majesty. **1603** HOLLAND *Plutarch's Mor.* 1120 Wherein he doth vilipend and mocke Socrates most, in that he demaundeth the question, What is man? **1651** C. CARTWRIGHT *Cert. Relig.* I. 76 You shall find Luther..vilipending those books of Scripture, which were received into the Canon. *a* **1806** C. J. FOX *Reign Jas. II* (1808) p. viii, Even Dryden, who speaks with proper respect of Corneille, vilipends Racine. **1848** THACKERAY *Van. Fair* xviii, Menacing the youth with maledictions..and vilipending the poor innocent girl as the basest and most artful of vixens. **1880** MEREDITH *Tragic Com.* (1881) 227, I am the object of her detestation..She will seize her opportunity to vilipend me.

Hence **'vilipended** *ppl. a.*; **'vilipending** *vbl. sb.* and *ppl. a.* Also **'vilipender**, one who vilipends; **vili'penditory** *a.*, abusive.

1836 HOR. SMITH *Tin Trump.* I. 9 Pleasant was the well-known revenge of the *villipended author. **1849** H. MAYO *Pop. Superst.* (1851) 197 The long-vilipended influence of Mesmer. **1832** *Westm. Rev.* July 133 He..would deserve to be laughed at with the mathematical *vilipender of Milton's poem. **1566** *Reg. Privy Council Scot.* I. 463 In manifest *vilipending of thair Hienessis autoritie. *a* **1626** BP. ANDREWES *Comm. Decalogue* 508 (T.), If it be to the scorning and vilipending of a man, it may be called the sin of the men of Succoth, who slighted Gideon. **1659** C. NOBLE *Answ. Immod. Queries* 6 What greater vilipendings..can be cast upon any man? **1884** *Manch. Exam.* 20 Feb. 4/7 An occasion for a wholesale vilipending of the Government. **1618** *Hist. Perkin Warbeck* 15 Neither security or presumption..of their owne greatnesse,..nor *vilipending and slight regard of the contrary. *a* **1722** FOUNTAINHALL *Decis.* I. 548 The Lords..considered his..vilipending expressions and carriage, and thought that deserved a fine. **1824** SCOTT *St. Ronan's* xii, Sir Bingo..was..in a thoughtless and vilipending humour. *a* **1849** H. COLERIDGE *Ess.* (1851) II. 195 The passionate Romeo, and the vilipending Mercutio. **1884** *Kendal Merc. & Times* 22 Feb. 5/3 If *vilipenditory rhetoric could overthrow a Government then Mr. Gladstone ought to have collapsed.

† **vili'pendency.** *Obs. rare.* [f. prec.: see -ENCY.] The expression of disparagement or contempt.

1653 WATERHOUSE *Apol. Learn.* 149 The mighty Goliahs of Rome, who by this way of vilipendency, hope to give our Clergies flesh to be food for the birds of the Air. *a* **1670** HACKET *Abp. Williams* I. (1692) 77 Some Lords,..not content with that vilipendency,..would have this contempt against the prelates inserted in their Journal Book.

† **vili'pendious,** *a. Obs. rare.* [f. as prec. Cf. Pg. *vilipendioso*.] Contemptible. Also **vili'pendiously** *adv.*, abusively, opprobriously.

1536 in Froude *Hist. Eng.* (1858) III. 168 [They inquired whether Cromwell,] whom they called most vilipendiously, [was put out of the king's council]. **1630** J. TAYLOR (Water P.) *Laugh & be Fat* Wks. II. 79/1 Thou ignoble horse-rubbing peasant,..being but a vilipendious mechanical Hostler.

† **vili'pension.** Chiefly *Sc. Obs.* Also 5-6 **vilipensioun**, 6 **-pentioun**, 7 **vilepension**. [a. OF. *vilipension*, *-pention*, or ad. med.L. *vilipensio*, noun of action f. L. *vilipendĕre* VILIPEND *v.* Cf. also It. *vilipensione*.] The action or fact of contemning or despising.

1456 SIR G. HAYE *Gov. Princes* (S.T.S.) 98 Mekle lauchter..engenderis vilipensioun and lichtlynes quhen it excedis. **1500-20** DUNBAR *Poems* ix. 116, I synnit in..he exaltit arrogance,..derisioun, scorne and vilipentioun. **1535** STEWART *Cron. Scot.* (Rolls) II. 512 With so grit schame and lak, In vilipentioun of the nobill blude. **1574** *Reg. Privy Council Scot.* II. 386 Committand heirthrow.. contemptioun and vilipensioun of his authoritie and lawis. **1602** *Ibid.* VI. 377 In grittar contempt and vilipensioun of his Majestie. **1651** in *Maitl. Cl. Misc.* III. 274 In vilepension of his precious blwd sched for me and mankynd.

b. The condition of being despised.

1538 ABP. BROWN in *St. Papers Hen. VIII* (1834) III. 6 The very occasioner and author off the vilipension and contempt that I am yn.

vili'pensive, *a.* [f. ppl. stem of L. *vilipendĕre*: see -IVE.] Abusive.

1824 *Blackw. Mag.* XVI. 3 Strains not simply laudative of Oporto, but vituperative and vilipensive of Bourdeaux. **1838** *Fraser's Mag.* XVII. 468 Southey..tacks vilipensive prefixes and postfixes to several of these.

vility ('vaɪlɪtɪ). *Obs.* exc. *arch.* Forms: 5-6 **vilite**, 6 **vylyte**, **vylite**, **vilitee**, 6-7 **vilitie**, 7, 9 **vility**. [a. OF. (also mod.F.) *vilité* (var. of *vilté* VILETY), ad. L. *vilitās*, f. *vilis* VILE *a.*: see -ITY. So It. *viltà*.]

1. Vileness of character or conduct; moral degradation or baseness.

1388 WYCLIF *Deut.* xxiv. 1 If..sche fyndith not grace bifor hise iȝen for sum vilite [L. *vilitatem*], he schal write a libel..of forsakyng. **1502** ATKYNSON tr. *De Imitatione* III. v. (1891) 199 That all vylyte or synne, specially thyn owne synne & foulenes, dysplease the. **1549** CHALONER *Erasm. on Folly* P iij, They coumpt it vilitee for theim to yelde theyr valiant soules to God, any where els than in a foughten fielde. **1599** SANDYS *Europæ Spec.* (1632) 209 Then surely have wee not now so great cause to dread him, as to blame our selves and our wranglings and vility.

1888 DOUGHTY *Arabia Deserta* I. 556 Zelots, who of their natural vility were busy-bodies, questioners of other men's religion.

† **2. a.** Mean or low estimate. *Obs.*⁻¹

c **1430** *Pilgr. Lyf Manhode* I. lxi. (1869) 37 For charitee holdeth in cheertee that that oothere holden in vilitee.

† **b.** Meanness or lowliness of condition. *Obs.*

1549 *Compl. Scotl.* xx. 170 Al ȝour gloire, veltht, and dignite, sal change in vilite. *c* **1550** *Disc. Common Weal Eng.* (1893) 123, I mervaile muche theare is anie (seinge a vilitie and contempte of the thinge) will occupie the feate of husbandrie at all. **1596** BELL *Surv. Popery* II. iv. 165 He suffered..in time of his infancie, baseness of his mothers womb, pouertie, asperitie, vilitie in the manger. *a* **1618** J. DAVIES (Heref.) *Witte's Pilgr.* lxxii, The Sunne..Disdaines not to behold the basest Worme, To glad his Soule and grace his vility. **1664** H. MORE *Myst. Iniq.* vi. 17 That idle mistake ..may probably be grounded upon the seeming vility of these figures. **1696** KENNETT *Rom. Antiq.* II. v. vi. 281 The Comedians wore these [sc. *socci*] to represent the vility of the Persons they represented.

† **c.** Lowness of value or price; cheapness. *Obs.*

1623 COCKERAM *Eng. Dict.* II, Cheapnes, *vility*. **1638** PENKETHMAN *Artach.* C ij, Such vilitie or cheapnesse of.. graine, as 6*d.* the Quarter. **1674** STAVELEY *Rom. Horseleech* (1769) 221 The vility of habits [i.e. dress] should be measured by the custom of every country.

† **3.** Impurity, filth. *Obs.*

1540 *Sc. Acts, Jas. V* (1814) II. 374/2 Becaus of þe vilite þat cumis be slaying of flesche, be the flescheouris. **1545** RAYNALD *Byrth Mankynde* 44 The refuce, drosse, & vilar part of the outher blud..separated from the purer for the vylite & euel qualite therin comprehendyd.

vill (vɪl). Also 6-8 (9) **ville**. [a. AF. *vill*, *vile*, OF. *vile*, *vylle*, *ville* farm, country-house, village, collection of villages around a city (mod.F. *ville* town):—L. *villa*: see VILLA *sb.*]

1. *Law* and *Hist.* A territorial unit or division under the feudal system, consisting of a number of houses or buildings with their adjacent lands, more or less contiguous and having a common organization; corresponding to the Anglo-Saxon tithing and to the modern township or civil parish.

1596 BACON *Maxims Com. Law* III. (1630) 14 If..part of the ville is his severall, and part his waste and common. *a* **1625** SIR H. FINCH *Law* (1636) 261 A plea of land which is for land or other such things in demesne..must alwayes bee brought in a ville, or place knowne out of any ville. And not in a hamlet which is parcell of a vill. **1672** MANLEY *Cowell's Interpr.*, *Vill*,..is sometimes taken for a Mannor, and sometimes for a Parish, or part of it. *a* **1676** HALE *Prim. Orig. Man.* (1677) 235 There are very many more Vills and Hamlets now than there were then, and very few Villages, Towns or Parishes then, which continue not to this Day. **1721** *Act Parlt.* in *Lond. Gaz.* No. 5927/6 Any Parish, Township, Vill, or Extraparochial Place. **1768** BLACKSTONE *Comm.* IV. 291 The party raising it must acquaint the constable of the vill,..and thereupon the constable is to search his own town, and raise all the neighbouring vills. **1799** E. HASTED *Hist. Canterbury* 106 This borough [i.e. Stablegate]..was some time past erected into a ville, in order to maintain its own poor. **1839** STONEHOUSE *Axholme* 316 One or two small houses have been built here, but they are hardly sufficient to constitute a hamlet or vill. **1874** STUBBS *Const. Hist.* I. iii. 54 The social organisation of the vill may be identical perhaps with that of the mark. **1891** ATKINSON *Moorland Par.* (ed. 2) 87 If..there were more than one [field] within the vill.

2. *poet.* A village.

a **1700** KEN *Hymnotheo* Poet. Wks. 1721 III. 383 Parochial Priests were fix'd in ev'ry Vill, Who under him should saving Truth instil. **1814** WORDSW. *Excurs.* VIII. 100 Among the tenantry of thorpe and vill, Or straggling burgh. **1821** CLARKE *Vill. Minstr.* II. 69 In every vill, at morning's earliest prime, To early-risers many a Hodge is seen. **1834** SIR H. TAYLOR *Artevelde* II. III. ii, So in field or forest, Or in wall'd town, by stipend lured, or vill Surprised and sack'd, by turns he lived at large.

† **3.** A villa. *Obs. rare.*

1684 tr. *Eutropius* x. 170 [Constantine] died in a publick Vill of the City Nicomedia. **1755** AMORY *Mem.* (1766) II. 61 He saw a vill, that seemed to him of wood, and consisted of ground-rooms. **1766** —— *Buncle* (1770) III. 203 The vill here was very odd, but a charming pretty thing. The house consisted of [etc.].

vill, obs. Sc. form of WILL *a.*

villa ('vɪlə). [Partly a. L. *villa* country-house, farm, etc., perhaps a diminutive from the stem of *vīcus* village, hamlet, country-seat; partly a. It. *villa* (whence also F., Sp., and Pg. *villa*) from the same source.]

1. Orig., a country mansion or residence, together with a farm, farm-buildings, or other houses attached, built or occupied by a person of some position and wealth; a country seat or estate; in later and more general use, a residence in the country, or in the neighbourhood of a town, usually of some size and architectural elegance and standing in its own grounds.

a. Among the ancient Romans, Greeks, etc.

1615 G. SANDYS *Trav.* IV. 274 Passing by Ciceros Villa, euen at this day so called, where yet do remaine the ruines of his Academy. **1644** STAPYLTON *Juvenal* I. 111 Who built so many villa's? when wast knowne Our Fathers with seven dishes supt alone? **1697** WALSH *Life Virgil* ¶3 The beautiful *Villa's* of the Roman Nobility, equalling the Magnificence of the greatest Kings. **1771** H. WALPOLE *Vertue's Anecd. Paint.* (1786) IV. 254 Pliny has left us descriptions of two of his villas. As he used his Laurentine villa for his winter retreat [etc.]. **1781** GIBBON *Decl. & F.* xxxvi. (1787) III. 443 The villa was pleasantly seated on the margin of the lake. **1797** S. LYSONS *Rom. Antiq. Woodchester* 16 The remains of a Roman house, or rather, perhaps, of a *villa*. **1832** G. R. PORTER *Porcelain & Gl.* xiii. 269 The ruins of a villa built by Tiberius in the island of Capri. **1838** THIRLWALL *Greece* V. 97 The dwellings which were thickly scattered in the neighbourhood of the capital..seem to have been chiefly villas of the more opulent Spartans. **1879** FROUDE *Cæsar* iv. 32 Their great men had country houses and villas, the surest sign of a settled state of society.

b. With reference to modern Italy or other Continental countries.

1611 CORYAT *Crudities* 139 A certaine Gentleman called Bassano..liued at a villa that he had in the country. **1636** MASSINGER *Gt. Dk. Florence* I. i, And how, I pray you, (For we, that never look beyond our villas, Must be inquisitive) are state affairs Carried in court? *a* **1700** EVELYN *Diary* 27 Feb. 1644, We went to see Cardinal Richelieu's villa at Ruell. *Ibid.* 10 Nov. 1644, We went to see Prince Ludovisio's villa... The house is very magnificent, and the extent of the ground is exceeding large. **1737** [S. BERINGTON] *G. di Lucca's Mem.* (1738) 238 Their Villa's, or Palaces of Pleasure, are scattered all over the Country. **1756-7** tr. *Keysler's Trav.* (1760) I. 510 The road from Pistoia to Florence..exhibits no villa's or plantations to the view, and consequently..there's the greater number of them in the neighbourhood of Florence. **1806** DALLAWAY *Observ. Eng. Archit.* x. 232 The capricious lightness of an Italian villa. **1838** *Murray's Handbk. N. Germ.* 320/1 On the borders of the Havel..is the little villa of Glienecke, once the residence of the minister Von Hardenberg. **1905** 'G. THORNE' *Lost Cause* iii, The gay villa at Nice by the old citadel of Mont-Albano.

c. In English use. Now merged in next.

1711 SHAFTESB. *Charac.* III. *Misc.* III. ii. 184 *note*, Behold the Disposition and Order of these finer sorts of Apartments, Gardens, Villa's! **1748** HARTLEY *Observ. Man* I. iv. § 1. 427 The Villas and Cabinets of the Noble, the Rich, and the Curious. **1799** *Med. Jrnl.* I. 338 The profits of some of whom are so extravagant, as to support them in enormous magnificent town-houses and country villas. **1830** PRAED *Poems* (1865) II. 227 Hurrying madly after marriage To some lord's villa. **1833** LOUDON *Encycl. Archit.* § 1677 A villa should always form part of a village, and be placed, if possible, on rather higher ground. **1842** GWILT *Archit.* § 3000 The villas at Foot's Cray and Mereworth, imitations of Palladio's Villa, Capra,..are the maxima of villas: beyond this the villa becomes a mansion.

fig. **1742** YOUNG *Nt. Th.* IX. 1732 What behold I now? A wilderness of wonders burning round;..Perhaps the villas of descending gods!

d. Hence, any residence of a superior or handsome type, or of some architectural pretension, in the suburbs of a town or in a residential district; also, any small better-class dwelling-house, usually one which is detached or semi-detached.

The word is frequently employed in the names given to particular houses of this type, as *Windsor Villa*.

1755 JOHNSON *Connoisseur* No. 81 ¶4, I cannot help observing, that persons polite enough to be fond of such exquisite refinements, are partly in the same case with the mechanic at his dusty Villa. 1781 COWPER *Retirem.* 481 Suburban villas, highway-side retreats, That dread th' encroachment of our growing streets. 1792 A. YOUNG *Trav. France* (1889) 114 To Havre de Grace,..the hills almost covered with little new built villas. 1825 C. M. WESTMACOTT *Eng. Spy* I. 318 Incongruous edifices called villas. 1849 MACAULAY *Hist. Eng.* iii. I. 349 No long avenues of villas, embowered in lilacs and laburnums, extended from the great centre of wealth. 1853 R. S. SURTEES *Sponge's Sp. Tour* ii. 6 The farm houses are dotted about as thickly as to look like inferior 'villas' falling out of rank. 1882 MISS BRADDON *Mt. Royal* II. ix. 167, I wish you would let me build you a villa at Torquay or Dartmouth.

†2. (See quot.) *Obs.*⁻¹

a 1700 EVELYN *Diary* 6 May 1645, In these [valleys] are faire Parks or Gardens call'd Villas, being onely places of recesse and pleasure, at some distance from the streetes, yet within the walls [of Rome].

3. *attrib.* and *Comb.* a. Simple attrib. (passing into adj.), as ***villa architecture, garden, -gate, style, -work***, etc.; **villa-house**, †(*a*) a house attached to a villa; (*b*) a villa residence; **villa dwelling, residence**, = VILLA 1 c, d.

a 1700 EVELYN *Diary* 10 Nov. 1644, In the villa-house is a man's body,..petrified. 1813 SCOTT *Let.* 13 Mar. in *Lockhart*, What I shall finally make of this villa-work I don't know. 1828 R. LUGAR (*title*), Villa Architecture. 1833 LOUDON *Encycl. Archit.* §1620 All the essential comforts of a villa dwelling. *Ibid.* §1624 Of the Choice of a Situation for a Villa Residence. 1844 DISRAELI *Coningsby* IV. iii, A.. dwelling-house, built in what is called a villa style, with a variety of gardens, and conservatories. 1855 BROWNING *Old Pict. in Florence* i, The aloed arch Of the villa-gate. 1876 'OUIDA' *Winter City* xii. 367 Mme. Mila was organising alfresco dinners in villa gardens.

b. In instrumental or similative combs., as ***villa-dotted, -haunted, -like***, adjs. Also in objective or obj. gen. combs., as ***villa dweller, owner***, etc.

1843 *Penny Cycl.* XXVI. 264/1 The houses are for the most part neat and villa-like. 1871 MISS CRAIK *Fair France* 154 Flat, tame, and villa-haunted, what we should call Cockneyfied. 1881 MISS BRADDON *Asphodel* III. 148 The smiling waters of Thun, with its villa-dotted shores. *a* 1894 STEVENSON *Lay Morals*, etc. (1911) 123 It is..from the villa-dweller that we hear complaints of the unworthiness of life. 1898 *Engineering Mag.* XVI. 35 This sort of villa-owner's selfishness.

Hence (in nonce-use) **villaette** (vɪlə'ɛt), **villa'rette**, a small villa; **villafy** ('vɪləfaɪ), *v. trans.*, (*a*) to turn into a villa; (*b*) to cover with villas.

1792 F. BURNEY *Jrnl.* 2 June (1972) I. 184 Mrs. & Miss ord & myself set off for Sudbury, near Harrow, where her very elegant Relation, Mr. Orde, has a *villarette. The House is half old, half new, but well fitted up. 1836 *Tait's Mag.* III. 563 Sweet nestling cottages and villaettes upon the shrubby braes. 1862 W. H. RUSSELL *Diary North & South* (1863) I. 274 Pretty villarettes [*sic*] in charming groves of magnolia, orange-trees, and lime oaks. 1865 C. M. YONGE *Clever Woman of Family* I. vii. 156 My sister lives..at Little Worthy, the next parish... It has a railroad in it, and the cockneys have come down on it and '*villafied' it. 1884 *Harper's Mag.* Aug. 338/1 [The château] has..been.. restored and villafied. 1887 *Oxford Mag.* 9 Mar. 129 A railway which would villa-fy the shores of Rydal.

villadom ('vɪlədəm). [f. VILLA + -DOM.] The world of villas; suburban villas or their residents collectively.

1880 *Macm. Mag.* May 76 Respectable and well-to-do villadom in the suburban counties. 1888 EARL OF DESART *Herne Lodge* I. i. 1 Oases in the desert of gorgeous villadom. 1897 S. S. SPRIGGE *Life Wakley* xxv. 233 The street still reserves many of the features of suburban villadom.

attrib. 1898 *Daily News* 2 Mar. 5/6 The roads..look to be of the lower villadom type.

'villaed, *a.* [f. VILLA + -ED².] Covered with villas.

1791 A. SEWARD *Let.* 30 July (1811) II. xxix. 95 A pretty little lawn..admits the near hill, so magnificently villaed. 1937 G. GREENE *Nineteen Stories* (1947) 51, I had forgotten too the turning to the left up a steep, villaed hill.

Villafranchian (vɪlə'fræŋkɪən), *a. Geol.* [ad. F. *villafranchien* (L. Pareto 1865, in *Bull. Soc. Géol. de France* XXII. 262), f. the name of *Villafranca* d'Asti in N. Italy, in the vicinity of which exposures of this series occur: see -IAN.] Of, pertaining to, or designating a stratigraphical stage in Europe variously assigned to the Upper Pliocene and the Lower Pleistocene (see quots.). Freq. *absol.*

1893 A. GEIKIE *Text-bk. Geol.* (ed. 3) 1016 (*table*) Villafranchian. 1955 G. G. WOODFORD tr. *M. Gignoux's Stratigraphic Geol.* x. 558 From the viewpoint of evolution of mammalian faunas, the Burdigalian..and Villafranchian mark important changes. 1972 *Gloss. Geol.* (Amer. Geol. Inst.) 778/2 *Villafranchian*, European stage: lower Pleistocene... It is the terrestrial equivalent (in France and Italy) of the marine Calabrian. Before 1948, it was used for the latest division of the Pliocene. 1973 *Nature* 15 June 391/2 Recent data have shown that the continental type Villafranchian is essentially late Pliocene (pre-Calabrian). 1974 *Encycl. Brit. Micropædia* X. 436/3 It is likely that the Villafranchian includes within it the Plio-Pleistocene boundary. *Ibid. Macropædia* XIV. 568/2 The Villafranchian fauna was..greatly modified by extinctions and new additions.

village ('vɪlɪdʒ), *sb.* Forms: 4- **village**, 5 **vylage, villach-**, 5-6 **vyllage**, 5-7 **vilage**, 6 **wylage**, *Sc.* **willage, -aige, welage**; also *pl.* 6 **vyllagies**, *Sc.* **willagies**. [a. OF. *village, vilage* (mod.F. *village*), = Pr. *vilatge*, Sp. *village*, Pg. *villagem* (fem.), It. *villaggio*:—L. *villāticum*, neut. sing. of *villāticus* of or pertaining to a villa, f. *villa* VILLA: see -AGE. Cf. late L. *villagium, vilatgium.*]

1. a. A collection of dwelling-houses and other buildings, forming a centre of habitation in a country district; an inhabited place larger than a hamlet and smaller than a town, or having a simpler organization and administration than the latter. (Cf. the note to TOWN *sb.* 4.)

c 1386 CHAUCER *Pard. T.* 225 Henne oure a myle, withinne a greet village. *a* 1400 *Sqr. lowe Degre* 491 He had not ryden but a whyle,..Or he was ware of a vyllage. 1422 YONGE tr. *Secreta Secret.* 184 A Candrede in frensh and in Irysh, is a Porcion of grovnde that may contene an hundrid villachis. 1477 *Rolls of Parlt.* VI. 184/1 In any Toune or other village not corporat. *c* 1515 *Cocke Lorell's B.* 14 They sayled England thorowe and thorowe, Vyllage, towne, cyte, and borowe. 1573 TUSSER *Husb.* (1878) 85 Much carting, ill tillage, makes som to flie village. 1600 SHAKS. *A. Y. L.* III. iii. 60 A wall'd Towne is more worthier then a village. 1600 J. PORY tr. *Leo's Africa* VII. 287 A large and ample village containing to the number of sixe thousand or mo families. 1617 MORYSON *Itin.* I. 51, I remember not to haue seene a more pleasant village than this [the Hague]. 1667 MILTON *P.L.* IX. 448 Forth issuing on a Summers Morn to breathe Among the pleasant Villages and Farmes,..The smell of Grain. 1725 WATTS *Logic* II. iii. §4 Consider also, that..the Customs of different Towns and Villages in the same Nation, are..contrary to each other. 1770 GOLDSM. *Des. Village* 1. 1806 *Gazetteer Scot.* (ed. 2), *Wallacetown*; a thriving and populous village in Ayrshire... The village nearly joins to the Newtown of Ayr, and contains about 960 inhabitants. 1860 MILL *Repr. Govt.* (1865) 115/1 A mere village has no claim to a municipal representation. 1882 T. COAN *Life in Hawaii* 43 When the meeting closed at one village, most of the people ran on to the next.

transf. 1604 E. G[RIMSTONE] *D'Acosta's Hist. Indies* II. vi. 94 There are whole villages of these Vros inhabiting in the Lake in their boates of Totora, the which are tied together and fastened to some rocke.

phr. 1770 *Gentl. Mag.* XL. 559 To express the Condition of an Honest Fellow and no Flincher, under the Effects of good Fellowship, he is said to..Come home by the Villages, this is Provincial, when a man comes home by the fields he meets nobody, consequently is sober, when he comes home by the Villages, he calls first at one house, then at another, and drinks at all.

b. Applied jocularly to a large town or city, esp. London.

1825 C. M. WESTMACOTT *Eng. Spy* I. 129, I used to keep a good prad here for a bolt to the village. ?*a* 1860 DU MAURIER in Moscheles *In Bohemia* (1897) 124 Living with Henley, No. 85, Newman Street... This is a very jolly little village, and I wish you were over here. 1860 HUGHES *Tom Brown at Oxf.* xxviii, You had much better come up to the little village at once, Brown, and stay there while the coin lasts. 1874 *Slang Dict.* 334 Birmingham is called 'the hardware village'.

c. *Cambr. slang.* (See quot.)

1865 *Slang. Dict.* 266 A Cambridge term for a disreputable suburb of that town, viz., Barnwell, generally styled 'the village'.

d. *U.S.* A minor municipality with limited corporate powers (see quots.).

1888 BRYCE *Amer. Commw.* II. II. xlviii. 240 A minimum population of three hundred, occupying not more than two square miles in extent, may by popular vote become incorporated as a 'village'. *Ibid.* 247 Of these villages and other minor municipalities there are various forms in different States. Ohio, for instance, divides her municipal corporations into (*a*) cities,..(*b*) villages, with two classes, the first of from 3000 to 5000 inhabitants, the second of from 200 to 3000,..and (*c*) hamlets.

e. A small self-contained district or community within a city or town; *spec.* †(*a*) see sense 1 c; (*b*) (with capital initial) = GREENWICH VILLAGE.

1865 [see sense 1 c]. [1924: implied in *Greenwich Villager* s.v. GREENWICH VILLAGE.] 1929 E. WILSON *I thought of Daisy* i. 16 Sue Borglum's pleasantry had been in the vein of the Village; Daisy's was in the taste of Broadway. 1931, etc. [see GREENWICH VILLAGE]. 1949 M. ALLINGHAM *More Work for Undertaker* xii. 156 London is made up of many villages. 1952 *N.Y. Times* 17 Aug. VIII–IX. 1W/5 (*caption*) Sketch of section of..cooperative multi-family for Holliswood, Queens, to be known as Hilltop Village. 1971 A. THORBURN *Planning Villages* iv. 24 The word 'village' has a pleasant and attractive connotation for most of us, sufficiently so for it to be borrowed by many estate agents regardless of the context, and to be applied to self-contained neighbourhoods in towns (e.g. at Banbury and Washington, Co. Durham). 1975 *Harper's & Queen* June 35/1 Hampstead—the loveliest of London's historical 'villages'. 1977 *Guardian Weekly* 25 Sept. 8/3 They call it a village but Skokie is geographically a middle-income suburb of Chicago with a population of 70,000. 1979 M. MCMULLEN *But Nellie was so Nice* I. iv. 23 She had grown up in the Village, on West Ninth Street between Fifth and Sixth.

2. The inhabitants or residents of a village; the villagers.

a 1529 SKELTON *Agst. Garnesche* iv. 25 The corte, the contre, wylage, and towne, Sayth..Of all prowde knauys thow beryst the belle. 1770 GOLDSM. *Des. Vill.* 207 The village all declar'd how much he knew. 1820 COMBE *Syntax, Consol.* I. (Chandos) 138 The Village on their Pastor gaz'd, At once afflicted and amaz'd. 1864 TENNYSON *Aylmer's F.* 35 A sleepy land,..Where almost all the village had one name.

3. *transf.* (from 1). A small group or cluster of the burrows of prairie-dogs. Cf. TOWN *sb.* 7 b.

1808 PIKE *Sources Mississ.* II. (1810) 156 *note*, The Wishtonwish of the Indians, prairie dogs of some travellers, ..reside on the prairies of Louisiana in towns and villages. 1814 BRACKENRIDGE *Jrnl.* in *Views Louisiana* 239, I happened on a village of barking squirrels, or prairie dogs. 1835 W. IRVING *Tour Prairies* xxxii. 295, I learned that a burrow, or village, as it is termed, of prairie dogs had been discovered.

4. *attrib.* and *Comb.* a. Simple attrib. passing into adj., = of or pertaining to, characteristic of, a village or villages; living in or belonging to a village; rural, rustic.

Freq. in poetry from the early 18th c.

1585 T. WASHINGTON tr. *Nicholay's Voy.* III. xiii. 95 The Voinuchz or Græcian village men. 1594 SHAKS. *Rich. III*, V. iii. 209 The early Village Cock Hath twice done salutation to the Morne. 1608 TOPSELL *Four-f. Beasts* 160 Of the Village dog or house-keeper. 1613 SHAKS. *Hen. VIII*, II. iv. 159 Enemies, that know not Why they are so; but like to Village Curres, Barke when their fellowes doe. 1634 MILTON *Comus* 346 Might we but hear..Or sound of pastoral reed.., or village cock Count the night watches to his feathery Dames. 1636 MASSINGER *Duke of Florence* II. iii. sig. E1, 'Tis a plaine Village Girle Sir, but obedient. 1697 DRYDEN *Ded. Æneis* Ess. (ed. Ker) II. 233 Those village words, as I may call them, give us a mean idea of the thing. 1703 ROWE *Fair Penit.* II. i, Faithful as the simple Village Swain. 1770 GOLDSM. *Des. Vill.* 327 She once, perhaps, in village plenty blest, Has wept at tales of innocence distrest. 1779 *Mirror* No. 42 ¶4 The village-surgeon being then absent. 1783 CRABBE *Village* II. 2 No longer truth..disdain, But own the Village Life a life of pain. 1803 G. COLMAN *John Bull* IV. ii. 46 One of the prettiest little village-churches you ever saw in your life. 1813 SCOTT *Rokeby* V. xxv, But village notes could ne'er supply That rich and varied melody. 1817 —— *Rob Roy* I. v. 111 The domestic chaplain, the village doctor.. and my uncle. 1818 T. G. FESSENDEN *Ladies Monitor* 124 Learning should never pose a woman's head,..Whose wealth and beauty sanction higher aims, Than those of village-school instructing aims. 1824 M. R. MITFORD *Our Village* I. 6 The village shop, like other village shops, multifarious as a bazaar; a repository for bread, shoes, tea, cheese..for every thing, in short. 1837 HT. MARTINEAU *Soc. Amer.* III. 91 Much might be said of village manners in America. 1841 DICKENS *Barnaby Rudge* xxv. in *Master Humphrey's Clock* III. 74 They hurried through the village street. 1842 TENNYSON *Poems* II. 201 He is but a landscape-painter, And a village maiden she. 1843 *Cumberland Pacquet* 1 Aug. 3/1 His [*sc.* a raven's] masterpiece was his correct repetition of the Lord's prayer; which..would have done no discredit to many a village schoolmaster. 1847 C. BRONTË *Jane Eyre* III. v. 121 To be a village-schoolmistress, free and honest. 1852 DICKENS *Bleak Ho.* (1853) vii. 61 A dark-eyed, dark-haired, shy, village beauty comes in. 1852 THACKERAY *Esmond* I. ii. 58 The village people began to be reconciled presently to their lady. 1853 C. M. YONGE *Heir of Redclyffe* I. vi. 94 A village boy, whom he caught misusing a poor dog. 1854 —— *Heartsease* I. i. 2 A party of village children..gathering cowslips. 1855 MRS. GASKELL *North & South* I. ii. 27 Mr. Hale..was anxious for the village postman, whose summons to the household was a rap on the back-kitchen window-shutter. *Ibid.* II. xxi. 281 The house fronted the village green. 1859 GEO. ELIOT *Adam Bede* I. ii. 28 Mr Rann's leathern apron and subdued griminess can leave no one in any doubt that he is the village shoemaker. *Ibid.* II. xvii. 5 That village wedding..where an awkward bridegroom opens the dance with a high-shouldered, broad-faced bride. *Ibid.* xviii. 36 An experienced eye would have fixed on him at once as the village blacksmith. 1860 in F. Galton *Vac. Tour.* (1861) 114 The literati of the southern Slaves are not to be found among a higher class than the village clergy, and masters of village-schools. 1860 C. M. YONGE *Hopes & Fears* I. viii. 316 The apartment was not much behind that at the village inn at Hiltonbury. *Ibid.* II. xviii. 347 It was..interesting to observe his impression of the English village-life at Hiltonbury. 1861 —— *Young Step-Mother* v. 58 The pleasures to which he had been introducing Gilbert, were not merely..the rabbit-shooting and rat-hunting of the farm, nor even the village cricket-match. 1871 MAINE (*title*), Village-Communities in the East and West. *c* 1873 C. RHODES *Let.* in J. Flint *Cecil Rhodes* (1974) ii. 24 Whether I become the village parson..remains to be proved. 1873 W. D. HOWELLS *Chance Acquaintance* 38 Under the porch of the village store some desolate idlers.. had clubbed their miserable leisure. 1883 SMILES in *Longm. Mag.* June 159 He was followed to the grave by a large number of the village labourers. 1890 W. BOOTH *In Darkest England* II. iii. 138 Every effort will be made to establish village industries, and I..hope..we may be able to restore some of the domestic occupations which steam has compelled us to confine to the great factories. 1891 J. L. KIPLING *Beast & Man in India* viii. 194 The village Elders stand before him with joined hands to learn his Lordship's commands. *Ibid.* xii. 316 The Eastern cat..is used in a frequently-quoted saying about doubtful matters. 'If the Punchayat (village council) says it's a cat, why, cat it is.' 1892 C. M. YONGE *Old Woman's Outlook* 167 The village shopkeeper, the maker of the 'vinosity' bread. 1894 KIPLING *Second Jungle Bk.* (1895) 34 As soon as the villagers saw the smoke in the deserted shrine, the village priest climbed up..to welcome the stranger. 1895 C. M. YONGE *Long Vacation* i. 5 An expedition to play the zither and sing at a village fête. 1907 G. B. SHAW *Major Barbara* 148, I myself have had a village idiot exhibited to me as something irresistibly funny. 1912 R. MARSH *Judith Lee* i. 10 Dickson was at my bedside..and Pierce, the village policeman. 1913 CHESTERTON *Victorian Age in Lit.* ii. 143 Hardy became a sort of village atheist brooding and blaspheming over the village idiot. 1915 J. BUCHAN *Salute to Adventurers* i. 9 She was presently driven out of the place by..the baillie, and the village dogs. 1920 'O. DOUGLAS' *Penny Plain* xxv. 296 The village women, with little girls in clean pinafores clinging to their skirts. 1923 M. KENNEDY *Ladies of Lyndon* ii. 70 I'm afraid..that Modern Art wouldn't be quite suitable... It's only simple village folk, Mr. Ervine. *Ibid.* 96 The Village Room is quite two miles off. 1924 H. DE SÉLINCOURT *Cricket Match* i. 10 Down by the Village Room, where pictures are shown on Friday evenings..and into the village square again. *Ibid.* ii. 27 Best cricket going, village cricket. 1926 L. ELMHIRST in M. Yonge *Elmhirsts of Dartington* (1982) vi. 138 Like the village community of earlier times,..the school community..must engage in many practical enterprises. 1929 C. DAY LEWIS *Transitional Poem* II. 24 It is high time to renounce This village idiocy. **1930** K. Boyle *Plagued by Nightingale* (1931) xi. 87 Tomorrow was the village *fête*. **1930** A. P. Herbert *Water Gipsies* xxiii. 350 She went many times..to the Chiswick Church in the little old village street beside the river. **1932** L. Golding *Magnolia Street* I. vi. 107 He would put up at the village pub until the moment to pounce was due. **1933** A. Thirkell *High Rising* i. 25 She had formed a habit of ordering groceries..on a gigantic scale, from the village store. **1939** L. Bemelmans *Life Class* III. v. 246 From the railroad station came crates and boxes with materials from New York and Vienna; the village children's hair was full of excelsior as they helped unpack them. **1939** F. Thompson *Lark Rise* x. 186 'Everybody who was anything'..kept a maid..stud grooms' wives, village schoolmasters' wives. *Ibid.* xii. 225 The position of a village schoolmistress was a trying one socially. **1942** M. Cable *Gobi Desert* 122 To buy the printed likeness of the kitchen god at a village fair. **1943** A. Christie *Moving Finger* vii. 82 Emily Barton..has a mental picture of men as..smoking cigars, and in the intervals dropping out to do a few seductions of village maidens. **1948** F. Thompson *Still glides Stream* ii. 18 At that time village houses had no numbers or names. **1949** D. Smith *I capture Castle* i. 5 He does nothing but read detective novels from the village library. **1950** *New Yorker* 23 Sept. 66/3 A lively, exalted young novice..was formerly a village schoolteacher. **1951** R. Firth *Elements of Social Organization* iv. 134 Such behaviour is a function of the social structure, with its emphasis on the village community and the kinship group. **1952** M. Laski *Village* i. 12 The village boys and girls still danced sedately. *Ibid.* iii. 52 The village people..normally had their radios on all day. **1953** G. E. & K. R. Fussell *Eng. Countrywoman* iv. 123 Farmhouse and cottage furniture was made by the village carpenter. **1953** S. Bedford *Sudden View* I. x. 94 In France, village *curés*..exact fees from their parishioners. **1954** A. Seton *Katherine* vii. 119 Celibacy might be asked of monk or friar but hardly from..a village parson. **1957** J. Cary in R. S. Surtees *Mr. Sponge's Sporting Tour* (1958) p. xi, The few hundred who..had been able to ..travel farther than the county town or the village fair. **1957** 'M. M. Kaye' *Shadow of Moon* xxi. 309 He called upon the Kotwal—the village headman. **1960** J. R. Ackerley *We think the World of You* 40 The small blank eyes mooned stolidly at me..it was like being gaped at by the village idiot. **1967** A. Cordell *Bright Cantonese* ii. 28 The village elders were waiting for me on the little airstrip at Hoon. **1969** R. Blythe *Akenfield* ii. 60 Texts in glass cases hang outside.. and can be read by passengers in the village bus, which just stops there. *Ibid.* iv. 89 When the village shopkeeper sends things to out-of-the-way cottages..he's going to charge.. something for the service. **1969** *Listener* 12 June 814/1 The village chief himself asked us to a dinner of dried deer and shrimp crackers. **1971** O. Norton *Corpse-Bird Cries* i. 3 Most of the fishing would probably be done in the company of a village bobby. *Ibid.* v. 96 Such a simple life, isn't it, being a village copper? **1973** *Stornoway Gaz.* 13 Jan. 7/2 The annual general meeting of Portree Village Council was held in the Portree Hotel, at which there was a fairly large attendance. *a* **1974** R. Crossman *Diaries* (1976) II. 157 Then we rushed him down to the village hall, which has been built by the energy of Len Edwards, our remarkable local inventor of laundry machinery. **1975** *Country Life* 9 Oct. (Suppl.) 26/1 (Advt.), Family house on village green. **1976** 'H. Carmichael' *False Evidence* ii. 25 The cottage was set in restful countryside, a quarter of a mile from the village inn. **1976** P. R. White *Planning for Public Transport* vii. 142 Local village shops may also substitute for day-to-day needs. **1978** P. Van Greenaway *Man called Scavener* ii. 21 Unhonoured assignations with village beauties. **1978** J. Porter *Dead Easy for Dover* ii. 25 We had the funeral on the Saturday... The village church was absolutely packed. **1978** 'J. Melville' *Axwater* ii. 57 The village girls used to go there at the new moon and wish. Like a wishing well. **1979** 'S. Kemp' *Goodbye Pussy* x. 125 The village doctor.. saw her once in a while for measles and mumps. **1980** G. Sims in *Winter's Crimes 12* 149 The village Postmistress, who delighted in gossip. **1981** M. Warner *Joan of Arc* i. 20 Women who..were ducked in village ponds to find out whether or not they were witches. **1981** E. Clark *Send in Lions* xiii. 121 The village postman..had seen Kemp that morning. **1981** A. Edwards *Sonya* xi. 175 On Christmas Eve the village priests came to hold a vespers service. **1981** C. Miller *Childhood in Scotland* 63 We wore heavy black boots made by the village shoemaker. **1983** *Times* (Saturday Suppl.) 29 Jan.–4 Feb. 4/4 (*caption*) Rekindling village life in Chelsea.

†**b.** Attrib., = village-like; of the size or constitution of a village. *Obs.*⁻¹

1642 Jer. Taylor *Episc.* (1647) 89 In populous Cityes, not in village Townes, for no Bishops were ever suffered to be in village Townes.

c. In objective and obj. genitive, instrumental, locative, or other combs., as ***village-founder***, ***-haunter***; ***village-based***, ***-born***, ***-dwelling***, ***-lit***, ***-made***, adjs.

1649 G. Daniel *Trinarch., Hen. V*, ccxcix, These.. wrought more With village-haunters. **1852** Badger *Nestorians* I. 343 The Jès were all *Igrâwy*, that is village-dwelling Arabs, who cultivate the soil. **1872** Howells *Wedd. Journ.* (1892) 270 The landscape of village-lit plain and forest-darkened height. **1880** *Cornh. Mag.* Jan. 35 The local hero or eponymous village-founder was the man who cut down the jungle. **1883** R. Jefferies *Nature near London* 221 Each village-made crook had an individuality, that of the blacksmith. **1891** *Daily News* 11 Sept. 3/4 The many village-born men in towns. **1976** P. R. White *Planning for Public Transport* vii. 140 In this situation the village-based independent may score over the larger operator.

d. Special combs.: **village burrow**, = sense 3; **village butler** *Cant* (see quot.); **village college** (see quot. 1981); **village constable**, (*a*) *Hist.*, in Papua, a local man through whom the orders of the Australian administration were transmitted; (*b*) a police constable stationed in a village; **village gossip**, (*a*) the idle talk of a village (see GOSSIP *sb.* 4); (*b*) a woman who gossips (see GOSSIP *sb.* 3); **village Hampden**, a person like John Hampden (1594–1643), one without means or influence who opposes a powerful local person or organization (in imitation of quot. 1751); **village-house**, the chief house of a Malay village; **village pump**, a village's communal water pump; freq. used allusively (cf. *parish pump* s.v. PARISH *sb.* 7 b).

1893 W. H. Hudson *Idle Days in Patagonia* i. 11 Like.. the vizcacha's village burrows, and the beaver's dam, it is made to last for ever. **1795** Potter *Dict. Cant* (ed. 2), *Village butlers*, old thieves, that would rather steal a dishclout than discontinue the practice of thieving. **1924** H. Morris (*title*) The village college. **1981** D. Rowntree *Dict. Educ.* 342 *Village colleges*, a UK scheme in community education initiated in rural Cambridgeshire in the 1930s, with a number of colleges each serving a village not only as a secondary school but also as a cultural and recreational centre for old and young alike out of school hours. The scheme was later adopted by several other largely-rural counties. **1924** 'R. Daly' *Outpost* xxvii. 259 'They say they will have no chief but the village-constable,' he said, 'and no sorcery except that of the white man.' **1943** F. Thompson *Candleford Green* vii. 115 The village constable was still regarded by many as a potential enemy. **1965** *Austral. Encycl.* VI. 468/1 In the period before World War II, for the carrying out of policy, Administrations to some extent relied on selected headmen (called luluais) in New Guinea and on village constables in Papua. **1981** B. Knox *Killing in Antiques* viii. 166 The village constable got there in ten minutes flat then ran for his car radio. **1847** C. M. Yonge *Scenes & Characters* xvi. 201 Jane sought for amusement in village gossip. **1952** M. Laski *Village* ix. 146 He'd tell her the village gossip. **1972** P. D. James *Unsuitable Job for Woman* iv. 143 The confiding relish of a village gossip about to relate the latest scandal. **1751** Gray *Elegy* 8 Some Village-Hampden that with dauntless Breast The little Tyrant of his Fields withstood. **1857** C. M. Yonge *Dynevor Terrace* I. i. 3 He stalked along like a village Hampden, muttering, 'The old tyrant shall see whether I'm to be trampled on!' **1957** D. Piper *English Face* iv. 111 Many of Johnson's portraits have now lost their names..yet some of them no doubt were 'village Hampdens'. **1978** A. Sanders *Victorian Historical Novel* i. 23 Reade is not mourning the silence of village Hampdens, for..he is aspiring to a history which is 'familiar rather than heroic'. **1862** S. St. John *Life Forests Far East* I. 7 A passage raised on posts three feet above the ground, led to the great village-house. **1925** V. Woolf *Common Reader* 112 The talk of old women round the village pump. **1953** G. E. & K. R. Fussell *Eng. Countrywoman* vi. Plate 48 (*caption*) The village pump at Fressingfield, Suffolk: still used. **1955** G. Gorer *Exploring Eng. Character* iv. 61 What a 20-year-old Hereford student calls 'the proverbial "village pump" attitude and conflicts' seems to bedevil the life of many. **1978** *Listener* 6 July 27/2 Officially, the village of Montaillou was subject to the bailiff of the local count of Foix... But Professor Ladurie is able to tell us about the exercise..of authority at the level of the village pump.

e. (With capital initial.) Of, pertaining to, or characteristic of Greenwich Village. *U.S.*

1950 T. Sterling *House without Door* iv. 41 She's not a Village artist... She was very wealthy once. **1979** M. McMullen *But Nellie was so Nice* I. i. 7 He wore a sort of Village uniform—corduroys and a turtle-necked dark jersey.

Hence **'village** *v. intr.*, (*a*) to settle down to a villeggiatura; (*b*) to visit a village in a pastoral capacity. **'villagedom**, the condition or status of a village; also, the system of village communities. **'villageful**, as many as a village contains; the whole of the people of a village. **'villagehood**, = *villagedom*. **'villageless** *a.*, having no village. **vi'llageous** *a.*, of or concerned with villages or village-life. †**'villageship**, ? a village community. **'villageward(s** *advs.*, in the direction of the village. **'villagism**, a mode of expression usual in villages; a rustic phrase.

1819 Byron *Let. to Hoppner* 6 June, I shall go back to Venice before I *village on the Brenta. **1871** F. Kilvert *Diary* 24 Feb. (1977) 130 Villaging about to Mrs Jones at the Infant School, Jo Phillips and Margaret Griffith. **1981** 'M. Innes' *Lord Mullion's Secret* 27 The Vicar of Mullion, an old man given to antique usages, sometimes described himself as having been 'villaging'—by which he meant going round the cottagers and chatting them up. **1867** McDowall *Hist. Dumfries* xiii. 144 William I. raised it [Dumfries] from humble *villagedom to be one of the King's own burghs. **1881** F. T. Palgrave *Visions Eng.* 4 O'er the land is wrought The happy villagedom by English tribes From Elbe and Baltic brought. *c* **1890** Stevenson *In South Seas* IV. (1900) 312 A *villageful of gay companions. **1897** Mary Kingsley *W. Africa* 401 They come down in villagefuls among the older tribes. **1890** *Murray's Mag.* May 662 Caudebec is only redeemed from pure *villagehood by its possession of a Mayor. **1889** Hissey *Tour in Phaeton* 169 An old and lonely country church, standing by itself, *villageless, on rising ground. **1858** Thoreau *Lett.* (1865) 171 Let it be a local and *villageous book. **1762** tr. *Busching's Syst. Geog.* IV. 72 The town contains some corporations of villages or *villageships. **1883** *Harper's Mag.* Sept. 493/2 We strolled *villageward. **1884** May Crommelin *Brown-Eyes* xix, Then the two groups..went back villagewards. **1772** Nugent *Hist. Fr. Gerund* VI. 169 To say, 'Command me, in every thing,' they would think a vulgarity and *villagism.

'village-like, *a.* [f. VILLAGE *sb.*] Like or resembling a village or that of a village.

1838 Ht. Martineau *West. Trav.* I. 251 The village-like character of some of the arrangements at Washington. **1840** Arnold *Hist. Rome* (1846) II. xxxv. 437 They lived mostly in villages, or in small village-like towns. **1864** A. McKay *Hist. Kilmarnock* 186 The town no longer presented a village-like aspect.

'villager. [f. VILLAGE *sb.* + -ER¹.] One who lives in a village; now usually, a working-class inhabitant or native of a village.

1570 Levins *Manip.* 80 A villager, *villicus*. **1601** Shaks. *Jul. C.* I. ii. 172 Brutus had rather be a Villager, Then to repute himselfe a Sonne of Rome Vnder these hard Conditions. **1634** Milton *Comus* 166 Som harmles Villager Whom thrift keeps up about his Country gear. **1718** Rowe tr. *Lucan* I. 59 No chearful Maid nor Villager is seen. **1752** Young *Brothers* II. i, Each villager Is queen of her affections. **1796** Morse *Amer. Geog.* II. 47 Vast districts, which the nearest villagers took possession of. **1841** Lytton *Nt. & Morn.* I. i, The desolate parsonage was committed to the charge of one of the villagers. **1876** Bancroft *Hist. U.S.* IV. i. 314 All Frenchmen, alike townspeople and villagers, were free.

transf. **1634** W. Wood *New Eng. Prosp.* (1865) 36 These waterie villagers [= fish] with thousands more, Doe passe and repasse neare the verdant shore.

Hence **'villageress**, a female villager, a village girl or woman.

1873 M. Collins *Miranda* II. 22 The villageresses were terribly jealous at first. **1894** A. D'Heristal *Discord. Life* 101 She was so indifferent about what the squiresses and villageresses might say about her.

villagery ('vɪlɪdʒrɪ, 'vɪlɪdʒərɪ). Also 6 **villagree**. [f. VILLAGE *sb.* + -(E)RY.] Villages collectively.

Now chiefly as an echo of the Shaksperian passage.

1590 Shaks. *Mids. N.* II. i. 35 Are you not hee, That frights the maidens of the Villagree. **1822** W. Tennant *Thane of Fife* III. l, Crowding they come from all her coasts so rife Of villagery. *a* **1839** Galt *Demon Destiny* (1840) 5 A vista bright appeared Of riant villagery. **1883** *Blackw. Mag.* Jan. 75/2 Unkempt mountain ponies startle the maidens of the villagery.

'villaget. *rare.* [f. as prec. + -ET¹. Cf. older F. *villagette* (Godef.).] A little village.

1781 *Twining Papers* Ser. II. (1887) 81 The mountains.. are, for some distance, so close to the river as scarcely to leave room for even a villaget. **1846** D. W. Pughe *Harlech Castle* 26 Naentwrog is a romantic villaget.

'villagey, *a.* [f. as prec. + -Y.] Somewhat village-like.

1882 *Advance* (Chicago) 21 Dec., Washington Street lays aside entirely the villagey aspect commonly ascribed to it. **1889** A. T. Pask *Eyes Thames* 100 The quiet waterside,..so villagey, and all that kind of thing, you know.

villagio, error or mispr. for *viliago* VILIACO.

1820 Scott *Monast.* xv, Truly, good villagio, your question hath in it somewhat of embarrassment.

villagi'zation. [f. VILLAG(E *sb.* + -IZATION.] In Africa and Asia, concentration of population in villages; the transfer of control of land to villagers communally; in Tanzania, *spec.* = UJAMAA. Cf. BHOODAN.

1963 *Punch* 10 July 42/1 'Villagisation' is the word. **1965** P. Fordham *Geogr. African Affairs* iv. 85 Part of the security measures during the Mau Mau rebellion was the forcible 'villagization' of the Kikuyu and the consolidation of fragmented holdings. **1970** *Guardian Weekly* 22 Aug. 2 The majority of land-owners in more than 140,000 Indian villages have declared themselves in favour of Gramadan (gift of village),..which involves the principle of villagisation (as distinct from nationalisation) of land. **1980** *Sci. Amer.* Sept. 152/1 A campaign of 'villagization' was begun, and over the next several years a massive transfer of rural population was accomplished.

villain ('vɪlən), *sb.* Forms: α. 4 **vyleyn**, 6 **villein(e**; 4 **vilaine**, 4–5 **vylayn** (5 **vil-**), 5–6 **vylayne**; 5 **vyllayn**, 6 **-ayne**, **-aine**, 5–7 **villayne** (7 **-ayn**), 6–7 **villaine**, 7– **villain**. β. 4 **velaun**, 6 **vyl-**, **vilane** (*Sc.* **veill-**, **vill-**, **willane**), **villan**, **wellantt-**, 7 **villiane**, 7–8 **villian**, 8 **villin**. [a. AF. and OF. *vilein*, *vilain*, *villain* (= Prov. *vilan*, It. and Sp. *villano*, Pg. *villão*):—pop.L. **villān-um*, acc. sing. of **villānus* (see VILLAINS *a.*), f. L. *villa* VILLA. See also VILLEIN.]

1. Originally, a low-born base-minded rustic; a man of ignoble ideas or instincts; in later use, an unprincipled or depraved scoundrel; a man naturally disposed to base or criminal actions, or deeply involved in the commission of disgraceful crimes: **a.** Used as a term of opprobrious address.

1303 R. Brunne *Handl. Synne* 11557 Goddys treytour, and ryȝt vyleyn! Hast þou no mynde of Marye Maudeleyn. **1320–30** *Horn Ch.* (Ritson) 857 The begger answered in that tide, Vilaine, cunestow nought ride? *c* **1380** Sir Ferumb. 5471 þanne he cryde and gan to sayn: 'Whar art þow, Charlis, þow vylayn?' **1501** Douglas *Pal. Hon.* I. lvii, Ane me fand, quhilk said, and greit disdenȝeit, 'Auant veillane, thow reclus imperfite'. *c* **1590** Marlowe *Faustus* vi, Villaine haue I not bound thee to tel me any thing? **1596** Shaks. *Tam. Shr.* I. ii. 20 Now knocke when I bid you: sirrah villaine. **1622** Massinger & Dekker *Virg. Martyr* IV. iii, *Theoph.* It matters not, We can discharge this work without his help... *Sap.* Villain! **1663** Cowley *Cutter Coleman St.* v. xii, Villain, Rebel, Traitor, out o' my sight. **1764** H. Walpole *Otranto* i, Presumptuous villain! cried Manfred, dost thou provoke my wrath? **1821** Scott *Kenilw.* xli, Drunken villain,..thy idleness and debauched folly will stretch a halter ere it be long. **1855** Kingsley *Westw. Ho!* v, 'Villain! give me your papers!' cried Amyas.

b. In descriptive use. (Common from *c* 1590.)

α. *c* **1400** *Rom. Rose* 2183 Thise vilayns arn withouten pitee, Frendship, love, and alle bounté. I nyl resseyve unto my servise Hem that ben vilayns of emprise. **1474** Caxton *Chesse* III. iii. (1883) 99 They..answerd to hym that he was a vylayne to requyre & desire of them thynge that was so peryllous. **1483** —— *G. de la Tour* h vij, For he is a chorle and a vylayne that of his mouthe sayth ony vylony. **1509** BARCLAY *Shyp of Folys* (1874) II. 182 In all the worlde nought vyler can I fynde Nor wors, than is a fals unkynde vylayne. *a* **1533** LD. BERNERS *Gold. Bk. M. Aurel.* (1546) E vij b, The greateste vyllany in a villayne is to be gyuen in largesse of lyes. **1590** SHAKS. *Com. Err.* V. i. 29 Thou art a Villaine to impeach me thus, Ile proue mine honor, and mine honestie Against thee presently, if thou dar'st stand. **1624** CAPT. SMITH *Virginia* III. 84 The two most exact villaines in all the Country. **1719** DE FOE *Crusoe* I. (Globe) 260 He told me there were two desperate Villains among them, that it was scarce safe to shew any Mercy to. **1769** *Junius Lett.* xv. (1788) 89 Every villain fancies himself a man of abilities. **1813** BYRON *Corsair* I. xi, He knew himself a villain—but he deem'd The rest no better than the thing he seem'd. *a* **1842** ARNOLD *Hist. Later Rom. Commw.* (1845) II. 56 The soldiers..told him that..if he played the villain he might win the throne. **1869** RUSKIN *Q. of Air* § 128 They are not made villains by the commission of a crime, but were villains before they committed it.

transf. **1691** HARTCLIFFE *Virtues* 241 Thus they slander Human Nature, and make a Villain of it. **1832** *Q. Rev.* Mar. 234 Perchance one hound in ten may throw his tongue as he goes to inform his comrades, as it were, that the villain is on before them.

β. **1535** COVERDALE *Job* xxx. 8 They were the children of fooles & vylanes, which are deed awaye from the worlde. **1570** *Satir. Poems Reform.* (S.T.S.) xiii. 95 Wa worth ȝow Uillanis that slew that Prince maist wise. **1573** *Nottingham Rec.* IV. 154 For be-callyng the Constabelles knaves and wellanttes. **1593** HARVEY *Pierce's Super.* Wks. (Grosart) II. 319 The Straunge Newes of the railing Villan. **1598** B. JONSON *Ev. Man in Hum.* (Q.[1]) v, *Gui.* I obey thee varlet; but for these villianes—. *Mus.* Keepe the peace I charge you sir. **1678** BUNYAN *Pilgr.* I. 132 He hath not been afraid to rail on you, my Lord,..calling you an ungodly Villian. **1704** BLAIR in W. S. Perry *Hist. Coll. Amer. Col. Ch.* I. 132 Several of them of the most noted good preachers he affronted and abused with the most opprobrious & villifying names as Dog, Rogue, Rascal, Villin, Jesuit. **1727** *Philip Quarll* (1816) 66 Those villians had most sacrilegiously rifled and ransacked his habitation.

c. Used playfully, or without serious imputation of bad qualities. Also applied to a woman.

1590 SHAKS. *Com. Err.* I. ii. 19 A trustie villaine sir, that very oft..Lightens my humour with his merry iests. **1601** —— *Twel. N.* II. v. 16 *Enter Maria*... Heere comes the little villaine: How now my Mettle of India? **1606** —— *Tr. & Cr.* III. ii. 35 Ile fetch her; it is the prettiest villaine. **1815** SCOTT *Guy M.* i, Jock, ye villain,..are ye lying routing there, and a young gentleman seeking the way to the Place? **1837** DICKENS *Pickw.* ix, 'Where's that villain Joe?' 'Here I am; but I han't a willin,' replied a voice. It was the fat boy's. **1908** R. BAGOT *A. Cuthbert* xxxiii. 300 If this afternoon's post does not bring me a letter from Jim,..I shall telegraph to the young villain.

d. (Usually with *the*.) The character in a play, novel, etc., whose evil motives or actions form an important element in the plot. Also *transf.*, esp. in phr. ***villain of the piece***.

1822 LAMB *Elia* I. *Old Actors*, The fact is, you do not believe in such characters as Surface—the villain of artificial comedy—even while you read or see them. **1854** A. C. MOWATT *Autobiogr. Actress* vii. 133 Ayesha, *the villain of the piece*,..had received a great wrong. **1867** FREEMAN *Norm. Conq.* I. iv. 252 Arnulf, as usual, appears as the villain of the piece. **1879** D. COOK *Nts. at the Play* (1883) II. 222 Mr. Vezin represented the villain, a welcher, pretending to be a Russian count. **1928** WODEHOUSE *Money for Nothing* ix. 200 I'm sure you're on the right track. This bird Twist is the villain of the piece. **1937** *Discovery* May 163/1 Fascism, in its ultra-national aspect, is the villain of the piece. **1978** P. SUTCLIFFE *Oxf. University Press* v. i. 173 Ernest Barker and others took on Nietzsche and Treitschke, who could be regarded as the ultimate villains of the piece.

e. A professional criminal. *slang.*

1960 [see BOGY[1], BOGEY[1] 4]. **1963** L. DEIGHTON *Horse under Water* xxxi. 125 This villain is doing a nice Cabinet Minister's home. **1975** *Sunday Tel.* 7 Dec. 1/2 A flying squad officer said: 'As far as we know these are no ordinary villains. We believe they are Irish IRA.' **1977** L. MEYNELL *Hooky gets Wooden Spoon* xiii. 156 There'll be a getaway car ..waiting close to the house with a villain in it... I don't like thieving villains.

†**2.** A bird (*esp.* a hawk) of a common or inferior species. *Obs.*

1480 CAXTON *Myrr.* II. viii. 85 Ther ben popengayes..of whom, as men saye, they that haue on eche foot fyue clawes been gentyl, and the vylayns haue but thre. **1575** TURBERV. *Faulconrie* 123 Of all kinde of hawkes.., as Sacres, Gerfalcons, peregrine Falcons, and Vilanes. *Ibid.* 124 The Vyllaine and the Lanerette may be sette vpon the stone incontinently, as soone as they be made.

3. A person or animal of a troublesome character in some respect. Const. *to* with inf.

1895 J. G. MILLAIS *Breath fr. Veldt* (1899) 201 The sable is a villain to run.

4. *Comb.*, as ***villain-like*** adv.

1605 SHAKS. *Lear* v. iii. 98 He..that names me Traitor, villain-like he lies. **1611** —— *Cymb.* v. v. 218 Villain-like, I lye.

villain, variant of VILLEIN.

villain (ˈvɪlən), *a.* Now *rare.* Forms: *α.* 4 vilein, 4–5 vil-, 5 vyleyn, 4 vyl-, 6 vileyne, villeine, 7 -ein; 5–6 vyl-, 6 vilayne, 5–6 vylayn, 6 vylaine, vilane; 5–6 vyllayne, 6 villayne, 6–7 -aine; 5 *Sc.* villayn, 5 *Sc.*, 7– villain. *β.* 5 veleyne, velaine, 6 velayn, velen. [a. AF. and OF. *vilein*, *vilain*: see prec. and cf. VILLAINS *a.*]

†**1.** Deficient in courtesy or good-breeding; boorish, clownish. *Obs.*

1340 *Ayenb.* 194 Zome þer byeþ zuo uyleyne to þe poure huanne hi ham yeueþ enye elmesse..þet wel is worþ þet zeluer. **1390** GOWER *Conf.* I. 319 Will seith..That such an herte is to vilein, Which dar noght love. *c* **1407** LYDG. *Reson & Sens.* 1508 And she [Venus] kan also, in certeyn, Hertys which that be vileyn Disposen hem to gentilesse.

2. Base in character or disposition; given to committing vile or criminal acts.

1340 *Ayenb.* 18 Vor-zoþe he is wel vileyn and ontrewe auoreye his lhord þet alle guod him heþ y-do,..and [he] yelt him kuead uor guod. **1390** GOWER *Conf.* III. 282 And whanne he hadde hem so forlein, As he the which was al vilein, He dede hem out of londe exile. **1447** BOKENHAM *Seyntys* (Roxb.) 226 To a cros of tre..naylyd was he And hangyd up betwyx thevys tweyne As mayster of hem and most veleyne. *c* **1450** *Merlin* xxxiii. 690 Thou art the moste vileyn knyght that euer I mette in my lif. *c* **1489** SKELTON *Death Earl Northumbld.* 24 Vilane hastarddis in their furious tene, Fulfylled with malice of froward entente. *a* **1500–34** *Cov. Corpus Chr. Pl.* I. 802 Owt! velen wrychis, har apon you I cry! **1540–1** ELYOT *Image Gov.* 170 Ye villaine generacion, full of pestiferous malice. **1598** *Min. Archdeaconry Colchester* (MS.) 211 b, He sayd that Thomas Reinoldes, senior, dyd call hym theefe and villaine thefe in the Church. **1605** ROWLANDS *Hell's Broke Loose* (Hunter. Club) 23 So these leawd wretches, sprung from Villain race, That had all Pietie in detestation. **1611** SHAKS. *Cymb.* IV. ii. 71 Soft, what are you That flye me thus? Some villaine-Mountainers? **1727–46** THOMSON *Summer* 269 Where gloomily retired The villain spider lives, cunning and fierce, Mixture abhorred! *c* **1750** SHENSTONE *Love & Hon.* 269 No! may the deep my villain corse devour. **1812** SHELLEY *Mexican* III. 8 Thousands wake to weep Whilst they curse a villain king. **1897** GUNTER *Ballyho Bey* x. 123 Go, leave me, villain-girl!

transf. **1591** SPENSER *Visions Bellay* xii, A troupe of Satyres in the place did rout, Which with their villeine feete the streame did ray.

3. Marked by baseness or depravity; partaking of the nature of villainy.

1340 *Ayenb.* 59 Þe zenne of yelpynge..is wel grat and wel uoul, wel uals and wel vileyn. *c* **1385** CHAUCER *L.G.W.* 1824 (Camb.), Allas of the this was a vileyn ded. **1474** CAXTON *Chesse* III. vi. (1883) 134 To thende that they shold kepe them and defende them fro that vyllayne and horrible synne. **1523** LD. BERNERS *Froiss.* I. lxxvii. 99 God yͤ father glorious be your conduct, and put you out of all vylayne thoughtes. *Ibid.* ccxxix. 308 To wasshe, clens, and purge hym of suche vyllayne dedes as he was gyltye in. **1689** PRIOR *Ep. F. Shephard* 118 When Lobb had sifted all his Text,..'Now to apply,' has plagu'd me more, Than all his Villain Cant before. **1850** TENNYSON *In Mem.* cxi, Narrowness or spite, Or villain fancy fleeting by. **1869** BLACKMORE *Lorna D.* xv, This villain job shall not have ending here.

†**b.** Bringing or casting opprobrium. *Obs.*

1338 R. BRUNNE *Chron.* (1810) 53 He did a grete outrage, His broþer a foule despite, him self vileyn skandre. *c* **1440** *Jacob's Well* 154 A vyleyn woord is scharpere þan a rasour, & more peryschande þan an allys-poynt. *a* **1450** *Knt. de la Tour* (1868) 128 Thre thinges distrained her for to eschewe diuerse plesauncez,..and tho were loue, drede, and shame; ..shame, to be auised and saued from velanie [*read* velaine] reproche. *c* **1530** LD. BERNERS *Arth. Lyt. Bryt.* (1814) 374, I ensure you I wyll shewe him these vylayne wordes that ye say of hym.

4. †**a.** Of occupations: Low, mean. *Obs.*

1456 SIR G. HAYE *Law Arms* (S.T.S.) 114 He suld nocht ..be na stewart, na procuratour, na advocate, or ony othir villayn craft. *a* **1533** LD. BERNERS *Gold Bk. M. Aurel.* (1546) Dd vij, Cursed bee soo vylaine an office.

b. Low or mean in respect of birth or position; belonging to the common herd.

1483 CAXTON *Cato* c v, Thou art of vylayn blood by the fadres syde. *Ibid.* i vj, Thou oughtest not to doubt neyther old nor yonge, pouer ne ryche, ne noble ne vylayne. *c* **1500** in Hazl. *E.P.P.* III. 36 Who can than holde hym selfe fro loue, nother fre nor vilayne? **1513** BRADSHAW *St. Werburge* I. 949 Nother of duke, erle, lorde, by auncetre, But of vylayne people. **1528** ROY *Rede Me* (Arb.) 106 This is a grett presumpcion For a villayne bochers sonne. **1816** SCOTT *Old Mort.* xxxv, Sweeping from the face of the earth some few hundreds of villain churles, who are born but to plough it.

†**c.** Of disposition: Mean-spirited, base. *Obs.*

1509 HAWES *Past. Pleas.* XII. (Percy Soc.) 48 The vylayne courage they do much refuse That is boystous and rude of governaunce. **1534** MORE *Comf. agst. Trib.* III. Wks. 1234/1 That seruante could skante be founden that were of suche an vnkynde vyllayne courage, that [etc.].

5. Of bad quality; vile. *rare.*

1607 COWELL *Interpr.*, *Villein fleeces*, are fleeces of wolle that are shorne from scabbed sheep. **1851** MITCHELL *Fresh Gleanings* 161 And carters shout to their mules in such villain *patois Lyonnais*.

†ˈ**villain**, *v.* *Obs.* Also 5 vileyn-, 6 vilayn-, villan-. [ad. OF. *vilainer*, *vil(l)aner*, etc., f. *vilain* VILLAIN *sb.*]

1. *trans.* To debase or degrade; to insult.

1412–20 LYDG. *Chron. Troy* I. 2492 For..it is to hygh a routhe A man tappere or dare do shewe his head When he hath ones his honour vyllanede. **1475** *Bk. Noblesse* (Roxb.) 74 Suffre ye not the prelates of the Chirche of that lande.. to be oppressed, revaled, ne vileyned. **1532** MORE *Confut. Tindale* Wks. 344/1 When they haue once vilayned the sacrament of matrimonye, then woulde they make vs vyolate the sacrament of the aulter too.

2. To call villain; to address as a villain.

1609 ROWLANDS *Crew Kind Gossips* E 2, Some Rascall told my wife,..And I was villaind for it sound at night.

villainage, var. VILLEINAGE.

ˈ**villaindom.** *rare*[−1]. [f. VILLAIN *sb.*] The class of villains.

1880 W. F. BUTLER *Far Out* 267 In the simple and unlettered Africander the educated villaindom of Europe and America has found a rich field for exploit.

villainess (ˈvɪlənɪs). [f. VILLAIN *sb.* + -ESS.] A female villain. (Common in recent use.)

1586 MARLOWE *1st Pt. Tamburl.* v. ii, My wife, my Queene and Emperesse,..Villanesse to shame, disdaine, and misery. **1865** *Reader* 20 May 563/3 Her villainess is a she-devil. **1872** M. COLLINS *Pr. Clarice* II. vii. 99 He can follow his hero and heroine, his villain and villainess, into holes and corners.

†ˈ**villainist.** *Obs.*[−1] [f. VILLAIN *sb.*] A confirmed villain.

1596 NASHE *Saffron Walden* Wks. (Grosart) III. 66 Some ..glicking Remembrancers (not with the multiplying spirite of the Alchumist, but the villanist).

villainize (ˈvɪlənaɪz), *v.* Also 7–8 villanize, 9 villainise. [f. VILLAIN *sb.*]

1. *trans.* To render villainous; to debase or degrade.

1623 tr. *Favine's Theat. Hon.* III. xii. 487 To blame or abuse Ladies..is..for a man to villanize and shame himselfe. **1700** DRYDEN *Wife of Bath's T.* 405 Were Virtue by Descent, a noble Name Could never villanize his Father's Fame. **1745** LAW *Consid. State World* III. 245 That those Writings which *villanize* Mankind have a pernicious tendency towards propagating and protecting Villany.

2. To treat or revile as a villain.

Cf. VILLAINIZER below.

1857 SIR F. PALGRAVE *Norm. & Eng.* II. 437 Here in Rouen had he been villainized, disgraced, hooted, imprisoned, bullied, degraded.

3. *intr.* To play the villain.

1882 *Echo* 11 Feb. 3 Let us hope that..these gentlemen [*sc.* actors], whose mission it is to dabble in crime.., will in future 'villainise' no more.

Hence ˈ**villainizing** *vbl. sb.* Also ˈ**villainizer**, one who reviles or defames.

1599 SANDYS *Europæ Spec.* (1605) P iij b, What renouncers of God, blasphemers of his onely begotten sonne, villanisers of his Saints. **1678** CUDWORTH *Intell. Syst.* I. v. § 31. 890 The foundation [of the atheistic ethics and politics] is first laid in the villanizing of Humane Nature. **1693** BENTLEY *Serm.* i. 13 In the debasing and villainizing of Mankind to the condition of Beasts.

†ˈ**villainly**, *adv.* *Obs.* Forms: *α.* 4 uilein-, vileyn-, vyleyn-, vilain-, vylaynliche; 4 vilayn-, 5–6 vylayn-, 6 villaynly. *β.* 4 vilanliche, 5 wylanlyche; 4 vilenlych, villenliche, 4 vylenly, 5 velenly. [f. VILLAIN *a.* + -LY[2].] After the manner of a villain; villainously, vilely.

α. *a* **1325** *MS. Rawl. B.* 520 fol. 49 b, *Homsokne*: þat is quite of amerciament for entre of houses uileinliche ant bi-þoute leue aȝen þe kinges pes. **1340** *Ayenb.* 64 Efterward huanne me zuereþ vileynliche by god and by his halȝen. *c* **1380** *Sir Ferumb.* 5345 How wer þou so hardy,..come armed on þy stede,..& þus vylayn[li]che on þy resoun þy message to me abede? **1483** CAXTON *G. de la Tour* e vij b, Within a lytell tyme after she deide vylaynly and sodenly of an euyll deth. *c* **1500** *Melusine* xxi. 130 Perceyue you not how this Dogges oppressen vylaynly these valyaunt & worthy crystens? *a* **1560** PHAER *Æneid* IX. Aa iij b, If but one harme Suffized had their sinne, and not with spyte all female kinds Thus villaynly disdain.

β. *c* **1330** *Arth. & Merl.* 5794 (Kölbing), So þai deden, sikerliche, Defuiland vilanliche, Toward..king Rion. *c* **1380** *Sir Ferumb.* 1825 To..presenty til him with such outrage þay heuedes bi-fore him selue, & so vylenly beode ys message. *c* **1400** *Laud Troy Bk.* 7499 Thow art now dede and ouer-throwen,..Velenly thow hast thi mede. *a* **1450** *Le Morte Arth.* 1156 Thou oughtiste with no Ryghte to gabbe on hym so wylanlyche, thus be-hynde hym, oute of hys syghte.

villainous (ˈvɪlənəs), *a.* Forms: *α.* 4 vylayneus, 5–6 vylaynous, 6 velaynous, vilaynouse; 6 vyllayn-, villayn-, 6– villainous (7 villainus, -einous). *β.* 4, 6–7 vilanous, 5–6 vylanous, 6 -ouse, vilanus, 4, 6–9 villanous (6 -ouse); 5 vilenous(e, 6 villenus, 7–8 -ous; 7 villonous. *γ.* 6 velanus-, velanous, 7 vealinous. [f. VILLAIN *sb.* + -OUS, or ad. OF. *vilenneus* insulting, defamatory.]

1. Of persons: †**a.** Churlish, ill-bred, unmannerly. *Obs. rare.*

13.. *Gaw. & Gr. Knt.* 1497 Ȝe ar stif in-noghe to constrayne wyth strenkþe, ȝif yow lykez, ȝif any were so vilanous þat yow devaye wolde. ? *a* **1366** CHAUCER *Rom. Rose* 178 Ful foule and cherlysshe semed she, And eek vylayneus for to be, And litel coude of norture.

b. Having the character or disposition of a villain; infamously depraved or wicked; vilely criminal.

c **1550** ROLLAND *Crt. Venus* IV. 281 Not for to say, Venus is velanous: Bot that hir warkis may na les be vndone Nor of befoir, bot Vesta is mair Famous. **1570** LEVINS *Manip.* 226 Villanouse, *flagitiosus*. **1596** SHAKS. *1 Hen. IV*, II. iv. 138 There is nothing but Roguery to be found in Villanous man. **1610** HOLLAND *Camden's Brit.* 475 The furious outrage of that most villanous Rebell Ket. **1623** in Foster *Eng. Factories Ind.* (1908) II. 244 A ploott of that vealinous strompitt Nahar Malle. **1698** FRYER *Acc. E. India & P.* 368 They are yet reckoned a Villanous sort of Breed. **1719** DE FOE *Crusoe* II. (Globe) 500 We have not half done yet, villainous Hell-hound Dogs! **1793** MRS. INCHBALD *Ev. One has Faults* III. ii, I repeat, he is the vilest, the most villanous of men. **1839** DARWIN *Voy. Nat.* iv. 83, I should think such a villanous, banditti-like army, was never before collected together. **1855** BREWSTER *Newton* II. xv. 56 The Elector of Hanover, whom the villanous English wished to deprive of the succession to the kingdom. **1869** D. COOK *Nts. at the Play* (1883) I. 116 Mr. Cowper gave a..careful portraiture of the villanous Stukely.

c. Miserable, wretched. *rare*[−1].

1582 STANYHURST *Æneis* II. (Arb.) 45 Oh, quod he, what region shal shrowd mee villenus owtcast?

2. a. Of actions: Of the nature of villainy; marked by depravity or vileness of conduct; deserving severe condemnation on moral grounds.

14.. *Chaucer's L.G.W.* 1824 (Fairf.), Allas of the thys was a vilenouse dede. **1573-80** BARET *Alv.* s.v., A Vilanous and shamefull act. **1599** DALLAM in *Early Voy. Levant* (Hakluyt Soc.) 84 He came but to speake with our Turke aboute their vilanus plott. **1664** H. MORE *Myst. Iniq.* 111 Which Figment is still the more vile, if we consider..with what villainous and barbarous injuries it must necessarily be conceived to be accompanied. **1681** H. HALLYWELL *Melamp.* 80 [They] have incorporated themselves into the Dark Society by all manner of villanous and flagitious actions. **1725** DE FOE *Voy. round World* (1840) 27 If their brutish rage led them to one villanous action, they would soon go on to another. **1772** PRIESTLEY *Inst. Relig.* (1782) I. 127 One villainous action is sufficient to imbitter a man's whole life. **1813** SHELLEY *Q. Mab* IV. 184 Their cold hearts blend Deceit with sternness, ignorance with pride, All that is mean and villanous. **1837** LYTTON *E. Maltrav.* IX. ii, I have done a villanous thing, but I thought it only a clever one. **1846** GREENER *Sci. Gunnery* 153 A villainous system of covering or plating barrels with fine iron, over a body of iron of the most inferior description.

b. Of looks, etc.: Indicative of villainy.

1828 SOUTHEY *Epistle to Allan Cunningham*, I shall show thee, Allan,..an array of villainous visages. **1840** DICKENS *Old C. Shop* xxix, Isaac [had] a very ill-favoured face, and a most sinister and villainous squint. **1841** BORROW *Zincali* I. iv. II. 284 With an expression so extremely villanous, that I felt uneasy. **1863** [see LEER *sb.*[2]].

3. Of words, etc.: Pertaining to or characteristic of a villain; vile, scurrilous; offensively opprobrious or profane.

α. **1470-85** MALORY *Arth.* I. xxvii. 74 The most vylaynous and lewdest message that euer man herd sente vnto a kynge. **1529** MORE *Dyaloge* IV. Wks. 261/2 Thus these wretched heretiques..lay more vilaynouse rebuke to the great maieste of god, than euer any one ribaude layd vnto a nother. **1532** —— *Confut. Tindale* Wks. 602/2 Wee fynde not that he called hym false wretche, nor no suche vylaynous word. *a* **1700** EVELYN *Diary* 28 Apr. 1696, A most villainous reviling book against K. James. **1782** MISS BURNEY *Cecilia* IX. viii, My heart swelled with indignation at so villainous a calumny. **1883** STEVENSON *Treas. Isl.* I. i, He at last broke out with a villainous, low oath.

β. **1523** LD. BERNERS *Froiss.* I. lxvi. 36/2 Whan the other commons sawe that, they began to sterre and sayde to the burgesses many euyll and vylanous wordes. **1559** *Homilies* I. *Agst. Contention* II. (1569) M viij b, Pericles being prouoked to anger with many vilanous wordes, answered not a worde. **1603** SHAKS. *Meas. for M.* V. i. 265 One that hath spoke most villanous speeches of the Duke. **1614** RALEIGH *Hist. World* V. i. 285 Princes doe rather pardon ill deedes, than Villanous words.

†**4. a.** Shameful, atrocious, horrible. *Obs.*

1526 *Pilgr. Perf.* (W. de W. 1531) 301 b, Euer conspyrynge for thy grace the moost vyllaynous & shamefull deth of the crosse. **1529** MORE *Dial. Concern. Heresyes* IV. vii. 106/2 To pyteouse and to abomynable were yt to reherse the vylanouse payne and tormentys that they deuysed on yᵉ sely women. *a* **1533** LD. BERNERS *Huon* lxx. 239 They are worthy to receyue a velaynous dethe. **1610** HOLLAND *Camden's Brit.* 359 Prince Edward..was there put to death and in most shamefull and vilanous maner his branes dashed out. **1616** *Barbour's Bruce* (Hart) 373 As Sir Dauid the good Brechyne..Was put to sa villanous a dead.

†**b.** ***villainous judgement***, a sentence of extreme severity (see quot. 1641) passed on one found guilty of conspiracy or other grave offence.

1607 COWELL *Interpr.*, *Villenous iudgement*..is that which casteth the reproch and shame vpon him against whom it is giuen, as a Conspiritour, &c. **1641** *Termes de la Ley* 264 Villeinous judgment is..that the party found guilty shall lose the benefit of the law,..that his lands, goods & chattels shall be seised into the Kings hands,..and his trees digd up, and his body imprisoned. **1769** BLACKSTONE *Comm.* IV. 136 It now is the better opinion, that the villenous judgment is by long disuse become obsolete; it not having been pronounced for some ages.

5. a. Extremely bad or objectionable; atrocious, detestable.

1596 SHAKS. *1 Hen. IV*, II. i. 15, I thinke this is the most villanous house in al London rode for Fleas. **1598** —— *Merry W.* III. v. 93 There was the rankest compound of villanous smell, that euer offended nostrill. **1607** B. BARNES *Divils Charter* v. ii. K 4, Out vpon thee, thou hast poysoned mee with thy stinking breath or with thy villonous powders. **1638** R. BAKER tr. *Balzac's Lett.* (vol. III) 123 Women are bound,..for the very interest of their beauty, to shun a passion, that makes such villanous faces, and sets so many wrinkles upon their countenances. **1672** MARVELL *Reh. Transp.* I. 5 The Press (that villanous Engine) invented much about the same time with the Reformation. **1706** ADDISON *Rosamond* I. ii, Thou art ugly and old, And a villainous Scold. **1806** J. BERESFORD *Miseries Hum. Life* I. 102 The only place..which by some villainous mischance you did not see. **1821** COBBETT *Rur. Rides* (1885) I. 20, I passed through that villanous hole, Cricklade, about two hours ago. **1853** KANE *Grinnell Exped.* xxvi. (1856) 214 This is the second I have killed with this villainous carbine. **1884** *Chr. World* 25 Sept. 719/2 The weather was villainous. It rained every day.

†**b.** As *adv.* Villainously, vilely. *Obs.*⁻¹

1610 SHAKS. *Temp.* IV. i. 250 We shall loose our time, And all be turn'd to Barnacles, or to Apes With foreheads villanous low.

†**6.** Low or base in respect of social position; servile. *Obs.* (Cf. VILLEIN.)

1607 COWELL *Interpr.* s.v. *Base*, Base tenents be they.. which do to their lords villeinous service. *Ibid.* s.v. *Villenage*, This villanous soccage is to cary the Lords dung into his feilds, to plow his ground [etc.]. **1645** USSHER *Bod. Div.* (1647) 143 The slavish and villanous estate of the parents is communicated unto all their off-spring. **1679** BLOUNT *Anc. Tenures* 155 *note*, I suppose..by *sanguinem suum emere*, was meant, that the Tenant being a Bondman, should buy out his Villainous blood, and make himself a Freeman. **1766** BLACKSTONE *Comm.* II. 62 These were the only free holdings or tenements; the others were villenous or servile.

7. *Comb.*, as ***villainous-looking*** adj.

1777 J. WOODFORDE *Diary* 22 July (1924) I. 209 The Hangman was an old Man and a most villainous looking Fellow indeed. **1842** BORROW *Bible in Spain* vii, They were villainous-looking ruffians. **1844** DICKENS *Pictures fr. Italy* (1846) 163 Seeing nothing but..a villanous-looking shepherd. **1897** MARY KINGSLEY *W. Africa* 271, I must admit my good friend was a villainous-looking savage.

Hence ˈ**villainousness** (Bailey, 1727, vol. II).

villainously (ˈvɪlənəslɪ), *adv.* Forms: (see prec.). [f. prec.] In a villainous manner, in senses of the adj.; atrociously, vilely, detestably.

α. **1484** CAXTON *Fables of Auian* ix, Better is to lyue in pouerte than to deye vylaynously and oppressyd of the ryche. *c* **1489** —— *Blanchardyn* vi. 26 Her true louer, þe whiche..ye haue betrayed & wounded vylaynously. **1555** EDEN *Decades* (Arb.) 86 Howe vylely, vylaynously, and violently he had byn vsed of owre men. **1585** T. WASHINGTON tr. *Nicholay's Voy.* I. xx. 25 They were thus villainously intreted, lying along the ground as halfe desperate. **1639** FULLER *Holy War* III. xvii. 137 His sonne was villainously strangled by Alexius Ducas. **1689** *Lond. Gaz.* No. 2443/3 On Sunday last Sir George Lockhart..was Villaniously [*sic*] Assassinated by one Cheeseley, who Shot him through the Back. **1749** FIELDING *Tom Jones* XVIII. xi, The Man whome Ruin he hath so villainously contrived. **1758** L. TEMPLE *Sketches* (ed. 2) 5 His Verses were what one may call most villainously bad. **1842** BORROW *Bible in Spain* xl, He had a villainously formed head. **1892** A. E. LEE *Hist. Columbus* I. 725 The drainage of the town was villainously bad.

β. **1490** CAXTON *Eneydos* Prol. 10 For a thynge more noble is to dye than vylanously to be subdued. **1533** MORE *Apol.* ix. Wks. 865/2 Agaynste the beste,..these blasphemous heretiques in theyr vngracyouse bookes so vilanouslye ieste and rayle. **1568** GRAFTON *Chron.* II. 355 They set nothing by them, but hated and spake shamefully, and vilanously of them. **1601** SHAKS. *Twel. N.* III. ii. 80 *Maria.* Hee's in yellow stockings. *Sir Toby.* And crosse garter'd? *Maria.* Most villanously. **1631** GOUGE *God's Arrows* III. §60. 296 They had Villanously entreated the Ambassadors..sent unto them. **1825** COBBETT *Rur. Rides* 66 Verily the most villanously ugly spot I ever saw in England. **1863** W. C. BALDWIN *Afr. Hunting* ix. 436, I have been living villanously since the death of my nags.

†ˈ**villains**, *a. Obs.* Forms: α. 4 **vyleyn(y)s, vileins, 4-5 vileyns** (**5 vileynes-**); **4 vilains-, 4-5 velaynes-, 5 vilayn(e)s-, vylayn(e)s, vyllayns, villaynis.** β. **4-5 vylens, vilens** (**5 vyl-, vilenis, vylence, velens-**); **4-5 vilans** (**5 velans, vilance-**), **5-6 vylans,** *Sc.* **welan(y)s, willans, 6 villanes; 5 uelonis, vilonis-, vilonys-, vyloyns-.** [a. OF. *vileins*, *vilains* (nom. sing. masc.):—pop.L. **villānus*: see VILLAIN *sb.* and *a.*] = VILLAIN *a.*, VILLAINOUS *a.*

a. Of actions, speech, etc.

a. **1303** R. BRUNNE *Handl. Synne* 1555 Many tyme a vyleynys [*v.r.* vylens] wurde Gadryþ foule pouþ to hurde. *Ibid.* 1847 For þat yche vyleyns synne, Ys here body partyd a-twynne. *c* **1386** CHAUCER *Melib.* ¶46 (Camb. MS.), He dede neuere synne ne neuere cam there a vileyns word out of his mouth. *c* **1450** *Merlin* ii. 26 Thow..haste putte oure frendes to so vileyns deth. **1456** SIR G. HAYE *Law Arms* (S.T.S.) 116 Quha ever strykis with wappin or othir villaynis manȝe. **1474** CAXTON *Chesse* III. iii. (1883) 97 For a man ought not to demande ner doo to be doon to his frende no vyllayns thynge that ought to be kept secrete.

β. *c* **1340** HAMPOLE *Pr. Consc.* 4412 Bot other þat wille noght do his rede Sal be done to vilans dede. *a* **1400-50** *Alexander* 4164 He..Come to a velans vale þare was a vile cheele. *c* **1400** *Destr. Troy* 527 Voidis me noght of vitius, ne vilans of tunge. *c* **1440** *Alph. Tales* 236 And at þe laste he sulde hafe a vylans dead. *a* **1450** *Knt. de la Tour* (1868) 25 With gret uelonis wordes, dispraising hym. **1460** CAPGRAVE *Chron.* (Rolls) 122 He said vilens wordis ageyn the Seint. **1523** LD. BERNERS *Froiss.* I. xxxiv. 48 He that dyde otherwyse, shulde be reputed as an euyll doer, and for a vylans dede.

b. Of persons.

1390 GOWER *Conf.* I. 28 Rome..laste so Long time amonges the Romeins Til thei become so vileins [etc.]. *c* **1400** tr. *Secreta Secret., Gov. Lordsh.* 104 Man ys hardy as a lyon,..vyleyns and boystous as asse, rebell as a rambe. *c* **1407** LYDG. *Reson & Sens.* 3800 A cowarde and of no renoun, And vileyns of condicion. *c* **1450** *Merlin* vi. 102 Yef he be fool, or fell, or vilenis, ye owe better to suffre hym than eny other. **1470-85** MALORY *Arthur* x. xxii. 450 He is the moost coward and the vylaynst kyng and knyght that is now lyuyng. **1556** OLDE *Antichrist* 92 Their regestres were neuer ful ynough of such myscheuous villanes popes.

†ˈ**villainsly**, *adv. Obs.* Forms: (see prec.). [f. prec.] = VILLAINLY *adv.*, VILLAINOUSLY *adv.*

α. ? *a* **1366** CHAUCER *Rom. Rose* 1498 That he shulde feele ..What sorowe trewe louers maken, That ben so velaynesly forsaken. *c* **1386** —— *Pars. T.* ¶12 Than was his visage.. vileynsly byspit. *c* **1400** LOVE *Bonavent. Mirr.* (1908) 225 Ʒit was hir sorwe moche more, seynge hir maister and lorde so vileynsly ferde with. *c* **1430** *Pilgr. Lyf Manhode* II. c. (1869) 112 Thou shalt neuere keepe thee so wel, that thou ne shalt be vileynesliche treted. **1456** SIR G. HAYE *Law Arms* (S.T.S.) 47 Thai war discomfyte rycht vilaynsly. **1483** CAXTON *Gold. Leg.* 191/3 Whan they had so vylaynsly beten hym they put hym out of the cyte.

β. **1388** WYCLIF *2 Sam.* x. 5 The men weren schent ful vilensly. *a* **1400** *Cast. Love* (Halliwell) 1628 How vylensli he wes ladde ȝet, With crowne of thornes on his hed set. *c* **1425** WYNTOUN *Cron.* IV. 165 þat þe commonys willansly Grewit sulde be throw þar mastry. *Ibid.* v. 1676 þat he..had supprysit hyr welansly. **1460** CAPGRAVE *Chron.* (Rolls) 233 Thei that were his rebelles he killid vilensly. **1470-85** MALORY *Arthur* x. liii. 503 Whanne syre Harre sawe hym doo so vyloynsly, he cryed traytour knyȝt leue of for shame. **1487** *Barbour's Bruce* v. 164 Thai nobill men and thai worthy Ar distroyit so vilonisly! *c* **1500** *Gest Robyn Hode* cxiii. in Child *Ballads* III. 62 The abbot lothely on hym gan loke, And vylanesly hym gan call.

villainy (ˈvɪlənɪ), *sb.* Forms: α. **3-4 vileinie** (**3 uil-**), **4 vileynye, vyleyny(e), vileyne; 4 vylaynye, vilaynie, 5 vilainy.** β. **4 vilani(ie, wilani(e, 6 vilanie, 4-5 vylanye** (**6 -ie**), **4-6 vylany, vilany(e; 4 velani(e, -ije, 4[5 velanye, 4-6 -any** (**5 -ane**), **6 welany; 5 villane, wyllanye,** *Sc.* **willany, 6 vyllany, 6-7 villanie, 6-9 villany** (**7 -ey**). γ. **4 vilenie, -ye, vylenye** (**fyl-**), **4-5 vi-, vyleny, 5 vylney,** *Sc.* **vilne; 5 veleni, -eny; 6 villeny(e, 6-7 -enie.** δ. **4-5 vilonie, -ony(e, 4-6 vylonye, 5 -ony; veloni, velonye, welonye; villonye.** ε. **7 villainie, 7- villainy.** [a. AF. *vile(i)nie*, *vilainye*, *vilanie*, OF. *vileinnie*, *villenie*, *vilanie*, *vilonie*, *vilenie* (so mod.F.), etc., = Pr. *vilania*, *-onia*, Sp., Pg., and It. *villania*, whence also med.L. *villania*: see VILLAIN *sb.* and -Y.

The present spelling was rare before the 18th c. and did not become established until the 19th, when it gradually displaced the more prevalent *villany*.]

1. Action or conduct befitting, characteristic or typical of, a villain; evil or wrongdoing of a foul, infamous, or shameful nature; extreme wickedness on the part of a person in dealing with others.

α. *a* **1225** *Ancr. R.* 216 Lechurs, þet habbeð so uorloren scheome þet ham nis nowiht of scheome, auh secheð hwu heo muwen mest uileinie wurchen. **1297** R. GLOUC. (Rolls) 1329 Vor it is ech prince iwis & king vileinie To defouli is kniȝtes þoru wam he aþ þe maistrie. **1340** *Ayenb.* 18 He is wel vileyn and ontrewe auoreye his lhord,..and yelt him kuead uor guod, and vileynye uor corteysye. **13..** *E.E. Allit. P.* B. 863 Dos away your derf dyn & derez neuer my gestes, Avoy! hit is your vylaynye, ȝe vylen your seluen.

β. *a* **1300** *Cursor M.* 2422 Bot godd hir [kept] þat was hir wit..þat moght naman o licherie Hir body neght wit wilanie. **13..** *E.E. Allit. P.* C. 71 For iwysse hit arn so wykke þat in þat won dowellez, & her malys is so much I may not abide, Bot venge me on hir vilanye & venym bilyue. **1396-7** in *Eng. Hist. Rev.* (1907) XXII. 297 We knowe wel þat euery lesyng opinli prechid turnith him to velanye þat euere was trewe and with oute defaute. *c* **1425** WYNTOUN *Cron.* II. 981 Tenelayus..mad hym cortasse welcummynge. .. Bot he did willany þar agayn: þis Tenelayus he walde haf slayn. *a* **1533** LD. BERNERS *Gold. Bk. M. Aurel.* (1546) E vij b, The greateste vyllany in a villayne is to be gyuen in largesse of lyes. **1538** ELYOT, *Obscœnitas*, villany in actes; rybauldrie. **1595** SHAKS. *John* III. i. 116 Thou little valiant, great in villanie, Thou euer strong vpon the stronger side. **1616** R. C. *Times' Whistle* (1871) 55 From thirst of wealth & golden villany I now am come to brutish gluttonie. **1679** *Hatton Corr.* (Camden) 199 He hath been twice pillor'd, and committed all manner of villaney. *a* **1716** BLACKALL *Wks.* (1723) I. 95 He will hardly ever be able to carry his Matters so cunningly, but that his Villany will at last be discover'd. **1771** *Junius Lett.* liv. (1788) 300 This may be logic at Cambridge,..but among men of sense and honour, it is folly or villany in the extreme. **1841** JAMES *Brigand* iii. 41 There is some mistake here, and I think some villany. **1855** MACAULAY *Hist. Eng.* xii. III. 217 He had been induced, by the villany of Tyrconnel, to trust himself at Saint Germains.

personif. ? *a* **1366** CHAUCER *Rom. Rose* 166 Another image, That Vilanye Y-cleped was, saugh I... Vilanye was lyk somdel That other image [*sc.* Felony]; and..She semed a wikked creature.

transf. and *fig.* **1611** SHAKS. *Cymb.* v. ii. 13 Nothing rowts vs, but The villany of oure feares. **1638** SIR T. HERBERT *Trav.* (ed. 2) 349 Ignorant of the deceits of men, and unused to the villany of powder.

γ. *c* **1315** SHOREHAM III. 328 Ac ys [deadly sin] þat uoule wyl al so To swyche fylenye. **1393** LANGL. *P. Pl.* C. VII. 433 Ich can nouht speke for shame The vylenye of my foule mouþe and of my foule mawe. *a* **1425** *Cursor M.* 4405 (Trin.), Here may men se þe vileny þat he souȝte on his lady. *a* **1450** *Knt. de la Tour* (1868) 36 He and y hadd gret communicacion diuerse tymes, but it was neuer in no ueleni, nor in no euell thought nor in dede. **1582** STANYHURST *Æneis* II. (Arb.) 61 In father his presence with spyghtful villenye cancred, Thee soon that murthrest, my sight with boucherye stayning. **1596** SPENSER *F.Q.* VI. vii. 23 The gentle knight Would not be tempted to such villenie.

δ. *c* **1380** WYCLIF *Tracts* Wks. (1880) 204 To be aschamyd of eche euyl speche, & namely of lecherie & euyl contenaunce of synne & ribaudrie & vilonye. *c* **1430** *How the Good Wife* in *Babees Book* (1868) 38 Kepe þee from synne, fro vilonye, & fro blame. **1485** CAXTON *Chas. Gt.* 44 Who wold haue thought that I shold haue had vylonye of Rolland?

ε. **1605** *1st Pt. Jeronimo* II. iii. 49 O, that villainy should be found in the great Chamber. **1722** WOLLASTON *Relig. Nat.* vi. 133 He may..endeavour to recover what has been by any kind of violence or villainy taken from him. **1772** PENNANT *Tours Scot.* (1774) 10 Murdered by assassins who crossed the moat to perpetrate their villainy. **1819** SHELLEY *Cenci* I. iii. 175 Manhood's purpose stern, And age's firm, cold, subtle villainy. **1843** BETHUNE *Sc. Fireside Stor.* 107 Jenny and his other friends declaimed loudly upon the villainy of Mr. M'Quiddit, in keeping him so long from his own. **1861** GEN. P. THOMPSON *Audi Alt.* cxlvi. III. 133 The same kind of villainy was meditated in China.

b. With *a* and pl., *this, that*, etc. An instance or case of this; a piece of wicked conduct or dealing; a vile act or deed.

13.. *Gaw. & Gr. Knt.* 634 Gawan was for gode knawen, & as golde pured, Voyded of vche vylany, wyth vertuez ennourned in mote. **1377** LANGL. *P. Pl.* B. XVIII. 94 For þis foule vyleynye veniaunce to ȝow alle. **1390** GOWER *Conf.* II.

133 Him thenkth it were a vilenie, Bot he rewarde him for his dede. *c* **1400** *Destr. Troy* 6912 Vlixes.. To venge of þat vilany vili dissirit. **1483** *Cath. Angl.* 400/1 A velany, *dedicus.* **1568** GRAFTON *Chron.* II. 755 Requiryng them therefore to studie how to reuenge and punishe so great a villanie. **1592** KYD *Sp. Trag.* III. viii. 12 Bought you a whistle and a whipstalke too, To be reuenged on their villanies? *c* **1618** MORYSON *Itin.* IV. (1903) 482 Though indeede they take it rather for a grace to be reputed actiue in any Villany, espetially Cruelty and theft. **1677** GILPIN *Demonol.* II. i. 187 Other Errours there are, that lead to beastly and unnatural Villanies. **1691** HARTCLIFFE *Virtues* 53 Under pretence thereof Wars might be raised, Robberies and all manner of Villanies committed. **1725** DE FOE *Voy. round World* (1840) 42 If they are honest men and would not appear in this villany. **1742** FIELDING *J. Andrews* I. x[i]v, The greatest villanies are daily practised to please thee. **1849** MACAULAY *Hist. Eng.* vi. II. 152 He was determined to keep his place, if it could be kept by any villany but one. **1860** GEN. P. THOMPSON *Audi Alt.* cxxviii. III. 86 But such is what the poor have to expect, when they assist in the villainies of the rich. **1867** FREEMAN *Norm. Conq.* I. 411 Æthelred, if he had not ordered this villany, at any rate made himself an accessory after the fact.

†**2.** Treatment of a degrading or shameful nature as suffered or received by a person; ill-usage, injury, indignity, insult. *Obs.*

Not always clearly distinct from sense 3.

a **1300** *Cursor M.* 17150 Befor mi moder eien.. Sufferd i al þis wilani [*v.r.* velani]. **13..** *K. Alis.* 2500 (Laud MS.), Þer dude Alisaunder curteisie; He kepte hem from vche vilenye, Darries moder, & darries wijf. *c* **1375** *Sc. Leg. Saints* i. (*Peter*) 548 He.. mad gret playnt of þe schame, of þe vilne, and of þe blame, þat lytil befor tholit he. *c* **1440** *York Myst.* xxii. 70 And gladly suffir I for thy sake swilk velany. **1567** *Trial Treas.* C iij b, Ye, ye they haue vsed me with to much vilanie. **1586** J. HOOKER *Hist. Irel.* in *Holinshed* II. 82/2 Kildare pursuing Ormond to the chapiter house doore, vndertooke on his honor that he should receiue no villanie. **1590** GREENE *Royal Exch.* Wks. (Grosart) VII. 263 To see villanie offered him, and to holde his peace.

†**b.** In the phr. *to put* (a person) *to villainy.*

1513 BRADSHAW *St. Werburge* II. 207 Wyddowes and wyues were put to vilany, Maydens were corrupt and slayne chamfully. **1548** UDALL, etc. *Erasm. Par. Mark* ix. 62 Syth menne shoulde se hym [*sc.* Jesus] sone after putte to so muche shame and villany. **1565** COOPER *Thesaurus, Conculco*,.. to treade vnder foote: to put to extreme vilanie.

†**c.** ? A punishment of a degrading or ignominious nature. *Obs.*$^{-1}$

a **1400–50** *Bk. Curtasye* 56 in *Babees Bk.*, Yf þou make mawes on any wyse, A velany þou kacches or euer þou rise.

†**3.** Disgrace, dishonour; ignominy; discredit. *Obs.* (freq. *c* 1400–*c* 1500).

c **1375** *Cursor M.* 803 (Fairf.), Þai clad ham þan for velane wiþ brade leues of fyge tree. **1375** BARBOUR *Bruce* IX. 545 Schir Amery.. Raid till Yngland, and purchast ther Of armyt men gret cumpany, To venge hym of the velany. *c* **1420** *Chron. Vilod.* 2384 Y þe mekely prey.. to correcty hit so þat y naue no vyleny þere-by. **1436** HEN. VI in *Rep. Hist. MSS. Comm.* Var. Coll. IV. 199 To caste this land oute of all reputacion into perpetual reprofe, vylonye and shame thorwgh the wordil. *a* **1470** HARDING *Chron.* VII. clxxxi, The kyng Edwarde had all the victorye, The kyng Philyp had all the vilanye. *c* **1530** LD. BERNERS *Arth. Lyt. Bryt.* (1814) 23 Dame Luke.. knew wel yᵗ her doughter Perron was no mayde, therfore she doubted greatly to haue vylonye. *a* **1533** —— *Huon* viii. 20 It shalbe greatly to your veleny and reproche yf I be thus slayne by you. **1565** JEWELL *Reply Harding* (1611) 371 They thought great villanie in that kind of Death. **1594** T. B. *La Primaud. Fr. Acad.* II. 327 For this cause there is in Shame not onely a feare of villanie, but indignation also, after the committing of some fault.

†**b.** Used predicatively: A fact or circumstance bringing disgrace or discredit *to* a person. Also without const. *Obs.*

c **1340** HAMPOLE *Prose Tr.* 27 It es a velany a man for to be curyously arrayede apone his heuede.. and all his body be nakede and bare as it ware a beggere. ? *a* **1366** CHAUCER *Rom. Rose* 1231 But she hym holpe his harme to aswage; Hir thought it elles a vylanye. *a* **1400** *Minor Poems fr. Vernon MS.* 533/173 Ʒif þat þou chyde þi soget, Hit is to þe vileynye gret. **1467** *Paston Lett.* II. 308, If I wer ther withought I had the mor sadder or wurchepfull persones abought me,.. it shuld be to me but a vylney. **1470–85** MALORY *Arthur* III. viii. 108 Ye haue doone a passynge fowle dede in the sleyinge of the lady, the whiche will be grete vylany vnto yow. *a* **1533** LD. BERNERS *Huon* lv. 185 It shal be to you grete velany [ed. 1601 dishonour].

†**c.** A person or thing that is the source of discredit or disgrace. *Obs. rare.*

1382 WYCLIF *Ecclus.* xxiii. 31 He shal ben vileny to alle; forthi that he vnderstod not the drede of the Lord. **1549** COVERDALE, etc. *Erasm. Par. Galat.* 21 The Gentiles.. coumpte his crosse for a vilanie and reproche.

†**4.** *to do villainy* or *a villainy*, esp. *to* (a person), in prec. senses. *Obs.*

a. **1303** R. BRUNNE *Handl. Synne* 6516 The syxte synne ys glotonye; þat ys a shameful vyleynye þat men doun of mete and drynk. *a* **1330** *Otuel* 358 King charles.. was hende & good, & nolde for his wordes heʒe Don otuel no vileinie. *c* **1380** WYCLIF *Sel. Wks.* III. 287 Þei.. don hym more dispite and vileyne þan diden Judas Scarioth and Jewis. *a* **1425** *Cursor M.* 20340 (Trin.), Þerfore þeron haue þou þi þouʒt.. þat þei me do no vilayne.

β. *a* **1300** *Cursor M.* 16306 Pilate said and badd þai ne suld do him [*sc.* Jesus] na vilani. *c* **1385** CHAUCER *L.G.W.* 1823 *Lucrece*, Whi hast thow don this lady vilanye? *c* **1450** *Mirk's Festial* 106 By helpe of þe fende, he made hym lyke an angyll, and come to dyuers maydyns,.. and soo lay by hom, and dude hom gret vylany. **1480** CAXTON *Chron. Eng.* ciii. 52 b, The kyng Osbright me hath done shame & vilanye ayens my wyll. **1526** *Pilgr. Perf.* (W. de W. 1531) 254 [They] spared not to do all the vylany & shame to the sone of god that they coude deuyse. **1597** SHAKS. *2 Hen. IV*, II. i. 130 Pay her the debt you owe her, and vnpay the villany you haue done her. *a* **1683** SIDNEY *Disc. Govt.* I. i. (1704) 8 A third sort of Men who would neither do Villanys, nor suffer more than the Laws did permit.

γ. *c* **1385** CHAUCER *L.G.W.* 2333 *Philomene*, This false thef Hath don this lady ʒit a more myschef For fere lyst she shulde his shame crye And don hym opynly a vilenye. **1422** YONGE tr. *Secreta Secret.* 136 In that he dothe to god ouergrete veleny.

δ. *c* **1380** *Sir Ferumb.* 2254 He wende wiþ is ferete [to] haue do þe vylonye. **1387** TREVISA *Higden* (Rolls) III. 389 Atthalus hadde despitousliche i-scorned þis Pausania, and i-doo hym grete vilonye. *c* **1449** PECOCK *Repr.* I. xvii. 100 Ther in thei doon foul vilonie to Cristis lawe of feith. **1474** CAXTON *Chesse* II. i. (1883) 20 Thanswer of a noble & debonair prynce That suffred that villonye don to his doughter.

†**5.** ***to say or speak*** (***a, no***, etc.) ***villainy***, to speak evil, to use wicked, low, obscene, or opprobrious language. Also, ***to speak villainy of***, to defame or throw discredit on (a person). *Obs.*

After OF. *dire vilonie* (Du Cange s.v. *Villania*).

(*a*) *a* **1300** *Cursor M.* 7832 For qua lais hand in feloni O king, or sais him vilani,.. wit-vten grith, He dei. **1303** R. BRUNNE *Handl. Synne* 1549 A nunne.. þat ʒede to helle for no þyng ellys But for she spake euer vyleyny. *c* **1386** CHAUCER *Prol.* 70 He neuere yet no vileynye ne sayde In al his lyf vn to no maner wight. **1419** in S. Bentley *Excerpta Historica* (1831) 38 That no man saye no vilony to non other, throughe the whiche vilony saynge, may falle sodenly man slaughter, or risinge of people. **1474** CAXTON *Chesse* II. i. (1883) 20 This prince had also a frende that.. sayd on a tyme as moche villonye unto the prynce as ony man miht saye. **1483** —— *Gold. Leg.* 424/1 She.. said many Iniuryes & vylonyes to fyacre contumeleyng & blasphemyng hym. **1611** BIBLE *Isaiah* xxxii. 6 The vile person wil speake villenie, and his heart will worke iniquitie.

(*b*) **1470–85** MALORY *Arthur* xx. xix. 832 Alle the world wylle speke of yow vylony. **1568** GRAFTON *Chron.* II. 285 Do not a thing that should blemishe your renowne, neither geue occasion for any to speake vilanie of you. **1581** A. HALL *Iliad* v. 83 Al men of vs great villany would say.

†**b.** So ***words of villainy***. *Obs.*

a **1300** *Cursor M.* 28531, I ha bene wont thoru lucheri Wordes to spek of vilany. *c* **1386** CHAUCER *Pars. T.* ¶22 If.. he be a talkere of ydil wordes of vanite or of vilonye. **1568** *Bk. Nurture* To Parents, Take heede they speake no wordes of vilany.

†**6.** Lack of courtesy or politeness; discourtesy, incivility, rudeness; boorishness, rusticity. *Obs.*

c **1340** HAMPOLE *Pr. Consc.* 1528 For þat somtyme men held velany Now yhung men haldes curtasy; And þat som tyme was curtasy cald, Now wille yhong men velany hald. *c* **1386** CHAUCER *Prol.* 740 Crist spak hym self ful brode in hooly writ, And wel ye woot no vileynye is it. **14..** *Voc.* in Wr.-Wülcker 590 *Inurbanitas*, vylonye. *c* **1480** in Hazl. *E.P.P.* I. 45 Syr erle, he seyd, take and begyn; He seyd: nay, be seynt Austyn, That was to me vylony. *c* **1481** CAXTON *Dialogues* 29 For I reffuse not The cuppe; That were vylonye [F. *villonie*].

a **1677** BARROW *Serm. Titus iii.* 2 Wks. (1687) I. 239 This practice [of railing and reviling] doth plainly signifie.. ill breeding and bad manners... In our modern languages it is termed *Villany*, as being proper for rustick Boors. **1694** DRYDEN *Love Triumph.* I. i, But this large courtesy, this overpraise You give his worth, in any other mouth Were villainy to me.

†**7.** The condition or state of a villein; bondage, servitude; hence, base or ignoble condition of life; moral degradation. *Obs.*

c **1386** CHAUCER *Pars. T.* ¶9 Certes wel aughte a man haue disdeyne of synne, and wiþdrawe him fro þat þraldom and vilenye. **1540** COVERDALE *Fruitful Less.* i. Wks. (Parker Soc.) I. 300 Jesus.. took upon himself the most extreme shame.. to deliver us from eternal villany. **1543** T. BECON *New Catech.* Wks. 1560 I. 415 b, These, these goo about to bring vs vnto vilany.

†**b.** Low or wretched condition. *Obs.*

1570 JEWEL *View Seditious Bull* (1582) 47 Haue not they spoiled & wasted those two noble Cuntries & brought them to such vilanie & miserie, as they neuer felt before?

†**8.** Imperfection, defect, or injury in things. *Obs.*$^{-1}$

c **1400** *Pilgr. Sowle* (Caxton) II. lviii. (1859) 56 The bones stoden vp, as men, in the same persones, ryght as they were byfore, withouten ony spot or vylonye.

9. Base, villainous, or wicked quality.

1702 ADDISON *Dial. Medals* ii. (1726) 101 Ingratitude.. can arise from nothing but a natural baseness and villany of soul.

Hence †**'villainy** (in 5 vylonye) *v. trans.*, = VILLAIN *v.* 1. *Obs.*$^{-1}$

1483 CAXTON *Gold. Leg.* 113/3 For as moche as they haue dyspyted and vylonyed the blood of Jhesu.

villakin ('vɪləkɪn). [f. VILLA + -KIN.] A little villa; a villa-residence.

Chiefly in familiar or jocular use, or with some degree of disparagement.

1730 SWIFT *Let. to Gay* 19 March, I writ lately to Mr. Pope: I wish you had a little Villakin in his neighbourhood. **1730** GAY *Let. to Swift* 31 March, I am every day building villakins and have given over that of castles. **1805** J. ALMON *Corr. Wilkes* V. 79 In this cottage (or *villakin*, as he usually termed it) he passed the pleasantest hours which he had enjoyed since the period of his adversities. **1841** *Tait's Mag.* VIII. 258 The *villakin* was transformed into a domestic paradise. **1883** MISS BROUGHTON *Belinda* II. 159 Spick and span villas and villakins, each with its half acre of tennis-ground and double daisies.

'villaless, *a.* [f. VILLA.] Having no villa or villas.

1833 *Fraser's Mag.* VIII. 481 The touch at the end, as to the villaless condition of Bulwer, is admirable.

villamaninite (vɪlə'mænɪnaɪt). *Min.* [f. *Villamanín*, name of the locality (north of León in NW. Spain) near which the mineral was found + -ITE¹.] A black isometric mineral, $(Cu,Ni,Co,Fe)S_2$, of the pyrite group.

1919 *Nature* 20 Nov. 326/1 Dr. W. R. Schoeller and A. R. Powell: Villamaninite, a new mineral. **1968** *Neues Jahrb. f. Mineral.: Monatshefte* 189 The conditions under which villamaninite formed must have been quite extreme. Investigations of Ni-Cu ores from Katanga, Carrol County in Maryland and So. Wisconsin.. where low temperature mineralizations are supposed to have occurred, failed to produce a new villamaninite locality. **1977** *Mineral. Abstr.* XXVIII. 205/1 Villamaninite breaks down to α-NiS, carrollite ($CuCo_2S_4$), and some Ni and Co sulphates at around 400°C.

'villan. Also 6–7, 9 **villane.** [ad. med.L. *villānus* villager, etc., f. L. *villa* VILLA.]

1. *Hist.* A villein; an occupier of land in the feudal vill.

1552 HULOET, Villan, *seruus*,.. *uillanus.* **1570** LEVINS *Manip.* 19 Villane, *verna.* **1609** SKENE *Reg. Maj.* 98 Gif ane over-lord causes marie the heires of his vassall, being in his custodie, with villans (or bondmen) or Burgesses, quhereby the heires are disparaged [etc.]. **1699** TEMPLE *Hist. Eng.* (ed. 2) 255 What Stock they were possessed of, and how many Villans upon their respective Estates. **1809** BAWDWEN *Domesday Bk.* 9 There are only two villanes there and four bordars having one plough and a half. **1851** T. H. TURNER *Dom. Archit.* I. iii. 105 To these woods [at Osterley, Middlesex] resorted moreover all lawless men, fugitive villans, and persons of the like description.

†**2.** A villager, a peasant. *Obs.*

1685 HEDGES *Diary* (Hakl. Soc.) I. 208 Vineyards stored with excellent good grapes, which the villanes carry every night to sell at Shirash.

villan, obs. f. VILLAIN.

villanage, variant of VILLEINAGE.

‖**villancico** (viʎan'θiko). *Mus.* [Sp.] A Spanish and Portuguese musical form (see quots.).

1822 J. B. WHITE *Lett. from Spain* ix. 327 The music.. was.. used in a species of dramatic interludes in the vulgar tongue, which were sung, not acted, at certain intervals of the service. These pieces had the name of *Villancicos*, from *Villano*, a Clown, shepherds and shepherdesses being the interlocutors in these pastorals. **1849** G. TICKNOR *Hist. Spanish Lit.* I. xxiii. 440 The 'Villancicos' that follow—songs in the old Spanish measure with a refrain and occasionally short verses broken in—are more agreeable, and sometimes are not without merit. **1876** STAINER & BARRETT *Dict. Mus. Terms* 446/2 *Villancico* (*Sp.*), a species of song of two or more stanzas, each containing seven lines, belonging to the poetry of the 15th century, which, like the madrigal, is of an epigrammatic form—formerly very popular in Spain... Those motets which are sung during high mass on Christmas-eve are always called Villancicos. **1937** M. N. HAMILTON *Music in 18th Cent. Spain* 5 In Eslava there were references to *villancicos*, which during the eighteenth century seemed to be the routine accomplishment of every chapel master. **1959** *Collins' Mus. Encycl.* 701/1 *Villancico*... (1) A type of song.. current in Spain in the late 15th and 16th cent. It is characterized by the fact that it begins with a refrain, which is subsequently repeated after each verse... (2) In the 17th and 18th cent. a cantata for soli and chorus with instrumental accompaniment, frequently on the subject of Christmas. (3) In modern Spanish a Christmas carol. **1968** *New Oxf. Hist. Mus.* IV. iv. 135 In earlier times courtly love had been a favourite theme for *villancicos*... In the later fifteenth century a more popular tone invaded *villancicos*... The increasing number of religious *villancicos* found in the sixteenth century points towards the transformation of the form in the seventeenth century into an extended sacred cantata. **1980** *Early Music Gaz.* Jan. 16/1 The three papers are:.. Manuel Carlos de Brito on 'A little-known collection of Portuguese Baroque Villancicos and Romances'; [etc.].

villane, obs. f. VILLAIN.

‖**villanella** (vɪlə'nɛlə). Pl. **-elle.** [It., fem. of *villanello* rural, rustic, f. *villano*: see VILLAIN *sb.* and *a.*] (See later quots.)

1597 MORLEY *Introd. Mus.* III. 180 Though many times the dittie be fine enough, yet because it carrieth that name *Villanella* they take those disallowances as being good enough for plow and cart. **1667** C. SIMPSON *Compend. Mus.* 139 Then, Cansonets, Vilanella's, Airs of all sorts; or what else Poetry hath contrived to be set and Sung in Musick. [Hence in R. Holme *Armoury* (1688) III. 159/2.] **1801** BUSBY *Dict. Mus.*, *Villanella*, the air of an old rustic dance, the time of which was gay and brisk, and the measure strongly marked. **1884** W. S. ROCKSTRO in Grove *Dict. Mus.* IV. 264 *Villanella*, an unaccompanied Part-Song, of light rustic character, sharing, in about equal proportions, the characteristics of the Canzonetta, and the Balletta.

villanelle (vɪlə'nɛl). Also 6 villanell, 7 -el. [a. F. *villanelle*, ad. It. *villanella*: see prec. In the first quot. perh. an Anglicizing of the Italian word.]

†**1.** = prec. *Obs.*

a **1586** SIDNEY *Arcadia*, etc. (1629) 535 To the tune of a Neapolitan Villanell. **1603** FLORIO tr. *Montaigne* I. liv. 170 The *Villanelles*, homely gigges, and countrie songs of Gasconie. **1685** COTTON tr. *Montaigne* (1711) I. liv. I. 472.

2. A poem of fixed form, usually of a pastoral or lyric nature, consisting normally of five three-lined stanzas and a final quatrain, with only two rhymes throughout.

The first and third lines of the first stanza are repeated alternately in the succeeding stanzas as a refrain, and form a final couplet in the quatrain.

1877 GOSSE in *Cornhill Mag.* July 65 It appears that villanelles may be any length, if only they retain this number and arrangement of rhymes. **1877–8** HENLEY in *Ballades & Rondeaus* (Canterb. Poets) 252 A dainty thing's the Villanelle. Sly, musical, a jewel in rhyme, It serves its purpose passing well. **1886** C. DICK *Model*, etc. 90 A Vacation Villanelle.

ˈvillaner. *rare.* [f. VILLAN + -ER[1].] = VILLAN. **1862** TOULMIN SMITH *Parl. Rememb.* Oct. 189 The 'Inquisitio Eliensis' states that book to have been the record of an inquisition made on the oaths of the priest, the provost and six villaners of every Vill.

Villanova (vɪləˈnəʊvə). *Archæol.* The name of a hamlet near Bologna, Italy, where archæological finds were made, used *attrib.* to designate an Italian culture of the early Iron Age.

1901 W. RIDGEWAY *Early Age Greece* I. ii. 237 After the Terramare came the Early Iron Age, usually termed the Villanova period by the Italian archaeologists, from the discovery of a large number of its characteristic remains at Villanova near Bologna. **1910** *Encycl. Brit.* V. 721/2 The next period..is known as the 'Villanova' period,..or as the period of pit-tombs (*a pozzo*), from the form of the graves in which the pottery has been found.

Villanovan (vɪləˈnəʊvən), *sb.* and *a.* *Archæol.* [f. prec. + -AN.] **A.** *sb.* An inhabitant of Italy during the Villanova period. **B.** *adj.* Of, pertaining to, or designating the Villanova period. Also *absol.*

1924 D. RANDALL-MACIVER *Villanovans & Early Etruscans* 3 In the fifth century the Villanovans disappear as a recognizable people, stifled no doubt..by the dominant Etruscans who had settled beside them. **1928** —— *Italy before Romans* v. 73 Villanovan helmets and girdles and Villanovan ossuaries..may be seen side by side with Hallstatt swords. *a* **1930** D. H. LAWRENCE *Etruscan Places* (1932) ii. 55 It seems as if the primitive inhabitants of this part of Italy always burned their dead, and then put the ashes in a jar, sometimes covering the jar with the dead man's helmet, sometimes with a shallow dish for a lid, and then laid the urn with its ashes in a little round grave like a little well. This is called the Villanovan way of burial, in the well-tomb. **1957** [see ATESTINE *a.* and *sb.*]. **1974** *Encycl. Brit. Micropædia* X. 438/3 During the first quarter of the 7th century an Orientalizing civilization..was superimposed on the Villanovan in Tuscany. The northern Villanovans of the Po valley..continued to produce a geometric art..as late as the last quarter of the 6th century. **1980** *Times Lit. Suppl.* 17 Oct. 1179/4 The Iron Age possessors of the material culture (or cultural material) conventionally known as 'Villanovan' ought at least to have been mentioned.

villar (ˈvɪlə(r)), *sb.* and *a.* *rare.* [ad. L. *villāris*, f. *villa* VILLA: see -AR.] **a.** *sb.* A peasant holding land in the feudal vill; a villein. **b.** *adj.* Pertaining or relating to, concerned with, the feudal vill or vills.

1874 A. P. FORBES *S. Ninian & S. Kentigern* Notes 313 Stephen gave his forest of Furness..a fishery at Lancaster, and one or two villars with their property. **1897** MAITLAND *Domesday & Beyond* 13 Manorial and fiscal geography interferes with physical and villar geography.

villarette, var. VILLAETTE.

villarsite (vɪˈlɑːsaɪt). *Min.* [a. F. *villarsite*, f. the name of the French botanist D. *Villars* (1745–1814): named in 1842 by Dufrenoy.] A hydrous silicate of magnesium occurring massive or in rounded grains at Traversella, Piedmont.

1846 WORCESTER (citing Dana). **1850** ANSTED *Elem. Geol., Min.*, etc. §429 *Villarsite*, silicate of magnesia with iron and manganese. **1855** *Orr's Circ. Sci., Geol.*, etc. 511 Villarsite, —Prismatic,..Translucent. Col[our], yellowish-green. **1889** A. IRVING *Metamorphism of Rock* 55 *Villarsite*, which agrees with olivine in crystal form and optical characters, contains 4 to 6.2 per cent. of water.

Villar y Villar (ˈvilar i ˈvilar). [Sp., = Villar (a surname) and Villar.] The proprietary name of a Havana cigar.

1878 *Army & Navy Stores Price List* 60 Cigars and tobacco... Villar y Villar. Reina Victoria... 62/- per 100. **1903** W. STEVENS *Let.* 20 Oct. (1967) 68 But to-night I've been polite..have..puffed a Villar y Villar.

villate (ˈvɪlət). *Hist.* [ad. med.L. *villata*, f. L. *villa* VILLA.] A feudal territorial division consisting of a number of vills.

The Latin term has had some currency in English historical works.

1897 LEADER *Rec. Burg. Sheffield* p. xxvi, Proceedings were taken against the constable and villate of Wakefield.

villatic (vɪˈlætɪk), *a.* [ad. L. *villātic-us*, f. *villa* VILLA.] Of or pertaining to a villa or villas, or the inhabitants; *esp.* (after the original sense of *villa*), rural, rustic; village-.

The Miltonic passage has been freely echoed in the 19th c.: see the first group of quots. and 1822–56 in (*b*).

(*a*) **1671** MILTON *Samson* 1695 The perched roosts, And nests in order rang'd Of tame villatic Fowl. **1822** LAMB *Corr.* (1870) 164 Widgeon, snipes, barn-door fowls, ducks, geese—your tame villatic things. **1889** *Gd. Words* Nov. 786/2 [Jacob] herding the tame villatic sheep of his father.

(*b*) **1751** JOHNSON *Rambler* No. 147 ¶8 He..consulted with her..how I might be..disencumbered from villatick bashfulness. **1771–2** *Ess. fr. Batchelor* (1773) I. 162 Two rebellious enchanters, whom villatic rusticity styled, Cow-herds,—or Cow-boys. **1822–56** DE QUINCEY *Confess.* App. 284 Little asteroids that formed ample inheritances for the wants of this or that provincial squire, of this or that tame villatic squireen. **1846** LOWELL *Biglow P.* Ser. I. ix. Introd., A feeling of villatic pride in beholding our townsman occupying so large a space in the public eye.

†**ville**[1]. *Anat.* *Obs.* [ad. L. *villus* VILLUS.] = VILLUS[2]. (Only in pl.)

c **1400** *Lanfranc's Cirurg.* 30 Þe corde whanne he entriþ into þe brawn is departid into many smale þredis, & þei ben clepid villes [*v.r.* vylles]—þat is to seie wrappingis. & þese villes ben of iij. manner. **1541** COPLAND *Guydon's Quest. Chirurg.* lj b, Of what villes is the stomacke composed? **1562** BULLEIN *Bulwarke, Dial. Sorenes & Chir.* 26 Iskyng [= yexing] procedyng of dryyng of the villes of the stomacke.

†**ville**[2], etc., varr. FILLE[1], chervil. *Obs.*

c **1265** *Voc. Plants* in Wr.-Wülcker 557 *Cerfolium*, i. cerfoil, i. villen. *a* **1387** *Sinon. Barthol.* (Anecd. Oxon.) 15 *Cerfolium*, i. villes. *Ibid.* 43 Ville, *cerefolium*.

ville[3] (vɪl, vaɪl). *slang* (now *U.S.*). Also 9 vile. [a. F. *ville* town.] A town or village.

1837 L. C. BOYNTON *Jrnl.* 11 Sept. in *Proc. Amer. Antiquarian Soc.* (1933) XLIII. 336 Amherst [Mass.] is a very pleasant little ville, but still and inactive. **1859** HOTTEN *Dict. Slang* 114 *Ville*, or *vile*, a town or village,—pronounced *phial*, or *vial*. *French.* **1891** 'F. W. CAREW' *No.* 747 xxxv. 416 We made a long round back to vile. **1939** JOYCE *Finnegans Wake* 130 The brick of the viled ville of Barnehulme. **1977** M. HERR *Dispatches* 10 Once we fanned over a little ville that had just been airstruck.

Ville[4] (vɪl). *slang.* Also 'Ville, (')ville. [Abbrev.] ***the Ville***, Pentonville Prison in London.

1903 'No. 77' *Mark of Broad Arrow* ii. 35 Before the notorious bank forgers had been in 'The Ville' a single hour they were located in different wings of the prison, thus rendering personal contact with each other impossible. **1936** [see *fly-paper* s.v. FLY *sb.*[1] 11]. **1962** *John o' London's* 25 Jan. 82/3 Pentonville Prison is *the ville*. **1962** D. WARNER *Death of Bogey* IV. iii. 146 A stretch in the Ville or on the Moor. **1967** C. DRUMMOND *Death at Furlong Post* xii. 152, I don't want to see your great face up against me in the 'ville for twenty years. **1972** L. HENDERSON *Cage until Tame* vi. 51 Yeah, that's right, he was in the 'Ville.

ville, obs. f. VILL; var. FILLE[2] *Obs.*

-ville (vɪl), *suffix.* *colloq.* [ad. F. *ville* town.] A terminal element appended to sbs. (which freq. have a pl. suff.) or adjs. to denote: (*a*) a fictitious place; (*b*) a particular quality suggested by the word to which it is appended.

In *U.S.* usage orig. as —— *from* ——*ville*.

1567 HARMAN *Caveat* (ed. 2) sig. G 3, Rome vyle London. **1843** G. CRUIKSHANK *Comic Almanack* sig. F 4[v], Tripe & Trotter Depôt..Meatville. **1891** *N.Y. Sporting Times* 11 July 3/4 Then he was as frisky as a young colt and a slugger from Sluggersville. **1906** F. H. BURNETT *Shuttle* (1907) xxxviii. 384 That girl is a winner from Winnersville. I take off my hat to her. **1932** *Magnet* 17 Sept. 13/3 I'm telling you you're the biggest bonehead from Boneheadville. **1939** [see *route march* s.v. ROUTE *sb.* 4]. **1956**, etc. [see SQUARESVILLE]. **1959**, **1961** [see *Cubesville* s.v. CUBE *sb.*[1] 1 c]. **1961** [see SQUARESVILLE]. **1962** P. MORTIMER *Pumpkin Eater* xiii. 118 Tiny bit boring, between you and me. Strict secrets of course. English Rose stuff. Deathville, as far as I'm concerned. **1964** [see RELOCATE *v.* 2]. **1967** J. AITKIN *Young Meteors* i. 35 University? Man, that's just dragsville. **1972** *Publishers' Weekly* 2 Oct. 56/1 There are some who will simply not get the fun of it out there in mass-marketville. **1979** *National Times* (Austral.) 13 Oct. 5/2 But there is a mite more to leadership, even here in Mediaville [*sc.* Washington], than looking pretty and carrying a resonant baritone voice.

‖**villeggiatura** (villeddʒaˈtura). Also (incorrectly) **villegiatura.** [It., f. *villeggiare* to live at a villa or in the country, f. *villa* VILLA.] Residence at a country villa or in the country; a holiday spent in this way.

1742 WALPOLE *Let. to Mann* 1 Nov., I don't wonder that she hates the country; I dare to say her child does not owe its existence to the Villeggiatura. **1765** SMOLLETT *Trav.* xxix. (1766) II. 80 The mountain of Viterbo is covered with beautiful plantations and villas belonging to the Roman nobility, who come hither to make the *villegiatura* in summer. **1822** SHELLEY *Prose Wks.* (1880) IV. 284 Lord Byron is in *villeggiatura*, near Leghorn. **1845** PRESCOTT in *Life Longfellow* (1891) II. 22 We keep our *villeggiatura* at Pepperell, not flitting at all to Nahant this summer. **1885** *Times* (wkly. ed.) 18 Sept. 15/3 [They] occasionally left the cares and dignity of the Vice-regal Lodge to come down for a quiet *villegiatura* here.

So ‖**villegiature.** *Obs.*[−1] [F. *villegiature.*]

1740 *Corr. betw. C'tess Hartford & C'tess Pomfret* (1805) II. 172, I am sorry the nobility of Florence did not defer their *villegiature* till Christmas.

villein (ˈvɪlən, -eɪn). Now *Hist.* Forms: α. 4 vilein, 4–5 vileyn, 5 veleyn, 6 vylleyne, 6–7 villeine, 6– villein, 8–9 villeyn; also 6–7 villen. β. 5 vylayn, 5–6 -ayne, 6 vyllayn(e, villayne, 6–7 villaine, 6– villain (7 vilain). [a. AF. *villein* (*vilein*, *-eyn*, *vyleyn*, etc.), var. *villain*, etc., VILLAIN *sb.* Both types of spelling have been freely employed for this special sense of the word, and the tendency to use the form *villein* has increased in recent years.]

1. One of the class of serfs in the feudal system; *spec.* a peasant occupier or cultivator entirely subject to a lord (*villein in gross* GROSS *sb.*[2] 2 e) or attached to a manor (***villein regardant*** REGARDANT *a.* 1); a tenant in villeinage; also applied to a person regarded as holding a similar position in other communities, a bondsman. †Hence formerly in general use, a peasant, country labourer, or low-born rustic.

α. *a* **1325** *MS. Rawl. B.* 520 fol. 56 b, Also lith assise after excepcion of villenage ȝif þat vileyn vnder his louerdes power purchasede ani lond. **1390** GOWER *Conf.* III. 325 Nou lete we this maiden hiere, And speke of Dionise ayein And of Theophile the vilein, Of whiche I spak of nou tofore. [Cf. p. 320, l. 1358.] *c* **1400** MAUNDEV. (1839) 191 Olifauntz ..that he makethe for to ben brought up amonges his Vileynes. *c* **1450** LOVELICH *Merlin* 11625 And while the veleyn hadde seyd al this, Evere stood sire Vlphyn and herkened, j-wys. **1587** HOLINSHED *Chron.* (ed. 2) III. 1109/1 In case my aduersaries villen or bondman be impaneled, I may lawfullie chalenge him. **1590** SWINBURNE *Testaments* 34 Amongest the second sort are comprehended such as lacke freedome, & full liberty, as bond-slaue, slaues, and villeines. **1620** J. WILKINSON *Courts Baron* 146 If any Villeine or Bondman of blood hath purchased any land within his Lordship, the Lord may seise both it and such villeines goods at his pleasure. **1648** D. JENKINS *Wks.* 10 The Villeine of a Lord, in the presence of the King cannot be seized. **1699** TEMPLE *Hist. Eng.* 65 The Villens, that held nothing but at the Will of the Landlord. **1765** BLACKSTONE *Comm.* I. 72 Villeins might be enfranchised by manumission. **1775** *Archaeol.* III. 80 Is it probable, that two day labourers, and at that time *villeins*, should have any fine to compound? **1818** CRUISE *Digest* (ed. 2) I. 256 After the conquest the estates of the great lords were cultivated by their villeins. **1848** LYTTON *Harold* I. v, The villeins are many and their hate is strong. **1875** K. E. DIGBY *Real Prop.* (1876) 51 If the villein could not depart from the land, no more could the lord remove him so long as he rendered the service due to the lord.

fig. **1607** HIERON *Wks.* I. 333 The scorner and scoffer at the word, is euen a villen to his own profanenes.

β. **1470–85** MALORY *Arthur* VIII. iii. 277 That..alle men of worship maye disseuer a gentylman fro a yoman, and from a yoman a vylayne. **1483** CAXTON *Gold. Leg.* 148/2 It happed upon a day that he tormented a vylayn or a carle for the couetyse of hys good. **1532** *Dial. Laws Eng.* II. xliii. P v, Yf a vyllayn be made a preste, yet neuertheles the lorde may sease his goodes. *a* **1548** HALL *Chron., Hen. VI*, 104 There were slain and taken foure hundred gentlemen and the villaines frankely let go. **1570** LAMBARDE *Peramb. Kent* 452 Bondseruants, which we do now sence call by a strained worde Villaines, ar not here talked of. **1600** HOLLAND *Livy* XLV. xliv. 1233 b, This K[ing]..was wont..to acknowledge & cal himselfe the freed villaine and vassaile of the people of Rome. **1622** BACON *Henry VII*, 156 John Cut,..Henry Wyat, and such other Caitifes and Villaines of Birth, have beene the principall Finders. **1698** FRYER *Acc. E. India & P.* 267 They are Preferred to no higher Employment than to Cultivate the Earth as Villains, not Inheritors. **1714** *Spect.* No. 607 ¶12 The Steward shall cause these two Neighbours to swear..if he be a Free-man, or a Villain. **1750** CARTE *Hist. Eng.* II. 602 An act for disabling the villains or copyholders of prelates and monasteries to purchase lands in fee. **1776** DALRYMPLE *Ann. Scot.* 320 A covenant between the Lord and the villain. **1839** KEIGHTLEY *Hist. Eng.* I. 168 They [the judges] were likewise required..to receive the oath of fealty from all persons from the earl down to the villain. **1866** ROGERS *Agric. & Prices* I. iii. 62 Time out of mind the services of the villains had been commutable for money payments. **1876** FREEMAN *Norm. Conq.* V. 478 The villain was not a slave, but a freeman minus the very important rights of his lord. As against all men but his lord, he was free.

†**b.** A servant, a retainer. *Obs.*[−1]

1535 *Goodly Primer Passion* iv. The villains had made a great fire beneath in the midst of the hall.

2. *attrib.*, as ***villein burgher***, ***class***, ***issue***, ***land***, etc.; **villein service**, service which a villein was bound to render to his lord as a condition of holding his land; **villein-socage**, socage or tenure by villein service (cf. quot. 1766); so ***villein-socman***.

1529 RASTELL *Pastyme* E iij b, Swanus..besegyd Canterbury, and wan it,..and slew the monkys; but euer kept the .x. monk alyue to do vylleyne seruyce, & slew .ix. of them. **1544** tr. *Littleton's Tenures* xi. 40 b, Lande holden in vyllenage or vyllayne landes. *a* **1625** SIR H. FINCH *Law* (1636) 23 A villein shall make free land to bee villein land, but villein land shall not make a free-man to be a villein. **1651** G. W. tr. *Cowel's Inst.* 9 There may be villain Issue between those which are our Captives. **1651** tr. *Kitchin's Jurisdict.* (1657) 327 If my Villain Infant be in ward of one, by reason that he holds of him by Knights service. **1766** BLACKSTONE *Comm.* II. 61 These villein-socmen do villein services. *Ibid.* 79 But socage..is of two sorts: free-socage,.. and villein-socage, where the services, though certain, are of a baser nature. **1776** DALRYMPLE *Ann. Scot.* 320 *Merchetum* ..was also used for expressing another *villain* custom. **1864** J. F. KIRK *Ch. the Bold* I. v. 244 For what purpose were the taille and the gabelle levied on the villain burghers, if the nobles derived no benefit from these exactions. **1875** K. E. DIGBY *Real Prop.* (1876) 51 Freemen sometimes held lands by villein services. **1878** STUBBS *Const. Hist.* xix. III. 367 The villein class..aspired to holy orders as one of the avenues to liberty.

†**3.** As *adj.* Of base or servile birth; belonging to the class of feudal villeins or serfs. *Obs.*

1551 in J. S. Leadam *Sel. Cases Crt. Requests* (Selden) 55 Your Oratour repplyede that he was Free and of Free estate and nott vyllayne.

villein, obs. f. VILLAIN *sb.* and *a.*

villeinage (ˈvɪlənɪdʒ, -leɪn-). Now *Hist.* Forms: α. 4–9 **villenage** (6 vyllenage, vyllynage, vellenage), 5 **vilenage.** β. 6–9 **villanage**, 7 villon-, villianage, 7–9 **villainage.** γ. 7– **villeinage** (9 vileinage). [a. AF. *vilenage*, *villenage*, OF. *vilenage*, *villenage*, *vila(i)nage*, = Pr. *vilanatge*, Sp. *villanage*, Pg. *villanagem*), or ad. med.L. *villenagium*, *vil(l)anagium*, *vileinagium*, from the same source: see VILLEIN and -AGE.]

1. The tenure by which a feudal villein held or occupied his land; tenure of lands by bond-service rendered to the lord or superior. Also called ***tenure in villeinage***.

α. *a* **1325** [see VILLEIN 1 *a*]. *c* **1450** *Godstow Reg.* (1905) 207, iiij. acres and an half acre and half a Rode of arable lond,.. the whiche he holdith in vilenage or bondage. **1523** FITZHERB. *Surv.* 12 All these tenauntes maye holde their landes by dyuers tenures..; as by..burgage tenures and tenure in vyllenage. **1544** tr. *Littleton's Tenures* xi. 40 Tenure in vyllenage is most properly whan a vylleyne holdeth of his lorde to whom he is vyllayne certayne landes & tenementes after the custome and maner or els at the wyl of his lorde, and to do his vyllayne seruyce. **1598** MARSTON *Sco. Villanie* I. ii. 176 Once Albion liu'd in such a cruell age Than men did hold by seruile villenage. **1602** FULBECKE *1st Pt. Parall.* 211 Villenage, is where a man holdeth of his Lord, either by doing vnto him some particular base seruice, and such a one is called a tenant by villenage, or by doing generally whatsoeuer base seruice his Lord will commaund and impose vpon him, and such a tenaunt is termed in our Law a villaine. **1607** COWELL *Interpr.* s.v., For euery one that houldeth in villenage, is not a villein, or a bond man. **1612** DAVIES *Why Ireland*, etc. (1787) 204 There was but one freeholder made in a whole country, which was the lord himself, all the rest were but tenants at will, or rather tenants in villenage. **1672** MANLEY *Cowell's Interpr.* s.v., Copy-holders is but a new Name, for anciently they were called Tenants in villenage, or, of base Tenure. **1766** BLACKSTONE *Comm.* II. 92 With regard to the folk-land, or estates held in villenage. **1818** CRUISE *Digest* (ed. 2) I. 308 Copyholds being derived from the tenure in villenage, they were not originally within the jurisdiction of the king's courts at Westminster. **1818** HALLAM *Mid. Ages* III. viii. (1819) III. 259 The tenements in villenage, whether by law or usage, were never separated from the lordship. **1875** STUBBS *Const. Hist.* xvi. (1896) II. 475 So villenage grew to be a base tenure, differing in degree rather than in kind from socage, and privileged as well as burdened.

attrib. **1679** BLOUNT *Anc. Tenures* 21 This was an usual restraint of old in Villenage Tenure.

β. **1565** COOPER *Thesaurus*, *Colonarii*,..rusticall people, tenantes in villanages. **1607** NORDEN *Surv. Dial.* II. 77 A matter almost out of vse, a tenure called Villanage: that is, where the Tenants of a Mannor were Bondmen and Bond-women. *a* **1618** RALEIGH *Rem.* (1644) 59 The bondmen.. were grievously prest by their Lords in their tenure of Villanage. **1681** H. NEVILE *Plato Rediv.* 133 Not only all Villanage is long since abollished, but the other Tenures are so altered and qualified, that they signifie nothing towards making the Yeomandry depend upon the Lords. **1776** ADAM SMITH *W.N.* III. ii. I. 473 Tenure in villanage gradually wore out. **1812** G. CHALMERS *Dom. Econ. Gt. Brit.* 23 It is extremely difficult to ascertain the time, when villainage ceased in England, or even to trace its decline. **1872** O. W. HOLMES *Poet Breakf.-t.* vi, We return to the state of villanage, holding our tenement-houses..of the State.

fig. *a* **1653** G. DANIEL *Idyll* v. 132 The Earth runs in one Tenure, and we but Prevent Repeals; Villainage is the Lott.

γ. **1641** *Termes de la Ley* 262 To hold in pure Villeinage, is to do all that the Lord will him command. **1845** S. AUSTIN *Ranke's Hist. Ref.* II. 225 The abolition of the punishment of death, of the lesser tithes, and of villeinage were especially insisted on. **1845** WILLIAMS *Real Property* III. 265 Villeinage is to hold part of the demesnes of any lord..by villein services.

†**b.** Land held by this tenure. *Obs.*

c **1450** *Godstow Reg.* (1906) 576 The tythes of the villenagis of medys and litell medis of the same towne. *c* **1460** *Oseney Reg.* (1913) 26 In cleydon, ij. hides of villenage, þe which my modur ȝafe to þe same church.

2. The state or condition of a feudal villein; complete subjection to a feudal lord or superior; bondage, serfdom, servitude.

α. **1531** *Star Chamber Cases* (Selden) II. 196 Ony maner of Entree into the seid Courte Rolles..Concernyng ony vyllenage agenst the seid defendauntes. **1551** in J. S. Leadam *Sel. Cases Crt. Requests* (Selden) 58 To dyscharge the vyllynage and bondage of the bloudde of the said complaynants. **1600** HOLLAND *Livy* XLI. viii. 1101 They that were to leave such yssue at home, gave their children as it were in villenage to some Romane citizen or other whom they liked of. **1643** MILTON *Sov. Salve* 26 Reduced to the terms of the Peasants of France, of villenage and slavery. **1699** TEMPLE *Hist. Eng.* 59 The Children that were born of these miserable People, belonged to the Lord of the Soil,.. and thus began Villenage in England. **1818** HALLAM *Mid. Ages* (1872) II. 57 The villenage of the peasantry in some parts of Catalonia was very severe. **1852** H. ROGERS *Ecl. Faith* 418 Mr. Newman says that it was *Christians*, not *men*, that the Church sought to enfranchise; it little matters; she sought to abolish all villenage. **1866** ROGERS *Agric. & Prices* I. iv. 70, I do not doubt that the social state of villenage existed.

fig. **1590** SPENSER *F.Q.* II. xi. 1 No wretchednesse is like to sinfull vellenage. **1604** HIERON *Wks.* I. 481 The continuall gamster is, as it were, in the state of villenage to his humor. **1644** MILTON *Divorce* II. iii. 36, I spake ev'n now, as if sin were condemn'd in a perpetual villenage never to be free by law, never to be manumitted.

β. **1589** WARNER *Albion's England* v. xxiii. 101 Thus Englands hope with Englands heire in one same Bark did saile: When desprat from their villanage was English bloud of baile. **1607** TOPSELL *Four-f. Beasts* 449 For those [ichneumons] that are ouercome in combates one with another, are branded with a warlicke marke of Villanage, or subiection to their Conquerors. **1700** DRYDEN *Wife of Bath's T.* 443 Their Glories shine; But Infamy and Villanage are thine. **1761** [see SERF 2 b]. **1796** MORSE *Amer. Geog.* II. 245 Joseph II rendered an essential service to humanity, in abolishing the servitude or villanage of the peasants of Bohemia. **1841** ELPHINSTONE *Hist. Ind.* II. 287 The original population..had..been conquered and reduced to a sort of villanage by certain Afghan tribes. **1876** FREEMAN *Norm. Conq.* xxiv. V. 480 While the churl sank to the state of villainage, the slave rose to it.

γ. **1641** *Termes de la Ley* 262 b, The division of Villeinage, is villeine of blood, and of tenure. **1832** HT. MARTINEAU *Demerara* ii. 22 Then came the bondage and villeinage of the Gothic nations. **1873** SPENCER *Stud. Sociol.* v. 103 When villeinage had passed away and serfs were no longer maintained by their owners. **1889** JESSOPP *Coming of Friars* ii. 66 A man or woman born in villeinage could never shake it off.

3. The body of villeins; villeins collectively.

1864 BURTON *Scot Abr.* I. i. 31 The French peasantry or villainage of the period.

'villeiness. *rare.* [f. VILLEIN + -ESS.] A female villein.

1611 COTGR. s.v. *Corps*, *Femme de corps*, a Villeinesse, a woman of a seruile condition. *Ibid.* s.v. *Femme.*

†**villeining.** *Obs.*$^{-1}$ = VILLEINAGE.

1471 in *Archaeol.* XLVII. 196 That..ye..paye yerely.. the sume of ten marcs according to the terms of th' endentures of Vilenyng between us and the said William.

villeinous, -en(o)us, obs. ff. VILLAINOUS *a.*

‖**ville lumière** (vil lymjɛr). [Fr., = town or city of light(s).] A brightly-lit city or town; an exciting modern city or town; ***la Ville Lumière***, Paris.

1920 W. J. LOCKE *House of Baltazar* xiv. 166 London ceased to be a city of dreadful night. In his enthusiastic eyes it had almost become a *ville lumière*. **1922** A. M. HYAMSON *Dict. Eng. Phrases* 353/2 *Ville Lumière, La*, (Fr., the light-city; the city of lights): Paris. **1923** W. J. LOCKE *Moordius & Co.* vii. 94 We are but nursing the lamp of la Ville Lumière till better times. **1955** E. WAUGH *Officers & Gentlemen* 137 Cape Town at the extremity of two dark continents was a *ville lumière* such as Trimmer had sought in vain. **1980** *Listener* 25 Sept. 389/1 The Eiffel Tower..proclaimed *la ville lumière* to be the modernist capital.

villenie, -enye, obs. varr. VILLAINY.

villi, pl. of VILLUS.

villiaco, -ago, varr. VILIACO *Obs.*

villiaumite ('vɪlɪəmaɪt). *Min.* [a. F. *villiaumite* (A. Lacroix 1908, in *Compt. Rend.* CXLVI. 215), f. *Villiaume*, name of a French explorer in whose collection the mineral was first identified: see -ITE¹.] Native sodium fluoride, NaF, occurring as red, pink, or orange transparent isometric crystals.

The symmetry is erron. described in quot. 1908.

1908 *Jrnl. Chem. Soc.* XCIV. II. 201 This new mineral, called villiaumite, is tetragonal and pseudo-cubic, with three perfect cleavages at right angles to one another. **1970** *Amer. Mineralogist* LV. 126 Thermodynamic calculations show that fluorite is to be expected as the common fluoride mineral in both silica-saturated and under-saturated igneous rocks; in calcium- and silica-poor assemblages villiaumite is favored, but in calcium-poor quartz-bearing rocks, cryolite will prevail.

†**'villicated,** *ppl. a. Obs.*$^{-0}$ [f. L. *villicāt-us*, pa. pple. of *villicāre* to act as bailiff.] (See quot.) Also **villi'cation** [ad. L. *villicātio*].

1623 COCKERAM I, *Villicated*, busied about husbandrie. *Ibid.*, *Villication*, husbandry. **1656** BLOUNT *Glossogr.* (copying Cooper), *Villication*, the rule of Husbandry under the Master or Owner of a Mannor.

villiche, obs. form of VILELY *adv.*

villiform ('vɪlɪfɔːm), *a. Zool.* [ad. mod.L. *villiform-is*: see VILLUS and -FORM. So F. *villiforme.*] Of the teeth of certain fishes: Having the form of villi; so numerous, slender, and closely set, as to resemble the pile of velvet.

Also *Bot.*, 'resembling villi'.

1846 [see *close-set* s.v. CLOSE C 1 and 2]. **1849–52** OWEN in *Todd's Cycl. Anat.* IV. 874/1 The teeth of the Sheat-fish.. present all the gradations between the villiform and raduliform types. **1859** MURCHISON *Siluria* (ed. 3) App. 562 The minute villiform teeth of osseous fishes. **1880** GÜNTHER *Fishes* 126 Very fine conical teeth arranged in a band are termed villiform teeth.

villify, obs. form of VILIFY *v.*

villin, obs. f. VILLAIN *sb.*

‖**villino** (vɪ'liːnəʊ). Pl. villini. [It., dim. of *villa* VILLA.] A small (rural, suburban, or urban) house in Italy (in quot. 1935, in France).

? **1863** MRS. GASKELL *Let.* 16 July (1966) 708 The pleasure of our intercourse at the Villino Trollope. **1923** A. HUXLEY *Let.* 12 Nov. (1969) 223 They have a Città Giardino just outside to the north and the number of horrible little villini ..is extraordinary. **1935** E. BOWEN *House in Paris* I. ii. 31 Though Mrs. Arbuthnot had not..been lent the villino at Beaulieu, she had been lent a flat at Mentone. **1958** 'M. INNES' *Long Farewell* I. 14 Then let's go up to the *villino*. The view's just as good from there. **1980** *Times* 11 Oct. 10/7 One restaurant..occupies a former *villino* or small house with a garden.

villipend, obs. f. VILIPEND *v.*

Villonesque (viːjɔ̃'ɛsk, viːlɒ'nɛsk), *a.* [f. the name of François *Villon* (1431–1480 or 1489), French poet + -ESQUE.] Characteristic of (the style of) Villon.

1932 E. RICKWORD tr. *Coulon's Poet Under Saturn* vi. 163 A name evocative of the cells, the Villonesque name of Pierre Duchâtelet. **1937** *Times Lit. Suppl.* 20 Mar. 222/1 The self-portrait..is of a somewhat Villonesque character. **1979** M. A. SCREECH *Rabelais* iii. 86 His Villonesque tricks against the university and church dignitaries.

villose (vɪ'ləʊs), *a. Bot.* and *Ent.* [ad. L. *villōs-us* hairy, rough, f. *villus* VILLUS. Cf. It. *villoso*, *velloso*, Sp., Pg. *velloso.*] = VILLOUS *a.*

a. *Bot.* **1727** BAILEY (vol. II), *Villose*, hairy. **1753** *Chambers' Cycl.* Suppl. s.v. *Leaf*, *Villose* Leaf. See *Pilose* Leaf, supra. **1812** *New Bot. Gard.* I. 29 The involucre remote and villose. **1844** *Florist's Jrnl.* (1846) V. 26 The various parts of plants, when clothed or furnished with hairs, are described as being downy, pilose, villose, tomentose. **1887** W. PHILLIPS *Brit. Discomycetes* 185 Margin fimbriate, villose-white.

b. *Ent.* **1819** SAMOUELLE *Entomol. Compend.* 156 *Dryp[ta] emarginata.* Blue, punctate, villose. **1826** KIRBY & SP. *Entomol.* IV. 39 The substance is unusually thick in the spinose caterpillars of butterflies; and in the pupa of one.. it is villose. **1847** HARDY in *Proc. Berw. Nat. Club* II. 235 Abdomen and elytra fulvo-pubescent, the last with a villose cinereous angulated band. **1861** HAGEN *Synop. Neuroptera N. Amer.* 153 *Libellula julia*... Fuscous, villose.

villosity (vɪ'lɒsɪtɪ). [ad. L. type **villōsitās*: see prec. and -ITY. So F. *villosité*, Sp. *vellosidad.*]

1. *Bot.*, *Zool.*, etc. The condition or fact of being villose or villous.

a. **1777** LIGHTFOOT *Flor. Scot.* II. 606 This villosity [of the leaf] soon wears off. **1823** SCORESBY *Jrnl.* 414 They differ from both in the form and villosity of the leaves. **1839** LINDLEY *Introd. Bot.* (ed. 3) 59 *Villosity*,..when they [*sc.* hairs] are very long, very soft, erect, and straight. **1857** DARWIN in F. Darwin *Life* (1887) II. 98, I find Moquin-Tandon treats in his 'Tératologie' on villosity of plants.

b. **1789** BENTHAM *Princ. Legisl.* xvii. 309 The villosity of the skin. **1852** DANA *Crust.* I. 200 But slight traces of any villosity can be detected. **1861** HAGEN *Synop. Neuroptera N. Amer.* 180 Thorax obscure brassy-brown, with brown villosity.

2. a. A villous formation or surface. **b.** A villus.

1828 STARK *Elem. Nat. Hist.* II. 229 This villosity is supposed to be composed of tubes adapted to taking up the surrounding fluids. **1857** BULLOCK *Cazeaux' Midwifery* 70 Its internal surface..exhibiting granulations, and some extremely delicate villosities. **1879** *De Quatrefages' Hum. Spec.* 50 The modifications of the hair and villosities.

vi'lloso-, comb. form of L. *villōsus* VILLOSE *a.*, as in ***villoso-scabrous*** adj.

1846 DANA *Zooph.* (1848) 390 Exterior finely striate and villoso-scabrous or spinulous.

‖**villotta** (vɪl'lɒtta). Also **villota**. Pl. **villot(t)e.** [It.] A type of villanella, originating in northern Italy.

1876 STAINER & BARRETT *Dict. Mus. Terms* 446/2 *Villotte* (*It.*). The name given to the first secular pieces in harmony after the rules of counterpoint were fixed. **1926** C. GRAY in Gray & Heseltine *Carlo Gesualdo* I. 10 They would spend whole nights out in the bay [of Naples], singing *villotte*, and madrigals. **1942** *Bull. Amer. Musicological Soc.* Apr. 9 The period of the *villota* is dated back by Torrefranca..to the first half of the 15th century... The theory is founded.. chiefly upon a group of eleven *villote*..now preserved in the Marciana in Venice. **1958** [see CANZONETTA]. **1980** *Early Music* Jan. 104/2 The *Libro primo* contains a wide variety of text forms including the madrigal, villotta, canzone, and ballata-madrigal.

villous ('vɪləs), *a.* [ad. L. *villōsus* VILLOSE *a.* Cf. F. *villeux.*]

1. *Anat.* Covered with numerous thick-set, slender projections resembling short hairs: **a.** Of the inner coat of the stomach or intestines.

c **1400** *Lanfranc's Cirurg.* 169 þe stomak & þe guttis is ordeyned a skyn, þat is clepid þe siphac; & is a syngle skyn & is not villous. **1731** ARBUTHNOT *Aliments* i. (1735) 7 The quick Sensation of the inward villous Coat of the Stomach. **1733** CHEYNE *Eng. Malady* II. vii. §1 (1734) 184 Either it [the stomach] is too thin and weak,..or the inner villous Membrane is worn off. **1769** HEWSON in *Phil. Trans.* LIX. 210 The lacteals in the cod..are remarkable for having a beautiful net-work of vessels between the muscular and villous coat of the intestines. **1842** COMBE *Digest.* 94 On examining the surface of the villous coat with a magnifying glass. **1881** MIVART *Cat* 183 There is thus a great contrast between its interior and the villous internal surface of the small intestine.

b. In general use.

1764 REID *Inquiry* ii. §1 The *membrana pituitaria*, and the olfactory nerves, which are distributed to the villous parts of this membrane. **1792** *Phil. Trans.* LXXXII. 179 The tongue itself is extremely villous, having some very long villi at the point, which act, I conceive, somewhat like capillary tubes. **1831** R. KNOX *Cloquet's Anat.* 555 The surface of the ciliary processes is reticulated and villous. **1846** CARPENTER *Man. Phys.* 192 The villous and vascular condition of a Mucous membrane. **1870** ROLLESTON *Anim. Life* 124 The pharynx has a coarsely villous exterior.

2. Of the nature of villi.

1664 POWER *Exp. Philos.* I. 22 An Appendent Proboscis or Trunk, consisting of many villous filaments in figure of a Cone. **1854** C. H. JONES & SIEV. *Pathol. Anat.* iv. 188 Rokitansky describes a variety of cancer, which he calls *villous*, from its consisting of a kind of delicate fibrous stalk branching at its end into villous processes. **1873** F. T. ROBERTS *Handbk. Med.* 44 The weak new vessels..in certain vascular cysts, or villous processes. **1876** BRISTOWE *Th. & Pract. Med.* (1878) 93 Fungous, papular, villous, or cystic formations.

Comb. **1869** G. LAWSON *Dis. Eye* (1874) 13 Covered with small red villous-looking granulations.

3. Of animals: Hairy, furry. *rare*$^{-1}$.

1661 LOVELL *Hist. Anim. & Min.* Isagoge b 1, Horses have most haire upon the mane, lions upon their shoulders, ..and the hare is most villous; in all they grow thick.

4. *Bot.* Of parts of plants: Thickly covered with long soft hairs.

1766 *Museum Rust.* VI. 444 The flowers..are succeeded by a swelling, villous pod. **1787** *Fam. Plants* I. 41 Stigmas two, villous on the side. **1808** ROXBURGH in *Asiat. Res.* VIII. 500 Leaves alternate, . . smooth above, villous underneath. **1844** *Florist's Jrnl.* (1846) V. 18 Its petals being far less taper-pointed, and not villous. **1881** *Gard. Chron.* XVI. 780 The whole plant is more or less villous.

b. Consisting of villi.

1821 W. P. C. BARTON *Flora N. Amer.* I. 37 The lower leaves . . invested beneath with a villous pubescence.

Hence **'villously** *adv.*

1870 HOOKER *Stud. Flora* 429 Empty glumes villously ciliate.

‖**villus** ('vɪləs). *Bot.* and *Anat.* Pl. villi ('vɪlaɪ). [L. *villus* tuft of hair, shaggy hair, etc.]

1. *Bot.* A long, slender, soft hair.

1704 J. HARRIS *Lex. Techn.* I, *Villi*, in Botany, are small Hairs like the Grain of Plush or Shag, with which, as with a kind of Excrescence, some Trees do abound. **1884** BOWER & SCOTT *De Bary's Phaner.* 90 The multicellular heads of the . . glandular hairs, villi, and scales.

2. *Anat.* A slender hair-like process or minute projection forming one of a number closely set upon a surface.

pl. **1728** CHAMBERS *Cycl.*, *Crusta Villosa*, . . the fourth Tunic . . of the Stomach. . . On the inner Surface of this Coat, are seen innumerable *Villi* or *Fibrillæ*. **1771** *Encycl. Brit.* I. 260/1 The villi of this intestine [*sc.* the duodenum] are thicker than in the stomach. **1792** [see VILLOUS *a.* 1 b]. **1848** CARPENTER *Anim. Phys.* 174 The lacteals originate in the numberless villi, or minute projections with which the mucous membrane that lines the alimentary tube is covered. **1861** J. R. GREENE *Man. Anim. Kingd.*, *Cœlent.* 31 The surface of this layer is often elevated into a number of villi, or conical processes. **1881** MIVART *Cat* 26 It may be produced into many, often relatively large, papillæ or villi. *sing.* **1848** CARPENTER *Anim. Phys.* 40 In the intervals of the digestive action, only a few granules . . can be seen at the end of the villus. **1880** BEALE *Slight Ailments* 89 Every villus of the intestinal canal is supplied with nerve fibres.

vilm(e, obs. varr. FILM *sb.*

vilne, vilony(e, etc., obs. varr. VILLAINY.

vilou, obs. f. WILLOW.

vilte, var. VILETY *Obs.*

vilthy, southern dial. var. FILTHY *a.*

vily(e, obs. varr. VILELY *adv.*

vilycoit, obs. f. WYLIECOAT.

vim[1] (vɪm). Orig. *U.S.* [Commonly regarded as a. L. *vim*, acc. sing. of *vis* strength, energy; but the early adverbial use (see quot. 1850) suggests a purely imitative or interjectional origin.] Force or vigour, energy, 'go'. †Also as *adv.*, vigorously, sharply.

1843 *Yale Lit. Mag.* VIII. 406 He would have acted out his real nature with all the *vim* and pathos which heroes always manifest in like circumstances. **1850** *Odd Leaves* 51 (Thornton), He thought of his spurs, so he ris up, an' drove them vim in the hoss's flanx. *Ibid.* 91. **1875** *New York Herald* 17 April (Bartlett), With a vim and determination that sometimes makes victory half assured. **1876** F. L. GALT in Orton *Andes & Amazons* II. xiv. 586 [The Portuguese] seem still to carry about the vim of a Vasco de Gama in their wanderings. **1880** JOHNSON *W. L. Garrison* 128 There was . . a Garrisonian grip and vim in the anti-slavery sentiment of the county. **1894** *Outing* XXIV. 259/1 He fought well and with a vim that I have never seen equaled.

Vim[2] (vɪm). Also vim. [Cf. VIM[1].] The proprietary name of a brand of detergent. Hence **vim** *v. trans.*, to clean with Vim.

1894 *Trade Marks Jrnl.* 6 June 484/1 *Vim*. . . All goods included in Class 48. Lever Brothers, Limited, Port Sunlight, near Birkenhead; soap manufacturers. **1926** R. MACAULAY *Crewe Train* II. x. 179 Denham looked vaguely at the vim. 'For the sink,' her aunt explained. 'And I've got you a . . brush. That's to scrub the vim in with.' 'Thank you very much,' said Denham, doubtfully; 'I don't know how much I shall vim the sink, though.' **1948** 'N. SHUTE' *No Highway* viii. 205 Shirley collected scrubbers and soap and Vim and a dustpan and brush. **1968** *Listener* 14 Mar. 359/1 The real battle, though, is with the Saturday-night dancers who put down French chalk to make the floor slippery. The badminton players retaliate—of old with Vim or a mixture of tea-leaves, sand and water. **1976** T. SHARPE *Wilt* ii. 11 She got the washing-up done . . and the bath Vimmed.

‖**vimana** (vɪ'mɑːnə). *India.* [Skr.]

1. The central tower enclosing the shrine in an Indian temple.

1863 *Chambers's Encycl.* V. 552/1 The temples consist of the temple or vimana, in front of which is the pillared porch or mantopa, [etc.]. **1891** J. FERGUSSON *Hist. Indian & Eastern Archit.* II. ii. 221 There is one other peculiarity common to both Jaina and Hindu architecture . . It is the form of the towers or spires called Sikras, or Vimanas, which invariably surmount the cells in which the images are placed. **1913** L. D. BARNETT *Antiquities of India* x. 233 When for the Buddhist relic is substituted the image or emblem of a god, the apse is changed into a closed cella, with a door, and its place as the holy of holies in the structure is marked by a spire or *śikhara*, forming with the cella a *vimāna*. **1969** *Hindu Weekly Mag.* (Madras) 3 Aug. p. ii/5 He made a bold departure by making the 'vimana', the tower over the sanctum sanctorum, dominate the entire scheme of temple construction.

2. *Mythol.* A heavenly chariot.

1946 S. KRAMRISCH *Hindu Temple* II. 344 Their bodies inflated by air race in giants across the atmosphere, support the Vimānas, the chariots of the gods. **1979** W. H. CANAWAY *Solid Gold Buddha* xv. 106 I've heard of a *vimana*, a sky chariot. Have you ever thought of using one of those things in the show?

†**vimaue.** *Obs.*[−1] [ad. OF. *vimauve*, mod.F. *guimauve*. Cf. MAW *sb.*[2]] Marsh-mallow.

c **1410** *Master of Game* xii. (MS. Bodl. 546) fol. 58, þenne take ȝe of þe mauys & of þe vimauys & of þe white lylyes.

'viminal, *a. rare*[−0]. [ad. L. *vīmināl-is*, f. *vīmin-*, *vīmen* osier.] (See quots.)

1623 COCKERAM I, *Viminal*, apt or fit to bind with. **1656** BLOUNT *Glossogr.* (copying Cooper), *Viminal*, apt to winde or binde, belonging to Osiers or Twigs. [Hence in later Dicts. with varying definitions.]

vimineous (vɪ'mɪnɪəs), *a.* Now *rare.* Also 7 viminious. [f. L. *vīmine-us* (f. *vīmin-*, *vīmen*: see prec.) + -ous.]

1. Made of pliable twigs or wickerwork.

1657 TOMLINSON *Renou's Disp.* 189 Chirurgions have invented an Æstuary of a vimineous texture like a bird-cage. **1664** EVELYN *Sylva* 37 The Timber is incomparable . ., because it is exceedingly light, for Vine, and Hop-props, and divers viminious works. **1717** PRIOR *Alma* III. 172 As in a Hive's vimineous Dome, Ten thousand Bees enjoy their Home. **1736** H. BROOKE *Univ. Beauty* VI. 309 Here lightly some vimineous burdens bear.

2. *Bot.* Producing long, flexible shoots or twigs.

1664 EVELYN *Sylva* 3 Willows, and all the Vimineous kinds, which are raised of Sets only. **1694** WESTMACOTT *Script. Herb.* 154 This vimineous Tree [poplar] is properly but of two kinds. *Ibid.* 222 This [the willow] is one of the Vimineous family. **1731** P. MILLER *Gard. Dict.* s.v. *Vegetation*, In some, it [the principle of life] is seated both in the Roots, and all over the Trunk and Branches; as, in the Vimineous or Willow Kinds. **1857** A. GRAY *First Less. Bot.* 236 *Vimineous*, producing slender twigs, such as those used for wicker-work. **1866** *Treas. Bot.* 1216/2.

‖**vin** (vɛ̃). [Fr.] Wine: used in various French phrases. **1.** Followed by *de*, *d'*, etc., designating a wine of a particular classification, district, or method of manufacture, etc., as *vin de Graves*, *de liqueur*, etc.

1699 M. LISTER *Journey to Paris* 161 Those Wines thus in the Must are called . . *Vin des Liqueurs*. **1777** P. THICKNESSE *Year's Journey* II. xxxvii. 38 Barren as the *Crau* appears to be, it . . produces such excellent wine . . that it is called *Vin de Crau*, by way of pre-eminence. **1833** C. REDDING *Hist. Mod. Wines* iii. 51 What are called in France *vins du liqueur*, are those in which the saccharine principle has not entirely disappeared during the process of fermentation, and been changed into alcohol. **1842** BROWNING *Dram. Lyrics* 15/2 For council dinners made rare havock With Claret, Moselle, Vin-de-Grave, Hock. **1911** Vin du Glacier [see FENDANT]. **1939** B. COLLIER *Catalan France* xii. 273 In the case of wines intended to be drunk as *apéritif* or dessert wines . . [the colour] is usually that indicated by the terms '*vin d'or*' or '*doré*'. **1955** *Times* 5 Aug. 7/4 The agreement also foresees an increase in the export of French vins d'appellation to the value of 350M. francs. **1967** A. LICHINE *Dict. Wines* 543/2 *Vin de liqueur*. This French term has two meanings. 1. A very sweet wine, such as a rich Sauternes. 2. Wine of approximately 18% of alcohol caused by the addition of brandy and added to Champagne prior to shipment. **1968** R. AMBERLEY *Incitement to Murder* i. 18 The wine . . was not an *appellation contrôlée*, or even a *vin de qualité supérieure*; it was . . an unpretentious local wine.

2. With (*ppl.*) *adjs.*, describing or purporting to describe wines of a certain quality or prepared in a certain way.

1833 C. REDDING *Hist. Mod. Wines* v. 176 At Moulins they make a species called *vin fou*, or mad wine, or rather . . 'drunkard's wine'. They fill a small, strong-bound cask, having no bung, with must; this they put into another cask, and plunge it into the vat, from which it is not withdrawn until the fermentation ceases. **1849** GEO. ELIOT *Let.* 22 Dec. (1954) I. 324 Dear Sara's letter is . . not at all physicky—rather an agreeable draught of *vin sucré*. **1920** G. SAINTSBURY *Notes on Cellar-Bk.* xi. 162 *Vin brulé*, a very popular beverage in Old France, and a regular Christmas and New Year tradition in the Channel Islands. **1952** V. WILKINS *King Reluctant* I. vi. 94 It is at least drinkable—a *vin bourgeois*. **1958** A. L. SIMON *Dict. Wines* 161/2 *Vin chaud*, mulled wine. **1966** P. V. PRICE *France: Food & Wine Guide* II. 238 The '*vin fou*' of the Jura is made by bottling either white or rosé wine at the peak of its first fermentation. **1974** *Times* 10 Aug. 11/2 A white Corbières. Vin Vert. Montagne d'Alaric.

3. Special collocations. **vin compris** [lit. 'understood']: (phrase denoting) wine included in the price of a meal or other entertainment; **vin cuit** = *wine cuit* s.v. CUIT, CUTE: an aperitif wine; **vin de paille** [lit. 'of straw'] = *straw wine* s.v. STRAW *sb.*[1] 14 (see quots.); **vin de table** = *table wine* s.v. TABLE *sb.* 22; cf. TAFELWEIN; **vin d'honneur**, a wine formally offered in honour of a person or persons; the reception at which the wine is offered; **vin doux (naturel)** [lit. 'sweet (unfortified)'], a sweet aperitif wine; **vin du pays** [lit. 'of the country'], a local wine; also *transf.* and *fig.*; **vin gris** [lit. 'grey'], a rosé wine of eastern France; **vin jaune** [lit. 'yellow'], (see quot. 1966); **vin mousseux** [MOUSSEUX], sparkling wine. See also VIN BLANC, ORDINAIRE, ROSÉ, ROUGE below as main entries.

1889 KIPLING *From Sea to Sea* I. xii. 308 The *vin ordinaire* which is *compris*, is good. **1910** G. B. SHAW *Let.* ?16 Apr. (1972) II. 921 Further excitement is provided by the institution of *vin compris* at meals. **1967** *Observer* 14 May 28/3 Vin compris in Camden. 'Free wine tasting,' promised the notice. **1833** C. REDDING *Hist. Mod. Wines* vi. 193 Their [*sc.* the Spaniards'] boiled wines, or vins *cuits*, as the French call them, are mingled with other growths. **1962** *Times* 21 Dec. 10/7 The bottle of *vin cuit* or unfermented wine. **1833** C. REDDING *Hist. Mod. Wines* iii. 51 The wines called *vins de paille* are so denominated from the grapes being laid for several months upon straw before they are taken to the press. **1964** A. SICHEL *Penguin Bk. Wines* III. 159 *Vins de paille*, the second of the unusual white wines of the Jura, get their name from the straw mats on which the black Poulsard and Trousseau grapes are dried for several weeks before being pressed. **1972** *Country Life* 14 Dec. 1660/1 Nowadays the grapes are normally laid not on mats but on trays. . . To produce a litre of *vin de paille* takes about 12–15 kilos of grapes. **1948** A. WAUGH *Unclouded Summer* vii. 142 They had treated it as a *vin de table*. **1981** *New Yorker* 28 Dec. 49/1, I took a half-litre bottle of Sichel le Cellier, *vin de table, rouge*. **1920** *Punch* 30 June 512/1 The Prime Minister was celebrating the longest—and pretty nearly the hottest—day by a *vin d'honneur* at Boulogne. **1947** E. WAUGH *Scott-King's Mod. Europe* 25 Vin d'honneur offered to the delegates by the Municipality of Bellacita. **1978** *Broadcast* 6 Mar. 4/1 A *vin d'honneur* at Television Centre for TFI's news director. **1958** A. L. SIMON *Dict. Wines* 162/1 *Vin doux*, grape-juice before it ferments and becomes wine; also used for a 'sweet' wine. **1959** W. JAMES *Word-bk. Wine* 197 *Vins doux naturels*, The Frenchman's logic has strange lacunae; . . the unnatural and fortified sweet wines made in the south-east [*read*: south-west] corner of his own country he blandly calls 'natural sweet wines'. **1981** *Country Life* 23 July 261/3 That delectable Muscat wine, a *vin-doux-naturel*. **1777** P. THICKNESSE *Year's Journey* II. xlix. 138, I could not help treating him with a bottle of *vin de païs*. **1822** L. SIMOND *Switzerland* I. 34 A well-seasoned veal pie, a boeuf-a-la-mode, plenty of the best *vin du pays*, and even a dessert. **1935** *Times Lit. Suppl.* 18 July 459 A renewed zeal for the land of England, and, especially for the savour of its products, of its beef and cheese and fruit and *vin du pays* or cider. **1965** Vin du pays [see PREMIER CRU]. **1833** C. REDDING *Hist. Mod. Wines* v. 176 A *vin gris*, a grey or rather brown wine, is made here [*sc.* at Gannat] by leaving the must to ferment for forty-eight hours. **1958** A. L. SIMON *Dict. Wines* 162/1 *Vin gris*, light red wine of Lorraine and Alsace, usually made of mixed black and white grapes. **1974** *Times* 18 May (Suppl.) p. i/4 The *vin gris* of the Jura. **1833** C. REDDING *Hist. Mod. Wines* iii. 51 The *mousseux* wines of Arbois are called *vins blanc de garde*, and when old, *vin jaune*. **1966** P. V. PRICE *France: Food & Wine Guide* II. 239 The two extraordinary wines of the Jura are the *vins jaunes* and *vins de paille*. . . *Vins jaunes* are made solely from the Sauvignon grape . . taste slightly like sherry, though . . they are not fortified in any way. **1981** *Times* 12 Dec. 12/4 The odd Jura wine, Château Chalon . . is a *vin jaune* . . staying long in cask, wherein a *veil* forms on the surface. **1789** Vin mousseux [see MOUSSEUX]. **1833** C. REDDING *Hist. Mod. Wines* ii. 30 Those wines which effervesce (*vins mousseux*) are impregnated deeply with carbonic acid gas. **1972** A. ROSS *London Assignment* 47, I . . pulled the napkin off the foil-topped bottle. It was a vin mousseux, and not a very good one.

vin, southern dial. variant of FIND *v.*

vina, var. VEENA.

vinaceous (vaɪ'neɪʃəs), *a.* [f. L. *vīnāce-us*, f. *vīn-um* wine: see -ACEOUS.] Of the (reddish) colour of wine; wine-coloured.

1688 HOLME *Armoury* II. 244 The Throat [is] tinctured with a lovely vinaceous, graplike colour. **1776** PENNANT *Brit. Zool.* (ed. 4) I. 267 The rump a fine cinereous: breast and belly, pale chesnut dashed with a vinaceous cast. **1802** BINGLEY *Anim. Biog.* (1805) II. 388 The fore part of the neck and breast are vinaceous. **1815** STEPHENS in *Shaw's Gen. Zool.* IX. I. 91 Throat and sides of the head vinaceous. **1889** P. L. SCLATER *Argentine Ornith.* II. 140 Beneath plumbeous, with a strong vinaceous tinge.

b. Qualifying names of colours.

1788 J. WHITE *Jrnl. Voy. N.S. Wales* (1790) 146 The general colour of the bird otherwise is brown, changing to vinaceous red on the breast. **1817** STEPHENS in *Shaw's Gen. Zool.* X. I. 5 Vinaceous-grey Coly, with a blue tail, crested head, and shining green occiput. *Ibid.* XI. I. 84 Pigeon with the head . . of a vinaceous purple. **1872** COUES *N. Amer. Birds* 226 Olive-gray with a reddish tinge, crown and under parts vinaceous-red. **1889** P. L. SCLATER *Argentine Ornith.* III. 140 Above pale vinaceous brown.

c. *ellip.* or as *sb.*

1819 STEPHENS in *Shaw's Gen. Zool.* XI. I. 126 The belly, sides, thighs, and under tail-coverts, of a reddish vinaceous. **1877** COUES & ALLEN *N. Amer. Rod.* 811 The prevailing tint of the dorsal surface varies from gray to pale vinaceous.

vinacre, vinager, obs. forms of VINEGAR.

†**vinager.** *Obs.*[−0] [Cf. med.L. *vinageria*, *vinacheria* (Du Cange).] ? A wine-vessel.

c **1440** *Promp. Parv.* 510/1 Vynagere (*K.* vynagre, *P.* vynegyr), *vinarium*.

vinaigrette (vɪneɪ'grɛt, vɪnɪ-). Also 7-8 vinaigret, 7, 9 vinegrette, 9 vinaigaret. [a. F. *vinaigrette* vinegar-sauce (also in senses 2 and 3), f. *vinaigre* VINEGAR *sb.*]

1. †**a.** A condiment prepared with vinegar. *Obs.*[−1]

1699 EVELYN *Acetaria* 20 Cucumber, . . tho' very cold and moist, the most approved Sallet alone, or in Composition, of all the Vinaigrets, to sharpen the Appetite.

b. Now *spec.* a dressing of oil and (wine) vinegar, sometimes with herbs (esp. tarragon), used esp. with salads and cold vegetables. In full ***vinaigrette sauce*** (also F. *sauce vinaigrette*). Also ***vinaigrette dressing***.

[**1877** *Cassell's Dict. Cookery* 1091 *Vinaigrette, Sauce à la.* This is a sauce much used in Paris for cold viands.] **1880** M. PARLOA *Appledore Cook Bk.* (new ed.) 235 (*recipe*) Vinaigrette sauce. **1906** MRS. BEETON *Bk. Househ. Managem.* xxxv. 1112 *Vinaigrette sauce* . . 4 tablespoonfuls of salad-oil, 2 tablespoonfuls of tarragon vinegar, [etc.]. **1936**

LUCAS & HUME *Au Petit Cordon Bleu* 136 *Sauce vinaigrette* ..tarragon vinegar..lemon..shallot..garlic..mixed herbs ..parsley..salad oil [etc.]. **1959** *Listener* 24 Dec. 1135/1 Mushrooms cooked and tossed in vinaigrette dressing. **1974** N. FREELING *Dressing of Diamond* 7 Colette..made vinaigrette for the avocadoes. **1982** T. FITZGIBBON *With Love* ix. 163 Calf's head with vinaigrette sauce, a dish seldom seen today.

2. A small two-wheeled carriage drawn or pushed by persons, formerly in use in France. Now only *Hist.*

1698 W. KING tr. *Sorbière's Journ. Lond.* 6, I saw a little Master in a little Vinegrette, drawn along by two Boys, much bigger then himself, and push'd behind by a Maid. **1698** M. LISTER *Journ. Paris* (1699) 13 The Vinegrette, a Coach on Two Wheels, dragg'd by a Man, and push'd behind by a Woman or Boy, or both. **1898** A. BALFOUR *To Arms* xxiv. 272 The vinegrettes plying hither and thither.. are like Sedans mounted on two thin wheels.

3. a. A small ornamental bottle or box usually containing a sponge charged with some aromatic or pungent salts; a smelling-bottle.

1811 MISS L. M. HAWKINS *C'tess & Gertr.* I. 55 She had no resource but silence, her fan and her *vinaigrette*. **1847** C. BRONTE *Jane Eyre* xviii, The matrons, meantime, offered vinaigrettes and wielded fans. **1866** GEO. ELIOT *F. Holt* xxxix, She..took up..a gold vinaigrette which Mrs. Transome often liked to carry with her.

b. *transf.* Applied to a person.

1836 T. HOOK *G. Gurney* I. iv. 140, I would not..have ventured to confess to my most exemplary parent, more especially in the presence of the fair vinaigrette,..the adventure at Twickenham.

vinaigrous, *a. rare*$^{-1}$. [f. F. *vinaigre* vinegar.] Vinegary; sour-tempered.

1837 CARLYLE *Fr. Rev.* I. VII. ix, Even the ancient vinaigrous Tantes admit it; the King's Aunts, ancient Graille and Sisterhood.

vinakir, obs. Sc. form of VINEGAR.

vinal (ˈvaɪnəl), *a.* [ad. L. *vīnāl-is* (rare), f. *vīn-um* wine, or directly f. *vīn-um* + -AL^1.]

†**1.** Addicted to, fond of, wine. *Obs.*$^{-1}$

1652 S. S. *Weepers* 6 His Vinal and Venereous temper opened the little Wicket for the five other Deadly Sinnes.

2. Produced by, originating in, wine.

1658 R. WHITE tr. *Digby's Powd. Symp.* (ed. 2) 110 The bodies..attract unto themselves..such as are of their nature ..; as wine doth the vinall spirits. *a* **1700** KEN *Edmund* Poet. Wks. 1721 II. 313 Their vinal Steams evaporating, they Felt of their usual Vigour a Decay. **1894** FROUDE *Erasmus* xi. 210 She drank it [the wine] to the last drop... Then she..tried to pitch him overboard. There is vinal energy for you.

vi'narious, *a. rare*$^{-0}$. [f. L. *vīnāri-us*, f. *vīnum* wine: see -ARIOUS.] Of or belonging to wine.

1656 BLOUNT *Glossogr.*

vina'torian, *a. rare*$^{-0}$. (See quot. and VINITORIAN *a.*)

1656 BLOUNT *Glossogr.*, *Vinatorian*, belonging to the dresser of a Vineyard.

vinaya (vinaˈja). *Buddhism.* [Skr., lit. 'leading (away)'.] The rules of conduct that regulate Buddhist monastic life. Also *attrib.*

1854 A. CUNNINGHAM *Ladák* xiii. 383 Vinaya, or 'Rules of Discipline'. **1881** RHYS DAVIDS & OLDENBERG (*title*) Vinaya texts. *Ibid.* p. xiii, Upâli is mentioned as the first among the custodians of the Vinaya. **1924** S. DUTT *Early Buddhist Monachism* i. 15 The Council of Vesali must be dated about the middle of the fourth century B.C., and the compilation of a complex codex of Vinaya rules not much earlier than that date. **1956** R. PIERIS *Sinhalese Social Organization* II. ix. 74 The monks themselves were prohibited by *vinaya* rules from performing these mundane duties. **1979** *Jrnl. Asian Studies* XXXVIII. 671 The *Vinaya*, or Code of Conduct.

‖**vin blanc** (vɛ̃ blɑ̃). [Fr.]

1. a. French white wine.

1792 A. YOUNG *Trav. France* I. 164 He gave me a bottle of excellent *vin blanc mouseux*, made in Auvergne. **1814** M. BIRKBECK *Journey through France* 29 Pouilly, [renowned] for its Vin Blanc. **1853** [see GOFER^1]. **1917** A. G. EMPEY *Over Top* 313 *Vin blanc*, French white wine made from vinegar. They forgot the red ink. **1958** 'E. DUNDY' *Dud Avocado* I. ix. 157 The vin blanc break around eleven o'clock. **1974** *Country Life* 31 Jan. 183/2 An enormous amount..must be sold not as burgundy at all but as plain *vin rouge* or *vin blanc*.

b. *vin blanc cassis* [CASSIS], (see quot. 1964).

1964 A. SICHEL *Penguin Bk. Wines* III. 173 A popular liqueur is made from blackcurrants..and is known as Cassis. Mixed with white wine, it is often used as an aperitif drink in France, called 'Vin Blanc Cassis'. **1982** 'R. GRAYSON' *Montmartre Murders* iv. 31 Gautier was sipping the vin blanc cassis which a waiter had brought him.

2. In various joc. and illiterate forms. Cf. PLONK *sb.*^{2} Chiefly *Mil. slang.*

1919 J. BUCHAN *Mr. Standfast* viii. 162 A pint and a dram for me. This is better than vongblong and vongrooge..in those estamints. **1933** F. RICHARDS *Old Soldiers never Die* vii. 83 An elderly Frenchman from Armentières..was soon selling beer and ving blong and doing a roaring trade. **1934** BLUNDEN *Choice or Chance* 31 In Pop. we banqueted no doubt On *vin-blong*, malaga-and-stout.

vinblastine (vɪnˈblæstiːn). *Pharm.* [f. mod.L. *Vin-ca*, former generic name (see PERIWINKLE^1) + *leuco*)*blast* s.v. LEUCO- + -INE^5.] A cytotoxic alkaloid, $C_{46}H_{58}N_4O_9$, obtained from the periwinkle *Catharanthus roseus* and administered intravenously (usu. as the sulphate) in the treatment of lymphomas and other cancers. Cf. VINCRISTINE.

1962 M. R. KARON et al. in *Pediatrics* XXX. 791/1 Several alkaloids were subsequently isolated from the crude extract [of *Vinca rosea*], two of which, leurosine and vinblastine (formerly called vincaleukoblastine), markedly inhibited this tumour. **1974** *Nature* 15 Mar. 239/1 The alkaloids colchicine and vinblastine interfere with the assembly of microtubules, yet they also affect several properties of the surface membrane of animal cells. **1983** *Oxf. Textbk. Med.* II. XIX. 96/1 Vincristine..is preferable to vinblastine..in the treatment of leukaemia.

vinca^1 (ˈvɪŋkə). Also **Vinca.** [mod.L.: see PERIWINKLE^1.] = PERIWINKLE^1 1; **vinca alkaloid**, any of several alkaloids (as vinblastine, vincristine) obtained from a periwinkle.

1868 D. THOMSON *Handy Bk. Flower-Garden* ix. 250 For forming permanent edgings to large beds, these Vincas are very effective. **1937** A. T. JOHNSON *Woodland Garden* vii. 70 The vincas as a tribe are either misused or not used at all. **1961** D. STUART *Driven* xvii. 170 There had been pride and delight in her eyes when first the oleanders she tended so carefully had bloomed, and all the outside of the camp was a blaze of vincas that same season. **1970** PASSMORE & ROBSON *Compan. Med. Stud.* II. xxix. 11/2 Effects peculiar to the vinca alkaloids..include paraesthesia (especially round the mouth), temporary mental depression, loss of deep tendon reflexes and more rarely headaches, psychoses and convulsions. **1978** R. B. SCOTT *Price's Textbk. Pract. Med.* (ed. 12) IV. 374/1 The vinca alkaloids vinblastine (VLB) and vincristine (VCR)..have a variety of toxic effects other than those on dividing cells.

Vinča^2 (ˈvɪntʃə). *Archæol.* The name of a village site near Belgrade, used *attrib.* to designate a central Balkan culture of the chalcolithic age. Also *absol.*

1925 V. G. CHILDE *Dawn European Civilization* 174 The sunken oval huts, the shoe-last celts, the rude clay idols.. and the spirals and meanders decorating the vases suffice to attach Vinča I to the contemporary culture of Moravia. **1940** C. F. C. HAWKES *Prehist. Foundations Europe* iv. 93 The early Vinča pottery shows Anatolian tradition. *Ibid.* 94 Some twenty other settlements of the Vinča culture have been identified along the Serbian bank of the Danube. **1974** *Encycl. Brit Macropædia* II. 613/1 The Vinča sequence is best documented at the eponymous site, situated..east of Belgrade, overlying the Starčevo levels excavated by the Yugoslav archæologist Miloje Vasić, intermittently from 1908 to 1932. Fine Vinča ceramic wares are burnished in orange or black and decorated with a shallow linear channeling. **1977** *Jrnl. R. Soc. Arts* CXXV. 486/1 The mask-like face certainly recalls the conventions of this period in southeast Europe, notably those of the Vinča culture, or Porodin.

†**vince**, *v. Obs.*$^{-1}$ [ad. L. *vincĕre.*] *intr.* To win the day, be victorious.

1530 CROMWELL in *St. Papers Hen. VIII*, I. 367 The Florentynes dothe styll continew and defende the power of the Pope, and it ys supposyd that they shall vynce.

Vincennes (vɛ̃sɛn). The name of a château in the town of *Vincennes* (now a suburb of Paris), used *attrib.* and *absol.* to designate porcelain produced there in the eighteenth cent., before the manufactory was transferred to Sèvres (see SÈVRES *a.*); also applied to colour characteristic of Vincennes porcelain.

1766 in F. A. Barrett *Worcester Porcelain* (1953) vi. 29 Great improvements in the Worcester manufactory of china... It is hardly surpassed by the Vincennes, and much cheaper. **1874** C. SCHREIBER *Jrnl.* 13 Aug. (1911) I. 276 A Vincennes cup all but unique. **1900** F. LITCHFIELD *Pottery & Porcelain* vii. 104 The pieces having rich grand colours in claret colour or crimson lake, and in rich deep Vincennes blue. **1925** W. W. WORSTER tr. *Hannover's Pottery & Porcelain* III. xiii. 279 In the biscuit figures and groups of Vincennes we find..traces of the growing neo-classical movement. **1949** W. B. HONEY *European Ceramic Art* I. 40 The incomparable Vincennes gilding, with its soft-looking delicately tooled surface. **1960** H. HAYWARD *Antique Coll.* 254/1 The earliest Vincennes..includes jardinières, jugs, ice-pails and trays of simple shape. **1978** *Times* 22 July 8/2 A massive white Vincennes pot-pourri vase.

†**vincent**^{1}. *slang. Obs. rare.* [Of obscure origin.] The dupe in a betting game of bowls or the like. Also *Vincent's law*, the art of cheating at bowls, etc.

1592 GREENE *Conny-catching* II. B ij b, The Vincents Law is a common deceit or cosenage vsed in Bowling-allies, amongst the baser sort of people. *Ibid.* II. B iij, The vincent, ..that is the simple man that stands by, and not acquainted with their cosenage.

Vincent^2 (ˈvɪnsənt). *Path.* The name of J. H. *Vincent* (1862–1950), French medical scientist, used in the possessive to designate a painful ulcerative condition of the inside of the mouth or the throat associated with infection with fusiform bacteria and spirochætes (described by him in 1896); also a similar condition of the gums that is accompanied by foul breath and bleeding.

1904 *Lancet* 16 July 135/2 Vincent's angina is a form of pseudo-diphtheria which is associated with, and is probably due to, certain characteristic micro-organisms. **1918** Vincent's disease [see *trench mouth* s.v. TRENCH *sb.* 9]. **1926** J. L. T. APPLETON *Bacterial Infection* xxiv. The condition.. goes under a great variety of names, *e.g.*, 'trench mouth', Vincent's gingivitis or stomatitis and ulcero-membranous stomatitis. **1935** *Motion Picture* Nov. 3/2 (Advt.), Keep gum disorders—gingivitis, pyorrhea and Vincent's disease far in the background. **1959** J. BLISH *Case of Conscience* i. 11 He saw few of the mixed bacilli and spirochetes which would have indicated a case of ordinary..Vincent's angina—'trench mouth'. **1962** BLAKE & TROTT *Periodontology* xvii. 173 The interdental cratering which follows longstanding Vincent's infection leads to interdental stagnation. **1983** *Oxf. Textbk. Med.* I. XII. 21/2 Acute ulcerative gingivitis.. At times there are shallow necrotic ulcers affecting the oropharyngeal mucosa which shows diffuse erythema, this has been referred to as Vincent's angina.

Vincentian (vɪnˈsɛnʃən), *sb.*^{1} and *a.*^{1} [f. *Vincent* (see def.) + -IAN.] **A.** *sb.* A member of an order of Roman Catholic mission-priests founded by St. Vincent de Paul (1576–1660). **B.** *adj.* Of or pertaining to St. Vincent or to this order.

1854 NEWMAN in W. Ward *Life* (1912) I. xi. 338 [I] went off to Cork to the Vincentians. **1896** W. J. FITZPATRICK *Mem. Fr. Healy* i. 10 The Vincentian Seminary, 34, Usher's Quay, Dublin. **1934** G. B. SHAW *Too True to be Good* 23 The latest rediscovery of the Vincentian principle has been made by Mr Ford, who has testified that if you want a staff of helpful persons..you must not give them either title, rank, or uniform. **1982** G. GREENE *Monsignor Quixote* I. v. 73 Marquez..did little entertaining apart from an occasional father from the Vincentian monastery. **1984** *New Yorker* 9 Apr. 52/3 St. John's is a Vincentian school... The Vincentians are trained missionaries.

Vincentian (vɪnˈsɛnʃən), *sb.*^{2} and *a.*^{3} [f. *Vincent* (see def.) + -IAN.] **A.** *sb.* A native or inhabitant of St. Vincent in the West Indies. **B.** *adj.* Of or pertaining to St. Vincent.

1933 *Vincentian* 4 Feb. 2/2 We have much pleasure in publishing in this issue the Report of the Installation of officers of the 'Vincentian Progressive Friendly Society'. *Ibid.*, Vincentians abroad are fondly thinking of home. **1944** *Minutes Legisl. Council St. Vincent 1943* 92 The parent.. was to all intents and purposes a Vincentian—who in turn was also from Vincentian parents. **1950** *Caribbean Q.* II. II. 18 In *Saraband* the light skinned Vincentian wants to marry a dark girl. **1974** *Advocate-News* (Barbados) 21 Feb. 2/1 Vincentians have temporarily thrown off cares of the current fuel crisis. **1980** *Oxf. Diocesan Mag.* Oct. 8/1 At Wycombe some 15% or more of the population is of immigrant origin —Pakistani, Vincentian, Indian, Jamaican, Polish, Italian, Yugoslav.

Vincentian (vɪnˈsɛnʃən), *a.*^{2} [f. *Vincent* (see def.) + -IAN.] Originating or associated with St. Vincent of Lerins (died *c* 450 A.D.).

The reference is to St. Vincent's test of orthodoxy: 'quod ubique, quod semper, quod ab omnibus creditum est'.

1875 LIDDON in Johnston *Life & Lett.* (1904) vii. 200 Your difficulty seems to be in the meaning of 'Semper' in the Vincentian Canon. **1887** LD. ACTON *Lett. Mary Gladstone* (1913) 182 No consensus, no Vincentian Rule, exists that can decide this question.

†**vincetoxic.** *Obs.*$^{-1}$ [ad. med.L. *vincetoxicum*, *-icus* (used as a plant-name), f. L. *vincĕre* to overcome + *toxicum* poison.] An antidote to poison.

1658 J. ROBINSON *Calm Ventilation* VII. in *Eudoxa*, etc. 151 Some Vincetoxicks [*printed* -toricks] are generall, and will be contrary to severall kinds [of poison].

vinch, obs. Sc. form of WENCH *sb.*

vinchuca (vɪnˈtʃuːkə). [Amer. Sp., f. Quechua *wihchuykuk.*] One of several blood-sucking triatomine bugs of Central and S. America, esp. *Triatoma infestans.*

1932 *Listener* 17 Aug. 227/1 The Vinchuca, a horrid looking beetle from half to an inch long..settles on its victims and draws their blood. **1971** P. C. C. GARNHAM *Progr. Parasitol.* ix. 189 In the opinion of Adler..Darwin contracted Chagas' Disease..when he landed on the coast of Argentina and was bitten by the 'vinchucas' (the triatomid bugs which convey the infection).

vincibility (vɪnsɪˈbɪlɪtɪ). [f. next + -ITY.] The state of being vincible; capability of being conquered or overcome.

1752 RICHARDSON *Corr.* (1804) III. 203 An instance of his favourite observation in behalf of the vincibility of a first love. **1753** —— *Grandison* (1781) VI. xii. 47, I don't know what to say to the vincibility of *such* a Love. **1807** *Ann. Rev.* V. 344 A belief in the vincibility of Frenchmen. **1856** J. STRANG *Glasgow & its Clubs* 141 In Egypt they had testified to the *vincibility* of the French *Invincibles*.

vincible (ˈvɪnsɪb(ə)l), *a.* [ad. L. *vincibilis*, f. *vincĕre* to overcome: see -IBLE. So obs. F. *vincible*, It. *vincibile*, Sp. *vencible*, Pg. *vencivel.*]

In the 15th cent. version of Higden (Rolls) IV. 167 *vincible* occurs as an error for *invincible*.

1. Of persons: That may be overcome or vanquished in battle or conflict, or in some contest; susceptible of defeat or overthrow.

1548 UDALL, etc. *Erasm. Par. Matt.* iv. 33 b, Christ ouercame hym to shewe vnto vs that he was vincible. **1590** R. ADAMS in *Harl. Misc.* I. 120 The English fleet..dispersed that invincible Navy, and made it vincible. **1630** J. HAYWARD *Edw. VI*, 75 He not easily vincible in spirit.. drew his sword and caused others to doe the like. **1680** C. NESSE *Ch. Hist.* 483 That Spanish Armado (which was stiled Invincible, but proved Vincible). **1736** AINSWORTH *Lat. Dict.* II, *Vincibilis*, vincible, conquerable. **1852** WILKS *Hist. Half Cent.* 68 The allies..could scarcely believe that the Napoleon who had so often conquered them was really vincible. **1899** S. E. HERRICK in W. H. Salmon *Culture Chr. Manhood* 240 And the heart is so exultant, so vigorous, and the man is so feeble and so vincible.

transf. **1882** *Atlantic Monthly* XLIX. 418 He [Peel] was vincible by the truth.

2. Of material or immaterial things, obstacles, arguments, etc.: That may be overcome; conquerable, surmountable.

a **1568** COVERDALE *Bk. Death* (1579) 110 To heare howe vnhurtfull, yea wholesome and vincible death is become thorow Christ. **1589** *Marprel. Epit.* Title-p., Very insufficiently furnished, with notable inabilitie of most vincible reasons. **1631** FULLER *David's Sin* xxxv. (1868) 49 Nought is so hard but vincible by paines. **1666** J. SMITH *Old Age* (1676) 153 All imminent evil is looked upon either as vincible or invincible. **1686** PLOT *Staffordsh.* 191 A Pox-stone, i.e. a stone scarce vincible by fire. **1753** RICHARDSON *Grandison* (1781) III. xxviii. 315 Were this great difficulty to be vincible. **1786** MRS. A. M. BENNETT *Juvenile Indiscr.* V. 130 He dreaded..her sense of duty, her obedience to her parents, had their objections been vincible. **1824** *Blackw. Mag.* XVI. 581 The form of faith that Lydia held (a vincible objection in other circumstances) was made a reason. **1872** *Chr. World Pulpit* II. 183 It is because these influences are vincible..that we are exhorted not to grieve the Spirit of God.

b. ***vincible ignorance***, an ignorance the means of overcoming which are possessed by the ignorant person himself. Cf. INVINCIBLE *a.* 1 c.

c **1626** DONNE *Serm.* lxxvi. (1640) 775 God forgives none of that which is left undone, out of a wilfull and vincible ignorance. **1689** *Dial. betw. Timothy & Titus* 5 Though I must tell you, Tim, 'tis vincible ignorance; for that you have not read them, is your own fault. **1724** A. SHIELDS *Life J. Renwick* Ep. Rdr. (1827) p. vii, Their Ignorance also proved vincible, when they had got that One Minister, whom he so reproaches. **1884** *Cath. Dict.* 424/2 All vincible ignorance of the things a man's duty requires him to know is in itself sinful. **1891** *Cath. News* 31 Jan. 3/4 Violation of duty attended by culpable or vincible ignorance.

Hence **'vincibleness; 'vincibly** *adv.*

1654 BRAMHALL *Just Vind.* vi. (1661) 157 Such Papists as they count vincibly ignorant of Roman errours. **1656** —— *Replic.* viii. 325 The Roman Church..doth not excommunicate all the Christians of Africk, Asia,..but only such as do erre vincibly or sinfully. **1727** BAILEY (vol. II), *Vincibleness*, Capableness or Liableness to be conquered or overcome.

vincristine (vɪn'krɪstiːn). *Pharm.* [f. as VINBLASTINE + *leuco*)*cristine* (former name of the drug), perh. f. LEU(KAEMIA + *-ro-* + CRIST(A + -INE[5].] A cytotoxic alkaloid, $C_{46}H_{56}N_4O_{10}$, obtained from the periwinkle *Catharanthus roseus* and administered intravenously (usu. as the sulphate) in the treatment of acute leukæmia and other cancers.

1962 M. R. KARON et al. in *Pediatrics* XXX. 791 (*heading*) A preliminary report on vincristine sulfate—a new active agent for the treatment of acute leukemia. **1977** *Lancet* 19 Feb. 433/1 Complete remission [of acute lymphocytic leukæmia] was achieved on a regimen of vincristine, prednisone, and daunomycin. **1983** [see VINBLASTINE].

'vincture. *rare*$^{-0}$. [ad. L. *vinctūra*, f. *vincīre* to bind.] 'A binding or tying.'

1656 BLOUNT *Glossogr.* [Hence in later Dicts.]

'vincular, *a. rare.* [f. L. *vincul-um* a bond or tie.] Of a vowel: Connective. Also *ellipt.* as *sb.* So **vincu'lation** (see quot.).

1871 KENNEDY *Public Sch. Lat. Gram.* 9 The weakest vowel is ĭ, for which reason it is used as a Vincular, to link parts in Flexion and Derivation. *Ibid.* 19 Vinculation, or insertion of a Vincular Vowell.

†**'vinculate,** *a. Obs.*$^{-1}$ [ad. L. *vinculāt-us*, pa. pple. of *vinculāre* to bind.] Bound.

1541 R. COPLAND *Galyen's Terap.* Dj, Yf the vlceres be nat bounde yᵗ thou mytygate the phlegmon. For it is necessary that they be nat vynculate.

‖**vinculum** ('vɪŋkjʊləm). Pl. vincula. [L., f. *vinc-*, stem of *vincīre* to bind + *-ulum* -ULE.]

1. A bond of union; a tie. Usually *fig.*

1678 CUDWORTH *Intell. Syst.* I. iv. 697 The Religion of an Oath is a Necessary *Vinculum* of Civil Society. **1699** *Phil. Trans.* XXI. 236 Which..does diffuse it self through the Whole, and breaking the Vinculum of the more solid Parts, does dissolve their Compages. **1710** T. FULLER *Pharm. Extemp.* (1730) 4 The gentle Intestine motion of Fermentation knocking asunder their *Vincula* of mixture, they naturally fall to pieces. **1831** BLAKEY *Free-will* 198 In material objects we do not see the connecting principle—the *vinculum*, as it is termed, which links causes and effects together. **1856** R. A. VAUGHAN *Mystics* (1860) II. VIII. iii. 279 The vincula of the Intellectual World are principally formulas of invocation. *a* **1871** GROTE *Eth. Fragm.* i. (1876) 13 Intimate connection drives us to conceive an ideal vinculum.

2. *Math.* A straight line drawn over two or more terms, denoting that these are to be considered as subject to the same operations of multiplication, division, etc., by another term.

1710 J. HARRIS *Lex. Techn.* II, *Vinculum*, is a Term in Fluxions, implying that some compound surd Quantity is multiplied into a Fluxion, &c. **1743** W. EMERSON *Fluxions* 24 The fluxionary Part may be divided by the Fluxion of the Root (or Part under the Vinculum). **1798** HUTTON *Course Math.* (1807) II. 292 When the Root under a Vinculum is a Compound Quantity; and the Index of the part or factor Without the Vinculum, increased by 1, is some Multiple of that Under the Vinculum. [**1842** BRANDE *Dict. Sci.*, etc. 1297 Vieta first used the bar or line over the quantities for a vinculum.] **1857** B. SMITH *Arith. & Algebra* (ed. 4) 5 The sign —— vinculum, placed over numbers,..[is] used to denote that all numbers under the vinculum..are equally affected by all numbers not under the vinculum. **1875** *Encycl. Brit.* I. 519/1 Each of these [quantities] has a line drawn over it called a vinculum.

fig. **1827** TATE *Grk. Metres* in *Theatre of Greeks* (ed. 2) 427 The words from τὸν to παῖδα are inclosed as it were in a vinculum of syntax. **1871** R. H. HUTTON *Ess.* (1877) I. 38 The other notion of unity..denotes the vinculum, or sheath, under which branches of thought or existence, really different in kind, are taken up into a single complex root or stem.

3. *Anat.* A ligament or frenum.

1859 MAYNE *Expos. Lex.* (and in later Dicts.).

vincus, obs. or dial. Sc. var. VANQUISH *v.*

vind, southern dial. var. FIND *v.*; obs. Sc. f. WIND *v.*

vindage, var. VENDAGE *Obs.*

vindak, obs. Sc. var. WINDOW.

vindaloo (vɪndə'luː). *Cookery.* Also bindaloo. [Prob. f. Pg. *vin d'alho* wine and garlic sauce, f. *vinho* VINHO + *alho* garlic.] An Indian curry dish made with meat, fish, or poultry in a sauce of garlic, wine (or vinegar), spices, etc.

1888 W. H. DAWE *Wife's Help to Indian Cookery* 65 Vindaloo or Bindaloo—A Portuguese Kárhí... The best Vindaloo is prepared in mustard-oil... Beef and pork, or duck can be made into this excellent curry. **1954** S. CHOWDHARY *Indian Cooking* 51 Chicken vindaloo is very tasty with peas pulao and other vegetable dishes. **1972** R. HILL *Fairly Dangerous Thing* I. iv. 39 A mouthful of Vindaloo prawn. **1982** BARR & YORK *Official Sloane Ranger Handbk.* 27/1 His macho-masochisms decree that he must order the hottest—Vindaloo, Madras or even Bangalore Phal. **1985** *Listener* 14 Mar. 15/3 Water is suggested as one option for Chinese food (expensive bottled water, of course), Guinness for oysters and lager for chicken vindaloo.

vinde, southern ME. var. FIND *v.*; obs. f. VINE *sb.*

vindemial (vɪn'diːmɪəl), *a. rare.* [ad. L. (post-classical) *vindēmiāl-is*, f. *vindēmia* VINDEMY.] Of or belonging to, associated with, the gathering of grapes.

1656 BLOUNT *Glossogr.* [Hence in Phillips, Kersey, etc.] **1819** H. BUSK *Dessert* 418 Yes, come, Lyæus, leave thy lucid rills, Thy ivy borders and vindemial hills.

vindemiate (vɪn'diːmɪeɪt), *v.* [f. L. *vindēmiāt-*, ppl. stem of *vindēmiāre*, f. as prec.] *intr.* To gather ripe fruit, esp. grapes. Hence **vin'demiating** *vbl. sb.*

1664 EVELYN *Kal. Hort.* Aug. 72 Now vindemiate and take your Bees towards the expiration of this Moneth. **1670** BLOUNT *Glossogr.* (ed. 3), *Vindemiate*, to gather grapes or ripe fruit in harvest. Hence in Phillips, etc.] **1728** CHAMBERS *Cycl.*, *Vindemiating*, the gathering of Grapes, or other ripe Fruits. **1831** WHEWELL in Todhunter *Acc. Writ.* (1876) II. 123 People will ask you to reckon your fruits: so vindemiate as fast as you can.

vindemiation (vɪndiːmɪ'eɪʃən). [ad. med.L. *vindēmiātio*, f. L. *vindēmiāre*: see prec.] The gathering of grapes or other fruits. Also *transf.* and *fig.*

1609 C. BUTLER *Fem. Mon.* x. (1623) Tij, Of the fruit and profit of Bees: Wherein is shewed first the Vindemiation or taking of Combes. **1653** W. G. *Bacon's Hist. Winds*, etc. 305 Let this be the first Vindemiation or inchoated interpretation of the Forme of heat. **1669** WORLIDGE *Syst. Agric.* 277 *Vindemiation*, the gathering of Grapes, or reaping the Fruit of any thing; as of Cherries, Apples, Bees, &c. **1727** BAILEY (vol. II), and in later Dicts.

vin'demiatory, *a. rare*$^{-0}$. [ad. L. *vindēmiātōri-us* (Varro).] (See quot.)

1656 BLOUNT *Glossogr.*, *Vindemiatory*, of or belonging to gathering Grapes, or ripe Fruit in Harvest.

‖**Vindemiatrix** (vɪndiːmɪ'eɪtrɪks). [med. or mod.L. fem. of *vindēmiātor* vintager, star in Virgo, f. L. *vindēmiāre*: see VINDEMIATE *v.*]

1. A bright fixed star in the constellation Virgo.

1704 J. HARRIS *Lex. Techn.* I, *Vindemiatrix*, a Fixed Star of the third Magnitude, in the Constellation Virgo, whose Longitude is 185 degr. 23 min. Latitude 16 degr. 15 min. [Hence in later Dicts.] **1728** CHAMBERS *Cycl.* s.v. *Virgo*, Stars in the Constellation Virgo [include].., Upper of North Wing, Vindemiatrix. **1843** *Penny Cycl.* XXVI. 373/1 Of the bright stars in this triangle, Vindemiatrix is the one nearest to the line joining Arcturus and β Leonis. **1860** OLMSTED *Mech. Heav.* 347 Twenty degrees north of Spica, is Vindemiatrix, in the arm of Virgo, a star of the third magnitude.

2. 'A female vintager' (Bailey, 1721).

†**'vindemy.** *Obs.*$^{-1}$ [ad. L. *vindēmia* vintage, fruit-gathering.] The taking of honey from beehives.

1609 C. BUTLER *Fem. Mon.* v. (1623) Kiij, At the Vindemie, in a fair calm morning, before any Bees be abroad, shut up close all the stalls in your Garden.

vinden, southern ME. variant of FIND *v.*

vindica'bility. *rare*$^{-0}$. [f. next.] 'The quality of being vindicable, or capable of support or justification.'

1828–32 WEBSTER (citing *Jrnl. of Science*).

vindicable ('vɪndɪkəb(ə)l), *a.* [ad. late L. *vindicābilis* (Du Cange), f. L. *vindicāre* to vindicate. Cf. OF. *vindicable* punishing.]

†**1.** Vengeful, vindictive. *Obs.*$^{-1}$

1632 LITHGOW *Trav.* I. 7 Any obuious obiect of disastrous misfortune: or perhaps any vindicable action, [which] might from an vnsetled ranckour be conceiued.

2. Capable of being vindicated; admitting of being justified or maintained.

1647 *Engl. Mountebank Cast. Sickly Water State* 5 Their freedoms, liberty of person, property of Estates given away and become meere Notions, and not vindicable, nor preservable by Law. **1713** *Lond. Gaz.* No. 5090/1 The most vindicable Quarrel can be imagin'd. **1736** CHANDLER *Hist. Persec.* 436, I think this manner of subscribing to Creeds.. is infamous in its nature, and vindicable upon no principles of conscience and honour. **1775** S. J. PRATT *Liberal Opin.* xlviii. (1783) II. 39, I think every work of God vindicable. **1836** J. HALLEY in W. Arnot *Mem.* (1842) 61 Feelings which were natural, but by no means vindicable. **1844** H. H. WILSON *Brit. India* II. 336 Hostilities in this campaign were generally prosecuted in a stern and inflexible spirit, vindicable, perhaps, by the cruelty and treachery of the Mahratta princes.

'vindicant. *Roman Law.* [ad. L. *vindicant-*, *vindicans*, pres. pple. of *vindicāre*: see next.] The claimant in a suit.

1880 MUIRHEAD *Gaius* II. §24 The praetor adjudges the thing to the vindicant. *Ibid.* IV. §16 The vindicant held in his hand a rod.

vindicate ('vɪndɪkeɪt), *v.* Also 6–7 as *pa. pple.* [f. L. *vindicāt-*, ppl. stem of *vindicāre* (also *vendicāre*: see VENDICATE *v.*) to claim, to set free, to punish, etc., f. *vim*, acc. sing. of *vis* force + *dic-*, stem of *dīcere* to say. Cf. It. *vindicare*, Sp. and Pg. *vindicar*, F. *vendiquer*.]

†**1.** *trans.* **a.** To exercise in revenge. *Obs.*$^{-1}$

1533 BELLENDEN *Livy* (S.T.S.) II. 326 Praying þam to provid þat þe peple vindicat na Ire nor wraith [*altered to* vse na vengeance nor punycioun] on þam.

†**b.** To avenge or revenge (a person, cause, wrong, etc.). *Obs.*

1623 COCKERAM I, *Vindicate*, to reuenge. **1655** STANLEY *Hist. Philos.* I. (1687) 17/2 Solon declared, that it behoved them..that they should vindicate the Gods cause. **1660** INGELO *Bentiv. & Ur.* II. (1682) 164 Resolving by God's assistance to vindicate his Wrongs. **1665** SIR T. HERBERT *Trav.* (1677) 67 News..being brought King Achbar that Mirza Sharoph..had been injured by the Ouzbeg Tartar; the King resolves to vindicate him. **1713** SWIFT *Cadenus & Vanessa* Wks. 1755 III. II. 18 But Cupid, full of mischief, longs To vindicate his mother's wrongs.

†**c.** To punish; to visit with punishment. *Obs.*

1632 LITHGOW *Trav.* VIII. 367 There are seuerall Seates of Iustice heere (though none to vindicate beastlinesse). **1659** PEARSON *Creed* i. 86 God is more powerfull to exact subiection, and to vindicate rebellion. **1665** MANLEY *Grotius' Low C. Wars* 974 Private Trespasses should be vindicated upon the Authors thereof themselves, or else where they lived. **1770** BURKE *Pres. Discont.* 8 Because our grievances are..not precisely those which we bore from the Tudors, or vindicated on the Stuarts.

†**2.** To make or set free; to deliver or rescue. Usually const. *from*. *Obs.* (common 1620–60).

1568–71 (*title*), The Warkis of..Schir Dauid Lyndesay... Newly correctit, and vindicate from the former Errouris quhairwith thay war befoir corruptit. **1570** BUCHANAN *Admon.* Wks. (S.T.S.) 22 How ȝe haue vindicat this realme out of thraldome of strangearis. **1613** SIR A. SHERLEY *Trav. Persia* 85 Nothing will giue you more honour then..First to vindicate those places, in which your religion is oppressed. **1620–51** I. JONES *Stone-Heng* (1655) 2 To vindicate, as much as in me lies, the Founders of this venerable Antiquity from oblivion. **1650** ASHMOLE *Arcanum* in *Fasc. Chem.* 166 A faithfull..Teacher, that may make the clear Sun conspicuous unto them, and vindicate their eies from darknesse. **1665** NEEDHAM *Med. Medicinæ* 267 The Liquor ferments, and is vindicated from Putrefaction and Stagnation. **1756** BURKE *Vind. Nat. Soc.* Wks. 1842 I. 21 We should renounce their dreams of society, together with their visions of religion, and vindicate ourselves into perfect liberty. **1761** HUME *Hist. Eng.* I. xiii. 328 His successful valour seemed to vindicate the nation from the ignominy into which it had fallen by its tame submission.

absol. **1628** GAULE *Pract. The.* (1629) 110 Cæsar vindicates from a knowne Enemie; Christ redeemes from a secret Aduersarie.

3. To clear from censure, criticism, suspicion, or doubt, by means of demonstration; to justify or uphold by evidence or argument.

a **1635** NAUNTON *Fragm. Reg.* (Arb.) 61 And so I shall onely vindicate the scandall of his death, and conclude him. **1651** BAXTER *Inf. Bapt.* 150 O that God would find out some way to vindicate his own honor, and clear his cause. **1691** LANGBAINE *Acc. Eng. Poets* Pref., I might be capable of doing them better Service, in vindicating their Fame. **1736** BUTLER *Anal.* II. viii. 389 The design of this treatise is not to vindicate the character of God. **1776** SIR J. REYNOLDS *Disc.* (1778) 280 Poussin..is said to have vindicated the conduct of Julio Romano for his inattention to the masses of light and shade. **1782** MISS BURNEY *Cecilia* v. ii, I don't mean to vindicate what has happened. **1817** JAS. MILL *Brit. India* I. II. ix. 413 Mr. Playfair admits that the Indian tables cannot be entirely vindicated in this respect. **1855** MACAULAY *Hist. Eng.* xvii. IV. 75 Those who had effected this Revolution thought it prudent to send a deputation to France for the purpose of vindicating their proceedings. **1884** *L'pool Mercury* 18 Feb. 5/2 He has no secret treaties to vindicate, no occult motives to gloss over in dubious pleadings.

b. With personal object.

1646 CRASHAW *Steps to Temple, Treatise Charity* 13 These learned leaves shall vindicate to thee Thy holiest, humblest, hand-maid Charitie. **1659** in *Burton's Diary* (1828) IV. 338, I rise up to vindicate the Committee. **1675** BAXTER *Cath.*

Theol. II. II. 238, I must be so far justified, that is, vindicated against Calumny by my innocency in those points. **1702** C. MATHER *Magn. Chr.* III. iii. (1852) 536 The mention of this gives me an opportunity..also to vindicate another great man unto the churches of our Lord Jesus Christ.

refl. **1639** MASSINGER *Unnat. Combat* IV. i, The torch that feeds them was not lighted at Thy altars, Cupid. Vindicate thyself, And do not own it! *a* **1648** LD. HERBERT *Hen. VIII* (1683) 232 It was thought, by some, he might haue Vindicated himself in great part. **1679** J. SMITH *Narr. Popish Plot* 19 There being no way left to vindicate themselves, or discredit their Accusers, save the making their recourse to lies. **1828** D'ISRAELI *Chas. I*, II. v. 130 He could have vindicated himself, if his enemies had chosen to be his listeners. **1849** MACAULAY *Hist. Eng.* v. I. 661 The wicked judge and the wicked king attempted to vindicate themselves by throwing the blame on each other.

c. Const. *from* (a charge, imputation, etc.).

1664 H. MORE *Apol.* in *Myst. Iniq.* 487 Those more notable Philosophick Truths in the Scripture doth.. vindicate her from that vile Imputation of Ignorance in Philosophy. **1675** J. HOWE *Living Temple* I. ii. 20 He makes Velleius highly vindicate from this imputation. **1700** LOCKE *Hum. Und.* (ed. 4) IV. viii. 367 But how that vindicates the making use of Identical Propositions for the Improvement of Knowledge, from the Imputation of Trifling, I do not see. **1723** J. DART *Westmonasterium* I. 87 This I here mention to vindicate my self from those Mistakes of which I am not guilty. **1798** FERRIAR *Illustr. Sterne*, etc. 37, I must vindicate Sterne from a charge of plagiarism. **1825** SCOTT *Betrothed* xxix, When he vindicated him from the suspicions thrown out by Guarine. **1845** M. PATTISON *Ess.* (1889) I. 18 He turned all his defence to vindicate himself from the charge of treason. **1891** *Speaker* 2 May 526/2 It is..the first serious attempt that has been made to vindicate Horace Walpole from the aspersions of Macaulay and his followers.

d. To provide justification for (something); to justify by facts or results. Also with personal object.

1702 FARQUHAR *Twin Rivals* IV. iv, For Heav'n's sake, Mr. Richmore, what have I ever shewn to vindicate this presumption of yours? **1749** FIELDING *Tom Jones* v. vi, The infidelity of Molly..would perhaps have vindicated a much greater degree of resentment than he expressed on the occasion. *a* **1763** SHENSTONE *Ess.* Wks. 1765 II. 203 One should not destroy an insect..without a reason sufficient to vindicate one through all the courts of morality. **1836** J. GILBERT *Christian Atonem.* vii. (1852) 205 The mere fact of voluntariness is insufficient to vindicate the justice of allowing the assumed responsibility. **1882** PEBODY *Eng. Journalism* xx. 150 No man has more brilliantly vindicated the sagacity which placed him in a position of power and responsibility.

4. To assert, maintain, make good, by means of action, esp. in one's own interest; to defend against encroachment or interference.

1650 MARVELL *Horatian Ode* 62 He nothing common did, or mean,..Nor called the gods with vulgar spite To vindicate his helpless right. **1654** BRAMHALL *Just Vind.* i. (1661) 4 That..they..vindicate that liberty left them as an inheritance by their Ancestours, from the incroachments.. of the Court of Rome. **1671** MILTON *P.R.* II. 47 Arise and vindicate Thy Glory, free thy people from thir yoke. **1738** WESLEY *Ps.* LXXX. ii, Stir up thy Strength, thine Arme make bare, And vindicate thy chosen Race. **1777** ROBERTSON *Hist. Amer.* VI. (1778) 196 He thought the happy period was at length come for vindicating his own rights. **1821** SYD. SMITH *Wks.* (1859) I. 394/2 Prevention of intrusion upon private property is a right which every proprietor may act upon, and use force to vindicate. **1875** STUBBS *Const. Hist.* II. 4 The liberties of the nation are not yet vindicated.

5. To claim as properly belonging *to* oneself or another; to assert or establish possession of (something) *for* oneself or another.

1680 DRYDEN *Ovid's Ep.* Pref., Ess. (ed. Ker) I. 235 It appears not from their writings, that any of the Grecians ever touched upon this way, which our poet therefore justly has vindicated to himself. **1737** *Gentl. Mag.* VII. 332 Though Christ's Appeal to the 110th vindicates that Psalm to David, it vindicates none else. **1822** T. TAYLOR *Apuleius* 218 Exciting a frivolous controversy about the boundaries of the fields, he vindicated the whole of the land to himself. **1855** PRESCOTT *Philip II*, I. (1857) 76 Paul the Fourth, one of those remarkable men, who..have vindicated to themselves a permanent place in history. **1858** HAWTHORNE *Fr. & It. Note-bks.* II. 42 Grand enough to vindicate for him all the genius that the world gave him credit for. **1884** *Schaff's Encycl. Relig. Knowl.* III. 2466/1 Robert Flint.. vindicates him [*sc.* Voltaire] an honorable place in the development of the philosophy of history.

b. Without const.: To claim for oneself or as one's rightful property.

1725 POPE *Odyss.* IV. 224 Affianc'd in your friendly power alone, The youth wou'd vindicate the vacant throne. **1733** —— *Ess. Man* III. 38 Is thine alone the seed that strews the plain? The birds of heav'n shall vindicate their grain. **1781** COWPER *Truth* 490 The soul..Can..Possess herself of all that's good or true, Assert the skies, and vindicate her due. **1807** J. BARLOW *Columb.* III. 850 The wide-beak'd hawk, that now beholds me die, Soon..my flesh shall tear, And wolves and tigers vindicate their share.

c. *spec.* in *Law*. Also *absol.*

a **1859** AUSTIN *Jurispr.* (1863) III. 207 A right to vindicate or recover the subject from any who may be in the possession of it. **1880** MUIRHEAD *Rules Ulpian* XXV. §17 The senate has decreed that he shall not be entitled to deduct his fourth, nor yet..to vindicate gifts under the testament that have become caducous. **1880** —— *Gaius* II. §24 When he has thus vindicated, the praetor asks the cedent whether he makes any counter-vindication.

Hence **'vindicated** *ppl. a.*; **'vindicating** *vbl. sb.* and *ppl. a.*; **'vindicatingly** *adv.*

1624 GATAKER *Transubst.* 42 The vindicating of this piece of antiquity to his right Author. **1642** DRUMM. OF HAWTH. *Skiamachia* Wks. (1711) 191 The equity of his taking of arms, for the vindicating of his crown and state from the implacable malice of those men. **1700** PRIOR *Carm. Sec.* xv, To rescu'd States, and vindicated Crowns His Equal Hand prescrib'd their ancient Bounds. **1724** A. SHIELDS *Life Renwick* (1827) 177 Instead of a reproached Minister, we got a vindicated Martyr. **1850** MRS. BROWNING *Sonn. fr. Portug.* xi, I obtain From that same love this vindicating grace, To live on still in love. **1891** MEREDITH *One of our Conq.* xii, Her mother required schooling to tell the story vindicatingly and proudly.

vindication (vɪndɪ'keɪʃən). Also 5 vyndi-, vyndycacion. [a. OF. (now F. dial.) *vindication* vengeance, or ad. L. *vindicātio* action of claiming, defending, punishing, etc., f. *vindicāre*: see prec. Cf. Sp. *vindicacion*, Pg. *-ação*, F. *vendication*, It. *vendicazione*.]

†**1. a.** The action of avenging or revenging. *Obs.*

1484 CAXTON *Fables of Æsop* I. xvi, An asse..smote hym [the lion] in the forhede with his feete by maner of vyndycacion. **1490** —— *Eneydos* xxii. 83 [She] pursued hym at alle houres, in alle places, for to distroye hym, in makynge vyndicacion of the deth of his sayd moder. **1658** PHILLIPS. **1690** NORRIS *Beatitudes* (1694) 77 As to private Vindication of Injuries, that which we more especially call Revenge, this I shall readily allow to be utterly unlawful.

†**b.** Retribution, punishment. *Obs.*$^{-1}$

1647 MAY *Hist. Parl.* I. ii. 17 Things carried so far on in a wrong way must needs..require a vindication so sharpe and smarting, as that the nation would groan under it.

†**2.** Deliverance; emancipation. *Obs.*$^{-1}$

1613 SIR A. SHERLEY *Trav. Persia* 7 So abhorred a neighbour, from whom their vindication, into liberty, must bee maintained by their own constancy.

3. The action of vindicating or defending against censure, calumny, etc.; justification by proof or explanation.

1647 CLARENDON *Hist. Reb.* I. §1 So the Memory of those ..may not lose the recompense due to their Virtue, but.. may find a vindication in a better age. *Ibid.* x. §85 The soldiers publish'd a Vindication, as they call'd it, of their Proceedings and Resolutions. **1669** GALE *Crt. Gentiles* To Rdr., The vindication of the Jewish and Christian Religion, against the Gentile Philosophers. **1705** ADDISON *Italy* (1733) 33 Pere Mabillon is now engaged in the Vindication of this Tear, which a learned Ecclesiastic..would have suppressed, as a false and ridiculous Relick. **1769** *Junius Lett.* ix. (1788) 65 The author of the vindication of your conduct..writes from his own mere motion. **1825** J. NEAL *Bro. Jonathan* I. 299 Leave the vindication of your character to your children. **1837** LYTTON *E. Maltrav.* I. xi, He enriched Mrs. Jones for life, in gratitude for her vindication of his lost and early love. **1870** DICKENS *E. Drood* vii, He begged to thank Miss Landless for her vindication of his character.

b. In the phr. *in vindication of*.

1660 COKE *Power & Subj.* 266 It will not ill become mee, sure, to add a word or two in vindication of Sir Edward Coke. *a* **1667** COWLEY *Ess., Obscurity*, This seems a strange Sentence,..and looks as if it were in vindication of the men of business. **1709** STEELE *Tatler* No. 39 ¶3, I can add other circumstances in Vindication of the Account of this Learned Body. **1752** BP. THOMAS in *10th Rep. Hist. MSS. Comm.* App. I. 307 Then Lord Sandwich spoke in Vindication of the Measure. **1845** MCCULLOCH *Taxation* I. iv. (1852) 114 It has been said, in vindication of this inequality, that the properties are of a different description.

c. A justifying fact or circumstance.

1846 TRENCH *Mirac.* Introd. 45 The position which it has won..is itself its vindication now. **1848** L. HUNT *Jar of Honey* x. 134 The great vindication of evil is, we could not manifest so much virtue without it. **1856** KANE *Arct. Expl.* II. xvii. 179 It must..stand..as my vindication for the step, in case we should be overtaken by disaster.

4. The action of asserting or maintaining.

1871 R. W. DALE *Commandm.* vi. 166 The Commandment 'Thou shalt not kill', is a Divine vindication of the greatness and sanctity of man. **1874** GREEN *Short Hist.* viii. §3. 490 The bulk of the members supported Eliot in his last vindication of English liberty.

5. *Roman Law.* (See quots.)

1880 MUIRHEAD *Gaius* II. §194 A legacy by vindication is so called because the thing bequeathed becomes the property of the legatee in quiritarian right the moment the inheritance has been entered upon. *Ibid.* IV. §5 Actions *in rem* are called vindications; while those in which we contend that something ought to be given to or done for us are called condictions.

vindicative (vɪn'dɪkətɪv, 'vɪndɪkeɪtɪv), *a.* Also 6 vendicatife, -yue, vindicatyfe, -iue. [ad. OF. *vindicatif* (also mod.F.), or med.L. *vindicātīvus*: see VINDICATE *v.* and -IVE. So Sp. *vindicativo*, It. *vendicativo*.]

†**1.** = VINDICTIVE *a.* 1. *Obs.* (Common *c* 1590–1690.) **a.** Of persons (or things personified).

1521 *Bradshaw's St. Werburge* (Chetham Soc.) 211 O cruell deth, o theffe vindicatyfe, To persons vertuous ennemy mortall. **1584** *Leycester's Commw.* (1641) 13 This his sonne, who..is..farre more insolent, cruell, vindicative, ..and fox-like then ever hee was. *a* **1637** N. FERRAR tr. *Valdes' 110 Consid.* (1638) 89 Understanding, that he doth not pardon, when hee is offended, wee hold him for cruell, inhumane, and vindicative. **1662** J. BARGRAVE *Pope Alex. VII* (1867) 53 Some people believe him vindicative; but his anger is only a soden impetus. **1693** DRYDEN *Disc. Satire* Ess. (ed. Ker) II. 80, I.., being naturally vindicative, have suffered in silence, and possessed my soul in quiet.

†**b.** Of nature, disposition, etc. *Obs.*

1549 *Compl. Scotl.* xii. 101 For thai ar of ane vendicatife nature. *Ibid.* xx. 177 My vendicatyue particular affectione. **1628** DONNE *Serm.* XXIX. (1640) 287 They discerned not between a zealous and a vindicative spirit. **1646** SIR J. TEMPLE *Irish Reb.* 68 They let loose the reins of their own vindicative humour and irreconcilable hatred. **1689** SHADWELL *Bury F.* IV, He is one of the Nobless, and his nature's vindicative in Honour's cause. *a* **1734** NORTH *Examen* III. vii. §79 (1740) 566 When Persons are fallen upon in our Heat, as upon the vindicative Turns of Parties.

2. = VINDICTIVE *a.* 2. Now *rare.* (Common in 17th cent.)

1610 BP. CARLETON *Jurisdict.* 31 Vindicative power or coaction belongs not to the Church. **1649** JER. TAYLOR *Gt. Exemp.* Disc. iv. 120 Repentance being in very many actions a primitive duty, afflictive, and vindicative. **1678** GALE *Crt. Gentiles* IV. III. vi. 200 That wherein he perpetually is mistaken, is the making of Non-election or Negative Reprobation a Vindicative act, the confounding it with the judicial Sentence of Damnation. **1812** *Ann. Reg., Gen. Hist.* 78 His act, which he always defended as vindicative of the injury he had sustained. **1854** TRENCH *Synon. N.T.* Ser. I. (1860) 27 The vindicative character of the punishment is the predominant thought.

b. *esp.* As an epithet of *justice*.

1626 J. YATES *Ibis ad Cæsarem* II. 30 God may separate from any creature in regard of his love,..and yet not be angry with them, which alwayes presupposeth vindicative iustice or fatherly castigations. **1647** N. BACON *Disc. Govt. Eng.* I. liii. 150 In proceedings in cases of vindicative justice delinquents might seem to be left rather to the fury then mercy of the law. **1679** MANSELL *Narr. Popish Plot* Addr. c2b, They will find it ill striving against the Stream and Current of Vindicative Justice.

3. Serving to vindicate by defence or assertion.

1660 T. WHITE (*title*), Religion and Reason mutually corresponding and assisting each other, a Reply to the Vindicative Answer lately published against a Letter [etc.]. **1863** H. COX *Instit.* I. ix. 204 We have to treat of the vindicative powers of each House; that is, its independent power to vindicate its authority.

Hence **vindicativeness**, vindictiveness.

1655 FULLER *Ch. Hist.* v. Ded., Whilest his ignorant auditors condemned their mutual vindicativeness, the wiser sort admired..their peaceable dispositions. **1711** SHAFTESB. *Charac.* III. 306 They..extol Voluptuousness, Wilfulness, Vindicativeness, Arbitrariness, Vain-Glory.

vindicator ('vɪndɪkeɪtə(r)). [a. late L. (eccl.) *vindicātor*, agent-n. f. *vindicāre* VINDICATE *v.* So OF. *vindicateur*, It. *vindicatore*, Pg. *vindicador*.] One who vindicates, in various senses of the verb.

1566 PAINTER *Pal. Pleas.* I. 68 For as Romulus was the first builder and peopler of that citie, so was Camillus the vindicator and deliuerer of the same. **1647** CLARENDON *Hist. Reb.* III. §3 A man, who in the memory of many present, had sate in that House an earnest vindicator of the Laws. **1651** BAXTER *Inf. Bapt.* 314 Dr. Twisse, and all our modern vindicators of grace. **1693** DRYDEN *Disc. Satire* Ess. (ed. Ker) II. 87 A noble soul is better pleased with a zealous vindicator of Roman liberty, than with a temporising poet. **1714** FORTESCUE-ALAND *Fortescue's Abs. & Lim. Mon.* Ded. 4 Our Author was so great a Lover and Vindicator of it [the English Constitution]. **1791** *Gentl. Mag.* Jan. 32/1 A certain vindicator of the Marbles..has taken occasion..to insult.. Le Clerc. **1827** SCOTT *Surg. Dau.* xiii. When this eager vindicator of betrayed innocence arrived in the capital of Hyder. **1849** ROBERTSON *Serm.* Ser. I. xi. (1855) 190 Job knew that God was the vindicator of wrongs. **1884** *Spect.* 4 Oct. 1320/2 Our author..has..entered the lists..as the vindicator of the claims of the Highland Crofters.

Hence **'vindicatorship**, the personality of a vindicator. *rare*$^{-1}$.

1695 J. SAGE *Fundam. Charter Presbyt.* Pref. (1697) 14, It was necessary for his Vindicatorship to justify this Separation.

vindicatorily, *adv.* [f. VINDICATORY *a.*] In a vindicatory or justifying manner.

1854 N. P. WILLIS in *Life & Lett. W. Irving* (1864) IV. 179 Thus vindicatorily of his friend spoke the just and kind Geoffrey Crayon. **1891** *19th Cent.* Dec. 1019 The vindicatorily personal denial of Councils of War in 1866.

vindicatory ('vɪndɪkeɪtərɪ), *a.* [f. VINDICATE *v.* + -ORY.]

1. Serving to vindicate; justificatory, defensive.

1647 *Royall & Royallist's Plea* 13 The warre on the Kings side is vindicatory and defensorie. **1755** JOHNSON, *Vindicatory*, defensory; justificatory. **1802** MRS. J. WEST *Infidel Father* III. 258 No proud aggression of vindicatory virtue would be visible in her manner. **1863** GEO. ELIOT *Romola* III. xxiii, A favourable magistracy..were writing urgent vindicatory letters to Rome on his behalf. **1884** *19th Cent.* May 869 The teaching of the parent Legislature does not end with the record of the famous contentions and vindicatory triumphs of the past from which it is derived.

2. Avenging; punitive, retributive.

1655 BRAMHALL *Def. True Liberty* 83 The afflictions of Job were no vindicatory punishments to take vengeance of his sins,..but probatory chastisements to make triall of his graces. **1765** BLACKSTONE *Comm.* I. 56 To make the sanction of their laws rather vindicatory than remuneratory, or to consist rather in punishments, than in actual particular rewards. **1800** *Ann. Reg.* 153 The laws should be vindicatory on such occasions. **1874** BUSHNELL *Forgiveness & Law* iii. 188 By the law..we are only held in terms of penal discipline and not of desert or vindicatory justice. **1882–3** *Schaff's Encycl. Relig. Knowl.* 1973 Every true philosophy of punishment must recognize the deterrent, and especially the vindicatory element, as well as the reformatory element.

vindicatress ('vɪndɪkeɪtrɪs). [f. VINDICATOR: see -ESS, and cf. OF. *vindicateresse*, med.L. *vindicatrix*.] A female vindicator.

1854 C. KNIGHT *Once upon a Time* II. 201 Had the vindicatress of the 'Rights of Women' lived in these days. **1878** GLADSTONE *Prim. Homer* 87 The Erinuës, afterwards called the Furies in a degenerated tradition, but more truly the vindicatresses of nature and the moral order.

†**vindict.** *Obs. rare.* [ad. L. *vindicta.*] Vengeance, revenge; retribution.

1639 GUILD in Spalding *Troubles* (1828) I. 314 As Simeon and Levi, pretending religion, but intending their own private vindict. **1675** R. BURTHOGGE *Causa Dei* 141 The Punishments annexed to them must be executed on offenders, they being Vindicts and concerning God.

vindictive (vɪnˈdɪktɪv), *a.* and *sb.* [f. L. *vindicta* vengeance, revenge + -IVE.]

A. *adj.* **1.** Of persons: Given to revenge; having a revengeful disposition. (Cf. VINDICATIVE *a.* 1.)

1616 BULLOKAR *Eng. Expos.*, *Vindictiue*, reuengefull, or apt to reuenge. **1770** LANGHORNE *Plutarch* (1851) II. 904/1 He was vindictive in his nature. **1787** BURKE *Corr.* (1844) III. 52 You have vindictive people to deal with, and you have gone too far to be forgiven. **1808** JEBB in A. Knox & Jebb *Corr.* (1834) I. 455 There exists in human nature.. a perturbed dread of some superior, powerful and most vindictive being. **1847** MRS. A. KERR tr. *Ranke's Hist. Servia* 206 He was not vindictive: when he had once pardoned an offender, he never recurred again to the offence. **1875** W. S. HAYWARD *Love agst. World* 18 He is as vindictive as a demon.

b. Of actions, qualities, etc.: Characterized by a desire for, or the exercise of, revenge.

1627 J. CARTER *Plain Expos.* 46 To forbeare irefull and vindictive courses, to say or doe nothing at all in anger, or hot bloud. **1629** J. MAXWELL tr. *Herodian* (1635) 430 Nor let any of you imagine that any vindictive resolution is harboured against you, either by us or the Romans. **1743** FRANCIS tr. *Horace, Odes* II. viii. 8 When..you engage To meet high Heaven's vindictive Rage. **1791** COWPER *Iliad* III. 450 Then with vindictive strides he rush'd again On Paris. **1807–8** W. IRVING *Salmag.* (1824) 305 This spirit of vindictive cowardice is not owing to any inherent depravity of soul. **1849** MACAULAY *Hist. Eng.* i. I. 80 After the fashion of oppressed sects, they mistook their own vindictive feelings for emotions of piety. **1863** GEO. ELIOT *Romola* II. xxx, With the first movement of vindictive rage awoke a vague caution.

2. Involving retribution or punishment; punitive, retributive; avenging. Now *rare.* **a.** As an epithet of *justice.* (Cf. VINDICATIVE *a.* 2 b.)

1623 R. CARPENTER *Consc. Chr.* 100 They are euer awaked with the remembrance of Gods presence, in all your actions and censures of vindictive or remuneratiue Iustice. **1660** JER. TAYLOR *Ductor* II. ii. rule 7 §5 For in all penal laws and inflictions, although there be much of Vindictive justice, yet this justice is but a handmaid to Government and Correction. *a* **1711** KEN *Div. Love* Wks. (1838) 313 Our sins, ..which are the vast debts we owe to thy vindictive justice. **1742** LD. CHOLMONDELEY in *Johnson's Deb.* (1787) II. 150 It has been unanswerably shewn..that vindictive justice is of the highest importance to the happiness of the public. **1824** SOUTHEY *Colloq. Soc.* (1887) 103 The shallow moralists who exclaim against vindictive justice, when punishment would cease to be just, if it were not vindictive.

b. In other contexts.

1656 BRAMHALL *Replic.* i. 11 The judgements of God in this life are more exemplary for the amendment of others, than vindictive to the delinquents themselves. **1695** BLACKMORE *Pr. Arth.* II. 436 Th' Almighty his Vindictive Arm makes bare. **1718** POPE *Iliad* XVI. 654 First to the fight his native troops he warms, Then loudly calls on Troy's vindictive arms. **1780** COWPER *Progr. Error* 44 Pleasure brings as surely in her train, Remorse, and Sorrow, and vindictive Pain. **1827** POLLOK *Course T.* II, He..Amidst vindictive thunders lets them try The stoutness of their heart. **1875** POSTE *Gaius* I. Introd., Sometimes the sanction is retributive or vindictive, the expression of the conscience or moral sentiments of the Society.

c. Of deities: Inflicting punishment for wrongdoing.

1703 ROWE *Ulysses* III. i, Vindictive Jove prepares his Thunder. Let the Wrong-doer and the Tyrant tremble. **1781** COWPER *Expost.* 407 The fast that wins deliv'rance, and suspends The stroke that a vindictive God intends, Is to renounce hypocrisy.

3. *vindictive damages*, damages awarded not only as compensation to the plaintiff but also as a punishment to the defendant.

1813 *Ann. Reg., Chron.* 67 It seemed established that there was no gross misconduct..on the part of the coachman, to call for vindictive damages.

†**B.** *sb.* An act of punishment. *Obs.*$^{-1}$

1726 DE FOE *Hist. Devil* I. i. 12 Who..could give a full.. account of the deluge, whether it was a meer vindictive, a blast from heaven?

vindictively (vɪnˈdɪktɪvlɪ), *adv.* [f. prec. + -LY².] In a vindictive manner; revengefully.

1727 BAILEY (vol. II). **1755** JOHNSON, *Revengingly*, with vengeance; vindictively. **1827** POLLOK *Course T.* x, Has He not..given at times Example fierce of wrath and judgment, poured Vindictively on nations guilty long? **1837** SYD. SMITH *Wks.* (1859) II. 287/2 Such a power might be maliciously and vindictively exercised. **1878** LECKY *Eng. in 18th C.* I. iv. 534 The leaders of fashion..steadily and vindictively derided them.

vindictiveness (vɪnˈdɪktɪvnɪs). [f. as prec. + -NESS.] The state or character of being vindictive; revengefulness.

1676 HALE *Contempl.* I. 476 If it found any corruptions within, either of Pride, Vain Glory, Insolence, Vindictiveness, or the like. **1679** PRANCE *Add. Narr.* 45 That which makes it more remarkable, is, That this Vindictiveness was exercised towards men of his own Religion. **1740** RICHARDSON *Pamela* (1824) I. 381 Here, to recapitulate my faults, is, in the first place, vindictiveness; I will not call it down-right revenge. **1800** COGAN *Passions* II. i. (1802) 195 There is a vindictiveness in fear, which may render it dangerous to its most innocent cause. **1844** H. H. WILSON *Brit. India* III. 180 The shield thrown over their dependants against their tyranny or vindictiveness. **1884** A. R. PENNINGTON *Wiclif* vii. 242 He tells us..that vindictiveness had mingled with his righteous indignation.

vindic'tivolence. *nonce-wd.* [f. L. *vindicta* vengeance, after *malevolence.*] The desire of revenging oneself or of taking vengeance.

1865 J. GROTE *Moral Ideals* (1876) 261 Ill-will is perhaps always a form or mode of vindictivolence, i.e. is connected with a feeling of ourselves as somehow wronged.

†**vin'dictor.** *Obs.*$^{-1}$ [Irreg. f. L. *vindicta.*] = VINDICATOR.

1677 GALE *Crt. Gentiles* IV. 6 It being a Science that teacheth the difference of good and evil; and the Conservator and Vindictor of al Laws.

vindo, obs. Sc. form of WINDOW.

vine (vaɪn), *sb.* Forms: *α.* 4 vygne (7 vigne), vinyhe, 5 vyny. *β.* 4–6 vyne (4–5 vyn, 5 viyn), 4–vine (5 vijne); 4, 6 wine, 5–6 wyne. *γ.* 6 vinde, vynde. [a. OF. *vigne* and *vine* (mod.F. *vigne*, = Pr. and Pg. *vinha*, Cat. *vinya*, Sp. *viña*, It. *vigna*):—L. *vīnea* vineyard, vine, etc., f. *vīn-um* wine.]

I. 1. a. The trailing or climbing plant, *Vitis vini-fera*, bearing the grapes from which ordinary wine is made (= GRAPE-VINE); also generally, any plant of the genus *Vitis.*

13.. *K. Alis.* 5758 (Laud. MS.), In eueryche felde rype is corne; þe grapes hongen on þe vyne. **1377** LANGL. *P. Pl.* B. XIV. 30 þough neuere greyne growed ne grape vppon vyne. *c* **1440** *Pallad. on Husb.* VI. 57 Now vyne and tre that were ablaqueate, To couer hem it is conuenient. **1535** COVERDALE *Judg.* ix. 12 Then sayde the trees vnto the vyne; Come thou and be oure kinge. **1562** TURNER *Herbal* II. 168 b, [It] is lyke vnto a gumme, and waxeth thicke aboute the bodye of the vinde. **1573** TUSSER *Husb.* (1878) 75 Get doong, friend mine, for stock and vine. **1591** SYLVESTER *Du Bartas* I. iii. 586 There, th' amorous Vine calls in a thousand sorts (With winding arms) her Spouse that her supports. **1600** SURFLET *Countrie Farme* VI. xxii. 774 Olde writers are not of one minde concerning the first originall and inuention of the vine. **1671** SALMON *Syn. Med.* III. xxii. 440 *Vitis*,..the Vine, the leeues bind strongly [etc.]. **1708** J. PHILIPS *Cyder* I. 16 Everlasting Hate The Vine to Ivy bears. **1776** GIBBON *Decl. & F.* ii. (1782) I. 64 In the time of Homer, the vine grew wild in the island of Sicily. **1811** SCOTT *Don Roderick* III. ii, The land..was rich with vine and flock. **1856** STANLEY *Sinai & Pal.* iii. (1858) 164 The elevation of the hills and table-lands of Judah is the true climate of the vine. **1867** H. MACMILLAN *Bible Teach.* ix. (1870) 186 The vine is one of the most graceful of plants.

b. A single plant or tree of this species or genus.

α. *a* **1300** *E.E. Psalter* civ. 31 He..smate þar vinyhes and figetres in-twa. *c* **1315** [see 2 a]. *c* **1440** *Promp. Parv.* 510/1 Vyny, or vyne, *vitis. Ibid.* 510/2 Vyny, þat bryngythe forþe grete grapys, *bumasta.* **1604** E. G[RIMSTONE] *D'Acosta's Hist. Indies* IV. xxxii. 296 Peru and..Chillé, where there are vignes that yeeld excellent wine.

β. **1303** R. BRUNNE *Handl. Synne* 882 Euery ȝere at þe florysyngge, whan þe vynys shulde spryngge, A tempest.. fordede here vynys alle. **1340** *Ayenb.* 43 Þe zenne of ham þet uor wynnynge..destrueþ þe vines oþer cornes. **1340–70** *Alex. & Dind.* 847 Ȝe telle vs þat ȝe tende nauht to tulye þe erþe,..no plaunte winus. **1390** GOWER *Conf.* II. 168 For he fond..how men scholden sette vines. **1422** YONGE tr. *Secreta Secret.* 244 In al regions the hettes bene encreschid, ..the wynes growyth, the cornes wixit rippe. *c* **1450** *Mirk's Festial* 20 He taketh a branche of a vyne, and puttyth yn Thomas hond. **1535** COVERDALE *Gen.* xl. 9, I dreamed that there was a vyne before me,..and the grapes therof were rype. **1562** WINȜET *Wks.* (S.T.S.) I. 45 The vnclene baris, quha..infectis the tender burgeounis of the ȝong wynis. **1590** SPENSER *F.Q.* II. xii. 54 A Porch with rare deuice, Archt ouer head with an embracing vine. **1610** HOLLAND *Camden's Brit.* (1637) 269 The vines..which we have had in Britaine..rather for shade than fruit. **1697** DRYDEN *Virg. Georg.* IV. 388 Raisins from the Grapes of Psythian Vines. **1731** MILLER *Gard. Dict.* s.v. *Vitis*, Those in the Plains.. sow a Hole of Melons between Vine and Vine. **1794** MRS. RADCLIFFE *Myst. Udolpho* xv, The vines were torn down from the branches that had supported them. **1830** M. DONOVAN *Dom. Econ.* I. 17 It is quite clear that wine could not have been first known at an Egyptian town, if the Egyptians had no vines. **1870** H. MACMILLAN *True Vine* v. (1872) 190 The celebrated vine of Hampton Court is a most productive bearer.

c. A representation of a vine in metal, embroidery, etc.; also, in mod. use, an ornamental figure cut by a skater on the ice.

a **1400** *Sqr. lowe Degre* 207 With vines of golde set all aboute Within your shelde,..Fulfylled with ymagery. *a* **1400–50** *Alexander* 3667 Be-twene þe pelers was piȝt with precious leuys, Gilden wynes with grapis of gracious stanes. **1506** *Lincoln Wills* (1914) I. 44 A whyte pece with a coveryng wroght with grapes or vynes on it. **1633** P. FLETCHER *Purple Isl.* XI. xlii, Agneia..spying Methos fenc't in 's iron vine, Pierc't his swoln panch. **1886** SHELDON tr. *Flaubert's Salammbô* 9 These cups were embellished on each of their six golden faces by an emerald vine. **1891** G. H. KINGSLEY *Sp. & Trav.* (1900) 460 When you have a pair of skates on, and an admiring circle of spectators to excite you into developing your most exquisite 'vines'.

d. *collect.* Vine-plants. *rare*$^{-1}$.

1779 FORREST *Voy. N. Guinea* 382 The Chinese keep the ground very clean between the rows of vine.

2. *fig.* **a.** Applied to Christ, in renderings or echoes of John xv. 1 and 5.

c **1315** SHOREHAM I. 804 For iesus seyþ þe vygne he hys, And eke þe greyn of wete. **13..** *E.E. Allit. P.* A. 628 In þe water of babtem þay dyssente, Þen arne þay boroȝt in-to þe vyne. **1382** WYCLIF *John* xv. 5, I am a vyne, ȝe ben the braunchis. *c* **1450** *Myrr. oure Ladye* 281, I as a vyne haue fruited the swetnesse of smelle... In this Chapyter, oure lorde ys lykened to a vyne. **1526** *Pilgr. Perf.* (W. de W. 1531) 222 b, For in that our lorde is as a vyne, and all chrystyans be as the braunches of the sayd vyne. **1568** LAUDER *Godlie Tract.* 395 Christ Iesus, the faithfull wine. **1597** HOOKER *Eccl. Pol.* v. lvi. (1611) 308 That true Vine whereof wee both spiritually and corporally are branches. **1870** H. MACMILLAN *True Vine* 26 Its full significance was not known until Christ, the True Vine, made it known.

b. In allusion to Ps. cxxviii. 3.

1787 M. CUTLER in *Life*, etc. (1888) I. 289 He..has married a wife, who bids fair to be a fruitful vine, for she has had three children in four years. **1807** CRABBE *Par. Reg.* I. 477 Now of that vine he'd have no more increase, Those playful branches now disturb his peace.

c. In miscellaneous uses.

1590 [see ELM *sb.* 3]. **1611** SHAKS. *Cymb.* IV. ii. 60 Grow patient, And let the stinking-Elder (Greefe) vntwine His perishing roote, with the encreasing Vine. **1639** S. DU VERGER tr. *Camus' Admir. Events* 149 Zotique..had like a furious wild Boare made a prodigious spoyle in the vine of many womens honesty. [Cf. Ps. lxxx. 8, 13.] **1643** [see ELM *sb.* 3]. **1784** COWPER *Task* VI. 969 He..recompenses well The state, beneath the shadow of whose vine He sits secure. [Cf. 1 Kings iv. 25.] **1820** SHELLEY *Prometh. Unb.* II. iv. 64 That vine Which bears the wine of life, the human heart. **1887** MEREDITH *Ballads & P.* 42 The training of Love's vine of flame Was writ in laws.

d. A suit of clothes; *pl.*, clothing. *U.S. slang.*

1932 *Evening Sun* (Baltimore) 9 Dec. 31/5 *Vine*, a suit of clothes. **1959** *Esquire* Nov. 70 J *Vines*, clothes. **1964** L. HAIRSTON in J. H. CLARKE *Harlem* 285, I..laid out my vine, a clean shirt and things on my bed. **1973** A. DUNDES *Mother Wit* 238 I'm going to lay a vine under the Jew's balls for a dime. **1975** *Amer. Speech 1972* XLVII. 152 Without your vines you're nothing but FBI [*sc.* Fat, Black, and Ignorant].

3. Applied, with distinguishing epithets, to some species of *Vitis* distinct from the ordinary grape-vine, and to many plants of other genera which in manner of growth, or in some other feature, resemble this: **a.** ***wild vine***, the fox-grape, *Vitis Labrusca* (now *rare* or *Obs.*); also, one or other of several wild climbing or trailing plants, esp. bryony and traveller's-joy.

In quot. 1382 (and similarly in later versions) *vine* is a literal rendering of the original text; the plant intended is app. the colocynth.

1382 WYCLIF *2 Kings* iv. 39 And oon..foond as a wijld vyne, and he gederde of it wijld gourdis of the feeld. *c* **1400** MAUNDEV. (Roxb.) vii. 26 Þai er lyke vnto wylde wynes. *Ibid.* xviii. 83 Pepre growez in maner of wilde wynes be syde þe treesse of þe forest. **14..** in Wr.-Wülcker 629 *Oliaster*, wyld vyne. *Labrusca*, wylde vyne. **1548** TURNER *Names Herbes* (E.D.S.) 45 Labrusca..may be called in englishe a wild vine. **1562** —— *Herbal* II. 168 Of the seconde kinde of *Vitis syluestris*, called wild vynde. **1600** SURFLET *Countrie Farme* VI. xxii. 774 Grapes..like vnto them which the wilde vine (called of vs *Labrusca*) doth now bring forth. **1607** TOPSELL *Four-f. Beasts* 372 Take of the stalkes of *Vitis alba*, otherwise called *Brioni*, or wilde Vine, two..handfuls. **1731** MILLER *Gard. Dict.* s.v. *Vitis*, The Wild Vine, commonly called the Claret Grape. This Sort of Grape is pretty well known in England. **1753** *Chambers' Cycl.* Suppl. s.v. *Vitis*, The species of Vine enumerated by Mr. Tournefort, are these: 1. The common, or wild Vine. **1796** WITHERING *Brit. Plants* (ed. 3) II. 67 Redberried Bryony. Wild Vine. **1814** SCOTT *Lord of Isles* I. xxviii, As the wild vine in tendrils spread, Droops from the mountain oak. **1855** MISS PRATT *Flower. Pl.* I. 18 *Clematis vitalba*... Country people call it.. Wild Vine. *Ibid.* II. 312 A very pretty climber is this Wild Bryony,.. called also Wild Vine.

b. In other special names, chiefly of non-British plants.

Alleghany vine, an American biennial plant (*Adlumia fungosa*), also called 'climbing fumitory'. **arbor vine**: see SPANISH *a.* 9. **balloon vine**, an Australian plant (see quots.). **bean vine**, *Phaseolus diversifolius* (see BEAN *sb.* 8). †**black vine**, black bryony. **Burdekin vine**, an Australian species of *Vitis* (see quot.). **caustic vine** (see quot.). **climbing vine**, †(*a*) the Virginian creeper; (*b*) a cinchonaceous plant, *Psychotria parasitica.* **condor vine**, *Gonolobus Cundurango.* **cypress vine**, quamoclit. **deer vine**, the twinflower (*Linnea*). **granadilla vine**: see GRANADILLA b. **Harvey's vine**, an Australian plant, *Sarcopetalum Harveyanum.* **hungry vine**, the green brier or cat-brier (*Smilax*). **india-rubber vine**, *Cryptostegia grandiflora.* **Isle of Wight vine**, bryony or black bryony. **lawyer vine**: see LAWYER 6. **link vine**, a West Indian species of vanilla (*V. articulata*). **Madeira** or **Mexican vine**, the climbing plant *Boussingaultia baselloides*, a native of the Andes. **matrimony vine**: see MATRIMONY 7. **mignonette vine**: see MIGNONETTE 3. **milk vine**, (*a*) the Southern European plant *Periploca græca*; (*b*) a Jamaican plant, *Forsteronia floribunda.* **negro vine**, a hairy-leaved species of *Vincetoxicum.* **pea vine**: see PEA-VINE. **pepper vine**: see PEPPER *sb.* 7. **pipe vine**: see PIPE *sb.*¹ 11 b. **poison vine**: see POISON *sb.* 5 b. **potato vine**: see POTATO 7. **red-bead vine**, *Abrus precatorius* (India). **rubber vine**: see RUBBER *sb.*¹ 12 b. **sand vine**, *Gonolobus lævis* (N. America). **scrub vine**, *Austr.* (*a*) the dodder laurel (*Cassytha*); (*b*) the native rose (*Bauera rubioides*). **seven-year vine**: see SEVEN-YEAR. **silk vine**, = *milk vine* (*a*). **sorrel vine**: see

SORREL *sb.*[1] 7 c. **Spanish arbor-vine**: see SPANISH *a.* 9. **strainer, Virginia(n, water, white vine**: see these words.

Many of these names appear to be first recorded in the *Treas. Bot.* (1866, and Suppl. 1874) and in American dictionaries. In *Chambers' Cycl.* Suppl. (1753) Tournefort's species of *Vitis*, twenty-one in number, are enumerated.

1889 MAIDEN *Useful Pl.* 13 *Cardiospermum halicacabum*, ..'Heartseed', 'Heart-pea', 'Winter-cherry', '*Balloon Vine'. *Ibid.* 161 'Balloon Vine' (because of its inflated membranous capsule). **1552** HULOET, *Blacke vyne, *apronia*. **1760** J. LEE *Introd. Bot.* App. 331 Vine, Black, *Tamus*. **1898** MORRIS *Austral Eng.* 490/1 *Burdekin Vine. Called also Round Yam, *Vitis opaca*. *Ibid.* 84/1 Caustic-Plant, or *Caustic-Vine,.. *Sarcostemma australis*. **1760** J. LEE *Introd. Bot.* App. 331 Vine, *Climbing five-leaved, of Canada, *Hedera*. **1846-50** A. WOOD *Class-bk. Bot.* 443 *Quamoclit vulgaris*. Bindweed. *Cypress Vine. *Ibid.* 449 *Lycium Barbarum*. *Matrimony Vine. **1866** *Treas. Bot.* 234/1 Some of the Australian species [of *Cassytha*] are called *Scrub-vines. **1898** MORRIS *Austral Eng.* 22/1 *Bauera rubioides*,.. the Scrub Vine, or Native Rose.

4. a. The stem of any trailing or climbing plant. Also *collect.* without article.

1563 HYLL *Art Garden* (1574) 124 And if not on this wise, then may you let their [*sc.* gourds'] vine run along on the earth, if you list. **1707** MORTIMER *Husb.* (1721) I. 179 On the outside of this Floor the Pickers [of hops] sit, and pick them into Baskets after the Vines are strip'd from the Poles. **1731** MILLER *Gard. Dict.* s.v. *Melon*, When your Melons begin to appear upon the Vines. **1779** FORREST *Voy. N. Guinea* 382 They do not let the vine, which bears the pepper, twist round a chinkareen tree, as is the custom on Sumatra. **1844** WELBY *Poems* (1867) 163 When sweet jasmine vines their wreaths were looping Around her bower. **1855** DELAMER *Kitchen Garden* (1861) 117 Leading points in growing frame cucumbers are, to pinch off the shoot.. to keep the frame clear of useless vine. **1898** JEAN A. OWEN *Hawaii* iii. 79 A hero.. who descended by means of a long rope, made of convolvulus vines, into the abyss.

b. *dial.* A straw rope.

1577 B. GOOGE *Heresbach's Husb.* 28 Rye.. strawe is gentle and flexible, seruing for Vines. **1884** JEFFERIES *Red Deer* v. 97 The farmers.. hang a vine of straw along from stake to stake... A vine is a rope of twisted straw.

c. *U.S.* A trailing or climbing plant.

1708 E. COOK *Sot-Weed Factor* 19 When sturdy Oaks, and lofty Pines Were level'd with Musmillion Vines. **1831** W. C. BRYANT *Marion's Men* 9 We know its walls of thorny vines, its glades of reedy grass. **1842** LONGF. *Slave in Dismal Swamp* ii, Where.. the cedar grows, and the poisonous vine Is spotted like the snake. **1856** A. GRAY *Man. Bot.* (1860) 2 Ranunculaceæ... Herbs (or woody vines) with a colorless acrid juice. **1879** BODDAM-WHETHAM *Roraima & Brit. Guiana* 9 Nearly every house has a garden, and passion-flowers, morning glory, and other vines creep up the pillars. **1886** C. D. WARNER *Summer in Gard.* 114 The bean is a graceful, confiding, engaging vine.

II. †**5.** A vineyard. *Obs.*

So AF. *vine, vyne* (Gower).

13.. *E.E. Allit. P.* A. 507 Þe lorde ful erly vp he ros To hyre werkmen to hys vyne. *Ibid.* 521 Gos in-to my vyne. **1382** WYCLIF *Prov.* xxxi. 16 She beheeld a feeld, and boȝte it; of the frut of hir hondis she plauntide a vyne. *c* **1400** MAUNDEV. (1839) x. 111 The cursed Queene.. that toke awey the Vyne of Nabaothe. **1430-40** LYDG. *Bochas* II. xxxi. (1554) 67 Trust [that] He will not refuse thyne axing, But thee receiue to labour in his vine. **1484** CAXTON *Fables of Æsop* I. x, A man was som tyme whiche fond a serpent within a Vyne. **1514** BAINBRIDGE in Ellis *Orig. Lett.* Ser. I. I. 227 Boith in the Citie and also in vynes and garthynges withoutt the Citie. **1560** BIBLE (Genev.) *Song Sol.* i. 5 Thei made me the keper of the vines: but I kept not mine owne vine.

6. A grape. *Obs.* or *poet.*

a **1425** tr. *Arderne's Treat. Fistula*, etc. 56 If þai be rede þai ar called uve,·i. grapez, and þai haue þe schap of a rede vyne or grape. **1697** DRYDEN *Virg. Past.* x. 54 Ah! that your birth and bus'ness had been mine—To pen the sheep, and press the swelling vine!

7. *Roman Antiq.* = VINEA. *rare.*

1563 GOLDING *Cæsar* (1565) 51 b, He made Vines [*marg.* an instrument of war made of timber & hurdles for men to go vnder safelye to the walles of a towne], and began to make prouision of thinges meete for the siege. *a* **1641** BP. MOUNTAGU *Acts & Mon.* (1642) 480 The Romans.. plyed their mines,.. their vines and other engines against the walls and gates. *a* **1656** USSHER *Ann.* (1658) 142 Some say, those Engines of Battrie, as Rams, and Vines, and Galleries, were there first invented. **1862** KINGTON *Fredk. II*, II. 191 Various warlike Machines... The Sow, the Vine, and the Cat.

III. *attrib.* and *Comb.* **8. a.** Simple attrib., as *vine-arbour, border, -bough, -bower, -bunch*, etc.

1731 MILLER *Gard. Dict.* s.v. *Vitis*, Care is to be taken.. not to mingle with them the Grapes of the *Vine-Arbour. **1839** tr. *Lamartine's Trav.* 147/1 Houses.. lying under the shade of vine-arbours or plane-trees. **1842** LOUDON *Suburban Hort.* 467 The most valuable manure that can be deposited in a *vine border. **1867** MORRIS *Jason* XIII. 222 A golden *vine-bough wreathed her golden head. **1848** tr. *Hoffmeister's Trav. Ceylon*, etc. xii. 462 A few *vine-bowers appear somewhat lower down. **1832** TENNYSON *Œnone* 177 Between the shadows of the *vine-bunches Floated the glowing sunlights. **1886** CONDER *Syrian Stone-lore* vi. (1896) 221 A door sculptured with vine-bunches. **1611** FLORIO, *Vineto*, a *vine-close, a vine-plot. **1865** J. H. INGRAHAM *Pillar of Fire* I. xiii. 152 There were wines from the *vine country of Helbona. **1888** *Encycl. Brit.* XXIV. 238/2 The success of *vine-culture in.. the Canary Islands. **1601** HOLLAND *Pliny* I. 530 Strengthned with the wood of *vine-cuttings. **1782** *Encycl. Brit.* (ed. 2) X. 8725/1 From whence Columella gives the title of *malleolus* to the vine-cuttings. **1857** MILLER *Elem. Chem., Org.* vi. 405 Each vat is filled with vine cuttings, and rapes. **1846** KEIGHTLEY *Notes Virg., Terms Husb.* 358 The cross-pieces in the *vine-espaliers. **1847** DARLINGTON *Amer. Weeds*, etc. (1860) 81 *Vitaceæ.* (*Vine Family.) **1600** SURFLET *Countrie Farme* VI. xxi. 769 To gather the greene grapes from of the *vine frames. **1565** COOPER *Thesaurus* s.v. *Pampinus*, A *vyne garlande. **1587** GOLDING *De Mornay* xxv. (1592) 382 Assigning to one.. the Corne countrie, and to another the *vinegrounds. **1818** LADY MORGAN *Autobiog.* (1859) 324 The vine-grounds being nothing but black earth and dry sticks until the middle of summer. **1611** COTGR., *Vendange*, ..vintage, *vine-haruest. **1733** TULL *Horse-Hoeing Husb.* 158 The Ancients were perfect Masters of *Vine-Husbandry. **1841** LEVER *C. O'Malley* lii. 262 A little weak wine savouring more of the borachio-skin than *vine-juice. **1886** MRS. CADDY *Footsteps Jeanne D'Arc* 25 One should make a point of seeing these *vine-lands in October. **1861** BENTLEY *Man. Bot.* 495 *Vitaceæ* or *Ampelideæ*.—The *Vine Order... Usually climbing shrubs with a watery juice. **1706** PHILLIPS (ed. Kersey), *Vitis*,.. the *Vine-plant. **1843** *Penny Cycl.* XXVI. 342/2 Some of the finest of the soil is put into each hole, and the vine-plants.. are carefully inserted. **1856** R. KNOX tr. *Edwards' Man. Zool.* §328 In the timber of the hedge-rows, of fruit-trees, and of *vine-poles. **1601** HOLLAND *Pliny* I. Table s.v., *Vine props and railes which be best. **1610** HEALEY *St. Aug. Citie of God* 251 First was carryed.. a pine apple, and a vine-prop. **1731** MILLER *Gard. Dict.* s.v. *Vitis*, Others make use of a Vine-prop, or some other Piece of Wood. **1815** KIRBY & SP. *Entomol.* xiv. (1816) I. 438 The upright putrescent espaliers or vine-props. *c* **1380** WYCLIF *Serm.* Sel. Wks. I. 99 Digge about þe *vyne rotis, and dunge hem wel. **1424** *E.E. Wills* (1882) 56 Also I wull he haue my maser of a vine rote. **1601** HOLLAND *Pliny* I. 545 To open a sluce.. for to overflow their Vine roots with the river. *c* **1440** *Pallad. on Husb.* Table (1896) 15 *Vyne sciouns, to sette. **1601** HOLLAND *Pliny* I. 529 In setting a nource-garden with vine-sions. *Ibid.* 527 A *vine-set or cutting, that hath joints standing thin. **1648** HEXHAM II, *Een wijngaerdt-scheute*, a *Vine-shoote, or Sprigge. **1793** HOLCROFT tr. *Lavater's Physiog.* i. 5 Though these vine-shoots look well, they will bear but few grapes. **1647** HEXHAM I, A *vine slip, *een Wijngaert-snijtsel*. **1725** *Fam. Dict.* s.v., Vine-slips.. being put into the Ground will easily take Root. **1854** WHITTIER *Poems Nature, Fruit-Gift* 22 Perchance our frail, sad mother plucked.. A single vine-slip. **1855** SINGLETON *Virgil* I. 48 Now on the merry *vine-spray swell the buds. **1872** HEAD *Sel. Grk. Coins in Electro-type Brit. Mus.* 38 Rose with bud, and vine-spray with bunch of grapes. **1611** COTGR. s.v. *Sarment*, To bridle himselfe with a *vine-sprig; be so drunke that he cannot speake. **1794** MRS. RADCLIFFE *Myst. Udolpho* xlix, She found the old woman within, picking *vine-stalks. **1888** *Encycl. Brit.* XXIV. 237 The conformation of the *vine stem has elicited a vast amount of explanatory comment. **1531** TINDALE *Exp. 1 John* (1537) 94 He yt is cut from ye *vynestocke.. can not but abyde vnfruteful. **1600** SURFLET *Countrie Farme* III. xxxiv. 497 The Italians graft it [*sc.* olive-tree] vpon the vine, boring the vine stocke neer vnto the earth [etc.]. **1690** TEMPLE *Ess. Anc. & Mod. Learn.* (1909) 19 A large Table at Memorancy cut out of the thickness of a Vine-stock. **1868** MORRIS *Earthly Par.* (1870) II. III. 3 Above them did they see the terraced way, And over that the vine-stocks, row on row. **1898** MANSON *Trop. Diseases* 462 The male worm is characterised.. by the peculiar *vine-tendril-like tail. **1846** LOUISA S. COSTELLO *Tour Venice* 192 There is.. no want of gardens and *vine-terraces. **1848** CLOUGH *Amours de Voy.* III. 16 Ah! that I were far away.. Under the *vine-trellis laid. **1694** MOTTEUX *Rabelais* IV. i. 3 A Golden *Vine-Tub of Mozaic work. **1727** BAILEY (vol. II), *Wicker*, a *Vine Twig, an Osier Twig. **1776** J. BRYANT *Mythol.* III. 229 The soft pliant vine-twigs, moving round In serpentine direction. **1883** BROWNING *Ferishtah's Fancies, Shah Abbas*, I weep like a cut vine-twig. **1601** HOLLAND *Pliny* I. 404 A great standing cup or boll to be seene of *Vine wood. **1700** tr. *Danet's Dict. Grk. & Rom. Antiq.* s.v. *Templum*, A Pair of Stairs made of Vine-wood. **1818** KEATS *Endym.* IV. 257, I saw Osirian Egypt kneel adown Before the *vine-wreath crown!

b. Objective and obj. genitive, with agent-nouns, as *vine-cutter, -grower, -planter*, etc., and vbl. sbs. or ppl. adjs., as *vine-bearing, -dressing, -growing*, etc.; also *vine-prop* adj.

(*a*) **1388** WYCLIF *2 Kings* xxv. 12 He lefte of the pore men of the lond vyntilieris, and erthetilieris. *a* **1586** SIDNEY *Arcadia* II. xv. (1912) 247 The King one morning.. saw a vine-labourer, that finding a bowe broken [etc.]. **1601** HOLLAND *Pliny* I. 501 Yet kind it is and wholesome for the Vine-planter and husbandman. **1611** COTGR., *Vendengeur*, a Vintager, or vine-reaper. **1648** HEXAM II, *Een.. wijngaerdenier*,.. a Vine-gardener. **1801** tr. *Gabrielli's Myst. Husb.* II. 119 One of our vine-cutters was telling yesterday [etc.]. **1835** T. MITCHELL *Acharn. of Aristoph.* App. 245 A metaphor which the vine-growers of Athens easily appreciated. **1884** KNIGHT *Dict. Mech.* Suppl. 928/1 *Vine puller*, a machine for extracting vines.

(*b*) *c* **1440** *Pallad. on Husb.* Table (1896) 16 Vyne coueryng and vindage apparayle. **1580** HOLLYBAND *Treas. Fr. Tong*, *Binement*, a vine working, weeding. **1590** SPENSER *F.Q.* I. i. 8 The sayling Pine, the Cedar proud and tall, The vine-prop Elme. **1601** HOLLAND *Pliny* Table s.v., Vine planting and pruning. **1791** COWPER *Iliad* II. 613 Arne claims A record next for her illustrious sons, Vine-bearing Arne. **1848** BUCKLEY *Iliad* 111 An enclosure of land,.. pleasant, vine-bearing, and arable. **1867** AUGUSTA WILSON *Vashti* i, Had Timour been trained to cabbage-raising and vine-dressing. **1888** *Encycl. Brit.* XXIV. 237/1 A vine-growing country hitherto free from *Phylloxera*.

c. With pa. pples. and adjs., chiefly in instrumental sense, as *vine-bordered, -clad, covered, -crowned*, etc.; also *vine-like* adj., *vine-wise* adv.

1868 MORRIS *Earthly Par.* (1870) I. II. 457 He saw a man draw nigh Along the dusty grey *vine-bordered road. **1824** LADY BLESSINGTON *Jrnl.* May in E. Clay *Lady Blessington at Naples* (1979) 102 The *vine-clad hills and fertile Campania. **1854** J. S. C. ABBOTT *Napoleon* (1855) I. ix. 162 The luxuriant valleys and vine-clad hillsides. **1856** R. A. VAUGHAN *Mystics* (1860) I. 115 Among the luscious slopes of vine-clad Burgundy. **1791** W. ROSCOE in H. Roscoe *Life* (1833) I. 108 The *vine-cover'd hills and gay regions of France. **1840** HOOD '*Ye Tourists & Trav.*' vi, Old Castles you'll see on the vine-covered hill. **1743** FRANCIS tr. *Horace, Odes* III. xxv. 27 When *Vine-crown'd Bacchus leads the Way. **1851** S. JACKSON tr. *Krummacher's Elisha* vi. 90 From the sea-coast to the vine-crowned banks of the Jordan. **1625** K. LONG tr. *Barclay's Argenis* IV. xviii. 306 Behold, with frolicke stirre comes Bacchus here, In's *Vine-deck't Chariot high. **1865** PRAED *Poems* (1865) II. 158 The merriest girl in all the land Of *vine-encircled France. **1746** FRANCIS tr. *Horace, Sat.* II. iv. 55 The *Vine-fed Goat's not always luscious Fare. **1871** PALGRAVE *Lyr. Poems* 90 Lines of white, *vine-garlanded. *a* **1835** MRS. HEMANS *Shepherd-Poet of Alps* 54 The cabin's *vine-hung eaves. **1835** WILLIS *Pencillings* II. lviii. 147 The same square, *vine-laced, perfectly green pastures and cornfields. **1855** SINGLETON *Virgil* I. 107 For thee, With *vine-leafed autumn laden blooms the field. **1822** *Hortus Anglicus* II. 208 *Vine-leaved Kitaibelia. **1727** P. BLAIR *Pharmaco-Bot.* v. 215 Viticulated, or *Vine-like Leaves. **1865** TYLOR *Early Hist. Man* 345 Stories.. of the climbing from earth to heaven by a tree or vine-like plant. **1740** DYER *Ruins Rome* 35 The *vine-mantled brows The pendent goats unveil. *a* **1593** MARLOWE *Ovid's Eleg.* II. xvi. 33 Although *vine-planted ground Conteines me. **1848** BUCKLEY *Iliad* 39 Vine-planted Epidaurus. **1809** J. MONTGOMERY *West Indies*, etc. (1810) 34 On pure Madeira's *vine-robed hills of health. **1839** BAILEY *Festus* 143 A *vine-shadowed cottage door. *a* **1869** ROSSETTI *House of Life* xc, Upon the broad *vine-sheltered path. **1876** LANIER *Psalm West* 183 O Stars wreathed *vinewise round yon heavenly dells. **1791** COWPER *Iliad* VI. 159 They their wands *Vine-wreathed cast all away. **1828** MISS MITFORD *Village* Ser. IV. (1863) 71 Working at her needle under the vine-wreathed porch.

9. Special Combs.: †**vine apple** (see SQUASH *sb.*[2] 1); **vine-bamboo**, a species of panic-grass (*Panicum divaricatum*); †**vine-bind** (see quots.); **vine-black** (see quot.); **vine-bower**, a species of clematis (*Clematis Viticella*); **vine-disease**, one or other disease attacking vines, esp. vine-mildew and the vine-pest (*Phylloxera*); †**vine dragon** [ad. F. *drageon*], (see quot.); **vine-feeder**, any insect living on vines; **vine-fly**, ? = *vine saw-fly*; **vine-fungus**, = *vine-mildew*; **vine gall-insect** (see quot.); **vine-garden**, †**-garth**, a vineyard; **vine-grub**, = VINE-FRETTER; **vine-hook, -knife**, implements used in pruning vines; **vine-leek**, round-headed garlic (*Allium ampeloprasum*); **vine-louse**, the phylloxera; †**vine-man, -master**, a vine-dresser or vine-grower; **vine-mildew**, a disease of vines caused by the fungus *Oidium Tuckeri*; the fungus or mould itself; **vine-moth**, a species of pyralis infesting vines; †**vine-pear** (see quots.); **vine-pest**, the phylloxera; †**vine-press**, a wine-press; **vine-rake** *U.S.* (see quot.); **vine-rod**, a rod of vine-wood, *spec.* as the staff of a Roman centurion; **vine-sawfly**, a species of sawfly, the larvæ of which feed on the vine; **vine-scroll**, an ornament representing a vine; **vine-scrub**, in Australia, scrub abounding in various species of *Vitis*; **vine-snail** [F. *escargot des vignes*], the Roman snail; †**vine-wand**, = *vine-rod*; †**vine-water**, the sap which issues from vines when pruned; **vine-weevil**, a small weevil destructive to vines; **vine-worm** (see quot.); **vine-worts**, the order *Vitaceæ*.

Also, in recent American dictionaries, ***vine-beetle, -borer, -chafer, -curculio, -flea-beetle, -gall, -gall-louse, -hopper, -inch-worm, -procris, -root-borer, -slug, -sphinx***, etc.

1871 KINGSLEY *At Last* viii, Overhead, sprawled and dangled the common *Vine-bamboo, ugly and unsatisfactory in form. **1483** *Cath. Angl.* 402/1 *Vynbynd, *cornubus*. **1601** HOLLAND *Pliny* I. 537 A certaine hearbe, which the Sicilians in their language call Ampelodesmos, (i. Vine-bind). **1860** *Ure's Dict. Arts* (ed. 5) III. 966 **Vine black*, a black procured by charring the tendrils of the vine and levigating them. **1852** JOHNSON *Gard. Dict.*, *Vine Bower, *Clematis Viticella*. **1854** FORRESTER in *Proc. Royal Soc.* VII. 156 On the *Vine-Disease in the Port-wine Districts of the Alto-Douro. **1601** HOLLAND *Pliny* I. 536 The manner of.. planting by a trees side a *Vine Dragon (for so we use to call the old braunch of a Vine past all service, which hath done bearing many a yeare, and is now growne to be hard). **1855** *Zoologist* XIII. 4680 Speyer gives Agrotis aquilina as a *vine-feeder. **1661** WALTON *Angler* (ed. 3) 97 Now for Flies;.. I will name you but some of them, as ..the cloudy, or blackish flie, the flag-flye, the *vine-flye. **1668** CHARLETON *Onomast.* 47 *Ips*,.. the Vine-Fly. **1728** CHAMBERS *Cycl.* s.v. *Fishing Fly*, Natural Flies are innumerable:.. the Tawny-Fly, the Vine-Fly, the Shell-Fly. **1857** HENFREY *Bot.* §636 The *Vine Fungus appears to be a plant of this tribe [*Oidium*], rarely producing perfect fruit. **1753** *Chambers' Cycl.* Suppl., **Vine Gallinsect*, an insect of the gallinsect class, principally found on the Vine, though capable of living on some other trees. *c* **1449** PECOCK *Repr.* III. xvi. 383 Whanne money is paied to.. a laborer in a *vyne gardein for his day labour in the same vyne gardein. **1839** W. CHAMBERS *Tour Rhine* 57/1 A tolerably long reach of the river, between banks richly clad with vine gardens. *c* **1440** *Alph. Tales* 201 When þai come þer, þe *vyne-garth, at no frute was in befor, was growyng full of rype grapis. **1687** MIÈGE *Gt. Fr. Dict.* II, Vine-fretter, or *Vine-grub. **1706** PHILLIPS (ed. Kersey), *Vine-grub*, a kind of Worm that gnaws the Vine. **1753** *Chambers' Cycl.* Suppl. s.v., Reaumur observes, that.. both the winged and the unwinged Vine-grubs are females. **1601** HOLLAND *Pliny* I. 547 Men are wont to take their *Vine hookes when they be newly ground & sharpened [etc.]. **1615** *Thomas' Dict.* (ed. 10), *Averrunco*,.. to purge vines with a vinehooke. **1483** *Cath. Angl.* 402/1 A *vyne knyfe, *falx, falcicula*. **1611** COTGR., *Serpette*, a Vine knife, or Gardeners knife. **1725** *Fam. Dict.* s.v. *Vintage*, You must also provide Paniers, Dressers, Vine-Knives, Shovels and Rakes. **1597** GERARDE *Herbal* I. lxxxviii. 139 The *Vine Leeke groweth of it selfe in vine-yards, and neere vnto vines in hot regions, whereof it both tooke the name Vine Leeke and French Leeke. **1852** G. W. JOHNSON *Cottage Gard. Dict.* 24/2 A[*llium*] *ampeloprasum* (vine-leek). **1882** *Gard.*

Chron. XVII. 20 The new *Vine-louse Convention, held at Berne. 1550 COVERDALE Spir. Perle vi. Wks. (Parker Soc.) I. 115 The heavenly *vineman bringeth the Christians unto the winepress. 1579–80 NORTH Plutarch (1612) 368 In the morning.. he went out.. with his vine-men to labour in his vineyard. 1588 FRAUNCE Lawiers Log. I. i. 2 b, The word.. is metaphoricall.., being borrowed of the *Vinemayster. 1855 OGILVIE Suppl. 283 Oidium tuckeri is the *vine-mildew, parasitical upon the leaves and green parts of vines. 1867 Chambers's Encycl. IX. 800/2 The vine disease, or vine mildew,.. has of late years made great ravages. 1840 J. & M. LOUDON tr. Köllar's Treat. Insects III. 172 This *Vine Moth is not the only species of the family Tortricidæ which selects the vine for its food. 1842 LOUDON Suburban Hort. 111 A.. very efficient mode of destroying the vine-moth in France. 1704 Dict. Rust. (1726), *Vine-Pear, or Damsel-Pear, is gray, reddish, round, and pretty big. 1731 MILLER Gard. Dict. s.v. Pyrus, Poire de Vigne, i.e. The Vine Pear. 1887 Westm. Rev. June 364 The ravages of the *vine-pest with the terrible name of Phylloxera vastatrix in France. 1897 Outing XXIX. 434/1 Then came the terrible vine-pest, and on its heels came ruin. 1587 GREENE Euphues Wks. (Grosart) VI. 237 Alaying the heate of Bacchus *vynepresse, with the sweete conserues fetcht from Myneruaes Library. 1632 LITHGOW Trav. x. 459 A Vine-presse house, standing alone amongst Vineyards. 1760–72 H. BROOKE Fool of Qual. (1809) II. 125 As grapes are squeezed in a vine-press. 1846 KEIGHTLEY Notes Virg., Georg. II. 4 The vinepress, or vat in which they trod the grapes. 1875 KNIGHT Dict. Mech. 2710/2 *Vine-rake, an implement for pulling sweet-potato or other vines off from the ridges preparatory to the digging of the ground. 1601 HOLLAND Pliny I. 406 For the Centurion hath the honour to carie in his hand a *Vine-rod. a1661 HOLYDAY Juvenal (1673) 263/1 They may get a vine-rod, that is, a centurion's place. 1856 MERIVALE Rom. Emp. xlii. (1871) V. 145 Some showed him the scars of their wounds, others the marks of the centurion's vine-rod. 1852 T. W. HARRIS Insects Injur. Veg. vi. (1862) 512 Fir Saw-Fly.—*Vine Saw-Fly.—Rose-bush Slug. [Ibid. 522 A kind of saw-fly which attacks the grape-vine,.. named Selandria Vitis. The saw-fly of the vine is of a jet-black color.] 1886 CONDER Syrian-Stone-Lore ix. (1896) 357 The *vine-scrolls and grape-bunches on the oldest mosaics of the Dome of the Rock. 1881 A. C. GRANT Bush-Life xxii, Impenetrable *vine-scrubs line the river-banks at intervals. 1889 LUMHOLTZ Among Cannibals 24 Along the streams vine-scrubs often abound. 1831 J. DAVIES Mat. Med. 413 Some animals of an inferior class, such as bull-frogs, the *vine-snail, turtle, viper, crayfish, &c. 1601 HOLLAND Pliny I. 406 The *Vine wand is now entred into the campe, and by it our armies are raunged into battaillons. 1736 BAILEY Household Dict. s.v., The *vine-water without distilling, will have the same effect. 1882 Garden 11 Mar. 172/1 Specimens of the black *Vine weevil (Otiorhynchus sulcatus), a very destructive insect. 1896 LODEMAN Spray. Plants 280 Fire-worm; Cranberry-worm; *Vine-worm; Blackhead (Rhopobota vacciniana). 1846 LINDLEY Veg. Kingd. 439 The propriety of placing Leea along with *Vineworts has been questioned. 1870 H. MACMILLAN True Vine vii. (1872) 296 note, The vine-worts, distinguished for their wholesome and nutritious qualities, seem closely allied to the Umbelliferæ.

Hence **vine** *v. trans.*, to graft (*in* or *into* a vine); *intr.*, to develop tendrils like a vine.

1579 W. WILKINSON Confut. Fam. Love 15 b, The vine braunch is to be vined in the vine. Ibid. 16 Neither doth the Greeke or Latin translation afford any such termes of vinyng into a vine, as ye seme to import. 1796 C. MARSHALL Gardening xv. (1813) 247 Sticking pease is to take place as soon as they begin to vine (or put forth tendrils).

vine, obs. Sc. form of WINE *sb.*

‖**vinea** ('vɪniːə). Also 7 vinia. [L. *vīnea*: see VINE *sb.*] A kind of protective shed or penthouse anciently used in siege-operations.

1601 HOLLAND Pliny I. 406 How to approch the walls of their enemies, to give an assault under a frame devised for the purpose, which thereupon took the name Vinea. 1614 GORGES tr. Lucan III. 106 Their Vinias to the wall they brought, Couerd with greene turfes all aloft. 1678 PHILLIPS (ed. 4). 1718 ROWE tr. Lucan III. 721 Beneath the Vinea close th' Assailant lies. 1783 W. GORDON tr. Livy's Rom. Hist. II. xvii. (1809) 130 The Vineae and other works were repaired. 1885 OMAN Art War 47 The vinea and testudo, the catapult onager and balista, were as well known in the tenth century as in the first.

vineal ('vɪniːəl), *a. rare.* [ad. L. *vīneālis*, f. *vīnea* VINE *sb.*] Of or pertaining to vines or wine; living on vines; consisting of wine.

1659 H. MORE Immort. Soul III. xii. 454 These exhalations of the Vineyards must spread.. from.. the Canaries to England... So that there will be an Hemisphere of vineall Atoms of an incredible extent. 1859 MAYNE Expos. Lex., Vinealis, applied by Mirbel to plants that grow spontaneously on the vines,.. vineal. 1908 Daily Chron. 30 Oct. 9/5 To obtain a 50 per cent. drop on Italian vineal exports to that country.

vineat, variant of VINET[1] *Obs.*

vine'atic, *a. rare*[−0]. [a. L. *vīneātic-us*, f. *vīnea* VINE *sb.*] (See quot.)

1656 BLOUNT Glossogr., Vineatick, belonging to Vines, apt, or that serves for Vines.

vine-branch. Also vine branch. [VINE *sb.*] A branch of a vine-tree.

c1400 Laud Troy Bk. 11201 The vyne-braunche with alle here grapes. c1440 Pallad. on Husb. Table (1896) 15 Vyne braunchis, to enoynte. 1535 COVERDALE John xv. 6 He that abydeth not in me, is cast out as a vyne braunche. 1560 BIBLE (Geneva) Nahum ii. 2 The emptiers haue emptied them out, & marred their vine branches. 1603 HOLLAND Plutarch's Mor. 685 He that gladly would in winter season weare a chaplet of vine branches. 1673–4 GREW Anat. Pl., Anat. Trunks i. §8 In Summer time,.. the Vessels also, in the Barque of a Vine-Branch, do Bleed a Sower Sap. 1691 RAY Creation II. (1692) 128 If in Summer-time you denude a Vine-branch of its Leaves, the Grapes will never come to maturity. 1731 MILLER Gard. Dict. s.v. Vitis, That Bulk which they have acquir'd upon the Vine-branches. 1770 LANGHORNE Plutarch (1851) II. 1107/1 He lifted up the vinebranch, with which the centurions chastise such as deserve stripes. 1818–22 Encycl. Metrop. (1845) XIV. 490/2 The vanilla is a plant of the thickness of a small vine branch. 1845 J. COULTER Adv. in Pacific xi. 133 Posts of wood, interlaced by vine branches.

vined, *a. rare.* [f. VINE *sb.*]

1. Ornamented with the representation of a vine.

1577 HARRISON England II. xxiii. (1877) I. 351 A table hauing at each hand an image vined and finelie florished both aboue and beneath. 1624 WOTTON Elem. Archit. 31 Other licentious inuentions, of Wreathed, and Vined, and Figured Columnes, which our Author himselfe condemneth.

2. Impregnated with the qualities of a vine.

1600 SURFLET Countrie Farme III. xxxiv. 498 These Oliues will tast both of the one and of the other, and become as it were vined Oliues.

†**vinedage**, variant of VENDAGE *Obs.*

1574 HELLOWES Gueuara's Fam. Ep. (1577) 237 Since your garden is blasted, your vinedage ended,.. your prime tyme finished.

vine-dresser. [VINE *sb.*] One occupied in the pruning, training, and cultivation of vines.

1560 BIBLE (Geneva) Joel i. 11 Houle, o ye vine dressers for the wheat, and for the barly. 1611 BIBLE Jer. lii. 16 Nebuzaradan.. left certaine of the poore of the land for Vine-dressers and for husbandmen. a1653 GOUGE Comm. Heb. vii. (1655) II. 131 The Apostle exemplifieth the equity of this.. by a Vine-dressers partaking of the fruit of it. 1709 Lond. Gaz. 4556/1 Of these there are, Husbandmen and Vinedressers, one thousand eighty three. 1763 MILLS Syst. Pract. Husb. IV. 341 That so the vine dresser may dig all round the vine. 1818 LADY MORGAN Autobiog. (1859) 123 When the vines were all gathered, the vinedressers came in procession under the castle windows. 1884 J. DE MILLE Castle in Spain iv, Shepherds, goatherds, and vine-dressers stared lazily up.

fig. 1770 BURKE Pres. Discont. Wks. 1808 II. 273, I do not mean those branches [of trade] which bear without the hand of the vine-dresser.

vine-fretter. Now *rare* or *Obs.* [VINE *sb.*] A grub or insect (in later use, a species of aphis) feeding upon vines.

1608 TOPSELL Serpents 105 After the manner of Vine-fretters, which are a kind of Catterpillers, or little hayrie wormes with many feete, that eate Vines when they begin to shoote. 1661 LOVELL Hist. Anim. & Min. Isagoge c 2, The butyri in vines, and ipes, and the vinefretter in the leaves thereof. 1725 Fam. Dict. s.v. Diseases of Trees, The Vine-fretter, a little black Animal, does a great deal of Mischief to Trees. 1762 MILLS Syst. Pract. Husb. I. 471 Almost all the peas in his neighbourhood were destroyed that year by a kind of vermin called vine-fretters. 1777 W. HOOPER Helvetius' Treat. Man I. 91 note, We should.. inclose a vine-fretter in a phial. 1848 BARTLETT Dict. Amer. 374 Vine-fretter,.. an insect very destructive to vines, rose bushes, cabbages, &c. in the Southern States. 1895 Dublin Rev. Oct. 444 He considered the generation of vine fretters from a new point of view.

vinegar ('vɪnɪgə(r)), *sb.* Forms: α. 4–6 vynegre (4 fyn-), 5–6 vynagre, 6 -ygre; 4–7 vinegre (5 uin-, win-, 6 winnegre), 7 vin'gre; 5 venagre, 5–7 venegre; 5 vyneygre, -aygre, 7 vinaigre. β. 5–6 vyneger, 6 -egyr, vynyger; 5–7 vineger (7 -ere, vinneger), 6–7 viniger (7 win-); 5 venegur, 6 -eger; 5, 7 vinager, 7 vinaiger, 5–6 vineager. γ. 6 vynegar, 6– vinegar (8 ven-). δ. 4 vynacre, 5, 7 vinacre, 7 vinaicre; 6 vinycare, vinyker, vyneker, venyker, -iker, *Sc.* vinakir, venaker, wynakar, -akir, 7 *Sc.* winiker. [a. OF. *vyn egre* (14th cent.), *vinaigre* (so mod.F.), f. *vin*:—L. *vīnum* wine + *egre*, *aigre* EAGER *a.* Cf. Pr. *vina(i)gre*, Sp. and Pg. *vinagre*, It. *vinagro*. Some of the spellings are influenced by the later F. form, or by mod.L. *vinum acre*.]

1. a. A liquid (consisting of acetic acid in a dilute form) produced by the acetous fermentation of wine and some other alcoholic liquors or special compounds and employed either pure or with various admixtures in the preparation of food (or as a relish to this) and in the arts, etc.

The chief sources of vinegar are indicated by the names *wine-*, *malt-*, *sugar-*, and *wood-vinegar*. *radical vinegar*: see RADICAL *a.* 9. *thieves' vinegar*: see THIEF 5.

α. a1300 Cursor M. 16762 + 13 Vinegre & gall þe jews blend And to his mouth put þore. c1315 SHOREHAM I. 829 Al so longe hyt hys blod, Ase lest þe forme of wyne, Nauȝt of fynegre kende [= kind] chald. 1362 LANGL. P. Pl. A. v. 70 Venim.., or vinegre, I trouwe, Walleþ in my wombe. a1425 tr. Arderne's Treat. Fistula, etc. 40 þe Iuyse of celidone y-medled wiþ vinegre and warmed at þe fire. 1489 CAXTON Faytes of A. I. xiv. 37 Flessh, benes, salt and vynaygre. a1500 Bale's Chron. in Six Town Chron. (1911) 118 Powles steple was sodenly on fire.. but it was holpen and quenched w[t] venegre. 1502 ARNOLDE Chron. a iij b/1 To make winnegre shortly if nede be. 1552 HULOET, Vynygre, and honye sodden together, oxymeli. 1561 HOLLYBUSH Hom. Apoth. 2 Let the same.. put a litle vinegre thereto. 1662 CHARLETON Myst. Vintners (1675) 164 Of which we have an instance in the making of Vinegre. a1699 J. BEAUMONT Psyche (1702) IX. 81 A flood, to which most fretful Vinaigre [1648 Vinaiger] Is gentle Oile.

β. c1408 Durham Acc. Rolls (Surtees) 52 In vinager et cepis emptis. 1409 Ibid. 53 In j quart de vineger empt. c1420 Liber Cocorum (1862) 6 Goode wyne schalle turne to venegur be dene. c1440 Gesta Rom. xxviii. 105 (Harl. MS.), Vyneger was gode,.. wyn is gode,.. and muste shalle be gode. 1502 ARNOLDE Chron. 72 b/1 To make veneger shortli if [ye] haue nede. 1539 ELYOT Cast. Helthe 22 Olyues.. dothe corroborate the stomake.. being eaten with vyneger. 1598 BARRET Theor. Warres V. iii. 133 Vineger to coole the Ordinance. 1608 ARMIN Nest Ninn. (1842) 20 The king calls for winiger to his sallet, because his sweet meate should haue sower sauce. 1612 WEBSTER White Devil IV. iii. 105 Best wine Dying makes strongest vinneger. 1647 COWLEY Mistr., Passions iii, Since Love by mixing Poyson there, Has made it worse than Vinegere. 1660 BOYLE New Exp. Phys. Mech. 189 Spirit of Vinager being try'd after the same manner, exhibited a moderate number of bubbles.

γ. 1577 B. GOOGE Heresbach's Husb. 148 Hard Cheese wrapped in cloutes wet in Vinegar.. returne to a softnesse. 1596 LODGE Wits Miserie M, One cast his paile of water at his head, another his oile, another his vinegar. 1612 WOODALL Surg. Mate Wks. (1653) 11 Vinegar I utterly mislike. 1652 in Gross Gild Merchant (1890) I. 133 In buying and selling a can of vinegar. 1732 POPE Ess. Man II. 138 As heav'ns blest beam turns vinegar more sowre. 1750 tr. Leonardus' Mirr. Stones 93 If it be drenched nine times in vinegar, it makes a fine eye-salve. 1789 W. BUCHAN Dom. Med. (1790) 109 They ought.. to keep the patient very clean, to sprinkle the room where he lies with vinegar, or other strong acids. 1815 J. SMITH Panorama Sci. & Art II. 386 Vinegar appears to have little or no effect upon iron, unless assisted by the air. 1838 T. THOMSON Chem. Org. Bodies 1033 The weaker the wine or the beer.., the more readily it is converted into vinegar. 1888 Encycl. Brit. XXIV. 241/1 All sources of alcohol may be regarded as possible materials for making vinegar.

δ. a1400 in Rel. Ant. I. 196 Seeth the rote in vynacre of wyne. 1497 Naval Acc. Hen. VII (1896) 88 Vinacre,.. j hoggshed. c1500 KENNEDY Passion of Christ 963 Intill wynakar þai soupit it full sone. 1533 GAU Richt Vay 41 Thay suld.. giff to hime vinakir and gal to drink. 1583 Shuttleworths' Acc. (Chetham Soc.) 8 A querte of vinycare, iiij[d]. 1583–4 Ibid. 16 For foure quartes of veniker, xvj[d]. 1586 Ibid. 26 A gallon of vyneker, xvj[d]. 1652 GAULE Magastrom. 44 The water of the wisemen, the philosophers vinacre, the minerall water. 1691 in Hawick Archæol. Soc. Trans. (1905) 13/2 I[tem] for osters and winiker, brandi and spis, [£]0. 6. 0.

fig. a1670 HACKET Abp. Williams I. (1693) 59 To stoop this Vinacre to the very Lees; some will say [etc.].

†**b.** *ellipt.* The accidental conversion of wine into vinegar. *Obs.*[−1]

1584 R. SCOT Discov. Witchcr. XII. xiv. (1886) 201 A charme against vineager. That wine wax not eager, write on the vessell [etc.].

c. With *a* and pl. A particular kind, or special preparation, of vinegar.

1839 URE Dict. Arts 13 The fallacy of trusting to the hydrometer for determining the strength of vinegars. 1875 H. C. WOOD Therap. (1879) 18 Vinegars are those preparations in which vinegar, or dilute acetic acid, is used as the menstruum.

2. In allusive use: **a.** With reference to the painful or harsh effect of vinegar on a wound, or on the teeth (after Prov. x. 26).

1548 UDALL Erasmus Par. Mark ii. 20 He that put in the vinegre of sorowe, dyd also giue him the oyle of good hope. 1590 NASHE Mart. Marprel. Wks. (Grosart) I. 224 It is vineger to his teeth, and maketh him very sawcie, with his g. of Cant. 1645 QUARLES Sol. Recant. III. xii, To qualify with oyle The soule-afflicting vin'gre of his toyle. 1656 in Clarendon Hist. Reb. XV. §109 Our desire is.. not to pour Vineger but Oyl into the wounds.

b. With reference to Hannibal's use of vinegar in making his way over the Alps, according to Livy XXI. 37 (cf. Juvenal x. 153).

Cf. the quotation for *vinegar-railing* in 6.

1636 QUARLES Elegie Wks. (Grosart) III. 11/1 We cut our way Through these our Alpine griefes, and sadly rise With the sharp vinegre of suffused eyes. 1776 in Boswell Johnson 12 Apr., Davies said of a well-known dramatick authour, that 'he.. made his way as Hannibal did, by vinegar; having begun by attacking people'. 1779 WARNER in Jesse Selwyn & Contemp. (1844) IV. 108 The Alps of your difficulties subside before you, and without vinegar.

3. *fig.* Speech, temper, etc., of a sour or acid character. (Cf. 5 b.)

1601 SHAKS. Twel. N. III. iv. 158 Heere's the Challenge, reade it: I warrant there's vinegar and pepper in't. 1681 CROWNE Hen. VI, Prol., A little Vineger against the Pope. 1848 DICKENS Dombey xlii, Mrs. Pipchin.. freshened the domestics with several little sprinklings of wordy vinegar. 1873 [see VERJUICE *sb.* 2].

†**b.** In the phr. ***to wish one at vinegar***. *Obs.*[−1]

1774 EARL CARLISLE in Jesse Selwyn & Contemp. (1844) III. 73 He will soon do something, and play some prank, which I dare say his uncle will wish him at vinegar for.

4. *slang.* (See quots.)

a1700 B. E. Dict. Cant. Crew, Vinegar, a Cloak. 1725 New Cant. Dict., Vinegar,.. the Fellow that makes a Ring, and keeps Order among Wrestlers, Cudgel-Players, &c. 1785 GROSE Dict. Vulg. T., Vinegar, a name given to the person, who with a whip in his hand, and a hat held before his eyes, keeps the ring clear at boxing matches and cudgel playings.

5. *attrib.* and *Comb.* **a.** Attrib., as ***vinegar-bottle*** (also *fig.*), ***-cask***, ***-cruet*** (also *fig.*), ***-manufactory***, ***-pot***, ***-poultice***, ***-powder***, ***-work***, ***-yeast***; obj. genitive, as ***vinegar-drawer***, ***-maker***, ***-making***; also ***vinegar-flavoured***, ***-tart*** adjs.

1459 Paston Lett. I. 490 Item, j. *venegre botell. 1593 NASHE Christ's T. To Rdr., It will bee some of their destinies to carrie the vineger bottle ere they die. 1602 2nd Pt. Return Parnass. I. ii. 1 What Ingenioso, carrying a Vinegar bottle about thee, like a great schole-boy giuing the world a bloudy nose? 1706 STEVENS Span. Dict. I, Vinagrera, a Vinegar-bottle, or Cruit. 1837 HEBERT Engin. & Mech. Encycl. II.

850 In some country districts, the people keep..a *vinegar cask, into which they pour such wine as they wish to acetify. **1713** *Lond. Gaz.* No. 5086/3 A Sett of Casters with *Vinegar Crewets. **1744** PARSONS in *Phil. Trans.* XLIII. 187 A little Piece of Camphire, exactly shaped like a common Vinegar-Crewet, having a round Bottom, and a long taper Neck. **1851** H. MELVILLE *Whale* xvii, Mrs. Hussey soon appeared with a mustard pot in one hand and a vinegar-cruet in the other. **1873** LELAND *Egypt. Sketch-Bk.* 113 A morose, narrow-minded, hide-bound set of vinegar-cruets. *a* **1704** T. BROWN *Laconics* Wks. 1711 IV. 12 He is a *Vinegar-drawer. **1601** HOLLAND *Pliny* II. 158 *Vinegre dregs are knowne to be verie good for to heale burnes. **1809** MALKIN *Gil Blas* VII. xiii. ¶18 A *vinegar-flavoured vintage of Parnassus. **1611** COTGR., *Vinaigrier*,..a *Vineger glasse, violl, or bottle. *Ibid.*, *Vinaigrier*, a Vineger-man, or *Vineger-maker. **1697** *Lond. Gaz.* No. 3283/3 All Malsters .., Brewers,..Victuallers, and Vinegar-makers. **1723** *Ibid.* No. 6134/4 John Gregory,..Distiller and Vinegar-maker. **1853** URE *Dict. Arts* (ed. 4) II. 905 This axiom cannot be too strongly inculcated into the minds of vinegar-makers. **1862** MILLER *Elem. Chem.*, *Org.* (ed. 2) 60 In the ordinary process of *vinegar-making from sugar and water. **1611** COTGR., *Vinaigrier*, a *Vineger-man, or Vineger-maker. **1839** URE *Dict. Arts* 1278 *Vinegar manufactory, by malt. **1842** *Penny Mag.* 29 Oct. 425/1 The vinegar-manufactories are but few in number. **1669** R. MONTAGU in *Buccleuch MSS.* (Hist. MSS. Comm.) I. 448 A *vinegar pot, oil pot, and sugar box. **1854** MAYNE *Expos. Lex.*, *Cataplasma Aceti*,..the *vinegar poultice; made of vinegar and bread crumb, or the like. **1753** *Chambers' Cycl.* Suppl. s.v., A sort of *Vinegar-powder, or Vinegar in a dry form. **1599** NASHE *Lenten Stuffe* Wks. (Grosart) V. 307 Let none of these scumme of the suburbs, be too *vinegar tarte with mee. **1608** [TOFTE] *Ariosto's Sat.* IV. (1611) 53 A viniger tart looke or clowdy brow. **1728** CHAMBERS *Cycl.* s.v. *Rape*, The Rape is..put into a Place to sour itself, before it is cast into the *Vinegar Vessel. **1839** URE *Dict. Arts* 3 When new vessels are mounted in a *vinegar work, they must be one third filled with the best vinegar that can be procured. *Ibid.* 2 Several azotized substances serve as re-agents towards the acetous fermentation,—such as vinegar ready-made, *vinegar-yeast, or lees.

b. Attrib., in the sense 'extremely sour in temper or disposition'; also in combs., as ***vinegar-faced***, ***-hearted*** adjs.

1596 SHAKS. *Merch. V.* I. i. 54 Other of such vineger aspect, That they'll not shew their teeth in way of smile. **1597** *Return fr. Parnass.* I. ii. 165 Such barmy heads wil alwaies be working, when as sad vineger wittes sit souring at the bottome of a barrell. **1654** H. L'ESTRANGE *Chas. I* (1655) 28 The Commons nothing mortified with these tart and vinacre expressions [of the king], kept close to their proper stations. **1662** *Rump Songs* (1874) I. 161 From a vinegar Priest on a Crab-tree stock,..Libera nos. **1694** MOTTEUX *Rabelais* v. iii. 11 More grum, vinegar-fac'd,.. than any kind whatsoever in the whole Island. **1824** MISS FERRIER *Inher.* xxix, The habitual vinegar expression of his long triangular visage. **1842** MIALL in *Nonconf.* II. 145 A peevish and vinegar-hearted step-mother. **1846** DE QUINCEY *Orthogr. Mutineers* Wks. 1860 XIV. 108 He was too vinegar a fellow for them; nothing hearty or genial about him. **1847** E. BRONTE *Wuthering Heights* ii, Vinegar-faced Joseph projected his head from a round window of the barn. **1850** MRS. CARLYLE *New Lett.* (1903) II. 13 You may fancy the vinegar looks of the Lady of the House and the visitors whom I had kept from their dinner one mortal hour.

6. Special Combs.: †**vinegar beer**, ? beer employed for conversion into vinegar; **vinegar Bible** (see quots.); **vinegar-eel**, a minute nematoid worm (*Anguillula aceti*) breeding in vinegar; **vinegar-field**, = *vinegar-yard*; **vinegar-fly**, a fruit-fly, *Drosophila melanogaster*; cf. DROSOPHILA; **vinegar mother**, = *vinegar-plant* (b); **vinegar-plant**, (*a*) the Virginian sumach, *Rhus typhina*; (*b*) a mould which grows on the surface of liquids undergoing acetous fermentation; **vinegar-railing** *fig.*, bitter abuse; **vinegar stick**, a sword or walking-stick with a vinaigrette (sense 3) fitted into the handle (now *Hist.*); also *transf.*; **vinegar-tree**, = *vinegar-plant* (a); **vinegar worm**, = *vinegar-eel*; **vinegar-yard**, a yard or open space in which vinegar-casks are arranged.

1677 *Act 29 Chas. II*, c. 2, For every Barrell of Beere commonly called *Vinegar beere brewed or made to be sold, Six pence. **1834** LOWNDES *Bibliogr. Man.* I. 180 A most magnificent edition, called 'The *Vinegar Bible', from an error in the running title at St. Luke, chap. xxii, where it is read 'the parable of the vinegar', instead of 'the parable of the vineyard'. **1868** MACRAY *Annals Bodl. Lib.* 147 Baskett, the printer, presented to the Library a magnificent copy on vellum of the 'Vinegar' Bible, printed by him in 1717. **1836–9** *Todd's Cycl. Anat.* II. 113/2 The *Anguillula aceti*, or common *Vinegar-eel. **1842** *Penny Mag.* 29 Oct. 426/2 Behind the store-house..is the **vinegar-field*, a remarkable feature in most vinegar-works. **1902** L. O. HOWARD *Insect Bk.* 185 They are also called '*vinegar flies', from the fact that their..larvae are frequently found in canned fruits and pickles which have been imperfectly sealed. **1937** *Discovery* Sept. 282/2 There is a type of cockroach found in vinegar breweries, at least two kinds of vinegar fly, and..the vinegar eel. **1979** P. L. G. BATEMAN *Household Pests* II. 19 The tiny red-eyed fruit fly *Drosophila melanogaster*, is one of several species associated with fermenting liquids or rotting fruit. They are also known as wine flies, yeast flies or vinegar flies. **1839** URE *Dict. Arts* 2 The Germans call it the *vinegar mother, as it serves to excite acetification in fresh liquors. **1853** *Ibid.* (ed. 4) I. 1 In the vinegar of wine..there appears a peculiar mould-plant, belonging to the genus *Mycoderma* Pers.; which is usually called vinegar mother. **1797** *Encycl. Brit.* (ed. 3) XVI. 228/1 The..Virginian sumach, or *vinegar plant, grows naturally in almost every part of North America. **1857** HENFREY *Bot.* §637 Flocculent or gelatinous masses, constituting the curious object called the Vinegar-plant. **1866** *Treas. Bot.* 1217/1 The exact mode in which the Vinegar-plant operates on the solution is not known. **1609** DEKKER *Gull's Horn-bk.* Wks. (Grosart) II. 203 Though, with Hanniball, you bring whole hogs-heads of *vinegar-railings, it is impossible for you to quench or come ouer my Alpine-resolution. **1935** A. J. POLLOCK *Underworld Speaks* 129/2 **Vinegar stick*, a stilletto; a long bladed knife; a sword. **1968** *Canadian Antiques Collector* Nov. 21/1 The forerunner of the vinaigrette was the vinegar stick, a walking stick with a hollow head for a vinegar-soaked sponge. **1979** 'J. GASH' *Grail Tree* vi. 60 You get them in all shapes, even as 'vinegar sticks', where the container is cleverly made into the handle of a sword or walking-stick. **1874** *Treas. Bot.* Suppl. 1350/2 *Vinegar-tree, *Rhus typhina*. **1896** tr. *Boas' Text Bk. Zool.* 163 *Anguillula aceti*, the *Vinegar worm, lives in sour paste and in vinegar. **1703** *Lond. Gaz.* No. 3893/4 A Distilling-house, Brew-house, and *Vinegar-yard. **1858** SIMMONDS *Dict. Trade*, *Vinegar-yard*, a place where vinegar is exposed to season.

vinegar ('vɪnɪgə(r)), *v.* [f. prec.] *trans.* To treat with vinegar in some way; to add or apply vinegar to; to restore by means of vinegar. Also *fig.* Hence **'vinegaring** *vbl. sb.*

1610 B. JONSON *Alch.* III. v, Then, to her Cuz, Hoping, that he hath vinegard his senses, As he was bid, the Faery Queene dispenses, By me this Robe. **1721** CIBBER *Rival Fools* v, Ev'n forgive her all... No, faith! I must crab her, she must be vinegar'd! **1804** W. IRVING in *Life & Lett.* (1864) I. 89 Where I should be detained, quarantined, smoked, and vinegared. **1831** BENTHAM *Memorandum-Bk.* Wks. 1843 XI. 73 You do as you do by a cucumber, when you cut it into slips to be eaten, when it has been peppered, salted, and vinegared. **1837** DICKENS *Pickw.* x, The landlady ..proceeded to vinegar the forehead, beat the hands, titillate the nose, and unlace the stays of the spinster aunt. **1841** —— *Barn. Rudge* xix, After..much damping of foreheads, and vinegaring of temples, and hartshorning of noses, and so forth. **1897** *Westm. Gaz.* 18 Feb. 2/1 Aurora rose and thrust a smelling-bottle under his nose, tapped his hands, vinegared him.

'vinegared, *ppl. a.* [f. VINEGAR *v.* + -ED[1].] Treated or flavoured with vinegar.

1861 [see SLAW]. **1892** A. CONAN DOYLE *Great Shadow* vi. 74 He set a dish of vinegared herrings before him. **1978** R. CONDON *Bandicoot* xiii. 54 And a little of the vinegared sparrows of Wakayama.

vinegarette, variant (after *vinegar*) of VINAIGRETTE.

1855 THACKERAY *The Almack's Adieu* i, And at parting I gave my dear Harry A beautiful vinegarette!

vinegarish ('vɪnɪgərɪʃ), *a.* Also 7 **vinegrish**. [f. VINEGAR *sb.*] Somewhat resembling vinegar (in taste); sourish. Also *fig.*

1648 HEXHAM II, *Azijnachtigh*, Vinegrish. **1669** W. SIMPSON *Hydrol. Chym.* 163 Animal juyces..degenerate into acid, sowre, vinegarish liquors. **1693** EVELYN *De la Quint. Compl. Gard.* I. 141 'Tis another fault to be sometimes so Vinous, as to contract from thence a Vinegarish sharp taste. **1845** TEMPLE in E. H. Coleridge *Life Ld. Coleridge* (1904) I. vii. 167, I expected that Scott.. would have given him rather a vinegarish reply; but [etc.]. **1867** C. J. SMITH *Syn. & Antonyms*, *Acid*, Syn... Acetose. Vinegarish.

Hence **'vinegarishly** *adv.* (In quots. *fig.*)

1890 'MARK TWAIN' in M. D. L. Landon *Kings of Platform & Pulpit* 354 My companion said vinegarishly, 'Well, well! What do you say now?' **1976** 'J. ROSS' *I know what it's like to Die* xviii. 122 'I never ever laid a finger on him. We were very good friends,' he said vinegarishly.

'vinegarist. *rare*[−1]. [f. as prec.] A vinegar-maker.

1676 WORLIDGE *Cyder* 146 The Rape our Vinegarists make use of, they have out of France.

vinega(r)roon (ˌvɪnɪgə'ruːn). *U.S.* Also **vinagron, vinegarone, vineg(e)rone**. [ad. Amer. Sp. *vinagrón*, f. Sp. *vinagre* VINEGAR *sb.* + (depreciatory) augmentative suffix *-ón*.] A large whip scorpion, *Mastigoproctus giganteus*, which is native to southern North America and Mexico, emits a secretion smelling like vinegar when alarmed, and is often wrongly believed to be venomous. Also *transf.*

1853 L. SITGREAVES *Rep. Exped. Zuñi & Colorado Rivers* 34 Frequently did I find in the road that disagreeable-looking object known to the Mexicans as the vinagron. **1889** *Cent. Dict.* 6758/3 Vinegerone..so called on account of the strong vinegar-like odor of an acid secretion noticeable when the creature is alarmed. **1914** *Blackw. Mag.* July 123/1 His late breaking-in, the lengthy vacation,..keep the 'vinegarone' in his [*sc.* a bronco's] composition. **1920** *Glasgow Herald* 8 July 4/2 His animal friends, the chief of whom seem to be vinegaroons, some species of bug. **1948** *Pacific Discovery* Mar. 8/2 The vinegaroons, those queer, eight-legged devils of the desert night, raced at top speed in and out of the shadows to gather insect prey. **1978** *Sci. Amer.* Mar. 36/3 Here are..the acetic-acid-secreting vinegarroons.

vinegary ('vɪnɪgərɪ), *a.* [f. VINEGAR *sb.* + -Y[1].] Resembling vinegar; sour like vinegar. Chiefly *fig.*

1730 BAILEY (fol.), *Acetous*, Vinegary, or being something like Vinegar. **1848** DICKENS *Dombey* xxxi, A vinegary face has Mrs. Miff. **1850** KINGSLEY *A. Locke* (1876) II. 33 So you'll just leave alone that vinegary, soul-destroying trash. **1870** FRISWELL *Mod. Men Lett.* viii. 143 Commonplace bishops and vinegary bishops' wives. **1879** MISS BRADDON *Vixen* iii, This is one of Miss Skipwith's servants,..rather a vinegary personage.

Comb. **1885** *Advance* (Chicago) 6 Aug. 509/3 A vinegary visaged lady. **1891** C. ROBERTS *Adrift Amer.* 116 The only person who was in the house was a vinegary-looking woman, who told me that I could not stay.

vi'neity. *rare*[−1]. [f. L. *vīne-us* vinous + -ITY.] Vinous quality or property.

1782 PRIESTLEY *Corrupt. Chr.* VI. II. 42 Innocent the third acknowledged that, after consecration, there did remain in the elements a certain pancity and vincity, as he called them, which satisfied hunger and thirst.

vine-leaf. [VINE *sb.*] A leaf of a vine.

c **1420** LYDG. *Assembly of Gods* 353 Of grene vyne leues he weryd a ioly crowne. *c* **1440** *Promp. Parv.* 510/2 Vyny leef, *pampinus*, *abestrum*. *c* **1475** *Pict. Voc.* in Wr.-Wülcker 810 *Hic pamplus*, a vyneleffe. *a* **1513** FABYAN *Chron.* VI. (1811) 160 They were fayne to take vyne leuys to couer with theyr secret membrys. **1601** HOLLAND *Pliny* I. Table s.v., Vine leaves to be cleansed once in the spring. **1634** PEACHAM *Compl. Gentl.* xii. (1906) 109 Whereby we are taught to know..Bacchus by his Vine-leaves. **1731** MILLER *Gard. Dict.* s.v. *Vitis*, That vile Taste of a rotten Vine Leaf. **1765** STERNE *Tr. Shandy* VII. xliii, There were two dozen of eggs covered over with vine-leaves at the bottom of the basket. **1818** SHELLEY *Rosal. & Helen* 1258 Its casements bright Shone through their vine-leaves in the morning sun. **1888** *Encycl. Brit.* XXIV. 238/2 The imago..shortly after lays its eggs upon the upper surface of the vine leaf.

attrib. **1874** H. H. COLE *Catal. Ind. Art S. Kens. Mus.* 258 Muslin. Figured; diaper vine-leaf pattern.

b. ***vine-leaf miner***, an insect infesting vine-leaves.

Also ***vine-leaf folder***, ***hopper***, ***roller***. (In recent Amer. Dicts.)

1830 *Insect Architecture* (L.E.K.) 238 The vine-leaf miner, when about to construct its cocoon, cuts..two pieces of the membrane of the leaf.

vineless ('vaɪnlɪs), *a.* [f. VINE *sb.*] Having no vines; destitute of vines.

1898 MEREDITH *Odes Fr. Hist.* 7 Broken hoops,..vineless poles, worm-eaten posts.

vinelet ('vaɪnlɪt). [f. VINE *sb.*] A young vine.

1881 BLACKMORE *Christowell* vii, A human form..rolled in upon a newly-potted platoon of those sensitive vinelets.

vinell, obs. variant of VENNEL.

vinello, obs. variant of VANILLA.

†**'viner**[1]. *Obs.* Forms: 4–5 **vyner** (4 **vigner**), 5 **viner, -ere**. [? ad. med.L. *vīnārium*, f. L. *vinum* wine. Cf. VINERY 1.] A vineyard.

a **1340** HAMPOLE *Psalter* lxxvii. 52 He sloghe in haghil þe vyners of þa. *Ibid.* Cant. Hab. 27 Burioyn sall noght be in þe vyners. **1382** WYCLIF *Luke* xiii. 7 Sum man hadde a fyge tree plauntid in his vyner. *c* **1449** PECOCK *Repr.* III. xvii. 389 The lord of the vyner..and of the werk doon in his Vyner.

†**'viner**[2]. *Obs.* Also 4 **vinour**, 5 **-oure, vyn-, vignour**; 6 **vyner**. [a. OF. *vignour*, *vigneur*, or AF. *viner* (Gower) vine-grower; with sense 2 cf. OF. *vinier*, *vignier* wine-merchant.]

1. A vine-grower or vine-dresser.

α. **1390** GOWER *Conf.* III. 148 The king and the vinour also Of wommen comen bothe tuo. **1398** TREVISA *Barth. De P.R.* XVII. cxciii. (Bodl. MS.), Vligo is þe kinde vinoure of þe erþe,..for þis tre rereþ vp and susteyneþ bowes, frute, & spraies of vines. *a* **1470** H. PARKER *Dives & Pauper* (W. de W. 1496) I. xxii. 58/1 Some ben shepeherdes,..some vynours, some of other craftes as the contre axeth. **1474** CAXTON *Chesse* II. iii. (1883) 41 Yf the smythes, the carpentiers, yᵉ vignours and other craftymen saye that it is most necessarye to studye for the comyn prouffit.

β. **1552** HULOET, Vyner, or orderer, or trymmer of vynes, *vinetor*. **1570** LEVINS *Manip.* 77 A viner, *vinitor*. **1611** FLORIO, *Vignaio*, a vineroll, a viner, a vine dresser.

2. A member of the Vintners' Company.

1674 MARVELL *Ld. Mayor & Crt. Aldermen* xviii, And now, worshipful sirs, Go fold up your furs, And Viners turn again, turn again.

'viner[3]. orig. *U.S.* [f. VINE *sb.* 4 c + -ER[1].] An implement for gathering the product of 'vines'; esp. one used to harvest peas.

1902 *Encycl. Brit.* (ed. 10) XXVI. 558/1 By the aid of modern machinery, the [pea-] pods are gathered by a viner. **1949** *Nat. Geogr. Mag.* Sept. 331/2 'Viners' that thresh out the peas were working day and night. **1963** *Times* 14 Jan. 13/1 Pea haulm silage, made under cover direct from the viners, plays a major part in the winter feeding. **1981** *Southern Horticulture* (N.Z.) Spring 36/1 In the 1950s the chore of hand-picking peas was removed with the development of a viner, to which the cut plants were cut and carted. **1982** *East Anglian Daily Times* 20 Nov. 5 The largest harvester around—the Mather and Platt SB8000 pea viner, soon to be produced in Suffolk.

Vinerian (vaɪ'nɪərɪən), *a.* [f. the name of Charles *Viner* (1678–1756), English jurist.] *Vinerian Professor*, the holder of the chair of English Common Law endowed by Viner at the University of Oxford; so ***Vinerian Professorship***. Also applied to other posts or studentships (and their holders) similarly endowed by Viner at Oxford, or to the fund administered for this purpose.

1759 (*public notice dated* 18 June), The Vinerian Professor gives this public Notice, that he proposes to begin his.. Course of private Lectures. **1765** BLACKSTONE *Commentaries* I. (title-page), Vinerian Professor of Law. *a* **1777** S. FOOTE *Devil upon Two Sticks* (1778) I. 3 Had you toil'd thro' the laborious page of the Vinerian professor. **1810** *Oxf. Univ. Calendar* 34 (*heading*) Vinerian Professorship of Common Law. **1846** *Ibid.* 58 Vinerian Professorship of Common Law. Charles Viner, Esq by his will..left about 12,000l. to the Chancellor, Masters, and Scholars of the University of Oxford, to establish a Professorship,..of the Common Law. **1934** *Law Q. Rev.* L. 196 Sir William Blackstone, the first

Vinerian Professor. **1954** *Wadham Coll. Gaz.* Trinity Term 124 Mr. Gotlieb came as a Rhodes Scholar from Manitoba to Christ Church and took a First Class in the B.C.L., also winning the Vinerian Scholarship. **1980** *Statutes, Decrees, & Regulations Univ. Oxf.* 111 Any surplus income of the Vinerian Fund which remains after paying the emoluments of the scholars shall be applied towards defraying the stipend of the Vinerian Professor of English Law.

†**vineroll**, alteration of *vineron* VIGNERON.

1598 FLORIO, *Vendemmiatore*, a vintager, a vineroll, a vintner, a maker of wines or a grape gatherer. **1611** *Ibid. Vignaio*, a vineroll, a viner, a vine dresser.

vineron, obs. variant of VIGNERON.

†**vinerous**, *a. dial. Obs.* (See quot.)

1674 RAY *N. Co. Words* 50 *Vinerous*, hard to please.

vinery (ˈvaɪnərɪ). Also 5 vinary, 6 vynery. [ad. med.L. *vinārium* (cf. VINER[1] and OF. *vignerie*) or f. VINE *sb.* + -ERY.]

†**1.** A vineyard. Also in fig. context. *Obs.*

c **1420** LYDG. *Commend. Our Lady* 45 Paradys of plesaunce, gladsom to all good,..Vinarye envermailyd. *a* **1513** FABYAN *Chron.* VII. (1811) 511 The kyng shuld haue in recompencement of his wrongys, the erledam of Bygorre, & the vynery of Ramer.

2. A glass house or hot-house constructed for the cultivation of the grape-vine. Also *attrib.*

1789 ABERCROMBIE (*title*), The Hot-House Gardener on the..Methods of forcing Early Grapes,..and other Choice Fruits, in Hot-Houses, Vineries, Fruit-Houses, Hot-Walls, &c. **1805** LOUDON *Improv. Hot-Houses* 34 A considerable depth [of flue] may generally be obtained..in vineries and peach houses. **1842** —— *Suburban Hort.* 215 A vinery twenty-five feet long by thirteen feet six inches wide in the roof. **1879** *Florist & Pomologist* Mar. 37/2 A three-quarters span or hipped roof vinery... For general purposes there is no better form of vinery than this.

3. Vines collectively.

1883 *Cent. Mag.* XXVI. 729 Overgrown with masses of vinery. **1895** *Outing* XXVI. 445/1 Its ruins..are overgrown with vinery and bushes.

†**vinet**[1]. *Obs.* Forms: α. 5 vynnett, vynette, -ett, 5–6 vynet, 5–7 vinet, 6 vinite, 7 vinnet; 5 venett(e, 7 venet. β. 6 vynyette, vyniet, viniet, vineyet, vineat, 7 vignet. [ad. OF. *vignete*, *vignette* (whence obs. It. *vignetta* (Florio), Sp. *viñeta*, Pg. *vinheta*) dim. of *vigne* VINE *sb.* Readopted in the 18th century as VIGNETTE *sb.*]

1. A running or trailing ornament or design in imitation of the branches, leaves, or tendrils of the vine, employed in architecture or decorative work.

1412–20 LYDG. *Chron. Troy* II. 656 And þe vowsyng ful of babewynes [= baboons], þe rich koynyng, þe lusty tablementis, Vynnettis rennynge in þe casementis. *c* **1420** *Life Alex.* (1913) 64 Bitwene þe pelers of golde, ware hyngande venettez of golde & syluere, wit leues of golde. And þe brawnchez of this venett ware sum of cristalle,..& sum of Onyches, and þay semed as þay hade bene verray vynes. *a* **1548** HALL *Chron., Hen. VIII*, 7 Appareyled in Crymosyn, satyne, and purpull, embrowdered with golde and by vynyettes [*Holinshed* viniet] ran floure delices of golde. *Ibid.*, Kyrtels of Crymosyne and purpul satyn, embroudered with a vynet of Pomegranettes of golde.

attrib. **1601** HOLLAND *Pliny* II. 93 The Pervincle.. Passing good and proper indeed for vinet and storie worke in borders.

2. = VIGNETTE *sb.* 1 b and 1.

α. **1467** *Paston Lett.* II. 336 For viij hole vynets,..prise the vynett, xii d. Item, for xxj demi vynets. **1573** *Art Limming* (1588) 2 Trace all thy letters, and set thy Vinets or flowres, and then thy imagery, if thou wilt make any. **1579** FULKE *Confut. Sanders* 691 Commonly such super-fluous vinites (I trowe they call them) bee not set to, vntill they presse the whole leafe. **1612** PEACHAM *Gentl. Exerc.* I. xv. (1634) 47 You may, if you list, draw..any kinde of wilde traile or vinet after your owne invention. **1637** *Star-Chamber Decree conc. Printing* 11 July §9 That no person shall hereafter print..vpon any booke or books, the name, title, marke or vinnet of the Company or Society of Stationers.

β. **1584** *Star Chamber Decree Printers & Stat.* (1863) 10 That everie founder of letter, cutter and pocher, be likewise bound not to cast any letter, vineyet, mark, singing notes, or such like. **1611** COTGR., *Vignettes*, Vignets; branches, or branch-like borders, or flourishes, in painting or Ingraverie.

b. An ornamental border on a page.

1630 BRATHWAIT *Eng. Gentlem.* Draught of Frontisp., Upon the other Border or Venet of the Picture, is presented a Summer Arbour. *Ibid.*, In the middle betwixt the Venets, is the Portraiture of a comely Personage.

3. An ornamental title-page or similar production containing various symbolical designs or figures.

1562 LEIGH *Armorie* (heading), The Description of the Viniet with the circumstaunce thereof, contayned in the fyrst Page of the booke. **1570** FOXE *A. & M.* (ed. 2) I. 688/2 Certaine there were which resorted to him, of whom some were drawers for his petygree and vyniet. **1625** F. MARKHAM *Bk. Honour* IV. iii. §3 Prudence..is to be esteemed aboue all other Vertues: for Philosophy cals it the Guide, and our Heraulds make it the first in the Vinet.

Hence †**vinetting (vignetting)** *vbl. sb. Obs.*

1611 COTGR., *Vignettement*, a vignetting; a bordering, or flourishing with the branches of Vines, or other plants.

†**vinet**[2]. *Obs.*[−1] In 5 vynet(te. [f. L. *vīnea.*] = VINEA.

1408 tr. *Vegetius' Art War* IV. xv. (MS. Digby 233) fol. 220/2 The vynet [*MS. Laud* vynette] is a gynne of werr & framed of liȝt tymber.

vineter, variant of VINTER.

ˈ**vine-tree.** Also 4 vintre, 4–5 vyntre, 4–6 vynetree (5–6 *Sc.* wyne-). [VINE *sb.*] A tree of the genus *Vitis* bearing grapes. Also *fig.*

a **1300** *Cursor M.* 7159 And sua þair corns did he brin, þair olives, wit þair vintres. *a* **1340** HAMPOLE *Psalter* cxxvii. 3 þi wife as vyntre haboundand in sides of þi house. *c* **1375** *Sc. Leg. Saints* vi. (*Thomas*) 401 Ensampil tane ma be sufficiandly be þe wyne-tre. **1483** *Cath. Angl.* 402/1 A vyne tree, *argitis*, *propago*, *vitis.* **1501** *Acc. Ld. High Treas. Scot.* II. 105 To the Franch man that set the wyne treis in Strivelin, xiiij s. **1576** FLEMING *Panopl. Epist.* 356 The Vinetree hath yeelded her purple grapes, by clusters. **1601** HOLLAND *Pliny* I. 519 The manner how to graffe a Vine tree. **1624** FISHER in F. White *Repl.* 340 The Saints being but branches of Christ Iesus, the true Vinetree. **1786** G. FRAZER *Fall of Man* 136 You will be as a fruitful vine-tree. **1786** ABERCROMBIE *Arrangem.* 43 in *Gard. Assist.*, Evergreen Trees and Shrubs, Proper for..shrubberies,..&c. [include] ..Vine tree, winged leaved. **1813** *Q. Rev.* IX. 159 Oft to mark, with curious eye, If the vine tree's time be nigh.

†**vinetry.** *Obs.*[−1] [App. f. VINET[1] + -RY.] Ornament, decoration. In quot. *fig.*

1622 PEACHAM *Compl. Gent.* 43 First your hearer coveteth to have his desire satisfied with matter, ere he looketh upon the form or vinetrie of words, which many times fall in of themselves to matter well contrived.

†ˈ**vinew**, *sb. Obs.* Also 6 vinue, 7 vinow, 8 vinnow. [var. of FINEW *sb.* Cf. mod. Hampshire dial. *vinny.*] Mould, mouldiness.

1538 ELYOT, *Mucor*, fylth, vinue, suche as is on bred or meate longe kept. **1601** HOLLAND *Pliny* II. 9 If it were not thus well followed, soone would it catch a vinow, begin to putrifie [etc.]. **1706** PHILLIPS (ed. Kersey), *Vinew*, Mouldiness, Hoariness, Mustiness. *a* **1722** LISLE *Husb.* (1757) 303 Two sorts of vinnow on cheese, one in the nature of mouldiness, or long downy vinnow, not blue.

†ˈ**vinew**, *v. Obs.* Also 6 venu-, 6–7 vinow. [var. of FINEW *v.* Cf. mod.Som. and Dev. dial. *vinny.*] *intr.* To grow mouldy.

1570 FOXE *A. & M.* (ed. 2) III. 2250/2 Which bread doth vinow, and mice oftentimes doe eate it. **1581** [see FINEW *v.*]. **1601** HOLLAND *Pliny* I. 364 Soone it vinoweth and catcheth a kind of mustines.

Hence †ˈ**vinewing** *vbl. sb.*

1552 [see FINEWING *vbl. sb.*]. **1565** COOPER *Thesaurus*, *Mucor*, filthe: vinewynge: hoarenesse. **1580** HOLLYBAND *Treas. Fr. Tong*, *Mucilage*, venuing, hoarinesse.

†ˈ**vinewed**, *a. Obs.* Also 6 venued, vynued, uinewed, 7 vinnewd, vinowed, vinnow'd. [f. VINEW *sb.* or *v.* Cf. FINEWED *a.* and VINNIED *a.*] Moulded, mouldy.

1538 ELYOT, *Mucidus*, fylthy: vinewed. **1558** WARDE tr. *Alexis' Secr.* (1580) 103 You must take first of the saied paste, that is not mouldie, vinewed or putrified. **1574** NEWTON *Health Mag.* 55 Sweete Almonds..decline to moysture, unlesse they be vinewed and restie for then they are drye. **1576** —— *Lemnie's Complex.* (1633) 179 Such a like hoary downe, or uinewed mouldinesse. **1601** HOLLAND *Pliny* I. 530 If it be let alone,..[the vine] would proove to be slender, vinewed, leane, and poore. **1654** GAYTON *Pleas. Notes* III. ii. 71 Like a mouldy Cheese, where three parts are blew and vinnow'd. **1668** WILKINS *Real Char.* 70 Mould, Horiness, Vinnewd.

fig. **1602** [see FINEWED *a.*].

Hence †ˈ**vinewedness.** *Obs. rare.*

1565 COOPER *Thesaurus*, *Situs*,..horenesse: mouldinesse: vinewednesse. **1611** COTGR., *Chansisseure*,..mouldinesse, vinewednesse. *Ibid.*, *Moisissure*, mouldinesse,.. vinowednesse.

†**vinewiness, -ewy**, varr. FINEWINESS, -EWY.

1727 BAILEY (vol. II), *Vinewiness*, Mouldiness, Hoariness, Mustiness. *Ibid.*, *Vinewy*, mouldy, hoary.

vineyard (ˈvɪnjəd, -jɑːd). Forms: 4 vinȝerd, 6 -yard(e, vinȝard, -yearde, 6 vyny(e)arde, wynyard, 7 viniard; 4–5 vyneȝerd(e, 5 -ȝorde, -ye(e)rd, 6 -yearde; 4 vineȝard, 5 -yerd, 6 -y(e)arde, 5– vineyard; *Sc.* 5 wyne-, 6 wineȝarde, wyneȝard, -yaird. [f. VINE *sb.* + YARD *sb.*, after the earlier *wineyard*, OE. *winȝeard.*]

1. A piece of ground in which grape-vines are cultivated; a plantation of vines.

a **1340** HAMPOLE *Psalter* civ. 31 He smate þaire vynȝerdis & þaire fige trese. **1398** TREVISA *Barth. De P.R.* XVII. cxli. (Bodl. MS.), þis tree..is beste in gardines to close hem wiþ and vineȝardes. **1432–50** tr. *Higden* (Rolls) I. 337 In þis lond is plente of hony and of mylk and of wyn, and nouȝt of vyneȝerdes. *c* **1450** *Mirk's Festial* 66 A husband-man.. hyryd men to his vyneȝorde for labour. **1483** CAXTON *G. de la Tour* f vj, A good man..whiche had an Aker of a vine yerd. **1535** COVERDALE *Job* xxiv. 6 They..gather the grapes out of his vynyarde, whom they haue oppressed by violence. *c* **1585** [R. BROWNE] *Answ. Cartwright* 45 Where no yarde is, there may be vynes growing, but there can bee no vineyarde. **1610** HOLLAND *Camden's Brit.* 171 There is a right learned man that feareth lest hee have inconsideratly put this down in writing, as if this land were unfit for vineyards. **1661** J. CHILDREY *Brit. Bacon.* 71 This Shire is very full of Vineyards. **1693** EVELYN *De la Quint. Compl. Gard.* II. 73 The good Grapes, which Compose part of our Gard'ning, and the common Grapes that grow in Vineyards. **1756–7** tr. *Keysler's Trav.* (1760) IV. 449 The vineyards begin to bear two years after their planting; and continue in heart fifty or sixty years. **1774** GOLDSM. *Nat. Hist.* IV. 211 When they [baboons] set about robbing an orchard or a vineyard,..they do not go singly to work. **1832** G. DOWNES *Lett. Cont. Countries* I. 218 We sought the elevated Cathedral, which stands without the town in the midst of vineyards. **1840** HOOD *Up Rhine* 162, I was rather disappointed at Bonn, by the first sight of what sounds so poetically, a vineyard. **1878** EMERSON *Misc., Fort. Republic* Wks. (Bohn) III. 387 The wine merchant has..also, I fear, his debts to the chemist as well as to the vineyard.

b. *fig.* A sphere of action or labour, esp. of an elevated or spiritual character.

Chiefly in allusion to passages of the New Testament, as Matt. xx. 1 and xxi. 28, 40.

c **1375** *Sc. Leg. Saints* xxvii. (*Machor*) 1293 Trawale þarfor all thi mycht in goddis wyne-ȝarde for to vyne feile folk þat bundine ar with syne. *c* **1380** WYCLIF *Serm.* Sel. Wks. I. 98 þis housbonde is God, and þis vyneȝerde is his Chirche. **1555** EDEN *Decades* (Arb.) 51 This noble and Catholyke prince..whom God raysed for a Capitayne..vnder whose banner they myght ouercome theyr enemies and pourge his vineyarde from suche wycked weedes. **1596** DALRYMPLE tr. *Leslie's Hist. Scot.* II. 467 Mr. Ninian..was a faithful labourer in the Lordes vinȝard, ernist, and bissie. **1618** BARET (*title*), An Hipponomie; or the Vineyard of Horsemanship deuided into Three Bookes. **1628** in Foster *Eng. Factories India* (1909) III. 295 Their principall merchants and factors, who are indeed the true labourers of their viniard, and th' other, if rightlie considred, no other then carriers. **1702** *Clarendon's Hist. Reb.* I. Pref. p. xviii, Every Man..that had laboured all the heat of the day in the Vine-yard..was not..recompenced immediately according to their Merit. **1771** SMOLLETT *Humph. Cl.*, *To Sir W. Phillips* 10 June, The vineyard of methodism lies before you. **1791** HAMPSON *Mem. Wesley* III. 110 The assiduity of the labourers in this vineyard was the chief visible cause of their success. **1804** *Med. Jrnl.* XII. 12 Sincerely wishing you success in your labours in the vine-yard of humanity. **1905** G. THORNE *Lost Cause* x, The League 'll go safe enough, there'll always be labourers in the vineyard.

¶**c.** = VINEA. *Obs.*[−1]

1650 R. STAPYLTON *Strada's Low C. Wars* IX. 58 The pioners, working under long and thick boards, in the form of a Tortois, covered with raw hides to secure them from Granadoes (anciently called Vineyards, and Galleries) to enter the ditch.

2. *attrib.* and *Comb.*, as ***vineyard-culture***, ***-dresser***, ***-ground***, etc.; †**vineyard leek**, a wild species of leek.

1562 TURNER *Herbal* II. 102 The wild or wynyard leke is more hurtfull for the stomack then the comon leke. **1577** tr. *Bullinger's Decades* (1592) 1121 The ministers of the Church are sometime called souldiers or vineyard-keepers. **1636** PRYNNE *Unbish. Tim.* (1661) 111 Like as an higher place is made for the Vineyardkeeper, to keep the Vineyard, so an higher place also is made for the Bishops. *a* **1704** T. BROWN *Declam. Def. Gaming* Wks. (1709) III. 146 Bacchus was made a God, a Vine-yard-keeper [etc.]. **1731** P. MILLER *Gard. Dict.* s.v. *Vitis*, I have seen in one Place in this Vineyard-Plot great Pieces of old Vines replanted after the aforesaid manner. **1733** TULL *Horse-Hoeing Husb.* (title-page), A Method of introducing a Sort of Vineyard-Culture into the Corn-Fields. *Ibid.* vii. 62 Without which they could not give it [*sc.* corn] the Vineyard-Hoeing. **1753** *Chambers' Cycl.* Suppl. s.v. *Porrum*, The wild vineyard leek. *c* **1820** S. ROGERS *Italy* (1839) 41 As I rambled through thy vineyard-ground. *Ibid.* 223 When on a vineyard-hill we lay concealed. **1848** CLOUGH *Amours de Voy.* II. 122 And we believe we discern some lines of men descending Down through the vineyard-slopes. **1849** K. H. DIGBY *Compitum* II. 361 Pope Urban I should be painted with grapes and a vine, being the patron of vineyardmen. **1884** KNIGHT *Dict. Mech.* Suppl. 928/1 A French double vineyard plow.

Hence ˈ**vineyarded**, *a.*, enclosed as a vineyard; covered with vineyards; ˈ**vineyarding**, the cultivation of vineyards; vine-growing; ˈ**vineyardist**, one who engages in vine-growing.

1820 KEATS *Isabella* xvii, In that land inspired, Paled in and *vineyarded from beggar-spies. **1886** MRS. CADDY *Footsteps Jeanne D'Arc* 83 One now walks from the train to the town by the side of vineyarded hill-slopes. **1870** *Congregationalist* 19 May (Cent.), Profits of *vineyarding in California. **1848** *Rep. Comm. Patents 1847* (U.S.) 199 A French wine maker and *vineyardist..from Kentucky. **1868** *Rep. U.S. Comm. Agric.* (1869) 267 The necessity of depending mainly upon professional vine-yardists. **1897** L. H. BAILEY *Princ. Fruit-growing* 291 Careful vineyardists are able to continue the practice [of girdling] year after year without apparent injury to the vine.

vineyet, var. VINET *Obs.*

vineyetour, var. VINITOR *Obs.*

vinger, southern ME. var. FINGER *sb.*

vingerpol (ˈfɪŋərpɔl). *S. Afr.* Also **fingerpoll**, **-pole.** [Afrikaans, f. Du. *vinger* FINGER *sb.* + *pol* tuft tussock.] One of several African species of *Euphorbia* producing succulent branches which resemble fingers.

1875 J. NOBLE *Descr. Handbk. Cape Colony* 178 The 'vingerpol' is another succulent plant in use: it has great fleshy fingers growing out of a crown, a foot in diameter. **1883** C. HOBSON *Farm in Karoo* 196 'Another very curious plant, circle within circle of things like fingers.' 'That is just what it is called... "Finger-pole".' **1889** H. A. BRYDEN *Kloof & Karroo* 258 Spent and foundered oxen,..when fed with fingerpoll, regained vitality. **1932** WATT & BREJER-BRANDWIJK *Medicinal & Poisonous Plants Southern Afr.* 104 *Euphorbia esculenta* Marl., Vingerpol, a drought-resisting plant of the Karroo; must not be confused with *Euphorbia caput medusae*, also known as Vingerpol. The former is a valuable fodder, the latter poisonous. **1966** E. PALMER *Plains of Camdeboo* xvi. 260, I dreamed I was struggling with a giant Vingerpol that bounced solidly and fleshily upon me.

vinȝhe, obs. form of VINE *sb.*

vingre, obs. f. VINEGAR *sb.*

‖**vingt-et-un** (vɛ̃t e œ̃), †**vingt-un** (vɛ̃tœ̃). Also 8 -une. [F., 'twenty-one'.] A round game of cards in which the object is to make the number twenty-one or as near this as possible without exceeding it, by counting the pips on the cards, court-cards counting as ten, the ace one or eleven as the holder chooses. (Cf. VAN JOHN.)

Also applied to a game at dominoes: see STONE *sb.* 13.

a. **1772** DUCHESS OF NORTHUMBERLAND *Diary* 7 June (1926) xxxiii. 186 We play'd..at Vingt et un till supper Time. **1842** DICKENS *Amer. Notes* (1850) 13/1 This passenger is reported to have lost fourteen pounds at Vingt-et-un..yesterday. **1853** 'C. BEDE' *Verdant Green* xi. 102 It was a very different thing to playing *vingt-et-un* at home. **1872** E. BRADDON *Life India* viii. 338 Happy gamblers, who look upon the scientific game much in the same way as they do *vingt-et-un*.

β. **1781** *Westm. Mag.* IX. 604 Give the Beau-monde impertinent advice, Proscribe *Vingt-une*! prohibit box and dice! **1790** A. C. BOWERS *Diaries & Corresp.* (1903) 109, I was sat down with every Miss in Winchester to play Vingt une. **1804** JANE AUSTEN *Watsons* (1879) 358, I have played nothing but vingt-un of late. **1868** E. F. PARDON *Card Player* 69 Vingt-un may be played by two or more players.

vingty ('væ̃tɪ). [-Y[6].] Slang abbrev. of prec.

1936 F. J. WHALEY *Trouble in College* viii. 129 Perhaps there was a game of poker or vingty on somewhere. **1946** M. DICKENS *Happy Prisoner* ii. 34, I asked her to come and play Vingty. **1954** N. BALCHIN *Last Recoll. my Uncle Charles* i. 16 As you see, a small school of vingty is in progress.

‖**vinho** ('viɲo). [Pg., wine: cf. VINO.] Portuguese wine. Used in various collocations, as ***vinho branco***, white wine; ***vinho corrente*** = *vino corriente* s.v. VINO 1 b; ***vinho da casa***, house wine; ***vinho de consumo***, cheap wine equivalent to *vin ordinaire*; ***vinho tinto***, red wine; ***vinho verde*** [lit. 'green wine'], young wine that is not allowed to mature.

1835 J. E. ALEXANDER *Sketches in Portugal* iii. 65 Some of the elders..went to a press in the wall and took from it a square bottle of vinho branco, with which they washed the dust from their throats in order that the chaunting might be more effective. *Ibid.* v. 112 In an outhouse were many pipes of 'vinho tinto'. **1955** M. MCCARTHY in *New Yorker* 5 Feb. 93/1 Hotel and boardinghouse keepers are required to serve a third of a litre of wine (the *vinho da casa*) with every lunch or dinner. **1958** K. AMIS *I like it Here* xii. 152 A few glasses of *vinho tinto*. **1962** 'D. WILSON' *Search for Geoffrey Goring* v. 118 Penny copied the men, drinking the white *vinho verde*. **1975** P. V. PRICE *Taste of Wine* v. 100/1 There are, however, some wines such as the *pétillant* and *vinhos verdes* ('green wines'), which have a natural 'liveliness' or inclination to sparkle. **1980** *Times* 27 Nov. 21/5 Outstanding wines include..the Beiramar *vinho corrente*. **1980** *Times* 10 June (Portugal Suppl.) p. vi/2 Prices of *vinho de consumo* (vin ordinaire) rosé. *Ibid.*, The northern Minho district which produces vinho verde. **1985** *Times* 26 Mar. 20/2 Organized tours from London will take tourists..to other regions such as the Dão, with its red and white table wines, and the regions of the *vinhos verdes* or green wines.

vinic ('vaɪnɪk), *a. Chem.* [f. L. *vīn-um* wine.] Obtained or derived from wine or alcohol.

1835 T. THOMSON in *R. D. & T. Thomson's Rec. Gen. Sci.* II. 98 The term racemic acid given by the French is preferable; because vinic is the name applied frequently on the Continent to tartaric acid. **1857** MILLER *Elem. Chem.*, *Org.* 28 Vinic Acids. *Ibid.* 119 Ethylic or Vinic Alcohol, Spirit of Wine. *Ibid.* 155 Ethylic or Vinic Ether. **1876** HARLEY *Royle's Mat. Med.* 330 Vinic æther prepared from alcohol.

'viniculture. [f. L. *vīni-*, *vīnum* wine + CULTURE *sb.*] The cultivation of grapes for the production of wine.

1871 *Echo* 3 Jan., The fair for the best and newest specimens of viniculture has been held in Florence last week. **1882** *Advance* (Chicago) 23 Nov., Viniculture from year to year is gaining ground in Southern Palestine. **1891** H. M. STEPHENS *Portugal* 368 He did not neglect to encourage agriculture and viniculture.

Hence **vini'cultural** *a.*; **vini'culturist.**

1888 *Voice* (N.Y.) 5 July, The Vinicultural Commission will establish in San Francisco..a Wine Exchange. **1888** *Sci. Amer.* 24 Nov. 327/2 The harvesting of the grape crop is the period of anxiety for the viniculturist.

viniet, variant of VINET[1] *Obs.*

vi'niferous, *a. rare.* [f. L. *vīni-*, *vīnum* wine: see -FEROUS.] Producing wine.

1832 G. DOWNES *Lett. Cont. Countries* I. 80 On the left lies the viniferous district of La Côte.

vinification (vaɪnɪfɪ'keɪʃən). [f. as prec.: see -FICATION.] The conversion of grape juice or the like into an alcoholic liquid by fermentation.

1880 *Lib. Univ. Knowl.* VII. 71 The vinification [of Greek wines] is very imperfect. **1894** THUDICHUM (*title*), A Treatise on Wines:..with Practical Directions for Viticulture and Vinification.

vining ('vaɪnɪŋ), *a.* [f. VINE *sb.*] Twining like a vine.

1814 LEWIS & CLARK *Trav. Missouri* xxvi. (1815) III. 124 Vining and whiteberry honeysuckle. **1897** *Voice* (N.Y.) 4 Mar. 5/3 The vining maples twined in so close about it that we had to get right in the water and follow up the stream.

vining ('vaɪnɪŋ), *vbl. sb.* [f. VINE *v.* + -ING[1].] The separation of certain leguminous crop plants from their vines and pods; ***vining pea***, a pea grown for mechanical vining.

1928 JONES & ROSA *Truck Crop Plants* xi. 215 The vines [of peas] are loaded onto racks and hauled to the cannery or a field vining station. **1944** *Sun* (Baltimore) 26 Apr. 5/5 Prisoners..will be employed in vining and husking operations and in handling the cans after processing. **1959** *Times* 7 Sept. 19/2 One large..herd is getting its sustenance mainly from kale and vining pea silage. **1968** *Times* 16 Dec. 7/3 Peas for vining and threshing. **1975** LOCKHART & WISEMAN *Introd. Crop Husbandry* (ed. 3) iv. 147 Vining and pulling peas are not so dependent on dry weather at harvest.

vinipote. *rare*[−0]. [f. L. *vīni-*, *vīnum* wine + *pōtus* having drunk.] (See quots.)

1623 COCKERAM I, *Vinipote*, a wine drinker. **1656** BLOUNT *Glossogr.*, *Vinipote*, a drinker of Wine, a Wine-bibber, a Drunkard.

viniter(ie, obs. forms of VINITER, VINTRY.

†**vinitor.** *Obs.* Also 7 **vinetor, vineyetour.** [a. L. *vīnitor*, f. *vīnum* wine.] A vine-grower.

1559 ABP. SANDYS *Serm.* iii. (1585) 48 Nowe it behoueeth the vinitor to take great heede what vine he planteth in this vineyard. **1595** CHARLDON *Fulfordo et Fulfordæ* 33 This skilfull vinitor..hath caused the stones that pestered the vineyard to bee gathered out. **1606** *True & Perf. Relat.* D dd 3, The branch beares fruit no longer then it continues in the naturall and proper Vine..cut and pruined by the same Vinetor. **1624** CAPT. SMITH *Virginia* IV. 155 The Vineyard our Vineyetours had brought to a good forwardnesse. **1631** R. H. *Arraignm. Whole Creature* xvi. 280 Had not Iezabel..made him a Potion and Caudell of the bloud of the Vinetor, and Grapes of the Vineyard.

vini'torian, *a. rare*[−0]. [f. L. *vīnitōri-us* (Columella), f. *vīnitor*: see prec.] (See quot.)

1656 BLOUNT *Glossogr.*, *Vinitorian*, of or belonging to the keeping a Vineyard or Vines.

vink (fɪŋk). *S. Afr.* [a. Afrikaans.] Var. FINK *sb.*[1]

1834 [see FINK *sb.*[1]]. **1913** D. FAIRBRIDGE *That which hath Been* 30 Yellow vinks shrieked and jabbered on their hanging nests. **1925** *Centenary Bk. S. Afr. Verse* 235 The bird referred to in the text..is evidently a weaver-bird, locally known as Vink. **1958** *Cape Times* 15 July 8/8 Vinks feed on many kinds of tiny parasites and insects.

vinnel, obs. variant of VENNEL.

vinnewed, variant of VINEWED *a. Obs.*

'vinnied, *a. dial.* [var. VINEWED *a.*] Mouldy.

1519 HORMAN *Vulg.* 162b, This breede is olde and venyed. **1670** H. STUBBE *Plus Ultra* 40 The moon is a Cheese..odly figured..(and perhaps a little vinnyed in some parts). **1787** GROSE *Prov. Gloss.*, *Vinnied*, fenny, mouldy. **1834-** in south-western dialects (*Eng. Dial. Dict.*).

vinnow, vinnowed, vinnowy, variants of VINEW *sb.*, VINEWED *a.*, FINEWY *a.*

vinny, dial. var. VENY[2], FENNY *a.*[2], FINNY *a.*[2]

'vinny, *v. Obs.* exc. *dial.* Also 6 **vynye.** [var. of VINEW *v.*, FINEW *v.*] *intr.* To become mouldy.

14.. *Voc.* in Wr. Wülcker 597 *Mucido*, to vynye. **1837-** in Somerset and Devon glossaries.

vino. [Sp. and It., wine; cf. VIN.] **I.** Non-naturalized forms ('vino). **1.** With various adjs. designating the quality, origin, etc., of a wine: **a.** ***vino blanco*** [Sp. = white], ***dolce*** [It. = sweet], ***dulce*** [Sp. = sweet], ***fino*** [Sp. = quality], ***locale*** [It. = local], ***rosso*** [It. = red], ***secco*** [It. = dry], ***tinto*** [Sp. = red] (cf. TINTO *sb.*[1]).

1673 J. RAY *Observations Journey Low-Countries* 487 We left Cordova... This day we first met with red wine again which they call *Vino tinto*. **1846** R. FORD *Gatherings from Spain* xiv. 155 This *amontillado*..is very scarce, since out of a hundred butts of *vino fino*, not more than five will possess its properties. **1901** F. W. MAITLAND *Let.* 23 Feb. (1965) 224 When Carnival came, our cook took herself off to spend her wages in *vino tinto*. **1902** BELLOC *Path to Rome* 317, I bought a bottle of a new kind of sweet wine called 'Vino Dolce'. **1911** *Encycl. Brit.* XXVIII. 725/2 Malaga is a sweet wine... It is generally..a blend made from *vino dulce* and *vino secco*, together with varying quantities of *vino maestro*, *vino tierno*, *arope* and *color*. **1949** E. POUND *Pisan Cantos* lxxvi. 47 Ex rum-runner (the rum being vino rosso). **1950** E. HEMINGWAY *Across River & into Trees* xxxvii. 226 A bottle of that *vino secco*, from Vesuvius, for the small soles. **1963** *House & Garden* Jan. 56/2 In little inns..you get a *vino locale* from the carafe. **1977** C. MCCARRY *Secret Lovers* xvi. 222 Mushrooms in one place..gazpacho in another..*vino tinto* in all. **1981** A. FRASER *Splash of Red* iv. 44 There's some lovely chilled *vino blanco* in the fridge.

b. Special collocations. **vino corriente** [Sp., lit. 'common, ordinary'], cheap wine equivalent to *vin ordinaire*; **vino cotto** [It., lit. 'cooked'], (see quot. 1965); cf. *vin cuit* s.v. VIN; **vino crudo** [It., lit. 'raw'], wine in its natural state, not boiled (cf. *vino cotto*); **vino de color** [Sp.], a rich sweet wine, used in the blending of sherry and other fortified wines; **vino de pasto** [Sp.], (see quot. 1965); **vino maestro** [Sp., lit. 'master'], (see quots.); **vino nero** [It., lit. 'black'], dark red wine; **vino santo** [It., lit. 'holy'], a sweet white dessert wine; = VINSANTO; **vino tierno** [Sp., lit. 'tender'], (see quots.).

1932 E. HEMINGWAY *Death in Afternoon* 338 *Vino corriente* is *vin ordinaire*. **1978** *Times* 21 Nov. 11/1 A humble *vino corriente*. **1673** J. RAY *Observations Journey Low-Countries* 387 The boil'd wine, which they call *Vin Cotto*, seemed to us much stronger than the wine unboil'd, which they call *Vin Crudo*. **1851** C. REDDING *Hist. Mod. Wines* (ed. 3) vii. 209 Their boiled wine, the Italian *Vino Cotto*, or *vin cuit*, as the French call it, is mingled with other growths, as well as with sherries, for the sake of deepening colour or improving flavour. **1965** O. A. MENDELSOHN *Dict. Drink & Drinking* 356 *Vino cotto*, Italian name of must.. concentrated to a syrup by evaporation (boiling) and used for sweetening Marsala..and similar fortified dessert wines. **1673** Vino crudo [see *vino cotto* above]. **1833** C. REDDING *Hist. Mod. Wines* ix. 241 At Bologna they boil most of their wines, which are then called *vino cotto*, the unboiled they call *vino crudo*. **1851** *Ibid.* (ed. 3) 205 All sherry wine is by nature of a pale colour, the darker shades are conferred by age, or by *vino de color*, or boiled wine. **1966** H. W. YOXALL *Fashion of Life* xxv. 239 P.X., the *vino de color*.., so sweet and heavy as to taste more like a liqueur than a wine. *c* **1870** in H. W. Allen *Number 3 St. James's St.* (1950) 184/1 *Sherry..Vino de pasto*—56/-. **1902** A. BENNETT *Grand Babylon Hotel* xxii. 251 The dry sherries of Spain..Manzanilla, and Amontillado, and Vino de Pasto. **1965** O. A. MENDELSOHN *Dict. Drink & Drinking* 357 *Vino de pasto*, this Spanish term, literally 'pasture wine', is variable in meaning. It can stand for a family wine, one for everyday use... But it is also used by English wine merchants for a mediocre kind of sherry, pale and not too dry. **1977** J. B. HILTON *Dead-Nettle* x. 85 For strong drink he had laid in..an octavo cask of Vino de Pasto. **1911** *Encycl. Brit.* XXVIII. 725/2 The *vino maestro* consists of a must which has only fermented to a slight degree and which has been 'killed' by the addition of about 17% of alcohol. **1965** O. A. MENDELSOHN *Dict. Drink & Drinking* 357 *Vino maestro*, Spanish name of the extra sweet and alcoholic wines used to top up the lesser breeds. Especially used in compounding malaga. **1968** *Listener* 29 Feb. 268/1 When the *vino nero* flows in village bars, songs are sung about Mesina (as they were about the late Sicilian bandit, Salvatore Guiliano). **1686** G. BURNET *Some Lett.* 122 There is near the Lake of Guarda a very extraordinary Wine which they call *Vino Santo*, which drinks like the best sort of Canary, it is not made till Christmas, and from thence it carries the name of Holy Wine. **1833** C. REDDING *Hist. Mod. Wines* ix. 241 On the shores of the Lake of Garda they make a sweet wine..of prime quality, called Vino Santo. **1981** B. HEALEY *Week of Scorpion* v. 81 Their *Vino Santo*, the traditional Tuscan wine of hospitality. **1911** *Encycl. Brit.* XXVIII. 725/2 The *vino tierno* is made by mashing raisins..with water..pressing, and then adding alcohol..to the must. **1965** O. A. MENDELSOHN *Dict. Drink & Drinking* 357 *Vino tierno*, Spanish wine made from partially dried grapes. Used in compounding malaga.

2. Also **bino.** An alcoholic liquor distilled from nipa-palm sap, drunk in the Philippines.

1901 *Army & Navy Jrnl.* 7 Dec. 341/3 The native drinks, ordinarily known as 'vino', manufactured in these islands, contain in a large amount the poisonous principle contained in wood alcohol. **1903** *Census of Philippine Islands* (1905) IV. 119 *Nipa* or *sasá* (*Nipa fructicans*) is a species of palm..from the sap or *tuba*..a liquor known as nipa wine, *vino*, or *bino*, is extensively distilled. **1964** J. M. GARVAN *Negritos of Philippines* vii. 90 The young fellow hies off and finds a present for his future father-in-law. A very acceptable form is a large bottle of Filipino *vino*.

II. Naturalized forms ('viːnəʊ). **3.** Also **veeno.** Wine, esp. of an inferior kind. *slang.*

1919 W. H. DOWNING *Digger Dial.* 56 *Vino*, wine. **1935** L. DURRELL *Spirit of Place* (1969) 31, I bear up very well under the stacks of local vino I am forced to consume. **1942** BERREY & VAN DEN BARK *Amer. Thes. Slang* § 100/14 *Wine*,..veeno, vino, wino. **1962** R. JEFFRIES *Exhibit No. 13* v. 50 We'd better use up the red vino. **1976** P. CAVE *High Flying Birds* i. 7, I was far too stoned to take much notice of Lloyd's vino-inspired ramblings.

vino- ('vaɪnəʊ), combining f. L. *vīnum* wine, employed in a few chemical terms, as ***vino-acetous***, ***-methylic***, ***-sulphureous***.

1730 *Phil. Trans.* XXXVI. 289 And the Retort being clapped in the Hand, there is found in the Receiver a Vino-sulphureous Gas. **1843** TIZARD *Brewing* 519 Vino-acetous fermentation. **1864** WATTS *Dict. Chem.* II. 542 Methylate of Ethyl; Ethylmethylic Methylethylic, or Vinomethylic Ether.

'vinolence. *rare.* [See next and -ENCE.] = next.

1430-40 LYDG. *Bochas* IV. ix. (1554) 106b, He..Through vynolence lost oft his reason. **1607** B. BARNES *Divils Charter* I. ii. A 4, Such odious Auarice and perfidie, Such vinolence and brutish gluttony. [**1727** BAILEY (vol. II), *Vinolence*, *Vinolentness*, Drunkenness.]

'vinolency. *rare.* [ad. L. *vīnolentia*, f. *vīnolentus*: see next and -ENCY.] Drunkenness.

1623 COCKERAM I. [Also Bailey (1721), etc.] **1804** TROTTER *Drunkenness* ii. 21 *note*, No bad assemblage of the phænomena of Vinolency.

vinolent ('vaɪnələnt), *a.* Also 4-6 **vyno-.** [ad. L. *vīnolent-us*, f. *vīnum* wine.] Addicted to drinking wine; tending to drunkenness.

1382 WYCLIF *Titus* i. 7 It bihoueth a bischop for to be withoute crime,..not proud, not wrathful, not vynolent. *c* **1386** CHAUCER *Wife's Prol.* 467 In wommen vinolent is no defence, This knowen lecchours by experience. *c* **1386** —— *Sompn. T.* 223 They ben..Al vinolent as botel in the spence. **1412-20** LYDG. *Chron. Troy* II. 5758 For man or woman pat is vinolent Is verreyly a beste vnresonable. *c* **1440** CAPGRAVE *Life St. Kath.* IV. 1533 Venus was lecherous and also vynolent. **1515** BARCLAY *Egloges* (1570) C vj/2 There is no secrete with people vinolent, By beastly surfeit, the life is breviate. **1556** LAUDER *Tractate* 286 ȝe sulde nocht chuse vnto that cure Ane Vinolent nor wod Pasture. **1656** BLOUNT *Glossogr.* **1837** WHEELWRIGHT tr. *Aristoph.* II. 80 *note*, The violent propensity of the Athenian females.

Hence **'vinolentness**, drunkenness. *rare*[−0].

1727 BAILEY (vol. II).

vi'nologist. *rare*[−1]. [f. L. *vīn-um* wine + -OLOGIST] A connoisseur in wines.

1845 FORD *Handbk. Spain* I. 309 The true vinologist should go down into one of the *cuevas* or cellars and have a goblet of the ruby fluid drawn from the big-bellied *Tinaja*.

vino'madefied, *a. rare*⁻¹. [f. L. *vīn-um* wine + *madefierī* to be soaked.] Soaked with wine.
1652 URQUHART *Jewel* Wks. (1834) 239 He, with his vinomadefied retinue, resolved to press in upon the page.

vi'nometer. [f. L. *vīn-um* wine + -OMETER.] An instrument for measuring the strength or purity of wine; an œnometer.
1863 ATKINSON tr. *Ganot's Physics* 81 Lactometers and vinometers.. are used for measuring the quantity of water which is introduced into milk or wine for the purpose of adulteration.

vinook, variant of VERNEUK *v.*

‖**vin ordinaire** (vɛ̃ ɔrdinɛr). [Fr.; cf. VIN and ORDINAIRE *sb.*] Simple French wine for everyday use.
1820 *Edin. Rev.* XXXIII. 344 And why should as large a duty be levied from the *vins ordinaires*, as from those of the first quality? **1852** E. TWISLETON *Let.* 9 Oct. (1928) iv. 56 You would laugh..if you saw me imbibing the Vin Ordinaire here! **1893** SOMERVILLE & 'ROSS' *Vine Country* viii. 159 A long array of dark-haired, white-coifed women and girls were to be seen..finishing their jugs of *vin ordinaire.* **1926** A. HUXLEY *Essays New & Old* 17 The red wines of Carthage are really delicious, and even the smallest of *vins ordinaires* are very drinkable. **1955** E. POUND *Classic Anthol.* II. 133 Our wine but vin ordinaire, We share spare Food but with jollity. **1975** *Woman's Jrnl.* Sept. 73/3 We drank a good *vin ordinaire* out of unlabelled bottles.

vinose (vaɪ'nəʊs), *a.* [ad. L. *vīnōs-us* full, or fond, of wine. Cf. It., Sp., and Pg. *vinoso*, Pg. *vinhoso.*] = VINOUS *a.*
1727 BAILEY (vol. II). **1732** *Hist. Litteraria* III. 382 The Acids..are divided by the Author into Vinose and Acetose. **1826** *Examiner* 187/2 Their salaried tutors, their rich professors, their vinose and indolent fellows.

vinosity (vaɪ'nɒsɪtɪ). Also 7 **vinocitie**. [ad. L. *vīnōsitās* (Tertullian), the flavour of wine, f. *vīnōs-us*: see prec. and -ITY. So OF. and F. *vinosité*, It. *vinosità*, Sp. *vinosidad*, Pg. *vinosidade.*]
1. The state or quality of being vinous; vinous character or flavour.
1658 SIR T. BROWNE *Hydriot.* 33 Vessels of Oyles and Aromaticall Liquors... And some yet retaining a Vinosity and spirit in them, which if any have tasted they have farre exceeded the Palats of Antiquity. [Hence in Blount *Glossogr.* (1661).] **1714** MANDEVILLE *Fab. Bees* (1733) II. 210 If we consider, how necessary fermentation is to the vinosity of the liquor. **1757** A. COOPER *Distiller* I. ii. (1760) 20 It is common with Distillers, in order to..give it a particular Flavour, or improve its Vinosity. **1843** TIZARD *Brewing* 465 The vinosity and mellowness [of vinous liquors] are at the same time improved. **1889** *Pall Mall G.* 20 July, A Médoc wine-taster can tell at a sip what sort of ground a bottle of wine has grown in;..that grown on a stony layer is marked by greater body and vinosity. **1890** O. CRAWFURD *Round Calendar* 195 All the rich and subtle chemistry of vinosity, which help to cheer and sustain the body.
2. Fondness for, addiction to, wine.
1624 HEYWOOD *Gunaik.* VII. 348 The souldiers.. reprooving his intemperate vinositie. *Ibid.* IX. 441 Riots, Reuels, Banquets, Pride, Surfets, Vinocitie, Voracitie. **1857** *Fraser's Mag.* LVI. 486 Aristophanes himself, notwithstanding his jokes on the vinosity of Cratinus, is said in Athenæus to have been well primed with wine when he sat down to write.

vinour(e, obs. variants of VINER².

vinous ('vaɪnəs), *a.* [ad. L. *vīnōs-us*, f. *vīnum* wine: cf. VINOSE *a.* and F. *vineux* (OF. *vineus*).]
1. Of the nature of wine; having the qualities of wine; tasting or smelling like wine; made of, or prepared with, wine.
1664 POWER *Exp. Philos.* I. 65 The fermentation and heat presently appears, with a kind of vinous steam. **1680** BOYLE *Exp. Chem. Princ.* I. 26 Fermentation rarefy's the oyly parts of the Juice of Grapes, and subtilizes them into vinous spirits. **1694** SALMON *Bate's Dispens.* (1713) 114/2 So will the Liquor be Vinous in Smell, and more delicious in Taste. **1713** J. WARDER *True Amazons* 156 The most wholesome of all the Vinous Liquors in the World. **1741** C. MIDDLETON *Cicero* I. iv. 324 He was obliged, he said, to take some vinous medicines. **1818** ACCUM *Chem. Tests* 72 All vinous fluids, even the mildest, contain a portion of a free acid. **1856** N. HAWTHORNE *Eng. Note-bks.* I. 242 They would perhaps have preferred a vinous potation. **1874** H. R. REYNOLDS *John Bapt.* iii. §2. 154 John was deprived from his birth of all vinous stimulus.
b. Producing wine or similar liquor. *rare.*
1676 WORLIDGE (*title*), Vinetum Britannicum: or, a Treatise of Cider;..Together with the Method of Propagating all sorts of Vinous Fruit-Trees. **1708** OZELL tr. *Boileau's Lutrin* 41 Burgundia's vinous Fields she hovers round.
2. Pertaining to, characteristic of, wine.
1708 J. PHILIPS *Cyder* II. 106 Water will imbibe The small Remains of Spirit, and acquire A vinous Flavour. **1719** LONDON & WISE *Compl. Gard.* 78 It has a vinous and delicious Taste. **1775** SIR E. BARRY *Observ. Wines Ancients* 9 A more rich and sweet taste than is natural to them in a recent true vinous state. **1834** J. FORBES *Laennec's Dis. Chest* (ed. 4) 173 An accumulation of blood..which..tinges the lungs of a livid or vinous colour.
b. *vinous fermentation*: (see quot. 1857).
1748 HARTLEY *Observ. Man* II. iii. §2. 220 All Liquors which have undergone vinous Fermentation..have a Mark set upon them as dangerous. *c* **1791** *Encycl. Brit.* (ed. 3) VII. 216/1 When the vinous fermentation was finished, the liquor..was found converted into vinegar. **1815** J. SMITH *Panorama Sci. & Art* II. 502 The vinous fermentation never takes place except in substances containing sugar, and it is most remarkable in those which contain the most of the saccharine principle. **1857** MILLER *Elem. Chem., Org.* 102 When spirit of wine is formed from sugar, the change is called the alcoholic or vinous fermentation.
fig. **1870** LOWELL *Among my Books* Ser. I. 147 The Reformation had passed the period of its vinous fermentation.
3. Caused or produced by, resulting from, indulgence in wine.
1776 JOHNSON in *Boswell* 12 Apr., I have heard none of those drunken,—nay, drunken is a coarse word,—none of those *vinous* flights. **1818** SCOTT *Rob Roy* xii, It has even been reported by maligners, that I sung a song while under this vinous influence. **1850** THACKERAY *Pendennis* xlvi, Frank and familiar..from vinous excitement. **1874** LD. LYTTON in Lady Balfour *Lett.* (1906) I. 318 On our way back to town I was seized with a vinous inspiration.
b. Affected by, showing signs of, the use of wine.
1847 L. HUNT *Men, Women, & B.* I. ix. 161 He was a shortish stout man, in powder, with a huge vinous face. **1848** THACKERAY *Van. Fair* xxxiv, Winking at his cousin with a pair of vinous eyes. **1882** 'F. ANSTEY' *Vice Versa* iii. 44 C. gave a vinous wink.
4. Addicted to wine.
1816 T. L. PEACOCK *Headlong Hall* ii, Indefatigable in his requisition for the proximity of his vinous Achates. **1820** BYRON *Juan* III. xlii, The vinous Greek to whom he had address'd His question, much too merry to divine The questioner, fill'd up a glass of wine. **1859** THACKERAY *Virgin.* x, Let us fancy them reeling to bed,..and their vinous General..conducted to his chamber by the young gentlemen of the house.
5. With names of colours: Like that of (red) wine; having a wine-coloured tinge.
1834 *Penny Cycl.* II. 79/2 The general colour of the body is a dark vinous red on the upper parts and silvery grey beneath. **1882** *Garden* 25 Mar. 203/2 The colour of the flowers is a yellow-green with blotches of deep vinous-purple at the basis of the flower-cup. **1887** W. PHILLIPS *Brit. Discomycetes* 65 Cup..rough, vinous-brown. **1894** R. B. SHARPE *Handbk. Birds Gt. Brit.* I. 65 Ear-coverts and throat vinous-chestnut.
b. Of the colour of wine; vinaceous. Also *Comb.*
1894 R. B. SHARPE *Handbk. Birds Gt. Brit.* I. 19 The white or vinous-throated birds. *Ibid.* 80 The median and lesser wing-coverts vinous.
Hence **'vinously** *adv.*; **'vinousness**.
1727 BAILEY (vol. II), *Vinousness*, winy Quality, Taste or Smell. **1836** *Fraser's Mag.* XIII. 733 He felt himself 'vinously inclined'. **1859** MEREDITH *R. Feverel* xvii, He determined to overbear his client vinously. **1891** —— *One of our Conq.* vi, His voice and words had a swing of conviction: they imparted vinousness to a heart athirst.

vinow, vinowed, variants of VINEW *sb.* and *v.*, VINEWED *a.*

vinquish, var. VANQUISH *sb.*

‖**vin rosé** (vɛ̃ roze). [Fr., f. as VIN + ROSÉ *a.*] = ROSÉ *sb.*²
1931 E. WAUGH *Remote People* 138 We dined on the roof; a delicious dinner; iced *vin-rosé.* **1958** A. L. SIMON *Dict. Wines* 162/1 *Vin rosé* (1) a pink wine made from very ripe black grapes, the skins of which are not allowed to ferment with the wine, so that they only impart to it a pink tinge instead of a dark red colour; (2) A pink wine made from black and white grapes mixed in the pressing; (3) A white wine coloured with cochineal to the degree of pink required. **1981** P. INCHBALD *Tondo for Short* xvi. 174 Bread and cheese, a salad, a bowl of fruit, a litre bottle of vin rosé.

‖**vin rouge** (vɛ̃ ruʒ). [Fr., f. as VIN + ROUGE *a.*]
a. French red wine; = ROUGE *sb.*¹ 6.
1917 A. G. EMPEY *Over Top* 313 *Vin rouge*, French red wine made from vinegar and red ink. **1922** E. E. CUMMINGS *Enormous Room* vii. 169 A good deal of color in his cheeks and a good deal of vin rouge in his guts. **1931** E. LINKLATER *Juan in America* II. iv. 79 Rumors of a Chianti racket or a corner in *vin rouge* are obviously premature. **1960** *Guardian* 31 Dec. 5/3 The working [French] man drinks..at each meal..a litre of vin rouge ordinaire. **1980** L. ST. CLAIR *Obsessions* iv. 105 A bottle of *vin rouge* and two glasses.
b. In joc. or illit. form. Cf. VIN BLANC 2. (In quot., *Mil. slang.*)
1919 [see VIN BLANC 2].

‖**vinsanto** (vin'santo). [It.] = *vino santo* s.v. VINO 1 b.
1965 A. SICHEL *Penguin Bk. Wines* III. 203 Although made all over Italy where fine-quality sweet wine can be made from dried grapes, the true Vin Santo Toscano should be made from grapes that have been left on the vine to dry... Fine Vin Santo is also made from grapes picked at the normal time in October and allowed to grape dry until January or February and then crushed. **1973** *Country Life* 28 June 1919/3 The sweet dessert Vin Santo, made from dried grapes..is made quite widely in Italy. **1981** M. NABB *Death of Englishman* I. i. 16 The Marshal drank half a litre of red every day..and a drop of *vinsanto* on Sundays.

vint, *sb. rare.* [Back-formation from VINTAGE *sb.* Cf. next.] Vintage.
1639 G. DANIEL *Ecclus.* xxiv. 88 Opulent As Gehon, in the season of the vint. **1895** SNAITH *Dorothy Marvin* vii, Such is the beauty of this rarest of vints [that, etc.].

vint (vɪnt), *v.* [Back-formation from VINTNER or VINTAGE.]
†**1.** *trans.* To sell or vend (wine). *Obs.*⁻¹
1728 NORTH *Mem. Music* (1846) 112 The taverner finding the sweets of vinting wine and taking money.
2. To make (wine, etc.); = VINTAGE *v.* 1.
1857 TROLLOPE *Barchester T.* xxi. II. 38, I wouldn't give a straw for the best wine that ever was vinted, after it had lain here a couple of years. **1908** *Academy* 11 April 666/1 Mr. Pickwick..drinks a brandy that was vinted and distilled in Sirius.

‖**vinta** ('vɪntə). [ad. Bisaya *binta.*] A kind of canoe used by the Moros in the Philippine Islands.
1900 F. H. SAWYER *Inhabitants of Philippines* xxxviii. 362 These vessels rendered good service, and to some extent checked the incursions of the pirates, but they had not the speed to follow up the fast-rowing *vintas* of the Moros, which could always escape from them unless caught in narrow waters. **1906** *Soldier Slang* in C. McGovern *Sarjint Larry an' Frinds, Parao*, a native canoe or row boat, usually a single hollowed-out log; propelled by one or two rude oars, with a paddle for a rudder. *Ibid., Vinta*, same as 'Parao'. **1946** G. STIMPSON *Bk. about Thousand Things* 47 Their *vintas*, fishing boats hewn from single long logs, were marvels of workmanship and efficiency. **1979** P. DRISCOLL *Pangolin* xvi. 127 The long, slender *vintas* of the Muslim fishermen lay at anchor.

vintage ('vɪntɪdʒ), *sb.* Also 5-6 **vyntage**. [a. AF. *vintage* (1353), altered f. of *vindage*, *vendage* VENDAGE, OF. *vendange*, by association with VINTER or VINTNER.]
1. The produce or yield of the vine, either as grapes or wine; the crop or yield of a vineyard or district in a single season. Now *rare* or *Obs.*
Quot. 1460 refers to the capture of large supplies of wine from the French.
c **1450** *Brut* II. 372 þere þay restid ham a while, and sette þe cuntre yn pees & rest tylle þe vyntage were redy to sayle. *a* **1460** CAPGRAVE *Chron.* 239 Than the vyntage of Ynglond took a othir felauchip, where thei had a thousand tunne wyn and V. hundred. **1523** LD. BERNERS *Froiss.* xxii. (1812) II. 55 And there he taryed tyll they had inned all their corne and vyntage. **1589** FLEMING *Virg. Georg.* II. 21 Not one and selfe same vintage hangs on our Italian trees. **1605** BACON *Adv. Learn.* I. iv. §11 By reason of their stirring and digging the mould about the roots of their vines, they had a great vintage. **1657** *Burton's Diary* (1828) I. 327 The commonwealth will be cheated; for most of the wine of this vintage is now in the vintners' cellars. **1697** DRYDEN *Virg. Past.* v. 109 Two Goblets will I crown with sparkling Wine, The gen'rous Vintage of the Chian Vine. **1713** YOUNG *Last Day* II. 348 Shine we in arms? or sing beneath our vine? Thine is the vintage, and the conquest Thine. **1748** GRAY *Alliance* 57 With grim delight the brood of winter view A brighter day..; Scent the new fragrance of the breathing rose, And quaff the pendent vintage as it grows. **1818** MRS. SHELLEY *Frankenst.* i. (1865) 62 Never did..the vines yield a more luxuriant vintage. **1818** SHELLEY *Euganean Hills* 221 Where..the milk-white oxen slow With the purple vintage strain, Heaped upon the creaking wain.
fig. **1586** WARNER *Alb. Eng.* IV. xxi. (1589) 89 The Vintage of my thriftles loue is blasted in the bloome. **1647** N. BACON *Disc. Govt. Eng.* I. ii. (1739) 19 This was the vintage of Kings and great men, but the gleanings of the People were much more plentiful. **1820** SHELLEY *Ode Liberty* xii. 7 How like Bacchanals of blood Round France, the ghastly vintage, stood Destruction's sceptred slaves, and Folly's mitred brood!
b. *poet.* Wine, esp. of good or rare quality.
1604 DEKKER *Honest Wh.* Wks. 1873 II. 51 We had excellent cheere, rare vintage, and were drunke after supper. **1725** POPE *Odyss.* IV. 67 In solid gold the purple vintage flows. **1820** KEATS *To a Nightingale* ii, O! for a draught of vintage, that hath been Cool'd a long age in the deep-delved earth. **1859** TENNYSON *Elaine* 266 The great knight,.. Whom they with meats and vintage of their best And talk and minstrel melody entertain'd. **1887** BOWEN *Æneid* I. 729 Soon for the goblet she asks,.. Then with the vintage fills it.
transf. **1856** B. TAYLOR *Summer's Bacchanal* 109 Where the crystal vintage of the mountain Runs in foam from dazzling fields of snow.
c. Used with reference to the age or year of a particular wine, usually connoting one of good or outstanding quality; now *spec.* a wine made from the grape-crop of a certain district in a good year and kept separate on account of its quality.
1746 FRANCIS tr. *Horace, Epist.* I. v. 6 Nor old,..nor excellent, my Wine, Of five Years Vintage, and a marshy Vine. **1760** JOHNSON *Idler* No. 97 ¶4 He may..regale his palate with a succession of vintages. **1817** BYRON *Manfred* II. i. 18 Taste my wine; 'Tis of an ancient vintage. **1864** TENNYSON *Aylmer's F.* 407 Honest Averill..fetch'd His richest beeswing from a binn reserved For banquets, praised the waning red, and told The vintage. **1888** *Encycl. Brit.* XXIV. 605 The principal claret vintages of the 19th century are considered to have been those of 1815, '25, '28 [etc.]. *Ibid.* 608 The last year when the wine was shipped as a vintage.
transf. **1874** L. STEPHEN *Hours in Library* (1879) III. 231 There are vintages, both material and intellectual, which are more frequently praised than heartily enjoyed.
d. A property yielding wine. *rare*⁻¹.
1840 HOOD *Up Rhine* 231 Last summer we purchased a small cask of wine from a woman who owns a little vintage.
2. a. The gathering of the ripe grapes in order to make them into wine, including the preliminary processes of wine-making, as pressing and placing the juice in the fermenting vats, etc.; the grape-harvest.
Also in the phrase †*to make vintage* (see *b*).
(*a*) **1540** *Act 32 Hen. VIII*, c. 14 §2 From Burdeux to London for everie tonne Wyne at the fyrst vintage,..xviij.s. **1550** NICOLLS *Thucydides* IV. 114 b, Sone after that, a lytle bifore the vintage, that selfe somer. **1560** BIBLE (Genev.) *Micah* vii. 1, I am as the somer gatherings, & as the grapes of the vintage. **1601** HOLLAND *Pliny* I. 405 The grape-gatherer in time of Vintage. **1656** BLOUNT *Glossogr.*, *Vintage*,..Vine-harvest, Grape-harvest, Grape-gathering,

Wine making. **1710** J. CLARKE tr. *Rohault's Nat. Philos.* (1729) I. 175 For if it rains a little before the Vintage, the Wine is sharper. **1790** BURKE *Fr. Rev.* 261 The produce of the vintage in Guienne and Languedoc. **1833** REDDING *Mod. Wines* iii. (1851) 53 The time of the vintage being fixed, the gathering is begun as early in the day as possible. **1863** T. G. SHAW *Wine, Vine & Cellar* xi. 285 The vintage is often delayed to such a late period of the season as to incur the danger of injury from frost. **1888** *Encycl. Brit.* XXIV. 605/1 The vintage in Médoc usually commences between the middle and end of September and lasts from two to three weeks. The process is a very simple one.

fig. **1860** PUSEY *Minor Proph.* 197 It was a vintage, not of wine, but of woe.

(*b*) **1600** NASHE *Summer's Last Will* F j b, My Lord askes thee, what vintage thou hast made? **1609** BIBLE (Douay) *Jer.* xxxi. 5 The planters shal plant, and til the time come they shal not make vintage. **1731** MILLER *Gard. Dict.* s.v. *Vitis*, My Conjecture is founded upon more than twenty-five Vintages, which I have seen made.

fig. **1609** BIBLE (Douay) *Lam.* i. 12 See if there be sorow like to my sorow: because he hath made vintage of me, as our Lord hath spoken.

b. The season or time when this is done. Also with *a* and pl.

1616 BULLOKAR *Eng. Expos.*, *Vintage*, the time of yeare when wine is made. **1651** R. CHILD in *Hartlib's Legacy* (1655) 148, I lived in Charanton two leagues from Paris, a whole Vintage, purposely to see how wine was made in France. **1764** HARMER *Observ.* i. §18. 43 If St. Jerome may be believed, the vintage of Judæa is not till the end of September or beginning of October. **1858** SIMMONDS *Dict. Trade*, *Vintage*, the season of gathering grapes. **1876** W. C. BRYANT in *St. Nicholas Mag.* Dec. 101/2 The cider-making season in autumn was, at the time of which I am speaking, somewhat correspondent to the vintage in the wine countries of Europe.

3. *transf.* and *fig.* **a.** The date or period when a person was born or flourished.

1883 *Sunday Mercury* (N.Y.) 23 Sept. 6/4 'I want to sue a man for breach of promise,' said a maiden of the vintage of 1842, coming into a lawyer's office. **1931** F. L. ALLEN *Only Yesterday* vi. 129 Harding had no sooner arrived at the White House than a swarm of practical politicians of the McKinley-Foraker vintage reappeared in Washington. **1945** A. L. ROWSE *West-Country Stories* 2 He was..a benevolent pluralist of a rich vintage. **1967** M. ARGYLE *Psychol. Interpersonal Behaviour* iv. 79 In many cases the hero has a well-defined style of social behaviour—compare ..the cowboy of 1890 vintage.

b. Hence, the date or period at which a thing was made or produced.

1929 R. S. & H. M. LYND *Middletown* xiv. 199 Examination questions of the two periods indicate so little change in method and emphasis in teaching that it is almost impossible simply by reading a history examination to tell whether it is of 1890 or 1924 vintage. **1939** E. S. GARDNER *D. A. draws Circle* vii. 105 Mrs Fermal drove up in a rattling car of ancient vintage. **1946** E. O'NEILL *Iceman Cometh* (1947) I. 11 His pointed tan buttoned shoes, faded pink shirt and bright tie belong to the same vintage. **1972** J. ROSSITER *Rope for General Dietz* iii. 31 Her accent was a creamy 1969-vintage Roedean.

4. *attrib.*, as ***vintage-ball, -day, -dinner, -eve, feast, -festival, -god, -home*** (after *harvest-home*), ***-man***, etc.

1876 'OUIDA' *Winter City* xiv, For the Palestrina *vintage balls. **1857** EMERSON *Poems* 51 'Twas the *vintage-day of field and wood. **1838** MISS PARDOE *River & Desert* II. 31 A *vintage-dinner, at which I have just assisted. **1826** MRS. HEMANS *Forest Sanctuary* I. xliii, The hour, the scene,.. came floating o'er my mind—A golden *vintage-eve. *a* **1820** S. ROGERS *Jacquel.* Poems (1839) 24 Thro' Provence had ceased The vintage and the *vintage-feast. **1846** GROTE *Greece* (1869) I. 36 Even the spontaneous joy of the vintage-feast was conferred by the favour..of Dionysos. **1833** *Philolog. Museum* II. 297 The difficulty of assigning a *vintage festival to the month of February. **1877** *Encycl. Brit.* VII. 247 The lesser Dionysia..were held..in the month of December. This was a vintage festival. **1873** SYMONDS *Grk. Poets* ix. 276 The cultus of the *vintage-god [*sc.* Dionysus]. **1657** THORNLEY tr. *Longus' Daphnis & Chloe* 65 The young gallants thinking to keep the *Vintage holy-dayes. **1839** T. MITCHELL *Frogs of Aristoph.* Introd. p. cxix, The ingathering of grapes, and, if we may be allowed such a term, the *vintage-home which followed. **1800** MOORE *Anacreon* lix. 12 The choral song, the *vintage hymn Of rosy youths and virgins fair. **1706** STEVENS I, *Vendimiador*, a *Vintage-man that gathers the Grapes. **1694** MOTTEUX *Rabelais* v. xix. 29 An infinite number of little pimping Wine-presses, all full of *Vintagemongers, who were picking, examining, and raking the Grapes. **1860** PUSEY *Min. Proph.* 197 Where aforetime was the *vintage-shout in thankfulness for the ingathering, there..should be wailing. *c* **1820** S. ROGERS *Italy* (1839) 280 From the first hour, when *vintage-songs broke forth. **1836** EARL CARNARVON *Portugal & Gallicia* I. 94 Groups of vintagers.. were gathering grapes, and singing the vintage song. **1601** HOLLAND *Pliny* II. 148 Staphis..waxeth ripe..at *vintage time. **1671** MILTON *P.R.* IV. 15 As a swarm of flies in vintage time. **1731** MILLER *Gard. Dict.* s.v. *Vitis*, Dew is rarely wanting in Vintage-Time. **1820** SHELLEY *Prometh. Unb.* I. i. 574 'Tis the vintage-time for death and sin. **1885** PATER *Marius* xxvii. II. 222 To see their emperor living there.., his hands red at vintage-time with the juice of the grapes.

b. In sense 1 c, as ***vintage claret, class, wine***, etc. Also ***vintage chart, year*** (in quots. *fig.*).

1888 *Encycl. Brit.* XXIV. 608/2 The cheaper wines are an exception.., also those of the so-called 'vintage' class, which are the finest wines of a good year kept separate and shipped as the produce of that..year. **1895** *Westm. Gaz.* 31 Dec. 1/1 There does not seem to be much 'depression' in the market for vintage wines. **1900** *Ibid.* 1 Sept. 2/1 We are allowed to make our little bids for fame with clean shirts, cut hair, sound coats, vintage clarets. **1933** T. E. LAWRENCE *Let.* 1 Aug. (1938) 773 Rather a vintage year, for books. **1964** A. LAUNAY *Caviare & After* xv. 104 If you arm yourself with a vintage chart—easily obtainable from most wine merchants—you can learn the best years for the best wines. **1973** *Country Life* 15 Nov. 1542/3 Characteristic and impish Lowry of a fine vintage year 1960. **1985** *Times* 1 May 23/5 Britain's offshore oil and gas industry achieved a vintage year in 1984.

c. *transf.* Denoting an old style or model of something, esp. a vehicle; **vintage car**, a motor car made between 1905 (or 1917) and 1930; cf. ***veteran car*** s.v. VETERAN *sb.* 3.

1928 M. ARLEN *Lily Christine* ii. 23 You should see mine in London—a vintage Buick. **1933** *Sat. Even. Post* 13 May 4/2 Alfred P. Sloan tries out a vintage model automobile. **1950** T. GUTHRIE in *Plays of Year 1949–50* III. 569 Goes on working at her vintage telephone. **1958** *Listener* 21 Aug. 261/2 The details of a vintage aircraft or an early locomotive. **1965** *Guardian* 6 Nov. 3/8 A 'veteran' is any car made before December 31, 1904. From January 1, 1905 to December 31, 1910, the definition..is 'Edwardian', and from then to December 31, 1930, cars are classified as 'Vintage'. **1979** J. LEASOR *Love & Land Beyond* iii. 32 The familiar vintage car smell of hot oil and old metal and carnauba wax polish. **1985** *New Yorker* 27 May 31/1 A debonair gentleman..wearing a vintage tweed jacket.

d. Characteristic of the best period of a person's work, etc.; classic.

1939 *Country Life* 11 Feb. 147/1 With a few minor reservations, this [play] may be recommended as vintage Coward. **1959** R. GANT *World in Jug* 7 My name is Larry Alden and maybe you'll only know it if you have a long memory or a stack of vintage jazz records. **1972** *Guardian* 25 Jan. 9/3 It was pure vintage Deauville to the background of Henry Hall type music. **1977** D. MACKENZIE *Raven & Kamikaze* i. 20 The Pole's..tone was compassionate. 'She is in love with me.' This was vintage Zaleski. 'Of course,' said Raven.

'vintage, *v.* [f. prec.]

1. *intr.* (See quot.) *rare.*

1598 FLORIO, *Vendemmiare*, to vintage, to gather grapes, to make wine. **1893** SOMERVILLE & 'ROSS' *Vine Country* viii. 153 A little, incredibly bowed woman, who had been vintaging here at Quinault for the last eighty years. **1923** F. STARK *Let.* 16 Sept. (1974) I. 77 The people here are vintaging... All the country from Cette to this place is vine. **1975** P. V. PRICE *Taste of Wine* v. 94/2 In many vintages, such as 1964, they can make wines quite different from those of the Medoc, because being further south they vintage a little earlier.

2. *trans.* **a.** To strip (vines or a vineyard) of grapes at the vintage. Also *fig.* ? *Obs.*

1618 BACON *Lett.* (1734) 87, I humbly beseech his Majestie that these royal boughs of forfeiture may not be vintaged or cropped by private suitors. **1648** tr. *Senault's Paraphr. Job* 222 They either carry away the corne which is not yet cut, or pillage the vines which are not yet vintaged. **1694** MOTTEUX *Rabelais* IV. xxiii. 99 The Devil take me..if the Close of Sevillé had not been all gather'd, vintag'd, glean'd and destroy'd.

b. To gather (grapes) in order to make wine; to make (wine) from gathered grapes.

Usually with special reference to the production of wine of fine quality (cf. VINTAGE *sb.* 1 c).

1888 *Encycl. Brit.* XXIV. 605/2 If..a first growth is vintaged a little too late and does not succeed so well as some second growths. **1890** *Pall Mall G.* 29 Sept. 3/2 The Department of the Marne, where the true sparkling champagne is vintaged.

'vintager. [f. VINTAGE *sb.* + -ER.]

1. One who gathers grapes in the vintage; a labourer or worker at the vintage.

1589 FLEMING *Virg. Georg.* II. 21 The grapes which Lesbian vintager doth crop from Methym vine. **1611** COTGR., *Vendengeur*, a Vintager, or vine-reaper. **1706** PHILLIPS (ed. Kersey), *Vintager*, a Vine-reaper, or Grape-gatherer. **1731** MILLER *Gard. Dict.* s.v. *Vitis*, Because there are green Grapes that the Vintagers ought not to gather and mingle with the others. **1796** H. HUNTER tr. *St.-Pierre's Stud. Nat.* (1799) II. 454 The basket of the vintager, and the apron of the reaper. **1806** W. TAYLOR in *Ann. Rev.* IV. 719 The annual dances of the vintagers, in which they smeared their faces with lees of wine. **1846** LANDOR *Story of Santander* Wks. II. 464 The officer was..threatening both vintagers and mules for their intractability. **1887** PATER *Imag. Portraits* 167 The sharp sound of a bell—death-bell, perhaps, or only a crazy summons to the vintagers.

fig. **1680** H. MORE *Apocal. Apoc.* 147 They are the same that are pressed here by Christ's Vintagers or Grape-pressers. **1865** MOZLEY *Mirac.* i. iii. 207 An element of prophecy..unfolding itself beneath the fostering care of the Divine vintager.

b. *transf.* Also *attrib.*

1607 TOPSELL *Four-f. Beasts* 6 A..hill, abounding in these beasts [*sc.* monkeys], who are a great hinderance to the poore vintagers of the countrey of Calechut, for they will climbe into the high palm trees,..breaking the vessels set to receiue the Wine. **1829** T. L. PEACOCK *Misfort. Elphin* 16 From the flower cups of summer on field and on tree Our mead cups are filled by the vintager bee. **1871** LOWELL *Study Wind.* 7 A dozen of these winged vintagers [*sc.* robins] bustled out from among the leaves.

2. (With capital initial.) A bright star in the constellation of Virgo.

After L. *vindēmiātor*: cf. VINDEMIATRIX.

1588 ASHLEY *Wagenar's Mariners Mirr.* B j, Præuindemiatrix, The Vintager. **1601** HOLLAND *Pliny* I. 604 Eleven daies before the Calends of September,..the star named in Latine Vindemiator, *i.* the Vintager, beginneth to shew in the morning.

'vintaging, *vbl. sb.* [f. VINTAGE *v.*] The action or process of gathering the grapes at the vintage.

1830 H. N. COLERIDGE *Grk. Poets* (1834) 218 Then follow successive representations of a city at peace,..of reaping, of sheaf-binding, of vintaging. **1870** MORRIS *Earthly Par.* III. 280 And timorous must he let the time go by For vintaging. **1890** O. CRAWFURD *Round Calendar in Portugal* 198 The maize-harvest..comes just after the vintaging of the grapes.

†vintaine. *Obs. rare.* Also 5 vintayne. [a. OF. *vintaine, -eine, -ene*, (also mod.F.) *vingtaine* (= Pr. and Pg. *vintena*, Sp. *veintena*), f. *vingt* twenty.] A company of twenty soldiers, etc.

13.. *Sir Beues* (A.) 3367 Make we þre vintaine, þat be gode and certaine! þe ferste ich wile me self out lede. *c* **1400** MAUNDEV. (Roxb.) xxv. 114 þai er wele arayd and ordaynd by thowsands, hundreths and vintaynes.

‖vintem (vintẽ). *Hist.* Forms: α. 6 vintiin (vinton), 7 ventin, vinteen, 8 vinten, 8–9 vintin. β. 8–9 vintain. γ. 8–9 vintem. [Pg. *vintem*, f. *vinte* twenty.] In the coinage of Portugal and countries subsequently colonized from there: A small silver coin of the value of 20 reis; also, a copper coin of the same value.

α. **1584** BARRET in Hakluyt *Voy.* (1599) II. I. 274, 5 vintons make a tanga, and 4 vintenas make a tanga of base money. **1598** W. PHILLIP tr. *Linschoten* I. xxxv. 69/1 There is likewise a reckoning of *Vintiins*, which is not likewise in coyne, but onely named in telling: of these foure good, and fiue badde doe make a *Tangas*. **1662** J. DAVIES tr. *Mandelslo's Trav.* II. (1669) 86 Eight of these *Basarucques* make a *Ventin*. **1698** FRYER *Acc. E. India & P.* 207 The *Tango*, 5 *Vinteens*. **1743** BULKELEY & CUMMINS *Voy. S. Seas* 206 We had hitherto been suppli'd at the Rate of eight Vintins each Man *per* Day. **1775** TWISS *Trav. Portug. & Sp.* 22 Exacting a *vinten*, or about three halfpence per head. **1805** T. LINDLEY *Voy. Brazil* 260 The ships..sell the beef on board by retail, at two vintins a pound.

β. **1728** CHAMBERS *Cycl.* s.v. *Coin*, Portuguese Coins... The Vintain, whereof they have two sorts, the one Silver, and the other Billon. **1819** J. H. VAUX *Mem.* I. 218 They stop, and empty their [water-] vessel, for which they receive a vintain.

γ. **1736** CHANDLER *Hist. Persec.* 183 Dr. Geddes tells us of one..who was allowed no more than three Vintems a day; a Vintem is about an English penny farthing. **1801** SOUTHEY in C. C. Southey *Life* (1849) II. 130 The ferry price varies ..from one vintem to nine,—that is, from a penny to a shilling. **1839** *Penny Cycl.* XV. 326/2 At Rio de Janeiro.. there are vintems of copper also current for 20 rees. **1856** H. OWEN *Here & There in Portugal* 122, I purchased..for three *vintems* (a trifle more than three-pence), a capital figure of a negro dandy.

†vintenary. *Obs. rare.* Also -are. [ad. med.L. *vintēnārius*, f. *vintēnum* twenty: cf. next.] A military officer in command of twenty men.

c **1450** *Contin. Brut* 540 Sir Iohn Ward, knyght, with x Centenaries..and viij vyntenaries. *Ibid.* 541 Sir Howell Griffith..with..ij C and iij vintenares, and iiij McCC Walsh-men.

†vintener. *Obs. rare.* [ad. OF. *vintenier* (*vingt-*), f. *vintene* VINTAINE.] = prec.

c **1450** *Contin. Brut* 541 The nombre of þe retenue.., that is to say, of erles,..Constables, Centeners, capteyns, vynteners, Archers on horsbak [etc.]. **1533** [see next].

†vinteney. *Obs. rare.* [f. OF. *vintene, vinteine* VINTAINE.] = VINTAINE.

1533 *Chron. Calais* (Camden) 156 One vintener with his hole vinteney shall kepe the stand watche. *Ibid.* 157 The saide vintener and constables..shall not depart more than fyve of the vinteney and iij of the constables at one tyme.

†'vinter. *Obs.* Forms: α. 3 viniter, 5 vineter. β. 5 vintere, vynter, 5 vinter. [a. AF. *viniter, vineter, vyn-, vinter*, OF. and early mod.F. *vinet(t)ier* (= Pr. *vinatier*, It. *vinattiere*, Sp. *vinatero*, Pg. *vinhateiro*, med.L. *vīnētārius, vīnātārius*) wine-seller, f. L. *vīnum* wine.] A vintner.

1297 R. GLOUC. (Rolls) 11226 In þe souþhalf of þe toune & suþþe þe spicerie, Hii breke fram ende to oþer & dude al to robberie. Vor þe mer was viniter, hii breke þe viniterie. **1428** *E.E. Wills* (1882) 77 Iohn Toker, Citezein and Vineter of London. *c* **1430** LYDG. *Min. Poems* (Percy Soc.) 192 The vintere tretethe of his holsom wynes, Of gentille frute bostethe the gardener. **1486** *Rec. St. Mary at Hill* (1905) 10 Iohn Walworth, late Citezein & vynter of london.

Hence **†'vinteress, 'vintress** = VINTNERESS.

1681 RYCAUT tr. *Gracian's Critick* 111 The Nobles..were served with Cups of Gold, which a pritty Nimph, the Vinteress of this Babylon, filled with much Courtesie. **1727** BAILEY (vol. II), *Vintress*, a Woman Tavern-keeper.

vintiin, obs. form of VINTEM.

vintir, obs. Sc. form of WINTER.

vintner ('vɪntnə(r)). Forms: α. 5 vyntenere, -tyner, 5–6 -tener, 6 -tenar (*Sc.* ventennar), 6–7 vintener; 6 vyntoner, 7 vintoner. β. 5–6 vyntner(e, 6– vintner (8 vinctner). [Alteration of VINTER.] One who deals in or sells wine; a wine-merchant; †an innkeeper selling wine.

α. *c* **1430** LYDG. *Min. Poems* (Percy Soc.) 211 Masouns, carpenterys, of Yngelond and of Fraunce, Bakerys, browsterys, vyntenerys, with fressh lycour. *c* **1440** *Promp. Parv.* 510 Vyntenere, *vinarius*. *c* **1470** *Cath. Angl.* 402/1 (Add. MS.), Vyntyner. **1526** *Pilgr. Perf.* (W. de W. 1531) 25 Or as the vyntenar gyueth frely to his customers or byers a taste of his wyne. **1530** in W. H. Turner *Select. Rec. Oxford* (1880) 91 No vyntoner shall set any wyne a broche. **1587** HARRISON *England* II. vi. (1877) I. 149 Such [wine] as was anie waies mingled or brued by the vintener. **1617** MORYSON *Itin.* III. 156 They had not our Vinteners fraud to mixe their Wines. **1636** J. TAYLOR (Water P.) *Trav. Signes Zodiack* A v b, All the worthy Company of Vintoners. **1669–70** MARVELL *Corr.* Wks. (Grosart) II. 301 One Mr. Wadlow, a vintener,..was represented as notoriously faulty.

β. *c* **1460** *Promp. Parv.* (Winch. MS.), Vyntnere, *vinarius*. **1483** *Cath. Angl.* 402/1 A vyntner.., *vinitor, merothecarius*.

1548 COOPER *Elyot's Dict.*, *Oenopola*,..a tauerner or vintner. 1570 B. GOOGE *Pop. Kingd.* IV. (1880) 54 Straight after this comes Vrban in, the Vintners God deuine. 1592 GREENE *Upst. Courtier* G ij, Now sir for the vintner, hee is an honest substantiall man, a friend to al good fellowes. 1605 BRETON *Old Man's Lesson* B ij, The Vintner, the Grocer, the Comfit-maker,..doe by the venting of their wares, the better maintaine their trades. 1657 TRAPP *Comm. Job* xxxiii. 3 They..may here learn..not to huckster the Word of God, or corrupt it with their own mixtures, as Vintners do their wines. 1687 *Lond. Gaz.* No. 2285/4 Charles Courtney.. Vintner and Innholder. 1725 W. HALFPENNY *Sound Building* List of Subs., Mr. Peter Hudson, of Richmond, Vinctner. 1772 JOHNSON in *Boswell* 6 April, Mr. Pitt might think it an advantageous thing for him to make him a vintner, and get him all the Portugal trade; but [etc.]. 1810 CRABBE *Borough* v. 195 Uncheck'd, the vintner still his poison vends. 1849 MACAULAY *Hist. Eng.* v. I. 633 Once, merely from a malignant whim, he staved all the wine in a vintner's cellar. 1880 DIXON *Windsor* III. xxxi. 306 A vintner was a big man in Elizabeth's time.

†**b.** ***merchant vintner.*** (Cf. MERCHANT *sb.* 1 and MERCHANT TAILOR, etc.) *Obs.*

1532-3 *Act 24 Hen. VIII*, c. 6 If at the tyme of any suche sale of Wyne purposed to be made, the merchaunt vyntener, or other owner..thereof, do..declare [etc.]. 1600 *Chester Pl.* Proëm. (Shaks. Soc.) 4 And you, worthy marchauntes vintners that nowe have plenty of wine, Amplifye the storie of those wise Kinges three.

Hence **'vintneress**, a female vintner. **'vintnership**, the occupation or position of a vintner. **'vintnery**, the trade of a vintner; wine-selling.

1641 J. JOHNSON *Acad. Love* 89 Hosts and Vint'neresses looke to your score. 1673 O. WALKER *Educ.* 67 He that lives abstemiously..needs not study the wholesomnes of this meat,..nor is critical in cookery and vintnership. 1816 STRUTHERS *Poet. Wks.* (1850) I. 148 Before engaging in the tempting career, let them consider..how they will enjoy a Vintnership. 1837 CARLYLE *Fr. Rev.* II. v. ii, Unless..the father of him did, in an unexceptionable manner, perform Cookery and Vintnery in the Village of Ouarville.

†**'vinton.** *Obs.* [Obscurely related to VINTENARY or VINTENER.] (See quots.)

1610 HOLLAND *Camden's Brit.* I. 275 The whole country [i.e. the Isle of Wight] is divided into eleven parts: and every of them hath their severall Centoner, as one would say Centurion, their Vintons also, leaders as it were of twenty. 1751 *Eng. Gazetteer* s.v. *Wight-Island*, The militia here is divided into 11 bands, over each of which is an officer, called a centurion, though he commands more than 100 men; and the inferior officers are called vintons.

vinton, obs. f. VINTEM.

vintre, obs. f. VINE-TREE.

vintress: see VINTERESS.

vintry ('vɪntrɪ). Now *arch.* or *Hist.* Forms: 3 **viniterie**, 5 **vyntrye**, 6 **vyntry**, 5-6 **vyntre** (6 **ventre**), 6 **vyne-**, **vintree**, **-trie**, 6, 8 **vintrie**, 6- **vintry**. [f. VINTER + -Y: see -ERY.] A place where wine is sold or stored; a wine-shop; a wine-vault, or a number of these.

1297 [see VINTER]. 14.. *Voc.* in Wr.-Wülcker 619/30 *Vinitria*, vyntrye. 1593 'P. FOULFACE' *Bacchus' Bountie* C j, Claudius Tiberius,..for the zeale hee had to the vintree, was merely termed *Caldius Biberius mero.* 1901 *Contemp. Rev.* May 728 In the markets, restaurants, and vintries, Jesus saw ..that men's faces were not joyful and friendly.

b. With *the* (and usually with initial capital): A large wine-store formerly existing in the City of London; also, the immediate neighbourhood of this as a part of the city.

The name survives in the designation of the church St. Martin Vintry, now united with St. Michael Paternoster Royal and All Hallows the Great and Less.

a 1456 *Scogan's Moral Ballad* (heading), At a souper of feorthe merchande in the Vyntre in London. *a* 1529 SKELTON *Replyc.* Wks. 1843 I. 208 They iuge them selfe able to be Doctours of the chayre in the Uyntre At the Thre Cranes. 1556 *Chron. Gr. Friars* (Camden) 86 Item the furst day of Februarij [1554] the qwenes grace came..un-to the yelde-halle of Londone,..& wente home agayne by watter at the Crane in the ventre. 1557 in Marsden *Court Adm.* (Selden) II. 98 Haye Wharf or the Three Cranes in the Vynetree. 1598 STOW *Surv.* 191 Then next ouer against S. Martins church, is a large house builded of stone and timber with vaults for, the stowage of wines, & is called the Vintry. [1687 MIÉGE *Gt. Fr. Dict.* II, Vintry, a great Place for selling of Wine. (Hence in Phillips and Bailey).] 1790 PENNANT *London* 310 In this neighborhood was the great house called the *Vintrie*, with vast wine-vaults beneath. 1826 SCOTT *Woodst.* vii, The bargain was made in a cellar in the Vintry. 1836 HERBERT *Livery Companies Lond.* II. 630 St. Martin in the Vintry was, in the reign of Edward I, called St. Martin Baremanne church.

attrib. 1598 STOW *Surv.* 189 The Vintry ward, so called of Vintners, and of the Vintrie.

vinue, variant of VINEW *sb. Obs.*

viny ('vaɪnɪ), *a.* Also 6-7 **vinie**, 7, 9 **viney**. [f. VINE *sb.* + -Y.]

1. Of or pertaining to, of the nature of, vines; composed or consisting of vines.

1570 B. GOOGE *Pop. Kingd.* IV. 54 Fast vpon his head a crowne of vinie leaues is wounde. 1600 SURFLET *Countrie Farme* III. xxxiv. 498 Both the nourishment and vinie qualitie of the stocke of the said vine. 1624 *Trag. Nero* I. iii. in Bullen *Old Pl.* (1882) I. 19 Not Bacchus drawn from Nisa downe with Tigers, Curbing with viny rains their wilful heads. 1712 tr. *Pomet's Hist. Drugs* I. 143/2 *Coloquintida* is a Fruit..that grows upon a climbing or viny Plant. 1715 POPE *Iliad* II. 701 Whom strong Tyrinthe's lofty walls surround, And Epidaure with viny harvests crown'd. 1816 *Ann. Reg., Chron.* 539 The cranberry is of the low and viny kind. 1848 BAILEY *Festus* (ed. 3) 213 Who enter are by kindest angels clad..in robes Woven of sunset clouds, while viny wreaths Gemberries bearing form their coronals.

b. *fig.* Of an embrace: Clinging, close.

a 1586 SIDNEY *Arcadia* IV. (1605) 395 These unfortunate louers..not forgetting with vinie embracements, to giue any eye a perfect modell of affection.

2. Abounding in, full of, or covered with vines; bearing or producing vines.

1612 DRAYTON *Poly-olb.* xv. 109 The Skeld, the goodly Mose, the rich and Viny Rheine, Shall come to meet the Thames. 1633 P. FLETCHER *Pisc. Ecl.* II. xiii, From thence he furrow'd many a churlish sea, The viny Rhene, and Volgha's self did passe. 1680 MORDEN *Geog. Rect., Germany* (1685) 115 Wurtzburg,..environed with Meadows, Gardens, and Vinie Downs. 1729 FENTON *Ded. Lady Harley* 104 Wks. (1790) 375 Trophies, atchiev'd on Gallia's viny plains. 1735 THOMSON *Liberty* I. 58 Baiæ's viny coast; where peaceful seas..ever kiss the shore. 1841 W. SPALDING *Italy & It. Isl.* I. 277 The steepest, but most lovely of pleasure-paths, conducts through viny woods and white villas to [etc.]. 1854 F. TENNYSON *Days & Hours* 87 Whisper of viny hills, and sands of gold.

3. *Comb.*, as ***viny-crowned*** adj.

1819 WIFFEN *Aonian Hours* 122 'Twas too sad For viny-crowned Thalia.

vinyl ('vaɪnɪl, -aɪl). *Chem.* [f. L. *vin-um* + -YL.]

1. The organic radical or group $CH_2 = CH-$, which is equivalent to a molecule of ethylene with one hydrogen atom removed. Usu. *attrib.*

1863 WATTS *Dict. Chem.* I. 675 Bromide of vinyl, C^2H^2Br. 1873 —— *Fownes' Chem.* (ed. 11) 611 Vinyl alcohol..is produced by combining ethine or acetylene with sulphuric acid, whereby vinyl-sulphuric acid..is formed. *Ibid.* 612 The univalent radical vinyl..may be supposed to exist in it [vinyl alcohol].

2. a. = POLYVINYL b. Freq. *attrib.*

1939 *Nature* 13 May 787/2 Resins more recently developed, such as vinyl and polystyrene, are slowly making headway. 1951 R. MAYER *Artist's Hand-bk. Materials & Techniques* iii. 152 The most promising synthetic varieties [of resin] at present are the alkyd, acrylic, and vinyl types. 1957 *Times* 18 Nov. 11/2 An unbreakable doll of vinyl, a glamorous young lady with elegant nylon-clad legs, costing 9 guineas. 1962 *B.B.C. Handbk.* 204 L.P. vinyl records giving basic pronunciation rules. 1969 J. H. STICKELMEYER in W. R. R. Park *Plastics Film Technol.* i. 7 Development of shrink wrapping techniques..has brightened the future for vinyls. 1976 P. LIVELY *Stitch in Time* viii. 98 There is paint that is non-drip and paint that is vinyl or emulsion and paint that is specially good for this, that or the other. 1982 *Sci. Amer.* July 54/1 Most synthetic organic materials such as vinyl or polyethylene are electrically insulating.

b. *spec.* a covering material or fabric made of or containing polyvinyl.

1959 *House & Garden* July 11/2 (Advt.), Dining-chairs upholstered in washable vinyl. 1970 *Interior Design* Dec. 753/3 The walls are papered with a pale grey vinyl. 1978 S. BRILL *Teamsters* vii. 263 The inside of the tractor..was lined along the doors, the seats, and the dashboard in brown vinyl.

c. As the material of which gramophone records are made (so ***piece of vinyl***). Also, a record. *colloq.*

1976 *New Musical Express* 31 July 27/1 A trio of knock out vinyl magnum opi, the like of which are not often to be heard on our sound systems. 1976 *Zigzag* Apr. 26/1 This is as depressing a piece of vinyl as I've listened to in many a full moon. 1977 *Ripped & Torn* VI. 6/2, I had rushed home, clutching this piece of shiny vinyl to my chest. 1980 *Musicians Only* 26 Apr. 12/3 He can continually judge the results on vinyl. 1984 *Sounds* 1 Dec. 24/2 When that song.. was released at the beginning of this month as the band's first single, the Immaculate Fools proved they could cut it equally well on vinyl.

3. *attrib.* and *Comb.*, as (sense 2), ***vinyl-coated, -covered, -faced, -surfaced*** adjs.; (sense 1) **vinyl acetate**, a colourless liquid ester, $CH_2CH{\cdot}O{\cdot}CO{\cdot}CH_3$, used in the production of polyvinyl acetate and other commercially important polymers; **vinyl chloride**, a colourless toxic gas, CH_2CHCl, used in the production of polyvinyl chloride and other commercially important polymers; **vinyl resin**, any resin (RESIN *sb.* 3) that is composed of polyvinyl compounds.

[1902 *Jrnl. Chem. Soc.* LXXXII. I. 256 Sodium vinyl-acetate is much less soluble in alcohol than sodium crotonate.] 1915 *Chem. Abstr.* IX. 2156 By acting with chem. rays on vinyl esters (vinyl acetate or vinyl chloracetate) solid masses are obtained..which..serve as a substitute for celluloid and like substances. 1974 *Encycl. Brit. Micropædia* VIII. 104/2 In addition to its conversion to polyvinyl acetate, vinyl acetate undergoes similar reactions with many other compounds. 1872 *Jrnl. Chem. Soc.* XXV. 891 Vinyl chloride undergoes a change by the action of sunlight, producing an isomeride. 1933 [see *polyvinyl chloride* s.v. POLYVINYL a]. 1978 *N.Y. Times* 30 Mar. A15/1 Fifty of the train's 116 cars left the tracks..and a tanker loaded with highly toxic vinyl chloride exploded soon afterward. 1967 *Jane's Surface Skimmer Systems 1967–68* 47/1 The structure is decked in vinyl-coated nylon fabric, which is also used for the skirt. 1970 A. ROSS *Manchester Thing* 148 Two vinyl-covered kitchen chairs. 1977 'E. CRISPIN' *Glimpses of Moon* i. 11 The furniture was all modern, from the oak counter..to the green glass-topped tables and the matching vinyl-covered chairs. 1960 *Times* 29 Nov. 2/4 Felt-backed vinyl-faced..flooring. 1934 W. DAVIS *Adv. of Sci.* xiii. 141 The great versatility of the vinyl resins was strikingly demonstrated in a house which the Carbide and Carbon Chemicals Corporation erected. 1942 GETTENS & STOUT *Painting Materials* 3 Chemically, they [*sc.* polyacrylic resins] are closely related to the vinyl resins. 1943 *Electronic Engin.* XVI. 216/3 The variation of dielectric properties with plasticiser content is examined for the vinyl resins. 1983 *Which?* Oct. 453/1 These are water-thinned paints usually based on vinyl resins. 1978 *Morecambe Guardian* 14 Mar. 6/6 Washable gloss paint and vinyl-surfaced wall coverings are immensely childproof.

vinylidene (vaɪ'nɪlɪdiːn, vaɪ'naɪlɪdiːn). *Chem.* [f. VINYL + -IDENE.] The bivalent radical $CH_2 = C<$; freq. *attrib.* Cf. POLYVINYLIDENE.

1898 *Jrnl. Chem. Soc.* LXXIV. I. 188 Acetic anhydride converts it first into oxanilide, and subsequently into vinylidene oxanilide. 1940 [see SARAN]. 1980 *Chem. in Brit.* XVI. 473/1 Vinylidene, indole or leuco crystal violet are used as the colour formers.., and carbon tetrabromide or iodoform as the activator.

Vinylite ('vaɪnɪlaɪt, -aɪl-). Also **vinylite**. [f. VINYL + -ITE[1].] A proprietary name for a vinyl resin used esp. in the manufacture of gramophone records.

1929 *Official Gaz.* (U.S. Patent Office) 28 May 852/2 Carbide & Carbon Chemicals Corporation, New York... *Vinylite* for artificial resins in powder form or in form of plates or sheets and molding mixtures containing such resins. 1929 *Trade Marks Jrnl.* 25 Sept. 1635/2 *Vinylite*... Synthetic resin sold in slabs, sheets, bars and tubes for industrial purposes and moulding materials made of synthetic resin. Carbide and Carbon Chemicals Corporation.., New York. 1936 [see PLEXIGLAS]. 1956 A. HUXLEY *Adonis & Alphabet* 123 We must depend on the vinylite record and the slow-speed phonograph for any large-scale revival of spoken literature. 1974 *Encycl. Brit. Macropædia* XVII. 53/2 In 1948, fine-groove records of clear Vinylite were introduced by two different manufacturers. 1977 *Gramophone* May 1762/3 The ace up the CBS sleeve, which really made the LP viable, was the changeover from noisy, abrasive, brittle shellac to quiet, soft, unbreakable vinylite for the new disc material.

vinylogous (vaɪ'nɪləgəs), *a. Chem.* [f. VINYL + -LOGUE + -OUS (or directly after *analogous*).] Of, pertaining to, or being compounds that have the same molecular structure except for one or more $-CH{:}CH-$ groups. Hence **'vinylogue** (U.S. **-log**), a vinylogous compound; **vi'nylogy**, the relationships between vinylogous compounds.

1935 R. C. FUSON in *Chem. Rev.* XVI. 2 It is proposed to term such a group of compounds a vinylogous series. The members of a vinylogous series will then be vinylogs of one another. *Ibid.*, In this series the operation of the principle of vinylogy may be illustrated by a comparison of the esters of saturated fatty acids with their vinylogs, the α, β-unsaturated esters. 1966 *McGraw-Hill Encycl. Sci. & Technol.* XIV. 326/2 The principle of vinylogy may be used to explain why *o-* and *p*-nitrochlorobenzene are readily hydrolyzed to the corresponding nitrophenols, whereas the meta isomer is not. 1977 *Nature* 14 Apr. 660/2 The reaction (21)→(22) is not, as stated, a vinylogous Norrish type I reaction. 1978 A. J. BIRCH in Porter & Fitzsimmons *Further Perspectives Organic Chem.* 15 The decarboxylation needs only very mild conditions, a fact which suggests intervention of a β-keto acid or a vinylogue during the processes.

Vinylon ('vaɪnɪlɒn). Also **vinylon**. [f. VINYL + *-on* (perh. after NYLON).] Any of a class of synthetic fibres made from polyvinyl alcohol treated with formaldehyde which are used esp. in the manufacture of water-resistant fabrics.

1952 *Chem. Abstr.* XLVI. 1260 (*heading*) Pilot-plant manufacture of the synthetic fiber 'Vinylon'. 1955 KIRK & OTHMER *Encycl. Chem. Technol.* XIV. 718 Fibers of polyvinyl alcohol, spun from water solution and treated with formaldehyde, as developed in Japan (Vinylon,..[etc.]), have good strength, abrasion resistance, and heat retention. 1965 *Economist* 23 Jan. 362/3 The plant will produce 50 tons of vinylon a day. 1975 *Textile Res. Jrnl.* XLV. 591/1 Tetoron is a polyester containing a benzene ring; Vinylon has no benzene ring.

Vinyon ('vɪnjən). [f. VINY(L + *-on*, after *rayon*, *cotton*.] Any of several synthetic fibres which are copolymers of vinyl chloride with other vinyl compounds.

1938 *Newsweek* 14 Nov. 10/2 An important company's chemists are experimenting with another silk-like yarn called 'Vinyon', for making hosiery, to rival du Pont's new 'nylon'. 1954 KIRK & OTHMER *Encycl. Chem. Technol.* XIII. 831 The low softening point made later Vinyon fibers suitable for the production of sculptured carpet fabrics, nonwoven fabrics, paper, felts, and other such specialized products... However, inability to withstand boiling water permanently relegated Vinyon fiber to specialized uses. 1965 A. J. HALL *Standard Handbk. Textiles* (ed. 6) i. 61 The original Vinyon having a low softening temperature has now been almost completely replaced by Vinyon N and dynel, especially for textile purposes. 1975 J. LABARTHE *Elem. Textiles* iv. 177 Vinyon fibers are made by three manufacturers in the United States at the present time.

viol ('vaɪəl), *sb.*[1] Forms: α. 5 **vyell**, 6-7 **viall**, **vyall** (6 **wyall**), 7 **vial**. β. 6 **veol**, 6-7 **viole** (7 **vyolle**), **vioII** (7 **wioll**), 7- **viol** (7 **vyol**). [Orig. ad. AF. and OF. *viele*, *vielle* (see VIELLE), but subsequently assimilated to, or replaced by, OF. and F. *viole* (= It., Sp., Pg. *viola*, Prov. *viula*).

That OF. *viole* and *vielle* represent earlier **vidule* and **videlle* (with variant forms of the diminutive suffix) is indicated by the med.L. *vidula*, *vitula*. On the relation of these to Germanic forms, see the note to FIDDLE *sb.*]

1. a. A musical instrument (in common use from the fifteenth to the eighteenth century) having five, six, or seven strings and played by means of a bow. Now *Hist.* or *arch.*

α. 1483 CAXTON *G. de la Tour* k vj, Syre Geffroy called hym before hym and demaunded hym where his vyell and clauy-cordes were. *a* 1500–34 *Cov. Corpus Chr. Pl.* I. 538 The whyle thatt I do resst, Trompettis, viallis and othur armone Schall bles the wakyng of my maieste. *a* 1533 LD. BERNERS *Huon* li. 170 He spyed lyeng beside hym an harp and a vyall wheron he coude well play. 1540 *Rutland MSS.* (Hist. MSS. Comm.) IV. 304 To a man to helpe to bryng the wyalls betwixt Croxton and Belwer, ij *d.* 1578 E. CLIFFE in Hakluyt *Voy.* (1600) III. 751 They were exceedingly delighted with the sound of the trumpet, and vialles. 1626 BACON *Sylva* §102 If any Man think that the String of the Bow, and the String of the Viall, are neither of them Equall Bodies, . . he is in an Errour. 1664 PEPYS *Diary* 28 Sept., So home, and find Mercer playing on her Vyall, which is a pretty instrument. 1684 BUNYAN *Pilgr.* II. (1847) 336 Christiana . . could play upon the Vial.

β. 1542 *Acc. Ld. High Treas. Scot.* VIII. 149 To be . . x pair of hois to the four playerris on the veolis, four trumpettis of ware, and twa taburnerris. 1560 BIBLE (Genev.) *Amos* v. 23 For I wil not heare the melodie of thy violes. 1581 MARBECK *Bk. of Notes* 545 Sing vnto him with Viole, and instrument of ten strings. 1604 DEKKER *King's Entertainm.* Wks. (1873) I. 307 Nine Boyes . . sang the dittie following to their viols and other instruments. *a* 1629 HINDE *J. Bruen* iii. (1641) 10 By occasion of Musitians and a chest of Viols kept in the house, he was drawn by desire and delight into the Dancing-schoole. 1676 T. MACE *Music's Mon.* 247 The Viol is an Instrument . . very much in use. 1742 YOUNG *Nt. Th.* VIII. 745 Dost call the bowl, the viol, and the dance, Loud mirth, mad laughter? 1776 HAWKINS *Hist. Music* IV. III. vii. 339 Compositions of many parts adapted to viols, of which there are many. 1801 BUSBY *Dict. Mus.* s.v., The viol was for a long while in such high esteem as to dispute the pre-eminence with the harp. 1839 LONGF. *Black Knight* v, Pipe and viol call the dances, Torch-light through the high halls glances. 1875 FORTNUM *Maiolica* x. 88 On another [cup] are the figures of a gentleman and a lady who plays the viol, in the costume of the 15th or early 16th century.

†**b.** One who plays a viol. *Obs. rare.*

1540 in *Vicary's Anat.* (1888) App. xii. 241 Item, or Hans Highorne, Viall, wagis, xxxiij s. iiij d. 1647 L. HAWARD *Crown Rev.* 25 Musicians and Players, . . Six Sackbuts: Eight Vials: Three Drumsteds.

2. a. With distinguishing terms, denoting esp. the form or tone of the instrument.

See also BASS-VIOL, gamba VIOL DA GAMBA² 1 (quots. 1598, 1710), *lyra viol* LYRA 5, and VIOL DA GAMBA.

1611 CORYAT *Crudities* 250, I heard much good musicke, . . especially that of a treble violl. 1662 [see VIOL DA GAMBA 1]. 1664 PEPYS *Diary* 5 Oct., The new instrument was brought called the Arched Viall, . . being tuned with lutestrings, and played on with kees like an organ. 1724 *Short Explic. For. Wds. in Mus. Bks., Viola Bastardo*, a Bastard Viol, which is a Bass Violin, strung and fretted like a Bass Viol. 1730 BAILEY (fol.), *Viola Tenoro*, a Tenor-Viol. Ital. 1836 DUBOURG *Violin* i. (1878) 9 The *viol* class—consisting of the *viol d'amore*, or treble viol; the *viol da braccia*, or tenor viol; and the *viol da gamba*, or great viol. 1889 *Grove's Dict. Mus.* IV. 267 *Viola di Fagotto* (Bassoon Viol), a name sometimes given to the Viola Bastarda.

b. *viol d'amore* or *d'amour* (see quot. 1801).

Cf. *viola d'amore* s.v. VIOLA². The F. form *viole d'amour* is also occasionally employed.

a 1700 EVELYN *Diary* 20 Nov. 1679, The *viol d'amore* of 5 wyre-strings plaied on with a bow. 1760–72 H. BROOKE *Fool of Qual.* (1809) III. 145 The psaltery, the *viol d'amor*, and other instruments. 1801 BUSBY *Dict. Mus.*, *Viol d'Amour*, or *Love Viol*, a viol, or violin, furnished with six brass or steel wires, instead of sheep's-gut, and usually played with a bow. [1856 MRS. C. CLARKE tr. *Berlioz' Instrumentation* 29 The viole-d'amour is peculiarly appropriate to chords of three, four, or more notes.] 1880 SHORTHOUSE *J. Inglesant* xxiii, If you could accompany me for some months, with your viol d'amore, across the mountains. 1889 *Daily News* 25 Jan. 2/2 Two performers upon that once obsolete but recently revived instrument, the viol d'amore.

†**3.** A variety of organ-stop. *Obs.*⁻¹

1688 BER. SMITH in Hopkins *Organ* (1870) 453 Choir Organ . . . A Violl and Violin, of mettle, . . 61 pipes, . . 12 foote.

4. *attrib.* and *Comb.*, as *viol bow, -case, class, -lesson, -play, species, -string*; *viol-maker, -tuning*.

a 1668 DAVENANT *Play-house to Let* Wks. (1673) 76 A man may bring a Pageant through the streets As privatly upon my Lord Mayor's day, As a burden of Viol-cases hither. 1674 PLAYFORD *Music* 101 In the choice of your Viol Bow, let it be proportioned to the Viol you use. 1676 T. MACE *Music's Mon.* 258 This . . may suffice for the Best Directions in Viol-Play. *Ibid.* 264 Viol-Lessons of all sorts of Forms, and Shapes; Suited to the Five Best of the Viol-Tunings. 1687 MIÈGE *Gt. Fr. Dict.* II, A Viol-Maker, *un Faiseur de Violes.* 1776 HAWKINS *Hist. Music* IV. III. vii. 342 That sweet and delicate tone, which distinguishes the viol species. 1836 [see 2]. 1849 D. G. ROSSETTI *Let.* 8 Oct. (1965) I. 71 The hand trails weak upon the viol-string That sobs. 1897 H. N. HOWARD *Footsteps Proserpine* 7 Life is the viol-string, Love is the melody.

Hence **viol** *v. intr.*, to play the viol. *rare*⁻¹.

1865 J. M. LUDLOW *Epics Mid. Ages* II. 212 A thousand dancing, and a thousand violling.

† **'viol**, *sb.*² *Naut. Obs.* Also 7 **vial, violl, vyoll**; 8–9 **voyol**, 9 **voyal**. [Of obscure origin.] (See later quots.)

1627 CAPT. SMITH *Seaman's Gram.* ii. 8 The violl is fastened together at both ends with an eye or two, with a wall knot, and seased together. *c* 1635 CAPT. BOTELER *Dial. Sea Services* (1685) 236. 1667 DAVENANT & DRYDEN *Tempest* I. i, *Must within.* Our vial's broke. *Vent. within.* Tis but our vial-block has given way. 1711 W. SUTHERLAND *Shipbuild. Assist.* 153 Viol cabl'd, as big as the Fore Stay. *Ibid.* 165 *Viol*, a large Hawser used to heave in the Cable. 1769 FALCONER *Dict. Marine* (1780), *Voyol*, a large rope used to unmoor, or heave up the anchors of a ship, by transmitting the effort of the capstern to the cables. 1841 R. H. DANA *Seaman's Man.* 133 *Viol*, or *Voyal*, a larger messenger sometimes used in weighing an anchor by a capstan. [Cf. 1867 SMYTH *Sailor's Word-bk.* 713 *Viol*, or *Voyal*, a large messenger formerly used to assist in weighing an anchor by the capstan.] 1869 W. M. THOMAS tr. *Hugo's Toilers of Sea* 191 Its chain was there, and . . might still be of service, unless the strain of the voyal should break away the planking.

b. *attrib.*, esp. in *viol-block*.

1667 [see above]. 1694 in *Navy Board Lett.* xxix. 833 Blocks. Vyoll, of 54 inch. 1751 SMOLLETT *Per. Pic.* lxxii, He may man his capstans and viol block, if he wool; but he'll as soon heave up the Pike of Teneriff, as bring his anchor aweigh! 1794 *Rigging & Seamanship* I. 157 *Voyol or Viol Block* is a large single-sheaved block . . . It is used in heaving up the anchor. [1867 SMYTH *Sailor's Word-bk.*, *Viol* or *Voyol Block*, a large single-sheaved block through which the messenger passed when the anchor was weighed by the fore or jeer capstan. *Ibid.*, This voyal-purchase.]

viol, obs. form of VIAL.

viola¹ ('vaɪələ). [a. L. *viola* violet.]

†**1.** The violet. Also *fig. Obs. rare.*

c 1430 LYDG. *Minor Poems* (1911) 300 Haile, fresshe Rose, planted in Iericho! Swettest viola, that neuer shal fade. *c* 1480 HENRYSON *Fables, Lion & Mouse* 16 The Rosis reid, . . The Prymeros, and the Purpour Uiola.

2. A large genus of herbaceous plants of the order *Violaceæ*, including violets and pansies; a plant or species of this genus.

1731 MILLER *Gard. Dict.* [as Latin generic name, and so in many later Dicts.] 1843 *Penny Cycl.* XXVI. 345/2 The principle . . has been separated by Boullay from some species of Viola. *Ibid.*, The capsule is like Viola. 1888 *Encycl. Brit.* XXIV. 241/2 The violas are credited with powerful emetic and diuretic properties. 1904 *Westm. Gaz.* 23 July 4/2 The Alpine viola, in wondrous shades of mauve and violet and purple, stands an inch above the grass.

b. A hybrid garden-plant of this genus, distinguished from the pansy by a more delicate and uniform colouring of the flowers.

1871 *Field* II. 250/2 There is still a good early-flowering white Viola wanted. 1888 *Encycl. Brit.* XXIV. 241/2 'Bedding violas,' which differ from pansies in some slight technical details, have been raised by crossing *V. lutea* with *V. calcarata.* 1897 *Westm. Gaz.* 22 Nov. 1/3 Patches of pale mauve and purple show where colonies of violas and pansies are in bloom.

attrib. 1871 *Field* II. 250/2 Another manifest want in the Viola tribe. 1896 *Daily News* 22 June 3/5 Viola Show.—The first show of the National Viola Society was held on Saturday afternoon.

3. *attrib.* In chemical terms denoting substances derived from the violet or pansy.

1868 WATTS *Dict. Chem.* V. 1001 *Violin*, or *Viola-Emetin*, an emetic substance contained, according to Boullay, in all parts of the common violet. 1887 *Buck's Handbk. Med. Sci.* V. 490/2 Little, if anything, of value has been found in pansy; a glucoside, violaquercitrin, of probably no active properties, and a little salicylic acid.

viola² (vɪ'əʊlə). [a. It. and Sp. *viola*, = F. *viole* VIOL *sb.*¹]

1. a. A four-stringed musical instrument slightly larger than a violin; the alto or tenor violin.

1797 SOUTHEY *Lett. Resid. Spain* xv. 265 The King of Spain wished to hear his daughter play on the viola, and an express was . . sent to Lisbon for her instrument! 1801 BUSBY *Dict. Mus.*, *Viola*, a tenor violin. . . The part it takes in concert is between that of the bass and the second violin. 1845 E. HOLMES *Mozart* 14 The father . . took the bass part on the viola, Wenzl played the first violin, I the second. 1891 MEREDITH *One of our Conq.* xxviii, Colney brought his viola for a duet.

attrib. 1856 MRS. C. CLARKE tr. *Berlioz' Instrumentation* 25 Viola players were always taken from among the refuse of violinists.

b. One who plays the viola.

1894 *Daily News* 25 Apr. 5 Herr Ludwig Strauss, for many years viola in the quartet at the Monday Popular Concerts.

c. A variety of organ-stop.

1876 HILES *Catech. Organ* ix. (1878) 65 *Viola*, an open stop of narrow measure, and a particularly soft and agreeable . . tone.

2. a. *viola da* (also *di*) *gamba*, = VIOL DA GAMBA 1. Also *viola da gambist*, one who plays this, a viol da gambist.

1724 *Short Explic. For. Wds. in Mus. Bks.*, *Viola Da Gamba*, is the same as *Viola Basso*, or Bass Viol. 1787 *Ann. Reg., Chron.* 210/1 The Viola di Gamba is not an instrument in general use; and will perhaps die with him, but his performance rendered it exquisitely charming. 1885 *Daily News* 17 Aug. 6/1 (Stanf.), The early 18th century room contains the spinet, the viola da gamba, and the viola d'amore. 1977 *Early Music* Apr. 274 For viola da gambists there will be individual tuition.

b. = VIOL DA GAMBA 2.

1876 HILES *Catech. Organ* ix. (1878) 66 *Viola di Gamba*, or *Gamba*, . . is of tin or metal, and the tone is soft, and somewhat cutting. 1889 E. J. PAYNE in Grove *Dict. Mus.* IV. 267 Under the incorrect title of Viola da Gamba it designates an organ stop of 8 ft. pitch, with open pipes, in the choir organ.

3. *viola d'amore* (or †*d'amour*): see VIOL¹ 2 b.

1724 *Short Explic. For. Wds. in Mus. Bks.*, *Viola D'Amour*, a kind of Treble Viol, strung with Wire, and so called because of its soft and sweet Tone. 1885 [see 2]. 1889 *Grove's Dict. Mus.* IV. 267.

4. With other distinguishing terms: **viola bastarda** = *lyra viol* s.v. LYRA 5; **viola da braccio** [lit. 'of the arm'], any member of the violin family, as opposed to a *viol da gamba*; *spec.* an alto violin, a viola; **viola pomposa**, an 18th-cent. viola with an additional string.

1724 Viola bastarda [see VIOL *sb.*¹ 2 a]. 1980 *Early Music* Apr. 250 (Advt.), The *viola bastarda* style of playing was a highly developed idiom that involved frequent changes of register. 1864 SANDYS & FORSTER *Hist. Violin* viii. 97 Vincentio Galilei, the father of the great astronomer, was an able writer on music, and in 1582 names the viola da braccio, which he says was called the lira not many years previously, the viola da gamba, and the violono, but not the violino. 1976 D. MUNROW *Instruments Middle Ages & Renaissance* 90/1 The name *viola da braccio*, which first occurs in 1543, was first used as a generic term like the older *viola*, but gradually came to refer to the members of the new violin family. 1864 SANDYS & FORSTER *Hist. Violin* xii. 164 John Sebastian Bach introduced an instrument he called the viola pomposa, in consequence . . of the heavy style of violon-cello performers in his time. 1954 GROVE *Dict. Mus.* VIII. 810/1 Sanford Terry has shown that Bach's 'viola pomposa' was really the violoncello piccolo. 1976 *Gramophone* Apr. 1607/2 The viola pomposa a cross between cello and a big Tertis-style viola, with a splendidly rounded sound.

violable ('vaɪələb(ə)l), *a.* [ad. L. (poet.) *violābilis*, f. *violāre* to violate. So OF. *violable*, It. *violabile*, Pg. *violavel.*]

†**1.** Destructive. *Obs.*⁻¹

a 1470 HARDING *Chron.* LII. ii, Yᵉ Pightes & fugitiues . . Destroyed the lande by warre full violable.

2. Capable of being violated, in senses of the vb.

1552 HULOET, Violable, or able to be defiled, . . or easy to be violated, *violabilis.* 1612 SELDEN *Illustr. Drayton's Poly-olb.* xvi. 255 Churches, Plough's and High-waies should haue liberties of Sanctuarie by no authoritie violable. 1633 MARMION *Fine Companion* III. i, Alas, my heart is Tender and violable with the least weapon Sorrow can dart at me. 1674 *Case of Bankers & Creditors* Introd. 4 The Subjects property is not violable but by his own consent. 1858 BUSHNELL *Serm. New Life* 347 If God had no violable sympathy he would be anything but a perfect character. 1885 J. MARTINEAU *Types Eth. Th.* I. I. II. 331 A rule which Spinoza treats as absolute, and will not allow to be violable, even to save one's life.

Hence **viola'bility** *rare* [-ITY], the condition of being violable; cf. INVIOLABILITY; **'violableness**, 'capableness of being violated' (Bailey).

1727 BAILEY II. Violableness. 1926 *Glasgow Herald* 1 Apr. 8/4 The suggestion . . raises the whole question of the violability of contracts.

vio'lacean, *a. rare*⁻¹. [-ACEAN.] = next.

a 1711 KEN *Edmund* Poet. Wks. 1721 II. 162 The Hyacinth of violacean Hue. The purple Amethyst, and Sapphire blue.

violaceous (vaɪə'leɪʃəs), *a.* [f. L. *violāce-us* violet-coloured, f. *viola* VIOLA¹: see -ACEOUS.]

1. Of a violet colour; purplish blue.

1657 TOMLINSON *Renou's Disp.* 498 Incrassated by coction to make it more violaceous. 1686 PLOT *Staffordsh.* 175 [A transparent stone] of an Amethystine violaceous colour, and a genuin luster. 1790 SHAW *Nat. Misc.* III. F 2, The Violaceous Partridge. 1819 STEPHENS in Shaw *Gen. Zool.* XI. I. 42 The inferior tail-coverts are whitish, with violaceous tinges towards the sides. 1844 *Florist's Jrnl.* (1846) V. 17 The flowers differ in having the violaceous tint . . mixed with the crimson in the texture of the flower. 1876 DUHRING *Dis. Skin* 247 In color they possess a dull red or even violaceous hue.

b. Qualifying names of colours.

1790 SHAW *Nat. Misc.* III. F 2, Violaceous-blackish Partridge with a cast of green. 1802 —— *Gen. Zool.* III. II. 521 Violaceous-brown Snake. *Ibid.* 549 Violaceous-green Snake. 1828 STARK *Elem. Nat. Hist.* I. 198 Violaceous black; sides of the wing and tail-feathers white. 1854 tr. *Pereira's Polarized Light* (ed. 2) 268 The extraordinary violaceous blue tint which immediately precedes the yellowish red.

2. *Bot.* Belonging to or resembling the order *Violaceæ.*

Hence **vio'laceously** *adv.*

1888 *Harper's Mag.* Aug. 336 The stricken flesh . . changes color, spots violaceously.

'violal, *a.* and *sb. Bot.* [f. VIOLA¹.] **a.** *adj.* Resembling or related to the genus *Viola*. **b.** *sb. pl.* The 'violal alliance' in Lindley's classification.

1846 LINDLEY *Veg. Kingd.* 320 They seem evidently to join the Violal Alliance. *Ibid.* 325 A perigynous form of Violals. *Ibid.* 338 Violal Exogens, with polypetalous flowers.

violan ('vaɪələn). *Min.* [f. L. *viola* VIOLA¹; named by A. Breithaupt, 1838.] (See quots.)

1850 ANSTED *Elem. Geol., Min.* etc. §407 Pistacite, . . Violane, Withamite, are either synonyms or varieties of Epidote. 1857 DANA *Min.* (1862) 182 Violan is a dark violet-blue mineral, resembling glaucophane. 1868 WATTS *Dict. Chem.* V. 1000 *Violan*, a silicate of aluminium, calcium, magnesium, and sodium . . . It occurs massive, and in indistinct, elongated, granular concretions.

violan(d, obs. variants of VIOLIN.

violant, obs. form of VIOLENT *v.*

violantin (vaɪə'læntɪn). *Chem.* Also -ine. [Blend f. L. *viola* VIOLA¹ + ALLOXANTIN.] 'A compound containing the elements of violuric and dilituric acids' (Watts).

1866 W. ODLING *Anim. Chem.* 128 Baeyer has increased the list of compounds by his discovery of pseudo-uric acid, hydantoine, violantine [etc.]. 1873 WATTS *Fownes' Chem.* (ed. 11) 939 Hydurilic acid . . with nitric acid of ordinary strength . . yields alloxan, together with violuric acid, violantin, and dilituric acid.

violar, variant of VIOLER.

violarite (vaɪə'lɑːraɪt). *Min.* [f. L. *violār-is* of violet + -ITE[1].] A rare isometric sulphide of nickel and iron, Ni_2FeS_4, occurring in massive form with a violet-grey colour and a metallic lustre.

1924 LINDGREN & DAVY in *Econ. Geol.* XIX. 318 It has been shown that the 'polydymite' from Vermilion, Ontario and Key West, Nevada, is not identical with polydymite... It might conveniently be designated as violarite. **1981** *Process Mineralogy* (Amer. Inst. Mining Engineers) 226 The close association of smythite with pentlandite indicates that its nickel content is derived from nickel liberated during the alteration of pentlandite to violarite.

†**'violary.** *Obs.*⁻¹ [ad. L. *violārium*, f. *viola* VIOLA[1].] A violet-bed.

1657 THORNLEY tr. *Longus' Daphnis & Chloe* 182 The Violaries, how are they spurned and trodden down!

vio'lascent, *a. rare*⁻⁰. [f. L. *viola* VIOLA[1].] 'Approaching a violet colour' (Smart, 1840).

†**violastre.** *Obs.*⁻¹ [a. OF. *violastre* (mod.F. *violâtre*) violaceous.] (See quot.)

c **1400** MAUNDEV. (1839) xiv. 160 There ben also Dyamandes in Ynde, that ben clept Violastres (for here colour is liche Vyolet, or more browne than the Violettes).

'violate, *pa. pple.* and *ppl. a.* Now only *poet.* Also 5 violatt, 6 -at, -ait, 6 vyolate, *Sc.* weolait. [ad. L. *violāt-us*, pa. pple. of *violāre*: see next.]

1. Characterized by impurity or defilement.

c **1485** *Digby Myst.* (1882) III. 1557 Now, lord of lordes, to þi blyssyd name sanctificatt, most mekely my feyth I recummend. Pott don þe pryd of mamentes violatt! **1513** DOUGLAS *Æneid* V. i. 12 For weill wist Eneas In violait [L. *polluto*] luif.. quhat thingis mycht be controvit By wemen in fury rage that stranglie lovit. **1594** *Warres Cyrus* C ij, The prince.. bare my daughter thence with violate hands Vnto his pallace. **1856** MRS. H. KING *Disciples, Agesilao Milano* (1873) 300 Take home the lesson to thee,.. Who makest of this lovely land, God's garden, A nation violate, corrupt, accurst.

2. As *pa. pple.* Violated, in various senses of the verb; subjected to violation or injury.

1503 HAWES *Examp. Virt.* vii. 112 Mayden and moder yet not vyolate. *a* **1513** FABYAN *Chron.* VII. 321 The peace.. was, by the kynge, vyolate and broken. **1555** EDEN *Decades* (Arb.) 317 Wherwith.. no parte of the maiestie of a kyng is vyolate. **1590** H. BARROW *Brief Discoverie* 4 That heauenly patterne left by the Apostles was soone violate. *a* **1619** FOTHERBY *Atheom.* II. ii. §5 (1622) 203 If Iustice may be violate, for any cause at all. **1675** MARVELL *Corr.* Wks. (Grosart) II. 479 It was declared and resolved to be an undouted ancient standing order, not to be violate. **1733** W. CRAWFORD *Infidelity* (1836) 159 The law of innocency.. being violate by man's apostacy. **1847** TENNYSON *Princ.* VI. 44 And now, O maids, behold our sanctuary Is violate, our laws broken.

b. = VIOLATED *ppl. a.*

1655 *Theophania* 169 My Fathers blood, Agnesias languishing griefs, my violate marriage,.. raised several passions.

violate ('vaɪəleɪt), *v.* Forms: 5 violatt, 6 -at, 5–6 vyolat(e, 6 voyolate, *Sc.* wiolate, violet; 5– violate. [f. L. *violāt-*, ppl. stem of *violāre* to treat with violence, to outrage, dishonour, injure, etc.]

1. *trans.* To break, infringe, or transgress unjustifiably; to fail duly to keep or observe:

a. An oath or promise, one's faith, etc.

1432–50 tr. *Higden* (Rolls) II. 347 His bloode be schedde in lyke wyse that dothe violate and breke this bonde of luffe. **1526** *Pilgr. Perf.* (W. de W. 1531) 187, I haue despoused you to a noble man, se yᵗ you violate not your fayth & spousage. **1558** KNOX *First Blast* (Arb.) 50 If any man be affraid to violat the oth of obedience, which they haue made to suche monstres. **1596** *Edw. III*, IV. iii. 27 Ah, but it is mine othe, my gratious Lord, Which I in conscience may not violate. **1624** CAPT. SMITH *Virginia* III. viii. 76 Your promise I find .. euery day violated by some of your subiects. **1651** HOBBES *Leviath.* I. xiv. 68 A Power set up to constrain those that would otherwise violate their faith. **1769** ROBERTSON *Chas. V*, VII. Wks. 1813 III. 53 The indecency of violating a recent and solemn engagement. **1777** R. WATSON *Philip II*, II. (1839) 25 Being convinced that Henry would never violate the truce of Vaucelles. **1835** THIRLWALL *Greece* I. 259 Fearing lest the sight of the fertile land.. might tempt the Heracleids to violate their compact with him. **1844** H. H. WILSON *Brit. India* I. 189 These arrangements were scarcely concluded when the Raja manifested a disposition to violate them. **1878** BROWNING *La Saisiaz* 18 She violates the bond.

b. A law, commandment, rule, etc.

1552 HULOET, Violate a lawe or custome, *soluere legem, uel morem.* **1579** LYLY *Euphues* (Arb.) 195 Thou praisest ye Empresse for instituting good lawes, and grieuest to see them violated by the Ladyes. **1611** BIBLE *Ezek.* xxii. 26 Her priests haue violated my law, and haue prophaned mine holy things. **1651** HOBBES *Leviath.* II. xxvii. 153 He which does Injury.. should suffer punishment without other limitation, than that of his Will whose Law is thereby violated. **1691** HARTCLIFFE *Virtues* 363 If we live contrary to this, we violate the Law of him that made us. **1726** SWIFT *Gulliver* II. vii, Power,.. liberty, and.. dominion. All which, however happily tempered by the laws of that kingdom, have been sometimes violated by each of the three parties. **1774** BURKE *Corr.* (1844) I. 485, I have not usually made any scruple to violate, in some degree, the strict letter and *summum jus* of decorum and propriety. **1836** J. GILBERT *Chr. Atonem.* vii. (1852) 204 It is of the essence of atonement, that while it protects all rights, it must not violate any. **1841** W. SPALDING *Italy & It. Isl.* III. 126 The sovereigns.. resolved to violate their own late precedents of non-intervention. **1875** MANNING *Mission H. Ghost* i. 11 The predestination of God in no way violates or takes away the perfect liberty of the human will.

c. Abstract and moral qualities, etc.

1588 KYD *Househ. Philos.* Wks. (1901) 253 First wold I that the parched earth did riue,.. Ere I to lose or violate my chastity beginne. **1671** MILTON *Samson A.* 893 An impious crew Of men.. violating the ends For which our country is a name so dear. **1722** WOLLASTON *Relig. Nat.* vi. 137 He that would not violate truth, must avoid all injustice. *a* **1745** SWIFT *Hen. I*, Wks. 1768 IV. 290 He was a strict observer of justice, which he seems never to have violated. **1794** PALEY *Evid.* III. vii. (1817) 369 Differences of opinion.. accompanied with mutual charity, which Christianity forbids them to violate. **1836** J. GILBERT *Chr. Atonem.* iii. (1852) 62 Let not the Rationalists be suffered, in the very name of justice, sacred as it is, to violate justice. **1892** TENNYSON *Dawn* iii, The press.. easily violates virgin Truth for a coin or a cheque.

2. To ravish or outrage (a woman).

c **1440** *Alph. Tales* 57, I hafe violatt & fylid many mens wyvis, & þer chuldre. *a* **1533** LD. BERNERS *Huon* cxiii. 398 He made it to be cryed in euere strete that no man shulde be so hardy on payne of dethe to vyolat any woman, or deflowre any mayd. **1585** T. WASHINGTON tr. *Nicholay's Voy.* I. xv. 16 [To] see his wife and his daughters rauished and violated. **1611** COTGR., *Forcer*,.. to violate, force, or rauish (as a woman). **1696** PHILLIPS (ed. 5). **1709** ADDISON *Tatler* No. 117 ¶4 She was discovered by Neptune, and violated after a long and unsuccesful Importunity. **1754** SHERLOCK *Disc.* (1759) I. xiii. 344 We gratify our Lust by violating his Wife or Daughter. **1841** ELPHINSTONE *Hist. Ind.* II. 509 This young man,.. having attempted to violate the wife of a Bramin, was imprisoned. **1879** FIFE-COOKSON *With Armies of Balkans* 38 It was alledged however that they [*sc.* the Cossacks] committed separate excesses of their own, violating all the Turkish women they could find.

absol. **1821** SHELLEY *Hellas* 951 Impale the remnant of the Greeks! despoil! Violate! make their flesh cheaper than dust!

3. a. To do violence to; to treat irreverently; to desecrate, dishonour, profane, or defile.

1490 CAXTON *Eneydos* xxi. 76, I haue not rented, vyolated ne broken, the pyramyde of his faders sepulture. ? *a* **1500** *Chester Pl.* (Shaks. Soc.) I. 217 This man.. Is not of God,.. Which doth voyolate the Saboath daye. **1513** DOUGLAS *Æneid* XI. xi. 127 Quha evir with wond dois hurt or violat Hyr haly body onto me dedicat. **1548** UDALL, etc. *Erasm. Par. John* xix. 115 A place perdye detestable and violated with dead bodyes. **1579** W. WILKINSON *Confut. Familye of Love* 13 Gods ministery is an holy and sacred thing, in thought not to be violated. **1635** PAGITT *Christianographie* I. iii. (1636) 129 If by chance any Catholicke Priest shall celebrate upon one of their Altars, they violate it and breake it. **1665** SIR T. HERBERT *Trav.* (1677) 17 They would commonly violate the graves of those dead men we buried. **1673** *Lady's Calling* II. i. §7 She that listens to any wanton discourse has violated her ears. **1797** MRS. RADCLIFFE *Italian* xvi, What sacrilegious footsteps thus rudely violate this holy place. **1846** ARNOLD *Hist. Later Roman Commw.* I. vii. 277 Some of the most famous and richest temples.. were violated and ransacked. **1849** JAMES *Woodman* ix, It would be searched, and the sanctuary violated.

refl. **1606** SHAKS. *Ant. & Cl.* III. x. 24 Experience, Manhood, Honor, ne're before, Did violate so it selfe.

b. To destroy (a person's chastity) by force.

1592 *Arden of Feversham* 38 That iniurious riball, that attempts To vyolate my deare wyues chastitie. **1610** SHAKS. *Temp.* I. ii. 347 Thou didst seeke to violate The honor of my childe. **1769** BLACKSTONE *Comm.* IV. 213 The civil law.. not allowing any punishment for violating the chastity of her, who hath indeed no chastity at all.

c. To interfere with by appropriation.

1823 LAMB *Elia* II. *Poor Relations*, A particular elbow-chair was appropriated to him, which was in no case to be violated. **1840** DICKENS *Old C. Shop* xxv, No boy attempted to violate the sanctity of seat or peg.

†**4. a.** To vitiate, corrupt, or spoil, esp. in respect of physical qualities. *Obs.*

1555 EDEN *Decades* (Arb.) 98 If wee.. consyder the largenes and wydenes of.. the mouthes of the famous ryuer of Ister.. and howe farre they violate or corrupte the salte water with their freshenes. **1598** YONG *Diana* 61 But this mischieuous absence doth violate and dissolue those things, which men thinke to be most strong and firme. **1620** VENNER *Via Recta* vii. 131 They breede phlegme, violate the lungs, and soone offend the stomack.. by their windie and cloying substance. **1656** STANLEY *Hist. Philos.* IV. iii. (1687) 141/2 He said, that Coals, when they forsake the nature of Wood, acquire a solidity not to be violated by moisture.

b. To damage or injure by violence. *Obs.*

1595 DANIEL *Civ. Wars* I. lxxxiii, Like to a River that is stopt his Course Doth violate his Banks. **1606** G. W[OODCOCKE] *Hist. Ivstine* XLIV. 136 For first it lieth not within the raging heate of the Sunne, as Affricke doth; neither is it violated with outragious windes like France. **1634** T. JOHNSON *Parey's Chirurg.* xv. xiv. (1678) 335 If the fracture violate.. the spinal marrow contained therein, then the Patient can scarce scape death. **1658** EVELYN *Fr. Gard.* (1675) 208 Couch it down without violating any of the leaves. **1675** J. ROSE *Eng. Vineyard Vind.* 41 Fear not your vessel if well made; since the force of the working.. will not violate it as some imagine.

c. To despoil *of* something. *Obs.*⁻¹

1646 G. DANIEL *Poems* Wks. (Grosart) II. 57 When the bleake Face of winter spreads The Earth, and violates the Meads Of all their Pride.

†**5.** To treat (a person) roughly or with violence; to assail or abuse. *Obs.*

a **1628** PRESTON *Breastpl. Love* (1631) 88 If a man should come and violate thee with ill termes thou wouldest be angry with him. **1629** CHAS. I *Declarations* Wks. 1662 II. 27 Precedents of former times were disobeyed, the Speaker violated [etc.]. **1635** R. N. tr. *Camden's Hist. Eliz.* III. 239 The Act was made against those which should violate the king by seditious writings.

6. To break in upon; to interrupt or disturb; to interfere with rudely or roughly.

1667 MILTON *P.L.* IV. 883 To question thy bold entrance on this place; Imploi'd it seems to violate sleep. **1697** DRYDEN *Æneid* XII. 474 O Trojans! cease From impious arms, nor violate the peace. **1722** WOLLASTON *Relig. Nat.* vi. (1724) 132 Since he, who begins to violate the happiness of another, does what is wrong. **1775** JOHNSON *Tax. no Tyr.* 31 Legislation passes its limits when it violates the purse. **1796** W. COMBE *Boydell's Thames* II. 3 [Pope's] garden has not yet been violated. It retains its early form. **1809** W. IRVING *Knickerb.* III. vi. (1849) 175 The dark forests which once clothed those shores had been violated by the savage hand of cultivation. **1819** SHELLEY *Cenci* V. i. 13 To violate the sacred doors of sleep.

7. To treat without proper respect or regard; to do violence or injury to (feelings, etc.) in this way.

1692 DRYDEN *St. Euremont's Ess.* 81 Never were they more careful of hindring the Majesty of the Roman People from being violated. **1705** ADDISON *Italy, Monaco* 15 They have never entertain'd a Thought of violating the Publick Credit. **1713** BERKELEY in *Guard.* No. 3 ¶1 A Body of Men, whom of all other a good Man would be most careful not to violate, I mean Men in Holy Orders. **1729** BUTLER *Serm.* Wks. 1874 II. 24 Man may act.. in a way disproportionate to, and violate his real proper nature. **1798** BLOOMFIELD *Farmer's Boy, Summer* 336 Ere tyrant customs strength sufficient bore To violate the feelings of the poor. **1817** SHELLEY *Rev. Islam* VIII. xxvii, Do ye thirst to bear A heart which not the serpent Custom's tooth May violate? **1822** LAMB *Elia* I. *Compl. Decay Beggars*, Do we feel the imagination at all violated when we read the 'true ballad', where King Cophetua woos the beggar maid?

8. To accuse or find (a prisoner on parole) guilty of violating the conditions of parole. *U.S. slang.*

1971 E. E. LANDY *Underground Dict.* 193 *Violate*,.. be returned to prison for a parole violation—eg. *I was violated.* **1973** J. MITFORD *Amer. Prison Business* (1974) xii. 222 If the parolee is 'violated' by his agent (this curious solecism is used, without any sense of irony, by everyone in Corrections, from the parole board to the convict), he is back to Square One. **1974** E. BRAWLEY *Rap* (1975) x. 133 My parole officer violated me on another phony beef and I wound up in the Joint again. **1978** H. B. FRANKLIN *Victim as Criminal & Artist* v. 191 Living outside Los Angeles, with life going reasonably well, Braly suddenly found himself with a zealous new parole officer, who threatened to violate him for driving a car, for having a woman spend the night in his apartment, or for writing anything he disapproved of.

Hence **'violating** *vbl. sb.*

1548 COOPER *Elyot's Dict.*, *Violatio*,.. a violatyng, a breakyng. **1581** NOWELL & DAY in *Confer.* I. (1584) C ij, Master Campion did vs wrong, to charge vs with violating of the Maiestie of the holy Bible. **1585** T. WASHINGTON tr. *Nicholay's Voy.* II. xiii. 48 b, The violating and deflouring of .. his daughters, & other Ladies. **1611** COTGR., *Violation*, a violation, or violating. **1671** PHILLIPS (ed. 3) s.v. *Sacrilegious*, A robbing of Churches, or violating of holy things. **1765–8** ERSKINE *Inst. Law Scot.* IV. iv. §52 The violating of a bride, or espoused virgin. **1769** in *Boston Gaz.* 8 Jan. (1770) 3/1 Since the Tories are so set upon ruining this continent, as not even to scruple the violating their own plighted faith.

violated ('vaɪəleɪtɪd), *ppl. a.* [f. prec. + -ED[1].] That has been subjected to violation.

1593 SHAKS. *Lucr.* 1059 Thou shalt not know The stained taste of violated troth. **1600** —— *A.Y.L.* III. ii. 141 Violated vowes, twixt the soules of friend, and friend. **1625** K. LONG tr. *Barclay's Argenis* III. xxi. 217 He foresaw the infamy of violated hospitality. **1645** MILTON *Tetrach.* Wks. 1851 IV. 164 They argue nothing to the continuance of a false or violated Mariage. **1697** DRYDEN *Æneid* XII. 221 Of ev'ry Latian fair, whom Jove misled To mount by stealth my violated bed. *c* **1760** SMOLLETT *Ode to Indep.* 6 Deep in the frozen regions of the north, A goddess violated brought thee forth. **1784** COWPER *Task* II. 340 By him the violated law speaks out Its thunders. **1828** TYTLER *Hist. Scot.* I. 118 In vindication of his violated rights. **1879** DIXON *Windsor* II. xii. 131 The violated charters were restored.

violater ('vaɪəleɪtə(r)). Now *rare.* [f. VIOLATE *v.*] = VIOLATOR.

1523 LD. BERNERS *Froiss.* I. ccxii. 107/1 We shall punysshe all such as violaters and brekers of the peace.. as the cas shall requyre. **1608** WILLET *Hexapla Exod.* 274 The punishment of the.. violater of the sabbath. **1645** GATAKER *God's Eye on Israel* 83 Amnon was an incestuous violater of his sister. **1665** MANLEY *Grotius' Low C. Wars* 914 They made a League, wherein it was agreed, That the King should give Assistance against the Violaters thereof. **1718** CHAMBERLAYNE *St. Gt. Brit.* (ed. 4) I. III. xi. 267 The Two Proctors.. assist in the Government of the University,.. punishing all Violaters of Statutes. **1767** R. BURN *Eccl. Law* (ed. 2) III. 31 Violaters of virgins consecrated to god. **1812** L. HUNT in *Examiner* 21 Dec. 801/2 Calling us libellers and violaters of the law. **1863** W. H. RUSSELL *Diary North & S.* I. 355 Here were seventy murderers, pirates, burglars, violaters, and thieves.

violation (vaɪə'leɪʃən). Also 5–6 vyolacion, violacion(e, 6 -acyon, -atioune. [a. OF. *violation* (F. *violation*, = Sp. *violacion*, Pg. *violação*, It. *violazione*), or ad. L. *violātiōn-*, *violātio*, noun of action f. *violāre* to violate.] The action of violating, in various senses.

1. a. Infringement or breach, flagrant disregard or non-observance, *of* some principle or standard of conduct or procedure, as an oath, promise, law, etc.; an instance of this.

1432–50 tr. *Higden* (Rolls) III. 291 An objeccion was made to hym of the violacion of his religion and beleve. *c* **1440** *Gesta Rom.* xxxiv. 133 (Harl. MS.), þe Emperour beynge in gret wrethe, for violacion of his precepte & comaundement. **1518** *Star Chamb. Cases* (Selden) II. 150 The further violacion and disordryng of the ordenaunces, vsages, and auncient custumes of the said towne. **1597** HOOKER *Eccl. Pol.* v. lxii. §15 The harme that groweth by violation of holie ordinances. **1611** SHAKS. *Wint. T.* IV. iv. 488 It cannot faile, but by The Violation of my faith. **1655** S. ASHE *Fun. Serm. Gataker* 18 It will be no violation of the Law of charity to affirm, that he was never truly good who doth not strive to be better. **1681** FLAVEL *Meth. Grace* xxxiii. 556 This is a sure rule, that the greatest violation of conscience is the greatest sin. **1711** ADDISON *Spect.* No. 99 ¶7 The great Violation of the Point of Honour from Man to Man, is giving the Lie. **1768** BLACKSTONE *Comm.* III. 153 The violation, or non-performance, of these contracts might be extended into as great a variety of wrongs, as the rights which we then considered. **1776** GIBBON *Decl. & F.* iii. (1782) I. 75 Without any violation of the principles of the constitution. **1824** L. MURRAY *Eng. Gram.* (ed. 5) I. 232 Of this rule there are many violations to be met with. **1863** KINGLAKE *Crimea* (1877) I. 360 It would be regarded by the Czar as a flagrant violation of treaty. **1875** JOWETT *Plato* (ed. 2) V. 11 Laws are passed concerning violations of military discipline.

b. Without const.

1481 *Coventry Leet Bk.* 475 Eny thyng..wherby the seid trewes & other conuencions passed betwen vs..myght fall in vyolacion or Ruptur in any wyse. *a* **1513** FABYAN *Chron.* VII. 472 The peas whiche then was proclaymed..whiche endured nat longe without vyolacion. **1640** GRIMSTON *Speech* 9 Nov. (1641) 5 To adjourne the house upon any command whatsoever, without the consent and approbation of the House it selfe, were breaches and violations that highly impeached our priviledges.

(*b*) In mod. use chiefly *U.S.*, esp. = an infringement of the law; an infringement of the rules in some sports.

1961 in WEBSTER. **1973** E. CALDWELL *Annette* (1974) VII. i. 155 Jack immediately began complaining that the police had no right to follow him and charge him with a traffic violation when he was certain he had not driven through any stop signs or red lights and had been careful to stay under the speed limit. **1976** *Honolulu Star-Bull.* 21 Dec. H-2/1, I only hope Big Brother can take as hard a line against those who transferred out of the VH program should they be equally as guilty of violations. **1982** L. BLOCK *Eight Million Ways to Die* (1983) iv. 47, I couldn't recall the last time I'd seen a cop ticket anyone for a moving violation.

†**2.** The action of treating or handling violently and injuriously. *Obs.*

c **1485** *Digby Myst.* (1882) II. 179 All..with furyous vyolacion..Thus shalbe subduyd. **1616** BULLOKAR *Eng. Expos.*, *Violation*, an offering of violence, a breaking. *a* **1656** USSHER *Ann.* VI. (1658) 424 Perseus..sent away the Rodians open Vessels, and Eudemus their President without Violation, nay even civilly entreated. **1699** EVELYN *Kal. Hort.* (ed. 9) 23 To apply the Collateral Branches of his Wall Fruits..(without violation and unnatural bending, and reverting) to the Earth or Borders.

3. a. Defilement *of* chastity, etc.; in later use esp. by means of violence.

1497 BP. ALCOCK *Mons Perfect.* D iij, In clennes of body & soule without voluntary pollucion or vyolacion. **1526** *Pilgr. Perf.* (W. de W. 1531) 182 Thou..conceyued thy chylde without corrupcyon or violacyon of thy virginite. **1696** PHILLIPS (ed. 5) s.v., A forcing of a Woman against her Will, is call'd a Violation of her Chastity. **1727** BAILEY (vol. II), *Rape*,..a Ravishing, or forcible Violation of the Chastity of a Woman, or Virgin.

b. Ravishment, outrage, rape.

1599 SHAKS. *Hen. V*, III. iii. 21 What is't to me, when you your selues are cause, If your pure Maydens fall into the hand Of hot and forcing Violation? **1728** CHAMBERS *Cycl.* s.v. **1769** BLACKSTONE *Comm.* IV. 81 By violation is understood carnal knowledge, as well without force, as with it. **1810** SOUTHEY *Kehama* IX. 126 When Arvalan, in hour with evil fraught, For violation seized the shrieking Maid. **1843** *Penny Cycl.* XXV. 171/2 The law [of treason] has been held to apply to a criminal connection by consent as well as to a forcible violation.

4. Desecration or profanation of something sacred.

1546 GARDINER *Detect. Devil's Sophistrie* 15 b, The breakyng of the most blessed sacrament, by the ministre in the masse, doth no violacion to christes most precious body there present. **1548** UDALL, etc. *Erasm. Par. Mark* iii. 26 They sawe the dumme beast might lawfully be drawen out of the hole, lest it shoulde peryshe, without anye violacion or breache of the sabboth. **1728** CHAMBERS *Cycl.* s.v. **1777** R. WATSON *Philip II* (1839) 221 The Spanish soldiers themselves..were afterwards..touched with remorse on account of their violation of the churches. **1849** JAMES *Woodman* ii, What he desires to do, that he will do—even to the violation of sanctuary. **1856** C. KNIGHT *Hist. Eng.* I. xxvii. 425 The violation of a sacred place by murder was considered a greater crime than the murder itself.

5. Improper use *of* something.

1822 SHELLEY *Chas. I*, II. 75 Look that those merchants.. take fullest compensation For violation of our royal forests.

Hence **vio'lational** *a. rare.*

1810 BENTHAM *Packing* (1821) 94 Something or other ..'injurious', 'prejudicial', 'hurtful', or 'violational'. **1876** J. J. G. WILKINSON *Hum. Sci. & Div. Rev.* 25 Medicine has made great strides of late, and this is owing noticeably to violational science. [*Violationism* and *violationist* are also used in this work, pp. 577, 579, etc.]

violative ('vaɪəleɪtɪv), *a.* Chiefly *U.S.* [f. VIOLATE *v.* + -IVE.] Involving or causing violation (*of* something).

1856 F. PIERCE *Message to Congress* 2 That no act shall remain on its statute book, violative of the provisions of the constitution. **1878** *Masque Poets* 26 Those Who have dared in violative wise To assault with strong and impious blows, The awful, slumbering Pharaohs. **1891** *Nation* (N.Y.) 24 Dec. 495/2 Four of the judges held that the act was violative of the amendments, and therefore invalid.

violator ('vaɪəleɪtə(r)). Also 6–7 -our. [a. L. *violātor*, agent-noun f. *violāre* to violate. So F. *violateur* (OF. *violatour*), It. *violatore*, Sp. and Pg. *violador*. Cf. VIOLATER.]

1. A ravisher or outrager of women.

1432–50 tr. *Higden* (Rolls) III. 33 Sardanapallus, a man hauenge grete delectacion of women, and a violator of þeim. **1603** SHAKS. *Meas. for M.* v. i. 41 That Angelo is an adulterous thiefe, An hypocrite, a virgin violator. **1748** RICHARDSON *Clarissa* VI. 327 If, by vowing love and honour at the altar to such a violator, I could sanctify..his unprecedented and elaborate wickedness. **1864** TENNYSON *Boadicea* 50 Me the sport of ribald Veterans, mine of ruffian violators!

2. A desecrator or profaner of something sacred or venerable.

1577 HOLINSHED *Chron.* II. 825/1 But Guye de Mountfort was excommunicate, as a violatour of the churche. **1591** in Jas. Campbell *Balmerino & Abbey* (1867) III. ii. 178 Ordanis the sessione of the kirk of Balmerinoch to cause violatoris of the Sabbath day publictlie to make publict repentance thairfor. **1638** BAKER tr. *Balzac's Lett.* (vol. II) 13 The persecuters of those who submit themselves are to me in equal execration with the violatours of sepulchers. **1665** MANLEY *Grotius' Low C. Wars* 30 Commanding the Inquisitors to execute judgement upon violators, and novelties in Religion. **1841** LYTTON *Nt. & Morn.* I. i, Now ..glared upon the startled violators of the sanctuary, with glassy eyes and horrent visage, a grim monster. **1865** BARING-GOULD *Were-Wolves* xv. 250 It is well known that Oriental romance is full of stories of violators of graves. **1898** MEREDITH *Odes Fr. Hist., Rev.* x, They, violators of home, dared hope an inviolate home.

3. An infringer, breaker, or transgressor (of a law, compact, etc.).

1642 C. VERNON *Consid. Exch.* 104 That due punishment be inflicted upon the violators thereof. **1644** MILTON *M. Bucer* Wks. 1851 IV. 331 They..are no more in bondage to such violators of Marriage. **1676** TEMPLE *Let. to Sir J. Williamson* 21 Mar., Nor could it easily be found out how the Violator of any such Passport should be punished. **1738** WARBURTON *Div. Legat.* I. 16 The Violator of the Laws of the Society. **1775** DE LOLME *Eng. Const.* II. xvi. (1784) 239 To give up the violators of these laws. **1809** W. IRVING *Knickerb.* (1820) 199 Whoever thought wrong,..was a flagrant violator of the inestimable liberty of conscience. **1881** JOWETT *Thucyd.* I. 76 Those who attack others, not those who defend themselves, are the real violators of treaties.

4. One who injures, disturbs, or interrupts violently.

1792 A. YOUNG *Trav. France* 31 The incendiaries, robbers, and violators of mankind. **1828–32** WEBSTER s.v., A violator of repose.

violatory, *a. rare.* [f. VIOLATE *v.* + -ORY.] = VIOLATIVE *a.*

1802 *Times* 13 July, Nothing was so violatory of the rules of ratiocination and eloquence. **1850** W. ANDERSON *Regeneration* 144, I contend, that the dogma is glaringly unphilosophical, and violatory of common sense.

violaxanthin (ˌvaɪələ'zænθɪn). *Biochem.* [a. G. *viola-xanthin* (Kuhn & Winterstein 1931, in *Ber. d. Deut. Chem. Ges.* LXIV. 327): see VIOLA[1] and XANTHIN.] A xanthophyll, $C_{40}H_{56}O_4$, occurring as a yellow pigment in daffodils and some other plants.

1931 *Chem. Abstr.* XXV. 3351 The petals of the yellow pansy contain..a pigment wax which can be extd. with petroleum ether and on sapon. yields a well-crystd. xanthophyll, viola-xanthin. **1965** [see LYCOPIN]. **1978** *Nature* 13 July 160/2 The photosynthetic pigments found in [the green alga] *C[odium] fragile* (β-carotene, zeaxanthin,.. violaxanthin,..and chlorophyll b).

viol da gamba ('vaɪəl də 'gæmbə). Also 6–7 **de gambo**, **7 di gambo**, **de gamboys**; 7– **de gamba**, **9 di gamba**. [ad. It. *viola da gamba* 'leg-viol': cf. VIOLA[2] and GAMBA[2].]

1. A viol held between the legs of the player while being played; in later use restricted to the bass viol corresponding to the modern violoncello.

1597 J. DOWLAND (*title*), The Firste Booke of Songes or Ayres of foure partes with Tableture for the Lute: So made that all..may be song to the Lute, Orpherian or Viol de gambo. **1599** B. JONSON *Ev. Man out of Hum.* III. iii, *Fast.* I doe more..admire your..predominate perfections, than ..euer I shall haue..facultie to expresse. *Saui.* Vpon the Violl *de Gambo* you meane? **1601** SHAKS. *Twel. N.* I. iii. 27 He playes o'th Viol-de-gamboys. **1611** CORYAT *Crudities* 252 Their instruments ten Sagbuts, foure Cornets and two Violdegambaes of an extraordinary greatnesse. **1662** PLAYFORD *Skill Mus.* II. (1674) 91 Of this Viol de Gambo there are three several sizes,..viz., Treble Viol, Tenor Viol, and Bass Viol... These three Viols agree in one manner of Tuning. **1774** 'J. COLLIER' *Mus. Trav.* 34, I think the effect was equal to any *viol di gamba* I ever heard. **1789** BURNEY *Hist. Mus.* III. vii. 361 Charles I..had been a scholar of Coperario on the viol da gamba. **1801** BUSBY *Dict. Mus.*, *Viol da Gamba*, or Greater Viol, a viol with six strings, formerly much used in Germany. **1843** *Penny Cycl.* XXVI. 343/2 Viol da Gamba..was the last survivor of the family of viols. **1908** '*Aberdeen Jrnl.*' *N. & Q.* I. 32/1 The music ceased, and died away in a long note, like the stroke of a viol-de-gamba.

2. An organ-stop having a tone resembling that of the above instrument.

1852 SEIDEL *Organ* 108 Viol di gamba, or simply gamba, is one of the finest registers. **1881** C. A. EDWARDS *Organs* 157 The Viol-di-Gamba is soft, reedy, and sweet.

Hence **viol da 'gambist**, one who plays the *viol da gamba*; a viola da gambist.

1915 E. S. J. VAN DER STRAETEN *Hist. Violoncello* iii. 32 The next viol da gambist whose name has been handed down to posterity is Vincenzo Galilei... He was the father of Galileo Galilei and an excellent lutenist, gambist, composer and a very learned master of musical theory.

†**viole**, *v. Obs. rare.* Also 5 **vyole**. [ad. OF. *violer*, ad. L. *violāre*: see VIOLATE *v.*] *trans.* To violate.

a **1450** *Knt. de la Tour* 75 He took fro them all that he couthe, and enforced their wyues, and vyoled their doughters. **1480** CAXTON *Ovid's Met.* XI. xxii, She moche enforced her for to flee for t'escape fro hyme, to th' ende that she were not vyoled ne defowled.

viole, obs. form of VIAL, VIOL *sb.*[1]

violence ('vaɪələns), *sb.* Also 4 **uiolence**, 4–6 **vyolence**, 5 *Sc.* **wyol-**, **wiolence**, 5–6 **violens** (7 **voyolence**). [a. AF. and OF. (also mod.F.) *violence*, ad. L. *violentia* vehemence, impetuosity, etc., f. *violentus* VIOLENT *a.* Cf. Pr. *violensa*, *-ansa*, Sp. and Pg. *violencia*, It. *violenza*.]

1. a. The exercise of physical force so as to inflict injury on, or cause damage to, persons or property; action or conduct characterized by this; treatment or usage tending to cause bodily injury or forcibly interfering with personal freedom.

c **1290** *Beket* 932 in *S. Eng. Leg.* I. 133 ȝif ani man hond on ov set, ich ov hote al-so þat ȝe þe sentence of holi churche, for swuche violence ȝe do. **1303** R. BRUNNE *Handl. Synne* 11142 Clerk to bete, or handes on ley yn vyolence, hyt ys grete eye. *c* **1340** HAMPOLE *Pr. Consc.* 1175 þe world es..a sted of mykel wrechednes,..Of filthe and of corrupcion, Of violence and of oppression. *c* **1380** WYCLIF *Wks.* (1880) 161 þei holden neuer neiþer lawe of god in dymes takynge, & taken hem bi vyolence & stronge curses aȝenst mennus goode wille. *c* **1420** *Prymer* 74 Lord! y suffre violence; answere þou for me! ? *a* **1445** [? GASCOIGN] *Life St. Bridget* in *New Leg. England* (Pynson) 123 When yᵉ cytezens sawe yᵗ by prayers they profyted nat, somwhat with vyolence, neuerthelesse reuerently they ledde hir out of hir house vnto the watersyde. **1504** ATKYNSON tr. *De Imitatione* I. xxiv. 174 They that by vyolence restrayne theyr selfe fro synne and euer be busy to make the bodye obedyent to the soule. **1560** DAUS tr. *Sleidane's Comm.* 38 Then might they also be in the more hope to give the repulse to the Turke, with all his violence. *a* **1596** *Sir T. More* II. iii. 14 They intend to offer violence To the amazed Lombards. **1617** MORYSON *Itin.* III. 47 Charles the fifth..was wont to say, that the King of Spaine ruled over Asses, doing nothing without blowes and violence. **1651** HOBBES *Leviath.* II. xx. 102 Promises proceeding from fear of death, or violence, are no Covenants. **1718** *Free-thinker* No. 58. 20 Almost all the Governments..had their Commencement in Violence. **1759** JOHNSON *Rasselas* xxxvii[i], The violence of war admits of no distinction. **1784** COWPER *Task* I. 604 In remote And barb'rous climes, where violence prevails, And strength is lord of all. **1844** H. H. WILSON *Brit. India* III. 524 The Government..protected them against the perils of violence and rapacity, and ensured them tranquillity and repose. **1876** BRISTOWE *Theory & Pract. Med.* (1878) 532 It occasionally originates..in the effects of very violent muscular exertion or of violence inflicted from without.

personif. **1609** DEKKER *Work Armourours* Wks. (Grosart) IV. 131 Violence hath borne many great offices, and Money hath done much for him. **1787** BURNS *Death R. Dundas* v, Mark ruffian Violence, ingrain'd with crimes, Rousing elate in these degenerate times.

b. In the phr. *to do violence to*, *unto* (or with indirect object): To inflict harm or injury upon; to outrage or violate. †Also ***to make violence***.

a **1300** *Cursor M.* 19325 þai durst na uiolence to þam do For þe folk þam helded to. **13..** *E.E. Allit. P.* B. 1071 When venkkyst was no vergynyte, ne vyolence maked. **1390** GOWER *Conf.* III. 340 He telleth hem the violence, Which the tretour Strangulio And Dionise him hadde do. **1535** COVERDALE *Luke* iii. 14 Do no man violence ner wronge. **1594** KYD *Cornelia* IV. i. 28 Iuba and Petreus, fiercely combatting, Haue each done other equall violence. **1602** SHAKS. *Ham.* I. ii. 171 Nor shall you doe mine eare that violence, To make it truster of your owne report Against your selfe. *a* **1619** FLETCHER, etc. *Knt. Malta* V. ii, They have done violence unto her Tomb, Not granting rest unto her in the grave. **1692** DRYDEN *St. Euremont's Ess.* 93, I make no question, but that in the violence of the Triumvirate, he did much Violence to himself. **1749** FIELDING *Tom Jones* XII. iii, To say the truth, we have.. often done great violence to the luxuriance of our genius. **1860** PUSEY *Min. Proph.* 474 They did violence to the majesty of the law,..and then, through profaning it, did violence to man.

c. In weakened sense: Improper treatment or use of a word; wresting or perversion of meaning or application; unauthorized alteration of wording.

1596 LAMBARDE *Peramb. Kent* (ed. 2) 143 But Master Camden with lesse violence..deriueth it [sc. *dele*] from the Bryttish *Dole*. **1659** PEARSON *Creed* ii. 294 Being in some places Adonai cannot be read for Jehovah, without manifest violence offered to the Text. **1662** EVELYN *Chalcogr.* 7 Neither the Paradigmatic..or any of the Plastic can be call'd Sculpture without a Catachresis and some Violence. **1749** FIELDING *Tom Jones* IV. vi, A passion which might without any great violence to the word, be called love. **1856** MAURICE *Gosp. St. John* vii. 94 Wherever violence is done to the truth of language, I believe more or less of violence is done to some higher truth. **1861** PALEY *Æschylus* (ed. 2) *Supplices* 510 *note*, But this is a reckless alteration. He might with less violence have written πατρὸς. **1875** E. WHITE *Life in Christ* IV. xxvii. (1878) 446 The violence of the proposed interpretation is..conspicuous.

d. Undue constraint applied to some natural process, habit, etc., so as to prevent its free development or exercise. Now used in political

contexts with varying degrees of appropriateness.
1715 tr. *Gregory's Astron.* (1726) I. 200 We must..not make our Reason and Philosophy perpetually offer violence to our Sight and other Senses. 1749 Fielding *Tom Jones* vi. iv, He was obliged to attend near a quarter of an hour, though with great violence to his natural impetuosity, before he was suffered to speak. 1847 J. Yeowell *Anc. Brit. Ch.* ix. 93 The first Christian missionaries in Ireland seem to have carefully avoided all unnecessary violence to the ancient habits of the aborigines. 1972 *Science* 23 June 1300/3 It is interesting that 58 percent of American men think that burning a draft card is violence, in and of itself; 38 percent think student protest is violence; and 22 percent feel sit-ins are violence. Clearly, many Americans consider acts of dissent, per se, to be violent. *Ibid.* 1301/1 Only 35 percent of American men define 'police shooting looters' as violence and only 56 percent define 'police beating students' in this manner. 1984 *Times* 2 July 1/8 Mr Scargill..said: '..My facts show to me..that the people guilty of intimidation and violence in this dispute have been the police.' 1984 *Daily Telegraph* 5 Oct. 20/2 [At the Labour Party Conference] much violence was done to the word violence, which it appears can be used to describe almost anything you do not care for.

e. *Law.* (See quot.)
1867 Smyth *Sailor's Word-bk.* 713 *Violence*, the question in tort, as to the amount of liability incurred by the owners for outrages and irregularities committed by the master.

2. a. With *a* and pl. An instance or case of violent, injurious, or severe treatment; a violent act or proceeding.
c 1375 *Sc. Leg. Saints* xxxiv. (*Pelagia*) 234 Þe feynde..can cry,..'Alace! I thole but defence of hyme þis ald gret wyolence. 1390 Gower *Conf.* III. 208 The tidinge of this violence..Sche sende anon ay wydewhere To suche frendes as sche hadde. 1435 Misyn *Fire of Love* ii. vii. 86 Well þis is cald a rauischynge als þe todyr, for with a violens it is doyne & als wer agayns kynde. 1508 Dunbar *Gold. Targe* 159 Curage in thame was noucht begonne to spring; Full sore thay dred to done a violence. 1596 Spenser *State Irel.* 510 b, She perhaps, for very compassion of such calamities, will not only stop the stream of such violences, and return to her wonted mildness, but [etc.]. 1649 Milton *Eikon.* Pref., A tedious..warr on his subjects, wherein he hath so farr exceeded his arbitrary violences in time of peace. 1682 Burnet *Rights Princes* ii. 64 He laments the Violences that were used in some Elections. 1704 *Col. Rec. Pennsylv.* II. 191 If they were clear of the violences done lately upon a family of the English. 1759 H. Walpole *Let. to G. Montagu* 23 Dec., Has your brother told you of the violences in Ireland? 1818 Cobbett *Pol. Reg.* XXXIII. 12 They saw nothing but the violences on Sir Francis's side. 1850 Kingsley *A. Locke* Pref., If the violences and tyrannies of American Democracy are to be really warnings to us [etc.]. 1864 Maine *Anc. Law* vi. (1870) 206 The violences inseparable from the best-ordered ancient society.

b. In weakened sense (cf. 1 c and 1 d).
1706 Estcourt *Fair Example* iv. i, I yielded to the Intreaty of my Friends, Acted a violence on my reluctant Heart, And gave my trembling Hand..to Another. 1777 Hume *Ess. & Treat.* I. 184 If he have but resolution enough ..to impose a violence on himself. 1793 Smeaton *Edystone L.* §119 It would yet be a violence to myself, to refrain from doing the Proprietors justice. 1818 Cruise *Digest* (ed. 2) IV. 371 Then a violence would be offered, as well to the words, as to the meaning of the party.

3. Force or strength of physical action or natural agents; forcible, powerful, or violent action or motion (in early use freq. connoting destructive force or capacity).
Now often merging into next, with an intensive sense.
c 1384 Chaucer *H. Fame* ii. 775 For whan a pipe is blowen sharpe, The aire ys twyst with violence. c 1386 —— *Can. Yeom. Prol. & T.* 355 Thise metals been of so gret violence, Oure walles mowe nat make hem resistence. c 1400 Maundev. (Roxb.) xxxiii. 151 Sum ware drouned by violence of þe wawes. 1426 Lydg. *De Guil. Pilgr.* 12210, I..sawh a whel..By vyolence tourne aboute Contynuelly tofor my face. 1560 Daus tr. *Sleidane's Comm.* 414 b, Than chiefly was the citie meruelouslye beaten with shot, the violence wherof was so great, that [etc.]. 1603 Shaks. *Meas. for M.* iii. i. 125 To be imprison'd in the viewlesse windes, And blowne with restlesse violence round about. 1610 Holland *Camden's Brit.* 513 The river Aufon..breaketh forth with more violence upon the flats adioyning. 1659 Leak *Water-wks.* 1 To make the Water enter therein with force,..the vessel..shall be made as high as may be, that it may give so much the more violence to the Water. 1703 Moxon *Mech. Exerc.* 84 The shorter the Stuff that the Tennant is made on, the less Violence the Tennant is subject to. 1793 Smeaton *Edystone L.* §61 *note*, The strokes of the sea may at the Edystone be so great as to wash the poison out again from the wood, that in a situation of less violence could ..slowly insinuate itself. 1841 Lane *Arab. Nts.* I. 104 He knocked a fourth time, and with violence. 1862 Darwin *Fertil. Orchids* ii. 57 The pollinia cannot be jarred out of the anther-cells by violence. 1895 *Law Times Rep.* LXXIII. 156/2 Two vessels..drifted through the violence of a storm on to the toe of a breakwater.

4. a. Great force, severity, or vehemence; intensity *of* some condition or influence.
1390 Gower *Conf.* I. 280 Wrathe.. Which hath hise wordes ay so hote, That all a mannes pacience Is fyred of the violence. c 1400 Maundev. (Roxb.) xv. 70 Oft tymes he fell by violence of þat sekeness. *Ibid.* xviii. 81 Þe grete violence of hete þat dissoluez þaire bodys. 1577 Googe *Heresbach's Husb.* 28 Rye..suffereth the violence of mystes and frostes. 1604 E. G[rimstone] *D'Acosta's Hist. Indies* ii. x. 103 Arabia, the which is burnt with the Sunne, having no showres to temper the violence thereof. 1658 Phillips s.v. *Intercident*, An extraordinary critical day,..being caused by the violence of the disease. 1702 J. Purcell *Cholick* (1714) 137 If an Inflammation arises,..Bleeding is to be order'd, and repeated according to its Violence. 1794 Mrs. Radcliffe *Myst. Udolpho* xli, She went off as peacefully as a child, for all the violence of her disorder was passed. 1809 *Med. Jrnl.* XXI. 518 The inflammatory complaints, particularly pneumonia, have recurred with considerable violence. 1874 J. L. Patterson *Ess. Relig. & Lit.* 3rd Ser. 134 It is yet obvious that..these laws apply with a far different and more grievous violence to the Catholic, than to any other..Church.

b. Intensity or excess *of* contrast.
1874 H. H. Cole *Catal. Ind. Art S. Kens. Mus.* 218 Violence of contrast either of light or dark colours, or gaudy, florid, and large ornament are among the common sources of error which ruin design.

5. Vehemence of personal feeling or action; great, excessive, or extreme ardour or fervour; also, violent or passionate conduct or language; passion, fury.
c 1430 Lydg. *Min. Poems* (Percy Soc.) 47 But arche wives, egre in ther vyolence, Fers as tygres for to make affray. 1563 Golding *Cæsar* (1565) 119 The enemy being not able to withstand the violence of oure fotemen,..toke them to flyght. 1604 Shaks. *Oth.* ii. i. 224 Marke me with what violence she first lou'd the Moore. 1654 *Nicholas Papers* (Camden) II. 84, I was trubled to see the violence it putt him into. 1696 Phillips (ed. 5), *Violence*,..figuratively spoken of Human Passions and Designs, when unruly, and not to be govern'd. 1735 Somerville *Chace* iii. 544 He vents the cooling Stream, and up the Breeze Urges his Course with eager Violence. 1818 Coleridge *Friend* (1865) 142 To expect that the violence of party spirit is never more to return. 1821 Scott *Kenilw.* xxxii, I said nothing to deserve such a horrid imputation as your violence infers. 1841 Elphinstone *Hist. Ind.* II. 321 It was concluded by Akber's reproving the mullahs for their violence.

†6. Violation *of* some condition. *Obs.*$^{-1}$
a 1754 Fielding *Remedy Afflict.* Wks. 1775 IX. 251 Nor is there any dissuasive from such contemplation [of the loss of friends]: it is no breach of friendship, nor violence of paternal fondness.

†'violence, *v. Obs.* [f. prec.]
1. *trans.* To do violence to; to violate.
Common in the 17th century.
1612 T. Taylor *Comm. Titus* iii. 1 The one was so farre from violencing the other, as one of them could not stand without the other. 1650 tr. *Caussin's Angel Peace* 6 The most Sacred things are violenced, and the most Profane are licenced. a 1677 Barrow *Serm.* (1686) III. 304 In doing otherwise he would thwart and violence his own conscience, and be self-condemned.

2. To compel or constrain; to force (a person) *to* or *from* a place, etc., or *to* do something, by violence.
1620 Brent tr. *Sarpi's Counc. Trent* vii. (1676) 618 Shewing there was a desire to violence the Fathers by weariness. 1647 Hammond *Power of Keys* ii. 8 Sure 'twill not be thought reasonable, that these two shall be forced and violenced to consent to that. 1648 Symmons *Vind. Chas. I* 296 They have done what they could to violence him from his Religion.

Hence **†'violencing** *vbl. sb. Obs.*
1612 T. Taylor *Comm. Titus* i. 6 Christ himself taxeth it as a violencing of the first institution. a 1615 Donne *Ess.* (1651) 82 The distortions and violencing of Scriptures. 1649 Hammond *Chr. Oblig.*, etc. 68 A kind of constraining and violencing of the spirit.

†'violency. *Obs.* Also 6 violensie, -cye, 6–7 -cie. [ad. L. *violentia*: see violence *sb.*] Violence, in various senses.
1545 Raynald *Byrth Mankynde* Y v, Accordynge to the aptitude or feoblenesse in resistence of the place receauyng it: and the force or violencye of nature..sendynge it. 1556 J. Heywood *Spider & Fly* xix. 25 My carte wheele catchth holde of the corner poaste Against my will, and by violencie, Asunder crussheth it. 1559–66 *Hist. Estate Scot.* in *Wodrow Soc. Misc.* (1844) 66 To resist the violencie of their adversaries. 1607 Walkington *Opt. Glass* i. (1664) 13 Such fare, as may banish and expel contagion and violencie from nature.

b. In pl. Cf. violence *sb.* 2.
c 1630 Sanderson *Serm.* (1681) II. 258 Although the text speaks expresly only of death; yet..all other violencies and injuries are intended. 1632 Sir T. Hawkins tr. *Mathieu's Unhappy Prosperitie* 199 Of all his violencies, the most execrable was the death of the Architect, who skilfully reedified..the..portall of Rome. 1660 Jer. Taylor *Ductor* iii. ii. rule 3 §2 He may do what is in his natural capacity to avoid these violencies and extremities of nature.

violent, obs. form of violon.

violent ('vaɪələnt), *a.* (*adv.*, *sb.*). Also 5 **wyolent**, 5–6 **vyolent**, **violente**. [a. OF. (also mod.F.) *violent*, or ad. L. *violent-us* (whence It., Sp., and Pg. *violento*) or *violent-*, *violens* (whence It. *violente*), forcible, impetuous, vehement, etc., f. *vis* strength.]

A. *adj.* **I. 1.** Of things: Having some quality or qualities in such a degree as to produce a very marked or powerful effect (esp. in the way of injury or discomfort); intense, vehement, very strong or severe: **a.** Of the sun, heat, etc. †*violent signs* (see quot. 1679).
c 1340 Hampole *Pr. Consc.* 852 It myght þe ayr swa corrumpud mak, þat men þarof þe dede suld take, Swa vile it es and violent. 1390 Gower *Conf.* III. 116 That planete which men calle Saturnus,..His climat is in Orient, Wher that he is most violent. c 1400 *Destr. Troy* 339 A playne, Full of floures fresshe,..With voiders vnder vines for violent sonnes. 1412–20 Lydg. *Chron. Troy* i. 2158 So violent and feruent was þe hete. 1585 T. Washington tr. *Nicholay's Voy.* iv. xxvi. 145 b, Vppon the coales..they cast a certaine seede, the smoke whereof was so violent, that foorthwith it made them..dissy. 1604 E. G[rimstone] *D'Acosta's Hist. Indies* ii. vii. 97 If the sunnebeames be weake, they draw vp no fogge from the rivers, if they be violent [etc.]. 1621 G. Sandys *Ovid's Met.* iv. (1626) 67 Signes onely vtter their vnwitnest loues: But hidden fire the violenter proues. 1679 Moxon *Math. Dict.* 161 *Violent Signs*, are those in which the Malefick Planets, viz. Saturn or Mars have any notable Dignitie... And also those in which there are any violent fixed Stars of note, and within the Zodiac. [Hence in Phillips, 1696]. 1719 London & Wise *Compl. Gard.* 171 Till such times as the violent Frosts are over. 1815 J. Smith *Panorama Sci. & Art* II. 380 Being again evaporated to dryness, it is..exposed to a violent heat in a crucible. 1864 Swinburne *Atalanta* 815 And thunder of storm on the sand, ..Fierce air and violent light.

b. Of poison, †the blood, etc.
c 1386 Chaucer *Pard. T.* 539 Sterue he shal, and that in lasse while. Than thou wolt goon a paas nat but a Mile; This poyson is so strong and violent. a 1400 *Stockholm Med. MS.* ii. 24 in *Anglia* XVIII. 308 Powdyr of betonye eke is good, Medelyd with hony, for vyolent blod. 1460–70 *Bk. Quintessence* 22 Discreet maistris seyn, þat þe feuere agu comounly is causid of a uyolent reed coler adust [etc.]. 1728 Chambers *Cycl.* s.v. *Sublimate*, Corrosive Sublimate..is then a violent Poison, which corrodes and destroys the Parts of the Body with much Violence.

c. Of pain, disease, etc.
14.. W. Paris *Cristine* 314 (Horstm. 1878), Foure men rokede hire to & froo, To make hire payne more violente. c 1450 *Mirk's Festial* 257 And þen was þys kyng smyton wyth a meselry þat was soo vyolent to hym, þat..he slogh hymselfe. 1607 Shaks. *Cor.* iii. i. 222 Those cold wayes, That seeme like prudent helpes, are very poysonous, Where the Disease is violent. 1728 Chambers *Cycl.* s.v. *Poison*, The Hyoscyamus [is successful] in Hæmorrhagies, violent Heats and Inflammations. 1749 Fielding *Tom Jones* xi. ii, The violent fatigue which both her mind and body had undergone. 1776 *Trial of Nundocomar* 23/1 Some days he has violent purgings, at other times he gets better. 1799 *Med. Jrnl.* II. 474 As the intestines had been sufficiently emptied..by a violent diarrhœa. 1803 *Ibid.* X. 102, I think the influenza distinguishable from a common catarrh, inasmuch as the symptoms are, in general, more violent, painful, and distressing. 1843 R. J. Graves *Syst. Clin. Med.* ix. 100 The patient..was attacked..by intensely violent maculated fever. 1899 *Allbutt's Syst. Med.* VIII. 739 The condition was associated with violent headaches and neuralgia of the tongue of the same side.

d. Of passions. (Cf. sense 8 c.)
1586 T. B. *La Primaud. Fr. Acad.* i. 291 Even the violentest and most common passions of mans nature. 1605 Shaks. *Macb.* ii. iii. 116 Th' expedition of my violent Loue Out-run the pawser, Reason. *Ibid.* iv. iii. 169 Alas poore Countrey,..Where violent sorrow seemes A Moderne ecstasie. 1697 Dryden *Æneid* i. 948 A love so violent, so strong, so sure, That neither age can change, nor art can cure. 1711 Addison *Spect.* No. 120 ¶10 This natural Love in Brutes is much more violent and intense than in rational Creatures. 1789 W. Buchan *Dom. Med.* (1790) 119 Love is perhaps the strongest of all the passions; at least, when it becomes violent, it is less subject to..control. 1797 Mrs. Radcliffe *Italian* i, She was of violent passions, haughty, vindictive, yet crafty and deceitful. 1808 W. Wilson *Hist. Dissent. Ch.* I. 272 Parker was a man of violent passions.

†e. Of taste or smell: Very strong. *Obs.*
1604 E. G[rimstone] *D'Acosta's Hist. Indies* iv. xxvii. 284 It hath a strong savour, and in my opinion, too violent. 1780 *Newgate Cal.* V. 232 In the morning she perceived a violent smell of sulphur.

f. Of colour: Intensely or extremely bright or strong; vivid. Also *fig.* of outline.
1768 Sterne *Sent. Journ.*, *Le Dimanche*. As the blue was not violent, it suited with the coat and breeches very well. 1873 B. Harte *Fiddletown* 11 Her hair, which was a very violent red, was [etc.]. 1886 Ruskin *Præterita* II. 204 The accurate study of tree branches..had more and more taught me the difference between violent and graceful lines. 1888 *Cent. Mag.* Feb. 539/1 Rouge, if too violent, by a natural law of color causes the planes of the cheeks to recede from the planes of the..whiter portions of the face.

2. a. Of natural forces: Possessed of or operating with great force or strength; moving, flowing, blowing, etc., strongly and impetuously.
c 1375 *Sc. Leg. Saints* xxxviii. (*Adrian*) 509 Of þe hewine a rayne gert fal, sa wyolent & fellonny, þat þe fyr slokit wes in hy. 1508 Dunbar *Gold. Targe* 238 Thay fyrit gunnis wyth powder violent. 1593 Shaks. *Rich. II*, ii. i. 34 For violent fires soone burne out themselues. 1600 E. Blount tr. *Conestaggio* 230 Hee knewe it [a river] was verie violent, running betwixte high mountaines without anie forde. 1610 Holland *Camden's Brit.* 680 It carrieth so violent a streame that presently it is able to driue a mill. 1658 T. Willsford *Nature's Secrets* 107 Venus and ☽,..increases the flowing of the Seas, causing violent Tides. 1712 E. Cooke *Voy. S. Sea* 382 The South and S.W. Winds, which are the violentest Winter Winds there. 1794 Mrs. Radcliffe *Myst. Udolpho* xxix, The accumulating clouds..assumed a red sulphureous tinge that foretold a violent storm. 1815 J. Smith *Panorama Sci. & Art* II. 46 In some places the time of change is attended with calms, in others..with violent tempests. 1854 *Poultry Chron.* II. 407/2 The circumstance of their having been in a violent storm and completely drenched. 1875 *Encycl. Brit.* III. 809/2 The violent explosives disintegrate the rock into a plastic mass.

b. Of noise: Extremely loud.
1602 *Kyd's Span. Trag.* iii. xii a. 131 Then, sir, after some violent noyse, bring me foorth..with my torch in my hand. 1761 *Encycl. Brit.* (ed. 3) X. 56/2 There appeared a prodigious smoke, attended with the same violent noise. 1815 J. Smith *Panorama Sci. & Art* II. 836 At the instant of its beginning to melt, it explodes with a violent report. 1852 Dickens *Bleak Ho.* vi, The stranger only answered with another violent snort.

3. a. Of persons: Acting with or using physical force or violence, esp. in order to injure, control, or intimidate others; committing harm or doing destruction in this way; †acting illegally, taking illegal possession.
1382 Wyclif *Matt.* xi. 12 The kyngdam of heuenes suffreth strengthe, or violence, and violent men rauyshen it. 1387 Trevisa *Higden* (Rolls) I. 87 Men þey acounteþ violent and wommen mylde, and euere þei beeþ vnesi to hir

neiheboures. c**1460** *Wisdom* 1101 in *Macro Plays* 71 With my syght I se þe people vyolent. **1533** MORE *Apol.* xl. 225 The man is bysyde so violent and so iubardouse, that none of theym dare be a knowen to speke of it. **1555** *Sc. Acts, Mary* (1814) II. 494/2 The actioun aganis the violent occupyaris and possessouris foirsaidis. **1560** BIBLE (Genev.) *Ps.* lxxxv. 14 The proude are risen against me, and the assemblies of violent men haue soght my soule. **1662** *Bk. Com. Prayer, For Restoring Public Peace*, The outrage of a violent and unruly people. **1687** *Assur. Abbey Lands* 195 A violent possessor of Church-lands. **1782** J. BROWN *Nat. & Rev. Relig.* I. i. 29 Violent injurers of others being public pests of society. **1849** MACAULAY *Hist. Eng.* v. I. 662 He had ..been very unwilling to employ as his deputy a man so violent and unprincipled as Goodenough.

absol. **1388** WYCLIF *Job* v. 15 God schal make saaf..a pore man fro the hond of the violent. **1535** COVERDALE *Matt.* xi. 12 Yᵉ kyngdome of heauen suffreth violence, and the violent plucke it vnto them.

b. Of the hand. Chiefly in the phr. ***to lay violent hands on*** or ***upon*** (also Sc. †*in*).

c**1375** *Sc. Leg. Saints* xxviii. (*Margaret*) 125 þan ware handis wyolent layd one þat cristis Innocent. **1529** MORE *Dyaloge* IV. Wks. 274/1 Al our dedes good or badde ascend or descende by the violent hande of God. **1588** SHAKS. *Tit. A.* III. ii. 22 Teach her not thus to lay Such violent hands vppon her tender life. **1597** in *Maitl. Cl. Misc.* I. 129 A. H. ..is fund..ane quha hes put violent handis in his father. **1605** SHAKS. *Macb.* v. viii. 70 His Fiend-like Queene, Who (as 'tis thought) by selfe and violent hands, Tooke off her life. **1662** *Bk. Com. Prayer, Burial Dead*, The Office ensuing is not to be used for any that..have laid violent hands upon themselves. **1749** FIELDING *Tom Jones* XII. iii, He laid violent hands on the collar of poor Partridge. **1753** *Chambers' Cycl.* Suppl. s.v. *Vices*, Staying him [*sc.* a horse], by degrees, with a steady, not a violent hand. c**1850** BRYANT *The Path* 70 What guilt is theirs who, in their greed or spite, Undo thy holy work with violent hands!

†**c.** With *to* (a person or thing). *Obs.*

1588 SHAKS. *Tit. A.* v. ii. 109, I pray thee doe on them some violent death, They haue bene violent to me and mine. **1645** MILTON *Tetrach.* 67 Colluders your selves, as violent to this law of God by your unmercifull binding, as the Pharises by their unbounded loosning!

4. Of actions: **a.** Characterized by the doing of harm or injury; accompanied by the exercise of violence.

13.. *E.E. Allit. P.* B. 1013 þis was a vengaunce violent þat voyded þise places, þat foundered has so fayre a folk & þe folde sonkken. c**1380** *Antecrist* in Todd *Three Treat. Wyclif* 116 þe first persecution of þe chirche was violent, whenne cristen men weren compellid bi exilyngis, betyngis, & deþis to make sacrifice to ydols. **1548** COOPER *Elyot's Dict.*, *Raptio*,..violent taking of a persone. **1598** SHAKS. *Merry W.* III. ii. 44 To these violent proceedings all my neighbors shall cry aime. **1606** —— *Tr. & Cr.* v. iii. 21 [To use] violent thefts, And rob in the behalfe of charitie. **1617** MORYSON *Itin.* III. 43 The more violent, at least more lasting persecution of them by fier under Marie, late Queene of England. a**1720** SEWELL *Hist. Quakers* I. Pref. a 3, They.. have at length Triumphed..by suffering,..and under violent Oppression from High and Low. **1809–10** COLERIDGE *Friend* (1865) 140 There could be no motive for a sudden and violent change of government. **1840** DICKENS *Old C. Shop* liii, Thus violent deeds live after men upon the earth. **1849** MACAULAY *Hist. Eng.* v. I. 546 The injustice with which he had been treated would have excused him if he had resorted to violent methods of redress.

b. Characterized by the exertion of great physical force or strength; done or performed with intense or unusual force, and with some degree of rapidity; not gentle or moderate.

In later use (*b*) tending to a weaker sense.

(*a*) **1398** TREVISA *Barth. De P.R.* III. xv. (1495) 60 By vyolent stoppyng of the throte and of the arteryes. **1526** *Pilgr. Perf.* (W. de W. 1531) 114 b, By the violent fall of the sayd crosse in to the morteys. a**1547** SURREY in *Tottel's Misc.* (Arb.) 27 The lofty pyne the great winde often riues: With violenter swey falne turrets stepe. **1595** SHAKS. *John* v. vii. 49 Oh, I am scalded with my violent motion And spleene of speede, to see your Maiesty. **1601** —— *All's Well* III. ii. 112 O you leaden messengers, That ride vpon the violent speede of fire. **1664** H. POWER *Exp. Philos.* 93 We perceived ..the little particles of air..on the suddain to become more visible by a violent and rapid dilatation. **1669** STURMY *Mariner's Mag.* v. xii. 69 The Piece is Level, and will carry the Bullet Horizontally in his violent Course. **1725** DE FOE *Voy. round World* (1840) 332 There was..some more violent motion at a distance. **1798** S. & HT. LEE *Canterb. T.* II. 133 Wine acted powerfully on a constitution already feverish with violent exercise. **1837** WHEWELL *Hist. Induct. Sci.* (1857) I. 7 Classifying them into Natural Motions and Violent Motions.

(*b*) **1857** MILLER *Elem. Chem., Org.* viii. 536 The action of bromine upon indigo is analogous to that of chlorine, though it is less violent. **1862** H. SPENCER *First Princ.* I. v. §32 (1875) 119 During those early stages..both political and religious changes..are necessarily violent; and necessarily entail violent retrogressions. **1868** BAIN *Mental & Mor. Sci.* IV. iii. 341 A certain impetus has been given,..and, if restrained outwardly, it seems to be more violent inwardly.

c. Tending to wrest or pervert the meaning.

1720 WATERLAND *Eight Serm.* 104 That we ought not to be wise beyond what is written, nor put a violent Construction on any Passages.

5. †**a.** *in violent*, by force or constraint. *Obs.*⁻¹

c**1440** *Alph. Tales* 148 þai..told hym þat þai tuke not his son & made him freer [= friar] in violent, bod he offerd hym þerto on his awn gude will.

†**b.** Due or subject to constraint or force; not free or voluntary; forced. *Obs.*

1560 DAUS tr. *Sleidane's Comm.* 124 They desyre the kynge to forsee, that there be no violent counsell called, in a place suspect & perillous, to the intent that vnder the name of a counsel, the true doctrine be not extinguished. **1574** HELLOWES *Gueuara's Fam. Ep.* (1577) 297 All violent marriages engender hatred betwixt the married. **1625** N. CARPENTER *Geog. Del.* II. v. (1635) 71 This conformity of the water dropps in a round figure is rather Violent, then Naturall. **1667** MILTON *P.L.* IV. 97 Ease would recant Vows made in pain, as violent and void.

c. Of death: Caused by or due to physical violence; not natural.

1588 SHAKS. *Tit. A.* v. ii. 108, I pray thee doe on them some violent death. **1593** —— *2 Hen. VI*, I. iv. 34 The Duke yet liues, that Henry shall depose: But him out-liue, and dye a violent death. **1651** HOBBES *Leviath.* II. xxi. 114 Though Soveraignty..is,..in its own nature, not only subject to violent death, by forreign war; but also [etc.]. **1790** PALEY *Serm.* Wks. (1834) 598/2 Sudden, violent, or untimely deaths..leave an impression upon a whole neighbourhood. **1822** SCOTT *Nigel* xxv, Men, who had both, within..less than half an hour, suffered violent death. **1836–7** DICKENS *Sk. Boz, Scenes* xxv, Whose miserable career will shortly terminate in a violent and shameful death. **1863** BOYD *Graver Thoughts Country Parson* Ser. I. iv. 67 The violent end of the martyr Stephen.

d. *Sc. Law.* Of profits: (see quot. 1765–8).

1594 *Sc. Acts, Jas. VI* (1816) IV. 69/1 In all tyme cuming the partie pursewit be ane vther for eiectioun sall find cautioun for the violent proffittis. **1606** *Ibid.* 286 The saidis decreittis..may bring þe danger of the ȝeirlie violent proffeittis vpoun the persones. **1678** SIR G. MACKENZIE *Crim. Laws Scot.* II. vi. §4 (1699) 190 When spoilzies or ejections are civilly pursued, the conclusion is violent profits (which is the double Rent of the Lands, and restitution of the thing craved). **1752** W. STEWART in *Scots. Mag.* (1753) 294/1 It can be no more than violent profits, which is often modified in inferior courts. **1765–8** ERSKINE *Inst. Law Scot.* II. vi. §54 Violent profits are so called, because they become due on the tenant's forcible or unwarrantable detaining the possession after he ought to have removed. **1814** SCOTT *Wav.* lxvi, Even when ye hae gotten decreet of spuilzie, oppression, and violent profits against them. **1838** W. BELL *Dict. Law Scot.* 1028 In rural tenements, the violent profits are held to be the full profits which the landlord could have made... In urban tenements, the violent profits are generally estimated at double the stipulated rent.

6. Of persons, their temper, etc.: Displaying or exhibiting passion, excessive ardour, or lack of moderation in action or conduct. Cf. sense 3.

1647 CLARENDON *Hist. Reb.* III. §149 If this Bill were once passed..the Violenter Party would be never able to prosecute their Designs. **1654** GATAKER *Disc. Apol.* 27 Some of the violenter sort of the other partie. **1706** HEARNE *Collect.* (O.H.S.) I. 291 Dunster, one of yᵉ Violentest Whiggs. **1715** BURNET *Hist. Own Time* (1766) I. 155 One of the violentest Ministers of the whole party. **1769** BURKE *Corr.* (1844) I. 215 He entertained me with an account of the present state of Lord Chatham's politics; violent, as before, against the ministry. **1858** LD. GRANVILLE in Fitzmaurice *Life* (1905) I. 306 Shaftesbury..is much more violent for you than he was against you. **1888** S. MAIMON *Autob.* ix. 59 In my passions I was violent and impatient.

absol. **1681** DRYDEN *Abs. & Achit.* To Rdr., The Violent on both sides will condemn the Character of Absalom. **1713** POPE *Lett.* (1735) I. 200, I am no way displeased that I have offended the Violent of all Parties already.

7. Of language, or writings: Resulting from, indicative or expressive of strong feeling.

1749 FIELDING *Tom Jones* XI. v, He..concluded by a very fond caress, and many violent protestations of love. **1818** SCOTT *Hrt. Midl.* xiv, The letter,..the contents of which were as singular as the expression was violent. **1826** DISRAELI *Viv. Grey* v. xi, He wrote violent letters, protesting his innocence. **1872** J. MORLEY *Voltaire* (1886) 5 The temperament which mistakes strong expression for strong judgment, and violent phrase for grounded conviction.

II. 8. In intensive use: Very or extremely great, strong, or severe. **a.** In legal use, chiefly *Sc.*, of suspicion or presumption.

1516 *Sc. Acts, Jas. V* (1875) XII. 36/2 All Lawis excludis þe said governour fra administracion and governance for suspicioun vehement and violent. **1678** SIR G. MACKENZIE *Crim. Laws Scot.* II. xxiv. §3 (1699) 256 Except the Presumptions be very violent, I cannot allow this Limitation. *Ibid.* xxv. §4. 263 Presumptions are divided, in Presumptions that are violent..and these that are not violent. **1768** BLACKSTONE *Comm.* III. 371 Violent presumption is many times equal to full proof.

b. In general use.

1578 TIMME *Caluine on Gen.* 30 It is too violent a cavill that Moses for instructions sake, distributeth all those thinges which he made at once, into sixe days. **1589** PUTTENHAM *Eng. Poesie* III. ii. (Arb.) 153 My Lord the simple woman is not so much to blame as her lewde abbettours, who by violent perswasions haue lead her into this wilfulnesse. **1607** SHAKS. *Cor.* IV. vi. 73 He and Auffidius can no more attone Then violent'st Contrariety. **1641** MILTON *Animadv.* v. Wks. 1738 I. 92 If your meaning be with a violent Hyperbaton to transpose the Text. **1807** SYD. SMITH *Lett. Catholics* Wks. 1859 II. 176/1, I cannot make use of so violent a metaphor. **1830** HERSCHEL *Study Nat. Phil.* 154 Ammonia is, however, a violent outstanding exception. **1891** FARRAR *Darkn. & Dawn* lxii, Judæa was in a state of violent revolt, and the presence of an able general was urgently needed.

c. Of feelings, etc.

1593 SHAKS. *Lucr.* 894 Thy violent vanities can never last. **1609** DEKKER *Gull's Horn-bk.* 27 That argues a violent impatience to depart from your money. **1638** JUNIUS *Paint. Ancients* 45 A blind fit of a most violent and irresistible fury. **1742** FIELDING *Jos. Andrews* I. iv, The violent respect he preserved for her. a**1770** JORTIN *Serm.* (1771) II. ii. 28 Repining and discontent arise from a violent affection for things here below. **1828** LYTTON *Pelham* I. xxiii, The duchesse was in a violent fright. **1846** MRS. A. MARSH *Father Darcy* II. xiii. 231 With that feeling of violent irritation which the slightest contradiction now produced. **1875** JOWETT *Plato* (ed. 2) V. 76 The intemperate life has violent delights, and still more violent desires.

†**B.** As *adv.* Violently. *Obs.*

1709 LADY M. W. MONTAGU *Let. to Mrs. Hewet* 12 Nov., These wars make men so violent scarce, that these good ladies take up with the shadows of them. **1712** W. ROGERS *Voy.* 39 This was a fair pleasant Day, but violent hot. **1719** LONDON & WISE *Compl. Gard.* 171 If it freezes so violent as that we are expos'd to danger.

C. *sb.* Something which acts with violence or force; a violent passion or person. *Obs.* after 17th c., but revived in recent use. Also in *Comb.*

1619 LUSHINGTON *Resurrect. Rescued* (1659) 21 All those Violents of the Soul which have mischiefs for their Objects, ..as sorrow, fear and despair. **1667** *Decay Chr. Piety* iv. 53 Did the Covetous extortioner observe that he is involv'd in the same sentence, [and] remember that such Violents shall take not heaven, but hell, by force. **1978** *Jrnl. Communication* XXVIII. 180 The number of roles in which characters were the perpetrators of violence (violents), its victims, or both. *Ibid.* 187 The violent-victim ratio ranged from −1.40 in 1973 to −1.06 in 1977, suggesting persistently negative but perhaps decreasing risks of general victimization. **1983** J. SCOTT *All Pretty People* ii. 12 The psychiatric wards are filled with violents, and they release them every day.

†**'violent**, *v.* *Obs.* [ad. OF. (also mod.F.) *violenter*, or ad. med.L. *violentāre* to compel by force: see prec.]

1. *trans.* To strain or wrest the meaning of (words, a passage, etc.). *rare.*

1549 LATIMER *5th Serm. bef. Edw. VI* (Arb.) 150 Thus they force and violent thys place to make for theyr purpose, wher no such thynge is mente.

2. To constrain or force by violence; to compel or coerce (a person).

Freq. in the 17th c., esp. in Scottish writers.

1598 FLORIO *Vehementare*, to vrge, to force, to constraine, to violent. **1634** LD. WARISTON *Diary* (S.H.S.) 200 My saule violented and urged God by this argumenting prayer. **1655** R. BAILLIE *Dissuas. Vindication* Pref., I could no longer be dumb, but so violented, I at last do open my mouth. **1678** SIR G. MACKENZIE *Crim. Laws Scot.* I. xxxiv. §7 (1699) 164 The civil Law in detestation of Force and Violence, did allow three several Remedies to the person violented. **1717** BOSTON in *Acc. Life* (1908) 227, I hope the Reverend Commission will not violent me, which they will do, if they transport me to Closeburn. **1725** WODROW *Corr.* (1843) III. 179 This matter would..be softly handled; and the woman and her brother look like cruel and inhuman..people, in violenting the good man in this matter.

refl. **1730** BOSTON *Mem.* (1899) 225, I would fain have caused draw the nail again, but because of one that was present I restrained and violented myself.

b. To compel or force (a person) *to* (*unto*, *into*) some action or *to* do something.

1655 FULLER *Ch. Hist.* XI. xvii. 157 When a great Adversary stepping in so violented his Majesty to a Tryall, that all was..frustrated. **1660** —— *Mixt Contempl.* xxxvii. (1841) 202 Surely many moderate men designed a good mark to themselves... But query whether,..in our late civil destruction, they were not violented to outrun the mark. **1710** BLACKWELL *Schema Sacrum* v. 103 Sin and Damnation violenting him (as it were) unto the same. **1721** WODROW *Hist. Suff. Ch. Scot.* I. 469 The Procedure of this Period, in violenting People into the Declaration.

3. To bring about (an action) by force or compulsion. *rare*⁻¹.

1650 R. GENTILIS *Considerations* 53 The free putting himselfe into his hands..being done willingly, not violented by any extrinsecall mover.

4. To perpetrate or attempt with violence.

a**1661** FULLER *Worthies, Anglesea* IV. (1662) 19 This Bishop Farrar was afterwards martyred in the raign of Queen Mary. I find not the least appearance, that his former adversaries violented any thing against him under that Queen.

5. *intr.* To act or rage with violence. *rare*⁻¹.

The 1st Folio reads 'no lesse'.

1606 SHAKS. *Tr. & Cr.* IV. iv. 4 (Q.), Why tell you me of moderation? The greife is fine, full, perfect, that I taste, And violenteth in a sence as strong As that which causeth it.

Hence †**'violented** *ppl. a. Obs.*

1642 HOWELL *Twelve Treat.* (1661) 90 It reaches to their very soules and consciences, by violented new coercive Oaths and Protestations. c**1643** *Observ. on his Majesty's late Answers* 24 A strange violented wrested conclusion.

violently ('vaɪələntlɪ), *adv.* [f. VIOLENT *a.* + -LY².]

1. By means of physical strength or violence; by the exercise of improper or unlawful force; forcibly. Now *Obs.* or *arch.*

1382 WYCLIF *Ezek.* xxii. 29 Puplis of the loond..violentli rauysheden the nedi man, and tourmentiden the pore man. c**1400** MAUNDEV. (1839) viii. 91 And there was oure Lord.. scourged and smytten and vylently entreted. c**1440** *Jacob's Well* 16 Be þis artycle are þey vnderstonde acursyd þat stelyn or beryn violently out of holy cherche holy cherch good. **1526** *Pilgr. Perf.* (W. de W. 1531) 254 How violently and without all..pite they racked that blessed body. **1535** COVERDALE *Lev.* v. 23 He shal restore agayne that he toke violently awaye, or gat wrongeously. **1582** N. T. (Rhem.) *John* vi. Annotations, Not compelling or violently forcing any against their will. **1631** GOUGE *God's Arrows* II. §7. 142 What is violently or fraudulently gotten, wilbe lavishly spent. **1695** LD. PRESTON *Boeth.* I. 32 If thou hadst rather be thought to have been violently remov'd, thou hast done thyself this Injury. **1786** BURKE *W. Hastings* Wks. 1842 II. 108 After he had..unjustly and violently expelled the rajah Cheyt Sing..from his said lordship. **1823** SCOTT *Quentin D.* xxxiii, To restore the banners of the community, which you took violently from the town.

b. With other than physical violence; in some illegal, unwarrantable, or improper manner.

1551 T. WILSON *Logike* (1580) 16 Neither can any Lawe bee able, violently to force the inwarde thought of man. **1560** DAUS tr. *Sleidane's Comm.* 216 Luther was in dede condemned at Rome, but his cause not heard, violently and tyrannically. **1626** GOUGE *Serm. Dignity Chivalry* §1 The forenamed point, The Dignity of Chivalry, is not violently wrested, but properly ariseth out of my Text. **1849** RUSKIN *Sev. Lamps* iv. §18. 108 You will infect that form itself with the vulgarity of the thing to which you have violently attached it.

2. By or with great or extreme force, strength, or vigour; with impetuous or violent motion or action; so as to produce a violent effect.

1387 TREVISA *Higden* (Rolls) II. 25 Þeyh al an oost stood by þe pond and torned þe face thiderward, þe water wolde drawe hem violentliche toward þe pond. ? *a* **1400** *Morte Arth.* 2571 With þe venymous swerde a vayne has he towchede! That voydes so violently þat alle his witte changede! *a* **1425** tr. *Arderne's Treat. Fistula*, etc. 54 Som tyme a man is smytyn som party of þe legge violently without wondyng of þe skynne. *Ibid.* 65 Þis [remedy].. wirkeþ noȝt so violently as puluis sine pari for þe vertgrez þat entreþ not here. **1495** *Trevisa's Barth. De P.R.* XI. xiii. (Caxton) 398 Though a bledder be lyghte yet it makyth grete noyse and sowne yf it be strongly blowen and afterwarde vyolently broken. *c* **1535** M. NISBET *Prol. Rom.* (S.T.S.) III. 339 The greattest appetite ouircumis the less, and charyis the man avay vyolently with hir. **1595** *Locrine* II. v. 66 The currents swift swimme violently with blood. **1597** A. M. tr. *Guillemeau's Fr. Chirurg.* 30/2 If the Arterye be greate, and violently beateth. **1613** PURCHAS *Pilgrimage* (1614) 351 The streame shooting violently ouer their heads without wetting them. **1669** STURMY *Mariner's Mag.* v. xii. 69 At 10 deg. mounture, [the gun] carries the Bullet violently 248 Paces. **1711** BUDGELL *Spect.* No. 161. ¶3 An huge brawny Fellow, who twirled him about, and shook the little Man so violently, that [etc.]. **1750** tr. *Leonardus' Mirr. Stones* 132 When it is kindled by fire, it rarifies, and is violently dilated. **1777** R. WATSON *Philip II*, xxi. (1839) 449 The ships were driven violently against each other. **1842** LOVER *Handy Andy* xxvi, The bells rang violently through the house. **1857** MILLER *Elem. Chem.*, *Org.* i. 48 The chlorinated derivatives of Dutch liquid are violently decomposed by potassium. **1860** TYNDALL *Glac.* I. xxvii. 211 The windows shook violently.

3. With great intensity or severity; to a high degree or pitch; intensely, severely.

14.. *Brut* II. 328 Grete..hetes, & þerewiþal a grete pestilens..destroyed & slow, violently & strongly, both men & wymmen without noumbre. **1697** DRYDEN *Virg. Georg.* I. 136 Lest soaking Show'rs shou'd pierce her secret Seat, Or scorching Suns too violently heat. **1724** *Lond. Gaz.* No. 6306/2 The Small Pox are come out very violently on the Queen Widow. **1745** *Life Bamfylde-Moore Carew* 34 Violently afflicted with the Sea-sickness. **1802** *Arab. Nts.* (1815) II. 172 He wept most violently. **1842** THACKERAY *Fitzboodle's Prof.* Misc. Wks. 1857 IV. 6 The consequence was that I became so violently ill as to be reported intoxicated. **1855** MACAULAY *Hist. Eng.* xiii. III. 351 The civil war..broke forth again more violently than before.

b. In intensive or emphatic use: To a very great or extreme degree or extent; very greatly, powerfully, or strongly.

1601 SIR W. CORNWALLIS *Disc. Seneca* (1631) 43 It is no charity to give so violently as to lay waste the maine of an estate. **1621** FLETCHER *Isl. Princ.* III. i, I may be mad, or violently drunk. **1817** JAS. MILL *Brit. India* I. I. i. 3 This splendid fortune had violently attracted the attention of Europe. **1845** DICKENS *Chimes* i. ¶1 A great multitude of persons will be violently astonished. **1869** *Eng. Mech.* 19 Nov. 224/3 We see it [an ellipse] violently foreshortened.

4. Strongly, in respect of feeling; with deep feeling or emotion; ardently, passionately, vehemently.

1617 MORYSON *Itin.* III. 55 My selfe weary of expecting companions, and violently carried with the desire to returne into my Countrey, did all alone..passe ouer the Alpes. **1682** NORRIS *Hierocles* 35 Not violently agitated by our domestick passions. **1726** SWIFT *Gulliver* II. vi, He then desired to know..how it came to pass that people were so violently bent upon getting into this assembly. **1780** *Mirror* No. 78, As I was not violently inclined towards literature. **1841** LANE *Arab. Nts.* I. 90 Upon which the man..became violently enraged. **1906** *Lit. World* 15 Nov. 492/1 Her work ..throws her in contact with a fiery young idealist,..and she falls violently in love with him.

5. *colloq.* In a flashy or showy manner; 'loudly'.

1782 MME. D'ARBLAY *Diary* 15 Dec., She was violently dressed,—a large hoop,..ribands and ornaments extremely shown.

ˈviolentness. ? *Obs.* [f. VIOLENT *a.*] The state or quality of being violent; violence.

1692 SIR W. HOPE *Fencing Master* 148 If all that take not away the violentness of his Pursuit. **1727** BAILEY (vol. II), *Violentness*, Violence, Forcibleness, Vehemence, Sharpness, Boisterousness, Outragiousness. **1737** BRACKEN *Farriery Impr.* (1756) I. 24 The Violentness of the Seasons. **1748** WASHINGTON *Jrnl.* 4 Apr., Writ. (1889) I. 5 This day our tent was blown by ye violentness of ye wind.

‖**violento.** *Obs.*$^{-1}$ [It.:—L. *violentus* VIOLENT *a.*] A violent person; one using or inclined to use violence.

a **1661** FULLER *Worthies*, *Cumberld.* I. (1662) 218 He..was no Violento in the Troubles of Francford, but with all meekness to his might, endeavoured a pacification.

violer (ˈvaɪələ(r)). Now *arch.* Also 6 *Sc.* veolar, 6- violar, 7 violler. [ad. OF. *violeur* (AF. *violour*): see VIOL *sb.*[1] and -ER[1].] A player of the viol, in early use esp. one attached to the household of the king, a noble, etc.; a fiddler.

Chiefly in Sc. use, and frequent in Scottish records and accounts of the 16th and 17th centuries.

1551 *Acc. Ld. High Treas. Scot.* X. 32 To the saidis violaris to by thame leveray. **1551-2** *Ibid.* 67 Be the lordis compositouris speciale command to my lord governouris veolaris. **1587** FLEMING *Contn. Holinshed* III. 1338/2 An other statelie pageant..made by an other companie of the rhetoricians, called painters or violers. **1617** in *3rd Rep. Hist. MSS. Comm.* 413/1 His Maiesties violeris that accompaneit the saidis knychtis to this burgh. **1678** SIR G. MACKENZIE *Crim. Laws Scot.* II. iv. §1 (1699) 185 James Johnstoun Violer, arraigned before the Magistrats of Edinburgh. *a* **1722** SIR J. LAUDER *Decisions* (1759) I. 364 A Violer..was serenading in the night-time with his fiddle. **1797** *Encycl. Brit.* XII. 491/2 At this period *violars*, or performers on the vielle or viol,..abounded all over Europe. **1801** BUSBY *Dict. Mus.* s.v. *Violars*, certain practical musicians much encouraged in Provence during the twelfth century; and so named because they performed on the vielle and viol. **1824** SCOTT *Redgauntlet* let. xii, They have brought another violer upon my walk! **1825** —— *Betrothed* xxx, I had forgot..the distance between an Armorican violer and a high Norman baron. **1843** JAMES *Forest Days* iv, Come, Master Violer, let us hear the notes of the catgut. **1931** M. BARING *In End is my Beginning* iv. 50 Her son was given..a band of four violars.

violescent (vaɪəˈlɛsənt), *a.* [f. L. *viol-a* VIOLA[1] + -ESCENT. Cf. VIOLASCENT *a.*] Tending to a violet colour; tinged with violet.

1847 WEBSTER. **1893** VIZETELLY tr. *Zola's Dr. Pascal* i, Under the sky of a fiery, violescent blue. **1896** —— tr. *Zola's Rome* 4 The yellow sunflashes..sharply outlined the violescent shadows.

violet (ˈvaɪəlɪt), *sb.*[1] Forms: 4- violet (6 *Sc.* violat), 4-7 violett, 5-6 vyolet (5 -ett, wyolet); 5-6 violette (5-6 -ete), vyolette (5 -ytte); 5 vyalett, vielet, 6 vilet, 7-9 vi'let. [In senses 1-2, a. OF. *violete*, *violette* (mod.F. *violette*, = It. *violetta*, Sp. and Pg. *violeta*), dim. of *viole* VIOLA[1]. In senses 3-4, a. OF. *violete*, *vielete*, *vilette* fem., or *violet*, *vielet*, *vilet* (mod.F. *violet*) masc., of similar origin.]

1. A plant or flower of the genus *Viola*, esp. *V. odorata*, the sweet-smelling violet, growing wild, and cultivated in gardens; the flowers are usually purplish blue, mauve, or white. **a.** In sing. without article or with *the*.

c **1330** *Arth. & Merl.* 3061 Mirie it is in time of June,.. Violet & rose flour Woneþ þan in maidens bour. **1387** TREVISA *Higden* (Rolls) I. 261 Of þat hille [the stones] smelleþ swete as violet. *c* **1400** *Pilgr. Sowle* (Caxton, 1483) IV. xxviii. 74 The white lely, the rede rose, the fresshe violet. *c* **1440** *Pallad. on Husb.* I. 1014 In busshis, treen, & herbis they may fynde Herbe origane, and tyme, and violette. *c* **1480** HENRYSON *Fables, Lion & Mouse* iii, The rosis reid.. and the purpour violat bla. *c* **1530** *Crt. of Love* ccvi, Eke eche at other threw the floures bright, The primerose, the violete, and the gold. **1589** GREENE *Menaphon* (Arb.) 36 There growes..the cowsloppe, the primrose, and the violet. **1667** MILTON *P.L.* IV. 700 Underfoot the Violet, Crocus, and Hyacinth with rich inlay Broiderd the ground. *a* **1718** PRIOR *Garland* i, The Pride of ev'ry Grove I chose, The Violet sweet, and Lilly fair. **1785** MARTYN *Lett. Bot.* xxxi. (1794) 477 Antirrhinum, Fumitory, Violet, Impatiens, and Orchis. **1838** T. THOMSON *Chem. Org. Bodies* 386 The violet is well known to be coloured by a blue matter which acids change to red. **1855** KINGSLEY *Heroes*, *Theseus* I. 199 The meadows [are sweet] with violet.

b. with *a* and pl.: A single flower, plant, or species of this.

c **1374** CHAUCER *Boeth.* I. met. vi. (1868) 25 Yif þou wilt gadre violettz, ne go þou not to þe purper wode whan þe felde chirkynge agriseþ of colde. *c* **1400** MAUNDEV. (1839) xiv. 160 Here colour is..more browne than the Violettes. **14..** *Nom.* in Wr.-Wülcker 712 *Hec viola*, a vyolytte. **1483** *Cath. Angl.* 402/2 A violett, *viola*. **1576** FLEMING *Panopl. Epist.* 352 What man is able to affirme, that he euer sawe the Spring tide without Marche Violettes? **1598** YONG *Diana* 469 Roses and vilets strowing. **1613** DEKKER *Strange Horse Race* Ep. Ded., It can bee no shame to gather a Violet, growing close to the ground. **1697** DRYDEN *Virg. Georg.* IV. 269 He spoils the Saffron Flow'rs, he sips the Blues Of Vi'lets. **1728-46** THOMSON *Spring* 448 Where purple violets lurk With all the lowly children of the shade. **1791** COWPER *Odyss.* v. 86 Meadows of softest verdure, purpled o'er With violets. **1811** A. T. THOMSON *Lond. Disp.* (1818) 408 Violets have an agreeable sweet odour, and a very slightly bitter taste. **1880** BESSEY *Bot.* 551 The genus *Viola*, the Violets, includes about half of the species of the order.

c. *collect.* and pl. The plant, or more usually the flowers, pulled or plucked for use in medicine or in making confections.

collect. *a* **1400-50** *Stockh. Med. MS.* 11 For to makyn surripe of violet. **14..** *Med. Rec.* in *Rel. Ant.* I. 52 For the stane: tak grummel, percel, rede nettil, violet, franken ensens, and chiristane kirnels. *a* **1425** tr. *Arderne's Treat. Fistula*, etc. 67 Oile of violette with white of iii. eiren well stired togidre. **1562** TURNER *Herbal* II. 164 The violet is better that is gathered in the morninge. **1811** A. T. THOMSON *Lond. Disp.* (1818) 688 Syrup of Violet.

pl. *a* **1425** tr. *Arderne's Treat. Fistula*, etc. 93 Oile of violettez may be made in þe same maner. *Ibid.*, Oile of violettz. **1562** TURNER *Herbal* II. 164 Violettes make a man to slepe, and they are good for the disease of the vuula. **1563** HYLL *Art Garden.* (1593) 83 The Violets ought especially to be gathered in March, and dryed in a shadowey place of the aire. **1631** JORDAN *Nat. Bathes* vi. (1669) 41 If Matthiolus his reason were good, then Roses and Violets, and Vinegar should be hot. **1718** QUINCY *Compl. Disp.* 181 Violets..are in every one's acquaintance, for their Use in Medicine. **1736** BAILEY *Housh. Dict.*, *Violets* are of a laxative quality, and are us'd medically in syrups, juleps, conserves, oils, &c. **1855** MAYNE *Expos. Lex.* 539 *Iosacchar*,..old name for the sugar of violets. **1861** BENTLEY *Man. Bot.* 458 The Violets generally, have been used on the Continent, as demulcent expectorants. **1887** *Lady* 20 Jan. 38/3 Small cut-glass dishes of pink and white bon-bons, together with candied violets.

d. *fig.* (Applied esp. to persons.)

1412-20 LYDG. *Chron. Troy* III. 4380 Somme also..With þe lillye of virginite And violettis of parfit chastite, Ascendid ben a-boue þe sterris clere. **14..** —— *To My Soverain Lady* 96 O violet, O *flour desiree*, Sith I am for you so amorous [etc.]. *c* **1440** *York Myst.* xxv. 498 Hayll! vyolett, vernand with swete odoure. **1593** SHAKS. *Rich. II*, v. ii. 46 Welcome my sonne: who are the Violets now, That strew the greene lap of the new-come Spring? **1842** TENNYSON *Will Waterproof* 147 How out of place she makes The violet of a legend blow Among the chops and steaks!

2. With specific epithets: **a.** Denoting species of *Viola*, or varieties of the common violet.

The number of these is very large, and only the older or more prominent are illustrated here. Tournefort's species (53 in all) are enumerated in *Chambers' Cycl.* Suppl. (1753) s.v. *Viola*; later lists may be found in Loudon *Encycl. Pl.* (1829-36) 186 and Johnson *Cottage Gard. Dict.* (1852) 912-3. American species are given by Gray *Man. Bot.* (1860, etc.) and in recent American dictionaries. See also DOG-VIOLET.

1753 *Chambers' Cycl.* Suppl. s.v. *Viola*, The purple *alpine Violet, with very small leaves. *c* **1710** PETIVER *Catal. Ray's Eng. Herbal* Tab. xxxvii, *Bog Violet. **1777** LIGHTFOOT *Flora Scot.* (1789) II. 1109 *Viola hirta*,..*Hairy Violet. **1578-1601** *March Violet [see MARCH *sb.*[2] 2 b]. **1728** BRADLEY *Dict. Bot.* s.v. *Viola*, Single March Violets. *Ibid.*, Double March Violets. **1731** MILLER *Gard. Dict.* s.v. *Viola*, Greater hairy March Violet, without Smell. **1753** *Chambers' Cycl.* Suppl. s.v. *Viola*, The round-leaved *marsh Violet. **1777** LIGHTFOOT *Flora Scot.* (1789) I. 506 *Viola palustris*,.. Marsh Violet. **1657** COLES *Adam in Eden* 175 *Mountain Violets with jagged Leaves. **1753** *Chambers' Cycl.* Suppl. s.v. *Viola*, The great flowered yellow mountain Violet. **1858** IRVINE *Handbk. Brit. Pl.* 688 *Viola lutea*, Yellow Mountain Violet, or Yellow Pansy. **1836-** *Neapolitan Violet [see NEAPOLITAN *a.* b]. **1856** DELAMER *Fl. Gard.* (1861) 106 The *Parma Violet has very light-blue double flowers. **1880** MISS BRADDON *Just as I am* xxi, A conservatory all abloom with snowdrops and Parma violets. *c* **1710** PETIVER *Catal. Ray's Eng. Herbal* Tab. xxxvii, Yellow *Rock Violet. **1856** DELAMER *Fl. Gard.* (1861) 106 Such are the *Russian and the Neapolitan Violets, amongst the singles. **1866** *Treas. Bot.* 1218/2 Large-flowered simple kinds—*e.g.*, the Russian Violet. **1578** LYTE *Dodoens* II. 148 The *sweete Violet is called..in Latine *Viola nigra*, *Viola purpurea*. **1785** MARTYN *Lett. Bot.* xxvi. (1794) 405 The Sweet Violet, that scents the banks, hedges, and borders of woods. **1853** ROYLE *Mat. Med.* (ed. 2) 327 The..Sweet Violet..is found wild on the borders of fields. **1731** MILLER *Gard. Dict.* s.v. *Viola*, White *sweet-scented Violet. **1831** DAVIES *Mat. Med.* 338 Sweet Scented Violet. *Viola odorata*. **1597** GERARDE *Herbal* 705 The vpright Pancie is called..*Viola assurgens*, ..*Tricolor*, that is to say Straight, or vpright Violet *three coloured. **1753** *Chambers' Cycl.* Suppl. s.v. *Viola*, The mountain three coloured Violet, or pansie, with variegated flowers. *Ibid.*, The *tree Violet, with blue and white flowers. *Ibid.*, The yellow-flowered tree Violet. **1851** GLENNY *Handbk. Fl. Gard.* 164 The tree-violet is a double-flowered, dark variety, which, if kept trained to a single stem, acquires the appearance of a miniature tree. **1846-50** A. WOOD *Class-bk. Bot.* 178 *Viola tricolor*. *Tricolored Violet. Pansey. Heart's-ease. **1597** GERARDE *Herbal* 700 *Viola canina syluestris*. Dogs Violets, or *wilde Violets. **1731** MILLER *Gard. Dict.* s.v. *Viola*, Wild or Dogs Violet. *c* **1710** PETIVER *Catal. Ray's Eng. Herbal* Tab. xxxvii, Hairy *Wood Violet. **1829** LOUDON *Encycl. Plants* 186 *Viola sylvestris*, wood violet. **1903** *Westm. Gaz.* 19 Feb. 4/2 Such pretty toques of wood violets are coming over from Paris! **1597** GERARDE *Herbal* 700 *Viola martia lutea*. *Yellow Violets. **1657** COLES *Adam in Eden* 175 Yellow Violets of Virginia. **1796** WITHERING *Brit. Pl.* (ed. 3) II. 263 *Viola lutea*. Yellow Violet or Pansies.

b. Applied to plants of other genera, as ***bulbous, dog's tooth, false, rock, toothed violet.***

See also BOG *sb.*[1] 3, CALATHIAN *a.*, CORN *sb.*[1] 11, DAME'S VIOLET, GUERNSEY, MARIAN *sb.*[1] 2, MERCURY *sb.* 11, QUEEN *sb* 14 c, RAPE *sb.*[5] 4, WATER *sb.*

1597 GERARDE *Herbal* 120 *Viola Bulbosa*, or *bulbed Violet... In English we may call it the Bulbose Violet. **1578** LYTE *Dodoens* liv. 216 White *bulbus violet. **1633** JOHNSON *Gerarde's Herbal* I. lxxxviii. 149 Touching the faculties of these bulbous Violets we haue nothing to say. **1688** R. HOLME *Armoury* II. 66/2 The bulbous Violet;..the Flower hangeth down its head. **1760** J. LEE *Introd. Bot.* App. 331 Violet, Bulbous, *Galanthus*. **1597** GERARDE *Herbal* 835 The Toothed Violet, or after some *Dogs tooth Violet, is commonly called *Dentaria*. **1760** J. LEE *Introd. Bot.* App. 331 Violet, Dog's Tooth, *Erythronium*. **1846-50** A. WOOD *Class-bk. Bot.* 253 *Dalibarda repens*. *False Violet. **1866** *Treas. Bot.* 1218/2 *Rock Violet, *Chroolepus Jolithus*. **1601** HOLLAND *Pliny* II. 85 In number of leaves this floure passeth the *Sea-violet aforesaid, which never exceedeth five. **1725** *Fam. Dict.* s.v., Mr. Chomel particularly distinguishes them into two sorts, *viz.* the Sea-Violet, or our Lady-Glove, and March-Violets. **1657** COLES *Adam in Eden* 333 Some have called the yellow Lupine *Spanish Violets, ..and..Virginia Roses. **1597** GERARDE *Herbal* 833 Of *toothed Violets, or Corallwoorts. **1728** BRADLEY *Dict. Bot.* s.v., *Dentaria*,..Toothed Violets, and Coral-Wort. *Ibid.*, Bulb-bearing toothed Violet.

3. Cloth, dress, or vestments of a violet colour.

Not always clearly separable from next.

1380 in *Test. Karleol.* (1893) 139, j cote de violett. *a* **1400** *Sir Degrev.* 625 Sche come in a vyolet, With whyȝthe perl overfret. *c* **1412** HOCCLEVE *De Reg. Princ.* 696 And where be my gounes of scarlet,..Grenes also, and þe fayre violet? **1483** in R. Davies *York Rec.* (1843) 142 The aldermen shalbe in vielet & the xxiiij[ti] in blew. *a* **1513** FABYAN *Chron.* VII. 523 He was mette with the prouost of ye marchantys with a company of xv. C. horse, ye cytezyns beyng cladde in whyte and vyolette. *c* **1580** in *Eng. Hist. Rev.* July (1914) 520 In every tene clothes you muste have ij light popengaye grenes, ij light violettes, ij light skye collers, ij azars and ij Blewes. **1598** STOW *Surv.* 130 The Maior with..the Aldermen are accustomed to be present in their Violets at Paules, on Good Friday, and in their Scarlets..at the Spittle in the Holy daies (except Wednesday in Violet). **1721** C. KING *Brit. Merch.* II. 96 What is become of our noble Manufacture of Plunkets, Violets, and Blues, formerly made in Suffolk? **1849** MACAULAY *Hist. Engl.* x. II. 599 He was well pleased that, in his own palace, an outcast..should, as king of France, dress in violet on days of court mourning. **1889** PATER *G. de Latour* (1896) 29 The mass said so solemnly, in violet, on Innocents' Day.

4. a. A purplish blue colour resembling that of the violet; a pigment or dye of this colour.

Partly a substantival use of the adj.

a **1400–50** *Alexander* 4336 Nouthire to toly ne to taunde transmitte we na vebbis, To vermylion ne violett ne variant littis. *c* **1400** MAUNDEV. (1839) xiv. 160 Here colour is liche Vyolet. *c* **1475** *Promp. Parv.* 510 (K.), Violet, coloure, *violaceus*. **1604** E. G[RIMSTONE] *D'Acosta's Hist. Indies* IV. xxvii. 284 There are other kindes which they call gilleflowers of the Indies, the which are like to a fine orange tawnie vellet, or a violet. *a* **1641** BP. MOUNTAGU *Acts & Mon.* (1642) 367 Of the same stuffe and colour that the Stole was of, that is, of a violet inclining to red. **1688** R. HOLME *Armoury* IV. ix. (Roxb.) 382/1 Cassocks of fine scarletted murrey (which is violett). **1730** BAILEY (fol.), *Purple*,..a red Colour, bordering on Violet. **1796** H. HUNTER tr. *St.-Pierre's Stud Nat.* (1799) I. 543 More than one Churchman considers violet as the most beautiful of colours, because his Bishop wears it. **1815** STEPHENS *Shaw's Gen. Zool.* IX. I. 56 The whole plumage is of a beautiful blue green, changing in certain lights to violet. **1852** THACKERAY *Esmond* II. ii, I think I never saw such a beautiful violet as that of her eyes. **1884** MARQ. DUFFERIN in Lyall *Life* (1905) II. 64 A tremendous thunderstorm had..dyed Olympus and his adjoining peaks with the deepest, blackest violet.

b. The scent of violets, esp. as used in cosmetics.

a **1850** in A. Davis *Package & Print* (1967) Pl. 8 Essence of Millefleur, Bouquet, Marechalle, Resida [*sic*], Violet, Tubereuse. **1890–1** *T. Eaton & Co. Catal.* Fall & Winter 42/2 Perfumes..white violet, Italian violet,..satchet powder,..violet. **1898** [see LILAC 2c]. **1928–9** *Army & Navy Stores Catal.* 496/3 Natural Flower Perfumes.. Muguet, Rose, Violet. **1982** *Christian Science Monitor* 26 Nov. B8/3, I stocked up on Roger & Gallet hand soaps in violet and sandalwood.

5. An onion; in *pl.* spring onions, sage and onions. *slang.*

In many dicts. of slang but no contextual examples found.

1890 BARRÈRE & LELAND *Dict. Slang* II. 397/1 *Violets* (common), an euphemism for sage and onions. **1903** FARMER & HENLEY *Slang* VII. 277/1 *Violet* (or *garden-violet*),.. 1. An onion: spec. in *pl.* = spring onions used as a salad. Also (2) in pl. = sage-and-onion stuffing. **1929** M. A. GILL *Underworld Slang*, *Violets*, onions. **1946** J. IRVING *Royal Navalese* 182 *Violets*, spring onions.

6. a. *attrib.*, in various senses, as ***violet bank***, ***-bed***, ***breath***, ***crown***, ***family***, ***flower***, etc.

Sometimes *fig.*, as *violet-virtue*, or in fig. context. *the city of the Violet Crown*, Athens (after Gr. ἰοστέφανοι Ἀθῆναι, used by Pindar and Aristophanes).

1801 SOUTHEY *Thalaba* VII. xiii, So on a *violet bank The Arabian Maid laid down, Her soft cheek pillow'd upon moss and flowers. *a* **1822** SHELLEY *Triumph Life* 72 Violet banks where sweet dreams brood. **1853** HICKIE tr. *Aristoph.* (Bohn) I. 267 The *violet-bed beside the well. **1862** MEREDITH *Mod. Love* xl, The *violet breath of maidenhood. **1834** MACAULAY *Ess.*, *Pitt* (1897) 308 Pitt..loved England, as an Athenian loved the City of the *Violet Crown. **1851** MRS. BROWNING *Casa Guidi Wind.* 37 Was the violet crown that crowned thy head So over-large..It slipped down? **1877** MORLEY *Crit. Misc.* Ser. II. 385 A thrill like that which the..sight of the dear city of the Violet Crown moved in an Athenian of old. **1849** BALFOUR *Man. Bot.* §768 *Violaceæ*, the *Violet Family. *a* **1400–50** *Alexander* 1539 He castis on a Cape of kastand hewes,..A vestoure to vise on of *violet floures. **1598** FLORIO, *Violina*, a little violet flowre. **1620** VENNER *Via Recta* vii. 147 Of Violet flowers with sugar, there is made a Conserue, and also a Syrupe. **1753** *Chambers' Cycl.* Suppl. s.v. *Viola*, Violet flowers, fresh gathered, are emollient, and gently purgative. **1814** SCOTT *Ld. Isles* VI. ix, When beams the sun through April's shower, It needs must bloom, the violet flower. **1658** ROWLAND tr. *Moufet's Theat. Ins* 908 Grape-honey, Bean-honey, Lilly-honey, *Violet-honey, &c. **1728** CHAMBERS *Cycl.*, *Populeum*, ..an Unguent prepared of the Buds of black Poplar, *Violet Leaves, Navel-wort [etc.]. **1857** HENFREY *Bot.* §416 *Violaceæ*. The *Violet Order. **1822** SHELLEY *Chas. I*, I. 46 Nor leave the broad..and beaten road..For the *violet paths of pleasure. **1611** COTGR., *Violier*,..a *Violet root or plant. **1728** CHAMBERS *Cycl.* s.v. *Oil*, Palm Oil [is]..a thick unctuous Liquor, of a yellow Colour, and a *Violet-smell. **1804** *Med. Jrnl.* XII. 230 The flowers have a violet smell. *a* **1814** *Intrigues of a Day* I. i. in *New Brit. Theatre* I. 76 That may soon be washed away. Only a little milk of roses, or *violet soap, and all will be well. **1828** MISS MITFORD *Village* Ser. III. (1863) 117 here I used to come almost every morning, during the *violet-tide. **1862** GOULBURN *Pers. Relig.* II. iv. I. 261 Here is the bosom-adder of vanity coiled up in the *violet-tuft of humility. **1628** FELTHAM *Resolves* II. vi. 12 It may seeme strange..that such a poore *violet Vertue [*sc.* humility] should euer dwell with Honour. **1620** VENNER *Via Recta* vii. 125 If there be neede of cooling with Rose, or *Violet-water and Sugar.

b. In adj. combs., chiefly instrumental, as ***violet-adorned***, ***-crowned***, ***-embroidered***, ***-garlanded***, ***-inwoven***, ***-scented***; also ***violet-dewy***, ***-hued***, ***-like***, ***-rippling***, ***-sweet***.

1953 C. DAY LEWIS *Italian Visit* iii. 37 *Violet-adorned beauties. **1837** B. D. WALSH *Aristoph.*, *Acharnians* II. vi, The envoys.., in order to cheat your Assemblies, Would call you all '*violet-crowned'. **1869** A. R. WALLACE *Malay Archip.* I. 366 A beautiful violet-crowned dove. **1932** BLUNDEN *Halfway House* 73 All fresh and *violet-dewy. **1637** MILTON *Comus* 233 In the *violet imbroider'd vale Where the love-lorn Nightingale Nightly to thee her sad Song mourneth well. **1836–48** B. D. WALSH *Aristoph.*, *Knights* V. i, He is dwelling now in ancient and fair and *violet-garlanded Athens. **1867** MISS BRADDON *R. Godwin* i, There were no tears in the large *violet-hued eyes. **1820** SHELLEY *Prometh. Unb.* IV. 197 Two runnels of a rivulet, Between the close moss *violet-inwoven, Have made their path of melody. **1825** *Greenhouse Comp.* I. 107 Purple *violet-like flowers on coriaceous roundish leaves. **1949** BLUNDEN *After Bombing* 29 And some have sung though never seen Melodious, voiceful, *violet-rippling, blushful Hippocrene. **1840** MRS. NORTON *Dream* 238 The *violet-scented lanes—the warm south-wall. **1859** GEO. ELIOT *A. Bede* xii, An afternoon in which destiny..poisons us with violet-scented breath. **1851** MRS. BROWNING *Casa Guidi Wind.* I. 411 Like some new bee-swarm leaving the old hive, Despite the wax..so *violet-sweet.

c. With vbl. sbs., as ***violet farming***, ***-plucking***, ***-poisoning***, ***setting***.

c **1440** *Pallad. on Husb.* (1896) 268 Violette settyng in Feuerer. **1833** T. HOOK *Parson's Dau.* I. i, Daisy-picking and violet-plucking [were now] the only pursuits she really loved. **1896** *Westm. Gaz.* 28 Oct. 8/2 The above case of violet-poisoning. **1902** *Daily Chron.* 17 July 6/3 Rose culture, violet farming, bee-keeping, or poultry rearing.

7. Special Combs.: †**violet-apple**, a violet-scented sort of apple; **violet-blind** *a.*, colour-blind as regards the violet rays of the spectrum; hence *violet-blindness*; **violet cream**, (*a*) a violet-scented cosmetic cream; (*b*) a violet-flavoured confection; †**violet-pear**, a violet-scented sort of pear; **violet powder**, a variety of toilet-powder; hence *violet-powder* vb.; †**violet tables**, lozenges made from violets and sugar; **violet tea**, an infusion made from dried violet flowers; **violet tree** (?); **violet-wood**, (*a*) kingwood; (*b*) the wood of the Australian *Acacia pendula*; (*c*) the wood of *Andira violacea*, a tree of Guyana; **violetworts**, Lindley's name for the *Violaceæ*.

1664 in Evelyn *Pomona* 47 Herefordshire affords several sorts of Cider-apples, as..the Gennet-moyle, the Summer-*violet or Fillet, and the Winter-fillet. **1676** WORLIDGE *Cyder* 163 The Violet-Apple is of a most delicate aromatick taste. **1894** ABNEY *Colour Vision* (1895) 70 The kind of colour that these colour blind imagine as white, whether they be red-, green-, or *violet-blind. *Ibid.* 73 So far I have only met with what appears to be one genuine case of *violet blindness. **1912** J. WEBSTER *Daddy-Long-Legs* 203, I started down town to-day to buy..a jar of *violet cream and a cake of Castile soap. **1965** A. CHRISTIE *At Bertram's Hotel* xxi. 194 They were lovely chocolates... There were some violet creams. That's the sort of chocolate that has a crystallised violet on top. **1683** EVELYN *Kal. Hort.* (ed. 7) 104 *Violet-pear, Petworth-pear, otherwise called the Winter-Windsor. **1856** DICKENS *Little Dorrit* (1857) II. ii. 338 She mended her complexion with *violet powder. **1858** SIMMONDS *Dict. Trade*, *Violet-powder*, powdered starch or flour scented, used..to powder the skin. **1859** *Habits of Gd. Society* i. 114 The use of violet-powder after shaving, now very common .., is one that should be avoided. **1876** MISS BROUGHTON *Joan* vi, She has, however, violet-powdered her fresh cheeks. **1620** VENNER *Via Recta* vii. 147 There is..made of Violets and Sugar, certaine Plates, called *Violet Tables, which are very pleasant to the taste. **1853** MRS. GASKELL *Ruth* III. iii. 115 She..brought her up a cup of soothing violet-tea. **1904** *Cassell's New Dict. Cookery* XVIII. 1033/1 *Violet tea*, this is a soothing beverage for persons suffering from bronchitis and similar affections. **1878** H. M. STANLEY *Dark Cont.* II. ix. 281 You may also see here [*sc.* Barundu] the *Strelitza vagina*, or the wild banana, or the *violet-tree, and the oil-berry tree. **1698** T. FROGER *Voy.* 129 Letter-wood (as they call it) and that of *Violet,..are very common in that country. **1843** HOLTZAPFFEL *Turning* I. 89 King-wood, called also Violet-wood, is imported from the Brazils. **1852** [see MYALL[2]]. **1866** *Treas. Bot.* 1218/2. **1846** LINDLEY *Veg. Kingd.* 338 The *Violet-worts are distinctly defined by their definite stamens.

†**'violet**, *sb.*[2] *Obs.*[−1] [ad. It. *violetta*, dim. of *viola* VIOLA[2].] (See quot. and cf. VIOLETTE.)

1688 R. HOLME *Armoury* III. xvi. (Roxb.) 58/1 The Violet or Violin, a diminitiue of the viol, being a very small Instrument, yet in all respects answereth to the forme of the Treble Viole in the body.

violet ('vaɪəlɪt), *a.* Also 4–6 violett, 5 vyolet(te, vyelett, vialet, 6 violitt. [a. OF. *violet*, *vielet*, *villet* (mod.F. *violet*) adj.: see VIOLET *sb.*[1] Cf. It. *violetto*, Pg. *violete*.]

1. a. Having the colour of violets; of a blue or bluish-purple colour.

In early use only of woven fabrics.

1370 *Bury Wills* (Camden) 5, j violett toga. *c* **1440** *Promp. Parv.* 509/2 Vialet, yn colowre, *violaceus*. **1464** *Maldon* (Essex) *Court Rolls* Bundle 40, No. 6, ii togas blewe et vyolette, 1 dobelet. *c* **1481** *Cely Papers* (Camden) 202 Item iij stykkes of tarny sateyn or els vyelett sateyn of Bruges. **1524** *Lincoln Wills* (1914) I. 130 A violitt reband with silver aglyttes. **1544** *Knaresborough Wills* (Surtees) I. 34 To Agnes Gill my violett kirtell. **1579** *Reg. Privy Council Scot.* III. 195 Thre single pandis, freinyeit with violet silk. *c* **1620** MORYSON *Itin.* IV. v. i. (1903) 438 Next rode some 20. of the Pope's Chamberlayns and cheefe officers, cloathed in gownes of violett Cloth. **1812** SIR H. DAVY *Chem. Philos.* 223 The luminous particles at the violet end of the spectrum. **1857** MILLER *Elem. Chem.*, *Org.* viii. 537 Boiling nitric acid colours it violet. **1884** MARQ. DUFFERIN in Lyall *Life* (1905) II. 64 Directly fronting you, rises a magnificent violet stretch of mountain.

b. Qualifying *colour*, *hue*, *tint*, etc.

c **1400** MAUNDEV. (Roxb.) xvii. 80 Men find dyamaundz of violet colour. **1548** COOPER *Elyot's Dict.*, *Violarius*, he that dieth violet colour. **1601** HOLLAND *Pliny* II. 621 There is not one of these Ameythysts, but it is transparent with a Violet colour. **1622–3** *Essex Archdeaconry Depositions Bk.* (MS.) 27 Feb. 26 One cloake for a man made of broade cloath and of a violett couler. **1648** HEXHAM II, *Een Violette verwe*, a Violet Dye or colour. **1706** LONDON & WISE *Retir'd Gard.* I. ix. 41 The Maugeron is [a plum] of a Violet Colour, large and round. **1750** tr. *Leonardus' Mirr. Stones* 79 The carbuncle brandishes its fiery rays, of a violet colour, on every side. **1800** tr. *Lagrange's Chem.* I. 419 Hydrogen gas alters the colour of bismuth, and gives it a violet tint. **1834** J. FORBES *Laennec's Dis. Chest* (ed. 4) 465 The lung..was of a violet hue, soft and flabby. *a* **1878** W. CARLETON *Farm Ballads* (1893) 84 The squire swore oaths of a violet hue.

c. Qualifying names of other colours, as ***violet black***, ***blue***, etc.

In later use frequently hyphened (cf. next), and in some cases (esp. *violet-blue*) also repr. the sb. used attrib.

1728 CHAMBERS *Cycl.* s.v. *Red*, In Limning, and Fresco, for a Violet Red,..they use a natural Earth found in England. **1782** LATHAM *Gen. Syn. Birds* I. II. 754 The quills of a violet brown. **1819** STEPHENS *Shaw's Gen. Zool.* XI. I. 3 The wings..are of a fine deep violet-blue. **1843** *Florist's Jrnl.* (1846) IV. 111 Flower-spike producing three to four flowers, and very handsome, of a beautiful violet-purple. **1882** *Garden* 17 June 418/1 The petals..bordered with violet-crimson.

d. Forming adj. combs., as ***violet-black***, ***-blue***, etc.

Many examples occur in Shaw's *Gen. Zool.*

1697 DRYDEN *Virg. Georg.* IV. 394 From one Root the rising Stem bestows A Wood of Leaves, and Vi'let-purple Boughs. **1753** *Chambers' Cycl.* Suppl. s.v. *Star-wort*, The tall hairy New England aster with very large violet-purple flowers. **1802** SHAW *Gen. Zool.* III. II. 423 Violet-black Snake, with the abdomen and sides crimson. **1819** STEPHENS *Ibid.* XI. I. 59 The upper parts of the body [are] violet-red. **1838** T. THOMSON *Chem. Org. Bodies* 746 The whole liquid assumes a very strong and fine violet-blue colour. **1887** W. PHILLIPS *Brit. Discomycetes* 70 Hymenium violet-brown; juice violet.

2. a. In names of varieties of fruits or plants, as ***violet clover***, ***maize***, ***plum***, etc. Also *ellipt.*

1706 LONDON & WISE *Retir'd Gard.* I. 147 The Fourth [kind is] the Violet Fig. *Ibid.*, The Violet ripens perfectly well. *a* **1722** LISLE *Husb.* (1757) 379 A violet-plum, a standard,..which is a plum that does not cleave from the stone. **1725** *Fam. Dict.* s.v. *Plum*, The Violet Damson or Maugeron Plum. **1760–72** tr. *Juan & Ulloa's Voy.* (ed. 3) II. 140 They first pulverize the cochineal by grinding, and after mixing four ounces of it, with twelve of violet maize, they form it into square cakes. **1786** ABERCROMBIE *Arrangem.* 13 in *Gard. Assist.*, Cherry plum, Violet plum, Apricot plum. **1860** HOGG *Fruit Man.* 72 Figs... Skin dark. Flesh red... Early Violet, Malta. *Ibid.* 251 Purple Gage (..Violet Gage). **1867** *Chambers's Encycl.* IX. 803/2 The Violet Moss (*Byssus Iolithus*)..was formerly in use as a popular remedy for feverish cutaneous eruptions. **1890** *Times* 22 Sept. 4/2 The cut of violet clovers in France is not likely to be large.

b. In names of birds, insects, etc., as ***violet bee***, ***cormorant***, ***crab***, ***creeper***, ***heron***, etc.; **violet-ear**, one or other species of the genus *Petasophora* of humming-birds; **violet-fly**, an artificial fly used in angling; **violet-green swallow**, a dark-coloured swallow with white patches, *Tachycineta thalassina*, found in western North America; **violet-tip**, an American butterfly (see quot.).

Latham's names are repeated in Shaw's *Gen. Zool.* (1811–26).

1845 *Encycl. Metrop.* XIV. 153/1 A *violet bee, which they now sent off [from the balloon], flew quickly away with its usual humming noise. *c* **1882** *Cassell's Nat. Hist.* V. 367 The Violet Carpenter Bee (*Xylocopa violacea*)..inhabits the south of Europe. **1785** LATHAM *Gen. Synop. Birds* III. II. 600 *Violet Corvorant... This bird is said to be wholly black, glossed with violet. **1826** STEPHENS *Shaw's Gen. Zool.* XIII. I. 86 Violet Cormorant, *Phalacrocorax violaceus*. **1774** GOLDSM. *Nat. Hist.* (1824) III. 86 The *Violet Crab of the Carribee Islands. **1895** *Pall Mall G.* 26 July 2/3 The much advertised land-crabs are precisely the same 'violet crab'.. found on similar tropical islands. **1782** LATHAM *Gen. Synop. Birds* I. II. 705 *Violet Creeper. **1861** GOULD *Trochilidæ* IV. Pl. 223 Brazilian *Violet-ear. *Ibid.* Pl. 226 Mexican Violet-ear. **1887** R. B. SHARPE *Gould's Trochilidæ* Suppl. V. Pl. 1 *Petasophora Germana*, Guiana Violet-ear. **1676** COTTON *Walton's Angler* II. vii. (1875) 255 A fly called the *Violet-Fly; made of a dark violet stuff; with the wings, of a grey feather of a mallard. **1787** BEST *Angling* (ed. 2) 101 The Violet fly... Dubbed with dark violet stuff, and a little dun bear's hair mixed with it. **1832** LYTTON *Eugene A.* I. ix, The old Corporal..busily employed in fixing to his line..what anglers..call the violet-fly'. **1858** S. BAIRD *Birds Pacific Rail Road* 311 *Violet-Green Swallow..Rocky Mountains to Pacific. **1972** L. HANCOCK *Sleeping Bag* viii. 205 A pair of violet-green swallows built a nest..above our bedroom window. **1815** STEPHENS *Shaw's Gen. Zool.* IX. II. 249 *Violet Grosbeak, with a streak above the eyes. **1785** LATHAM *Gen. Synop. Birds* III. I. 97 *Violet Heron,..of a blueish black, glossed with violet. **1782** *Ibid.* I. II. 756 *Violet Humming Bird;..the whole head, the neck, back, breast, and belly, of a violet purple. **1864–5** J. G. WOOD *Homes without H.* iv. (1868) 88 The *Violet Land Crab of Jamaica (*Gecarcinus ruricola*) is the most familiar of these creatures. **1832** J. RENNIE *Consp. Butterfl. & M.* 205 The *Violet Pygmy (*Microsetia violaceella*). Wings:..first pair deep black, with a tinge of violet. **1785** LATHAM *Gen. Synop. Birds* III. II. 600 *Violet Shag. Violet Corvorant. **1858** BAIRD *Cycl. Nat. Sci.* 307/2 *Janthina*. The *Violet Shells.—A genus of molluscous animals belonging to the class *Gasteropoda*. **1845** GOSSE *Ocean* vii. (1849) 343 The *Violet-snail (*Janthina fragilis*),..whose shell..is of a pearly white above, and beneath violet. **1873** DAWSON *Earth & Man* iv. 76 Those singular molluscous swimmers by fin or float known to zoologists as violet-snails. **1783** LATHAM *Gen. Synop. Birds* II. II. 574 *Violet Swallow,..general colour of the plumage deep blue, reflecting violet in different tints. *Ibid.* I. 222 *Violet Tanager,..colour of the plumage a deep violet. *Ibid.* 57 *Violet Thrush,..the whole plumage of a changeable violet blue. **1881** S. H. SCUDDER *Butterflies* 167 The most conspicuous case [of dimorphism] is in the largest, the *Violet-Tip (*Polygonia interrogationis*), where the two forms were once universally considered distinct species.

c. With names of minerals, etc.

1796 KIRWAN *Elem. Min.* (ed. 2) II. 280 Violet Cobalt ore. **1839** DE LA BECHE *Rep. Geol. Cornwall*, etc. xv. 497 The violet rock crystal, or amethyst, seems scarce. **1867** *Chambers's Encycl.* IX. 803/2 *Violet Stones*,..certain stones found upon high mountains, as in Thuringia,..which, in consequence of being covered with..Violet Moss, emit a smell like that of violets. **1871** *Routledge's Ev. Boy's Ann.* June 335 Violet ebony is used for making inlaid chairs.

d. *violet ray*: (*a*) a ray of violet light; (*b*) a ray of ultra-violet light. Also *attrib.* Now *rare*.

1803 *Jrnl. Nat. Philos.* V. 255 He placed muriate of silver without the solar spectrum and next to the violet rays. This oxide became blackened in a short time, it became still deeper in the violet rays, still more in the blue, and so on. **1903** *Sci. Amer.* 20 June 473/1 The so-called 'violet ray', which is now so common in literature, should be dropped, and 'blue ray' should be substituted in its place. **1925** A. Bennett *Jrnl.* 7 Feb. (1933) III. 74 He went to lie down under the light of his violet-ray lamp (equivalent of sunlight or some such thing) over his bed. **1929** *Proc. IRE* XVII. 1388 The real difficulty lies in the modernization of household equipment such as electric fans..and violet ray machines. All of these must be designed with elimination of radio interference in mind. **1933** *Amer. Speech* VIII. II. 55/2 *Nature-ray*, all right, or O.K., as in the phrase, *I'm feeling nature-ray*. It evidently is based on violet rays. **1966** J. S. Cox *Illustr. Dict. Hairdressing & Wigmaking* 79/2 *High frequency*, an electric current of high voltage and very low amperage, used in scalp treatment. Also called Violet Ray because of the violet light produced in the glass applicator.

3. In parasynthetic combs., as ***violet-eared***, ***-headed***, ***-hooded***, ***-horned***, ***-ringed***, etc.

1782 Latham *Gen. Synop. Birds* I. II. 767 *Violet-Eared Humming Bird;..beneath the ears, is a very splendid violet spot. **1898** *Daily News* 12 Feb. 6/3 Violet-eared waxbills, African firefinches, black-crested yellow bulbuls. **1782** Latham *Gen. Synop. Birds* I. II. 718 *Violet-Headed Creeper, *Certhia violacea*. **1815** Stephens *Shaw's Gen. Zool.* IX. I. 8 Violet-headed Curucui (*Trogon violaceus*). **1847** Tennyson *Princ.* II. 354 With scraps of thundrous Epic lilted out By *violet-hooded Doctors. **1822** *Hortus Angl.* II. 10 *Violet-horned Poppy. **1880** A. H. Swinton *Insect Variety* 4 A *violet-ringed Oak Eggar caterpillar. **1821** Shelley *Epipsych.* 69 Art thou not..A *violet-shrouded grave of Woe? *a* **1882** —— *Death Adonis* 4 Wake *violet-stoled queen, and weave the crown Of Death. **1786** Abercrombie *Arrangem.* 77 in *Gard. Assist.*, White, *violet striped [tulip]. **1803** Shaw *Gen. Zool.* IV. II. 382 Violet-striped Acanthurus. *Acanthurus Sohal.* **1782** Latham *Gen. Synop. Birds* I. II. 754 *Violet Tailed Humming Bird. **1811** Shaw *Gen. Zool.* VIII. I. 208 *Violet-throated Creeper. *Certhia affinis*.

4. Special collocation: ***violet shift*** (*Astr.*), displacement of spectral lines towards the violet end of the spectrum; decrease in the wavelength of electromagnetic radiation; usu. called a *blue shift*; cf. red shift *sb.*

1959 *Listener* 3 Dec. 971/1 The spectroscope will reveal a violet shift for one component, and a red shift for the other, according to the familiar Doppler principle. **1977** J. Narlikar *Struct. Universe* iii. 76 Hence negative *z* is interpreted as 'blue-shift' or 'violet-shift'.

violet (ˈvaɪəlɪt), *v.* [f. violet *sb.*[1] or *a.*]

1. *trans.* To tinge with a violet hue.

1623 tr. *Favine's Theat. Hon.* I. iv. 35 For the Noble Kings of France mourne in Scarlet violetted. **1832** [R. Cattermole] *Beckett*, etc. 192 The sea, Yet darklier violeted, almost frowned With splendor. **1895** Meredith *Amazing Marriage* v, One flank of the white in heaven was violetted wonderfully.

2. *intr.* To gather violets.

1813 Miss Mitford in L'Estrange *Life* (1870) I. 226 Tomorrow I shall go violeting. **1827** Mrs. Hemans in H. F. Chorley *Mem.* (1836) I. 151 Having accompanied you again, and again, as I have done, in 'violetting' and seeking for wood-sorrel. **1873** *Argosy* XVI. 270 How delightful was that day among the Kentish Downs! We began it by violeting in the woods.

violet-coloured, *a.* [violet *sb.*[1] or *a.*] Having the blue or bluish-purple colour of a violet.

1552 in *Rep. Hist. MSS. Comm., Var. Coll.* IV. 221 The xlviij and other onneste men in violet collord gownes. **1653** H. Cogan tr. *Pinto's Trav.* lxxii. 253 Six or seven pieces of Violet coloured Damask. **1671** Woodhead *St. Teresa* II. 276 A longer Coffin in fashion of a Tomb was provided, which they covered with violet-coloured Silk. **1721** Mortimer *Husb.* (ed. 5) II. 244 The Violet coloured Tulip striped with White. **1753** *Chambers' Cycl.* Suppl. s.v. *Star-wort*, The broad-leaved paniculated aster with deep violet-coloured flowers. **1800** Herschel in *Phil. Trans.* XC. 516 A violet-coloured glass..stops 955 rays of light. **1857** Miller *Elem. Chem.*, *Org.* vii. §1. 447 The liquid..deposits beautiful violet-coloured prismatic crystals. **1886** Froude *Oceana* ii. 27 Looking round us and down into nothing but the violet-coloured ocean.

violetish (ˈvaɪəlɪtɪʃ), *a.* [f. violet *sb.*[1] + -ish.] Somewhat violet in colour.

1871 *Routledge's Ev. Boy's Ann.* June 359 A grey partaking of a violetish tone. **1906** *Westm. Gaz.* 24 Feb. 16/3 Its flesh is a violetish black or a blackish violet, overrun by a thin network of white veins.

‖**violetta** (vioˈlɛtta). Pl. violette. [It.]

1. = violet *sb.*[2] and violette.

1740 J. Grassineau *Mus. Dict.* 327 *Violetta*, or little viol, is in reality, our triple Viol. **1876** Stainer & Barrett *Dict. Mus. Terms* 447/2 *Violetta*, a little viol. **1979** *Early Music* Jan. 137/3 Kolneder also points out that even violins, violas and *violette* are regularly written in the bass clef in the lower octave.

2. *violetta marina* (see quots.); cf. *viol d'amore* s.v. viol *sb.*[1] 2 b.

1801 Busby *Dict. Mus.*, *Violetta Marina*, a stringed instrument not now in use. Supposed to have been similar in shape and tone to the *Viol d'Amour*. It was first introduced in England by Signior Castrucci in the year 1732. **1889** Grove *Dict. Mus.* IV. 267/2 *Violetta marina*, a name found occasionally in the scores of Handel and his contemporaries, probably to designate the Viola d'Amore. **1963** *Listener* 21 Feb. 354/1 The use of the violetta marina in *Orlando*.

vioˈlette. *rare*[−1]. [ad. It. *violetta*.] = violet *sb.*[2]

1884 Haweis *My Musical Life* I. 239 The smaller viols or violettes of the seventeenth century fell into violins.

‖**violette de Parme** (vjɔlɛt də parm). [Fr.] = *Parma violet* (*b*), (*c*) s.v. Parma[1].

1904 E. Nesbit *Phoenix & Carpet* xii. 232 A little scent sachet labelled 'Violettes de Parme'. **1913** 'Saki' *When William Came* (1914) xiv. 243 All the hangings, *violette de Parme*, all the furniture, rosewood. *c* **1938** *Fortnum & Mason Price List* 55/1 Violette de Parme Toilet [soap]. **1968** M. Kay *Masha* xxv. 252 She..left, the smell of *Violette de Parme* perfume trailing behind her.

violety (ˈvaɪəlɪtɪ), *a.* [f. violet *sb.*[1] + -y.] Of or belonging to violets; more or less violet in colour.

1831 Keightley *Mythol. Anc. Greece & It.* 399 His mother called him Iamus, *Violety*. **1891** T. Hardy *Tess* (1900) 96/2 Dark eyelashes and brows,..and large eyes violety-bluey-blackish.

violin (vaɪəˈlɪn, ˈvaɪəlɪn), *sb.* Forms: 6 violine, 7 vyoline, viallin, 7– violin. [ad. It. *violino* (Pg. *violino*, Sp. *violín*), f. *viola* viola[2]. Cf. violon.]

1. a. A musical instrument in common use, having four strings tuned in fifths and played with a bow; a fiddle.

In general structure the violin is composed of a resonant box of elaborately curved outline, and a neck or handle from the end of which the strings are stretched over a bridge to a tail-piece.

1579 Spenser *Sheph. Cal.*, *April* 103, I see Calliope speede her to the place, where my Goddesse shines: And after her the other Muses trace, with their Violines. **1589** R. Harvey *Pl. Perc.* (1590) 6 Then were it high time for..all Peace-Makers, to put vp their pipes, or else in steed of the soft violine, learne to sound a shrill trumpet. **1608** B. Jonson *Masques* Wks. (1616) 964 The first [dance] was to the Cornets, the second to the Vyolines. **1618** Bolton *Florus* (1636) 115 Some excellently pleasing lesson plaid upon soft winde-instruments, or Violins. **1660** Pepys *Diary* 6 Mar., I played upon a viall, and he a viallin, after dinner. **1711** Steele *Spect.* No. 258 ¶4 Violins, Voices, or any other Organs of Sound. **1756–7** tr. *Keysler's Trav.* (1760) II. 10 Orpheus or Amphion in bronze, playing upon a violin. **1842** Lytton *Zanoni* I. i, He was not only a composer, but also an excellent practical performer, especially on the violin. **1884** Haweis *My Musical Life* I. 237 The violin is not an invention, it is a growth.

transf. **1670** Eachard *Cont. Clergy* 62 People..presently phansi'd the Moon, Mercury, and Venus to be a kind of violins or trebles to Jupiter and Saturn.

b. With distinguishing terms.

1601 B. Jonson *Poetast.* III. iv, Come, we must haue you turne fiddler againe, slaue, 'get a base violin at your backe. *c* **1670** Wood *Life* (O.H.S.) I. 212 Before the restoration of K. Charles 2 and especially after, viols began to be out of fashion, and only violins used, as treble-violin, tenor and bass-violin. **1685** Playford (*title*), The Division-Violin: containing a Collection of Divisions upon several Grounds for the Treble-Violin. **1728** Chambers *Cycl.* s.v., The Word Violin, alone, stands for Treble Violin. *Ibid.*, The Counter-Tenor, Tenor, or Bass-Violin. **1888** *Encycl. Brit.* XXIV. 245/1 The tenor violin, in compass a fifth lower than the treble violin, appears to have preceded the latter.

c. *to play first violin*, to take the leading part. (Cf. fiddle *sb.* 1 b.) Similarly (*rare*), *to play second violin*, to take the subordinate part.

1780 Mme. D'Arblay *Diary* May, [He] seemed to think nobody half so great as himself, and..chose to play first-violin without further ceremony. **1902** G. B. Shaw *Let.* 20 May (1972) II. 273, I dont see Janet playing a silly second moral violin like Judith.

2. One who plays on the violin; a violinist.

1667 Pepys *Diary* 20 Feb., They talked how the King's viallin, Bannister, is mad. *c* **1670** Wood *Life* (O.H.S.) I. 485 Thomas Baltzar, one of the violins in the king's service. **1699** J. Jackson *Let. to Pepys* 25 Dec., Corelli the famous violin playing, in concert with above 30 more. **1843** *Penny Cycl.* XXVI. 346/2 At the early age of twenty he was chosen to fill the situation of first violin in the royal chapel of Turin. **1878** Miss Fothergill (*title*), The First Violin.

3. A variety of organ-stop. *rare*[−1].

1688 [see viol *sb.*[1] 3].

4. *attrib.* and *Comb.*, as ***violin-bow***, ***-case***, ***class***, ***concerto***, ***family***, ***sonata***, ***-stand***, etc.; ***violin-maker***, ***-making***, ***-player***, ***-playing***; ***violin-like -shaped*** adjs.; **violin spider** [see quot. 1969[2]], a small brown and orange spider, *Loxosceles læta*, whose bite can be fatal to man and which is chiefly found in South America.

1858 Simmonds *Dict. Trade*, **Violin-bow*, a bow strung with horse-hair, for playing on a violin. **1875** Knight *Dict. Mech.* 2711/1 The Hindus claim to have invented the violin-bow. **1685** *Lond. Gaz.* No. 2041/4 Lost.., a black Leather *Violin-Case, with a Violin in it. **1840** Dickens *Old C. Shop* xxxiv, She might as well have been dressed in a violin-case. **1864** Engel *Mus. Anc. Nat.* 86 Two other Hindoo instruments..belonging to the *violin class. **1876** Stainer & Barrett *Dict. Mus. Terms* 449/1 **Violin clef*, the G clef placed upon the first line of the stave. **1889** Grove *Dict. Mus.* IV. 293/2 Mozart in his younger years was hardly less great as a violinist than a piano-player, and his *Violin Concertos,..are the most valuable compositions in that form. **1934** Violin concerto [see *pianoforte concerto* s.v. pianoforte b]. **1865** J. Hullah *Transition Period Music* 34 Of these instruments it would easily be found that incomparably the most important were the *Violin family. **1837** *Penny Cycl.* VIII. 198/1 *Cruth*,..a musical instrument of the *violin kind. **1884** 'Edna Lyall' *We Two* xix, *Violin-like sensitiveness of nature. **1683** *Lond. Gaz.* No. 1862/8 Mr. Aggttar, *Violin-Maker in the Strand. **1843** *Penny Cycl.* XXVI. 346 The same author [M. Otto] also gives the names of many German violin-makers. **1875** Knight *Dict. Mech.* 2711/2 Antonio Stradivarius..stands, by common consent, at the head of all violin-makers. *Ibid.*, The art of *violin-making.. appears to have reached its culminating point in the productions of the Cremonese school. **1861** Adams *5000 Mus. Terms* 108 *Corde vuide*, in *violin music, indicates the open string. **1875** Knight *Dict. Mech.* 2712/1 **Violin-piano*,..a form of the pianoforte patented..in England by Todd. **1797** *Encycl. Brit.* XII. 493 The most celebrated *violin players of Italy..have been Farina, M. Angelo Rossi, [etc.]. **1814** Jane Austen *Mansfield Park* I. xii. 243 The late acquisition of a violin player in the servants' hall. **1865** Baring-Gould *Werewolves* ix. 137 A violin-player, who..confessed to thirty-four murders. **1815** J. Mayne *Jrnl.* 23 Jan. (1909) x. 250 The Romans have no idea of what good *violin playing is. **1976** Y. Menuhin in D. Villiers *Next Year in Jerusalem* 335 The technical points of violin-playing common to the Jew and the gypsy. **1888** *Encycl. Brit.* XXIV. 242/2 *note*, *Violin rosin is called in French *colophane*. **1862** *Catal. Internat. Exhib.*, *Brit.* II. No. 5438, *Violin school for joint practice of the elementary and advanced classes. **1802** R. Hall *Elem. Bot.* 158 Panduriform, *panduriformis*, *violin-shaped. **1889** Grove *Dict. Mus.* IV. 288/2 Towards..1630, we find the first compositions containing rudimentally the form of the classical *Violin Sonata. **1969** *Daily Colonist* (Victoria, B.C.) 8 June 14/1 War on a colony of deadly South American *violin spiders in Sierra Madre Memorial Park was intensified Saturday when the city of Sierra Madre called a commercial exterminator into the battle. **1969** *Pest Control* Oct. 54/2 The violin spider is so named because in most instances it has the discernible shape of a violin on its head. The handle of the violin points toward the abdomen. **1979** *Daily Tel.* 15 Dec. 15/3 Hundreds of thousands of poisonous violin spiders, whose bite can be lethal and for which there is no known antidote, have invaded Johannesburg. **1915** D. H. Lawrence *Rainbow* iii. 80 A drawing-room..with a piano and a *violin-stand. **1841** Spalding *Italy & It. Isl.* III. 160 Among the manufactures, those of the fine arts, leather, and *violin-strings, are alone industriously practised. **1871** tr. *Schellen's Spectr. Anal.* App. 433 The motion of a point near the end of a violin string. **1884** Thompson *Tumours of Bladder* 82 A very small écraseur, with violin-string ligature. **1843** *Penny Cycl.* XXVI. 346 A lyre, or lute,..may be considered..as the parent of all instruments of the *violin tribe.

Hence **vioˈlinic** (*rare*), **violiˈnistic** *adjs.*; **violiˈnistically** *adv.*

1776 J. Hawkins *Gen. His. Sci. & Pract. Mus.* III. IV. i. 431 The Violini piccoli alla Francese must in often spoiling the phrasing and making violinistic rather than musical effects. **1963** V. Nabokov *Gift* iv. 231 He had no real understanding of the real, violinic essence of the anapaest. **1976** Y. Menuhin *Unfinished Journey* (1977) 376 Violinistically I can point to an understanding of my instrument which has grown day by day, year by year. **1978** *Gramophone* Aug. 348/3 The violinistic 'treatments' applied to every phrase are at first startling because people don't dare to play like this any more.

violin, *v.* *rare.* [f. prec.]

†**1.** *trans.* To entice by violin-playing. *Obs.*[−1]

1713 *Gentl. Instructed* (ed. 5) I. Suppl. iv. p. xlii, Was not Madam W. plaid out of her Reputation, and violin'd into a Match below her Quality?

2. *intr.* To play the violin; *fig.*, to play a leading part.

1895 Meredith *Amazing Marriage* xxx, How does he enjoy playing second fiddle with the maid while Mr. tall brown-face Taffy violins it to her ladyship?

Hence **violining** *vbl. sb.*

1899 *Daily News* 15 Feb. 5/2 The songs..and the violining..all perfect in their degree.

violin, var. violine[1].

‖**vioˈlina.** *Chem.* [-ina[1].] = next.

1836 Smart. **1838** T. Thomson *Chem. Org. Bodies* 293 Violina..is more soluble in water..than emetina. **1843** *Penny Cycl.* XXVI. 345/2 The principle on which this property seems to depend has been separated by Boullay from some species of Viola, and has been called Violina.

violine[1] (ˈvaɪəlaɪn). *Chem.* Also -in. [a. F. *violine*, f. *viole* viol[1] + -ine[5]. Cf. prec.] A bitter emetic principle found in the common violet.

1831 J. Davies *Man. Mat. Med.* 338 An alkaloid principle, nearly related to emetine, discovered by M. Boulay, who has called it *Violine*. **1861** Bentley *Man. Bot.* 458 The emetic property is due to a peculiar alkaloid named *violine*, which greatly resembles, if it be not identical with, *emetine*. **1887** *Buck's Handbk. Med. Sci.* V. 490/2 *Viola odorata* contains a gastric irritant called violin.

violine[2] (ˈvaɪəlaɪn). *Chem.* [f. L. *viol-a* viola[1] + -ine[5].] A violet-blue colouring matter or colour. Also *attrib.*

1859 D. G. Price in *Repertory Patent Invent.* (1860) XXXV. 159 The colouring matters I produce embrace shades of purple and pink. Three of these I name respectively, 'violine', 'purpurine', and 'roseine'. **1862** *Chambers's Encycl.* III. 721/2 Violine is very slightly soluble in water, is readily dissolved by alcohol. **1903** *Daily Chron.* 31 Oct. 8/4 Green is a dye that has receded from the affections of the smart, while violine is one that is equally ascending the scale of success. *Ibid.* 5 Dec. 8/4 A model in violine beaver, trimmed with a plume to match.

ˈviolinism. *rare*[−1]. [f. violin *sb.*] Violin-playing.

1844 H. F. Chorley *Music & Manners* III. 61 Royalty thus did its part in fostering a school of violinism.

violinist (vaɪəˈlɪnɪst, ˈvaɪ-). Also 7 violinest. [ad. It. (also Sp.) *violinista*, f. *violino* violin *sb.* Cf. F. *violoniste*.] A player of, or performer on, the violin.

c 1670 WOOD *Life* (O.H.S.) I. 274 Nathaniel Crew, M.A., fellow of Linc. Coll.; a violinist and violist, but alwaies played out of tune. 1696 AUBREY *Misc.* xii. 98 Mr. Davys Mell (the famous Violinist, and Clock-maker). 1773 *Phil. Trans.* LXIII. 270 Our ablest violinist conceived that it was too difficult to be performed. 1845 E. HOLMES *Mozart* 121 A natural surprise that.. the most striking acquirements of great players in our own time should be found in a violinist of that early date. 1888 *Buck's Handbk. Med. Sci.* VI. 36 Violinist's cramp may attack the right hand which holds the bow, or the left hand which fingers the strings. 1899 *Allbutt's Syst. Med.* VIII. 12, I have been informed that in violinists.. the bow arm is always considerably longer than the left arm.

‖**violino piccolo** (viːəˈliːnəʊ ˈpɪkələʊ). [It.; cf. PICCOLO.] A small variety of violin.

1776 J. HAWKINS *Gen. Hist. Sci. & Pract. Mus.* III. IV. i. 431 The Violini piccoli alla Francese must in strictness signify small violins; and of these there are none now known but that contemptible instrument called the Kit. 1889 GROVE *Dict. Mus.* IV. 813/1 *Violino piccolo*, a violin of small size, but of the ordinary parts and proportions, differing in this respect from the pochette or kit. 1961 *Times* 24 July 7/6 Mr. Carl Pini had taken the trouble to use a *violino piccolo* for the performance. 1979 *Early Music* Jan. 3 The instruments ..include..violino piccolo (with its characteristically scalloped outline) theorbo-lute, and bass viol.

violist (ˈvaɪəlɪst). [f. VIOL *sb.*[1] + -IST.] A player on the viol or the viola. (Also as the title of a book.)

c 1670 WOOD *Life* (O.H.S.) I. 274 He was a violinist, and the two former violists. *a* 1699 B. HELY (*title*), The compleat Violist, or An Introduction to the Art of Playing on the Bass Viol. 1705 *Phil. Trans.* XXV. 2069 Upon these, a Sonata was perform'd by those two most eminent Violists. *a* 1734 NORTH *Lives* I. 13 He outdid all his teachers and became one of the neatest violists of his time. 1782 BURNEY *Hist. Music* (1789) II. iv. 266 The Minstrels..were at all times the best Violists of their age. 1894 *Daily News* 5 Feb. 5/3 A large viol, so large that a boy was placed inside to sing the air while the violist played the bass. 1977 *Gramophone* Nov. 860/2, I prefer some details of phrasing and the greater warmth of the old Tchaikovsky Quartet which has Rudolf Barshai as violist. 1978 *Oxford Times* 3 Feb. 14 The splendid viola part reminds one of the fact that the composer was a violist.

violl, obs. form of VIAL *sb.*, VIOL *sb.*

viologen (vaɪˈəʊlədʒən). *Chem.* [f. VIOL(ET *sb.*[1] + -O + -GEN.]

Any of several salts of the 1,1′-dialkyl-4,4′-bipyridylium ion, $(-C_5H_4\overset{+}{N}.R)_2$, which are used as redox indicators.

1933 MICHAELIS & HILL in *Jrnl. Gen. Physiol.* XVI. 859 The new indicators will be designated as viologens... They differ from other indicators in several respects; in the first place, the color is exhibited by the reduced form, whereas usually the oxidized form is the colored one. 1964 J. W. LINNETT *Electronic Struct. Molecules* vii. 109 The viologens ..can be formed by reducing γγ′-dipyridyl, or its derivatives, with zinc dust. 1980 *Nature* 27 Nov. 321/1 Methyl viologen (paraquat)..acts as electron carrier. 1984 *New Scientist* 17 May 23/1 New electrochromic displays (ECDs) based on viologens—close relatives of..paraquat that turn purple when electrochemically reduced—look set for commercialisation.

violon (ˈvaɪələn). Also 6 **violan, -and,** 7 **-ent, vyolon, phialon.** [a. F. *violon* (16th c.) violin, or (in sense 2) It. *violone* bass-viol. Cf. Sp. *violon* violoncello.]

†**1.** A violin. Also, a violinist. *Obs.*

α. 1552 *Househ. Exp. Princess Eliz.* 38 in *Camd. Misc.* (1853) II, Paid in rewarde unto sondrie persons at S. James, her grace then beyng there—..to the warderobe, xl.s.; the violans, xl.s. 1594 PLAT *Jewell-ho.* I. 39, Were it not,..I coulde finde in my hearte to commaunde the Violands to cease. 1610 GUILLIM *Heraldry* IV. vi. 200 Hee beareth gules, three treble violents transposed argent stringed sable.

β. 1593 DRAYTON *Eclogues* iii. 113 Tune the Taber and the Pipe to the sweet violons. 1602 CAREW *Cornwall* 139 b, He could not only turne, and make Virginals, Organes, Vyolons,..but also tune, and handsomely play vpon them. 1603 in *10th Rep. Hist. MSS. Comm.* App. I. 32 Gifin to a sat of phialonis when they played at my chamber dor, xi s. 1606 SYLVESTER *Du Bartas* II. iv. *Tropheis* 436 In Argos the chaste Violon For's absent Soveraign doth grave-sweetly grone.

2. A variety of organ-stop.

1852 SEIDEL *Organ* 108 Violon..is one of the finest and most common pedal-registers. 1876 HILES *Catech. Organ* ix. (1878) 63 *Violon* or *Violone*, Double Bass. An open flue-stop; the tone is penetrating and fine, in imitation of the Double Bass.

violonˈcellist. [f. next + -IST.] One who plays the violoncello.

1835 G. HOGARTH *Musical Hist.* 423 As a violoncellist, Lindley has, for many years, been unrivalled. 1881 *Macm. Mag.* XLIII. 435 It chanced on one occasion that the violoncellist's instrument did not arrive.

‖**violoncello** (vaɪələnˈsɛləʊ, vaɪələnˈtʃɛləʊ; violonˈtʃɛllo). Also 8–9 **violincello.** [It. *violoncello*, dim. of *violone*: see VIOLON. Hence also Pg. *violoncello*, Sp. *-celo*, F. *-celle.*]

1. a. A large four-stringed instrument of the violin class; a bass violin. Cf. ′CELLO.

α. 1724 *Short Explic. For. Wds. in Mus. Bks.*, *Violon-cello*, is a Small Bass Violin, just half as big as a common Bass Violin, in Length, Breadth, and Thickness. 1742 FR. BARSANTI (*title*), A Collection of Old Scots Tunes, with the Bass for Violoncello or Harpsichord. 1795 MASON *Ch. Mus.* i. 73, I know and confess that this and the violon-cello are the most perfect of all stringed Instruments. 1867 TROLLOPE *Chron. Barset* II. xlix. 55 Of all the works of his life this playing on the violoncello had been the sweetest to him. 1881 C. A. EDWARDS *Organs* 149 If the bass string of a Violoncello be vibrated, other sounds besides that proper to the string may be detected.

β. 1773 BARRINGTON in *Phil. Trans.* LXIII. 271 *note*, Mr. Zeidler, who plays the violincello at Covent-Garden theatre. 1797 MRS. BERKELEY *Poems G. M. Berkeley* p. ccccxii, Dr. Berkeley was esteemed the finest gentleman-performer on the violincello in England. 1852 DICKENS *Bleak Ho.* vi, Mr. Skimpole could play on the piano and the violincello.

b. A player on the violoncello. Cf. VIOLIN *sb.* 2.

1861 GEO. ELIOT *Let.* 6 Oct. (1954) III. 456 We have our violoncello, who is full of sensibility.

2. An organ-stop having a tone similar to that of a violoncello.

1876 HILES *Catech. Organ* ix. (1878) 63 *Violoncello*, an 8 feet stop, resembling in construction the Violone.

3. *attrib.* and *Comb.*, as ***violoncello bow, player, species.*** ‖**violoncello piccolo**, a small variety of violoncello; cf. VIOLINO PICCOLO.

1788 J. WOODFORDE *Diary* 12 Sept. (1927) III. 46 There is not perhaps a better Violencello [*sic*] player in the Kingdom. 1818 BLAQUIERE tr. *Panant's Resid. Algiers* 267 The *arabebbah*, of the violincello species, with one string. 1888 *Encycl. Brit.* XXIV. 246/1 One of his best violoncello bows, which are rarities, was recently sold in Paris for £44. 1889 GROVE *Dict. Mus.* IV. 813/1 *Violoncello piccolo*, a violoncello of the ordinary pitch, but of smaller size and having thinner strings. 1899 *Allbutt's Syst. Med.* VIII. 12 In the violoncello players who perform solos..there is very great strain. 1959 *Collins Mus. Encycl.* 706/1 *Violoncello piccolo*,..a small-sized cello for which Bach wrote obbligato parts in 9 of his cantatas. 1977 *Gramophone* Oct. 672/1 It falls short in the provision of a cello rather than Bach's own stipulation of a violoncello piccolo.

Hence **violonˈcelloing** *ppl. a.*

1830 MISS MITFORD *Village* Ser. IV. (1863) 266 One fluting brother; one fiddling ditto; a violoncelloing music-master; and a singing papa.

‖**violon d'Ingres** (vjɔlɔ̃ dɛ̃gr). [Fr., lit. 'Ingres' violin'; cf. INGRES.] An occasional pastime, an activity other than that for which one is well-known or at which one excels.

[1931 *Larousse du XX*[e] *Siècle* IV. 68/1 *Violon d'Ingres.* Une légende, assez suspecte, prétend que le peintre Ingres était plus fier de son jeu sur le violon, jeu qui était fort ordinaire, que de sa peinture, qui l'avait rendu illustre. 1964 ROBERT *Dict. Langue Française* VI. 1004/1 *Violon d'Ingres*, le fait, pour un artiste, de pratiquer un art qui n'est pas le sien (le peintre Ingres aurait excellé au violon).] 1963 E. HYAMS *New Statesmanship* 255 President Eisenhower's *violon d'Ingres* being golf, it fell to..John Foster Dulles to follow N. S. Kruschev into the pages of the *New Statesman.* 1968 J. M. WHITE *Nightclimber* v. 31 Fame, if we achieve it, is thrust upon us for a minor attribute that we rather despise. For example..Ingres..preferred to play his violin—badly —to visitors..instead of showing them his pictures. Night-climbing was my *violon d'Ingres.* 1973 *Listener* 13 Sept. 345/2, I suspect that music was no more than Rousseau's *violon d'Ingres*..and that the composition of *The Village Soothsayer* was a happy fluke.

‖**violone** (vioˈlone). [It., f. *viola* VIOLA[2].] The double-bass viol.

Also as the name of an organ-stop: see VIOLON 2.

1724 *Short Explic. For. Wds. in Mus. Bks.*, *Violone*, is a very large Bass Violin, or Double Bass. 1730 *Treat. Harmony* 35 This Error is daily run into, by giving Divided Basses to be play'd on the *Violone* or Double Bass. 1824 *Mechanic's Mag.* 31 July 335 Having made a violin, a viola, and a violoncello, I have long since conceived the idea of making a violono [*sic*], or double bass also. 1865 J. HULLAH *Transition Period Music* 118 Those Gothic abominations, the violin, the viola, the violoncello, and the violone. 1873 H. C. BANISTER *Music* 221 The Contra-basso, or Double-Bass (also termed *Violone*), is the largest of the stringed instruments.

†**violous**, irreg. variant of VIOLENT *a.*

1623 FLETCHER & ROWLEY *Maid in Mill* III. i, *Fra.* The.. Count shall pay for it! *Gil.* You are so violous.

violurate (vaɪəˈljʊərət). *Chem.* [f. VIOLUR-IC *a.* + -ATE[1] c.] A salt produced by the action of violuric acid on a base.

1868 WATTS *Dict. Chem.* V. 1001 Hydurilic acid is warmed with water and nitrate of potassium, whereby deep-blue violurate of potassium is formed. *Ibid.* 1002 Violurate of Ammonium.

violuric (vaɪəˈljʊərɪk), *a. Chem.* [f. VIOL(ET + URIC *a.*] ***violuric acid***, an acid produced by the action of nitric on hydurilic acid.

1866 ODLING *Anim. Chem.* 128 Baeyer has increased the list of compounds by his discovery of pseudo-uric acid,.. and the violuric and barbituric acids. 1868 WATTS *Dict. Chem.* V. 1001 Violuric acid crystallises in shining, yellowish, rhombic octahedrons.

viomycin (vaɪəʊˈmaɪsɪn). *Pharm.* [f. *vio-*, of unkn. origin + -MYCIN.] A bacteriostatic antibiotic, $C_{25}H_{43}N_{13}O_{10}$, produced by several species of bacterium which has been given as an alternative drug in the treatment of tuberculosis, usu. by intramuscular injection of the sulphate.

1950 *Sun* (Baltimore) 22 Apr. 15/1 The company [*sc.* Chas. Pfizer & Co.] just announced a new anti-biotic drug called viomycin, hoped to be effective in the treatment of tuberculosis. 1983 *Oxf. Textbk. Med.* I. v. 254/2 Kanamycin, capreomycin, and viomycin are aminoglycosides which can be used as alternatives to the more potent streptomycin in patients hypersensitive to the streptomycin or who are infected with strains resistant to first-line drugs.

†**viorne.** *Obs.*[−1] [a. F. *viorne* (16th c.):—L. *vīburna*, pl. of *vīburnum.*] The wayfaring-tree.

1637 HOLLAND *Camden's Brit.* 421 *Inter viburna Cupressus*, that is, the Cypresse tree amongst the Viornes [1610 among smal twigges].

viosterol (vaɪəʊˈstɪərɒl). *Biochem.* [f. ULTRA)VIO(LET *a.* and *sb.* + -STEROL.] Calciferol (vitamin D_2) obtained by the irradiation of ergosterol with ultraviolet light.

1929 *Jrnl. Amer. Med. Assoc.* 31 Aug. 693/1 The Council [on Pharmacy and Chemistry] has adopted the term viosterol to designate irradiated ergosterol. 1933 *Discovery* May 160/1 The daily dose of yeast milk required for the prevention of rickets is approximately 24 ounces (120 rat units) of cod liver oil, 3 teaspoonful (200 rat units) and of viosterol 10 drops (800 units). 1971 A. A. MICHELE *You don't have to Ache* vii. 162 Today rickets is rare. Vitamin D and viosterol have done much to eliminate the disease.

V.I.P., VIP (viː aɪ ˈpiː). **1. a.** An abbrev. f. the initial letters of 'very important person', esp. a high-ranking guest. Freq. *Mil. slang* in early use.

1933 C. MACKENZIE *Water on Brain* viii. 111 'At the moment he has a V.I.P. with him'... Miss Glidden seemed to divine his perplexity, for..she turned round and whispered through a pursed up mouth, 'Very Important Personage'. 1945 *Daily Mirror* 11 Aug. 5/4 Then they started pouring buckets of water on the crowds below.. until a very important person happened along. The VIP got a bucketful all to himself... The VIP was a brigadier. 1946 E. WAUGH *Diary* 31 Mar. (1976) vi. 645, I found I had been categorized VIP—Very Important Person. It seemed odd to be asked 'Are you a VIP?' 1953 J. PUDNEY *Ring for Luck* 19 A sophisticated traveller, something of a V.I.P., expecting to be met and seen off wherever he went. 1964 MRS. L. B. JOHNSON *White House Diary* 24 Mar. (1970) 98 There were about three hundred people in front of the platform—VIP's from Huntsville. 1980 J. DITTON *Copley's Hunch* III. 221 For their own safety—as with all VIPs—their going had to be kept secret.

b. Spelt vip (vip), as an acronym. Now *rare.*

1945 *Fortune* Aug. 161 Very important persons, or 'Vips', usually travel in plush C-54's. 1968 *Listener* 22 Aug. 243/1 'Provided you are a Vip,' he added, joining the initials so that they formed a word. I was rather intrigued by this and asked him to explain what he meant by Vip, the meaning of which I feigned ignorance of. 'A Vip,' he said, 'is what in the days of you British used to be called a *bara sahib*, a senior official, but now we have been ordered to use this new Hindi word.'

2. *attrib.*, esp. as ***V.I.P. lounge, treatment.***

1945 *Yank* 24 Aug. 6 The private was told by a general who had just left the VIP mess hall that 'I had a wonderful dinner'. 1958 *New Statesman* 22 Feb. 242/3 Mr Nutting, for example, was given the alpha-plus VIP treatment. 1967 MRS. L. B. JOHNSON *White House Diary* 3 Aug. (1970) 552 We drove up to an entrance and went quickly into a small VIP lounge where they shut the door. 1980 G. MCDONALD *Snatched* i. 8, I explained the situation to the head stewardess in the V.I.P. lounge.

viˈparious, app. a mistake or misprint for *vivacious* 'tenacious of life'.

1849 LYTTON *Caxtons* XII. ii, A cat the most viparious is limited to nine lives.

viper (ˈvaɪpə(r)). Also 6 **vyper, vypar, veper.** [a. OF. *vipere, vipre* (mod.F. *vipère*, = Pr. *vipera, vipra, vibra* fem., *vibre* masc., Sp. and Pg. *vibora*, It. *vipera*) or ad. L. *vīpera* viper, snake, serpent, contracted from *vīvi-pera*, f. *vīvus* alive, living, and *parĕre* to bring forth. See also WIVER.]

1. a. The small ovo-viviparous snake *Pelias berus* (formerly *Coluber berus* or *Vipera communis*), abundant in Europe and the only venomous snake found in Great Britain; the adder; in general use, any venomous, dangerous, or repulsive snake or serpent.

The flesh of the viper was formerly regarded as possessing great nutritive or restorative properties, and was frequently used medicinally.

1526 TINDALE *Acts* xxviii. 3 When Paul had gaddered a boundle of stickes, And putt them into the fyre, a viper (be cause off the heet) creept out. 1545 BRINKLOW *Lament.* 116 The vypar aboue all other..serpentes is most fullest of poyson. 1551 TURNER *Herbal* (1568) I. B v, Garlyke.. helpeth the bytyng of a veper. 1583 GREENE *Mamillia* I. Wks. (Grosart) II. 74 The Elephant being enuenomed with the Viper, eateth him vp, and is healed. 1616 BULLOKAR *Eng. Expos.*, *Viper*, a venemous serpent in some hot countries lying much in the earth, hauing a short taile, which grateth and maketh a noise as he goeth. 1634 PEACHAM *Compl. Gentl.* (ed. 2) xii. 109 Some mortals also are knowne by their cognisances, as..Cleopatra by a viper. 1697 DRYDEN *Virg. Georg.* III. 629 With that rank Odour from thy Dwelling-place To drive the Viper's Brood, and all the venom'd Race. 1750 tr. *Leonardus' Mirr. Stones* 65 The proper virtue of the Sicilian is, to subdue the poison of vipers. 1769 PENNANT *Brit. Zool.* III. 17 Vipers are found in many parts of this island. 1805 BINGLEY *Anim. Biog.* (ed. 3) III. 95 The Viper is the only one, either of the Reptile or Serpent tribes, in Great Britain, from whose bite we have any thing to fear. 1857 BORROW *Romany Rye* App. ix, The duty of the true critic is to play the part of a leech, and not of a viper.

transf. and *fig.* 1535 JOYE *Apol. Tindale* 24 Ar not these the venomouse tethe of vepers that thus gnawe a nother mannis name? 1555 EDEN *Decades* (Arb.) 193 These blind and swalowyng sandes, the Spaniardes caule Vypers: And that by good reason, bycause in them many shyppes are entangled. **1606** SHAKS. *Tr. & Cr.* III. i. 145 Hot bloud, hot thoughts, and hot deedes, why they are Vipers, is Loue a generation of Vipers? **1713** WATERLAND *Serm. Assizes Cambr.* 13 Special care therefore must be taken to find out this lurking Viper [*sc.* pride] in our Bosoms, and to cast it far from us. **1819** SCOTT *Ivanhoe* xxvii, Then comes remorse, with all its vipers, mixed with vain regrets for the past.

b. *Zool.* Applied with distinguishing terms to other species of the genus *Vipera*, the sub-order *Viperina*, or snakes resembling the common viper.

For *horned, pit, red, sand, water, yellow viper*, see those terms.

1736 MORTIMER in *Phil. Trans.* XXXIX. 254 *Vipera fusca*: the brown Viper in Virginia. In Carolina it is called the Truncheon-Snake. **1743** CATESBY *Nat. Hist. Carolina* (1771) II. 44 The Black Viper..is short and thick, of slow motion. *Ibid.* 45 The Brown Viper..is..in length about two feet, and large in proportion. **1778** *Encycl. Brit.* (ed. 2) III. 2096/1 The Vipera, or common viper of the shops... It is a native of Egypt, and other warm countries. **1802** SHAW *Gen. Zool.* III. II. 377 Egyptian Viper. *Ibid.* 382 Swedish Viper. **1834** MCMURTRIE *Cuvier's Anim. Kingd.* 185 *Vip[era] brachyura*, Cuv. (The Minute Viper.) **1843** *Penny Cycl.* XXVI. 347/2 Variegated Viper—that described by Mr. Bell from Hornsey Wood. **1845** *Encycl. Metrop.* XXV. 1099–1101 [Various species]. **1861** HULME tr. *Moquin-Tandon* II. v. i. 250 The *Vipera Berus* (Daud) or Small Viper (*Coluber Ammodytes*, Linn.). **1881** Nose-horned viper [see VIPERLING].

c. *Zool.* One or other of the snakes belonging to the genus *Vipera*, of which the common viper is the type, or to the family *Viperidæ*.

The vipers were formerly classified (following Linnæus) under the order *Coluber*, from which they are now separated (cf. quot. 1834). The *Viperidæ* form one of the four families into which the suborder *Viperina* (or *Solenoglypha*) is now divided.

1802 SHAW *Gen. Zool.* III. II. 364 The species [of Coluber] differ greatly in size and habit, according to their respective tribes; some, as the Vipers, having large, flattish, and sub-cordate heads, with rather short than long bodies and tails. **1834** MCMURTRIE *Cuvier's Anim. Kingd.* 185 The vipers, most of which were confounded with the Colubers by Linnæus, on account of their double sub-caudal plates, require to be separated from them from the circumstance of their having poisonous fangs. *c* **1882** *Cassell's Nat. Hist.* IV. 311 The Vipers (*Viperidæ*)..have a large broad head, a vertical and long pupil in the eye, and the top of the head is covered with very little plates and scales.

2. *fig.* A venomous, malignant, or spiteful person; a villain or scoundrel.

In some quots. the influence of sense 3 or 3 b is perceptible.

[**1526** TINDALE *Matt.* iii. 7 He sayde vnto them: O generacion of vipers, who hath taught you to fle from the vengeaunce to come?] **1591** GREENE *Conny Catch.* Wks. (Grosart) X. 39 These villanous vipers, vnworthy the name of men, base roagues,..being outcasts from God, vipers of the world. **1607** SHAKS. *Cor.* III. i. 265 Where is this Viper, That would depopulate the city, & be euery man himself? **1613** J. TAYLOR (Water P.) *Watermen's Suit* Wks. (1630) 173, I will regard such Vipers and their slander so little, that their malice [etc.]. **1642–4** VICARS *God in Mount* (1844) 149 That most mischievous Viper of our Church & State too, Mathew Wren Bp. of Elie. **1693** DRYDEN *Juvenal* VI. 836, I (she confesses) in the Fact was caught; Two Sons dispatching, at one deadly Draught. What Two, Two Sons, thou Viper, in one day? **1819** SHELLEY *Cenci* I. iii. 165 *Cenci* (*to Beatrice*). Thou painted viper! Beast that thou art! Fair and yet terrible! **1832** WARREN *Diary Late Physic.* II. ii. 88 'Cannot this infamous scoundrel be brought to justice?' I inquired. 'If he were, he may prove, perhaps, not worth powder and shot, the viper!' **1846** MRS. A. MARSH *Father Darcy* II. iv. 85 'What a generation of vipers!' thought he, 'what a hydra brood of oppressors!' **1850** MARSDEN *Early Purit.* (1853) 403 The seditious carriage of some vipers of the lower house.

3. In other figurative or allusive uses: †**a.** In allusion to the supposition that the female viper was killed by her young eating their way out at birth. *Obs.*

Cf. Pliny *Nat. Hist.* x. lxii. 82.

1601 B. JONSON *Poetaster* v. iii, Out viper, thou that eat'st thy parents, hence! **1608** SHAKS. *Per.* I. i. 64, I am no viper, yet I feed On mother's flesh which did me breed.

b. In allusion to the fable of the viper reared or revived in a person's bosom: One who betrays or is false to those who have supported or nourished him; a false or treacherous person. Cf. SNAKE *sb.* 2 a.

Partly after the similar L. uses *in sinu viperam habere* (Cicero) and *viperam nutricare sub ala* (Petronius).

1596 *Edward III*, I. i. 105 Degenerate Traytor, viper to the place Where thou was fostred in thine infancy. *a* **1688** BP. S. PARKER in H. Coleridge *North. Worthies* (1852) I. 68 Tenderness and indulgence to such men were to nourish vipers in our bowels. **1689** *Muses Farew. to Popery* 28 Ev'n thy Royal Patron was not spar'd..O strange return to a forgiving King, But the warm'd Viper wears the greatest Sting. **1749** FIELDING *Tom Jones* XVIII. viii, He is the brother of that wicked viper which I have so long nourished in my bosom. **1821–2** SHELLEY *Chas. I*, II. 214 Mark the consequence of warming This brood of northern vipers in your bosom. **1911** RIKER *Ld. Holland* I. iii. 164 The Newcastles had been in terror lest they had raised a viper in their midst.

4. One who smokes marijuana or opium, esp. habitually. Also, a heroin addict. Now *rare*.

1938 M. BERGER in *New Yorker* 12 Mar. 36/1 They play special recordings of viper, or weed, songs with weird ritualistic themes. *Ibid.*, I was not a viper, which is the Harlem word for a marijuana smoker. **1943** I. LANG *Background of Blues* 21 The addict is a 'viper' who 'likes to smoke' or 'climbs the bush'. **1956** D. WEBB *Line-Up for Crime* iv. 69 Three good shots of heroin and you're a viper for life. A viper is an addict. **1959** MURTAGH & HARRIS *Who live in Shadow* (1960) I. iv. 54 They said I wasn't just a viper but also scumpteen of a pusher. **1977** *Canadian* 8 Jan. 15/1 He wrote that song in the late Thirties, back when people who smoked marijuana used to be called vipers.

5. *attrib.* and *Comb.* **a.** Comb., as ***viper-curled, -green, -haunted, -headed, -mouthed, -nourished*** adjs.; ***viper-catcher, -hunter, -hunting.***

a **1593** MARLOWE *Ovid's Elegies* III. xi. 26 Our verse great Tityus a huge space out-spreads, And giues the viper curled Dogge three heads. **1607** TOPSELL *Four-f. Beasts* 526 If it happen that..any man chaunce to light vpon these Viper-nourished blinde-Dormise. **1702** R. MEAD *Poisons* 29 Our Viper-Catchers have a Remedy,..in which They do place..great Confidence. **1774** GOLDSM. *Nat. Hist.* (1776) VII. 199 The seeming rashness of one Tozzi, a viper-catcher. **1802** SHAW *Gen. Zool.* III. II. 465 Viper-headed snake. *Coluber Viperinus.* **1804** *Ibid.* V. I. 120 Viper-mouthed Pike. *Esox Stomias.* **1843** *Penny Cycl.* XXVI. 349/1 In England these reptiles were caught with a cleft or forked stick, which the viper-catcher drove down immediately behind the head. **1851** BORROW *Lavengro* iv, When a person is timid in viper-hunting he had better leave off. *Ibid.*, Besides being a viper-hunter, I am what they call a herbalist. **1904** W. M. GALLICHAN *Fishing Spain* 102 These viper-haunted spots. **1958** L. DURRELL *Mountolive* xvi. 300 Among the thickets of reed and sedge, in places polished to black or viper-green by the occasional clinging frosts, you could hear the chuckling ..of..duck. **1976** *Star* (Sheffield) 3 Dec. 25/9 (Advt.), 1975 (N) VW *Passat* 1300... Attractively finished in viper green.

b. Simple attrib., as ***viper bite, fat, flesh, group, kind, oil, spirit, virus.***

1721 BAILEY, *Viperous*, of the Viper kind or belonging to Adders. **1754** BARTLET *Gentlem. Farriery* Index, Viper bite, how to be treated. **1767** GOOCH *Treat. Wounds* I. 199 Viper oil or fat, which shou'd be fresh, is a sovereign remedy against the stinging of bees..and other venomous insects. **1776** G. WHITE *Selborne* 29 April, This little fry [of fifteen vipers] issued into the world with the true viper spirit about them. **1843** *Penny Cycl.* XXVI. 349/1 Pliny, Galen, and others praise the efficacy of viper flesh in the cure of ulcers [etc.]. **1870** GILLMORE tr. *Figuier's Reptiles & Birds* ii. 88 Such are the terrible weapons of the Viper group. **1891** 'SON OF MARSHES' *On Surrey Hills* 61 Viper-oil..you would find in all the woodmen's cottages. **1894** *Daily News* 8 Feb. 5/4 By heating some viper virus at a temperature of 85 degrees Centigrade.

c. With intensive force (passing in later use into adj.), = Venomous, extremely bitter, viperous.

1591 SYLVESTER *Du Bartas* I. vi. 95 York and Lancaster, Ambitious broachers of that Viper-War. **1605** *Ibid.*, *Sonn. Late Peace* xxviii, All the tempests of our Viper-Warre. **1788** BURNS *Poet's Progr.* 30 Viper-critics cureless venom dart. **1876** SIR E. M. THOMPSON *Chron. A. de Usk* 221 The viper race of Lombardy, split up into Guelphs and Ghibellines. **1899** MISS B. HARRADEN *Fowler* 75, I can't abide the little viper man. *Ibid.* 83 He don't like that little viper gentleman any more than I.

6. a. Special combs., as **viper-broth**, broth made from vipers, or in which a viper has been boiled, formerly supposed to possess nutritive or invigorating properties; **viper-fish**, a deep-sea fish of the family *Chauliodontidæ*, esp. *Chauliodus sloani* (*Cent. Dict.* 1891); **viper-gourd**, an East Indian climbing gourd, *Trichosanthes colubrina*, remarkable for its ugliness (*Treas. Bot.* 1866); **viper-grass**, = viper's grass; also *attrib.*; **viper-jelly** (cf. *viper-broth*); †**viper-mouth** (see quot. and cf. *viper-fish* above); †**viper-stone**, = SERPENTINE *sb.* 3; **viper-weever**, the lesser weever, *Trachinus vipera*; **viper-wine**, wine medicated by an extract or decoction obtained from vipers, formerly drunk on account of its supposed restorative or vitalizing properties; †**viper-worm**, = VIPER 1.

1707 FLOYER *Physic. Pulse-Watch* 327 Hunted Venison, Stale Meats, *Viper Broths, or Wine. **1732** ARBUTHNOT *Rules of Diet* in *Aliments*, etc. I. 509 Viper-broth is both anti-acid and nourishing. **1843** *Penny Cycl.* XXVI. 349/1 The lingering belief in the wonderfully invigorating qualities of 'viper broth' is not yet quite extinct in some places. **1656** J. SMITH *Pract. Physick* 238 Topicals must be Specifical Resolvers, as *Viper-grasse. **1711** C. CLEVE tr. *Cowley's Plants* III. C.'s Wks. III. 347 Viper-grass, full of a milky Juice Good against Poison. **1757** A. COOPER *Distiller* III. xv. (1760) 170 Of Viper-grass ten Ounces. **1771** *Encycl. Brit.* III. 102/2 A decoction made of barley,..viper-grass root, and liquorice. **1796** WITHERING *Brit. Plants* (ed. 3) II. 232 Wall Viper-grass. *Ibid.*, Common Viper-grass. **1863** PRIOR *Brit. Pl.* 234 Viper-grass,..*Scorzonera edulis.* **1702** R. MEAD *Poisons* 34 The Patient ought to eat frequently of *Viper Gelly; or Broth. **1743** CATESBY *Nat. Hist. Carolina* (1771) II. 119 *Vipera Marina*, the *Viper-Mouth. This Fish is eighteen inches in length. **1738** *Phil. Trans.* XL. 442 Speaking of the Serpentine or *Viper-Stone, he relates a very extraordinary Accident. **1863** COUCH *Brit. Fishes* II. 48 The *Viper Weever, however, is common on most of the shores of Britain and Ireland. **1631** MASSINGER *Beleeve as You List* IV. i, Your *viper wine, So much in practise with gray bearded gallants, [is] But vappa to the nectar of her lippe. **1631** QUARLES *Hist. Samson* Wks. (Grosart) II. 149/2 Their Viper-wines, to make old age presume To feele new lust, and youthfull flames agin. **1745** ELIZA HEYWOOD *Female Spect.* No. 12 (1748) II. 292 Lady Frolick pouring a glass of viper wine down his throat. **1802** SHAW *Gen. Zool.* III. II. 372 Galen..relates very remarkable cures of this disease [*sc.* elephantiasis] performed by means of viper wine. **1896** *Academy* 28 Nov. 467/3 The legend that Lady Digby died of drinking viper-wine. **1591** SYLVESTER *Du Bartas* I. vi. 199 Th' innamel'd Scorpion, and the *Viper-worm. **1592** —— *Tri. Faith* IV. v, The deadly sting of th' ugly Viper-Worm.

b. Special collocations with *viper's*, forming names of plants, as **viper's bugloss**, the plant *Echium vulgare* or a variety of this; **viper's grass**, a plant of the genus *Scorzonera*, esp. *S. hispanica*; †**viper's herb**, viper's bugloss; **viper's plant**, viper's grass.

1597 GERARDE *Herbal* II. cclxxii. 658 *Vipers Buglosse, or wall Buglosse. **1678** PHILLIPS (ed. 4), *Vipers Buglosse*, a Solar herb, the roots and seeds whereof are Cordial and Expellers of Melancholy. **1698** PETIVER in *Phil. Trans.* XX. 402 In Texture very much resembling our Vipers Bugloss. **1777** JACOB *Catal. Plants* 33 *Echium anglicum*, English Viper's Bugloss. *Echium vulgare*, Viper's Bugloss. **1840** *Florist's Jrnl.* (1846) I. 106 A flinty soil nourishes the Three-leaved Speedwell and the Viper's Bugloss. **1869** RUSKIN *Queen of Air* §87 It [the serpent spirit] enters into the forget-me-not, and the star of heavenly turquoise is corrupted into the viper's bugloss. **1597** GERARDE *Herbal* II. ccxlii. 596 There be diuers sorts of plants conteined vnder the title of *Viperaria, Scorzonera*, or *Vipers grasse. **1629** PARKINSON *Paradisus* 301 This Spanish Vipers grasse hath diuers long, and somewhat broad leaues. *Ibid.*, This purple flowred Vipers grasse hath long and narrow leaues. **1718** OZELL tr. *Tournefort's Voy.* I. 174 A Flower of an inch and half diameter, yellow, like that of the common Vipers-grass. **1842** J. B. FRASER *Mesopot. & Assyria* xv. 359 East of Mosul, a species of vipers'-grass..abounds, and affords a plentiful nutriment. **1855** DELAMER *Kitchen Gard.* (1861) 32 Scorzonera, Viper's-Grass, or Spanish Salsify. **1597** GERARDE *Herbal* II. cclxxii. 659 It is called..in English vipers Buglosse, Snakes Buglosse, and of some *vipers herbe, and wilde Buglosse the lesser. **1884** tr. *De Candolle's Orig. Cultivated Pl.* 45 *Scorzonera hispanica*..was formerly supposed to be an antidote against the bite of adders, and was sometimes called the *viper's plant.

Hence (chiefly in nonce-use) *v. intr.*, to have an effect like that of a viper's venom; **'viperan**, †**vi'pereal**, †**'vipered**, **vi'perian** *adjs.*, of or pertaining to a viper; viperine, viperous; **vi'periform** *a.*, having the form of a viper; viperine.

1953 DYLAN THOMAS *Under Milk Wood* (1954) 63 Mr Pugh..mixes especially for Mrs Pugh a venomous porridge unknown to toxicologists which will scald and viper through her. **1877** TALMAGE *Serm.* 338 The acid of a soured life, the *viperan sting of a bitter memory. **1748** *Phil. Trans.* XLV. 662 Hence perhaps the *vipereal Venom..may derive its Force. **1560** FITZWILLIAM *Let.* in Froude *Hist. Eng.* (1863) VIII. 16 There was not under the sun a more craftier *vipered undermining generation. **1866** J. B. ROSE tr. *Ovid's Met.* 115 And Perseus triumphant homeward brings *Viperian spoils. *c* **1882** *Cassell's Nat. Hist.* IV. 301 The poisonous Snakes are divided into two groups—the *Viperiform Snakes and the Venomous Colubrines.

†**'viperal.** *Obs.*$^{-1}$ [ad. L. *vīperāl-is*, f. *vīpera* VIPER.] A medicament derived from the viper.

1716 M. DAVIES *Athen. Brit.* II. 352 The great Pox which can scarce ever be cur'd without Viperals or Mercurials.

†**vi'pereous,** *a. Obs.*$^{-1}$ [f. L. *vīpere-us* (hence It. *vipereo*), f. *vīpera* VIPER: see -EOUS. Cf. VIPERIOUS *a.*] Viperous, venomous.

In the first quot. after Ovid *Metam.* IV. 490; in the second translating Virgil *Æneid* VII. 349–51.

c **1620** ROBINSON *Mary Magd.* 547 A dreary hagge of Acheron..in the palaces of Pleasure stood, Shakinge ye frie of her vipereous brood. *Ibid.* 565 And one vpon ye wretched mayd shee slunge, That..glided on her brest with gentle hast, And there vipereous cogitations plac't.

'viperess. *rare*$^{-1}$. [f. VIPER + -ESS.] A female viper. In quot. *fig.*

1647 R. STAPYLTON *Juvenal* 102 But Pontia did confesse, 'My sons I would have poyson'd'. Viperesse!

viperid ('vaɪpərɪd), *sb.* and *a. Zool.* [ad. mod.L. *Viperid-æ*, f. L. *vīpera* VIPER: see -ID³.] **A.** *sb.* A snake of the family Viperidæ, which comprises the true vipers and in most modern classifications the pit vipers, all venomous snakes having hinged maxillary bones, that are toothless except for a fang that is folded back in the mouth when not in use. **B.** *adj.* Of or pertaining to this family.

1909 WEBSTER, Viperid *a. & n.* **1956** L. M. KLAUBER *Rattlesnakes* II. xi. 716 The viperids were evolved directly from primitive aglyphous ancestors, rather than from either opisthoglyphs or proteroglyphs. **1965** R. & D. MORRIS *Men & Snakes* iv. 97 Generally speaking, the viperids are not as dangerous to man as the cobras and mambas, yet in some ways the symptoms of viperine poisoning are even more alarming. **1969** A. BELLAIRS *Life of Reptiles* I. v. 193 It has been suggested that the viperid or solenoglyph type of jaw was derived from that of opisthoglyphs. **1977** A. HALLAM *Planet Earth* 272 The elapids..and the viperids..are both first known from the Miocene.

'viperine, *sb.*¹ *rare.* [f. VIPER + -INE⁵.] (See quot.)

1861 HULME tr. *Moquin-Tandon* II. v. ii. 284 Prince Lucien Bonaparte has shown that the poison of the Viper consists essentially of a principle to which he has given the name Echidnine or Viperine.

viperine ('vaɪpəraɪn, -ɪn), *a.* and *sb.*² Also 8 -in. [ad. L. *vīperīn-us* (hence OF. *viperin*, F. *vipérin*, It., Sp., and Pg. *viperino*), f. *vīpera* VIPER: see -INE¹.]

1. Resembling a viper or that of a viper; having the nature or character of a viper; venomous, viperous; viper-like. Chiefly in fig. or allusive use (cf. VIPER 3).

a **1550** *Image Hypocr.* II. 291 in *Skelton's Wks.* (1843) II. 426 His county pallantyne Haue coustome colubryne, With codes viperyne And sectes serpentyne. **1604** R. CAWDREY *Table Alph.* (1613), *Viperine*, like a viper, or of a viper. **1648** E. SIMMONS *Pref. to Wodenote's Herm. Theol.* A 8 b, If ever the Title of Rex diabolorum was rightly applyable to the King of this land, 'tis since the viperine birth of these miscreants. **1657** J. SERGEANT *Schism Dispach't* 22 Lingua viperea! Viperine tongue! **1697** EVELYN *Numism.* ix. 299 Cæsar Borgia's Viperine Aspect. **1716** M. DAVIES *Athen. Brit.* II. 150 Of all the Poetick Salts,.. the Satyrical [is] most Viperin and Piercing, the Eclogist and Idilian the most Country-wise and Native. **1873** *Routledge's Yng. Gentl. Mag.* June 401/1 He [a grass-snake] raised himself up in true viperine fashion.

†**b.** *fig.* Of glosses (see VIPER 3 a). *Obs.*

1647 TRAPP *Comm. Matt.* v. 22 Our Saviour.. taking away their viperine glosses that did eat out the bowels of the text. **1648** *Commoner's Liberty* 18 Had he any other way to weaken what must of necessity be inferred from them, but by such viperine glosses.

c. Of persons.

1652 GAULE *Magastrom.* 362 Archilocus, a viperine satyrist, and not onely so, but a petulant obscure poet. **1716** M. DAVIES *Athen. Brit.* II. To Rdr. 40 Implacable Enemies of the most invenemated Viperin, or rather Draconick kind, who are.. continually gnawing and corroding the very Bowels.. of the Church of England. **1845** BROWNING *Lett.* (1899) I. 48 A viperine she-friend of mine who, I think, rather loves me, she does so hate me. **1903** *Times* 16 Dec. 11/5 The convention of the virtuous heroine and the viperine adventuress.

2. Of or pertaining to a viper; obtained from or natural to vipers.

1608 TOPSELL *Serpents* 286 They [tortoises] eate Origan, for that herbe is an antidote against Viperine poyson for them. **1684** tr. *Bonet's Merc. Compit.* x. 347 Viperine Medicines are good in the Itch and Leprosie. **1702** R. MEAD *Poisons* 33 The main Efficacy of the Viperine Flesh is to quicken the Circle of the Blood. **1728** CHAMBERS *Cycl.* s.v. *Viper*, The Virus.. proves a nimble Vehicle to carry the Viperine Spicula almost every where suddenly. **1851** W. J. BRODERIP *Leaves fr. Note Bk. Nat.* (1852) 224 The viperine remedy had classical authority for its ministration. **1904** *Brit. Med. Jrnl.* 17 Sept. 670 These two being examples of mixed colubrine and viperine poisons.

3. *Zool.* Of snakes: Resembling or related to the common viper; now *spec.* belonging to the suborder *Viperina* (*Solenoglypha*).

1802 SHAW *Gen. Zool.* III. II. 355 Viperine Boa. *Boa Viperina.* **1870** GILLMORE tr. *Figuier's Reptiles & Birds* ii. 41 His Venomous Colubrine Snakes have certainly a much nearer resemblance in other respects to the *Colubridæ* than they have to the Viperine Snakes. *Ibid.* 47 The Viperine Snake (*Tropidonotus viperinus*)... This is the smallest of all the European *Colubridæ.* **1887** GÜNTHER in *Encycl. Brit.* XXII. 191/1 The poison of Viperine snakes invariably destroys its coagulability.

4. *sb. Zool.* A snake belonging to the *Viperina.*

1887 GÜNTHER in *Encycl. Brit.* XXII. 191/1 In the other venomous snakes (Viperines and Crotalines) the maxillary bone is very short. *Ibid.* 198/2 The Death Adder.. differs from the other Viperines in having the poison-fang permanently erect.

†**viperious**, *a. Obs. rare.* [f. VIPER + -IOUS. Cf. VIPEREOUS *a.*] Viperous, venomous. Hence †**viperiously** *adv. Obs.*$^{-1}$

c **1520** *Treat. Galaunt* (1860) 12 If ye beholde the galauntes progenye vyperyous That out of France be fledde. **1538** *St. Papers Hen. VIII* (1834) III. 2 He made there.. a comment on the saide letter,.. with sousch a stomake, as I thinke the three mouthed Cerberous of Hell coulde not have uttered it more viperiously. *a* **1670** HACKET *Abp. Williams* I. (1692) 92 Our viperious countrymen, the English Jesuits in France,.. retorted that argument upon us.

viperish (ˈvaɪpərɪʃ), *a.* [f. VIPER + -ISH.]

1. *fig.* Venomous, viperous, spiteful.

1755 SMOLLETT *Quix.* (1803) II. 40 Tell me, you viperish scoffer, what you think hath won this kingdom? **1860** W. COLLINS *Wom. White* III. narr. W. Hartwright vii, She cast one viperish look at me as I entered the hall. **1880** MISS BRADDON *Just as I am* xlv, He listened to her viperish speech. **1889** *Spectator* 14 Dec. 839 All sorts of characters, from the most malignant and viperish to the noblest and most self-forgetful.

2. Somewhat resembling a viper; viper-like.

1863 MISS BRADDON *Aurora Floyd* xv, It seemed as if her footfall had startled some viperish creature. **1873** SYMONDS *Grk. Poets* vii. 218 [Medea's] viperish loose hair and throbbing skin.

Hence ˈ**viperishly** *adv.*, with the rapid and sinuous motion of a viper.

1870 *Temple Bar Mag.* XXIX. 180 Men.. with lissom wrists that can make a foil curl viperishly round an antagonist's blade.

ˈ**viper-like**, *adv.* and *a.* [f. VIPER.]

A. *adv.* In or after the manner of a viper. Only in allusive use (see VIPER 3).

1630 DRAYTON *Muses Eliz.* x. 117 This cruell kinde thus Viper-like deuoure That fruitfull soyle which them too fully fed. **1646** J. HALL *Poems* I. 43 Had not thy mother born thee toothlesse thou Hadst eaten Viper-like a passage through. **1677** HORNECK *Gt. Law Consid.* iv. (1704) 141 If Absalom had not had a kingdom in his eye, he would hardly have,.. viperlike, preyed upon the bowels that did feed him. *a* **1700** DRYDEN *P.S. to Hist. League* Wks. 1821 XVII. 162 The government in which they live, and which, viper-like, they would devour. **1729** MADDEN *Themistocles* IV. i. (ed. 3) 44 Can I live By Athens' Ruin, working out my Way Into the World, most Viper-like, by gnawing E'en thro' my Mother's Bowels? **1771** KELLY *Clementina* III. i, They'll else blast all the comforts of your life, And, viper-like, with death return your fondness. **1897** FLANDRAU *Harvard Episodes* 277 He couldn't bring himself at that late day to arise, viper like, from the hearthstone and smite.

B. *adj.* Like or resembling a viper.

1888 *Encycl. Brit.* XXIV. 247 The genus *Echis* consists of but one species (*E. carinata*)... It is a viper-like snake. **1903** *Westm. Gaz.* 3 Mar. 2/1 The noise of the little brass viper-like being in the corner as it whirred and hissed and snapped its teeth.

ˈ**viperling.** [f. VIPER + -LING.] A young viper.

1847 *Blackw. Mag.* LXII. 299 Young viperlings come into the world in full maturity of malice. **1881** *Daily News* 28 Dec. 3/2 About three weeks ago the nose-horned viper.. distinguished herself by presenting the Gardens at one fell swoop with six-and-forty viperlings. **1897** G. C. BATEMAN *Vivarium* 222 The Viper produces, at one time, from thirty to fifty little Viperlings.

viperous (ˈvaɪpərəs), *a.* Also 6 vyperos, -ouse, viperouse, 7–8 viporous; 6 vipros, 7 viprous, 7–8 *poet.* vip'rous. [f. VIPER + -OUS.]

1. Of or pertaining to a viper or vipers.

Rarely in literal use.

fig. **1535** STEWART *Cron. Scot.* (Rolls) II. 144 With vipros vennum inwart in his mynd,.. Dissaitfullie that tyme he gart him trow, That he wrocht ay for his plesour and prow. **1602** ROWLANDS *Tis Merrie when Gossips meete* (Hunter. Cl.) 13 No viperous tongue thy pleasant vayne will strike. **1608** D. T[UVILL] *Ess. Pol. & Mor.* 130 With the filthy slime of their malicious and viperous iawes. *a* **1665** J. GOODWIN *Filled w. the Spirit* (1867) 55 Men of a viperous spirit, and desperately set upon their own ruin and destruction. **1765** BEATTIE *Judgm. Paris* ciii, Censure spreads the viperous hiss around. *a* **1859** MACAULAY *Hist. Eng.* xxv. (1861) V. 304 Papers about the brazen forehead, the viperous tongue, and the white liver of Jack Howe. **1886** *Daily News* 8 April 5/3 What viperous venom and what rat-like rage.

lit. **1614** GORGES *Lucan* IX. 391 But when she [Medusa] comb'd her crawling crowne, The viprous venome trailed downe. **1706** DE FOE *Jure Divino* XII. 268 In vain supplies of vip'rous Blood they bring.

†**b.** In allusive use (see VIPER 3 a). *Obs.*

1561 T. NORTON *Calvin's Inst.* III. v. (1634) 319 Out of that ancient custome the confessions and satisfactions that are at this day used, tooke their beginning. Truly very viperous births. **1603** J. DAVIES (Heref.) *Wits Pilgr.* Wks. (Grosart) II. 52/2 The Viperous Iron Teeth of Time may gnaw away, to wrack, through my Works Wombe. **1638** SIR T. HERBERT *Trav.* (ed. 2) 127 Whether [it be].. from vapors ingendred in the bowels of the earth, and loth to bee imprisoned in a wrong orb, [the subterranean fire] rends its passage by a viperous horrid motion; or [etc.].

2. Composed or consisting of vipers. Freq. with admixture of sense 4.

Chiefly in fig. use or as a term of opprobrium, esp. in ***viperous brood*** or ***generation***; freq. in the 17th c., now *rare* or *arch.*

fig. **1538** BALE *Thre Lawes* 1754 Oh ragynge serpentes and vyperouse generacyon. **1586** J. HOOKER *Hist. Irel.* in *Holinshed* II. 42/1 The loose life of that viperous nation. **1601** DENT *Pathw. Heaven* 152 This viperous brood [of liars] doe but watch their times and opportunities. **1643** QUARLES *Loyal Convert* Wks. (Grosart) I. 142/2 A viperous Generation (which hath long nested in this unhappie Island). **1670** *Devout Commun.* (1688) 124 That the Lord of all should.. take into his bosom the viperous brood, that have so often spit their venom in his face? **1706** E. WARD *Hud. Rediv.* (1707) II. vii. 13 For in this pious Christian Nation There is a vip'rous Congregation [etc.]. **1714** L. MILBOURNE *Traitor's Reward* Pref., His way of extolling his viperous generation is so very impudent and rediculous, that [etc.]. **1814** SOUTHEY *Roderick* v. 115 These were Witiza's hateful progeny; And in an evil hour the unhappy King Had spared the viperous brood. **1874** FARRAR *Christ* viii. (1884) 53 A formalism and falsity which made them vipers of a viperous brood.

lit. **1648** J. BEAUMONT *Psyche* II. 128 She.. rent from thence, before Psyche's astonish'd eyes, that viperous fry Which her snarl'd soul in unfelt bands did ty. **1688** *Phil. Trans.* XVIII. 128 Vipers, and all the Viperous Brood.

†**b.** In allusive use (cf. 4 b, and see VIPER 3 a).

1615 W. HULL *Mirr. Maiestie* 39 Sinne is a viperous brood: the life of the daughter, is the death of the mother. **1627** in Rushw. *Hist. Coll.* (1659) I. 514 This forwardness of you is the more remarkable, when that Viperous Generation .. do, at ease, with tooth and nail, essay to rend the Bowels of their Mother. **1648** *Canterburie March* B 2, Hence Viprous Brood! what make you heare, Who thus the Kingdomes Bowels teare?

†**c.** Of hair, etc. Cf. SNAKY *a.* 1. *Obs. rare.*

1633 P. FLETCHER *Purple Isl.* XII. xxx, Her viperous locks hung loose about her eares; Yet with a monstrous snake she them restrains. **1648** J. BEAUMONT *Psyche* XI. 8 Then from his own viperous Tresses He Pluck'd three large handfuls of his longest Snakes.

3. Of actions, qualities, etc.: Worthy of or befitting a viper; malignant, treacherous, venomous.

Very common in the 17th c.; now *rare* or *arch.*

1542 BRINKLOW *Compl.* xxiii. 48 b, How haue thei bewitched the Parlament howse in making such vyperos actys as the beast of Rome neuer made him selfe! **1555** in Strype *Eccl. Mem.* (1721) III. App. xlvi. 142 Their wicked lyves, and viperouse behaviour toward the said bishope. **1604** COKE *2 State Trials* 26, I want words sufficient to express your viperous treasons. **1631** WEEVER *Anc. Funeral Mon.* 252 The viperous malice of this Monkish broode. **1646** J. HALL *Poems* I. xi. 27 Wee'l suffer viperous thoughts and cares To follow after silver hairs. *a* **1716** SOUTH *Serm.* (1744) X. 285 Let us now see into how many cursed consequences, this viperous piece of villany is like to spread itself. **1824** JEFFERSON *Writ.* (1830) IV. 399 Passions so vehement and viperous.

b. Of language, writings, etc.

1605 CAMDEN *Rem.* Epit. 34 Vpon Stigand.. I finde this most viperous Epitaph in an old Manuscript. **1611** SHAKS. *Cymb.* III. iv. 41 'Tis Slander,.. whose tongue Out-venomes all the Wormes of Nyle;.. the Secrets of the Graue this viperous slander enters. **1632** LITHGOW *Trav.* I. 3 The viperous murmurings of miscreant villaines. **1728** P. WALKER *Life Peden* (1827) 270 This is a viporous, groundless wicked Story. **1809–10** COLERIDGE *Friend* (1865) 58 In one of those viperous journals, which deal out profaneness, hate, fury, and sedition throughout the land. **1860** MOTLEY *Netherl.* (1868) I. ii. 37 Wit.. expended in darting viperous epigrams at Court-ladies. **1905** *Athenæum* 12 Aug. 217/1 Lockhart was.. annoyed.. especially by the viperous notes from a Whig hand.

4. Of the nature of a viper; resembling a viper in character or action; having the attributes or evil qualities of a viper.

Freq. in the 17th c.; now *rare.*

1593 G. HARVEY *Pierce's Super.* Wks. (Grosart) II. 20 Good Sir, arise, and confound those Viperous Cryticall monsters. **1607** SHAKS. *Cor.* III. i. 287 Speake breefely then, For we are peremptory to dispatch This Viporous Traitor. **1621** in Foster *Eng. Factories Ind.* (1906) I. 347 These viprous, dessemblinge, and crockadillike currs. **1680** *Spirit of Popery* 24 The Viperous Author of the Reformed Bishop. **1760** H. BROOKE *Fool of Qual.* (1809) I. 130 No step-dames, nor viporous instruments, shall ever hereafter insinuate between us. **1821** SHELLEY *Adonais* xxxvi, What deaf and viperous murderer could crown Life's early cup with such a draught of woe?

†**b.** In allusive use (see VIPER 3 a). *Obs.*

1591 SHAKS. *1 Hen. VI*, III. i. 72 Ciuill dissention is a viperous Worme That gnawes the Bowels of the Common-wealth. **1603** J. DAVIES (Heref.) *Microcosmos* Wks. (Grosart) I. 56/2 Woe woorth such vip'rous Cousins that wil rend Their Mother's wombe (the Common-wealth) to raigne. **1648** *Hunting of Fox* 11 Such viperous Schismaticks as would eate out their way. **1652** BENLOWES *Theoph.* XII. ix, Twas vip'rous Nero slew his own indulgent Mother.

c. *fig.* Of things.

1805 WORDSW. *Prelude* IX. 576 The stings of viperous remorse, Trying their strength, enforced him to start up, Aghast and prayerless. **1880** *Sat. Rev.* No. 1311. 734/1 Considering how much damage these viperous little craft are likely to do in war. **1885–94** R. BRIDGES *Eros & Psyche* April xi, A savage beast, The viperous scourge of gods and humankind.

Hence ˈ**viperously** *adv.*, in or after the manner of a viper; venomously; ˈ**viperousness**, viperous nature or character; venomosity. *rare.*

1587 HOLINSHED *Chron.* III. 419 In that copious treatise hauing spoken as maliciouslie & *viperouslie as he might.. of Wickliffes life. **1648** J. BEAUMONT *Psyche* III. 210 O how the peevish and reluctant elves (Mad with their own birth,) viperously contend The worried bowels of the heart to rend! **1649** COCKAYNE *Found. Freedom Vind.* 1 Whose seeming sugered words are mixed with wormwood, promising fairnesse, but viperously stinging the poore despised Army. **1728** P. WALKER *Life Peden* To Rdr. (1827) p. xxv, Mr. William Vetch,.. in his dotted old Age, wrote so viporously and maliciously against him. **1651** *Mr. Love's Case* 37 Is it possible that such virulency and *viperousness of words as these should proceed from any other Principle? **1727** BAILEY (vol. II), Viperousness.

ˈ**vipery**, *a. rare*$^{-1}$. [f. VIPER + -Y.] Consisting of vipers; viperous.

1909 R. BRIDGES *Paraphr. Virg. Æneid* VI. Poems (1913) 458 On those convicted tremblers then leapeth avenging Tisiphone with keen flesh-whips and vipery scourges.

†**vi-politic.** *Obs.* [VI- *pref.*] (See quot.)

1632 B. JONSON *Magn. Lady* I. vii, [He is] a Vi-politique! Or a sub-aiding Instrument of State! A kind of laborious Secretary To a great man!

vipoma (vaɪˈpəʊmə). *Path.* [f. VIP s.v. V 5 b + -OMA.] A tumour which secretes vasoactive intestinal polypeptide (VIP).

1973 S. R. BLOOM et al. in *Lancet* 7 July 15/2 We suggest that tumours containing V.I.P., and reacting with no other hormone antisera, should be called vipomas. **1980** *Brit. Med. Jrnl.* 15 Nov. 1323/2 This patient's symptoms were unequivocally the result of a functioning vipoma of the left kidney.

†**vi-ˈpresident.** *Obs.*$^{-1}$ [f. VI- + PRESIDENT *sb.*] A vice-president.

c **1668** DAVENANT *Masque* Poems (1672) 364 We have had new orders read in the Presence-Chamber, by the Vi-President of Parnassus.

†**vipseys**, obs. var. of or error for GIPSIES.

1610 HOLLAND *Camden's Brit.* 715 Those famous waters which commonly are called Vipseys, rise out of the earth from many sources not continually, but every second yeere, and being growne unto a great bourne runne downe by the lower grounds into the sea. **1674** BLOUNT *Glossogr.* (ed. 4). **1727** [see GIPSIES]. **1777** *Ann. Reg.* II. 146 Vipseys or gypseys in Yorkshire.. mean a torrent which flows only now and then or once in a few years.

vi-queen. *rare.* [VI- *pref.*] A vice-queen.

1862 H. MARRYAT *Year in Sweden* I. 327 There Lina lies like a vi-queen in her grave.

vir, variant of VIRR *Sc.*

viræmia (vaɪˈriːmɪə). *Med.* Also (*U.S.*) viremia. [f. VIR(US + *-æmia*, after *anæmia*, *leukæmia*, etc.] The condition in which viruses are present in the bloodstream. Hence **viˈræmic** *a.*

1947 DORLAND & MILLER *Med. Dict.* (ed. 21) 1619/1 Viremia. **1954** *Jrnl. Pediatrics* XLIV. 20/1 Little is known about the presence of viremia during the course of the disease [*sc.* poliomyelitis] in man. *Ibid.* 25/2 The infectious process is now almost generally regarded as one which begins with a viremic stage. **1964** M. HYNES *Med. Bacteriol.* (ed. 8) xxv. 383 Infection with poliovirus leads first to proliferation in the intestinal mucosa. A viraemia follows and it is probably thus that the virus usually reaches the central nervous system. **1977** *Lancet* 23 Apr. 884/1 The possibility that this illness is a consequence of early viræmia should not be overlooked. **1979** *Nature* 17 May 200/2 Chickens, mice or cats neonatally infected with oncornaviruses become viraemic, develop low or no anti-tumour immunity and usually succumb to their tumours.

†viragin. *Obs. rare.* [ad. L. *virāgin-*, stem of *virāgo*. Cf. It. *viragine*.] = VIRAGO.

1576 FOXE *A. & M.* (ed. 3) 2005/2 This most rough brake (wherwith this Viragin rather then Virgin..boasted her selfe to be sent of God to ryde and tame the people of England). **1655** FULLER *Ch. Hist.* VI. 364 The aforesaid two Virgins, or rather Viragins, travelled to Rome with three the most beautifull of their society.

viraginian (vɪrəˈdʒɪnɪən), *a.* and *sb.* [f. L. *virāgin-* (see prec.) + -IAN.] **a.** *adj.* = VIRAGINOUS *a.* **b.** *sb.* The language of a virago.

1642 MILTON *Apol. Smect.* Wks. 1851 III. 292 The remembrance of his old conversation among the Viraginian trollops. **1869** O. W. HOLMES *Old Vol. Life, Cinders fr. Ashes* (1891) 242 Her face..showed itself capable of something resembling what Milton calls the viraginian aspect. **1899** B. CAPES *Lady of Darkness* ii. 12 She was rating him in voluble viraginian.

viraˈginity. *rare*⁻⁰. [f. as prec. + -ITY.] The character or qualities of a virago.

1846 WORCESTER (citing *Q. Rev.*).

viraginous (vɪˈrædʒɪnəs), *a.* [f. as prec. + -OUS.]

Of the nature of, having the characteristics of, a virago.

1666 *Third Adv. Painter* 24 She dry'd no tears, for she was so Viraginous, But only snufling her trunk Cartilaginous. **1825** BROCKETT *N.C. Gloss.* s.v. *Stang*, He is carried through the whole hamlet, with a view of exposing or shaming the viraginous lady. **1886** *Sat. Rev.* 10 July 58 Besides the viraginous loves of Fanny Douglas there is much other love-making in the novel. **1890** *Ibid.* 16 Aug. 214 Virile was exactly what Mme. de Staël was not, though she may have been viraginous.

Hence **viˈraginously** *adv.*

1644 R. CULMER *Cathedral News fr. Canterb.* 21 In comes a Prebend's wife, and pleaded for the Images there, and jeered the Commissioners *viraginously*.

virago (vɪˈrɑːgəʊ, vɪˈreɪgəʊ). Also 6 virragoo, 7 ver-, vyr-, firago. [a. L. *virāgo* a man-like or heroic woman, a female warrior, etc., f. *vir* man. Hence also OF., F., and Sp. *virago*.]

†**1.** Woman. (Only as the name given by Adam to Eve, after the Vulgate rendering of Gen. ii. 23.)

c **1000** ÆLFRIC *Hom.* I. 14 Beo hire nama Uirago, þæt is, fæmne, forðan ðe heo is of hire were ȝenumen. *a* **1300** *Cursor M.* 633 Virago gaf he hir to nam; þar for hight sco virago, for maked o þe man was sco. **1388** WYCLIF *Gen.* ii. 23 And Adam seide..This schal be clepid virago, for she is takun of man. **1483** CAXTON *Gold. Leg.* 37 b/1, And Adam gaf here a name lyke as her lord and said, she shal be called Virago, whiche is as moche to saye as made of a man and is a name taken of a man. ? *a* **1500** *Chester Pl.* I. 150 Shee shalbe called, I wisse, Viragoo, nothing amisse, For out of man tacken shee is. **1547** BOORDE *Brev. Health* ccxlii. 82 b, First when a woman was made of God she was named Virago because she dyd come of a man. **1576** GASCOIGNE *Droome Doomes Day* I. ¶6 Before Eva sinned, she was called *Virago*, and after she sinned she deserved to be called Eva.

2. a. A man-like, vigorous, and heroic woman; a female warrior; an amazon. Now *rare.*

1387 TREVISA *Higden* (Rolls) VI. 413 The strong virage [L. *virago potentissima*] Elfleda..halp moche her broþer þe kyng in ȝevynge of counsaile. *a* **1513** FABYAN *Chron.* VI. clxxx. (1811) 178 Elfleda,..this noble venquerersse Virago and made, whose vertue can I nat expresse. **1513** DOUGLAS *Æneid* XII. viii. 56 The mynd..Of Juturna, the verray virago; Quhilk term to expone, be myne avis, Is a woman exersand a mannis office. **1553** EDEN *Treat. New Ind.* (Arb.) 24 One of his wiues..decketh her selfe moste gorgiously.. and procedeth like a *Virago* stoutly and cherefully to the fire, where the corps of her husbande was burnte. **1582** STANYHURST *Æneis* I. (Arb.) 34 No swarms or trouping horsmen can apale the virago. **1613** PURCHAS *Pilgrimage* (1614) 383 This Sultan presented him with the head of that Virago Periaconcona vpon the top of a Launce. *a* **1641** BP. MOUNTAGU *A. & M.* (1642) 361 Shee so ruled as Queene eight yeers and better: a man-like virago of a stout and noble spirit. **1677** W. HUBBARD *Narrative* (1865) II. 20 That young Virago kept the door fast against them. **1712–4** POPE *Rape Lock* v. 37 To arms! to arms! the fierce virago cries, And swift as lightening to the combate flies. **1781** COWPER *Let.* 5 Mar., And as to the neutralities, I really think the Russian virago an impertinent puss for meddling with us. **1831** CARLYLE *Sart. Res.* III. xi, Did not the same virago boast that she had a Cavalry Regiment, whereof neither horse nor man could be injured. **1885** *19th Cent.* May 472 She [Vittoria Colonna] was a virago, a name which, however misapprehended now, bore a different and worthy signification in her day.

†**b.** Applied to a man. *Obs. rare.*

c **1600** DAY *Begg. Bednall Gr.* IV. i. (1881) 78 Come then, my mad Viragoes,..now I'll turn swaggerer myself. **1601** SHAKS. *Twel. N.* III. iv. 300 Why man, hee's a verie diuell, I haue not seen such a firago... They say, he has bin Fencer to the Sophy.

3. A bold, impudent (†or wicked) woman; a termagant, a scold.

c **1386** CHAUCER *Man of Law's T.* 359 O Sowdanesse, roote of Iniquitee, Virago, thou Semyrame the secounde [etc.]. **1680** C. NESSE *Ch. Hist.* 178 God sets this black brand upon this virago Jezabel. **1724** SWIFT *Quiet Life* Wks. 1755 IV. I. 48 He saw virago Nell belabour, With Dick's own staff, his peaceful neighbour. **1770** BURKE *Corr.* (1844) I. 230 No heroine in Billingsgate can go beyond the patriotic scolding of our republican virago. **1838** JAS. GRANT *Sk. Lond.* 175 It now devolved on her to act the part of a wife who played both the tyrant and virago at home. **1865** TROLLOPE *Belton Est.* xxvii. 329, I believe Lady Aylmer to be an overbearing virago, whom it is good to put down. **1891** C. ROBERTS *Adrift Amer.* 90 Three women—a mother and two daughters. These were the greatest viragoes I ever saw.

transf. **1713** WARDER *True Amazons* (ed. 2) 23 But the Numbers are not great of these forward Viragos [= young bees]. **1793** G. WHITE *Selborne* lii, Every hen is in her turn the virago of the yard.

4. a. *attrib.*, chiefly appositive, as ***virago family, girl, heroine***, etc.; also ***virago-strain.***

1598 FLORIO, *Brifalda*, a..mankinde, virago woman. **1621** J. TAYLOR (Water P.) *Superb. Flagellum* C vi, Like shamelesse double sex'd *Hermaphrodites*, Virago Roaring Girles. **1639** G. DANIEL *Vervic.* 161 But the Virago Queene ..doth aggravate Th' aggreived Lords. **1746** FRANCIS tr. *Hor., Sat.* I. i. 131 But a bold wench, of right virago strain, Cleft with an axe the wretched wight in twain. **1760–2** GOLDSM. *Cit. W.* lxii, Petticoated philosophers, blustering heroines, or virago queens. *a* **1843** SOUTHEY *Comm.-pl. Bk.* (1851) I. 470 Edward III's queen Philippa was of a virago family. **1862** ANSTED *Channel Isl.* 360 Montfort was taken prisoner; his countess, one of the virago heroines of the time, was besieged in Hennebon. **1891** FARRAR *Darkn. & Dawn* i, If she had not made Galba and his virago-mother feel the weight of her vengeance, it was only because they were too insignificant.

b. *Comb.*, as ***virago-like.***

1602 MARSTON *Ant. & Mel.* Induct., Wks. 1856 I. 4 An Amazon should have such a voice, virago-like. **1615** BRATHWAIT *Strappado* (1878) 92 He doth renew his battery, and stands too't, And she, Vyrago-like, yeelds not a foote.

Hence **viˈragoish** *a.*, somewhat resembling, or characteristic of, a virago; **viˈragoship**, the character of a virago.

1666 KILLIGREW *Siege of Urbin* I. ii, How shall we answer at the Resurrection? for our Viragoships? for our own, and others blood, thus shed! **1887** E. BERDOE *St. Bernard's* 288 The over-dressed, robust, viragoish lady patient. **1888** LADY D. HARDY *Dang. Exper.* I. iii. 59 Mrs. Brown's rather viragoish, coarse-featured face.

†viragon, irreg. f. VIRAGIN or VIRAGO.

1641 *Vox Borealis* C j b, Wherein Women against the Laws of God, Nature, Nations, they act Man, and play the very Viragons.

viral (ˈvaɪərəl), *a.* [f. VIR(US + -AL¹.] Of the nature of, caused by, or pertaining to a virus or viruses.

1948 *Diagnostic Procedures for Virus & Rickettsial Diseases* (Amer. Public Health Assoc.) 15 Viral agents belonging to the psittacosis group. **1955** [see *parrot fever* s.v. PARROT *sb.* 4]. *a* **1974** R. CROSSMAN *Diaries* (1977) III. 371 She said the viral pneumonia seemed to have cleared up, and the only area of danger was his bronchial tubes. **1976** EDINGTON & GILLES *Path. in Tropics* (ed. 2) xi. 577 Although many viruses may cause hepatitis there are two main types—infectious hepatitis and homologous serum jaundice. It is now recommended that these conditions be redesignated viral hepatitis type A and viral hepatitis type B respectively (WHO, 1973). **1983** *New Scientist* 10 Mar. 642/1 If chemicals can be found that inhibit the activity of these viral enzymes, while leaving cellular enzymes unaffected, then the path to anti-viral drugs will have been cleared.

Hence **ˈvirally** *adv.*, by a virus or viruses.

1968 *Biochem. & Biophys. Res. Communications* XXXIII. 563 The normal and the virally transformed cells differ in regard to the quantity of glycolipids. **1977** *Proc. R. Soc. Med.* LXX. 559/1 Gradually interest in the viral theory was restored as examples of virally-induced tumours were discovered in mammals. **1982** *Proc. Nat. Acad. Sci.* LXXIX. 6822/1 Virally transformed rat embryo cells.

virall, obs. f. VIRL.

virallay, obs. f. VIRELAY.

viranda, etc., obs. f. VERANDA.

virandoed, var. VERANDA(H)ED *a.*

virchippe, obs. f. WORSHIP.

Virchow-Robin space (f-, ˈvɜːkəʊ ˈrɒbæ̃). *Anat.* [Named after R. L. K. *Virchow* (1821–1902), German pathologist, and C. P. *Robin* (1821–85), French histologist.] An extension of the subarachnoid space surrounding a blood vessel for a short distance as it enters the brain or the spinal cord.

1890 A. HILL tr. *Obersteiner's Anat. Central Nervous Organs* III. 137 Between the adventitia and the muscularis a considerable space is seen in all isolated arteries, the adventitial lymph-space (Virchow-Robin space). **1976** *Path. Ann.* XI. 298 (*caption*) Cryptococcosis involving a Virchow-Robin space in the cerebral cortex.

virdingal, obs. var. FARTHINGALE.

†vire, *sb.*¹ *Obs.* Also 4 fyre, 4–6 vyre, 5 *Sc.* **wyr, wyir.** [a. OF. *vire* (= Prov., Sp., Pg. *vira*), f. *virer* to turn.] A form of quarrel or bolt for a cross-bow. (Cf. VIRETON.)

1375 BARBOUR *Bruce* v. 595, I haf a bow, bot and a vyre. *Ibid.* 623 He tasit the vyre and leit it fle. **1390** GOWER *Conf.* I. 164 As a fyre Which fleth out of a myhti bowe, Aweie he fledde for a throwe. *c* **1400** *Laud Troy Bk.* 4802 Thei fauȝt vn-armed in here atyres With longe Arwes and scharpe vires. *c* **1425** *Cast. Persev.* 2113 in *Macro Plays* (1904) 140, I schal slynge at þee many a vyre, & ben a-vengyd hastely here. *c* **1500** *Lancelot* 1092 The red knycht, byrnyng in loues fyre, Goith to o knycht, als swift as ony vyre. **1513** DOUGLAS *Æneid* v. xi. 16 This virgine sprent on swiftlie as a vyre.

†vire, *sb.*² *Obs.*⁻¹ In 5 wire. [ad. L. *vīrus.*] = VIRUS.

c **1400** *Lanfranc's Cirurg.* 77 For euery olde wounde hauynge rotnes or wire, þat is þinne venymous quyttir or ony oþir þing.

†vire, *v.*¹ *Obs. rare.* Also 5 *Sc.* **wyre, vyre.** [ad. OF. *virer* to turn: cf. VEER *v.*²]

1. *trans.* To whirl or throw.

1375 BARBOUR *Bruce* XVII. 702 Iohne Crab..In his fagattis has set the fyre, And our the wall syne can thame wyre.

2. *intr.* To turn; to wind about.

1456 SIR G. HAYE *Law Arms* (S.T.S.) 119 As the dure turnis about apon the herre,..and vyris and revyris. *a* **1586** SIDNEY *Arcadia* (1622) 436 No, no, hee hath vired all this while, but to come the sooner to his affected end.

†vire, *v.*² *Obs. rare*⁻¹. (Origin and meaning doubtful: cf. VIRE *sb.*¹)

c **1400** *Laud Troy Bk.* 5448 Many a Gregey was euel atyred, With brode arwes al to-vired; Thei wounded hem with arwes brode.

vire, southern dial. var. FIRE; obs. Sc. f. WIRE.

virelay (ˈvɪrəleɪ). Now *Hist.* or *arch.* Forms: 4–7, 9 virelai (5 virallay, 7 virilai, 9 -lay), 5–6 vyrelay; 4 verelai, 6–7, 9 verilay, 6 ver(re)lay. [a. OF. *virelai* (14th c.), an alteration (prob. after *lai* LAY *sb.*⁴) of *vireli*: see VIRLY.] A song or short lyric piece, of a type originating in France in the 14th century, usu. consisting of short lines arranged in stanzas with only two rhymes, the end-rhyme of one stanza being the chief one of the next.

Chiefly current in the Chaucerian period, from *c* 1575 to 1610, and in the 19th cent.

c **1385** CHAUCER *L.G.W.* 423 *Balade*, He made..manye an ympne for your halydayis That hightyn baladis, roundelys, & vyrelayes. **1390** GOWER *Conf.* I. 133 Ek he can carolles make, Rondeal, balade and virelai. **14..** LYDG. *To Soverain Lady* 40 Thus many a roundel and many a virelay In fresshe Englisshe..I do recorde. **1483** CAXTON *G. de la Tour* A j, For in that time I made..vyrelayes in the mooste best wyse I cowde. *a* **1500** *Chaucer's Dreme* 975 Som to make verelaies & laies, And som to othere diverse pleyes. **1525** LD. BERNERS *Froiss.* II. xxvi. 30/1 Whiche boke was called the Melyader, conteyninge all the songes, baladdes, rundeaux, and vyrelayes, whiche the gentyll duke had made in his tyme. **1579** SPENSER *Sheph. Cal.* Nov. 21 But if thou algate lust light virelayes, And looser songs of loue to vnderfong. **1593** DRAYTON *Ecl.* iii. 55 With daintie and delightsome straynes of dapper Verilayes. **1614** J. DAVIES (Heref.) *Eclogue* 34 Let thy Virilaies Kill enuious cunning swaines..With enuy. **1700** DRYDEN *Flower & Leaf* 365 And then the Band of Flutes began to play, To which a Lady sung a Virelay. **1795** H. WALPOLE *Let. to Mrs. H. More* 13 Feb., I received your letter and packet of lays and virelays. **1812** D'ISRAELI *Calam. Auth.* (1867) 76 Thus he lived, like some old troubadour, by his rhymes, and his chants, and his virelays. **1851** MRS. BROWNING *Casa Guidi Wind.* I. 233 O Dead, ye shall no longer..Drag us backward by the garment thus, To stand and laud you in long-drawn virelays! **1880** F. HUEFFER in *Macm. Mag.* No. 253. 51 Every one will admit that a halting rondel or virelai is simply an abomination.

transf. **1642** H. MORE *Song of Soul* II. I. iii. 5 You chearfull chaunters of the flowring woods,..To mournfull note turn your light verilayes, Death be your song, and Winters hoary sprayes. **1818** MILMAN *Samor* 171 The merry birds.. spring-tide virelays carolling.

virelle, obs. form of VIRL.

virement (‖ˈvirmɑ̃, ˈvaɪəmənt). [a. F. *virement*, f. *virer* to turn (cf. VEER *v.*²).] A strictly regulated process of transferring items, esp. public funds, from one financial account to another.

[**1873** *Ann. Reg. 1872* I. 272 A dubious financial transaction, of the nature of what the French call a *virement*, had been the cause.] **1902** *Rep. Select Committee on National Expenditure* in *Parl. Papers* (H.C. 387) VII. 15 This temporary power of *virement* is vested in the Treasury by the Appropriation Act, and its exercise is conditioned by Mr Monk's Resolution of 4th and 5th March 1879. **1917** A. J. V. DURELL *Princ. & Pract. System of Control over Parliamentary Grants* I. ii. 39 In the case of the army and navy the powers of virement enable surplus appropriations in aid under one army or navy vote to be applied in making good a deficiency under another army or navy vote. **1921** W. S. CHURCHILL in M. Gilbert *Winston S. Churchill* (1977) IV. Compan. III. 1625 A supplementary estimate will not be necessary if the powers of *virement* are used to the full. **1936** W. I. JENNINGS *Cabinet Government* vii. 133 Virement is thus of two kinds, according as it is between sub-heads or between votes. **1946** *Erskine May's Law of Parl.* (ed. 14) xxv. 677 There is no definite statutory authority for this long standing facility, but it is implied by the still larger power of *virement.* **1958** *Times* 30 May 15/6 Criticism of the practice of virement whereby the Treasury allow Service Departments to use surpluses on Votes to meet deficits on other Votes is made by the Committee of Public Accounts in their second report. **1960** A. H. MARSHALL *Financial Administration in Local Govt.* xxi. 305 Most local authorities allow *virement* either formally or informally. **1975** *Language for Life* (Dept. Educ. & Sci.) xxi. 309 At one extreme, expenditure is rigidly controlled under specific 'heads', with no virement of any kind.

viremia, -ic, varr. VIRÆMIA, -IC.

virent (ˈvaɪərənt), *a.* [ad. L. *virent-*, *virens*, pres. pple. of *virēre* to be green. Cf. It. *virente*.]

†**1.** Verdant; fresh, not faded. *Obs.*

1595 *Locrine* III. ii. 11 By reason of the fatall massacre Which shall be made vpon the virent plaines. **1606** N. BAXTER *Sidney's Ourania, Song* E iv b, Then comes the Deaw, and doth them recreate: Making them fresh, virent, and fortunate. **1646** SIR T. BROWNE *Pseud. Ep.* 94 In these [roots] yet fresh and virent, they carve out the figures of men and women. **1646** G. DANIEL *Poems* Wks. (Grosart) I. 23 For through yᵉ Place is nothing witherd; but still-virent Bayes..Appeare.

2. Green in colour.

1830 J. Wright *Retrospect* ii. 89 Let not the virent snake entwine thee round. **1837** *Tait's Mag.* IV. 107 The sun.. illuminated its virent tints. **1852** Bailey *Festus* (ed. 5) 490 One hand a staff of virent emerald held.

vireo (ˈvɪrɪəʊ). *Ornith.* [a. L. *vireo*, *-ōnis* (Pliny) some small bird, perhaps the greenfinch.] Any small American bird belonging to the genus *Vireo* or the family *Vireonidæ*; a greenlet, a fly-catcher.

Many species are distinguished by special epithets, as *black-capped*, *black-headed*, *blue-headed*, *gray*, *mountain*, *plumbeous*, *red-eyed*, *white-eyed*, *yellow-throated*, etc.

1834 Audubon *Ornith. Biogr.* II. 287 The Vireos quench their thirst with the drops of dew or rain that adhere to the leaves or twigs. **1845** Hirst *Com. Mammoth* etc. 155 In yon oak a vireo shrills. **1869** J. Burroughs in *Galaxy Mag.* Aug. 170 The Vireos, or Greenlets, are a sort of connecting-link between the Warblers and the true Fly-catchers. **1878** Coues *Birds Colorado Valley* 485 The Vireos were long supposed to be in the curious case, that some species possessed ten primaries, and others only nine.

ˈvireonine, *sb.* and *a.* [f. L. *vireōn-*, *vireo* (see prec.) + -ine.] **a.** *sb.* A vireo or bird related to this. **b.** *adj.* Characteristic of the vireo and related birds.

1878 Coues *Birds Colorado Valley* 484 The genus *Icteria* is still associated by some leading ornithologists with the Vireonines. *Ibid.* 523 The nest is always built after the usual Vireonine style of architecture.

virescence (vɪˈrɛsəns). [See next and -ence.]
a. *Bot.* Regular or abnormal development of a green colour in leaves or flowers. **b.** Greenness.

1888 *Cassell's Encycl. Dict.* **1904** R. J. Farrer *Garden Asia* 167 The fields, whose wealth of virescence glimmers ghostly.

virescent (vɪˈrɛsənt), *a.* [ad. L. *virescent-*, *virescens*, pres. pple. of *virescĕre* to become green.] Greenish; turning or becoming green. Also *fig.*

1826 *Blackw. Mag.* XX. 324 In the most flourishing and virescent condition of any pool, ditch, or otherwise in the empire. **1844** *Fraser's Mag.* XXX. 326/2 Virescent juvenility or green old age. **1881** T. Hardy *Laodicean* v. ii, The summer.. tipping every twig with a tiny sprout of virescent yellow. **1882** *Garden* 1 July 12/3 He also exhibited .. some virescent flowers of Auricula.

†**vireton.** *Obs. rare.* In 6 vyre-. [a. OF. *vireton* (= Prov. *viraton*), f. *virer* to turn: cf. vire *sb.*¹, and Sp. and Pg. *virote*.] A cross-bow bolt so constructed as to rotate on its axis while flying.

c **1500** *Melusine* 269 They.. saylled foorth by such wyse that it semed as it had be the vyreton of a Crosbow. *Ibid.* 287 No sarasyn durste hym abyde, but casted at him fro ferre sperys, darts, stones & arowes, vyretons & quarelles, with theire crosbowes.

†**viretote.** *Obs.* [app. of OF. origin, f. *virer* to turn.] An unsettled state or condition.

c **1386** Chaucer *Miller's T.* 584 (Ellesm.), What eyleth yow? som gay gerl, god it woot, Hath broght yow thus vp on the viritoot. [For variants see meritot.] [**1822** Scott *Nigel* xviii, Here you come on the viretot, through the whole streets of London, to talk some nonsense to a lady.]

virga (ˈvɜːgə). Pl. -ae. [a. L. *virga* rod.]
‖**1.** *Mus.* A symbol used in plainsong notation; the note designated by this (see quots.).

1908 R. Dunstan *Cycl. Dict. Mus.* 439/2 *Virga*, one of the signs in Neum notation. **1925** *Ibid.* (ed. 4) 555/2 *Virga* (*L.*) 'A twig'. A square note with a stem or tail... The plainsong Virga is interpreted as a quaver. **1948** M. Pierek *Song of Church* vii. 213 Among the Latin neums ten have Greek names.., while eight have Latin names, *clivis*, *pes*, *punctum*, *virga*, *torculus*, [etc.]. **1954** A. Hughes *Early Medieval Music* xi. 380 The essential difference between the pre-Franconian mensural notation.. and the modal notation which preceded it lies in the fact that there is a definite sign (..the *virga* of plainsong) for a long note. **1978** *Gramophone* Aug. 365/2 But worst of all, these singers had introduced a new notion of their own, gleaned from goodness knows where, the idea that every *virga* is a long note, worth two beats.

2. *Meteorol.* Streaks of precipitation that appear to be attached to the undersurface of a cloud and usually evaporate before reaching the ground. Also *pl.* in same sense.

1947 M. A. Garbell *Trop. & Equatorial Meteorol.* iii. 48/1 Streaks of falling cloud mass, or virgae.., are then observed under that part of the cloud base where showers are occurring. **1959** R. E. Huschke *Gloss. Meteorol.* 611 Virga is frequently seen trailing from altocumulus and altostratus clouds. **1968** *New Scientist* 4 Jan. 22/1 (*caption*) An untreated cap cloud which characteristically has little if any virga or snow plumes. **1979** L. J. Battan *Fund. Meteorol.* viii. 151 When the water or ice particles evaporate before reaching the ground, the precipitation is called virga.

ˈvirgal, *a. rare.* [f. L. *virga* rod.] Made of twigs or rods.

1732 Fielding *Convent Gard. Trag.* i. iii, Oh! would'st thou bear.. To see the hangman lift the virgal rod? **1880** *Daily Tel.* 23 Feb., The terrible 'Croquemitaine' and his frightful spouse.. flourish their virgal sceptres to the terror of insubordinate juveniles.

virgalieu, virgaloo, varr. vergaloo.

virgate (ˈvɜːgət), *sb. Hist.* [ad. med.L. *virgāta* (sc. *terræ*), f. L. *virga* rod, used as a rendering of OE. *ȝierd-land* yard-land.]
1. An early English land-measure, varying greatly in extent, but in many cases averaging thirty acres.

1655 Fuller *Ch. Hist.* vi. 337 Indeed, it is beneath a Prince.. to stoop to each Virgate and rod of ground. **1661** Blount *Glossogr.* (ed. 2), *Virgate of Land*, See Yard-land. **1688** R. Holme *Armoury* iii. 137/2 Virge, or Virgate of land is 20, in some places 24 Acres, or in some 30 Acres. **1710** Hearne *P. Langtoft's Chron.* (1810) II. 600 The town, according to Domesday Book, consisted of VIII. virgats of Land. *Ibid.*, Each virgat comprehending fourty acres. **1747** Carte *Hist. Eng.* I. 436 The survey was made by.. carucates, virgates and acres. **1781** Warton *Hist. Kiddington* (1783) 45, I have discovered that lady Elisabeth Montacute.. possessed one virgate, about the year 1330. **1840** *Penny Cycl.* XVI. 173/2 Reckoning four virgates in each hide and thirty acres to make a virgate. **1868** Freeman *Norm. Conq.* II. App. 548 In Sussex we find a virgate of land at Apredoc which Harold [etc.]. **1895** Pollock & Maitland *Eng. Law* I. 347 The hide is generally regarded as made up of four, but it may well be of six virgates.

2. As a linear measure: A rod or pole.

1772 Shrubsole & Denne *Rochester* 42 The first land pier .. shall be built.. by the bishop of Rochester; to plank three virgates or Yards, and to lay three sullivas or large beams on the bridge. **1809** Bawdwen *Domesday Bk.* 152 Wood pasture three quarentens long, and one quarenten and one virgate broad.

virgate (ˈvɜːgət), *a. Bot.* and *Zool.* [ad. L. *virgātus*, f. *virga* rod.]
1. Rod-like; long, slender, and straight.

1821 W. P. C. Barton *Flora N. Amer.* I. 17 Branches virgate, elongated, one-flowered. **1832** Lindley *Introd. Bot.* 47 From this kind of branch [sc. *vimen*], that called a virgate stem, *caulis virgatus*, differs only in being.. more rigid. **1846** Dana *Zooph.* (1848) 652 Branchlets.. long before branching, and virgate.

2. 'Twiggy; producing many weak branchlets or twigs' (*Treas. Bot.*, 1866).

ˈvirgated, *a. rare.* [f. L. *virgāt-us*: see prec.]
1. Rod-shaped; long and narrow.

1752 J. Hill *Hist. Anim.* 543 The Felis, with an elongated tail, and virgated spots. The Tyger.

2. *Bot.* (See quots.)

1776 J. Lee *Introd. Bot.* Explan. Terms 380 *Virgatus*, virgated, with many slender Twigs. *c* **1789** *Encycl. Brit.* (ed. 3) III. 444/2 *Virgated*, having small weak pliant branches of unequal length.

3. Streaked, striped.

1803 Shaw *Gen. Zool.* IV. ii. 420 Virgated Sparus. *Sparus Virgatus.*

ˈvirgater. *Hist.* [f. virgate *sb.* + -er¹.] A person holding or cultivating a virgate of land.

1897 Maitland *Domesday & Beyond* 416 Even the villein virgater on the monastic manors of the thirteenth century is often expected to have four oxen. **1900** *N. & Q.* 9th Ser. VI. 382/1 Next above the four virgaters just mentioned are.. four bovators.

virˈgation. *Geol.* [f. L. *virga* twig + -ation.] A system of faults branching out like twigs from a bough.

1897 *Geogr. Jrnl.* (R.G.S.) IX. 87 The Western Balkans form in their southern part six ranges, the orographical expression of a geological 'virgation'.

†**virge.** *Obs.* [var. of verge *sb.*¹, after L. *virga*.]
1. = verge *sb.*¹ 10.

1540 *Act 32 Hen. VIII*, c. 20 §7 Within the virge lymited and accustumed to his Graces Courte. **1596** Bacon *Max. & Use Com. Law* ii. (1635) 5 Controversies arising within the Virge. Which is within xii. miles of the chiefest Tunnell of the Court. **1671** F. Philipps *Reg. Necess.* Table, The Kings granting Protections under the Great Seal of England to such as are his Servants.. when especially imployed by him .. out of his Palace or Virge thereof.

b. *transf.* = verge *sb.*¹ 12.

a **1639** T. Carew *Poems, To Ben Jonson* 48 Thou art not of their ranke, the quarrell lyes Within thine owne virge. **1671** F. Philipps *Reg. Necess.* 385 Within the Virge and compass of loyalty and modesty.

2. A rod or wand; *esp.* a rod of office.

1610 G. Fletcher *Christ's Vict.* ii. lvi, A hundred Kings, whose temples wear impal'd In goulden diadems,.. And of their golden virges none disceptred wear. *a* **1646** M. Prideaux *Introd. Hist.* (1648) 102 Hadrian the second.. kept a greate stirre to bring the Bulgarians under his virge. *a* **1668** Davenant *Poems* (1672) 230 Therefore my Robe, that in his Altar lay, My Virge, my Wreath, I took; and thus did pray. **1727** Swift *Horace* i. Ep. vii. 97 Suppose him now a dean complete.., The silver virge, with decent pride, Stuck underneath his cushion side.

b. = verge *sb.*¹ 4 b.

1635 Calthrope *Relat. betw. Lord & Copy-holder* 51 Although some bee called Coppy-holders, some Customary, some Tenants by the Virg [*sic*],.. yet doe they all agree in substance and kinde of Tenure.

3. = verge *sb.*¹ 9 b.

1688 [see virgate *sb.* 1]. **1706** Phillips (ed. Kersey) s.v. *Yard-Land*, In the Statute of Wards, *An.* 28, *E.* 1, it is call'd a *Virge of Land*.

4. = verge *sb.*¹ 1 a.

1608 Topsell *Serpents* 252 They suffer also vomiting with a spasme or crampe, and inflamation of the virge. **1698** Fryer *Acc. E. India & P.* iv. v. 177 Many of these Apes fell by our hands;.. opening them I found.. their seminary Vessels turgid, their Virge White and Nervous.

†**virge,** obs. variant of verge *v.*²

1693 W. Freke *Sel. Ess.* v. 38 True Vertue is a Streight line, that neither virges for Laziness nor Glory.

virgean, *a. rare.* [f. L. *virgē-us*, f. *virga* virge.] Twig-like. (Applied to a variety of the Ogham alphabet.)

1793 Hely tr. *O'Flaherty's Ogygia* II. 104, I find these seven vowels A. O. U. E. I. Æ. Oi. thus decyphered in Virgean characters.

virgenite, obs. form of virginity.

ˈvirger. *Obs.* exc. at certain cathedrals, such as St. Paul's and Winchester. [var. of verger², after virge or med.L. *virgārius*.] An official rodbearer; a verger.

1671 F. Philipps *Reg. Necess.* 176 The Virgers or Tipstaves attending upon the said Courts. **1704** South in T. Warton *Life Bathurst* (1761) 185 You may deposit it with Mr. Thomas Rooks, virger of Christ-church. **1776** *Ann. Reg.* ii. 8 The archbishop.. came to visit us at the convent, .. attended by a virger. **1832** *Index Rolls of Parlt.* 1001/1 Office of Virger, or Usher to the Order of the Garter,.. confirmed to William Pope. **1975** M. Sullivan *Watch How You Go* x. 174 The Canons' Virger on duty always virges the Canons in procession. **1978** *Church Times* 1 Sept. 8/2 If the Dean were still preceded by a wanded virger on his way to the divine office. **1983** *Ibid.* 11 Mar. 17/5 The Dean and Chapter of Winchester invite applications for a virger.

So †**ˈvirgerer**, = vergerer (*obs. rare*); [as back-formation] **virge** *v. trans.*, to conduct (cathedral dignitaries, etc.) in the manner of a virger.

1581 [A. Gilby] *Pleas. Dial. Soldier & Chapl.* L vij b, 9. The Cannon. 10. The pettie Canon. 11. The Virgerer. **1663** Wood *Life* (O.H.S.) I. 482 After them came the virgerer and six bedells. **1975** [see virger]. **1977** *Church Times* 25 Nov. 8/5 The Deacon is virged from his place to the Altar for the Gospel during the Fanfare.

virgie (ˈvɜːdʒɪ), *a.* and *sb.* Colloq. abbrev. of virgin *sb.* and *a.* Cf. -ie.

1930 [see mucked *ppl. a.*]. **1965** H. Gold *Man who was not with It* xxvii. 251 How do you know? A virgie like you were.

†**ˈvirgifer.** *Obs.*⁻¹ [a. med.L. *virgifer*, f. L. *virga* virge + *-fer* bearing.] A verger.

1629 *Acts Durham High Commission Crt.* (Surtees) 17 Examinate.., being one of the Virgifers, did goe unto him and tooke holde of him and soe carried him forth.

Virgilian (vəˈdʒɪlɪən), *a.* and *sb.* Also 6 *Sc.* **Virgiliane**, 6, 8 **Virgillian**. [ad. L. *Virgiliān-us*, f. *Virgili-us*: see -an, and cf. OF. and F. *Virgilien*.]
A. *adj.* **1.** Of or pertaining to, characteristic of, the poet Virgil; agreeing with, or suggestive of, the style of Virgil.

1513 Douglas *Æneid* Concl., Completit was this wark Virgiliane, Apon the fest of Marie Magdelane. *c* **1590** J. Stewart *Poems* (S.T.S.) II. 78 Heirfoir to vichts venerian I quyt To form in verse virgilian perfyt Thair facund fassons. **1635–56** Cowley *Davideis* iv. Note 38 In emulation of the Virgilian Verse, *Quadrupedante putrem* [etc.]. **1718** J. Trapp tr. *Virgil* Pref. to Æneis (1735) I. p. lxxxvii, What could be more well-manner'd, more delicate, and truly Virgillian? *c* **1754** Warton in Boswell *Johnson* (1904) I. 180, I told him, I thought it a very sonorous hexameter. I did not tell him, it was not in the Virgilian style. **1782** V. Knox *Ess.* lxiii. (1819) I. 26 The style [of the poem] is beautiful and Virgilian. **1846** Keightley *Notes Virg., Georg.* ii. 485 This mode of supplying the ellipse.. is certainly the more Virgilian. **1886** Swinburne *Misc.* 151 An instinctive dignity and precision not unworthy to be called Virgilian.

b. *Virgilian lots* [tr. L. *sortes Virgilianæ*], a method of divination consisting in taking a passage of Virgil at random.

1838–45 *Encycl. Metrop.* XXIV. 737/1 It is said that Charles I. and Lord Falkland made trial of the Virgilian lots a little before the commencement of the great civil war.

2. Of agriculture: Practised according to the methods described in the Georgics of Virgil. Also of persons following these methods.

1724 W. Benson *Virgil's Husb.* ii. Pref. p. xvi, I am certain the Husbandry of England in general is Virgilian. **1731–3** Tull *Horse-Hoeing Husb.* xix. 271 The Virgilian Farmer must be content to have only his Labour for his Travel. **1764** J. Randall (*title*), The Semi-Virgilian Husbandry, deduced from various Experiments.

B. *sb.* **1.** One who is specially devoted to, or skilled in, the study of Virgil's works.

1577 Grange *Golden Aphrod.*, etc. Q iij b, You would a good Virgillian be.

2. One who practises agriculture after the methods laid down by Virgil.

1731–3 Tull *Horse-Hoeing Husb.* xix. 272 The Virgilian is commonly late in his sowing. *Ibid.* 279 This puts the Virgilians upon a Necessity of using Dung.

Hence **Virˈgilianism**, the characteristic style of Virgil; a Virgilian expression.

1850 L. Hunt *Autobiog.* x. (1860) 164 When I had the pleasure of hearing him [Campbell] afterwards, I forgot his Virgilianisms.

†**Virgils**, *sb. pl. Obs.*⁻¹ [ad. L. *Virgiliæ*.] The Pleiades.

c **1440** *Pallad. on Husb.* x. 154 In somer tyme hym liketh wel to glade, That whan Virgilis doun goth, gynneth fade.

virgin (ˈvɜːdʒɪn), *sb.* and *a.* Forms: *α.* 3, 5 **uirgine**, 3–7 **virgine** (6 wir-), 4, 6 **virgyne** (5 wir-), 4–5 **vyrgyne** (4 wyr-), 5 **vyrgine**. *β.* 4 **uirgin**, 4–6 **virgyn** (5 uirgyn, 6 wirgynne), 5–6 **vyrgyn** (6 wyr-), 5- virgin (5 wyr-, 6 wirgin). γ. 4 vergyne, 4–5 vergine (4 uer-), vergyn. δ. 5 vyrgene (wyr-), 5–6 virgen(e. [a. AF. and OF. *virgine*, *virgene*, *viergene*, etc. (= It. *vergine*, Sp. *virgen*, Pg. *virgem*), ad. L. *virginem*, acc. of *virgo* maiden. OF. also had the reduced forms *virge*, *vierge*, mod.F. *vierge*.]

I. 1. *Eccl.* An unmarried or chaste maiden or woman, distinguished for piety or steadfastness in religion, and regarded as having a special place among the members of the Christian church on account of these merits.

Chiefly used with reference to early Christian times.

c1200 *Trin. Coll. Hom.* 185 Ðar haueð..martirs, and confessors, and uirgines maked faier bode inne to wunien. a1225 *Leg. Kath.* 2310, I þe feire ferreden of uirgines in heouene. c1290 *Beket* 2302 in *S. Eng. Leg.* I. 172 Fair was þat processioun..Of Martirs and of confessours and of virgines þer-to. 1303 R. Brunne *Handl. Synne* 8270 And she ys callede Seynt Iustyne, A martyr and an holy vyrgyne. 13.. *E.E. Allit. P.* A. 1098 Þis noble cite..Was sodanly ful ..Of such vergynez in þe same gyse þat was my blysful anvnder croun. 1389 in *Eng. Gilds* (1870) 8 Seint Katerine þe gloriouse virgyne and martyr. c1430 *Life St. Kath.* (1884) 59 Þe wykked tyraunt.. saat in hys astat and bad þat þe holy virgyn schold be presented to hym. 1500–20 Dunbar *Poems* xxv. 46 Patriarchis, profeitis, and appostillis deir, Confessouris, virgynis and marteris cleir. c1610 *Women Saints* (1886) 92 Modwene..became the mistresse of verie many like professed and holie virgins. 1652 J. Taylor (Water P.) *Short Relat. Long Journ.* (1859) 10 The pious and chaste virgin Winifrid. 1728 Chambers *Cycl.* s.v., In the Roman Breviary, there is a particular Office for Virgins departed. 1810 E. D. Clarke *Trav. Russia* (1839) 56/1 A host of saints, virgins, and bishops, whose pictures covered the walls. 1862 Burton *Bk. Hunter* iv. 326 St. Ursula and her eleven thousand virgins.

2. a. A woman (esp. a young woman) who is, or remains, in a state of inviolate chastity; an absolutely pure maiden or maid.

In early use chiefly of the Virgin Mary: cf. 4 and 5.

a1310 in Wright *Lyric P.* xxx. 88 When y lygge on dethes bed,..On o ledy myn hope is, moder ant virgyne. c1375 *Sc. Leg. Saints* Prol. 50 Til scho consawit godis sone,..scho beand altyme vergine chaste. a1400–50 *Alexander* 4665 Voide & vacand of vices as virgyns it ware. c1430 Lydg. *Min. Poems* (Percy Soc.) 8 Alle clad in white, in tokyn of clennes, Lyke pure virginis as in ther ententis. c1485 *E.E. Misc.* (Warton Cl.) 36 When he dyssenddyt..Into a chast wombe of a wyrgene clene. 1536 Bellenden *Cron. Scot.* (1821) II. 163 He that revisis ane virgine, bot gif scho desire him in mariage, sal be heidit. 1568 *Satir. Poems Reform.* xlvii. 58 Remember first ȝour former qualitie, And wrak na virgenis with ȝour wilfull weir. 1601 Shaks. *All's Well* i. i. 146, I will stand for't a little, though therefore I die a Virgin. 1634 W. Tirwhyt tr. *Balzac's Lett.* (vol. I) 318 Nor am I ignorant that never any woman was so vicious, who hath not heretofore bin a Virgin. 1671 Milton *P.R.* i. 138 Then [thou] toldst her doubting how these things could be To her a Virgin, that on her should come The Holy Ghost. 1737 Whiston *Josephus, Antiq.* iii. xii. §2 Moses..permitted him [*sc.* the high-priest] only to marry a virgin. 1807 *Med. Jrnl.* XVII. 494 Ruysch's subject, though not a virgin, may have yet been troubled with this complaint. 1845 Day tr. *Simon's Anim. Chem.* I. 230 The venous blood of virgins gave, in 1000 parts [etc.].

fig. 1526 Tindale *2 Cor.* xi. 2 For I coupled you to one man, to make you a chaste virgen to Christ. 1860 Pusey *Min. Proph.* 107 God regarded as a virgin, the people whom He had made holy to Himself; He so regards the soul which He has regenerated and sanctified.

b. An old maid, a spinster.

1759 Johnson *Idler* No. 53 ¶6 Lady Biddy Porpoise, a lethargick virgin of seventy-six.

c. *transf.* Of things.

1620 Capt. Smith *New-Eng. Trials* Wks. (Arb.) I. 243 From which blessed Virgin [i.e. the colony of Virginia].. sprung the fortunate habitation of Somer Iles. *Ibid.*, This Virgins sister (called New England, *An.* 1616, at my humble suite). 1756 Nugent *Gr. Tour, France* IV. 303 They give it [*sc.* Peronne] the name of *Virgin*, because it was never taken. 1837 Whewell *Hist. Induct. Sci.* iv. iii. 292 In the language of the New Platonists, the number seven is said to be a virgin, and without a mother. 1897 *Westm. Gaz.* 18 Jan. 8/3 Similarly, in Africa, the highest mountain is still a virgin.

d. Virginity. (After 1 Cor. vii. 37.) *rare.*

1649 Jer. Taylor *Gt. Exemplar* Disc. iv. §12 S. Jerome affirms that, to be continent in the state of widowhood is harder, then to keep our virgin pure.

e. *Entom.* A female insect producing fertile eggs by parthenogenesis. (Cf. 13 g.)

1883 *Imperial Dict.* (and in later Dicts.).

f. *transf.* A naïve, innocent, or inexperienced person. Freq. with adj. indicating sphere of activity. *colloq.*

1953 A. Moorehead *Rum Jungle* iv. 53 A new player [at two-up]..is known as a 'virgin'. 1964 L. Deighton *Funeral in Berlin* xxxii. 173 He had no strong political ideas... He described himself as a 'political virgin'. 1970 *Daily Tel.* (Colour Suppl.) 15 May 10/3 There was a competition.. called 'Be a Millionaire'... I was an industrial virgin in those days but friends told me to have a go. I entered and won. 1976 E. Stewart *Launch!* 89 'That's a violation of security.' 'Stop being a virgin. People in this town bat secrets around like ping-pong balls.'

3. a. A young woman, a maid or maiden, of an age and character affording presumption of chastity.

13.. *Sir Beues* (A.) 2689 A wende, a miȝte leue namore, And ȝet him þouȝte, a virgine Him brouȝte out of al is pine. c1380 Wyclif *Wks.* (1880) 330 God..seiþ bi Iob þat a man shuld make couenaunt wiþ hise wittis to þenke not on a virgyne. 1432–50 tr. *Higden* (Rolls) III. 37 Whiche commaundede also virgynes to be mariede with owte eny dowery. c1450 *Mirk's Festial* 16 Then was scho so meke yn all hor doyngys, þat all othyr vyrgenes called hor qwene of maydens. 1538 Starkey *England* ii. i. 151 The wych some schold..be dystrybutyd..partely to the dote of pore damosellys and vyrgynys. 1579 Gosson *Sch. Abuse* (Arb.) 20 The Harpies haue Virgins faces, and vultures Talentes. 1596 Shaks. *Tam. Shr.* iv. v. 37 Yong budding Virgin, faire, and fresh, & sweet, Whether away? 1697 Dryden *Æneid* i. 440 She seemed a virgin of the Spartan blood. a1700 Evelyn *Diary* 25 May 1645, Rare pieces, especialy of Guido, Domenico, and a virgin named Isabella Sirani. 1757 Burke *Abridgm. Eng. Hist.* Wks. X. 252 Vortigern was struck with the beauty of a Saxon virgin, a kinswoman of Hengist. 1790 Wolcot (P. Pindar) *Rowland for Oliver, Ode to Affectation* ii, Say, virgin, where dost thou delight to dwell? With maids of honour, startful virgin? 1806 W. Herbert *Sel. Icel. Poetry* i. 119 Two of the Valkyriæ or virgins of slaughter. 1838 Dickens *Old C. Shop* ix, The beautiful virgin took another pinch [of snuff]. 1871 R. Ellis *Catullus* lxiv. 87 A royal virgin, in odours silkily nestled.

b. In allusions to the parable of the wise and foolish virgins (Matt. xxv. 1–13).

1620 Gataker *Spirituall Watch* 62 Either you are a wise Virgin or a foolish one: if a wise one, the company hath need of you; if an unwise one, you of it. 1756–7 tr. *Keysler's Trav.* (1760) I. 182 On the sides of this entrance are seen the five foolish and the five wise virgins, in stone. 1826 Scott *Woodst.* ii, Why shouldst thou not talk like one of the wise virgins? 1873 Carleton *Farm Ball.* 22 Next mornin' an ancient virgin took pains to call on us, Her lamp all trimmed and a-burnin' to kindle another fuss.

4. a. ***the Virgin Mary***, the mother of Christ. Also, an image or picture representing her.

a1300 *Cursor M.* 24977 Conceiud o þe hali gast, born o þe virgine marie. c1380 Wyclif *Wks.* (1880) 21 He is þe sone of þe vergyne marie. c1400 Maundev. Prol. (1839) 1 The seyd blessed and gloriouse Virgine Marie. 1470–85 Malory *Arthur* xvii. v. 697 Also the holy ghoost shewed hym the comynge of the gloryous vyrgyne marye. 1533 Gau *Richt Vay* (S.T.S.) 39 Quhen the virgine Maria hard the salutatione of the angel. 1547 *Homilies* i. *Obedience* iii, And let vs not forget the blessed virgyn Maries obedience. 1611 Bible *Matt.* i. (heading), Christ..was..borne of the Virgin Mary when she was espoused to Ioseph. 1655 Vaughan *Silex Scint.* Ded., Jesus Christ, The Son of the living God, and the sacred Virgin Mary. 1717 [see madonna 2]. 1776 Ld. Hailes *Ann. Scotl.* I. 134 He ascribed his deliverance to the Virgin Mary. 1823 Scott *Quentin D.* v, He wore his national bonnet,..with a Virgin Mary of massive silver for a brooch. 1885 J. King *Angl. Hymnology* 3 The hymn of Hannah is the prototype of the Virgin Mary's 'Magnificat'.

b. *attrib.*, or in possessive, in popular names of plants (see quots.); also (after Gaelic use) ***Virgin Mary's nut***, the Bonduc or Molucca nut.

1703 M. Martin *Western Islands* 39 If she would but take the White Nut, called the Virgin Maries Nut, and lay it in the Pale into which she was to milk the Cows. 1823 E. Moor *Suffolk Wds.*, *Virgin Mary thistle*, the beautiful and magnificent *Carduus Benedictus*, or Blessed Thistle. 1855 Miss Pratt *Flower. Pl.* III. 230 Milk Thistle... This very handsome stately plant, the Virgin Mary's Thistle [etc.]. 1869 *N. & Q.* 4th Ser. III. 414/2 In some parts of Berkshire the spotted persicaria..is known as 'The Virgin Mary's pinch', from the dark thumb-like mark in the centre of its leaves. 1873 *Gard. Chron.* 26 April 579/3 *Pulmonaria officinalis.*—This plant is known in Cheshire as Virgin Mary's Honeysuckle. 1880 Miss Jackson *Shropsh. Wordbk.* 464 Virgin-Mary's-cowslip, *Pulmonaria officinalis*, common Lungwort.

c. ***Virgin Mary*** [after *bloody Mary* s.v. bloody *a.* and *adv.* C. 2], a glass of tomato juice (see quots.). Chiefly *U.S.*

1976 W. Goldman *Magic* ii. 90 Some girl wanted a Virgin Mary. The waiter nodded. 1977 J. Philips *Five Roads to Death* i. 11 A waitress approached the table. 'A Virgin Mary... A Bloody Mary without the vodka.' 1981 T. Heald *Murder at Moose Jaw* ix. 103 Crombie ordered himself a straight tomato juice with..Worcester. The Colonel did not, Bognor noted with approval, refer to the drink as 'a Virgin Mary'.

5. a. ***the Virgin*** (also ***the blessed, holy,*** etc., ***Virgin***), = sense 4.

c1330 R. Brunne *Chron. Wace* (Rolls) 5873 Syn Crist cam of þe vyrgyne, Nyne score ȝer euene, & nyne. c1340 Hampole *Pr. Consc.* 4370 Þis was þat Iohan saw in a vision Of hym þat semed þe virgyn son. 1390 Gower *Conf.* II. 186 For be that cause the godhede Assembled was to the manhede In the virgine. c1489 Caxton *Sonnes of Aymon* i. 37 God, that of the vyrgyn was borne in bedeleym. 1526 *Pilgr. Perf.* (W. de W. 1531) 10 b, Hymselfe sayenge in the gospell, Excepte ye eate the flesshe of the sone of the virgyn [etc.]. 1555 Eden *Decades* (Arb.) 139 Desyringe almyghtie God and the blessed virgin to fauour his beginninges. 1623 Cockeram iii, *Valentineans*, a certaine heretiques, who held opinion that our Sauiour receiued not his flesh from the blessed Virgin. 1643 Caryl *Expos. Job* xx. 17 And this is the food which the Virgins son our Immanuel was prophesied to eat. 1704 [see annunciation 2]. 1756–7 tr. *Keysler's Trav.* (1760) I. 286 The church of the holy virgin at Lireyo. 1797 Coleridge *Christabel* i. 139 Praise we the Virgin all divine Who hath rescued thee from thy distress! 1801 Scott *Eve St. John* xl, 'Alas! away, away!' she cried, 'For the holy Virgin's sake!' 1867 Jas. Campbell *Balmerino* ii. ix. 122 A full length figure of the Virgin and Holy Child standing within a Gothic niche. 1876 Bancroft *Hist. U.S.* II. xxxiii. 329 Uttering a special prayer to the immaculate Virgin.

b. A picture or image of the Virgin Mary; a madonna.

a1700 Evelyn *Diary* 23 April 1646, There are two Sacristias, in one of which is a fine *Virgin* of Leonardo da Vinci. 1823 Galt *R. Gilhaize* ix, My grandfather..seized the Virgin's timber leg, and flung it with violence at them. 1840 *Penny Cycl.* XVII. 140/1 A most exquisite Virgin in a tabernacle in the open street at Prato. 1883 *Parker's Guide to Oxford* 87 The niches have been filled with the Virgin and Child [etc.].

6. A person of either sex remaining in a state of chastity. Usually in pl.

a1300 *Cursor M.* 24685 He ledis lijf lik til angels, For uirgins all ar þai. 1390 Gower *Conf.* III. 277 Hou that Adam and Eve also Virgines comen bothe tuo Into the world and were aschamed [etc.]. c1440 *Alph. Tales* 297 When þe Emperour Henrie and Ranegunde his wyfe abade alway clene virgyns. 1451 Capgrave *Life St. Gilbert* xxxi. 107 Fro þat tyme in whech he was take fro þe world, a-non was he set a-mongis þe dauns of virgynes.

7. A youth or man who has remained in a state of chastity.

c1330 *Arth. & Merl.* 8913 (K.), Þis Naciens..bicome prest, messe to sing; Virgine of his bodi he was. c1386 Chaucer *Pars. T.* ¶950 Virginitee baar oure lord Ihesu crist, and virgine was hym selue. c1450 Lovelich *Grail* xxxix. 559 A virgyne evere schal he be alle dayes of his lyve certeinle. 1470–85 Malory *Arthur* xvii. xviii. 715 Thow arte a clene vyrgyn aboue all knyghtes. a1513 Fabyan *Chron.* vi. ccxiv. 232 This kynge Edwarde lafte after hym no childe, for he was accompted for a virgyn whan he dyed. 1585 T. Washington tr. *Nicholay's Voy.* iii. xvi. 101 These Calenders..say themselues to be virgins. 1613 J. Hayward *Norm. Kings* 296 It is certaine also that Anselme, the most earnest enforcer of single life, died not a Virgine. 1653 H. Cogan tr. *Scarlet Gown* 14 It is held for certain, by them which know him, that he is still a Virgin. 1700 Tyrrell *Hist. Eng.* II. 785 He was reputed a Pure Virgin. 1847 tr. *Bacci's Life St. Philip Neri* ii. xiii. 253 A famous harlot,.. having heard it said that Philip was a virgin,..audaciously boasted that she would cause him to fall. 1880 A. I. Ritchie *Ch. St. Baldred* 49 King Malcolm [IV] is universally said to have died a virgin.

fig. 1798 Lamb *Rosamund Gray* iv. 498 His temper had a sweet and noble frankness in it, which bespake him yet a virgin from the world.

8. *Astr.* = Virgo.

c1480 Henryson *Fables, Fox & Wolf* iv, Mercurius, the God of Eloquence, Into the Uirgyn maid his residence. c1491 *Chast. Goddes Chyld.* 11 Whan the sonne in tyme of yere begynneth to wythdrawe dounwarde thenne reigneth he in a planete that we call Virgyne. 1509 Hawes *Past. Pleas.* xliv. (Percy Soc.) 216 Tyll peace and mercy made right to encline, Out of the Lyon to enter the Vyrgyne. c1550 Rolland *Crt. Venus* Prol. 43 The Virgin, Libra, and the Scorpion. 1596 Spenser *F.Q.* v. i. 11 The Virgin, sixt in her degree. 1667 Milton *P.L.* x. 676 Thence down amaine By Leo and the Virgin and the Scales, As deep as Capricorne. 1697 Creech *Manilius* ii. 70 The Twins, Vrn, Virgin force his Sign to bend By Nature's Law. 1730–46 Thomson *Autumn* 23 When the bright Virgin gives the beauteous days, And Libra weighs in equal scales the year. 1762 Falconer *Shipwr.* i. 197 Now, in the southern hemisphere, the sun Thro' the bright Virgin and the Scales had run. 1868 Lockyer *Guillemin's Heavens* (ed. 3) 326 The Virgin and Boötes are, with the Lion, the most important constellations in view.

9. a. *ellipt.* Applied to varieties of apple and pear.

1664 Evelyn *Kal. Hort.* 80 The Squib-pear, Spindle-pear, Virgin, Gascogne-Bergamot. 1886 *Cheshire Gloss.* 378 *Virgins*, a kind of apple.

b. *Ent.* Applied to species of moths and butterflies.

1832 J. Rennie *Consp. Butterfl. & M.* 49 The Virgin (*Triphæna Innuba.*) Wings two inches to two inches one-third, of uniform colour. *Ibid.* 100 The Virgin (*Brepha Parthenias*) appears the end of March.

10. A cigarette made of Virginia tobacco. *slang.* Now *Obs.* or *rare.*

1923 J. Manchon *Le Slang* 329. 1935 C. Brooks *Frame-Up* iv. 34 You gave me a virgin; I hadn't smoked one for nearly a fortnight. 1940 Graves & Hodge *Long Week-End* iii. 43 In the early Twenties..in offering a cigarette-case one would say, 'I hope you don't mind: it's only a Virgin.'

11. *attrib.* and *Comb.*, as ***virgin-birth***, ***-born*** adj., ***-produced*** adj., ***-violator***, ***-worship***; **virgin-bower**, = virgin's bower; **virgin-stock**, the Virginia stock; **virgin-tree**, Oriental sassafras.

1652 Crashaw *Carmen Deo Nostro* Poems (1904) 271 The *virgin-births with which thy soveraign spouse Made fruitfull thy fair soul. 1864 Pusey *Lect. Daniel* viii. 484 That announcement of the Virgin-birth of Him, of whom it is said, she shall call His Name Emmanuel. 1899 *Daily News* 16 Sept. 7/1, I fail to see how those who deny the virgin birth of Our Lord can in any way claim part in the Christian Church. 1671 Milton *P.R.* iv. 500 Then hear, O Son of David, *Virgin-born. 1846 Trench *Mirac.* 46 The Virgin-born, the Son of the Most Highest. 1725 *Fam. Dict.*, **Virgin-bower*, a Plant of which there are two sorts [etc.]. 1810 Scott *Lady of Lake* i. xxvi, The clematis, the favour'd flower Which boasts the name of virgin-bower. 1861 *N. Syd. Soc. Year-bk. Med. & Surg. 1860*, 377 They are altogether equivalent to *virgin-produced 'zooids'. 1786 Abercrombie *Gard. Assist.* 55 Sweet peas, pansies, *virgin-stock. 1891 *Cent. Dict.* s.v. *Stock*, The somewhat similar *Malcolmia maritima*,..in England called *Virginia* or *virgin stock*. 1866 *Treas. Bot.* 1219/1 *Virgin-tree, *Sassafras Parthenoxylon*. 1603 Shaks. *Meas. for M.* v. i. 41 That Angelo is an adulterous thiefe, An hypocrite, a *virgin violator. 1848 Kingsley *Saint's Trag.* Introd. p. xviii, I should..have copied the introduction of *Virgin-worship into the original tale.

12. In possessive collocations: **virgin's garland**, a garland of flowers and coloured paper formerly carried at the funeral of a maiden; † **virgin's honey**, **-oil**, = *virgin honey*, *oil* (see 18 b); † **virgin's sea**, = *Virginian sea* Virginian *a.*[1] 1 d; **Virgin's spike** (see spike *sb.*[1] 1 b); † **virgin's thread** (see quot.).

1825 Brockett *N.C. Gloss.*, **Virgin's garland*, many country churches in the North are adorned with these garlands; in token, says Bourne, of esteem and love, and as an emblem of reward in the heavenly Church. 1828 *Craven Gloss.*, *Virgin's Garlands*. Many of the Churches in the Deanery of Craven are adorned with these garlands. [Description follows.] 1879–81 Miss Jackson *Shropsh. Wordbk.* 465 Virgins-garlands still exist; as..at Minsterley, where there are several, the most recent of them being of the date 1764. **1611** COTGR., *Miel vierge*, *Virgins honie, the honie which of it selfe, and without pressing, distills from the combe. **1725** *Fam. Dict.* s.v. *Empyema*, They mix a quartern of Virgins Honey, with two Paris Pints thereof. **1611** COTGR., *Huile Virginal*, *Virgins Oyle; the Oyle that comes from the Oliue of it selfe, and without pressing. **1603** in *Shirburn Ballads* lxxvii. 7 His Empyre.. Halfe which her beseme foorth doth lay from German to the *Virgin's [*v.r.* Virginian] sea. **1704** *Dict. Rust.* (1726), **Virgin's-Thread*, a sort of Dew, which flies in the Air, like small untwisted Silk or Yarn, and falling upon the Ground or Plants, changes it self into a form like a Spider's web.

II. ***attrib.*** passing into *adj.* **13. a.** Of persons (usually of the female sex): Being a virgin or virgins; remaining in a state of chastity.

Virgin Queen, a name for Queen Elizabeth I of England.

1560 BIBLE (Genev.) *Jer.* xiv. 17 For yᵉ virgine daughter of my people is destroyed.. with a sore grieuous plague. **1599** SHAKS. *Much Ado* v. iii. 13 Pardon, goddesse of the night, Those that slew thy virgin knight [*sc.* Hero]. **1611** SPEED *Theat. Gt. Britain* I. xi. 21/1 Ursula,.. with her companie of canonized Virgin-Saints. **1633** FORD *Broken Heart* Prol., The virgin-sisters then deserv'd fresh bays. *Ibid.* III. v, To virgin-wives, such as abuse not wedlock By freedom of desires. **1652** BENLOWES *Theoph.* VI. xxv, Hail, blessed Virgin-Spouse, who didst bequeath Breath unto him, who made thee breathe! **1697** DRYDEN *Æneid* XI. 754 The Volscians, and their virgin leader, wait His last commands. *a* **1718** PARNELL *Hesiod* 34 In such a shape.. As virgin-goddesses are proud to wear. **1738** tr. *Guazzo's Art Convers.* 45, I am, with Respect to any concern with Women, as true a Virgin-man as I came from my Mother's womb. **1786** POLWHELE tr. *Idyllia of Theocritus*, etc. (1792) II. 38 And still the Arabian maids have their hair inwreathed with hyacinths, like the virgin companions of Helen. **1827** POLLOK *Course T.* x, Stars, the virgin daughters of the sky. **1834** L. RITCHIE *Wand. by Seine* 40 The virgin-martyr St. Honoria.

b. In predicative use. Also *fig.*, and const. *of* and *to*. *rare.*

1667 MILTON *P.L.* IX. 396 Likest she seemd.. to Ceres in her Prime, Yet Virgin of Proserpina from Jove. **1849–50** ALISON *Hist. Europe* XIV. xcvi. §21. 218 Germany, alike virgin to revolutionary passions, and unused to revolutionary suffering, has had a firebrand tossed into its bosom. **1859** TENNYSON *Guinevere* 553 Yet not less, O Guinevere, For I was ever virgin save for thee.

c. ***the Virgin Mother***, the Virgin Mary.

[*a.* **1711** KEN *Sion* Poet. Wks. 1721 IV. 321 His Virgin-Mother had Angelick Grace]. **1720** WELTON *Suffer. Son of God* I. x. 242 The Humble Deference of the sacred Virgin-Mother in Regard to Him, who was her Son, and her God too. **1817** SCOTT *Monks of Bangor's March* ii, On the long procession goes,.. And the Virgin-mother mild In their peaceful banner smiled. **1846** MRS. A. MARSH *Father Darcy* II. i. 11, I.. would fain enlist every holy saint in the calendar, and implore the virgin mother herself. **1860** TENNYSON *Sea Dreams* 234 The Virgin Mother standing with her child High up on one of those dark minster-fronts.

d. ***virgin widow***, a widow who has been deprived of her husband before the consummation of the marriage.

a **1644** QUARLES (*title*), The Virgin Widow. A Comedie. **1700** DRYDEN *Pal. & Arc.* III. 927 A Virgin-Widow and a Mourning Bride. **1882** STEVENSON *Men & B.* 243 Isabella, virgin-widow of our Richard II. **1887** J. GAIRDNER in *Dict. Nat. Biog.* IX. 291/1 On 2 April [1502].. he [Prince Arthur] died at Ludlow, and Catherine was left a virgin widow.

e. *transf.* (See quots.)

1674 JEAKE *Arith.* (1696) 663 Seven, the old Magi called a Virgin Number, supposing the Force thereof great, as a Virgin in her full strength. **1725** *Fam. Dict.*, *Virgin-Vine*, a Plant reckon'd by many among the sorts of Snake-Weed... 'Tis call'd the Virgin-Vine, because, if it may be so said, it is a Maid, and has hitherto brought forth nothing. **1849** OWEN *Parthenogenesis* 76 The development of an *Aphis* in the body of a virgin parent. **1888** F. R. CHESHIRE *Bees & Bee-Keeping* II. 330 The cage may be used in introducing both laying and virgin queens.

f. Of a fortress, city, etc.: That has never been taken or subdued.

1780 BURKE *Œcon. Reform* Wks. III. 240 That household, which has been the stronghold of prodigality, the virgin fortress which was never before attacked. **1856** *N. Brit. Rev.* XXVI. 103 She stands and grows and thrives, a virgin land for now eight hundred years. **1868** *Chambers's Encycl.* X. 186/1 Widdin.. is called by the Turks the Virgin Fort, from its never having been taken. **1873** TRISTRAM *Moab* v. 78 Ibrahim.. was never able to take Kerak, whose proud boast is that it yet remains a virgin city.

g. ***virgin generation***, ***procreation***, or (***re***)***production***, parthenogenesis.

1849 OWEN *Parthenogenesis* 28 The structures.. which Reaumur.. cited in order to solve the problem of the alleged virgin procreation. **1859** *Todd's Cycl. Anat.* V. 37/2 Professor Owen has given the name of Parthenogenesis, or Virgin-production, to this mode of generation. **1881** *Encycl. Brit.* XII. 574/2 While.. *Hymenoptera* reproduce by the union of the two sexes, yet parthenogenesis or virgin reproduction is of not uncommon occurrence.

14. Composed or consisting of virgins.

c **1586** C'TESS PEMBROKE *Ps.* LXVIII. iv, Taught by thee, in this tryumphant song, A virgin army did their voices try. **1596** SHAKS. *Merch. V.* III. ii. 56 Yong Alcides, when he did redeeme The virgine tribute, paied.. To the Sea-monster. **1698** FRYER *Acc. E. India & P.* 290 The Graces Adorn our Parks and Malls Crowned with Virgin-Garlands. *a* **1711** KEN *Psyche* Poet. Wks. 1721 IV. 306 Psyche then left the lovely virgin-choir. **1820** KEATS *To Psyche* 30 Though temple thou hast none,.. Nor virgin-choir. **1857** EMERSON *Poems* 13 The lover watched his graceful maid, As mid the virgin train she strayed. **1885–94** R. BRIDGES *Eros & Psyche* April 22 And next the virgin tribe in white forth sail'd.

15. Of or pertaining to a virgin; appropriate to, or characteristic of, virgins: **a.** Of parts of the body, articles of dress, etc.

1588 SHAKS. *L.L.L.* v. ii. 816 Come challenge me,.. And, by this Virgin palme, now kissing thine, I will be thine. **1608** —— *Per.* IV. ii. 160 Untied I still my virgin knot will keep. **1616** DRUMM. OF HAWTH. *Madrigals* xlv, This virgine Lock of Haire To Idmon Anthea giues. **1650** BULWER *Anthropomet.* Pref., The Midwives do the Virgin Zone cashere. **1684** BUNYAN *Pilgr.* II. Introd. Lines 182 Come see her in her Virgin Face, and learn Twixt Idle ones, and Pilgrims to discern. **1725** POPE *Odyss.* IV. 1050 Iphthima the fair,.. whose blooming charms Allured Eumelus to her virgin-arms. **1807–8** WORDSW. *Eccl. Sonn.* II. xxv, Mother! whose virgin bosom was uncrost With the least shade of thought to sin allied. **1810** SCOTT *Lady of Lake* III. v, Yet ne'er again to braid her hair The virgin snood did Alice wear. **1819** S. ROGERS *Hum. Life* Poems (1839) 10 Moves in her virgin-veil the gentle bride. **1846** PROWETT *Prometheus Bound* 31 Thou favoured maiden, Why in thy virgin-zone still braced?

fig. **1855** THACKERAY *Newcomes* xxxix, Whenever you found him he seemed watchful and serene, his modest virgin-lamp always lighted and trim.

b. Of qualities, feelings, etc.

a **1586** SIDNEY *Arcadia* II. xvii. (1622) 165 Though the purenesse of my virgin-mind be stained, let me keepe the true simplicity of my word. **1611** *2nd Maiden's Trag.* III. i. in Hazl. *Dodsley* X. 433 Hast thou.. overcome Thy honour's en'mies with thine own white hand, Where virgin-victory sits. **1633** FORD *Broken H.* II. iii, The virgin-dowry which my birth bestow'd Is ravish'd by another. **1651** HOBBES *Govt. & Soc.* xviii. §14. 362 Hither also in some respect tends the Virgin-life of Ecclesiasticall Persons. **1667** MILTON *P.L.* IX. 270 To whom the Virgin Majestie of Eve.. With sweet austeer composure thus reply'd. **1713** ADDISON *Cato* I. vi, *Lucia*. Was ever virgin love distress'd like mine! **1720** WELTON *Suffer. Son of God* I. iv. 67 Without the least Injury to her Virgin-Purity. **1757** GRAY *Bard* 118 Her.. face Attemper'd sweet to virgin-grace. **1762** GOLDSM. *Cit. W.* lxxxviii, A lady in the virgin bloom of sixty-three. **1808** HELEN ST. VICTOR *Ruins of Rigonda* I. 55 These.. are mere virgin scruples. **1839** DE QUINCEY *Recoll. Lakes* Wks. 1862 II. 201 The honourable election of a self-dependent virgin seclusion, by preference to a heartless marriage! **1848** THACKERAY *Van. Fair* iii, The picture of youth, unprotected innocence, and humble virgin simplicity. **1885** 'MRS. ALEXANDER' *Valerie's Fate* ii, We must not disturb her virgin thoughts with a question of marriage.

16. a. Comparable to a virgin in respect of purity or freedom from stain; pure, unstained, unsullied. In early use in fig. context.

13.. *E.E. Allit. P.* A. 426 We leuen on marye.. þat ber a barne of vyrgyn flour. *c* **1450** *Godstow Reg.* 20 With blessyd Seynt Cuthburge, þat virgyn flour. **1596** SPENSER *Prothalamion* 32 The Virgin Lillie, and the Primrose trew. **1596** SHAKS. *Merch. V.* II. vii. 23 What saies the Siluer, with her virgin hue? **1610** —— *Temp.* IV. 55 The white cold virgin Snow vpon my heart. **1633** FORD *Broken H.* v. i, The virgin-bays shall not withstand the lightning With a more careless danger, than my constancy The full of thy relation. **1641** MILTON *Reform.* I. Wks. 1851 III. 19 These that must be call'd the ancientest, and most virgin times between Christ and Constantine. **1655** VAUGHAN *Silex Scint.* I. *Search* 70 What shades, and cells, Faire virgin-flowers, and hallow'd Wells I should rove in. **1743** FRANCIS tr. *Hor.*, *Odes* I. xxvi. 9 Sweet Muse, who lov'st the virgin Spring, Hither thy sunny Flowrets bring. **1819** S. ROGERS *Hum. Life* Poems (1839) 14 A funeral garland hung Of virgin-white. **1818** KEATS *Endym.* II. 113 My veined pebble-floor, that draws A virgin light to the deep. **1839** DE QUINCEY *Recoll. Lakes* Wks. 1862 II. 23 A glittering expanse of virgin snow. **1861** THACKERAY *Four Georges* iv. 225 To lead a pure life, to keep your honour virgin. **1885** R. BUCHANAN *Annan Water* iii, The garden was covered with a sheet of virgin white.

b. Not yet touched, handled, or employed for any purpose; still undisturbed or unused; perfectly fresh or new.

1590 SHAKS. *Mids. N.* I. i. 70 The Rose.. which withering on the virgin thorne.. dies in single blessednesse. **1638** DRUMM. OF HAWTH. *Exequies A. Alexander* 66 How oft have we Some Chloris Name graven in each Virgin tree? **1785** CRABBE *Newspaper* 29 Unbought, unbless'd, the virgin copies wait In vain for fame. **1799** WORDSWORTH *Nutting* 21 The hazels rose Tall and erect, with tempting clusters hung, A virgin scene. **1823** D'ISRAELI *Cur. Lit.* Ser. II. I. 415, I propose to give what.. may be called the Philosophy of Proverbs—a topic which seems virgin. **1838** THIRLWALL *Greece* II. xii. 108 A.. Samian, named Colæus, reached Tartessus, and found, as Herodotus says, a virgin mart. **1867** F. FRANCIS *Angling* ix. (1880) 307 Salmon.. hatched in perfectly virgin waters. **1882** FLOYER *Unexpl. Baluchistan* 176 It was at least a virgin country which.. had never yet been entered by white man. **1879** *Allbutt's Syst. Med.* II. 258 The ravages of Small-pox in a virgin race.

c. Perfectly free or clear *of* something.

1889 *Harper's Mag.* May 878/2 The Sierra Madres in Mexico are still virgin of sportsmen and skin-hunters.

17. a. Employed for the first time.

1627 DRAYTON *Agincourt*, etc. 87 When th' Earle of March.. His Virgine valour on that day bestowes. **1725** POPE *Odyss.* I. 389 His virgin sword Ægysthus' veins imbru'd. **1760** STERNE *Tr. Shandy* I. ix, But [it] is honestly a true Virgin-Dedication untried on, upon any soul living. *a* **1839** PRAED *Poems* (1864) II. 16 As on the day that saw him wield His virgin sword in battle field.

b. Forming a first essay or attempt; coming at the beginning or outset.

1627 E. F. *Hist. Edw. II* (1680) 8 The first Virgin-works of his greatness. *a* **1628** F. GREVILLE *Sidney* (1652) 225 Her Virgin-triumph over that.. invincible Navy. **1652** N. CULVERWEL *Treat.* I. xi. (1661) 76 Instincts.. the first-born faculties.. that are presently espoused to their Virgin-objects. **1708** OZELL tr. *Boileau's Lutrin* 121 A Youth.. entring the Lists, his Virgin-Motion makes. **1771** SMOLLETT *Humph. Cl.*, *To Sir W. Phillips* 10 June, Tim Cropdale.. had happily wound up the Catastrophe of a virgin-Tragedy, from the Exhibition of which [etc.]. **1857** HEAVYSEGE *Saul* (1869) 27 Now quit thee well on this thy virgin field. **1873** HAMERTON *Intell. Life* v. iii. 191 That interest you preserve in all its virgin force, and this force carries a man far. **1891** *Daily News* 21 Feb. 3/2 That any measure dealing with.. the House of Lords could only be undertaken by the virgin energy of the session.

18. Special collocations: **a.** ***virgin bush***, bush land not brought under cultivation; ***virgin country***, country that has not yet been opened up to the outside world for trade, etc.; ***virgin earth***, ***soil***, etc., soil which has not hitherto been brought into cultivation, and retains all its natural power of producing vegetation; ***virgin forest***, a forest of natural growth as yet untouched by man; ***virgin land***, previously uncultivated land, *spec.* [tr. Russ. *tselinâ*] in Western Siberia and Kazakhstan, land made the subject of an intensive agricultural programme by the Soviet government since 1954; ***virgin rock***, etc., native rock not yet cut into or quarried.

1905 W. B. *Where White Man Treads* 297 A heroic dare-all to share her children's father's toil to build up a home in the *virgin bush. **1982** *Times* 15 Feb. 6/2 The Pope.. celebrated Mass at a huge open space.. which had been bulldozed out of the virgin bush a few days earlier. **1709** T. ROBINSON in *Vind. Mosaick System* 103 A small Parcel of *Virgin-Clay, digged some Fathoms under Ground. **1929** *Daily Express* 7 Nov. 8/4 Great tractors that will take heavy loads over *virgin country where there are no roads. **1652** FRENCH *Yorksh. Spa* ii. 13 Helmonts *sabulum* or *virgin-earth, which he saith is a certain sand continued from the Center of the earth in divers places, even to the superficies of the same. **1692** BOYLE *Hist. Air* 44 Hoping to find in the salt of what he supposed to be Virgin-earth, the true receptacle of an universal spirit. **1744** BERKELEY *Siris* §141 Virgin earth becomes fertile, crops of new plants ever and anon shew themselves. **1799** J. ROBERTSON *Agric. Perth* 280 Hence the astonishing fertility of all new soil, or what is called virgin earth. **1812** *New Botanic Gard.* I. 64 A third part of fresh virgin earth, from a pasture ground. **1886** J. BARROWMAN *Sc. Mining Terms* 69 **Virgin field*, a mineral field untouched or solid. **1851** G. F. RICHARDSON *Geol.* (1855) 443 A *virgin forest of the Isle of Gouahan, one of the Mariana Islands. **1955** *Britannica Bk. of Year* 460/2 New state farms were to be set up at once mainly in Kazakhstan and western Siberia, where there were said to be many millions of acres of *virgin or neglected, but fertile, land. **1959** *Listener* 10 Sept. 378/2 Mr. Khrushchev's virgin-lands scheme in Siberia and Kazakhstan. **1967** C. COCKBURN *I, Claud* xxxv. 438 Hardly anyone can be packed off to some social equivalent of the Russian 'virgin lands' for lousing things up. **1981** O. BERNIER *Pleasure & Privilege* xiii. 222 Every day men were claiming and enclosing new, virgin land. Homesteaders were at work all over the Eastern states. **1813** SIR H. DAVY *Agric. Chem.* (1814) 358 Strawberries and potatoes at first produce luxuriantly in *Virgin Mould, recently turned up from pasture. **1877** J. NORTHCOTE *Catacombs* I. i. 10 They choose rather to excavate in their own fashion in the *virgin rock below. **1828** WEBSTER *Virgin*,.. fresh; new; unused; as **virgin* soil. **1837** H. MARTINEAU *Soc. Amer.* II. 106 The slave population.. is killed off.. on the virgin soils to which alone it is, in any degree, appropriate. **1847** DICKENS *Dombey* (1848) xi. 104 We shall impart a great variety of information to our little friend... Quite a virgin soil, I believe you said. **1857** LIVINGSTONE *Trav.* xix. 372 Virgin soil does not give such a heavy crop as an old garden. **1888** BRYCE *Amer. Commw.* III. lxxvi. 6 No event, no speech or article, ever falls upon a perfectly virgin soil. **1868** *Rep. U.S. Commissioner Agric.* (1869) 18 It [*sc.* present practice] will doubtless continue in vogue till our *virgin wheat lands are run over by pioneers.

b. In special names of various substances (usually denoting one in a pure unmixed state or obtained as a first product), as ***virgin barm***, ***breccia***, ***comb***, ***copper***, ***dip***, ***gold***, ***wool***, etc. (see quots.).

1893 R. WELLS *Mod. Pract. Bread Baker* 10 *Virgin barm, or bastard barm, as it is sometimes called, is made in somewhat the same way as Parisian barm. **1839** *Civil Eng. & Arch. Jrnl.* II. 454/1 *Seme Santo*, or **Virgin Breccia*. Very small red, chocolate,.. white and yellowish angulous fragments. **1891** *Cent. Dict.*, **Virgin clay*, in industrial arts, .. clay that has never been molded or fired, as distinguished from the ground substance of old ware, which is often mixed with it. **1639** G. DANIEL *Ecclus.* xxiv. 65 My Memory Is pleasant as the Honey, and my ffee Is sweeter then *Virgin-Combes. **1666** DRYDEN *Ann. Mirab.* cxlv, With glewy wax some new Foundations lay Of Virgin-combs, which from the Roof are hung. **1867** *Tomlinson's Cycl. Arts* App. 693/2 Some virgin comb that had never seen the light was placed in clean linen. **1728** CHAMBERS *Cycl.*, **Virgin Copper*, is that which has never been melted down. **1796** MORSE *Amer. Geog.* I. 167 Remarkable for the abundance of virgin copper. **1725** *Fam. Dict.*, **Virgin-Cream*, a Dish for which having the Whites of five Eggs, let them be well whip'd and put into a Pan, with Sugar [etc.]. **1856** OLMSTED *Slave States* 343 The flow of the first year.. is of higher value than the ordinary dip. It is called '*virgin dip.' **1884** C. S. SARGENT *Rep. Forests N. Amer.* 517 'Virgin dip,' or 'Soft white gum turpentine'— the product of the first year the trees are worked. **1673** E. BROWNE *Acc. Trav. Hungary*, etc. 99 There have been pieces of pure or *virgin Gold found in this Mine. **1728** CHAMBERS *Cycl.* s.v. *Gold*, *Virgin Gold*, is Gold, just as it is taken out of the Mines before it have undergone any Action, or Preparation of Fire. **1777** ROBERTSON *Hist. Amer.* VII. (1778) II. 343 A late governor of Sante Fé brought with him to Spain a lump of virgin gold. **1837** LOCKHART *Scott* (1839) IV. 141 Sir John Malcolm had given him some Indian coins to supply virgin gold for the setting of this relic. **1733** TULL *Horse-Hoeing Husb.* xiv. 182 This came out of the Ricks at Winter with a much finer Colour, and as fine a smell as the *Virgin-Hay. *a* **1648** DIGBY *Closet Opened* (1677) 4 It is of three sorts, *Virgin-honey, Live-honey, and Stock-honey. **1679** M. RUSDEN *Further Discov. Bees* 64 The ignorance of many Country people not knowing which is right Virgin-Hony, and which is not. **1707** MORTIMER *Husb.* (1721) I. 283 The Honey which first flows of it self from the Combs is called Virgin Honey (as is also the Honey which comes from the first Years Swarm). **1772** FLETCHER *Appeal* Wks. 1795 I. 204

note, Some poor hungry hearts will say, 'One thing is needful for us. We cannot have too much virgin-honey'. **1867** *Tomlinson's Cycl. Arts* App. 695/1 Any experiments on this subject must be with virgin honey, or that drained from the new comb. *a* **1728** WOODWARD *Nat. Hist. Fossils* I. (1729) I. 297 Lead-Grains so pure as nearly to approach the Fineness of *Virgin Lead. **1669** *Phil. Trans.* IV. 1080 *Virgin-Mercury they call that, which discovers itself without the help of fire. **1757** tr. *Keysler's Trav.* (1760) IV. 144 Virgin mercury..is that which is entirely prepared by nature. **1668** *Phil. Trans.* III. 821 Yet sometimes there are great Masses found all of pure Silver, which is call'd *Virgin-mettal. **1740** SOMERVILLE *Hobbinol* I. 202 With his Plant Of toughest *Virgin Oak in rising [he] aids His trembling Limbs. **1719** BOYER *Dict. Royal* I, *De l'huile vierge*,..sweet, or pure Oyl, *Virgin Oyl. **1853** URE *Dict. Arts* II. 284 In the district Montpellier, they apply the term virgin oil to that which spontaneously separates from the paste of crushed olives. **1857** MILLER *Elem. Chem., Org.* 359 The ripe olives are first subjected to pressure without the application of heat; in this manner the finest oil, or virgin oil, is obtained. **1758** BORLASE *Nat. Hist. Cornw.* 199 The most perfect copper..is the Malleable (from its purity called in Cornwall the *Virgin-ore). **1821** BYRON *Sardanap.* IV. i, The miner lights Upon a vein of virgin ore. **1611** COTGR., *Parchemin verri*, Cleere Parchment, *virgine Parchment. **1706** PHILLIPS (ed. Kersey), *Virgin Parchment*, a sort of fine Parchment made of the Skin of a young Lamb. **1823** SCOTT *Quentin D.* xiii, It was fastened round his middle by a broad belt of virgin parchment. **1839** URE *Dict. Arts* 897 The best [olive oil], called *virgin salad oil, is obtained by gentle pressure in the cold. **1888** *Buck's Handbk. Med. Sci.* VI. 297/1 In this way the bubbles and sour odor are developed, and what is known as '*Virgin Scammony' is produced. **1726** SHELVOCKE *Voy. round World* 167, 1300 dollars weight in ingots of *virgin silver. **1776** ADAM SMITH *W.N.* I. xi. II. I. 182 Silver is very seldom found Virgin. **1806** FORSYTH *Beauties Scotl.* IV. 10 It had the appearance of metallic, malleable, or what is called, virgin silver. **1873** E. SPON *Workshop Receipts* Ser. I. 238/2 The silver found in the trade, even under the name of virgin silver, retains traces of copper. **1833** J. HOLLAND *Manuf. Metal* II. 39 Run, or *virgin steel;—which, indeed, in the proper sense of the term, is no steel at all, but rather good cast metal. **1668** CHARLETON *Onomast.* 235 *Sulphur Virgineum*... *Virgin Sulphur. **1672** *Compl. Gunner* xv. 16 This is called Sulphur Vivum, and by some Virgin Sulphur. **1752** CHAMBERS *Cycl.* s.v. *Sulphur*, *Sulphur vivum*, *native* or *virgin sulphur*, is that which is dug in this form out of the earth. **1706** *Art of Painting* (1744) 283 On this they laid their *virgin tints, with light strokes of the pencil. **1753** HOGARTH *Anal. Beauty* xiv. 190 Let us then..call class 4 of each colour 'bloom-tints', or, if you please, 'virgin tints', as the painters call them. **1799** G. SMITH *Laboratory* I. 430 Take the first, or *virgin wine, which runs of itself from the grapes. **1921** *Daily Colonist* (Victoria, B.C.) 5 Oct. 7/6 (Advt.), Pure *virgin wool socks at 45 c a pair. **1952** *Amer. Speech* XXVII. 262 Woolens and worsteds may be manufactured from *virgin wool*—any wool that has never before been spun, woven, knitted, felted, or otherwise made into a manufactured product. **1977** *New Yorker* 12 Sept. 106/3, 100% virgin shetland wool from the Shetland-Isles. Hand-loomed and fully-fashioned in the U.S.A.

19. *Comb.*, as ***virgin-eyed***, ***-minded***, ***-vested*** adjs.

1848 B. D. WALSH *Aristoph.* 365 *note*, Jove's virgin-eyed daughter. **1867** EARL LYTTON *Lett.* (1906) I. 224 There exists nowhere..a more virgin-minded community of young men. **1871** SWINBURNE *Songs bef. Sunrise*, *Quia Multum Amavit* 18 Thou wast fairest and first of my virgin-vested daughters.

Hence **'virgin** *v.* (*a*) *intr.* with *it*. To remain a virgin. (*b*) *trans.* To speak of, mention (virgins).

1607 SHAKS. *Cor.* v. iii. 48 That kisse I carried from thee deare; and my true Lippe Hath Virgin'd it ere since. **1625** MASSINGER *New Way* III. ii, *Marg.* You'll have me, sir, preserve the distance that Confines a virgin? *Over.* Virgin me no virgins! I must have you lose that name, or you lose me.

virginal ('vɜːdʒɪnəl), *sb.* Forms: 6 **virginalles**, **-ynal(le)s**, 6–7 **virginall(s**, 6– **virginal(s**, 7–8 **virginelles**. [App. of the same formation as VIRGINAL *a.*, but the reason for the name is obscure.]

1. A keyed musical instrument (common in England in the 16th and 17th centuries), resembling a spinet, but set in a box or case without legs.

a. In plural form, applied to a single instrument.

1530 PALSGR. 711/1 Set my virgynalles, *entonnez mes espinettes*. *a* **1548** HALL *Chron., Hen. VIII*, 8 Exercisyng hym self dayly in..plaiyng at the recorders, flute, virginals, and in setting of songes. **1591** FLORIO *2nd Fruites* 129 He plaies also upon the cittarn, virginals, violine and flute. **1601** B. JONSON *Ev. Man in Hum.* (Q.) II. iii. 161, I can compare him to nothing more happely, then a Barbers virginals; for euery one may play vpon him. **1660** PEPYS *Diary* 8 Dec., Her daughter played after dinner upon the virginals. **1662** PLAYFORD *Skill Mus.* I. i. 4 But Lessons for the Organ, Virginals, or Harp, two staves of six lines together are required. **1710** J. CHEIN in E. Dunbar *Soc. Life* (1865) 15, I can..play on the Treble and Gambo, Viol, Virginelles and Manicords. **1786** *Lounger* (1787) II. 192, I could play pretty well on the Virginals at home. **1823** ROSCOE tr. *Sismondi's Lit. Eur.* (1846) I. v. 128 The claricord was a sort of spinet resembling the virginals. **1841** BARHAM *Ingol. Leg.* Ser. II. *Nell Cook*, And fine upon the virginals is that gay Lady's touch. **1873** DIXON *Two Queens* XII. iii. II. 298 Himself a player on the virginals and organ.

b. ***a pair of virginals***, in the same sense. (Cf. PAIR *sb.*[1] 6.)

1542 *Test. Ebor.* (Surtees) VI. 159 A paire of virginals. **1545** *Lanc. Wills* (Chetham Soc.) II. 67 My best paire of virginalls. **1630** DEKKER *2nd Pt. Honest Wh.* H iv, No, for she's like a paire of Virginals, Alwaies with Iackes at her taile. **1666** PEPYS *Diary* 2 Sept., Hardly one lighter or boat in three that had the goods of a house in, but there was a pair of Virginalls in it. **1684** BUNYAN *Pilgr.* II. 93 The Dining-Room, where stood a pair of excellent Virginals. **1755** J. COLLIER (Tim Bobbin) *Let.* Wks. (1775) 177 You know I have a pair of rusty old Virginals in a Corner of the School, which have about eight Strings left out of forty-five.

c. As a singular, with plural denoting more than one instrument.

The plural use (*a*) prob. preceded the singular.

(*a*) **1566** STERNHOLD & HOPKINS *Ps.* cl. 14 Praise him with Tymbrell and with flute, orgaines and virginals. **1598** SYLVESTER *Du Bartas* II. i. *Handycrafts* 567 Wiery Cymbals, Rebecks sinnews twin'd, Sweet Virginals, and Cornets curled winde. **1630** *R. Johnson's Kingd. & Commw.* 187 Those [teeth] that are left, leaping in their heads, like Iacks in Virginals. **1644** DIGBY *Nat. Bodies* vii. (1658) 57 Artificial musical instruments (as organs and virginals that playd by themselves). **1694** *Patent Specif.* (1856) No. 337. 1 Harpsichords, virginalls or the like. **1833** HT. MARTINEAU *Three Ages* i. 7 Large and airy study..ornamented with books, manuscripts, maps, viols, virginals, and other musical instruments.

(*b*) **1570** LEVINS *Manip.* 15 Virginall, *cymbala*. **1597** BRETON *Wit's Trenchmour* Wks. (Grosart) II. 14/1 Let me euer loue musicke, though I cannot tune a virginall. **1625** GILL *Sacr. Philos.* II. 188 In an Organ or Virginall, all manner of tunes, all concords, and discords are, which are possible to bee made or conceived by any Musician. **1667** PEPYS *Diary* 23 Jan., He and I did see the organ, but I do not like it, it being but a bauble, with a virginal joining to it. **1694** *Phil. Trans.* XVIII. 73 He shews the best way how to have an Organ or Virginal tuned. **1709** ADDISON *Tatler* No. 157 ¶8 That ancient serious Matron-like Instrument the Virginal. **1789** BURNEY *Hist. Mus.* III. i. 5 *note*, The Virginal is a keyed instrument of one string, jack, and quill, to each note, like a spinet. **1843** *Penny Cycl.* XXVI. 360/2 The compass of the virginal was from the second added line below the base to the second added line above the treble —or four octaves. **1889** BRINSMEAD *Hist. Pianoforte* 91 The instrument which gradually superseded the clavichord in England was the virginal.

transf. **1593** HARVEY *New Lett.* Wks. (Grosart) I. 266 Is not the Verse of M. Spencer in his braue Faery Queene, the Virginall of the diuinest Muses, and gentlest Graces?

2. *attrib.* and *Comb.*, as ***virginal book***, ***jack*** (JACK *sb.*[1] 14), ***-maker***, ***master***, ***music***, ***music-book***, ***string***, ***wire***.

1663 PEPYS *Diary* 16 Mar., Thence home by coach, buying at the Temple the printed *virginall-book for her. **1604** *Virginal jack [see JACK *sb.*[1] 14]. **1622** F. MARKHAM *Bk. War* IV. vii. 146 Men should not like virginall Iacks be skipping up here and there, and in every corner. *c* **1638** G. PLATTES in Worlidge *Syst. Agric.* (1669) iv. §6. 44 These may be made to play up and down like Virginal Jacks. **1551** *Acts Privy Counc.* (1891) III. 306 Robert Gundet of Westminster, *virginall maker. *c* **1580** MUNDAY *View Sundry Examples* (Shaks. Soc.) 93 A Virginal maker that came to look Ravens quils found the man slain. **1640** in Sir C. Sharp *Chron. Mirab.* (1841) 44 Thomas Forcer, *Virginall master. **1874** OUSELEY *Musical Form* 48 It was very commonly employed three hundred years ago for *virginal music. **1889** BRINSMEAD *Hist. Pianoforte* 93 Queen Elizabeth must..have performed music that would be considered exceedingly difficult even now, if she really played the pieces that are in her *virginal music-book. **1626** BACON *Sylva* §13 The sound of a *Virginall String, as soone as the Quill of the Jack falleth from it, stoppeth. **1743** EMERSON *Fluxions* 265, I took a virginal String 29..Inches long. **1662** *Ireland, Stat. at Large* (1765) II. 418 *Virginal and ghittern wire, the pound, 4*l.* **1698** *Phil. Trans.* XX. 433 It was a Piece of small Virginal Wire. **1812** J. SMYTH *Pract. of Customs* (1821) 279, 1 Cask, 63 lbs. Brass Virginal Wire.

Hence †**'virginal** *v. intr.*, to tap with the fingers as on a virginal. *Obs.*$^{-1}$

1611 SHAKS. *Wint. T.* I. ii. 124 To be padling Palmes, and pinching Fingers,..Still Virginalling Vpon his Palme?

virginal ('vɜːdʒɪnəl), *a.* Forms: 5– **virginal** (5 **-alle, -el, -ele**), 6–7 **virginall** (6 **-eall**); 5 **virgynal**, 5–6 **-all**, 6 **vyrginall**; 5 **vyrgynal**, 5–6 **-all**. [a. OF. (also mod.F.) *virginal* (= Sp. and Pg. *virginal*, It. *virginale*), or ad. L. *virginal-is*, f. *virgin-*, *virgo*: see VIRGIN *sb.* and -AL[1].]

1. Of or pertaining to a virgin or to virginity.

14.. in *Tundale's Vis.* (1843) 129 For of hur wombe the cloysture vyrgynall Euer was lyke bothe fyrst and last Closed and schytt as castell principall. *c* **1440** CAPGRAVE *Life St. Kath.* v. 1314 He hath stodied with al herte and meende Thi virgynal body to destroye and shende. **1513** BRADSHAW *St. Werburge* I. 2973 In the vyrgynall wombe of blessed marye. **1579** FULKE *Heskins' Parl.* 170 The Virginall bowels of his vndefiled mother. **1592** R. D. *Hypnerotomachia* 78 This honourable Nymph had her virgineall..body covered with a.. stuffe of greene silke. **1612** FIELD *Woman's a Weathercock* III. ii. in Hazl. *Dodsley* II. 53 And thy Bellafront presents herself, Lav'd in a bath of contrite virginal tears. **1650** JER. TAYLOR *Holy Living* 395 The load was too great, and did sink thy tender and virginal body to the earth. **1721** R. KEITH tr. *T. à Kempis, Solil. Soul* xxii. 294 Thanks also be to holy Mary thy Mother, from whose virginal Flesh thou didst take the holy Members of thy Body. **1846** LANDOR *Imag. Conv.* Wks. I. 537/1 Can the calmest face,..or can the most virginal apron, do away with or cover this? **1854** CDL. WISEMAN *Fabiola* (1855) 201 One ..whose brides never put off their virginal wreaths. **1878** H. M. STANLEY *Dark Cont.* I. xv. 400 They are all comely and brown, with fine virginal bosoms.

b. ***virginal generation***, parthenogenesis.

1879 tr. *Haeckel's Evol. Man* I. ii. 28 The so-called parthenogenesis, or virginal generation, of Bees.

2. Of qualities, actions, etc.: Proper to, characteristic of, a virgin.

c **1411** HOCCLEVE *De Reg. Princ.* 3584 O humble maide! who is it þat can The debonaire humblesse tellen al, Restynge in þy clennesse virginal? **1483** CAXTON *Gold Leg.* 195 b/1 There ben twelue vertues vyrgynal..wyth out whiche no vyrgyne may be agreeable to god. **1493** *Petronilla* 58 (Pynson), She fulfylled his byddynge in certeyn Withoute grutchinge of virgynall mekenesse. *a* **1529** SKELTON *Replyc.* 32 Whiche is the most clere christall Of all pure clennesse virgynall. **1590** SPENSER *F.Q.* II. ix. 20 Gentle court and gracious delight She to them made, with mildnesse virginall. **1608** SHAKS. *Per.* IV. vi. 62 Without any more virginal fencing, will you use him kindly? **1627** DONNE *Serm.* Wks. 1839 V. 613 Where is that Soul?.. Is it come back in the virginal integrity in which I made it? **1640** BP. HALL *Christian Moderation* I. §8. 76 Virginall chastity is a grace worthy of our fervent prayers, worthy of our best endeavors. **1850** KINGSLEY *A. Locke* i, No foundlings educated in a nunnery ever grew up in a more virginal and spotless innocence. **1873** DORAN *Lady of last Cent.* iii. 73 The..affected virginal coyness with which [she]..received ..their rather audacious gallantry. **1891** FARRAR *Darkn. & Dawn* xxx, That beautiful mixture of manly courage and virginal modesty.

transf. **1862** S. LUCAS *Secularia* 133 Many..were privileged to behold the West in all its virginal freshness and splendour. **1868** J. H. NEWMAN *Verses Var. Occas.* 271 He lifts his hands, there issues forth A fragrance virginal and rare.

3. Of persons: Continuing in a state of virginity; having the chastity or purity of a virgin.

1483 CAXTON *Gold. Leg.* 99 b/2 The vyrgynal companye of thynnocentes. **1500–20** DUNBAR *Poems* lxxxv. 79 Bricht ball cristall, ross virginall,..Aue Maria. *a* **1513** FABYAN *Chron.* I. xxvii. 19 Most virgynall flour, of al most excellent. **1546** BALE *Eng. Votaries* I. (1550) 5 Ye shall easely perceyve by their actes, that these virginall votaries hath bene the verye Angels of darkenesse. **1567** ABP. PARKER *Corr.* (Parker Soc.) 304, I would it were indifferently credited to understand, whether the married sort or the virginal pastors had done most spoil to the church. **1867** E. F. BOWDEN *Fathers of Desert* 267 O Virginal Mother, arouse my soul to penance and guide me to the way of salvation. **1886** W. ALEXANDER *St. Aug. Holiday* 14 Such virgin gifts for spirits virginal. **1905** G. THORNE *Lost Cause* xii, She was pure but not virginal in temperament.

4. *transf.* Fresh, pure, unsullied, untouched.

a **1659** OSBORN *Observ. Turks* Wks. (1673) 344 Learning.. resembling dead Honey, which is stale, coorse, and less useful, none being pure and Virginal, but what is sucked from every Flower that may be found in the wild Field of a general Commerce. [**1767** A. CAMPBELL *Lexiph.* I A novel exhibition which is purely virginal.] **1811** W. R. SPENCER *Poems* 152 Shall the earth, 'mid the roses of June, May's virginal violets scorn? **1866** M. ARNOLD *Empedocles* I. ii, The grass is cool, the seaside air Buoyant and fresh, the mountain flowers More virginal and sweet than ours. **1889** JOS. THOMSON *Trav. Morocco* 24 From no point of view..does Tangier look so beautiful and virginal..as from this particular gateway.

virginalist ('vɜːdʒɪnəlɪst). [f. VIRGINAL *sb.* + -IST.] A player on the virginals; a composer for the virginals.

1913 J. E. MATTHEW tr. *C. van den Borren's Sources of Keyboard Mus. in Eng.* iv. 66 After Tallis, John Bull is the only virginalist who still used faux-bourdon as a means of figuration. **1924** M. H. GLYN *About Eliz. Virginal Mus. & its Composers* ii. 22 Had Orlando Gibbons lived out his span instead of dying in his early prime..the English Keyboard school must have attained publication... This music contains seeds which will yet fructify, unknown even to the later seventeenth century musicians, who were not true descendants of the virginalists. **1942** E. BLOM *Mus. in Eng.* xi. 183 The Elizabethan virginalists, for example, liked to base variations on them. **1960** *Times* 4 Mar. 4/6 The Elizabethan virginalists discovered that possibility and exploited it. **1979** *Early Music* Jan. 3 Clearly, there is no reason why the virginalist absolutely *must* have music, but there is a reason in this case why she should not.

virgi'nality. *rare.* [f. VIRGINAL *a.* + -ITY.] The state or quality of being virginal.

a **1450** *Knt. de la Tour* 149 Within her pure uirginalite of her flesshe, blode, and bone, the Sone of God toke humanite. **1721** BAILEY, *Virginality*, Maidenliness. **1965** F. SARGESON *Memoirs of Peon* iv. 67, I was at first a little awed ..by the room's too severe and uncompromising air of virginality.

virginally ('vɜːdʒɪnəlɪ), *adv.* [f. VIRGINAL *a.* + -LY[2].] In a virginal manner; like a virgin.

1882 STEVENSON *Men & B.* 35 Virginally troubled at the fluttering of her dress in the spring wind. **1882** MISS C. P. WOOLSON *Anne* 101 Young ladies, dancing virginally by themselves.

†**vir'gineous**, *a. Obs. rare.* [f. L. *virgine-us* (f. *virgin-*, *virgo* virgin) + -OUS.] Virginal, virgin.

1585–7 ROGERS *39 Art.* Pref. (1607) ¶3 Her Faith, her wisedome,..her virgineous and chast behauiour he would euer celebrate. **1694** MOTTEUX *Rabelais* v. 248 Your Phrase, robustly propt, with ease produces Fractions in many weak Virgineous Cruises.

†**virginet**, var. of (or error for) VIRGINAL *sb.*

?*c* **1680** ASHMOLE *Mem.* (1717) 4 Mr. Henry Hinde, Organist of the Cathedral,..taught me the Virginetts and Organ.

†**virginhead.** *Obs.* [-HEAD.] = next.

1598 SYLVESTER *Du Bartas* II. i. *Eden* 662 Unlike it is, Such blessed state the noble flowr should miss Of Virginhead. **1611** J. DAVIES (Heref.) *Sco. Folly* Ep. cxxv, Two foes of honord name in Honors bed, (The field) desirde (like virgins newly wiues) To lose their valours lusty virgin-head.

'virginhood. [f. VIRGIN *sb.* + -HOOD.] The condition or state of a virgin; virginity.

1636 DAVENANT *Platonick Lovers* 111, To live in sweet unskilfull virgin-hood, The Angels life, for they no sexes know. **1871** BROWNING *Balaust.* 821 But thou, my girl, how will thy virginhood Conclude itself in marriage fittingly?

1874 Withrow *Catacombs of Rome* (1877) 527 The abandonment of the lofty vantage ground of virginhood.

Virginia (və'dʒɪnɪə). [f. L. *virgin-*, *virgo* VIRGIN *sb.* (in honour of Queen Elizabeth) + -IA[1].]

With the various applications of the word cf. those of Virginian *a.*[1]

1. a. The name of that part of North America in which the first English settlement was made in 1607, subsequently one of the original thirteen States of the North American Union, used attrib. in ***Virginia colony, company, landscape, trade***, etc.

1609 in Capt. Smith *Wks.* (Arb.) p. xcviii, I am bold to write the truth of some late accidentes, be falne his Maiesties Virginia collonye. **1611** *Ibid.* 641 It came to be apprehended by some of the Virginia Company. **1773** in *Nairne Peerage Evidence* (1874) 170 Copertners in a Virginia trade carryed on by them under the firm of Oswald Dennistoun and Company. **1781** *Ann. Reg., Hist.* 47/1 The Virginia militia gave the British troops a warm reception. **1855** Kingsley *Westw. Ho!* xxix, [They] joyfully unloaded their Virginia goods, and replaced them with powder and shot. **1888** *Encycl. Brit.* XXIV. 256/2 The most striking feature of thousands of square miles of Virginia landscape.

b. In names of plants and trees, as ***Virginia cedar, corn, ivy, pea, tobacco, wheat***; **Virginia bluebell, cowslip**, a perennial herb, *Mertensia virginica*, of the family Boraginaceæ, native to eastern North America and bearing clusters of blue flowers; cf. *Virginian cowslip* s.v. COWSLIP 2 e; **Virginia creeper**, *Ampelopsis hederacea* and *quinquefolia*, common climbing plants of the family *Vitaceæ*; **Virginia vine** (see quots.).

Also ***Virginia snake-root, spiderwort, stock, sumach, witch-hazel***: see the sbs.

1934 Webster, *Virginia bluebell. **1939** *Nat. Geogr. Mag.* Aug. 236/2 The pale-blue flowers and rosy-pink buds of the Virginia bluebells . . are clustered on slender branches. **1978** *Detroit Free Press* 16 Apr. (Gardening Guide) 12/2 Virginia bluebells . . can be purchased from special wild-flower nurseries. **1731** Miller *Gard. Dict.* s.v. *Juniperus*, The three Sorts of *Virginia Cedars . . afford excellent Timber for many Uses. **1888** *Encycl. Brit.* XXIV. 258/2 The principal timber trees . . are . . yellow or pitch pine; red or Virginia cedar. **1621** in Capt. Smith *Wks.* (Arb.) 564 Whatsoeuer is said against the *Virginia Corne, they finde it doth better nourish than any prouision is sent thither. [**1826** W. Darlington *Florula Cestrica* 23 Pulmonaria . . virginica . . Virginian Cowslip.] **1901** N. L. Britton *Man. Flora Northern States & Canada* 771 *Virginia cowslip... In low meadows and along streams. **1944** G. L. Nute *Lake Superior* 293 By July 1 the Virginia cowslips are coming into bloom. **1968** Peterson & McKenny *Field Guide to Wildflowers* 322 Virginia cowslip... The nodding, trumpetlike flowers are pink in bud. **1704** Petiver *Gazophyl.* II. xiv, This adheres to Trees by its hoary fibres, as our *Virginia Creeper does to Walls by its tendrels. **1786** Abercrombie *Gard. Assist.* 153 Train and nail climbers—to walls, &c. as virgin's bower, passion flower, Virginia creeper, &c. **1857** Henfrey *Bot.* §452 The species of *Ampelopsis* known as 'Virginia Creepers' exhibit some interesting phænomena. **1870** Dickens *E. Drood* ii, The Virginia creeper on the cathedral wall has showered half its deep-red leaves down on the pavement. **1629** Parkinson *Parad.* 612 *Vitis, seu potius Hedera Virginensis*, the *Virginia Vine, or rather Iuie. **1607** in Capt. Smith *Wks.* (Arb.) 97 We daily feasted with good bread, *Virginia pease, pumpions, and putchamins. **1657** Coles *Adam in Eden* 333 Some have called the yellow Lupine Spanish Violets, . . and . . *Virginia Roses. **1706** Phillips (ed. Kersey), **Virginia-Tobacco*, the Tobacco-Plant growing in those Parts. **1786** Abercrombie *Gard. Assist.* 115 Sow . . cape-marigold, yellow sultan, Virginia tobacco, &c. **1629** Parkinson *Parad.* 564 The *Virginia Vine . . beareth small Grapes without any great store of iuice therein. *Ibid.* 612 This slender, but tall climing Virginia Vine (as it was first called; but Iuie, as it doth better resemble). **1651** R. Child in *Hartlib's Legacy* (1655) 36 The hill where their Corn is planted, called *Virginia-Wheat. **1688** *Phil. Trans.* XVII. 978 English Wheat (as they call it, to distinguish it from Maze, commonly called Virginia Wheat).

c. In names of birds, insects, etc., as ***Virginia bat, chafer, didapper, frog, goatsucker, rail*** (cf. RAIL *sb.*[3]), ***red-bird, snap-beetle, squirrel***; **Virginia nightingale**, the cardinal grosbeak.

1688 *Phil. Trans.* XVII. 991 The Night Raven, which some call the *Virginia Bat, is about the bigness of a Cuckow. **1704** Petiver *Gazophyl.* Dec. III. Tab. xxvii, Marshal's *Virginia Chaffer. **1688** *Phil. Trans.* XVII. 997 Teale, Wigeon, . . *Virginia-Didapers. **1706** Phillips (ed. Kersey), **Virginia-Frog*, a kind of Frog, that . . makes a noise like the bellowing of a Bull. **1783** Latham *Gen. Synop. Birds* II. II. 595 *Virginia Goatsucker . . inhabits Virginia in summer; arrives there towards the middle of April. **1688** *Phil. Trans.* XVII. 995 Of *Virginia Nightingale, or red Bird, there are two sorts. **1695** *Lond. Gaz.* No. 3108/4 A Parcel of choice Virginia Nightingales, with choice Mock-Birds, . . are to be sold by Tho. Bland. **1706** Phillips (ed. Kersey), *Virginia-Nightingale*, a Bird of a pure scarlet Colour, with a tuft on the Head. **1731** [see RED *a.* and *sb.*[1] 17 b]. **1808** A. Wilson *Amer. Ornith.* (1831) II. 273 Numbers . . having been carried over both to France and England, in which last country they are usually called Virginia nightingales. **1783** Latham *Gen. Synop. Birds* II. II. 777 *Tetrao Virginianus*, *Virginia Partridge, smaller than the Common Partridge. **1828** C. L. Bonaparte *Genera N. Amer. Birds* 334 The *Virginia Rail . . inhabits throughout North America. **1914** *Chambers's Jrnl.* July 439/1 The Virginia rail . . is rare. **1945** *Bull. Mass. Audubon Soc.* Mar. 63 At the Sanctuary on this date we might get the Virginia Rail. **1808** A. Wilson *Amer. Ornith.* (1831) II. 276 They are generally known by the names of red-bird, *Virginia red-bird, . . and crested red-bird. **1702** Petiver *Gazophyl.* I. § 10 The Velvet-eyed *Virginia Snap-Beetle. **1609** in Capt. Smith *Wks.* (Arb.) p. c, I tould him of the *Virginia squirills which they say will fly.

d. Miscellaneous combs., as ***Virginia cigarette, ham, tobacco*** (cf. 2); **Virginia fence**, a rail fence made in a zig-zag manner; ***to make a V. fence*** (see quot. 1861); **Virginia reel**, a country-dance.

1919 *Honey Pot* I. 1. Advt. facing p. 1, The best *Virginia cigarette I have ever smoked. **1745** Franklin *Drinker's Dict.* Wks. 1887 II. 26 He [being drunk] makes a *Virginia fence. **1789** Anburey *Trav.* II. 324 The New Englanders have a saying when a man is in liquor, he is making Virginia fences. **1826** T. Flint *Recollections* 206 The universal fence split rails, laid in a worm trail, or what is known in the North by the name of Virginia fence. **1844** P. H. Gosse in *Zoologist* II. 708 The fences, which are almost wholly made of rails set up in the zig-zag fashion so general in the north, commonly called a Virginia fence. **1861** Lowell *Biglow P.* Ser. II. Introd., Poet. Wks. (1912) 285 'Virginia fence, to make a:' to walk like a drunken man. **1833** *Virginny ham [see MUDLARK *sb.* 1]. **1908** Virginia ham [see *chicken gumbo* s.v. CHICKEN *sb.*[1] 8]. **1976** Virginia ham [see *Virginia tobacco* below.]. **1859** Bartlett *Dict. Amer.* (ed. 2) 497 **Virginia reel*, the common name throughout the United States for the old English 'country-danse'. **1694** Salmon *Bate's Dispens.* (1713) 14/1 If you steep good *Virginia Tobacco in the Water, . . it will be much more effectual. **1747** W. Douglas *Brit. Settlements N. Amer.* (1760) I. 116 Virginia tobacco, and Brazil, and Varinas tobacco, differ upon this account. **1976** *Times* 3 Jan. 11/6 Smells of herbs and Virginia tobacco fill the air . . the menu offered . . Virginia ham steak from Surrey County.

2. *ellipt.* A variety of tobacco grown and manufactured in Virginia. Hence, a cigarette made of Virginia tobacco. Cf. VIRGIN *sb.* 10. Also *attrib.*

1618 in Capt. Smith *Wks.* (Arb.) 541 There are so many sofisticating Tobaco-mungers in England, were it neuer so bad, they would sell it for Verinas, and the trash that remaineth should be Virginia. **1650** B. *Discolliminium* 47 My bare purse will reach no higher then to Democraticall Virginia, which many times tasts like some Levellers old leathern linings. **1681** T. Flatman *Heraclitus Ridens* No. 9 (1713) I. 53 The Reforming Troops . . offering the Incense of Virginia, and the Drink-offering of the Bottle, to their Idol of the Long-sword. **1712** Addison *Spect.* No. 329 ¶6 He bid him stop by the way at any good Tobacconist's, and take in a Roll of their best Virginia. **1803** Sir A. Boswell *Spirit of Tintoc* xix, He's ta'en his spleuchan frae his breeks For a quid o' the right Virginia. **1864** Hawthorne *S. Felton* (1883) 301 A . . German pipe . . puffed out volumes of smoke, filling the pleasant western breeze with the fragrance of some excellent Virginia. **1964** D. E. Middleton in C. K. Stead *N.Z. Short Stories* (1966) 205 Now we can enjoy another of Blackie's virginias. **1971** R. Dentry *Encounter at Kharmel* ix. 171 Do you mind if I smoke my Virginias?

3. *Astr.* One of the minor planets.

1868 Lockyer *Elem. Astron.* 328 Minor Planets [include] . . 48. Doris. 49. Pales. 50. Virginia. **1875** *Encycl. Brit.* II. 807/2 Virginia [discovered] 1857, October 4 [by] Ferguson [at] Washington.

Virginian (və'dʒɪnɪən), *sb.* and *a.*[1] [f. prec. + -AN.]

A. *sb.* **a.** One of the aboriginal natives or inhabitants of Virginia.

1588 Hariot *Brief Rep. Virginia* B 1 b, [If mulberry trees are planted] there will rise as greate profite in time to the Virginians, as . . doth now to the Persians. **1607–12** in Capt. Smith *Wks.* (Arb.) 79 Of the manner of the Virginians governement. **1619** Middleton *Love & Antiq.* in Bullen *O. Pl.* VII. 321 The civilly instructed Irishman, and that kind savage the Virginian. **1719** De Foe *Crusoe* I. (Globe) 209 The Brasilians, and Virginians, and other Natives of America. **1859** Thackeray *Virginians* xl, A young savage Iroquois, Choctaw, or Virginian, who has lately been making a little noise in our quarter of the globe.

b. A white settler in Virginia; a native or inhabitant of the modern State of Virginia.

1654 in *Colonial Rec. N. Carolina* (1886) I. 18 Sir, if you think good to acquaint the States with what is done by two Virginians born, you will honour our country. **1755** W. Smith *Brief State Province of Pennsylvania* 15 'Tis true our Neighbours, the Virginians, have taken the Alarm, and called on our Assistance. **1797** *Encycl. Brit.* (ed. 3) XVIII. 659/1 The Virginians who are rich, are in general sensible, polite, and hospitable and of an independent spirit. **1843** *Penny Cycl.* XXVI. 372/2 Parts of the Navigation Laws were deemed highly injurious to the interests of the Virginians. **1876** Bancroft *Hist. U.S.* III. xiii. 208 Two regiments composed of Pennsylvanians, Marylanders, and Virginians, remained as a garrison.

B. *adj.* **a.** Of, belonging or relating to, the State of Virginia; connected with or interested in Virginia.

With the various applications of the adj., cf. the attributive uses of Virginia.

1609–12 in Capt. Smith *Wks.* (Arb.) 169 For the honorable and better sort of our Virginian adventurers, I think they vnderstand it as I haue writ it. **1614** Chapman *Masque Inns of Court* A ij, On their heads high sprig'd-feathers, compast in Coronets, like the Virginian Princes they presented. **1781** *Ann. Reg., Hist.* 46/2 The second line [was composed] of Virginian militia. *a* **1797** H. Walpole *Geo. II* (1822) I. 346 An Indian half king, . . who in the Virginian accounts is called a very considerable monarch. **1839** Thackeray *Virginians* vi, The scanty pay and patronage of the Virginian government. **1876** Bancroft *Hist. U.S.* I. xx. 545 Virginian and Maryland volunteers joined together, and . . besieged the fort.

b. In names of plants and trees, as ***Virginian anemone, azarole, bindweed, cowslip, date plum, dogwood, fir, grape, guelder-rose, hemp, ivy, jasmine, poplar***, etc.; † **Virginian climber**, = MARACOCK; **Virginian creeper**, = *Virginia creeper.*

Also ***Virginian poke, snake-root, spider-wort, stock, sumach, witch-hazel***: see the sbs.

1822 *Hortus Angl.* II. 50 *Virginian Anemone... Petals green; flower-stalks long; seeds shaggy. **1785** Martyn *Lett. Bot.* xxi. (1794) 290 *Virginian Azarole has oval leaves wedge-shaped at the base, shining and deeply serrate. **1731** Miller *Gard. Dict.* s.v. *Smilax*, Rough *Virginian Bindweed, with a smooth Ivy Leaf, commonly call'd Zarzaparilla. *Ibid.* s.v. *Juniperus*, Red *Virginian Cedar *Ibid.*, The White-berry'd Virginian Cedar. **1861** Bentley *Man. Bot.* 660 *Juniperus virginiana*, the Virginian Red Cedar. **1688** Holme *Armoury* II. 68/2 The *Virginian Climber; . . these Flowers are of a whitish colour, thick spotted with a Peach colour. **1704** *Dict. Rust.* (1726), *Virginian Climber*, or *Maracac*, comes out of the Ground in May with long round winding Stalks. **1856** A. Gray *Man. Bot.* (1860) 323 *Mertensia Virginica*, *Virginian Cowslip or Lungwort. **1882** *Garden* 20 May 352/1 The Virginian Cowslip . . attains true development in semi-shady spots. **1856** A. Gray *Man. Bot.* (1860) 78 *Ampelopsis*, . . *Virginian Creeper. **1871** H. Macmillan *True Vine* ii. (1872) 41 The Virginian creeper is known to botanists by the generic name of Ampelopsis, derived from its vine-like habit of growth. **1866** *Treas. Bot.* 411/2 *Diospyros virginiana* is the *Virginian Date Plum or Persimon, a native of the United States. **1725** *Fam. Dict.*, **Virginian-Dogwood*, a Tree of the natural growth of Virginia, about the size of the common Cherry-Tree, blossoming early in the Spring. **1731** Miller *Gard. Dict.* s.v. *Abies*, The *Virginian Firr Tree, with small roundish Cones. *Ibid.* s.v. *Vitis*, The wild *Virginian Grape. **1829** T. Castle *Introd. Bot.* 95 The *Virginian gelder-rose, a common garden shrub, affords a very perfect specimen of this kind of inflorescence. **1829** Loudon *Encycl. Plants* 834 *Acnida*, . . *Virginian Hemp. [Cf. HEMP 5.] **1731** Miller *Gard. Dict.* s.v. *Hedera*, Round-leav'd *Virginian Ivy. **1664** Evelyn *Kal. Hort.* Sept. 75 Yellow *Virginian Jasmine. **1882** *Garden* 29 April 297/1 The pure blue of *Virginian Lungwort combines happily with alpine Auriculas. **1731** Miller *Gard. Dict.* s.v. *Acer*, The *Virginian flowering Maple was rais'd from Seeds which were brought from Virginia. **1669** Evelyn *Kal. Hort.* (ed. 3) Aug. 23, Single flowers, Shrub Spiræa, *Agnus Castus*, the *Virginian Martagon, *Malva arborescens*. **1725** *Fam. Dict.* s.v., *Virginian-Myrtle, otherwise call'd Candle-Berry-Tree. **1843** *Penny Cycl.* XXV. 341/2 *Tulip-tree*, the English name of the *Liriodendron tulipifera*: . . in America, where it is a native, it is also known by the names White wood, . . *Virginian Poplar, and the Poplar. **1731** Miller *Gard. Dict.* s.v. *Rubus*, The *Virginian Raspberry-bush with black Fruit. *Ibid.* s.v. *Rosa*, The Wild *Virginian Rose. **1629** Parkinson *Parad.* 444 *Virginian Silke. **1731** Miller *Gard. Dict.*, *Periploca*, Virginian Silk... The Flower consists of one Leaf. **1860** *Chambers's Encycl.* I. 468/1 *Asclepias Syriaca*, Syrian or Virginian Swallow-wort, sometimes called Virginian Silk, appears to be a native of North America... It is frequently cultivated in flower-gardens. **1866** *Treas. Bot.* 1219/1 Virginian Silk, *Periploca græca*. **1731** Miller *Gard. Dict.* s.v. *Veronica*, Tall *Virginian Speedwell, with many Spikes and white Flowers. **1829** Loudon *Encycl. Pl.* (1839) 196 *Asclepias syriaca*, *Virginian Swallow-wort. **1860** [see *Virginian silk* above]. **1842** *Penny Cycl.* XXIV. 217/2 *T. Virginiana*, the *Virginian Tephrosia, . . is a handsome plant with reddish flowers. **1844** Stephens *Bk. Farm* I. 393 The cock's-spur-thorn (*Cratægus crus galli*) and the *Virginian thorn (*C. Virginiana*) have been proposed. **1741** *Compl. Fam.-Piece* II. iii. 386 There are several other Trees and Shrubs which are now in Flower, as . . *Virginian Trumpet-flower. Olives, . . Capers. **1640** Howell *Dodona's Gr.* 180 In this *Virginian-Vine, the saying of the wisest of Kings may be verifyed, That a good Wife is a Tree of life. **1731** Miller *Gard. Dict.* s.v. *Vitis*, The Virginian Vine or Common Creeper. **1725** *Fam. Dict.*, **Virginian Wild Crab-tree*, a Plant that blossoms somewhat like the Apple, but very pleasant to the Smell.

c. In names of birds, quadrupeds, etc., as ***Virginian colin, deer, nightingale, owl***, etc.

1843 Yarrell *Brit. Birds* II. 348 *Ortyx Virginiana*, *Virginian Colin. **1781** Pennant *Quad.* I. 104 *Virginian Deer with slender horns... A quite distinct species, and peculiar to America. *c* **1880** *Cassell's Nat. Hist.* III. 68 The Virginian Deer . . is the 'Common' Deer of North America, and is slightly smaller than the Fallow Deer. *Ibid.* 301 The Eagle Owl . . and its relative, the *Virginian Eared Owl of America, are the largest of all the family. **1801** Shaw *Gen. Zool.* II. I. 155 *Virginian Flying Squirrel. *Sciurus Volucella.* **1817** Stephens *Ibid.* X. I. 153 *Virginian Goatsucker. *Caprimulgus virginianus.* **1809** *Ibid.* VII. I. 215 *Virginian Horned Owl. *Strix Virginiana.* **1668** Charleton *Onomast.* 85 *Coccothraustes Virginiana*, . . the *Virginian Nightingale. **1753** *Chambers' Cycl.* Suppl. s.v. *Nightingale*, *Virginian Nightingale*, . . the common, but improper, name of a bird of the gross-beaked kind. **1775** Sheridan *Duenna* II. i, She is a nightingale—a Virginian nightingale. **1896** P. A. Bruce *Econ. Hist. Virginia* I. 119 The cardinal or red bird, which was always described as the Virginian nightingale, on account of the clearness and strength rather than the variety of its notes. **1800** Shaw *Gen. Zool.* I. II. 473 *Didelphis Virginiana*. *Virginian Opossum. **1843** Yarrell *Brit. Birds* II. 348 *Perdix Virginiana*, *Virginian Partridge. **1884** *St. James' Gaz.* 28 Apr. 6/2 The so-called Virginian partridge . . has unaccountably failed to adapt himself to the English climate. **1867** *Chambers's Encycl.* IX. 809 *Virginian Quail, or Colin (*Ortyx*), a genus of birds of the family *Tetraonidæ*, closely allied to quails and partridges. *c* **1880** *Cassell's Nat. Hist.* IV. 144 Some of the American Partridges are familiar to us in this country, such as the Virginian Quail (*Ortyx virginianus*). **1785** Latham *Gen. Synop. Birds* III. I. 228 *Rallus Virginianus*, *Virginian Rail. [Hence in Pennant (1792) and Stephens (1824).] *a* **1700** Evelyn *Diary* 19 Sept. 1657, 2 *Virginian rattle-snakes. **1774** Goldsm. *Nat. Hist.* (1824) II. 71 The grey *Virginian squirrel . . is larger than a rabbit, and of a greyish colour. **1783** Latham *Gen. Synop. Birds* II. II. 546 *Parus Virginianus*, *Virginian Titmouse. [Hence in Pennant (1792) and Stephens (1817).]

d. Miscellaneous uses, as **Virginian plate, silver** (see quot.); **Virginian sea**, that part of the Atlantic Ocean lying off the coast of Virginia; † **Virginian vapour**, tobacco-smoke.

In quot. 1617 (and under VIRGIN *sb.* 12) *Virginian* is an error for *Vergivian*, an epithet (derived from Ptolemy) of the Irish Sea.

1864 STRAUSS, etc. *Eng. Workshops* 60 This new compound to which the inventors have given the name of *Virginian plate or Virginian silver. **1612** CAPT. SMITH *Map of Virginia* Map, The *Virginian Sea. [**1617** MORYSON *Itin.* III. 156 This famous Iland in the Virginian Sea, is by olde Writers called Ierna,..by the English at this time Ireland.] **1888** *Encycl. Brit.* XXIV. 256/1 On the S. it is bounded by North Carolina and Tennessee,..and on the E. by the Virginian Sea of the Atlantic Ocean. **1631** LENTON *Charact.* F 7, He..then liues by *Virginian vapour a week after.

†**vir'ginian,** *a.*² *Obs.* [f. VIRGIN *sb.* + -IAN.] Virginal; virgin.

1613 PURCHAS *Pilgrimage* (1614) 754 Whether it be Virginian modestie, and after the vse of Virgins, shee would say nay at first. **1758** *Elaboratory laid Open* 319 The best virginian honey.

†**vir'ginic,** *a. Chem. Obs.* Also **virgineic.** [f. VIRGIN-IAN *a.*¹ + -IC.] ***virginic acid,*** an acid obtained from the fat-oil of Virginian snake-root.

1837 R. D. THOMSON in *Brit. Ann.* 350 *Virginic acid*... Quevenne considers the whole of the oil to constitute the acid to which he has applied a name from Virginia, from whence the plant was originally sent by Dr. Tennant..in 1738. **1868** WATTS *Dict. Chem.* V. 1002.

'Virgin 'Islander [f. *Virgin Island(s* + -ER¹.] A native or inhabitant of (one of) the Virgin Islands, the westernmost islands of the Lesser Antilles, which are divided between Great Britain and the United States.

1931 *Ann. Rep. Governor Virgin Islands* 1 In replacing Navy personnel of the former administration, more than 40 per cent Virgin Islanders have been appointed to office. **1955** A. A. ALEXANDER in *Ibid.* 4 There are no colleges or schools of business administration here, and many Virgin Islanders who go to the continental United States for such training do not return. **1975** M. ORR *Rich Girl, Poor Girl* xix. 259 The lilting tones of the native Virgin Islander.

virginity (və'dʒɪnɪtɪ). Forms: 4–5 **virgynyte**, 6 **-ite**; 4–6 **vyrgynyte**, 5 **-enyte**, 6 **-inite**; 4–6 **virginite** (**-itee**, 4 **wirginite**, 5 *Sc.* **verginite**), 5 **-yte**, 5–7 **-itie**, 6– **virginity**. [a. AF. and OF. *virginite* (mod.F. *virginité*, = It. *verginità*, *virginità*, Sp. *virginidad*, Pg. *-idade*), ad. L. *virginitāt-*, *virginitas*, f. *virgin-*, stem of *virgo*: see VIRGIN *sb.* and -ITY.]

1. The condition of being or remaining in a state of chastity; abstinence from or avoidance of all sexual relations; bodily chastity, as a virtue of great commendation, or as conferring especial merit or sanctity; the mode of life characterized by this, esp. as adopted from religious motives.

a. Of persons of either sex (or without special limitation of sex).

a **1300** *Cursor M.* 24681 Man or wornman, queþer it be, þat liues in wirginite, Quat fanding þat þai fele. **1377** LANGL. *P. Pl.* B. XVI. 203 Wedloke and widwehode with virgynyte ynempned, In toknynge of þe Trinite was taken oute of o man. *c* **1386** CHAUCER *Wife's Prol.* 62 When sawe ye in eny maner age That highe God defendid mariage By expres word?..Or wher commaunded he virginite? **1526** *Pilgr. Perf.* (W. de W. 1531) 83 Well may virginite be compared to a floure. Nothynge is more fayre, more beautefull, ne more pleasaunt than is virginite. **1547–64** BAULDWIN *Mor. Philos.* (Palfr.) VII. vii, The first degree of chastity is pure virginity, and the second faithfull matrimony. **1570** ASCHAM *Scholem.* (Arb.) I. 85 Commonlie they cum home, common contemners of mariage..: not because they loue virginitie, nor yet because they hate prettie yong virgines, but [etc.]. **1651** CARTWRIGHT *Cert. Relig.* I. 174 Origen..saith that such as live in virginity, doe not that which is commanded, but above what is due. *a* **1711** KEN *Psyche* Poet. Wks. 1721 IV. 256 Virginity's a Heav'nly tender Grace, Connatural to the angelick Race. **1837** HALLAM *Hist. Lit.* I. vi. §7 The faculty of theology at Paris, censured the Colloquies for slighting the fasts of the church, virginity, monkery, pilgrimages, and other established parts of the religious system. **1840** NEWMAN *Par. Serm.* V. vii. 103 Therefore marriage was in repute and virginity in disesteem. **1871** FREEMAN *Norm. Conq.* (1876) IV. xix. 422 An exaggerated reverence for virginity had been growing up in the Church from the beginning.

b. Of men (esp. ecclesiastics or other religious persons).

c **1375** *Sc. Leg. Saints* xxxvi. (*Baptist*) 14 Angele als callit wes he [John the Baptist], fore kepyng of verginite. **1382** WYCLIF *John* Prol., Double witnesse of virgynyte is 3ouun to hym..in this that he is said loued of God byfor othere disciplis. **1430–40** LYDG. *Bochas* I. (Bodl. MS.) 58/2 He lyued euer in virgynyte. **1456** *Coventry Leet Bk.* 288 *John Euaungelist*. Holy Edward, crownyd kyng, brothur in virgynyte. **1585** T. WASHINGTON tr. *Nicholay's Voy.* III. xvi. 101 Hee that wil enter into this religion must..obserue..virginitie and abstinence. **1615** BEDWELL *Moham. Impost.* II. §68 By this perfection, that is, by virginitie, it is knowne that he was of God accepted for his perfection. **1657** FARINDON *Serm.* (1672) II. 1191 Some have placed Perfection in Virginity,..making themselves eunuchs for the kingdom of heaven; and have laid an imputation upon the state of Matrimony as most imperfect. **1658** BROMHALL *Treat. Specters* v. 307 [He] defended the married Priests against the Monks, which observed the vow of Virginity. **1868** FREEMAN *Norm. Conq.* (1877) II. App. 538 The resolution of Eadward..to devote himself to a life of perpetual virginity. **1884** *Cath. Dict.* 556/2 Catholic feeling..has attached itself strongly to the virginity of St. Joseph.

c. Of women. Also in phrases ***flower, gem,*** etc., ***of virginity,*** chiefly with reference to the Virgin Mary.

c **1386** CHAUCER *Pars. T.* ⁋948 The thridde manere of chastitee is virginitee, and it behoueth þat she be hooly in herte and clene of body, thanne is she spouse of Ihesu crist and she is the lyf of Angeles. **1390** GOWER *Conf.* II. 336 And thus cam this Calistona Into the wode of Tegea, Wher sche virginite behihte Unto Diane. *c* **1410** HOCCLEVE *Mother of God* 65 Wel oghten we thee worsshipe & honure, Paleys of Cryst, flour of virginitee. **1432–50** tr. *Higden* (Rolls) VI. 91 Seynte Etheldreda,..whiche contynuede in virginite thauȝhe sche was mariede twyes. **1447** BOKENHAM *Seyntys* Introd. (Roxb.) 6 Whan I gan inwardly to remembre..Of hyr that is gemme of virgynyte. **1500–20** DUNBAR *Poems* lxxxvi. 17 Roiss Mary,..O chast conclaif of clene virginite, That closit Crist but crymes criminale. **1540** HYRDE tr. *Vives' Instr. Chr. Wom.* I. vi. (1541) 15 b, Virginite was euer an holy thinge euen amonge theues, breakers of Sayntuary, vngratious liuers [etc.]. **1603** DEKKER *Patient Grissill* 816 Master Farneze, sweet virginitie is that inuisible God-head, that turns vs into Angells, that makes vs saints on earth, and starres in heauen. **1634** MILTON *Comus* 738 List Lady,..be not cosen'd With that same vaunted name Virginity. **1711** ADDISON *Spect.* No. 164 ⁋5 That Vow of Virginity in which she [a novice] was going to engage herself. **1911** *Edin. Rev.* July 62 Jacqueline aspired to the veil, dedicated herself to virginity and the spiritual life.

d. Personified.

c **1400** *Pilgr. Sowle* (Caxton, 1483) IV. iv. 60 This noble lady was suster to Aungels and was cleped vyrgynyte. *c* **1420** LYDG. *Assembly of Gods* 842 Many pety capteyns aftyr these went, As..Clennesse, Continence, and Virginite.

2. a. The state or condition of a virgin or chaste woman; chastity, as the natural or normal condition of an unmarried woman; maidenhood. Also, a condition affording presumption of chastity; spinsterhood.

1303 R. BRUNNE *Handl. Synne* 2875 Graunte me two moneþes ar y dye, þat y may wepe my virginite. **13..** *E.E. Allit. P.* B. 1071 By how comly a kest he was clos þere, When venkkyst was no vergynyte, ne vyolence maked. *c* **1400** *Laud Troy Bk.* 18560 For me is leuere in my contre Be sclayn in my virginite, That I falle not in 3oure handis, þan go with 3ow. *c* **1425** WYNTOUN *Cron.* III. 130 þat scho mycht murnand be Twa moneth hir virginite. **1500–20** DUNBAR *Poems* lxxxiv. 13 Evin so women wairis thair virginitie On thame that maist ar holdin onworthie. **1588** SHAKS. *L.L.L.* I. i. 298, I denie her Virginitie: I was taken with a Maide. **1634** SIR T. HERBERT *Trav.* 20 The [Malagasy] youth scarce knowing twelue, the maid ten years in the World, the title of Virginity. **1709** ADDISON *Tatler* No. 102 ⁋1 Some pleaded their unspotted Virginity; others their numerous issue. **1750** JOHNSON *Rambler* No. 39 ⁋5 The reproach and solitude of antiquated virginity. **1796** H. HUNTER tr. *St.-Pierre's Stud. Nat.* (1799) II. 543 They dispense premiums on virginity! **1825** SCOTT *Lett.* 24 Aug. in *Lockhart*, The celebrated 'Ladies'..who..selected this charming spot for the repose of their time-honoured virginity. **1884** *Cath. Dict.* 556/2 Mary, then, was the Virgin Mother of God. She remained in perpetual virginity.

b. Freq. in phrases, esp. with possessives, as ***to ravish, rob,*** etc. (a woman's) ***virginity***; ***to keep, lose,*** etc. (one's) ***virginity***; sometimes with approximation to a concrete sense.

1390 GOWER *Conf.* II. 316 Thus this tirant there Beraft hire such thing as men sein Mai neveremor be yolde ayein, And that was the virginite. *Ibid.* 339 To robbe the virginite Of a yong innocent aweie. ?**1402** QUIXLEY *Ballade* xii. in *Yorksh. Archæol. Jrnl.* (1908) XX. 46 This Tereus kyng, The virginite rauysht by treson Of Philomene. *c* **1440** *Gesta Rom.* ix. 23 (Harl. MS.), Whan he was ded, þer come a knyȝt, and spoiled me of my virginite. **1485** CAXTON *St. Wenefr.* 9 She chase leuer the smytynge of of her hede than to lose her vyrgynyte. **1563–83** FOXE *A. & M.* 94/2 Her heare hanging about her shoulders in two parts deuided (wherewith her shamefast chastitie and virginitie was couered). **1599** SHAKS. *Much Ado* IV. i. 49 If you..Haue vanquisht the resistance of her youth, And made defeat of her virginitie. **1622** ROWLANDS *Good Newes & B.* 21 Since Nans Virginity past help is lost, They'l teach him what a maidenhead will cost. *c* **1706** PRIOR *True Maid* 1 For my Virginity, When I lose that, says Rose, I'll dye. **1728** CHAMBERS *Cycl.* s.v., That the next Relation..of the Maid's, shall undertake to enjoy her before him, and take away her Virginity. **1759** A. BUTLER *Lives Saints* (1821) X. 489 These holy martyrs seem..to have met a glorious death in defence of their virginity from the army of the Huns. **1866** B. TAYLOR *On Leaving California* Poems 272 Mother of mighty men, thou shalt not mourn Thy lost virginity.

fig. **1652** CRASHAW *Carmen Deo Nostro, 3rd Elegy* 6 O had he nere been at that cruell cost Nature's virginity had nere been lost.

†**c.** With *a* or pl. *Obs.*

1604 E. G[RIMSTONE] *D'Acosta's Hist. Indies* v. xv. 367 Some were appoynted to serve the Guacas and Sanctuaries, keeping their virginities for ever. **1632** LITHGOW *Trav.* IV. 157 The men..and the Virgines..both shall haue their Virginities renewed, as fast, as lost. **1634** W. TIRWHYT tr. *Balzac's Lett.* 269 Nor was every any virginity so brittle, as that she brought into the world.

d. Used as a title: A virgin or unmarried woman. *rare*⁻¹.

1755 MRS. F. BROOKE *Old Maid* No. 9. 64 You must know then, my good sister virginity, that [etc.].

3. a. *fig.* The state of being virgin, fresh, or new.

1610 G. FLETCHER *Christ's Vict.* II. lix, See, see the flowers that..blowe, And of all, the virgin rose,..How they all unleavied die, Loosing their virginitie. **1639** FULLER *Holy War* xix. (1647) 31 Cana the less.., where he shewed the virginity of his miracles, turning water into wine. **1692** SOUTH *Serm.* (1744) XI. 8 As the purest water.., when it slides into a dirty and a muddy Kennel, it immediately loses its clearness and virginity. **18..** WHITTIER *Pr. Wks.* (1889) II. 187 What avail your abstract theories, your hopeless virginity of democracy, sacred from the violence of meanings? **1896** *Daily News* 14 Feb. 5/4 Pretty well for what Lord Rosebery would call the virginity of the Session. **1915** J. KELMAN *Salted with Fire* ix. 121 Men's prejudices..had destroyed what Ruskin calls the virginity of the eye, and it was the main endeavour of Jesus to restore it.

b. *transf.* (The appearance of) virtue or integrity; innocence, inexperience. Also with adj. indicating a sphere of activity. Cf. VIRGIN *sb.* 2 f.

1975 *Listener* 10 Apr. 468/1 She turned down £20,000 for half-a-day's advertising work. 'I'm selling my virginity,' she said. 'At least, that's what they're bidding for.' **1978** T. L. SMITH *Money War* I. 21 The President does not want to know... They all want it handled discreetly. And they all wish to maintain their virginity. **1982** *Times* 15 Feb. 4/2 He could claim no political virginity since he..had been an elected delegate at both Conservative and Labour conferences.

Hence **vir'ginityship**, spinsterhood.

1741 MRS. MONTAGU *Lett.* I. 299 Old Virginityship is certainly Milton's Hell 'Where hope ne'er comes that comes to all.'

virginium (və'dʒɪnɪəm). *Obs.* exc. *Hist.* [f. VIRGINIA, name of a state of the U.S. + -IUM.] = FRANCIUM.

1932 F. ALLISON et al. in *Jrnl. Amer. Chem. Soc.* LIV. 615 We suggest the name virginium and the symbol Va for element 87. **1936** [see ALABAMINE]. **1938** *Encycl. Brit. Bk. of Year* 145/1 The discovery of element No. 87 has again been announced, this time with the name of Mavadium instead of Virginium. **1975** *Jrnl. Chem. Educ.* LII. 585/2 These two new elements he called virginium, after his native state, and alabamine, after the institute and state in which he worked.

'virgin-like, *a.* and *adv.* [f. VIRGIN *sb.*]

A. *adj.* Resembling a virgin or that of a virgin; characteristic of or befitting a virgin; maidenlike.

1586 T. B. *La Primaud. Fr. Acad.* I. 432 Oh cursed and furious envie!..seeing by thee man was first beguiled, and induced afterward..to water the earth, being yet virgine-like, with his brothers blood. *a* **1593** MARLOWE & NASHE *Dido* III. iii, And here we met faire Venus virgine like, Bearing her bowe and quiuer at her backe. **1603** FLORIO *Montaigne* III. v. 520 When I heare them bragge to have so virgin-like a will and colde minde. **1611** SHAKS. *Cymb.* III. ii. 22 Oh damn'd paper,..Art thou a Fœdarie for this Act, and look'st So Virgin-like without? **1721** STRYPE *Eccl. Mem.* II. 376 [To] restore unto it again that Virgin-like Attire. *a* **1794** SIR W. JONES *Enchanted Fruit* Wks. 1799 VI. 189 Rich bowls.., Some virgin-like in native pride, And some with strong Haldea dyed. **1848** THACKERAY *Van. Fair* iii, She had previously made a respectful virgin-like curtsey to the gentleman.

B. *adv.* = VIRGINLY *adv. rare.*

1595 J. WEEVER *Epigr.* (1599) Evj, Chaste Lucretia virgine-like her dresses.

†**'virginly,** *a.* *Obs.*⁻¹ [f. as prec. + -LY¹.] Virgin, virgin-like.

1548 UDALL, etc. *Erasm. Par. Luke* xxiv. 88 Dooe ye not knowe the menyng of it to bee the enclosure & tabernacle of the virginly chastitee, whiche neither any mortall man entreyng vnto it, ne the soonne of God..hath violated or defoiled?

'virginly, *adv.* [f. as prec. + -LY².] As or like a virgin; in or after the manner of a virgin; in a way becoming to a virgin or virgins.

1483 CAXTON *Gold. Leg.* 194/1 The holy ghoost shewed unto saynt germayn of ancerre how she shold serue god holyly & virgynely. **1823** MOORE *Rhymes on Road* v. 34 Whose beginnings are virginly pure as the source Of some mountainous rivulet. **1895** MEREDITH *Amazing Marriage* I. xv. 161 Virginly sensible of treasures of love to give.

virgin's bower. [VIRGIN *sb.* 12.] The British climbing shrub *Clematis Vitalba*, traveller's joy.

1597 GERARDE *Herbal* II. cccxiii. 741 Vpright Clamberer or Virgins Bower, is also a kinde of Clematis. **1688** HOLME *Armoury* II. 68/2 The Virgins Bower groweth like the Honysuckle. **1796** WITHERING *Brit. Plants* (ed. 3) II. 500 Traveller's-joy. Great Wild Climber. Virgin's Bower. **1818** KEATS *Endym.* II. 417 Virgin's bower, trailing airily. **1842** *Florist's Jrnl.* (1846) III. 36 The twisting or bending back of the petioles over any horizontal body,..as in the Virgin's bower. **1870** MORRIS *Earthly Par.* III. IV. 261 And woodbine, and the odorous virgin's-bower, Hung in great heaps about that undyked tower.

b. Applied to other species of *Clematis*, esp. to the American species *C. virginiana*, or employed as book-name for the whole genus.

1668 WILKINS *Real Char.* II. iv. §6. 111 *Clematis*, Virgins-bower. **1753** *Chambers' Cycl.* Suppl., *Virgins Bower*,..in botany, the name of a genus of plants;..The flower is of the rosaceous kind. **1760** J. LEE *Introd. Bot.* App. 331 Virgin's Bower, *Clematis*. **1771** J. R. FORSTER *Flora Amer. Septentr.* 25 Clematis viorna. Virgin's bower, violet. Virg. Car. **1845–50** MRS. LINCOLN *Lect. Bot.* 65 One of our most beautiful climbing plants is the *Clematis virginica*, or virgin's bower. **1856** DELAMER *Fl. Garden* (1861) 158 Virgin's Bower—*Clematis montana*, *Viticella*, and its varieties, are hardy climbers, pretty when trained over lattice-work. **1866** WHITTIER *Maids of Attitash* 15 Hardhack, and virgin's-bower, And white-spiked clethra-flower. **1880** BESSEY *Bot.* 564 *Clematis*, the Virgin's Bower, of many species.

c. With distinguishing terms.

1704 *Dict. Rust.* (1726) s.v., The Purple Virgin's-Bower... The Double-purple Virgin's-Bower. **1707** MORTIMER *Husb.* (1721) II. 190 Double Virgin Bower is a climbing Tree, fit to cover some place of Repose. **1731** MILLER *Gard. Dict.* s.v. *Clematitis*, Purple creeping Climber, or Single Virgins Bower. *Ibid.*, Blue Climber with a double Flower, or Double Virgins Bower. **1822** *Hortus Anglicus* II. 39 *Clematis Cirrhosa*. Evergreen Virgin's Bower. **1862** *Chambers's*

Encycl. III. 73/2 *Clematis flammula*, a native of the south of Europe and north of Africa,..is the species known as Sweet Virgin's Bower.

'virginship. *rare.* [f. as prec. + -SHIP.] The personality of a virgin. Used with possessives as a title or form of address.

1642 H. MORE *Song of Soul* I. III. xlvii, And Gabriel sware he would wait upon Her Virginship. **1673** DAVENANT *Distresses* v. i, Will your vex'd Virginship Vouchsafe to stay here, till you be well swadled.

'virgin's milk. ? *Obs.* [transl. med.L. *lac virginis.*] A chemical preparation having a milky appearance: **a.** A cosmetic preparation or wash for cleansing or purifying the face or skin (see quots.). Cf. LAC VIRGINIS I.

1600 SURFLET *Countrie Farme* III. lxxiii. 604 Virgins milke is thus made with a filtre. *Ibid.*, This virgins milke is good to heale ringwormes, and saucie and red faces. **1694** SALMON *Bate's Dispens.* (1713) 289/1 The Tincture [of Benjamin] made with the Alcohol of Wine, being mixt with a great deal of Water, makes a kind of Milk, which by some is call'd Virgins Milk, which serves for a Wash for the Face and Skin. **1712** tr. *Pomet's Hist. Drugs* I. 187 This Tincture of Benjamin and Storax is call'd Virgin [*sic*] Milk. **1721** BAILEY, *Virgin's milk*, a sort of Chymical Composition, called Benjamin water. **1835** *Penny Cycl.* IV. 257/1 A solution of benzoin in alcohol, added to twenty parts of rose-water, forms the cosmetic called Virgin's milk.

†**b.** (See quot.) *Obs. rare*$^{-0}$.

1704 J. HARRIS *Lex. Techn.* I, *Virgin's Milk*, is made of dissolving *Saccharum Saturni* [i.e. lead acetate] in a great deal of Water: It will turn white as Milk; whence the Name. [Hence in Bailey.]

†**virginty.** *Obs. rare.* In 4 vergynte. [f. VIRGIN *sb.*: see -TY.] Virginity.

13.. *E.E. Allit. P.* A. 767 In hys blod he wesch my wede on dese, & coronde clene in vergynte.

virgin wax. Also virgin-wax; 5–8 virgin's wax. [tr. med.L. *cera virginea*: cf. VIRGIN 17 b and 11. So F. *cire-vierge.*] Orig., fresh, new, or unused bees-wax, sometimes that produced by the first swarm of bees; in later and more general use, a purified or fine quality of wax, esp. as used in the making of candles; white wax.

α. **13..** *K. Alis.* 334 (Linc. MS.), After, he tok virgyn wax, And made a popet after þe quene. *a* **1400** *Sqr. lowe Degre* 688 She sered that body with specery, With wyrgin waxe and commendry. *a* **1425** tr. *Arderne's Treat. Fistula*, etc. 30 þan putte to a litle oyle of olyue,..wiþ als miche virgine wax togidre dissolued at þe fire by it self. *c* **1440** *Promp. Parv.* 510/2 Vyrgyne wex, *cera virginea*. **1502** *Acc. Ld. High Treas. Scot.* II. 37 Payit to Robert Bertoune for virgyne wax that he brocht hame to the King. **1538** in W. M. Williams *Ann. Founders' Co.* (1867) 55 The Herse to be garnyshed with xxx other great Tapers with ij Branches of Virgyn waxes. **1594** PLAT *Jewell-ho.* 57 An excellent cement for broken glasses. Take one part of Virgin-wax [etc.]. **1626** T. H[AWKINS] tr. *Caussin's Holy Crt.* 9 He hath imprinted all his perfections vpon our Sauiour..as one should impresse a golden seale vpon virgin-waxe. *c* **1645** HOWELL *Lett.* (1650) I. 33 They say, the young King's picture was found in her closet in virgin-wax. *a* **1711** KEN *Hymnotheo* Poet. Wks. 1721 III. 310 Like Virgin-Wax, he soft'ned the hard Bone, And wrought it till to female shape 'twas grown. **1795** W. BLAKE *Lett.* (1906) 54 Take a cake of virgin wax..and stroke it..over the surface of a warm plate. **1821** SCOTT *Kenilw.* vi, Besides lesser lights, the withdrawing-room was illuminated by four tall torches of virgin wax. **1861** HULME tr. *Moquin-Tandon* II. III. ccix, Wax which has been completely deprived of its colour is called virgin or white wax.

fig. *a* **1586** SIDNEY *Arcadia* II. xii. (1912) 229 You use vile Vulcans spight..to melt that Virgin-waxe, Which while it is, it is all Asias light.

attrib. **1599** NASHE *Lenten Stuffe* Wks. (Grosart) V. 256 The most intenerate Virgine wax phisnomy. **1654** GAYTON *Pleas. Notes* IV. viii. 223 The convoy presently departed, leaving him..with a Virgin-waxe-light, in a golden Candle-stick.

β. **1495** *Trevisa's Barth. De P.R.* XIX. lxi. 897 The more newe wexe is the more able it is to take inpressyon and pryntynge of dyuers fygures and shapes, and suche wex is callyd vyrgyns wexe. **1535** *Wardr. Kath. Arragon* 41 in *Camden Misc.* III, Item, seevyn hoolle tapers of vyrgyn's waxe. **1567** MAPLET *Gr. Forest* 37 Cerfolie..being wrought & tempered with Virgins Waxe, remedieth all kinde of swelling. **1607** WALKINGTON *Opt. Glass* 39 The purest virgins wax. **1658** ROWLAND tr. *Moufet's Theat. Ins.* 915 Simple and natural Wax is the thicker part of the combs that contains the honey; and it is either virgins wax, or of a second sort; virgins wax is that the younger swarms of Bees make from the young branches of flowers. (That is the first Swarm put into a new Hive.) **1660** BOYLE *New Exp. Phys. Mech.* x. 76 Slender Tapers of white Wax (commonly called Virgins Wax). **1736** BAILEY *Househ. Dict.* s.v. *Eye-salve*, Take one ounce of May butter, half an ounce of virgins wax [etc.].

Virgo ('vɜːgəʊ). *Astr.* and *Astrol.* [L.: see VIRGIN *sb.*]

1. a. The zodiacal constellation lying between Leo and Libra; the Virgin. **b.** The sixth sign of the zodiac, which the sun enters about Aug. 20–23.

a **1000** in *Saxon Leechd.* III. 244 An þæra tacna ys ȝehaten *aries*,..fifta *leo*; syxta *uirgo*, þæt is mæden. **1390** GOWER *Conf.* III. 121 After Leo Virgo the nexte Of Signes cleped is the sexte. *c* **1391** CHAUCER *Astrol.* II. §28 Alle signes in thy zodiak fro the heued of aries vnto the ende of virgo. **1588** SHAKS. *Tit. A.* IV. iii. 64 *Tit.* Good Boy in Virgoes lap... *Marc.* My Lord, I aime a Mile beyond the Moone, Your letter is with Iupiter by this. *c* **1600** W. FOWLER *Wks.* (S.T.S.) I. 269 Leo [may] lye of al the beastes forlorne, as virgo may with gemini bewar. **1664** BUTLER *Hud.* II. iii. 534 Quoth Wizard, So! In Virgo? Ha! quoth Whachum, No. Has Saturn nothing to do in 't. **1697** CREECH *Manilius* II. 70 Against the Crab and Bull the Goat declares, And Virgo too, and Libra feels his Wars. **1771** *Encycl. Brit.* I. 469/2 In 14 days afterwards, the moon comes to Virgo and Libra, which are the opposite signs to Pisces and Aries. **1787** BURNS *Let. to Moore* 2 Aug., Yet I went on with a high hand with my geometry, till the sun entered Virgo, a month which is always a carnival in my bosom. **1843** *Penny Cycl.* XXVI. 373/1 Virgo,..the sixth constellation in the zodiac... It is best known by two remarkable stars: the first, Spica (α Virginis);..the other, Prævindemiatrix, or Vindemiatrix (ε Virginis). **1868** LOCKYER *Guillemin's Heavens* (ed. 3) 395 This zone..is known under the name of the nebulous regions of Virgo.

2. a. *attrib.* or as *adj.*, born under or ruled by the sign of Virgo.

1894 E. KIRK *Influence of Zodiac* xiv. 121 With proper training these Virgo people may grow into the most powerful spiritual healers. **1928** E. ADAMS *Astrol.* 74 The mercurial type of Virgo native is a very different object. **1964** L. MACNEICE *Astrol.* i. 16 'Are you Virgo?' 'Oh, no, I'm Leo.' **1970** 'D. HALLIDAY' *Dolly & Cookie Bird* ii. 15, I ..said to Austin, 'When is your birthday?'.. We got it worked out that he was Virgo.

b. A person born under the sign of Virgo.

1917 H. T. WAITE *Compend. Natal Astrol.* 45 The good type of Virgo is the most conscientious, methodical..man. **1924** C. E. O. CARTER *Conc. Encycl. Psychol. Astrol.* 114 Virgo, however, is frequently extremely given over to foibles and personal idiosyncrasies which warp the mental outlook. **1938** D. ANRIAS *Man & Zodiac* vii. 82 Virgos are often witty but seldom positive. **1968** T. WOLFE *Electric Kool-Aid Acid Test* xxi. 294 'When were you born?'.. 'I'm a Virgo.' **1976** *Reader's Digest* June 75, I don't believe in this astrology business. We Virgos aren't easily taken in.

Hence **'Virgoan** = VIRGO 2 b.

1946 'STELLA COELI' *Your Fate* xi. 70 The high type of Virgoan makes a good statistician, efficiency expert, [etc.]. **1960** E. CHATELHERAULT *You & Your Stars* ii. 16 Virgoans are among the most fascinating of the Zodiac tribes. **1978** *TV Times* 28 Jan.–3 Feb. 69/3 There may be a special link with a Virgoan.

‖**virgo intacta** ('vɜːgəʊ ɪn'tæktə). [L.] A woman of inviolate chastity (in quot. 1922, *transf.* of a man); one who has never had sexual intercourse, a virgin. Freq. in legal contexts.

1726 J. AYLIFFE *Parergon Juris Canonici Anglicani* 228 The wife of one Bury was divorc'd from him upon the Score of Frigidity, it appearing that for three years after the Marriage she remain'd *Virgo Intacta* on the Account of the Husband's Impotency. **1829** J. HAGGARD *Rep. Cases Eccl. Courts* I. 728 If the parties lay together in one bed for so many years, of such ages, and the woman is certified to remain *virgo intacta*, there cannot be a stronger presumption that impotency existed, and that it was incurable. **1898** W. S. CHURCHILL *Let.* 31 Mar. in R. S. Churchill *Winston S. Churchill* (1967) I. Compan. II. 908 She too is to be pitied.. as she was not originally *virgo intacta*. **1922** JOYCE *Ulysses* 483, I declare him to be *virgo intacta*. **1932** G. B. SHAW *Let.* 16 Apr. in *B. Shaw & Mrs. Campbell* (1952) 300 Ellen, though she came through with me *virgo intacta*, gave herself away heart and soul without a thought of reserve. **1968** 'A. GILBERT' *Night Encounter* iv. 48 It was later shown that she was *virgo intacta*. **1980** J. B. HILTON *Anathema Stone* x. 107 She may have teased his patience... Hence my uncertainty as to whether she was *virgo intacta*.

†**Virgoule(e.** *Obs.* Also 7 vergoule. [a. F. *Virgoulée*, the popular pronunciation of *Villegoureix*, the name of a village in the province of Limousin (Hatzf.).] = next.

1699 EVELYN *Kal. Hort.* (ed. 9) 18 Pears. Winter Musk,.. Vergoules, the great Surrein. *Ibid.* 134 Ice-Pear, Dove-Pear, Virgoule, Deadman's-Pear. **1719** LONDON & WISE *Compl. Gard.* 53 *La Virgoulee*. The Virgoulee, otherwise call'd the Bujaleuf, Chambrett, the Ice-Pear [etc.]. *Ibid.* 160 Autumn, and Winter Pears, especially the largest; as the *Beurees*, *Virgovles*, and *Bon-Cretiens*. **1741** *Compl. Fam.-Piece* II. iii. 406 These Pears; [Nov.] Martin Sec,..Virgoule, Sucrevert.

‖**Virgouleuse** (virguløz). Also 7 Virguleus, 7, 9 Vergouleuse, 8 Virgoleuse. [F. *virgouleuse*, f. *Virgoulée* (see prec.).] A juicy variety of winter pear. Also *attrib.* with *pear*. Cf. VERGALOO.

1698 M. LISTER *Journ. Paris* (1699) 159 The Virguleus Pears were admirable. **1699** EVELYN *Kal. Hort.* (ed. 9) 167 Pears. Bergamot de Busy. Vergouleuse. **1706** *Gentil's Jardinier Solitaire* 40 The Marquise, the Easter Bergamot, the Virgouleuse. **1725** *Fam. Dict.* s.v. *Pears*, Pears which become ripe in November.—The Virgouleuse is an old Pear, well known for its Goodness. **1828–32** WEBSTER, *Vergouleuse*, a species of pear; contracted to *vergaloo*. **1845** A. J. DOWNING *Fruits & Fruit trees Amer.* 450 Virgouleuse. .. An excellent old French variety [of winter pear]... It is, however, a very different pear from the Virgalieu of New-York, which is the White Doyenné. **1860** HOGG *Fruit Man.* 219 Virgouleuse... Fruit large and pyriform. Skin smooth and delicate, pale lemon colour... November till January.

‖**virgula** ('vɜːgjʊlə). [L., small rod or twig, critical mark, dim. of *virga* twig, rod, wand, etc.]

1. *Zool.* A small rod-like growth or formation: †**a.** One of the spines of a ray. *Obs.*

1661 LOVELL *Hist. Anim. & Min.* b 5 b, They [*sc.* rays] take their prey, by hiding themselves in the mudde and putting out their virgulæ, and so alluring the small fishes, comming to them as weeds.

b. The rod-like axis of a graptolite.

1907 *Fossil Invertebr. Anim. Brit. Mus.* 47 The colony acquired a median supporting rod or virgula; this ended often in a disk.

2. †**a.** *virgula divina* or *divinatoria*, a divining- or dowsing-rod. *Obs.*

1656 COWLEY *Pindar. Odes, To Mr. Hobs* Note 28 *Virgula Divina* [see DIVINING *vbl. sb.* 2]. **1669** WORLIDGE *Syst. Agric.* vi. §3. 80 It is the onely Plant for the *Virgula Divina*, for the discovery of Mines. **1674** BLOUNT *Glossogr.* (ed. 4), *Virgula divinatoria*, is a Rod of Hazel, wherewith Miners pretend to discover where the Ores of Metalls lie. **1691** LOCKE *Lower. Interest* 40 Not of the nature of the deusing-rod, or virgula divina, able to discover mines of gold and silver.

b. = ROD *sb.* 6 b.

1826 PEACOCK in *Encycl. Metrop.* (1845) I. 411 Of this description are the *virgulæ*, or *rods* of Napier, which were formerly much celebrated and very generally used.

3. a. = VIRGULE I. *rare.*

1728 CHAMBERS *Cycl.* s.v. *Point*, A Point with a Virgula, call'd a Semicolon. *Ibid.* s.v. *Comma*. **1934** PRIEBSCH & COLLINSON *German Lang.* II. x. 380 The full stop or, instead, a virgula, i.e. a short slanting strike (/) is used..to mark the end of a sentence or of a portion of a sentence followed by a pause.

b. *Mus.* (See quots.)

1801 BUSBY *Dict. Mus.*, *Virgula*, the name of one of the ten notes used in the middle ages. **1876** STAINER & BARRETT *Dict. Mus. Terms* 450/1 *Virgula*, (1) The stem or tail of a note. (2) A neume.

virgular ('vɜːgjʊlə(r)), *a.* [f. L. *virgula* (see prec.) + -AR^{1}.]

†**1.** Of musical syncopation: Denoted by a small dash or stroke. *Obs.*$^{-1}$

1609 DOULAND *Ornith. Microl.* 51 To the same Signe there may belong a double Diminution, to wit; virgular and numerall, thus: ₵ 2. Virgular syncopation is much used.

2. Of Ogham characters, etc.: Having the shape of small thin rods; consisting of slender rod-like lines or strokes.

1827 G. HIGGINS *Celtic Druids* 3 Another example of an Irish character called a virgular ogham. *Ibid.* 35 The virgular alphabets of the Druids.

'virgulate, *a.* [ad. L. *virgulāt-us*, f. *virgula*: see -ATE.] (See quots.)

1840 SMART *Walker's Dict.*, *Virgulate*,..shaped like a little rod. **1892** CROZIER *Dict. Bot. Terms* 199 *Virgulate*, diminutive of *virgate*, shaped like a little twig or rod.

virgule ('vɜːgjʊl). [a. F. *virgule*, or ad. L. *virgula* VIRGULA.]

1. A thin sloping or upright line (/, |) occurring in mediæval MSS. as a mark for the cæsura or as a punctuation-mark (frequently with the same value as the modern comma). Now also in more general use with various functions (see quots.). Cf. SLASH *sb.*^{1} 5.

1837 HALLAM *Hist. Lit.* I. viii. §26 In the manuscripts of Chaucer, the line is always broken by a cæsura in the middle, which is pointed out by a virgule. **1895** HOFFMAN *Beginnings of Writing* 111 According to Orozco y Berra these virgules or commas represent the verb to blow or to hum. **1946** G. STIMPSON *Bk. about Thousand Things* 487 The technical name of the short slanting stroke between *and* and *or* in the device is *virgule*. **1962** *Gen. Systems* VII. 299/2 Its mate is suffixed with a slant (virgule), thus: 4006 How to Silence. 4006/ How to Sound. **1980** O. M. RICCIO *Intimate Art Writing Poetry* v. 138 The vertical lines (virgules) separate the feet that make up the line.

2. *Clockmaking.* (See quot.)

1884 F. J. BRITTEN *Watch & Clockm.* 284 [A] Virgule ..[is] an escapement having points of resemblance to the verge and to the horizontal.

†**virguler,** error for prec. or VIRGULA.

1610 MARCELLINE *Triumphs Jas. I*, C j b, Let them measure the Syllables, weigh the Words, controule the points and Virgulers.

†**virgult.** *Obs.* [ad. L. *virgulta* (neut. pl.), bush, thicket, copse, slips or cuttings of trees, f. *virgula* VIRGULA.]

1. A bush or shrub; a set of young shoots; a branch or twig.

1501 DOUGLAS *Pal. Hon.* I. Prol. xii, Amyd the virgultis all in till a fary, As feminine sa feblit fell I down. **1656** BLOUNT *Glossogr.*, *Virgult*,..a company of young shoots, or many young tender Sprigs and Sprouts growing together out of the ground. **1657** TOMLINSON *Renou's Disp.* 240 Certain red berries adhere to its virgults.

2. A thicket or copse.

1736 *Drake's Eboracum* I. vii. 334 A toft and a virgult, and three other measures of land.

vir'gultate, *a.* *rare*$^{-0}$. [f. mod.L. *virgult-um* (see next) + -ATE.] Virgulate.

1888 *Cassell's Encycl. Dict.*

‖**virgultum** (və'gʌltəm). *Bot.* [mod.L.: see VIRGULT.] A young slender branch or twig.

1866 *Treas. Bot.* 1219/2; and in recent Dicts.

virguncule (və'gʌŋkjuːl). *nonce-wd.* [ad. L. *virguncula*, dim. of *virgo* VIRGIN *sb.*] = VIRGIN *sb.* 3 a; a young virgin.

1911 BEERBOHM *Zuleika D.* vii. 94 There are the virguncules of Somerville and Lady Margaret's Hall; but beauty and the lust for learning have yet to be allied.

†**vir-hirne,** southern ME. var. FIRE-IRON I.

c **1325** *Gloss. W. de Bibbesw.* in *Rel. Ant.* II. 81 Flint, *cailleun*: vir-hirne, *le fusil*.

virial ('vɪrɪəl). *Physics.* [a. G. *virial* (Clausius), f. L. *vīr-*, pl. stem of *vīs* force, strength.] **a.** In Clausius' kinetic theorem of gases: (see quots.). ***virial theorem***, the theorem that for a steady-state system of particles obeying an inverse square law of force, the time-average of the kinetic energy equals the time-average of the virial; or equivalently, that the potential energy is twice the total energy and the kinetic energy is the negative of the total energy.

1870 tr. *Clausius* in *Lond.*, etc. *Philos. Mag.* Aug. 123 We will therefore give to the mean value which this magnitude has during the stationary motion of the system the name of *Virial* of the system. **1875** *Encycl. Brit.* III. 39 When an attraction or repulsion exists between two points, half the product of this stress into the distance between the two points is called the *virial* of the stress. **1904** J. H. JEANS *Dynamical Theory of Gases* vi. 144 The virial depends solely on the forces acting upon the molecules, and not upon the motion of the molecules. **1925** *Phil. Mag.* L. 414 By the extended theorem of the virial, the effect of the pressure of radiation can be ignored, and thus all consequences of the virial theorem which hold in the absence of radiation hold also when radiation is taken into account. **1965** PHILLIPS & WILLIAMS *Inorg. Chem.* I. i. 11 A useful theorem known as the Virial Theorem, which holds for all coulombic potential energy systems.., states that the equilibrium binding energy is equal to $\frac{1}{2}\bar{V}$ or $-\bar{T}$, where $\bar{V}$ and $\bar{T}$ are time-average potential and kinetic energies. **1974** *Encycl. Brit. Macropædia* VI. 852/2 Under such conditions the total potential energy of the cluster is exactly twice as great as the combined kinetic energy of all the cluster stars. This relation is known as the virial theorem. **1980** *Nature* 29 May 305/1 The virial theorem is often used to calculate a [galaxy] system's mass from its size and velocity dispersion.

b. ***virial coefficient*** [tr. G. *virialcoefficient* (H. K. Onnes 1901, in *Arch. neérlandaises des Sci. exactes & nat.* VI. 874)], each of the (temperature-dependent) coefficients of inverse powers of *V* in a polynomial series used to approximate the quantity pV/RT in the equation of state of an ideal gas or similar collection of particles; so ***virial equation, expansion***.

1902 *Sci. Abstr.* V. 364 The series development $pv = A + B/v + C/v^2 + D/v^4 + E/v^6 + F/v^8$ is applied... The coefficients A, B, &c., are termed virial coefficients, and are functions of the temperature. **1955** H. B. G. CASIMIR in W. Pauli *Niels Bohr* 121 In the theory of an ideal gas interaction between atoms is neglected, but it is possible to calculate successive approximations, the so called virial coefficients. **1967** CONDON & ODISHAW *Handbk. Physics* (ed. 2) v. iv. 49/2 The virial expansion is one of the cleanest-cut developments in the subject of statistical mechanics. **1967** MARGERISON & EAST *Introd. Polymer Chem.* ii. 63 Some idea of the deviations from ideality in these dilute solutions can be obtained by evaluation of the second virial coefficients. **1978** P. W. ATKINS *Physical Chem.* i. 39 Conclusions can be drawn from the virial equation of state only by inserting specific values of the coefficients and taking note of their temperature dependence.

viricidal (vaɪrɪˈsaɪdəl), *a.* [f. VIR(US + -I- + -CIDE + -AL.] Fatal to viruses. So **ˈviricide**[2], a viricidal agent.

1924 *Brit. Jrnl. Exper. Path.* V. 341 Spots in which no naked-eye change whatever has taken place owing to complete neutralization by viricidal serum have been removed for study. **1946** J. R. PORTER *Bacterial Chem. & Physiol.* iv. 225 The ideal disinfectant or viricide has not been discovered. **1970** M. SKINNER *Old Rectory* 2 Who'd bred a virus which no viricide Could cope with. **1981** *Appl. & Environmental Microbiol.* XLII. 469 The results indicate that CAT may be an effective viricide against poliovirus type 2 in an acid medium. *Ibid.*, The viricidal properties of CAT [*sc.* chloramine-T] and chlorine are compared.

ˈviricide[1]. *nonce-wd.* [f. L. *vir* man, husband + -CIDE 2.] The slaying of men or of husbands.

1766 G. CANNING *Anti-Lucretius* I. 71 The impious Danaides, Grecian stories tell, For barbarous viricide condemn'd to hell.

†**viricund**, *a.* *Obs.*$^{-1}$ [Irreg. f. L. *viri-dis* (see next), after *rubicund*.] In a green state.

1599 A. M. tr. *Gabelhouer's Bk. Physicke* 191/2 Take hoppes with the stalckes, and roote, ether viricunde, or exsiccated.

ˈvirid, *a.* *poet.* and *rhet.* Also 7 viride. [ad. L. *virid-is* green, blooming, vigorous.] Green, verdant.

1600 FAIRFAX *Tasso* XII. xciv, Her tombe was not of viride Spartane greet, Nor yet by cunning hand of Scopas wrought. **1658** H. CROMPTON *Pierides* 82 The virid Marjoram Her sparkling beauty did but see. **1794** T. TAYLOR *Pausanias' Descr. Greece* I. 61 There is, also, a temple of Earth the nurse of youths, and of virid Ceres. **1812** H. & J. SMITH *Rej. Addr.* x. (1873) 97 The pillars.. blooming in virid antiquity, like two massy evergreens. **1866** J. B. ROSE tr. *Ovid's Met.* 341 And as he spoke the virid bough upon Wound as he was, the dragon turned to stone.

‖**viriˈdarium.** *Roman Antiq.* [L. *viridārium* plantation of trees, pleasure-garden, f. *viridis* VIRID *a.*] A pleasure-garden or green court of an ancient Roman villa or palace.

a **1700** EVELYN *Diary* 10 Nov. 1644, We went to see Prince Ludovisio's villa where was formerly the *Viridarium* of the poet Sallust. **1832** W. GELL *Pompeiana* I. viii. 168 A sort of court, probably planted with flowers, and sometimes called a *viridarium*. **1848** LYTTON *Harold* I. i, The wide space between the columns, which had once given ample vista from graceful awnings into *tablinum* and *viridarium*. **1891** FARRAR *Darkn. & Dawn* x, As Titus went across the viridarium, or chief green court of the Palace.

†**viridary**, *sb.* *Obs. rare.* [In sense 1 ad. med.L. *viridarius* verderer, f. L. *viridis* VIRID *a.*; in sense 2 ad. L. *viridārium* VIRIDARIUM.]

1. A verderer.

?**13..** in Arnolde *Chron.* (1502) p. lxxx/1 And moreouer euerych xl. daies bi al the yere forestirs and virydaries shall come togedurs to see [etc.]. **1601** W. WATSON *Sparing Discov.* a 3 Being but aduanced to the dignitie..of a vice-president, nay but of a viceprotonotary, nay but of a vice-uiridary.

2. A viridarium or garden.

1657 THORNLEY tr. *Longus' Daphnis & Chloe* 190 Seeing how fair and flourishing the Viridarie [was].

†**viridary**, *a.* *Obs.* (Of obscure meaning.)

Perh. an attrib. use of the sb. (see sense 1, quot. 1601), but the allusion is not obvious.

1600 W. WATSON *Decacordon* (1602) 147 [The Jesuits] haue a new tricke of a viridary post or current of time to gaine time withall, in keeping Nobles, State and all the people in suspence of euents, vntil they haue what they looke for.

ˈviridate, *sb.* *Chem.* [f. VIRID-IC + -ATE[1].] A salt formed by the action of viridic acid.

1868 WATTS *Dict. Chem.* V. 1002 Coffee-beans owe their green colour to a small quantity of calcic viridate. *Ibid.*, The blue precipitate of lead-viridate is decomposed by sulphydric acid.

†**ˈviridate**, *v.* *Obs.*$^{-0}$ [f. late L. *viridāre* to grow green, f. *viridis* VIRID *a.*] (See quots.)

1623 COCKERAM I, *Viridate*, to wax or make greene. **1656** BLOUNT *Glossogr.*, *Viridate*, to make green and lusty.

†**virideer.** *Obs.*$^{-1}$ [ad. med.L. *viridarius* (see VIRIDARY *sb.*), after words ending in *-eer*.] A verderer.

1609 SKENE *Reg. Maj.*, *Stat. K. William* 12 Gif he be found the third time with grene wode, he sall be presented to the virideer (the keiper of the grene wode and grasse).

†**viˈrideous**, *a.* *Obs.*$^{-1}$ [Irreg. f. L. *virid-is* VIRID *a.*] Virid.

1688 HOLME *Armoury* II. 313/2 *Viridis*, virideous, green-colour.

viriˈdescence. [Cf. next.] The quality of being viridescent.

1841 *Blackw. Mag.* L. 697 An artist of this school..is signalized by the flatness and viridescence of his canvass in a moment. **1912** *Nation* 25 May 282/2 More like potatoes than the tender viridescence that we like best. **1961** G. DURRELL *Whispering Land* v. 123 Here were the vivid greens of the tropics, so many shades and some of such viridescence that they make the green of the English landscape look grey in comparison.

viriˈdescent, *a.* [ad. ppl. stem of late L. *viridescĕre* to become green, f. *viridis* VIRID *a.*: see -ESCENT.] Somewhat green or virid. Also *fig.*

1847 DARLINGTON *Amer. Weeds*, etc. (1860) 433 *Viridescent*, greenish. **1889** STEVENSON *Lett.* (1899) II. 158 The front of the mountain ivied and furred with clinging forest, one viridescent cliff. **1907** *Sat. Rev.* 5 Oct. 420/2 Philosophers, like gods, may have a crude and viridescent old age. **1938** S. BECKETT *Murphy* viii. 152 The..kites rode steadily..flown by the child. She could just discern them... For a moment they stood out motionless and black, in a glade of limpid viridescent sky. **1980** P. HILL *Savages* iv. 57 The mainly deciduous trees joined branches overhead so that Leo was walking in a viridescent gloom.

‖**viˈridia.** *Chem.* [mod.L., f. L. *viridis* VIRID *a.* Cf. VIRIDINE 3.] A vegetable alkaloid obtained from the rootstock of *Veratrum viride*, an American variety of white hellebore; jervine.

1874 GARROD & BAXTER *Mat. Med.* 383 The researches of Dr. H. C. Wood have led him to conclude that Viridia and Veratroidea both exert a depressant influence on the heart.

viˈridian, *sb.* and *a.* Also veridian. [f. L. *virid-is* VIRID *a.*] **a.** *sb.* Veronese green. **b.** *adj.* Of or pertaining to this colour.

1882 W. T. SUFFOLK in *Science Gossip* Mar. 49 The following list of colours contained in my own box may prove useful... Viridian. [*Note.*] A transparent oxide of chromium, perfectly permanent, of great use both by itself and in compounding other greens. **1902** R. FRY *Let.* 13 Oct. (1972) I. 197 The trees [are] strawy green, the glass almost veridian. **1903** *Sat. Rev.* 21 Mar. 356/2 The patch of green bank shimmering up to viridian pitch encouraged by.. greys. **1950** M. PEAKE *Gormenghast* lxiii. 355 The waters became stained with evergreen from the softest olive to veridian. **1974** R. RENDELL *Face of Trespass* viii. 70 A new name..in veridian neon, stuck up above the portico.

viˈridic, *a.* *Chem.* [f. as prec. + -IC.] ***viridic acid*** (see quot.).

1868 WATTS *Dict. Chem.* V. 1002 *Viridic acid*,..an acid produced by the oxidation of caffetanic acid in presence of ammonia.

viridin (ˈvɪrɪdɪn). *Pharm.* [f. L. *virid-us* VIRID *a.*, specific epithet + -IN[1].] A crystalline antibiotic with antifungal properties, $C_{20}H_{16}O_6$, derived from the mould *Trichoderma viride*.

1945 BRIAN & MCGOWAN in *Nature* 4 Aug. 144/2 We have recently found a number of strains which produce another substance, which we propose to name 'viridin', characterized by remarkably high fungistatic activity. **1970** *Nature* 18 July 300/2 *T. viride* may retard the development of other fungi by producing the antibiotics gliotoxin or viridin, although attempts to demonstrate this with plate cultures have been unsuccessful. **1978** T. KORZYBSKI et al. *Antibiotics* III. II. 1970 Viridin is inactive against staphylococci, colon bacilli, and typhoid bacilli in concentrations up to 100μg/ml.

viridine (ˈvɪrɪdaɪn). Also -in. [f. as VIRIDIC *a.* + -INE. Cf. F. *viridine*.]

1. *Bot.* = CHLOROPHYLL, CHROMULE.

1837 P. KEITH *Bot. Lex.* 59 The pulp constituting the parenchyma of the leaves was at one time designated by the appellation of *viridine*, because it is generally of a green colour. **1859** MAYNE *Expos. Lex.* s.v.

2. *Dyeing.* A green aniline dye (see quots.).

1875 *Ure's Dict. Arts* (ed. 7) I. 720 Viridine. A green dye has been obtained..by acting on rosolic acid with aniline and benzoic acid. **1882** *Nature* XXV. 546 R. Meldola.. investigates the action of benzyl chloride upon diphenylamine, and the action of oxidising agents upon the product. The substance thus produced is a green dye, 'viridin'.

3. *Chem.* = VIRIDIA, JERVINE.

1877 H. WATTS *Fownes' Chem.* (ed. 12) II. 610 Parvoline, ..Coridine,..Rubidine,..Viridine. ($C_{12}H_{19}N$.) **1886** *Buck's Handbk. Med. Sci.* III. 604/1 The viridine and veratroidine of Bullock are now supposed to have been impure conditions of jervine and rubijervine respectively. **1888** H. C. WOOD *Therap.* (ed. 7) 392 The root-stock of Veratrum viride..contains two alkaloids, *jervine* and *veratroidine*... Dr. George B. Wood named them *viridine* and *veratroidine*.

viridite (ˈvɪrɪdaɪt). *Min.* [f. as prec. + -ITE[1] 2 b. Named *viridit* by H. Vogelsang, 1872.] A mineral compound occurring in certain rocks in the form of minute greenish particles.

1879 RUTLEY *Stud. Rocks* x. 166 Viridite includes mineral matter which is probably referable to different varieties of chlorite and serpentine. **1883** *Science* II. 111/1 Yellowish-green needles of epidote and viridite. **1892** J. D. DANA *Min.* 664 *Viridite*,..A collective name... They are generally in scaly or fibrous forms and are often the result of the decomposition of amphibole, pyroxene, chrysolyte, etc.

viridity (vɪˈrɪdɪtɪ). Now *rare*. Also 5 **vyridite**, 6–7 **viriditye**. [ad. OF. (also mod.F.) *viridité* (= It. *viridità*), or L. *viriditāt-*, *viriditās*, f. *viridis* VIRID *a.*]

1. The quality or state of being virid or green; greenness, verdancy. Also in fig. context.

c **1430** LYDG. *Min. Poems* (Percy Soc.) 78 God Almyghti.. Hath florissched the erthe on every side, The woodes and the medowes wyde, Withe grete habundance of vyridite. **1597** A. M. tr. *Guillemeau's Fr. Chirurg.* 29/2 Ther remayneth somtimes a viriditye or greenes about the apertione. *Ibid.* 53/2 The matter of our woundes resolveth it selfe into viriditye. **1605** J. DOVE *Confut. Atheism* 90 The Bush bore the heat of the fire without losse of viriditye. **1661** FELTHAM *Resolves* (ed. 8) II. lvii. 304 The Soul of Man..was planted in the Element of Vertue, and while 'tis nourisht by it, it spreads and thrives with fruit and fair viridity. **1670** EVELYN *Sylva* (ed. 2) 238 This deification of their Trees, and amongst other things, for their Age and perennial viridity,.. might spring from the manifold use which they afforded. **1875** *Sat. Rev.* XL. 553/1 To mark more clearly the distinction between black and green tea, the practice has arisen of imparting to the latter 'an obvious viridity' by means of various pigmentary substances.

2. *fig.* †**a.** (See quot.) *Obs.*$^{-0}$

1656 BLOUNT *Glossogr.* (copying Cooper), *Viridity*,.. lustiness, strength, manliness. [Hence in Phillips, etc.]

b. = VERDANCY 2.

1825 T. HOOK *Sayings* Ser. II. *Passion & Princ.* iv, What intellectual viridity that exemplary creature possesses! **1858** *Chamb. Jrnl.* IX. 99 A desire to extenuate..my dear parent's viridity and trustfulness in the matter. **1859** HELPS *Friends in C.* Ser. II. I. viii. 264 The next in innocency;—may we say, in viridity?

†**viridour.** *Obs. rare.* In 6 virydour. [ad. med.L. *viridarius* verderer, with ending assimilated to VERDOUR[2].] = VERDERER[2] 1.

?**13..** *Charter of Forests* in Arnolde *Chron.* (1811) 212[That] euerych forester of our fee from hensforth attache plees of forest as wele of grasinges as of our veneri and them presente to yᵉ virydour of yᵉ prouince.

viˈrific, *a.* *rare*$^{-1}$. [f. L. *vīr-us* VIRUS + -(I)FIC.] Virulent, poisonous.

1885 *Pall Mall G.* 20 Jan. 4/1 It was further ascertained that the maximum of virific effect is produced in the medulla oblongata.

virile (ˈvɪraɪl, -ɪl, ˈvaɪəraɪl, -ɪl), *a.* (and *sb.*). Also 5 viryle, 6 vyryll, 6–8 viril (7 -ill). [a. OF. *viril* or ad. L. *virīlis*, f. *vir* man: see -ILE. So F., Sp., Pg. *viril*, It. *virile*.]

1. Of, belonging to, or characteristic of a man; manly, masculine; marked by strength or force.

a. Of things, qualities, etc.

1490 CAXTON *Eneydos* ix. 36 O the fortytude viryle of wymmen, or loos & pryce of chastyte femynyne. **1604** T. WRIGHT *Passions*, *Clymact. Years* 3 The next clymactericall yeere in them of solide and virile constitution is an 100. **1651** N. BACON *Disc. Govt. Eng.* II. iii. (1739) 17 And yet the power of this grew as virile and Royal, as it would acknowledge no Peer but the Parliament. **1679** J. GOODMAN *Penit. Pard.* III. ii. (1713) 292 There is a virile state of vertue attainable when duty is turned into nature. **1728** CHAMBERS *Cycl.* s.v., The Virile Age..is the Strength and Vigour of a Man's Age, *viz.* from thirty to forty-five Years. **1822** T. TAYLOR *Apuleius* VIII. 175 Stammering words of an uncertain meaning, she breathed out her virile soul. **1858** GEN. P. THOMPSON *Audi Alt. Part.* II. lxviii. 7 It was an act not reconcileable with virile sense, on the part of either the proposers or the accepters. **1875** G. MACDONALD *Malcolm* III. xv. 199 She punished her husband for the virile claim to greater freedom.

absol. **1876** STEDMAN *Victorian Poets* (1887) 407 Only the virile and heroic can fully satisfy her own nature and master it for good or evil.

b. Of dress: Denoting the attainment of man's estate; distinctively belonging to men in contrast to youths (or women).

1603 HOLLAND *Plutarch's Mor.* 51 Having put on your virile robe and growen to mans estate. **1631** BRATHWAIT *Eng. Gentlew.* (1641) 340 One of this ranke.. forbore not to unwoman herselfe, by assuming not onely a virile habit, but a virago's heart. **1728** CHAMBERS *Cycl.* s.v. *Robe*, At Rome, they gave the Name Virile Robe, *Toga Virilis*, to a plain kind of Gown which their Youth assumed when arrived at Puberty. **1761** *Acc. of Books* in *Ann. Reg.* 298/2 Girls wore it [i.e. the *prætexta*] till they were married, and youths till they took the viril robe. **1848** THACKERAY *Van. Fair* xliv. The assumption of the virile jacket and pantaloons.

2. Of persons: **a.** Full of masculine energy or strength; not weak or effeminate.

1512 *Helyas* in Thoms *Prose Rom.* (1828) III. 51 He semed almost a man viril in his force. **1880** *Scribner's Mag.* May 124/1 His instrument broke for want of a firm and even hand to use it—a virile, devoted master to prolong the strain. **1890** HOSMER *Anglo-Sax. Freedom* 319 All had.. been disciplined and made strongly virile by that priceless polity ..which had been inherited from Anglo-Saxon ancestors. **1893** J. STRONG *New Era* 102 The more virile a man is the more positive are his defects.

†**b.** Of a woman: Nubile. *Obs.*⁻¹

1648 HEXHAM II, *Manbaer*,.. a maide that is Mariageable or ripe for a Husband, or Virill.

c. Of sex: Male.

1697 EVELYN *Numism.* viii. 287 A Treatise of Illustrious Women showing how far they surpass the Virile Sex in all sorts even of Martial undertakings and Affairs.

d. *absol.* as *sb.* A virile person.

1903 *Critic* XLIII. 374/1 It is the fashion of the 'viriles' —to coin a word—to stigmatize the poetry.. as 'decadent.'

3. ***virile member*** (or ***yard***), the male organ of generation. Also ***virile part***.

1541 R. COPLAND *Guydon's Quest. Chirurg.* Kj, It is the yerde vyryll that is the cultyuer and labourer of the felde of mankynde. **1607** TOPSELL *Four-f. Beasts* 89 But it is good to leaue as many of the vaines and nerues of the virile member vntouched and whole as may be. **1610** HOLLAND *Camden's Brit.* I. 135 Frico, whose image they devise and pourtray with a great viril member. **1728** CHAMBERS *Cycl.* s.v. *Penis*, The Member, or virile Member,.. one of the principal Organs of Generation in the Male Kind. **1856** MAYNE *Expos. Lex.* 672/1. **1967** W. STYRON *Confessions Nat Turner* III. 372, I felt my virile part stiffen again beneath my trousers.

Hence **'virileness**, 'manhood, manliness'.

1727 BAILEY (vol. II).

virilescence (vɪrɪ'lɛsəns). [See next and -ENCE.] The condition of becoming virile, *spec.* of assuming physical characteristics of the male.

1836–9 *Todd's Cycl. Anat.* II. 716/2 The change to virilescence in the former [*sc.* birds] being more marked and striking than in the latter [*sc.* mammalia]. **1853** DUNGLISON *Med. Lex.* 908 *Virilescence*,.. the state of the aged female in which she assumes certain of the characteristics of the male. —Mehliss. **1912** A. HARRISON in *Eng. Rev.* Feb. 493 The virilescence of women would seem to imply the emasculation of men.

virilescent (vɪrɪ'lɛsənt), *a.* [f. VIRILE *a.* + -ESCENT.] Assuming characteristics of the male.

1836–9 *Todd's Cycl. Anat.* II. 716/2 Two cases in which a virilescent type was shewn principally in the hair of the female deer.

virilia (vɪ'rɪlɪə). *rare.* [L. *virīlia* penis.] The male genitals; the penis.

1962 V. NABOKOV *Pale Fire* 123 When stripped and shiny in the mist of the bath house, his bold virilia contrasted harshly with his girlish grace.

virilify (vɪ'rɪlɪfaɪ), *v.* [f. VIRILE *a.* + -IFY.] *trans.* To make virile or manly.

1849 J. WILSON in *Blackw. Mag.* LXVI. 647 It is merely his manhood that quails, which his wife has to virilify.

†**vi'riliously**, *adv. Obs. rare.* [Irreg. f. L. *virīlis* VIRILE *a.*] Manfully.

1632 LITHGOW *Trav.* v. 178 [The] Knights of St. Iohn.. viriliously expulsed the Saracens from thence. **1637** —— *Siege of Breda* 25 The Enemy did divers times sally forth upon them, but they were ever viriliously repulsed backe to their owne repugnable limits.

virilism ('vɪrɪlɪz(ə)m). [f. VIRILE *a.* + -ISM.]

1. A form of hermaphroditism.

1896 *Nat. Science* Sept. 154 They can be referred to infantilism.. and virilism.

2. The state, of a female, of having some male sexual characteristics; also, = VIRILIZATION.

1922 MASON & AYRES tr. *Lereboullet's Endocrine Glands* 164 Virilism may appear either in young girls after puberty, or in women after the menopause. **1945** [see FEMINISM 3]. **1983** *Oxford Textbk. Med.* I. x. 87/1 Congenital adrenal hyperplasia can present in adult life with hirsutism, virilism, and often disturbed menstrual cycles.

virilist ('vɪrɪlɪst), *sb.* (and *a.*). *nonce-wd.* [f. VIRILE *a.* + -IST.] A hearty, excessively 'manly' person; one who makes a cult of conventional masculine virtues. Also *attrib.* or as *adj.*

1910 C. E. MONTAGUE *Hind let Loose* viii. 145 To give.. to the pedant and virilist their several rights of stark rigidity and of jolly brutishness. **1922** —— *Disenchantment* v. 69 Your virilist chaplain was apt to overdo.. his jolly implied disclaimers.

virility (vɪ'rɪlɪtɪ). Also 6–7 -tie, -tye. [ad. F. *virilité* (OF. *virilite*) or L. *virīlitas*, f. *virīlis* VIRILE *a.*: see -ITY. So It. *virilità*, Sp. *virilidad*, Pg. *-idade*.]

1. The period of life during which a person of the male sex is in full vigour; mature or fully developed manhood or masculine force.

1586 T. B. *La Primaud. Fr. Acad.* I. 531 The parts are these; infancie, childhood, youth, adolescencie, virilitie, and old age. **1623** J. WODROEPHE *Marrow Fr. Tongue* 373/2 The first Aage of Man is called Virilitie, in which hee is in his Best Force, Vnderstanding and Disposition. **1652** J. WRIGHT tr. *Camus' Nat. Paradox* I. 4 At such years as but just passing out of Virility he saluted only the first and freshest time of Old-Age. **1728** CHAMBERS *Cycl.* s.v. *Virile*, For which Reason some compare Youth to Summer, and Virility to Autumn. **1757** BURKE *Abridgm. English Hist.* Wks. X. 329 When a young man approached to virility, he was not yet admitted as a member of the State. **1822–7** GOOD *Study Med.* (1829) II. 27 At puberty it [the pulse] is only 80; about virility 75. **1859** MAYNE *Expos. Lex.* 1333/2.

b. *transf.* or *fig.*

1622 A. COURT *Constancie* I. 41 The ruine of Townes is still at hand;.. they haue their Youth, their virility, their Olde age, like men. **1627** DONNE *Serm.* 214 Our Virility, our holy Manhood, our religious Strength consists in a faithfull Assurance [etc.]. **1671** E. PANTON *Spec. Juventutis* 89 In the Youth and Virility of our Empire our Nobles handled all affairs of State. **1875** MAINE *Hist. Inst.* xiii. 395 During the virility of his intellect.

c. Masculine vigour; masculinity of sex.

1890 *Amer. Naturalist* Nov. 1030 We may infer, therefore, that sexual power and high sexual characters go hand in hand, and that in proportion to the advance toward organic perfection virility increases. **1898** *Allbutt's Syst. Med.* V. 839 Both these men were literary men of more sensitiveness than virility.

2. †**a.** The generative organs. *Obs.* **b.** The power of procreation; capacity for sexual intercourse.

1597 A. M. tr. *Guillemeau's Fr. Chirurg.* 2 b/2 That suture or seame which passeth along the virilitye. **1611** SPEED *Hist. Gt. Brit.* IX. iii. §23 William of Anco was punished with losse of both his eyes and his virilitye. **1650** BULWER *Anthropomet.* 205 He never after would trust any of his Eunuchs with any part of their virility. **1659** MILTON *Civ. Power* Wks. 1851 V. 316 No less then the amercement of thir whole virilitie. **1721** G. ROUSSILLON tr. *Vertot's Rev. Portugal* 136 The King.. was for bringing half the prostitutes of Lisbon to prove his virility. **1756–7** tr. *Keysler's Trav.* (1760) III. 194 Such mutilated persons as have voluntarily and deliberately deprived themselves of their virility. **1859** MAYNE *Expos. Lex.* 1333/2 *Virility*,.. more particularly the generative power of man.

†**c.** *pl.* = prec. *Obs.*

1646 SIR T. BROWNE *Pseud. Ep.* III. ix. 124 Castrated animals in every species are longer lived then they which retaine their virilities. **1650** BULWER *Anthropomet.* 206 Sealing up his Virilities in a Box, delivered it unto the King.

3. Manly strength and vigour of action or thought; energy or force of a virile character.

1603 HOLLAND *Plutarch's Mor.* 1275 Yet could they never observe and keepe the virilitie of visage, and lion-like looke of his [*sc.* Alexander]. **1632** LITHGOW *Trav.* v. 211 Thus.. discharged he the function of his calling.. with prudent and magnanimous virilitie. **1716** ADDISON *Freeholder* No. 26. ¶7, I have lately been told of a Country-Gentlewoman, pretty much famed for this Virility of Behaviour in Party-Disputes. **1768** TUCKER *Lt. Nature* I. 262 Etymologists derive virtue from virility, supposing it to denote a manly strength and vigour of mind. **1845** FORD *Handbk. Spain* I. 2 Thus the virility and vitality of the noble people has been neutralised. **1855** MOTLEY *Dutch Rep.* II. i. (1866) 118 The famous moustache upon her upper lip was supposed to indicate authority and virility of purpose. **1891** FARRAR *Darkn. & Dawn* xix, A mind in which every spark of virility was dead, and which was rapidly degenerating into a mass of sensuous egotism.

b. *transf.*

1597 MORLEY *Introd. Mus.* 177 These motions be more masculine causing in the song more virilitie then those accidentall cordes. **1889** W. WILSON *State* §1195 The result some day to be reached will be normal liberty, political vitality and vigor, civil virility. **1894** E. BROOKS in *Educator* (Philad.) Oct. 159 Those universal and comprehensive principles of education which unite the parts of the science into an organic unity of power and virility.

virilization (vɪrɪlaɪ'zeɪʃən). [f. VIRIL(E *a.* + -IZATION.] The pathological development of male sexual characteristics, esp. in a female. Also **'virilized** *ppl. a.*, exhibiting virilization; **'virilizing** *ppl. a.*, causing virilization.

1951 L. J. SOFFER *Dis. Endocrine Glands* xxi. 689 The virilizing syndrome is an affliction essentially of females and preadolescent males. *Ibid.* 699 The Leydig cell tumours produce pseudosexual precocity in the male and virilization in the female. **1964** *Steroids* IV. 140 A virilized woman.. with Cushing's syndrome due to an adrenal adenoma, had 390μg/day of testosterone in her urine. **1974** PASSMORE & ROBSON *Compan. Med. Stud.* III. xxviii. 50/1 This virilizing ovarian tumour.. occurs in young adults. **1976** *Lancet* 13 Nov. 1081/1 This hormone stopped her menses and produced all the features of virilisation. **1983** *Oxf. Textbk. Med.* I. x. 85/2 Excessive hair growth is among the commoner endocrine afflictions of women. The complaint may exist in isolation or it may be one of a constellation of abnormalities found in the virilized state.

virilocal (,vɪrɪ'ləʊkəl), *a. Anthrop.* [f. L. *virī-lis* VIRILE *a.* + LOCAL *a.* 2.] Pertaining to or designating a woman's residence after marriage in the domicile of her husband. Cf. PATRILOCAL, UXORILOCAL *adjs.*

1948 [see UXORILOCAL *a.*]. **1957** V. W. TURNER *Schism & Continuity Afr. Soc.* p. xviii, It is possible that hunting, a purely masculine pursuit, and virilocal marriage, which binds together male kin in local descent groups, are parallel expressions of structural opposition between men and women in this matrilineal society. **1969** in Halpert & Story *Christmas Mumming in Newfoundland* 137 A consequence of the rigidly virilocal marriage and settlement pattern.

Hence **virilo'cality**; **viri'locally** *adv.*

1957 V. W. TURNER *Schism & Continuity Afr. Soc.* p. xviii, Within villages the dominant principles influencing residence were maternal descent and virilocality. *Ibid.* ii. 55 Women are often brought up patrilocally, marry virilocally, and after divorce reside avunculocally until remarriage. **1974** G. H. GOSSEN in N. Hammond *Mesoamerican Archaeol.* 219 Chamulas live virilocally in dispersed hamlets.

†**viring-rope.** *Obs.*⁻¹ [app. f. VIRE *v.*] ? A warping rope.

1336 *Acc. Exch. K.R.* 19/31 m. 4 (Publ. Rec. Off.) In lx. petris cordis de canabo.. pro tribus viryngropes inde faciendis.

†**Virinus**, obs. var. VERINAS, VARINAS.

1666 J. DAVIES *Hist. Caribby Isles* 192 It is made more excellent than that which commonly goes under the name of Virinus-Tobacco.

virion ('vɪrɪɒn). *Microbiology.* [a. F. *virion* (A. Lwoff et al. 1959, in *Ann. de l'Inst. Pasteur* XCVII. 286), f. *vir-us* VIRUS + *-i-* + *-on* -ON¹.] The complete, infective form that a virus has outside a host cell, with a core and a capsid.

1959 *Ann. de l'Inst. Pasteur* XCVII. 288 The viral infective system, the virion, may be considered as a clathrate type of compound in which the genetic component is enclosed in a coat or capsid formed of subunits or capsomeres. **1967** K. M. SMITH *Insect Virol.* i. v The virion is, structurally and physiologically, different from any cellular organelle and from any microorganism. **1975** *Sci. Amer.* May 25/2 An electron micrograph of the polio-virus virion (the virus particle) reveals a sphere 17 nanometers (millionths of a millimeter) in diameter... The virion consists only of protein and the nucleic acid RNA.

†**vi'ripotence.** *Obs.*⁻⁰ [f. VIRIPOTENT *a.*¹: see -ENCE.] 'Marriageableness' (Bailey, 1727). So †**vi'ripotency.** *Obs.*⁻¹

1652 PEYTON *Catastr. Ho. Stuarts* (1731) 6 Mary Stuart.. when she attained to viripotency, was sought for a Consort to the Dauphine of France.

†**vi'ripotent**, *a.*¹ *Obs.* [ad. late L. *viripotent-*, *viripotens*, f. *vir* man, husband + *potens* able.] Of a woman: Physically fit for marriage; of a marriageable age.

1587 HOLINSHED *Chron.* (ed. 2) III. 38/1 The kings daughter affianced.. vnto him, and being now viripotent or mariable. *Ibid.* 101/2 He would not suffer his sonne to marrie hir, being not of ripe yeares nor viripotent or mariable. **1623** COCKERAM I. **1656** BLOUNT *Glossogr.*

†**vi'ripotent**, *a.*² *Obs.*⁻¹ [ad. L. *vīripotent-*, *vīripotens* (Plautus), f. *vīrēs* strength.] Possessed of strength or energy.

1646 GAULE *Cases of Conscience* 113 Of giving Potions to make people love or hate as they please. Making the strength of youth impotent, and dead Bodies viripotent.

†**viritrate.** *Obs.*⁻¹ [Of obscure origin: cf. ME. *trate*, *trat* TROT *sb.*²] An abusive term applied to an old woman.

c **1386** CHAUCER *Friar's T.* 284 This Somonour clappeth at the wydwes gate Com out quod he, thou olde virytrate, I trowe thou hast som frere or preest with thee.

virk, dial. var. FIRK *v.*

virk(e, obs. Sc. ff. WORK *v.*

virkin, dial. var. FIRKIN.

virking, obs. Sc. f. WORKING *vbl. sb.*

virl. Now only *Sc.* Forms: α. 5–6 vyroll (5 vyrolfe), virol. β. 5–6 vyral, 6 wyrall, viral(l. γ. 5 vyrille, vyr-, virelle, 6 wirrell, 9 virrel, 8– virl. [a. OF. *virol(e* and *virelle*: see VIROLE, VERREL, and FERRULE.] A band of metal, ivory, or bone, placed round the end or some other part of a piece of wood, etc., to keep it from splitting or wearing; a ferrule.

α. *c* **1440** *Promp. Parv.* 510/2 Vyrolfe, of a knyfe (*K.* uirol, *P.* vyroll.), *spirula.* *c* **1450** *Medulla* (Cant. MS.), *Toius est summitas templi eminens rotunditas*, a bolle or a toppe or els a rownde vyrolle. **1530** PALSGR. 285/1 Vyroll, *uirolle.* **1580** *Reg. Privy Council Scot.* III. 319 Ane battirt.. montit upoun ane auld stok, and hir axtre and quhelis garnysit with foure virols of irn.

β. **1496** *Acc. Ld. High Treas. Scot.* I. 289 Item, for iij^c nalis to the wyndbandis and the vyralis, iiij s. **1503** *Ibid.* II. 389 Item, for sevin score viralis and diamandis for speris, ilk pece vj d. **1547** in *N. & Q.* 9th Ser. IX. 109/2 Item three staves, every of theym having a picke with two graynes at the nether end and a wyrall of Iron tynned. **1552** in Strype *Eccl. Mem.* (1721) II. 539 One of the king's canes,.. garnished with gold; and having at the end a viral of gold.

γ. **14..** in Wr.-Wülcker 735 *Hec spirula*, a vyrille. **1482–4** *Acc. Exch. K.R.* 496/28 (Publ. Rec. Off.) Virelles Plates pro diversis poleys. **1483** *Cath. Angl.* 402/1 A vyrelle of a knyfe. **1511** *Acc. Ld. High Treas. Scot.* IV. 272 Foure dusson of wirrellis with diamontis. **1725** RAMSAY *Gentle Sheph.* I. i, A winsome flute, O' plum-tree made, wi' iv'ry virles round.

1787 Burns *Brigs Ayr* 84 Five taper staves as smooth's a bead, Wi' virls an' whirlygigums at the head. **1813** W. Tennant *Anster Concert* in *Life* (1861) I. 25 Braw flute, wi' ivory virls, man. **1890** Service *Notandums* 115, I gaed in to Willie Gaud's as I cam bye and got him to put a new virrel on my staff.

transf. **1823** Galt *Gilhaize* xii, He walked with slow and tottering steps, wearing a virl of fur round his neck.

Hence **virled** *ppl. a.*, furnished with a virl or ferrule. Also **'virlet**, a small virl.

1793 *Statist. Acc. Scot.* IX. 371 The blade is..set in a haft of Tortoise-shell, or stained horn, girt with silver virlets. **1822** Galt *Sir A. Wylie* III. v. 35 An ivory headed cane virled with gold. **1842** D. Vedder *Poems* 227 A staff..Cut frae the gallows wood, Weel virled about wi' murderer's banes.

virlat, obs. Sc. form of VARLET.

†**virly.** *Obs.*[−1] [ad. OF. *virely*, *vireli*, in origin probably a meaningless refrain employed in dancing songs.] A light dance, or sport accompanied by dancing.

c **1430** *Pilgr. Lyf Manhode* III. xxx. (1869) 152 Boistows j am, and haltinge, and wronge. To the virly j go hippinge.

virm, obs. Sc. f. WORM *sb.*

virmet, obs. Sc. var. WORMWOOD.

virmilion, obs. f. VERMILION.

virmin, obs. or U.S. f. VERMIN *sb.*

viro- ('vaɪrəʊ), comb. form of VIRUS (sense 2 b), as in **'virogene**, a gene sequence corresponding to the genome of a tumour virus but occurring, normally repressed, in a cell; **viro'genesis**, the formation or production of viruses; **viroge'netic**, **-'genic** *adjs.*, giving rise to viruses; **viro'pexis** [after *colloidopexis*, f. Gr. πῆξις fixing], the process by which a virus particle becomes attached to a cell wall and incorporated into the cell by phagocytosis; **'virosome** [-SOME[4]], (*a*) a particle of ribonucleoprotein and virus DNA found in the cytoplasm of certain virus-infected cells; (*b*) a liposome into which viral proteins have been introduced.

1969 Virogene [see ONCOGENE]. **1971** *Nature* 27 Aug. 620/2 [This] suggests that activation of this sarcoma oncogene in the tumour cells is often accompanied by activation of the gs antigen of the virogene. **1976** *Ibid.* 13 May 101/1 African Old World monkeys..and African apes ..possess virogenes that are useful in the taxonomic classification of these animals. **1961** Virogenesis [see *virogenetic* adj. below]. **1982** *Virology* CXXI. 296 (*heading*) The nuclear matrix is involved in herpes simplex virogenesis. **1961** *Jrnl. Insect Path.* III. 195 Inasmuch as the virogenetic network (strands) spreads over the entire cell, the viro-genesis is neither confined to the cytoplasm nor to the nucleus. **1982** *Jrnl. Urol.* CXXVII. 646/2 The improved graft survival..may be an additional manifestation of unresponsiveness, not only to immunologic but also to virogenetic stimulation. **1956** *Nature* 25 Aug. 412/1 In the midgut cells of Hymenoptera infected with nuclear polyhedroses proteinaceous virogenic stromata form *de novo* in the nuclear sap... They are networks, and virus rods differentiate within vesicles in their cords. **1982** *Jrnl. Invertebrate Path.* XXXIX. 205/2 The hypertrophy is evident at a very early stage and before any obvious sign of a virus infection, such as the virogenic stroma. **1948** S. F. de St. Groth in *Nature* 21 Aug. 295/1 This phenomenon strongly recalls the uptake by cells of colloidal dyes, and may ..be termed 'viropexis'. **1981** *Jrnl. Gen. Virol.* LII. 329 Virosomes were taken up by Vero cells by viropexis with no evidence of fusion. **1970** Dahl & Kates in *Virology* XLII. 453/2 Since viral DNA complexes are quite poorly defined biochemically it seems appropriate to refer to such structures by the general term 'virosomes'.., in analogy with chromosomes, in order to avoid more restricted nomenclature (e.g., viral DNA, DNA 'factories', etc.), which may..create a misleading impression concerning their composition and function. **1975** J. D. Almeida et al. in *Lancet* 8 Nov. 899/2 The surface hæmagglutinin and neuraminidase projections of influenza virus were removed from the viral envelope..and relocated on the surface of unilamellar liposomes. The resulting structures were.. found to resemble the original virus... The name virosome is proposed for these new bodies. **1981** *Jrnl. Gen. Virol.* LII. 329 Virosomes constitute a model system for studies on the organization of virus membrane proteins and lipids and interaction between virus particles and membranes.

viroid ('vaɪərɔɪd). *Biol.* [f. VIR(US + -OID.]

1. A virus-like particle. Also *attrib.* or as *adj.* Now *disused* in favour of next sense.

1946 E. Altenburg in *Amer. Naturalist* LXXX. 559 It is conceivable that there exist ultra-microscopic organisms which are akin to viruses but which are useful symbionts, and that these symbionts occur *universally* within the cells of larger organisms. We might call these supposed symbionts viroids. **1953** S. E. Luria *Gen. Virol.* xviii. 361 Mutations of viroids could also give rise to nontransmissible, abnormal plasmagenes and be responsible..for the tumoral transformation of cells. **1959** *Oxf. Mag.* 26 Feb. 286/2 The relationship between viruses and other 'viroid' particles. **1963** *New Scientist* 20 June 652/1 If blind natural selection could conjure man out of a viroid in a couple of billion years, what could not man's conscious and purposeful efforts achieve?

2. An infectious entity similar to a virus but smaller and consisting of a strand of nucleic acid only, without the protein coat characteristic of a virus.

1971 T. O. Diener in *Virology* XLV. 426/1, I propose the term 'viroid' for such entities. Altenburg (1946) introduced this term to designate hypothetical symbionts, akin to viruses... If, however, the 'viroid' is redefined operationally and in modern terms to encompass nucleic acid species with the properties discussed here, the term serves a useful function. To distinguish pathological conditions incited by viroids from those incited by viruses, the term 'viroid disease' is proposed. **1979** *Nature* 4 Jan. 60/2 Viroids are the smallest replicating pathogenic agents known. **1981** *Times* 2 Apr. 16 There is a parallel class of agents which infect plants, the viroids, which consist solely of strands of RNA.

‖**virole.** *Her.* Also **virolé.** [a. F. *virole* ring, ferrule (see VIRL), and *virolé* provided with a ferrule.] (See quots.)

1722 A. Nisbet *Her.* 226 From Vires, are the Terms Viroles, and Virole, in the Blazons of Figures, that have Hoops and Rings round them. **1780** Edmondson *Her.* II *Virolé*, is the hoop, ring, or mouth-piece of the bugle or hunting horn.

Hence **viroled** *a.*

c **1828** Berry *Encycl. Her.* I. Gloss., *Virolled*, this term is sometimes used for the garnishings of the bugle-horn, being the rings or rims, which surround it at various parts.

virology (vaɪ'rɒlədʒɪ). [f. VIR(US + -OLOGY.] The branch of science concerned with the study of viruses.

1935 in Dorland & Miller *Med. Dict.* (ed. 17) 1502/2. **1937** *Ann. Reg. 1936* 59 In virology, two discoveries overshadowed all others. **1957** *New Scientist* 9 May 11/1 This will be the first chair in virology in this country, and its creation marks a stage in the development of virology from the young brother of bacteriology to a fully grown science in its own right. **1978** H. McLeave *Borderline Case* x. (1979) 96 She no longer looked like a virology professor but an attractive, seductive woman.

Hence **viro'logic** (chiefly *U.S.*), **-'logical** *adjs.*; **viro'logically** *adv.*; **vi'rologist**, a specialist in virology.

1946 *Nature* 14 Sept. 363/1 One of the main objects of the symposium, the finding of common grounds of interest between virologists, bacteriologists, mycologists and geneticists, was fully achieved. **1953** S. E. Luria *Gen. Virol.* p. ix, In spite of many important additions to virological literature, no single volume suitable for class-room use has appeared. **1955** *Proc. Soc. Exper. Biol. & Med.* LXXXIX. 438/1 The Detroit-6 strain fulfills certain criteria..for a useful cell strain for virologic research. **1963** *Guardian* 10 Apr. 20/3 Virologists in the research laboratories at Mill Hill were exploring the possibility that some forms of human cancer may be caused by viruses. **1970** *Sci. Jrnl.* Apr. 3/3 The history of virological research is one of the continual discovery of new viruses or of new facts about old viruses. **1972** *Arch. Neurol.* XXVII. 103 (*heading*) Herpes simplex encephalitis. The course in five virologically proven cases. **1977** M. Sokolinsky tr. *Merle's Virility Factor* xii. 248 He was a virologist without great clinical experience. **1980** *Brit. Jrnl. Dermatol.* CIII. Suppl. No. 18. 24 Virological studies were performed on stools and throat swabs in all patients. **1980** *Amer. Jrnl. Epidemiol.* CXII. 487 There were two virologically confirmed cases with complications. **1983** *Amer. Jrnl. Veterinary Res.* XLIV. 64/1 The serologic and virologic responses of all cattle were monitored for 1 year.

†**viron**, *sb. Obs.* Also 4 viroun, 5 vyroun, vyrown, vyrne. [a. OF. *viron* (f. *virer* to turn), used as prep. or in the phr. *en viron* ENVIRON.]

1. Circuit, compass; a circling course. *in the viron of*, round about.

a **1380** *St. Augustine* 1221 in Horstm. *Altengl. Leg.* (1878) 82 þe viroun [L. *circulum*] of þe wattres wondurliche He schewed. **1382** Wyclif *Judg.* ii. 12 The sones of Yrael.. folweden alien goddis, goddis of the puple that dwelten in the viroun of hem. *c* **1400** *Arth. & Merl.* (L.) 1616 þe rede dragoun..Drof þeo white feor adoun In to þe pleynes a gret vyroun. *c* **1440** *Promp. Parv.* 510/2 Vyrne, or sercle,..*girus, ambitus, circulus.*

2. *in viron*, round about; = ENVIRON *adv.*

c **1380** Wyclif *Sel. Wks.* II. 311 In viroun and wiþinne þei weren ful of iȝen. **1447** Bokenham *Seyntys* (Roxb.) 107 Summe blewe so sore that the flaume up sprong Aboutyn hyr sydys even in vyroun. *c* **1450** Lovelich *Merlin* 3196 [He must] serchen jn market & town Abowtes al this contre jn vyrown. *c* **1450** —— *Grail* xlii. 46 ȝit he loked he bothe vppe and down Al abowtes that schipe in vyrown.

†**viron**, *v. Obs.* Also 5 vyroun, 5-6 viron (6 vyron); 5 vyrnyn. [ad. OF. *vironner*, f. *viron*: see prec. and cf. ENVIRON *v.*]

1. *trans.* To go round; to make the circuit of.

1382 Wyclif *Pref. Epist. St. Jerome* i, We han redde in olde stories, sum men to han vyrounde [L. *lustrasse*] prouynces.

2. To environ or encircle, to surround (*with* something).

c **1440** *Promp. Parv.* 510/2 Vyrnyn a-bowte, or closyn (*K.* closyn abowtyn), *vallo, circumvallo. Ibid.*, Vyrnyn a-bowte, or gon a-bowte, *ambio, circumdo.* *c* **1440** *Psalmi Penit.* (1894) 10 Thu art my refute yn my woo, That hath vironed me aboute. **1523** Ld. Berners *Froiss.* I. ccccviii. 711 They vyroned rounde aboute the towne. *c* **1530** —— *Arth. Lyt. Bryt.* (1814) 139 The curtaynes were of grene sendall vyroned wyth golde & asure. **1587** Turberv. *Trag. T.* (1837) 40 We may presume the service there was rare, Because the board was vironed round with states.

†**vironry.** *Obs.*[−1] [Cf. prec. and ENVIRONRY.] Environment.

1600 Tourneur *Transf. Metam.* lxxxv. Dvj, Her streaming rayes haue pierc'd the cloudie skies, And.. Cleared the world of her blacke vironries.

virose (vaɪ'rəʊs), *a.* Now *rare.* [ad. L. *vīrōs-us*, f. *vīrus* VIRUS.] Poisonous; suggestive of poisonous qualities; rank and unwholesome:

a. Of things, esp. plants.

1680 Morden *Geogr. Rect., Germany* (1685) 124 The virose streams and particles of Mercury, or other Minerals descending from off their Mountains. **1702** *Phil. Trans.* XXIII. 1167 Most of them are of an Aromatic Smell and Taste, but some are fœtid, virose, and fervid in their Taste. **1767** *Nat. Hist.* in *Ann. Reg.* 98/2 The root of the œnanthes that is like hemlock, with virose juice. **1845-50** Mrs. Lincoln *Lect. Bot.* App. 205 *Virose*, nauseous to the smell, poisonous. **1866** *Treas. Bot.* 1219/2.

b. Of smell or flavour.

1756 P. Browne *Jamaica* 174 This plant..is of a virose heavy smell. **1761** *Phil. Trans.* LII. 92 By that time the plants will..have acquired an highly virose smell. **1817** J. E. Smith in *Encycl. Brit.* (ed. 4) Suppl. II. 405/1 Some [leaves] have a virose or nauseous flavour about them. **1831** J. Davies *Manual Mat. Med.* 309 Its smell is virose and nauseous. **1840** *Penny Cycl.* XVII. 206/1 The virose and nauseous odour which characterises crude opium.

virosis (vaɪə'rəʊsɪs). Pl. **-oses** (-'əʊsiːz). [f. VIR(US + -OSIS.] A virus disease.

1927 *Phytopathology* XVII. 161 Certain aggregates of symptoms in potatoes (*Solanum tuberosum*) are considered to be due to corresponding degeneration diseases or viroses. [*Note*] A name for 'virus diseases' proposed on December 28, 1925, at Lincoln, Nebraska, by Dr. L. R. Jones. **1963** G. Benz in E. A. Steinhaus *Insect Path.* I. x. 325 The most intimate association between the pathogen and its host is found in viroses. **1972** *Biol. Abstr.* LIII. 3729/2 The 'spindle virosis' of *M. melolontha* is characterized by the coexistence of 2 types of cytoplasmic inclusions: spindles and spherules.

†**virour.** *Obs.*[−1] [ad. late L. *viror*, f. *virēre* to be green.] Green growth, verdure.

1657 Tomlinson *Renou's Disp.* I. VII. xiii. 403 Ivy.. circumvests..vicine Plants; which it kills with its multifarious convolutions and virour [L. orig. *virore*].

virous ('vaɪrəs), *a. rare.* = VIROSE *a.*

1661 Lovell *Hist. Anim. & Min.* 240 They are pleasant to the pallate; but of evil juyce, and virouse. **1887** A. M. Brown *Anim. Alkaloids* 26 The liquid ptomaines possess a virous, cadaveric odour, occasionally suggestive of musk or odoriferous plants.

virr (vɪr). *Sc.* Also vir. [Of obscure origin.] Force, vigour, energy.

c **1575** *Balfour's Practicks* (1754) 493 Making of the course of the water to be of greiter force or strenth than of befoir, or ȝit to be of greiter force or virre than of befoir. **1710** Ruddiman *Gloss. Douglas' Æneis, Bir*, force, noise which an arrow, or such like makes in the air. *Scoti boreales* Vir *pronunciant.* **1742** R. Forbes *Jrnl. fr. London* (1755) 31 Syne we laid our heads together, an' at it wi' virr. **1790** Shirrefs *Poems* 141 Bessy ran, and brought some whins, wi' vir, Frae out the nook. **1808-92** in *Eng. Dial. Dict.*

virre, southern ME. var. FIR; var. VERRE *Obs.*

virrok (obs. Sc.): see WIRROCK.

virry, obs. Sc. f. WORRY *v.*

virschepe, virschip, obs. Sc. ff. WORSHIP.

virschypful, obs. f. WORSHIPFUL.

virse, southern ME. var. FURZE.

virsling, obs. Sc. var. WRESTLING.

virst, southern ME. var. FIRST *sb.* and *a.*, FRIST *sb.*

virste, obs. var. WRIST *sb.*

virsute, obs. var. VERSUTE *a.*

virtiginous, obs. f. VERTIGINOUS.

virtigo, obs. f. VERTIGO.

†**virtival.** *Obs.*[−1] [ad. F. *vertivelle*: cf. VARTIWELL.] A bush or metal support for an axle.

1794 *Ann. Reg., Chron.* 32 The lightning..finally threw the axis of one of the clock hammers out of the bouches or virtivals, by which it was supported.

‖**virtu, vertu** (vɜː'tuː, 'vɜːtuː). Also vertù, virtù. [a. It. *virtù*:—L. *virtūt-em*, acc. sing. of *virtus* VIRTUE. The form *vertu* follows French spelling without justification, as the Italian sense of the word has never been current in French.]

1. a. A love of, or taste for, works of art or curios; a knowledge of, or interest in, the fine arts; the fine arts as a subject of study or interest.

α. **1722** Richardson *Statues*, etc. *in Italy* 290 The whole Nation have a sort of Love to what they call the *Virtù*, and know Something of it. **1752** Foote *Taste* Prol., Virtù to such a height is grown, All artists are encourag'd—but our own. **1782** Han. More *Let.* in W. Roberts *Mem.* (1834) I. 248 Mr. Locke, a man of fashion,..and so deep in virtú, that every artist of every sort allows Mr. Locke to beat him even in the secrets of his own art. **1820** Scott *Let.* in *Lockhart* (1837) IV. xi. 358 It may be the foundation of a set of bronzes, if stout Lord Walter should turn to *virtu*. **1858** Carlyle *Fredk. Gt.* III. viii. I. 266 No noble Nation sunk from virtue to virtù, ever offered such a spectacle before.

personif. **1841** Lytton *Nt. & Morn.* Introd., A lumber-room; Lumber, indeed! what *Virtù* double-locks in cabinets is the real lumber to the boy!

β. **1742** Pope *Dunc.* IV. 569 Her children..Who study Shakespeare at the Inns of Court, Impale a Glow-worm, or Vertù profess. **1771** Mackenzie *Man Feel.* (1886) 147 Fashion, Bon ton, and Vertù, are the homes of certain idols, to which we sacrifice the genuine pleasures of the soul. **1815**

W. H. Ireland *Scribbleomania* 118 A Walpole for love of vertù far renown'd. **1830** Cunningham *Brit. Paint.* I. 236 This country at that period..exported swarms of men with the malady of vertu upon them. **1871** Smiles *Charact.* ix. (1876) 262 There [at Rome], the virtus or valour of the ancient Romans has characteristically degenerated into vertu, or a taste for knicknacks.

b. ***man*** (or ***gentleman***) ***of virtu***, a virtuoso.

1749 Fielding *Tom Jones* xiii. v, They..may be called men of wisdom and vertù (take heed you do not read virtue). **1787** *Gentl. Mag.* 1163/1 Being in company lately with several gentlemen of virtù, I found in their conversation frequent use of the word Taste in a sense I was unaccustomed to. **1811** Jeffrey in *Edin. Rev.* May 31 There are few things, about which men of *virtu* are more apt to rave, than the merits of the Grecian architecture.

c. ***article, object, piece***, etc., ***of virtu***, an article such as virtuosos are interested in; a curio, antique, or other product of the fine arts.

α. **1771** Goldsm. *Haunch of Venison* 8, I had thoughts in my chambers to place it in view, To be shown to my friends as a piece of virtù. **1825** T. Hook *Sayings* Ser. ii. *Man of Many Fr.* (Colburn) 148 Soon were they doomed to withdraw their eyes from the innumerable bits of virtù which surrounded them. **1857** C. Sumner in S. Longfellow *Life Longf.* (1891) II. 343 Stirling's house is full of the choicest articles of virtù. **1879** S. C. Bartlett *Egypt to Pal.* iv. 74 An immense number of articles of virtu from Egypt are now scattered through the world.

β. **1815** J. Scott *Vis. Paris* (ed. 2) 116 The manufacture of some decoration, some piece of vertù, some elegant trifle. **1848** Thackeray *Van. Fair* xlix, Bareacres Castle was theirs,..with all its costly pictures, furniture, and articles of vertu. **1902** Snaith *Wayfarers* ii, Every object of *vertu* that I ever possessed.

2. A special branch of this study or interest.

1745–6 Mrs. Delany in *Life & Corr.* (1861) II. 429 Last Tuesday Mr. Bristowe, an uncle of Miss Dashwood's, dined here; he is a great virtuoso, understands all the *virtus* to perfection.

3. *collect.* Objects of art; curios.

Not always clearly distinguishable from sense 1.

1746 H. Walpole *Let. to G. Montagu* 17 June, My books, my *virtu*, and my other follies and amusements take up too much of my time to leave me much leisure to think of other people's affairs. **1768** *Let.* in J. H. Jesse *Selwyn & Contemp.* (1843) II. 308 My longing to see my own collection of *virtu* at Castle Howard is wonderful. **1773** W. Mason *Heroick Ep. Sir W. Chambers* 7 Whose orb collects, in one refulgent view, The scatter'd glories of Chinese Virtù. **1839** Barham *Ingol. Leg.* Ser. i. *Acc. New Play*, Some Vandal or Jew, With a taste for virtu, Has knock'd off his toes, to place, I suppose, In some Pickwick Museum. **1858** D. Costello *Millionaire of Mincing Lane* ii, Pictures, crockery, gimcracks of all kinds—what is generally known as *virtù*.

attrib. **1792** J. Wolcott (P. Pindar) *Ep. Sir W. Hamilton* Postscr. 4 What Britons, *knowing* in the *Virtú* trade, Soon as a grand discov'ry shall be made, Are near thee,..prepar'd to bite?

4. The distinctive qualities inherent in a thing or person.

1934 E. Pound *Eleven New Cantos* xxxvi. 27 Or say where it had birth What is its virtu and power. **1949** —— *Pisan Cantos* lxxiv. 11 In the light of light is the virtù. **1969** *Listener* 14 Aug. 214/3 Cromwell was shown in the same light—of a *de facto* sovereign come into power thanks to his *virtù*—by Clarendon. **1973** *Times Lit. Suppl.* 1 June 601/3 The pagan *virtù*, the 'civic humanism' of Machiavelli, had become the proud Christian freedom of the Huguenots.

virtual (ˈvɜːtjuːəl), *a.* (and *sb.*). Forms: 4, 7–8 **vertual** (7 **-all**); 5 *Sc.* **wertual(e, -all**; 5–7 **virtuall** (5 **-alle**), 6– **virtual**. [ad. med.L. *virtuālis*, f. L. *virtus* virtue, after L. *virtuōsus*. Hence also It. *virtuale*, Sp. and Pg. *virtual*, F. *virtuel*.]

1. a. Possessed of certain physical virtues or capacities; effective in respect of inherent natural qualities or powers; capable of exerting influence by means of such qualities. Now *rare*.

1398 Trevisa *Barth. De P.R.* xix. viii. (Bodl. MS.), But vertual liȝt igadered in a litel place or in a pointe is cleped moche liȝt. **1477** Norton *Ord. Alch.* v. in Ashm. (1652) 62 But our chiefe Digesture for our intent, Is virtuall heate of the matter digerent. *a* **1593** Marlowe *Hero & Leander* iii. 89 So to all objects..his senses' flame Flowd from his parts with force so virtuall, It fir'd with sence things weere insensuall. **1626** Bacon *Sylva* §326 See if the Virtuall Heat of the Wine, or Strong Waters will not mature it. **1657** R. Ligon *Barbadoes* (1673) 106 Though the virtual beams of the Sun, give growth and life to all the Plants and Flowers it shines on. **1675** E. Wilson *Spadacrene Dunelmensis* Pref., Even ordinary water admits of a virtual mixture at least, as Experience evidenceth in Chalybeate waters. **1898** Meredith *Odes Fr. Hist.* 91 It was the foreign France the unruly feared,..Not virtual France, the France benevolent, The chivalrous.

b. Of herbs: Possessing specific virtues. *rare*.

1660 F. Brooke *Le Blanc's Trav.* 364 To Rivers they sacrifice the shels that come from them, to fountains fruits and vertual herbs. **1830** T. Aird *Captive of Fez* iii, She knew..every virtual plant, and every sovereign flower Beneath the moon.

†**2.** Morally virtuous. *Obs.*

c **1425** Wyntoun *Cron.* vii. 1218 His awyn oysse to lif wertual, May mirroure and ensample be Til alkyn statis. *Ibid.* vii. viii. 2206 Iohun of Salerne, prest cardynale, Commendit a lorde wertuale. **1607** Dekker *Wh. of Babylon* Wks. 1873 II. 216 You by your heauenly Influence change his vilenes Into a vertuall habit fit for vse.

†**3. a.** Capable of producing a certain effect or result; effective, potent, powerful. *Obs.*

1432–50 tr. *Higden* (Rolls) II. 177 For a man and the worlde be assimilate in iij. thynges, in dimension diametralle.., in disposicion naturalle, and in operation virtualle. *Ibid.* 185. **1526** *Pilgr. Perf.* (Pynson) iii. ix. 47 b, That is called after Saynt Thomas virtuall attencyon which causeth a person in the begynnyng of his prayer to haue an actuall consideracion of the prayer or duety that he hath to do. **1619** W. Sclater *Exp. 1 Thess.* (1630) 37 So vertuall was the speech of Paul a Prisoner, in the heart of his Judge. **1640** Shirley *Arcadia* iv. iii, I meant it A draught for false Zelmane, it being virtual To increase affection. **1672** Josselyn *New Eng. Rarities* 12 The Loone is a Water Fowl, alike in shape to the Wobble, and as virtual for Aches. **1683** Moxon *Mech. Exerc., Printing* i, Dr. Dee..as a vertual Proof of his own Learned Plea, quotes two Authentique Authors.

b. *Mech.* (See quots.)

1815 J. Smith *Panorama Sci. & Art* II. 124 Whatever is the real length of the leg *b a* [of a siphon], the virtual or acting length when in use, only extends from *b* to the surface of the fluid. **1825** J. Nicholson *Oper. Mech.* 67 The velocity ..due to a head of 15 inches; and this we call the *virtual* or *effective head*.

4. a. That is so in essence or effect, although not formally or actually; admitting of being called by the name so far as the effect or result is concerned.

1654 Jer. Taylor *Real Pres.* 21 We affirm that Christ is really taken by faith,..they say he is taken by the mouth, and that the spiritual and the virtual taking him in virtue or effect is not sufficient, though done also. **1664** —— *Dissuas. Popery* ii. §8 But even this attention is not necessary that it should be actual, but it suffices to be virtual. **1697** Burghope *Disc. Relig. Assemb.* 166 We shall find it to amount to no less than a vertual renunciation of our baptism. **1734** Waterland *Diss. Exist. First Cause* 30 Every Proof *a priori* proceeds by Causes either real or virtual. **1769** Burke *Obs. Pres. St. Nat.* Wks. 1842 I. 112 One part of it could not be yielded..without a virtual surrender of all the rest. **1787** Bentham *Def. Usury* viii. 73 *Heading*, Virtual Usury allowed. **1820** Milner *Suppl. Mem. Eng. Cath.* 132 To prevent the virtual choice of a Catholic Bishop by an A-Catholic Ministry. **1844** H. H. Wilson *Brit. India* III. 211 He had reigned thirty-three years, during the first ten of which he was virtual sovereign of the greater part of Hindustan. **1883** A. Barratt *Phys. Metempiric* 157 The simplest conscious action involves actual or virtual thought.

b. ***Virtual Church***, a council or similar body acting in the name of the whole church. Also *ellipt.* as *sb.*

1646 J. Maxwell *Burden of Issachar* 20 Whatsoever power..the Catholike Church, or her virtuall and Representative, an œcumenical Councel, justly challengeth, this general Assembly vindicateth to it selfe. *Ibid.* 45 It was not consented to by the Church: that is, the Virtuall Church, the Generall Assemblie. **1654** Bramhall *Just Vind.* viii. (1661) 230 In all which..they understand..the virtual Church which is inuested with Ecclesiastical power, that is, the Pope with his Cardinals and Ministers.

c. *Optics.* Applied to the apparent focus or image resulting from the effect of reflection or refraction upon rays of light.

(*a*) **1704** J. Harris *Lex. Techn.* I, *Virtual Focus*, or *Point of Divergence* in a Concave Glass. **1728** Chambers *Cycl.*, *Point of Dispersion*, is that wherein the Rays begin to diverge; usually call'd the Virtual Focus. **1808** J. Webster *Nat. Philos.* 185 They issued from the virtual focus in the axis of the lens. **1831** Brewster *Optics* i. 11 The point A′, behind the mirror..is called their *virtual focus*, because they only tend to meet in that focus. **1874** *Lommel's Light* 90 The lenses of the second group have virtual foci.

(*b*) **1831** Brewster *Optics* ii. 18 In convex mirrors the image is always a virtual one formed behind the mirror. **1859** Parkinson *Optics* (1866) 130 A familiar instance of a *virtual* image is that formed by a common looking-glass of an object in front of it:—the image of an object under water is *virtual*. **1885** *Buck's Handbk. Med. Sci.* I. 39/1 If their direction, after the refraction, be prolonged backward, their prolongations meet to form a virtual image.

d. *Dynamics.* Of velocity or moment (see quot. 1867). ***virtual displacement***, any notional, infinitesimal displacement in a mechanical system that is consistent with the constraints of the system; ***virtual work***, the work done by a force making a virtual displacement.

1818 Barlow in *Encycl. Metrop.* (1845) III. 41/1 [The] principle..of virtual velocities..is now, by most foreign writers, made the foundation of the whole theory of statics. **1843** *Penny Cycl.* XXVI. 373/2 The name of the principle of virtual velocities..is very ill fitted to express the idea which is to be conveyed. [Full account follows.] **1867** Thomson & Tait *Nat. Phil.* I. i. §237 If the point of application of a force be displaced through a small space, the resolved part of the displacement in the direction of the force has been called its Virtual Velocity. *Ibid.*, The product of the force, into the virtual velocity of its point of application, has been called the Virtual Moment of the force. **1877** G. M. Minchin *Treat. Statics* iv. 61 The virtual work of a force is the product of the force and the projection along its direction of the virtual displacement of its point of application. **1897** A. E. H. Love *Theoret. Mech.* viii. 139 Principle of Virtual Work. The sum of the virtual works of all the forces on a system in equilibrium vanishes in every infinitesimal displacement. **1942** Synge & Griffiths *Princ. Mech.* ii. 60 Although the chief merit of the principle of virtual work lies in the fact that it does not involve the reactions of constraints, nevertheless it can be used to find these reactions should they be required. **1981** R. R. Craig *Structural Dynamics* ii. 28 Use the principle of virtual displacements to derive the equation of motion of the idealized system shown below.

e. *Nucl. Physics.* Applied to an excited state of an atomic nucleus which has energy in excess of that needed for the emission of a particle but a lifetime sufficiently long for it to be regarded as a quasi-stationary state.

1931 *Proc. R. Soc.* A. CXXXIII. 228 According to the theory..the emission of α- particles by radio active nuclei is to be explained by the assumption that there exists in the nucleus a 'virtual' level of positive energy, which is occupied by an α- particle. **1955** I. Kaplan *Nucl. Physics* xvi. 368 Each excited state of the compound nucleus, whether bound or virtual, has a certain mean lifetime. **1963** W. E. Burcham *Nucl. Physics* ix. 372 All nuclear levels, except the ground state, can in principle emit radiation, leaving the nucleus in a less highly excited state, and virtual levels can in addition emit particles.

f. *Particle Physics.* Applied to particles and processes that cannot be directly detected and occur over very short intervals of time and space with correspondingly indefinite energy and momenta, which are not necessarily conserved within the time involved.

1949 *Physical Rev.* LXXV. 1305/2 These divergent terms must now be interpreted as renormalization or modification of the electric charge of the proton due to virtual mesons. **1961** W. S. C. Williams *Introd. Elementary Particles* xiii. 341 If the incident photon is 140 Mev and the positron is emitted at 90° with an energy of 100 Mev, then the four-momentum of this virtual electron is about 140 Mev/c. **1971** *Sci. Amer.* June 71/3 Although it may seem that virtual particles violate fundamental conservation laws, the violation is closely delimited to those areas where the uncertainty principle applies. **1973** L. J. Tassie *Physics Elementary Particles* viii. 15 The electron now consists of its 'bare' self together with all its virtual interactions with the electromagnetic field, corresponding to the electron emitting and re-absorbing virtual photons. **1973** *Sci. Amer.* Oct. 110/1 The scattering of the two electrons is described by saying that these particles exchange a virtual photon that transfers momentum from one particle to the other. **1979** D. R. Hofstadter *Gödel, Escher, Bach* (1980) v. 146 To understand how a real, physical electron propagates..the physicist has to be able to take a sort of average of all the infinitely many different possible drawings which involve virtual particles.

g. *Computers.* Not physically existing as such but made by software to appear to do so from the point of view of the program or the user; *spec.* applied to memory that appears to be internal although most of it is external, transfer between the two being made automatically as required.

1959 *Proc. Eastern Joint Computer Conf.* xvi. 82/2 The sole function of the virtual memory is to increase machine speed. **1966** R. Adair et al. *IBM Cambridge Scientific Center Rep.* No. G320-2007 (*title*) A virtual machine system for the 360/40. **1966** *IBM Systems Jrnl.* V. 79 A virtual-storage computer (vsc) can decode addresses that are longer than those of its memory. The longer address is treated..as a virtual address that must be transformed to the actual, shorter memory address... The virtual addressing of the word in external storage triggers a procedure that automatically brings the addressed word into memory. **1972** *Computer Jrnl.* XV. 199/2 Our system runs in a virtual machine, which is implemented by an interpreter. We can therefore easily add new instructions to our virtual hardware, merely by extending the interpreter. **1973** P. B. Hansen *Operating System Princ.* i. 3 An operating system makes a virtual machine available to each user... The simultaneous presence of several users makes the virtual machines much slower than the physical machine. **1981** Pohl & Shaw *Nature of Computation* vi. 198 The Algolic language defines an Algolic virtual machine that may be implemented on a variety of computers. The Algolic machine could be constructed with the following software on a particular machine. **1982** G. Lee *From Hardware to Software* xxvi. 444 In a multi-programming system, several programs are being executed 'at once'... Thus the operating system has to make available to each user a virtual store, of which he appears to be the sole user. **1983** *80 Microcomputing* Feb. 232/2 Virtual-memory systems have been prevalent in main-frames and large minicomputers for at least a decade. **1985** *Which Computer?* Apr. 54/1 No doubt this is a side effect of using the disc as a virtual memory.

h. Other collocations: ***virtual cathode*** (Electronics), a part of a space charge or electron beam where the potential is a minimum, so that electrons are repelled and positive ions attracted; ***virtual height***, the height of an imaginary reflecting plane surface which in free space would give rise to the same travel time for reflected radio waves as an actual ionospheric layer; ***virtual temperature*** (Meteorol.) [tr. F. *température virtuelle* (Guldberg & Mohn *Études sur les Mouvements de l' Atmosphère* (1876) i. i. 6)], the temperature that dry air would have to have in order to have the same density as a given body of moist air when at the same pressure.

1937 *Virtual cathode [see suppressor 3]. **1964** *New Scientist* 1 Oct. 29/1 It was found that a virtual cathode could be obtained with a beam current of 3·5 milliamperes or more, and that its relaxation time was in fact inversely proportional to pressure. **1928** *Proc. IRE* XVI. 85 The heights as given in this paper are *virtual heights. They are calculated on the assumption that ordinary reflection takes place and that the layer is parallel to the earth's surface. **1967** [see ionogram 1]. **1975** D. G. Fink *Electronics Engineers' Handbk.* xviii. 107 The reflection process for plane ionosphere is equivalent to mirror-type reflection at a height equal to the virtual height *h′* of reflection of the equivalent vertical frequency. **1910** C. Abbe tr. Guldberg & Mohn in *Smithsonian Misc. Collections* LI. No. 4. 124 We call the quantity *T* the *virtual temperature; for dry air the virtual temperature is the same as the absolute temperature. **1957** G. E. Hutchinson *Treat. Limnol.* I. vii. 468 *C* represents the virtual temperature of isothermal circulation prior to the development of stratification in the early summer. **1979** L. J. Battan *Fund. Meteorol.* v. 83 The effects of humidity can be taken into account by employing a quantity called the virtual temperature.

virtualism (ˈvɜːtjuːəlɪz(ə)m). [f. prec. + -ism.] The Calvinistic doctrine of Christ's virtual presence in the Eucharist.

1883 *Ch. Times* XXI. 775 The haze and cloud of Genevan Virtualism. **1905** *Treasury* Oct. 5 Charles Wordsworth.. a learned exponent of 'virtualism' in Eucharistic doctrine.

virtualist ('vɜːtjuːəlɪst). [f. as prec. + -IST.] One who holds or advocates virtualism.

1897 *Month* Sept. 331 Without devoting much space to the attempt to prove that St. Thomas was a Virtualist. **1908** *Sat. Rev.* 12 Sept. 322/2 Our countrymen.. knowing their Church Catechism, are neither Zwinglians nor Virtualists.

virtuality (vɜːtjuː'ælɪtɪ). Also 5 **vertualyte**. [f. VIRTUAL *a.* + -ITY, perh. after med.L. **virtualitas*. Cf. F. *virtualité*, It. *virtualità*, Sp. *virtualidad*, Pg. *virtualidade*.]

†**1. a.** The possession of force or power. *Obs.*$^{-1}$

1483 CAXTON *Gold. Leg.* 25 b/1 Now we may saye that Jhesus in his ascension was right hye of iiii maners of heyght that is to wyte of place, of remuneracion or reward, of knowleche, and of vertualyte or strengthe.

†**b.** Something endowed with virtue or power.

1614 RALEIGH *Hist. World* I. i. 7 This omnipotent Spirit of God.. St. Augustine sometimes taketh.. for the holy Ghost; sometimes for a winde or breath,.. or.. for a created virtuality.

2. Essential nature or being, apart from external form or embodiment.

1646 SIR T. BROWNE *Pseud. Ep.* VII. ii. 343 In one graine of corne.. there lyeth dormant the virtuality of many other, and from thence sometimes proceed an hundred eares. **1688** R. L'ESTRANGE *Brief Hist. Times* II. Pref., The Two Main Pillars of the Old Cause were the Protestation (that was afterwards Emprov'd into a Covenant) and the Virtuality of the Sovereign Power in the Two Houses. **1843** tr. *Custine's Empire of Czar* II. 272 When the church abdicates its liberty, it loses its moral virtuality. **1858** H. BUSHNELL *Nat. & Supernat.* xiii. (1864) 418 The government of the world is waiting on Christianity, and is thus in highest virtuality a supernatural kingdom.

3. A virtual (as opposed to an actual) thing, capacity, etc.; a potentiality.

1836–7 SIR W. HAMILTON *Metaph.* xxxviii. (1870) II. 357 Our inclinations, dispositions, natural habitudes or virtualities. **1843** CARLYLE *Past & Pr.* IV. i, A Virtuality perfected into an Actuality. **1885** MRS. H. WARD tr. *Amiel's Jrnl.* II. 263 Is not mind the universal virtuality, the universe latent?

virtually ('vɜːtjuːəlɪ), *adv.* Also 5 **vertualliche**, 5, 7 **vertually**. [f. VIRTUAL *a.* + -LY². Cf. F. *virtuellement*, It., Sp., Pg. *virtualmente*.]

1. In respect of essence or effect, apart from actual form or specific manner; as far as essential qualities or facts are concerned.

Passing into next by a slight weakening of the sense, the idea of simple equivalence becoming more prominent than that of essential qualities.

c **1430** *Pilgr. Lyf Manhode* I. lxxxvii. (1869) 49 Serteyn, quod she, localliche j vnderstonde not, but oother weys; vertualliche j vnderstonde summe, ymaginatyfliche summe. **1495** *Trevisa's Barth. De P.R.* VIII. i. S viij b/1 The vertue of god made and ordeyned primordyall matere in yᵉ whiche as it were in a massy thynge the foure elementes were vertually and not dystyngued in tale and nombre as they arne now. **1639** FULLER *Holy War* I. xxiv. 40 But these and many more voluminous engines (for the ramme alone had an hundred men to manage it) are now virtually epitomized in the cannon. **1673** [R. LEIGH] *Transp. Reh.* 22 He defeated.. the other ten nations virtually and inclusively. **1690** C. NESSE *O. & N.T.* I. 206 All the lesser pearls.. are contain'd vertually in this one diamond. *a* **1768** SECKER *Serm.* (1770) III. xvi. 378 If the Jews had prevailed, they would have imagined their Success a full Proof, that the Messiah was yet virtually, though not corporally, amongst them.

b. In effect, though not formally or explicitly; practically; to all intents; as good as.

a **1600** HOOKER *Disc. Justification* (1612) 32 No man is ignorant of their first principles, which doe vertually containe whatsoever by naturall meanes, is, or can be knowne. *a* **1626** BP. ANDREWES *Serm.* (1856) I. 237 That was but virtually as good as born, this actually born indeed. **1642** FULLER *Holy & Prof. St.* III. iv. 160 Continue correspondencie with.. some Professour or Secretary, who virtually is the whole University, or State. **1651** BAXTER *Inf. Bapt.* 92 It is sufficient that the parent be virtually and dispositively at present a believer. *a* **1718** PRIOR *Alma* II. 183 By the Peep-holes in his Crest, Is it not virtually confest That there his Eye took distant Aim. **1748** HARTLEY *Observ. Man* II. ii. §34. 170 As far as this is virtually included in the Precepts for loving God above all and our Neighbour as ourselves. **1791** BURKE *App. Whigs* Wks. 1842 I. 497 It is virtually a begging of the question. **1817** W. SELWYN *Law Nisi Prius* (ed. 4) II. 1152 The seamen may sue.. the owners, as the persons virtually contracting with them through the agency of the master. **1856** FROUDE *Hist. Eng.* (1858) I. ii. 160 The cause was virtually transferred to Rome, where Henry.. was unlikely to consent to plead. **1878** LECKY *Eng. in 18th C.* I. ii. 301 Before the middle of the 18th century the laws against Catholic worship were virtually obsolete.

2. Virtuously, morally. *rare.*

1539 in Strype *Eccl. Mem.* (1721) I. App. cx. 296 [All persons shall] virtually and devoutly.. hear their divine services and masses. **1812** CARY *Dante, Purg.* xxx. 118 This man Was.. So gifted virtually, that in him All better habits wonderously had thrived.

3. In respect of (physical) virtues. *rare*$^{-1}$.

1660 BURNEY *Κέρδ. Δῶρον* (1661) 75 The Prince is not placed in his Chair of State, as the Sun has its spherical collocation amidst the Planets, and is chiefest vertually.

4. With virtue or power; effectively. *rare*$^{-1}$.

1604 DEKKER *King's Entertainm.* Wks. 1873 I. 302 Beames from thine eyes So vertually shining, that they bring, To England's new Arabia, a new Spring.

†'**virtuate**, *v.* *Obs.* [f. VIRTUE + -ATE.] *trans.* To render efficacious; to invest with a particular virtue or quality.

1632 G. SANDYS *Ovid's Met.* VII. *Note* 254 Medea.. now likewise invokes the Earth, Aire, Winds, Mountaines, &c. as either producing or virtuating magicall ingredients. **1657** W. MORICE *Coena quasi Κοινὴ* xi. 132 None but God could.. sanctifie, and virtuate the Signs and Elements [etc.]. **1689** G. HARVEY *Curing Dis. by Expect.* v. 35 The preparation.. is virtuated with an abstersif quality.

virtue ('vɜːtjuː), *sb.* Forms: α. 3–6 **uertu, vertu** (4 **vertw-, vartu**), 3–8 (9 *Sc.*) **vertue** (4 **uertue**, 5 **vertuwe**), 4–5 **wertu** (5 **wertw-**); 4–7 **verteu**, 4–6 **vertew** (4 **-ewe**), 5– 7 **wertew** (5 **-ewe**); 4 **ver-, wertow**, 5 **wertou-**, 9 *north. dial.* **varter**, *Sc.* **verter**. β. 3–4 **uirtu**, 4–5, 7 **virtu**, 6– **virtue**; 6 **virtew**. [a. AF. and OF. *vertu* (F. *vertu*, = It. *virtù*, Sp. *virtud*, Pg. *virtude*), ad. L. *virtūt-*, *virtus* manliness, valour, worth, etc., f. *vir* man.]

I. As a quality of persons.

1. a. The power or operative influence inherent in a supernatural or divine being. Now *arch.* or *Obs.*

c **1250** *Kent. Serm.* in *O. Eng. Misc.* 30 Besech ure lorde þet he do ine þe his uertu. **1303** R. BRUNNE *Handl. Synne* 5852 'Pers', he seyd, '.. þou art weyl with Ihesu; He sheweþ for þe grete vertu.' **1338** —— *Chron.* (1810) 184 If ȝour God be so clere, & of so grete vertewe, As ȝe precne oft tide. *c* **1386** CHAUCER *Knt.'s T.* 1391 For though so be that Mars is god of Armes Youre vertu is so greet in heuene aboue That [etc.]. *a* **1425** tr. *Arderne's Treat. Fistula*, etc. 37 Þat it [Bubo] may neuer be cured.. but if it plese god.. for to help wiþ his vnspekeable vertu. *a* **1450** *Mirk's Festial* 6 Hopyng þat þe vertu of Cryst schull put away his temptacyon. **1483** CAXTON *Gold. Leg.* 19/2 After the passion of Jhesu Cryst.. he was transported from Infirmyte to Vertu. **1557** *N.T.* (Genev.) Epist. *iiii, In his owne vertue he rose agayne. **1570** T. NORTON tr. *Nowel's Catech.* 25 b, All things would runne to ruine, and fall to nothyng, vnlesse by hys vertue, & as it were by hys hand, they were vpholden. **1594** DRAYTON *Idea* 489 All unclean Thoughts, foule Spirits cast out in mee, Onely by Vertue that proceeds from thee. **1655** STANLEY *Hist. Philos.* I. I. 14 That the world is animated, and that God is the soul thereof,.. whose divine moving vertue penetrats through the element of water. **1738** WESLEY *Ps.* LXXX. xx, Look on them with thy flaming Eyes, The Sin-consuming Virtue dart. **1850** NEALE *Med. Hymns* (1867) 27 Michael, who in princely virtue Cast Abaddon from on high.

b. An embodiment of such power; esp. *pl.*, one of the orders of the celestial hierarchy.

a **1300** *Cursor M.* 19523 Godds virtu or gret prophet, Or angel elles þai him let. **13..** *E.E. Allit. P.* A. 1125 Þe steuen moȝt stryke þurȝ þe vrþe to helle, Þat þe vertues of heuen of Ioye endyte. **1382** WYCLIF *Mark* xiii. 25 Vertues that be in heuenes, schulen be mouyd. **1398** TREVISA *De P.R.* II. xvi. (1495) c j b/2 The seuenth ordre [of angels] is Vertues. **1533** GAU *Richt Vay* 4 And siclik thay dremit and maid innumerabil pouers and vertus and laid to siclik orisons. **1575** TIMME tr. *Marlorat's Expos. John* 146/2 Hee hath committed these partes in charge, to the Angell. For the which cause the Angelles are called, powers, or vertues. **1584** R. SCOT *Discov. Witchcr.* XV. ii. (1886) 315 Two and twentie legions of divels, partlie of the order of vertues, & partlie of the order of thrones. **1620** QUARLES *Pentæologia, Gloria Cœli* 13 Where troups of Powers, Vertues, Cherubins,.. Are chaunting praises to their heauenly King. **1667** MILTON *P.L.* x. 460 Thrones, Dominations, Princedoms, Vertues, Powers. *a* **1711** KEN *Hymnotheo* Poet. Wks. 1721 III. 200 Virtues, who turn the orbs celestial round. **1812** CARY *Dante, Par.* XXVIII. 113 Dominations first; next them, Virtues; and powers the third. **1880** *Encycl. Brit.* XI. 792/1.

†**c.** An act of superhuman or divine power; a 'mighty work'; a miracle. *Obs.*

a **1300** *Cursor M.* 19566 (Edin.), Þe haligaste, it was sa gode, þate þa men þat it undirfange moȝte do suilc uirtuz and sua strange. *c* **1305** *St. Christopher* 127 in *E.E.P.* (1862) 63 On such god, he seide, ȝe schulde bileoue: þat such virtu mai do. *c* **1375** *Sc. Leg. Saints* x. (*Matthew*) 232, I traste þat þu ma do þe sammyne-lyke vertu fore his sake. **1382** WYCLIF *Matt.* xi. 20 Thanne Ihesus began for to seie repreue to citees, in whiche ful manye vertues of hym ben don. *c* **1400** *Apol. Loll.* (Camden) 28 Crist in a coost of þe Jewes miȝt not do ani vertu þer, for þe vntrouþ. **1526** TINDALE *Mark* vi. 2 What wysdom is this that is geven vnto him? and such vertues that are wrought by his hondes?

2. a. Conformity of life and conduct with the principles of morality; voluntary observance of the recognized moral laws or standards of right conduct; abstention on moral grounds from any form of wrong-doing or vice.

a **1225** *Ancr. R.* 268 Nu hit is vertu.. uor to wakien, uor hit greueð þe. **1390** GOWER *Conf.* I. 7 Tho was vertu sett above And vice was put under fote. **1399** LANGL. *Rich. Redeles* III. 206 So vertue wolde fflowe whan vicis were ebbid. *c* **1410** HOCCLEVE *Mother of God* 9 Modir of mercy,.. Þat of al vertu art superlatyf. **1484** CAXTON *Fables of Æsop* IV. xx, The roote of alle vertue is obedynce and humylyte. **1531** ELYOT *Gov.* II. x, If vertue be an election annexed unto our nature, and consisteth in a meane, which is determined by reason. **1545** BRINKLOW *Lament.* 79 Reformacion or redresse.. wherby to expulse vice, and encreace vertu. **1585** T. WASHINGTON tr. *Nicholay's Voy.* III. ii. 71 b, [They] haue enclined, & finally returned vnto their naturall and primitiue vertue. **1621** BURTON *Anat. Mel.* I. i. II. xi, The principall Habits are two in number, Vertue, and Vice. **1655** STANLEY *Hist. Philos.* I. III. 107 He describes morall vertu in his discourses and writings. **1691** HARTCLIFFE *Virtues* 9 There were also those, who taught, That Virtue was that excellent thing, in which we should find our chiefest Good. **1736** BUTLER *Anal.* I. iii. §4 Virtue consists in a regard to what is right and reasonable, as being so; in a regard to veracity, justice, charity, in themselves. **1751** CHATHAM *Lett. Nephew* ii. 7 Lessons of honour, courage,.. humanity, and in one word, virtue in its true signification. **1791** BURKE *Corr.* (1844) III. 200 Vice is never so odious.. as when it usurps and disgraces the natural place of virtue. **1828** CARLYLE *Misc.* (1857) I. 89 He thinks that to propose a reward for virtue is to render virtue impossible. **1850** F. W. ROBERTSON *Lect.* 73 That alone is virtue which has good placed before it and evil, and seeing the evil, chooses the good. **1875** JOWETT *Plato* (ed. 2) V. 179 Unless we know whether virtue is one or many, we shall hardly know what virtue is.

phr. [**1669** DRYDEN *Tyrannic Love* II. i, To follow Vertue, as its own reward.] **1697** VANBRUGH *Relapse* V. iii, Virtue is its own Reward: There's a Pleasure in doing good, which sufficiently pays it self. **1756** HOME *Douglas* III. i. **1771** SMOLLETT *Humph. Cl., To D. Lewis* 12 June, I shall be content with the reflection, that virtue is its own reward. **1850** SMEDLEY *F. Fairlegh* xxxviii, Supposing this iniquitous engagement.. broken off by your exertions, is Virtue to be its own reward?

b. Personified, or regarded as an entity.

1402 HOCCLEVE *Let. Cupid* 457 Vertu so digne is and so noble in kynde, That Vice and she wol not in feere abide. *c* **1420** LYDG. *Assembly of Gods* 2074 Then may ye say ye have a sure staff To.. walke by the waye of Vertu hys loore. *a* **1586** SIDNEY *Arcadia* III. xx, If ever Vertue tooke a bodie to shewe his (else unconceaveable) beautie. **1593** SHAKS. *3 Hen. VI*, III. ii. 63 That loue which Vertue begges, and Vertue graunts. **1607** DEKKER *Northw. Hoe* V. Wks 1873 III. 73 Virtue glories not in the spoil, but in the victory. **1660** INGELO *Bentiv. & Ur.* II. (1682) 68 If Virtue be so happy when it is afflicted. **1692** PRIOR *Ode Imit. Horace* viii, Virtue is her own Reward, With solid Beams and Native Glory bright. **1726–46** THOMSON *Winter* 1039 Virtue sole survives, Immortal never-failing friend of man. **1770** GOLDSM. *Des. Vill.* 108 But on he moves to meet his latter end, Angels around befriending Virtue's friend. **1799** CAMPBELL *Pleas. Hope* I. 530 So Virtue dies, the spouse of Liberty! **1818** COLERIDGE *Friend* (1865) 72 A wound in feelings which virtue herself has fostered. **1860** *All Year Round* No. 64. 322 Man may bow before virtue, but virtue never bows before man.

c. *spec.* Chastity, sexual purity, esp. on the part of women. ***of easy virtue***: see EASY *a.* 12.

1599 SHAKS. *Much Ado* IV. i. 84 Hero it selfe can blot out Heroes vertue. **1706** ESTCOURT *Fair Example* V. i, Ne'er let the fair one boast of Virtue prov'd Till she has well refus'd the Man she lov'd. **1740** RICHARDSON *Pamela* (1824) I. xiv. 252, I say not this.. to excuse the lady's fall: Nothing can do that; because virtue is.. preferable to all considerations. **1749** FIELDING *Tom Jones* II. iii, That order of females whose faces are taken as a kind of security for their virtue. **1819** SHELLEY *Peter Bell 3rd* III. viii, There are mincing women, mewing.. Of their own virtue. **1885** MABEL COLLINS *Prettiest Woman* ii, She played the woman of virtue—and played it well.

transf. **1845** McCULLOCH *Taxation* I. iv. (1852) 121 The tax will then fall with its full weight upon men of integrity, while the millionaire of 'easy virtue' may well-nigh escape it altogether.

d. *Sc.* Industry, diligence. *rare.*

1546 *Reg. Mag. Sig. Scot.* 757/2 Quhairthrow all virtew and marchandice within the said burgh is abusit, ceissit and dekeyit. **1641** *Sc. Acts, Chas. I* (1817) V. 657/2 It is necessar that in everie schyre at leist thair be ane schooll or hous of vertue erected. *Ibid.* 658/2 Any parcellis of cloth, seyis, &c., .. made in the saidis houses of vertew. **1803** SCOTT *Let.* in *Lockhart* (1837) I. xi. 386 In many parts of Scotland the word *virtue* is limited entirely to *industry*.

3. a. With *a* and pl. A particular moral excellence; a special manifestation of the influence of moral principles in life or conduct.

a **1225** *Ancr. R.* 368 Þet oðer þing is.. deuociun, reoufulnesse, merci, pite of heorte.., edmodnesse, & oðre swuche uertuz. *c* **1230** *Hali Meid.* 13 Þis is ȝet þe uertu þat halt.. ure feble flesch.. in hal halinesse. *a* **1300** *Cursor M.* 571 Alle virtus has [that] saul i-wis, þat vte o sin vnsaked is. *a* **1325** *Spec. Gy Warw.* 71, I wole þe teche, Faire uertuz for to take And foule þewes to forsake. **1377** LANGL., *P. Pl.* B. XI. 370 Suffraunce is a souereygne vertue. *c* **1400** *Destr. Troy* 4017 Ho.. voidet all vanities, & virtus dissyret. **1422** YONGE tr. *Secreta Secret.* 147 The beste good of all is good of vertues and grace. *c* **1440** *Jacob's Well* 82 Oþere synnes arn contrarye to on vertew, as pride is contrarye to lownesse. **1526** *Pilgr. Perf.* (W. de W. 1531) 2 All maner of goostly matter, concernynge the perfeccyon of graces and vertues. **1589** PUTTENHAM *Eng. Poesie* III. xxiii. (Arb.) 274 The word became not.. her sex, whose chiefe vertue is shamefastnesse. **1601** SHAKS. *All's Well* IV. iii. 84 Our crimes would dispaire if they were not cherish'd by our vertues. **1644** MILTON *Areop.* (Arb.) 44 How great a vertue is temperance, how much of moment through the whole life of man? **1682** BUNYAN *Greatness of Soul* Wks. 1853 I. 138 It is a sport now to some to taunt and squib and deride at other men's virtues. **1705** STANHOPE *Paraphr.* III. 207 They confess too, that Self-Denial is a Christian Vertue. **1761** HUME *Hist. Eng.* II. xxviii. 136 Courage, preferably to equity or justice, was the virtue most valued. **1797** GODWIN *Enquirer* I. ii. 9 Human virtues without discrimination are no virtues. **1835** THIRLWALL *Greece* I. 321 Thousands.. proclaimed the virtues of the deceased prince superior to those of all his predecessors. **1865** LUBBOCK *Preh. Times* xiv. (1869) 553 Neither faith, hope, nor charity enters into the virtues of a savage.

transf. **1680** MORDEN *Geog. Rect., China* (1685) 423 Their chief practice or special Virtues are Theft, Murder and Adultery. **1719** YOUNG *Busiris* I. i, When rage and rancour are the proper virtues, And loss of reason is the mark of men. **1820** BYRON *Mar. Fal.* IV. ii, But they were not aware that there are things Which make revenge a virtue by reflection.

b. In enumerations of certain moral qualities regarded as of special excellence or importance, as the four cardinal virtues (see CARDINAL *a.* 2), the three theological virtues (see THEOLOGICAL *a.* 1), or the seven virtues opposed to the seven deadly sins.

c 1320 *Cast. Love* 827 þat beþ þe seuen vertues wiþ winne To ouercome þe seuen dedly sinne. **1387** Trevisa *Higden* (Rolls) I. 5 Þe metynge of þe þre waies of þe þre vertues of deuynyte, and þe metynge of foure weies of þe foure chief vertues. **c 1400** *Cursor M.* 25391 (Cott. Galba), Now haue I sayd þir askinges seuyn..whilk seuyn vertue vntill us wins, and als fordose seuyn dedly sins. **1411–2** Hoccleve *De Reg. Princ.* 4755 Prudence, attemperance, strengthe, and right, Tho foure ben vertues principal. **c 1425** *Cast. Persev.* 1694 Þe seuene synnys I forsake & to þese vij vertuis I me tak. **1552** Abp. Hamilton *Catech.* (1884) 7 The twa principal vertewes callit Faith and Hoip. **1590** Spenser *Let. W. Raleigh* in *F.Q.* Pref., The twelve private Morall Vertues, as Aristotle devised. **1693** *D'Emilianne's Hist. Monast. Orders* 249 Of the Order of the ten Virtues, or Delights of the Virgin Mary, called also of the Annunciade. **1753** Challoner *Cath. Chr. Instr.* 2 To nourish..in our Souls the three Divine Virtues of Faith, Hope and Charity.

c. ***all the Virtues***, a name given to the Opposition in the House of Commons in 1815–16.

On the model of 'All the Talents' applied to the Grenville Ministry of 1806–7: see talent *sb.* 6 d.

1816 Sir G. Bingham *Lett.* 1 Jan., in *Cornh. Mag.* (1900) Jan. 34 Bonaparte..has heard that 'All the Virtues', with Sir Francis Burdett at their head, were to advocate his cause and recall.

d. A personified moral quality, or a representation of this in painting, sculpture, etc.

1851 E. J. Millington tr. *Didron's Chr. Iconogr.* I. 84 Each Virtue bears a characteristic attribute... Liberty, like ..the twelve sister Virtues..is decorated with a large nimbus. **1885** J. R. Allen *Early Chr. Symbolism* 277 Crowned figures armed with shields..to symbolise the Virtues trampling on the Vices overcome.

4. a. ***to make (a) virtue of necessity*** (or †***need***), to do with apparent willingness, or as if performing a meritorious action, what one in reality cannot help doing; to submit to circumstances with a good grace.

After OF. *faire de necessité vertu*, L. *facere de necessitate virtutem* (Jerome *In Rufinum* 3, n. 2).

(*a*) **c 1374** Chaucer *Troylus* iv. 1586 Thus makeþ vertue of necessite By paciens, and þenk þat lord is he Of fortune ay, þat nought wole of here recche. **c 1386** —— *Sqr's. T.* 593 That I made vertu of necessitee And took it wel syn þat it moste bee. **1411–2** Hoccleve *De Reg. Princ.* 1252 Make of necessite, reed I vertu; For better rede can I non. **c 1480** Henryson *Test. Cresseid* 478, I counsall the mak vertew of ane neid. **1578** Whetstone *2nd Pt. Promos & Cass.* v. v, Good Maddame way, by lawe, your Lord doth dye, Wherefore make vertue of necessity. **1646** Earl Monm. tr. *Biondi's Civil Wars* v. 115 Villandras weighing the danger made vertue of necessity, hee went to Toulosse. **1652** J. Wright tr. *Camus' Nat. Paradox* x. 245 However, I will have patience, and making Vertue of Necessity, I will forbear.

(*b*) **1583** Stocker *Civ. Warres Lowe C.* I. 28 b, They were enforced to behaue themselues..and of necessitie, to make a vertue. **1588** Greene *Pandosto* (1607) 10 Shee was faine to make a vertue of her neede. **1614** Day *Festivals* x. (1615) 297, I wil make a Vertue of this Necessitie. **1639** S. Du Verger tr. *Camus' Admir. Events* 46 They make a vertue of that necessity. **1677** W. Hughes *Man of Sin* ii. ix. 144 Their Modern Doctors, whom the Arguments of the Protestants have compelled to make a Vertue of Necessity. **a 1708** [see necessity *sb.* 5]. **1764** tr. *Gil Blas* i. v. I. 21 And making a virtue of necessity, I put the best face I could upon it, and went about the work she set me upon. **1837** [see necessity *sb.* 5]. **1980** 'J. Melville' *Chrysanthemum Chain* 38 We'll make a virtue of necessity. I'll take charge of the case myself.

b. ***to make a virtue of***, to make a merit of, to gain credit by.

1842 Lover *Handy Andy* xiii, Mat, who saw Furlong was near the mark, thought he might..make a virtue of telling him.

5. a. Superiority or excellence, unusual ability, merit, or distinction, in some respect.

1382 Wyclif *Wisd.* x. 2 God..ladde hym out fro his gilte, ..and ʒaf to hym vertue of hauynge alle thingus. **c 1384** Chaucer *H. Fame* ii. 18 Now shal men se Yf any vertu in the be To tel al my dreme aryght. **c 1400** *Brut* i. 229 Miche peple wer out of here mynde, & God haþ sent ham her mynde aʒeyn þrouʒ vertu of þat holy martr'. **c 1450** Holland *Houlate* 264 Thir fowlis..weraly awysit, full of wirtewe, The maner, the mater, and how it remanyt. **c 1475** *Rauf Coilʒear* 162 Thow hes walkit, I wis, in mony wyld land, The mair vertew thow suld haue, to keip the fra blame. **1484** Caxton *Fables of Auian* xii, For what vertue that ony man hath none oughte to preyse hym self. **1602** *Speght's Chaucer* (ed. 2) c iv, Vertue flourisheth in Chaucer still, Though death of him hath wrought his will. **1631** Markham *Cheap Husb.* (ed. 6) i. ii. 10 Our English Gentry..aime for the most part at no more skill than the riding of a ridden and perfect horse, which is but onely the setting forth of another mans vertue. **1828** Macaulay *Ess., Hallam's Constit. Hist.* (1897) 85 That unsparing impartiality which is his [*sc.* Hallam's] most distinguishing virtue.

b. An accomplishment. Now *rare* or *Obs.*

15.. *Aberdeen Reg.* (Jam.), The singeir to pas & remane in Pareis for ane yeir to ler wertews. **1591** Shaks. *Two Gent.* iii. i. 313 *Sp.* Item, she can wash and scoure. *La.* A speciall vertue. **1608** —— *Per.* iv. vi. 195 Proclaim that I can sing, weave, sew, and dance, With other virtues, which I'll keep from boast. **1615** Markham (*title*), The English Hus-Wife, Contayning, The inward and outward vertues which ought to be in a compleat woman. As, her skill in Physicke,.. Cookery, [etc.]. **1656** Duchess of Newcastle *True Relation* in *Life* (1886) 280 Tutors..for all sorts of virtues, as singing, dancing, playing on music, reading, writing, working, and the like. **1808** Scott *Autobiog.* in *Lockhart* i. (1842) 4/1 Robert sung agreeably–(a virtue which was never seen in me).

c. = virtu 1. *rare.*

1709 *Tatler* No. 38 ¶ 12 He has by rote, and at second-hand, all that can be said of any man of figure, wit, and virtue in town. **1828** *Edin. Rev.* XLVIII. 61 The Italians commonly call a taste for the fine arts, or skill in them, by the name of Virtue.

†**6. a.** Physical strength, force, or energy. *Obs.*

Common *a* 1325–1420 as a rendering of L. *virtus*.

a 1325 *Prose Psalter* xxviii. 10 Our Lord shal ʒeue vertu to his folk. **a 1340** Hampole *Psalter* xxxii. 16 Geaunt sall noght be safe in multitude of his vertu. **1382** Wyclif *Luke* x. 19, I hau ʒouun to ʒou power of..tredinge, on serpents, and scorpiouns, and on al the vertu of the enemy. **c 1400** *Laud Troy Bk.* 9291 He myʒt not wel his breth blowe, He was In poynt to ouer-throwe; His vertu hadde he clene lore. **1422** Yonge tr. *Secreta Secret.* 242 Hit servyth to the stomake and to the entraill, and than thay gederith hare streynth and vertu, wyche was amenuset and febelit. **c 1450** tr. *De Imitatione* iii. ix. 76 Þou art oure helpe, our vertu, & our strengþe. **c 1500** *Melusine* xxx. 226 He..smote Zelodius vpon his helmet, by suche strengthe & vertue that he made hym to enclyne vpon his hors neck.

†**b.** An armed force. *Obs. rare.*

1382 Wyclif *1 Macc.* i. 4 And he gadride vertu, and ful stronge oost. *Ibid.* xiii. 54 And Symont seeʒ Joon, his sone, that he was a man of bateil, and he putte hym duyk of alle vertues.

†**c.** Flourishing state or condition. *Obs.*

c 1400 *Three Kings Cologne* (1886) 8 Whan þe citee of Acon ..florisshed and stode in his vertue, Ioye and prosperite. **1484** Caxton *Fables of Æsop* iii. xvi, He that gouerneth not wel his bely withe grete payne he may hold the other lymmes in theyr strengthe and vertue.

7. The possession or display of manly qualities; manly excellence, manliness, courage, valour.

In later use tending to pass into sense 2.

13.. *Coer de L.* 2810 A baroun of gret vertewe. **a 1400–50** *Alexander* 5324 Quat may þi vertu now a-vaile & all þine vayn pride? **c 1420** Lydg. *Assembly of Gods* 1092 Syres, put no dowte, Vertu shall retorne & haue hys entente. Thys felde shalbe our. **c 1450** *Merlin* xxxii. 656 The Bretouns hem diffended as peple of grete vertu. **1523** Ld. Berners tr. *Froiss.* I. cxcii. 228 The lord Pynnand his company defended themself by great vertue. **1549** *Compl. Scotl.* Ep. 2 Quhar for ʒour heroyque vertu is of mair admiratione. **1579** Fenton *Guicciard.* ii. 104 The bastard of Burbon was made prisoner, notwithstanding he fought with great vertue. *Ibid.* Yet his vertue defended his person. **a 1668** Lassels *Voy. Italy* (1698) II. 86 Marius..from a common soldier came by his warlike vertue to be seven times consul. **1710** Shaftesb. *Advice to Author* ii. §1. 67 They [*sc.* the Muses] were more to him than his Arms or military Virtue. **1758** Johnson *Let. to B. Langton* 21 Sept. in *Boswell*, A man that languishes with disease, ends his life with more pain, but with less virtue. **1817** Jas. Mill *Brit. India* II. iv. ii. 70 The English were called upon for the utmost exertions of their virtue.

II. As a quality of things.

8. In the prepositional phrases ***in*** or ***by*** (also †***through*** or ***with***) ***virtue of***, by the power or efficacy of (something aiding or justifying); hence, in later use, by the authority of, in reliance upon, in consequence of, because of. (Cf. 10 e.)

(*a*) **c 1230** *Hali Meid.* 13 Engel & meiden beon euening in uertu of meidenhades mihte. **c 1330** R. Brunne *Chron.* (1810) 18 Þe Kyng with þe maistrie went in to þe toun, Þe pris he had wonnen in vertew of Criste's passioun. **1617** *Fortescue Papers* (Camden) 29 They should talke of the points of religion but by way of discourse, and not as in vertue of the commission [etc.]. **1660** Jer. Taylor *Worthy Commun.* i. iv. 75 Christ in heaven perpetually offers and represents that sacrifice to his heavenly Father and in vertue of that obtaines all good things for his church. **1703** Maundrell *Journ. Jerus.* (1707) 105 In vertue of which perswasion, the Olives, and Olive stones, and Oyl which they produce, became an excellent commodity in Spain. **1754** Sherlock *Disc.* (1759) I. ii. 77 He was the Head of all Creatures in Virtue of having created them. **1793** Smeaton *Edystone L.* §344 The experiment..was ordered in virtue of an observation that had occurred in the course of the work. **1833** Ht. Martineau *Three Ages* ii. 39 In virtue of an office which he held, he had liberty to pass through the palace garden. **1879** Froude *Cæsar* xiii. 188 He remained a senator in virtue of his quæstorship.

(*b*) **c 1350** *Will. Palerne* 284, I þe coniure..bi vertu of þing þat þou most in þis world louest. **c 1380** Wyclif *Wks.* (1880) 32 Bi vertue of þis cheef domesman he owiþ to be excused fro þis somonynge of worldly prelat. **c 1386** Chaucer *Parson's T.* ¶ 340 It may wel wexe fieble and faille by vertu of baptesme and by the grace of god thurgh penitence. **1425** *Rolls of Parlt.* IV. 290/1 That they mowe be vertue of the same lokett, be fully excused att alle tymes. **1495** *Act 11 Hen. VII*, c. 53 §1 Noo..persone the whiche..therwith entermedlede to your use or by vertu of your letters patentes. **1553** in Feuillerat *Revels Q. Mary* (1914) 149 By vertue of a warraunte sygned with her Maiesties oune handes. **1587** Fleming *Contn. Holinshed* III. 1376/2 They shall loose the fiue shillings that they should receiue..by vertue of my will. **1617** Sir T. Wentworth in *Fortescue Papers* (Camden) 25 When indeed he was in effect out of the Commission before, by vertu of that direction. **1663** Heath *Flagellum* (1672) 47 Upon some pretence of private business of the Colonels and by vertue thereof in a Disguise of a Servant [etc.]. **1681–6** J. Scott *Chr. Life* (1747) III. 283 So we Christians by vertue of our Covenant with God in Christ, are separated from all other Societies. **1695** *Enq. Anc. Const. Eng.* 44 Violating the Fundamental Laws and constitutions of the Government by vertue of which he became King. **1785** Burke *Sp. Nabob Arcot* Wks. 1842 I. 318 No others, by virtue of general powers, can obtain a legal title..to exercise those special functions. **1838** Thirlwall *Greece* III. 287 The refugees who retired by virtue of the treaty from Amphipolis, found shelter at Eion. **1868** Lockyer *Elem. Astron.* §374 The planets, when they are visible, appear as stars, and, like the stars, they rise and set by virtue of the Earth's rotation.

(*c*) **c 1290** *S. Eng. Leg.* I. 11/346 And þoruʒ vertue of þe holie croiz he ouer-cam alle is fon. **c 1320** *Sir Tristr.* 1894 Hole sche was & sounde þurch vertu of his gle. **c 1380** *Sir Ferumb.* 157 Þe barouns..prayede god þorw vertue of hem Schold sauye hem thar fro heþe men. **c 1400** *Brut* ccviii. 237 He come to þe Gildehall of London, and axede þe keies of þe ʒates of þe citee þrouʒ vertue and strengh of his commission.

(*d*) **1586** Marlowe *1st Pt. Tamburl.* v. ii, So..Must Tamburlaine by their resistlesse powers, With vertue of a gentle victorie, Conclude a league of honor to my hope.

9. Without article: †**a.** Of precious stones: Occult efficacy or power (as in the prevention or cure of disease, etc.); in later use, great worth or value. *Obs.*

a 1272 *Luue Ron* 170 in *O.E. Misc.* 98 Hwat spekstu of eny stone þat beoþ in vertu oþer in grace. **c 1340** Hampole *Pr. Consc.* 9198 Þus may a man..Alle þe cete of heven lyken.. to precyouse stanes of vertow [etc.]. **c 1350** *Will. Palerne* 4425 Þe ston..was of so stif vertu, þat neuer man vpon mold miʒt it hium on haue, ne schuld he with wicche-craft be wicched neuer-more. **c 1400** *Melayne* 978 His helme & his hawberke holde, Freth ouere with rede golde, With stones of vertue dere. **1470–85** Malory *Arthur* vii. xxvii. 254 A coronal of gold besette with stones of vertue to the valewe of a thousand pound. **1503** Hawes *Examp. Virt.* xiii. 242 The roof was set with stones of vertue. **1509** —— *Past. Pleas.* xxvii. (Percy Soc.) 127 With perles and rubies rubicond, Mixte with emeraudes so full of vertue.

b. Of plants, waters, etc.: Efficacy arising from physical qualities; esp. power to affect the human body in a beneficial manner; strengthening, sustaining, or healing properties.

a 1300 *Cursor M.* 34 Bot be the fruit may scilwis se O quat vertu is ilka tre. *Ibid.* 1016 Treis o frut þan es þar sett þat serekin vertu has at ette. **1390** Gower *Conf.* III. 129 His herbe is Anabulla named, Which is of gret vertu proclamed. **c 1430** Lydg. *Min. Poems* (Percy Soc.) 16 Ʒe schall draw wateris..Oute of wellis of oure Saviour, Wiche have vertu to curen alle langueres. **1562** Turner *Herbal* ii. 31 It is sayde that there is an other Magadaris in Lybia... It hath like vertu with Laserpitio. **1602** Shaks. *Ham.* iv. vii. 145 No Cataplasme..Collected from all Simples that haue Vertue Vnder the Moone, can saue the thing from death. **1655** Culpepper, etc. *Riverius* i. xiii. 48 This following Fomentation is of wonderful Vertue. **1678** Lady Chaworth in *12th Rep. Hist. MSS. Comm.* App. V. 48 A wolfes tooth for my pritty godson, that Lady Fingall gave me as a thinge of much vertu..and antidotal against convulsions. **1706** Phillips (ed. Kersey), *Birds-Eye*, an Herb..of singular Virtue against the Palsey. **1778** Johnson *Let. to Mrs. Thrale* 15 Oct., The second [night]..not so much better as that I dare ascribe any virtue to the medicine. **1841** Myers *Cath. Th.* iii. §27. 102 Distilling healing virtue into better waters. **1865** Parkham *Huguenots* i. (1875) 6 There was a fountain of such virtue that, bathing in its waters, old men resumed their youth.

c. Efficacy of a moral nature; influence working for good upon human life or conduct. †Also, in early use, miraculous power (of the cross, etc.).

c 1300 *St. Margarete* 316 Of gret vertu is hire lyf, ho so þeron þoʒte. **c 1305** in *E.E.P.* (1862) 99 If þu woldest þat soþe ihure..Gret vertu ic wole þe telle of þe suete holi rode. **c 1425** *Hampole's Psalter* Metr. Pref. 12 In þis boke is muche vertu, to reders wiþ deuocyown. **c 1430** Lydg. *Min. Poems* (Percy Soc.) 9 Thes rialle gifftes been of verteu most, Gostly coragis most sovereignly delyte. **1549** Latimer *Ploughers* (Arb.) 32 Purposinge to euacuate Christes death, and to make it of smal efficacitie and vertue. **1567** *Gude & Godlie B.* (S.T.S.) 14 Our Baptisme dotit with sanctitude, And greit vertew, to wesche our sinfulness. **1841** Myers *Cath. Th.* iii. §17. 64 Few questions..could well be more important, if Divine virtue is to be ascribed to every letter of Scripture.

d. Superiority or excellence in respect either of nature or of operation; worth or efficacy of any kind.

1390 Gower *Conf.* III. 16 Selden get a domb man lond. Tak that proverbe, and understond That wordes ben of vertu grete. **c 1400** *Destr. Troy* 8388 The walles [were] vp wroght..With stones full stoute, stithest of vertue. **1423** Jas. I *Kingis Q.* xx, In vere, that full of vertu is and gude, Quhen nature first begynneth hir enprise. **1596** Spenser *F.Q.* v. i. 10 The blade..was of no less virtue, then of fame. **1665–6** *Phil. Trans.* I. 282 Yet have these two Load-stones no connexion or tye, though a Common Center of Virtue according to which they joyntly act. **1669** Bunyan *Holy Citie* 153 Gold is the choice and chief of all Metals both for worth, colour, and vertue. **1779** Forrest *Voy. N. Guinea* 339 The latter [*sc.* cinnamon] is vastly superior in richness, sweetness, and virtue. **1812** Cary *Dante, Par.* vii. 132 The elements Are by created virtue inform'd. **1830** Herschel *Study Nat. Phil.* 59 There is virtue in a bushel of coals properly consumed, to raise seventy millions of pounds weight a foot high. **1883** *N. York Chr. Union* 21 June, The new Sound steamer 'Pilgrim' is regarded as a model of mechanical and constructional virtue.

†**e.** Of laws, etc.: Operation, vigour. *Obs.*

c 1450 *Harl. Contin. Higden* (Rolls) VIII. 511 Whiche statute was ordeynede to take vertu and begynnynge at the feste of the Purificacion. **1472–5** *Rolls of Parlt.* VI. 162/1 That the said late Ordenaunce..be and stond in strenght and vertue, unto the xxvi day of May. **1652** Needham *Selden's Mare Cl.* 59 The Sea-Laws which were used and in full force and virtue in both the Empires were borrowed from the Rhodians. **1686** *Col. Rec. Pennsylv.* I. 171 All those laws shall and are hereby Continued to Stand and be in full force and Vertue untill yᵉ End of the first Session.

†**f.** ***in virtue***, virtually. *Obs.*

a 1633 G. Herbert *Priest to Temple* xxi, A most plain and easy framing the question, even containing, in virtue, the answer also.

10. With limitation to special instances (usually ***the virtue of***.., or with possessives):

a. In senses 9 a and 9 b.

c 1290 *S. Eng. Leg.* I. 312/428 Also man, ʒwane he is i-bore, onder heore [*sc.* the planets'] power i-wis, Schullen habbe diuers lijf, euere ase heore vertue is. **a 1300** *Leg. Rood* (1871) 32 Þat water hi honurde muche..Ac hi nuste noþing of þe tre þat al þe vertu made. **1320–30** *Horn Ch.* 567 Rimneld..bi-tauʒt him a ring þe vertu wele sche knewe. **13..** *Guy Warw.* (A.) 1660 Thilke monk Sorgien was, þe vertu, he knewe of mani a gras. c 1400 Maundev. v. (1839) 50 Who so kutte hem [sc. balm-branches] with Iren, it wolde destroye his Vertue and his Nature. 1450 *Myrr. our Ladye* 37 A drynke.. whiche is swete to taste, and effectuall to hele the woundes of synners by hys verteu. 1593 Earl of Shrewsbury in Ellis *Orig. Lett.* Ser. i. III. 39, I would your Lordship wolde once make trial of my Oyle of Stags blud, for I am strongly persuaded of the rare and great vertu thereof. 1626 Bacon *Sylva* §17 It is an Errour in Phisicians, to rest simply vpon the Length of stay, for encreasing the vertue. But if you will haue the Infusion strong [etc.]. 1640 Nabbes *Bride* i. ii, Like those pills which an unwilling patient Doubting their vertue takes. 1757 A. Cooper *Distiller* i. i. (1760) 6 Till at last the whole Virtue or saccharine Sweetness of the Malt is extracted. 1759 Mills *Duhamel's Husb.* i. ix. (1762) 52 By this means the sun.. will be prevented from exhaling the virtue of your manure. 1769 Mrs. Raffald *Eng. Housekpr.* (1778) 1 It will draw all the virtue out of the roots or herbs, and turn it to a good gravy. 1845 M. Pattison *Ess.* (1889) I. 11 The virtue of St. Martin's precious relics was in the most active operation during the fifth and sixth centuries.

b. In sense 9 c.

c 1250 *Meid. Maregrete* xlv, Sclawen was þe dragun þoru þe uertu of þe rod. c 1340 Hampole *Pr. Consc.* 3821 Pardon .. es of þe tresur of haly kirke, þat es gadirde.. Of þe vertu of Crestes passion. 1382 Wyclif *Rom.* i. 16 Forsoth I schame not the gospel, for it is the vertu of God in to helthe to ech man bileuynge. c 1450 *M.E. Med. Bk.* (Heinrich) 138, I coniure ȝow fyue croppes in þe verteu of þe v woundes, þat crist suffred on þe roode treo. 1473 Warkw. *Chron.* 18 Kynge Edwarde.. requyrede hyme by the vertu of sacrament that he schulde pardone alle tho whos names here folowe. 1526 *Pilgr. Perf.* (Pynson) i. vii. 20 Hauyng grace and werkyng therafter.. by the vertue of the same he may meryt and deserue the crowne of glory. 1557 N.T. (Genev.) *Phil.* iii. 10 That I may knowe him, and the vertue of his resurrection. a 1617 Bayne *On Eph.* (1658) 23 A thing wrought not by any power of nature but by the vertue of Gods Spirit. a 1629 Hinde *J. Bruen* li. (1641) 168 Doth not the vertue of the death and resurrection of Christ require it, that henceforth wee die unto sin..?

c. In sense 9 d.

a 1340 Hampole *Prose Tr.* 2 It falles the flesche may noghte of his vertu noghte defaile ay whils þe saule in swylk joyes is rauyste for to joye. c 1386 Chaucer *Sqr.'s T.* 302 But fynally the kyng asked the knight The vertu of this stiff courser, and the might, And prayd him tellen of his governaunce. 1477 Norton *Ord. Alch.* i. in Ashm. (1652) 19 For cause efficient of Mettalls finde ye shall Only to be the vertue Minerall. 1535 Coverdale *Wisd.* xix. 19 The fyre had power in the water (contrary to his awne vertue). 1584 Sir T. Chaloner *(title)*, A shorte Discourse of the most rare.. Vertue of Nitre, wherein is declared the.. cures by the same effected. 1592 Daniel *Compl. Rosamond* Wks. (1717) 47 Pleasure had set my well-school'd Thoughts to play, And bid me use the Vertue of mine Eyes. a 1628 Preston *Effectual Faith* (1631) 118 It if bee the vertue of a horse to goe well; If it be the vertue of a knife to cut well, if it be the vertue of a Souldier to fight well. 1634 Sir T. Herbert *Trav.* 209 At the top [of the date palm].. is a soft pith, in which consists the soule and vegetatiue vertue of that tree. 1759 Franklin *Lett.* Wks. 1840 V. 364 Both these stones have evidently the two properties;.. the virtue seems strongest towards one end of the face. 1815 J. Smith *Panorama Sci. & Art* II. 170 A piece of soft iron.. capable of supporting as much as the magnet from which it derives its virtue. 1841–4 Emerson *Ess., Spir. Laws* Wks. (Bohn) I. 57 The virtue of a pipe is to be smooth and hollow. 1878 Browning *La Saisiaz* 370, I shall.. bless each kindly wrench that wrung From life's tree its inmost virtue.

d. In similar use of immaterial things. †Also in sense 9 e.

c 1325 *Spec. Gy Warw.* 658 If þu couþest knowe and se þe uertu of humilite. 1340–70 *Alisaunder* 513 Þe uertue of il uictorie.. Is noght stabled in strength of no stiff prese. 1390 Gower *Conf.* III. 30 The vertu of hire goodly speche Is verraily myn hertes leche. 1450 *Rolls of Parlt.* V. 196/2 That the seid Letters Patentes,.. aftre the strengthe, forme and vertue of the same,.. stonde and abide in the force and vertue. c 1477 Caxton *Jason* 21 b, Fayr lordes displese yow not yf the uertue of my corage knowe not now the feblesse of my body. 1563 Man *Musculus' Commonpl.* 28 The Apostle witnesseth, that the law is the vertue of sinne. 1579 Lyly *Euphues* (Arb.) 112 The old verse standeth as yet in his old vertue. 1607 *Puritan* iii. i. 74 The amazd widdow Will .. wonder at the vertue of my words. 1642 J. M[arsh] *Argt. conc. Militia* 18 The name of a Parliament onely, and not the power and vertue of it. 1691 T. H[ale] *Acc. New Invent.* 41 Whether the Harwich.. suffered any thing from her said sheathing, in her virtue of Sailing. 1746 Wesley *Princ. Methodist* 63 Works beyond the Virtue of Natural Causes, wrought by the Power of Evil Spirits. 1818 Scott *Hrt. Midl.* xliii, David.. came, through the great virtue of *if*, to be of opinion that he might safely so act in that matter. 1852 Robertson *Serm.* Ser. iii. xvii. (1882) 227 He hath imparted to us the virtue of his wrestlings. 1872 Morley *Voltaire* (1886) 4 A collective religious tradition that had lost its virtue.

†**e.** *by* (or *in*) *the virtue of*, = sense 8. *Obs.*

c 1380 Wyclif *Wks.* (1880) 32 He schal be excused fro þe lasse bi þe vertue of þe heiȝere iuge. 1654 R. Codrington tr. *Iustine* xvi. 254 [Many of them] delivered themselves from their.. calamities by the virtue of an ingenious shame. 1656 Bramhall *Replic.* vii. 292, I confess persons deputed.. by the King doe often excommunicate and absolve.. but this is by the vertue of their own habit of Jurisdiction. 1681–6 J. Scott *Chr. Life* (1747) III. 201 By interceding for us as Priest in the vertue of his Sacrifice. 1695 Dryden *Ess.* (ed. Ker) II. 124 The painters, by the virtue of their outlines, colours, lights, and shadows, represent the same things and persons in their pictures.

11. With *a* and pl. A particular power, efficacy, or good quality inherent in, or pertaining to, something: **a.** Of plants, medicines, precious stones, etc. (Cf. 9 a, 9 b, and 10 a.)

1377 Langl. *P. Pl.* B. xiv. 37 Vitailles of grete vertues, for al manere bestes. a 1400 *Stockholm Med. MS.* 26 The vertuis of violet. c 1400 Maundev. vi. (1839) 69 Many othere Vertues it [an oak-tree] hathe: where fore Men holden it fulle precyous. c 1425 *Cursor M.* 1011 (Trin.) Mony vertues þere is sene þe erbes euer I-liche grene. 1470–85 Malory *Arth.* xvii. v. 696 This Salamon was wyse and knewe alle the vertues of stones and trees. 1551 Turner *Herbal* Prol. A iij, I declare also the vertues of euery herbe. 1585 T. Washington tr. *Nicholay's Voy.* ii. ii. 32 b, Wild asses, whiche haue in their head a stone, hauing the vertue against the falling sicknes. 1597 Gerarde *Herbal* i. ii. 4 These kindes of grasses do agree as it is thought, with the common Medow grasse, in nature and vertues. 1607 Topsell *Four-f. Beasts* 34 There are sundry vertues confected out of this beast. 1649 Bp. Reynolds *Hosea* i. 22 Wine draweth a nourishing vertue from the flesh of Vipers. 1699 Dampier *Voy.* (1729) III. i. 379 The Sulphurousness or other Vertue of this Water. 1762 H. Walpole *Vertue's Anecd. Paint.* (1786) I. 280 It is said in the note that Sir Nathaniel was famed for painting plants, and well skilled in their virtues. 1796 Withering *Brit. Plants* (ed. 3) I. 324 The plants of this class are supposed to have various specific virtues. 1806 *Med. Jrnl.* XV. 327 Have practitioners yet proved the full virtues of the digitalis? 1838 *Murray's Hand-bk. N. Germ.* 374/2 The hot mineral springs.. owe their virtues to the presence of sulphur and alkaline salts. 1856 R. A. Vaughan *Mystics* viii. iv. (1860) II. 53 Each planet, according to its mind or mood, shed virtues healing or harmful into minerals and herbs.

b. Of animal bodies, the elements, or other physical entities.

expulsive virtue: see expulsive *a.* 1.

c 1384 Chaucer *H. Fame* ii. 42 For so astonyed and a-sweved Was every vertu in my heved. c 1386 —— *Prol.* 4 Whan that Aprille.. hath.. bathud every veyne in swich licour, Of which vertue engendred is the flour. c 1400 *Lanfranc's Cirurg.* 15 Þe vertues of lymes þou must knowe, þat he se, whanne þe worchinge of ony vartu failith in ony lyme. 1451 Capgrave *Life St. Gilbert* 120 Hir left arme had lost þe vertue of felyng. 1480 Caxton *Myrr.* iii. viii. 145 The sterres that ben in heuen whiche haue vertues on therthe. 1544 Phaer *Regim. Life* (1560) S v, When a childe neseth out of measure, that is to say with a long continuance & therby the brayn & virtues animal be febled, it is good to stop it. 1585 T. Washington tr. *Nicholay's Voy.* iv. xxix. 151 The sacred fountayne.. is of such a vertue, that putting into it any burning thing [it] is sodainly extinguished. 1604 E. G[rimstone] tr. *D'Acosta's Hist. Indies* iii. xxi. 188 This moisture from heaven hath such a vertue, that ceasing to fal vpon the earth, it breedes a great discommoditie and defect of graine and seedes. a 1628 Preston *Effectual Faith* (1631) 59 If the Loadstone be of such a vertue, let it show it by attracting the Iron to it. 1684 R. Waller *Nat. Exper.* 46 The imperceptible pores of those passages by which the attractive Virtue issues out. 1709 T. Robinson *Nat. Hist. Westmoreld.* v. 26 A very active Principle, or Virtue, that operates in the Generation of Stones. 1755 B. Martin *Mag. of Arts & Sci.* 389 What seems most wonderful, is, that the magnetic Virtue should not be interrupted by the Glass.

c. In miscellaneous uses.

1486 *Bk. St. Albans, Her.* a j, Ther ben here the vertuys of Chyualry. 1568 Grafton *Chron.* II. 206 Money is of so great a vertue that it corrupteth Popes. 1629 Hobbes *Thucyd.* (1822) 70 For a great and a little claim imposed.. by way of command hath one and the same virtue to make subject. 1676 Hobbes *Iliad* Pref. (1686) 1 Concerning the Vertues of an Heroick Poem. 1702 *Rouse's Heav. Univ.* Advert. 4 They may inwardly perceive by a most powerful and most secret Vertue imprinted in their Souls and Hearts. 1815 J. Smith *Panorama Sci. & Art* I. 276 It is not meant that there is any peculiar virtue or charm in the point called the centre. 1872 Ruskin *Eagle's N.* §18 Over these three kingdoms of imagination, art, and science, there reigns a virtue or faculty.. the appointed ruler and guide of every method of labour.

III. 12. *Comb.*, as ***virtue-binding***, ***-proof***, ***-wise*** adjs.

1667 Milton *P.L.* v. 384 No vaile Shee needed, Vertue-proof, no thought infirme Alterd her cheek. 1691 *Satyr agst. French* 21 And she must be but little Vertue-proof, Who can be taken with such fulsom Stuff. 1816 L. Hunt *Rimini* iii. 6 The holy cheat, the virtue-binding sin. 1838 S. Bellamy *Betrayal* 49 And wisdom's self revealings, virtue-wise, Thy darkness comprehending not.

†**virtue**, *v. Obs.*$^{-1}$ In 4 vertue. [f. prec.] *refl.* To exert (oneself).

1390 Gower *Conf.* I. 372 For schrifte stant of no value To him that wol him noght vertue To leve of vice the folie.

'virtued, *a. rare.* [f. virtue *sb.*] Endued with virtue or efficacy.

1609 Heywood *Brit. Troy* iv. xi, He discends unto his knees Taking the vertued chaplet from his head. 1635 Quarles *Embl.* v. iv. 21 But has the virtu'd Steele a pow'r to move? Or can the untouch'd Needle point aright? 1897 J. Primmer *J. Primmer in Rome* (1903) 110 The old woman.. rubs her hand on the toes and passes the virtued hand across the child's forehead.

'virtuefy, *v. rare.* [f. as prec. + -fy.] *trans.* To render virtuous.

1834 Chalmers *On Const. Man* ii. ii. II. 244 It is this which *virtuefies* emotion, even though there be nothing virtuous, which is not voluntary. 1884 H. James *Let.* 8 Mar. (1980) III. 36, I am sorry that the divine Daudet is going to virtuefy his *souillon*.

†**'virtuehead.** *Obs.*$^{-1}$ In 5 vertued, -hede. [f. as prec. + -head.] Virtuousness.

c 1450 in *Archiv Stud. neu. Spr.* (1900) CIV. 308 In taryeng is oft full grete drede, Where a begynnyng causith vertued [*v.r.* vertuhede].

'virtueless, *a.* Also 4–7 vertu-, 6–7 vertue-. [f. virtue *sb.* + -less.]

1. Destitute of efficacy or excellence; ineffective, worthless.

c 1374 Chaucer *Troylus* ii. 344 Wo worth þe faire gemme vertules. Wo worth þat herbe also þat doth no bote. 1390 Gower *Conf.* III. 129 The seconde is noght vertules, Clota or elles Pliades It hatte. 1548 Udall, etc. *Erasm. Par. Mark* ix. 58 In the presence of the disciples they depraued the name of Jesu, as a thing vertuelesse, and of no efficacie. 1600 Fairfax *Tasso* vi. lxviii, And vertuelesse she wisht all herbes and charmes, Wherewith false men encrease their patients harmes. 1627 Hakewill *Apol.* ii. v. §3, I do not consent with them who would make those glorious Creatures of God vertuelesse. c 1642 *Observ. his Majesty's late Answ. & Expresses* 9 Parliaments are thus vertuelesse and void Courts. 1824 *New Monthly Mag.* X. 264 The winds of March.. are far from being virtueless. 1856 Ruskin *Mod. Paint.* III. iv. v. §4 The architecture of Palladio is wholly virtueless and despicable.

2. Destitute of virtue or moral goodness; immoral, vicious.

1402 Hoccleve *Let. of Cupid* 262 But swyche filthes [= low women] as weren vertulesse, they quytten thus, this olde clerkis wisse. 1407 Scogan *Mor. Balade* 133 That, whan ye come in your juges presence, Ye be not set as vertules behynde. 1533 More *Apol.* x. Wks. 867/2 Howe badde so euer they reken me, I am not yet fullye so vertuelesse, but that [etc.]. 1594 O. B. *Quest. Profit. Concern.* 23 The strange and monstrous life and death, of a vertulesse recreant. 1602 *How Choose Good Wife* i. i. in Hazl. *Dodsley* IX. 9 O, too unkind unto so kind a wife, Too virtueless to one so virtuous. 1650 Fuller *Pisgah* ii. (1869) 112 We know the wicked man's.. name, and yet.. his virtueless name shall rot. 1803 Mary Charlton *Wife & Mistress* I. 307 You are not to become a worthless, virtueless, shameless fine lady. 1847 G. Harris *Life Ld. Hardwicke* xiii. III. 222 Sallies of indignation, possibly not altogether virtueless, which on special occasions were wont to emanate from this monarch's lips.

Hence **'virtuelessness.**

1891 H. S. Constable *Horses, Sport & War* 221 The cowardice, imbecility, and virtuelessness of the other classes.

†**virtuifi'cation.** *Obs.*$^{-1}$ [Cf. virtuefy *v.*] The action of enduing with virtue.

1652 Urquhart *Jewel* 17 The Bonification and virtuification of Lully, Scotus's Hexeity, and Albedineity of Suarez.

virtuize ('vɜːtjuːaɪz), *v. nonce-wd.* [f. virtu(e *sb.* + -ize.] *intr.* To behave with conscious propriety; to act in a virtuous manner.

1920 D. H. Lawrence *Touch & Go* ii. 52 If you want me to virtuise and smug with you, you had [better have stayed away].

‖**virtuosa** (vɜːtjuː'əʊsə). Now *rare.* [It., fem. of *virtuoso* virtuoso.] A female virtuoso.

1668 Shadwell *Sullen Lovers* ii, D'ye think, I that am a *Virtuosa* understand no better, then to leave you now you are not well? 1675 Plume *Life of Hacket* (1865) 20 Pope Gregory XV. had canonised Ignatius Loyola.. and Madam Teresia, a Spanish Virtuosa. 1754 Chesterf. in *World* No. 98 ¶8 Consequently those respectable titles of virtuoso and virtuosa have not the least relation to the moral characters of the parties. 1796 Burney *Mem. Metastasio* II. 161 This *virtuosa*, being unemployed, will doubtless have offers from other quarters. 1826 Margravine of Anspach *Mem.* I. viii. 310 The Virtuosa the other day had sung a Hebrew air, which began at the end. 1847 Leitch tr. *C. O. Müller's Anc. Art* §425. 505 A musical virtuosa playing at the same time on a standing and lying stringed instrument.

†**virtuose**, *sb. Obs.*$^{-1}$ In 8 vertuose. [Anglicized form of virtuoso: cf. next.] A virtuoso.

a 1721 Prior *Ess. Learning* ¶6 The Gentleman who likes Medals very well will always be desirous to possess the best of them, and the Antiquary or Vertuose will be sure to top false ones upon him.

virtuose (vɜːtjuː'əʊs), *a.* [ad. It. *virtuoso*: cf. prec.] Having or exhibiting the characteristics of a virtuoso; of or pertaining to virtuosi.

1890 *Academy* 17 May 346/1 Mme. Carreno is essentially a virtuose player, and it was in pieces by Liszt that she astonished her audience. 1906 *Athenæum* 8 Sept. 281/3 The virtuose element is prominent, but thought, feeling, and a poetical atmosphere are evident in the music.

virtuose, obs. form of virtuous *a.*

virtuosi, pl. of virtuoso.

virtuosic (vɜːtjuː'əʊsɪk), *a.* [f. virtuos-o + -ic.] = virtuose *a.*

1889 *Academy* 13 April 261/3 Of late we have had only fugitive pieces of the romantic, and even virtuosic, schools. 1899 *Scotsman* 13 Nov. 9/4 The Capriccio, on the other hand, can only be described as a piece of virtuosic music.

virtuosity (vɜːtjuː'ɒsɪtɪ). Also 5 vertuosyte, 7 vertuositie. [In sense 1 ad. med.L. *virtuōsitas*, f. late L. *virtuōsus* virtuous *a.* In other senses f. virtuos-o + -ity: cf. F. *virtuosité*.]

†**1. a.** Manly qualities or character. *Obs.*$^{-1}$

a 1470 Harding *Chron.* lix. i, For his wyt and virtuosyte, Able he was, as Chronycles coulde fele, To haue ruled all the emperalyte.

†**b.** Virtuousness. *Obs.* (Bailey, 1721).

2. The pursuits, interests, or temperament, characteristic of a virtuoso; interest or taste in the fine arts, esp. of a fastidious, finical, dilettante or trifling nature.

1673 H. Stubbe *Further Vind. Dutch War* 82 We are regenerated from the School of Aristotle to that of Epicurus, from all Moral Gallantry and Virtue, to a most impertinent and effeminate Virtuosity. 1676 Wood *Life* (O.H.S.) II. 360 Edward Bendlowes,.. a great poet.. spent about 7 hundred a yeare in vertuositie and on flattering poets. 1823 W. Taylor in *Monthly Mag.* LV. 408 Charles-Augustus had imbibed.. a taste for merit, a virtuosity in human excellence, to employ his preceptor's phrase. 1840 *Blackw. Mag.* XLVIII. 491 The Viennese, by their wise virtuosity, do the thing [*sc.* eating and drinking] gently, and like gentlemen. 1886 SYMONDS *Renaiss. It., Cath. React.* (1898) VII. xii. 189 This..state of things..was due rather to the abuse of science and of virtuosity.

b. *spec.* Excessive attention to technique, or to the production of special effects, in vocal or instrumental music (also *transf.* in art or literature).

1865 *Reader* 18 Mar. 321/3 For this sentiment, this type of art, as applied to matters musical, there is a special name. It is called 'virtuosity'. 1877 E. PROUT in *Academy* 17 Feb. 150 We have a short sketch of the history of piano virtuosity. 1884 HAWEIS *Musical Life* II. 608 It is doubtful whether two such extraordinary personalities as those of Paganini and Liszt have ever appeared in the world of virtuosity.

c. With *a* and pl. A special study or interest of the kind affected by virtuosi.

1883 *Century Mag.* XXVI. 280 I've been cultivating some virtuosities, among other things.

3. Virtuosi collectively.

1831 CARLYLE *Sart. Res.* I. iii, Where all the Virtuosity and nearly all the Intellect of the place assembled of an evening.

‖**virtuoso** (vɜːtjuːˈəʊsəʊ). Also 7–8 vertuoso. Pl. **virtuosi** (7 vert-) and **virtuosos**. [It. *virtuoso* (also *vertuoso*) 'learned, skilled, skilful, full of learning' (Baretti):—L. *virtuōsus*: see VIRTUOUS *a.* Hence also F. *virtuose*, †*virtuoso.*]

It is frequently difficult in particular instances to decide which of the senses is intended.

†**1.** One who has a general interest in arts and sciences, or who pursues special investigations in one or more of these; a learned person; a scientist, savant, or scholar. *Obs.*

Sometimes tending towards a depreciatory sense, as in 2.

α. 1651 in Brent tr. *Sarpi's Counc. Trent* (1676) xxv, There have happened to come to Venice..divers Virtuosi in several professions. 1660 BOYLE *New Exp. Phys. Mech.* Proem 2 Perceiving by Letters from..Paris, that several of the Virtuosi there, were very intent upon the examination of the Interest of the Ayr in hindring the descent of the Quick-silver. 1684–5 —— *Min. Waters* 73 The little Bodies that the ingenious Mr. Lewenhoeck, and since him divers other Virtuosi, have observ'd in Water wherein Pepper has been infus'd. 1709 T. ROBINSON *Nat. Hist. Westmoreld.* xii. 69 That new Hypothesis so stiffly maintained by some of our learned *Virtuosi.* 1739 *Dublin Soc. Weekly Observ.* I. No. 26. 172 Some Virtuosi tell you that continued Fermentation and repeated racking certainly spoil your Cyder. 1754 FIELDING *Voy. Lisbon* ¶16 The former receives the thanks of mankind; the latter [i.e. the antiquary] of that valuable part, the virtuosi. [1855 KINGSLEY *Westward Ho!* xvi, Philip Sidney..has given up his rightful place toward the head of the table that he may have a knot of virtuosi all to himself.]

β. 1656 EARL MONM. tr. *Boccalini's Advts. fr. Parnass.* I. v. 8 The gallant Dispute which arose..between some Letterati of the State, deserves to be written; every one of these Vertuosie defended their own Opinion as the best. 1665 GLANVILL *Scepsis Sci.* xi. 58 As great Wits, as it may be e're saw the Sun, such as Pythagoras, Des-Cartes, Copernicus, Galileo, More, Kepler, and generally the vertuosi of the awakened world. 1700 T. BROWN tr. *Fresny's Amusem.* 36 The Projectors who are generally broken Citizens, were coop'd up in the Counters and Ludgate;..the Vertuosi were confined to Gresham-College.

γ. 1656 BLOUNT *Glossogr.*, *Virtuoso*,..a learned or ingenious person, or one that is well qualified. 1660 INGELO *Bentiv. & Ur.* II. (1682) 22, I must not offend these Virtuoso's with laughing at them. 1676 GLANVILL *Ess.* III. 30 Another excellent Virtuoso of the same Assembly, Mr. John Evelyn, hath very considerably advanced the History of Fruit and Forest-Trees. 1706 E. WARD *Wooden World Diss.* (1708) 60 He's no Digbian Virtuoso,..for he knows not how to sympathize with any mans Wounds whatever. 1732 BERKELEY *Alciphr.* II. §14 Certain particularities discovered in that animal by a modern virtuoso. 1788 *Eng. Gazetteer* (ed. 2) s.v. *Comb-Martin*, They were neglected till the reign of queen Elizabeth, when Sir Beavis Bulmer, a virtuoso in refining metals, got great quantities of silver from them. [1834 SOUTHEY *Doctor* vi. (1862) 19 There were in him undeveloped talents which might have raised him to distinction as..a virtuoso of the Royal Society.]

δ. 1656 EARL MONM. tr. *Boccalini's Advts. fr. Parnass.* I. ii. 5 Appearing much displeased at the affront done this man, he first honoured him with the name of Vertuoso [etc.]. 1683 KENNETT tr. *Erasm. on Folly* 60 To these are to be added those plodding Vertuoso's that plunder the most inward recesses of Nature. 1691 WOOD *Ath. Oxon.* I. 852 He was afterwards an eminent Physician, Vertuoso, and Knight. 1700 T. BROWN tr. *Fresny's Amusem.* ix. (1709) 89 The *Vertuoso* despises the Rich for making such a bustle about so foolish and pale-fac'd a Metal as Gold.

2. One who has a special interest in, or taste for, the fine arts; a student or collector of antiquities, natural curiosities or rarities, etc.; a connoisseur; freq., one who carries on such pursuits in a dilettante or trifling manner.

α, β. 1662 EVELYN *Chalcogr.* iii. 34 The Greeks and inventive Romans, who..publish'd so many thousands of medails, and coynes as are in the hands and collections of the *Virtuosi.* 1675 HOBBES *Iliad* To Rdr., There be many men called critiques; and wits, and vertuosi, that are accustomed to censure the poets, and most of them of divers judgements. *a* 1711 SHAFTESB. *Charac.* III. 157 A Worse thing than this happens commonly to these inferior *Virtuosi.* In seeking so earnestly for Raritys, they fall in love with Rarity, for Rareness-sake. 1781 J. MOORE *View Soc. Italy* (1790) II. lxxi. 367 The beautiful head of Alexander is universally admired by all the virtuosi. 1839 HALLAM *Hist. Lit.* II. viii. §61 The well-known word virtuosi, applied to these lovers of what was rare and beautiful in art or nature. 1851 D. WILSON *Preh. Ann.* (1863) I. v. 153 The virtuosi to whose inspection it was submitted. 1876 MORLEY *Crit. Misc.* Ser. I. (1877) 349 For intellectual dilettanti and moralising virtuosi.

γ, δ. *c* 1665 COWLEY *Queen's repairing Somerset-house* 86 If any prouder Virtuoso's sense At that part of my Prospect take offence. 1667 DRYDEN & DK. NEWCASTLE *Sir M. Marall* III. (beginning), I am sure, in all companies I pass for a virtuoso. *a* 1700 EVELYN *Diary* 1 Mar. 1644, One of the greatest virtuosos in France, for his collection of pictures, achates, medalls, and flowers. 1729 MANDEVILLE *Fab. Bees* II. 414 Look upon the mighty labours of antiquaries, botanists, and the vertuoso's in butterflies, cockle-shells, and other odd productions of nature. 1749 FIELDING *Tom Jones* VIII. x, A great number of nicknacks and Curiosities, which might have engaged the attention of a virtuoso. 1787 MME. D'ARBLAY *Diary* June, Virtuosos being next.. named, Colonel Manners inveighed against them quite violently. 1825 *Gentl. Mag.* XCV. I. 332 The Virtuoso will appreciate justly this small volume as a very instructive and agreeable manual. 1858 MERIVALE *Rom. Emp.* liii. (1865) VI. 324 For painting and sculpture, as Grecian arts, he may have acquired the taste of a virtuoso. 1885 J. PAYN *Talk of Town* I. 183 He was a *virtuoso* and antiquary himself, and therefore recognised the full extent of his danger.

transf. 1829 LYTTON *Devereux* II. vi, Salter is a shaving virtuoso. 1837 LOCKHART *Scott* IV. v. 161 Excellent dishes, —such..as Scotland borrowed from France before Catherine de Medicis brought in her Italian *virtuosi* to revolutionize the kitchen like the court.

3. a. One who has special knowledge or skill in music; *spec.*, in modern use, one who excels in, or devotes special attention to, technique in playing or singing.

1743 BP. BERKELEY in Fraser *Life* viii. (1871) 289 Such virtuosi as the country affords; I mean in the way of music. 1764 *Advert.* in *N. & Q.* 3rd Ser. IV. 386 The late famous Vertuoso Handel, received during his Life-time, such particular protection. 1834 BECKFORD *Italy* II. xxxi. 222 *note*, All these *virtuosi*..were either *contraltos* of the softest note, or *sopranos* of the highest squeakery. 1859 WRAXALL tr. *R. Houdin* xi. 155, I had often heard a nightingale sing, which I thought was the 'star' among the virtuosi. 1900 *Daily News* 19 June 4/7 A piece of little or no musical merit ..has of late years come again into fashion with violin virtuosi.

b. *transf.*

1921 H. CRANE *Let.* 1 Nov. (1965) 69 [Ben] Hecht is a virtuoso and arouses suspicions that one would never feel for Dreiser or Anderson. 1950 E. H. GOMBRICH *Story of Art* xviii. 268 For him to be an artist was no longer to be a respectable and sedate owner of a workshop: it was to be a 'virtuoso' for whose favour princes and cardinals should compete. 1952 A. HUXLEY *Let.* *c* 20 July (1969) 647 On the basis..of what I have seen done..by a man who is probably the greatest living virtuoso in the field of hypnosis..I would advise you very strongly to try hypnosis.

4. *attrib.*, as ***virtuoso collection, country, expression, kind, scheme***, etc. Now also passing into adj.

1668 COWLEY *Ess. Verse & Prose, Of Avarice*, As if thou No other Use of precious Gold didst know, But that of curious Pictures to delight With the fair stamp thy *Virtuoso* Sight. 1700 T. BROWN tr. *Fresny's Amusem.* x. (1709) 100 The Philosophical, or Virtuosi Country. 1710 SHAFTESB. *Charac.* (1711) I. 157 In Philosophy, Matters answer exactly to this *Virtuoso*-Scheme. *Ibid.* 333 To the Academys of Painters, Statuarys, and to the rest of the *Virtuoso*-Tribe. 1727 GAY *Fables* I. xvi. 24 Her head's of virtuoso kind. 1775 S. J. PRATT *Liberal Opin.* civ. (1783) III. 251, I would peep into the..opinions of men, with a sort of virtuoso vigilance. 1835 WILLIS *Pencillings* I. vi. 38 About his mouth and eye there was the proper virtuoso expression of inquisitiveness and discrimination. 1856 KANE *Arct. Expl.* II. ix. 93 Near these is a virtuoso collection of cups grouped in a tumulus or cairn. 1882 ANNIE EDWARDES *Ballroom Repent.* I. 52 With her Stradivarius tucked, in true virtuoso style, under her chin. 1947 A. EINSTEIN *Mus. Romantic Era* xi. 225 These compositions are intimate confessions, often difficult but never virtuoso. 1952 S. KAUFFMANN *Tightrope* v. 82 'Look,' he said, staring intently into her eyes, giving a virtuoso performance of sincerity, 'I can't say all this makes me happy.' 1978 J. UPDIKE *Coup* (1979) iv. 129 The virtuoso arabesques of her sullen profile. 1984 *Times* 7 Sept. 20/8 Another virtuoso set of interim figures from Bunzl left the share price up 2p at 305p.

virtu'osoship. [f. prec. + -SHIP.] The state or condition of being a virtuoso; the profession of a virtuoso.

a 1711 SHAFTESB. *Charac.* III. 160 Let us view Philosophy, like mere Virtuoso-ship, in its usual Career. 1749 MRS. MONTAGU *Lett.* (1813) III. 98 Vanity and virtuosoship go hand in hand. 1778 *Phil. Surv. S. Irel.* 34 Too refined..by Italian virtuosoship, for the relish of his country neighbours. 1831 CARLYLE *Misc. Ess., Schiller* (1872) III. 65 Apart from virtuosoship, or any technical object, what a hold have such things on our universal curiosity as men. 1887 E. GURNEY *Tertium Quid* II. 110 The most brainless and soulless form of virtuosoship.

virtuous (ˈvɜːtjuːəs), *a.* Forms: *α.* 4–5 vertuos, 4–6 -uose, 4–7 -uouse, 4–8 -uous (4 -ouous, -uuus, -ueous), 5 -uus, -uows(e, -ueux (*Sc.* wertuo(u)sse, -uwisse, -uus, 6 vertwus); 5 vertues (wert-), vertuys (*Sc.* -uyse, -uise), 5–6 -uis; 5 vertus (*Sc.* -use), wertuz (*Sc.* -us); 4 vertiuus, 5–6 *Sc.* verteous, 6 *Sc.* -ewous, -ewus, -eus, werteous. Also *superl.* 5 vertues, 6 vertuest, vertuost. *β.* 4 uirtuous, virtuus, 5 virtuose, 7– virtuous. [a. AF. and OF. *vertuous*, OF. *vertuos, vertuus*, (also mod.F.) *vertueux*, etc., = Pr. *vertuos*, Cat. *virtuos*, Sp. and Pg. *virtuoso*, It. *ver-, virtuoso*, late L. *virtuōsus*, f. L. *virtus* VIRTUE *sb.* See -OUS.]

I. Of persons, personal qualities or actions, etc.

†**1. a.** Distinguished by manly qualities; full of manly courage; valiant, valorous. *Obs.*

13.. *K. Alis.* 2408 (Laud MS.), Alisaunder and tholomeus, Mid her men þat weren so vertuous, þat hij weren passed ostes two. *Ibid.* 3319 Ne seiȝ ich neuer so hardy kniȝth..So stronge on hors ne so vertuouse. *c* 1330 *Arth. & Merl.* 4310 For alle hem werreþ Galcus, þe riche king so vertouous. *c* 1450 *Merlin* xxix. 595 The slaughter [was] grete on bothe sides. Neuertheles whan Merlin saugh the saisnes so vertuouse, he [etc.]. 1474 CAXTON *Chesse* IV. vi. 178 Ye shalle vnderstande that they ben stronge and vertuous in bataylle. *c* 1489 —— *Sonnes of Aymon* xx. 451 'Brother', sayd reynawde, 'I praye you that ye shewe yourselfe vertuous & stronge agenste our enmyes'. 1606 CHAPMAN *Gent. Vsher* I. i, My Lord, I know too well your vertuous spirit; Take heede for God's loue if you rowse the bore You come not neere him. *c* 1611 —— *Iliad* XIII. 148 With this all strengths and minds he mov'd; but young Deiphobus, Old Priam's son, amongst them all was chiefly virtuous. 1611 BEAUM. & FL. *King & No K.* I, Must all men that are vertuous Think suddenly to match themselves with me.? I conquered him and bravely, did I not?

†**b.** Of an act: Evincing a manly spirit; brave, heroic, courageous. *Obs. rare.*

1560 WHITEHORNE tr. *Machiavell's Arte Warre* 85 Thei had appointed rewardes to euery worthie acte: as he that faighting, saued the life of one of his Citezeins,..to him that had..slaine the enemie, and so euery vertuous act, was of the Consulles knowen and rewarded. 1653 COGAN *Diodorus Siculus* V. ii. 174 The child,..catching them [*sc.* two Dragons] by the throat, strangled them both; for which his vertuous act, the Argives called him Hercules.

†**c.** Capable, able. *Obs.*[−1]

1483 CAXTON *Cato* e viij, It happeth oftymes that they to whome nature hath denyed..her forces or strengthes been better and more vertuous to gyue a good counceyl than the other.

2. a. Possessing or showing virtue in life and conduct; acting with moral rectitude or in conformity with moral laws; free from vice, immorality, or wickedness; good, just, righteous.

The prevailing sense. In some early quots. as a general term of commendation (cf. sense 3).

α. *c* 1340 HAMPOLE *Prose Tr.* 14 Þe mare þat a saule es.. joynede to oure Lorde Godd, þe mare stabill it es and myghty,.. gude, peyseble, luffande, and mare vertuous. 1390 GOWER *Conf.* II. 78 Bot if a man of bothe two Be riche and vertuous also, Thanne is he wel the more worth. *c* 1400 *Apoll. Loll.* 91 Crist is more exellent & vertuosar þan oþer createris. *a* 1475 G. ASHBY *Active Policy* 480 Looke that youre servauntes be of the best,..And eueriche in his degre vertuest. 1509 FISHER *Funeral Serm. C'tess Richmond* Wks. (1876) 301 All the vertuous and deuoute persones to whome she was as a louynge syster. 1534 CROMWELL in Merriman *Life & Lett.* (1902) I. 375 Diuerse other vertuose prestes men of good lernyng and reputation, shuld so testifie of her. 1563 *Homilies* II. *Peril Idol.* III. Ss iij b, The vertuest and best learned..auncient fathers. 1567 PAYNELL tr. *Treas. Amadis of Gaule* E ij b, I neuer saw a wiser, vertuouser or a more temperate prince. 1611 BIBLE *Transl. Pref.* ¶8 A man may be counted a vertuous man, though hee haue made many slips in his life. 1640 QUARLES *Enchiridion* xci, If a Prince expect vertuous Subjects, let his Subjects have a vertuous Prince. 1695 LD. PRESTON *Boeth.* IV. 172 The Reward of vertuous Men. 1701 ROWE *Amb. Step-Moth.* Ep. Ded., Two Vertuous (or at least Innocent) Characters. 1706 STANHOPE *Paraphr.* III. 206 Approving ourselves vertuous in our Behaviour as well as orthodox in our Belief.

transf. 1426 LYDG. *De Guil. Pilgr.* 22098 Byholde ȝonder a Chartrehous, An ordur that is full vertuous. 1539–40 WRIOTHESLEY *Chron.* (Camden) I. 109 The howse of Sion.. which was the vertues [= most virtuous] howse of religion that was in England.

β. 1487 *Barbour's Bruce* IV. 742 He had beyn fals and couatus; Bot his vit maid him virtuous. 1660 INGELO *Bentiv. & Ur.* II. (1682) 72 When that which is worse hath cunningly contriv'd the destruction of Virtuous persons. 1691 HARTCLIFFE *Virtues* 397 It were impossible so long as Men..have a desire of their own Happiness, but they should be virtuous. 1707 *Curios. in Husb. & Gard.* 7 *Ecclesiasticus* injoins Labour and Agriculture as a Duty of virtuous Men. 1777 R. WATSON *Philip II* (1839) 23 Thus did this monarch, who was not less virtuous than most of his cotemporary princes, deliberately resolve to add treachery to the perjury and falsehood into which he had been betrayed. 1826 DISRAELI *V. Grey* v. xiii, I have been too weak to be virtuous: but I have been..tried most bitterly. 1859 GEO. ELIOT *A. Bede* xvii, Let your most faulty characters always be on the wrong side, and your virtuous ones on the right. 1881 *Jrnl. Inst. Bankers* II. IX. 563 The virtuous debtor, whose insolvency was attributable to unavoidable losses and misfortune.

b. Of women. Freq. = CHASTE *a.*

In quot. *c* 1400 merely an epithet of commendation.

c 1386 CHAUCER *Man of Law's T.* 526 They can not gesse That sche had doon so gret a wikkednesse, For they han seyen hir so vertuous. *c* 1400 *Destr. Troy* 2432 Venus the vertuus was verely the fairest. *c* 1420 *Chron. Vilod.* 1573 Þer nasse A wysor wommon..Ny vertuoser in levyng,..þen was þis holy mayde. 1536 CROMWELL in Merriman *Life & Lett.* (1902) II. 21 Soo hath his grace I thinke chosen the vertuost lady and the veriest gentlewoman that lyveth. *a* 1578 LINDESAY (Pitscottie) *Chron. Scot.* (S.T.S.) I. 157 Quene Margarit was werie wyse and werteous in hir husbandis tyme, bot sune efter his deid..scho became leichorous of hir body. 1598 SHAKS. *Merry W.* IV. ii. 136 Mistris Ford, the honest woman, the modest wife, the vertuous creature, that hath the iealious foole to her husband. 1611 BIBLE *Prov.* xii. 4 A vertuous woman is a crowne to her husband. 1632 *High Commission Cases* (Camden) 265 That she being a vertuous and a chaste lady, he called her whore often tymes. 1712 STEELE *Spect.* No. 286 ¶1 In my Opinion, and in that of many of your virtuous Female Readers. 17.. *Suffolk Miracle* ii. in Child *Ballads* V. 66/1 Her beauty was beyond compare, She was both virtuous and fair. 1796 H. HUNTER tr. *St.-Pierre's Stud. Nat.* (1799) III. 77 'She will be virtuous', said she, 'and she will be happy: I knew calamity only in ceasing to be virtuous'. **1837** LYTTON *E. Maltrav.* II. i, Madame D'Epinay's memoirs are of this character. She was not a virtuous woman—but she felt virtue and loved it. **1843** BETHUNE *Sc. Fireside Stor.* 35 A virtuous woman, who has given her heart..to one whom [etc.].

†**c.** Used as a title of courtesy in addressing or referring to persons, esp. ladies of rank or emimence. *Obs.*

c **1532** DU WES *Introd. Fr.* in *Palsgr.* 896 Most illustre, ryght exellente & ryght vertuouse lady my lady Mary of Englande. **1588** KYD *Househ. Philos.* Ded., To the Worshipfvll and Vertvovs Gentleman Maister Thomas Reade, Esqvier, Health and all Happines. **1616** SIR W. MURE *Misc. Poems* xvii. *title*, Epitaph of the wery excellent, vertuouse..trulie honoured Lady, the Lady Arnestoun. *a* **1700** EVELYN *Diary* 4 Feb. 1668, I saw the tragedy of 'Horace' (written by the virtuous Mrs. Phillips).

d. *absol.* (as pl.), chiefly with *the.*

1390 GOWER *Conf.* III. 226 He putte awey the vicious And tok to him the vertuous. *c* **1425** WYNTOUN *Cron.* VII. 832 He chastit þa þat war wiciousse, And rewardit þa þat war vertuousse. **1589** NASHE *Anat. Absurd.* Wks. (Grosart) I. 35 The acts of the ventrous, and the praise of the vertuous. **1597** MORLEY *Introd. Mus.* Ded., A second being..causing vs liue in the mindes of the vertuous, as it were, deified to the posteritie. **1651** HOBBES *Leviath.* IV. xlvi. 373 As if the Vertuous, and their Vertues could be asunder. *a* **1711** KEN *Urania* Wks. 1721 IV. 498 They priz'd an humble modest Air, Sang more the Virtuous than the Fair. **1759** JOHNSON *Rasselas* xxxvii[i,] But the angels of affliction spread their toils alike for the virtuous and the wicked. *c* **1805** LEYDEN in *Life & Poems* (1875) 195 The soft descending dews of sleep, That bathe the virtuous in serene repose. **1846** MRS. A. MARSH *Father Darcy* II. viii. 137 The esteem of the noble and virtuous I would still retain.

e. Of the disposition or mind.

1584 POWEL *Lloyd's Cambria* 398 Of a good and vertuous disposition. **1598** SHAKS. *Merry W.* I. i. 189 *Slen.* If I be drunke, Ile be drunke with those that haue the feare of God, and not with drunken knaues. *Euan.* So got-udge me, that is a vertuous minde. **1602** *Ld. Cromwell* IV. i. 20 He was my Maister, And each vertuous part, That liued in him, I tenderd with my hart. **1634** MILTON *Comus* 211 These thoughts may startle well, but not astound The vertuous mind. **1660** INGELO *Bentiv. & Ur.* II. (1682) 196 Many Vertuous Dispositions are fair Resemblances of the Divine Perfections. **1780** A. HAMILTON *Let. to Miss Schuyler* Wks. 1850 I. 187 A virtuous mind cannot long esteem a base one. **1784** COWPER *Tiroc.* 436 The most disint'rested and virtuous minds. **1816** SHELLEY *Dæmon of World* II. 136 The bliss..Which..Dawns on the virtuous mind.

f. *Sc.* Diligent or industrious in work.

Perhaps due to Prov. xii. 4: see b. above, quot. 1611.

1725 RAMSAY *Gentle Sheph.* I. ii, I've heard my honest uncle aften say, That lads should a' for wives that's vertuous pray. *a* **1825** SCOTT in Jamieson *Sc. Dict.* Suppl. s.v., Her daughter was the most virtuous woman in the parish, for that week she had spun sax spyndles of yarn.

g. ***virtuous circle*** [after *vicious circle* s.v. VICIOUS *a.* 9], a recurring cycle of events, the result of each one being to increase the beneficial effect of the next.

1953 E. SIMON *Past Masters* III. 156 It will be a virtuous circle of publicity attracting helpers and, I trust, supplementary donations, and these begetting more publicity. **1958** *Brit. Jrnl. Sociol.* IX. 163 The child's..range and expression of discriminating verbal responses is fostered by the social structure... A virtuous circle is set up which is continually reinforced. **1982** *Times* 6 May 18/4 The rating reflects the company's virtuous circle—years of store building and modernization leading to productivity gains, which allow it to hold prices lower than its rivals but still make a better margin of 4·5 per cent.

3. a. Of acts, life, manners, etc.: Characterized by, of the nature of, virtue; according with, or conforming to, moral law or principles; morally good or justifiable.

Occas. in a weakened sense: 'estimable, commendable, praiseworthy.'

c **1375** *Sc. Leg. Saints* xix. 634 God to christofore gafe sic grace of vertuyse lare. *Ibid.* xxxvi. 424 Aganis þaim..þat awantis þaim-selfe of uertuise lif. *a* **1393** CHAUCER *Gentilesse* 17 Ther may no man..beqweythe his heyre his vertuous noblesse. *a* **1400** *Apol. Loll.* 36 In meknes, pouert, paciens, & labour, & oþer vertuus dedis. **1450** *Lett. Marg. of Anjou,* etc. (Camden) 97 The womanly and vertuouse governance that ye be renowned of. **1484** CAXTON *Fables of Auian* xi, None oughte to preyse hym self but oughte to doo good and vertuous werkes whereof other may preyse hym. **1509** FISHER *Serm.* Wks. (1876) 271 Blessyd are tho whiche haue made vertuous ende and conclusyon of theyr lyfe in our lorde. **1585** T. WASHINGTON tr. *Nicholay's Voy.* II. vii. 37 [They] are much giuen too musick and all other vertuous & honest exercises. **1607** SHAKS. *Timon* III. ii. 44 If his occasion were not vertuous, I should not vrge it halfe so faithfully. **1667** MILTON *P.L.* VIII. 550 That what she wills to do or say, Seems wisest, vertuousest, discreetest, best. **1712** STEELE *Spect.* No. 500 ¶3 There is one thing I am able to give each of them, which is a virtuous Education. **1759** JOHNSON *Rasselas* xxxiii, The present reward of virtuous conduct. **1782** J. BROWN *Compend. View Nat. & Rev. Relig.* I. 25 To constitute an act truly virtuous, it must originate from a virtuous principle or habit. **1836** J. S. GILBERT *Chr. Atonem.* ix. (1852) 297 Can pride be virtue, or can any act be truly virtuous, if done in pride? **1838** DICKENS *Nickleby* i, My Father has got it [*sc.* my uncle's money] now, and is saving it up for me, which is a highly virtuous purpose. **1871** R. W. DALE *Commandm.* Introd. 11 It is only the virtuous man who knows what is virtuous.

†**b.** Of writings: = MORAL *a.* 3 b. *Obs.*$^{-1}$

1509 HAWES *Past. Pleas.* XIV. (Percy Soc.) 53 He made also the tales of Caunterbury; Some vertuous, and some glad and mery.

c. Of a blush: Chaste, modest.

1818 BYRON *Juan* I. Ded. vii, Your bays made hide the baldness of your brows—Perhaps some virtuous blushes.

†**4.** Belonging to the virtuosi. Also *absol.* with *the. Obs. rare.*

c **1680** BUTLER *Rem.* (1759) I. 10 Most excellent and virtuous Friends, This great Discovery makes amends For all our unsuccessful Pains. **1685** PETTY *Will* in Ld. Fitzmaurice *Life* (1895) 319, I obtained my degree of Doctor of Phisick in Oxford, and forthwith thereupon to be admitted into the College of Phisitians, London, and into severall clubbs of the virtuous.

II. Of things, their operations, etc.

5. a. Producing, or capable of producing, (great) effect; powerful, potent, strong.

In some quots. influenced by or approximating to sense 6.

13.. *K. Alis.* 5228 (Laud MS.), Hij maden fyres vertuous Fyue hundreþ, vche gret als an hous. **1390** GOWER *Conf.* III. 137 That word above alle erthli thinges Is vertuous in his doinges, Wher so it be to evele or goode. **1598** CHAPMAN *Iliad* IV. [VIII.] 22 Then wil I to Olimpus top our vertuous engine binde, And by it euerie thing shall hang. **1616** J. LANE *Contn. Sqr.'s T.* IX. 394 Till happelie her ffather slewe the snake, and by his virtuous wordes did th' venom slake.

b. Of actions, qualities, etc.

1387 TREVISA *Higden* (Rolls) II. 185 Touchynge þe pridde liknesse, þat is vertuous worchynge. **1422** YONGE tr. *Secreta Secret.* 246 Therfor the dygestion is the bettyr and more vertuose in wyntyr than in any othyr tyme. **1426** LYDG. *De Guil. Pilgr.* 3427 And ye may ther..Maken thynges fresshe of hewe, And whan ye lyst, transforme hem newe, Your power ys so vertuous. **1578** LYTE *Dodoens* I (heading), Plantes..their temperature, complexions, and vertuous operations. **1590** SHAKS. *Mids. N.* III. ii. 367 Then crush this herbe into Lysanders eie; Whose liquor hath this virtuous propertie, To take from thence all error. **1644** [H. PARKER] *Jus Populi* 18 Such causes as remain more vertuous then their effects, as the water heated is lesse hot then the fire. **1667** MILTON *P.L.* III. 608 With one vertuous touch Th' Arch-chimick Sun, so farr from us remote..Produces..so many precious things. **1797** COLERIDGE *Christabel* I. xxi, It is a wine of virtuous powers; My mother made it of wild flowers. **1813** SCOTT *Rokeby* I. ix, Yet the soil..Had depth and vigour to bring forth The hardier fruits of virtuous worth.

6. Endowed with, or possessed of, inherent or natural virtue or power (often of a magical, occult, or supernatural kind); potent or powerful in effect, influence, or operation on this account; *spec.* having potent medicinal properties or qualities; efficacious or beneficial in healing. Now *arch.* **a.** Of precious stones, etc.

13.. *Gaw. & Gr. Knt.* 2027 His cote, wyth þe conysaunce of þe clere werkez, Ennurned vpon veluet vertuuus stonez. **13..** *E.E. Allit. P.* B. 1280 þe vyoles & þe vesselment of vertuous stones. **1398** TREVISA *Barth. De P.R.* XVI. liii. (Bodl. MS.), [The more] þat Jacinctus is liche to þe Saphire in coloure,..þe more vertuous it is. *c* **1400** MAUNDEV. (Roxb.) xvii. 80 If þe dyamaund be gude and vertuous, þe adamand drawes noȝt þe nedill to him. **1483** CAXTON *Gold. Leg.* 214/2 A Margaryte, whyche gemme is white lytyl and vertuouse... The virtu of thys Stone is sayd to be ayenst effusyon of blood. **1503** HAWES *Examp. Virt.* iv. 40 Of vertuous turkeys there was a cheyr. *a* **1533** LD. BERNERS *Huon* cxlix. 562 The stone was so vertuous that none coud esteme the value therof. **1626** BACON *Sylva* §499 There is a virtuous Bezoar and another without virtu which appear to the show alike.

b. Of things in general.

1340 *Ayenb.* 113 Me zayþ þet hit [sacramental bread] is ope substance þet is uirtuous and substanciel aboue onderstondigge. *c* **1440** *Gesta Rom.* lxii. 264 (Add. MS.), This knyght than had a vertuous welle beside his bedde. *c* **1510** *Gesta Rom.* (W. de W.) A iij, All my temporall rychesse I haue expended, & almoost no thynge is lefte me, excepte a vertuous tre..in the myddes of myne empyre. **1527** BRUNSWYKE (*title*), The vertuose boke Of the distyllacyon of all maner of waters of the herbes in this present volume expressed. **1586** MARLOWE *1st Pt. Tamburl.* III. i, For neither rain can fall vpon the earth, Nor Sun reflexe his vertuous beames thereon. **1590** SPENSER *F.Q.* II. xii. 86 Streight way he with his vertuous staffe them strooke And streight of beasts they comely men became. **1629** A. SYMMER *Spir. Posie* I. iii. 13 Behold the timely vertuous presence of Gods Providence. **1632** MILTON *Penseroso* 113 Canace.., That own'd the vertuous Ring and Glass.

c. Of herbs, etc.

1390 GOWER *Conf.* III. 129 And ek his herbe in special The vertuous Fenele it is. *c* **1407** LYDG. *Reson & Sens.* 4433 The erbys..be so vertuous, That no beste venymous..Ne may in no Wyse aproche. *c* **1460** *Wisdom* 92 in *Macro Plays* 38 The drede of God,..þat makyst..swete wertuus herbys in þe sowll [to] sprynge. **1578** LYTE *Dodoens* V. xxv. 584 The leaves [of mallow] are good for all the greefes afore-sayde,.. yet they be nothing so vertuous as the roote. **1609** C. BUTLER *Fem. Mon.* (1634) 108 Where the flowers are most fragrant and vertuous,..there the Honey dews..are most fine and pure. **1614** W. B. *Philosopher's Banquet* (ed. 2) 81 Fylberds ..are vertuous in Medicine. **1632** J. HAYWARD tr. *Biondi's Eromena* 84 These our mountaines are full of vertuous herbes. **1700** DRYDEN *Flower & Leaf* 418 The Ladies sought around For virtuous herbs. **1853** G. JOHNSTON *Nat. Hist. E. Bord.* I. 264 Twenty-five 'elegant' copper-plates containing the figures of many of the most virtuous herbs. **1871** BROWNING *Balaust.* 2124 Cutting the roots of many a virtuous herb To solace overburdened mortals! **1884** —— *Ferishtah* Wks. (1896) II. 665/1 By application of a virtuous root The burning has abated.

d. Of drugs, etc.

1600 ROWLAND *Lett. Humours Blood* VI. 77 Strong sodden Water is a vertuous thing. ? *c* **1614** J. DAVIES *Let.* Wks. 1876 I. p. xlviii, Least the intention of to much Reading hinder the working of those vertuous drugs. **1615** CHAPMAN *Odyss.* X. 283 Before her gates hill-wolves, and lions, lay; Which with her virtuous drugs so tame she made, That [etc.]. **1694** SALMON *Bate's Dispens.* (1713) 43/1 By that means you will have a very strong and virtuous Spirit. **1871** HAWTHORNE *S. Felton* (1879) 99 It is the most virtuous liquor that ever was.

†**7.** Of great excellence or worth. *Obs.*

c **1400** *Laud Troy Bk.* 9460 For now is non so glorious, Ne non in this world so vertuous, As Ilion was the while it stode. *c* **1420** *Chron. Vilod.* 1171 Harp he couthe & syng welle þerto, & carff welle ymagus, & peyntede bothe—Suche virtuose werkus he wolde welle do. *c* **1430** LYDG. *Min. Poems* (Percy Soc.) 80 The douffe..Unto the erthe she toke hir flight, And sang a song ful gracious, Of al songes most vertuous.

III. 8. *Comb.* (in sense 4), as ***virtuous disposed, -like, -making, -minded, -seeming*** adjs.

1450 *Rolls of Parlt.* V. 206/1 By ther Founders and other vertuous disposed persones. **1654** WHITLOCK *Zootomia* 347 Becoming..as virtuous-making a Pattern among Wives, as she was before among Virgins. **1699** SHAFTESB. *Charac.* (1711) II. 36 If that which restrains the Person, and holds him to a virtuous-like Behaviour, be no Affection towards.. Virtue it-self,..he is not in reality the more virtuous. **1807** *Europ. Mag.* LII. 469/2 Those, on whom the virtuous-minded Muse Ne'er breath'd a portion of her hallow'd fire. **1959** S. SPENDER tr. *Schiller's Mary Stuart* III. iv. 63, I did not hide my sinful deeds behind The false show of a virtuous-seeming face.

'virtuously, *adv.* Forms: (see VIRTUOUS *a.*). [f. prec. + -LY².]

1. In a virtuous manner; according to or in conformity with moral laws; uprightly, righteously; chastely, purely.

c **1380** WYCLIF *Sel. Wks.* III. 46 Qwikenynge hem wiþ my grace, to lyve in mekenes vertuously. **1422** YONGE tr. *Secreta Secret.* 236 How that ye shal kepe youre sowle fro vices and ill maners, and vertuosly to lywe. **1463** *Bury Wills* (Camden) 36 A rememberaunce of oold love vertuously set at alle tymes to the pleseen of God. **1509** *Paternoster, Ave & Creed* A ij, To dyspose men to be vertuously occupyed in theyr myndes and prayers. **1597** HOOKER *Eccl. Pol.* V. lxvii. §12 How should a vertuously disposed minde better resolue with it selfe then thus? **1604** SHAKS. *Oth.* IV. i. 7 They that meane vertuously, and yet do so, The Diuell their vertue tempts, and they tempt Heauen. **1682** NORRIS *Hierocles* 22 The denial of Honour to our Parents wherein we think we doe vertuously. **1691** HARTCLIFFE *Virtues* 105 To be vertuously Magnificent, is with daily Provisions to feed the Hungry. **1709** STEELE *Tatler* No. 33 ¶6 This Woman, who could be so virtuously impertinent, as to admonish one she was hardly acquainted with. **1838** DICKENS *Nickleby* xxviii, Here Mrs. Wititterley tossed her head—not passionately only virtuously. **1847** CARLYLE *Misc.* IV. 223 This we say the present editor has virtuously forborne.

†**2.** Bravely, courageously, valiantly. *Obs. rare.*

1422 YONGE tr. *Secreta Secret.* 162 Therfor the troians vertuosly the grecans into hare tentis fleynge suyt. *c* **1530** LD. BERNERS *Arth. Lyt. Bryt.* (1814) 109 Hector encountred the fyrst so vertuously, yᵗ he ran him thrugh out with his spere.

†**3.** With great skill or excellence. *Obs.*$^{-1}$

c **1425** WYNTOUN *Cron.* VIII. 981 (Cott.), þat buk Qwhar Master Iohun Barbere..His dedis ditit mar wertusly þan I can thynk in al study.

†**4.** Virtually. *Obs. rare.*

1426 LYDG. *De Guil. Pilgr.* 6030 Somme vnderstonde certeynly That he ys ther vertuously; Somme seyn 'ymaginatiue', And somme 'representatiue'. **1502** *Ord. Crysten Men* (W. de W. 1506) II. viii. 104 Also this fourth commaundement yˢ is the fyrst of yᵉ seconde table conteyneth in hym vertuously yᵉ .vii. werkes of mercy.

†**5.** Powerfully, strongly. *Obs.*$^{-1}$

In quot. used affectedly.

1588 SHAKS. *Timon* I. ii. 232, 1. *Lord.* We are so vertuously bound. *Tim.* And so am I to you. 2. *Lord.* So infinitely endeer'd.

'virtuousness. Also 5 vertuosenes, 5–6 -uousnes (6 -uouseness), 6–7 -nesse, 6–8 -ness; 6 vertousnes, -usnes, *Sc.* -eousnes. [f. as prec.]

†**1.** The condition of being endowed with inherent virtue or power. *Obs.*$^{-1}$

1398 TREVISA *Barth. De P.R.* VIII. xvi. (1495) v vij b/1 The sonne..hath a vertu of plente [1535 plentiful] vertuousnes for he yeuyth vertu of generacion to thyse nether thynges.

2. The state or condition of being virtuous; virtuous quality or character; moral rectitude; goodness, probity.

c **1449** PECOCK *Repr.* I. xvii. 96 Thei laborid euere in mekenes for to haue it in greet mesure, whilis thei myȝten haue laborid forto haue had kunnyng of moral vertuosenes. **1528** ROY *Rede me* II. (Arb.) 72 They are slaunder of vertousnes, Occasion vnto viciousnes. **1576** NEWTON *Lemnie's Complex.* (1633) 39 Behaviour, countenance, rayment,..all smells of vertuousnesse. **1608** L. MACHIN *Dumbe Knight* III, I know you hate me for my vertuousnesse. **1650** BAXTER *Saints' R.* III. xi. (1662) 471 And so their chief Virtuousness lieth in that Will or Love which is contained in them. **1736** BUTLER *Anal.* I. iii. §4 The pleasure or advantage in this case is gained by the action itself, not by the morality, the virtuousness or viciousness of it. **1754** EDWARDS *Freed. Will* III. vi. (1762) 178 In order to the Vertuousness of an Act, the Heart must be indifferent in the Time of the Performance of that Act. **1833** CHALMERS *Const. Man* (1835) I. i. 100 He meddles not with the virtuousness either of humanity or justice. **1865** J. GROTE *Moral Ideals* viii. (1876) 117 But that is a very low degree of virtuousness where conscience does no more than guard from wrong action. **1879** H. SPENCER *Data of Ethics* iii. 38 Perfection of nature, or virtuousness of action.

†**3.** High or worthy character; excellence, merit. *Obs.*$^{-1}$

1525 LD. BERNERS tr. *Froiss.* II. xxvi. 71 *heading*, Of the great vertuousnesse and largesse that was in therle of Foiz.

‖**virtute officii** (vɜːˈtjuːtɪ ɒˈfɪʃiː), *adv. phr. Law.* [L.] By virtue of (one's) office.

1800 M. HALE *Hist. Pleas of Crown* II. xvii. 147 The court of King's bench may *virtute officii* bail any person brought before them, of what nature soever the crime is, even for treason or murder, as hath been before shewn. **1939** HENTY

& Redfern *Lewin's Pract. Treat. Law of Trusts* (ed. 14) iv. 298 The powers of trustees may be divided into (1) powers incident to the office of trustee *virtute officii*, including such powers as powers of maintenance and advancement formerly conferred by express proviso but now implied by statute, and (2) such general powers, including powers of appointment, as the settlor may expressly confer upon the trustees. **1982** *Law Q. Rev.* XCVIII. 403 He is a judge of the High Court *virtute officii*.

virucidal (vaɪərʊˈsaɪdəl), *a.* [f. viru(s + -cide + -al.] = viricidal *a.* So **ˈvirucide** = viricide².

1925 *Jrnl. Exper. Med.* XLII. 533 Animals inoculated with this strain do not become refractory to skin infection with Virus III and their sera do not become virucidal. **1975** *Water Res.* IX. 872/1 The results obtained in this present study did not confirm the greater efficiency of the OCl- ion as a virucide as compared with hypochlorous acid. **1977** *Lancet* 8 Oct. 760/1 Effective treatment will have to include good nursing and the use of steroids.., besides virucidal agents.

virulence (ˈvɪrjʊləns). [ad. L. *vīrulentia*: see next and -ence. So OF. and F. *virulence*.]

1. Extreme acrimony or bitterness of temper or speech; violent malignity or rancour.

1663 Jer. Taylor *Fun. Serm. Bramhall* Wks. 1831 IV. vii. 75 It was also such honor, that it is greater than the virulence of tongues, which his worthiness and their envy had armed against him. **1696** Tate & Brady *Ps.* cxl. 3 Their sharpen'd Tongue the Serpent's sting In Virulence exceeds. **1728** Young *Love Fame* vi. 150 Our virulence is thrown On others' fame, thro' fondness for our own. **1748** Richardson *Clarissa* (1811) I. iv. 28 My sister, who had treated Mr. Lovelace with virulence, came into me and insulted me as fast as I recovered. **1796** Bp. Watson *Apol. Bible* 322, I have been frequently shocked at the virulence of your zeal. **1838** Dickens *Nickleby* xxi, The ill will of Miss Knag had lost nothing of its virulence. **1867** Smiles *Huguenots Eng.* xi. (1880) 194 The persecution..was carried on with increased virulence, until resistance almost disappeared.

b. An instance of this.

a **1774** Tucker *Lt. Nat.* (1834) II. 295 The leaders, however they may sometimes encourage these virulences to serve a turn, do not enter into the same sentiments themselves.

2. The property or quality of being physically virulent or full of virus; extreme poisonousness or venomousness; malignity or violence (of disease).

1748 *Anson's Voy.* i. x. 106 A general dejection prevailed amongst us, which added much to the virulence of the disease. **1789** W. Buchan *Dom. Med.* (1790) 519, I have frequently known the disease return with all its virulence after a course of goat-whey. **1815** J. Smith *Panorama Sci. & Art* II. 48 The wind is salubrious, stopping infection, and removing the virulence of distemper. **1834** Mrs. Somerville *Connex. Phys. Sci.* xxvii. 283 Venomous snakes ..decrease..in the virulence of their poison with decrease of temperature. **1878** H. M. Stanley *Dark Cont.* II. xii. 361 The itch disease was rabid;..about a dozen of the men were fearful objects of its virulence.

attrib. **1896** *Allbutt's Syst. Med.* I. 721 Whether..the virulence test is satisfactory and exclusive is a doubtful matter.

virulency (ˈvɪrjʊlənsɪ). [ad. L. *vīrulentia*, f. *vīrulentus*: see next and -ency. So Sp. and Pg. *virulencia*, It. *virulenza*.]

1. = virulence 1.

a **1617** Hieron *Wks.* (1620) II. 487 Men of corrupt minds shall..bee as it were moued..to goe on in their virulency and spite, and scorne of good Profession. **1647** N. Ward *Simp. Cobler* (1843) 6 The zeale of the one, the virulency of the other, must..kindle combustions. **1672** Clarendon *Ess.* Tracts (1727) 269 Those differences which are debated between Roman Catholics themselves with so much virulency and animosity. **1738** Birch *Milton* in *M.'s Wks.* I. 28 He was always remarkable for an Haughtiness of Temper and Virulency of Style. **1847** E. Brontë *Wuthering Heights* ii, Several incoherent threats of retaliation that, in their indefinite depth of virulency, smacked of King Lear.

2. = virulence 2.

1651 French *Distill.* v. 135 The powder..is very good to be strewed upon old ulcers, for it doth much correct the virulency of them. **1669** W. Simpson *Hydrol. Chym.* 73 The Hyacinth..becomes the infallible indication of the Plague, by which afterward..the virulency..is driven forth. **1694** Salmon *Bate's Dispens.* (1713) 561/2 Lest the Particles of the Mercury..should..create Pains, Aches, Rottenness, or a Virulency never to be taken away. **1710** T. Fuller *Pharm. Extemp.* 283 The Particles of the Quick-Silver..oftentimes impress an indelible Virulency upon the Brain.

virulent (ˈvɪrjʊlənt), *a.* Also 5 verelent, 6 vyrulent. [ad. L. *vīrulentus* poisonous, f. *virus* virus. So OF. and F. *virulent*, It., Sp., and Pg. *virulento*.]

1. *Med.* †**a.** Of wounds or ulcers: Characterized by the presence of corrupt or poisonous matter. *Obs.* (passing into next).

c **1400** *Lanfranc's Cirurg.* 77 *marg.*, Off olde verelent woundes. *Ibid.* 80 If þe vlcus be virulent, þat is to seie venemi, loke if þat venym þat goiþ out be redisch or ȝelowisch. **1541** R. Copland *Guydon's Form.* Riv, The gouernall accomplysshynge the entencyon after the vlceracyon is to drye the rottenesse that is thycke and flesshy, blody, and vyrulent. **1578** Lyte *Dodoens* 28 Chamaepitys..layd upon great woundes, and virulent.. healeth the same. **1600** Surflet *Countrie Farme* ii. xlii. 266 A certaine person, well knowen vnto me, hauing a virulent vlcer, in manner of a Polipus in his nostrils. **1728** Chambers *Cycl.*, *Ulcers* are..Virulent, which instead of Pus, or Sanies, yield a malignant *Virus*, &c.

b. Of diseases, etc.: Characterized by extreme malignancy or violence.

1563 T. Gale *Antidot.* 22 b, Yf the desease be malygne or Virulent,..put in more of the *Argentum Viuum.* **1694** Salmon *Bate's Dispens.* (1713) 28/1 It may be us'd..in the Cure of virulent Gonorrhœa's. **1748** *Anson's Voy.* i. x. 102 The scars of wounds which had been for many years healed, were forced open again by this virulent distemper. **1799** *Med. Jrnl.* I. 203 They deny that the contagion has become more frequent..while the disease itself has thus been rendered less virulent and fatal. **1866** Rogers *Agric. & Prices* I. iv. 66 Scurvy in its most virulent form, and leprosy, were common disorders. **1871** Tyndall *Fragm. Sci.* (1879) I. v. 178 Germs..which may be pushed by foul air into virulent energy of reproduction.

transf. **1860** Emerson *Cond. Life, Fate* Wks. (Bohn) II. 327, I find the like unity in human structures rather virulent and pervasive. **1865** Merivale *Rom. Emp.* lxv. VIII. 170 A virulent insurrection was still glowing throughout a large portion of the empire. **1871** Tyndall *Fragm. Sci.* (1879) II. xiii. 299 There is often virulent contagion in a confident tone.

2. a. Of serpents, material substances, plants, etc.: Possessing venomous or strongly poisonous qualities; highly injurious or fatal to life; extremely noxious.

1577 Stanyhurst *Descr. Irel.* 7/2 in *Holinshed* II, Ireland bred no snake before S. Patrick was borne: *ergo*, it engendered no toade, no Adder, no Frogge, nor any other virulent worme. **1634** Sir T. Herbert *Trav.* 196 They giue the too forward maydens a virulent potion. **1657** W. Cole *Adam in Eden* c, The Viper and all other virulent Creatures whatever. **1671** R. Bohun *Wind* 132 Herbs or minerals, with Virulent, and Deleterious Qualities. **1807** J. E. Smith *Phys. Bot.* 216 How the same soil..should in a leaf of the vine or sorrel produce a wholesome acid, and in that of a spurge or manchineel a most virulent poison. **1839** Carlyle *Chartism* i. (1858) 4 While the virulent humour festers deep within, poisoning the sources of life. **1877** F. T. Roberts *Handbk. Med.* (ed. 3) I. 8 In certain cases it contains specific agents in the causation of disease, and promotes their development or renders them more virulent.

fig. **1894** P. Pinkerton *Adriatica, On Asolan Hills*, Jealousy's virulent darts, Fortune's opprobrious thrusts.

†**b.** Potent, powerful, effective. *Obs.*⁻¹

1599 A. M. tr. *Gabelhouer's Bk. Physicke* 2/2 A very excellent water for the payne of the heade... It wilbe very good and virulent for the heade.

c. Obnoxiously violent or strong. *nonce-use.*

1771 Smollett *Humph. Cl.*, *To Sir W. Phillips* 6 May, Nay, I am convinced that she has likewise a most virulent attachment to his person; though her love never shows itself but in the shape of discontent.

3. *fig.* Violently bitter, spiteful, or malignant; full of acrimony or enmity: **a.** Of action or feeling.

1607 Hieron *Wks.* I. 325 Where hee rules, there is a rancourous heart and a rayling tongue, there malicious and virulent courses cannot bee wanting. **1632** Massinger *Maid of Hon.* iii. iii, I bring you..the sting Of virulent malice, festering your fair name, Plucked out and trod on. **1726** Dk. Wharton in Ellis *Orig. Lett.* Ser. ii. IV. 339 Every virulent vote, every passionate reproach..are so many real commendations of my conduct. **1769** *Junius Lett.* xv. (1788) 89 The virulent exaggeration of party must be employed, to rouse..the passions of the people. **1815** W. H. Ireland *Scribbleomania* 98 On my head I may draw down your virulent spite. **1855** Brewster *Newton* II. xviii. 165 We have failed, like Mr. Baily, to discover the ground of Flamsteed's virulent antipathy to Halley. **1867** 'Ouida' *C. Castlemaine's Gage* i She was hated by Whig beauties with virulent wrath.

b. Of speech or writing.

1631 *Star Chamb. Cases* (Camden) 29 He is greatly faulty in his virulent termes and charging the same upon my Lord Falkland. **1689** Wood *Life* (O.H.S.) III. 313 A virulent pamphlet..wherein he foolishly reflected on King William. **1713** Steele *Englishm.* No. 15. 101 It is impossible..to escape the virulent Pen of that Rascal the Examiner. **1777** Priestley *Disc. Philos. Necess.* 172 Your virulent censures of myself..are abundantly too severe. **1840** Macaulay *Ess.*, *Clive* (1851) II. 526 The meetings were large, stormy, even riotous, the debates indecently virulent. **1868** Freeman *Norm. Conq.* II. App. 540 He stops twice in the course of his history to apostrophize..Harold..in terms of virulent abuse.

c. Of persons, their dispositions, etc.

1613 Purchas *Pilgrimage* (1614) 215 Let him take heed of striking his wife, said another, or to be virulent in termes against her. **1647** Clarendon *Contempl. Ps.* Tracts (1727) 472 Let the virulent tongues of ill men traduce us with what calumnies they please. **1693** J. Edwards *Author. O. & N. Test.* 150 (Appion), a virulent writer against the Jews. **1714** Swift *Pres. St. Aff.* Wks. 1841 I. 495 Since the virulent opposers of the queen..have so far prevailed..as to make [etc.]. **1792** Gouv. Morris in Sparks *Life & Writ.* (1832) II. 227 His enemies here are as virulent as ever. **1833** I. Taylor *Fanat.* i. 3 The deluded religionist, even when virulent in an extreme degree. **1855** Macaulay *Hist. Eng.* xiii. III. 276 He had since disgusted some virulent fanatics by his humanity and moderation. **1883** F. M. Peard *Contrad.* I. 42, I am glad you don't consider me very virulent.

4. *Microbiology.* Of a phage: causing lysis of the host cell immediately after replicating within it, without a period as a prophage; lytic, not lysogenic. [The sense is due to F. Jacob et al. 1953, in *Ann. de l'Inst. Pasteur* LXXXIV. 223, who used F. *virulent*.]

1953, etc. [see temperate *a.* 8]. **1969** A. M. Campbell *Episomes* i. 2 Phage types which are able to establish lysogenic systems and to reproduce as prophage are called temperate phages, as distinguished from virulent phages which are unable to do so. **1973** R. G. Krueger et al. *Introd. Microbiol.* xviii. 506/1 This type of virus is called a virulent virus, the agent functioning continuously as a lethal intracellular parasite.

Hence **ˈvirulent** *v. trans.*, to render virulent.

1661 Feltham *Resolves* (ed. 8) ii. lvi. 301 They say, Certain spirits virulented from the inward humor, darted on the object, convey a Venom where they point and fix.

virulently (ˈvɪrjʊləntlɪ), *adv.* [f. prec. + -ly².] In a virulent manner; with virulence or violence:

a. Of actions, language, etc.

1599 *Broughton's Lett.* xi. 38 The raising of whose bones, more virulently, then truly, you obiect to this our *Apostaticall land.* **1607** R. C[arew] tr. *Estienne's World Wond.* 274 There was neuer yet controuersie in Christian religion so stoutly, so vehemently, nor so virulently canuased and ventilated. **1647** Clarendon *Hist. Reb.* ii. §101 Which, it may be, made the other to be the more virulently remembered. **1709** Hearne *Collect.* (O.H.S.) II. 306 Sacheverell..levell'd his..Anathemas most virulently against him. **1783** Hailes *Anc. Chr. Ch.* ii. 23 The device of forging acts of Pilate, in which Christ was virulently defamed. **1816** Scott *Bl. Dwarf* iv, Sentiments so virulently misanthropic. **1856** Miss Mulock *J. Halifax* xxvi, Catholics were hunted down both by law and by public opinion, as virulently as Protestant nonconformists.

b. Of poisons, diseases, etc.

1632 Massinger & Field *Fatal Dowry* iii. i, This potion that hath wrought so virulently! **1858** Copland *Dict. Pract. Med.* III. ii. 1341/2 The..effects of the malady having become thus virulently contagious. **1867** H. Macmillan *Bible Teach.* vi. 112 Though some kinds are virulently poisonous, yet a large number are highly useful to man. **1876** *Jrnl. R. Geog. Soc.* XLVI. 54 Several are pitted with small-pox, which ranged virulently..about ten years ago.

ˈvirulentness. *rare.* [f. as prec. + -ness.] Virulence.

a **1676** Hale *True Relig.* iii. (1684) 43 These bitternesses and virulentnesses..have been commonly of two kinds. **1727** Bailey (vol. II), *Virulentness*, poisonous Nature; also Maliciousness.

viruliferous (vɪrʊˈlɪfərəs), *a.* [f. L. *vīrul-entia* virulence + -iferous.] Containing a virus: said esp. of an insect vector.

1933 K. M. Smith *Introd. Study Viruses* 409 Viruliferous. **1937** *Jrn. Bacteriol.* XXXIV. 132/2 Viruliferous leafhoppers held at..about 32°C. a few days frequently transmit mild strains instead of typical severe yellows. **1967** K. M. Smith *Insect Virol.* xi. 208 Viruliferous aphids were colonized on a virus-immune plant such as Chinese cabbage for 7 days, hemolymph from these aphids was then injected into a series of known virus-free aphids. **1982** *Jrnl. Gen. Virol.* LXI. 187 The planthopper vector..became viruliferous after injection with nB.

virus (ˈvaɪərəs). [L. *vīrus* slimy liquid, poison, offensive odour or taste. Hence also F., Sp., Pg. *virus*.]

In *Lanfranc's Cirurgie* (*c* 1400) 77 the word, explained as 'a thin venomy quitter', is merely taken over from the Latin text.

1. Venom, such as is emitted by a poisonous animal. Also *fig.*

1599 *Broughton's Lett.* iv. 14 You..haue..spit out all the *virus* and poyson you could conceiue, in the abuse of his.. person. **1702** Mead *Poisons* 26 The Story of Cleopatra.. pouring the Virus of an Asp into a Wound made in her Arm by her own Teeth. **1728** Chambers *Cycl.* s.v. *Viper*, By the Microscope, the Virus [of the viper] was found to consist of minute Salts in continual Motion. **1867** Dk. Argyll *Reign of Law* i. 37 That the deadly virus shall in a few minutes curdle the blood. **1879** R. T. Smith *Basil Gt.* ix. 111 He it was who hollowed the minute sting of the bee to shed its virus through.

2. *Path.* **a.** A morbid principle or poisonous substance produced in the body as the result of some disease, esp. one capable of being introduced into other persons or animals by inoculations or otherwise and of developing the same disease in them. Now superseded by the next sense.

1728 Chambers *Cycl.*, *Virulent*, a Term apply'd to any thing that yields a *Virus*; that is, a corrosive or contagious Pus. **1771** Smollett *Humph. Cl.*, *To Sir W. Philip* 3 Oct., When he examined the *egesta*, and felt his pulse, he declared that much of the *virus* was discharged. **1799** *Med. Jrnl.* I. 448 Whether opium applied externally, may or may not prove an antidote to the canine virus. **1800** *Ibid.* III. 352 The pustules..contain a perfect Small-pox virus. **1826** S. Cooper *First Lines Surg.* (ed. 5) 165 In consequence of the virus being mixed with the saliva of the rabid animal. **1878** T. Bryant *Pract. Surg.* I. 79 It should never be forgotten that it is the virus which infects the system. **1899** *Allbutt's Syst. Med.* VIII. 602 Possibly there is some virus acting on the nerve-centres. **1910** Hiss & Zinsser *Text-bk. Bacteriol.* xlvii. 639 Virus dried for eight days was no longer regularly infectious. **1922** *Jrnl. Amer. Med. Assoc.* 11 Feb. 411/1 It was quickly found that the virus floats in a suspending fluid of specific gravity 1·14, while it sinks in a suspending fluid of specific gravity 1·11... To purify it,..it seems best to wash it and centrifugalize it in a suspending fluid just heavier than itself.

b. Pl. **viruses.** An infectious organism that is usu. submicroscopic, can multiply only inside certain living host cells (in many cases causing disease) and is now understood to be a non-cellular structure lacking any intrinsic metabolism and usually comprising a DNA or RNA core inside a protein coat (see also quot. 1977).

Formerly referred to as filterable viruses, their first distinguishing characteristic being the ability to pass through filters that retained bacteria.

[**1880** Pasteur in *Compt. Rend.* XCI. 673 Le virus est constitué par un parasite microscopique qu'on multiplie aisément par la culture, en dehors du corps des animaux que le mal peut frapper.] **1881** *Sci. Amer. Suppl.* 4 June 4516/1

M. Pasteur writes: '.. The virus is a microscopical parasite, which may be multiplied by cultivation outside of the body of an animal.' **1899** G. Newman *Bacteria* vii. 260 The vaccination in small-pox is an inoculation of the virus of the disease;..the plague and cholera vaccinations are inoculations of pure cultures of living virus from out-side the body. **1900** *Jrnl. Compar. Path. & Therapeutics* XIII. 16 The virus of foot-and-mouth disease passes through a Berkefeld filter when it is suspended in a watery liquid. **1906** *Philippine Jrnl. Sci.* I. 583 The length of time during which the virus may remain viable in the soil and in stables is not determined. **1908** *Jrnl. Compar. Path. & Therapeutics* XIII. 59 Filters which are efficient for the arrest of the smallest of the known visible microbes allow the viruses of these diseases to pass through their pores. **1912** *Jrnl. Med. Res.* XXVII. 20 The probable nature of filterable viruses, whether protozoan or bacterial. **1912**, etc. [see FILTERABLE *a.*]. **1915** *Lancet* 4 Dec. 1242/2 We do not know for certain the nature of an ultra-microscopic virus. It may be a minute bacterium that will only grow on living material, or it may be a tiny amœba which..thrives on living micro-organisms... It is quite possible that an ultra-microscopic virus belongs somewhere in this vast field of life more lowly organised than the bacterium or amœba. **1929** *Jrnl. Amer. Med. Assoc.* 6 Apr. 1147/1 Throughout this paper the terms filtrable viruses and viruses will be used interchangeably. **1931** *Nature* 10 Oct. 599/2 But a few years ago I think that we should have had no difficulty in accepting three cardinal properties as characterising a virus, namely, invisibility by ordinary microscopic methods, failure to be retained by a filter fine enough to prevent the passage of all visible bacteria, and failure to propagate itself except in the presence of, and perhaps in the interior of, the cells which it infects. **1935** *Science* 28 June 644/1 A crystalline material, which has the properties of tobacco-mosaic virus, has been isolated from the juice of Turkish tobacco plants infected with this virus. *Ibid.* 8 Nov. 443/2 The defining characters of filterable viruses appear to be ultramicroscopic size and obligate parasitism. **1963** J. H. Burn *Drugs, Med. & Man* xix. 188 One view is that these cells contain a virus and the cancer begins when the virus is no longer kept under control. **1972** N. Calder *Restless Earth* iv. 95/2 The Moon was declared free of viruses or spores that might infect the Earth. **1973** [see MYCOPLASMA]. **1977** S. S. Hughes *Virus* 112 The term 'virus' as used by bacteriologists of the 1880s and 1890s meant simply 'an agent of infectious disease'. This is the usage in Pasteur's dictum: 'Every virus is a microbe.' (1890). **1982** *Sci. Amer.* Apr. 22/3 Viruses..are not included; noncellular, they are mere genetic recipes and are not alive. **1983** W. A. Stevens *Virol. Flowering Plants* i. 3 Bawden (1956) defined a virus as an obligate parasitic pathogen with dimensions less than 200nm. Although possibly adequate in its day, such a definition does not exclude naked nucleic acid pathogens—the viroids, or some mycoplasmas.

c. *colloq.* A virus infection.

1954 C. S. Lewis *Lett. to Amer. Lady* (1969) 24 We mustn't let these modern doctors get us down by calling a cold a *virus* and a sore throat a *streptococcus*.

3. *fig.* A moral or intellectual poison, or poisonous influence. Also in weakened use, an infectious fear, anxiety, etc.

1778 Warner in Jesse *Selwyn & Contemp.* (1844) III. 317 Venice is a stink-pot, charged with the very virus of hell! **1807** Southey *H. K. White* 12 As if there were not enough of the leaven of disquietude in our natures, without inoculating it with this dilutement—this vaccine virus of envy. *a* **1834** Coleridge *Shaks. Notes* (1875) 189 The corrosive virus which inoculates pride with a venom not its own. *a* **1884** M. Pattison *Mem.* (1885) 239 The clerical virus would have lingered in the system. **1982** *Economist* 25 Dec. 83/1 The virus quickly spread. First Canada extracted a promise of restraint from Japan. Then West Germany's mercurial economics minister..hastened to Tokyo.

4. Violent animosity; virulence.

1866 Alger *Solit. Nat. & Man* iv. 360 Two classes of men, however, he did hate with especial relish and virus.

5. *attrib.* and *Comb.*, as (sense 2 b) ***virus disease, infection, particle***; ***virus-carried, -containing, -free, -induced, -infected, -like*** adjs.; **virus pneumonia**, pneumonia caused by a virus rather than a bacterium.

1958 *Times* 12 June 11/3 The great diversity of *virus-carried diseases. Influenza, poliomyelitis, cholera, Australian Q-fever, [etc.]. **1968** *Times* 3 Oct. 13/6 Antiserum..was found to react positively with a *virus-containing extract prepared from dahlias. **1860** W. T. Fox in *Trans. Obstetr. Soc.* II. 228 This latter action is alike common to all forms of *virus disease. **1926** *Jrnl. Trop. Med. & Hygiene* XXIX. 19/2 The intricate processes involved in 'virus' diseases of plants and vertebrates. **1978** J. Gardner *Dancing Dodo* xvii. 126 Rift Valley Fever..a virus disease... Usually transmitted to humans by cattle, sheep, other animals: and usually in Asia. **1946** *Nature* 26 Oct. 569/2 The great work of East Malling Research Station in raising and distributing *virus-free clonal stocks. *Ibid.* 17 Aug. 217/2 M. B. Shimkin is also critical of the wide extrapolation of observations made on the relatively few *virus-induced tumours to the whole range of cancer. *Ibid.* 23 Nov. 735/2 We have grown many thousands of seedlings from seeds which were obtained from *virus-infected plants..and in not a single instance have we found the seedlings diseased. **1924** *Jrnl. Exper. Med.* XL. 773 (*heading*) A filterable *virus infection of rabbits. **1965** A. Roudybush *Season for Death* (1966) xxviii. 165 Mrs. Tor was suffering from a virus infection. **1982** R. Rendell *Master of Moor* xv. 165 He was ill, he had a virus infection. **1946** *Nature* 17 Aug. 218/1 They found no evidence of the presence of a rapidly acting *virus-like principle associated with the Jensen rat sarcoma. **1972** *Science* 16 June 1225/2 Electron microscopy initially revealed that HBAg consists of virus-like particles approximately 20 nanometers in diameter. **1968** *Brit. Med. Bull.* XXIV. 244/2 They [*sc.* the results] are consistent with the inactivation of a *virus particle by a single interaction with radiation. **1929** *Public Health Rep.* (U.S.) XLIV. 2635 (*heading*) Vaccine *virus pneumonia in rabbits. **1977** 'J. Bell' *Such Nice Client* xix. 189 She died of a virus pneumonia caught in an epidemic at the hospital. **1971** *New Scientist* 8 Apr. 82/2 The surface antigens also appear to be *virus-specific. **1936** *Discovery* Oct. 329/1 Investigation of ten *virus strains.

† **vis**, *sb.*[1] *Obs. rare.* [ad. L. *vīs-us* sight, f. ppl. stem of *vidēre* to see.] Vision, sight.

c **1340** Hampole *Prose Tr.* 34 If a mane lufe anoþer whilke es absent he desyris gretly his presence for to hafe þe vys of his lufe and his likynge... þare-fore we may noghte hafe þe vis of His lufe here in fulfilling.

‖ **vis** (vɪs), *sb.*[2] Pl. vires ('vaɪriːz). [L. *vīs* (pl. *vīrēs*).]

1. Strength, force, energy, vigour.

c **1630** T. Goodwin *Serm.* Wks. 1681 I. iii. 39 [Christ] Who then must be the immediate Uniter, by his own *Vis* or Power exerted in it. **1650** Hubbert *Pill Formality* 104 There is a certain vis, a power infused into the soul. **1788** *Trifler* No. 17. 231 Charmed with the prospect which the vis of combined effects presented to him, he resolved to investigate the springs of action. **1882** Dr. J. Brown *John Leach*, etc. 183 His verses..had more imaginative *vis*, more daintiness of phrase [etc.]. **1888** Abp. Benson in A. C. Benson *Life* (1899) II. v. 200 There is no *vis* and there is also no learning, among them [*sc.* Reformers], out of Germany. **1907** P. T. Forsyth *Positive Preaching* v. 163 The great moral *vis* of the Reformation subsided into the renewed intellectualism of the seventeenth century dogmatists.

2. In special collocations with other Latin words.

In addition to those illustrated below, various others are or have been in use, as *vis acceleratrix, centrifuga, centripeta, impressa, insita,* etc. A number of these appear in dictionaries from about 1700 onwards.

a. ***vis major***, such a degree of superior force that no effective resistance can be made to it.

1601 Holland *Pliny* I. 599 Hailes, stormes of wind and raine, and such like impressions of the aire, which whensoever they doe light, are tearmed by the Lawyers, *Vis major, i.* the greater violence. **1866** Ld. Blackburn in Hurlstone & Coltman *Rep.* IV. 271 He can excuse himself by shewing that..the escape was the consequence of vis major or the act of God.

b. ***vis inertiæ***, the resistance naturally offered by matter to any force tending to alter its state in respect of rest or motion; also *transf.*, tendency on the part of persons, etc., to remain inactive or unprogressive.

1706 [see INERTIA 1]. **1710** J. Harris *Lex. Techn.* II. s.v., This *Vis Inertiæ* is no where more conspicuous, than in the sudden Motion of a Vessel full of Liquor upon a Horizontal Plane. **1748** Hartley *Observ. Man* II. i. §6. 31 Matter is a mere passive thing, of whose very essence it is, to be endued with a *Vis inertiae*. **1781** *Phil. Trans.* LXXI. I. 312 Not so much owing to the smallness of the quantity of powder that takes fire in that case as to the *vis inertiæ* of the generated fluid. **1836** I. Taylor *Phys. The. Another Life* ii. 32 This power of the mind in overcoming the *vis inertiæ* of matter. *transf.* **1755** Chesterf. *Let. to Bp. of Waterford* 26 June, Writing seems to be acting..which my *vis inertiæ* will not suffer me to undertake. **1780** H. Walpole *Lett.* (1858) VII. 405 By the time absolute power is attained, it will..be charming in speculation, but prove to be nothing but the *vis inertiæ*. **1818** *Edin. Rev.* XXIX. 361 The *vis inertiæ* which strengthens the subject in repelling the aggressions of his rulers. **1878** Sir G. Scott *Lect. Med. Archit.* vii. I. 272 There is a *vis inertiæ* in Art which is not easily overcome.

c. ***vis viva***, the operative force of a moving or acting body, reckoned as equal to the mass of the body multiplied by the square of its velocity.

1780 *Encycl. Brit.* (ed. 2) V. 3317/1 The *vis viva*, or absolute apparent strength of the stroke. **1808** *Edin. Rev.* XII. 122 The proposition on which the whole theory of the *vis viva* is actually founded. **1849** Sir W. Thomson *Math. & Phys. Papers* (1882) I. 107 Notes on Hydrodynamics. On the Vis-viva of a liquid in motion. **1870** *Lond.* etc. *Philos. Mag.* Sept. 210 But a part only of the vires vivæ produced during the efflux has been transformed into heat. **1875** Croll *Climate & T.* App. 546 The vis viva of vibration depends upon the force of the stroke.

d. ***vis vitæ***, vital force.

1752 *Gentl. Mag.* 67/1 All medicines whatever, which tend to lessen the *vis vitæ*, are pernicious. *a* **1817** T. Dwight *Trav. New Eng.*, etc. (1821) I. 385 A pungency, entirely peculiar, accompanied the smell; and appeared to lessen the *vis vitae* in a manner, different from any thing, which I had ever experienced before.

e. ***vis a fronte***, a force operating from in front (as in attraction or suction). ***vis a tergo***, a force operating from behind; a propulsive force.

1822 Good *Study Med.* II. 15 Hence arose another hypothesis, which ascribed the propulsive power to a progressive *vis à tergo*. **1825** *Ibid.* (ed. 2) II. 18 The secernents or extreme arteries..operate by a kind of suction, which may be regarded as a *vis à fronte*. **1873** T. H. Green *Introd. Pathol.* (ed. 2) 19 The combined effect of the diminished *vis à tergo* and of the arterial degeneration may, in some cases, be alone sufficient to cause arrest of the circulation.

f. ***vis comica***, humorous energy; comic force or effect.

1757 S. Foote *Author* I. i. 6 My disposition has, at present, very little of the Vis Comica. **1798** T. Holcroft *Jrnl.* 12 Oct. in *Mem.* (1925) II. v. ii. 184 This character has ..not enough of the *vis comica*. **1887** G. M. Hopkins *Lett. to R. Bridges* (1955) 261 In *vis comica*, in fun,..it is not strong: still there is enough to make me laugh aloud sometimes. **1911** Brereton & Rothwell tr. *Bergson's Laughter* ii. 71 In the scene..between Sganarelle and Pancrace, the entire *vis comica* lies in the conflict set up between the idea of Sganarelle..and the obstinacy of the philosopher. **1979** F. Felsenstein in Smollett *Trav.* p. xxv, Smollett's *vis comica* is..sufficiently broad to allow him to laugh at himself.

g. ***vis medicatrix*** (***naturæ***), the healing power of nature.

1804 *Edin. Rev.* Apr. 186 In this position arose the *vis medicatrix naturæ*, like a fairy queen, to put the wheel in motion. **1904** W. H. Hudson *Green Mansions* xxii. 295 The *vis medicatrix* with which nature helps our weaknesses. **1949** A. Huxley *Let.* 30 July (1969) 601 The news of your mishap was forwarded to us... I do hope that by this time the enforced rest will have given the *vis medicatrix naturae* a chance to get busy.

† **vis**, *sb.*[3] *Obs. rare.* [Arbitrary shortening of VISIT *sb.*: see first quot.] A short visit or call.

1754 *World* No. 62 ¶8 When a fine gentleman chuses to signify his intention of making a short Visit..I am for an abridgment of the word, and only calling it a Vis. *Ibid.* ¶9, I may observe..that the Vis seems to be chiefly confined within the bills of mortality. **1807** Southey *Life A. Bell* (1844) II. 562 If you cannot make me a *visit*, at least make me a *vis*, if you can, before your return to Swanage.

Hence † **vis** *v. trans.*, to pay a short visit to. (Cf. VIZ *v.*) *Obs.*

1754 *World* No. 62 ¶8 Lady Changeherfriend's compliments to Lady Fiddlefaddle, and intends to Vis her ladyship this evening.

† **vis**, *sb.*[4] *Obs. rare.* Abbreviation of VIS-À-VIS 1. Also *attrib.*

1809 *Sporting Mag.* XXXIII. 276 The Vis Landau will be the fashionable vehicle among the Members of the Whip Club. **1814** Byron *Let. to Moore* 9 April, In utter contempt of a hackney-coach and my own *vis*, both of which were deemed necessary for our conveyance.

vis, var. VICE *sb.*[3]; obs. f. VISS; obs. Sc. f. WISE *sb.* and *a.*

vis., abbrev. f. VISCOUNT.

visa ('viːzə), *sb.* [a. F. *visa*, a. L. *vīsa*, fem. pa. pple. of *vidēre* to see.] **1.** = VISÉ *sb.*[3]

This has now replaced VISÉ *sb.*[3] as the normal term for an entry or note on a passport.

1831 *Edin. Rev.* LIV. 200 No trust whatever..can be placed in the simple certificate given by conscience... Beyond this..its *visa* does not reach. **1859** B. Jerrold *Life D. Jerrold* 309 On going to the Austrian Consul in London for the visa of my father's passport. **1885** *Field* 4 April 439/3 We had hoped to..return through Finland, but were unable to obtain the Russian visa at Stockholm. **1898** *Daily News* 19 Dec. 5/2 Notification of the witness list was made yesterday to the Parquet, which began by refusing its visa.

2. (With capital initial.) A proprietary name for an international bank credit-card service (formerly *BankAmericard*), or a card issued to users of this service. orig. *U.S.*

1976 *N.Y. Times* 11 Sept. 27/5 Starting some time next year, according to National BankAmericard Inc., the name of this credit card will be changed all over the world to Visa. **1977** *Official Gaz.* (U.S. Patent Office) 17 May TM140/1 Visa... For financial services involving the use of plastic cards by cardholders at merchant and banking outlets for payment to merchants, loans to cardholders, or transfer of cardholder funds. **1977** *Trade Marks Jrnl.* 27 July 1459/1 *Visa*.. Printed cards related to banking and to credit services. **1979** *United States 1980/81* (Penguin Travel Guides) 40 Major bank cards are Visa (formerly BankAmericard) and Mastercharge. **1983** J. Valin *Natural Causes* ix. 57 It'll cost more. And in cash. I don't take Visa. **1986** [see *PIN* s.v. P II].

Hence **'visa** *v. trans.*, to visé. Also **'visaed** *ppl. a.*

1847 Webster s.v. *Visé*, Hence, travelers speak of getting their passports *visaed*. **1858** Homans *Cycl. Commerce* 1500/2 For each passport so *visaed*. **1896** *Westm. Gaz.* 2 Mar. 3/2 For want of the same readily visaed passport.

† **'visable**, *a. Obs.*[−1] [f. VISE *v.*[1] + -ABLE.] Able to plan or act wisely.

c **1440** Lovelich *Merlin* ix. 9544 [They] seiden he was a worthy knyht, vayllaunt & vysable jn every fyht.

visage ('vɪzɪdʒ), *sb.* Forms: 4–6 **vysage** (4 *fysage*), uisage, 4– **visage** (4, 5 *Sc.*, **wisage, wysage**), 5 **visache**, 6 **visadge**, 6 *Sc.* **visag** (**wissag**), **vissage**; 4 **vysege**, **fisege**, 5 **fyssege**; 5 **vesage, -ayge**, *Sc.* **wesage**, 6 *Sc.* **vessage**. [a. AF. and OF. (also mod.F.) *visage*, = Sp. *visage, visaje*, Pg. *visagem*, It. *visaggio*, f. L. *vīs-us* face (cf. VIS *sb.*[1]): see -AGE.]

1. The face, the front part of the head, of a person (rarely of an animal).

1303 R. Brunne *Handl. Synne* 5887 He hydde hys vysege al þat he myȝt, Out of knowlych of here syȝt. **13..** *Coer de L.* 827 Sche gahchyd herself in the vysage. *c* **1340** *Nominale* (Skeat) 14 Forhede, visage, and browes. *c* **1380** *Sir Ferumb.* 1162 þe bond þat is fysage was bounde wyþ. *c* **1400** *Lanfranc's Cirurg.* 141 To treten of anotamie of þe visage. *a* **1450** *Mirk's Festial* 141 Then had þis Vaspasyan..a maledy yn hys vysage. *c* **1489** Caxton *Sonnes of Aymon* ix. 230 They scratched theyr vysages & pulled theyr heeres. **1568** Grafton *Chron.* II. 296 He was sore hurt in the bodye and in the visage. **1588** Shaks. *L.L.L.* v. ii. 144 Vpon the next occasion that we meete, With Visages displayd to talke and greete. **1632** J. Pory in Ellis *Orig. Lett.* Ser. II. III. 272 One out of the house dischardged haile shot upon Mr. Atturnies sonnes face, which..pitifully mangled his visage. **1653** W. Ramesey *Astrol. Restored* 297 Rubbing their feet about their visage and head, whence the vulgar usually say at such times, the cat washeth her face. **1697** Dryden *Æneid* ix. 1019 Scalp, face, and shoulders, the keen steel divides; And the shared visage hangs on equal sides. **1715** Pope *Iliad* ii. 331 Shrunk in abject fears, From his vile visage [he] wiped the scalding tears. **1784** *Cook's Voy.* II. iv. i. 273 Sometimes the orator of the canoe would have his face covered with a mask, representing either a human visage, or that of some animal. **1797** Godwin *Enquirer* i. xii. 108 There are no wrinkles in his visage. **1842** Borrow *Bible in*

Spain vi, The sun burnt my visage, but I heeded it not. **1847** C. BRONTE *J. Eyre* xxvi, The maniac bellowed: she parted her shaggy locks from her visage. **1860** TYNDALL *Glac.* I. v. 41 The ruddy fire-light..lending animation to the visages sketched upon them [*sc.* the walls] with charcoal.

†**b.** *in one's* (or *the*) *visage*, in or to one's face.

1430–40 LYDG. *Bochas* v. x. (1554) 120b, On a day, the story telleth us, With Affricans and folkes of Chartage, Siphax the Romaines met in the visage. **1470–85** MALORY *Arthur* I. xi. 61 But euer the xj Kynges and their hooste was euer in the vysage of Arthur. **1483** CAXTON *Gold. Leg.* 18/2 That the moneye..he tooke and dyde with all his prouffyt, and [it] was prevyd in his vysage that [etc.]. **1521** *Burgh Rec. Stirling* (1887) 12 Frier Wynssent..protestit solemnitly in presens of the saidis ballies, and in the vesiagh [*sic*] of the haill court, that [etc.].

2. The face with reference to the form or proportions of the features.

a **1300** *Cursor M.* 18858 O suilk a moder, wel slik a child, Wit fair wisage. **13..** *K. Alis.* 6425 (Laud MS.), Anoþer folk bisiden is, Wiþ brode visage, & pleyn, I wys. **1375** BARBOUR *Bruce* I. 383 In wysage wes he sumdeill gray. *c* **1386** CHAUCER *Prol.* 110 A not-heed hadde he, with a broun visage. **1422** YONGE tr. *Secreta Secret.* 228 Tho that haue grete visachys and fleschy bene dysposyd to concupyscence. *c* **1470** *Gol. & Gaw.* 88 With vesage lufly and lang, Body stalwart and strang. **1480** CAXTON *Myrr.* I. xiv. 46 They be dyuerse in somme caas or of body or of membres..or of the visage. *a* **1533** LD. BERNERS *Huon* xxiv. 71, I neuer sawe..soo fayre a creture in yᵉ visage. **1550** J. COKE *Eng. & Fr. Heralds* §5, Saynt Gregory..writeth..howe the vysages of Englande resemble more unto aungelles than earthly creatures. **1592** R. D. *Hypnerotomachia* 34b, With a visage adulterated betwixt a mans and a Goates. **1625** B. JONSON *Staple News* II. i, *Shun.* And such a parboil'd visage! *Fit.* His face looks like a dyer's apron, just. **1697** DRYDEN *Æneid* IX. 890 Old Butes' form he took,.. His wrinkled visage, and his hoary hairs. **1712** STEELE *Spect.* No. 518 ¶9 The intrinsick Worth..is ordinarily calculated from the Cast of his Visage, the Contour of his Person [etc.]. **1769** E. BANCROFT *Guiana* 133 The visage of this animal is erect, & pretty much resembles that of the Quato. **1775** ADAIR *Amer. Ind.* 5 Their faces are tolerably round, contrary to the visage of the others, which inclines much to flatness. **1820** W. IRVING *Sketch Bk.* I. 72 Their visages, too, were peculiar: one had a large head, broad face, and small piggish eyes. **1863** GEO. ELIOT *Romola* iii, A visage like mine, looking no fresher than an apple that has stood the winter. **1866** G. MACDONALD *Ann. Q. Neighb.* xxxii. (1878) 554 The form of her visage was altered.

3. The face or features as expressive of feeling or temperament; the countenance.

1338 R. BRUNNE *Chron.* (1810) 308 Boldely þei bed bataile with visage fulle austere. *c* **1380** WYCLIF *Wks.* (1880) 307 ȝif þei froþen bi irose fisege aȝen men þat tellen hem treuþe, noo drede þei froþen heere owen confusion. *c* **1400** *Rom. Rose* 7402 Of her estat she her repented, As her visage represented. **1448** HEN. VI *Will* in J. W. Clark *Cambridge* (1880) 158 As they wol answere before the blessed and dredeful visage of our Lord Jhesu in his..last dome. *c* **1500** *Lancelot* 460 The king stondith heuy cherith, And to the clerkis his visag so apperith, That all thei dred them of the kingis myght. *a* **1533** LD. BERNERS *Huon* lxiv. 221 He was so ouercome with ire.., that his vysage became lyke a flame of fyer. *a* **1547** SURREY in *Tottel's Misc.* (Arb.) 29 A visage, stern, and myld: where bothe did grow, vice to contemne, in vertue to reioyce. *a* **1578** LINDESAY (Pitscottie) *Chron. Scot.* (S.T.S.) II. 58 Mr. George..without stope of toung ansuering, nocht moveing his continance nor changing his vessage. **1603** SHAKS. *Meas. for M.* III. i. 90 This outward sainted Deputie, Whose setled visage, and deliberate word Nips youth i'th head. **1652** C. B. STAPYLTON *Herodian* XIX. 158 A mighty Bulke he had and Visage grim. **1667** MILTON *P.L.* II. 989 Him thus the Anarch old With faultring speech and visage incompos'd, Answer'd. **1728** YOUNG *Love of Fame* I. 219 Hence aching bosoms wear a visage gay. **1771** GOLDSM. *Haunch Venison* 109 A visage so sad, and so pale with affright, Wak'd Priam in drawing his curtains by night. **1810** SCOTT *Lady of L.* III. iv, His grisled beard and matted hair Obscured a visage of despair. **1834** HOGG *Domestic Manners Scott* (1882) 31 He looked up to me with a visage as stern as that of a judge. **1860** MOTLEY *Netherlands* (1868) I. i. 2 A plodding invalid..with..dreary visage.

†**b.** *to make good visage*, to appear cheerful or composed; to make oneself pleasant or agreeable *to* others. *Obs.*

c **1386** CHAUCER *Shipman's T.* 230 We may wel make cheer and good visage, And dryve forth the world, as it may be. **1390** GOWER *Conf.* III. 211 A king schal make good visage, That noman knowe of his corage. *a* **1450** *Knt. de la Tour* (1868) 3 There be suche men that lyethe and makithe good visage and countenaunce to women afore hem, that scornithe and mockithe hem in her absence. **1525** LD. BERNERS *Froiss.* II. xcix. [xcv.] 291 Than the duke and these two knyghtes rode along their batayle and made good vysage.

4. *transf.* The face or visible side of the sun or moon.

1390 GOWER *Conf.* III. 109 The Mones cercle so lowe is, Wherof the Sonne out of his stage Ne seth him noght with full visage. *c* **1480** HENRYSON *Fables, Fox & Wolf* ii, Hesperous put up his cluddie heid, Schawand his lustie wisage in the sky. **1500–20** DUNBAR *Poems* xxxiii. 2 As ȝung Awrora,..In orient schew hir visage paile. **1590** SHAKS. *Mids. N.* I. i. 210 To-morrow night when Phœbe doth behold Her siluer uisage, in the wat'ry glasse. **1634** MILTON *Comus* 333 And thou fair Moon..Stoop thy pale visage through an amber cloud, And disinherit Chaos. **1667** —— *P.L.* v. 419 Earth and the Sea feed Air, the Air those Fires Ethereal, and as lowest first the Moon; Whence in her visage round those spots. **1794** G. ADAMS *Nat. & Exp. Philos.* IV. xxxix. 88 Sometimes she looks full upon us, and her visage is all lustre. **1847** WHEWELL *Hist. Induct. Sci.* (ed. 2) I. 137 *note*, Aratus says of the moon,..As still her shifting visage changing turns By her we count the monthly round of morns.

†**b.** The face or surface *of* the earth. *Obs.*⁻¹

c **1500** *Lancelot* 1374 He distroys by vengance of his suerd The synaris fra the vysagis of the Erde.

5. In various figurative uses. (Cf. 7.)

c **1374** CHAUCER *Troylus* v. 899 Dowble wordes slye, Swich as men clepe, 'a word with two visages'. *c* **1557** ABP. PARKER *Ps.* lxxx. 234 Visite thy vyne O Lorde..that it may be reuiued continually by the brighte visage of thy presence. **1602** SHAKS. *Ham.* III. iii. 47 Whereto serues mercy, But to confront the visage of Offence? **1611** —— *Wint. T.* I. ii. 266 Beseech your Grace Be plainer with me, let me know my Trespas By it's owne visage. **1646** J. HALL *Horæ Vac.* 10 To propose his adversaries arguments with their edge blunted; nor..to set them out in more horrid visages then they truly carry. **1818** SHELLEY *Eug. Hills* 173 The tattered pall of time, Which scarce hides thy [i.e. Venice's] visage wan.

†**6.** An image or likeness; a portrait. *Obs.*

c **1375** *Cursor M.* 1971 (Fairf.), I made mon ofter myne awen visage. *a* **1400–50** *Alexander* 3362 (Dubl.), Who-someuer in þat ilke hys vysage [*v.r.* ymage] behaldes, þe face is to þe foldward þe fete into þe welkyn. **1570–6** LAMBARDE *Peramb. Kent* (1826) 395 This is the lively visage in deede, both of the one and the other.

7. An appearance or aspect. †*by the first visage*, at first sight.

1422 YONGE tr. *Secreta Secret.* 157 Ofte tymes verite hath a vysage of lesynge, and ofte tymes a lesynge hath a coloure of verite. **1456** SIR G. HAYE *Law Arms* (S.T.S.) 193 As be the first visage it semys that he suld nouthir obey to the tane na to the tothir. **1531** ELYOT *Gov.* I. x, To here thinges merueilous and exquisite, whiche hath in it a visage of some thinges incredible. **1692** RAY *Creation* I. (ed. 2) 103 The sad and melancholick Visage of their Leaves, Flowers and Fruit. **1811** PINKERTON *Petral.* I. 351 Noble serpentine..is generally of a dark leek green, and of an unctuous visage. **1905** *Times, Lit. Supp.* 27 Jan. 28/3 Freeman..tries to reconstitute the visage of the towns Pippin..took and the towns he passed by.

†**8.** An assumed appearance; an outward show; a pretence or semblance. *Obs.*

1390 GOWER *Conf.* III. 227 Thing which men nevere afore knewe He broghte up thanne of his taillage, And all was under the visage Of werkes which he made tho. **1524** *St. Papers Hen. VIII*, VI. 280 Demonstracions and colorable dealinges..sounding more to a shewe and visage then to any parfite frute. **1534** MORE *Comf. agst. Trib.* III. Wks. 1211/2 They see him so many times make a great visage of warre, whan he myndeth it not. **1604** SHAKS. *Oth.* I. i. 50 Others there are Who trym'd in Formes, and visages of Dutie, Keepe yet their hearts attending on themselues. *a* **1684** LEIGHTON *Comm. 1 Pet.* iii. 15 'Be not deceived; God is not mocked.' He looks through all visages and appearances, in upon the heart.

†**b.** *to give a visage*, to create an appearance or impression. *Obs.*

1549 BONNER in Foxe *A. & M.* (1563) 717/1 Lest that they tarieing with such preachers should..gyue a vysage to the encouragement of their errors. *Ibid.* 718/1 Your tarieng with him still..shal geue a visage, that there doctrin is tollerable.

9. *Comb.*, as *visage-burner*, *-changed* adj.

1625 K. LONG tr. *Barclay's Argenis* II. viii. 88 As once in Tyre Pale, guilty, visage-chang'd Penthevs appear'd. **1824** J. BOWRING *Batavian Anthol.* 158 Beast—annoyer—visage-burner—Fair-one's spoiler—maiden's hate.

†**'visage**, *v. Obs. rare.* [f. prec. F. *envisager* is recorded only from 1583, and there is no independent evidence for Palsgrave's *visager*.]

1. *trans.* To face or confront.

c **1386** CHAUCER *Merch. T.* 1029 Al hadde man seyn a thyng with bothe hise eyen, Yit shul we wommen visage it hardily, And wepe and swere and chide subtilly.

2. To look upon or at; to regard or observe.

1450 *Paston Lett.* I. 150 My Lord was with the Kynge, and he vesaged so the mater that alle the Kynges howshold was and is aferd ryght sore. **1530** PALSGR. 765/2 This man hath vysaged me well sythe I came in a dores. **1531** ELYOT *Gov.* II. ii, The theues..humbly approched to Scipio, who visaged them in suche fourme that they..made humble reuerence.

Hence †**'visaging** *vbl. sb.*, meeting, encountering. *Obs.*

a **1500** *Gough Chron.* in *Six Town Chron.* (1911) 159 The duke of Somersett and Sir John Nevyle knyght son of the Erle of Salisbury had grete visagyng to gidder at London.

visaged ('vɪzɪdʒd), *a.* [f. VISAGE *sb.*] Having a visage of a specified kind.

Frequent (from the 15th c.) as the second element in combs., e.g. *black-*, *close-*, *double-*, *grim-*, *hard-*, *long-*, *sharp-visaged*: see these adjs.

13.. *K. Alis.* 6351 (Laud MS.), Anoþer folk bisyde is Visaged after hounde I wys. **1607** WALKINGTON *Opt. Glass* 65 By reason of his sad heavy humor, always stoically visaged. **1612** *Two Noble K.* v. iii. 52 Arcite is gently visagd. **1638** MAYNE *Lucian* (1664) 132 Before his arrivall he made a linnen head to his Dragon, visaged like a Man, and painted like one. **1865** H. BUSHNELL *Vicar. Sacr.* II. ii. (1868) 153 Christ passes before us visaged in sorrow. **1894** HESLOP *Northumbld. Wds.* 375 *Hickory-fyeced*, pock-marked, ill visaged.

‖**visagiste** (vizaʒist). Also anglicized as **visagist** ('vɪzədʒɪst). [Fr.] A cosmetic artist.

1958 *Observer* 14 Sept. 11/3 Elizabeth Arden..has brought over to Bond-street from Paris her *visagist.* **1965** *Harper's Bazaar* Aug. 48/2 Guy Nicolet, visagiste supreme from Revlon, designed for her the Leprechaun Look. **1979** *Courier-Mail* (Brisbane) 16 Apr. 16 (Advt.), Our visiting visagists are: [etc.]. **1981** *Times* 10 Nov. 9/1 In our pictures, visagiste Christina Saunders used Estee Lauder's shimmering bronze face powder. **1984** *Listener* 12 Jan. 26/2 The latest..has for heroine a just-post-punk visagiste.

Visakha, var. VESAK.

visar, obs. Sc. form of VISOR.

visard(e, obs. forms of VIZARD.

‖**visarga** (viː'sɑːgə). Also 9 **viserga**. [Skr., lit. 'emission'.] A sign in the Sanskrit alphabet representing a hard (voiceless) aspiration; also, the sound itself.

1819 H. H. WILSON et al. *Dict. Sanscrit & Eng.* p. xlii, A final *Viserga* or its omission, and a final nasal mark or its omission, are always optional. **1886** *Encycl. Brit.* XXI. 270/1 The Sanskrit alphabet consists of the following sounds...visarga (ḥ) a hard aspirate, standing mostly for original *s* or *r*. **1939** *Year's Work Eng. Stud. 1937* 29 It is a pity that Flasdieck consistently uses the *visarga* (transliterated as *ḥ*) for the final letter of Sanskrit words originally ending in *s*; for only the reader familiar with Sanskrit and its rules of *sandhi* will at once realize that the first person plural of the substantive verb given as Sanskrit *smaḥ*..is to be taken for etymological purposes as equivalent to *smas*. **1953** W. S. ALLEN *Phonetics in Anc. India* II. 50 Since these variants [sc. *-ḥ*, *-x*, and *-ɸ*] are not included in the alphabet, special names are devised for them [by the old Indian phoneticians], viz. *visarjanīya* (or later *visarga*) for *-ḥ*, etc... We shall perhaps be giving the most direct and phonetically appropriate translation if we render it by 'off-glide', as referring to the breathy transition from the vowel to silence. **1975** *Language* LI. 120 The first of these rules obligatorily assimilates a dental stop or continuant before any following coronal (dental, palatal, or retroflex) stop... The third converts *s* to visarga before word boundary.

‖**vis-à-vis** (ˌvɪzɑː'viː, -æ-, 'viːz-), *sb.*, *prep.*, and *adv.* Also 8 **viz-a-viz**, 8–9 **vis-a-vis**. [F. *vis-à-vis* face to face, f. *vis*:—L. *visum*, acc. of *visus* sight, face: see VIS *sb.*[1]]

A. *sb.* **1.** A light carriage for two persons sitting face-to-face. *Obs.* exc. *Hist.*

1753 H. WALPOLE *Let. to G. Montague* 17 July, He was walking slowly..with..two pages, three footmen and a *vis-à-vis* following him. **1768** J. BYRON *Narr. Patagonia* (ed. 2) 230 The common vehicle here is a calash, or kind of vis-à-vis, drawn by one mule only. **1781** W. HAYLEY *Triumphs of Temper* II. 98 Her quick eyes sparkle with surprise to see The glories of a golden viz-a-viz. **1831** SIR J. SINCLAIR *Corr.* II. 357 It is necessary to purchase a very strong carriage... A vis-a-vis is the best shape, made so that it can be converted into a bed. **1844** *Act 7 & 8 Vict.* c. 91. Sched., Every horse..drawing any coach..chaise, phaeton, vis-a-vis, calash, curricle.

plur. **1775** MME. D'ARBLAY *Early Diary* (1889) II. 13 Not being much in town, the new vis-à-vis were not familiar to him. **1787** in *Sixth Rep. Dep. Kpr. Publ. Rec.* II. 177 A new method of hanging Coaches, Vis à Viss, and other Bodies. **1802** *Sporting Mag.* XX. 41 The number of coaches..vis-à-vis..and nondescripts. **1834** in J. Tomlinson *Doncaster* (1887) 265 Mrs. Belcher for Chaises and visivis [*sic*].

2. a. One or other of two persons or things facing, or situated opposite to, each other.

c **1757** *Let.* in J. H. Jesse *Selwyn & Contemp.* (1843) I. 158 We are reduced to Miss Wylde, who has a most charming vis-à-vis, Mr. Ward, who sings like a nightingale. **1766** G. WILLIAMS *Ibid.* II. 56 My *vis-à-vis* thinks you have done wrong to let even the music-meeting go off unattended. **1840** HOOD *Up Rhine* 113 There you are, at an Innkeeper's ordinary, with all kinds of low company, and a common soldier for your vis-a-vis. **1865** W. G. PALGRAVE *Arabia* II. 204 Menamah, though larger in extent than Moharrek, has a less showy appearance: it is a centre of commerce, as its vis-à-vis is of government. **1893** MARTIN in Barrows *Parl. Relig.* II. 1142 Does it make no difference to us, whether we have for our vis-a-vis on the other shore of the ocean a Christian or a pagan power?

b. *esp.* in dancing. Also as *pl.*

1808 MISS BERRY *Jrnls. & Corr.* II. 371 It seems perfectly indifferent to them [the peasant men and women dancing] who is their vis-à-vis. **1834** MARRYAT *P. Simple* (1863) 231 Miss Eurydice had but a sorry partner, but she undertook to instruct me. O'Brien was our *vis-à-vis* with Miss Euterpe. **1841** THACKERAY *Gt. Hoggarty Diamond* v, Lady Jane Preston..asked me to dance with her. We had my Lord Tiptoff and Lady Fanny Rakes for our *vis-à-vis*. **1877** MISS GRANT *Sun-Maid* xiv, Partners were scrambling for vis-a-vis and places.

c. A counterpart, an opposite number.

1900 J. K. JEROME *Three Men on Bummel* xii. 273 The Vosges peasant has not the unromantic air of contented prosperity that spoils his *vis-a-vis* across the Rhine. **1975** *Publishers Weekly* 21 July 67/1 Middleton's admiration ..[for the U.S. armed services] extends to their vis-à-vis, the Russian military.

3. A meeting face to face; an encounter.

1867 BAKER *Nile Trib.* ii. 41 This being my first *vis-à-vis* with a hippo, I was not certain whether I could claim the victory. **1871** 'M. LEGRAND' *Cambr. Freshm.* 345 Every minute brought him nearer the dreaded *vis-à-vis* with an omniscient M.A.

B. 1. *prep.* Over against, in comparison with, in relation to; also *lit.*, facing, face to face with.

1755 H. WALPOLE *Let. to R. Bentley* 16 Nov., What a figure would they..make *vis-à-vis* his manly vivacity and dashing eloquence. **1759** CHESTERF. *Lett.* (1792) IV. 161, I allow his army will be what you say; but what will that be *vis-à-vis* French, Austrians, Imperialists, Swedes, and Russians, who must amount to double that number? **1847** E. BRONTE *Wuthering Heights* i, His master dived down to him, leaving me *vis-à-vis* the ruffianly bitch. **1907** *Westm. Gaz.* 24 July 10/1 He is responsible vis-à-vis the Government for their efficiency.

2. a. *adv.* Opposite, so as to face (another or each other).

1807 BYRON *Let.* in Moore *Life* (1830) I. 111 Even the hero of my Cornelian (who is now sitting *vis-à-vis*, reading a volume of my Poetics) passed me in Trinity walks. **1816** *Gentl. Mag.* LXXXVI. I. 6 The captivating air and fascinating manners of a French lady, who sat *vis-a-vis*. **1871** NESBITT *Catal. Slade Coll. Glass* 75 A pair of doves are poised *vis-a-vis*.

b. Const. *to* or *with*.

1814 SCOTT *Wav.* lxi, Waverley..found himself in the desired vehicle, *vis-à-vis* to Mrs. Nosebag. **1841** MRS.

MOZLEY *Lost Brooch* II. xx. 142 Only too well pleased to find myself once again *vis a vis* to Constance Duff. **1870** DISRAELI *Lothair* xxi, Lothair was there vis-à-vis with Miss Arundel.

Hence **vis-à-vis** *v.*; **vis-à-visness**.

1839 LEVER *H. Lorrequer* vi, The hissing kettle on the hob was *vis à vis'd* by a gridiron with three newly-taken trout. **1887** E. GURNEY *Tertium Quid* I. 371, I doubt whether it would involve anything like the sense of vis-à-vis-ness or parallelism, suggested to me now by such a phrase as 'posited myself in space'.

visc., abbrev. form of VISCOUNT.

viscacha (vɪˈskætʃə). Also 8 viscacho, 8–9 viscaccia, 9 vizcacha, vischacha. [a. Sp. *viscacha* (also *biscacha* BISCACHA), ad. Quichuan *(h)uiscacha*. Hence also F. *viscaque*.] One or other of two large burrowing rodents of South America, related to the chinchilla.

a. The *Lagidium cuvierii*, inhabiting the upper Andes from Chile to Ecuador; the Alpine viscacha.

1604 E. G[RIMSTONE] *D'Acosta's Hist. Indies* IV. xxxviii. 314 There are other small animalles which they call Viscachas, and are like to hares, although they be bigger. **1781** PENNANT *Hist. Quadrup.* II. 376 Allied to this [Cape Hare] seems the *Viscachos*, or *Viscachas*, mentioned by Acosta and Feuillée, in their accounts of Peru. **1801** SHAW *Gen. Zool.* II. I. 209 *Viscaccia*... This species is said to have the general appearance of a Rabbet. **1811** W. WALTON *Peruv. Sheep* 175 They afford furs and ornamental skins, .. particularly the *viscacha*, which is a species of rabbit. **1849** *Sk. Nat. Hist., Mammalia* IV. 126 The general colour of the viscacha of the western acclivities of the Peruvian Andes.. is grayish ash, clouded here and there with a tint of brown. **1879** E. P. WRIGHT *Animal Life* (Cassell) 196 The Alpine Viscacha (*Lagidium cuvierii*) inhabits the lofty Andes of Chili, Bolivia, and Peru.

b. The *Lagostomus trichodactylus* of the southern Argentine pampas.

1836 *Partington's Brit. Cycl. Nat. Hist.* II. 26 The Viscacha (*Lagostomus trichodactylus*) is about the size of a rabbit. **1855** *Orr's Circ. Sci., Org. Nat.* III. 464 The Viscacha.. inhabits the great plains of Buenos Ayres, where it digs burrows for itself. *c* **1882** *Cassell's Nat. Hist.* III. 138 The Viscacha lives on the Pampas from Buenos Ayres to the borders of Patagonia.

So **viscache**. *rare*⁻¹.

1847–9 *Todd's Cycl. Anat.* IV. I. 373 In the viscache the squamous portion of the temporal bone is.. deeply indented.

†**viscate**, *ppl. a. Obs.*⁻¹ [ad. L. *viscāt-us*: cf. next and INVISCATE *v.*] Inviscated.

c **1400** *Lanfranc's Cirurg.* 136 þilke blood is not viscat in þe substaunce of dure matris, as þe mater is in empostymes.

viscated, *ppl. a.* [f. L. *viscāt-us*, pa. pple. of *viscāre*, f. *viscus*, *viscum* birdlime.] (See quots.)

1623 COCKERAM I, *Viscated*, taken with Bird-lime. **1656** BLOUNT *Glossogr.*, *Viscated*, dressed, or taken with Bird-lime.

‖**viscera** (ˈvɪsərə), *sb. pl.* [L. *viscera* internal organs, pl. of *viscus* VISCUS². Cf. It. *viscere*, Sp. and Pg. *visceras*, F. *viscères*.]

1. *Anat.* The soft contents of the principal cavities of the body; *esp.* the internal organs of the trunk; the entrails or bowels together with the heart, liver, lungs, etc.

1651 BIGGS *New Disp.* ⁋174 Exhausting the stock of aliment from the *vasa* and *viscera*. **1667** *Phil. Trans.* II. 545 Also lifting up the Viscera of the lower Belly. **1718** QUINCY *Compl. Disp.* 111 For in the Intentions, the Seat of the Complaint is most commonly in the Viscera. **1750** *Phil. Trans.* XLVII. 83 [It is] to keep them from touching the abdominal viscera of this animal. **1801** *Med. Jrnl.* V. 500 Instancing its powerful effects in obstructions of the viscera, especially in liver cases. **1845** BUDD *Dis. Liver* 32 Great stress is laid on the case of the mollusca, animals whose liver is generally immense in proportion to their other viscera. **1878** W. H. DALL *Later Preh. Man* 18 The viscera had evidently been removed, but the muscular and cutaneous tissues were in tolerable preservation.

†**b.** *fig.* = BOWEL *sb.*¹ 3. *Obs.*

1652 N. CULVERWEL *Treat.* II. vi. (1661) 141 Do you think now that God will trust these with his more special mercies, with his viscera and tender mercies?

2. *transf.* The interior; the inner parts: = BOWEL *sb.*¹ 4.

1709 T. ROBINSON *Vind. Mosaick Syst.* 41 If the Atheist will venture himself into the Interior Viscera or Bowels of the Earth. **1828** *Lights & Shades* I. 210, I dived into the viscera of Newgate-market.

visceral (ˈvɪsərəl), *a.* [ad. med.L. *viscerālis* (Du Cange) internal, f. *viscera*: see prec. So OF. *visceral* (fig.), F. *viscéral*, Sp. *visceral*, It. *viscerale*.]

1. a. Affecting the viscera or bowels regarded as the seat of emotion; pertaining to, or touching deeply, inward feelings. *Obs.* after 17th c. and revived in the 20th.

1575 FENTON *Gold. Epist.* (1582) 117 Thys warre is called Viscerall, for that it is bredde and begon in the hearte, and dissolueth and takes ende in the hearte. **1626** T. H[AWKINS] tr. *Caussin's Holy Court* 288 He is vnited to all men, as oftentymes as they receyue him, by a viscerall transfusion of himselfe, as one should melt one waxe within another. **1627** DONNE *Serm.* (1640) 285 Christ here sends Paracletum in a more entire and a more internall and more Viscerall sense—a Comforter. **1640** BP. REYNOLDS *Passions* xi. 109 Love is of all other the inmost and most visceral affection; and there-fore called by the apostle, 'Bowels of love'. **1949** *Scrutiny* XV. 152 A tendency to borrow the mantle of Mr. Wyndham Lewis in attacking the visceral and the formless in art and poetry. **1969** *Listener* 31 July 162/3 Hardly any of them fall into the tragic error of modern straight music, which eschews visceral appeal entirely. **1976** *Publishers Weekly* 1 Mar. 93/1 By accumulating a mass of homely details he gives his story of the death of Sgt. Mullen great visceral power and emotional impact. **1978** J. IRVING *World according to Garp* xvi. 321 Hoping that the visceral reality of Garp's language.. somehow rescued the book from sheer soap opera.

†**b.** *fig.* Lying in the entrails or inward parts.

1624 DONNE *Serm.* xvii. (1640) 167 There is the land of Gold, centricall Gold, viscerall Gold, gremiall Gold, Gold in the Matrice and womb of God.

2. *Phys.* Of disorders or diseases: Affecting the viscera or internal organs.

1794 in Morse *Amer. Geog.* I. 500 The Lebanon pool is famous for having wrought many cures.. even in visceral obstructions and indigestion. **1845** FORD *Handbk. Spain* II. 919 A spring.. much frequented for visceral disorders. **1862** SMILES *Engineers* III. 247 Disease also fell upon him,—first fever, and then visceral derangement. **1876** BRISTOWE *Th. & Pract. Med.* (1878) 288 The visceral lesions and cachexiæ which supervene on ague.

3. *Anat.* Of or pertaining to, consisting of, situated in or among, the viscera.

1826 KIRBY & SP. *Entomol.* xxxviii. IV. 62 The *bronchiæ* .. may be considered as consisting in general of.. visceral ones which enter the cavity of the body, and are lost amongst the viscera and the caul [etc.]. **1853** KANE *Grinnell Exp.* xxx. (1856) 259 The lost art of petrified visceral monstrosities seen at the medical schools. **1870** ROLLESTON *Anim. Life* Introd. p. xix, In the sub-kingdom vertebrata.. visceral systems exist in specialized and differentiated forms. **1880** BASTIAN *Brian* 34 Such communicating branches are especially numerous in the course of the visceral nerves.

b. *visceral cavity*, that part of an animal body in which the viscera are contained.

1846 DANA *Zooph.* (1848) 11 A visceral cavity closed below. **1851** S. P. WOODWARD *Mollusca* I. 31 Sea-water is admitted to the visceral cavity of many of the mollusks by minute canals. **1868** DUNCAN *Insect World* Introd. 14 It is the unoccupied portions of the great visceral cavity which serve as conductors to the blood.

c. *visceral hump*, the dorsal enlargement, containing the viscera, of snails and other gastropod molluscs in which the ventral part is a foot.

1883 *Encycl. Brit.* XVI. 635/2 As the ventral foot is clearly separate from the projecting head, so is this dorsal region, and it is conveniently spoken of as the visceral hump or 'dome' (cupola). **1927** E. STEP *Shell Life* (new ed.) i. 23 Within the shell [of the Snail] is.. the 'visceral hump' containing most of the internal organs. **1972** M. S. GARDINER *Biol. Invertebrates* xi. 58/2 This and the coiling of the visceral hump has led, in a number of species, to the suppression of organs on one side (usually the right).

4. Pertaining to the viscera of animals used as a means of divination.

1833 MRS. BROWNING *Prometh. Bound* Poems 1850 I. 161, I.. taught what sign Of visceral lightness, coloured to a shade, May charm the genial gods. **1861** COL. HAWKER in C. E. Byles *Life & Lett.* (1905) xvii. 382, I have visceral augury.

5. *Anat.* **a.** *visceral layer*, a portion of the arachnoid membrane.

1840 G. V. ELLIS *Anat.* 13 That portion of it.. which covers the brain, or the visceral layer, is separated from the brain by a considerable interval. **1875** SIR W. TURNER in *Encycl. Brit.* I. 865/1 Many anatomists regard the arachnoid as the visceral layer of a serous membrane.

b. *visceral arch*, one of a set of parallel ridges in the region of the mouth in the embryonic skull. *visceral cleft*, one of the intervals between the visceral arches.

1870 ROLLESTON *Anim. Life* Introd. p. xlvii, The malleus of Mammalia.. being developed out of the proximal elements of the first visceral arch. **1872** MIVART *Elem. Anat.* i. (1873) 5 These arches are separated by temporary apertures termed 'visceral clefts'. **1875** SIR W. TURNER in *Encycl. Brit.* I. 831/1 Immediately below each maxillary lobe four arches, called branchial or visceral, arise in the ventral aspect of the head.

c. *visceral brain*, those parts of the brain which mediate bodily activity, esp. visceral activity, in response to emotion.

1949 P. D. MCLEAN in *Psychosomatic Med.* XI. 340 (*caption*) The shaded area of cortex represents what was formerly known as the limbic lobe of Broca and subsequently termed the rhinencephalon by Turner. It corresponds to what is arbitrarily referred to in this paper as the visceral brain. **1972** H. J. EYSENCK *Psychology is about People* i. 35 Emotionality-stability seems indissolubly linked with the *autonomic* nervous system, which regulates the expression of the emotions, and which in turn is organized and governed by the 'visceral brain'.

Hence ˈ**viscerally** *adv.*

a **1636** C. FITZGEFFREY *Comp. tow. Captives* iii. (1637) 38 Then shall your compassion extend it selfe more viscerally towards your afflicted brethren. **1965** H. KAHN *On Escalation* vi. 119 Most individuals.. conclude, at least viscerally, that the dangers are simply too great. **1970** T. ROETHKE *Sel. Lett.* 173, I teach viscerally: I try to make up for ignorance by energy and enthusiasm. **1982** *Wall St. Jrnl.* 13 Aug. 16/2 Viscerally, your friends recognize that what is involved here is not one issue, but your capacity to govern.

visceralization (ˌvɪsərəlaɪˈzeɪʃən). *Path.* [f. VISCERAL *a.* + -IZATION.] The spreading of an infection to the viscera; the movement of a pathogen towards the viscera.

1963 *Ann. N.Y. Acad. Sci.* CXIII. 410 Visceralization of the parasites occurs as a further complication. **1969** *Current Topics in Microbiol. & Immunol.* XLVIII. 30 Subinoculation of the organisms responsible for these conditions into laboratory animals is often followed, even in cutaneous types, by extensive visceralization of the infection. **1980** *Jrnl. Exper. Med.* CLII. 605 BALB/c mice have an exceptional susceptibility to *Leishmania tropica* infection such that cutaneous lesions grow without restraint in all cases leading to fatal metastasis and visceralization in normal and x-irradiated.. animals.

Also ˈ**visceralize** *v. intr.*, to spread to or attack the viscera.

1969 *Current Topics in Microbiol. & Immunol.* XLVIII. 32 Sudanese or some East African infections of *L. donovani* derived from wild rodents may fail to visceralise, while the purely human kala-azar of India is usually fatal. **1974** W. H. R. LUMSDEN in *Trypanosomiasis & Leishmaniasis* (Ciba Symp.) 8 Organisms tending to 'visceralize' in man (i.e. with a predilection for infecting cells in the viscera, particularly in the spleen). **1981** *Ann. Trop. Med. & Parasitol.* LXXV. 139 The primary lesions of kala-azar may be confused with oriental sore and.. some strains with the capacity to visceralize may fail to do so, causing only dermal lesions.

ˈ**viscerate**, *v. rare.* [f. VISCERA + -ATE³, after *eviscerate*.] *trans.* To eviscerate, disembowel. Also *fig.*

1727 BAILEY (vol. II), *Viscerated*, having the Bowels taken out. **1798** *Sporting Mag.* XII. 53 A butcher was employed one evening to viscerate a mare. **1830** *Examiner* 659/1 A vain pretender, who.. falls a victim to his temerity and is dissected;—viscerated to the edification of the profession.

viscеˈration. *rare*⁻⁰. [ad. L. *viscerātio*, f. *viscera* VISCERA.] (See quots.)

1623 COCKERAM I, *Visceration*, a dole of raw flesh. **1656** BLOUNT *Glossogr.* (after Cooper), *Visceration*.. good chear, a dole or distributing raw flesh at the death of rich men, or when hogs are killed; also the garbage that Hunters give their Dogs.

viscero- (ˈvɪsərəʊ), combining form, on Greek models, of L. *viscera* VISCERA, employed in anatomical terms, as ***viscero-branchial***, ***-pericardial***, ***-pleural*** (etc.), adjs. Also **visceroˈcranium** = *splanchnocranium* s.v. SPLANCHNO-; ˌ**visceropˈtosis** *Path.* (see quot. 1897); **visceroˈtropic** *a. Med.* [-TROPIC], tending to attack or affect the viscera; hence **visceroˈtropism**.

The more correct combining form *visceri-* is given in some dictionaries, as *viscericardial*, etc.

1888 W. HERDMAN in *Encycl. Brit.* XXIII. 613/1 A third great sinus, the *viscero-branchial vessel. **1925** J. S. KINGSLEY *Vertebrate Skeleton* 58 Recently the terms *neurocranium* and **viscerocranium* have been introduced. **1980** *Gray's Anat.* (ed. 36) 141/2 The trabeculae cranii may largely be derived from branchial arch (neural crest) mesoderm, i.e. from the viscerocranium, having been adapted into the cartilaginous or basal part of the neurocranium, or 'brainbox'. **1888** HOWES & SCOTT *Huxley & Martin's Biol.* i. 108 **Viscero-motor nerves*; seen to arise from both sympathetic and lumbo-sacral plexus for distribution to the pelvic viscera. **1883** E. R. LANKESTER in *Encycl. Brit.* XVI. 667/1 The pericardium is extended so as to form a very large sac passing among the viscera dorsal wards.. the *viscero-pericardial sac. *Ibid.* 679/2 The visceral nerves of the *viscero-pleural ganglion-pair. **1897** *Allbutt's Syst. Med.* III. 587 The names enteroptosis or *visceroptosis have been applied to cases in which various abdominal organs have become displaced from their normal positions. **1905** H. D. ROLLESTON *Dis. Liver* 11 In other cases the symptoms are due to visceroptosis. **1935** M. HOSKINS in *Amer. Jrnl. Trop. Med.* XV. 675 The term '*viscerotropic virus' is used to designate the strain of yellow fever virus which has been carried in *M. rhesus*. **1940** *Nature* 2 Nov. 596/1 Man ordinarily suffers only the viscerotropic attack [in yellow fever]—in his liver, kidneys and heart. **1976** *Ann. Rev. Microbiol.* XXX. 443 In the 17D strain of virus both the viscerotropic and neurotropic properties of the natural virus were markedly reduced. **1940** *Viscerotropism [see NEUROTROPISM 2]. **1973** *Acta Virologica* XVII. 241 Street strains displaying a higher viscerotropism can actively multiply in the internal organs.

†**visceˈrose**, *a. Obs.*⁻¹ [-OSE.] = VISCEROUS *a.*

1690 J. EDWARDS *Demonstr. Exist. God* II. (1696) 83 This viscerose sort of flesh is most suitable.. to those vessels and parts of the body which are composed of it.

viscerotome (ˈvɪsərəʊtəʊm). *Med.* [f. VISCERO- + -TOME.] An instrument for obtaining post-mortem samples of liver tissue through a puncture in the abdominal wall (avoiding necropsy), used esp. when yellow fever is suspected. Hence **visceˈrotomy**, the use of a viscerotome.

1934 *Amer. Jrnl. Hygiene* XIX. 553 The attempt.. led one of us (E. R. R[ickard]) to attempt the design of an instrument for the removal of liver tissue without autopsy. This instrument, later christened the 'viscerotome' by Dr. Mario Bião, reached a practicable stage of development within a few weeks. *Ibid.* 555 The opposition of relatives and friends to autopsy is greatly reduced in the case of viscerotomy. **1940** VAN ROOYEN & RHODES *Virus Dis. of Man* xxxv. 472 The viscerotome is a metal instrument.. resembling a trocar, about 1 cm. square, possessing a sharp, hollow, pointed extremity fitted with a mechanically operated guillotine blade. *Ibid.*, Viscerotomy has revealed the existence of yellow fever in places in which it had hitherto passed unrecognized. **1971** P. C. C. GARNHAM *Progr. Parasitol.* iii. 24 The disease was scarcely recognized until 1934, when the introduction by Penna.. of a viscerotomy service for the diagnosis of fatal cases of yellow fever revealed its presence in Brazil. *Ibid.*, The brutal instrument, the viscerotome, is plunged through the abdominal wall of the cadaver into the liver.

viscerotonic (ˌvɪsərəʊˈtɒnɪk), *a.* and *sb.* [f. VISCERO- + TONIC *a.*] **A.** *adj.* Designating or characteristic of a type of personality which is comfort-loving, sociable, and easy-going, classified by Sheldon as being associated with an endomorphic physique. **B.** *sb.* One having this type of personality. So **viscero'tonia** (-'təʊnɪə), viscerotonic personality or characteristics. Cf. CEREBROTONIC, SOMATOTONIC *adjs.* and *sbs.*

1937 [see CEREBROTONIC *a.* and *sb.*]. **1938**, etc. [see SOMATOTONIC *a.* and *sb.*]. **1956** GOACHER & WHIGHAM in E. Pound tr. *Sophocles' Women of Trachis* 60 Stigmatized as a sex crank, as a maniacal visceratonic [*sic*], he [*sc.* D. H. Lawrence] in fact made an extraordinary effort to re-establish the 'whole' man. **1969** V. DE S. PINTO *City that Shone* iii. 68, I suppose that in modern psychological jargon, as a child in those distant Edwardian days, I could be described as an introvert and cerebrotonic living in a world of extroverts, somatotonics and viscerotonics. **1980** F. J. BRUNO *Behav. & Life* xi. 379 As might be expected, viscerotonia is said to be correlated with endomorphy. The extreme endomorph with a viscerotonic personality would be a self-indulgent person.

† **'viscerous,** *a. Obs.* [f. VISCER-A + -OUS.] Of the nature of, resembling that of, the viscera.

1657 W. COLES *Adam in Eden* xlix, It [fumitory] prevaileth in Chronicall diseases arising from stoppings of the viscerous parts. **1668** CULPEPPER & COLE *Barthol. Anat.* Introd., Viscerous flesh or the flesh of the Bowels. **1728** CHAMBERS *Cycl.* s.v. *Flesh*, The Antients made five different kinds of Flesh:.. The third, Viscerous, as the Flesh of the Stomach and Intestines.

viscid ('vɪsɪd), *a.* [ad. late L. *viscid-us*, f. L. *viscum* birdlime (see VISCOUS *a.*). Hence also OF. *viscide*, It. *viscido*.]

1. Of fluid or soft substances: Having a glutinous or gluey character; sticky, adhesive, ropy. (Cf. VISCOUS *a.* 1.)

1635 BRATHWAIT *Arcad. Pr.* 235, I meane by sweatings and suffumigations to extract all those viscid and oily humours. **1657** *Physical Dict.*, *Viscid phlegm*, clammy tough phlegm, roping like birdlime. **1672** GREW *Anat. Roots* I. iii. §21, I call it a Balsame;.. Yet not a Terebinth; because, nothing near so viscid or tenaceous as that is. **1742** *Lond. & Country Brew.* I. (ed. 4) 46 By which the spirituous Particles are set loose and free from their viscid Confinements. **1777** FORSTER *Voy. round World* I. 104 Whenever we lamed any of them, they disgorged a quantity of viscid food. **1804** ABERNETHY *Surg. Obs.* 131, I could not see the surface [of the ulcer] for a very viscid discharge, which adhered to it like mucus. **1845** BUDD *Dis. Liver* 268 In persons who die of phthisis, the bile in the gall-bladder.. is often very dark-coloured, and viscid. **1875** DARWIN *Insectiv. Pl.* i. 13 The secretion from the glands is extremely viscid.

2. Of surfaces: Covered with a glutinous or sticky secretion. Chiefly *Bot.* of leaves.

1760 J. LEE *Introd. Bot.* III. v. (1765) 182 *Viscid, Clammy*; when they are smeared over with a Juice that is not fluid but tenacious, sticky. **1793** MARTYN *Lang. Bot.* s.v. *Viscidum*, A Viscid or clammy leaf. **1812** *New Bot. Gard.* I. 42 The panicle is upright and viscid. **1823** STARK *Elem. Nat. Hist.* I. 421 Head.. covered with large and hard plates, or a viscid skin. **1870** HOOKER *Stud. Flora* 207 *Senecio viscosus*; annual, glandular-pubescent, viscid. **1874** LUBBOCK *Wild Flowers* iii. 164 Close behind the stigma is a projection which terminates in a very viscid disk.

viscidity (vɪ'sɪdɪtɪ). [f. prec. + -ITY. Cf. obs. F. *viscidité* (16th c.).]

1. The quality of being viscid; glutinousness, stickiness, ropiness.

1611 COTGR., *Viscidité*, visciditie;.. viscositie. **1658** PHILLIPS, *Viscidity* or *Viscosity*, a clamminesse, a sticking to any thing like glue or bird lime. **1686** PLOT *Staffordsh.* 100 The Sulphur by its viscidity, does.. sweeten the pungency of the Salt. **1707** FLOYER *Physic. Pulse-Watch* 189 Then we must dilute the Viscidity of the Humours if it be sizy. **1758** *Descr. Thames* 170 Salmon.. offends the Stomach by its Viscidity. **1773** *Phil. Trans.* LXIV. 30 The density, viscidity, and other qualities of this matter. **1836–9** *Todd's Cycl. Anat.* II. 101/2 The viscidity of the solution of sugar.. is very little above that of pure water. **1876** BARTHOLOW *Mat. Med.* (1879) 469 Castor-oil has a pale amber-color,.. and is quite viscid. Cold increases the viscidity.

2. A collection or accumulation of viscid humours; viscid matter or substance.

c **1720** GIBSON *Farrier's Guide* II. xxxix. (1738) 144 The cure consists in all those things that are proper to destroy the Viscidities in the Bowels. **1743** tr. *Heister's Surg.* 193 For by this means all Viscidities in the Blood will be diluted. **1774** GOLDSM. *Nat. Hist.* (1862) I. xvi. 90 The parts of the fluid rubbing against each other, destroy all viscidities. **1846** LANDOR *Imag. Conv.* Wks. II. 237/1 They must have honey, sugar, cinnamon... Dante and Ariosto, different as they are, equally avoided these sweet viscidities.

'viscidize, *v. rare.* [f. VISCID *a.* + -IZE.] *intr.* To become viscid.

1859 R. F. BURTON *Centr. Afr.* in *Jrnl. Geog. Soc.* XXIX. 437 It viscidizes in the solution used for washing the true copal. **1876** —— *Gorilla L.* II. 56, I was assured that it does not viscidize in the potash-wash.

'viscidly, *adv.* [f. as prec. + -LY².] In a viscid manner.

1821 W. P. C. BARTON *Flora N. Amer.* I. 83 Plant fetid,.. all over viscidly pubescent.

'viscidness. [-NESS.] = VISCIDITY.

1710 T. FULLER *Pharm. Extemp.* 218 Honey.. from its Viscidness, digesteth and healeth. **1755** *Phil. Trans.* L. 876, I have already observed, that Cassia is found in chewing to have a viscidness, which Cinnamon has not.

visciere, obs. form of VIZIER.

viscin ('vɪsɪn), *Chem.* [a. F. *viscin* (Macaire), f. L. *viscum* birdlime (see VISCOUS *a.*) + -IN.] A substance which forms the main constituent of birdlime, chiefly obtained from the berries and other parts of the mistletoe.

1838 T. THOMSON *Chem. Org. Bodies* 917 The berries.. yield to alcohol a brown extractive matter soluble in water, which smells like viscin. **1887** *Buck's Handbk. Med. Sci.* V. 12/1 Mistletoe.. contains sugar,.. and a peculiar, very sticky substance, viscin. Viscin is also contained in a few other plants.

,viscoela'sticity. [f. VISCO(US *a.*, VISCO(SITY + ELASTICITY.] The property of a substance of exhibiting both elastic and viscous behaviour, the application of a constant stress causing an immediate deformation that disappears if the stress is quickly removed but increases for a time and becomes permanent if the stress is maintained.

1944 *Q. Jrnl. Appl. Math.* II. 119 The solution of the first and second boundary value problems of visco-elasticity is reduced to the solution of equivalent boundary value problems of elasticity, and the determination of the response of the visco-elastic material under consideration to a simple shearing stress or a simple shearing strain. **1963** *Times* 27 Mar. 1/6 Viscosity and visco-elasticity of glasses. **1972** *Science* 2 June 1041/3 The viscoelasticity of the solutions would decrease upon continued stirring. **1976** *Nature* 12 Aug. 573/1 The explanation for the observed increase in cavitation erosion rate in polymer solution may still have its origin in polymer viscoelasticity.

So **viscoe'lastic** *a.*, exhibiting or pertaining to viscoelasticity.

1944 [see above]. **1949** *Proc. Internat. Congr. Rheology 1948* II. 24 Flow birefringence in aluminium soap solutions, considered here as a typical visco-elastic system. **1963** *New Scientist* 22 Aug. 382/3 Polymer solutions.. generally show some elasticity, or tendency to preserve their shape, and are therefore called 'viscoelastic'. **1970** P. SHERMAN *Industr. Rheology* iv. 236 The Instron tester has been used to study the viscoelastic properties of potatoes, peas, and apples. **1973** J. R. RICE in A. C. Palmer *Symposium Role Plasticity in Soil Mech.* 263 Viscoelastic creep of the soil. **1978** *Sci. Amer.* Nov. 145/1 Silicone putty.. is such a viscoelastic fluid.

'viscoid, *a. rare*⁻¹. [-OID.] Of a viscid or viscous nature.

1877 LE CONTE *Elem. Geol.* (1879) 55 A glacier moves like a fluid, though a very stiff, viscous-fluid: its motion may therefore be rightly called viscoid.

vi'scometer. [f. L. *viscōs-us* VISCOUS *a.*: see -METER.] An instrument for measuring the viscosity of liquids.

1883 SIMMONDS *Dict. Trade*, *Viscometer*, a standard measurer for ascertaining the viscosity of oils for cotton-mill and other spindles. **1886**, etc. [see SAYBOLT]. **1946** *Nature* 2 Nov. 614/2 Graphs showing the flow characteristics of a grease at medium rates of shear (plunger viscometer) and at high rates of shear (pendulum viscometer) were displayed. **1967** M. CHANDLER *Ceramics in Mod. World* ii. 61 The commonest instrument for testing the fluid properties of a slip is the torsion viscometer. **1970** *British Printer* June 70/2 Mr Bisset described the functions of viscometers and tack-meters.

Hence **vi'scometry**, the measurement of viscosity; the use of a viscometer; **visco'metric** *a.*, **-'metrically** *adv.*

1886 B. REDWOOD in *Jrnl. Soc. Chem. Industry* 29 Mar. 121/2 (*heading*) On viscosimetry, or viscometry. **1931** G. BARR *Monogr. Viscometry* iii. 48 In practical viscometry it is rarely necessary for the investigator to undertake the labour involved in the evaluation of the constants of his instrument ab initio. **1938** *Chem. Abstr.* XXXII. 1091/1 The viscometric results were in excellent agreement with those obtained by using a photoelec. nephelometer. **1946** *Chem. Rev.* XXXIX. 161 The process can be followed viscometrically, polarimetrically, or by chemical determination of the aldose end group produced. **1978** *Nature* 1 June p. xi/2 Further applications are in the field of interface rheology and viscometric determination of the molecular weight of plastic material solutions. **1982** *Lebensmittel-Wissensch. und Technol.* XV. 242 (*heading*) Viscometric study of the dispersion of whole and gelatinised cassava starch. *Ibid.*, The solubilisation of cassava starch in aqueous dimethyl-sulphoxide has been followed viscometrically. **1982** *Jrnl. Exper. Bot.* XXXIII. 1248 The enzyme procedure and assay, using citrus pectin, described here have enabled us to assay endo-PG by viscometry during a 6 h incubation period.

† **viscontal,** *a. Obs.*⁻¹ [f. *viscont* VISCOUNT.] Of or pertaining to a viscount.

1742 J. CLERK in *Bibl. Topogr. Brit.* (1790) III. 71 What you write of the Viscontal seal, found in an urn with bones.

viscontial (vaɪ'kɒntɪəl), *a. rare*⁻¹. [f. *viscont* VISCOUNT + -IAL; cf. VISCONTAL, VISCOUNTIAL *adjs.*] Reminiscent of a viscount.

a **1916** R. ASQUITH in M. Asquith *Autobiogr.* (1920) I. xiv. 276 You beat your tangled music out Lofty, aloof, viscontial.

viscontiel, variant of VICONTIEL *a.*

viscose ('vɪskəʊs, -z), *sb.* [f. VISC(OUS *a.* + -OSE².] **1.** A viscid, orange or brown solution of sodium cellulose xanthate obtained by treating cellulose successively with sodium hydroxide and carbon disulphide, and used to make regenerated cellulose by extruding it into dilute acid and either spinning it into rayon or casting it as film.

1896 *Westm. Gaz.* 10 April 8/2 A.. contract for sacks in this new cotton pulp, to which the name of viscose is given. **1896** C. F. CROSS *Brit. Pat.* 4713 Cellulose.. requires a very much smaller proportion of alkali to convert it into alkali-cellulose suitable for use in other manufactures such.. as that of the substances now known as 'viscose' and 'viscoid'. **1913** CARRIER & MARTIN in G. Martin *Industr. & Manuf. Chem.: Organic* IV. i. 189 Viscose is reconverted into cellulose (1) spontaneously, on long standing; (2) by heating; (3) by treatment with oxidising agents. **1927** T. WOODHOUSE *Artificial Silk* 30 By far the greater percentage of artificial silk is made from Viscose. **1968** *Kirk-Othmer Encycl. Chem. Technol.* (ed. 2) XVII. 179 After filtration, the viscose is transferred to a ripening tank system.., where it is deaerated and ripened to the desired level of xanthation. **1981** *Chem. Abstr.* 17 Aug. 544/1 Emulsion sausages were made in the usual way. Pork and beef casings and synthetic casings (protein, viscose, and polyamide) were used.

2. Rayon made by the viscose process.

1932 A. HUXLEY *Brave New World* iii. 58 Her jacket was made of bottle-green acetate cloth with green viscose fur at the cuffs and collar. **1949** W. GARNER *Textile Lab. Man.* iii. 77 Acetate is sometimes partly saponified, especially for the printing of mixed fabrics of viscose and acetate. **1960** *Guardian* 28 Sept. 8/6 Lilian, helion, terital and viscose are blended with wool in textiles by the high fashion houses. **1972** *Vogue* June 113/3 Candy pink and white cotton and viscose shirtwaister. **1980** GOHL & VILENSKY *Textile Sci.* ii. 32 Viscose and the other two rayon fibres have similar thermal properties to cotton.

3. Special Combs.: **viscose process**, the process for making rayon with viscose as an intermediate product; **viscose rayon**, † **silk** = sense 2 above.

1913 CARRIER & MARTIN in G. Martin *Industr. & Manuf. Chem.: Organic* IV. ix. 214 (*heading*) *The viscose process. **1981** *Kirk-Othmer Encycl. Chem. Technol.* (ed. 3) XVI. 108 Considerable research is underway to replace the viscose process and to improve rayon fiber properties. **1930** *Chem. Abstr.* XXIV. 5153 *Viscose rayons of 120 and 150 denier were treated with Na_2S solns. of various concns. **1957** *Woman* 16 Nov. 25/3 Viscose rayon is quite easy to do [*sc.* dye] at home. **1974** *Sci. Amer.* Apr. 57/3 The largest single use for dissolving pulp is as the raw material for the viscose-rayon process. **1913** CARRIER & MARTIN in G. Martin *Industr. & Manuf. Chem.: Organic* IV. ix. 214 The viscid solution is then spun into a solution of ammonium chloride which separates out the cellulose again, and gives.. '*viscose silk'. **1925** *Good Housekeeping* Apr. 142/3 The remaining variety [of artificial silk], Viscose silk, is now being made in enormous quantities.

† **viscose,** *a. Obs.* [ad. L. *viscōs-us*: see VISCOUS *a.*] Viscid, viscous.

c **1400** *Lanfranc's Cirurg.* 33 (Addit. MS.), Synwys by kynde buþ nessche and viscose. *a* **1425** tr. *Arderne's Treat. Fistula*, etc. 78, It avoideþ souerenly ventosenez, and wonderfully putteþ out viscose fleume & putrified. **1526** *Pilgr. Perf.* (W. de W. 1531) 118 The nature of a passyon of ire or fylthy pleasure of the body is so viscose & cleuynge, that harde it is for a begynner in perfeccyon to put it away whan he wolde. **1727** BAILEY (vol. II), Viscose, clammy, sticky, glewy. **1775** *Phil. Trans.* LXV. 224 A viscose matter, like that which is seen on fish newly caught, issues from them.

visco'simeter, variant of VISCOMETER.

1868 WATTS *Dict. Chem.* V. 1003 *Viscosimeter.* This name is given by Dollfus to an apparatus for measuring the viscosity of colouring liquids thickened with gum, &c. **1882** CROOKES *Dyeing & Tissue-Printing* 381 To test the strength of a sample, it is dissolved in water,.. and tested with the viscosimeter. **1886**, **1925** [see SAYBOLT]. **1944** *Acta Med. Scand.* CXVII. 227 The determinations with viscosimeters having varying dimensions of the capillaries gave no real differences even in sera with very high viscosity. **1974** *Nature* 13 Dec. 572/2 This unexpected phenomenon was further investigated in a modified Couette viscosimeter device.

Hence **visco'simetry** = *viscometry*; **,viscosi'metric** *a.*, **-'metrically** *adv.*

1886 B. REDWOOD in *Jrnl. Soc. Chem. Industry* 29 Mar. 121/2 It is my intention.. to treat the subject of viscosimetry, or the determination of viscosity, as related to the valuation of oils intended for the lubrication of machinery. **1895** BENEDIKT & LEWKOWITSCH *Chem. Anal. Oils, Fats, Waxes* xii. 621 Viscosimetric constants as determined with the new apparatus. **1904** J. LEWKOWITSCH *Chem. Technol. & Anal. Oils, Fats, & Waxes* (ed. 3) II. xv. 933 It if is desired to examine the unsaponifiable portion of a blended oil viscosimetrically. **1944** *Acta Med. Scand.* CXVII. 227 With the aid of this modified instrument it seems, as if viscosimetry would be a simple and useful clinical method. **1956** *Nature* 17 Mar. 517/1 A viscosimetric investigation into the influence of pH and ionic strength on molecular shape of a structural muscle protein. **1975** *Welding Production* May 11/1 A method is proposed of examining electrode coating mixtures by means of capillary viscosimetry. **1976** *Jrnl. Polymer Sci.* (Polymer Physics Ed.) XIV. 309 (*heading*) Abnormal viscosimetric behavior of homopolymers in mixed solvents and preferential solvation.

viscosity (vɪ'skɒsɪtɪ). Also 5–6 viscosite, 6 -tye, 6–7 -tie. [a. OF. *viscosite* (F. *viscosité*) or ad. med.L. *viscōsitās*, f. L. *viscōs-us* viscous: see -ITY. So It. *viscosità*, Sp. *viscosidad*, Pg. *-idade*.]

1. a. The quality or fact of being viscous; viscidity.

a **1425** tr. *Arderne's Treat. Fistula*, etc. 65 Bole with his drynes and viscosite consumiþ þe moistenes. *c* **1530** *Judic. Urines* III. vi. 50b, Suche maner of froth sheweth alway more viscosite.. of humours in yᵉ body, than doyth ony other maner of froth. **1582** HESTER *Secr. Phiorav.* III. iv. 9 It taketh awaie the viscositie in the Stomacke, and openeth the powres. **1620** VENNER *Via Recta* iv. 80 The Perch is.. a little inferiour.., by reason of some viscosity in it. **1669**

BOYLE *Contn. New Exp.* II. (1682) 140 That liquor is very thin, and hath no viscosity to resist the pervading body. **1686** GOAD *Celest. Bodies* I. ix. 31 Rarity is nothing but a Privation of Density,.. Friability of Viscosity. **1733** CHEYNE *Eng. Malady* III. iv. (1734) 304 The phlegm in the Glands.. is nothing but the Viscosity of the Serum of the Blood. **1771** T. PERCIVAL *Ess.* (1777) I. 190 To dissolve a general lentor and viscosity of the whole mass of fluids. **1821** W. P. C. BARTON *Flora N. Amer.* I. 65 The extreme viscosity of its pubescence, has caused it to receive the specific name it bears. **1899** *Allbutt's Syst. Med.* VII. 245 The resistances due to the viscosity of the blood in the arteries.

fig. **1662** M. W. *Marriage-Broaker* v. i, So I, by my viscosity, Labouring for life in love-lime [am] drown'd in Cupid's galli-pot. **1902** *Spectator* 29 Nov. 825/1 Vehicular traffic.. will.. block itself from its inherent viscosity.

attrib. **1898** *Allbutt's Syst. Med.* V. 461 The determination of the viscosity coefficient of the blood.

b. ***magnetic viscosity***, tendency on the part of a magnetic medium to retard the magnetizing force.

1892 *Electrical Engineer* 16 Sept. 287/1 Up to the frequency tried—*i.e.*, about 125 per second—there is no sign of magnetic viscosity; the magnetic cycle is unaffected [etc.].

c. In scientific use, the tendency of a liquid or gas to resist by internal friction the relative motion of its molecules and hence any change of shape; the magnitude of this, as measured by the force per unit area resisting a flow in which parallel layers unit distance apart have unit speed relative to one another; also called ***absolute*** or ***dynamic viscosity***; ***kinematic viscosity***, the dynamic viscosity divided by the density of the fluid.

1866 J. C. MAXWELL in *Phil. Trans. R. Soc.* CLVI. 249 The viscosity of a body is the resistance which it offers to a continuous change of form, depending on the rate at which that change is effected. *Ibid.* 254 Suppose that this friction is equal to a tangential force f on every square foot, then $f = \mu v/a$, where μ is the coefficient of viscosity, v the velocity of the upper plane, and a the distance between them. **1880** *Proc. London Math. Soc.* XI. 58 If ν be the kinematic viscosity. **1913**, etc. [see POISE *sb.*[2]]. **1921** A. W. JUDGE *Automobile & Aircraft Engines* viii. 309 The kinematical viscosity of air is thirteen times that of water. **1927** SCHODER & DAWSON *Hydraulics* xvi. 275 The unit of absolute viscosity is called a poise. **1943** R. C. BINDER *Fluid Mech.* v. 50 Viscosity = shearing stress/*rate* of shearing strain. Sometimes the foregoing term is called absolute viscosity. Probably a better term would be dynamic viscosity. **1962** J. M. MCKELVEY *Polymer Processing* ii. 41 In general, liquid viscosities decrease and gas viscosities increase with increasing temperature. **1964** [see STOKE(S *sb.*[4]]. **1979** C. A. MARCHAJ *Aero-Hydrodynamics of Sailing* ii. 169 The kinematic viscosity of water.. needed for Reynolds Number computation at the 'normal' temperature of 15°C is.. $1{\cdot}23 \times 10^{-5}$ ft^2/sec.

2. A viscous substance; a collection of viscous matter. Cf. VISCIDITY 2.

1545 RAYNALD *Byrth Mankynde* 56 Linesede oyle, or oyle of fenegreke, or the viscosite of holioke, and suche other. **1597** A. M. tr. *Guillemeau's Fr. Chirurg.* 27b/2 When the stomacke is burthened with anye crudityе of vndigested meat or drincke, or with anye other viscositye whatsoever. **1646** SIR T. BROWNE *Pseud. Ep.* 80 As is observable in drops of syrup, oyle and seminall viscosities. **1651** FRENCH *Distill.* v. 143 It openeth obstructions, and purgeth viscosities of the stomack and bowells. **1707** FLOYER *Physic. Pulse-Watch* 297 These Viscosities depend on Heat. **1794** R. J. SULIVAN *View Nat.* I. 493 The sand.. has, by the means of a calcareous viscosity infiltrated by the sea, become so hard, as to become stone.

3. Special Comb.: **viscosity index**, a number expressing the degree to which the viscosity of an oil is unaffected by temperature.

1929 DEAN & DAVIS in *Chem. & Metallurgical Engin.* XXXVI. 618/1 This system of classification permits expressing the viscosity-temperature coefficient of an oil as a simple function of its Saybolt Universal viscosities at 100 and 210 deg. F. This function, hereafter referred to as the 'viscosity index', is independent of the actual viscosity of the oil. **1977** *Lubricants Business* (Shell Internat. Petroleum Co.) 3 These [additives] are chemical compounds which supplement the properties of the mineral base oil; for example, to reduce wear of moving parts.. and to improve viscosity index.

viscount ('vaɪkaʊnt). Forms: α. 3–6 viscounte (4 vescownte), 5– viscount (6 viscont). β. 5 vycounte, vicounte, vicound, 6 *Sc.* vecount, 6–8 vicount (7 vicont). [a. AF. *ves-*, *viscounte* (*-cunte*, *-conte*), OF. *visconte*, *viconte* (F. *vicomte*), f. *vis-*, VICE- + *counte* COUNT *sb.*[2], after med.L. *vicecomes*: cf. VICE-COUNT. So It. *visconte*, Pg. *visconde*, Sp. *vizconde*.]

1. *Hist.* One acting as the deputy or representative of a count or earl in the administration of a district; in English use *spec.* a sheriff or high sheriff.

1387 TREVISA *Higden* (Rolls) VIII. 37 The erle Pictaveuse.. ravesched his owne viscountes wyf. *Ibid.* 165 Oon Wydomarus, viscounte of Lemovik.. foond greet tresour of gold. ? *a* **1400** *Morte Arth.* 1984 Sir Valyant of Vyleris.. made siche avowez, To venquyse by victorie the vescownte of Rome! **1484** CAXTON *Chivalry* 23 Kynges oughte to haue under them dukes, Erles, vycountes and other lordes. *a* **1513** FABYAN *Chron.* VII. (1811) 287 Otho.. pursued after yᵉ vaungarde of the kyng, of yᵉ which were capitayns yᵉ vicounte of Mylyon, and one named fryer Garny. **1568** GRAFTON *Chron.* II. 113 The Vicount of Melun, a verye noble man of the realme of Fraunce. **1579** *Expos. Termes Law* 181b, Viscount is a magistrate, and officer, of grat authoryty whom wee commonly call (Sherife). **1630** WADSWORTH *Pres. Estate Spain* 32 Vicountes of Spayne, and the value of their Lordships, of which they are Vicounts. **1710** J. HARRIS *Lex. Techn.* II, *Viscount*,.. *Vicount*, signifies as much as Sheriff. **1861** LD. BROUGHAM *Brit. Const.* iii. 42 All the freeholders assembled under the viscount or sheriff. **1867** FREEMAN *Norm. Conq.* (1877) I. v. 302 Neal, the valiant Viscount of the district.

Comb. **1611** COTGR., *Vicomptier*, of a Vicount, Vicountlike.

b. In the island of Jersey: (see quots.).

1694 FALLE *Jersey* ii. 65 Before whom rideth the Viscount, or Sheriff, with his Staff of Office erected, one End thereof on the Pommel of his Saddle. **1862** ANSTED *Channel Isl.* IV. xxiii. 525 In Jersey there is an officer called Vicomte, or Viscount, who represents the High Sheriff of an English county.

2. A member of the fourth order of the British peerage, ranking between an earl and a baron. Occas. contracted *Visc.*, *Visct.*

This use of the title dates from the reign of Henry VI, when John, Baron Beaumont, was created Viscount Beaumont by letters patent of 12th February, 1440.

1450 *Rolls of Parlt.* V. 189/2 Notwithstondyng that Viscountes were not erecte nor create, in the tyme of.. oure Fadre. *c* **1475** *Contin. Brut* 602 þe Duke of Northfolke, þe Erle of Warwyk, Lord Facounbryge, & Vicound Bowser. *a* **1548** HALL *Chron., Rich. III*, 25b, Fraunces lorde Louell was then made Vicount Louell, and the kynge his chamberlain. *Ibid., Hen. VIII*, 190 The kyng.. created the vicount Rochforth Earle of Wilshire, and the vicount Fitzwater was created Earle of Sussex. **1628** BURTON *Anat. Mel.* (ed. 3) I. ii. III. xi, A Knight would be a Baronet, and then a Lord, and then a vicount, and then an Earle. **1631** MILTON *Ep. M. Win.* 3 The honour'd Wife of Winchester, A Viscounts daughter, an Earls heir. *a* **1700** EVELYN *Diary* 17 Oct. 1664, I went with my Lord Visct. Cornebury to Cornebury in Oxfordshire. **1765** BLACKSTONE *Comm.* I. 385 All degrees of honour are not of equal antiquity. Those now in use are dukes, marquesses, earls, viscounts, and barons. **1840** *Penny Cycl.* XVII. 369/2 Peers of the Realm;.. the persons who fall under this description are the dukes, marquesses, earls, viscounts, and barons. **1882** CUSSANS *Her.* (1893) 180 The privilege of wearing Coronets was accorded to Viscounts by James the First.

3. In Continental usage: The son or younger brother of a count.

1848 THACKERAY *Van. Fair* xxviii, The postillion who drove us [to Waterloo] was a *Viscount*, a son of some bankrupt Imperial General.

viscountcy ('vaɪkaʊntsɪ). [f. prec. + -CY.] The title, dignity, or rank of a viscount.

1868 *Daily News* 6 July, He exchanges a barony in the peerage of Ireland.. for a viscountcy, the fourth order in the peerage of the United Kingdom. **1884** *L'pool Mercury* 3 Mar. 5/1 Her Majesty has conferred the dignity of a viscountcy upon Sir Henry B. W. Brand. **1887** *Twin Soul* I. xvi. 169 Neither Baronetcy nor Viscountcy rewarded his zeal.

viscountess ('vaɪkaʊntɪs). [See VISCOUNT and -ESS. So F. *vicomtesse*, It. *viscontessa*, Sp. *vizcondesa*, Pg. *viscondessa*.]

1. The wife of a viscount; a peeress of the fourth order of nobility.

1475 *Rolls of Parlt.* VI. 134/1 Margaret Viscountesse Lisle, wyfe of the said Henry Bodrugan, which is a grete estate of this Reame. **1525** LD. BERNERS *Froiss.* II. lxi. 80b/2 The erle then sent letters.. desyrynge the kynge to suffre his cosyn the vycountes to be in peas. **1529** *Act 21 Hen. VIII*, c. 13. §17 Any Chapeleyne of any Duches Marques Countesse Vyscountesse or Baronesse. **1578** *Chr. Prayers* in *Priv. Prayers* (1851) 521 *The Viscountess.* Viscountesses I do not spare; For of them I have no care. **1643** *Docq. Lett. Pat. at Oxf.* (1837) 377 A Lease made.. to the said Viscountesse of parcell of the lands. **1689** *Lond. Gaz.* No. 2444/1 A Pursuivant, a Vicountess, Vicounts. **1728** CHAMBERS *Cycl.* s.v. *Vicount*, A Viscountess may have her Gown bore up by a Woman, out of the Presence of her Superiors; and in their Presence by a Man. **1753** GRAY *Long Story* 134 Why, what can the Viscountess mean? **1805** in A. Duncan *Nelson* (1806) 333 His relict Lady Viscountess Nelson. **1876** T. HARDY *Ethelberta* (1890) 317 Rather disappointed at this aspect of a viscountess's life. **1890** FROUDE *Ld. Beaconsfield* xiv. 211 Mrs. Disraeli became Viscountess Beaconsfield.

2. A particular size of slate.

1878 D. C. DAVIES *Slate & Slate Quarrying* 136 Princesses.. Duchesses.. Marchionesses.. Countesses.. Viscountesses 18 × 9.. Ladies.

viscountial (vaɪ'kaʊntɪəl), *a. rare.* [f. VISCOUNT + -IAL.] = VICONTIEL *a.*

1751 *Eng. Gazetteer* s.v. *Lincoln*, This city is a Co. of itself, and has a viscountial jurisdiction for 20 m. round.

†**viscountry.** *Obs.*[−1] [-RY.] = next.

a **1661** FULLER *Worthies, Westminster* II. (1662) 242 He forgot that he was but Lord Verulam. A Viscountry that began and ended in him dying issu'less.

'**viscountship.** Also 7 vicount-. [f. VISCOUNT + -SHIP.] The dignity of a viscount; a viscountcy.

1611 [see VISCOUNTY 2]. *a* **1647** HABINGTON *Surv. Worcs.* (Worcs. Hist. Soc.) I. 33 Concearninge the Devereuxes, in whom are included the Earldome of Essex and vicountshyp of Hereford. **1651** HOWELL *Venice* 25 Crema was a long time under the Vicountship of Milan untill the yeer 1405. **1881** MRS. LYNN LINTON *My Love* I. xii. 215 The few years of his Viscountship.

viscounty ('vaɪkaʊntɪ). Also 6–7 vicountie, 8 -ty. [f. VISCOUNT + -Y. Cf. OF. *vis-*, *viconte(i*, etc., F. *vicomté*, It. *viscontado*, Sp. *viz-*, Pg. *viscondado*, and med.L. *vicecomitatus*.]

†**1.** A viscount. *Obs.*[−1]

1586 J. HOOKER *Hist. Irel.* in *Holinshed* II. 131/2 From thense by iourneies he marched and went to Corke, being met in the waie by the vicounties of Roch and Barrie, and by sir Corman Mac Teege.

2. *Hist.* The office or jurisdiction of, the territory under the authority of, a viscount.

1611 COTGR., *Vice-conte*, a vicountie, a vicountship. **1706** PHILLIPS (ed. Kersey), *Viscounty*, the Territory of a Viscount; a sort of Lordship, or Jurisdiction in France; as The Viscounty of Turenne is very considerable. **1756** NUGENT *Gr. Tour, France* IV. 286 Caen has a provostship, a presidial, a vicounty, an office of the finances of the admiralty, and other royal tribunals. **1792** A. YOUNG *Trav. France* 6 Mons. Colmar, a Jew, bought the seignory and estate, including the viscounty of Amiens, of the Duke of Chaulnes. **1859** JEPHSON *Brittany* xviii. 288 The Viscounty of Dinan.. became.. the heritage of a young lady. **1868** FREEMAN *Norm. Conq.* (1876) II. viii. 252 William was now at a point in Neal's own viscounty, at no great distance from his own castle. **1898** S. EVANS *Holy Graal* 46 Five brothers shared among them the viscounty of that city [Marseilles].

3. = VISCOUNTCY.

1859 LEVER *Dav. Dunn* lxxii, 'But the title?' 'The Viscounty goes with the English property.' **1874** DIXON *Two Queens* XVIII. vii. III. 353 About the time when he received the viscounty of Rochford. **1905** *Westm. Gaz.* 9 Nov. 10/2 His Majesty has.. been pleased to confer the dignity of a Viscounty upon Lord Iveagh, K.T.

viscous ('vɪskəs), *a.* Forms: 5–7 viscouse, 6 vyscous, 6– viscous; 6 vys-, viscus. [a. AF. *viscous* (Gower), or ad. L. *viscōsus* (cf. VISCOSE *a.*), f. *viscum* (also *viscus*) mistletoe, birdlime made from mistletoe-berries. Cf. F. *visqueux*, It., Sp., Pg. *viscoso*.]

1. a. Of substances: Having a glutinous or gluey character. Cf. VISCID *a.* 1.

c **1400** *Lanfranc's Cirurg.* 33 Senewis bi kynde ben neische & viscouse. **1533** ELYOT *Cast. Helthe* (1541) 8b, Flewme,.. thycke, viscouse lyke byrde lyme and heuy. **1542** BOORDE *Dyetary* xii. (1870) 264 The whyte of an egge is viscus and colde. **1547** —— *Brev. Health* §207 By eatynge of euyl & vyscus meates & euyl drinkes. **1578** LYTE *Dodoens* 721 The fruit is.. of a viscus or clammie substance. **1605** TIMME *Quersit.* I. x. 39 He cast up from his stomacke all impurity, tough and viscous. **1664** POWER *Exp. Philos.* I. 52 A Nitt is an Egge glewed by some viscous matter to the sides of the hair it sticks to. **1686** GOAD *Celest. Bodies* I. xviii. 120 Gossamere.. is nothing else but the viscous misty vapour, furled up by the warm alteration of the Air. **1718** J. CHAMBERLAYNE *Relig. Philos.* I. ix. §3 A viscous Liquor like Turpentine. **1756** C. LUCAS *Ess. Waters* I. 37 Some sustain, that the Chaos.. was a mass of a certain kind of viscous or mucous water. **1822** IMISON *Sci. & Art* I. 107 Water and Mercury may be considered as among the most perfect fluids. Others as oil &c. are viscous or imperfect fluids. **1859** W. H. GREGORY *Egypt* II. 72 The rocky walls were black and sticky, and seemed to sweat a thick, fatty, viscous liquor. **1897** *Allbutt's Syst. Med.* II. 800 The blood drawn during life is dark and viscous.

transf. **1899** *Allbutt's Syst. Med.* VI. 158 Contact with the abnormal surface sets up an immediate viscous metamorphosis of the platelets.

b. *Physics.* Imperfectly fluid; intermediate between solid and fluid; adhesively soft. Also used with abstract sbs. (as *state*, etc.).

(*a*) **1847** WHEWELL *Hist. Induct. Sci.* (ed. 2) XVIII. III. 683 The ice of a glacier is.. supposed to be a plastic or viscous mass. **1863** BARING-GOULD *Iceland* 194 The edges of the molten [lava] stream cooling and resisting the tension of the still viscous centre. **1872** C. KING *Mountain. Sierra Nev.* xii. 261 The water converted into steam, blew up the viscous rock in such forms as we find. **1880** *Times* 1 Dec. 10 His researches on tidal retardation from the action of a satellite on a viscous planet.

(*b*) **1830** HERSCHEL *Study Nat. Phil.* 223 The solid, liquid, and aëriform state, to which, perhaps, ought to be added the *viscous*, as a state intermediate between that of solidity and fluidity. **1853** KANE *Grinnell Exp.* viii. (1856) 57 Forbes' beautifully simple views of a viscous movement. **1860** TYNDALL *Glac.* II. xvi. 311 The inquiry as to what Professor Forbes really meant when he propounded the viscous theory. **1863** —— *Heat* ii. §34. (1870) 36 The viscous character of the space between the poles instantly disappears.

c. ***viscous flow***, laminar flow (see LAMINAR *a.* 2a).

1930 [see TURBULENT *a.* 2c]. **1973** FOX & MCDONALD *Introd. Fluid Mech.* viii. 311 (*caption*) Details of viscous flow around an airfoil. **1979** [see STREAMLINE *sb.* 1b].

2. *fig.* Adhesive, sticky.

1605 BACON *Adv. Learn.* II. xxiii. §33. 100 These graue solemne wittes.. haue more dignity then fœlicity: But in some it is nature to bee somewhat viscouse and inwrapped, and not easie to turne. **1660** in *Harl. Misc.* (1809) I. 276 Our magistracy and judicatures.. have.. been intrusted in such viscous and birdlimed fingers.

3. *Bot.* Of leaves: = VISCID *a.* 2.

1712 tr. *Pomet's Hist. Drugs* I. 37 Leaves, like those of Linseed, but.. more viscous. **1857** A. GRAY *First Less. Bot.* Gloss., *Viscous*,.. having a glutinous surface.

Hence '**viscously** *adv.*

1878 ABNEY *Photogr.* 55 Note if the collodion flows freely, viscously, or lumpily.

'**viscousness.** Now *rare* or *Obs.* [f. prec.] The quality of being viscous; viscosity.

1594 PLAT *Jewell-ho., Soyle* 28 It is an erronious opinion to thinke that Marle.. is to be knowne from other moulds by the fattiness, or viscousness thereof. **1612** WOODALL *Surg. Mate* Wks. (1653) 238 The thicknesse and viscousnesse of Sulphur. **1674** GREW *Anat. Pl., Disc. Mixture* v. vi. §3 The very Cause of the said Viscousness of Phlegm, is chiefly some great Acidity in the Blood. **1706** STEVENS *Span. Dict.* I, *Viscosidad*, Viscousness, Clamminess. **1757** T. BIRCH *Hist. Royal Soc.* IV. 256 Dr. Lister.. added, that holly might turn [into stone] suddenly by reason of its viscousness and tenacity.

'viscuous, *a. rare.* [Irreg. f. L. *viscum, -us* + -OUS.] Viscous. Also *transf.*
In quot. 1936 perhaps a misprint.
1603 HOLLAND *Plutarch's Mor.* 618 They testifie..a repletion of grosse, viscuous or slimy humours, and a great perturbation of the spirits within. **1635** SWAN *Spec. M.* v §2 (1643) 135 When the Exhalation by reason of the want of viscuous matter is not enflamed. **1655** T. VAUGHAN *Euphrates* 24 It is even so with the World, for it was originally made of a seed, of a seminall viscuous Humidity or Water. **1705** *Phil. Trans.* XXV. 1977, I expected Water, but there was only a viscuous darkish Humour. **1706** LONDON & WISE *Retir'd Gard'ner* I. ii. 8 The coldest and most viscuous Dungs or Soil, such as Cows-Dung. **1771** *Encycl. Brit.* II. 468 The albumen is a cold, viscuous, white liquor in the egg. **1932** S. GIBBONS *Cold Comfort Farm* iii. 32 Growing with the viscuous light that was invading the sky. **1936** *Jrnl. R. Aeronaut. Soc.* XL. 11 Heat generated in the blades in overcoming viscuous drag also plays a part in determining the distribution of ice.
Hence **'viscuousness**.
1644 DIGBY *Nat. Bodies* xxiii. (1658) 262 The solidness and viscuousness of the substance will not permit it to evaporate.

‖**'viscus^{1}**. *Obs. rare.* [app. a. L. *viscus* birdlime, glue.] A soft viscous substance or mass.
1643 J. STEER tr. *Exp. Chyrurg.* viii. 36 This following Viscus..incarnateth all sorts of corrupt ulcers. **1673** RAY *Journ. Low C.* 457 Snails taken alive shells and all, and pounded in a mortar till they become a perfect pap or *viscus*.

‖**viscus^{2}** ('vɪskəs). *Anat.* [L. *viscus*, usually in pl. *viscera* VISCERA.] One or other of the soft internal organs of the body.
1728 CHAMBERS *Cycl.*, *Liver*, a large glandulous Viscus, of a red sanguine Colour [etc.]. **1754–64** SMELLIE *Midwif.* I. 144 A tension of the part ensues affecting the nerves of that Viscus. **1771** *Encycl. Brit.* I. 238/1 It passes next behind the liver, through the great sinus of that viscus. **1804** ABERNETHY *Surg. Obs.* 236, I felt the bladder, and could puncture that viscus. **1839–47** *Todd's Cycl. Anat.* III. 208/2 In other parts of the body they assume various appearances peculiar to each viscus or organ. **1879** SPENCER *Data Ethics* iii. 33 Imperfection of any viscus, as lungs, heart or liver. *transf.* **1829** T. CASTLE *Introd. Bot.* 260 Sap or lymph.. must either be intermediately conveyed to some viscus proper to give it elaboration, or immediately distributed throughout the whole body of the plant.

visdamme, obs. variant of VIDAME.

visdome, obs. Sc. form of WISDOM.

†**vise**, *sb.*^{1} *Obs.*$^{-1}$ [Cf. VISE *v.*^{1}] View, contemplation, regard.
a **1450** MYRC *Par. Pr.* 66 Thus thys worlde þow moste despyse, And holy vertues haue in vyse.

vise, *sb.*^{2} *Coalmining.* Also 7 **weyse**. [Of obscure origin. Cf. VEISE.] (See quots.)
1672 G. SINCLAIR *Misc. Observ. Hydrostat.* (1683) 281 That which the coal-hewers term the vise, or some of them the weyse of the gae..which in effect is..but a dark vestige of the dipp or rise, that the body which now constitutes the gae, should have had naturally, if it had been perfected. **1789** J. WILLIAMS *Min. Kingd.* I. 13 Your conductor, with the point of a pick, can open up a little of the vise or fissure in the pavement. *Ibid.* 14 The mine has been made in the vise or fissure of the slip. [See also VESTIGIA.] **1886** J. BARROWMAN *Sc. Mining Terms* 69 *Veize, vees, vise*, the line of fracture of a fault or hitch.

‖**visé** ('vize, 'viːzeɪ), *sb.*^{3} [F. *visé*, pa. pple. of *viser* to examine, view: see VISE *v.*^{1}] An entry or note on a passport, certificate, or other official document signifying that it has been examined and found correct; a formal official signature or entry of this nature: = VISA. Now superseded by VISA *sb.*
1842 E. LAWES *Scamper through Italy & Tyrol* iii. 32 It became necessary to obtain the *visé* of the English Consul, who demands a fee of five francs and six sous. **1858** HAWTHORNE *Fr. & It. Note-bks.* (1883) 36 The *visé* of a minister carries more weight than that of a consul. **1904** *Times* 26 Aug. 11/6 The..system..requires Consular visés and certificates for all exports to their country.

vise, var. (now usually *U.S.*) of VICE *sb.*^{2} (see also *sb.*^{1}, etc.); obs. f. VISS; obs. Sc. f. WISE *sb.* (manner); obs. f. WISE *a.*

†**vise**, *v.*^{1} *Obs.* Forms: 4–5 **vise**, 5 **wyse**, 5–6 **vyse**, 6 *Sc.* **vyiss**, **wys**. [Partly (1) aphetic f. of *avise* ADVISE *v.* or DEVISE *v.*: partly (2) a. OF. (mod.F.) *viser*:—pop.L. **visare*, f. *vis-*, ppl. stem of L. *vidēre* to see. Cf. VIZY *v.*^{1}]
1. *trans.* To devise, contrive, make.
c **1325** *Song of Yesterday* 14 in *E.E.P.* (1862) 133 Þis day as leef we may be liht With alle þe murþes þat men may vise To reuele with þise buyrdes briht. *a* **1400–50** *Alexander* 4686 Ȝe vise ȝow þar-of [*sc.* gold] vessell for vanyte & pride. *Ibid.* 5651 Þe names of all þe prouynces & þe places þat he was prince ouire..ware visid all in versis in variant letters.
2. *refl.* To bethink oneself (*well* or *better*); = ADVISE *v.* 5.
a **1330** *Syr Degarre* 542 Nou I schal vise me bette. *c* **1375** *Sc. Leg. Saints* xliii. (*Cecile*) 345 For-þi is gud ȝe wyse ȝu weile, or ȝe tyne al varldis sele. *a* **1400–50** *Alexander* (D.) 751 Þan ayres hym forth alexander & hys aynde takes.., wysez hym how he say wald or he aunswer ȝheldes. *a* **1500** in *Ratis Raving*, etc. 81 Thar ȝha is ȝhai, thar nay is nay, Thai wys thaim weill, ore at thai say. *a* **1568** *'This Warldis joy'* in *Bannatyne MS.* (Hunter. Cl.) 202 Dreid God, do weill;.. Seik weill at weill, and vyiss the voundir weil.
b. *trans.* To think of as useful or necessary.
a **1400–50** *Alexander* 126 Þen takis to him tresour & trusses in baggis,..And oþire necessari notis as nedis to his craftis, To sike salmary dangell as him self vyses.
3. To advise, counsel, direct (a person); = ADVISE *v.* 9.
a **1529** SKELTON *Replyc. agst. Yng. Scolers* 297 Therfore I vyse you to forsake Of heresy the deuyllysshe scolcs. *a* **1553** UDALL *Royster D.* I. iv. (Arb.) 26 Well mocke muche of hir, and keepe hir well I vise ye. **1587** MASCALL *Govt. Cattle, Horses* (1600) 101 To trust all currant horse-coursers, I vise thee to beware.
b. With clause as object; = ADVISE *v.* 9 c.
1581 A. HALL *Iliad* v. 98, I am content answerd the God, but in your place I vise For better end, that Pallas she do take the enterprise.
4. *intr.* To look *on* (something).
a **1400–50** *Alexander* 1539 A vestoure to vise on of violet floures. *Ibid.* 3945 Þan come a fliȝtir in of fowls as fast as it dawid, To vise on as vowtres as vermeon hewid.
b. To reflect *on*; to consider, contemplate.
1568 T. HOWELL *Newe Sonets* (1879) 118 Within whose troubled head, such thronge of thoughts doth rise, That now on this and then on that, I cease not oft to vise.
5. *trans.* To look at or regard attentively or closely; to observe. *rare.*
1550 BALE *Eng. Votaries* II. 88 She loked smothely vpon him (the storye sayth) and he as gentyllye vysed her agayne. *a* **1557** ABP. PARKER *Ps.* cxix. 352 Inure my hart; I purpose yet all whole thy lawes to vyse.
Hence †**vised** *ppl. a.*, = ADVISED *ppl. a.* 1; †**'vising** *vbl. sb.*, advice, counsel.
c **1375** *Sc. Leg. Saints* xxxvi. (*Baptista*) 496 Scho gluterit hyme rycht ofte With wysing fare & wordis softe. **1422** YONGE tr. *Secreta Secret.* 130 Yf thou wolte largely lyue.. thre thyngis thou moste beholde... The thyrde that ye can be viside, and see the Services and Meritis of thy Subiectes.

‖**visé** ('vize, 'viːzeɪ), *v.*^{2} Now *arch.* [See VISÉ *sb.*^{3}] *trans.* To put a visé on (a passport or other document); to endorse or sign as correct and in due order.
1810 B. SILLIMAN *Jrnl. Trav.* (1820) III. 33 This passport had not been indorsed, 'viséd' as they termed it. **1842** BORROW *Bible in Spain* viii, An officer..despatched a soldier with me to the police office, that my passport might be viséed. **1858** *Merc. Marine Mag.* V. 24 Foreign vessels are bound to have their ship papers *viséd* by these..Consular Agents. **1892** *Nation* (N.Y.) 19 May 372/2 The information given to Intendente Viel, who viséed the cablegram.
transf. and *fig.* **1854** *Tait's Mag.* XXI. 166 The same ages visé'd other poets who wrote worse, and better. **1917** J. AGATE *Buzz, Buzz!* 59 Every member of the audience would appear to be in possession of a passport of respectability visé'd by the police. **1927** P. HAMMOND *But —is it Art* 102 Since these New York premières are so important, let us try to attend one, carefully passported and viséd by a regular New Yorker.

vise, obs. Sc. var. WISE *v.* (to direct).

Viséan (vɪ'zeɪən), *a. Geol.* Also **Visean**. [ad. F. *viséen* (E. F. Dupont 1883, in *Bull. de l' Acad. R. des Sci.*, etc., *de Belgique* V. 223), f. *Visé*, name of a town in Belgium: see -AN.] Of, pertaining to, or designating the upper of the two divisions of the Lower Carboniferous (Dinantian) in Europe. Also *absol.*
1905 *Q. Jrnl. Geol. Soc.* LXI. 264 If I am correct in correlating the Lower Viséan of the Belgian Geological Survey with the *Syringothyris*-Zone of the Bristol area, the terms Tournaisian and Viséan, as employed by me in this paper, do not bear their original connotation. *Ibid.* 265 The Tournaisian and Viséan facies are essentially distinct. **1956** W. EDWARDS in D. L. Linton *Sheffield* 22 The imposing scarp along the north side of the outcrop at Castleton, with its reef-aprons..referred to movements of the Derbyshire 'massif' in relation to the 'basin' north of it, during Visean times. **1969** BENNISON & WRIGHT *Geol. Hist. Brit. Isles* ix. 207 Goniatites have shown that only the Lower Limestone Group belongs to the Viséan. **1983** *Rep. Inst. Geol. Sci.* No. 82/12. 1/1 The Carboniferous rocks [exposed at Benburb, County Tyrone] fall within the Viséan Series of the Dinantian.

viseire, obs. form of VIZIER.

viseite ('viːzeɪaɪt). *Min.* Also **viséite**. [a. F. *viséite* (J. Mélon (after G. Cesàro) 1942, in *Ann. Soc. géol. Belgique* LXVI. B53), f. as VISÉAN *a.*: see -ITE^{1}.] A hydrous basic calcium and aluminium silicophosphate occurring as translucent isometric crystals of a white, bluish, or yellowish colour.
1944 *Chem. Abstr.* XXXVIII. 6244 In the examn. of the minerals which occur with delvauxite at Visé, a new mineral was found to which the name viseite was given. **1975** *Nature* 27 Feb. 722/1 Among the minerals described to have any significant degree of P(V)–Si(IV) partial substitution are viseite, nagatelite and wilkeite.

†**'visely**, *adv. Obs.*$^{-1}$ [Aphetic f. of *avisely* ADVISEDLY *adv.*] Carefully, attentively, prudently.
c **1380** WYCLIF *Wks.* (1880) 278 Þat þe sotil amortasynge of seculer lordischipis þat is don bi menene hondis in fraude of þe kyngis statute be visely enquyred.

†**'visement**. *Obs.* In 5–6 **vyse-**, **vysment** (5 *Sc.* **viss-**, **wys-**). [Aphetic f. of *avisement* ADVISEMENT, or directly a. OF. *visement* (rare) f. *viser* VISE *v.*^{1}] Consideration, deliberation, reflection, thought.
? **1414** *26 Pol. Poems* (1904) 58 Wiþ wit and vysement all amende. Lete werk be witnes ȝe can ȝoure Crede. *c* **1440** *Jacob's Well* 170 Þe ferst spanne muste be forthowȝt in thynkyng of þi synnes be-forn, wyth a full vysement, to brynge hem to þi mynde. *c* **1500** *Debate Carpenters Tools* 25 in Hazl. *E.P.P.* I. 80 Thou arte a fole in that case: For thou spekes without vysment. **1535** W. STEWART *Cron. Scot.* (Rolls) II. 353 And syne agane to him so said this king, Without lang vysment in so grit ane thing. *a* **1568** *Be Gratious Ground* 85 in *Bannatyne MS.* (Hunter Cl.) 242 With vertewous vyssment counsall gude reasoun.

†**'visenage**. *Obs.*$^{-1}$ [Of obscure origin.] A term of abuse applied to a woman.
14.. *Beryn* 1012 'Go home, lewde visenage, þat evil must þowe the!' Quod Beryne to the damesell, & gan hir fray & feer.

visenomy, obs. variant of VISNOMY.

viser, *v. rare.* [a. F. *viser*: see VISÉ *v.*^{2}] *trans.* = VISÉ *v.*^{2}
1833 L. RITCHIE *Wand. by Loire* 105 At Tours, they refused..to viser our passports. **1905** *Daily Chron.* 3 July 5/1 The consulates are overwhelmed with applications to viser passports for people going abroad.

viser(e, obs. forms of VISOR *sb.*, VIZIER.

†**'visern**, *sb. Obs.* In 5 **vy-**, 5–6 **viserne**, 6 *Sc.* **vis(s)orne** (7 *Sc.* **vizerne**). [Altered form of *viser* VISOR *sb.*^{1}] A visor or vizard. Also *fig.*
c **1400** *Anturs of Arth.* xxxii, Then he auaylet vppe his viserne fro his ventalle. **1483** *Cath. Angl.* 402/1 A vyserne, *larva.* **1561** DAUS tr. *Bullinger on Apoc.* (1573) 30b, Thus the very sonne of God plucketh of the viserne from these varlets. *a* **1572** KNOX *Hist. Ref.* IV. Wks. 1848 II. 406 For I see the pure flock in no less daunger nor it hes bene at ony time befoir, except that the Devill hes gottin a visserne upon his face.
Hence †**'visern** *v.*, †**'viserned** *ppl. a.*, = VISOR *v.*, VISORED *ppl. a.*
1483 *Cath. Angl.* 402/1 To vyserne, *larvare.* *a* **1598** ROLLOCK *Serm.* ix. Wks. (1849) I. 406 All ar visorned folk: he cummis out, scho cummis out, all masked and disaguysed.

†**visevase**. *Obs.*$^{-1}$ In 5 **vyseuase**. [a. obs. Du. and Flem. *vise-*, *viese-vase* (Kilian; W.Flem. *viezeveze*) phantom; mod.Du. has *viezevaas*, *-waas* prank, trick, grimace.] A vain or empty matter.
1481 CAXTON *Reynard* iv. (Arb.) 8 Now maketh kywaert the hare a complaynt also, that thynketh me a vyseuase.

†**'visgee**. *Obs. rare.* Also 7 *pl.* **vysgeis**. [app. ad. Sp. and Pg. *fisga* in the same sense.] (See quot. 1620 and FIZGIG 4.)
1593 *Sir F. Drake Revived* (1628) 45 Such poore weapons as they had: viz. a broken pointed Rapier, one old Visgee and a rustie Caliuer: Iohn Drake took the Rapier, and..Richard Allen the Visegee. **1622** R. HAWKINS *Voy. S. Sea* 42 The Dolphins and Bonito's are taken with certaine instruments of Iron, which we call Vysgeis, in forme of an Eelespeare, but that the blades are round, and the poynts like vnto the head of a broad Arrow.

visgy ('vɪzgɪ). Also **visgie**. *Cornish* and *Devon dial.* = BISGAY.
1777 in *Eng. Dial. Dict.* (1905) VI. 348/2. **1880** COURTNEY & COUCH *Gloss. Cornwall* 62/1 *Visgie*, an agricultural implement, in shape between a mattock and a hammer, for beating down hedges. *Ibid.* 105 Visgy. **1899** 'Q.' *Ship of Stars* iv. 35 A knife lay between his wide-planted feet, and a visgy close behind him on a heap of disturbed sand. **1915** *Blackw. Mag.* Apr. 546/1 The day being Sunday, he could not dare to risk outraging public opinion by carrying shovel or visgy through the open streets. **1954** L. WALMSLEY *Golden Waterwheel* v. 91 For the roots I had a kind of double-bladed mattock, a combination of pick-axe, chopper, adze and hoe, known in Cornwall as a visgy.

Vishnu ('vɪʃnuː). Also 7 **Vistney**, 8 **Wistchnu**, 8–9 **Vishnoo**, **Vishnou**. [Skr. *Vishnu*, prob. f. the root *vish*, and meaning 'all-pervader' or 'worker' (Monier-Williams).] One of the principal Hindu deities, holding the second place in the great triad, but by his worshippers identified with the supreme deity and regarded as the preserver of the world.
1638 SIR T. HERBERT *Trav.* (ed. 2) 42 Bremaw..has power to create all other creatures. Vistney has order given to preserve them. **1763** ORME *Hist. Mil. Trans. Indostan* I. 182 That identical image of the god Wistchnu, which used to be worshipped by the god Brahma. *c* **1790** SIR W. JONES *Hymn to Nárâyena* Wks. 1799 VI. 368 The evil beings, who are feigned to have sprung from the ears of Vishnu. *c* **1791** *Encycl. Brit.* (ed. 3) VIII. 516/1 Many of these enthusiasts will throw themselves in the way of the chariots of Vishnou or Sheevah. *c* **1813** MRS. SHERWOOD *Stories Ch. Catech.* x. 72 At the foot of this tree was a little stone figure of Vishnoo (that is, one of this country's gods). **1877** J. E. CARPENTER tr. *Tiele's Hist. Relig.* 147 In the cultus of Krishna the worship of Vishnu reaches its climax.

Vishnuism ('vɪʃnuːɪz(ə)m). [f. prec. + -ISM.] The worship of Vishnu.
1871 ALABASTER *Wheel of Law* 250 Veneration of holy foot-prints is not a peculiarly Buddhist idea, but is also found in other religions, and particularly in Vishnuism. **1875** SIR W. W. HUNTER in P. E. Roberts *Life* xiii. (1901) 238 Brahma-worship..is a strange mixture of Vishnuism, Sivaism, and something much older. **1882** *Athenæum* 17 June 759/1 Prof. Weber's theory that Christianity shaped to a certain extent Vishnuism.

Vishnuite ('vɪʃnu:aɪt). [f. as prec. + -ITE.] A worshipper of Vishnu; an adherent of Vishnuism. Also *attrib.* or as *adj.*

1871 TYLOR *Prim. Cult.* II. 364 A Vishnuite who has inadvertently killed a monkey..may expiate his offence by a mock sacrifice. **1882** *Athenæum* 17 June 758/3 The great Çivaite and Vishnuite systems of more recent times.

Vishnuvite ('vɪʃnu:vaɪt). [f. as prec., with *v* from the Skr. adj. *vaishṇavá* belonging to Vishnu.] = prec.

The form *Vishnavite* has had some currency.

1883 *Encycl. Brit.* XV. 185/1 The Vishnuvites are chiefly found in the northern districts [of the Madras Presidency]. **1896** *Mission. Herald* (Boston) Oct. 395 This evangelist.. saw a Vishnuvite mendicant approaching..singing a Christian hymn. *Ibid.*, He was singing them in place of his old Vishnuvite hymns.

‖**visibilia** (vɪzɪ'bɪlɪə), *sb. pl.* [L., neut. pl. of *vīsibilis* VISIBLE *a.* and *sb.*] Things seen; visual images.

1936 C. S. LEWIS *Allegory of Love* ii. 45 On the one hand you can start with an immaterial fact, such as the passions which you actually experience, and can then invent *visibilia* to express them. **1982** *Times Lit. Suppl.* 29 Jan. 97/1 Some people see things that they describe as ghosts; we can dispute the name and nature of these visibilia, but not the fact that they are seen. **1982** *PN Rev.* No. 26. 40/1 A theology of the material world..which can offer us a convincingly spiritual account of the *visibilia*.

visibility (vɪzɪ'bɪlɪtɪ). [ad. late L. *vīsibilitāt-*, *vīsibilitās* (Tertull.), f. L. *vīsibilis*: see next and -ITY. So F. *visibilité* (OF. *visibleté*), It. *visibilità*, Sp. *visibilidad*, Pg. *-idade*.]

1. The condition, state, or fact of being visible; visible character or quality; capacity of being seen (in general, or under special conditions).

a. Of the Church, a kingdom, etc.

1581 W. FULKE in *Confer.* II. (1584) H ij b, What visibilitie could there be in those daies.., when there was no face at all of an outward Church? *a* **1591** H. SMITH *God's Arrow* (1593) L j, And consequently visibility (which the Papists make a marke of the Church) is no perpetuall marke thereof. **1629** LYNDE *Via Tuta* Ep. Ded. 1 That the world may know, it is no difficult matter for a meane Lay-man to prooue the ancient visibilitie of the Protestant profession. *a* **1662** HEYLIN *Laud* (1668) 53 He maintained the constant and perpetual visibility of the Church of Christ. **1667** POOLE *Dial. betw. Protest. & Papist* 49 If Christ did indeed promise the perpetual visibility of his Church. **1699** BURNET *39 Art.* xix. 183 Another question may arise out of the first words of this Article, concerning the Visibility of this Church. **1841** MYERS *Cath. Th.* IV. §29. 315 The visibility of the Theocracy gradually grew fainter and fainter from the first establishment of a visible monarchy. **1866** J. G. MURPHY *Comm., Exod.* xv. 18 The kingdom thus rising into visibility never again disappears from the earth.

b. Of things in general.

1614 JACKSON *Creed* III. xxx. §5 The actual visibility of colours wholly depends upon the light as well for existence as duration. **1651** BAXTER *Inf. Bapt.* 74 Where there is not so much as a seeming or visibility, there is no evidence. **1678** CUDWORTH *Intell. Syst.* 407 The Sun gives to things not only their Visibility, but also their Generation. **1737** WHISTON *Josephus, Hist.* v. v. §4 This gate had no doors, for it represented the universal visibility of heaven. **1772** H. BARNES *Pract. Cas. C.P.* (ed. 2) 322 The Affidavits as to Defendant's Visibility were fully answered, and his total Absconding proved. **1794** G. ADAMS *Nat. & Exp. Philos.* III. xxv. 53 They considered the visibility of matter not a necessary consequence of its creation. **1813** SHELLEY *Q. Mab* VII. 13 *note*, But the God of Theologians is incapable of local visibility. **1867** J. HOGG *Microsc.* I. ii. 44 The visibility of the effect depends on the distance of the object from the object-glass. **1882** PROCTER *Fam. Sci. Stud.* 35 The comet.. attracted more attention when it had passed from view than ..during the brief period of its visibility.

c. *spec.* The possibility of (a vessel, etc.) being seen under the conditions of distance, light, atmosphere, etc., existing at a particular time; hence conversely, the possibility of seeing, or the range of vision, under such conditions.

Cf. Harbord *Gloss. Navig.* (1863), s.v. *Weather notation.*

1914 tr. *Baudry's Naval Battle* 265 The radius of visibility must fix the maximum time allowable for final preparations. **1916** SIR J. JELLICOE *Disp.* 24 June, in *Battle of Jutland* 62 The visibility early on 1st June (three to four miles) was less than on 31st May.

d. *fig.* The degree to which something impinges upon public awareness; prominence.

1958 MARCH & SIMON *Organizations* iv. 103 The greater the prestige of the organization..the greater the visibility of the organization. **1975** *New Yorker* 26 May 28/1 These are busy times, and our report doesn't have so very much visibility. **1981** *Nordic Skiing* Jan. 10/3 The purpose of the team is to increase skiing's visibility in this country. **1984** *Observer* 5 Aug. 15/1 From a business standpoint, the visibility Carl receives during the Olympic Games can enhance his value to the companies.

2. a. With *a* and pl. A visible thing or object.

1628 FELTHAM *Resolves* II. [I.] xcii. 269 St. Paul grants, that they may know God, through the visibilities in his Workes. **1646** SIR T. BROWNE *Pseud. Ep.* I. iii. 9 The beatitude of that part which earth and visibilities too weakly affect. **1660** JER. TAYLOR *Worthy Commun.* i. §1. 27 It cannot be natural flesh, however altered in circumstance and visibilities. **1828** CARLYLE *Misc.* (1857) I. 162 Mind, by being modelled in Men's imaginations into a Shape, a Visibility. **1843** —— *Past & Pr.* II. xvi, The Highest God dwells visible in that mystic unfathomable Visibility, which calls itself 'I' on the Earth.

†**b.** = SIGHT *sb.* 1 c. *Obs.*$^{-1}$

1775 JOHNSON in Boswell *Life* (1904) I. 624 Sir, I have seen all the visibilities of Paris, and around it.

†**3.** Appearance, aspect, look. *Obs.*$^{-1}$

1669 BUNYAN *Holy Citie* 114 'And the City lieth four square'... Now both the City, Gates and Wall, were exactly in their Visibility according to the Word.

†**4.** The faculty or power of seeing; the exercise of this; sight, vision. *Obs. rare.*

1616 BULLOKAR *Eng. Expos.*, *Visibilitie*, the abilitie or powre of seeing. **1641** MILTON *Ch. Govt.* v. Wks. 1851 III. 120 Why they choose to live by custome and catalogue, or as S. Paul saith by sight and visibility, rather then by faith. **1733** W. ELLIS *Chiltern and Vale Farm.* 42 The Fibers of Corn or Trees.., that in Clays and Loams have firm and holding Bottoms, and will lie two or three Years to visibility.

'**visibilize**, *v. rare*$^{-1}$. [f. next + -IZE.] *refl.* To make visible.

1899 S. L. WILSON *Theol. Mod. Lit.* 243 Its spirit visibilised and exemplified itself in priests, rabbis, scribes.

visible ('vɪzɪb(ə)l), *a.* and *sb.* Forms: 4 visibil(e, 4–6 visyble, 5–6 **vysyble**, 4– visible (5 visibal, visebill, 6 viscible, *Sc.* vissabill). [a. OF. *visible* (12th c.; F. *visible* = Sp. *visible*, Pg. *visivel*, It. *visibile*), or ad. L. *vīsibilis* f. *vīs-* ppl. stem of *vidēre* to see.]

A. *adj.* **1. a.** Capable of being seen; that by its nature is an object of sight; perceptible by the sense of sight.

a **1340** HAMPOLE *Psalter* ix. 1 Bot i sall loue þe in all þi werkis, and tell all þi wondirs: þat is bath þat ere sen & þat ere noght sene, visibiles & invisibils. *Ibid.* xxxiv. 3 Multiply vengaunce agayns my foes visibils & invisibils. *c* **1383** in *Eng. Hist. Rev.* Oct. (1911) 744 The sacrament of þe auteer which is whiȝt & round visible & palpable. **1426** AUDELAY *Poems* (Percy Soc.) 22 Use vertuys, and leve visibal vayne and vanetė. **1483** CAXTON *Cato* C j b, One onely god..the whyche hath myght and preemynence upon alle thynges vysyble and unuysyble. *c* **1532** DU WES *Introd. Fr.* in *Palsgr.* 920 Colour is lyght incorporate in a body visyble pure & clene. **1550** COVERDALE tr. *Calvin's Treat. Sacram.* Pref. A ij b, He was neuer visyble to the mortall eye, and yet wyll they make him appere at euerie knaues requeste that wyl.. paye theyr..shote. **1597** HOOKER *Eccl. Pol.* v. lviii. §1 It was of necessitie that words..should be added vnto visible elements. **1601** B. JONSON *Poetaster* v. ii, A humane soule made visible in life. **1651** HOBBES *Leviath.* I. x. 46 Put some eminent and visible mark upon the Crest of their Helmets. **1667** MILTON *P.L.* I. 62 Yet from those flames No light, but rather darkness visible Serv'd only to discover sights of woe. *a* **1721** PRIOR *Ess. Opinion* ¶2 All Visible and Audible objects are properly within their Connoissance. **1764** REID *Inquiry* vi. §8 The mathematical consideration of visible figure, which we shall call the geometry of visibles. **1803** IMISON *Sci. & Art* I. 1 Some sorts of matter are visible, or capable of being seen. **1851** ROBERTSON *Serm.* Ser. IV. x. (1876) 124 The visible world presents a different aspect to each individual man. **1871** TYNDALL *Fragm. Sci.* (1879) I. ii. 46 The sun's invisible rays far transcend the visible ones in heating power.

transf. **1646** SIR T. BROWNE *Pseud. Ep.* I. ix. 36 Painters who are the visible representers of things..are not inculpable herein.

b. Of actions, processes, etc.

1560 DAUS tr. *Sleidane's Comm.* 221 Of baptisme, which they saye is a visible and an outward sygne. **1615** T. ADAMS *Two Sonnes* 69 Onely service hath neither ease nor concealment allotted to it, because it consists in a visible action. **1653** W. RAMESEY *Astrol. Restored* 214 [It] denoteth such accidents as are visible in this World. **1664** JER. TAYLOR *Dissuas. Popery* i. 5 This method is the best, the most certain, visible and tangible. **1782** J. BROWN *View Nat. & Rev. Relig.* IV. iii. 362 The Holy Ghost in a visible manner descended upon him at baptism. **1878** STEWART & TAIT *Unseen Univ.* iii. §114. 127 The conversion of visible energy into heat.

c. Of association, organizations, etc., *spec.* of the Church (see CHURCH *sb.* 4 c).

1590 R. ALISON (*title*), A Plaine Confutation of a Treatise of Brownisme,..entitled, a Description of the Visible Church. **1651** C. CARTWRIGHT *Cert. Relig.* I. 109 For Visibility, it is granted that ordinarily the Church is visible, i.e. that there is a visible company of such as professe the truth. **1691** G. KEITH (*title*), The Presbyterian and Independent Visible Churches in New England. **1739** BUTLER *Serm.* Wks. 1874 II. 217 It pleased God to unite Christians in communities or visible churches. **1841** MYERS *Cath. Th.* IV. §29. 315 The first establishment of a visible monarchy. **1839** YEOWELL *Anc. Brit. Ch.* iv. (1847) 35 The Christian Church was intended to be a visible Society. **1879** A. W. HADDAN *Apost. Succession Ch. Eng.* iv. 97 That the Church to which Christians are 'to be added' was a visible organized body upon earth.

d. *visible speech*, (*a*) the distinctive name of a system of phonetic notation devised by A. Melville Bell, consisting of characters or symbols intended to represent the actual position of the vocal organs in the production of speech-sounds; also *attrib.*; (*b*) speech rendered into a visible record by spectrography.

1865 A. MELVILLE BELL (*title*), Visible Speech: a new fact demonstrated. **1883** *Science* I. 474/1 An important immediate use might be made of a few of the Visible-speech symbols. **1886** *Buck's Handbk. Med. Sci.* II. 379/2 Each letter of the Visible Speech Alphabet..is a picture of the vocal organs placed in the proper position for producing the sound indicated. **1947** R. K. POTTER et al. *Visible Speech* i. 4 A sound spectrographic record for the words 'Visible Speech' is shown... The pattern is a new form of visible speech, a system of natural phonetic symbols translated from speech itself. **1953** [see SONOGRAPH 1].

†**e.** Similar or comparable in appearance *to* something. *Obs.*$^{-1}$

1412–20 LYDG. *Chron. Troy* I. 290 Eke of her eyen þe lokys moste horible To a furneis the stremys wer visyble.

2. a. That may be mentally perceived or observed; clearly or readily evident or perceptible; apparent, manifest, obvious.

In earlier use sometimes passing into the sense 'very great, eminent, etc.'

a **1613** SIR T. OVERBURY *A Wife*, etc. (1638) 95 His courting language, visible bawdy jests. **1672** BAXTER *Bagshaw's Scand.* ii. 16 His next subject..is one of the visiblest lyes that ever I saw written by a man. **1676** D'URFEY *Mme. Fickle* IV. ii, 'Tis above the common rate of wonders, and doubtless portends some visible Calamity that threatens the Nation. **1710** LUTTRELL *Brief Rel.* (1857) VI. 597 The majority being so visible, as at least two to one, they declined insisting thereon. **1764** HARMER *Observ.* i. §15. 38 There is a visible opposition betwixt this account..and those words of our Lord [etc.]. **1796** H. HUNTER tr. *St.-Pierre's Stud. Nat.* (1799) II. 391 Whatever charms may appear in..the human figure, there is no visible reason why it's physical effect should exert an influence over animals. **1835** T. MITCHELL *Acharn. of Aristoph.* 445 *note*, A visible decrease in the offences which had been previously committed. **1908** *Animal Managem.* 313 Pneumonia..may ..arise without any visible cause.

†**b.** In the phr. ***it is visible*** followed by clause.

1693 EVELYN *De la Quint. Compl. Gard.* I. 38, I..say, That in case such a Place full of ill Earth, were too low,..it is visible that half the Expence would be sav'd. **1712** SWIFT *Rem. Barrier Treaty* 9 To which if we add the many Towns since taken, [etc.].., it is visible what Forces the State may be able to keep. **1716** ADDISON *Freeholder* No. 32 ¶2 It is visible that great Numbers of them have of late eloped from their Allegiance. **1751** R. PALTOCK *P. Wilkins* xix. (1883) 56/1 So that it was visible he could never fly.

c. Of means, or revenue.

1779 *Mirror* No. 45 ¶7 But all these things a man of fashion can do, without possessing any visible revenue whatever. **1824** *Act 5 Geo. IV*, c. 83 §24 Every Person wandering abroad..not having any visible Means of Subsistence.. shall be deemed a Rogue and Vagabond. **1895** S. R. HOLE *Tour America* xv. 210 He ought to have been apprehended as a vagrant having no visible means of support.

3. a. That can be seen under certain conditions, at a certain time, or by a particular person; in sight; open or exposed to sight or view.

visible horizon: see HORIZON 1.

1667 MILTON *P.L.* XI. 321 On this Mount he appeerd, under this Tree Stood visible. *a* **1677** BARROW *Serm. Jer.* li. 15 Wks. 1686 II. 92 As for example, what would an eye.. signifie, if there were not light prepared to render things visible thereto. **1704** J. HARRIS *Lex. Techn.* I. s.v. *Horizon*, The Sensible or Visible Horizon, is that Circle which limits our Sight. **1713** STEELE *Englishm.* No. 55. 353 This elevated Machine was visible to all the People. **1784** COWPER *Task* III. 232 Philosophic tube, That brings the planets home into the eye Of observation, and discovers, else Not visible, his family of worlds. **1812–16** PLAYFAIR *Nat. Phil.* (1819) II. 281 The disturbance of Jupiter might have so altered its original orbit, as to render the Comet for a time visible from the Earth. **1860** TYNDALL *Glac.* I. ii. 21 The whole glacier was visible to us from its origin to its end. **1868** LOCKYER *Elem. Astron.* §330 When a star is so situated that it is just visible on the eastern horizon.

b. *Comm.* Of stocks or supply: Actually in hand or to be seen.

1882 *Times* 22 Feb., If the statistics relating to the visible supply of grain are to be trusted. **1891** *Daily News* 3 Dec. 2/3 Messrs...report deliveries of copper in England and France last month as 2,095 tons in excess of the supplies, and 'visible' stocks are reduced accordingly.

c. *Econ.* Descriptive of or denoting actual goods exported or imported, as opposed to 'invisible' items such as services rendered or received (cf. INVISIBLE *a.* 1 d).

1882 R. GIFFEN *Use of Import & Export Statistics* vii. 58 As to the increase of our shipping business as a means of accounting for the non-increase of our apparent exports. It is because our invisible exports have been increasing so enormously, that there is less increase of the visible. **1917** J. A. TODD *Mech. Exchange* xiv. 184 Visible and invisible exports alike go to the debit side of the account. **1957** A. C. L. DAY *Outl. Monetary Econ.* xxviii. 365 In this way we get a balance of visible trade: quite literally 'visible', because it only includes goods that can actually be seen as they are put on board ship. **1976** *Economist* 16 Oct. 22/2 In August, 1976, Britain ran a visible trade deficit at an annual rate of £3½ billion, compared with a 1970 deficit of £25m.

d. ***visible index***: an index so arranged that each item is visible.

1916 E. R. HUDDERS *Indexing & Filing* (1919) ii. 26 It is not anticipated that the visible index in any of its forms will ever supersede the card index. **1955** V. GEORGE in W. Ashworth *Handbk. Special Librarianship* iii. 45 The system most usually employed..is some form of visible index.

4. a. Of persons: Capable of being seen or visited; accessible to others; now *esp.*, disposed or prepared to be seen or visited, 'at home' to visitors. (Cf. F. *visible.*)

1722 DE FOE *Plague* (1754) 224 Spreading from that House to other Houses, by the visible unwary conversing with those who were sick. **1772** H. BARNES *Pract. Cas. C.P.* (ed. 2) 322 Objected, on the Part of Defendant, That he was a publick visible Man, and Plaintiff had not endeavoured to arrest him. **1835** LYTTON *Rienzi* II. i, A foreign signor is with him—but to you he is of course visible. **1848** THACKERAY *Van. Fair* lxvii, Jos wasn't up yet; Becky not visible (though she looked at them through the blinds). **1889** F. M. CRAWFORD *Sant' Ilario* ix, He..inquired if he could see the princess. The porter replied that she was not visible, and that the prince had gone out.

b. Of a way of life: Free from any concealment or mystery.

1885 'MRS. ALEXANDER' *At Bay* vii, He has been pretty steady in his attendance at the Bourse, and done well in a quiet way, but his life has been visible and regular.

5. ***visible direction***, in *Optics*, the apparent direction in which an object is seen.

1829 *Nat. Philos., Optics* 42/2 (U.K.S.) These perpendiculars must all pass through one point, which may be called the centre of visible direction.

6. *fig.* In a position of public prominence; well known. Cf. VISIBILITY 1 d.

1977 *Chicago Tribune* 2 Oct. II. 28/1 (Advt.), National leader in health care field has highly visible position available on its corporate headquarters consulting staff. **1978** *Guardian Weekly* 12 Feb. 14/2 The Wilmington Ten affair makes Chavis the most visible of American political prisoners today.

B. *sb.* **1. a.** A visible thing or entity. Chiefly in pl.

1614 JACKSON *Creed* III. xxvii. §5 Our bodily sight, which sees diuers visibles all immediately, not one after, or by another. **1650** H. MORE *Observ.* in *Enthus. Tri.*, etc. (1656) 77 For it is alike easie to see visibles without eyes, as to see invisibles with eyes. *a* **1674** TRAHERNE *Poet. Wks.* (1903) 18 All that in visibles is good Or pure, or fair, or unaccurst. **1721** R. KEITH tr. *T. à Kempis, Solil. Soul* xii. 200 When thou..beholdest the visibles of this whole Creation. **1748** RICHARDSON *Clarissa* (1811) III. 248 That the most charming woman on earth..can excel the meanest in the customary visibles only. **1871** W. H. GILLESPIE *Argt. Being & Attrib. Absolute One* III. §2 (ed. 5) 54 Narrow is their horizon: within it, themselves the only visibles. **1872** *Ibid.* (ed. 6) 188 The things which are seen, were not made of phenomenal visibles. **1895** ZANGWILL *Master* III. i. 277 The flux of centuries, the visibles of Art, the invisibles of Religion.

b. *pl.* Visible exports or imports.

1962 H. O. BEECHENO *Introd. Business Stud.* xv. 143 A country which is running an adverse balance of trade may still have a favourable balance of payments because the gain on 'invisible' items exceeds the loss on 'visibles'. **1968** *Economist* 23 Mar. 64/1 The current account (that is on 'visibles' and 'invisibles' but leaving out movements of investment funds).

2. ***the visible***, that which is visible, esp. the visible world.

1742 YOUNG *Nt. Th.* VI. 246 The visible and present are for brutes, A slender portion! and a narrow bound! **1836** J. GILBERT *Chr. Atonem.* iv. (1852) 102 In his operations in the material universe, God has seen fit..to make known to us the invisible by the visible. **1851** MRS. BROWNING *Casa Guidi Wind.* I. 1159 The last chain-link By which he had drawn from Nature's visible The fresh well-water.

3. The visible part of the electromagnetic spectrum.

1962 [see NERNST a]. **1973** WILLIAMS & FLEMING *Spectrosc. Methods Org. Chem.* (ed. 2) i. 21 The n→π* transitions of α-diketones in the diketo form give rise to two bands, one in the usual region near 290 nm..and a second ..which stretches into the visible in the 340–440 nm region.

'visibleness. [f. prec. + -NESS.] The quality of being visible; visibility.

1581 W. FULKE in *Confer.* II. (1584) I ij, There was a time when visiblenes was no note of the Church. **1605** A. WOTTON *Answ. Pop. Articles* 14 We easily grant a perpetuall continuance of the church, though we denie a necessity of visiblenesse. **1620** T. GRANGER *Div. Logike* 66 Also visiblenesse, touchablenesse, which are inseparable. **1727** BAILEY (vol. II). **1842** MANNING *Serm.* (1848) I. xiv. 195 We have yet to regain the visibleness and consciousness of unity. *Ibid.* xxvi. 392 There is an inwardness and a retirement about it [*i.e.* the Church] even in its visibleness. **1890** *Spectator* 11 Jan. 45/2 The owners feel..as if the visibleness of their wealth constituted a danger.

visibly ('vɪzɪb(ə)lɪ), *adv.* Forms: 4–5 **visibely**, 5 **visibilly**, 5–6 **vysybly**, 6 **visybly**, 5– **visibly** (7 **vissiblie**); also 5 **visablelyche**. [f. prec. + -LY².]

1. In a visible manner (†or form); so as to be visible to the eye or sight.

Passing insensibly into next.

c **1380** WYCLIF *Sel. Wks.* III. 522 Þat same body and blood invisibly, and not þe same visibely. *c* **1400** MAUNDEV. (Roxb.) xvii. 79 Þai growe ilk a ȝere visibilly, so þat þe smale waxez grete. *c* **1420** *Chron. Vilod.* 2141 As þus visablelyche to hurre modur he dude aper. **1484** CAXTON *Fables of Alfonce* xii, The goddesse Venus vysybly shewed her self to me. **1526** *Pilgr. Perf.* (W. de W. 1531) 124 b, Somtyme as it were an aungell of lyght, somtyme visybly, somtyme fantastically. **1591** SHAKS. *Two Gent.* II. vii. 4 The Table wherein all my thoughts are visibly Character'd and engrau'd. **1612** W. COLSON *Gen. Tresury* Advt. A iij b, The other faults escaped in printing, or figures not visibly printed are..corrected with the pen. **1617** J. TAYLOR (Water P.) *Obs. & Trav. fr. Lond. to Hamburgh* Wks. (1630) III. 87/2 If it were possible that the hand of mortall men.. could visibly set forth the magnificent glory of the immortal Creator. **1736** BUTLER *Anal.* I. vii. Wks. 1874 I. 145 A moral scheme of government then is visibly established. **1781** COWPER *Truth* 390 Solyma's interior shrine, Where..Dwelt visibly the light-creating God. **1817** SHELLEY *Rev. Islam* XII. xxxiii. 6 Down that mighty stream..The boat fled visibly —three nights and days. **1825** SCOTT *Betrothed* vi, The mouth visibly arranged itself into a smile of inexpressible sweetness. **1857** W. K. LOFTUS *Trav. Chaldæa & Susiana* 270 Traces of which were still visibly adhering to many of the tablets.

2. So as to be clearly evident, manifest, or perceptible; to an extent which can be (readily) seen or observed; evidently, plainly; manifestly, obviously.

1631 GOUGE *God's Arrows* III. §81. 337 God hath oft visibly shewed himselfe by extraordinary meanes to fight for his. **1647** CLARENDON *Hist. Reb.* I. §9 The Envy..was visibly the cause of the Murther. **1690** LOCKE *Hum. Und.* I. iii. 17 God, having..made the Practice thereof..visibly beneficial to all, with whom the vertuous Man has to do. **1713** BERKELEY *Hylas & Phil.* I. Wks. 1871 I. 282 It being too visibly absurd to hold that pain or pleasure can be in an unperceiving Substance. **1719** DE FOE *Crusoe* I. (Globe) 278, I saw my Deliverance indeed visibly put into my Hands. **1839** JAMES *Louis XIV*, III. 308 A war which had been visibly overhanging them for more than two years. **1856** FROUDE *Hist. Eng.* (1858) I. v. 400 The cardinals were visibly afraid of the position which had been taken by the French king. **1885** 'MRS. ALEXANDER' *At Bay* iv, Lambert was visibly relieved, and his daughter reflected her father's mood.

†**3.** By actual sight. *Obs.*⁻¹

1600 E. BLOUNT tr. *Conestaggio* 314 He cast anchor at Saint Sebastian, beginning visiblie to finde, that the Iland was no lesse fortified then had beene described vnto them.

visie, var. VIZY *Sc.*

visier, var. VIZIER.

†**visiere.** *Obs.*⁻¹ In 5 vysiere. [a. OF. *visiere*: see VISOR *sb.*¹] A visor or vizard.

1485 CAXTON *Chas. Gt.* 226 Tofore the Sarasyns that were on horsback they had ordeyned men on fote whyche had vysieres counterfeyted all black & rede.

Visigoth ('vɪzɪgɒθ). Also **Wisigoth**. [ad. late L. *Visigoth-us*, usually in pl. *Visigothi* (late Gr. *Οὐισίγοτθοι*); the contrast with *Ostrogothi* (OSTROGOTH) has suggested that the first element is to be taken as meaning 'West'.]

1. A member of that branch of the Gothic race which entered Roman territory towards the end of the fourth century and subsequently established a kingdom in Spain, overthrown by the Moors in 711–2; a West-Goth. Chiefly in *pl.*

1647 COTTERELL *Davila's Hist. France* I. I. 4 The famous incursions of..the Visigoths,..and the Longbeards. **1763** SMOLLETT *Trav.* x, This amphitheatre [at Nismes] was fortified as a citadel by the Visigoths. **1780** *Encycl. Brit.* (ed. 2) V. 3349/2 The Romans distinguished the Goths into two classes, the Ostrogoths and Visigoths... The Visigoths settled in Spain in the time of the Emperor Honorius. **1841** W. SPALDING *Italy & It. Isl.* I. 106 The West Goths (Visigoths)..were followed across the Alps in 405 by a new army of the same nation. **1867** E. F. BOWDEN tr. *Fathers Desert* 258 Julian was by birth a Visigoth, and had fallen into slavery through the fortune of war. **1889** J. B. BURY *Hist. Later Rom. Emp.* II. i. I. 64 The event which at length brought him into contact with Stilicho was the rising of the Visigoths. **1906** W. H. HUTTON *Ch. & Barbarians* vi. 73 The Wisigoths identified their heresy with their nationality.

2. *transf.* An uncivilized or barbarous person. Cf. GOTH 2.

1749 H. WALPOLE *Lett.* (1846) II. 307 He..had entirely forgot what Visigoths his countrymen are. **1764** FOOTE *Patron* II. 47 *Sir Thomas.* She [a careless housemaid] merits impaling. Oh, the Hun! *Dactyl.* The Vandal! *All.* The Visigoth.

Visigothic (vɪzɪ'gɒθɪk). Also **Wisi-**. [f. prec. + -IC.] Of or belonging to the Visigoths.

1788 *Encycl. Brit.* (ed. 3) I. 496/1 With regard to the alphabets derived from the Latin, the Lombardic relates to the manuscripts of Italy; the Visigothic to those of Spain. **1818** HALLAM *Mid. Ages* (1872) I. 278 Especially as regards the Visigothic and Burgundian partitions. **1855** KINGSLEY *Westw. Ho!* ix, He was an exceedingly tall and graceful personage, of that *sangre azul* which marked high Visigothic descent. **1884** *Encycl. Brit.* XVII. 655/2 The money of the Iberian Peninsula begins with the Visigothic series, which consists of gold pieces. **1906** W. H. HUTTON *Ch. & Barbarians* vi. 75 The Wisigothic possessions.

visile ('vɪzaɪl), *a.* and *sb.* [f. L. *vīs-us* sight + -ILE, after *tactile*, *audile*.] **A.** *adj.* Responding most readily to visual sensations; thinking predominantly in visual images. **B.** *sb.* A person of this kind; = VISUAL *sb.* 2, VISUALIST I.

1909 [see AUDILE *a.*]. **1927** J. ADAMS *Errors in School* 74 This does not imply that the visiles get their knowledge entirely through the eye. **1940** *Brit. Jrnl. Psychol.* XXXI. 56 The theory of the existence of a 'visile' type. *Ibid.* 60 A theory that adolescents who draw men well tend to be of high..intelligence, to be 'visiles' in their thinking. **1954** J. EVANS *John Ruskin* 411 He [*sc.* John Ruskin] had..a visile mind. **1960** MENON & PATEL *Teaching of Eng. as Foreign Lang.* (ed. 2) iv. 26 Galton classified individuals, with reference to the sense that dominated his memory, into *visiles*, *audiles* and *kinaesthetic*.

visinage, obs. form of VICINAGE.

vision ('vɪʒən), *sb.* Forms: 3–6 **visioun**, 4 **-iun**, **-iowne**, **-eoun**, **vysyoun**, 5 **vysyoune**, 5–6 *Sc.* **wisioun**; 4–5 **vysione**, **vysyon**, 5 **vyssyon**, 5–6 **vysion**; 4– **vision** (5 **uision**, **visionne**), 4–6 **vysioun** (6 *Sc.* **vesyne**). [a. AF. *visiun*, *visioun*, OF. *vision* (= Sp. *vision*, It. *visione*), or ad. L. *vīsiōn-*, *vīsio* sight, seeing, thing seen, f. *vīs-*, ppl. stem of *vidēre* to see.]

1. a. Something which is apparently seen otherwise than by ordinary sight; *esp.* an appearance of a prophetic or mystical character, or having the nature of a revelation, supernaturally presented to the mind either in sleep or in an abnormal state. ***beatific vision***: see BEATIFIC *a.* b.

In early texts *a vision* cannot always be clearly separated from *avision*.

c **1290** *S. Eng. Leg.* I. 52 Seint Edward cam al-so aniȝht ase in a visioun To an holi man þat þere was neiȝ. *a* **1300** *Cursor M.* 4454 Als þai lai in þat prisun, A-naght þam mete a visiun. **1338** R. BRUNNE *Chron.* (1810) 65 Who so lokes his life, & redis his vision, What vengeance ordeyned was on Inglond to be don. *c* **1340** HAMPOLE *Pr. Consc.* 4369 Þis was þat Iohan saw in a vision Of hym þat semed þe virgyn son. **1387** TREVISA *Higden* (Rolls) III. 113 Þat ȝere byfel þe secounde siȝt and visioun of Daniel, of þe aungel þat delyuerede þe children out of þe ouene. *c* **1430** LYDG. *Min. Poems* (Percy Soc.) 98 This prophete.. Be a visioune so hevenly and divyne, Toke a chalice. *c* **1450** *Mirk's Festial* 17 When he had told þe kyng of þys vysion, þe kyng made preche hit ouer all þe reme. **1526** *Pilgr. Perf.* (W. de W. 1531) 3 The seruaunt of god Moyses had moost hye reuelacyons & visyons. **1560** DAUS tr. *Sleidane's Comm.* 65 Secrete teachers that fayned themselves to see visions, and to have talke with God. **1584** LYLY *Sappho* IV. iii. 56, I haue had many phantastical visions, for euen now slumbring by your beddes side, mee thought I was shadowed with a clowd. **1615** G. SANDYS *Trav.* 227 But behold an accident, which I rather thought at the first to haue bene a vision, then (as I found it) reall. **1669** DRYDEN *Tyrannick Love* I. i, *Char.* What did the Vision shew? *Placid...* A Town besieg'd; and on the neighb'ring Plain Lay heaps of visionary Souldiers slain. **1711** ADDISON *Spect.* No. 159 ¶8, I then turned again to the Vision which I had been so long contemplating. **1757** GRAY *Bard* 107 Visions of glory, spare my aching sight. **1802** LEYDEN *Mermaid* xxvi, Like one that from a fearful dream Awakes,..Yet fears to find the vision true. *a* **1859** DE QUINCEY *Dream Fugue* Wks. 1897 XIII. 319 On the ocean, ..the unknown lady from the dreadful vision, and I myself are floating. **1860** PUSEY *Min. Proph.* 80 In the vision, God is understood to have represented things to come, as a picture to the prophet's mind.

b. Without article. (Cf. AVISION 2.)

13.. *Seuyn Sages* (W.) 3809 Als he lay opon a nyght In a dreme, than thoght him right That he was warned in visiowne [etc.]. *a* **1340** HAMPOLE *Psalter* lxxxviii. 19 When þou sayd þat, þou spak in visyon, þat is, in pryue reuelacioun til prophetis. *c* **1420** LYDG. *Assembly of Gods* 1621 To vndyrstand..the mater of Morpheus hys shewyng As he hath the ledde aboute in vysyon. **1508** KENNEDIE *Flyting w. Dunbar* 298 Ȝit of new tressone I can tell the tailis, That cumis on nycht in visioun in my sleip. **1671** MILTON *P.R.* I. 256 Just Simeon and Prophetic Anna, warn'd By Vision, found thee in the Temple. **1723** POPE *Let. to Mrs. Cowper* 26 Sept., Wks. 1769 IX. 431, I could wish you tried something in the descriptive way on any subject you please, mixed with vision and moral. **1732** WATERLAND *Script. Vind.* III. 52 Upon the Foot of this Construction, it is supposed, that Isaiah in prophetic Dream or Vision, heard God speaking to him. **1813** SCOTT *Rokeby* III. xix, Not do I boast the art renown'd, Vision and omen to expound. **1856** STANLEY *Sinai & Pal.* ii. (1858) 132 Such, not in vision, but in the most certain reality, was that double view of Jerusalem from Mount Olivet.

c. A mental concept of a distinct or vivid kind; an object of mental contemplation, esp. of an attractive or fantastic character; a highly imaginative scheme or anticipation.

1592 TIMME *Ten Eng. Lepers* E iv, In the sayde hypocriticall Pharisei then, we see a certaine phantasticall vision, shewing that in forme which it hath not in trueth. **1668** TEMPLE *Wks.* (1720) II. 60, I wish some of his Visions may not give it another Face than what it ought..to receive from the true present State of the Spanish Affairs. **1784** COWPER *Task* I. 451 Upon the ship's tall side he stands, possess'd With visions prompted by intense desire. **1809** CAMPBELL *Gert. Wyom.* III. 5 And, in the visions of romantic youth, What years of endless bliss are yet to flow. **1855** *Poultry Chron.* II. 582/2 Visions of success floated before me all day. **1872** YEATS *Growth Comm.* 212 The Dutch were not excited by those visions of American gold and silver which had inflamed the imagination of the Spaniards. **1876** GLADSTONE *Glean.* (1879) II. 314 The splendid visions which his fancy shaped had taken possession of his mind.

d. A person seen in a dream or trance.

1611 BIBLE *Wisd.* xvii. 4 Sadde visions appeared vnto them with heauie countenances. **1667** MILTON *P.L.* VIII. 367 The vision bright, As with a smile more brightn'd, thus repli'd. **1697** DRYDEN *Æneid* VII. 139 A more than mortal sound Invades his ears; and thus the vision spoke. **1727** DE FOE *Syst. Magic* I. iv. (1840) 105 Ali..failed not to ask the vision how he should obtain his promised assistance in the like cases of difficulty. **1817** SCOTT *Harold* VI. xi, And thou, for so the Vision said, Must in thy Lord's repentance aid.

e. *transf.* A person, scene, etc., of unusual beauty. (Cf. DREAM *sb.*² 3 b.)

1823 SCOTT *Quentin D.* xii, Dost thou think it makes thee fit to be the husband of that beautiful vision? **1896** *Westm. Gaz.* 30 Apr. 2/1 The big dining room is..a vision of walnut and mahogany. **1901** *Daily Chron.* 29 June 8/3 One girl was a remarkable vision in a creamy white cloth Empire coat.

2. a. The action or fact of seeing or contemplating something not actually present to the eye; mystical or supernatural insight or foresight.

1382 WYCLIF *1 Sam.* iii. 1 In tho dais was noon opyn visioun. *c* **1420** *Chron. Vilod.* 2512 Þe same nyȝt þat seynt Dunstone to Salesbury come, He saw by vysione alle þat he saw here, & myche more. *c* **1491** *Chast. Goddes Chyld.* D iv a, The seconde kynde of vysion is callid Spyrytual vysion or Imagynatyf. *Ibid.* D iv b, In yᵉ thirde vision yᵗ is callid Intellectual. **1560** BIBLE (Genev.) *Isaiah* xxviii. 7 Thei faile in vision: thei stomble in iudgement. **1594** HOOKER *Eccles. Pol.* I. xi. 82 The first..beginning here with a weake apprehension of things not seen, endeth with the intuitiue vision of God in the world to come. **1604** E. G[RIMSTONE] *D'Acosta's Hist. Indies* VII. xxiii. 567 It may be, that what the laborer reported, had happened vnto him by imaginary vision. **1657** J. WATT *Vind. Ch. Eng.* 153 Ministers..neither have vision to foretell, nor power to confer, blessing. **1676** DRYDEN *Aurengzebe* I. i, If Love be Vision, mine has all the Fire Which in first Dreams, young Prophets does inspire. *a* **1745** SWIFT *Th. on Var. Subj.* Wks. 1745 VIII. 273 Vision is the art of seeing things invisible. **1836** MACGILLIVRAY *Trav. Humboldt* i. 18 That truths faithfully extracted from the book of nature are alone calculated to enlarge the sphere of mental vision. **1871** FARRAR *Witn. Hist.* iii. 97 It needed, let us say, the divine vision of a Peter, and the inspired eloquence of a Paul, to burst the intolerable yoke. **1899** W. R. INGE *Chr. Mysticism* i. 14 Ecstasy or vision begins when thought ceases, to our consciousness, to proceed from ourselves.

b. Ability to conceive what might be attempted or achieved, esp. in the realm of politics; statesmanlike foresight.

[**1904** CHESTERTON *Napoleon of Notting Hill* II. iii. 107, I fight for your royal vision, for the great dream you dreamt of the League of the Free Cities.] **1926** FOWLER *Mod. Eng. Usage* 695/2 *Vision*, in the sense of statesman-like foresight or political sagacity, is enjoying a noticeable vogue. **1960** M. SPARK *Ballad Peckham Rye* v. 86 'How do you find Weedin?' 'Totally,' Dougal said, 'lacking in vision. It is his fatal flaw. Otherwise quite sane.' **1965** A. J. P. TAYLOR *Eng. Hist. 1914–45* xvi. 593 Truman, the new president, had none of Roosevelt's vision as international leader. **1973** E. F. SCHUMACHER *Small is Beautiful* i. 243 A lack of vision on the part of the socialists themselves. **1982** D. FRASER *Alanbrooke* ix. 217 Churchill had enormous vision. He could and often did impressively surpass his supporters in his imaginative span.

3. a. The action of seeing with the bodily eye; the exercise of the ordinary faculty of sight, or the faculty itself. Also *transf.* (quot. 1854).

c **1491** *Chast. Goddes Chyld.* D iv a, The fyrst is callyd a corporal vision be cause it is seen outwarde bi bodely eye wittes. *c* **1510** MORE *Picus* Wks. 20/2 Because that our felicitie is fulfilled in the vision and fruicion of the humanitie of Christ. *c* **1600** SHAKS. *Sonn.* cxiii, For it [*sc.* my eye] no forme deliuers to the heart..Nor his owne vision houlds what it doth catch. **1644** HAMMOND *Pract. Catech.* I. iii. (1646) 14 *Faith* here is turned into *Vision* there. **1676** HALE *Contempl.* I. 71 A means whereby he might be restored..to blessedness and the vision of his Creator. **1704** NORRIS *Ideal World* II. iii. 201 Vision in itself is the having or perceiving an idea representatively material in consequence of a certain impression made by light upon that expansion of the optick nerve which is at the bottom of the eye. **1718** J. CHAMBERLAYNE *Relig. Philos.* (1730) I. xii. §25 Whether he ever considered the manner how Vision is performed. **1774** M. MACKENZIE *Maritime Surv.* 58 The Distance of the Eye and the Thickness of the Lines should, be previous Trial, be suited to distinct Vision. **1832** BREWSTER *Nat. Magic* iii. 48 Even the vision of natural objects presents to us insurmountable difficulties. **1854** —— *More Worlds* xi. 180 The globular nebulæ of Sir W. Herschel have disappeared as globes under the sharp vision of Lord Rosse's telescope. **1879** HARLAN *Eyesight* iii. 31 To understand anything of the physiology of vision, it is necessary to have a general idea of the way in which images of objects are formed by refracting surfaces.

b. An instance of seeing; a look.

1855 BAIN *Senses & Int.* II. ii. §11 With the blind the case is different;..their visions of the surfaces of all things are visions of touch. *a* **1861** T. WOOLNER *My Beautiful Lady, Tolling Bell* ix, Our visions met, when pitiyingly she flung Her passionate arms about me.

†**4.** A visage or vizard. *Obs. rare.*

In both instances perh. a misprint for *visor.*

1563 *Homilies* II. *Excess of Apparel* Ggg iiij b, As thoughe a wyse, and a christian husband, should delyte to see his wife in such paynted, and florished visions [1623 visages], which common harlots mostly do vse. *a* **1701** SEDLEY *Tyrant of Crete* v. ii, Methinks, till this day the times had Likewise a vision on, and look'd not with A true face before.

5. A thing actually seen; an object of sight.

1611 SHAKS. *Wint. T.* I. ii. 270 Ha' not you seene Camillo? (But that's past doubt: you haue,..For to a Vision so apparant, Rumor Cannot be mute.)

6. The visual part of a television broadcast, television images collectively; the transmission or reproduction of such images; also, the signal corresponding to them.

1910 H. N. CASSON *Hist. Telephone* ix. 287 Some future Carty..may transmit vision as well as speech. **1930** MOSELEY & CHAPPLE *Television* i. 9 On 9th February, 1928, the public were startled to learn that the Atlantic had been spanned by vision. **1934** J. H. REYNER *Television* x. 109 The radio transmission of sound or vision is usually accomplished by modulating a high-frequency carrier-wave. **1939** *Jrnl. Television Soc.* III. 8/1 Vision is amplified at an intermediate frequency of 13.2 m.c. (vision carrier). **1955** 'J. CHRISTOPHER' *Year of Comet* i. 5 He had followed the usual practice of leaving sound switched on as well as vision. **1959** G. FREEMAN *Jack would be Gentleman* i. 8 The sound came on a full minute before the vision. **1973** E. G. M. ALKIN *Sound with Vision* i. 3 In any entertainment medium in which sound and vision are combined there is a tendency to consider sound as the poor relation.

7. *attrib.* and *Comb.* **a.** *gen.*, as ***vision-field, -literature, machinery, -monger, poem, -world; vision-haunted, -seeing, -seeking, -struck*** adjs.; **vision quest** *N. Amer.*, the attempt to achieve a vision traditionally undertaken by mature men of the Plains Indian peoples, usu. through fasting or self-torture; **vision splendid**, the dream of some glorious imagined time; **vision-telephone** = *videophone* s.v. VIDEO-.

1880 *Academy* 3 July 7 *Vision-field contraction is illustrated by the case of a patient [etc.]. *c* **1823** MRS. HEMANS *Valkyriur Song*, The Sea-king woke from the troubled sleep Of a *vision-haunted night. **1929** T. S. ELIOT *Dante* 67 The *Vita Nuova*,..a sequence of beautiful poems connected by a curious *vision-literature. **1895** A. NUTT *Voy. Bran* I. x. 250 Early Christian literature likewise supplies similar descriptions without employing the Vision machinery. **1718** *Entertainer* Ded. A iij, The Atheist and the Infidel..are reinforc'd by the Quaker, the *Vision-monger and the Seeker. **1961** A. CLARKE *Later Poems* 91 The *Aisling*, or *Vision poem, in which Ireland was personified, reached its pitch in the eighteenth century. **1922** R. BENEDICT in *Amer. Anthropol.* XXIV. 3 Three patterns of wide distribution are sometimes taken to characterize the *vision quest of the Plains. **1966** D. ABERLE *Peyote Relig. among Navaho* xx. 340 Anthropologists have been impressed by the similarities between peyotism and the Plains vision quest. **1971** E. SHORRIS *Death of Great Spirit* iv. 40 He is a Uwipi, a medicine man and practitioner of the traditional vision quest, and there is not a Sioux Indian within two hundred miles of Pine Ridge who does not regard him with a certain amount of awe. **1827** PUSEY *Let.* in Liddon *Life* (1893) I. vi. 131 A half-distracted, visionary and *vision-seeing mystic. **1922** W. B. YEATS *Trembling of Veil* II. xiv. 129 Politics, for a *vision-seeking man, can be but half achievement. **1807** WORDSWORTH *Poems* II. 151 The youth, who..still is Nature's priest, And by the *vision splendid Is on his way attended. **1895** A. B. PATERSON *Man from Snowy River* (1896) 21 And he sees the vision splendid of the sunlit plains extended, And at night the wond'rous glory of the everlasting stars. **1959** X. HERBERT *Seven Emus* x. 110 Such was his acting that he took in his audience along with himself, made them share his optimism, his vision splendid. **1972** I. MOFFITT *U-Jack Soc.* xii. 199, I sat obediently and listened, and Sir Philip spread his vision splendid of electricity extended—with nuclear power. **1708** SHAFTESB. *Charac.* (1711) I. 50 Whether the matter of Apparition be true or false, the Symptoms are the same..in the Person who is *Vision-struck. **1966** *Guardian* 22 Dec. 3/3 The Post Office is exploring the possibility of..a *vision-telephone for calls between individuals. **1969** *New Scientist* 16 Oct. 146/3 Big industrial concerns might..find vision telephones helpful for conferences between executives. **1915** D. H. LAWRENCE *Rainbow* xi. 267 In the *vision-world He spoke of Jerusalem, something that did not exist in the everyday world.

b. In sense 6; *spec.* **vision-mixer**, a person whose job is to switch from one camera to another in television broadcasting or recording; so **vision-mixing** *vbl. sb.*

1935 *Illustr. London News* 23 Feb. 307/1 (*in figure*) Vision control [of a television receiver]. **1937** *Discovery* Nov. 330/1 The incoming vision signal..carries the time-sequence of light-and-shade in the original image. **1938** *Times* 7 Jan. 13/6 Behind him is the key-man, the vision-mixer. **1951** I. ASIMOV *Stars like Dust* (1958) i. 7 He jabbed at the vision control and the small screen was alive with light. **1953** AMOS & BIRKINSHAW *Television Engin.* I. i. 17 The composite signal obtained by combining a picture with a synchronising signal is known as a vision [1957: video] signal. **1956** *B.B.C. Handbk. 1957* 59 This unit..has its own VHF sound and vision transmitters. **1960** *Daily Tel.* 17 June 13/4 The present [television] centre runs more than 100 vision and 400 sound circuits. **1961** G. MILLERSON *Technique Television Production* xvi. 296 The television director is his own editor. He may himself carry out the mechanical operation of the video switching console (vision mixing desk), or have..a switcher (vision mixer), follow his instructions. **1972** D. LEES *Zodiac* 30 Zodiac's director, vision mixers, audio-men and camera men were obviously tops. **1979** ZARACH & MORRIS *Television Princ. & Pract.* ii. 8 The signal from the camera, together with the synchronising pulses.., modulate the vision carrier. **1982** A. ROAD *Dr. Who* 45/2 To the director's..right [in the gallery] are the vision mixer, the producer..and..the technical manager.

vision ('vɪʒən), *v.* [f. prec.]

1. *trans.* To show as in a vision; to display to the eye or mind. Also with *out.*

1594 NASHE *Unfort. Trav.* Wks. (Grosart) V. 129 Euen as the age of goates is knowen by the knots on their hornes, so think the anger of God apparently visioned or showne vnto thee in the knitting of my browes. **1802** H. MARTIN *Helen of Glenross* III. 254 Should I return and behold the tomb you have affectingly visioned. **1887** RIDER HAGGARD *She* 192 Mankind asks ever of the skies to vision out what lies behind them.

b. To call *up* a vision of.

1902 *Academy* 25 Jan. 100/1 Those eyes, that hair, vision up Spanish princes.

2. To see as in a vision; to bring before the eye of the mind. Also with *forth.*

1795 SOUTHEY *Joan of Arc* VIII. 135 We in the morning eyed the pleasant fields Vision'd before. **1816** J. WILSON *City of Plague* II. i. 63, I too am his brother, though his face Was only vision'd sweetly in my soul. **1856** RUSKIN *Mod. Paint.* III. IV. iv. §5 That we may be able to vision forth the ministry of angels beside us. **1876** MEREDITH *Beauch. Career* xxxiii, Gentlemen of an unpractised imaginative capacity cannot vision for themselves exactly what they would.

3. *intr.* To take a view; to look.

1898 MEREDITH *Odes Fr. Hist.* 6 Up that midway We vision for new ground.

visional ('vɪʒənəl), *a.* [f. VISION *sb.* + -AL[1].]

1. Connected or concerned with, relating to, based upon, a vision or visions.

1588 J. HARVEY *Disc. Probl.* 35 Is not true and pure diuinitie according to the diuision of some learned, and reuerant autors, either Expositiue, and Interpretatiue: or else Visionall, and Propheticall? **1644** JESSOP *Angel of Eph.* 8 In visionall speeches Daniel..saith to Nebuchadnezzar [etc.]. **1668** CLARENDON *Contempl. Ps.* Tracts (1727) 574 That this Psalm was composed upon the visional deliberation of the defeat of that army. **1732** WATERLAND *Script. Vind.* III. 53 And therefore this visional Interpretation appears to be preferable to the other. *Ibid.* 78 So much in Favour of the visional Construction. **1908** J. ORR *Resurrect. Jesus* viii. 214 May it not at least be possible to show that the appearance of Jesus can be explained.. either by subjective hallucinations, which is the older form of the visional theory, or [etc.]?

2. Of the nature of, seen or occurring in, forming part of, a vision; visionary, unreal.

1647 R. H. *Trial & Exam. Serm. by Haslewood* 2 There was no materiall house at all, nor any gate; unless he will make the visionall ladder the gate or house. **1681** FLAVEL *Meth. Grace* xxii. 376 The teaching of God, and our hearing and leaving of him, is not to be understood of any extra-ordinary visional appearances. **1690** C. NESSE *O. & N. Test.* I. 295 A real and corporal combat not visional or imaginary. **1708** *Brit. Apollo* No. 11. 1/1 We cannot..suppose, that Visional Representations wou'd be exhibited to us under the Notion of Realities. *a* **1767** BOSTON *Serm.* (1850) 41 What sort of wrestling was it? and how could worm Jacob prevail over an uncreated angel? Some make it visional, and in a dream. **1827** G. S. FABER *Sacr. Cal. Prophecy* (1844) II. 70 The interpreting angel..does not superfluously enter into any description of the visional conflict beheld by Daniel. **1858** H. BUSHNELL *Nat. & Supernat.* ii. (1864) 41 Some apparition or visional wonder.

3. Pertaining to sight; visual. *rare*$^{-1}$.

1790 *Bystander* 201 With an ardent brand Ulysses deprived him of his only visional organ.

Hence **'visionally** *adv.*, as or in a vision.

1647 TRAPP *Comm. Rev.* xi. 14 The second woe is past: Visionally past, not eventually. *a* **1679** POOLE *Annot.*, *Ezek.* xxxvii. 1 The Spirit of God carrying him visionally not corporally. **1708** *Brit. Apollo* No. 11. 1/1 We esteem the whole as Really, and not Visionally perform'd. **1847** H. MILLER *Test. Rocks* (1857) 169 The reason why the drama of creation has been optically described seems to be, that it was in reality visionally revealed.

'visionarily, *adv. rare*$^{-1}$. [f. as next.] In a vision; visionally.

1677 GILPIN *Demonol.* III. vi. 37 Nay how impossible is it, to make that expression..to agree to an imaginary Temptation, except we also say, that we are only tempted visionarily and not really.

'visionariness. [f. next + -NESS.]

1. The quality of being visionary in respect of mind or views.

c **1806** D. WORDSWORTH *Jrnl.* (1941) I. 286 That visionariness which results from a communion with the unworldliness of nature. **1809–10** COLERIDGE *Friend* (ed. 3) III. 72 Visionariness seems the tendency of the German;.. fanaticism of the French. **1831** *Blackw. Mag.* XXX. 104 The conceptive faculty delights at times in half-formed and hazy visionariness. **1840** DE QUINCEY *Style* Wks. 1859 XI. 256 Books..labouring with the same two opposite defects.. dulness from absolute monotony, and visionariness from the aërial texture of the speculations. **1880** PATER *Coleridge* Wks. 1901 V. 83 A kind of languid visionariness, deep-seated in the very constitution of the 'narcotist'.

2. The quality of being visionary in respect of reality, fulfilment, or practical value.

1817 BENTHAM *Parl. Reform.* Introd. 317 Annuality—with all its wildness and visionariness..would be far less intolerable. **1837** *Blackw. Mag.* XLII. 98 He..wrote instantly,..against the new alarmist, pledging his own head upon the visionariness of his alarms. **1876** MOZLEY *Univ. Serm.* i. 16 This project of a Universal Empire..may.. justly be charged with utter visionariness.

visionary ('vɪʒənərɪ), *a.* and *sb.* [f. VISION *sb.* + -ARY. Cf. F. *visionnaire*, It., Sp., Pg. *visionario.*]

A. *adj.* **1.** Able or accustomed to see visions; capable of receiving impressions, or obtaining knowledge, by means of visions.

1651 HOBBES *Leviath.* III. xxxvi. 231 Such quarrells amongst the Visionary Prophets. **1697** DRYDEN *Æneid* III. 576 Thus, many not succeeding, most upbraid The madness of the visionary maid. *a* **1721** SHEFFIELD (Dk. Buckhm.) *Wks.* (1753) I. 79 So visionary brains ascend the sky, While on the ground entranc'd the wretches lie. **1771** BEATTIE *Minstr.* I. xxix, See, in the rear of the warm sunny shower The visionary boy from shelter fly. **1792** S. ROGERS *Pleas. Mem.* I. 161 What spells entrance my visionary mind. **1817** SCOTT *Harold* v. xvii, O, think upon the words of fear Spoke by that visionary Seer. **1850** MRS. JAMESON *Leg. Monast. Ord.* (1863) 383 And as she grew up, she became a strange, solitary, visionary child, to whom a unseen world had revealed itself. **1883** F. GALTON *Hum. Faculty* (1910) 125 A large natural gift of the visionary faculty might become characteristic..of certain families.

b. Given to fanciful and unpractical views; having little regard to what is actual or possible; speculative, dreamy.

1727 SWIFT *Let. Eng. Tongue* Wks. 1755 II. I. 183 Supplying our wants, faster than the most visionary projector can adjust his schemes. **1770** BURKE *Pres. Discont.* Wks. 1842 I. 124 If a man happens not to succeed in such an enquiry, he will be thought weak and visionary. **1786–7** BONNYCASTLE *Astron.* i. 17 We laugh at the absurdities of a visionary pretender. **1817** W. BROUGHAM in *Parl. Deb.* 298 Mr. Spence, the visionary author of the new system, lived 20 years ago. **1827** LYTTON *Falkland* I. 13, I grew by degrees of a more thoughtful and visionary nature. **1902** W. L. MATHIESON *Politics & Relig. Scot.* I. iii. 100 Knox was no visionary enthusiast.

2. Of the nature of a vision; presented or apprehended in a vision. Cf. VISIONAL 2.

1648 BOYLE *Seraph. Love* xvi. (1700) 103 The sole Hymn (except a Visionary one) I find recorded of the Celestial Quire, was sung for a Blessing to Mankind. **1681** DRYDEN *Abs. & Achit.* I. 656 Some things like Visionary flights appear; The Spirit caught him up, the Lord knows where, And [etc.]. *a* **1701** MAUNDRELL *Journ. Jerus.* (1721) 80 Which, they say, is the Mountain into which the Devil took our Blessed Saviour, when he tempted him with that visionary scene of all the Kingdoms and Glories of the World. **1720** WELTON *Suffer. Son of God* I. viii. 161 These Divine Illapses of Revelation, which become Visionary in our Sleep. **1784** COWPER *Task* v. 400 There, like the visionary emblem seen By him of Babylon, life stands a stump. **1838** MRS. BROWNING *Seraphim* I. 205 One of those Whom the loving Father chose, In visionary pomp to sweep O'er Judæa's grassy places.

b. Seen only in a vision; unreal, non-existent, phantom, spectral.

1697 DRYDEN *Æneid* II. 365, I wept to see the visionary man, And, while my trance continued, thus began. **1700** —— *Theod. & Hon.* 280 The hounds at nearer distance hoarsely bayed; The Hunter close pursu'd the visionary Maid. **1725** POPE *Odyss.* x. 633 Sudden shall skim along the dusky glades Thin airy shoals, and visionary shades. **1781** GIBBON *Decl. & F.* xxxviii. (1787) III. 619 The visionary fabric melted into air. **1820** LAMB *Elia* I. *South-sea House*, The shade of some dead accountant, with visionary pen in ear, would flit by me, stiff as in life. **1852** MRS. STOWE *Uncle Tom's C.* xiv, There was not a corner or nook..where those fairy footsteps had not glided, and that visionary golden head..fleeted along. **1865** DICKENS *Mut. Fr.* III. viii, By what visionary hands she was led along upon that journey to escape from the Samaritan.

c. Connected with, or pertaining to, visions.

1727-46 THOMSON *Summer* 556 Here frequent, at the visionary hour, When musing midnight reigns, or silent noon, Angelic harps are in full concert heard. **1775** ADAIR *Amer. Ind.* 313 Having intimidated themselves apart from the rest, with visionary notions. **1818** SCOTT *Br. Lamm.* xxxi, Meanwhile, this mysterious visionary traffic had its usual effect, in unsettling Miss Ashton's mind.

d. Disturbed by visions.

1807 J. BARLOW *Columb.* I. 49 When from a visionary short repose, That nursed new cares and temper'd keener woes, Columbus woke.

3. Existing in imagination only; imaginary; not actual or real.

1725 POPE *Odyss.* IV. 246 Vanish'd are all the visionary joys. **1745** J. MASON *Self Knowl.* I. xiv. (1853) 105 Suffer not your Thoughts..to give you a visionary Pleasure in the Prospect of what you have not the least Reason to hope. **1798** S. & HT. LEE *Canterb. T.* II. 308 So deep a hold had this..visionary delight taken on Emily, that the days hung heavily with her. **1844** H. H. WILSON *Brit. India* III. 364 With the consolidation of the supremacy, the apprehension of its visionary evils recurred. *a* **1859** MACAULAY *Hist. Eng.* xxiii. (1861) V. 11 The danger which seemed so terrible to many honest friends of liberty he did not venture to pronounce altogether visionary. **1876** BESANT & RICE *Gold. Butterfly* i, The power of the penniless twins was a shadowy and visionary thing.

b. Of schemes, plans, etc.: Incapable of being carried out or realized; purely ideal or speculative; fantastic, unpractical.

1727 SWIFT *Modest Proposal* Wks. 1755 II. II. 67 Vain, idle, visionary thoughts. **1751** EARL ORRERY *Remarks Swift* (1752) 75 A miserable example of an ill-spent life, fantastic wit, visionary schemes, and female weakness. **1777** ROBERTSON *Hist. Amer.* v. (1778) II. 130 The crews of three of his ships..insisted on relinquishing the visionary project of a desperate adventurer. **1815** STEPHENS in *Shaw's Gen. Zool.* IX. I. 77 Those [opinions] of the ancients appear to be either visionary or erroneous. **1834** MARRYAT *P. Simple* xlvi, These were wild and visionary notions, and with little chance of ever arriving at any successful issue. **1855** BREWSTER *Newton* I. xi. 265 Kepler abandoned for a while his visionary speculations. **1883** *Manch. Exam.* 30 Oct. 5/5 The quiet of the land is being disturbed to suit the visionary theories of well-meaning but unpractical men.

c. Characterized by fantasy or imagination without corresponding reality.

1777 J. RICHARDSON *Dissert. East. Nations* 3 On this visionary field, learned and pious men have disputed with much want of temper. **1794** MRS. RADCLIFFE *Myst. Udolpho* xxx, Emily sought to lose the sense of her own cares, in the visionary scenes of the poet. **1840** THIRLWALL *Greece* VII. lvi. 141 Lycurgus..had not learnt..to withdraw from active life into a visionary world. **1863** KINGLAKE *Crimea* I. 228 If Louis Napoleon was going to be content with a visionary life [etc.]. **1874** L. STEPHEN *Hours in Library* (1892) I. v. 194 [He] sought refuge from the hard facts of commonplace life by retiring into a visionary world.

4. Pertaining to (physical or mental) vision.

1814 WORDSW. *Excurs.* IV. 111 It may be allowed me to remember What visionary powers of eye and soul In youth were mine.

B. *sb.* **1.** One who has visions; one to whom unknown or future things are revealed in visions.

1706 PHILLIPS (ed. Kersey), *Visionary*, one that is subject to Dreams, silly Notions and extravagant Fancies; a fantastical Pretender to Visions and Revelations. **1711** ADDISON *Spect.* No. 56 ¶3 One of their Countrymen descended in a Vision to the great Repository of Souls... The Visionary..arrived at length on the Confines of this World of Spirits. **1778** T. HARTLEY *Pref. Swedenborg's 'Heaven & Hell'* p. xi, Of such honourable repute was the name Seer, or visionary, in those times. **1830** SCOTT *Demonol.* i. 6 It becomes almost in vain to argue with the visionary against the reality of his dream. **1850** MRS. JAMESON *Leg. Monast. Ord.* (1863) 253 On one side kneels the visionary, with features wan and worn. **1870** BALDW. BROWN *Eccl. Truth* 262 Forms of perfect beauty and purity, of which the keenest visionary has had but feeble dreams.

2. One who indulges in fantastic ideas or schemes; an unpractical speculator or enthusiast.

1702 ADDISON *Dial. Medals* i. (1726) 28 This science has its visionaries as well as all others. **1796** H. HUNTER tr. *St.-Pierre's Stud. Nat.* (1799) I. p. xii, We must therefore respect the Man, even while we smile at the Visionary. **1834** HT. MARTINEAU *Demerara* x. 122 He had laid his accounts for being treated as a visionary, and for his own plans being laughed at as absurd. **1868** PEARD *Waterfarm.* xiv. 140 The agriculturist..will not be deemed a visionary, because he calculates on the coming harvest with certainty. **1880** HOWELLS *Undisc. Country* v, He's a visionary, but he's a good man.

visioned ('vɪʒənd), *ppl. a.* [f. VISION *sb.* or *v.*]

1. Seen in a vision.

1510 CLEREVILLE (*title*), The Copye of the letter folowynge which specifyeth of ye greatest and meruelous visyoned batayle that euer was sene.

1803 SCOTT *Cadyow Castle* xxix, Whose cheek is pale, whose eyeballs glare, As one some vision'd sight that saw. **1807** J. BARLOW *Columb.* I. 19 Till vision'd ages, opening on his eyes, Cheer'd his sad soul. **1838** CHALMERS *Introd. Ess. Chr. Def. agst. Infidelity* Wks. 1849 XIII. 298 The battles of the faith against the dark and the visioned spectres of geology. **1863** LD. LYTTON *Ring Amasis* II. III. xiii, As..he pressed that solemn kiss upon the visioned thing I could not see.

2. Associated with, arising from, a vision or visions.

1817 SCOTT *Harold* VI. xii, Trembling at first,..Had Gunnar heard the vision'd tale. **1822** BEDDOES *Bride's Trag.* IV. iv, I dreamed and in that visioned agony 'Twas whispered by strange voices [etc.]. **1853** JERDAN *Autobiog.* III. 170 In her inmost abstract and visioned moods..she was the Poet. **1891** C. DAWSON *Avonmore* IV. 79 Braver from that visioned thought, I duty did and duty sought.

3. Gifted with vision; having the power of seeing visions.

1813 SHELLEY *Q. Mab* I. 68 The visoned poet in his dreams, When silvery clouds float through the 'wildered brain. **1830** MOIR *Tower of Ercildoune* iv, Methinks the visioned bard I see..Piercing the mazy depths of Time. **1866** R. S. STORRS *Serm.* in *Bible Soc. Rec.* Feb. (1894), Of such a majestic teacher as Ezekiel, the visioned prophet,..we know almost nothing.

4. Full of visions.

1815 SHELLEY *Alastor* 682 The dream Of dark magician in his visioned cave.

visioner ('vɪʒənə(r)). [f. VISION *sb.*] One who has visions; a visionary.

1716 M. DAVIES *Athen. Brit.* II. 184 He should exalt his Character by playing the Vissioner with a superannuated Superintendant. **1902** FR. THOMPSON in *Academy* 12 April 378/1 The dreams..He half made possible; for that he was Visioner of vision in a most sordid day.

visionic (vɪʒɪ'ɒnɪk), *a. rare.* [f. VISION *sb.*] Of the nature of a vision.

1857 *Tait's Mag.* XXIV. 363 Which, if it does not assert, yet strongly suggests, the visionic character of the revelation of the creation to Moses.

visioning ('vɪʒənɪŋ), *vbl. sb.* [f. VISION *sb.* or *v.*] The action or fact of seeing visions; an instance of this.

a **1835** MOTHERWELL *Poet. Wks.* (1847) 35 But still the present is o'ercast with visionings of yore. **1838** MRS. BROWNING *Felicia Hemans* vii, Such visionings have paled in sight. **1843** CARLYLE *Past & Pr.* II. viii, Such guessing, visioning, dim perscrutation of the momentous future. **1880** W. WATSON *Prince's Quest* Poems (1892) 13 By potence wrought of Mortal Visionings In that dark house of which Sleep hath the Keys.

visionist ('vɪʒənɪst). [f. VISION *sb.*]

1. One who has, or professes to have, visions; a professed visionary.

1665 J. SPENCER *Vulg. Proph.* 43 The many gross fallacies put, even upon wise men, by such frequent Visionists. **1666** BP. S. PARKER *Free & Impart. Censure* (1667) 66 We are so far from attaining any certain and real knowledge of Incorporeal Beings (of an acquaintance with which these Visionists [*sc.* Platonists] do boast). **1700** HICKES *Let. to Pepys* 19 June, P.'s Diary (Chandos) 696, I asked this question, to know..whether these Second-Sight folks were Seers or Visionists. **1727** DE FOE *Syst. Magic* iii. Wks. 1840 XII. 312 This Jacob Behemen..was a kind of visionist. He pretended to see things invisible. **1809** W. TAYLOR in *Monthly Mag.* XXVIII. 188 Joanna Southcott, a fanatical visionist of the present day. **1841** D'ISRAELI *Amen. Lit.* (1867) 185 The visionist had deeper thoughts and more concealed feelings than these rhapsodical phantoms. **1877** J. A. CHALMERS *Life Tiyo Soga* xviii. (1878) 347 The third class is that of dreamers or visionists, who discover the nature of the disease.

2. One who supports the view that the Biblical account of creation was revealed to the writer in a vision or series of visions.

1888 A. CAVE *Inspir. O. Test.* iii. 129 A third class, the Visionists, also maintain the literal character of the days mentioned... In their view the days..refer to..the actual days of the revelation of the creation.

visionless ('vɪʒənlɪs), *a.* [f. VISION *sb.*]

1. Destitute of vision; sightless, blind.

1820 KEATS *Hyperion* I. 243 Half-closed, and visionless entire they seem'd Of all external things. **1848** ELIZA COOK *Song for Dog* iv, Tis my Dog that I trust to,..And he ministers well to my visionless eyes. **1874** G. MACDONALD *Malcolm* III. xxii. 294 Her eyes rolled stupid and visionless.

2. Having no vision of unseen things; devoid of higher insight or inspiration.

1856 R. S. VAUGHAN *Mystics* (1860) II. x. ii. Notes 316 Theresa might, in the abstract, rate the visionless altitude above the valley of vision. **1859** BP. S. WILBERFORCE *Addr. Ordination* ix. 182 The hindrances to our delivering simply our message may lead us to suppress or tamper with it until we become visionless and dumb. **1891** N. LORAINE *Battle of Belief* 181 His cheerless, shoreless, visionless system of negations.

'visionlike, *adv.* [f. VISION *sb.*] After the manner of a vision.

1824 MISS L. M. HAWKINS *Annaline* I. 78 As if some thoughts had visionlike swept across her mind.

visiophone ('vɪzɪəʊfəʊn). [f. L. *vīsio* VISION *sb.* + -PHONE.] = *videophone* s.v. VIDEO-.

1971 *New Scientist* 15 July 140/2 It is estimated that 125 Visiophones will be in use in that area [*sc.* Paris] within four years. **1978** *Jrnl. Communication* XXVIII. 151 The audio and video (visiophone) two-way link was reserved..each day for consultations..between staff in Nairobi and Paris.

visir(ate, obs. forms of VIZIER(ATE.

visit ('vɪzɪt), *sb.* Also 7 **visite, visitt, visette, vizet.** [ad. F. *visite* (= It., Sp., Pg. *visita*), or f. VISIT *v.*]

1. a. An act of visiting a person; a friendly or formal call upon, a shorter or longer stay with, a person as a feature of social intercourse.

1621 G. SANDYS *Ovid's Met.* XIII. (1626) 274 To Nymphs of Seas,..She beares her vizets. **1638** R. BAKER tr. *Balzac's Lett.* (vol. II) 228 You know well, I have appointed you here a chamber, and that you are my debter of a visite, now a whole year. **1648** *Nicholas Papers* (Camden) 94 To..undertake..for a visitt to him by the Lord Jarmin (who I beleeve visited none else there). **1681** V'TESS CAMPDEN in *12th Rep. Hist. MSS. Comm.* App. V. 56 My Lady Skidmore and her lord was at Mr. Conisbys house upon a visette. **1711** ADDISON *Spect.* No. 102 ¶8 Like Ladies that look upon their Watches after a long Visit. **1753** *Scots Mag.* XV. 36/1 Guilty of that most atrocious crime, the owing a visit. **1774** GOLDSM. *Nat. Hist.* (1776) V. 246 If the monkey ventures to offer a visit of curiosity, the toucan gives him such a welcome, that he..is glad to escape. **1848** THACKERAY *Van. Fair* i, On the solemn occasions of the visits of parents. **1887** *Brit. Med. Jrnl.* 2 April 754/1 To call twice in one week, under the pretence..of a social visit. **1907** *Verney Mem.* I. 99 He is looking forward to a visit from Ralph in the summer.

fig. **1781** COWPER *Table T.* 411 'Tis not..despondence and dismay Will win her [*sc.* Mercy's] visits or engage her stay.

b. Freq. in the phrases *to make*, or *pay* (also †*give*) *a visit, to return a visit.*

(*a*) **1644** T. PRUJEAN *Aurorata* II. Ej, Romeo..going to give her a visit meetes Tybalt her kinsman. **1674** *Essex Papers* (Camden) I. 179 My Ld Shaftsbury did me ye honour ye other day to give me a visit. **1699** R. L'ESTRANGE *Erasm. Colloq.* (1725) 227 An Abbot gives a Lady a visit. **1709-10** STEELE *Tatler* No. 128 ¶7 He came to give our Family a formal Visit.

(*b*) **1643** CARYL *Expos. Job* I. 636 There is no obligation but that of love, to make a visit. *a* **1699** LADY HALKETT *Autobiog.* (Camden) 3, I doe nott remember that I made a visitt to ye neerest neibour. **1710** STEELE *Tatler* No. 124 ¶1, I went on Saturday last to make a Visit in the City. **1753** E. MOOR in *World* I. No. 11. 87 She made him a visit of a month, and at his entreaty would have settled with him for ever. **1779** FORREST *Voy. N. Guinea* 224 Making him a visit, I found him in the great hall. **1823** J. SIMPSON *Ricardo the Outlaw* I. 241 She promised that in two years, at longest, she would make them a visit. **1885** W. W. STORY *Fiammetta* 195 You promised you would make me a visit in the autumn.

(*c*) **1654-66** EARL ORRERY *Parthen.* (1676) 503 Surena, by this visit, was in a few days able to pay me one. **1711** STEELE *Spect.* No. 24 ¶6 Let us pay Visits, but never see one another. **1725** DE FOE *Voy. round World* (1840) 38 The Dutch captain came off in his shallop..to pay his visit to me. **1781** COWPER *Conversat.* 399 The visit paid, with ecstasy we come, As from a seven years transportation, home. **1835** *Court Mag.* VI. 186/1, I quitted Oxford, and paid a visit to a maiden lady dwelling in the Orange Grove. **1855** TENNYSON *To Rev. F. D. Maurice* xii, When the wreath of March has blossom'd,..Or later, pay one visit here, For those are few we hold as dear.

fig. **1770** GOLDSM. *Des. Vill.* 3 Where smiling spring its earliest visit paid.

(*d*) **1677** LADY CHAWORTH in *12th Rep. Hist. MSS. Comm.* App. v. 37, I missed my nephew Anthony the other day who Lady Shaftesbery sent to see me, and I am now going to returne his visit. **1718** LADY M. W. MONTAGU *Let. to C'tess Mar* 10 March, I returned my visits at three weeks' end. **1766** [see RETURN *v.*^{1} 21 b].

c. *transf.* A place to which one goes only as a visitor.

1784 COWPER *Task* I. 251 Society for me! thou seeming sweet, Be still a pleasing object in my view, My visit still, but never mine abode.

d. An excursion *to* a place for the purpose of sight-seeing; a short or temporary stay at a place. Also *transf.* of animals or birds (cf. VISIT *v.* 10 d).

1800 (*title*), Visits to the Aviary. For the instruction of youth. **1839** MISS MITFORD in L'Estrange *Life* III. vii. 97 There is an account of a visit to Lyme in Miss Austen's exquisite 'Persuasion'. **1860** CLOUGH *Poems*, etc. (1869) I. 245 We had a visit to Fryston in Yorkshire, and after passing through the Highlands to Oban, made a three week's stay in Morven. **1872** RUSKIN *Fors Clav.* xxi. 20, I spend five hundred in Paris in the two visits I make there.

transf. **1831** T. NUTTALL in *Mem. Amer. Acad. Arts & Sci.* (1833) I. 101 Crossbills..pay irregular visits to the northern and middle States. **1843** *Penny Cycl.* XXV. 7/1 [The black-cap titmouse] probably extending its visits into Mexico.

e. An occasion of going *to* a dentist, doctor, etc., for examination or treatment.

1884 THOMPSON *Tumours of Bladder* 10 After two or three visits [to a hospital], he took a sea voyage for his health. **1902** R. BAGOT *Donna Diana* xxviii. 356 He felt that he would far prefer a visit to the dentist to the interview before him.

f. *Dog-Breeding.* A bitch's journey to and her stay with a dog for breeding purposes. Cf. VISIT *v.* 8 b.

1867 *Field* 5 Jan. 5/3 The following bitches have been on a visit to Patent. **1887** G. STABLER *Pract. Kennel Guide* xii. 125 Dogs..refuse food during the time of the bitch's visit. **1910** R. LEIGHTON *Dogs* I. 320 A proper mating should be considered at the outset... It is customary for the bitch to be the visitor, and it is well that her visit should extend to two or three days at the least.

2. a. An instance of going to see, and assist or comfort, persons in distress.

1709 (*title*), A charitable Visit to the Prisons, containing counsel to those who are confined there. **1792** [R. CECIL] (*title*), A Friendly Visit to the House of Mourning.

b. A call made by a clergyman as part of his pastoral duties.

1724 A. SHIELDS *Life J. Renwick* 114 No place did more desire his frequent Visits than those that were most persecuted for him. **1727** HURRION *Funer. Serm. J. Nesbit* 41 His visits were generally short, but very agreeable, and useful.

c. A professional call made by a doctor on a patient.

1719 BOYER *Dict. Royal* I. s.v., The visit of a Physitian, or Surgeon. **1858** SIMMONDS *Dict. Trade, Visit*, the attendance of a surgeon or physician, inspector, etc. **1861** FLOR. NIGHTINGALE *Nursing* 35 For a doctor..to leave the patient and communicate his opinion on the result of his visit..

within hearing..of the patient [etc.]. **1890** J. W. MARTIN *Quest. & Answ. Nursing* 92 To report anything that may appear unusual to the Doctor at his next visit.

3. a. Surgical examination (of a wound). *rare*⁻¹.

1796 CHARLOTTE SMITH *Marchmont* IV. 17, I am faint after a visit to my wound.

b. An instance (or the action) of going to a place, house, etc., for the purpose of inspection or examination.

1787 BURNS *Let. to M. Chalmers* Wks. (Globe) 352, I have been at Dumfries, and at one visit more shall be decided about a farm in that country. **1815** J. C. HOBHOUSE *Substance Lett.* (1816) I. 291 The Emperor..examined the new manufacture of Arms... Napoleon was accompanied only by three officers when he made his visit. **1861** M. PATTISON *Ess.* (1889) I. 48 Sir Thomas More made, as Chancellor, a domiciliary visit in search of heretical books. **1897** J. S. RISLEY *Law of War* III. viii. 265 (*heading*) The right of visit and search. A belligerent has the right..to visit and search every merchant ship at sea in time of war.

c. *Billiards* and *Snooker*. A turn of play at the table.

1927 *Times* 22 Feb. 16/3 At his second visit to the table he made a break of 111.

†**4.** An occurrence of menstruation. *Obs.*

1653 T. BRUGIS *Vade Mecum* (ed. 2) 112 Philonium Persicum..is good against the overmuch flowing of womens naturall visits. *Ibid.* 127 Myrrhe..procureth womens monthly visits. **1721** BRADLEY *Philos. Acc. Wks. Nat.* 95 The Females of these have periodical Visits like Females of the Human Race.

5. *attrib.* and *Comb.*, as *visit-day*, *-paying*; †**visit-leg**, a posture of politeness in paying a visit (cf. LEG *sb.* 4).

1673 WYCHERLEY *Gent. Dancing-Master* IV. i, *Blackamoor (teaching postures to M. de Paris)*. Now let me see you make your visit-leg—thus. *a* **1717** PARNELL *Elegy to old Beauty* 29 With better Strength, on Visit-days she bears To mount her fifty Flights of ample Stairs. **1849** THACKERAY in *Scribner's Mag.* I. 522/2, I have been most remiss in visit-paying.

visit (ˈvɪzɪt), *v.* Forms: 3 uisiti, 3–4 visiten, 4–6 visyte, 4–7 visite (4 uisite, visitte, 5 vissite), 5– visit (4 wisit, 6 vizit, visyt), 5–7 visitt (5 visytt), 6–7 vissit; 4 vysyty, 4–6 vysyte (5 usyte, vycyte), vysite (4 uys-), 4 vysitte, 5 vysid, 5–6 vysit, vysyt; 4–6 visete, 4–6 viset (5 viss-, 6 visett), vyset (5 -ed, ett, 6 -ette); 4–5 vesete (5 -ette, *Sc.* -eit), 5 vecyte, vesyte, -ite; *Sc.* 5 wesit, 6 vesit. Also *pa. t.* (*north.* and *Sc.*) 4–5 wisit, 5 vyset, vised; *pa. pple.* 4–5 visit, -yt, 5 -ide, 6 -itt. [ad. OF. *visiter* (also mod.F., = Sp. and Pg. *visitar*, It. *visitare*) or L. *vīsitāre* to go to see, to inspect, etc., frequentative of *vīsāre*, f. *vīs-*, ppl. stem of *vidēre* to see. In early use largely due to the frequent use of *visitare* in passages of the Vulgate, from which senses 1–7 are directly derived.]

I. 1. a. *trans.* Of the Deity: To come to (persons) in order to comfort or benefit.

Sometimes passing into senses 7 or 8. In *Alexander* 1964 used of pagan deities.

a **1225** *Ancr. R.* 154 Me ivint þet heo fluwen monne sturbinge, & wenden bi ham one: & tet God visitede ham & ȝef ham hore bonen. *a* **1300** *Cursor M.* 5789 Sai þam i sal þam son visete,..I sal þam bring vte of thain-hede. *a* **1325** *Prose Psalter* cv. (cvi.) 4 Þenche, Lord, on vs in þe wele-likand of þy folk, and visit vs in þyne helþe. **1340** *Ayenb.* 128 Þet is þet uerste guod þet þe holy gost deþ to þe sene-ȝere, huanne he him uisiteþ. **1382** WYCLIF *Jer.* xv. 15 Lord, recorde thou of me, and visite me, and delyuere me fro them that pursuen me. *c* **1412** HOCCLEVE *De Reg. Princ.* 914 God, as him list, visitith folk, & smyt. *c* **1440** *Alph. Tales* 269 Almighti God hase forsaken me, becauce He vissettis not me as He was wunt. **1535** COVERDALE *Ruth* i. 6 She had herde ..yᵗ the Lorde had visited his people & geuen them bred. **1553** *Primer* in *Lit. & Doc. Edw. VI* (1844) 399 Visit him, O Lord, as thou didst visit Peter's wife's mother, and the captain's servant. **1645** CARYL *Expos. Job* I. 636 When God comes in kindness and love to do us good, he visiteth us. **1676** HALE *Contempl.* I. 526 But art thou come, dear Saviour? hath thy Love Thus made thee stoop..and thus thy self to dress In dust to visit Mortals? **1727** DE FOE *Hist. Appar.* i. (1840) 9 Thus Adam was frequently visited in Eden. **1784** COWPER *Task* VI. 743 For He..Shall visit earth in Mercy.

transf. **1830** TENNYSON *Ode to Memory* 4 Oh, haste, Visit my low desire! Strengthen me, enlighten me!

b. *spec.* (See quots.)

1382 WYCLIF *Gen.* xxi. 1 God forsothe visitide Sara,..and fulfillide that that he spak. And she conseyuede. [Similarly in later versions.] **1390** GOWER *Conf.* I. 190 The hihe makere of nature Hire hath visited in a throwe, That it was openliche knowe Sche was with childe be the king.

c. To come to (persons) in order to judge of their state or condition. (Cf. sense 9.)

1382 WYCLIF *Exod.* iii. 16 Visitynge Y haue visitid ȝow, and Y haue seen alle thingis that haue fallun to ȝow in Egipte. **1645** CARYL *Expos. Job* I. 637 In this sense, Job saith, that God visits man every morning, as a shepherd his flock, lest any should be hurt or straid.

†**2.** To come to (persons) in order to observe or examine conduct or disposition; to make trial of; to subject to test or scrutiny. *Obs.*

a **1300** *Cursor M.* 3195 (Cott.) Godd has þe [Abraham] visited here to-dai, þi dede in minnyng sal last ai. *a* **1325** *Prose Psalter* xvi. 4 (xvii. 3), Þou prouedest myn hert, and uisited it on niȝt. *Ibid.* lviii. 6 (lix. 5), Ȝif entent to uisiten al folkes; ne haue þou nouȝt mercy on alle þat wirchen wickednes. **1382** WYCLIF *Job* vii. 18 Thou visitist hym the morntid, and feerli [1388 sudeynli] thou prouest hym. *c* **1450** tr. *De Imitatione* II. ix. 51 Wherfore saiþ Iob: 'Thou visitist him by tyme,..& sodenly þou preuest him'. **1535** COVERDALE *Job* xxxi. 14 But seynge that God wil sytt in judgment, what shal I do? And for so moch as he wil nedes vyset me, what answere shal I geue him? **1645** CARYL *Expos. Job* I. 637 The eye of God is alway upon us:..he visiteth us so, that we can turn no way but he is with us. **1667** MILTON *P.L.* XII. 48 But God who oft descends to visit men Unseen, and through thir habitations walks To mark thir doings.

absol. **1611** BIBLE *Job* xxxi. 14 What then shall I do, when God riseth vp? and when hee visiteth, what shall I answere him?

3. a. To inflict hurt, harm, or punishment upon (a person); to deal severely or hardly with (persons or things); †to cut off, cause to die.

1382 WYCLIF *Isa.* xxvi. 14 Therfore thou hast visityd, and to-brosedest hem, and lost al the mynde of hem. **1485** *Cov. Leet Bk.* 528 If your wisdomes..woll please..to chese me.. Recorder of your Citie, if God visite your Recorder that nowe is. **1535** COVERDALE *Amos* iii. 2 Therfore will I vyset you in all youre wickednesses. **1541** *Test. Ebor.* (Surtees) VI. 152 Beinge visitt with the hande of God. **1594** T. B. *La Primaud. Fr. Acad.* II. 312 Let vs alwayes looke to the first cause of our affliction, and to God who visiteth vs iustly. **1611** BIBLE *Amos* iii. 14, I will also visite the altars of Bethel, and the hornes of the altar shall be cut off. **1645** CARYL *Expos. Job* I. 636 When God visits our bodies, our estates, our families, or the kingdom where we live. *a* **1770** JORTIN *Serm.* (1771) I. iii. 52 We haue mentioned several reasons why God doth not immediately visit the disobedient. **1781** COWPER *Expost.* 248 If vice receiv'd her retribution due When we were visited, what hope for you? **1788** GIBBON *Decl. & F.* xlviii. V. 67 Her life was spared by the clemency of the emperor, but he visited the pomp and treasures of her palace.

b. To afflict or distress *with* sickness, poverty, or the like.

1424 HEN. VI in Ellis *Orig. Lett.* Ser. II. I. 100 Oure bel Uncle of Excestre, whom oure Lord now late visitid with seknesse. *c* **1430** LYDG. *Min. Poems* (Percy Soc.) 127 Som withe povert hym list to visite. **1526** *Pilgr. Perf.* (W. de W. 1531) 134 b, Euery chylde that he receyueth, he chastiseth & visiteth with payne & tribulacyon. **1581** PETTIE *Guazzo's Civ. Conv.* I. (1586) 2 God..hauing visited mee with a long, and perchaunce a curelesse disease. **1582** N. LICHEFIELD tr. *Castanheda's Cong. E. Ind.* I. vii. 19 b, Before his departure ..he ment to visit the town of Mousambick, and the dwellers therein, with some sufficient reuenge. **1624** J. USHER in *Lett. Lit. Men* (Camden) 131 It pleased God to visite me with a quartan. **1748** SMOLLETT *R. Random* xxvii, His indignation ought to be directed to Cot Almighty, who visited his people with distempers. **1862** BOYD *Graver Thoughts* 52 Holy Scripture sets before us two men,..each of whom was visited with a thorn in the flesh to keep him down.

c. To deprive *of* something. *rare*⁻¹.

c **1585** *Faire Em* III. iv, Good father, giue me leaue to sit where I may not be disturbed, sith God hath visited me both of my sight and hearing.

4. a. Of sickness, etc.: To come upon (a person or persons), to assail or afflict. Freq. in passive and const. *with* or *by*.

c **1340** HAMPOLE *Pr. Consc.* 1980 Als we suld ilk day þeded fele, And byde noght til þe dede us vyset. **1382** WYCLIF *Numb.* xvi. 29 If [there]..visyte them a veniaunce, with the which and other ben woned to be visytid, the Lorde hath not sente me. *a* **1548** HALL *Chron., Hen. VI*, 95 The kyng his father, so visited with sickenesse was not personable. *a* **1578** LINDESAY (Pitscottie) *Chron. Scot.* (S.T.S.) I. 156 He was hestelie vissitit with the heot feweris. **1596** SHAKS. *1 Hen. IV*, IV. i. 26, I would the state of time had first beene whole, Ere he by sickenesse had beene visited. **1645** CARYL *Expos. Job* I. 636 When a house hath the Plague,..we use to say, Such a house is visited. **1657** R. LIGON *Barbadoes* (1673) 21 So grievously visited with the plague,..that before a month ..the living were hardly able to bury the dead. **1662** E. HOOKES in *Extr. St. P. rel. Friends* II. (1911) 154 In the White Lyon prisson..about 23 of them vissitted with sicknesse and a high feever. **1727** SWIFT *God's Rev. agst. Punning* Wks. 1755 III. I. 171 One Samuel an Irishman, for his forward attempt to pun..hath been visited all his life after with bulls and blunders. **1754** *Med. Observ.* (1776) I. 43 Being visited by a gentle attack [of gout] in both feet. **1832** R. & J. LANDER *Exped. Niger* I. iii. 120 Since leaving Jenna, we have met an incredible number of persons visited with the loss of one eye. **1855** *Poultry Chron.* III. 148/1 Some which were..tended with constant care, all died: and similar mortality has visited others also. **1866** ROGERS *Agric. & Prices* I. xxiii. 602 Cornwall must have been more lightly visited with the Plague than most English counties.

b. *spec.* in *pass.* Bewitched.

1820 *Sporting Mag.* VII. 101 On account of their stock thus 'visited', as the term is, the infatuated peasantry almost invariably have recourse to charms.

5. a. To punish or requite (wrongdoing). Also const. *with*.

a **1325** *Prose Psalter* lxxxviii. (lxxxix.) 32 Y shal uisite in chasteing her wickednesses, and her synȝes in vengeaunce. **1382** WYCLIF *Exod.* xxxii. 34 Y in the day of veniaunce shal visite this synne of hem. [Also *Jer.* xiv. 10, *Lam.* iv. 22, etc.; similarly in later versions.] **1535** COVERDALE *Jer.* xxiii. 2 Therfore, now will I vyset the wickednes of youre ymaginacions, saieth yᵉ Lorde. **1833** I. TAYLOR *Fanat.* ii. 41 So jealous is Nature of her constitutions that she rigorously visits every infringement of them. *Ibid.* 49 The instinct of Retribution or the vehement desire to see wrong visited with punishment. **1849** MACAULAY *Hist. Eng.* iv. I. 496 What, he often said, could be more unjust, than to visit speculations with penalties which ought to be reserved for acts? **1879** FROUDE *Cæsar* xix. 310 Mild offences were visited with the loss of eyes or ears.

b. To avenge, or inflict punishment for (wrongdoing) *on* or *upon* (also †*in*, *into*) a person.

1382 WYCLIF *Exod.* xx. 3 Visitynge the wickidnes of fadris in sones into the thridde and the ferthe generacioun. —— *Jer.* xxiii. 2 Y shal visite vp on ȝow the malice of ȝoure studies. **1535** COVERDALE *Numb.* xiv. 18 The Lorde.. vysiteth the myszdede of the fathers vpon the children. **1595** SHAKS. *John* II. i. 179 Thy sinnes are visited in this poore childe. **1596** —— *Merch. V.* III. v. 16 So the sins of my mother should be visited vpon me. **1611** BIBLE *Jer.* xxiii. 2 Behold I will visite vpon you the euill of your doings. **1667** MILTON *P.L.* x. 955, I to that place Would speed before thee,..That on my head all might be visited. **1813** SHELLEY *Q. Mab.* VIII. 181 Which doubly visits on the tyrants' heads The long-protracted fulness of their woe. **1831** KEBLE *Serm.* v. (1848) 118 Thus, reversing the Scripture rule most unfairly, men visit the sins of the children on the fathers. **1866** G. MACDONALD *Ann. Q. Neighb.* xiii. (1878) 266 He visited the daughter's fault upon the son.

c. To inflict (punishment) *on* one. *rare*.

1836 J. GILBERT *Chr. Atonem.* ix. (1852) 292 It is said to be of the essence of legal penalty to visit punishment on the person of the offender.

6. *absol.* To take vengeance or inflict punishment. †Also const. *on* or *over*.

1382 WYCLIF *Isa.* x. 12, I shal visite vpon the fruyt of the gret doende herte of the king of Assur. *Ibid.* xxvii. 1 In that dai viseten shal the Lord in his harde swerd..vp on leuyathan. **1609** BIBLE (Douay) *Isa.* xiii. 11 And I will visite over the evils of the world, and against the impious their iniquitie. **1840** DE QUINCEY *Essenes* III, When the vilest outrages were offered by foreigners to their women, probably they [*sc.* the Sicarii] 'visited' for such atrocities.

II. 7. a. To make a practice of going to (persons in sickness or distress) in order to comfort or assist them.

c **1250** *Kent. Serm.* in *O.E. Misc.* 28 For þo luue of gode wakie, go ine pelrimage, uisiti þe poure, and to sike. *c* **1315** SHOREHAM I. 1032 [To] Vysyty syke and prysone, And helpe pouere at nede. *c* **1375** *Lay Folks' Catech.* 1133 Whi schuld venym or stynk lette vs to visite men in presun. **1377** LANGL. *P. Pl.* B. v. 412, I visited neuere fieble men, ne fettered folke in puttes. *c* **1430** LYDG. *Min. Poems* (Percy Soc.) 68 Visite the pore, with intyre diligence, On al nedy have thow compassioun. *c* **1450** *Mirk's Festial* 231 Helpe þe seke, and vysed hom þat be in prison. *c* **1491** *Chast Goddes Chyld.* 13 Also it is good to visite seke folke that ben holden goostly lyuers. **1526** TINDALE *Jas.* i. 27 To vysit the frendlesse and widdowes in their adversite. **1588** SHAKS. *L.L.L.* v. ii. 861 You shall this tweluemonth terme from day to day, Visite the speachlesse sicke. **1603** —— *Meas. for M.* II. iii. 4 Bound by my charity,..I come to visite the afflicted spirits Here in the prison. **1687** J. RENWICK in A. Shields *Life* (1724) 219 Ye must visit the Sick and these who are in Distress. **1795** PALEY (*title*), The Clergyman's Companion in Visiting the Sick. **1862** *Chambers' Encycl.* IV. 541/1 The deplorable condition of the female prisoners in Newgate attracted her [Elizabeth Fry's] attention, and she resolved upon visiting them.

absol. *a* **1591** H. SMITH *Wks.* (1867) II. 22 The devil goeth a-visiting, he will teach the sick how they shall recover their health.

b. Similarly with reference to individual cases.

a **1300** *Cursor M.* 16013 Til his felaus he yede He went him for to wisit þaim, for þar-of had þai nede. **1303** R. BRUNNE *Handl. Synne* 4388 He lay yn hys bedde long Sone aftyr betydde a lytte þe kyng come, hym to vysyte. **13..** *Seuyn Sages* (W.) 1138 He let of-sende..Hise neyebours him to visite, And told..Hou his deth was comen him on. **1389** in *Eng. Gilds* (1870) 50 Þere shal no broþir ne sister sene othir in prison, [but] þat he shal comyn and vesyten hym and comfordyn hym. **1530** PALSGR. 766/1 It is an almesse dede to visyte the poore man, he hath ben long sycke. *a* **1533** LD. BERNERS *Huon* I. 167 It pleaseth me well that this caytyue Huon, who endureth myche payne, be vysytyd by thee. **1548–9** (Mar.) *Bk. Com. Prayer, Vis. Sick*, If the person visited bee very sicke, then the curate may end his exhortacion at this place. **1607** SHAKS. *Cor.* I. iii. 85 Come, you must go visit the good Lady that lies in. **1645** CARYL *Expos. Job* I. 636 Christ pronounceth the blessing on them who, when he was in prison, visited him. **1712** N. SPINCKES (*title*), The Sick Man Visited; and furnished with Instructions, Meditations, and Prayers. **1808** MRS. E. HAMILTON *Cottagers of Glenburnie* x, The minister..had been sent for..to visit a sick parishioner.

8. a. To go to see (a person) in a friendly or sociable manner; to call upon as an act of friendliness or politeness, or for some special purpose; also, to stay with for a short time as a guest.

13.. *Arth. & Merlin* 701 Biside þer woned an ermite, þat þider com, þis [= these] to visite. **13..** *Guy Warw.* (A.) 4450 Whende ichil in-to mi cuntre, Mine frendes to visite & to se. **1387** TREVISA *Higden* (Rolls) II. 325 Þat tyme whanne Moyses visited his breþeren in þe lond of Iessen, he slowȝ a man of þe Egipcians. *c* **1400** MAUNDEV. (1839) v. 39 And whan the Soudan wille, he may go visite him. **1412–20** LYDG. *Chron. Troy* III. 3764 Hector in herte cauȝte an appetite..þe same day Grekis to vesite. **1474** CAXTON *Chesse* II. iv. (1883) 47 The knyght enulphus which cam the same nyght with his squyer for to visite his lord. *a* **1548** HALL *Chron., Rich. III*, 46 As though he had gone secretely to visite a familiar frende of his. **1580** E. KNIGHT *Trial Truth* To Chr. Rdr., A friend of myne viziting me at my chamber, and finding me so solitary exercised [etc.]. **1656** EARL MONM. tr. *Boccalini's Pol. Touchstone* (1674) 268 This Duke visited..Prospero Colonna, of whom he was received with all sorts of Honour. **1676** LADY CHAWORTH in *12th Rep. Hist. MSS. Comm.* App. v. 29 Lady Cleaveland is not, they say, much satisfied in France because the greatest ladies doe not visit her. **1706** E. WARD *Wooden World Diss.* (1708) 61 He's too lazy and proud to visit common Sailors. **1749** FIELDING *Tom Jones* xv. ix, Who, though some overnice ladies will not be seen with her, is visited (as they term it) by the whole town. **1797** MRS. RADCLIFFE *Italian* xxvi, Vivaldi was visited in his prison by a man whom he had never consciously seen before. **1848** THACKERAY *Van. Fair* xlvii, Had he not been so great a Prince very few possibly would have visited him. **1860** WARTER *Sea-board* II. 461 How many of the friends I was on my way to visit are no more seen! **1870** DICKENS *E. Drood* vii, He comes here visiting his relation, Mr. Jasper.

fig. **1591** SHAKS. *Two Gentl.* I. i. 60 Let me heare from thee by Letters..And I likewise will visite thee with mine. **1683** *Pennsylv. Archives* I. 72, I have long promised my-self to visit thee wᵗʰ a Letter.

b. To have cohabitation with (one of the opposite sex). *rare* exc. in *Dog-Breeding*: To be put to mate with (a dog) or at (a kennel).

c **1400** *Destr. Troy* 10820 Now the maner was most of þo mylde wemen, Thre mones with mirthe þo men for to viset. **1553** EDEN *Treat. Newe Ind.* (Arb.) 24 The men are accustomed to vysyte the women once in the yeare. **1867** *Field* 5 Jan. 5/3 The following bitches have visited Good Idea at the Blundell Arms Kennels. **1877** G. STABLES *Pract. Kennel Guide* xii. 122 In your correspondence with the owner of the bitch that is going to visit your kennel, be sure to let him know that he is to send her..as soon as there are the slightest signs of her coming in season. **1922** R. LEIGHTON *Compl. Bk. Dog* iii. 34, 40 per cent. of prize-bred bitches which visit prize-bred dogs are unproductive.

c. Of a medical man: To attend (a patient) professionally.

1585 T. WASHINGTON tr. *Nicholay's Voy.* III. xii. 93 [The physician] is bound to visite him foure times a daye, vntill suche time as he haue recouered his health. **1607** *Peele's Jests* 7 The gentlewoman..sent one of the men to desire the Doctor to come and visit her Husband. **1707** FLOYER *Physic. Pulse-Watch* 253 The Physicians themselves in China are Apothecaries, and when they Visit their Patients, they carry a Servant loaded with their Medicines. **1728** CHAMBERS *Cycl.* s.v. *Physician*, Clinical Physicians were those who visited their Patients a-bed, to examine their Cases. **1768** *Med. Observ.* (1772) IV. 5 About four o'clock I visited her again, and found that the vomiting had ceased. **1800** *Med. Jrnl.* III. 409 The District, in which the Patients of the Finsbury Dispensary are visited. **1840** *Penny Cycl.* XVIII. 133/1 For visiting a patient out of his own city he [Petrus de Abano] charged..about six pounds per day. **1886** in *Brit. Med. Jrnl.* (1887) 486/1 In cases of urgent necessity, patients will be visited at their own houses.

d. *transf.* To go to (a person, etc.) with hostile intentions.

a **1533** LD. BERNERS *Huon* lviii. 196 Syr, cause your men too be armed, and let vs go vysyte the Admyrall Galaffer. **1596** SHAKS. *1 Hen. IV*, IV. iv. 37 For if Lord Percy thriue not, ere the King Dismisse his power, he meanes to visit vs. **1602** MARSTON *Antonio's Rev.* III. i, Before I touch The banks of rest, my ghost shall visite her. **1607** SHAKS. *Cor.* IV. v. 148 Set downe..thine own waies, Whether to knocke against the Gates of Rome, Or rudely visit them in parts remote.

e. *absol.* To make a call or calls; to pay calls; to maintain friendly or social intercourse by this means; also, to spend a short time with one as a guest; to pay visits of this kind.

In the first quot. app. 'to go canvassing'.

1626 MEADE in Ellis *Orig. Lett.* Ser. I. III. 230 Hereupon on Tuesday morning..some durst be so bold as to visitt for the contrary in publick. **1645** CARYL *Expos. Job* I. 636 It is ..more extraordinary to visit in a morning, and most, early in the morning. **1711** STEELE *Spect.* No. 24 ¶5 They are qualify'd rather to add to the Furniture of the House (by filling an empty Chair) than to the Conversation they come into when they visit. **1798** S. & HT. LEE *Canterb. T.* II. 546, I found myself very sad, and lonely,..so all my kindred made it a point to have me a visiting among them. **1826** DISRAELI *Viv. Grey* I. vii, Busied with his studies, and professing 'not to visit'. **1841** THACKERAY *Gt. Hoggarty Diam.* xiii, Her ladyship knows my address, having visited here. **1894** L. ALMA-TADEMA *Wings of Icarus* 41 A spinster ..who spends her life visiting from place to place.

fig. **1837** DICKENS *Pickw.* xxii, You rayther want somebody to look arter you, sir, wen your judgment goes a visitin'.

(*b*) Const. *at*.

1753 MISS COLLIER *Art Torment.* I. ii. (1811) 54 Unless.. she happens to receive any particular address from the young gentlemen who visit at your house. **1836** DICKENS *Let.* 31 Mar. (1965) I. 144, I cannot..visit at a relation's house from which my father is excluded. **1976** *Stillwater* (Montana) *News* 1 July 2/1 Ruthie Braunstadter of Billings visited at the home of her grandmother. **1978** *Times* 1 Feb. 15/5 If it were only a friendly meal around a common table, I am sure that Catholics would be only too happy to visit at the tables of their friends whenever they were invited.

f. *to visit with*: = sense 8a. Now *U.S.*

1850 E. RUSKIN *Let.* 18 Jan. in M. Lutyens *Effie in Venice* (1965) II. 117 They visit with everybody in Venice. **1872** GEO. ELIOT *Middlem.* I. I. i. 8 The small group of gentry with whom he visited. **1903** F. NORRIS *Pit* v. 150 Almost every evening nowadays the Dearborn girls came..to visit with the Cresslers. **1927** C. A. LINDBERGH *We* iv. 57 Perryville, Missouri, where we visited with some of Klink's friends. **1949** M. LOWRY *Let.* 1 July (1967) 179 Margerie is flying..to visit—to visit *with*, I believe I should say— her family for a week. **1973** *Black Panther* 16 June 2/1 Seale visited with David Hilliard at Vacaville (Medical Facility) Prison. **1981** C. POTOK *Bk. Lights* (1982) vii. 227 He took Karen to a movie, then visited for a while with her family. **1985** *New Yorker* 11 Feb. 70/1 A young man of Ved's age and grade level is visiting with him.

g. *intr.* To talk or chat; to exchange conversation. *U.S.*

1856 M. D. COLT *Diary* 21 Oct. in *Went to Kansas* (1862) xii. 195 Have visited some, but am now in my room again to rest. **1879** A. TOURGÉE *Fool's Errand* xix. 111 He..stopped at the Mission-House, visiting with the teachers. **1898** M. DELAND *Old Chester Tales* 75 You can eat it while I get out and visit with the minister. **1929** *N.Y. Times Mag.* 20 Oct. 1 Having disposed of a batch of correspondence he was willing to visit in informal..fashion. It was good talk. **1967** 'P. KRUGER' *Weave Wicked Web* xi. 94, I called to see her around eight... Stella and I visited until close on eleven. **1979** N. MAILER *Executioner's Song* I. xviii. 304 Nicole drove down to the Preliminary Hearing..but they let her visit with Gary for only a moment.

9. a. To go to look at (†or explore); to inspect or examine; to look into or see to (something); in later use *esp.* to examine (vessels, goods, baggage, etc.) officially.

Rarely with clause as object, as in Milton *P.L.* VIII. 45.

13.. *K. Alis.* 6081 (Laud MS.), Whan hij han rested a lyte, þe lande hij wenden to visite. Hij founden narewe paþes, & liȝtt fen. **13..** *Coer de L.* 645 Thus they vysyted the Holy Land How they myght wynne it to her hand. **1338** R. BRUNNE *Chron.* (1810) 4 þe kyng Ine gart crie Home forto wend to childe & to wife, To visitte þer londes, to solace þer life. **1388** WYCLIF *Job* v. 24 And thou visityinge thi fairnesse [*gloss*, that is, biholding thi prosperite] schalt not do synne. **14..** *Tretyce* in *W. of Henley's Husb.* (1890) 58 Loke þat ye viset your þynges wisely & often..also loke you visite often tymis your servauntes. **1474** CAXTON *Chesse* III. iii. (1883) 94 Also ought they to rede visite and to knowe the statutes..of the contre. *c* **1500** *Melusine* xxi. 139 There he made come.. all the Captayns & chieftayns..to behold & vysyte theire harneys, yf eny thing wanted. **1514** BARCLAY *Cyt. & Uplondyshm.* (Percy Soc.) 8 Faustus, aryse thou out of thy lyttre hote, Go se and vysyte our wethers in the cote. **1530** PALSGR. Introd. 5 When they had thorowly visyted my said two bokes. **1585** T. WASHINGTON tr. *Nicholay's Voy.* I. xix. 21 b, Visiting afterwards theyr teeth and eyes, as though they had been horses. **1601** MOUNTJOY *Let. to Cecil* 13 Nov., in Moryson *Itin.* (1617) II. 157 It groweth now about foure a clocke in the morning at which time I lightly chuse to visit our Guards my selfe. **1654** BRAMHALL *Just Vind.* vii. (1661) 199 All Bulls and Missives which come from Rome to France are to be seen and visited, to try if there be nothing in them prejudicial [etc.]. **1687** A. LOVELL tr. *Thevenot's Trav.* I. 182 We were introduced into the City by the Trucheman of the Convent, who came with a Turk belonging to the Basha, that visited our Baggage. **1730** T. BOSTON *Mem.* viii. (1899) 161 The synod-book was once a year to be filled up for the General Assembly to visit it. **1737** *Gentl. Mag.* VII. 685/1 That no British Vessels shall be visited or molested..by the Judges of Contraband. **1772** *Regul. H.M. Service at Sea* 17 A Captain..is immediately to repair on board, and visit her through-out, in Company with his Officers. **1778** ORME *Hist. Milit. Trans. Indostan* VI. II. 21 A passport, or *dustuck*...should exempt the goods it specified from being visited or stopped by the officers. **1822** SHELLEY *Fragm. Unfin. Drama* 155, I rose, and went, Visiting my flowers from pot to pot. **1897** [see VISIT *sb.* 3 b].

b. *spec.* To go to (an institution) for the purpose of seeing that everything is in due order; to exercise a periodic surveillance or supervision over, or make a special investigation into (management or conduct).

c **1325** *Poem Times Edw. II* (Percy Soc.) x, The erchedeknes that beth sworn To visite holy cherche,..welle begynne Febleche to wyrche. **1533-4** *Act 25 Hen. VIII*, c. 21 §14 Provyded alway that the seid Archebisshopp of Canterburye..shall have noo power or auctoritie..to vysite or vexe any Monasteries. **1535** in *Lett. Suppress. Monasteries* (Camden) 76 Whan I have visite hys see, this nyght I wilbe at Feversham Abbay. **1558** BP. WATSON 7 *Sacram.* 148 Bishoppes haue power..to call synodes..to visit theyr diocesanes. *a* **1578** LINDESAY (Pitscottie) *Chron. Scot.* (S.T.S.) I. 159 The said Bischope went to wissit ewerie kirk withtin his diosie four tymes in the ȝeir. **1640** in J. Campbell *Balmerino & Abbey* III. iii. (1867) 191 The Presbyterie of Cupar did visitt the kirk. **1690** WOOD *Life* (O.H.S.) III. 334 Jonathan Trelawney, bishop of Exon visited Exeter College July 26. Dr. Arthur Bury, the rector, expelled. **1726** AYLIFFE *Parergon* 96 The Bishop ought to visit his Diocess every Year in his own Person. **1849** MACAULAY *Hist. Eng.* vi. II. 91 To appoint a commission with power to visit and govern the Church of England. **1868** J. H. BLUNT *Ref. Ch. Eng.* I. 52 A faculty empowering Wolsey to visit those English monasteries.

absol. **1575-85** ABP. SANDYS *Serm.* xiii. 217 His orderly proceeding appeareth in this, that he first visited and then reformed. **1621** BAYNES *Diocesan's Tryall* Pref. A 2 b, When Arch. Bancroft sent M. Harsenet to Visite as they call it, that is..to suppresse those that are not friends to the Bishops Kingdome. **1691** *Case of Exeter Coll.* 46 This is every whit as rational, as that a Bishop, being a Visitor of a College, &c. should take his Episcopal Authority along with him when he goes to Visit. **1713** GIBSON *Codex* XLII. viii. 1009/1 To enable Archdeacons to Visit with greater Authority and Effect. **1721** in *Cath. Rec. Soc. Publ.* VIII. 304 The said Lord Arch-Bishop..may visit once every year conformable to the Rule.

†**c.** To examine medically. *Obs.*

1484 CAXTON *Fables of Alfonce* i, When the medecyns had sene and vysyted hym..they sayd that he had no bodyly sekeness. *c* **1500** *Melusine* xxxvi. 288 Your woundes and soores must be vysyted and ouersene. *a* **1533** LD. BERNERS *Huon.* x. 28 He sent for his surgens, causyng them to serche his wounde;..and when they hadde well vysytyd the wounde, they sayde [etc.].

10. a. To go to (a temple, shrine, etc.) for the purpose of worship or as a religious duty.

a **1340** HAMPOLE *Psalter* xxvi. 8 þat i see þe will of lord & visite his tempile. **1387** TREVISA *Higden* (Rolls) VIII. 53 Whan Kyng Henry had i-visited mekeliche Thomas þe martires tombe. *c* **1420** *Chron. Vilod.* 3094 þer was a lady dwellyng in þat abbay þat wold vysed hurre tombe everyche day. **1465** *Paston Lett.* II. 233, I pray you voysyt the Rood of Northedor and Seynt Savyour,..and lat my sustyr Margery goo with yow to pray to them. *c* **1482** J. KAY tr. *Caoursin's Siege of Rhodes* (1870) ¶11 Hys entente..was: to uysyte deuoutely the blessed and holy sepulchre..in Jerusalem. **1509** BP. FISHER *Funeral Serm. C'tess Richmond* Wks. (1876) 300 Her legges and fete [had been occupied] in vysytynge the aulters and other holy places. *a* **1533** LD. BERNERS *Huon* lx. 209 We are goynge a pylgremage..to vysyt the holy sepulcure. **1613** PURCHAS *Pilgrimage* (1614) 614 In Thagia is visited the Sepulchre of a holy man. **1697** DRYDEN *Virg. Georg.* IV. 792 His Mother's Precepts he performs with Care; The Temples visits, and adores with Pray'r. **1728** CHAMBERS *Cycl.* s.v. *Sepulcher*, The Eastern Pilgrimages are all made with Design to visit the Holy Sepulcher. **1825** SCOTT *Betrothed* xxxii, The pilgrim.. carried a palm branch in his hand, to shew he had visited the Holy Land. **1885** *Encycl. Brit.* XIX. 92/1 Chinese converts [to Buddhism]..came to visit the holy places and to collect the sacred books.

b. To go to (a place) for the purpose of sightseeing or pleasure, or on some special errand.

c **1400** *Rom. Rose* 7619 This knowe ye, sir, as wel as I, That lovers gladly wole visiten The places ther her loves habiten. *c* **1400** MAUNDEV. (Roxb.) xv. 70 þe whilk in swilk maner visitez all rewmes fer to aspie þe maners of vs Cristen men. *c* **1420** *Chron. Vilod.* 3428 Bot in short tyme after þis His owne contrey visitede he wold. **1535** COVERDALE *Ezra* vii. 14 Beynge sent of the kynge and of the seuen lordes of the councell, to vyset Iuda and Ierusalem. *a* **1578** LINDESAY (Pitscottie) *Chron. Scot.* (S.T.S.) I. 240 They had seine and visitit the maist pairt of scotland. **1593** NORDEN *Spec. Brit., Cornw.* (1728) 35 A like hamlet..moste visited with Tynners, where they lodge and feede, being nere their mynes. **1632** LITHGOW *Trav.* VIII. 364 A French Lapidator, ..intending to visit Fez, ioyned company with me. **1657** R. LIGON *Barbadoes* (1673) 7 We were to have visited a small Island called Soll; by the intreating of a Portugal we carried with us. **1693** DOWDALL in Ingleby *Shaksp. Cent. of Praise* 417 The 1st Remarkable place in this County y^t I visitted was Stratford super avon. **1797** MRS. RADCLIFFE *Italian* vi, He designed to visit again, at midnight, the fortress of Paluzzi. **1837** LOCKHART *Scott* I. vii. 210 It was also..at this time that Scott visited for the first time Glammis. **1854** *Poultry Chron.* II. 249/2 About 4000 persons visited the poultry tent in the course of the day. **1863** LYELL *Antiq. Man* 2, I have visited..many parts of England, France and Belgium.

transf. **1894** NEWTON *Dict. Birds* 554 One tree after another is visited by the active little rovers, and its branches examined.

c. *transf.* Of things.

Sometimes with suggestion of sense 8.

1593 SHAKS. *Rich. II*, I. iii. 275 All places that the eie of heauen visits. **1601** —— *Jul. C.* II. i. 290 You are..As deere to me, as are the ruddy droppes That visit my sad heart. **1604** E. G[RIMSTONE] *D'Acosta's Hist. Indies* III. xxvii. 201 There are partes whereas the sea enters far within the land, as comming to visite it. *Ibid.* IV. viii. 230 Forasmuch as those places are never visited with the sunne. **1667** MILTON *P.L.* IV. 240 How from that Saphire Fount the crisped Brooks.. Ran Nectar, visiting each plant. **1757** GRAY *Bard* 40 Dear, as the light that visits these sad eyes. **1796** MORSE *Amer. Geog.* II. 351 The Seine..runs to the northwest, visiting Troyes, Paris, and Rouen, in its way. **1816** SHELLEY *Mont Blanc* 50 Some say that gleams of a remoter world Visit the soul in sleep. **1847** EMERSON *Musketaquid* 12 For me in showers, in sweeping showers, the spring Visits the valley.

d. Of birds, etc.: To resort to or frequent (land or sea, a country, etc.) for a limited period or at certain seasons.

1774 GOLDSM. *Nat. Hist.* (1776) VI. 93 As they never visit land,..their feathers take a colour from their situation. **1802** MONTAGU *Ornith. Dict.* s.v. *Blackcap*, The blackcap is a migrative species visiting us early in the spring. **1840** *Cuvier's Anim. Kingd.* 199 The Mountain Chaffinch.. which visits Britain in Winter. **1887** NEWTON in *Encycl. Brit.* XXII. 577 In winter the Storks of Europe retire to Africa,..while those of Asia visit India.

absol. **1831** T. NUTTALL in *Mem. Amer. Acad. Arts & Sci.* (1833) I. 96 [The] Canada Jay..regularly visits, if it does not breed, in Maine or New Hampshire.

†**11.** To come to (a person) *with* some accompaniment; to supply or enrich *with* some benefit.

a **1300** *Cursor M.* 18158 (Cott.) þe lem þat come wit him, Brast all þe bandes of ur site, And visite vs wit grett delite. ? *a* **1400** *Morte Arth.* 1726 Thynk one þe valyaunt prynce þat vesettez us ever With landez and lordscheppez, whare us beste lykes. **1591** SHAKS. *Two Gentl.* III. ii. 83 Visit by night your Ladies chamber-window With some sweet comfort. **1645** CARYL *Expos. Job* I. 637 God visiteth his [people] with mercies.

visitable ('vɪzɪtəbl(ə)l), *a.* [f. prec. + -ABLE.]

1. Of institutions, etc.: Liable to visitation by some competent authority; subject to official supervision or inspection.

1605 COKE *Reports* v. 15/2 All religious or Ecclesiastical houses, whereof the king was founder, are..only visitable and corrigible by the kings ecclesiasticall Commission. **1661** J. STEPHENS *Procurations* 40 When those Religious persons..had relinquished their habit, rule, and order, for which they were visitable, then..the Visitation ceased. **1726** AYLIFFE *Parergon* 295 All..Hospitals..built since the Reformation are Visitable by the King or Lord-Chancellor. **1767** BURN *Eccl. Law* (ed. 2) IV. 12 Free chapels..being visitable only by commission from the king. **1873** *Act 36 & 37 Vict.* c. 39 §4 In all cases such holder shall be visitable by the Visitor of the Chapter. **1895** PHILLIMORE *Eccl. Law* (ed. 2) 1061 Donatives and free chapels used to pay no procurations to any ecclesiastical ordinary, because they were not visitable by any.

2. Of places or persons: Capable of being visited; readily admitting of a visit; worth visiting.

a **1701** MAUNDRELL *Journ. Jerus.* (1732) 104 In order to see the Sanctuaries, and other visitable places. **1837** *New Monthly Mag.* LI. 192 Richmond..might..thus be rendered visitable by tourists. **1842** SIR J. GRAHAM in *Illustr. Lond. News* 14 May 7/1 The children easily visitable by their parents. **1876** RUSKIN *St. Mark's Rest* i. §2 The most beautiful columns at present extant and erect in the conveniently visitable world. **1896** *Advance* (Chicago) 4 June 811/1 The tropics are visitable in the winter only, and then the preacher is busiest. **1953** *John o' London's Weekly* 12 June 519/1 He was also known as a charming and eminently visitable old gentleman. **1972** *Maclean's Mag.* Mar. 57/3 While it has it share of visitable old buildings Rijeka is more European than most Yugoslav cities. **1983** R. MUIR in Muir & Welfare *Nat. Trust Guide Prehistoric & Roman Britain* ii. 27/2 There are few exciting and visitable relics of [Mesolithic] human life apart from caves.

transf. **1866** MISS MULOCK *Noble Life* vi, His rank lifted him above the small proprietors who lived within visitable distance of the Castle.

3. Of persons: **a.** Capable of being visited on more or less equal terms by those of some standing in society; having some social position in a neighbourhood.

1765 COWPER *Let.* 18 Oct., In about two months time after my arrival, I became known to all the visitable people here. **1835** *Court Mag.* VI. 186/1 The Orange Grove! I was not aware that visitable people ever resided there! **1851** TUPPER *Castle Cornet* 309 The landlords, having no visitable neighbours, no society within many miles, are necessarily absentees. **1876** GEO. ELIOT *Dan. Der.* v, In a select party of thirty..few visitable families could be entirely left out.

b. Capable of being visited by a clergyman in the discharge of his pastoral duties.

1904 R. SMALL *Hist. U.P. Congregations* I. 474 In the southern division..there were only ninety visitable families at that time.

4. Such as admits of receiving visitors.

1864 KEBLE *Let.* in J. T. Coleridge *Mem.* (1869) 486 Charlotte was not very much in visiting, or visitable order, during a great part of the time. **1876** MRS. WHITNEY *Sights & Ins.* II. xxv. 538 Her cold, or whatever it was, had affected her face and eyes; she was not really in visitable condition.

‖**visita'dor.** *rare.* [Sp. and Pg., f. *visitar* to visit.] An official visitor, inspector, or superintendent.

1698 FRYER *Acc. E. India & P.* 311 The Father Visitador of the Carmelites, a Spaniard, and a good Scholar. **1777** ROBERTSON *Hist. Amer.* VI. (1778) II. 231 He authorised Francisco Tello de Sandoval to repair to Mexico as Visitador or superintendent of that country. **1846** G. GARDNER *Brazil* 200 Soon afterwards the Visitador's troop overtook us, consisting of eight or nine horses.

Visi'tandine. [F., irreg. f. L. *vīsitand-*, gerundial stem of *vīsitāre* to visit + -INE.] **a.** A nun belonging to the Order of the Visitation, founded in 1610 by Mme. de Chantal (St. Frances) under the direction of St. Francis de Sales.

1747 *Gentl. Mag.* 571/1 There is near the same number of Congregants, Ursulines, Visitandines, and other sorts of Beguines. **1872** W. H. JERVIS *Gallican Ch.* I. v. 247 A kindred institution took its rise, whose history is one of special interest, namely the Order of Visitandines, founded by François de Sales. **1888** EMILY BOWLES *Mme. de Maintenon* 128 Madame de Maintenon wisely made choice of some Visitandines..to train the community.

b. *attrib.* or as *adj.*

1871 A. J. C. HARE *Walks in Rome* I. vi. 277 It has been decided that some remains which exist in the garden of the Villa Mills (now a Convent of Visitandine Nuns) are those of the House of Hortensius. **1888** *Dublin Rev.* Oct. 313 Miss Giberne..who afterwards became a Visitandine nun.

visitant ('vɪzɪtənt), *sb.* and *a.* [a. F. *visitant*, pres. pple. of *visiter*, or ad. L. *vīsitant-*, *vīsitans* pres. pple. of *vīsitāre* to visit.]

A. *sb.* **1.** One who pays a visit to another; a visitor.

Very common in 17–18th cent.; now *rare* or *Obs.*

1599 B. JONSON *Cynthia's Rev.* II. i, Hee has a rich wrought wast-coat to entertaine his visitants in. **1623** MASSINGER *Dk. Milan* I. iii, For the most part she hath kept her private chamber, No visitants admitted. **1664** PEPYS *Diary* 22 Nov., Being sick, and full of visitants, we could not speak with him. **1697** DRYDEN *Virg. Georg.* II. 644 No Palace, with a lofty Gate he wants, T' admit the Tydes of early Visitants. **1722** POPE *Lett.* (1737) 127 As a visitant, a lodger, or a friend you are always welcome to me. **1760** JOHNSON *Idler* No. 101 ¶3 His chamber was filled by visitants, eager to catch the dictates of experience. **1825–9** MRS. SHERWOOD *Lady of Manor* I. v. 151 She calmly explained to her visitant the motives of her conduct. **1826** LAMB *Elia* II. *Popular Fallacies* xii, It is not of guests that we complain, but of endless, purposeless visitants. **1832** R. & J. LANDER *Exped. Niger* I. xi. 81 He was shy and bashful..and really appeared agitated and afraid of his white-faced visitants.

transf. **1807** J. E. SMITH *Phys. Bot.* 260 The services rendered by such visitants [*sc.* insects] will be understood when we have described all the parts of a flower. **1862** R. VAUGHAN *Eng. Nonconformity* 357 Rulers who deserve that an avenger should be upon their path, cannot always resist the impression that such a visitant may be at hand. **1868** GLADSTONE *Glean.* (1879) III. 44 To the absolutely stereotyped forms both of faith and scepticism,..the author of 'Ecce Homo' has been a most unacceptable visitant.

b. Applied to supernatural beings or agencies, etc., esp. as revealing themselves to mortals.

1667 MILTON *P.L.* XI. 225 Adam..to Eve, While the great Visitant approachd, thus spake. **1782** J. BROWN *Nat. & Revealed Relig.* II. ii. 133 We are commended to hear him, as infinitely superior to Moses and Elias, his then visitants. **1813** COLERIDGE *Remorse* III. i. 85 Thou sainted spirit, Burst on our sight, a passing visitant! **1847** DISRAELI *Tancred* II. xi, I would ask those mountains..why they no longer received heavenly visitants! **1873** M. ARNOLD *Lit. & Dogma* (1876) 248 The spiritual visitant, indeed, which rejoiced the wise poet of Asera, was not the Paraclete of Jesus.

c. One who visits from charitable motives.

1661 WITHER *Improv. Imprisonment* (title-p.), A few Crums & Scraps Lately found in a Prisoners-Basket at Newgate, And Saved together, by a Visitant of Oppressed Prisoners.

d. One who makes a short stay at a friend's house.

1769 WESLEY *Wks.* (1872) III. 365, I found a young gentlewoman there, a visitant. **1822** SCOTT *Peveril* xii, An attachment, which lulled..to pleasing dreams, though of a character so different, her charge and her visitant. **1838** LYTTON *Alice* II. ii, She was transferred from the little chamber,..to an apartment..usually appropriated to the regular Christmas visitant, the Dowager Countess of Chipperton.

2. One who visits some place or object of interest.

1677 PLOT *Oxfordsh.* 238 Being often used by way of sport to wet the Visitants of the Grot. **1710** HEARNE *Collect.* (O.H.S.) II. 382 Visitants of the Library. **1815** W. H. IRELAND *Scribbleomania* 88 *note*, Which fact the visitant is given to understand from a long inscription upon a brass plate. **1839** *Civil Eng. & Arch. Jrnl.* II. 194/1 Some of the earliest and most extensive specimens of painted glass, well worthy of the attention of the visitant. **1894** MRS. DYAN *Man's Keeping* (1899) 61 This gallery had frequent visitants.

b. One who visits a place, shrine, etc., from religious motives.

1698 FRYER *Acc. E. India & P.* 45 Some of the Visitants count it meritorious to be trod to death under a weighty Chariot of Iron. *a* **1797** H. WALPOLE *Mem. Geo. III* (1845) I. x. 147 The father would accept no money from the various visitants, for which he was promised an adequate recompense by the chiefs of his sect. **1812** CARY *Dante, Par.* xxv. 20 Behold the peer of mickle might, That makes Galicia throng'd with visitants. **1844** KINGLAKE *Eothen* xvi. (1845) 228 The caution is said to be as applicable to the visitants of Jerusalem as to those of Mecca.

c. One who visits a strange town or country; a stranger who spends a short time in a place; a temporary resident.

1751 SMOLLETT *Per. Pic.* (1779) III. lxxxi. 183 Ghent.. was much crowded with these new visitants. **1762** GOLDSM. *Nash* 24 The lodgings for visitants were paltry, though expensive. **1801** J. JONES tr. *Bÿgge's Trav. Fr. Rep.* i. 22 This town has very little to invite the eye of a visitant. **1823** JEFFERSON *Writ.* (1830) IV. 361 The paper..was not written by a Virginian, but a visitant from another State. **1857** G. MUSGRAVE *Pilgr. Dauphiné* I. ii. 34 A splendid specimen.. was continually surrounded by the French visitants. **1863** HAWTHORNE *Our Old Home* (1879) 144 To show..the absurdity of a new visitant pretending to hold any opinion whatever on such subjects.

d. One who enters a country in hostile fashion; an invader.

1765 BLACKSTONE *Comm.* I. 93 The antient and christian inhabitants of the island retired to those natural intrenchments, for protection from their pagan visitants.

3. A thing which comes to one in a casual or temporary manner.

1742 YOUNG *Nt. Th.* v. 723 When your neighbour's knell (Rude visitant!) knocks hard at your dull sense. *a* **1774** GOLDSM. *Surv. Exp. Philos.* (1776) II. 135 However irregular we find the wind.., they have it a more constant and more grateful visitant. **1833** WHEWELL in Todhunter *Acc. Writ.* (1876) II. 160 Digby..is still ill of a rheumatic fever, his not unusual visitant. **1849** MISS MULOCK *Ogilvies* xvi, Chasing away sleep and making the faint daylight a welcome visitant. **1876** GEO. ELIOT in Cross *Life* (1885) III. 297, I am never in that mood of sadness which used to be my frequent visitant.

4. A migratory bird, etc., as temporarily frequenting a particular locality.

1770 J. LOGAN *Cuckoo* iii, Delightful visitant! with thee I hail the time of flowers. **1774** GOLDSM. *Nat. Hist.* (1776) VI. 29 Such are our visitants. With regard to those which.. breed here [etc.]. **1834** MUDIE *Brit. Birds* (1841) I. 19 Those [birds] which come in the spring and depart in the autumn are called summer visitants. **1883** *Fisheries Exhib. Catal.* (ed. 4) 97 Fresh-water fishes may be..merely visitants from the ocean for the purpose of depositing their spawn. **1894** R. B. SHARPE *Handbk. Birds Gt. Brit.* I. 13 The Hooded Crow ..being..in some localities a winter visitant only, in others a resident.

B. *adj.* Paying a visit or visits; having the position or character of a visitor.

1653 H. COGAN tr. *Scarlet Gown* 67 One shall never see any visitant Coches there, he being no otherwise accounted of, then as of a forelorn Cardinal. **1676** D'URFEY *Mme. Fickle* III. ii, I begin to have a knowledge of the visitant kinsman that us'd to molest us. **1726** DE FOE *Hist. Devil* (1822) 247 An intimate Devil, or a Devil visitant. **1794** PIOZZI *Synon.* I. 125 The snappish housekeeper gives short answers to the poor visitant niece. **1807** WORDSW. *Song Feast Brougham Castle* 129 He knew the rocks which Angels haunt Upon the mountains visitant. **1864** TENNYSON *Aylmer's F.* 166 And Edith's everywhere; And Edith ever visitant with him. **1887** RUSKIN *Præterita* II. 281 Mr. Melvill was entirely amiable in the Church visitant, though not formidable in the Church militant.

'visitating, *ppl. a. rare*⁻¹. [f. L. *vīsitāt-*, ppl. stem of *vīsitāre* to visit.] Visiting.

1612 *Two Noble K.* I. i, But our Lords Lie blist'ring 'fore the visitating Sun, And were good Kings, when living.

visitation (vɪzɪ'teɪʃən). Forms: 4 **vysytacyun,** 5–6 **vysytacyon** (5 **-acyone,** 6 **-acion**), **vysitacyon, visytacion;** 4–5 **visitacioun** (6 *Sc.* **-atioun**), 4–7 **visitacion** (7 **-acyon**), 4– **visitation;** 6 **vesyt-, ffessyt-, fecytacyon.** [a. AF. *visitacioun* (Gower), OF. and F. *visitation* (= Sp. *visitacion*, Pg. *visitação*, It. *visitazione*), or ad. L. *vīsitātiōn-*, *vīsitātio*, noun of action f. *vīsitāre* to visit.]

I. 1. The action, on the part of one in authority, or of a duly qualified or authorized person, of going to a particular place in order to make an inspection and satisfy himself that everything is in order; an instance of such inspection or supervision.

a. A visit by an ecclesiastical person (or body) to examine into the state of a diocese, parish, religious institution, etc.; *spec.* in English use, such a visit paid by a bishop or archdeacon; a meeting or gathering of persons concerned in such a visit.

Quotations for an archdeacon's visitation are placed separately under (*b*).

(*a*) **1303** R. BRUNNE *Handl. Synne* 2103 He [an abbot] went hys wey To Palestyne, þat ys an abbey, To make hys vysytacyun As falleþ yn relygyun. **1401** *Pol. Poems* (Rolls) II. 21 Why be ye not under your bishops visitations, and leege men to our king? **1526** *Pilgr. Perf.* (W. de W. 1531) 64 Abbot Pyor, whiche among a great multitude of fathers and bretherne gathered together in maner of a vysytacyon..dyd in this wyse. *a* **1548** HALL *Chron., Hen. VIII*, 143 The Cardinall by Visitacions, makyng of Abbottes,..and other pollynges..had made his threasore egall with the kynges. **1591** SPENSER *M. Hubberd* 569 All their Parishners..to the Ordinarie of them complain'd,..Till at the length he published to holde A Visitation, and them cyted thether. **1661** J. STEPHENS *Procurations* 17 For what are Visitations other then laborious travellings from place to place? **1739** BP. HERRING in J. Duncombe *Lett.* (1773) II. 132 It was the year of my primary visitation, and I determined to see every part of my diocese. **1761** WARBURTON in *W. & Hurd's Lett.* (1809) 326, I fancy my Visitation..will be the last week in June and the first in July. **1827** HALLAM *Const. Hist.* ii. (1876) I. 70 Wolsey, as papal legate,..commenced a visitation of the professed as well as secular clergy in 1523.

(*b*) **1536** *Dunmow Churchw. MS.* fol. 22 b, Item payd at the ffessytacyon, iiii^d. **1537** *Ibid.* fol. 23 Item payd at Chelmsford at the Vesytacyon for howr costs, xviiid. **1566** *Eng. Ch. Furniture* (Peacock, 1866) 56 Imprimis a box made of bone sold to Jho Wattes sens the last visitacion who keeps yt to put monney in. **1603** *Constit. & Canons* cxi, In all Visitations of Bishops and Archdeacons, the Church-wardens..shall..present the names of all those which behaue themselues rudely..in the Church. **1692** PRIDEAUX *Lett.* (Camden) 152, I have yours of the 16th, but it came not to my hands till last Friday, for I was absent at Ipswich on a visitation. **1713** GIBSON *Codex* 999 If any Archdeacons are entituled to require Exhibits in their Visitations, it can only be upon the foot of Custom. **1726** AYLIFFE *Parergon* 96 For the Bishop ought to visit his Diocess every Year in his own Person, unless he thinks fit to omit the same,..and then in such a Case he ought to send his Archdeacon, which was the Original of the Archdeacons Visitation. **1842** *Words to Churchwardens* (Camb. Camd. Soc.) I. 3 The Archdeacon at his Visitation seldom ends his charge without a few words to us Churchwardens. **1857** TOULMIN SMITH *Parish* 94 The articles of Visitation issued by him, when archdeacon in 1713, as to be answered by all churchwardens.

(*c*) **1727** P. WALKER *Life Semple* Biog. Presbyt. (1827) I. 158 There were few parochial Visitations..but he was at them, for encouraging of laborious godly Ministers, and censuring of such as were scandalous.

b. A visit of inspection made by one or more persons having civil authority or jurisdiction or specially appointed to exercise supervision within a certain sphere; the making of such visits; †the body of persons making an inspection of this kind.

†*visitation of maners*: see quot. 1607 and MAINOUR.

1533–4 *Act 25 Hen. VIII*, c. 21 §14 Redresse visitacion and confirmacion shalbe had by the Kynges Highnes. **1556** *Chron. Gr. Friars* (Camden) 54 Item the v. day after in September [1547] beganne the kynges vysytacion at Powlles, and alle imagys pullyd downe. **1607** COWELL *Interpr.*, *Visitation of maners*..was wont to be the name of the Regarders office in auncient time. **1665** in W. Campbell *Ch. & Par. Kirkaldy* 84 The visitation present appoynts the school to be visited four times in the year. **1691** WOOD *Ath. Oxon.* I. 327 On the 8. of Nov...the Visitation of his Library is commonly made. **1773** *Gentl. Mag.* XLIII. 349 Sir Thomas Pye..has it in command from the King to acquaint [certain admirals, captains, etc.] that he is pleased with their attention during his visitation at Portsmouth. **1845** POLSON in *Encycl. Metrop.* II. 826/1 It was held, that in default of.. a special visitor appointed by the founder or charter, the king, in the person of his chancellor, had the right of visitation. **1874** BUCKNILL & TUKE *Psychol. Med.* (ed. 3) 2 The bill of 1828, by which the Secretary of State was allowed to appoint fifteen Commissioners annually, for the license and visitation of those houses which had been previously licensed by the College of Physicians.

c. A periodic visit made to a district by heralds to examine and enrol arms and pedigrees. Now only *Hist.*

1572 N. ROSCARROCKE *Prelim. Verses* in Bossewell *Armorie*, Of dubbing knights, the orders ther they haue;.. With visitacions, which allottes to eche desert his right. **1640** YORKE *Union Hon.* To Rdr., For the Armes of our Lincolnshire Gentlemen, I haue taken their knowledge from themselues, and by Visitations. **1849** R. SIMS (*title*), An Index to the Pedigrees and Arms contained in the Heralds' Visitations. **1864** BOUTELL *Her. Hist. & Pop.* xiii. (ed. 3) 133 The Records of these Visitations are preserved in the College of Arms.

d. In general use: Examination, inspection.

1583 MELBANCKE *Philotimus* E iij b, The old huddle missing his monye at his next visitation, toke the haulter and hanged himselfe. **1643** SIR T. BROWNE *Relig. Med.* I. §16, I cannot tell by what Logick we call a Toad, a Beare, or an Elephant, ugly, they..having past that generall visitation of God, who saw that all that he had made was good.

e. *spec.* Examination of goods by a customs officer or similar official; the action on the part of a belligerent vessel of ascertaining, by entry or close examination, the character of a merchant ship belonging to a neutral state.

1755 MAGENS *Insurances* II. 513 Where these Goods shall be subject to Visitation in the same manner, as those which are made in the Kingdom. **1826** KENT *Comm.* I. 31 Maritime states claim upon a principle just in itself and temperately applied, a right of visitation. **1867** SMYTH *Sailor's Word-bk.* 714 The law of nations gives to every belligerent cruiser the right of visitation and search of all merchant ships.

2. a. The action of going to a place, either for some special purpose or merely in order to see it; an instance of this.

c **1386** CHAUCER *Wife's Prol.* 555 Therfore I made my visitacions To vigilies, and to processions To prechyng eek and to thise pilgrimages. **1654** CODRINGTON tr. *Justin* xxxviii. (1672) 377 The Ambassadors of the Romans..made a visitation into those parts to observe the condition and Kingdoms of their Confederates. **1687** A. LOVELL tr. *Thevenot's Trav.* I. 172 We took the way by Tor, partly to see it, and partly to take a Monk to guide us in our visitations. **1720** WELTON *Suffer. Son of God* II. xviii. 495 The Blessed Jesus..found Time enough to make His Circular Visitation thro' all those Towns in and about Palestine. *a* **1774** GOLDSM. *Surv. Exp. Philos.* (1776) I. 395 In this manner we find, that no part of nature is wholly secluded from human visitation. **1829** LYTTON *Devereux* I. viii, The town was a favourite place of visitation with all the family. **1832** G. DOWNES *Lett. Cont. Countries* I. 311 We proceeded from hence to the Church of St. Mary Segreta, and terminated our visitation at that of the Holy Sepulchre. **1866** ROGERS *Agric. & Prices* I. xxvii. 654 As they possessed estates in widely distant places, it was an object to them that they should have easy and convenient means of visitation.

transf. **1821** SCOTT *Kenilw.* xxix, Lambourne, on whom his last draught, joined to repeated visitations of the pitcher upon former occasions began to make some innovation.

b. *poet.* The object of a visit. *rare*$^{-1}$.

1667 MILTON *P.L.* XI. 275 O flours,..My early visitation, and my last At Eev'n, which I bred up with tender hand.

c. The action, on the part of animals, of resorting to a particular place at certain seasons, or of exceptionally appearing in places which are not their usual habitat.

1774 GOLDSM. *Nat. Hist.* (1776) VI. 330 Along the coasts of Norway,..these animals are found punctual in their visitations.

3. a. The action or practice of visiting sick or distressed persons as a work of charity or pastoral duty.

c **1430** LYDG. *Min. Poems* (E.E.T.S.) 79 Whan Abackuk.. Broughte potage in to Babyloun,..Affter figure this mater to conveye, How almesse-dede and vysytacyoun Gretly avaylleth to sowlys whan they deye. **1474** CAXTON *Chesse* III. v. (1883) 120 And as to them that ben seke contynuell visitacion of them. **1548–9** (Mar.) *Bk. Com. Prayer, Offices* 18 The Order for the visitacion of the sicke. **1583** in *Wodrow Soc. Misc.* (1844) 460 As tuitching the Visitatioun of the seik, he declairit he was..glad to wissie the puirest creatour. **1777** BRAND *Pop. Antiq.* 379 In performing..the Service appropriated to the Visitation of the Sick with one of these Men (who died a few Days after). **1795** PALEY *Clergym. Comp.* Pref., The offices of Public and Private Baptism, though no ways relating to the visitation of the Sick, are retained. **1862** *Chambers's Encycl.* III. 180 The Church of England..retains private confession in the rubric for visitation of the sick. **1886** KINGTON OLIPHANT *New English* I. 160 An office for the Visitation of the sick, which dates from about 1390.

b. The action of pastoral visiting on the part of a clergyman.

1546 *Yorks. Chantry Surv.* (Surtees) 253 The curate beinge of visitacion in the one parte of his paroch, cannot com to the church by the space of ij dayes. **1818** SCOTT *Rob Roy* iii, Country parsons, jogging homewards after a visitation. **1911** T. B. KILPATRICK *N. Test. Evangelism* III. ii. §2. 167 The Work of Visitation. Every minister knows that this may be the most profitable part of his pastoral duty. .. The work of visitation can never be stereotyped.

4. a. ***the Visitation*** (***of our Lady***), the visit paid by the Virgin Mary to Elizabeth, recorded in Luke i. 39 ff.; hence *ellipt.*, the day on which this is commemorated, July 2; also, a picture representing the event.

1498 *Coventry Leet Bk.* 588 This ȝere the Chaptur of blak monkes was kept at Couentre aboute þe visitacion of our Lady. **1547** BOORDE *Introd. Knowl.* xiv. (1870) 161, I haue seen snowe in somer on saynct Peters day and the Vysytacion of our Ladye. **1611** COTGR. s.v., The feast of the Visitation of our Ladie. *a* **1700** EVELYN *Diary* 10 Nov. 1644, There are in it divers good pictures, as the Assumption..; the Crucifix; the Visitation of Elizabeth. **1753** *Chambers' Cycl.* Suppl. s.v., The Visitation of the Virgin Mary is a feast instituted first by pope Urban IV. in the year 1389. **1880** F. MEYRICK in *Dict. Chr. Antiq.* II. 1140/1 Among the black-letter or second-class festivals [in the Anglican calendar] occur:—1. The Visitation, July 2nd. **1880** tr. *Woltmann & Woermann's Hist. Paint.* I. 420 The Visitation..in which.. the expression of Elizabeth surprises by its individuality.

b. ***the*** (***order of the***) ***Visitation***, the Visitandine order of nuns.

1701 in *Cath. Rec. Soc. Publ.* VII. 94 We were at the Nuns of the Visitation, St. Frances de Sales' Festivall. **1745** A. BUTLER *Lives Saints* (1845) VIII. 277 He [St. Francis of Sales] then mentioned his project of forming a new establishment of a congregation of the Visitation of the Virgin Mary. **1864** NEWMAN *Apol.* iv. (1904) 143/1 There was a lady, now a nun of the Visitation, to whom at this time I wrote the following letters. **1899** A. SHIELD in *Dublin Rev.* July 64 To visit the Nuns of the Visitation in their convent at Chaillot, founded by Queen Henrietta Maria.

5. a. The action of making a friendly or formal call or calls; social intercourse of this nature; visiting.

a **1586** SIDNEY *Arcadia* III. xviii. (1912) 463 He..so much abhorred all visitation or honour,..that he besought his two noble friends to carrie him away to a castle not far of. **1588** PARKE tr. *Mendoza's Hist. China* 190 Many of the Gentlemen of the cittie did go vnto the Spaniards to visite them..in the which visitation they spent all the whole day. **1605** *Journ. of Earl of Nottingham* 50 Sunday, Munday and Tuesday were..spent onely in visitation and matters of complement with one or other. **1631** MAY tr. *Barclay's Mirr. Mindes* II. 81 Because there was acquaintance betweene the two families, this youth was brought by way of visitation to the Ladies lodging. **1643** BAKER *Chron., Edw. III*, 169 The King of Scots came for businesse and visitation. **1819** CRABBE *T. of Hall* IX, How much she grieved to lose the given day In dissipation wild, in visitation gay. **1899** *Allbutt's Syst. Med.* VIII. 411 Family visitation [of the insane] should be prohibited.

b. An instance of such visiting; a visit.

1581 PETTIE *Guazzo's Civ. Conv.* III. (1586) 157 b, The chaunces of these visitations in deede are so often, and so many, that they spend six daies of the week in them. **1588** PARKE tr. *Mendoza's Hist. China* 176 He..was more familiar than at his first visitation. **1617** MORYSON *Itin.* III. 17 Men of best quality will easily beleeve, that their name is knowne among strangers, and they take these visitations for honours done them. **1629** WADSWORTH *Pilgr.* viii. 83 Which Letters and visitations I entertained vntill my Mother had paid my debts. **1642** EGLISHAM *Forerunner of Revenge* 14 Hee knowing Buckinghams visitation to proceed of dissimulation, requested your petitioner..to finde the meanes to get him away quickly. **1786** MRS. A. M. BENNETT *Juvenile Indiscr.* I. 180 As he attended Mr. Orthodox to the door, to press his early visitation next morning. **1798** S. & HT. LEE *Canterb. T.* II. 509 Feasts and visitations occupied the Duke. *a* **1817** JANE AUSTEN *Watsons* (1879) 337 In the occurrences of the visitation..she heard Mr. Howard spoken of as the preacher. **1877** BLACK *Green Past.* ii, Her father hearing that she contemplated some charitable visitation of the kind had strictly forbidden it.

c. A prolonged visit, or one which is disagreeable to the recipient.

1819 *Metropolis* I. 231 She now went on a visitation (for her visits are far beyond the common length) to Lord ——.

d. A gathering at the home of a deceased person before the funeral takes place; a wake. *U.S.*

1974 *Amer. Speech 1971* XLVI. 70 Another interesting Boston area universal was the use, even among Protestants, of *wake* for what is elsewhere in the state often called a *visitation*. **1976** N. THORNBURG *Cutter & Bone* iii. 75 'The goddamn funeral,' he explained. 'Or what do they call it the day before—visitation?' **1983** *Chicago Sun-Times* 27 Sept. 18 An acquaintance in the life insurance business showed up at the visitation and proceeded to solicit business... What kind of a person would latch onto an opportunity to solicit business at a wake?

II. 6. The action, on the part of God or some supernatural power, of coming to, or exercising power over, a person or people for some end:

a. In order to encourage, comfort, or aid.

c **1340** HAMPOLE *Prose Tr.* 19 If he..halde it a specyalle vesytacyon of oure Lorde, and thynke it mare þan it es. *c* **1430** LYDG. *Min. Poems* (Percy Soc.) 72 Whan God of his grete visitacioun, List out of this worlde for hym to sende. *c* **1450** *Mirk's Festial* 41 Syr, ȝe mowe blesse þe tyme þat ȝe wer borne, forto haue suche vysitacion, as I now haue herde. *a* **1513** FABYAN *Chron.* (1811) 306 Now drawe ye therfore holefull water of lore of my wellys, & that wt ioy, for ye tyme of your vysytacyon is comyn. **1597** HOOKER *Eccl. Pol.* V. xxiii, For which cause we see that the most comfortable visitations, which God hath sent men from above have [etc.]. **1643** CARYL *Expos. Job* I. 636 Mercies are visitations; when God comes in kindness and love to do us good, he visiteth us. **1667** MILTON *P.L.* IX. 22 My Celestial Patroness, who deignes Her nightly visitation unimplor'd. *a* **1741** CHALKLEY *Wks.* (1766) 86 The merciful Visitations of that High and Lofty One who inhabits Eternity! **1814** WORDSW. *Excurs.* I. 212 In such high hour Of visitation from the living God, Thought was not. **1841** MYERS *Cath. Th.* III. §9. 34 In such a high hour of religious visitation and in this etherial region..the Divine Spirit may mingle with the Human.

b. In order to test, try, examine, or judge.

1382 WYCLIF *Luke* xix. 44 And thei schulen not leeue in thee a stoon on a stoon, for thou hast not knowe the tyme of thi visitacioun. **1382** —— *1 Pet.* v. 6 Therfor be ȝe mekid vndir the miȝty hond of God, that he reise ȝou in the day of visitacioun. *a* **1450** *Mankind* 281 in *Macro Plays* 11 Lyke as þe smyth trieth ern in þe feer, So was he triede by Godis vysytacyon. **1526** *Pilgr. Perf.* (W. de W. 1531) 134 b, It maketh hym..glad to receyue the visitacion of our lorde what so euer it be. **1551** ABP. HAMILTON *Catech.* 24 b, For na vther cause..bot yat thai wald nocht knaw the tyme of thair uisitatioun. **1560** BIBLE (Genev.) *Isaiah* x. 3 What wil ye do now in the daie of visitation, & of destruction. **1645** CARYL *Expos. Job* I. 636 Jerusalem is threatned to be searcht with candles, and that was the time of Jerusalems visitation. **1801** SOUTHEY *Thalaba* I. xxvii, In the Day of Visitation, In the fearful hour of Judgement, God will remember thee!

c. So as to afflict with sickness or other trouble, esp. by way of punishment for wrong-doing.

c **1380** WYCLIF *Sel. Wks.* III. 207 And in alle þingis bewar of grucchyng aȝens God and his visitacion, in gret labour and long, and gret sikenesse, and oþer adversities. **1421** HOCCLEVE *Complaint* 382 My sycknesse, which came of god[de]s visytacion. **1439** *Rolls of Parlt.* V. 33/1 That notorie sekenesse or impediment by Gods visitation. **1455** *Ibid.* 313/2 John Banham Squier,..which is blynde by Goddes visitation. **1485** *Coventry Leet Bk.* 524 And any Casualtes of disease by Godes visitacion com vnto the Recourder. *a* **1529** SKELTON *Magnyf.* 2016 Pray to God your sorowes to asswage: It is foly to grudge agaynst his vysytacyon. **1603** (*title*), Certaine Prayers..most necessary to be vsed at this time in the present Visitation of Gods heauy hand for our manifold sinnes. **1635** *Life & Pranks of Long Meg of Westminster* (Hindley II) 45 'Tis the visitation of the Lord for the great sins you have committed. **1645** CARYL *Expos. Job* I. 636 If God in affliction visit us,..let us answer his visitation of us with our visitation of him. **1820** *John Bull* 31 Dec. 24/2 A verdict of 'died by the visitation of God' was recorded. **1898** J. ARCH *Story of Life* xiii. 312 A visitation of the Almighty..upon a luxurious and dissipated aristocracy.

d. A similar action on the part of an evil power or disembodied spirit.

1844 DICKENS *Christmas Carol* ii. 14 The ghost had warned him of a visitation when the bell tolled one. **1861** GEO. ELIOT *Silas M.* i. 7 He observed that, to him, this trance looked more like a visitation of Satan than a proof of divine favour.

7. A heavy affliction, blow, or trial, regarded as an instance of divine dispensation; retributive punishment operating by this means.

a **1450** *Mankind* 721 (Brandl), Yt were to me solace, þe cruell vysytacyone of deth. **1567** *Trial Treas.* (1850) 37 Enter God's Visitation. I am God's minister, called Visitation... Sometime I bring sickness; sometime perturbation. *c* **1585** *Faire Em.* V. i, Put case I had beene blinde, and could not see—As often times such visitations falles That pleaseth God. **1639** *Bury Wills* (Camden) 172 My late wives kinsman..at the late heavy visitacion did take great paines about me in the time of my trouble. **1642** EARL OF EGLINTON *Let.* in *10th Rep. Hist. MSS. Comm.* App. I. 52, I am sorrowfull from my heart for your lordships great losse and heavie visitatioun. **1706** PHILLIPS (ed. Kersey), *Visitation*,..the great Sickness with which the People of this Kingdom were sorely afflicted during..1665 and 1666. **1798** S. & HT. LEE *Canterb. T.* II. 544 [I] now can account for the severe visitation on me, and mine. **1806** *Med. Jrnl.* XV. 287 You boast an intimate knowledge of the decrees of Heaven, and shew what is ordained for the visitation of man. **1865** SEELEY *Ecce Homo* vi. (1866) 55 Jehovah was considered.. as punishing by providential visitations and by mysterious pains inflicted on the dead. **1885** DUNCKLEY in *Manch. Weekly Times* 21 Feb. 5/5 War is here regarded..as a punitive visitation, as a form of retribution for our sins.

8. The fact of some violent or destructive agency or force coming or falling upon a people, country, etc.

1535 COVERDALE *Prov.* xix. 23 The feare of the Lorde preserueth the life, yee it geueth plenteousnes, without the visitacion of any plage. **1593** SHAKS. *2 Hen. IV*, III. i. 21 In the visitation of the Windes, Who take the Ruffian Billowes by the top. **1757** CHESTERF. *Lett.* cclxxxix, The Austrians always leave behind them pretty lasting monuments of their visits, or rather visitations. **1833** LYELL *Princ. Geol.* III. viii. (1835) III. 116 In Arabia and India, and other countries, their [*sc.* locusts] visitations have been periodically experienced. **1838** ARNOLD *Hist. Rome* I. 187 The period.. was marked by the visitations of pestilence, as well as those of war. **1844** KINGLAKE *Eothen* xv, Thanks to Ibrahim Pasha's terrible visitation the men of the tribe were wholly unarmed.

9. The fact of some immaterial power or influence acting or operating on the mind.

1791 MRS. INCHBALD *Simple Story* I. Pref. p. iii, In justice to their heavenly inspirations, I believe they have never yet favoured me with one visitation. **1819** SHELLEY *Ye Gentle Visitations* 1 Ye gentle visitations of calm thought. **1841** EMERSON *Ess.* Ser. I. *Love* (1901) 100 But be our experience ..what it may, no man ever forgot the visitations of that power to his heart and brain. **1866** GEO. ELIOT *F. Holt* xiv, His voice was what his uncle's might have been if it had been modulated by delicate health and a visitation of self-doubt. **1873** BLACK *Pr. Thule* xvi, Or was he moved by some visitation of compunction?

III. 10. *attrib.* (chiefly in special senses), as ***visitation acquaintance***, ***book***, ***court***, ***day***, ***dinner***, ***fee***, ***nun***, ***office***, ***sermon***, ***work***.

1822 GALT *Sir A. Wylie* xc, Mary would fain hae had me to cultivate a *visitation-acquaintance with him. **1768** BLACKSTONE *Comm.* III. 105 Their original *visitation-books, compiled when progresses were solemnly and regularly made into every part of the kingdom, to enquire into the state of families,..are allowed to be good evidence of pedigrees. **1870** F. R. WILSON *Ch. Lindisf.* 80 The visitation books show us the old edifice once more. **1841** (*title*), Report of the *Visitation Court of the Archbishop of York. **1708** J. CHAMBERLAYNE *St. Gt. Brit.* (1710) 292 This day still continues to be the *Visitation-day, when the Curators..do inspect the Library and call over all the Books. **1900** *Daily News* 27 June 6/5 Chocolate is the time-honoured beverage on visitation day at Greenwich Observatory. **1848** THACKERAY *Van. Fair* xi, There was not ..a ball, nor an election, nor a *visitation dinner..but he found means to attend it. **1850** J. H. NEWMAN *Diffic. Anglic.* I. ii. (1891) I. 61 Was it a subject..discussed and denounced ..in episcopal charges and at visitation dinners? **1791** J. WOODFORDE *Diary* 6 Dec. (1927) III. 316 Recd. of Ditto, my last *Visitation Fee, 0.2.6. **1880** *Wyclif's Wks.* 249 *marg.*, Visitation fees. *a* **1700** *Visitation nun [see *Blue Nun* s.v. BLUE *a.* 13]. **1899** *Dublin Rev.* Oct. 273 Three visitation nuns from the monastery of Chaillot, near Paris. **1795** PALEY *Clergym. Comp.* v, Prayers for a sick Child. (*Visitation office.) **1676** GLANVILL *Ess. Philos. & Relig.* Pref. a 3, The Fifth [Essay] of the Agreement of Reasons and Religion, was at first a *Visitation Sermon. **1782** C. SIMEON in W. Carus *Life* (1847) 28 There is a Visitation Sermon preached every month at my own parish-church at Reading. **1747** BP. SHERLOCK *Let.* 27 Aug., in *10th Rep. Hist. MSS. Comm.* App. I. 297 As the *visitation work is divided between me and the Bp. of L. we have got thro' it with great ease.

Hence **visi'tational**, of or pertaining to a visitation. †**visi'tationer**, one who performs, or takes part in, a visitation.

1670 EACHARD *Cont. Clergy* 91 A money-renouncing clergy, that can abstain from seeing a penny a month together, unless it be when the collectors and visitationers come. **1791** *Gentl. Mag.* 20/2 Without impairing the utility or expediency of visitational charges.

'visitator. Now *rare.* [a. late L. *vīsitātor*, f. *visitāre* to visit. Cf. It. *visitatore*, Sp. and Pg. *visitador*.] An official visitor.

1536 *Act 28 Hen. VIII*, c. 10 §5 If any ecclesiasticall Judge or Visitatour do voluntaryly concele..any presentment. **1545** *Act 37 Hen. VIII*, c. 17 Censures ecclesiasticall made by your Highnes and your Vicegerent, officialls, commissaries, and Judges and visitators. **1606** W. CRASHAW *Rom. Forgeries* F j b, The reuerend Andreas Vander Rijt,.. Canon of Antwerpe, and the censor or visitator appointed to ouerlooke and allow bookes before they be printed. **1676** in *Essex Papers* (Camden) 68 James Darcy, now Guardian of Dublin, but then Comm[i]ssary visitator. **1897** J. McCABE *Twelve Yrs. in Monastery* 178 The usual course is for the General..to send a deputy to the province which is about to hold its elections. The deputy or visitator visits all the monasteries in succession.

visitatorial (vɪzɪtə'tɔərɪəl), *a.* [See next and -ORIAL.]

1. Pertaining to, connected with, involving or implying, official visitation: **a.** Of power, authority, etc.

1688 N. JOHNSTON (*title*), The King's Visitatorial Power asserted. Being an impartial relation of the late visitation of St. Mary Magdalen College in Oxford. **1711** BENTLEY *Corr.* (1842) I. 417 The Crown has, for a century and half, been in sole possession of the Visitatorial power. **1765** BLACKSTONE *Comm.* I. 470 In one of our colleges, (wherein the bishop of that diocese.. has immemorially exercised visitatorial authority). **1770** (*title*), The Conduct of.. the Lord Bishop of Winchester.. with brief Observations on visitatorial Power. **1834** *Edin. Rev.* LVIII. 476 Deriving the visitatorial power from the property of the donor. **1849** MACAULAY *Hist. Eng.* vi. II. 90 The enactment which annexed to the crown an almost boundless visitatorial authority over the Church. **1874** STUBBS *Const. Hist.* I. xiii. 596 The visitatorial jurisdiction by which the first.. regulated, and remodelled the second.

b. With other sbs.

1771 *Gentl. Mag.* XLI. 19 When I wrote my remarks upon the defence of the visitatorial decision I was ignorant of the Presidents of Magdalene College being favoured with the indulgence you mention. **1868** J. H. BLUNT *Ref. Ch. Eng.* I. 53 The Pope.. left the visitatorial question undecided. **1884** *Manch. Exam.* 16 May 4/7 In his visitatorial address to the churchwardens.. Mr. Chancellor Christie went a little out of his way. **1890** DUCKETT *Visit. Eng. Cluniac Found.* 5 Formulæ for visitatorial duties.

2. Having the power of visitation; exercising authority of this kind.

1880 *Daily News* 10 Nov. 5/3 He [a professor at Oxford] may be brought before a Visitatorial Board, admonished, fined, and deprived. **1881** *Nature* XXIII. 471 Leave of absence granted by visitatorial boards.

† **visitatory**, *a. Obs.*⁻¹ [ad. L. type **vīsitātōrius*, f. *vīsitāt-*, ppl. stem of *vīsitāre* to visit: see -ORY.] = prec. 1 a.

1651 N. BACON *Disc. Govt. Eng.* II. xxvii. 208 It is a visitatory, or a reforming Power which is executed by inquiry of offences against Lawes established, and by executing such Lawes.

visite (vɪˈziːt). [F. *visite* VISIT *sb.*]

1. A light cape or short sleeveless cloak worn by ladies.

c **1847** J. S. COYNE *How to settle Accounts with your Laundress* 4 I'll come in my blue *visite* and my native innocence. **1852** SMEDLEY *L. Arundel* xxxvi. 303 A *visite*, of light blue *glacé* silk. **1864** *Daily Tel.* 1 July, She wore a white dress with a black silk visite, and a white bonnet. **1885** *Pall Mall G.* 11 May 4/2 We have a 'visite' without arms or any proper accommodation for those useful appendages.

2. Short for CARTE-DE-VISITE, in attrib. use.

1891 *Anthony's Photogr. Bull.* IV. 302 A stereoscope camera which can be used to make.. 24 visite negatives.

‖**3.** ***visite de digestion***, a formal call paid in return for hospitality received.

1908 J. CHURCHILL *Reminisc.* (1973) iii. 44 The writing of ceremonious notes, the leaving of cards, not to speak of *visites de digestion*, which even young men were supposed to pay, took up most afternoons. **1971** L. P. HARTLEY *Mrs Carteret Receives* 17, I thought it only civil to ask Madame Carteret if we could pay her a farewell visit, not a *visite de digestion*, but just an acknowledgment of her kindness.

visited (ˈvɪzɪtɪd), *ppl. a.* Also 6 vysset, vysyted. [f. VISIT *v.*]

† **1.** Afflicted with illness; attacked by plague or other epidemic. *Obs.*

1537 *Nottingham Rec.* III. 375 This towne, the wheche dothe kepe the vysset folke at Bradmar. **1553** S. CABOT *Ordinances* in Hakluyt *Voy.* (1589) 261 The sicke, diseased, weake, and visited person within boord to be.. comforted and holpen. **1575** *Nottingham Rec.* (1889) IV. 159 Payd more for the charges of the vysyted woman at Hye Crosse xxiij d. **1604** F. HERRING *Mod. Defence* B 2, He will not rush rashly into euery infected and visited house. **1640** SOMNER *Antiq. Canterb.* 16 Convenient Pest-houses, and Receptacles for the poore visited people of the City. **1722** DE FOE *Plague* (1896) 33 If any person visited do fortune.. to come.. from a place infected to any other place.

2. That is the object of a visit or visits.

1673 O. WALKER *Educ.* II. i. 223 In receiving visits.. the Gentlemen meet them at the bottom. It is alwaies observed that the visiteds Gentlemen attend one degree at least further then the Patron. **1754** *World* No. 62 ¶9 The Visited in these cases.. have invented on their parts several curious hints towards shortning the length of a Visitation. **1873** SMILES *Huguenots France* III. i. (1881) 383 Dauphiny is one of the least visited of all the provinces of France.

visitee (vɪzɪˈtiː). [f. VISIT *v.* + -EE.] The person to whom a visit is paid.

1710 W. KING *Let.* 16 Sept. in Swift *Corr.* (1963) I. 176 There are great men here as much out of humour, as you describe your great visitee to have been. **1825** *New Monthly Mag.* XVI. 181 A very necessary convenance interposed between visitor and visitee in those numerous calls of etiquette. **1842** MRS. CARLYLE *Lett.* (1883) I. 174 To suit the more fashionable hours of our visitees. **1886** *Cornh. Mag.* July 39, I should think that angels (and their visitees) were very lucky.

visiter (ˈvɪzɪtə(r)). Now *rare.* Also 6 vycytar. [f. VISIT *v.* + -ER.]

1. = VISITOR 2 a and 2 b.

1382 WYCLIF *2 Macc.* iii. 39 He that in heuens hath dwellyng, is visiter and helper of that place. **1608** WILLET *Hexapla Exod.* 822 He is also a visiter and punisher of sinne vpon the wicked.

2. = VISITOR 1.

1612 BREREWOOD *Lang. & Relig.* 185 These Jacobites.. be esteemed to make about 160000 families, or rather 50000, as Leonard the bishop of Sidon, the popes visiter in those parts hath recorded. **1691** BAXTER *Nat. Ch.* v. 21 The Scots had at first a General visiter, that was really a General Bishop. **1830** DE QUINCEY *Bentley* Wks. 1863 VI. 75 Her Majesty was the true visiter of Trinity College.

3. = VISITOR 3.

1592 GREENE *Conny Catch.* III. 30 Country Gentlemen haue many visiters both with neere dwelling neighbours, and freends that iourney from farre. **1638** JUNIUS *Paint. Ancients* 13 We doe moreover shorten our own time, fooling the greatest part of our best houres away among a company of pratling visiters. **1668** LADY CHAWORTH in *12th Rep. Hist. MSS. Comm.* App. V. 10 She yesterday.. kept her bed yet admitted visiters in the afternoone. **1727** SWIFT *What passed in Lond.* Wks. 1755 III. I. 184 It was observed too, that he had few visiters that day. **1766** GOLDSM. *Vic. W.* v, Tell me, Sophy, my dear, what do you think of our new visiter? **1773** MRS. CHAPONE *Improv. Mind* (1774) II. 44 The empty compliments of a visiter. **1796–7** JANE AUSTEN *Pride & Prej.* xi. (1813) 225 On the very morning after their own arrival at Lambton these visiters came. **1836–7** DICKENS *Sk. Boz, Scenes* xxv, A squalid-looking woman [in Newgate prison] .. was communicating some instructions to her visiter—her daughter evidently.

fig. **1799** SICKELMORE *Agnes & Leonora* I. 90 The sudden and unwelcome intrusion of his old visiter, the gout, obliged him to alter his determination.

transf. **1756** (*title*), The Universal Visiter and Memorialist.

4. = VISITOR 4 and 4 b.

1843 YARRELL *Brit. Birds* III. 386 The Terns.. are summer visiters to this country. **1851** *Catal. Gt. Exhib.* III. 729 Immense mirrors.. occupy a prominent position, which must render them appreciable to every visiter. **1883** *Encycl. Brit.* XV. 671/2 The chief object of every Meccan.. being to pillage the visiter in every possible way.

visiting (ˈvɪzɪtɪŋ), *vbl. sb.* [f. VISIT *v.*] The action of coming or going to a person or place for some special purpose.

1. On the part of supernatural beings, esp. the Deity in order to comfort, try, or punish persons.

a **1300** *Cursor M.* 6189 Ioseph.. praid þe folk and badd þat quen godd sent þaim visiting, þai suld his banes þeþen bring. *Ibid.* 11266 Feird war þaa hirdes for þat light.. For þai sagh neuer.. sli visiting be-for þat night. **1382** WYCLIF *Jer.* li. 18 Veyne ben the werkus, and wrthi scornyng; in tyme of ther visityng thei shul pershe. *c* **1425** AUDELAY *XI Pains Hell* 359 in *O.E. Misc.* 222 God haþ me chastyst fore my leuyng, I þonke my god my grace treuly Of his gracious vesityng. **1645** CARYL *Expos. Job* I. 637 We may apply it.. either to Gods visiting of us in afflictions, or in mercies.

2. a. On the part of persons, in various senses of the verb; *esp.* the action of calling upon others in a social or friendly way.

c **1374** CHAUCER *Troylus* II. 41 Yn some lond were al the game yshent, If that men ferd with love as men do here,.. In visityng, in forme, or seying here sawis. **1377** LANGL. *P. Pl.* B. II. 176 Denes and suddenes, drawe ȝow togideres,.. To bere bischopes aboute, abrode in visytynge. *c* **1380** *Antecrist* in Todd *Three Treat. Wyclif* (1851) 140 Þei discoumforten treu men & putten hem in prison for visityng of cristen men. **1497** *Acc. Ld. High Treas. Scot.* I. 344 Item, to ane cowpar for mending and visiting of thir pipis,.. viijd. **1530** PALSGR. 285/1 Vysityng, *uisitance, uisitation.* **1565** COOPER *Thesaurus, Visitatio*, a visitynge, or commyng to see. **1617** MORYSON *Itin.* I. 234 Our Consuls burning with desire of returning homeward, appointed the next day for the visiting of the Sepulcher. **1658** *Whole Duty Man* xvi. 137 Visiting the sick and imprisoned; by which visiting is meant .. so coming as to comfort and relieve them. **1727** SWIFT *To Very Yng. Lady* Wks. 1755 II. II. 43, I hope your husband will interpose his authority to limit you in the trade of visiting. **1749** FIELDING *Tom Jones* XIII. iv, Mrs. Fitzpatrick, .. though it was a full hour earlier than the decent time of visiting, received him very civilly. **1806** H. K. WHITE *Let.* 6 Jan., Visiting and gayety are very well by way of change, but there is no enjoyment so lasting as that of one's own family. **1820** BYRON *Blues* II. 8 What with driving and visiting, dancing and dining. **1890** *Science-Gossip* XXVI. 68/2 It requires great care before any one can assert that a plant has disappeared, and some years' visiting of the station. **1911** *Act 1 & 2 Geo. V*, c. 55 §14 Every such rule relating to the visiting of insured persons by visitors appointed by the society.

b. An instance of this; a visit.

a **1586** SIDNEY *Ps.* XLI. iii, Their courteous visitings are courting lyes. **1628** in Foster *Eng. Factories India* (1909) III. 211 By often visitings, presents, and invitacions. **1754** RICHARDSON *Grandison* (1781) VII. xi. 54 We shall be favoured with the company of Lord and Lady L. as soon as her visits and visitings are over. **1770** WILKES *Corr.* (1805) IV. 36, I begin to recover the fatigue of visitings and great dinners, which I abominate. **1817** MAR. EDGEWORTH *Ormond* xvi, Say I'm too old and clumsy for morning visitings.

3. a. Of things. (Cf. VISIT *v.* 10 c.)

1382 WYCLIF *Prov.* xix. 23 In plenteuousnesse it shal abide stille, withoute visiting of the werste. **1822** MRS. HEMANS *Siege of Valencia* iv. (1823) 160, I have swept o'er the mountains of your land, Leaving my traces, as the visitings Of storms, upon them! *a* **1851** MOIR *Hymn Night Wind* Poet. Wks. (1852) II. 379 But not alone to inland solitudes,.. Are circumscribed thy visitings.

b. Of influences affecting the mind.

c **1449** PECOCK *Repr.* I. xvii. 96 Thei mowe be verrified in manye othere wisis and for manye other visitingis, than ben the visitingis and the ȝiftis of Kunnyng. **1605** SHAKS. *Macb.* I. v. 46 Stop vp th'accesse and passage to Remorse, That no compunctious visitings of Nature Shake my fell purpose. **1807** WORDSW. *White Doe* I. 332 A Spirit,.. In soft and breeze-like visitings, Has touched thee. **1834** J. H. NEWMAN *Par. Serm.* I. ix. 141 Let not those visitings pass away. **1836** *Ibid.* III. i. 6 They cannot be 'as the heathen': they are pursued with gracious visitings, as Jonah when he fled away. **1867** PARKMAN *Jesuits N. Amer.* vii. (1875) 81 Some of them seemed to have visitings of real compassion.

4. *attrib.*, as ***visiting acquaintance, dress, relations, terms, way***; † **visiting-bell**, ? a bell used in visiting a sick person; **visiting-book**, (*a*) a book containing the names of persons to be visited; (*b*) = *visitors' book* s.v. VISITOR 6; **visiting-card**, (*a*) a small card bearing a person's name, to be left or presented on paying a visit; (*b*) in (orig. *Mil.*) *slang* phr. ***to leave one's visiting-card***, to leave unpleasant evidence of having been at a place; † **visiting-day**, a day set apart for receiving visitors; an at-home day; **visiting hours**, hours when visitors may call, *spec.* to see a person in a hospital or other institution; **visiting-list**, a list of persons to be visited; **visiting rights**, the right to pay or receive visits (to or from a child in the custody of a divorced spouse) or to receive them (while in an institution of any kind); **visiting-society**, a society formed for the purpose of visiting the poor or sick; † **visiting-ticket**, a visiting-card.

1775 SHERIDAN *Rivals* IV. i, But they are the last people I should choose to have a *visiting acquaintance with. **1808** SCOTT *Marm.* II. xix. *note*, His [St. Cuthbert's] carrying on a visiting acquaintance with the Abbess of Coldingham. **1552–3** *Inv. Ch. Goods, Staffs.* in *Ann. Lichfield* (1863) IV. 41 It[e]m a *veseting bell, and a peare of sensors of brasse. **1818** LADY MORGAN *Autobiog.* (1859) 157 All my great and small names in my old French *visiting-book. **1848** THACKERAY *Van. Fair* lv. 500 The Bishop went and wrote his name in the visiting-book at Gaunt House that very day. *Ibid.* lx, Before long Emmy had a visiting-book, and was driving about regularly in a carriage, calling upon [etc]. **1782** MISS BURNEY *Cecilia* I. iii, Why, a ticket [for an assembly] is only a *visiting card with a name upon it. **1820** LADY GRANVILLE *Lett.* (1894) I. 158 The Duke of Beaufort's pocket was picked of.. his visiting-cards. **1859** *All Year Round* No. 30. 79 People are photographed on their visiting cards. **1899** *Daily News* 26 Jan. 5/3 The New Year's visiting-card.. is one of the survivals of old-fashioned French politeness. **1945** PARTRIDGE *Dict. R.A.F. Slang* 60 *Visiting-card*, a bomb. Mostly in *Leave one's visiting card*... As the civilian drops visiting cards into tray or salver, so the airman drops bombs on.. enemy-occupied territory. **1953** 'E. CRISPIN' *Fen Country* (1979) 68 All he had to do was to .. leave his visiting card [*sc.* an explosive device] and collect his fee. **1972** V. CANNING *Rainbird Pattern* vi. 116 He should have brought Albert [*sc.* the dog] in from the car, he at least could have left a visiting card in self-defence. **1709** STEELE *Tatler* No. 80 ¶3, I had the Misfortune to drop in at my Lady Haughty's upon her *Visiting-Day. **1717** PRIOR *Dove* ix, With one great Peal They rap the Door, Like Footmen on a Visiting-Day. **1768** (*title*), The Visiting Day: a Novel. **1825** E. WEETON *Jrnl.* 20 June (1969) II. 397, I am .. as neat in my *every day apparel*, as any of my acquaintances; they many of them exceed me in *visiting dresses. **1859** *Habits Gd. Society* iv. (new ed.) 177 Shawls,.. belong rather to the carriage or visiting dress. **1851** *London at Table* I. 36 A cigar is not the indispensable companion of *visiting hours. **1897** *Scribner's Mag.* Sept. 384/1 Formal visiting-hours were ignored in the village of Sewanee. **1947** 'G. ORWELL' *Let.* 31 Dec. in *Coll. Ess.* (1968) IV. 386 I'd love it if you did come & see me... They don't seem very lavish with their visiting hours... I've only been in the hospital abt 10 days. **1979** 'D. KYLE' *Green River High* ii. 15, I scribbled a note giving hospital visiting hours. **1825** LADY GRANVILLE *Lett.* (1894) I. 368 Sitting in judgment over a *visiting list. **1870** MISS BRIDGMAN *R. Lynne* II. iii. 66 Who would have been unexceptionable wives as regarded their dress and their visiting-list. **1884** YATES *Recoll.* I. 279 *Visiting relations had, in the mean time, been established between us and the Dickens family. **1971** *Deb. House of Commons* (Canada) 14 Dec. 10 460/1 Has the minister or his department investigated allegations that *visiting rights were denied to members of the Black United Front? **1972** H. KEMELMAN *Monday the Rabbi took Off* xxiv. 159, I was divorced from his mother—he was ten at the time—I had visiting rights, of course. **1982** G. WAGNER *Children of Empire* viii. 138 All the homes were surrounded by high walls to keep intruders out and the children in. Visiting rights were restricted. **1844** [W. HARNESS] (*title*), *Visiting Societies and Lay Readers. **1876** LOWELL *Among my Bks.* Ser. II. 301 No one had stood on these *visiting terms with heaven. **1770** CUMBERLAND *West Indian* I. vi, Here, give me your direction; write it upon the back of this *visiting ticket —Have you a pencil? **1824** MISS L. M. HAWKINS *Mem.* II. 253 Finding the visiting-ticket of Mr. Harris on his return home one morning. **1859** THACKERAY *Virgin.* lxxxiii, A gigantic footman.. delivered their ladyships' visiting tickets at our door. **1779** T. HUTCHINSON *Diary* 26 Feb., Called on Mrs. Burnet and Colonel Leland—which is doing a great deal for me in the *visiting way.

visiting (ˈvɪzɪtɪŋ), *ppl. a.* [f. VISIT *v.*]

1. a. That visits; that pays visits or is engaged in visiting.

1606 SHAKS. *Ant. & Cl.* IV. xv. 68 There is nothing left remarkeable Beneath the visiting Moone. **1710** STEELE *Tatler* No. 151 ¶2 The Memory of an old Visiting-Lady is so filled with Gloves, Silks, and Ribands. **1807** J. HARRIOTT *Struggles through Life* II. 41 Should any visiting company wish to see the infant.. I have known the child brought to the door of the apartment. **1859** LEVER *Davenport Dunn* iii, To think you're a visiting governess in an Aldermans' family. **1895** *Daily News* 26 Oct. 3/1 None of the visiting teams were on the winning side.

b. ***visiting ant*** (see quots.).

1855 *Orr's Circ. Sci., Org. Nat.* II. 394 One of these species, the *Atta cephalotes*, which inhabits the West Indies, is there known as the Visiting Ant. *c* **1882** *Cassell's Nat. Hist.* V. 382 The Driver Ants, or Visiting Ants, of West Africa, generally referred to the species *Anomma arceus*. **1899** MARY KINGSLEY *W. African Stud.* i. 27 These ants are sometimes also called 'visiting ants', from their habit of calling in quantities at inconvenient hours on humanity.

c. ***visiting fireman*** (U.S. slang): a person given especially cordial treatment while visiting an organization or place; a tourist expected to spend freely.

[**1855** *Sun* (Baltimore) 25 Oct. 1/6 A company of firemen from Rochester, N.Y.,.. continue to receive the attentions of their brother firemen of Baltimore... This evening the visiting firemen will be the guests of the Washington Hose Company.] **1926** S. LEWIS *Mantrap* xxi. 265, I.. couldn't keep my hooks off any he-male that blows into town with the visiting firemen! **1936** H. BERNSTEIN *Choose Bright Morning* ii. 20 He never sees people who might have legitimate business with him... But he receives all the visiting firemen. **1945** H. S. TRUMAN in M. Truman *Harry S. Truman* (1972) x. 202 Naturally got pointed out as the visiting fireman and had a kind of reception between acts and afterwards. **1962** A. DAVISON *In Wake of Gemini* 115 Members of the firm, whose business it was to look after visiting firemen, had the same happy knack. **1964** *Economist* 25 Jan. 313/2 The marked-up tickets are usually sold to 'visiting firemen'. **1972** K. BENTON *Spy in Chancery* i. 19 Don't they know the form for visiting firemen?.. As the British delegate.. I shall make a courtesy visit to the Embassy.

d. ***visiting fellow, lecturer, professor***: an academic who accepts an invitation to work at another institution for a fixed term; so ***visiting fellowship***, etc.

1950 *Univ. London Gaz.* 28 Oct. 178 (*heading*) Appointment of Visiting Professor of Belgian Studies. *Ibid.*, The Visiting Professorship of Belgian Studies. **1960** A. HUXLEY *Let.* 12 Nov. (1969) 898, I am here for the moment working as a Visiting Professor at MIT. **1962** *St. Edmund Hall Mag. 1961–2* 3 Mr. Allen was Visiting Lecturer at the University of Iowa. **1963** *Cambridge Univ. Reporter* 24 Apr. 1450 The Board of Managers of the Smuts Memorial Fund invite applications for Smuts Visiting Fellowships in Commonwealth Studies. *Ibid.*, The emoluments of a Visiting Fellow will be a sum not exceeding £1,500. **1973** *Oxf. Mag.* 1 June 2/2 Professor Levitch.. has accepted a Visiting Fellowship at University [College]. **1980** A. COPPEL *Hastings Conspiracy* viii. 59 Langton enjoyed a visiting lectureship at the London School of Economics. **1980** M. DRABBLE *Middle Ground* 156 A visiting professor.. on his way to an excavation. **1982** C. MONTEITH in A. Thwaite *Larkin at Sixty* 41 All Souls—a College where he later stayed in his own right as a Visiting Fellow.

2. That visits officially for the purpose of inspection or examination.

1713 GIBSON *Codex* XLII. viii. 1009/1 In the Council of Laodicea, ann. 360, it was Ordained, That no Bishops should be placed in Country Villages, but only.. Itinerant or Visiting Presbyters. **1802** JAMES *Milit. Dict.*, *Visiting Officer*, he whose duty it is to visit the guards, barracks, messes, hospital, etc. **1818** SIR S. ROMILLY in *Parl. Debates* 30 That the royal prerogative should be interposed.. between them and the visiting magistrates. **1822** SYD. SMITH *Prisons* Wks. 1859 I. 361 Are visiting justices to doom such a prisoner to bread and water? **1868** (*title*), The Visiting Justices and the Troublesome Priest.

'visitment. *nonce-wd.* [f. VISIT *v.* + -MENT.] A visit or visitation.

1754 *World* No. 62 ¶9, I may very shortly send you a few necessary remarks upon each of these three Visitments.

visitor ('vɪzɪtə(r)). Also 5 **visitur, -oure,** 6–7 **visitour** (6 *Sc.* **vesit-, vesatour**). [a. AF. *visitour* (Gower), = OF. *visiteor, visiteur* (F. *visiteur*), f. *visiter* to visit.]

1. One who visits officially for the purpose of inspection or supervision, in order to prevent or remove abuses or irregularities:

a. An ecclesiastic, or a lay commissioner, appointed to visit religious establishments, churches, etc., for this end, either at regular intervals or on special occasions.

1426 LYDG. *De Guil. Pilgr.* 23985 Our noble Visitour, Which doth his peyne and his labour to looke for lucre and fals guerdoun. *c* **1440** *Alph. Tales* 272 þe Abbott.. oppynlie in þe chapitr.. putt forth all þies trispas of þis yong man, when þer visitur was þer. **1483** *Cath. Angl.* 402/2 A Visitoure, *reformator proprie in religione, visitator.* *a* **1513** FABYAN *Chron.* VII. 416 The maister of yᵉ Templers, with an other great ruler of the sayd ordre, which was named visitour of the same. **1550** CROWLEY *Epigr.* 749 These visitours found many stout priestes, but chieflye one That had sondrye benefices. **1585** *Holinshed's Chron.* II. *Scotl.* 440/1 After they had discharged bishops, they agreed to haue superintendents, commissioners, and visitors. **1628** COKE *On Litt.* 96 Where a speciall Visitor is appointed vpon the foundation, the complaint must be made to that Visitor. **1676** DEGGE *Parson's Counsellor* II. xv. 201 The Clergy and Religious Houses came to this composition, every one to pay such a proportion to their visitors to be freed of that great oppression. **1721** in *Cath. Rec. Soc. Publ.* VIII. 305 Whatever the Visitor ordains, the Mother Abbesse and all her Religious shall receive and execute with respect and obedience. **1732** NEAL *Hist. Purit.* I. 18 The management of which was committed to the Lord Cromwel with the title of Visitor General. **1788** GIBBON *Decl. & F.* xlix. V. 102 The formidable name and mission of the *Dragon* his visitor-general. **1849** MACAULAY *Hist. Eng.* vi. II. 90 An Act was.. passed, which.. took away from the Crown the power of appointing visitors to superintend the Church. **1872** JERVIS *Gallican Ch.* I. Introd. 18 An officer, called the Visitor, usually one of the bishops of the province, was appointed to preside over the proceedings.

b. One who has a right or duty of supervision (usually exercised periodically) over a university, college, school, or similar institution.

1553 ASCHAM in *Lett. Lit. Men* (Camden) 16 The Visitors have taken this ordre, that every man shall professe the studie eyther of divinitie, law, or physick. **1587** LD. BURLEIGH in *Collect.* (O.H.S.) I. 204 The Archbishop of Canterburie youre Visitor. **1643** CARYL *Expos. Job* v. I. 480 And over Colledges, Hospitals, and such publick Foundations, Visitors are appointed, to see [etc.]. **1691** *Case of Exeter Coll.* 14 In order to which he gets an Appeal drawn up, and carries it to the Lord Bishop of Exeter, visitor of the Colledge, then at London. *a* **1700** EVELYN *Diary* 9 Aug. 1682, The Council of the R. Society had it recommended to them to be trustees and visitors, or supervisors, of the Academy which Monsieur Faubert did hope to procure to be built. **1709** SWIFT *Adv. Relig.* Wks. 1755 II. I. 106 Whatever abuses.. have crept into the universities.. they might in a degree be reformed by strict injunctions.. to the visitors and heads of houses. **1808** W. WILSON *Hist. Dissent. Ch.* I. 229 He was appointed by the Protector Oliver, one of the New Visitors of that University. **1829** R. GILBERT *Liber Scholast.* 306 The appointment of the mastership [of Sedberg] is vested in the Master and Fellows of St. John's College, Cambridge, who are the Visitors to the school. **1832** WHATELY in *Life* (1866) I. 155 In certain Colleges.. fundamental statutes can only be changed by visitors.

c. In other connexions.

1555 *Burgh Rec. Edinb.* (1871) II. 228 Thomas Boyis vesitour of the baxter craft within this burgh. **1574** in *Maitl. Cl. Misc.* I. 104 Superflowis bankatting,.. as the baillies and eldaris than vesatouris presentlie declarit. **1600** HAKLUYT *Voy.* III. 862 An expert mariner or two called Visitors of the shippes, to know whether the ships be well tackled; whether they haue sufficient men. **1624** BEDELL *Lett.* vi. 94 The French discourse printed at Antwerp *cum priuilegio*, and approbation of the Visitor of bookes. **1654** tr. *Martini's Conq. China* 154 This Governour, by reason of some corruption, and Avarice of the Visitor of the Country, had some difficulties with him. **1765** BLACKSTONE *Comm.* I. 468 The founder [i.e. the King], his heirs, or assigns, are the visitors of all lay-corporations. **1766** ENTICK *London* IV. 170 The visitor (now called the ordinary of Newgate). **1897** *Daily News* 1 Feb. 7/5 Visitor.. is the.. name given to those vigilant officers of the Board whose business it is to run truants to earth. **1901** *Daily Chron.* 29 Aug. 7/1 In 1899 four ladies were appointed as health visitors.

2. a. One who visits from charitable motives or with a view of doing good.

c **1430** LYDG. *Min. Poems* (Percy Soc.) 205 Vertuous visitour to folkys in prisoun. **1536** *Lett. Suppress. Monast.* (Camden) 133 Most gracyus lord and most worthyst vycytar that ever cam amonckes us. **1610** SHAKS. *Temp.* II. i. 11 *Seb.* He receiues comfort like cold porredge. *Ant.* The Visitor will not giue him ore so. **1833** J. TUCKERMAN (*title*), Visitor of the Poor. **1863** *Biogr. Sk. E. Fry* 45 The cheerfulness visible in their [*sc.* prisoners'] countenances.. conspired to excite the.. admiration of their visitors. **1870** [see DISTRICT *sb.* 6].

b. One who visits with punishment. *rare.*

1545 JOYE *Exp. Dan.* i. 12, I am.. the visitour and seker out of the wykednes of the fathers in their childern.

3. One who pays a visit to another person or to a household; one who is staying for a time with friends.

1607 SHAKS. *Timon* I. i. 42 You see this confluence, this great flood of visitors. **1662** J. STRYPE in *Lett. Lit. Men* (Camden) 177, I hear also my brother Sayer is often a visitor. **1693** DRYDEN *Juvenal* VI. 620 She hires Tormentors, by the Year; she Treats Her Visitours, and talks. **1697** COLLIER *Ess. Moral Subjects* II. (1698) 137 They do not care to be crowded with Visitors,.. and to be always yoaked in Ceremony. **1797** MRS. RADCLIFFE *Italian* Prol., Too singular in his conduct, to pass unnoticed by the visitors. **1838** LYTTON *Alice* I. iv, She filled the rooms of the visitors with flowers. **1856** KANE *Arct. Expl.* I. xxx. 407 After sharing the supper of their hosts, the visitors stretched themselves out and passed the night in.. slumber. **1871** GRENVILLE-MURRAY *Member for Paris* I. 287 'Oh, I'm only a visitor', answered Horace modestly.

transf. **1576** FLEMING *Panopl. Epist.* 130 What is done heere shalbe reuealed vnto you by mine Epistles, whiche shall not be your sealdome visitoures. **1784** COWPER *Task* VI. 570 The creeping vermin, loathsome to the sight,.. A visitor unwelcome.

attrib. **1857** DICKENS *Dorrit* xxxii, The visitor-wife and the unseasoned prisoner still lingered.

4. a. One who visits a place, country, etc., esp. as a sightseer or tourist.

1728 CHAMBERS *Cycl.* s.v. *Cynics*, The Novelty of the Thing drew abundance of Visitors to the Village. **1841** LANE *Arab. Nts.* I. 71 Sometimes the visitors.., after having hired a person to perform a longer recitation, go away before he commences. **1860** TYNDALL *Glac.* II. xvii. 315 It is usual for visitors to the Montauvert to descend to the glacier. **1895** *B'ham Y.M.C.A. Record* Oct. 3/2 The usual time of year for the arrival in India of visitors is the middle of October.

b. An animal or bird which occasionally or at regular seasons frequents a certain locality or area.

1859–62 SIR J. RICHARDSON, etc. *Mus. Nat. Hist.* (1868) I. 425 The Puffin.. is a summer visitor to our shores. **1863** LYELL *Antiq. Man* 15 The presence of the wild swan, now only a winter visitor. **1870** N. F. HELE *Aldeburgh* vii. 71 The Glead or Kite.. is a very rare visitor.

c. *Sport.* A member of a visiting team. Usu. in *pl.*

1900 W. J. FORD *Cricketer on Cricket* xiv. 162 Setting aside one unpleasant incident of the present trip.. our visitors can hardly complain of the treatment they have received at the hands of the players, the public, or the press. **1916**, **1930** [see HOME *a.* 2 c]. **1976** G. L. GREAVES *Over Summers Again* xvi. 105 September 1966 saw Yorkshire once again.. needing an outright win over Kent to give them yet another championship... Trueman and Nicholson.. soon had Kent in trouble and the visitors, all out for 119, closed 91 behind.

5. A menstrual discharge; = VISIT *sb.* 4. *slang.*

1980 *Quarto* June 3/2 It was shortly before my thirteenth birthday that I first had 'Visitors'. Mother.. had told me about the monthly cycle... My first 'visitor' was a light one. **1983** *Maledicta 1982* VI. 26 Menstruation (females):.. visitor. **1984** *New Yorker* 29 Oct. 45/3 Girls used to say they had the curse. Or they had a visitor.

6. *Comb.*, as **visitor centre** orig. *U.S.*, a building in a tourist area in which exhibitions, slide-shows, etc., are displayed as an introduction to the locality; **visitors' book**, a book in which visitors may write their names and addresses, and, sometimes, comments; **visitors' list**, a public list of those making a visit to a place, esp. to a resort; in quot. 1864, a list of official visitors (VISITOR 1 b).

1964 P. JENSEN *National Parks* i. 18 Park headquarters is also here. A *visitor center explains the features of the area. **1979** *Farmington* (New Mexico) *Daily Times* 27 May 3c/6 Visitor centers will tell tourists the speed limits will be enforced. **1979** *United States 1980/81* (Penguin Travel Guides) 239 A 25-minute movie about the Battle of Shiloh is shown in the Visitor Center. **1983** *Leisure, Recreation & Tourism Abstr.* VIII. IV. 205/2 A new accommodation concept, and an existing visitor centre facility. **1846** *Punch* 20 June 278/2 (*heading*) Ibrahim Pacha's *visitors' book. **1870** *Ibid.* 1 Oct. 138/2 The Emperor Nicholas.. 'expressed himself much pleased', as the visitors' books have it. **1910** BELLOC *Pongo & Bull* vii. 96 The Duke.. had very properly insisted upon the retention of the visitors' book. **1976** L. DEIGHTON *Twinkle, twinkle Little Spy* xvi. 157 There was a visitors' book.. a beautiful leather-bound volume.. dutifully signed by the Reid-Kennedys' guests. **1984** *Times* 25 May 7/5 (*caption*) All smiles: the Queen leaving the town hall.. after signing the visitors' book. **1864** MRS. GASKELL *Wives & Daughters* (1866) I. i. 8 Though my name has been down on the *visitors' list these three years, the countess has never named me in her note... Her ladyship would be as hurt as any one when she did not see Phœbe among the school visitors. **1904** A. E. W. MASON *Truants* II. vi. 105 She.. bought a visitors' list at the kiosk. **1907** E. GLYN *Three Weeks* iv. 53 The simplest thing.. seemed to descend into the hall and look at the Visitors' List... There were only a few people in the hotel. **1927** E. BOWEN *Hotel* iii. 27 Victor.. took up the local paper and began to read the visitors' list.

Hence **'visitoress,** = VISITRESS.

Also *visitorish, visitorless* (nonce-words).

a **1843** SOUTHEY *Comm.-Pl. Bk.* Ser. II. (1849) 30/2 Their superior was called the Prepostress, and they had Visitoresses, Rectresses, and other dignitaries.

visitorial (vɪzɪ'tɔərɪəl), *a.* [f. prec. or VISIT *v.*: see -ORIAL.]

1. = VISITATORIAL *a.* 1.

1813 *Examiner* 24 May 332/1 We held it to be beneath our visitorial functions. **1843** *Lett. Suppress. Monast.* (Camden) 71 One of the visitorial injunctions, in allusion to this class of students, directs [etc.]. **1873** B. GREGORY *Holy Catholic Ch.* xv. 153 The visitorial authority of the itinerant Apostolate.

2. Capable of visiting.

1853 *Tait's Mag.* XX. 486 The more terrible and supposed visible, or at least visitorial deities of the hideous Pantheon of the Hindoos.

'visitorship. [f. VISITOR 1 + -SHIP.] The office or dignity of an official visitor.

1886 L. O. PIKE *Yearbks. 13 & 14 Ed. III*, Introd. p. lxvii, The visitorship was in the Treasurer on the King's behalf. **1894** *Nation* (N.Y.) 19 July 49/1 Thus Balliol stands alone among the twenty-one Oxford Colleges in having the power to bestow the visitorship was given to Mr. Peel.

visitress ('vɪzɪtrɪs). [f. VISITOR: see -ESS.]

1. A female visitor. Also *transf.*

1827 E. W. BARNARD *Swallow* i, The visitress of man, on earth She resteth not her flagging wing. **1832** *Fraser's Mag.* V. 173 Our importunate visitress. **1847** C. BRONTË *J. Eyre* xxxii, Keenly, I fear, did the eye of the visitress pierce the young pastor's heart. **1869** W. R. GREG *Lit. & Soc. Judgm.* (ed. 2) 25 It is highly proper that by such an act at this time, you express your contradiction of our importunate visitress.

2. *spec.* A woman who undertakes regular visiting of the poorer households of a district in order to help or advise.

1861 M. ARNOLD *Pop. Educ. France* 104 If she ceases to be a schoolmistress, she becomes a visitress or a nurse, or she gives her labours in the dispensary. **1894** *Westm. Gaz.* 5 Oct. 2/3 There is an understanding.. that district visitresses have a.. vested right to the society of curates.

visive ('vɪzɪv), *a.* ? *Obs.* [ad. med.L. *visīv-us*, f. L. *vīsus* seeing, sight: see -IVE. So F. *visif, -ive* (15th c.), It., Sp., Pg. *visivo.*] Of or pertaining to sight or to the power of seeing; visual.

1. ***visive faculty, power, virtue***, etc.: The faculty of sight, the power of vision.

In early use *virtue visive*, after med.L. *virtus visiva*; cf. F. *virtu, faculté, puissance visive* (15–16th cent.).

1543 TRAHERON *Vigo's Chirurg.* IV. 136 Remotion of the matter conjoynt, by evaporation, and confortacyon of the vertue visive. **1576** G. BAKER tr. *Gesner's Jewell of Health* 82 b, A water.. with a notable comforting of the virtue visive or seeing. **1609** BIBLE (Douay) *Deut.* xxxiv. *comm.*, God elevated his visive powre above nature to see so farre. **1614** JACKSON *Creed* III. xxix. §5 As oft as he is disposed to exercise his visive facultie. **1653** CULPEPPER *Pharm. Londin.* 306 Ocular Medicines are two fold, viz. such as are referred to the Visive Vertues, and such as are referred to the Eyes themselves. **1666** SPURSTOWE *Spir. Chym.* (1668) 34 A principle, which is as necessary to goodness, as a visive power to the eye, to enable it to discern its object. **1709** BERKELEY *Th. Vision* §59 For this end chiefly the visive sense seems to have been bestowed on animals. **1733** tr. *Belloste's Hosp. Surgeon* II. 263 This man's eye was fair and sound to all appearance, yet was it utterly deprived of the visive faculty. **1804** *Something Odd* II. 54 The neat simplicity of Eloisa's dress.. struck on the visive faculty of 'my Lord'. **1836** *Blackw. Mag.* XL. 337 He had thrown a new and important light on the true character of these visive sensations.

fig. **1660** S. FISHER *Rusticks Alarm* Wks. (1679) 597 He hath given an understanding,.. and this all men have, the inward visive faculty. *a* **1679** T. GOODWIN *Work of Holy Spirit* v. ii. Wks. 1704 V. I. 178 This new Spiritual visive Power, with which the Understanding is endowed. **1728** E. ERSKINE *Serm.* Wks. (1791) 229/2 You bid me open my eyes, but alas! I want a visive faculty. **1830** T. TAYLOR *Argts. Celsus* 31 If, closing the perceptive organs of sense, we look upward with the visive power of intellect. *a* **1838** JAMIESON *Influence Spirit* (1844) 82 Ignorance of such a description that it cannot receive the light; a want of the visive faculty.

b. Serving as a means by which sight or vision is made possible. Now *rare* or *Obs.*

1634 T. JOHNSON tr. *Parey's Wks.* I. x. 26 That [spirit] which causeth the sight, is named the Visive. **1655** CULPEPPER, etc. *Riverius* II. Pref., In curing Diseases of the Eyes.. we must alwaies mingle those things which comfort the visive spirits with other Medicines. **1657** *Physical Dict.*, *Visive-nerve*, the nerve that is the instrument of the visive faculty, or of seeing. **1686** SNAPE *Anat. Horse* III. vii. 119 The Optick or Seeing Nerves; so called..because they carry the visive spirits to the Eyes. **1812** CARY *Dante, Parad.* xxx. 49 The lightning..dashes from the blinding eyes The visive spirits dazzled and bedimm'd.

c. ***visive organ***, the organ of vision; the eye. *a* **1652** J. SMITH *Sel. Disc.* IV. iii. (1660) 79 Lucretius.. believes the *Idolum* in his own Visive organ to be adequate to the Sun it self. **1682** SIR T. BROWNE *Chr. Mor.* III. §14 Let intellectual Tubes give thee a glance of things, which visive Organs reach not. **1704** NORRIS *Ideal World* II. iii. 110 Vision is here taken materially for that impression which is made upon the visive organs by the rays of light.

d. Having the power of vision; able to see. **1681–6** J. SCOTT *Chr. Life* (1747) III. 641 God.. impressed three Phantasms on the sensitive or visive Soul.. of Abraham. **1793** T. TAYLOR *Orat. Julian* 22 We infer his perfective power from the whole phænomena, because he gives vision to visive natures.

2. Forming the object of vision; capable of being seen. **1598** R. HAYDOCKE tr. *Lomazzo* II. 196 It looseth the corporal visiue form. **1647** A. ROSS *Mystag. Poet.* x. (1675) 249 For open and solid bodies are not fit to receive or transmit the visive species.

b. *Optics.* Falling upon or appearing to the eye. **1646** SIR T. BROWNE *Pseud. Ep.* 156 This doth happen when the axis of the visive cones, diffused from the object, fall not upon the same plane. **1670** E. R. *Ne Plus Ultra* 23 The visive rays. **1690** LEYBOURN *Curs. Math.* 456 b, If the Sight-hole be..any whit large, it admitteth too many visive Rays.

3. Sent out from the eyes. **1622** MABBE tr. *Aleman's Guzman d'Alf.* II. 283 It seeming ..that the visiue beames in both..strucke home vpon our soules.

visk, variant of WHISK (whist).

Visking (ˈvɪskɪŋ). Also **visking**. A proprietary term for seamless cellulose tubing used as membranes in dialysis and as edible casings for sausages.

1931 *Trade Marks Jrnl.* 29 July 1050/1 *Visking casing*... sausage casings made of cellulose. The Visking Corporation,..Chicago, Illinois, United States of America; manufacturers. **1941** *Official Gaz.* (U.S. Patent Office) 15 Apr. 550/1 The Visking Corporation, Chicago... *Visking* for merchandise protectors—namely seamless cellulose tubes, and artificial sausage casings made of cellulose. **1956** *Nature* 25 Feb. 381/1 These compounds were removed..by dialysis of aqueous solutions of 2–3 mgm. of the venom, in Visking tubing. **1970** *Ibid.* 26 Dec. 1336/2 The oxidized form dialysed through visking tubing. **1977** *Times Educ. Suppl.* 21 Oct. 29/1 This apparatus was designed to simplify the setting up of experiments using visking tubing.

visna (ˈvɪznə). *Vet. Sci.* Also **Visna**. [a. ON. *visna* to wither.] A fatal disease of sheep in which there is progressive demyelination of neurones in the brain and spinal cord. Freq. *attrib.*

1957 *Jrnl. Neuropath. & Exper. Neurol.* XVI. 389 (*heading*) Visna, a demyelinating transmissible disease of sheep. *Ibid.* 393 This experiment obviously does not prove conclusively that Visna-sera will specifically neutralize Visna-virus but it is consistent with such an explanation. **1970** JUBB & KENNEDY *Path. Domestic Animals* (ed. 2) I. 269/2 The virus of visna can be transmitted by intra-pulmonary injection. **1982** *Jrnl. Neuro-immunology* III. 140 Icelandic sheep are free of natural infection since visna virus has been eradicated from the whole country.

visnamy, variant of VISNOMY.

visne (ˈviːnɪ). *Law* or *Hist.* Also 5 **visnee**, 6 **vysne**. [a. AF. and OF. *visné* (earlier *visnet*: see next), f. *vesin, visin, veisin* (F. *voisin*):—L. *vicinus* neighbour: see VICINE *a.*]

1. A neighbourhood or vicinage, esp. as the area from which a jury is summoned.

1449 *Rolls of Parlt.* V. 150/1 Triable by Enquest, in the same Shire and Visne where the said action shall be taken. **1464** *Ibid.* 565/2 Of the visnee where the seid seyser shall be had. **1531** *Dial. on Laws Eng.* I. vii. 15 All yssues..muste be tryed by .xii. fre & lawful men of the vysne. **1620** J. WILKINSON *Coroners & Sherifes* 3 A Coroner hath a fee belonging to his office viz. of every visne 1 d. **1625** SIR H. FINCH *Law* (1636) 411 In euery suit betweene an Alien and a Demesne..the one halfe of the Iurie shall be the Aliens, if so many be in that visne. **1651** tr. *Kitchin's Jurisdictions* (1657) 574 The sherif returns a Jury of the Visne of D., and the new sherif returns no such visne. **1769** BLACKSTONE *Comm.* IV. xxvii. 344 The sheriff of the county must return a panel of jurors.., without just exception, and of the *visne* or neighbourhood. **1832** *Index of Rolls of Parlt.* 952/1 The Inquest taken by Men of the Visne of the County where the Plaintiffs were born. **1867** SMYTH *Sailor's Wordbk.* 714 *Visne*, a neighbouring place; a term often used in law in actions of marine replevin.

2. A jury summoned from the neighbourhood in which the cause of action lies.

1633 SIR J. BOROUGH *Sov. Brit. Seas* (1651) 103 Replevin was brought of a Ship taken upon the wast of Scarborough ..to which Mutford tooke two exceptions, one because no certaine Towne, or place was named from whence the visne should come. **1832** SIR F. PALGRAVE *Eng. Commw.* II. 156 It did not occur to the Vehmic Judges to put the offender upon his second trial by the visne, which now forms the distinguishing characteristic of the English law. **1863** H. COX *Instit.* II. iii. 347 *note*, If the visne appeared on the record to be from a wrong place, it was a good ground for arresting or reversing the judgment.

†**3.** = VENUE 5. *Obs. rare.*

1641 [see VENUE 5]. **1665** EVER *Tryals per Pais* viii. 85 Where the Visne is laid to be in a City, in an Action brought in a superior Court [etc.]. **1768** [see VENUE 5 b].

ˈ**visnet.** *rare.* [a. OF. *visnet* (see prec.) or Anglo-L. *visnetum* (also *vicinetum*).]

†**1.** A trial by jury. *Obs.*

14.. in *Sc. Acts Parlt.* (1814) I. 378/2 Na Galowa man aw to haf visnet bot gif he refus þe law of Galowa and ask visnet.

2. *Hist.* = VISNE 1.

1872 ROBERTSON *Hist. Essays* 122 The Twelve-hides appears to have been usually regarded as a small *visnet*, or neighbourhood. *Ibid.* 137.

†**visney.** *Obs. rare.* [ad. Turk. *vishneh*, Pers. *wishneh* cherry (with corresponding forms in the Slavonic and other languages of eastern Europe: cf. the note to GEAN).] A liqueur of the nature of cherry brandy.

1733 W. ELLIS *Chiltern & Vale Farm.* 143 Cherry Brandy ..to come up very near to the Liquor called Turkish Visney, that used to be sold at London for twenty Shillings per Gallon. **1736** BAILEY *Household Dict.*, *Visney.* Fill a large bottle or cask with morello cherries..and fill up the bottle or vessel with brandy [etc.].

visnomy (ˈvɪznəmɪ). Now *arch.* or *dial.* Also 6 **vyse-, vice-, visnamy, visenomy, visnomye, -nomie**, 9 **viznomy** (*dial.* **visomy**). [var. of ME. *fisnomye*: see PHYSIOGNOMY.]

1. = PHYSIOGNOMY 3.

1509 HAWES *Past. Pleas.* (1555) R iij b, For you are euill fauoured, and also vgly, I am the worse, to se your visnamy. **1556** OLDE *Antichrist* 70 The..Prophet Daniel, and the Apostle Paule: which paynt out Antichristes visnomye unto us wyth suche lyght and euidence. **1591** SPENSER *Muiopot.* 311 Each of the Gods by his like visnomie Eathe to be knowen. **1605** CHAPMAN *All Fools* II. i. 159 Then with a bell regard advant mine eye With boldnes on her verie visnomie. **1640** BROME *Sparagus Gard.* III. v, You seldom see a Poet look out at a good Visnomy. **1818** SCOTT *Br. Lamm.* xvi, The loon has woodie written on his very visnomy. **1821** —— *Kenilw.* x, My own ugly viznomy. **1822** LAMB *Elia* Ser. I. *Distant Correspondents*, Who would consult his sweet visnomy, if the polished surface were two or three minutes..in giving back its copy. **1838** J. P. KENNEDY *Rob of Bowl* ii, A thick gray moustache gave a martial and veteran air to his visnomy.

†**2.** = PHYSIOGNOMY 2. *Obs.*$^{-1}$

c **1540** COPLAND *Hye Way to Spyttel Ho.* 452 For all the seuen scyences surely he can; And is sure in physyk and palmestry, In augury, sothsayeng and vysenamy.

viˈsometer. *rare.* [f. L. *vīs-us* sight + -OMETER. Cf. VISUOMETER.] (See quot.)

1856 *N. Brit. Rev.* Nov. 178 The first person..who constructed and used an apparatus, which he calls a *visometer*, for determining the focal length of each eye, was Mr. Salom of Edinburgh.

vison (ˈvaɪsən). [a. F. *vison* (Buffon), of obscure origin.] The American mink.

By some writers *Vison* has been used as the name of the genus *Lutreola*, to which the mink belongs.

1781–5 SMELLIE *Buffon's Nat. Hist.* (1791) VII. 308 The pekan has so strong a resemblance to the pine weasel, and the vison to the martin, that they may be regarded as varieties of these species. **1800** SHAW *Gen. Zool.* I. II. 448 Vison, Lutra Vison... This animal appears to approach.. extremely near to the L. Lutreola, or Smaller Otter. **1843** T. E. GRAY *List Spec. Mammal. Brit. Mus.* 64 The Mink, or Nurek Vison, *Vison Lutreola*. **1864–5** J. G. WOOD *Homes without H.* i. (1868) 22 The Mink, the Vison and other weasels of Northern America are in the habit of retiring to holes and crevices.

attrib. **1839** *Penny Cycl.* XV. 253/2 Minx, a name for the Vison-weasel.

visor, vizor (ˈvaɪzə(r)), *sb.* Forms: *α.* 4–7 **viser, vyser** (6 **wesser**); 5 **visere, vysere**, *Sc.* **veseir, -ere**. *β.* 5–6 **visar**, *Sc.* **wysar**, 6 **vysar**, 6–7 (9) **vizar**; *Sc.* 5–6 **wesar**, 6 **vesar, vezar**. *γ.* 5 **vesoure**, 6 **visoure, vysour(e), vizour**, 6–7 (9) **visour**; 6– **visor, vizor** (7 **vizzor**). [a. AF. *viser*, f. F. *vis* face, VICE *sb.*³ Cf. VISIERE and VISURE.]

1. a. The front part of a helmet, covering the face but provided with holes or openings to admit of seeing and breathing, and capable of being raised and lowered; sometimes spec. the upper portion of this. Also *transf.*

α. **13..** *Coer de L.* 323 Hys pusen therwith gan gon, And also hys brandellet bon, Hys vyser and hys gorgere. *c* **1330** R. BRUNNE *Chron. Wace* (Rolls) 8552 By þe vyser he hym hent, & held it til he had sesed his nekke. *c* **1400** *Destr. Troy* 7092 He..voidet his viser, auentid hym seluyn. **1412–20** LYDG. *Chron. Troy* I. 4185 Lamedoun, with a despiteous chere, From his face raced his visere. **1464** *Mann. & Househ. Exp.* (Roxb.) 194 My mastyr lent hym..a salat wyth a vesere of meleyn. **1470–85** MALORY *Arthur* v. xii. 181 Thenne the kyng aualyd his vyser with a meke & noble countenaunce. *a* **1533** LD. BERNERS *Huon* cxliv. 540 Then Gloryand and Malabrone lyft vp theyr wessers and shewyd theyr faces. **1611** COTGR., *Visiere*, the viser, or sight of an helmet.

β. *c* **1470** HENRY *Wallace* VIII. 830 Ane other awkwart apon the face tuk he; Wysar and frount bathe in the feild gert fle. *Ibid.* x. 386 Graym..smate that knycht in teyn, Towart the wesar, a litill be neth the eyn. **1507** *Acc. Ld. High Treas. Scot.* III. 367 Item, for ane vesar to ane gret hewmond and ane litill gard that beris the gret gard,..lvj s. **1508** DUNBAR *Poems* vii. 76. **1530** PALSGR. 285/1 Vysar of harnes, *uisiere dung armet.*

γ. **1459** *Paston Lett.* I. 487 Item, viii. saletts, white, withe out vesoure. **1590** SPENSER *F.Q.* III. vii. 42 She..made him low incline his lofty crest, And bowd his battred visour to his brest. **1599** SHAKS. *Much Ado* II. i. 99 Why then your visor should be thatcht. **1728** CHAMBERS *Cycl.* s.v. *Helmet*, Dukes and Princes have their Helmet, damask'd, fronting, the Vizor almost open, and without Bars. **1796** WITHERING *Brit. Plants* (ed. 3) II. 35 In this state nearly globular,.. resembling in figure an antique helmet with a vizor. **1803** SCOTT *Cadyow Castle* xxxix, From the raised vizor's shade, his eye, Dark-rolling, glanced the ranks along. **1836** THIRLWALL *Greece* xvi. II. 336 He was pierced with a shaft of a javelin through the visor of his helmet. **1879** GREEN *Read. Eng. Hist.* xvii. 82 They were in mail with their vizors down. **1957** *Time* 2 Sept. 37/2 Simons quickly clamped shut the visor of his space helmet. **1962** W. SCHIRRA in *Into Orbit* 51 Once we are up..we can open up our visor and breathe the cabin air for a bit.

b. *U.S.* The stiff rounded part on the front of a cap; = PEAK *sb.*² 1 e.

1864 WEBSTER. **1892** BIERCE *In Midst of Life* 95 His cap was worn with the visor a trifle askew.

c. A shade for protecting the eyes from unwanted light while not impeding the vision; *spec.* one attached to the top of the wind-screen of a motor vehicle or aircraft.

1925 J.-L. HUDON *Lexique Technique* 109 Windshield visor. **1936**, etc. [see *sun visor* s.v. SUN *sb.* 13 a]. **1952** *Times* 9 Jan. 3/3 Canberra pilots at Binbrook are testing a new type of visor for protecting crews against the glare at high altitudes. **1957** RAWNSLEY & WRIGHT *Night Fighter* 57, I peered into the visor [of a radar], trying to accustom my eyes to the dim light. **1973** 'E. MCBAIN' *Let's hear It* iii. 41 The visor on the driver's side was down.

2. A mask to conceal the face; a vizard.

α. **13..** *Seuyn Sages* (W.) 2779 A viser he made more, Two faces bihinde and two before. *c* **1380** WYCLIF *Sel. Wks.* II. 226 Siche fendis wiþ þer visers maken men to flee pees. *c* **1485** *Wisdom* 755 in *Digby Myst.* (1896) 166 Here entre vj womane in sute, thre disgysede as galauntes, and thre as matrones, with wonderfulle vysers. **1509** BARCLAY *Shyp of Folys* (1570) 232 The one hath a viser vgly set on his face, Another hath on vile counterfaite vesture. *a* **1548** HALL *Chron., Hen. VIII*, 16 Thei were appareled in garmentes long and brode..with visers and cappes of gold.

β. **1530** PALSGR. 285/1 Vysar for a mummar, *faulx uisaige.* **1539** *Act 31 Hen. VIII*, c. 12 Any person..with his face hyde or covered withe hoode or vysar. **1547** in Feuillerat *Revels Edw. VI* (1914) 14 Vezars or maskes for men & women. **1570** GOOGE *Pop. Kingd.* IV. 48 Their faces hid alone, With visars close. **1628** DONNE *Serm.* (1640) 231 In the Resurrection, God shall put of that Vizar, and turne away that picture, and shew his own face. *a* **1689** MRS. BEHN tr. *Cowley's Plants* VI. 1426 His Image..Breaks through the Cloud of Darkness; and a Shine Gilds all the sooty Vizar!

γ. **1511–12** *Act 3 Hen. VIII*, c. 9 Preamble, Dyvers persones have disgysed and appareld theym, and covert theyr fayces with Vysours. **1555** EDEN *Decades* III. (Arb.) 184 The fouler in the meane tyme, disguysinge hym selfe as it were with a visour. **1578** T. N. tr. *Conq. W. India* 205 Each of those Idolles had a counterfaite visor with eies of glasse. **1628** WITHER *Brit. Rememb.* II. 7 Lines, therefore, over-darke, or over-trimm'd, Are like a Picture with a Visour limm'd. **1682** FLAVEL *Fear* 78 There are some things which are..scarecrows and vizors which children fear. **1693** *Humours Town* 127 You can never think an Amour began in a Vizor in the Play-house, will ever end in the Church. **1719** YOUNG *Busiris* III. i, The rest in vizors, fearing to be known, Have ventur'd thro' the streets for your protection. **1797** MRS. RADCLIFFE *Italian* vi, They were disguised in cloaks and visors. *a* **1839** PRAED *Poems* (1864) II. 436 With a fearful vizor on his face, And a bright axe in his hand. **1906** B. CAPES *Loaves & Fishes* 146 The eyelets in its woollen visor were like holes scorched through by the burning gaze behind.

3. *fig.* (or in fig. contexts). **a.** An outward appearance or show under which something different is hid; a mask or disguise.

1532 MORE *Confut. Tindale* Wks. 354/2, I shall so pull of theire gaye paynted visours, that euery man..shall plainlye perceiue and beholde the bare vgly gargyle faces of their abhominable heresie. **1590** SPENSER *F.Q.* I. vii. 1 The crafty cunning traine, By which deceipt doth maske in visour faire. **1606** SYLVESTER *Du Bartas* II. iv. *Magnif.* 590 All discover'd lies, The vizor's off. **1653** HOLCROFT *Procopius, Vand. Wars* I. 4 He concealed his dislike (their enmity being covered yet under a fair visour). **1692** WASHINGTON tr. *Milton's Def. Pop.* ii. M.'s Wks. 1851 VIII. 41 I'll make it appear that you have only put on a Knaves Vizor for the present. **1766** FORDYCE *Serm. Yng. Wom.* (1767) I. iv. 132 A person proceeds by little and little to take off the visor. **1798** BRAGGE in *Anti-Jacobin* 12 Feb. (1852) 61 But soon the vizor dropp'd. **1822** SHELLEY *Chas. I*, I. 76 When lawyers masque 'tis time for honest men To strip the vizor from their purposes. **1831** SCOTT *Chron. Canongate* Introd., It appeared to him that it would have been an idle piece of affectation to attempt getting up a new *incognito*, after his original visor had been thus dashed from his brow. **1855** BREWSTER *Newton* II. xv. 81 Nor can we justify his personal retreat from the battle-field, and his return under the vizor of an accomplished champion.

b. Const. *of* (the quality, etc., serving as a mask or disguise).

1390 GOWER *Conf.* I. 258 Under the viser of Envie, Lo, thus was hid the tricherie, Which hath beguiled manyon. **1547** J. HARRISON *Exhort. Scottes* D viij b, So apperyng to theim with a visor of simplicitie and holines..gat credite of vertue and Godlinesse. **1581** J. BELL *Haddon's Answ. Osor.* 144 There is scarse any substaunce at all in Free will,.. except a glorious visour of Title onely. **1614** RALEIGH *Hist. World* III. 65 This Vizzor of holie and zealous reuenge falling off, discouered the face of couetousnesse so much the more ouglie. *a* **1656** BP. HALL *Rem. Wks.* (1660) 122 Those that are meer outsides and visors of Christianity. **1677** W. HUBBARD *Narrative* II. 32 He pulled off his Vizour of a friend, and discovered what he was. **1857** C. BRONTE *Professor* x, I had buckled on a breast-plate of steely indifference, and let down a visor of impassible austerity. **1860** WARTER *Sea Board* II. 19 She put on the vizar of religion.

†**4.** A face or countenance; an outward aspect or appearance. Also *fig.* of immaterial things. *Obs.*

1575 VAUTROLLIER *Luther on Ep. Gal.* 158 They looke onely vpon the outward visour of the lawe. *a* **1586** SIDNEY *Arcadia* I. iii. (1912) 21 This lowtish clowne is such, that you never saw so ill favourd a visar. *a* **1591** H. SMITH *Restit. Nebuchadn.* 17 They which vnderstand not yet what is the booke of God, are but horse and mule, though they beare the visors of men. **1654** WHITLOCK *Zootomia* 15 Sicknesse, Poverty, Exile, Death,..by expectation lessen the terror of their visors. **1693** CONGREVE *Old Bach.* III. vi, Lay by that Worldly Face and produce your natural Vizor.

5. A variety of pigeon (see quots.).

1879 L. WRIGHT *Pigeon Keeper* 179 Vizors are another and the last introduced of the short-billed Frilled Pigeons. **1881** J. C. LYELL *Fancy Pigeons* 236 The Vizor. This variety was produced by crossing the domino with the satinette tribe, the object being to have coloured headed satinettes. **1892** —— *Pigeon-keeping* 102 The Vizor may be called a Bluette with coloured head, as in the Domino.

6. a. *attrib.* and *Comb.*, as *visor-clasp*, *-helm*, *-smile*; *vizor-faced*, *-like* adjs.; **visor-bearer**, a Brazilian bird having head-feathers arranged like a visor.

1546 J. HEYWOOD *Prov. & Epigr.* (1867) 42 With visor-lyke visage, suche as it was, She smirkt. **1598** E. GUILPIN *Skial.* (1878) 36 This vizar-fac't pole-head dissimulation, This parrasite. **1797** T. PARK *Sonn.* 106 O! that the world would by her ways improve,..Nor wear the vizor-smile of feigned love. **1798** LANDOR *Gebir* I. 51 His vizor-helm, His buckler and his corset [1803 corslet] he laid by. **1814** SCOTT *Lord of Isles* VI. xxvii, Strong Egremont for air must gasp, Beauchamp undoes his visor-clasp. **1861** GOULD *Monogr. Trochilidæ* IV. Pl. 221 *Augastes Scutatus*, Natterer's Vizor-bearer. *Ibid.* Pl. 222 *Augastes Lumachellus*, Hooded Vizor-bearer.

b. visor-mask, (*a*) a form of disguising mask; a domino; (*b*) a prostitute. Cf. VIZARD-MASK.

(*a*) **1672** [H. STUBBE] *Rosemary & Bayes* 11 *Personam induere* doth also signifie to put on a perruke and visor-mask. **1679** DRYDEN *Limberham* v. i, I will put on my vizor-mask, however, for more security. **1700** T. BROWN *Amusem. Ser. & Com.* v. 50 A Whore [is known] by a Vizor-Mask: And a Fool by Talking to her. **1713** *Guardian* No. 4 ¶1 Even Truth itself in a Dedication is like an Honest Man in a Disguise, or Vizor-Mask.

(*b*) **1693** *Humours Town* 105 The Orange-Wenches, and the Vizor-Masks. **1694** CONGREVE *Double Dealer* Epil., The Vizor-Masks, that are in Pit and Gallery, Approve, or Damn the Repartee and Rallery.

ˈvisor, ˈvizor, *v. rare.* Also 6 viser. [f. prec.]

1. *refl.* To disguise (oneself) with a visor.

a **1548** HALL *Chron., Hen. VIII*, 80 b, In secrete places euery one visered himselfe, so that they were vnknowen.

2. *trans.* To cover *up* with a visor.

1872 TENNYSON *Gareth & Lynette* 1012 The Sun.. vizoring up a red And cipher face of rounded foolishness.

visored, vizored (ˈvaɪzəd), *ppl. a.* [f. as prec. + -ED.]

1. a. Of persons: Having the face covered or hid with a visor or mask. Also *fig.*, and of things.

c **1380** WYCLIF *Wks.* (1880) 99 þus in stede of cristis apostlis ben comen in viserid deuelis, to disceyuen men in good lif. **1571** GOLDING *Calvin on Ps.* xvi. 4 There is no cause why theis visord Nicodemusses should coker themselves with this fond pretence. **1634** MILTON *Comus* 698 Hast thou betrai'd my credulous innocence With visor'd falshood, and base forgery? **1827** HALLAM *Const. Hist.* iv. (1876) I. 205 Martin Mar-prelate, a vizored Knight of those lists, behind whose shield a host of sturdy puritans were supposed to fight. **1876** MEREDITH *Beauch. Career* III. xv. 260 There was the enemy hard in front, mailed, vizored, gauntleted.

b. In predicative use. (Cf. VISOR *v.*)

c **1460** *Wisdom* 727 in *Macro Plays* 59 Here entrethe vj. Jorours..with hodis abowt her neckis, hattis of meyntenance þer-vp-on, vyseryde dyuersly. *a* **1470** GREGORY *Chron.* in *Hist. Coll. Cit. Lond.* (Camden) 78 The Schottys came in to Inglonde in to the parke of Stanhope. And ther they were vyseryde for knowynge. **1813** HOGG *Queen's Wake* Concl. 325 The lofty brows of stern Clokmore Are visored with the moving cloud. **1830** MRS. BRAY *The Talba* xx. 170 Did you not come, you and your companion, visored and shrouded,..to waylay our path. **1883** SWINBURNE *Les Casquettes* iii, Like heads of the spirits of darkness visored That see not for ever, nor ever have heard.

2. a. Of a helmet: Furnished with a vizor.

1834 PLANCHÉ *Brit. Costume* 136 The improued visored bascinet and camail. **1862** H. MARRYAT *Year in Sweden* I. 271 A soldier in a vizored helmet. **1898** *Archaeol. Jrnl.* LV. 119 The head-piece, which is a visored salade.

b. Of a cap: peaked.

1950 *Manch. Guardian Weekly* 5 Oct. 15/2 The General left the 'plane, dressed in field jacket and visored, brass-encrusted cap. **1961** M. BEADLE *These Ruins are Inhabited* (1963) ii. 30 The salesman spread out an impressive..array of..red-bound black blazers, visored caps, red bordered black Rugby socks. **1983** P. CHEVALIER *Shaft* xvii. 119 He was wearing exquisite yachting whites and a Navy-style visored cap.

visorless, vizorless (ˈvaɪzəlɪs), *a.* [f. VISOR *sb.* + -LESS.] Having no visor.

1848 LYTTON *Harold* III. v, There were the small round shield and spear of the earlier Saxon with his vizorless helm. **1889** *Harper's Mag.* July 188/1 He wore a round visorless cap of astrakhan.

†**ˈvisorly**, *a. Obs.*⁻¹ In 5 viserly. [f. as prec. + -LY¹.] Resembling a visor or mask.

1421 HOCCLEVE *Learn to Die* 678 Hir viserly faces, grim & hydous Me putte in thoghtful dreedes encombrous.

visorne, Sc. variant of VISERN *Obs.*

†**viˈsorum.** *Obs.* [For *visorium* (so in F.), aphetic for *divisorium* (so in G.), a special use of med.L. *divisorium* a dividing thing or part.] A device formerly used by compositors while setting up, to indicate the line on the copy.

1659 C. HOOLE tr. *Comenius' Vis. World* (1672) 190 The Compositor..(according to the Copy, which he hath fastened before him in a Visorum) composeth words in a composing-stick. **1683** MOXON *Mech. Exerc., Printing* xxii. ¶4. 212 Some Compositers use Visorums,..pricking the point of the Visorum..upon the Border or Frame of the Case. **1770** LUCKOMBE *Hist. Printing* 383 When our Copy is very wide we use a Divisorium (commonly called Visorum), we chuse to move it each time downwards, to compose what by that means appears from under the Visorum.

†**ˈvisory**, *a. Obs.* [f. L. *vīs-* (ppl. stem of *vidēre* to see) + -ORY.] Visive, visual.

1633 T. ADAMS *Exp. 2 Pet.* i. 19 The serpent stroke him dead, infecting his visory spirits with her unprevented poison. **1650** BULWER *Anthropomet.* 20 Let them endeavour untill they perceive where the visory rayes do come. **1684** tr. *Bonet's Merc. Compit.* XVIII. 627 Fænil and Seseli seed.. attenuate the visory Spirits.

†**visoˈtactile**, *a. Obs.*⁻¹ [f. L. *vīs-us* sight + *tact-us* touch.] Involving both sight and touch.

1652 URQUHART *Jewel* Wks. (1834) 236 By vertue of the intermutual unlimitedness of their visotactil sensation.

visour(e, obs. forms of VISOR.

‖**viss** (vɪs). Also 7 **vise, vyse**, 8 **vis.** [ad. Tamil *visai*. Cf. It. *byza*, Pg. *biça*, in 16th c. writers.] A weight used in Southern India and Burmah equal to about 3¼ lbs.

[**1588** HICKOCK tr. *Federici's Voy. & Trav.* 32 b, This Ganza goeth by weight of Byze..and commonly a Byza of a Ganza is worth..halfe a ducket.] **1626** METHOLD in Purchas *Pilgrimage* (ed. 4) 1003 His peremptory demand of a Vyse of the fairest Diamonds. **1665** SIR T. HERBERT *Trav.* (1677) 87 The annual Tribute i.e. three pound weight being a Vise of the fairest Stones or Diamonds. **1766** T. BROOKS *Coins E. Indies* 7, 40 Pollams weight is equal to 1 Vis, or 3⅛ lb. Avoirdupoise. *Ibid.* 11, 4 Putas is 1 Viss. **1800** *Misc. Tr.* in *Asiat. Ann. Reg.* 319/2 From the wells the oil is carried in small jars, by cooleys,..to the river; where it is delivered to the merchant exporter at 2 tecals per hundred viss. **1829** CRAWFURD *Jrnl. Emb. to Crt. of Ava* (1834) II. 203 The King [of Burma] lays claim to all [stones] that exceed in value a viss of silver, or one hundred ticals. **1876** J. ANDERSON *Mandalay to Momien* 336 In 1872, no less than one hundred and fifty thousand viss of royal cotton were stored at Manwyne.

viss, southern ME. var. FISH; obs. Sc. f. WISH *v.*

vissage, obs. f. VISAGE.

vissare, southern ME. var. FISHER¹.

visse, obs. var. VIZY *v. Sc.*

†**vissep**, southern var. of ME. *fisheth* (OE. *fiscaþ*), fishing.

1297 R. GLOUC. (Rolls) 5341 A day as he weri was..& is men were ywent a vissep.

vissett, obs. f. VISIT *v.*

vissie, var. VIZY *v. Sc.*

†**vissier.** *Sc. Obs.*⁻¹ [f. *vissy* VIZY *v.*] An inspector.

1566 *Inv. R. Wardr.* (1815) 175 The said Sir James Balfour of Pettindreich knycht..vissier and ressaver.

vissill, Sc. f. WISSEL *v. Obs.*

vissite, obs. f. VISIT *v.*

vissorne, Sc. var. VISERN *Obs.*

vissy, var. VIZY *v. Sc.*

vist, obs. Sc. form of *wist* WIT *v.*

vista (ˈvɪstə), *sb.* Also 7–9 **visto.** [It. (also Sp. and Pg.) *vista*, f. L. *vīs-*, ppl. stem of *vidēre* to see. The form *visto* exhibits the common tendency to substitute *-o* for *-a* in adoptions of Romanic words: cf. -ADO 2.]

1. A view or prospect, especially one seen through an avenue of trees or other long and narrow opening.

α. **1657** R. LIGON *Barbadoes* 97 This is one of the pleasantest Vistos in the Iland. **1727** A. HAMILTON *New Acc. E. Ind.* I. xii. 136 The Churches..standing gradually higher than one another, make the Visto from the Sea admirably pleasant. **1742** tr. *Algarotti on Newton's Theory* I. 122 A Landskip drawn by Claude Lorrain, or a Visto by Canalleto. **1798** T. GREEN *Diary Lover of Lit.* (1810) 83 We caught a grand view of it, extending in a long visto, and bounded by the opposite projecting points of Cary Sconce and Hurst Castle. **1817** J. SCOTT *Paris Revisit.* (ed. 4) 49 It was impossible to look in any direction but along the narrowing *visto* of canal.

β. **1686** BURNET *Trav.* 222 On several hands one sees a long Vista of streets. **1711** POPE *Temple Fame* 263 The Temple ev'ry moment grew, And ampler Vista's open'd to my view. **1735** SOMERVILLE *Chase* IV. 480 The flow'ry Landskip, and the gilded Dome, And Vistas op'ning to the wearied Eye. **1770** GOLDSM. *Des. Vill.* 298 But verging to decline, its splendours rise, Its vistas strike, its palaces surprise. **1832** G. DOWNES *Lett. Cont. Countries* I. 379 Near the tomb is obtained a splendid vista of Naples in all its glory. **1850** KINGSLEY *A. Locke* xi, I stood looking wistfully over the gate..at the inviting vista of the green embroidered path. **1873** HIGGINSON *Oldport Days* x. 252 A piny dell gave some vista of the broad sea we were leaving.

2. a. A long narrow opening (esp. one made on purpose) in a wood, etc., through which a view may be obtained, or which in itself affords a pleasant prospect; an avenue or glade.

α. **1671** R. BOHUN *Wind* 29 A Mountaine in Provence which had a *Visto* thorough it. **1711** *Hermit* 25 Aug. 2/2 A Visto cut thro' a Hill for which the Workmen have not seen their Money. **1733** W. ELLIS *Chiltern & Vale Farm.* 90 An old House that stood at the End of a Visto. **1756** TOLDERVY *Hist. 2 Orphans* IV. 214 Humphry employs himself..in hunting..cutting vistoes through the woods, or gardening. *a* **1774** GOLDSM. *Hist. Greece* II. 131 A fine park..[with] spacious vistoes, under which those who walked were shaded from the sun-beams. **1809** *Child 36 Fathers* (N.Y.) I. 182 My eyes..were suddenly attracted by a small visto of trees, which appeared to me well suited to the indulgence of meditation.

fig. **1790** BURKE *Fr. Rev.* 115 In the groves of *their* academy, at the end of every visto, you see nothing but the gallows.

β. **1686** PLOT *Staffordsh.* 37 The woods lye disperst at due distance, and if any thing large, have lawnes or vista's cut through them. **1732** MRS. DELANEY *Life & Corr.* (1861) I. 376 Below the house and between the lakes is a little copsewood which is cut into vistas and serpentine walks. **1741** RICHARDSON *Pamela* (1824) I. xiii. 251 He employed hands to cut a vista through a coppice. **1791** W. GILPIN *Forest Scenery* II. 64 A winding road through a wood has undoubtedly more beauty than a vista. **1827** D. JOHNSON *Ind. Field Sports* 75 The tops of the grass are cut away with a sickle so as to form a narrow vista for the passage of an arrow. **1868** NETTLESHIP *Ess. Browning* i. 36 A many-columned vista of a wood. **1895** RIDER HAGGARD *Heart of World* xiv, Everywhere stretched vistas that brought to my mind memories of the dimly-lighted nave of the great cathedral of Mexico.

b. An open corridor or long passage in or through a large building; an interior portion of a building affording a continuous view.

α. **1708** *Lond. Gaz.* No. 4414/3 Newington House built with Stone after the Italian manner, with a Visto through,.. to be let. *c* **1710** CELIA FIENNES *Diary* (1888) 112 An abundance of good sizeable roomes leading one out of another in Visto's through the house, something Like our new way of building. **1735** W. STUKELEY *Mem.* (Surtees) II. 36 They have opened a visto from the lodg through the gallery, to the library.

β. **1726** SWIFT *Gulliver* IV. ii, Beyond this Room there were three others, reaching the length of the House, to which you passed through three Doors, opposite to each other, in the manner of a Vista. **1806** A. DUNCAN *Nelson's Funeral* 37 The central aisle..forming in itself the grandest architectural vista in Europe. **1858** HAWTHORNE *Fr. & It. Note-bks.* (1871) I. 15 The whole [*sc.* galleries of the Louvre] extended into infinite vistas by mirrors that..multiplied everything for ever. **1876** MISS BRADDON *J. Haggard's Dau.* II. 15 The door at the end of the narrow little passage stood open, and the westward-fronting casement was shining like a jewel at the end of the vista.

†**c.** An opening or passage-way. *Obs.*⁻¹

1737 A. HAMILTON *New Acc. E. Ind.* I. xiii. 155 To search well, that there should be no subterraneous Communication ..[but] finding no Visto that might be suspected, they ordered the Jougies to remove their great Water Jar.

3. *fig.* **a.** A mental view or vision of a far-reaching nature.

1673 *Lady's Call.* II. iii. §8 It must infinitly more do so.. if they please to open a visto into the other world. **1704** NORRIS *Ideal World* II. Pref. 3, I pretend only to make a kind of visto into the intelligible world. **1848** R. J. WILBERFORCE *Doctr. Incarnation* iii. (1852) 28 Those occasional intimations which open vistas into the mighty depths of God's counsels. **1876** MOZLEY *Univ. Serm.* viii. 178 The human heart takes in all the great vistas and reaches of human reason. **1887** *Pall Mall G.* 29 Dec. 6/1 The use of reading is to lighten the load of life, and to open vistas of thought which otherwise would be closed to us.

attrib. **1809** MALKIN *Gil Blas* v. i. ¶17 Catching every now and then a vista vision of ten thousand ducats.

b. A view or vision, in prospect or retrospect, of an extensive period of time or series of events, experiences, etc.

1742 YOUNG *Nt. Th.* VI. 117 Through the long visto of a thousand years, To stand contemplating our distant selves. **1780** BURKE *Œcon. Reform* Wks. 1906 II. 307 They might see a long, dull, unvaried visto of despair and exclusion, for half a century, before them. **1834** MARRYAT *P. Simple* i, A sort of vision of future grandeur passed before me, in the distant vista of which I perceived a coach with four horses and a service of plate. **1839** MURCHISON *Silur. Syst.* I. Introd. 12 As yet we can gaze but dimly into the obscure vista of these early periods. **1861** M. PATTISON *Ess.* (1889) I. 39 Dr. Pauli..to whose strong historical vision a vista of a few centuries is nothing. **1888** BRYCE *Amer. Commw.* lxxx. III. 50 They see a long vista of years stretching out before them in which they will have time enough to cure all their faults.

4. *in vista*, in continuous view.

1758 J. KENNEDY *Curios. Wilton House* (1786) p. xxxvii, The Rooms lie in Visto as a great Gallery. **1815** W. H. IRELAND *Scribbleomania* Pref. p. viii, Like a monotonous and undeviating route to the traveller, who..beholds the object constantly in vista. **1887** RUSKIN *Præterita* II. 259 The level road with its aisles of poplars in perspective vista.

5. Comb.: **vista-dome** *U.S.*, a high glass-sided railway carriage that enables passengers to look at the view from above the normal level of the train. Freq. *attrib.*

1945 *Time* 18 June 78/3 For travelers who like to watch the country go by, Chicago, Burlington & Quincy Railroad announced a new 'Vista Dome' car, to be put in operation next week. **1948** *Sun* (Baltimore) 6 Jan. 6/5 (Advt.), The Vista-Dome affords a wonderful opportunity for camera fans. **1973** [see RHEINGOLD].

Hence **'vistal** *a.*, of the nature of a vista. **'vistaless** *a.*, devoid of any vista or prospect.

1860 MAYNE REID *Wild Huntress* i, The squatter's clearing..is a mere vistal opening in the woods. **1890** *Lippincott's Mag.* Feb. 242 Was Bombin's life more aimless quite Than the vistaless one of the Sybarite?

'vista, *v. rare*⁻¹. [f. the sb.]

1. *trans.* To make into vistas.

1832 LYTTON *Eugene A.* xxxiii, The night had now closed in, and its darkness was only relieved by the wan lamps that vistaed the streets.

2. In *pa. pple.* Seen in vistas.

1848 LYTTON *K. Arthur* VII. xxviii, And all the galleries vista'd through the wave.

vistaed ('vɪstəd), *a.* [f. VISTA *sb.*]

1. Placed or arranged so as to make a vista or avenue.

1835 LYTTON *Rienzi* v. iii, They..extending far down the vistaed streets..awaited the orders of their leader. **1862** —— *Str. Story* v, I did not pass through the lane..but up the broad causeway, with vistaed gas-lamps. **1882** J. HAWTHORNE *Fort. Fool* xxxviii, She moved slowly and saunteringly along the vistaed aisle.

2. Provided with vistas.

1862 CALVERLEY *Verses & Transl.*, *Dover to Munich* 105 Lawns, and vista'd gardens, Statues white, and cool arcades. **1881** MRS. C. PRAED *Policy & P.* II. 258 They would ride on and on through the many-vistaed forest.

3. *fig.* Seen as it were in prospect by the imagination.

1849 W. M. W. CALL *Reverberations* II. 85 Gazing steadfastly Thro' vistaed centuries. *a* **1851** MOIR *Poems* (1852) I. 64 To her appear The vista'd joys of Heaven's eternal year. **1893** F. THOMPSON *Poems*, *Hound of Heaven* 6 Up vistaed hopes I sped.

Vistavision ('vɪstəvɪʒən). Also **vista-**. [f. VISTA *sb.* + VISION *sb.*] A form of wide-screen cinematography employing standard 35 mm. film in such a way as to give a larger projected image with ordinary methods of projection. Also *fig.*

A proprietary name in the U.S.

1954 *Newsweek* 15 Mar. 104/3 A new filming process in which Paramount Pictures will produce all its films beginning with 'White Christmas'..was demonstrated last week in Hollywood. Called VistaVision, it..is designed primarily to improve wide-screen clarity. **1955** *Official Gaz.* (U.S. Patent Office) 25 Jan. TM 138/2 Paramount Pictures Corporation... *Vistavision* for motion picture films and cameras and parts therefor. **1961** *Guardian* 20 Jan. 7/3 Passion and vistavision ideas are not enough. **1976** *New Musical Express* 12 Feb. 27/5 I'll direct you to a copy of Diana Ross's 'An Evening With' (Motown) a vistavision affair on which Berry Gordy's favourite movie star provides a medley of Motown oldies.

visual ('vɪʒjuːəl, 'vɪz-), *a.* and *sb.* Also 6–7 **visuall**. [a. OF. *visual* (16th c., = Sp. and Pg. *visual*, It. *visuale*, OF. and F. *visuel*), or ad. late L. *vīsuālis* (rare) attained by or belonging to sight, f. L. *vīsus* sight, VISION *sb.*]

A. *adj.* **1. a.** Of beams: Coming, proceeding, or directed from the eye or sight. *Obs.* or *arch.*

1412–20 LYDG. *Chron. Troy* I. 1697 þat of oure si3t þe stremys visual May nat be-holde, nor I-sen at al,.. How Appollo is in his chare schynende. **1603** HOLLAND *Plutarch's Mor.* 1362 It fareth with us in this case, as with those who would see a thing very farre distant; for of necessitie the visual beames of his sight doe faile before they can reach thereto. **1612** DRAYTON *Poly-olb.* To Rdr., Trusting Authorities at second hand, and rash collecting..from visuall beam's refracted through anothers eye. **1671** MILTON *Samson* 163 For inward light alas Puts forth no visual beam.

b. *visual line*, the direct line from the eye to the object or point of vision; the line of sight.

1571 DIGGES *Pantom.* I. xx. F ij b, Agayne my line visuall proceeding from D to H the subtill notche in the subtendente side of the angle, extendeth to my fifte staffe G. **1602** DOLMAN *La Primaud. Fr. Acad.* (1618) III. 696 By meanes of the shadowes, or visuall lines, representing the said shadowes. **1667** SIR R. MORAY in *Phil. Trans.* II. 474 The Visual line that passeth from the Eye to the upper-side of the Mark. **1755** *Dict. Arts & Sci.* s.v. *Perspective*, In drawing a perspective figure, where many lines come together, you may..draw the diagonals in red; the visual lines in black. **1850** NICHOL *Archit. Heav.* II. iv. 135 Merely to indicate that they lie in almost the same visual line, or that their proximity is optical only, and not real.

c. *visual ray*, a ray proceeding from the eye to the object seen (cf. *visual beam* above), or in later use from the object to the eye.

1625 N. CARPENTER *Geogr. Del.* I. vi. (1635) 154 The visuall Ray wherein the sight is carried is alwaies a right line. **1667** MILTON *P.L.* III. 620 The Aire, No where so cleer, sharp'nd his visual ray To objects distant farr. **1755** *Dict. Arts & Sci.* s.v. *Perspective*, The point of sight..is the point where all the other visual rays..unite. **1779** *Phil. Trans.* LXIX. 649 The great and varying refractions of the visual rays. **1815** J. SMITH *Panorama Sci. & Art* II. 710 Visual rays, are those which, passing through the transparent plane, render original objects visible. Principal visual ray, is that which passes through the axis or centre of the eye. **1840** LARDNER *Geom.* 203 If the visual ray from the upper extremity A' coincide with the visual ray from the upper extremity of the other. **1868** LOCKYER *Guillemin's Heavens* (ed. 3) 475 The instrument will give us the angle formed by the visual ray with our base-line.

2. a. Of power or faculty: Pertaining or relating to, concerned or connected with, sight or vision. *visual acuity*, sharpness of vision; *spec.* as measured or expressed in terms of a definite scale (see quot. 1974).

1603 HOLLAND *Plutarch's Mor.* 1345 As the one [*sc.* the sun] kindles, bringeth foorth and stirreth up the visuall power and vertue of the sense. **1798** WORDSW. *Peter Bell* 918 The Spirits of the Mind Are busy..Upon the rights of visual sense Usurping. **1874** CARPENTER *Ment. Phys.* I. i. (1879) 13 That part of the Brain which is the instrument of our Visual Consciousness. **1889** *Buck's Handbk. Med. Sci.* VII. 665/2 Comparative researches upon the visual acuity of different parts of the retina. **1938** R. L. REA *Neuro-Ophthalmology* iv. 86 In the early stages [of papillœdema] there may be..full central visual acuity. **1974** *Encycl. Brit. Macropædia* VII. 104/1 A visual acuity of unity indicates a power of resolving detail subtending one minute of arc at the eye; a visual acuity of two indicates a resolution of one-half minute..of arc.

fig. **1828** MACAULAY *Misc. Writ.* (1860) I. 197 Language.. when it becomes too copious,..altogether destroys the visual power [of the imagination]. **1849** W. A. BUTLER *Serm.* vii. 114 Faith is the realizing power. Its the visual sense of the Spirit.

b. *visual purple* [tr. G. *sehpurpur* (app. first used by W. Kühne 1877, in *Verh. d. Naturhist.-med. Verein zu Heidelberg* I. 484)]: = RHODOPSIN.

[**1877** *Nature* 1 Feb. 296/1 These first observations of Kühne on the vision-purple (*Sehpurpur*), as he terms it.] **1878** M. FOSTER *Text Bk. Physiol.* (ed. 2) III. ii. 415 For the restoration of the visual purple, after it has been destroyed by light, the maintenance of the circulation of the blood through the tissues of the eye is not essential. **1921** *Proc. R. Soc.* B. XCII. 232 A highly dilute visual purple may suffice for the requirements of photopic vision. **1953** *Sci. News* XXX. 116 Although as many as six visual pigments have been recognized in different species, only one, visual purple, has been obtained from the human retina. **1983** *Guardian* 4 Aug. 17/2 Retinaldehyde..is present in the retina of the eye combined with the visual pigment known as visual purple.

3. a. Of organs: Endowed with the power of sight; having the function of producing vision. Cf. OPTIC *a.* 2.

1626 BACON *Sylva* §400 An Eye..hath beene thrust forth, so as it hanged a pretty distance by the Visuall Nerue. **1667** MILTON *P.L.* XI. 414 Michael..then purg'd with Euphrasie and Rue The visual Nerve [of Adam], for he had much to see. **1704** SWIFT *T. Tub* xi, The virtue of the Visual nerve, which every little accident shakes out of order. **1837** P. KEITH *Bot. Lex.* 228 An assemblage of several organs, all concurring to the production of a single result, constitutes an apparatus,—the visual apparatus, the digestive apparatus [etc.]. **1874** tr. *Lommel's Light* 1 The visual organ, like every other special sense, possesses a peculiar form of sensibility. **1880** HUXLEY *Cray-Fish* iii. 121 Each of these visual pyramids consists of an axial structure—the visual rod invested by a sheath.

b. Of the eye, or in phrases denoting this, as *visual orb*. Chiefly *poet.*

1725 POPE *Odys.* I. 90 Neptune..Afflicts the chief, to avenge his giant son Whose visual orb Ulysses robbed of light. *Ibid.* IX. 454 Urged by some present god, they swift let fall The pointed torment on his visual ball. **1801** *Lusignan* IV. 177 [She] complained that the light,..hurt the visual optic. **1877** L. MORRIS *Epic Hades* II. 221 By night when visual Eyes are blind.

4. a. Of knowledge: Attained or obtained by sight or vision.

In early use app. contrasted with book-knowledge.

1651 BIGGS *New Disp.* ¶74 Mathiolus,..and other Herbalists, have hitherto been busied only about the features, and visuall knowledge of Plants, but all of them.. describe vertues out of Dioscorides. **1903** CONRAD & HUEFFER *Romance* IV. v. 270 These..were the only two men of whom she could be said to have more than a visual knowledge.

b. Carried out or performed by means of vision.

1849 ROBERTSON *Serm.* Ser. I. x. (1866) 155 The visual perception of His Form would be a small blessing. **1882** PROCTOR *Fam. Sci. Stud.* 8 The visual test however is independent.

c. Of impressions, etc.: Received through the sense of sight; based upon something seen.

1833 SIR C. BELL *Hand* (1834) 327 Were the eye fixed in the head..we should still be capable of comparing the visual impression with the experience of the body. **1840** MILL *Diss. & Disc.* (1859) II. 103 The visual ideas, which thus become our main symbols of tangible objects. **1877** M. FOSTER *Physiol.* III. ii. (1878) 397 These two things we will briefly distinguish as visual sensations and visual judgments. **1879** HARLAN *Eyesight* iii. 37 All parts of the retina are not equally sensitive to visual impressions.

5. a. Of or pertaining to vision in relation to the object of sight; = OPTIC *a.* 5, OPTICAL *a.* 2. Chiefly in special collocations as *visual angle*, *axis*, *field*, *focus*, *point*, *range*.

1710 J. HARRIS *Lex. Techn.* ii, **Visual-angle*, is the same with the Optick-Angle. *c* **1790** IMISON *Sch. Arts* I. 205 The Visual or Optic Angle, is that which is contained under the two right lines drawn from the extreme points of an object to the eye. **1858** O. W. HOLMES *Aut. Breakf.-t.* xii. 110 To-day's dinner subtends a larger visual angle than yesterday's revolution. **1873** W. LEES *Acoustics* II. iv. 66 The size of an object depends upon the magnitude of the visual angle. **1874** HARTWIG *Aerial World* xiii. 198 If the sun rises, the *visual axis sinks, and with it the rainbow. **1880** W. JAMES *Coll. Ess. & Rev.* (1920) 169 He perceives correctly the position of objects in the *visual field. **1927** B. RUSSELL *Anal. Matter* xii. 111 The sort of relation that will not do is illustrated if we take $xy = zw$ to mean that xy and zw have the same apparent dimensions in the visual field of a certain observer. **1961** G. E. M. ANSCOMBE tr. *Wittgenstein's Notebks. 1914–16* 45 What is a uniformly coloured part of my visual field composed of? **1837** GORING & PRITCHARD *Microgr.* 63 What may be called the *visual focus of a lens, or its distance from an object upon which we have adjusted its focus as a magnifier. **1867** J. HOGG *Microsc.* I. ii. 156 The making of the actinic and visual foci coincident. **1679** MOXON *Math. Dict.* s.v., The *Visual Point in Perspective,..is a point in the Horizontal Line, wherein all the Occular Rays unite. [Hence in Phillips, Harris, etc.] **1755** *Dict. Arts & Sci.* s.v. *Perspective*, Let the object you intend to delineate..be placed also on the right-hand of the visual point. **1842** FRANCIS *Dict. Arts*, *Visual Point*, the point of vision from which an object is viewed, synonymous with the point of sight. **1953** R. CHISHOLM *Cover of Darkness* iii. 36 Reading the faces of cathode-ray tubes was a small part of the Observer's task. By description and instruction he had to get his Pilot to *visual range. **1965** *Observer* 31 Oct. 1/1 'Visual range'—the distance one can see along the runway —is measured and passed to the pilot.

b. In general use.

1812 WOODHOUSE *Astron.* xi. 91 Certain smaller corrections belonging..to some change in the position of the poles of the earth: or to causes merely visual and optical. **1869** J. MARTINEAU *Ess.* II. 158 It is indeed quite conceivable that, in beings of another race, the visual scale may be much larger than ours.

6. a. That is an object of vision or sight; capable of being seen; perceptible, visible.

1756 BURKE *Subl. & B.* III. xxvi, A clear and settled idea of visual beauty. *Ibid.* IV. xv, Among many remarkable particulars that attended his first perceptions and judgments on visual objects. *c* **1810** COLERIDGE in *Lit. Rem.* (1838) III. 295 The second commandment expressly makes the worshipping of God in or before a visual image of him.. idolatry. **1853** KANE *Grinnell Exp.* xxxv. (1856) 313 Refraction, with its preternatural augmentation of the visual hemisphere, revisited us. **1869** TYNDALL in *Fortn. Rev.* 1 Feb. 237 Of all the visual waves emitted by the sun, the shortest and smallest are those which correspond to the colour blue. **1871** —— *Fragm. Sci.* (1879) I. vi. 223 The spectrum embraces three classes of rays—the thermal, the visual, and the chemical. **1892** *Photogr. Ann.* II. 240 Which from the visual aspect of colour should appear almost black.

b. Of actions, conditions, etc. Also, characterized by visibility.

1828 CARLYLE *Misc.* (1840) I. 307 (*Goethe*) Everything has form, everything has visual existence; the poet's imagination bodies forth the forms of things unseen. **1840** —— *Heroes* ii. (1904) 69 That this so solid-looking material world..is a visual and tactual Manifestation of God's power and presence. **1849** RUSKIN *Sev. Lamps* v. §10. 145 The inclination may be seen by the eye, by bringing it [the wall] into visual contact with the upright pilasters. **1867–77** G. F. CHAMBERS *Astron.* I. i. 11 The period required to make a whole visual rotation.

c. Of signalling or a signal.

1876 VOYLE & STEVENSON *Milit. Dict.* 424/1 Visual signalling was formerly carried on by semaphores. **1895** *Outing* (U.S.) XXVI. 396/2 Visual signaling embraces flags, heliograph, torch, flash light, etc. **1906** *Times* 20 Aug. 5/1, I proceeded as far..as ensured my being able to use visual signals to the signal station.

d. *visual aid*, illustrative matter designed to supplement written or spoken information; *spec.* in *Educ.* with reference to pictures, models, films, etc., as an aid to learning. orig. *U.S.*

1911 P. MONROE *Cycl. Educ.* V. 734/2 The last century of schoolroom practice has been marked by a great increase in the use of natural objects, models, pictures, maps, charts, and other visual aids. **1938** *Rep. Physical Educ. & Film* (Brit. Film Inst.) 1 The function of the film in education has been defined as that of a visual aid. **1958** *Economist* 29 Nov. 764/1 The visual aids which the party's television programme used to good effect. **1967** MRS. L. B. JOHNSON *White House Diary* 14 Mar. (1970) 497 In one room they were using visual-aid machines for faster reading. **1980** E. BLISHEN *Nest of Teachers* I. ii. 11 That most familiar of visual aids, an extremely tatty blackboard.

e. *visual display* (Computers) = DISPLAY *sb.* 1 c; *visual display unit*, a device for displaying on its screen data stored in a computer, and usu. incorporating a keyboard for manipulating the data; abbrev. VDU, vdu s.v. V 5 b.

1954 *Jrnl. Assoc. Computing Machinery* I. 57/1 Cathode ray tube equipment for providing external visual displays of information stored internally in the computer. **1967** KLERER & KORN *Digital Computer User's Handbk.* I. 77 The importance of the use of machine-produced graphs and other types of visual displays can hardly be over emphasized. **1969** *Computers & Humanities* IV. 83 For those interested in on-line text manipulation, there is special temptation in newer devices like cathode ray tubes (CRTs) or visual displays, or 'scopes', as they are variously called. **1971** J. ANDERSON in B. de Ferranti *Living with Computer* vii. 59 With..the introduction..of visual display units.. there has been a resurgence of interest in applying such techniques to medical recording. **1977** *R.A.F. News* 11–24 May 7/2 When can we have our visual display unit? **1983** *Brit. Med. Jrnl.* 23 July 271 Most of the comments relating to paper records apply to visual displays for data entry. **1984** *Times* 16 Nov. 12/4 The latest scare comes from reports of women who worked on visual display units (VDUs) during pregnancy and went on to deliver handicapped babies or suffer miscarriages.

7. a. Of the nature of a mental vision; produced or occurring as a picture in the mind.

1817 COLERIDGE *Biog. Lit.* I. iv. 76 The change of one visual image for another involves in itself no absurdity. **1845** CARLYLE *Cromwell* I. 88 Let the reader try to make a visual scene of it as he can. **1851** HELPS *Comp. Solit.* x. 192 When we are thinking or talking of a person, we recall some visual image of that person. **1875** E. WHITE *Life in Christ* I. v. (1876) 46 The deeper is the sense of incompetence even to imagine as a visual conception the mass of human beings who have tenanted it.

b. Carrying or conveying a mental vision or image.

1868 GLADSTONE *Juv. Mundi* xiii. (1870) 469 The Greek Catalogue is charged throughout with what I may call local colour and visual epithets; epithets which..raise up a prospect or scene before the mental eye of a reader or a hearer.

B. *sb.* **1. a.** A visual ray: see VISUAL *a.* 1 c.

1726 LEONI *Alberti's Archit.* III. 2/2 Certain Rays which minister to the sight..are called Visuals. **1779** *Phil. Trans.* LXIX. 649 The quantity of effects and of errors in the visuals proceeding from this last cause must be very different at different times.

2. = VISUALIST 1.

1886 *Mind* July 415 This division of men into visuals, audiles, motiles and indifferents, as we may respectively call them, if of great interest and importance. **1899** *Allbutt's Syst. Med.* VII. 440 These variations depend..upon the question whether the patients are 'auditives' or 'visuals'.

3. A visual image or display, a picture; *spec.* the visual element of a film or television production. Usu. *pl.*

1951 *Brit. Kinematogr.* XIX. 110/1 A good deal has been done by..'visuals'. **1959** *Times* 4 Mar. 11/7 Exposition is particularly difficult on television—it gets confused by the visuals and the speaker's loose words. **1961** *Listener* 19 Oct. 622/3 As the commentator's voice announced that allocations for shelters by the U.S. Government had been currently increased 700 per cent, we saw a visual of President Kennedy roaring with laughter. **1966** J. DERRICK *Teaching Eng. to Immigrants* vii. 229 The Language Master ..is a new transistorized machine into which can be fed visuals and reading matter on long cards. **1972** *Observer* 16 Apr. 34/6 Written entries..should be typed, visuals (a maximum of 3ft square) carefully packed. **1974** 'D. CRAIG' *Dead Liberty* xxi. 125 The Finance lads liked your economics piece... We're getting some graphs and other visuals done. **1984** *Times* 23 Jan. 7/1 There is more porn in the [cinema] subtitles than in the visuals.

visualist ('vɪʒjuːəlɪst, 'vɪz-). [f. VISUAL *a.* + -IST.]

1. (See quot.)

1895 *Pop. Sci. Monthly* Apr. 731 Charcot, who classified people into 'visualists' those whose recollections were chiefly of things seen, who had to read a name in order to remember it; 'audists' [etc.].

2. = VISUALIZER.

1902 *Amer. Jrnl. Psychol.* XIII. 544 The visualist probably proceeds more from the standpoint of the object and the enumeration of qualities.

3. (See quot.)

1903 G. M. STRATTON *Exp. Psych.* 128 There are the visualists, who maintain that sight is the only sense that gives us a knowledge of these things.

visu'ality. [f. VISUAL *a.* + -ITY. Cf. late L. *vīsuālitas.*]

1. The state or quality of being visual or visible to the mind; mental visibility.

1840 CARLYLE *Heroes* iii. (1904) 92 Every compartment of it is worked-out, with intense earnestness, into truth, into clear visuality. **1858** —— *Fredk. Gt.* x. viii. II. 685 The image he has of his Burial, we perceive, is of perfect visuality, equal to what a Defoe could do in imagining.

2. With *a* and pl. A mental picture or vision.

1841 CARLYLE *Misc. Ess.* (1857) IV. 242 We must..catch a few more visualities. **1845** —— *Cromwell* I. 154 We have a pleasant visuality of an old summer afternoon 'in the Queen's Court' two hundred years ago. **1912** H. BRADLEY *Let.* in *Corr. Bridges & Bradley* (1940) 96, I do not think I can even say or hear 'bread and butter', or 'dog and cat', without an accompanying under-consciousness of the way in which these words are commonly spelt. (It may be deplorable that any human soul should have got into this degraded state of subjection to black and white visualities.)

3. Vision, sight.

1923 D. H. LAWRENCE *Birds, Beasts & Flowers* 27 You are everywhere, and I am blind, Sightless among all your visuality, You staring caryatids. **1941** *Illustr. London News* CXCVIII. 37 Immediately in front of the driver is a movable periscope, shown reflecting the other tanks ahead, whereby he can obtain full visuality when the armoured cowl has to be closed when in action.

4. Visual aspect or representation; physical appearance.

1938 R. G. COLLINGWOOD *Princ. Art* vii. 144 His [*sc.* Cézanne's] landscapes have lost almost every trace of visuality. **1975** *Physics Bull.* Apr. 165/3 Regretfully, the printed word can hardly do justice to the visuality of the afternoon. **1976** *Times Lit. Suppl.* 5 Mar. 251/1 Notable among the elements of visuality which lead to the effect of amenity is that of scale.

visualizable (ˌvɪzjuːə'laɪzəb(ə)l), *a.* [f. VISUALIZE *v.* + -ABLE.]

a. Capable of being visualized. **b.** Capable of being rendered visible.

1956 E. H. HUTTEN *Lang. Mod. Physics* v. 202 The models may overlap, in part, and they may become more 'abstract', i.e. less visualisable. **1968** *Amer. Speech* XLIII. 5 In the world of reality for which the elements of language are symbols, there are no visualizable objects which correspond to adjective symbols. **1980** *Nature* 8 May 100/1 We think it unlikely that the large visualizable deposits in the older birds are more than epiphenomenal.

visualization (ˌvɪʒjuːəlaɪ'zeɪʃən, ˌvɪz-). [f. next + -ATION.] **1.** The action or fact of visualizing; the power or process of forming a mental picture or vision of something not actually present to the sight; a picture thus formed.

1883 *Academy* 14 July 31 Investigations into the phenomena of visualisation. **1884** GURNEY & MYERS in *19th Cent.* July 72 In the next stage of visualisation the percipient sees a face or figure projected or dejected, as it were, on some convenient surface. **1894** *Athenæum* 10 Nov. 638/2 [The book had] a power of visualization that gave it a claim to real originality.

2. The action or process of rendering visible.

1926 [see CHOLECYSTOGRAPHY]. **1936** *Amer. Jrnl. Cancer* XXVII. 49 The hexagonal tube..offers distinct advantages with its flat sides permitting good visualization. **1960** *New Scientist* 28 July 305/3 Echo sounding..is now being applied to the visualization of structures within the body. **1973** *Nature* 17 Aug. 410/1 Direct visualization of biological material at this level would tell us much about the structure and mode of action of macromolecules. **1982** *Listener* 23/30 Dec. 42/3 The cinematic visualisation of the script.. belongs entirely to Welles and his technicians.

visualize ('vɪʒjuːəlaɪz, 'vɪz-), *v.* Also **visualise.** [f. VISUAL *a.* + -IZE.]

1. *trans.* To form a mental vision, image, or picture of (something not visible or present to the sight, or of an abstraction); to make visible to the mind or imagination.

Freq. in recent use, sometimes in connexion with special branches of psychology or psychical research.

1817, 1831 [implied in *visualized* ppl. a.] **1863** TYNDALL *Heat* x. 350 We can hardly help attempting to visualise the atoms themselves. **1899** J. SMITH *Chr. Charac.* 165 Bunyan, in his immortal allegory, visualised the progress from justification to glory.

2. *absol.* or *intr.* To form a mental picture of something not visible or present, or of an abstract thing, etc.; to construct a visual image or images in the mind.

1871 J. A. SYMONDS in H. F. Brown *Biog.* (1895) II. 52 For numbers I have..no head. I do not visualise except in the most rudimentary way. **1882** *Macm. Mag.* XLVI. 485 This answers to the way in which I visualize for them. **1897** A. LANG *Dreams & Ghosts* ii. 58 A novelist of my acquaintance can 'visualise' so well that [etc.].

3. *trans.* To render visible.

1912 *Moving Picture World* 17 Aug. 646/2 The printed volumes of ancient history have been carefully preserved and why not the film, which is more accurate and which, supplementing the printed story, would visualize the actual occurrences so that all may readily understand? **1925** D. H. LAWRENCE in *Calendar Mod. Lett.* Dec. 269 And the camera will *visualize* the sunflower far more perfectly than Van Gogh can. **1938** *Q. Jrnl. Med.* XXXI. 462 Inflating the stomach with gas by means of an effervescing drink, a procedure we have found of great help in visualizing the apex [of the heart in radiography]. **1958** *Arch. Neurol. & Psychiatry* LXXIX. 59/1 The dorsal root axons..may then be stained and visualized. **1971** *Daily Tel.* 18 Nov. 5 (Advt.), Research has led to the building of an ultra-sensitive Schlieren apparatus, in which pulsed ultrasound may be visualised both in water and in solids.

So **'visualized** *ppl. a.*, made visual or visible to the mind; formed in the mind; **'visualizing** *vbl. sb.* (also *attrib.*) and *ppl. a.*

Carlyle's use of *visualized* was objected to by Sterling (see Carlyle *Life Sterling* II. ii).

1817 COLERIDGE *Biog. Lit.* I. ii. 48 *note*, The images are at least consistent, and it was the intention of the writers to mark the seasons by this allegory of *visualized puns. **1831** CARLYLE *Sart. Res.* I. viii, A Voice, a Motion, an Appearance:—some embodied, visualised Idea in the Eternal Mind? **1883** F. GALTON *Hum. Faculty* (1910) 112 A third..abiding fantasy of certain persons is invariably to connect visualised pictures with words. **1880** E. WHITE *Cert. Relig.* 43 A pictorial *visualizing imagination, which can faithfully depict the scenes recorded. **1881** *Sat. Rev.* 30 July 142/1 Mr. Francis Galton's interesting illustrations of the power of visualizing. *a* **1901** F. W. H. MYERS *Human Personality* (1903) I. p. xli, It involves at least a great increase in his ordinary visualising power.

'visualizer. [f. VISUALIZE *v.* + -ER.] **1.** One who visualizes or has the faculty of forming mental images of invisible things, abstract ideas, conditions, etc.

1886 GURNEY, etc. *Phantasms of Living* I. 195 Mrs. Bettany is by nature a good visualiser. **1894** *Contemp. Rev.* Aug. 266 One may be a visualiser when thinking of music. *a* **1901** F. W. H. MYERS *Human Personality* (1903) I. 125 For those who are already good visualisers such phenomena as these..present no quite unique experience.

2. *spec.* in *Advertising*, a commercial artist employed to design lay-outs.

1921 R. S. DURSTINE *Making Advertisements* ii. 23 Several arrangements suggest themselves immediately if the visualizer has a natural or a trained imagination. **1948** [see LAY-OUT 1 b]. **1968** M. BUTTERWORTH *Walk Softly* ii. 30 She worked as a visualiser in an ad agency. **1981** *West Lancs. Evening Gaz.* 5 June 24 (Advt.), Visualisers/finished artists ..required by a rapidly-expanding studio.

visually ('vɪʒjuːəlɪ, 'vɪz-), *adv.* Also 5 visuu-, 6 viswally. [f. VISUAL *a.* + -LY².] In a visual manner; in relation to vision; by sight.

1448–9 J. METHAM *Wks.* (E.E.T.S.) 19/525 The ouer cerkyl..so vysuually, to yche mannys syte, Abouyn this spere enchauntyd apperryd. **1516** *Lett. & Pap. Hen. VIII*, II. I. 514 [That they might..] viswally aperceeyve [that there was money actually there]. **1821** COLERIDGE in *Blackw. Mag.* X. 249 Outness is but the feeling of otherness (alterity), rendered intuitive, or alterity visually represented. **1831** FARADAY *Exp. Res.* (1859) 295 When..the wheels were visually superposed then the appearance of cogs or teeth was seen. **1878** ABNEY *Photogr.* 86 That when the picture is visually in focus the position of the sensitive plate shall be chemically in focus.

visuo- ('vɪʒjuːəʊ, 'vɪz-), combining form on Gr. models of L. *vīsu-s* sight, vision, employed in a few terms, chiefly *Anat.*, as *visuo-auditory, -kinæsthetic, -psychic, -sensory, -spatial, tactual*, adjs.; *visuo-spatially* adv.; **'visuometer** (see quot. 1847 and cf. VISOMETER); **'visuomotor** *a.*, pertaining to or involving motor activity as guided by or dependent on sight; **ˌvisuo'psychic** *a.*, an epithet of two cortical areas adjacent to the striate cortex, orig. regarded as sites of mental elaboration of visual sense impressions; **ˌvisuo'sensory** *a.*, pertaining to or involving the visual perception of sensory signals; *spec.* an epithet of the striate cortex (see STRIATE *a.* 2), as the part of the brain that receives sensory nerve impulses from the eye.

1899 *Allbutt's Syst. Med.* VIII. 445 The other [commissure] conducts impressions from the visual to the auditory word-centre (the *visuo-auditory commissure). *Ibid.* VII. 415 Destruction of the *visuo-kinæsthetic commissure. **1847** A. SMEE *Vision in Health & Dis.* iii. 37 The adjustment of the exact centre of the glass to the optical centres is so important in practice, that I have contrived an instrument to measure the width accurately between these centres... I have called the instrument itself the *visuometer. **1942** *Anat. Rec.* LXXXIV. 470 (*heading*) Reestablishment of *visuomotor coordination by optic nerve regeneration. **1972** *Science* 5 May 536/2 This difference could be observed in splitbrain monkeys executing a visuomotor task with one eye covered. **1900** *Phil. Trans.* CXCIII. Ser. B. 168 Measurements taken from the whole of the visuo-sensory area and from the neighbouring *visuo-psychic cortex. **1954** S. DUKE-ELDER *Parsons' Dis. Eye* (ed. 12) xxix. 500 A lesion of this vessel thus causes a crossed homonymous hemianopia often with disturbances of the visuopsychic areas. **1980** *Gray's Anat.* (ed. 36) VII. 1010/2 Not only the striate cortex (area 17, visuosensory area), but also the para- and peri-striate areas around it (areas 18 and 19—the 'visuopsychic' cortex) receive projection fibres. **1900** *Visuo-sensory [see *visuo-psychic* adj. above]. **1907** J. H. PARSONS *Dis. Eye* v. 90 This area, which is the primary visual or visuo-sensory area.., is the cortical projection of the corresponding halves of both retinæ. **1980** Visuo-sensory [see *visuopsychic* adj. above]. **1962** *Jrnl. Speech & Hearing Research* Dec. 359/2 Factor 3 is a clear-cut *visuospatial factor. Tests..include matching, copying, drawing, and object-assembly tests. *Ibid.* 367/1 Visuo-spatial behavior..involved both visual and sensory processes. **1977** *Lancet* 10 Dec. 1227/2 Intelligence tests indicated severe intellectual deterioration on subtests measuring visuospatial perception. **1939** *Mind* XLVIII. 360 We touch surfaces of things optically known to us, and when we pass from one thing to another we leave them *visuo-spatially related behind us. **1932** H. H. PRICE *Perception* ix. 277 Let us call it a *visuo-tactual solid. **1959** J. L. AUSTIN *Sense & Sensibilia* (1962) ii. 8 Visuo-tactual solids.

†**visure**, *sb. Obs.* Also 5–6 vysur(e. [a. AF. **visure* (cf. *visuré* pa. pple. in Godef.), alteration of AF. *viser* VISOR, after forms ending in -URE. Cf. med.L. *visura* view, inspection.]

1. Face, visage. *rare*⁻¹.

c **1400** *Laud Troy Bk.* 14608 Alle that coude of surgerye.. Hadde Achilles in that cure To hele his woundes & his visure.

2. A visor of a helmet. (See also quot. 1688.)

1470–85 MALORY *Arthur* VIII. x. 289 Now gentyl knyght ..put vp thy vysure. **1509** HAWES *Past. Pleas.* xxxvii. (1555) Aa j b, The hote fyre was so intollerable Aboue me fleying that vnneth I might Through my visure cast abrode my sight. **1523** LD. BERNERS *Froiss.* I. ccclxxiii. 616 They.. were afote, armed at all peces with bassenettes and vysures and good speres. **1688** R. HOLME *Armoury* III. xvii. (Roxb.) 109/1 The Visures or holes in the Bever to see through.

b. A mask. Also *fig.*

c **1460** *Wisdom* 756 in *Macro Plays* 60 Here entreth vi women, in sut, thre dysgysyde as galontis..with wondyrful vysurs conregent. **1531** TINDALE *Exp. 1 John* (1538) 96 He ..kepeth it [*sc.* bitter speech] vntyll he come & be present wyth hym, for than doth he threaten he wyll pull awaye hys vysure.

3. *fig.* A mere outward show or appearance (*of* something); a pretence or mask. Cf. VISOR *sb.* 3.

1531 TINDALE *Exp. 1 John* (1537) 53 The fayth & hope of the Romane byshop..are no true fayth & hope: but vayne wordes and vysures only. **1548** UDALL, etc. *Erasm. Par. Mark* vii. 51 They haue a certayne counterfayte apparaunce or visure of holines. **1585** FETHERSTONE tr. *Calvin on Acts* ix. 10 He hath in deed suffered Satan to deceiue the vnbeleeuers with false imaginations and visures.

4. a. A sight or vision. *rare*⁻¹.

1535 COVERDALE *Isaiah* xxxiv. 14 There shal straunge visures and monstruous beastes mete one another.

b. Appearance; sight. *rare*⁻¹.

1545 COVERDALE *Def. Chr. Man* A ij, A man, who nether in name ner visure hath bene knowne vnto me till this present daye.

Hence †**'visure** *v. trans.*, to deceive or impose upon. †**'visured** *ppl. a.*, wearing a visor; only *fig.*, masked, false, specious. *Obs.*

1570 FOXE *A. & M.* (ed. 2) II. 1426/2 If kyng Henry the vij. had lyued vnto this day,..it had bene past my Lorde of Wynchesters power, to haue visured the kynges highnes as he did. **1577** H. BULL tr. *Luther's Comm. Ps.* 50 This is rightly to behold the temple, and not as the visured Bishops [L. *larvarum Episcopi*] behold their idolatrous temple when they consecrate it. **1585** FETHERSTONE tr. *Calvin on Acts* xvii. 11 This is not spoken of any visured [L. *larvato*] councell, but of a small assembly of men.

†**vi'suriency.** *Obs. nonce-wd.* [f. L. type **vīsurīre*, desiderative vb., f. L. *vīsĕre*, freq. of *vidēre* to see + -ENCY.] The desire of seeing.

1652 URQUHART *Jewel* 125 The visuriency of either, by ushering the tacturiency of both, made the attrectation of both consequent to the inspection of either.

visy(e, obs. ff. VIZY *v. Sc.*

vit, obs. Sc. f. WIT *sb.* and *v.*; southern dial. f. FIT *v.*

Vita[1] ('vaɪtə). Also **vita**. [L., = 'life'.] A proprietary term for glass which transmits most of the ultraviolet rays of sunlight. Usu. as *Vitaglass*, *Vitaglass*.

1925 *Trade Marks Jrnl.* 29 July 1649 Vita... Glass. Francis Everard Lamplough, 47, Bunbury Road, King's Norton, Birmingham; chemist. **1925** *Spectator* 14 Nov. 869/1 A substitute for quartz... This vitaglass is what I asked for. **1939** O. LANCASTER *Homes Sweet Homes* 60 The small tight-shut windows..will be replaced by a wide expanse of hygienic vita glass. **1948** J. BETJEMAN *Coll. Poems* (1958) 227 And many a cultivated hour they pass In a fine school with walls of vita-glass. **1957** *Oxford Mag.* 17 Oct. 18/2 The well-intended propaganda of Sir Leonard Hill and others about 1930..gave it a new lease of life by preaching that the sun was the best preventative of rickets provided that 'vitaglass' windows were used. **1981** *Times* 21 Feb. 22/3 The old Marine Spa..contained..a Vita-glass sun lounge.

vita[2] ('viːtə). **1.** ‖*vita nuova* [It., = new life]. The title of a work by Dante describing his love for Beatrice, used to denote a fresh start or new direction in life, usu. after some powerful emotional experience.

1934 A. J. A. SYMONS *Quest for Corvo* xii. 164 There seemed no impediment to his *vita nuova*. **1939** L. MACNEICE *Autumn Jrnl.* 43 A cultured accent alone will not provide A season ticket to the Vita Nuova. **1975** P. ORGAN *House on Cheyne Walk* xviii. 163 Not a very good way to begin *la vita nuova*, with more lies.

2. [a. L. *vīta* life.] A biography, the history of a life; *spec.* = *curriculum vitæ* s.v. CURRICULUM.

1949 WYNDHAM LEWIS *Let.* 3 Sept. (1963) 505 You ought to cut out *cleanly* and implacably the *vita* material from this typescript. **1960** *Encounter* Mar. 82/2 Clifton Fadiman.. whose credentials include..a *vita* which concludes as follows:..master of ceremonies on the popular radio programme *Information Please*, and on the television show *This is Show Business*. **1974** H. L. FOSTER *Ribbin', Jivin', & Playin' Dozens* i. 18 As far as children and their schools are concerned, the reports were simply another exercise for academicians to contribute, primarily, as a source for an additional listing on a vita or a source for citations for future papers, lectures, books, and speeches. **1979** *Amer. Speech* LIV. 257 All these observations..are summarized in the vitas of the informants.

vita'bility. *rare*$^{-1}$. [f. L. *vīta*: see VITAL *a.*] = VIABILITY[1].

The adj. *vitable*, in place of *viable*, was suggested by F. Hall *Mod. Eng.* (1873) 181.

1889 *Nature* 26 Sept., If the modification is of service, then presumably it will add to the vitability of the individual.

vitail(e, vitaill(e, vitail(e)er, etc., obs. ff. VICTUAL *sb.* and *v.*, and VICTUALLER.

†**vitaillement**. *Obs. rare.* [a. OF. *vitaillement*, f. *vitail* VICTUAL *sb.*] The provision of victuals; victualling.

1453 *Rolls of Parlt.* V. 235/2 For wages and vitaillement of the Soudeours. **1464** *Ibid.* 509/2 The payment of wages and vitaillement of Caleis.

†**vitaillous**, *a.* *Obs.*$^{-1}$ [f. *vitail* VICTUAL *sb.* + -OUS.] Of the nature of victual.

c **1475** *Partenay* 987 Ther all peple preuilage had echon,.. Euery of that which thai wold demaund Off wynes and of uitaillous viand.

vital ('vaɪtəl), *a.* and *sb.* Also 5 **vytalle**, 5–6 **vytall**, 5–7 **vitall**, 6 **vitalle** (**vytail**, *Sc.* **wettal**). [a. OF. (also mod.F.) *vital* (14th c.; = Sp. and Pg. *vital*, It. *vitale*) or ad. L. *vītāl-is* f. *vita* life. Cf. VITALS.]

A. *adj.* **I. 1. a.** Consisting in, constituted by, that immaterial force or principle which is present in living beings or organisms and by which they are animated and their functions maintained. Now chiefly *Phys.* or *Biol.*

c **1386** CHAUCER *Knt.'s T.* 1944 In hise armes two The vital strengthe is lost, and al ago. **1426** LYDG. *De Guil. Pilgr.* 24220 And thus my silf, I consume al The vertu that called is vital. **1597** HOOKER *Eccl. Pol.* v. liv. §9 For though it [i.e. Christ's body] had a beginning from us, yet God hath giuen it vitall efficacie. **1603** HOLLAND *Plutarch's Mor.* 1019 For that in each of us that which is mortall and subject to dissolution, containeth within it the power which is vitall. **1647** H. MORE *Song of Soul* I. Pref. B viij b, He..shapes us from an inward vitall Principle..into a new life and shape. **1719** DE FOE *Crusoe* I. (Globe) 321 Men..spent their strength in daily Strugglings for Bread to maintain the vital Strength. **1784** COWPER *Task* VI. 134 Where now the vital energy that mov'd,..the pure and subtile lymph Through th' imperceptible meand'ring veins Of leaf and flow'r? **1799** *Med. Jrnl.* I. 372 Due attention ought always to be paid to the presence and activity of vital power in the animal body. **1843** SIR C. SCUDAMORE *Med. Visit Gräfenberg* 92 The higher importance and still greater influence of vital force and nervous energy, as compared with simple chemical action. **1887** BENTLEY *Man. Bot.* (ed. 5) 24 This internal energy, which is peculiar to living protoplasm, is frequently spoken of as vital force.

b. *vital spark* (†or *flame*). Cf. SPARK *sb.*[1] 3.

(*a*) **1704** J. HARRIS *Lex. Techn.* I, *Flamma Vitalis*; some do suppose, that there resides in the Heart of Animals such a fine and kindled, but mild Substance, as they call a *Vital Flame*. **1744** BERKELEY *Siris* §156 The calidum innatum, the vital flame, or animal spirit in man.

(*b*) **1712** POPE *Dying Christian to his Soul* i, Vital spark of heav'nly flame! Quit, oh quit this mortal frame. **1826** F. REYNOLDS *Life & Times* II. 341 For some moments it was supposed, that the vital spark was extinct. **1862** BOYD *Graver Th. Country Parson* xv. 250 The multitudinous machinery of animal life is there, but the vital spark to set it in motion is wanting.

2. Maintaining, supporting, or sustaining life. †**a.** *vital spirit, spirits*. Cf. SPIRIT *sb.* 16. *Obs.*

Freq. in the 16th c., chiefly in pl.

(*a*) *c* **1450** *Mankind* 805 in *Macro Plays* 30 He ys so tymerouse; me semyth hys vytall spryt doth expyre. **1477** NORTON *Ord. Alch.* v. in Ashm. (1652) 82 The Spirit Vitall in the Hert doth dwell. **1539** ELYOT *Cast. Helthe* (1541) 12 b, Spirit vitall procedeth from the harte, and by the arteries or pulses is sente into all the body. **1577** tr. *Bullinger's Decades* (1592) 500 Paule calleth him the naturall man which liueth naturally by the vitall spirit. **1671** SALMON *Syn. Med.* III. iv. 334* The vital spirit resides in the heart, is dispersed by the arteries [etc.]. **1715** POPE *Iliad* III. 366 The vital spirit issued at the wound.

(*b*) **1531** ELYOT *Gov.* I. xvi, Continual studye, without somme maner of exercise, shortely exhausteth the spirytes vytall. *a* **1548** HALL *Chron., Hen. IV*, 32 b, He lay as though all his vital spirites had bene from hym departed. **1606** BRYSKETT *Civ. Life* 48 The heart, wherein all the vitall spirits are forged, and receiue their strength. **1626** BACON *Sylva* §30 As for liuing creatures it is certaine, their Vital Spiritts are a Substaunce Compounded of an Airy and Flamy Matter. **1667** MILTON *P.L.* v. 484. **1707** FLOYER *Physic. Pulse-Watch* 134 The vital Spirits are the Animal, as they are commonly call'd; I call them vital, because they move the Heart and Respiration.

b. Of blood, heat, etc., or in general use.

vital fluid, in *Bot.*, = LATEX 2.

1558 BULLEIN *Govt. Health* A v, Apoplexia and Vertigo will neuer fro the[e] starte, Untill the vitall blode be killed in the harte. **1563** B. GOOGE *Eglogs*, etc. (Arb.) 71 He..Gaue Onset fyrst vpon his Foes, and lost his vitall blud. **1598** BARCKLEY *Felic. Man* (1631) 707 The vitall moysture of his body [is] so consumed that he cannot be known to be the same man. **1611** CORYAT *Crudities* 365 + 3 For whose sake ..he ought not doubt to powre out his vitall bloud. **1667** MILTON *P.L.* VII. 236 The Spirit of God..vital vertue infus'd, and vital warmth throughout the fluid Mass. **1697** DRYDEN *Virg. Georg.* II. 555 To unload the branches, or the leaves to thin, That suck the vital moisture of the vine. **1713** ADDISON *Cato* IV. iii, The vital blood, that had forsook my heart, Returns again in such tumultuous tides. **1797** BURKE *Regic. Peace* iii. Wks. VIII. 409 Let us..watch the systole and diastole, as it now receives, and now pours forth the vital stream through all the members. **1837** P. KEITH *Bot. Lex.* 354 A fluid secreted from the crude sap which M. Schultz designates by the name of the *latex* or 'vital fluid'. **1861** FLOR. NIGHTINGALE *Nursing* ii. (ed. 2) 13 A careful nurse will keep a constant watch over her sick..to guard against the loss of vital heat by the patient himself.

transf. and *fig.* **1602** MARSTON *Antonio's Rev.* IV. iv, She was my vitall blood.

c. Of breath or air. Chiefly *poet.*

Merging into sense 5.

(*a*) **1565** COOPER *Thesaurus*, s.v. *Vitalis, Halitus vitalis*, vitall breath. **1598** *Mucedorus* I. iv. 27 Vnworthy I to beare this vitall breath! **1610** HOLLAND *Camden's Brit.* (1637) 814 [He] dashed out his own braines, and at last yeelded up his vitall breath. **1697** DRYDEN *Virg. Georg.* IV. 699 Longing the common Light again to share, And draw the vital breath of upper Air. **1717** PRIOR *Engraven on a Column* 5 While yet We draw this vital Breath. **1738** WESLEY *Psalms* CXXXIX. II. ii, Should I suppress any vital Breath. **1817** WORDSW. *Vernal Ode* 47 To every draught of vital breath, Renewed throughout the bounds of earth.

(*b*) **1590** SPENSER *F.Q.* II. vii. 66 All so soone as his enfeebled spright Gan sucke this vitall aire into his brest. **1697** DRYDEN *Æneid* XII. 876 Mad with her anguish,..she loaths the vital air. **1704** POPE *Pastorals, Spring* 74 The sun's mild lustre warms the vital air. *a* **1721** PRIOR *Colin's Mistakes* vii, All that under sky breathe vital Air. **1821** SHELLEY *Adonais* iii, Dream not that the amorous Deep Will yet restore him to the vital air. **1863** HAWTHORNE *Our Old Home* (1879) 35 If the missing Doctor still breathed this vital air.

†**d.** *vital air*, in *Old Chem.*, = OXYGEN 1.

1791 W. HAMILTON *Berthollet's Dyeing* I. I. I. iii, I placed [it] in contact with vital air over mercury. **1793** T. BEDDOES *Calculus*, etc. 213 Venous blood exposed to vital air acquires the vermilion colour of arterial blood. **1806** *Med. Jrnl.* XV. 582 Dr. Thornton has laid before the public some cases, which show the efficacy of vital air, or, as it is usually called, oxygen gas, in the cure of fits. **1837** P. KEITH *Bot. Lex.* 135 It appears that oxygen gas,..indispensable to the life of animals, is also indispensable to the life of vegetables, on both which accounts it seems to have well merited the appellation of *vital air*, by which it was at one time designated. **1880** HUXLEY *Crayfish* ii. 75 A new supply of the needful 'vital air', as the old chemists called it.

3. a. Of parts, organs, etc.: Essential or necessary to life; performing the functions indispensable to the maintenance of life.

In modern use also of parts of plants: *vital node* (see quot. 1861); *vital vessels*, those containing or conveying the vital fluid or latex.

1482 *Monk of Evesham* (Arb.) 111 Onethe laste myghte be perseuyd yn hym a ful smalle meuyng as a thynne drede yn hys vytalle veynys. **1565** COOPER *Thesaurus* s.v. *Vitalis*, The vitalle partes. **1615** CROOKE *Body of Man* 23 Of the Naturall parts, he disputeth in the fourth and fift Bookes; of the Vitall in the sixt and seuenth. **1667** DRYDEN *Ind. Emperor* IV. x, It streams, it streams from every vital Part. **1696** PHILLIPS (ed. 5) s.v., The Vital Parts are the Heart, Brain, Lungs and Liver. **1718** PRIOR *Solomon* III. 112 Hoary with Cares, and Ignorant of Rest, We find the vital Springs relax'd and worn. **1732** BERKELEY *Alciphr.* IV. §5 The heart and brain, and other vital parts. **1832** LINDLEY *Introd. Bot.* 13 The *Vital* vessels of Schultz. **1861** BENTLEY *Man. Bot.* 119 The part where the stem and root diverge has been called the *neck* or *collum*, or formerly, the *vital node*, because it was erroneously supposed to be the seat of the life of the plant.

b. *transf.* (In modern use denoting especially those parts of a machine, ship, etc., essential to its proper working.)

1647 CLARENDON *Hist. Reb.* I. §76 Their submiss Reverence to their Princes being a vital part of their Religion. **1698** KEILL *Exam. Th. Earth* (1734) 181 If these he has mentioned be the substantial and vital parts [of his theory]. **1866** CRUMP *Banking* v. 134 Erasure of any vital part of the bill..would justify the banker in refusing payment. **1873** J. RICHARDS *Wood-working Factories* 12 The piston, cross-head connecting rod, and main bearings, are the vital parts to be looked after. **1889** WELCH *Naval Archit.* 141 To preserve intact such vital parts as the machinery, magazines, and steering gear.

4. a. Of, pertaining, or relating to, accompanying, or characteristic of life; inherent in or exhibited by living things or organic bodies.

1565 COOPER *Thesaurus* s.v. *Vitaliter*, To haue liuely or vitaille motion. **1599** SHAKS. *Hen. V*, III. vi. 49 Let not Bardolphs vitall thred bee cut with edge of Penny-cord. **1604** —— *Oth.* v. ii. 14 When I haue pluck'd thy Rose, I cannot giue it vitall growth againe. **1652** FRENCH *Yorksh. Spa* ii. 13 In which as in a vital abode, and natural place, the water, whilest it remains, is living. **1697** DRYDEN *Æneid* VI. 1075 There mighty Cæsar waits his vital hour, Impatient for the world. **1705** J. DUNTON *Life & Errors* 311 The last sands in his Life were run, and there was no turning the Vital-glass. **1784** COWPER *Task* III. 509 When the temper'd heat, Friendly to vital motion, may afford Soft fomentation. **1816** SHELLEY *Alastor* 238 Red morning..Shedding the mockery of its vital hues Upon his cheek of death. **1844** G. BIRD *Urin. Deposits* (1857) 47 In every case in which we endeavour to explain vital phenomena by the physical or chemical laws governing dead matter. **1873** H. SPENCER *Stud. Sociol.* xiv. 330 All actions of individuals being vital actions that conform to the laws of life at large.

b. Of faculties, functions, powers, etc.

1593 SHAKS. *2 Hen. VI*, III. ii. 41 Came he right now to sing a Rauens Note, Whose dismall tune bereft my vital powres. **1634** SIR T. HERBERT *Trav.* 169 It immediatly ouer-charged my vitall sences, and put mee..into a deadly trance. **1696** PHILLIPS (ed. 5), *Vital* Faculty, an Action whereby a Man lives..as the Motions of the Heart, Respiration, Nutrition, &c. **1805** WORDSW. *Prelude* VIII. 299 Whose truth is not a motion or a shape Instinct with vital functions. **1826** S. COOPER *First Lines Surg.* (ed. 5) 38 By a gradual decay of the vital powers from old age. **1857** HENFREY *Bot.* §782 The vital forces appear to be of more than one kind. **1878** HUXLEY *Physiogr.* xvii. 275 The whole mass has been constructed..of the products of denudation, or of those of vital processes.

c. *Geol.* Produced or formed by vital action or force; of vital or organic origin.

1855 J. PHILLIPS *Man. Geol.* 49 Proportions of Chemical, Vital, and Mechanical Deposits. **1880** HAUGHTON *Phys. Geogr.* iii. 164 *note*, It is converted into Chemical and Vital work done by the vegetable and animal organisms that clothe the surface of the earth.

d. Of statistics: (*a*) concerned with or relating to the facts of life, e.g. birth, marriage, death, etc.; also *transf.*; (*b*) *colloq.*, the measurements of a woman's figure, *spec.* bust, waist, and hips (cf. STATISTICS 2 b); similarly *vital measurements*. (Occas. of a man's figure.)

1837 [W. FARR] in McCulloch *Acc. Brit. Emp.* II. 567 Vital Statistics; or, the Statistics of Health, Sickness, Diseases, and Death. **1885** J. NICOL (*title*), Vital, Social, and Economic Statistics of the City of Glasgow, 1881–85. **1949** *Brit. Birds* XLII. 147 Vital statistics from ringed Swallows. **1956** *Newsweek* 23 Jan. 60 New eyes open on a bright wonderful world—and photography makes identification positive, records vital statistics in life's first few minutes. **1958** J. TOWNSEND *Young Devils* ii. 19 A short history of the school plus its vital statistics—i.e. number of boys, teachers, classrooms, subjects and educational standards. **1971** *Brit. Med. Bull.* XXVII. 13/2 The epidemic of iatrogenic deaths in asthmatic children shows the need for continuous monitoring of vital statistics. **1974** *Nature* 22 Mar. 306/1 The vital statistics of this second edition command respect—94 of the 1,562 pages are needed to index its 64 chapters!

1958 *Observer* 18 May 10/4 To control and vary our vital measurements with changing fashion. **1968** G. KENT *Pictorial Hist. Wrestling* v. 119/1 *Height* 6ft. 1 in. *weight* 15 st. *chest* 48 ins. *biceps* 15 ins. *thigh* 26½ ins. Donald Dinnie and his vital measurements. **1952** C. R. COOPER *Teen-Age Vice* (1959) viii. 125 Regina..wrote haphazardly to men, giving her age and vital statistics. **1957** *Times* 1 Aug. 5/5 Those feminine measurements which have become known, in the entertainment world, as vital statistics. **1966** WODEHOUSE *Plum Pie* 60 A book like yours always involves a serious risk for the publisher owing to the absence of the Sex Motif, which renders it impossible for him to put a nude female of impressive vital statistics on the jacket. **1975** C. WESTON *Susannah Screaming* (1976) xxv. 135 I have her phone number and vital statistics.

e. In special collocations:

vital affinity (see quot. and AFFINITY 9). *vital capacity*, in *Phys.*, the breathing or respiratory capacity of the lungs (cf. quot. 1852). *vital contractility*, in *Phys.* = IRRITABILITY 3. *vital germ theory* = *germ theory*, GERM *sb.* 6 (1891 *Cent. Dict.*). †*vital indication* (see quot.). *Obs.*$^{-1}$ †*vital line*, in palmistry, the line of life: see LINE *sb.* 8 b. *vital sister* (see quot.). *vital statistics*, (see sense 4 d). *vital union*, a union involving common life; also *fig.*

1850 DAUBENY *Atom. The.* xi. (ed. 2) 359 *Vital affinity —a force, which is supposed to come in aid of common chemical attraction, and to render the union between the particles of a body more stable. **1852** J. HUTCHINSON *Spirometer* §4 The most complete voluntary expiration immediately following the most complete inspiration, which we denominate the '*vital capacity'. **1876** BRISTOWE *Th. & Pract. Med.* (1878) 372 The vital capacity of women is much less that of men. **1830** R. KNOX *Béchard's Anat.* 216 These vessels are extensible, and are even possessed of a high degree of retractility... Their irritability or *vital contractility is not less evident. **1704** J. HARRIS *Lex. Techn.* I, **Vital Indication*, in the Art of Medicine, is such an one as requires the restoring and reserving of the Natural Strength of the Body. **1653** R. SANDERS *Physiogn.* 100 The *Vital line forked in the end, towards the wrist. *Ibid.* 102 The Liver line at a distance, and not touching the Vital line. **1824** *Encycl. Metrop.* (1845) XVI. 602/2 The Vital line thicker than ordinary..denotes a laborious old age. *Ibid.* 604 Of the Via Martis, the way or Line of Mars, or the *Vital-sister. **1662** STILLINGFL. *Orig. Sacræ* III. iii. §6 Those inferiour terrestrial Beings with which it [i.e. the soul] communicates through the *vital union which it hath with the body. **1690** LOCKE *Hum. Und.* II. xxvii. §25 Several substances..which, whilst they continued in a vital union with that,..made a part of the same self. **1742** YOUNG *Nt. Th.* II. 57 Is this our duty, wisdom, glory, gain? (These heav'n benign in vital union binds). **1746** WESLEY *Princ. Methodist* 49, I believe there was a supernatural Power..which occasion'd their Bodies to be so affected by the natural Laws of the vital Union.

f. Of biological stains or their use: used or carried out on living tissue. Cf. *intra vitam* s.v. INTRA *prep.* 2, INTRAVITAL *a.*

1907 *Chem. Abstr.* I. 734 The character of the vital staining and apparent deposition of the carmine as particles in the body cells of the rabbit was found under physiological conditions to be essentially as earlier described. **1912** *Ibid.* VI. 2453 (*heading*) The resorption of vital coloring matters in the stomach and alimentary canal. **1926** H. M. CARLETON *Histol. Technique* xiii. 194 Janus Green.—This dye..may almost be regarded as a specific vital stain for mitochondria. **1946** A. FISCHER *Biol. Tissue Cells* iii. 68 A staining of the nucleus by ordinary vital dyes is..always a sure sign of the death of the cell. **1948** *New Biol.* V. 28 Some dyestuffs do not kill the cell, and if they stain specific structures, this process of vital staining can give important information on the living cell. **1956** *Nature* 25 Feb. 387/1 A large body on one side of the nucleus stains directly..with 0.1 per cent aqueous vital red. **1974** *Ibid.* 18 Oct. 572/1 By staining with vital dyes, Bonner..showed that the cells in the anterior third of the grex become stalk cells.

5. Conferring or imparting life or vigour; invigorating, vitalizing; life-giving. Chiefly *poet.*

1590 SPENSER *F.Q.* II. i. 12 Liues he yet..that wrought this act, And doen the heauens afford him vital food? **1601** HOLLAND *Pliny* I. 56 The whole temperature of the aire is evermore so vitall, healthie, and holesome. **1608** WILLET *Hexapla Exod.* 245 Vitall and comfortable heate..from the bodie of the sunne. **1667** MILTON *P.L.* III. 22 Hail holy light, ofspring of Heav'n first-born..: thee I revisit safe, And feel thy sovran vital Lamp. **1719** YOUNG *Revenge* III. i, O Joy, thou welcome stranger! twice three years I have not felt thy vital beam. **1744** AKENSIDE *Pleas. Imag.* I. 72 Till in time complete, What he admir'd and lov'd, his vital smile Unfolded into being. **1865** NEALE *Hymns Paradise* 8 There they quaff the vital sweetness of the Well of Quickening. **1872** HUXLEY *Physiol.* vii. 156 The vital foods are derived directly, or indirectly, from the vegetable world.

6. Affecting life; fatal to or destructive of life.

1612 ROWLANDS *Knaue of Harts* (Hunter. Cl.) 46 This Picke-pocket suffer'd vitall losse, Betweene the Court-gate hang'd, and Charing-crosse. *a* **1645** MILTON *Arcades* 65 The celestial Sirens..That sit upon the nine enfolded sphears, And sing to those that hold the vital shears, And turn the Adamantine spindle round. **1776** S. J. PRATT *Pupil of Pleas.* II. 238 The surgeon, to whom I went myself, in defiance of danger, assures me the wound is vital. **1812** CALHOUN *Speech* 24 June, Wks. 1864 II. 29 Throw him into battle, and he is scarcely sensible of vital gashes.

7. *fig.* **a.** That is essential to the existence of something expressed or implied in the context; constituting or involving an essential part or feature; absolutely indispensable, necessary, or requisite. Also, in wider sense, of supreme importance.

Common in recent use, freq. const. *to* something (*b*).

(*a*) **1619** LUSHINGTON *Resurrect. Rescued* (1659) 70 The three vital circumstances of a well-ordered Action, Person, Time and Place. **1692** ATTERBURY *Serm. bef. Queen* 29 May 3 The weakness and worthlessness of external Performances, when compar'd with more vital and substantial Duties. **1708** —— *Serm. bef. Queen* 31 Oct. 8 A thorough Sense, and Vital Experience of his Paternal Care over us, and Concern for us. **1809–10** COLERIDGE *Friend* (1865) 169 At a time when the views of France became daily more and more incompatible with our own vital interests. **1849** MACAULAY *Hist. Eng.* ii. I. 273 If one of them differs from the rest on a vital point. **1879** F. HARRISON *Choice Bks.* (1886) 10 The really vital books for us we also know to be a very trifling portion of the whole.

(*b*) **1742** YOUNG *Nt. Th.* VI. 506 A competence is vital to content. **1856** STANLEY *Sinai & Pal.* iv. 215 Hence it was that the raising of the siege of Gibeon..was so vital to the conquest of Canaan. **1860** MOTLEY *Netherl.* vi. (1868) I. 289 A cause which was so vital to both nations. **1893** A. CAWSTON *Street Improv. London* 1 Doubtless many will gladly take up a work so vital to the welfare of the whole community.

b. Of questions, problems, etc.

1822 HAZLITT *Table-T.* xxxiii. II. 389, I should like to live to see the downfall of the Bourbons. That is a vital question with me. **1825** COBBETT *Rur. Rides* 278 He and I never agreed upon this subject; and this subject was, with him, a vital one. **1850** CARLYLE *Latter-d. Pamph.* i. (1872) 31 The 'Organisation of Labour'..is the universal vital Problem of the world. **1865** RUSKIN *Sesame* ii. §54 Respecting this question—quite vital to all social happiness.

c. Paramount, supreme, very great.

1810 WELLINGTON in Gurw. *Desp.* (1838) V. 529 In order to concentrate our troops on other points of greater and more vital importance. **1849** MACAULAY *Hist. Eng.* vii. II. 233 Questions respecting postures, robes, festivals and liturgies, he considered as of no vital importance. **1850** GLADSTONE *Glean.* (1879) V. viii. 180 This inquiry..is indeed of vital moment to those who [etc.].

II. 8. a. Endowed with, or possessed of, life; animate, living. Now *poet.* or *rhet.*

1513 BRADSHAW *St. Werburge* I. 3470 Than this vitall glebe [*sc.* the body of St. Werburge] by divine ordinaunce voluntary permytted naturall resolution. **1561** DAUS tr. *Bullinger on Apoc.* (1573) 185 b, For who soeuer shew not themselues obedient,..onto this beast..are accompted for dead and rotten members, and therfore to be cut of from this vitall body. **1621** T. WILLIAMSON tr. *Goulart's Wise Vieillard* 30 Of the dismall day, that doth threaten with death, Things vitall feele the smart, and things without breath. **1667** MILTON *P.L.* VI. 345 For Spirits that live throughout Vital in every part..Cannot but by annihilating die. **1745** WATTS in *Trans. & Paraphr. Scripture* XXXVII. vii, Out of the Deep, th' Almighty King did vital Beings frame. **1774** J. BRYANT *Mythol.* II. 206 He called the winds, and made them breathe into each, and render them vital. **1817** SHELLEY *Rev. Islam* II. xxvi. 6 Some monument Vital with mind. **1820** —— *Witch Atl.* xxxv, That bright shape of vital stone which drew the heart out of Pygmalion.

transf. **1667** *Decay Chr. Piety* v. ¶25 That mind..that can be free when the body is fast bound..is never more strong and vital, than when that languishes and expires.

fig. **1837** J. H. NEWMAN *Par. Serm.* (ed. 2) III. xiv. 219 His creed may be orthodox, but his religion is not vital. **1842** MRS. BROWNING *Grk. Chr. Poets* (1863) 97 The live grasshopper, called..an emblem of the vital Greek tongue. **1873** SYMONDS *Grk. Poets* x. 320 Every line of Theocritus is vital with a strong passion for natural beauty.

b. Of places: Full of life or activity.

1742 YOUNG *Nt. Th.* I. 115 This is the desart, this the solitude: How populous! how vital, is the grave! **1817** SHELLEY *Rev. Islam* II. vi. 1 This vital world, this home of happy spirits.

c. Endowed with spiritual life. *rare.*

1807 SYD. SMITH *Lett. Catholics* (1808) 81 Those groaning and garrulous gentlemen, whom they denominate ..Gospel preachers and Vital clergymen.

9. Employed as an epithet of *life.*

1597 J. PAYNE *Royal Exch.* 13 You must be changed you know not when, from your ritches, from this vitall lyfe and the whole worlde vnto a nother place paynefull or Joyfull. **1633** BP. HALL *Occas. Medit.* §61 I cannot tell whether I should say those Creatures live which doth nothing; Sure I am their life is not vital. **1645** —— *Rem. Discontents* 122 Neither indeed is any other life truly vitall, but this; for hereby we enjoy God in all whatsoever occurrences.

†**10.** Having the qualities essential to life; capable of living; = VIABLE *a.*[1] *Obs.*

1608 TOPSELL *Serpents* 108 When the Butterflyes do ioyne together very late,..they doe lay or cast theyr eggs which will continue vitall, and that may liue till the next Spring. **1615** CROOKE *Body of Man* 336 The nine-moneth birth is of all other the most vitall and legitimate. **1646** SIR T. BROWNE *Pseud. Ep.* IV. xii. 218 Pythagoras, Hippocrates,..and others ..affirming the birth of the seventh month to be vitall.

B. *sb.* †**1.** The vital spirit or principle. *Obs.*$^{-1}$

1670 CAPT. J. SMITH *Eng. Improv. Reviv'd* v. 246 When the ulcerous Lungs cannot with dexterity enough perform their Office of cooling the Heart, the Vital is generated more hot than it should be.

2. A vital part or organ. *rare.*

Formed from the collect. pl. VITALS.

1710 OLDISWORTH tr. *Quillet's Callipœdia* I. 492 A florid Bloom with Blushes decks the Face,..And every Vital breathes the sweets of Love. **1847** C. BRONTË *J. Eyre* xxxiv, Forced to keep the fire of my nature continually low, to compel it to burn inwardly..though the imprisoned flame consumed vital after vital.

3. *Palmistry.* The vital line.

1824 *Encycl. Metrop.* (1845) XVI. 602/2 This also frequently shows a most perilous Saturnine disease in that part wherein it touches the Vital.

vitale, vitale(e)r, obs. forms of VICTUAL *sb.* and *v.*, VICTUALLER.

vi'talic, *a. rare*$^{-1}$. [f. VITAL *a.*] Vital.

1848 POE *Eureka* Wks. 1865 II. 173 The successive geological revolutions which have attended,..these successive elevations of vitalic character.

vitalism (ˈvaɪtəlɪz(ə)m). *Biol.* [a. F. *vitalisme*, or independently f. VITAL *a.* + -ISM.] The doctrine or theory that the origin and phenomena of life are due to or produced by a vital principle, as distinct from a purely chemical or physical force.

1822 W. TAYLOR in *Monthly Rev.* XCIX. 514 His perfect knowledge of anatomy..succeeded in erecting..the vitalism of Bichot. **1877** SHIELDS *Final Philos.* 267 Leading biologists also have maintained a duality of matter and life known as vitalism. **1889** *Nature* 26 Sept. 525 But even at the height of this movement there was a reaction towards vitalism, of which Virchow,..was the greatest exponent.

vitalist (ˈvaɪtəlɪst). [Cf. prec. and F. *vitaliste.*] An advocate of or believer in vitalism. Also in recent use as *adj.*, = next.

1860 LAYCOCK *Mind & Brain* I. Contents p. xviii, Conflicting theories of Life and Mind resulting from the Dogmas of the Vitalists. **1870** MAUDSLEY *Body & Mind* 169 The obvious refuge of the vitalist is to the facts that it is impossible now to evolve life artificially out of any combination of physical and chemical forces [etc.]. **1884** *Pop. Sci. Monthly* XXIV. 763 Cuvier..was a vitalist, and thought the vital properties of the body a kind of entity.

vitalistic (vaɪtəˈlɪstɪk), *a.* [f. prec. + -IC.]

1. Of or pertaining to, involving or denoting, vitalism or a hypothetical vital principle.

1865 *Englishm. Mag.* Feb. 158 Though Homer assures us that..Polybius and Machaon excelled in the healing art, nothing..remains to throw any light upon their vitalistic theories. **1871** TYLOR *Prim. Cult.* I. 395 The Karen doctrine of the là is indeed a perfect and well-marked vitalistic system. **1889** DUNCAN *Clin. Lect. Dis. Women* (ed. 4) xxviii. 224 The great question implied in vitalistic doctrine.

2. Pertaining to or denoting the germ-theory (see GERM *sb.* 6), esp. in its relation to fermentation.

1891 *Nature* 26 Mar. 482/1 It was no easy thing for him to justify the study of fermentation on the lines suggested by what was called the vitalistic or germ-theory.

vitality (vaɪˈtælɪtɪ). Also 6–7 vitalitie. [ad. L. *vītālitāt-, vītālitās* (Pliny) vital force, life, f. *vītālis* VITAL *a.*: see -ITY. Cf. F. *vitalité*, It. *vitalità*, Sp. *vitalidad*, Pg. *-idade.*]

1. Vital force, power, or principle as possessed or manifested by living things (cf. VITAL *a.* 1); the principle of life; animation.

1592 *Soliman & Pers.* v. iii. 65 Death..Hath depriued Erastus trunke from breathing vitalitie. **1614** RALEIGH *Hist. World* I. i. §6. 6 Whether that motion, vitality and operation, were by incubation, or how else, the manner is only knowne to God. **1628** FELTHAM *Resolves* II. [I.] xxxii. 102 When a man shall exhaust his very vitalitie, for the hilling vp of fatall Gold. **1659** PEARSON *Creed* iv. 432 When by an act of his will he had submitted to that death,..it was not in the power of his soul to continue any longer vitality to the body. **1700** ROWE *Amb. Step-Moth.* III. ii, Let thy vitality impart New Spirits to his fainting Heart. **1812** *Times* 6 Mar. 2/2 They perceived that vitality had been actually extinct in two of them for some time, the bodies being perfectly cold. **1844** G. BIRD *Urin. Deposits* (1857) 338 Those which we have now to investigate are organic substances, often possessing organization, and sometimes enjoying an independent vitality. **1873** SYMONDS *Grk. Poets* i. 1 The mysteries of organized vitality remain impenetrable.

transf. **1652** FRENCH *Yorksh. Spa* ii. 13 Which sand hath in it a vitality, and in which..the water, whilest it remains, is living. **1816** BYRON *Ch. Har.* III. xxxiv, There is a very life in our despair, Vitality of poison. **1831** CARLYLE *Sart. Res.* I. v, Not Mankind only, but all that Mankind does or beholds, is in continual growth, re-genesis and self-perfecting vitality. **1837** WHEWELL *Hist. Induct. Sci.* IV. i. I. 240 All such writers..have in them no principle of philosophical vitality.

b. Of plants or vegetative organisms. Also *spec.* of seeds: Germinating power.

(*a*) **1829** T. CASTLE *Introd. Bot.* 262 Vitality of Plants. **1842** WORDSW. *Sonn.*, '*A Poet!*' i, And so the grandeur of the Forest-tree Comes..from its own divine vitality. **1848** LINDLEY *Introd. Bot.* (ed. 4) II. 150 The experiments.. prove indeed conclusively that whatever the true seat of vegetable vitality may be, it is similar in its nature to that of the Animal Kingdom.

(*b*) **1832** LINDLEY *Introd. Bot.* 271 The power [in seeds] of preserving their vitality is also extremely variable. **1861** BENTLEY *Man. Bot.* 767 By retaining vitality we mean preserving their power of germinating.

2. *fig.* The ability or capacity on the part of something of continuing to exist or to perform its functions; power of enduring or continuing.

Merging insensibly into next.

1844 H. H. WILSON *Brit. India* III. III. ix. 563 The dependance of ministerial vitality upon parliamentary majorities. **1866** R. W. DALE *Disc. Spec. Occas.* viii. 275 There is terrible vitality both in truth and error. **1874** L. STEPHEN *Hours in Library* I. 113 The vitality of Pope's writings, or at least of certain fragments of them, is remarkable.

3. *fig.* Active force or power; mental or physical vigour; activity, animation, liveliness.

Common from *c* 1860.

1858 O. W. HOLMES *Aut. Breakf.-t.* xii. 110 Which shows that their minds are in a state of diminished vitality. **1860** MOTLEY *Netherl.* I. ii. 45 Such was the intense vitality of the Béarnese prince. **1869** TOZER *Highl. Turkey* I. 358 A country whose vitality is strong, and where the administrative power is active and vigorous. **1884** *Manch. Exam.* 9 May 5/4 To the strong vitality which distinguishes his race, he united intellectual power of the highest order.

4. With *a* and pl. Something possessed of vital force. Also *fig.*

1851 CARLYLE *Sterling* II. iii, He was full of bright speech and argument; radiant with arrowy vitalities. **1853** KANE *Grinnell Exp.* v. (1856) 36 There was no vegetation to define its course, not even the green conferva, that obscure vitality, which follows water at home. **1898** MEREDITH *Odes Fr. Hist.* 91 Shall, then, the great vitality, France, Signal the backward step once more?

vitali'zation. Also -isation. [f. VITALIZE *v.* + -ATION.] The action or process of vitalizing, or the state of being vitalized; an instance of this.

1846 J. HUDSON in *Rep. & Papers Bot.* (Ray Soc.) 306 The phenomenon of the vitalization of cells is brought about only by an excessive endosmose or nutrition. **1891** T. HARDY *Tess* xxxvi, Her love..might result in vitalisations that would inflict upon others what she had bewailed as a misfortune to herself. *a* **1901** F. W. H. MYERS *Human Personality* (1903) I. p. xxxiv, An increased subliminal vitalization of the organism.

vitalize (ˈvaɪtəlaɪz), *v.* Also 9 -ise. [f. VITAL *a.* + -IZE.]

1. *trans.* To give life or animation to (the body, etc.); to endow with vital force or principle.

1678 CUDWORTH *Intell. Syst.* I. v. 784 By the Idol of the soul Plotinus seems to mean an airy or spirituous Body, quickned and vitalized by the soul, adhering to it after death. **1813** T. BUSBY *Lucretius* I. III. 797 Seeds which now the body vitalise. **1846** J. HUDSON in *Rep. & Papers Bot.* (Ray Soc.) 305 How does it happen that a cell is so vitalized as to be able to produce a phyton? **1868** PEARD *Water-farm.* xi. 113 Every year..millions of eggs are regularly vitalised and transmitted over the Continent.

transf. **1858** J. H. BENNET *Nutrition* ii. 43 The intellectual man..who has vitalized..his brain by brain exercise.

b. *Path.* To excite activity in (an ulcer, etc.).

1884 M. MACKENZIE *Dis. Throat & Nose* II. 277 For the purpose..of 'vitalizing' the borders of an indolent ulcer within the nasal cavity.

2. *fig.* To make living or active; to infuse vitality or vigour into (something); to animate.

1805 FOSTER *Ess.* I. iv. 50 A malignant quality appears vitalized into a powerful demon. *a* **1853** ROBERTSON *Lect.* (1859) 124 What he wanted was to vitalize the system—to throw into it not a Jewish, but a Christian feeling. **1873** SYMONDS *Grk. Poets* v. 111 The Greek genius was endowed with the faculty of distinguishing, differentiating, vitalizing, what the Oriental nations left hazy and confused and inert.

b. To put life into (a literary or artistic conception); to present or depict in a lifelike manner.

1884 *Athenæum* 8 March 319/3 Lord Tennyson..always allows himself room not only to vitalize his characters, but to let them grow. **1907** *Ibid.* 16 March 313/1 He is not an artist. He cannot vitalize his material.

Hence **'vitalized** *ppl. a.*

1843 R. J. GRAVES *Syst. Clin. Med.* xxvii. 350 The seminal fluid of the male is a highly vitalized product. **1868** PEARD *Water-farm.* xiii. 127 The largest quantity of this vitalised seed was sown in the rivers of France. **1874** H. R. REYNOLDS *John Bapt.* viii. 505 Those who..regard Christianity as an etherealized or vitalized morality.

'vitalizer. [f. prec. + -ER.] One who or that which vitalizes.

1882 J. BROWN *John Leech*, etc. 375 He was not only..an organiser and vitaliser of hunting, he was a great breeder. **1888** *Advance* (Chicago) 21 June 385 Life is the revealer and vitalizer of truth.

'vitalizing, *ppl. a.* [f. VITALIZE *v.*] That vitalizes or endues with vitality; animating, invigorating.

1813 T. BUSBY *Lucretius* I. III. *Comm.* p. xxvii, The seeds ..do not possess..any vitalizing quality. **1857** MILLER *Elem. Chem.*, *Org.* 742 The principal change is that described by Prout as the vitalizing action of the stomach. **1880** BROWNING *Dram. Idylls* II. 149 Not one flower-dust fell but straight its fall awoke Vitalizing virtue.

vitall, -er, obs. ff. VICTUAL, -ALLER.

Vitallium (vaɪ'tælɪəm). Also **-alium** and with small initial. [f. *vitall-*, of unkn. origin + -IUM.] A proprietary term for an alloy of cobalt, chromium, and molybdenum that has a high resistance to abrasion, corrosion, and heat and is used in surgery, dentistry, and engineering.

1935 *Official Gaz.* (U.S. Patent Office) 18 June 520/2 *Vitallium* for cobalt, chromium alloy. Claims use since July 8, 1934. **1947** *Richmond* (Va.) *Times-Dispatch* 13 Sept. 15/1 Short pieces of tubes made of the metal vitallium have been tried [to replace the missing link in arteries]. **1948** *Jrnl. R. Aeronaut. Soc.* LII. 16/2 The ease with which large quantities of these small supercharger blades could be produced to finished size by means of the 'lost wax' casting process, turned attention to 'Vitallium', an alloy which had been used for making special small castings by this method. **1951** *Trade Marks Jrnl.* 1 Aug. 713/2 *Vitallium*... Common metal alloys in the form of nuggets. Austenal Laboratories Incorporated.., New York, United States of America; manufacturers. **1961** *Lancet* 30 Sept. 757/1 At first a vitallium tube was used for the anastomosis. **1979** *Courier-Mail* (Brisbane) 21 July 3/1 Two teeth in the three-year old German Shepherd guard dog's armour now are capped with vitalium one of the toughest of alloys... It was Taz's enthusiasm for his work which tooks its toll on his teeth.

vitally ('vaɪtəlɪ), *adv.* [f. VITAL *a.* + -LY².]

†**1.** In a manner which imparts life or vitality; so as to cause or produce life. *Obs.*

1661 RUST *Origen & Opin.* 78 The Body wherewith she [the Soul] is vitally united. **1664** H. MORE *Apology* 499 What Body more radiant and refulgent then the Sun in his greatest brightness can be vitally organized? **1690** LOCKE *Hum. Und.* II. xxvii. §4 Though that Life be communicated to new Particles of Matter vitally united to the living Plant. *a* **1791** WESLEY *Serm.* lxxx. Wks. 1811 IX. 395 You are not now vitally united to any of the members of Christ.

†**2.** By means of vital force or power. *Obs. rare.*

a **1676** HALE *Prim. Orig. Man.* I. ii. (1677) 50 The Mixt sort of Reason seems to be when a thing concurrs actively and from an internal principle, and (in things that have life) vitally, to the production of a reasonable effect. *Ibid.*, This reasonable work [of ploughing] is performed actively and vitally by my Brute in the virtue of my direction.

†**3.** In a living state; alive. *Obs.*⁻¹

1692 BENTLEY *Boyle Lect.* v. 174 Nature may bring forth the young infants vitally into the world.

4. In a way or to an extent which is vital or absolutely essential; essentially, indispensably.

1770 BURKE *Pres. Discont.* Wks. II. 303 The first franchise of an Englishman, and that on which all the rest vitally depend. **1795** —— *Scarcity* Wks. VII. 381 Affairs that vitally concern the agriculture of the kingdom. **1852** MISS YONGE *Cameos* II. xxxi. 325 It was vitally necessary to Henry to keep himself respected and feared. **1861** FLOR. NIGHTINGALE *Nursing* ii. (ed. 2) 11 Due attention would be bestowed on this vitally important matter. **1881** MASSON in *Macm. Mag.* Dec. 150/1 His Edinburgh life during those five years divides itself, however, very vitally, in the retrospect of it now, into two portions.

b. In an important or high degree; intensely, powerfully. *rare.*

1787 JEFFERSON *Writ.* (1859) II. 187 The effect of this operation was vitally felt by every farmer in America.

5. With life-like or vivid realization; vividly.

1865 RUSKIN *Sesame* ii. §72 She should be taught to enter with her whole personality into the history she reads; to picture the passages of it vitally in her own bright imagination.

6. So as to affect or destroy life; fatally, mortally.

1891 *Cent. Dict.* s.v., The animal was vitally hit or hurt.

vitals ('vaɪtəlz), *sb. pl.* [ad. L. *vītālia*, neut. pl. of *vītālis*, or directly f. VITAL *a.*]

1. Those parts or organs of the body, esp. the human body, essential to life, or upon which life depends; the vital parts.

Usually as a vague or general term, but sometimes applied specifically to the brain, heart, lungs, and liver.

For the phr. *stop my vitals*, see STAP *v.* and STOP *v.* 9c.

a **1610** HEALEY *Cebes* (1636) 134 Now hee.. purgeth away the causes and nutriment of the maladie, and then corroborates the vitals. **1641** TATHAM *Distracted State* IV. i. (1651) 24, I feel my vitals fail me. **1690** C. NESSE *O. & N. Test.* I. 52 Like the wound in the heel, far from the vitals, the head or heart. **1708** SWIFT *Sacram. Tests* Wks. 1755 II. I. 125 If..you think a poultice made of our vitals will give it any ease, speak the word. **1760–72** H. BROOKE *Fool of Qual.* (1809) III. 117 The weapon has missed your vitals. **1791** COWPER *Odyss.* IX. 347 Me, then, my courage prompted to approach The monster..And to transfix him where the vitals wrap The liver. **1861** PALEY *Aeschylus* (ed. 2) *Choeph.* 264 *note*, The notion in the mind of the speaker is that of a cold chill at the vitals. **1897** MARY KINGSLEY *W. Africa* 246 A miscellaneous collection of bits of broken iron pots and lumps of lead frisking among their vitals.

b. *fig.* or in fig. context.

1641 MILTON *Reform.* II. 64 Now heare how they [i.e. the prelates] strike at the very heart and vitals [of monarchy]. **1671** TRENCHFIELD *Cap Gray Hairs* (1688) 32 The dainty Tooths of some corroding so far into their estates, as to reach the very vitals. **1719** W. WOOD *Surv. Trade* 56 The truest Sign of our Vitals not being tainted, and that we are not wounded in any Noble Part, but go on increasing in Trade. **1790** BURKE *Fr. Rev.* 350 Such immense sums, drawn from the vitals of all France. **1802–12** in Bentham *Ration. Judic. Evid.* (1827) V. 536 The very life and vitals of the cause lies in secreting the evidence. **1853** MERIVALE *Rom. Rep.* i. (1867) 7 Tiberius..continued to brood over the plague-spot he had discovered in the vitals of his country. **1868** FARRAR *Seekers* I. iii. (1875) 37 To have fastened upon the very vitals of the national existence.

2. *transf.* Parts or features essentially necessary to something; essential points, essentials.

1657 J. WATTS *Vind. Ch. Eng.* 30 So long as the vitals and fundamentals of faith and truth abide. **1657–8** in *Burton's Diary* (1828) II. 433 If the vitals were preserved, I should not differ for the rest. **1689** *Myst. Iniq.* 9 Tho all English Protestants have ever been at an Accord in all the Essentials and Vitals of Religion. **1702** C. MATHER *Magn. Chr.* III. II. xxviii. (1852) 504 Of pernicious consequence to the very vitals of religion. **1887** *Pall Mall G.* 4 May 11/1 When the Parnellite leaders approached the vitals of the issue.

b. The vital parts of a ship. Cf. VITAL *a.* 3b.

1884 *Pall Mall G.* 13 Nov. 5/1 *Riachuelo*... Speed 17 knots; 6,200 tons; 8½ in. armour over vitals. **1894** C. N. ROBINSON *Brit. Fleet* 288 The armour..shielding the gun, the machinery, and 'vitals' of the vessel.

†**vitaly.** *Obs.*⁻⁰ In 5 **vytaly**. [var. of ME. *vitaille* VICTUAL *sb.* Cf. obs. Flem. *victalie* (Kilian).] Victual, victuals.

c **1440** *Promp. Parv.* 511/1 Vytaly, or vytayl, *victuale.*

vitalyge, obs. f. VICTUALAGE.

vitamin ('vɪt-, 'vaɪtəmɪn). orig. **vitamine** ('vaɪtəmɪn, 'vɪt-, -iːn). [f. L. *vīt-a* life + AMINE, from a mistaken belief about the chemical nature of the compounds (cf. quot. 1920).]

1. a. Any of a diverse group of organic compounds of which small quantities are needed in the diet because they have a distinct biochemical role, often as coenzymes, and cannot be adequately synthesized by the body, so that in most cases a deficiency produces characteristic symptoms or disease.

1912 C. FUNK in *Jrnl. State Med.* XX. 342 It is now known that all these diseases, with the exception of pellagra, can be prevented and cured by the addition of certain preventive substances; the deficient substances, which are of the nature of organic bases, we will call 'vitamines'; and we will speak of a beri-beri or scurvy vitamine, which means a substance preventing the special disease. **1915** *Times Lit. Suppl.* 11 Nov. 400/3 The point about vitamines is that without them the animal ceases to grow or becomes diseased on a physiologically pure diet. **1916** MCCOLLUM & KENNEDY in *Jrnl. Biol. Chem.* XXIV. 493 We would.. suggest the desirability of discontinuing the use of the term vitamine, and the substitution of the term fat-soluble A and water-soluble B for the two classes of unknown substances concerned in inducing growth. **1920** J. C. DRUMMOND in *Biochem. Jrnl.* XIV. 660 The criticism usually raised against Funk's word Vitamine is that the termination '-ine' is one strictly employed in chemical nomenclature to denote substances of a basic character, whereas there is no evidence which supports his original idea that these indispensable dietary constituents are amines... The suggestion is now advanced that the final '-e' be dropped, so that the resulting word Vitamin is acceptable under the standard scheme of nomenclature..which permits a neutral substance of undefined composition to bear a name ending in '-in'. If this suggestion is adopted, it is recommended that the somewhat cumbrous nomenclature introduced by McCollum (Fat-soluble A, Water-soluble B), be dropped, and that the substances be spoken of as Vitamin A, B, C, etc. **1932** METCALF & FLINT *Princ. Insect Life* xii. 465 Green plants can..manufacture complicated proteins, carbohydrates, fats, and vitamines from the nitrates, phosphates, sulfates, and water of the soil. **1966** V. B. WIGGLESWORTH *Life of Insects* iv. 75 Cockroaches whose symbionts have been killed out by treatment with antibiotics must have extra vitamins in their diet. **1974** *Daily Tel.* 15 Feb. 17/4 Vitamins have received so much publicity as an essential factor for healthy living that there has been a tendency to forget that in excess some of them at least can be harmful. **1982** F. UNGAR in T. M. Devlin *Textbk. Biochem.* xv. 719 Since the rat has this enzyme and ascorbic acid can be synthesized in its tissues, ascorbic acid is not a vitamin for this species.

b. *fig.*

1921 *Spectator* 16 Apr. 492/2 A book..so full of the vitamines of literature. **1971** *Where* Nov. 334/1 A diet only of football annuals would be deficient of almost every known reading vitamin.

2. With following (or occas. preceding) capital letter, denoting a particular vitamin or group of vitamins.

Some designations were abandoned when the substance concerned was shown to be a mixture, was not confirmed as a new vitamin, or became known under a chemical name.

vitamin A, either or both of two closely related fat-soluble vitamins, A_1 and A_2, esp. the former; = RETINOL²; ***vitamin*** A_1, an alcohol that is present (as fatty acid esters) in egg-yolk, liver, butter, and milk, is also formed in the body from carotenoids present in green vegetables and stored in the liver, and is a component of the visual pigment rhodopsin; a deficiency of vitamin A_1 leads to night blindness and anæmia and ultimately xerophthalmia and blindness, ***vitamin*** A_2, the analogous component of the visual pigment porphyropsin in freshwater fish; **vitamin B**, any or all of several chemically unrelated water-soluble vitamins mostly occurring together in liver, cereals, and yeast and discovered by separation from the original 'vitamin B'; so ***vitamin B complex*** or ***group***; ***vitamin*** B_1 = THIAMINE 3a; ***vitamin*** B_2 = RIBOFLAVIN; ***vitamin*** B_6, any or all of the compounds pyridoxine, pyridoxal, and pyridoxamine, esp. the first (the dietary form of the vitamin), deficiency of which is accompanied by symptoms that can include irritability, nervousness, or convulsions; ***vitamin*** B_{12}, cobalamin or any of several derivatives of it, cobalt, containing compounds synthesized by micro-organisms and present in food of animal origin (esp. meat, eggs, and dairy products), a deficiency leading to pernicious anæmia and neuropathy; cf. *extrinsic factor* s.v. EXTRINSIC *a.* 3c; **vitamin C**, ascorbic acid; a water-soluble sugar, $C_6H_8O_6$, which is present in citrus fruits, green vegetables, and tomatoes, and in man is required for the synthesis of collagen and the maintenance of connective tissue, its deficiency leading to scurvy; **vitamin D**, each or all of the fat-soluble vitamins that cure or prevent rickets in children and osteomalacia in adults, one or other being required for the correct metabolism of calcium; *spec.* ***vitamin*** D_2 [named in Ger. by A. Windaus et al. 1931, in *Ann. d. Chem.* CDLXXXIX. 269], a compound, $C_{28}H_{44}O$, made by the ultraviolet irradiation of ergosterol and added to dairy products; also called *calciferol* or *ergocalciferol*; ***vitamin*** D_3 [named in Ger. by A. Windaus et al. 1936, in *Zeitschr. f. physiol. Chem.* CCXLI. 102], a closely related compound, $C_{27}H_{44}O$, formed in the skin by ultraviolet light and present in egg-yolk, liver, and fish-liver oils; also called *cholecalciferol*; **vitamin E** = TOCOPHEROL; **vitamin G** chiefly *U.S.* = *vitamin* B_2 above; now *rare*; **vitamin H** [named in Ger. by P. György 1931, in *Zeitschr. f. ärztliche Fortbildung* XXVIII. 379/2, f. *haut* skin] = BIOTIN; **vitamin K**, either or both of two related fat-soluble derivatives of naphthoquinone, ***vitamin*** K_1 (= PHYLLOQUINONE) and ***vitamin*** K_2 (menaquinone, $C_{41}H_{56}O_2$), one or other of which is required for proper clotting of the blood, the former occurring in green vegetables and the latter being synthesized by intestinal bacteria; **vitamin P**, any or all of the flavonoids present in food plants, formerly thought to be necessary in the diet for the integrity of the capillaries.

1920 Vitamin A [see sense 1a above]. **1937** J. R. EDISBURY in *Nature* 7 Aug. 234/1 A substance apparently identical with the 693 mμ chromogen can replace the vitamin A of rhodopsin without loss of physiological function... It.. seems desirable provisionally to designate as 'vitamin A_2' the 693 mμ chromogen. **1950** [see RETINENE]. **1960**, etc. [see RETINOL²]. **1968** A. WHITE et al. *Princ. Biochem.* (ed. 4) xl. 906 Vitamin A_2 differs from A_1 by having one additional conjugated double bond in the ring. **1976** H. R. SCHIFFMAN *Sensation & Perception* xii. 184/2 When the eye is kept in the dark, vitamin A joins with opsin to reconstitute rhodopsin. **1982** S. G. CHANEY in T. M. Devlin *Textbk. Biochem.* xxvi. 1202 Vitamin A is also apparently required for mobilization of iron from the liver.

1920 *Brit. Med. Jrnl.* 31 July 151/1 The water-soluble B vitamine in rice polishings is very stable. **1920** [see sense 1a above]. **1934** *Nature* 31 Mar. 498/2 The view has already been considered..that these two classes of dissimilar skin changes are to be ascribed to a deficiency not only of vitamin B_2 but also of another component of the vitamin B complex. **1953** D. M. DUNLOP et al. *Textbk. Med. Treatment* (ed. 6) 398 Three other components of the vitamin B complex have been reported to have therapeutic effects; pantothenic acid

.., pyridoxin..and biotin. **1967** *Martindale's Extra Pharmacopoeia* (ed. 25) 122/1 Dried yeast is used for the prevention and treatment of vitamin B deficiency. **1969** R. F. CHAPMAN *Insects* v. 74 The B vitamins thiamine, riboflavin, nicotinic acid, pyridoxine and pantothenic acid are essential to most insects. **1983** A. TULL *Food & Nutrition* i. 22/2 Like the other B vitamins..nicotinic acid is also an important factor in the release of energy from food..by oxidation.

1928 CHICK & ROSCOE in *Biochem. Jrnl.* XXII. 790 Experiments..confirmed the conclusion of Goldberger and his colleagues..that the water-soluble B vitamin..had two components. (1) Vitamin B_1, or the antineuritic, less heat-stable vitamin... (2) Vitamin B_2, a more heat-stable vitamin..in the absence of which the animal fails to grow. **1955** *Sci. News Let.* 26 Mar. 194/1 In each group some mothers got vitamin C (ascorbic acid) pills; some got thiamine, or vitamin B-1 pills; some got pills containing thiamine, iron, and riboflavin and niacinamide which are B vitamins; and some got placebos. **1974** PASSMORE & ROBSON *Compan. Med. Stud.* III. xxiv. 26/2 Both wet and dry beriberi occur among chronic alcoholics whose diet can be deficient in vitamin B_1.

1928 Vitamin B_2 [see *vitamin B_1* above]. **1933** *Jrnl. Amer. Chem. Soc.* LV. 2927 Several similarities suggest its close relationship [*sc.* that of pantothenic acid] to vitamin G (B_2). **1934** [see *vitamin B* above]. **1967** H. A. GUTHRIE *Introd. Nutrition* xii. 236/1 Riboflavin, which has also been known as vitamin B_2, vitamin G, and the yellow vitamin, was recognized in 1917 when it became clear that vitamin B retained some growth-promoting properties after its anti-beriberi properties had been destroyed by heat.

1934 P. GYÖRGY in *Nature* 31 Mar. 499/1 We have for the time being named this 'rat pellagra preventive factor' in its narrow sense vitamin B_6. **1955** D. M. HEGSTED in F. C. Blanck *Handbk. Food & Agric.* ix. 292 The natural occurring deficiency of vitamin B_6 has probably not been seen in any species other than recent reports of its development in infants fed certain prepared formulas. **1970** [see PYRIDOXINE]. **1970** [see PYRIDOXAMINE]. **1974** [see PYRIDOXAL]. **1983** J. KATZ in Kaye & Rose *Fund. Internal Med.* cxxxvi. 904/1 Dietary and primary pyridoxine (vitamin B_6) deficiencies are rare.

1948 M. S. SHORB in *Science* 16 Apr. 397/1 A crystalline compound, vitamin B_{12}, has been isolated from liver..and has been shown to be highly active hematopoietically..upon cases of pernicious anemia. **1950**, etc. [see COBALAMIN]. **1961** *New Scientist* 23 Feb. 457/2 The cobalt..had a selective action. Experiments showed that it was taken up by the flora of the rumen of sheep and cattle in the synthesis of vitamin B_{12}. **1982** S. G. CHANEY in T. M. Devlin *Textbk. Biochem.* xxvi. 1225 The liver stores up to a 6-year supply of vitamin B_{12}. Thus, deficiencies..are extremely rare.

[**1919** J. C. DRUMMOND in *Biochem. Jrnl.* XIII. 77 The diet has been seriously, if not totally, deficient in the antiscorbutic factor or 'water-soluble C'.] **1920** [see sense 1 a above]. **1921** *Jrnl. Industr. & Engin. Chem.* Dec. 1115/1 We know that the antiscorbutic vitamine is water-soluble; indeed, it has been called the water-soluble C vitamine. **1942** *Ann. Reg. 1941* 344 Work on prothrombin, vitamins C, K, and P,..greatly advanced knowledge of haemorrhagic diseases. **1966** E. BIRNEY *Selected Poems* II. 61 A hotelroom all to myself with a fan and a box of Vitamin C. **1983** *Oxf. Textbk. Med.* I. VIII. 24/2 There is no convincing evidence for the claims that large doses of vitamin C (4 g or more daily) prevent or decrease severity of the common cold; the evidence for protection against cancer is stronger, but not conclusive.

1921 FUNK & DUBIN in *Proc. Soc. Exper. Biol. & Med.* XIX. 15 It is possible in most cases to effect an almost quantitative separation of the B-vitamine..from another substance, which we provisionally have called vitamine D. **1928** [see ERGOSTEROL]. **1932** *Chem. Abstr.* XXVI. 1015 The isolation of cryst. vitamin D_1. *Ibid.*, An added note states that vitamin D_2 has been isolated. **1936** *Ibid.* XXX. 6423 The name vitamin D_3 is proposed for this substance. **1953** FRUTON & SIMMONDS *Gen. Biochem.* xxxviii. 903 The term vitamin D_1 has been discarded since the material to which it was first applied has been found to be a mixture of calciferol and several sterols. **1976** H. CAMPION et al. in B. E. C. Nordin *Calcium, Phosphate & Mineral Metabolism* XII. 445 The compounds known as vitamin D have in common a unique arrangement of three carbon-carbon double bonds, two of which connect a hydroxylated cyclohexane ring to a substituted hydrindane system. **1983** *Oxf. Textbk. Med.* I. x. 44/2 In most respects these vitamin Ds are comparable in their metabolism and their actions.

1925 H. M. EVANS in *Proc. Nat. Acad. Sci.* XI. 373 The evidence..is thus conclusively in favor of the existence of a new vitamine or food accessory to which the designation of fat soluble E may be given. [*Note*] We have adopted the letter E as the next serial alphabetic designation, the antirachitic artanine now being known as D. **1948** MARTIN & HYNES *Clin. Endocrinol.* viii. 157 Vitamin E deficiency..produces loss of sperm-motility in rats and is followed by atrophy of spermatogenic tissue and final loss of the sex instincts. **1968**, etc. [see TOCOPHEROL]. **1983** *Oxf. Textbk. Med.* II. XIX. 75/2 Vitamin E is necessary to prevent auto-oxidation of the unsaturated fatty acids in the red cell membrane.

1929 SHERMAN & SANDELS in *Proc. Soc. Exper. Biol. & Med.* XXVI. 536 Experiments with reference to the more heat-stable factor of the vitamin B group (factor P-P, vitamin B_2 or G). **1934** *Jrnl. Biol. Chem.* CVI. 433 The vitamin G concentrate..was prepared by extracting hog livers with boiling water, [etc.]. **1949** R. A. & W. A. GORTNER *Outl. Biochem.* (ed. 3) xxxvi. 925 Riboflavin (lactoflavin or ovoflavin or vitamin G) is 6,7-dimethyl-isoalloxazine-9-D-riboside. **1967** Vitamin G [see *vitamin B_2* above].

1937 L. E. BOOHER in *Jrnl. Biol. Chem.* CXIX. 223 The vitamin concerned..is a relatively heat-stable component of the vitamin B complex... It will be referred to here as vitamin H. **1959** Vitamin H [see EGG-WHITE].

1935 H. DAM in *Nature* 27 Apr. 653/1, I therefore suggest the term vitamin K for the antihæmorrhagic factor. **1939** *Jrnl. Amer. Chem. Soc.* LXI. 1295/1 (*heading*) The isolation of vitamins K_1 and K_2. **1939**, etc. [see PHYLLOQUINONE]. **1947** *Radiology* XLIX. 304/1 Vitamin K and transfusions of whole blood were ineffective in reducing clotting time. **1975** J. MARKS *Guide to Vitamins* 71 Domestic animals suffering from warfarin poisoning should be treated with vitamin K_1. **1983** J. KATZ in Kaye & Rose *Fund. Internal Med.* cxxxvi. 905/2 A deficiency of vitamin K cannot occur solely from an inadequate diet. Intestinal bacteria synthesize the vitamin.

1936 RUSZNYÁK & SZENT-GYÖRGYI in *Nature* 4 July 27/2 We propose to give the name 'vitamin P' to the substance responsible for the action on vascular permeability. **1949** [see FLAVONOID]. **1955** [see CITRIN]. **1969** *Brit. Med. Jrnl.* 25 Jan. 235/1 No condition representing lack of vitamin P has ever been satisfactorily demonstrated. **1978** F. H. MEYERS et al. *Rev. Med. Pharmacol.* (ed. 6) xli. 449/1 The flavonoids or vitamin P are of interest in relation to the question of how drug efficacy is evaluated rather than because of any nutritional effect.

3. *attrib.* and *Comb.*, as ***vitamin capsule, cream, deficiency, pill, shot*** (SHOT *sb.*[1] 7 g(a)), ***tablet, therapy; vitamin-containing, -enriched, -free, -poor, -rich*** adjs.

1958 *Listener* 2 Oct. 523/1 Perhaps all those compact references at the foot of the page..are vitamin capsules of chapter for verse to insatiable scholars. **1965** M. SPARK *Mandelbaum Gate* iii. 61 Freddy..carried small red vitamin capsules about with him to swallow after meals taken outside the British Isles. **1921** *Conquest* Sept. 498/2 The only safe rule is this..eat vitamine-containing food on every possible occasion..and avoid, as far as practicable, vitamine-free foods. **1938** *Encycl. Brit. Bk. of Year* 588/1 Preparations that have but recently come to the fore include..the group of hormone and vitamin creams, etc., known collectively as 'biological' preparations. **1979** P. FERRIS *Talk to me about England* III. 133 She took the vitamin cream. **1920** *Brit. Med. Jrnl.* 31 July 147/1 It is..still a hypothesis that the particular disease depends upon vitamine deficiency. **1946** R. LEHMANN *Gypsy's Baby* 149 My *brain*..just doesn't *function* any more. Don't you think it's some vitamin deficiency? **1980** *Times* 15 Dec. 1/3 One of the hunger strikers..is in danger of irreversible loss of sight because of a vitamin deficiency. **1961** *Which?* Oct. 270/1 Wholemeal biscuits with a vitamin-enriched filling. **1921** Vitamin-free [see *vitamin-containing* above]. **1956** *Nature* 11 Feb. 271/1 Aerated cultures of *B. cereus* 569H were grown at 36° on..vitamin-free casein hydrolysate. **1945** N. MITFORD *Pursuit of Love* xv. 121 A packing-case full of vitamin pills. **1981** D. UHNAK *False Witness* (1982) xi. 90 The customers..gulped down vitamin pills with swallows of juice. **1973** T. PYNCHON *Gravity's Rainbow* (1975) I. 170 Nasty little fangs achop and looking to ulcerate the vitamin-poor tissue they came from. **1923** *Jrnl. Biol. Chem.* LVI. 333 The fat-soluble, vitamin-rich ration. **1944** J. S. HUXLEY *On Living in Revolution* 31 Sweeping measures of social security and welfare—..subsidized housing and vitamin-rich food for the under-privileged,..and so on. **1971** J. PHILIPS *Escape a Killer* (1972) I. ii. 25, I always feel as if I'd had a vitamin shot when you turn up. **1980** J. GARDNER *Garden of Weapons* II. iii. 139 Mistochenkov looked in startlingly good health. 'It's the vitamin shots they're giving me,' he told Herbie. **1951** M. KENNEDY *Lucy Carmichael* II. i. 76 She..ended by saying I didn't look very well and she would send me some vitamin tablets. **1982** M. MCMULLEN *Better Off Dead* II. xiv. 171 A little saucer was placed before him with his vitamin tablets, the B-complex and the C. **1969** *Listener* 1 May 627/2 He thinks the cure of Tobit's blindness must have been either a colossal coincidence or a primeval case of vitamin therapy, by the liberal administration of fish-guts. **1972** Vitamin therapy [see PERCEPTUAL *a.*].

Hence **vita'minic** *a.*, pertaining to or containing a vitamin or vitamins; **'vitaminless** *a.* (*rare*); **vi'taminous** *a.* (*rare*), vitaminic; also *fig.*

1914 *Nature* 12 Mar. 42/1 Vitaminous foods are fresh milk.., whole grains, potatoes, [etc.]. *Ibid.*, Such vitamineless foods as sterilised milk,..starch, and sugar. **1926** *Chambers's Jrnl.* Apr. 291/2 The milk tends to become less and less valuable from the point of view of vitaminic value. **1931** C. J. HOLMES *Gram. Arts* iii. 27 Life..is the essential thing..and we must not starve ourselves of this vitaminous element. **1980** *Acta Vitaminologica et Enzymologica* II. 75 Drug induced avitaminoses are produced more easily and are more severe if the devitaminizing power of the drug and its dosage are high..and the vitaminic status of the patient is not optimal.

vitaminize ('vɪtəmɪnaɪz), *v.* [f. prec. + -IZE.] *trans.* To add a vitamin or vitamins to (food, esp. food that lacks the vitamin concerned). Also *absol.* and *fig.* Chiefly as **'vitaminized** *ppl. a.* Also ,**vitamini'zation**, the treatment of food in this way; **'vitaminizing** *ppl. a.*

1930 *Observer* 13 Apr. 7 Adventure, we are told, is the 'vitaminizing element' in history. **1940** *Economist* 27 Apr. 762/2 A diet of vegetables..milk, butter or vitaminised margarine..brown bread and cheese. **1942** *Endeavour* Jan. 30/2 The compulsory 'vitaminization' of margarine that has taken place since the war has merely been an extension to the whole margarine output of a practice already in partial operation. **1944** *Ourselves in Wartime* 153 Margarine was 'vitaminized', so that all categories, even the cheapest varieties, were equal in vitamin value to butter. **1960** 'R. GORDON' *Doctor in Clover* xi. 92 He has taken his vitaminised milk and played *Clair de Lune* twice on the piano. **1968** M. PYKE *Food & Society* iii. 32 Government regulations enforcing the fluoridization of drinking water or the vitaminization of margarine. **1968** M. WOODHOUSE *Rock Baby* iii. 25 You've a home-grown, vitaminized, tall-walking, all-American boy. **1970** *R. Soc. Health Jrnl.* XC. 24/1 It had been decided to vitaminize to such a level that in respect of A and D the margarine would be equal to summer butter. **1975** *Islander* (Victoria, B.C.) 3 Aug. 8/2 Vitaminized canned juices.

Vitaphone ('vaɪtəfəʊn). Chiefly *U.S.* Also **vitaphone.** [f. L. *vita* life + PHONE *sb.*[1]] A process of sound film recording in which the sound track is recorded on discs and played in synchronization with the projection of the film; also, sound films made by this method. Now *disused.*

1926 *Westm. Gaz.* 20 Sept. 7/2 A method of talking-motion pictures has been developed in America. The invention is called the vitaphone... It is claimed that the synchronisation of picture and voice..is perfect. **1948** M. QUIGLY *Magic Shadows* xvii. 160 Thirty years later, magic shadow history was made... The event was the premiere of 'The Jazz Singer', starring Al Jolson and presenting the Vitaphone system of talking motion pictures. **1976** *Islander* (Victoria, B.C.) 8 Aug. 13/2 To begin with two types of sound pictures were made—Movietone and Vitaphone. **1977** *Amer. Film* Oct. 27/1 Warner theaters in every major American city were wired for Vitaphone.

vitascope ('vaɪtəskəʊp). *U.S.* [f. L. *vīta* life + -SCOPE.] A variety of kinematograph.

1896 *Columbus* (Ohio) *Dispatch* 4 Apr. 1/2 The vitascope throws upon a screen by means of bright lights and powerful lenses the moving life size figures of human beings and animals. **1896** *N. Amer. Rev.* Sept. 380 As yet, vitascope exhibitions are confined to episodes lasting from two to five minutes. **1897** *Pop. Sci. Monthly* Dec. 180 In some forms of apparatus, such as the vitascope,..the shutter is omitted.

†**vi'tation.** *Obs.*$^{-0}$ [ad. L. *vītātio*, f. *vītāre* to avoid.] 'An eschewing, voiding, or shunning' (Blount).

1623 COCKERAM I. [Hence in Blount and Phillips.]

vi'tativeness. *Phren.* [Irreg. f. L. *vīta* life.] The love of life, the desire to live, regarded as a special faculty of the mind or brain.

1843 G. COMBE *Syst. Phrenol.* (ed. 5) I. 292 Dr. Spurzheim was disposed to admit the existence of this faculty, which he calls Vitativeness. **1884** G. COHEN *Mod. Self-Instr. Phrenol.* 131 To cultivate Vitativeness people should lead a natural and healthy life.

vitayle, -ayll(e, obs. forms of VICTUAL.

vitayler, -lour, obs. forms of VICTUALLER.

†**vitch**, obs. var. FITCH *sb.*[1] (Cf. VETCH.)

1598 FLORIO, *Vezza*, the pulse Veccie, or Vitches.

viteilour, vitel, obs. ff. VICTUAL(LER.

†**vitele.** *Obs.*$^{-1}$ [a. obs. Pg. *vitele.*] = BETEL.

1582 N. LICHEFIELD tr. *Castanheda's Conq. E. Ind.* I. xvii. 44 In this was yᵉ Vitele which the king doth chaw in his mouth.

viteler, vitell, obs. ff. VICTUAL(LER.

vitellarian (vɪtɛ'lɛərɪən), *a. Anat.* [f. next.] Of or belonging to the vitellarium.

1877 HUXLEY *Anat. Inv. Anim.* i. 67 The function of the vitellarian gland may be taken on by cells of the ovary, or oviduct. *Ibid.* iv. 199 Passing between the anterior vitellarian masses.

‖**vitellarium** (vɪtɛ'lɛərɪəm). *Anat.* Pl. **-aria.** [mod.L., f. *vitell-us* VITELLUS.] An accessory gland in the female productive organs of some worms, by which the vitellus for the eggs is secreted; a yolk-gland.

1865 *Nat. Hist. Rev.* July 336 There is added a highly specialised yolk-forming apparatus, or 'vitellarium'. **1877** HUXLEY *Anat. Inv. Anim.* iv. 178 The two vitellaria, which are long and simple or branched tubes, open into the oviduct.

vitellary ('vɪtələrɪ, vɪ'tɛlərɪ, vaɪ-), *sb.* and *a.* [f. L. *vitell-us* VITELLUS + -ARY.]

A. *sb.* †**1.** The place or part where the yolk of an egg is formed. *Obs.*

1650 SIR T. BROWNE *Pseud. Ep.* (ed. 2) III. xxviii. 151 A greater difficulty..is, how the sperm of the Cock..attaineth unto every egg, since the vitellary or place of the yelk is very high. **1687** *Phil. Trans.* XVI. 482 Now this Fecundation seems to be in the Vitellary, and not in the Uterus.

†**2.** (See quot.) *Obs.*$^{-0}$

1736 BAILEY (fol.) Pref., *Vitellary*..the Yolk of an Egg; but some use it to signify a Cluster of Eggs.

B. *adj.* Of or belonging to the vitellus; vitelline.

1846 *Proc. Amer. Philos. Soc.* IV. 307 There can be no mammiferous germ independent of vitellary matter. **1854** S. P. WOODWARD *Mollusca* II. 161 The contractions of this caudal vesicle and of the vitellary vesicle alternate. **1877** HUXLEY *Anat. Inv. Anim.* vi. 323 A caecal process, the remains, according to Rathke, of one lobe of the vitellary sac of the embryo.

viteller, obs. form of VICTUALLER.

vitelli-, combining form of L. *vitellus* VITELLUS, employed in a few scientific terms, as **vite'lliferous, vite'lligenous, vite'lligerous, vi'telligine** *adjs.*, producing the vitellus or yolk.

1819 LINDLEY tr. *Richard's Obs. Fruits & Seeds* 52 The most simple *vitelliferous embryo. *Ibid.* 59 This embryo is composed, like those which are called vitelliferous, of two distinct bodies. **1859** *Todd's Cycl. Anat.* V. 121*/1 The ova, as they continue to descend in the *vitelligenous part of the tube,..assume the form of sub-triangular flattened bodies. **1870** ROLLESTON *Anim. Life* p. cxxv, A complicated reproductive apparatus, in which..vitelligenous exist independently of germigenous glands. **1877** HUXLEY *Anat. Inv. Anim.* vii. 442, I am inclined to believe that..these epithelial cells..play the part of vitelligenous cells. **1898** *Proc. Zool. Soc. London* 555 The larvæ of many Teleosteans ..in the *vitelligerous condition. **1864** COBBOLD *Entozoa* 214 The female organs..consist of two masses of *vitelligine glands occupying a limited space.

vi'tellicle. *Biol.* [f. L. *vitell-us* VITELLUS + dim. ending *-icle*.] A vitelline sac; a yolk-sac.

1852 BRANDE *Dict. Sci.*, etc. (ed. 2) Suppl. s.v., In man and mammalia the vitellicle is called the 'umbilical vesicle'.

vitellin (vɪ'tɛlɪn, vaɪ-). *Chem.* Also **-ine**. [f. VITELL-US + -IN¹.]

1. The albuminoidal substance in the yolk of egg, a mixture of albumin and casein.

1857 MILLER *Elem. Chem., Org.* 647 These bodies of minor importance, such as globulin and vitellin. **1867** BLOXAM *Chem.* 614 Yolk of egg contains a modification of albumen termed vitelline. **1886** *Buck's Handbk. Med. Sci.* II. 640/1 The yolk..is a bright yellow mixture of about sixteen per cent. of vitellin, a substance resembling albumen.

2. A related substance found in the seeds of plants. Also *attrib.*

1882 BENTLEY *Man. Bot.* (ed. 4) 35 The proteids exist in these grains as globulins, which hitherto have been known only to occur in animals, that is, as myosin-globulin and vitellin-globulin. **1885** GOODALE *Physiol. Bot.* (1892) 364 Weyl..holds that legumin is a mixture of vegetable vitellin and casein.

vitelline (vɪ'tɛlaɪn, -ɪn, vaɪ-), *a.* and *sb.* Also 5-6 **vitellyn(e**, 6 **vytellyn**, 7 **vitellin**. [ad. med.L. *vitellīn-us*, f. L. *vitell-us* VITELLUS. Cf. OF. *vitellin* (in sense 1).]

A. *adj.* **1.** Coloured like the yolk of an egg; deep-yellow with a tinge of red. In early use *spec.* of bile.

?*a* **1412** LYDG. *Two Merchants* 307 Yif of colre he take his groundement Pure or vnpure, citryn or vitellyne. *c* **1530** *Judic. Urines* II. viii. 33 Color Prassyn is gendred of a color vitellyn. *Ibid.* ix. 36 b, Coler citrin & Coler vytellyn be all one. **1596** BARROUGH *Meth. Physick* (ed. 3) 393 Matter cholericke and filthie (as one would say) vitelline, the which causeth feuers. **1666** G. HARVEY *Morbus Angl.* xxv. (1672) 56 If we should commit the first of these, namely yellow, or vitellin choler to the test. **1684** tr. *Bonet's Merc. Compit.* VI. 244 A yellow colour arises, which indicates vitelline Bile. **1887** W. PHILLIPS *Brit. Discomycetes* 144 Hymenium vitelline; stem rather long.

2. *Biol.* Of or belonging to the vitellus or yolk of an egg.

1835-6 *Todd's Cycl. Anat.* I. 545/1 Only the..oily particles of the vitelline nidus could be expected to be seen. **1849** OWEN *Parthenogenesis* 73 An ovum..may contain a supplementary nutrient vitelline mass, properly called yelk. **1883** *Science* I. 451/2 This sac..was connected with the foetal vascular system by a vitelline artery and two veins.

b. ***vitelline membrane, sac***, the transparent membrane which surrounds the yolk of an egg; the yolk-sac; the investing membrane of the embryo.

1845 TODD & BOWMAN *Phys. Anat.* I. 48 The first, or the vitelline membrane of the ovum, is the wall of a cell. **1861** J. R. GREENE *Man. Anim. Kingd., Cœlent.* 15 In addition to these parts, many ova are provided with an outer envelope, known as the yolk-sac or 'vitelline membrane'. **1880** GÜNTHER *Fishes* 166 Generally the vitelline sac of the embryoes is free.

B. *sb.* The yolk, the vitellary substance.

1891 *Cent. Dict.*

Hence † **vitellinous** *a.* (See quot.) *Obs.*

1786 ABERCROMBIE *Arr.* 35 in *Gard. Assist.*, Vitellinous, or yellow barked [willow-tree].

vi'tello-, combining form (cf. VITELLI-) of VITELLUS, used in a few terms (*Biol.* and *Chem.*), as **vitello-duct, -intestinal** *a.*, **-lutein, -rubin** (see quots.); **vi,tello'genesis**, the formation of the vitellus; **vi,telloge'netic, -'genic, -genous** *adjs.*, producing the vitellus or yolk; **vi,tello'genin** [-IN¹], a blood-borne protein from which the substance of the vitellus is made; **vi'tellophag** (-fæg), **-phage** (-feɪdʒ) *Ent.* [Gr. -φαγος eating], a nucleus or energid which, during cleavage and the formation of blastoderm, remains in or moves into the vitellus and assimilates it.

1888 ROLLESTON & JACKSON *Anim. Life* 647 Internally it opens, when single, into the *vitello-duct, or germ-duct. **1956** *Nature* 11 Feb. 277/1 (*in table*) All [honey-bee ovaries] fully regressed; no commencement of *vitellogenesis. **1974** *Ibid.* 4 Jan. 72/2 Some fish are not fully regressed and have ovaries in early stages of vitellogenesis. **1961** *Biol. Abstr.* XXXVI. 1333/1 (*heading*) *Vitellogenetic processes of *A. depilans* observed by electron microscopy with further considerations on the Golgi apparatus. **1978** *Nature* 23 Mar. 351/2 The last female revealed no chorionated eggs and only four late vitellogenetic proximal oocytes..in the ovarioles. **1964** *Symp. R. Entomol. Soc.* II. 37 In *Drosophila*, one *vitellogenic oocyte is normally found in each ovariole. **1974** *Nature* 4 Jan. 71/2 The induction of sexual behaviour in female goldfish..by injection of ovulated eggs into the ovarian lumen of individuals with vitellogenic ovaries. **1969** *Jrnl. Insect Physiol.* XV. 1279 Two immunochemically discrete protein yolk precursors or *vitellogenins appear in the blood of adult *Periplaneta americana* on day 4 or 5 after emergence. **1973** *Nature* 13 July 103/2 Insect yolk proteins, or vitellogenins, are synthesized and secreted by the fat body. **1982** *Sci. Amer.* Nov. 139/3 In the liver [of the garter snake] the phospholipids are incorporated into a lipophosphoprotein known as vitellogenin. **1872** E. R. LANKESTER *Advancem. Sci.* (1890) 265 The others disappear as..*vitellogenous cells. **1878** F. J. BELL *Gegenbaur's Comp. Anat.* 301 This vitellogenous layer occupies the portion of the chamber behind the egg-cell. **1854** BUSHMAN in *Orr's Circ. Sci.* II. 84 A communication is found to have arisen between the yolk and the intestine, by a wide duct termed the *vitello-intestinal duct. **1886** *Buck's Handbk. Med. Sci.* II. 247/2 In the red eggs of *Maja squinado* R. Maly found two kinds of coloring matter, which he named *vitellolutein and vitellorubin. *Ibid.* 248/1 Vitellolutein is soluble in alcohol to a clear yellow solution. **1892** J. P. MCMURRICH in *Zool. Anzeiger* XV. 274 In the same manner the endoderm cells are excluded from the surface of the egg, but in this case there is an actual immigration, the cells sinking down into the interior of the yolk, and becoming '*vitellophags'. **1904** *Science* 8 April 588/2 There is no satisfactory evidence to show that the cells..are really such, and not dividing cleavage cells or possibly vitellophags. **1935** [see PRESUMPTIVE *a.* 3 b]. **1978** R. J. ELZINGA *Fund. Entomol.* iv. 86 Some of these nuclei remain behind to become vitellophags, cells for metabolizing yolk for embryonic use. **1886** *Buck's Handbk. Med. Sci.* II. 248/1 *Vitellorubin occurs in an amorphous form, soluble in alcohol to a brown fluid.

‖**vitellus** (vɪ'tɛləs, vaɪ-). [L. *vitellus* yolk of an egg.]

1. *Embryol.* The yolk of an egg; the germinative contents of an ovum-cell.

1728 CHAMBERS *Cycl.* s.v. *Egg*, In the middle of the inner White, is the *Vitellus* or Yelk. **1826** GOOD *Bk. Nat.* (1834) I. 165 In this respect the albumen of the cotyledon corresponds with the vitellus of the hen's egg. **1857** BERKELEY *Cryptog. Bot.* xv. 26 Nothing can be more close than the mode of development in these..and of the vitellus in the eggs of certain *Mollusca*. **1877** HUXLEY *Anat. Inv. Anim.* 367 In certain Amphipods..the vitellus undergoes complete division.

2. *Bot.* A fleshy sac situated between the albumen and the embryo in a seed.

1807 J. E. SMITH *Phys. Bot.* 292 The *Vitellus* is esteemed by Gærtner to compose the bulk of the seed in Fuci, Mosses and Ferns. **1829** T. CASTLE *Introd. Bot.* 245 The vitellus is an organ of a fleshy but firm texture, situated, when present, between the albumen and embryo. **1861** BENTLEY *Man. Bot.* 444 Embryo minute, enclosed in a vitellus, and outside of abundant fleshy albumen.

b. (See quot.)

1900 B. D. JACKSON *Gloss. Bot. Terms*, *Vitellus*,..an oily substance adhering to the spores of Lycopodium.

viterde, variant of VITTERED *a. Obs.*

† **viteroke.** *Obs.*⁻¹ [app. related to VITTERED, FITTERED *a.*] A ragged upper garment.

a **1225** *Ancr. R.* 328 Heo hudet eke hore ihole cloðes, & doð an alre vuemeste on viterokes al to torene.

vitex ('vaɪtɛks). [L. name used by Pliny for *Vitex agnus-castus* or a similar shrub, later adopted as a generic name by Linnæus and earlier botanists.] A deciduous shrub or small tree, often aromatic, of the genus of the same name, belonging to the family Verbenaceæ. Cf. AGNUS CASTUS.

1608 TOPSELL *Serpents* 37 The leaves of *Vitex*..being cast on the coales for a fumigation, doe with theyr vapour chase away venomous beastes. **1829** [see CLERODENDRUM]. **1955** E. POUND *Classic Anthol.* I. 71 Vitex in swamp ground, Branched loveliness..Vitex negundo, casting thy flowers in air. **1976** *Hortus Third* (L. H. Bailey Hortorium) 1161/2 Vitexes do well in any good soil.

vith, ME. form of WITH.

viþele, southern ME. var. FIDDLE *sb.*

viti-, combining form of L. *vītis* vine, occurring in a few forms, as **vi'tiferous** *a.* [L. *vītifer*], † **viti'gineous** *a.* [L. *vītigineus*] (see quots.).

Also (in recent dicts.) ***viticide*** something which kills or destroys vines; ***viticolous*** adj., living on or in vines.

1656 BLOUNT *Glossogr.*, *Vitiferous*, that bears Vines. **1721** BAILEY, *Vitigineous*, that cometh of a Vine. **1753** *Chambers' Cycl.* Suppl. s.v. *Porrum*, The vitigineous wild leek of Gerrard.

† **vitial**, *a. Obs.*⁻¹ [f. L. *viti-um* + -AL¹.] Vicious.

1614 T. ADAMS *Sinners Passing Bell* Wks. (1629) 253 There is nothing on it [*sc.* earth] that is of it, which is not become more vitiall, then vitall.

vitiate ('vɪʃɪət), *ppl. a.* Now *rare.* Also 5-6 **viciat(e**, 6 **vicyate, vycyat(e**. [ad. L. *vitiāt-us* (med.L. also *viciāt-us*), pa. pple. of *vitiāre*: see next.]

1. Vitiated, depraved, infected, spoiled: **a.** In predicative use.

1432-50 tr. *Higden* (Rolls) IV. 427 Peple viciate and pollute, to whom hit was not lawefulle to offre. *Ibid.* V. 213 A man viciate of body scholde not receyve ordres. **1539** ELYOT *Cast. Helthe* I. (1541) 1 b, Fyre..is the clarifyer of other elementes if they be vicyate or out of theyr naturall temperaunce. **1545** RAYNALD *Byrth Mankynde* 79 Yf the matrice be perysshed or otherwyse viciate. **1737** BRACKEN *Farriery Impr.* (1756) I. 14 The Blood is..vitiate or corrupt.

b. Const. *by* or *with*.

c **1450** tr. *De Imitatione* III. lx. 140 Nature sliden & viciat by þe first man Adam þoruȝ synne. **1460** CAPGRAVE *Chron.* Ded. 1 For the elde bokes..thouȝ thei were mad ful treuly, ȝet be thei viciat be the writeres. **1533** MORE *2nd Pt. Confut. Tindale* II. Wks. 636/2 The scripture adulterate and viciate with false gloses & wronge exposicions. **1572** BOSSEWELL *Armorie* III. 7 Neyther with the sonne beame is viciate the sterre, Nor yet by the bearing of a sonne, the mother.

c. Used attributively.

1551 ROBINSON tr. *More's Utopia* II. (1895) 202 In their viciate and corrupt taste. **1665** G. HARVEY *Advice agst. Plague* 15 Add thereunto the vitiate disposition of the air. **1913** A. NOYES *Tales of Mermaid Tavern, Raleigh*, He never stooped, Never once pandered to that vitiate hour.

† **2.** *Sc. Law.* Rendered null or void; interfered or tampered with. *Obs.*

1586 in *Dunfermline Regr.* (Bann. Cl.) 449 Ye auld assumptioun of ye said thrid is vitiat be ye said commendatouris proper deidis. **1593** *Sc. Acts Parlt., Jas. VI* (1816) IV. 25/2 As ony pairt of the rent of dumfermling now viciat salbe recoverit. **1678** SIR G. MACKENZIE *Crim. Laws Scot.* I. xxvii. §2. (1699) 135 It is said to be suspect, if ..it appear vitiat by ocular inspection.

vitiate ('vɪʃɪeɪt), *v.* Also 6-8 **viciat(e**, 7 **vitiat, vitiatt**. [f. L. *vitiāt-* (med.L. also *viciāt-*), ppl. stem of *vitiāre* (whence It. *viziare*, Sp. and Pg. *viciar*, F. *vicier*), f. *vitium* VICE *sb.*¹ Cf. prec.]

1. *trans.* To render incomplete, imperfect, or faulty; to impair or spoil.

1534 MORE *Treat. Passion* Wks. 1303/1 Hym must we serue, though specially wyth the mynde (whych if it be not good, viciateth all together) yet..also wyth body and goodes and al. *a* **1631** DONNE *Serm., Matt. v. 16* (1640) 82 A superstitious end, or a seditious end vitiates the best worke. **1665** MANLEY *Grotius' Low C. Wars* 453 Other Advices were prefer'd, which..do many times vitiate, if not ruine, the most noble and valiant Undertakings. **1678** BARCLAY *Apol. Quakers* vii. §2. 197 This Doctrine of Justification hath been, and is greatly vitiated in the Church of Rome. **1711** ADDISON *Spect.* No. 25 ⁋5 A continual Anxiety for Life vitiates all the Relishes of it, and casts a Gloom over the whole Face of Nature. **1738** WARBURTON *Div. Legat.* I. 166 Time, which naturally and fatally viciates and depraves all things. **1794** HUTTON *Philos. Light*, etc. 124 It would only lead us into error, and thus vitiate the science or philosophy in which it were employed. **1808** J. HASLAM *Observ. Madness & Mel.* i. (1809) 31 It might be urged, that in these instances, the perception was vitiated. **1851** NICHOL *Archit. Heav.* (ed. 9) 60 Considering that a deviation from truth by the fraction of a hairbreadth, would vitiate the figure.

b. To corrupt (*a*) literary works or (*b*) language by carelessness, arbitrary changes, or the introduction of foreign elements.

(*a*) **1659** BP. WALTON *Consid. Considered* 198 The Septuagint..which we now have is the same for substance with that anciently used, though..by the injury of time, and frequent transcriptions vitiated. **1788** REID *Aristotle's Logic* i. §1. 5 There is reason to doubt whether what [works] are his be not much vitiated and interpolated.

(*b*) **1690** TEMPLE *Ess., Poetry* Wks. 1720 I. 243 Where-ever the Roman Colonies had remained, and their Language had been generally spoken, the common People used that still, but vitiated with the base Allay of their Provincial Speech. **1742** *De Foe's Tour Gt. Brit.* (ed. 3) III. 4 It is observable, that the Normans could not well pronounce Lincoln, but vitiated it to Nichol. **1756** JOHNSON *Dict.* Pref., Many barbarous terms and phrases, by which other dictionaries may vitiate the style, are rejected from this. **1790** 'CASSANDRA' (J. Bruckner) *Crit. Tooke's Purley* 55 Those who consider how much the language had been vitiated at the time they lived, by the importation of foreign words.

2. To render corrupt in morals; to deprave in respect of principles or conduct; to lower the moral standard of (persons).

1534 MORE *Treat. Passion* Wks. 1311/2 We shulde note well and marke thereby, that the vice of a vicious personne, viciateth not the company or congregacion. **1658-9** in *Burton's Diary* (1828) IV. 59 This will not vitiate persons, but your nature and your posterity. **1682** BURNET *Rights Princes* Pref. 13 Mankind is not so vitiated with prejudice. **1751** JOHNSON *Rambler* No. 177 ⁋12 The suppression of those habits with which I was vitiated. **1770** *Junius Lett.* xxxvii. (1788) 199 If any part of the representative body be not chosen by the people, that part vitiates and corrupts the whole. **1853** C. L. BRACE *Home Life Germany* 258 In 1806, the army had become thoroughly vitiated by luxury. **1880** E. KIRKE *Garfield* 55 In short, he had only one fault, but that was radical, and in the end, vitiated the whole man. He was thoroughly selfish.

b. Similarly with impersonal objects.

1584 R. SCOT *Discov. Witchcr.* v. v. (1886) 80 He being a spirit, may with Gods leave and ordinance viciat and corrupt the spirit and will of man. **1598** MARSTON *Pygmal., Sat.* ii, Many spots my mind doth vitiate. **1634** HABINGTON *Castara* Pref. (Arb.) 12, I encounter'd there..Innocencie,..not vitiated by conversation with the world. **1675** TRAHERNE *Chr. Ethics* 324 So doth one vice cherished and allowed corrupt and viciate all the vertues in the whole world. **1714** R. FIDDES *Pract. Disc.* II. 93 Sufferings vitiate the best tempers. **1751** JOHNSON *Rambler* No. 172 ⁋2 Many vitiate their principles in the acquisition of riches. **1837** HT. MARTINEAU *Soc. Amer.* III. 263 The encouragement of an amusement which does seem to be vitiated there. **1847** HAMILTON *Rewards & Punishm.* viii. (1853) 362 One sin of youth vitiates a protracted life. **1861** MILL *Utilit.* i. 4 To what extent the moral beliefs of mankind have been vitiated ..by the absence of any distinct recognition of an ultimate standard.

c. To pervert (the eye, taste, etc.), so as to lead to false judgements or preferences.

1806 A. HUNTER *Culina* (ed. 3) 120 Stomachs may be so far vitiated as to lose all relish for plain roast, or boiled meat. **1821** CRAIG *Lect. Drawing*, etc. ii. 103 This practice has such a tendency to vitiate the eye and to mislead the mind. **1845** MCCULLOCH *Taxation* I. vi. (1852) 245 It had the mischievous effect of vitiating the public taste and stimulating the consumption of ardent spirits.

† **3.** To deflower or violate (a woman). *Obs.*

1547-50 [see *vitiating* vbl. sb.]. **1624** HEYWOOD *Gunaik.* I. 35 Till she returned into her owne naturall forme, in which he vitiated her, and of her begat Achilles. *c* **1645** HOWELL *Lett.* (1650) I. 49 This beutious Maid [Venice] hath bin often attempted to be vitiated. **1675** BAXTER *Cath. Theol.* I. 107 Being not..moved by him (as David to murder Urias, and to vitiate his wife). **1710** STEELE *Tatler* No. 198 ⁋8 He confessed his Marriage, and his placing his Companion on Purpose to vitiate his Wife. **1769** BLACKSTONE *Comm.* IV. 81 It was a felony and attended with a forfeiture of the fief, if the vasal vitiated the wife or daughter of his lord. **1791** BURKE *Let. Member Nat. Assembly* Wks. VI. 36 Pedagogues, who betray the most awful family trusts, and vitiate their female pupils.

4. To corrupt or spoil in respect of substance; to make bad, impure, or defective.

1572 J. JONES *Bathes Buckstone* 15 For blood is the treasure of lyfe, not viciated. **1599** SANDYS *Europæ Spec.* (1632) 103 As a dead Flie doth vitiate a whole boxe of sweet oyntment. **1608** TOPSELL *Serpents* 125 Euen as women in their monthly courses doe vitiat their looking-glasses. **1652** L. S. *People's Liberty* iii. 6 As much water cannot so soon be viciated as a lesser quantity. **1674** R. GODFREY *Inj. & Ab. Physic* 33 The very texture of his Stomach and other vital bowels was vitiated. **1759** MILLS tr. *Duhamel's Husb.* I. xvi. 93 Farmers distinguish the wheat thus vitiated by saying that it is blacked in the point. **1789** W. BUCHAN *Dom. Med.* (1790) 465 When the saliva is vitiated,..the curing of the disorder is the cure of this symptom. **1863** GEO. ELIOT *Romola* xxxiv, The oncoming of a malady that has permanently vitiated the sight. **1882** *Med. Temp. Jrnl.* No. 52. 177 As I shall endeavour to show you, it vitiates the blood.

b. *esp.* To render (air) impure and so inadequate for, or injurious to, life.

1715 DESAGULIERS *Fires Impr.* 34 The ill Humours which go out of their Bodies..vitiate the Air more and more. **1793** BEDDOES *Consump.* 137 Only a very small portion of the air was vitiated, i.e. converted into fixed air. **1869** E. A. PARKES *Pract. Hygiene* (ed. 3) 118 The impurity of the air vitiated by respiration. **1878** HUXLEY *Physiogr.* 84 This gas would unduly accumulate, and..vitiate the entire bulk of the atmosphere.

5. To render of no effect; to invalidate either completely or in part; *spec.* to destroy or impair the legal effect or force of (a deed, etc.).

1621 SANDERSON *Serm.* I. 170 An earthly judge is subject to misprision, mis-information, partiality, corruption, and sundry infirmities that may vitiate his proceedings. **1726** AYLIFFE *Parergon* 104 A Transposition of the Order of the Sacramental Words, does, in some Mens Opinion, vitiate Baptism. **1790** BURKE *Fr. Rev.* 37 If all the absurd theories of lawyers and divines were to vitiate the objects in which they are conversant, we should have no law, and no religion left in the world. **1827** JARMAN *Powell's Devises* II. 21 If an undefined portion of a bequest is to be applied to a purpose void by the statute, it vitiates the whole. **1853** LYTTON *My Novel* XII. xxvii, I told them flatly..that, as Mr. Egerton's agent, I would allow no proceedings that might vitiate the election. **1883** *Law Rep. 11 Q.B. Div.* 568 The plaintiff is engaged in carrying out the illegal objects of the association; ..and this circumstance alone vitiates the contract for repayment.

b. To render (an argument, etc.) inconclusive or unsatisfactory.

1748 HARTLEY *Observ. Man* I. iii. §1. 308 This will not vitiate the foregoing Conjectures. **1846** MILL *Logic* I. v. §3 The theory of that intellectual process has been vitiated by the influence of these erroneous notions. **1866** HERSCHEL *Fam. Lect. Sci.* (1867) 73 His proof is vitiated by an enormous oversight: and the thing..is a physical impossibility. **1878** STEWART & TAIT *Unseen Univ.* ii. §84. 94 It is this eternity of atom which vitiates the hypothesis.

†**6. a.** To adulterate. *Obs.*$^{-1}$

1728 SHERIDAN tr. *Persius* ii. (1739) 35 It was Luxury first made us vitiate our Oyl with Cassia.

†**b.** To alter feloniously. *Obs.*$^{-1}$

1753 *Scots Mag.* Aug. 420/1 And William Taylor, for vitiating a bank-note.

Hence **'vitiating** *vbl. sb.* and *ppl. a.*

1547 HOOPER *Declar. Christ & Office* xii. L viij, The deathe of his chyldre, the conspyricie of Absolon, the uiciating of his wiues. *a* **1550** LELAND *Itin.* (1769) V. 21 The Collegiate Church..was translatid to Aberguili for vitiating of a Maide. **1647** CLARENDON *Contempl. Ps.* Tracts (1727) 392 The yielding to every corrupt affection and passion is as great a vitiating and weakening of the mind. **1669** BOYLE *Certain Physiol. Ess.* (ed. 2) *Absol. Rest Bodies* 27 Finding its passage obstructed..by the vitiating of the Pores of the Glass. **1832** J. S. MILL in *Monthly Repos.* VI. 658 After all which has been done to break down these vitiating, soul-debasing prejudices,..where are we now? **1858** J. MARTINEAU *Stud. Chr.* 275 A certain vitiating unsoundness of mind. **1859** GEO. ELIOT *A. Bede* xxix, No man can escape this vitiating effect of an offence against his own sentiment of right.

vitiated (ˈvɪʃɪeɪtɪd), *ppl. a.* [f. the vb.] That has undergone vitiation; corrupted, spoiled, impaired: **a.** In respect of substance.

1620 VENNER *Via Recta* vii. 135 Those [almonds] that ..[are] reserued all the yeare, so that they waxe not too dry, or in their colour and substance vitiated [etc.]. **1644** MILTON *Areop.* (Arb.) 43 Wholesome meats to a vitiated stomack differ little or nothing from unwholesome. **1688** BOYLE *Vitiated Sight* 271 Some may think that [such] a man has rather an excellent, than a vitiated sight. **1747** tr. *Astruc's Fevers* 285 These cells becoming turgid with this viciated matter, raise the *cuticula*. **1770** *Phil. Trans.* LX. 400 It might..seem possible, that blood-letting had only let out the vitiated part. **1813** J. THOMSON *Lect. Inflam.* 648 When the vesications pass into the state of sloughing, or vitiated ulcers. **1826** S. COOPER *First Lines Surg.* (ed. 5) 38 Certain deleterious kinds of food, such as the ergot or vitiated rye. **1867** A. BARRY *Sir C. Barry* vi. 166 The smoke and vitiated air of every room in the building. **1892** *Photogr. Ann.* II. 213 Confinement in the vitiated atmosphere of an ill-ventilated dark room.

b. In some abstract quality or principle.

1660 R. COKE *Power & Subj.* 189 No affliction, or the keeping the thing detained, ought to injure the Appellant, or the vitiated Cause ayded by remedy of the Appeal. **1719** DE FOE *Crusoe* I. 201 To have no other Guide than that of their own abominable and vitiated Passions. **1740** CIBBER *Apol.* iv. 68 It is..to the vitiated and low Taste of the Spectator, that the Corruptions of the Stage..have been owing. **1790** BURKE *Fr. Rev.* 100 It is in us the degenerate choice of a vitiated mind. **1833** I. TAYLOR *Fanat.* i. 1 Vitiated religious sentiments have too much connexion with the principles of our physical constitution to [etc.]. **1841** D'ISRAELI *Amen. Lit.* (1867) 97 This vulgar or corrupt Latin..was the vitiated mother of the sister-languages of Europe. **1871** DARWIN *Desc. Man* II. xiv. 115 Vitiated instincts may also account for some of the hybrid unions above referred to.

vitiation (vɪʃɪˈeɪʃən). [ad. L. *vitiātio* (rare), or f. VITIATE *v.*] The action of vitiating, the fact or state of being vitiated, in senses of the verb.

1635 JACKSON *Creed* VIII. xx. §5 No addition is forbidden, but such as includeth a vitiation of the text. **1658** PHILLIPS, *Vitiation*, a corrupting or defiling; also a deflowring. **1666** G. HARVEY *Morb. Angl.* xvii. (1672) 35 The cause of the foresaid extenuation of body..is imputed to..the bloods vitiation by malign putrid vapors, smoaking throughout the vessels. **1802** PALEY *Nat. Theol.* xxvi. (1819) 429 That vitiation of taste which frequently occurs in fevers, when every taste is irregular and every one bad. **1809** W. IRVING *Knickerb.* (1861) 61 The original name of the island..has already undergone considerable vitiation. **1843** MILL *Logic* I. ii. §5 With the least vitiation of the truth of any propositions. **1863** GEO. ELIOT *Romola* xxv, No man ever struggled to retain power over a mixed multitude without suffering vitiation.

'vitiator. *rare*$^{-1}$. [ad. L. *vitiātor* (rare) or f. VITIATE *v.*] One who or that which vitiates.

1846 LANDOR *Imag. Conv.* Wks. I. 68/2 The worst vitiator and violator of the Muses and the Graces.

vi'ticulated, *a. Bot. rare*$^{-1}$. [f. L. *vīticula*, dim. of *vītis* vine.] (See quot.)

1727 P. BLAIR *Pharmaco-Bot.* v. 215 Viticulated, or Vine-like Leaves.

vi,ticu'lose, *a. Bot.* [ad. mod.L. *vīticulōsus*, f. L. *vīticul-a* (see prec.).] (See quot.)

1866 *Treas. Bot.* 1222/1 *Viticulose*, furnished with trailing stems or viticulæ.

vi'ticulous, *a. rare*$^{-1}$. [See prec. and -OUS.] Resembling the shoots of a vine.

1657 TOMLINSON *Renou's Disp.* 264 Out of which [*sc.* the root of scammony] slender and viticulous branches [L. *viticulosi surculi*] issue.

viticultural (vɪtɪˈkʌltjʊərəl, vaɪtɪ-), *a.* [f. VITICULTURE + -AL[1].] Of or pertaining to viticulture; connected with the growing of vines.

1865 *Pall Mall G.* 7 Nov. 9 All viticultural operations not requiring the muscular strength of a man. **1888** *Encycl. Brit.* XXIV. 610/2 Hungary, from a viticultural point of view, forms by far the most important part.

viticulture (ˈvɪtɪkʌltjʊə(r), vaɪtɪ-). [f. VITI- + CULTURE.] The cultivation of the vine; vine-growing.

1872 THUDICHUM & DUPRÉ (*title*), A Treatise on the Origin, Nature, and Varieties of Wine: being a complete Manual of Viticulture and Œnology. **1881** *Spectator* 12 March 345 Viticulture can only be successfully followed by those who give to it constant personal attention. **1902** A. DOBSON *S. Richardson* iii. 66 His latest idea was to establish viticulture in England.

Hence **viti'culturer, viti'culturist**, one who is engaged in the cultivation of the vine; a vine-grower.

1882 *St. James' Gaz.* 29 March 6/1 A process of elimination..turned to account by the viticulturists. **1890** *Nature* 13 Nov. 38/2 To aid in these researches, relations have already been opened with horticulturists and viticulturists. **1907** *Westm. Gaz.* 20 June 2/2 Then the viticulturers tried to carry on the trade themselves.

vitiliginous (vɪtɪˈlɪdʒɪnəs), *a.* [f. L. *vitilīgin-*, stem of *vitilīgo* (see next) + -OUS.] Of or connected with, of the nature of, vitiligo.

1898 P. MANSON *Trop. Diseases* xxvi. 392 They [leprosy spots] may be mere vitiliginous patches.

‖**vitiligo** (vɪtɪˈlaɪgəʊ). *Path.* [L. *vitilīgo* tetter.] Formerly, a skin disease characterized by the presence of smooth white shining tubercles on the face, neck, and other parts of the body; in mod. use, a skin disease whose only manifestation is the post-natal development of sharply defined white patches that tend to grow in size.

1657 *Physical Dict., Vitiligo*, a foulness of the skin with spots of divers colours. Morphew. **1693** tr. *Blancard's Phys. Dict.* (ed. 2), *Vitiligo*, a sort of Leprosie; there are Three kinds of them [etc.]. **1814** BATEMAN *Cutaneous Dis.* (ed. 3) 274 The disease, which is here intended to be designated by the term *Vitiligo*, is..somewhat rare. **1842** E. WILSON *Pract. & Theoret. Treat. Dis. Skin* xii. 280 Vitiligo is the designation applied to partial leucopathia, or the diminution or absence of pigmentary secretion upon one or more parts of the body. **1855** G. B. WOOD *Treat. Pract. Med.* (ed. 4) II. 460 Vitiligo.—This term..has received various applications. Celsus embraced under it different forms of what are now known as lepra and psoriasis, and another affection which is probably identical with the *lupus non exedeus* of modern writers. **1864** W. T. FOX *Skin Dis.* 21 Albinism, vitiligo, deformities of vascular and sebaceous structure. **1874** W. TAY tr. *Hebra & Kaposi's Dis. Skin* III. xli. 174 The want of pigment at one time represents a substantive anomaly of formation, or a morbus *sui generis* and a wholly insignificant condition (Vitiligo alba levior, Celsus), and, at another time, forms a part of the phenomena of a very intense, constitutional disease, namely, Elphantiasis Græcorum (Vitiligo alba gravior, Celsus). *Ibid.* 176 According to the latter expressions [of Celsus], we might consider vitiligo to mean Psoriasis or Eczema.., or Elephantiasis Græcorum. In fact, these words have led to the great confusion which has existed even up to the present time..as to this matter. *Ibid.* 177 Most writers..have not been able to ignore the original meaning of Vitiligo as indicating a want of pigment, and make use of the expression to designate partial Achroma. **1887** T. M. ANDERSON *Treat. Dis. Skin* 28 Some cases of true Leprosy may be mistaken for Vitiligo. **1889** *Buck's Handbk. Med. Sci.* VIII. 604/1 The dark-skinned races are rather more subject to vitiligo than those of fair skin and light hair. **1907** *Lancet* 16 Feb. 407/2 Leucoderma or vitiligo is doubtless familiar to you all. **1976** *Ibid.* 4 Dec. 1248/1 Since 1974 she had had psoriasis, vitiligo, and recurrent herpes labialis. **1979** E. L. RHODES *Dermatology for Physician* ii. 9/1 Although pale patches on the skin may follow eczema, psoriasis, pityriasis rosea and pityriasis versicolor, the patches of vitiligo are absolutely white.

Hence ‖**vitili'goidea**, a skin-disease resembling vitiligo.

1873 F. T. ROBERTS *The. & Pract. Med.* 779 A peculiar enlargement [of the liver] associated with vitiligoidea. **1899** *Allbutt's Syst. Med.* VIII. 767 Two cases are..discussed by Addison and Gull..in relation to vitiligoidea.

viti'litigate, *v. rare.* [f. ppl. stem of L. *vitilītigāre.*] (See quot.) Hence **viti'litigating** *ppl. a.*

1670 BLOUNT *Glossogr.* (ed. 3), *Vitilitigate*,..to backbite, to detract, to wrangle, or make bate. *Hudebras.* [Cf. next.] **1819** H. BUSK *Vestriad* III. 717 In heaven yclept Alecto.. But Discord called by mortals here on earth; A vitilitigating horrid girl.

vitiliti'gation. *rare.* [See prec. and -ATION.] Contention, wrangling.

1647 N. WARD *Simple Cobler* 14 It is a most toylsome taske to runne the wild-goose chase after a well breath'd Opinionist: They delight in vitilitigation. **1663** BUTLER *Hud.* I. iii. 1262 I'll force you by right ratiocination To leave your Vitilitigation.

†**vitili'tigious,** *a. Obs.*$^{-1}$ [f. L. *vitilītig-āre* (see above), after *litigious.*] Contentious, quarrelsome.

1683 E. HOOKER *Pref. Pordage's Mystic Div.* 19 Most inevangelicly malevolous, vitious, vitilitigious.

vitiosity (vɪʃɪˈɒsɪtɪ). Also 6–7, 9 viciosity (6 -itie, -itee), 7 visiositie. [ad. L. *vitiōsitās*, f. *vitiōsus*: see next and -ITY. So OF. *viciosité* (*vicieusité, -eté*), It. *viziosità.*]

†**1.** A defect or fault; an imperfection. *Obs.*

1538 ELYOT *Dict.* Addit., *Cacia*, viciositie, or that whiche we commonly do calle, a faute in a thynge. **1563** ABP. PARKER *Corr.* (Parker Soc.) 199 With my natural viciosity of overmuch shamefastness I am so babished..that [etc.]. **1589** PUTTENHAM *Eng. Poesie* (Arb.) 167 It may come to passe that what the Grammarian setteth downe for a viciositee in speach may become a vertue and no vice. **1665** JER. TAYLOR *Unum Necess.* vi. §16 Any person that hath a fault or a legal impurity, a debt, a vitiosity, defect, or imperfection.

2. The state or character of being morally vicious.

1603 HOLLAND *Plutarch's Mor.* 247 Reason by little and little doth illuminate, purge and cleanse the soule in abating and diminishing evermore the visiositie thereof. **1643** SIR T. BROWNE *Relig. Med.* I. §42 My untamed affections and confirmed vitiosity makes mee dayly doe worse. **1678** CUDWORTH *Intell. Syst.* I. iii. Contents 104 It is not only moral vitiosity which inclines men to atheize. **1782** J. BROWN *Compend. View Nat. & Rev. Relig.* I. 13 An inconceivable vitiosity of nature absolutely inconsistent with godhead. **1836** GILBERT *Chr. Atonem.* Notes (1852) 380 The vitiosity of sin and public injury are here correlative.

†**b.** An instance of this; a vice. *Obs.*

1643 SIR T. BROWNE *Relig. Med.* II. §7 There are certaine tempers of body, which..doe hatch and produce viciosities, whose..monstrosity of nature admits no name. **1657** GAULE *Sap. Just.* 9 That, after Baptism, it is no real viciosity, but only a penalty.

†**3.** The quality of being physically impaired or defective. *Obs.*

1647 A. ROSS *Mystag. Poet.* i. (1672) 9 In this Gum [*sc.* myrrh] Venus is much delighted, as being a help to..the vitiosity of the Matrix. **1651** N. BIGGS *New Disp.* ⁋223 If the more waterish and yellow bloud doth denote its vitiosity.

4. *Sc. Law.* The quality of being faulty or improper in a legal aspect.

1765–8 ERSKINE *Inst. Law Scot.* III. ix. §52 Such confirmation..purges the vitiosity of his former intromissions. **1838** W. BELL *Dict. Law Scot.* 529 It infers an intention on the part of the intromitter to account for his intromissions, which takes off the vitiosity, and renders him liable only to the extent of his intromissions.

vitious(ly, -ness, varr. VICIOUS(LY, -NESS.

vitivert, var. VETIVER.

vitle, vitler, obs. ff. VICTUAL(LER.

vitles, obs. Sc. f. WITLESS *a.*

vitnes, obs. Sc. f. WITNESS.

vitoll, obs. f. VICTUAL.

vitraell, obs. f. VITRIOL.

‖**vitrage** (vitraʒ). [F. *vitrage* glass-windows, f. *vitre* glass.] ***vitrage net*** (also ***cloth***), a lace-net or thin fabric suitable for window-curtains.

1886 *Daily News* 14 June 2/7 Window-blinds, vitrage nets, and other goods made upon curtain-machines are only in moderate request. **1894** *Times* 19 April 4/3 A steady business is being done in curtains, antimacassars, vitrage nets, &c.

'vitrailed, *a. rare*⁻¹. [f. F. *vitrail* (usu. in pl. *vitraux*) a glass-window.] Having glazed windows or compartments (of a specified colour).

1884 RUSKIN *Bible Amiens* iv. §10 This Lord's House and blue-vitrailed gate of Heaven.

'vitraillist. *rare.* [f. as prec.] A maker of glass; an artist in glass-work for windows, etc.; a designer in stained-glass.

1607 B. BARNES *Divils Charter* III. v. F3, Th' Italian Vitraillist, Which in the fierie Phlegitonian flames, Did worke strange vitriall dildidoes for Dames. **1904** *Daily News* 28 July 4/1 In the inner gallery is a large and ambitious picture,..and some drawings by the young artist. But it is as a vitraillist that he excels.

vitrain ('vɪtreɪn). [f. L. *vitr-eus* VITREOUS *a.* + *-ain* in FUSAIN (sense 2).] A black, highly lustrous, and often brittle type of coal.

1919, etc. [see CLARAIN]. **1930** [see DURAIN]. **1975** D. G. MURCHISON et al. tr. *E. Stach's Textbk. Coal Petrol.* v. 334 The first step..is the crushing of the run-of-mine coal... When a seam contains thick layers of bright coal, the soft and mostly brittle vitrain concentrates in the smalls, below 10 mm.

† **vitre**, *sb. Obs. rare.* Also 5 **vytre**. [a. F. *vitre*, ad. L. *vitrum* VITRUM.] Glass.

c **1420** LYDG. *Ballad Commend. Our Lady* 113 O glorious viole, O vitre inviolate! **1599** A. HUME *Hymnes* iii. 55 The glansing thains, and vitre bright, Resplends against the sunne.

† **vitre**, *a. Obs. rare.* [ad. F. *vitré*, or L. *vitreus*, f. *vitrum* glass.] = VITREOUS *a.* 2 a.

c **1530** *Judic. Urines* II. v. 24 The .v. spice of flewme is called fleume vitrium..anglice a flewme vitre. *Ibid.* II. ix. 36 b A fleume vitre, and a whyte fleume be all one.

vitre, variant of VITRY *Obs.*

† **vitreal**, variant of VITRIAL *a. Obs.*

1658 PHILLIPS, *Vitreal*, or *Vitrine*, belonging to, or made of glasse.

† **'vitrean**, *a. Obs. rare.* [f. L. *vitre-us* vitreous + -AN.] Of or resembling glass.

1656 BLOUNT *Glossogr.*, *Vitrean*, *Vitrine*,..belonging to Glass, glassie, glassie-green; clear like glass, or resembling glass. **1778** W. PRYCE *Min. Cornub.* 60 Vitrean Ore of an irregular figure.

vitrectomy (vɪ'trɛktəmɪ). *Surg.* [f. VITRE(OUS *a.* + -ECTOMY.] The operation of removing the vitreous fluid from the eyeball and replacing it with another fluid.

1968 D. KASNER in *Highlights Ophthalm.* XI. 304 (*heading*) Vitrectomy: a new approach to the management of vitreous. **1975** *Courier-Mail* (Brisbane) 5 Nov. 18/6 She is the first woman in Western Australia to have the operation, known as a vitrectomy, which restored her sight. **1983** *Oxf. Textbk. Med.* I. IX. 32/2 Recently, vitrectomy has developed as a treatment for blindness from unresolved vitreous haemorrhage and as a treatment of retinal detachment subsequent to vitreous haemorrhage.

vitree, variant of VITRY *Obs.*

vitrefacture. *rare*⁻¹. [Cf. VITRI- and FACTURE.] (See quot.)

1842 R. PARK *Pantology* (1847) 478 Under the head of *Vitrefactures*, we include glass, pottery, and porcelain. [Hence *vitrifacture* in Worcester (1846), and later Dicts.]

Vitremanie ('viːtrəmæniː). [f. F. *vitre* window-pane + *manie* fad.] A process of decorating window panes by the application of coloured designs in imitation of stained glass, popular in the Victorian period.

1881 *Sylvia's Bk. Artistic Knicknacks* 324 The art of vitremanie—the decoration of glass windows, &c., by the application of coloured designs so as to resemble stained-glass—is a modern invention. *Ibid.* Vitremanie may be applied to exclude unpleasing views seen through staircase or other windows. **1961** J. GLOAG *Victorian Comfort* ii. 36 A form of window decoration called 'Vitremanie', which was applied to glass 'to exclude unpleasing views'.

† **vitremyte.** *Obs.*⁻¹ (Of obscure meaning.)

c **1386** CHAUCER *Monk's T.* 382 And she that helmed was in starke shoures..Shal on hir heed now were a vitremyte [*Harl.* wyntermyte].

vitreo-, combining form, on Greek models, of L. *vitreus* VITREOUS *a.*, employed in a few special terms having little or no currency.

1828–32 WEBSTER, *Vitreo-electric*, containing or exhibiting positive electricity, or that which is excited by rubbing glass. *c* **1840** *Encycl. Metrop.* (1845) VI. 496 Lustre [of thraulite] vitreo-resinous. **1875** KNIGHT *Dict. Mech.* 2713/2 *Vitreograph*, a photograph on glass. **1891** *Cent. Dict.* s.v., Vitreo-dentinal, -dentine.

vitreole, obs. form of VITRIOL.

Vitreosil ('vɪtrɪəʊsɪl). Also **vitreosil**. [f. VITREO(US *a.* + SIL(ICA.] A proprietary name for vitreous silica.

1909 *Trade Marks Jrnl.* 15 Dec. 2050 *Vitreosil*... Fused silica articles included in Class 15 in the form of tubes, plates, basins..and other shapes for chemical, electrical, ornamental and other similar purposes. The Thermal Syndicate, Limited,..Wallsend-on-Tyne. **1921** *Chambers's Jrnl.* 26 Mar. 272/1 Vitreosil..is composed of pure silica fused in the electric furnace by a special process. **1938** *Jrnl. R. Aeronaut. Soc.* XLII. 822 Hollow tubes of vitreosil were wound internally with spiral heating coils. **1973** *Nature* 27 July 233/1 Each portion was placed on defatted lens paper on a stainless steel mesh grid in a vitreosil dish containing Trowell's T-8 medium.

vitre'osity. *rare.* [f. L. *vitre-us* (see next) + -OSITY.] The state or quality of being vitreous.

1889 A. IRVING *Metamorphism of Rock* 110, I have been led to recognise vitreosity as a phenomenon occasionally exhibited by water.

vitreous ('vɪtrɪəs), *a.* Also 8 **vitrious**. [f. L. *vitre-us* of glass, glassy, bright, etc., f. *vitrum* glass, VITRUM: see -OUS. Cf. F. *vitreux*, *-euse*.]

1. a. Of or belonging to, consisting or composed of, glass; of the nature of glass; glassy. ***vitreous silica***, an amorphous, translucent or transparent form of silica obtained by rapid quenching from the molten state.

1646 SIR T. BROWNE *Pseud. Ep.* II. i. 51 Calcination or reducing it by Arte, into a subtile powder, by which way and a vitreous commixture, glasses are sometime made hereof. **1711** SHAFTESB. *Charac.* III. 15 The tumid Bladder bounds at every Kick, bursts the withstanding Casements, the Chassys, Lanterns, and all the brittle vitrious Ware. **1784** COWPER *Task* v. 161 Mirrour needed none Where all was vitreous. **1791** W. HAMILTON *Berthollet's Dyeing* II. II. IV. iv. 275 A vessel of earthenware with a vitreous coat. **1827** FARADAY *Chem. Manip.* vii. (1842) 224 Glass would then be easily acted upon, and..the product obtained would not be pure, but a combination, with part of the vitreous matter. **1852** DICKENS *Repr. P.*, *Plated Article*, Of course, you saw the glaze—composed of various vitreous materials—laid over every article. **1882** GEIKIE *Text-bk. Geol.* II. II. §4. 105 The final stiffening of a vitreous mass into solid stone. **1925** J. W. MELLOR *Comprehensive Treat. Inorg. & Theoret. Chem.* VI. xl. 288 Various names are applied to the vitrified quartz—thus, quartz-glass, vitreous-silica, fused quartz,.. etc. **1971** *Materials & Technol.* II. i. 22 Transparent vitreous silica is used for the production of lenses..and other optical elements which are required to transmit ultraviolet or infra-red rays.

fig. **1836** *New Monthly Mag.* XLVI. 206 He had left the vitreous and mercurial clime of France..for the voluptuous and indolent air of Italy.

b. *Geol.* and *Min.* Resembling glass in brittleness, hardness, lustre, and mode of cleavage.

1774 in Forster *Voy.* (1777) I. 587 Some of them carried arms,..which were headed with a black vitreous lava. **1796** KIRWAN *Elem. Min.* (ed. 2) I. 409 All real lavas except those of the vitreous kind affect the magnetic needle, unless the iron they contain be much oxygenated. **1811** PINKERTON *Petral.* I. 45 There are..evidences of a vitreous lava in one of the isles of Faroe. **1849** MURCHISON *Siluria* iii. 38 It is often intersected by veins of vitreous quartz. **1855** *Orr's Circ. Sci., Geol.*, etc. 498 Redruthite.—Vitreous Copper. Prismatic Copper Glance. **1868** WATTS *Dict. Chem.* V. 306 *Vitreous Silver.* Native argentic sulphide. **1882** GEIKIE *Text-Bk. Geol.* II. II. §4. 100 Crystallites..seem to be earlier or peculiar forms of crystallization developed..in many vitreous rocks.

c. *Chem.* Resembling glass in composition.

1800 tr. *Lagrange's Chem.* I. 369 There remains in the retort a vitreous mass,..which is very pure arsenic acid. **1826** HENRY *Elem. Chem.* I. 363 Equal parts of potassium and very pure and vitreous boracic acid were put into a copper tube. **1866** ROSCOE *Elem. Chem.* xiv. 122 Like sulphur, it is capable of existing in various allotropic modifications, one of which is crystalline, the other vitreous.

d. *Anat.* and *Zool.* (See quots.)

(*a*) **1858** HUMPHRY *Hum. Skeleton* 206 The separation of the outer and inner tables of the skull by the intervening diploë... The inner, or 'vitreous' table, which is the most dense. **1866** *Chambers's Encycl.* VIII. 759 An inner dense, brittle, and somewhat glass-like layer, known as the vitreous table or layer.

(*b*) **1873** C. W. THOMSON *Depths of Sea* vii. 422 When the first specimen of *Hyalonema* was brought home, the other vitreous sponges..were unknown. **1879** CARPENTER in *Encycl. Brit.* IX. 378/2 The Vitreous *Foraminifera* may be grouped into three families. *Ibid.* 385/1 The material of their 'porcellanous' or 'vitreous' skeletons. **1896** tr. *Boas' Text Bk. Zool.* 121 Vitreous sponges (*Hexactinellidæ*) are silicious forms, characterised by the striking beauty of the skeleton, which is like spun-glass.

e. ***vitreous enamel***: = ENAMEL *sb.* 1 a, ***porcelain enamel*** s.v. PORCELAIN 5. So ***vitreous-enamelled*** adj., ***vitreous enamelling***.

1916 *Chem. Abstr.* X. 261 (*heading*) Vitreous enamels or glazes for pottery, etc. **1939** BURNS & SCHUH *Protective Coatings for Metals* xvi. 381 Vitreous or porcelain enamels are essentially fused silicates or glasses holding in suspension a colloidal dispersion of color oxides, opacifiers and gases. **1963** G. S. BRADY *Materials Handbk.* (ed. 9) 281 Vitreous enameled metals are used for cooking utensils, signs, chemical tanks and piping, [etc.]. **1977** R. B. ROSS *Handbk. Metal Treatments & Testing* 389 Vitreous enamelling was very popular in late nineteenth and early twentieth centuries. With the advent of new materials, for example, aluminium in cooking ware,..the use of vitreous enamel declined and was confined very largely to articles such as baths. **1984** WORTHINGTON & KNIGHT *Home Plumbing* 96/1 Modern materials are less resistant to abrasives than the traditional vitreous enamel.

2. † **a.** *Med.* Of phlegm: Having the thick viscid consistency of molten glass. *Obs.*

1661 LOVELL *Hist. Anim. & Min.* 437 Of phlegme, if salt, from thirst... If vitreous, from fixed paine. **1684** tr. *Bonet's Merc. Compit.* III. 98 She voided much vitreous phlegm and bilious humours. **1707** FLOYER *Physic. Pulse-Watch* 75 A moderate degree of cold produces a sweet Phlegm..and the greatest an *Acerbe* vitrious slime towards the coldest time of Winter.

b. ***vitreous humour*** (or ***body***), the transparent gelatinous substance occupying the posterior and larger part of the eyeball. † ***vitreous tunicle*** (see quot. 1704).

1663 BOYLE *Usef. Exp. Nat. Philos.* I. 96 We have sometimes..speedily frozen Eyes, and thereby have turn'd the Vitreous humor into very numerous and Diaphanous Films. **1676** *Phil. Trans.* XI. 747 As to the Vitreous humor, he judges it to be of that nature, that being once lost, it can never be repaired. **1704** J. HARRIS *Lex. Techn.* I, *Vitrious Tunicle*, a thin Film, or Coat, which is said to separate the Glassie Humour from the Chrystalline. **1710** J. CLARKE tr. *Rohault's Nat. Philos.* (1729) I. 237 The Vitreous Humour ..being one of the most transparent Things that we know of in the World. **1793** *Phil. Trans.* LXXXIII. 175 Its elasticity will assist the cellular texture of the vitreous humour..in restoring the indolent form. **1831** R. KNOX *Cloquet's Anat.* 559 The Vitreous Body is a soft, perfectly transparent, tremulous mass, occupying the three posterior fourths of the cavity of the ball of the eye. **1877** M. FOSTER *Physiol.* III. ii. (1878) 398 The rays of light traverse in succession the cornea, the aqueous humour, the lens and the vitreous humour.

c. *ellipt.* as *sb.* = *vitreous humour* above.

1869 G. LAWSON *Dis. Eye* (1874) 144 He has succeeded in thus extracting the lens without the loss of any vitreous. **1879** *St. George's Hosp. Rep.* IX. 479 A quantity of the thin fluid vitreous escaped.

3. ***vitreous electricity***, positive electricity obtained from glass by friction.

1759 *Phil. Trans.* LI. 308 Experiments..respecting the vitreous and resinous electricities, as they are called. **1799** [see ELECTRICITY 1 b]. **1840** CARLYLE *Heroes* i. (1904) 18 Thunder was not then mere Electricity, vitreous or resinous. **1860** EMERSON *Cond. Life, Wealth* Wks. (Bohn) II. 357 The genius of reading and of gardening are antagonistic, like resinous and vitreous electricity. **1879** PROCTOR *Pleas. Ways Sc.* xi. 238 If glass is briskly rubbed with silk it becomes charged..with positive electricity, formerly called vitreous electricity for this reason.

4. a. Resembling that of glass; characteristic of glass.

1811 A. T. THOMSON *Lond. Disp.* (1818) 196 The tears are ..brittle, and break with a vitreous fracture. **1841** BRANDE *Chem.* (ed. 5) 130 This change from the vitreous to the crystalline state sometimes takes place suddenly. **1854** RONALDS & RICHARDSON *Chem. Technol.* (ed. 2) I. 42 They form a..perfectly black mass,..generally possessing a fatty or vitreous lustre. **1863** A. C. RAMSAY *Phys. Geog.* i. (1878) 20 Modern lavas have often a vitreous structure (glassy) such as obsidian.

b. Having the colour or appearance of glass.

1874 R. BUCHANAN *Pan* Poet. Wks. I. 90 What time the pallid sickle wax'd Blue-edged and vitreous o'er the black'ning West. **1882** —— *Annan Water* i, The vitreous rays of the moon began playing on the window panes. **1900** B. D. JACKSON *Gloss. Bot. Terms, Vitreous*,..transparent, hyaline; formerly used for the light green of glass.

5. *Comb.*, as ***vitreous-like***, ***-shelled*** adjs.

1879 CARPENTER in *Encycl. Brit.* IX. 378/1 The vitreous-shelled *Foraminifera* constitute the most elevated division of the group. **1902** *Westm. Gaz.* 22 Sept. 6/3 Some of the finer wares will break showing a vitreous-like substance.

Hence **'vitreousness.**

1727 BAILEY (vol. II), and later Dicts.

vitreously ('vɪtrɪəslɪ), *adv.* [f. prec. + -LY².] In a vitreous manner: **a.** With positive electricity.

1794 G. ADAMS *Nat. & Exp. Philos.* IV. xlvi. 264 Those attracted by excited wax, are vitreously..electrified. **1844** NOAD *Electricity* (ed. 2) 9 We are led to the inference that the cloth is vitreously electrified. **1885** WATSON & BURBURY *Math. The. Electr. & Magn.* I. 75 The outside of the vessel will be found to be vitreously electrified.

b. Glassily; like glass.

1904 HOWELLS *Son of Royal Langbrith* 62 In the moonlight Hawberk's face had a greenish hue, and his eyes shone vitreously.

vitrescence (vɪ'trɛsəns). [f. VITRESCENT *a.*: see -ENCE.] The state of becoming vitreous or glassy; vitrified or vitreous condition.

1796 KIRWAN *Elem. Min.* (ed. 2) I. 279 Mineral alkali promotes their [*sc.* zeolytes] vitrescence most, next borax, microcosmic salt least. **1888** *Encycl. Brit.* XXIV. 264/1 The vitrescence was produced by beacon fires lighted during times of invasion. **1903** *Academy* 24 Jan. 75/2 The difficulty in most cases arises from the high vitrescence of surface [of Chinese porcelain].

So **vi'trescency.** *rare.*

1756 F. HOME *Exper. Bleaching* 116 Their junction with oils, and their vitrescency. **1847** H. MILLER *Rambles Geol.* (1858) 365 They are artificial structures, in which vitrescency was designedly induced.

vitrescent (vɪ'trɛsənt), *a.* [f. L. *vitr-um* glass + -ESCENT. Cf. It. *vitrescente*.] Tending to become glass; susceptible of being turned into glass; glassy.

1756 P. BROWNE *Jamaica* 48 They seem to be formed chiefly of the vitrescent fluor, debased by a less agitated or divided clay. **1767** *Phil. Trans.* LVII. 440 The stone is of an extreme hardness, and almost a petrifaction..of many different stones, but all vitrescent. **1778** PRYCE *Min. Cornub.* 262 The nitre and tartar are..rendered still more vitrescent by the borax. **1825** J. NICHOLSON *Oper. Mech.* 756 Iron ores ..require calcareous additions, and the copper ores, rather slags or vitrescent stones, than calcareous earth. **1885** tr. *Labarte's Arts Mid. Ages* viii. 289 A vitrescent coating.

vitrescible (vɪ'trɛsɪb(ə)l), *a.* [f. L. type **vitrescĕre* to become glass + -IBLE, or directly a. F. *vitrescible* (*a* 1762), = It. *vitrescibile*, Pg. *-ivel*.] That can be vitrified; vitrifiable.

1754 HUXHAM in *Phil. Trans.* XLVIII. 841 Loosely combined with the vitrescible earth. **1786** WEDGWOOD *Ibid.* LXXVI. 400 This effect is constant in certain clays, and begins earliest in those which are most vitrescible. **1794** R.

J. SULIVAN *View Nature* I. 450 They have likewise been ranked among vitrescible stones. **1825** HIBBERT in *Trans. Soc. Antiq. Scot.* (1831) IV. 166 The interstices between them being filled full of this vitrescible iron ore. **1872** YEATS *Techn. Hist. Comm.* 266 Vitrescible colours..are now laid on the glass, and burned into it.

Hence **vitresci'bility**. [Cf. F. *vitrescibilité*.]

1786 WEDGWOOD in *Phil. Trans.* LXXVI. 401 Enabling us to ascertain the degree of vitrescibility of bodies that cannot actually be vitrified by any fires which our furnaces are capable of producing.

†**'vitrial**, *a. Obs.* [f. L. *vitr-um* glass + -IAL.] Composed of glass; glassy, vitreous.

1605 TIMME *Quersit.* I. xii. 50 Their fixed heauen, or vitriall and chrystalline circles, is a salt body. **1608** TOPSELL *Hist. Serpents* 161 As for the flesh, it is of a vitriall or glassie colour. **1609** ARMIN *Maids of More-Cl.* (1880) 125 Place your plate, and pile your vitriall boales Nest vpon nest.

vitrial(l, obs. forms of VITRIOL.

†**'vitriary**, *a. Obs.*⁻¹ [f. L. *vitr-um* glass. Cf. L. *vitreārius* glass-worker.] Relating to the making of glass.

1668 SIR T. BROWNE *Let. Merritt* 29 Dec., Wks. (Bohn) III. 508 Though I have not been a stranger unto the vitriary art, both in England and abroad.

†**'vitriate**, *v. Obs.*⁻¹ [f. as prec.] *trans.* To make clear like glass.

1631 A. WILSON *Swisser* II. i. 106 An ownce of Honestie, Cleare, Pure, well vitriated.

†**'vitriature**. *Obs.*⁻¹ [f. as prec.] (See quot.)

1569 R. ANDROSE tr. *Alexis' Secr.* IV. III. 32 It helpeth maruelouslye to take a dramme of the vitriature or glasing of vessels made in pouder.

vitric ('vɪtrɪk), *a. Geol.* [f. L. *vitr-um* glass + -IC.] Of tuff: composed chiefly of glassy material.

1915 L. V. PIRSSON in *Amer. Jrnl. Sci.* CXC. 193 The use of 'vitric' and 'lithic' is suggested instead of the more common 'glassy' and 'stony' in order to avoid the misapprehension that the outward appearance of the material is referred to. **1976** *Nature* 5 Aug. 461/2 The other vertebrate remains are confined to the uppermost 30 m of aeolian tuffs beneath a widespread pale yellow vitric tuff.

'vitrics. *rare*⁻⁰. [f. L. *vitr-um* glass + -IC 2.] (See quot.)

1875 KNIGHT *Dict. Mech.* 2713/2 *Vitrics*, this term includes the fused compounds in which silex predominates, such as glass and some of the enamels; in contradistinction to the ceramics, in which alumina predominates.

†**'vitrid**, *a. Obs.*⁻¹ [f. as prec. + -ID¹.] Glass-like, vitreous.

1777 J. WILLIAMS *Acc. Anc. Ruins* 11 In some others, the stones seem to have been partly run down, and partly enveloped by the vitrid matter.

vitrie, variant of VITRY *Obs.*

vitrifaction (vɪtrɪ'fækʃən). [See VITRIFY *v.* and -FACTION.] = VITRIFICATION.

1728 CHAMBERS *Cycl.*, *Vitrification*, or *Vitrifaction*, the Act of converting a Body into Glass, by Fire. **1840** VYSE *Oper. Pyramids Gizeh* I. 228 In some instances the glaize was of an extremely brilliant colour, and a perfect vitrifaction. **1845** LADY EASTLAKE *Jrnls. & Corr.* I. 163 We now come nearer into granite Edinburgh: such petrifactions or vitrifactions, of houses. **1888** *Encycl. Brit.* XXIV. 264/2 In Scandinavia, where there are hundreds of ordinary forts, ..no trace of vitrifaction has yet been detected.

vitrifacture: see VITREFACTURE.

vitrifiable (vɪtrɪ'faɪəb(ə)l), *a.* [f. VITRIFY *v.* + -ABLE. Cf. F. *vitrifiable* (1734).] Capable of being vitrified; admitting of conversion into a glassy substance by means of heat.

1646 SIR T. BROWNE *Pseud. Ep.* II. iii. 69 Vitrification is the last or utmost fusion of a body vitrifiable, and is performed by a strong and violent fire, which keeps the melted glasse red hot. **1684** BOYLE *Porousn. Anim. & Solid Bod.* vii. 98 We are wont to add to the vitrifiable matter, either some prepared metal, as calcined Copper [etc.]. **1709** *Phil. Trans.* XXVI. 382, I believe that with this Oil there is mixed a great deal of the earthy, vitrifiable part of the Metal. **1756** C. LUCAS *Ess. Waters* I. 3 The primary, or vitrifiable, earth..he looks upon as the basis or matrix of all other earths. **1796** KIRWAN *Elem. Min.* (ed. 2) I. 53 Mr. Achard found a mixture of two parts calcareous earths and one part magnesia vitrifiable. **1839** URE *Dict. Arts* 574 The same mixture of vitrifiable materials will yield very different results. **1878** MISS J. J. YOUNG *Ceramic Art* 182 The compartments are then filled with vitrifiable enamels.

Hence **vitrifia'bility**. [Cf. F. *vitrifiabilité*.]

1891 *Cent. Dict.*

'vitrificable, *a. rare*⁻⁰. [Cf. VITRIFICATE and -ABLE. So Sp. *vitrificable*, Pg. *vitrificavel*, It. *vetrificabile*.] Vitrifiable.

1727 BAILEY (vol. II), and in later Dicts.

†**vitrifi'cacious**, *a. Obs.*⁻¹ [Cf. next and -ACIOUS.] Resembling glass.

1794 R. J. SULIVAN *View Nat.* II. 105 A black, compact, hard bitumen; brittle and vitrificacious in breaking.

†**vitrificate**, *pa. pple. Obs.* [ad. med.L. *vitrificāt-us*, pa. pple. of **vitrificāre* to vitrify.] Vitrified. Also †**vitrificate** *v. trans.*, to vitrify.

1471 RIPLEY *Comp. Alch.* v. xviii. in Ashm. (1652) 152 And make thy fyre so temperat, That by the sydys thy Water be never vytryfycate. **1626** BACON *New Atl.* (1635) 162 We have..crystals likewise, and glasses of divers kinds, and among them some of metals vitrificated. **1721** BAILEY, *Vitrificate*, to turn into Glass.

vitrification (vɪtrɪfɪ'keɪʃən). [ad. med. or mod.L. **vitrificātio*, f. **vitrificāre* to vitrify. Cf. F. *vitrification* (16th c.), Sp. *vitrificacion*, Pg. *-ação*, It. *vit-*, *vetrificazione*.]

1. The action or process of vitrifying; conversion into a glassy substance by fusion due to heat; the fact of being so converted.

1612 WOODALL *Surg. Mate* Wks. (1653) 274 Vitrification is Combustion, converting Calk and Cineres into transparant glasse. **1643** SIR T. BROWNE *Relig. Med.* I. §50 The last and proper action of that element [fire] is but vitrification, or a reduction of a body into Glasse. **1661** BOYLE *Scept. Chem.* v. 322 Cuppels..ought to be Destitute of Salt, lest the Violence of the Fire should bring them to Vitrification. **1709** *Phil. Trans.* XXVI. 378 We may look on it as the beginning of Vitrification, or a middle state between Metal and Glass. **1773** FRANKLIN *Lett.*, etc., Wks. 1840 V. 454 There is no earth known so vitrifiable as not to require some auxiliary solvent to facilitate its vitrification. **1804** P. F. TINGRY *Paint. & Varnish. Guide* 301 This vitrification is facilitated by the addition of a certain quantity of carbonate of potash.., or carbonate of soda. **1851** D. WILSON *Preh. Ann.* II. III. iii. 416 Sandstone, though *per se* infusible, is perfectly capable of vitrification. **1863** A. C. RAMSAY *Phys. Geog.* xxxv. (1878) 613 Stones originally separate, get, so to speak, glued together in the process of vitrification.

b. With *a* and pl.: An instance of such conversion.

1626 BACON *Sylva* §291 Likewise in their Putrefactions, or Rusts; as Vermilion, Verdegrease, Bise, Cirrus, &c. and likewise in their Vitrifications. **1646** SIR T. BROWNE *Pseud. Ep.* II. i. 53 Crystall..is not onely triturable, and reduceable into powder, by contrition, but will subsist in a violent fire, and endure a vitrification. **1759** DELAVAL in *Phil. Trans.* LI. 86 Because all vitrifications must proceed from previous calcinations.

2. The result or product of vitrifying; a vitrified substance or body.

1651 BIGGS *New Disp.* ¶136 We yet more detest the precipitations, vitrifications, and preparations of Mercury, Antimony, Tuty, Sulphur, &c. **1762–71** H. WALPOLE *Vertue's Anecd. Paint.* (1786) III. 235 Sir Theodore.. communicated to them the process of the principal colours which ought to be employed in enamel, and which surpassed the famous vitrifications of Venice and Limoges. **1769** *Phil. Trans.* LX. 17 Both abound with pyrites and crytallizations, or rather vitrifications. **1845** PETRIE *Eccl. Archit. Irel.* 89 This is also observable in the interior of the building, where there is a slight superficial vitrification. **1860** SMILES *Self Help* ii. 41 He had but to cover this material with a vitrification of transparent glaze.

†**vitrificatory**, *a. Obs.*⁻¹ [Cf. prec. and -ORY.] Causing, or resulting in, vitrification.

1678 R. R[USSELL] tr. *Geber* II. i. II. vii. 54 Having no good Fusion in Heat of Fire but a vitrificatory Fusion only.

vitrified ('vɪtrɪfaɪd), *ppl. a.* [f. VITRIFY *v.*]

1. Converted into glass or a glassy substance by exposure to heat; rendered glassy; glazed.

1646 SIR T. BROWNE *Pseud. Ep.* II. i. 53 Vitrified and pellucide bodyes are of a clearer complexion in their continuities, then in their powders and Atomicall divisions. **1690** T. BURNET *Theory Earth* II. 49 The sun..would.. convert it at length either into an heap of ashes, or a lump of vitrified metal. **1777** J. WILLIAMS *Acc. Anc. Ruins* 15 It was all one heap of vitrified ruins from top to bottom. *a* **1787** G. WHITE *Selborne* iv, The sand..fluxes and runs by the intense heat, and so cases over the whole face of the kiln with a strong vitrified coat like glass. *a* **1817** T. DWIGHT *Trav. New Eng.*, etc. (1821) II. 80 At a little distance from the pit there was a large pile of calcined and vitrified ore. **1857** TOULMIN SMITH *Parish* 349 Glazed or vitrified pipes should only be used in or under buildings. **1869** J. PHILLIPS *Vesuv.* ii. 37 That foul vitrified matter called lava.

b. *fig.* Icy, frozen.

c **1779** CRABBE *Midnight* 216 The winds that in converging Furrows plough The freezing pool..Are arm'd with pain, and vitrified their Wings.

2. ***vitrified fort***, a hill-fort of a type occurring in Scotland and some parts of the Continent, the stones of which have been converted into a vitreous material by the action of fire.

1777 J. WILLIAMS *Acc. Anc. Ruins* 25 The largest vitrified fort I ever saw, is on the south side the Grampians, in the shire of Angus. **1791** NEWTE *Tour Eng. & Scot.* 115 Upon the top of an insulated hill adjoining, there appears to have been what some would call a vitrified fort; though others will have it to be the vestiges of a volcano. **1825** HIBBERT in *Trans. Soc. Antiq. Scot.* (1831) IV. 180 The name of *vitrified fort* may with much advantage be exchanged for the more comprehensive and untheoretical one of *vitrified site*. **1851** D. WILSON *Preh. Ann.* II. III. iii. 413 One of the most remarkable specimens of a vitrified fort in Scotland. **1879** LUBBOCK *Addr. Pol. & Educ.* ix. 173 The vitrified fort on the Hill of Noath.

vitriform ('vɪtrɪfɔːm), *a.* [f. L. *vitr-um* glass.] Having the form or appearance of glass.

1796 KIRWAN *Elem. Min.* (ed. 2) II. 449, 120 [grains] of the Vitriform Phosphoric Acid. **1800** tr. *Lagrange's Chem.* I. 431 You will obtain a vitriform matter, of the colour of an animal's liver. **1834** J. FORBES *Laennec's Dis. Chest* (ed. 4) 217 The tuberculous induration is semi-transparent, vitriform, and humid. **1857** BULLOCK *Cazeaux' Midwif.* 176 The space between the amnios and chorion..principally filled with a liquid called by M. Velpeau the reticulated or the vitriform body.

vitrify ('vɪtrɪfaɪ), *v.* [ad. F. *vitrifier* (16th c.), or med.L. **vitrificāre* (Sp. and Pg. *vitrificar*, It. *vit-*, *vetrificare*), f. *vitr-um* glass: see -FY.]

1. *trans.* To convert into glass or a glass-like substance; to render vitreous by fusion due to heat.

1594 PLAT *Jewell-ho.* I. 25 Stones which..endure the strength of fire, and are not consumed therewith, but rather vitrified. *c* **1645** HOWELL *Lett.* I. I. xxix, Surely, that grand Universal-fire..at the day of judgment may by its violent ardor vitrifie and turn to one lump of Crystal, the whole Body of the Earth. **1665** HOOKE *Microgr.* 45 Sometimes also is that heat so very intense, as further to melt it and vitrifie it. **1690** BURNET *Theory Earth* II. 46 Clayey soils, and such like, may by the strength of fire be converted into brick, or stone, or earthen metal, and so melted down and vitrified. **1728** in *6th Rep. Dep. Kpr. Rec.* App. II. 118 Vitrifying the dross of metals so as to mould the same like Bricks or Tiles. **1750** FRANKLIN *Lett.*, etc., Wks. 1840 V. 239 The metal appeared to have been not only melted, but even vitrified. **1800** tr. *Lagrange's Chem.* I. 418 This glass pierces crucibles and vitrifies them. **1863** A. C. RAMSAY *Phys. Geog.* iv. (1878) 39 Shales, sandstones, &c., are often..vitrified at the points of junction with greenstone, basaltic, and felspathic rocks. **1866** LIVINGSTONE *Last Jrnls.* (1873) I. iii. 79 The clay pipes ..are met with everywhere, often vitrified.

fig. *a* **1618** RALEIGH *Rem.* (1644) 155 Every ordinary wit can vitrifie, and make transparent pieces, and discern their corruptions. *a* **1678** MARVELL *Appleton House* Wks. 1786 III. 221 By her flames, in heaven try'd, Nature is wholly vitrify'd. **1846** MRS. GORE *Eng. Char.* (1852) 102 The soys, ketchups,..and other..compounds, with whose astringent juices we vitrify the coats of our stomachs.

absol. **1664** POWER *Exp. Philos.* I. 54 That..so small a fire can vitrify, will be better understood by him that knows how small a heat at a Lamp-Furnace will melt Glass.

2. *intr.* To become vitreous; to turn into glass or a substance resembling this.

a **1626** BACON *Physiol. Rem.* (1679) 101 We see Metals will vitrify. **1712** tr. *Pomet's Hist. Drugs* I. 103 These are apt to vitrifie, and make Glass and Crystal withal. **1770** *Phil. Trans.* LX. 226, I imagined that metals might not calcine or vitrify except in the same circumstances. **1813** SIR H. DAVY *Agric. Chem.* (1814) 328 Such lime easily vitrifies, in consequence of the affinity of lime for silica and alumina. **1876** PAGE *Adv. Text-bk. Geol.* xiv. 252 Resisting heat without slagging or vitrifying.

Hence **'vitrifying** *vbl. sb.* and *ppl. a.*

1674 BOYLE *Grounds Corpusc. Philos.* 32 So strictly united ..as to maintain their union in the vitrifying violence of the fire. **1756** F. HOME *Exper. Bleaching* 155 The heat was just below the vitrifying point. **1839** URE *Dict. Arts* 1019 White vitrifying pastes, fit for receiving all sorts of metallic colours. *Ibid.* 1159 The vitrifying colours are laid on by means of larger hair pencils.

vitrine ('vɪtriːn), *sb.* [a. F. *vitrine*, f. *vitre* glass.] A glass show-case for specimens or for objects of art. (Also *attrib.* in ***vitrine table***.)

1880 C. SCHREIBER *Jrnl.* 19 Nov. (1911) II. 328 A small ornament... I believe it to be Spanish, [but]..I only saw it as it lay in the vitrine at the Exposition. **1886** *Athenæum* 27 Mar. 430/2 Four large vitrines in the Vase Room are now appropriated to the display of the Greek examples.

†**vitrine**, *a. Obs.*⁻⁰ [ad. med.L. *vitrīn-us*, f. L. *vitrum* glass.] Vitreous.

1656 [see VITREAN *a.*].

vitrinite ('vɪtrɪnaɪt). [f. VITR(AIN + *-inite* (f. -IN¹ + -ITE¹).] One of the three major kinds of maceral that go to make up humic coal, rich in oxygen and characteristic of vitrain.

1935 M. C. STOPES in *Fuel* XIV. 11 It is now proposed to give to the individual 'macerals' a distinctive set of descriptive names with the termination *-inite*... The basis of the grouping is very simple and the names logical; and the whole therefore can easily be built up from: Rock types... Vitrain..Fusain..Clarain..Durain. Macerals... Vitrinite ..Fusinite..[etc.]. **1955** *Sci. Amer.* July 62/1 The broadest attack on the problem was launched in 1951 by the British Coal Utilization Research Association, which set out to analyze..a series of vitrinites—bright black coal particles —from typical coals. **1964** *Fuel* XLIII. 123 It is..suggested that the reflectance of vitrinite A occurring in the whole coal may provide the best available index of rank. **1978** *Nature* 7 Dec. 598/1 The most common methods of estimating the degree of thermal alteration [of petroleum source rocks] are based on measurements of the residual insoluble organic material in rocks. Some of the more common methods use ..electron spin resonance, kerogen coloration and vitrinite reflectance.

vitrinopal: see VITRITE.

vitriol ('vɪtrɪəl), *sb.* Forms: 4–5 vitriole, 5 vit-, vytreole, 5–6 vytryol(e, 6–7 vitrioll (6 -olle), 5– vitriol; 5–7 vitriall, 6–7 vitrial, 7 vitraell. [a. OF. (also F.) *vitriol* 13th c.; = Sp. and Pg. *vitriolo*, It. *vetriolo*, *-iuolo*, *vitriolo*, *-iuolo*, *-ivuolo*) or directly ad. med.L. *vitriolum* (Albertus Magnus) f. *vitrum* glass.]

1. One or other of various native or artificial sulphates of metals (see 2 and 3) used in the arts or medicinally, esp. sulphate of iron: **a.** Used in *sing.* without article.

c **1386** CHAUCER *Can. Yeom. Prol. & T.* 255 Vnslekked lym, chalk,..Poudres diuerse, asshes,..Cered pottes, sal peter, vitriole. **14..** *Voc.* in Wr.-Wülcker 579 *Draganti*, vytryole, or coporose. *a* **1425** tr. *Arderne's Treat. Fistula*, etc. 40 Pulueres of alume, zucarine brent, of attrament, and of vitriol. **1471** RIPLEY *Comp. Alch.* Adm. iv. in Ashm. (1652) 190 Also I wrought in Sulphur and in Vitriall, Whych folys doe call the Grene Lyon. **1527** ANDREW *Brunswyke's Distyll. Waters* F j b, Halfe an ounce of vytryol wherof the ynke is made. **1599** A. M. tr. *Gabelhouer's Bk. Physicke* 317/1 Bloodstenchinge. Take of the best Vitriolle, beate it smalle, and boulte it through a fine cloth. **1612** WOODALL *Surg. Mate* Wks. (1653) 210 Copperas or Vitriol..is a mineral salt which..doth farre excel many other kinds of salts. **1681** tr. *Belon's Myst. Physick* Introd. 38 Those Acides, and acrimonious Particles of the Salt and Vitriol which had caused its Sublimation. **1718** QUINCY *Compl. Disp.* 8 The last is what is forced from Vinegar, Vitriol, and such like acid Substances. **1728** CHAMBERS *Cycl.* s.v., The Antients give the Name *Chalcitis*, or Chalcite, to native Vitriol;..which is a kind of mineral Stone, of a reddish Colour. **1756-7** tr. *Keysler's Trav.* (1760) III. 124 Besides sulphur, vitriol is also made here, of a sapphire colour. **1854** RONALDS & RICHARDSON *Chem. Technol.* (ed. 2) I. 359 The chloride of calcium melting easily in the still, enables the whole of the acetic acid to be evolved at a lower temperature than when vitriol is employed. **1879** MCCARTHY *Own Times* xviii. II. 26 The use of vitriol was recommended among other destructive agencies.

b. In *pl.* (or with *a*).

a **1425** tr. *Arderne's Treat. Fistula*, etc. 79 Of atramentez, i. of vitriolez, bene many kyndez. **1605** TIMME *Quersit.* I. ix. 37 Some of these salts are bytter as wormewood, some sharpe as vitriolls. **1656** J. SMITH *Pract. Physick* 6 They that drink of them purge forth black excrements by reason of the vitrials. **1728** CHAMBERS *Cycl.* s.v., According to Boerhaave, Vitriols consist of a metallic Part with a Sulphur adhering, a menstruous Acid, and Water. **1799** KIRWAN *Geol. Ess.* 395 Vitriols have been discovered buried in the ancient sandy bed of that sea. **1868** WATTS *Dict. Chem.* V. 1004 The several vitriols being distinguished by their colours, or by the metals which they contain.

2. With distinguishing epithets: **a.** With adjs. of colour. ***blue, green, red, white vitriol***, sulphate of copper, iron, cobalt, and zinc respectively.

c **1400** tr. *Lanfranc's Cirurg.* 14 Grene vitriol, & he be do to a man of a drie complexioun, engendrith fleisch. [*a* **1425** tr. *Arderne's Treat. Fistula*, etc. 79 Þer is a spice of vitriol þat is called vitriolum romanum, i. coporose; And it is of ȝalow colour in reward of þe grenner vitriol. And þer is one of white colour bot noȝt schynyng.] **1611** COTGR., *Marcassin iaulne*, Red vitrioll. **1676** *Phil. Trans.* XI. 617 A salt that had some resemblance to white Vitriol. **1728** CHAMBERS *Cycl.* s.v., In Blue Vitriol, the Metal, where-with the Acid, etc. is join'd, is Copper. **1751** GIBSON *Diseases Horses* III. iii. 193 In some cases it [*sc.* the horse's eye] may be touched with the blue Vitriol stone, or the Lunar caustic. **1758** REID tr. *Macquer's Chym.* I. 66 Green Vitriol hath a saltish and astringent taste. **1819** BRANDE *Chem.* 247 Copper and Sulphuric Acid—Oxysulphate of Copper—Blue Vitriol. **1837** DANA *Min.* 180 Cobalt Vitriol..Red Vitriol. Sulphate of Cobalt. **1858** SIMMONDS *Dict. Trade* s.v., White vitriol is a combination of sulphuric-acid and oxide of zinc. **1887** *Buck's Handbk. Med. Sci.* IV. 224/2 Ferrous sulphate is the salt so well known as green vitriol, and also in the impure state as copperas.

b. With other adjs., as ***English, German, Hungarian, Roman vitriol.***

1573 *Art of Limming* 7 Then put in it two unces of greene Coporas, or els of Romayne Vitrial, which is beste. **1611** COTGR., *Vitriol d'Allemagne*, German Vitrioll. *Ibid.*, *Vitriol d'Hongrie*, Hungarie Vitrioll. **1617** MORYSON *Itin.* III. 134 The English bring into France..Leade, Tynne, English Vitriall, or Shoemakers blacke. **1651** FRENCH *Distill.* iii. 66 Take of Hungarian, or the best English Vitriall. **1728** CHAMBERS *Cycl.* s.v., Roman Vitriol is made by exposing these Pyrites to the Air, till such time as they calcine. **1741** *Compl. Fam.-Piece* I. i. 46 Take Hungarian Vitriol, Allum, of each half a Pound, Phlegm of Vitriol 10 Pounds. **1837** *Penny Cycl.* VII. 505/1 Sulphuric acid and copper form sulphate of copper, blue vitriol, or Roman vitriol, or blue copperas.

3. With term indicating the base, as ***vitriol of cobalt, copper, iron, lead, silver***, etc.

1695 W. W. *New Light Chirurg. Put out* 61 The Pouder consists of a Vitriol of Copper. **1699** SALMON *Bate's Dispens.* (1715) 453/1 Of this opened Sol, to make Vitriol of Gold. **1704** HARRIS *Lex. Techn.* I, *Vitriol of Copper* or *Venus*, is Blue Chrystals made by a Solution of Copper in Spirit of Nitre, Evaporation, and Chrystallization in a cool place. *Ibid.*, *Vitriol of Silver*, or of the *Moon.* **1753** *Chambers' Cycl.* Suppl. s.v., Of this kind are the Vitriols of gold, silver, copper, iron, lead, and tin. *Ibid.*, Vitriol of Quicksilver, the name of a chemical preparation of quick-silver, with acid spirits. *Ibid.*, Another method of making the Vitriol of mercury. **1791** *Phil. Trans.* LXXXI. 381 Fused..on a plate of platina, with the vitriols of tartar and soda, it appeared entirely to resist their action. **1796** KIRWAN *Elem. Min.* (ed. 2) II. 90 If they are considered..as Vitriols of Cobalt and Nickel, they are ranged among Ores. **1800** *Med. Jrnl.* IV. 288 The patient bore large doses of the vitriols of copper and of zinc.

†**b.** ***vitriol of Mars, Moon, Venus***, etc. (see quots. and 1704 in prec.). *Obs.*

1678 SALMON *Pharm. Lond.* 836/2 Filings of Steel are digested in Spirit of Vitriol, to make Vitriol of Mars. **1696** PHILLIPS (ed. 5), *Vitriol of Mars*, Iron and Spirit of Vitriol mix'd and distill'd together. **1704** J. HARRIS *Lex. Techn.* I, *Vitriol of Mars*, or *Salt of Steel*, is made by dissolving Steel in some proper Acid Menstruum then Evaporating and Chrystallizing to gain the Salt as above in Copper. **1758** REID tr. *Macquer's Chym.* I. 66 These crystals are called Green Vitriol, and Vitriol of Mars.

4. a. ***oil of vitriol***, concentrated sulphuric acid.

1580 FRAMPTON tr. *Monardes' Med. agst. Venome* 117 b, In our time there hath been compounded and drawen out an Oyle, which they call Oyle of Vitrioll or Coporace. **1611** COTGR., *Huile de vie*, Oyle of Vitrioll. **1660** BOYLE *New Exp. Phys. Mech.* xxii. 176 This we fill'd with Oyl of Vitriol and fair water. **1728** CHAMBERS *Cycl.* s.v., Oil of Vitriol, which comes out after the Spirit, by heightning the Fire wherewith that had been rais'd. **1779** *Phil. Trans.* LXX. 31 Add, by a little at a time, as much vitriolic acid, commonly sold by the name of oil of vitriol, as will re-dissolve the whole. **1827** FARADAY *Chem. Manip.* xv. (1842) 391 Pouring in so much concentrated oil of vitriol as shall moisten the fragments. **1878** HUXLEY *Physiogr.* 102 Water made slightly sour by addition of a little oil of vitriol.

b. ***spirit(s) of vitriol***, a distilled essence of vitriol.

1671 R. BOHUN *Wind* 175 Such as Oyl of Tartar and spirit of Vitriol. **1674** *Phil. Trans.* IX. 44 As for the Acid Saline Principle, I suppose no person who hath tasted the Spirit of Vitriol,..will question its abounding in that subject. **1728** CHAMBERS *Cycl.* s.v. *Salt*, Spirit of Nitre,..Spirit of Salt,..and Spirit of Vitriol. **1771** *Encycl. Brit.* II. 72/1 If the vitriolic acid contain much water, it is then called spirit of vitriol. **1789** W. BUCHAN *Dom. Med.* (1790) 223 This may be sharpened with the spirits of vitriol. **1859** MAYNE *Expos. Lex.* 1336 *Vitriol, Sweet Spirit of*,..a term for..sulphuric ether.

fig. **1679** ALSOP *Melius Inq.* II. i. 174 The Medicine is the same; only Rome has added a few drops of the Spirits of Vitriol.

†**c.** ***colcothar, earth, salt, of vitriol***: see quots. Also *elixir of vitriol*: see ELIXIR *sb.* 4.

1684 tr. *Bonet's Merc. Compit.* I. 21 Comatous children are ..cured by Vomitive Salt of Vitriol. **1699** SALMON *Bate's Dispens.* (1715) 453/2 *Terra Vitrioli dulcis*, sweet Earth of Vitriol. **1753** *Chambers' Cycl.* Suppl. s.v. *Sulphur*, Colcothar, or fixed salt of vitriol. **1755** *Dict. Arts & Sci.* s.v., A fine purple matter, called colcothar of vitriol. **1799** G. SMITH *Laboratory* I. 95 Take red calcined vitriol, or colcothar of vitriol.

5. *fig.* (In allusion to the corrosive properties of vitriol.) Virulence or acrimony of feeling or utterance.

1769 *Junius Lett.* xv. (1788) 90 Flat and insipid in your retired state, but brought into action you become vitriol again. **1872** SPURGEON *Treas. David* Ps. lv. 3 They..cast the vitriol of their calumny over me. **1895** *Literary World* (Boston) 8 Nov. 359/1 This introduction, with its mixture of genius, shrewdness, and vitriol, is a piece of prose not to be missed.

6. *attrib.* and *Comb.*, as ***vitriol bath, chamber, -maker, marcasite, -thrower, -throwing, water***; **vitriol ochre**, a former name of glockerite; †**vitriol stone**, a native vitriol or sulphate.

1669 BOYLE *Certain Physiol. Ess.* (ed. 2) *Absol. Rest Bodies* 15 A bulky Marchasite that I procur'd from a Virtuoso that lives just by a Vitriol-work, whither these among other Vitriol-Stones are brought. **1670** [see VITRIOLIC *a.* 1]. **1675** E. WILSON *Spadacr. Dunelm.* 43 Two vitriol waters in the Copper Mine of Herongrundt. **1676** WISEMAN *Surg. Treat.* v. ix. 378 If in the incarning the Wound the Flesh grows luxurious, touch it with a Vitriol-stone, and it will..dispose it to cicatrize. **1755** *Dict. Arts & Sci.* s.v., The old iron, picked up by the poor people about our streets, is sold to the vitriol or copperas makers. **1843** THACKERAY *Irish Sk.-bk.* viii, We had a talk about the vitriol-throwers at Cork, and the sentence just passed upon them. **1849** HT. MARTINEAU *Hist. Peace* v. v. (1877) III. 263 They mourned over the murders, and vitriol-throwing of the operatives, who were enslaved by mercenary delegates. **1867** BLOXAM *Chem.* 203 Reactions in the Vitriol Chambers. **1867** AUGUSTA WILSON *Vashti* iv, Compassion is about as welcome to my feelings as a vitriol bath to fresh wounds.

Hence **'vitriol** *v. trans.*, to injure (a person) by means of vitriol; to expose (a thing) to the effects of vitriol.

1897 *Westm. Gaz.* 16 Dec. 5/2, I do not want to be killed, and I have a particular objection to being vitrioled.

† **'vitriolate**, *a. Obs.* Also 7 vitriolet. [ad. med. or mod.L. **vitriolāt-us*, f. *vitriolum* vitriol. Cf. It. *vitriolato*, Sp. and Pg. *vitriolado*, F. *vitriolé*.]

1. Of or belonging to, resembling that of, vitriol.

1646 SIR T. BROWNE *Pseud. Ep.* VI. xii. 336 A vitriolate or copperose quality conjoyning with a terrestrious and astringent humidity. **1665-6** *Phil. Trans.* I. 323 This had some-what of a Vitriolate taste. **1672** BOYLE *Ess. Gems* 159 Particles which..I observ'd to be of a Vitriolate nature.

2. Treated with vitriol. ***vitriolate tartar*** (see VITRIOLATED 3 a).

1665 NEEDHAM *Medel. Medicinae* 513 As we see in Tartar Vitriolate. **1671** SALMON *Syn. Med.* III. lxxxiv. 730 Vitriolate Tartar taken in Broath,..extract of Hellebore [etc.]..are here good. **1684** tr. *Bonet's Merc. Compit.* III. 95, I gave him Spring-water corrected with Vitriolate Syrup of Rasberries. **1704** [see TARTAR¹ 3 b]. **1782** KIRWAN in *Phil. Trans.* LXXIII. 40 The same double decomposition will be produced if, instead of tartar vitriolate, glauber's salt be used.

3. Affected by, impregnated with, vitriol.

1666 BOYLE *Orig. Forms & Qual.* 339 This Vitriolate Nitre (if I may so call it). **1670** H. STUBBE *Plus Ultra* 131 It is also..manifest, that there are in the bodies of men.. solutions or liquors imbued with sundry salts, as aluminous, acid, and vitriolate, etc. **1684** BOYLE *Porousn. Anim. & Solid Bod.* viii. 125 So that their Texture was spoiled by the saline and vitriolate Corpuscles.

b. Of water, springs, etc.

1666 *Phil. Trans.* I. 359 That Pool..seems to be of Vitriolate water. **1667** *Ibid.* II. 469 The Iron, that is said to be turned into Copper, by the Vitriolate Springs at Cremnitz..in Hungary. **1670** *Ibid.* V. 1043 There are also two Springs of a Vitriolat water, which are affirm'd to turn iron into Copper. **1751** *Eng. Gazetteer* s.v. *Worton-Lower*, A vitriolate ferrugineous spring.

'vitriolate, *v. rare.* [Cf. prec. and -ATE³.] *trans.* To affect or treat with vitriol; to render vitriolic.

1605 TIMME *Quersit.* I. vii. 27 By reason of a singular temper of sharpness vitriolated by sweet and sulphurus spirits. **1828-32** WEBSTER, *Vitriolate*, to convert, as sulphur in any compound, into sulphuric acid, formerly called vitriolic acid.

'vitriolated, *ppl. a.* [f. prec. or VITRIOLATE *a.*]

†**1.** = VITRIOLATE *a.* 1. *Obs.*⁻¹

1651 BIGGS *New Dispens.* ¶ 144 The acid saline vitriolated qualities of wine, vineger, or juice of Limons.

2. Impregnated with vitriol: **a.** Of liquids.

a **1626** MEVEREL in *Bacon's Physiol. Rem.* (1679) 125 Iron may be dissolved by any tart, salt, or vitriolated Water. **1670** H. STUBBE *Plus Ultra* 154 The vitriolated Serum would not flame; the vitriolated blood did burn with a brisk but short flame. **1756** F. HOME *Exper. Bleaching* 185 The liquor more acid than the vitriolated liquor in the foregoing experiment.

b. Of minerals, etc., affected by native sulphates.

1794 R. J. SULIVAN *View Nat.* I. 250 Vitriolated clay, or alum, is rarely found. **1796** KIRWAN *Elem. Min.* (ed. 2) II. 113 Mr. Bergman..deduces the origin of Vitriolated Silver, from the withering and Acidification of the Sulphurated Silver Ores. **1802-3** tr. *Pallas's Trav.* (1812) I. 87 The vitriolated layers of mire still exhibit traces of sea-weeds and marshes. **1805** W. SAUNDERS *Min. Waters* 49 Any spring of water that flows in the neighbourhood, will hence contain both alum and vitriolated iron.

3. Treated with vitriol: **a.** ***vitriolated tartar***, sulphate of potassium. (Cf. TARTAR¹ 3 b.)

1694 SALMON *Bate's Dispens.* (1713) 628/1 Antimonial Tartar vitriolated. **1728** CHAMBERS *Cycl.* s.v. *Tartar*, Tartar Vitriolated, which some call Magistery of Tartar, is Oil of Tartar mix'd with rectify'd Spirit of Vitriol. **1758** REID tr. *Macquer's Chym.* I. 25 Vitriolated Tartar is almost as hard to dissolve in water as the Selenites. **1789** *Trans. Soc. Arts* I. 183 An innocent neutral salt, vitriolated tartar. **1836** BRANDE *Chem.* (ed. 4) 36 The residuum in the retort furnishes vitriolated tartar. **1887** *Buck's Handbk. Med. Sci.* V. 795/2 Potassic sulphate..is the salt formerly called vitriolated tartar and *sal de duobus*.

b. With other sbs., as ***ammonia, iron***, etc.

1788 *Phil. Trans.* LXXVIII. 395 Of vitriolated natron (Glauber's salt) four parts. **1799** *Monthly Rev.* XXX. 67 Eight grains of myrrh, a grain and a half of vitriolated iron. **1801** *Encycl. Brit.* Suppl. I. 360/1 Sulphat of ammonia.. was also called vitriolated ammoniac. **1804** ABERNETHY *Surg. Obs.* (1827) 169, I gave her emetics of vitriolated zinc and copper. **1823** CRABB *Technol. Dict.*, *Vitriolated Alkali* (Chem.), the sulphate of potash.

vitrio'lation. [f. VITRIOLATE *v.*] (See quot.)

1828-32 WEBSTER, *Vitriolation*, the act or process of converting into sulphuric acid or vitriol.

†**vitrio'lescent**, *a. Obs.*⁻¹ [f. VITRIOL *sb.* + -ESCENT.] Passing into a vitriolated state. Hence **vitrio'lescence**.

1757 tr. *Henckel's Pyritol.* 60 Dissolved, crumbled, vitriolescent copper-pyrites. *Ibid.* 296 The spontaneous vitriolescence of pyrites.

vitriolet, variant of VITRIOLATE *a.*

vitriolic (vɪtrɪ'ɒlɪk), *a.* and *sb.* Also 7-8 vitriolick, 7 -ike, -iq(ue. [ad. F. *vitriolique* (16th c., = It., Sp., Pg. *vitriolico*), or f. VITRIOL *sb.* + -IC.]

A. *adj.* **1.** Of or belonging to vitriol; having the nature or qualities of vitriol; impregnated with vitriol.

1670 W. SIMPSON *Hydrol. Ess.* 62 The solution of the vitriol marcasite..precipitates the same vitriolick oaker. **1676** GREW *Anat. Pl.*, *Exper. Luctation* ii. §4 Irish Slat.. seems to be nothing else but a Vitriolick Bole. **1707** FLOYER *Physic. Pulse-Watch* 257 In the Quartans, the..Pain is from the vitriolic Cacochymia. **1760** *Phil. Trans.* LI. 470 It is of a subacid taste, and very nauseously vitriolic. **1774** GOLDSM. *Nat. Hist.* (1862) I. xi. 215 A mucous substance, which had something of a vitriolic quality, settled under the reticular membrane. **1802** PLAYFAIR *Illustr. Hutton. The.* 33 This compound of metal and sulphur..is destroyed by the contact of moisture and resolved into a vitriolic salt. **1844** *Civil Eng. & Arch. Jrnl.* VII. 108/1 If the pit water be vitriolic..it becomes necessary to use every means to procure better water. **1899** F. T. BULLEN *Log Sea-waif* 49 A fiery white spirit, fresh from the still... This vitriolic stuff seemed to meet every emergency.

b. ***vitriolic acid***, oil of vitriol.

1747 WALL in *Phil. Trans.* XLIV. Suppl. 588, I acidulated the Liquors with the vitriolic Acid. **1778** W. PRYCE *Min. Cornub.* 54 It entirely resists the vitriolick acid, which dissolves or corrodes every other known metallick body, except Gold. **1802** MAR. EDGEWORTH *Moral T.*, *Forrester*, *Banknotes*, The large bottle of vitriolic acid was broken. **1842** ORDERSON *Creol.* xiii. 137 The gas was generated from steel filings and vitriolic acid.

2. *fig.* Of language, persons, etc.: Extremely sharp, caustic, or scathing; bitterly ill-natured or malignant.

1841 H. F. CHORLEY *Music & Mann.* III. 31 Venting a flood of vitriolic sarcasm, or a flight of high-toned poetry. **1866** E. P. WHIPPLE *Characters & Charac. Men* 5 Robespierre..[and] Frederick of Prussia..were both bitter and vitriolic natures. **1879** MCCARTHY *Hist. Own Times* II. 197 He never became more than a great Parliamentary critic of the acrid and vitriolic style. **1903** COLEMAN *C. Reade* III. v. (1904) 324 For vitriolic vigour this epistle excels anything in the language.

B. *sb.* A vitriolic substance. *Obs.*⁻¹

a **1700** EVELYN *Diary* 7 Nov. 1651, It had a taste of a strong vitriolíq, and smelt like aqua fortis.

vitriolico-, combining form of prec., employed in a few chemical terms, as ***vitriolico-antimoniated, -muriated, -neutral.***

1782 KIRWAN in *Phil. Trans.* LXXIII. 49 Whenever a vitriolico-neutral salt..is evaporated to a certain degree, the vitriolic expels these acids in its turn. **1796** —— *Elem. Min.* (ed. 2) II. 113 [Silver] Vitriolico muriated, or Corneous Silver Ore. *Ibid.* 122 Vitriolico Antimoniated Silver Ore.

vitri'olify, *v. rare*$^{-0}$. [f. VITRIOL *sb.* + -(I)FY.] *trans.* To vitriolize. Hence **vitri'olifying** *ppl. a.*
1674 *Phil. Trans.* IX. 71 The expansion of some of those prodigiously active Springy particles..which together with the Aerial Salt were arrested by the Vitriolifying principle.

†**'vitrioline**, *a. Obs.* [f. VITRIOL *sb.* + -INE[1].] Resembling vitriol; vitriolic.
1652 FRENCH *Yorksh. Spa* iii. 34 Astringing waters, as Alluminous, and Vitrioline almost every where. *a* **1661** FULLER *Worthies, Yorks.* (1662) III. 188 In a morish boggy ground ariseth a spring of a Vitrioline tast and odour. **1684** tr. *Bonet's Merc. Compit.* III. 52 The Bath waters, wherein the vitrioline virtue is most eminent. **1703** *Phil. Trans.* XXV. 1573 How far these Stones are the effect of a Vitrioline Juice, I will not determin.

vitrio'lizable, *a.* [f. VITRIOLIZE *v.* + -ABLE.] That may be vitriolized; capable of being converted into vitriol.
1796 KIRWAN *Elem. Min.* (ed. 2) II. 82 That the Iron, in Pyrites, [is] spontaneously Vitriolizable. **1828–32** WEBSTER. [Hence in later Dicts.]

vitrioli'zation. [f. next + -ATION.] The process of converting, or of being converted, into a vitriol.
1757 tr. *Henckel's Pyritol.* 109 The vitriolisation of pyrites. **1782** KIRWAN in *Phil. Trans.* LXXIII. 74 As Mr. Monnet has observed in his excellent Treatise on Vitriolization. **1804** *Ibid.* XCIV. 318 The magnetical pyrites ..seems to be liable to oxidizement, but not to vitriolization.

vitriolize ('vɪtrɪəlaɪz), *v.* [f. VITRIOL *sb.*]
1. a. *trans.* To convert into vitriol; to vitriolate. Also *absol.*
1694 SALMON *Bate's Dispens.* (1713) 453/1 Dissolve again in fair Water and crystallize or vitriolize as before. **1799** KIRWAN *Geol. Ess.* 395 By long exposure to the air and moisture they are at last vitriolized.
b. *intr.* To become vitriolated or vitriolic.
1757 tr. *Henckel's Pyritol.* 327 Such pyritæ as vitriolise sparingly and leisurely. **1796** KIRWAN *Elem. Min.* (ed. 2) II. 80 There are some that spontaneously effloresce and vitriolize.
2. *trans.* To injure with vitriol; to throw vitriol at (a person) with intent to injure.
1886 *Daily News* 15 March (Cassell's), The jury did not believe that the child from the same motive vitriolized himself. **1901** *Daily Chron.* 24 July 4/6 The painful case of a handsome girl who was 'vitriolised' by a rival.
Hence **'vitriolized** *ppl. a.* Also **'vitriolizer**, one who throws vitriol with intent to injure.
1882 *Pall Mall G.* 13 Nov. 2 Thinking he had to deal with a vitriolizer the servant ran down to call a policeman. **1891** *Ibid.* 9 Nov. 7/1 Vitriolized spices and arsenicated coffee. **1894** *Westm. Gaz.* 17 Oct. 6/3 With vitriolised drink supplied to you at fabulous prices.

†**'vitriolous**, *a. Obs.* [f. VITRIOL *sb.* + -OUS. Cf. OF. *vitrioleux.*] Of the nature of vitriol; vitriolic.
1646 SIR T. BROWNE *Pseud. Ep.* III. xxii. 164 Some attrition from an acide and vitriolous humidity in the stomack. *Ibid.* VI. xii. 336, I say, a vitriolous or copperous quality; for vitrioll is the active or chiefe ingredient in Inke. **1707** *Curios. in Husb. & Gard.* 56 Vitriolous, nitrous, &c. Spirits.

vitrious, obs. form of VITREOUS *a.*

vitrisch, variant of VITRY *Obs.*

vitrite ('vɪtraɪt). *Min.* [f. L. *vitr-um* glass + -ITE[1].] (See quots.)
1866 LAWRENCE tr. *Cotta's Rocks Class.* (1878) 341 Opal, as a rock, usually only forms very subordinate masses, e.g. the so-called vitrite, which occurs at Meronitz, in Bohemia. **1868** WATTS *Dict. Chem.* V. 1004 *Vitrinopal, Vitrite*, the matrix of Bohemian pyrope, related to pitchstone.

'vitro-, combining form on Gr. models of L. *vitrum* glass, used in a few terms, as **vitro-'dentine**, the hard external layer of dentine in a tooth; **'vitrophyre**, a subdivision of porphyritic rocks; hence **vitrophyric** *a.*; **'vitrotype** (see quot. 1875).
1849–52 *Todd's Cycl. Anat.* IV. 882/1 The dental plate consists..of a central mass of coarse osseous substance.. and an external sheath of very hard 'vitro-dentine'. **1870** tr. *Stricker's Man. Histology* xv. (N. Syd. Soc.) 471 The central portion [of a tooth] consists of vaso-dentine, which is covered with true dentine; external to which again is a thin layer of vitro-dentine. **1875** KNIGHT *Dict. Mech.* 2713/2 *Vitro-type* (Photography), a name given to the processes which involve the production of collodion film pictures on glass. **1882** GEIKIE *Text-Bk. Geol.* II. II. iii. 90 Vogelsang has proposed to classify this type [Porphyritic] in three divisions: 1st, Granophyre,..2nd, Felsophyre,..3rd, Vitrophyre, where the ground-mass is a glassy magna. **1890** *Philos. Mag.* March 288 Among the pyroxenic rocks the most noticeable varieties are the labradorite-audesites, the pyroxene-audesites—of which both 'trachytoid' and 'vitrophyric' forms occur.

Vitrolite ('vɪtrəʊlaɪt). Also vitro-. [f. L. *vitr-um* glass + -O + -LITE.] A proprietary name for opal glass.
1937 *Times* 19 Oct. 11/3 A glass floor has been laid, and glass pictures have been hung, and a bathroom lined with vitrolite is being built. **1939** *Trade Marks Jrnl.* 1 Feb. 147/1 *Vitrolite*... Opal and opaline glass. Pilkington Brothers Limited,..Liverpool, 2; glass manufacturers. **1954** *Archit. Rev.* CXVI. 268/1 Such an atmosphere is not created by stove-enamelled hardboard, vitrolite and chromium-plated barrier rails, the language of the cafeteria. **1975** [see OPALITE].

†**vitrose**, *a. Obs.*$^{-0}$ [ad. L. type **vitrōs-us*, f. *vitrum* glass.] 'Glassy, full of glass.'
1727 BAILEY (vol. II).

'vitrous, *a. rare.* [f. L. *vitr-um* glass. Cf. F. *vitreux*, and med.L. *vitrus* adj.] Vitreous.
1657 *Physical Dict.*, *Vitrous humor*, a moisture like to molten glass or chrystal, which is a part of the eye. **1779** SIR W. HAMILTON in *Phil. Trans.* LXX. 51 *note*, A flexible, capillary, yellow glass,..wih small vitrous globules at a little distance one from the other. **1859** MAYNE *Expos. Lex.* 1336 Omalius admitted a genus of vitrous rocks comprehending the silicated, vitrified stones or rocks.

†**'vitrum.** *Obs. rare.* [L.] Glass; a glassy substance; a glass vessel.
1657 *Physical Dict.*, *Vitrum*, glass: it's used to signifie glass distilling vessels, or any other vessels made of glass. **1665** HOOKE *Microgr.* 51 A certain thin Lamina of a vitrum or vitrified part of the Metal. **1694** SALMON *Bate's Dispens.* (1713) 547/1 Le Febure makes the Salt..of the Glass.., but he mingles the Vitrum with its equal Weight of Sulphur in Pouder.

Vitruvian (vɪ'truːvɪən), *a.* [f. the name of M. *Vitruvius* Pollio, a Roman architect and writer on architecture (*c* 10 B.C.).] Of, relating to, or in the style of Vitruvius.
1762 H. WALPOLE *Vertue's Anecd. Paint.* (1765) I. 116 Our buildings must be as Vitruvian, as writings in the days of Erasmus were obliged to be Ciceronian. **1835** R. WILLIS *Archit. Mid. Ages* ii. 23 *note*, The later [Alberti] published the first treatise on the Vitruvian architecture, in 1485. **1893** SYMONDS *Michelangelo* xiii. II. 217 Church, cupola, and spires are built up by a succession of Vitruvian temples.
b. ***Vitruvian scroll***, a convoluted scroll-pattern employed as an architectural ornament.
1837 *Antiq. Athens* 19 A sort of thatch of laurel leaves, surrounded by an ornamental edge, usually termed a Vitruvian scroll. **1886** G. SCHUMACHER *Across the Jordan* iii. 173 A lintel-stone..which is..ornamented with the seven-branched candlestick and a sort of vitruvian scroll.
Hence **Vi'truvianism**, the style or principles of architecture favoured by Vitruvius.
1859 JEPHSON *Brittany* viii. 115 Going straight from the debased flamboyant or perpendicular to Vitruvianism.

†**'vitry.** *Obs.* Forms: 5 **vettris**, *Sc.* **vitrisch**; 6 **vitre**, 7 **vitree**, **vitrie**, **vittry**, 8 **vitry**; 6–7 **vittery**, 9 **vittory**. [ad. F. *Vitré*, the name of a town in Brittany. The early forms in *-is*, *-isch* prob. represent F. *Vitrées* pl., canvas cloths made at Vitré.] ***Vitry canvas***, a kind of light durable canvas. (Cf. VANDELAS.) Also *ellipt.*
c **1425** *Foreign Accts.* 59 m. 23 a (P.R.O.), [A ship's bonnet containing] iiij di' uln' canab' de vettris. **1497** *Acc. Ld. High Treas. Scot.* I. 345 For xiiij elne of vetrisch cammas to ane litil palʒoune of the Kingis, xiiij s. **1534** *Exch. Acc.* 58/13 Vittery canvas. **1599** NASHE *Lenten Stuff* 27 For which is alwaies paide ready Golde, with salt, Canuas Vitre, and a great deale of good trash. **1612** *Ledger A. Halyburton* (1867) 319 Vandolose or Vitrie canves the eln, x s. **1617** MORYSON *Itin.* III. 134 And they bring from thence Linnen cloathes, called white Roanes and Vitree Canvas. **1640** in Entick *London* (1766) II. 167 Linnens,..narrow vandales, or vittry canvas. **1721** C. KING *Brit. Merch.* I. 181, 17000 Hund. of Vitry and Noyals Canvas. *Ibid.* 284 Canvas Vitry,..Canvas Norman. **1757** J. H. GROSE *Voy. E. Indies* 176 Holland's duck, or vitry, is whilst in use, more pliant, and less apt to split. **1867** SMYTH *Sailor's Word-bk.* 714 *Vitry*, a light and durable canvas. *Ibid.*, *Vittory*, a fine canvas, of which the waist-cloths were formerly made.

Vitsonday, obs. Sc. form of WHITSUNDAY.

‖**vitta** ('vɪtə). Pl. **vittæ** ('vɪtiː). [L. *vitta* a band, fillet, chaplet, esp. one worn round the head.]
†**1.** *Anat.* (See quot.) *Obs.*$^{-0}$
1693 tr. *Blancard's Phys. Dict.* (ed. 2), *Vitta*, that part of the Coat call'd *Amnion*, which sticks to the Infants Head when 'tis just Born. [Hence in Phillips, 1706, etc.]
2. *Rom. Antiq.* (See quots.)
Neither of the applications rests upon L. usage.
1726 A. GORDON *Itin. Sept.* 77 He [*sc.* a Roman soldier] has a Sash or Vitta coming over his Breast, reaching to his Middle. **1847** *Kitto's Cycl. Bibl. Lit.* I. 227/2 The objects above denominated appendages and vittæ..were straps of leather secured to the lower rim of the barrel of a suit of armour, and to the openings for arm-holes.
3. *Zool.* A band or stripe of colour.
1819 STEPHENS in *Shaw's Gen. Zool.* XI. II. 346 The hypochondria [of the Guernsey Partridge] marked with a double black vitta. **1849** JOHNSTON in *Proc. Berw. Nat. Club* II. 365 Mite..marked on the back with a dark vitta or line forming two sigmoid flexures. **1875** G. N. LAWRENCE *Birds S.W. Mexico* 51 *Larus californicus*..bill grayish-white, behind the yellowish-white tip a black vitta.
b. *Bot.* (See quot.)
1843 *Penny Cycl.* XXVI. 403/2 The term vittæ is also sometimes applied to the various stripes which are found upon leaves, and which either arise from irregular distribution or entire deficiency of colouring-matter.
4. *Bot.* **a.** One of a number of elongated club-shaped canals or tubes occurring in the pericarp of the fruit of most umbelliferous plants and containing their characteristic oil. Usually in pl.
1830 LINDLEY *Nat. Syst. Bot.* 4 The ridges are separated by channels, below which are often placed, in the substance of the pericarp, certain linear receptacles of coloured oily matter, called *vittæ*. **1847** STEELE *Field Bot.* 30 Vittæ on the upper half of the fruit only..*Heracleum.* Vittæ as long as fruit... *Peucedanum.* **1870** HOOKER *Stud. Flora* 156 Trinia ..primary ridges subequal, thick, smooth, rugose or plaited, with a large *vitta* inside each.
b. One of a number of internal projections occurring in the valves of diatomaceous plants.
1888 *Cassell's Encycl. Dict.* **1900** JACKSON *Gloss. Bot. Terms.*

vittail(e, obs. forms of VICTUAL *sb.* and *v.*

vittandly, obs. Sc. variant of WITTINGLY *adv.*

vittate ('vɪtət), *a.* [ad. L. *vittāt-us* bound with a fillet or chaplet, f. *vitta* VITTA + -ATE[2].]
1. *Zool.*, *Bot.*, etc. Marked or striped with vittæ. Cf. VITTATED *a.*
1826 KIRBY & SP. *Entomol.* IV. xlvi. 290 Vittate (*Vittata*), painted with several such stripes. **1866** *Treas. Bot.* 1224/1 *Vittate*, striped lengthwise.
2. *Bot.* Having a vitta or vittæ (sense 4 a).
Chiefly in combination, *1-vittate*.
1870 HOOKER *Stud. Flora* 153 Eryngium;..primary ridges obscure 1-vittate.

'vittated, *a. Zool.*, *Ornith.*, etc. *rare.* [f. as prec. + -ED[2].] = prec. 1.
Only in the specific names of a few birds, reptiles, etc.
1790 LATHAM *Ind. Ornith.* II. 827 *Procellaria vittata*,.. Vittated Petrel. **1802** SHAW *Gen. Zool.* III. II. 533 Vittated Snake. *Coluber Vittatus.* **1804** *Ibid.* V. I. 22 Vittated Silure. *Silurus Vittatus.*

vitte, obs. f. WIT *sb.*

vittee, dial. var. FITTY *a.*[1]

Vittel (viː'tɛl). The proprietary name of a type of mineral water obtained from springs in the neighbourhood of the town of *Vittel* in the Vosges department of France. Also ***Vittel water***.
1895 *Army & Navy Co-op. Soc. Price List* 23 Natural mineral waters..Vichy..Vittel..Wiesbaden. **1909** *Trade Marks Jrnl.* 26 May 901 *Vittel*... A natural mineral water. Société Générale des Eaux Minérales de Vittel,..Vittel, Vosges, France. **1974** N. FREELING *Dressing of Diamond* 76 Carafe of Beaujolais and a bottle of Vittel. **1975** —— *What are Bugles blowing For?* i. 4 He..drank a little Vittel water and went to bed. **1979** 'M. HEBDEN' *Death set to Music* iii. 29, I ought to have had Vittel water, not wine.

vittel(l, obs. ff. VICTUAL *sb.* and *v.*

vitteller, -lour, etc. obs. ff. VICTUALLER.

vittely, obs. Sc. f. WITTILY *adv.*

vitten, dial. var. FITTEN *sb.* and *a.*

†**vittered**, variant of FITTERED *ppl. a. Obs.*
a **1400** *Minor Poems fr. Vernon MS.* 335/265 Viterde hodes and Clokes also, Al þat vile pride schal don hem ful wo. **1578** LYTE *Dodoens* 609 The wilde Ache or Parseley hath large leaves, al jagged, cut, and vittered, much like the leaves of the wilde Carrot.

vittering, Sc. form of WITTERING.

vitterly, Sc. form of WITTERLY *adv. Obs.*

vittery, var. VITRY *Obs.*

vittie-vayr: see VETIVER.
[**1843** *Penny Cycl.* XXVI. 403 *Vittie-vayr*, the Tamool name, sometimes written *Woetiwear*, of the highly fragrant roots of a grass which is found in many parts of India.] **1861** BENTLEY *Man. Bot.* 699 *Andropogon muricatus*, Vittie-vayr or Cuscus, yields a fragrant oil according to Dr. Hooker.

vitting, obs. Sc. form of WITTING *vbl. sb.*

vittle, obs. or dial. f. VICTUAL *sb.*; obs. f. VICTUAL *v.*

†**vittorin.** Anglicized f. VETTURINO. *Obs.*
1613 SIR A. SHERLEY *Trav. Persia* 24 He brought me to a Vittorin, of whom he had already hired Horses, Camels, and Moiles for me.

vittory, vittry, var. VITRY *Obs.*

vitty, dial. or slang var. of FITTY *a.*; obs. Sc. f. WITTY *a.*

vittyng, obs. Sc. f. WITTING *vbl. sb.*

†**'vitulate**, *v. Obs.*$^{-0}$ [f. L. *vītulāt-* ppl. stem of *vītulārī* to celebrate a festival, keep holiday, be joyful.] *intr.* 'Wantonly to rejoice' (Cockeram I, 1623).

†**vitu'lation.** *Obs. rare.* [ad. late L. *vītulātio* (Macrobius), noun of action f. L. *vītulārī*: see prec.] A public thanksgiving or festival.
In quots. erroneously associated with L. *vitulus* a calf.
1607 TOPSELL *Four-f. Beasts* 90 The auncients called Victoria by the name of the Goddesse Vitula, bycause they sacrificed vnto hir calues, which was termed a Vitulation: and this was vsuall for victory and plenty. **1623** COCKERAM, *Vitulation*, a reioicing like a calfe.

vituline ('vɪtjʊlaɪn), *a. rare.* [ad. L. *vitulīn-us*, f. *vitulus* calf. Cf. F. *vituline* (Balzac).] Of or belonging to a calf or calves; resembling that of a calf.
vitular, *vitulary*, with similar sense, are recorded in the *Cent. Dict.* and other recent Dicts.
1656 BLOUNT *Glossogr.* **1786–1805** TOOKE *Purley* (1829) II. 444. **1860** WRAXALL *Life in Sea* ii. 27 In spite of their [i.e.

seals'] clumsy form, the vituline countenance wears an expression of calmness and peace. **1870** LOWELL *Among my Bks.* Ser. I. (1873) 167 If a double allowance of vituline brains deserve such honor, there are few commentators on Shakespeare that would have gone afoot.

† **vituper**, *sb. Obs.* Also 5 vi-, vytupere, 6 *Sc.* **wituper**. [a. OF. *vituper*, *-ere* (obs. or arch. F. *vitupère*, = Pr. *vetupier*), ad. late or med.L. *vituperium* VITUPERY.] Vituperation.

1456 SIR G. HAYE *Law Arms* (S.T.S.) 188 Thir fals Jowis ..revy[l]is thame and dois all the vituper thai may to haly kirk and to the sacrament. **1484** CAXTON *Fables of Auian* xv, Suche is now in grete honour and worship that herafter shalle falle in to grete vytupere shame and dishonour. *c* **1500** *Melusine* xxxiii. 233 To the moost vytupere & shame of the Catholycal feyth. **1571** *Satir. Poems Reform.* xxvii. 109 Mark als þe wite, vise, wituper, and the waige Off wntried traisoun and of tyrannye.

† **vituper**, *v. Obs. rare.* In 5 vytuper. [a. OF. *vituperer* (10th c.; obs. or arch. F. *vitupérer* = Pr., Sp. and Pg. *vituperar*, It. *-are*), ad. L. *vituperāre* to VITUPERATE. Cf. prec.] *trans.* To vituperate or revile; to dishonour or disgrace.

1484 CAXTON *Fables of Æsop* III. vii, Men preysen somtyme that that shold be blamed & vytupered And ofte men ..vytuperen that that shold be preysed. *c* **1489** —— *Sonnes of Aymon* xiv. 337 O, gode lord..deliver me from the handes of my enmyes that I be not vytupered nor brought to shame.

vi'tuperable, *a.* ? *Obs.* Also 6 **vytuperable**. [a. OF. *vituperable* (obs. F., Sp. *vituperable*, Pg. *vituperavel*, It. *vituperabile*), ad. L. *vituperābil-is* (rare) blameworthy, censurable, f. *vituperāre* to VITUPERATE.] That deserves or merits vituperation; blameworthy, censurable, reprehesible; disgraceful, shameful.

c **1450** tr. *De Imitatione* I. xix. 22 Yf an accustumed exercise..be liȝtly forsaken þorugh hevynes o' soule or negligence, it is vituperable, & wol be founde noyous. **1481** BOTONER *Tulle on Old Age* (Caxton) C vij, Cecilyus saide of olde age a thyng is no more vituperable and lothyng, thenne is the same that he seeith here before. *c* **1510** BARCLAY *Mirr. Gd. Manners* (1570) G v, But a famous merchaunt, great, riche, and habowndant, And rightwisely dealing, is not vituperable. **1547** BOORDE *Brev. Health* §163. 58 b, There be many other myrthes & consolacions, some beynge good & laudable & some vytuperable. **1586** DAY *Eng. Secretary* I. (1625) 61 To ouercome others by vertue is a thing most honourable, but in pursuite thereof to be conuinced of any other, is a thing most vituperable. **1603** H. CROSSE *Vertues Commw.* (1878) 99 Nothing doth more corrupt and wither greene and tender wits, then such vnsauoury and vituperable bookes. **1822** T. TAYLOR *Apuleius* 357 Of vituperable men there are four species; of which the first consists of the ambitious.

vi'tuperant, *a.* and *sb. rare.* [ad. L. *vituperant-*, *vituperans*, pr. pple. of *vituperāre* to VITUPERATE. Cf. OF. *vituperant* (Godef.).] **a.** *adj.* Abusive, vituperative. **b.** *sb.* A vituperator.

1864 *Realm* 17 Feb. 7 We do not think..that the most vituperant colonel would express such strong opinions. **1889** *Pall Mall G.* 16 Oct. 5/1 Whilst Lord Salisbury came here as your most exalted vituperant, you are journeying hither as his most obedient and faithful adulator!

vi'tuperate, *ppl. a. rare*⁻¹. [ad. L. *vituperātus*, pa. pple. of *vituperāre*: see next.] Vituperated; worthy of vituperation.

1832 *Westm. Rev.* XVI. 7 Wealth was to be discreditable, unmanly, vituperate, because it was found greatly to indispose men to be active thieves.

vituperate (vaɪ'tjuːpəreɪt, vɪ-), *v.* [f. L. *vituperāt-*, ppl. stem of *vituperāre* to censure, blame, disparage, find fault with, etc., f. *vitu-* for *viti-*, stem of *vitium* blemish, fault, VICE *sb.*[1] + *parāre* to prepare. See also VITUPER *v.*] *trans.* To blame, speak ill of, find fault with, in strong or violent language; to assail with abuse; to rate or revile.

Not in common use until the beginning of the 19th c.

1542 BOORDE *Dyetary* xvi. (1870) 273 They louyth not porke nor swynes flesshe, but doth vituperat & abhorre it. **1611** COTGR., *Vituperer*, to vituperate, dispraise, discommend. [Hence in Cockeram, Blount, Bailey, etc.] **1638** PENKETHMAN *Artach.* C ij, Whatsoever transcends their sedulous apprehension..without any favourable expostulation..they will unworthily and unwittingly vituperate and reprehend. **1819** SCOTT *Ivanhoe* xxxiii, The incensed priests.. continued to raise their voices, vituperating each other in bad Latin. **1826** LAMB *Elia* Ser. II. *Pop. Fallacies* iv, A speech from the poorest sort of people which always indicates that the party vituperated is a gentleman. **1860** FROUDE *Hist. Eng.* V. 477 He vituperated from the pulpit the vices of the court. **1883** A. FORBES in *Fortn. Rev.* 1 Nov. 671 Englishmen are not in the habit of vituperating Monk as a traitor.

refl. **1812** H. & J. SMITH *Rej. Addr.* x. (1873) 96 Deviation from scenic propriety has only to vituperate itself for the consequences it generates.

b. *absol.* or *intr.* To employ abusive language.

1856 R. A. VAUGHAN *Mystics* VIII. v. 46 Vituperated and vituperating, he became a wanderer throughout Germany. **1877** MRS. OLIPHANT *Makers Flor.* vi. 168 He loses his temper and begins to vituperate.

Hence **vi'tuperated** *ppl. a.*

1841 EMERSON *Conservative* Wks. (Bohn) II. 272 You are yourself the result of this manner of living, this foul compromise, this vituperated Sodom.

vituperation (vaɪˌtjuːpə'reɪʃən, vɪ-). Also 5 -acyon. [a. OF. *vituperaciun*, *-acion*, *-ation* (obs. F. *vituperation*, = Sp. *vituperacion*, Pg. *vituperação*, It. *vituperazione*), or ad. L. *vituperātiōn-*, *vituperātio* blaming, censuring, etc., noun of action f. *vituperāre*: see prec. and -ATION.]

1. The action, fact, or process of vituperating; blame, censure, reproof, or (esp. in later use) the expression of this, in abusive or violent language; abuse, railing, rating. Also, vituperative or abusive language.

There are few instances of the use of the word before the beginning of the 19th c.: cf. VITUPERATE *v.*

1481 BOTONER *Tulle on Old Age* (Caxton) C viij, The third part..which Caton answerith,..repreuith them of the seconde defaulte of uituperacyon opposed ayenst olde age. **1602** (*title*), Ane Satyre of the thrie Estaits, in commendation of Vertew and Vituperation of Vyce; maid be Sir Dauid Lindesay. **1633** J. DONE *Hist. Septuagint* 155 When a man becomes vntractable, and inaccessible, by fiercenesse and pride:..then vituperation comes vpon him, and priuation of honour followes him. **1656** STANLEY *Hist. Philos.* v. (1687) 165 Of Rhetoric are six kinds..[6] Vituperation, when we declare a Man to be wicked. **1821** SCOTT *Kenilw.* xx, It was one of these old women who..answered his petition..with a volley of vituperation. **1845** FORD *Handbk. Spain* I. 35 Few nations can surpass the Spaniards in the language of vituperation. **1887** RUSKIN *Præterita* II. 193 A rhyme written..in vituperation of the idle people at Conflans.

† **2.** A cause of blame or censure. *Obs.*⁻¹

1726 AYLIFFE *Parergon* 305 (*bis*) Such a Writing ought to be clean and free from any Cavil or Vituperation of Rasure.

† **vitupe'ratious**, *a. Obs.*⁻¹ [f. prec.: see -IOUS.] Vituperative.

1797 SOUTHEY *Let. to J. Cottle* 13 Mar. in *Life* (1849) I. 306 Language is not vituperatious enough to describe the effect of its downward elongation.

vituperative (vaɪ'tjuːpərətɪv, vɪ-), *a.* [ad. L. type **vituperātīv-us*, f. *vituperāt-*, ppl. stem of *vituperāre*, or directly f. VITUPERATE *v.* + -IVE. Cf. obs. F. *vituperativement* adv. (Godef.), It. *vituperativo*.]

1. Of words, language, etc.: Containing, conveying, or expressing strong depreciation; violently abusive or fault-finding; contumelious, opprobrious. Also, of or pertaining to vituperation.

Freq. in the 19th c.

1727 POPE, etc. *Art of Sinking* 115 The vituperative partition will as easily be replenished with a most choice collection [of arguments]. **1759** STERNE *Tr. Shandy* I. xix, Tristram!—Melancholy dissyllable of sound! which, to his ears, was unison to Nincompoop, and every name vituperative under heaven. **1816** SCOTT *Antiq.* xxx, In utter despair at this vituperative epithet. **1856** KANE *Arct. Expl.* II. xii. 129 His eloquence becoming more and more licentious and vituperative. **1859** MILL *Liberty* ii. (1865) 32/1 It is far more important to restrain this employment of vituperative language than the other.

b. Const. *of* (a person). *rare*⁻¹.

1823 SCOTT *Quentin D.* viii, Had I..heard by report that a question vituperative of my Prince had been asked by the King of France, I had..instantly mounted and returned.

2. Characterized or accompanied by vituperation or abuse.

1754 CHESTERFIELD in *World* No. 101 ¶3 The torrents of their [*sc.* female] eloquence, especially in the vituperative way, stun all opposition. **1844** DISRAELI *Coningsby* II. i, The indignant, soon to become vituperative, secession of a considerable section of the cabinet. **1871** 'HOLME LEE' *Miss Barrington* I. ix. 129 When they have been most in fault themselves, they are most prone to shower a general vituperative blame and condemnation on the other side.

3. Of persons: Given to vituperation; employing or uttering abusive language.

1819 *Blackw. Mag.* V. 90 A Whig is a vituperative animal. **1843** CARLYLE *Past & Pr.* III. v, Quietly hearing all manner of vituperative able editors speak. **1904** H. PAUL *Hist. Mod. Eng.* I. xii. 208 The violent and vituperative champion of the Protestant religion.

Hence **vi'tuperatively** *adv.*, in a vituperative manner; with vituperation or abuse.

1831 CARLYLE in Froude *First 40 Years* (1882) II. 159 The critical republic will cackle vituperatively, or perhaps maintain total silence. **1852** *Fraser's Mag.* XLVI. 456 [He] continues his vituperatively shrill demands. **1884** J. PARKER *Apost. Life* III. 115 They would not speak their mother tongue if they did not speak vituperatively.

vituperator (vaɪ'tjuːpəreɪtə(r), vɪ-). [a. L. *vituperātor*, agent-noun f. L. *vituperāre* to VITUPERATE. Cf. Sp. and Pg. *vituperador*, OF. *vitupereur*.] One who vituperates; an abuser.

1837 *Chambers' Jrnl.* 19 Aug. 239 To stigmatise the vituperators would be now of little service. **1841** HOR. SMITH *Moneyed Man* II. iv. 116, I was tempted to chastise the vulgar vituperator. **1884** *Manch. Exam.* 9 May 5/1 That indignant declamation which is a favourite weapon with the vituperators of the Government.

vi'tuperatory, *a.* ? *Obs.* [f. L. type **vituperātōri-us*, f. *vituperāre*: see VITUPERATE *v.* and -ORY[2].] Expressive of blame or censure; vituperative, violently abusive.

1586 DAY *Eng. Secretary* I. (1625) 20 Laudatorie [Epistles] wherein is specially praised any thing, and Vituperatorie, in which is misliked or condemned whatsoeuer may be thought worthy either to be abhorred or dispraised. **1660** *Charac. Italy* To Rdr. A 5, For that [proverb] hath two ends..the one Vituperatory, and the other Laudatory. *a* **1832** BENTHAM *Deontol.* (1834) I. 315 The very same desire having ordinarily three designations, one laudatory, one vituperatory, and the other neutral. **1843** *Tait's Mag.* X. 343 A fluent array of vituperatory and laudatory phrases.

† **vitu'perious**, *a. Obs.* [a. OF. *vituperieus* (implied in the adv. *vituperieusement*; cf. Sp. *vituperioso*), or ad. late or med.L. *vituperiōsus* (Diefenbach), f. *vituperium* VITUPERY: see -IOUS.]

1. Vituperative, strongly abusive or censorious.

1604 DRAYTON *Moyses* I. 2 Muse, I inuoke the vtmost of thy might,..Gainst the vile Atheists vituperious sting. **1632** LITHGOW *Trav.* x. 490 To confound the calumnious and vituperious Papists. **1667** WATERHOUSE *Fire Lond.* 88 Vituperious Sarcasms, Secret rejoycings at their ruins.

2. Worthy of blame, vituperable; hence, shameful, discreditable, disgraceful, ignominious.

1612 tr. *Benvenuto's Passenger* I. iv. 281 O what doe I see, and what doe I heare in my dayes, what vituperious crimes? **1624** *Gag for Pope* 12 Clothed with the Sambenito, a punishment as vituperious as the carting of Bawdes in England. **1688** R. HOLME *Armoury* II. 15/2 The bearing of these Hellish Vituperious, horrid and vile things, is to deter ..the beholder from becoming like them.

Hence † **vitu'periously** *adv.*, vituperatively; shamefully. *Obs.*

1632 LITHGOW *Trav.* I. (1906) 3 The name and fame of the most righteous alive,..be thus diversly taxed and vituperiously calumniated. **1650** HOWELL *Giraffi's Rev. Naples* I. 130 So they concluded to die sooner,..then to live so vituperiously in such a basenesse and servitude.

vi'tuperize, *v. nonce-word.* [irreg. f. L. *vituperāre* + -IZE.] *trans.* To vituperate.

1894 T. WRIGHT *Life Defoe* 52 Whoever vituperised 'The True-born Englishman', it is not to be supposed that the ladies did.

vi'tuperous, *a.* [ad. obs. or arch. F. *vitupéreux* (= Pr. *vituperos*), or Sp. (also It. and Pg.) *vituperoso*, ad. late or med.L. *vituperōsus*, f. *vituperium* VITUPERY: see -OUS.]

1. = VITUPERIOUS *a.* 1.

1588 PARKE tr. *Mendoza's Hist. China* 33 Then they returne againe with vituperous and vile words. **1914** R. M. JONES *Spiritual Reformers 16th & 17th Cent.* v. 69 Schwenckfeld was denounced in the most vituperous language of the period.

2. = VITUPERIOUS *a.* 2.

1610 *Chester's Tri.* To Rdr. A 2 b, Let him be prest without pity.., and like a vituperous offender, be stamped and stared at. **1651** CULPEPPER *Astrol. Judgem. Dis.* (1658) 173 White clouds in the Urine, and neer the bottome, are commendable; black clouds, and neer the top, are bad and vituperous. **1959** *Times Lit. Suppl.* 10 July 409/3 Venetia.. watches with relief Karlo's vituperous and vulgar exit.

Hence **vi'tuperously** *adv.*, vituperatively.

1892 E. L. WAKEMAN in *Columbus* (Ohio) *Dispatch* 18 Aug., Authorities differ not only widely but vituperously as to the origin of practical effort for their betterment.

† **vi'tupery**. *Obs.* Also 5 vituperye, 6 -ie. [a. AF. *vituperie* (Gower), OF. **vituperie* (= Pr. *vituperi*, Sp., Pg., and It. *vituperio*), ad. late or med.L. *vituperium* (Diefenbach), blame, dishonour, shame, f. L. *vituperāre* to VITUPERATE. Cf. VITUPER *sb.*] Dishonour, reproach, shame; blame, vituperation.

1489 CAXTON *Faytes of A.* IV. i. P iiij, It may be yᵗ som.. wolde gladly vse therof [*sc.* a safe-conduct], whiche ought to tourne them in to grete vituperye and blame. **1572** BOSSEWELL *Armorie* II. 105 He ought..to defende the same (euen to the death) from all challenge or vituperie. **1590** BARROW & GREENWOOD in *Coll. Lett. & Confer.* 36 The rest of the vituperie wherwith you haue laden vs. **1608** H. CLAPHAM *Errour Left Hand* 35 Emulations, heart-burnings, vituperies, bloudy practises. **1620** SHELTON *Quix.* II. liii. 357 At whose perswasions & vitupery, the poore Gouernour tried if he could mooue himselfe.

Vitus, in *St. Vitus's Dance*: see DANCE *sb.* 6 b. Similarly *St. Vitus' fits*.

a **1845** HOOD *Sniffing a Birthday* xv, Ring Tom of Lincoln till he splits, And dance into St. Vitus' fits.

viue, southern ME. variant of FIVE.

viurie *Her.*: see VIVRY.

‖ **viva** ('viːvə), *sb.*[1] and *int.* [It., lit. 'live', 3rd pers. sing. pres. subj. of *vivere* (:—L. *vīvĕre*) to live. So Sp. and Pg. *viva*. Cf. VIVAT.] A cry of 'long live' as a salute or greeting; a shout of applause; a cheer or hurrah: **a.** As a sb., in the pl. **vivas**.

a **1700** EVELYN *Diary* 23 Nov. 1644, The multitude..were ..looking out of their windows and houses, with loud *viva's* and acclamations of felicity to their new Prince. **1728** [? DE FOE] *Capt. Carleton's Mem.* 268 The Cavaliero..received the repeated *Vivas* of that vast Concourse. **1818** LADY MORGAN *Autobiog.* (1859) 53 He kept bowing and scraping, ..answering the paid vivas of the populace with one of his *jolis mots.* **1851** MRS. BROWNING *Casa Guidi Wind.* I. 490 Whereat the popular exultation drunk With indrawn 'vivas' the whole sunny air. **1882** 'OUIDA' *Under Two Flags* (1890) 411 Lifting her, with wild vivas that rent the sky, on to the shoulders of the four tallest men.

b. As an exclamation.

1841 BARHAM *Ingol. Leg.* Ser. II. *Auto-da-Fé*, How they shouted, and fired the great guns in the square, Cried 'Viva!' and rung all the bells in the steeple.

viva ('vaɪvə), *sb.*² *Univ. colloq.* [Abbrev. of VIVA VOCE.] = VIVA VOCE *sb.*

1891 *Athenæum* 19 Dec. 825/2 The description of his *vivâ* will bring vivid recollections of similar tortures to many minds. **1897** *Westm. Gaz.* 27 July 1/3 If a man has done his paperwork either very well or very badly, the 'viva' is almost entirely formal.

Hence **'viva** *v. trans.*, to subject to a viva voce examination; also *intr.*, to examine viva voce.

1893 in J. B. Firth *Minstrelsy of Isis* (1908) 190 We shall laugh at our Tutors and leave them to 'viva' themselves and be free. **1907** 'BARBARA BURKE' *Barbara goes to Oxford* 122 Facing them..sat the youth who was being vivâed.

†**vivace**, *a.* *Obs.*⁻¹ [ad. L. *vīvāc-*, *vīvāx* VIVACIOUS *a.*, after F. *vivace*.] Vivacious, lively.

1721 RAMSAY *Content* 356 Another beau, as fine, but more vivace.

‖**vivace** (vi'vatʃe), *adv.* (and *sb.*) *Mus.* [It. *vivace* brisk, lively:—L. *vīvāc-*, *vīvāx*: see next.]

a. A direction indicating brisk or lively performance (see quots.). Also with the *adv.* used quasi-adjectivally to characterize musical composition.

1683 PURCELL *3-Pt. Sonnatas* To Rdr. (1893), Allegro, and Vivace [import] a very brisk, swift or fast movement. **1724** *Short Explic. For. Wds. in Mus. Bks.*, *Vivace*, is as much as to say with Life and Spirit. By this Word is commonly understood a Degree of Movement between *Largo* and *Allegro*, but more inclining to the latter than the former. **1801** BUSBY *Dict. Mus.*, *Vivace*, a word implying that the movement to which it is prefixed is to be sung, or played, in a brisk and animated style. **1922** D. H. LAWRENCE *Aaron's Rod* xiii. 187 Lady Franks started with a *vivace* Schumann piece. *Ibid.* 188 'I always prefer Schumann in his *vivace* moods,' said Aaron.

b. as *sb.* A passage intended to be performed in this manner (see also quot. 1889).

1683 [see ALLEGRO B, C]. **1889** *Grove's Dict. Mus.* s.v., The Vivace in the latter case would imply an absence of passion or excitement, an even rate of speed, and a bright and cheerful character. **1922** D. H. LAWRENCE *Aaron's Rod* xiii. 188 Our Colonel began to..bounce in his chair,..doing a sitting-down jig to the Schumann *vivace*. **1959** *Times* 11 Sept. 10/6 He moved into the ensuing *vivace* with unhurried moderation. **1976** *Gramophone* Sept. 410/1 The movement's main *vivace* is a good deal less mettlesome.

vivacious (vaɪ'veɪʃəs, vɪ-), *a.* Also 7–8 -eous. [f. L. *vīvāci-*, *vīvāx* (whence F. and It. *vivace*, Sp. and Pg. *vivaz*), tenacious of life, long-lived, lively, vigorous, f. *vīvĕre* to live: see -ACIOUS.]

1. Full of, characterized by, or exhibiting vivacity or liveliness; animated, brisk, lively, sprightly. **a.** Of persons, the mind, disposition, etc.

In quot. 1647 the reference is to the soul.

c **1645** HOWELL *Lett.* (1650) I. II. xv. 26 When people of a more vivacious and nimble temper com to mingle with them. **1647** H. MORE *Song of Soul* III. App. xiv, This is that nimble quick vivacious Orb All ear, all eye, with rayes round shining bright. *a* **1700** EVELYN *Diary* 20 Mar. 1692, The Pr. of Wales,..seeming..very much to resemble..his mother, and of a most vivacious countenance. **1711** STEELE *Spect.* No. 43 ⁋10 If the Poet had not been Vivacious, as well as Stupid, he could not [etc.]. **1785** BURKE *Nabob of Arcot's Debts* Wks. IV. 266 With all the reachings and graspings of a vivacious mind. **1798** EDGEWORTH *Pract. Educ.* (1811) I. 130 Vivacious pupils should from time to time be accustomed to an exact enumeration of particulars. **1861** GEO. ELIOT *Silas M.* xi, Here the vivacious doctor made a pathetic grimace. **1900** *Longm. Mag.* March 438 The.. question of assigning the palm of beauty to the vivacious.. little mother or to the tall, slim, grave daughter.

absol. **1752** JOHNSON *Rambler* No. 204 ⁋5 The young, the fair, the vivacious, and the witty.

b. Of birds.

1773 BARRINGTON in *Phil. Trans.* LXIII. 291 The scholar pitched upon may not only be more vivacious, but will continue in song. **1817** STEPHENS in *Shaw's Gen. Zool.* X. II. 363 It is a vivacious bird, and frequently utters the notes *sic sic sáic*.

c. Of qualities, conditions, etc.

1670 MAYNWARING *Vita Sana* xvi. 159 These Passions.. whose propensities are to..steal away from the Soul, that vivacious enlivening power. **1681–6** J. SCOTT *Chr. Life* (1747) III. 522 A most vivacious and everlasting Sense of Pain. *a* **1711** KEN *Hymns Festiv.* Poet. Wks. 1721 I. 294 Your Love the more vivacious grew, The nearer it to Glory drew. **1814** SCOTT *Diary* 12 Aug., in *Lockhart*, He looks very poorly,..but seems to retain all the quick, earnest, and vivacious intelligence of his character and manner. **1838** DICKENS *Nich. Nick.* xxx, Mr. Snevelicci..proposed 'The Ladies! Bless their hearts!' in a most vivacious manner. **1853** C. BRONTE *Villette* xxxvi, She invited affection by her beauty and her vivacious life.

d. Of writings, language, etc.

1788 V. KNOX *Winter Even.* (1790) I. xxv. 211 If, instead of collecting ideas, it [i.e. the mind] had been indulging its own pride in uttering vivacious nonsense. **1826** F. REYNOLDS *Life & Times* II. 202 The vivacious anecdotes related..rendered the whole scene peculiarly amusing. **1884** *Macm. Mag.* Nov. 3/1 The new work is more vivacious than the old.

2. Continuing to live; remaining alive for a long time; long-lived. Now *rare* or *Obs.*

1655 FULLER *Ch. Hist.* IX. iii. §27 Hitherto the English Bishops had been vivacious almost to wonder. **1682** SIR T. BROWNE *Chr. Mor.* III. §1 Their longevity swelling their impieties, the longanimity of God would no longer endure such vivacious abominations. **1692** BENTLEY *Boyle Lect.* viii. 282 They will never be able to prove, that therefore Men would be so vivacious as they would have us believe. **1742** YOUNG *Nt. Th.* IV. 30 [One sees] Vivacious ill; good dying immature. *Ibid.* v. 851 He gave an old vivacious usurer His meagre aspect, and his naked bones.

transf. *a* **1661** FULLER *Worthies*, *Northampton.* (1662) II. 293 By Gods blessing on his vivacious frugality he got so great an Estate. **1693** J. O. tr. *Cowley's Plants* I. 13 Though I the Oaks vivacious Age should live, I ne'er to all, their Names in Verse should give.

b. Of plants; †*spec.*, perennial.

1676 GREW *Anat. Flowers* II. v. §7 As if the other [plant], because it contains a far greater Proportion of the above-said Particles,..is able to beget a more Numerous, Vivaceous, or Gigantick Birth. **1721** BRADLEY *Philos. Acc. Wks. Nat.* 34 These..may again be distinguished by being Annual, or Perennial and Vivaceous. **1725** *Fam. Dict.* s.v. *Foxglove*, This Plant is one of those called the vivacious Plants, and consequently..may also be raised by the Roots. **1827** J. COLDSTREAM in J. H. Balfour *Biog.* (1865) ii. 24 Such foreign vivacious plants as pass the winter without shelter in our climate. **1854** THOREAU *Walden* (1906) 237 Still grows the vivacious lilac a generation after the door and lintel and sill are gone.

3. Possessing or exhibiting tenacity of life; difficult to kill or destroy. *rare.*

1660 BOYLE *New Exp. Phys. Mech.* Digress. 373 The particular and vivacious Nature of this sort of Fishes [i.e. eels]. **1667** *Decay Chr. Piety* ii. ⁋3 A late statesman said.. of England, that it was a vivacious animal that could never die except it kill'd it self. **1822–7** GOOD *Study Med.* (1829) I. 345 The long round worm,..body transparent,.. gregarious and vivacious.

vi'vaciously, *adv.* [f. prec. + -LY².] In a vivacious or lively manner; with vivacity or sprightly animation; †vigorously.

a **1711** KEN *Hymnarium* Poet. Wks. 1721 II. 40 The more of Spirit things contract, The more vivaciously they act. **1816** J. SCOTT *Vis. Paris* (ed. 5) 19 In the French crowd,.. vivacity is every where apparent;—the soldiers are vivaciously surly; the ladies vivaciously charming [etc.]. **1847** C. BRONTE *J. Eyre* xviii, While she is so vivaciously accosting him. **1880** 'OUIDA' *Moths* I. 40 'By the bye,' said her mother vivaciously, 'didn't you bring a maid?'

Comb. **1859** *Westm. Rev.* Oct. 594 A vivaciously-written narrative of a vacation voyage.

vi'vaciousness. [f. VIVACIOUS *a.* + -NESS.]

1. Tenacity of life; longevity. *rare.*

a **1661** FULLER *Worthies*, *Devon.* I. (1662) 248 Such their Fleetnesse, they will outrun many Horses; Vivaciousnesse, they out live most men. **1806** SYMMONS *Life Milton* (1810) 433 The shameless vivaciousness with which it refused to remit its grasp of political existence. **1849** *Southey's Comm.-pl. Bk* II. 605 Vivaciousness of the Acacia Tree.

2. Vivacity of manner or speech; liveliness, sprightliness.

1727 BAILEY (vol. II), *Liveliness*, vivaciousness, &c. **1807** S. TURNER *Hist. Anglo-Sax.* (ed. 2) IV. v. 279 There is a vivaciousness in his despair, which no danger can intimidate. **1872** J. C. JEAFFRESON *Woman in Spite of Herself* I. v, He had achieved a reputation for humour and vivaciousness. **1882** J. HAWTHORNE *Fort. Fool* I. xix, One whose equanimity is not to be upset by the sallies of feminine vivaciousness.

vivacity (vaɪ'væsɪtɪ, vɪ-). Also 5–6 vivacite, 6–7 -tie, 7 vivassity. [a. OF. *vivacite* (F. *vivacité*, = It. *vivacità*, Sp. *vivacidad*, Pg. *-idade*), or ad. L. *vīvācitāt-*, *vīvācitās* natural vigour, vital force, or liveliness, f. *vīvāci-*, *vīvāx* VIVACIOUS *a.*: see -ITY.] The state or condition of being vivacious.

1. Intellectual or mental animation, acuteness, or vigour; quickness or liveliness of conception or perception.

In the first group const. *of* (mind, spirit, thought, etc.).

(*a*) **1432–50** tr. *Higden* (Rolls) VII. 337 Lanfrancus.. restorede specially to monkes possessions taken from theyme; whom vivacite of mynde and favor of seynte Dunstan made bolde to do soe. **1526** *Pilgr. Perf.* (W. de W. 1531) 216 b, He hath this viuacite or quycknes of wytte. **1598** ROB. BARRET *Theor. Warres* v. ii. 143 The Harqubutiers..inuring their horse, both to the crack and fire..wherein consisteth fine skill with viuacitie of spirite. **1632** J. HAYWARD tr. *Biondi's Eromena* 57 In the vivacity of spirit there is none can paragonize or equall her. **1649** OGILBY tr. *Virg. Georg.* II. (1684) 80 The Invention, Light, and Vivacity of Mind. **1694** ATTERBURY *Serm.*, *Prov. xiv. 6* (1726) I. 186 Wit indeed, as it implies a certain uncommon Reach and Vivacity of Thought, is an excellent Talent. **1796** MORSE *Amer. Geog.* II. 456 What is wanting in the robust frame of their bodies..is in a great measure made up to them by the vivacity of their minds. **1849** MACAULAY *Hist. Eng.* vii. II. 217 That amplitude and acuteness of intellect, that vivacity of fancy,..belonged..to Halifax alone.

(*b*) **1604** E. G[RIMSTONE] *D'Acosta's Hist. Indies* VI. ii. 433 Wherein..wee may well perceive the great signes of their vivacitie and good vnderstanding. **1607–12** BACON *Ess.*, *Young Men* (Arb.) 256 Heat and vivacity in age is an excellent Composicion for busines. **1682** BURNET *Hale* 122 He had great vivacity in his Fancy, as may appear by his Inclination to Poetry. **1728** POPE *Dunc.* I. Notes (1736) 110 Mr. Colly Cibber, an author..of a good share of wit, and uncommon vivacity. **1763** COLE in *Coll. Top. & Gen.* (1837) IV. 48 A fine youth,..of great parts and vivacity, at Eton School. **1836–7** SIR W. HAMILTON *Metaph.* (1877) I. xiv. 254 How many several objects can the mind simultaneously survey, not with vivacity, but without absolute confusion.

b. Of conceptions or ideas.

a **1704** T. BROWN *Eng. Sat.* Wks. 1730 I. 27 His conceptions were..full of fire and vivacity. **1746** in *10th Rep. Hist. MSS. Comm.* App. I. 295, I greatly apprehend that the Weakness of his Lordships Body will not be able to keep pace with the Vivacity of his conceptions. **1764** REID *Inquiry* ii. §5 Sensation, memory, belief and imagination when they have the same object are only degrees of strength and vivacity in the idea.

†**2.** Vital force or power; vitality. *Obs.*

This sense and sense 3 tend to merge into one another and are not always clearly distinguishable.

1611 COTGR., *Vivaceté*, viuacitie, liuelinesse, lustinesse, vigor, strength. **1635** HEYWOOD *Hierarchy* III. 156 Aire,..of all the Elements the most noble, and fullest of vivacitie and liuelyhood. *a* **1699** BEAUMONT *Psyche* XII. 189 Ah, dead and rotten Faith, which can display No fruit to prove the Root's vivacity! **1724** R. WELTON *Chr. Faith & Pract.* 12 The grave shall surrender our crumbled ashes, redintegrated into a more perfect vivacity than ever. **1747** tr. *Astruc's Fevers* 130 This fever is much more dangerous in young persons..than in old people; for the vivacity of the former..contribute[s] ..to foment it constantly.

b. *transf.* and *fig.* Active force, power, vigour.

1649 JER. TAYLOR *Gt. Exemp.* Exhort. §13. 9 Many cases do occurre, which need a president, and the vivacity of an excellent example. **1663** PATRICK *Parab. Pilgr.* (1687) 75 It is an active and busie affection; having as much Vivacity as it hath strength. **1746** HERVEY *Medit.* (1748) II. 8 See! how languishingly it [the departing sunlight] trembles on the leafy Spire... The little Vivacity, that remains, decays every Moment..While I speak, it expires. **1753** N. TORRIANO *Gangr. Sore Throat* 66 To prevent the Vivacity of the Fever and other Symptoms. **1793** W. ROBERTS *Looker-on* No. 36 (1794) II. 33 While this principle was in its full vivacity, all was sure to go well.

3. The property or fact of living for a long time; longevity. Now *rare*.

1616 BULLOKAR *Eng. Expos.*, *Viuacitie*, long life, liuelinesse. **1646** SIR T. BROWNE *Pseud. Ep.* III. ix. 123 Fables are raised concerning the vivassity of Deere; for neither are their gestation or increment such as may afford an argument of long life. **1655** FULLER *Ch. Hist.* VI. 347 The vivacity of some of these Pensioners is little lesse than a Miracle, they survived so long. **1684** T. BURNET *Theory Earth* I. 181 In their topical paradises also, they [the ancients] always suppos'd a great vivacity or longævity in those that enjoy'd them.

fig. **1853** TRENCH *Proverbs* 119 The vivacity of the truth, as contrasted with this short-lived character of the lie.

†**b.** Tenacity of life. *Obs.*

1663 BOYLE *Usef. Exp. Nat. Philos.* II. i. 16 The strange vivacity we have sometimes..observed in Vipers: Since.. their Hearts clearly sever'd from their Bodies may be observ'd to beat for some hours. **1664** POWER *Exp. Philos.* I. 6 Many more observables there are in Common Flyes, as their Vivacity; for, when they appear desperate..they will be revived into life, and perform its functions again.

4. Vigorous or energetic action; activity, energy, vigour; spirit. Now *rare*.

1652 KIRKMAN *Clerio & Lozia* 137 He himself killed the Prince of Doudonne, who for a time defended himself with much vivacity. *a* **1656** BP. HALL *Rem. Wks.* (1660) 35, I was enabled with much..vivacitie to perform that service. **1736** LEDIARD *Life Marlborough* II. 494 They were charg'd with a great deal of Vivacity by the Enemy. **1750** H. WALPOLE *Lett.* (1846) II. 359 Robbing is the only thing that goes on with any vivacity. **1787** JEFFERSON *Writ.* (1859) II. 301 The preparations were pushed with such vivacity on the part of England, that it was believed she had other objects in view. **1815** J. SMITH *Panorama Sci. & Art* II. 65 The vivacity with which sounds are transmitted through solid substances, is very remarkable. **1863** KINGLAKE *Crimea* II. 337 Of course, the vivacity of France and England tended to place Austria at her ease. **1885** BANCROFT *Hist. U.S.* III. 61 The promise ..stimulated their irregular vivacity to enforce laws which had become obsolete.

5. The quality, condition, or fact of being animated or lively; esp. lively or spirited conduct, manner, or speech; animation or liveliness of demeanour or disposition; briskness, sprightliness.

Also (*b*) const. *of* (the disposition, etc.).

(*a*) **1647** CLARENDON *Hist. Reb.* I. §7 Whoever considers the Acts of power and injustice..in those intervals of Parliament, will not be much scandalized at the warmth and vivacity of those meetings. **1654** LD. BROGHILL *Parthenissa* 209 He had a look so spiritual and full of vivacity, that no effeminate Beauty was comparable to it. **1711** ADDISON *Spect.* No. 128 ⁋1 As Vivacity is the Gift of Women, Gravity is that of Men. **1766** FORDYCE *Serm. Yng. Wom.* (1767) I. v. 173 Is not extreme vivacity a near borderer on folly? **1791** MRS. RADCLIFFE *Rom. Forest* vii, Her natural vivacity resumed its long-lost empire. **1828** D'ISRAELI *Chas. I*, II. vi. 156 The noisy vivacity which the French usually assume when they would carry their point. **1847** S. AUSTIN *Ranke's Hist. Ref.* III. 511 The ambassador remarked, with all the vivacity consistent with his respect for the pope, how important the affair was. **1879** DIXON *Windsor* III. viii. 74 A man with the vivacity of a boy.

(*b*) **1702** W. J. *Bruyn's Voy. Levant* xxix. 109 The Oppression under which they groan has extinguish'd all the Vivacity of their Minds. **1716** POPE *Lett.* (1735) I. 286 There is a Vivacity and Gaiety of Disposition almost peculiar to him. **1800** *Charac.* in *Asiat. Ann. Reg.* 32/2 The natural ardour and gay vivacity of his disposition. **1826** SCOTT *Woodst.* i, The vivacity of his eye indicated some irascibility of temperament. **1835** *Jas. Martin's Disc.* Memoir p. xliii, The spring and vivacity of his spirit became almost like those of a boy discharged from school.

b. As a literary or artistic quality.

1762 H. WALPOLE *Vertue's Anecd. Paint.* (1765) II. 126 An admirable half length..painted and finished with the greatest vivacity and clearness. **1824** L. MURRAY *Eng. Gram.* (ed. 5) I. 195 When narration is full of images or events, the omission of connectives may..give a sort of picture of hurry and tumult, and so heighten the vivacity of description. **1827** SCOTT *Chron. Canongate* Introd., The reckless play of raillery which gave vivacity to his original acting. **1855** MACAULAY *Hist. Eng.* xiii. III. 308 The first great painter of life and manners has described, with a vivacity which makes it impossible to doubt that he was copying from nature, the effect [etc.].

c. A vivacious or lively act, expression, scene, etc. Usu. in *pl.*

1692 DRYDEN tr. *St. Euremont's Ess.* 375 The most fertile Spirits come to exhaust themselves,..the most enlivened Vivacities either repulse you or weary you. **1712** STEELE *Spect.* No. 448 ¶2 Persons who fall into that Way purely to recommend themselves by their Vivacities. **1756** H. WALPOLE *Lett. to Mann* (1846) III. 217, I have read..the Pucelle,..throughout there are many vivacities; but so absurd, perplexed a story is intolerable. **1847** L. HUNT *Jar Honey* v. (1848) 58 The Scotch, appear to have been driven by a jovial desperation into the vivacities inspired by the sunshine of the south. **1851** CARLYLE *Sterling* II. iii, He was full of bright speech and argument; radiant with arrowy vitalities, vivacities and ingenuities.

6. Brightness, brilliancy (of light or colour).

1734 tr. *Rollin's Anc. Hist.* (1827) I. Pref. 19 The splendour and vivacity of whose colours charm the eye. **1735** *Dict. Polygraph.* s.v. *China*, The vivacity of this colour appears no less in glass of lead than in crystal. **1808** SIR W. HERSCHEL in *Phil. Trans.* XCVIII. 157 The vivacity of the light of the comet..had a much greater resemblance to the radiance of the stars.

† **ˈvivacy,** variant of or error for VIVACITY.

1637 SIR A. JOHNSTON *Diary* (S.H.S.) 278 Quhat dumplies, deadens the vivacie, vigor, livlenes of man's spirit, bot sin? **1719** F. HAUKSBEE *Phys.-Mech. Exper.* (ed. 2) Supp. xvi. 305 Those Gudgeons..now began considerably to abate of their Vivacy.

† **ˈvival,** *a. Obs.*⁻¹ [f. L. *vīv-us* alive, living, etc. + -AL¹.] Vital.

1636 W. BELLAS in *Ann. Dubrensia* (1877) 38 Draw forth the vivall substance of your spring, You Sisters nine.

† **ˈvivand,** *pres. pple. Obs.*⁻¹ In 5 **wywande.** [ad. OF. *(mal-)vivant*, pr. pple. of *vivre* to live.] *ill vivand*, ill-living.

c **1460** *Wisdom* 786 in *Macro Plays* 61 He þat ys yll wywande, Wo hys hym, by þe bone.

‖ **vivandier** (vivɑ̃dje). [F. *vivandier* masc. (= Sp. *vivandero*, Pg. *vivandeiro*, It. *vivandiere*) a supplier of victuals or provisions, f. pop.L. **vivanda* for *vivenda*: see VIAND¹. Cf. VIANDER¹.] In the French or other continental armies: A person who supplies victuals to troops in the field; a sutler.

The feminine *vivandière* occurs freq. in 19th cent. works relating to Continental wars.

1591 *Garrard's Art Warre* 13 Another doth visite Vivandiers and Victualers (if any follow the Campe). **1691** *Lond. Gaz.* No. 2694/2 They seized several hundreds of Vivandier's Boats. **1802** JAMES *Milit. Dict.* **1813** WELLINGTON in Gurwood *Desp.* (1838) X. 321 Operations so near to the enemy, as that the *vivandiers* and other attendants on the troops cannot with safety remain near them. **1848** H. GREVILLE *Diary* 29 June (1883) I. 278 Women went about disguised as *vivandières*, giving poisoned brandy to the soldiers. **1896** D. BINGHAM *Recoll. Paris* I. xiii. 221 Madame de Beaulieu..joined the Mobiles of her native province in the capacity of *vivandière*. **1963** P. FLEMING *Kolchak* xiii. 149 They were often companioned by their own or other men's wives or by ladies who played, sometimes usefully, a role roughly corresponding to the *vivandière's*.

vivarium (vaɪˈvɛərɪəm, vɪ-). Pl. **vivaria,** also **-iums.** [L. *vīvārium* enclosure for live game, warren, fish-pond, etc., neut. sing. of *vīvārius*, f. *vīvus* alive, living.]

1. A place where living animals, esp. fish, are maintained or preserved for food; a fish-pond or fish-pool; = VIVARY 2. Also *fig.*

1600 HOLLAND *Livy* 1389 Whereupon it commeth, that those places or parkes which are set out and appointed for feeding of Deere, we use to call Vivaria. **1653** JER. TAYLOR *Serm. for Year* I. xxvi. 328 The face of the Sea is our Traffique, and the bowels of the Sea is our Vivarium, a place for fish to feed us. **1845** GOSSE *Ocean* ii. (1849) 80 In some of the Hebrides, there are large pools for the preservation of sea-fishes, hollowed out of the solid rock... Great numbers of cod-fishes are kept in these vivaria. **1888** D. BEVERIDGE *Between Ochils & Forth* v. 80 The dry hollow..in former days served the monks as a *vivarium*, or fish-pool.

2. a. A place or enclosure, a piece of ground or stretch of water, specially adapted or prepared for the keeping of living animals under their normal conditions, either as objects of interest or for the purpose of scientific study; freq. in later use, an aquarium; = VIVARY I.

1684 tr. *Combes' Versailles*, &c. 87 In the *Vivarium* are seen many kinds of Animals which have been caused to be brought from Forein Countries. *a* **1700** EVELYN *Diary* 17 Nov. 1644, There is also adjoining to it a vivarium for estriges, peacocks, swanns, cranes, &c. **1853** *Athenæum* 28 May, The new Fish house..has received the somewhat curious title of the 'Marine Vivarium'. **1853** *Guide Zool. Gard.*, Aquatic Vivarium. **1880** A. R. WALLACE *Isl. Life* xiv. 297 Forming a kind of natural museum or vivarium in which ancient types..had been saved from..destruction. **1900** L. HUXLEY *Life Huxley* I. xii. 155 The bay was calm and suitable both for the dredge and for keeping up a vivarium.

b. A glass bowl, case, etc., in which fish or other aquatic animals are kept, esp. for purposes of scientific study; = VIVARY I b. Now usu. = TERRARIUM.

1853 GEO. ELIOT *Let.* 13 June (1954) II. 103, I was at the Zoological gardens..and saw..the marine queerities in the Vivarium. **1855** *Zoologist* XIII. 4849 Those who would view vivariums merely as interesting subjects for their drawing-room windows. **1856** GEO. ELIOT in Cross *Life* (1885) I. 396 We set out for Ilfracombe with our hamper of glass jars, which we meant for our sea-side vivarium. **1858** H. N. HUMPHREYS *Butterfly Vivarium* i. 2, I am about to describe a novel kind of Vivarium, by means of which another and very distinct class of animal life—that of the 'world of insects'—may be made to exhibit its wonders. **1890** DK. ARGYLL in *Mem.* xlv. (1906) II. 464 Your old vivarium is still standing in its old place. **1914** W. P. WESTELL *Boys' Bk. Pets* xvi. 217 Another type of vivarium may be constructed on similar lines to the rectangular aquarium, only making it a few inches deeper. **1978** *Nature* 19 Oct. 646/2 Lizards were housed in vivaria in a constant temperature room.

vivars, obs. form of VIVERS.

vivary (ˈvaɪvərɪ). Also 7 **vivarie.** [ad. L. *vīvārium* VIVARIUM: see -ARY¹. Cf. also VIVER¹ and VIVIER.]

1. = VIVARIUM 2. Also *fig.* Now *rare* or *Obs.*

1601 DONNE *Progr. Soul* iii, That swimming Colledge, and free Hospitall Of all mankinde, that cage and vivarie Of fowles, and beasts. **1660** F. BROOKE tr. *Le Blanc's Trav.* 140 Slaves..who have no other office then to hunt the Woods and Marshes for triple-coloured tortoises for the Kings Vivary. **1699** EVELYN *Acetaria* (1729) 118 Of Aviaries, Apiaries, Vivaries, Insects, &c. **1865** *Reader* No. 139. 233/1 Our marine-water vivaries.

b. = VIVARIUM 2 b. *rare*⁻¹.

1781 G. WHITE *Selborne* xcviii, I spent a fortnight at the house of a friend, where there was such a vivary.

2. = VIVARIUM I. Also *fig.*

1628 COKE *Inst.* (1642) II. 100 Vivarium..in Law..signifieth Parks, Warrens, and Pischaries or Fishings... They might imprison such as they should take in their Parks or Vivaries. **1659** C. NOBLE *Inexpediency Exped.* 4 The Remedy that is prescribed is the very Seed and Sperm, the very Nursery, and Fomenter, and Vivary of that difference. **1670** BLOUNT *Glossogr.* (ed. 3). [Hence in Phillips, Bailey, etc.] **1851** T. H. TURNER *Dom. Archit.* I. iii. 140 There was a pond, or vivary, in the garden, and the bailiff expended eight shillings..to feed the pikes in it. **1858** W. JOHNSON *Ionica* 60 In stagnant vivaries they lie Forgetful of their ancient haunts. **1863** J. R. WALBRAN *Mem. Fountains Abbey* (Surtees) I. 191 The monks converted a marsh into a vivary which may still be traced.

‖ **vivat** (ˈvaɪvæt, ˈviː-), *int.* and *sb.* [a. L. *vīvat*, lit. 'may he (or she) live', 3rd pers. sing. pres. subj. of *vīvĕre* to live; perh. partly a. F. *vivat*, of the same origin. Cf. VIVA *sb.*¹]

A. *int.* A word of acclamation wishing a person (long) life and prosperity, or expressing applause or approval.

The L. phrases *vivat regina, vivat rex* have had some currency in English books.

1663 COWLEY *Cutter Coleman St.* II. viii, *Joll.* Here's a Health to the Royal Travailer... *Wor.* Come on Boys, *Vivat*; have at you agen then. **1852** C. BARTER *Dorp & Veld* xiii. 103 Dingaan..was succeeded by Panda, the present king [of the Zulus], of whom we have every reason to say 'vivat'.

B. *sb.* An utterance of this word by way of acclamation or applause.

1821 SCOTT *Kenilw.* xxxii, These donations were accepted with the usual clamour and *vivats* of applause common on such occasions. **1823** —— *Quentin D.* xix, The multitude..greeted Meinheer Pavillon with a loud *vivat*, as he ushered in his distinguished guest. **1840** THACKERAY *Paris Sk.-bk.* (1872) 31 The king was received with shouts and loyal vivats. **1895** MEREDITH *Amazing Marriage* xxxiv, Followed by the vivats of the whole Principality.

‖ **viva voce** (ˈvaɪvə ˈvəʊsiː, ˈvəʊtʃiː), *adv. phr., a.,* and *sb.* Also **vivâ voce.** [med.L., lit. 'by or with the living voice', f. L. *vīvā*, abl. sing. fem. of *vīvus* living, and *vōce*, abl. sing. of *vox* voice.

The expression *viva vox* is employed by classical Latin authors, but the use of the ablative phrase appears to be of later date. Cf. OF. *par vives voix* (1258 in Du Cange), F. *de vive voix*.]

A. *adv.* By word of mouth; in speech; orally. (Freq. in parenthetic use.) **a.** As distinct from writing. Also *in* or *with viva voce.*

(*a*) **1581** W. CHARKE in *Conf.* IV. (1584) Bb ij, The Apostles taught *viua voce*, by liuely voyce. **1594** in *Cath. Rec. Soc. Publ.* V. 243 Confessyd by Thomas Walpoole and by John Ingram (*viua voce*) That [etc.]. **1611** MIDDLETON & DEKKER *Roaring Girl* D.'s Wks. 1873 III. 138 Yes, sir, she's there, *viua voce*, to deliuer her auricular confession. **1697** COLLIER *Ess. Mor. Subj.* II. (1703) 66 Instruction from books, strikes the imagination more faintly than that which is delivered *viva voce*. **1748** J. LIND *Lett. Navy* ii. (1757) 94 The manner of giving in the evidence in writing privately, and not viva voce in court,..gives room for great partiality. **1797** MRS. BERKELEY *Poems G. M. Berkeley* Pref. p. ccccxxxviii, The good lady has frequently, *vivâ voce*, said to the Editor, 'Ah!' [etc.]. **1802** M. CUTLER in *Life*, etc. (1888) II. 102 But I must leave the accounts until I can give it to you *viva voce*. **1848** G. STRUTHERS *Orig. Secession Ch.* 63 They were now required to answer separately and *viva voce* to the question. **1861** *Two Cosmos* I. 297 Let's hear ye *viva voce* now, man!

(*b*) **1621** R. COCKS *Diary* (Hakl. Soc.) II. 174 Whoe all 4 with viva voce accused the said Roan to doe the acte in their sight. **1760** FOOTE *Minor* I. Wks. 1799 I. 234, I thought it was proper for you to examine him in *viva voce*.

b. As distinct from silent reading or repetition: = ALOUD *adv.* ? *Obs.*

1665 R. JOHNSON *Scholars Guide* 7 Read the best Authors by periods, *vivâ voce*, thereby their stile will be secretly instilled into your minds. **1711** SHAFTESB. *Charac.* I. 159 We might peradventure be less noisy and more profitable in Company, if at convenient times we discharg'd some of our articulate Sound, and spoke to ourselves *vivâ voce* when alone. **1834** in J. A. Henderson *Ann. Lower Deeside* (1892) 221 On the petition being read *viva voce* the Petitioner was desired, and required, to retire.

B. *adj.* Conveyed or expressed in speech instead of writing; given or stated by word of mouth; spoken; oral.

a **1718** PRIOR *'Lie, Philo'* 10 Pursue me with Satyr:..But from all *vivâ voce* Reflection forbear. **1816** SINGER *Hist. Cards* 165 This *viva-voce* testimony of a cotemporary witness places the matter beyond doubt. **1852** LATHAM *Ethnol. Brit. Isl.* vii. 119 For Lincolnshire he had *viva voce* information from Cynebert. **1901** *N. & Q.* 9th Ser. VIII. 54 When *vivâ voce* news and gossip were eagerly sought from fresh arrivals from the country.

b. Of an examination, etc.: Carried on or conducted by speech.

In University use applied to a supplementary oral examination following upon one or other of the ordinary written examinations.

1815 SCOTT *Guy M.* xxxv, But there are cases in which a *viva voce* conference [etc.]. **1840** *Penny Cycl.* XVIII. 135/1 The *vivâ voce* part of each [examination] is carried on in Latin. **1845** [PYCROFT] *Collegian's Guide* 265 In that case the *vivâ voce* examination and a second paper of questions may set all right.

C. *sb.* A viva voce examination. Freq. abbrev. VIVA *sb.*²

1842 ABP. TEMPLE in *Mem.* (1906) II. 433 When the day for Vivâ Voce came I was in no small fright. **1872** H. KINGSLEY *Hornby Mills*, etc. II. 52 His papers were simply admirable, and his 'viva voce' was as good as he had ever heard. **1888** *Temple Bar* Jan. 29 He was in for the terrible ordeal of a *vivâ-voce* before the Bishop.

ˈviva-voce, *v.* [f. VIVA-VOCE *sb.*] *trans.* To subject to a viva voce examination; to examine orally. Freq. abbrev. VIVA *v.*

1880 W. W. R. B[ALL] *Orig. & Hist. Math. Tripos* 11 Every candidate was liable to be taken aside to be vivâ-voced by any M.A. who wished to do so.

vivax (ˈvaɪvæks). *Med.* [L., = 'long-lived'.] The specific name of a protozoon of the genus *Plasmodium*, used *absol.* and *attrib.* to denote the organism and *attrib.* with reference to the relapsing type of malaria it causes, in which paroxysms occur every third day and which is usually not fatal. Freq. printed in italic.

1930 [see FALCIPARUM]. **1946** *Jrnl. Amer. Med. Assoc.* 20 July 964/1 The patients were military personnel who had acquired vivax infections in the Pacific or Mediterranean theaters of operation. **1955** *Sci. News Let.* 23 July 52/1 The Negro seems to have a general resistance to strains of vivax from all areas. **1958** N. F. LEOPOLD *Life plus 99 Years* xxi. 321 *Vivax* malaria is also known as tertian malaria because, once the trophozoites have fallen into step and got synchronized, they sporulate every forty-eight hours. **1983** *Oxf. Textbk. Med.* I. v. 394/2 The vivax resistance factor [in many black Africans] is a blood group determinant.

† **ˈvivda.** *Ork.* and *Shetl. dial. Obs.* Also **vifda.** [perh. ad. ON. *vǫðva* (nom. *vǫðve, -vi*) muscular flesh.] (See quots.)

a **1688** J. WALLACE *Descr. Orkney* (1693) 94 *Vivda*, Flesh dried in a Skeo without being salted. **1809** EDMONDSTON *State Zetland Isl.* x. II. 49 They seldom salt their meat, but either smoke it in the house, or dry it in the air. When preserved in this latter manner, it is known by the name of *vivda*. **1821** SCOTT *Pirate* xxx, Here, Laurie, bring up the *vifda*. **1822** HIBBERT *Descr. Shetl. Isl.* 470 Vivda, or unsalted mutton, hung up in their buildings until it was hardened and dried, is no longer known.

† **vive,** *sb. Obs.*⁻¹ [ad. L. *vīvum*, neut. of *vīvus*: see next.] = LIFE *sb.* 7.

1555 W. WATREMAN *Fardle Facions* I. v. 53 The image of death, caruen out of wodde, or drawen with the pencille as niere to the vive as is possible.

vive, *a.* Now only *Sc.* or *arch.* Also 5 **vyue,** 6–7 **viue;** *Sc.* 6 **viwe,** 7 **wieve,** 9 **veive, veev, veef.** [a. OF. (also mod.F.) *vive* fem. of *vif*:—L. *vīv-um, vīv-us* living, alive (whence also It., Sp., Pg. *vivo*), or a direct adaptation of the L. word.]

1. Physically lively, forcible, or brisk. *rare.*

c **1477** CAXTON *Jason* 31 b, He dyde so well that by vyue force with his trenchaunt swerde he brake the wardes and Araye of the Esklauons. **1638** SIR T. HERBERT *Trav.* (ed. 2) 43 Thou shalt not sinne in any of thy five senses:..thy pallat hating wine, flesh, and all other vive things. **1808** JAMIESON, *Vive*, brisk, vigorous.

† **b.** Of minerals: Having active properties.

See also ARGENT VIVE, *calx vive* CALX 2, and SULPHUR VIVE.

1669 BOYLE *Contn. New Exp.* II. (1682) 166, I exposed Vive Sulpher to the Beams of the Sun. **1670** W. SIMPSON *Hydrol. Ess.* 101 Take a mineral sulphur, whether vive, or in a marcasite. **1671** J. WEBSTER *Metallogr.* xv. 224 Being a perfect metal..containing in itself vive-spermatick sulphur, and vive immature Mercury.

2. Affecting or impressing the mind in a lively or vivid manner.

In various applications: see groups of quots.

(*a*) **1528** in Burnet *Hist. Ref.* (1679) I. *Records* xxii. 53 Ye may declare the Premises unto him;..[and] in as effectual and vive manner as ye can, open it unto his Holiness. **1624** BACON *War w. Spain* (1629) 22 By a viue and forcible perswasion, he moued him to a warre vpon Flanders. **1665** SIR T. HERBERT *Trav.* (1677) 4 Sylvester gives it this true and vive description.

(*b*) *c* **1614** SIR W. MURE *Dido & Æneas* II. 521 What woes so vive, charact'red in thy face, Thus overcloud the rayes of princely grace. **1629** H. BURTON *Truth's Triumph* 116 None of the Israel of God is healed..but by his speciall, cleare, viue faith. **1675** R. BURTHOGGE *Causa Dei* 168 It being Another to which I am proceeding, that it seems awakens in you far more feeling and more vive Resentments.

(*c*) **1650** GENTILIS *Considerations* 1 As if oblivion were not by some much more to bee desired, than to have the memory of them to vive. 1652 KIRKMAN *Clerio & Lozia* 98 We receive in our hearts all the various and vive impressions of so fair and divine objects.

3. Of images, pictures, etc.: Life-like, suggestive of life or reality; closely reproducing or representing the actual person or thing.

1585 JAS. I *Ess. Poesie* (Arb.) 13 Heir surely lyes, Of seasons fowre, the glasse and picture viue. 1588 A. KING tr. *Canisius' Catech.* 81 A maist vive repræsentation of our lords death. 1596 DALRYMPLE tr. *Leslie's Hist. Scot.* I. 169 Mogallie, Galdies sister sone, .. the viue and perfyte Jmage of King Galdie. 1621 ARCHBOLD *Beauty Holines* 16 As a father delighteth to looke upon the expresse and vive Image of himselfe in his sonne. 1637 J. WILLIAMS *Holy Table* 35 That sacred Oratory, the vivest resemblance I know upon the Earth of the Harmony of the Cherubims. 1669 R. FLEMING *Fulfilling Script.* (1726) 74 There is a vive portraicture of providence in the affairs of the church held forth in that vision [of Ezechiel].

4. Of colours: Bright, vivid.

1591 JAS. I *Lepanto* 436 The Painter mixes colours viue, The Printer Letters sets. 1596 DALRYMPLE tr. *Leslie's Hist. Scot.* I. 267 The Croce, .. suddanlie appeirit, in viue and bricht colouris. 1633 *Epitaph A. Munday* in *Stow's Surv.* 869/2 He .. ore them laid Such vive and beauteous colours with his Pen. 1671 [R. MACWARD] *True Nonconf.* 373 It hath been my endeavour so to draw and design in vive collours, that naming would appeare superfluous.

b. *Sc.* Of things seen (actually or mentally): Clear, distinct.

1825 JAMIESON *Suppl.*, *Vive*, applied to what may be seen clearly; as, 'vive prent', letter-press which may be read easily. 1861 J. DAVIDSON *Poems Buchan Dial.* 119 In thought as veev as fan't took place, I see anither scene. 1886 D. M. SMITH *Glen Ogil* in R. Ford *Harp Perthshire* (1893) 327 The hills abune Glen Ogil! I see them a' the day As veive as when I speel'd them in summer days lang-syne.

†**5.** Alive; in a living state. *Obs.*

c 1590 J. STEWART *Poems* (S.T.S.) II. 245 Guid Elias .. Quhom Eliseus vith his ies beheld Viwe reft till heawen. *Ibid.* 23 He did suddane sie The veirray viwe formosit figure frie Of Angelique. 1673 A. WALKER *Lees Lachrymans* 3 Shrunk into Decrepidness, and a Living Death, made a vive Skeleton before he Dyed.

†**b.** Of the voice: (cf. VIVA VOCE). *Obs.*

1616 SYMSON *Short Compend.* VII. ii. II. 9 To y^e singing of Psalmes in the Church by viue voyce, he added Organes. 1675 J. SMITH *Chr. Relig. Appeal* III. 38 Reveiled by the vive-voyce of the Gods themselves.

†**vive**, *v. Obs.*$^{-1}$ [f. prec., or directly f. L. *vīv-us.*] *trans.* To endue with life.

1637 G. DANIEL *Genius of Isle* 295 But I forget this now, viv'd by the Beams Of such a maiestie.

‖**vive** (viv), *int.* [Fr., lit. 'may he (she, it) live': cf. VIVA *sb.*[1] and *int.*]

1. a. ***vive le roi*** (viv lə rwa) = *long live the king* s.v. LIVE *v.*[1] 9, used as a general acclamation to or for a sovereign. Similarly ***vive l'empéreur***.

?1594 MARLOWE *Massacre at Paris* sig. B7, *Sound trumpets within, and then all crye* Viue le Roy. *a* 1700 EVELYN *Diary* an. 1651 (1955) III. 42 The King .. saluting the Ladys & Acclamators who had fill'd the Windos with their beauty, & the aire with *Vive Le Roy.* 1768 STERNE *Sentimental Journey* I. 114 Here's a couple of sous for thee—*Vive le Roi!* said the old soldier. 1815 F. BURNEY *Let.* Mar. in *Jrnls. & Lett.* (1980) VIII. 76 There was no species of enthusiasm, but .. moderate cries of *Vive le roi.* 1848 E. B. BROWNING *Let.* 4 July (1897) I. v. 375 How did you feel when the cry was raised, 'Vive l'Empereur'? 1861 G. MEREDITH *Let.* 19 Nov. (1970) I. 115 The Emperor allows her £1000 a year: her mother gets £2000. *Vive l'Empereur!* 1896 C. M. YONGE *Release* II. iii. 104 Ecstatic cries of '*Vive le Roi*' broke from the populace.

b. ***vive la bagatelle*** (viv la bagatɛl), 'success to frivolity or nonsense', an exclamation denoting a carefree attitude to life.

1732 SWIFT *Let.* 10 July in *Lit. Corr.* (1741) 150 All for want of my Rule, *Vive la bagatelle!* 1760 STERNE *Tristram Shandy* I. xix. 121 The footing of mere whims, and of a *vive la Bagatelle.* 1880 *Girl's Own Paper* 27 Nov. 144/3 *Vive la bagatelle* means 'Success to trifling'. Not a good sentiment. 1915 J. WEBSTER in *Century Mag.* Sept. 492/1, I seem to have covered a lot of paper without telling you much. *Vive la bagatelle!* 1948 M. ALLINGHAM *More Work for Undertaker* xxiii. 260 (*heading*) Vive la bagatelle!

c. Used in other phrases denoting extreme approval or enthusiasm or as a cry of acclamation. Also *joc.*

1865 G. MEREDITH *Let.* 11 Aug. (1970) I. 315 My mind is free, and vive la liberté! 1889 E. DOWSON *Let.* 24 Mar. (1967) 55 Have just finished my poulet. Vive la jeunesse: it has actually lasted 3 weeks. 1906 [see BAN *sb.*[3]]. 1914 'BARTIMEUS' *Naval Occasions* xi. 81 Well! .. *Vive le sport!* If there were no fools there'd be no fun. 1922 E. E. CUMMINGS *Enormous Room* viii. 176 *Vive la bourgeoisie*, I said to myself. 1965 V. CANNING *Whip Hand* viii. 89 We all want to know where Mrs Vadarci is going, and you have—*vive l'amour*—a special contact there. 1980 C. ROSS *Case for Compensation* v. 29 *Vive La France. Vive le sport* and where's my passport. I'm going.

d. ***vive la différence*** (viv la diferɑ̃s), a *joc.* expression denoting approval of the difference between the sexes. Also in extended use. Occas. as *attrib. phr.*

1963 H. SLESAR *Bridge of Lions* (1964) xi. 164 It's your stock-in-trade, isn't it, youth and beauty? *Vive la différence*, and all that jazz. 1964 *Guardian* 21 Apr. 18/4 'Vive là difference' Tories are recognizably Tories, and Socialists are demonstrably Socialists. 1969 [see JOCKETTE]. 1970 G. GREER *Female Eunuch* 29 Frenchmen may well cry 'Vive la différence', for it is cultivated unceasingly in all aspects of life. 1978 *Country Life* 3 Aug. 341/3 The control layout extends Citroen's *vive la différence* attitude.

2. *absol.* and as *sb.*

1919 D. H. LAWRENCE in *Athenæum* 11 Apr. 167/2 There is a new régime, sound of a new *Vive! vive!* 1922 JOYCE *Ulysses* 303 The even more excitable foreign delegates cheered vociferously in a medley of cries .. *hiphip, vive, Allah.*

'**vively**, *adv.* Now *Sc.* or *Obs.* Also 5 **vyvelyche**; *Sc.* 6 **uif-**, **vife-**, **viwe-**, **vivelie**, **vivly**, 6–7 **viuelie**, **-ly**. [f. VIVE *a.* + -LY[2].]

†**1.** In a lively, animated, or energetic manner; with lively action. *Obs.*

1471 RIPLEY *Comp. Alch.* Prol. iii. in Ashm. (1652) 118 After them vyvelyche therefor thou crave. *c* 1590 J. STEWART *Poems* (S.T.S.) II. 11 Thow fyrie vulcane .. My sensis schairpe, And viwelie tham vpsteir. 1648 *Polexena* IV. II. 219 He .. did so vively resent it, that the most of his wounds opened againe. 1673 O. WALKER *Educ.* (1677) 257 Give no man just cause of offence nor resent too vively injuries towards yourself.

†**b.** Sharply; to the quick. *Obs.*$^{-1}$

c 1590 A. HUME *Poems* (S.T.S.) 77/318 And sick as are with wickednes bewitched, I sussie not how viuely they be tuitched.

2. Clearly, distinctly, vividly.

1537 CDL. POLE in Strype *Eccl. Mem.* (1721) I. App. lxxxii. 199 There be divers places .. that cannot so vively be perceived by writing as they should be by conferring the same presently with the writer. *a* 1564 BECON *Policy of War* Wks. I. 125 Whom would it not animate .., seing so many goodly examples viuely described and liuishely set forth in histories before his face? 1593 B. BARNES *Parthenophil & Parth.* Sonn. xxv, If she vively Could see my sorrow's maze, which none can tread. 1630 B. JONSON *New Inn* Argt. 77 Lovel .. describing the effects of Love, so vively, as she .. confesseth herself enamour'd of him. 1632 —— *Magn. Lady* II. [i.] vii. *Chorus*, If I see a thing vively presented on the stage. 1663 BLAIR *Autobiog.* vii. (1848) 97, I supposed the thing had been actually done, when it was so vively represented unto me. 1673 O. WALKER *Educ.* 124 So Polus the Actor, that he might more vively represent the grief of a Father upon the body of his deceased Son, brought in an Urn the ashes of his own Son newly dead. 1789 Ross *Helenore* (ed. 3) 69 But gin ye like to ware the time, then ye How a' the matter stoode, shall vively see.

vivency ('vaɪvɪnsɪ). *rare.* [f. L. *vīv-ĕre* to live + -ENCY.] Manifestation of the principle of life; vitality.

1646 SIR T. BROWNE *Pseud. Ep.* II. i. 55 Not in a distinct and indisputable way of vivency, or answering in all points the properties or affections of plants. [1656 BLOUNT *Glossogr.*, *Vivency*, a living, or injoying life. 1755 JOHNSON, *Vivency*, manner of supporting or continuing life, or vegetation.] 1823 *New Monthly Mag.* VII. 312, I used to enjoy a spring day, its redolence, its vivency, its thrilling sensations of pleasure.

'**viver**[1]. Now *dial.* or *Obs.* Forms: 4 **viuere**, 5 **vyvere**, **wywere**; 4–5 **viuer** (5 **vever**, *Sc.* **wewar**), 5 **vyuer**, 6 **vyver**, 9 **viver**. [a. AF. *viver*, OF. (also mod.F.) *vivier* (= Sp. *vivero*, Pg. *viveiro*), ad. L. *vīvārium* VIVARIUM.] A fishpond.

a 1300 *Cursor M.* 13764 Þis ilk water als þe stori sais, Was mikel renumed in þaa dais, Als it war a gode viuere [*printed* vinere]. *c* 1330 *Durham Acc. Rolls* (Surtees) 519 In j fossato facto de Molend[ino] usque le viuer, vijs. iijd. *c* 1375 *Sc. Leg. Saints* ii. (*Paul*) 344 Sanct paulis hed eftir his discese In a depe vewar warpit was. *c* 1400 MAUNDEV. (Roxb.) xxiii. 105 Withouten þaim er many vyuers and stankes, whare on er many fewles of riuer. *c* 1425 *Voc.* in Wr.-Wülcker 652 *Hoc uiuarium*, wywere. 1511 in *Pat. Roll* III. m. 1 (P.R.O.), Parkes, chaces, warennes, vyvers, pondes. 1875 PARISH *Sussex Gloss.* 128 Vivers, fish-ponds.

†'**viver**[2]. *Obs.* Also 7 **viuer**. [ad. OF. *vivre* (var. *guivre*) serpent:—L. *vīpera* VIPER.] (See quots.)

1611 COTGR., *Poignastre*, the Viuer, a little sea-Dragon. *Ibid.*, *Traigne*, the sea Dragon, Viuer, Quauiuer. [1674 T. P., etc. *Eng. & Fr. Cook* 412 Potage of Vives (*sic*) or Sea-dragons.]

viver[3] ('vaɪvə(r)). *dial.* [Alteration of *fiver* FIBRE.] A fibre or rootlet.

1877 E. LEIGH *Cheshire Gloss.*, *Vivers*, small roots, fibres. 1906 KIPLING *Puck of Pook's Hill* 250 But the vivers of her roots they hold the bank together.

‖**viverra** (vɪ'vɛrə, vaɪ-). *Zool.* [L. *viverra* ferret.] †**a.** The ferret. *Obs.* **b.** The civet-cat (*Viverra civetta*), or other species of the type-genus of the civet family (*Viverridæ*). Also *attrib.*

1706 PHILLIPS (ed. Kersey), *Viverra*, the Ferret, a little Creature that runs into the Burroughs of Rabbits. 1772–84 *Cook's Voy.* (1790) I. 217 Of quadrupedes, there are goats, wolves, pole-cats, a spotted animal of the viverra kind, and several kinds of serpents. 1813 PRICHARD *Phys. Hist. Man* iii. §3. 113 Of the Viverra family. 1815 KIRBY & SP. *Entomol.* ix. (1817) I. 280 Another species of Viverra (*V. prehensilis*) is also reputed to be an eager insect-hunter.

viverrid (vɪ'vɛrɪd), *a.* and *sb. Zool.* [ad. mod.L. *Viverrid-æ*, f. L. *viverra* ferret: see -ID[3].]

A. *adj.* Belonging or pertaining to the family Viverridæ, which comprises civets, genets, and mongooses. **B.** *sb.* A viverrid animal.

1910 H. F. OSBORN *Age of Mammals* iii. 197 Still more striking is the presence [in the Oligocene] of the fierce viverrid carnivores (*Amphicitis*, *Herpestes*) of the modern civet and mongoose types. *Ibid.* iv. 259 The mustelids were becoming more numerous .. while the Asiatic civets or viverrids (*Viverra*) are becoming somewhat more rare [in the Miocene]. 1964 PARKER & HASWELL *Text-bk. Zool.* (ed. 7) II. 795 The aberrant *Proteles*, the Aard-wolf or Earth-wolf of Africa is insectivorous... Like the hyænas it is obviously a highly specialised viverrid offshoot. 1976 *Nature* 5 Aug. 464/1 The carnivore fauna [of the Laetolil beds in Tanzania] is characterised by a high percentage of viverrids, constituting 32% of all the carnivore specimens.

vi'verridous, *a. Zool.* [f. mod.L. *Viverrid-æ* (see VIVERRA) + -OUS.] Of or belonging to the *Viverridæ* or civet family.

1833 E. T. BENNETT in *Trans. Zool. Soc.* I. 137 Notice of a Mammiferous Animal from Madagascar, constituting a New Form among the Viverridous Carnivora. 1834 *Proc. Zool. Soc.* I. 46 Description of a Viverridous Animal from Madagascar.

viverrine (vɪ'vεraɪn, vaɪ-), *a.* and *sb. Zool.* [ad. mod.L. *viverrin-us*, f. *viverra* VIVERRA: see -INE[1].]

A. *adj.* Resembling or related to the civet, or the civet family; *spec.* belonging to the sub-family *Viverrinæ.* **a.** In specific names, as ***viverrine cat, dasyurus, opossum***, etc.

1800 SHAW *Gen. Zool.* I. II. 491 Viverrine Opossum. *Didelphis Viverrina.* 1810 *Encycl. Brit.* (ed. 4) XII. 497 *Dasyurus Viverrinus*, Viverrine Dasyurus. Black, spotted with white; tail without spots. *c* 1880 *Cassell's Nat. Hist.* II. 53 The Viverrine Cat, *Felis viverrina.* 1885 *Athenæum* 28 Mar. 412/1 A viverrine phalanger (*Phalangista viverrina*) from Australia.

b. In general use.

1874 WOOD *Nat. Hist.* 47 A small, but rather important, group of the Viverrine animals. 1883 *Encycl. Brit.* XV. 436/2 *Cynogale benettii* .. is a curious Otter-like modification of the Viverrine type.

B. *sb.* An individual of the sub-family *Viverrinæ.*

c 1880 *Cassell's Nat. Hist.* II. 86 The skull has all the essential characters of that of a Viverrine.

vivers ('vaɪvəz), *sb. pl.* Chiefly *Sc.* Forms: α. 6 **veveres**, **wewers**, 7 **vievers**, **viewers**. β. 6 **viwers**, **wivers**, **wiwors**, **wiuerse**, 6–7 **viuers**, 6, 8–9 **vivers** (6 **vivars**). See also VIVRES. [ad. OF. (also mod.F.) *vivres*, pl. of *vivre* food, sustenance, substantive use of *vivre* to live.] Food, provisions, victuals, eatables.

Only Sc. till the 19th century; its later literary currency is probably due to its frequent occurrence in the Waverley Novels.

α. 1536 QUEEN MARGARET in *St. Papers Hen. VIII* (1836) V. 43 þa ma be portative be wattyr for carying of þar veveres and uthyres necyssares. *a* 1578 LINDESAY (Pitscottie) *Chron. Scot.* (S.T.S.) I. 78 Ane armie .. weill furnischit witht all kynd of weweris and munitioun. 1609 SKENE *Reg. Mag.*, *Stat. Rob. I*, 20 b, He sall cume .. weill furnished with siluer to bye vievers for his sustentation.

β. 1551 *Reg. Privy Council Scot.* I. 114 The greit .. derth .. of all kynd of victuallis and viveris. 1582–8 *Hist. James VI* (1804) 168 The stoir of thair victualles being daylie scand, they directit, as afore, sum horsmen to scour the fields for viuers. 1622 in *10th Rep. Hist. MSS. Comm.* App. I. 108 Viuers are very chepe heere and thay are dere with the enimy. 1725 *Records of Elgin* (New Spald. Cl. 1903) I. 420 The prices of fyring, fewell, fish, flesh and other vivers are latelie arisen to an exorbitant hight. 1756 MRS. CALDERWOOD in *Coltness Collect.* (Maitl. Club) 149 Every thing of vivers is dear in Holland but vegetables. 1814 SCOTT *Wav.* xlii, I'll join you at three, if the vivers can tarry so long. 1860 MOTLEY *Netherl.* xiii. (1868) II. 164 He bitterly complained of the unwillingness of the country-people to furnish vivers, waggons, and other necessaries. 1887 BEATTY-KINGSTON *Music & Manners* II. 18 You shall have your beer, vivers, and tobacco cheap.

fig. 1588 A. KING tr. *Canisius' Catech.* 87 This is our viuers during the pilgramedg of this transitorie lif.

vives (vaɪvz), *sb. pl.* Also 6 **vyves**, 6–8 **viues**, 7 **uiues**, **vies**. [Aphetic form of AVIVES. Cf. FIVES[1], VEES[1], and YVES.] Hard swellings of the submaxillary glands of a horse; the presence of these regarded as a specific morbid condition in a horse.

1523 FITZHERB. *Husb.* §91 The viues is a sorance vnder a horse ere, bytwene the ouer ende of the chall-bones and the necke, and are rounde knottes bytwene the skyn and the fleshe. 1566 BLUNDEVIL *Horses* IV. xxxvi. (1580) 17 b, The Vives be certaine kirnels growing vnder the horses eare. 1577 B. GOOGE *Heresbach's Husb.* III. (1586) 123 There is a disease that is common in Horses, called the Viues. 1639 T. DE GRAY *Compl. Horsem.* 79 It is a disease which growes under the eares, and secundum vulgus it is called the fives or vives. 1681 *Lond. Gaz.* No. 1605/4 One a Bay Horse above thirteen hands high, .. has been burned in the Head for the Vies. *c* 1720 W. GIBSON *Farrier's Dispens.* xiii. (1734) 263 This is particularly of service in the Vives and Strangles. 1754 BARTLET *Gentlem. Farriery* 104 The vives or ives differs from the strangles only in this, that the swelling of the kernels under the ears of the horse .. seldom gather. 1831 YOUATT *Horse* 149 Several distinct kernels are to be felt under the jaw... The farriers call them vives.

‖**viveur** (vivœr). [Fr., lit. 'a living person'.] One who lives a fashionable and social life; a man of pleasure. Cf. *bon viveur* s.v. BON *a.*

1845 THACKERAY in *Fraser's Mag.* Nov. 591/2 He became a *viveur* and jolly dog about town. 1901 'L. MALET' *Hist. Sir Richard Calmady* III. x. 261 He has the credit of being something of a *viveur.* He knew not only his Paris, but his Baden-Baden, and his Naples, and various other warm corners where great and good men .. congregate. 1921 L. STRACHEY *Queen Victoria* iii. 70 The middle-aged, hard-faced *viveur* was addressed by his young hostess. 1943 *Burlington Mag.* Aug. 201/1 Boulestin was secretary to Willy, the well-known Parisian author, journalist and *viveur*, husband to Colette.

vivi- ('vɪvɪ), combining form of L. *vīvus* alive, living, employed in a few terms, as †**vivicom'bustion**, = next; **vivicre'mation**, the action of burning, or the fact of being burned, alive; †**vividi'ssection** = VIVISECTION 2; **vivi'sepulture**, burying alive.

a **1711** G. GREY *Life M. Robinson* in Mayor *Autobiogr.* (1856) 31 He was invited by some learned persons in other colleges to shew them vividissections of dogs. **1827** G. S. FABER *Sacr. Cal. Prophecy* (1844) I. 220 The horrid penalty of vivi-cremation which a corrupt Church has specially appropriated to those whom she denominates heretics. **1852** J. W. BLAKESLEY *Herodotus* I. 87 Many centuries afterwards ..human sacrifices appear to have been offered to Mithras, but then not by vivi-combustion. **1861** R. F. BURTON *City of Saints* 580 They are a superstitious brood and have many cruel practices—human sacrifices and vivisepulture. **1863** LIDDELL in *Archaeol.* XL. 243 Pliny speaks of the practice of vivisepulture as continued to his own time.

vivianite ('vɪvɪənaɪt). *Min.* [f. the name of the discoverer, John Henry *Vivian* (1785–1855), of Truro and Swansea; named by Werner, 1817.] A phosphate of iron usually occurring in crystals of blue and green colour.

1823 W. PHILLIPS *Elem. Introd. Min.* 238 Phosphate of Iron, Vivianite,..is of various shades of blue and green, sometimes bluish-green. **1867** BLOXAM *Chem.* 324 The phosphates of protoxide and sesquioxide of iron are found associated in the mineral known as vivianite or native Prussian blue. **1884** *Times* (weekly ed.) 19 Sept. 3/3 A small gold coin, doubled up, was found within a lump of bone and vivianite.

Hence **'vivianitized** *a.*, encrusted with vivianite.

1870 *Illustr. Lond. News* 1 Jan. 12/3 Great quantities of vivianitised bones..were found.

vivid ('vɪvɪd), *a.* [ad. L. *vīvid-us* living, animated, lively, f. *vīvĕre* to live. Cf. It. *vivido.*]

1. Full of life; vigorous, active, or energetic on this account; lively or brisk: **a.** Of persons (or animals), their attributes, etc.

1638 JACKSON *Creed* IX. xxix. §2 In my old and decaying days to publish the fruits of my former labours in these mysteries which to my apprehension had been well set in my flourishing and vivid years. **1658** W. BURTON *Itin. Anton.* 80 His whole body was vivid and strong. **1769** E. BANCROFT *Guiana* 254 They have a sprightly vivid countenance. **1799** CORRY *Sat. Lond.* (1803) 45 When the fine lady returns home fatigued after a succession of important morning visits and the exhaustion of her vivid spirits. **1858** HAWTHORNE *Fr. & It. Note-bks.* (1871) II. 13 Mr. Browning was..a most vivid and quick-thoughted person. **1876** GEO. ELIOT *Dan. Der.* xxxv, Mr. Vandernoodt,..as good a foil as could well be found to the intense colouring and vivid gravity of Deronda. **1878** BROWNING *Poets Croisic* clix, His hope be in the vivid horse Whose neck God clothed with thunder.

fig. **1876** BLACKIE *Songs Relig. & Life* 234 Let sweet fragrance flow from thee, Vivid breath of pure emotion.

b. Of material things or substances, or their qualities.

1650 BULWER *Anthropomet.* 230 The vertue that was ordained to be in that matter, cannot be so vivid and effectual. **1670** W. SIMPSON *Hydrol. Ess.* 99 Elementary fire ..produced from a vivid nitrous or hermetick salt. **1818** BUSBY *Gram. Mus.* 481 This vivid and volatile instrument [*sc.* the violin]. **1897** MARY KINGSLEY *W. Africa* Introd. 6 Things emitting at unexpectedly short notice vivid and awful stenches.

c. Of feelings, etc.: Lively, strong, intense.

1853 C. BRONTE *Villette* xix, His passions were strong, his aversions and attachments alike vivid. **1859** DARWIN *Orig. Spec.* xi. (1860) 366 We might have remained in this same belief, had not Agassiz and others called vivid attention to the Glacial period. **1860** W. COLLINS *Wom. White* I. narr. W. H. vi, Her face expressed vivid interest and astonishment, nothing more. **1873** H. ROGERS *Orig. Bible* i. (1875) 35 The first is clearly proved by..the vivid indignation he evoked. **1905** G. THORNE *Lost Cause* viii, There is a sterling and vivid Christianity among them.

2. a. Of actions or operations: Proceeding, or taking place, with great vigour or activity.

1702 *Rouse's Heav. Univ.* Adv. 2 More vivid Operations of the Internal Light of souls. **1815** J. SMITH *Panorama Sci. & Art* II. 472 The combustion that ensues is exceedingly vivid and beautiful. **1842** A. COMBE *Physiol. Digestion* (ed. 4) 257 Whenever any living part is called into vivid action, an increased flow of blood and of nervous energy towards it immediately commences. **1858** LARDNER *Hand-bk. Nat. Phil.* 392 A thin cylinder of oily vapour..is kept in a state of vivid and constant combustion.

b. Of utterances: Strongly or warmly expressed.

1806 J. BERESFORD *Miseries Hum. Life* (ed. 3) VI. xiii, Being mounted on a beast who..proceeds very coolly to repose himself in the middle of the pond without..paying the slightest attention to your vivid remonstrances on the subject. **1838** PRESCOTT *Ferd. & Is.* (1846) III. x. 10 The Spanish government..made the most vivid remonstrances through its resident minister. **1981** *Observer* 15 Nov. 2/8 The famous are shown off-guard—for example,..Sue Lawley using vivid language.

c. Of intellectual faculties: Capable of ready and clear creation of ideas or concepts.

1814 SCOTT *Wav.* iii, Edward's power of imagination.. was vivid. **1836** HOR. SMITH *Tin Trump.* I. 14 Vivid conception, and keen sensibility, will not of themselves make a good actor. **1863** TREVELYAN *Compet. Wallah* (1866) 318 Every page teems with the vivid thought, the glowing fancy [etc.]. **1885** 'MRS. ALEXANDER' *At Bay* i, I suspect your fancy is tolerably vivid still.

d. Of description, etc.: Presenting subjects or ideas in a clear and striking manner. Freq. with *picture* in fig. use.

(*a*) **1837** LOCKHART *Scott* IV. v. 157, I mean especially a power of vivid painting—the true and primary sense of what is called Imagination. **1864** PUSEY *Lect. Daniel* vi. 339 Nehemiah himself relates,..in one consecutive vivid narrative, the history of the rebuilding of the walls of Jerusalem. **1868** FREEMAN *Norm. Conq.* (1877) I. iv. 149 A most vivid history of the time. **1872** LOWELL *Milton* Prose Wks. 1890 IV. 72 Mr. Masson's unhappy infection with the vivid style. **1876** FREEMAN *Norm. Conq.* V. xxiii. 296 We have..a no less vivid report of the real or imaginary speeches.

(*b*) **1847** GROTE *Greece* II. xvii. III. 320 It is not from them however that Herodotus draws his vivid picture of the people, with their inhuman rites and repulsive personal features. **1879** FROUDE *Cæsar* xx. 349 These letters give a vivid picture of the uncertainties which distracted public opinion.

3. a. Of colour, light, etc.: Brilliant, fresh, lively, bright.

1665 BOYLE *Occas. Refl.* VI. v. (1848) 354 Many of the Ladies wear in their Ribbands little less vivid colours, than those of their faces. **1667** —— in *Phil. Trans.* II. 582 A piece of such Wood..that gave a vivid light (for rotten Wood). **1704** NEWTON *Optics* I. II. x. (1721) 157 Such Bodies ought to be chosen as have the fullest and most vivid Colours. *c* **1750** SHENSTONE *Ruin'd Abbey* 180 The vivid vermeil fled his fady cheek. **1791** MRS. RADCLIFFE *Rom. Forest* i, Upon the vivid glow of the western horizon. **1815** J. SMITH *Panorama Sci. & Art* II. 413 In a little time it becomes of a deep vivid blue. **1867** HOWELLS *Ital. Journ.* 114 The lavish delight in color found expression in the vividest hues upon the walls. **1875** J. H. BENNET *Winter Medit.* (ed. 5) 408 The love of vivid colours seems to increase as we descend south.

b. Of things in respect of colour or brightness.

1686 GOAD *Celest. Bodies* II. iv. 212 The Sun alone makes not any Rainbow that is vivid or Illustrious. **1718** POPE *Iliad* VIII. 691 Around her throne the vivid planets roll. *a* **1763** SHENSTONE *Elegies* xi. 42 Then glows the breast..More free, more vivid, than the linnet's wing. **1794** R. J. SULIVAN *View Nat.* II. 381 The best glasses have no other effect than the making them [the stars] more vivid in their appearance. **1837** *New Monthly Mag.* L. 407 A wreath of laurel, intensely vivid, inclosed..the auburn splendours of the head. **1860** TYNDALL *Glac.* I. ii. 21 Like a vivid circular rainbow quite round the sun. **1874** HOLLAND *Mistr. Manse* 114 The brooding, threatning bank of mist Grows into groups of vivid isles.

4. a. Clearly or distinctly perceived or perceptible; appealing strongly to the mind or eye.

1690 LOCKE *Hum. Und.* II. xix. 112 Those Motions made on the Organs of Sense, which at other times produce very vivid and sensible Ideas. **1710** J. CLARKE tr. *Rohault's Nat. Philos.* (1729) I. 248 This immaterial Image, ought to be so much the more vivid or clear, as the Object sends forth more Rays of Light. **1774** J. BRYANT *Mythol.* II. 214 We shall find the traces of this event more vivid and determinate than those of Greece. **1806** JEBB in Knox & J. *Corr.* (1834) I. 297 Sweet sounds awaken latent harmonies within us, and thus produce a vivid idea of the beautiful. **1848** W. K. KELLY tr. *L. Blanc's Hist. Ten Y.* I. 320 At a moment when the part played by the people in July was still fresh and vivid in recollection. **1869** FARRAR *Fam. Speech* ii. (1873) 79 *note*, No book gives a more vivid impression of the growth of Russian influence. **1883** H. WACE *Gosp. & Witnesses* ii. 34 Its vivid internal marks of genuineness.

absol. **1876** LOWELL *Among my Bks.* Ser. II. 261 Whether the cause lie not rather in a besetting velleity of the picturesque and vivid.

b. Intensely or strongly felt.

1704–5 ATTERBURY *Serm., Matt. xiv. 23* (1726) I. 357 Tempting Objects, by their Number and Nearness, make the most Vivid and Lasting Impressions upon us. **1715** DESAGULIERS *Fires Impr.* 41 A more vivid Sensation of Cold. **1835** I. TAYLOR *Spir. Despot.* ii. 55 Seasons..in which the clergy are exposed to vivid anxieties or endure actual privations. **1850** ROBERTSON *Serm.* Ser. III. viii. (1857) 111 When the recollection of his sin is most vivid and most poignant. **1874** GREEN *Short Hist.* viii. §1. 454 The vivid sense of a Divine Purity close to such men made the life of common men seem sin.

5. Life-like; resembling life.

1852 HAWTHORNE *Blithedale Rom.* xi, He carried a stick with a wooden head, carved in vivid imitation of that of a serpent.

6. Quasi-*adv.* Vividly, brightly.

1819 KEATS *Fall Hyperion* I. 245 The scenes Still swooning vivid through my globed brain. **1865** CARLYLE *Fredk. Gt.* XX. iii. (1872) IX. 44 The Prussian camp-fires, they too are all burning uncommonly vivid.

vividity (vɪ'vɪdɪtɪ). [f. prec. + -ITY.]

†**1.** Living force, vitality. *Obs.*$^{-1}$

1616 T. ADAMS *Soul's Sickness* 28 Corrupt affections, which like vicious humours gnaw and suck the conscience dry of all viuiditie.

2. The quality or state of being vivid; vividness.

1772 W. CULLEN *Lect. Pathol.* in J. Thomson *Life* (1832) I. 378 A degree of Vividity, of Alacrity, and Levity, or a disposition to change..can only be considered as states of morbid Irritability..in the Brain. **1780** BENTHAM *Princ. Legisl.* vi. §12 (1789) 45 Clearness of discernment,..vividity and rapidity of imagination. **1813** T. BUSBY *Lucretius* II. v. Comm. p. xl, A vast mass of illumined matter, in the general glow and vividity of which the opaque spots are almost lost. **1880** *Daily News* 15 April 6/1 Being of life size, the vividity of the flesh tints and the extraordinary modelling give to it a startling appearance of reality.

vividly ('vɪvɪdlɪ), *adv.* [f. VIVID *a.* + -LY[2].]

1. Brightly, brilliantly, in respect of colour or light.

1667 BOYLE in *Phil. Trans.* II. 587, I..found it to shine vividly. **1815** J. SMITH *Panorama Sci. & Art* II. 220 The light is still seen, but not so vividly. **1842** JOHNSTON in *Proc. Berw. Nat. Club* II. 36 The shell is strongly ribbed and rather vividly streaked..with yellow or red. **1860** TYNDALL *Glac.* I. vi. 255 While the former semicircle remains white, the latter one is vividly coloured. **1878** HUXLEY *Physiogr.* 103 It bursts suddenly into flame and burns vividly.

2. Clearly, strongly, intensely, in respect of mental impression or effect.

a **1677** BARROW *Serm. Prov. iv. 23* Wks. 1686 III. 46 He will not be so forward to engage himself upon such occasions; danger and mischief being so vividly pre-represented to his sight. **1748** HARTLEY *Observ. Man* I. iii. §5. 385 If they rise up quick and vividly one after another, as Subjects, Predicates, and other Associates use to do. **1832** R. & J. LANDER *Exped. Niger* III. xviii. 142 Oh how vividly did early impressions return to my soul. **1862** M'COSH *Supernat.* II. i. §4. 159 The word seraphic..is vividly descriptive of the flights of Isaiah. **1868** FREEMAN *Norm. Conq.* (1877) II. viii. 287 The way in which treason is spoken of sets vividly before us the difficulties with which William had still to contend.

'vividness. [f. as prec. + -NESS.] The state or quality of being vivid, in senses of the adj. **a.** Of colour, light, etc.

1667–8 BOYLE in *Phil. Trans.* II. 593 To examine..the Conjecture,..That the durableness of the Light..might proceed in great part from the Vividness of it. *a* **1700** EVELYN *Diary* 22 June 1664 With such lively colours, that for splendour and vividness we have nothing in Europe that approches it. **1794** G. ADAMS *Nat. & Exp. Philos.* IV. xliv. 190 In the vividness of its lustre..it exceeded any thing he had ever seen before. **1836** MACGILLIVRAY *Trav. Humboldt* xviii. 256 Numerous palms are reflected by the surface of the river with a vividness almost as bright as that of the objects themselves. **1859** GEO. ELIOT *A. Bede* ii, The delicate colouring of her face seemed to gather a calm vividness, like flowers at evening. **1883** MISS M. BETHAM-EDWARDS *Disarmed* xxxiv, For a few minutes the flashes of lightning were awful in their vividness.

b. Of ideas, conceptions, impressions, etc.

1768 TUCKER *Lt. Nat.* II. I. xiii. 189 A variety of ideas afford us no notion of succession unless we perceive one come before the other; nor can it be imagined that their degrees of vividness or faintness will do the job. **1812** SIR H. DAVY *Chem. Philos.* 17 The notions of fairies and of genii, which have been depicted with so much vividness of fancy and liveliness of description. **1858** J. MARTINEAU *Stud. Chr.* 207 The very vividness of the conception may have rendered him insensible to the precariousness of the proof. **1873** SYMONDS *Grk. Poets* xi. 356 Death at sea touched the Greek imagination with peculiar vividness.

c. Of description, narrative, etc.

1828 MISS MITFORD in L'Estrange *Life* (1870) II. xi. 257 She has a mastery of the subject, and a truth and vividness of expression, second only to Cowper. **1845** M. PATTISON *Ess.* (1889) I. 7 His graphic narrative has all the vividness that art can give to description of what the describer has not himself actually witnessed. **1884** R. W. CHURCH *Bacon* ix. 220 In the essay on Friendship he describes the process with a vividness which tells of his own experience.

‖ **vivier** (vivje). In 5 vyuier. [OF. and mod.F. *vivier*: see VIVER[1].] A fishpond; a tank for storing live fish, etc.

c **1450** *Merlin* xix. 308 He lete make a maner to repeire to, that was right feire and riche by the vyuier.

b. In mod. use. Also *attrib.*

1964 F. WHITE *West of Rhone* ii. 31 Viviers, an old town, ..was once the fish-ponds, the *viviers*, of the bishop. **1973** *Alderney Jrnl.* 8 Oct. 4 Much has been said about the politics of building vivier tanks at the end of the harbour jetty. **1979** *Guardian* 10 Oct. 12/6 The Dutch lorries..that buy shellfish from Harveys, are vivier lorries. They have huge water tanks full of sea water.

vivific (vɪ'vɪfɪk), *a.* Also 6 viuifike, 7–8 vivifick. [ad. L. (post-classical) *vīvific-us*, f. *vīv-us* living: see -FIC. So OF. and F. *vivifique*, Sp., Pg., It. *vivifico.*] Life-giving, enlivening, vivifying.

1551 BP. GARDINER *On Sacram.* I. 13 b, Wherby they might vnderstand him verie God, whose fleshe..geuen spiritually to be eaten of vs..[is] viuifike and geueth life. **1669** GALE *Crt. Gentiles* I. III. iii. 324 Chrysostome cals it.. a vivifick Energie. **1694** *Phil. Trans.* XVIII. 39 A Vivifick Spirit or Aura, generated out of the Blood by the Brain. **1709** T. ROBINSON *Vind. Mosaick Syst.* 19 Light was the Active and Vivifick Principle of Generation. **1788** T. TAYLOR *Proclus* I. 118 The zoogonic, or vivific goddess, pours through these into the universe, an inexplicable and efficacious power. **1809** SOUTHEY in *Q. Rev.* I. 194 There is, however, in all religious communities a vivacious and vivific principle not to be found in the same degree in political bodies. **1852** A. BALLOU *Spirit Manifest.* i. 15 Matter inert and passive, spirit vivific and active. **1877** W. R. COOPER *Egypt. Obelisks* v. (1878) 25 [The name] 'The Eternal Generator' contains an allusion to the vivific power of Ra, as the creator of life.

†**vi'vifical,** *a. Obs.* [f. as prec. + -AL[1].] = prec.

1632 L. ROWZEE *Qveenes Welles* i. 2 Vivificall moisture.. maketh them [plants] all to grow and prosper. **1665** J. WEBB *Stone-Heng* (1725) 104 That Vivifical Heat, which..gives Life to all Things. *a* **1686** T. WATSON *Body of Div.* (1692) 215 Christ is so full of Sap and vivifical Influence, that he makes all, inoculated into him, grow Fruitful.

†**vivificant,** *a. Obs.* [ad. L. *vīvificant-*, *vīvificans*, pres. pple. of *vīvificāre*: see next.] = VIVIFIC *a.*

1576 FLEMING *Panopl. Epist.* A 3, The temperature of the ayre, which is viuificant, quickening, and full of life. **1603** HOLLAND *Plutarch's Mor.* 992 Every sense findeth benefit of fire as of a vivificant power and quickening vertue. **1653** H. COGAN *Diod. Sic.* 4 The one..having a vivificant and fierce, the other a cold and moist nature. **1660** tr. *Amyraldus' Treat. conc. Relig.* III. viii. 464 That admirable splendor and vivificant virtue which is in the Sun.

vivificate (vɪˈvɪfɪkeɪt), *v.* Also 5–7 viuificat(e, 6 vivifycate. [ad. L. *vīvificāt-*, ppl. stem of *vīvificāre* (Tertullian, etc.; hence It. *vivificare*, Sp. and Pg. *vivificar*), f. *vīv-us* alive: cf. VIVIFIC *a.* and -ATE[3].]

1. *trans.* To give life to, to animate, to enliven or quicken; = VIVIFY *v.* 1.

1432–50 tr. *Higden* (Rolls) I. 189 In the pleyne þer of is a pitte where thei ȝafe to viuificate the myndes of philosophres. *a* **1500** *Colkelbie Sow* 887 Lyk [fr]o sede sawin in erd mortificat Flouris mony fructis viuificat. **1547** BOORDE *Brev. Health* lxxxvi. 35 The herte dothe vivifycate all other members. **1565** HARDING *Confut.* II. xiv. 109 b, God the Wordes owne body, that hath power to viuificate and quicken all thinges. **1609** BIBLE (Douay) *Ezek.* xiii. 18 When they caught the soules of my people, they did vivificate their soules. **1653** H. MORE *Conject. Cabbal.* 31 Even as God vivificates and actuates the whole world. **1675** O. WALKER, etc. *Paraphr. St. Paul* 161 The sensitive..soul or faculty continues meanwhile in the body..vivificating it. **1819** H. BUSK *Vestriad* I. 217 Whose blood vivificates thy veins.

†**2.** *intr.* To become endued with life. *Obs.*$^{-1}$

1660 STANLEY *Hist. Philos.* IX. (1687) 551/2 This beam penetrates to the Abyss, and thereby all things vivificate.

Hence **viˈvificating** *ppl. a.*

a **1688** CUDWORTH *Immut. Mor.* III. ii. §3. (1731) 89 The Compound..of the Body and a certain Vivificating Light, imparted from the Soul to it.

vivification (ˌvɪvɪfɪˈkeɪʃən). Also 6–7 viui-, 7 uiui-. [ad. L. *vīvificātio* (Tertullian), n. of action f. *vīvificāre*: see prec. and -ATION. So F. *vivification*, Sp. *vivificacion*, Pg. *-ação*, It. *vivificazione*.]

1. The process or fact of being vivified in a spiritual sense. (Cf. Eph. ii. 1–5.)

a **1548** in Ellis *Orig. Lett.* Ser. III. III. 262 We muste receyve the sacraments and have contrition..and then viuification, whiche is to aryse agayne by feithe. **1589** T. L. *Advt. to Q. Elizabeth* (1651) 48 That Holinesse and trewnesse of life,..under the names Vivification, renovation spirituall, and the first resurrection. **1606** S. GARDINER *Bk. Angling* 116 An auersion from sinne, a conuersion to God: the mortification of the olde Adam, and the viuification of the newe man. **1653** BAXTER *Worc. Petit. Def.* 9 O the sweet comfort that I have..in the Mortification and Vivification of my godly Friends! **1690** C. NESSE *O. & N. Test.* I. 63 The new man..must be put on by the grace of vivification.

2. The action or fact of enduing with life; the fact of being vivified physically.

1626 BACON *Sylva* §329 If that Motion be in a certain Order, there followeth Vivification and Figuration. **1631** A. B. tr. *Lessius' De Prov. Num.* II. viii. 315 The vnion of the Soule of man with the body, as also the informing and the viuification (as I may tearme it) of the whole body decayeth no lesse, then in beasts. **1678** CUDWORTH *Intell. Syst.* 805 The Divine Spirit..which was the Efficient Cause of the Vivification of our Saviour's Body at his Resurrection. **1797** *Monthly Mag.* III. 515 The gods call the soul..a drop from the whole of vivification. **1871** TYLOR *Prim. Cult.* II. 44 The vivification of ghosts by sacrifices of blood.

b. *concr.* That which vivifies. *rare*$^{-1}$.

1631 MABBE *Celestina* I. 20 O reliever of my torment, and vivification of my life.

c. *Phys.* The process of converting, or of being converted, into living tissue.

1872 F. G. THOMAS *Dis. Women* (ed. 3) 128 Vivification of the edges not being necessary, the procedure is simpler and less dangerous.

†**3.** Restoration of a metal to its original state.

1610 B. JONSON *Alch.* II. v, *Sub.* And when comes Viuification? *Fac.* After Mortification. **1649** QUARLES *Virgin Widow* IV. i, He can bring an Artificiall Resurrection, and Vivification to Mercury. **1728** CHAMBERS *Cycl.*, *Vivification*, ..The Chymists also use the Word in speaking of the new Force, Vigour, and Lustre which by this Art they give to natural Bodies, particularly to Mercury, which after having been fix'd or amalgamated, they restore to its first State.

4. The action or fact of investing with an air of vitality or reality.

1858 BAGEHOT in *Nat. Rev.* Oct. 468 A second most wonderful special faculty which Mr. Dickens possesses is what we may call his vivification of character. **1890** *Sat. Rev.* 15 March 333/1 [He] is an industrious scholar..but we do not know that he has the gift of vivification.

†**vivificative,** *a. Obs.* [f. VIVIFICATE *v.* + -IVE. Cf. OF. *vivificatif, -ive*, Sp., Pg., It. *vivificativo*.] Life-giving, vivifying.

c **1550** ROLLAND *Crt. Venus* II. 852 The sweit smell, and the suaue odour..Sa weill sawrit, and viuificatiue. **1647** H. MORE *Song of Soul* Notes 353 Psyche cannot issue out into any externall vivificative act, unlesse you suppose a body. **1661** RUST *Origen's Opin.* 122 The operations of the Spirit of life, or quickning Spirit, are all vivificative. **1755** AMORY *Mem.* (1766) II. 194 *note*, By touching them with faith, we may attract the sanctification and vivificative virtue which resideth in them.

†**vivificator.** *Obs.* [f. as prec. + -OR. Cf. OF. *vivificateur*, Sp. and Pg. *vivificador*.] One who or that which gives life, a vivifier.

a **1555** BRADFORD *Wks.* (Parker Soc.) 280 We..believe.. the Holy Spirit to be the only Comforter, vivificator, counsellor, and master of all truth. **1648** HEXHAM II, *Levendigh maker*, a Vivificatour. **1677** GALE *Crt. Gentiles* IV. II. viii. 449 If they had believed that this Spirit is both Lord, and Creator and Vivificator,..they might have had some convenient accesse to life.

†**vivificent,** *a. Obs.* [irreg. f. L. *vīv-us* alive: cf. -FIC and -ENT.] Living.

1597 A. M. tr. *Guillemeau's Fr. Chirurg.* 33 b/1 It is necessarye that the vivificent parte drive from it the mortified, or else the mortifiede allso cause mortificatione in the vivificent partes. **1599** —— *Gabelhouer's Bk. Physicke* 39/1 Take a vivificent Cocke, and vse him on that sorte. **1604** R. CAWDREY *Table Alph.*, *Viuificent*, liuely, or full of strength.

vivified (ˈvɪvɪfaɪd), *ppl. a.* [f. VIVIFY *v.* + -ED[1].] Endued with life, animated, living.

Also *transf.* of metals: cf. VIVIFICATION 3.

1767 S. PATERSON *Another Trav.* II. 113 Are we not all originally..sprung from the same vivified mass? **1833** N. ARNOTT *Physics* (ed. 5) II. 120 Charcoal..heated with an oxid-ore..leaves at the bottom of the furnace or crucible the vivified or pure metal. **1858** PIRIE *Inq. Hum. Mind* vii. 339 A physical feeling of pain, appertaining to the vivified machine. **1893** F. ADAMS *New Egypt* 179, I looked back.. and saw him still standing there in the dark frameway, strangely like some vivified portrait by Velasquez.

vivifier (ˈvɪvɪfaɪə(r)). [f. as prec. + -ER[1].] One who or that which gives life.

1860 PUSEY *Min. Proph.* 310 God's love for us is the great incitement, constrainer, vivifier of His creature's love. *c* **1865** WATSON in *Circ. Sci.* I. 427/2 The oxygen of the air is the great vivifier of nature. **1879** CHR. G. ROSSETTI *Seek & F.* 26 Light and heat, to our apprehension the great vivifiers of the material world.

vivify (ˈvɪvɪfaɪ), *v.* [ad. F. *vivifier* (OF. from 12th c.), ad. L. *vīvificāre*: see VIVIFICATE *v.*]

1. *trans.* To give life to; to endue with life; to animate; to quicken.

1545 RAYNALD *Byrth Mankynde* 42 Throughe these artyres liuely spirite, and fresshe aere, is diriuied out of the mother into the childe, wherwith the naturall hete of the chylde is viuified and refresshed. **1597** A. M. tr. *Guillemeau's Fr. Chirurg.* *iij, Let us consider on the Sunne ..what doth she effect?..[she doth] warme us, vivifye and administre lyfe vnto vs. **1615** CROOKE *Body of Man* 263 Mercurius Trismegistus saide well, that it was the spirite which viuifieth or quickneth euery forme in the whole world. **1653** W. RAMESEY *Astrol. Restored* 86 [They] placed a fiery sign first, for that heat ruleth in fire, by which all things are quickened and vivifyed. *a* **1693** *Urquhart's Rabelais* III. iii. 39 The great Soul of the *Universe*..vivifyeth all manner of things. **1799** *Monthly Rev.* XXX. 568 In this explosion of lite, every particle of native soil was vivified; and numberless races of vegetables and animals were produced. **1859** KINGSLEY *Misc.* (1860) I. 359 An instinct of the dynamic and supernatural laws which underlie and vivify this material universe. **1881** TYNDALL *Ess. Floating Matter of Air* 224 An indraught—slight no doubt, but still sufficient to contaminate or vivify the infusion.

b. *transf.* and *fig.* (Common in 19th c.)

1603 FLORIO *Montaigne* I. xix. 30 As in nature one contrarie is vivified by another contrarie. **1713** POPE *Guardian* No. 11 ¶3 It [an elixir] restores and vivifies the most dejected Minds. **1776** SIR J. REYNOLDS *Disc.* vii. (1876) 408 That Promethean fire, which animates the canvass and vivifies the marble. **1788** GIBBON *Decl. & F.* xlix. V. 144 Their execution would have vivified the empire. **1832** HT. MARTINEAU *Each & All* iv. 59 The utmost that education can do is to extend his views, to exalt his aims, and vivify his powers. **1833** ALISON *Hist. Europe* (1849) I. iii. §68. 322 His plan was to vivify the State by vigorous measures. **1865** MOZLEY *Mirac.* i. 4 It vivifies the stock we have, but does not add one item to it. **1905** *Sat. Rev.* 29 April 545/2 It enables its 'supers' to shout.. and thereby vivify a languishing enthusiasm.

c. *Phys.* To convert into living tissue.

1897 *Allbutt's Syst. Med.* IV. 416 An incision..to lay open any sinuous track, vivify callous edges, or remove spongy granulations..must be tried.

2. To make brighter or more brilliant.

1791 MRS. RADCLIFFE *Rom. Forest* ii, The sun appeared in all his glory,..vivifying every colour of the landscape. **1821** CRAIG *Lect. Drawing*, etc. ii. 127 This covering..vivifies the most brilliant colours. **1885** 'MRS. ALEXANDER' *Valerie's Fate* i, The bright..autumnal sunshine was vivifying the many-tinted trees of the Bois de Boulogne.

b. To render more animated or striking.

1833 HT. MARTINEAU *Three Ages* i. 26 His ready wit seldom failed to interpose to illustrate and vivify what was said. **1853** FELTON *Fam. Lett.* xi. (1865) 100, I always try to vivify an idea by embodying it in some manner. **1885** *Manch. Exam.* 25 Feb. 3/3 This little volume is..vivified throughout by the sympathetic yet discriminating appreciation which pays all due honour to the hero.

3. *absol.* To impart life or animation.

1626 BACON *Sylva* §696 Which should shew, that Snow hath in it a secret Warmth; For else it could hardly Viuifie. **1655** VAUGHAN *Silex Scint.* II. *Quickness*, 'Tis such a blissful thing, that still Doth vivifie. **1852** L. HUNT *Day by the Fire, Rainy Day* (1870) 294 It [a fire] talks to us;..it is vivified at our touch; it vivifies in return. **1871** TYNDALL *Fragm. Sci.* (1879) II. xiv. 359 The one may vivify, while the other kills.

4. *intr.* To acquire life; to become alive.

1737 BRACKEN *Farriery Impr.* (1757) II. 277 The Ova will vivify or come to Life sooner. **1768** FOOTE *Devil* III. Wks. 1799 II. 276 They quit their torpid state, and vivify. **1842** LOUDON *Suburban Hort.* 113 The egg begins to vivify and swell with the heat of the spring. **1867** *Routledge's Ev. Boy's Ann.* May 277 A sign that the eggs have vivified, and that they will probably hatch out. **1899** *Daily News* 1 July 8/7 When the eggs have vivified, the young salmon will be tended until the two-year-old stage.

Hence **ˈvivifying** *vbl. sb.*

1860 PUSEY *Min. Proph.* 2 The calf was the symbol..of.. His continued vivifying of all which lives. **1884** EARL GREY in *Life Mandell Creighton* (1904) I. viii. 247 The ripple which sprung from the vivifying of the waters of Embleton spread over a large surface.

ˈvivifying, *ppl. a.* [f. prec. + -ING[2].]

1. That vivifies or animates physically; life-giving, quickening.

1635 HEYWOOD *Hierarchy* VI. 374 The second Adam, sleeping in a vivifying death. **1671** J. WEBSTER *Metallogr.* viii. 127 That vivifying and incombustible sulphur that is Natures true fire and agent. **1707** *Curios. in Husb. & Gard.* 59 The vivifying Juice, with which the Earth is impregnated. **1776** PRIESTLEY in *Phil. Trans.* LXVI. 231 In other places..he explodes the doctrine of a vivifying spirit in the air. **1799** *Monthly Rev.* XXX. 570 The vivifying action of the atmosphere. **1828** STEUART *Planter's G.* (ed. 2) 321, I have repeatedly tried it on all sorts of subjects,..and its vivifying powers have proved extraordinary in every instance. **1836** *Penny Cycl.* V. 246/2 The monads, and the vivifying animalcules of flowering plants. **1871** TYNDALL *Fragm. Sci.* (1879) II. xii. 275 The vivifying gas cannot penetrate to the centre of the film.

†**b.** Of medicines: Restorative. *Obs.*

1665 MANLEY *Grotius' Low C. Wars* Pref., Whose Aid was not onely as a Hand to uphold, but a vivifying Medicine to a fainting Body. **1727** SWIFT *Further Acc. E. Curll* Wks. 1755 III. I. 160 That all our members..be provided with a sufficient quantity of the vivifying drops, or Byfield's *sal volatile.* **1762** GOLDSM. *Cit. W.* lxviii, It may sometimes happen that..a countryman who cannot read, dies without ever hearing of the vivifying drops.

2. That vivifies spiritually or mentally; imparting interest or energy.

1768 TUCKER *Lt. Nat.* (1834) I. 45 That vivifying ingredient which gives life and vigour to our motives. **1770** BURKE *Pres. Discont.* Wks. 1842 I. 134 Without it,..the people cannot long enjoy..the vivifying energy of good government. **1809–10** COLERIDGE *Friend* (ed. 3) III. 85 The vivifying influences of the altar, the censer, and the sacrifice. **1838** PRESCOTT *Ferd. & Is.* (1846) III. xiv. 105 The vivifying impulse of patriotic sentiment. **1884** *Athenæum* 7 June 722/2 Human beings..cannot dispense with some such vivifying element in their religion.

3. *vivifying ink*, a liquid which brings out what has been written in sympathetic ink.

1823 J. BADCOCK *Dom. Amusem.* 42 Soak a double paper in the vivifying ink.

†**viˈviparal,** *a. Obs.*$^{-1}$ [f. L. *vīvipar-us* (see VIVIPAROUS) + -AL[1].] = VIVIPAROUS.

1660 R. COKE *Justice Vind.* 5 All viviparal creatures (although born blind privitively) yet in their very first production find a way to their dams papps.

viˈviparism. [Cf. F. *viviparisme*.] Viviparous reproduction.

1876 G. B. BUCKTON *Monograph Brit. Aphides* (Ray Soc.) I. 78 Viviparism continued uninterruptedly through the whole winter.

viviparity (vɪvɪˈpærɪtɪ). *Zool.* and *Bot.* [f. L. *vīvipar-us* (see next) + -ITY.] The condition or character of being viviparous.

1864 SPENCER *Princ. Biol.* I. 211 This homogenesis..in reptiles and fishes..is always essentially oviparous, though there are cases..in which viviparity is simulated. **1888** ROLLESTON & JACKSON *Anim. Life* 358 Instances of viviparity occur among *Lacertilia*, *Ophidia* [etc.].

viviparous (vɪˈvɪpərəs, vaɪ-), *a.* [f. L. *vīvipar-us* (Appuleius), f. *vīv-us* alive, living + *parĕre* to bring forth: see -OUS. Cf. F. *vivipare*, Sp., Pg., It. *viviparo*.]

1. Involving the production of young in a living state.

1646 SIR T. BROWNE *Pseud. Ep.* III. xxi. 158 We cannot from them expect a viviparous exclusion. **1861** HULME tr. *Moquin-Tandon* II. I. 48 This constitutes the viviparous reproduction of the Mammalia. **1890** *Science-Gossip* XXVI. 259 This..corresponds to the viviparous habit in some fishes and reptiles.

2. Of animals: Bringing forth young in a live state. (Usually in contrast with *oviparous*.)

1651 BIGGS *New Disp.* ¶267 Quadrupedes..together with us are viviparous, and hitherto more familiar to us, then birds, fishes, and animals oviparous. **1668** WILKINS *Real Char.* II. v. §3. 133 Viviparous cartilagineous fish, whose bodies are not long and round. **1692** BENTLEY *Boyle Lect.* 160 That uniform warmth, which is so necessary even in the incubation of birds, much more in the time of gestation of viviparous animals. **1768** G. WHITE *Selborne* xvii, Though they [*sc.* vipers] are oviparous, yet they are viviparous also, hatching their young within their bellies, and then bringing them forth. *c* **1791** M. CUTLER in *Life*, etc. (1888) I. 469 The Sea-anemone is said to be viviparous. **1827** G. HIGGINS *Celtic Druids* 138 The oviparous quadrupeds are found..in more ancient strata than those of the viviparous class. **1858** LEWES *Sea-side Stud.* 249 The Pedicellina is viviparous, as well as oviparous, and gemmiparous. **1870** ROLLESTON *Anim. Life* p. xliii, The true *Cetacea*..are always viviparous.

b. With specific names.

1681 GREW *Musæum* I. v. i. 95 The Viviparous Eel-Pout. .. 'Tis well pictur'd by Adam Olearius, who calls it a Sea-Wolf. **1774** GOLDSM. *Nat. Hist.* (1824) III. 11 The viviparous blenny..brings forth two or three hundred at a time, all alive. **1838** T. BELL *Brit. Reptiles* 17 Viviparous Lizard. Nimble Lizard. Common Lizard. *Zootoca vivipara.* **1890** *Cent. Dict.*, *Perch*,..2. Any surf-fish or member of the *Embiotocidæ*: more fully called *viviparous perch.*

3. *Bot.* Reproducing from seeds or bulbs which germinate while still attached to the parent plant. Also in specific names.

1777 LIGHTFOOT *Flora Scot.* I. 101 Viviparous-Fescue-Grass. **1794** PALEY *Nat. Theol.* xx. (1819) 322 Grasses abound which are viviparous and consequently able to propagate themselves without seed. **1812** *New Bot. Garden* I. 58 The pericarps viviparous. **1846–50** A. WOOD *Class-bk. Bot.* 475 *Polygonum viviparum*, Viviperous [*sic*] Bistort. **1855** DELAMER *Kitchen Garden* (1861) 48 A few roots [of

Rocambole] may be allowed standing-room as a curiosity, and as examples of viviparous plants. **1889** A. R. WALLACE *Darwinism* (1890) 24 The buttercup is replaced by the little poisonous yellow oxalis with its viviparous buds.

b. Characterized by this mode of reproduction.

1802 R. HALL *Elem. Bot.* 196 Viviparous Fructification, .. when the rudiment of the germen grows out into leaves. **1906** *Athenæum* 12 May 581 The viviparous habit, now represented by the seedling hanging from the mangrove, was once nearly universal.

Hence **vi'viparousness.**

1855 SPENCER *Princ. Psychol.* I. IV. vii. 575 Creatures having large brains were seen to have other characteristics than that of intelligence: as .. viviparousness.

vi'viparously, *adv.* [f. prec. + -LY².] In a viviparous manner; by viviparous reproduction.

1822-7 GOOD *Study Med.* (1829) I. 338 The latter are .. succeeded .. by hosts of the young insects produced viviparously; for .. the aphis breeds both ways. **1861** H. MACMILLAN *Footn. Page Nat.* 133 The plant is propagated viviparously. **1877** HUXLEY *Anat. Inv. Anim.* vii. 447 Aphides kept in a warm room .. have continued to propagate viviparously for four years.

vi'vipary. *Bot.* and *Zool.* [f. L. *vīvipar-us* viviparous + -Y, or ad. F. *viviparie.*] = VIVIPARITY.

1900 B. D. JACKSON *Gloss. Bot. Terms* 289. **1906** *Times* (Lit. Suppl.) 30 March 117/2 The lost habit is at times revived in the abnormal vivipary of some inland plants. **1963** DAVIS & GOLLEY *Princ. Mammalogy* v. 118 Another approach is .. to infer from changes in skull and jaw morphology the presence or absence of homeothermy .. and vivipary. **1981** *Entomologica Generalis* VII. 13 Nothing .. is known about the time when in the evolution of Aphidina vivipary has developed.

vivisect ('vɪvɪsɛkt, vɪvɪ'sɛkt), *v.* [Back-formation from VIVISECTION.]

1. *trans.* To dissect (an animal) while living; to perform vivisection upon.

1864 *Daily Tel.* 1 Aug., Much as they vivisect live animals at Alfort. **1876** RUSKIN *Fors Clav.* lxx. 320 Modern naturalists, not being able to vivisect the Psyche, have .. resolved that animals are to be classed by their bones. **1890** G. A. SMITH *Isaiah* II. xii. 202 We do not vivisect our murderers nor kill them off by gladiatorial combats.

transf. **1892** W. H. HUDSON *Naturalist in La Plata* 180 These insects .. house them in cells where the grubs can vivisect them at leisure. **1893** SELOUS *Trav. S.E. Africa* 413 The piteous cries .. of a donkey being vivisected by hyænas.

b. *fig.* To investigate as if by vivisection; to examine or criticize minutely or mercilessly.

1876 RHODA BROUGHTON *Joan* I. xx, On the contrary, I live in hopes of seeing a successor or two [i.e. suitors] vivisected. **1880** RUSKIN in *19th Cent.* June 950 The modern novelist .. cannot easily, in a city population, find a healthy mind to vivisect.

2. *intr.* To practise vivisection.

1883 S. COLERIDGE *Vivisection* 13 Surely a man must be at his wits' end before he could gravely put forward such an argument .. in defence of a claim to vivisect by wholesale.

Hence **vivisected** *ppl. a.*; **vivisecting** *vbl. sb.* and *ppl. a.*; also **vivisec'tee**, that which is vivisected; **vivi'sectible** *a.*, capable of being, liable to be, vivisected.

1859 *Todd's Cycl. Anat.* V. 317/2 The artificial vomiting of *vivisected animals. **1880** MEREDITH *Tragic Com.* v, The vivisected youth received the caress which quickened him to wholeness at a touch. **1886** *Pall Mall G.* 3 June 5/2 Whether any attempt at the absolute prohibition of vivisection would not react to the disadvantage of the unhappy '*vivisectees'. **1875** HOGGAN *Let.* in *Morn. Post* 2 Feb., I am inclined to look upon anæsthetics as the greatest curse to *vivisectible animals. **1876** J. J. G. WILKINSON *Hum. Sci. & Div. Rev.* 21 The *vivisecting scalpel is all human cruelty. *Ibid.* 67 Facts of life .. which must for ever escape the vivisecting mind. **1890** 'R. BOLDREWOOD' *Miner's Right* (1899) 59/2 The Doctor .. looks at Cyrus with a vivisecting eye. *Ibid.* 65/2 He did not choose to adopt the vivisecting process permitted to counsel in the higher courts. **1897** *Our Dumb Animals* (Boston) Nov. 70/2 The angel conducted him from one laboratory to another, from one vivisecting table to another.

vivisection (vɪvɪ'sɛkʃən). [f. L. *vīvī* gen. sing. neut. (and masc.), or *vivi-* combining form, of *vīvus* living + *sectio* cutting. Hence F. *vivisection.* Cf. *vividissection* s.v. VIVI-.]

1. The action of cutting or dissecting some part of a living organism; *spec.* the action or practice of performing dissection, or other painful experiment, upon living animals as a method of physiological or pathological study.

1707 SLOANE *Jamaica* I. 2 How sensible those nervous parts are, need not be told any who have seen vivisections, where the least .. touches .. will cause a sensible motion. **1736** *Phil. Trans.* XXXIX. 260 Small Parts of large Objects cannot easily be applied to the Microscope without being divided from their Wholes which in the case of Vivi section defeats the Experiment.

1842 DUNGLISON *Med. Lex.* 735 *Vivisection*, .. the act of opening or dissecting living animals. **1852** LEWIS *Meth. Obs. & Reas. in Pol.* I. 161 Of late years in particular vivi-section, or anatomical investigation of the living subject, has often been practised upon some of the smaller mammalia. **1879** BROWNING *Tray* 43 By vivisection, .. How brain secretes dog's soul, we'll see!

b. An operation of this nature.

1859 *Todd's Cycl. Anat.* V. 317/1 The vivisections which many experimenters have practised, agree in carrying this investigation further. **1881** MIVART *Cat* 311 Such a conclusion seems to result from pathological facts and vivisections.

fig. **1895** BALFOUR in *Daily News* 15 Nov. 2/4 The vivisection of the British Empire—was that a constructive policy?

2. *fig.* Excessively minute examination or criticism.

1880 SWINBURNE *Study Shaks.* i. (ed. 2) 23 This vivisection of a single poem is not defensible as a freak of scholarship.

3. *attrib.* and *Comb.*, as ***vivisection act, bill, experiment.***

1876 *Nature* XIV. 65/1 Lord Carnarvon's vivisection bill. **1883** *Encycl. Brit.* XV. 799/2 The Act restricting the practice of physiology is the Vivisection Act of 1876. **1894** *Westm. Gaz.* 26 Feb. 2/1 The atrocious character of many vivisection experiments.

vivisectional (vɪvɪ'sɛkʃənəl), *a.* [f. prec.]

1. Of or belonging to, of the nature of, vivisection.

1866 *Westm. Rev.* Jan. 148 It is impossible by vivisectional experiment to know which microscopical elements of the nervous tissues of the animal we destroy. **1876** *Nature* XIV. 65/2 For the purpose of demonstrating physiological facts to students, vivisectional experiments are .. not absolutely necessary. **1896** *Daily News* 21 Aug. 6/3 The licensing for vivisectional purposes of the British Institute of Preventive Medicine.

2. Performing vivisection. Also *fig.*

1882 W. JAMES in *Amer. Ann. Deaf & Dumb* April (1883) 116 Vivisectional physiologists. **1881** *Times* 17 Jan. 6/1 A few lively touches, which were the first to vanish under the vivisectional hands of the cleaner.

Hence **vivi'sectionally** *adv.*

1899 J. W. EBSWORTH in *Roxb. Ball.* IX. p. clxxx*, 'The Maid's Comfort' and 'The Merry Cuckold' can be studied vivisectionally on pp. cxxix* and cxxxii*.

vivisectionist (vɪvɪ'sɛkʃənɪst). [f. as prec. + -IST.] One who practises or defends vivisection.

1879 LD. SHAFTESBURY *Sp. Ho. Lords* 15 July, The contradictions of vivisectionists were surprising. **1887** 'EDNA LYALL' *Knight-Errant* (1889) 133 Without a deep, living sympathy, the artist surely degenerates into a species of vivisectionist.

vivisective, *a.* [f. as prec. + -IVE.] = VIVISECTIONAL *a.* 2. In quot. *fig.*

a **1876** M. COLLINS *Pen Sketches by Vanished Hand* (1879) II. 249, I am not surprised that Mr. Browning, himself a vivisective poet, likes the diagnosis of human malady which Euripides supplies.

vivisector ('vɪvɪsɛktə(r), vɪvɪ'sɛktə(r)). [f. as VIVISECT *v.* + -OR. Hence F. *vivisecteur.*] One who vivisects or practises vivisection.

1863 *Times* 2 Aug., That is the extent of the tender mercies of French vivisectors. **1876** J. J. G. WILKINSON *Hum. Sci. & Div. Rev.* 20 No man not interested personally, but humanely, can doubt what the vivisectors are doing.

fig. **1874** BLUNT *Dict. Sects* 237/2 Pascal was the vivisector rather than the anatomist. **1899** BEATRICE HARRADEN *Fowler* 115 He had plunged deep into inquiry, and was in fact a theological and historical vivisector.

vivotoxin ('vaɪvəʊtɒksɪn). *Biochem.* [f. *vivo-* (cf. VIVI-) + TOXIN.] A substance produced in an infected plant and involved in the disease process (see quot. 1953).

1953 DIMOND & WAGGONER in *Phytopathology* XLIII. 229/2 To clarify this situation a new term is suggested. A vivotoxin is defined as a substance produced in the infected host by the pathogen and/or its host, which functions in the production of disease, but is not itself the initial inciting agent of disease. **1971** *Agric. & Biol. Chem.* XXXV. 618/2 Vivotoxins are considered to be usually nonspecific to plant species. **1981** R. J. GREEN in M. E. Mace et al. *Fungal Wilt Dis. Plants* i. 11 Acceptance of the concept of the vivotoxin directed investigators to attempt to demonstrate toxins in the vascular tissues of the infected plants.

‖**vivres** ('viːvəz, ‖vivr). [F. *vivres*: see VIVERS.] Victuals, provisions.

a **1650** in Grose *Milit. Antiq.* (1788) II. 222 There are yet .. two quarters more; the one of noblemen strangers, and the other the magazines of the vivres. *Ibid.*, The general of the vivres. **1800** A. CARLYLE *Autobiog.* (1860) 160 The marketplace [of Yarmouth] .. is very spacious, and remarkably well provided with every kind of vivres for the pot and the spit. **1819** *Blackw. Mag.* VI. 279 So much for demand and supply of vivres, and good substantial vivres too. **1852** JERDAN *Autobiog.* II. 142 He got into some debt for the vivres and tipple.

†**vivry,** *a. Her. Obs.* In 6–7 viurie. [ad. F. *vivré*, f. *vivre* serpent.] Serpentine, tortuous.

1572 BOSSEWELL *Armorie* II. 34 The seconde beareth Vert, a Bende Viurie, Dargent. **1611** COTGR. s.v. *Vivré*, A bend Viurie.

vix, abbrev. form of VIXEN.

1828 *Sporting Mag.* XXII. 23 Mr. Russell killed a fat unfortunate soil-running vix.

vix, ME. variant of *wex* WAX *v.*

vixen ('vɪks(ə)n), *sb.* and *a.* Forms: 5–8 **fixen** (5 **fixene**), 6– **vixen** (7 **vixinge**, 8 **vixin**), 7–8 **vixon.** [repr. OE. **fyxen* (= MHG. *vühsinne*, G. *füchsin*), fem. of *fox* FOX. Cf. OE. *fyxen* adj. 'of a fox' (= OHG. *fuhsîn*, MHG. *vühsîn*). The word is one of the few in which the southern *v* for *f* has definitely established itself.]

1. The female of the fox; a she-fox.

c **1410** *Master of Game* (MS. Digby 182) vii, Þe fixene [*v.r.* fixen] of þe foxe bereth as longe, as þe bicche of þe wolfe bereth hir whelpes. **1605** VERSTEGAN *Dec. Intell.* x. (1628) 334 Fixen .. is the name of a she-fox otherwise and more anciently foxin. **1706** PHILLIPS (ed. Kersey), *Vixen* or *Fixen*, a Fox's Cub. **1719** D'URFEY *Pills* (1872) II. 270 The vixen's just now earthed, see here's the Hole. **1796** *Grose's Dict. Vulgar T.* (ed. 3), *Vixen*, .. a she fox, who, when she has cubs, is remarkably fierce. **1828** *Sporting Mag.* XXII. 23, I must confess, I felt rather spoony upon that vixen. **1867** TROLLOPE *Chron. Barset* I. xxxiii. 286 A vixen was trapped just across the field yonder. **1880** *Times* 2 Nov. 4/5 They are familiar as the craftiest old vixen with the country they have been born and bred in.

fig. **1705** WYCHERLEY in *Pope's Lett.* (1735) I. 22 You may see a Pack of Spaniels, called Lovers, in hot Pursuit of a two-legg'd Vixen.

2. An ill-tempered quarrelsome woman; a shrew, a termagant.

1575 *Gamm. Gurton* III. ii, That false fixen .. that counts her selfe so honest. **1590** SHAKS. *Mids. N.* III. ii. 324 O when she's angry, she is keene and shrewd, She was a vixen when she went to schoole. **1621** BURTON *Anat. Mel.* III. ii. v. ii. 636 She is a foole, a nasty queane, a slut, a fixen, a scolde. *a* **1644** QUARLES *Virgin Widow* v. i, She's a pestilent vixen when she's angry, and as proud as Lucifer. *a* **1677** BARROW *Serm. Prov. x. 18* Wks. 1687 I. 247 Those fiery Vixons, who .. really do themselves embroil things, and raise miserable combustions in the world. **1721** AMHERST *Terræ Fil.* No. 8 (1726) 36 Since they [Oxford and Cambridge] have come to woman's estate they have been a couple of the arrantest vixens. **1787** *Minor* 68 Perverseness hurried him to marry a young vixin. **1801** MAR. EDGEWORTH *Contrast* (1832) 108 Mrs. Betterworth was a vain, foolish vixen. **1855** MACAULAY *Hist. Eng.* xv. III. 565 'That may be very honourable in you', answered the pertinacious vixen, 'but it will be very poor comfort to the Princess.' **1879** 'E. GARRETT' *House by Works* II. 160 His unhappy secret marriage with the foreign vixen.

transf. **1861-2** G. H. K. in *Vac. Tour.* (1864) 136 There are the sixteen of them [*sc.* hinds] .. quarrelling and fighting, rising perfectly upright on their hind legs, .. and striking at each other with their sharp fore hoofs. What vixens!

†**b.** In the phrase *to play the vixen. Obs.*

1596 NASHE *Saffron Walden* Wks. (Grosart) III. 164 A Gentlewoman; who, howsoeuer shee scolds and playes the vixen neuer so, wilbe borne with. **1597** LYLY *Wom. in Moon* I. i. (stage direction), She playes the vixen with euery thing about her.

†**c.** Applied to a child or a man. *Obs. rare.*

a **1700** B. E. *Dict. Cant. Crew*, *Fixen*, a froward, peevish Child. **1702** S. PARKER tr. *Cicero's De Finibus* II. 151 He's the veriest Vixin of a Stoick. **1731-8** SWIFT *Pol. Conversat.* i. 95 Well, if that Child was mine, I'd whip it till the Blood came; Peace, you little Vixen!

3. *attrib.* (passing into *adj.*). **a.** Appositive with *fox*, = sense 1.

c **1410** *Master of Game* (MS. Digby 182) vii, The fixene fox whelpeth vnder þe erthe. **1845** YOUATT *Dog* iv. 102 The mouth of the earth in which a vixen fox—a fox with her young ones—has taken up her abode. **1883** E. PENNELL-ELMHIRST *Cream Leicestersh.* 274 A little vixen fox jumping out among listless idlers of the pack.

b. Appositive, of persons, = VIXENISH *a.* 1.

a **1660** *Contemp. Hist. Irel.* (Ir. Archæol. Soc.) III. 80 O shame of soe greate a peere, imitatinge herin the vixinge calleaghs. **1842** BORROW *Bible in Spain* i, The fury which the old vixen queen displayed.

c. Of looks, actions, etc., = VIXENISH *a.* 2.

1700 CONGREVE *Way of World* IV. 54 Pshaw, what a Vixon trick is this? **1816** SCOTT *Antiq.* xxii, Disturbing us with his vixen brawls, and breaking God's peace and the king's. **1820** KEATS *Cap & Bells* lxxix, She .. Castled her King with such a vixen look, It bodes ill to his Majesty. **1850** E. BRONTE *Wuthering Heights* x, Begone, for God's sake, and hide your vixen face!

4. *Comb.*, as ***vixen-faced, -visaged.***

1836 *Boston Herald* 20 Dec. 1/6 A Mrs. Vaughton was summoned by a vixen-visaged girl, named Susan Jones. **1840** BARHAM *Ingol. Leg.* Ser. II. *Black Mousquetaire*, Nervous folks still, when they come in their way, shun Old vixen-faced tramps of the Hebrew persuasion.

vixenish ('vɪks(ə)nɪʃ), *a.* [f. prec. + -ISH¹.]

1. Resembling a vixen in disposition; cross, ill-tempered, snappish.

1828 MISS MITFORD *Village* Ser. III. 109 My friend Daphne, the vixenish pug. **1841** LEVER *C. O'Malley* lxvii, Others are married and have vixenish wives. **1880** MISS BRADDON *Just as I am* xlv, He could hardly endure existence in the house that held his vixenish sisters.

Comb. **1837** DICKENS *Pickw.* xlvi, Two small vixenish looking ladies.

2. Characteristic of, appropriate to, a vixen.

1838 DICKENS *O. Twist* iv, A short, thin, squeezed-up woman, with a vixenish countenance. **1865** *Dublin Univ. Mag.* I. 261 She .. rang the bell with vixenish violence. **1889** *Sat. Rev.* 23 Feb. 208/2 The trashy verbiage, the vixenish tattle, .. to which they are treated.

Hence **'vixenishness.**

1820 *Examiner* No. 651. 633/1 Madge is too apt to think that vixenishness and virtue go together. **1865** MRS. WHITNEY *Gayworthys* I. 117 She would never sharpen or narrow to vixenishness.

vixenishly, *adv.* [f. prec. + -LY².] In a vixenish or ill-tempered manner.

1845 *Bachelor of Albany* (1848) 174 'Barker of the Albany! .. is he the man?' cried the termagant Mrs. Harry, vixenishly and exultingly. **1880** MEREDITH *Tragic Com.* xviii, Her mother treated her vixenishly, snubbing her for a word. **1891** BARING-GOULD *In Troubadour-Land* ii. 28 [He] endeavoured to get hold of her hand. She snatched it away vixenishly.

vixenly ('vɪks(ə)nlɪ), *adj.* and *adv.* Also 7 **vixonely.** [f. as prec. + -LY.] **a.** *adj.* Resembling a vixen in disposition. **b.** *adv.* Crossly, ill-naturedly.

a **1677** BARROW *Pope's Suprem.* Wks. 1687 I. 225 It was onely, which in such a vixonely Pope was a great favour, a forbearance to quarrel with him. **1850** HAWTHORNE *Scarlet L.* Introd. (1852) 3 Nevertheless, vixenly as she looks, many people are seeking, at this very moment, to shelter themselves under the wing of the federal eagle. **1895** MEREDITH *Amazing Marriage* xlv, Our female government asks it vixenly of our impotent male.

Viyella (vaɪ'ɛlə). Also **viyella**. The proprietary name of a fabric made from a twilled mixture of cotton and wool; also, a garment made of this material. Freq. *attrib.*

1894 *Trade Marks Jrnl.* 6 June 471 *Viyella*... Yarns of wool, worsted or hair. William Hollins and company (Nottingham), Limited,..Nottingham; spinners. **1912** G. FRANKAU *One of Us* v. 41 No impious fingers groped in his Viyella. **1921** 'K. MANSFIELD' *Let.* 29 Aug. (1977) 229 That's the kind of stuff I meant, too. They had both better be lines with silver grey *viyella* or cashmere. **1932** R. LEHMANN *Invitation to Waltz* I. iii. 46 Cream viyella blouses, white piqué tennis skirts. **1942** *R.A.F. Jrnl.* 16 May 33 The pilot was wearing thick vest and pants, a Viyella shirt ..and Mae West. **1969** E. MCGIRR *Entry of Death* iii. 51 She wears thick Viyella pyjamas. **1977** *Lancashire Life* Feb. 23/1 William Hollins' famous collection of mice, dressed in Viyella, that fabulous mixture of wool and cotton that keeps both mice and human mites warm in winter.

‖**viz.**, *adv.* and *sb.* Also 6 vz., 7 vizt. [Abbrev. of VIDELICET. Cf. VIDZ(T.

The *z* represents the ordinary med.L. symbol of contraction for *et* or *-et*. For the various forms in which the abbreviation occurs in med.L. manuscripts, see Chassant *Dict. des Abréviations* and Cappelli *Dizionario di Abbreviature*. In reading aloud usually rendered by 'namely'.]

A. *adv.* = VIDELICET *adv.*

a **1540** J. LONDON in Ellis *Orig. Lett.* Ser. III. III. 132 Thyder resortyd suche as..hadde any slottiche wydowes lockes, viz. here growen to gether in a tufte. **1596** BLAGRAVE *Uran. Astrolabe* H 2 b, If the question..be of the night (vz. you shall finde it about 8¼ of clocke in the morning) and vnto that houre (vz. 8¼)..set the fiducialI line of the Planetary scale. **1642** ROGERS *Naaman* 28 The stupid King..mistakes the letter..and construes it to a sinister sense viz. that a quarrel was pickt with him. **1645** in Ellis *Orig. Lett.* Ser. III. IV. 250 His Ma^tye had opportunity to effect his designe, vizt. the releife of Westchester. *a* **1700** in *Cath. Rec. Soc. Publ.* (1911) IX. 335 In the time of the first Lady-Abbesse of that house viz Dame Francis Gawen. **1728** SWIFT *Mullinix & Tim.* Wks. 1755 III. II. 213 Observe my counsel, (viz.) Adapt your habit to your phyz. **1788** COWPER *Let. Lady Hesketh* 6 May, The ingenious contriver of it, viz. myself. **1841** BARHAM *Ingol. Leg.* Ser. II. *Auto-da-fé* 11, The vestment aforesaid, perhaps, from its hue, *viz.* yellow. **1861** PALEY *Aeschylus* (ed. 2), *7 agst. Thebes* 740 *note*, To fall..on several devoted heads successively, viz. Laius, Oedipus, and his sons. **1896** BADEN-POWELL *Matabele Campaign* xi, Took with me three of Plumer's men as escort, viz. Troopers Abrahamson, White, and Parkin.

B. *sb.* = VIDELICET *sb.* Also, a special clause in a deed introduced by *viz.*

17.. *Modern Reports* VI. 228 *marg.*, If a bond bear date at any place abroad, that place must be stated in the declaration, with a viz. at such a place in England. **1797** MRS. M. ROBINSON *Walsingham* IV. 76 If I won't give you a viz and a settlement. **1805** *East Reports* V. 253 The date which gave rise to such repugnancy was laid under a *viz.*

†**viz.**, *v. Obs.*⁻¹ [For *vis*, abbrev. of VISIT *v.* Cf. VIS *v.*] *intr.* To pay a visit.

1767 GRAY *Let. Mason* Wks. (1884) III. 277 Tomorrow I go Vizzing to Gibside to see the new married Countess.

†**vizament**, alteration of ADVISEMENT or VISEMENT.

1601 SHAKS. *Merry W.* I. i. 34 The Councell (looke you) shall desire to heare the feare of Got, and not to heare a Riot: take your viza-ments in that.

vizar, obs. f. VISOR *sb.*

vizard ('vɪzəd), *sb.* and *a.* Now *arch.* Forms: α. 6 vysard(e, visarde, viserde, 6–9 visard (8 *Sc.* vissart). β. 6 vi-, vyzarde, 6–8 vyzard, 7–8 vizzard, 6– vizard. [Altered form of *vysar, viser, vizar* VISOR by confusion of ending: see -ARD.]

1. A mask; = VISOR *sb.* 2.

Very common from *c* 1560 to *c* 1700. Also †*case of vizards.*

α. **1558** in Feuillerat *Revels Q. Eliz.* (1908) 95, i dozen of viserdes with shorte berdes. **1579** LYLY *Euphues* (Arb.) 38 Not the carued visarde of a lewde woman, but the incarnate vysage of a lasciuious wantonne. **1600** DEKKER *Fortunatus* Wks. 1873 I. 104 She [Vice] and others wearing gilded visards. *a* **1668** LASSELS *Voy. Italy* (1698) I. 93 In Modena are made the best visards for masquerades. **1718** *Free-thinker* No. 80. 179 The Fairy applied an enchanted Visard to her Face.

β. **1558** in Feuillerat *Revels Q. Eliz.* (1908) 12 Warderobe stuffe, vizardes, heare. **1572** *Ibid.* 183 For ffoyle for vyzardes & ffawchins. **1588** KYD *Househ. Phil.* Wks. (1901) 256 Artificiall Oyles, and dawbings..for vizards, pageants, and poppets. **1601** B. JONSON *Poetaster* v. iii, Gag him: And put a case of vizards o're his head. **1655** STANLEY *Hist. Philos.* III. (1687) 91/2 Some wild young Men..lay in wait for him, attired like furies, with vizards and torches. **1692** WASHINGTON tr. *Milton's Def. Pop.* M.'s Wks. 1738 I. 456 He complains that Executioners in Vizards (*personati Carnifices*) cut off the King's Head. **1711** STEELE *Spect.* No. 32 ⁋ 3 Wits were privileged to wear what Masks they pleased in all Ages; and..a Vizard had been the constant Crown of their Labours. **1760–72** H. BROOKE *Fool of Qual.* (1809) III. 151 Let me see what you have got under that vizard of yours. **1821** SCOTT *Kenilw.* xxiv, A little diminutive urchin, wearing a vizard with a couple of sprouting horns. **1851** THACKERAY *Eng. Hum.* iii. (1858) 115 A gentleman on a grey mare, with a black vizard on his face.

b. *transf.* or *fig.*

1621 G. SANDYS *Ovid's Met.* IV. (1626) 83 The silent Virgin..modestly had made A visard of her hands. **1632** LITHGOW *Trav.* III. 81 When the welkin had put aside the vizard of the night. *a* **1680** BUTLER *Rem.* (1759) I. 177 A Beard is but the Vizard of a Face. **1682** WHELER *Journ. Greece* v. 356 It was hard to conjecture what their Natural Complexion was, by reason of the thick Vizard of Paint they had on. *c* **1715** RAMSAY *Vision* ii, The Thunder crakt, and Flauchts did rift, Frae the blak vissart of the lift. **1827** CARLYLE *Misc. Ess., Richter* (1840) I. 18 All Nature is gone forth mumming in the strangest guises. Yet the anarchy is not without its purpose: these vizards are not mere hollow masks.

†**c.** A mask as used to protect the face or eyes.

1614 RALEIGH *Hist. World* I. 176 They vsed to wear a vizard of defence, with one sight in the middle to serue both eyes. **1669** PEPYS *Diary* 25 June, I to my office,..to write down my journal..and did it, with the help of my vizard, and tube fixed to it, and do find it mighty manageable, but how helpful to my eyes this trial will show me.

2. *fig.* or in fig. context. = VISOR *sb.* 3.

Very common from *c* 1560 to *c* 1700. The various types of context are illustrated by the different groups of quotations.

(*a*) **1572** *Tindale's Wks., Sacraments* 442/1 The hypocrites that haue put a visard [*ed. c* 1550 visare] on the face of the law. **1586** T. B. *La Primaud. Fr. Acad.* I. 66 Vice putteth on a vizard, and goeth disguised and covered with goodly shewes that belong onely to vertue. **1653** H. MORE *Def. Moral Cabbala* iii. *heading*, That..it is only the halting and hypocrisie of men that generally have put so soure and sad a vizard upon it [i.e. Religion]. *a* **1680** BUTLER *Rem.* (1759) I. 71 For those..Wore Vizards of Hypocrisy, to steal And slink away, in Masquerade, to Hell. **1833** G. S. FABER *Recapit. Apostasy* p. x, Popery, whatever vizard the theological Proteus may wear,..is still..a form of recapitulated Roman apostasy.

(*b*) *a* **1555** PHILPOT in Strype *Eccl. Mem.* (1721) III. App. xlviii. 155 Put off your shameles vyzards, O ye unbelevyng Arrians. *a* **1569** KINGESMYLL *Conflict w. Satan* (1578) 27 We will bring him to the tryall particularly that we may plucke of his maske and vysarde. **1629** H. BURTON *Truth's Triumph* Pref., We haue assayed to pull off Romes vizard. **1654** WHITLOCK *Zootomia* 93 What are they but the Scum of the people, take off their Visards, and underneath appeare Wicked Jewes,..&c. **1682** SIR T. BROWNE *Chr. Mor.* III. §20 Men are glad to pull of their Vizards, and resume themselves again.

(*c*) **1579** GOSSON *Sch. Abuse* (Arb.) 74 Trueth can neuer be Falsehoods Visarde. **1633** G. HERBERT *Temple, Ch. Militant* 185 He took fine vizards to conceal his crimes. **1653** A. WILSON *Jas. I* 70 A sober and fair outside, the true vizard of Hypocrisie. **1680** H. MORE *Apocal. Apoc.* 349 The participation of the promised Spirit of Christ, without which all Religion is but a mere Mask or dead Vizard. **1704** SWIFT *T. Tub* xi, He would make use of no other vizard than a long prayer.

(*d*) **1589** R. HARVEY *Pl. Perc.* (1860) 11 For all that fatherly countenance and graue vizard which sometimes thou vsest to plead the cause of thy Reformation vnder. **1607** R. C[AREW] tr. *Estienne's World of Wonders* 67 The impietie that lay masked vnder this vizard. **1656** W. HOWARD in Clarendon *Hist. Reb.* XV. §121 Having long since, by peeping a little..under the vizzard of the Impostor, got such glimpses, though but imperfect ones, of his ugly face. **1678** MARVELL *Def. J. Howe* (Grosart) 141 To outlaw Mr. Howe ..from all Protestant protection, is to represent him under a Popish Vizard.

(*e*) **1567** JEWEL *Def. Apol.* 4 But who they be, that..with a painted Visarde, or emptie name of the Churche, haue feared al the cattel of the fielde, it is needelesse to speake it.

b. = VISOR *sb.* 3 b.

1562 COOPER *Answ. Priv. Masse* (1850) 170 That by this means your doctrine..might have a face or vizard of antiquity. **1576** FLEMING *Panopl. Epist.* 316 Those things which put on a pretended shewe and vizard of felicitie. **1612** WOODALL *Surg. Mate* Pref., Wks. (1653) 10 Whereby every unworthy ignorant impostor (as under a vizard of hidden skill) made use of the art of Surgery. **1636** FEATLY *Clavis Myst.* xxiv. 314 Heresie and schism have the vizard, but not the face of holinesse. **1684** J. RENWICK in *Biogr. Presbyt.* (1827) II. 263 Another Sort of Folk cover over their Pride with a Vizard of Humility. **1725** WATTS *Logic* Introd. 3 So Knavery puts on the Face of Justice, Hypocrisy and Superstition wear the Vizard of Piety. **1743** E. ERSKINE *Serm.* Wks. (1871) III. 91 It has put on the name and vizard of Presbyterian. **1855** MOTLEY *Dutch Rep.* IV. v. (1906) III. 55 The Spaniards seemed to cast off even the vizard of humanity.

†**3.** In depreciatory use: A face or countenance suggestive of a mask. *Obs.*

1568 T. HOWELL *Arb. Amitie* (1879) 58 With hatefull hawtie haunt not, For dainefull vizards daunt not. **1603** BRETON *Packet Mad Lett.* Wks. (Grosart) II. 12 For my Fan, it keepes me sometimes from the sight of such a vizard as your good face. *a* **1625** FLETCHER *Custom of Country* I. i. This little beauty you are pleased to honour Will be so chang'd, so alter'd to an uglinesse To such a vizard, ten to one, I dye too.

†**4.** A phantasm or spectre. *Obs.*⁻¹

a **1591** H. SMITH *Seven Godly Serm.* vi. 229 If thou thinkest that it is such a mans bodie which thou seest, look in ye graue..and there thou shalt see the body where it was laid, euen while this vizard walkes in thy sight.

†**5.** A person wearing a visor or mask; *spec.* a woman of loose character wearing a mask in public, a prostitute. *Obs.* (Cf. VIZARD-MASK 2.)

1652 H. BELL *Luther's Colloq.* 283 For the world cannot live without such vizards and shrove-tide-fools. **1660** *Trial Regic.* 164 Afterwards I saw the Vizards going into a Chamber there. **1676** ETHEREDGE *Man of Mode* I. i, This business of yours Dorimant has been With a Vizard at the Play-house. **1719** D'URFEY *Pills* (1872) II. 75 Or if you find me with a vizard prattle Do you the same with any other man.

†**6.** = VISOR *sb.* 1. *Obs. rare.*

1704 SWIFT *Batt. Bks.* Misc. (1711) 252 The Stranger desir'd a Parley; and lifting up the Vizard of his Helmet, a Face..appeared [etc.]. **1768** STERNE *Sent. Journ., Paris*, Helmets which had lost their vizards.

†**b.** *Bot.* (See quot.) *Obs.*⁻¹

c **1789** *Encycl. Brit.* (ed. 3) III. 446/2 *Galea-ringentis*, the vizard or upper lip of a ringent corolla.

7. *attrib.* and *Comb.*, as **vizard bead, -maker, -making, -manufacture, -monger, vice; vizard-faced, -like** adjs.

1573 in Feuillerat *Revels Q. Eliz.* (1908) 218 The vyzard-maker John Owgle for xiiii Beardes. **1593** SHAKS. *3 Hen. VI*, I. iv. 117 But that thy Face is Vizard-like, vnchanging, Made impudent with vse of euill deedes. **1615** BRATHWAIT *Strappado* (1878) 4 Bacchus cares not for outward signes a rush, Good wine needs not the hanging of a bush. Dost not thou vizzard-fac't ingratefull Elfe? **1650** B. *Discolliminium* 47 My Recreations [are]..Metamorphosing and Vizard-making. **1678** BUTLER *Hud.* III. I. 1012 Strive who shall be ..the most genteelly bred At sucking of a Vizard Bead. **1682** SIR T. BROWNE *Chr. Mor.* II. §7 The old Philosophers and great pretenders unto Virtue, who well declining the gaping Vices of Intemperance, [etc.]..were envious, malicious, contemners,..and stufft with Vizard Vices. **1684** OTWAY *Atheist* v. i, A Way to revenge my self on that Vizard-monger. **1856** R. A. VAUGHAN *Mystics* (1860) II. 116 [Loyola's] order..claimed and merited the monopoly of the vizard manufacture.

vizard, obs. or dial. form of WIZARD.

'**vizard**, *v.* Now *rare.* Also 7 visard. [f. the sb.]

†**1.** *trans.* To conceal or disguise (something) under a false outward show or appearance; to represent falsely or speciously. *Obs.*

1628 PRYNNE *Brief Survay* 48 Their dangerous and infectious plague-soares, which are onely vizarded and palliated, not clothed nor warmed with the sacred Robes. **1631** WEEVER *Anc. Funeral Mon.* 51 Cloakes to hide their knauery, and beards to visard their hypocrisie. **1660** SHIRLEY *Andromana* IV. vii, Plangus who hath vizarded his ends With vertue.

2. To cover or disguise (the face, etc.) with or as with a vizard or visor; to mask.

c **1609** WEBSTER *Appius & Virginia* v. iii, See these Monsters, whose fronts the fair Virginias innocent blood hath visarded with such black ugliness, that they are loath-some to all good mens souls. **1662** HIBBERT *Body Divinity* I. 279 Jobs comforters..vizarding themselves under the cloke of amity. *a* **1669** H. FOULIS *Hist. Rom. Treasons* (1681) 255 They vizarded their members and meetings. **1872** CLARK RUSSELL *Repr. Actors* (Chandos) p. xiii, Women mockingly vizarded themselves to conceal the only blushes their cheeks could exhibit—that of the paint-pot.

Hence '**vizarding** *vbl. sb.*, the action of disguising with or as with a vizard; also *concr.*, that which serves as a vizard or disguise.

1609 *Ev. Woman in Hum.* v. i. in Bullen *O. Pl.* IV, Now for the cunning vizarding of them and tis done. **1694** CROWNE *Married Beau* I. i, I'm angry with 'em for their vizarding. **1861** J. MURRAY *Songs Covenant Times* 77 Skulking from cot to cot, from cave to cave,..In quaint disguise and vizarding uncouth They shunned pursuit.

'**vizarded**, *ppl. a.* [f. VIZARD *v.*]

1. Disguised with a vizard; wearing a vizard; visored, masked. Used (*a*) predicatively or (*b*) attributively. Also *fig.*

(*a*) **1593** NASHE *Christ's T.* 71 b, Your mornelike christall countenances shall be netted ouer, and (Masker-like) cawle-visarded, with crawling venomous wormes. **1598** MARSTON *Sco. Villanie* II. vii. (1599) 207 She is so vizarded,..I cannot see her face. **1606** SHAKS. *Tr. & Cr.* I. iii. 83 Degree being vizarded, Th'vnworthiest shewes as fairely in the Maske. **1650** R. STAPYLTON *Strada's Low C. Wars* VII. 64 These two prostrated Figures..were armed with Petitions,..their faces Vizarded; their Eares and Necks hung with little dishes [etc.]. **1756** MRS. F. BROOKE *Old Maid* No. 29. 243 The obsequious lover approaches in a mask: to say the truth, the lady is generally as well vizarded as he can be.

(*b*) *a* **1637** B. JONSON *Love Restored* Wks. (Rtldg.) 588/1 *Masq.* Have you recovered your voice to rail at me? *Plu.* No, vizarded impudence. **1658** W. SANDERSON *Life K. Charles* 1138 He..humbly bowed down his generous neck to God, to be cut off by the vizarded Executioner. **1691** tr. *Emilianne's Frauds Romish Monks* 400 Many Vizarded Lackeys came forth with Flambeaus to Light them in. **1715** tr. *C'tess D'Anois' Wks.* 410 Four vizarded Ruffians.

2. *fig.* Assumed, pretended.

1663 J. H. *Hist. O. Cromwell* xi. 16 Oliver.., in a passion, and transported beyond his vizarded sanctity, with an oath ..dissolved them. *a* **1688** G. STRADLING *Serm. & Disc.* (1692) 350 Bodily worship..which usually concluded like the Turkish Lents after the vizarded austerity of a few spare hours in nightly Bacchanals.

'**vizardless**, *a. rare.* [f. VIZARD *sb.*] Having no vizard; visorless.

1674 C. F. *Wit at Venture* 76 Like a Vizardless Miss that peeps under her hood.

vizard-mask. Now *arch.* [f. VIZARD *sb.* Cf. *visor-mask* VISOR *sb.* 6 b.]

1. A mask worn to conceal or disguise the face; a domino; = VIZARD 1.

1667 DRYDEN & DK. NEWCASTLE *Sir Martin Mar-all* v. iii, Fetch me down two Indian-gowns and Vizard-masks. **1688** R. HOLME *Armoury* III. 13/1 The Visard Mask..covers the whole face,..being only held in the Teeth by means of a round bead. **1693** WOOD *Life* (O.H.S.) III. 438, 3 hackney coaches rob'd at Wheatley bridge by 4 Oxford scholars (as 'tis said) with vizard maskes. **1704** *Lond. Gaz.* No. 3985/1 That no Woman be allowed..to wear a Vizard-Mask in either of the Theatres. **1760** *Ann. Reg., Chron.* 73/2 A man habited like a sailor with a vizard mask on.

2. A woman who wears such a mask; a prostitute. (Cf. VIZARD *sb.* 5.)

1670 DRYDEN *2nd Pt. Conq. Granada* Prol. 25 As those Vizard Masks maintain that Fashion, To soothe and tickle sweet Imagination. **1672** WYCHERLEY *Love in Wood* v. ii, There are as grave men as your worship..that adjourn their cares and businesses, to come and unbend themselves at night here with a little vizard-mask. **1710** STEELE *Tatler* No. 193 ¶3 His dexterous Insinuations, which prevailed upon a few deluded Women, especially the Vizard Masks, to believe that the Stage was in danger. **1740** CIBBER *Apol.* (1756) II. 143 The play-houses are so extremely pestered with Vizard-masks and their trade. [**1823** SCOTT *Peveril* xxviii, Billets-doux, my lord... This left at the porter's-lodge by a vizard mask.]

vizaret, -iat, -it, varr. VIZIERATE.

vizariat, -it, varr. VIZIERATE.

viz-a-viz, obs. f. VIS-À-VIS.

vizcacha, var. VISCACHA.

vize, dial. var. VICE *sb.*^{4}

Vizeeree, var. WAZIR^2.

vizeroye, obs. f. VICEROY.

vizet, obs. f. VISIT *sb.*

vizier (vɪˈzɪə(r), ˈvɪzjə(r), ˈvɪzɪə(r)). Now *Hist.* Forms: *α.* 6 (*pl.*) vesiri, 7 vesir, 7–9 vezir; 6–8 visir (8 wizir), 6–9 vizir; 9 vizeer, vuzeer. *β.* 6 vizeare, 7 -ear, viseire, -ere, visciere, vizeere, 7–9 visier (7 visiar), 7– vizier. *γ.* 7 viser, vizer, visur. [ad. Turk. *vezīr*, a. Arabic *wazīr*, *wezīr*, orig. a porter, hence one who bears the burden of government, a minister or lieutenant of a king, f. *wazara* to carry, carry on. Cf. F. *visir*, *vizir*, Sp. *visir*, Pg. *visir*, *vizir*, It. *visire*. See also ALGUAZIL.]

1. In the Turkish empire, Persia, or other Muslim country: A high state official or minister, freq. one invested with vice-regal authority; a governor or viceroy of a province; subsequently esp. the chief minister of the sovereign (see 2).

α. **1562** J. SHUTE tr. *Cambini's Turk. Wars* II. 13 b, The Turcke called vnto him all his consellours called in the Turckishe tonge Vesiri, & all his Bassas. **1614** SELDEN *Titles Honor* 377 The Vezirs are Counsellors of State. **1662** J. DAVIES tr. *Mandelslo's Trav.* 12 The Governour of the City hath the quality of Sulthan, and hath under him, not a Calenter, but a Visir or Secretary. **1662** —— tr. *Olearius' Voy. Ambass.* 371 The conversation he had with a Persian Visir. **1728** MORGAN *Algiers* I. vi. 170 Abou Yezid, his ambitious and too powerful Wizir, or Prime Minister, revolted. **1753** HANWAY *Trav.* III. xxxii. (1762) I. 145 He immediately ordered his vizir to take me up behind him. **1763** SCRAFTON *Indostan* (1770) 47 The march of Monsur Ally Caun, Visir of the empire, into the province of Bahar. **1815** ELPHINSTONE *Acc. Caubul* (1842) II. 251 This rule was departed from by Shauh Zemaun, who made a Suddozye vizeer. **1841** —— *Hist. Ind.* II. 9 His vizir..had been long in one of the highest employments under the calif. **1847** *Gentl. Mag.* March 299/2 The Vuzeer Lall Singh..has been deposed... Unable to select a Vuzeer from among their own number [etc.]. **1909** *Athenæum* 4 Sept. 262/3 It was..the rivalry of jealous vezirs that invited the interference of Nur-ad-din.

β, γ. **1599, 1601** [see b. below]. **1613** SIR A. SHERLEY *Trav. Persia* 47 The place of the Viseire comprehending in it, the office of Chancellor, and high Treasurer. *c* **1618** MORYSON *Itin.* IV. (1903) 21 The Visers or Viceroyes residing in Constantinople being 4. of old, were 7 at this tyme. **1634** SIR T. HERBERT *Trav.* 28 Nassuf Bashaw, the Visier and Generall to Sultan Schmat. **1696** tr. *Du Mont's Voy. Levant* xiv. 177 The seven Visiers of the Bench brought up the Rear of this Magnificent Troop. **1707** *Lond. Gaz.* No. 4363/1 The Janisaries have depos'd the Grand Seignior, and set his Nephew upon the Throne, who..is to act under the Direction of Four Visiers during his Minority. **1722** *Ibid.* No. 6023/1 The Venetian Bailo has not yet been with the Vizier. **1786** BURKE *Art. agst. W. Hastings* Wks. XI. 371 A certain prince called Sujah ul Dowla, Nabob of Oude, and Vizier of the empire. **1819** T. HOPE *Anastasius* I. Notes 331 All Pashas, before whom are carried the three horse-tails, have the title of Visier. **1847** MRS. A. KERR tr. *Ranke's Hist. Servia* 369 In a great council of Viziers and Ulemas assembled at the house of Scheik-ul-Islam. **1888** *Encycl. Brit.* XXIV. 268/1 The office of vizier, which spread from the Arabs to the Persians, Turks, Mongols, and other Oriental peoples, arose under the first Abbasid caliphs.

transf. **1848** THACKERAY *Van. Fair* li, His Lordship's vizier and chief confidential servant..Mr. Wenham.

†**b.** With the title *bashaw* added or prefixed. (See quot. 1819 in *β* above). *Obs.*

1599 DALLAM in *Early Voy. Levant* (Hakl. Soc.) 60 Our imbassader Delivered a presente to the Vizeare Basha at his house. **1601** R. JOHNSON *Kingd. & Commw.* (1603) 57 When the counsell hath sitten seauen or eight houres, the Bassa visur maketh true relation to the Prince, of all that hath bene handled. **1648** W. L. *Newes fr. Turkie* 25 A translate of the Imperiall Commandement, directed to the Vizeere-Bassa of Egypt.

c. *transf.* One holding a position analogous to that of a Muslim vizier; a vicegerent, viceroy, or chief minister.

1709 SWIFT *Adv. Relig.* Wks. 1755 II. I. 113 The arbitrary will of an unlimited monarch, or his vizier. **1820** SHELLEY *Œd. Tyr.* II. ii. 8 Emperors, kings, and priests and lords, Who rule by viziers, sceptres, bank-notes, words. **1869** RAWLINSON *Anc. Hist.* 211 Perdiccas' own office [in Macedonia] was that of vizier or prime minister.

2. ***grand*** (also formerly ***chief***, ***great***, ***head***, or ***prime***) ***vizier***, the chief minister or administrator of a Muslim ruler, esp. of the Sultan of Turkey.

(*a*) **1597** WRAG in Hakluyt *Voy.* (1599) II. I. 304 At the departure of Sinan Bassa the chiefe Vizir..there was another Bassa appointed in his place. *Ibid.* 305 This reconciliation with the great Vizir thus made [etc.]. **1615** G. SANDYS *Trav.* 44 Aladin..dying, Sahib the head *Vezir* vsurped the soueraigntie. **1686** tr. *Chardin's Trav. Persia* 16 The High Dignity of Prime Vizier. **1825** *Arab. Nts.* II. 240 The King was at that time in discourse with his prime vizier.

(*b*) **1642** HOWELL *For. Trav.* (Arb.) 85 Neither the Gran Visiar, or the Emperour Himselfe will question his [i.e. the Mufti's] sentence. *c* **1645** —— *Lett.* (1650) I. 70 By the advice of his grand Visier..he intended to erect a new Soldiery in Asia about Damasco. **1687** A. LOVELL tr. *Thevenot's Trav.* I. 63 He hath his chief Minister, who is the Grand Visier; for he hath commonly seven Visiers, whereof the first hath all the Authority and does all. **1756–7** tr. *Keysler's Trav.* (1760) IV. 311 When the grand vizir takes the field, the mufti generally makes him such a valuable present. **1802** JAMES *Milit. Dict.* s.v., The Grand Vizir possesses great powers, especially with regard to military affairs. **1848** W. K. KELLY tr. *L. Blanc's Hist. Ten Y.* II. 205 To save Syria, perhaps Constantinople, Mahmoud turns to his grand vizier, Reschid Mehemet. **1881** TROTTER *Visit Crt. Marocco* xiii. 191 The Grand Vizier,..together with his colleagues, looked as black as thunder. **1897** *Whitaker's Alm.* 561/1 Morocco, Empire of. Sultan.., Grand Vizier.. Minister of For. Affairs.

b. *transf.*

1855 MACAULAY *Hist. Eng.* xi. III. 13 They would rather ..be subject to an usurper like Oliver,..than to a legitimate King who referred them to a Grand Vizier.

3. *attrib.* and *Comb.*, as ***vizier-craft***, ***-slave***.

1833 *Edin. Rev.* LVII. 141 Into whatever untried vanities of being Faust and his Vizier-slave may pass. **1880** MEREDITH *Tragic Com.* vii, He is for kingcraft to match his viziercraft.

vizieral (vɪˈzɪərəl), *a.* [f. prec. + -AL^1.] = VIZIERIAL.

1870 R. ANDERSON *Miss. Amer. Board* III. xxi. 373 The American Ambassador also procured a strong vizieral letter to the Pasha in the Tripoli district. **1901** *Daily Chron.* 11 Nov. 5/4 That is why he held the Grand Vizieral office longer than any of his predecessors.

vizierate (vɪˈzɪərət). Forms: *α.* 7, 9 visirate, 8–9 vizirate, 9 vizierate. *β.* 8 vizariat, 8–9 vizarit. *γ.* 8 vizirat, 9 vizierat. [ad. Arab. *wizārat*, *-et*, f. *wezīr*, etc. VIZIER; or refashioned on VIZIER + -ATE^3. Cf. F. *vizirat*, *viziriat*.]

1. The dignity, position, or authority of a vizier or grand vizier; also, the period during which a particular vizier held office.

α. **1687** A. LOVELL tr. *Thevenot's Trav.* I. 80 Zornesan Mustapha..who had been made Caymacam before the Visirate of Chiaoux Basha. **1732** *Hist. Litteraria* III. 10 What an ardent and restless desire Asado'ddin had conceived for the Vizirate of Egypt. **1820** T. HOPE *Anastasius* (ed. 2) III. 145 This man..had served the Capitan-Pasha during his short Visirate. **1882** *Daily Tel.* 4 May, The change in the Vizierate is supposed to indicate an early settlement of the war indemnity question with Russia. **1895** *Times* 9 Nov. 5/1 Kiamil Pasha was dismissed from the Grand Vizierate last night.

β. **1768** DOW *Hist. Hindostan* II. II. *Decline* 52 Ahmed Shaw..degraded Seifdar Jung from the vizarit. **1787** BECKFORD *Italy* (1834) II. 44 During the grand vizariat of Pombal. **1817** JAS. MILL *Brit. India* I. III. ii. 503 In the reign of Musaood he was raised to the dignity of lord of requests; and in that of Mahmood obtained the vizarit.

γ. **1815** J. C. HOBHOUSE *Substance Lett.* (1816) I. 347 It is ..clear that for some years the power of the crown, or the vizirat (it is the same), has been increasing. **1864** *Spectator* 24 Dec. 1464/1 They will rather..fling up a vizierat, as Ouseley did, because the King asked him to impede a British design.

transf. **1795** W. TAYLOR in *Monthly Rev.* XVI. 539 France has had four religions in four years: catholic at the opening of the States General;..deistical in the vizirat of Robespierre.

2. A province or district governed by a Turkish vizier.

1876 A. J. EVANS *Through Bosnia* v. 189 When the Vizierate of Bosnia stretched itself over Slavonia to the Drave. *Ibid.* viii. 346 The Vizierate of Herzegovina.

3. The department, establishment, or political residence of a (grand) vizier.

1908 *Times* 15 Sept. 3/6 A communication from the Grand Vizierate followed the Bulgarian's receipt.

vizie'ress. *rare*$^{-1}$. [f. VIZIER.] A female vizier.

1884 J. PAYNE *Bk. of 1001 Nights* VIII. 340 The queen entreated Abdallah's wife with honour..and made her her vizieress.

vizierial (vɪˈzɪərɪəl), *a.* Also vizirial, vizerial. [f. VIZIER + -IAL. Cf. F. *vizirial* and VIZIERAL *a.*]

1. Of a letter or rescript: Issued by or under the authority of a vizier or grand vizier.

α. **1849** LAYARD *Nineveh* I. v. 130, I received the vizirial letter procured by Sir Stratford Canning, authorising the continuation of the excavations. **1883** *Times* 21 Aug. 3/5 The question will now be arranged on the basis of the Imperial firman to the exclusion of the Vizerial letters.

β. **1870** C. WARREN *Recov. Jerus.* i. (1871) 50 In July another vizierial letter was received, but it only enforced the former one. **1876** R. F. BURTON in Lady Burton *Life* (1893) II. 518 In June 1869 vizierial letters were addressed especially to the Hejaz.

2. Of or pertaining to a vizier.

1876 A. J. EVANS *Through Bosnia* v. 189 Omer Pasha in 1850..transferred the Vizierial residence once more to the Serai. *Ibid.* viii. 347 The Vizierial palace of Moskar.

viziership (vɪˈzɪəʃɪp). Also 8 visier-, 9 vizirship. [f. VIZIER + -SHIP.]

1. The office or function of a vizier; rule or government as a grand vizier. Also *transf.* Cf. VIZIERATE 1.

1655 *Nicholas Papers* (Camden) II. 344 [There are] perhaps others in other courts, that aime at a Viziership in Christendome to the height of that in Turky. **1719** BOYER, *Visirat*, (Office de Visir), Visiership. **1824** *New Monthly Mag.* X. 523 The viziership of the Prince of Peace. **1840** *Ibid.* LVIII. 183 It is our gracious intention to promote you to the viziership. **1878** SEELEY *Stein* II. 456 Unnecessary odium falls upon him, and his power gets the appearance of a Vizirship.

2. = VIZIERATE 2. *rare*$^{-1}$.

1715 J. STEVENS *Hist. Persia* 163 Dividing them [*sc.* his dominions] all into four Wazir, or Vizierships, that is, Governments.

viznomy, variant of VISNOMY.

vizor, vizour: see VISOR *sb.* and *v.*

†**vizrey.** *Obs. rare.* In 6 viz rée, vizrea. [ad. Pg. *vicerei* (also arch. *visorei*), Sp. *visorey* (*virey*): see VICEROY.] A viceroy.

1583 in Purchas *Pilgrims* (1625) II. 1644 To bee at the will and pleasure of the Vizrea. **1588** R. PARKE tr. *Mendoza's Hist. China* I. vii. 13 Some doo esteeme those cities to be metropolitans, where as is resident, the gouernors, presidents, or viz Rées.

vizroy, vizt., obs. forms of VICEROY, VIZ.

vizsla (ˈvɪʃlə). Also Vizsla. The name of a town in Hungary used *absol.* to designate a golden-brown pointer with large pendent ears belonging to a breed developed in the region.

1945 C. L. B. HUBBARD *Observer's Bk. Dogs* 153 Of the five national breeds of dogs of Hungary, the Vizsla is the sole sporting dog. **1971** F. HAMILTON *World Encycl. Dogs* 208 The Vizsla has a lively, elegant and graceful gait. **1976** *Shooting Times & Country Mag.* 9–15 Dec. 52/1 Vizsla pups, excellent pedigree. **1977** J. WAMBAUGH *Black Marble* (1978) viii. 103 Letter openers bearing the likenesses of Vizslas and Brittany spaniels.

vizy (ˈvɪzɪ), *sb.* *Sc.* Also 8–9 vizzy, 9 vizzie, vizzey, vissie, visie, visey, etc. [f. the vb., or ad. F. *visée* (OF. *visee*), look, sight, aim, etc.]

1. An aim at an object which it is desired to hit; esp. in the phr. ***to take a vizy*** (cf. F. *prendre visée*).

1720 RAMSAY *Marr. Earl Weymss* vi, The Thane of Fife, wha lately wi' his flane, And vizy leel, made the blyth bowl his ain. **1808** J. MAYNE *Siller Gun* IV. xlviii, Roused at the thought, [he] charged his fuzee, Took but ae vizzy wi' his e'e —The bullet flies Clean through the target to a tee. **1822** GALT *Steam-boat* vii, Logan took a vizy, and fired. **1884** PAE *Eustace* 143 The gun was run into the desired position, the sailor called it a 'vizzey'.

b. The sight of a gun.

1828 *Blackw. Mag.* Sept. 288/2 Thus too, the vizy (*Anglice* sight) generally inclined unduly to one side or the other.

2. A look or view; a sight *of* something; a glimpse.

1785 MACKENZIE *Lounger* No. 6 ¶2 He tried to see the stage, and got a flying vizzy now and then. **1818** SCOTT *Br. Lamm.* xvi, But ye had best take a visie of him through the wicket before opening the gate. **1834** *Tait's Mag.* I. 429/1 It unfortunately never was his forte to take a steady fixed vizzy of any one thing.

Hence **'vizyless,** *a.*

1828 *Blackw. Mag.* Sept. 300/1 Oh! that our passion could restore thee [i.e. Mons Meg], butless, lockless, vizyless,.. though thou be'st, to the light of day.

vizy (ˈvɪzɪ), *v.* *Sc.* Forms: *α.* 5–6 vesy, wesy, 6 wese, wessie, vese, vesie. *β.* 5–6, 8 visy, 5 wysy, 6 wis(s)y, -ie, vis(s)e, visye, 6–7 visie, 6, 9 vissie, 8 vizzey, 8–9 vizzy, 8– vizy. [ad. ONF. *viseer* (Wace):—L. *vīsitāre* VISIT *v.*]

†**1.** *trans.* To go to see; to pay a visit or visits to; to visit. *Obs.* **a.** a person.

Freq. in the 16th c.

c **1375** *Sc. Leg. Saints* v. (*John*) 631 He vent to vesy þe kinge, & tel hym of his travalinge. *c* **1425** WYNTOUN *Cron.* v. 3899 Scho oyssit to wesy bodely Al pur folk þat was nere by. **1500–20** DUNBAR *Poems* ix. 28, I confess me, Lord! that I.. To hungre meit, nor drynk to thristy gaif, Nor veseit the seik. **1550** in *Exch. Rolls Scotl.* XVIII. 502 *note*, Ane sair leg, quharthrouch I mycht nocht cum west tyll wisy þe and uthir freyndis. **1583** in *Wodrow Soc. Misc.* (1844) 460 He was.. maist wiland to wissie the puirest creatour, being aduertisit or requyreit thairunto, in the verray nicht seson. **1600** HAMILTON in *Cath. Tractates* (S.T.S.) 231 Elizabeth..sayd, ..how is this commit to me, that the Mother of my lord suld come to visie me.

b. a place.

1535 LYNDESAY *Satyre* 504, I mak ane vow,..Richt reuerentlie thy Tempill to visie. **1549** *Compl. Scot.* Prol. 13 Thir tua princis vsit oft to visye the feildis to tak ther recreatione. *Ibid.* vi. 38 Quhen titan vas visiand antepodos.

2. To look at closely or attentively; to regard, see, view.

c **1470** HENRY *Wallace* III. 103 The worthi Scottis..Send twa skowrrouris to wesy weyll the playne. *c* **1470** *Golagros & Gaw.* 243 The king stude vesiand the wall. *a* **1500** *Bernardus de cura rei fam.* (E.E.T.S.) 212 Haffand a gret delyte For to wesy..oculatouris or trumpouris. **1533** BELLENDEN *Livy* IV. xv. (S.T.S.) 100 Frequent nowmer of pepill þat come to vesy þir playis. *a* **1568** A. SCOTT *Poems* (S.T.S.) xxvii. 33 Quhen scho growis heich, I draw on dreich, To vesy and behald the end. **1724** RAMSAY *Vision* vii, I vizyt him then round about. **1725** —— *Gentle Sheph.* III. ii. Prol., 'Tis Symon's house, please to step in, And visy 't round and round. **1790** SHIRREFS *Poems* 256 When first your Castles I did vizzey. **1867** J. GRANT *White Cockade* I. 60 An eye was seen to vizzy them carefully.

†**b.** To examine, inspect, survey, or view formally or officially. *Obs.*

1496 *Acc. Ld. High Treas. Scot.* I. 321 To pas to Borthuik ..to vesy tymmyre for gun paraling. **1512** *Ibid.* IV. 459 To xxxvj marynaris for ij dais quhen the Franchmen passit to vesy the schippis. **1561** *Exch. Rolls Scotl.* XIX. 265 *note*, Thir our lettres being anis producit thairin and vesyt be the lordis auditouris therof. **1597** SKENE *Acts of Parlt.* Table s.v. *Prenters*, Prenters suld not prent ony buikes, or vther thing, bot that quhilk is visied and tryed, havand the Kingis licence.

†**c.** With clause as object, or with *to* and inf. *Obs.*

c **1375** *Sc. Leg. Saints* xl. (*Ninian*) 559 Ȝet wald he [i.e. a bishop] mekly on fete ga..to visy in quhat wyse þe kirkmen did þar seruice. **1497** *Acc. Ld. High Treas. Scot.* I. 380 To the man that ȝeid to vesy to se gif he could wyn sclait, ij½ vnicornis. **1535** STEWART *Cron. Scot.* (Rolls) III. 431 The erle of Marche..and mony lordis mo, Come to his tent to visie how he did. **1556** *Peebles Burgh Rec.* (1872) 235 The thesaurare to vesy gif ony timber be to by to mak portis of.

d. To visé. *rare*$^{-2}$.

1867 J. GRANT *White Cockade* I. 54 Letters..signed and vizzied by the conservator of Scottish privileges at Campvere, and the British ambassador.

†**3. a.** To afflict or visit (a person) *with* sickness or harm. *Obs.*

c **1470** HENRY *Wallace* VII. 381 His fadyr..wes wesyed with seknes. *a* **1500** *Colkelbie Sow* 595 Throuch the will of God, so as it was, Thay war weseit with suddane soir seikness. **1549** *Compl. Scot.* ii. 24, I sal visee you vitht dreddour, vitht fyir, ande vitht suellieg (*sic*).

†**b.** To punish (a sin or wrong). *Obs.*

1552 ABP. HAMILTON *Catech.* (1884) 58, I will visie and punis the synnis quhilk the fatheris dois..on thair sonnis. **1562** A. SCOTT *Poems* (S.T.S.) i. 151 To wisy all þir wrangus workis..God gife þe grace.

4. *intr.* (or *absol.*). To look or gaze.

1513 DOUGLAS *Æneid* III. ix. 113 And weseand all about, I se at last This navy of ȝouris drawand hiddir fast. **1536** BELLENDEN *Cron. Scot.* (1821) I. p. xliv, And sine thay luke and visies throwe the cleir and purifyit watter, quhill thay se the mussilis. **1899** in *Eng. Dial. Dict.* (Shetland dial.).

5. To take aim with a gun, etc.; to aim *at*.

1582–8 *Hist. James VI* (1804) 75 He..cuttit ane small hole in the tarlies, quhairby he might vissie with his hagbute. **1818** HOGG *Brownie of Bodsbeck* viii, They'll maybe hae been trying how weel they could vizy at the wild ducks. **1824** MACTAGGART *Gallovid. Encycl.* 457 Some raw hands, when vizzying first at the nail in the bull's eye of the target with loaded ball [etc.].

Hence **'vizying**, *vbl. sb.* (also *attrib.*).

1552 *Acc. Ld. High Treas. Scot.* X. 148 The lairdis of Corswell, Auchyngassill, Cowhill, commissioneris for veseing of the futemen to be rasit withtin the Sherefdomes quhair thai dwell. **1825** R. CHAMBERS *Trad. Edinb.* I. 236 Sometimes the rod was simply stretched across the *vizzying hole*, a convenient aperture through which the porter could take cognizance of the person applying.

vizzard, -or, obs. forms of VIZARD, VISOR *sb.*

VJ (viː dʒeɪ). [f. the initial letters of *V*ictory over *J*apan.] Used *attrib.* and *absol.* to denote the victory of the Allied forces over those of Japan during the war of 1939–45; esp. as *VJ-day*, designating either the day upon which Japan ceased fighting (14 August 1945) or the day of Japan's formal surrender (2 September 1945).

1944 [see VE]. **1945** *Sun* (Baltimore) 15 June 1/8 (*heading*) 'V-J by Christmas' amazes Carlson. **1945** *Yank* 7 Sept. 9 The GIs had managed to keep their VJ spirit bottled up through most of the phony rumors, but when the real thing was popped, the cork popped with a vengeance. **1956** *B.B.C. Handbk.* 1957 169 VJ-day was recalled by the Overseas Services in a series of talks. **1968** *Listener* 19 Dec. 811/3 (*caption*) Revellers on V-J night. **1974** J. WAINWRIGHT *Hard Hit* 87 My memories ended with the war... Then—less than a week after V.J.—I married James. **1977** [see VE]. **1978** *Jrnl. R. Soc. Arts* CXXVI. 252/1 On VJ night I was Station Duty Officer. **1982** T. FITZGIBBON *With Love* xi. 176 A little under a month after the first bomb on Hiroshima being dropped, VJ-Day as it was called was officially celebrated on 2 September 1945.

vl-, southern ME. and dial. var. of FL-; occas. ME. and older Sc. spelling for UL-.

Vlach (vlæk). Also 9 Vlache. [a. Bulg. *vlakh* or Serb. *vlah*, = OSlav. *vlakhŭ* Romanian, Italian, Czech *vlach* Italian, Pol. *włoch* Italian, *wołoch* Walachian, ORuss. *volokh* Walachian, Italian; these terms are Slavonic adoptions of the Germanic *walh* (OHG. *walh*, *walah*, MHG. *walch*; OE. *wealh*) foreigner, applied especially to Celts and Latins. See WALACH and WELSH *a.*] A member of the Latin-speaking race occupying portions of south-eastern Europe; a Walachian or Romanian.

1841 *Penny Cycl.* XXII. 246/2 The Vlaches, or Wallachians, only live in the most south-western angle of the empire [of Russia]. **1886** *Encycl. Brit.* XXI. 16/1 They call themselves 'Romani' or 'Rumeni', but by their neighbours..they are universally known by one or other form of the word 'Vlach'. **1901** *Speaker* 21 Sept. 683/2 The alliance..would array the scattered Vlachs of Macedonia once more on the Greek side.

attrib. **1886** *Encycl. Brit.* XXI. 16/1 This Vlach or Rouman race occupies a far wider area than that included in the present Roumanian kingdom. **1905** *Speaker* 23 Sept. 580/1 The Greek bands..fell to murdering the leaders of the Vlach movement.

Hence **Vlachian** ('vleɪkɪən), *a.*

1886 *Encycl. Brit.* XXI. 19/1 The officials bearing for the most part Slavonic titles derived from the practice of the Bulgaro-Vlachian czardom. **1909** *Q. Rev.* April 681 Not the least interesting constituent of this chaotic population is the Vlachian.

vladimirite (vlædɪ'mɪəraɪt). *Min.* [ad. Russ. *vladimirit* (E. I. Nefedev 1953, in *Zap. Mineral. Obshch.* LXXXII. 317), f. the name *Vladimir*: see -ITE[1].] A hydrated arsenate of calcium, $Ca_5H_2(AsO_4)_4.5H_2O$, occurring as colourless acicular monoclinic crystals.

1954 *Mineral. Abstr.* XII. 352 Vladimirite... Found in the zone of oxidation of ore deposits. **1972** [see SAINFELDITE]. **1978** *Mineral. Rec.* IX. 73 Vladimirite... Fine, acicular, brilliant, colorless crystals in quartz cavities or with talmessite crusts were found in 1963 at the Irthem mine [in Morocco].

vlaȝe, southern ME. pa. pple. of FLAY *v.*

vlai, var. VLEI.

vlakte ('flaktə). *S. Afr.* Pl. **vlaktes**, †**-en**, [Afrikaans, a. Du.] An extent of flat open country; a plain. Freq. *pl.*

1785 G. FORSTER tr. *Sparrman's Voy. Cape Good Hope* II. xiv. 222 Animals (probably of the gazel kind) two feet in height, which used..to herd together on the *vlaktens*, or plains. **1852** C. BARTER *Dorp & Veld* 82 The plains, or *vlakten*, occupy more than two-thirds of the whole extent of the Sovereignty. **1938** E. CAMPBELL *'Die ou Pad' & Other Rhymes* 5 The vlakte is tamed and strange. **1975** *Sunday Times* (Johannesburg) 21 Sept. 20 There was everyone wondering why the men from the vlaktes, usually so docile, suddenly seemed so fractious.

vlanck, var. WLONK *a. Obs.*

vlanker, var. FLANKER (spark of fire). *dial.*

vlaske, southern ME. var. FLASK *v.*

vlat, southern dial. var. FLAT *a.*

1602 *Contention betw. Liberality & Prodigality* II. ii, Chil goe boldly to her, that's a vlat case.

vlatsum, Sc. f. WLATSOME *a. Obs.*

vleau, southern ME. var. *flew*, p.t. of FLOW *v.*

‖**vlei** (vlaɪ). Also 8 valley; 9– vley, vly, vlie, vlaie. [Du. dial. *vlei*, reduced form of Du. *vallei* valley.]

1. In South Africa: A shallow pool of water; a piece of low-lying ground covered with water during the rainy season.

1793 C. R. HOPSON tr. *Thunberg's Trav. Europe, Afr., & Asia* II. p. xii, A *valley* is nothing more than a rivulet, which is sometimes over-grown with rushes, and is broad in some places, and narrow in others. **1801** TRUTER & SOMERVILLE in G. M. Theal *Rec. Cape Colony* (1899) IV. 369 We afterwards passed two other vleis or ponds about two hours distant one from another. **1849** E. E. NAPIER *Excurs. S. Africa* II. 179 The Hottentots look anxiously around for the well known 'vlei'. **1850** R. G. CUMMING *Hunter's Life S. Afr.* (ed. 2) I. 97, I came full in view of the vley or pool of water beside which I had been directed to encamp. **1863** W. C. BALDWIN *Afr. Hunting* vi. 226 We found the vley, where we fully expected water, dried up. **1899** RIDER HAGGARD *Swallow* viii, A large vlei, or pan, where were many ducks and also some antelope.

2. *local U.S.* A swamp.

1880 *Amer. Jrnl. Sci.* Ser. III. XIX. 432 To the same settlers [the Dutch] are due the geographical appellations of *kill* for stream,..and *vly* or *vlaie* for swamp, so frequently met with in the Catskills. **1889** BYNNER *Begum's Dau.* i, Up over the grassy edge of the basin which formed the vly..the children came bounding pell-mell. **1904** R. W. CHAMBERS in *Harper's Mag.* May 933/1 Have you reason to believe that an attempt has been made to fire the Owl Vlaie?

3. vlei lourie, loerie, one of several species of coucal of the genus *Centropus*, esp. *C. superciliosus*, found in southern Africa.

1864 T. BAINES *Expl. S.-W. Afr.* xv. 391, I shot one of the loosely-feathered birds called in the colony Vlei Lories, or Reed Hawks. **1908** [see LOERIE]. **1936** E. L. GILL *First Guide S. Afr. Birds* 108 Burchell's Coucal, Vlei Lourie (Loerie). **1973** *Weekend Post* 28 Apr. 4 Some are just fascinating in their own right, like the vlei louries..and the Diederick cuckoo. **1978** MCLACHLAN & LIVERSIDGE *Roberts' Birds S. Afr.* (ed. 4) 253 White-browed Coucal. Vleiloerie. *Centropus superciliosus.*

vleoin, vleon, vlesche, vleys(s, vlex, southern ME. varr. FLY *v.*[1], FLEE *v.*, FLESH, FLAX.

vlie, southern ME. var. FLEA, FLY *sb.*; var. VLEI.

vliht, southern ME. var. FLIGHT.

vlindre, southern ME. var. FLINDER (butterfly).

vlouting, dial. var. FLOUTING *vbl. sb.*

vly, vlycche, southern ME. varr. FLY *v.*, FLITCH.

vm-, vn-, common ME. spelling for UM-, UN-.

vo., abbrev. of VOCE[2]. (Cf. VOC.)

1808 JAMIESON s.v. *Gowk's Errand*, Grose's Class. Dict. vo. *April Fool.* **1825** —— Suppl. s.v. *Custumable*, Skene, Ind. to Acts, vo. *Customers.*

vo, *sb. nonce-wd.* [f. the last syllable of *octavo.*] A size of book.

1847 *Chambers's Jrnl.* 6 Feb. 87/2 Duodecimo, postoctavo, eighteenmo, sixteenmo, and a hundred other vos and mos, bewildered the aged members of the profession.

vo, southern ME. var. FO *v.*, FOE.

Vo-Ag (vəʊ'æg). *U.S. colloq.* Also Vo. Ag. Short for *Vocational Agriculture*, agriculture considered as a subject of study for those who intend to make it their profession. Also *attrib.*

1953 *Manch. Guardian Weekly* 5 Feb. 15/2 At Milton, Georgia, the 'Vo. Ag.' instructor took me to see Gill Brown as an example of a leading F.F.A. member... In the cultivation of the 'management' attitude..Vo. Ag. achieves distinctive success. **1976** *Columbus* (Montana) *News* 17 June 1/2 The Montana Vo-Ag teachers have selected Don Owen as the Outstanding Teacher of the 1975–76 year. *Ibid.* 1 July 4/2 Lyle has accepted a position teaching Vo-Ag at a Junior College.

voar (vɔə(r)). *Orkn.* and *Shetl. dial.* Also 7, 9 vore, 9 vor, vour. [a. Norw. *vaar* (vɔːr), = Da. *vaar*, Sw. *vår*, ON. and Icel. *vár* spring: see WARE *sb.*] The spring; seed-time. Also *vore-time.*

1629 *Orkney Witch Trial* in *County Folk-Lore* III. (1903) 76 Being accusit thairupoun be the said Michaell in vore tyme. *Ibid.* 78 Sex yeiris sene or thairby in vore. **1806** P. NEILL *Tour* 58 If a man and a dog land upon some of the islands in *vor*-time, i.e. Spring. **1825** JAMIESON Suppl., *Vor, Voar, Vour*, the spring-time. **1856** ELIZA EDMONDSTON *Sk. & Tales Shetland* xi. 135, I ought to go to help our poor father and mother to get their voar finished. **1871** R. COWIE *Shetland* II. viii. 159 The operations of 'Vore' (as the seed-time is called in Shetland) do not commence until the end of March.

voc., abbrev. of VOCE[1]. (Cf. VO.)

1725 T. HEARNE *R. Brunne's Chron.* (1810) I. p. ccxiii, See the Glossary to this Work, voc. *Kampedene.* **1753** *Chambers' Cycl.* Suppl. s.v. *Calkins*, Savar. *Dict. Com.* T. I. p. 1598. voc. crampon. **1870** ALLIBONE *Dict. Eng. Lit.* (1888) II. 1532 See, also, Collier's Bibl. Acct. of Early Eng. Lit., 1865, voc. Paynell.

voc., abbrev. of VOCATIVE.

vocab ('vəʊkæb). Also voc. Abbrev. of VOCABULARY.

1900 FARMER *Public School Word-Bk.* 215 *Vocab*, ..(Charterhouse)..a vocabulary. **1971** 'M. INNES' *Awkward Lie* v. 94 Beadon should have said 'tailed', not 'trailed'. He hasn't got the vocab right. **1980** K. FOLLETT *Key to Rebecca* xvii. 195 'Have you done your prep?' 'Yes —French vocab.'

voca'bility. [f. next + -ITY.] A spoken or shouted remark or sentence.

1846 MRS. GORE *Eng. Char.* (1852) 54 At the time of the Reform Bill, their [*sc.* the linkmen's] vocabilities had a still more personal tendency.

vocable ('vəʊkəb(ə)l), *sb.* [a. F. *vocable* (16th c., = Pr. *vocable*, Sp. *vocablo*, Pg. *vocabulo*, It. *vocabolo*, *-ulo*), or directly ad. L. *vocābul-um*, f. *vocāre* to call, name.]

1. A word or term.

App. reintroduced in the 18th century; mentioned as a Scotticism by Beattie in 1787.

1530 PALSGR. Introd. p. xxii, The great nombre of theyr vocables be evidently deryved forth of latin. **1542** UDALL *Erasm. Apoph.* 9 This sillable, εὖ, in composicion of greke vocables betokeneth a certain facilitee. **1577** GRANGE *Golden Aphrod.* Ij, N.O. perceyuing this deuision of vocables, thought good to note the sense thereof. **1600–9** ROWLANDS *Knaue of Clubbes* 19 He to coniure goes, With characters, and vocables, and diuers antique shewes. **1638** A. READ *Chirurg.* ix. 60 It is not amisse sometimes to coine vocables of art to expresse the matter which is in hand.

1786 GEDDES *Prospectus New Transl. Bible* 61 There is no language so compleatly copious and distinctive as to have a different *vocable* for every different idea. **1787** —— *Let. to Bp. of London* 82, I had ventured to use the word *vocable.* Some have approved of it, as a term we wanted; others have objected to it, as an innovation. **1797** *Encycl. Brit.* (ed. 3) XIV. 527/1 Even some of the American jargon dialects contain vocables which indicate an Asiatic or European original. **1807** BOUCHER *Suppl. Johnson's Dict.* s.v. *Ay*, The simple annals, or history, of this vocable in our own language..would probably be not less curious than its general history is. **1852** BLACKIE *Study Lang.* 30 If you love the book..you will master the vocables it contains in a speedy and agreeable way. **1875** E. WHITE *Life in Christ* IV. xxiv. (1878) 348 Dreamers, for whom..every vocable is surrounded with an aureola or many-tinted halo of mysteries and 'inner senses'.

†**2.** A name or designation. *Obs. rare.*

c **1550** *Disc. Common Weal Eng.* (1893) 76 Therof to this daie remaineth these vocables of coine, as libra, pondo, dipondium,..vocables of weight; that afterward weare gyven to coines pretending the same weight. *a* **1623** BUCK *Rich. III*, v. (1646) 133 We will next endeavour to understand that Vocable, or term, *Tyrannus* (that is, a Tyrant, or an evil King) cast upon King Richard.

'vocable, *a. rare*⁻¹. [f. L. *voc-āre* to call + -ABLE.] Capable of utterance.

1901 MEREDITH *Poems, With the Persuader* 174 Cunninger than the numbered strings,.. For mastered discords and the things Not vocable, whose mysteries Are inmost Love's.

Hence **'vocably** *adv.*

1906 J. A. HOBSON *Canada To-day* i. 3 Canada is conscious, vocably, uproariously conscious, that her day has come.

†**vo'cabula.** *Obs.*⁻¹ [pl. of L. *vocābulum* VOCABLE *sb.*] A vocabulary.

1698 FRYER *Acc. E. India & P.* 360 They have their Grammars, Dictionaries, and Vocabulaes, in which are the Roots of the Arabick Tongue.

†**vo'cabular,** *sb. Obs.*⁻¹ [See VOCABULARY *sb.* and -AR².] A vocabulary.

1530 PALSGR. 10 By what meanes it shalbe knowen in the frenche vocabular whan *i* and *u* be vowels and whan they be consonantes. **1659** W. JACOB in Somner *Dictionarium*, To list your names in this Vocabular.

vocabular (vəʊ'kæbjʊlə(r)), *a.* [f. L. *vocābulum* VOCABLE *sb.* + -AR¹.] Of, pertaining to, or concerning words.

1608 TOPSELL *Serpents* 282 Which wordes in their seuerall Languages, haue other significations, as are to be found in euery vocabular Dictionary. **1647** M. HUDSON *Div. Right Govt.* II. ii. 75 To unscruple all vocabular doubts and difficulties, let us but look into the fourteenth Ch. of Gen. and there we shall find a King of Gods own making. **1824** J. GILCHRIST *Etym. Interpreter* 61 This is the most prolific origin of verbal multiplication or vocabular augmentation; for thus an indefinite number of nouns are produced by a few verbs and adjectives. **1848** CLOUGH *Bothie* ix, Leaving vocabular ghosts undisturbed in their lexicon-limbo. **1867** LYTTON in *Ld. Lytton's Lett.* (1906) I. iv. 206 Too many images and vocabular effects make the sense of the whole obscure.

vocabu'larian, *a.* [Cf. prec. and -IAN.] One who gives much or undue attention to words.

1899 *Pall Mall G.* 20 July 4/1 He is not a vocabularian; he uses, as none but a poet can, the old poetic materials.

vo'cabularize, *v. rare*⁻¹. [Cf. prec. and -IZE.] *trans.* To furnish with a vocabulary.

1851 SIR F. PALGRAVE *Norm. & Eng.* I. 51 The vernacular French of the Capital,.. amply vocabularized from the other languages of the mixed hosts whom Napoleon had assembled.

vocabulary (vəʊ'kæbjʊlərɪ), *sb.* Also 6 **-arye,** 7 **-arie.** [ad. med.L. *vocābulāri-us, -um*, f. L. *vocābulum* VOCABLE *sb.*: see -ARY¹. Hence also It., Sp., Pg. *vocabulario*, F. *vocabulaire* (1481). Cf. VOCABULAR *sb.*, VOCABULER.]

1. a. A collection or list of words with brief explanations of their meanings; now *esp.* a list of this kind given in an elementary grammar or reading-book of a foreign language.

Longer vocabularies are usually arranged alphabetically or according to subject-headings. In philological grammars and readers the vocabulary is commonly termed a *glossary*.

1532 MORE *Confut. Tindale* Wks. 427/1 Then must he with his translacion make vs an Englishe vocabularye of his own deuise too. **1579** FULKE *Heskins' Parl.* 55 Maister Heskins fareth as hee were halfe madde, sending vs to the Vocabularies, Calepines, and Dictionaries. **1611** COTGR., *Vocabulaire*, a Vocabularie, Dictionarie. **1646** SIR T. BROWNE *Pseud. Ep.* VII. ix. 355 This is the proper signification of the word, [it is] thus used in Scripture by the Septuagint, [and] Greeke vocabularies thus expound it. **1690** LOCKE *Hum. Und.* III. xi. 260 A vocabulary made after this fashion, would, perhaps, with more ease, and in less time, teach the true signification of many Terms. **1741** WATTS *Improv. Mind* (1801) 41 It is necessary that we should be furnished with Vocabularies and Dictionaries of several sorts. **1816** TUCKEY *Narr. Exped. R. Zaire* ii. (1818) 65 From our visitors I procured a vocabulary of their language. **1857** T. WRIGHT (*title*), A Volume of Vocabularies. *Ibid.* Pref., One of the most valuable of the later vocabularies here printed. **1884** BRADLEY *Latin Prose Composition* 353 General Vocabulary. *Ibid.*, The Latin words in this Vocabulary are not necessarily equivalent to the English.

fig. **1532** MORE *Confut. Tindale* Wks. 598/1 As I wene it is expounded in god almightes vocabulary.

transf. **1662** STILLINGFL. *Orig. Sacrae* I. i. §3 Otherwise all the use of words is to be a meer vocabulary to the understanding, and an Index to memory.

b. Const. *of*. (Passing into the sense of 'list'.)

1821 J. Q. ADAMS in C. Davies *Metric Syst.* (1871) III. 145 A vocabulary of new denominations was annexed to every weight and measure belonging to it. **1825** T. HOOK *Sayings* Ser. II. *Man of Many Fr.* (Colburn) 137 He heard a vocabulary of dishes enumerated with grace and fluency [by the French cook]. **1862** STANLEY *Jew. Ch.* (1877) I. xvi. 309 The most complete vocabulary of arms..in the Old Testament is taken from the panoply of a Philistine warrior.

c. *Naut.* (See quot.)

1867 SMYTH *Sailor's Word-bk.* 714 *Vocabulary*, the system of naval signals based on Sir Home Popham's improvements.

2. a. The range of language of a particular person, class, profession, or the like.

Used with limiting terms (possessives, adjectives, etc.).

1753 H. WALPOLE *Lett.* (1846) III. 20, I wore out..my vocabulary with commending. **1782** MISS BURNEY *Cecilia* VIII. v, Let nerves be discarded from the female vocabulary. **1815** J. CORMACK *Abol. Fem. Infanticide Guzerat* x. 196 The almost infinite labours of an individual, from whose vocabulary the word impossible seems to have been excluded. **1851** PALGRAVE *Norm. & Eng.* I. 2 An Innocent, in Shakesperian vocabulary, signifies an Idiot. **1891** FARRAR *Darkn. & Dawn* xxix, The actor..had erased the words 'ought' and 'ought not' from his vocabulary as completely as most of his contemporaries.

b. Const. *of* (some quality, feeling, etc.).

1770 CUMBERLAND *West Indian* IV. x, In the vocabulary of modern honour there is no such term. **1856** KANE *Arct. Expl.* II. xii. 129 His eloquence becoming more and more.. vituperative, until it has exhausted either his strength or his vocabulary of invective. **1872** MORLEY *Voltaire* (1886) 5 The rank vocabulary of malice and hate. **1884** J. SHARMAN *Hist. Swearing* v. 80 The more religion appeals to the senses, the more fecund has been the vocabulary of oaths.

c. With *a*, or without article.

1837 EMERSON *Addr., Amer. Schol.* Wks. (Bohn) II. 181 If it were only for a vocabulary, the scholar would be covetous of action. **1892** C. TAYLOR *Witness of Hermas to Four Gosp.* 130 On the principle that vocabulary is an indication of an author's literary sources. **1898** WATTS DUNTON *Aylwin* v. i, 'To repeat one's words', I said quietly, shows a limited vocabulary.

3. The sum or aggregate of words composing a language.

1782 V. KNOX *Ess.* cxiv. (1819) II. 285 The Latin Fathers ..wrote..well enough to preserve a skill in the construction and vocabulary of the language. **1841** BORROW *Zincali* II. ii. III. 107 It is no longer a sealed language, its laws, structure, and vocabulary being sufficiently well known. **1868** FREEMAN *Norm. Conq.* (1877) I. i. 4 The largest infusion that the vocabulary of one European tongue ever received from another. **1882** A. W. WARD *Dickens* vii. 206 He recognised his responsibility..in keeping the vocabulary of the language pure.

4. *fig.* A set of artistic or stylistic forms, techniques, movements, etc.; the range of such forms, etc., available to a particular person, etc.

1917 G. B. SHAW *How to become Musical Critic* (1960) 291 As far as mere grammar and vocabulary go, there is nothing more in the statue scene from Don Juan, which threw open the whole magic realm of modern orchestration..than in the exquisite little song of Cherubino. **1949** *Ballet Ann.* III. 109/2 Repetitions, lengthy passages, obscure symbols and movements..which ever aim not only at enriching the classic vocabulary..but at uplifting the mind. **1959** *Listener* 10 Dec. 1042/2 The extraordinary vocabulary of the latest works with their untrammelled blossoming in space, their hectic and at times almost hysterical proliferations of bumps, bulges, bags. **1960** *Economist* 22 Oct. 369/2 No country is likely to be able to rely purely on its own 'vocabulary' of styling; but British manufacturers..might be glad to escape the dependence on Italian and Swiss fashion leadership in car bodies. **1967** 'LA MERI' *Spanish Dancing* (ed. 2) vii. 86 Important is the fact that with the Pavane a vocabulary of steps appeared for the first time in dance history. **1972** E. LUCIE-SMITH in Cox & Dyson *20th-Cent. Mind* II. xiv. 474 Cubism is no longer 'analytic' but 'synthetic'. That is, it aims to create, by means of a consistent vocabulary of form, a universe which parallels the real one. **1977** *New Yorker* 25 July 62/2 Together the two enlarged the vocabulary of lawn tennis and laid the foundation for the all-court game. **1977** M. GIROUARD *Sweetness & Light* vii. 176 During the 1880s the Bedford Park vocabulary was being taken up by speculative builders and put to every kind of use. **1980** *Jrnl. R. Soc. Arts* Feb. 165/1 The vernacular building, employing the simple vocabulary of wall, sloping roof, door and small window, results in a national display of tranquil richness.

vo'cabulary, *a. rare.* [f. L. *vocābul-um* VOCABLE *sb.* + -ARY.] Of or pertaining to words; composed of, or concerned with, words.

1616 BULLOKAR *Eng. Expos.*, *Vocabularie*, of or belonging to words, which consisteth onely of words. **1903** *Daily Chron.* 21 April 6/3 The vocabulary code compiled by the International Bureau of Telegraphic Administrations. **1909** *Westm. Gaz.* 28 May 2/1 Treating it as a vocabulary quarrel to which it would be childish to attach any importance.

vocabu'lation. *rare*⁻¹. [f. as prec. + -ATION.] The use or choice of words.

1891 E. EGGLESTON *Faith Doctor* xiii. 162 A mind.. felicitous in vocabulation and ingenious in the construction of sentences.

†**vo'cabuler.** *Obs. rare.* [Cf. VOCABULARY *sb.* and -ER² 2.] A vocabulary.

1530 PALSGR. 150 By the helpe of the frenche vocabuler. **1706** STEVENS I, *Vocabulario*, a Dictionary, a Vocabuler.

vo'cabulist. Also 6 **-iste, -yst(e.** [ad. L. type **vocabulista*: see VOCABLE and -IST. So F. *vocabuliste* (1731) in sense 2.]

†**1.** A vocabulary. *Obs.*

1530 BAYNTON in *Palsgr.* Introd. p. xiii, Theyr vocabulistes, which have ben of so many yeres, and by so sondry clerkes agatheryng. **1530** PALSGR. 150 Some fewe sentences whiche the lernar shall fynde before the begynnyng of the sayd vocabulyst.

2. A compiler of a vocabulary.

1545 BALE *Myst. Iniq.* 2 After the vocabulystes Tortellius ..Calepinus, Guarin' & soche other vocabulystes. **1800** in *Spirit Pub. Jrnls.* IV. 147 This is an obsolete phrase, and is not to be found in any vocabulist I know of.

vo'cabulize, *v. rare*⁻¹. [Cf. prec. and -IZE.] *trans.* To put into words, to utter.

1873 LELAND *Egypt. Sketch-Bk.* 233 He was too much disgusted to speak—too much revolted at me and the ring and all mankind, to vocabulise anything.

vocal ('vəʊkəl), *a.* and *sb.* [ad. L. *vōcāl-is* uttering voice, speaking, etc., f. *vōc-*, *vox* voice + -AL¹. So F., Sp., Pg. *vocal*, It. *vocale*.]

A. *adj.* **I. 1.** Uttered or communicated by the voice; spoken, oral: **a.** Of prayer. (Opposed to *mental*.)

a **1395** HYLTON *Scala Perf.* I. xxvii. (W. de W. 1494), This manere of prayer whiche is callid vocal. **1526** *Pilgr. Perf.* (W. de W. 1531) 159 Bycause this prayer is for the hole chirche, necessary it is that it be vocall, that is to say, eyther songe or distinctly sayd with voyce. **1563** *Homilies* II. *Com. Prayer* Ppp iiij, Let vs se whether the Scriptures..wyll allow any vocall prayer, that is, when the mouth vttereth the peticions with voyce. **1641** 'SMECTYMNUUS' *Answ.* ii. (1653) 8 Which Prayers were so farre from being Prescript Formes or Liturgies that they were not vocall but mentall Prayers. **1671** WOODHEAD *St. Teresa* I. vi. 314 If Vocal Prayer be made, as it should, even Mental is an ingredient into it. **1766** FORDYCE *Serm. Yng. Wm.* (1767) II. xi. 148 Vocal prayer, whether more or less articulate, will be found..by far the most proportioned to the human..faculties. **1782** PRIESTLEY *Corrupt. Chr.* II. IX. 151 Instead of the ancient severities [of penance], vocal prayers came to be all that was enjoined. **1862** *Lond. Rev.* 26 July 84 The dangers of unreality and self-delusion with which *vocal* prayers were beset. **1884** *Cath. Dict.* 569 St. Benedict supposes that some of his monks will pray after the vocal prayers of the office with tears and application of heart.

b. In other contexts.

1579 W. WILKINSON *Confut. Fam. Love* 53 b, Why then do they make accompt of it, but as a vocall word, and outward sounde? **1642** FULLER *Holy & Prof. St.* IV. ix. 278 He is diligent and faithfull in preaching the Gospel: either by his pen..or by his vocall sermons. **1660** F. BROOKE tr. *Le Blanc's Trav.* 232 Messengers, who deliver their missives by vocal relation. **1667** MILTON *P.L.* IX. 198 Forth came the human pair, And joynd thir vocal Worship to the Quire Of Creatures wanting voice. **1725** POPE *Odyss.* VIII. 42 When high he sings The vocal lay responsive to the strings. **1757** GRAY *Bard* 120 What strains of vocal transport round her play. **1818** STODDART in *Encycl. Metrop.* (1845) I. 90/1 It is quite enough that we have one vocal sign, one organic articulation, to advertise the hearer, that what we say is not in the subject of which we speak. **1874** SPURGEON *Treas. Dav.* Ps. xcii. 1 Silent worship is sweet, but vocal worship is sweeter. **1887** RUSKIN *Præterita* II. 191 John Hobbs, called always..George, to distinguish him, in vocal summons, from my father and me.

†**c.** Expressed in words. *Obs.*⁻¹

1610 W. FOLKINGHAM *Art of Survey* III. i. 65 The Propriety of Possessions..may be deuided into Vocall and Evidential. Vocall Propriety denotates the Properties of particulars by due Appellation.

d. Of sound: Produced by the voice; *spec.* of the nature of words or speech.

1623 MASSINGER *Bondman* I. iii, If a virgin..Presume to clothe her thought in vocal sounds, Let her find pardon. **1669** HOLDER *Elem. Speech* 23 A vibration of those Cartilaginous Bodies which forms that Breath, into a Vocal sound or Voice. **1693** DRYDEN *Ovid's Met.* XII. 571 Her Words were in her Clamour drown'd; For my stun'd Ears receiv'd no vocal Sound. **1839** *Penny Cycl.* XIII. 305/1 If any two human beings can by vocal sounds mutually convey to each other their desires. **1860** FARRAR *Orig. Language* i. 19 The mere possession of vocal cries not different from those of animals. **1864** BOWEN *Logic* ii. 31 Vocal sound is the Matter of speech.

2. a. Of music: Performed by, composed for, the voice; that is sung or intended for singing. (Opposed to *instrumental*.)

c **1586** C'TESS PEMBROKE *Ps.* XCVIII. ii, O sing,.. Make lute a part with vocall musique beare. **1603** HOLLAND *Plutarch's Mor.* 486 Giving herselfe to learne poesie, and likewise vocall musicke. **1650** BULWER *Anthropomet.* 161 Vocal-Musick, performed by Instruments which Nature hath invented for delight, ought not to be set at naught. **1698** FRYER *Acc. E. India & P.* 276 The Morning being ushered in with Vocal and Instrumental Musick. **1712** ADDISON *Spect.* No. 405 ⁋8 Vocal and Instrumental Musick were made use of in their Religious Worship. **1795** MASON *Ch. Music* i. 24 When the Greek and Latin writers treat of Instrumental Music..they seldom, if ever, consider it as separated from Vocal. **1840** *Penny Cycl.* XVI. 22/1 In the accompaniment to vocal music, much greater freedom of imitation is allowable than in the voice part. **1864** ENGEL *Mus. Anc. Nat.* 9 Vocal music, regarded historically, takes precedence by its antiquity of instrumental music.

b. Connected with singing. ***vocal score*** (see quot. 1876); ***vocal line*** [LINE *sb.*² 7 h].

1799 *Monthly Rev.* XXX. 535 The vocal taste of Spain must be very much degenerated, or that of France improved, if the same singer can excite equal rapture in the capitals of both countries. **1822** C. BUTLER *Hist. Mem. Eng. Cath.* IV. xcviii. 464 [Ancient Greek music] was governed by rhythm and quarter tones made a part of its regular vocal scale. **1857** CANON AINGER in E. Sichel *Life & Lett.* (1906) 43, I..shall place myself in a snug corner of the hall, with the vocal score in my hands. **1876** STAINER & BARRETT *Dict. Mus. Terms* 388/2 A vocal score is (or was formerly understood to be) one in which the voice-parts are written out in full, and the accompaniment (if any) is indicated by a figured bass. **1934** C. LAMBERT *Music Ho!* III. 190 The disparity between the vocal line and its harmonic background [in *Les Noces*]. **1961** [see LINE *sb.*² 7 h]. **1963** *Listener* 7 Feb. 264/3 The orchestral skill..the command of texture and expressive colour, and the judging of instrumental comment on the vocal line.

3. a. Having the character of a vowel; vocalic.

1589 PUTTENHAM *Eng. Poesie* II. xv[i]. (Arb.) 141 The foote (*Tribrachus*) of three short times is very hard to be made by any of our trissillables vnles they be compounded of the smoothest sort of consonants or sillables vocals. **1631** WEEVER *Anc. Funeral Mon.* To Rdr. 7 Also E vocall, for E dipthong. **1736** AINSWORTH *Lat. Dict.* II. s.v. *I*, They give it [*sc.* i, j] a name from its consonant use, we from the vocal. **1807** SOUTHEY *Espriella's Lett.* I. 279 As their delicate ears could bear none but vocal terminations.

b. Actually uttered or sounded. *rare.*

1751 JOHNSON *Rambler* No. 88 ⁋11 There is reason to believe that the silent e which our ancestors added to the most of our monosyllables,..was once vocal. **1755** JOHNSON s.v. *E*, Afterwards it [the letter *e*] was in poetry either mute or vocal, as the verse required.

c. *Phonetics.* Uttered with voice (as distinguished from *breath*); voiced, sonant.

1668 WILKINS *Real Char.* III. xii. §2. 369 (*Zh*) the sonorous Consonant, and (*Sh*) its correspondent mute, are framed by a percolation of the breath, betwixt the tongue rendered concave, and the teeth both upper and lower: The first being vocal, the other mute. **1669** W. HOLDER *Elem. Speech* 53 B. is Vocal, Labial, Occluse. *Ibid.* 58 L. and R... are not easie.. to be pronounced spiritally,.. but are apt to get a tincture of Vocal sound. **1824** L. MURRAY *Eng. Gram.* (ed. 5) I. 35 The semi-vowels may be subdivided into *vocal* and *aspirated*. The vocal are those which are formed by the voice; the aspirated, those formed by the breath. **1847** *Proc. Philol. Soc.* III. 72 Examples beginning with a vocal letter are found both in the Chinese and in other languages. **1874** SWEET in *Trans. Philol. Soc.* 538 There can be no doubt that the *f* in Early Old English was vocal like the Welsh *f*.

II. 4. a. Endowed with a voice, possessed of utterance; exercising the power of speech or of uttering sounds.

1601 HOLLAND *Pliny* I. 233 Brought there were thither.. such [frogs] as would crie in the water: and that whole kind still remaineth vocall. **1654** WHITLOCK *Zootomia* 199, I am sure neither are Canonicall, neither the meere vocall Preacher, nor the Preaching Auditor. **1668** H. MORE *Div. Dial.* III. xxxiv. (1713) 271 As probable as the black Hunter ranging the Forest with his vocal, but invisible, Hounds in Fountainbleau. **1733** POPE *Essay on Man* III. 157, In the same temple, the resounding wood, All vocal beings hymn'd their equal God. **1774** GOLDSM. *Nat. Hist.* (1776) VII. 339 These insects are generally vocal in the midst of summer. *c* **1792** *Encycl. Brit.* (ed. 3) IX. 529/1 The organs of all vocal animals are so formed, as, upon any particular impulse, to utter sounds. **1877** TYNDALL in *Daily News* 2 Oct. 2/5 Though the mechanical theory of a vocal Heavenly multitude proves untenable.

b. *transf.* Of inanimate things, places, etc.

1646 J. HALL *Poems* 57 Were but this Marble vocall, there such an Elogium would appeare As [etc.]. **1667** MILTON *P.L.* IX. 530 He.. with Serpent Tongue Organic, or impulse of vocal Air, His fraudulent temptation thus began. **1710** W. KING *Heathen Gods & Heroes* x. (1722) 40 How these Oracles were deliver'd, is a Controversie, whether by two Doves that spoke, or by the Leaves of the Oaks themselves, which became Vocal. **1784** COWPER *Task* IV. 159 The poet's or historian's page, by one Made vocal for th' amusement of the rest. **1796** SOUTHEY *Lett. fr. Spain* (1799) 160 Many a stream That from the neighbouring hill descended clear Wound vocal thro' the valley. **1825** LAMB *Elia* II. *Superannuated Man*, Stones of old Mincing Lane,.. to the footsteps of what toil-worn clerk are your everlasting flints now vocal? **1837** WILKINSON *Mann. & Cust. Anc. Egypt* ii. (1841) I. 59 *note*, The vocal statue of the supposed Memnon is of Amunoph III. **1890** W. J. GORDON *Foundry* 156 There are seven steam-hammers.. and a remarkably vocal saw for cutting red-hot iron.

c. Of musical instruments. Chiefly *poet.*

a **1700** EVELYN *Diary* 5 Oct. 1664, There was brought a new invented instrument of musiq,.. made vocal by a wheele, and a zone of parchment that rubb'd horizontaly against the strings. **1738** WESLEY *Ps.* CXXXVII. ii, Our Harps, no longer vocal now, We cast aside. **1743** FRANCIS tr. *Hor., Odes* III. i. 23 Nor chaunt of birds, nor vocal lyre To him can sleep afford. **1760** FAWKES tr. *Anacreon, Ode* i. 5 Rapt I strike the vocal Shell—Hark—the trembling Chords rebel.

5. a. *fig.* Conveying impressions or ideas as if by speech; expressive, eloquent.

1608 TOPSELL *Serpents* 134 By a mute and silent way it ascendeth, and bringeth all things mortall to a vocall iustice, which speaketh in action though not in voyce. **1608–11** BP. HALL *Epist.* (1643) 328 Accusations are vocall, Apologies dumbe. **1697** EVELYN *Numism.* Introd. 1 Medals.. (give me leave to call them) Vocal Monuments of Antiquity. **1720** WELTON *Suffer. Son of God* I. xiii. 343 The Multitude of my successive Miseries might become Vocal, and never cease to Importune Thy Mercy. **1724** R. WELTON *Christ. Faith & Pract.* 209 That vocal blood and those speaking wounds. **1897** *Garden* 24 April 294/3 Every leaf is vocal, and the air is full of the moist fragrance of the earth.

Comb. **1649** OWEN *Shaking & Transl. Heav. & Earth* 36 The works of God.. are vocall-speaking works: the minde of God is in them.

b. *spec.* (See quot.) *rare*$^{-0}$.

1728 CHAMBERS *Cycl.* s.v. *Arms*, Speaking, or Vocal Arms, are those wherein the Figures bear an Allusion to the Name of the Family.

6. a. Operative or concerned in the production of voice. Freq. in ***vocal chord, fold, organs, tract***, etc.

1644 DIGBY *Nat. Bodies* xxxvi. §14. 318 Who would looke curiously into the motions of the dispositions of a beastes vocal instruments. **1656** BLOUNT *Glossogr.* s.v., Vocal nerves are those noble sinews, which have the vertue of forming the speech. **1704** J. HARRIS *Lex. Techn.* I, *Recurrent Nerves*, by some called *Vocal*, because they are spent upon the Instruments of Speech. **1751** HARRIS *Hermes* Wks. (1841) 208 What these vocal organs precisely are, is not in all respects agreed by philosophers and anatomists. **1842** *Penny Cycl.* XXII. 429/2 The upward current of air passing through the larynx produces an effect on the vocal ligaments. **1872** HUXLEY *Physiol.* vii. 178 These sharp free edges of the glottis are the so-called vocal chords or vocal ligaments. **1887** *Buck's Handbk. Med. Sci.* IV. 391/2 The vocal bands deserve a separate notice on account of their great physiological importance. **1936** *Summ. Doct. Diss. Northwestern Univ.* IV. 183 Many investigations have been carried on to determine how the vocal folds vibrate. **1940** *Bell System Techn. Jrnl.* XIX. 496 Message waves are produced as muscular motions in the vocal tract. **1960** *Jrnl. Speech & Hearing Res.* III. 159/1 An investigator observed the image of the subject's vocal folds in the laryngeal mirror. **1961** *Jrnl. Acoustical Soc. Amer.* XXX. 1725/2 The generally accepted theory of speech production views the speech wave as the result of acoustic excitation of the vocal tract by one or more sources... The characteristics of the glottal source are to a large extent independent of the vocal-tract configuration anterior to the glottis. **1977** D. FRY *Homo Loquens* iii. 30 The process of articulation.. depends on continual changes in the shape of the vocal tract, and hence in its acoustic properties. **1981** *Word 1980* XXXI. 152 The disruptions.. due to the effects of coupling between the larynx and the supraglottal tract on the rate of vibration of the vocal folds.

b. *spec.* Connected with the utterance of vowel-sounds; = VOCALIC *a.* 2.

1788 *Asiatick Res.* I. 13 This is the simplest element of articulation, or first *vocal* sound, concerning which enough has been said: the word *America* begins and ends with it; and its proper symbol therefore is A. **1818** *Trans. Amer. Philos. Soc.* I. 246 The vocal sounds are those which are represented in alphabets by the letters we call vowels. **1887** *Alien. & Neurol.* VIII. 7 The vocal (vowel) mechanism is the first that is manifested in the child.

7. a. Of or belonging to the voice (†or sound). Also comb., as ***vocal-auditory*** adj.

1644 BULWER *Chirol.* 4 In the report of a Piece, the eye being the nimbler sense, discernes the discharge before any intelligence by conduct of the vocal Wave arrive at the eare. **1654** H. L'ESTRANGE *Chas. I* (1655) 1 Though his [Charles's] vocall impediment accompanyed him till the fatall stroke. **1795** MASON *Ch. Music* ii. 154 They must still endeavour to hit that precise medium in the vocal faculty, which pronounces and sings at the same time. **1840** DICKENS *Old C. Shop* lxii, Mr. Quilp was certainly entertaining himself with vocal exercise. **1862** H. W. FULLER *Dis. Chest* I. iii. 18 This 'vocal fremitus' is more pronounced in adults than in children. **1881** LADY HERBERT *Edith* 6 Indifferent to everything but his child's beauty and vocal talents. **1958** *Proc. 8th Internat. Congr. Linguists* 754 Despite eloquent pleas,.. that writing can and should be considered as basically a visual system independent of the vocal-auditory process, is it likely that any system of writing would be seriously proposed to-day that was not based on some attempt at a systematic correlation with the spoken language? **1981** *Amer. Speech* LVI. 130 Sign language is as adequate for the deaf as any vocal-auditory language is for a hearing person.

b. Of the nature of voice or sound.

a **1826** HEBER *Transl. Pindar* II. 158 Of vocal shafts.. that wildly fly. **1844** MRS. BROWNING *Lady Geraldine's Courtship* xliv, 'Tis the eyes that shoot out vocal light.

8. Full of voice or sound; sounding, resounding. Also const. *by*, *with*.

1667 MILTON *P.L.* V. 204 Hill, or Valley, Fountain, or fresh shade Made vocal by my Song. **1697** DRYDEN *Virg. Past.* IV. 4 Sicilian Muse prepare To make the vocal Woods deserve a Consul's care. **1717** POPE *Eloisa* 140 Such plain roofs as Piety could raise, And only vocal with the Maker's praise. **1746** HERVEY *Medit.* (1818) 247 She flies the vocal grove, and shuns the society of all the feathered choir. **1823** BYRON *Age of Bronze* xi, This was not the method of old Rome, When Tully fulmined o'er each vocal dome. **1834** PRINGLE *Afr. Sk.* viii. 288 The inland streams.. are vocal in spring with the shrill chirping of millions of frogs. **1868** FARRAR *Silence & V.* i. (1875) 8 When all the air is vocal with whispering trees, and singing birds.

9. Readily or freely expressing oneself in speech; giving vent to one's views or opinions.

1871 SMILES *Charac.* ix. (1876) 256 The modern English, as compared.. with their nimbler more communicative and vocal.. neighbours, the modern French and Irish. **1881** *Pall Mall G.* 10 Feb. 1/1 That policy [of coercion in Ireland] may have done something to pacify.. an influential and highly vocal class in England. **1887** *Ibid.* 4 March 1/2 The most vocal class in the whole community, as the legal profession may fairly be described.

B. *sb.* **1. a.** A vowel. *Obs.*

1582 STANYHURST *Æneis* To Rdr. (Arb.) 14 Where the next woord following beginneth with a vocal. **1586** —— *Treat. Irel.* 9/2 in *Holinshed* I, In corruption of common talke we find that (u) with his vocale is easilie lost and suppressed; so we saie ere for euer [etc.].

†**b.** A voiced consonant. *Obs.*

1669 HOLDER *Elem. Speech* 78 To soften the Occluse Gingival Consonants, by a kind of.. addition of a Spirital.. to a Vocal producing the Vowel.

2. Vocal faculty; power of speech.

1838 MRS. BROWNING *Seraphim* II. 112 Hath language left thy lips, to place Its vocal in thine eye?

3. A member of a Roman Catholic body who has a right to vote in certain elections.

a **1660** *Contemp. Hist. Irel.* (Ir. Archæol. Soc.) II. 109 In Conaght, on the 15th of August, 1650, all the vocalls of the whole province there apeeringe, and of Carons faction.. were the undernamed (though not all, but some, before theire transgression were vocalls). **1728** CHAMBERS *Cycl.* s.v., A Man must have been a Religious a certain number of Years, to be a Vocal. **1811** W. JACOB *Trav. S. Spain* 64, I am afraid I should only create disgust were I to dwell on other characters among the vocals, as they are designated.

4. a. Vocal music; singing.

1928 S. LEWIS *Man who knew Coolidge* I. 30 She felt more kind of called to the music line, and she was taking vocal and piano. **1968** *Blues Unlimited* Sept. 26 For strange vocal try to hear Daniel Brown's version.

b. A musical composition written for, or including a part for, the voice; a vocal part.

1934 S. R. NELSON *All about Jazz* iv. 84 A succession of vocals in radio music is sometimes tiresome. **1938** D. BAKER *Young Man with Horn* IV. 171 He had them pretty heavily arranged, with a transitional passage before every vocal. **1957** R. HOGGART *Uses of Literacy* viii. 203 Almost all [the records] are 'vocals' and the styles of singing much advanced beyond what is normally heard on the Light Programme of the B.B.C. **1975** A. AYCKBOURN *Norman Conquests* 14 He does a dance to the music and sings as the vocal starts. **1983** *Sunday Tel.* 9 Oct. 24/2 The cost of a machine with a complete package of 400 songs with the vocals edited out, is £600.

vocalese (vəʊkəˈliːz). *Jazz.* [f. VOCAL *a.* and *sb.* + -ESE, perh. partly after VOCALISE.] A style of singing in which singers put words to jazz tunes, esp. to solos previously improvised by jazz musicians. Also = SCAT *sb.*[6] a.

1955 L. FEATHER *Encycl. Jazz* 248 Annie Ross, Eddie Jefferson and others imitated his idea of translating ad lib jazz into 'vocalese'. **1963** *Guardian* 5 July 11/1 Her unusual talent for simulating orchestral sounds (the jazz singing style called 'vocalese'). **1978** [see SCAT *sb.*[6] (and *a.*) b]. **1981** *Times* 15 Apr. 16/8 King Pleasure, a pioneer of the style of modern jazz singing known as 'vocalese', has died... Vocalese is the process of putting words to improvized jazz solos.

vocalic (vəʊˈkælɪk), *a.* [f. VOCAL *a.* + -IC. Cf. F. *vocalique.*]

1. Rich in vowels; composed mainly or entirely of vowels.

1814 SCOTT *Wav.* xxii, The Gaelic language being uncommonly vocalic is well adapted for sudden and extemporaneous poetry. **1846** GROTE *Greece* I. xvi. I. 473 Its richness, its flexibility and capacity of new combinations, its vocalic abundance and metrical pronunciation. **1859** PATTESON in Miss Yonge *Life* (1874) I. 439 Their language is all vocalic and so easy to put into writing.

b. Characterized by a vowel or vowels.

1874 SAYCE *Compar. Philol.* ii. 92 The varying vocalic forms of the Imperfect [tense]. **1887** A. S. COOK *Sievers' O.E. Gram.* 129 Vocalic or strong declension.

2. Consisting of a vowel or vowels; of the nature of a vowel.

1852 in *Jrnl. Ethnol. Soc.* (1854) III. 264 The series of vocalic and consonantal sounds. **1868** G. STEPHENS *Runic Mon.* I. 25 The sing. accusative ending in a vowel or a vocalic consonant. **1874** A. B. DAVIDSON *Introd. Hebr. Gram.* 101 Sometimes the vocalic termination is written with *yod.* **1891** A. L. MAYHEW *O.E. Phonology* 19 In final unaccented syllables e was developed from a vocalic liquid or nasal.

3. Of or pertaining to, affecting or concerning, a vowel or vowels.

1861 GRAHAM *Eng. Word-Bk.* Introd., In words of Gothic origin we more frequently find that internal vocalic and consonantal changes are employed to produce the new word. **1876** DOUSE *Grimm's Law* 171 Of the corresponding vocalic affections, the palatal.. is as much European as Aryan. **1876** BLACKIE *Lang. & Lit. Scot. Highl.* i. 63 No man with an ear will deny vocalic depth.. to the following lines.

vocalion (vəʊˈkeɪlɪən). [f. VOCAL *a.* + -ION[1].] A musical instrument of the nature of a harmonium with broad reeds, producing sounds somewhat resembling the human voice.

Invented in 1882 by J. Baillie Hamilton.

1882 *Daily News* 17 Apr. 2/2 The vocalion resembles in form a small organ, and is constructed of various dimensions, some having but one row of keys (or manuals), others having two keyboards and pedals. **1889** GROVE *Dict. Mus.* IV. 320 A main peculiarity of the Vocalion is that the reeds are placed above the pallets and below the slides.

vocalise (vəʊkəˈliːz, ˈvəʊkəliːz). *Mus.* Also (in imitation of VOCALIZE *v.* 5 b) **vocalize.** [a. F. *vocalise*, f. *vocaliser* VOCALIZE *v.*] **a.** A singing exercise using individual syllables or vowel sounds. **b.** A vocal passage consisting of a melody without words.

1872 *Scribner's Monthly* Feb. 481/2 When the *vocalise* was ended, I expressed my gratification and my admiration of his method to the maestro. **1949** *Scrutiny* XVI. 77 The Sonata Vocalise is an experiment in the combination of a wordless coloratura part with Medtner's habitual intricate pianism. **1959** *Listener* 2 July 37/3 The second movement.. is very much in the spirit of a vocalize. **1972** J. L. DILLARD *Black English* vi. 262 If the preacher slows or hesitates, one of the older women may pick up the tempo and propel the performance forward in a *vocalise* which is strikingly like the 'breaks' utilized by New Orleans jazzmen. **1980** *Early Music* Jan. 18/2 For the virtuoso repertory of the 16th and 17th centuries exercises are available. They belong on the music stand for daily vocalises, and not on a bookshelf for theoretical research.

vocalism (ˈvəʊkəlɪz(ə)m). [f. VOCAL *a.* + -ISM. Cf. F. *vocalisme*, mod.L. *vocalismus*, in sense 2 b.]

1. a. The exercise of the voice or vocal organs in speech.

1864 WEBSTER, *Vocalism*, the exercise of the vocal organs. **1866** FELTON *Anc. & Mod. Gr.* I. i. 11 Rough and violent intonations embodied in mimetic vocalism the harsh, the painful, the agitating passions. **1873** F. HALL *Mod. Eng.* 19 We should now be talking in monosyllables, and eking out our scantiness of vocalism by nods, shrugs, winks, and other resources of pantomime.

b. The art of exercising the voice in singing.

1884 SALA *Journ. due South* I. xx. (1887) 255 Italian vocalism seems to me to be extremely beautiful everywhere save in Italy itself, where singing out of tune.. seem[s] to be the rule. **1889** *Daily News* 28 June 2/3 A professor of vocalism to the family of the Prince and Princess of Wales. **1903** *Sat. Rev.* 16 May 614/2 When vocalism is wanted.. her vocal art is sufficient for the purpose.

2. a. A vocal sound or articulation.

1873 EARLE *Philol. Eng. Tongue* (ed. 2) §126 In the schools, children are allowed to utter such thick-lipped vocalisms as *Mosos.*

b. A system of vowels; the use of vowels.

1854 T. AUFRECHT in C. Bunsen *Christianity & Mankind* III. 93 The vowels have.. been well preserved... The final consonants in the flexions have remained. The vocalism and consonantism stand in good organic relation to each other. **1873** EARLE *Philol. Eng. Tongue* (ed. 2) §109 There is one dialect of our family which is distinguished for such a vocalism, and that is Mœso-Gothic. **1891** A. L. MAYHEW *O.E. Phonology* Pref. p. v, The subject of my book is the Vocalism and Consonantism of Old English or Anglo-Saxon.

vocalist (ˈvəʊkəlɪst). [f. as prec. + -IST. Cf. F. *vocaliste* in sense 2.]

†**1.** An utterer of words; a speaker. *Obs.*$^{-1}$

1613 JACKSON *Creed* II. iv. §6 The ciuill Magistrates facilitie to countenance euery prating Discontent, or forthputting Vocalist.

2. A vocal musician; a singer.

1834 AINSWORTH *Rookwood* II. i, Preparing himself, like certain other accomplished vocalists, with a few preliminary hems and haws. **1858** H. SPENCER *Ess.* I. 370 Now, in singing, this tremulousness of voice is very effectively used by some vocalists in highly pathetic passages. **1885** STEVENSON *Prince Otto* II. iv. 102 She was a good vocalist; and, even in speech, her voice commanded a great range of changes.

transf. **1897** G. ALLEN *Type-writer Girl* viii. 86 Little vocalists..carolled songs without words in the sky overhead.

Hence **voca'listic** *a.*, pertaining to vocal music or musicians.

1884 *Bazaar* 12 Dec. 629/2 Vocalistic feats..which would put to shame most of the public singers of the day.

vocality (vəʊˈkælɪtɪ). [f. VOCAL *a.* + -ITY.]

1. The quality of having voice or utterance; the possession or exercise of vocal powers.

1597 J. KING *On Jonas* (1618) 34 Sentences of scripture, expressing the loudnesse and vocality of sinne. **1657** *Divine Lover* 27 Now as concerninge the maner of exercising these Deuotions, it ought cheifly to be done in Spirit and mind, and without any vocalitie at all. **1794** E. DARWIN *Zoon.* I. xvii. 192 The movements of her eyes and eyelids, and of the intricate muscles of vocality. **1818** *Monthly Mag.* XLVI. 321 If you consider attentively the proportion of vocality needed in articulating each consonant. **1829** MARRYAT *F. Mildmay* xxiv, Fearing she might not confine herself to vocality. **1865** CARLYLE *Fredk. Gt.* xx. vi. (1872) IX. 122 Cats do execution for a time, but cannot stand the confinement..and object (think with what vocality).

2. The quality or fact of being uttered or utterable; vocal quality or nature.

1623 COCKERAM I, *Vocalitie*, the tune or sound of the voice. **1863** A. MELVILLE BELL *Princ. Speech* 197 When the Stammerer can..keep the tongue and jaw steady during the continuous flow of the vocality of *l*.

b. *pl.* Vocal properties or sounds, *spec.* as displayed in singing.

1667 PEPYS *Diary* 30 Dec., Not understanding the words, I lose the benefit of the vocalitys of the musick, and it proves only instrumental. **1774** 'J. COLLIER' *Mus. Trav.* (1775) 91, I was informed..that I could not see him, as he was then busied in performing his vocalities. **1833** J. RUSH *Philos. Human Voice* iii. (ed. 2) 55 The five tonic sounds to which the vocalities of the subtonics bear a resemblance, are *ee*-l, *oo*-ze, *e*-rr, *e*-nd, *i*-n. **1884** *Century Mag.* XXVIII. 510 What in all the vocalities of Nature is there to compare with ..this cloistered melodist?

3. *Phonetics.* The quality of being (*a*) voiced or (*b*) vocalic.

1669 HOLDER *Elem. Speech* 58 L. and R. being in extreams, one of Roughness, the other of Smoothness and freeness of Vocality, are not easie..to be pronounced spiritally. **1748** *Phil. Trans.* XLV. 402 My present Design.. is to give a List of Vowels, whereby to discriminate, as conveniently as may be, all the Instances of Vocality that occur, distinctly, in the English Language. **1874** SWEET in *Trans. Philol. Soc.* 538 Even in the present literary English we find initial vocality still preserved in the words *véin* (from *fana*), *væt* and *vixen*.

vocalization (vəʊkəlaɪˈzeɪʃən). [f. next + -ATION, or ad. F. *vocalisation* (1835).]

1. The action of vocalizing or the fact of being vocalized; utterance with the voice.

1842 *Penny Cycl.* XXII. 431/2 In this stammer the difficulty is not to produce voice, but to control its quantities. Vocalization freely takes place, but [etc.]. **1856** KANE *Arct. Expl.* I. xxx. 410 His vocalization is something between the mooing of a cow and the deepest baying of a mastiff. **1865** TYLOR *Early Hist. Man.* iv. 73 Mere vocalizations of the movements of the mouth. **1899** *Allbutt's Syst. Med.* VII. 450 A break will at once occur in the vocalisation of the letter *f*.

b. Mode of utterance or pronunciation, esp. of vowel sounds.

1855 PALEY *Æschylus* 167/1 It is of course uncertain whether the word..is a Greek vocalisation of a Persian word. **1868** BLACKIE in *Athenæum* 12 Dec. 797/2 In the gamut of the vowels..the English have set up a vocalization of their own. **1873** EARLE *Philol. Eng. Tongue* (ed. 2) §179 Its French vocalisation has resulted in *toil*.

c. Expression in words or speech.

1887 *Spectator* 5 Nov. 1473 Sir George Trevelyan has this week contributed largely to this vocalisation of the Home-rulers' case.

2. *Mus.* The action or art of producing musical sounds with the human voice; exercise of the voice in singing.

1852 SMEDLEY *L. Arundel* xxv. 215 It is not every one who is gifted with the..talent of vocalization. **1863** E. C. CLAYTON *Queens of Song* II. 386 Mlle. Piccolomini..bore a certain similitude to the great German singer, though in point of vocalization she was very inferior. **1883** *19th Cent.* May 867 On a visit to the Zoological Gardens,..I heard.. illustrations of nearly all the principal subjects belonging to the repertoire of technical vocalisation.

b. *spec.* The action of singing upon a vowel to one or more notes.

1889 *Grove's Dict. Mus.* IV. 321 Vocalisation is therefore one part of the operation of pronunciation, the other being articulation.

3. The insertion of vowel-signs in forms of writing consisting mainly or entirely of consonants.

1845 PITMAN *Man. Phonography* (ed. 7) 27 Vocalization of double Consonants. **1847** *Ibid.* (ed. 8) 35 Vocalization of Words. **1848** *Athenæum* 10 June 571/2 The question of vocalization..is one of the highest importance in Biblical criticism. **1883** A. ROBERTS *O.T. Revision* vii. 145 The important subject of vocalization..here falls to be more particularly considered.

4. *Phonetics.* Conversion into a voiced sound.

1874 SWEET in *Trans. Philol. Soc.* 539 It seems, therefore, that the vocalization of initial (and also medial) *s* in English is merely a case of levelling, caused by the analogy of the vocal ð and *v*.

5. The utterance of vowel sounds.

1887 *Alien. & Neurol.* VIII. 7 Vocalization (vowelizing) is the expression of an emotion, an indistinct sensation, not an idea.

vocalize (ˈvəʊkəlaɪz), *v.* [f. VOCAL *a.* + -IZE. Cf. F. *vocaliser* (1835), Pg. *vocalisar, -izar*, Sp. *-izar*, It. *-izzare*.]

1. a. *trans.* To form into voice; to make audible by utterance; to utter or articulate.

1669 HOLDER *Elem. Speech* 30 It is one thing to Breath, or give an Impulse to breath alone; another thing, to vocalize that breath, *i.e.* in its passage through the Larynx to give it the sound of Humane Voyce. *Ibid.* 80 The Vowels are made by a free passage of Breath Vocalized through the cavity of the Mouth. **1673** [R. LEIGH] *Transp. Reh.* 119 Every breath of moving air may continue articulate, especially if vocaliz'd in Sir S. Moreland's trumpet. **1867** A. MELVILLE BELL *Visible Speech* 91 A faithful copy of the native pronunciation which readers in all countries will vocalize alike. **1899** *Allbutt's Syst. Med.* VII. 65 A similar inability to control the tongue can be demonstrated by making the patient vocalise *r*.

b. To sing.

1798 in *Spirit Pub. Jrnls.* (1799) II. 146 Our small company had vocalized all the songs in the opera, in such a manner as I never heard them executed upon any theatre in London. **1851** E. FITZGERALD *Lett.* (1889) I. 213 How would you like to see me..scoring up semibreves on a staff for half a dozen Rustics to vocalize?

2. *Phonetics.* **a.** To convert into a vowel.

1844 *Proc. Philol. Soc.* I. 249 It is true that the objectionable sound might be..got rid of..by vocalizing the second consonant, especially if a labial. **1871** KENNEDY *Public Sch. Lat. Gram.* 8 §12 Poets sometimes vocalize v-consonans before a vowel: as *sil-u-æ* for *sil-væ*. **1891** A. L. MAYHEW *O.E. Phonology* 67 Ēa = au, the u of which is the w vocalized when standing at the end of a syllable.

b. To utter with voice (as distinguished from *breath*); to render sonant.

1836 SMART *Pronouncing Dict.* p. xxx, *s* is always vocalized, that is, pronounced as *z*, when, in forming the plural of a noun..it can be so pronounced. **1848** *Proc. Philol. Soc.* III. 169 If we were asked why the Cochin-Chinese vocalized the *p*, it would be difficult to give any other reason than that some languages are distinguished.. by the softness of their pronunciation.

3. To endow with voice; to render vocal or articulate.

1858 W. IRVING in *Life & Lett.* (1864) IV. 219 In this way, by turns, you vocalize the whole Union, and make the growing chorus of the Revolution rise from every part of it. **1872** SYMONDS *Introd. Study Dante* 226 It was not merely the painting of his age that Dante absorbed into himself and vocalized.

4. To furnish with vowels or vowel-signs.

1845 PITMAN *Man. Phonography* (ed. 7) 27 These series of double consonants are vocalized in the following manner. **1889** *Amer. Jrnl. Philol.* X. 232 Arabic books, especially Arabic poetry, are vocalized in the East as well as in the West.

5. a. *intr.* To perform vocal music; to sing.

1830 *Fraser's Mag.* II. 503 He..would therefore endeavour to vocalize, if an auditory were to be found. **1879** H. JAMES *Daisy Miller* ii. I. 69 The young lady, who was still strolling along in front of them, softly vocalising.

b. *spec.* (See quots.)

1873 H. C. BANISTER *Music* 254 *Vocalise*, to sing with several notes to one vowel, as distinguished from Sol-faing, or Sol-misation. **1889** *Grove's Dict. Mus.* IV. 321 To vocalise is..to sing upon a vowel, whether one note or a series of notes, in contradistinction to singing to separate syllables.

c. To utter any vocal sound.

1960 R. D. LAING *Divided Self* i. 20 Studying verbal behaviour in terms of neural processes and the whole apparatus of vocalizing. *a* **1961** W. LA BARRE in *Webster* (1961) s.v., The gorilla is just as likely to thump upon the upper chest..as he is to vocalize. **1972** *Sci. Amer.* Aug. 29/1 The female mallard generally vocalizes at the rate of from zero to four calls per one-minute interval.

Hence **'vocalized** *ppl. a.*; also *spec.* in *Jazz*, of the tone of an instrument: made to resemble that of the human voice; **'vocalizing** *vbl. sb.* and *ppl. a.*; **'vocalizer**, one who vocalizes or gives expression (to something).

1855 tr. *Lepsius' Standard Alphabet* 35 *French j.* This letter is the soft and *vocalised sound. **1882** A. MACFARLANE *Consanguinity* 17 Vocalised equivalent fayoyo. **1898** *Westm. Gaz.* 7 Oct. 3/1 The sweetest and most delicately vocalised dialect in Britain. **1961** *John o' London's* 7 Dec. 637/1 The great jazz instrumentalists have based their styles on what is known as the 'vocalised' tone. **1970** P. OLIVER *Savannah Syncopators* 18 Emphasis is placed on the quality of blues singing and the 'vocalised tone' of jazz instrumentation. **1901** H. MURRAY *R. Buchanan* 81 Browning and Tennyson, ..as the typical *vocalisers of modern religious thought. **1863** A. MELVILLE BELL *Princ. Speech* 164 The glottis is in the *vocalizing position, and the breath in passing through it creates sonorous vibration. **1899** *Allbutt's Syst. Med.* VII. 452 There is great danger of vocalising with the short inspiration.

vocalize, var. VOCALISE.

'vocaller. *rare*⁻¹. [f. VOCAL *a.*] = VOCALIST 2.

1876 BESANT & RICE *Gold. Butterfly* xviii, Presently that young lady discovers that she is not likely to get cracked up as a vocaller.

vocally (ˈvəʊkəlɪ), *adv.* [f. VOCAL *a.* + -LY².]

1. In a vocal manner, by or with the voice; in spoken words.

1483 CAXTON *Gold. Leg.* (1892) 15 As to the thirde [name] vocally, for as moche as by the voys he was callyd Jhesus. **1616** A. ROBERTS *Treat. Witchcraft* Title-p., Her contract vocally made between the Deuill and her, in solemne termes. **1656** S. H. *Golden Law* 74 Neither Moses nor Joshua were Usurpers, though not vocally chosen by the people. **1659** B. JONES *Hermælogium* 42 In that the first and second persons of the Verb be aswell digitally as vocally notified. **1726** DE FOE *Hist. Devil* II. iii. (1840) 198 By whispering to her vocally when she was asleep. **1782** ELIZ. BLOWER *Geo. Bateman* II. 136 The valet, though he durst not vocally express his admiration.., yet leered familiarly. **1848** R. J. WILBERFORCE *Doctr. Incarnation* xii. (1852) 301 That which we in all our prayers and thanksgivings do vocally,..the ancient Church..did visibly. **1847** EMILY BRONTE *Wuthering H.* i, I 'never told my love' vocally. **1897** S. CRANE *Third Violet* ii. 8 The dog..gave vent to little sobs in a wild attempt to vocally describe his gladness.

b. Contrasted with *mentally*.

a **1638** MEDE *Wks.* (1672) 366 That which every Christian doth mentally and vocally, when he commends his prayers to God the Father through Jesus Christ. **1671** WOODHEAD *St. Teresa* I. vi. 315 Whence it falls out, that those, who in this manner pray vocally, are very often by God exalted..to Contemplation. **1738** WATERLAND *Chr. Sacrifice Expl.* App. 59 In Baptism..we represent and commemorate mentally, vocally, and manually, (in Mind, and by Mouth, and by significant Actions) the Death and Burial of Christ our Lord. **1872** SPURGEON *Treas. Dav.* Ps. xxi. 2 Jesus prayed vocally as well as mentally.

2. By means of singing; in vocal music.

1716 in *Lond. Gaz.* No. 5487/3 Mr. Purcell's Te Deum will be vocally and instrumentally performed. **1724** *Ibid.* No. 6324/2 An Anthem..will be vocally and instrumentally performed. **1872** SPURGEON *Treas. Dav.* lvii. 8 Vocally and instrumentally will I celebrate thy worship. **1901** *Athenæum* 27 July 134/3 Madame Suzanne Adams was successful vocally.

3. In respect of vowels.

1873 EARLE *Philol. Eng. Tongue* (ed. 2) §647 Those syllables which are vocally of the lowest consideration.

'vocalness. [f. VOCAL *a.*] (See quot.)

1727 BAILEY (vol. II), *Vocalness*, a vocal Quality. [Hence in later Dicts.]

†**vocate**, *sb.* *Obs.* Forms: *α.* 4–5 **voket**, 4–5 **vokett-**, 5 **vokett, vokyte.** *β.* 4 **vok-, vocate**, 5 **vocat.** [Aphetic f. *avoket, avocat* ADVOCATE *sb.*] An advocate, in various senses.

α. **1303** R. BRUNNE *Handl. Synne* 5402 3yf þou yn falsehede so moche 3ede,..To consente to a fals Iuggyng, Or hyredyst a voket to swyche þyng. **13..** *Propr. Sanct.* (Vernon MS.) in Herrig *Archiv Stud. neu. Spr.* LXXXI. 315/113 We han euer a good voket To foren his holi fader set. **1393** LANGL. *P. Pl.* C. III. 61 Were bede to þat brudale..vytailers and vokettus of þe Arches. **14..** in Wr.-Wülcker 680/31 *Hic causidicus*, a vokyte. *c* **1440** *Gesta Rom.* lii. 372 (Add. MS.), Bi the foxe are vndirstondyn vokettes, prelates of causes temporall, courteers, Iurrours, and wily men. *c* **1475** *Cath. Angl.* 404/1 (A.), A Vokett, *vbi* A plettere.

β. **13..** *Cursor M.* 20927 (Gött.) Paule, þat saul had first to nam.. First he was þe iuus vocate [*Cott.* auocate], And syden he come till postil state. **1377** LANGL. *P. Pl.* B. II. 60 Were boden to þe bridaile..vitaillers and vokates of þe arches. **1426** LYDG. *De Guil. Pilgr.* 4847 My wondys I geue ..To plete for hem when they ha nede..I make ther vocat of my blood. ?**14..** in *Wars Eng. in France* (Rolls) II. 525 Receyvoures, Procutours, Vocatis. **1509** FISHER *Wks.* (1876) 282 Our sauyour Ihesu is..a suffycyent vocate for vs before the face of his fader. *a* **1513** FABYAN *Chron.* VII. 516 A vocat named Peter Puyssour, and a felowe of his named maister John Godarde.

†**vocate**, *v.* *Obs.*⁻¹ [f. L. *vocāt-*, ppl. stem of *vocāre* to call.] *trans.* To call or summon.

a **1548** HALL *Chron., Hen. VII*, 40 Your realme to the which you be bothe (as you saye) inheritoure, and by your people accercited and vocated vnto.

vocation (vəʊˈkeɪʃən). Forms: 5–7 **vocacion**, 5 **-cioun**, 5–6 **-cyon, -tioun**, 6 **wocatioun**, 6– **vocation.** [a. OF. *vocacion, -ation* (F. *vocation*, = Sp. *vocacion*, Pg. *vocação*, It. *vocazione*), or ad. L. *vocātiōn-, vocātio*, noun of action f. *vocāre* to call summon.]

1. a. The action on the part of God of calling a person to exercise some special function, especially of a spiritual nature, or to fill a certain position; divine influence or guidance towards a definite (esp. religious) career; the fact of being so called or directed towards a special work in life; natural tendency to, or fitness for, such work.

1426 LYDG. *De Guil. Pilgr.* 10808 Thapostles..By choys & by elleccioun And also by vocacioun,..kam to hym. **1526** TINDALE *1 Cor.* i. 1 Paul by vocacion the Apostle of Jesus Christ thorowe the will of god. **1528** ROY *Rede me* (Arb.) 107 Of Saynt Thomas of Cantourbury..I beleve and..trust yf that he were..of oure lordes vocacion [etc.]. **1649** F. ROBERTS *Clavis Bibl.* 92 His Vocation or calling by God to be Governour of Israel in Moses stead, is repeated. **1660** F. BROOKE tr. *Le Blanc's Trav.* 128 A Cordelier,..being at Goa, moved with a pious vocation, went to preach the Gospel in these parts. **1728** CHAMBERS *Cycl.* s.v., 'Tis a Rule, that none are to enter the Ecclesiastick or Monastick State, without a particular Vocation, or Call. **1753** *Diary Blue Nuns* in *Cath. Rec. Soc. Publ.* VIII. 126 Peggy Johnson [a postulant] left our house haveing no vocation. **1840** CARLYLE *Heroes* iv. (1904) 117 Luther and Knox were by express vocation Priests, and did faithfully perform that function in its common sense. **1852** LD. COCKBURN *Jeffrey* I. 353, I wish I had more of the inward vocation to the holy office. **1888** BERNARD *Fr. World to Cloister* i. 5 You see, it is a question of vocation—where I am called there must I go.

b. The action on the part of God (or Christ) of calling persons or mankind to a state of salvation or union with Himself; the fact or condition of being so called. (Cf. CALLING *vbl. sb.* 9.)

1502 *Ord. Crysten Men* (W. de W. 1506) IV. v. P vj, As the deuyll blyndeth the synner, so he hym maketh to lose the herynge of the vocacyon that our lorde vnto hym maketh. **1526** *Pilgr. Perf.* (W. de W. 1531) 262 b, That vnspekable mercy that thou shewed in theyr vocacyon or callynge. **1561** T. NORTON *Calvin's Inst.* III. 306 As by vocation and election God maketh his elect. **1609** BIBLE (Douay) *Amos* comm., Foreshewing.. the vocation of al Nations to Christ. **1646** E. F[ISHER] *Marrow Mod. Divin.* (ed. 2) 186 Therefore sayth he you must not look for sanctification, till you come to Christ in vocation. **1672** *Disc. Evangelical Love* 33 There is Vocation, or an effectual Calling to the knowledg of Christ by the Gospel. *a* **1771** J. GILL *Expos. O.T.* Ps. cxiv. 1 (1810) IV. 192/1 An emblem of the Lord's people in effectual vocation, coming out of bondage into liberty. **1826** G. S. FABER *Diffic. Romanism* (1853) 262 He calls with a saving and beatifying vocation. **1898** C. BELL tr. *Huysman's Cathedral* xi. 233 The vocation of the Jewish nation is set forth in these three doorways.

c. *vocation of the Gentiles* (cf. Acts x. 45, etc.). So F. *la vocation des Gentils* (Calvin).

1649 F. ROBERTS *Clavis Bibl.* 611 Vocation of the Gentiles, and many spirituall Priviledges of the Church. **1662** J. DAVIES tr. *Olearius' Voy. Ambass.* 129 They pitch on Twelf-day, as that on which sometime happened the vocation of the Gentiles.

2. a. The particular function or station to which a person is called by God; a mode of life or sphere of action regarded as so determined. (Cf. CALLING *vbl. sb.* 10.)

1487 CAXTON *Bk. Good Manners* d vi b (Stanf.), The pryncipal of theyr vocacyon is for to defende the fayth. **1502** *Ord. Crysten Men* (W. de W. 1506) I. iv. D iiij, Yf they [*sc.* kings] gouerne truely the realme of theyr conscyence and the estate of theyr vocacyon. **1545** BRINKLOW *Compl.* iii. 15 He wil gyue grace to the kyng, to walke in his vocacyon. **1565** STAPLETON *Fortr. Faith* 129 Gregory Naziansen leaving the bishoprick of Constantinople, much.. serche was made to finde a worthy man to occupy that high vocation. **1642** FULLER *Holy & Prof. St.* IV. ix. 281 Heaven is his vocation, and therefore he counts earthly employments avocations. *a* **1792** V. KNOX *Serm.* xxiii. 507 Let us go forth to our various employments, resolved to walk worthy of our Christian vocation. **1847** C. BRONTË *Jane Eyre* xxii, 'I shall probably take the veil.'.. 'The vocation will fit you to a hair', I thought. **1888** LIDDON in *Chr. World Pulpit* XXXIV. 388 In some quarters, the missionary's life.. is regarded as a profession rather than as a vocation.

b. One's ordinary occupation, business, or profession. (Cf. CALLING *vbl. sb.* 11.)

1553 T. WILSON *Rhet.* 95 b, By vocation of life a souldiour is counted a great bragger, and a vaunter of hymselfe. **1566** PAINTER *Pal. Pleas.* I. Ded. 5 The same hath.. commended suche unto her highnes.. as officers right worthy their vocations. **1596** SHAKS. *1 Hen. IV*, I. ii. 114 Why, Hal, 'tis my Vocation Hal: 'Tis no sin for a man to labour in his Vocation. **1610** ROWLANDS *Martin Mark-all* 13 If there bee any in our vocation or calling, that liue disorderly and out of compasse, what trade can you name that doe not the like. **1622** PEACHAM *Compl. Gentl.* i. 12 Vsefull necessaries for our vocations, and callings. **1672** MARVELL *Reh. Transp.* I. 118, I cannot but be sorry that he hath under-taken this desperate vocation. **1712** STEELE *Spect.* No. 304 ¶3 Your Petitioner's Ancestor.. was the first of that Vocation in Britain; who.. was by way of Eminency called the Stationer. **1762–71** H. WALPOLE *Vertue's Anecd. Paint.* (1786) II. 242 It is idle to write a panegyric on the greatest man in any vocation. **1820** W. IRVING *Sketch Bk.* II. 356 In addition to his other vocations, he was the singing-master of the neighbourhood. **1871** AINSWORTH *Tower Hill* I. i, A droll-looking wight, whose vocation was proclaimed by his motley garb. **1879** *St. George's Hosp. Rep.* IX. 554 The vocations of the women.. expose them to sudden changes of temperature.

c. *collect.* Those who follow a particular business or profession.

1587 HARRISON *England* II. v. (1877) I. 132 Euerie function and seuerall vocation striueth with other. **1589** PUTTENHAM *Eng. Poesie* III. xxix. (Arb.) 289 It is comely that euery estate and vocation should be knowen by the differences of their habit. **1651** HOBBES *Leviath.* II. xxvi. 137 Some Lawes are addressed.. to particular Provinces; some to particular Vocations; and some to particular Men.

3. a. A call *to* a public position.

1553 Q. MARY in Strype *Eccl. Mem.* (1721) III. App. vi. 10 Speciallye synce the tyme of her vocation to the crowne.

b. The action, on the part of an ecclesiastical body, of calling a person to the ministry or to a particular office or charge in the Church. (Cf. CALLING *vbl. sb.* 3 b.)

1578 *2nd Bk. Discipline* iii, Vocatioun or calling.. is ane lauchfull way, be the quhilk qualifeit personis is promotit to ane spirituall office within the kirk of God. **1588** UDALL *Demonstr. Discipl.* (Arb.) 67 The gouernors of the Church may not meddle, but onely in church-matters, as for example, vocation, and abdication. **1637** GILLESPIE *Eng. Pop. Cerem.* III. viii. 195 As the vocation of Ministers pertaineth to the whole Church, so to the same also pertaineth the removing of Ministers. **1847** tr. *Bunsen's Ch. of Future* v. 116 Here the natural and historical form, that of call (or vocation) meets us at once. It is recognised as belonging to the congregation. **1860** HOOK *Lives Abps.* I. i. 2 A vocation to pastoral duty in the manufacturing districts demanded.. his energies for five and thirty years.

†**4.** ? Designation, title. *Obs.*⁻¹

c **1477** CAXTON *Jason* 116 Knowest not thou wel that euery man of noble name or vocacion is holden & bounden to paye and holde his promesse.

†**5.** The action of summoning an assembly or its members. *Obs. rare.*

c **1480** HENRYSON *Test. Cress.* 272 Befoir Cupide.. [he] Speiris the caus of that vocatioun. **1772** *Hartford Merc.* Suppl. 18 Sept. 1/1 The letters of vocation for the new Senators appointed by the King of Sweden.

†**6.** Appeal, entreaty, petition. *Obs. rare.*

1574 in *Maitl. Cl. Misc.* (1840) I. 98 That ane publict humiliatioun and fast, togidder with an ernest vocatioun and prayar, be institutit. **1587** M. GROVE *Pelops & Hipp.* (1878) 18 Some on Venus, some to Luna make their vocation.

Hence **vo'cationless** *a.*

1924 *Blackw. Mag.* Apr. 445/2 Apparently we were all vocationless. **1939** A. CLARKE *Sister Eucharia* iii. 27, I stood beneath the iron gate, unveiled, Vocationless.

vocational (vəʊ'keɪʃənəl), *a.* [f. VOCATION + -AL¹.] Of, pertaining or relating to, a vocation or occupation.

1652 GAULE *Magastrom.* 204 It [i.e. prophecy] was a gift, or grace, not so much personal as vocational; pertaining not to ordinary duty so much as extraordinary occasion. *a* **1732** T. BOSTON *Crook in Lot* (1805) 16 It may fall in the vocational part. Whatever is men's calling or station.. the crook in their lot may take its place therein. **1865** *Athenæum* 27 May 715/3 With these appear the Tilewrights, a vocational name of Saxon Origin, and the Mayers. **1875** WHITNEY *Life Lang.* ix. 159 The classes, whether social, vocational, or educational. **1910** *Proc. 1st Congr. National Conservation* 164 In conclusion.. the remedies:.. *Vocational training* in high schools. **1927** W. E. COLLINSON *Contemp. Eng.* 106 The enlistment of the psychologist's help for vocational guidance. **1951**, **1957** [see GUIDANCE 1 c]. **1977** *New Statesman* 2 Sept. 294/3 The IBA is attracted to the.. Open College concept—courses in numeracy and literacy, vocational training for school-leavers, and other forms of further education.

Hence **vo'cationally** *adv.*; **vo'cationalism**, training for a vocation; educational emphasis on this; **vo'cationalize** *v. trans.*, to direct towards vocational training.

1890 CLARK RUSSELL *Nelson* xvi. 229 The seamanship of those days, the strategies, the devices,.. are no longer of the least value vocationally. **1912** J. H. MOORE *Ethics & Education* 33 Schools should not be industrialized merely, nor commercialized, nor professionalized, but vocationalized. **1924** *Glasgow Herald* 1 May 8/6 The primary function of education is wider than mere vocationalism. **1959** *Oxf. Mag.* 11 June 458/2 We are so vocationalised now that we have begun to believe it is our true function to train professional scholars, professional critics and even professional readers. **1971** *Black Scholar* June 65 (Advt.), Vocationalizing higher education. **1979** *Yale Alumni Mag.* Apr. 12/2 Of all the areas in colleges and universities that will feel.. the growing vocationalism of the young, the humanities will be hardest hit. **1980** [see SUBSIDIARITY].

vocative ('vɒkətɪv), *a.* and *sb.* Also 5 vocatyf, 6 vocatyve, 6–7 vocatiue (6 foc-). [a. OF. *vocatif, -ive* (mod.F. *vocatif* = Sp., Pg., It. *vocativo*), or ad. L. *vocātīv-us* (sc. *casus*; also as sb.), f. *vocāt-*, ppl. stem of *vocāre* to call.]

A. *adj.* **1.** *vocative case*: That case of nouns, adjectives, or pronouns, which in inflected languages is used to express address or invocation.

c **1440** *Gesta Rom.* xci. 418 (Add. MS.), The fyfte is the vocatyf case. **1520** WHITINTON *Vulg.* (1527) 1 The verbe shall accorde with his nominatiue or vocatiue case. **1549** LILY *Introd. Gram.* B ij, The seconde person is spoken to: as Tu, thou: vos, ye. And of this person is also euery vocatiue case. **1598** SHAKS. *Merry W.* IV. i. 54 What is the Focatiue case (William ?). **1612** BRINSLEY *Lud. Lit.* 101 In construing.. we begin commonly of a Vocatiue case if there be one. **1668** WILKINS *Real Char.* IV. vi. 448 Interjections, divers of which are said to govern the Nominative, Dative, Accusative, Vocative Case. *c* **1791** *Encycl. Brit.* (ed. 3) VIII. 42/1 Thus the nominative case would pass into a vocative, of which the use is always to solicit attention. **1867** BRANDE & COX *Dict. Sci.*, etc. III. 959 Vocative Case... In strictness of speech it is not a case at all. *a* **1892** D. FRASER *Autobiog.* i. 14 Reasoned and didactic prayers—what I once heard well stigmatised as 'sermons in the vocative case'.

b. In fig. context. (Cf. next.)

14.. *Piers of Fulham* 370 in Hazl. *E.P.P.* II. 15 To knowen folke that ben datyff: Their purches be called ablatif: They haue their ȝen vocatif.

2. Characteristic of, pertaining to, calling or addressing.

1644 BULWER *Chirol.* 55 To this vocative, alluring and inticing compellation of the Hand. **1827** G. S. FABER *Sacr. Cal. Prophecy* (1844) III. 112 Pope Gregory, in his first epistle to the Emperor Leo Isauricus,.. salutes him with the vocative title of Βασιλεῦ. **1871** EARLE *Philol. Eng. Tongue* 162 As to the sense: the O prefixed merely imparts to the title a vocative effect.

B. *sb.* **1.** The vocative case.

a **1522** LILY *Gram. Rudim.* in *Colet's Æditio* (1537) A viij, Whan the nominatiue endeth in us, the vocatiue shal ende in e. **1549** —— *Introd. Gram.* A vi b, All nounes of the neuter gendre.. haue the nominatiue, the accusatyue, and the vocatiue lyke in both numbers. **1647** JER. TAYLOR *Lat. Gram.* 5 [In neuter nouns] the nominative, accusative, and vocative are alike in both numbers. **1719** *Lat. Gram.* 6 These Nouns following make their Vocative in *e* or in *us.* **1736** AINSWORTH *Lat. Dict.* II, *O*.. is often understood both before an accusative and vocative. **1751** HARRIS *Hermes* I. viii. (1786) 145 *note*, The Vocative.. was nothing more than the Form of address in front of names, titles, and epithets. *Ibid.* II. iv. 276 The Vocative.. being not only unknown to the modern Languages, but often in the ancient being supplied by the Nominative. *c* **1792** *Encycl. Brit.* (ed. 3) IX. 541/2 Those [Latin nouns] in *um*, whose nominative, accusative, and vocative.. are alike. **1818** STODDART in *Encycl. Metrop.* (1845) I. 33/1 The vocative or ablative, which latter some writers have considered as the primary and original case of the noun. **1872** GEO. ELIOT *Middlem.* xxxv, O endless vocatives that would still leave expression slipping helpless from the measurement of mortal folly!

2. An invocation or appeal. *rare*⁻¹.

1747 RICHARDSON *Clarissa* (1811) II. v. 27 The two latter will hardly come neither, if they think it will be to hear your whining vocatives.

Hence **'vocatively** *adv.*

1662 BP. PEARSON *Creed* (ed. 2) 145 The Nominative may as well stand vocatively without an Article. **1904** BRADLEY *Making of English* 192 To use the word [fellow] vocatively to an equal in the sense of 'comrade'.

voce¹ ('votʃe). *Mus.* [It. = voice.] Used with qualifying phrases to designate various qualities or registers of the voice, as ***voce di gola*** (di 'gola), a throaty or guttural voice; ***voce di petto*** (di 'pɛtto), the chest register; ***voce di testa*** (di 'tɛsta), the head register; formerly, the falsetto voice.

1742 tr. *Tosi's Observations on Florid Voice* i. 22 *Voce di Petto* is a full Voice, which comes from the Breast by Strength. *Ibid.*, *Voce di Testa* comes more from the Throat, than from the Breast. **1771** Voce di petto [see PORTAMENTO]. **1801** BUSBY *Dict. Mus.*, *Voce di Testa*,.. a falsetto, or feigned voice. **1876** STAINER & BARRETT *Dict. Mus. Terms* 450/2 *Voce di gola*, a guttural or throaty voice. **1889** G. B. SHAW *London Music in 1888–89* (1937) 229 You are singing with your chest voice, or *voce di petto*, or long reed register, whichever you please to call it. *Ibid.*, You are singing falsetto, or in *voce di gola*, or throat voice, or short reed register. *Ibid.* 230 This high voice is what used to be called *voce di testa* or head voice. **1951** P. A. DUEY *Bel Canto in its Golden Age* xi. 124 Tenducci, the Italo-Anglican voice teacher writes briefly:.. Never force the Voice, in order to extend its compass in the *Voce di petto* upwards; but rather to cultivate the *Voce di testa* in what is called *Falsetto.* **1980** *New Grove Dict. Mus.* XVIII. 690/1 Until the late 18th and even early 19th centuries most tenors in the Italian tradition emphasized the lyrical quality of their top range and, when required, carried their voices with ease into the falsetto register (treatises of the 18th century and earlier call the falsetto range the *voce di testa*). During the first half of the 19th century, however, this traditional Italian manner of singing in the top range fell into disuse, and the expression *voce di testa* came to refer to the normal, much stronger head voice, falsetto being reserved as a special effect only for the very highest notes.

‖**voce²**. [L. *vōce*, abl. of *vox* voice, word.] Under the word or heading. (Cf. VO, VOC.)

1838 BELL *Dict. Law Scotl.* 866 What regards the calling lists has been explained, *voce* Calling a Summons.

voce, obs. Sc. and north. variant of VOICE.

†**voche**, *v. Obs.*⁻¹ [app. ad. OF. *vocher, -ier*: see VOUCH *v.*] *trans.* ? To call or summon.

13.. *E.E. Allit. P.* 1221 Legyounes of aungelez togeder uoched þer kesten ensens of swete smelle.

vochette, error for *rochette* ROCHET.

a **1548** HALL *Chron., Hen. VIII*, 7 Ouer their garmentes were vochettes of pleasantes, rouled with Crymsyne veluet, and set wᵗ letters of golde. [Hence in Holinshed.]

vociferance (və(ʊ)'sɪfərəns). [f. next: see -ANCE.]

a. Clamour or noise of shouting. **b.** Vociferant quality.

1838 S. BELLAMY *Betrayal* 168 From darkness came The hydra tongued vociferance. **1855** BROWNING *Master Hugues of Saxe-Gotha* xv, All now is wrangle, abuse and vociferance. **1889** *Pall Mall G.* 28 May 2/3 Alternating between a hoarse whisper and a painfully pitched vociferance.

vociferant (və(ʊ)'sɪfərənt), *a.* and *sb.* [ad. L. *vōciferant-*, *vōciferans*, pres. pple. of *vōciferārī*, *-āre*: see next.]

A. *adj.* Clamouring, bawling, vociferating.

1609 J. DAVIES (Heref.) *Holy Roode* Wks. (Grosart) I. 19/2 For, all his Wounds, with voice vociferant, Crie out they can more than supply each want! **1659** GAUDEN *Tears Ch.* 214 The most vociferant vulgar.. do least know what the matter is. **1685** H. MORE *Paralip. Prophet.* vi. 38 That Themistocles came to Artaxerxes, not to Xerxes,.. he proves from a plain narrative, where there is no mention of any vociferant Ecstatical Olbius. **1836** *Westm. Rev.* XXIV. 82 A new race of parsons sprung up, half political leaders, half-fanatical fire-brands.. now declaiming in the pulpit, now vociferant in the tavern [etc.]. **1850** BROWNING *Christmas Eve* iv. 28 My mind was full of the scene I had left, That placid flock, that pastor vociferant. **1863** MRS. WHITNEY *Faith Gartney's Girlh.* xiv, She.. shook first him and then his frock.. and carried him, vociferant, to the door.

B. *sb.* A clamorous or noisy person.

1890 *Atlantic Monthly* May 675/2 Strange as it may appear to earnest but misguided vociferants.

vociferate (və(ʊ)'sɪfəreɪt), *v.* [f. *vōciferat-*, ppl. stem of L. *vōciferārī* (rarely, *-āre*), f. *vōci-*, *vox* voice + *ferre* to carry. Cf. F. *vociférer*, Sp. and Pg. *vociferar*, It. *vociferare.*]

1. *intr.* To cry out loudly; to bawl, to shout.

1623 COCKERAM I, *Vociferate*, to bray or crie out. **1672** MARVELL *Reh. Transp.* II. 270 You do so insult and vociferate upon it, like one of your bulky Princes [etc.]. **1768** MARQ. ROCKINGHAM in G. Harris *Life Ld. Hardwicke* (1847) xvi. III. 427 He vociferated beyond even his usual pitch. **1791** COWPER *Iliad* XII. 335 So they vociferating to the Greeks, Stirr'd them to battle. **1824** MISS L. M. HAWKINS *Annaline* II. 196 His passion was somewhat exhausted and he ceased to vociferate. **1856** KANE *Arct. Expl.* I. xvii. 202 They were vociferating as if to attract our attention.

2. *trans.* To utter in a loud voice; to shout out clamorously; to declaim or assert with loud vehemence.

The object may be either the words uttered (*a*), or a descriptive noun (*b*).

(*a*) **1748** RICHARDSON *Clarissa* VI. 99 Damn'd, damn'd doings! vociferated the Peer. **1797** MRS. RADCLIFFE *Italian* xvi, 'You shall not separate me from my master, though', vociferated Paulo. **1816** SCOTT *Old Mort.* xxxi, They vociferated loudly, that those who were not with them were against them. **1852** MRS. STOWE *Uncle Tom's C.* vii, He therefore rode along..vociferating occasionally that 'twas 'desp't rough, and bad for Jerry's foot'. **1871** *Member for Paris* I. 233 'You shall apologize,' vociferated the Bench. (*b*) **1758** JOHNSON *Idler* No. 2. ¶6 The cook warbles her lyrics in the kitchen, and the thrasher vociferates his heroicks in the barn. **1782** V. KNOX *Ess.* lxxxi. (1819) II. 127 The ignorant plebeian, though he may vociferate the word Liberty in a riot, knows not how to give it an effectual support. **1802** MRS. E. PARSONS *Myst. Visit* I. 89 The nursery-maid..loudly vociferated the dreadful accident to the astonished servants. **1848** EMILY BRONTË *Wuthering H.* ix, He entered, vociferating oaths dreadful to hear. **1860** F. WINSLOW *Diseases Brain & Mind* iv. 53, I then began to vociferate a number of most incoherent expressions.

3. To drive by means of clamour.

1880 *Daily Tel.* 9 April, It would be worse than disappointing..if Lord Beaconsfield should have been vociferated out of office merely in order to please Montenegro and Bulgaria.

Hence **vo'ciferated** *ppl. a.*; **vo'ciferating** *vbl. sb.* and *ppl. a.*

1617 FLETCHER *Mad Lover* II. ii, Beef we can bear before us..And tubs of pork; vociferating veals. **1728** POPE *Dunc.* II. *Argt.*, Then follow the Exercises for the Poets, of tickling, vociferating, diving. **1781** COWPER *Conversat.* 113 Vociferated logic kills me quite.

vociferation (vəʊ)sɪfə'reɪʃən). Also 5 voce-, 5-6 vocyferacion, 6 -cyon, 6 vociferacion. [a. OF. *vociferacion* (mod.F. *vociférations* pl., = Sp. *vociferacion*, Pg. *-ação*, It. *-azione*), or ad. L. *vōciferātiōn-*, *vōciferātio*, noun of action f. *vōciferārī*: see prec. and -ATION.]

1. An act or instance of loud speaking or shouting; a clamour or outcry.

c **1400** *Sc. Trojan War* II. 145 Þe vocyferacions Of the gret glawmours & þe sownes War herd in entring of þe place. **1541** R. COPLAND *Galyen's Terap.* 2 C ij, Ye ought to haue cure of all the body in strengthyng it with dyuers exercytacyons, testynges, and vociferacions. **1603** HOLLAND *Plutarch's Mor.* 619 Howbeit, in this exercise we must beware of over-loud vociferations and clamours. **1709** STEELE *Tatler* No. 54 ¶5 When our young Heralds are exercis'd in the Faculties of making Proclamation, and other Vociferations. **1750** JOHNSON *Rambler* No. 18 ¶4, I can hear the vociferations of either sex without catching any of the fire from those that utter them. **1837** HT. MARTINEAU *Soc. Amer.* II. 167 How mean and trivial are the vociferations in defence of property. **1865** LIVINGSTONE *Zambesi* xxvii. 550 Without paying any attention to his vociferations we went on.

2. The action of vociferating; the utterance of loud outcries or shouts; loud and vehement exercise of the voice.

1528 ROY *Rede me* (Arb.) 43 With terrible vociferacion They made wonderfull exclamacion The worde of god to subverte. *a* **1548** HALL *Chron., Rich. III*, 29 b, The people.. woulde openly crye and make vocyferacion that God dyd take vengeance. **1590** BARROUGH *Meth. Physick* III. xxviii. (1639) 148 It is manifest that vociferation and crying out.. doth greatly helpe in this evill. **1650** BULWER *Anthropomet.* 188 Such exercises as gently dilate and extend the Breast, as shooting, vociferation, commotion of the Arms. **1712** ADDISON *Spect.* No. 407 ¶2 Violent Gesture and Vociferation naturally shake the Hearts of the Ignorant. **1753** HANWAY *Trav.* VII. lxxxvi. (1762) I. 400 They modulate their voices to a tone consistent with pious thoughts, without that extravagant vociferation practised in some churches. **1820** SCOTT *Let.* in *Lockhart* (1837) IV. xi. 368 The whole mob of the Middlesex blackguards..almost drive me mad with their noise and vociferation. **1862** BORROW *Wales* iv, There was plenty of vociferation, but not one single burst of eloquence. **1867** LADY HERBERT *Cradle L.* ii. 58 That wonderfully busy scene of embarkation and disembarkation, and of noisy Arab vociferation.

b. Const. *of* (the words uttered).

1780 JOHNSON in *Boswell* (1904) II. 325 Having after some confused vociferation of 'Hear him—hear him!' obtained a silent attention.

vo'ciferative, *a. rare.* [f. as VOCIFERATE *v.* + -IVE.] Vociferous.

1593 NASHE *Christ's T.* (1613) 50 With dismall crying and vociferatiue inculcating vnto her. **1889** G. B. SHAW *London Music in 1888-89* (1937) 167 The riot in the second act would have been better if it had either been sung note for note as written, or, as usual, frankly abandoned as impossible and filled up according to the vociferative fancy of the choristers.

vociferator (vəʊ)'sɪfəreɪtə(r)). [f. VOCIFERATE *v.*, or ad. L. *vōciferātor* (Tertullian). Cf. F. *vociférateur*, Sp. and Pg. *vociferador*.] One who or that which vociferates; a clamorous or noisy shouter.

1814 MOORE *Mem.* (1853) II. 50, I dare say I shall put up with their noises till spring, when certainly you shall have the advantage of at least one of the little vociferators. **1824** *Ann. Reg.* 172 A numerous herd of vociferators in favour of arbitrary power. **1887** *Daily Tel.* 27 Oct. (Cassell's), He defied the vociferators to do their worst.

vocife'rosity. *rare*⁻¹. [f. next: see -OSITY.] The quality or state of being vociferous.

1837 CARLYLE *Misc., Mirabeau* (1857) IV. 90 Shall we give poor Buffière's testimonial in mess-room dialect; in its native twanging vociferosity?

vociferous (vəʊ)'sɪfərəs), *a.* [f. L. *vōcifer-ārī* (see VOCIFERATE *v.*) + -OUS.]

1. Uttering loud cries or shouts; clamorous, bawling, noisy.

c **1611** CHAPMAN *Iliad* II. 83 Thrise three vociferous heralds rose to checke the rout, and get Eare to their Ioue-kept gouernors. **1700** T. BROWN tr. *Fresny's Amusem.* 121, I sailed into a Presbyterian Meeting..where the vociferous Holder-forth was as bold and saucy, as if the Deity and all Mankind had owed him Money. **1749** FIELDING *Tom Jones* II. ix, Mr. Allworthy had been before silent, from the same cause which had made his sister vociferous. **1784** COWPER *Task* I 299 The boorish driver leaning o'er his team Vocif'rous, and impatient of delay. **1816** SOUTHEY *Poet's Pilgr.* Proem xviii, The restless joy Of those glad girls, and that vociferous boy! **1834** JAMES *J. Marston Hall* vii, My companions were very vociferous. **1875** JOWETT *Plato* (ed. 2) V. 56 The whole audience instead of being mute became vociferous.

transf. **1850-1** LONGF. *Gold. Leg.* Prol., Sp. iv, Hover downward! Seize the loud, vociferous bells, and..to the pavement Hurl them from their windy tower.

fig. **1883** *Harper's Mag.* Sept. 565/1 Mr. Cody..could scarcely design a vulgar and vociferous work if he tried.

b. Applied to birds.

1809 SHAW *Gen. Zool.* VII. 94 Vociferous Eagle, *Falco Vocifer.* **1809** W. IRVING *Knickerb.* III. ii. (1820) 170 Flocks of vociferous geese cackled about the fields.

2. Of the nature of vociferation; uttered with or accompanied by clamour; characterized by loud declamation.

1631 BRATHWAIT *Whimzies, Piper* 144 All he reedes, he puts into his pipe: which consisting of three notes breaks out into a most vociferous syllogisme. **1740** CIBBER *Apol.* (1756) II. 59 Though candour and benevolence are silent virtues, they are as visible as the most vociferous ill-nature. **1828** D'ISRAELI *Chas. I*, II. v. 126 Popular gratitude is as vociferous as it is sudden. **1837** W. IRVING *Capt. Bonneville* II. 283 Jealousy of their good name now prompted them to the most vociferous vindications of their innocence. **1873** BLACK *Pr. Thule* i, Showing by his answers that he was but vaguely hearing the vociferous talk of his companions.

vociferously (vəʊ)'sɪfərəslɪ), *adv.* [f. prec. + -LY².] In a vociferous manner; with great noise or vehemence.

1816 'QUIZ' *Grand Master* VII. 162 Meantime the Hammalls and Goulaub, Vociferously call'd to 'Sahib'. **1847** DISRAELI *Tancred* IV. xi, The little dog began barking vociferously. **1863** E. C. CLAYTON *Queens of Song* II. 115 All Paris thronged to admire..and applauded vociferously.

vociferousness (vəʊ)'sɪfərəsnɪs). [f. as prec. + -NESS.] The quality or character of being vociferous.

1842 MACGILLIVRAY *Man. Brit. Ornith.* II. 93 The Tattlers..being equally remarkable for their timidity, vociferousness, and the balancing motion of their bodies. **1882** J. HAWTHORNE *Fort. Fool* I. xxix, The voice..came in deep tones, more feminine than any shrillness, and more impressive than vociferousness.

†**vocification.** *Obs. rare.* [f. L. *vōci-*, *vox* voice + -FICATION. Cf. L. *vōcificāre* to shout.] Articulate speech or utterance.

1631 R. H. *Arraignm. Whole Creature* iii. 19 He breathes and pathetically bleeds out this vocification. **1758** *Phil. Trans.* L. 744 You, Sir,..are not to be informed, that vocification is performed in the *aspera arteria*.

'vocitate, *v. rare*⁻¹. [f. ppl. stem of L. *vocitāre* (frequentative of *vocāre* to call), after *vociter* in Rabelais.] *trans.* To name or call.

1653 URQUHART *Rabelais* II. vi, From the alme, inclyte, and celebrate Academie, which is vocitated [F. *que l'on vocite*] Lutetia.

voci'tation. *rare*⁻¹. [f. as prec. + -ATION.] Shouting, outcry.

1819 H. BUSK *Vestriad* V. 518 With lungs Stentorian here, affrights the crowd, And Ilium scares with vocitations loud.

†**vockeel**, obs. variant of VAKEEL 1.

1698 FRYER *Acc. E. India & P.* 115 In Town there are many private Merchants that bear a Port equal to our Europe Companies, being only Vockeels or Factors for money'd Men up the Country.

vocoder (vəʊ'kəʊdə(r)). [f. VO(ICE *sb.* + CODE *sb.*¹ + -ER¹.] Any of various devices or systems for analysing speech or other sounds to obtain information that may be transmitted in a much reduced frequency band and used to reconstruct the sounds or synthesize new ones.

1939 H. DUDLEY in *Jrnl. Acoustical Soc. Amer.* XI. 169/1 Speech has been remade..by analyzing a talker's speech for the fundamental speech information and then using this information to remake the speech with a synthesizing device... The apparatus used has been called a 'vocoder'. **1955** *Sci. Amer.* Feb. 95/1 The Vocoder reduces to about one tenth the band width necessary to send speech. **1956** *Jrnl. Acoustical Soc. Amer.* XXVIII. 160/1 In the Scan Vocoder, we scan the envelope of the short time-frequency spectrum, for example, 30 times per second. The scan voltage is then transmitted through only one narrow band frequency channel as an envelope curve. **1970** *Sci. Jrnl.* Mar. 12/4 The main advantage of vocoders is that they require only very low digit rates of the order of 1·2- 2·4 kilobits/second. **1976** *New Musical Express* 12 Feb. 24/5 The song's bridge section follows as a motley collection of barks, yelps and whines are fed through the vocoder, a device which synthesises sounds into eerie echo and resonance. **1980** *Musicians Only* 26 Apr. 13/6 The keys line-up includes..a Korg vocoder.

Hence (as a back-formation) **vo'code** *v. trans.*, to transform by means of a vocoder; **vo'coded** *ppl. a.*, produced by a vocoder.

1973 *Lang. & Speech* XVI. 293 The fundamental frequency contour of a 700-msec. vocoded utterance..was systematically varied to produce 72 contours. **1976** *New Musical Express* 12 Feb. 24/5 'Pigs' is the strongest slice of straight ahead rock the Floyd have recorded and the vocoded pig gruntings are fittingly hideous. *Ibid.* 24/6 Waters' voice is again vocoded and emerges sounding unpleasantly cybernetic. **1981** R. BROWN *Megalodon* i. 15 An electronic translator that could handle the full range of dolphin whistles and vocode them out as an ersatz humanoid voice.

vocoid ('vəʊkɔɪd), *a.* and *sb. Linguistics.* [f. VOC(AL *a.* and *sb.* + -OID.] **A.** *adj.* Vowel-like; articulated with no obstruction of the air-stream; contrasted with CONTOID *a.* **B.** *sb.* A speech sound of this type.

1943 K. L. PIKE *Phonetics* v. 78 Vocoid and contoid groups are strictly delineated by the articulatory and acoustic nature of sounds. *Ibid.* vii. 143 The sounds which as a group function most frequently as syllabics are vocoids. .. Vocoids include practically all sounds which are usually called 'vowels'.., except that 'fricative vowels' are excluded, while 'vowel glides' such as [r], [w], and [y] are included. **1957**, **1958** [see CONTOID *a.* and *sb.*]. **1965** *Language* XLI. 476 This results in a variety of unrounded vocoid transitions between labials and following vowels. **1977** *Word 1972* XXVIII. 307 Vocoid symbolism is at most an extremely vague feeling for the appropriateness of certain vocoids to a particular meaning. **1984** *Amer. Speech* LIX. 342 One violation of (most) native English phonotactics was the *r*, which was usually a tap, even word-initially, rather than a vocoid.

vocular ('vɒkjʊlə(r)), *a. rare.* [f. L. *vōcula* VOCULE + -AR.]

1. Vowel, vocalic.

1813 J. C. HOBHOUSE *Journey* (ed. 2) 1056 The vocular sound in bread.

2. Vocal.

1838 DICKENS *O. Twist* vii, Something which would render the series of vocular exclamations so designated [*sc.* howling], an involuntary process.

vocu'lation. *rare*⁻⁰. [ad. L. *vōculātio*, f. *vōcula*: see next.] (See quot.)

1656 BLOUNT *Glossogr.*, *Voculation*, the accent of every word, the due moderation and measuring the voice in pronouncing a word.

vocule ('vɒkjʊl). [ad. L. *vōcula*, dim. of *vox* voice.] The faint final sound produced in pronouncing certain consonants.

1833 J. RUSH *Philos. Human Voice* iii. 55, I have called this last vented sound of the subtonics the Vocule. *Ibid.* xlii. 273 When the articulative occlusion..is removed, there is a slight momentary issue of voice which completes the structure of these sounds. This is called the Vocule.

vod, obs. Sc. f. WOOD *sb.* and *a.*

vodder, southern ME. var. FODDER *sb.*; obs. Sc. f. WEATHER.

vode, southern ME. var. FOOD *sb.*; obs. Sc. var. VOID *a.*, WOOD *a.*

vodeness, obs. Sc. f. WOODNESS (madness).

vo-de-o-do, var. VO-DO-DEO-DO.

vodka ('vɒdkə). Also β. **vodki, -ky, wodky**; γ. **votku, votky.** [a. Russ. *vódka* (gen. sing. *vódki*), pronounced ('votka).] **a.** An ardent spirit used orig. esp. in Russia, chiefly distilled from rye, but also from barley, potatoes, or other materials. Also, a glass or drink of this.

α. **1802-3** tr. *Pallas's Trav.* (1812) II. 484 The principal imports are..Sekiskaya-Vodka, or brandy distilled from fruit. **1833** R. PINKERTON *Russia* 74 The peasantry..still prefer their national brandy, called vodka. **1883** C. READE in *Harper's Mag.* Jan. 253/1 A young fellow..brings..me a flask of vodka. **1969** M. PUGH *Last Place Left* xxix. 209 Pardoe decided to pour himself a vodka. **1981** 'J. Ross' *Dark Blue & Dangerous* xvi. 89 'Another?' he asked her. 'Thank you. A vodka and mixer.'

β. **1830** *Edinb. Encycl.* XVII. 514/2 The Russian nobles do not drink ardent spirits, *vodki*, in the morning. **1875** R. H. R. *Rambles in Istria* 271 A glass of wodky. **1885** HARE *Russia* i. 24 Vodki (corn brandy) is the chief means of intoxication. **1891** *Blackw. Mag.* Oct. 470/2 Anything which his understanding failed to connect directly with the price of bread and 'vodky'.

γ. **1855** *Englishwoman in Russia* 86 The government revenues are in great part acquired by the sale of votku. **1891** *Pall Mall G.* 27 Aug. 7/1 A large tame bear, which had been trained..to drink votky..entered a village tavern.

b. *attrib.*, as ***vodka bottle, flask, glass***, etc.; **vodka Collins**: see COLLINS²; **vodka gimlet** [GIMLET *sb.* 1 c], a cocktail made of vodka and lime-juice; **vodka martini**, a martini cocktail in which vodka is substituted for gin; **vodka-tonic**, a drink consisting of vodka and tonic water.

1876 MARY M. GRANT *Sun-Maid* xxxiii, He hastily searched the room and found a vodka flask. **1883** O'DONOVAN *Merv* i. 1 After the fashion of Russia generally, the majority of these [houses] consisted of rum and vodka shops. **1903** *Times* 8 Sept. 7/2 The establishment of the vodka monopoly..strained the resources of Russian credit. **1953** R. & A. LONDON *Cocktails & Snacks* 46 (*heading*) Vodka martini. **1958** 'J. BYROM' *Or be he Dead* viii. 117 The vodka glasses were genuine ones. **1965** 'P. QUENTIN' *Family Skeletons* i. 4, I ordered a vodka martini. **1969** 'P. KAVANAGH' *Such Men are Dangerous* i. 13 The desk men.. drink.., in the summer, vodka collinses. **1974** R. B. PARKER *God save Child* ix. 61 Can I get you a drink?.. Would you take a vodka gimlet? **1976** J. HAYES *Missing* (1977) iii. 61 She poured another vodka-tonic.

vodkatini (ˌvɒdkəˈtiːnɪ). Contr. of *vodka martini* s.v. VODKA b.

1955 WILLIAMS & MYERS *What, When, Where & How to Drink* 146 (*heading*) Vodkatini (Vodka Martini). **1969** 'J. MORRIS' *Fever Grass* x. 97 You go on and get a table and order a couple of drinks. Mine is a vodkatini, a double. **1979** *Listener* 18 Jan. 80/1 'You're fighting ten pints of beer in every man.'.. The remark applies in essence (be it beer, whisky or vodkatinis) from the roughest club to the plushiest cabaret.

vodnes, vodure, obs. Sc. ff. WOODNESS, VOIDER.

vo-do-deo-do (ˌvəʊdəʊdiːəʊˈdəʊ). Also vo-do-de-o, vo-de-o-do, vo-do-deo-vo, etc. A meaningless jazz refrain, used *attrib.* to designate a style of singing or a song characterized by speed, energy, and the repetition of such a refrain or insistent rhythm. Also *fig.*

[**1927** J. YELLEN *Crazy Words, Crazy Tune* (song), Sings the same words to ev'ry song. Vo-do-de-o. Vo-do-do-de-o-do.] **1934** C. LAMBERT *Music Ho!* iii. 209 The most irritating quality about the Vo-dodeo-vo, poop-poop-a-doop school of jazz song is its hysterical emphasis on the fact that the singer is a jazz baby going crazy about jazz rhythms. **1937** N. COWARD *Present Indicative* VIII. 335 Slick American 'Vo do deo do' musical farces, in which the speed was fast, the action complicated, and the sentimental value negligible. **1946** MEZZROW & WOLFE *Really Blues* viii. 120 All the hi-de-ho, vo-de-o-do, and boop-boop-a-doo howlers that later sprouted up. **1958** V. BELLERBY in P. Gammond *Decca Bk. Jazz* xvii. 214 At quick tempos some of her tricks can sound a little dated and imbued with the 'vo-do-de-o-vo' style of the late 'thirties.

vodun (ˈvəʊduːn). Also vodu. [W. Afr. (Dahomey) *vodu* (see quot. 1890).] A fetish, usu. one connected with the snake-worship and other rites practised first in Dahomey, then introduced by slaves esp. to Haiti and Louisiana. Also *attrib.* and *Comb.*, esp. in **vodunhwe, -kwe,** fetish-house. Cf. VOODOO.

1874 J. A. SKERTCHY *Dahomey as it Is* iii. 54 The name is derived from *Danh*, a snake, and Hweh, a residence. It is sometimes called *Vodun-hweh, i.e.*, the fetiche house. *Ibid.* vii. 154 This shrine is the Vodun-no-Demen, or fetiche-house of Demen. **1890** A. B. ELLIS *Ewe-Speaking Peoples* ii. 29 The term *vōdu*.. is still used.. in the so-called Vaudoo, or Vaudoux worship of the negroes of Hayti..where the old python *culte* of Whydah still survives. *Ibid.*, Vōdu appears to be derived from *vō* (to be afraid), or from *vō* (harmful). **1920** *Encycl. Relig. & Ethics* XI. 400/2 The Voodoo serpent-cult in Haiti and elsewhere reproduces these W. African cults, one of the names of Dañh-sio being Vodunhwe. **1953** *Caribbean Q.* III. i. 39 The compound began with one house ..a chapel or vodunkwe (house of the gods), and a tent. **1956** M. STEARNS *Story of Jazz* (1957) ii. 20 A photograph by Earl Leaf of a Haitian *vodun* altar. **1963** [see OBEAH 2]. **1973** E. BULLINS *Theme is Blackness* 9 Black..vodun ritual-ceremony. **1985** *Times Lit. Suppl.* 11 Jan. 28/3 It is fashionable at present to argue that such African legacies as Santeria, Shango, Vodun or Camboulay provide a more promising basis for a Caribbean identity than imported European religions.

voe (vəʊ). *Orkn.* and *Shetl. dial.* [ad. Norw. *vaag* (vɔːg), ON. and Icel. *vág-r* (mod. Icel. *vog-r*), bay, inlet.] A bay, creek, or inlet.

a **1688** J. WALLACE *Descr. Orkney* (1693) 93 *Voe*, a Creek or Bay, or firth, or inlet. *a* **1733** *Shetland Acts* 33 in *Proc. Soc. Ant. Scot.* (1892) XXVI. 201 That none fish with haddock lines within voes from Belton to Martinmas. **1791** *Statist. Acc. Scotl.* I. 389 The voes, by which the parish [*sc.* Delting] is intersected. **1821** SCOTT *Pirate* i, A comfortable roadstead..with the house situated on the side of an inland voe. **1841** *Penny Cycl.* XXI. 384/1 Tracts of cultivated and fertile land, generally near the voes and the sea-coasts. **1872** BLACKIE *Lays Highl.* 60 In the voes of Orkney, Haco, Thou didst spread thy prideful sail.

attrib. **1898** J. NICHOLSON *Sprigs Hedder* 25 He was not long in walking round the voe-head.

voel (vɔɪl), *rare.* [W., mutation of *moel* bald.] A bare hill or mountain.

1876 [see ROPED *ppl. a.* 2a].

voertsek, var. VOETSAK *int.*

voetganger (ˈfuːtxaŋə(r)). *S. Afr.* Also foot-ganger. [Afrikaans, f. Du. 'pedestrian', f. *voet* foot + *ganger* one who goes.]

1. A locust in its immature wingless stage. Cf. HOPPER[1] 2.

1824 *S. Afr. Jrnl.* I. 70 The flying locusts are..less dreaded in this colony, than those which have not quite reached that stage of maturity, and are..vulgarly called 'voetgangers'. **1873** F. BOYLE *To Cape for Diamonds* 300 We drove through a host of foot-gangers on the trek. These are the larvæ of locust. **1913** J. J. DOKE *Secret City* 119 The locusts, the voetgangers, came in their countless millions. **1936** R. CAMPBELL *Mithraic Emblems* 79 See there, and there it gnaws, the Rust—Voet-ganger of the coming swarm. **1966** E. PALMER *Plains of Camdeboo* xv. 244 All the world turns out to devour the voetgangers, but I remember only the white storks which appeared in numbers, and the fowls. When the first voetganger column appeared, our domestic fowls went berserk.

2. A pedestrian; also, (in quot. 1902) an infantryman.

1902 C. R. DE WET *Three Years' War* 410 It was exceedingly difficult for Colonials to rise, for they knew that not only would they have to be *voetgangers*, but also that if they were captured they would be..punished. **1950** L. G. GREEN *In Land of Afternoon* 144 In some ways the voetganger of a century ago fared better than the modern tramp.

voetsak (ˈfuːtsæk), *int. S. Afr.* Also footsack, voertsek, and other varr. [ad. Afrikaans *voertsek, voetsek*, f. Du. *voort zeg ik* be off I say.] A command to leave (addressed esp. to a dog).

1837 J. E. ALEXANDER *Narr. Voy. Observation W. Afr.* I. 351 Dogs attacked us as we approached; but on the cry of '*voortzuk*!' from the master..they left us. **1871** *Cape Monthly Mag.* III. 332 Cries of *foot-sek* with the slashing of a whip and the yelping of a defeated cur. **1890** *Digger's Doggerel* 22 'Bonzela Baas, Inkos!' He tell me 'Hamba, footsack!' **1899** A. WERNER *Capt. of Locusts* 194 Be off with you! How dare you annoy a lady like this? *Voetsak*! **1918** C. GARSTIN *Sunshine Settlers* 50 He learned that when he heard the word 'Mike' he was wanted, and when he heard the word 'footsack' he was not. **1949** O. WALKER *Wanton City* 74 What's White civilization in South Africa?.. Social inhibitions imported from Europe? Broken accents from the world's ghettos? Fooie! Voetsak. **1950** *Cape Argus* 3 May 9/5 Betsy's only response was: 'Voetsek, you skollie.' **1963** A. DELIUS *Day Natal took Off* 9 He heard Bloubakkies yell to Sobisa, 'Hardloop! Run! Go! Voertsek!' **1969** A. FUGARD *Boesman & Lena* 42 Few dops and a guitar and its voetsek yesterday and to hell with tomorrow.

Hence **ˈvoetsak** *v.*, (*a*) *trans.* to chase (a dog) away, (*b*) *intr.* to leave, to go away.

1897 E. GLANVILLE *Tales from Veld* 227, I jes' drop in t'ask you *voetsack* all the dogs outer the place, 'fore I bring him in. **1958** *Cape Times* 4 Dec. 13/8 De La Fontaine said: 'You had better give me my money back.' I told him to *voetsak*. **1971** *The 1820* Apr. 11 But be careful who you tell to 'voetsak'..or be prepared for the consequences!

‖**vœu** (vø). Pl. vœux (vø). [Fr., lit. 'vow, wish': see VOW *sb.*] A recommendation made by an international conference, which is not mandatory.

1917 E. SATOW *Guide to Diplomatic Practice* II. xxvi. 142 A recommendation (*vœu*)..respecting the liquor trade was adopted. **1936** R. C. K. ENSOR *England, 1870–1914* xii. 420 A preamble like that..enacts nothing. It is only a *vœu*. **1939** H. NICOLSON *Diplomacy* 250 *Voeux.* It sometimes happens that a conference wishes to add to its treaty certain 'recommendations' for future good conduct. These are called 'wishes' or 'voeux'. Thus the Hague Peace Conference of 1899 emitted six 'voeux'. These have no binding force upon the signatories. **1961** A. MARDER *From Dreadnought to Scapa Flow* I. vi. 133 Sir Edward Fry.. presented a pious *voeu*,..declaring it was 'highly desirable that the Governments should resume the serious study of this question'.

voff, voful, obs. Sc. ff. WOLF *sb.*, WOEFUL *a.*

vogal, vogle. *Cornish mining.* [ad. Cornish *vooga* cavern. Another variant is *fogo*.] = VUG.

1855 J. R. LEIFCHILD *Cornwall Mines* 278 Vugh, or *vogal* ..a cavity. **1860** WORCESTER (citing Ansted), *Vogle.*

vogesite (ˈvəʊdʒɪzaɪt). *Petrogr.* [ad. G. *vogesit* (C. H. F. Rosenbusch *Mikrosk. Physiogr.* (1887) II. 315), f. *Vogesen*, G. name of the Vosges Mountains in N.E. France: see -ITE[1].] A lamprophyre consisting essentially of phenocrysts of hornblende (or augite) in a groundmass containing potash feldspar.

1891 F. H. HATCH *Introd. Stud. Petrol.: Igneous Rocks* v. 97 A second type of syenitic lamprophyre, containing hornblende instead of mica, is termed vogesite by Rosenbusch. **1937** A. JOHANNSEN *Descr. Petrogr. Igneous Rocks* III. 37 The vogesites are greenish, grayish, or black melanocratic rocks when fresh, and reddish or brownish when weathered. **1976** *Nature* 5 Aug. 462/2 The vogesite lava is composed of approximately 85–90% olivine and augite.

voȝel, voȝte, southern ME. varr. FOWL *sb.*, *fought* FIGHT *v.*

voghte, obs. variant of VAULT *sb.*[1]

vogie (ˈvəʊgɪ), *a. Sc.* Also 8 vougy, 9 vogey. [Of obscure origin.]

1. Vain, proud, conceited.

1719 RAMSAY *Epist. Hamilton* Answ. II. ii, 'Whisht', quoth the vougy jade. **1788** BURNS *My Hoggie* 4 My only beast, I had nae mae, And vow but I was vogie! **1789** ROSS *Helenore* (ed. 3) 112 Of your consent, he says, I'm mair nor fain, And vogie that I can ca' you my ain. **1830** GALT *Lawrie T.* VII. xi. (1849) 350, I was somewhat vogie of the valour I had shown her so handsomely off-hand.

2. Merry, cheerful, delighted, gay.

1715 in Hogg *Jacobite Relics* (1819) 81 We took a spring, and danc'd a fling, And wow but we were vogie! *a* **1774** FERGUSSON *Ode to Bee* Poems (1845) 18 The Muse Scuds ear' and heartsome owre the dews, Fu' vogie and fu' blythe to crap The winsome flowers frae nature's lap. **1822** GALT *Provost* xlii, Many among us thought..that we had got a great catch, and they were both blythe and vogie when he was chosen. **1896** in Proudlock *Borderland Muse* 323 He's harmless as yon vogie lamb That loups beside its sleeping dam.

‖**vogt** (*Du.* voːxt, *G.* foːkt). Also 7 vooght, vaught. [a. G. *vogt* (and Du. *voogd*, †*voogt*), MHG. *voget*, OHG. *fogat*, ad. med.L. *vocāt-us*: cf. VOCATE *sb.*] A steward, bailiff, or similar official.

1694 PENN *Trav. Holland & Germ.* 91 The Inspector of the Calvinists hath injoined the Vooght, or chief Officer, not to suffer any preaching to be among our Friends. *Ibid.* 109 The Vaught or chief Officer. **1762** tr. *Busching's Syst. Geog.* IV. 252 He acknowledged them to be hereditary vogts of his church. **1874** STUBBS *Const. Hist.* I. iii. 57 The rights of the archbishop being guarded by an advocatus or vogt,..the state was governed by its own landrath.

vogue (vəʊg), *sb.* Also 6 vog(e, *Sc.* wogue, 7 voag, vouge. [a. F. *vogue* rowing, course, success, f. *voguer*, ad. It. *vogare* to row. So It. and Pg. *voga*, Sp. *boga*.]

I. †**1.** *the vogue*, the principal or foremost place in popular repute or estimation; the most pronounced success or general acceptance; the greatest currency or prevalence. Chiefly in phrases *to have, bear, carry, get* (etc.) *the vogue*. Now *Obs.*

(*a*) **1571** *Satir. Poems Reform.* xxvii. 123 Quha hes þe wogue [*printed* wogne], him all þe warld dois wew. *c* **1590** J. STEWART *Poems* (S.T.S.) II. 12/24 As mychtie Monarck rair,..He onlie hes the vog armipotent. **1643** HOWELL *Twelve Treat.* (1661) 290 These are the men that now have the vogue, and..seem to have quite swallowed up both the King's Prerogatives, and those of the Lords. **1678** CUDWORTH *Intell. Syst.* 17 Democritus having had for many ages almost the general cry and vogue for Atoms. **1731** MEDLEY *Kolben's Cape G. Hope* I. 65 They have the vogue above all the other Hottentot nations for strength and dexterity in throwing the Hassagaye. **1738** *Observ. Brit. Wool* 9 English Woollen Manufactures have had the Vogue and Name for many Years past, all over Europe. **1788** FRANKLIN *Autobiog.* Wks. 1840 I. 210 He had published a theory of electricity, which then had the general vogue.

(*b*) *c* **1610** SIR J. MELVIL *Mem.* (1735) 380 Such scornful and such partial Persons, as have oftest possessed your Ear and carried the Vogue in your Court. **1664** POWER *Exp. Philos.* I. 47 Though Mustard-seed do carry the Vogue amongst the People. **1698** FRYER *Acc. E. India & P.* 123 It bears the Vogue for altering the Blood. **1722** W. HAMILTON *Wallace* 152 McFadzean that most bloody Rogue, Who for his Villany did bear the Vogue. **1741** BETTERTON *Eng. Stage* i. 9 Notwithstanding the Industry of the Patentee and Managers, it seems the King's House then carried the Vogue of the Town.

(*c*) **1685** *Choice Coll. Songs*, '*Fill up the Bowl*' v, While you can find one Factious Rogue, To sway the Poll, and get the Vogue. **1710** SWIFT *Tatler* No. 230 ¶7 Some of which [words] are now struggling for the Vogue, and others are in possession of it. **1725** RAMSAY *Gentle Sheph.* I. ii, I'll..win the vogue at market, tron, or fair, For halesome, clean, cheap and sufficient ware. **1732** SWIFT *Beast's Confession* Pref., London is seldom without a dozen of their own educating, who engross the vogue for half a winter together.

2. a. Without article: Popularity; general acceptance or currency; success in popular esteem.

1604 WILCOCKS in *Golding's De Mornay* Ded. Pr. Wales (1617) A2b, This booke being countenanced, vnder your Patronage and defence, shall haue more vogue, and better acceptance with all sorts. **1653** A. WILSON *Jas. I*, 121 So long as you permit the Schisms of Arminius to have such vogue..in the principal Towns of Holland. **1694** W. FREKE *Sel. Ess.* 2 An Author not Licensed by Common Vogue, as well as Authority, looks like one with the Plague-sore upon him. **1704** SWIFT *T. Tub* vii. Wks. 1768 I. 116 Having observed how little invention bears any vogue, besides what is derived into these channels. **1716** WATERLAND *Serm. bef. Cambridge Univ.* 21 A good Man has no Security..but by examining carefully what is true, right, and just in it self, separate from common Vogue, or popular Opinion. **1752** HUME *Ess. & Treat.* (1777) I. 248 To convince you that fashion, vogue,..and law, were the chief foundation of all moral determinations. **1858** HAWTHORNE *Fr. & It. Notebks.* I. 154 Mr. ——..seems to have a good deal of vogue as a sculptor. **1879** FARRAR *St. Paul* I. 351 Astrologers, magians, soothsayers,..acquired such vogue, as to attract the indignant notice of both satirists and historians.

b. In phr. *in* (or *out of*) *vogue*. Also with adjs. (usually intensive), as *in full vogue*, etc.

(*a*) **1643** CHAS. I in Ellis *Orig. Lett.* Ser. I. III. 297 Though Mars be now most in voag, yet Hymen may bee some tymes remembred. **1653** H. COGAN tr. *Pinto's Trav.* lix. 242 The Idol which is most in vogue amongst them, and most frequented. *a* **1676** HALE *Prim. Orig. Man.* II. iv. (1677) 165 The same Words and Phrases that were not used, in former Ages, become in Fashion, Reputation and Vogue in another Age. **1726** SWIFT *Gulliver* IV. xii, It is highly probable, that such travellers..may, by detecting my errors,..justle me out of vogue and stand in my place. **1738** —— *Pol. Conversat.* Introd. 42 My Book would be out of Vogue with the first Change of Fashion. **1747** BUTLER *Serm.* Wks. 1874 II. 297 Corruptions of the grossest sort have been in vogue, for many generations. **1787** BENTHAM *Def. Usury* x. 98 A method much in vogue was, to let the Jews get the money.. and then squeeze it out of them as it was wanted. **1820** W. IRVING *Sketch Bk.* I. 274 The writers whom you suppose in vogue,..have long since had their day. **1842** NEWMAN *Par. Serm.* (ed. 2) V. ix. 141 The influence of some system of religion which is in vogue. **1879** PROCTOR *Pleas. Ways Sc.* ii. 30 The system of lunar weather wisdom in vogue to this day among seamen.

(*b*) **1687** A. LOVELL tr. *Thevenot's Trav.* I. 101 Letters are in no vogue in that Country, and profound Ignorance reigns among them. **1692** SPRAT *Wicked Contrivance* II. 15 The Popish-Plot having been just before in full vogue there, as well as here. **1741** BETTERTON *Eng. Stage* i. 8 During this Interval, many Plays were brought upon the Stage written in Heroic Rhime: and..in 1668..it became still in greater Vogue. **1798** *Anti-Jacobin* No. 35 The following popular song is said to be in great vogue. **1838** JAMES *Louis XIV*, IV. 83 As the system of conversion [to the Roman Catholic faith] was at that time in high vogue.

c. In phr. *to bring* or *put*, *to come* or *start*, etc., *into* (or *in*) *vogue*.

a **1700** EVELYN *Diary* 29 Nov. 1694, It had been brought into vogue by Mr. Tudor an apothecary. **1702** ADDISON *Dial. Medals* Misc. Wks. 1736 III. 15 To bring the study of Medals in vogue. **1750** CHESTERF. *Lett.* ccxviii. (1792) II. 341 Without which they..would be vilified by those very gallantries which put them in vogue. **1768** TUCKER *Lt. Nat.* (1834) I. 176 What would the mathematician give to know the newest fashions as they start into vogue, or be let into all the scandal and tittle-tattle of the town? **1844** THIRLWALL *Greece* VIII. lxii. 148 Austere doctrines..seem to have come into vogue in the higher circles. **1845** FORD *Handbk. Spain* I. 13 Travelling in a carriage with post-horses was brought into vogue by the Bourbons. **1876** GLADSTONE *Homeric Synchr.* 134 It had still more recently come into vogue as the national name.

d. In phr. *to give vogue* (to something).

c **1688** [? BURNET] *Enquiry into Reasons Abrog. Test* 7/1 The main things that gave it Popular Vogue and Reputation with his Party. **1770** GRAY *Lett.* Poems (1775) 385 That childish nation, the French, have given him vogue and fashion. **1799** in *Med. Jrnl.* (1800) III. 14 Those artifices that have so often given Medical Men vogue in the great world. **1824** BYRON *Juan* XV. xlviii, Although her birth and wealth had given her vogue, Beyond the charmers we have already cited. **1837** HALLAM *Hist. Literature* I. I. vii. §27. 402 It contains several feigned letters of the Emperor Marcus Aurelius, which probably in a credulous age passed for genuine, and gave vogue to the book. **1877** E. R. CONDER *Basis Faith* ii. 69 To give vogue to a phrase by which he hopes to make the idea..ridiculous.

†**e.** *of vogue*, holding a prominent place in popular estimation or notice; fashionable.

1678 GALE *Crt. Gentiles* IV. III. iv. 137 Is it not strange then, that Reformed Divines, yea some of great vogue for Pietie and Learning should espouse an error so grosse. **1703** STEELE *Tender Husb.* I. i, The Great Beauties, and Short-liv'd People of Vogue, were always her Discourse and Imitation. **1709** —— *Tatler* No. 14 ⁋5 There are Two who frequent this Place, whom she takes for Men of Vogue.

3. a. With *a*: A prominent place in popular favour or fashion; a course or period of success or distinction in this connexion.

1673 *Lady's Call.* I. v. §25 That impudence of profaneness which has given it such a vogue in the world. **1704** SWIFT *Mech. Operat. Spir.* Misc. (1711) 274, I do not find any [Title] which holds so general a Vogue as that of A Letter to a Friend. **1752** HUME *Ess. & Treat.* (1777) I. 248 Authority ..may give a temporary vogue to a bad poet. **1753** HOGARTH *Anal. Beauty* viii. 45 Paltry imitations of Chinese buildings have a kind of vogue, chiefly on account of their novelty. **1818** *Sporting Mag.* III. 118 The carriages called caterpillars acquired a temporary vogue. **1832** LEWIS *Use & Ab. Pol. Terms* xiv. 136 A theory which, in its day, had a sufficient vogue to transfer its peculiar and technical expressions into common language. **1880** H. JAMES *Hawthorne* 37 The Universal History had a great vogue and passed through hundreds of editions.

b. In similar use with *the* or other limiting terms.

c **1645** HOWELL *Lett.* I. v. xxxiii. 169 The Lord Treasurer Weston is he who hath the greatest vogue now at Court, but many great ones have clash'd with him. **1674** BOYLE *Excell. Theol.* II. v. 202 The present success..ought not to make him so sure..that the same Opinions will be always in the same, or greater Vogue. **1697** BENTLEY *Phal.* (1699) 351 The Milesian Cloths had the greatest Vogue in the Greek Markets. **1709** O. DYKES *Eng. Prov. & Refl.* (ed. 2) 18 Prodigality is a jolly Vice, and of the most popular Vogue in the World. **1743** FIELDING *J. Wild* I. iv, Whisk and swabbers was the game then in the chief vogue. **1834** MACAULAY *Ess., Pitt* ⁋24 The vogue which it has obtained may serve to show [etc.]. **1881** *Athenæum* 15 Jan. 88/3 The vogue which mountaineering has acquired of late years.

c. With possessives (or *of*).

a **1683** OLDHAM *Art of Poetry* Wks. (1686) 7 Others.. Shall be revived, and come again in force If custom please: from whence their vogue they draw. **1737** L. CLARKE *Hist. Bible* (1740) II. 316 James, in regard of his great Vogue with the populace, for sincerity, virtue, and judgment. **1771** SMOLLETT *Humph. Cl.* Let. 4 July, All these places, Bath excepted, have their vogue, and then the fashion changes. **1780** MISS WILKES in *Corr. J. Wilkes* (1805) IV. 298 The vogue of this employment occasions a great many presents being made. **1835** *Court Mag.* VI. p. x/2 Tartan shawls have entirely lost their vogue; they are replaced by Egyptian shawls, which are now more fashionable than any other. **1855** N. HAWTHORNE in *Life Longfellow* (1891) II. 287 No other poet has anything like your vogue. **1886** *Ch. Times* 730/1 Its defects, not its merits are the source of its vogue.

II. †**4. a.** Natural bent or capacity. *Obs.*$^{-1}$

1590 SIR R. WILLIAMS *Disc. Warre* 25 If they finde any of great qualitie that carries a voge, to command popular or men of war.

†**b.** General course or tendency; general character or condition. *Obs.*

1626 T. H[AWKINS] *Caussin's Holy Crt.* 74 They seing all things are permitted them, do instantly take that vogue, which depraued nature doth present vnto them, they follow the track of pleasure. **1633** G. HERBERT *Temple, Bunch of Grapes* i, One vogue and vein, One aire of thought usurps my brain. **1647** LILLY *Chr. Astrol.* cxiii. 543 The Native.. shall live gallantly..above the ordinary Vogue of his Birth. **1660** GAUDEN *Slight Healers* 76 They go with the vogue and stream of times. **1702** *Eng. Theophrast.* 195 Mens merit is generally judg'd of by the Vogue of the Fortune they are in. **1729** LAW *Serious C.* xvii. 308 According to the spirit and vogue of this world, whose corrupt air we have all breath'd, there are many things that pass for great, and honourable.

†**c.** Vigour or energy. *Obs.*$^{-1}$

1674 *Ch. & Court of Rome* 5 This is at large inculcated.. with great vogue and ostentation by the Bishop of *Condom*.

†**5. a.** The approbation, approval, or popular favour *of* some class of persons, etc. *Obs.*

1606 BIRNIE *Kirk-Buriall* ix, For many to eternize their soone forgot memory, and to gaine the vogue of this vaine world, hes prepared Pyramides of pomp. **1646** G. DANIEL *Poems* Wks. (Grosart) I. 75 Wouldst Thou wooe a Feature In a glasse?.. Or resigne what you may claime To the vogue of vulgar ffame. **1662-3** SOUTH *Serm.* (1843) II. xviii. 305 A King..not owing his Kingdom to the vogue of the populace but to the suffrage of nature. **1681** CHETHAM *Angler's Vade-m.* x. §1. (1689) 97 For that the Trout is the most Excellent Fish, by the Vogue of the most curious Palates. **1720** WELTON *Suffer. Son of God* II. xx. 565, I would fain Recollect and Obtain the Universal Approbation and Vogue in my own Favour.

†**b.** The current opinion or belief; the general report or rumour. *Obs.*

1626 in Birch *Crt. & Times Chas. I* (1848) I. 131 Some affirm the Earl of Suffolk..goes general of the fleet... Captain Pennington hath the vogue to go to his vice-admiral. **1661** SIR P. TYRILL in *Essex Rev.* (1909) XVIII. 95 The generall vogue of the towne is yt yesterday the Portugall match was agreed upon at the Counsell. **1685** J. CHAMBERLAYNE *Coffee Tea & Choc.* 49 Indeed 'tis the common vogue and opinion of this Country, that there is nothing more Soveraign then this plant. **1721** PERRY *Daggenh. Breach* 79 The Opinion of my Assistants being urg'd, and the general vogue of Men that my Work was carried on in a sufficient Manner. **1730** SWIFT *Let. to Gay* 19 Nov., The vogue of our few honest folks here is that Duck is absolutely to succeed Eusden in the laurel.

6. a. The prevailing fashion or tendency; *esp.* that which is in favour at a particular time.

1648-9 *Eikon Bas.* xi. (1662) 46 The common Sewer or stream of the present vogue and humor. **1660** STILLINGFL. *Iren.* II. vi. §11. (1662) 266 If Jerome speak according to the general vogue, this solution may be sufficient. **1834** MARRYAT *P. Simple* lxv, His mustachios, bad French, and waltzing..were quite the vogue. **1860** SALA *Lady Chesterf.* Pref. p. iii, An age when burlesque is the vogue.

b. Without article or with *a*.

1689-90 TEMPLE *Ess. Health & Long Life* Wks. 1720 I. 283 As Diseases have changed Vogue, so have Remedies in my Time and Observation. **1738** FIELDING *Hist. Register* III, There is a vogue, my Lord, which if you will bring me into, you will lay a lasting obligation on me. **1905** *Westm. Gaz.* 10 June 15/3 Others..at once took the thing up and made it a vogue.

7. *attrib.* or as *adj.* Fashionable; currently in vogue; esp. in *vogue word*.

c **1669** HOWARD & VILLIERS *Country Gentleman* (1976) I. i. 66 Pox on your Bourdeaux, Burgundie..no more of these vogue names,..get me some ale. **1915** H. L. WILSON *Ruggles of Red Gap* (1917) iii. 49 Decidedly he was not vogue. His hat was remarkable, being of a black felt with high crown and a wide and flopping brim. **1926** FOWLER *Mod. Eng. Usage* 697/1 *Vogue-words*. Every now & then a word emerges from obscurity, or even from nothingness or a merely potential & not actual existence, into sudden popularity. **1947** PARTRIDGE *Usage & Abusage* 351/1 *Brave new world* is perhaps as much a cliché as it is a vogue-term. **1958** *Listener* 16 Oct. 621/2 Psychosomatic is the vogue-word of today. **1960** PATRIDGE *Charm of Words* I. 47 One of the main differences between vogue-phrase and cliché: the majority of clichés last for generations. **1972** P. D. JAMES *Unsuitable Job for Woman* iii. 106 Typical of the worst kind of academic writing. Contempt for logic; a generous sprinkling of vogue names; spurious profundity. **1978** *Forum on Med.* Apr. 84/1 Clichés and vogue expressions are equally plentiful. **1981** W. SAFIRE in *N.Y. Times Mag.* 22 Feb. 9/1 Vogue words are his specialty [*sc.* Alexander Haig's]. The academic joyword of the 70's was 'exacerbate'. **1982** *Sunday Times* 5 Dec. 55 It was Chinese orders that made the mining machinery companies vogue stocks in the late seventies.

†**vogue**, *v.*^{1} *Obs.* [f. the sb.]

1. *trans.* To cry *up* or *down*.

c **1661** in *Harl. Misc.* (1746) VIII. 31/2 He procured an awe and reverence to himself, by being vogued up by the Clergy, and rendered to the Vulgar as a Pattern of Piety. **1710** T. FULLER *Pharm. Extemp.* 408 Thus may a good Medicine be vogu'd down by a groundless fancy!

b. To bring into, or keep in, vogue.

1687 J. REYNOLDS *Death's Vis.* Pref. (1713) 2 [That] those Poets shou'd be chiefly Applauded and Vogued, whose sole use of Religion..is to Undermine and Lampoon it.

2. To repute or reckon (as something).

1675 R. BURTHOGGE *Causa Dei* 251 Pythagoras..might put this Honorary Mark upon the Ternary Number, and Vogue it Sacred and Divine. **1682** T. FLATMAN *Heraclitus Ridens* No. 78. (1713) II. 228 Hellish Rage, which, forsooth, must be vogued Protestant Zeal. **1691** T. H[ALE] *Acc. New Invent.* p. xlii, Some who would take it ill not to be vogued for first-rate Politicians.

†**vogue**, *v.*^{2} *Obs.*$^{-1}$ [ad. F. *voguer*: see VOGUE *sb.*] *intr.* To float.

1687 RYCAUT *Hist. Turks* II. 316 The Turks brake it [the bridge] the preceeding day, letting the materials vogue with the stream into the Danube.

‖**vogue la galère** (vɔg la galɛr), *int.* [Fr., lit. 'let the galley be rowed'.] Let's get on with it! Let's give it a go!

[*c* **1525** WYATT *Coll. Poems* (1969) 59 My fearful trust, 'en vogant la Galère'.] **1744** LADY HERVEY *Let.* 20 Oct. (1821) 86 As long as Mrs. Phipps is well, and Mr. Phipps happy, *vogue la galère*. **1822** SCOTT *Peveril of Peak* IV. xi. 258 '*Vogue la Galere*!' he exclaimed, as the carriage went onward; 'I have sailed through worse perils than this yet.' **1850** THACKERAY *Pendennis* II. vi. 63 Eh, *vogue la galè re*, I say. It's good sport, Warrington—not winning merely, but playing. **1909** L. STRACHEY *Let.* 13 Oct. in *V. Woolf & L. Strachey: Letters* (1956) 35 My health seems still to be something of a Mahomet's coffin. However, vogue la galère! *a* **1918** D. H. LAWRENCE *Phoenix* (1936) v. 594 We'll embark on a new course of education, and *vogue la galère*.

voguey ('vəʊgɪ), *a.* [f. VOGUE *sb.* + -Y^1.] = next.

1928 *Observer* 22 July 9/2 An achievement..which steers a happy course between the 'arty' and the 'voguey'. **1980** *Listener* 21 Feb. 228/1 'Don't have' has become voguey and displaced 'haven't got'.

voguish ('vəʊgɪʃ), *a.* [f. VOGUE *sb.* + -ISH^1.] That is in vogue or temporarily fashionable.

1927 *Daily Express* 26 Mar. 8 (Advt.), Hundreds of the voguish Jumper Suits await your selection. **1951** G. GREENE *End of Affair* I. ii. 18 A voguish choice of reading matter in the waiting-room..*Harper's Bazaar* and *Life*. **1960** *News Chron.* 11 Oct. 4/3 An obsessive interest in [James] Dean.. is voguish. **1980** *Times Lit. Suppl.* 31 Oct. 1220/1 Couples steer impeccably towards 'the smart upper floor' of a voguish restaurant.

Vogul ('vəʊgʊl). Also 8 Vogoul, Wougoul, 9 Wogul, Wogule, Vogule. [Russian *vogul*, G. *Wogul*, etc.] **a.** A member of a Ugrian people inhabiting Tobolsk and and Perm.

[**1698** tr. *Brand's Jrnl. Embassy* 21 Wogultzoi.] **1780** W. TOOKE *Russia* I. 157 The Vogouls. **1796** MORSE *Amer. Geog.* II. 84 A Wougoul village is commonly composed of one family. **1880** A. H. SAYCE *Introd. Sci. Lang.* II. x. 325 The Hungarians were once the neighbours of the savage Voguls of the Ural. **1887** *Encycl. Brit.* XXII. 8/2 The Voguls..on the eastern slopes of the Urals. **1948** D. DIRINGER *Alphabet* 483 The Voguls in the Ural mountains. **1975** [see OSTYAK].

b. The language of this people, belonging to the OB-UGRIAN group.

1908 T. G. TUCKER *Introd. Nat. Hist. Lang.* 133 Ugric, which comprises..Vogul and Ostiak, dialects of a few thousands scattered over a wide region eastward from the Northern Ural and about the Obi River. **1933**, etc. [see OB-UGRIAN]. **1951** W. K. MATTHEWS *Languages U.S.S.R.* iii. 21 The 'primitive' or East Ugrian languages, Ostyak and Vogul. **1980** *Amer. N. & Q.* Oct. 29/1 Marianne Sz. Bakró-Nagy..has pulled together some 500 terms..on the bear as a tabu animal in the Urals among the Ostyak (Khanty) and Vogul (Mansi) speaking peoples.

Hence †**Wogulian** (-olian); †**Wogulic** *a.* [G. *Wogulisch*].

1796 MORSE *Amer. Geog.* II. 84 The Wogolians are rather below the middle stature. **1813** *Q. Rev.* Oct. 256 Classes.. of Languages... Siberian, Permian, Wogulic. **1925** P. RADIN tr. *Vendryès's Language* II. iii. 118 In Wogulian *mini* 'he goes'..[is] formed like *puri* 'taking'.

voiadge, obs. form of VOYAGE *sb.*

voice (vɔɪs), *sb.* Forms: α. 3-4 voiz (4 uoyz), 3-5 voys (5 uoys, 5-6 woys), 4-5 voise (4 uoise), 4-6 (7) voyse (5 woyse); 4-7 voyce (4 voysce, 5 voyc, 5-6 *Sc.* woyce), 4- voice (4 uoice, 4, 5-6 *Sc.*, woice, 6 voic); also 5 wyce, 8-9 *dial.* vice. β. *Sc.* and *north.* 4-7 voce (5 uoce, 5-6 woce), 5, 7 vose, 6 vox, wox. [a. AF. *voiz*, *voice*, OF. *voiz*, *vois*, *voix* (mod.F. *voix*, = Pr. *votz*, Sp. and Pg. *voz*, It. *voce*):—L. *vōc-em*, *vox* voice, sound.]

I. 1. Sound, or the whole body of sounds, made or produced by the vocal organs of man or animals in their natural action; esp. sound formed in or emitted from the human larynx in speaking, singing, or other utterance; vocal sound as the vehicle of human utterance or expression. Also occas., the faculty or power of producing this; or concretely, the organs by which it is produced.

a. With *the*, or with limiting terms as *man's*.

a **1300** *Cursor M.* 11420 Þis ilk stern..said to þaim wit mans woice, þat þai suld wend to Juen land. *c* **1350** *Will. Palerne* 40 Þe son of þe cry com to þe cowherde euene, þat he wist witerly it was þe voys of a childe. **1387** TREVISA *Higden* (Rolls) I. 83 Þe voys þat þey makeþ is liker to an houndes berkynge þan to a manis voys. **1398** —— *Barth. De P.R.* v. xxiii. (Bodl. MS.), To schape þe voice aier is ifonge in þe leues of þe lungen. **1580** J. HAY *Demandes* §17 in *Cath. Tract.* (S.T.S.) 39 The trew intelligence..and nocht the outward sounding of the woce. **1587** GOLDING *De Mornay* v. 59 There is..a dubble Speech; the one in the mynd,..the other the sounding image thereof,..vttered by our mouth and..termed the Speech of the Voyce. **1603** HOLLAND *Plutarch's Mor.* 838 Plato defineth the Voice to be a spirit. **1606** SHAKS. *Tr. & Cr.* III. ii. 95 They that haue the voyce of Lyons, and the act of Hares: are they not Monsters? **1655** VAUGHAN *Silex Scint., Holy Script.* ii, Thou [the Bible] art the great Elixir rare and choice; The Word in Characters, God in the Voice. **1710** M. HENRY *Disputes Reviewed* Wks. 1853 II. 464/1 When the temper is not kept within due bounds, commonly the voice is not. **1780** W. SHAW (*title*) A Galic and English Dictionary. Containing all the Words in the Scotch and Irish Dialects of the Celtic, that could be collected from the Voice, and Old Books and MSS. **1831** YOUATT *Horse* viii. 152 The voice of animals is produced by the passage of air through this aperture. **1842** *Penny Cycl.* XXIV. 154/1 Speaking-pipes, or tubes to convey the voice from one place to another. **1889** RUSKIN *Præterita* III. 162 The Voice is the eternal musical instrument of heaven and earth, from angels down to birds.

b. Without article.

Occas. put for 'musical voice', 'power of singing': cf. quots. 1667 and 1697.

a **1300** *Cursor M.* 17840 And als sun þai spak wit woice. *c* **1380** WYCLIF *Serm.* Sel. Wks. I. 75 Among alle þingis vois is a freel þing. *c* **1400** *Pilgr. Sowle* (Caxton 1483) IV. xx. 67 See howe my sone..bymeneth hym in herte chere and voys. **1444** *Aberdeen Regr.* (1844) I. 12 He sal vphald the ladymesse with uoce on Twisdai, Thurisdai, and Fridai ilke owke for a yher. *c* **1450** tr. *De Imitatione* III. xlviii. 119 So I teche wiþoute voice of wordes, wiþoute confusion of opinyons. **1500-20** DUNBAR *Poems* xlviii. 162 Thane all the birdis song with voce on hicht. **1588** A. KING tr. *Canisius' Catech.* 124 Seing wraith without ony voce of worde is appointed to iudgement, wraith in voce is appointed to a councel quhairin sentence is pronunced. **1594** KYD *Cornelia* III. i. 132 These are..melancholie showes, That.. counterfet the dead in voyce and figure. **1608** TOPSELL *Serpents* 134 A vocal iustice, which speaketh in action though not in voyce. **1666-7** PEPYS *Diary* 12 Feb., I confess

I was mightily pleased with the musique. He pretends not to voice; though it be good, but not excellent. 1697 DRYDEN Virg. Georg. IV. 70 Hollow Rocks that render back the Sound, And doubled Images of Voice rebound. 1697 —— Virg. Past. v 10 Your merit and your years command the choice: Amyntas only rivals you in voice. 1721 BAILEY, Aphony, a want of voice. 1728 CHAMBERS Cycl. s.v., That Canal,..which at first pass'd for the principal Organ of Voice. ? 1780 COWPER Cricket 17 Though in voice and shape they be Form'd as if akin to thee. 1828 WHATELY Rhet. in Encycl. Metrop. I. 295/1 To observe all the modulations, &c. of voice, which take place in such a delivery. 1872 HUXLEY Physiol. vii. 184 Thus, voice may exist without speech, and ..speech may exist without voice, as in whispering. 1884 F. M. CRAWFORD Rom. Singer I. 2 He had so much voice that he did not know what to do with it.

transf. and fig. 1815 SCOTT Waterloo i, We yet may hear the hour Peal'd over orchard and canal, With voice prolong'd and measured fall. 1817 —— Harold III. vi, From realms afar Comes voice of battle and of war.

c. With adjs. denoting the quality or tone. Chiefly *with* or *in..voice*. Cf. 6c.

13.. K. Alis. 3850 (Laud MS.), And hem he seide wiþ voice clere Ich bidde frendes þat ȝe me here. c1330 Arth. & Merl. 4853 (Kölbing), Ten com bihinde.. Wiþ loude voice & to hem gradde. 1377 LANGL. P. Pl. B. xv. 584 With styf voys [he] hym called, Lazare, veni foras. 1422 tr. Secreta Secret., Priv. Priv. 140 Therfor criet the pepill, har kynge and his good werkes with hey woyce commendid and preisit. c1460 Oseney Reg. 18 Hit shall be lefull to yow..in lowe voice to saye diuine seruice. a1500 Lancelot 13 Throw birdis songe with opine wox one hy, That sessit not one luffaris for to cry. 1552 LYNDESAY Monarche 5588 [An angel shall cry] With hydous voce, and vehement,—Ryse, [etc.]. a1609 ALEX. HUME Poems (S.T.S.) 15 When I waill with weeping vose, Lord, to my plaint give eare. 1667 MILTON P.L. v. 37 Methought Close at mine ear one call'd me forth to walk With gentle voice. 1812 CARY Dante, Purg. xxv. 24 At the hymn's close They shouted loud, 'I do not know a man'; Then in low voice again took up the strain. 1819 SHELLEY Cenci v. iv. 9 Muttering with hoarse, harsh voice.

d. *in* (..) *voice*. Of persons: Having the voice or vocal organs in fit or good condition for speaking or singing. So *out of voice*.

1757 FOOTE Author Epil., O! Such a Sustinuto upon B! Ma'am, when she's quite in Voice she'll go to C. 1760–2 GOLDSM. Cit. W. lxxi, You know very well..that I am not in voice [for singing] to-day. 1826 COBBETT Rur. Rides (1885) II. 285 Owing to a cold..I was, as the players call it, not in very good voice. 1868 DICKENS Lett. (1880) II. 391, I was in wonderful voice last night, but croak a little this morning. 1884 'EDNA LYALL' We Two xxvi, I am afraid my wife is quite out of voice.

transf. 1883 PENNELL-ELMHIRST Cream Leicestersh. 253 Hounds were in full voice, and several foxes in full flight almost immediately.

e. The sound of voices. (In quot., of birds.)

1831 JAMES Phil. Augustus I. ii, The earth was full of flowers, and the woods full of voice.

f. Utterance or expression (of feeling, etc.). Chiefly in phrases, as *to give voice to*, *to find voice in*.

1855 ARNOLD Haworth Churchyard v, Hail to the courage which gave Voice to its creed. 1885 'E. GARRETT' At Any Cost xiv. 255 Tom had been unable to suppress sundry conjectures.., but he had never given them voice. 1906 SINTON Poetry Badenoch Introd. p. xxxv, There was always plenty of hero-worship, which found voice in song.

g. *Phonology*. Sound uttered with vibration or resonance of the vocal chords, as distinguished from BREATH 10.

1842 Penny Cycl. XXII. 429/2 The consonants are conveniently classed into those with and those without voice. 1888 SWEET Eng. Sounds 18 The relations of breath and voice in consonants are mainly determined by their surroundings. Ibid. 89 The intermediate change of voice to whisper is very common.

2. †**a.** The supremacy or upper hand in a struggle. *Obs.*⁻¹

Employed merely for the sake of rime.

a1300 Cursor M. 21694 Quen þai þai faght..And moises held his hand o-loft, To-quils he heild his hend on croice, Ai haid his aun folk þe voice.

b. The right or privilege of speaking or voting in a legislative assembly, or of taking part in, or exercising control or influence over, some particular matter; part or share in the control, government, or deciding of something. Chiefly in phr. *to have* (or †*bear*)..*voice in*. Cf. 10d.

App. not in common use from the end of the 17th c. to the latter part of the 19th.

1433 Rolls of Parlt. IV. 479/2 Not to be made free, ne herde, ne bere no voice in no maner assemble of the seid Comyns. 1503–4 Act 19 Hen. VII, c. 27 §11 No merchaunt ..[shall] bere eny voyce ne have eny sayngs in eny Courte.. wythin oure seid Staple. 1525 in Reg. Mag. Sig. Scot. 1527 (1883) 97 That he be chosin be fremen, and na servandis till have voce amangis maisteris in ony materis. 1581 ALLEN Apologie 38 b, The Parliament is a mere temporal Court, the Bishops them selues hauing voice there no otherwise but as Barons of the Realme. 1666 in J. Bulloch Pynours (1887) 70 The Master of Impost..to have voce and consent of the distribution of the moneyes belonging thervnto. 1697 View Penal Laws 323 Persons having Voice or Vote to such Election. 1780 COWPER Progr. Error 45 Man, thus endued with an elective voice, Must be supplied with objects of his choice. 1873 HELPS Anim. & Mast. v. (1875) 114 If we had more voice in the management of affairs. 1884 Manch. Exam. 28 May 5/2 Some voice Europe will insist upon having in the political disposal of Egypt. 1889 JESSOPP Coming of Friars iv. 185 The parishioners had more voice in the matter than they have now.

†**c.** *to give voice to*, to vote for. *Obs.*

1566 in Fowler Hist. C.C.C. (O.H.S.) 112 Item, he gave voyce to himselfe in the graunte of lease to him selfe, for the which lease he gave no fine at all.

3. a. The expressed opinion, judgement, will, or wish *of* the people, a number of persons, a corporate body, etc., occas. as indicated or shown by the exercise of the suffrage; now freq. in the names of radio stations supposedly representing national or local opinion. Cf. 10.

In some instances not clearly distinct from 4.

1390 GOWER Conf. Prol. I. 7 The world is changed overal, ..And that I take to record Of every lond for his partie The comun vois, which may noght lie. c1412 HOCCLEVE De Reg. Princ. 2886 For peples vois is goddes voys, men seyne. c1470 HENRY Wallace VI. 909 With the great seill, and woice off hys parliament. 1528 in 10th Rep. Hist. MSS. Comm. App. IV. 426 [Order made] by the consent of Mr. Recordar, and the ballyffes with the holl voyce of the town then being present. a1548 HALL Chron., Hen. V, 62 The whole voice of the commons was to yelde, yeld, rather then starue. 1613 SHAKS. Hen. VIII, II. ii. 88 A President..in committing freely Your scruple to the voyce of Christendome. 1651 HOBBES Leviath. I. xvi. 82 The voyce of the greater number, must be considered as the voyce of them all. 1653 W. RAMESEY Astrol. Restored To Rdr. 3 Let no man..be so weak as..[to] conclude ought against it either by Tradition or the common Voice of the World. 1711 SWIFT Cond. Allies 78 It is the Folly of too many, to mistake the Eccho of a London Coffee-house for the Voice of the Kingdom. 1775 W. H. DRAYTON in R. W. Gibbes Doc. Hist. Amer. Revol. (1855) I. 181 These men..have practised every art, fraud, and misrepresentation, to raise in this Province an opposition to the voice of America. 1780 Mirror No. 77 Before the trial of an atrocious criminal, the unanimous voice of the Public is, that he should be led out to punishment. 1837 CARLYLE Fr. Rev. I. IV. i, It is the voice of all France, the Sound that rises. 1849 MACAULAY Hist. Eng. ii. I. 167 Recalled by the voice of both the contending factions, he was the very man to arbitrate between them. 1877 TENNYSON Harold II. ii, I will be king of England by the laws, The choice, and voice of England. 1925 Country Gentleman 22 Aug. 14/1 If you tune in on WSB any evening at 8 or 10:45, you hear 'The voice of the South'—the Atlanta Journal. 1932 G. B. SHAW Platform & Pulpit (1962) 246 Mussolini is the most responsible ruler in Europe because he gives his orders with his own voice and not through an imaginary megaphone called 'The Voice of the Italian People'. Mr MacDonald's voice is a National Voice. 1942 N.Y. Times 9 Oct. 19/1 With all the short-wave stations under control of two Federal agencies.., it is expected that 'the Voice of America' will tell more nearly the same story. 1956 B.B.C. Handbk. 1957 132 The violently anti-British station, 'The Voice of the Arabs'. 1959 Listener 24 Sept. 490/2 In war time the Continental European and British colleagues broadcasting from Bush House, London, to Europe, represented not only 'the voice of London' but the true voice of the nations under Hitler's occupation. 1962 E. SNOW Other Side of River (1963) vi. 51 The main building had a hundred large rooms, each with modern bath and each with an all-wave radio set; on mine I heard the Voice of America from Manila and United States Army broadcasts from Tokyo. 1970 D. CAUTE Fanon iv. 51 In 1956 the Voice of Free Algeria came on the air and within twenty days..the entire stock of radio sets was sold out. 1982 T. KENEALLY Schindler's Ark xxxvii. 397 The radio technicians..listened with an earphone to the 2 p.m. news, from the Voice of London.

b. Without *of*. Now usually with defining adj., as *general*, *popular*, *public*, prefixed (*b*).

(*a*) 1338 R. BRUNNE Chron. (1810) 17 Hakon, Hernebald sonne, of best he bare þe voice, In stede of Kynges banere he did him bere þe croice. 1599 SHAKS. Hen. V, II. ii. 113 Whatsoeuer cunning fiend it was That wrought vpon thee so preposterously Hath got the voyce in hell for excellence. 1603 B. JONSON Sejanus IV. v, I feare, you wrong him. He has the voyce to be an honest Romane. 1628 EARLE Microcosm. (Arb.) 70 [He] cries Chaucer for his Money aboue all our English Poets, because the voice ha's gone so. 1703 ROWE Ulyss. II. i, So shall the Voice in Ithaca be for you. 1787 WASHINGTON Lett. Writ. 1891 XI. 181 note, Thus stands the matter at present in this State. I think nevertheless the voice is for it.

(*b*) 1588 SHAKS. Tit. A. v. iii. 140 Lucius our Emperour: for well I know, The common voyce do cry it shall be so. 1746 FRANCIS tr. Horace, Epist. II. ii. 150 Much I endure, when writing I would bribe The public Voice. 1749 FIELDING Tom Jones III. vii, The public voice..seldom reaches to a brother or a husband, though it rings in the ears of all the neighbourhood. 1773 MRS. CHAPONE Improv. Mind (1774) II. 212, I believe the general voice will direct you to Hume. 1832 TENNYSON Œnone 82 To me, by common voice Elected umpire, Herè comes to-day. 1849 MACAULAY Hist. Eng. vi. II. 123 While the king was thus trying to terrify the lords of articles into submission, the popular voice encouraged them to persist.

†**4. a.** That which is generally or commonly said; general or common talk; rumour or report. *Obs.*

Freq. in the 16th c., often with *common*.

c1400 MAUNDEV. (Roxb.) vii. 27 Þe comoun voice es þare þat þai er þe bernes of Joseph. ? 1462 Paston Lett. II. 107 It is my part to enfourme youre maistirshyp as the comoun voyse is,..for it is half a deth to me to here the generall voyse of the pepyll, whiche dayli encreassyth. 1523 LD. BERNERS Froiss. I. ccclxxxiv. 651 In this meane tyme voyce and bruyte ranne through London, howe these vnhappy people were lykely to sle the kynge [etc.]. a1568 Satir. Poems Reform. xlvii. 12 Grit foulis ȝe were with fallowis to defeme hir, Havand na causs bot commoun voce and sklander. 1577 F. de L'isle's Legendarie K viij, The voyce went the same time..that there was a letter..sent into Normandy, conteining these wordes. 1607 in Birch Crt. & Times Jas. I (1848) I. 70 All Sunday it was current that the parliament did hold, but now the voice runs otherwise. a1639 WOTTON Let. in Reliq. (1651) 429 Doctour Belcanquel..shall (as the voice goeth) be removed to the Deanrie of Durham. 1652 HOWELL Giraffi's Rev. Naples II. 100 The next day the voice went up and down, that..they intended to introduce Forreign force.

†**b.** A piece of common or general talk; a report or rumour. *Obs.*

1463 in Sc. Acts, Jas. III (1874) XII. 30/1 Þe kingis declaratioun..quhilk..þai hald sufficiant to purge þe said Alexander..of þe said voice and Rumor. 1538 in Ellis Orig. Lett. Ser. I. II. 98 Ther ys a voyce that yt shulde be the Duchys of Myllayn. a1540 BARNES Wks. (1573) 330/1 There runneth a great voyce of mee, that I haue maried a wife. 1619 in Birch Crt. & Times Jas. I (1848) II. 156 There is a voice, that my Lord North sets forth four ships. 1639 WOTTON Lett. (1907) II. 410 We have a new strange voice flying here, that the Prince Palatine is towards a marriage. 1652 HOWELL Giraffi's Rev. Naples II. 100 The sound of this voice went up to the Castle.

†**c.** Fame or renown *of* something. *Obs.*

c1470 HENRY Wallace VIII. 1138 Sum off thaim said, the queyn luffyt Wallace, For the gret woice off his hie nobilnes. 1600 HOLLAND Livy XXVIII. xlvi. 707 His power increased dayly; for that the Frenchmen flocked unto him from all parts, upon the noyse and voyce of his name.

5. *Gram.* The form of a verb by which the relation of the subject to the action implied is indicated; one or other of the modes of inflecting or varying a verb according to the distinctions of *active*, *passive*, or *middle*.

In quot. 1591 used instead of 'person'.

1382 WYCLIF Prol. 57 A participle of a present tens, either preterit, of actif vois, eithir passif. 1591 PERCIVAL Span. Dict. C 2 By changing *e* of the future of the Indicatiue into *ia*, you make the third voice of the preterimperfect tense of the Subiunctiue. 1612 BRINSLEY Pos. Parts (1615) 20 b, Giue the terminations of the first Persons of the Actiue voice alone. a1653 GOUGE Comm. Heb. vi. 1 The word φερώμεθα, translated 'Let us go on', is of the passive voice. 1678 [see PASSIVE *a.* 3]. 1706 J. STEVENS Sp. Dict., Sp. Gram. 15 Participle of the Present Tense and Active Voice. 1765– [see ACTIVE *a.* 3]. 1772 A. ADAM Gram. (1793) 20 Voice expresses the different circumstances in which we consider an object, whether as acting, or being acted upon. 1841 LATHAM Eng. Lang. 12 The characteristic..of..the Scandinavian languages is the possession of a Passive Form, or a Passive Voice, ending in *st*. 1858 C. P. MASON Eng. Gram. §180 By means either of a verb in the active voice, or of a verb in the passive voice. 1871 [see MIDDLE *a.* 4a].

II. 6. In limited sense: The sounds naturally made by a single person or animal in speech or other form of vocal utterance; these sounds regarded as characteristic of the person and as distinguishing him from another or others; also freq., the individual organic means or capacity of producing such sounds.

a. In usages where this sound is taken to represent the person or being who utters it, or is regarded apart from the utterer. Freq. with verbs of saying, introducing the words uttered.

c1290 St. Francis 54 in S. Eng. Leg. I. 55 Þo spac a voiz þare-inne [the cross] wel Mildeliche and solte, And seide, 'Fraunceys, go þe forth' [etc.]. 1297 R. GLOUC. (Rolls) 5750 A voys sede as hym þoȝte þes wordes..as he vel adoun. c1330 R. BRUNNE Chron. Wace (Rolls) 16633 Til þe kyng Alayn he spak, And teld hym what þe vois had seyd. 1377 LANGL. P. Pl. B. XVIII. 260 A voice loude in þat liȝte to lucifer cryeth. 1423 JAS. I Kingis Q. lxxxiii, And there-with-all apperit vnto me A voce, and said, 'tak hede, man, and behold'. 1470–85 MALORY Arthur XI. vi. 580 He herd a voys that said go hens thow syre Bors. 1526 TINDALE Acts x. 13 And a voyce spake vnto hym from heven: Ryse Peter Kyll and eate. a1548 HALL Chron., Hen. VII, 2 Men commonly reporte that..it was by a heauenly voyce reueled to Cadwalader..that [etc.]. 1594 SHAKS. Rich. III, III. vii. 36 Some..hurld vp their Caps, And some tenne voyces cry'd 'God saue King Richard'. 1611 BIBLE Transl. Pref. ¶2 A voyce forsooth was heard from heauen, saying: Now is poison poured down into the Church, &c. 1637 MILTON Lycidas 132 Return Alpheus, the dread voice is past, That shrunk thy streams. 1667 —— P.L. IV. 167 There had I fixt Mine eyes till now..Had not a voice thus warnd me. 1718 ROWE tr. Lucan I. 462 In secret murmurs thus they sought relief, While no bold voice proclaim'd aloud their grief. 1725 WATTS Logic II. v. §1 Proof of divine Revelation by Visions, Voices, or Miracles. 1794 MRS. RADCLIFFE Myst. Udolpho xxx, 'It is I', replied the voice. 1820 SHELLEY Prometh. Unb. II. i. 191 In the world unknown Sleeps a voice unspoken. 1848 W. K. KELLY tr. L. Blanc's Hist. Ten Y. I. 423 'I second that proposal', exclaimed a voice. 1871 TENNYSON Last Tourn. 756 About his feet A voice clung sobbing till he question'd it, 'What art thou?' and the voice about his feet Sent up an answer, sobbing, 'I am thy fool'.

b. In ordinary use, with *a*, *the*, *this*, etc., or more freq. with possessives.

The Biblical passage illustrated by quot. 1382 has had some echo in recent use.

a1300 Cursor M. 8904 And þan bigan sco for to cri Als wit a voce o propheci. 1303 R. BRUNNE Handl. Synne 7490 As sone as he hadde made þe croyce, Þe bryde flegh furþ, and left hys voys. 1382 WYCLIF Gen. xxvii. 22 The vois forsothe is the voys of Jacob, but the hondis ben the hondis of Esau. 1399 LANGL. Rich. Redeles III. 56 Þan cometh and crieth her owen kynde dame, And þey [the young partridges] ffolwith þe vois at þe ffrist note. c1400 Apol. Loll. 31 Crie, cese not, vphauns þi vois os a trompe. c1470 HENRY Wallace II. 218 Compleyne your woice unto the God abuffe. 1513 DOUGLAS Æneid I. vi. 173 Quhy grantis thou nocht we may joine hand in hand, And for to heir and rendir vocis trew? 1577 GOOGE tr. Heresbach's Husb. 149 Though the Swyne wil roame at the knowen voyce of theyr swyneheard. 1609 DOULAND Ornith. Microl. 5 The sound of a sensible creature is properly called a Voyce, for things without sence haue no Voyce. 1647 COWLEY Mistr., Despair i, Beneath this gloomy shade, By Nature only for my sorrows made I'll spend this voyce in crys. 1697 DRYDEN Virg. Past. x. 111 Now let us rise, for Hoarseness oft invades The Singer's Voice, who sings beneath the Shades. 1726 SWIFT Gulliver II. viii, I admired as much at the voices of him and his men who seemed to me only to whisper. 1791 COWPER Odyss. XII. 214 When with rapid course we had arriv'd Within such distance as a voice may reach. 1820 KEATS Isabella vi, He inwardly did pray For power to speak; but still the ruddy tide Stifled his voice. 1831 JAMES Phil. Augustus I. iii, He felt sure that he had stammered like a schoolboy, and spoken below his voice, like a young squire to an old knight. 1853 M. ARNOLD *Forsaken Merman* 12 Call her once before you go.—Call once yet! In a voice that she will know. 1897 *Allbutt's Syst. Med.* III. 872 The extremities become cool, ..the voice sunk to a whisper, and the countenance Hippocratic.

c. With adjs. denoting the quality or tone (sometimes *spec.* in respect of musical quality or power).

1382 WYCLIF *1 Kings* xviii. 28 Thanne thei crieden with a greet voys. 1398 TREVISA *Barth. De P.R.* XIX. cxxxi. (1495) nn iv b/1 The voyce that is dysposid to songe and melody hath thyse proprytees as Isyder sayth. Voyces he sayth ben smalle, subtyll, thicke, clere, sharpe & shylle. *c* 1400 *Destr. Troy* 12040 Vlixes..declaret hom þe cause with his clere voyc. *c* 1420 LYDG. *Assembly of Gods* 439 And on a rewde maner he salutyd all the rout, With a bold voyse, carpyng wordys stout. 1500–20 DUNBAR *Poems* xlvi. 105 Than sang thay both with vocis lowd and cleir. 1560 BIBLE (Genev.) *Ezek.* xxxiii. 32 A iesting song of one that hathe a pleasant voice. 1598 BARRET *Theor. Warres* 105 To talke modestly, stilly, and with low voices. 1600 SHAKS. *A.Y.L.* II. vii. 161 His bigge manly voice, Turning againe toward childish trebble. *Ibid.* v. iii. 14 The onely prologues to a bad voice. 1623 COCKERAM II, A *Voyce* as strong as if it were the noise of 100 men, stentorian voice. 1637 *Scotch Prayer Bk., Morn. Prayer*, Then shall the Presbyter or Minister begin the Lords prayer with a loud voyce. 1746 FRANCIS tr. *Horace, Epist.* I. viii. 20 And then..with a gentle Voice Instil this Precept at his list'ning Ear. 1762–71 H. WALPOLE *Vertue's Anecd. Paint.* (1786) III. 39 Besides painting [he] had a talent for music and a good voice. 1819 STEPHENS *Shaw's Gen. Zool.* XI. I. 127 White-bellied Goura..: it has a very disagreeable and mournful voice, which is repeatedly uttered. 1846 MRS. A. MARSH *Father Darcy* II. i. 32 'Come here, both of you', says the lady, in a deep, awful voice. 1863 KINGSLEY *Water-Bab.* iii. 102 He..began chatting away in his squeaking voice.

transf. 1635 A. STAFFORD *Fem. Glory* (1869) 3 Whose due Praise the Catholike Church doth at this day solemnely sing, but with a more elevated Voyce.

d. In or after Biblical phraseology, esp. ***the voice of God***. Chiefly in fig. use and freq. = 'the expressed will or desire *of* God, etc.; the divine command, ordinance, or word'.

a 1325 *Prose Ps.* cv. 24 [cvi. 25] And hij..gruched in her tabernacles, and hij ne herd nouȝt þe voice of our Lord. 1390 GOWER *Conf.* III. 174 And there I herde and understod The vois of god with wordes cliere. *c* 1400 *Rule St. Benet* Prol. 70 [= Hebr. iii. 7, 8] If þat ȝe here hys vose þis day, Turn noght ȝoure hertes fro hym oway—Bott tyll hys voce ȝe tak gude hede. 1563 WINȜET *Wks.* (S.T.S.) II. 7 That ony sentence in the haly Wreit is the voce and mynd of Christe. 1667 MILTON *P.L.* IX. 653 God so commanded, and left that Command Sole Daughter of his voice. 1691 HARTCLIFFE *Virtues* 371 The Voice of Nature is the Voice of God. 1730 THOMSON *Hymn* 11 And oft thy voice in dreadful thunder speaks. 1781 W. HAWKINS *Ode St. Cecilia's Day* i. *Chorus* 63 Music, essence holy, high,..Daughter of the voice of God. 1860 PUSEY *Min. Proph.* 474 They did violence to the majesty of the law, which was the very voice of God. 1870 J. H. NEWMAN *Gram. Assent* II. x. 398 As prayer is the voice of man to God, so Revelation is the voice of God to man.

e. Used in reference to the expression of opinion or protest, or the issuing of a command.

1667 MILTON *P.L.* I. 337 Yet to their Generals Voyce they soon obeyd Innumerable. 1720 *Humourist* 23 All the Time the Business of Scandal was handling, there was not one dissenting Voice to be heard in the whole Assembly. 1796 MORSE *Amer. Geog.* I. 329 A convention..ratified the constitution without a dissenting voice. 1827 SCOTT *Highl. Widow* v, Here I will abide my fate; nor is there in Scotland a voice of power enough to bid me stir from hence, and be obeyed. 1849 MACAULAY *Hist. Eng.* ix. II. 435 When the voice of a single powerful member of the Batavian federation might have averted an event fatal to all the politics of Lewis, no such voice was raised. 1871 FREEMAN *Norm. Conq.* (1876) VI. xviii. 140 The voice..from Exeter was a voice raised on behalf of the House of Godwine.

f. ***to lose the*** (or ***one's***) ***voice***, to be (temporarily) deprived of the power of using the voice for singing or speaking.

1749 LAVINGTON *Enthus. Meth. & Papists* II. (1754) 34 A religious Nun,..famed for Skill in Music and a fine Voice, had her Voice lost by a Hoarseness for ten Years. 1822–7 GOOD *Study Med.* (1829) I. 546 In one case..the voice was merely much weakened;..in the other,..the voice was lost altogether. 1877 ROBERTS *Handbk. Med.* I. 353 Voice is completely lost, and cough becomes aphonic.

7. In phrases. **a.** ***with one*** (†***o***, †***a***) ***voice***, unanimously. †Also Sc. ***in one voice***.

(*a*) *c* 1330 R. BRUNNE *Chron. Wace* (Rolls) 15030 Alle wyþ o voys Songen þey þe Letanie. 1375 BARBOUR *Bruce* XII. 200 Vith ane voce all can thai cry—'Gud king [etc.]. *a* 1400–50 *Alexander* 1000 þan answard him with a voice all his proud princes. 1485 CAXTON *Chas. Gt.* ii. 26 Al wyth one voys gaf to hym laude and honour. *a* 1500 *Lancelot* 3473 With o woys thay cry al, 'sir knycht' [etc.]. 1568 GRAFTON *Chron.* II. 258 They with one minde and voyce gave a determinate aunswere. 1606 SHAKS. *Tr. & Cr.* I. iii. 221 All the Greekish heads, which with one voyce Call Agamemnon Head and Generall. 1669 DRYDEN *Tyrannic Love* v. i, We, with one voice, salute you emperor. 1772 *Junius Lett.* lxviii. (1788) 357 With one voice they all condemn you. 1820 SHELLEY *Prometh. Unb.* I. 651 The nations..cried aloud, As with one voice, Truth, liberty, and love! 1845 M. PATTISON *Ess.* (1889) I. 23 All the members demanded with one voice who it was who was charged with the crime.

(*b*) 1550 *Abst. Protocols Town Clerks Glasgow* (1894) I. 18 We the saidis devyderis..all in ane voce devyidis the said land and tenement as eftir followis. 1569 *Reg. Privy Council Scot.* II. 21 Sic boittis as the Lieutenentis in ane voce sall find gude to hald on the watter. 1604 in *Chron. Perth*, etc. (Maitl. Club) 69 The Session all in one voice finds the said Mr. William's proceedings orderly done.

†**b.** ***at a voice***, in accord or agreement, unanimous. *Obs.*$^{-1}$

1338 R. BRUNNE *Chron.* (1810) I. 144 Bes boþe at a voice, in one ȝour wille be mynde, To help þe Cristen men..Ageyn þe oste paen.

†**c.** ***in my voice***, in my name. *Obs. rare.*

1600 SHAKS. *A.Y.L.* II. iv. 87 But what is, come see, And in my voice most welcome shall you be. 1603 —— *Meas. for M.* I. ii. 185 Implore her, in my voice, that she make friends To the strict deputy.

8. a. The sound *of* prayer, etc.

a 1325 *Prose Ps.* cxxxix. 7 [cxl. 6] Here, Lord, þe voice of my prayere. 1388 WYCLIF *Ps.* vi. 9 [8] The lord hath herd the vois of my wepyng. 1390 GOWER *Conf.* I. 15 The vois of his preiynge, Which herd was to the goddes hihe. 1551 BIBLE *Lev.* v. 1 When a soule hath synned and herde yᵉ voyce of cursing. 1611 BIBLE *Ps.* xxxi. 22 Thou heardest the voice of my supplications when I cryed vnto thee. 1784 COWPER *Task* v. 887 'Tis the voice of song—A loud hosanna sent from all thy works. 1791 —— *Iliad* XVIII. 617 And sweet was heard The voice around of Hymenæal song. 1817 JAS. MILL *Brit. India* II. v. ix. 714 From that very moment, complaint was extinguished; and the voice of praise..occupied the vacant air.

b. *transf.* A sound or sounds produced or emitted by something inanimate, as (*a*) a stream, thunder, the wind, etc., or (*b*) musical instruments.

(*a*) *a* 1325 *Prose Ps.* xcii. 4 [xciii. 3] þe flodes an-heȝed her voice. *Ibid.* 5 [4] Fram þe voices of mani waters. *Ibid.* ciii. 8 [civ. 7] Hij shul douten of þe voice of þy þonder. 1382 WYCLIF *Ps.* xcii[i]. 3 The flodis rereden vp ther vois. Flodis rereden vp ther flowingis; fro the voises of manye watris. 1539 BIBLE (Great) *Ps.* lxxvii. 18 The voyce of thy thonder was hearde rounde aboute. 1611 BIBLE *Isaiah* lxvi. 6 A voice of noyse from the city, a voice from the Temple. 1697 DRYDEN *Virg. Georg.* I. 443 With a roaring sound The rising Rivers float the nether Ground; And Rocks the bellowing Voice of boiling Seas rebound. 1784 COWPER *Task* I. 191 Upon the roar Of distant floods, or on the softer voice Of neighb'ring fountain. 1801 SCOTT *Glenfinlas* lx, The voice of thunder shook the wood. 1807 WORDSW. *Sonn., Thought of a Briton*, Two Voices are there; one is of the sea, One of the mountains; each a mighty Voice. 1853 KANE *Grinnell Exp.* xxvi. (1856) 211 The voices of the ice..are at this moment dinning in my ear.

(*b*) 1535 COVERDALE *2 Chron.* v. 13 Whan the voyce arose from yᵉ trompettes, cymbales and other instrumentes of musick. 1551 BIBLE *Exod.* xix. 16 The voyce of yᵉ horne waxed exceadynge lowde. 1606 SHAKS. *Tr. & Cr.* I. iii. 257 Trumpet blow loud, Send thy Brasse voyce through all these lazie Tents. 1607 TOPSELL *Four-f. Beasts* 313 They must bee such as wil reioyce and gather stomacke at the voice of musicke, or trumpets. 1713 ADDISON *Cato* III. iii, O Marcus, I am warm'd; my heart Leaps at the trumpet's voice, and burns for glory. 1820 SHELLEY *Hymn Merc.* lxxvii, The liquid voice Of pipes, that fills the clear air thrillingly. 1825 LONGF. *Sunrise on Hills* ii. 26 The wild horn, whose voice the woodland fills, Was ringing to the merry shout. 1841 WHITTIER *Merrimac* 66 Clearly on the calm air swells The twilight voice of distant bells.

c. In figurative use.

In the second group with reference to conscience or duty.

(*a*) 1382 WYCLIF *Gen.* iv. 10 The vois of the blood of thi brother crieth to me fro the erthe. 1533 GAU *Richt Vay* 104 Ye voce of his blwid cryis..to ye hewine. 1732 POPE *Hor. Sat.* II. ii. 99 Unworthy he, the voice of Fame to hear. 1750 GRAY *Elegy* 43 Can Honour's voice provoke the silent dust? *Ibid.* 91 E'en from the tomb the voice of Nature cries. 1802 MAR. EDGEWORTH *Moral T.* (1816) I. xix. 162 He dreaded that the voice of truth should be heard. 1839 YEOWELL *Anc. Brit. Ch.* ix. (1847) 90 Where the voice of tradition has been strong, unvarying, and continued. 1843 CARLYLE *Past & Pr.* III. ii, Came it never,..like the voice of old Eternities, far-sounding through thy heart of hearts?

(*b*) 1784 COWPER *Task* v. 685 The still small voice is wanted. 1796 BURKE *Corr.* (1844) IV. 389, I advised, that you should obey the voice of what we considered an indispensable duty. 1810 tr. *Mme. Cottin's Chevalier de Versenai* II. 110 That interior voice, that inflexible judge which speaks within us. 1870 J. H. NEWMAN *Gram. Assent* I. v. 104 We are accustomed to speak of conscience as a voice. 1875 JOWETT *Plato* (ed. 2) I. 419 The voice of conscience, too, was heard, reminding the good man that he was not altogether innocent.

d. A call or cry. *rare*$^{-1}$.

1657 S. PURCHAS *Pol. Flying-Ins.* I. v. 12 With two or three loud voyces Ceaseth all their disports,..untill the next morning when by a like voyce they have liberty given them to play.

e. (The utterance of) an invisible guiding or directing spirit (merging with fig. uses as sense 8c). Chiefly *pl.* ***direct voice***: see DIRECT *a.* 7.

1911 G. B. SHAW *Doctor's Dilemma* I. 12 When my patients tell me that theyve made a greater discovery than Harvey, and that they hear voices, I lock them up. 1924 —— *St. Joan* p. xv, Joan must be judged a sane woman in spite of her voices because they never gave her any advice that might not have come to her from her mother wit. 1924 W. HOLTBY *Crowded Street* xxxv. 260 Things happen against our will. Always being driven and we follow—voices. 1956 'C. BLACKSTOCK' *Dewey Death* vii. 166 Do you think, perhaps, I am mad? Will I hear voices? 1973 A. MORICE *Death & Dutiful Daughter* vi. 65, I ought to check up... My voices tell me that all is not..plain sailing there... Still, I may be wrong. 1975 'J. LYMINGTON' *Spider in Bath* ii. 30 A voice come to me in the night... Me Mum used to 'ave voices. Told 'er all sort er things.

†**9. a.** A word or number of words uttered or expressed in speech; a phrase, sentence, or speech; a discourse or report. *Obs.*

13.. *Cursor Mundi* 3806 (Gött.), And oyle he putt apon þat ston, And made to godd a voice [*Cotton* voo (= vow)] anon. *c* 1440 *Alph. Tales* 17 It had bene mor expedient vnto þe þis day for to hafe etyn flessh in þi cell, þan for to hafe made þis voyce of þine abstinence emange so many of þi brethir. 1598 Q. ELIZ. *Plutarch* 130 [The] busy man..go he wyl to Jugis seates, to markets and to portz; Vsing this vois, 'have you no newes to-day?' 1608 *Yorksh. Trag.* I. ii, In thy change, This voice into all places will be hurl'd: Thou and the deuill has deceaved the world. 1781 H. BLAIR in *Sc. Paraphr.* XLIV. iii, 'Tis finish'd, was his latest voice.

†**b.** An articulate sound; a vocable, term, or word. *Obs.*

1526 *Pilgr. Perf.* (W. de W. 1531) 291 Some coude not saye so moche, but onely expresse suche voyces, that be not in vse to signyfye ony thynge. 1542 UDALL *Erasm. Apoph.* 164 b, The Greke voice κλεὶς signifieth bothe a keye..and also the canell bone. 1586 FERNE *Blaz. Gentrie* 4 A gentleman or a nobleman..(for I do wittingly confound these voices). 1614 RALEIGH *Hist. World* I. viii. §9 *Cethim* is a voice plurall..and signifieth *percussores*. 1654 JER. TAYLOR *Real Pres.* 129 For as Aquinas said, in all sciences words signifie things, but it is proper to Theologie, that things themselves signified or expressed by voices should also signifie something beyond it. 1697 tr. *Burgersdicius' Logic* I. xxiv. 98 Of Voices.. That we call Articulate which consists of so many Syllables, or Letters.. So that it may be written, as, Man, Animal, &c.

10. a. An expression of opinion, choice, or preference uttered or given by a person; a single vote, esp. one given in the election of a person to some office or position or on a matter coming for decision before a deliberative assembly. In Parliament, etc., *spec.* a vote given with the voice, esp. by like-minded voters in unison; esp. in phr. ***to collect the voices***, to take a vote by noting the relative strength of the calls of *ay* and *no* (cf. *voice vote*, sense 14a below). †***dumb voice*** (see quot. *c* 1618).

Very common from *c* 1540 to *c* 1770.

1380 in Horstm. *Altengl. Leg.* (1881) 150/1 Paschasius gaf his voice in hy To him he wist was les wurthy. 1390 GOWER *Conf.* I. 103 Thus grante I yow myn hole vois. Ches for ous bothen, I you preie. 1444 *Rolls of Parlt.* V. 105/1 Officers have ben chosen at the said Staple, by the voyces of Marchauntz, havyng goodes. 1489 *Ibid.* VI. 432/1 If in the said Eleccions..the Voises be divided and equall for sundry parties, then the Voise of the Maire..to stand and be reputed for two Voices in the same Election. 1523 LD. BERNERS *Froiss.* I. cccxlvi. 547 Than the cardynals all of one acorde assembled togyder, and their voyces rested on sir Robert of Genesue. 1549 THOMAS *Hist. Italie* 79 This maner of geuyng theyr voyces by ballotte is one of the laudablest thynges vsed amongest theim. 1581 PETTIE tr. *Guazzo's Civ. Conv.* II. (1586) 108 b, The new Academikes that were before chosen by priuie voyces. 1606 in Birch *Crt. & Times Jas. I* (1848) I. 62 Upon long debate in the House, and put to the question,..Oxford won it by many voices. *c* 1618 MORYSON *Itin.* (1903) 118 Agayne 24 are by lott selected, who being shutt up in a chamber, may not depart till by dumb voyces, that is by divers little balls, they have chosen eight Protectours. 1691 WOOD *Ath. Oxon.* I. 846 In the year 1626 was a greater Canvas than this, there being then 1078 voices given on all Sides. 1727 POPE, etc. *Art of Sinking* 123 If it should happen, that three and three should be of each side, the president shall have a casting voice. 1776 J. ADAMS *Wks.* (1854) IX. 376 A motion is made, and carried by a majority of one voice. 1802–12 BENTHAM *Ration. Judic. Evid.* (1827) V. 470 *note*, The number of persons..having a voice, as the phrase is, meaning a vote, in any assembly invested with the form of a body corporate. 1844 ERSKINE MAY *Law of Parl.* viii. 179 It must be well understood by members that their opinion is to be collected from their voices in the house, and not by a division; and if their voices and their votes should be at variance, the former will be held more binding than the latter. 1855 J. S. WATSON tr. *Xenophon's Anab.* I. x. §9 *note*, But on the whole, the other interpretation seems to have most voices in favour of it. 1898 *Times* 12 Feb. 9/1 The speaker said he had already collected the voices, and it was now too late for the hon. member to intervene. 1924 [see *voice vote*, sense 14 below]. 1976 S. LLOYD *Mr Speaker, Sir* 179 He then 'collects the voices' by saying, 'As many as are of that opinion say aye: of the contrary noe'.

fig. 1781 COWPER *Conversat.* 663 Though common sense, allowed a casting voice, And free from bias, must approve the choice.

†**b.** ***to put to voices***, to put to the vote. *Obs.*

1585 in *Eng. Hist. Rev.* Jan. (1914) 111 Th' act..being put to voices..past as an acte with consent of the hole howse. 1603 KNOLLES *Hist. Turkes* (1621) 859 After this..matter had been thus..debated on both sides in the Senat, it was at last put to voices. *a* 1604 HANMER *Chron. Irel.* (1633) 123 When Herveie had made an end of his speech, they put it to voyces, and the voyces went on Herveis side.

†**c.** Support or approval in a suit or petition. *Obs. rare.*

1598 SHAKS. *Merry W.* I. iv. 167 There's money for thee; Let mee haue thy voice in my behalfe. 1599 —— *Mids. N.* I. i. 54 In this kind, wanting your fathers voyce The other must be held the worthier. 1611 —— *Cymb.* III. v. 115 Thou should'st neither want my meanes for thy releefe, nor my voyce for thy preferment.

d. A right or power to take part in the control or management of something. Chiefly in the phr. ***to have a voice in***. Cf. 2 b.

1835 MALDEN *Orig. Universities* 169 The appointments to the remaining five [professorships] are of a mixed nature, but the town-council has a voice in all. 1865 J. S. MILL in *Even. Star* 10 July, It was a matter of the utmost importance that they should have a voice in the thing that was to be decided. 1888 *Echo* 21 April (Cassell's), The one thing which the labourer wants is a voice in the management of the workhouse.

11. *Mus.* **a.** The vocal capacity of one person in respect of its employment for musical purposes, esp. in combination with others; a person considered as the possessor of a voice so employed; a singer. Chiefly in pl.

1607 in Nichols *Progr. Jas. I* (1828) II. 107 Sixe cornets and sixe chappell-voyces were seated almost right against them. 1664 PEPYS *Diary* 2 Aug., [He] hath sent for voices and painters and other persons from Italy. *a* 1700 EVELYN *Diary* 16 Nov. 1650, A concert of French music and voices. 1731 in *Penny Cycl.* (1840) XVI. 468/1 An oratorio in

English..composed by Mr. Handel,..to be performed by a great number of voices and instruments. **1840** *Ibid.* 467/2 Dialogues in verse..which he caused to be performed by the most beautiful voices in Rome. **1862** *Chambers' Encycl.* III. 9/2 Another Chorus of hundreds of voices, and eighty harps, which had been assembled and trained for the same occasion.

b. A vocal part in music.

1666–7 PEPYS *Diary* 24 Jan., Mrs. Anne Jones,..who dances well,..and danced with great pleasure;..and then sung many things of three voices. **1706** A. BEDFORD *Temple Mus.* iii. 55 This one Voice or Part is mentioned as the greatest Excellency of the Temple Musick.

12. a. The agency or means by which something specified is expressed, represented, or revealed.

c **1600** SHAKS. *Sonn.* lxix. 3 All toungs (the voice of soules) giue thee that due, Vttring bare truth. **1691** HARTCLIFFE *Virtues* 371 The Consent of Mankind is the Voice of Nature. *a* **1854** H. REED *Lect. Brit. Poets* ii. (1857) 45 Poetry is the voice of imagination. **1867** J. H. NEWMAN in B. Ward *Life* (1912) II. xxvii. 223 Doctrine is the *voice* of a religious body. **1872** MORLEY *Voltaire* (1886) 3 The scientific reason urgently seeks instruments and a voice.

b. Applied to persons.

1597 SHAKS. *2 Hen. IV*, IV. ii. 19 To vs [you were] th' imagine Voyce of Heauen it selfe. **1603** —— *Meas. for M.* II. iv. 61 I (now the voyce of the recorded Law) Pronounce a sentence. **1850** TENNYSON *In Mem.* cxiii, A potent voice of parliament, A pillar steadfast in the storm. **1876** LOWELL in *New Princeton Rev.* March 173 This no doubt is one of the chief praises of Gray, as of other poets, that he is the voice of emotions common to all mankind. **1903** *Q. Rev.* April 602 They met with no contradiction from Lord Cranborne, the present voice of the Foreign Office in the House of Commons.

III. *attrib.* and *Comb.* **13. a.** Comb., chiefly objective, as *voice-breaking*, *-producer*, *-production*, *-training* sbs.; *voice-crazing*, *-feigning*, *-ordering*; *voice-like*; *voice-activated*, *-matched*, *-operated* adjs.

c **1440** *Jacob's Well* 295 To stodye more in voys-brekyng in cherche þan in deuoute syngynge. *a* **1593** MARLOWE *Ovid's Elegies* II. vi. 23 No such voice-feigning bird was on the ground. **1593** NASHE *Christ's T.* Wks. (Grosart) IV. 249 With reiterated solicitings, and prostrate voyce-crazing vehemencie. **1598** SYLVESTER *Du Bartas* II. ii. II. *Babylon* 575 David's the next, who, with the melody Of voyce-matcht fingers, draws sphear's harmony. *Ibid.* IV. *Columns* 715 All these Harps and Lutes..Plac't round about her, prove in every part This is the noble, sweet, Voyce-ord'ring Art. **1842** FABER *Styrian Lake* 71 And the chattering voicelike sounds that came On the breath of the tempest swelling. **1889** G. B. SHAW in *Star* 13 Dec. 2/4 Teacher of voice production. **1895–6** *Cal. Univ. Nebraska* 110 The development of the voice-producing muscles. **1896** *Godey's Mag.* Feb. 165/2 We have methods of voice-training to overcome this. **1897** *Allbutt's Syst. Med.* IV. 791 The patient must be instructed in the proper method of voice-production. **1931** H. NICOLSON *Diary* 6 May (1966) 73 He told me that Joseph Chamberlain was the best voice-producer he had ever heard. **1937** *Bell Telephone Q.* Apr. 113 This voice operated gain adjusting device operates on the speech coming into the control office to iron out the differences between loud voices and weak ones. **1972** *Computers & Humanities* VII. 50 Another hardware development used in teaching languages with computers is ..a highly sophisticated (and rather expensive) tape recorder... It features the ability to stop a tape automatically for learner control decisions, voice-activated starting and stopping of recording, and automatic replay after each exercise. **1976** K. BENTON *Single Monstrous Act* i. 11, I want Clancy's room bugged. Use a voice-operated mike. **1983** *Listener* 11 Aug. 33/2 It can't be long before voice-activated equipment enters the modern home, making remote controls a thing of the past.

b. Simple attrib., as *voice-accompaniment*, *-gesture*, *-pitch*, *-quality*, *-range*, *-stammer*, *tune*, etc. Also in sense 1 g, as *voice-glide*, *sound*, *stop*, etc.

(*a*) **1842** *Penny Cycl.* XXII. 431/2 Voice stammer is of two kinds. **1876** LIDDON in J. O. Johnston *Life* (1904) 211 The voice-accompaniment was beautiful. **1879** WHITNEY *Sanskrit Gram.* 369 The utterances which may be classed as interjections are..in part voice-gestures, in part onomatopœias. **1897** MARY KINGSLEY *W. Africa* 181 In all cases the tunes are only voice tunes, not for instrumental performance. **1932** D. JONES *Outl. Eng. Phonetics* (ed. 3) vi. 23 Some sounds are more sonorous than others, that is to say they carry better or can be heard at a greater distance, when pronounced with the same length, stress, and voice-pitch. *Ibid.* xxxi. 282 When there is more than one stressed syllable, the fall of the last stressed syllable generally begins at a pitch near to that of the initial unstressed syllables, and falls to the lower limit of the voice-range. **1946** K. L. PIKE *Intonation Amer. Eng.* iv. 100 These characteristics—relaxed vocal cords, open throat..—are the goals of the trainer of voices... Voice quality..is comprised of such characteristics plus some..other differences. **1964** J. C. CATFORD in D. Abercrombie et al. *Daniel Jones* 29 Phoneticians should be able to classify 'voice-qualities' and other phonatory activities in as systematic a way as they classify supralaryngeal articulation. **1977** *Early Mus.* Oct. 492/2 It is actually a difficult piece, requiring..voice-ranges quite different from our standard choral division into soprano, alto, tenor, bass. **1977** P. STREVENS *New Orientations Teaching of Eng.* xi. 144 Range of voice pitch, voice quality, and several more dimensions.

(*b*) **1888** SWEET *Eng. Sounds* 21 In North Welsh all long high vowels are followed by an obscure voice-glide. **1890** —— *Primer Spoken Eng.* 1 In the formation of voice sounds, such as *aa* in 'father'. *Ibid.* 9 Initial voice stops..have hardly any vocality in the stop itself.

14. a. Special combs., as †**voice-asker**, one who asks for the opinion of others; **voice-box**, (*a*) the larynx; (*b*) = *speak-box* s.v. SPEAK *v.* 36; **voice channel** *Telecommunications*, a channel with a bandwidth sufficiently great to accommodate speech; **voice coil** = *speech coil* s.v. SPEECH *sb.* 13; also, a similar coil with the converse function in a moving-coil microphone; **voice-figure**, a figure or graphic representation of a vocal sound; **voice frequency**, a frequency within the range required for the transmission of speech (commonly taken as 200 or 300 Hz to 3000 Hz or higher); usu. *attrib.*; **voice leading** *U.S.*, = *part-writing* s.v. PART *sb.* (*adv.*) 29; **voice level**, the volume of a voice measured for recording purposes; **voice-part**, *Mus.*, a part or melody written for the voice, a vocal part; **voice-pipe, -tube**, a pipe or tube for conveying the voice, a speaking tube, esp. as used on ships; **voice radio**, a two-way radio; = TRANSCEIVER; **voice synthesizer**, a synthesizer for producing sounds in imitation of human speech; **voice vote** (orig. *U.S.*), a vote taken by noting the relative strength of the calls of *ay* and *no* (cf. sense 10 above).

1593 BILSON *Govt. Christ's Ch.* xiv. 317 Much lesse did Paul make him [Timothy] *voice-asker, to knowe whether it should please the Presbyters to haue these things done, or no. **1912** A. KEITH *Human Body* i. 16 The windpipe has already been exposed, and is seen issuing from the *voice-box or larynx below the chin. **1971** 'K. ROYCE' *Concrete Boot* i. 18, I rang the bell and a voicebox crackled in my ear. I told him who I was and pushed the door. **1959** *Listener* 18 June 1057/2 Current costs of this means of trans-oceanic telephone communication is about £70 per *voice channel per mile. **1971** E. F. SCHOETERS in B. de Ferranti *Living with Computer* viii. 67 To every terminal must be assigned.. equipment able to transform computer signals into a form suitable for long-distance transmission over what the Post Office calls 'voice channels'. **1934** *Discovery* Oct. 301/2 Goodmans' new '12 Watt' permanent magnet moving coil speaker..has a totally enclosed *voice coil. **1961** G. A. BRIGGS *A to Z in Audio* 126 The moving coil or dynamic microphone has been widely used... With low impedance voice coil windings..a wide frequency response with good sensitivity can be achieved. **1977** *Rolling Stone* 7 Apr. 87/3 (Advt.), With voice-coils wound with hi-temp wire on aluminum heat-sinking formers to handle the power of modern amps without burnout. **1891** MARG. WATTS HUGHES in *Century Mag.* May 37/1 The peculiar forms shown in the illustrations of this article, and which I call *Voice-Figures. **1903** *Daily Chron.* 3 June 5/2 The range and variety of the Voice Figures correspond to the scope of the human voice. **1925** *Telegraph & Telephone Jrnl.* XI. 151/2 *Voice frequency telegraph. 200 to 2,000. **1944** *Electronic Engin.* XVI. 360 The transmitters are keyed by means of voice-frequency tone signals. **1975** R. L. FREEMAN *Telecommunication Transmission Handbk.* viii. 389 In practice voice frequency carrier telegraph techniques handle data rates up to 1200 bps. **1934** WEBSTER, *Voice leading. **1942** [see FAUX-BOURDON]. **1980** *Dædalus* Spring 198 The upward gap of a sixth..has here been masked by voice-leading. **1984** *Listener* 30 Aug. 30/4 With the increasingly frequent appearance of tonal triads and ever more connected voice-leading, something very much akin to the use of commonplace words has been creeping into his music. **1962** A. NISBETT *Technique Sound Studio* 258 **Voice level* is the acoustic volume produced by a voice in the studio. **1981** P. NIESEWAND *Word of Gentleman* xxvi. 180 Will you read a couple of sentences so we can get a voice level. **1600** J. PORY tr. *Leo's Africa* III. 144 Certaine minstrels and singers, which by turnes sometimes vse their instruments and sometimes *voice-musicke. **1776** J. HAWKINS *Hist. Music* I. p. lxxix, Instrumental aids to the *voice-parts. **1869** GORE OUSELEY *Counterp. Canon & Fugue* xv. 111 When the canon is produced simply between two voice-parts, it is called 'two in one'. **1897** SIR A. SULLIVAN in *Strand Mag.* Dec. 654/1 Then the voice parts are written out by the copyist, and the rehearsals begin. **1893** *Daily News* 20 Feb. 5/5 *Voice pipes have, according to this authority, 'failed utterly on board ships'. **1959** C. OGBURN *Marauders* (1960) iv. 132 Tom Senff..had..got hold of a *voice radio. **1962** *Sunday Express* 25 Nov. 3/2 Back in the cockpit, Harvey called George Bell on the voice radio. **1974** G. JENKINS *Bridge of Magpies* ii. 39 I've got a special transceiver—voice radio—laid on. RCA Navy job. [**1939**, **1958** Speech synthesizer: see SYNTHESIZER 2.] **1967** *Electronics* 3 Apr. 266/1 A *voice synthesizer that Fujitsu Ltd. has developed as an audible output for its computers... When 'good morning' is fed into the computer by typewriter, the printed-out response is 'ohayo gozaimasu' and at the same time the robot-sounding voice of the synthesizer says it in Japanese. **1975** *Minicomputer Forum* 333 A voice synthesizer driven by a minicomputer and coupled to a telephone answering device and an automatic calling unit is an economical way of providing online computer services to the general public. **1979** *Personal Computer World* Nov. 58/3 On show will be two new line printers, a voice synthesizer, a P2 Quick printer and the new TRS- 80 Model II. **1985** *Listener* 30 May 23 (Advt.), You won't have to ask the computer for essential information updates. The voice synthesiser will offer them. **1895** *Review of Rev.* Aug. 219 Receiving orders only by *voice-tube transmitted from the deck. **1899** F. T. BULLEN *Way Navy* 91 Electric wires, telephones, voice tubes, and engines of every sort. **1924** E. W. HUGHES *Man. Amer. Parl. Law* x. 241 If the voices and vote on division be at variance, do not agree, the *voice vote will bind. **1955** H. W. DONAHUE *How to manage your Meeting* v. 217 In the *voice vote* all those in favor of the motion say *aye* and those opposed say *no*. This is the method usually used in deliberative assemblies. **1976** H. WILSON *Governance of Britain* iii. 55 Perhaps after suggesting a formula which appears to command assent, the prime minister asks 'Cabinet agree?'—technically a voice vote, sometimes just a murmur.

b. voice-over, narration spoken by an unseen narrator on a film or television broadcast; also, the unseen person whose voice is heard; also *attrib.*

1947 H. C. GIPSON *Films in Business & Industry* 284 *Voice-over*, narration-type recording as opposed to live sound. **1964** *Listener* 16 Apr. 629/1 The BBC..trying to find a way of avoiding naturalistic dialogue by the use of images with 'voice over' narration. **1964** *Punch* 21 Oct. 594/1 How would you like to do some voice-overs? **1966** G. N. LEECH *Eng. in Advertising* iv. 37 In the scripts, the speaker of commentaries is variously designated 'commentator', 'announcer' and 'voice over'. **1968** *Listener* 19 Sept. 379/2 In slow motion she loped muzzily through sylvan glades, and it was a matter of judgment whether the voice-over announcer would come on to plug the sexual properties of petrol, hand lotion or tooth-paste. **1974** K. MILLETT *Flying* II. 225 What I'm trying to do is to supply the voiceover for the pictures I make. **1983** *Daily Tel.* 18 Aug. 13/1 The minister gives up the cloth and takes off..to earn modest fame as a voice-over for TV commercials. **1984** *Daily Mail* 17 May 3/1 His [*sc.* Prince Andrew's] recorded voiceover will be heard by a total of around 300,000 spectators and a TV audience of millions.

voice (vɔɪs), *v.* Also 5 voyse, voise, 6–7 voyce, 7 *Sc.* woyce. [f. prec.]

I. *trans.* **1.** In passive: To be commonly said or stated; to be spoken of generally or publicly; to be reported, rumoured, or bruited *abroad*. ? *Obs.*

a. With *for*, *as*, *to be*, or simple complement.

1453 *Paston Lett.* Suppl. (1901) 49 Johane, the wyfe of Robert Iclyngham, chapman, quich ys voysed for a mysse governyd woman. **1626** in Birch *Crt. & Times Chas. I* (1848) I. 148 Here is much lamentation for the King of Denmark, whose disaster is voiced by all to be exceeding great. **1638** MAYNE *Lucian* (1664) 206 Nor are they..to be pointed at by passengers, and voiced the most Valiant among equalls. **1659** HEYLIN *Certamen Epist.* 33 A Book of mine called Respondit Petrus..was publiquely voyced abroad, to have been publiquely burnt in London. **1698** FRYER *Acc. E. India & P.* 63 About the House was a delicate Garden, voiced to be the pleasantest in India. **1810** SCOTT *Lady of L.* II. xxv, Not long should Roderick Dhu's renown Be foremost voiced by mountain fame. **1822** —— *Nigel* xxix, Your father was voiced generally as..one of the bravest men of Scotland.

†**b.** In impersonal use, *it is voiced*. Usually introduced by *as*, or const. *that*, *how*. *Obs.*

(*a*) **1458** *Paston Lett.* I. 425 The King's safe conduct is not holden but broken, as it is voiced here. **1475** *Bk. Noblesse* (Roxb.) 71 Which grevous offence, as it is voised accustumablie,..hathe be more usid under..youre obeisaunce..than in othir straunge regions. **1599** HAKLUYT *Voy.* I. 605 A prayer.. made by her Maiestie, as it was voyced. **1659** RUSHW. *Hist. Coll.* I. 176 Pennington hasted to Oxford where the Parliament was reassembled, but as was voiced, was there concealed till the Parliament was dissolved.

(*b*) **1606** DEKKER *Sev. Sins* II. (Arb.) 20 After it was voyc'd that Monsieur Mendax came to dwell amongst them. **1629** MAXWELL tr. *Herodian* (1635) 95 When it was voyced, how graciously he had spoken to the Senate. *a* **1648** LD. HERBERT *Hen. VIII* (1683) 138 The Duke of Albany..made it to be voiced abroad, that he had no purpose to stir out of France this year. **1652** C. B. STAPYLTON *Herodian* VI. 52 When it was voic'd how Graciously he spoke,..All men were pleas'd.

†**c.** Const. *upon* (a thing or person). *Obs.*

1599 SANDYS *Europæ Spec.* (1632) 5 For one miracle reported to be wrought by the Crucifix, not so few perhaps as an hundred are voiced upon those other Images. **1638** FEATLY *Strict. Lyndom.* II. 54 If the Church groundeth not the canonization of Saints upon the report of miracles voyced on them.

†**d.** In miscellaneous uses. *Obs.*

1600 HOLLAND *Livy* XLV. xxvii. 1219 Giving no credite to the fame that was voiced of the Romans victorie, they cruelly handled certaine Romane souldiours. **1628** HOBBES *Thucyd.* (1822) 13 The causes of the breach of the league publickly voiced, were these. *a* **1648** LD. HERBERT *Hen. VIII* (1683) 473 And now these Articles being published in the neighbourhood, and thence voiced abroad, drew many to them.

†**2.** Similarly in active use: To speak of, state, report, proclaim, etc. *Obs.*

Used (*a*) with or (*b*) without complement. Cf. sense 1.

(*a*) **1597–8** BACON *Ess., Suitors* (Arb.) 46 Secrecie in Sutes is a great meane of obtaining, for voycing them to bee in forwardness may discourage some kinde of suters, but doth quicken and awake others. **1609** DANIEL *Civ. Wars* III. lxxxiii, Many sought to feed The easie creditours of nouelties, By voycing him aliue. **1644** FEATLY *Roma Ruens* 2 So you papists generally, though you are a medly or cento of many hereticks,..yet you voyce your selvs Catholikes. **1672** MARVELL *Reh. Transp.* (1673) II. 53 He voiced my book all over as a most pernicious engine against the whole body of the clergy.

(*b*) **1623** MIDDLETON & ROWLEY *Span. Gipsy* II. ii, He, as report Was bold to voice, retir'd himself to Rhodes. **1628** FORD *Lover's Mel.* II. i, With much joy [she] returned home, and, as report voiced it at Athens, enjoyed her happiness. **1633** —— *Love's Sacr.* II. i, Yet for the friendship 'twixt my lord and you, I have not voic'd your follies.

†**3. a.** To speak much or highly of; to praise or cry *up* (a person or thing). Usually in the passive.

1603 HOLLAND *Plutarch's Mor.* 498 The publike calamities of her countrey..caused her to be well knowne and voiced in the world. **1654** W. JENKYN *Fun. Serm.* Ep. Ded. A ij b, Nothing is more ordinary than for the wicked to voice up dead Ministers for..blessed men, whom in their life-time..they bitterly opposed. **1673** HICKERINGILL *Greg. F. Greyb.* 149 Such was this advancement of Abbot to the Arch-Bishoprick, voic'd and carried up so high by the Cabal of the Puritans.

†**b.** To speak of (one) in a certain way. *Obs.*[−1]

1607 SHAKS. *Timon* IV. iii. 81 Is this th' Athenian Minion, whom the world Voic'd so regardfully?

†4. a. To elect (a person) by voice or vote; to name, nominate, or appoint to an office. Also with *out*. *Obs.*
1606 Bacon *Let. Ld. Salisbury* Several Lett. (1657) 40 Because I have been voiced to it [*sc.* the Solicitor's place], I would be glad it were done. 1623 Bp. Sanderson *Serm.* I. 96 We may well voice him for a magistrate;..that hath the fewest and least [defects]. 1624 Heywood *Gunaik.* iv. 186 Praxaspes begins his oration,..Then told them whom in his [*sc.* Cyrus's] stead they had voyced into the Sacred Empire. *a*1670 Spalding *Troub. Chas. I* (Spalding Cl.) II. 363 He desyrit the moderatour to voice out tuelf of thair bretheren to sit..at thair committee.

†b. With complement. *Obs.*$^{-1}$
1607 Shaks. *Cor.* ii. iii. 242 Say..that Your Minds preoccupy'd..made you against the graine To Voyce him Consull.

†c. To vote for (something). *Obs.*$^{-1}$
1642 Sir E. Dering *Sp. on Relig.* v. 20 They that were present had voyce, they who voyced the Canons, joyned in the decree.

5. a. To speak or utter (a word, etc.); †to sound or pronounce in utterance *like* (something).
1638 Sir T. Herbert *Trav.* (ed. 2) 18 Some words I gather'd from one of the gravest of them, which (being voyced like the Irish) if I give it hardly to be pronounced, you may excuse mee. 1848 Bailey *Festus* (ed. 3) 167 Again that name hath knelled upon mine ear, Though I have never voiced it. 1866 Lowell *Biglow Papers* Ser. ii. Introd., The Americanisms with which we are faulted and which we are in the habit of voicing. 1904 Weyman *Abb. Vlaye* xxiii, He was more than content if the little fool would..voice no cries.
fig. 1875 Lanier *Symphony* 265 And man shall sing thee a true-love song, Voiced in act his whole life long.

†b. To announce (something) *to* a person. *Obs.*
1629 R. Hall in *Bp. Hall's Wks.* (1839) XI. 407 Was it lately voiced to thee from heaven, concerning these wretched animals stabling in France, 'Arise, Pope Urban, kill and eat?'

c. To inform or tell (a person) *that* (etc.).
1898 T. Hardy *Wessex Poems* 134 Till chance had there voiced me That one I loved vainly in nonage Had ceased her to be.

d. = narrate *v.* 1 b.
1961 *Listener* 14 Dec. 1044/2 Scripted by Roger Fulford ..voiced by Andrew Cruickshank in sub-Dimbleby, it recaptured little of the emotion of the Abdication crisis. 1969 *Radio Times* 6 Feb. 31/1 The films we want to see are prized out of Continental cutting rooms by our multi-lingual production team who make translations of the original commentaries. The English versions are then voiced by nationals of each appropriate country.

6. a. To give voice, utterance, or expression to (an emotion, opinion, etc.); to express in words or with the voice; to proclaim openly or publicly.
Common from *c* 1880 in both Eng. and U.S. use.
1607–12 Bacon *Ess.*, *Gt. Place* (Arb.) 286 Rather assume thie right in silence and *de facto*, then voyce it with claimes and Challenges. 1852 *Fraser's Mag.* XLVI. 429 None daring to give utterance to a thought, or to voice the thrill of emotion which even every coward's heart must have felt. 1880 Kinglake *Crimea* VI. ix. 264 The will of a united and resolute people was voiced by our great English journal. 1898 G. W. E. Russell *Coll. & Recoll.* xx. 258 St. Aldegonde..voiced the universal sentiment of his less fortunate fellow-citizens.
refl. 1848 Bailey *Festus* (ed. 3) 203 Again the world-soul voiced itself, and I Drank in the fruitful glories of her words.

b. *poet.* Of birds, the wind, etc.
1822 B. W. Proctor *Misc. Poems, Mids. Madness*, But I may hear..the lost nightingale, Voice her complaint. 1829 Southey *Young Dragon* iv. 57 Wherefore, ye happy Birds, your mirth Are ye in carols voicing? 1881 *Scribner's Mag.* XXI. 516 The windy forest, rousing from its sleep, Voices its heart in hoarse, Titanic roar.
absol. 1868 Tennyson *Lucretius* 101 The bird Makes his heart voice amid the blaze of flowers.

c. Of words, writings, etc.
1850 Blackie *Æschylus* I. 88 Words in vain shall voice my sorrow. 1889 W. M. Thayer *Life A. Lincoln* xxv. 337 These earnest words voice his abiding interest in the loyal army. 1892 *Times* 13 June 6/2 This letter voices the opinion of my church in Ireland.

d. To act as the mouthpiece or spokesman of, to express the opinions of (a body of persons).
1893 *Westm. Gaz.* 8 July 4/3 The leader of the South German Democrats rose to voice the Opposition. 1893 *Programme World's Congress* 3 A series of popular congresses..voiced by the ablest living representatives.

7. a. *poet.* or *rhet.* To endow with voice, or the faculty of speech or song. Cf. voiced *ppl. a.* 1.
*a*1711 Ken *Hymns Evang.* Poet. Wks. 1721 I. 33 The God of Harmony voic'd all their Throats, And sweetly harmoniz'd their various Notes. 1731 A. Hill *Adv. Poets* xvi, Th' Almighty God, who gave the Sun to blaze, Voic'd the Great Poet, for his Maker's Praise. 1853 D. Jerrold *Chron. Clovernook* Wks. VI. 298 Upon the shore are beautiful shells, red-lipped as Venus, and voiced with wondrous singing.

b. *Organ-building.* To give the correct quality of tone to (an organ or organ-pipe). Cf. voicing *vbl. sb.* 4. Also *transf.*
1708 in Willis & Clark *Cambridge* (1886) II. 580 Agreed.. y^t Mr Christopher..do finish the Organ by tuning and voicing it. 1715 *Ibid.* 581, 30 pounds for cleaning and voicing ye Chapel Organ. 1801 Busby *Dict. Mus.*, *To voice*, an expression applied by organ-builders to the regulating the tone of a pipe. *To Voice a Pipe*, is to bring it to its intended tone and power. 1858 J. Baron *Scudamore Organs* 27 Such an organ, if properly voiced and played, will have a clear, ringing, truthful tone. 1881 W. E. Dickson *Pract. Organ-building* ix. 121 The skill, taste, and judgment with which it is finally voiced and regulated. 1933 *Metronome* Mar. 34 Voicing ensembles should be considered entirely differently from voicing separate sax or brass trios.

c. To sound (a musical instrument). *rare*$^{-1}$.
1728 R. North *Mem. Music* (1846) 26 It is said the tibia had four foramina.., by which I guess it was voiced either by the lipps, as a cornett, or els by some reedall.

8. *Phonology.* To utter (a sound) with vibration of the vocal chords. Cf. voiced *ppl. a.* 3. Also, to cause (a sound) to become voiced, and *intr.* for *pass.*
1877 [see voiced *ppl. a.*]. 1888 Sweet *Eng. Sounds* 18 Dutch still voices final *s* in stressless words such as *is* and *was* when a vowel follows. 1959 A. Campbell *OE. Gram.* viii. 163 A system by which a voiceless spirant was voiced if the preceding vowel did not bear the main stress. 1964 *Language* XL. 26 The sibilant affricated in close juncture with /l/ but did not voice.

9. *Mus.* To write the voice-parts for (a piece of music).
1873 Hiles *Dict. Mus. Terms* (ed. 2) 227 To voice, also means, writing the voice parts, regard being had to the nature and capabilities of each kind of voice.

II. *intr.* †10. To use the voice; to cry out, exclaim, make outcry. Also *to voice it*. *Obs.*
1627 W. Sclater *Exp. 2 Thess.* (1629) 225 The siluer-Smith at Ephesus made a head of such good fellowes, voycing it as strongly as their Captaine against the Apostle. 1632 Quarles *Div. Fancies* ii. xxvii, If thou wilt give me David's heart, Ile voyce, Great God, with David; and make David's choyce. 1682 Southerne *Loyal Brother* iii. i, Were those soft slaves of leachery..To head an Army;..How wou'd they voice it o're and o're for Tachmas To come, and blunt the edge of War agen!

†11. a. To vote; to give a vote or votes. *Obs.*
*a*1639 Spottiswood *Hist. Ch. Scot.* vi. (1677) 386 Mr. Thomas and the rest abode in the place, and according as they had voiced, appointed Mr. Patrick Weimes..to be received Minister. 1642 Jer. Taylor *Episc.* §41. 290, I remember also that this place is pretended for the peoples power of voycing in Councells.

†b. With complement. *Obs.*$^{-1}$
1638 *Act Gen. Assembly Ch. Scot.* (1682) 14 In this pretended Assembly..the voicers were threatned to voice *affirmativè*, under no lesse pain nor the wrath of authoritie.

voiced (vɔɪst), *ppl. a.* [f. voice *sb.* and *v.*]
1. Endowed with or possessing a voice; having a voice *like* that of some other person or being.
In some instances perhaps the passive participle.
*a*1600 Montgomerie *Misc. Poems* xxxvii. 10 Sen we ar voced, whairfor suld we refrane, To suffer pain for ony bodies bost? 1642 Denham *Sophy* iv. 34 That's Erythæa, Or some Angell voyc't like her. *a*1821 Keats *Wks.* (1889) II. 15 Where the germs take buoyant root in stormy Air, suck lightning sap, and become voiced dragons. 1861 Ld. Lytton & Fane *Tannhäuser* 11 God to her rescue sends Voiced seraphims.
transf. 1834 Ld. Houghton *Mem. Tour Greece* 138 How were ye voiced, ye Stars,—how cheerily Castor and Pollux spoke to the quivering seaman. 1849 *Tait's Mag.* XVI. 108/2 All was silence and all was solitude, and yet all was voiced and all was full. 1861 Ld. Lytton & Fane *Tannhäuser* 34 Oft have you flooded this fair space with song, Waked these voiced walls, and vocal made yon roof.

b. Having a voice of a specified kind, quality, or tone.
For *clear-*, *faint-*, *gentle-*, *hoarse-*, *hollow-*, *loud-*, *low-*, †*nine-*, †*rank-* (1513), *rough-*, *shrill-*, *soft-*, *sweet-voiced*, etc., see the adjs.
1637 Austin *Hæc Homo* v. 128 Ovid..advised women (who are so angel-like voyced) to learne by musicks rules, to order it. 1884 W. C. Smith *Kildrostan* 61 Never were rills and fountains So merrily voiced as these.

†2. Much or highly spoken of; commended, famed. *Obs.*$^{-1}$
1661 *Life T. Fuller* 14 He continued his pious endeavours of preaching in most of the voyced pulpits of London.

3. *Phonology.* Uttered with voice (or vibration of the vocal chords) as opposed to breath; sonant. Said esp. of certain consonants, as opposed to those which are *voiceless* (see voiceless *a.* 5).
1867 A. M. Bell *Visible Sp.* 67 The initially voiced *v* sinks imperceptibly into its voiceless correspondent *f*—as if the word were written *leavf*. 1876 Douse *Grimm's L.* App. D. 195 The action of the chordae in the production of voiced sounds. 1899 *Allbutt's Syst. Med.* VII. 64 The pronunciation of certain letters is also somewhat indistinct, especially the voiced explosives such as *b*, *d*, *g*.

b. Of breath.
1877 Sweet *Handbk. Phonetics* 74 As stops can only be voiced by driving voiced breath into an air-tight chamber, they cannot be continued for any length of time.

voiceful (ˈvɔɪsfʊl), *a.* Chiefly *poet.* or *rhet.* [f. voice *sb.* + -ful.]
1. Endowed with, or as if with, a voice; having voice or power of utterance; vocal.
*c*1611 Chapman *Iliad* xviii. 459 The Seniors then did beare The voicefull Heralds scepters. 1842 Faber *Styrian Lake*, etc. 100 And for the voiceful Church and poor mute world Doth he not keep his potent Cross unfurled? 1869 Farrar *Fam. Speech* i. 11 As they supposed that Song had been learned by man first, and by all voiceful creatures.
transf. 1842 Faber *Styrian Lake*, etc. 43 Man's voiceful destinies, Like the surge of meeting seas, Are to them but a wild song. 1860 Ruskin *Mod. Paint.* V. ix. ix. §24. 301 Death, not silent or patient, waiting his appointed hour, but voiceful, venomous.

b. Of a stream, the sea, etc.
Also in the sense of 'full of sound or sounds'.
1613–16 W. Browne *Brit. Past.* ii. iii. 70 To take the kinde ayre of a wistfull morne Neere Tauies voycefull streame. 1818 Coleridge *Fancy in Nubibus* 14 That blind Bard, who..Beheld the Iliad and the Odyssee Rise to the swelling of the voiceful sea! 1859 Sala *Gas-light & D.* xxviii. 316 Our green lanes and voiceful woods. 1891 Miss Dowie *Girl in Karp.* 202 The trumpeters..blew long notes of inconsequent music, which the Czeremosz caught in its voiceful waters.

c. Vocal *with*, expressive *of*, something.
(*a*) 1856 Ruskin *Mod. Paint.* III. iv. xiv. §10 The mountains were thus voiceful with perpetual rebuke. 1863 Goulburn *Office H. Comm.* I. 79 A law..every statute of which..is voiceful with condemnation. 1879 Farrar *St. Paul* I. 520 He sailed along shores of which every hill and promontory is voiceful with heroic memories.
(*b*) 1868 *Contemp. Rev.* IX. 76 Blake's poems..run on a sort of parallel of contrast—the one creative, the other voiceful of revolt and self-consciousness.

2. Of or pertaining to the voice; uttered by the voice or voices.
1821 L. Hunt *Indicator* No. 75. (1822) II. 177 He has less of the oracular or voiceful part of his art. 1867 Howells *Ital. Journ.* 62 In clamorous Italy, whose voiceful uproar strikes to the summits of her guardian Alps. 1876 Farrar *Marlb. Serm.* xxxi. 308 Every silent, every voiceful appeal to that which each of us has in him of purest and sweetest.

3. Involving much speech or argument; contentious. *rare*$^{-1}$.
1879 Meredith *Egoist* II. vi. 137 Dr. Middleton assented and entered on the voiceful ground of Greek metres.

Hence ˈ**voicefulness**.
1849 Ruskin *Sev. Lamps* vi. §10. 172 That deep sense of voicefulness..which we feel in walls that have long been washed by the passing waves of humanity.

ˈ**voiceless**, *a.* [f. voice *sb.* + -less.]
1. Having no voice; destitute of the power of utterance; uttering no words or speech; dumb, mute.
In group (*b*) applied to immaterial things.
(*a*) 1535 Coverdale *Acts* viii. 32 As a lambe voycelesse before his sherer so opened he not his mouth. 1817 Shelley *Rev. Islam* x. xii, Peace in the silent streets! save when the cries Of victims to their fiery judgement led, Made pale their voiceless lips. 1849 De Quincey *Eng. Mail-Coach* iii. iv. Wks. 1890 XIII. 325 Clinging to the horns of the altar, voiceless she stood. 1859 Tennyson *Enid* 1115 Mute As creatures voiceless thro' the fault of birth. 1873 Black *Pr. Thule* ii, Lavender did not care to remain among those voiceless monuments of a forgotten past.
absol. 1855 Singleton *Virgil* II. 108 He of the voiceless both a council calls And gains the knowledge of their lives. 1893 Max Pemberton *Iron Pirate* xxiv, The men waited for some seconds silent as the voiceless.
(*b*) 1816 Byron *Monody on Sheridan* 10 Who hath not shared that calm so still and deep, The voiceless thought which would not speak but weep. 1883 *Fortn. Rev.* Dec. 766 It is the public good which is so often powerless and voiceless in presence of the audacity of private wrong. 1891 Farrar *Darkn. & Dawn* liv, The deadly wrong..had excited an indignation..which, though it was voiceless, had made itself felt.

b. Having no voice in the control or management of affairs.
*a*1634 Coke *Inst.* iv. i. (1648) 5 The Proctors of the Clergy ..were voicelesse Assistants;..and having no voices, and so many learned Bishops having voices, their presence is not now holden necessary.

c. Failing, unable, or not attempting, to express one's feelings or opinions; silent, mute. Also *absol.*
1863 J. G. Holland *Lett. to Joneses* ix. (1864) 129 The world will never come to you..you must go to the world or die voiceless. 1884 *Pall Mall G.* 28 June 1/1 The surrender of the voiceless, helpless masses of the population to their Turkish taskmasters. 1890 C. W. R. Cooke *4 Y. in Parl.* 69 By the voiceless I mean the men who have the capacity to speak, and the desire, but have missed their opportunities.

2. Characterized by the absence of sound; in or on which no voice or sound is heard; silent, still.
In this and the two following senses chiefly *poet.* or *rhet.*
1815 Shelley *Alastor* 662 Motionless, As their own voiceless earth and vacant air. 1820 Byron *Juan* iii. lxxxvi, On thy voiceless shore The heroic lay is tuneless now. 1850 S. Dobell *Roman* viii. 27 The sweet content of voiceless woods After the nightingale. 1868 Lockyer *Guillemin's Heavens* (ed. 3) 156 To an inhabitant of the Earth, our light-giver by night would appear..but a silent and voiceless desert.

3. Not expressed or uttered by the voice or in speech; unspoken, unuttered.
1816 Byron *Ch. Har.* iii. xcvii, I live and die unheard, With a most voiceless thought, sheathing it as a sword. 1839 Longf. *Footsteps of Angels* ix, Uttered not, yet comprehended, Is the spirit's voiceless prayer. 1862 T. C. Grattan *Beaten Paths* II. 218 A dead silence followed the fall of the curtain; and I felt..the voiceless verdict of 'damnation'. 1865 C. Stanford *Symb. Christ* xi. (1878) 296 Secret as the voiceless language of the soul.

4. Characterized by, or causing, loss of speech or vocal utterance; speechless.
1818 Byron *Ch. Har.* iv. lxxix, The Niobe of nations! there she stands, Childless and crownless, in her voiceless woe. 1843 *Chambers's Edin. Jrnl.* 47/2 Her lips parted with a voiceless agony. 1879 Tourgee *Fool's Err.* xxxiv. 225 Dumb mouths which spoke of the voiceless agony of death.

5. *Phonology.* Produced or uttered without voice or vocalic tone; surd. Said esp. of certain consonants in opposition to voiced *ppl. a.* 3.
1867 A. M. Bell *Visible Sp.* 67 Where the voiceless correspondent of a vocal consonant is separately heard. 1874 Ellis *E.E. Pronunc.* iv. xi. 1333 The great relations between voiced and voiceless consonants. 1877 Sweet *Handbk. Phonetics* 75 Consonants with voiceless stop and breath off-glide are called 'breath' or 'voiceless' stops.

ˈvoicelessly, *adv.* [f. prec.] In a voiceless manner; without speech or utterance; silently.
1851 MEREDITH *Daphne* lii, Voicelessly the forest Virgin Vanished! **1887** T. HEMPSTEAD in *Harper's Mag.* April 677 The river sliding there, Voicelessly, slowly down. **1890** D. C. MURRAY *J. Vale* xxviii, The engineer, accustomed to rough fare, attacked it cheerfully; but Snelling waved it voicelessly away.

ˈvoicelessness. [f. as prec.] The fact or condition of being voiceless, in various senses.
1843 *Blackw. Mag.* LIV. 74 Dreadful as if distilled from the voicelessness of the graves of a buried world. **1874** ELLIS *E.E. Pronunc.* III. 1126 To indicate voicelessness, prefix (ʻ) to a whispered, or (ʻʻ) to a voiced letter. **1877** *Fraser's Mag.* XV. 38 The utter voicelessness of the common people in any point when the Law or the Senate had spoken.

ˈvoicelet. [f. VOICE *sb.* + -LET.] A little voice.
1844 *Blackw. Mag.* LVI. 209 The voicelets of the Dwarfs sounded only like a light whisper.

ˈvoiceprint. [f. VOICE *sb.* + PRINT *sb.*, after *fingerprint.*] A sonogram of a person's voice. Also *attrib.*
1962 *New Scientist* 14 June 598/2 'Voiceprint' identification may eventually supplement that from fingerprints. **1968** M. GUYBON tr. *Solzhenitsyn's First Circle* xxxiii. 198 This was really something quite new—tracing a criminal by his voice-print. **1973** *Daily Tel.* 5 Apr. 15/3 A Californian appeal court has ruled after years of controversy that voiceprints are acceptable as evidence in criminal cases. **1981** I. ST. JAMES *Balfour Conspiracy* ii. 49 The voice print library is still limited.
Hence **ˈvoiceprinter, voice printer**, an apparatus for producing voiceprints; **ˈvoice-printing** *vbl. sb.*, the production or use of voiceprints.
1962 *Nature* 29 Dec. 1253/1 Voiceprinting uses the spectrographic impressions of the utterances of ten words frequently used in telephone conversations. **1966** *Economist* 20 Aug. 734/2 A young Negro.. has been brought to trial in Los Angeles.. on evidence provided by an electronic device known as a 'voiceprinter'. **1978** S. BRILL *Teamsters* iv. 144 Nine days after the voice printing Faugno disappeared. **1979** J. CROSBY *Party of Year* (1980) i. 13 If you'd just state your name again, for the Voice Printer.

voicer (ˈvɔɪsə(r)). [f. VOICE *v.*]
†**1.** *Sc.* One who votes or has the right to do this; a voter. *Obs.*
1638 [see VOICE *v.* 11 b]. **1641** R. BAILLIE *Lett. & Jrnls.* (1841) I. 350 They.. will force the King either to be our agent, and formall voycer to his death, or else doe the world knows not what. **1651** in Cramond *Ann. Banff* (1893) II. 32 He wes.. a voicer in Parliament for that ingagement.
2. *Organ-building.* One who voices the pipes of an organ; esp. a skilled workman whose special task it is to do this.
1879 *Organ Voicing* 12 Touching the manufacture of all pipes, it is of paramount importance to the voicer, that they should be thoroughly well made. **1881** W. E. DICKSON *Pract. Organ-building* ix. 119 Thus completed and cleaned over, the pipes are handed to the voicer. **1889** STAINER in Grove *Dict. Mus.* IV. 335/2 Few are equally good voicers both of reed and flue-pipes.

voicespond (ˈvɔɪspɒnd), *v.* [f. VOICE *sb.* + CORRE)SPOND *v.*] *intr.* To correspond by means of recorded oral messages. So **ˈvoicespondence, ˈvoicespondent**.
1954 *Sun* (Baltimore) 1 Feb. 4/1 A new type of friend-to-friend communication—'voicespondence'—is gaining fans in Europe. To 'voicespond' you have to own.. a wire or tape recorder. *Ibid.*, Some 'voicespondents' collect recordings of famous voices... These they exchange by re-recording them for others. **1960** *Guardian* 9 Nov. 11/1 The amateur tape recording enthusiast.. [may] 'voicespond' and 'tapespond'.. with others at home and abroad. **1973** *Britannica Bk. of Year* (U.S.) 732/3 *Voicespondence*, communication between persons by an exchange of tape-recorded messages; *voicespond*, vb.; *voicesponder*.

voicing (ˈvɔɪsɪŋ), *vbl. sb.* [f. VOICE *v.*]
†**1.** The action, fact, or process of voting by voice; voting; election, nomination, or decision by vote. *Obs.*
1623 SANDERSON *Serm.* I. 94 We must confer our voices.. upon those whom.. we conceive to be the fittest; and the greater the place is.. the greater ought our care in voycing to be. **1649** BP. GUTHRIE *Mem.* (1702) 119 It was not the Custom in Assemblies for any Man.. to interrupt Voicing by Discourses; every one was to answer to the Question, Yea, or Nay, and no more. *a* **1670** SPALDING *Troub. Chas. I* (Spalding Cl.) II. 292 It gois to voiceing, and, be pluralitie of voices, found, no man sould be raisit aganes the countrie.
2. The action or fact of uttering with the voice; the speaking or utterance *of* something; also, †mentioning, speaking about.
?*c* **1615** BACON *Wks.* (1879) I. 493/1 That the very voicing or suspect of the raising of the price of silver.. would make.. a deadness and retention of money. **1631** MABBE *Celestina* VI. 72 Being wounded with that golden shaft, which at the very voycing of your name, had struck her to the heart. **1657** J. WATTS *Vind. Ch. Eng.* 18 The one professeth by their due hearing, and the other by their due voicing (*i.*), Preaching the word of Faith. **1871** EARLE *Philol. Eng. Tongue* xii. 517 Poetry.. makes great efforts to express.. this finest part of the voicing of language. **1878** *Scribner's Mag.* Oct. 896/1 When Bryant's sweet and solemn voicing of nature's meanings and life's mysteries will fail in their music to the ears of men.
3. a. Speech, vocal utterance; enunciation.
1822 B. W. PROCTER *Juan* i, Be silent.., ye ministers Of death and darkness (for your voicing doth Bespeak ye terrible agents). **1860** EMERSON *Cond. Life, Beauty* Wks. (Bohn) II. 430 The clergy have bronchitis.. Macready thought it came of the falsetto of their voicing.
b. With *a* and pl.
1849 M. ARNOLD *New Sirens* 47 Till at evening we descry At a pause of Siren voicings These vext branches and this howling sky. **1873** W. S. MAYO *Never Again* xi. 145 Expound me, then, these mystic voicings.
c. Expression or utterance. *rare.*
1888 *Advance* (Chicago) 29 Nov. 772 How much of all that is best in our modern life had voicing and in some manner organic formulation in this little town.
4. a. *Organ-building.* The operation or process of obtaining the correct quality of tone in an organ-pipe or stop, or of obtaining the same tone in a series of these; the tone so obtained.
1840 *Penny Cycl.* XVII. 2/1 The tone of the pipes.. depending on what is technically called the voiceing. **1879** *Organ Voicing* 28 The only difference in the voicing consists in keeping the mouth a trifle lower. **1889** STAINER in Grove *Dict. Mus.* IV. 335/2 In testing the voicing of an organ-stop.
attrib. **1879** *Organ Voicing* 25 If.. the voicing operations [are] cleanly and correctly done.
b. *Jazz.* The tonal quality of a group of musical instruments in an ensemble; a blend of instrumental sound; harmonization.
1946 MEZZROW & WOLFE *Really Blues* ix. 152 We wrote.. figuring out the right voicing by playing clarinet duets until it sounded good to us. **1949** L. FEATHER *Inside BeBop* i. 6 He was a third horn, blending the guitar with the tenor and trumpet for three-part voicings that produced a sound new to jazz. **1958** S. RACE in P. Gammond *Decca Bk. Jazz* x. 127 A technique of voicing for one clarinet and four saxes. **1977** *Zigzag* Mar. 5/1 What I do now is get a piano player who I really like and show him how the song was written, what kind of voicings, etc.
5. *Phonetics.* The action or process of producing or uttering with voice or sonancy; the change of a sound from unvoiced to voiced.
1874 ELLIS *E.E. Pronunc.* III. 1113 In middle Germany, where the distinctions (p b, t d) are practically unknown,.. recourse is had to what Brücke and M. Bell consider as whispering instead of voicing. **1959** A. CAMPBELL *OE. Gram.* ix. 180 The voicing of medial spirants was followed by the unvoicing of final spirants.

void (vɔɪd), *a.* and *sb.*[1] Forms: 3–7 voyde (5–6 woyde, 6 wyde), 4–7 voide (6 woide); 4–8 voyd (6 voyed, 6–7 *Sc.* woyd), 4– void (5 voied, 6 woid); *Sc.* 6 vode (9 vodd). [a. AF. and OF. *voide* (OF. also *vuide, veude*, etc.; mod.F. *vide*), fem. of *voit, vuit, vuis*, etc.:—pop.L. **vocit-um, -us*, replacing L. *vacuus*. Cf. Pr. *voit, voig*, It. *voto.*]
A. *adj.* **I. 1. a.** Of a see, benefice, etc.: Having no incumbent, holder, or possessor; unoccupied, vacant.
c **1290** *Beket* 594 in *S. Eng. Leg.* I. 123 Þat no bischopriche ne non Abbeie also, þat were voyde with-oute prelat, In þe kingus hond were I-do. *c* **1450** *Contin. Brut* II. 360 Ser Roger Walden, that King Richard had made Archebischop of Caunterbury, he made Bischop of London, for þat time it stode voyde. **1473–5** in *Cal. Proc. Chanc. Q. Eliz.* (1830) II. Pref. 61 They beyng so seased, the chirch fell voyde. **1503–4** *Act 19 Hen. VII*, c. 25 §2 Whensoever.. any of ther Sees to be voyde be eny other ways. **1568** GRAFTON *Chron.* II. 36 The See was voyde fiue yeres, and the goodes of the Church spent to the kinges vse. **1596** DRAYTON *Legends* iv. 705 If some Abbey hapned void to fall, By death of Him that the Superiour was. **1628** BURTON *Anat. Mel.* II. iii. VII. (ed. 3) 324, I know not.. in what Cathedral Church, a fat Prebend fell voide. **1655** FULLER *Ch. Hist.* II. iv. §45 Winchester lay void six, and Sherburn seven years. **1691** WOOD *Ath. Oxon.* II. 684 In the said See, after it had laid void till Nov. 1688, did succeed Dr. Tho. Lamplugh. *a* **1715** BURNET *Own Time* (1766) I. 248 He was removed to Winchester void by Duppa's death. **1785** PALEY *Mor. Philos.* III. I. xx, The advowson of a void turn, by law, cannot be transferred from one patron to another. **1835** *Penny Cycl.* IV. 223/2 If a donative is the second living taken without a dispensation, the first is not made void by the statute. **1848** LYTTON *Harold* III. iii, The chairs of the prelates of London and Canterbury were void.
b. Similarly of secular offices.
1387 TREVISA *Higden* (Rolls) II. 109 Norþhumberlonde was voyde wiþoute kyng eiȝte ȝere. *c* **1435** *Chron. London* (Kingsford, 1905) 43 Hit was knowyn that thurh the deposicion,.. and causes fforseyd,.. the Rewme off Englond was voyde ffor the tyme. *c* **1500** *Melusine* xix. 67 Your fader.. lefte hys landes and possessyons voyde, without lord. **1535** CROMWELL in Merriman *Life & Lett.* (1902) I. 398, I am acerteynyd that the Rowmes of your foure Clarkes are now furnyshyd & non of theym voide. **1560** DAUS tr. *Sleidane's Comm.* 158 b, This office had bene for ever voyde synce the death of the Duke of Bourbon. **1617** MORYSON *Itin.* II. 54 To bee Lord President of Mounster, which place had layen void some few moneths. **1670** WALTON *Lives* II. 123 The Provostship of His Majesties Colledge of Eaton became void by the death of Mr. Thomas Murray. **1708** J. CHAMBERLAYNE *St. Gt. Brit.* I. I. iii. (1710) 6 Seventy Queen's Scholars are.. sent yearly to King's College in Cambridge, as Places become void. **1867** FREEMAN *Norm. Conq.* (1877) I. App. 660 This last was evidently the earldom made void by the death of Ælfhelm.
†**c.** *void money*, money which has accumulated during the vacancy of an office. *Obs.*
1513 *MS. Acc. St. John's Hosp., Canterb.*, Rec. off voyd money at þe payment off Lomas. Rec. off voyd money off þe payment off Phelyp and Jacobe. **1539** *Ibid.*, Rec. of the voyd money vs. ij d.
2. a. Of a seat, saddle, etc.: Having no occupant; in which no one is sitting, lying, etc.; empty.
13.. *Coer de L.* 5079 Ther was a many a voyd sadyl. *a* **1350** *St. Stephen* 286 in Horstm. *Altengl. Leg.* (1881) 31 Þaire graues er both voyd & bare. **14..** *Tundale's Vis.* 2243 Tundale saw.. A sige that was full bryght schynand, But hyt was voyde wen he saw hyt. *c* **1450** *Merlin* iii. 59 At this table was euer a voyde place, that betokeneth the place of Iudas. **1474** CAXTON *Chesse* IV. ii. (1883) 165 He may put hym in the voyde space to fore the phisicyen. **1483** —— *Gold. Leg.* 289/1 Whan her fader & moder sawe her chare come home empty & voide thenne they did do seke their douȝter oueral. **1565** COOPER *Thesaurus, Transtrum vacuum*, a seate voyde or emptie. **1695** SIBBALD *Autobiog.* (1834) 127 She was interred in her father's grave in the isle of Torphichen upon the part of the through stone that was voyd. *a* **1713** ELLWOOD *Autobiog.* (1765) 20, I stept in and sate down on the first void Seat. **1851** MRS. BROWNING *Casa Guidi Wind.* I. 42 Behold, instead, Void at Verona, Juliet's marble trough. **1886** KIPLING *Departm. Ditties*, etc. (1899) 120 'We know the Shrine is void,' they said, 'The Goddess flown'.
†**b.** Of a horse: Having no rider. *Obs. rare.*
1470–85 MALORY *Arthur* IV. viii. 129 Accolon mounted vpon a voyde hors. **1565** COOPER *Thesaurus* s.v. *Inanis, Inanis equus*, a voyde or emptie horse: a leere horse.
c. Of a house or room: Unoccupied; untenanted. Now chiefly *dial.*
1479–81 *Rec. St. Mary at Hill* (1905) 96 A howse at fayster lane, voyd by iij quarters. **1502** ARNOLDE *Chron.* (1811) 127 The same ten[emen]t.. stood wyde without ani tenant many yeres afore. **1603** HARSNET *Pop. Impost.* 10 Happily they slipped into some Noble mans voide house in London. **1610** HOLLAND *Camden's Brit.* (1637) 471, 720. mansions: whereof 224. stood void. **1700** DRYDEN *Cock & Fox* 217 Eu'ry Inn so full, That no void Room in Chamber, or on Ground,.. was to be found. **1866–** in dial. glossaries (Shetland, Shropshire, Worc., Herts., Glouc.).
3. a. Of places: Destitute of occupants or inhabitants; not occupied or frequented by living creatures; deserted, empty.
1338 R. BRUNNE *Chron.* (1810) 192 Tille Acres þei him led, better hele to haue In þey way ilk dele þei fond voide als hethe. *Ibid.* 305 Alle voide was þe place, þe bataile slayn & done all within þat space. **1340** HAMPOLE *Pr. Consc.* 390 Sen þat place in heven bright Was made voyde thurgh þe syn of pride. *c* **1380** *Sir Ferumb.* 3221 Wel two Mile to loke aboute a stryde voide þer nas, þat of þat ilke heþenene route al ful was euery plas. **1422** tr. *Secreta Secret., Priv. Priv.* 129 Otheris sayde that hit was to drede that thay sholde fynde the Cite of grece woyde. **1423** JAS. I *Kingis Q.* clxiv, On the quhele was lytill void space. *a* **1513** FABYAN *Chron.* II. (1811) 25 Ye kyng wt thaduyce of his Barons graunted vnto them a voyde and wast countre. **1535** COVERDALE *1 Macc.* iii. 45 As for Ierusalem, it laye voyde, and was as it had bene a wyldernesse. There wente no man in nor out at it. **1578** TIMME *Calvin on Gen.* 209 That he might know that the world.. should not be a desert and voyde place for ever. **1596** DALRYMPLE tr. *Leslie's Hist. Scot.* I. 184 Finding it [the realm] than voyd in a maner and bair of strang handes to defend it. **1653** JER. TAYLOR *Serm. for Year* (1678) 79 An appetite keen as a Wolf upon the void plains of the North. **1697** DRYDEN *Æneid* IX. 675 Where void spaces on the walls appear, Or thin defence, they pour their forces there. **1813** SCOTT *Rokeby* II. xvii, In the void offices around Rung not a hoof, nor bay'd a hound. **1899** CROCKETT *Kit Kennedy* 197 The scanty pasture-fields were void and empty.
b. Not occupied by buildings or other useful structures; unutilized, vacant.
1442 in Willis & Clark *Cambridge* (1886) I. 387 For cariage of xxxj lodes of lome fro the fundacion of the College.. in to a woyde place. **1473** *Rolls of Parlt.* VI. 90/1 A cotage, and a voide place conteignyng by estimation a Rode. **1519** *Churchw. Acc. St. Giles, Reading* (ed. Nash) 3 A void grownd in the North side of the said mill lane. **1548** *Nottingham Rec.* IV. 93 A tenement late in the tenure of John Alestre and a voide peyce of grownde with a gardeyn. **1611** BIBLE *1 Kings* xxii. 10 The King of Iudah sate.. in a voyd place in the entrance of the gate of Samaria. **1665** G. HAVERS *P. della Valle's Trav. E. India* 50 Near this Castle Gate, in a void place of the street are two pulpits handsomely built of stone. **1687** A. LOVELL tr. *Thevenot's Trav.* II. 72 Hamadan is a very large Town, but contains many void places, Gardens, and even ploughed Fields within it. **1734** tr. *Rollin's Anc. Hist.* (1827) II. 143 In the middle of each square was likewise all void ground. **1759** B. MARTIN *Nat. Hist.* I. 113 There is a great Deal of void Ground, within the Walls [of Winchester]. **1871** FREEMAN *Norm. Conq.* (1876) IV. xviii. 191 Most likely it stood in the void space between the mound, the gateway, and the later Castle.
†**c.** Unproductive, uncultivated. *Obs.*
1398 TREVISA *Barth. De P.R.* XIV. xlviii. (Bodl. MS.), A feelde þat is yered hatte Noualis oþer feelde þat lieþ voide euer þe oþer ȝere to renewe his vertu. **1615** W. LAWSON *Country Housew. Gard.* (1626) 6 Men and cattell (that haue put trees thence, from out of Plaines to void corners) are better then trees.
4. Not occupied by visible contents; containing no matter; empty, unfilled: **a.** Of receptacles, or things of similar form.
1390 GOWER *Conf.* II. 191 We.. With voide handes schul appiere, Touchende oure cure spirital. *c* **1400** MAUNDEV. (1839) v. 53 Ȝif þei weren sepultures, þei scholden not ben voyd with inne. *c* **1440** *Gesta Rom.* lxi. 255 (Harl. MS.), Hit is a woyde tonne, caste oute with sum men fro sum shippe. *c* **1500** *For to serve a Lord* in *Babees Bk.* (1868) 370 Cutte away the nekke in a voyde plate. **1523** LD. BERNERS *Froiss.* I. xviii. 25 All there Cariagis were sette in voyde granges and barnes. *a* **1533** —— *Huon* xlv. 150 Incontynent the cuppe was voyde, and ye wyne vanysshyd away. **1617** MORYSON *Itin.* III. 83 They vse to serue in sower crawt or cabbage vpon a voide circle of carued Iron standing on three feete. **1791** COWPER *Iliad* III. 447 But Venus, foam-sprung Goddess,.. snapp'd short the brace,.. And the void helmet follow'd as he pull'd.
b. In general use. (Freq. of place or space.)
1523 FITZHERB. *Husb.* §36 The small corne lyeth in the holowe and voyde places of the greate beanes. **1598** BARRET *Theor. Warres* III. ii. 82 With their shot bestowed, in the 4 voyde angles or corners. *a* **1639** T. CAREW *Truce in Love entreated* i, For see my heart Is made thy Quiver, where remaines No voyd place for another Dart. *a* **1680** BUTLER

Rem. (1759) I. 88 Nor can endure to fill up a void Place, At a Line's End, with one insipid Phrase. **1697** J. POTTER *Antiq. Greece* I. viii. (1715) 39 The Spaces between.. left void to admit the Light. **1794** HUTTON *Philos. Light*, etc. 49 It therefore passes as freely through a transparent body as through the voidest space. **1796** MORSE *Amer. Geog.* II. 182 There are no void spaces among the basaltes. **1821** SHELLEY *Adonais* xlvii, Dart thy spirit's light Beyond all worlds, until its spacious might Satiate the void circumference. **1865** SWINBURNE *Atalanta* 428 An eagle wrought in gold That.. with void mouth gapes after emptier prey.

Comb. **1857** G. MACDONALD *Poems* 140 The air is as the breath From the lips of void-eyed Death.

†**c.** ***void room***, an unfurnished or unoccupied room serving as an entrance or waiting hall. *Obs.*

1577 B. GOOGE *Heresbach's Husb.* I. (1586) 12 You see a voyd roome before the Kitchin, whiche is an entrie both to the Kitchin.. and to the Oxhouses. **1586** J. HOOKER *Hist. Irel.* in *Holinshed* II. 123/2 Betweene which & the lower end of the house is a void roome seruing for the lower house, and for all sutors.

†**d.** Of paper, etc.: Blank, not written on; containing no writing or lettering. *Obs.*

1551 ASCHAM *Lett.* Wks. 1865 I. II. 286 Because this paper is void, I cannot leave talking with you. **1610** HOLLAND *Camden's Brit.* (1637) 728 A mangled Inscription.. broken heere and there with voide places betweene. **1669** STURMY *Mariner's Mag.* IV. xvii. 202 Keep the left side of your Book void, that you may write all the Passages of the Voyage. **1748** *Anson's Voy.* III. vii. 360 He had every head of enquiry separately wrote down on a sheet of paper, with a void space opposite to it.

e. *spec.* Having the centre empty or not filled in.

1597 MORLEY *Introd. Mus.* Annot., There were in old time foure maners of pricking, one al blacke which they tearmed blacke full, another which we vse now which they called black void. **1704** J. HARRIS *Lex. Techn.* I, *Bastions Void* or *Hollow*, are those that have a Rampart and Parapet ranging only round about their Flanks and Faces, so that a void Space is left toward the Centre.

†**5. a.** Empty-handed; destitute. *Obs.*

c **1374** CHAUCER *Boeth.* II. pr. v. (1868) 50 Yif þou haddest entred in þe paþe of þis lijf a voide wayfaryng man, þan woldest þou synge by-fore þe þeef. **1382** WYCLIF *Mark* xii. 3 The erthe tilieres.. beten him takun, and leften him voyde. *c* **1425** *Found. St. Bartholomew's* (E.E.T.S.) 25 He wolde not go from hym voyde. **1532** MORE *Confut. Barnes* VIII. Wks. 759/1 My sonne.. shall not returne againe to me voyde or emptie. For he shall bring with him the fathers out of Limbus.

†**b.** ***void (of) course***, said of a planet: (see quot. 1679). *Obs.*

c **1374** CHAUCER *Compl. Mars* 114 Now fleeth Venus unto Cylenius tour, With voide cours, for fere of Phebus light. **1679** MOXON *Math. Dict.*, *Void of Course.* A Planet is said to be so, when he is separated from one Planet, and doth not during his being in that Sign, Apply to any other, either by Body or Aspect.

6. †**a.** Of persons, etc.: Empty or destitute of good qualities; worthless. *Obs.*

c **1380** WYCLIF *Wks.* (1880) 36 He þat seiþ to his broþer þat haþ þe holi gost.. þat he is voide & wiþ-oute kunnynge. **1382** —— *2 Peter* i. 8 Thei shulen not ordeyne ȝou voyde, ne with outen fruyt, in the knowinge of oure Lord Jhesu Crist. *c* **1440** *Gesta Rom.* xcii. 421 (Add. MS.), Ye dreme, or ellys ye han fastid to mych, that your hede is voyde. **1563** FOXE *A. & M.* 1346/1 They that do persecute, be voyde and without all truth. **1728** POPE *Dunc.* II. 45 Empty words she gave, and sounding strain, But senseless, lifeless! idol void and vain!

b. Of speech, action, etc.: Ineffective, useless, leading to no result.

1382 WYCLIF *Isaiah* lv. 11 My wrd.. shal not be turned aȝeen voide to me, but shal do what euere thingus I wolde. **1422** tr. *Secreta Secret., Priv. Priv.* 154 In voyde wordis onely is hare memory makyd. *c* **1450** tr. *De Imitatione* I. xx. 23 Wiþdrawe þiself fro voide spekinges & idel circuites. **1513** BRADSHAW *St. Werburge* I. 1453 In certaynte haue I All worldely pleasures,.. and honour, With all voyde busynesse, and cures transytory. *Ibid.* 1809 O gloryous vyrgyn, replete with synguler grace,.. Refusynge voyde pleasures. **1557** *Tottel's Misc.* (Arb.) 145 For all was ioy that I did fele: And of voide wandering I was free. **1597** HOOKER *Eccl. Pol.* v. lx. §5 Despaire I cannot, nor induce my minde to thinke his faith voide. **1605** BACON *Adv. Learn.* I. v. §11 The end ought to be, from both philosophies to separate.. whatsoever is empty and void, and to preserve.. whatsoever is solid and fruitful. **1611** BIBLE *1 Cor.* ix. 15 It were better for me to die, then that any man should make my glorying voyd. **1847** TENNYSON *Princ.* VII. 19 Void was her use, And she as one that climbs a peak to gaze O'er land and main. **1871** 'STONEHENGE' *Brit. Rur. Sports* (ed. 9) III. 629/2 Void end means that neither side can score a cast. *Ibid.* 630/1 A void end shall be included in this provision. **1881** DUFFERIN in Lyall *Life* (1905) II. i. 13 Any serious communication we may make to the Ministers is as void as though it had been confided to the winds.

†**c.** Of material things; Superfluous, waste. *Obs. rare.*

c **1440** *Pallad. on Husb.* VI. 23 This mone is ek for pampinacioun Conuenient: void leves puld to be. **1494-5** *Rec. St. Mary at Hill* (1905) 215 For makyng of j ole in the chirche for voyde water. *c* **1530** H. RHODES *Bk. Nurture* 293 in *Babees Bk.* (1868) 79 Wyth bones & voyd morsels fyll not thy trenchour, my friend, full.

d. Of looks: Vacant. *rare*[−1].

1796 COLERIDGE *Destiny of Nations* 253 Her flushed tumultuous features.. now once more Naked, and void, and fixed.

7. a. Having no legal force; not binding in law; legally null, invalid, or ineffectual.

null and void: see NULL *a.* 1 b.

1433-4 *Rolls of Parlt.* V. 437/2 This thaire assent and grant for to stande in strengthe, and ellus to be as voide and of noe valeure. *c* **1475** *Harl. Contin. Higden* (Rolls) VIII. 511 That parliamente of kynge Ricardus was made voyde & as of noo valoure. **1496** *Rolls of Parlt.* VI. 513/1 An Acte for making voyde of a Statute concerning artificers. **1527** in *Trans. Cumbld. & Westmoreld. Archæol. Soc.* (1914) XIV. 80 This obligacione to be woide and of non effect. **1560** DAUS tr. *Sleidane's Comm.* 106 What soever is there done to be voyde and of none effect. **1592** WEST *1st Pt. Symbol.* §B, Then the said couenant touching the paiment of &c. and the deliuering of the said bond to be cancelled, and either of them shalbe utterly void. **1625** DONNE *Serm. 24 Feb.* (1626) 43 If the Bill were interlinde, or blotted, or dropt, the Bill was voyd. **1651** HOBBES *Leviath.* II. xxi. 111 Covenants, not to defend a mans own body, are voyd. **1672** DRYDEN *Conq. Granada* I. i, The Force us'd on me made that Contract void. **1713** STEELE *Englishm.* No. 41. 265 She immediately made void certain Grants she had made. **1774** JEFFERSON *Autobiog.* App., Wks. 1859 I. 130 The true ground on which we declare these acts void, is, that the British Parliament has no right to exercise authority over us. **1838** THIRLWALL *Greece* II. 46 All statutes which they deemed void, contradictory, or superfluous. **1861** LD. BROUGHAM *Brit. Const.* xiv. 202 The Parliament declared that the same marriage had from the beginning been void. **1879** MᶜCARTHY *Own Times* xviii. II. 35 The election was declared void, and a new writ was issued.

b. In general use: Null, invalid.

1526 *Pilgr. Perf.* (W. de W. 1531) 5 Ceremonyes.. whiche all were euacuate and made voyde by the passyon of our sauyour Jesu Chryst. **1530** RASTELL *Bk. Purgat.* Prol., That repentaunce that he had before shuld be but voyde. **1604** JAS. I *Counterbl. to Tobacco* (Arb.) 102 Of this Argument, both the Proposition and Assumption are false, and so the Conclusion cannot but be voyd of it selfe. *a* **1682** SIR T. BROWNE *Tracts* (1683) 99 This makes void that common conceit and tradition of the Fish called *Faber marinus.* **1746** HOYLE *Games, Quadrille* 36 If there happen to be two Cards of the same sort, and found out before the Deal is ended, the Deal is void, but not otherwise. **1801** STRUTT *Sports & Past.* IV. 225 The cast is void if the ball does not enter any of the holes. **1812** CARY *Dante, Parad.* III. 57 Our vows Were, in some part, neglected and made void.

8. a. Of time: Free from work or occupation; unemployed, idle, leisure. Now *rare.*

c **1450** *Myrr. our Ladye* 23 Therefore though.. a lesson be red but of one alone, yet thinke not that that is a voyde tyme to all the other to do what they wyll. **1538** STARKEY *England* II. i. 161 To haue a commyn place appoyntyd.. wherin they myght at voyd tymys exercyse themselfys. **1551** ROBINSON tr. *More's Utopia* IV. (1895) 142 All the voide time, that is betwene the houres of woorke, slepe, and meate. **1598** R. BERNARD tr. *Terence, Heautontim.* I. i, Haue you so much leasure and voide time from your owne priuate affaires, that [etc.]. **1634** MASSINGER *Very Woman* III. i, I'll chain him in my study, that a void hours I may run o'er the story of his country. **1853** C. BRONTE *Villette* xxiv, That void interval which passes for him so slowly.. teems with events for his friends.

†**b.** Vacant in respect of office; marked by a vacancy or interregnum. *Obs.*

1480 *Waterf. Arch.* in *10th Rep. Hist. MSS. Comm.* App. V. 316 They that be chosen ballyffs one yere, shal not be chosen.. without they have one yere voied betwxt. **1496** *Ibid.* 324 The eldest that have borne the office of Mairaltie shall have the same voide day, if he have noo daye before. **1591** SAVILE *Tacitus, Hist.* II. lxxi. 94 That Valens and Cæcina might obtaine some voide moneths that yeare to be Consuls in. **1614** RALEIGH *Hist. World* II. vi. §8. 329 There can be no void years found betweene Iosua and Othoniel. *Ibid.* xxii. §11. 558 Yet some coniectures there are made, which tend to keepe all euen, without acknowledging any voide time.

†**c.** Of persons: Unemployed. In quot. *fig.*

c **1450** tr. *De Imitatione* III. lix. 137 Nature loueþ idelnes,.. but grace can not be voide ner idel, but gladly takiþ upon him labour & traueile.

†**9.** Lacking, wanting. *Obs.*[−1]

1554-9 *Songs & Ball. Phil. & Mary* (Roxb.) 4 In Chryst all fullness of power and myght dothe dwell; In hyme voyd was nothyng that was nydfull and fytt.

†**10.** Powerless, unable. *Obs.*[−1]

1578 ROYDON in T. Procter *Gorg. Gallery* A ij b, But Sicophantes will neuer cease to swell Though (learnedly) themselues be voyde to write.

11. *Cards.* Of a hand: having no cards in a given suit.

1934 F. D. COURTENAY *System Experts Play* (ed. 3) 17 A void suit at a trump declaration is equivalent to an A. **1958** *Listener* 6 Nov. 753/3 One never lives to enjoy the double, for either dummy or partner will be void and will remove the double. **1972** R. MARKUS *Aces & Places* 25 When West showed void he went into a huddle. **1980** [see sense B. 8 below].

II. Const. *of* (occas. †*from*).

12. a. Devoid of, free from, not tainted with (some bad quality, fault, or defect).

c **1374** CHAUCER *Former Age* 50 The lambish peple, voyd of alle vyce. *c* **1385** —— *L.G.W.* Prol. 167 Thus thise foweles, voide of al malice.. songe alle of oon acorde. *c* **1430** LYDG. *Min. Poems* (Percy Soc.) 11 And Musik had, voyde of alle discord, Boece her clerk, withe hevenly armony. *c* **1470** HENRY *Wallace* VIII. 1624 A ryoll king.. herd off Wallace gouernance.. and off his pruvyt prys, Off honour, trewth, and woid off cowatis. *a* **1529** SKELTON *Calliope* 18 Yet is she fayne, Voyde of disdayn Me to retayne Her seruiture. **1560** DAUS tr. *Sleidane's Comm.* 231 b, They oughte to be free and voyde from anger. **1595** *Locrine* II. ii. 3 We Coblers lead a merie life:.. Void of all enuie and of strife. **1605** EARL STIRLING *Alexandr. Trag.* IV. i, All love a courteous count'nance, voyd of Art. **1617** MORYSON *Itin.* II. 75 The said point could not be thought void of that cunning, wherein the writer excelled. **1718** *Free-thinker* No. 66. 84 Let your Deliberations be void of Animosities. **1815** W. H. IRELAND *Scribbleomania* 260 Our code void of quirks in a Blackstone is seen. **1832** G. R. PORTER *Porcelain & Gl.* xi. 253 A piece of flint glass,.. by no means void of imperfections. **1862** TROLLOPE *Orley F* i, He was a man void of mystery, and not given to secrets.

b. Free from, untouched by, not affected or impaired by (something unpleasant or hurtful).

c **1420** LYDG. *Assembly of Gods* 809 On a camell rydyng, as voyde of all care. **1509** FISHER *Funeral Serm. C'tess Richmond* Wks. (1876) 305 A lyfe voyde of all sorow & encombraunce. **1522** MORE *De quat. Noviss.* Wks. 81/1 So yᵗ neuer any of them had euer in their liues knowen or herd, either themself or any other voyd of those disseases. **1560** DAUS tr. *Sleidane's Comm.* 101 A place myght be assigned for the counsell, voyde of all daunger and suspicion. *c* **1586** C'TESS PEMBROKE *Ps.* LIX. vi, They prate and bable voide of feare. **1607** TOPSELL *Four-f. Beasts* 350 Some would haue him kept in a close, darke and quiet house, voyde from all noise. **1655** MARQ. WORCESTER *Cent. Inv.* iv. 6 Never clogging the memory with several figures for words.. which with ease and void of confusion, are thus speedily.. letter for letter set down. **1697** DRYDEN *Virg. Georg.* I. 585 Next Day, nor only that, but all the Moon,.. Are void of Tempests. *Ibid.* II. 688 My next Desire is, void of Care and Strife, To lead a soft, secure, inglorious Life. **1753** RICHARDSON *Grandison* (1781) III. xxviii. 330, I, sanguine in my hopes, had expressed myself as void of all doubt but you would become a Catholick. **1828** SCOTT *F.M. Perth* xxxiv, Eachin alone had left it [the battle-ground] void of wounds. **1878** MARIE A. BROWN tr. *Runeberg's Nadeschda* III. 37 And void of fear.. She goes to Woldmar.

†**c.** Clear or quit of (a person); vacant in respect of. *Obs.*

a **1548** HALL *Chron., Rich. III*, 48 b, Nowe nothinge was contrariant.. to his pernicious purpose, but that his mancion was not voide of his wife. **1560** DAUS tr. *Sleidane's Comm.* 293 b, In the countrey round about were forces of Spanyardes and Italians. Of whome to be voyde and free, they.. payde thirty thousand.. crownes. **1651** N. BACON *Disc. Govt. Eng.* II. xxiv. 188 The Parliament.. declared the Throne void of Edward the Fourth, and Henry the Sixth King.

13. a. Destitute of, not graced or ennobled by (some virtue or good quality).

c **1400** *Pilgr. Sowle* (Caxton) IV. xxix. (1859) 62 Thou arte veyne, and voyde of al maner of vertue. **1467** *Songs Costume* (Percy Soc.) 56 Ye poope holy prestis full of presomcion,.. voyd of discrecion. **1508** DUNBAR *Flyting* 61, I se the haltane in thy harlotrie,.. Off every vertew woyd. **1553** EDEN *Treat. New Ind.* (Arb.) 24 The inhabitantes are.. vtterly voyde of all godly knowledge. **1555** —— *Decades* (Arb.) 52 O vnthankefull Englande and voyde of honest shame. **1590** SIR J. SMYTH *Disc. Weapons* Ded. 3 They haue been so voide of the orders and exercises of war of their forefathers. **1612** *Two Noble K.* III. i, O thou most perfidious That ever gently lookd; the voydest of honour That eu'r bore gentle Token. **1667** MILTON *P.L.* IX. 1074 Bad Fruit of Knowledge,.. Which leaves us naked thus, of Honour void. **1686** in *Verney Mem.* (1907) II. 410, I am not so void of reson at this age bot that I can refran from doing myself and family any damag by play. **1706** ESTCOURT *Fair Example* V. i, Beauty, tho' void of Virtue, has the Power To make as well the Wise as Fools adore. **1743** BULKELEY & CUMMINS *Voy. S. Seas* 136 But Hunger is void of all Compassion. **1782** MISS BURNEY *Cecilia* VI. iv, She was totally void of judgment or discretion. **1817** JAS. MILL *Brit. India* II. v. viii. 660 Whom he represents as too void of character, to write anything of himself. **1831** MACKINTOSH *Hist. Eng.* II. 44 He was as void of manly as of kingly virtues. **1861** LD. BROUGHAM *Brit. Const.* xiv. 206 A person void of capacity, without any experience.

b. Destitute or deprived of, lacking or wanting (something desirable or natural).

The groups of quotations illustrate different types of context.

(*a*) *c* **1420** LYDG. *Assembly of Gods* 1382 Came thedyr Attropos, voyde of all gladness, Wrappyd in hys shete. **1533** BELLENDEN *Livy* (S.T.S.) I. 298 Þai war vode of all gude esperance. **1567** *Gude & Godlie Ball.* (S.T.S.) 33 Woide of all ioy, but full of painfulnes. **1592** TIMME *Ten Eng. Lepers* K iij, They find that they are utterly void of all helpe. **1612** DRAYTON *Poly-olb.* v. 341 Voyd of all delight, cold, barren, bleake and dry. **1690** CHILD *Disc. Trade* (1698) 14 The people poor, despicable, and voide of commerce. **1697** DRYDEN *Virg. Georg.* IV. 676 He took his way, thro' Forrests void of Light. **1709** BERKELEY *Th. Vision* §90 It would not at first view be altogether void of probability. **1742** YOUNG *Nt. Th.* VII. 643 Life void of joy, Sad prelude of Eternity in pain! **1812** CRABBE *Tales* II. 394 By various shores, he passed, on various seas, Never so happy as when void of ease. **1862** BURTON *Bk. Hunter* (1863) 309 The records of endurance and martyrdom for conscience sake, can never be void of interest.

(*b*) **1422** tr. *Secreta Secret., Priv. Priv.* 240 Ryghtful houre of ettynge is, whan the stomake is purchet and clenset, and voyde of the mette. **1563** B. GOOGE *Eglogs* v. (Arb.) 47 Thy face good Egon [is] voide of blud, thine eies amased stare. **1581** W. FULKE in *Confer.* III. (1584) O iij b, Nay, hee saith plainely, they are not *Expertes corporis*, voyde of body. **1656** STANLEY *Hist. Philos.* v. (1687) 185/2 If matter it self be in it self void of measure, it is necessary that it receive measure from some superiour. **1728** T. SHERIDAN tr. *Persius* v. (1739) 68 A white Shield void of any Figures in it. **1794** R. J. SULIVAN *View Nat.* I. 378 This water, when newly melted, is totally void both of air, and of the aerial acid. **1815** J. SMITH *Panorama Sci. & Art* II. 489 It is colourless and void of smell, but intensely saline and bitter. **1829** *Chapters Phys. Sci.* 124 Leaving 1727 cubic inches void of any material substance. **1859** JEPHSON & REEVE *Brittany* 237 The surface of the water was perfectly void of any ripple.

(*c*) **1432-50** tr. *Higden* (Rolls) III. 339 Philippus, kynge of Macedony, scholde destroye sone the cite if that hit were vacuate and voide of discrete men. **1500-20** DUNBAR *Poems* lxxii. 97 Methocht Compassioun, vode of feiris, Than straik at me with mony ane stound. *a* **1513** FABYAN *Chron.* VII. (1533) II. 8 b/2 To espye when he were voyde of his company, and then to take hym. **1600** J. PORY tr. *Leo's Africa* VIII. 298 He marched through wilde and desert places voide of inhabitants. **1632** LITHGOW *Trav.* x. 505 The Inhabitants being left void of a Gouernour, or solid Patrone.

(*d*) **1513** *Life Henry V* (Kingsford, 1911) 126 Whereby the Englishmen, voide of there requests, returned to there lodges. **1670** G. H. *Hist. Cardinals* III. I. 240 He was depos'd, and declar'd void of the Papacy.

B. *sb.*[1] **1.** †**a.** One who is devoid *of* something. *Obs.*[−1]

1614 SYLVESTER *Bethulia's Rescue* IV. 186 Their immodest flame Fires none but Fools, Frantiks, or Voids of shame.

b. A state or condition devoid *of* something; a lack or want. *rare.*

1786 *Phil. Trans.* LXXVI. 274 On account of the impossibility of making a perfect void of air by means of the pump. 1788 WESLEY *Wks.* (1872) VI. 352 Men in whom pride..supplies the void of sense. 1789 JEFFERSON *Writ.* (1859) II. 559 Nor has the society he has kept been such as to supply the void of education. 1875 JOWETT *Plato* (ed. 2) IV. 273 Space is the void of outward objects.

2. Emptiness, vacancy, vacuity, vacuum.

a 1618 SYLVESTER *Trag. Hen. Gt.* 602 Who, from the Ocean, Motion can recall, Heat from Fire, Void from Air, Order from All. 1781 LOFFT *Eudosia* VI. 349 In perfect void, the medium lost,..All substances with like velocity Descend. 1871 B. TAYLOR *Faust* (1875) II. I. v. 67 Naught shalt thou see in endless void afar. 1878 STEWART & TAIT *Unseen Univ.* iv. §121. 133 But there is also void in things, else they would be jammed together.

fig. 1860 PUSEY *Min. Proph.* 471 It leaves the feeling of void and forsakenness.

3. a. *Arch.* A space left in a wall for a window, or door; the opening of an arch; any unfilled space in a building or structure.

1616 *Extr. Aberdeen Reg.* (1848) II. 341 The said Thomas ..sall build ane voyd hard be the said passage for letting doun the paissis frome the knock. 1723 CHAMBERS tr. *Le Clerc's Treat. Archit.* I. 138 Massive is found over Massive, and Void under Void. 1742 *De Foe's Tour Gt. Brit.* (ed. 3) II. 120 The Thickness of each Pier is not one Third Part of the Void of each Arch. 1844 H. STEPHENS *Bk. Farm* I. 163 A very loose mode of..measuring *voids*, as the openings of doors and windows are termed. 1889 HISSEY *Tour in Phaeton* 124 The windows are both prominent and graceful features in the building, not merely glazed voids.

b. An empty or vacant space; an unoccupied place or opening in something or between things; a vacancy caused by the removal of something.

Examples of the singular with *the* (cf. sense 4) are placed under (*a*). The use is often *fig.*, esp. in the phrase *to fill the void.*

(*a*) 1697 DRYDEN *Æneid* x. 634 From the forbidden space his men retired... He said, and to the void advanced his pace. 1737 [S. BERINGTON] *G. di Lucca's Mem.* (1738) 161 In the middle of this Concave is a golden Sun, hanging in the Void. 1784 COWPER *Task* IV. 209 All the tricks That idleness has ever yet contriv'd To fill the void of an unfurnish'd brain. 1817 MOORE *Lalla R.* Wks. (1910) 415/1 A wide, deep, and wizard glen, So fathomless, so full of gloom, No eye could pierce the void between. 1861 MAINE *Anc. Law* iv. 99 The mind of a Roman lawyer..would instantly fill the void with the ordinances of Nature.

(*b*) 1708 CHAMBERLAYNE *St. Gt. Brit.* II. I. ii. (1710) 353 There is..a Void within for the Soldiers Lodgings. 1712 BLACKMORE *Creation* 84 The Stars..At a vast distance from each other lye, Sever'd by spacious voids of liquid sky. 1822 BYRON *Heaven & Earth* I. iii. 310 Without Him, even eternity would be A void. 1849 JULIUS HARE *Sermons* II. 469 We learn that the courts of heaven are not a bare void, but that..innumerable beings are there. 1882 VINES *Sachs' Bot.* 932 If..a severe frost..destroys half the plants..the voids are again filled up by the dispersion of the seeds.

c. *spec.* An absolutely empty space; a vacuum.

1727 SWIFT *Wonder of Wond.* Wks. 1755 II. II. 53 He is an atomic philosopher, strongly maintaining a void in nature. 1785 REID *Intell. Powers* II. xix. 262 It [*sc.* space] is only an immense, eternal, immoveable, and indestructible void or emptiness. 1834 MRS. SOMERVILLE *Connex. Phys. Sci.* xiv. (1840) 123 It is utterly incomprehensible that the celestial bodies should exert a reciprocal attraction through a void. 1837 WHEWELL *Hist. Induct. Sci.* (1857) I. 33 Whether there was or was not a Void, or place without matter, had already been debated among rival sects of philosophers. 1905 *Times* 31 Aug. 7/4 Does not..the Democritean void..again emerge?

fig. 1732 POPE *Ess. Man* I. 243 On superior pow'rs Were we to press, inferior might on ours: Or in the full creation leave a void. 1868 TENNYSON *Lucretius* 37 It seem'd A void was made in Nature; all her bonds Crack'd.

d. One of the small unoccupied spaces in a heap or mass which is not perfectly solid.

1837 J. T. SMITH tr. *Vicat's Mortars* 87 It is then easy to judge by the quantity of water used, what proportion the voids bear to the whole bulk of the sand. 1868 TENNYSON *Lucretius* 254 The very sides of the grave itself shall pass, Vanishing, atom and void, atom and void, Into the unseen for ever. 1884 *Century Mag.* XXIX. 48 How large we could determine by filling its voids with water and measuring its quantity. 1900 *Engineering Mag.* XIX. 774/1 Strength of Concrete with Different Per Cent. of Voids Filled.

spec. (*a*) A defect in a crystal lattice consisting of a space larger than a single vacancy. (*b*) An interatomic space in any crystal lattice.

(*a*) 1947 *Trans. Amer. Inst. Metallurgical Engineers* CLXXI. 136/2 Supposedly these voids do not equal in volume the sum of lattice-volume change plus the direct zinc transfer. 1952 *Proc. Physical Soc.* B. LXV. 522 It remains now to discuss the generation and removal from the lattice of the large number of vacancies which do not form voids. 1965 J.-I. TAKAMURA in R. W. Cahn *Physical Metallurgy* xiv. 722 In these crystals voids are formed at grain boundaries as a result of large amount of strain. 1974 *Physics Bull.* Dec. 582/3 A nice illustration..was the discovery by Evans of the void lattice in molybdenum, voids of a few tens of Å in radius being ordered on a lattice with a spacing of one or two hundred Å.

(*b*) 1964 WERT & THOMSON *Physics of Solids* ii. 32 The fcc structure has small voids (called interstices) between the atoms. 1982 J. V. SMITH *Geom. & Structural Cryst.* v. 145 (*caption*) Tetrahedral and octahedral voids in (*a*) cubic closest-packing and (*b*) hexagonal closest-packing.

4. a. *spec.* With *the*: The empty expanse of space.

1667 MILTON *P.L.* II. 829 With lonely steps to tread Th' unfounded deep, & through the void immense To search with wandring quest a place foretold. 1697 DRYDEN *Virg. Past.* VI. 51 He sung..How Seas, and Earth, and Air, and active Flame, Fell through the mighty Void. 1697 —— *Æneid* XII. 994 Prone through the void the rocky ruin shoots. 1707 *Curios. in Husb. & Gard* 229 This rich variety of Creatures, that fill the Void, in which the Earth in the Beginning was said to bc. 1774 BEATTIE *Minstr.* II. xxiii, For now no cloud obscures the starry void. 1820 SHELLEY *Liberty* i, The ray Of the remotest sphere of living flame Which paves the void was from behind it flung. 1854 BREWSTER *More Worlds* x. 163 The immense void which lies between our system and the nearest system of the stars. 1871 B. TAYLOR *Faust* (1875) I. iv. 65 The scattered Fragments into the Void we carry.

b. Const. *of* (heaven, etc.).

1667 MILTON *P.L.* II. 438 The void profound Of unessential Night receives him next Wide gaping. 1697 DRYDEN *Virg. Georg.* I. 47 In the Void of Heav'n a Space is free, Betwixt the Scorpion and the Maid, for thee. 1726–46 THOMSON *Seasons, Winter* 576 If Nature's boundless frame Was call'd, late-rising from the void of night, Or sprung eternal from th' Eternal Mind. 1743 FRANCIS tr. *Hor., Odes* I. iii. 38 Thus did the venturous Cretan dare To tempt with impious wings the void of air.

fig. 1709 POPE *Ess. Crit.* 210 Pride, where wit fails,..fills up all the mighty void of sense. 1746 FRANCIS tr. *Horace, Epist.* I. ii. 43 Mere Outside all, to fill the mighty Void Of Life, in Dress and Equipage employ'd. 1795 BURKE *Regic. Peace* i. Wks. 1842 II. 275 To lose ourselves in the infinite void of the conjectural world. 1829 I. TAYLOR *Enthus.* iv. 84 The dark void of infidelity. 1866 GEO. ELIOT *F. Holt* i, To fill up the great void of life with giving small orders to tenants.

5. *fig.* **a.** An unsatisfied feeling or desire.

1779 COWPER *Hymns* i, They have left an aching void, The world can never fill. 1850 TENNYSON *In Mem.* xiii. 6 [Tears] Which weep a loss for ever new, A void where heart on heart reposed. 1899 DOYLE *Duet* (1909) 15/1 You talk about my happiness before I met you,..but what a void there was!

b. A blank in a record.

1866 ROGERS *Agric. & Prices* Introd., They are an attempt to satisfy a total void. 1869 FREEMAN *Norm. Conq.* (1875) III. xiv. 329 A void is left which history cannot fill.

6. A period during which a house or farm is unoccupied or unlet. (Cf. VOID *a.* 2 c.)

1885 *Daily News* 23 Jan. 3/3 For some years it went reasonably well; but with frequent voids and losses of rent. 1905 —— 20 Feb. 3 The [income tax] authorities would only allow 'voids' or 'empties' within the financial year in which they occurred.

7. In the game of skat: The seven, eight, or nine, which have no value in counting.

1891 DIEHL *Skat* 58 By leading the void of the plain suit, you will very likely be enabled to make two tricks in that suit.

8. *Cards.* The absence of any cards in a particular suit in a player's holding.

1933 C. VANDYCK *Contract Contracted* ii. 20 The Short Suits are the Doubletons, Singletons and Voids. 1944 *Times* 17 May 6/3 Provision was made for revaluation after the first round of bidding to count three points for a void. 1980 M. DUMMETT *Twelve Tarock Games* vii. 125 Singleton Kings are usually even better than voids, unless..there is a danger that one of the opponents is void in [that suit].

9. *Med.* An emptying of the bladder.

1980 *Brit. Med. Jrnl.* 29 Mar. 889/2 Residual urine was estimated..by catheterisation after a normal void.

Hence **'voidward** *adv.* (*rare*).

1927 JOYCE *Nightpiece* in *Pomes Penyeach*, As the bleak incense surges, cloud on cloud, voidward from the adoring Waste of souls.

†**void**, $sb.^2$ *Obs.* An abbrev. of VOIDEE, prob. through misunderstanding the spelling *voide.*

1461–83 *Househ. Ord.* (1790) 36 The King never taketh a voyd of comfittes and other spices, but standing. 1587 HOLINSHED *Chron.* III. 934/1 To whome the earle of Sussex in a goodlie spice plate brought a void of spice and comfets. 1616 LANE *Contn. Sqr.'s T.* III. 91 After the void, praeserves in silvern plate Set suche a postscripte to ann antedate, As not a common penn knowes to define.

void (vɔɪd), *v.* Forms: 4–5 voyden, 4–7 voyde (4 woyde, 5 uoyde, voyede), voyd (5 woyd, voyed, 6 *Sc.* woyid); 4, 6 voiden, 4–6 voide, 4– void (5 woid); 4 vewd-, 6 *Sc.* woud. [Partly (1) ad. AF. and OF. *voider, vuider* (OF. also *voidier, vuidier*; mod.F. *vider*, = Pr. *voidar, vojar, vujar*, etc., Cat. *vuydar*, It. *votare*):—pop.L. **vocitare* to make empty: see VOID *a.* Partly (2) an aphetic form of AVOID *v.*]

I. 1. *trans.* To clear (a room, house, place) *of* occupants; to empty or clear (a place, receptacle, etc.) *of* something. †Also const. *from.* Now *arch.*

13.. *K. Alis.* 373 (Linc.), He voidud þeo chaumbre of many vchon. *c* 1380 *Sir Ferumb.* 3131 By þat wern þe feldes alle of þe Sarsyns y-vewdid wel. *c* 1385 CHAUCER *L.G.W.* 2625 *Hypermnestra*, Whan that the house voyded was of alle. *c* 1400 *Beryn* 1951 þere was no thing, þat eny man myȝte se, ..For hanybald had do void it [*sc.* his house] of al thing þat was there. *c* 1482 J. KAY tr. *Caoursin's Siege of Rhodes* ⁋7 Anon with grete dylygence they voyded theyr shippes of the men of werre and of their ordonnances. 15.. *Aberdeen Reg.* (Jam.), To woud the said biging of the gudis. 1578 LYTE *Dodoens* 232 Penny royal..clenseth the Lunges, and voydeth them and the breast from all grosse and thicke humors. 1654 FULLER *Wounded Consc.*, etc. (1867) 187 Bondi..causeth the room to be voided of all company. 1786 *Phil. Trans.* LXXVI. 280 The cavity of the cylinder and globe containing the thermometer was completely voided of air with mercury. 1861 LD. LYTTON & FANE *Tannhäuser* 73 And, voided now Of all his multitudes, the mighty Hall.. laid bare His ghostly galleries to the mournful moon.

b. To rid, to make free or clear, *of* (or †*from*) some quality or condition.

1338 R. BRUNNE *Chron.* (1810) 247 þe barons alle said, ..þe lond þei wild voide of þat herisie. 1375 BARBOUR *Bruce* I. 26 þai suld weill hawe pryss þat..war woydyt off cowardy. 1526 *Pilgr. Perf.* (W. de W. 1531) 79 Excepte it be fyrst voyded from all..elacyon, pryde and contradiccyon. 1545 *Primer* A ij, That our hartes be voyded quyte, From phansy, and fond delighte. 1576 GASCOIGNE *Kenelworth Castle* Wks. 1910 II. 94 Your thrice comming here doth bode thrise happy hope and voides the place from feare. 1641 MILTON *Reform.* II. 74 The Parliament shall void her Upper House of the same annoyances. 1668 HOWE *Bless. Righteous* (1825) 273 Having voided thy mind of what is earthly and carnal. 1861 BERESF. HOPE *Eng. Cathedr. 19th C.* i. 2 It is neither possible nor desireable so wholly to void either nature of the presence of the other.

†**c.** To bereave or deprive *of* life. $Obs.^{-1}$

a 1400–50 *Alexander* 3980 If I be vencust in þe vaile & voidid of my lyfe, Lat all my seggis & soile be to þi-selfe ȝolden.

2. Without const. †**a.** To clear (a table) of dishes, remains of food, etc. after a meal. *Obs.*

a 1400 *Sqr. lowe Degre* 468 Full lowe he set hym on his kne, And voyded his borde full gentely. 1513 *Bk. Keruynge* in *Babees Bk.* (1868) 271 Now this feest is done, voyde ye the table. 1586 WARNER *Alb. Eng.* IV. xxi. (1589) 89 The Traine and table voyded, then he..Directs her by his tongue and teares, vnto his louing heart. 1621 QUARLES *Argalus & P.* III. Wks. (Grosart) III. 273/1 The board was voided, and the Sewer Had now resign'd his office with the Ewer. 1657 THORNLEY tr. *Longus' Daphnis & Chloe* 119 Dinner was done, and the Table voided.

fig. 1638 QUARLES *Hieroglyphikes* xiii. Wks. (Grosart) III. 195/2 Time voids the table, dinner's done.

b. To evacuate (the stomach); to clear or blow (the nose); to clean out (slaughtered animals). Also *refl.* *rare.*

c 1410 *Master of Game* (MS. Digby 182) vi, And whan þei be ful or seeke, þei fedeth hem with gras, as an hounde doth, forto voyed hem. 1422 tr. *Secreta Secret., Priv. Priv.* 240 To kepe kynde hete, and to voyde the stomake, good is hit afor mette sumwhate to walke or ryde. 1535 in W. H. Turner *Select. Rec. Oxford* (1880) 133 The bochers..shall voyd and kyll noe moe ware in the sayd howses. 1594 R. ASHLEY tr. *Loys le Roy* 49 They would neither..spit, nor void their noses into the riuers, but reuerenced them aboue all things. 1876 *Fur, Fin & Feather* Sept. 167 They [*sc.* squirrels] should be voided..and kept several days in cold weather.

†**c.** To make void or empty; to clear or empty (some thing or place) of its contents or occupants. *Obs.*

1506 in *Mem. Hen. VII* (Rolls) 288 A little before..my lord Herberd voided all the King's chamber except lords and officers..which remained there still. 1580 LYLY *Euphues* (Arb.) 227 The chamber being voyded, he brake with him in these tearmes. 1600 HOLLAND *Livy* VII. v. 252 So the roume being voided, and all commaunded to depart farre ynough out of the way, he draweth out his skeine. 1616 *Marlowe's Faustus* III. iv, Good Fredericke see the roomes by voyded straight, His Maiesty is comming to the Hall. 1658 EVELYN *Fr. Gard.* (1675) 4 Thus when your Trench is voided and emptied to the depth which you desire, you shall cast in long dung.

d. To render (a benefice) vacant; to vacate. *Obs.*

1660 R. COKE *Power & Subj.* 217 When any Archbishoprick or Bishoprick shall be voided. 1677 W. MOUNTAGU in *Buccleuch MSS.* (Hist. MSS. Comm.) I. 327 His living..being voided by his own act, though it would have been otherwise if voided by death. *a* 1703 BP. KIDDER in Cassan *Bps. Bath & Wells* II. (1830) 126 After I had entered upon this living, and thereby voided that in Essex.

†**e.** To exhaust (a subject) by discussion or exposition; to deal with exhaustively or thoroughly.

1659 H. THORNDIKE *Epil. Trag. Ch. Eng.* I. xx. 155 Not to insist here, what the respective interests of publick and private persons in the Church are and ought to be, because it is a point that cannot here be voided. 1687 TOWERSON *Baptism* 273 A question which will best be voided by considering the force of those Arguments, which the condemners..have produc'd.

3. To deprive (something) of legal validity; to make legally void or invalid; to annul or cancel.

a 1325 *MS. Rawl. B. 520* fol. 30b, The parties of þulke fins..ope suuche fins to voiden ant for te anenden weren i suffred. *Ibid.*, On suuche manere þe fins..oftesiþes beþ ivoided. 1487 *Rolls of Parlt.* VI. 394/1 That..it be lefull to the said Roger..to enter,..and enjoye all that comprised in the same Lettres Patentes so voided. 1535 CROMWELL in *State Papers Hen. VIII* (1849) VII. 586 [To] desire the Bisshop..to revoke and denounce voyd and frustrate the injust and slaunderous sentence. 1641 H. THORNDIKE *Govt. Churches* 132 In some cases they void excommunication that is grounded upon particular interesse. 1647 DIGGES *Unlawf. Taking Arms* §4. 147 His obstinate refusall voides the Parliament. 1691 LOCKE *Lower. Interest* Wks. 1727 II. 7 Unless you intend to..void Bargains lawfully made. 1762–71 H. WALPOLE *Vertue's Anecd. Paint.* (1786) II. 79 A contract voided by the death of the Prince. 1863 H. COX *Instit.* I. viii. 98 The giving meat and drink, exceeding £5 in value, to electors, shall void an election. 1883 *Ch. Times* 9 Nov. 812/4 On the principles of Roman Canon law, the Papal succession has been voided many times over.

b. To deprive of efficacy, force, or value; to render inoperative or meaningless; to set aside or nullify. Now *rare.*

a 1340 HAMPOLE *Psalter* cvi[i]. 11 þe counsaile of þe heghest þai voidyd [L. *irritaverunt*]. 1396–7 in *Eng. Hist. Rev.* (1907) XXII. 304 For þou þese to [= two] craftis nemlid were michil more nedful in þe elde lawe, þe newe testament hath voydid þese and manie othere. ? 1462 *Paston Lett.* II. 115 That th' effect of the old purpose of the seid Sir Iohn Fastolff schuld not be voided. 1483 CAXTON *G. de la Tour* (1868) 176 Yf one begynne to..talke with you of suche mater, lete hym alone..And thus ye shalle voyde and breke his talkynge. 1513 *Life Hen. V* (Kingsford, 1911) 20 By whose departure the intent of this victorious Kinge was vtterly empesshed and voyded in that Cause. **1533** More *Answ. Poysoned Bk.* Wks. 1057/1 By yᵉ marking of thys one poynt, ye may voyde almost all the craft, with which master .. Frith and Tyndall.. labour to deceiue you. **1597** Hooker *Eccl. Pol.* v. lxii. §12 Baptisme.. is by a fourth sort of men voided for the onely defect of ecclesiasticall authoritie in the Minister. **1655** Stanley *Hist. Philos.* iii. (1687) 105/1 Now tell me if thy adversary Sue thee, and thou art like to be overthrown For want of witnesses, how wilt thou void His suit? **1675** O. Walker, etc. *Paraphr. Hebrews* 3 The former religion of the Law.. voided and annulled by that farr more preeminent of Christ. *a* **1688** W. Clagett *17 Serm.* (1699) 197 They voided the commandments of God, and made his word of none effect. **1742** Young *Nt. Th.* iv. 467 O how is man inlarg'd, Seen thro' this medium [i.e. Redemption].. How voided his vast distance from the skies! **1874** S. Cox *Pilgr. Ps.* iv. 83 We defeat our own hope and void our own prayer.

†**c.** To confute or refute. *Obs.*

1570 Foxe *A. & M.* (ed. 2) II. 926/1 With these and such other like reasons, the Gray Franciscans voyded their Aduersaries. **1630** M. Godwyn tr. *Bp. Hereford's Ann. Eng.* (1675) 184 He by such witty answers voided the accusation of his Adversary, that the Jurors found him not guilty. **1645** Milton *Colast.* 19 After waiting and voiding, hee thinks to void my second Argument. **1699** Bentley *Phal.* xiv. 479 His Design was.. To account for the Low Sicilian Talent, and to void all that Mr. B. had written about it before.

II. †**4.** To send or put (a person) away; to cause or compel to go away from or leave a place; to dismiss or expel. *Obs.*

Freq. const. *out of*, also more rarely *from* or *of* the place. Also (*b*) with advs. as *out* or *aloof*.

(*a*) **13..** *Gosp. Nicodemus* (A.) 285 Pilate gart voyde þame alle þat were within þat house. *c* **1386** Chaucer *Can. Yeom. Prol. & T.* 1136 Voyde youre man and lat hym be ther oute. *c* **1400** Maundev. (1839) xii. 137 He let voyden out of his Chambre alle maner of men. **1418** *E.E. Wills* (1882) 29, Y wille that the same Jonet be vtterliche excluded & voyded fro the forsaide Manere of Staverton. *c* **1450** Capgrave *Life St. Augustine* 11 þe bischop was compelled to voyde hir with swech wordys: Go fro me, woman. **1483** Caxton *G. de la Tour* fj/b, The pryour that was voyded and hydde under the bed. *a* **1539** in *Archaeologia* XLVII. 57 That ye voide out of your house Robert laurence and he nomore to resorte to the same. **1553** Grimalde *Cicero's Offices* iii. (1558) 164 Al hearers being voided out of the place, he commaunded, the yongman shoulde come to hym. **1608** Dekker *Dead Tearme* Wks. (Grosart) IV. 57 Not to keepe any single woman in his house on the Holy-dayes, but the Bailiffe to see them voyded out of the Lordship. **1644** Milton *Areop.* (Arb.) 62 Now the Bishops abrogated and voided out of the Church.. the Episcopall arts begin to bud again.

(*b*) **1430-40** Lydg. *Bochas* viii. xx. (1554) 190 b/1 Let him also voyde out at his gate, Ryotous people. **1553** Brende *Q. Curtius* Q vij, [He] appointed certaine to waite whiles he slept, which shoulde voide al men a loufe, to the entent he should not be disquieted wᵗ any noise. **1575-85** Abp. Sandys *Serm.* xiii. 206 In his pastorall care he visited it [*sc.* the Temple], and in the zeale of God voided them out which did defile it.

†**b.** With double object. *Obs.*

1402 Hoccleve *Let. of Cupid* 468 Voide hem our court, and banyssh hem for euer. **1483** *Presentmts. of Juries* in *Surtees Misc.* (1890) 28 We wyll pᵗ schoy be woydyd the ton [= town]. **1529** Rastell *Pastyme* (1811) 126 He warryd oft agaynst the Danys, but at the last by agrement he voydyd them the West contrey. **1583** Melbancke *Philotimus* A a ij, I knowe one Antiochus well,.. but as for this fellowe, I perceiue he is a counterfeit, and therewith commaunded him to be voided his lodging.

†**c.** To dismiss or remove from a situation or position. *Obs.*

1502 Arnolde *Chron.* (1811) 95 Yf that yeman be from you soo voyded ye shal take awey the lyueri of the said Sherefs. *c* **1515** Barclay *Egloges* iii. (1570) Cij b/2 If thou chaunge some better for to haue, Thou voydest a lubber to haue agayne a knaue.

†**d.** *refl.* To remove or withdraw (oneself) *from* or *out of* a place. *Obs.*

1387 Trevisa *Higden* (Rolls) III. 391 Also he voidede and wiþ-drow hym from þat place. **1467** *Maldon* (Essex) *Crt. Rolls* (Bundle 43, No. 3ʳ), The said Gilbert voided hymself owt of the same place without rent or ferme paying.

†**5.** Of persons or animals: To go away, depart, retire, or withdraw from, to leave or quit (a place); to give (ground); to move out of (the way); to get out of (one's sight); = avoid *v.* 7. *Obs.*

Very common from *c* 1400 to *c* 1645; now *Obs.* (cf. d).

13.. *Gaw. & Gr. Knt.* 345 Bid me boȝe fro þis benche, & stonde by you þere þat I wyth-oute vylanye myȝt voyde þis table. *c* **1330** R. Brunne *Chron. Wace* (Rolls) 5388 Bot whare so euere he hem [the Romans] fond He dide hem sone voyde þe lond. *c* **1374** Chaucer *Boeth.* i. pr. iv. (1868) 16 He comaunded but þat þei voided þe citee of Rauenne by certeyne day assigned þat men scholde.. chasen hem out of toune. *c* **1410** *Master of Game* (MS. Digby 182) xxxv, Smale deer be kynde will rather voyde his couert þan will a gret herte. *c* **1440** *Generydes* 3335 He sent the word,.. To voyde his grownde and tary not to long. *c* **1440** *Alph. Tales* 236, I sulde sla þe with my hynder fete becauce þou wolde not voyde þe way, & giff me rowm to pass by þe. *c* **1500** *Melusine* xxxvii. 297 Goo your way & voyde my syght. **1523** Ld. Berners *Froiss.* I. xxv. 36 So this syr Robert was fayne to voyde the realme of Fraunce, and went to Namure. **1577** Hanmer *Anc. Eccl. Hist.* (1619) 140 Paulus would not depart the Church, neither void the house. **1631** Weever *Anc. Funeral Mon.* 716 They voyded the Church, falling.. as they sought to get out of the same. **1654** tr. *Martini's Conq. China* 36 They.. withall commanded them speedily to voyd the City. **1732** Sir C. Wogan *Let.* 27 Feb. in *Swift's Wks.* (1841) II. 670 The whole shoal of virtuosoes were sensible to the stroke, and voided the room at once.

†**b.** To dismount from (a horse). *Obs.*

1470-85 Malory *Arthur* i. xvi. 58 Thenne the kynge of the C knyghtes voyded the hors lyghtly.

†**c.** To cover, move over (ground) in progression. *Obs.*⁻¹

1608 Topsell *Serpents* 218 They are slow of pace, and voyde ground very sluggishlie, and therfore it is iustly termed a heauy and slothfull beast.

d. To vacate (a seat). *rare.*

1853 Miss E. S. Sheppard *Chas. Auchester* II. 38 Before I could gather with my glance who had left them, several seats were voided beneath us. **1885** *Daily Tel.* 17 Dec. (Cassell's), A wholesale system of voiding seats.

6. To remove (something) so as to leave a vacant space; to take, put, or clear away; occas., to remove by emptying or taking out. Now *rare.*

c **1386** Chaucer *Frankl. T.* 1159 For with an apparence a clerk may make To mannes sighte þat alle the Rokkes blake Of Britaigne weren yvoyded euerichon. **1390** Gower *Conf.* I. 231 Afterward hem stant no doute To voide with a soubtil hond The beste goodes of the lond. *c* **1400** *Beryn* 1898 Let al yeur marchandise Be voidit of yeur Shippis. *c* **1440** *Jacob's Well* 12 þe Abbot & þe priour togydere seydin to þe scolere þat god had voydyd his synnes out of þat lettere, in counfortyng him þat his synnes ben forgeuyn. **1466** in Leland *Collect.* (1715) VI. 11 The Sewer geveth a voyder to the Carver, and he doth voyde into it the Trenchers.. and so cleanseth the table cleane. **1474** Caxton *Chesse* ii. iv. (1883) 51 He voyded the mete and toke the vayssell. **1530** Palsgr. 769/1, I voyde a thyng out of the way, or out of syght, *je oste.* **1596** Spenser *F.Q.* vi. vii. 43 A roll of linen,.. With which his locks,.. Were bound about, and voyded from before. **1629** Hobbes *Thucyd.* (1822) 113 The earth being drawn away below and settling over the part where it was voided. **1653** Holcroft *Procopius, Goth. Wars* iv. 129 And having voyded away much earth from beneath those timbers, they shook.. the Wall, and a part of it suddenly sunk. *a* **1700** Evelyn *Diary* 18 Dec. 1685, The spectators.. were exceedingly pleas'd to see in what a moment of time all that curious work was demolish'd, the comfitures voided, and the tables clear'd. **1855** Browning *Epistle* 40 'Sooth, it elates me, thus reposed and safe, To void the stuffing of my travel-scrip And share with thee whatever Jewry yields.

phr. *c* **1430** Lydg. *Min. Poems* (1911) 78, I shal.. Voyde the chaff, & gadryn out the corn. **1430-40** —— *Bochas* ix. xxxviii. *Lenvoye* (1558) 37/1 Voyde [ye] the wede, of vertue take the corne.

†**b.** To clear away by destruction or demolition. *Obs.*

13.. *E.E. Allit. P.* B. 1013 þis was a vengaunce violent þat voyded þise places, þat foundered has so fayr a folk & þe folde sonkken. *Ibid.* C. 370 *a* **1400-50** *Alexander* 1338 He blisches to þe burȝe & sees his bild voidid, Als bare as a bast his baistell a-way. **1464** *Rolls of Parlt.* V. 569/2 That all such Weres, Milles and Demmynges,.. should be voided and clene beten downe.

†**c.** With immaterial object. *Obs.*

Not always clearly distinguishable from sense 11.

1382 Wyclif *Job* xv. 4 As myche as in thee is, thou hast voidid drede. *c* **1399** *Pol. Poems* (Rolls) II. 13 Bot who that is of charité perfit, He voideth alle sleightes ferr aweie. *c* **1440** *Jacob's Well* 287 þis mynde schal voyde fro þe suche euyll demynges, & euyll thouȝtys, woordys, and dedys. *a* **1500** *Chaucer's Dreme* 2184, I find ne might.. thing that kerved,.. Wherewith I might my woful pains Have voided with bleeding of my vains. *c* **1530** *Crt. of Love* 628, I me bethought.. Myne orison right goodly to devyse, And plesauntly.. Beseech the goddes voiden my grevaunce. *a* **1553** Udall *Royster D.* Prol. (Arb.) 10 Mirth recreates our spirites and voydeth pensiuenesse. **1656** J. Smith *Pract. Physick* 12 The cause that is joyned with it [the carbuncle] must be voided, with scarification deep enough.

†**d.** To remove or take off (a helmet, etc.). *Obs.*

c **1400** *Destr. Troy* 7092 He was glad of the gome, & o gode chere Voidet his viser, auentid hym seluyn. *c* **1407** Lydg. *Reson & Sens.* 1208 Thilke tyme, as I took hede, Her helme was voyded from hir hede. **1470-85** Malory *Arthur* vii. xxiii. 249 He stroke doune that knyghte and voyded his helme and strake of his hede.

†**e.** To cast, fling, or throw away (a sword); to bring or blow *down* (leaves). *Obs.*

a **1400-50** *Alexander* 4145 Vulturnus þe violent þat voidis doun þe leuys. *c* **1400** *Melayne* 1069 And Charles voydede his broken brande, Owte he hent a knyfe in hande.

7. Of persons, animals, or their organs: To discharge (some matter) from the body through a natural vent or orifice, esp. through the excretory organs; to eject by excretion or evacuation; †also, to spit or pour forth (venom).

Now the usual sense. †Also (*b*) formerly with *out.*

(*a*) *c* **1386** Chaucer *Knt.'s T.* 1893 The vertu expulsif or animal.. Ne may the venym voyden ne expelle. **1398** Trevisa *Barth. De P.R.* v. xli. (Bodl. MS.), For humours þat comeþ of þe melte.. mowe not be yuoided att þe fulle. **1551** Robinson *More's Utopia* ii. (1895) 203 Sumetymes whyles those thynges be.. voided, wherof is in the body ouer great abundaunce. **1577** B. Googe *Heresbach's Husb.* iii. (1586) 124 The more filth he voides at the mouth, the better will it be for him. *a* **1617** Hieron *Wks.* (1620) II. 15 What good will a mans meate doe him, if he void it vp, through weaknesse of stomake, as fast as it is eaten? **1617** Moryson *Itin.* i. 215 My brother.. fell, and voided much blood at the nose. **1684** Boyle *Porousn. Anim. & Solid Bod.* vi. 53 The Purulent matter hath been voided by Siege and Urine. **1738** *Gentl. Mag.* VIII. 548/2 Mr. D.. took the Medicines, voided three small Stones, and became perfectly well. **1766** *State, D. Macdonald v. Dk. Gordon* Pursuer's Proof 7 The he-fish they carried off with them, and [he] has seen them often voiding the melt at their bellies. **1804** Abernethy *Surg. Obs.* 243 The patient voided his urine by the natural channel. **1815** Kirby & Sp. *Entomol.* iv. (1816) I. 91 A white line, which.. he found to consist of innumerable Acari, precisely the same with those that he had voided. **1867** F. Francis *Angling* iii. (1880) 100 It is astonishing what a vast number of eggs the female perch will void.

transf. and *fig.* **1599** Shaks. *Hen. V*, iii. v. 52 The Valleyes, whose low Vassal Seat, The Alpes doth spit, and void his rhewme vpon. **1651** Cleveland *Hecatomb Mistress* 69 Thou man of mouth,.. whose Musk-cat verse Voids nought but flowers for thy Muses herse. **1655** Vaughan *Silex Scint.* i. *Rules & Lessons* xiii, That's base wit, That voyds but filth and stench. **1664** Butler *Hud.* ii. iii. 742 For Anaxagoras.. Believ'd the Heavens were made of Stone, Because the Sun had voided one. **1883** Villari *Machiavelli* ii. ii. III. 274 No sooner were the Tarquins dead than the nobles began to void their venom on the people.

(*b*) **1587** Golding *De Mornay* ii. (1592) 15 By one part the things that are needfull are taken in, and by another the things that are superfluous are voyded out. **1645** Pagitt *Heresiogr.* (1661) 167 We read of Arrius an Arch-heretick, that voided out his bowels at the Jakes.

b. *absol.* To evacuate; to empty the bladder; to vomit.

c **1410** *Master of Game* (MS. Digby 182) vi, Whan þe wolfe sees [the greyhounds] and he be fulle, he voydeth both before and behynde alle in his rennynge. **1598** Sylvester *Du Bartas* ii. i. *Furies* 296 Still her monstrous maw Voyds in devouring. **1655** Culpepper, etc. *Riverius* ix. vii. 267 It is not good to void sparingly in a crisis. **1731** Swift *Strephon & Chloe* Wks. 1755 IV. i. 154 The bride must either void or burst. **1832** W. Motherwell *Poet. Wks.* (1847) 44 While one and all Hissed, fought, and voided on their thrall. **1947** Stafford & Diller *Textbk. Surg. for Nurses* xlix. 500 The patient's bladder must be empty; therefore.. she should void before being draped for examination. **1966** *Amer. Jrnl. Obstetrics & Gynecol.* XCIV. 796/1 Sixteen patients were investigated who were unable to void following operations. **1977** *Lancet* 21 May 1072/2 The patient voided, was catheterised, and then lay comfortably on a.. couch.

†**8.** To carry off or drain *away* (water, etc.); to discharge or let out. *Obs.*

14.. *Sir Beues* (O.) 1320 A water thorough that preson ranne, To voyde the ffilth from any man. **1412-20** Lydg. *Chron. Troy* ii. 699 Euery hous.. With spoutis þoruȝ, & pipes.. Voyding filþes low in-to þe grounde. *c* **1450** *Merlin* ii. 38 When the water was all voided thei saugh the two stones. **1577** B. Googe *Heresbach's Husb.* 142 You must looke.. that where they [*sc.* sheepcots] stande, the grounde be made fayre and euen.. that the vrine may be well voyded away. *Ibid.* 173 The water being voyded and kept out by Sluses and Bankes. **1601** Holland *Pliny* II. 586 The mountaine that was digged through.. to void away the water out of the lough or meere Fucinus. **1610** —— *Camden's Brit.* (1637) 213 Under this Middleton, there is voided also another river. **1648** Wilkins *Math. Magic* ii. xv. (1707) 166 Every Circumvolution voiding only so much [water] as is contained in one Helix. **1707** Mortimer *Husb.* (1721) I. 91 One of these Pumps.. will void a vast Quantity of Water in an Hour, with a great deal of ease.

†**b.** To empty out (water, etc.) from a vessel.

1460-70 *Bk. Quintessence* 5 Aftir þat þis erþly water be voydid, putte [etc.]. **1530** Palsgr. 769/1, I voyde, I emptye, *je vuyde. Ibid.*, Voyde this water. *a* **1577** Sir T. Smith *Commw. Eng.* (1609) 60 As a water held in a close and dark vessel issueth out, & is voyded and emptied.

†**c.** Of a river or stream. Also *refl.* and *absol.*, to discharge *into* the sea or another river. *Obs.*

1598 Sylvester *Du Bartas* ii. ii. *Colonies* 62 Ob, the King of Rivers.. In Scythian Seas voyding his violent load. **1600** J. Pory tr. *Leo's Africa* 44 Finally it voideth into the sea at two mouths, one of which mouthes is a mile broad. **1610** Holland *Camden's Brit.* i. 466 A little above it, the river Blith voideth it selfe into the sea. **1633** Bp. Hall *Occas. Medit.* (ed. 3) §19. 45 When the little rivulets have once voyded themselves into the mayne streames.

†**9.** To make by excavation; to cut or hollow out (a hole, etc.). *Obs.*

1575 Laneham *Let.* (1871) 51 Holez wear thear also, and cauerns,.. voyded intoo the wall.

III. †**10.** To leave alone, set aside; to abstain or refrain from; to have nothing to do with. *Obs.*

a. A thing, action, course of conduct, etc. = avoid *v.* 8 b.

13.. *E.E. Allit. P.* B. 744 Nay þaȝ faurty forfete ȝet fryst I a whyle, & voyde away my vengaunce, þaȝ me vyl þynk. **1390** Gower *Conf.* I. 105 For he doth al his thing be gesse, And voideth alle sikernesse. *c* **1400** *Destr. Troy* 4017 Ho.. voidet all vanities, & virtus dissyret. **1412-20** Lydg. *Chron. Troy* iv. 1072 Be wisdam lete vs voide pride And wilfulnes. **1435** Misyn *Fire of Love* 12 þai haue wodid old vnthriftynes of venemus lyfe. **1534** More *Comf. agst. Trib.* ii. Wks. 1190/2 He fyrmely purposeth vpon it, no lesse glad to do it, then a nother man wolde be glad to voyde it. **1681** R. L'Estrange *Tully's Offices* 64 Beware.. to void things that look Harsh, Rough, and Uncivil.

b. A person or persons: = avoid *v.* 8 a.

c **1374** Chaucer *Anel. & Arc.* 295, I voyde companye, I fle gladnesse. **1387** Trevisa *Higden* (Rolls) VII. 249 William.. was i-corowned kyng at Westmynstre of Aldredus archebisshop of York, and voydede Stygandus archebisshop of Caunterbury. *c* **1400** *Beryn* 2456 Good sir,.. why do yee voide me?.. I woll ȝewe no more harm. **1607** Shaks. *Cor.* iv. v. 88 For if I had fear'd death, Of all the Men i th' world I would haue voided thee.

†**11.** To keep clear of, to escape from or evade (something injurious or troublesome); = avoid *v.* 9. *Obs.*

In later use containing a mixture of sense 6 c.

c **1380** Wyclif *Sel. Wks.* III. 30 We þat hoten grete avowis to voiden angus and siiknessis of þis liif. **1387** Trevisa *Higden* (Rolls) V. 347 And for þe Romayns scholde somdel voide þe cruelnesse, he made trompoures blowe. *a* **1400-50** *Alexander* 2424 (Dubl.), Bot whilke of yow as foundes frist on fote vs agayns, Sall neuer voyde my dysdane ne my derfe Ire. **1444** *Rolls of Parlt.* V. 127/2 To eschewe and voyde the perils in thes seid Articles.. expressed. **1513** More *Rich. III* (1883) 48 A merveilous case it is to here, either the warninges of that he should haue voided, or the tokens of that he could not voide. *c* **1520** Skelton *Magnyf.* 300 Let se this checke yf ye voyde canne. *c* **1580** in *Eng. Hist. Rev.* July (1914) 524 He may rise or fall his price accordinglye and void manye inconveniences wiche the unskillfull fall in to. **1606** Bryskett *Civ. Life* 16 The labyrinth which I desire most to eschew and voide. **1620** *Frier Rush* 18 For to voyde all tribulations and misfortunes that might fall in time to come. *a* **1677** Barrow *Serm.* Wks. 1682 I. 15 For voiding which prejudices.. I shall.. propose some of those innumerable advantages.

†**b.** To get out of the way of (a blow, person, etc.); to avoid in this way. *Obs.*

c **1450** *Merlin* x. 159 He..leide a-boute hym on bothe sides, and slow all that he raught with a full stroke, so that thei voyded hys strokes and made hym rome. **1596** Spenser *F.Q.* iv. vi. 3 As soone as th' other nigh approaching, vewed The armes he bore, his speare he gan abase, And voide his course. **1606** Holland *Sueton.* 106 He had given streight commandement..that no man should trouble him, and all the way voided as many as were comming towards him. **1639** Fuller *Holy War* v. ix. (1840) 258 A patron of pilgrimages, not able to void the blow yet willing to break the stroke of so..plain a testimony.

†**12.** To prevent or obviate; to keep or ward *off*; = avoid *v.* 10. *Obs.*

c **1400** *Destr. Troy* 12109 Hit hade doutles ben done, and hire deth voidid, Had not Calcas þe cursit carpit before. **1509** *Parl. Devylles* xxxviii, If I tempte hym wt lechery, I must me hyde, He voydeth me of with chastyte. **1528** More in *St. Papers Hen. VIII*, I. 285 Hym selfe and Your Grace, if it may be voided, wold be as lothe to have eny warre with theym. **1605** Sylvester *Du Bartas, Sonn. Late Peace* xl, Henry our King, our Father, voyds our dangers, And..planteth Peace in France. **1722** W. Hamilton *Wallace* 4 To void a bloody Civil War, The two Contendants should submit the Thing, To the Decision of the English King.

IV. 13. *intr.* To go away, depart, withdraw from or leave a place or position; to retire or retreat; to give place, make way; to vanish or disappear: = avoid *v.* 6. Now *Obs.* or *arch.*

Also const. (*b*) with advs., as *aside, away, hence, thence, out*, or (*c*) with preps. as *from, of, out of, to*.

a. Of persons or animals.

(*a*) **13..** *Coer de L.* 2192 The folk of the countre gan renne, And were fain to void and flenne. c **1374** Chaucer *Troylus* ii. 912 So whan it liked hire to gon to reste, And voyded were þey þat voyden oughte. c **1400** *Beryn* 2285 'Nay, thou shalt nat void', he seid, 'my tale is nat i-do'. c **1430** Lydg. *Beware of Doubleness* 52 What man may..holde a snake by the tail, Or a sliper eel constraine That it nil voide, withouten fail. **1470–85** Malory *Arthur* i. xvi. 58 Yonder I see the moste valyaunt knyght of the world.., wherfore we must nedes voyde or deye. **1534** More *Treat. Passion* Wks. 1275/2 He voyded not at Gods commyng, but abode to see the sentence of theyr dampnacion. a **1553** Udall *Royster D.* iii. iii. (Arb.) 48 Voyde sirs, see ye not maister Roister Doister come? Make place my maisters. **1568** Grafton *Chron.* II. 756 Whose warres whoso well consider, he shall no lesse commend his wisedome where he voyded, then his manhood where he vanquished. **1606** Holland *Sueton.* 102 He caused all his traine and company to void. [**1896** J. H. Wylie *Hist. Engl. Hen. IV*, lxxxvii. III. 477 As he almost got knocked down in a crowd, he very soon voided.]

(*b*) **1387–8** T. Usk *Test. Love* i. iii. (Skeat) I. 140 Although I might hence voyde, yet wolde I not. c **1410** *Master of Game* (MS. Digby 182) xi, For whann a wilde boore is in a stronge hate of wode, peraventure..he wolde not voyed þens for þe rennynge houndes. **14..** W. Paris *Cristine* 435 (Horstm. 1878), She bade the serpens voyde awaye In to deserte. **1570** Foxe *A. & M.* (ed. 2) I. 89/1 The brethren voyded a side, and withdrew themselues. **1609** Holland *Amm. Marcell.* 349 Erecthius and Aristomenes..voided aside to farre remote and hidden corners.

(*c*) a **1400–50** *Alexander* 1113 Þan waynest him þis vayne God & voidis fra þe chambre. c **1450** *Merlin* vii. 108 Thei..dide hem wele to wite..that he sholde in all haste voide oute of the londe and the contree. **14..** in *Hist. Coll. Citizen London* (Camden) 208 The quene hyrrynge thys she voydyde unto Walys. c **1540** *Order in Battayll* B iij b, [To] remowe hys hoste..& voyde to some sure forteresse. **1548** Udall, etc. *Erasm. Par., Luke* xi. 107 b, Jesus..commanded the deuil to voide out of hym, and he voided. **1587** Mascall *Govt. Cattle, Hogges* (1627) 290 The strong sauor thereof wil cause the moules to void from those places. **1600** Holland *Livy* xxiv. xxix. 529 So they went their waies and voided clean out of Sicilie.

b. Of things, material and immaterial.

13.. *E.E. Allit. P.* B. 1548 Þenne hit [*sc.* the hand] vanist verayly & voyded of sy3t, Bot þe lettres bileued ful large vpon plaster. **1387–8** T. Usk *Test. Love* ii. x. (Skeat) I. 34 So thilke bodily goodes at the laste mote awaye, and than stinge they at her goinge, wherthrough entreth and clene voydeth al blisse of this knot. c **1400** *Destr. Troy* 7029 And the duke with a dynt derit hym agayn, þat the visere & the ventaile voidet hym fro. *Ibid.* 7133 Wen þe day vp drogh, & þe dym voidit. c **1430** *Hymns Virgin* (1867) 65 Þi fleischeli lustis þou muste spare, For vicis and vertues wole voide atwynne. **1579** Spenser *Sheph. Cal., Aug.* 164 Let all that sweete is, voyd; and all that may augment My doole, drawe neare. **1586** T. B. *La Primaud. Fr. Acad.* i. (1594) 44 So when the soule filleth it selfe with certaine and true goods, vanitie voideth and giveth place. **1607** Topsell *Four-f. Beasts* 567 Least that the smell or fume doe fade, and voide away.

†**c.** To give up possession or occupancy of a place. *Obs.*−1

1518 *Yorkshire Deeds* (Yorks. Archæol. Soc. 1914) II. 92 If the said Cristofer haue nede..to com and dwell vpon the said fermehold..then the said John to wode of it vpon resonable warnyng.

†**14.** To give oneself up *to*, devote one's time *to*, something. *Obs.*−1

1382 Wyclif *Esther* ix. 17 Thei ordeyneden..that in that time eche 3er therafter thei shulden voiden [L. *vacarent*] to plenteuous metis..and to io3e, and to festis.

†**15.** To form an interval *between*. *Obs.*−1

1387 Trevisa *Higden* (Rolls) I. 41 Dayes and monþes þat voydede bytwene tweie Kynges were forgendred.

†**16.** Of a benefice, etc.: To become, fall, or remain vacant. *Obs.*

a **1380** *St. Ambrose* 204 in Horstm. *Altengl. Leg.* (1878) 204 Hit befel afturward sikerliche þat in a cite voyded a bisschopriche. **1387** Trevisa *Higden* (Rolls) V. 109 After þe passioun of Marcellinus þe pope, þe see voydede meny dayes. **1421** Hen. V in Ellis *Orig. Lett.* Ser. iii. I. 71 Hit is wel oure entent whanne any succhе benefice voydeth of oure yifte yat ye make collacion to him yrof. **1444** *Rolls of Parlt.* V. 75/1 When sumever hit happen the said House or Hospitall here after to void by deth..or any other wise. **1531** *Dial. on Laws Eng.* ii. xxxvi. N ij b, It ys sayd that benefyces, dygnytyes, and personages, voydynge in the court of Rome may not be gyuen but by the Pope.

†**17.** Of matter, etc.: To come, flow, or pass out, esp. in or by evacuation or excretion; to issue. *Obs.*

1558 Warde tr. *Alexis' Secr.* (1568) 41 b, To the intent that al the venom may comme out and voide from the heart. **1561** Hollybush *Hom. Apoth.* 33 The..gut through the whyche the ordure voydeth. **1596** Danett tr. *Comines* (1614) 213 By meanes whereof all fumes voided that troubled his head. **1607** Topsell *Four-f. Beasts* 433 Presently the filth and excrements will void cleane away. **1678** Moxon *Mech. Exerc.* v. 83 Knock hard upon it, till..the Basil of The Chissel will no longer force the chips out of the Mortess: then..work..till the Chips will void no longer. **1774** Goldsm. *Nat. Hist.* (1776) V. 244 It feeds chiefly upon pepper, which it devours very greedily, gorging itself in such a manner, that it voids crude and unconcocted.

voidable (ˈvɔɪdəb(ə)l), *a.* [f. void *v.* + -able. Cf. avoidable *a.*]

1. Capable of being annulled or made legally void; *spec.* (as distinguished from *void*), that may be either voided or confirmed.

1485 *Rolls of Parlt.* VI. 285/2 The same Feoffments, States, Leases..be..not in anie wise voided ne voidable by reason of Coverture. **1544** in I. S. Leadam *Sel. Cases Crt. Requests* (1898) 68 Their coppie holldes beynge allwayes voydable in the lawe at the wyll of the lord. **1590** Swinburne *Testaments* 241 The testament made by feare is not voide *ipso iure*, but voidable by the helpe of exception. **1602** Fulbecke *1st Pt. Parall.* 3 In the one case the gift or conueyance is voidable onely, in the other it is void to all intents. **1643** Prynne *Sov. Power Parl.* ii. 78 Even as a Marriage, Bond, or deed made by Duresse or Menace, are good in Law, and not meerly void, but voidable only upon a Plea and Tryall. **1726** Ayliffe *Parergon* 38 If the Metropolitan..grants Letters of Administration, such Administration is not void, but voidable, by a Sentence. **1765** Blackstone *Comm.* I. 423 These civil disabilities make the contract void *ab initio*, and not merely voidable. **1809** G. Rose *Diaries* (1860) II. 428 Whether the Vicarage..cannot be opened to a new presentation as voidable but not void. **1821** Scott *Kenilw.* v, I have but a poor lease of this mansion under you, voidable at your honour's pleasure. **1875** K. E. Digby *Real Prop.* x. §1. (1876) 369 His [*sc.* an infant's] conveyances are voidable, subject, that is, to be ratified or avoided by him when he comes of age.

†**2.** *Her.* That may be made void: (see quot. and voided *ppl. a.* 2 c). *Obs.*−1

1610 Guillim *Heraldry* ii. v. (1611) 48 Voiding..is the exemption of some part of the inward substance of things voidable by occasion whereof the Field is transparent thorow the charge. [Hence in Phillips, Harris, etc.]

3. Capable of being voided or evacuated. *rare.*

1663 Boyle *Usef. Exp. Nat. Philos.* ii. iii. 79 He had..so broaken the Stone, partly by crumbling it, and partly by dissolving the Cement, as to make if voidable by Urine.

Hence **voidaˈbility**; **ˈvoidableness**.

1727 Bailey (vol. II), *Voidableness*, capableness of being voided or emptied. **1823** *Ann. Reg., Hist. Eur.* 90 In some cases there must be a nullity, but that there should be a voidability was most objectionable. *Ibid.* 91/2 A medium between the entire dereliction of parental authority on the one side and entire voidability on the other. **1883** *Sat. Rev.* 16 June 755 Despite the quibble about voidness and voidableness.

voidage (ˈvɔɪdɪdʒ). [f. void *sb.*1 + -age.] Voids collectively; the proportion of a volume occupied by voids.

1946 *Nature* 17 Aug. 236/1 At 1,000°C. and with an inlet total gas rate of 200 litres/hr., sufficient to expand the bed of coke particles to a voidage of 0·7 so that the whole bed was agitated, the exit gas analyses..were [etc.]. **1966** R. D. West in P. Hepple *Petroleum Supply & Demand* 70 Injection wells scattered across the reservoir to inject the relatively large volumes of water required, not only to replace new oil, but also to fill the voidage left by the natural depletion. **1970** *Nature* 11 Apr. 158/2 The variation in local voidage occurring near the wall of a large cylindrical container filled with a mixture of spheres. **1983** *Chem. & Engin. Sci.* XXXVIII. 350/1 There is little difference between the surface settling rate of a bubbling bed and of a uniformly expanded bed of the same voidage.

voidance (ˈvɔɪdəns). Also 4–5 voydaunce, 5 -ans, 5, 7 -ance, 5 voidaunce, -ans. [a. AF. *voidaunce, vuedance*, OF. *vuidance, voydance*, etc., f. *voider* void *v.*, or aphetic f. avoidance.] The action of voiding or making void.

1. The action or process of emptying out the contents of something; = avoidance 1. **a.** The discharge or evacuation of something through a natural vent, esp. from the human body by excretion; = evacuation 1 b. Now *rare.*

1398 Trevisa *Barth. De P.R.* v. xlvi. (Bodl. MS.), Þis wombe is ofte igreued by greete fulnes and replecion and þat is nought þanne iholpe but by voidans þat is contrary to replecion. c **1440** *Promp. Parv.* 511/2 Voydaunce (or voydynge), *vacacio, evacuacio*. c **1460** *Vrbanitatis* 20 in *Babees Bk.* (1868) 13 Fro spettyng & snetyng kepe þe also; Be priuy of voydance, & lette hit go. **1528** More *Dyaloge* i. Wks. 137/1 By the longing for mete with voidance of yt she had eten..she was perceiued for no saint. **1654** Gataker *Disc. Apol.* 58 This voidance of blood doth at times stil surprize me, tho not with such vehemency. **1668** Culpepper & Cole *Barthol. Anat.* i. vi. 14 The Second Action follows upon the former, viz. the voidance of Excrements. **1671** Grew *Anat. Plants* vi. §2 In the bark the same thing is effected by..a meer voydance of the Sap. **1829** Landor *Imag. Conv.* Ser. ii. I. 491 The reception, concoction, and voidance, of nutriment.

b. The emptying out, carrying off or away, of water, etc., esp. by drainage. Now *rare.*

1398 Trevisa *Barth. De P.R.* xiv. lvii. (Tollem. MS.), For parties of þe erþe ben digged and holowid..with crepynge wormes and bestes..or with voydaunce and oute castynge. **1442** *Rolls of Parlt.* V. 44/1 As well for passage of all maner Shippes comyng therto, and voidaunce of water under the seid Brigg, as for passage of Man. **1861** Smiles *Engineers* II. 160 To provide for the drainage of the Fen districts..by means of proper cuts and conduits for the voidance of the Fen waters.

†**2.** The action or fact of removing, clearing away, or getting rid of something; removal. *Obs.*

c **1400** *Sowdone Bab.* 1106 The Barons made hem at one with grete prayer and instaunce,..Of the more myschiefe to make voydaunce. **1530** Palsgr. 285/2 Voydaunce, *uidance, deslegement.* **1610** Bp. Hall *Apol. Brownists* liii. 128 Succeeding times found these Canaanites to be prickes and thornes, and therefore both by mulctes and banishments sought eyther their yeeldance or voydance. **1631** J. Burges *Answ. Rejoined, Lawfuln. Kneeling* 70 Before the Transubstantiation, or voydance of the substance of bread was resolued of. a **1677** Barrow *Serm.* Wks. 1686 III. 213 What pains..they require, in the voidance of fond conceits, in the suppression..of froward humours.

3. *Eccl.* The fact of a benefice, etc., becoming or being void or vacant; = avoidance 4.

1422 *Rolls of Parlt.* IV. 194/1 That tyme of the voidaunce of the same Prebend. c **1440** *Jacob's Well* 28 Alle þo, þat vsurpyn of newe tyme þe kepyng or þe amonicyoun of ony cherch in tyme of voydaunce, & ocupye þe godys. **1449** *Rolls of Parlt.* V. 158/1 Of the sayd Wardes, mariages, Relevis, voydaunces abovesayd. **1531** *Dial. on Laws Eng.* ii. xxxvii. N iij b, If the patron presented not within the halfe yere after suche voydance:..That than the kynge shold haue also the presentement. **1570** Foxe *A. & M.* (ed. 2) I. 347/1 That prouision should be made for iij hundred Romanes in the chiefest and best benefices in al Englande, at ye next voydance. **1607** Cowell *Interpr., Voydance*, is a want of an Incumbent vpon a benefice: and this voydance is double: either in law, as when a man hath more benefices incompetible: or indeed, as when the Incumbent is dead, or actually depriued. a **1645** Featly *Abbot* in *Fuller's Abel Rediv.* (1867) II. 282 One of his hearers, having a benefice of great value in his gift,..took a resolution upon the next voidance of it to confer it upon him. **1709** Strype *Ann. Ref.* I. ii. 73 This voidance of so many bishopricks happened well for the furthering of the reformation of religion. **1766** Entick *London* IV. 126 The parishioners present twice and the king once in three voidances. **1899** J. Vincent *1st Bp. Bath & Wells* 10 How could the occasion arise, except by the voidance of the See? **1909** *Westm. Gaz.* 10 March 5/1 By an Order in Council the lectureship attached to the parish church of Dedham..will be merged in the benefice at the next voidance.

4. Annulment; = avoidance 2.

1488 *Rolls of Parlt.* VI. 419/1 This Acte of Adnullacion or Voidans of Lettres Patentes. **1691–8** Norris *Pract. Disc.* (1711) III. 105, I have argued against the Voidance, and for the Establishment of the Law upon Rational Principles. **1736** *Col. Rec. Pennsylv.* IV. 177 The first part of those Proposals..directly infers a Voidance of the Agreement. **1756** *Monitor* No. 30. I. 276 There are men who blush not to promote a voidance of that part of the same act. **1884** *Law Times* 19 Jan. 205/1 It was held that the purchaser was not entitled in equity to obtain a voidance of the contract.

†**5.** A verbal evasion or subterfuge; an evasive answer or argument. *Obs.*−1

1621 Bacon *Lett.* (1734) 137 Therefore I am resolved, when I come to my answer, not to trick my innocency..by cavillations, or voydances, but to speak to them the language that my heart speaketh to me.

†**6.** *concr.* Matter voided or cleared away; the clearings *of* a table. *Obs.*−1

1740 *Propos. Prov. Poor* 6 Bones and other Voidance of the Table, Dish-water.

ˈvoided, *ppl. a.* [f. void *v.*]

†**1.** Made void or empty; emptied or cleared of contents. *Obs.*

1382 Wyclif *Job* xiv. 11 What maner if watris gon awei fro the se, and flod voided [L. *fluvius vacuefactus*] waxe drie. **1426** Lydg. *De Guil. Pilgr.* 6177 Humblely I yow be-seke,.. My voyded herte to fulfylle, Wych so longe..hath voyde be. c **1440** *Promp. Parv.* 512/1 Voydy[d], or avoydyd (*K.* voydid,..auoyded), *evacuatus.* c **1482** J. Kay tr. *Caoursin's Siege of Rhodes* (1870) ¶10 [The bridge] was made with voyded pypes and with bords strongly nayled upon them. **1563** A. Neville *Seneca's Œdipus* i. A iij, The corne..Nowe to the voided Barnes nought els but emptie stalkes doth bring.

2. Having a part or portion cut out so as to leave a void or vacant space: †**a.** Of shoes: Made with the front or uppers cut away or left open. *Obs.*

a **1539** in *Archaeologia* XLVII. 53 That noon of the said religious susters doo use..eny such voyded shoys. **1555** W. Watreman *Fardle Facions* ii. ii. 121 They vse a kinde of voided shoes (which afterwarde the Grieques toke vp, and called sandalium). **1565** Cooper *Thesaurus, Crepida*, a low voyded shoe with a latchet.

†**b.** Of a garment: Cut so as to show the skin or another garment beneath. *Obs. rare.*

a **1548** Hall *Chron., Hen. VIII*, 6 b, Doblettes of Crimosin veluet, voyded lowe on the backe and before to the cannell bone. a **1623** G. Buck *Rich. III*, i. (1646) 26 The King and Queene..then ascended to the high Altar shifting their Robes, and putting on other open and voyded in sundry places for their Anoynting.

c. *Her.* Of a charge or ordinary (see quots. 1704, 1780). *voided per cross* (see quot. c 1828).

1572 Bossewell *Armorie* 26 There are also to bee..seene in armes Crosses doble partited,..persed, graded, & voyded, &c. *Ibid.* ii. 126 He beareth Argent, on a Bende Gules, thre Mascles de Or, voyded... Whensoeuer ye shall see eyther Losenge, Mascle, or other thynge voyded of the fielde, Fesse, bende, &c., whereon theye stande, it is sufficient to saye, voyded, onelye. **1704** J. HARRIS *Lex. Techn.* I, *Voided*, a Term in Heraldry, when there are Lines drawn within, and Parallel to the out Lines of any Ordinary: This expresses an Exemption of something of the thing Voidable, and makes the Field appear transparent thro' the Charge. **1780** EDMONDSON *Her.* II, *Voided*, is a term applied to any ordinary, as a fesse, chevron, pale, etc. when it is pierced through, so that the field appears, and nothing remains of the charge but its edge. *c* **1828** BERRY *Encycl. Her.* I. Gloss., *Voided per cross* is a voiding in the form of a cross, such as a cross moline, and the like, voided, or cut out in the middle in the shape of a plain cross, through which the field is seen. **1864** BOUTELL *Her. Hist. & Pop.* xxxi. (ed. 3) 460 A cross gu., voided of the field. **1883** C. F. KEARY in S. L. Poole *Coins & Medals* (1894) 114 The pennies of Alexander II. have short and long voided crosses, like those of Henry III.

3. Emitted by evacuation; evacuated. *rare.*

1784 COWPER *Task* v. 95 Their nauseous dole..Of voided pulse and half-digested grain.

voidee (ˈvɔɪdiː). Now only *Hist.* Forms: 4–5 voide, 6 voyde; 5–6 (9) voidee (7 voydee); 5 voidie, 6 voidy(e, voydye. [a. AF. *voidé or *voidée, pa. pple. masc. or fem. of *voider* VOID *v.*, with reference app. to the withdrawing from a hall or chamber of those who were not to sleep there.] A collation consisting of wine accompanied by spices, comfits, or the like, partaken of before retiring to rest or the departure of guests; a repast of this nature following upon a feast or fuller meal; a parting dish. (Cf. VOID *sb.*²)

c **1374** CHAUCER *Troilus* III. 674 Ther nys no more, but here efter soone, The voide dronke and traueres drawe anon, Gan euery wight þat hadde nought to done More in þat place out of þat chamber gon. **1440** J. SHIRLEY *Dethe K. James* (1818) 13 Withyn an owre the Kyng askid the voidee, and drank, the travers yn the chambure edraw, and every man depairtid and went to rist. **1494** in *Lett. & Papers Rich. III. & Hen. VII.* (Rolls) I. 390 When they wer dry in their beddes they were revested.., and soo departed to the chappell, where they had spices, and their voidie. **1533** *Coronation of Anne Boleyn* (1884) 33 There was a voyde of spyce plates and wyne. **1546** *St. Papers Hen. VIII*, XI. 262 That night there was a greate bancket..and after that, two riche maskes..And after that, a voydye. *a* **1548** HALL *Chron., Hen. VIII*, 99 When they had daunced, then came in a costly banket and a voidy of spices, and so departed to their lodgyng. **1587** HOLINSHED *Chron.* III. 849/1 The king and the ambassadours were serued at a banket with two hundred and sixtie dishes, and after that a voidee of spices with sixtie spice plates. **1650** WELDON *Crt. Jas. I*, 19 He..made him the most sumptuous Feast..that ever was seen before,..and after that a costly Voydee, and after that a Maske.

attrib. **1881** ROSSETTI *King's Trag.* xci, And the King paused, but he did not speak. Then he called for the Voidee-cup.

voider (ˈvɔɪdə(r)). Also 5 woider, 5–7 (9) voyder, 6 -iar, vodyer; 5, 6–7 *Sc.*, voydour, *Sc.* 5 vyd-, 6 vod-, voidour. [f. VOID *v.* + -ER¹, or ad. OF. *vuideur, vuideor, voideor*, etc. (obs. F. *videur*), f. *voider* VOID *v.* Cf. AVOIDER.]

†**1.** That which keeps off or away; a screen or defence; a remover or driver away *of* something.

c **1400** *Destr. Troy* 339 Vmbe the sercle of the Citie was sothely a playne,..With lef-sales vppon lofte lustie and faire,..With voiders vnder vines for violent sonnes. *c* **1520** *Everyman* B v, A precious iewell I wyll gyue the Called penaunce, voyder of aduersyte. ? *a* **1550** in *Dunbar's Poems* (S.T.S.) 329 The sterne of day, voyder of dirknes.

†**2.** A piece of armour covering an exposed or unprotected place (see quot. 1880). *Obs.*

c **1330** R. BRUNNE *Chron. Wace* (Rolls) 10028 Doublet & quysseux, wiþ poleyns ful riche, Voydes [*sic*], breche of maille, wyþ paunz non liche. **1412–20** LYDG. *Chron. Troy* III. 50 [They] did on firste, after her desires, Sabatouns, grevis, cusschewis, & voideris. *Ibid.* 64 On his armys, rynged nat to wyde, þer wer woiders frettid in þe maille. *c* **1425** J. HILL in *Illustr. Anc. State & Chivalry* (Roxb.) 5 First behoveth sabatouns, greevis, and cloos qwysseux with voydours of plate or of mayle, and a cloos breche of mayle. [**1880** *Encycl. Brit.* XI. 697/1 The voider in defensive armour was a gusset-piece either of plate or of mail, used to cover a void or unprotected space at the elbow or knee joints.]

3. A receptacle into which something is voided or emptied: **a.** A tray, basket, or other vessel in which dirty dishes or utensils, fragments of broken food, etc., are placed in clearing the table or during a meal. Also *ellipt.*, the carrying round or use of this (quot. 1659). *Obs.* exc. *dial.*

1466 in Leland *Collect.* (1715) VI. 11 In the meane tyme the Sewer geveth a voyder to the Carver, and he doth voyde into it the Trenchers that lyeth under the knyves poynt,..and so cleanseth the table cleane. *c* **1475** *For to serve a Lord* in *Babees Bk.* (1868) 371 The kerver muste..have a voyder to geder in all the broke brede, trenchours, cromys lying upon the tabill. **1513** DOUGLAS *Æneid* I. xi. 58 Eftir the first paws, and that cours neir gane, And voduris and fat trunschoouris away tane, The goblettis greit with mychty wynis in hy Thai fillit. **1594** in *Archaeol.* (1884) XLVIII. 131 Item ij pewter voyders, xs. **1607** HEYWOOD *Wom. killed w. Kindn.* (1617) D 3 b, Enter 3 or 4 seruingmen, one with a Voyder and a woodden Knife to take away. **1620** SIR R. BOYLE in *Lismore Papers* (1886) I. 265, I sent my old silver voyder..to be exchandged for a new. **1659** EVELYN *Char. Eng.* 64 Their ceremony at the Table, and to see the formality of the Voider, which our Withdrawing roomes in France are made to prevent. **1703** R. NEVE *City & C. Purchaser* 90 The Butler..disposes..his Napkin-press.., Spoons, Knives, Forks, Voider, or Basket, and all other Necessaries appertaining to his Office. **1739** 'R. BULL' tr. *Dedekindus' Grobianus* 114 See now, the Stripling, with his Voider, waits To bear away the greasy Load of Plates. **1755** *Gentl. Mag.* XXV. 190 Ten waiters..Produce vast voiders, and a load of bread. **1823** E. MOOR *Suffolk Wds.*, *Voider*, a pail-like article, of wood or wicker, into which bones, etc. are shelved or thrown, during a meal. **1854** MISS BAKER *Northampt. Gloss.*, *Voider*, a butler's Tray.

attrib. **1610** *Althorp MS.* in Simpkinson *Washingtons* (1860) App. p. vii, Item voyder knives, whereof one is steele with a case. **1688** HOLME *Armoury* III. xiv. (Roxb.) 16/2 He beareth sable a Voyder Baskett, or a night Baskett Or.

b. *fig.* or in fig. context.

Very common in the first half of the 17th c.

1609 DEKKER *Gull's Horn-bk.* i. 7 Piers ploughman layd the cloth, and Simplicity brought in the voyder. **1615** T. ADAMS *Leaven* 112 You may as well..set him the voyder of abstinence instead of his table of surfeits. **1655** GURNALL *Chr. in Arm.* verse 13. vii. (1669) 139/1 Death comes with a Voider to carry away all thy carnal enjoyments.

†**c.** *fig.* A receptacle for refuse or rubbish. *Obs.*

1613 PURCHAS *Pilgrimage* VIII. v. 631 Haply some conceiued indignitie..that our Britannia should make her Virginian lap to bee the voider, for her lewder and more disordered Inhabitants. **1615** S. WARD *Coal fr. Altar* 79 How are his Sabaoths made the voider and dung-hill for all refuse businesse.

†**d.** A tray, basket, or large plate, esp. one of ornamental pattern or design, for holding, carrying, or handing round sweetmeats. Also *transf.* a quantity or amount carried in this. *Obs.*

1676 LADY FANSHAWE *Mem.* (1829) 164 Several times we saw the Feasts of Bulls [at Madrid] and at them we had great voiders of dried sweetmeats brought us upon the King's account. **1677** *Lond. Gaz.* No. 1249/1 And many Voiders of Sweetmeats were thrown among the People. **1686** tr. *Chardin's Trav. Persia* 259 Every one of the Guests were serv'd..with a Voider of Sweet-Meats Dry and Wet,.. the Voiders themselves being of Wood Painted and Gilt. **1706** PHILLIPS (ed. Kersey), *Voider*,..Among Confectioners, a wooden painted Vessel to hold Services of Sweet-meats.

†**e.** *Brickmaking.* (See quot.) *Obs.*⁻¹

1683 J. HOUGHTON *Collect. Lett. Improv. Husb.* II. VI. 188 Then we have a Mould or Frame made of Beech, because the Earth will slip easiest from it. This Mould, Frame, or Voyder is made of the thickness of the Brick abovesaid, only half inch deeper.

f. *dial.* A large basket or receptacle of wickerwork for holding soiled clothes, etc.; a clothesbasket; a wicker basket of any kind.

1707 in Boyle *Ch. of St. Nicholas, Newcastle* 94 Paid for a voider for ye sirplices. **1788** W. H. MARSHALL *Yorksh.* II. 362 *Voider*, a kind of open-work basket. **1879** *Saunterer's Satchel* 25 (E.D.D.), I catched a lad running off wi' ahr voider. **1880** *West Cornwall Gloss.* 62 *Voyder*, a clothes basket; a large basket for holding unmended linen sold by gipsy women.

†**4.** *Sc.* **a.** An empty barrel, cask, or the like.

1482 in *Charters* (etc.) *Edinb.* (1871) 168 All the tym vydouris of gudis ventit or temyt in the..toun of Leith. **1603** *Reg. Mag. Sig. Scot.* 516/1 All the twme voydouris of guidis [etc.].

†**b.** Packing or wrappers removed from bales or bundles of goods. *Obs.*

1511 *Burgh Rec. Edin.* (1869) I. 134 It is ordanit be the provest baillies and counsale anent the voydour callit cord and canves..of pakkis of lint [etc.]. *Ibid.*, To deliuer the cords and canves thairof as voidouris.

5. *Her.* As the name of an ordinary (see quots.).

1562 LEGH *Armory* (1597) 70 b, He beareth Tenné, two voyders, Or. This is the rewarde of a Gentlewoman for seruice by her done to the prince or princes, but then the voiders shoulde be of one of the nine furs or doublings. **1610** GUILLIM *Heraldry* II. vi. (1611) 64 Last of all in our ordinaries, cometh the voider, consisting of one arch line moderately bowing from the corner of the chiefe by degrees towards the nombrile of the escocheon and from thence in like sort declining untill it come unto the sinister base. **1780** EDMONDSON *Her.* II, *Voider*, is an ordinary much resembling the flanch, but is not quite so circular towards the centre of the field. **1882** CUSSANS *Her.* 71 Flasques and Voiders are Flanches which encroach less on the Shield.

6. a. One who or that which voids, clears away, or empties; an emptier. *rare.*

1589 ? LYLY *Pappe w. Hatchet* (1844) 25 We are..in all cases alike, till we haue brought Martin to the ablatiue case, that is, to be taken away with a Bulls Voyder. **1598** FLORIO, *Vuotatore*, an emptier, a voider. **1607** MARKHAM *Cavel.* III. (1617) 39 Purgations which are the emptiers and voiders of all superfluous humours.

b. *Med.* One who passes urine.

1969 *Radiology* XCII. 1178/1 Two of the patients were troubled by fecal retention and soiling and were thus infrequent defecators as well as infrequent voiders. **1974** *Amer. Jrnl. Roentgenol.* CXX. 407/1 We can enlarge the clinical application of these observations to patients with so-called megacystis syndrome..and the 'infrequent voider' syndrome.

†**7.** A servant or attendant who clears the table after a meal. Freq. *fig.* or in fig. context. *Obs.*

Often indistinguishable from senses 3 a and b.

1609 DEKKER *Lanth. & Candle Lt.* Wks. (Grosart) III. 221 The voider hauing cleered the table, Cardes and Dice..are serued up. **1644** CLEVELAND *Char. London Diurnall* 6 O brave Oliver! Times voyder, Sub-sizer to the Wormes. **1651** —— *Poems* 8 Thou that art able To be a Voider to King Arthurs Table.

†**8.** *pl.* Castings, ejections (of worms). *Obs.*⁻¹

a **1683** OLDHAM *Wks.* (1686) 83 Hither are loads from emptied Channels brought, And Voiders of the Worms from Sextons bought.

voidie (cunning): see VOISDIE.

ˈ**voiding**, *vbl. sb.* [f. VOID *v.* + -ING¹.] The action of the verb, in various senses.

1. The discharging, emitting, or evacuation *of* something (now only of the bladder or bowel); = VOIDANCE 1 a.

In quot. 1976 perh. *concr.* (cf. sense 8 a).

c **1400** *Destr. Troy* 304 Thurgh voidyng of venym with vomettes grete. *a* **1425** tr. *Arderne's Treat. Fistula*, etc. 26 So by tuo hole natural daies be it noȝt moued, bot if voydyng of þe wombe make it. **1545** RAYNALD *Byrth Mankynde* Hh iij, Betwene each voydynge of these lumps of blud. **1611** COTGR., *Vuidement*, a voyding, emptying, euacuating. **1671** GREW *Anat. Plants* iv. §19 It still gives way to the voyding of the Sap in these, for the mounting of that in the Root. **1727** BAILEY (vol. II), *Exgurgitation*, a casting or voiding up. **1926** J. S. HUXLEY *Ess. Pop. Sci.* 281 Underlying the voiding of the bladder is a reflex mechanism. **1972** *Jrnl. Urol.* CVIII. 259/2 During voidings, rectal pressure was monitored. **1976** *Lancet* 9 Oct. 773/1 Urine from each voiding was poured into a funnel and allowed to drip. **1980** *Brit. Med. Jrnl.* 29 Mar. 889/2 Radiographic screening of the outflow tract was carried out during voiding.

†**2.** The emptying out, clearing or sending away, removing, etc., of things or persons. *Obs.*

c **1435** *Chron. London* (Kingsford, 1905) 36 The same kyng..hath Juggid Thomas Arundell..to perpetuel exile and voydyng oute off the Rewme. **1477–9** *Rec. St. Mary at Hill* (1905) 82 For voyding of ij Tonne owte of a pryve. **1513** *Bk. Keruynge* in *Babees Bk.* (1868) 272 Keruynge of brede, layenge, & voydynge of crommes. *c* **1530** H. RHODES *Bk. Nurture* ibid. 67 Then if so be ye haue any more courses then on or two, ye may make the more hast in voyding. **1622** BACON *Hen. VII*, 101 The voiding of all Scottishmen out of England. **1688** SIR E. HERBERT *Hales' Case* 24 The Statutes for Voiding of Aliens out of the Kingdom.

†**3.** = VACATION 2. *Obs.*⁻¹

1468 *Liber B.* (Maldon, Essex) fol. 14 Ner noon a-rest make with-oute a warant of the court, but in the tyme of voydyng.

†**4.** The avoidance *of* something. *Obs.*

1398 TREVISA *Barth. De P.R.* XVIII. i. (1495) Yj/1 Beestes ..haue redynesse of wytte in..flyghte and voydynge of harme. **1519** *Interl. Four Elem.* (Percy Soc.) 35 And therfore thou shalt have another, For voydynge of stryfe. **1538** STARKEY *England* I. ii. 30 The wyl of man euer commynly folowyth that to the wych opynyon of perseuying the gud or voydyng of the yl ledyth hyt.

†**5.** The action of leaving or going away from a place, etc. *Obs.*

1597 BEARD *Theatre God's Judgem.* (1612) 33 Yet notwithstanding for all their voyding and shifting, the pestilence followed them whither soeuer they went. **1661** MORGAN *Sph. Gentry* IV. iii. 39 The whiche..at their voiding and going out shall abide and go in order, so as they sate at the table.

6. *Her.* (See quot. 1610 and VOIDED *ppl. a.* 2 c.) Also, the vacant space made in the voided charge or ordinary.

1610 GUILLIM *Heraldry* II. v. 49 Voiding..is the exemption of some part of the inward substance of things voidable, by occasion whereof the Field is transparent thorow the Charge. [Hence in subsequent glossaries and Dicts.] **1722** A. NISBET *Her.* 48 If the Voiding be of a different Tincture from the Field. **1828** [see VOIDED *ppl. a.* 2 c].

7. The action of rendering void or invalid; = VOIDANCE 4.

1649 BP. HALL *Cases Consc.* IV. x. 488 Now you inquire of the annulling or voiding of marriages made unlawfully. **1707** *Col. Rec. Pennsylv.* II. 145 That the voiding of one part might void the whole.

8. That which is voided or evacuated: **a.** *pl.* Excrements *of* persons or animals; castings *of* worms. *rare.*

1599 HAKLUYT *Voy.* II. II. 69 Here be solde the voydings of close stooles. **1864** *Morn. Star* 14 Oct., It was manured year after year by the voidings of sheep only. **1880** *Libr. Univ. Knowl.* (N.Y.) VI. 582 Voidings and trails of worms.

†**b.** Fragments or remains of food removed from the table. = VOIDANCE 7. *Obs.*

1680 OTWAY *Caius Marius* IV. ii, He..fed upon the voidings of my table. **1713** ROWE *Jane Shore* v, Oh! bestow Some poor remain, the voiding of thy table, A morsel to support my famish'd soul.

9. *attrib.*, as †**voiding beer**, beer given or drunk immediately before departing (cf. VOIDEE); †**voiding knife**, a knife used to clear away fragments of food from the table; †**voiding plate** = VOIDER 3 a.

1520 WHITINTON *Vulg.* (1527) 42 b, Set down a charger or a voyder & gadre vp the fragmentes therin, & wᵗ the voydynge knyfe gadre vp the..cromes clene. *a* **1600** DELONEY *Gentle Craft* II. ix. Wks. (1912) 193, I must be constrained to call my Maid for a cup of voyding beere ere you will depart. **1607** *Lingua* v. xiii. K iij [*Stage direction*] Gvstvs with a voiding knife in his hand. **1610** GUILLIM *Heraldry* II. vi. 64 These are called Voiders, either because of the Shallownesse wherein they doe resemble the accustomed voiding Plates with narrow brims vsed at Tables, or [etc.]. **1649** in *Archaeol.* (1806) XV. 281, 2 Voyding knives with christall handles.

ˈ**voidless**, *a. rare* [f. VOID *v.*]

a. That cannot be made void or annulled; not voidable.

1642 tr. *Perkins' Prof. Bk.* i. §12. 6 Some grants of some persons are voidlesse by themselves, by their heires, and by those which shall have their estates for ever.

b. *poet.* Unavoidable.

1908 HARDY *Dynasts* III. III. i. 382 All must prepare to grip with gory death In the now voidless battle.

† **'voidly**, *adv. Obs.* Also 5 **voidli, voydely,** 6 **-lye.** [f. VOID *a.* + -LY². Cf. OF. *vuidement* (Godef.).] Vainly, uselessly; to no purpose.

c **1400** *Destr. Troy* 4384 At Vaxor þe vayn pepull voidly honourit Bachian..as a blist god. **1402** *Pol. Poems* (Rolls) II. 103 Thanne was the memento put fal[s]ly in the masse, and hooli chirche voidli or madli biddith preye. **1493** *Festivall* (W. de W. 1515) 157 b, Of Christ thou takest thy name... And beware that thou bere not thy name voydely. **1544** BETHAM *Precepts War* I. cxcvi. I iv, By whych policie he shal neuer attempte, ne enterpryse anye matter voydelye, ..but by all wayes he shall haue hys owne desyre.

'voidness. [f. VOID *a.* + -NESS.]

† **1.** Freedom from work; leisure. *Obs.*⁻¹

1382 WYCLIF *Ecclus.* xxxviii. 25 Wisdom wrijt in tyme of voydenesse [1388 *marg.*, That is, in the tyme, in which thou art voide of other werkis of nede].

† **2.** The quality of being devoid or destitute of value or worth; inanity, vanity, futility.

1388 WYCLIF *Wisd.* xiv. 14 For whi the voidnesse of men [L. *supervacuitas*] foond these idols in to the world. **1552** HULOET, Voydenes, *inanitas, uanitudo.* **1603** FLORIO *Montaigne* I. I. 165 We are not so full of evill, as of voydnesse and inanitie.

3. The state or condition of being void, empty, or unoccupied; emptiness, vacancy, vacuity.

c **1400** *Lanfranc's Cirurg.* 116 þe brayn haþ sum substaunce of marie þe which fulfilliþ þe voidenes [*c* 1430 voydenesses] of þe forseid panniclis. *c* **1430** *Pilgr. Lyf Manhode* IV. xviii. (1869) 185 If þou be void þou shalt breke, oþer sowne hye; In voydnesse is but murmure whan men smyte it with an hard thing. **1561** HOLLYBUSH *Hom. Apoth.* 20 b, But if the voydnesse or emptinesse is in the nethermost membres, then tye hys vpper membres. **1595** SPENSER *Col. Clout* 850 Through him..began..the hungry t' eat, And voydnesse to seeke full satietie. **1603** HOLLAND *Plutarch's Mor.* 839 The Stoicks say, that the aire..admitteth no voidnesse at all. *a* **1693** *Urquhart's Rabelais* III. xiii. 105 There is nothing in the Body but a kind of Voidness and Inanity. **1727** BAILEY (vol. II), *Voidness*, emptiness. **1801** *Lusignan* I. 74 They seemed robbed of attraction, and to her preoccupied mind presented only the voidness of a desert. **1840** *Blackw. Mag.* XLVII. 775 The state of mind we have slightly depicted—so auspicious, one should think, from its troubled voidness, to the reception of religious convictions. **1888** *Harper's Mag.* July 210 The perfect transparency and voidness about us make the immense power of this invisible medium seem something ghostly.

b. A void or vacant space, esp. = VACUITY 8 b.

c **1430** [see *c* **1400** above]. **1603** HOLLAND *Plutarch's Mor.* 820 The schoole of Pythagoras holdeth that there is a voidnesse without the world,..out of which the world doth draw breath. *Ibid.* 1336 It is not likely that this world floteth ..in a vast and infinit voidnesse. **1642** H. MORE *Song of Soul* II. *Infin. Worlds* l, This precious sweet Ethereall dew..God ..did distill..thorough all that hollow Voidnesse.

† **4.** The state or condition of being without something; freedom *from*, absence or lack *of*, something. *Obs.*

1534 WHITINTON *Tullyes Offices* I. (1540) 33 The valyaunce of stomake is to be gyue to them and voydeness from angre and grefe. *a* **1569** KINGESMYLL *Confl. Satan* (1578) 25 This is our Crimosin, no less then voidnesse of all goodnesse. **1579** TOMSON *Calvin's Serm. Tim.* 286/2 He hardeneth himselfe in his impudencie, and voidnes of shame. *a* **1586** SIDNEY *Arcadia* IV. (1605) 406 In whom a man might perceiue what small difference in the working there is, betwixt a simple voidnesse of euill, and a iudiciall habite of vertue.

5. The state or condition of being legally void; nullity.

1883 *Sat. Rev.* 16 June 755 The existing system of prohibition (which, despite the quibble about voidness and voidableness, has notoriously been recognized in England from time immemorial).

† **voil.** *Cant. Obs. rare.* [prob. ad. F. *ville.*] A town.

1821 *Life D. Haggart* (ed. 2) 67 The whole voil was in an uproar. **1823** EGAN *Grose's Dict. Vulg. T.*, *Voil*, a town.

‖ **voilà** (vwala), *imp.* as *prep.* and *int.* [Fr., f. imp. of *voir* to see + *là* there.] There is, are, etc. As *int.*: there it is! there you are! lo! *voilà tout* (tu) [= all], that is all, there is nothing more to do or say.

1739 GRAY *Let.* 12 Apr. (1971) I. lx. 102 The minute we came, voila Milors Holdernesse, Conway, and his brother. **1778** H. WALPOLE *Let.* 12 Feb. (1955) XXVIII. 356 *Voilà* a truly long letter. **1801** JANE AUSTEN *Let.* 11 Feb. (1952) 121 Mr Bramston called here the morning before,—et voila tout. **1824** B. HAYDON *Jrnl.* 20 July in *Autobiogr.* (1926) I. 352, I have..no thoughts; I am painting portraits; *voilà tout.* **1858** LYTTON *What will he do with It?* (ed. 2) II. VI. i. 236 Ah, *voilà!* there he comes, the laggard! **1910** W. J. LOCKE *Simon* vi. 78 Dale asked me if he could call. I said 'Yes.' Perhaps I was wrong. Anyhow, *voilà!* **1920** D. H. LAWRENCE *Let.* in C. Mackenzie *My Life & Times* (1966) V. 169 One of F's diamond rings was stolen... One shouldn't have diamonds voila tout! **1973** *Philadelphia Inquirer* (Today Suppl.) 7 Oct. 5/1 Plain junk that becomes—voila!—a memento when a 'Historic Philly' decal is affixed. **1980** *Quilt World* Sept./Oct. 42/3 The batting and backing were then trimmed and the edges of the quilt sewn shut. Voila! a completed quilt. **1981** 'D. JORDAN' *Double Red* xxxiv. 156 Live all your life! That is all I know, *voilà tout.*

voile (vɔɪl, ‖vwal). [a. F. *voile* VEIL *sb.*] A thin semi-transparent cotton or woollen material much used for blouses and dresses.

1889 *Pall Mall G.* 25 June 6/1 Another dress was made of a material called voile, in biscuit colour. **1898** *Westm. Gaz.* 5 May 3/2 The term 'voile' covers a variety of makes of stuff, some like muslin, some like cloth. **1899** *Daily News* 29 April 8/4 The veiling that was so popular some years since, but which is now called 'voile'.

attrib. **1898** *Westm. Gaz.* 9 Sept. 3/3 A charming dress of white voile cashmere.

‖ **voilette** (vwalɛt). [F., dim. of prec.]

1. A little veil.

1842 C. RIDLEY *Let.* 9 Oct. in *Cecilia* (1958) viii. 101 She had on..a blue silk bonnet with a long veil (not a *voilette*). **1862** *Eng. Wom. Dom. Mag.* IV. 237/2 The bonnet is of white terry velvet, made with a voilette of lace. **1902** *Westm. Gaz.* 16 Oct. 3/1 The American whimsical, graceful draping of a veil of velvet-spotted chiffon has given rise to a remarkably pretty voilette in the shops there.

2. A kind of thin dress material.

1908 *Westm. Gaz.* 29 June 10/2 A gown made in fine voilette, trimmed with lace insertion.

† **voillance.** *Obs.*⁻¹ In 5 **woillaunce.** [a. OF. (*bien*)*voillance* (mod.F. *-veillance*), ad. L. (*bene*)*volentia* benevolence.] (Good)will.

1422 tr. *Secreta Secret., Priv. Priv.* 123 Than gouerne ye hame wyth good Woillaunce and bonerte.

† **voine,** obs. (southern dial.) var. FOIN *v.*

1596 HARINGTON *Metam. Ajax* Prol. B v b, For to voine or strike below the girdle, we counted it base and too cowardly.

† **voirably,** *adv. Obs.*⁻¹ [f. OF. *voirable*, f. *voire* true.] Truly, veritably.

1501 in *Lett. Rich. III & Hen. VII* (Rolls) I. 165 The king of Ro[mains] may voirably saye that the same amytee in as [much] as it is persevtuall..oughte not to be availlable to the said rebelles.

‖ **voir dire** (vwar dir). *Law.* Also **voire.** [OF. *voir* true, the truth + *dire* to say.] (See quots. 1701 and 1768). Also, an investigation into the truth or admissibility of evidence, held during a trial. Also *attrib.*

1676 T. W. *Office of Clerk of Assize* G j, Such person so produced for a witness, may be examined upon a *Voire Dire.* **1701** *Cowell's Interpr.* s.v., When it is pray'd upon a Trial at Law, that a Witness may be sworn upon a *Voir dire*; the meaning is, he shall upon his Oath speak or declare the truth. **1768** BLACKSTONE *Comm.* III. 332 If however the court has, upon inspection, any doubt of the age of the party, ..it may..examine the infant himself upon an oath of *voir dire, veritatem dicere*, that is, to make true answer to such questions as the court shall demand of him. **1834** *Edin. Rev.* Apr. 232 All the persons most intimately connected with Ireland are examined on the *voir dire.* **1968** *Daily Colonist* (Victoria, B.C.) 13 Sept. 42/3 Police testimony was called and a voir-dire—a trial within a trial—was held to determine whether a statement from one of the accused was admissible evidence. Immediately after the voir-dire, Magistrate Fraser questioned Dr. Carpenter. **1973** *N.Y. Law Jrnl.* 19 July 12/3 The voire dire examination as to the qualifications of this witness..revealed that he lacked the background which would qualify him as an expert. **1980** *Times* 18 Jan. 10/4 His Lordship was prepared to assume that the voire dire (trial within a trial) and the verdict taken together did constitute a final judgment on the same issues. **1981** *Daily Tel.* 26 June 6/3 The purpose of the 'trail within a trial' known to lawyers as a *voir dire*, had been to decide whether Brophy had been induced to make a number of alleged statements [etc.].

vois, obs. f. VOICE *sb.*

† **voisdie.** *Obs. rare.* Also 5 *Sc.* **woidie.** [a. OF. *voïsdie, voidie*: see VAIDIE.] Cunning, stratagem, sleight.

1375 BARBOUR *Bruce* IX. 747 3he suld press till deren3e 3our richt, And nocht with woidie [*MS.* woidre] na with slicht. [*Ibid.* x. 516 the correct reading is probably *voidy.*] **1390** GOWER *Conf.* III. 217 Nou schalt thou hiere a gret mervaile, With what voisdie that he wroghte.

† **voisin,** *a. Obs.*⁻¹ [a. F. *voisin*:—L. *vīcīn-um, -us* VICINE *a.*] Neighbouring.

1527 in Ellis *Orig. Lett.* Ser. III. II. 129 The voisin Realmes and Lordships shuld be in hassarde.

† **'voisinage.** *Obs.* Also 6–7 **voicinage,** 7 **voysinage.** [a. F. *voisinage*, f. *voisin*: cf. prec. and VICINAGE.]

1. The fact of being neighbouring or near.

1665 SIR T. HERBERT *Trav.* (1677) 283 Erzirum is a Town of great strength..and by reason of its voicinage to the Persian Dominions usually made the place of rendezvous, when the Turks have any design against that Empire. **1681** BURNET *Hist. Ref.* II. I. 203 Worcester and Glocester had been united, by reason of their Voicinage.

2. The neighbourhood; the adjoining district.

1642 JER. TAYLOR *Episc.* xxi. 114 All the Presbyters that came from Ephesus and the voisinage. **1647** —— *Lib. Proph.* Ep. Ded. 5, I had no Books of my own here, nor any in the voisinage. **1673** H. STUBBE *Further Vind. Dutch War* 4 We in the City and Country do repine, complain and rage, till the whole Voisinage prove Male-content. **1678** SANCROFT in Bp. Wake *Charge* (1706) 43 Three Priests.., who are of the Voisinage where the Person testified of, resides.

b. The neighbourhood *of* a place.

1649 JER. TAYLOR *Gt. Exemp.* II. Sect. x. 2 There hapned to be a marriage in Cana of Galilee in the voisinage of his dwelling. **1660** —— *Ductor* I. iv. rule 2 § 13 It occasioned the death of all the little babes in the city and voisinage of Bethlehem. **1720** S. PARKER *Biblioth. Bibl.* I. 415 A City came to be built in the Voisinage of this Holy Place.

† **'voisom.** *Obs. rare.* Also 6 **voysom.** [ad. OF. *avoëson*, var. of *avoueson*: see VOWSON.] An advowson.

1538 *Test. Ebor.* (Surtees) VI. 77 The voysom of one benifice. **1560** DAUS tr. *Sleidane's Comm.* 154 b, Pope Paule by his deputes ordeyned a reformation, touching the abuses of the Church, as permutations, voisomes, benefices incompatibles.

† **voisour.** *Obs.*⁻¹. [ad. OF. *voisure*, var. *vosure, vousure*, etc. (mod.F. *voussure*): cf. VOUSSOIR.] Vaulting.

c **1375** *Cursor M.* 2278 (Fairf.) Thorow þe grundwal of þis tour flum rennis wiþ grete voisour.

voist, variant of FOIST *v.*¹, VOUST *v.*

voit, obs. Sc. form of VOTE *sb.*

‖ **voiture** (vwatyr). [F. *voiture*:—L. *vectūra*, f. *vect-*, ppl. stem of *vehĕre* to convey. Cf. VETTURA.] A carriage or conveyance; a vehicle.

1698 W. KING tr. *Sorbière's Journ. Lond.* 6, I drew these Surprising Conclusions. First that a Hackney is a miserable *Voiture* [etc.]. **1698** M. LISTER *Journ. Paris* (1699) 13 Hackneys and Chairs, which here are the most nasty and miserable Voiture that can be. **1716** LADY M. W. MONTAGU *Let. to C'tess of Mar* 3 Aug., I..went in the longboat to Helvoetsluys, where we had voitures to carry us to the Brill. **1750** H. WALPOLE in *Phil. Trans.* XLVII. 46 Having caused an easy voiture to be made, I undertook the journey in it. **1779** WARNER in Jesse *Selwyn & Contemp.* (1844) IV. 32 But it rained hard, and I could get no *voiture* till I was forced to go to my engagement with Lady Lambert. **1814** *Sporting Mag.* XLIV. 60 To say a few words, in the way of compliment, to the driver of another voiture. **1840** ARNOLD in *Life & Corr.* (1844) II. App. C. 418 We are again in *voiture*, going along the edge of the sea in the port of Naples.

b. *transf.* and *fig.*

1718 LADY M. W. MONTAGU *Let. to Abbé Conti* 31 July, I hired an ass (the only voiture to be had there). **1725** DE FOE *Voy. round World* (1840) 347 This was the voiture with which they conveyed themselves quite down to the sea, and one of these boats it was that we spied..coming to us in the bay. **1746** CHESTERF. *Lett.* 9 Oct. (1774) I. 197 In this journey, the understanding is the *voiture* that must carry you through.

‖ **voiturette** (vwatyrɛt). [F., dim. of prec.] A small motor vehicle.

1897 *Daily News* 26 July 5/5 Three motor bicycles, thirteen tricycles, eight voiturettes or quadricycles with one wheel fore and aft and two in the middle and with one or two seats. **1901** *Contemp. Rev.* Jan. 107 It is far better to get a small car or a voiturette.

‖ **voiturier** (vwatyrje). [F., f. *voiture* VOITURE: see -IER.] The driver of a carriage or coach.

1763 SMOLLETT *Trav.* v, I have hired a berlin and four horses to Paris, for fourteen Louis d'ors; two of which the *voiturier* is obliged to pay for a permission from the farmers of the post. **1782** J. DOUGLAS *Trav. Anecd.* I. 41 The *voiturier* said he was in haste, and opened the door of the diligence. **1818** MRS. SHELLEY in Dowden *Shelley* (1887) II. 188 After dinner our voiturier comes. **1849** J. FORBES *Physic. Holiday* iv. (1850) 44 We arranged..with a voiturier, to take us to Schaffhausen the following day. **1878** BOSW. SMITH *Carthage* 434 A few shopkeepers, indeed, and most of the voituriers are Italian.

‖ **voiturin.** [F., f. *voiture* (cf. prec.), after It. *vetturino* VETTURINO.]

1. The driver of a voiture; a voiturier.

1768 STERNE *Sent. Journ.*, *Case of Delicacy*, I contracted with a *voiturin* to take his time with a couple of mules. **1790** H. WALPOLE *Let. to Miss Berry* 9 Nov., I am not surprised at your finding voiturins, or anybody, or anything dearer. *c* **1832** MRS. SHERWOOD in *Life* xxx. (1847) 524 We have to thank our landlord, who hurried us away under the pretence that the voiturin we had hired to drive us to Nice was obliged to be off that very morning.

2. A carriage for hire, a voiture.

1768 STERNE *Sent. Journ.*, *Case of Delicacy*, A *voiturin* arrived with a lady in it, and her servant-maid. **1768** BARETTI *Acc. Mann. Italy* II. 315 Mr. Sharpe's advice..of hiring voiturins through Savoy.

voivode ('vɔɪvəʊd). Forms: *α.* 6 **voy-, voiuoda, voivoda.** *β.* 7 **uoiuod,** 7, 9 **voyvode,** 9 **voivode.** *γ.* 9 **woivode, -wode, woywod.** [ad. Bulg. and Serb. *vojvoda*, Czech. *vojevoda*, Pol. *wojewoda*, Russ. *voevoda*, whence also Rom. *voevoda, -vod*, mod.L. *voivoda*, mod.Gr. βοεβόδα(ς).] = VAIVODE.

α. **1570** in Hakluyt *Voy.* (1599) I. 401 When we should haue deliuered him with the rest of his felowes vnto the Voiuodaes officers. *Ibid.*, Kneze Yoriue your Maiesties Voiuoda at Plasco. **1599** *Ibid.* II. I. 198 Voyuoda of Bogdania, & Valachia.

β. **1614** SELDEN *Titles Honor* 249 That of Vaiuod or Uoiuod, vsd in other parts of the Eastern Europe, being, I think, a Slauonig, or Windish word. **1686** W. HEDGES *Diary* (Hakl. Soc.) I. 232, I went to visit and present yᵉ Voyvode & Musellim of Diarbikeer. **1833** R. PINKERTON *Russia* 111 Now but an insignificant-looking place, though formerly the residence of a Voivod. **1869** TOZER *Highl. Turkey* I. 141 The protectorate..passed into the hands of the Hospodars or Voyvodes of Wallachia and Moldavia. **1884** W. CARR *Montenegro* 22 By repeated efforts the voivode maintains with difficulty a position on the coast.

γ. **1847** S. AUSTIN *Ranke's Hist. Ref.* III. 31 He encouraged Francis I. to keep alive the agitation in Germany,..and to support the Woiwode of Transylvania. **1847** MRS. A. KERR tr. *Ranke's Hist. Servia* xvi. 303 Amongst those executed before Belgrade were venerable Senators..and aged and renowned Woiwodes. **1868** *Daily Tel.* 1 Sept., To be prince of its park, lord of its lake, ruler of its river, and woiwode of its woods.

attrib. **1888** E. GERALD *Land beyond Forest* xxxiii. II. 84 Only such Tziganes are supposed to be eligible as are descended from a Woywod family.

'voivodeship. Also woiwod-, woywod-. [f. prec. + -SHIP.]

1. The district or province governed by a voivode.

1792 MORSE *Amer. Geog.* (1794) 662 Great Poland..is subdivided into 12 districts, called woiwodships. **1793** *State Papers* in *Ann. Reg.* 228 Following the border of the voivodship of Vilna. **1837** *Penny Cycl.* VIII. 133/1 Cracow, a republic..formerly part of the woywodship or palatinate of the same name in the Kingdom of Poland.

2. The office or dignity of a voivode.

1886 *Encycl. Brit.* XXI. 16/2 Multiplying the candidates for the voivodeship. *Ibid.* 17/2 Serban..was raised to the voivodeship of Walachia.

‖**voix** (vwa). [Fr. = voice.] Used in various phrases, as ***voix blanche*** (blɑ̃ʃ) [lit. 'white voice'], a toneless voice; ***voix céleste*** (selɛst) [lit. 'heavenly voice'] = *vox angelica* s.v. VOX 2; also *fig.*; ***voix d'or*** (dɔr) [lit. 'voice of gold'], a rich dramatic voice; ***voix grave*** (grav), a low-pitched or deep voice; ***voix moyenne*** (mwajɛn) [lit. 'middle voice'], a voice of middle range.

1876 STAINER & BARRETT *Dict. Mus.* 452/2 *Vox angelica.* .. Called also *Voix céleste*, unda maris, &c. **1895** G. B. SHAW *Our Theatres in Nineties* (1932) I. 137 The inevitable stale, puerile love scene is turned on to shew off that 'voix céleste' stop which Madame Berhardt, like a sentimental New England villager with an American organ, keeps always pulled out. **1897** *Ibid.* III. 210 Sarah Bernhardt's *voix d'or*. **1907** Voix celeste [see SUABE]. **1920** D. H. LAWRENCE *Lost Girl* x. 232 The muted *voix blanche* came through his lips. **1935** JOYCE *Let.* 19 Mar. (1966) III. 351, I sent The Dupan collection. There is none for *voix grave*. So I sent the best I could: *voix moyenne*. **1962** *Listener* 8 Nov. 779/2 Her verse has always lacked intellectual content, and..the later and more ambitious manner comes to seem one-tenth genuine poem-making to nine-tenths *voix d'or* and delphic vapour.

voiz, obs. form of VOICE *sb.*

vok(e, obs. variants of FOLK *sb.*

†**voke.** *Sc. Obs.*$^{-1}$ [Of obscure origin.] Arrogance, vanity, conceit.

a **1508** in Laing *Golagrus & Gawane* (1827) III. 20 Thou schryne secrete of stinkand voke & pride.

voky, vokie ('vəʊkɪ), *a. Sc.* Also 8 vowkie. [f. prec.] Proud, vain, elated. (In first quot. as *sb.* personified.)

a **1510** DOUGLAS *K. Hart* II. 523 To Vant and Voky ȝe beir this rowm slef. **1599** JAMES MELVILL *Diary* (1842) 459 That gossope..was na litle vokie for getting of the bern's name. **1755** R. FORBES *Jrnl. fr. London* in *Ajax's Sp.* 30, I was fidgin fain an' unco vokie fan I gat out oner her. **1768** ROSS *Helenore* III. 108 Of your consent..I'm mair nor fain, And vowkie [*ed. 2* vokie] that I can ca' you my ain. **1871** ALEXANDER *Johnny Gibb* xxxvii, He was met at the door by his mamma, who was in the mood described as 'vokie'.

vol (vɒl). *Her.* Also 8 vole, voll. [F. *vol* flight, f. *voler*:—L. *volāre* to fly.] Two wings displayed and joined at the base.

1722 NISBET *Syst. Her.* II. v. I. 363 When two Wings are joined together, they are then called a Vole, or two Wings in Lure. **1742** *Ibid.* IV. v. II. 14 A Crown relevant with Flowers, and issuing out of it a Demi Lion between two Volls for Crest. **1780** EDMONDSON *Her.* II, *Vol*, in the French blazon, is two wings conjoined and expanded. **1864** BOUTELL *Heraldry Hist. & Pop.* x. (ed. 3) 64 The two wings of an Eagle displayed, when conjoined and borne as a charge, are blazoned as a Vol. *Ibid.* xxxii. 466 Out of a crest-coronet a vol az. and or.

vol, southern ME. var. FULL *a.* and *adv.*; var. VOLE *sb.*¹; obs. Sc. var. WELL *sb.*, WOOL.

vol., abbrev. of VOLUME.

(*a*) **1682** (*title*), An Impartial Collection of the Great Affairs of State,..By John Nalson, LL.D. Vol. I. *Ibid.*, Vol. II. **1725** T. HEARNE *R. Brunne's Chron.* (1810) I. p. xcii, At the End of the first Vol. of Leland's Itin. **1790** J. WILLIAMS *Shrove Tuesday* in *A Cabinet* etc. (1794) 33 I'll purchase Sherlock, Drelincourt and Dodd, Thomas Aquinas and old Jerome's vols. **1806** BERESFORD *Miseries Hum. Life* VI. i, A few odd vols. of the Racing Calendar. *a* **1883** FAGGE *Princ. & Pract. Med.* (1886) I. 980 A coloured plate in vol. xxx of the 'Pathological Transactions'.

(*b*) **1864** WATTS *Dict. Chem.* II. 533, 2 vol. chlorine with 1 vol. hydride of ethyl.

‖**vola** ('vəʊlə). *Anat.* [L. *vola*, in the same sense.] The hollow of the hand or foot.

1693 tr. *Blancard's Phys. Dict.* (ed. 2), *Vola*, the Palm of the Hand; also the Cavity of the Foot. **1728** CHAMBERS *Cycl.* s.v. *Hand*, The Metacarpus, which is the Body of the Hand, including the Dorsum and Vola. **1808** BARCLAY *Muscular Motions* p. xx, An aspect towards the side on which the radius is situated is radial,..and if towards the side on which the vola or θεναρ is situated, thenal.

†**vo'lacious,** *a. Obs.*$^{-1}$ [f. L. *vol-āre* to fly + -ACIOUS.] Fitted for, given to, flying.

1653 H. MORE *Antid. Atheism* II. xi. (1712) 73 But the reason is, because they are Birds less volacious. **1706** PHILLIPS (ed. Kersey), *Volacious*, apt or fit to fly; as A Volacious Creature.

volage, *a.* Also 6 *Sc.* vollage. [a. OF. and F. *volage* (vɔlaʒ), f. *voler*:—L. *volāre* to fly.] Giddy, foolish; fickle, inconstant. (In later literary use reintroduced from mod. French.) Also in comb. ***volage-brained.***

? *a* **1366** CHAUCER *Rom. Rose* 1284 She fulfilled of lustynesse, That was not yit twelve yeer of age, With herte wylde, and thought volage. *c* **1386** —— *Manc. T.* 135 Whan phebus wyf had sent for hir lemman Anon þay wrouȝten al her wil volage. ? **1402** QUIXLEY *Ballades* xvii. in *Yorksh. Arch. Jrnl.* (1909) XX. 49 Vnto Gawayn may he be resemblyng, Curteys of loue, bot he was ouer volage. **1480** CAXTON *Ovid's Metam.* XIV. ii. (Roxb.) 56 b, He [Eneas] hath the herte harde, volage & more orageo[us] than the see. **1509** BARCLAY *Shyp of Folys* (1570) 194 A woman, variable as the winde Being of hir love unstable and volage. *c* **1520** BARCLAY *Jugurtha* (1557) 66 As a volage brained man he fullye determined agayne to begynne and continue the warre..rather then to yelde hym selfe to deathe or captivitie. **1549** *Compl. of Scotlande* i. 22 Oure vit is ouer febil, oure ingyne ouer harde, oure thochtis ouer vollage, ande oure ȝeiris ouer schort. *a* **1722** LD. FOUNTAINHALL *Decisions* (1759) I. 484 Some doubted how far such volage expressions inferred treason, being but *lubricum linguæ*. *a* **1773** MRS. E. MONTAGU in *Garrick's Private Corr.* (1832) II. 375 Lord Lyttelton is more *volage*, more difficult to fix, than any of Messieurs les Maccaronis. [**1825** JAMIESON *Suppl.* s.v., He's unco volage o' his siller.] **1845** JANE ROBINSON *Whitehall* xxii, As naturally alluring as beds of flowers to the volage butterfly. **1859** MEREDITH *R. Feverel* xxxvi, Both [parties] are volage: wine, tobacco, and the moon, influence both alike. **1865** 'OUIDA' *Strathmore* vi. I. 94 The volage, and somewhat indiscreet Princesse de Lurine.

Hence †**'volageness.** *Obs.*

1633 LD. WARISTON *Diary* (S.H.S.) 179 The fear of folks speaking, rayling, and jesting at my sudaine chainge and volagnes disuaded me.

volageous, *a. Sc.* ? *Obs.* Also 5 walageous. [a. AF. *volag(e)ous*, f. *volage*: see prec.] = VOLAGE *a.*

1375 BARBOUR *Bruce* VIII. 455 He wes bath ȝoung, stout, and fellоun, Richt ioly als, and volageous [*MS. E.* walageous]. *Ibid.* x. 553, I was sum dele volageous [*MS. E.* walageous], And lufit ane vench her in the toune. **1882** *Jamieson's Sc. Dict.* IV. 699 *Volageous*, adj., very light, giddy, or boastful. Clydes[dale].

†**volaille.** *Obs.*$^{-1}$ In 5 vollayle. [a. OF. *volaille*:—late L. *volātilia* fowls, neut. pl. of L. *volātilis*, f. *volāre* to fly.] Poultry; fowls.

1444 *Maldon Bye-law* in *Essex Herald* (188.) 11 April 6/2 There shall be no man on the market day..selle, ne bye ne flesh, ne fyshe, vollayle, ne other vytayle,..tyl the hour of pryme.

†**vol'alkali.** *Chem. Obs.* [f. VOL(ATILE) *a.* + ALKALI.] Volatile alkali; ammonia.

[*c* **1789** *Encycl. Brit.* (ed. 3) IV. 438/2 Vol. alkali.] **1796** KIRWAN *Elem. Min.* (ed. 2) II. 7 As pure Volalkali consists of mephitic..air and inflammable air concreted together. **1799** —— *Geol. Ess.* v. 142 Margraff.. found it to yield volalkali from some remains of the putrid wood that were still contained in it.

volant ('vəʊlənt), *a.* and *sb.* Also 6 wolant. [a. F. *volant*, pres. pple. of *voler*, also as sb.; or ad. L. *volant-*, *volans*, pres. pple. of *volāre* to fly. Cf. also It., Sp., Pg. *volante*. In 1 b and 3 placed after the noun.]

A. *adj.* †**1. a.** Riding at full gallop. *Obs. rare.*

a **1548** HALL *Chron., Hen. VIII*, 57 They ranne volant one as fast as he might ouertake the other. *Ibid.* 58 b, After that yᵉ king & his aides had performed their courses, thei ranne volant at al commers. [Hence in Holinshed and Baker.]

†**b.** *Mil.* So constituted as to be capable of rapid movement or action. (Cf. FLYING *ppl. a.* 4 d.)

a **1548** HALL *Chron., Hen. VIII*, 167 b, Certain Frenchmen..came before Alexandrie & there kept a siege volant. **1560** MAITLAND in E. Russell *Maitland of L.* (1912) ii. 57 For lack of money the camp volant cannot continue. **1577** HOLINSHED *Hist. Scot.* 479/1 in *Chron.* I, The French army in Scotland..determined with a siege volant to keepe the Englishmen in Hadington from vitayles and all other reliefe. **1617** MORYSON *Itin.* II. 160 Out of these Regiments was raised a squadron *volante* (or flying Regiment) which onely was to annoy the Rebels with continuall Alarums. *Ibid.* 176 Sir Henrie Powers squadron volant (or flying Regiment). **1633** T. STAFFORD *Pac. Hib.* II. xxi. (1821) 415 The Regiment volant (commanded by Sir Harvie Power). **1647** CLARENDON *Hist. Reb.* VI. §268 He sent Charles Cavendish.., with a Party Volant of Horse and Dragoons, into Lincolnshire.

†**c.** Hovering between two sides. *Obs.*$^{-1}$

a **1734** NORTH *Examen* I. ii. §25 (1740) 42 He was not, like the Party volant, waiting for Profers to determine him.

†**2.** ***volant piece***, an addition to the front of a helmet as a protection for the face, used especially in tournaments. *Obs.*

1509–10 in Meyrick *Anc. Armour* (1824) II. 251 These four knights shall present themselves..in harneys for the tylt without tache or breket, wolant pece on the hedde [etc.]. *a* **1548** HALL *Chron., Hen. VIII*, 123 To whiche coyffe or bassenet neuer armorer taketh hede, for it is euermore couered with the viser, barbet and volant pece. [**1824** MEYRICK *Anc. Armour* II. 263 The grand-guard, volant piece and gard de bras were put on with nuts which rendered pincers necessary.]

3. *Her.* Of birds, etc.: Represented as flying; having the wings expanded as if in flight.

Many special varieties, as *volant descendant*, *displayed*, *expansed*, etc., are explained in Berry's *Encycl. Herald.* (*c* 1828) I. Gloss.

1572 BOSSEWELL *Armorie* II. 29 b, R. beareth Sable and Argente..two Faucons volante, and a Greyhounde cursante. **1599** R. LINCHE *Fountain Anc. Fiction* F iij b, Downe from his shoulders depended a vestement, wherein was curiously proportioned the head of Medusa,..on the one side of him were placed certaine Eagles volant. **1610** GUILLIM *Heraldry* III. xxiii. 172 Heere also you see one gesture of a Fowle-volant. **1684** *Lond. Gaz.* No. 1980/4 A Coat of Armes being a Faulcon volant between 3 Mullets with distinction of a half Moon. **1728** CHAMBERS *Cycl.*, *Volant*, in Heraldry, is when a Bird in a Coat of Arms is drawn flying, or having its Wings spread out. **1838** *Penny Cycl.* XII. 143/2 Birds, according to their attitudes, are blazoned Volant, Displayed, Preying, etc. **1864** BOUTELL *Her. Hist. & Pop.* iii. (ed. 3) 66 Az. three butterflies volant or.

4. a. Flying; able to fly, capable of flight.

1665 SIR T. HERBERT *Trav.* (1677) 385 This is the onely four-footed Beast that's volant. **1698** *Phil. Trans.* XX. 167 As to the Fire-Flies,..I take them to be a Glow-Worm Volant. **1708** *Brit. Apollo* No. 90. 3/1 With Engine fatal to the Volant Kind. **1759** JOHNSON *Rasselas* vi, I have considered the structure of all volant animals. **1789** MRS. PIOZZI *Journ. France* I. 366 A kind of volant beetle. **1822** T. TAYLOR *Apuleius* 300 In every part of the world there are animals adapted to the several parts, the volant living in the air, and the gradient on the earth. **1830** *Fraser's Mag.* I. 222 The volant, bright-plumaged birds of heaven. **1876** FARRAR *Marlb. Serm.* xv. 142 Then shall thousands of volant angels bear us down upon their wings.

fig. **1655** FULLER *Ch. Hist.* v. i. §50 English silver now was current, and our gold volant in the Popes Courts. **1789** E. DARWIN *Bot. Gard.* II. (1791) 60 The first..Weighs with nice ear the vowel, liquid, surd, And breaks in syllables the volant word. **1796** BURNEY *Mem. Metastasio* I. 351 Let me in volant thought Ideal bliss renew. **1818** BP. J. JEBB *Life & Lett.* lxvii. 619 But, alas, my paper wings are very rarely volant. **1840** MRS. TROLLOPE in *New Monthly Mag.* LX. 40 A sort of volant admiration that seemed ready to take wing, and fly off in whatever direction he might please to indicate. **1898** MEREDITH *Poems, Napoleon* i. 11 Reverberant notes and long blew volant Fame.

b. *transf.* Connected with flying.

1748 RICHARDSON *Clarissa* VI. 3 But here,..to carry on the volant metaphor.., is a pretty little Miss [etc.].

5. a. Of things: Passing rapidly through the air or space, as if by flight; floating lightly in the air.

1603 HOLLAND *Plutarch's Mor.* 639 Alexander the Great, ..who..lanced himselfe in maner of a starre volant in the aire, leaping out of the East into the West. *Ibid.* 791 The intelligent nature of heaven, he [Plato] calleth, a Chariot volant, to wit, the harmonicall motion and revolution of the world. **1687** A. LOVELL tr. *Thevenot's Trav.* II. I. xii. 54 It may be thought that these fires volant proceed from sulphurous exhalations that rise out of the Earth. **1789** MRS. PIOZZI *Journ. France* II. 286 The volant shadows that cross our British hills. **1798** in *Spirit Pub. Jrnls.* (1799) II. 167 The eddying smoke, quick flame, and volant spark. **1813** T. BUSBY *Lucretius* II. IV. Comm. p. vii, The poet distinguishes the volant films of substances from other portions of bodies. **1831** CAMPBELL *View fr. St. Leonard's* 75 Men's volant homes that measure liquid space On wheel or wing. **1840** MRS. F. TROLLOPE *Widow Married* xxii. 150 She had always some volant ribbon or floating scarf to attend to and arrange. **1865** *Athenæum* 15 July 78/2 The car volant of Armida.

b. Moving rapidly or lightly; active, nimble. Also *fig.* of discourse.

1650 WELDON *Crt. Jas. I*, 176 Now have I brought this great Kings Reign to an end, in a volant discourse, and shall give you his Character in briefe. **1667** MILTON *P.L.* XI. 561 His volant touch Instinct through all proportions low and high Fled and pursu'd transverse the resonant fugue. **1708** J. PHILIPS *Cyder* II. 75 Bards with volant touch Traverse loquacious strings. **1753** RICHARDSON *Grandison* (1781) I. xxxvi. 251 Yes, my volant, my self-conducted quill, begin with the Sister. **1759** [H. DALRYMPLE] *Woodstock* (1761) 13 Their volant fingers o'er the chorded lyre, With modulating touch the artists ply. **1805** H. K. WHITE *Rem.* (1825) 95, I could..in the caverns of the ocean flood, thrid the light mazes of thy volant foot. **1828** *Lights & Shades* II. 277 Those dexter fingers, such volant summoners of sound. **1897** DOWDEN *French Lit.* v. iii. 367 He knew how to wing his verses with a volent [*sic*] refrain.

†**c.** Of colours: Changing, iridescent. *Obs.*$^{-1}$

1616 LANE *Contn. Sqr.'s T.* XI. 204 *note*, All colors vaunced, save white,..with all new volant dies of gallant dresse.

6. Characterized by, of the nature of, flight.

1818 MRS. ILIFF *Corfu* Poems (ed. 2) 98 The games, the race, the wrestlers meed; The discus urged with volant speed. **1831** *Blackw. Mag.* XXIX. 263 What godlike grace in that volant motion! **1863** LYELL *Antiq. Man* xxii. 446 A change from..volant to non-volant habits of living. **1891** C. E. CRADDOCK *In 'Stranger People's' Country* xvi. 312 He turned to catch through the trees a flitting glimpse of her light dress, her volant attitude, as she sped silently and secretly back to the waiting group on the porch.

7. Flounced; frilled. (Cf. sense 3 below.)

1902 *Daily Tel.* 2 Aug. 3/2 The seamed skirt..has the preference over the volant skirt.

B. *sb.* †**1.** ***to act, to keep (upon), the volant,*** to hover between two parties, sides, or opinions. *Obs.*

a **1734** NORTH *Examen* I. ii. §64. (1740) 63 And so they kept the Volant a good While, and did not declare on which Side they would fall. *Ibid.* III. vi. §69. 474 The Dutch had acted the volant, and done enough, on the one Side or the other, to have kept the Fire alive. *a* **1734** —— *Lives* (1826) III. 336 He..chose to keep upon the volant, free to discourse and censure as he from time to time thought fit.

2. = ***volant piece*** (see sense A. 2 above). *rare*$^{-0}$.

1867 SMYTH *Sailor's Word-bk.* 714 *Volant*, a piece of steel on a helmet, presenting an acute angle to the front.

3. A flounce or frill.

1851 *Harper's Mag.* Jan. 288/1 Five volants are set on full, each being trimmed at a little distance from the edge by a narrow guimpe. **1882** CAULFEILD & SAWARD *Dict. Needlew.* 515/1 *Volant*, the French term denoting either a flounce, or a frill; both of which are descriptions of dress trimmings. **1908** *Daily Chron.* 17 June 6/5 Her muslin Empire dress had a deep white cloth 'volant'.

4. = VOLET 2.

1898 *Daily News* 14 July 6/2 The most interesting of the late acquisitions is the pair of volants or shutters to Lionardo's Holy Family.

Hence 'volantly *adv.*, in a volant manner.

1876 J. Ellis *Caesar in Egypt* 98 Two seraphs hovering o'er the fragile ark, Its puny canvas fanning volantly.

‖**volante** (vo'lante). [Sp.: see volant *a.*] A two-wheeled covered carriage drawn by a horse ridden by a postilion (freq. with another horse attached at the side), used in Spanish countries. Mod. examples refer chiefly to Cuba.

1791 J. Townsend *Journ. Spain* (1792) I. 105 You pay for a volanté with a good mule, attended by a guide, five shillings a day. 1817 Keatinge *Trav.* I. 55 He is an author for the closet (a snug parlour we should say in England), and not for a volante. 1854 Bartlett *Mex. Boundary* I. i. 8 Towards evening..we took a volante and drove out to the bishop's palace. 1878 *Masque Poets* 185 Drawn (behind a jaunty Black-faced postilion) in a gay volante.

Hence **volantier**, the owner or driver of a volante.

1791 J. Townsend *Journ. Spain* I. (1792) 77, I left Montpellier at five in the morning with a volantier of Barcelona.

volante, variant of volunty *Obs.*

‖**volapié** (volapi'e). [Sp., lit. 'flying foot', f. *volar* to fly + *pie* foot.] In *Bullfighting*, a manner of killing in which the bullfighter runs in to kill a stationary or slowly-moving bull. Also *à volapié* adv. phr., in this manner.

1838 *Q. Rev.* LXI. 418 The 'volapie'..is dangerous but beautiful; the bull is met half way. 1910 *Encycl. Brit.* IV. 790/1 The stroke..is usually given *à volapié* (half running), the *espada* delivering the thrust while stepping forward, the bull usually standing still. 1932 E. Hemingway *Death in Afternoon* xix. 244 The volapié to be properly executed demands that the bull be heavy on his feet. 1967 McCormick & Mascareñas *Compl. Aficionado* ii. 58 This time a three-quarter sword follows a good *volapié*.

Volapük, -puk ('vɒləpʊk). [f. *vol* world (alteration of E. *world*) + *a* connecting vowel, + *pük* speech (alteration of E. *speak*).] An artificial language, chiefly composed of materials from European tongues, invented in 1879 by a German priest, Johann M. Schleyer, as a means of international communication. Also *transf.*

1885 *Sat. Rev.* 3 Jan. 15/1 Volapük is the name of the recently invented world-language, or universal tongue. 1888 *Contemp. Rev.* Sept. 434 In his shop-fronts the Russian mercifully interprets his Cyrillian characters by that original volapuk of the world's infancy, the picture. 1890 O. W. Holmes *Over Tea-cups* v. 99 Music will be the universal language—the *Volapük* of spiritual being.

Hence 'Volapüker, 'Volapükist, an advocate or student of Volapuk.

1886 *Pall Mall G.* 30 Dec. 4/1 It seems that the Volapükists have published a directory giving the names and addresses of its disciples. 1887 *Scott. Leader* 28 Nov. 4 As much practice..as in the case of a living language, would be needed to give the Volapuker facility in dialogue.

volar ('vəʊlə(r)), *a.*[1] *Anat.* [f. vola + -ar.] Of or belonging to the palm of the hand or the sole of the foot; palmar.

1814 Wishart tr. *Scarpa's Treat. Hernia* Explan. p. xvi, The term *volar* in the atlantal extremities is restricted, as in common anatomical language, to the parts within the palm of the hand. 1870 Rolleston *Anim. Life* 9 Any bone of similar function in connection with the tendons on the volar side of the hand. 1885 *Buck's Handbk. Med. Sci.* I. 353 Superficial volar [artery]: Very often of small size, so small that it terminates in the muscles of the thumb.

'**volar**, *a.*[2] *rare*$^{-1}$. [f. L. *vol-āre* to fly.] Employed in flying.

1840 *Cuvier's Anim. Kingd.* 69 The volar membrane is attached more or less near to the middle of the back, in some of the Roussettes.

volary ('vəʊlərɪ). Now *rare*. Also 7 volarie, vollary, 7–8 volery. [app. ad. F. *volière*, after types in -ary, -ery.]

1. A large bird-cage; an aviary. Also *fig.* and in fig. context.

1630 B. Jonson *New Inn* v. i, She..now sits penitent and solitary, Like the forsaken turtle, in the volary Of the light Heart, the cage, she hath abused. 1654 Flecknoe *Ten Years Trav.* 110 In lieu of imagining it flying about the world, we may imagin it rather pent up, and fluttering about some narrow Bird-cage or volary. 1687 A. Lovell tr. *Thevenot's Trav.* ii. 105 On the left hand before a Garden on the River-side, there is a Volary full of rare Fowl, as Estradges, Peacocks and others. 1718 Ozell tr. *Tournefort's Voy.* II. 235 The gardens, the volaries, the dog-kennel, the falconry, the square and bazar..are worth seeing. ? 1743 Lady M. W. Montagu *Lett., to Mrs. Forster* (1893) II. 124, I find myself so improperly lodged as if I inhabited a volery. 1756 Mrs. Calderwood in *Coltness Coll.* (Maitland Club) 186 Here is a flat, laid out like a parterre,..and a volary, which is a little place with the face of it wire. 1892 *Daily News* 3 Sept. 5/3 Birds..living happily in..confinement in very large cages, in spacious volaries.

transf. a 1637 B. Jonson *Underwoods* xvi. Wks. (Rtldg.) 694/1, I thought thee then our Orpheus, that wouldst try, Like him, to make the air one volary. 1640 Carew *Poems* Wks. (1824) 34 Yet thou hadst daintyes, as the skie Had only been thy volarie.

attrib. 1720 Strype *Stow's Surv.* vi. iii. II. 624/1 Edward Story, Esq; Volary-keeper to King Charles II. 1684.

2. *collect.* The birds kept in an aviary. Also *fig.*

1693 Locke *Educ.* §94 An old Boy, at his first Appearance, with all the Gravity of his Ivy-Bush about him, is sure to draw on him the Eyes and Chirping of the whole Town Volery. 1745 tr. *Columella's Husb.* viii. x, These things wipe off and remove the nauseating of such of them [thrushes] as sit loitering in the aviaries, and make the whole volary more greedy and voracious.

†**volate.** *Obs. rare.* (Meaning uncertain.)

c 1460 *Oseney Reg.* 27, j. crofte and a volate [L. *volatam*] þat Hemmying preste was i-wonyd to have.

volatic (və'lætɪk), *sb.* and *a.* Now *rare* or *Obs.* [ad. L. *volātic-us*, f. *volāt-*, ppl. stem of *volāre* to fly.]

A. *sb.* A winged creature.

a 1643 W. Cartright *On Mr. Stokes* vi, How would they vex their Mathematicks, Their Ponderations, and their Staticks, To skew the Art of these Volaticks? 1657 Angier *Elegy* in S. Purchas *Pol. Flying-Ins.*, I've sometimes viewed thy small Volaticks flye Like golden atom's hov'ring in the sky.

B. *adj.* That flies or flits about; *spec.* in *Path.* of a variety of itch.

1684 tr. *Bonet's Merc. Compit.* iii. 71, I ordered a Cupping-glass..to get out that Volatick Spirit, which daily ranged the whole body. *Ibid.* xvi. 549 This Remedy is of so great efficacy, that..presently the volatick Itch falls off dead. 1762 Falconer *Shipwr.* iii. 292 Amidst the gloom volatic meteors blaze. 1860 Mayne *Expos. Lex.* 1336/2 *Volaticus*,..flying; flitting; inconstant; volatic.

So vo'latical *a. rare*$^{-0}$.

1656 Blount *Glossogr.*, *Volatical*, that flyes or goes away suddenly, flitting, inconstant.

†**vo'latify**, *v. Obs.*$^{-1}$ [f. L. *volāt-* (cf. next) + -(i)fy.] *trans.* To render volatile.

1666 J. H. *Treat. Gt. Antid.* 4 Poure thereon a pint and half of volatile Salt of Tartar volatified with spirit of Wine.

volatile ('vɒlətaɪl, -ɪl), *sb.* and *a.* Forms: 4, 7–8 volatil, 5 -tille, 6–7 -till, 7 -tle; 4– volatile (4 -tyle). [a. OF. and F. *volatil, -ile* (= Sp. and Pg. *volatil*, It. *volatile*), or ad. L. *volātilis* (also late L. *volātile* sb.), f. *volāt-*, ppl. stem of *volāre* to fly.]

A. *sb.* †1. *collect.* Birds, *esp.* wild-fowl. *Obs.* (So OF. *volatil.*)

a 1300 *Cursor M.* 6386 Volatil sent þaim þat king. 13.. *Coer de L.* 4225 Off..Partryhches, plovers, and heroun, Off larkes, and smale volatyle. 1382 Wyclif *Gen.* vii. 14 Al that moueth vpon the erthe in his kynde, and al volatile after his kynde. a 1400–50 *Alexander* 4637 Of all þe frutis on þe fold we fange at oure will, Bath venyson & volatile & variand fisches. c 1475 *Promp. Parv.* 512/1 (K.), Volatile, wyld fowle,..*volatile*. 1501 Douglas *Pal. Hon.* iii. xv, To noy the small the greit beistis had na will, Nor rauenous foulis the lytill volatill. 1572 *Satir. Poems Reform.* xxxviii. 36 As the fals fowler..Deuoiris the pure volatill he wylis to the net. a 1660 *Contemp. Hist. Irel.* (Ir. Archæol. Soc.) I. 164 Espiing that greate mortalitie not yett interred, disfigured by volatle and other wilde beastes.

2. A winged creature; a bird, butterfly, or the like; a fowl. Usually in plural.

a 1325 *Prose Psalter* lxxvii. 31 [lxxviii. 27] He rained vp hem pudre, flesshes, and volatils feþered as grauel of þe se. 1382 Wyclif *Matt.* xxii. 4, I haue made redy my mete, my boles and volatilis ben slayn. 1398 Trevisa *Barth. De P.R.* xii. v. (Bodl. MS.), Alle oþer volatiles bringeþ forþe burþe vnneþe in a ȝeere. 1632 Guillim *Heraldry* (ed. 2) iii. xxi. 234 No lesse than other Volatiles, or flying Animals. 1651 Biggs *New Disp.* ⁋294 Nor is a volatile contrary to a Reptile. 1666 J. Davies tr. *Rochefort's Caribby Isles* 230 As to the Volatiles of this Country, there are Turkeys, Pintadoes, Parrots, Woodquists. 1716 *Phil. Trans.* XXIX. 530 That the Tongue of this Volatile was much commended..will appear from the following Quotations. 1750 G. Hughes *Barbados* 61 By Animals I would be understood to mean..such only as are generally termed Quadrupeds, Volatiles, and Insects. 1819 H. Busk *Vestriad* ii. 390 From that first ball where Orpheus, first of lutes, Drew reptiles, volatiles, pantiles, and brutes. c 1876 R. F. Burton in Lady I. Burton *Life* (1893) I. iii. 40 A dove not being procurable, its place was supplied by a turkey-cock, and the awful gabbling of the ill-behaved volatile caused much more merriment than was decorous.

3. A volatile matter or substance.

1686 W. Harris tr. *Lemery's Chym.* i. xvii. (ed. 3) 408 These volatiles ought to be taken always in some cold liquor and not in hot broth. 1709 T. Robinson *Vind. Mosaick Syst.* 16 The Earth..was only a confus'd Mass of Matter, consisting of Solids, Fluids, and Volatiles, all jumbled together. 1748 Hartley *Observ. Man* i. ii. §7. 248 Applying Volatiles to the Nose. 1782 E. Gray in *Med. Comm.* I. 33 Volatiles..which had been given..in order to encourage perspiration. 1810 S. Green *Reformist* II. 2 The excessive heat of the place..rendered the use of volatiles..requisite to the delicate fair ones who composed this religious group. 1840 L. Hunt *Legend Florence* ii. ii, Applying a volatile to her temples. 1883 *Times* 6 June 5/2 The machine is fitted with a volatile the fumes of which cause instantaneous death.

B. *adj.* †1. Of meal: So fine or light as readily to fly about. *Obs.*

1597 A. M. *Guillemeau's Fr. Chirurg.* 46/2 An astringent Plaster, made of Bolus, flower, or volatill meale, of whytes of Egges [etc.]. 1599 —— *Gabelhouer's Bk. Physicke* 54/1 Sift them till they resemble volatile meale.

2. a. Flying, capable of flying, volant.

1626 Bacon *Sylva* §728 The Catterpiller toward the End of Summer waxeth Volatile, and turneth to a Butterflie, or perhaps some other Fly. 1653 H. Cogan *Diodorus Siculus* 94 It produceth likewise all kinde of creatures both terrestrial and volatile, greater and stronger then other regions. a 1676 Hale *Prim. Orig. Man.* iv. ii. (1677) 304 The production of Animals aquatil and volatil preceded the production of terrestrial Animals. 1719 J. T. Philipps tr. *Thirty-four Confer.* 308 Their Souls will be re-committed into Bodies two-footed, four-footed, or volatile. 1786 tr. *Beckford's Vathek* (1868) 64 One of those beautiful blue butterflies of Cashmere, which are at once so volatile and rare. 1825 Hone *Every-day Bk.* I. 292 Pheasants by all that's volatile! 1865 *Athenæum* 21 Oct. 535/1 Conveyed by some volatile insect.

transf. 1796 H. Hunter tr. *St.-Pierre's Stud. Nat.* (1799) II. 135 The seeds of the largest mountain-trees are no less volatile. That of the maple has two membranous pinions similar to the wings of a fly. 1812 J. Cutler *Descr. Ohio* 81 The cotton wood tree..has been supposed to be the same as the lombardy poplar, but..differs, at least, in the very large quantity of volatile, capillary pappus attached to the seeds.

b. Moving or flitting from one place to another, esp. with some degree of rapidity.

1654 Vilvain *Epit. Ess.* v. lii, Two Meteors, Thunder and Lightning volatil. 1660 Jer. Taylor *Ductor* i. iii. rule 1 §5 It is like a fire-stick which in the hand of a child being gently mov'd, gives a volatile and unfixed light. 1856 *N. Brit. Rev.* XXVI. 169 M. De la Hire..describes these muscæ as of two kinds, some permanent and fixed,..and others as volatile, or flying about and changing their place, even though the eye be fixed.

c. Characterized by rapid passage. *rare*$^{-1}$.

1655 *Marrow Complements* 8 With volatile haste let us set forward to the temple.

3. a. Of substances: Characterized by a natural tendency to dispersion in fumes or vapour; liable to, or susceptible of, evaporation and diffusion, at ordinary temperatures.

1605 Timme *Quersit.* Ded., Of which foure elements two are..volatil, as water and ayre. 1610 B. Jonson *Alch.* ii. iii, Infuse vinegar, To draw his volatile substance and his tincture. 1656 J. Smith *Pract. Physick* 252 Nitre is commended because it fixeth volatil things. 1671 J. Webster *Metallogr.* iv. 74 Sulphur is fixt and not volatile. 1708 J. Philips *Cyder* i. 21 How with heavy Bulk Volatile Hermes, fluid and unmoist, Mounts on the Wings of Air. 1764 Reid *Inquiry* ii. §1 These volatile particles do probably repel each other. 1789 W. Buchan *Dom. Med.* (1790) 437 A bit of sugar dipped in compound spirits of lavender, or the volatile aromatic tincture. 1813 Sir H. Davy *Agric. Chem.* i. (1814) 6 As soon as dung begins to decompose it throws off its volatile parts. 1854 Ronalds & Richardson *Chem. Technol.* (ed. 2) I. 49 The volatile or organic portion of coal is composed of the same elements as wood, peat and brown coal. 1876 Routledge *Discov.* 28 This preliminary treatment removes all the volatile matters, expelling the whole of the carbonic acid.

transf. 1769 E. Bancroft *Guiana* 234 They afford a very strong, volatile, disagreeable smell.

b. *volatile salt* or *salts*.

1639 G. Plattes *Discov. Subterr. Treas.* 39 The fixed salt of any vegetable is different from the volatill or fugitive salt of the same. 1662 R. Mathew *Unl. Alch.* 20 Thy Salt doth also consist of three sorts, a fixed Salt, and a Nitrous, and a Volatil. 1670 W. Simpson *Hydrol. Ess.* 30 The neatness and novelty of the word volatile salt. 1712 tr. *Pomet's Hist. Drugs* I. 4 It affords a great deal of volatile Salt. 1765 Sterne *Tr. Shandy* vii. ii, The nervous juices, with the fix'd and volatile salts, are all jumbled into one mass! 1813 J. Thomson *Lect. Inflam.* 95 After smelling to volatile salts, or eating too much strong mustard,..a pain is often felt above the eye-brows. 1837 Carlyle *Fr. Rev.* i. i. iii, Few are so happy as the Duke d'Orleans and the Prince de Condé; who can themselves, with volatile salts, attend the King's antechamber.

ellipt. 1683 J. Reid *Scots Gardiner* (1756) 80 Some have sown it [*sc.* salt] on moist muirish land to great advantage, for being far from the sun they have little volatile.

c. *volatile alkali*, ammonia. (See alkali 3.) Hence *volatile-alkaline* adj.

1728 Chambers *Cycl.* s.v. *Alkali*, No body hath hitherto produced a volatile Alkaly from the Acids of the Mineral Kingdom. 1766 *Phil. Trans.* LVI. 98 The tincture produced did not effervesce with acids, but retained a volatile-alkaline smell. 1800 Henry *Epit. Chem.* (1808) 121 Carbonate of ammonia retains, in a considerable degree, the pungent smell of the pure volatile alkali. 1854 J. Scoffern in *Orr's Circ. Sci.*, *Chem.* 327 Ammonia was formerly denominated the volatile alkali.

d. *volatile oil*: (see essential 5 b.).

1800 tr. *Lagrange's Chem.* II. 229 Volatile oils are distinguished from the fixed oils by their acrid taste, their volatility, their aromatic odour, and their solubility in alcohol. 1836–41 Brande *Man. Chem.* (ed. 5) 1143 The volatile or essential oils are generally obtained by distilling the vegetables, or the parts of the plants which afford them, with water, in common stills. 1880 Haughton *Phys. Geogr.* vi. 301 Its flora is characterized by bulbous plants and those yielding volatile oils.

e. Connected with volatilization.

1807 T. Thomson *Chem.* (ed. 3) II. 403 The inside of the volatile tube is coated with charcoal in the state of a fine black.

4. Readily changing from one interest or mood to another; changeable, fickle; marked or characterized by levity or flightiness: a. Of the mind, disposition, etc.

1647 Clarendon *Hist. Reb.* iv. §146 If the Volatile, and Unquiet Spirit of the Lord Digby had not prevailed with the King. 1665 Glanvill *Scepsis Sci.* xiv. 81 If we consider the volatile nature of those officious assistants, and the several causes which occur..to scatter and disorder them. 1719 De Foe *Crusoe* ii. (Globe) 330 The French..Temper is allow'd to be more volatile,..and their Spirits more fluid than in other Nations. 1759 Johnson *Idler* No. 58 ⁋3 Sometimes occasions will be wanting to tempt the mind, however volatile, to sallies and excursions. 1796 Mme. D'Arblay *Camilla* I. 115 Her spirits were volatile, but her heart was tender. c 1850 *Arab. Nts.* (Rtldg.) 527 Neither kindness nor the fear of punishment was able to restrain his volatile and restless disposition. 1861 Ld. Brougham *Brit. Const.* App. 461 The fickle, inconstant, volatile temper of the people.

b. Of persons.

1719 Vanbrugh in *Athenæum* (1890) 6 Sept. 322/1 To think, that such a volatile gentleman..shou'd turn his thoughts & application to the duty of a Surveyors business, is a monstrous project. 1745 J. Mason *Self-Knowledge* iii. i. (1853) 167 What is it, but a Want of Self-Knowledge and

Self-Government, that makes us so unsettled and volatile in our Dispositions? **1791** BOSWELL *Johnson* an. 1769 (1816) II. 108, I was volatile enough to repeat to him a little epigrammatick song of mine. **1830** D'ISRAELI *Chas. I*, III. vii. 129 Henrietta was nothing more than a volatile woman. **1852** MRS. STOWE *Uncle Tom's C.* xxvii, Volatile, fickle, and childish as they generally were, they were soft-hearted and full of feeling. **1878** BOSW. SMITH *Carthage* 55 Either of these stories..may among a people so volatile as the Carthaginians, perhaps be true.

ellipt. **1756** C. SMART tr. *Horace, Epist.* I. xviii. (1826) II. 259 The melancholy hate the merry,..the volatile dislike the sedate.

c. Of markets, shares, etc.: showing sharp changes in price or value (merging with uses of sense 5).

1931 *Daily Express* 31 Jan. 2/6 Some volatile issues.. recorded..advances. **1977** *Time* 19 Dec. 10/1 It stabilized the volatile lira. **1981** *Times* 25 Sept. 1/6 The pound slipped further against all leading currencies on nervous and volatile foreign exchange markets. *Ibid.* 26 Sept. 23/6 Leading shares..remained volatile until after-hours trading when prices steadied a little. **1985** *Times* 26 Jan. 23/1 It has been one of the most volatile [Stock Exchange] accounts in recent history.

5. a. Evanescent, transient; readily vanishing or disappearing; difficult to seize, retain, or fix permanently.

1665 JER. TAYLOR *Unum Necess.* v. §6 Those transient acts of devotion, or other volatile and fugitive instances of Repentance, are not the proper and proportion'd remedy to the evil of vicious habits. **1661** K. W. *Conf. Charac.* (1860) 58, I cannot give a more substantiall expression to such a violatile subject. **1686** HORNECK *Crucif. Jesus* xvii. 499 Will you prefer a few airy, volatile joys before their safety? **1711** SHAFTESB. *Charac.* III. 234 Whatever Interpretations might have been made of this fragil and volatil Scripture. **1756** BURKE *Subl. & B.* Introd., This delicate and aërial faculty, which seems too volatile to endure even the chains of a definition. **1791** BOSWELL *Johnson* Introd. (1816) I. 9 The incidents which give excellence to biography are of a volatile and evanescent kind. **1844** KINGLAKE *Eothen* i, In the Ottoman dominions..wealth..is a highly volatile blessing, not easily transmitted. **1863** —— *Crimea* (1877) I. xiv. 239 He was a buyer and seller of those fractional and volatile interests in trading adventures which go by the name of 'shares'. **1876** MOZLEY *Univ. Serm.* xi. 214 These are..mere volatile day dreams.

b. *Computers.* Of a memory: retaining data only as long as there is a power supply to it.

1950 W. W. STIFLER et al. *High-Speed Computing Devices* xiv. 305 In a volatile storage medium, like a delay line, retransmission of each signal once during each storage cycle period is required. **1970** O. DOPPING *Computers & Data Processing* x. 136 The flip-flop register is a fast, expensive, volatile memory. **1979** R. MUTCH *Gemstone* viii. 95, I need two microprocessors, read-only and volatile memories,.. and a battery.

†**6.** Of the air: Light; not oppressive. *Obs.*⁻¹

1698 FRYER *Acc. E. India & P.* 328 The Air is Serene and Volatile, which..is highly serviceable to the Respiration of all Living Creatures.

'volatileness. [f. prec.] The character or state of being volatile; volatility. Chiefly *fig.*

a **1676** HALE *Prim. Orig. Man.* I. i. (1677) 19, I do not see the Animal or Vital Spirits, neither can they, by reason of their subtilty and volatileness, be discovered immediately to the Sense. *a* **1690** HOPKINS *Expos.* etc. (1692) 314 This would fix that Volatileness and Flittiness of our Memories, and make every truth as indelible, as it is necessary. **1727** BAILEY (vol. II), *Volatileness*, volatile Nature, Fleetingness; also a Property of Bodies whose Particles are apt to evaporate with Heat. **1766** *Life Quin* xii. (1887) 48 Many mistakes which our immortal bard Shakespeare had by oversight, or the volatileness of his genius, suffered to creep into his works. **1849** *Tait's Mag.* XVI. 314/1 With the volatileness of youth, he turned to his own amusements.

volatility (vɒlə'tɪlɪtɪ). [ad. mod.L. *volatilitas*, f. L. *volātilis* VOLATILE *a.* Cf. F. *volatilité* (1641), It. *volatilità*, Sp. *volatilidad*, Pg. *-idade*.] The quality, state, or condition of being volatile, in various senses.

1. Readiness to vaporize or evaporate, tendency to be readily diffused or dissipated in the atmosphere, especially at ordinary temperatures.

1626 BACON *Sylva* §294 Heat causeth the Spirits to search some Issue out of the Body, as in the Volatility of Metals. **1657** G. STARKEY *Helmont's Vind.* 311 Essentiall or distilled Oyls,..by reason of their volatility, not abiding decoction, are with difficulty made into a Sapo. **1684-5** BOYLE *Min. Waters* 29 Of the fixity or volatility of the Saline part in strong fires. **1718** QUINCY *Compl. Disp.* 7 By Spirit is understood the most fine and subtile Parts of Bodies, which is discoverable by its Volatility and Quickness to the Smell and Taste. **1757** *Phil. Trans.* L. 427 From one or more of which principles, I apprehend, the volatility or fixity of all minerals..takes its origin. **1800** tr. *Lagrange's Chem.* II. 45 Ammonia warm has less action on zinc, on account, no doubt, of its volatility. **1857** MILLER *Elem. Chem.*, *Org.* iii. 157 From its great volatility..it [*sc.* ether] is frequently employed for producing cold artificially. **1880** MACCORMAC *Antiseptic Surgery* 103 The volatility of the acid renders any but recently prepared gauze untrustworthy.

2. Tendency to lightness, levity, or flightiness; lack of steadiness or seriousness.

1655 FULLER *Ch. Hist.* xi. ii. §33 Those [recreations], which..must needs be preacted by the fancy (such the volatility thereof) all the day before. *a* **1700** KEN *Edmund* Poet. Wks. 1721 II. 78 Consideration..Fixes the Volatility of Thought, Till to itself the wandring Soul is brought. **1759** JOHNSON *Rasselas* xvi, Such sprightliness of air and volatility of fancy as might have suited beings of a higher order. **1792** A. YOUNG *Trav. France* 279 Volatility and changeableness are attributed to the French as national characteristicks. **1811** SHELLEY in Hogg *Life* (1858) I. 379 Volatility of character evinces no capabilities for great affections. **1870** EMERSON *Soc. & Solit.* viii. 171 The imagination infuses a certain volatility and intoxication. **1871** MOZLEY *Univ. Serm.* vi. 132 The inner life of man is a struggle with volatility and disorder.

3. Adaptability for flight. Also *fig.*

1722 WOLLASTON *Relig. Nat.* ix. (1724) 212 [The soul must] be capable of mounting upwards, in proportion to the volatility of its vehicle. **1841** SYD. SMITH in Lady Holland *Mem.* (1855) I. 125 The volatility of the butterfly.

4. Capacity for ready or rapid movement. *rare*⁻¹.

1797 *Monthly Mag.* III. 226 Musical pretensions..are so much more calculated to promote unmeaning volatility of finger, than grace, taste, or expression.

5. *Computers.* The property of a memory of not retaining data after the power supply is cut off.

1969 *IEEE Trans. Magnetics* V. 583/1 Progress in the overall field of semiconductor memories to date is surveyed. .. The problems of power, reliability, and volatility are yielding to practical solutions. **1981** *Appl. Solid State Sci.* Suppl. II. A. 122 Many investigations into lessening the impact of the volatility of the semiconductor memory have been made.

Hence **vola'tilityship** [-SHIP 3 b], used to designate a volatile person. *rare.*

1771 P. PARSONS *Newmarket* II. 134, I repeat my wishes that this may come to the hands of your volatilityship.

volatilizable (vɒlæti'laɪzəb(ə)l), *a.* [f. VOLATILIZE *v.*] Capable of being volatilized; that may be rendered volatile.

1818 W. PHILLIPS *Min. & Geol.* (ed. 3) 30 There is another Alkali,..which, being volatilizable at moderate heat, is therefore termed Volatile Alkali. **1841** *Civil Engin. & Arch. Jrnl.* IV. 63/2 The portion of the coal, which in common parlance is called 'bituminous', is in a solid or fixed state while in the coal,..though, subsequently, it is volatilizable and assumes the form of gas. **1876** BARTHOLOW *Materia Med.* (1879) 6 Iodine in vapor, iodoform, sal-ammoniac, bromine, and other volatilizable solids and gases.

volatilization (vɒlətɪlaɪ'zeɪʃən). [f. next + -ATION. Cf. F. *volatilisation*, Sp. *-izacion*, Pg. *-ização*, It. *-izzazione*.] The action or process of making volatile; the state of being volatilized.

1661 BOYLE *Scept. Chem.* VI. (1680) 420 Multitudes of Chymists have..attempted in Vain the Volatilization of the Salt of Tartar. **1663** —— *Usef. Exp. Nat. Philos.* II. App. 373 This volatile red Balsam (especially if by this volatilization the Antimony have lost its Emetick property) we cannot but think endowed with more then ordinary Vertues. **1744** *Phil. Trans.* XLIII. 143 The Contagion of pestilential Fevers proceeds from a Subtilization and Volatilization of the perspirable Humours. **1782** *Ibid.* LXXIII. 55 Nor can this be attributed to the volatilization of the acid by heat. **1827** FARADAY *Chem. Manip.* iv. (1842) 130 At higher temperatures, the volatilization and decomposition of these bodies would occasion inconvenience. **1873** E. SPON *Workshop Rec.* Ser. I. 11 In fusing the three metals together there is always a loss of zinc by volatilization.

fig. **1882** *Cent. Mag.* Sept. 783 Analyses of humor are apt to leave one rather serious, and to result in an entire volatilization of the humor.

volatilize ('vɒlətɪlaɪz), *v.* [f. VOLATILE *a.* + -IZE. Cf. F. *volatiliser* (1611), Sp. and Pg. *-izar*, It. *-izzare*.]

1. *trans.* To render volatile; to cause to evaporate or disperse in vapour.

1657 G. STARKEY *Helmont's Vind.* To Rdr., Salt of Tartar volatilized, or made into a spiritual Elixir, with any essential oyle, is an absolute corrector of all vegetal poysons. **1672-3** GREW *Anat. Pl., Anat. Roots* (1682) 89 The Air-Vessels, or rather, the Aery Ferment contained in them, volatilizing only a smaller portion of the Sap. **1755** *Phil. Trans.* XLIX. 341 Hence we see how necessary heat is, to volatilize the rancid oil. **1778** PRYCE *Min. Cornub.* 253 The Glass..is likely to detain any of the nobler Metals, which the arsenick might otherwise volatilize. **1807** T. THOMSON *Chem.* (ed. 3) II. 254 The acids belonging to the first order are crystallizable, and they may be volatilized by heat without undergoing decomposition. **1849** D. CAMPBELL *Inorg. Chem.* 221 When the protochloride of uranium is carefully heated, so as not to volatilize it,..this compound remains. **1874** tr. *Lommel's Light* 153 If a fragment of zinc be volatilised between the carbon poles a series of beautifully coloured striæ are seen.

b. *fig.* To render light, airy, unsubstantial, etc.

1664 POWER *Exp. Philos.* Concl. 184 The greatest part of Humanity is [so] lost in Earth..that nothing can volatilize them, and set their Reasons at Liberty. **1822-56** DE QUINCEY *Confess.* (1862) 198 Beyond a certain point it is sure to volatilise and to disperse the intellectual energies. **1856** MERIVALE *Rom. Emp.* xli. (1865) V. 121 Propertius is deficient in that light touch and exquisitely polished taste which volatilize the sensuality and flattery of Horace. **1882** FARRAR *Early Chr.* I. 274 On the other hand [in Philo's philosophy] angels are sometimes volatilised into ideas.

2. *intr.* To become volatile; to evaporate.

1728 CHAMBERS *Cycl.* s.v. *Volatilisation*, To dispose the fix'd Salts of Plants to volatilise, the Process is to be begun by making them into a Sapa. **1796** KIRWAN *Elem. Min.* (ed. 2) II. 33 It does not give out its Acid in any heat, but rather volatilizes. **1822** *Imison's Sci. & Art* II. 125 It easily fuses and Volatilizes before the blow-pipe. **1842** E. A. PARNELL *Chem. Anal.* (1845) 21 The chlorine is expelled almost before the acid begins to volatilize. **1880** MACCORMAC *Antiseptic Surgery* 152 The solution must be renewed from time to time as the carbolic acid volatilises.

fig. **1892** *Nation* (N.Y.) 15 Dec. 454/2 To those who know pictures as very tangible things..it is puzzling to find them volatilizing before their eyes and evaporating into a haze of words.

Hence **'volatilized, 'volatilizing** *ppl. adjs.* Also **'volatilizer**, an apparatus for volatilizing.

1727 BAILEY (vol. II), *Volatilizing*, making volatile. *c* **1789** *Encycl. Brit.* (ed. 3) IV. 513/1 To bring vinegar therefore nearer the state of tartar, we must deprive it of its fine volatilizing phlogiston. **1825** J. NICHOLSON *Operat. Mechanic* 724 The volatilised mercury is again condensed. **1869** E. A. PARKES *Pract. Hygiene* (ed. 3) 87 The volatilising turpentine may..carry into the air particles of plumbic carbonate. **1878** ABNEY *Photogr.* 282 The spectrum of the volatilised metal falls on the sensitive plate. **1897** KELLOGG in *Voice* (*N.Y.*) 23 Dec. 5/2 The employment of medicinal vapors by means of a suitable volatilizer or vaporizer.

vo'lation. *rare.* [f. L. *vol-āre* to fly: see -ATION, and cf. the earlier TRANSVOLATION.] The action of flying, volitation.

1755 JOHNSON, *Flight*,..the act of using wings; volation. ? **187.** COWES (Cent.), The muscles of volation.

†**volative,** *a. Obs. rare.* [f. L. *volāt-*, ppl. stem of *volāre* to fly + -IVE.] Capable of flying.

1613 R. CAWDREY *Table Alph.* (ed. 3). **1673** O. WALKER *Educ.* 148 For example, an Eagle. Is..it a substance created? corporeal? volative? wilde? that flies single, not in flocks.

†**volati'zation.** *Obs. rare.* [f. next + -ATION.] = VOLATILIZATION.

1669 W. SIMPSON *Hydrol. Chym.* 76 A vital ferment, out of which the Archeus by a further volatization hews forth these spirits. **1818** ACCUM *Chem. Tests* 110 One hundred grains dried fully, but short of volatization.

†**'volatize,** *v. Obs.* [f. VOLAT-ILE *a.* + -IZE. Cf. VOLATILIZE *v.*]

1. *trans.* = VOLATILIZE *v.* 1.

1650 ASHMOLE *Chym. Coll.* 96 If thou wouldst Volatise or Imbibe thy prepared Elixer. **1671** J. WEBSTER *Metallogr.* xii. 170 As easily as snow is volatized and melted in warm water. **1693** tr. *Blancard's Phys. Dict.* 75/1 A Lymphatick Juice, which it discharges into the gut..to ferment and volatize the Meat. **1790** BURKE *Fr. Rev.* 277 By this means the spirit of money jobbing and speculation goes into the mass of land itself, and incorporates with it. By this kind of operation, that species of property becomes (as it were) volatized. **1826** HENRY *Elem. Chem.* I. 6 The common still..can only be employed for volatizing substances that do not act on copper.

2. *intr.* = VOLATILIZE *v.* 2. *rare.*

1685 [Implied in *Volatizing* ppl. a.]. **1812** SIR H. DAVY *Chem. Philos.* 271 It fuses at about 220° Fahrenheit, and volatizes slowly even before it fuses.

Hence †**'volatized, 'volatizing** *ppl. adjs.*

1671 J. WEBSTER *Metallogr.* iii. 45 Æther, which some hold to be nothing else but pure volatiz'd Salt. **1685** BOYLE *Salubr. Air* 111 Some Mineral Bodies of a very volatizing nature.

†**'volatory.** *Obs.*⁻¹ [Cf. VOLARY and -ATORY.] An aviary.

1656 HEYLIN *Surv. France* 61 Here we saw the Volatory full of sundry forain birds.

†**volature.** *Obs.*⁻¹ [ad. L. *volātūra*, f. *volāre* to fly.] A fluttering movement.

1633 J. DONE tr. *Aristeas's Hist. Septuagint* 62 A little Wind..entring within the vayle, running from low to high, making volatures and replies like waves.

‖**vol-au-vent** (vɔlovɑ̃). [F., lit. 'flight in the wind'.] A kind of raised pie, formed of a light puff paste filled with meat, fish, or the like.

1828 LYTTON *Pelham* I. xxiv, The..landlady,..regaled him with cold *vol-au-vent*, and a glass of Curaçoa. *Ibid.* To think she should serve me so cruelly, after I had eaten so plentifully of the *vol-au-vent*. **1846** SOYER *Cookery* 24 Serve [the sauce] in a vol-au-vent or wherever directed. **1899** DOYLE *Duet* (1909) 90/1 Oyster patties or oyster vol-au-vents.

volbet, obs. Sc. form of WOUBIT.

volborthite. *Min.* [Named (1837) after its discoverer, Alexander von *Volborth*, a Russian scientist.] 'Hydrous vanadate of copper, barium and calcium, found in small, yellowish-green crystals' (Chester).

1844 DANA *Min.* (1868) 611. **1878** LAWRENCE tr. *Cotta's Rocks Classified* 41 Volborthite occurs as an accessory ingredient in many sandstones of the Permian formation of Russia.

volc, southern ME. variant of FOLK.

volcan ('vɒlkən). Now *rare.* [a. F. and Sp. *volcan* (Pr. *volca*), ad. L. *Volcān-us*, *Vulcān-us*: see VULCAN.] = VOLCANO *sb.* 1. Also *attrib.*

1577 FRAMPTON *Joyful News* 31 Other Sulphur..founde nigh vnto the Volcan of Nicaragua. **1604** E. G[RIMSTONE] *D'Acosta's Hist. Indies* III. xxiv. 193 Of the Volcans or Vents of fire. *a* **1676** HALE *Prim. Orig. Man* 190 The like Volcans or Fiery Eruptions happen sometimes in the Land subjected to the Sea. **1697** DAMPIER *Voy.* I. viii. 225 Then..the Volcan of Guatimala appeared in sight. **1850** LOWELL *New Year's Eve* ii, If we..our faces turned When volcan glares set all the east aglow. **1893** RIDER HAGGARD *Montezuma's Dau.* xv, Those that have seen the sun rise over the volcans of Tenoctitlan. *Ibid.* xxiii, Within fifteen years..the volcan Popo had ceased to vomit smoke and fire.

vol'canean, *a. rare*⁻¹. [Cf. VOLCANIST.] Maintaining the igneous origin of certain geological formations.

1852 TH. ROSS tr. *Humboldt's Trav.* I. i. 36 A mountain in Saxony,..celebrated on account of the disputes of volcanean and neptunean geologists.

‖**volca'nello.** Pl. volcanelli. [It., dim. of *volcano* VOLCANO *sb.*] A small volcano, esp. as forming one of a group.

1888 DOUGHTY *Arabia Deserta* I. 395 The volcanelli appeared standing so thick that bye and bye..I counted above thirty at once.

vol'canian, *a. rare.* [f. VOLCAN-O *sb.* + -IAN. Cf. VULCANIAN *a.*] Of or pertaining to, resembling that of, a volcano.

1820 KEATS *Lamia* I. 155 A deep volcanian yellow took the place Of all her milder-mooned body's grace. **1869** J. PHILLIPS *Vesuv.* viii. 203 This safety-valve for the volcanian pressure.

volcanic (vɒl'kænɪk), *a.* (and *sb.*). Also 8-9 -ick. [a. F. *volcanique* (= Sp. and Pg. *volcanico*), f. *volcan* VOLCAN *sb.*; or directly f. VOLCAN-O + -IC. Cf. VULCANIC *a.*]

1. Of ashes, etc.: Discharged from, produced or ejected by, a volcano or volcanoes.

1774 in G. Forster *Voy. round World* (1777) I. 591 The country being strewed with volcanic cinders. **1777** *Ibid.* I. 568 Our road was intolerably rugged, over heaps of volcanic stones. **1796** KIRWAN *Elem. Min.* (ed. 2) I. 402 Of Volcanic Scoriæ... Their texture cavernous,..but never fibrous. *Ibid.* 410 Of Volcanic Ashes, Sand, Pouzzolana [*sic*], Trass, Tufa, and Piperino. **1832** LYELL *Princ. Geol.* (1835) II. 243 This volcanic dust when it fell was an impalpable powder. **1841** W. SPALDING *Italy & It. Isl.* I. 19 The winds and the birds clothe its volcanic soil with vegetation. **1877** HUXLEY *Physiogr.* xii. 191 In some cases, the lava is broken into such fine particles that it is known as *volcanic dust* or sand.

b. Used *spec.* with names of rocks, minerals, etc.

1811- *Volcanic tufa, tuff* [see TUFA 1 b, TUFF 1 b]. **1815** AIKIN *Min.* (ed. 2) 99 Volcanic or Specular Iron occurs in very compressed and irregular crystals. **1850** ANSTED *Elem. Geol., Min.* etc. §413 Pumice or Volcanic-ash, is a light spongy modification of obsidian. **1852** BRANDE *Dict. Sci.* (ed. 2) App. 1421 *Vulcanite*, a mineralogical synonym of the pyroxene, or volcanic garnet. **1856** EMERSON *Eng. Traits* xiii. *Religion* Wks. (Bohn) II. 96 As volcanic basalts show the work of fire which has been extinguished for ages. **1867** BLOXAM *Chem.* 267 The ammonia which is evolved from the Tuscan boracic acid employed in this process is known in commerce as Volcanic ammonia. **1868** WATTS *Dict. Chem.* V. 528 Sulphur..occurs native,..in opaque, lemon-yellow, crystalline masses (volcanic sulphur).

c. ***volcanic bombs, glass*** (see quots.).

1798 R. JAMESON *Mineral. Shetl. Isl.* etc. 56 Any appearance of..what the Volcanists call volcanic bombs. **1833** LYELL *Princ. Geol.* III. Gloss. 83 *Volcanic Bombs*, volcanos throw out sometimes detached masses of melted lava, which, as they fall, assume rounded forms (like bomb-shells), and are often elongated into a pear shape. *c* **1840** *Encycl. Metrop.* (1845) VI. 527/2 Volcanic Glass. Obsidian. **1850** ANSTED *Elem. Geol., Min.* etc. §413 Obsidian or Volcanic-glass..is also a well-known volcanic product.

d. *sb. pl.* Rocks due to volcanic action.

1894 *Cosmopolitan* XVII. 128 These volcanics..in most cases..have been subjected to deforming pressures which have converted them into schists.

2. Due to or caused by a volcano or volcanoes.

1776 SIR W. HAMILTON *Campi Phlegræi* 11 Many Islands ..whose Volcanick origin seems to be evidently pointed out. *c* **1790** *Encycl. Brit.* (ed. 3) VI. 286/1 Six days after the immense volcanic eruption in Iceland had ceased. **1817** LADY MORGAN *France* VIII. (1818) II. 347 The cause of those volcanic shocks, which finally overwhelm the island Atlantis. **1833** N. ARNOTT *Physics* (ed. 5) II. 135 Examining its structure as exposed to view by volcanic or other convulsions. **1876** PAGE *Adv. Text-bk. Geol.* xvi. 304 Thought by some geologists to be of volcanic origin.

b. Of or pertaining to a volcano or volcanoes.

1797 *Encycl. Brit.* (ed. 3) XVIII. 687/1 To account for the volcanic fire, Dr. Woodward and others have had recourse to the hypothesis of a central fire. **1828-32** WEBSTER s.v., Volcanic heat. **1833** LYELL *Princ. Geol.* III. 362 That great masses of subterranean lava in the volcanic foci may remain in a red hot or incandescent state. **1856** EMERSON *Eng. Traits* x. *Wealth* Wks. II. 72 Steam..vies with the volcanic forces which twisted the strata. **1877** HUXLEY *Physiogr.* 189 At the mouth of the volcanic pipe, there is usually a funnel-shaped opening known as the crater.

c. Relating to volcanoes.

1828 DUPPA *Trav. Italy*, etc. 94 Vesuvius..makes a great feature in volcanic history.

3. Characterized by the presence of volcanoes; composed of volcanoes; consisting of materials produced by igneous action.

c **1789** *Encycl. Brit.* (ed. 3) IV. 461/1 That species of ore.. is to be met with only in volcanic countries. **1794** R. J. SULIVAN *View Nat.* II. 171 In America, particularly the Southern America, what a volcanic chain!..with Cotopaxi for its principal link. **1832** DE LA BECHE *Geol. Man.* (ed. 2) 19 Hot springs are common to the volcanic districts of different parts of the world. **1837** W. IRVING *Capt. Bonneville* II. 80 A volcanic tract of similar character is found on Stinking river. **1855** *Orr's Circ. Sci., Inorg. Nat.* 180 The lava itself is seen where it has burst through the sides of volcanic hills.

b. Of the nature of a volcano.

1833-4 *Encycl. Metrop.* (1845) VI. 740/1 Constitution of a Volcanic Mountain in General. **1872** RAYMOND *Statist. Mines & Mining* 235 The great volcanic vent of the last-mentioned mountain.

4. *fig.* Resembling or characteristic of a volcano, or the attributes of this; violently explosive, or latently capable of sudden and violent activity.

a **1854** H. REED *Lect. Eng. Lit.* iii. (1855) 96 The revolutions were not sudden, devastating, volcanic eruptions. **1862** 'SHIRLEY' (J. Skelton) *Nugæ Crit.* ix. 407 The military despotism of Napoleon was a volcanic power, which..perpetually threatened the tranquillity of Europe. **1882** J. H. BLUNT *Ref. Ch. Eng.* II. 486 His [*sc.* Charles I's] gentleness and love of peace were ill-fitted for the volcanic age in which his lot was cast.

b. Of the mind, passions, etc.: Intensely fervid or violent; full of latent or suppressed violence. Also occas. of persons.

1807 D'ISRAELI *Cur. Lit.* (ed. 5) II. 71 His volcanic head flamed with imagination. **1870** SPURGEON *Treas. Dav.* Ps. xxxix. 3 His volcanic soul was tossed with an inward ocean of fire. **1872** LIDDON *Elem. Relig.* i. 4 The tremendous force of the volcanic passions latent in human nature. **1883** *Harper's Mag.* July 243/2 *Besant*. But Hugo reaches as high and goes as deep as anybody... *Spencer*. But isn't he rather —rather volcanic.

5. = VOLCANEAN *a. rare*⁻¹.

1793 [EARL DUNDONALD] *Descr. Estate Culross* 31 It is a field well worth being explored by a volcanic Mineralist.

6. *Comb.*, as ***volcanic-like, -looking*** adjs.

1800 LEYDEN *Tour Highlands* (1903) 132 The red conical top of the volcanic-like hill. **1854** A. R. WALLACE in *My Life* (1905) I. xx. 335 A coarse, volcanic-looking gravel.

Hence **volcanico-**, combining form, in the sense 'volcanic and——', as in ***volcanico-marine*** adj.

1822 J. PARKINSON *Outl. Oryctol.* 260 The Brecciæ of Nice, the volcanico-marine valley, as it is called by St. Fond.

vol'canically, *adv.* [See prec. and -ICALLY.]

1. In an explosive, eruptive, or fiery manner; with sudden violence.

1840 CARLYLE *Heroes* iv. (1858) 274 The accumulation of offences is..too literally exploded, blasted asunder volcanically. **1873** SYMONDS *Gk. Poets* v. 127 The energies ..were restrained by the Aeolians within the sphere of individual emotions, ready to burst forth volcanically. **1891** T. HARDY *Tess* xxv, Here, in this apparently.. unimpassioned place, novelty had volcanically started up.

2. In respect of a volcano or volcanoes; with regard to volcanic nature.

1886 *Daily News* 2 Sept. 4/7 Astronomically, it [the earth] is solid in its relations; volcanically, it is of liquid or plastic character. **1892** *Ibid.* 26 Mar. 2/1 Cotopaxi..comports itself, volcanically speaking, in a regular and well-behaved manner.

volcanicity (vɒlkə'nɪsɪtɪ). [ad. F. *volcanicité*, or f. VOLCANIC *a.* + -ITY. Cf. VULCANICITY.] Volcanic action, activity, or phenomena.

1836 MACGILLIVRAY *Trav. Humboldt* xxvii. 411 Volcanicity, or the influence which the interior of our planet exercises upon its external envelope. **1883** *Athenæum* 25 Aug. 245 One of those earthquakes called perimetric, that are due to a local volcanicity.

volcaniclastic (vɒl,kænɪ'klæstɪk), *a.* and *sb. Geol.* Also ,volcano-. [Blend of VOLCANIC *a.* (and *sb.*) and CLASTIC *a.*] **A.** *adj.* Both volcanic and clastic. **B.** *sb.* A volcaniclastic rock.

1961 R. V. FISHER in *Bull. Geol. Soc. Amer.* LXXII. 1409/1 Only recently..have attempts been made to group all volcanic clastic (termed *volcaniclastic* in this paper) rocks into a single system... Rocks of pyroclastic origin are only one category of volcaniclastic rocks. **1972** F. J. PETTIJOHN et al. *Sand & Sandstone* vii. 261 The erosional volcaniclastics are comparable—in sedimentary structures, geometry, and thickness—to other terrigenous sandstones. **1975** *Nature* 17 Apr. 581/2 The rock types include..a variety of reworked volcanic ashes, volcaniclastic and fluviatile sediments. **1980** *Ibid.* 29 May 289/2 The Savage Mountain Formation consists of up to 5,000 m of..pillow basalt and massive subaerial flows with associated volcanoclastics.

volcanism ('vɒlkənɪz(ə)m). [a. F. *volcanisme*: see VOLCANO *sb.* and -ISM, and cf. VULCANISM.] The state, condition, or character of being volcanic; volcanic action or phenomena.

1869 J. PHILLIPS *Vesuv.* v. 150 Even if no other indication of former volcanism be traceable. **1882** GEIKIE *Geol. Sk.* 276 The vast number of fissures..appeared hardly to connect themselves with any known phase of volcanism. **1895** *Pop. Sci. Monthly* Mar. 577 Much more attention than formerly is now paid to the study of volcanism.

volcanist ('vɒlkənɪst). [f. VOLCAN-O *sb.* + -IST, or a. F. *volcaniste.*]

1. An asserter of the igneous origin of certain geological formations; a Plutonist or Vulcanist. Cf. VULCANIST 3.

1796 KIRWAN *Elem. Min.* (ed. 2) I. 445 This theory having appeared unsatisfactory to many of the volcanists themselves, they next devised [etc.]. **1815** W. PHILLIPS *Min. & Geol.* 68 Two distinct parties, distinguished according to the notion they embrace, by the appellations of Volcanists and Neptunists. **1850** ANSTED *Elem. Geol., Min.* etc. Gloss., *Volcanist*... A term of reproach belonging now only to the history of geology. **1971** H. KONDO *Moon* (1972) 14 The volcanists have three main arguments for believing that their theory is correct.

2. One who studies or is versed in volcanoes.

1828-32 WEBSTER. **1848** DAUBENY *Descr. Volcanos* 142 The neighbouring country to the north of Vicenza is interesting to the volcanist.

'volcanite[1]. *Min. rare*⁻⁰. [f. VOLCAN-O *sb.* + -ITE, or a. F. *volcanite.*] (See quot. and cf. VULCANITE 1.)

1828-32 WEBSTER, *Volcanite*, a mineral otherwise called augite. [Hence in later Dicts.]

'volcanite[2]. *Min.* [f. *Volcan-o* one of the Lipari Islands + -ITE[1] 4.] (See quot.)

1868 WATTS *Dict. Chem.* V. 1004 *Volcanite*, selenide of sulphur.

vol'canity. *rare.* [f. VOLCAN-IC *a.* + -ITY. Cf. VOLCANICITY.] **a.** Volcanic nature, quality, or character. **b.** Volcanic phenomena; volcanicity.

1796 KIRWAN *Elem. Min.* (ed. 2) I. 433 Their volcanity is ..established by their colour, grain, and the scoriæ,..that accompany them. **1892** *Literary World* 22 July 70/1 Some such work..in which the general principles of Volcanity can be studied.

†**volcani'zation.** *Obs.*⁻¹ [Cf. next, and F. *volcanisation.*] The process of undergoing, or the state of having undergone, change by volcanic heat or action.

1798 tr. *Spallanzani's Trav. Sicilies* vi. I. 191 The limits of the volcanization of the Phlegrean fields.

'volcanized, *ppl. a. rare.* [ad. F. *volcanisé* (Buffon, etc.), f. *volcan* VOLCAN: see -IZE.] Affected or altered by volcanic action or heat.

1792 A. YOUNG *Trav. France* 286 The French naturalists, ..assert the depth to be twenty feet of beds of earth, formed of the ruins of what they style the primitive (granite) and volcanized mountains. **1798** tr. *Spallanzani's Trav. Sicilies* vi. I. 190 So as to form a soil entirely volcanized. *Ibid.* vii. I. 200 In a volcanized country, where stones of any other than a volcanic nature are not to be found.

Hence **'volcanize** *v. trans.* (Cf. VULCANIZE *v.*)

1828 WEBSTER (citing Spallanzani), and in later Dicts.

volcano (vɒl'keɪnəʊ), *sb.* Also 7-9 **vulcano**. Pl. volcanoes (7-9 -os, -o's). [a. It. *volcano* (Florio, 1598), *vulcano* (Florio, 1611):—L. *Vol-, Vulcānum*, acc. of *Volcānus* VULCAN. Cf. VOLCAN.]

1. a. *Physiogr.* A more or less conical hill or mountain, composed wholly or chiefly of discharged matter, communicating with the interior of the globe by a funnel or crater, from which in periods of activity steam, gases, ashes, rocks, and freq. streams of molten materials are ejected.

See also *mud-, pseudo-volcano* s.v. MUD *sb.* 5, PSEUDO- 2.

α. **1613** PURCHAS *Pilgr.* VIII. xiv. 686 A Vulcano or flaming hill, the fire whereof may be seene..aboue 100 miles. **1663** J. SPENCER *Prodigies* (1665) 85 They regarded those mighty Vulcanos as the Courts of Pluto. **1710** PALMER *Proverbs* 25 He that would needs peep into mount Vesuvius, and search the depth of its vulcano's. **1788** GIBBON *Decl. & F.* xxxix. IV. 42 The vulcano of Lipari, one of the flaming mouths of the infernal world. **1830** W. TAYLOR *Hist. Surv. Germ. Poetry* II. 467 Unusual events, earthquakes, inundations, and vulcanoes altered the face of the planet.

β. **1690** T. BURNET *Theory Earth* II. 55 The burning mountains or volcano's of the earth. **1692** BENTLEY *Boyle Lect.* 271 The seeds of subterraneous minerals..sometimes cause earthquakes and furious eruptions of volcano's. **1725** DE FOE *Voy. round World* II. 66 A volcano, or burning vent among the hills. **1742** YOUNG *Nt. Th.* III. 220 Volcano's bellow ere they disembogue. **1773** BRYDONE *Tour Sicily* ii. (1809) 16 Of all the volcanoes we read of, Strombolo seems to be the only one that burns without ceasing. **1781** COWPER *Heroism* 85 Some heav'n-protected isle, Where no volcano pours his fiery flood. **1868** LOCKYER *Elem. Astron.* §221 Hill country [in the moon] broken up in the most tremendous manner by volcanoes of all sizes. **1877** HUXLEY *Physiogr.* 198 Submarine volcanoes occasionally give rise to new land. *fig.* **1856** EMERSON *Eng. Traits* xiv. *Literature* Wks. (Bohn) II. 113 The island is a roaring volcano of fate, of material values,..glutted markets, and low prices. **1898** D. C. MURRAY *Tales* 207 You're going to offer your old second-hand volcano of a heart to that fresh innocence?

b. An eruption or discharge *of* flame.

1716-20 *Lett. Mist's Jrnl.* (1722) I. 65 The very Eruptions, or Vulcano's of Flame, which..are observed to burst out from it on all Sides.

c. *transf.* (See quots.)

1784 COWPER *Task* III. 737 The eclipse That metropolitan volcano's [*sc.* chimneys] make, Whose Stygian throats breathe darkness all day long. **1890** *Cent. Dict., Fizgig*, a firework, made of damp powder, which makes a hissing or fizzing noise when ignited; in one form called by boys a *volcano*.

2. *fig.* **a.** A violent feeling or passion, esp. one in a suppressed state.

1697 SIR T. P. BLOUNT *Ess.* 143 Blow him into a Flame, and you may see Vulcano's, Hurricans and Borasco's in him. **1852** MRS. STOWE *Uncle Tom's C.* ii, A whole volcano of bitter feelings burned in his bosom, and sent streams of fire through his veins. **1872** BLACK *Adv. Phaeton* xxv. 352 Nursing this volcano of wrath in his breast. **1883** MEREDITH *Woods of Westermain* iii, Love, the great volcano, flings Fires of lower Earth to sky.

b. A state of things liable to burst out violently at some time, esp. in phr. ***to sit on a volcano*** and varr.

1853 C. BRONTE *Villette* ix, On the edge of a moral volcano that rumbled under my feet. **1890** *Spectator* 10 May, An outburst of the social volcano which some think exists below modern society. [**1908** L. MITCHELL *New York Idea* I. 32, I feel as if we were all taking tea on the slope of a volcano.] **1909** GALSWORTHY *Silver Box* I. iii. 16 You're sitting upon a volcano, John. **1930** G. B. SHAW *Apple Cart* I. 26 The more I see of the sort of prosperity that comes of leaving our vital industries to big business men as long as they keep your constituents quiet with high wages, the more I feel as if I were sitting on a volcano. **1954** J. WHITING *Marching Song* II. 42 Is it a volcano I'm sitting on and not, as I'd supposed, a dung-hill? **1983** *Listener* 27 Jan. 28/3 As in Ragtime, he exposes to white, middle-class America the nature of the volcano (racism; social injustice; competition; aggression) on which it blithely sits.

3. *attrib.*, as *volcano-fire*, *immortality*, *land*, *-mountain*, etc.; **volcano rabbit**, a small, dark brown rabbit, *Romerolagus diazi*, found only in the mountains of central Mexico and very similar to the pika, having short ears and no tail; **volcano-ship**, a kind of fire-ship.

1772–84 *Cook's Voy.* (1790) VI. 2174 The next, a volcano-mountain, may readily be known by the smoke issuing from the top. **1804** WOLCOT (P. Pindar) *Ep. to Ld. Mayor* Wks. 1812 V. 208 A great city orator..and *elève* of John Wilkes, Of volcano immortality. **1821** SHELLEY *Hellas* 589 Like mountain-twins that from each other's veins Catch the volcano-fire and earthquake-spasm. **1845** BAILEY *Festus* (ed. 2) 133 As these scenes, Fire-fountains, and volcano-utterances,..evince. **1860** MOTLEY *Netherl.* xiii. II. 157 York..had distinguished himself..by..having sprung on board the burning volcano-ship at the seige of Antwerp. **1880** MEREDITH *Tragic Com.* (1881) 62, I have seen the other face of it..It is the old volcano land. **1969** J. FISHER et al. *Red Bk.* 54/2 The volcano rabbit is covered with fur, which is a uniform dark brown on its back and dark brownish-grey beneath. **1972** G. DURRELL *Catch me a Colobus* ix. 173 The Volcano rabbit lives at a very high altitude..in the pine forests.

vol'cano, *v. rare.* [f. prec.] **a.** *trans.* To attack (a person) in a manner suggestive of a volcano. **b.** *intr.* To blaze or belch fire like a volcano.

1866 MEREDITH *Vittoria* xxix, Manœuvre your cigar. The plan is, to give half-a-dozen bright puffs, and..when you see an Italian head, volcano him like fury. **1878** *Harper's Mag.* Feb. 432 The great cannon volcanoing through all.

volcano-. The sb. used as a formative element: **volcanoclastic**, var. VOLCANICLASTIC *a.* and *sb.*; **ˌvolcano'genic** *a.* [-GENIC], of volcanic origin; **volˌcanotec'tonic** *a.*, involving or pertaining to both volcanic and tectonic processes.

1965 E. LEHNER et al. in G. J. Williams *Econ. Geol. N.Z.* xix. 353/2 Their survey left little doubt that the marine late Eocene and Oligocene strata which overlie the basement cover..are..intercalated with volcanogenic beds. **1977** A. HALLAM *Planet Earth* 59/2 Glacial or volcanogenic sediments contain coarse particles which can be very unstable. **1907** W. H. HOBBS in *Beiträge zur Geophysik* VIII. 224 The seismotectonic lines often intersect lines of volcanoes (volcanotectonic lines) at volcanic vents. **1941** *Univ. Calif. Publ. Geol. Sci.* XXV. 242 Calderas are volcanic and therefore centric forms of destruction, volcano-tectonic engulfments of the roofs of magma reservoirs, regardless of the number of vents involved. **1965** G. J. WILLIAMS *Econ. Geol. N.Z.* xv. 235/2 The relatively high permeability of the pumiceous volcanics deposited in the large volcano-tectonic basins so typical of this active tectonic and volcanic zone. **1979** *Nature* 26 July 286/2 Zukwala volcano..lies on an isolated (non-WFB) volcanotectonic line that projects NNE via a Holocene basalt lava cone.

vol'canoism. *rare*⁻¹. [f. VOLCANO *sb.* + -ISM.] The action of a volcano; eruption.

1843 CARLYLE *Past & Pr.* II. x, Not blaze out, or the seldomest possible blaze out, as wasteful volcanoism to scorch and consume!

volcanological (ˌvɒlkənəʊ'lɒdʒɪkəl), *a.* [f. VOLCANOLOG(Y + -ICAL.] = VULCANOLOGICAL *a.* Also **ˌvolcano'logic** *a.*

1889 *Cent. Dict.*, Volcanological. **1931** G. W. TYRRELL *Volcanoes* i. 12 With the establishment of volcanological observatories on Vesuvius and Etna..the study of volcanoes has entered upon a new phase. **1961** WEBSTER, Volcanologic. **1974** *Encycl. Brit. Macropædia* XIX. 98/2 Numerous stations have been set up [on Vesuvius] at various heights for making volcanologic measurements. **1982** *Encycl. Brit. Bk. of Year* 307/2 Mt. St. Helens remained active,..providing an excellent volcanological laboratory.

volca'nologist. [See VOLCANOLOGY and -OLOGIST.] = VULCANOLOGIST.

1890 *Smithsonian Rep.* 216 A result worthy of examination by volcanologists. **1905** W. J. SOLLAS *Age Earth* iii. 72 Signor Sambon, an experienced and intrepid volcanologist.

volca'nologize, *v. rare*⁻¹. [See next and -IZE.] *intr.* To prosecute studies in volcanic phenomena.

1826 WHEWELL in Todhunter *Acc. Writ.* (1876) II. 69 He has gone to geologize and volcanologize and so forth in Auvergne.

volca'nology. [f. VOLCANO *sb.* + -(O)LOGY.] = VULCANOLOGY.

1886 *Athenæum* 14 Aug. 210/3 The Progress in volcanology and seismology for 1885. **1889** *Pall Mall G.* 23 Oct. 3/2 Students..will find comparatively little that is new to them, as volcanology, in this..easy-going volume.

volck, southern ME. variant of FOLK.

vold(e, southern ME. varr. of FOLD *sb.* and *v.*

volde, obs. form of *would* WILL *v.*

vole (vəʊl), *sb.*¹ Also 7, 9 vol. [a. F. *vole* (1642), app. f. *voler*, ad. L. *volāre* to fly.] The winning of all the tricks in certain card-games, as écarté, quadrille, or ombre. Freq. *to win the vole.*

1679 DRYDEN *Limberham* IV. i, Pug has sent me to you..to bring you down to Cards again;..She'll never forgive you the last Vol you won. **1712–13** SWIFT *Jrnl. to Stella* 7 Mar., I..played at ombre..for three hours. There were three voles against me,..but [I] came off for three shillings and sixpence. **1728** VANBR. & CIB. *Prov. Husb.* v. iii, Unless..sometimes winning a great Stake; laying down a Vole, *sans prendre* may come up, to the profitable Pleasure you were speaking of. **1741** MRS. E. MONTAGU *Lett.* (1813) II. 111 Many there would have gone twice as far to have saved a vole at quadrille. **1778** *Camp Guide* 12 To win a great—battle—I think from my soul, Is rather more dubious, than Quadrille the vole. **1810** CRABBE *Borough* xvi. 224 Cards answer'd to her call..'A vole! a vole!' she cried, 't'is fairly won.' **1861** *Macm. Mag.* Dec. 131 Unless the winners should choose to undertake to make all the ten tricks [in Quadrille], which is called the vole. **1894** WILKINS & VIVIAN *Green Bay Tree* I. 21 'A gentle flutter at ecarté.' 'In which you began with King and vol each game, I wager.'

b. *to go the vole*, to run every risk in the hope of great gain; to try all shifts.

1816 SCOTT *Antiq.* iv, Who is he?—why, he has gone the vole—has been soldier, ballad-singer, travelling tinker, and is now a beggar. **1827** —— *Jrnl.* (1890) II. 62 He thinks Cadell's account must turn up trumps, and is for going the vole. **1895** *Daily News* 27 May 8/3 In the old phrase he 'went the vole,' he would be colossal, or a blank failure.

Hence **vole** *v. intr.*, to win the vole. *rare*⁻¹.

1735 POPE *Donne's Sat.* IV. 146 Shortly no lad shall chuck, or lady vole, But some excising Courtier will have toll.

vole (vəʊl), *sb.*² [Orig. *vole-mouse*, ad. Norw. **vollmus* (Icel. *vallarmús*), f. *voll* (Icel. *völlr*, Sw. *vall*) field + *mus* mouse.] One or other of various rat- or mouse-like quadrupeds, esp. the short-tailed field-mouse, *Microtus* (formerly *Arvicola*) *agrestis*; the water-rat, *M. amphibius*; and the red or bank vole, *Evotomys glareolus*; also, the genus or genera to which these belong. Also †*vole-mouse.*

1805 BARRY *Orkney* III. i. 314 The Short-tailed Field Mouse,..which with us has the name of the *vole mouse.* **1828** J. FLEMING *Brit. Anim.* 23 Arvicola. Vole.—No subsidiary incisors. Roots of the grinders simple... Tail round and hairy. **1840** *Cuvier's Anim. Kingd.* 114 The Voles..have three grinders above and below. *Ibid.*, The Musk-quash,..which is a Vole with semi-palmated hind-feet. *c* **1880** *Cassell's Nat. Hist.* III. 115 The true Voles..number about fifty known species.

attrib. **1896** *Daily News* 21 Apr. 6/2 May the vole-plague ravage the land of those who neglect this plain-featured fact! **1906** *Country-Side* 6 Jan. 100/3 A committee of gentlemen who had come specially to investigate the 'vole' question.

b. With distinguishing terms (see quots. and prec.; also WATER-VOLE).

1840 *Cuvier's Anim. Kingd.* 114 The *Alsacian Vole..lives under ground like the Mole. **1843** *Zoologist* I. 72 The *bank vole or bank mouse. **1888** *Encycl. Brit.* XXIV. 278/1 The Bank-Vole (*Arvicola glareolus*). **1840** *Cuvier's Anim. Kingd.* 114 The *Economic Vole..inhabits a sort of oven-shaped chamber. **1828** J. FLEMING *Brit. Anim.* 23 The *field vole is most destructive in gardens to seeds. **1864** [H. W. WHEELWRIGHT] *Spring Lapl.* 239 Besides these we had another species of field vole (the *Lemmus medius*, Nilss.) which is peculiar to the north. **1840** *Cuvier's Anim. Kingd.* 114 *Meadow Vole..Size of a Mouse, reddish ash-colour. **1896** LYDEKKER *Brit. Mammals* 308 The *northern Vole (*Microtus ratticeps*), and the *Siberian Vole (*M. gregalis*). **1875** *Encycl. Brit.* I. 633/1 Fauna of the Alps..[includes] the *snow-vole (*Arvicola nivalis*).

Hence **voledom**, the world of voles. *rare*⁻¹.

1892 *Chambers's Jrnl.* 25 June 407/2 The young mice being greedily gulped down by the black bogies, whose appearance must be the prevailing terror of voledom.

vole, southern dial. variant of FOAL.

vole, volee, obs. forms of VOLLEY *sb.*

†**'volency.** *Obs. rare.* [ad. L. (post-class.) *volentia* will, inclination.] The power of willing or determining to act in a certain way.

1686 H. MORE in J. Norris *Lett.* (1688) 208 Nor can [I] conceive but that the free Agency we are conscious to ourselves of, is placed in the soul as Volent as much as Intelligent, because this Volency, as I may so speak, is implyed in her Attention or Advertency. **1768** TUCKER *Lt. Nat.* (1834) I. 552 This is another kind of agency,..and for distinction sake we shall beg leave to call it free volency (for the speculative will allow one another to coin a word upon occasion): so the question is not whether a man be a free agent but a free volent.

volens ('vəʊlɛnz), *ppl. a. Law.* [L., f. *velle* to will.] Consenting to a dangerous course of action. Cf. VOLENTI NON FIT INJURIA.

1872 *Law Jrnl.* (Court of Exchequer) XLI. II. 101/2 Then comes the great difficulty; it is said 'volenti non fit injuria'. It is true that he was 'volens', in the sense that he entered the employment voluntarily. **1951** *Law Rep. House of Lords* (Appeal Cases) 765 He was not volens or careless. **1965** *Mod. Law Rev.* XXVIII. v. 519 A finding that a workman was *sciens* was sufficient to defeat his claim as an invitee, even if he was not *volens.*

†**volens nolens**, var. NOLENS VOLENS. *Obs.*

1602 W. WATSON *Quodlibets* 58 Yet must they keepe such a..strait watch..continually, as *volens nolens* their will must not be theirs, but their superiors. **1620** SHELTON *Quix.* II. lx. 404 If I should whip Sancho, *volens nolens.* **1634** W. WOOD *New Eng. Prosp.* (1865) 59 A wronged servant shall have right *volens nolens* from his injurious master.

volent ('vəʊlənt), *a.* and *sb.* [a. L. *volent-*, *volens*, pres. pple. of *velle* to will, wish, desire.]

A. *adj.* Exercising, or capable of exercising, will or choice in respect of one's conduct or course of action.

1654 VILVAIN *Theol. Treat.* ii. 47 They say the appetit confined to good is volent, and therefore free. **1686** [see VOLENCY]. **1701** NORRIS *Ideal World* I. vi. 358 Nor do they [*sc.* eternal truths] depend upon the mind of God as decretory or volent,..but only..as intelligible or exhibitive. **1849** J. WILSON in *Blackw. Mag.* LXVI. 388, I leave the body to moulder, and I go sentient, volent, intelligent, whithersoever I am called.

†**B.** *sb.* One who freely chooses or determines the course of action which he follows. *Obs. rare.*

1768 TUCKER *Lt. Nat.* (1834) I. 552 Upon this supposition man is a free agent, and a free volent. [See also VOLENCY.]

Hence †**'volently** *adv.*, willing. *Obs.*⁻¹

1614 T. ADAMS *Diuells Banket* iv. 183 Into the pit they runne against their will, that ranne so volently, so violently to the brinkes of it.

volente, variant of VOLUNTY *Obs.*

†**volentine.** *Obs. rare.* In 4 vilentyne, 5–6 *Sc.* walentyne, valantene. [Alteration of OF. *volatile*, *voletile* (see VOLATILE *sb.*), perh. influenced by *volant* VOLANT *a.*] *coll.* Birds, fowls.

c **1380** *Sir Ferumb.* 3555 He made him murie al þilke day, For vilentyne [F. *volatisses*] he fond ynow On ryuer and on lake. *c* **1450** HOLLAND *Howlat* 918 All birdis he rebalkit, that wald him nocht bowe,..Thus wycit he the walen-tyne [*v.r.* valantene]..That all the fowlis [etc.].

‖**volenti non fit injuria** (vəʊ'lɛntɪ nəʊn fɪt ɪn'dʒʊrɪə). *Law.* [L.] No injury is done to a willing person: a defence to an action whereby it is claimed that a person who sustained an injury agreed to risk such injury.

1658 E. WINGATE *Maximes of Reason* cxxii. 482 If the Tenant in an Assise of an house desire the Plaintiffe to dine with him in the house, which the Plaintiffe doth accordingly, but doth not clame the house at that time; this is no entry or possession to cause the Assise to abate; because if he had been a stranger, he had been no trespasser for *volenti non fit injuria.* **1743** C. CIBBER *Egotist* 6 *Volenti*, you know, *non fit injuria.* The publick is not obliged to buy. **1872** [see VOLENS *ppl. a*]. **1933** *Law Rep.* (*King's Bench Division*) II. 299 We are at present disposed to take the view that the respondent is precluded from recovering on the principle volenti non fit injuria. **1980** *Oxf. Compan. Law* 1280/1 *Volenti non fit injuria*.., the principle that an injured person cannot complain of harm done him if he knew of and voluntarily incurred the risk of that harm... The plea is practically excluded in employment cases but is still relevant to cases of participation in dangerous sports.

volero, obs. variant of BOLERO.

volery, obs. form of VOLARY.

‖**volet** (vɒlɛ). Also 8 *dial.* volleat. [a. OF. *volet*, *vollet* kerchief, or mod.F. *volet* shutter, etc., f. *voler*:—L. *volāre* to fly.]

†**1.** A kerchief or veil worn at the back of the head by ladies. *Obs.*

1398 *Will J. Asshebom* (Comm. Crt. London), Unam flamiolam parisiam vocatam volet. **1407** *Nottingham Rec.* II. 52 Pro ij. volets de Northfolk-thred, xd.

†**b.** *dial.* A handkerchief. *Obs.*

1788 VALLANCEY *Voc. Bargie* in *Trans. R. Irish Acad.* II. 34 *Volleat*, a handkerchief.

2. One of the wings or side-compartments of a triptych. (Cf. VOLANT *sb.* 4.)

1847 WORNUM *Hist. Paint.* xxiii. 317 This picture was painted in 1410,..It consists of a centre and two volets or revolving doors, which close upon it. **1848** MRS. JAMESON *Sacr. & Leg. Art* (1850) 227 On the volet to the right is the supper in the house of Levi.

volewen, southern ME. var. FOLLOW *v.*

voley, obs. f. VOLLEY.

volf(e, obs. Sc. ff. WOLF *sb.*

Volga ('vɒlgə). The name of a Russian river used *attrib.* in **Volga German**, a member of an ethnic minority living near the Volga from the seventeenth century until the Second World War; also *adj.*, of or pertaining to this people.

1941 *Times* 9 Sept. 3/3 (*heading*) Volga Germans to go. *Ibid.*, The Volga German region is an autonomous republic, with its own supreme council. **1947** W. BACZKOWSKI *Towards Understanding of Russia* v. 199 The following Autonomous Republics were liquidated: the Republic of Volga Germans, the Kalmyk Republic, [etc.]. **1973** A. PRICE *October Men* xi. 176 Korbel deserted to the Wehrmacht... Told 'em he was a Volga German. **1985** *Observer* 28 July 17/1 Muscovites say this is to keep out troublemakers (Volga Germans? Crimean Tartars?).

†**volge.** *Obs. rare.* [ad. L. *volgus*, *vulgus* VULGUS.] The mob; the common crowd.

1639 FULLER *Holy War* IV. xxix. (1647) 219 He would prefer to fight with any mean person, if cried up by the volge for a tall man. **1655** —— *Ch. Hist.* XI. iv. §32 One had as good be dumb, as not speak with the Volge. **1663** HEATH *Flagellum* (1672) 29 Nor did the Volge know when, nor could their Boutefeus tell where to cease.

†**'volger.** *Obs.*⁻¹ [ad. obs. F. **volgere*, *vulgere*, var. of *voglaire*, *veuglaire*, etc.: see Godefroy s.v.

vouglaire and cf. FOWLER 3.] A species of ordnance, longer and less powerful than the bombard.

a **1548** HALL *Chron., Hen. VIII*, 121 The ordinaunce of bombardes, curtawes, and demy curtaux, slinges, canons, volgers and other ordinaunce.

Volgian ('vɒlgɪən), *a. Geol.* [f. as VOLGA + -IAN.] Of, pertaining to, or designating a stage of the Upper Jurassic and Lower Cretaceous in Russia. Also *absol.*

1893 A. GEIKIE *Text-bk. Geol.* (ed. 3) 919 Some of the recognized [Jurassic] life-zones of western Europe can be detected in Russia... [These include] Volgian, consisting of green, brown and dark sandstones and sands. **1955** E. NEAVERSON *Stratigraphical Palaeont.* (ed. 2) xii. 473 The lower beds of the Russian Volgian stage.. may be correlated with the Upper Kimmeridge Clay of England. **1978** *Nature* 13 July 132/2 The fault-controlled stepwise submergence of the block-faulted basin culminated in Middle Volgian times with the most important Mesozoic phase of block-faulting in the region.

† **volgivagant**, *a. Obs.*$^{-0}$ [f. L. *volgi-, vulgivag-us* roving + -ANT.] (See quot.)

1656 BLOUNT *Glossogr.*, *Volgivagant, Vulgivagant*, pertaining to the common people, poor, base, mean, incertain, inconstant.

† **'volible**, *a.*^{1} *Obs. rare.* [ad. L. *volūbilis*, f. *volvĕre* VOLVE *v.*: see -IBLE.] Capable of turning or of being turned round.

1382 WYCLIF *Ezek.* x. 13 He clepide the ilk wheelis volible, or turnynge about. **1607** TOPSELL *Four-f. Beasts* 279 This beast [*sc.* the hedgehog].. is called red, sharp, maryne, volible, and rough.

† **'volible**, *a.*^{2} *Obs.*$^{-1}$ [f. L. *vol-*, stem of *volo* I wish.] Capable of being wished or desired.

1675 BAXTER *Cath. Theol.* II. I. 76 As sensible good is apprehended by the Intellect, and made volible.

'volipresence. *rare.* [f. as prec.: see PRESENCE.] (See quots.) So **'volipresent** *a.*

1882-3 *Schaff's Encycl. Relig. Knowl.* III. 2415 The glorified body is.. volipresent, that is, its presence was subject to the will of Christ. **1892** *Mag. Chr. Lit.* Apr. 3/1 (Stand.), The Saxon Churches generally acknowledged a potential presence (volipresence, multipresence) of the human nature of Christ.

† **'volitable**, *a. Obs.*$^{-1}$ [f. L. *volit-āre*: see VOLITATE *v.* and -ABLE.] Volatile.

a **1690** HOPKINS *Serm. John* iii. 5 Disc. (1694) III. 120 Their Prayers may be so importunate and earnest as if they would take no denial from God: But yet this Vollitable Spirit is soon spent.

volitant ('vɒlɪtənt), *a.* [ad. L. *volitant-, volitans*, pres. pple. of *volitāre*: see next.]

1. Flitting, flying, or constantly moving about.

1847 EMERSON *Repr. Men, Montaigne* Wks. (Bohn) I. 340 We are golden averages, volitant stabilities,.. houses founded on the sea. **1858** LEWES *Sea-side Studies* 358 That snowy mass of cloud.. rose from the surface of this brilliant, buoyant, volitant, sea. **1891** *Cent. Dict.* s.v., The bat is a volitant quadruped.

2. Characterized by flitting or flying to and fro.

1857 *Fraser's Mag.* July 65/1 The tremulous volitant motion of breeze upon wave.

volitate ('vɒlɪteɪt), *v.* [f. L. *volitāt-*, ppl. stem of *volitāre-*, freq. of *volāre* to fly.]

1. *intr.* (See quots.) ? *Obs.*

1623 COCKERAM I, *Volitate*, still to wander or flie vp and downe. **1656** BLOUNT *Glossogr.*, *Volitate*, to flie often, to run in and out, or to and fro often.

2. To fly with a fluttering motion.

1866 J. B. ROSE tr. *Virg. Ecl. & Georg.* 67 Then straws and leaves will volitate in air. **1890** *Illustr. Lond. News* 26 July 120/2 When a few weeks old they take wing, and if from an acclivity volitate down hill for a short distance.

volitation (vɒlɪ'teɪʃən). [a. med.L. *volitātiōn-, volitātio* (Diefenb.), noun of action f. L. *volitāre*: see prec.] Flying, flight.

1646 SIR T. BROWNE *Pseud. Ep.* IV. i. 180 Birds or flying animals.. are almost erect, advancing the head and breast in their progression, and onely prone in the act of their volitation. **1706** PHILLIPS (ed. Kersey), *Volitation*, a flying or fluttering about, or up and down. **1864** *Soc. Sci. Rev.* I. 382 The practical means of Volitation are to be sought for in the same mechanical means as those by which Birds fly. **1895** S. R. HOLE *Tour Amer.* 193 The young rook.. exercises in brief migrations.. his powers of volitation.

transf. **1823** *Blackw. Mag.* XIII. 175 The additional volitation acquired by such a stumble is rather apt to make you run your head plump against the next person.

vo'litient, *a. rare*$^{-1}$. [Irreg. f. VOLITI-ON + -ENT.] Of one's own free will or choice; voluntary.

1844 MRS. BROWNING *Drama of Exile* 92, I elected it Of my will, not of service. What I do, I do volitient, not obedient.

volition (və'lɪʃən). [a. F. *volition* (16th c., = Sp. *volicion*, Pg. *volição*, It. *volizione*), ad. med.L. *volitiōn-, volitio* (Diefenbach), noun of action f. L. *volo* I wish, will.]

1. With *a* and pl. An act of willing or resolving; a decision or choice made after due consideration or deliberation; a resolution or determination.

1615 JACKSON *Creed* IV. vi. §4. Wks. III. 61 That such acts, again, as they appropriate to the will, and call volitions, are essentially and formally intellections, is most evident. **1640** BP. REYNOLDS *Passions* xvii. 180 They are onely Velleities and not Volitions: halfe and broken wishes, not whole desires. **1678** CUDWORTH *Intell. Syst.* I. v. 851 They suppose .. humane volitions.. to be mechanically caused and necessitated from those effluvious images of Bodies, coming in upon the willers. **1740** CHEYNE *Regimen* 314 We may have vehement Willings, Longings, Volitions and Velleities. **1777** PRIESTLEY *Phil. Necessity* i. 6 A determination to suspend a volition is, in fact, another volition. **1777** —— *Matt. & Spir.* (1782) I. Introd. p. v, Every human volition is subject to certain fixed laws. **1830** R. KNOX *Béclard's Anat.* 9 When the animal has received a sensation, and this sensation determines a volition in it, it is by the nerves that the volition is transmitted to the muscles. **1844** MRS. BROWNING *Drama of Exile* 1190 Grant me such pardoning grace as can go forth From clean volitions toward a spotted will. **1864** BOWEN *Logic* ix. 300 No one can tell how a mere volition moves the arm. *Ibid.* 310 Unless some new volition of a power capable of controlling the universe should supervene.

fig. **1854** EMERSON *Lett. & Soc. Aims, Poet. & Imag.* Wks. (Bohn) III. 148 Good poetry.. heightens every species of force in nature by giving it a human volition.

b. Used with reference to the will of God.

1654 WARREN *Unbelievers* 145 Gods gracious volitions towards them. **1675** BAXTER *Cath. Theol.* II. II. 27, I doubt all sides are over temerarious in their distribution of Gods Decrees and Volitions. **1700** C. NESSE *Antid. Armin.* (1827) 26 We.. make the volitions of God to come behind the created and temporary volitions of man.

2. The action of consciously willing or resolving; the making of a definite choice or decision with regard to a course of action; exercise of the will.

Very common from *c* 1830.

1660 JER. TAYLOR *Ductor* IV. i. rule 3 §8 The external act does superadd new obligations beyond those which are consequent to the mere internal volition, though never so perfect and complete. *a* **1676** HALE *Prim. Orig. Man.* I. ii. (1677) 58 The Acts of this Faculty are generally divided into Volition, Nolition, and Suspension. **1690** LOCKE *Hum. Underst.* II. xxi §5 This Power the Mind has to prefer the Consideration of any Idea;.. the actual preferring one to another, is that we call Volition, or Willing. **1713** BERKELEY *Hylas & Phil.* I. Wks. 1871 I. 287 By the motion of my hand, which was consequent upon my volition. **1751** JOHNSON *Rambler* No. 166 ¶12 That when we find worth faintly shooting in the shades of obscurity, we may let in light and sunshine upon it, and ripen barren volition into efficacy and power. **1794** GODWIN *Caleb Williams* 231, I shifted my situation with a speed that seemed too swift for volition. **1828** SCOTT *F.M. Perth* xxix, In this answer the citizen saw something not quite consistent with his own perfect freedom of volition. **1843** GLADSTONE *Glean.* (1879) V. 14 Do not let us suppose that.. we are contemplating an affair of mere individual volition. **1874** SAYCE *Compar. Philol.* i. 37 Human volition is the result of so many obscure and complicated causes, as to appear at first sight mere caprice and chance.

b. The power or faculty of willing.

1738 *Gentl. Mag.* VIII. 22/2 The Traveller, as he hath Volition, may will to go to the Right or the Left before he comes to the Guide-Post. **1764** FOOTE *Patron* II. Wks. 1799 I. 345 To this cabinet volition, or will, has a key. **1794** PALEY *Evid.* III. viii. (1800) 412 The individuality of a mind.. or its volition, that is, its power of originating motion. **1839** BARHAM *Ingol. Leg.* Ser. I. *St. Gengulphus*, For Saints, e'en when dead, still retain their volition. **1848** MRS. JAMESON *Sacr. & Leg. Art* (1850) 46 That sort of angel-beings supposed to have a volition of their own. **1895** G. MACDONALD *Lilith* xx, Despair restored my volition,.. I ran and overtook her.

c. Will-power.

1844 DISRAELI *Coningsby* I. ii, The four votes.. had been increased, by his intense volition and unsparing means, to ten. **1847** —— *Tancred* I. ii, Montacute.. acted upon a stronger volition than his own.

Hence **vo'litionless** *a.*, lacking volition.

1881 J. OWEN *Even. w. Skeptics* x. II. 415 The volitionless will of the former [*sc.* Schopenhauer] is an instinct with purpose.. as the most personal conception of Deity ever evolved from the brain of a theologian.

volitional (və'lɪʃənəl), *a.* [f. prec. + -AL^{1}.]

1. Of or belonging to volition; pertaining or relating to the action of willing.

1816 BENTHAM *Chrestom.* 197 Whatsoever influence.. the prospects of them may have upon the will or volitional faculty. **1853** R. DUNN in *Jrnl. Ethnol. Soc.* (1856) IV. 43 The exercise of perception, memory, and volitional power. **1857** GRINDON *Life* xviii. (ed. 2) 215 The conscious, volitional exercise of our noblest capabilities. **1897** *Hutchinson's Arch. Surg.* VIII. 223 It was conceivable that the absolute volitional rest imposed by the severe pain might have acted on the muscle.

b. Affecting or impairing the will-power.

1854 BUCKNILL *Unsoundness of Mind* 28 Insanity may thus be Intellectual, Emotional, or Volitional.

2. Possessed of, endowed with, the faculty of volition; exercising or capable of exercising this.

1802-12 BENTHAM *Ration. Judic. Evid.* (1827) V. 229 Besides the argument you present to the intellectual part of their frame, you present to its neighbour the volitional part another sort of argument. **1864** ALGER *Hist. Doctrine Fut. Life* v. viii. 627 The essence of mind must be the common ground and element of all different states of consciousness. What is that common ground and element but the presence of a percipient volitional force, whether manifested or unmanifested, still there? **1887** M. ROBERTS *Western Avernus* 5, I began to feel alive, volitional, not dead and most basely mechanical as at home in England.

3. Of the nature of a volition.

1831 *Fraser's Mag.* IV. 361 It cannot move of itself, but a volitional thought is sufficient to raise it.

4. Of forces: Leading or impelling to action.

1863 KINGLAKE *Crimea* (1877) I. Pref. p. xiii, The volitional forces which acted upon Russia in 1853. **1874** SIDGWICK *Meth. Ethics* I. iii. 22 There seem to be two grounds of objection,.. one relating to the cognitive function, and the other to the motive or volitional influence, of the Practical Reason.

5. Of actions, etc.: Arising from, due to, characterized by, the exercise of volition.

Freq. from *c* 1875.

1859 *Todd's Cycl. Anat.* V. 675/1 The case of the respiratory muscles constitutes an example of mixed movements wherein volitional can be superadded to unconscious rythmic motion. **1875** POSTE *Gaius* I. Introd., Such actions are both Volitional (for the motor organs are set in motion by Volition) and Intentional. **1878** *Smithsonian Rep.* 419 The impulse causing the animal to make volitional movements comes from the peripheral centres. **1889** *Buck's Handbk. Med. Sci.* VII. 689/2 There is probably one portion of the cerebrum in which volitional work is especially performed, viz., the frontal lobes.

b. Depending on volition or free choice.

1890 'R. BOLDREWOOD' *Col. Reformer* (1891) 119 A mode of life more irregular, more volitional, than the daily mechanical regularity.. at Garrandilla proper.

Hence **volitio'nality**, the quality or state of being volitional.

1895 *Funk's Stand. Dict.*

vo'litionally, *adv.* [f. prec. + -LY^{2}.] With respect to volition; in a volitional manner.

1872 W. R. GREG *Enigmas of Life* (1873) 101 They were morally and volitionally more vigorous. **1875** *Contemp. Rev.* XXV. 941 Whether they be performed volitionally or automatically.

vo'litionary, *a.* [f. as prec. + -ARY.] = VOLITIONAL *a.* 5.

1890 *Nature* 13 Feb. 358/2 Some experiments which extend our knowledge of volitionary movement.

volitive ('vɒlɪtɪv), *a.* and *sb.* Also 7 **volutive**. [ad. med. or mod.L. **volitivus* (whence It., Sp. *volitivo*), or f. VOLIT-ION + -IVE.]

A. *adj.* **1.** Of or pertaining to the will; volitional.

1660 JER. TAYLOR *Ductor* I. i. rule 2 §4 The Volitive or chusing faculty cannot [take the name of conscience], but the intellectual may. *a* **1676** HALE *Prim. Orig. Man.* (1677) 29 The Command that is given by the volitive Faculty of the Soul. **1677** GALE *Crt. Gentiles* II. 359 The ordinate and actual power of God.. which some terme Gods Volutive Power. **1799** SIR H. DAVY in Beddoes *Contrib. Phys. & Med. Knowl.* 139 The perceptive and volitive powers depend.. on the constant supply of.. phosoxydated blood to the nervous and muscular systems. **1811-31** BENTHAM *Logic* Wks. 1843 VIII. 280 The volitional, or volitive faculty, or, in one word, the will. **1878** MACCALL tr. *Letourneau's Biol.* 386 In effect the deep cells of the cortical layers are motory, or rather volitive.

2. Originating in, arising from, the will.

1675 BAXTER *Cath. Theol.* II. II. 32 So that no man ever sinned by meer Action as such, whether Vital, Intellectual, or Volitive.

3. Performed deliberately or with express intention; designed, deliberate.

1839 J. ROGERS *Antipopopr.* II. 321 [The clergy's] intentional barbarity and cruelty, their volitive despotism and oppression, their willed persecution.. in reference to Luther and the like.

4. *Gram.* Expressive of a wish or desire; desiderative.

1846 MONIER WILLIAMS *Elem. Gram. Sanscrit Lang.* vi. 129 Certain roots.. take a desiderative form, without exactly yielding a volitive signification. **1864** WEBSTER s.v., A volitive proposition. **1894** W. G. HALE in *Classical Rev.* Apr. 167/2 The Greek.. Subjunctives of Will (volitive) and.. of Anticipation (anticipatory or prospective).

B. *sb.* A desiderative verb, mood, etc.

a **1813** MURRAY *Hist. European Lang.* (1823) II. 280 Volitives or desideratives.. are formed by using the future consignificative sa with the doubled verb. **1894** W. G. HALE in *Classical Rev.* Apr. 167/2 The volitives never have ἄν.

voli'torial, *a.* [f. mod.L. *Volitor-es* birds capable of flight + -IAL.] Of or pertaining to flying; having the power of flight.

1872 COUES *N. Amer. Birds* 178 The swifts, goatsuckers, and hummingbirds.. are birds of remarkable volitorial powers. **1875** C. C. BLAKE *Zool.* 93 The Hornbills are.. instances of the volitorial and the Kamichi in the grallitorial order.

voliwis, southern var. ME. *fuliwis* FULL *adv.* 2d.

‖ **Volk, volk** (fɔlk). [G., Du., Afrikaans = nation, people: see FOLK.]

1. *S. Afr.* **a.** The Afrikaner people.

1880 G. HUDSON *Let.* 1 Dec. in B. Bellairs *Transvaal War* (1885) 424, I met with a very sullen reception, and Mr Paul Kruger appeared.. very anxious that I should keep out of sight of the 'volk' (people) as much as possible. **1928** E. A. WALKER *Hist. S. Afr.* xiii. 515 The *Afrikaner Volk* proceeded to find itself along cultural and then along political lines. The Old Colony led the way. **1948** *Press Digest* (S. Afr. Jewish Board of Deputies) No. 2. 16 What the nationally-minded Afrikaner wishes for himself and for his volk, he wishes also for other peoples, namely a national home. **1953** P. ABRAHAMS *Return to Goli* 175 It is not only the Afrikaans-speaking Whites, not only 'Die Volk', who believe in the colour bar. **1979** J. DRUMMOND *Patriots* iii. 24 We have to throw out white privilege... That's being said.. in the.. strongholds of the Afrikaner volk.

b. The Coloured employees of an Afrikaner.

1882 *Cape Q. Rev.* 317 The water to be utilised for medicinal purposes in a bathing-house adjacent, which at present serves as a habitat for the 'volk' (workmen) of the farm. **1900** B. MITFORD *Aletta* 79 Come this way. My *volk* will see to your horse. **1939** J. S. MARAIS *Cape Coloured People* i. 5 In the western Cape a farmer calls his labourers his 'volk'—the same word that Adam Tas used for his slaves, as distinguished from his Hottentot labourers, in the early eighteenth century. **1968** K. MCMAGH *Dinner of Herbs* 30, I get the volk to drag away the carcasses and skin them.

2. The German people, esp. in the ideology of National Socialism.

1933 C. B. HOOVER *Germany enters Third Reich* vii. 175 *Das Volk* is thought of not as a juridical organization to which one might belong by obtaining citizenship rights through naturalization, but as a community held together by the sacred ties of common blood. **1937** *N.Y. Times Mag.* 21 Nov. 2/3 Like most nations of today, what is known as the Deutsche Volk is in itself a hybrid people composed of Germanic, Celtic, Slavic and Lithuanian elements.

3. *Comb.* **a.** In sense 1 (of the Afrikaner people): **'volkspele** (-spiələ) *pl.*, Afrikaner folk dances; hence **'volkspeler**, a dancer of these; **'volkswil** (-vil), the will of the people.

1949 *Cape Times* 24 Sept. 9/2 There would be volkspele demonstrations, recitations and singing. **1972** *Evening Post* (Port Elizabeth) 5 Feb., Dancing that night will be confined to volkspele and other typically South African dances. **1953** *Cape Times* 17 Apr. 9/8 The group of *volkspelers*.. will sail on an oversea tour in to-day's mailship. **1948** *Cape Argus* 2 Dec. 1/5 The numerical question apparently no longer applies, and it is now just a question of 'volkswil' and the support of the people. **1956** *Star* (Johannesburg) 23 Feb. 12/7 South Africa.. has heard much sanctimonious talk of the 'volkswil' from members of a minority government.

b. (In English some of these words are used without proper regard for the inflexional endings customary in German itself.) In the possessive in sense 2 (of the people): **Volksdeutsch** ('fɔlksdɔitʃ) *a.*, fem., pl., **-deutsche** (-tʃə), belonging to or characteristic of the *Volksdeutsche*, ethnically German; **Volksdeutsche** *sb. pl.*, people of German origin resident outside Germany and Austria; ethnic Germans; **Volksdeutscher**, a member of the *Volksdeutsche*, an ethnic German; also *attrib.*; **Volksgeist** ('fɔlksgaist), the spirit or genius which marks the thought or feeling of a nation or people; **Volkskammer** ('fɔlkskamər), the parliament of the German Democratic Republic; **Volksoper** ('fɔlksɔːpər), the light opera house in Vienna; also *transf.*; **Volkspolizei** ('fɔlkspolitsai), a police force of the German Democratic Republic; members of this; **Volkspolizist** ('fɔlkspolitsist), a member of the *Volkspolizei*; **Volkssturm** ('fɔlksʃturm) a territorial army established in Germany during the last years of the Third Reich; also *attrib.*; **Volkswanderung** ('fɔlksvandəruŋ) = VÖLKERWANDERUNG.

1952 E. F. DAVIES *Illyrian Venture* x. 177 The house-keeper matron, a fat, grim *Volksdeutsche* woman. **1962** *Listener* 7 June 1004/2 The old Volksdeutsch grannie who has nothing left to do except learn to die. **1981** I. BOLAND tr. *Ginzburg's Within Whirlwind* I. x. 83 She.. expostulated in her *Volksdeutsch* dialect that people must be fed before they are turned out to work. **1937** *N.Y. Times Mag.* 21 Nov. 16/3 The Germans of foreign citizenship are called 'Volksdeutsche', or 'racial Germans'. **1944** I. ORIGO *Diary* 7 June in *War in Val d'Orcia* (1947) 193 The Italian patriots.. are.. to give shelter to *Volksdeutsche* who have deserted from the German Army. **1961** R. KEE *Refugee World* iii. 20 Ethnic Germans (*Volksdeutsche*) living in east and south-east Europe. **1961** WEBSTER, Volksdeutscher. **1978** H. WOUK *War & Remembrance* xlvi. 463 A tall thin horribly pimpled *Volksdeutscher* burglar from Prague. **1981** I. BOLAND tr. *Ginzburg's Within Whirlwind* I. xiii. 108 He was a German. A Crimean *Volksdeutscher*. **1936** WIRTH & SHILS tr. *Mannheim's Ideology & Utopia* ii. 59 During this period the *Volksgeist*, 'folk spirit', comes to represent the historically differentiated elements of consciousness. **1977** D. WATKIN *Morality & Archit.* III. i. 79 Our fundamental concern is.. with the impression left by the emphasis on national character or *Volksgeist* as a determinant of artistic style. **1949** *Times* 8 Oct. 4 The German 'People's Council' proclaimed itself in Berlin yesterday to be the provisional Volkskammer, or Lower House, of the Parliament of the new 'German Democratic Republic'. **1977** *Whitaker's Almanack 1978* 865/1 Further amendments came into force on October 7, 1974 after adoption by the *Volkskammer* on September 27, 1974. **1928** J. A. MAHAN *Vienna of Yesterday & Today* ix. 210 Two opera houses, the Staatsoper.. and the Volksoper.. are in use every day of the season. **1968** *Vogue* 15 Apr. 23/1 Theoretically, the difference between the Wells and the Garden is that between *Volksoper* and *Staatsoper* in Vienna. **1980** *Times* 31 Dec. 3/5 The report rejects the idea that the D'Oyly Carte company should be built up.. to become a British 'Volksoper', performing light music and operetta. **1964** L. DEIGHTON *Funeral in Berlin* vi. 38 A volkspolizei troop carrier was parked at the roadside. **1967** R. V. BESTE *Repeat Instructions* (1968) ix. 94 He walked past *Volkspolizei*, who eyed him suspiciously. **1980** A. COPPEL *Hastings Conspiracy* vii. 52 Two uniformed officers of the Volkspolizei.. had hurried him to the military airfield at Bützow. **1974** J. D. WHITE *Leipzig Affair* vii. 63 There was a volkspolizist waiting outside my room. **1944** *Nation* (N.Y.) 25 Nov. 653 The *Volkssturm* is necessarily largely composed of men between fifty and sixty, with a sprinkling of sixteen- and seventeen-year-old boys. **1969** A. MARIN *Rise with Wind* ii. 12 He could still remember the.. day when a Volkssturm officer dug him out of the rubble. **1855** GEO. ELIOT *Let.* 9 Jan. (1954) II. 190 The subject I now propose is 'Women in Germany'.. through the periods of the Volkswanderung and the romantic.. life of the Middle Ages up to our own day.

volk, southern ME. or dial. var. FOLK *sb.*

‖**Volka'meria.** *Bot.* Also Volc-. [mod.L., f. the name of Johann G. *Volckamer*, a German botanist (1616–93).] A Linnean genus of verbenaceous shrubs, characterized by their fleshy or corky fruit; a shrub or plant of this genus.

1753 *Chambers' Cycl. Suppl.*, *Volkameria*, in botany, the name of a genus of plants... The fruit is a roundish bilocular capsule. **1823** CRABB *Technol. Dict.* s.v., The species are shrubs, as—*Volkameria aculeata*,.. Prickly Volkameria, &c. **1833** B'NESS BUNSEN in Hare *Life* (1879) I. ix. 403, I have replanted with roses, oleanders, volcamerias, and geraniums. **1866** *Treas. Bot.* 1225.

‖**Völkerwanderung** ('fœlkərˌvandəruŋ). Pl. **-ungen.** [G., f. *völker* pl. of VOLK + *wanderung* migration.] A migration of a people or peoples *en masse*, *spec.* that of Germanic and other peoples in Europe during the later Roman Empire and the early Middle Ages. Also *attrib.*

[**1885**: see *Volkswanderung* s.v. VOLK 3 b.] **1934** A. TOYNBEE *Study of Hist.* II. 97 The last convulsion of the post-Minoan Völkerwanderung along the west coast of Anatolia. **1946** PRIEBSCH & COLLINSON *German Lang.* (ed. 2) II. ii. 24 Subsequent encroachments.. by Goths, Franks and others during the Age of Migration (Völkerwanderung) are discussed. **1961** L. F. BROSNAHAN *Sounds of Language* iii. 52 The Germanic expansion of the Völkerwanderung period. **1969** J. MANDER *Static Society* i. 46 The Germanic *Völkerwanderungen* after the fall of the Roman Empire.

‖**völkisch** ('fœlkiʃ), *a.* [Ger.: see VOLK, -ISH[1].] Populist, nationalist, racialist.

1939 *Times Lit. Suppl.* 7 Jan. 8/3 Saratoga and Yorktown are more familiar to the British schoolboy than a more *völkisch* school of history would tolerate. **1962** *Listener* 26 Apr. 739/3 As Franco grew strong enough to disembarrass himself of any kind of *völkisch* institutions, he encouraged the Falange to fade away. **1975** *Times Lit. Suppl.* 21 Nov. 1392/2 Whether the *völkisch* ideology and antisemitic sentiment suffered a similar setback or penetrated to other parties... There was much less personal.. continuity of this older generation of *völkisch* leaders.

volkonskoite (vɒl'kɒnskəʊait). *Min.* Also 9 wolch-, wolk-; volch-. [ad. G. *wolchonskoit* (A. Kämmerer 1831, in *Jahrb. f. Mineral.*, etc. II. 420), f. the name of Prince 'Wolchonskoy' (? i.e. Volkonsky): see -ITE[1].] A green or bluish-green amorphous clay mineral of the montmorillonite group in which there is some substitution by chromium, now regarded as a variety of nontronite.

1844 J. D. DANA *Syst. Min.* (ed. 2) VI. 533 Wolchonskoite. Amorphous. Dull-shining. **1852** *Amer. Jrnl. Sci.* LXIV. 62 Silicated Chrome (Wolchonskoite?). **1892** E. S. DANA *Dana's Syst. Min.* (ed. 6) 696 Wolchonskoite... Volchonskoite. **1953** R. E. GRIM *Clay Mineral.* iv. 58 Substitutions within the octahedral sheet [of montmorillonite] may vary from few to complete... Replacement of aluminum by iron yields nontronite; by chromium, volkonskoite; by zinc, sauconite. **1973** *Norsk Geol. Tidsskr.* LIII. 329 The Cr_2O_3 content of volkonskoite may vary within wide limits, and values up to 15–20% have been reported from Russian occurrences.

Volkslied ('fɔlksliːt). Also volkslied. Pl. **-lieder** (-liːdər). [Ger. and Du., f. *volks* gen. of VOLK + LIED, LIED.] **1.** A German folk song; a popular song in a German folk idiom.

1858 GEO. ELIOT *Jrnl.* 23 May in *Life* (1885) II. viii. 41 His wife.. sang us some charming Bavarian *Volkslieder*. **1882** F. A. KEMBLE *Rec. Later Life* II. 8 Dr. Charles Follen, known in his own country as Carl Follenius.. wrote some fine spirited Volkslieder. **1934** C. LAMBERT *Music Ho!* iii. 159 The second [*sc.* Glinka's wedding song in five-four time].. freed music from the restricting and lumbering rhythms of the German Volkslied. **1977** *Early Music* Apr. 213/1 Only two songs are true 'volkslieder' with the usual upbeat opening and steady chorale-like melody.

2. *S. Afr.* **a.** *Hist.* The national anthem of the 19th-century Transvaal Republic. **b.** A simple popular folk song.

1874 *Cape Monthly Mag.* 254 We should, in the pages of the *Magazine*, from time to time collect some of the.. 'Volks-liedjes' written in the Cape Dutch patois. **1898** C. RAE *Malaboch* 217 *Volkslied*, the Transvaal National Anthem. **1921** *Eastern Province Herald* 18 Jan., The singing of the Volkslied and a vote of thanks to General Hertzog closed the meeting. **1954** H. GIBBS *Background to Bitterness* II. ix. 149 So they had ridden off, farmers, shop assistants, civil servants, lawyers, singing the *Volkslied* as they camped close to the southern frontier with Natal. **1961** *Sunday Times* (Johannesburg) 19 Mar. 10/7 The 16 girls and 14 boys in the choir will give Volksliedjie recitals and volkspele performances.

‖**Volksraad** ('vɔlksraːt). [Du., Afrikaans, f. Du. *volk* people, FOLK *sb.* + *raad* senate, council, REDE *sb.*]

1. The House of Assembly of the Republic of South Africa; formerly the chief legislative assembly in either of the former South African republics of the Transvaal or the Orange Free State.

1840 in J. C. Chase *Natal* (1843) II. 127 On the 14th [Feb. 1840], the Chief Commandant.. caused the following Proclamation to be read..:—I, Andries Wilhelmus Jacobus Pretorius, Chief Commandant.. of all the Burghers of the.. Volks-Raad of the South African Society of Port Natal.. &c &c &c. **1852** BARTER *Dorp & Veld* xiii. 194 A resolution of the *Volksraad*, that no additional natives should be allowed to take up their residence within the colony. **1865** *Chambers's Encycl.* VII. 25/2 While the volksraad, or peoples' council [of Orange River Free State], exercise legislative functions. **1881** EARL SELBORNE in *Personal & Pol. Mem.* (1898) II. 5 The Volksraad must yield, or the war be renewed.

2. *Netherlands East Indies.* A council advisory to the Governor-General.

1920 *Manual Netherlands India* (Admiralty) viii. 248 This council, under the name of the *Volksraad*.. is a representative body of 38 members. **1948** A. J. BARNOUW *Making of Mod. Holland* xi. 210 By an act of December 16, 1916, a *Volksraad* or People's Council was set up. **1974** *Encycl. Brit. Macropædia* IX. 488/1 At the end of World War I the Dutch.. created the Volksraad (People's Council). Composed of a mixture of appointed and elected representatives of the three racial divisions defined by the government—Dutch, Indonesian, and 'foreign Asiatic'—the Volksraad provided opportunities for debate and criticism but no control over the government of the Indies.

†**voll**, shortened f. of, or error for, VOLLEY *sb.*

1574 B. RICH *Dial. betw. Mercury & Soldier* A 4, Too my farewell, certayne voll of shot discharged in hope of my good speede.

vollary, obs. f. VOLARY.

volle, southern ME. var. FILL *sb.*[1], FULL *v.*[1] (to baptize), FULL *a.* and *adv.*

†**vollenge.** *Obs.*[−1] [Cf. VALANCHE and It. *valanga*.] An avalanche.

1830 W. TAYLOR *Hist. Surv. Germ. Poetry* II. 456 The vollenge, which overwhelms the whole village, was at first but a little snowball.

'voller, 'vollier. *s. dial.* Forms: 7 vallor, vallow, 9 valler; 8 voler, 9 voller, vollier. [Southern dial. var. of FOLLOWER (5 a).] That part of a cheese-press (or cider-press) to which pressure is applied.

1675 WORLIDGE *Syst. Agric.* (ed. 2) 323 *Vallor*, or *Vallow*,.. a Concave-Mold wherein a Cheese is pressed. [Hence in some later Dicts.] **1730** BUDGEN *Hurricane fr. Bexhill to Newingden-level* 2 A Cheesebail and Voler were taken from a Shelf in a Chamber. *Note*, The Voler is a round Piece of Inch Board, fitted into the Bail, that communicates the Force of the Press upon the Cheese. **1853** COOPER *Sussex Gloss.* 84. **1891** *Hartland Gloss.* 82 *Voller*,.. that part of a cider or cheese press to which the pressure is applied by screw or lever.

vollere, southern ME. variant of FULLER *sb.*[1]

volley ('vɒlɪ), *sb.* Forms: α. 6 volée, volee, (valee), vole, 7 vollee, volle. β. 6 vallew, 6–7 volue. γ. 6–8 vollie (6 vallie, *Sc.* wollie), 7 volie, 7–9 *pl.* vollies; 6 voly, 6–7 volly, 7 *Ir.* voylly. δ. 6–7 voley, 7 wolley, valley, 6– volley. [ad. F. *volée* (12th c. in Godef. *Compl.*), = Pr. and Sp. *volada*, It. *volata*:—Romanic *volāta*, fem. sb. f. L. *volātus*, pa. pple. of *volāre* to fly.

The spellings *volue*, *vallew*, are prob. on the analogy of *venue*, *vinew* beside *veny*, *vinny*.]

1. a. A simultaneous discharge of a number of firearms or artillery; a salvo.

α. **1587** HOLINSHED *Chron.* III. 1219/2 The whole fire began to plaie in such sort, that within foure volées both sides of the house were battered through. **1591** *Garrard's Art Warre* 48 They must abide at ye least a volee of Canons.

γ. **1573** *Satir. Poems Reform.* xxxix. 93 For ordinance thay dung at day and nycht By weirlyk volyis. *a* **1578** LINDESAY (Pitscottie) *Chron. Scot.* (S.T.S.) I. 143 The king.. commandit to charge all the gunnis to gif the castell ane new wollie. **1617** MORYSON *Itin.* II. 163 The enemy played all the night upon them with great vollyes, but hurt onely three men. **1688** HOLME *Armoury* III. xix. (Roxb.) 214/2 In grand Battalia's or feild service the souldier fires by Vollies or as some terme it, by Salves of shot. **1700** S. L. tr. *Fryke's Voy. E. Ind.* 318 A Dutch Company that conducted us out of Town gave three Vollies and went back again. **1745** P. THOMAS *Jrnl. Anson's Voy.* 282 We then kept a continual Fire upon her of both great and small Arms, not firing in set Broadsides and Vollies. **1826** J. F. COOPER *Mohicans* (1829) I. viii. 101 Rifles which sent their leaden messengers across the rock in vollies.

δ. **1591** in *Lyly's Works* (1902) I. 440 But from the Snailmount and the Ship-Ile in the Pond.. there was a long volley of Chambers discharged. **1600** E. BLOUNT tr. *Conestaggio* 203 They forced the gallions with a fewe volleies. **1625** MARKHAM *Souldiers Accid.* 9 Let the first Ranke onely giue their volley,.. and the second to passe through it, and so giue their volley. **1662** J. DAVIES tr. *Olearius' Voy. Ambass.* 169 We made some stay before the City,.. and saluted it with a Volley both of all our great Guns, and of small shot. **1719** DE FOE *Crusoe* I. (Globe) 304 We were by this Method able to fire six Volleys, half of us at a Time. **1817** J. SCOTT *Paris Revisit.* (ed. 4) 293 A loud coarse laugh burst out from each,—united as a volley of musquetry, and ending as abruptly. **1844** H. H. WILSON *Brit. India* II. 219 After firing a volley, the troops charged and put the enemy to the rout. **1879** BROWNING *Martin Relph* 103 They level: a volley, a smoke and the clearing of smoke.

b. Const. *of* (shot, etc.).

α. **1583** STOCKER *Civ. Warres Lowe C.* III. 83 b, The valee of an 150. Canon shot. **1590** SIR J. SMYTH *Disc. Weapons* 12 If our.. Mosquettiers would giue their volees of Mosquet shot uppon these shipboates full of men. **1623** in Foster *Eng. Factories Ind.* (1908) II. 231 At his putting into the grave 3 volles of smale shotte.

β. **1579** DIGGES *Stratiot.* 105 These Troupes.. hauing deliuered their Volue of Shot, shall marche away. *c* **1595** CAPT. WYATT *Dudley's Voy.* (Hakl. Soc.) 19 Givinge whole vallews of shott at our meetinge. *Ibid.* 45 Wyatt..receaved his Generall with a vallew of small shott.

γ. **1584** Lyly *Campaspe* v. iii. 37 There is more pleasure in tuning of voyce, then in a volly of shotte. **1599** Dallam in *Early Voy. Levant* (Hakl. Soc.) 59 Betwyxte everie greate shott a vallie of smale shott. **1650** R. Stapylton *Strada's Low C. Wars* vii. 76 A great joy expressed by three Vollyes of shot, and the cheerfull sound of Drums. *a* **1660** *Contemp. Hist. Irel.* (Ir. Archæol. Soc.) I. 261 The relife gaue a voylly of foure score shott amonge them. *a* **1700** Evelyn *Diary* 8 Oct. 1641, From whence we received many vollies of shot in compliment to my Lord Marshall.

δ. **1591** Raleigh *Last Fight Revenge* (Arb.) 20 After many enterchanged voleies of..small shot. **1604** T. Wright *Passions* v. §4. 192 Resembling a volley of shot speedily deliuered. **1625** in Ellis *Orig. Lett.* Ser. i. III. 199 Which gave her a volley of fifteen hundred great shot. **1725** De Foe *Voy. round World* i. 143 His Men fell..as flat to the Ground, as if they had been Shot to Death with a Volley of our Shot. **1748** *Anson's Voyage* ii. v. 186 He fired a volley of small shot between the masts. **1803** Scott *Let.* in *Lockhart* (1837) I. xi. 390 A volley of small shot fired through the window. **1847** James *Convict* xvi, Another volley of shot rang from behind the gateway of the town.

c. *transf.* (*spec.* in *Physiol.*), *fig.*, and in fig. context. Also without article (quot. 1749); cf. next.

1629 H. Burton *Truth's Triumph* 232 Thus haue we..spent a small volley vpon the Pontifician forces. **1738** Mrs. Delany *Life & Corr.* (1861) II. 15 Every one was pleased with your..compliments, and volleys have been shot off in return this afternoon, when I said I was coming to my room to write to you. **1749** Smollett *Regicide* iii. viii, I will pour My vengeance in full volley; and the earth Shall dread to yield you succour or resource! **1749** Fielding *Tom Jones* ix. v, She discharged a volley of small charms at once from her whole countenance in a smile. **1817** Byron *Beppo* xlv, Large black eyes that flash on you a volley Of rays. **1836–7** Dickens *Sk. Boz, Scenes* xii, Ginger-beer corks go off in volleys. **1928** *Jrnl. Physiol.* LXV 276 The rhythmic discharge is due to a more or less synchronous activity in a large number of the optic nerve fibres. The different ganglion cells have given up their usual independent fire of impulses and have taken to firing volleys. **1968** *Brit. Med. Bull.* XXIV. 253/2 Small localised changes in cortical potential, such as may follow the arrival of a sensory volley from the periphery, are completely lost in the background of much larger voltages produced by the rest of the cortical surface.

†**d.** ***in volley***, by simultaneous firing. *Obs.*$^{-1}$

1598 Barret *Theor. Warres* iii. i. 42 There is yet another order of discharging of troupes of Muskets in vollie.

e. *Mining.* 'The act of exploding blasts in sections.'

1895 *Funk's Stand. Dict.*

2. a. A shower or simultaneous flight of many missile weapons, as arrows, stones, etc. Also in fig. context.

1598 Barret *Theor. Warres* i. i. 3 Our bowmen may shoot by vollies, as thick as hayle. **1611** Speed *Hist. Gt. Brit.* vi. xiv. §11. 91 The Britaines..auoided the volue of the Romans, showring downe withall great store of theirs vpon them. **1667** Milton *P.L.* vi. 213 Over head the dismal hiss Of fiery Darts in flaming volies flew. **1697** Dryden *Æneid* i. 215 Stones and brands in rattling volleys fly. **1808** Scott *Marm.* vi. xxxiv, The English shafts in volleys hail'd. **1820** — *Abbot* xviii, Even thus fly all your shafts.., but a breath of foolish affection ever crosses in the mid volley, and sways the arrow from the mark.

b. Const. *of*.

1590 Sir J. Smyth *Disc. Weapons* 31 b, The Archers with their volees of arrowes did breake both horsmen and footmen. **1600** Holland *Livy* xxviii. xxxvi. 696 The Romans..at the first onset and volie of shot..put them to flight. **1625** Bacon *Apophth.* §126 It was told him, that the enemie had such volleyes of arrowes, that they did hide the Sunne. **1686** tr. *Chardin's Trav. Persia* 210 The People..ply'd the Top of the Mosque with..Volleys of Stones. **1734** tr. *Rollin's Anc. Hist.* (1827) I. 345 Numerous volleys of arrows and stones. **1788** Gibbon *Decl. & F.* xlvi. IV. 520 Their engines discharged a perpetual volley of stones and darts. **1850** Marsden *Early Purit.* (1853) 437 The mob rushed upon them with a volley of stones.

c. *poet.* A storm or shower of hail, rain, etc.

1737 *Gentl. Mag.* VII. 630 Wintry clouds, Surcharg'd with vollies of tumultuous hail, Or stores of sounding rain. **1784** Cowper *Task* v. 141 The gloomy clouds find weapons, arrowy sleet, Skin-piercing volley, blossom-bruising hail.

†**3. a.** A company or troop of birds, etc., in flight; a flight. *Obs. rare.*

1601 Dolman *La Primaud. Fr. Acad.* (1618) III. 760 The ringe doues are seene to come euery yeere in great vollies ouer the sea. *Ibid.* 843 Birds of prey doe not flie togither in vollies or troopes. **1610** G. Fletcher *Christ's Vict.* ii. lxi, But to their Lord, now musing in his thought, A heavenly volie of light Angels flew.

†**b.** A crowd or large number *of* persons or things. *Obs.*

1595 Daniel *Civil Wars* v. cvii, Therefore easily great Sommerset..With all the vollie of disgraces met. **1639** Fuller *Holy War* ii. xxxvii. 94 King Almerick himself wearied with whole volleys of miseries, ended his life of a bloudy flux. *a* **1656** Ussher *Ann.* vi. (1658) 564 The Souldiers..finding their return intercepted by a valley of Archers. **1693** *Humours Town* 27 The Vollies of Duns, of believing Vintners, Tailors, Sempstresses.

4. a. An uttering or outpouring *of* numerous words, oaths, shouts, etc., in smart or rapid succession. Also without const.

1590 Nashe *Pasquil's Apol.* i. C ij b, He giues vs a voley of Scriptures against Non Residents. **1591** Shaks. *Two Gent.* ii. iv. 30 A fine volly of words, gentlemen, & quickly shot off. **1620** [G. Brydges] *Horæ Subs.* 455 Whatsoeuer by them is performed, shall be sure to finde whole vollies of praises. **1647** N. Ward *Simple Cobler* (1843) 54, I am resolved..to storme you with volyes of Love and Loyalty. **1649** Milton *Eikon* x. Wks. 1851 III. 412 Those thousands of blaspheming Cavaliers about him, whose mouthes let fly Oaths and Curses by the voley. **1710** Steele & Addison *Tatler* No. 254 ¶5 We heard a Volley of Oaths and Curses, lasting for a long while. **1779** Sheridan *St. Patrick's Day* i. i, Let him have our grievances in a volley. **1782** Miss Burney *Cecilia* v. vii, [He] poured forth..a volley of compliments. **1820** W. Irving *Sketch Bk.* I. 64 This, however, always produced a fresh volley from his wife. **1847** *Illustr. Lond. News* 2 Oct. 219/2 Between them continuous volleys of what is called 'chaff' were kept up. **1874** Lisle Carr *J. Gwynne* I. v. 163 A volley of dire anathemas against those scoundrelly insurance chaps.

b. Similarly of sighs, groans, cheers, laughter, etc. Also without const.

1589 Greene *Tullies Love* Wks. (Grosart) VII. 189 After a vole of broken sighes tempered with some teares, hee fell a sleepe. **1640** Sandys *Christs Passion* iv. 270 Cries Of weeping Women, in lowd Vollies rise. **1648** Crashaw *Music's Duel* 63 A Throng Of short thicke sobs, whose thundring volleyes float..In panting murmurs. **1727** Gay *Begg. Op.* i. xii, What vollies of sighs are sent from the windows of Holborn. **1786** tr. *Beckford's Vathek* (1868) 103 They burst out into volleys of laughter. **1877** Talmage *Serm.* 334 Let this religion of Christ go down under a volley of merriment. **1882** B. D. W. Ramsay *Recoll. Mil. Serv.* II. xv. 65 Giving a volley of British cheers.

c. A succession of words of command rapidly or smartly delivered.

1796 *Instr. & Reg. Cavalry* (1813) 27 The repetition of them by every other individual concerned, must not be strictly successive, but as much as can be in a volley.

†**5.** ***at*** (***the*** or ***a***) ***volley***, ***on*** (or ***o'***) ***the volley***, at random, without consideration. Usu. with verbs, esp. *speak*. *Obs.*

After F. *à la volée*.

(*a*) **1578** H. Wotton *Courtlie Controv.* 252 The king..they knew loued hir feruently,..although it were begun at the volue. **1596** Harington *Metam. Ajax Apol.* Aa vj b, The sundrie censures I shoulde incurre, by letting such a pamphlet fly abroad at such a time, when euerything is taken at the voley. *c* **1620** Z. Boyd *Zion's Flowers* (1855) 125 Like those who speake at random at a voleye. **1625** B. Jonson *Staple of N.* iv. i, 'Tis like a Ball at Tennis..When we doe speak at volley, all the ill we can one of another. **1686** F. Spence tr. *St. Euvremont's Misc.* Pref., Otherwise we cannot lay hold of him, he speaks at volley and universally. [**1820** Scott *Monast.* xvii, I have always known you..prompt to speak at the volley and without reflection.]

(*b*) **1629** Massinger *Picture* iii. vi, What we spake on the voley begins to work. **1630** B. Jonson *New Inn* i vi, You must not giue credit To all that Ladies publiquely professe, Or talke, o'th vollee, vnto their seruants. **1831** *Fraser's Mag.* Sept. 161/1 He never speaks 'on the *voley*' (that is to say, at random).

6. a. *Tennis.* The flight of a ball in play before it has touched the ground. Cf. fly *sb.*² 2 b.

1596 Nashe *Saffron Walden* To Rdr. 24 One that stands, as it were, at the line in a Tennis-court, and takes euerie ball at the volly. **1878** Marshall *Ann. Tennis* 112 He frequently takes a difficult service (at the volley) off the pent-house.

b. *Tennis*, *Lawn-tennis*, *Cricket*, etc. A return stroke or hit at a ball before it has touched the ground; the action of so returning the ball. (Cf. *half-volley* half- II. i.)

1851 J. Pycroft *Cricket Field* v. 79 At Woolwich he hit a volley to long field for *nine*. **1862** *Temple Bar* VI. 282 [Mr. Budd] is said to have hit a volley to long-field for nine. **1884** *Marshall's Tennis Cuts* 124 The match was..loudly applauded every now and then by the spectators, when a brilliant volley was called, or a smash was declared. **1902** *Sat. Rev.* 12 July 51/1 Instruction is given in the underhand volley [in lawn-tennis].

c. = volleyer.

1878 Marshall *Ann. Tennis* 112 He was a powerful *force*, and a capital volley.

7. *attrib.* and *Comb.*, as ***volley-boast***, ***loophole***, †***-shot***, ***system***; **volley-ball**, **volleyball** orig. *U.S.*, a game in which a ball is struck from alternate sides of a high net without touching the ground (*Cent. Dict.* Suppl.); also *attrib.*; also, the ball used in this game; **volley-firing**, simultaneous firing at the word of command by successive parties of soldiers; also *fig.*; **volley gun**, a form of machine-gun which fires bullets successively or in a volley (Knight, 1884).

1896 *Physical Education* V. 50/1 Mr. W. G. Morgan of Holyoke, Mass., has developed a game..which is called *Volley Ball... The play consists in keeping a ball in motion over a high net,..thus partaking of the character of two games,—tennis and hand ball. **1936** P. Fleming *News from Tartary* vii. i. 325 In the evening we played tennis with the Russians, or football or volley-ball with the Hunza guard. **1949** *Dziennik Zwiazkowy* (Chicago) 19 Nov. 6/3 Last year two of our volleyball teams finished in a tie for second place. **1976** *Milton Keynes Express* 4 June 39/7 Stoke Mandeville has told the club that any money raised for them will be used to purchase table tennis nets and volleyballs for the National Spinal Injuries Centre. **1878** Marshall *Ann. Tennis* 197 He would generally return it by a *volley boast against the main-wall. **1859** *Musketry Instr.* 62 Every file is to have its own target, and the hits are to be counted as in *volley firing. **1879** *Cassell's Techn. Educ.* III. 267 The superior efficacy of volley-firing and reserved fire. **1891** *Daily News* 2 Oct. 5/5 In the..Town Hall of Newcastle the representative fighting men of the Liberal party were assembled for volley firing. **1898** Sir G. S. Robertson *Chitral* xxiii. 225 *Volley loopholes are good against an enemy that attacks with a masterful rush. **1689** *Lond. Gaz.* No. 2433/3 The Night concluded with Dancing, Bells Ringing, Bonfires, *Volly-shots. **1702** *Ibid.* No. 3793/3 The 2 Companies of Foot..gave a Volley Shot at each Proclamation. **1899** *Westm. Gaz.* 15 Sept. 2/3 There has for some time been a feeling in the air that the *volley system was going.

volley ('vɒlɪ), *v.* Forms: 7 volly (8–9 *pa. t.* vollied); 6– volley. [f. prec.]

1. *trans.* **a.** To utter (words, etc.) rapidly or impetuously. Usually with advs., as *forth*, *off*, *out*.

1591 *Troub. Raigne K. John* i. (1611) 62 A prophet new sprung up, whose diuination volleis wonders foorth. *Ibid.* ii. 73 If sobs would helpe,..My heart should volley out deepe piercing plaints. **1593** Shaks. *Ven. & Ad.* 921 Another flapmouthd mourner, blacke, and grim, Against the welkin volies out his voyce. **1754** P. H. *Hiberniad* 37 She raves, and vollies off an horrid Cry. **1824** Scott *St. Ronan's* xx, The bursts of applause which were vollied towards the stage. **1859** Meredith *R. Feverel* xxxviii, Sir Julius turned one heel, and volleyed out silver laughter. **1885–94** R. Bridges *Eros & Psyche* Aug. xii, She saw an uncouth form ..whose parted lips Volley'd their friendly warning in a storm.

b. To discharge (arrows, shot, etc.) in a volley.

Cf. volleyed *ppl. a.* 3.

1839 Bailey *Festus* 139 When the storm bends his bow, And volleys all his arrows off at once.

c. *Tennis*, etc. To return (a ball) in play before it touches the ground; to reply to (a service) in this way. Also, *Association Football*, to kick (the ball) before it touches the ground; to score (a goal) in this way.

1875 'Stonehenge' *Brit. Rur. Sports* (ed. 12) iii. i. v. 690/1 The service must not be volleyed. **1878** [see 2 b]. **1902** *Sat. Rev.* 12 July 51/2 It is bad policy to give the advice not to volley a lob. **1909** in Webster. **1972** G. Green *Great Moments in Sport: Soccer* viii. 85 He vollied [*sic*] in Bowen's clever lob with half an hour left. **1976** *Scotsman* 25 Nov. 25/1 In 52 minutes Somner volleyed a goal from McQuade's cross. **1976** *Norwich Mercury* 10 Dec., It was he who provided the perfect pass for Mann to volley the ball against the St. Andrews crossbar before the interval.

d. *Cricket.* To bowl or deliver (a ball) which reaches the batsman before bouncing. ? *U.S.*

1909 *Cent. Dict.* Suppl.

e. To fire a volley or volleys at.

1908 Hardy *Dynasts* III. vii. ii. 489 Kempt's brigade..volleys murderously Donzelot's columns..and repulses them.

2. *absol.* **a.** To fire a volley (or volleys). Also in fig. context.

Common in 19th-cent. journalistic use, prob. after quot. 1854.

1606 Shaks. *Ant. & Cl.* ii. vii. 119 Then the Boy shall sing, The holding euery man shall beate as loud, As his strong sides can volly. **1854** Tennyson *Lt. Brigade* v, Cannon behind them Volley'd and thunder'd. **1899** *Westm. Gaz.* 2 Jan. 2/1 A large line of guerillas..decided swiftly that their presence and position were discovered, and swiftly they volleyed.

b. *Tennis*, etc. To hit or return the ball before it bounces; to make a volley-stroke.

1819 in Hone *Every-day Bk.* (1825) I. 867 He never *volleyed* [i.e. at fives], but let the balls hop. **1878** Marshall *Ann. Tennis* 197 A young player, if he fancies he can volley well, will always be apt to volley balls which would come well off the end-walls. **1892** *Pall Mall G.* 20 July 7/2 F. Rooke..volleyed more effectively than his opponent.

3. *intr.* **a.** To emit or produce sounds simultaneously or continuously, in a manner suggestive of firearms or artillery.

In 19th-cent. use freq. in 'to volley and thunder', after quot. 1854 in sense 2 a.

1810 Southey *Kehama* xxiii. xi, When its thunder broke, ..while it vollied round the vault of Hell, Earth's solid arch was shaken with the shock. **1875** L. Morris *Children Street* i, Every day come they there, Afternoon foul or fair, Shouting and volleying. **1886** Stevenson *Kidnapped* xxix, For some time Alan volleyed upon the door, and his knocking only roused the echoes of the house.

b. To rush, roll, or stream with simultaneous motion; to shoot rapidly.

1853 C. Bronte *Villette* vii, About a hundred thoughts volleyed through my mind in a moment. **1880** Blackmore *Mary Anerley* I. x. 129 The crest of the wave volleys up the incline.

c. To issue or be discharged in, or after the manner of, a volley.

1887 Bowen *Æneid* i. 150 Firebrands fly, stones volley, the weapons furnished of wrath. *Ibid.* iii. 577 Molten masses of stone to the skies with a groan and a roar Volley in showers.

volley, southern dial. var. follow *v.*

volleyed ('vɒlɪd), *ppl. a.* Forms: 7 volied, 7–9 vollied; 8 volly'd, 8–9 volley'd, 9 volleyed. [f. volley *v.* + -ed.]

1. Shouted or uttered in the manner of a volley.

a **1616** Beaum. & Fl. *Bonduca* iii. v, Heark..how the air Totters and reels, and rends apieces, Drusus, With the huge vollied clamours. **1813** Scott *Rokeby* v. xxxiii, He strove, with vollied threat and ban,..To rally up the desperate fight.

2. Of thunder or lightning: Discharged with the noise or continuous effect of a volley.

Very common in poetry of the 18th cent.

1667 Milton *P.L.* iv. 928 When in Battel to thy aide The blasting volied Thunder made all speed. **1726** Pope *Odyss.* xx. 212 Some pitying God..With vollied vengeance blast their towering pride! **1744** Akenside *Pleas. Imag.* i. 188 She springs aloft Thro' fields of air; pursues the flying storm; Rides on the volley'd lightning thro' the heav'ns. **1812** H. & J. Smith *Rej. Addr.* 38 The vollied flame rides in my breath, My blast is elemental death. **1821** Clare *Vill. Minstr.* II. 60 While skies in vollied rolls are rent.

b. Of the nature of a volley.

1835 J. HARRIS *Gt. Teacher* (1837) 25 He discharged its tremendous contents in one volleyed and prolonged explosion.

3. Of missiles, etc.: Discharged or cast in or as in a volley. Also in fig. context.

1759 W. MASON *Caractacus* Poems 1830 II. 127 Our vollied darts, That thick as hail fell on their helms. **1791** COWPER *Iliad* VIII. 78 The vollied weapons on both sides their task Perform'd effectual. **1797** PARK *Sonn.* 78 Then will we fire a vollied round, And uncharg'd goblets shall resound. **1856** BRYANT *Winter Piece* 122 And bounding on the frozen earth Shall fall their [*sc.* clouds'] volleyed stores rounded like hail.

4. *Tennis.* Returned by volleying.

1878 MARSHALL *Ann. Tennis* 226/2 Volleyed service.

volleyer ('vɒlɪə(r)). *Tennis.* [f. as prec. + -ER.] One who returns the ball before it bounces.

1878 MARSHALL *Ann. Tennis* 196 When the ball is judged and met by the racket of the volleyer. **1879** in *Marshall's Tennis Cuts* (1884) 36 A generation of volleyers will rise up who will volley from the service-line.

'volleying, *vbl. sb.* [f. as prec. + -ING[1].] The action of returning the ball (in tennis and other ball games) before it bounces. Also *attrib.*

1837 D. WALKER *Games & Sports* 256 (Rackets), This last stroke is termed volleying. **1882** *Daily Tel.* 18 July 2 The volleying and low play gaining repeated rounds of applause. **1883** *Pall Mall G.* 1 Sept. 8/2 He exhibited splendid volleying ability, and won by three sets to one.

'volleying, *ppl. a.* [f. as prec. + -ING[2].] That volleys, in senses of the verb.

(*a*) **1796** COLERIDGE *Destiny of Nations* v. 53 Some drive the mutinous clouds to clash in air, And..Yoke the red lightning to their volleying car. **1805** SCOTT *Last Minstrel* IV. ii, When the volleying musket play'd Against the bloody Highland blade. **1849** J. GRANT *Kirkaldy of Grange* xxvi. 301 The booming cannon, the volleying harquebusses. **1852** TENNYSON *Ode Wellington* 62 Let..the volleying cannon thunder his loss.

(*b*) **1816** BYRON *Siege Corinth* ii, There the volleying thunders pour, Till waves grow smoother to the roar. **1822** —— *Juan* VIII. vi, The volleying roar, and loud Long booming of each peal on peal, o'ercame The ear far more than thunder. **1894** *Outing* (U.S.) XXIV. 50/2 The volleying boom of giant trees, uprooted from their rocky foundations, sounded above the shriek of the wind.

(*c*) **1844** HOOD *Forge* I. 170 The Forge..With volleying smoke, and many a spark, Vomiting fire. **1866** M. ARNOLD *Thyrsis* vi, So have I heard the cookoo's parting cry,..Come with the volleying rain and tossing breeze.

volliche, southern ME. var. FULLY *adv.*

vollier. *s.w. dial.* Also volyer. [dial. var. of FOLLOWER: cf. VOLLER.] (See quot. 1855.)

1855 *Househ. Wds.* 23 Sept. 130/1 [In pilchard fishing] there is a second or assisting boat, called the volyer, which carries another net, called the tuck-seine. *a* **1870** J. COUCH *Hist. Polperro* vi. (1871) 106 A second boat, the *volyer*,..has another sean-net of a hundred or more fathoms in length, and eighteen in depth.

vollier, variant of VOLLER *dial.*

†**volliere.** *Obs. rare.* Also -yere, -ier. [a. F. *volière*, f. *voler* to fly.] = VOLARY.

1638 SIR T. HERBERT *Trav.* (ed. 2) 148 His Gardens are.. prettily contrived into grotts, mazes, vollieres, and the like. *Ibid.* 156 [The] ayery Citizens..returne their thankfull notes in a more swift melodious consort, than if they were in the exactest vollyere in the Vniverse.

vollit, obs. Sc. form of WOOLLED *a.*

†**vollouth,** variant of FULLOUGHT *Obs.*

c **1330** HEREBERT in *Rel. Ant.* I. 87 Crist..so com to seynt Jon, And of hym was y-wasȝe.., To halewen our vollouth water, that sunne havet vor-don.

volly, southern dial. var. FOLLOW *v.*, FOLLY *sb.*[1] and *sb.*[2]

Volnay ('vɒlneɪ). Also 7 Volne. [Name of a commune in the department of Côte-d'Or, France.] A red wine of Burgundy, produced near Beaune (formerly also a white wine).

1699 M. LISTER *Journey to Paris* 161 Volne, a pale Champagne, but exceeding brisk upon the Palate...is said to grow upon the very borders of Burgundy, and to participate of the Excellency of both Counties. **1833** [see POMARD]. **1889** [see CORTON]. **1961** A. WILSON *Old Men at Zoo* i. 48 'They've got two good burgundies here,' he said, 'this and the Volnay '57.' **1979** R. LEWIS *Violent Death* v. 140 A good lunch of roast beef with an excellent Volnay.

†**volo-nola.** *Obs.*[−1] [f. L. *volo* I am willing + *nolo* I am unwilling.] A vacillation or wavering in decision.

1672 MARVELL *Reh. Transp.* I. 14 His story of the Bookseller, and all the Volo-Nola's, and shall-I, shall-I's betwixt them, was nothing but fooling.

volontary, obs. form of VOLUNTARY.

volonteer(e, obs. forms of VOLUNTEER.

‖**volost** ('vɒlɒst). [a. Russ. *volost'*.] The smallest rural administrative subdivision in Imperial Russia and the U.S.S.R. (abolished in 1930).

1889 in G. N. Curzon *Russia in Central Asia* v. 114 There are forty *volosts*, or sub-districts, in the Merv circuit. **1920** B. RUSSELL *Pract. & Theory Bolshevism* I. v. 75, I asked in the villages how they were represented on the Volost (the next larger area) or the Gubernia. **1948** J. TOWSTER *Political Power in U.S.S.R.* iv. 66 The Baltic republics..are still divided into *uyezds* and *volosts* as in Imperial Russia. **1959** *Chambers's Encycl.* XIV. 102/2 The terms *okrug* (national enclave), *uyezd* (district) and *volost* (rural area) are obsolescent. **1974** *Encycl. Brit. Macropædia* XVI. 59/1 Kiselev..provided for a measure of self-government under which the mayor of the *volost* (a district grouping several villages or peasant communes) was elected by male householders.

†**volow,** var. of *folowe* FULL *v.*[1] Hence †**volower,** one who baptizes; †**volowing** *vbl. sb.*, baptism. *Obs. rare.*

1528 TINDALE *Obed. Chr. Man* 107 b, Baptism is called volowinge in many places of Englonde. *Ibid.*, The child was well volowed (saye they); yee and our vicare is as fayre a volower as ever a prest within this twenty myles. **1530** —— *Answ. More* Wks. (1573) 277/1 They brought them to confirmation straight from Baptisme: so that now oftymes they be volowed and bishopped both in one day.

volowynge, error for *bolnynge* BOLNING *ppl. a.*

c **1450** tr. *De Imitatione* III. xiv. 82 Be wrothe ayeins thi selfe, and suffre no volowynge pride [L. *tumorem*] to lyve in the.

volplane ('vɒlpleɪn), *sb.* [Orig. two words, *vol plane*, properly *vol plané*, f. F. *vol* flight + *plané*, pa. pple. of *planer* PLANE *v.*[2]] A dive, descent, or downward flight at a steep angle on the part of an aeroplane under control, and with the engine stopped or shut off.

1910 in Hamel & Turner *Flying* (1914) 17 The 'vol plané', or aerial dive. **1911** GRAHAME-WHITE & HARPER *Aeroplane* 121 He was diving down from an altitude of about 1,000 feet. It was not a *vol plane* that he was making, as he had his engine running.

'volplane, *v.* [f. the *sb.*] To make a volplane. Also *transf.* (esp. with bird as subj.) and *fig.* Hence **'volplaning** *ppl. a.*

1911 *Daily News* 21 July 1 He volplaned from about 200 feet to 20 feet of the ground, which he skimmed for about a hundred yards. **1922** 'KLAXON' *Heather Mixture* xi. 223 Two cocks [*sc.* pheasants] came over the brow.., and with steady wings volplaned down the line from the right. **1929** E. BOOTH *Stealing through Life* x. 243, I..volplaned down a flight of steps and hit the..sidewalk on my hands and knees. **1936** D. MCCOWAN *Animals Canad. Rockies* xx. 182 You may be fortunate enough to see one of these [*sc.* flying] squirrels as it volplanes gracefully from a high branch to the ground. **1937** *Discovery* Dec. 364/1 Volplaning marsupials. **1970** 'E. LINDALL' *Gathering of Eagles* v. 46 They could all ..die together..watched by the eagles, seeing..the huge birds volplaning in.

†**vol'pone.** *Obs.* Also vulpone, -ony. [The name of the chief character in B. Jonson's play *Volpone, or the Fox*, a. It. *volpone*, f. *volpe* fox; the forms in *vulp-* are after L. *vulpis.*] A cunning schemer or miser. Also *Comb.*

1672 G. THOMSON *Let. to H. Stubbe* 25 To observe their Vulpone-like windings, intrigues and nimble diversions. **1685** SOUTH *Serm.* (1715) I. 408 Come to an old, rich, professing Vulpony, and tell him, that there is a Church to be built [etc.]. **1709** SACHEVERELL *Serm. 5 Nov.* 21 In what ..lively Colours does the Holy Psalmist paint out the crafty Insiduousness of such wilely Volpones? **1710** *Acc. Last Distemper Tom Whigg* I. 4 Certain Beasts of Prey, Vultures and Vulpones.

†**Volsce.** *Obs.* Also 4 Vulce, 6 *Sc.* Wolche, 7 Volce (*pl.* -es, -ies). [ad. L. *Volscus*, pl. *Volscī*: cf. next.] = VOLSCIAN *sb.* 1.

1387 TREVISA *Higden* (Rolls) III. 159 He ouercame þe Vulces and þe Gabies, and made pees wiþ Tuscans. **1533** BELLENDEN *Livy* I. xx. (S.T.S.) I. 114 To seik supporte of þe pepill namyt Wolchis [*v.r.* Wolches]. **1579–80** NORTH *Plutarch* (1612) 234 Vpon returne of the Volsces ambassadors..Tullus caused an assembly generall to be made of the Volsces. **1607** SHAKS. *Cor.* I. i. 228 The newes is, sir, the Volcies are in Armes. *Ibid.* 253 The Volces haue much Corne. *Ibid.* iv. 28 He that retires, Ile take him for a Volce.

Volscian ('vɒlʃən), *sb.* and *a.* Also 6 *Sc.* Volscan, 7 Volcian, Volcean. [f. L. *Volscī* + -AN. Cf. prec.]

A. *sb.* **1.** *Hist.* One of an ancient warlike people formerly inhabiting the east of Latium, subdued by the Romans in the 4th century B.C.

1513 DOUGLAS *Æneid* XI. xi. 29 Wyth armyt men and wageouris the Volscanis So neir almost by lappit hym at anis. **1607** SHAKS. *Cor.* v. iii. 178 This Fellow had a Volcean to his Mother. *Ibid.* vi. 116 Like an Eagle in a Doue-coat, I Flatter'd [*sic*] your Volcians in Corioles. **1697** DRYDEN *Virg. Georg.* II. 233 Volscians armed with iron-headed darts. **1770** LANGHORNE *Plutarch* II. 163 Corioli was the capital of the country of the Volscians. **1841** *Penny Cycl.* XX. 105/2 M. Valerius, who, with an army of 40,000 plebeians, defeated the Volscians, Aequians, and Sabines.

2. The Italic language spoken by the Volscians.

1859 B. W. DWIGHT *Mod. Philol.* I. 187 The Umbro-Samnite Dialects: Umbrian; Samnite or Oscan; Volscian; Marsian. **1897** R. S. CONWAY *Italic Dialects* I. 272 The majority of scholars incline to regard them as borrowed from Oscan. From geographical considerations I think Volscian is a more likely source. *Ibid.* 288 The Osco-Umbrian family of dialects (to which Volscian belonged).

B. *adj.* Of, pertaining or belonging to, the Volscians; that is a Volscian.

1601 HOLLAND *Pliny* I. 58 The towne Tarracina, called in the Volscian tongue Anxur. **1607** SHAKS. *Cor.* v. iii. 3 My partner in this Action, You must report to th' Volcian Lords. **1700** DRYDEN *Pal. & Arc.* II. 639 The Volscian Queen extended on the Plain. **1770** LANGHORNE *Plutarch* II. 186 This proclamation exasperated the whole Volscian nation against the Romans. **1841** W. SPALDING *Italy & It. Isl.* III. 289 The Pontine Marshes..were once covered with Volscian towns. **1880** *Encycl. Brit.* XIII. 443/1 The volcanic region of Terra di Lavoro is separated by the Volscian mountains from the Roman district.

‖**vol'sella.** *rare.* Also 7 **vulsella.** [L. *volsella*, *vulsella* tweezers, forceps, f. *vols-*, *vuls-*, ppl. stem of *vellĕre* to pluck.] (See quot. 1693 and next.)

1693 tr. *Blancard's Phys. Dict.* (ed. 2), *Volsella*, or *Vulsella*, an Instrument to pull up Hairs with by the Root, Tweezers: Or a Chyrurgions little Tongs, which are of different shape according to the Diversity of their Use. [Hence in Harris, Phillips, etc.] **1728** CHAMBERS *Cycl.*, *Acanthabolus*, a Surgeon's Instrument; called also *Volsella.* **1889** DUNCAN *Clin. Lect. Dis. Women* (ed. 4) ii. 5 A Volsella is fixed in the cervix.

‖**vol'sellum.** *Surg.* [mod.L., perhaps from mistaking L. *volsella* (see prec.) for a neuter pl. Cf. VULSELLUM.] A kind of forceps used in surgical operations. Also *attrib.*

1876 CURLING *Dis. Rectum* 53 The hæmorrhoidal growths are to be seized separately with the volsellum forceps. *Ibid.* 75 A fold of membrane..is to be seized with a volsellum, or the hæmorrhoidal forceps. **1898** *Baldy's Amer. Text-Bk. Gynecol.* (ed. 2) 375 A double tenaculum or volsellum forceps.

Volstead ('vɒlstɪd). The name of Andrew J. *Volstead* (1860–1947), American legislator, originator of the legislation to enforce prohibition (sense 4) which was passed in 1919 by the U.S. Congress, used *attrib.* to designate this legislation or the period during which prohibition was in force.

1920 *Current Opinion* Apr. 451/1 The Wet leaders..will wage a campaign for the election..of Congressmen favorable to changes in the Volstead Act. **1935** A. G. MACDONELL *Visit to Amer.* xiii. 229 The Volstead amendment led to some pretty confusion, but the repeal of the Volstead amendment seems to be almost worse. **1949** *Chicago Tribune* 8 Sept. 22/2 In the Volstead era, corrupt politicians talked to exactly the same effect with the leaders of the Anti-Saloon league. **1977** H. FAST *Immigrants* III. 179 The Congress of the United States was overriding President Wilson's veto of the Volstead Act and making Prohibition the law of the land. *Ibid.* 203 This is the finest wine country in the world, and some day the world is going to discover that—if we ever rid ourselves of this lousy Volstead thing.

Hence **'Volsteadism,** the policy of the Volstead Act; prohibition.

1920 *Harvey's Weekly* 27 Mar. 11/2 The Republicans would have to stand for Volsteadism or incur defeat. **1947** *Chicago Daily News* 23 Jan. 14/1 Volstead didn't write the law. Nor was he an apostle of the fanaticism called 'Volsteadism'.

volt (vɒlt, vəʊlt), *sb.* [f. the name of *Volta*: see VOLTAIC *a.*[1]] The practical unit of electromotive force; the difference of potential capable of sending a current of one ampere through a conductor whose resistance is one ohm.

1873 F. JENKIN *Electr. & Magn.* x. §2 There is already a unit of electromotive force in practical use called a *volt.* The volt is intended to represent 10^8 absolute units. **1881** SIR W. THOMSON in *Rep. Brit. Assoc.* 518 Nothing above 200 volts ought..to be admitted..where safeguards against accident cannot be made absolutely..trustworthy. **1892** *Electr. Engin.* 16 Sept. 283/1 The small glow lamp requires from 0·6 to 0·8 amperes and four volts to fully light it.

b. *attrib.* (with numeral preceding).

1881 SIR W. THOMSON in *Rep. Brit. Assoc.* 518 To take energy direct from the electric main with its 80,000 volts, and supply it by secondary 200-volt dynamos or 100-volt dynamos. **1890** *Anthony's Photogr. Bull.* III. 223 Five cells of this battery will light the six volt lamp.

volt, obs. var. VAULT *sb.*[1] and *v.*[1]; var. VOLTE *sb.*; var. obs. Sc. VULT (face).

volt (vɒlt, vəʊlt), *v.*[1] [ad. F. *volter* (f. *volte* VOLTE or ad. It. *voltare*); or (in sense 4) variant of VAULT *v.*[2] under the influence of this.]

†**1.** *refl.* To turn or roll over. *Obs.*[−1]

1658 FRANCK *North. Mem.* (1694) 67 See where he comes tumbling and tossing, and volting himself in the stiffest Streams.

†**2.** *intr.* (See quot.) *Obs.*[−1]

1688 HOLME *Armoury* II. 150/1 [A horse is said to] Voult, when he Raires, or stands upright.

3. *Fencing.* To make a volte. Also *fig.*

1692 SIR W. HOPE *Fencing Master* 101 You must Volt, or leap with both your feet in the Air at once, quite by your Adversaries left shoulder. **1696** R. H. *Sch. Recreat.* 72 Fourthly, you may Volt, and in your so doing, give him the Thrust, which being clearly done, will mainly surprize him. **1771** LONNERGAN *Fencer's Guide* 215, I parry you with a Prime, and cut at your head with a Medium as I volt. **1897** *Westm. Gaz.* 14 July 3/2 When Mr. Chamberlain volts, it is not only his face, but his whole personality he turns round.

†**4.** = VAULT *v.*[2] 2. *Obs. rare.*

1753 YOUNG *Brothers* III. i, This pass'd, as suits his Wisdom, Macedonians! Who volts o'er elder Brothers to a Throne. **1757** —— *Love Fame* v. 124 Some nymphs affect a more heroic breed, And volt [*earlier edd.* vault] from hunters to the manag'd steed.

Hence **'volting** *vbl. sb.*

1692 SIR W. HOPE *Fencing Master* 10 Volting is the leaping by your adversaries left side, quite out of his measure. **1823** G. ROLAND *Treat. Art Fencing* 151 The same may be said of volting, or any manœuvre that does not give the opponent a fair opportunity of hitting the right breast. **1861** G. CHAPMAN *Foil Practice* 34 Volting is prohibited in teaching with the foil, and condemned in fencing.

volt (vəʊlt), *v.*[2] *literary*. [f. the sb.] **a.** *trans.* To charge (something) as with electricity; to energize; to shock. **b.** *intr.* To travel like an electric current. Hence **'volted** *ppl. a.*

1930 R. CAMPBELL *Adamastor* 48 Dainty one, deadly one.. Whose coils are volted with electric power. *Ibid.* 61 A starved mongrel... Fierce tremors volted through his bony notches. **1936** —— *Mithraic Emblems* 21 The volted ecstasy outglows A dolphin dying in the noon. **1936** *Times Lit. Suppl.* 28 Mar. 266/4 Give man the grace to find a firm abode,.. Not in power's seat that volts the sitter dead. **1942** S. SPENDER *Ruins & Visions* II. 38 Driven by intolerance and volted with lies. **1962** N. COGHILL in Davis & Wrenn *Engl. & Medieval Stud.* 207 All that is finest and most central in this figure is 'made' by a coalescence or fusion of allegory, parable, and symbol, and that is the poetic fact that volts it with imaginative power.

‖**volta** ('vɔlta). [It. *volta* turn, etc., fem. pa. pple. of *volgere*, *volvere* to turn, employed as a sb.] = LAVOLTA.

1642 KYNASTON *Leoline & Sydanis* 1905 These with ten Satyrs danc'd an antique round With Volta's, and a Saraband. **1656** BLOUNT *Glossogr.*, *Volta*,.. a turning Dance so called. **1753** *Chambers' Cycl.*, Suppl. s.v., Volta is also a sort of dance of Italian origin, in which the man turns the woman several times, and then assists her to make a leap or jump; it is a species of galliard. **1823** CRABB *Technol. Dict.*, *Volta*, an old three-timed air, peculiar to an Italian dance of the same name. **1910** *Times* 8 Aug. 10/4 At His Majesty's Theatre.. the court dances will include a 'volta' with its light-hearted leaps into the air.

volta- ('vɒltə), combining form of VOLTAIC *a.*[1] used in a few technical terms, as ***volta-electric***, ***-electrometer***, ***-inductric***; **voltaplast** (see quot.); **voltatype** *sb.*, an electrotype; *v. trans.*, to electrotype.

voltagraphy, given in some Dicts. as a synonym of 'electrotypy', after *Penny Cycl.* (1843) XXVI. 434/2, was coined specially for use in that work, and appears to have had no real currency.

1834 MRS. SOMERVILLE *Connex. Phys. Sci.* xxxiii. 338 *Volta-electric induction is instantaneous. **1862** *Catal. Internat. Exhib.*, *Brit.* II. No. 3578, The instantaneous generation of volta-electric currents of intensity. **1834** FARADAY in *Phil. Trans.* CXXIV. 85 On a new Measure of *Volta-electricity. *Ibid.* 93 The instrument offers the only actual measurer of voltaic electricity which we at present possess... I have therefore named it a *Volta-electrometer. **1839** NOAD *Electricity* iii. 130 Its terminal wires are soldered to a Faraday's volta-electrometer. **1875** KNIGHT *Dict. Mech.* 2714/1 *Voltaelectrometer*, an instrument for indicating the degree of electrical excitation. **1849** NOAD *Electricity* (ed. 3) 491 The manner in which this machine acts will be clearly understood by reference to the general principles of *volta-inductric action. **1842** FRANCIS *Dict. Arts*, **Voltaplast*. Such is the name given to that form of galvanic battery which is adapted to the electrotype. **1842** BRANDE *Dict. Sci.* 1309/2 Gold, silver, and other metals may.. be substituted for copper, and thus a variety of *volta-types may be obtained. *Ibid.*, It often happens that the article to be *voltatyped*, as this process is now called, is not a conductor of electricity. **1875** KNIGHT *Dict. Mech.* 2714/2 *Volta-type*, a cast of an object obtained by the gradual deposition of a metal from a metallic solution, through the agency of electric action.

†**'voltage**[1]. *Obs.*[−1] [f. F. *volte* VOLTE + -AGE.] The action of causing a horse to move in voltes.

1606 FORD *Fame's Mem.* xxxii, He assaies, Which way to manage an vntamed horse When, how, to spur, and rayn, to stop, and raise, Close sitting, voltage of a manlike force.

voltage[2] ('vɒltɪdʒ, 'vəʊltɪdʒ). [f. VOLT *sb.* + -AGE.] **a.** Electromotive force reckoned or expressed in volts. Also *fig.*

1890 *Pall Mall G.* 8 Aug. 4/3 The voltage varied between 700 and 1,300 volts. **1894** BOTTONE *Electr. Instr.* 111 In calculating the voltage, the desired current must also be considered, and allowance made both for the internal and external resistances. **1898** *Allbutt's Syst. Med.* V. 855 It is difficult to say what voltage is fatal to man.

fig. **1904** *Spectator* 30 Apr. 670/1 Pope.. was seldom the subject of currents of high voltage like.. the emotional Hazlitt. **1949** E. POUND *Pisan Cantos* lxxx. 85 Whoi didn't he [*sc.* Padraic Colum] keep on writing poetry at that voltage. **1961** *Times* 24 Mar. 18/4 Walton's first symphony is a work of extraordinarily high voltage. **1978** F. OLBRICH *Desouza pays Price* xx. 125 Beaming the full voltage of her smile at Habib.

b. *attrib.* (esp. with adj. preceding). Also in *fig.* use.

1890 *Daily News* 4 Jan. 6/7 There is as much danger from the low voltage as there is from the high voltage system, as far as fire is concerned. **1894** *Ibid.* 22 Jan. 2/8 The question of high voltage electricity. **1959** *Listener* 8 Oct. 590/1 Synge's brief but high-voltage career. **1966** N. FREELING *King of Rainy Country* 128 Her high-voltage emotions injected into the situation would doubtless tangle things still further.

c. *Comb.*, as ***voltage doubler***, ***-regulation***, ***regulator***; ***voltage-doubling*** adj.; **voltage clamp** *Physiol.*, (the application of) a constant voltage maintained across a cell membrane by artificial means; so **voltage-clamped** *a.*, **-clamping** *vbl. sb.*; **voltage-controlled** *a.*, controllable by varying the applied voltage; **voltage divider**, a linear resistor or series of resistors which can be tapped at any intermediate point to obtain a voltage equal to a desired fraction of the voltage applied between its ends.

1952 *Jrnl. Physiol.* CXVII. 504 (*heading*) Mathematical description of membrane current during a voltage clamp. **1964** G. H. HAGGIS et al. *Introd. Molecular Biol.* vi. 159 These ionic permeability changes associated with the action potential have been studied in squid axons and frog muscle cells.. with the very elegant 'voltage clamp' technique. **1979** *Acta Protozoologica* XVIII. 183 Instantaneous I/V plots of voltage-clamped deciliated cells lack the negative resistance property characteristic of ciliated cells. **1981** *Nature* 15 Oct. 517 Although the principle is simple enough—to keep the voltage across a cell membrane constant—the technology of voltage-clamping has become a sophisticated exercise in electrical engineering. **1962** SIMPSON & RICHARDS *Physical Princ. Junction Transistors* xiv. 359 External methods of gain control usually employ auxiliary diodes.. to act as a voltage-controlled potential divider. **1976** *Electronic Engin.* Nov. 27/1 It [*sc.* a waveform generator circuit] can be used.. in many other applications where a voltage controlled waveform is required. **1930** *Sci. Abstr.* B. XXXIII. 846 (Index), Voltage dividers, capacity and resistance types. **1932** *Bureau of Standards Jrnl. Res.* (U.S.) IX. 81 (*heading*) Theory of voltage dividers and their use with cathode ray oscillographs. **1983** *IEEE Trans. Instrumentation & Measurement* XXXII. 33/2 The attenuation reference standard in this system is a high class.. inductive voltage divider. **1947** R. LEE *Electronic Transformers & Circuits* iii. 51 (*heading*) Voltage doublers. *Ibid.* (*caption*) Relation of peak sine voltage to d-c voltage in voltage-doubling circuit. **1956** *Nature* 18 Feb. 298/1 Electrical characteristics are next treated, including.. descriptions of.. voltage-regulation methods and apparatus. **1902** *Encycl. Brit.* XXVIII. 90/2 (*heading*) Voltage regulators. **1962** SIMPSON & RICHARDS *Physical Princ. Junction Transistors* 496 We consider a voltage regulator whose input voltage.. and output voltage and current.. are connected by the equation [etc.].

voltaic (vɒl'teɪɪk), *a.*[1] [From the name of the Italian physician and scientist, Alessandro *Volta* (1745–1827) + -IC.]

1. Of apparatus: Used in producing electricity by chemical action after the method discovered by Volta; esp. ***voltaic battery*** (BATTERY 10), ***voltaic pile*** (PILE *sb.*[3] 5).

(*a*) **1813** SIR H. DAVY *Agric. Chem.* (1814) 41 It has been shown by Experiments made by means of the Voltaic battery.. that compound bodies in general are capable of being decomposed by Electrical powers. **1850** GROVE *Corr. Phys. Forces* (ed. 2) 81 A voltaic battery, which consists usually of alternations of two metals, and a liquid capable of acting chemically upon one of them,.. is incapable of acting. **1879** G. PRESCOTT *Sp. Telephone* 1 When galvanism was discovered, at the beginning of the present century, and the voltaic battery invented.

(*b*) **1815** J. SMITH *Panorama Sci. & Art* II. 275 The Voltaic pile, as well as the battery last described, are now but little used. **1839** NOAD *Electricity* iii. 97 To Volta's experiments we are indebted for the first galvanic instrument, namely, the voltaic pile; it was described by him in the Philosophical Transactions of 1800. **1896** *Allbutt's Syst. Med.* I. 352 After the discovery of the voltaic pile the use of the electrical machine gradually fell into disuse.

(*c*) **1812** SIR H. DAVY *Chem. Philos.* 54 Without the Voltaic apparatus, there was no possibility of examining the relations of electrical polarities to chemical attractions. **1827** FARADAY *Chem. Manip.* xvii. 460 Voltaic arrangements, consisting of a few large plates rather than many small ones. **1855** BAIN *Senses & Int.* I. ii. §22 In a voltaic cell, an energy is generated and transmitted along a wire with inconceivable rapidity. **1884** KNIGHT *Dict. Mech.* Suppl. 930/2 A voltaic pencil, by the use of which designers and draughtsmen may be enabled to dispense entirely with the aid of the engraver.

2. Of electricity: Generated by chemical action.

1816 ACCUM *Chem. Tests* 223 When the precipitation of the metallic lead takes place in the surface of the zinc, voltaic electricity is evolved. **1836** MRS. SOMERVILLE *Connex. Phys. Sci.* (ed. 3) xxviii. 305 Voltaic electricity is of that peculiar kind which is elicited by the force of chemical action. **1890** *Nature* 4 Sept., The application of voltaic electricity to the welding and fusion of metals.

b. Of a current: Consisting of voltaic electricity.

1834 MRS. SOMERVILLE *Connex. Phys. Sci.* xxxi. 324 The magnetic and electric fluids,.. arising from all possible positions of the conducting wire, and every direction of the voltaic current. **1860** PIESSE *Lab. Chem. Wonders* 180 The effect of a continued voltaic current.

3. Of or pertaining to, connected with, caused by, electricity due to chemical action.

1820 FARADAY *Exp. Res.* (1859) 65 The little bars.. evidently produced voltaic action. **1827** —— *Chem. Manip.* xvii. 461 This formed a voltaic combination with the platina and the fluid. **1855** BAIN *Senses & Int.* II. ii. §23 The voltaic shock is very different, in consequence of the altered character of the discharge. **1879** *Cassell's Techn. Educ.* IV. 309/1 The invention of voltaic deposition.. created a new era for the manufacture of silver-plated wares.

b. ***voltaic brass***, brass deposited by the action of electricity.

1860 *Ure's Dict. Arts* (ed. 5) II. 94 Voltaic brass does not appear to have been obtained in a solid distinct form, but has been successfully produced as a coating upon a copper surface.

c. *fig.*

1920 D. H. LAWRENCE *Lost Girl* iii. 45 A superhuman, voltaic force filled her.

Hence **vol'taically** *adv.*, by means of, in respect of, voltaic electricity; after the manner of a voltaic battery.

1843 GROVE *Corr. Phys. Forces* etc. (1874) 303 Besides employing the usual chemical tests, I analysed it voltaically. **1844** NOAD *Electricity* (ed. 2) 144 When a series of some hundred couples of zinc and copper cylinders are arranged voltaically, and charged with common water, a battery is obtained. **1865** MANSFIELD *Salts* 12 One of these, the Chlorine, is said to be voltaically or chemically negative.

Vol'taic, *sb.* and *a.*[2] [f. the name of the West African river *Volta* + -IC.] **A.** *sb.* **a.** A group of Niger-Congo languages of West Africa. **b.** A speaker of one of these languages; a citizen of the Republic of Upper Volta. **B.** *adj.* Of or pertaining to this group of languages, or to this republic or its citizens. Cf. UPPER VOLTAN *a.* and *sb.*

1939 L. H. GRAY *Foundations of Lang.* xii. 402 The divisions of Sudano-Guinean, according to Delafosse, may now be enumerated:.. Voltaic (fifty-three languages).. apparently possessing inclusive and exclusive pronouns for the first person plural. **1949** L. HOMBURGER *Negro-African Languages* i. 22 The people who speak Voltaic languages number about 3,000,000. **1967** M. SCHLAUCH *Language* ii. 39 Suffixes are also used to indicate nominal classes (e.g. in Voltaic). **1969** [see SENUFO]. **1970** P. OLIVER *Savannah Syncopators* 66 The use of a drone or continuous humming between sung phrases is also a vocal feature shared by Voltaic peoples and some blues singers. **1976** *New Society* 11 Nov. 293/3 Doing their military service by teaching in Voltaic schools. *Ibid.* 294/3 Educated Voltaics like to discount the CIA theory with one of their own. **1979** *Observer* (Colour Suppl.) 17 June 56/3 France for example in 1976 exported 64 million dollars worth of goods to Upper Volta (43 per cent of Voltaic imports). **1984** *Chicago Sun-Times* 9 Jan. 18 The government is treated with some skepticism by older Voltaics.

Voltairean, Voltairian (vɒl'tɛərɪən), *sb.* and *a.* [f. the later name of the French author François Marie Arouet (1694–1778), who from 1718 styled himself *de Voltaire*.]

A. *sb.* A follower or adherent of Voltaire in respect of opinions or the manner of expressing them; one whose views on social and religious questions are characterized by a critical and mocking scepticism.

α. **1871** MORLEY *Condorcet* in *Crit. Misc.* Ser. I. (1878) 51 He [Condorcet] was a Voltairean in the intensity of his antipathies to the Church. **1885** *Athenæum* 2 May 567/1 His father, a country squire, and, as the fashion then was, a thorough-going Voltairean, had married one of his own serfs.

β. **1842** J. S. MILL *Let.* 10 Jan. in *Wks.* (1963) XIII. 497 We are all either bigots or Voltairians. **1875** GLADSTONE *Glean.* (1879) VI. 225 We are now engaged in training a nation to consist of Voltairians and of Clericals. **1883** M. PATTISON *Mem.* (1885) 212 If it is against the Church it is a fiction of the Voltairians.

B. *adj.* Of, belonging to, or resembling Voltaire; holding opinions like those of Voltaire, or expressing them in his style.

α. **1846** BP. OF MEATH in J. O'Connor *Hist. Ireland 1798–1924* (1925) I. viii. 249 Voltairean newspapers. **1879** MORLEY *Burke* viii. 176 The eager, bustling, shrill-tongued crowd of the Voltairean age. **1885** 'MRS. ALEXANDER' *At Bay* i, A shrewd, worldly, voltairean woman.

β. **1833** J. S. MILL *Lett.* (1910) I. 75 The little *feuilles* which one buys as one goes into a theatre, are the representatives of the Voltairian philosophy at present. **1876** L. STEPHEN *Hours in Library* 189 Walpole must be reckoned as belonging both in his faults and his merits to the Voltairian school of literature. **1896** W. K. LEASK *H. Miller* v. 125 There is still the Voltairian type of thinker.

Hence **Vol'tairianism** (also **-ean-**), = VOLTAIRISM.

1848 W. K. KELLY tr. *L. Blanc's Hist. Ten Y.* II. 187 In order not to offend the Voltairianism of several of his friends, he had forborne to base his constitution on religion. **1890** *Athenæum* 19 July 92/2 He interprets Voltairianism as 'a school based on destructive irony,.. and incapable of raising or fortifying the human mind'. **1901** *Q. Rev.* CXCIV. 599 Sir Henry Craik pounces with perhaps unnecessary severity upon the flippant Voltaireanism, the dapper self-assurance, and the 'slovenly omniscience' of Jeffrey and his allies. **1942** *Scrutiny* X. 400 Dostoyevsky's denunciation of the deracinated nobility who despised their own language and national character and lived in a froth of Voltaireanism and French *bons mots*.

Vol'tairianize, *v. rare.* [f. VOLTAIREAN, VOLTAIRIAN *sb.* and *a.* + -IZE.] *trans.* To render Voltairian. Hence **Vol'tairianized** *ppl. a.*

1872 LIDDON *Elem. Relig.* ii. 49 It was.. quite another [thing] permanently to control the heart and convictions even of the Voltairianized multitudes of Paris. **1902** *Academy* 3 Jan. 7/2 Hamlet is completely Voltairianised, in the most audacious fashion.

Vol'tairish, *a. rare* [f. *Voltaire* (see above) + -ISH.] Resembling Voltaire.

1842 MRS. BROWNING *Bk. Poets* Poet. Wks. (1904) 639/2 We will not.. set up its grand, luxurious, melancholy devil against Goethe's subtle, biting, Voltairish devil. *a* **1846** B. R. HAYDON *Autobiogr.* (1927) III. xiii. 252 '*Ah*,' shrugged out monsieur le valet, with a sparkling Voltairish look which every Frenchman has when convicted, as if planning a repartee, '*c'est très vrai*.'

Voltairism (vɒl'tɛərɪz(ə)m). Also **-eism**. [f. as prec. + -ISM.]

1. Something characteristic of Voltaire.

1776 MICKLE tr. *Camoens' Lusiad* Introd. p. cxxvi, The error confessed, and still retained, is a true Voltairism.

2. The body of opinions or views expressed by Voltaire; the mocking and sceptical attitude characteristic of these.

1840 CARLYLE *Heroes* i. (1904) 14 Truly, if Christianity be the highest instance of Hero-worship, then we may find here in Voltaireism one of the lowest! **1872** MORLEY *Voltaire*

(1886) 1 We may think of Voltairism in France, somewhat as we think of Catholicism or the Renaissance or Calvinism.

voltaism (ˈvɒltəɪz(ə)m). [f. *Volta* (see VOLTAIC *a.*[1]) + -ISM.] The production of an electric current by the chemical action of a liquid on metals; galvanism as produced by Volta's methods.
1811 R. TURNER *Arts & Sci.* xxix. 271 In voltaism, it is necessary that the bodies by which it is exhibited should have some chemical agency on each other. **1826** GOOD *Bk. Nat.* (1834) I. 219 Every one has now some knowledge of Galvanism and Voltaism. **1844** NOAD *Electricity* (ed. 2) 132 That remarkable form of Electricity, known by the name of Galvanism or Voltaism.

voltaite (ˈvɒltəaɪt). *Min.* [f. as prec.; named by A. Scacchi in 1840.] A hydrous sulphate of iron occurring in green, black, or brown crystals.
1846 WORCESTER (citing Dana). **1852** DANA *Min.* 228 Voltaite is a double sulphate of iron, alumina, potash and water crystalising like alum in octahedrons. **1868** WATTS *Dict. Chem.* V. 1005 *Voltaite*, a ferroso-ferric sulphate, containing alumina, occurring at the Solfatara, near Naples.

voltameter (vɒlˈtæmɪtə(r)). [See VOLTA- and -METER.] An instrument used for the quantitative measurement of electricity by means of the results of electrolysis.
1836 BRANDE *Chem.* (ed. 4) 385 When the quantity of products was examined by the voltameter, the oxygen..was always in the same proportion as from water. **1866** R. M. FERGUSON *Electr.* (1870) 140 To measure one or other of these is the object of a galvanometer or voltameter. **1881** S. P. THOMPSON *Electr. & Magnetism* 179 The voltameter gives us the 'time integral' of the current.
attrib. **1844** NOAD *Electricity* (ed. 2) 222 One equivalent of lead was reduced in the voltameter tube.

voltammetry (vɒlt-, vəʊlˈtæmətrɪ). *Physical Chem.* [f. VOLT *sb.* + AM(PERE + -METRY.] An electroanalytical technique for establishing the identities and concentrations of various ions in solution (see quot. 1978). Hence **voltaˈmmetric** *a.*, by means of or employing voltammetry; **voltaˈmmetrically** *adv.*
1940 KOLTHOFF & LAITINEN in *Science* 16 Aug. 152/1 (*heading*) The voltammetric determination of oxygen. *Ibid.*, By the term 'voltammetry' we mean the determination and interpretation of current-voltage curves obtained in electrolysis experiments using a suitable microelectrode as an indicator electrode. *Ibid.* 153/1 Oxygen can also be determined voltammetrically by using a platinum wire microelectrode. **1976** *Nature* 8 July 146/1 An efflux of 5-hydroxyindole acetic acid..into the CSF was observed by the voltammetric monitoring. **1978** *Kirk-Othmer Encycl. Chem. Technol.* (ed. 3) II. 618 Voltammetry is the general procedure of studying the current-voltage behavior of a microelectrode in a system which also contains a large nonpolarizable reference electrode and a large excess of an electrolyte... Polarography is a special case of voltammetry in which the small, polarizable electrode is a capillary tube from which small mercury droplets emerge at regular intervals... The plot of current vs voltage..provides qualitative and quantitative information about the solution composition. **1983** *Jrnl. Chem. Soc. Dalton Trans.* 991 (*heading*) Electron-transfer processes and electrode-position involving the iron hexacyanoferrates studied voltammetrically.

volte, volt (vɒlt, vəʊlt). [a. F. *volte*, ad. It. *volta*: see VOLTA.]
†**1.** A kind of dance; = VOLTA, LAVOLTA. *Obs.*
1586 SIR E. HOBY tr. *Cognet's Polit. Disc. Truth* xi. 39 The Voltes, courantes, and vyolent daunses proceede from furie. **1597** T. MORLEY *Introd. Mus.* 181 Like vnto this [the Bransle] (but more light) be the voltes and courantes which being both of a measure, are notwithstanding daunced after sundrie fashions. **1610** DOWLAND *Var. Lute-lessons* R 2, Voltes for the Lute.
2. *Fencing.* A sudden dexterous movement to avoid a thrust.
1688 HOLME *Armoury* III. xix. (Roxb.) 160/1 A Volt..is when thy adversarie doth thrust at thee which thou perceiueing, dost first put by his thrust; and just turne [*sic*] thy body round about, with thy back towards thine adversarie thrusteth him with a quarte in his right brest. **1765** ANGELO *Sch. Fencing* 44 You must..with swiftness and agility perform this turn of the body called volte. **1771** LONNERGAN *Fencer's Guide* 104 When I disengage a Quarte, single your body from the thrust, by quickly forming a Volt. **1861** G. CHAPMAN *Foil Practice* 34 The volt or spring to the right or left [being] occasionally put in practice. **1889** A. HUTTON *Cold Steel* 90 Make a complete volte or turn about on the toe of the right, bringing the left foot well behind it.
†**b.** *volt-coupe*, a feint in fencing.
1692 SIR W. HOPE *Fencing Master* 46 The Volt-coupe, single and double. *Ibid.* 65 Then make use of the Double Volt-Coupe..after you have made your Feint. **1696** R. H. *Sch. Recreat.* 87 Lesson 12. Of Volt Coupe.
3. In the manège, a circular movement executed by a horse. (Cf. the earlier DEMI-VOLTE.)
1727 BAILEY (vol. II), *Volte* (in Horsemanship) signifies a round or a circular Tread. **1728** CHAMBERS *Cycl.* s.v., A Renversed Volt, is a Track of two Treads, which the Horse makes with his Head to the Centre, and his Croup out. **1884** E. L. ANDERSON *Mod. Horsem.* II. xvii. 148 The school gallop is employed in traversing, and for voltes and pirouettes. The horse may be made to traverse and to do the voltes in the ordinary gallop.
4. Turn, change. *rare*[−1].
1901 MEREDITH *Hueless Love* viii, So has there come the gust at South-west flung By sudden volt on eves of freezing mist.

†**ˈvolted**, *ppl. a. Obs.* (Meaning not clear.)
1613–39 I. JONES in Leoni *Palladio's Archit.* (1742) II. 45 The Roses fretted, not volted.

‖**volte-face** (vɔltəfas). [Fr., ad. It. *volta faccia*, f. *volta* turn + *faccia* face.] The act of turning so as to face in the opposite direction; *fig.* a complete change of attitude or opinion.
1819 SCOTT *Leg. Montrose* xvi, Your Excellency has only to hint that the M'Aulays are going in that direction, and my friends of the Mist will instantly make volteface, and go to the right about. **1822** —— *Peveril* xxxiv, At last we were obliged to make volte-face. **1883** *Athenæum* 20 Oct. 493/2 He is getting to believe in evolution and has to make some curious *voltes-face* in order to retain at the same time his belief in theism. **1889** *Spectator* 9 Nov. 627/1 The sudden *volte-face* which Mr. Gladstone and Sir William Harcourt performed in 1886.

volter, variant of WALTER *sb. Obs.*

Volterra (vɒlˈtɛrə). The name of a town in the Tuscany region of Italy, used *attrib.* to designate alabaster quarried there. Hence also **Volˈterran** *a.*
1924 D. H. LAWRENCE in M. Magnus *Mem. Foreign Legion* 20 So at last coming down to the Mercato Nuovo we saw little bowls of Volterra marble, a natural amber colour, for four francs. *a* **1930** —— *Etruscan Places* (1932) vi. 183 Everybody knows Volterra marble—so called—nowadays, because of the translucent bowls of it which hang under the electric lights, as shades, in half the hotels of the world. *Ibid.*, There is no love lost between a Volterran alabaster worker and the lump of pale Volterran earth he turns into pale marketable form.

‖**voltigeur** (vɔltiʒœr). [F., agent-n. f. *voltiger* to flutter, hover, vault, etc.] Formerly in the French army, a member of a special skirmishing company attached to each regiment of infantry.
1807 *Hist. Europe* in *Ann. Reg.* 25/1 They were received at the mouth of the musket by the voltigeurs. [*Note.* Sharp-shooters, or marksmen, mounted on horseback, whose business it is to hover around the enemy,..and annoy him (etc.).] **1827** SOUTHEY *Hist. Penins. War* III. 430 The enemy's chasseurs and voltigeurs advanced in considerable bodies under General Lorset.
attrib. **1805** JAMES *Milit. Dict.* (ed. 2) s.v., They submitted to a long..training, before they were admitted in the voltigeur companies. **1824** DE QUINCEY *Pol. Econ. Dial.* vi. Misc. (1854) 259 Go on,..and skirmish with him a little more in this voltigeur style.
transf. **1809** W. IRVING *Knickerb.* (1861) 221 The Van Bunschotens..would have been put to utter rout but for the arrival of a gallant corps of voltigeurs. **1817** KEATINGE *Trav.* I. 155 The most active and habituated voltigeurs of the community..contrive to anticipate, and *font main basse* on whatever can be found.

voltmeter (ˈvɒltmiːtə(r), ˈvəʊlt-). [f. VOLT *sb.*[2] + METER.] An instrument for measuring the pressure of electricity in volts.
1882 *Eng. Mech.* 10 Mar. 4/3, I have two instruments devised by Prof. Perry and myself, an Am-meter, and a Volt-meter, the one for measuring a strong current, and the other a large electromotive force. **1884** C. G. W. LOCK *Workshop Rec.* Ser. III. 132/1 This can be verified by connecting one terminal of a voltmeter to the negative brush. **1898** *Engin. Mag.* XVI. 139/2 Plan of the plant is given, showing how the dynamo, voltmeter, switchboards, and tanks should be connected.

‖**ˈvolto.** [It. *volto* = *volta* vault (the same word as VOLTA).] = VAULT *sb.*[1] 1.
a **1700** EVELYN *Diary* 22 Oct. 1644, Entring the Church [St. Peter's, Rome], admirable is the bredth of the volto or roofe. *Ibid.* 18 Jan. 1645, The Consistory, a noble roome, the volto painted in grotesq. **1880** SHORTHOUSE *J. Inglesant* xxvi. 375 The garden [at Rome] was entered by a portico or door-case adorned with ancient statues, the volto or roof of which was painted with classic subjects.

ˈvoltzine. *Min.* Also volz-. [-INE[5].] = next.
1836 T. THOMSON *Min., Geol.*, etc. I. 540 *Voltzine.* Oxysulphuret of zinc. This mineral occurs at Rosiers. **1850** ANSTED *Elem. Geol., Min.*, etc. §470 Volzine. **1855** *Orr's Circ. Sci., Geol.*, etc. 503 *Voltzine*..Found in a vein of quartz..and in some zinc furnaces.

voltzite (ˈvɒltzaɪt). *Min.* [f. the name of P. L. *Voltz*, inspector of mines; named by Fournet, 1833.] A native oxysulphide of zinc.
1835 *R. D. & T. Thomson's Rec. Gen. Sci.* I. 274 Voltzite. This mineral is found at Pont Gibaud, in Puy de Dome. It possesses a pearly lustre; colour rose-red, or yellow. **1852** DANA *Min.* 252 *Voltzite.* A compound of sulphuret and oxyd of zinc. Occurs in implanted globules of a dirty rose-red color.

voˈlubilate, *a. Bot.* [f. next + -ATE.] = next.
1819 REES *Cycl.*, *Volubile*, or *Volubilate* Stem or Stalk,..a name given to those of many plants, as all those the stems or stalks of which are of a twining or winding climbing nature.

volubile, *a. Bot. rare.* [ad. L. *volūbilis.* So F. *volubile.*] = VOLUBLE *a.* 4.
1819 [see prec.]. **1838** J. MURRAY *Econ. Veg.* 48 Some stems are volubile; or 'twine' as the hop and honeysuckle, convolvolus, and 'scarlet runner.' **1849** BALFOUR *Man. Bot.* §66 Stems have usually considerable firmness and solidity, but sometimes they..twist round other plants in a spiral manner like Woodbine, becoming volubile.

‖**voˈlubilis.** *Bot. Obs.* [L.; see prec. So F. *volubilis.*] Convolvulus.
1664 EVELYN *Kal. Hort.* Mar. 63 Sow on the Hot-bed such Plants as are late bearing Flowers or Fruit in our Climate; as Balsamine,..Volubilis, Myrrh, Carrobs, [etc.]. **1712** tr. *Pomet's Hist. Drugs* I. 132 This Pod is the Fruit of a Kind of Volubilis.

volubility (vɒljuːˈbɪlɪtɪ). Also 6–7 -itie, 7 -itye. [ad. F. *volubilité* (15–16th cent.; = It. *volubilità*, Sp. *-idad*, Pg. *-idade*), or ad. L. *volūbilitās*, f. *volūbilis*: see next and -ITY.]
I. †**1.** Quickness in turning from one object to another; versatility. *Obs. rare.*
1579 FENTON *Guicciard.* I. (1599) 3 The wisedome and reputation of the man, togither with the naturall volubilitie of his wit. **1605** BACON *Adv. Learn.* II. xviii. §5 Orators..by the obseruing their well graced fourmes of speech..leese the volubilitie of Application.
†**b.** Ready variation of expression. *Obs.*[−1]
1659 HARRINGTON *Valerius & Publicola* 18 If you speak of Israel, Athens, Rome, Venice, or the like, they hear you with volubility of countenance.
2. The capacity of revolving, rolling, or turning round; aptness to rotate about an axis or centre.
1594 HOOKER *Eccl. Pol.* I. iii. §2 If Celestiall Spheres should forget their woonted Motions, and by irregular volubilitie turne themselues any way as it might happen. **1601** HOLLAND *Pliny* I. 31 The world with continuall volubilitie and turning about it, driveth the..globe thereof into the forme of a round ball. **1656** STANLEY *Hist. Philos.* VIII. (1687) 432/2 He who thrust the Cylinder, gave it the beginning of motion, but did not give it volubility. **1687** A. LOVELL tr. *Bergerac's Com. Hist.* 86 It began to be out of my power any more to discern the Diversity of their several Motions by reason of their extream Volubility. **1705** PURSHALL *Mech. Macrocosm* 296 They lose their Fluidity, which depends upon the Volubility of Globular Particles at liberty. **1740** CHEYNE *Regimen* 75 Blood Globules, by their Rotundity, Volubility, and Elasticity, resist Trituration, that is, Digestion. **1754** *Dict. Arts & Sci.* s.v. *Needle*, In the construction of the horizontal needle a piece of pure steel is provided, of a length not exceeding six inches, lest its weight impede its volubility. **1871** BROWNING *Pr. Hohenst.* 1920 Under pretence of making fast and sure The inch [of ascent] gained by late volubility.
b. Of the eye: Readiness in moving. *rare*[−1].
1603 HOLLAND *Plutarch's Mor.* 1275 The cheerefull cast & amiable volubility of his quicke eie.
†**3.** Capacity for moving in an easy or gliding manner. *Obs.*
1605 BACON *Adv. Learn.* II. xxi. §9 Except men know exactly all the conditions of the serpent;..his volubility and lubricity. **1610** GUILLIM *Heraldry* III. xviii. 153 Such Creatures..which..as it were slide from place to place, some more slowlie, but othersome with a certaine Volubility and flexible Agitation of the Bodie. **1653** T. WATSON *Art Div. Contentm.* xi. (1668) 185 The Poets painted Time with wings, to shew the volubility and swiftness of it.
†**4.** Tendency to change or turn from one condition to another; changeableness, mutability, inconstancy. *Obs.* **a.** Of persons.
1603 FLORIO *Montaigne* II. i. 195 Whosoever shall heedefully survay and consider himselfe, shall finde this volubilitie and discordance to be in himselfe. **1613** SHIRLEY *Trav. Persia* 136 The world by taking notice of your infirmitie will alwayes feare volubilitie in all your actions. *a* **1660** *Contemp. Hist. Irel.* (Ir. Archæol. Soc.) I. 204 All the lawe, phisicke, and poetrie in the world canot cure or amende the flexibilitie, volubilitie, inconstancie, and treacherie of this man.
b. Of fortune or affairs.
1609 HOLLAND *Amm. Marcell.* 286 The volubilitie of inconstant fortune produceth these occurrences in the East parts. **1670** *Moral State Eng.* 1 All affairs do resemble the great Machines of Heaven and Earth, in their motion and volubility. **1699** T. C[OCKMAN] tr. *Tully's Offices* (1706) 88 The great Volubility and Changeableness of Fortune.
II. 5. Ready flow *of* speech, etc.
1589 PUTTENHAM *Eng. Poesie* II. v. (Arb.) 91 Which flowing of wordes with much volubilitie smoothly proceeding from the mouth is in some sort harmonicall. **1653** JER. TAYLOR *Serm. for Year* I. ii. 15 Some men..explicate our praying in the Spirit, by a mere volubilty [*sic*] of language. **1656** STANLEY *Hist. Philos.* V. (1687) 228/2 Cicero being at Athens heard him, and was much taken with the eloquence and volubility of his discourse. **1670** CLARENDON *Hist. Reb.* XVI. §122 The General was not a Man of Eloquence or Volubility of Speech. **1729** BUTLER *Serm.* Wks. 1874 II. 43 This unrestrained volubility and wantonness of speech is the occasion of numberless evils. **1791** COWPER *Odyss.* XVIII. 32 Gods! with what volubility of speech The table hunter prates. **1823** LAMB *Elia* II. *Old Margate Hoy*, A..young man..with..an insuppressable volubility of assertion. **1836** THIRLWALL *Greece* III. 11 The sweetness of voice, and the volubility of utterance, with which both [Pisistratus and Cimon] expressed themselves.
b. Smooth, easy, or copious flow of verse or poetic utterance.
1589 NASHE in Greene *Menaphon* Pref. (Arb.) 6 The spacious volubilitie of a drumming decasillabon. **1751** JOHNSON *Rambler* No. 92 ¶11 The verse intended to represent the whisper of the vernal breeze, must be confessed not much to excel in softness or volubility. **1779** —— *L.P., Pomfret* (1838) 113 In his other poems there is an easy volubility.
6. The character or state of being voluble in speech; great fluency of language; readiness of speech; garrulousness.
1596 SHAKS. *Tam. Shr.* II. i. 176 Say she be mute, and will not speake a word; Then Ile commend her volubility. **1602** MARSTON *Ant. & Mel.* II. Wks. 1856 I. 23 You have the most gracefull presence,..amazing volubility,..delicious affabilitie. **1670** G. H. tr. *Hist. Cardinals* I. I. 13 It was my fortune to hear a Franciscan Preach.., but with more Volubility than Virtue. **1710** STEELE *Tatler* No. 115 ¶5 His great Volubility and inimitable Manner of Speaking. **1751** JOHNSON *Rambler* No. 157 ¶8 Long familiarity with my subject enabled me to discourse with ease and volubility.

1781 R. KING *Mod. Lond. Spy* 118 The following account, which she delivered with great volubility. **1826** F. REYNOLDS *Life & Times* II. 11 He took the lead in conversation, and his natural volubility, increased by sudden joy, carried all before it. **1855** MACAULAY *Hist. Eng.* xi. III. 25 Before he had been a member three weeks, his volubility, his asperity, and his pertinacity had made him conspicuous. **1875** H. JAMES *Mme. de Mauves* i, Her volubility was less suggestive than the latter's silence.

7. Extreme readiness *of* the tongue in respect of speech or discourse.

1612 W. MARTYN *Youths Instr.* 99 The volubilitie of a smooth tongue is nothing profitable. **1650** R. STAPYLTON *Strada's Low C. Wars* III. 67 A Counsellour of great subtilty and volubility of tongue. **1699** GARTH *Dispens.* III. 36 Both had the Volubility of Tongue, In Meaning faint, but in Opinion strong. **1711** STEELE *Spect.* No. 252 ¶3 You have mentioned only the Volubility of their Tongue. **1755** SMOLLETT *Quix.* (1803) II. 6 All this preamble was uttered ..with such volubility of tongue,..that they admired her good sense as much as her beauty.

b. Similarly of the throat, voice, etc.

1740 CIBBER *Apol.* (1756) I. 282 In volubility of throat the former [singer] had much the superiority. **1769** GOLDSM. *Hist. Rome* (1786) II. 225 Nero..used all those methods which singers practice either to mend the voice, or improve its volubility. **1884** *Encycl. Brit.* XVII. 98/2 These [harmonics on horns and trumpets] they executed with volubility akin to that displayed on fingered instruments.

†**vo'lubilous**, *a.* *Obs.*⁻¹ [f. L. *volūbil-is*: see next.] Apt to roll or turn.

1658 ROWLAND tr. *Moufet's Theat. Ins.* 1059 It hath a broad round volubilous body.

voluble ('vɒljʊb(ə)l), *a.* Also 7 volubil. [a. older F. *voluble* (= Sp. *voluble*, Pg. *voluvel*, It. *volubile*) or ad. L. *volūbilis*, f. *volū-*, *volvĕre* to turn: see -BLE.

In some instances the use of the word echoes Horace *Ep.* I. ii. 43 (Amnis) in omne volubilis ævum.]

I. 1. Liable to change; inconstant, variable, mutable. Now *rare*.

1575 FENTON *Gold. Epist.* (1582) 21 As of all voluble things there is nothyng more light than renown. **1578** WOTTON *Courtlie Controuersie* 29 Poets, and Painters.. testifye the loue of men to be voluble and vnconstant lyke a birde. **1604** T. WRIGHT *Passions* VI. 339 Perceive how vain fancies, and voluble crosses vanish away as little cloudes before the northerne winds. **1647** J. CARTER *Nail & Wheel* 71 Nothing abides at a stay; all things are unstable, and voluble. **1652** N. CULVERWEL *Lt. Nat.* I. xii. (1661) 104 The noblest Perfections..are but voluble, and uncertain. **1678** ALSOP *Melius Inq.* II. v. 243 The Lot, wherein the..Alruling God Controuls the Contingency of the voluble Creature. **1898** MEREDITH *Odes Fr. Hist.* 28 He waves, and the voluble scene is a quagmire shifting block.

2. Capable of ready rotation on a centre or axis; apt to revolve or roll in this manner. Now *rare*.

1589 PUTTENHAM *Eng. Poesie* II. xi. (Arb.) 111 He [the round or sphere] is euen and smooth, without any angle, or interruption, most voluble and apt to turne, and to continue motion. **1609** BIBLE (Douay) *Ezek.* x. 13 And these wheeles he called voluble, my self hearing it. **1637** GILLESPIE *Eng. Pop. Cerem.* A ij b, Like Diogenes turning about the mouth of his voluble hoggeshead. **1667** MILTON *P.L.* IV. 594 Or this less volubil Earth By shorter flight to th' East had left him there. **1726** LEONI *Alberti's Archit.* III. 2/1 A Sphere is ..a round body voluble on every side. **1784** COWPER *Task* III. 490 Thrice must the voluble and restless earth Spin round upon her axle. **1812** CARY *Dante, Purg.* XXII. 41, I had met The fierce encounter of the voluble rock. **1822** HAZLITT *Table-T.* Ser. II. xvii. 397 Go thy ways old world, swing round in blue ether, voluble to every age; you and I shall no more jostle!

fig. **1598** DALLINGTON *Meth. Trav.* B j b, His imagination shall be carried in the voluble Sphere of diuers mens discourses. **1605** BACON *Adv. Learn.* II. xxiii. §33 Nothing is more politique then to make the wheels of our mind concentrique and voluble with the wheel of fortune. **1632** J. HAYWARD tr. *Biondi's Eromena* 106 Fortune (Sister) is unstable, and her wheele voluble.

†**b.** Of the eye: Moving readily. *Obs.*⁻¹

1661 LOVELL *Hist. Anim. & Min.* 91 He hath..high eye-browes, eyes not very voluble or prominent.

c. Capable of being rolled up.

1662 EVELYN *Chalcogr.* 19 Which from the German *Bucher*..were called Books, to whatever voluble or folding matter applyed.

3. Moving rapidly and easily, esp. with a gliding or undulating movement.

1589 PUTTENHAM *Eng. Poesie* III. iv. (Arb.) 156 A broad and voluble tong, thinne and mouable lippes, teeth euen and not shagged. **1608** TOPSELL *Serpents* 11 The Tongue of a Serpent..is also thinne, long, and black of colour, voluble; neither is there any beast that moueth the tongue so speedily. **1667** MILTON *P.L.* IX. 436 Neerer he drew, and many a walk travers'd Of stateliest Covert, Cedar, Pine, or Palme, Then voluble and bold, now hid, now seen. **1695** WOODWARD *Nat. Hist. Earth* III. 131 The parts of it [*sc.* water] being very voluble and lubricous, as well as fine and small, it easily..distends the Tubes and Vessels of Vegetables. **1836** BRYANT *Summer Air* 25 Why so slow, Gentle and voluble spirit of the air?

fig. **1862** THACKERAY *Philip* xvii, Would you like to hear yesterday's sermon over and over again—eternally voluble?

4. *Bot.* Twining, twisting. Cf. VOLUBILE *a.*

1753 *Chambers' Cycl.* Suppl. s.v. *Stalk*, *Voluble stalk*, that which twists round other things. **1789** E. DARWIN *Bot. Gard.* II. (1791) 108 *note*, Some of the plants with voluble stems ascend other plants spirally, east—south—west. **1835** KIRBY *Power, Wisd. & Goodn. God* II. 247 Some with a climbing or voluble stem, constantly turn one way, and some as constantly turn another. **1857** A. GRAY *First Less. Bot.* (1866) 37 *Twining*, or *voluble*, when stems rise by coiling themselves spirally around other stems or supports. [Also in later botanical works.]

II. 5. Characterized by fluency or glibness of utterance; rapid and ready of speech; fluent:

a. Of persons.

1588 SHAKS. *L.L.L.* III. i. 69 A most acute Iuuenall, voluble and free of grace. **1604** —— *Oth.* II. i. 242 A knaue very voluble... A slipper, and subtle knaue, a finder of occasion. **1621** T. WILLIAMSON tr. *Goulart's Wise Vieillard* 14 There be found men aboue a hundred yeares old, that are very voluble and fluent in talke and discourse. [**1704** STEELE *Lying Lover* V. i, Oh this unhappy Tongue of mine! Thou lawless voluble destroying Foe.] **1726** POPE *Odyss.* XXII. 319 There end thy pompous vaunts and high disdain; Oh sharp in scandal, voluble and vain! **1807** CRABBE *Par. Reg.* II. 158 Fierce in his air, and voluble of tongue. **1840** THIRLWALL *Greece* lvi. VII. 138 A school of oratory, which produced a long series of voluble sophists. **1890** M. WILLIAMS *Leaves of Life* II. xvii. 150 Of all the voluble men I have encountered in the course of my career, he is the most voluble.

absol. **1762** FOOTE *Orator* II. Wks. 1799 I. 219 You will have at one view, the choleric, the placid, the voluble,..and the clamorous.

b. Of the tongue.

1608 MIDDLETON *Trick to catch Old One* I. ii, 'Tis a fine little voluble toung mine Hoste, that wins a widdow. **1650** R. STAPYLTON *Strada's Low C. Wars* III. 63 A man naturally eloquent, of a voluble fluent tongue. **1699** BURNET *39 Art.* xxiii. 257 Hot-headed Men of warm Fancies, and voluble Tongues..would be apt to thrust themselves on to the Teaching and Governing others. **1720** PRIOR *Truth & Falsehood* 45 Her tongue, so voluble and kind, It always runs before her mind. **1791** COWPER *Iliad* XX. 309 The tongue of man is voluble, hath words For every theme. **1817** CHALMERS *Life Churchyard* 8 Churchyard was, plainly, a plausible man, who had many tales to tell, with a voluble tongue.

Comb. **1604** DEKKER *Honest Wh.* v, A notable-voluble tongde villaine.

transf. **1820** KEATS *Eve St. Agnes* xxiii, But to her heart, her heart was voluble, Paining with eloquence her balmy side.

6. Of discourse, words, etc.: Characterized by great fluency or readiness of utterance.

1588 SHAKS. *L.L.L.* II. i. 76 Aged cares play treuant at his tales..So sweet and voluble is his discourse. **1590** —— *Com. Err.* II. i. 92 If voluble and sharpe discourse be mar'd, Vnkindnesse blunts it more then marble. **1649** MILTON *Eikon.* 32 A discours, voluble anough, and full of sentence. **1690** *Lond. Gaz.* No. 2612/4 One John Waterhouse of full middle Stature,..and of a large Voice, and voluble Speech. **1782** J. WARTON *Ess. Pope* II. xiv. 473 *note*, The style of which is certainly not so melodious and voluble as that of Dryden's enchanting prose. **1791** BOSWELL *Johnson* an. 1750, His periods, though not diligently rounded, are voluble and easy. **1849** ROBERTSON *Serm.* Ser. I. ii. (1855) 25 In such persons words are ever at command—voluble and impassioned words. **1870** L'ESTRANGE *Life Miss Mitford* I. vi. 170 At length 'madame' began a very voluble oration, intended to express the extent of our delinquency.

transf. *a* **1721** PRIOR *Dial. betw. Locke & Montaigne* ¶5, I find the same strain run with a most voluble impetuosity almost thro every Chapter of your Book. **1802** MAR. EDGEWORTH *Moral T., Forester, Catastrophe*, The joy of the poor dancing-master..was rapturous and voluble. **1849** MISS MULOCK *The Ogilvies* xvi, The good woman went on in her voluble grief. **1871** MACDUFF *Mem. Patmos* xxii. 308 Oh, the jarring discord of voluble sympathy!

†**b.** (See quot.) *Obs.*⁻¹

1745 P. THOMAS *Jrnl. Anson's Voy.* 243 They [the Chinese] have contrived a fourth Kind of Writing, the Strokes whereof..are made with more Ease and Expedition; on which Account they are called Voluble Letters.

Hence **'volubleness**, the quality or character of being voluble.

1610 GUILLIM *Heraldry* III. xxii. 168 Such Reptiles as hauing no feet doe with a kind of volublenesse make their way in the waters with many intricate doublings. **1727** BAILEY (vol. II), *Volubleness*, an Aptness to roll; also a round Delivery or Utterance, an easy Pronunciation. **1895** *Advance* (Chicago) 10 Oct. 517/3 In general there is..a certain volubleness among the ministers, and forgetfulness ..to give the laymen a chance [to speak].

volubly ('vɒljʊblɪ), *adv.* [f. prec. + -LY².] In a voluble manner; fluently, glibly.

1615 CHAPMAN *Odyss.* XVIII. 41 O Gods (saide he) how volubly doth talke This eating gulfe. **1663** BUTLER *Hud.* I. i. 105 This he as volubly would vent As if his stock would ne'er be spent. **1671** CLARENDON *Dial.* Tracts (1727) 339 A Secretary of State who..spoke French as volubly and as exactly as he needed to do, without ever having been in France. **1765** JOHNSON in *Shaks. Wks.* (1778) X. 489 *note*, One that discourses fearlessly and volubly. **1796** MME. D'ARBLAY *Camilla* III. i, She talked volubly of what she was about, as if it were the sole subject of her thoughts. **1852** MRS. STOWE *Uncle Tom's C.* xiv, He was listening to Haley, who was very volubly expatiating on the quality of the article for which they were bargaining. **1862** GOULBURN *Pers. Relig.* i. (1873) 3 Every body can speak volubly upon controversial subjects.

'volucrary. *rare*⁻¹. [f. L. *volucr-is* bird + -ARY¹.] A treatise on birds.

1897 DOWDEN *Fr. Lit.* iii. 40 The earliest versified Bestiary, which is also a Volucrary.

'volucrine, *a.* *rare*⁻¹. [f. as prec. + -INE.] Of or pertaining to, arising from, birds.

1881 P. S. ROBINSON *Under Punkah* 23 The volucrine clamour continued unabated... The passage was filled with bird-cages.

volue, obs. var. VOLLEY *sb.*; obs. Sc. f. WOLF *sb.*

volume ('vɒljuːm), *sb.* Forms: α. 4–6 volym, 5 volom, 5–8 volum (5–6 vollum, 5 *Sc.* wolum). β. 5 volyme, velome, volome, 5– volume (6 *Sc.* wollume). γ. 7 volumne, 7–9 volumn. [a. OF. *volum*, *volume*, *volumme* (F. *volume*, = It. and Pg. *volume*, Sp. *volumen*), ad. L. *volūmen* coil, wreath, roll, etc., f. *volvĕre* to roll. The chief senses of the English word also exist in French.]

I. 1. *Hist.* **a.** A roll of parchment, papyrus, etc., containing written matter; a literary work, or part of one, recorded or preserved in this form, which was customary in ancient times. Also *fig.*

1382 WYCLIF *Deut.* xvii. 18 He shal discriue to hym a declaracioun of this lawe in a volym. **1387** TREVISA *Higden* (Rolls) V. 27 He expownede Ypocras his bookes as it were, and..also he made meny veleyns [*v.rr.* volyms, volums] of his owne. **1587** GOLDING *De Mornay* vi. (1592) 65 Hee wrote sixe and thirtie thousand, fiue hundred, and fiue and twentie Volumes, that is to say, Rolles of paper, as Iamblichus reporteth. **1611** BIBLE *Ps.* xl. 7 In the volume of the booke it is written of me. **1623** LISLE *Ælfric on O. & N. Test.*, *Esdras*, Esdras the Scribe wrote a volume, how the people returned from Chaldea to Jury. **1790** BURKE *Fr. Rev.* I. Sel. Wks. 1898 II. 166 In history a great volume is unrolled for our instruction. **1865** J. HANNETT *Bibliopegia* 23 Two strings.., attached to the last sheet or cover of the volume, round which, when it was rolled up, they were fastened. **1881** G. W. MOON *King's English* II. 99 The rolls, or volumes, were composed of several sheets, fastened to each other, and rolled upon a stick; the whole making a kind of cylinder, which was to be managed by the stick, as a handle.

†**b.** A roll or scroll containing a legal document. *Obs.*⁻¹

1530 *Will T. Broke, Ld. Cobham* (Somerset Ho.), This my present testament and laste will in two volumes.

2. a. A collection of written or printed sheets bound together so as to form a book; a tome.

α. *c* **1380** WYCLIF *Serm.* Sel. Wks. II. 61 Men algatis don worse now, for in stede of philateries men maken gret volyms of newe lawes. **1387** TREVISA *Higden* (Rolls) I. 15 þat þey mowe be enformed by þis schort tretys, þat haueþ nouȝt i-seie þe grete volyms and large, þat beeþ of stories i-write. *c* **1425** WYNTOUN *Cron.* IV. Prol. 25, I haf set me..to tret in þis wolum Qwhen biggit was be Romule Rome. **1445–50** METHAM *Wks.* (1916) 157, I rede in elde volummys this matere subsequent. **1513** DOUGLAS *Æneid* Wks. 1874 IV. 228 Virgillis volum of hir sonne Enee. **1590** *Lydgate's Serpent of Division* Concl. C iv, Thus by the large writings and golden vollums of that woorthye Chaucer, the froward Dame of Chaunce hath no respecte of persons. **1651** *Burton's Anat. Mel.* (ed. 6) III. iv. II. ii. 692 To describe them in particular..would require a just volum. **1652** CULPEPPER *Eng. Physic.* 180 It being sufficient for a Volum by itself to speak fully of them. **1698** KEILL *Exam. Th. Earth* (1734) 19 Mr. Erasmus Warren, who has wrote the greatest Volum against it. **1700** MAIDWELL in *Collectanea* (O.H.S.) I. 313 Never to be bound up in the last volum.

β. *c* **1386** CHAUCER *Wife's Prol.* 681 Ouides Art and bookes many on And alle thise were bounden in o volume [*v.rr.* volome, velome]. *c* **1440** *Promp. Parv.* 512/1 Volyme, booke, *volumen*. **1480** CAXTON *Myrr.* III. xii. 160 Boece..compiled in his lyf plente of fair volumes aourned of hye and noble philosophye. *a* **1513** FABYAN *Chron.* VI. (1811) 145 Of his notable dedis myght I make a great volume. **1555** EDEN *Decades* (Arb.) 278 It wolde requyre rather a hole volume then a booke. **1594** SOUTHWELL *St. Peters Complaint* (1602) 15 Sweet volumes stoard with learning fit for Saints. **1605** BACON *Adv. Learn.* I. vi. §16 You erre not knowing the Scriptures, nor the power of God: laying before vs two Bookes or Volumes to studie, if we will be secured from errour. **1646** CRASHAW *Poems* (1858) 61 Lo, here a little volume, but great book! **1691** HARTCLIFFE *Virtues* 225 The Lawyers..in those infinite and immense Volumes, which they have written. **1719** DE FOE *Crusoe* I. (Globe) 170 It would take up a larger Volume than this whole Work is intended to be, to set down all the Contrivances I hatch'd. **1769** *Junius Lett.* xx. (1788) 115 The writer of the volume in question meets me upon my own ground. **1808** *Med. Jrnl.* XIX. 109 The great number of pages, I might perhaps say, volumes, which have been written on the subject. **1849** MACAULAY *Hist. Eng.* iii. I. 394 The shops of the great booksellers..were crowded..and a known customer was often permitted to carry a volume home. **1893** *Bookman* June 85/2 Some writers would have gathered their fugitive pieces into volumes and called them books.

γ. **1648** PAGITT *Heresiogr.* (ed. 4) Ep. Ded., A Uolumn wil hardly containe the hurt that these Sectaries have..done to this poore Church. **1649** J. H. *Motion to Parl.* 10 The best man upon earth..did so many things as all the Volumnes in the world could scarce containe. **1672** MARVELL *Reh. Transp.* I. 211 He cannot answer without reading over eight or ten large Volumns in Folio. **1693** SOUTH *Serm., Rom. i. 32* 288 In every volumn there is a nursery..of vice.

b. *the sacred volume*, the Bible. *the Christian volume*, the New Testament.

1785 BURNS *Cotter's Sat. Nt.* xv, Perhaps the Christian Volume is the theme. **1850** FORSHALL & MADDEN *Wycliffite Bible* I. Pref. p. iii, Aelfric..added greatly to the knowledge of the sacred volume [among the Anglo-Saxons]. **1863** *Biogr. Sk. E. Fry* 75 Fifty copies of the entire Sacred Volume, and twenty-five New Testaments, were promptly forwarded for her use.

3. *fig.* **a.** Something which in character or nature is comparable to a book; *esp.* something which may be studied after the manner of a book.

1592 SHAKS. *Rom. & Jul.* I. iii. 81 This night you shall.. Read ore the volume of young Paris face, And find delight, writ there with Beauties pen. **1593** —— *Rich. II*, I. iv. 18 Would the word Farwell haue lengthen'd houres, He should haue had a volume of Farwels. **1605** TIMME *Quersit.* Ded. p. iii, This philosophy natural, both speculatiue and actiue, is not only to be found in the volume of nature. **1638** R. BAKER tr. *Balzac's Lett.* (vol. II) 19 The publick prosperities would be less deare unto me if yours were not bound up in one volume with them. **1663** SIR G. MACKENZIE *Religio Stoici* 96 It is as strange that man, having that huge volumn of the Creation to revolve [etc.]. **1709** PRIOR *Carm. Sec.* 338 Be kind, and with a milder Hand, Closing the Volume of the finish'd Age,..A more delightful Leaf expand. **1814** BYRON *Lara* i. ix, Books, for his volume heretofore was Man, With eye more curious he appear'd to scan. **1869** FARRAR *Fam. Speech* i. 7 Thought which so completely permeates the whole of language as to render it one vast volume of compressed allegories.

b. In the phrase ***to speak*** (also ***express, tell***) ***volumes***, to be highly expressive or significant.

1803 M. Wilmot *Let.* 3 May in *Russ. Jrnls.* (1934) I. 13 A sentimental story that speakes Volumes in favour of the Count and his Daughter. **1810** Shelley *Zastrozzi* iv. Pr. Wks. 1888 I. 23 A pause ensued, during which the eyes of Zastrozzi and Matilda spoke volumes to each guilty soul. **1833** Whittier *Abolitionists* Pr. Wks. 1889 III. 86 The late noble example of the eloquent statesman..speaks volumes to his political friends. **1867** Freeman *Norm. Conq.* (1877) I. vi. 444 Something which speaks volumes in favour of the King. **1891** 'J. S. Winter' *Lumley* xv, Mrs. Jock's tone expressed volumes.

4. A separately bound portion or division of a work; one of two or more portions into which a work of some size is divided with a view to separate binding; one of a number of books forming a related set or series.

1523 Ld. Berners *Froiss.* I. 322/2 Thus endeth the first volume of sir Johan Froissart: of the cronycles of England, Fraunce, Spayne [etc.]. **1549** Coverdale (*title*), The second tome or volume of the Paraphrase of Erasmus vpon the newe testament. **1684** *Scanderbeg Rediv.* vi. 155 To Attempt his Character would require another Volumne. **1706** London & Wise (*title*), The Retir'd Gard'ner. In Two Volumes. *Ibid.*, To this Volume is added [etc.]. **1796** H. Hunter tr. *St.-Pierre's Stud. Nat.* (1799) III. 11, I have given, in the advertisement to my first Volume, the origin of this error. **1798** Ferriar *Illustr. Sterne*, etc. i. 4 When the first volumes of Tristram Shandy appeared. **1855** *Poultry Chron.* III. 555 The 'Poultry Chronicle'..being now complete in three volumes.

5. *attrib.* and *Comb.*, as ***volume form***, ***-swollen***, ***-trophied*** adj.

a **1661** Holyday *Juvenal* (1673) 1 Mighty Telephus..Or volume-swolne Orestes, that does fill The margin of an ample book. **1831** Howitt *Seasons* (1837) 325 The lamp lights the volume-trophied wall. **1880** *Gentl. Mag.* CCXLVI. 80 A volume Hansard is still published at the end of the session. **1897** *Daily News* 13 May 6/2 Mr. Nimmo.. will publish the whole series immediately in volume form.

II. †**6. a.** Size, bulk, or dimensions (of a book).

1530 Palsgr. 285/2 Volym for the largenesse of a boke, *uolume.* **1555** in *Lydgate's Chron. Troy* A vi/1 After he had wryt his booke to the iuste volume, filled then the mergentes and outwarde sydes with his madnes. **1577** *Vicary's Anat.* To Rdr., And albeit this Treatise be small in Volume, yet in commoditie it is great and profitable. **1612** Brinsley *Lud. Lit.* iv. (1627) 30 The fittest volume for their writing booke is, to haue them in quarto. **1638** Sir T. Herbert *Trav.* (ed. 2) 254 The Alcoran or Bible..is in volume twice so big as the Psalmes of David. **1683** Moxon *Mech. Exerc. Printing* xxii. ¶7 There are four Volumns in use that are differently Imposed, viz. Folio, Quarto, Octavo and Twelves... The places of these Pages for all Volumns the Compositer has always in his memory.

†**b.** In phr. ***of the largest volume***, with reference to copies of the Bible. *Obs.*

1538 Cromwell in Merriman *Life & Lett.* (1902) II. 152 That ye shall prouide..one boke of the hole bible of the largest volume in english. **1540** (*title*), The Byble in Englyshe of the largest and greatest volume. **1569** Parkhurst *Injunct.* A iv, 3. Item, whether you haue in your Churche a Bible, of the largest volume. **1605** *Min. Archdeaconry Colchester* (MS.) fol. 183 They want the saulter, the byble of the largest volume. *a* **1629** Hinde *J. Bruen* xl. (1641) 123 He set up..two goodly faire Bibles of the best Edition, and largest Volume (as then they were Printed). **1753** *Chambers' Cycl.* Suppl. s.v. *Bible*, Cranmer's Bible..was printed by Grafton, of the largest volume, and published in 1540.

7. a. A particular bulk, mass, or quantity as an attribute of a thing. Also *fig.*

1621 Quarles *Div. Poems, Esther* (1638) 101 So shall his people euen as well as He Princes (though in a lesser volume) be. *a* **1668** Lassels *Voy. Italy* (1698) II. 31 It [the great hall] is beautified with rare pictures in a great volume. **1815** Shelley *Alastor* 540 The stream, that with a larger volume now Rolled through the labyrinthine dell. **1862** Spencer *First Princ.* II. iv. §52 (1875) 173 Certain gases, which, in assuming a larger volume, have caused the explosion. **1863** Kinglake *Crimea* I. 376 The torrent had so great a volume that it was worthy to be turned against a foreign State.

b. *concr.* A quantity or mass (esp. a large one) regarded as matter occupying space. Also *fig.*

1647 Clarendon *Hist. Reb.* iv. §98 It was now evident enough..what Use they would make upon occasions, of those Volumes of Votes they had often poured out upon all accidental Debates. **1794** R. J. Sulivan *View Nat.* I. 331 The prodigious volumes of water which have from the beginning of the world been falling into [the ocean]. **1806** J. Beresford *Miseries Hum. Life* ii. xviii, Volume upon volume of black, heavy clouds suddenly rising. **1833** Macaulay *Ess., Walpole* (1897) 272 Every noble sharper whose vast volume of wig and infinite length of riband had figured at the dressing. **1863** Lyell *Antiq. Man* 32 Both in England and Ireland..bogs have burst, and sent forth great volumes of black mud. **1871** B. Stewart *Heat* (ed. 2) §24 The volume of mercury in the stem of a thermometer.

c. *Chem.* A determinate quantity or amount, in terms of bulk, of any substance.

1812 Sir H. Davy *Chem. Philos.* 65 Solids differ in degrees of hardness, in color, in density, or in the weight afforded by equal volumes. **1820** Faraday *Exp. Res.* (1859) 51 A mixture of equal volumes of oxygen and hydrogen was made, and two volumes of it detonated..by the electric spark. **1857** Miller *Elem. Chem., Org.* 316, 1 equivalent yields 4 volumes of vapour. **1877** Huxley *Physiogr.* 79 Instead of a given volume or measure, a given weight of air is examined.

attrib. **1866** Odling *Anim. Chem.* 152 The atomic weights or volume-weights of chlorine, bromine, and iodine. **1881** J. C. Maxwell *Electr. & Magn.* I. 134 The volume-density at any point is determined by the equation. **1885** Watson & Burbury *Math. Th. Electr. & Magn.* I. 53 We call the distribution superficial in distinction from the volume distribution hitherto considered.

8. a. The bulk, size, or dimensions *of* a thing. Also *concr.*, the mass or solid body *of* something.

1792 *Munchausen's Trav.* xxxi. 143 Wawau..made several violent darts against the volume of the balloon, so fierce as at length to tear open a great space. **1809** *Med. Jrnl.* XXI. 462 It is sufficient the volume of the muscular elements be augmented sufficiently to enlarge the fibres while the volume of the interstices, and of the superficial parts diminishes. **1830** Lyell *Princ. Geol.* I. 249 Considerable labour has been bestowed in computing the volume of lava-streams. **1868** Lockyer *Elem. Astron.* §103 The volume of the Sun is 1,200,000 times greater than that of the Earth. **1877** Huxley *Physiogr.* 185 The volume of the sea is very much greater than that of the land which rises above the sea-level.

fig. **1876** J. Parker *Paracl.* I. v. 63 Inspiration increases as well as sanctifies the volume of a man's being.

b. The amount or quantity *of* something.

1882 D. A. Wells *Our Merch. Marine* 112 So small a matter apparently as the civility or neglect of conductors.. will sensibly influence the volume of travel. **1886** *Manch. Exam.* 13 Mar. 5/2 It would be a good thing to enlarge the volume of the currency; to make money more plentiful. **1892** *Daily News* 24 Dec. 7/2 The volume of business, as is usual at this season of the year, has undergone considerable diminution.

9. Without article: Bulk, mass, dimensions.

1794 R. J. Sulivan *View Nat.* I. 71 It is not true, that the seas diminish in volume, or sink gradually beneath their level. **1800** tr. *Lagrange's Chem.* I. 110 A mixture of three parts in volume of hydrogen gas, and one part of sulphurous acid gas. **1834** Marryat *P. Simple* xlvi, The waves, which every moment increased in volume, washed up to us. **1868** Peard *Water-farm.* xiv. 139 The brook is clear, of average purity, and moderate volume. **1871** A. Meadows *Man. Midwifery* (ed. 2) 96 There is usually some increase of volume and vascularity of the uterus itself.

fig. **1873** Symonds *Grk. Poets* v. 112 The Iambic did not carry weight enough or volume to sustain a lengthy narrative. **1876** Geo. Eliot *Dan. Deronda* lxi, The soul of man may know in fuller volume the good which has been.

10. a. *Mus.* (See first quots.)

1801 Busby *Dict. Mus., Volume*, a word applied to the compass of a voice from grave to acute; also to its tone, or power: as when we say, 'such a performer possesses an extensive or rich volume of voice'. **1876** Stainer & Barrett *Dict. Mus. Terms* 451/2 *Volume*, a term applied to the power and quality of the tone of a voice or instrument. **1881** *Athenæum* 10 Sept. 348/1 The voice of Herr Reichmann is a bass of great volume and richness. **1901** *Scotsman* 6 Mar. 8/6 The solo voices were not quite of professional volume.

b. Quantity, strength or power, combined mass, of sound.

1822 Byron *Werner* v. i. 134, I heard.., Distinct and keener far upon my ear Than the late cannon's volume, this word—'Werner!' **1868** Milman *St. Paul's* xvii. 428 The new organ pealed out its glorious volume of sound. **1897** Mary Kingsley *W. Africa* 249 The row when we reached the town redoubled in volume.

III. 11. *poet.* **a.** A coil, fold, wreath, convolution, esp. of a serpent. (Freq. in Dryden and Pope.)

1648 Crashaw *Delights Muses, Foule Morning* 25 Hee.. will trim And brush her Azure Mantle, which shall swim In silken Volumes. **1666** Dryden *Ann. Mirab.* cxxiii, So glides some trodden Serpent on the Grass, And long behind his wounded Volume trails. **1695** Blackmore *Pr. Arth.* ii. 164 The Crested Snake rolls on the flowry Plain, The shining Volumes of his Spiral Train. **1703** Pope *Thebais* 728 Th' Inachians view the slain with vast surprise, Her twisting volumes and her rolling eyes. **1762** Falconer *Shipwr.* iii. 60 The wounded serpent, agoniz'd with pain, Thus trails his mangled volume on the plain. **1784** Cowper *Task* iii. 499 The overcharg'd And drench'd conservatory breathes abroad, In volumes wheeling slow, the vapour dank. **1805–6** Cary *Dante, Inf.* ix. 42 Around them greenest hydras twisting roll'd Their volumes. **1821** Shelley *Epipsych.* 501 In the place of it The ivy and the wild-vine interknit The volumes of their many-twining stems.

b. A winding of a stream.

1716 Fenton *Ode Ld. Gower* iii, Where Thames's fruitful Tides, Slow thro' the Vale in silver Volumes play.

IV. 12. Special Combs.: **volume control**, (*a*) control of the volume of sound, esp. when reproduced or transmitted; (*b*) a knob or other device for achieving this; **volume-density**, the number *of* anything per unit volume; **volume indicator** *Electronics*, a device for measuring the power of a complex electrical signal corresponding to a sound pattern, so as to indicate the volume of the sound that is represented; **volume table** *Forestry*, a set of empirically derived figures relating the volume of timber in a given type of tree or log to measurable parameters such as height and girth, thus enabling such measurements to be used in estimating timber volumes in the field; **volume unit** = *VU*, *vu* s.v. V 5 b.

1927 *Star* 4 June 6/4 Volume Control... Noises, etc. in the loud speaker can be very easily reduced. **1931** T. H. Pear *Voice & Personality* 78 It [*sc.* a preacher's voice] should be articulate, but with an efficient and graded volume-control. **1933** *Boys' Mag.* July 108/2 One of the all-important components..is the volume control. **1956** *B.B.C. Handbk.* 1957 100 They are also responsible for the volume control and technical quality of programmes leaving studios. **1977** 'E. Crispin' *Glimpses of Moon* viii. 152 Titty ..was wearing the hearing-aid, so Ling..addressed himself ..to her, while she fiddled with volume control. **1956** *Nature* 4 Feb. 226/1 These photographs have been useful for determining..the area-density and volume-density of the flying locusts. **1968** R. A. Lyttelton *Mysteries Solar Syst.* v. 155 The time that an individual particle would take to cross the cylinder..would be of the order of $2s/V$, and for this time the particle would be contributing to the average volume-density within the cylinder. **1923** *Trans. Amer. Inst. Electr. Engineers* XLII. 77/2 There has been developed a device which is called a 'volume indicator'. This consists of an amplifier detector working into a direct-current meter. **1961** G. Millerson *Technique Television Production* i. 16 His [*sc.* the sound mixer's] attention is divided mostly between the flickering needle of his volume indicator and his picture monitor. **1895** W. Schlich *Man. Forestry* III. 39 (*heading*) Estimate of volume by means of volume tables. **1902** *Forestry Q.* I. 6 The Bavarian government, in 1846, instituted a very extended study..of the stems of the more important forest trees of that country. The volume tables which resulted..involved a complete analytical measurement of over forty thousand trees. **1981** *Southern Jrnl. Appl. Forestry* V. 186/2 Users of volume tables are cautious about applying them outside the region from which they were derived, because the effects of geographic location are unknown. **1940** *Chambers's Techn. Dict.* 897/1 *VU*, the number of volume-units above or below zero power-level.. indicated by the standardised volume-indicator. **1960** *McGraw-Hill Encycl. Sci. & Technol.* XIV. 374/2 Meters which give readings in volume units, called VU meters, are widely used for monitoring radio broadcasts and for sound recording.

volume (ˈvɒljuːm), *v.* [f. prec.]

1. a. *trans.* To send up, pour out, in volumes.

1815 Scott *Waterloo* viii, Through the war-smoke, volumed high, Still peals that unremitted cry. **1865** Meredith *Farina* 194 More and more the nightingales volumed their notes.

b. *intr.* To rise or roll in a volume or cloud.

1824 Byron *Def. Transf.* i. i, The mighty steam, which volumes high From their proud nostrils, burns the very air. **1884** Howells *Silas Lapham* (1891) I. 65 Shutting the registers, through which a welding heat came voluming up from the furnace. **1891** Meredith *Fragm. Iliad* in *Illustr. Lond. News* 18 Apr. 507/1 Up from under them volumed the dust cloud, Up off the plain.

2. *trans.* To collect or bind in a volume.

1853 G. J. Cayley *Las Alforjas* II. 119 It must have a bouquet of chemically prepared sentiment, and then it is fit to be volumed from the rough cask of MS., and decanted into the reviews. **1895** *Punch* 5 Jan. 1/1 For it's always been my practice, Sir,..Since the day that I was volumed, until now I'm fifty four.

volumed (ˈvɒljuːmd), *a.* [f. volume *sb.* and *v.*]

1. Made into a volume or volumes of a specified size, number, etc.

1596 Nashe *Saffron Walden* L j b, A little epitomizd *Bradfords Meditations*, no broader volum'd than a Seale at Armes. **1609** F. Grevil *Mustapha* i. Chorus, There, as in margents of great volum'd bookes The little notes. **1875** A. R. Hope *My Schoolboy Fr.* Pref. 4 Full of the horrors of three volumed novels.

b. Filling a volume or volumes.

1746 Francis tr. *Horace, Sat.* i. x. 89 Whose volumed works..Kindled around thy corse the funeral fire. —— *Epist.* i. iv. 5 Do you..Some rhiming Labours meditate, That shall in volum'd Bulk arise.

c. Furnished with volumes.

1897 Howells *Landlord at Lion's Head* 225 The room.. was volumed round by the collections of her grandfather.

2. Formed into a rolling, rounded, or dense mass.

1803 Scott *Cadyow Castle* xxiv, For the hearth's domestic blaze, Ascends destruction's volumed flame. **1812** Byron *Ch. Har.* ii. xlviii, The distant torrent's rushing sound Tells where the volum'd cataract doth roll. **1813** —— *Corsair* ii. v. 18 His breath choked gasping with the volumed smoke. **1855** Bailey *Mystic* 31 They in his hands the volumed lightnings laid. **1887** Meredith *Appeasement of Demeter* ix, The volumed shades enfold An earth in awe before the claps resound.

volumeless (ˈvɒljuːmlɪs), *a.* [f. volume *sb.* + -less.] Occupying no volume; *spec.* applied to an idealized polymer chain having this property.

1946 *Nature* 26 Oct. 571/1 An ideally flexible and volumeless [polymer] chain. **1967** Margerison & East *Introd. Polymer Chem.* i. 17 Certain configurations open to the 'volumeless' chain are not available to the real polymer chain. **1974** *Jrnl. Polymer Sci.: Polymer Symposia* No. 46. 97 An expression for Γ, suggested by a well known equation for a regular cubic network of freely jointed volumeless chains, is derived. **1983** [see voluminal *a.*].

‖**volumen** (vəˈljuːmɛn). [L. *volūmen*: see volume *sb.*]

†**1.** A volume, a book. *Obs.*$^{-1}$

1536 Bellenden *Cron. Scot.* (1821) II. 163 He drew all the confusit lawis of Scotland in ane compendius volumen.

2. A roll (*of* parchment, etc.).

1851 Millington tr. *Didron's Chr. Iconogr.* I. 32 A volumen of parchment unfolded in the centre. **1904** W. M. Ramsay *Lett. Seven Ch.* xix. 262 A small bronze coin, which showed the poet sitting, holding a volumen on his knees.

voˌlumeˈnometer. [f. L. *volūmen* (cf. prec.) taken in the sense of volume *sb.* 7 + -ometer.] (See quot. 1868.) Also **voˌlumeˈnometry**, 'the art of determining the volumes or spaces occupied by bodies' (*Imp. Dict.* 1884).

1857 Miller *Elem. Chem., Org.* 765 Their apparatus or volumenometer consists of a globular flask provided with a long narrow neck..graduated from below upwards, to indicate grains of water. **1868** Watts *Dict. Chem.* V. 1005 *Volumenometer*, or *Stereometer*... Instruments for measuring the volume of a solid body by the quantity of a liquid or of air which it displaces, and thence also determining its specific gravity.

'volumescope. [f. VOLUME *sb.* 7 c + -SCOPE.] An instrument for measuring the volume of various compounds.

1829 HARE in *Philos. Mag.* VI. 171 An instrument which I have advantageously employed, in order to illustrate the experimental basis of the theory of volumes,.. I shall call this instrument a Volumescope.

vo'lumeter. [f. VOLU-ME *sb.* 7 c + -METER.] An instrument for measuring the volume of a gas.

1829 HARE in *Philos. Mag.* VI. 173 Afterwards by means of a volumeter or sliding-rod gas measure, add at once three volumes of nitric oxide.

volumetric (vɒljuːˈmɛtrɪk), *a.* [Cf. prec. and METRIC *a.*²] Of, pertaining to, or noting measurement by volume. ***volumetric efficiency*** (Mech.), the ratio of the volume of fluid actually displaced by a piston or plunger to its swept volume.

1857 H. E. ROSCOE tr. *R. Bunsen's Gasometry* 170 The saturated solution.. becomes sufficiently diluted.. to allow the ammonia to be determined by a volumetric analysis with sulphuric acid. **1862** *Catal. Internat. Exhib., Brit.* II. No. 2904, Containing everything necessary for the preparation of the test liquors, or their use in volumetric analysis. **1864** GARROD *Mat. Med.* (ed. 2) 352 In making use of the volumetric solutions a graduated tube or alkalimeter is employed. **1880** PROCTOR *Rough Ways made Smooth* 100 Professor Newcomb has, I conceive, omitted to consider the enormous volumetric expansion. **1912** *Proc. Inst. Automobile Engineers* VI. 78 In the writer's opinion, volumetric efficiency is almost entirely a function of port area. **1930** *Engineering* 11 July 31/2 The standard valve tuning of the E.35 engine is arranged for the best possible volumetric efficiency at 1,500 r.p.m. **1973** A. PARRISH *Mech. Engineer's Ref. Bk.* II. 51 Leakage tends to be greater than in a reciprocating design but as they [*sc.* rotary positive displacement pumps] are often used for viscous fluids such as oil, this effect may be reduced to give a volumetric efficiency of 95%.

volumetrical (vɒljuːˈmɛtrɪkəl), *a.* [f. as prec. + -AL¹.] = VOLUMETRIC *a.*

1853 *Pharmac. Jrnl.* XIII. 285 The volumetrical determination of silver or chlorine. **1862** R. H. SCOTT *(title)*, A Handbook of Volumetrical Analysis. **1870** MAUDSLEY *Body & Mind* 183 Perhaps it might once for all be stated, as a law of vital action, that the dignity of the force is in an inverse ratio to its volumetrical display.

Hence **volu'metrically** *adv.*

1863 W. O. MARKHAM tr. *Neubauer & Vogel's Anal. Urine* 305 The determination of the albumen volumetrically by means of ferrocyanide of potassium. **1864** WEBSTER, *Volumetrically*, in a volumetric manner. **1878** ABNEY *Photogr.* 135 The metallic deposit was dissolved off in nitric acid, and estimated volumetrically. **1889** *Anthony's Photogr. Bull.* II. 435 Acetic acid is, therefore, better tested volumetrically with a standard solution of alkali.

vo'lumetry. *rare*⁻¹. [Cf. VOLUMETRIC *a.* and -METRY.] The scientific measurement of volume.

1863 SUTTON *Handbk. Volumetric Anal.* p. vi, The main feature of volumetry is not so much analysis.. as the quantitative determination of one principal constituent of a substance.

volumette (vɒljuːˈmɛt). [f. VOLUME *sb.* 2 + -ETTE.] A small volume.

1857 SIR F. PALGRAVE *Norm. & Eng.* II. 397 The conventional pictorial embellishment which adorns the hide-bound educational volumette. **1885** W. ANDREWS *Mod. Yorksh. Poets* 194 He has already published two volumettes.

voluminal (vəˈljuːmɪnəl), *a.* [f. L. *volūmin-, volūmen* (see VOLUME *sb.*) + -AL.] Of, pertaining to, or possessing volume.

1872 *Proc. R. Soc.* XX. 5 The remarkable phenomena of the voluminal conditions at and near the critical point of temperature and pressure. **1925** J. JOLY *Surface-Hist. Earth* vii. 113 A small upward displacement must then be attended with voluminal expansion. **1983** *Nucl. Instruments & Methods* CCV. 211/1 Many works.. have been published for volumeless sources such as point isotropic and beam sources. But only a few papers deal with voluminal sources in which self-absorption and self-scattering of gamma rays cannot be disregarded.

voluminosity (vəljuːmɪˈnɒsɪtɪ). [See next and -OSITY.]

1. The state of being voluminous in respect of literary production.

1782 T. TWINING in R. Twining *Recreat. & Stud.* (1882) 115 Last night I received the Virg. MSS. Thanks again. I was astonished at our voluminosity. **1881** *Academy* 5 Mar. 163/3 A reasonable mean is kept between the voluminosity of Kinglake and the curtness of Livy's 'this year there was war with the Hernicans and Volscians.' **1902** *Ibid.* 16 Aug. 167/1 In point of voluminosity the *Manchester Guardian* easily outdid all competitors.

2. The fact of turning or winding; an instance of this.

1841 *Blackw. Mag.* L. 149 With what sublime.. voluminosities it winds, and wreathes, and whirls, and rolls.

voluminous (vəˈljuːmɪnəs), *a.* Also 7 volluminous. [ad. late L. *volūminōsus* (Sidonius), f. L. *volūmin-, volūmen* VOLUME *sb.* Cf. F. *volumineux*, It., Sp., Pg. *voluminoso.*]

1. Full of turnings or windings; containing or consisting of many coils or convolutions.

1611 CORYAT *Crudities* 501 The manifold turnings and windings of the way, like a company of voluminous meanders. **1667** MILTON *P.L.* II. 652 Many a scaly fould Voluminous and vast, a Serpent arm'd With mortal sting. **1781** COWPER *Heroism* 15 Dark and voluminous the vapours rise, And hang their horrors in the neigh'ring skies. **1792** D. LLOYD *Voy. Life* III. 46 When the serpents twain From Tenidos voluminous and vast, Him and his sons with poisonous jaws devour'd. **1802** PALEY *Nat. Theol.* 180 These voluminous bowels, this prolixity of gut, seems in no wise necessary. **1831** R. KNOX *Cloquet's Anat.* 429 These lateral portions [of the cerebellum] are a little flattened, and more voluminous than the middle region.

2. Writing so much as to fill volumes; producing numerous or extensive literary works; writing or discoursing at great length.

1611 SPEED *Hist. Gt. Brit.* VI. ix. §4. 73 Cæsar Baronius, that voluminous Historian. **1654** 'PALÆMON' *Friendship* 30 If I were to recapitulate all the Motives.. I should be Voluminous. **1656** COWLEY *Misc., Chron.* xiii, I more voluminous should grow.. Than Holinshead or Stow. **1711** ADDISON *Spect.* No. 124 ¶1 The most severe Reader makes Allowances for many Rests and Nodding-places in a Voluminous Writer. **1782** V. KNOX *Ess.* lix. (1819) II. 10 For the very learned and voluminous Grotius was engaged in public life. **1822** SCOTT *Nigel* Introd. Epist., It is some consolation to reflect, that the best authors in all countries have been the most voluminous. **1851** HELPS *Comp. Solit.* xi. 225 You should be good-natured and voluminous in your replies. **1907** *Verney Mem.* I. 118 They were all.. voluminous correspondents.

3. Forming a large volume; extending to, or consisting of, many volumes; extensive, copious.

1612 DEKKER *Lond. Tri.* Wks. 1873 III. 251 Erect thou then a serious eye, and looke What worthies fill vp Fames voluminous booke. **1665** BOYLE *Occas. Ref.* I. III. ii. 34 Those Voluminous Romances that are too often the only Books which make up the Libraries of Gallants. **1686** PLOT *Staffordsh.* I Voluminous Works have but few Buyers, and much fewer Readers. **1756** C. LUCAS *Ess. Waters* III. 331 Let the voluminous records of the numerous apothecaries' shops at Bath be examined. **1794** R. J. SULIVAN *View Nat.* II. 309 Why should we be so obstinately wedded to the infallible correctness of voluminous writings? **1840** HOOD *Up Rhine* 167 He will tell you that the folly of the day.. is recorded in voluminous documents. **1865** KINGSLEY *Herew.* viii, Questions which.. produced a voluminous literature for several centuries. **1878** NEWCOMB *Pop. Astron.* Index 54 A recent and complete edition of Kepler's voluminous writings.

fig. **1671** MILTON *P.R.* IV. 384 By what the Stars Voluminous, or single characters, In thir conjunction met, give me to spell.

b. Containing many volumes. *rare*⁻¹.

1690 TEMPLE *Ess. Anc. & Mod. Learn.* (1909) 5 The account of this Library at Alexandria, and others very Voluminous in the lesser Asia and Rome.

4. Of matter of discourse: Extremely full or copious; forming a large mass or collection.

1647 CLARENDON *Hist. Reb.* II. §108 They made great and voluminous expressions of their affection to the Kingdom and People of England. **1672** *Essex Papers* (Camden) I. 45, I have now prepar'd Aunswers to the objections.., but they are so voluminous as they will require some time to transcribe. **1701** NORRIS *Ideal World* I. iii. 162 Unless they [these passages] were less numerous and voluminous than they are. **1742** YOUNG *Nt. Th.* IX. 1628 One firmament, enough for man to read! O what voluminous instruction here! **1775** ADAIR *Amer. Ind.* 434 It is difficult to impress them with a favourable opinion of the wisdom and justice of our voluminous laws. **1821** HAZLITT *Table-T.* viii. ¶1. 162 The impressions of real objects, stripped of the disguises of words and voluminous roundabout descriptions. **1821** J. Q. ADAMS in C. Davies *Metric Syst.* III. (1871) 247 The assize of casks has been in Maryland,.. a subject of frequent and voluminous legislation.

b. In general use: Extensive, vast.

a **1652** J. SMITH *Sel. Disc.* i. 14 Truth is not, I fear, so voluminous, nor swells into such a mighty bulk as our books do. **1658** SIR T. BROWNE *Hydriot.* Introd., Many have taken voluminous Pains to determine the State of the Soul upon Dis-union. **1870** J. BRUCE *Life Gideon* xiii. 239 These matters are too varied and too voluminous for any further notice here. **1899** *Times* 31 Oct. 9/5 Not that.. all our splendid English history [is] one voluminous mistake.

c. Expressing volumes. *rare*⁻¹.

1804 *Something Odd* III. 96 He.. cast a most voluminous look on Clara.

5. Of great volume or size; massive, bulky, large, swelling.

The different groups of quotations illustrate some varieties of application.

(*a*) *a* **1635** CORBET *Poems* (1807) 11 When now Thy observations with thy brain ingendered, Have stuft thy massy and voluminous head. *a* **1637** B. JONSON *Underwoods, Poet to Painter*, I am not so voluminous, and vast, But there are lines, wherewith I might b' embrac'd. **1664** POWER *Exp. Philos.* Pref. b 2 b, The larger and more voluminous sort of Animals, as Bulls, Bears, Tygers, &c. **1800** tr. *Lagrange's Chem.* I. 211 It swells up a great deal, and presents an exceedingly voluminous light mass. **1830** LYELL *Princ. Geol.* I. 248 The most voluminous current of lava which has flowed from Etna within historical times, was that of 1669. **1872** BLACK *Adv. Phaeton* xxx. 397 That young lady with the voluminous light brown hair.

(*b*) *a* **1680** BUTLER *Rem.* (1759) II. 84 His Legs are stuck in his great voluminous Britches. **1809** W. IRVING *Knickerb.* 75 The voluminous skirts turned up at the corners. **1849** C. BRONTE *Shirley* vi, On no account would Mademoiselle have appeared in her own house without the thick handkerchief and the voluminous apron. **1883** O'DONOVAN *Merv* xii. 134 The men, with their voluminous turbans. *Ibid.* xix. 218 A long, striped crimson tunic, girt with voluminous white sash.

(*c*) **1836–9** *Todd's Cycl. Anat.* II. 386/2 In *Phasianella* the stomach is very voluminous and sacculated internally. **1846** BRITTAN tr. *Malgaigne's Man. Oper. Surg.* 386 When you fear wounding any rather voluminous vessel, arterial or venous, you may embrace it beyond the diseased parts in a ligature. **1881** MIVART *Cat* 15 The neck is a little shorter and less voluminous than the head.

Comb. **1872** CALVERLEY *Fly Leaves* (1903) 116 Now Law steps in, bigwigg'd, voluminous-jaw'd.

(*d*) **1855** BAIN *Senses & Int.* II. ii. §7 The thundery discharge, the howling winds, are voluminous sounds. **1873** BLACK *Pr. Thule* xvi. 259 The voluminous noise of this opening passage. **1885** *Manch. Exam.* 20 Feb. 5/7 Tory cheers, which from the first were more loud than voluminous, rather fell away.

b. Large in numbers; numerous. *rare*⁻¹.

1650 FULLER *Pisgah* II. xiv. 303 Judas Maccabeus in that place got an eminent conquest, and defeated the voluminous army of Lysias.

c. Extensive in area or in time. *rare.*

a **1661** FULLER *Worthies, Lincoln.* II. (1662) 144 [Lincolnshire] being too Volluminous to be managed entire is divided into three parts. **1662** GURNALL *Chr. in Arm.* verse 17. II. ii. (1669) 285/1 The Earth was thin sown with People, and the Age of man so voluminous as to contain many centuries of years.

vo'luminously, *adv.* [f. prec. + -LY².] In a voluminous manner, in senses of the adj.

1. At great length; with abundant or copious discourse; to the extent of volumes.

1633 HEYWOOD *Eng. Trav.* To Rdr., It neuer was any great ambition in me, to bee in this kind Volumniously [*sic*] read. **1651** BAXTER *Inf. Bapt.* Apol. 12 Lest we should write voluminously and without end or profit. **1672** —— *Bagshaw's Scand.* ii. 17 When I had not only said the contrary, but told where I had voluminously proved it. **1704** SWIFT *Batt. Bks.* Bookseller to Rdr., The doctor falls hard upon a new edition of Phalaris,.. to which Mr. Boyle replied.. with great learning and wit, and the doctor voluminously rejoined. *a* **1751** BOLINGBROKE *Fragm. Ess.* xxxiii. Wks. 1754 V. 262 They insisted on them so constantly and so voluminously, that natural religion held but the second place in their system. **1841** D'ISRAELI *Amen. Lit.* (1867) 464 Elizabeth exercised her poetical pen more voluminously than we have hitherto known. **1880** MUIRHEAD *Gaius* Introd., On the Edict, both urban and provincial, he wrote voluminously.

2. In swelling wreaths or rolls; in turns or windings.

1742 YOUNG *Nt. Th.* IX. 559 Clouds.. Thy flowing mantle form, and, heav'n throughout, Voluminously pour thy pompous train. **1823** D'ISRAELI *Cur. Lit.* Ser. II. III. 248 The transparent lake.. voluminously winding by banks covered with olives and laurels.

3. In a large mass or quantity.

1834 DE QUINCEY *Autob. Sk.* Wks. 1854 II. 175 Stowing away.. the snowy folds of a lady's gown.. so voluminously, that a very small portion of it, indeed, remained for the lady's own use. **1846** POE *L. G. Clark* Wks. 1864 III. 111 His hair and whiskers are dark, the latter meeting voluminously under the chin. **1864** E. BURRITT *Walk* 313 A mineral spring at which the visitors.. drink most voluminously.

vo'luminousness. [f. as prec. + -NESS.]

1. The character or state of being voluminous or bulky; copiousness, extensiveness.

1664 H. MORE *Myst. Iniq.* ii. 6 The Christian worship being so pure as to abhor from the voluminousness of Judaizing ceremonies. **1687** WINSTANLEY *Lives Eng. Poets* 147 Here he did begin and finish the translation of so many authors, that considering their voluminousness, a man would think he had done nothing else. **1764** D. E. BAKER *Companion Playh.* II. s.v. *Beaumont*, Our Admiration might fix itself in the opposite Extreme,.. when we look back on the Voluminousness of his Works, and then enquire into the Time allowed him for them. **1802–12** BENTHAM *Ration. Judic. Evid.* (1827) I. 443 Having.. been wrought up to the highest possible pitch of voluminousness, indistinctness, and unintelligibility. **1877** OWEN *Wellesley's Desp.* p. xvii, The distressing voluminousness of the materials is undoubtedly a difficulty in the way of the enquirer.

2. The quality of forming many coils or folds.

1820 SHELLEY *Vision of Sea* 141 The jar, and the rattle Of solid bones crushed by the infinite stress Of the snake's adamantine voluminousness.

'volumist. *rare*⁻¹. [f. VOLUME *sb.* 2 + -IST.] One who writes a volume; an author.

1641 MILTON *Animadv.* Wks. 1851 III. 245 Yee write them in your closets, and unwrite them in your Courts, hot Volumists and cold Bishops.

volu'mometer. [f. VOLUME *sb.* + -OMETER.] = VOLUMENOMETER.

1879 ATKINSON *Ganot's Physics* (ed. 9) 141 [The] Volumometer.. consists of a glass tube with a cylinder C at the top.., the edges of which are carefully ground [etc.].

volumo'metrical, *a.* = VOLUMETRICAL *a.*

1863 *Jrnl. R. Agric. Soc.* XXIV. II. 315 Fehling's volumometrical copper test.

'volumy, *a. rare*⁻¹. [f. VOLUME *sb.*] Swelling, rounded.

1827 DARLEY *Sylvia* 170 Clouds under clouds with volumy wombs.

†volunt. *Obs. rare.* [a. late AF. *volunt* for earlier *volunte* VOLUNTY.]

a. (See first quot.) **b.** One's own will.

1592 *Termes of the Law* 191 b, *Volunt* is, when the tenant holdeth at the will of the lessor, or of the Lord, and that is in two manners. [Hence in Harris (1704), etc.] **1611** SPEED *Hist. Gt. Brit.* IX. xvi. 666/1 This I haue here promised and sworne, proceedeth of mine owne desire and free volunt.

†voluntaire, *a. Obs. rare.* [a. F. *voluntaire*, obs. f. *volontaire*: see VOLUNTARY *a.*] Free, voluntary; of one's own choice.

1615 SYLVESTER *Tobacco Battered* 835 Woe to the World because of such Offences; So voluntaire, so voyd of all pretences. **1671** R. MACWARD *True Nonconf.* 27 His unimitable example, in this his free and voluntaire suffering.

† **voluntar**, *sb. Obs.* [Cf. next.] One who rules arbitrarily; a despot.

1650 B. *Discolliminium* 12 Such..may..fitlier be called Masters then Magistrates, Voluntar's then Potentat's.

† '**voluntar**, *a. Sc. Obs.* [ad. older F. *voluntaire* or L. *voluntār-ius* VOLUNTARY *a.*: see AR[2].] Freely undertaken or given; voluntary.

1581 J. HAMILTON in *Cath. Tract.* (S.T.S.) 80 [He] hes.. sufferit voluntar baneisment out of his natiue cuntrie thir monie yeris bypast. **1619** *Burgh Rec. Aberdeen* (1845) II. 361 That a voluntar contributioun be crawit to that effect. **1640–1** *Kirkcudbr. War-Comm. Min. Bk.* (1855) 75 The voluntar contribution that is..collected within your bounds. **1678** SIR G. MACKENZIE *Crim. Laws Scot.* I. i. §4 (1699) 5 Seing man can only offend in what is voluntar to him.

volun'tariate. [ad. F. *volontariat* (1866), f. *volontaire* VOLUNTARY *a.*] Voluntary service, *spec.* of a military character. Also *attrib.*

1881 *Daily News* 7 June 6/4 To the [German] army at large the one year voluntariate has rendered the most precious service. **1888** *Times* 20 Nov. 5/3 In Vienna the medical students have drawn up a petition to the Reichsrath against the proposed changes in the one-year voluntariate.

voluntarily ('vɒləntərɪlɪ), *adv.* Forms: 4–5 uoluntariely, 5– voluntarily, 6 -ilye, -ile, 6–7 -ilie; 6 -elie, -ely; 6 -yly(e, 6–7 -ylie. [f. VOLUNTARY *a.* + -LY[2].]

1. Of one's own free will or accord; without compulsion, constraint, or undue influence by others; freely, willingly.

In very frequent use from *c* 1530.

c **1374** CHAUCER *Boeth.* III. pr. xii. (1868) 103 þer may no man douten, þat þei ne ben gouerned uoluntariely. **1432–50** tr. *Higden* (Rolls) III. 163 Wherefore sche thouȝhte..men wolde haue seide that sche consente to hym voluntarily. **1440** DK. GLOUCESTER *Manifesto* in Rymer *Fœdera* (1710) X. 766/2 To see the Worship, that God soe long hath eured hym with..shuld so voluntarily be put in likelyhed of total Perdition. *a* **1513** FABYAN *Chron.* VII. (1811) 299 Kyng Richarde..voluntaryly tooke vppon hym, and promysed to warre vpon Crystis enemyes. **1560** DAUS tr. *Sleidane's Comm.* 196 b, Duke Maurice of Saxonye served in thys warre voluntarily. **1583** STUBBES *Anat. Abus.* II. (1882) 84 If the other churches..will voluntarily impart any thing to the supplie of his necessities. *c* **1610** *Women Saints* (1886) 37 To these mariages, albeit with a king, she was rather haled perforce than voluntarilie assenting. **1663** BP. PATRICK *Parab. Pilgr.* xiii. (1687) 87 At last he voluntarily, and without any compulsion but that of his Love, died upon a Cross. **1711** STEELE *Spect.* No. 149 ¶7 The happy Marriage is, where two Persons meet and voluntarily make Choice of each other. **1754** EDWARDS *Freed. Will* II. ix. 76 When Men act voluntarily, and do what they please, then they do what appears most agreable to them. **1808** PIKE *Sources Mississ.* III. 215, I know you do not go voluntarily, but I will give you a certificate..of my having obliged you to march. **1858** MASSON *Milton* I. 605 Milton..either voluntarily offered a contribution, or was invited to send one. **1875** JOWETT *Plato* (ed. 2) I. 160 Him who does no evil, voluntarily I praise and love.

b. Said of animals.

1607 TOPSELL *Four-f. Beasts* 161 Euery night..an assembly of dogs..meete voluntarily at an appointed houre, for the custody of the Temple. *Ibid.* 669 They vse to harden their ribs by rubbing them voluntarily vppon Trees. **1831** YOUATT *Horse* iv. 55 It..does sometimes happen, that..the horse..voluntarily presses on, until..he falls and dies.

2. Without other determining force than natural character or tendency; naturally, spontaneously.

1562 BULLEIN *Bulwarke, Sicke Men* (1579) 21 The first of them is naturall, as when men do voluntarily sweat, without force of medicine. **1575** TURBERV. *Faulconrie* 318 They plume themselues oftentimes, yea and the pendant feathers of their thighes..fal off voluntarily. **1613** PURCHAS *Pilgrimage* IV. i. 291 The Earth voluntarily and liberally yeeldeth her store. **1700** C. NESSE *Antid. Armin.* (1827) 68 Man being left to the mutability of his own will..would voluntarily incline to evil.

† **3.** At will, at pleasure; extempore. *Obs.*[−1]

1676 T. MACE *Mus. Mon.* Pref., The Hints and Directions which I have given, as towards the Procuring of Invention, or Playing Voluntarily.

'**voluntariness.** [f. VOLUNTARY *a.* + -NESS.] The state or condition of being voluntary, free, or unconstrained; absolute freedom or liberty in respect of choice, determination, or action; spontaneity: **a.** Of actions.

1612 T. TAYLOR *Comm. Titus* ii. 14 Vnto both which branches of his obedience, if you adde the voluntarinesse and freedome of both, the whole will appeare most perfectly meritorious. **1644** HAMMOND *Will-Worship* §16 The voluntarynesse of an action is not able to defame it, if there be..no irregularity imputable to the action it selfe abstracted from the voluntarinesse. **1728** CHAMBERS *Cycl.* s.v. *Voluntary*, There are two Things..requir'd to the Voluntariness of an Action. **1782** J. BENSON in MacDonald *Mem.* (1822) 134 The Author attempts to show that liberty is voluntariness... We are said to be free when we act from choice. **1865** *Churchman* 14 Dec. 1400/2 The bare voluntariness which attaches to every act of a layman's religious life. **1881** J. MACPHERSON *Conf. Faith* xii. (1882) 73 The voluntariness of Christ's service is everywhere throughout the Scriptures made most clear.

b. Of persons.

1643 R. BAKER *Chron., Edw. I*, 125 This voluntarines in Prince Edward, won the King of France againe to grant quietly unto him, all the Lands [etc.]. **1650** R. HOLLINGWORTH *Exerc. Usurped Powers* 7 Doth not their voluntarinesse and free complyance make the Usurpation compleater? *a* **1672** STERRY *Freed. Will* (1675) 47 God, where the highest Voluntariness and the highest Necessity meet. **1727** BAILEY (vol. II), *Voluntariness*, the doing a Thing voluntarily, or without Constraint. **1856** OLMSTED *Slave States* 490 All the faculties..will be developed..by any man,..in proportion to the voluntariness—the good will with which they are exercised. **1892** *Quiver* July 695/2 Liberty and voluntariness..had no existence in the ancient world.

c. With pl. An instance of this. *rare.*

1612 H. AINSWORTH *Annot. Ps.* cx. 3 Thy people shall be voluntaries in the day of thy power,..a people of voluntarinesses or of liberalities. **1681** FLAVEL *Meth. Grace* iv. 71 They shall be voluntarinesses, as willing as willingnesses itself.

† **volun'tarious**, *a. Obs.*[−1] [ad. L. *voluntārius* VOLUNTARY *a.*] Free, voluntary.

1387–8 T. USK *Test. Love* II. viii. (Skeat) l. 116 Men, of voluntarious wil, withsitte that hevens governeth.

Hence † **volun'tariously** *adv. Obs. rare.*

1550 PAYNELL *Pithy Sayings Scripture* Pref., A diligent ensuer of his wil and steppes, moste pleasaunt and voluntariously to beare the yoke of his most comfortable.. commaundementes. **1553** —— tr. *Dares Phryg. Destr. Troy* H vij b, I opened my gate vnto him & voluntariously communicated al y[t] I had.

voluntarism ('vɒləntərɪz(ə)m). [Irreg. f. VOLUNTAR-Y *a.* + -ISM. Cf. VOLUNTARYISM.]

1. = VOLUNTARYISM 1.

1838 G. S. FABER *Inquiry* 586 Here..we behold, painted to life, the genuine workings of coarse tyrannical Voluntarism!

2. *Philos.* One or other theory or doctrine which regards will as the fundamental principle or dominant factor in the individual or in the universe.

1896 *Advance* (Chicago) 3 Sept., This voluntarism [of Alf. Weber] differs essentially from that of Schopenhauer, according to whom will strives for being and nothing else. **1902** CASE in *Encycl. Brit.* (ed. 10) XXX. 671/2 On the whole, his [Wundt's] voluntarism, though like that of Schopenhauer and Hartmann, is not the same.

3. orig. *U.S.* **a.** The principle of relying on voluntary action rather than compulsion; *spec.* with reference to political and trade-union activities. Cf. VOLUNTARYISM 2.

1924 S. GOMPERS in *Rep. Proc. 44th Ann. Convention Amer. Federation Labor* 5/2, I want to urge devotion to the fundamentals of human liberty—the principles of voluntarism. **1948** *Sun* (Baltimore) 6 Dec. 12/3 There is reason to think that voluntarism is preferable to compulsion on racial matters as on everything else. **1973** *Times* 15 Jan. 18/6 From an almost exclusive reliance on 'voluntarism', *ie.* the promotion of negotiating procedures drawing at most indirectly upon law, Great Britain has now imposed upon the conduct of unions and employers more formal.. regulations. **1983** *Listener* 22 Sept. 5/1 So much for voluntarism, the golden rule of the British TUC.

b. Denoting the involvement of voluntary organizations in social welfare. Also *spec.* in U.K. use = VOLUNTEERISM 2.

1957 *Observer* 8 Sept. 15/4 This is the essence of the American economic achievement to-day: an emphasis on the importance of the individual... And an increasing knowledge of the techniques by which men can co-operate in 'free collectivism'—voluntary private organisation. Voluntarism in our social structure is tremendously important. Without it the whole system would break down. **1969** *Wall St. Jrnl.* 21 Mar. 1/1 'Voluntarism'—President Nixon's program to enlist the help of private groups in solving social problems. **1979** *Guardian* 10 Aug., Voluntarism is one of the central characteristics of a number of organisations with which the Prince of Wales has specific connections. **1981** *Times Lit. Suppl.* 7 Aug. 911/2 When their representatives attained some municipal power, they clung to a weedy sort of voluntarism and missed their chance of creating active local democracy. **1981** *Times* 7 Sept. 2/4 The Government's emphasis on the role of volunteers in providing social services could be counterproductive... Some Labour councils connected the twin themes of public spending cuts and the strong emphasis on voluntarism. **1982** *Chicago Sun-Times* 31 Aug. 30 Bernardin could be the key to the rebirth of a larger sense of community—at a time when its implicit sense of voluntarism would be in keeping with the Reagan era and with the voluntaristic spirit alive today. **1984** *Listener* 14 June 12/2 We are going back to reliance on 'voluntarism' in this vital field.

voluntarist ('vɒləntərɪst). [f. as prec. + -IST.] An advocate or adherent of the voluntary principle or method in the Church or in philosophy.

Also, an advocate of voluntary military service as opposed to conscription.

1841 *Fraser's Mag.* XXIV. 361 'Bread for nothing'..is the hope of every Voluntarist, from sweet Mr. Gadsby's chapel to dear Mr. Fletcher's meeting. **1903** *Harvard Psychol. Stud.* I. 643 Phenomenalist and voluntarist thus do not see anything under the same aspect, neither the ideas nor the will.

volunta'ristic, *a.* [f. prec. + -IC.] **1.** Pertaining or belonging to the philosophical theory of voluntarism.

1903 *Athenæum* 30 May 694/1 Voluntaristic Idealism, on the contrary, lays primary stress on purpose and relevancy of purpose.

2. Pertaining to voluntary action.

1961 B. R. WILSON *Sects & Society* I. iv. 89 Where voluntaristic activities are concerned the sectarian's feud with society remains latent. **1969** A. STEWART in Ionescu & Gellner *Populism* 194 Populist movements which are basically protest movements are threatened by the anti-institutional, voluntaristic character of grass-roots populism. **1974** B. PEARCE tr. *Amin's Accumulation on World Scale* I. 29 Being voluntaristic in character, development policy draws upon new techniques of economic planning in order to work out the series of choices involved. **1977** *Dædalus* Summer 72 The obligatory component in social relationship yields to the optional or voluntaristic, status gives way to contract. **1982** [see VOLUNTARISM 3 b].

† **volun'tarity.** *Obs.* [f. VOLUNTARY *a.*: see -ITY.] Voluntariness, willingness, spontaneity.

1794–6 E. DARWIN *Zoon.* (1801) I. 94 The propensity to action, whether it be called irritability, sensibility, voluntarity, or associability. **1805** *Monthly Mag.* XX. 111 He was likely to make the surrender..with apparent complacence, equanimity, and voluntarity. **1819** *Ibid.* XLVIII. 43 A proof that great voluntarity of idea usually accompanies the individual.

† **voluntarly**, *adv. Sc. Obs.* [f. VOLUNTAR *a.* + -LY[2].] Voluntarily.

c **1568** REGENT MURRAY in H. Campbell *Love-lett. Mary Q. Scots* (1824) App. 21 Sho..constituted me..Regent to his Grace;..and that voluntarlie. **1580** *Reg. Privy Council Scot.* III. 325 Frelie, voluntarlie, and with thair awin gude-will. **1637–50** ROW *Hist. Kirk* (Wodrow Soc.) p. xliv, The saids ministers doe voluntarly expon..ane portion of Scriptur. **1639** DRUMM. OF HAWTH. *Conv. w. B. Jonson* Wks. (1711) 224 He [Ben Jonson]..voluntarly imprisoned himself with Chapman and Marston.

voluntary ('vɒləntərɪ), *a.*, *adv.*, and *sb.* Also 5–7 voluntarye, -arie, 8 -erie; 7 volontarie. [ad. OF. *voluntaire* (14th c.), *volontaire* (16th c.; mod.F. *volontaire* = It. *volontario*, It., Sp., Pg. *voluntario*), or ad. L. *voluntārius*, f. *voluntas* VOLUNTY.]

A. *adj.* **I. 1. a.** Of feelings, etc.: Arising or developing in the mind without external constraint; having a purely spontaneous origin or character.

1387–8 T. USK *Test. Love* I. vi. (Skeat) l. 146 Moche comune meyny, that have no consideracion but only to voluntary lustes withouten reson. *a* **1450** *Mankind* 187 in *Macro Plays* 8 Yf we wyll mortyfye owur carnall condycyon, Ande owur voluntarye dysyres. **1595** SHAKS. *John* V. ii. 10 Albeit we sweare A voluntary zeale, and an vn-urg'd Faith. **1633** R. HALL in *Bp. Hall's Occas. Medit.* Ded., The expressions of these voluntary and sudden thoughts of his. **1644** MILTON *Educ.* Wks. 1851 IV. 380 That voluntary Idea, which hath long in silence presented it self to me. **1728** CHAMBERS *Cycl.* s.v. *Liberty*, Tho' all natural Inclinations be voluntary, yet they are not all free. **1822** J. MACDONALD *Mem. J. Benson* 167 It requires much voluntary faith to be an infidel. **1875** JOWETT *Plato* (ed. 2) V. 74 Unfaithfulness is the voluntary love, as ignorance is the involuntary reception, of a lie. **1884** RUSKIN *Pleas. Learn.* 78 Were faith not voluntary, it could not be praised.

b. Of actions: Performed or done of one's own free will, impulse, or choice; not constrained, prompted, or suggested by another.

Sometimes denoting 'left to choice', 'not required or demanded of one'.

c **1449** PECOCK *Repr.* I. iv. 18 Before that..eny voluntarie or wilful assignement of God was ȝouen to the Iewis. *a* **1513** FABYAN *Chron.* VII. (1811) 548 The archebysshop..shewyd vnto them seryously the voluntary renounsynge of the kyng. **1534** MORE *Comf. agst. Trib.* II. Wks. 1206/2 Restitucion is ..a thing of such necessitie, that in respect of restitucion, almes dede is but voluntary. **1551** T. WILSON *Logike* D v b, That is called voluntarie, which doth betoken any thing done freely. **1596** SHAKS. *Merch. V.* II. i. 16 The lottrie of my destenie Bars me the right of voluntarie choosing. **1632** LITHGOW *Trav.* I. 7 Thy voluntary wandring, and vnconstrayned exyle. **1673** DRYDEN *Amboyna* Ded., This voluntary Neglect of Honours has been of rare Example in the World. **1736** BUTLER *Anal.* I. v. Wks. 1874 I. 84 All wickedness is voluntary, as is implied in its very notion. **1780** BENTHAM *Princ. Legisl.* viii. (1789) 79 *note*, By a voluntary act is meant sometimes, any act, in the performance of which the will has had any concern at all; in this sense it is synonymous to *intentional.* **1784** COWPER *Task* VI. 333 The horse..throwing high his heels, Starts to the voluntary race again. **1849** ROBERTSON *Serm.* Ser. IV. ix. (1876) 82 There must be some voluntary act transgressing some known law or there is no sin. *a* **1871** GROTE *Eth. Fragm.* v. (1876) 187 Every action is voluntary, wherein the beginning of organic motion is the will of the agent.

(*b*) ***Voluntary Service Overseas***, an organization promoting voluntary work by young people (in education, social welfare, etc.) in developing countries; the service so offered or the scheme itself.

1960 *Voluntary Service Overseas* 1 Voluntary Service Overseas enables as many as possible of these young people to have this opportunity—and, in meeting the needs of others, to deepen their own experience. *Ibid.*, Governments and agencies overseas are asking for volunteers to serve as temporary auxiliaries in many fields—social welfare, schools, youth clubs... It is in response to these requests that Voluntary Service Overseas is sending selected volunteers. **1964** M. DICKSON *World Elsewhere* 11 In September 1958 ten young men left Britain for Sarawak. Three flew to Nigeria and two set off for Ghana. All were eighteen years old... They were the spearhead of the scheme which was Voluntary Service Overseas. **1965** *Listener* 7 Jan. 21/2 One finds British young people doing voluntary service overseas in all sorts of out-of-the-way places.

c. Of oaths, etc.: Proceeding from the free, unprompted, or unconstrained will of a person; voluntarily made or given; *spec.* in *Law* (cf. next).

1595 SHAKS. *John* III. iii. 23 Thy voluntary oath Liues in this bosome, deerely cherished. **1607** COWELL *Interpr.*,

Assumpsit, is a voluntarie promise made by word. **1729** JACOB *Law Dict.* s.v. *Oath*, A voluntary Oath, by the Consent and Agreement of the Parties, is lawful as well as a compulsory Oath. **1769** BLACKSTONE *Comm.* IV. 137 [The perjury] is no more penal than in the voluntary extra-judicial oaths. **1782** MISS BURNEY *Cecilia* v. iv, The next day Miss Belfield was to tell her everything by a voluntary promise. **1828–32** WEBSTER, *Voluntary affidavit* or *oath*, is one made in an extra-judicial matter. **1840** *Penny Cycl.* XVI. 382 Oaths may be either voluntary or may be imposed by a political superior. **1883** *Cassell's Encycl. Dict.* s.v. *Confession*, There existed also an ancient practice of voluntary confession in public of private offences and secret sins.

d. *Law.* Of documents, proceedings, etc. (see quots.).

1625 GLANVILLE *Voy. Cadiz* (1883) 29 A voluntary certificate from some of the officers..to prove her a defective Shipp. **1724** SALKELD *Reports* III. 174 He, as a Purchaser, shall avoid this Conveyance, because it was voluntary, and therefore fraudulent. **1765–8** ERSKINE *Inst. Law Scot.* I. ii. §4 Voluntary [jurisdiction] was that which was exercised in matters that admitted of no opposition. *Ibid.* II. viii. §17 If the wadsetter receive his money upon this intimation without compulsion,.. the redemption is voluntary. **1781** J. T. ATKYNS *Rep. Cases* (ed. 2) II. 89 Even in voluntary settlements, if the words lean more strongly to the one construction than to the other, it must likewise prevail. **1818** CRUISE *Digest* (ed. 2) II. 521 The third mode of voluntary partition is, when the eldest makes the division of the lands; in which case she shall choose last. *Ibid.* IV. 401 Edward Bussey being possessed of a term for 59 years, by voluntary deed, conveyed it to trustees. **1845** POLSON in *Encycl. Metrop.* II. 848/1 A voluntary charter is granted by a superior *ex mero motû*. **1860** WHARTON *Law Lex.* (ed. 2) 757/2 *Voluntary Answer*, one filed by a defendant to a bill in equity, without being called upon to answer by the plaintiff. **1875** K. E. DIGBY *Real Prop.* (1876) 373 Voluntary conveyances of estates in land, that is, conveyances without any consideration, such as money or marriage.

e. *Naut.* (See quot.)

1867 SMYTH *Sailor's Word-bk.* 714 *Voluntary charge*, a document delivered with the purser's accounts respecting provisions.

2. *Physiol.* Of bodily actions: Regulated or governed by the volitional faculty; subject to the will. (Cf. INVOLUNTARY *a.* 1 b.)

c **1400** *Lanfranc's Cirurg.* 29 Brawn is maad of fleisch, senewe, & ligamentis, & þei ben instrument [of] voluntarie meuynge. **1650** BULWER *Anthropomet.* 6 Voluntary motion depends upon the Nerves. **1651** HOBBES *Leviath.* I. vi. 23 Imagination is the first internal beginning of all Voluntary Motion. **1728** CHAMBERS *Cycl.* s.v. *Muscle*, The Muscles of Voluntary Motion..have each of 'em their Antagonist Muscles. **1843** GRAVES *Syst. Clin. Med.* xv. 184 The muscles of voluntary life. **1855** BAIN *Senses & Int.* I. ii. §17 The Spinal Cord..is necessary to sensation and to voluntary movement (movement from feeling). **1881** MIVART *Cat* 124 Amongst the voluntary movements are the various movements of the several members.

3. a. Of conditions, etc.: Assumed or adopted voluntarily or by free choice; freely chosen or undertaken.

1426 LYDG. *De Guil. Pilgr.* 22714 Kome fforthe, and se an exanplayre Off poverte not voluntarye. **1474** CAXTON *Chesse* II. v. (1883) 65 Scipion of affrique..was so poure of voluntarie pouerte yᵗ..he was buried at yᵉ dispencis of yᵉ comyn good. **1581** PETTIE tr. *Guazzo's Civ. Conv.* I. (1586) 45 b, The companie which we come into by chance, consisteth of many persons, but yᵗ which is voluntarie, which we ought to couet, containeth but few folke in it. **1585** T. WASHINGTON tr. *Nicholay's Voy.* IV. xxxi. 154 Hee ended hys dayes in voluntarie exyle. **1611** BIBLE *Col.* ii. 18 Let no man beguile you of your reward, in a voluntarie humilitie. **1622** T. SCOTT *Belg. Pismire* 1 The Creatures subjected to his gouernment, in their voluntarie obedience. **1752** YOUNG *Brothers* III. i, I pretend 'twas voluntary flight To save a brother's blood. **1759** JOHNSON *Rasselas* xxviii, They discover what nothing but voluntary blindness before had concealed. **1847** S. AUSTIN *Ranke's Hist. Ref.* III. 85 The inhabitants of the town and country took a voluntary share in all the changes. **1877** MRS. OLIPHANT *Makers Flor.* xv. 386 His exile was voluntary, not forced like Dante's.

transf. **1638** SIR T. HERBERT *Trav.* (ed. 2) 10 The dead are ..laid to sleep in a neat..dormitory, his Armolets, Bracelets, and voluntary shackles accompany him. *Ibid.* 38 Many voluntary rings and fetters of Brasse.

b. Brought about by one's own choice or deliberate action; self-inflicted, self-induced.

1548 ELYOT s.v. *Voluntarius, Mors voluntaria*, voluntarie death. **1576** FLEMING *Panopl. Epist.* 246 *marg.*, Voluntarie death ought not to be attempted of any wise man. **1601** HOLLAND *Pliny* I. 126 These make profession of voluntarie death: and..when they are disposed to die at any time, they make a great funeral fire [etc.]. **1601** SHAKS. *Jul. C.* II. i. 300, I haue made strong proofe of my Constancie, Giuing my selfe a voluntary wound Heere, in the Thigh. **1781** COWPER *Truth* 101 His voluntary pains, severe and long, Would give a barb'rous air to British song. **1878** BROWNING *La Saisiaz* 61 A law to contravene Voluntary passage from this life. **1891** FARRAR *Darkn. & Dawn* ix, One of those creatures.. who, in that age, so often took refuge from a depraved life in a voluntary death.

c. Entered into of free choice; also *spec.* (see quot. 1889).

1612–13 SIR H. HOBART *Reports* (1650) 149 We know well that the Primitive Church..were but voluntary Congregations of beleevers. **1849** MACAULAY *Hist. Eng.* ii. I. 158 In some districts..the ministers formed themselves into voluntary associations, for the purpose of mutual help and counsel. **1889** *Cent. Dict.* s.v. *Association, Voluntary association*, in *law*, a society which is unincorporated, but is not a partnership, in that the members are not agents for one another.

4. a. Done of deliberate intent or purpose; designed, intentional.

(*a*) **1495** *Rolls of Parlt.* VI. 488/1 She theryn [*sc.* in lands devised to her] doyng noe voluntary Waste ne Destruccion. **1544** tr. *Littleton's Tenures* (1574) 15 b, If the lessee at wil make voluntarye wast, as in pullinge downe of houses, or in cuttinge or fellinge of trees. **1766** BLACKSTONE *Comm.* II. 281 Waste is either voluntary, which is a crime of commission, as by pulling down a house; or it is permissive. **1867** SMYTH *Sailor's Word-bk.* 714 *Voluntary stranding*, the beaching or running a vessel purposely aground to escape greater danger.

(*b*) **1530–1** *Act 22 Hen. VIII*, c. 9 §1 Consyderyng that.. voluntary murders [are] moste highly to be detested and abhorred. ? *a* **1600** PERKINS (J.), If a man be lopping a tree and his ax-head fall from the helve,..and kills another passing by; here is indeed manslaughter, but no voluntary murther.

b. *Law.* Of escapes: Deliberately permitted or connived at.

1660 YOUNG *Vade Mecum* (ed. 6) 94 Voluntary [escape] is when one hath arrested another for felony or other crime, and doth afterwards suffer him to go whither he will. **1769** BLACKSTONE *Comm.* IV. 130 Voluntary escapes, by consent and connivance of the officer, are a much more serious offence. **1797** TOMLINS *Jacob's Law Dict.* s.v. *Escape*, If the marshal of the King's Bench..or any other who hath the keeping of prisons in fee, suffer a voluntary escape, it is a forfeiture of the office.

5. Of gifts, etc.: Freely or spontaneously bestowed, rendered, or made; contributed voluntarily or by reason of generous or charitable motives.

1580 G. HARVEY *Let. Spenser* S.'s Wks. (1912) 627/2 A small voluntarie Supplement of his owne..in commendation of hir..thrice excellent Maiestie. **1614** RALEIGH *Hist. World* II. xvii. §8. 490 He exhorted all others to a voluntary contribution. **1651** HOBBES *Leviath.* III. xlii. 287 A common stock of mony, raised out of the voluntary contributions of the faithfull. **1682** PENN in Clarkson *Mem.* (1813) I. 321 Let the Lord have a voluntary share of your income for the good of the poor. **1728** CHAMBERS *Cycl.*, *Charity Schools*, are Schools erected and maintain'd in various Parishes, by the voluntary Contributions of the Inhabitants. **1797** BURKE *Regic. Peace* iii. Wks. VIII. 359 Nor is it every contribution, called voluntary, which is according to the free will of the giver. **1800** *Asiatic Ann. Reg., Misc. Tracts* 335/1 Neither shall any subsidy be exacted from them,..what they furnish shall be voluntary. **1818** CRUISE *Digest* (ed. 2) III. 46 The clergy were supported by the voluntary offerings of their flocks. **1845** *Encycl. Metrop.* XIII. 918/2 Voluntary contributions in aid of the national resources. **1897** *Westm. Gaz.* 2 Mar. 2/3 You have got to go to the school whether you like to or not, whilst the 'voluntary' part of the maintenance is just twopence out of every shilling.

II. 6. †**a.** Of the will, etc.: Free, unforced, unconstrained. *Obs.*

1508 FISHER *7 Penit. Ps.* cxxx. Wks. (1876) 230 We knowe ..that almyghty god of his owne voluntary wyll and gracyous volunty..redemed vs. **1560** DAUS tr. *Sleidane's Comm.* 206 Duke Maurice served themperour..of hys oune voluntarye mynde. **1563** GOLDING *Cæsar* I. (1565) 33 b, Consideryng he offered of his own voluntary wil, the thing he hadde before denied when it was requested.

b. *voluntary faculty*, the will.

1867 ALDEN *Elem. Intell. Philos.* xxvi. 261 By the voluntary faculty, or the will, we mean simply the capacity of the mind to perform acts of volition.

7. a. Of persons: That is such of one's own accord or free choice; acting voluntarily, willingly, or spontaneously in a specified capacity; also, endowed with the faculty of willing.

1594 HOOKER *Eccl. Pol.* I. iii. §2 God did not worke as a necessary but a voluntary agent. **1611** SHAKS. *Cymb.* III. v. 158 That thou wilt be a voluntarie Mute to my designe. **1642** FULLER *Holy & Prof. St.* III. xx. 205 No pity is to be shown to such voluntary cripples. **1667** MILTON *P.L.* x. 61 Sending thee Mans Friend, his Mediator, his design'd Both Ransom and Redeemer voluntarie. **1754** EDWARDS *Freed. Will* II. iv. 50 The Soul is an active Being in Nothing further than it is a voluntary or elective Being. **1776** GIBBON *Decl. & F.* ii. I. 43 These voluntary exiles were engaged, for the most part, in the occupations of commerce. **1868** HUXLEY *Lay Serm.* iii. (1870) 46 The greatest voluntary wanderers and colonists the world has ever seen.

†**b.** Serving as a volunteer soldier; that is a volunteer; also, composed of volunteers. *Obs.*

1586 *Acts Privy Council* N.S. XIV. 55 A Commission..to levie..the number of 150 voluntarie footemen. **1590** SIR J. SMYTH *Disc. Weapons* Ded. 5 b, The souldiors thereby being made voluntary, haue obeyed their Captaines no otherwise than hath pleased themselues. **1604** E. GRIMSTONE *Siege Ostend* 30 The Arch-duke had caused..a volontarie Gentleman..to be put in prison. **1632** LITHGOW *Trav.* VIII. 350, I left Mr. Bruce with a Galley Captaine a voluntary Souldier. **1647** CLARENDON *Hist. Reb.* VI. §249 Sʳ Nicholas Slanning's, and Colonel Trevannion's Voluntary Regiments.

c. *poet.* Of a sword: Offered freely or willingly in aid of some cause.

1761 GRAY *Epit. Sir W. Williams* ii, At Aix his voluntary sword he drew, There first in blood his infant honor seal'd. **1808** SCOTT *Marm.* IV. Introd., Eleven years we now may tell, Since..our hand First drew the voluntary brand.

d. *voluntary patient*, one who enters a mental hospital without being committed to it.

1930 *Daily Express* 6 Sept. 9/4 Instructions sent by the Board of Control to local authorities regarding the working of the Mental Treatment Act (1930) stipulate that 'mental hospital' is to be substituted for 'asylum', and 'voluntary patient' is to be used instead of 'voluntary boarder'. **1943** G. GREENE *Ministry of Fear* III. i. 167 If only someone would complain—they are all voluntary patients. **1979** J. THOMSON *Deadly Relations* xiii. 189, I had a nervous breakdown... I ..was sent to a clinic..as a voluntary patient.

†**8.** Favourably inclined or disposed (*to* do something); willing, ready. *Obs.*

1597 A. M. *Guillemeau's Fr. Chirurg.* f iv, I am so voluntarye to communicate the same vnto certayne of my goode frendes. **1638** in Picton *L'pool Munic. Rec.* (1883) I. 133 The greater parte of the Common Councell..beinge all voluntary tendered to lend [to] the towne for the expedicion of the towne's business att London. **1668** MARVELL *Corr.* Wks. (Grosart) II. 263 He should be so much more at liberty to show how voluntary and affectionate he was to your Corporation. **1741–2** GRAY *Agrippina* 36 When yet a stranger To adoration,..and obsequious vows From voluntary realms. **1768** H. WALPOLE *Hist. Doubts* Pref. p. xv, When a successful king is chief justice, historians become a voluntary jury.

absol. **1611** BIBLE *Ps.* xlvii. 9 *marg.*, The voluntarie of the people are gathered vnto the people of the God of Abraham.

transf. **1621** G. SANDYS *Ovid's Met.* I. (1626) 11 Other Creatures tooke their numerous birth And figures, from the voluntary Earth. **1652** CRASHAW *Carmen Deo Nostro, Mary Magdalene* xxi, That King..That thus can boast to be Waited on by a wandring mine, A voluntary mint, that strowes Warm sylver showres where're he goes!

9. a. Of institutions: Maintained or supported solely or largely by the freewill offerings or contributions of members or subscribers, and free from State interference or control; *spec.* in *Educ.* with reference to schools, etc., maintained by voluntary bodies.

1745 BUTLER *Serm.* Wks. 1874 II. 277 The education of poor children was all along taken care of by voluntary charities. **1837** MCCULLOCH *Acc. Brit. Empire* II. 491 Private or Voluntary Schools. **1867** *Chambers's Encycl.* IX. 647/1 The United Presbyterian Church is..not only in practice, but also in theory, a voluntary church. **1868** *Ibid.* X. 651/1 They held that the same objections did not apply to voluntary organisations [for educational purposes]. **1944** *Act 7 & 8 Geo. VI* c. 31 §8 Primary and secondary schools maintained by a local education authority, not being nursery schools or special schools, shall, if established by a local education authority..be known as county schools and, if established otherwise than by such an authority, be known as voluntary schools. **1969** L. TINKHAM in Cockburn & Blackburn *Student Power* 84 There are now about one hundred Local Education Authority colleges and half as many independent voluntary colleges. **1976** *Star* (Sheffield) 29 Nov. 9/1 Pupils will be transferred to the Perlethorpe Church of England Voluntary Aided Primary School.

b. Of or pertaining to, concerned or connected with, voluntaryism in respect of the Church or educational institutions.

1834 GRAHAM in C. S. Parker *Life & Lett.* (1907) I. 198, I cannot favour in the least 'the Voluntary Principle'. **1867** *Chambers's Encycl.* IX. 646/1 A great controversy..known as the Voluntary Controversy (1829–1834). **1868** *Ibid.* X. 23/2 An important article in the Voluntary creed. **1891** E. KINGLAKE *Australian at Home* 51 The voluntary system..is almost universal in Australia. The clergyman is the servant of his congregation, and must please them or go.

c. Of persons: Advocating or supporting the voluntary principle as opposed to State establishment and control.

1835 C. J. BROWN *Ch. Establishm.* iv. 15 Voluntary Churchmen, out of an Establishment, talk of the independence of the Church—our forefathers, within one, bled and died for it. **1868** *Chambers's Encycl.* X. 24/1 Those known as Voluntary educationists reject the idea of any national system.

10. a. Of muscles, etc.: Acting or moving in response to the volition; directing or controlling voluntary movements.

1788 *Encycl. Brit.* (ed. 3) I. 702/1 The motions.., in a natural and healthy state, are subject to the will, and for this reason they are called voluntary muscles. **1843** GRAVES *Syst. Clin. Med.* xv. 186 A debility of the voluntary muscles. **1864** WEBSTER, *Voluntary nerve*, nerve distributed to voluntary muscle. **1884** *Pop. Sci. Monthly* June 174 We see here that atrophy begins in the most voluntary limb, the arm.

b. *Physiol.* (See quot.)

1860 MAYNE *Expos. Lex.* 1337/1 *Voluntary Motor Power*, ..the power exercised by the brain and nerves in volition, in distinction from the excito-motor power, or that which is peculiar to the spinal marrow and its nerves.

III. †**11.** Growing wild or naturally; of spontaneous growth. *Obs. rare.*

1620 VENNER *Via Recta* vii. 130 The wilde or voluntary Strawberries, that I may so terme them. **1633** BP. HALL *Hard Texts, N.T.* 4 Feeding on such homely and voluntary diet as that wild place would afford. **1718** POPE *Iliad* XIV. 396 Glad earth perceives, and from her bosom pours Unbidden herbs and voluntary flowers.

B. *adv.* = VOLUNTARILY *adv.*

In early use perh. partly after L. *voluntāriē*.

1480 *Cov. Leet Bk.* 435 All þe forseid persones..cam voluntarye, & seid openly ther to þe seid Maire, þat [etc.]. **1562** *Child-Marriages* 75 The said Henrie did neuer lye with the said Mavde, nor did cohabete voluntarie together. *c* **1595** CAPT. WYATT *Dudley's Voy.* (Hakl. Soc.) 34 One of them voluntarie profered to goe with him into Englande. **1609** HOLLAND *Amm. Marcell.* d 4 b, He did this voluntarie, according to the example of the ancient Decii. **1632** J. HAYWARD tr. *Biondi's Eromena* To Rdr., In excuse of my not voluntary undergoing..the burthen of this Translation. **1671** MILTON *P.R.* II. 394 If of that pow'r I bring thee voluntary What I might have bestow'd on whom I pleas'd. **1710** PRIDEAUX *Orig. Tithes* iii. 145 All should voluntary pay them in their Offerings at the Church. **1769** SIR J. REYNOLDS *Disc.* ii. (1876) 322 To go voluntary to a tribunal where he knows he must be humbled.

C. *sb.* **I.** †**1.** Free will or choice; = VOLUNTY. In the phrases ***of, out of, upon,*** or ***at*** (a person's) ***own voluntary, at voluntary.***

(*a*) **1585** T. WASHINGTON tr. *Nicholay's Voy.* I. xix. 23 b, Of theyr owne voluntarie [they] came to surrender themselues. *Ibid.* I. xx. 25 The offer [was] made vppon his owne voluntary. **1590** GREENE *Mourn. Garm.* Wks. (Grosart) IX. 168 If you were to chuse husbands at your owne voluntary. **1606** G. WOODCOCK *Hist. Ivstine* II. 16

After this the Spartans,..out of their own voluntary, inuaded the borders of their Empire. *a* **1617** BAYNE *On Eph.* (1643) 317 How canst thou,..out of thy voluntary, converse with them who are not sanctified? **1633** J. DONE tr. *Aristeas' Hist. Septuagint* 59 Uppon his owne voluntary, he came often to visite the workes.

(*b*) **1590** GREENE *Neuer too late* Wks. (Grosart) VIII. 71 Womens flatteries [were] too forceable to resist at voluntarie. **1591** —— *Conny Catch.* II. 11 He began to..rap out gogs Nownes, and pronounes, while at voluntarie he had sworne through the eight parts of speach in the Accidence.

2. † **a.** Music added at the will of the performer to a piece played or sung. *Obs.*

1565 JEWEL *Reply Harding* (1611) 113 This is the plaine song, and may well stand for the ground: the rest is altogether descant and vaine voluntary, and the most part out of tune. **1597** MORLEY *Introd. Mus.* 126 To make two parts vpon a plainesong is more hard then to make three parts into voluntary. *Ibid.*, Rules which may serue him both for descant and voluntary.

b. A musical piece or movement played or sung spontaneously or of one's free choice, esp. by way of prelude to a more elaborate piece, song, etc.

1598 FLORIO, *Preludio*, a proheme in musicke, a voluntary before the song. **1628** FORD *Lover's Mel.* I. i, Upon his instrument he plays so swiftly, So many voluntaries, and so quick, That [etc.]. **1662** PLAYFORD *Skill Mus.* I. 60 He with his Harp..ending his excellent Voluntary with some choice Fancy upon this Phrygian Mood. **1688** HOLME *Armoury* III. xix. (Roxb.) 154/2 The seuerall Beates or points of warre are these... 4. A Voluntary before the March. **1754** R. NEWTON *Char. Theophrastus* 7 Something in the nature of a flourish, or of a voluntary before the tune. *a* **1785** T. POTTER *Moralist* II. 134 He took up his flute, and touched a few notes of the voluntary he had heard the night before. **1848** THACKERAY *Van. Fair* xlviii, Sitting down to the piano, she rattled away a triumphant voluntary on the keys.

fig. and *transf.* **1603** HYND *Mirrour Worldly Fame* v, Dancing is the voluntary, which is played before a passage is made to unlawful desires. **1629** GAULE *Holy Madn.* 155 Like a fantasticke Musician, he chiefly pleases himselfe; while he leaues the Grounds, to run upon the Voluntaries. **1686** GOAD *Celest. Bodies* II. viii. 255 The Lark and the Thrush sung their Voluntaries. **1712** STEELE *Spect.* No. 504 ¶1 These can..say you are dull to-day, and laugh a Voluntary to put you in humour. **1795** BURKE *Let. to W. Elliot* Wks. 1842 II. 240, I have been told of the voluntary, which, for the entertainment of the house of lords, has been lately played by his Grace. **1814** SCOTT *Wav.* xliii, He..ran off in a wild voluntary of fanciful mirth. *a* **1881** ROSSETTI *House of Life* ix, This harp still makes my name its voluntary.

c. *esp.* A piece or solo, usu. consisting of two or more movements, played upon the organ before, during, or after any office of the Church; also, the music for this.

in-, *out-voluntary*, those respectively played at the beginning and close of a religious service.

1712 STEELE *Spect.* No. 503 ¶2 Now the Organ was to play a Voluntary, and she..kept time..with some Motion of her Head. **1731** in *Abridgm. Specif. Patents, Music* (1871) 2 All psalm tunes, fuges, volunteries, and anthems that are usually sung in churches or chappells. **1779** *Phil. Trans.* LXIX. 193 Several voluntaries which he heard..the organist play at the Cathedral. **1801** BUSBY *Dict. Mus.* s.v., The voluntary was originally so called, because its performance, or non-performance, was at the option of the organist. **1837** HOOD *Ode R. Wilson* 398 Let the solemn, swelling, organ greet, With Voluntaries meet, The willing advent of the rich and poor. **1870** ANDERSON *Missions Amer. Bd.* II. xxxviii. 344 A voluntary skillfully played..on the powerful organ belonging to the church.

fig. **1863** COWDEN CLARKE *Shaks. Char.* xvii. 448 This scene..will form a choice voluntary as conclusion to our homily.

† **3.** A voluntary oath. *Obs.*$^{-1}$

1593 BILSON *Govt. Chr. Ch.* 270 In matters of religion that touch the peace and safetie of the whole Church of Christ, do you looke your voluntarie should bee receiued without all authoritie or testimonie to warrant it?

† **4.** An occurrence or event due to some person's voluntary action. *Obs. rare.*

1652 GAULE *Magastrom.* 83 Casualties and voluntaries, whose events are not so much as probable, as not having any such causes as aforesaid.

5. An extempore, optional, or voluntary piece of writing or composition.

1690 TEMPLE *Ess., Poetry* Wks. 1720 I. 245 The *Priapeia* ..were little Voluntaries or Extemporaries, written upon the ridiculous Wooden Statues of Priapus. **1801** W. TAYLOR in Robberds *Mem.* (1843) I. 387 If I get Phillips to receive his voluntaries in the Monthly Magazine, he..will take the less pains. **1860** MANSFIELD *School-life at Winchester* (1870) 107 Præfects and Senior part also were encouraged to write ..a copy of verses on any subject selected by themselves, which was called a 'Voluntary'. **1876** LOWELL *Among my Books* Ser. II. 206 At school he wrote some task-verses..and also some voluntaries of his own.

6. A voluntary contribution.

1837–8 J. KEEGAN *Leg. & Poems* (1907) 80 [The heap of stones] at last assumed a size sufficiently large to attract the attention of every person who went the way, who, in their turn, added their 'voluntary' to the pile.

7. A parting of a rider from his horse without sufficient cause; an unwarranted fall. Freq. *to cut a voluntary.*

1863 G. A. LAWRENCE *Border & Bastille* ii. 33 A conscript, who could keep his saddle, through an entire day, without 'taking a voluntary', was considered..a credit to the regiment. **1883** MRS. KENNARD *Right Sort* xxi, They will say I cut a voluntary... The stirrup-leather alone was to blame. **1890** *Field* 8 Feb. 177 The number of 'voluntaries' which are ever taking place in the hunting field.

8. A voluntary examination.

1894 J. PAYN *Gleams of Memory* 75 As an initial step to my becoming a divine, it was..necessary to pass 'the Voluntary' —a theological examination in my case very inappropriately named.

II. † **9.** One voluntarily, and usually without pay, serving as a soldier in a campaign, battle, etc.; = VOLUNTEER *sb.* 1. *Obs.*

In very frequent use from 1600 to 1645.

1595 SHAKS. *John* II. i. 67 Rash, inconsiderate, fiery voluntaries,..Haue sold their fortunes at their natiue homes,..To make a hazard of new fortunes heere. **1601** MOUNTJOY in Moryson *Itin.* II. (1617) 138 Diuers worthy men..haue followed the wars here as voluntaries to their very great expence. **1622** F. MARKHAM *Bk. War* I. vii. 25 Those Souldiers, which we call by the name of Voluntaries, being a ranke of men which voluntarily, and of their owne meere motion without any constraint at all, doe betake themselues vnto the Warres. **1636** WINTHROP *New Eng.* (1825) I. 195 The soldiers who went were all voluntaries, and had only their victuals provided, but demanded no pay. **1670** MILTON *Hist. Eng.* v. 219 Turkitel the Dane..got leave of the King, with as many voluntaries as would follow him, to pass into France.

fig. **1612** T. TAYLOR *Comm. Titus* ii. 6 Let them now serue as voluntaries vnder the Captaine Iesus Christ.

transf. **1627** J. TAYLOR (Water P.) *Navy Land Ships* A ij b, There were 7. other needlesse Ships which were in the nature of voluntaries, or hangers on vpon the Nauy.

10. One who undertakes or engages in any kind of service, enterprise, etc., of his own choice or free-will; = VOLUNTEER *sb.* 3.

1609 BIBLE (Douay) *1 Macc.* ii. 42 Then there was gathered to them the synagoge of the Assideans.., everie voluntarie in the law. **1612** H. AINSWORTH *Annot. Ps.* cx. 3 Thy people shall be voluntaries in the day of thy power. **1628** WITHER *Brit. Rememb.* III. 1507 That none durst become a voluntary, In such a Fire, for conscience sake, to tarie. *a* **1641** BP. MOUNTAGU *Acts & Mon.* (1642) 146 Unto Esdras was granted..licence to goe up unto Jerusalem, to carry with him all such voluntaries as would goe.

† **11.** One who is willing or ready to give way or withdraw. *Obs.*$^{-1}$

1620 [G. BRYDGES] *Horæ Subs.* 25 If..they..could haue beene content to withdraw..it would haue expressed an excellent temper, and moderation. But few such voluntaries bee found.

12. One who holds or advocates that the Church (or educational institutions) should be maintained by voluntary contributions and be independent of State connexion or support. Cf. VOLUNTARYIST.

1834 *Tait's Mag.* I. 418/1 The Governor was a Voluntary; but Lord Goderich granted [the congregation] the L. 100 from the colonial revenue. **1843** E. MIALL in *Nonconf.* III. 241 Where the truth has got hold of a man it makes him a real voluntary. **1868** *Chambers's Encycl.* X. 651/1 Obstacles to the establishment of a national system [of education] more formidable than the opposition of the Voluntaries.

voluntaryism (ˈvɒləntərɪɪz(ə)m). [f. prec.]

1. The principle or tenet that the Church and educational institutions should be supported by voluntary contributions instead of by the State.

Freq. from *c* 1850. (Cf. VOLUNTARISM.)

1835 (*title*), Picture of Slavery in the United States of America, with a Practical Illustration of Voluntaryism and Republicanism. **1845** J. MARTINEAU *Misc.* (1852) 146 The voluntaryism of the Independents,..the National endowment of Coleridge and Chalmers. **1866** GEO. ELIOT *F. Holt* Introd. 8 They had not at least given in to schismatic rites, and were free from the errors of Voluntaryism. **1869** M. ARNOLD *Cult. & An.* (1882) 70 Abolition of church-rates, voluntaryism in religion and education.

2. Any system which rests upon voluntary action or principles. Now usu. with reference to voluntary labour. Cf. VOLUNTEERISM 2.

Also with reference to military service.

1883 CHALMERS & HOUGH *Bankruptcy Act* Introd. p. ix, Official assignees..were..totally abolished, and the public entered once more on a system of voluntaryism. **1946** *Organisation & Finance Adult Educ.* (Min. Educ.) 36 We are unanimously of the opinion that voluntaryism as exemplified by the Workers' Educational Association is essential if the spirit of adult education is to be preserved. **1967** *Listener* 1 June 709/2 In the light of the present arguments about the prices and incomes policy, Bevin's insistence on what he called 'voluntaryism' is most significant... Bevin resisted strong pressures in parliament to conscript labour on the home front.

voluntaryist (ˈvɒləntərɪɪst). [f. as prec. + -IST.] One who advocates or upholds the voluntary system of support and control in religious or (latterly esp.) educational institutions.

Also, an advocate of voluntary military service. (Cf. VOLUNTARIST.)

1842 E. MIALL in *Nonconf.* II. 305 The proceedings of voluntaryists hitherto..have not been on a commanding scale. **1869** *Spectator* 24 July 861 We are not Voluntaryists, ..but his Grace of Canterbury's remarks seem to us thoroughly intolerant..in the head of a national Church. **1888** T. W. REID *Life W. E. Forster* I. 311 A vigorous attack upon the voluntaryists,..showing how complete had been the failure of the voluntary system to meet the educational wants of the people.

attrib. **1893** *Daily News* 7 Apr. 3/5 At present parents of all children in School Board districts are contributors to the local rates, and voluntaryist parents receive nothing for what they contribute.

voluntative, *a.* and *sb.* [ad. med.L. *voluntativus*, f. L. *voluntāt-*, *voluntas* VOLUNTY.]

A. *adj.* † **a.** (See quot. 1656.) *Obs.*$^{-0}$ **b.** *Hebrew Gram.* Of a verbal form: Expressive of a desire; desiderative. **c.** Having the ability to act or accomplish at will; voluntary.

1656 BLOUNT *Glossogr.*, *Voluntative*, that proceeds from the Will, wilfull, or full of desire. **1870** tr. *Lange's Comm.*, *Song Sol.* viii. 3 The following voluntative or jussive future. **1883** *Amer. Jrnl. Philol.* IV. 425 The simple solution seems to be that the conditioning of a purpose destroys its absolute voluntative power.

B. *sb. Hebrew Gram.* A verbal form expressive of a desire to do the action denoted by the verb; a desiderative.

1870 J. F. SMITH *Ewald's Introd. Hebr. Gram.* 160 The voluntative, or the expression of the desire that something may be, arises from the imperf. [etc.]. **1874** A. B. DAVIDSON *Introd. Hebr. Gram.* 50 By some grammarians this form is called Cohortative; others embrace both the long and short forms under the name voluntative.

volunteer (vɒlənˈtɪə(r)), *sb.* and *a.* Forms: α. 7 volunteir(e, 7–8 voluntier, 8 volontier. β. 7– volunteer (7 -eere), 7–8 volenteer. [ad. F. *volontaire*, †*voluntaire* (= It. *volont-*, *voluntario*, Sp. and Pg. *voluntario*), ad. L. *voluntārius* VOLUNTARY *a.* The ending has been assimilated to the suffixes -IER and -EER[1].]

A. *sb.* **1.** *Mil.* **a.** One who voluntarily offers or enrols himself for military service, in contrast to those who are under obligation to do so, or who form part of a regular army or military force.

In early use freq. implying service without the pay given to the regular troops.

α. *a* **1618** RALEIGH *Mahomet* (1637) 80, 6000 horse and voluntiers infinite accomodated with all provisions. **1654** H. L'ESTRANGE *Chas. I* (1655) 68 The enemy being about one thousand Horse and Foot besides Voluntiers, made a very gallant impression upon us. **1654–66** EARL ORRERY *Parthen.* (1676) 25 The Prince honor'd me with the leading of 2000 Horse, all Voluntiers. *a* **1715** BURNET *Own Time* ix. (1766) I. 306 The earl of Montague..was then a voluntier and one of the Duke's Court. **1769** ROBERTSON *Chas. V*, VIII. Wks. 1813 III. 85 To every standard that was erected, voluntiers flocked from all quarters.

β. *c* **1600** DRAYTON *Miseries Q. Margaret* clxxvi, And with fiue thousand valient Volunteers, Of natiue French, put vnder her Command, With Armes well fitted she towards Scotland steeres. **1627** *Lisander & Cal.* I. 14 With a handfull of Volenteers he defeated manie thousands of Reisters. **1653** H. COGAN tr. *Pinto's Trav.* lxiv. (1663) 261 He resolved by the means of ten thousand Volunteers, who had offered themselves unto him,..to attacque this fort. **1677** W. HUBBARD *Narrative* 18 A Company of Volunteers, under the Command of Captain Samuel Moseley. **1747** *Gentl. Mag.* 321 Certain burgesses and inhabitants of the city, offering to serve as volunteers in defence of the city, against the rebels. **1788** *Encycl. Brit.* (ed. 3) I. 599/2 All this time the American army was increasing by the continual arrival of militia and volunteers from all parts. **1841** CATLIN *N. Amer. Ind.* lviii. (1844) II. 242 He is then a volunteer, like all of their soldiers in war, and bound by no compulsive power. **1870** J. BRUCE *Gideon* xxii. 399 These discouraged Israelites who had deserted were here seen returning and flocking as volunteers now, round the triumphant standard of that mighty man of valour.

b. *spec.* A member of an organized military company or force, formed by voluntary enrolment and distinct from the the regular army. In later use, a civilian forming part of the 'auxiliary forces' of a country as a member of such a body.

1642 *Exceeding Welcome Newes fr. Beverley* (title-p.), The Resolution of the Gentry and Commonalty of Yorkshire to joyn with the London Voluntiers, for the defence of the King and Parliament. **1643** in *10th Rep. Hist. MSS. Comm.* App. IV. 435 To warne the watch of the voluntiers of the said Town whoe did dutie of watch twice 24 howres every weeke. **1712** E. COOKE *Voy. S. Sea* 74 The Volunteers march'd before the Army, daring the Enemy in a very haughty Manner. **1797** *Encycl. Brit.* (ed. 3) XVIII. 689/2 Making their object known to government, they were, in 1794, embodied in a regiment, called The Royal Edinburgh Volunteers. **1801** *Farmer's Mag.* Nov. 418 At his house we met with the poet-laureat of the Inverness volunteers. **1818** MRS. ILIFF *Poems Sev. Occas.* (ed. 2) 23 Our tars shall keep the sea—our coast Be guarded by our volunteers. **1860** DICKENS *Lett.* (1880) II. 115 Every other man..I know..is a volunteer though. **1888** *Encycl. Brit.* XXIV. 295/2 The personal equipment of the volunteers,..as a rule, is deficient for field service.

† **c.** In the phrase *to go* (also *serve*) *a volunteer*.

1650 R. STAPYLTON *Strada's Low C. Wars* I. 24 Octavio Forneze..served a Volunteer against the French. **1685** CROWNE *Sir C. Nice* I, They will go volunteirs into a battle, but must be prest to marriage. **1718** PRIOR *Poems Sev. Occas.* Ded., In the first Dutch War He went a Voluntier under the Duke of York. **1760** *Cautions & Adv. Officers Army* 23 Whilst Suspicions only are against him, there is a possibility of wiping them out, and that is by desiring to go a Voluntier with the Grenadiers the first desperate Attack they are ordered on. **1770** LANGHORNE *Plutarch* (1879) I. 215/2 He endeavoured to prevent the young men who offered to go volunteers from giving in their names. **1870** L'ESTRANGE *Miss Mitford* I. i. 2 He had the resolution to part from what he loved, and to go a volunteer into the army.

† **d.** One voluntarily serving in the Navy. *Obs.*

1706 E. WARD *Wooden World Diss.* (1708) 18 What Discouragement gives not this to right-bred Tars from entering Volunteers. **1708** *Lond. Gaz.* No. 4440/1 The Trumpeters, Quarter-Gunners,..Volunteers by Letter, and Marine-Soldiers. *a* **1720** SEWEL *Hist. Quakers* (1795) I. II. 122 King Charles II. then in exile, asked the Dutch to be received in their navy as a volunteer.

2. *fig.* (With direct allusion to sense 1.) **a.** Of things.

1636 QUARLES *Elegie* Wks. (Grosart) III. 11/2 But stay! what need, what need we presse a teare, When every eye becomes a Volunteire? **1650** FULLER *Pisgah* III. i. 359 More probable it is, that Hirams fancy..was not pressed in all particulars, but was left a volunteire for some descants of

Art. 1715 CHAPPELOW *Right Way to be Rich* (1717) 167 There are abundance of full texts.. which offer themselves as voluntiers in this service. 1733 POPE *Ess. Man* III. 88 Reason.. Cares not for service, or but serves when prest,.. But honest Instinct comes a volunteer. 1733 DUCHESS OF QUEENSBERRY *Let. to Swift* 3 Nov., I.. have not time to think of answering your letters. This is only a volunteer.

b. Of persons.

1650 BAXTER *Saints' R.* III. ii. 295 They wilfully and obstinately persisted in their Rebellion, and were meer Voluntiers in the service of the Devil. 1667 *Decay Chr. Piety* v. ¶25 They have generally gone higher, exhorted men to become voluntiers in vertues warfare. 1671 SHADWELL *Humourists* IV, If it be the Devil, Mr. Parson, we'll turn you loose to him; you take pay to fight against him, we are but voluntiers. 1755 YOUNG *Centaur* ii. Wks. 1757 IV. 150 The clergy are voluntiers; the aged are pressed by nature into the service of wisdom.

3. One who voluntarily offers his services in any capacity; one who of his own free will takes part in any enterprise.

α. 1638 *Penit. Conf.* xi. (1657) 301 He comes in as a voluntier upon his own confession. 1648 GAGE *West Ind.* i. 3 Yearly are sent thither Missions.. either of Voluntiers, Fryers Mendicants, Priests or Monkes, or else of forced Jesuites. 1677 *Auth. Life* in *Cleveland's Gen. Poems* A6b, Perceiving the Ostracism that was intended, he became a Voluntier in his Academick Exile. 1688 PENN in *Life* Wks. 1782 I. 112 Voluntiers are Blanks and Cyphers in all Governments. 1755 *Connoisseur* No. 70 ¶19, I do not know the names of any of the Voluntiers, to whom I have been greatly indebted. 1765 BLACKSTONE *Comm.* I. 257 Such unauthorized voluntiers in violence are not ranked among open enemies.

β. 1655 FULLER *Hist. Cambr.* 104 More probably he was a Volunteer in his Lecture, having no Salary for the reading thereof. 1712 STEELE *Spect.* No. 526 ¶2 Our Hackney-Coachmen.. do still ply as Volunteers Day and Night for the Good of their Country. 1768 TUCKER *Lt. Nat.* (1834) II. 415 There is a multitude of labourers in the vineyard, as well volunteers in dissertations and essays, as retained servants entered upon the steward's roll. 1794 SOUTHEY *Botany Bay Eclogues* ii, Anon the morning came, And off I set a volunteer for fame. 1820 SCORESBY *Acc. Arctic Reg.* II. 50 Another party, likewise consisting of seven volunteers, were landed in Jan Mayen Island. 1833 *Tracts for Times* No. 17. 3 Are they duly authorised and commissioned from the Court; are they come as volunteers, or have they been sent by their master? 1873 MOZLEY *Univ. Serm.* (1876) 168 The peculiar nature of the agency concerned in the Act.. is.. a guarantee to the willingness of the victim.. as being that of a volunteer from the first.

4. A flower or tree which grows spontaneously, (cf. B. 2b); a self-sown plant.

1657 THORNLEY tr. *Longus' Daphnis & Chloe* 172 Flowers,—some the Earth's own Voluntiers, some the structure of the Artist's hand. 1960 *Jrnl. Forestry* LVIII. 402/3 The stand was planted on a 6 × 6-foot spacing, with some interspersed volunteers. 1978 *New Yorker* 3 July 42/1 Around the buildings.. are some of the tallest volunteers in New York, top-heavy plants.

†**5. a.** A deliberate lie. **b.** A voluntary gift.

1678 DRYDEN *Kind Keeper* III. i, Now will he lie three or four rapping Voluntiers, rather than be thought ignorant in any thing. 1757 MRS. GRIFFITH *Lett. Henry & Frances* (1767) I. 154, I think myself vastly obliged to dear Harry for his obliging voluntier.

6. *Law.* One to whom a voluntary conveyance is made; one who benefits by a deed made without valuable consideration.

1744 JACOB *Law Dict.* (ed. 5) s.v. *Voluntary*, Remainders limited in Settlements, to a Man's right Heirs, etc. are deemed Voluntary in Equity, and the Persons claiming under them are called Volunteers. 1818 CRUISE *Digest* (ed. 2) II. 135 There seemed no reason.. why these general incidents.. should be saved in favour of a devisee, or other volunteer, and not in favour of a wife. *Ibid.* IV. 276 Equity will relieve, even in favour of a volunteer.

B. *attrib.* or as *adj.*

1. a. Of troops, etc.: Consisting or composed of persons undertaking military service as volunteers.

1662 *Extr. St. Papers rel. Friends* (1911) II. 158 A Company of 100 Voloncteere Horse which I drew together. 1662 DK. BUCKHM. in *Slingsby's Diary* (1836) 363, I have sent orders.. to get the volontier troopes in as great a readinesse as they can. 1798 HINDERWELL *Hist. Scarborough* 236 A Volunteer Corps of one hundred and eighty, raised in the town. *Ibid.*, Five Companies of Volunteer Infantry. 1811 *Regul. & Orders Army* 5 Officers of Yeomanry Cavalry and Volunteer Corps rank as juniors of their respective Ranks. 1822 *Act 3 Geo. IV*, c. 126 §32 No Toll shall be demanded.. for any Carriage conveying Volunteer Infantry. 1852 SIR C. NAPIER *Def. Eng.* 13 With regard to your volunteer corps, I think each should consist of from one to four companies. 1886 C. E. PASCOE *London of To-day* xviii. (ed. 3) 169 The military spirit of the 'Volunteer' corps of London.

b. Of persons: Voluntarily performing military service; serving as a volunteer in the army (†or navy). Also in predicative use (*b*).

(*a*) 1649 G. DANIEL *Trinarch., Hen. V*, ccxcix, They dance and rore The expectation of a Muster; where they 'nroule themselves, Gentlemen volunteire. 1653 URQUHART *Rabelais* I. xlvii, Nine thousand dragoons and a hundred and fourty thousand voluntier adventurers. 1698 T. FROGER (*title*), A Relation of a Voyage made.. by the Sieur Froger, Voluntier-Engineer on board the English Falcon. 1710–11 SWIFT *Lett.* (1767) III. 127, I doubt the scoundrel was broke, and got a commission, or perhaps is a voluntier gentleman. 1782 V. KNOX *Ess.* cxxxi. (1819) III. 64 Compare the limbs of the volunteer soldiers in the metropolis with those of the rustic militia, or regulars.

(*b*) 1722 DE FOE *Col. Jack* xiv, I was not only insensibly drawn in, but was perfectly volunteer in that dull cause. 1724 —— *Gt. Law Subordination* 145 You will blame the gentleman, perhaps, for engaging thus voluntier with his servant. 1728 —— *Compl. Eng. Gent.* (1890) 14 The modern Lord was a Man of Spirit, had serv'd Voluntier under the Fountain of Glory Gustavus Adolphus. 1744 M. BISHOP *Life & Adv.* 57 There is a wide Difference between being press'd and going Voluntier.

c. Of or pertaining to a volunteer or volunteers.

1724 DE FOE *Mem. Cavalier* (1840) 136 Indeed it will be a volunteer war, said the king, for the northern gentry have sent me an account of above four thousand horse they have already. 1779 SHERIDAN *Critic* I. i, If you had the least spirit you would have been.. trailing a volunteer pike in the Artillery ground. 1837 ALISON *Hist. Europe* (1847) VI. 118 This was the Volunteer system and the general arming of the people.

d. *Volunteer State*, a nickname for Tennessee (see quot. 1950).

1853 J. C. M. RAMSEY *Ann. Tennessee* 116 Thus early did the 'Volunteer State' commence its novitiate in arms. 1950 *Newsweek* 20 Mar. 96/2 A call for 2,800 volunteers [in the Mexican War of 1847] in Tennessee brought out 30,000 men and gave Tennessee its nickname, 'The Volunteer State'. 1973 *Guardian* 14 June 13/2 There was a spectacular .. murder deep in the hills of Tennessee.. as could only happen in the deepest by-ways of the Volunteer State.

2. a. Voluntarily performing any action or service; undertaking a service of one's own free will.

The predicative use (quot. 1727) is freq. in De Foe's works.

1661 BOYLE *Style of Script.* 195 He is such a Volunteer Sinner, that he hath neither the Wit nor the Excuse of declining his Conscience in Complement to his Senses. 1727 DE FOE *Hist. Apparit.* Introd. 7 It was a most incongruous Suggestion that the devil should come Voluntier to an Atheist. 1759 DILWORTH *Pope* 71 It was natural for them to be the volunteer-heralds of the expedition which translation's merit they had some share in bringing to perfection. 1762–71 H. WALPOLE *Vertue's Anecd. Paint.* (1786) III. 179 Probably a volunteer artist. 1812 H. & J. SMITH *Horace in Lond.* 125 How many a volunteer muse.. Has met with her death in reviews. 1858 J. MARTINEAU *Stud. Chr.* 249 James and John and Peter, who never heartily recognized the Volunteer Apostle.

transf. 1713 STEELE *Englishm.* No. 55. 353 There were many hundreds of Volunteer Links brought into this Protestant Illumination.

b. Of vegetation: Growing spontaneously.

1794 VANCOUVER *Agric. Cambridge* 44 A remarkably fine growth of volunteer ash, has lately been cut down. 1882 *Contemp. Rev.* Aug. 233 They had the year before last 80 acres of volunteer or self-sown oats. 1883 *Century Mag.* Oct. 804/1 Crops are raised sometimes for twenty successive years, on the same fields, without the soils showing exhaustion, and what are called volunteer crops.

3. Of services, actions, etc.: Rendered or performed voluntarily.

1724 DE FOE *Mem. Cavalier* (1840) 55 The king desires no man's service but what is purely volunteer. 1779 BURKE *Corr.* (1844) II. 284, I am not very fond of any volunteer modes of raising money for public service. 1794 MATHIAS *Purs. Lit.* (1798) 252 Mr. Reeves will deter any man from volunteer effusions in favour of any Minister. 1873 MOZLEY *Univ. Serm.* viii. (1876) 167 It cannot be said that it is.. contrary to justice to accept a volunteer offer of suffering.

volun'teer, *v.* [Back-formation from VOLUNTEERING *vbl. sb.*]

1. a. *intr.* To undertake military service voluntarily, esp. on a special occasion. Freq. const. *for*.

1755 JOHNSON, *To volunteer*, to go for a soldier. 1802 JAMES *Milit. Dict.* s.v., In some instances soldiers volunteer for a limited period, and within certain boundaries. 1849 EASTWICK *Dry Leaves* 163 The Bengáli sipáhis.. being asked, 'Do you volunteer?' replied, 'Yes, Saheb, we volunteer, but we don't go willingly'. 1859 THACKERAY *Virginians* lxii, Sir John had volunteered for the expedition which is preparing. 1874 STUBBS *Const. Hist.* I. ii. 15 They volunteered and were bound by honour to their leaders.

b. Const. *to* with inf. (esp. *to serve*).

1802 JAMES *Milit. Dict.* s.v., The drafts from the militia in 1798, who volunteered to serve in Europe only. 1849 MACAULAY *Hist. Eng.* iii. I. 301 John Sheffield, Earl of Mulgrave,.. volunteered to serve at sea against the Dutch.

c. Const. *into* (a particular regiment).

1841 E. COSTELLO *Adv. Soldier* i, At Londonderry.. I volunteered into the 95th, since made the 'Rifle Brigade'.

2. a. To offer of one's own accord *to* do something.

1840 HOOD *Up Rhine* 192 Our old acquaintance volunteering to be our guide, we made the round of the sights of the town. 1860 TYNDALL *Glac.* II. xi. 292 My guide volunteered to cut the steps for me up to the pickets. 1881 FROUDE *Short Stud.* (1883) IV. II. ii. 180 No dean or tutor ever volunteered to help our inexperience.

b. To be thrown from a horse without sufficient cause. (Cf. VOLUNTARY *sb.* 7.)

1890 *Field* 8 Feb. 177 There is scarcely a horseman of experience who will not confess to have been at some time or other taken unawares, and to have 'volunteered' in consequence.

3. a. *trans.* To offer (one's services) for some special purpose or enterprise.

1800 *Med. Jrnl.* IV. 127 When I first volunteered my services on this important subject. 1820 SCORESBY *Acc. Arctic Reg.* II. 49 Seven men volunteered their services. 1857 DICKENS *Dorrit* I. vi, Mrs. Bangham.. had volunteered her services as.. general attendant.

b. With vbl. sb. as object, or *refl.*

1806 SCOTT *Let.* in *Lockhart* (1837) II. iii. 94 One of the kindest was Lord Somerville, who volunteered introducing me to Lord Spencer. 1825 T. HOOK *Sayings* Ser. II. *Passion & Princ.* xii. III. 270 He.. gravely volunteered himself as silk-holder, while Miss Harriet.. wound off, I know not how many skeins.

4. To offer to undertake or perform (something).

1818 SCOTT *Hrt. Midl.* vi, Mr. Lindsay.. volunteered the perilous task of carrying a verbal message. 1863 COWDEN CLARKE *Shaks. Char.* x. 271 One of the soldiers volunteers the office of interpreter. 1876 MISS YONGE *Womankind* vi, I had rather make Latin the schoolroom lesson, and leave German to be volunteered afterwards.

5. To communicate (information, etc.) on one's own initiative.

1805 JANE AUSTEN *Let.* 27 Aug. (1952) 166 She volunteers, moreover, her love to little Marianne, with the promise of bringing her a doll. 1813 —— *Let.* 14 Oct. (1952) 354, I talk to Cassy about Chawton; she remembers much but does not volunteer on the subject. 1839 DICKENS *Nickleby* vii, He had grown thoughtful and appeared in nowise disposed to volunteer any observation. 1841 MRS. MOZLEY *Lost Brooch* II. xiii. 99 This was what I call forward in a servant, to volunteer explanations. 1860 W. COLLINS *Wom. White* III. xi. (1861) 411, I did not feel called on to volunteer any statement of my own private convictions. 1866 GEO. ELIOT *F. Holt* ii, He volunteered no information about himself and his past life at Smyrna.

ellipt. 1893 H. CRACKANTHORPE *Wreckage* 178 When he started out late at night, he never volunteered where he was going.

6. To offer to give or supply. Also *fig.*

1814 JANE AUSTEN *Mansfield Park* II. ix. 200 Thursday.. opened with more kindness to Fanny than such.. unmanageable days often volunteer. 1873 TRISTRAM *Moab* i. 6 A delegate of the Ta'amirah.. volunteered a guard of his tribe.

7. With *away*: To surrender voluntarily.

1807 JEFFERSON *Writ.* (1830) IV. 82, I.. do not wish to volunteer away that portion of tranquillity, which a firm execution of my duties will permit me to enjoy.

Hence **volun'teered, volun'teering** *ppl. adjs.*

1797 J. SYMONDS in *A. Young's Autobiog.* xii. (1898) 304 You justly reprobate volunteering infantry. 1845 *Times* 1 Nov. 4/4 The members of the press retired.. from the hall, into which they had been invited by the volunteered cards of admission from the benchers. 1864 MEREDITH *Sandra Belloni* xiv, In the end they deputed the volunteering Adela to sit with him in the library. 1879 GEO. ELIOT *Theophrastus Such* i. 7 The fellow-feeling which should restrain us from turning our volunteered and picked confessions into an act of accusation against others. 1886 *Encycl. Brit.* XXI. 791 With Godwin Shelley had opened a volunteered correspondence late in 1811. 1903 MORLEY *Gladstone* II. v. ii. 20 He was not forbidden to proceed upon his volunteered mission.

volun'teering, *vbl. sb.* [f. VOLUNTEER *sb.* and *v.*] The action of serving, or offering one's services, as a volunteer.

1691 DRYDEN *K. Arthur* Prol. 47 If you Gallants lose, to all appearing You'll want an Equipage for Volunteering. 1706–7 FARQUHAR *Beaux' Strat.* I. i, I warrant you, our Friends imagine that we are gone a volunteering. 1758 H. WALPOLE *Corr.* (1837) I. 381 Has he stolen to Southampton and slipped away a-volunteering.. to conquer France in a dirty shirt and a frock? 1789 MRS. PIOZZI *Journ. France* I. 199 Numbers of young nobility were willing to run a-volunteering in her defence. 1805 W. TAYLOR in *Ann. Rev.* III. 316 We encourage volunteering to prevent enlisting. 1840 DICKENS *Barn. Rudge* xli, How strange it is of you to run down volunteering, when it's done to defend you.. in case of need. 1858 *Merc. Marine Mag.* V. 112 The law permitting the volunteering from the merchant ship to a ship of war should be altered.

volun'teerism. [f. VOLUNTEER *sb.* + -ISM.]

1. The system of having volunteer military forces.

1844 P. HARWOOD *Hist. Irish Reb. 1798* 26 The effects of volunteerism on national morals and manners.

2. *N. Amer.* The use of volunteer labour, esp. in the social services. Cf. VOLUNTARISM 3b, VOLUNTARYISM 2.

1977 *New Yorker* 1 Aug. 48/2 Still another productivity proposal is that as the city work force shrinks, volunteerism should be encouraged; citizen volunteers could serve as auxiliary policemen, park attendants, case-workers, and school aides, for instance. 1979 *Globe & Mail* (Toronto) 28 May S14 A closer examination of voluntary action or 'volunteerism' as it relates to volunteer support staffs in amateur sport. 1983 *United Airlines Mag.* June 48 Minnesota's Corporate Volunteerism Council, a clearinghouse designed to help match community needs with people willing and able to give some time to others.

†**volun'teerly,** *adv. Obs.*$^{-1}$ [f. as prec. + -LY^2.] As a volunteer.

1715 *Battle of Sheriffmuir* iii. in *Jacobite Songs* (1871) 30 Volunteerly to ramble With Lord Loudoun Campbell.

volun'teership. [f. as prec. + -SHIP.] The condition of being a volunteer.

1796 A. BELL in Southey *Life* (1844) I. 527 His brother Verry has served me from his earliest volunteership.

voluntive, *a. rare*$^{-1}$. [Cf. next and -IVE.] Volitional.

1832 J. THOMSON *Life W. Cullen* I. 170 Comprehending the vegetative, sentient, and voluntive faculties of the mind .. under the common term Soul.

,volunto-'motory, *a. Biol.* [Cf. next and MOTORY *a.*] Associated with voluntary motion.

1878 *Encycl. Brit.* VIII. 167/2 The outer division [of the middle layer of the blastoderm], the *volunto-motory*, corresponding to the body-wall or somatopleure of more recent authors.

†**volunty.** *Obs.* Forms: *α.* 4–6 volunte (5 -ee), 6 wolunte, volounte; 5 voluntie, 6–7 volunty. *β.* 5–6 volente (5 uol-, voulente), volante, 6 volenty. [a. OF. *volonte* (*voulonte*, *-unte*), *volente* (mod.F.

volonté = It. *voluntà*, Sp. *voluntad*, Pg. *vontade*), ad. L. *voluntāt-*, *voluntas* will, f. *vol-*, *velle* to will.] Will, desire, pleasure; that which one wishes or desires.

Rarely, the faculty of willing, volition.

α. *c* **1330** *Arth. & Merl.* 681 (Kölbing), A forseyd deuel liȝt adoun & of þat wiif made a couioun, To don alle his volunte. *c* **1400** *Rom. Rose* 5276 For that he May not fulfille his volunte Fully, as he hath requered. *c* **1449** Pecock *Repr.* II. xi. 210 That this answere is a feyned and forgid thing bi pure volunte withoute eny for him sufficient evidence, Y proue thus. **1490** Caxton *Eneydos* iv. 19 O cursid and false deceyuable auaryce whiche blyndeth the voluntees humayn. *c* **1525** *Doctr. Gd. Servaunts* (Percy Soc.) 7 Seruauntes ought not to ensue Theyr owne wyll nor volunte. **1649** Evelyn tr. *Le Vayer's Lib. & Servit.* Misc. Writ. (1825) ii. 11 Our volunty cannot (after some sort) embrace the evill, considering it as evill. **1652** —— *St. France* 15 The handsomer to disguise and apparell these his volunties, and render them at the least specious proceedures of Justice.

β. **1418–20** J. Page *Siege Rouen* in *Archaeologia* XXI. 48 Byfore Rone that reche cyte Fore that he lovyde as hys own volante. *c* **1450** *Merlin* i. 22 Neuer shall I make the do thynge that shal be ageyn the volente of oure lord Ihesu Cryste. *c* **1477** Caxton *Jason* 134 But as sone as I was leyd in my bedd an euill volente or wil surprised me. **1518** H. Watson *Hist. Oliver of Castile* (Roxb.) E 4 b, The knyght..sayd that al his volente was for to go there as he had specyfyed. **1525** Ld. Berners *Froiss.* II. xliv. 143 Syth it is your pleasure and volante yt I shall pursewe my wordes, I shall shewe you euery thynge as I knowe.

b. In the phrases *of* (*free*) *volunty*, *of* or *at one's* (*own*) *volunty*.

(*a*) *c* **1402** Lydg. *Compl. Bl. Knt.* 299 The whiche..Of volunte, withoute more trespas, Myn accusurs hath taken vnto grace. **1426** —— *De Guil. Pilgr.* 23031 The space of xxxix yere I was bound of volunte, to obedience. *c* **1430** —— *Min. Poems* (Percy Soc.) 79 The kyng..That..Into a virgyns wombe immaculate, Descendid..of fre volunte.

(*b*) *c* **1407** Lydg. *Reson & Sens.* 4453 Thow sholdest chese here tabyde..Of thin ovne volunte, Syth thou hast swich lyberte. **1459** *Rolls of Parlt.* V. 347/1 This that I here have promitted and sworn, procedeth of myne owne desire and fre volunte. *c* **1485** *Digby Myst.* (1882) III. 3 Of my most hyest and mytyest wolunte, I woll it be knowyn to al þe word vnyversal. **1508** Fisher 7 *Penit. Ps.* cxxx. Wks. (1876) 230 Almyghty god of his owne voluntary wyll and gracyous volunty..redemed vs. **1533** Bellenden *Livy* III. xii. (S.T.S.) I. 295 Þis Iulius, of his fre volunte & benevolence, remittit certane thingis to þe Iugement of pepill.

(*c*) **1426** Lydg. *De Guil. Pilgr.* 20335 Bothe to shette and ek vnclose And as hym lyst, for to dyspose At ther owne volunte. *c* **1450** *Merlin* iii. 58 They shall neuer haue power over me at her volunte. **1461** *Rolls of Parlt.* V. 492/1 The same Letteres Patentes..to endure and be of force..at our pleasure and voluntie.

†volupe. *Obs.*⁻¹ [app. a. L. *volup* with pleasure; but perh. a misprint for *volupt*.] = volupt.

1669 *Address Yng. Gentry Eng.* 38 It becomes manna to all the guests by yielding the tast he put upon it, and he may easily be understood to have the volupe of his palat extended in all theirs.

†voluper. *Obs.* Forms: 4–5 voluper(e, 5 -peer, 6 veluper; 5 voly-, volipere, voly-, wolyper, wulpere. [a. AF. *volupier* (Gower), f. OF. *voluper* (*voleper*, *veloper*, etc.), to wrap up: see envelop *v.* OF. *envelopeur* occurs (in 1361) in a similar sense.] A form of head-dress worn especially by women; a kerchief.

c **1386** Chaucer *Miller's T.* 55 The tapes of her white voluper Were of the same suyte of hir coler. —— *Reeve's T.* 383 Whan she gan the white thyng espye, She wende the clerk hadde wered a volupeer. **14..** *Voc.* in Wr.-Wülcker 569 *Calamandrum*, a volupere. *c* **1440** *Promp. Parv.* 512/1 Volypere, kerche, *teristrum, caliendrum*. *c* **1475** *Pict. Voc.* in Wr.-Wülcker 776/27 *Hoc caliandrum*, a wulpere. **1483** *Cath. Angl.* 404/1 A volyper, *caliendum*. **1552** in *Rep. MSS. Ld. Middleton* (1911) 404 For a hede lace and veluper for Mris. Margarett..xij d.

†volupt. *Obs. rare.* [ad. OF. *volupte* or L. *voluptas*: see volupty.] Pleasure. Also *attrib.*, sensuous.

14.. *Trevisa's Barth. De P.R.* v. xxxix. (Bodl. MS.), In þe lyuour is þe place of volupt. **1582** *Ibid.* VIII. xxvi. 131/1 In mans body he disposeth to fairenesse, volupt and lyking. **1585** T. Washington tr. *Nicholay's Voy.* II. xxi. 59 [They frequent the baths] aswel for their volupt pleasure as bodily health. *c* **1590** J. Stewart *Poems* (S.T.S.) II. 205 It is the bontie of ane mychtie spreit, Vith monie guidlie qualiteis repleit In vincusing voluptis ewell and vaine.

†voluptable, *a.* *Obs.*⁻⁰ [ad. L. (ante-classical and late) *voluptābilis*, f. *voluptas* volupty.] (See quots.) Hence **voluptableness**.

1623 Cockeram I, *Voluptable*, which brings pleasure. **1656** Blount *Glossogr.*, *Voluptable*, which brings pleasure, pleasurable, that causeth delight. **1727** Bailey (vol. II), *Voluptableness*, Delightfulness.

†voluptary. *Obs.*⁻¹ [ad. L. *voluptāri-us*, f. *voluptas* pleasure.] = voluptuary *sb.*

1599 B. Jonson *Cynthia's Rev.* v. iv, *Hed.* An excellent confection. *Cri.* And most worthie a true voluptarie.

‖**volupté** (vɔlypte). [Fr.: see volupty.] = voluptuousness.

1712 M. W. Montagu *Let.* 12 Aug. (1965) I. 155 All things would have contributed to make your Life passe in (the true volupté) a smooth Tranquillity. **1937** L. Bromfield *Rains Came* III. xxxvi. 435 The lingam, symbol of creation, of *volupté* and strange desires and pleasures. **1962** W. Nowottny *Lang. Poets Use* viii. 216 The elements of *volupté* and masochism in a fervent devotional tradition. **1981** *Times Lit. Suppl.* 13 Feb. 158/3 The narrative's need to shock, its dedicated oscillatings between *volupté* and vomit, are adolescent.

volupte(e, variants of volupty.

†volupteous, *a.* *Obs.* Also -ious. [Alteration of voluptuous *a.*, probably after *volupte(e* volupty.] Voluptuous.

1513 More *Rich. III* (1883) 70 He set his volupteous pleasure before his honor. **1562** T. Wilson *Rhet.* 37 b, The vnstedfastnes..and wickednes of volupteous desire. **1596** Dalrymple tr. *Leslie's Hist. Scot.* I. 242 False hartednes, volupteous litherie, and al kynd of Viciousness.

Hence **†volupteousness.** *Obs.*

1526 Tindale *Jas.* iv. 3 Youre volupteousnes that rayneth in youre members. *a* **1548** Hall *Chron., Edw. V*, 3 b, A private mannes fantesy or volupteousnesse. **1559** W. Cunningham *Cosmogr. Glasse* 82 There be some that suppose..Paradise, to be situated vnder th' Equinoctiall, as a place of pleasure, voluptiousnes, voide of Alteration, and contrary qualities. **1596** Dalrymple tr. *Leslie's Hist. Scot.* II. 91 To satisfie the volupteousnes of the ryche.

†voluptibility. *Obs. rare.* [Cf. voluptable *a.*] Voluptuousness.

1631 J. Done *Polydoron* 28 The Stoickes and Pharises [held] that by voluptibility [*printed* -tillity] heere, wee lost the future ioyes of the other life. **1633** —— *Hist. Septuagint* 129 To the end that perseuering in that manner, you shall..shewe your selfe inuiolable against all Voluptibilities.

voluptie, variant of volupty *Obs.*

volup'tific, *a.* *rare*⁻⁰. [ad. late L. *voluptificus*.] 'Making pleasure or delight' (Bailey, 1721).

voluptu'arian, *sb.* or *a.* [f. next + -ian.] = next.

1879 *Tinsley's Mag.* XXIV. 53 The feeblest and least reputable of his brothers, the voluptuarian Joseph.

voluptuary (vəˈlʌptjuːərɪ), *sb.* and *a.* [ad. L. *voluptuārius*, post-classical form of *voluptārius* voluptary, f. *voluptas* pleasure, volupty. Cf. F. *voluptuaire* adj.]

A. *sb.* One who is addicted to sensuous pleasures; one who is given up to indulgence in luxury or the gratification of the senses; a sybarite.

a **1610** Healey *Cebes* (1636) 126 Here are professed voluptuaries also. **1647** R. Stapylton *Juvenal* 13 His very name signifies a favourer of learning, and (as it appeares by this allusion) it may likewise signifie a voluptuary. **1668** Bp. Hopkins *Serm., Vanity* (1685) 47 The most artificial voluptuaries have always allowed themselves an intermission in their pleasures, to recruit nature, and sharpen their sensual desires. *a* **1734** North *Lives* (1826) I. 314 He was a great voluptuary, and companion of the high court rakes. **1776** Gibbon *Decl. & F.* vi. I. 149 A rational voluptuary adheres with invariable respect to the temperate dictates of nature. **1819** Scott *Ivanhoe* xxix, The admiration which her charms excited, when accident threw her into the power of that unprincipled voluptuary. **1840** Carlyle *Heroes* ii. (1858) 238 We shall err widely if we consider this man as a common voluptuary, intent mainly on base enjoyments. **1869** McLaren *Serm.* Ser. II. vii. 126 Remember that this cruel voluptuary is the sweet singer of Israel.

transf. **1852** Mrs. Stowe *Uncle Tom's C.* xv. 138 St. Clare, who was in his heart a poetical voluptuary, smiled as Miss Ophelia made her remark on his premises.

B. *adj.* Of, pertaining to, characterized by, sensuous or luxurious pleasures.

1605 Bacon *Adv. Learn.* II. x. §13 The Arts which florish ..while vertue is in declination, are voluptuarie:..with Arts voluptuarie, I couple practises Iocularie. **1609** Holland *Amm. Marcell.* E 3 b, Leading a wanton and voluptuary life. **1662** Hibbert *Body Divinity* I. 308 Art is twofold, of 1. Body. 2. Soul. Either 1. Cosmetick,..2. Medicinal,..3. Athletick,..4. Voluptuary. **1779** Johnson *L.P., King* ¶8 He did not love..any kind of business which interrupted his voluptuary dreams.

vo'luptuate, *v.* *rare.* [f. voluptu-ous *a.*]

1. *trans.* To make luxurious and pleasant.

1661 Feltham *Resolves* II. xliv. 270 'Tis watching and labour, that voluptuates repose and sleep.

2. *intr.* To delight voluptuously; to luxuriate.

1836 *New Monthly Mag.* XLVII. 143 The eye voluptuates, if I may coin a word, on peach, and almond, and orange blossoms.

vo'luptuize, *v.* *rare*⁻¹. [Cf. prec. and -ize.] *intr.* = prec. 2.

1831 Trelawny *Adv. Younger Son* II. 136 If you would voluptuize in the full luxuriance of its perfect flavour.

voluptuosity (vəˌlʌptjuːˈɒsɪtɪ). Now *rare* or *Obs.* Forms: 4–6 voluptuosite (5 -itee, 5–6 -yte, 6 -ytee), 5–6 voluptuositie (5 -itye), 7– voluptuosity. [a. OF. *voluptuosité* (= Sp. *voluptuosidad*, Pg. *-idade*), or ad. med.L. *voluptuōsitas*, f. L. *voluptuōs-us*: see next.] The quality or state of being voluptuous; voluptuousness.

a **1380** *St. Augustine* 741 in Horstm. *Altengl. Leg.* (1878) 74 But þat paas is voluptuosite. **1390** Gower *Conf.* III. 280 Thurgh sotie and thurgh nycete, Of his voluptuosite He spareth no condicion Of ken ne yit religion. **1432–50** tr. *Higden* (Rolls) III. 349 Thei scholde not ȝiffe theire myndes to voluptuosite, but to theire doctrine. *c* **1440** *Alph. Tales* 99 Epicurus,..if all he was a sewer of voluptuosite,..neuer-þe-les he..said, þat appyls & oþer vile meatis sulde be vsid. **1483** Caxton *Cato* I ij, Thou oughtest to flee dronkeship, and lechery and al her voluptuosites. **1515** Barclay *Egloges* ii. (1570) B iv/2 Voluptuositie Will haue of dishes chaunge & diwersitie. *c* **1520** —— *Jugurth* (1557) 44 This discorde and takyng of parties bytwene them..began amonge them..by superfluous habundance of richesse, voluptuosite, and of other worldely delectations. *a* **1678** Woodhead *Holy Living* (1688) 113 The same action, that now is lawful, if continued, presently becomes unlawful (as..particular affection, into concupiscence; recreations, into voluptuosity).

voluptuous (vəˈlʌptjuːəs), *a.* Also 5 voluptuouse, -tuose, *Sc.* woluptous. [ad. OF. (also mod.F.) *voluptueux*, *-euse* (= Sp. and Pg. *voluptuoso*, It. *voluttuoso*), or L. *voluptuōsus* (Pliny, etc.), f. *voluptas* pleasure, volupty. Cf. volupteous *a.*]

1. Of or pertaining to, derived from, resting in, characterized by, gratification of the senses, esp. in a refined or luxurious manner; marked by indulgence in sensual pleasures; luxuriously sensuous:

a. Of desires or appetites.

c **1374** Chaucer *Troylus* IV. 1573 Love ne drof yow nought to don this dede, But lust voluptuous, and cowarde drede. *c* **1407** Lydg. *Reson & Sens.* 4714 To soiourne in the Erbere ..Oonly ordeyned for delyte And voluptuouse appetyte. **1491** Caxton *Vitas Patr.* (W. de W. 1495) I. i. 5/1 This techith us our sauyour for to kepe us from voluptuous desyres. **1526** *Pilgr. Perf.* (W. de W. 1531) 82 b, Abstynence from the carnall voluptuous appetyte of the flesshe. *c* **1540** in Prance *Addit. Narr. Pop. Plot* (1679) 36 The supporters of our voluptuose and Carnal Appetite. **1697** South *Serm.* I. 32 God..has corrected the Boundlessness of his Voluptuous desires, by stinting his strengths, and contracting his Capacities. **1796** Morse *Amer. Geog.* II. 546 [Dancing girls, who] communicate, by a natural contagion, the most voluptuous desires to the beholders.

b. Of pleasure or pleasurable sensations.

c **1407** Lydg. *Reson & Sens.* 2022 Venus..goddesse is of al plesaunce, Of lust, and fleshly appetyte, And of voluptuous delyte. **1603** Knolles *Hist. Turks* (1638) 242 Solyman..lay in great securitie,..passing his time in all voluptuous pleasure. **1663** S. Patrick *Parab. Pilgr.* xiv, Because I believe you are desirous to know, how they receive and take in those voluptuous enjoyments. **1756** Burke *Subl. & B.* I. v, That smooth and voluptuous satisfaction which the assured prospect of pleasure bestows. **1820** Shelley *Prometh. Unb.* I. 426 If thou might'st dwell among the Gods the while Lapped in voluptuous joy? **1869** J. Phillips *Vesuv.* i. 10 The long voluptuous dream came to a startling end. **1888** *Buck's Handbk. Med. Sci.* VI. 397/2 Excessive voluptuous sensations may be the result of peripheral or central causes.

transf. **1614** Donne *Lett.* (1651) 173 Out of a voluptuous loathnesse to let that taste go out of my mouth. **1815** Shelley *Alastor* 11 Spring's voluptuous pantings when she breathes Her first sweet kisses, have been dear to me.

c. Of modes of life or conduct.

1432–50 tr. *Higden* (Rolls) VI. 79 The luffe of the cuntre and elegancy voluptuous deceyvide his grevous labors. **1553** Brende *Q. Curtius* x. 209 Hauing in these and suche other like voluptuous vanities consumed a great part of the treasure. *a* **1578** Lindesay (Pitscottie) *Chron. Scot.* (S.T.S.) I. 82 They subornit him quyitlie to dissobedience,..for by it they thocht they had ane woluptous lyfe. **1582** Bible (Genev.) *2nd Alph. Direct., Voluptuous* liuing, one of the thornes that choke the worde. **1600** Holland *Livy* XXXVI. ii. 925 The very souldiours were let loose and given over to take voluptuous waies. **1634** W. Tirwhyt tr. *Balzac's Lett.* 211 He as easily surmounteth all his voluptuous irregularities, as he doth his most violent revels. **1685** Otway *Windsor Castle* 124 The Priests who humble Temp'rance should profess, Sought silken Robes and fat voluptuous Ease. *a* **1734** North *Lives* (1826) II. 95 By his voluptuous unthinking course of life he ran in debt. **1809** W. Irving *Knickerb.* (1861) 75 The gallant warrior starts from soft repose, from golden visions, and voluptuous ease. **1817** Shelley *Constantia* iv, The breath of summer night, Which..suspends my soul in its voluptuous flight. **1838** Thirlwall *Greece* xxxviii. V. 29 A man of voluptuous habits, who desired power as an instrument of sensual indulgence.

d. Of fare or feasting.

1544 *Exhort.* in *Priv. Prayers* (1851) 569 Wholesome abstinence..from all delicious living in voluptuous fare. **1585** Lupton *Thous. Notable Th.* (1675) 77 Cleopatra, the last Queen of Egypt,..did drink one so voluptuous a draught as never any did before. **1638** Penkethman *Artach.* K 3 Excessive consumption and abuse of Wheat and other Victuals in voluptuous Feasts. **1727** [Dorrington] *Philip Quarll* (1816) 14 These provisions being somewhat too voluptuous for an hermit. **1759** B. Martin *Nat. Hist.* I. 78 The most voluptuous Part of Cookery. **1796** Morse *Amer. Geog.* II. 589 That dissolving jelly which is so voluptuous a rarity at European tables.

e. Of places.

1687 A. Lovell tr. *Thevenot's Trav.* I. 39 They tell a thousand other Fopperies of this voluptuous Paradise. **1820** Shelley *Prometh. Unb.* I. 171 Foodless toads Within voluptuous chambers panting crawled. **1832** W. Irving *Alhambra* I. 4 A soft southern region, decked out with all the luxuriant charms of voluptuous Italy. **1839** Thirlwall *Greece* l. VI. 227 The army was permitted to revel for some time in the enjoyments which the most splendid and voluptuous of Eastern cities offered in profusion.

2. Addicted to sensual pleasure or the gratification of the senses; inclined to ease and luxury; fond of elegant or sumptuous living.

c **1440** *Gesta Rom.* xviii. 333 (Add. MS.), The voluptuous flessh, that bereth the fire of glotonye and lechery. **1577** tr. *Bullinger's Decades* (1592) 20 Voluptuous and daintie louers of this world..doo without any fruite at al heare Gods worde. **1594** T. B. *La Primaud. Fr. Acad.* II. 121 Our Lord Iesus Christ himselfe, who was neither nice nor voluptuous. **1612** T. Taylor *Comm. Titus* ii. 12 The voluptuous person, is a louer of his pleasure more then of God. **1638** Sir T. Herbert *Trav.* (ed. 2) 240 The poore are not so voluptuous: they content themselves with drie ryce, herbs, roots. **1670** Clarendon *Ess.* Tracts (1727) 166 The lustful and voluptuous Person, who sacrifices the Strength and Vigour of his Body to the Rage and Temptation of his Blood. *a* **1734**

NORTH *Lives* (1826) II. 411 The bey was a merry fellow, and, like other voluptuous Turks, had his buffoons to divert him. **1783** JOHNSON *Lett.* (1788) II. 298 A friend of mine, who courted a lady of whom he did not know much, was advised to see her eat, and if she was voluptuous at table, to forsake her. **1838** THIRLWALL *Greece* II. 172 The voluptuous and unwarlike people were protected by impregnable walls. **1848** LYTTON *Harold* I. i, A large building that once had belonged to some voluptuous Roman.

absol. *a* **1680** BUTLER *Characters* (1908) 266 The voluptuous is very hard to be pleas'd. **1682** BURNET *Rights Princes* v. 160 As if it had been the Rich and Voluptuous, and not the Poor and the Hungry. **1762** *Charac.* in *Ann. Reg.* 13 His high relish of social enjoyment soon brought him into request with the voluptuous of all ranks. **1802** *Gentl. Mag.* Jan. 3/1 To the.. Splenetic—the Voluptuous—the Petulant—and the Proud.

transf. *a* **1822** SHELLEY *Calderon* III. 56 And, voluptuous Vine, O thou Who seekest most when least pursuing.

3. Imparting a sense of delicious pleasure; suggestive of sensuous pleasures, esp. of a refined or luxurious kind.

1816 BYRON *Ch. Har.* III. xxi, And when Music arose with its voluptuous swell, Soft eyes look'd love to eyes which spake again. **1820** HAZLITT *Lect. Dram. Lit.* 71 The poet succeeds less in the voluptuous and effeminate descriptions. **1844** LEVER *T. Burke* xli. 307 The seigneur.. had.. mixed in the voluptuous fascinations of the period. **1877** DOWDEN *Shaks. Primer* vi. 87 The voluptuous moonlit nights are only like a softer day.

b. Suggestive of sensuous pleasure by fulness and beauty of form.

1839 HALLAM *Hist. Lit.* (1847) II. 101 We recognise his spirit in the sylvan shades and voluptuous forms of Albano and Domenichino. **1841** MACAULAY *Ess., Hastings* (1851) 649 There appeared the voluptuous charms of her to whom the heir of the throne had in secret plighted his faith. **1875** JOWETT *Plato* (ed. 2) III. 144 The voluptuous image of a Corinthian courtezan. **1891** FARRAR *Darkn. & Dawn* xxvi, She was now twenty-six, but had lost none of her voluptuous loveliness.

transf. **1852** TENNYSON *Ode Wellington* 208 He shall find the stubborn thistle bursting Into glossy purples, which outredden All voluptuous garden-roses.

vo'luptuously, *adv.* [f. prec. + -LY².] In a voluptuous manner; so as to gratify or indulge the senses; luxuriously; sensually.

1387-8 T. USK *Test. Love* II. x. (Skeat) l. 18 Heritykes, sayn they, chosen lyf bestial, that voluptuously liven. **1549** LATIMER *4th Serm. bef. Edw. VI* (Arb.) 128 To eate and drincke in the forgetfulnes of goddes commaundement, voluptuously, in excesse and glotonnie. **1602** FULBECKE *Pandects* 78 The people of Sodom and Gomorra voluptuously mingling themselues with the women of the Moabites. *a* **1639** W. WHATELEY *Prototypes* II. xxvi. (1640) 21 It is a sin to live voluptuously, to have none other calling but pastimes and vaine sports. **1670** MILTON *Hist. Eng.* v. 212 Alfred enjoying three years of peace, by him spent, as his manner was, not idlely or voluptuously, but in all vertuous emploiments. **1749** FIELDING *Tom Jones* XIII. vi, The Hopes of seeing Sophia at the Masquerade, on which.. he had voluptuously feasted during the whole Day. **1786** tr. *Beckford's Vathek* 82 Vathek (voluptuously reposed in his capacious litter upon cushions of silk..) was soundly asleep. **1805** WORDSW. *Prelude* I. 251 Ah! better far than this, to stray about Voluptuously through fields and rural walks. **1857** DICKENS *Dorrit* I. xx, She.. composed herself voluptuously, in a nest of crimson and gold cushions, on an ottoman. **1891** FARRAR *Darkn. & Dawn* xlv, The cool, well-shaded, voluptuously-furnished room.

vo'luptuousness. Also 7 voluptousnes, -tusnesse. [f. as prec. + -NESS.] The quality of being voluptuous.

1. Addiction to sensuous pleasures; indulgence in pleasure and luxury.

1508 FISHER *7 Penit. Ps.* vi. Wks. (1876) 11 Our prophete.. ferynge to offende almyghty god, syth that afore tyme he was ouercomen by his owne voluptuousnesse. **1531** TINDALE *Expos. 1 John* (1537) 48 Some call themselues dead, which lyue in all voluptuousnesse. **1560** DAUS tr. *Sleidane's Comm.* 56 b, They take your goodes and spende them wickedly in pride, riot and voluptuousnes. **1614** PURCHAS *Pilgrimage* IV. v. (ed. 2) 365 As their liues were burthened with voluptuousnesse, so they prepared for their deaths. **1638** SIR T. HERBERT *Trav.* (ed. 2) 340 They delight excessively in all sorts of games and voluptuousnesse. *a* **1701** MAUNDRELL *Journ. Jerus.* (1721) 122 No place in the World can promise the Beholder at a distance greater voluptuousness. **1782** PRIESTLEY *Corrupt. Chr.* II. x. 275 Complaints of their voluptuousness are without end. **1812** G. CHALMERS *Dom. Econ. Gt. Brit.* 329 We became more luxurious, and, as our voluptuousness increased, our industry diminished. **1860** ADLER *Prov. Poet.* xv. 328 The man who was tormented by voluptuousness was declared incapable of love. **1873** HAMERTON *Intell. Life* v. i. 170 Men of the English race are often grandly strong in resistance to every form of voluptuousness.

personif. **1603** J. DAVIES (Heref.) *Extasie* Wks. (Grosart) I. 91/1 In summe shee was such as Voluptuousnesse With all her coulors cannot well expresse. **1639** N. N. tr. *Du Bosq's Compl. Woman* I. 15 There are more who haunt the Schoole of Voluptousnes, then that of vertue.

transf. **1768** *Woman of Honor* III. 243, I could with great voluptuousness of scorn have spit in his face.

b. The quality of expressing voluptuous ideas.

1873 SYMONDS *Grk. Poets* v. 129 The voluptuousness of Æolian poetry is not like that of Persian or Arabian art.

2. Luxuriance, luxury, or refinement tending to gratify the senses or to impart sensuous pleasure.

1652 HEYLIN *Cosmogr.* III. 11 The Countrey very plentifull of all manner of fruites, even unto voluptuousnesse. **1729** SHELVOCKE *Artillery* v. 354 He celebrated the Decennia with new Sorts of Games, with a new Kind of Pomp, and with the most exquisite Voluptuousness. **1800** S. & HT. LEE *Canterb. T.* IV. 380 The species of rustic voluptuousness his garden otherwise afforded. **1832** LYTTON *Eugene A.* I. vi, Softened by the quiet beauty and voluptuousness around him, Walter's thoughts assumed a more gentle dye. **1893** E. F. HOWE in *Voice* (N.Y.) 21 Sept., We have.. the desert brought into voluptuousness by the development of great irrigation enterprises.

† **voluptuousty.** *Obs.* In 4 -ouste, -oste, 5 -ostee. [f. as prec. + -TY. Cf. obs. F. *voluptueuseté.*] = VOLUPTUOSITY.

1382 WYCLIF *Eccl.* xi. 10 Waxende age and voluptuouste ben veyn. **1382** —— *Jer.* xxii. 28 Whether [is he] a vessel withoute al voluptuoste? *c* **1450** *Mirour Saluacioun* 4243 Ȝe sold joye eternale for vayne voluptuostee.

volupty. Forms: 4-6 volupte(e, 6 voluptie, 6-volupty. [a. OF. *volupte* (mod.F. *volupté*), or ad. L. *voluptāt-*, *voluptas* pleasure. Cf. VOLUPT.] Pleasure, delight. Freq. (esp. in earlier use) in pl.

(*a*) *c* **1380** WYCLIF *Sel. Wks.* II. 380 So volupteis and rychesse of þe worlde maken þei to be loved. **1382** —— *Titus* iii. 3 We weren sum tyme vnwyse, vnbileueful, erringe, and seruynge to desyris, and dyuerse voluptees. *c* **1450** tr. *De Imitatione* II. x. 52 Spiritual consolacions passiþ all þe delices of þe worlde, & all fleshly voluptes. **1483** CAXTON *Cato* 7 b, Seneque sayth that by voluptees and excesse comen foure euylles. **1540** HYRDE tr. *Vives' Instr. Chr. Wom.* (1592) C j, It is so, because they bee ever among volupties & pleasures, & banketing. **1541** PAYNELL *Catiline* xlii. 68 b, Syth ye at home giue your selfes to volupties and pleasures.

(*b*) **1382** WYCLIF *Ezek.* xxxi. 9 Alle the trees of voluptee [1388 lust], that veren in paradise of God, sueden hym. **1508** FISHER *7 Penit. Ps.* xxxviii. Wks. (1876) 55 Whan Adam was set in paradyse a place of grete pleasure volupty & rest. **1526** *Pilgr. Perf.* (W. de W. 1531) 232 To haue the fruicyon, that is full volupte & pleasure of yᵉ same. **1542** UDALL *Erasm. Apoph.* 137 For that the same caused in deede.. delicious pleasure & voluptee. **1716** BOLINGBROKE *Refl. on Exile* (1752) 475 *note*, The doctrine of volupty taught by Epicurus. *c* **1730** —— *Fragm.* Wks. 1777 V. 402, I will crayon out a picture in imitation of those Cleanthes used to draw when he disputed against the partizans of volupty. **1799** W. TAYLOR in Robberds *Mem.* (1843) I. 251 His poems are the sweetest blossoms of the rose-garden of volupty. **1929** S. LESLIE *Anglo-Catholic* xv. 216 Edward could see every brick in position with that strange microscopic vision which makes seeing a volupty of the eye.

personif. *c* **1590** J. STEWART *Poems* (S.T.S.) II. 206 Dame voluptie vith proud pernicious spreit.

‖ **voluta** (və'ljuːtə). *Arch. Obs.* [L. *volūta* scroll, properly fem. of *volūtus*, pa. pple. of *volvĕre* to turn. In later use also from It. *voluta* (Sp. and Pg. *voluta*), of the same origin.] = VOLUTE *sb.* 1.

1563 SHUTE *Archit.* D ij, The Abacus, that lieth vpon Voluta, is.. flat like to a trencher. **1598** R. HAYDOCKE tr. *Lomazzo* I. 93, 9 partes and an halfe: whereof one and an halfe makes abacus, and the other 8 downwards make voluta or the scrowle M. **1624** WOTTON *Archit.* in *Reliq.* (1651) 231 The Capitall dressed on each side, not much unlike womens Wires, in a spirall wreathing, which they call the Ionian Voluta. **1664** EVELYN tr. *Freart's Archit.* 128 The Voluta, or as we tearm it properly enough, the Scroul,.. is the principal, and only appropriate member of the Ionic Capital in imitation of a femal Ornament. **1711** W. SUTHERLAND *Shipbuild. Assist.* 6 Cupolo's, Pilasters, Voluta's, Columns in several noble Structures. **1715** LEONI *Palladio's Archit.* (1742) I. 19 The hollow.. of the Voluta is even with the body of the Column. **1753** HOGARTH *Anal. Beauty* ii. 17 The scroll or voluta, gradually lessening to its center.

transf. **1658** SIR T. BROWNE *Gard. Cyrus* iii. 57 In the parts thereof [*sc.* of plants] we finde Heliacall or spirall roundles, voluta's, conical sections,.. and frustrums of Archimedes.

† **volutate**, *v. Obs.*$^{-0}$ [ad. L. *volūtāt-*, ppl. stem of *volūtāre* to roll or wallow.] (See quot.)

1623 COCKERAM I, *Volutate*, to wallow vp and downe.

volutation (vɒljuː'teɪʃən). ? *Obs.* [ad. L. *volūtātiōn-*, *volūtātio*, noun of action f. *volūtāre* (see prec.), f. *volūt-*, *volvĕre* to roll.]

1. The action of rolling or causing to roll; revolution combined with progression.

c **1610** SIR C. HEYDON *Astrol. Disc.* (1650) 42 For whatsoever moveth another, it doth it either by impulsion, attraction, volutation, or vection. **1658** SIR T. BROWNE *Gard. Cyrus* iii. 53 Every globular Figure placed upon a plane, in direct volutation, returns to the first point of contaction. **1665** GLANVILL *Def. Van. Dogm.* 47 In Volutation the whole circumference moves by a motion both progressive and circular; but the centre by the progressive only. **1755** JOHNSON, *To roll*, to move any thing by volutation, or successive application of the different parts of the surface, to the ground.

b. Applied to the motion of liquids or sound.

1640 BP. REYNOLDS *Passions* xxi. 220 In the Sea when a storme is over, there remaines still an inward working and volutation. **1671** R. BOHUN *Wind* 192 When as the volutation of the waves so often changes the Superficies of the water. **1692** RAY *Disc.* II. v. (1693) 205 The ebullition and volutation of the melted Materials. **1713** DERHAM *Phys. Theol.* IV. iii. 120 But being hard, and curiously smooth and tortuous, sounds find an easy passage, with a regular Volutation and Refraction.

c. The action of rolling or turning over in a prostrate position; wallowing. Also *fig.*

1655 VAUGHAN *Silex Scint.* I. Pref. (1858) 6 A constant sensual Volutation or wallowing in impure thoughts and scurrilous conceits. **1678** CUDWORTH *Intell. Syst.* I. iii. §37. 161 Not only our nictations.. when we are awake, but also our nocturnal volutations in sleep, are performed with very little or no consciousness. **1721** BAILEY, *Volutation*, a rolling, tumbling, or wallowing.

2. *fig.* (See quots.)

1623 COCKERAM I, *Volutation*, a tossing in the minde. **1649** J. H. *Motion to Parl. Adv. Learn.* 35 Considering the.. activity of his understanding, and the strange volutations of his affaires. **1806** H. K. WHITE *Let. to R. W. A.* 18 Aug., If these æthereal, aeronautical, mathematical volutations should displease you, perhaps it would not be amiss to saunter a few weeks on the site of Troy.

volute (və'ljuːt), *sb.* [ad. L. *volūta* VOLUTA, or a. F. *volute* from the same source.]

1. *Arch.* A spiral scroll forming the chief ornament of the Ionic capital and employed also in those of the Corinthian and Composite orders.

1696 PHILLIPS (ed. 5), *Volute*, a part of the Capital of the Ionick, Compound, and Corinthian Order. **1728** CHAMBERS *Cycl.* s.v., There are also eight angular Volutes in the Corinthian Capital. **1753** *Phil. Trans.* XLVIII. 34 On the top is an apex, with a volute on each side. **1789** SMYTH tr. *Aldrich's Archit.* (1818) 96 The volutes of the capital were generally by the ancients made elliptic. **1823** P. NICHOLSON *Pract. Build.* 377 To produce graceful effects in the foliage and contour of the volutes. **1841** W. SPALDING *Italy & It. Isl.* I. 174 Complete Doric fronts, with volutes and other decorations foreign to the order. **1879** BARING-GOULD *Germany* II. 344 The English capital was circular; the volute disappeared at once.

2. A spiral conformation; a convolution, twist, or turn; a thing or part having a spiral form.

1756 in *Shenstone's Wks.* (1793) I. p. lxiii, The smooth volutes of Ammon's horn. **1769** FALCONER *Dict. Marine* (1780), *Cagouille*, a sort of volute or ornament. **1794** *Phil. Trans.* LXXXV. 93 You may perceive by the drawing that they do not take such beautiful forms and volutes as a fine dry smoke usually does. **1851** MAYNE REID *Scalp Hunt.* xxvii. 203 We carefully pare off the volutes and spikelets [of the cacti]. **1885** E. J. PAYNE in Grove *Dict. Mus.* IV. 286 The carving of the volute, and the double grooving of its back, are among the most difficult branches of the violin-maker's art. **1895** HOFFMAN *Begin. Writing* 129 Near the top of these are short volutes or commas, similar in type to the speech or voice commas.

attrib. **1875** KNIGHT *Dict. Mech.* 2714/2 *Volute-compasses*, a draftsman's compasses in which the legs are gradually expanded, so as to trace a spiral.

3. The spiral shell of a gastropod of the genus *Voluta*; also, the animal itself.

1753 *Chambers' Cycl.* Suppl. s.v., The Volute, variegated with two reticulated zones. **1775** *Phil. Trans.* LXV. 238 These anemonies had been found on old volutes, called spindle-shells. **1835** KIRBY *Hab. & Inst. Anim.* I. ix. 282 The cowries are said to have eyes exhibiting both iris and pupil, as have some volutes. **1847** ANSTED *Anc. World* iii. 48 The numerous groups of flesh-eating gasteropoda (the murex, the cone, the volute, the cowry, and many others). **1874** J. G. WOOD *Nat. Hist.* 637 When young, the shell is very like that of a volute, having a prominent spire and a rather wide-spreading lip.

volute (və'ljuːt), *a.* [ad. L. *volūtus*, pa. pple. of *volvĕre* to roll; or attrib. use of prec.] Having the form of a volute; forming a spiral curve or curves.

volute spring, *wheel*, are described by Knight *Dict. Mech.* 2714/2 and Suppl. 931/1.

1845 DARWIN *Voy. Nat.* xiii. 288 Another was killed in the act of carrying to its hole a large volute shell. **1847** LEITCH tr. *C. O. Müller's Anc. Art* §108. 67 The Corinthian capital.. was unfolded by an ingenious combination of the volute forms of the Ionic with freer and richer vegetable ornaments. **1859** DARWIN *Orig. Spec.* vi. (1872) 161 The beautiful volute and cone shells of the Eocene epoch. **1879** PRESCOTT *Sp. Telephone* 302 This plate has a volute spiral groove cut in its surface.

Comb. **1862** *Catal. Internat. Exhib., Brit.* II. No. 6460, Cast-steel tyres, volute spring buffers.

vo'luted, *a.* [f. as prec. + -ED.]

1. Spirally twisted or grooved.

1801 CHARLOTTE SMITH *Lett. Solit. Wand.* I. 39 A table covered with green plush, the voluted legs of which seemed to have been produced as a great effort of art. **1806** ANNA SEWARD *Lett.* (1811) VI. 281 Its voluted wreaths are doubtless in the natural horn; art could not produce them. **1836** *Blackw. Mag.* XXXIX. 201 An old high-backed arm chair, its voluted oak legs and framework blackened by Time.

2. *Arch.* Furnished with a volute or spiral scroll.

1810 *Rudim. Anc. Archit.* 15 (Jod.) The boldness of the voluted capital with the beauty of the shaft makes it eligible for porticoes, frontispieces, entrances to houses, etc. *a* **1878** SIR G. SCOTT *Lect. Archit.* (1879) II. 302 The voluted capital was an accidental introduction from the East. **1887** *Pall Mall G.* 18 Aug. 14/1 This thing, with its huge voluted buttresses,.. should serve as a warning to all who contemplate bridge building.

vo'lutiform, *a. rare*$^{-1}$. [f. L. *volūta* VOLUTE *sb.* + -(I)FORM.] Shaped like a volute.

1843 *Penny Cycl.* XXVI. 447/1 Glabella.. Volutiform: the spire more or less conic.

volutin ('vɒljuːtɪn). *Biochem.* Also †-ine. [a. G. *volutin* (A. Meyer *Practicum der bot. Bakterienkunde* (1903) xiii. 80), f. L. *volūt-ans* (pres. pple. of *volūtāre* to roll), specific epithet of the bacterium *Spirillum volutans*: see -IN¹.] A basophilic compound containing polyphosphate found in metachromatic granules in the cytoplasm and vacuoles of various micro-organisms and fungi.

1908 *Q. Jrnl. Microsc. Sci.* LIII. 298 The granules ('metachromic granules', 'red granules', 'volutine granules', etc.) probably consist of some reserve material. **1947** *Nature* 11 Jan. 63/2 Volutin is a cytological entity which has long been recognised as an important constituent of the yeast cell. **1970** PASSMORE & ROBSON *Compan. Med. Stud.* II. xviii. 14/1 Volutin granules..have a special significance in the genus *Corynebacterium* since they are produced typically by the diphtheria bacillus.

volution (vəˈljuːʃən). [f. L. *volūt-*, ppl. stem of *volvĕre* to turn, after *revolution*, etc.]

1. A rolling or revolving movement. Also *fig.*

1610 J. MASON *Turke* II. iii. E 3, This..shall conduct him to the bed of Borgias: amidst whose waking plotts & state volutions, the amorous youth must needs be hartyly welcome. **1741** H. BROOKE *Constantia* 804 Wks. 1789 I. 306 Yet these the inanimate volution keep, And roll eliptic thro' the boundless deep. **1762** FALCONER *Shipwr.* II. 43 The [water-spout's] swift volution, and the enormous train, Let sages versed in nature's lore explain. **1819** SHELLEY *Ess. & Lett.* (1852) II. 216 To bear them over the earth, as the rapid volutions of a tempest have the ever-changing trunk of a water-spout. **1831** [MARY BERRY] *Soc. Life England & France* 395 The art of quickening..the motion of his heart he certainly possessed, as he made his pulse keep pace with the volutions of the divining rod.

2. A spiral turn or twist; a coil or convolution.

1752 J. HILL *Hist. Anim.* 152 At the head there stands a small conic clavicle, formed of about four volutions. **1766** *Phil. Trans.* LVI. 208 The crane..has such a turning of the aspera arteria in the keel of the sternum; but the volution of this bird is round within the bone. **1786** *Ibid.* LXXVI. 161 It is generally coiled up into four volutions. **1842** POE *Marie Roget* Wks. 1864 I. 220 Two circular excoriations, apparently the effect of ropes, or of a rope in more than one volution. **1854** S. P. WOODWARD *Mollusca* II. 191 Nidamental ribbon rather wide, forming a spiral coil of few volutions.

3. A whorl of a spiral shell.

1884 *Proc. Zool. Soc.* 262 Four specimens of a small Melania were collected..all eroded at the upper part of the spire, leaving only four volutions remaining.

volutite (ˈvɒljʊtaɪt). *Palæont.* [f. VOLUTE *sb.* 3 + -ITE.] A fossil volute.

1802–3 tr. *Pallas's Trav.* (1812) I. 70 Whole strata full of ..turbinates.., as well as single volutites, entalites, and pieces of bone.

volutive, obs. variant of VOLITIVE *a.*

vo'lutor. *rare.* [f. L. *volūt-*: cf. VOLUTION.] (See quots.)

1859 J. BOOTH (*title*), Description of the Volutor, an Instrument for Describing Spirals and Volutes. **1862** *Catal. Internat. Exhib., Brit.* II. No. 2920, Volutors for tracing spiral curves.

'volutory, *a. rare*$^{-1}$. [Cf. prec. and -ORY.] Revolving, rolling.

1839 URE *Dict. Arts* 218 This second roller being hardened, and placed in an appropriate volutory press, is employed to engrave..the whole of its intended pattern.

voluwe, ME. variant of FOLLOW *v.*

‖**volva**[1] (ˈvɒlvə). *Bot.* [L. *volva* (Pliny), f. *volvĕre* to roll, wrap.] The membranous covering which completely encloses many fungi in the early stage of growth.

1753 *Chambers' Cycl.* Suppl., *Volva*,..a membranous matter surrounding the bases of many of the fungi. **1784** *Phil. Trans.* LXXIV. 423 This..vegetable production arises from a volva, which is buried six or eight inches deep in dry sandy banks. **1856** HENSLOW *Bot. Terms* 159 *Ring*,.. the debris left round the stipes of some agarics by the bursting of the volva. **1874** COOKE *Fungi* 28 In Phalloidei the hymenium is at first enclosed within a sort of peridium or universal volva, maintaining a somewhat globose or egg-shape.

Hence **'volvate** *a.* (In recent Dicts.)

volva[2] (ˈvɒlva). [ad. ON. *völva* (also used) (Norw. *volve*) prophetess, sibyl.] In Scandinavian mythology, a prophetess, a soothsayer, a witch.

1889 P. B. DU CHAILLU *Viking Age* I. iv. 27 The Völuspa was an inspired poem of a Völva or Sibyl, and embodies the records of the creation of the present world. **1927** E. V. GORDON *Introd. Old Norse* v. 40 It is the most complete description extant of the volva or sibyl of Scandinavian heathen times. **1966** S. WAVELL et al. *Trances* xvi. 133 The priestesses of Freyja known as *volva* were the shamans of their time. They wore animal skins, their boots made of calf skin, their gloves lined with the fur of arctic cats, their goddess being drawn in a cat carriage.

volve (vɒlv), *v.* Also 5–7 volue. [ad. L. *volvĕre* to turn, roll, etc., or obs. F. *volver* (= Sp. and Pg. *volver*, It. *volvere*, *volgere*) from the same source.]

1. *intr.* To turn over, to roll. *Obs.* exc. *nonce-use.*

c **1480** HENRYSON *Fables, Lyon & Mouss* 204 (Bann. MS.), Voluand [*v.r.* Welterand] about with hiddouss rowmissing, Quhyle to, quhyle fro, gif he mycht succour get. **1910** GALSWORTHY *Inn Tranq.* in *Nation* 12 Nov. 266/2 If It did not volve and revolve on Itself, It would peter out at one end or the other.

†**2.** *trans.* To turn over the pages of (a book). Also *absol.* (Cf. REVOLVE *v.* 5.) *Obs.*

1523 LD. BERNERS *Froiss.* I. Auth. Pref. 2 Whan this ymaginacyon came to me, I volued, tourned, and redde many volumes and bokes, conteyning famouse histories. **1625** DARCIE *Ann.* To Rdr., I sedulously volued and reuolued Characters of Kings and Peers, Letters, Consultations. **1638** R. CHAMBERLAIN *Noct. Lucubrations* Ep. Ded., Many..Peeces of learning your Worship hath volved and revolved. **1677** P. A. *Pref. Poem* in *Cary's Chronol.*, Even so our studious Friend..is intent On Books and Reading, so doth chuse and pick, Volve and Revolve, and finally doth stick.

†**3.** To turn over in the mind; to consider. *Obs.*

c **1520** BARCLAY *Jugurtha* (1557) 65 b, Somtyme he volued in mynd rather to subdue hymselfe..than to begyne war agayn. **1616** J. LANE *Contn. Sqr.'s T.* IV. 257 Cambuscan.. volvd, revolvd, in diepe perplexitie How to fitt love and iustice remedie. **1760** STERNE *Tr. Shandy* VII. xx. I have been volving and revolving in my fancy..by what clean device I might..modulate them.

volvelle (ˈvɒlvɛl). *Obs.* exc. *Hist.* Also 5–6 voluell(e, 6 (9) volvell. [ad. med.L. *volvella* or *volvellum*, app. f. *volvĕre* to turn.] An old device consisting of one or more movable circles surrounded by other graduated or figured circles, serving to ascertain the rising and setting of the sun and moon, the state of the tides, etc.

14.. *MS. Ashmole 191* fol. 199 The Rewle of the Voluelle. Now folowiþ here þe voluelle that sum men clepen a lunarie. *c* **1440** *Astron. Cal.* (MS. Ashm. 391), Now folowiþ þe thrid table þ[t] is cleepid a voluelle or a lunary. **1501** in Kingsford *Chron. Lond.* (1905) 239 A Costlew pagent w[t] a volvell by the which the xii signes moved aboute the Zodiak..and ouer that voluell Sat, in a stage or pynnacle, Raphaell the Arch angell. **1523** SKELTON *Garl. Laurel* 1517 He turnyd his tirikkis, his voluell ran fast. *a* **1529** —— *Sp. Parrot* 137 Tholomye and Haly were cunnyng and wyse In the volvell, in the quadrant, and in the astroloby. **1843** in Dyce *Wks. Skelton* II. 336 A curious description of the volvell, with directions for its use. **1865** *Athenæum* 18 Feb. 233/2 One volvelle and an accompanying table do the work quickly enough. **1884** *Manch. Exam.* 16 Sept. 6/2 A curious Kalender, with an astronomical volvelle of which the stylus had been preserved.

'volvent, *ppl. a.* [ad. L. *volvent-*, *volvens*, pres. pple. of *volvĕre* to turn.] Turning round.

1898 MEREDITH *Odes Fr. Hist.*, *Napoleon* xi, Now had the Seaman's volvent sprite..Slung northward.

volvoci'naceous, *a. Bot.* [Cf. next and -ACEOUS.] Resembling or related to the *Volvocineæ* (see next).

1874 H. C. WOOD *Fresh Water Algæ* 235 A peculiar condition of the Volvocinaceous Algæ.

volvo'cinean, *a. Bot.* Also -ian. [f. mod.L. *Volvocineæ*, f. *Volvoc-*, VOLVOX.] Of or pertaining to the *Volvocineæ*, a family of microscopic confervaceous plants.

1885 E. R. LANKESTER in *Encycl. Brit.* XIX. 836/1 Other Protozoa are known which are provided with chlorophyll corpuscles and..nourish themselves as do green plants. Such are the Volvocinean Flagellata and some of the Dinoflagellata. **1890** *Nature* 6 Feb. 318/2, I have cited the two Volvocinean genera Pandorina and Volvox as examples of the differentiation of homoplastids into the lowest heteroplastids.

‖**volvox** (ˈvɒlvɒks). *Bot.* [mod.L., f. L. *volvĕre* to roll.] A genus of fresh-water organisms having a spherical form and provided with cilia which enable them to roll over in the water; an individual of this genus.

Volvox as the name of a vine-fretter in Holland *Pliny* (1601) I. 547 is derived from old editions of the *Nat. Hist.* XVII. xxviii, which have *volvocem* in place of *volucre(m)*.

1798 *Tilloch's Philos. Mag.* I. 212 Girod Chantram..even distinguished in one species of *conferva* a real *volvox*, which had some similarity to the *rotator* of Gmelin. **1864** H. J. SLACK in *Intell. Observer* V. 183 In one of my specimens I found a small volvox apparently uninjured. **1884** *Edin. Rev.* Oct. 373 It would now seem that the celestial spaces have also their volvoxes and diatoms.

†**'volvulous**, *a. Obs.*$^{-1}$ [f. L. *volv-ĕre* to turn, after *pendulous*, etc.] Twining.

1657 TOMLINSON *Renou's Disp.* 264 It is a lacteous, volvulous, scansory and smooth plant.

‖**volvulus** (ˈvɒlvjʊləs). *Path.* [med. or mod.L., f. L. *volvĕre* to turn, twist.] A form of intestinal obstruction caused by a twisting or knotting of the bowel. †Also in pl. *volvuli*.

1679 J. SMITH *Eng. Improv. Reviv'd* 247 When the Entrals are stopt that they cannot void, it is the Volvuli or wringing of the Guts. **1704** J. HARRIS *Lex. Techn.* I. s.v. *Ileum*, Sometimes the Coats being doubled inward, the upper part of an Intestine sinks or falls with the lower, which makes the Iliack-Passion, or Volvulus. **1755** A. MONRO in *Ess. Phys. & Lit.* (1756) II. 353 Remarks on..Intussusceptio,.. Inflammation, and Volvulus of the Intestines. **1799** *Med. Jrnl.* I. 429 Pneumonic Inflammation,..Peritoneal Inflammation,..Volvulus. **1846** BRITTAN tr. *Malgaigne's Oper. Surg.* 396 The exact seat of the foreign body, volvulus, or strangulation. **1885** *Buck's Handbk. Med. Sci.* I. 22/1 Volvulus is sometimes induced by violent muscular exertions, as in jumping or lifting. **1897** *Allbutt's Syst. Med.* III. 815 Under the general name 'volvulus' are included two distinct modes of obstruction. In one the bowel is so twisted about its mesenteric axis that it becomes occluded; in the other form two suitable coils of intestine are so intertwined or knotted together as also to cause an obstruction in their canals.

b. With *a*: An instance of this.

1758 J. S. *Le Dran's Observ. Surg.* (1771) 187 There might be a *Volvulus*. *Ibid.* 189 A *Volvulus* may be the Consequence of that Inflammation, and of the antiperistaltick Motion that succeeds it. **1887** *Buck's Handbk. Med. Sci.* IV. 156/2 Once a volvulus has become fairly established, it cannot spontaneously relieve itself. **1891** F. TAYLOR *Pract. Med.* (ed. 2) 587 Occasionally the small intestine forms a volvulus of the same kind as that described in the sigmoid.

volwyshe, obs. Sc. form of WOLFISH.

voly, obs. form of VOLLEY *sb.*

volyer, variant of VOLLIER.

volym, obs. form of VOLUME *sb.*

†**volymare**, var. *folmare*, etc., FOUMART.

c **1450** *Bk. Hawkyng* in *Rel. Ant.* I. 305 The mewe in this maner schal be sette, that no fucher no volymare enter in.

volyper(e, obs. forms of VOLUPER.

volzine, variant of VOLTZINE *Min.*

voman, obs. Sc. f. WOMAN.

vomating, obs. Sc. f. VOMITING *vbl. sb.*

vomative, variant of VOMITIVE *Obs.*

†**vome**, *sb. Obs. rare.* Also voom, woom. [f. next.] Vomit.

1382 WYCLIF *Isaiah* xxviii. 8 Alle forsothe boordis ben fulfild with the vome and filthis, so that ther were no more place. **1382** —— *2 Pet.* ii. 22 An hound turned aȝen to his woom [*v.r.* vome, voom].

†**vome**, *v. Obs. rare.* [ad. L. *vomĕre*: see VOMIT *v.*] *trans.* and *absol.* To vomit. Also *fig.*

1382 WYCLIF *Lev.* xviii. 25 Whos hidows synnes Y shal visite, that it caste [*early MSS.* vome] out his dwellers. —— *Jer.* xxv. 27 Drinketh, and beth drunken, and vometh, and falleth. **1407** *Exam. W. Thorpe* in *MS. Rawl. C. 208* lf. 24 He & hise felowis mowen sore drede,..last þei ben sodeynli vomed out of þe noumbre of goddis chosen peple. **1549** *Compl. Scotl.* vi. 67, I sau brume, that prouokis ane person to vome ald feume.

Hence †**'voming** *vbl. sb.* and *ppl. a. Obs.*

1382 WYCLIF *Isa.* xix. 14 To erren thei maden Egipt..as erreth a drunke man and a vomende. —— *Jer.* xlviii. 26 He shal hurtle the hond of Moab in his vomyng. —— *2 Pet.* ii. 22 A sowe waschun [returned] in the walewinge [*v.r.* vomyng].

vome, southern ME. var. FOAM *sb.* and *v.*

†**voment.** *Obs. rare.* [Alteration of *vomet* VOMIT *sb.*] Vomit.

1482 *Monk of Evesham* xxi. (Arb.) 51 He drew out of his mowthe an horrable voment of venyne and cast hit al abrode. *c* **1510** *Gesta Rom.* (W. de W.) xxviii. (1879) 443 As a dogge whiche maketh a voment, and casteth out the mete that he hathe eten before.

vomer (ˈvəʊmə(r)). [a. L. *vōmer* ploughshare.]

1. *Anat.* A small thin bone forming the posterior part of the partition between the nostrils in man and most vertebrate animals.

1704 J. HARRIS *Lex. Techn.* I, *Vomer*, is a Bone situated in the middle of the lower part of the Nose. **1726** MONRO *Anat. Bones* 158 The Vomer divides the Nostrils, [and] enlarges the Organ of Smelling. **1758** J. S. *Le Dran's Observ. Surg.* (1771) 26, I..found that the Roots of the Polypus adhered to the *Vomer*. **1831** R. KNOX *Cloquet's Anat.* 66 The *Vomer* is an azygous bone, situated in the median line,..forming the posterior part of the septum of the nasal fossæ. **1870** ROLLESTON *Anim. Life* 25 The skull of the Common Fowl differs from that of the Common Pigeon..in its possession of a rudimentary vomer.

2. *Ichthyol.* A bone forming the front part of the roof of the mouth, and often bearing teeth.

1828 STARK *Elem. Nat. Hist.* I. 405 Many pointed teeth along both jaws, the palate, and the tongue, but none on the vomer. **1854** BADHAM *Halieut*, 170 The next, or fourth family of the Acanthopterygii..differ in not having teeth on either vomer or palate. **1888** GOODE *Amer. Fishes* 469 Brook Trouts,..distinguished from the true Salmons by a peculiar arrangement of teeth on the vomer.

3. *Ornith.* The large terminal bone in the tail of most birds; the pygostyle.

1872 COUES *N. Amer. Birds* 37 The bones are few..and short, not projecting beyond the general plumage, and the last one, called *coccyx* or *vomer*,..is large and singularly shaped.

vomerine (ˈvəʊməraɪn), *a.* [f. VOMER + -INE.]

1. Of or belonging to the vomer (esp. of fishes); composing the vomer.

1854 OWEN in *Orr's Circ. Sci.*, *Org. Nat.* I. 194 The natural segment which..is formed by the vomerine, prefrontal, and nasal bones, is very distinct in the ophidians. **1858** W. CLARK *Van der Hoeven's Zool.* II. 252 Teeth in vomerine bones in a transverse row. **1881** *Encycl. Brit.* XII. 647/2 An extremely large basal bone, which extends from the vomerine region on to the anterior part of the spinal column.

2. Of teeth: Situated on the vomer.

1863 DANA *Man. Geol.* 345 *note*, The species of Europe want these vomerine teeth. **1889** NICHOLSON & LYDEKKER *Palæont.* II. 985 Here the vomerine teeth of the middle row are larger than the teeth of the other rows.

vomero-, combining form of VOMER, as in *vomero-nasal*, *-palatine* adjs. (In recent Dicts.)

†**vomic**, *a. Obs. rare.* Also 6 vomike, 8 -ick. [ad. mod.L. *vomicus* in *nux vomica*.] *vomic nut*, = NUX VOMICA.

The sense of 'purulent, ulcerous' given in later Dictionaries (from *c* 1884) appears to have been evolved from VOMICA 2.

1563 TURNER *Herbal* III. 49 First I wil rehearse what he writeth of the vomike nut. **1751** J. HILL *Mat. Med.* 505 Vomick nut is the nucleus of a fruit of an East-Indian tree. **1794** WOODVILLE *Med. Bot.* Suppl. 29 *Strychnos Nux vomica.* Vomic nut, or Poison-nut.

‖**vomica** (ˈvɒmɪkə). Pl. **vomicæ** (-ɪsiː), and **vomicas**. [L. *vomica* boil, ulcer, f. *vomĕre* to eject, vomit. Hence also It., Sp., Pg. *vomica*, F. *vomique*, in sense 2.]

1. †**a.** A vent or opening. *Obs.*⁻¹

1572 J. Jones *Bathes of Bath* II. 15 b, It should followe, that where such hote bathes were, there should bee vomica and a chimney, out of whiche that flame should bee expelled.

b. A place at which water issues.

1838 *Civil Eng. & Arch. Jrnl.* I. 273/1 It is obvious that the conflux of the springs in the Beck, is greater than the unvarying quantity gauged at the vomica or source of each Spring.

2. *Path.* **a.** An ulcerous cavity or abscess in the substance of the lungs or (more rarely) some other internal organ.

1693 tr. *Blancard's Phys. Dict.* (ed. 2), *Vomica*, a fault in the Lungs, from Heterogeneous Blood. **1732** Arbuthnot *Rules of Diet* in *Aliments*, etc. I. 387 If the Ulcer is not broke it is commonly call'd a Vomica. **1775** T. Percival *Ess.* (1776) III. 104 The lungs become inflamed, a cough ensues, tubercles or a vomica are formed. **1822–7** Good *Study Med.* (1829) I. 639 Vomicas or indurated tumours of whatever kind in the substance of the lungs. **1879** *St. George's Hosp. Rep.* IX. 156 A vomica in the middle lobe of the right lung. **1880** A. Flint *Princ. Med.* 196 The ulcerative cavities, vomicæ, result from a softening of the tuberculous and inflammatory cheesy material and its removal through the bronchi.

b. A sudden and profuse expectoration of purulent or putrid matter.

1895– in American dicts.

vomicene, -in(e. *Chem.* [f. (nux) vomica.] = brucine. (In recent Amer. dicts.)

vomiˈcose, *a. Path.* [f. vomica 2 a.] Abounding in ulcerous cavities.

†**ˈvomish**, *v. Obs.*⁻¹ [ad. F. *vomiss-*, lengthened stem of *vomir* to vomit.] *trans.* To vomit.

1536 *Stories & Proph. Scripture* S vj, And the Lorde hath commaunded the whayle, and he hath vomished out Jonam vpon the lande.

†**vomishment.** *Obs.*⁻¹ In 5 vomysch-. [ad. OF. (also mod.F.) *vomissement*, f. *vomir* to vomit.] The act or fact of vomiting.

a **1450** Myrc *Par. Pr.* 1888 He schalt not þenne hys hosul take, For vomyschment & castynge sake.

vomit (ˈvɒmɪt), *sb.* Forms: 4–5 **vomyt** (5 **womyt, vomyght**), 5–6 **vomyte**, 5–7 **vomite**, 6 **vomitte**, 6– **vomit** (6 **womit**), 7–8 **vomitt**; 4–6 **vomet**, 5 **-ete, -ette**, 6 **womeit**, 7 **vomett**. [a. AF. *vomit, -ite*, OF. *vomite* (= It., Sp., Pg. *vomito*), or ad. L. *vomitus*, f. *vomĕre*: see next.]

1. The act of ejecting the contents of the stomach through the mouth: **a.** With *a* and pl.

1387 Trevisa *Higden* (Rolls) VII. 85 Duke Edrik.. feynynge a vomet or brakynge, seide þat he was seek. *c* **1400** *Destr. Troy* 13545 The salt water sadly sanke in my wombe, þat I voidet with vomettes by vertu of goddes. **1484** Caxton *Curial* 3 b, We ete so gredyly..that otherwhyle we caste it up agayn and make vomytes. *a* **1548** Hall *Chron., Hen. VIII*, 194 b, For very feblenes of nature caused by purgacious and vomites he dyed. **1579** Langham *Gard. Health* 437 Nvx vomica..causeth a strong vomite. **1601** B. Jonson *Poetaster* v. iii, I haue pills about me Would giue him a light vomit. **1681** Rycaut tr. *Gracian's Critick* 123 It gave them immediately such a Vomit, that they speued forth most vile Corruption. **1707** Floyer *Physic. Pulse-Watch* 158 They soon grow old, they have..Phrensies, choleric Vomits, and Fluxes. **1740** Cheyne *Regimen* p. v, Vomits drive forcibly out of the upper part of the chyliferous Tube ..its noxious contents. **1794** T. Taylor *Pausanias' Descr. Greece* III. 172 He afterwards threw it up by a vomit. **1897** *Allbutt's Syst. Med.* III. 901 Vomiting in perityphlitis.. may occur repeatedly, or there may be only an initial vomit.

fig. **1411–2** Hoccleve *De Reg. Princ.* 272 Vnwise is he þat besy þoght ne dredeþ. In whom þat he his mortel venym schedeþ, But if a vomyt after folwe blyue, At þe port of despeir he may arryue. *a* **1635** Naunton *Fragm. Reg.* (Arb.) 55 Others..stirred up the dregs of those rude humours, which by time..he sought to repose, or to give them all a vomit.

b. Without article.

c **1386** Chaucer *Knt.'s T.* 1898 Hym gayneth neither for to gete his lif, Vomyt vpward, ne dounward laxatif. **1422** tr. *Secreta Secret., Priv. Priv.* 247 Vomyte purgyth the stomake of ill humours aboue, as a medecyne laxatyfe benethe. *c* **1440** *Promp. Parv.* 512/1 Vomyte, or evomyte, brakynge, *vomitus*. **1528** Paynell *Salerne's Regim.* D iij, He shulde eate no maner of meates without his stomake be net, and purged of all yl humours by vomet. **1555** Eden *Decades* (Arb.) 293 They remedy that surfecte by vomyte whiche they prouoke by eatynge of antes. **1564** Harding *Answ. Jewel* 46 When the deacon had forced her to receiue a litle of the cuppe, the yexe and vomite followed. *a* **1610** Healey *Cebes* (1636) 135 Which purgeth out all their ingulphed evils, as by vomit or ejection. *c* **1610** *Women Saints* 40 As often as she eate of the ..meate, she by vomite cast it vp againe. **1694** Salmon *Bate's Dispens.* (1713) 331/2 It is said to be Diaphoretick, and gently to provoke Vomit.

†**c.** With *the*, in specific use. *Obs.*⁻¹

a **1585** Montgomerie *Flyting* 318 The weam-eill, the wild-fire, the vomit and the vees.

d. (See quot.)

1898 Morris *Austral Eng.* 20/1 *Barcoo Vomit*, a sickness occurring in inhabitants..of the interior of Australia. It is characterized by painless attacks of vomiting.

2. a. Matter ejected from the stomach by vomiting; = spew *sb.* 1.

c **1390** *Wycliffite Bible* 2 Pet. ii. 22 An hound turned aȝen to his woom [*v.rr.* vomyt, womyt]. *c* **1440** *Gesta Rom.* lxiv. 278 (Harl. MS.), He may be likenide to an hound þat turnith aȝen to his vomyt. **1535** Coverdale *Isaiah* xxviii. 8 All tables are so ful of vomyte and fylthynes, yᵗ no place is clene. **1578** H. Wotton *Courtlie Controv.* 205 The Image of Bacchus with fat red cheekes, begrimed wyth vomets. **1631** R. Bolton *Comf. Affl. Consc.* (1635) 307 As a loathsome vomit is to the stomacke of him that casts it out so are luke-warme Professours to the Lord Jesus. **1643** Trapp *Comm. Gen.* vi. 11 The vomit of a dog. **1820** Shelley *Œdipus* I. 353 Here The Gadfly's venom..Is mingled with the vomit of the Leech. **1876** Bristowe *Th. & Pract. Med.* (1878) 655 The character of the vomit depends on circumstances. Generally, however, it comprises mucus..and bile. **1882** Ballantine *Exper. Barrister's Life* II. 10 A physician.. who was present when the vomit was analysed.

b. *black vomit*, a blackish matter, resembling coffee grounds and due to hæmorrhage, vomited in severer cases of yellow fever; also, the disease of yellow fever itself.

1749 *Phil. Trans.* XLVI. 137 The black Vomit was not known at Cartagena..until the Years 1729 and 1730. *c* **1793** *Encycl. Brit.* (ed. 3) XI. 146/2 The Yellow Fever..is the same with that called, from one of its worst symptoms, the *black vomit*. **1833** *Cycl. Pract. Med.* II. 295 A fever, with yellow skin and black vomit in some of the cases, appeared among a party of forty men. **1876** Bristowe *Th. & Pract. Med.* (1878) 199 On the third or fourth day, or later, the vomited matters..begin to contain blood..and they soon assume..a coffee-ground character, constituting the so-called 'black vomit'. **1883** *Century Mag.* July 427/1 Hands sent aboard..left on the next day, believing they had detected 'black vomit' in her hospital.

attrib. **1833** *Cycl. Pract. Med.* II. 265 A black-vomit epidemic. *Ibid.*, The black-vomit fever of the West Indies.

c. (See quots.)

1886 *Fagge's Princ. & Pract. Med.* II. 808/1 Coffee-ground vomit in cancer of stomach. **1895** *Funk's Stand. Dict.*, *Bilious vomit*, bile forced back into the stomach and ejected with vomited matter.

3. a. *fig.* (Chiefly in allusion to Prov. xxvi. 11 and 2 Pet. ii. 22).

(*a*) **1575** Gascoigne *Glasse Govt.* Argt., Wks. 1910 II. 5 The eldest (turning to their vomit) take their cariage with them, and travaile the worlde. **1579** Northbrooke *Dicing* (1843) 80 Turne no more to the puddle and vomit of your filthye, ydle life. **1601** F. Godwin *Bps. of Eng.* 7 They likewise returned to the filthie vomite of their abominable idolatrie. **1642** Milton *Apol. Smect.* Wks. 1851 III. 290 Now that ye have started back from the purity of Scripture ..to the old vomit of your traditions. **1677** W. Hubbard *Narrative* 14 Returning back to his old vomit, he was at last prevailed with to forsake Philip. **1706** Stevens *Span. Dict.* I, *Bolver al vomito*, to return to the vomit, to relapse into sin.

(*b*) *a* **1583** Polwart *Flyting* 564 in *Montgomerie's Poems* (S.T.S. 1910) 170 The loun man lik his womeit, and deny His schameles sawis. **1597** Shaks. *2 Hen. IV*, I. iii. 99 Now thou would'st eate thy dead vomit vp, And howl'st to finde it. **1602** Marston *Antonio's Rev.* I. iv, Dog! I will make thee eate thy vomit up. **1655** Vaughan *Silex Scint.* I. *Misery* 20, I..Feed on those vomits of my heart.

b. Applied with contemptuous force to persons or things of a vile, loathsome, or disgusting character.

1610 B. Jonson *Alch.* I. i, Out you dog-leach, The vomit of all prisons. **1650** T. Vaughan *Anthroposophia* To Rdr., It is not the primitive Trueth of the Creation.., but a certaine preternaturall upstart, a vomit of Aristotle. **1880** L. Wallace *Ben-Hur* 531 The vomit of Jerusalem is coming. **1889** J. Dickie *Words Faith, Hope & L.* (1892) 272 Jesus speaks of him as a vomit, which He will have to spue out.

c. *transf.* Substance cast out by discharge or eruption.

1695 Blackmore *Pr. Arth.* III. 65 The lab'ring Mounts Belch drossy Vomit out. **1914** *Blackw. Mag.* Oct. 473/1 Four companies..had to be detailed to capture it under cover of a mountain battery's vomit.

4. A powder, draught, or other medicine which causes vomiting; an emetic.

Freq. from *c* 1600 to *c* 1800.

a **1400** *Stockholm Med. MS.* ii. 51 in *Anglia* XVIII. 309 3if þou of vomites wylt hawe bote. *c* **1400** *Lanfranc's Cirurg.* 18 Laxatiues & vometis ben nedeful to hem, þat han olde rotid woundis. **1522** More *De quat. Noviss.* Wks. 100 Fain wold we haue some medicins, as purgacions & vomites, to pul down & auoid yᵗ we cram in to much. **1580** Hester tr. *Fioravanti's Disc. Chirurg.* 37 The first thing that I gaue him was a vomitte that purged the stomacke. **1605** Timme *Quersit.* I. xiii. 53 The extraction whereof maketh a very good and gentle vomit. **1664** Wood *Life* (O.H.S.) II. 19 A vomitt that I took of Mʳ. Alport, 1s. 6d. **1712** Swift *Jrnl. to Stella* 18 Sept., I have taken a vomit to-day, and hope I shall be better. **1753** *Chambers' Cycl.* Suppl. s.v. *Emetic*, The great practice of the antient Egyptian physicians consisted in glysters, vomits, and abstinence. **1785** Trusler *Mod. Times* II. 161, I told the scoundrel to make up a vomit, and he has made up a purge. **1803** Beddoes *Hygeia* IX. 155 The state of the stomach had been changed by absorbents, vomits or bitters. **1822–7** Good *Study Med.* (1829) I. 452 He saw from thirty to fifty gall-stones voided after taking only an oil vomit. **1860** Mayne *Expos. Lex.* 1337/2 *Vomit*, common term for an emetic draught or powder.

fig. **1589** Nashe *Pasquill & Marf.* 20 Martin..poysoned her [*sc.* Divinity] with a vomit which he ministred vnto her, to make her cast vppe her dignities and promotions. **1643** Trapp *Comm. Gen.* vi. 13 The earth..is burdened with them, and cryes to me for a vomit to spue them out.

5. The hood or cover of a vomiting boiler.

1880 J. Dunbar *Practical Paperm.* (1881) 19 [Rags] boiled with steam..for 10 hours in stationary boilers without vomit. **1885** *Encycl. Brit.* XVIII. 220/1 [The] hot liquid.. is dispersed all over the boiler by striking against a hood E at the top. This is technically known as the 'vomit'.

6. *Comb.*, as *vomit-green* adj.; **vomit bag** = *sick-bag* s.v. sick *a.* 12.

1975 D. Lodge *Changing Places* i. 42 The passengers swallow to relieve the pressure on their eardrums, close their eyes, finger their passports and vomit-bags. **1978** D. Murphy *Place Apart* i. 6 The sleazy plastic Lounge Bar had a vomit-green carpet.

vomit (ˈvɒmɪt), *v.* Forms: 5–6 **vomyte**, 6–7 **vomite**, 6 **vomyt, -itte, womit**, 6– **vomit**; 6 **vomete, womet**. [a. L. *vomit-*, ppl. stem of *vomĕre* (whence It. *vomire*, F. *vomir*: see vome *v.*), or ad. L. *vomit-āre* (whence It. *vomitare*, Sp., Pg., and Pr. *vomitar*, obs. F. *vomiter*), frequentative of *vomĕre* to vomit. Cf. evomit *v.*]

1. *intr.* To bring up and eject the contents of the stomach by the mouth; to cast or throw up; = spew *v.* 1.

1422 tr. *Secreta Secret., Priv. Priv.* 245 If a man haue nede to vomyte, lete hit be done atte myde-day. **1529** More *Suppl. Soulys* Wks. 322/1 Then shall ye sometime see..al their bodye shiuer for paine, and yet shall neuer vomete at all. **1553** Eden *Treat. New Ind.* (Arb.) 16 Some..are prouoked to vomitte, euen as they were tossed on the sea. **1592** Kyd *Murder J. Brewen* ¶5 Immediatlie after he began to vomet exceedingly. *c* **1643** Ld. Herbert *Autobiog.* (1824) 127 Sir Herbert Croft..met him upon the water vomiting all the way. **1675** E. Wilson *Spadacr. Dunelm.* 79 In case the Stomach be fowl, and the Patient..be apt to Vomit. **1722** De Foe *Plague* (1754) 67 The young Lady complained she was not well; in a Quarter of an Hour more she vomited. **1774** Goldsm. *Nat. Hist.* (1776) VII. 294 The belly was always greatly swollen, when the animal began to vomit. **1804** Abernethy *Surg. Obs.* 231 She complained..of extreme sickness, which produced frequent efforts to vomit. **1872** Darwin *Emotions* xi. 259 The monkeys in the Zoological Gardens often vomit whilst in perfect health.

2. a. *trans.* To bring up and discharge (swallowed food or drink) through the mouth; to cast out (a matter or substance) in this way; = spew *v.* 2. Also *fig.*

1560 Bible (Geneva) *Prov.* xxiii. 8 Thou shalt vomit thy morsels that thou has eaten. **1565** Cooper *Thesaurus* s.v. *Vomitus*, Matter of diuers colours vomited. **1588** Shaks. *Titus A.* III. i. 232 My bowels cannot hide her woes, But like a drunkard must I vomit them. **1611** —— *Cymb.* I. vi. 45 Sluttery..Should make desire vomit emptinesse, Not so allur'd to feed. **1804** *Med. Jrnl.* XII. 149 His stomach became uneasy, and he vomited a small portion of the last dose. **1845** *Encycl. Metrop.* VII. 552/1 The matters vomited are merely the contents of the stomach, half digested. **1898** J. Hutchinson in *Arch. Surg.* IX. 109 A lady vomited the contents of a very large swelling which had formed.

b. Freq. with advs., as *forth, out, up*.

1541 Elyot *Image Gov.* 23 Yf by chance he espied any of them, he was therwith so greued, that he immediately wolde vomite vp colar. **1565** Cooper *Thesaurus, Reijcere sanguinem*, to vomite out bloudde. *a* **1591** H. Smith *Wks.* (1866) II. 59 Then might the poor be fed with that which he oftentimes..loathsomely vomits forth. **1609** Bible (Douay) *Jonah* ii. 11 The Lord spoke to the fish: and it vomited out Jonas upon the dry land. **1663** Cowley *Cutter Coleman St.* II. viii, I ha' vomited out..all my entrails. **1693** Evelyn *De la Quint. Compl. Gard.* II. *Treat. Orange Trees* 43 The Juggler, who..Vomits up so many several sorts of Water, all differing in Colour, Taste, and Smell. **1756** Mrs. Calderwood in *Coltness Collect.* (Maitl. Cl.) 174 You must know it is a mortall sin to vomit up this morsell. **1818–20** E. Thompson *Cullen's Nosol. Method.* (ed. 3) 247 Desire of food in great quantity, which is immediately vomited up. **1845** Birch in *Classical Museum* III. 420 The Jason vomited up by the serpent of the Fleece. **1904** Spencer & Gillen *North. Tribes Cent. Austral.* xiv. 472 The natives say that once some men..became so ill that they vomited forth their livers.

3. *fig.* **a.** To eject, reject, cast *out* or *up*, esp. with abhorrence or loathing.

1562 Winȝet *Wks.* (S.T.S.) II. 54 That thai mot..womet out agane fra the ground thai bittir and tribulous seis of errouris. **1582** N. T. (Rhem.) *Rev.* iii. 16 Because thou art.. neither cold nor hote, I wil begin to vomite thee out of my mouth. **1602** Marston *Antonio's Rev.* v. iii, They faine would cast And vomit him from off their governement. **1636** Sir R. Baker *Cato Variegatus* 94 Praise not too much; lest thou be forc'd in th' end To eate thy words, and vomit up thy friend. *a* **1704** T. Brown *Dial. Dead, Belgic Hero* Wks. 1711 IV. 67 A haughty Tyrant..was obliged to vomit up numberless Provinces and Towns, which he had dishonourably stolen. **1839** T. Mitchell *Frogs of Aristoph.* Introd. p. xcii, A stern admonition, that where such vices are practised, the very earth shall vomit out its inhabitants.

b. To give vent to, belch out, or utter (abusive or objectionable language); = spew *v.* 2 c. Chiefly with advs. (as *forth, out, up*) or preps.

1592 Breton *Pilgr. Paradise* Wks. (Grosart) I. 12/2 Vp did start the heade of Gluttonie, Vomiting out theese wordes of villany. **1611** B. Jonson *Catiline* IV. ii, I hope This Senate is more graue, then to giue credit Rashly to all he vomits. **1639** S. Du Verger tr. *Camus' Admir. Events* 270 He..made him vomit out a thousand outragious speaches against the perfidie..of Babilas. **1675** Cotton *Scoffer Scoft* 96 All these abominable names Thou vomits forth so fluently. **1865** Parkman *Champlain* viii. (1875) 289 The Frenchman vomited against him every species of malignant abuse.

absol. **1640** Sir E. Dering *Carmelite* iv. (1641) 52 How basely..is unfit for any man to foul his pen with; more unfit for you..so to vomit against your dead Prince.

4. *transf.* **a.** To discharge, to give, send, or throw out (flames, water, etc.) copiously or with force.

1552 Huloet, Vomitynge or castynge out water, *vndiuomus*. **1634** Milton *Comus* 655 He and his curst crew ..like the sons of Vulcan, vomit smoke. **1635** Quarles *Emblems* I. xi. (1718) 45 Sol's hot-mouth'd steeds, whose nostrils vomit flame. **1697** Dryden *Æneid* v. 894 The silent plague [*sc.* fire] through the green timber eats, And vomits out a tardy flame by fits. **1748** Melmoth *Fitzosborne Lett.* li. (1749) II. 47 Those grotesque heads..which the ingenious architect has represented in the act of vomiting out the rain, which falls through certain pipes. **1820**

SHELLEY *Prometh. Unb.* I. i. 552 Many a million-peopled city Vomits smoke in the bright air. **1851** KINGSLEY *Yeast* xv, That huge black-mouthed sewer, vomiting its pestilential riches across the mud. **1871** PALGRAVE *Lyr. Poems* 84 The roar Of the dead salt sea that vomits Wrecks of the past ashore.

b. To discharge or emit, to send *out* or pour *forth* (persons or things, esp. in numbers) in a manner suggestive of vomiting.

1594 SHAKS. *Rich. III*, v. iii. 318 A scum of Brittaines,.. Whom their o're-cloyed Country vomits forth To desperate Aduentures. **1819** C'TESS SPENCER in *Lady Lyttelton's Corr.* viii. (1912) 213 If I find any Englishwoman going home by a diligence,.. Mrs. Bishop may be vomitted out at the Black Bear, Piccadilly. **1820** *Ibid.* 222 All such as you see vomited out of the steam-vessel upon Ramsgate or Margate piers. **1834** S. E. BRYDGES *Autobiog.* I. 108 An incredible quantity of nonsense is vomited from the press. **1850** DICKENS *Dav. Copp.* xvii, There was Uriah's blue bag lying down and vomiting papers. **1922** JOYCE *Ulysses* 750 If there was a row on you vomit a better face. **1946** E. O'NEILL *Iceman Cometh* III. 182 You'll be saying something soon that will make you vomit your own soul like a drink of nickel rotgut that won't stay down! **1955** E. BOWEN *World of Love* x. 185 Bent in two, she vomited laughter; though also, mortified by the exhibition, she let out penitent sobs and moans.

c. To eject or cast out by volcanic action; = SPEW *v.* 4 c. Also with advs., as *forth, up.*

1614 EARL STIRLING *Doomsday* II. lviii, The earth.. Doth vomit mountaines, and doth swallow Townes. **1687** A. LOVELL tr. *Thevenot's Trav.* I. 107 A little Rockie Island, which.. vomited up incredible Flames. **1713** *Lond. Gaz.* No. 5128/8 Mount Vesuvius had vomited violent Streams of Sulphur. **1770** W. HODSON *Ded. Temp. Solomon* 4 Ætna vomits forth her livid Fires. **1794** R. J. SULIVAN *View Nat.* I. 76 A mouth of fire is opened in a low place..: that mouth vomits a quantity of burning matters. **1837** CARLYLE *Fr. Rev.* III. III. iv, Mentz is changing into an explosive crater, vomiting fire, bevomited with fire! **1866** HERSCHEL *Fam. Lect. Sci.* (1867) 33 The opening of a chasm vomiting fire and red-hot stones and ashes. **1878** HUXLEY *Physiogr.* 218 The fused rocks.. which are vomited forth by volcanoes.

5. a. *absol.* Of emetics: To cause vomiting.

1651 FRENCH *Distill.* v. 172 You may have a Liquor in the morning which will vomit. **1681** tr. *Belon's Myst. Physick* Introd. 50 Which Tincture does variously operate, sometimes purging, sometimes (though rarely) vomiting. **1737** BRACKEN *Farriery Impr.* (1756) I. 284 The Mineral Bezoar will sometimes vomit. **1762** *Gentl. Mag.* 274 It [hemlock] seldom purges, very rarely vomits. **1822–7** GOOD *Study Med.* (1829) II. 57 Emetic tartar, when introduced into the jugular vein, will vomit in one or two minutes. **1843** R. J. GRAVES *Syst. Clin. Med.* iv. 50 When chemistry reveals why Tartar Emetic vomits.

b. *trans.* To cause (a person) to vomit.

1662 R. MATHEW *Unl. Alch.* 3 Yet will it vomit some, purge others, and make others sweat out of measure. **1753** N. TORRIANO *Gangr. Sore Throat* 34 We gave some Ipecacuanha, which vomited our Patient, and made her discharge several Membranes and Fragments of Eschars. **1756** C. LUCAS *Ess. Waters* II. 141 Some having taken this water in a mistake,.. it has vomitted and purged them. **1799** UNDERWOOD *Dis. Childhood* (ed. 4) I. 21 It is true, vinum antimoniale does not always vomit children. **1843** R. J. GRAVES *Syst. Clin. Med.* xii. 131 Almost every dose vomited him.

c. Said of the person administering the emetic; or in passive of the patient.

1684 tr. *Bonet's Merc. Compit.* VIII. 298 We presently proceeded to vomit him: for he was easy to vomit. **1727** SWIFT *Further Acc. E. Curll* Wks. 1755 III. I. 158, I have taken involuntary purges, I have been vomited. **1756** *Med. Obs. & Inq.* (1776) I. xxi. 271, I proposed.. to relieve her, by vomiting her in the most gentle manner. **1790** J. C. SMYTH in *Med. Commun.* II. 478 He was vomited with tartar emetic. **1810** BYRON *Let. to Hodgson* 3 Oct., The English Consul.. forced a physician upon me, and in three days vomited and glystered me to the last gasp. **1841** CATLIN *N. Amer. Ind.* lviii. (1844) II. 248 He is vomiting and purging his patients with herbs.

fig. **1682** DRYDEN & LEE *Dk. Guise* III. ii, I took thee for my Soul's Physician, And dost thou vomit me with this loath'd Piece? **1798** *Anti-Jacobin* No. 10 We'll vomit his purse, And make it the guineas disgorge.

6. *intr.* To issue, or come out, with force or violence; to rush *out*, to spout *up*.

1632 LITHGOW *Trav.* IX. 392 It impetuously vomiteth out, in an outragious Torrent. **1844**, **1904** [see VOMITING *ppl. a.*]

Hence **'vomited** *ppl. a.*

1846 DAY tr. *Simon's Anim. Chem.* II. 393 A case in which urea was detected in the vomited fluid. **1873** RALFE *Phys. Chem.* 46 In certain forms of dyspepsia they have been obtained from the vomited matters.

vomit-, the stem of VOMIT *v.* used in a few combinations, as †**vomit-grass**, a grass causing vomiting in dogs; **vomit-nut**, = VOMIC NUT (Simmonds *Dict. Trade*, 1858); **vomit-wort** *U.S.*, Indian tobacco (*Lobelia inflata*).

1808 JEFFERSON *Writ.* (1830) IV. 119 Your presence will be to them what the vomit-grass is to a sick dog.

vomitary, variant of (or misprint for) VOMITORY *sb.*

1651 WITTIE tr. *Primrose's Pop. Err.* 448 Much lesse vomitaries; for of all evacuations a vomit is the most grievous and dangerous. [*But p.* 338 vomitories.] **1833** SIR C. NAPIER *Colonies* 3 The innumerable tributary rivers which send their waters through these mighty vomitaries into the ocean.

'vomiter. [f. VOMIT *v.* + -ER. Cf. L. *vomitor.*] **1.** One who spews or vomits.

1565 COOPER *Thesaurus, Vomitor*, a vomiter. **1648** HEXHAM II, *Een braker*, a Vomiter, or a Spewer. **1739** 'R. BULL' tr. *Dedekindus' Grobianus* 266 The Vomiter in no small Passion flew, But all in vain: 'Twas nothing but his Due, Instead of Laurel to be crown'd with Spue. **1962** 'R. GORDON' *Doctor in Swim* xxiii. 160 'Also,' he added, 'one is being sick into the swimming pool.' 'All right,' I told him wearily. 'I'll do my best. Perhaps we'd better start with the little vomiter,' I suggested, putting professional things first.

†**2.** = VOMITORY *sb.* 1. *Obs.*

1634 P. LOWE *Chirurg.* 265 Purging the grosse phlegmatique humors by laxatives and vomiters. **1681** W. WALWYN *Physick* 4 Without any disturbance of Nature, by Loosners, Vomiters, Bleedings, Issues. **1717** WODROW *Corr.* (1843) II. 262 Let blood if your stitch continue, and take a vomiter. **1743** *Scott. Forfeited Estates Papers* (S.H.S.) 190 To Mary Strang, a vomiter, [£]0. 10. 0.

'vomiting, *vbl. sb.* [f. VOMIT *v.* + -ING[1].]

1. The act of ejecting the contents of the stomach through the mouth; an instance of this.

1495 *Trevisa's Barth. De P.R.* XVII. xxi. O ij b/1 This floure balaustia.. hath also vertue to staunche spewyng & vomytynge. **1555** W. WATREMAN *Fardle Facions* I. v. 73 When they are sicke, they heale them selues, eyther with fasting or vomiting. *a* **1568** in *Bannatyne MS.* (Hunt. Cl.) 196 Oppin thy crop at morrowing, Cast out flowme, mak vomating. **1603** HOLLAND *Plutarch's Mor.* 781 Inordinate passion of vomiting.. is nothing different from a keckish stomacke and a desire to cast. **1663** BOYLE *Usef. Exp. Nat. Philos.* II. v. xiv. 249 The Water.. has upon the gazer the operation of a rapid stream, and by making him giddy, hastens and facilitates his Vomiting. **1706** STANHOPE *Paraphr.* III. 323 Such a nauseating and indigestion that great Numbers.. dyed.. by violent Vomitings. **1742** in *Cath. Rec. Soc. Publ.* (1914) XIV. 137 A Sudden Vomiting seiz'd her, which deprived her of yᵉ Benefit of her Viaticum. **1813** J. THOMSON *Lect. Inflam.* 599 A mild vegetable aliment, where aliment can be taken without inducing sickness, or exciting vomiting. **1885** PATER *Marius* I. vii, A painful vomiting, which seemed to shake his body asunder.

b. Const. *of* (the matter ejected).

1601 HOLLAND *Pliny* II. Table, s.v., Vomiting of bloud out of the stomacke, how to bee cured. **1622** VENNER *Via Recta* viii. (ed. 2) 194 It.. induceth vomitings of bloud. **1728** CHAMBERS *Cycl.* s.v. *Colic*, A Vomiting of bilious green Liquor. **1765** WESLEY *Jrnl.* 27 May (1827) III. 215 A young man, brought near death by a vomiting of blood. **1822–7** GOOD *Study Med.* (1829) II. 183 Gangrene.. accompanied with a vomiting of matter resembling coffee-grounds. **1859** MAYNE *Expos. Lex.* 1337/2 *Vomiting of Blood*,.. common term for the disease *Hæmatemesis.*

c. With defining terms. (See quots.)

1794 B. RUSH *Acc. Yellow Fever* (ed. 2) 56 Several persons died without a black vomiting of any kind. **1836** MACGILLIVRAY *Trav. Humboldt* xxi. 300 The yellow fever or black vomiting is prevalent. *a* **1883** FAGGE *Princ. & Pract. Med.* (1886) II. 130 'Irritability of the stomach,' or 'hysterical vomiting.' **1895** *Funk's Stand. Dict., Morning vomiting*, the vomiting of drunkards, due to alcoholism; also, the vomiting of pregnant women.

2. *concr.* Matter which is vomited; = VOMIT *sb.* 2.

1727 SWIFT *Poisoning E. Curll* Wks. 1755 III. I. 149 The contents of his vomiting being as green as grass. **1794** B. RUSH *Acc. Yellow Fever* (ed. 2) 56 The matter which constitutes the fatal black vomiting.

3. *techn.* (See quot. and VOMITING *ppl. a.*)

1881 *Spons' Encycl. Industr. Arts* IV. 1486 The steam from the pipe A heats the liquor.. and forcing it up the wide pipe C, causes it to strike against the dome or bonnet D... This is technically called 'vomiting'.

4. *attrib.*, chiefly in the sense 'causing vomiting, emetic', as ***vomiting drink, julep, pap, tartar***, etc.; †**vomiting nut**, = NUX VOMICA I.

(*a*) **1575** BANISTER *Chyrurg.* 106 b, *Nux vomica*, the vomiting nutte. **1587** *Wills & Inv. N.C.* (Surtees 1860) 155, iij vomitinge nottes of puther. **1668** CULPEPPER & COLE *Barthol. Anat.* I. xviii. 49 They are no bigger than a large vomiting Nut. **1681** GREW *Musæum* II. I. iv. 210 The true Methel; or the Vomiting-Nut commonly so call'd. **1712** tr. *Pomet's Hist. Drugs* I. 137 The Vomiting Nuts are round, flat Nuts, of divers Colours. **1723** *Pres. St. Russia* II. 53 They.. pour strong Vinegar upon vomiting Nuts.

(*b*) **1647** HEXHAM I, A vomiting drinke or potion, *een dranck die over-geven doet.* **1663** BOYLE *Usef. Exp. Nat. Philos.* II. v. viii. 189 That violent Vomiting Medicine.. called.. Mercurius Vitæ. **1694** W. SALMON *Bate's Dispens.* (1713) 363/2 A Vomiting Pappe. *Ibid.* 527/2 *Tartarum Emeticum*, Emetick, or Vomiting Tartar. **1737** *Med. Ess. & Observ.* IV. 33 An Essay towards ascertaining the Doses of vomiting and purging Medicines. **1789** W. BUCHAN *Dom. Med.* (1790) 191 A few spoonfuls of the vomiting julep, will generally answer this purpose.

(*c*) **1651** WITTIE tr. *Primrose's Pop. Err.* 44 He that first found out the vomiting vertue of antimony. **1899** *Allbutt's Syst. Med.* VII. 650 Again vomiting.. is suggestive.. of a tumour in the region of the vomiting centre.

'vomiting, *ppl. a.* [f. as prec. + -ING[2].] That vomits or causes to vomit.

vomiting-boiler: (see quot. 1844).

1844 G. DODD *Textile Manuf.* ii. 76 A 'vomiting-boiler', that is, a boiler so constructed that the water is made to vomit upwards from a pipe, and then to fall down on the cloth in the boiler. **1879** *Cassell's Techn. Educ.* III. 14/2 Fixed kiers with a vomiting-pipe. **1880** J. DUNBAR *Pract. Paperm.* (1881) 19 [Esparto grass] boiled for 10 hours in stationary vomiting boilers with 10 lb. steam pressure. **1904** R. J. FARRER *Gard. Asia* 248 From the wide plain leapt a vomiting cone of fire.

'vomitingly, *adv. rare*[−1]. [f. as prec. + -LY[2].] In a manner suggestive of vomiting.

1609 DEKKER *Gull's Horn-bk.* 24 Take occasion (pulling out your gloues) to haue some Epigram.. or Sonnet fastned in one of them, that may (as it were vomittingly to you) offer it selfe to the Gentlemen.

vomition (və'mɪʃən). [a. obs. F. *vomition* (16th c.), or ad. L. *vomitiōn-is, vomitio*, noun of action f. *vomĕre* to vomit.] The action of vomiting.

1656 BLOUNT *Glossogr., Vomition*, a vomiting, casting, or parbreaking. **1676** GREW *Musæum, Anat. Stomach & Guts* vi. 25 The use hereof with Vndulation, is for Vomition. **1701** —— *Cosm. Sacra* III. ii. 98 If the Stomack had wanted the Faculty of Vomition, they had inevitably died. *c* **1714** ARBUTHNOT, etc. *M. Scriblerus* I. x, He attended Dr. Woodward through a twelve months course of vomition. **1800** *Med. Jrnl.* III. 585 Prof. Hufeland distinguishes two species of vomition of the milk observed in infants. **1822–7** GOOD *Study Med.* (1829) II. 619 An emetic which.. has the additional benefit of emulging the meseraic or mesenteric vessels by the act of vomition. **1908** *Edin. Rev.* July 200 Some of these.. were relieved by a copious vomition and survived.

†**vomitive**, *a.* and *sb. Obs.* Also 7 **vomitif**, **womitive**; 6 *Sc.* **womatiue**, 7–8 **vomative**. [a. F. *vomitif, -ive* (= Sp., Pg., It. *vomitivo*), ad. med.L. **vomitīv-us*: see VOMIT *v.* and -IVE.]

A. *adj.* **1.** Of medicines, etc.: Causing vomiting; vomitory; emetic.

1580 *Well of Woman Hill, Aberdeen* a 2 b, To vtheris it is womatiue. **1635** J. HAYWARD tr. *Biondi's Banish'd Virg.* 142 Being therein helped by certaine vomitive pils. **1646** SIR T. BROWNE *Pseud. Ep.* VI. xii. 337 From this vitriolous quality *Mercuries dulcis*, and vitriol vomitive occasion black ejections. **1682** *Hist. Thee* in *Harl. Misc.* I. 532 Now Thee itself, when given in a large dose,.. does often prove vomitive. **1725** SLOANE *Jamaica* II. 186 These nuts grow in Jamaica; they are not vomitive,.. but called and eaten as Wallnuts. **1754** *Phil. Trans.* XLVIII. 846 [Antimony] being in substance most violently vomitive.

2. Of or pertaining to vomiting.

1657 G. STARKEY *Helmont's Vind.* Ep. Rdr. 10 The true preparation of all Vegetals, takes away.. the vomitive quality of them, except only in Opium. **1663** BOYLE *Usef. Exp. Nat. Philos.* II. v. viii. 189 That Vomitive faculty, of Antimonial Glass. *a* **1691** —— *Hist. Air* (1692) 233 *Antimonium Diaphoreticum*, being kept some Years,.. acquir'd a Vomitive Quality.

B. *sb.* An emetic; = VOMITORY *sb.* I.

1611 COTGR., *Vomitif*, a Vomitiue, or Vomitorie; any thing that prouokes vomiting. **1677** HORNECK *Gt. Law Consid.* vii. (1704) 422 Physicians.. make him sicker than he is.. by vomitives. **1697** *Phil. Trans.* XIX. 403 They gave her also Vomitives and Deobstruents. **1728** CHAMBERS *Cycl.*, The *Ipecacuanha*.. is also a gentle Vomitive. **1747** tr. *Astruc's Fevers* 71 The second indication is to evacuate the morbid humour by vomitives or purgatives, or a catharticoemetic. **1756** C. LUCAS *Ess. Waters* III. 337 Vomits may be rendered purgatives, and purges vomitives.

fig. **1685** *Gracian's Courtier's Orac.* 192 Slowness in believing is a Vomitive that brings up secrets.

‖**vomito** ('vomito). [Sp. (and Pg.) *vómito*, ad. L. *vomitus*, f. *vomĕre* to VOMIT.] The yellow fever in its virulent form, when it is usually accompanied by black vomit. Cf. VOMIT *sb.* 2 b.

1833 *Cycl. Pract. Med.* II. 290/2 He even says that during the eight years preceding 1794, there was not a single example of the *vomito.* **1843** PRESCOTT *Mexico* (1850) I. 2 The season of the bilious fever,—*vomito*, as it is called,—which scourges these coasts. **1869** E. A. PARKES *Pract. Hygiene* (ed. 3) 472 When paroxysmal fever and the true yellow fever or vomito were thought to own a common cause.

vomi'torial, *a.* [f. L. *vomitōria* (see VOMITORIUM) + -AL[1].] **1.** Of or pertaining to a vomitorium or vomitoria. *rare*[−1].

1850 DOBELL *Roman* v. Poet. Wks. (1875) 59 From these wide And vomitorial windows, belched your tumult To me transgressing.

2. = VOMITORY *a.* (in quot. *fig.*). *rare.*

1868 SWINBURNE *Let.* 1 Jan. (1959) I. 284 What abject and vomitorial rot of Tennyson's is this in Once a Week!

‖**vomi'torium.** *Roman Antiq.* Pl. **vomitoria** (also 8 **-iums**, *erron.* **-iæ**). [Neuter sing. of L. *vomitōrius* (cf. next); recorded only in pl. (Macrobius *Sat.* VI. iv).] **1.** A passage or opening in an ancient amphitheatre or theatre, leading to or from the seats. Usu. pl.

1754 *Dict. Arts & Sci.* I. 129/2 They were entered by avenues, at the end of which were gates, called vomitoriæ. **1766** SMOLLETT *Trav.* II. 228 The remains of two galleries one over another; and two vomitoria or great gateways at opposite sides of the arena. **1837** *Antiq. Athens* 48 Those numerous corridors and vomitoria which gave such free.. access to all parts of a Roman theatre.

2. *erron.* A room in which ancient Romans are alleged to have vomited deliberately during feasts.

1923 A. HUXLEY *Antic Hay* xviii. 252 There strode in, like a Goth into the elegant marble vomitorium of Petronius Arbiter, a haggard and dishevelled person. **1965** R. EBERHART *Sel. Poems* 40 Good Boy Man! Your innards are put out, From now all space will be your vomitorium.

vomitory ('vɒmɪtərɪ), *sb.* [ad. L. *vomitōri-um* (whence F. *vomitoire*, Sp., Pg., It. *vomitorio*): see prec. and next.]

†**1.** A medicine or the like which causes or induces vomiting; an emetic. *Obs.*

1601 HOLLAND *Pliny* II. 252 This Tithymall is nothing so strong a vomitorie as the former. **1666** G. HARVEY *Morb. Angl.* xix. (1672) 38 Having a power to force themselves a vomiting.. by straining, or by other means in taking Vomitories privately. **1694** SALMON *Bate's Dispens.* (1713) 332/1 A most gentle Vomitory, Dejectory, and

Diaphoretick. **1753** *Chambers' Cycl.* Suppl. s.v. *Anacatharsis*, Vomitories, sternutatories or masticatories. *fig.* **1651** WITTIE tr. *Primrose's Pop. Err.* IV. xxxiv. 338 So infirme..are all those things which are prescribed against this sort of poyson, but especially vomitories who do..offer great violence to Nature.

2. An opening, door, or passage in a theatre, playhouse, or the like, affording ingress or egress to the spectators; originally (and usually) = VOMITORIUM.

1730 A. GORDON *Maffei's Amphith.* 274 He had made the number of the Vomitories in the Middle full in the second Line. **1776** GIBBON *Decl. & F.* xii. I. 351 Sixty-four *vomitories* (for by that name the doors were very aptly distinguished) poured forth the immense multitude. **1847** PRESCOTT *Peru* (1850) II. 54 Low ranges of buildings, consisting of spacious halls with wide doors or vomitories opening into the square. **1850** *Tait's Mag.* XVII. 629/1 Yonder are the vomitories through which..the tide of eager population flowed. **1861** MISS E. A. BEAUFORT *Egypt. Sepulchres & Syrian Shr.* II. xxiv. 320 Near this are the remains of a once fine theatre..: some of the vomitories still remain.

3. A funnel, vent, or other opening through which matter is emitted or discharged.

1822 *Blackw. Mag.* XI. 427 A low building, which is almost all chimney—it has indeed a wide-throated vomitory ..for so tiny an edifice. **1863** LYELL *Antiq. Man* xv. 307 From this vomitory, the old glacier poured into the plains.. that wonderful accumulation of mud. **1904** R. G. FARRER *Gard. Asia* 165 Those roaring vomitories [*sc.* volcanoes] of the underworld.

b. In fig. use.

1826 J. WILSON *Noct. Ambr.* Wks. 1855 I. 270 His tongue struck dumb in his cheek, and the vomitory of vociferation hermetically sealed. **1829** *Blackw. Mag.* XXVI. 917 Our three great theatres, which Mr. Prynne..proved long ago to be vomitories of vice. **1830** *Fraser's Mag.* I. 236 The great vomitory of the London press. **1878** J. THOMSON *Plenip. Key* 25 Your shameless charlatans whose dirty tricks And frothy gab defile all politics..Retard sure progress—damn such vomitories!

vomitory (ˈvɒmɪtərɪ), *a.* [ad. L. *vomitōri-us*, f. *vomĕre* to VOMIT: see -ORY².]

1. Of or pertaining to vomiting.

1620 VENNER *Via Recta* vi. 103 Their heating, cutting, attenuating and vomitorie facultie. **1646** SIR T. BROWNE *Pseud. Ep.* II. v. 86 Its Regulus will manifestly communicate unto water, or wine, a purging and vomitory operation. **1672** GREW *Idea Philos. Hist. Plants* §7 Whence one [faculty] becomes Purgative, another Vomitory, a third Diaphoretick. **1701** WOLLEY *Jrnl. New York* (1860) 61 If we will believe the ingenious Dr. Carr,..there is an Emetick Vomitory vertue in the Sea-water it self. **1849** *Blackw. Mag.* LXVI. 684 Vomitory agonies, and spasms of the diaphragm.

2. Efficacious in promoting vomiting; causing vomiting; emetic.

1634 T. JOHNSON *Parey's Chirurg. Wks.* xxvi. v. (1678) 632 Agarick, and other nauseous and vomitory Medicins. **1662** J. CHANDLER *Van Helmont's Oriat.* 228 A Physitian of the City offers him a vomitory potion, whereby he vomited twice every day. **1684** tr. *Bonet's Merc. Compit.* VI. 212 After taking a Medicine, whether sudorifick or vomitory. **1706** PHILLIPS (ed. Kersey). **1859** MAYNE *Expos. Lex.* 1337/2 *Vomitorius*,..causing vomiting; emetic;..vomitory.

'vomitous, *a. U.S.* [f. VOMIT *sb.* + -OUS.] Repugnant, loathsome, nauseating.

1952 S. KAUFFMANN *Tightrope* xiv. 241 What kind of world is this..having to trudge back from bad restaurants in sickening heat to face mountains of vomitous, meaningless, commercial tripe? **1976** *Publishers Weekly* 24 May 57/2 Those descriptions of methods of murdering human beings as dishes for the table end up being more than a little vomitous.

†**vomiture.** *Obs.*⁻¹ [f. VOMIT *sb.* + -URE.] Matter ejected by or as by vomiting.

1598 BP. HALL *Sat.* IV. i. 42 Long as the craftie Cuttle lieth sure In the blacke cloude of his thicke vomiture.

†**vomiturient,** *a. Obs.*⁻¹ [Cf. next and -URIENT.] Characterized by a desire to vomit.

1666 H. STUBBE *Mirac. Conformist* 43 He was sick at Stomach, and seemed to be in a very vomiturient condition.

vomitu'rition. [a. F. *vomiturition* or ad. med. or mod.L. *vomiturītiōn-*, *vomituritio*, noun of action f. **vomiturīre* to desire to vomit.] (See first quot.)

1842 DUNGLISON *Med. Lex.*, *Vomiturition*,..ineffectual efforts to vomit. Some authors mean..the vomiting of but little, or..without effort. [Hence in Worcester (1846) and later Dicts.] **1872** THUDICHUM *Chem. Phys.* 6 This can be collected in quantity by irritating the fauces with a feather, and producing vomituritions.

vomitus (ˈvɒmɪtəs). [L.] = VOMIT *sb.* 2 a. Also *fig.*

1904 J. M. FRENCH *Text-bk. Pract. Med.* III. 724 The presence of HCl, pepsin, and rennet is generally sufficient evidence that the vomitus has come from the stomach. **1948** *Diagnostic Procedures for Virus & Rickettsial Diseases* (Amer. Public Health Assoc.) 11 The material available for examination may be blood, sputum, vomitus, or pleural fluid obtained during illness, or tissues, etc., collected at autopsy. **1973** *Nature* 23 Mar. 265/1 Stools, urine and vomitus were collected for a total of 48 h. **1978** J. UPDIKE *Coup* (1979) v. 211 Fighting down the vomitus of superstitious terror rising in my craw.

'vomity, *a. U.S.* [f. VOMIT *sb.* + -Y¹.] Redolent of vomit.

1951 J. D. SALINGER *Catcher in Rye* xii. 106 The cab I had was a real old one that smelled like someone'd just tossed his cookies in it. I always get those vomity kind of cabs if I go anywhere late at night. **1967** I. A. BARAKA in W. King *Black Short Story Anthol.* (1972) 125 Oh, I am drunk and vomity in my room, with only Charley Ventura to understand my grace. **1984** *Listener* 20–27 Dec. 68/3, 80 per cent of the material is American, vomity kind of lampoons of great American institutions such as Advertising and the Presidency.

von, ME. var. WONE *sb. Obs.*

vond(e, southern ME. var. *fond*, pa. t. of FIND *v.*

vonde(n, -di-, -dy, southern ME. varr. FAND *v.*

vondir, vondit, vone, obs. Sc. ff. WONDER, WOUNDED, WONE *v.*

vonge, southern ME. var. FANG *v.*

vonnyn, obs. Sc. pa. pple. WIN *v.*

vonnyt, obs. Sc. pa. t. WONE *v.*

von Recklinghausen's disease (fɒn ˈrɛklɪŋhaʊzən). *Path.* [Named after Friedrich *von Recklinghausen* (1833–1910), German pathologist.] **1.** A familial disease in which numerous neurofibromas develop on various parts of the body, esp. the skin, the nerve trunks, and the peripheral nerves (described by von Recklinghausen in 1882). Also **Recklinghausen's disease.**

1899, etc. [see NEUROFIBROMATOSIS]. **1900** H. A. THOMSON *Neuroma & Neuro-Fibromatosis* iv. 55 There is not even a good general name for the group which will include all its members, unless we adopt that suggested by certain French authors, viz.—'von Recklinghausen's Disease'. **1935** [see NEURILEMOMA, NEURILEMMOMA]. **1969** S. JABLONSKI *Illustr. Dict. Eponymic Syndromes & Dis.* 256/1 (*caption*) Recklinghausen's disease. **1976** *Path. Ann.* XI. 371 A total of 15 schwannomas were studied ultrastructurally. Of these, two were classified as neurofibromas by light microscopy and were associated with von Recklinghausen's disease.

2. A disease in which bones are weakened by diffuse resorption and fibrous replacement of the bone substance as a result of hyperparathyroidism, leading to bowing of long bones and sometimes deformities of the chest and spine (described by von Recklinghausen in 1891); osteitis fibrosa cystica.

1910 *Ann. Surg.* Aug. 163 Crile and Hill interpret..as multiple giant-cell sarcoma, but it seems to me that it belongs to the group of Von Recklinghausen's disease. **1949** *New Gould Med. Dict.* 862/1 Generalized osteitis fibrosa cystica is called von Recklinghausen's disease of the bone. **1966** WRIGHT & SYMMERS *Systemic Path.* II. xxxii. 1129/1 Some forty years elapsed before it was recognised that von Recklinghausen's disease of the bones was..directly due to an excess of circulating parathyroid hormone. **1984** TIGHE & DAVIES *Pathology* (ed. 4) xxi. 209 These changes produce the 'brown tumours' of osteitis fibrosa cystica (von Recklinghausen's disease of bone) which may be misdiagnosed as giant cell tumours of bone (osteoclastoma).

vonsenite (ˈvɒnsənaɪt). *Min.* [f. the name of Marcus *Vonsen* (1879–1954), U.S. amateur mineralogist who collected the original material + -ITE¹.] A borate of ferrous and ferric iron, $Fe^{II}{}_2Fe^{III}BO_5$, that occurs as black, lustrous, orthorhombic crystals and is the magnesium-free end-member of a series with ludwigite.

1920 A. S. EAKLE in *Amer. Mineralogist* V. 143 Its distinctive difference in composition, and its manifest difference in structural and optical characters from ludwigite, justifies the writer in proposing the new name vonsenite. **1976** *Mineral. Abstr.* XXVII. 279/2 The first Spanish occurrence of vonsenite, end-member of the magnesium and iron borate series, is reported from the 'Monchi' mine [Badajoz].

vont, obs. Sc. f. WONT *a.*

von Willebrand (vɒn ˈwɪləbrænd). *Path.* The name of E. A. von *Willebrand* (1870–1949) Finnish physician, used *attrib.* and in the possessive to designate a hereditary disease described by him that is characterized by prolonged bleeding, chiefly caused by abnormalities of the capillaries and mucous membranes.

1941 *Q. Jrnl. Med.* XXXIV. 18 It [*sc.* athrombocytopenic purpura] has also been called Von Willebrand's disease, Glantzmann's disease, and 'hemogenia'. **1966** WRIGHT & SUMMERS *Systemic Path.* I. iv. 190/1 In von Willebrand's disease the platelets are morphologically and functionally normal, but the capillaries show both structural and functional changes. **1977** [see *replacement therapy* s.v. REPLACEMENT 3].

vonyng, obs. Sc. pa. pple. WIN *v.*

voo, obs. Sc. f. WOE *a.*

voodoo (ˈvuːduː), *sb.* Also vodoo, voodu, voudon, voudoo, voudou, voudoun, vudu, and VAUDOUX. (Cf. HOODOO.) [African (Dahomey) *vodu.*]

1. A form of religious witchcraft prevalent among Blacks in the West Indies, esp. Haiti, and the southern United States, and ultimately of African origin.

1880 G. W. CABLE *Grandissimes* xiv, Do this much for me this one time and then I will let voudou alone as much as you wish. **1884** *Lisbon* (Dakota) *Star* 20 Sept., The Voudoos of Louisiana..were recently viewed at the funeral of a negress, one of the Queens of Voudoo. **1888** *Daily News* 15 June 5/1 As generally understood, Voodoo means the persistence, in Hayti, of abominable magic, mysteries, and cannibalism, brought originally by the negroes from Africa. **1953** M. DEREN *Divine Horsemen* 15 Voudoun is the religion, primarily African in origin, of the vast majority of the Republic of Haiti in the West Indies.

2. One who practises voodoo; a Black sorcerer or witch; a voodoo spirit.

1880 G. W. CABLE *Grandissimes* xii, She practised the less baleful rites of the voudous. **1880** *New Orleans Picayune* 20 May, The fool spends all her money to do us harm, thinking she is a voudou. **1888** *Daily News* 15 June 5/2 Accused, like the Voodoos, of serpent-worship. **1953** M. DEREN *Divine Horsemen* 60 Voudoun (which is the Fons word for god) includes the loa (the Congo word for the spirits) of many nations. **1953** *Times Lit. Suppl.* 2 Aug. 510 A Voudoun, as some purists insist, with little basis, in spelling it. **1958** J. SYKES *Quakers* I. i. 34 Almost any gathering of English citizenry could run to a pitch one associates more with a Haitian voudoun possessed by 'the loa'.

3. *attrib.*, as ***voodoo adorer, dance, doctor, king, pantheon, priest, queen***, etc.

1868 *De Bow's Rev.* Aug. 724 But may not the agent be met, then, by some such valid objection, on the part of the *Vodoo* adorers? **1872** *New Orleans Times* 28 June, Soon there arrived a skiff containing ten persons, among which was the Voudou queen. **1885** *Boston* (Mass.) *Jrnl.* 17 Aug. 2/4 Under the influence of some withered old mummy of a voodoo-doctor. **1887** LANG *Myth, Rit. & Relig.* II. 240 The Voodoo-dance is consecrated as the 'Jerusalem Jump'. **1888** *Pall Mall G.* 4 July 13/2 An old negro woman who claims to be a great voudoo doctor. **1905** DU BOIS *Souls Black Folk* x. 198 The witch-woman and the voodoo-priest became the centre of Negro group life. **1939** M. STEEDMAN *Unknown to World: Haiti* xvii. 159 The gods and goddesses of the Voudon pantheon are known as the 'Lois'. **1974** A. MURRAY *Stomping Blues* ii. 10 Some specific..charm, or talisman, which can be counteracted only with the aid of a voodoo queen or madam (or somewhat less often, a voodoo king, doctor, witchdoctor, or snakedoctor).

Hence **'voodoo** *v. trans.*, to bewitch, to cast a spell over, by means of voodoo arts.

1880 G. W. CABLE *Grandissimes* xxix, It is true, as he says, that he is voudoued. **1880** *New Orleans Picayune* 20 May, She flung this over into my yard to voudou me... She would spend her last dollar to voudou me. **1885** C. F. HOLDER *Marvels Anim. Life* 117 Averring that they had been 'voudoued' and nearly killed by the..fish.

voodooism (ˈvuːduːɪz(ə)m). Also **voudouism, vooduism,** and VAUDOUISM. [f. prec. + -ISM.] The system of beliefs and practices constituting voodoo; the belief in, or practice of, voodoo as a superstition or form of religous witchcraft.

1871 *N. & Q.* 4th Ser. VII. 210/2 What is Voodouism? **1880** *New Orleans Picayune* 20 May, Finding that no affidavit could be made for voudouism. **1883** *Philadelphia Times* No. 3023. 3 His mission is to supplant Voodooism and its kindred superstitions among the colored population. **1897** *Church Progr.* (St. Louis, U.S.A.) 18 April, A sort of refined Voodooism disguised in Christian phraseology.

voodooist (ˈvuːduːɪst). [f. VOODOO *sb.* + -IST.] A practitioner of voodoo. Also *fig.*

1929 W. B. SEABROOK *Magic Island* 289 The connection which Haitian Voodooists believe exists between Dangbé and Ayida-Ouédo. **1935** *Sun* (Baltimore) 2 Jan. 10/1 Full payment of the bonus will be accomplished..by the addition of the strength of the miracle workers in finance, the monetary voodooists, to the strength of the veterans' bloc. **1958** *Times* 18 Sept. 13/2 On the one side are set a young American officer, his wife..and others of his race, and, on the other, well, the others: the dark, the alien, the voodooists. **1966** G. GREENE *Comedians* I. ii. 57 Joseph was a good Catholic as well as a good Voodooist.

voog, variant of VUG.

vool, -ish, southern dial. varr. FOOL, FOOLISH *a.*

1569 PRESTON *Cambyses* D iv b, I think the vool be mad. *Ibid.*, Has he plaid zuch a volish [*sic*] deed?

voom (vuːm), *int. U.S.* [Echoic.] Indicating the sound of an explosion; usu. in *fig.* contexts. Occas. redupl. as *sb.*, the roar of an engine being revved. Cf. VROOM.

1964 in Hamblett & Deverson *Generation X* 115 Ideally, according to them, young people should be seen and not heard. The moment they do something to draw attention to themselves, voom: trouble. **1968** S. J. PERELMAN in *New Yorker* 23 Nov. 58/1 The inspiration came to me—*voom.* **1978** *New York* 3 Apr. 56/1 The screeching car brakes, honking horns, the voom-voom of motorcycles, and the thundering of First Avenue buses exhausted me. **1985** *Observer* 12 May 1/1, I thought someone had let off a smoke bomb, then voom it all went off.

voom, variant of VOME *sb. Obs.*

voor. *dial.* [var. VORE².] A furrow.

1669 WORLIDGE *Syst. Agric.* (1681) 334 A Voor, or Furrow of Land. [Hence in Ray, Phillips, etc.] **1889**- in southwestern dialects (*Eng. Dial. Dict.* s.v. FOOR *sb.*¹).

‖**voorbok** (ˈfʊərbɔk). *S. Afr.* Pl. voorbokke. [Afrikaans.] A goat which acts as bell-wether to a flock of sheep. Also *fig.* Cf. BELL-WETHER 2.

1913 C. PETTMAN *Africanderisms* 540 *Voorbok*... A goat.. is generally used on South African sheep-farms, instead of a bell-wether as in England. **1947** *Cape Argus* 29 Mar. 6 Many English-speaking South Africans regarded him as a man wielding a moderating influence upon racial politics. Why then should he not be useful as a bell-wether ('voorbok') leading United Party sheep into the Herenigde kraal? **1951** *Cape Times* 15 Aug. 2/6 A delivery van ran into a flock of sheep.., killing 25 sheep and the voorbok. **1972** *Daily Dispatch* (East London) 6 May 10 It reminds me of days long ago when farmers trekked their sheep from the Free State to the better winter grazing of the Natal lowveld. Each flock was led by a goat, the voorbok. The sheep..would never cross a river or enter a gate unless led by the more clever voorbok. **1976** *Evening Post* (Port Elizabeth) 20 Nov., The woman..was described in court as one of the 'voorbokke' of the riots who incited children to throw stones at White people's cars.

‖**voorhuis** (ˈfʊərhœys). *S. Afr.* [Cape Du., a. Du. *voorhuis* fore-part, hall of a house.] In a Cape Dutch house, an entrance hall, or a room into which the front door opens; a front room or sitting-room.

1822 W. J. BURCHELL *Trav. Interior S. Afr.* I. vi. 118 At about half an hour after nine, all retired to rest; some to a mat on the floor in the *voorhuis* (entrance-room, or hall). **1867** E. L. LAYARD *Birds S. Afr.* 118 Perhaps one or two would have found their way into the *voorhuis*, or entrance-hall. **1923** [see RIEMPIE]. **1946** *Cape Times Week-end Mag.* 16 Nov. 4 The thatched cottage..had only two rooms; a *voorhuis* and bedroom. **1981** *N. & Q.* June 193/2 The *voorhuis* was the large central space or hall, often running right through the house, off which the other rooms opened.

‖**voorkamer** (ˈfʊərkɑːmər). *S. Afr.* [Afrikaans.] = prec. Occas. partially anglicized as fore-kamer.

1775 S. PIGOT *Let.* Aug. in 'V. M. Fitzroy' *Dark Bright Land* (1955) i. 16 Papa and Leonora..are at Whisk in mijnheer's fore-kamer as they style it. **1827** G. THOMPSON *Trav. & Adv. S. Afr.* (ed. 2) I. i. iii. 49, I slept this night in the outer apartment (voorkamer) or sitting-room of the house. **1896** *Cape Argus* 2 Jan. 5 The flash entered at the front doorway, and the shock was felt by all the occupants of the *voorkamer*, fourteen in number. **1940** 'B. KNIGHT' *Piping on Wind* IV. xx. 298 The voorkamer had been cleared of its furniture for dancing. **1981** *N. & Q.* June 193/2 The sitting-room or *voorkamer* appears to have been most often one of the smaller rooms, and with a fireplace.

‖**voorloper** (ˈfʊərlʊəpər). *S. Afr.* Also voorlooper. [Du., Afrikaans, f. Du. *voor-* before + *loopen* to run (see LEAP *v.*).] A native boy who walks with the foremost pair of a team of oxen in order to guide them. Also *fig.*

1837 J. E. ALEXANDER *Western Afr.* I. xiii. 323 Then a long wagon would pass..drawn by a span of ten or fourteen oxen under the guidance of a *voorlooper*, a brown boy, holding occasionally a small rope attached to the horns of the leading bullocks. **1852** C. BARTER *Dorp & Veld* vii. 49 Our driver and leader, or *voor looper*, were both Hottentots. **1878** AYLWARD *Transvaal of To-day* ii. 18 *note*, Every team of bullocks has a leader, generally a native boy, who holds a tow-line fastened to the horns of the front oxen, hence the word 'Voorlooper'. **1885** RIDER HAGGARD *K. Solomon's Mines* i, A wagon, with a driver, a voorlooper, and a Kafir hunter. **1899** G. H. RUSSEL *Under Sjambok* 50 But, have you not got me a driver and voorloper? **1947** *Cape Argus* 22 Feb. 4 We in the pilot train are at first sight everywhere mistaken for the royal train itself. In time..the fact that we are merely the 'voorloper' of royalty will become more generally known. **1974** *Weekend Post* 21 Dec. 2 Clandestine trips were made across the Great Fish River, and it was on these that George Wood became a 'voorloper' of the oxen.

‖**voorskot** (ˈfʊərskɔt). *S. Afr.* [Afrikaans, f. *voorskiet* to advance (money).] The advance payment for a crop, wool clip, etc., by a farmers' co-operative society or similar body to its members. Also *transf.* Cf. AGTERSKOT.

1948 *Cape Times* 22 Nov. 14 The Land Bank had fixed the *voorskot* price for first grade lucerne at 3s. for 100 lb. **1958** *Ibid.* 6 Nov. 1/1 Importers of raw materials and machinery would..receive 33⅓ per cent. of 1958 issues as *voorskot*. **1961** *Ibid.* 15 Feb. 9/7 A figure of R50m. is being mentioned as a *voorskot* for Bantu homelands. **1974** *Eastern Province Herald* (Port Elizabeth) 9 Sept., The Voorskot for the 1974/75 wool season has been fixed at an average of R1.50 a kilogram for clean wool.

‖**voorslag** (ˈfʊərslax). [Afrikaans.] The lash of a whip.

1833 *Graham's Town Jrnl.* 4 Apr. 3 He then took his whip and in endeavouring to frighten them began using the 'voor slach' of the whip. **1852** C. BARTER *Dorp & Veld* v. 43 Putting a new *voorslag* (lash) to the wagon-whip, that its smack might be clear and loud. **1910** J. BUCHAN *Prester John* iii. 59 He roared with laughter at my way of tying a *voorslag*. **1939** 'D. RAME' *Wine of Good Hope* I. v. 71 The great twelve foot driving whip with its thong of eland hide..and its thin, cutting voorslag. **1973** *Farmer's Weekly* (Suppl.) 30 May 37 Voorslags 86c doz.

‖**Voortrekker** (ˈfʊərtrɛkər). *S. Afr.* [Du., Afrikaans, f. Du. *voor-* before + *trekken* TREK *v.*] One of the original Dutch emigrants into the Transvaal; a pioneer.

1878 AYLWARD *Transvaal of To-day* i. 3 Mr. Oliphant,..in speaking of the Voortrekkers (advanced pioneers), says [etc.]. **1883** *Pall Mall G.* 26 Nov. 2/1 To prevent a large and respected portion of the English people from ever doing justice to the Transvaal Voortrekkers. **1899** RIDER HAGGARD *Swallow* Introd. §2 Sympathy with the Voortrekkers of 1836 is easy.

attrib. **1885** J. G. MILLAIS *Breath fr. Veldt* (1899) 61 In those days the 'voor-trekker' Dutchmen shot them [the natives] down like rabbits. **1899** FITZPATRICK *Transvaal* 26 The active party among the Boers, i.e. the Voortrekker party, the most anti-British and Republican.

Vopo (ˈfəʊpəʊ). [a. Ger., f. *volkspolizei* people's police.] (A member of) the *Volkspolizei* (see VOLK 3 b).

1954 *Ann. Reg. 1953* 216 Members of the 'people's police', or *Vopos*, threw away their weapons. **1959** *News Chron.* 9 July 4/6 The Vopo—the People's Police. **1966**, **1967** [see GREPO]. **1978** L. HEREN *Growing up on The Times* vi. 237 The young Vopo returned with a sergeant.., who returned our passports with an apology.

vor, southern var. FOR *prep.* and *conj.*, southern ME. pa. t. FARE *v.*

vor-, southern ME. variant of FOR- *prefix*.

voracious (vɒˈreɪʃəs), *a.* [f. L. *vorāci-*, *vorax*, f. *vorāre* to devour + -OUS. Cf. F. *vorace*, It. *vorace*, Sp. and Pg. *voraz*.]

1. Of animals (rarely of persons, or of the throat): Eating with greediness; devouring food in large quantities; gluttonous, ravenous. Also const. *of*.

1693 CONGREVE in *Dryden's Juvenal* xi. (1697) 283 Well may they fear some miserable End,..Whose large voracious Throats have swallow'd All. **1699** DAMPIER *Voy.* II. 68 The King Carrion Crows..are very voracious, and will dispatch a carkass in a trice. **1725** DE FOE *Voy. round World* (1840) 231 The Spaniards are..cruel, inexorable, uncharitable, voracious. **1750** G. HUGHES *Barbados* 81 These [Cockroaches] are very troublesome, being voracious of most kinds of dressed victuals. **1796** MORSE *Amer. Geog.* I. 88 All the Indians of South America..are in general excessively voracious. **1819** STEPHENS in Shaw's *Gen. Zool.* XI. II. 616 All the species being extremely voracious. **1855** *Orr's Circ. Sci., Inorg. Nat.* 69 At the earliest introduction of fishes we find the voracious and highly organized tribe of sharks fully represented. **1861** J. R. GREENE *Man. Anim. Kingd., Cœlent.* 229 Yet are the *Ctenophora* very voracious, feeding on a number of floating marine animals.

transf. **1850** CARLYLE *Latter-d. Pamph.* ii. (1872) 45, I had seen him about a year before,..and had noted well the unlovely voracious look of him.

b. *fig.* Of persons: Excessively greedy or eager in some desire or pursuit. Also const. *of*.

1746 FRANCIS tr. *Horace, Epist.* I. ii. 34 Circe's Cups..Which with his Mates, voracious of their Woe, If he had blindly tasted [etc.]. **1812** *Examiner* 7 Sept. 571/2 A..most voracious believer he is. **1851** CARLYLE *Sterling* I. iv, A voracious observer and participator in all things he likewise all along was. **1883** *Evangelical Mag.* Sept. 419 Mr. Rowlands..was a voracious reader.

c. *transf.* Of things.

1767 A. YOUNG *Farmer's Lett. to People* 111 He will abhor the practice of sowing so voracious a vegetable after wheat. **1784** COWPER *Task* IV. 450 Twitch'd from the perch, He gives the princely bird, with all his wives, To his voracious bag.

2. Characterized by voracity or greediness. Also *fig.*

1635 J. TAYLOR (Water P.) *Very Old Man* in Hindley III. 12 All Creatures are Made for mans use, and may by Man be us'd, Not by voracious Gluttony abus'd. **1720** WELTON *Suffer. Son of God* II. xxvii. 709 This Miscreant thought of nothing else but how to glut his Voracious Appetite. **1800** *Med. Jrnl.* III. 62 He had such a voracious appetite that he would take with indifference either medicine or food. **1875** *Chambers's Jrnl.* 2 Jan. 45/2 [The snail's] appetite is as voracious as its means of indulging it are perfect.

b. *fig.* Of desires, interests, etc.: Insatiable.

1712 ADDISON *Spect.* No. 452 ¶5 They have a Relish for every thing that is News, let the matter of it be what it will; or, to speak more properly, they are Men of a Voracious Appetite, but no Taste. **1852** H. ROGERS *Ess.* (1874) I. vii. 342 He took revenge for his transient fit of scepticism by a subsequent most voracious dogmatism. *a* **1854** H. REED *Lect. Brit. Poets* x. (1857) II. 22 His appetite for argument was as voracious as his physical appetite.

voraciously (vɒˈreɪʃəslɪ), *adv.* [f. prec. + -LY².] In a voracious manner; greedily, gluttonously, ravenously.

1752 J. HILL *Hist. Anim.* 381 All four of the species of this singular genus are fond of pepper, but this eats it most voraciously. **1776** MRS. DELANY *Life & Corr.* (1862) II. 208 They came starved,..and eat their little dinner voraciously. **1839** DICKENS *Nickleby* v, The boys began to eat voraciously, and in desperate haste. **1864** C. GEIKIE *Life in Woods* xi. (1874) 191 Even the bush people..eat it voraciously. **1902** J. BUCHAN *Watcher by Threshold* 73, I was voraciously hungry.

fig. **1840** MRS. CARLYLE *Lett.* (1883) I. 126 Carlyle is reading voraciously, great folios.

voˈraciousness. [f. as prec. + -NESS.] = next.

1710 ADDISON *Tatler* No. 255 ¶3 Distinguishing himself by Voraciousness of Appetite. **1774** GOLDSM. *Nat. Hist.* (1776) VI. 362 For some days before their change, the animal discontinues its usual voraciousness. **1786** tr. *Beckford's Vathek* 29 The Caliph..found himself incommoded by the voraciousness of his guest. **1974** R. HELMS *Tolkien's World* iv. 80 The Orcs are covered with hair, in part to represent their sexual voraciousness and animality.

voracity (vɒˈræsɪtɪ). Also 6–7 voracite, -itie. [a. F. *voracité* (14th c., = It. *voracità*, Sp. *voracidad*, Pg. *-idade*), or ad. L. *vorācitas*, f. *vorāci-*, *vorax*: see VORACIOUS *a.* and -ITY.] The quality or character of being voracious; greediness in eating.

1526 *Pilgr. Perf.* (W. de W. 1531) 99 b, Voracite or gredynesse in eatyng,..sayth, O, how hungry I am. **1584** LODGE *Alarm agst. Usurers* F iij, What though you cloath your selues in simplicitie of Doues, and your inwarde habite be worse then the voracite of Wolues. **1615** G. SANDYS *Trav.* 18 Those that with the rarities of the earth do pamper their voracities. **1638** SIR T. HERBERT *Trav.* (ed. 2) 241 No people in the world have better stomacks, drinke more, or more affect voracity. **1652** EARL MONM. tr. *Bentivoglio's Hist. Relat.* 64 This Army is like a great Animall which lives in continual voracity. **1774** GOLDSM. *Nat. Hist.* (1776) III. 399 The animal's voracity is greater than its feelings, and it never seizes without bringing down its prey. **1833** J. RENNIE *Alph. Angling* 6 To me it appears much more probable, that ..fishes have intervals more or less extended of fasting, after which they eat with great voracity. **1868** PEARD *Water-farm.* xvi. 164 Innumerable Anecdotes have been related regarding the voracity of this fish [the pike]. **1891** FARRAR *Darkn. & Dawn* xxvi, Who is that extremely stout personage..who is devouring his dainties with such brutal voracity?

b. *transf.* and *fig.* Also const. *of*.

1601 HOLLAND *Pliny* I. 47 What a Nature is that which feedeth the most greedie voracitie in the whole world [*sc.* that of fire] without losse of it selfe? **1638** SIR T. HERBERT *Trav.* (ed. 2) 274 In Iberia also and Armenia they entred with no lesse voracity. **1664** H. MORE *Apology* 496 The fierceness and voracity of what we ordinarily call *Fire*. *a* **1701** MAUNDRELL *Journ. Jerus.* (1721) 62 The voracity of time..has left nothing but a few Foundations remaining. **1779** JOHNSON *L.P.*, *Pope* Wks. IV. 46 Pope's voracity of fame taught him the art of obtaining the accumulated honour both of what he had published, and of what he had suppressed. **1860** EMERSON *Cond. Life, Wealth* Wks. (Bohn) II. 358 The eating quality of debt does not relax its voracity. *Ibid.*, *Consid.* 421 Afflicting other souls..with ministrations to its voracity of trifles.

†**vorage.** *Obs. rare.* [a. OF. *vorage*, or ad. L. *vorāgo* VORAGO.] A whirlpool, gulf, chasm.

1490 CAXTON *Eneydos* x. 39 On that other syde cam vpon theym Neptunus wyth all his vorages and wawes alle full of scume. *a* **1533** LD. BERNERS *Gold. Bk. M. Aurel.* (1537) A iv b, The famous Romayn: whiche for to delyuer the towne of Rome..yelded hym selfe to the same vorage, that as than was sene in Rome. [**1623** COCKERAM, *Vorage*, a Quagmire.]

†**vorageous**, *a.* *Obs.*⁻¹ In 5 voraygeouse. [ad. OF. *voragieux*.] = next 1.

1490 CAXTON *Eneydos* xviii. 67 The wyndes ben in their furye, the see full of tempest and of grete voraygeouse wawes.

†**voˈraginous**, *a.* *Obs.* [ad. L. *vorāginōs-us*, f. *vorāgin-*, *vorāgo* VORAGO. Cf. obs. F. *voragineux*, It., Sp., Pg. *voraginoso*.]

1. Of or belonging to an abyss or whirlpool; resembling a chasm or gulf.

1624 T. SCOTT *Belg. Souldier* 8 More dangerous then the gaping and voraginous caue, wherein Curtius leapt. **1654** COKAINE *Dianea* III. 233 A voraginous place, about the banks of which those men appeare that have perished by a violent death. **1675** E. WILSON *Spadacr. Dunelm.* 23 The bottom of the Sea..is perforated with sundry voraginous inlets and patent mouths. **1747** MALLET *Amyntor & Theod.* I. 219 His secret seat,..deep amidst A cavern's jaws voraginous and vast.

b. *transf.* and *fig.*

1624 *Gag for Pope* 15 The Countrey villages know not what a Sermon meaneth, onely Mass and Mattens, with some voraginous deliuery of wonders. **1642** H. MORE *Song of Soul* II. III. II. xlviii, For course of time voraginous With rapid force is violently just.

2. Having the receptive or swallowing power of a gulf or abyss; devouring, voracious.

1653 A. WILSON *Jas. I*, 165 This Voraginous appetite gaped after the possession of the Countrie. **1657** REEVE *God's Plea* 85 How it doth grieve me..that we think to get our admission under God with voraginous paunches, and soaked gullets. **1665** SIR T. HERBERT *Trav.* (1677) 376 No Nation in the World be more idle and voraginous than they. **1691** in C. R. Wilson *Old Fort William* (1906) I. 11 Provisions..being extremely deer, made so by the Voraginous great Armyes near us.

Hence †**voˈraginousness**. *Obs.*⁻¹

1654 R. CODRINGTON tr. *Iustine* IV. 74 Those Waves did bark, which the voraginousness of the devouring Sea did commit and clash together.

†**voragious**, *a.* *Obs.*⁻¹ [Cf. VORAGEOUS *a.*] = prec. 2.

1665 D. DUDLEY *Mettall. Martis* (1854) 38, I do not wholly compute the vast quantities of charcoles and wood spent in these voragious works.

‖**vorago** (vɒˈreɪgəʊ). Now *rare.* [L. *vorāgo*, f. *vorāre* to devour. Cf. VORAGE.] An abyss, gulf, or chasm.

1654 HOWELL *Parthenop.* To Rdr. A ij b, The great *Vorago* or fiery Gulph..which rageth in the head of that Mountain [Vesuvius]. **1656** S. H. *Gold. Law* 91 Earth-quakes, Chasmaes, and Voragoes were at his command. **1669** *Phil. Trans.* IV. 1028 The top of Ætna must about the same time have sunk down into its old Vorago or hole.

fig. **1836** LANDOR *Imag. Conv.* Wks. 1876 VI. 450 Adultery and concubinage did you mention! Another vorago, two voragoes, Scylla and Charybdis, of national wealth. **1895** J. J. RAVEN *Hist. Suffolk* 151 Five years more, and Blythburgh Priory perishes in the general vorago.

vorant (ˈvɔərənt), *a.* [ad. L. *vorant-*, *vorans*, pres. pple. of *vorāre* to devour.]

†**1.** Devouring. *Obs. rare.*

1618 DEKKER *Owles Almanack* 18 Lofty Lion (said Jove) I will thee claspe thy jawes, and shut the portall of that vorant grave. **1639** G. DANIEL *Ecclus.* xxviii. 72 As the fierce Lyon from his cunning ward, It shall Surprise him; as the Vorant Pard, It shall destroy them.

2. *Her.* Of animals: (see quots.).

1766 PORNY *Heraldry* Dict., *Vorant*, this term..is used in Blazonry to express the action of any Animal, Fish, Bird, or Reptile, devouring or swallowing up another creature. **1780** EDMONDSON *Her.* II. s.v., A serpent erect, in pale, vorant an infant. **1864** BOUTELL *Her. Hist. & Pop.* x. (ed. 3) 60 A Lion ..may be Vigilant, or Vorant. **1868** CUSSANS *Her.* (1893) 95 *Trussing* has the same signification when applied to birds, as *Vorant* has to animals.

†**vo'ration.** *Obs.*⁻⁰ [ad. L. *vorātio*, f. *vorāre*.] 'A devouring, or eating up greedily.'
1656 BLOUNT *Glossogr.*

†**vo'raulite.** *Min. Obs.* [f. *Vorau* in Styria + -LITE. Named in 1806.] = LAZULITE.
c **1840** *Encycl. Metrop.* (1845) VI. 481/1 Azurite. Klaprothite. Tyrolite. Voroulite... Occurs in attached crystals and massive. **1852** BRANDE *Dict. Sci.* (ed. 2) App. 1421 *Voraulite*, a mineralogical name of the ferro-magnesian phosphate of alumina,..a species of *blue-spar*, or *lazulite*.

†**vorax,** *a. Obs.*⁻¹ [a. L. *vorax* devouring.] Voracious, ravenous.
1535 STEWART *Cron. Scot.* III. 442 This Alexander,..Of Badzenoch wes callit all his dais The vorax wolf.

vorbarn, -bede, -bisne, southern ME. varr. FORBURN *v.*, FORBID *v.*, FORBYSEN *sb.*

vorbroide, -broyde, southern pa. pple. of FORBRAID *v. Obs.*

vord, southern ME. var. FORD *sb.*; obs. Sc. f. WORD *sb.*

vordan, vordily, obs. Sc. ff. WARDEN, WORTHILY *adv.*

vordrye, southern ME. var. FURTHER *v.*

vordy, obs. Sc. f. WORTHY *a.*

†**vore¹.** *Obs.* [South-western var. FORE *sb.* 2. Used to render L. *vestigium*.] Track, trace.
1387 TREVISA *Higden* (Rolls) VI. 373 þe pore man þonked hym, and vansched sodenly awey, and noon wey [*MS. γ*, non vore] was i-sene of his goynge. **1393** LANGL. *P. Pl.* C. VII. 118 Freres folowen my vore fele tyme and ofte, And prouen vnparfit prelates of holy churche. **1398** TREVISA *Barth. De P.R.* VIII. viii. (Tollem. MS.), By þe opinion of þe comyn peple þis cercle, Galaxias, is þe vore of þe passynge of þe sonne. *Ibid.* III. xix. (1495) d vj b/2 Hondes..folowyth the vores of bestes by smellinge.

vore². *dial.* [South-western var. (still in use) of *fore, fure* FURROW *sb.* Cf. VOOR.] A furrow.
c **1380** *Sir Ferumb.* 1565 þay..ne spared rigges noþer vores til þay mette þat pray. **1582** BATMAN *Barth. De P.R.* Catal. hard Words, *Vores*, forowes of land.

vore, voregoer, voreward(e, southern ME. varr. FORE *adv.*, FOREGOER, FOREWARD *sb.*¹

vorfare, -fret, -gon, -gulte, southern ME. varr. FORFARE, -FRET, -GO, -GUILT.

vorie, aphetic f. AVOWRY 2.

vorke, obs. Sc. f. WORK *sb.*

vorlage ('fɔːlɑːgə, ‖'fɔːrlaːgə). [a. Ger. (both senses). Cf. G. *vorlegen* to lean forward.]
1. a. *Skiing.* (see quot. 1939.) **b.** *pl.* Skiing trousers. Also **vorlagers.**
1939 WEBSTER Add., *Vorlage*... A position in which one leans forward from the ankles without lifting the heels from the skis, keeping the body, as a rule, at least perpendicular to the slope. **1958** *Vogue* Jan. 1 (Advt.), The Winter Sports Shop..has everything for the skier:..Luis Ebster designs and cuts the vorlages. *Ibid.* 35/1 Tattersall checks of black and caramel match caramel vorlagers. **1959** H. LANTSCHNER *Ski-ing for Beginners* 89 One must..have the necessary Vorlage to take the weight off the skis when necessary. **1961** *Times* 27 Nov. 13/2 'Tailormade' vorlagers in a large range of sizes. **1963** C. GLYN *Don't knock Corners Off* xxii. 184 Our beanies, vorlages, ankle-length tomato coloured pants.
‖**2.** An original version of a manuscript or a book from which a copy is produced.
1965 K. MALONE in Bessinger & Creed *Medieval & Linguistic Stud.* 120, I conceive that our scribe copied as *heol* the *hleo* of his *vorlage*. **1975** *Times Lit. Suppl.* 25 Apr. 462/4 This was first published in a French translation..in 1930 and was not followed by the Amharic original till more than thirty-five years later... More than one Amharic original was in existence, and the published text was not the *Vorlage* used for the 1930 French edition.

‖**vorlaufer** ('fɔːrlaʊfər). [G. *vorläufer* precursor, forerunner, f. *vorlaufen* to run on ahead.] A skier who travels a course before a race in order to establish a standard by which the competitors are marked.
1961 *Times* 11 Jan. 16/1 As a result of the *vorlaufers's* times, the announcer..foresaw a winning time in the region of '1·55, 1·60'. **1964** *Times* 4 Feb. 4/1 Miss T. Hecher..had followed down the *vorlaufers*.

vorlese, southern ME. var. FORLESE *v.*

vorloffe, obs. var. FURLOUGH.

vorme, southern ME. var. FORME *a.*

vorne, southern ME. var. FERN *a.*; obs. Sc. f. WORN *pa. pple.*

vorold, southern ME. var. FOROLD *v.*

-vorous, *suffix*, forming adjs., after L. *-vorus* devouring, eating (cf. *vorāre* to devour) in *carnivorus, omnivorus* (both used by Pliny). The commoner English examples mainly date from the 17th cent., as *carnivorous, herbivorous, omnivorous, phytivorous* (also *granivorous, ossivorous, piscivorous*); later instances are *graminivorous* (1739), *metallivorous, offivorous* (1713), *serpentivorous* (1882), and *terrivorous*.
1837 MURRAY *Vital Princ.* 5 A very singular appetite..at once terrivorous and metallivorous.

vorow, vorre, southern ME. varr. FURROW *sb.*, FAR *adv.*

vorpal ('vɔːpəl), *a.* A word invented by 'Lewis Carroll' app. with the sense 'keen, deadly'; also in subsequent allusive uses.
1871 'L. CARROLL' *Through Looking-Glass* i. 22 The vorpal blade went snicker-snack! **1941** AUDEN *New Year Let.* II. 44 Wave at the mechanized barbarian The vorpal sword of an agrarian. **1970** [see FRABJOUS *a.*].

vorschalde, southern ME. var. FORSCALD (see FOR- *pref.*¹ 5).

vorshipfull, obs. Sc. f. WORSHIPFUL.

‖**vorspiel** ('foːrʃpiːl). *Mus.* Pl. **-e.** [Ger., f. *vor* before + *spiel* (see SPIEL *sb.*²).] A prelude.
1876 STAINER & BARRETT *Dict. Mus. Terms* 452/2 *Vorspiel* (*Ger.*), prelude, introductory movement, overture. **1889** G. B. SHAW *London Music 1888–89* (1937) 66 It was not surprising to find a charm in this 'Vorspiel' that is wanting in the empty and violently splendid overture to Rienzi. **1895** G. KOBBÉ *How to understand Wagner's Ring* (ed. 6) 66 This vorspiel is a masterly representation..of a storm gathering. **1974** *Encycl. Brit. Macropædia* XIII. 680/1 By the time of Bach, the written *Choral-Vorspiel*, or chorale prelude (as opposed to the improvised prelude to the chorale within the Lutheran service), prelude and fugue..were firmly established forms for the organ. **1983** *New Oxf. Compan. Mus.* II. 1949/2 *Vorspiel* (Ger.), 'prelude'. Wagner called the introductions to his operas *Vorspiele*, and described *Das Rheingold* as a *Vorspiel* to the *Ring*.

vorst(e, southern ME. varr. FIRST *a.*, FROST *sb.*

vorsted, obs. f. WORSTED.

‖**vorstellung** ('foːrʃtɛlʊŋ). *Psychol.* Pl. **-en.** [Ger.] An image, idea, mental picture, or presentation.
1807–8 COLERIDGE *Notebks.* (1962) II. I. 3217 Emptiness & absence, silence, darkness as Spinoza observed whose pocket Mr Locke picked of it without after confession, are as positive Vorstellungen as Light, Sound, Image. **1865** J. GROTE *Exploratio* I. iv. 60 Knowledge as acquaintance..is the kind of knowledge which we have of a thing by the presentation of it to the senses or the representation of it in a picture or type, a 'vorstellung'. **1890** W. JAMES *Princ. Psychol.* I. ix. 236 A permanently existing 'idea' or 'Vorstellung' which makes its appearance before the footlights of consciousness at periodical intervals, is as mythological an entity as the Jack of Spades. **1959** J. L. AUSTIN *Sense & Sensibilia* (1962) vi. 61 In Berkeley's doctrine there are *only* ideas, in Kant's only *Vorstellungen* (things-in-themselves being not strictly relevant here).

vort(e, southern ME. var. FORT(E *conj.*

vortex ('vɔːtɛks). Pl. **vortices** ('vɔːtɪsiːz). [a. L. *vortex* (var. of *vertex* VERTEX) an eddy of water, wind, or flame, a whirlpool, whirlwind, f. *vort-, vertĕre* to turn. Cf. F. *vortex* (Anat.), Pg. *vortices* pl., It. *vortice*.]
1. a. In older theories of the universe (esp. that of Descartes), a supposed rotatory movement of cosmic matter round a centre or axis, regarded as accounting for the origin or phenomena of the terrestrial and other systems; a body of such matter rapidly carried round in a continuous whirl.
1653 H. MORE *Philos. Cabbala* App. i. (1713) 113 That there are infinite numbers of Atoms or Particles, different in magnitude and figure;..and that they are moved in the Vniverse after the manner of vortices. **1662** GLANVILL *Lux Orient.* xiv. 141 That great orb of fire..shall fly away out of this vortex, and become a wandring Comet. **1665** —— *Def. Van. Dogm.* 69 The Cartesian Vortices will serve to account for the Phænomena, and teach a way of Theory not unserviceable to experiment. **1698** KEILL *Exam. Th. Earth* (1734) 283 It is no hard matter to prove, that the Vortices can never be the cause of the Cœlestial motions. *a* **1714** M. HENRY *Expos. O. & N. Test., Eccles.* i. 14 (1737) II, He saw ..all within this vortex (to use the modern gibberish) which has the sun for its centre. **1785** SIR W. HERSCHEL *Sci. Papers* (1912) I. 223 These will vanish like the Cartesian vortices, that soon gave way when better theories were offered. **1833** COLERIDGE *Table-t.* 29 June, Descartes' vortices were not an hypothesis: they rested on no facts at all. **1869** LECKY *Europ. Mor.* I. 389 The false theory of the vortices or the true theory of gravitation.
b. In fig. context or use.
1704 SWIFT *Batt. Bks.* Misc. (1711) 251 Death, like a Star of superior Influence, drew him [Descartes] into his own Vortex. *a* **1721** PRIOR *Dial. Dead, Locke & Montaigne* ad fin., Those very Ideas changing, Lock may be led into a new Labyrinth, or sucked into another Vortex; and may write a Second Book in order to Disprove the first. **1790** CATH. GRAHAM *Lett. Educ.* 401 Our benevolence extends at last to the whole race of mankind, like so many different vortices; the center of them all is self love. **1809–10** COLERIDGE *Friend* (1865) 140, I was a sharer in the general vortex, though my little world described the path of its revolution in an orbit of its own. **1855** BRIMLEY *Ess., Poetry & Crit.* (1858) 197 That mighty ocean of intermingling, interacting vortices [*sc.* Time]. **1879** GEO. ELIOT *Theo. Such* xvii. 304 The spiral vortices fundamentally concerned in the production of epic poems.
(*b*) *spec.* (with capital initial) a group of artists practising vorticism (see VORTICISM).
1913 E POUND *Let.* 19 Dec. (1950) I. 28 You may get something that you would miss in *The Vortex*. **1914** *Blast* 20 June 8 Do you think Lloyd George has the Vortex in him? **1969** *Listener* 30 Jan. 138/1 The so-called Great English Vortex, i.e. the group of painters, sculptors and writers who ..formed and represented the Vorticist movement.
c. In modern scientific use: A rapid movement of particles of matter round an axis; a whirl of atoms, fluid, or vapour.
1847 EMERSON *Repr. Men, Swedenborg* Wks. (Bohn) I. 316 Descartes, taught by Gilbert's magnet, with its Vortex, spiral, and polarity. **1862** J. C. MAXWELL *Sci. Papers* (1890) I. 489 The theory of molecular vortices applied to statical electricity. **1872** PROCTOR *Ess. Astron.* xix. 230 Friction between vortices of meteoric vapours and the Sun's atmosphere must be the immediate cause of solar heat. **1882** MINCHIN *Unipl. Kinemat.* 184 If there is not vortical motion throughout the whole area, but only local vortices, this integral will reduce to a simple sum of terms equal in number to the number of vortices.
2. An eddying or whirling mass of fire or flame.
1652 J. HALL *Height of Eloquence* p. lxv, The Pits and vortices of the Aetna, whose eructations throw whole stones from its depths. **1827–39** DE QUINCEY *Murder* Wks. 1854 II. 62 Men, of course, read in this hurrying overhead of scintillating and blazing vortices, the annunciation of some gigantic calamity going on in Liverpool. **1869** J. PHILLIPS *Vesuv.* iii. 67 It continued to vomit forth from five different openings vortices of flame.
3. a. A whirl or swirling mass of water; a strong eddy or whirlpool.
1704 J. PITTS *Acc. Moham.* 77 In this place is much Danger without a fresh Gale of Wind, because it is a kind of Vortex, the Water whirling round, and is apt to swallow down a Ship. **1759** STERNE *Tr. Shandy* II. ix, [A coach] splashing and plunging..with such a vortex of mud and water moving along with it, round its axis. **1774** GOLDSM. *Nat. Hist.* (1776) I. 268 The noise of this dreadful vortex still farther contributes to encrease its terror. **1816** TUCKEY *Narr. Exped. R. Zaire* iv. (1818) 143 In crossing the river we passed through several whirlpools... These vortices are formed in an instant..and subside as quickly. **1839** T. BEALE *Nat. Hist. Sperm Whale* 181 Leaving nothing but a white-and-green looking vortex in the disturbed blue ocean. **1864** C. GEIKIE *Life in Woods* xxiii. (1874) 366 The poor wretch was kept revolving, with each end of his support sunk in the vortex by turns.
b. Applied to a waterspout.
1762 FALCONER *Shipwr.* II. 37 Still round and round the fluid vortex flies, Scattering dun night and horror thro' the skies.
c. *ellipt.* A vortex water-wheel (see 7).
1853 URE *Dict. Arts*, etc. (ed. 4) II. 914 The vortex admits of several modes of construction. *Ibid.* 915 A low pressure vortex constructed for another mill near Belfast.
4. a. A violent eddy or whirl of the air; a whirlwind or cyclone, or the central portion of this.
a **1700** KEN *Edmund* Poet. Wks. 1721 II. 24 Now the North Wind the crazy Vessel sweeps, And in its rapid Vortex pris'ner keeps. **1728** CHAMBERS *Cycl.*, *Vortex*, Whirlwind, in Meteorology, a sudden, rapid, violent Motion of the Air, in Gyres or Circles. **1838** REDFIELD in *Amer. Jrnl. Sci.* XXXIII. 59 A direct circuit of rotation in the form of a vortex or active whirlwind. **1845** A. THOM *Nat. Storms* 48 The *Margaret*, on the opposite side of the vortex, still had the 'hurricane strong' from S.W. by W. with a heavy sea. **1860** MAURY *Phys. Geog.* (Low) xix. 439 The vortex of a cyclone is often and aptly compared to a meteor. **1870** TYNDALL *Fragm. Sci.* (1879) I. vi. 198 We seemed crossing the vortex of a storm.
transf. **1871** B. TAYLOR *Faust* (1875) II. II. 123 The vortex of this night Hath whirled him hither to my sight.
b. In fig. context or use.
1788 MME. D'ARBLAY *Diary* 13 Feb., The whirlwind of his eloquence nearly drew me into its vortex. **1854** EMERSON *Lett. & Soc. Aims, Poet. & Imag.* Wks. (Bohn) III. 160 In their rhythm is no manufacture, but a vortex, or musical tornado. **1856** R. A. VAUGHAN *Mystics* I. 145 Bernard.. began life by drawing after him into the convent all his kindred..with the irresistible vortex of his own religious fervour.
5. *fig.* **a.** A state or condition of human affairs or interests comparable to a whirl or eddy by reason of rush or excitement, rapid change, or absorbing effect.
1761 HUME *Hist. Eng.* (1806) IV. lv. 273 The distant parts of the kingdom, being removed from that furious vortex of new principles and opinions which had transported the capital. **1793** BURKE *Obs. Conduct Minority* Wks. 1842 I. 611 No man..may be justly suspected of secretly abetting this French Revolution, who must not be drawn into its vortex. **1806** A. HUNTER *Culina* (ed. 3) 243 Lecturers, who delight in being continually whirled round in the vortex of new opinions. **1838** W. IRVING in *Life & Lett.* (1866) III. 124, I value my peace of mind too highly to suffer myself to be drawn into the vortex of New York politics. **1860** MILL *Repr. Govt.* (1865) 137/1 The appointments are kept out of the vortex of party and parliamentary jobbing. **1883** S. WADDINGTON *A. H. Clough* 83 The vortex of religious excitement and discussion kept him idly moving in its ceaseless gyrations.
b. A constant round *of* excitement or pleasure.
[**1766** FORDYCE *Serm. Yng. Wm.* (1767) I. vii. 268 That whirl of dissipation, which, like some mighty vortex, has swallowed up in a manner all conditions and characters.] **1792** A. YOUNG in *Mme. D'Arblay's Lett.* (1842) V. 329 A person who is constantly moving in a vortex of pleasure, brilliancy, and wit. **1802** MAR. EDGEWORTH *Moral T.*, *Breakfast*, I feel that I cannot be at ease in the vortex of dissipation. **1877** MRS. FORRESTER *Mignon* I. 191 She and her husband lived in a vortex of gaiety.

c. A situation into which persons or things are steadily drawn, or from which they cannot escape. (Chiefly after sense 3.)

1779 J. MOORE *View Soc. Fr.* I. i. 8, I thought it most prudent to remove.., that no chance might remain of my being..whirled round again in the vortex of dissipation and gaming. **1833** MRS. BROWNING *Prometh. Bound* Poet. Wks. (1904) 159/2 Let him hurl me anon, into Tartarus,..With Necessity's vortices strangling me down. **1850** KINGSLEY *Alt. Locke* x, I looked with horror on the gulf of penury before me, into the vortex of which not only I, but my whole trade, seemed irresistibly sucked. *a* **1862** BUCKLE *Civiliz.* (1869) III. v. 356 Generation after generation passes away, successively absorbed in one mighty vortex.

†**6.** A design or figure representing or suggesting vortical movement. *Obs.*$^{-1}$

1665 HOOKE *Microgr.* Time Table, The Figures of Hoar Frost, and the Vortices on windows.

7. *attrib.*, chiefly in terms of physical science, as ***vortex-atom***, ***-filament***, ***-line***, ***-matter***, ***-motion***, ***-ring***; **vortex shedding**, the periodic detachment of vortices from an object in a fluid flow, causing a varying force to be experienced by the object; **vortex sheet**, a region of vortices that is created at the interface of two masses of fluid having different velocities along the interface; **vortex street**: see STREET *sb.* 2 g; **vortex turbine** or **(water-)wheel**, a turbine in which the water enters tangentially at the circumference and is discharged at the centre.

1867 SIR W. THOMSON in *Phil. Mag.* Ser. IV. XXXIV. 15 (*heading*), On *Vortex Atoms. **1876** P. G. TAIT *Rec. Adv. Phys. Sci.* i. 24 Sir W. Thomson's splendid suggestion of Vortex-atoms..will enable us thoroughly to understand matter. **1867** —— (tr. Helmholtz) in *Phil. Mag.* Ser. IV. XXXIII. 486 By **vortex-filaments*..I denote portions of the fluid bounded by vortex-lines drawn through every point of the boundary of an infinitely small closed curve. **1878** W. K. CLIFFORD *Dynamic* III. 203 The part of the body inside the tube is called a vortex-filament. **1867** TAIT (tr. Helmholtz) in *Phil. Mag.* Ser. IV. XXXIII. 486 By **vortex-lines*..I denote lines drawn through the fluid so as at every point to coincide with the instantaneous axis of rotation of the corresponding fluid element. **1878** W. K. CLIFFORD *Dynamic* III. 200 A curve such that its tangent at every point is in the direction of the spin at that point is called a vortex-line. *a* **1721** KEILL *Maupertuis' Diss.* (1734) 21 As each Planet describes equal Area's in equal Times, it follows that the Beds of the *Vortex Matter have their Velocities in a reciprocal Proportion to their distances from the Center. **1867** TAIT (tr. Helmholtz) in *Phil. Mag.* Ser. IV. XXXIII. 491 We may..call the motions which have no velocity-potential, generally, **vortex-motions*. **1876** —— *Rec. Adv. Phys. Sci.* xii. 290 The peculiar properties of vortex-motion were mathematically deduced..by Helmholtz. **1867** —— (tr. Helmholtz) in *Phil. Mag.* Ser. IV. XXXIII. 510 These *vortex-rings travel on,..and are widened or contracted by other vortex-rings. **1878** W. K. CLIFFORD *Dynamic* III. 205 Suppose that in a mass of fluid there is a single vortex ring of any form (i.e. a vortex-filament returning into itself). **1953** A. ROSHKO *Devel. Turbulent Wakes from Vortex Streets* (U.S. Nat. Advisory Comm. Aeronaut. TN 2913) 45 There is yet no adequate theory of the periodic *vortex shedding and it is not clear what is the principal mechanism which determines the frequency. **1975** *Offshore Engineer* Dec. 42/1 Vortex shedding can impose periodic forces on a pipeline. **1982** *New Scientist* 27 May 566/1 Vortex shedding is quite harmless until it begins to interfere with the safety or the function of man-made structures. **1879** H. LAMB *Treat. Math. Theory Motion Fluids* vi. 154 Let us suppose we have a series of vortex-filaments arranged in a thin film over a surface... The infinitely thin film is then called a '*vortex-sheet'. **1926** [see SEPARATION 15]. **1983** *Jrnl. Fluids Engin.* CV. 53 Nascent vortex strength and position are determined from the Kutta condition so that the nascent vortex has the same strength as a vortex sheet of uniform strength. **1877** *Iron* 27 Oct. 516 The turbine manufactured by them is termed the '*Vortex'. **1884** *Athenæum* 16 Aug. 212/1 A description of the vortex turbine or inward-flow water-wheel. **1853** GLYNN *Treat. Power Water* 146 Several machines derive their power from the reaction of water-pressure: such as Dr. Barker's mill,..the *Vortex-wheel, and others. **1860** *Ure's Dict. Arts*, etc. (ed. 5) III. 928 The name of Vortex Wheel has been given to a modification of the turbine by Mr. James Thomson of Belfast.

vorth, southern ME. var. FORTH *adv.*; obs. Sc. f. WORTH *sb.* and *v.*

vorþere(more, southern ME. varr. FURTHER(MORE.

vorthy, dial. var. FORTHY *a.*; obs. Sc. form of WORTHY *a.*

vortical (ˈvɔːtɪkəl), *a.* and *sb.* [f. L. *vortic-*, *vortex* VORTEX + -AL[1].]

A. *adj.* **1.** Of motion: Like that of a vortex; rotating, eddying, whirling.

1653 H. MORE *Conject. Cabbal.* (1713) 191 The Matter being coagulated..and set upon Vortical Motion, Light dawned out in infinite parts of the World. **1692** BENTLEY *Boyle Lect.* 226 This universal attraction or gravitation is.. not a magnetical power, nor the effect of a vortical motion; those common attempts toward the explication of gravity. **1746** *Phil. Trans.* XLIV. 43, I have never been able to discern that vortical Motion, by which this Effect was said to be brought about. **1847** EMERSON *Repr. Men, Swedenborg* Wks. (Bohn) I. 316 Descartes, taught by Gilbert's magnet, ..had filled Europe with the leading thought of vortical motion, as the secret of nature. **1881** G. MACDONALD *Mary Marston* II. ii. 10 She made a sudden vortical gyration, and walked from the vile place. **1882** MINCHIN *Unipl. Kinemat.* 155 Twice the product of the area of the curve and the vortical spin inside it.

2. Moving in a vortex; whirling round.

1728 PEMBERTON *Newton's Philos.* 231 The vortical fluid, by which he explains the motion of the planets. **1792** D. LLOYD *Voy. Life* 23 Till all their brain is vortical;—and wreck'd They sink o'erladen with anxiety. **1860** GOSSE *Rom. Nat. Hist.* 165 Vibrating cilia..are more developed on these organs, which are only pushed out at the will of the little animal, when they form strong vortical currents.

B. *sb.* A vortical motion.

1864 *Athenæum* 8 Oct. 465/2 The summary of the author's theories is:—..That the magnetic vortical can be excited by means of spiral currents of electricity generally.

Hence ˈ**vortically** *adv.*, in a vortical manner.

1872 PROCTOR *Ess. Astron.* xix. 230 If meteoric matter came in vortically around the equatorial parts of the sun. **1882** MINCHIN *Unipl. Kinemat.* 183 Energy of Vortically moving Liquid.

†**vortice**, *sb. Obs.*$^{-1}$ [ad. stem of L. *vortex*.] A vortex.

1661 BOYLE *Spring of Air* (1662) 97 Particles, agitated or whirled round,..whereby they are each of them enabled to drive or force out of their Vortice all such other agitated particles.

ˈ**vortice**, *v. rare*$^{-1}$. [Cf. prec.] *trans.* To bring by vortical motion.

a **1843** SOUTHEY *Comm.-pl. Bk.* (1851) IV. 213 The heavier bodies..became outermost, and in their whirling vorticed the evil spirits into the centre.

vorticel (ˈvɔːtɪsɛl). *Zool.* [ad. mod.L. *vorticella*: see next, and cf. F. *vorticelle*.] = next.

1835 KIRBY *Hab. & Inst. Anim.* II. xvii. 97 Some, as the vorticels, the wheel-animals by way of eminence, appear to have two wheels.

‖**vorticella** (vɔːtɪˈsɛlə). *Zool.* [mod.L., dim. f. L. *vortic-*, *vortex* VORTEX.] The typical genus of *Vorticellidæ* (cf. next); an individual belonging to this genus; a bell-animalcule. Also *attrib.*

1787 G. ADAMS (*title*), Essays on the Microscope, containing..an account of the various species and singular properties of the Hydræ and Vorticellæ. **1806** PRISCILLA WAKEFIELD *Dom. Recreat.* vi. 86 A most curious animalcule, called the wheel animal, or vorticella. **1875** HUXLEY & MARTIN *Elem. Biol.* (1877) 90 Sometimes a rounded body, encircled by a ring of cilia but having otherwise the characters of a *Vorticella* bell, is seen to be attached to the base of the bell of an ordinary *Vorticella*.

vorticellid (vɔːtɪˈsɛlɪd). *Zool.* [Cf. prec. and -ID[3].] An individual of the *Vorticellidæ*, a family of sedentary infusorians.

1865 *Intell. Observ.* No. 38. 101 The jerk of a Vorticellid. **1888** ROLLESTON & JACKSON *Anim. Life* 837 Encysted Vorticellids with many nuclei have been observed.

Hence **vortiˈcellidan** *a. rare.*

1865 H. JAMES-CLARK in *Mem. Boston Soc. Nat. Hist.* I. 127 This singular appendage of the Vorticellidan group. **1880** SAVILLE KENT *Infusoria* I. 68 Members of the Vorticellidan family.

vorˈticial, *a. rare*$^{-1}$. [Cf. next.] = VORTICAL.

1848 POE *Eureka* Wks. 1865 II. 205 Cyclic and seemingly gyrating or vorticial movements.

†**vorˈtician**, *a. Obs.* [f. L. *vortici-*, *vortex*: see VORTEX and -IAN.] Of or belonging to the theory of a vortex or vortices.

a **1721** KEILL *Maupertuis' Diss.* (1734) 23 This is all one of the greatest Men of the Age could say in Defence of the Vortician System. *Ibid.* 27.

vorˈticiform, *a. rare*$^{-1}$. [f. as prec.: see -FORM.] Having the form of a vortex.

1849–52 *Todd's Cycl. Anat.* IV. 1228/1 When the vibratile cilia..are simultaneously effecting their vorticiform movements with rapidity and perfect harmony.

vorticism (ˈvɔːtɪsɪz(ə)m). Also **Vorticism**. [f. L. *vortex*, *vortic-* VORTEX + -ISM.] A British art-movement of the early twentieth century, characterized by abstractionism and machine-like forms. Also applied to similar tendencies in literature.

1914 E. POUND in *Fortn. Rev.* Sept. 470 The image is not an idea. It is a radiant node or cluster; it is what I can.. call a *Vortex*, from which..ideas are constantly rushing... And from this necessity came the name 'vorticism'. **1915** *Drawing* July 56/1 Vorticism..is in reality our old and amusing friend Cubism, but Cubism heavily charged with electricity. **1926** F. V. P. RUTTER *Evolution in Mod. Art* v. 105 Impressionism..was succeeded by Fauvism, Cubism, Expressionism, Futurism, Vorticism, and what not. **1962** *Listener* 5 Apr. 599/1 He [*sc.* Ezra Pound] was fighting under the banner of 'vorticism'. **1977** P. L. FERMOR *Time of Gifts* iii. 69 Pale woods and plastics were juggled together with stale and pretentious vorticism. **1980** *Daily Tel.* 6 Feb. 18 Nevinson was one of the first artists to use the contemporary techniques of vorticism and futurism for depicting the war [of 1914–18].

vorticist (ˈvɔːtɪsɪst). [f. as VORTICIFORM *a.* + -IST.] **1.** An advocate of the theory of vortices.

1866 DE MORGAN in *Athenæum* 26 May 706/3 Giordano Bruno..was, as has been said, a vorticist before Descartes, an optimist before Leibnitz, a Copernican before Galileo.

2. a. An exponent of vorticism in art.

1914 *Daily News* 7 July 6 My Scot one morning preached me a fiery sermon on the poetry of lawn tennis, and..I became a Vorticist. **1914** E. POUND *Let.* 10 Nov. (1971) 47 While the vorticists are well-represented, the College does not bind itself to a school. **1915** [see FAUVE]. **1930** J. W. MACKAIL *Largeness in Lit.* 15 Imagists, contortionists, vorticists..have had their little day. **1970** *English Studies* LI. 269 This period [*sc.* 1910–1922] also saw the birth and death of other more obviously revolutionary groups such as the Vorticists, Imagists and Futurists. **1980** *Illustr. London News* Mar. 58/1 Even the brief and feeble spark of abstraction in England, fanned by the Vorticists and almost immediately snuffed out by the First World War, became the subject of intensive investigation.

b. *attrib.* or as *adj.*

1914 *Blast* 20 June 8 We will convert the King if possible. A Vorticist King! Why not? **1914** E. POUND in *Fortn. Rev.* Sept. 461, I shall be..more lucid if I give..the history of the vorticist art with which I am most intimately connected, that is to say, vorticist poetry. **1923** *Daily Mail* 3 Mar. 12 Mr Wadsworth has all the qualifications of a tempera painter. In his vorticist past he was inclined to transform the world and its people into rigid, machine-like shapes. **1962** *Listener* 5 Apr. 599/1 The imagist and vorticist movements of less than fifty years ago. **1966** A. L. COBURN *Autobiogr.* ix. 102 It was in 1914 that Wyndham Lewis..founded the *avant-garde* movement named by..Ezra Pound 'Vorticist', the ideas of which derived partly from Futurism and partly from Cubism. **1981** V. GLENDINNING *Edith Sitwell* v. 83 Wyndham Lewis..was five years older than Edith herself; his Vorticist period, the editorship of *Blast*..already lay behind him.

vorticity (vɔːˈtɪsɪtɪ). [f. as prec. + -ITY.] The condition of a fluid, etc., with respect to vortical motion. In mod. use, a vector quantity equal at any given point in a fluid to twice the angular velocity of a small element of fluid about the point.

1888 A. B. BASSETT *Treat. Hydrodynamics* I. 75 Let P be any point on the axis of one of these [vortex] filaments, dm the mass of the filament which contains P, ω and dS the molecular rotation and cross section of the filament... Then the quantity $\omega dS/dm$ is called the vorticity of the fluid at the point P. **1895** *Athenæum* 23 Nov. 722/2 [Math. Soc.] On the Propagation of Waves upon the Plane Surface separating Two Portions of Fluid of Different Vorticities. **1896** *Proc. London Math. Soc.* XXVII. 14 The component velocities ..u and v, are connected with a stream-function Ψ by the relations $u = d\Psi/dy$, $v = -d\Psi/dx$. The vorticity is represented by $\frac{1}{2}\nabla^2\Psi$. **1916** H. LAMB *Hydrodynamics* (ed. 4) iii. 30 The component angular velocities of the rotation being $\frac{1}{2}\xi$, $\frac{1}{2}\eta$, $\frac{1}{2}\zeta$. The vector whose components are ξ, η, ζ may conveniently be called the 'vorticity' of the medium at the point (x, y, z). **1938** L. M. MILNE-THOMSON *Theoret. Hydrodynamics* xix. 511 Either sense of rotation can be obtained according as the bath is filled with the hot or the cold tap, the fluid from one or the other acquiring opposite vorticities as it moves near the boundary. **1958** *Science* 4 Apr. 731/3 On the surface of a fluid, the vorticity may be observed by following a cork marked with a cross... If the arms of the cross do not rotate, the vorticity is zero; if they do rotate, there is vorticity. **1976** *Nature* 1 Apr. 457/1 A motor vehicle or any other projectile in air produces vortices in its wake, but no net vorticity.

†ˈ**vorticle**. *Obs. rare.* [f. L. *vortic-*, *vortex*, after diminutives in *-cle*.] A little vortex.

1766 G. CANNING *Anti-Lucretius* IV. 309 In the vast Vortex, that surrounds the Whole, Examine how the Vorticles must roll. *Ibid.* 317.

†**vortiˈcordious**, *a. Obs.*$^{-1}$ [f. L. *Vorti-*, *Verticordia*: see VERTICORDIOUS *a.*] Turning the heart.

1669 T. G[ALE] *True Idea Jansenisme* 135 Then cap. 24 he proves more largely, That this medicinal Grace is Vorticordious or most potent.

vorticose (vɔːtɪˈkəʊs), *a.* [ad. L. *vorticōs-us* (It. *vorticoso*), f. *vortic-*, *vortex* VORTEX: see -OSE.]

1. Of motion: = VORTICAL *a.* 1.

1783 *Phil. Trans.* LXXIII. p. ii, At times..the motion was undulatory, and at others vorticose. *Ibid.* 194 The first shock..was lateral, and then vorticose, and exceedingly violent. **1830** LYELL *Princ. Geol.* I. 418 The wave-like motions, and those which are called vorticose or whirling in a vortex. **1839** DARWIN *Voy. Nat.* xvi. 376 The displacement at first appears to be owing to a vorticose movement beneath each point thus affected. **1881** C. A. YOUNG *Sun* 173 Only a very small percentage of the spots show any trace of vorticose motion.

2. Resembling a vortex.

1870 MATT. WILLIAMS *Fuel of Sun* §326. 214 The..orb would be twisted bodily into a huge vorticose crater. **1893** HOWLETT in Sir R. Ball *Story Sun* 147 They are illustrative of the development of two different and remarkable groups [of sun-spots]. The first is the elegant vorticose group.

Hence **vortiˈcosely** *adv.*, in the manner of a vortex; vortically.

1882 *Nature* XXV. 291 There is a strong inflow of the air along the surface of the ground all round vorticosely towards the base of the whirlwind. **1883** *Encycl. Brit.* XVI. 131/2 The strong air currents which..converge vorticosely round the base of the column [of the dust storm].

vorticular (vɔːˈtɪkjʊlə(r)), *a.* [Cf. prec. and -ULAR.] Of motion: Vortical, vorticose.

1838 REDFIELD in *Amer. Jrnl. Sci.* XXXIII. 59 Were there no vorticular or whirling action already excited,..there could then be no inequality of pressure to produce rotation. **1864** DE PENNING *Meteorol.* 65 This inward vorticular movement can only arise from the constant lateral pressure that is always maintained towards the partial vacuum of the vortex. **1891** *Atlantic Monthly* LXVIII. 68/2 They [*sc.* tornadoes] possess truly vorticular motion.

vortiginous (vɔːˈtɪdʒɪnəs), *a.* [f. L. *vortīgin-*, *vortigo*, var. of *vertigo*: see VERTIGINOUS *a.*]

1. Of motion: Vortical, vorticular.

1671 R. BOHUN *Wind* 230 The spirit or Wind..whirls about in a Circle: for.. the density and resistence of the Cloud, gives it an oblique or Vortiginous Motion. **1774** PENNANT *Tour Scot. in 1772*, 75 Great circular hollows, the work of the Vortiginous Motion of the Water. **1784** COWPER

Task II. 102 The fixt and rooted earth..with vortiginous and hideous whirl Sucks down its prey insatiable.

2. Moving in a vortex or vortices; rushing in whirls or eddies.

1791 COWPER *Iliad* XXI. 2 Where Xanthus winds His stream vortiginous. **1804** C. B. BROWN tr. *Volney's View Soil U.S.* 168 In the same manner may water-spouts be explained, which are vortiginous masses of air and water, seen only in cloudy weather. **1813** *Edin. Rev.* XXI. 137 The great, deep, and vortiginous Scamander had dwindled into a scanty rivulet.

vortograph ('vɔːtəgrɑːf, -æ-). Also Vortograph. [f. VORT(EX + -O + -GRAPH.] An abstract photograph taken with a camera and a vortoscope.

1917 E. POUND *Let.* 24 Jan. (1971) 104 The vortographs are perhaps as interesting as Wadsworth's woodcuts, perhaps not quite as interesting. **1963** *Times* 29 Apr. 7/2 Mr. Coburn..went on to show the parallels between his photography and the work of painters and sculptors at a later period with his astonishing series of 'vortographs'—photographic abstractions very close in feeling to the vorticist paintings of Wyndham Lewis and such early Epstein sculptures as 'The Rock Drill'. **1966** A. L. COBURN *Autobiogr.* ix. 102 Photography depends upon pattern..as well as upon quality of tone and luminosity, and in the Vortograph the design can be adjusted at will. **1982** M. WEAVER *Alvin Langdon Coburn* 26 Prismatic, triangular effects appeared in the Vortographs in which abstraction and conception superseded observation and perception.

vortoscope ('vɔːtəskəʊp). Also Vortoscope. [f. VORT(EX + -O + -SCOPE.] A mirror device used for producing abstract photographs (see quot. 1966).

1917 E. POUND *Let.* 24 Jan. (1950) 104 The vortescope [*sic*] isn't a cinema. It is an attachment to enable a photographer to do sham Picassos. That sarcastic definition probably covers the ground. **1918** —— *Pavannes & Divisions* App. IV. 252 The vortoscope is useless to a man who cannot recognise a beautiful arrangement of forms on a surface. **1966** A. L. COBURN *Autobiogr.* ix. 102, I aspired to make abstract pictures with the camera. For this purpose I devised the Vortoscope late in 1916. This instrument is composed of three mirrors fastened together in the form of a triangle... The mirrors act as a prism splitting the image formed by the lens into segments. **1982** M. HARKER in M. Weaver *Alvin Langdon Coburn* 2 He made a Vortoscope in 1916. Based on the principles of the kaleidoscope the instrument was composed of three mirrors fastened together in the form of a triangle.

vorty, south-western dial. form of FORTY.

1602 *Contention betw. Lib. & Prod.* I. iv. Bij, Cham sure chaue come, vorty miles and twenty. *a* **1642** SUCKLING *Poems* (1646) 37 And there did I see comming down Such folks as are not in our Town Vorty at least, in Pairs.

vorwe, southern ME. var. *forwe* FURROW *sb.*

vory, obs. f. WORRY *v.*

voryef (-yif), -yet (-yit), southern ME. varr. FORGIVE *v.*, FORGET *v.*

vose, obs. Sc. and north. f. VOICE *sb.*

Vöslauer (fœs'laʊər). Also Voslauer. [a. Ger., f. *Vöslau* name of a district in Lower Austria: see -ER¹.] An Austrian red or white table wine from Vöslau in the Vienna Woods.

1920 [see CARLOWITZ]. **1960** *Times* 11 June 11/6 A local red wine, Voslauer, which is among the best in the country.

Vosne Romanée (von romane). The name of a commune in the department of Côte-d'Or in France, used *absol.* to designate the wines produced there. Cf. ROMANÉE.

1930 G. KNOWLES tr. *P. de Cassagnac's French Wines* vi. 140 The Côte-de-Nuits begins at Dijon. It includes... Flagey, with Grands-Echezeaux; Vosne-Romanée and the estates of Romanée [etc.]. **1952** A. LICHINE *Wines of France* 126 Wines from Les Verroilles..are never sold under their own name..while the third *cuvées* are sold simply as Vosne-Romanée. **1963** N. FREELING *Gun before Butter* III. 164 We'll have some burgundy. I've a Vosne Romanée; just the trick. **1980** E. LEATHER *Duveen Letter* xiv. 160 Rupert..ordered a bottle of Vosne-Romanée 1961.

vostre, vot, southern ME. varr. FOSTER *v.*, FOOT *sb.*

'votable, *a. rare*⁻¹. [f. VOTE *v.* + -ABLE.] Capable, or having the right, of voting.

1754 in *New Princeton Rev.* (1887) IV. 253 The votable inhabitance convened in His Majesties name.

votal ('vəʊtəl), *a.* [f. L. *vōt-um* vow, wish (see VOTE *sb.*) + -AL¹.]

†**1.** Existing in will or wish, though not carried out in fact. *Obs.*

1610 BOYS *Wks.* (1622) 361 When not so much as priuate [baptism] may be well obtained, votall is enough. **1618** T. ADAMS *God's House* Wks. (1629) 624 He is not like those Debters, that haue neither meanes, nor meaning to pay. But though he wants actuall, he hath votall retribution. **1624** SANDERSON *Serm.* I. 243 Retribution and requital...must be real, if it be possible: but at the least, it must be votal in the desire and endeavour.

2. Of the nature of a vow or solemn engagement.

1632 LITHGOW *Trav.* I. 5 And teare-rent Sophyre, Synon-like betrayd What votall oathes, loues sterne fort, ne'er bewrayd. *a* **1638** MEDE *Wks.* (1672) 286, I will shew how far and in what sort these Eucharistical and Votal Offerings have been used in the first ages of the Church. **1855** R. BOYLE in *B. versus Wiseman* 47 My reasons for leaving the Society were purely conscientious, arising solely from strong objections to take any further votal obligations.

†**3.** Bound by vows; devoted to a religious life; appropriate to one under vows. *Obs.*

1636 R. JAMES *Iter Lanc.* (Chetham Soc.) 159 Lord Thebith's daughter, whoe had promised..to liue aye A votall virgin till hir dying daye. **1656** *Artif. Handsom.* 123 Threatned with speedy death, if she did not restore her daughter to the former mode of votall habiliments.

4. Of offerings: Associated with a vow; votive.

1846 R. HART *Eccl. Rec. Gt. Brit.* 230 The mariner preserved from shipwreck presented a votal tablet on which was depicted the story of his escape.

Hence **'votally** *adv.*, with a vow, solemnly.

1632 LITHGOW *Trav.* x. 484 He votally vndertooke..that ..I should haue all my money..restored me agayne.

votaress ('vəʊtərɪs). Also 6 -isse, 7 -esse, voteress. (Cf. VOTRESS¹.) [f. VOTAR-Y + -ESS.] A female votary; *esp.* a woman devoted to a religious life or to a special saint.

1589 WARNER *Alb. Eng.* VI. xxx. (1592) 133 The wrong must then by Phœbe be excused, Who, rescuing her Votarisse, did so preuent her brother. **1610** HEALEY *St. Aug. Citie of God* 887 Neare this place, at Caspalia, dwelt a Votaresse, who beeing sicke and past recouery, sent her garment to the shrine. **1654** R. CODRINGTON tr. *Iustine* XLIII. 503 She seemed not so much to be a person condemned, as a Voteress elected. **1670** COVEL in *Early Voy. Levant* (Hakl. Soc.) 114 If a poor Votaresse there..should by chance steal a taste of forbidden pleasure. **1798** SOTHEBY tr. *Wieland's Oberon* (1826) I. 85 Thou heavenly maid Who bad'st this knight thy votaress defend. **1810** SCOTT *Lady of L.* II. xiii, Rather will Ellen Douglas dwell A votaress in Maronnan's cell. **1853** LYTTON *My Novel* IX. iii, The same [book] which had charmed the circle at Hazeldean—..charmed now the wearied and tempted votaress of the world. **1879** DIXON *Windsor* I. iii. 25 At length the votaress yielded to these prayers.

attrib. **1897** F. THOMPSON *New Poems* 138 Ruled lips Befit a votaress Muse.

†**vo'tarious,** *a. Obs.*⁻¹ [Cf. VOTARY and -ARIOUS.] Vowed to a religious life.

a **1581** CAMPION *Hist. Irel.* xii. (1633) 39 Where hee erected many Celles and Monasteries, replenished with votarious men and women.

votarist ('vəʊtərɪst). [Cf. next and -IST.] One bound by a vow; a devotee, a votary.

1603 SHAKS. *Meas. for M.* I. v. 5 Wishing a more strict restraint Vpon the Sisterhood, the Votarists of Saint Clare. *a* **1639** SPOTTISWOOD *Hist. Ch. Scot.* I. (1677) 12 Divers Virgins..did in like sort apply themselves to the solitary life; not as the Votarists did that in after-times rose up, for they did not bind themselves by vows. **1656** S. HOLLAND *Zara* (1719) 44, I believe the Lady..is of too noble..a temper to welcome her Votarist with an affront. **1782** ELIZ. CARTER *Lett.* (1809) IV. 322 One of the nuns was kneeling very near the grate... If one of our fine drest ladies had been placed near this charming votarist [etc.]. **1782** R. CUMBERLAND *Anecd. Emin. Painters* I. 60 In the fore ground of the groupe of Bachanals there is a young female votarist asleep. **1813** SHELLEY *Q. Mab* Notes v. 189 The language of the votarist is this. **1844** R. P. WARD *Chatsworth* II. 188 Like a spotless heifer..surrounded by the proud priests and senseless votarists in whose sight..it is presently to die. **1869** BROWNING *Ring & Bk.* VII. 1506 So kneels a votarist, Weeds some poor waste traditionary plot Where shrine once was.

transf. **1806** H. SIDDONS *Maid, Wife, & Widow* II. 187 He is but a lukewarm votarist in the cause of truth and virtue, if he is to be thus ridiculed out of his integrity. **1831** W. GODWIN *Thoughts Man* 202 There is still further advantage that belongs to the poet and the votarist of polite literature, which ought to be mentioned.

votary ('vəʊtərɪ), *sb.* Also 7–8 vot'ry. [f. L. *vōt-*, ppl. stem of *vovēre* to vow + -ARY.¹]

I. 1. One who is bound by vows to a religious life; a monk or nun.

1546 BALE (*title*) The first two partes of the Actes or unchast examples of Englysh votaryes. **1560** DAUS tr. *Sleidane's Comm.* 90 b, The controversie was..especially for the Masse, and Votaries, for herein woulde the Catholikes nothyng at all relent. **1594** WEST *2nd Pt. Symbol.* §17 Persons civilly dead, as monks, fryers, canons, professed nuns, and such other superstitiouse votaries. **1607** *Merry Devil Edmonton* v. ii. 166 Sirra, ride strait to Chesson Nunry,..the house, I know, By this time misses their yong votary. **1654** EARL MONM. tr. *Bentivoglio's Wars Flanders* 89 The hereticks..growing more outragious then ordinarily against Ecclesiasticks, and especially against Votaries. **1662** OWEN *Animadv. Fiat Lux* v. Wks. 1855 XIV. 68 Monasteries of votaries under special and peculiar vows and rules. **1705** ADDISON *Italy* 494 The Abuse of Indulgencies, the Folly and Impertinence of Votaries, and in short the Superstition..of the Roman Catholick Religion. **1856** R. A. VAUGHAN *Mystics* (1860) I. 16 So Christianity, corrupted by Gentile philosophy, has in like manner its privileged and its inferior order of votaries.

b. One who has made, or is bound by, a special vow.

1588 SHAKS. *L.L.L.* II. i. 37 Who are the Votaries my louing Lords, that are vow-fellowes with this vertuous Duke? *a* **1596** *Sir T. More* III. ii. (orig. draft), The votarie that will not cut his haire, Vntill the expiration of his vow. **1643** TRAPP *Comm. Gen.* xxviii. 20 [*And Jacob vowed a vow*] The first holy votary that ever we read of. **1872** SPURGEON *Treas. Dav.* Ps. lxvi. 14 God in answer to his vow removed the distress, and now the votary desires to make good his promise.

2. One who is devoted to a particular religion, or to some form of worship or religious observance; a devotee.

1704 LOCKE *Toleration* iv. Wks. 1727 III. 464 Nor is there among the many absurd Religions of the World, almost any one that does not find Votaries to lay down their Lives for it. **1754** SHERLOCK *Disc.* (1759) I. i. 16 No other Religion can give any Security of Life and Happiness to its Votaries. **1777** R. WATSON *Philip II*, VIII. I. 296 That method of justifying iniquity, of which the votaries of the Romish church have so often availed themselves. **1794** PALEY *Evid.* I. i. (1817) 32 The ancient religion of a country has always many votaries. **1847** EMERSON *Repr. Men, Swedenborg* Wks. (Bohn) I. 334, I think of him as of some transmigrating votary of Indian legend. **1860** —— *Cond. Life, Worship* ibid. II. 395 The religion cannot rise above the state of the votary.

b. A devout worshipper. (Cf. next.)

1823 PRAED *Poems* (1864) II. 291 A happier votary at a holier fane. **1842** BARHAM *Ingol. Leg.* Ser. II. *Lay St. Cuthbert*, In fact, when the votaries came there to pray All said there was nought to compare with it. **1863** KINGLAKE *Crimea* I. 41 In order to keep these convents up, the priests imagined the plan of causing the votary to pay according to his means at every shrine which he embraced.

3. A devoted or zealous worshipper of God, Christ, one of the saints, etc.

a **1700** KEN *Sion* Poet. Wks. 1721 IV. 388 True Christ-like Love all other Loves exceeds, By which to save a soul Christ's Vot'ry bleeds. —— *On the Temptation* Poet. Wks. 1721 I. 92 Jesus Satan of his Force bereft, And Conquest easy to his Vot'rys left. **1742** YOUNG *Nt. Th.* III. 53 In propitious dreams (For dreams are thine) transfuse it thro' the breast Of thy first votary. **1779** J. MOORE *View Soc. Fr.* (1789) II. xcv. 421 A supposed connection between the characters of the Saints and the votaries. **1825** SCOTT *Betrothed* xxvii, The Virgin of the Garde Doloureuse, that never failed a votary. **1840** BARHAM *Ingol. Leg.* Ser. I. *St. Odille*, I don't see, as a Saint, how she well could do less Than to get such a votary out of her mess. **1869** FREEMAN *Norm. Conq.* (1875) III. xiv. 360 Harold implored the help of the relic whose sworn votary he was.

b. Used with reference to ancient or heathen deities, partly in fig. use.

? *a* **1690** PRIOR *To Earl of Dorset* i, Hear, Goddess, hear thy Votary. The meanest of thy Sons inspire. **1726** POPE *Odyss.* XVII. 288 Daughters of Jove!..your votary restore: Oh be some God his convoy to our shore! **1766** [ANSTEY] *Bath Guide* iii. 14 Come the Nymph of various Mien, Vot'ry true of Beauty's Queen. **1778** BP. LOWTH *Transl. Isaiah* Notes (1812) 340 Nor can they [the idols] answer, or deliver their votaries, when they cry unto them. **1877** L. MORRIS *Epic Hades* III. 242, I did not envy any goddess of all The Olympian company her votaries. **1878** BROWNING *Poets Croisic* xxxi, Silence and solitude Befit the votary of the Muse.

II. 4. One who is devoted or passionately addicted to some particular pursuit, occupation, study, aim, etc.

1591 SHAKS. *Two Gentl.* III. ii. 58 We know (on Valentines report) You are already loues firme votary. **1738** GRAY *Propertius* I. 2 Before the Goddess' shrine we too, love's vot'ries bend. **1764** REID *Inquiry* i. §8 If philosophy befools her Votaries,..let her be sent back to the infernal regions. **1771** BEATTIE *Minstr.* I. ix, The boundless store Of charms which Nature to her votary yields! **1806** H. K. WHITE *Lett.* (1837) 319, I am..a rejected votary at the shrine of Health. **1830** HERSCHEL *Study Nat. Phil.* I. i. 14 One of the great sources of delight which the study of natural science imparts to its votaries. **1873** HAMERTON *Intell. Life* VI. iv. 218 Science requires a certain inward heat and heroism in her votaries.

b. Const. *to* (now rare) or *of*.

(*a*) **1591** SHAKS. *Two Gentl.* I. i. 52 But wherefore waste I time to counsaile thee That art a votary to fond desire? **1594** *Selimus* Dj, I haue liu'd Almost a votarie to wantonnesse. **1742** *Lond. & Country Brew.* I. (ed. 4) 79, I cannot be a Votary to this practice. **1811** SHELLEY *St. Irvyne* iii, He became..even a more devoted votary to gambling than before.

(*b*) **1595** SPENSER *Col. Clout* 766 They..do themselues for want of other worke, Vaine votaries of laesie loue professe. **1690** TEMPLE *Ess., Heroic Virtue* Wks. 1720 I. 233 The usual Acceptation takes Profit and Pleasure for two different Things, and..calls the Followers or Votaries of them by several Names of busy and of idle Men. **1732** BERKELEY *Alciphr.* I. §5 Are you then in earnest a votary of truth? **1766** FORDYCE *Serm. Yng. Wm.* I. iii. 90 Is it surprising to see the daughters of such become very early the votaries of Folly? **1783** COWPER *Valediction* 71 Vot'ries of bus'ness and of pleasure prove Faithless alike in friendship and in love. **1801** HAMILTON *Wks.* (1886) VII. 218 The patriotic votaries of whiskey in Pennsylvania and Virginia. **1825** MACAULAY *Ess., Milton* (1851) I. 21 That an enthusiastic votary of liberty should accept office under a military usurper seems..extraordinary. **1869** FREEMAN *Norm. Conq.* (1875) III. xi. 40 Ground from which the votaries of devotion and art and history are bidden to turn away.

5. A devoted adherent or admirer of some person, institution, etc.

1647 CLARENDON *Hist. Reb.* VI. §36 It was not safe for any to live at their Houses, who were taken notice of as no Votaries to the Parliament. **1678** BUTLER *Hud.* III. i. 183, I come to prove How much I've suffer'd for your Love, Which (like your Votary) to win, I have not spar'd my tatter'd skin. **1682** VILLIERS (Dk. Buckhm.) *Chances* v. iii, I shall not be asham'd to own my self a Votary to all your Commands. **1713** STEELE *Guard.* No. 18 ¶4 One of the most successful Stratagems whereby Mahomet became formidable, was the assurance that Impostor gave his votaries, that [etc.]. **1817** CHALMERS *Life* in Churchyard *Chippes* 46 He endeavoured to cultivate the patronage of Essex, even after it had ceased to be of any value to his votaries. **1868** FREEMAN *Norm. Conq.* II. x. 464 The same virtues gained him a still nobler and more powerful votary; he became, as we have seen, the special friend of Earl Harold.

†**'votary,** *a. Obs.* [Cf. prec.]

1. Of persons: Consecrated by a vow; devoted to a religious life.

1564 *Brief Exam.* Bivb, The salarie..consecrated..to theyr holy votaries virgins. **1611** SPEED *Theat. Gt. Brit.* xix. (1614) 27/2 Elie, had in account for the repute and holinesse of votary-nunnes there residing. **1656** *Artif. Handsom.* 122 Having designed her daughter to be a votary virgin.

b. Of mode of life: Subject to vows.

1642 (*title*), The English Nunne, being a Dialogue, wherein the Author endeavoureth to draw young and unmarried Catholike Gentlewomen to embrace a Votary and Religious Life.

2. Of the nature of a vow.

1582 STANYHURST *Æneis* IV. (Arb.) 95 Had not I foresnaffled my mynde by votarye promise,..Haplye this oane faulty trespas might bring me toe bending. **1607–12** BACON *Ess., Custom & Educ.* (Arb.) 368 Onely Superstition is now so well advaunced that..votarie resolucion is made equipollent to Custome.

votation (vəʊˈteɪʃən). [f. VOTE *v.* + -ATION.] The action of voting in an election or at a meeting.

1816–30 BENTHAM *Offic. Apt. Maximized, Extr. Const. Code* 28 Modes of votation, two: the secret mode; then, before the result of the secret mode has been disclosed or ascertained, the open mode. **1848** *Times* 15 Jan. 4/6 A nominal votation was demanded,..that is, that each member should stand up in his place and give his vote,..at the same time calling out his name. **1877** T. A. TROLLOPE *Life Pius IX*, II. IV. i. 113 The result of the votation of the population of Umbria.

votcloth, southern ME. var. FOOTCLOTH.

vote (vəʊt), *sb.* Also 7 voate; *Sc.* 6 voit, voitt, vott, 6–7 voite; 6 wote, woit, wott, 7 woatt. [ad. L. *vōtum* vow, wish, properly the pa. pple. neut. of *vovēre* to vow, desire. Hence also It., Sp., Pg. *voto*; mod.F. *vote* in sense 5 is from English. Before 1600 only in Sc. use.]

I. †**1.** A vow; a solemn promise or undertaking. *Obs.*

1533 BELLENDEN *Livy* V. x. (S.T.S.) II. 182 Nochtwithstanding þat þai made solempne vote to appollo, ȝit þai tuke mare regarde of ony vthir thing þan to..fulfil þe said vote. **1536** —— *Cron. Scot.* (1821) II. 141 King Hungus ..maid solempnit vote, that he and his posterite sall use na ansenye in times cuming..bot the croce of Sanct Andro. **1715** M. DAVIES *Athen. Brit.* I. 152 A Temporal Religious Pensioner, or what is vulgarly call'd a Galloping-Nun, without any Votes.

†**2. a.** A prayer or intercession. *Obs.*

1626 B. JONSON *Fort. Isles, Song* Wks. (Rtldg.) 651/1 All the heavens consent, With harmony to tune their notes, In answer to the public votes, That for it up were sent. **1633** COWLEY *Constantia & Philetus* 146 Now at last the pitying God, o'recome By his constant votes and teares, fixt in her heart A golden shaft. **1656** J. PRIDEAUX *Euchologia* 226 Here may be taken in those interchangeable Votes of Priest and People, which are interposed, 'O Lord, arise, help us and deliver us for thy Names sake!' **1664** FULLER *Triana & Paduana* in *Wounded Consc.*, etc. (1867) 223 Being assigned but three hours of three several days, for the begging of the votes of mankind to help her in her extremity.

†**b.** A petition, a request. *Obs.*⁻¹

1645 *Unholsome Henbane betw. two Fragr. Roses* 1 A most humble Vote, and serious desire to our..Assembly of Divines.

†**3.** An aspiration; an ardent wish or desire. *Obs.* (Common 1630–60.)

*a***1626** BACON *Hist. Gt. Brit.* Wks. (Bohn) 498 Queen Elizabeth..carrying a hand restrained in gift, and strained in points of prerogative, could not answer the votes either of servants or subjects to a full contentment, especially in her latter days. **1640** HABINGTON *Edw. IV*, 169 Nothing was more in the vote of the English; then to preserve King Lewys safe in his estate at home. **1656** SANDERSON *Serm.* (1689) 541 The Glory of God, is to be the Alpha and Omega of all our votes and desires. **1667** *Decay Chr. Piety* v. ¶29 To breath out Moses's wish, O that men were wise; or if that be too hopeless a vote, O that men were not so destructively foolish.

II. †**4. a.** *Sc.* A formal expression of opinion by a member of a deliberative assembly on a matter under discussion; a decision or verdict. *Obs.*

1533 BELLENDEN *Livy* I. xiii. (S.T.S.) I. 76 Quhen þe maist parte & nowmer of senatouris war foundin of þe samyn votis as þe first has schewin,..it is accustumyt [etc.]. **1562** WINȜET *Wks.* (S.T.S.) II. 76 Quhat..wes the woceis and woteis of al [the bishops in council], bot that the thing quhilk wes techeit of auld suld be haldin? **1581** BURNE in *Cath. Tract.* (S.T.S.) 154 Thair is na ressoune quhy he sould follou rather the voittis of your ministeris, nor ye the voittis of his bischopis.

†**b.** *Sc. in one vote*, with one consent, of one accord, unanimously. *Obs.*

1546 *Reg. Privy Council Scot.* I. 28 Tha all in ane vote conselit and consentit that my Lord Governour suld cause the said hous to be deliverit to the said Lord Maxwell. *c* **1550** ROLLAND *Crt. Venus* II. 494 All in ane voit set thair Felicitie On future thingis, and Predestination. **1582–8** *Hist. James VI* (1804) 81 They all in ane voite [1825 voce], voittit, declarit, and testified, that [etc.].

5. a. An indication, by some approved method, of one's opinion or choice on a matter under discussion; an intimation that one approves or disapproves, accepts or rejects, a proposal, motion, candidate for office, or the like.

casting vote: see CASTING *ppl. a.* 2.

c **1460** in *Liber Pluscardensis* (Skene) I. 394 Be eleccioune chosin men of gude,..Quhilkis has the votis of al the commonis hale. **1552** in *Rec. Convent. Roy. Burghs* (1870) I. 3 To woit about throw that haill nowmer,..and he that gettis monyest woittis to be chosin and sworn incontinent. *a* **1578** LINDESAY (Pitscottie) *Chron. Scot.* (S.T.S.) I. 18 Lyk as he haid beine suppreme magistratt apprivit be the vottis of this realme. **1596** DALRYMPLE tr. *Leslie's Hist. Scot.* I. 246 Malduin the fourt sone of King Donalde,..with al votis, is declaired king. **1609** SKENE *Reg. Maj.* II. 132 The crime being lawfully provin,..be the suffrages and voites of the estaites in parliament..he may be condemned. **1651** HOBBES *Govt. & Soc.* vii. §14. 119 The civill Person sinnes not, but those subjects only by whose votes it was decreed for sinne. **1681** WOOD *Life* 5 July (1848) 231 Both his dispensations for terms and absence from lectures were denied but by one vote. **1756–7** tr. *Keysler's Trav.* (1760) I. 192 A young Prussian nobleman..was very near undergoing the same fate.., two votes only saving him from losing his head. **1823** *Local Act 4 Geo. IV*, c. iii. §8 Where the Number of Votes upon any Question shall be equal (including the Chairman's Vote) the Chairman shall have the casting Vote. **1855** TENNYSON *Maud* I. VI. vi, That so, when the rotten hustings shake In another month to his brazen lies, A wretched vote may be gain'd. **1884** tr. *Lotze's Logic* 394 It is sometimes done by simply counting the single vote of the preferred person as equal to several votes.

b. In the phrase ***to give*** (in recent use also ***to record***) ***a*** or ***one's vote***.

a **1578** LINDESAY (Pitscottie) *Chron. Scot.* (S.T.S.) I. 269 Lord Patrick Lyndsay that hes gevin the first wott. *a* **1654** SELDEN *Table-T.* (1689) 6 Bishops give not their Votes by Blood in Parliament, but by an Office annext to them. **1727** BAILEY (vol. II), *Voting*, giving his Vote or Suffrage at the Election of a Magistrate, or making a Law, etc. **1765** BLACKSTONE *Comm.* I. 165 If it were probable that every man would give his vote freely and without influence. *a* **1856** [see RECORD *v.*¹ 9 b].

c. *transf.* (Cf. sense 9.)

1652 CRASHAW *Poems* (1904) 189 Twixt pen and pensill rose a holy strife Which might draw vertue better to the life. Best witts gave votes to that. **1667** JER. TAYLOR *Dissuas. Popery* II. I. §7. 217 But the events of salvation and damnation (blessed be God) do not depend upon the votes and sentences of men. **1746** FRANCIS tr. *Horace, Art of Poetry* 467 Profit and Pleasure, then, to mix with Art, T' inform the Judgement, nor offend the Heart, Shall gain all Votes. **1829** LYTTON *Devereux* I. iv, You run, ride, leap too, better than anyone else, according to the votes of your comrades.

d. A means of signifying choice, approval, etc.; a voting tablet or ticket.

1817 SHELLEY *Rev. Islam* IV. xxii, Her voice, whose awful sweetness doth repress All evil,..And cast the vote of love in hope's abandoned urn. **1838** F. A. P[ALEY] tr. *Schömann's Assemb. Athen.* I. xi. 129 The citizens of each tribe cast their votes of condemnation or acquittal into one urn.

6. a. The collective opinion or assent of an assembly or body of persons. ***to take a vote***, to ascertain the opinion of a meeting by formal reference.

1582 *Reg. Privy Council Scot.* III. 482 To beare the chargeis of provest, baillies, eldermen, and counsale of the said burgh, not being electit thairto be commoun consent and voit of the haill inhabitantis. **1597–8** *Rec. Earldom Orkney* lxxix. (S.H.S.) 173 Patrik, Erle of Orkney..sittand in judgement at the head court callit the Harmanstein.. befoir the haill woit of the countrie. **1624** MASSINGER *Renegado* Ded., With a full vote and suffrage it is acknowledged that the patronage and protection of the dramatic poem is your's. **1632** *Chron. Perth* (Maitl. Cl.) 33 Mr John row wes admittit master of the gramer scole, be the provest, baillies, and counsall, without consent or woatt of ony wtheris. **1667** MILTON *P.L.* II. 313 For so the popular vote Inclines, here to continue, and build up here A growing Empire. **1721** RAMSAY *Prospect of Plenty* 133 Nor can we wyt them, since they had our vote. **1821** BYRON *Two Foscari* v. i, Why would the general vote compel me hither? **1848** W. K. KELLY tr. *L. Blanc's Hist. Ten Y.* I. 76 The law of the double vote had been..an implement of war directed against the throne. **1875** JOWETT *Plato* (ed. 2) V. 88 One is to be chosen by lot out of ten who are elected by vote. **1884** tr. *Lotze's Logic* 394 A number of groups in each of which a separate vote is taken.

b. In the phrase ***to put to the vote***, to submit to the decision of a meeting. Similarly (of a question), ***to go to the vote***.

1599 *Hist. Writers to Signet* (1890) 234 It being put to vote .., the maist part voteit to the said incorporatioun. **1681** in *Acts Parlt. Scotl.* (1875) XII. 45/2 It was putt to the vote, If the Act should be delayed or not, and was carried in the negative. **1770** LANGHORNE *Plutarch* V. 87 Cato, however, before it was put to the vote, ascended the rostrum. **1823** *New Monthly Mag.* IX. 244/1 He implored the House not to let the question go to the vote. **1857** TOULMIN SMITH *Parish* 58 He must then put it to the Vote whether the meeting 'approve' and 'confirm' the minutes. **1888** [see PUT *v.*¹ 22 b].

c. The collective support of a special number or class of persons in a deliberative decision, election, etc. (Cf. 7 c.)

1851 GALLENGA *Italy* 391 We must not, indeed, allow that it was the result of the Lombard vote that turned Sardinia's allies into enemies. **1884** *Nation* (N.Y.) 3 July 1/3 Mr. Blaine will get the following 'votes'. The Hebrew vote, because he spoke severely about the persecution of the Jews by Russia; the Dynamite vote, because he is down on the English.

7. a. The right or privilege of exercising the suffrage; esp. in the phrase ***to have a vote***.

a **1585** MONTGOMERIE *Cherry & Slae* 683 (Laing MS.), Thay say pat wayage neuir luckis, quhair ilk ane hes ane woit. **1624** in *Eng. Hist. Rev.* Jan. (1913) 130 It is to be carryed by most voyces, because every Councillor hath equall vote there. **1660** R. COKE *Power & Subj.* 109 If every man of England has not a like vote and power in electing Members for the House of Commons, then cannot the House of Commons be the Representative of the Nation. **1686** tr. *Chardin's Trav. Persia* 5 Who has sufficient to drive a Trade that will bear an Imposition of Eight Crowns, has as good a Vote as he that Trades for an Hundred Thousand. **1765** BLACKSTONE *Comm.* I. 165 Every member of the community..should have a vote in electing those delegates. **1782** PRIESTLEY *Corrupt. Chr.* II. x. 229 The common people ceased to have votes. **1829** MACAULAY *Mill on Govt.* in *Edin. Rev.* Mar. 177 On these grounds Mr. Mill recommends that all males of mature age, rich and poor, educated and ignorant, shall have votes. **1835** THIRLWALL *Greece* I. 379 Each tribe, however feeble, had two votes in the deliberation of the congress. **1866** GEO. ELIOT *F. Holt* xi, He..was already a forty-shilling freeholder, and was conscious of a vote for the county.

b. A person regarded merely as an embodiment of the right to vote; also, a person possessing the right to vote; a voter.

1737 POPE *Hor. Ep.* II. ii. 197 That from a Patriot of distinguish'd note, Have bled and purg'd me to a simple Vote. ? *a* **1800** *Devonshire's Noble Duel* ii. in Child *Ballads* VII. 114/2 Then away to the Parliament these votes all went again, And there they acted like just and honest men. **1806** WOLCOT (P. Pindar) *Tristia* Wks. 1812 V. 298 Oh! had I been a vote, a borough vote, Then Fortune would have squeezed me by thy hand. *Ibid.* 299 To enter the votes' houses up and down. **1852** R. S. HAWKER in C. E. Byles *Life* xiii. (1905) 220, I am not a vote, but a Man. The reverse is the general fact. People are not Men but votes.

c. The aggregate of voters, esp. of a certain class. (Cf. 6 c.)

1888 *Daily Chron.* 26 April (Cassell's) Alluding to the large amount of the illiterate vote in Ireland.

8. a. A resolution or decision passed by, or carried in, an assembly as the result of voting; an expression of opinion formally adopted by a meeting of any kind.

1641 *Jrnls. Ho. Comm.* II. 230/2 Resolved..That these Votes shall be printed; and attested under the Clerk's Hand. **1648** *Hamilton Papers* (Camden) 192 The distempers of the Houses (to see their former votes eluded and Presb[yterians] lately excluded now so numerous to carie all votes with a high hand) will grow suddenly to a great fire. **1682** A. MUDIE *Pres. St. Scotl.* ii. 26 The Prerogatives of the Crown are great, as Power of..giving the Votes of Parliament, the Authority of Laws. **1713** STEELE *Englishm.* No. 2 ¶7 That's the Gentleman who gained the first Vote [in the Senate] against Hannibal. **1724** SWIFT *Drapier's Lett.* Wks. 1738 IV. 62 Several smart Votes were printed. **1809** *Med. Jrnl.* XXI. 170 Pursuant to a Vote of the House of Commons, passed in the last Session. **1855** in Blaikie *Livingstone* ix. (1881) 185, I need not say that the award was made by an unanimous and cordial vote. **1874** GREEN *Short Hist.* ix. §9. 700 Marlborough was..charged with peculation, and condemned as guilty by a vote of the House of Commons.

(*b*) ***vote on account***, a resolution at the close of the financial year to assign a sum of money to a government department as an advance payment before its full annual expenditure is authorized by law.

1859 ERSKINE MAY *Law of Parl.* (ed. 4) 531 Votes on account. The entire sums proposed to be granted for particular services, are not always voted at the same time, but a certain sum is occasionally voted on account of such grants. **1910** W. S. CHURCHILL *Let.* 11 Mar. in R. S. Churchill *Winston S. Churchill* (1969) II. Compan. II. xiii. 992 The Vote on account is the most powerful and the most simple Parliamentary engine by which the House of Commmons is assured of its influence upon the Executive Government. **1963** *Economist* 24 Feb. 71/3 Part of the central government's expenditure, as recorded in the 'vote-on-account', is simply of a transfer kind; it includes, for instance, not only such personal payments as family allowances but also grants to local authorities made out of the central tax pool. *a* **1974** R. CROSSMAN *Diaries* (1977) III. 332, I am worried about this year's Vote on Account.

b. Const. *of.* ***vote of confidence***, a resolution showing majority support for a government, policy, etc. Similarly ***vote of no*** (or ***want of***) ***confidence***. Also *fig.*

1837 DICKENS *Pickw.* xiii, Then a vote of thanks was moved to the mayor for his able conduct in the chair. **1846** G. BENTINCK in *Hansard Commons* 8 June 182, I should certainly have preferred an Amendment which took the shape of a direct vote of want of confidence in Her Majesty's Ministers. **1863** H. COX *Instit.* I. vi. 44 Subsequently in the session a further vote of public money has been required. **1870** LD. RUSSELL *Sel. Speeches* I. 154 Institutions..whose ministers resign on a vote of want of confidence. **1881** *Sat. Rev.* 30 July 125/1 A majority, if it is good for anything, may be relied upon to reject a vote of censure. **1955** *Times* 10 May 14/4 The Government are asking for a vote of confidence. **1962** *Listener* 13 Dec. 1002/1 Why is it that grown men and women, no less than teenagers, are registering this unmistakable vote of no confidence in a society which has in so many ways improved their physical and material conditions of life? **1963** *Ibid.* 14 Feb. 281/2 The government survived..a vote of no confidence in the Parliament. **1976** *Glasgow Herald* 26 Nov. 1/8 Derby County's Scottish manager, Dave Mackay, was dismissed last night after three years at the Baseball ground. He had asked the club's directors for a vote of confidence.

†**9. a.** A declaration or statement of opinion. *Obs.*

1634 SIR T. HERBERT *Trav.* 206 [China] is by common vote, reputed the greatest Empire in the Orient. **1650** BULWER *Anthropomet.* 228 The Vote of the Proverb, for a handsome Woman, would have her English to the Neck, French to the Waste, and Dutch below. *a* **1680** GLANVILL *Sadducismus* I. App. (1681) 179 That a thing should be, and yet not be anywhere in the whole Universe, is so wild and mad a vote..that it cannot be said by any man in his wits.

†**b.** Reckoning, estimate. *Obs.*

1639 G. DANIEL *Ecclus.* The End 30, I blush to see our great Siracides ffall to the Vote of a low Paraphrase.

10. *attrib.* and *Comb.*, as ***vote-begging***, ***-catcher***, ***-collector***, ***-getter***, ***-getting***, ***-loser***, ***-monger***, ***-rigging***, ***-seeker***, ***-splitter***, ***-splitting***, ***-winner***; ***vote-catching***, ***-convicted***, ***-orientated***, ***-proof*** adjs.; ***vote-wise*** adv.; **vote bank**, in India, a group of people who can be relied upon to vote together in support of the same party; **Vote Office**, the office from which Parliamentary bills and papers are issued to members of the House of Commons; **vote-recorder**, a mechanical contrivance for registering votes.

1963 H. TINKER *Democratic Ideal in Asia* 17 The tribe, caste, or other association represents a '*vote bank'. **1982** *Jrnl. Commonwealth & Comparative Politics* XX. 9 The kinship group became an important vote-bank. **1923** *Weekly Dispatch* 13 May 2/2 The wild men pin their faith to the Capital Levy as a *vote-catcher. **1977** *Cork Examiner* 6 June 1/7 Mr Leddin felt that Ald. Lipper was being victimised because he was a 'vote catcher' for the party in Limerick. **1887** HUXLEY in *Darwin's Life & Lett.* (1887) II. 195 In the form of a *vote-catching resolution. **1859** MILL *Parl. Reform* 32 Why should the *vote-collector make a distinction where the tax-gatherer makes none? **1643** SIR J. SPELMAN *Case of Affairs* 28 Making them *Vote-convicted State Heretickes. **1906** *Springfield* (Mass.) *Weekly Republ.* 1 Nov. 3 He is also a strong campaigner, and has proved himself a *vote-getter. **1981** *Times* 13 June 16/7 Mrs Williams..is..the party's outstanding vote-getter. **1984** *Listener* 4 Oct. 5/1 Margaret Thatcher has held doubting Conservatives loyal by a mixture of unrelenting leadership and a formidable reputation as a vote-getter. **1892** *Courier-Jrnl.* (Louisville, Kentucky) 3 Oct. 3/3 Mr. Needy..was made a victim of the *vote-getting machine. **1929** *Daily Tel.* 8 Jan. 10/4 Acidulated suggestions of a lack of moral principle one day, want of suppleness the next, and ignorance of the elementary arts of vote-getting the day after do not help the cause. **1963** A. HOWARD in Sissons & French *Age of Austerity* I. 16 The Conservatives..seem to have based their whole vote-getting strategy on a fundamental misreading of the nation's mood. **1963** *Guardian* 25 Feb. 8/1 Nationalisation is a fully certified *vote-loser when it comes to election campaigning. *a* **1974** R. CROSSMAN *Diaries* (1975) I. 150 Immigration can be the greatest potential vote-loser for the Labour Party. **1887** *Amer. Missionary* July 195 Made tools of..by corrupt *vote-mongers. **1844** MAY *Treat. Parl.* xx. 312 The *Vote-office is charged with the delivery of printed papers to members of the house. **1852** DISRAELI *Ld. G. Bentinck* viii. (1872) 103 The interview by appointment took place in the Vote Office. **1971** H. WILSON *Labour Government* xxxvi. 744 *Vote-orientated promises to increase most individual spending programmes. **1928** G. B. SHAW *Intelligent Woman's Guide Socialism* lxiii. 291 Those who do understand it will never be unanimous in resisting it; consequently it is *voteproof at the parliamentary elections. **1875** KNIGHT *Dict. Mech.* 2715/1 *Vote-recorder. **1890** *Pall Mall G.* 5 Feb. 6/1 To expedite business by an electrical vote recorder. **1958** *New Statesman* 22 Feb. 230/3 He also ignored the detailed figures I gave of 10 other branches which recorded votes in excess of the number of members entitled to vote in September 1948; nor does he deal..with any other of the numerous illustrations I gave of *vote-rigging. **1983** *Listener* 20 Dec. 32/2 A 1981 BBC play about the famous ETU vote-rigging scandal of the Fifties. **1931** *Economist* 17 Oct. 723/1 *Vote-splitting will be avoided as far as possible. **1950** W. S. CHURCHILL *In Balance* (1951) 391 Great harm was done to national interests at the General Election by the policy of the Liberal Party in running hopeless or vote-splitting candidatures in hundreds of constituencies. **1959** *Punch* 16 Sept. 158/2 The wing-collared politicians who emancipated women *vote-wise probably had minds awhirl. **1969** G. KIRKLAND in R. Blythe *Akenfield* iv. 86 We are all mainly Socialists vote-wise.

vote (vəʊt), *v.* Also 6 *Sc.* **voitt, woit, wott**; 8 **whoat.** [f. L. *vōt-*, ppl. stem of *vovēre* to vow, to desire, or ad. med.L. *vōtāre* to devote by a vow, from the same stem. Cf. It. *votare*, Sp. and Pg. *votar*, to devote, to vote, F. *voter* to vote (in older use from It., in mod. use from English). Before 1600 almost exclusively a Sc. word.]

†**1.** *intr.* To vow (to do something). *Obs. rare.*

1533 BELLENDEN *Livy* I. xv. (S.T.S.) I. 86 He votit to consecrate þe harnes and armoure of his Inemyis to þe god vulcane. *Ibid.* II. ix. 163 Þe dictator..votit to edifie ane tempil in þe honoure of þe god Castor.

2. a. *refl.* and *trans.* To assign by a vow; to devote religiously. Now *rare.*

1533 BELLENDEN *Livy* v. xix. (S.T.S.) II. 211 All þe agit pepill..votit þame self wilfully to þe deith for þe wele of þere cuntre. **1589** WARNER *Alb. Eng.* Prose Add. (1592) 195 The Queene..voted, euen in her better part, to the loue of Æneas. **1652** GAULE *Magastrom.* 55 In an impiety, or (at least) temerity, of invoking, provoking, voting, devoting, imprecating. **1865** J. H. INGRAHAM *Pillar of Fire* I. xi. 123 To enumerate what met my eyes in the vases, which the common soldiers in their piety voted to the god,..would fill the page on which I write.

†**b.** To devote or consign *to* destruction. *Obs.*

1676 GLANVILL *Ess. Philos. & Relig.* IV. 1 The Books of curious Arts, that were voted to Destruction by Apostolick Authority and Zeal.

3. a. *intr.* To give a vote; to exercise the right of suffrage; to express a choice or preference by ballot or other approved means. Also *fig.* Cf. sense 3 c below.

1552 in *Rec. Convent. Roy. Burghs* (1870) I. 3 Thair sall convene in the Tolbuyth the auld counsale and new,..and thair to begyn at the litis of provestre, and to woit about throw that haill nowmer. **1637–50** ROW *Hist. Kirk* (Wodrow Soc.) 191 Because the brethren could not be fullie resolved for the present concerning the office of him who should vote in Parliament. **1651** HOBBES *Govt. & Soc.* vii. §1. 110 A Councell..of all the Citizens, (insomuch as every man of them hath a Right to Vote..) or of a part onely. **1727** STUKELEY in *Mem.* (Surtees) 194 It will enable you however to whoat at our elections. **1765** BLACKSTONE *Comm.* I. i. ii. 167 The statutes..direct..that no person shall vote in right of any freehold granted to him fraudulently to qualify him to vote. **1790** BURKE *Fr. Rev.* 100 With a compelled appearance of deliberation, they vote under the dominion of a stern necessity. **1845** GLADSTONE *Corr. Ch. & Relig.* (1910) I. 343 The question on which they voted was chosen for them by the Board of Heads. **1887** LOWELL *Democr.* 31 The right to vote makes a safety-valve of every voter. **1970** *Globe & Mail* (Toronto) 26 Sept. 23/1 They said its auditorium was poorly designed—dead acoustics, too many seats too distant. But the audiences, voting at the box-office, have continued to come for almost 40 weeks of every season.

b. Const. *against*, *for* (†*to*), or with inf.

1599 [see VOTE *sb.* 6 b]. **1651** HOBBES *Leviath.* II. xviii. 88 Every one, as well he that Voted for it, as he that Voted against it, shall Authorise all the Actions and Judgements of that Man. **1681** PRIDEAUX *Lett.* (Camden) 119 The fellows almost unanimously payd their obedience to his Majestys commands and voted for Finch. **1697** DRYDEN *Æneid* III. 86 All vote to leave that execrable shore. **1749** FIELDING *Tom Jones* I. iv, Mrs. Wilkins..would have voted for sending the child..immediately out of the house. **1806** *Med. Jrnl.* XV. 244, I would humbly propose that each subscriber..be qualified to vote for the election of a surgeon to a county hospital. **1831** SIR J. SINCLAIR *Corr.* II. 451, I vote for the Abbé Sieyes,—whom do you vote for? **1863** GEO. ELIOT *Romola* Introd. I. 8 Men..were conscious of having not only the right to vote, but the chance of being voted for.

c. With the name of a political party or of a candidate as quasi-*adv.*

1918 [see LABOUR *sb.* 2 c]. **1926** *Socialist Rev.* Oct. 48 There are still hundreds of thousands of voters who cannot bring themselves to vote Conservative. **1938** *Sun* (Baltimore) 6 Sept. 20 (*caption*) Vote Lewis. **1949** C. P. SNOW *Time of Hope* I. iv. 42 He voted radical and she was a vehement tory. **1977** R. BARNARD *Blood Brotherhood* i. 11 The parishioners..voted Conservative, when they did not vote National Front.

d. In *fig.* phr. ***to vote with one's feet***, to indicate an opinion by presence in or absence from a country, institution, activity, etc.

1965 *Listener* 16 Dec. 983/1 Politically, emigration provided a useful safety valve, anyone who hated the regime ..could just vote with his feet and get out. **1968** *Ibid.* 31 Oct. 567/2 The McCarthy supporters began to realise that if the only choice was Nixon or Humphrey, perhaps the streets were the only true political arenas... On and after 5 November there will be plenty of voting with the feet. **1970** *Guardian* 30 July 9/6 The children..just vote with their feet and join in. **1972** M. JONES *Life on Dole* vii. 56 Welshmen, in fact, were voting with their feet against the hopelessness that surrounded them. Those who were qualified scattered themselves across England. **1982** *Christian Order* Nov. 546 Uncounted thousands have 'voted with their feet', i.e., have left the Church. **1985** *Times* 7 Jan. 15/1 With another 16,000 to 20,000 miners returning to work an effective majority would have voted with its feet to end the strike.

†**4. a.** To declare one's opinion. *Obs.*$^{-1}$

a **1578** LINDESAY (Pitscottie) *Chron. Scot.* (S.T.S.) I. 268 [When] the lord Lyndsay had wottit in this maner, the haill lordis was contentit of this conclusioun.

†**b.** To decide, to judge. *Obs. rare.*

1643 CHAS. I *Lett.* Wks. (1650) 230 Some finde fault with too much kindnesse to thee (thou maist easily vote from what constellation that comes).

5. a. *trans.* Of assemblies, etc.: To choose, elect, enact, or establish by vote; to ratify or determine by formal expression of will.

1568 *Peebles Burgh Rec.* (1872) 74 The saidis baillies votit the samin be fre electioun of the haill communite. **1593** in *Spalding Club Misc.* I. Pref. 44 [The council] voitit, thocht guid and expedient, that the Grey freiris place thairof, sal be resignit. *a* **1648** LD. HERBERT *Henry VIII* (1683) 550 The Cardinal..was remoued to a Chamber apart..till the main question of the marriage was voted and agreed. **1665** in Picton *L'pool Munic. Rec.* (1883) I. 317 It is generally voted, agreed, thought fit, and so ordered, that the keeping of the fair here on St. Martin's day..shall..for this year be absolutely forborne and forbidden. **1697** DRYDEN *Æneid* IX. 298 They vote a message to their absent chief. **1781** GIBBON *Decl. & F.* xxviii. III. 73 Four respectable deputations were sucessively voted to the Imperial court. **1817** W. SELWYN *Law Nisi Prius* (ed. 4) II. 1071 Having in common council voted a petition to the king. **1841** W. SPALDING *Italy & It. Isl.* II. 180 Next year a parliament was summoned which.. voted a new balia. **1865** *Jrnl. Anthropol. Soc.* III. 19 The following list of presents were read, and thanks were voted for the same.

b. Const. with inf., expressing the result of the decision.

1648 WINYARD *Midsummer-Moon* 4 Thus Oxford, like the house of office at Westminster, is voted to bee reformed by those who sould it. **1648** *Hamilton Papers* (Camden) 168 Yett in hope of a party, they haue voted the Papists to compound. **1675** F. LD. AUNGIER in *Essex Papers* (Camden) 25 The House of Commons after a long debate vote the said persons to be sent to ye Tower. **1729** in Picton *L'pool Munic. Rec.* (1886) II. 91 The motion..for voteing the aforenam'd persons to be free.

c. Const. *away*, *from*, *in*, *into*, *off*, etc.

1641 SIR E. DERING in Rushw. *Hist. Coll.* (1692) III. I. 295 You have done exceeding well to vote away this Bishop. **1647** N. BACON *Disc. Govt. Eng.* I. xlvii. 126 Notwithstanding the Canon that had long before this time voted the Laity from having to do with Church matters. **1649** MILTON *Observ. Peace Ormond* Wks. 1851 IV. 576 They had no privilege to sit there, and vote home the Author ..of all our Miseries. **1835** T. MITCHELL *Acharn. of Aristoph.* 530 *note*, Previous to his voting Agyrrius into office. **1870** ROGERS *Hist. Gleanings* Ser. II. 162 The House met..and voted away their privilege in cases of libel by 258 votes to 133. **1890** *Longm. Mag.* July 255 My name has been voted off the list of your committee.

refl. **1914** *Times* (weekly ed.) 13 Mar. 218 The.. delimitation of the areas which may vote themselves out of Home Rule.

d. With appositive predicate.

1649 in *Verney Mem.* (1907) I. 443, I heare the Lords on Tuesday last voted all null since ye army siezed ye members. **1660** R. COKE *Power & Subj.* 52 All the Kings commands in prosecution of the Laws, were Voted breaches of the Priviledges of Parliament. **1730** *Lett. to Sir W. Strickland rel. to Coal Trade* 21 The House of Commons, after an Enquiry..voted both Lightermen, Masters and Owners guilty of a Combination.

e. With cognate object.

1871 BROWNING *Pr. Hohenst.* Wks. 1897 II. 304/1 Divers hundred thousand fools may vote A vote untampered with by one wise man.

f. ***to vote stock*** or ***shares***, to cast votes representing stock held in a company. *U.S.*

1957 R. A. HEINLEIN in *Mag. of Fantasy & Sci. Fiction* Oct. 30/2, I had assigned the stock to her but she knew..that I always voted it, that I had had no intention of parting with control of the company. **1978** *N.Y. Times* 29 Mar. D10/1 The state pension agencies can vote the stock but the banks must confer with others first.

†**6.** To submit (a matter) to a vote; to vote upon. *Obs. rare.*

1582–8 *Hist. Jas. VI* (1804) 130 Eftir the reeding of the quhilk supplicatioun, the heads quhairoff being reassonit and voitted, it was fund..that the Queene was compellit.. to subscryve the said comissioun. **1689** in *Acts Parlt. Scotl.* (1875) XII. 57/1 It was voted if the Committie should be named be the plurality of the whole house or be the plurality of each of the three benches.

7. ***to vote down***, to defeat, to put down or suppress, by a vote.

1642 LAUD *Wks.* (1854) IV. 10 About the tenth of this month, the bishops were voted down in the Upper House. **1644–7** CLEVELAND *Char. Lond. Diurn.* 2 And, since the Stages were voted down, the only Play-house is at Westminster. **1682** SIR T. BROWNE *Chr. Mor.* II. §5 (1716) 53 Old Truths voted down begin to resume their places. **1858** in Herndon *Life A. Lincoln* (1892) II. 115 The idea put forth by Judge Douglas, that he 'don't care whether slavery is voted down or voted up.' **1882** A. BAIN *Jas. Mill* vi. 268 It is the aristocracy that must, in the House, vote down the Ministry.

8. To grant, allow, or confer by vote.

1710 in *14th Rep. Hist. MSS. Comm.* App. IX. 352 The Tories are preparing complaints, among them one against the Admiralty for spending 500,000*l.* more than was voted. **1711** SWIFT *Examiner* No. 46 ¶4 The Parliament voted Subsidies, and the willing People chearfully paid them. **1838** THIRLWALL *Greece* IV. 91 They voted 1000 heavy infantry, 100 horse, and 50 galleys. **1849** MACAULAY *Hist. Eng.* iv. I. 510 Some among them talked of voting the revenue only for a term of years. **1873** C. ROBINSON *N.S. Wales* 83 The amount voted for public works in 1872 was £642,856; and this is about the amount voted by Parliament every year for public improvements.

transf. **1871** E. F. BURR *Ad Fidem* iii. 41 All the proprieties vote him a rest.

9. a. To declare by common assent; to characterize by an expression of opinion; to pronounce. Const. with simple compl. or inf.

1663 PATRICK *Parab. Pilgr.* xx, The old ways are much decried, and the last invention is voted to be altogether Divine. **1695** J. EDWARDS *Perfect. Script.* 395 We may.. safely vote him a true penitent. **1718** *Free-thinker* No. 61. 36 Last Night, I was voted a very Impudent Fellow. **1781** MME. D'ARBLAY *Diary* May, He..spoke no more during the whole debate, which I am sure he was ready to vote a bore. **1812** COL. HAWKER *Diary* (1893) I. 40 Shooting and sport of this kind being voted a rarity at Atworth. **1826** DISRAELI *Viv. Grey* v. xv, Receiving some not very encouraging response,..they voted her ladyship cursedly satirical. **1881** *Punch* 31 Dec. 309/1 The fair lady's dresses ..were voted charming.

b. *colloq.* To propose, suggest.

1814 SCOTT *Wav.* lxxi, I vote we should go to meet them. **1820** SHELLEY *Œd. Tyr.* II. 122, I vote, in form of an amendment, that Purganax rub a little of that stuff Upon his face. *Ibid.* 127, I vote Swellfoot and Iona Try the magic test together. *c* **1850** J. M. MORTON *Box & Cox* 23, I vote, Box, that we stick by her. **1880** TROLLOPE *Duke's Children* I. xviii. 222 We've got the trap and the horses..and I vote we make a start. **1927** E. BOWEN *Hotel* ii. 15, I vote we take those two on again.

c. To agree in, decide on, sending (a person) to a place.

1863 COWDEN CLARKE *Shaks. Char.* xvii. 432 So far are we from voting him to Coventry,..there are few of us who would refuse to march through Coventry with him.

10. a. To influence or control in voting; to cause to vote in a particular way.

1895 *Standard Dict.* s.v., He votes his employees.

b. To present for voting; to record the votes of (electors). *U.S.*

1859 BARTLETT *Dict. Amer.* (ed. 2) 98 They..are taken to the polls, and 'voted', as it is called, for the party. **1884** E. W. NYE *Baled Hay* 217, I believe they vote people there who have been dead for centuries. **1904** *N.Y. Even. Post* 8 Nov. 1, 25 men were in line in many places, and they were voted at a rate of nearly one a minute.

ˈ**voted,** *ppl. a.* [f. prec. + -ED¹.]

†**1.** Vowed, devoted. *Obs. rare.*

1586 WARNER *Alb. Eng.* I. ii, His wife and Sister..with Vesta seeke to shunne The voted fathers deadly doome. **1621** G. SANDYS *Ovid's Met.* XII. (1626) 244 Of a voted Hart The Antlers from a pine he puls.

2. Established or assigned by vote.

1644 MILTON *Areop.* (Arb.) 33 More gently brooking writt'n exceptions against a voted Order, then other Courts. **1884** *Pall Mall G.* 25 April 10 The right hon. gentleman estimated the expenditure..for the voted services £54,188,000.

voteen (vəʊˈtiːn). *Irish.* [prob. f. DEVOTE *sb.*¹ or DEVOTEE; the equivalent Ir. *móidín* is however connected with Ir. *móidim* I dedicate or devote.] A very religious person; a devotee.

1830–2 W. CARLETON *Traits* (1843) I. 16 Up near the altar ..you might perceive a voteen, repeating some new prayer or choice piece of devotion. **1856** P. KENNEDY *Banks of Boro* (1867) 184 One of the class that is called in Scotland 'The unco guid', and 'Voteens' among ourselves. *Ibid.* 333 He had considered his neighbour a voteen and twaddler.

voteless ('vəʊtlɪs), *a.* [f. VOTE *sb.* + -LESS.] Having no vote. (Common from 1880.)

1672 H. MORE *Brief Reply* 87 The Lay Courtiers.. were enabled to vote, when so many of the Reverend Clergy were by devices made vote-less. **1866** GEO. ELIOT *F. Holt* xi, There was a way of using voteless miners and navvies at Nominations and Elections. **1884** *Fortn. Rev.* Feb. 212 Many artisans live voteless outside boroughs. **1888** *Co-operative News* 15 Dec. 1261 We only refer to their voteless condition in order [etc.].

voter ('vəʊtə(r)). Also 6 *Sc.* **wottar**. [f. VOTE *v.*]

1. a. One who has a right to vote; *esp.* an elector.

a **1578** LINDESAY (Pitscottie) *Chron. Scot.* (S.T.S.) I. 267 The lordis devyssit and chargit Lord Patrick Lyndsay of the Byaris to be chancellor and first wottar in the consall. **1637–50** ROW *Hist. Kirk* (Wodrow Soc.) 191 As to the number of voters, that there should be fifty-one. **1767** T. HUTCHINSON *Hist. Mass.* II. 10 Every freeholder of forty shillings sterl. a year is a voter. **1841** DICKENS *Barn. Rudge* xlvii, He usually drove his voters up to the poll with his own hands. **1855** MACAULAY *Hist. Eng.* xx. IV. 458 In the towns in which he wished to establish an interest, he remembered, not only the voters, but their families. **1880** MᶜCARTHY *Own Times* lix. IV. 311 Voters were dragged to the poll like slaves or prisoners.

b. One who gives a vote. *rare*$^{-1}$.

1701 SIR D. HUME *Diary Parl. Scot.* (Bann. Cl.) 78 So by vote it was carried (Halcraig and I being no voters,) to send a macer.. to require them to attend the Council.

c. *attrib.*, as ***voter registrar, registration***. *U.S.*

1960 *Nation* (N.Y.) 23 Jan. 72/3 HR7597, introduced by Congressman Powell.. provides for the establishment of a Federal Voter Registration Commission. **1964** *Federal Suppl.* CCXXIX. 933/2 The suits filed by the United States against several county voter registrars.. were matters of common knowledge throughout the State of Mississippi. **1976** *National Observer* (U.S.) 10 July 5/5 He hopes to raise all he can—$3 million—for the Carter campaign, and raise even more, maybe $8 million, for voter registration and training schools for candidates and things like that.

†**2.** One who is bound by an oath or vow. *Obs.*$^{-1}$

a **1660** *Contemp. Hist. Irel.* (Ir. Archæol Soc.) I. 240 The Generall would passe noe other way than Balimore, as enformed of the said oath to try whether nowe or neuer they did proue true voters.

voteress, obs. var. VOTARESS.

votesave, obs. var. VOUCHSAFE.

voth, var. WOTHE *Obs.*

vother, southern ME. var. FOTHER *sb.*

Votiak, var. VOTYAK.

Votic ('vəʊtɪk). [Origin uncertain.] A language of the Finnish group of the Finno-Ugrian family of languages, used by a small number of speakers in the Ingrian region, now in the north-west part of the U.S.S.R. Also '**Votian**.

1908 T. G. TUCKER *Introd. Nat. Hist. Lang.* 132 Tchudic and the cognate dialects Vepsic and Votic, about Lake Onega. **1933** [see LUDIAN]. **1939** L. H. GRAY *Foundations of Language* 369 The languages of the Uralic family are as follows:.. *Finnish* group: Finnish proper.., Karelian.., Olonetzian, Ingrian, Lüdish, Vepsian, Votian, Esthonian, etc. **1954** PEI & GAYNOR *Dict. Linguistics* 229 *Votian*, a member of the Finnish group of the Finno-Ugric (or Uralic) sub-family of the Ural-Altaic family of languages. **1964** *Language* XL. 98 The Veps, Votic, and Estonian cognates.. are hardly necessary. **1977** *Ibid.* LIII. 477 The last ten are Yurak Samoyed, Lapp, Judeo-Spanish, Vepsian, Kashubian, Karaim, Ingrian, Livonian, Votic, and Manx Gaelic.

voting ('vəʊtɪŋ), *vbl. sb.* Also 6 *Sc.* **votting**; 7 *Sc.* **woitting**. [f. VOTE *v.* + -ING[1].]

1. The action of giving a vote.

1575 in *Maitl. Cl. Misc* (1840) I. 113 After lang ressonyng, with votting past thairin... the last kirk hes ordanit [etc.]. **1633** *Sc. Acts, Chas. I* (1870) V. 95/2 To haue voitt in parliament.. and in all vther lawfull meittings.. quhair burghes royall.. hes place of sitting and woitting. **1649** OGILBY *Æneis* XI. (1684) 364 Let him not threaten, and make Voting free. **1711** in *10th Rep. Hist. MSS. Comm.* App. V. 121 The Commons's voteing of the throne of England vacant. **1765** BLACKSTONE *Comm.* I. 165 Some, who are suspected to have no will of their own, are excluded from voting. **1822** A. RANKEN *Hist. France* IX. x. §2. 259 The sittings and votings of the states should be together, or separately. **1861** LD. BROUGHAM *Brit. Const.* App. III. 438 The voting was generally by the bean, or ballot in later times. **1885** *Manch. Exam.* 20 May 4/7 The voting for the Chancellorship of Dublin University took place yesterday.

2. *attrib.*, as ***voting age, -place, urn***; **voting machine**, a vote-recorder; **voting-paper**, a paper on which a vote is recorded; a ballot-paper.

1846 KEIGHTLEY *Notes on Virgil* Bucol. I. 34 *Saeptum* was originally any inclosure, whence the *Saepta* or voting-place of the tribes at Rome. **1858** SIMMONDS *Dict. Trade, Voting-paper*, a balloting-paper; a proxy. **1861** MILL *Repr. Govt.* 140 It is therefore provided that an elector may deliver a voting paper containing other names. **1880** MᶜCARTHY *Own Times* lii. IV. 109 The voting-paper principle was abandoned. **1900** *Daily News* 28 Nov. 7/7 The adoption of the voting machine would do away with all the delay in counting and checking the ballot papers. **1937** V. BARTLETT *This is my Life* x. 165 That mass of people.. saluting with religious intensity the dustbin-like voting urns. **1966** M. WOODHOUSE *Tree Frog* viii. 60 He must have reached voting age, but you couldn't tell by looking at him. **1978** *Listener* 2 Feb. 145/2 Those recently reaching voting age. **1978** K. J. DOVER *Greek Homosexuality* III. 111 The funnel of the voting-urn used in a lawcourt.

'**voting**, *ppl. a.* [-ING[2].]

†**1.** Votive, dedicatory. *Obs.*$^{-1}$

1630 HAKEWILL *Apol.* (ed. 2) 293 With Scythicke piety their aged Sier Let striplings tumble from the voting bridge.

2. That possesses or exercises the right of suffrage.

1830 JAS. MILL in A. Bain *Life* vii. (1882) 351 They are the class by whom chiefly the moral character of the voting classes is formed. **1837** W. E. FORSTER in T. W. Reid *Life* (1888) I. 93, I saw some dreadful cases of voting drunken people, both Whig and Tory. **1888** BRYCE *Amer. Commw.* v. lxxxviii. III. 194 The voting population seemed determined to give its whole attention to the Ring for one day at least.

†'**votist**. *Obs. rare.* [f. VOTE *sb.* or *v.* + -IST.] One who makes a vow; a votary.

1613 CHAPMAN *Revenge Bussy D'Ambois* III. Plays 1873 II. 137 Trie If a poore woman, votist of reuenge, Would not performe it. **1700** G. HICKES *To Rdr.* in *Devot. Anc. Way Offices*, Those stiff, morose, and saturnine Votists, who are so sparing of bodily Adoration, in our most solemn Services. **1711** —— *Two Treat. Chr. Priesth.* (1847) II. 107 A religious mystery, exhibiting one thing to the sense, and another to the understanding of the votist.

votive ('vəʊtɪv), *a.* and *sb.* [ad. L. *vōtīv-us* performed, offered, etc., in consequence of a vow, f. *vōt-um* vow VOTE *sb.* Hence also It., Sp., Pg. *votivo*, F. *votif, -ive*.]

A. *adj.* †**1.** Of persons: Carrying out a vow; devout. *Obs. rare.*

1593 NASHE *Christ's T.* (1613) 57 That Sepulchre you see is but a thing built vp by Saracens to get mony with, and beguile votiue Christians.

2. a. Dedicated, consecrated, offered, erected, etc., in consequence of, or in fulfilment of, a vow.

1611 SPEED *Hist. Gt. Brit.* VI. xxx. §2. 126 Which votiue Altar was erected by the Troupe of Horsemen surnamed Augusta Gordiana. **1616** B. JONSON *Poetaster, Dial. Hor. & Treb.* 57 So that the old man's life described, was seen As in a votive table in his lines. **1678** CUDWORTH *Intell. Syst.* I. iv. §23. 400 Those Last Dying words.. wherein he required his friends to offer a Votive Cock for him to Æsculapius. **1702** ADDISON *Dial. Medals* (1726) 136 Sacred to Mars these votive spoils proclaim The fate of Asdrubal, and Scipio's fame. **1756–7** tr. *Keysler's Trav.* (1760) II. 230 A marble boat placed before the church, and said to be a votive piece, as an acknowledgement for deliverance in a storm. **1789** MRS. PIOZZI *Journ. France* I. 152 The jewels given as votive offerings. **1820** W. IRVING *Sketch Bk.* I. 233 It is a pious custom,.. to honour the memory of saints by votive lights burnt before their pictures. **1841** W. SPALDING *Italy & It. Isl.* II. 343 In a third class, which embraces most of the votive pictures, the Virgin and Child are exhibited in glory. **1853** HUMPHREYS *Coin-coll. Man.* xxiv. 357 The altars for Apollo were besieged with votive offerings for the staying of the pestilence.

b. Observed, practised, undertaken, etc., in consequence of a vow.

1628 FELTHAM *Resolves* II. [I.] lxxxv. 246 Votiue Abstinence, some cold constitutions may endure. **1805** WORDSW. *Prelude* I. 181 Whence inspiration for a song that winds Through ever changing scenes of votive quest Wrongs to redress. **1876** STEDMAN *Victorian Poets* 397 A knight tilting at a wayside tournament as he rides on his votive quest.

c. Of the nature of a vow. *rare*$^{-1}$.

a **1626** A. LAKE *Serm.* (1641) 116 The King bindeth himselfe to make good his duty with a Votive Oath.

3. a. Consisting in, expressive of, a vow, desire, or wish.

1597 MIDDLETON *Wisd. Solomon* ix. 8 When I command, the people do obey, Submissive subjects to my votive will. **1629** J. GAULE (*title*), Practiqve Theories: or, Votiue Speculations upon Christs Prediction, Incarnation, Passion, Resurrection. **1641** SANDERSON *Serm.* (1689) 537 The sence hangeth unperfect, unless we take in the former verse too. Both together contain a Votive Prayer or Benediction. **1824** WORDSW. '*O for a dirge*' 9 No tears of passionate regret Shall stain this votive lay. **1835** —— *To Moon* 34 The fanes Extinct that echoed to the votive strains.

†**b.** = VOTAL *a.* 1. *Obs.*$^{-1}$

1664 JER. TAYLOR *Dissuas. Popery* I. ii. §1 80 A man, by contrition is not reconcil'd to God, without their Sacramental or Ritual penance, actual or votive.

4. ***votive mass*** (see quot. 1881).

1738 CHAMBERS *Cycl.* s.v. *Mass*, Votive Mass, is an extraordinary Mass besides that of the day, rehearsed on some extraordinary occasion. **1853** ROCK *Ch. of Fathers* III. 161 The Catholic priest will find in his Missal.. those votive Masses as they were.. allotted each one to its own day of the week, by Alcuin. **1881** BRIDGETT *Hist. Holy Eucharist* I. 200 Masses have also been composed for special occasions, and are called votive masses, because said according to the votum, i.e. the intention or desire of the celebrant.

B. *sb.* A votive offering.

1646 SHIRLEY *To T. Stanley*, A palsy shakes my pen while I intend A votive to thy muse. **1975** Y. YADIN *Hazor* iv. 61 We found.. an elevated rectangular platform that looked like an open high place, or *bamah*, where the votives.. were laid. **1976** *Scotsman* 27 Dec. 7/4 Archaeologists have recently dug up 8395 such terra cotta votives, as they are called.

Hence '**votively** *adv.*, in a votive manner.

1847 *Proc. Berw. Nat. Club* II. 237 Fruits placed votively on the shrine.

votmen, southern ME. var. pl. of FOOTMAN.

'**votograph, vo'tometer**, U.S. names for special types of voting-machines.

'**votress**[1]. Also 8–9 **vot'ress**. [var. of VOTARESS, after forms like *enchantress, protectress*.] A female votary.

1590 SHAKS. *Mids. N.* II. i. 125 His mother was a Votresse of my Order. *Ibid.* ii. 164 The imperiall Votresse passed on, In maiden meditation, fancy-free. **1607** *Barley-Breake* (1877) 21 What Nymph, what Nun, or what disdainefull Votresse, Shall not plucke downe and strike to thee the Sayle? **1647** R. STAPYLTON *Juvenal* 105 Ceres, the goddesse of husbandry, whose votresses none but chast women durst presume to be. **1700** DRYDEN *Pal. & Arc.* III. 225 Thy Votress from my tender Years I am. **1739** *Corr. betw. C'tess Hartford & C'tess Pomfret* (1805) I. 149, I do not wonder that you shed tears at the profession of the unhappy votress at Genoa, since I could scarcely restrain mine at the recital of her sufferings. **1758** JOHNSON *Idler* No. 18 ¶6 Every one.. has the pleasure.. of hoping to be numbered among the votresses of harmony. **1825** SCOTT *Talism.* iv, Surprise at the sudden appearance of these votresses, and the visionary manner in which they moved past him. **1866** J. B. ROSE tr. *Ovid's Met.* 27 A votress of the power Ortygian.

'**votress**[2]. [f. VOTER + -ESS.] A female voter.

1894 *Daily Tel.* 23 Nov. 5/4 The votress insisted that she must plump for 'Annie Sinclair'. **1895** *N. Amer. Rev.* Sept. 267 Unable to conjecture what the results may be when women shall have become not only votresses but.. alderwomen.

Votyak ('vəʊtjæk, ‖ va'tjak), *sb.* (*a.*) Also **Votiak**. [Russ.]

1. A member of a Finno-Ugrian people inhabiting the Udmurt republic in the northwestern region of the U.S.S.R. Also *attrib.* or as *adj.*

1841 *Penny Cycl.* XX. 247/1 The Votiakes are settled west of the Permians, on both sides of the upper course of the river Viatka, and in the country about the source of the Kama. **1845** *Encycl. Metrop.* XXV. 866/2 Near Perm.. are the Votyaks, who call themselves 'Uhdmurd, *i.e.*, Hospitable men. **1938** *N. & Q.* 23 Apr. 291/2 Votyak folklore is influenced by the Persians. **1948** D. DIRINGER *Alphabet* II. viii. 482 The Votiaks,.. living in the Vyatka region. **1968** BETHELL & BURG tr. *Solzhenitsyn's Cancer Ward* (1971) I. viii. 110 Now, as he paced up and down the ward, he remembered how the old folk used to die back home on the kama—Russians, Tartars, Votyaks or whatever they were. **1974** *Encycl. Brit. Macropædia* VII. 313/1 In the *lud* sanctuaries of the Votyaks.. worship was performed by members of the family.

2. The language of this people, belonging to the Permian branch of the Finno-Ugrian family.

1878 *Encycl. Brit.* VIII. 700/1 *Finnic* or *Ugrian* represented by.. (*b*) Karelian.. (*m*) Votiak. **1908**, etc. [see PERMIAN *a.* (*sb.*) 2]. **1932** W. L. GRAFF *Language & Languages* 406 Votyak (about 400,000) is situated between the Viatka and the Kama. **1951** W. K. MATTHEWS *Languages U.S.S.R.* iii. 24 The Permian branch, which comprises two languages, Zyryan and Votyak (Udmurt). **1977** [see VEPSIAN].

vou, obs. var. Sc. WOW *int.*

voubet, obs. Sc. form of WOUBIT.

vouch, *sb.* [f. next.]

†**1.** = VOUCHER *sb.*[1] 1. *Obs.*$^{-1}$

1621 BP. MOUNTAGU *Diatribæ* 128 Tell mee, if hee will not stand amazed at your Vouches in Fines and Recoueryes.

2. An assertion, allegation, or declaration; a formal statement or attestation of truth or fact. Now chiefly *colloq.*

1603 SHAKS. *Meas. for M.* II. iv. 156 My vouch against you, and my place i' th' State, Will so your accusation ouerweigh. [Also *Oth.* II. i. 147, etc.] **1610** W. FOLKINGHAM *Art of Survey* To Rdr. p. iii, An Arte-lesse Agent can.. with the bare vouch of the generall goodnesse of the Ground.. haile on the poore Pesant. **1621** BP. MOUNTAGU *Diatribæ* 14 Discrediting their vouches, by empairing their credits, and calling their Honesty into question. **1631** HEYLIN *St. George* 5 For having in the generall vouche and confession of the Church, beene reckoned with the Saints departed.

vouch (vaʊtʃ), *v.* Forms: 4 **voch-** (5 *Sc.* **woche**), **fouche**, 4 **wowche**, 5–6 **vowch**, 4–6 **vouche**, 5– **vouch**. [a. AF. and OF. *vocher, voucher* (OF. also *voch-, vouchier, vougier, voukier*), to call, summon, invoke, claim, etc., obscurely f. L. *vocāre* to call. Cf. AVOUCH *v.*]

1. *trans. Law. **to vouch to warrant*** or *to* (also †*for*) ***warranty***, to cite, call, or summon (a person) into court to give warranty of title. (After AF. and OF. *voucher a garant.*)

a **1325** *MS. Rawl. B.* 520 fol. 47 ȝif þilke þat is i voched to warant be in present ant mid wille wolle waranti þe tenaunt. **1485** *Rolls of Parlt.* VI. 324/2 And over that, caused theym.. to vouche by covyn to warrant one John Smyth, whiche also by covyn entred into warrant. **1509–10** *Act 1 Hen. VIII* c. 19 *Preamble*, Margaret vouched to warranty your said Suppliant. **1544** tr. *Littleton's Tenures* 34 Yf such tenaunt be impleded by a Precipe quod reddat &c. and he voucheth hys lorde to warranty. **1594** WEST *2nd Pt. Symbol.* §136 The vouchee is he, whom the tenant voucheth, or calleth to warranty for the land in demaund. **1628** COKE *On Litt.* 102 When the Tenant being impleaded within a particular iurisdiction.. voucheth one to warranty. **1741** T. ROBINSON *Gavelkind* I. vi. 130 If the Heir at Common Law be vouched for Warranty. **1766** BLACKSTONE *Comm.* II. 380 If the vasal's title to enjoy the feud was disputed, he might vouch, or call, the lord or donor to warrant or insure his gift. **1818** CRUISE *Digest* (ed. 2) V. 382 When a person is vouched to warranty, and enters of his own accord into the warranty, the law presumes that he parted with his possession with warranty. **1875** K. E. DIGBY *Real Prop.* (1876) 78 *note*, The person vouched to warranty might in his turn vouch a second person, and the second vouchee a third.

absol. **1531** *Dial. on Laws Eng.* II. i. Fivb, When the tenaunte in tayle hath vouched to warrauntye. **1865** F. M. NICHOLS *Britton* II. 258 If the deforciant vouches to warranty, then the like process shall hold [etc.].

b. *ellipt.* (with omission of *to warrant*).

1544 tr. *Littleton's Tenures* 12 The wyfe of the feoffour bryngeth an accyon of Dower gaynst the yssue of the feoffe, and he vouched the heyre of the feoffour. **1625** SIR H. FINCH *Law* (1636) 370 If the tenaunt vouch a dead man, the demandant may auerre he is dead, or there is none such. **1628** COKE *On Litt.* 386 b, If two men make a Feoffment.., and the one die, the Feoffee cannot vouche the survivor only, but the heir of him that is dead also. **1766** BLACKSTONE *Comm.* II. 359 If Edwards therefore be tenant of the freehold in possession,.. Edwards doth first vouch Barker, and then Barker vouches Jacob Morland the common vouchee. **1818** CRUISE *Digest* (ed. 2) V. 325 This person being tenant to the *præcipe*, vouches the tenant in tail. **1875** K. E. DIGBY *Real Prop.* (1876) 78 *note*, If at the time of the claim the vouchee were dead, the possessor of the thing claimed could 'vouch the tomb' of the vendor.

absol. **1523** FITZHERB. *Surv.* 20 If their copies were lost they may vouche and resort to the lordes court rolles. **1628** COKE *On Litt.* 101 b, The partie, if he hath a Warrantie, shall not vouche, but haue his action of couenant, if [etc.]. **1642** tr. *Perkins' Prof. Bk.* I. §49. 23 If a bastard eigne is impleaded and vouch and the vouchee enters into warranty. **1672** [see VOUCHER *sb.*[2] 4].

c. With *over*. Of a vouchee: To cite (another person) into court in his stead. Also *absol.*

1511–2 *Act 3 Hen. VIII*, c. 18 *Preamble*, In whiche.. accione the seid tenauntes vouched to warrante Syre John Rysley Knyght and he vouched over to Warantie Thomas Fysshe. **1628** [see VOUCHER *sb.*[1] 1 b]. **1741** T. ROBINSON *Gavelkind* I. vi. 130 If the Heir at Common Law be vouched for Warranty, who vouches the Heirs in Gavelkind because of the Possession, they all shall vouch over. **1766** BLACKSTONE *Comm.* II. 359 He vouches the tenant in tail, who vouches over the common vouchee. **1818** CRUISE *Digest* (ed. 2) V. 451 If a *præcipe* is brought against a tenant in tail, and his wife,..and they both vouch over in the usual manner, it will bar the estate tail. *Ibid.*, A common recovery, in which he and his wife vouched over the common vouchee.

2. To take or call (a person) to witness. †In early use with *to record*. Also *transf.* (quot. 1700).

c **1412** HOCCLEVE *De Reg. Princ.* 1838 God of heuen vouch I to record, þat.. Thow schalt no cause haue more þus to muse. **1425** *Rolls of Parlt.* IV. 267/2 And yat ye same Wauter voucheth Baronez to recorde whiche bene present in yis Parlement, and wer present in yat Counseill. **1676** W. LONGUEVILLE in *Hatton Corr.* (Camden) I. 125 Clarke.. quoted Basset's man, a bookseller in Fleet-streete; and ye yong bookseller vouch't Mr. Freake, a yong barrister of ye Middle Temple. **1700** DRYDEN *Ovid's Met.* XIII. 22 The Sun and Day are Witnesses for me, Let him who fights unseen relate his own, And vouch the silent Stars, and conscious Moon. *Ibid.* 101 That it is not a Fable forged by me,.. I vouch ev'n Diomede.

b. To cite or appeal to (authority, example, doctrine, etc.) in support of one's views or statements or as justification for a course of action.

1531 ELYOT *Gov.* III. xxv, But the most catholike and renoumed doctours.. vouche (as I mought say) to their ayde the autoritie of the writars. **1581** J. BELL *Haddon's Answ. Osor.* 30 Bycause I sayd that our Preachers do alleadge Scriptures onely: and yet within a whiles after I added, that they did vouche the authoritie of the Fathers also. **1641** J. SHUTE *Sarah & Hagar* (1649) 195 He voucheth the example of Elias, how God, upon his prayer, shut and opened heaven. **1660** BONDE *Scut. Reg.* 363, I vouch every mans experience to warrant this truth. **1692** LOCKE *Toleration* III. ix. 215 So that you cannot vouch the Intention of the Magistrate, where his Laws say nothing. **1884** *Law Rep. 14 Q.B.D.* 799 There is no such doctrine as that.. which has been vouched in order to take away the effect of this deed. **1885** LD. ESHER in *Law Times' Rep* (N.S.) LIII. 445/2 A solicitor cannot vouch his privilege in such a case as this.

c. Similarly with reference to the citation of authors, works, etc.

1599 THYNNE *Animadv.* (1875) 71 In the catalogue of the auctors, you haue omytted manye auctors vouched by chawcer. **1611** SPEED *Hist. Gt. Brit.* IX. x. (1623) 651 For more credit to which assertion hee vouched sundry bookes and acts. **1630** PRYNNE *Anti-Armin.* 239 We have truly vouched well nigh two hundred that consent with us. **1651** H. L'ESTRANGE *Smectymnus-mastix* 17 When he is vouched to serve their turns, he is set out with a more honorable encomium, he is then stiled A learned Jew, the famous Rabbi Maymonides. **1722** WOLLASTON *Relig. Nat.* iii. 43 For the truth of this I vouch the mathematicians. **1744** HARRIS *Three Treat.* Wks. (1841) 45, I am not certain.. whether you will admit such authorities as it is possible I may vouch. **1831** *Westm. Rev.* Jan. 73 No one now regards such writers as Ascham, Burton, Chapman.. as obsolete, or would hesitate to vouch them to justify a word and keep its memory from oblivion. **1866** *Q. Rev.* July 261 As he vouches another person for his former charge, and speaks allusively only of the second, it is difficult to say how much weight he attaches to either of these.

d. To cite, quote, or adduce (a passage, etc.) out of a work in support of a view or statement.

1581 J. BELL *Haddon's Answ. Osor.* 25 b, You recite at the last certeine of my wordes, vouched out of Augustine, which be as followeth. **1583** H. HOWARD *Defensative* Ooj b, Since I find a sorte of godly verses vouched out of theyr vessels, by the learned fathers of the church. **1596** DANETT tr. *Comines* (1614) 79 Neither will I vouch examples out of the ancient histories. **1631** HEYLIN *St. George* 155 His testimony vouch'd by Authors of that antiquity,.. assure[s] mee.. that such a worke was in their times, receiv'd as his. **1656** SANDERSON *Serm.* (1689) 488 It would be too long to vouch Texts for each particular. **1842** S. R. MAITLAND *Remarks* 72 A statement, that Philpot vouched the major of his argument 'out of Vigilius, an ancient writer'.

†**3. a.** To put in evidence, to display. *Obs.*

13.. *E.E. Allit. P.* B. 1358 Þis bolde Baltazar biþenkkes hym ones, To vouche on [= an] avayment of his vayne glorie.

†**b.** To announce or declare (a vow). *Obs.*

13.. *E.E. Allit. P.* C. 165 Vchon glewed on his god þat gayned hym beste, Summe to Vernagu þer vouched a-vowes solemne.

†**c.** To cast the responsibility of (something) *on* a person. *Obs.*

c **1395** *Plowman's Tale* 945 On hir bishop their warant [to] vouche, That is law of the decre.

4. To allege, assert, affirm or declare. Also const. *upon* or *against* (a person). Now *rare* or *Obs.*

1390 GOWER *Conf.* I. 295 Bot I spak nevere yit.. That unto Cheste mihte touche, And that I durste riht wel vouche Upon hirself as for witnesse. *Ibid.* II. 24 For.. sche myn herte toucheth, That for nothing that Slowthe voucheth I mai foryete hire. **1425** *Rolls of Parlt.* IV. 267/2 Thenne.. ye same Wauter seyth and voucheth, ye Parlement yat King Richard held at Westm' [etc.]. **1581** J. BELL *Haddon's Answ. Osor.* 228 b, From whence shall this mylde & charitable allegation.. appeare at the length to be truly vouched agaynst Luther? **1603** SHAKS. *Meas. for M.* v. i. 326 What can you vouch against him, Signor Lucio? Is this the man that you did tell vs of? **1604** —— *Oth.* I. iii. 103 *Bra.* I therefore vouch againe, That with some Mixtures, powrefull o're the blood,.. He wrought vp on her. *Duke.* To vouch this, is no proofe. **1662** SOUTH *Serm.* (1697) I. 52 In that Power and Dominion that God gave Adam over the Creatures: In that he was vouched his immediate Deputy upon Earth. **1817** SHELLEY *Rev. Islam* IX. xxxi. 5 What we have done None shall dare vouch, though it be truly known.

†**b.** With complement. *Obs.*[−1]

1601 SHAKS. *All's Well* II. v. 87 But like a timorous theefe, [I] most faine would steale What law does vouch mine owne.

5. To assert or affirm to be true or according to fact; to guarantee the truth or accuracy of (a statement, etc.); to attest or certify. Also const. *against* (a person).

1591 SAVILE *Tacitus, Hist.* I. 49 Diuerse miracles vowched by sundry persons terrifyed the mindes of men. **1601** SHAKS. *All's Well* I. ii. 5 Nay tis most credible, we heere receiue it, A certaintie, vouch'd from our Cosin Austria. **1700** LOCKE *Hum. Und.* (ed. 4) IV. xvi. §8 When any particular matter of fact is vouched by the concurrent Testimony of unsuspected Witnesses, there our Assent is also unavoidable. *a* **1703** BURKITT *On N.T.* Matt. xxviii. 15 What an improbable and unlikely lie this was, which they put into the soldiers' mouths to vouch. **1750** tr. *Leonardus' Mirr. Stones* 117, I believe the saying of Pliny is very true, that there is no lie so impudent which is not vouched by authority. **1774** REID *Aristotle's Logic* vi. §2. 237 They will.. respect nothing but facts sufficiently vouched. **1827** HALLAM *Const. Hist.* xv. II. 496 *note*, Boyer, in his History of the Reign of Queen Anne, p. 12, says [etc.].. I should be glad to have found this vouched by better authority. **1841** W. SPALDING *Italy & It. Isl.* II. 99 Other legends were vouched by grave citations from a certain Book of Martyrdoms. **1879** M. PATTISON *Milton* 153 An idle story that Milton died a Roman Catholic.. is not well vouched, being hearsay three times removed.

absol. **1814** SCOTT *Lord of Isles* I. vi, Further vouches not my lay, Save that such lived in Britain's isle. **1878** BROWNING *La Saisiaz* 66 Go and see and vouch for certain.

b. With subordinate clause: To bear witness, to testify, *that* (etc.).

1604 SHAKS. *Oth.* I. iii. 262 Vouch with me Heauen, I therefore beg it not To please the pallate of my Appetite. *a* **1806** BP. HORSLEY *9 Serm.* (1815) 138 Some few hours after, Peter vouches that he had seen our Saviour. **1828** SCOTT *F.M. Perth* xxxiv, The Prior of the Dominicans will vouch for me, that they are more than half heathen. **1884** *Marshall's Tennis Cuts* 24 That there are now occasional complaints on this score we can vouch from personal knowledge.

c. With complement to the object.

1684–5 SOUTH *Serm., Prov. xvi. 33* (1697) I. 358 If a man succeeds in any attempt, though undertook with never so much folly and rashness, his success shall vouch him a politician. **1693** —— *Serm., Eccl. i. 18* (1842) V. 3 His [*sc.* Solomon's] judgment, whom God has hitherto vouched the wisest of men. **1903** *Times* 29 Jan. 13/4 The girl.. had vouched the man Waugh as having been present.

6. To support or uphold by satisfactory evidence; to back with proofs of a practical or substantial character.

1579 TOMSON *Calvin's Serm. Tim.* 3/1 That all they that teache, may vouch in deede, and of a trueth, that Iesus Christ speaketh by their mouth. *Ibid.* 458/1 To vouch our Godlinesse, that is to say, to shewe in deede & without dissembling that wee labour to serue God. **1662** GLANVILL *Lux Orient.* i. 3 Let us take some account of what the 2 first opinions alledge one against another..: now, if they be found unable to withstand the shock of one anothers opposition; we may reasonably cast our eies upon the third, to see what force it brings to vouch its interest. **1667** MILTON *P.L.* v. 66 Mee damp horror chil'd At such bold words voucht with a deed so bold. **1697** C. LESLIE *Snake in Grass* (ed. 2) 281 If G. Whitehead cannot, by some better Miracles than these, vouch that Curse and Prophecy. *a* **1704** T. BROWN *Sat. French King* Wks. 1730 I. 59 A change so monstrous I cou'd ne'er have thought, Tho' Partridge all his stars to vouch it brought. **1778** *Hist. Eliza Warwick* I. 29 Say, Madam, how can I possibly relieve you.. and my zeal in serving you will best vouch the sincerity of my words. **1828** D'ISRAELI *Chas. I*, II. ii. 49 He afterwards honourably vouched his words by his deeds. **1830** SCOTT *Demonol.* x. 394 The extreme antiquity of the building is vouched by the immense thickness of the walls. **1911** E. BEVERIDGE *North Uist* vii. 239 The general character of this site is fully vouched by traces of five or six old dwellings.

b. To attest or substantiate by written evidence.

1745 POCOCKE *Descr. East* II. III. i. 126 When I arrived at Scutari, they took my slave from me, as I had not the original writing by me to vouch the property of him. **1796** MORSE *Amer. Geog.* I. 462 Either party may appeal to the superior court.. except on bonds or notes vouched by two witnesses. **1886** *Law Times Rep.* LXXX. 197/1 All expenses so claimed must be strictly vouched.

7. To support by recommendation; to become sponsor for (a person or thing). *rare.*

1590 GREENE *Never too Late* Ep. Ded., Knowing you are such a Mæcenas of learning, that you will as soone vouch with Augustus a few verses, giuen by a poor Greeke, as of the Arabian Courser. **1659** T. PECKE *Parnassi Puerp.* i, I want no Patrons for to vouch my Books. **1775** C. JOHNSTON *Pilgrim* 212 It was impossible to object to such a scheme, especially as the magistrate vouched the fellow's sagacity. **1906** A. NOYES *Drake* I. 82 Leicester vouched him; 'This man's tale is true!'

b. To affirm or guarantee (the truth of a statement).

1607 SHAKS. *Cor.* v. vi. 5 Bid them repayre to th' Market place, where I.. Will vouch the truth of it. **1670** COVEL in *Early Voy. Levant* (Hakl. Soc.) 112 One of our English Merchants there (of good repute, though I shall not vouch the truth of his story).. told us [etc.]. **1741** C. MIDDLETON *Cicero* II. vi. (ed. 3) 149 The three Tribuns.. terrifying the City with forged stories.. produced their creatures in the Rostra to vouch the truth of them to the people. **1771** MRS. GRIFFITH *Hist. Lady Barton* III. 131 She had framed a novel against me,.. so guarded at all points, that each part of it seemed to vouch the truth of the rest. **1805** EUGENIA DI ACTON *Nuns of Desert* II. 179 Willet.. should be summoned to vouch the truth of his own despatches.

c. To give or pledge (one's word of honour) *for* something.

1898 *Daily News* 10 Nov. 4/7 M. Cavaignac has.. insulted France by vouching his personal honour for a gross, clumsy, .. forgery.

8. *intr.* With *for*. **a.** To speak or bear witness in behalf of (a person); to be surety or sponsor for.

1687 A. LOVELL tr. *Thevenot's Trav.* Pref. c, As to the Englishing of this Work, since the Translator has no body to Vouch for him, he must e'en leave it to take its chance. **1698** COLLIER *Immor. Stage* 215 The Salvo of Sir John Friendly's appearing at last, and vouching for Lord Foplington, won't mend the matter. **1728** CHAMBERS *Cycl.* s.v., A Person is said to Vouch for another, when he undertakes to maintain or warrant him in a thing, or passes his Word in his behalf. **1781** COWPER *Lett.* 19 Feb., Mr. Hill knows me well enough to be able to vouch for me that I am not over-much addicted to compliments and fine speeches. **1820** SCOTT *Monast.* xviii, I dispute not the lad's qualities, for which your reverence vouches.

b. Of things: To supply evidence or assurance of (some fact).

1755 YOUNG *Centaur* v. Wks. 1757 IV. 222 What year, nay, what day, has passed unimpowered to vouch for his clement, and absolute reign? **1757** W. WILKIE *Epigon.* Pref. p. xxxv, The stories.. would have appeared.. altogether ridiculous,.. till antiquity had procured them credit, or a tradition been formed afterwards to vouch for them to the world. **1826** DISRAELI *Viv. Grey* v. viii, The very incident vouches for its sweet seclusion. **1867** FREEMAN *Norm. Conq.* (1877) I. v. 324 The plan which he formed, though not successful, seems to vouch for his generalship. **1884** tr. *Lotze's Metaph.* 276 The certainty of the law.. is vouched for.. by the results of experiment.

c. To give personal assurance of the truth or accuracy of (a statement or fact). Also with *accuracy*, *truth*, etc., as object.

1777 SHERIDAN *Sch. Scand.* IV. iii, A very clear account, truly! and I dare swear the Lady will vouch for the truth of every word of it. **1798** in Nicolas *Disp. Nelson* (1846) VII. p. clx, I do not vouch for what I have said of the Bellerophon and Majestic. **1800** *Med. Jrnl.* IV. 510, I cannot vouch for the accuracy of every minute particular, but am certain that the general statement will be found to be correct. **1841** LANE *Arab Nts.* I. 24 When he relates anything for the truth of which he can not vouch. **1865** W. G. PALGRAVE *Arabia* II. 176, I can vouch for the great frequency of these sources. **1882** MISS BRADDON *Mt. Royal* II. iv. 54, I love the country better than ever, I can vouch for that.

†**9.** *trans.* To assert a claim to (something). *Obs. rare.*

1488 *Acta Dom. Conc.* (1839) 108/1 Becauss þe said thomas clamit þe said landes to pertene to alane kynnard.., and that he walde woche thaim wiþ the perell: The lordis þarefore ordanis þe said maister William to woche samekle of þe said landis as he plessis. **1491** *Ibid.* 216/2 The said Johne allegiit þat all þe saidis landis wer his fee & heretage, & wochit þe samyn wiþ þe perell of law in presens of þe lordis. **1549** COVERDALE, etc. *Erasm. Par. 1 Cor.* 39 Howebeit this labor of myne, I vouche not as myne, but gyue al to goddes goodnes, by whose helpe all was wrought.

†**10.** To guarantee the title to, or legal possession of (something). *Obs. rare.*

1602 SHAKS. *Ham.* v. i. 117 Will his Vouchers vouch him no more of his Purchases? *a* **1661** FULLER *Worthies* (1662) I. 64 If one ignorantly buyeth stolen Cattel, and hath them fairly vouched unto him,.. he cannot be damnified thereby.

11. †**a.** To deign or think fit *to* do something; = VOUCHSAFE *v.* 6. Also with simple object. *Obs.*

1589 GREENE *Menaphon* (Arb.) 51, I was.. drawne.. to.. affoord you such companie as a poore swaine may yeeld without offence, which if you shall vouch to deigne of, I shall be.. glad of such accepted seruice. **1590** LODGE *Euphues' Gold. Leg.* F 3 b, Marry, if you want lodging, if you vouch to shrowd your selues in a shepheards cotage, my house (for this night) shalbe your harbour. *c* **1590** GREENE *Fr. Bacon* vii, Then must we all make suit.. To Friar Bacon, that he vouch this task, And undertake to countervail in skill The German.

b. To condescend to grant or give; to allow or permit; = VOUCHSAFE *v.* 2 a.

1594 LODGE & GREENE *Looking Gl.* II. iii. 855 If that I meant not, Rasni, to forgiue,.. I would not vouch her presence in my Courts. **1612** *Two Noble K.* v. iv. 123 Our master Mars Hath vouch'd his Oracle, and to Arcite gave The grace of the Contention. **1848** BAILEY *Festus* (ed. 3) 200

Power And means vouched heretofore to some, and now To him who words the wonders he hath seen.

†**12.** *intr.* To deign to accept *of* something; = VOUCHSAFE *v.* 6 d. *Obs. rare.*

1589 GREENE *Tullies Love* Ded., Then..if my worke, treating of Cicero, seeme not fit for Cicero..yet I craue your Honour will vouch of it, only for it is written of Cicero. **1590** —— *Never too Late* (1600) 6 This Palmer..returning me many thanks, voucht of my proffer, and was willing to take my house for his Inne. **1602** ROWLANDS *Greenes Ghost* 6 But you kind friends, that loue your countries wealth, Vouch of my labours.

Hence **vouched** *ppl. a.*, **ˈvouching** *vbl. sb.*

1573–80 BARET *Alv.* s.v. *Vouch*, Such vouching or constant affirmance. **1610** SHAKS. *Temp.* II. i. 60 *Gon.* But the rariety of it is, which is indeed almost beyond credit. *Seb.* As many voucht rarieties are. **1611** COTGR., *Vouchement*, a vouching in law. **1657** W. MORICE *Coena quasi Κοινὴ* xi. 127 By the vouching of Theophylact I conceive they have gotten nothing. **1757** MRS. GRIFFITH *Lett. Henry and Frances* (1767) IV. 76 A Gentleman had bought a Horse, some Time ago, which happened not to answer his Vouchings. **1816** SCOTT *Antiq.* xxxvi, Aymer de Geraldin..who, by the less vouched, but plausible tradition ..of the country, is said to have been descended from the Marmor of Clochnaben. **1832** *Rolls of Parlt.* Index 955/2 Collusive Sale of Land, and vouching by Warranty. **1894** A. BIRRELL *Ess.* i. 4 This side of the account needs no vouching; but there is another side.

†**ˈvouchable,** *a.* *Obs.*$^{-1}$ [f. prec. + -ABLE.] Able to be cited or quoted in support of a statement, etc.

a **1641** BP. MOUNTAGU *Acts & Mon.* (1642) 544 For this opinion elder Authors are vouchable.

vouched-safe, *ppl. a.* [f. VOUCHSAFE *v.*] Vouchsafed, granted.

1839 BAILEY *Festus* xxx. 347 His is the vice-royed, vouched-safe, sway of God.

vouchee (vaʊˈtʃiː). [f. VOUCH *v.* + -EE[1].]

1. *Law.* The person vouched or summoned into court to give warranty of a title. ***common vouchee***: (see quot. 1766).

1485 *Rolls of Parlt.* VI. 293/2 The said Recoveries and Judgments.., and the Vouchees in the same and theire heires. **1531** *Dial. on Laws Eng.* II. i. F i b, And that vouche shal appere, and the demaundantes shall declare agaynst hym. **1594** WEST *2nd Pt. Symbol.* §52 A fine betweene the vouchee and the demaundant is good,..for that the vouchee is as it were tenant in law. **1607** COWELL *Interpreter* s.v., The party that voucheth in this case, is called the Tenent, the partie vouched is tearmed the Vouchee. **1625** SIR H. FINCH *Law* (1636) 372 In an assise of nouell disseisin and nusance, voucher lyeth not, vnlesse the vouchee be present in Court, and will by and by enter into warrantie. **1653** in Somers *Tracts* I. 503 By any Recovery or Recoveries had against him as Tenant or as Vouchee in any common Recovery. **1752** MCDOUALL *Inst. Law Scot.* II. 244 The writ is brought against the tenant in tail himself, who vouches the common vouchee. **1766** BLACKSTONE *Comm.* II. 353 Upon this, Jacob Morland, the vouchee, appears, is impleaded, and defends the title. *Ibid.* 359 The cryer of the court (who, from being frequently thus vouched, is called the common vouchee). **1802–12** BENTHAM *Ration. Judic. Evid.* (1827) V. 492 A.. man of straw, under some such name as that of the common witness, or common vouchee. **1818** CRUISE *Digest* (ed. 2) V. 451 Because the wife was named..and appeared and vouched as joint tenant; and the vouchee entered into the warranty, admitting that he ought to warrant to them. **1875** [see VOUCH *v.* 1].

2. A person cited or appealed to as an authority for some fact or statement, or in evidence of some assertion. Occas. ***common vouchee***, after prec.

1654 GATAKER *Disc. Apol.* 29 His Vouchee, Autor, or Advocate (cal him which you please). **1673** HICKMAN *Quinquart. Hist.* 439 Making also the immortal Grotius his Vouchee for this opinion. **1809** MAR. EDGEWORTH *Manœuvring* xiv, He had wisely determined to obtain accurate and positive evidence from Captain Lightbody, who seemed in this case to be the common vouchee. **1851** *Fraser's Mag.* XLIII. 271 Some respectable names are occasionally attached as vouchees. **1890** *Pall Mall G.* 23 June 3/1 Poor Nausicaa! She is the common vouchee of every writer on every game of ball.

†**b.** A fact or circumstance cited in evidence or justification. *Obs. rare.*

1657 W. MORICE *Coena quasi Κοινὴ* Pref. 8 Importunity of friends (the common vouchee to warrant publications). **1665** GLANVILL *Scepsis Sci.* Addr. p. xi, Conceiving Reason and Philosophy sufficient vouchees of Licentious practices.

†**3.** An avouchment or assertion. *Obs. rare.*

1625 BP. MOUNTAGU *App. Cæsar* 119 It insisteth but upon some points only; and that not by or with a generall vouchee neither, but thus only, I see no cause. *a* **1641** —— *Acts & Mon.* (1642) 256 Of what credit or authority this his vouchee is, I cannot tell.

voucher (ˈvaʊtʃə(r)), *sb.*[1] [a. AF. *voucher* VOUCH *v.*: see -ER[4].]

1. a. *Law.* The summoning of a person into court to warrant the title to a property. ***voucher over*** (cf. VOUCH *v.* 1 c).

1531 *Dial. on Laws Eng.* II. iv. G v b, If suche a recouerye be had of rente with a voucher ouer, then it shalbe taken to be of lyke effecte as recoueryes of landes be in suche maner as we haue treated of before. **1544** tr. *Littleton's Tenures* 12 And he vouched the heyre of the feoffour, and duringe the voucher and not termyned, the wyfe of the feoffe bryngeth an accyon of Dower agaynst the heyre of the feoffe. **1570** *Act 13 Eliz.* c. 5 §5 Any Estate..by reason whereof any Person ..shall use any Voucher in any Writ of Formedon. **1621** SANDERSON *Serm.* I. 184 When thou..hast nayled all these with all the appurtenances, by fines, and vouchers, and entayls, as firm as law can make them, to thy child. **1625** [see VOUCHEE 1]. **1766** BLACKSTONE *Comm.* II. 358 This is called the voucher..or calling of Jacob Morland to warranty. **1768** *Ibid.* III. 299 Voucher also is the calling in of some person to answer the action, that hath warranted the title to the tenant or defendant. **1818** CRUISE *Digest* (ed. 2) I. 425 To the intent that a common recovery should be had and suffered against them, with voucher of the lessor. [**1865** F. M. NICHOLS *Britton* II. 4 In this writ neither view nor voucher lies. *Ibid.* 98 In such case the tenant shall fail in his voucher.]

b. ***double voucher***: (see quot. 1628).

1594 WEST *2nd Pt. Symbol.* §136 In a recouerie with double voucher, the fine must be sued first to make him tenant at the time of the writ of Entre brought. **1602** SHAKS. *Ham.* v. i. 114 His recognizances, his Fines, his double Vouchers. **1628** COKE *On Litt.* 102 You shall finde in bookes a recouery with a single Voucher, and that is when there is but one Voucher, and with a double Voucher, and that is when the Vouchee voucheth over. **1752** MCDOUALL *Inst. Law Scot.* II. 244 The above is the procedure in a Common Recovery with a double voucher, and is the most common and safe way. **1766** BLACKSTONE *Comm.* II. 359 It is now usual always to have a recovery with double voucher at the least. **1818** CRUISE *Digest* (ed. 2) V. 325 In a recovery with double voucher.

2. a. *transf.* A piece of evidence; a fact, circumstance, or thing serving to confirm or prove something; a guarantee.

1611 SHAKS. *Cymb.* II. ii. 39 Heere's a Voucher, Stronger than euer Law could make. **1696** WHISTON *The. Earth* II. (1722) 191 Plutarch and Pliny attest it,..the last bringing Augustus's own Words for his Voucher. **1699** BENTLEY *Phal.* 37 It has no Voucher but the Epistles of Phalaris, the very Book that's under debate. **1719** R. WODROW *Corr.* (1843) II. 436 The vouchers and proofs are such as will, I hope, be found sufficient. **1744** T. BIRCH *Life Boyle* 112 The philosophy of Des Cartes..had not the necessary vouchers of repeated experiments, purposely tried, to make it good. **1788** PRIESTLEY *Lect. Hist.* IV. xxix. 217 The collection of records..supplies good vouchers of the truth of all he advances. **1807** G. CHALMERS *Caledonia* I. II. vi. 302 *note*, The Register of St. Andrews is the most ancient voucher for the death of Alpin. **1856** KANE *Arct. Expl.* II. xxiv. 237 The destruction of the vouchers of the cruise..the log-books, the meteorological registers, the surveys, and the journals. **1885** *Manch. Exam.* 3 June 5/2 The strength of the bias which these letters reveal..[is] a sufficient voucher for their genuineness.

b. A written document or note, or other material evidence, serving to attest the correctness of accounts or monetary transactions, to prove the delivery of goods or valuables, etc.

1696 LUTTRELL *Brief Rel.* (1857) IV. 28 At last it ended in appointing a committee to repair to the East India house and search their books, if they can find vouchers for the said accounts. **1731** in W. Hale *Prec. Causes of Office* (1841) 68 The vouchers and an estimate of the necessary expenses..to be laid before the vestry. **1760** *Cautions & Advices to Officers of Army* 35 Keep all the Serjeant's Pay-Notes, and all Receipts, to be produced as your Vouchers when you settle Accompts with your Captain. **1780** JEFFERSON *Corr.* Wks. 1859 I. 245 The arms you have to spare may be delivered to General Gates's order, taking and furnishing us with proper vouchers. **1828** D'ISRAELI *Chas. I*, I. xi. 309 At his death, his family discovered that he..had kept no vouchers or any accounts whatever. **1857** TOULMIN SMITH *Parish* 183 When they have regularly to produce accounts, with vouchers, of all receipts and expenditure. **1866** CRUMP *Banking, &c.* iv. 96 Disputing the payment of a particular cheque, and alleging that all his paid vouchers had been destroyed.

c. A written warrant or attestation.

1796 *Trans. Soc. Arts* XIV. 274. I send along with this a voucher signed by the Mayor..who saw me make Net on this machine. **1862** R. H. GRONOW *Remin.* I. 49 No one could obtain a box or a ticket for the pit without a voucher from one of the lady patronesses. **1884** *Manch. Exam.* 12 Sept. 5/1 The report..appears to have been sent direct from the Mudir to Cairo, without a voucher from Major Kitchener, who is at Dongola.

d. A document which can be exchanged for goods or services as token of payment made or promised by the holder or another (see also quot. 1947).

1947 *Sun* (Baltimore) 12 May 2/5 Stefan has gone through a stack of vouchers—expense accounts—from the American Embassy. **1955**, etc. [see LUNCHEON 3]. **1960** S. UNWIN *Truth about a Publisher* II. xix. 353 The New Zealand Company had not given me an actual ticket..but a voucher instructing their agent to issue me a ticket.

3. *attrib.*, as ***voucher-card, form, number, plan, scheme, system.***

1881 MISS BRADDON *Asph.* xvii, Where the voucher system is so thoroughly carried out. **1891** *Pall Mall G.* 21 Sept. 7/2 As I get into the train the guard rushes up and hands me a voucher-card. **1898** *Engineering Mag.* XVI. 46 The voucher form is printed on white paper for the office, and on tinted green paper for the agents. *Ibid.*, The 'Key' to this voucher number. **1970** *Phi Delta Kappan* LII. 49 For some time Christopher Jenks has believed that voucher plans offer an exit from the bureaucratic morass in which many major school systems are mired. **1980** *Jrnl. R. Soc. Arts* July 475/1 It could be done through some kind of voucher scheme.

Hence †**ˈvoucher** *v. trans.*, = VOUCH *v.* 5 b.

1609 SKENE *Reg. Maj., Stat. Rob. III*, 59 The tenant..sall woucher, that is, affirme, that he halds that land..be the tenour of the chartour quhilk is tynt.

voucher (ˈvaʊtʃə(r)), *sb.*[2] [f. VOUCH *v.* + -ER[1]. Cf. VOUCHOR.]

1. One who vouches for the truth or correctness of a fact or statement or corroborates another person in this respect; an author or literary work serving this purpose.

1612 WOODALL *Surg. Mate* Wks. (1653) 290 Without painting of phrases or collecting of great Authours for my Vouchers. **1679** PENN *Addr. Prot.* I. vi. (1692) 22 They would make him a Voucher of all their Falshood. **1698** FRYER *Acc. E. India & P.* 252 Whether the Beams were of Cedar, it is not so fortunate as to have a Voucher of its own Nation. **1715** M. DAVIES *Athen. Brit.* I. 96 For the authenticalness of his Chymical MS. he produces no other Voucher than one Reinesius. **1754** EDWARDS *Freed. Will* II. v. 53 The Use he makes of Sayings of the Fathers, whom he quotes as his Vouchers. **1826** SCOTT *Woodst.* xiv, Tomkins ..was in the habit of being voucher for his master. **1836–7** SIR W. HAMILTON *Metaph.* (1859) I. iii. 47 Heraclides and Sosicrates, the two vouchers of this story. **1853** J. H. NEWMAN *Hist. Sk.* (1873) II. I. ii. 81 But here I am only concerned with its wealth, for which grave writers are the vouchers.

b. One who vouches for the respectability or good faith of another, or who undertakes to guarantee some procedure.

1667 WATERHOUSE *Fire Lond.* 105 Deteining suspicious persons till they brought good vouchers and cleared themselves. **1711** ADDISON *Spect.* No. 253 ¶3 All the great Writers of that Age..stand up together as Vouchers for one another's Reputation. **1732** SWIFT *Let. to Barber* 14 Dec., Mr. Pilkington..says you will be his voucher that he still continues his modest behaviour. **1791** MRS. INCHBALD *Next door Neighb.* III. ii. 66 Mr. Manly, notwithstanding you are these people's voucher, this appears but a scheme. **1820** HAZLITT *Lect. Dram. Lit.* 94 The only way that I know of is to make these old writers, as much as can be, vouchers for their own pretensions. **1829** SCOTT *Jrnl.* 9 Mar., The Solicitor was voucher that they would keep the terms quite general. **1871** R. ELLIS tr. *Catullus* lxiv. 362 Voucher of him last riseth a prey untimely devoted E'en to the tomb.

c. *transf.* Of things, in preceding senses.

1718 ROWE tr. *Lucan* IV. 820 The Seas, and Earth, our Virtue shall proclaim, And stand eternal Vouchers for our Fame. **1742** YOUNG *Nt. Th.* IV. 553 Religion! the sole voucher man is man; Supporter sole of man above himself. **1835** J. H. NEWMAN *Par. Serm.* (1837) I. xiii. 195 Nothing but past acts are the vouchers for future. **1838** EMERSON *Addr. Cambridge, Mass.* Wks. (Bohn) II. 192 Speak the truth, and all things alive or brute are vouchers..to bear you witness. **1856** —— *Eng. Traits, Aristocr.* Ibid. 84 The grand old halls scattered up and down in England, are dumb vouchers to the..broad hospitality of their ancient lords.

†**2.** A supporter or upholder of some practice or theory. *Obs.*

1677 W. HUGHES *Man of Sin* II. iii. 56 This Practice must needs declare it self a notorious moral Wickedness;..and so bids fairer still for its great Vouchers claim unto that Title of the Man of Sin. **1684** tr. *Bonet's Merc. Compit.* I. 31 A stout Voucher of the 4 Humours, tells how he read..that the Gout arose from Vapours.

†**3.** *Cant.* One who utters counterfeit coin. *Obs.*

1673 R. HEAD *Canting Acad.* 69 Gilts,..Runners, Padders, Booth-heavers, Vouchers and the like. *Ibid.* 191 The first was a Coyner that stampt in a Mould, The second a Voucher to put off his Gold. *a* **1700** B. E. *Dict. Cant. Crew*, *Vouchers*, that put off False Money for Sham-coyners.

†**4.** *Law.* **a.** = VOUCHEE 1. **b.** = VOUCHOR. *Obs.*

1596 BACON *Use Com. Law* (1635) 52 Which I. H. is one of the Cryers of the Common Pleas, and is called the Common Voucher. **1637** COWELL *Interpreter* s.v., The partie that voucheth in this case, is called the Tenent, the partie vouched is termed the Voucher. **1672** MANLEY *Cowell's Interpreter* s.v., He that voucheth is called Voucher, (*vocans*) and he that is [vouched is] called Vouchee, (*Warrantus*).

ˈvoucheress. *rare*$^{-1}$. [ad. AF. *voucheresce*: see prec. and -ESS[1].] A female voucher.

1865 F. M. NICHOLS *Britton* II. 272 The warrant is bound to defend the voucheress against the plaintiff.

vouching *vbl. sb.*: see VOUCH *v.*

†**vouchment.** *Obs.*$^{-1}$ [a. OF. *vouchement* (15th c.), or f. VOUCH *v.* + -MENT.] The action of vouching; a solemn assertion or affirmation.

a **1670** HACKET *Abp. Williams* I. (1693) 77 The Peers..lay not their Hand upon the Book, but upon their Breast; which is a Sign that their vouchment by their Honour in that Tryal is not an Oath.

vouchor. *rare.* [AF., f. *voucher* VOUCH *v.* Cf. VOUCHER *sb.*[2] 4 b.] One who calls another into court to warrant a title.

1628 COKE *On Litt.* 101 b, Hee that voucheth is called the Vouchor.., and he that is vouched is called Vouchee. **1768** BLACKSTONE *Comm.* III. 299 If the vouchee appears, he is made defendant instead of the vouchor. **1865** F. M. NICHOLS *Britton* I. 59 If the warrant makes good his case, then let both the vouchor and his warrant be acquitted. *Ibid.* 116, etc.

vouchsafe (vaʊtʃˈseɪf), *v.* Forms: *α.* 4–5 vowche-, 5 vowch-, 4–6 vouche- (4–5 voche-, 5 woche-, vousshe-), 4– vouch-, 6 voutchsafe, etc.; also 4 votesave, 6 voutsalfe, vousalf, vowt-, voult-, 6–8 voutsafe, 7 vouchafe. *β.* 4–5 fowche-, fouche-, 5 ffouch-, foche-, fuch(e)safe, etc.; also 5 fuchesef. *γ.* 4–5 woche- (5 woches-; whoche-), 5 woch-, 4–6 wouche- (5 woushe-), 6 wouchsafe, etc.; also 5 wot-save, 7 wow-, wouchaife, wouchaiffe. *δ.* 4 weche-, 5 wych(e-, wiche-, 6 wichsafe, etc.; also 5 wet-saffe, wytsaff, *Sc.* witsaufe, 6 -save, -saffe, -safe, wytsaue, -save, -saufe; 5 *Sc.* wichauf, wiche-, wichsauf, -saif, 5–6 witschaif, 6 withsaif, -save, -schaif, wythsaue, -save; 5 witeselfe, 6 -safe, 6 wytesave (5 wyȝt-). (For usual variants of the second element see SAFE *a.*, and for special illustration of forms see sense 6 b.) [f. VOUCH *v.* (in the sense of 'warrant') + SAFE *a.* In early use still treated as two words, with normal inflection of the verb, and occasional inversion (*safe vouch*), or insertion of words between the verb and adj.]

I. †**1.** *trans.* To confer or bestow (some thing, favour, or benefit) *on* a person: **a.** With separable vb. and adj. (Freq. in 14th cent. romances.) *Obs.*

1303 R. BRUNNE *Handl. Synne* 6345 He vouchede hyt [*sc.* his property] saufe on vs, he seyd, þat we ȝave hyt whan he deyde. *a* **1400** *Sir Amadace* (Camden) liii, And ȝe be a mon that wille wedde a wife, I vouche hur safe, be my life, On ȝo that fayre may. *c* **1425** *Seven Sag.* (P.) 453, I vowch hym wylle save on the, To do what thy wylle bee. **1456** SIR G. HAYE *Law Arms* (S.T.S.) 103 Quhy suld man tak it fra thame sen God vouchis it sauf on thame. **1457** HARDING *Chron.* I. in *Eng. Hist. Rev.* Oct. (1912) 742 Seth that prynce is gone.. I vouche it sauf, wyth all benyvolence, On yow, gode lorde, hys sonne and hayre that bene. **1508** *Gest Robyn Hode* ccclxxxi. in Child *Ballads* III. 75/1 But yf I had an hondred pounde, I wolde vouch it safe on the.

†**b.** With vb. and adj. in juxtaposition or combination. *Obs.*

c **1330** *King of Tars* 336 Ich fouchesaf on him my blod, To him heo nis not to good, Though heo weore ten so briht. *c* **1374** CHAUCER *Anel. & Arc.* 254 Is þer now neyþer worde ne chere Ye vowchensauff vpon myn hevynesse? *a* **1440** *Sir Eglam.* 222 Lorde, y have servyd yow many a day, Vowchesafe ye hur on mee. *c* **1475** *Babees Bk.* 175 For yt ys nouhte ywys conveynent,.. Alle forto holde that vnto yow ys brouhte, And as wrecches on other vouchesauf nouhte. *c* **1485** *Digby Myst.* (1882) I. 624 But syth þou wytyst saff a dyner on me, with pes and grace I entyr þi hows. **1560** ROLLAND *Seven Sages* 10 Na rewaird desire I of ȝour grace Bot to witchaif on me sa greit credence [etc.]. **1599** HAKLUYT *Voy.* I. Pref. **2, You may see.. what gracious priuileges and high prerogatiues were by diuers kings vouchsafed vpon them. **1671** MILTON *P.R.* II. 210 What woman will you find .. On whom his leisure will vouchsafe an eye Of fond desire?

2. To give, grant, or bestow in a gracious or condescending manner: **a.** Without const.

13.. *Gaw. & Gr. Knt.* 1391 Tas yow þere my cheuicaunce, I cheued no more; I wowche hit saf fynly, þaȝ feler hit were. *a* **1400** *Sir Amadace* (Camden) xxxii, Sadyll, brydyll, and oder geyre, Fowre so gud thoffe hit were I woch hit save, bi Sen Jon! **1424** in R. R. Sharpe *Lond. & Kingd.* (1895) III. 369 Of þat þat your lordly clemence so beningly voucheþ sauf.. it excedeth inestimablich our power.. to yeve you thankynges. **1594** KYD *Cornelia* Ded., And so vouchsafing but the passing of a Winters weeke with desolate Cornelia, I [etc.]. **1611** SHAKS. *Cymb.* II. iii. 45, I haue assayl'd her with Musickes, but she vouchsafes no notice. **1642** CHAS. I in *3rd Rep. Hist. MSS. Comm.* 420/2 There is hardly any-thing.. that we shall not finde in our hart a willingnesse and readinesse to voutsafe it. **1667** MILTON *P.L.* v. 881 Those indulgent Laws Will not now be voutsaf't, other Decrees Against thee are gon forth without recall. **1781** COWPER *Hope* 487 Nature indeed vouchsafes, for our delight, The sweet vicissitudes of day and night. **1838** TALFOURD *Athenian Captive* II. i, Wilt thou not join thy fellows at the feast, And taste a cup of wine the king vouchsafes For merriment to-day? **1856** R. A. VAUGHAN *Mystics* (1860) II. IX. iii. 138 Forms of glory come and go: gifts of subtlest discernment are vouchsafed. **1881** BESANT & RICE *Chapl. of Fleet* I. 2 They ought not to lessen the glad song of praise for blessings formerly vouchsafed of love, of joy, and of happiness.

b. With indirect object. †Also (quot. 1595), to make a grant *of* something.

1587 GOLDING *De Mornay* xxxii. (1592) 515 Men voutchsafed them not so much as a Tombe to be buried in. **1592** G. HARVEY *Four Lett.* iii. 19 Not Tubulcain,.. but Tuball, whom Genesis voutsafeth honourable mention. **1595** SPENSER *Col. Clout* 484 But say, who else vouchsafed thee of grace? They all (quoth he) me graced goodly well. **1605** SHAKS. *Lear* II. iv. 158 On my knees I begge That you'l vouchsafe me Rayment, Bed, and Food. **1610** HOLLAND *Camden's Brit.* To Rdr. *4 b, As for obscure Etymologies,.. I have vouch-safed them no place in this worke. **1659** HAMMOND *On Ps.* lxxii. 1 They are vouchsafed that dignity. **1778** MISS BURNEY *Evelina* (1791) II. xxi. 136 Should I once more remind you of the promise you vouchsafed me yesterday? **1791** COWPER *Iliad* IV. 466 Them Tydeus vanquish'd easily, such aid Pallas vouchsafed him. **1848** W. K. KELLY tr. *L. Blanc's Hist. Ten Y.* I. 315 Men who are not always vouch-safed the use of a church steps or stones of the street for their bed. **1867** 'OUIDA' *C. Castlemaine's Gage* (1879) 13 That is all you vouchsafe me.

c. Const. *to* (or *unto*).

a **1660** *Contemp. Hist. Irel.* (Ir. Archæol. Soc.) III. 40 His Lordship may be pleased.. to voutchafe a meetinge.. to Sir Walter Dungan. **1671** MILTON *P.R.* I. 490 Thy Father.. vouchsaf'd his voice To Balaam Reprobate, a Prophet yet Inspir'd. **1756–7** tr. *Keysler's Trav.* (1760) I. 20 Whether they will vouchsafe any new memorial to their benefactor time must discover. **1781** COWPER *Table-t.* 699 Nature.. But seldom.. Vouchsafes to man a poet's just pretence. **1818** SCOTT *Br. Lamm.* xxvii, I will be true to my word, while the exercise of my reason is vouchsafed to me. **1856** KANE *Arct. Expl.* II. iii. 47 We have marked every dash of color which the great Painter in his benevolence vouchsafed to us. **1880** SWINBURNE *Stud. Shaks.* 4 It is as yet but a partial revelation that has been vouchsafed to them.

d. To deign or condescend to give (a word, answer, etc.) in reply or by way of friendly notice.

1597 HOOKER *Eccl. Pol.* v. lxiv. §2 Vouchsafe me hereunto some short answer, such as.. may.. instruct me in the cause thereof. **1603** SHAKS. *Meas. for M.* III. i. 152 Vouchsafe a word, yong sister, but one word. **1648** MILTON *Tenure Kings* 22 Yet to a tyrant we hear him not voutsafe an humble word. **1732** BERKELEY *Alciphr.* II. §12 Lysicles.. smiled at Crito, without vouchsafing any answer. **1836** W. IRVING *Astoria* II. 163 So saying, he flung out of their presence without vouchsafing any further conversation. **1848** LYTTON *Harold* I. v, Twice the Duke paced the chamber without vouchsafing a word to either. **1872** BLACK *Adv. Phaeton* iv. 40 All the reply that Tita vouchsafed was to wear a pleased smile of defiance.

ellipt. **1598** B. JONSON *Ev. Man in Hum.* I. v, *Bob.* You were wish'd for, and drunk to, I assure you. *Mat.* Vouchsafe mee, by whom, good Captaine.

†**3. a.** To condescend to engage in (some pursuit). *Obs.*

c **1581** LODGE *Repl. Gosson's Sch. Abuse* (Shaks. Soc. 1853) 10 Ask Josephus, and he wil tel you that Esay, Job and Salomon, voutsafed poetical practises, for.. theyre verse was Hexameter, and Pentameter. **1667** MILTON *P.L.* VI. 823 Nor other strife with them do I voutsafe.

†**b.** To receive (a thing) graciously or condescendingly; to deign to accept. *Obs.*

1589 GREENE *Tullies Love* Wks. (Grosart) VII. 156 Considering it [a letter] came from so honourable a personage as Lentulus, shee vouchsafed it. **1599** ? GREENE *George a Greene* D j, *Geo.* Why then, to honour G. a Greene the more, Vouchsafe a peice of beefe at my poore house. **1599** *Broughton's Let.* iii. 11 Whose singular affabilitie and clemencie.. [is] such, that shee will vouchsafe the speech of the meanest. **1601** SHAKS. *Jul. C.* II. i. 313 Vouchsafe good morrow from a feeble tongue. **1607** —— *Timon* I. i. 152 Vouchsafe my Labour, And long liue your Lordship.

†**c.** To be prepared to bear or sustain. *Obs.*

1613 SHAKS. *Hen. VIII*, II. iii. 43 If your backe Cannot vouchsafe this burthen, 'tis too weake Euer to get a Boy.

†**4.** To acknowledge (a person) in some favourable relationship or manner. *Obs.*

1582 in *T. Watson's Poems* (Arb.) 34 Let Britan beare your spring.. That it hence foorth may of your fauour boast, And him, whome first you heere voutsafe for hoast. **1584** LODGE *Hist. Forbonius & Prisceria* K 4 b, He which whilome hated Forbonius, now vouchsafeth him his son in lawe. **1615** T. ADAMS *Two Sonnes* 73 It is no ordinary favour that God will vouchsafe thee his Servant; yet hath hee made us his Sonnes. **1634** FORD *Perk. Warbeck* I. ii, If my princely mistress Vouchsaf'd me not her servant, twere as good I were reduc'd to clownery.

II. †**5.** To grant, permit, or allow, as an act of grace or condescension. Usually const. with clause introduced by *that*. *Obs.*

1338 R. BRUNNE *Chron.* (1810) 260 Homage vp to ȝeld, lordschip to forsake,.. As ȝe haf mad present, þe Kyng vouches it saue. *c* **1350** *Will. Palerne* 1449 He prayeth, lord, vowche-sauf þat his sone hire wedde. *Ibid.* 4152 Þat þe quen be ofsent sauf wol i fouche. *c* **1386** CHAUCER *Frankl. T.* 315 Now voucheth sauf, that I may you devise How that I may be holpe. *c* **1400** *Rom. Rose* 2002 My mouthe.. to no vilayn was never couthe.. For saufF of cherlis I ne vouche That they shulle never neigh it nere. **1430–40** LYDG. *Bochas* III. v. (1554) 74 Rehearce I wil, so that ye sauf it vouch, A mortal wronge which the and me doth touch. **1539** ELYOT *Cast. Helthe* Proheme a ij b, Truely yf they wyll call hym a physition,.. I wytsaufe they so name me. **1560** ROLLAND *Seven Sages* 72 War I gyltie or ȝit committit crime, I wald witschaif ȝe held me out this time. **1594** KYD *Cornelia* III. i. 50 Doe ye vouchsafe that thys victorious title Be not expired in Cornelias blood. **1601** SHAKS. *Jul. C.* III. i. 130 If Brutus will vouchsafe, that Anthony May safely come to him. **1639** SIR W. MURE *Psalm* xvii. 2 Wouchaife furth from before thy face, My sentence may proceid.

b. To permit or allow (a person) *to* do something. †Also *ellipt.*, to allow to speak.

14.. LYDG. *Lyfe our Ladye* (1484) a viij b, And lord also on me saue thou vouche.. That holy mayde to handyl and touche. **1590** SHAKS. *Com. Err.* v. i. 282 Most mighty Duke, vouchsafe me speak a word. **1599** —— *Much Ado* III. ii. 3 *Clau.* Ile bring you thither my Lord, if you'l vouchsafe me. **1608** CHAPMAN *Byron's Conspir.* v. Plays 1873 II. 244, 2. Truely we are not of his counsaile of warre. *Sau.* Nay but vouchsafe me. 3. Vouchsafe him, vouchsafe him, else there is no play in't. **1827** KEBLE *Chr. Y., St. Luke* xx, Be it vouchsaf'd thee still to see Thy true, fond nurslings closer cling.

6. To show a gracious readiness or willingness, to grant readily, to condescend or deign, *to* do something: †**a.** In earlier types of usage (with verb and adj. still distinct).

(*a*) *a* **1350** *St. Stephen* 207 in Horstm. *Altengl. Leg.* (1881) 30 Gamaliell wouched safe To lay þat body in his awyn graue. *c* **1380** WYCLIF *Sel. Wks.* III. 339 For as Crist vouchiþ-saaf to clepe þis Chirche his spouse, so he clepiþ curside men fendis. *c* **1400** *Prymer* in Maskell *Mon. Rit.* (1847) II. 23 The maker of mankynde takynge a bodi.. fouchide saaf to be born. *c* **1450** tr. *De Imitatione* III. vi. 69, I blesse þe, heuenly fader,.. for þou vouchist saaf to haue mynde on me. **1483** CAXTON *Gold. Leg.* 376/1 Thou haste vouched sauf to comforte me poure caytyf. **1545** UDALL *Erasm. Par. Luke* (1548) 21 Who.. hath vouchedsafe to cast a fauourable iye on me. **1555** W. WATREMAN *Fardle Facions* Ded. 3 The Emperours Maiestie.. vouchedsaulfe to receiue the presentacion therof. **1565** GOLDING *Ovid's Met.* IV. (1593) 81 In vouching safe to let Our sayings to our friendly eares thus freely come and go.

(*b*) *c* **1380** WYCLIF *Serm.* Sel. Wks. II. 73 ȝit he fouchide nevere saaf to fede hem þus wiþ a kide. *c* **1400** *Prymer* in Maskell *Mon. Rit.* (1847) II. 29 Fouche thou saaf to liȝtne our hertis and bodies. **14..** LYDG. *Lyfe our Ladye* lviii. (1484) i ij, Glad mayst thou be that sauf [he] list to vouche .. To have plesaunce thy brestis for to towche. **1540–1** ELYOT *Image Gov.* Pref., He wouched not saufe to loke on them. **1565** GOLDING *Ovid's Met.* I. (1593) 6 As Satyres.. Whom into heaven since that as yet we vouch not safe to take.

b. In ordinary later forms.

α[1]. *c* **1380** WYCLIF *Sel. Wks.* III. 55 Lord, vouchesaaf to kepe us þis day wiþouten synne. **1387** TREVISA *Higden* (Rolls) VI. 373, I þonke God.. þat he wole vouchesauf þis day to axe me þat he haþ i-yeve me. **1411** *Rolls of Parlt.* III. 650/2 He besought the Kyng of grace, And that he wold vouchesauf to praye the Lord the Roos, that he wold chese two Lordes of hys kyn. **1447** BOKENHAM *Seyntys* Introd. (Roxb.) 7, I yow beseche frend ryht enterly That ye vouchesaf for me to preye. *c* **1489** CAXTON *Blanchardyn* v. 24 Blanchardyn.. prayed hym that he vousshesauff to helpe hym that he were doubed knyght wyth his armes. *c* **1539** in Ellis *Orig. Lett.* Ser. I. II. 126 The most bountiful gifts.. wich your Grace hath vouchsavid to bestowe upon us. **1542** UDALL *Erasm. Apoph.* 83 b, Diogenes.. would not vouchesalve so muche as ones to aryse up from his taille. **1579** W. WILKINSON *Confut. Fam. Love, Brief Desc.* ☞ iij b, For the testimony of the truth hereof vouchsafe good reader to read the booke. **1624** *Trag. Nero* II. iii. in Bullen *O. Plays* I. 37 O Piso, that vouchsafest To grace our headlesse partie with thy name. **1648** J. BEAUMONT *Psyche* XI. 17 The only Thing Which Heav'n's peculiar Hand vouchaf'd to frame. **1661** *Papers on Alter. Prayer-Bk.* 88 We had a conceit that you would have vouchsaved to treate with us personally in presence. *a* **1713** ELLWOOD *Autobiog.* (1714) 2 The many Deliverances and Preservations, which the Lord hath vouch-safed to work for me. **1765** GOLDSM. *New Simile* 31 Lastly, vouchsafe t' observe his hand Filled with a snake-encircled wand. **1807** WORDSW. *White Doe* III. 75 A Maid o'er whom the blessed Dove Vouchsafed in gentleness to brood. **1862** CHR. WORDSW. *Misc.* (1879) I. 280 The Pope vouchsafed to give bulls of institution to the ecclesiastics named by the crown to fill the vacant sees. **1880** MRS. FORRESTER *Roy & V.* I. 177 She did not even vouchsafe to answer him.

α[2]. **1546** *Supplic. Poore Commons* (E.E.T.S.) 85 Onles your Hyghnes wyll voultsafe to take our cause in hand. **1565** STAPLETON tr. *Bede's Hist.* 116 That most louely geast,.. who was wonte to visit our bretherne, hath voutsafed this day to come to me also. **1577** FULKE *Answ. True Christian* Pref., If any one of these.. shall voutsalfe to reade this answere. *c* **1597** SIR J. HARINGTON *On Play* in *Nugæ Ant.* (1804) I. 206 Her Highnes can vowtsafe to play somtyme with her servantes. **1642** MILTON *Apol. Smect.* Wks. 1851 III. 303 We count it ample honour when God voutsafes to make man the instrument and subordinate worker of his gracious will. **1667** —— *P.L.* VII. 80 Since thou hast voutsaf't Gently for our instruction to impart Things above Earthly thought. **1704** N. N. tr. *Boccalini's Advts. fr. Parnass.* III. 176 They besought her Imperial Majesty, that she would voutsafe to acquaint 'em [etc.].

β. *c* **1380** WYCLIF *Sel. Wks.* III. 359 ȝif þat God wolde fouchesafe to ȝyve þes preestis of his grace, þat þei wolden mekeli leeve þis. **1393** LANGL. *P. Pl.* C. XIX. 18 Ich þonke ȝow a þowsend sythes.. þat ȝe fowche-saue to seye me what hit hihte. *c* **1420** *Chron. Vilod.* 2195 ȝyff God wold fouchesave to consent þerto. **1432–43** in *Cal. Proc. Chanc. Q. Eliz.* (1827) I. Introd. 24 That ye wold fuchesef of your benygne grace to graunte a writ of sub pena. *c* **1440** *Gesta Rom.* iv. 9 (Harl. MS.) Thei prayd him.. that he wold fuch-saffe to helpe hem ayenst theyre enemeys.

γ. *c* **1420–30** in *Hampole's Wks.* (1895) I. 171 Þis syght is bot be tymes, wen god will woches-sawf forto gif it vnto a wyrkande saule. **1448** *Paston Lett.* Suppl. (1901) 18 My mastres.. pray yow that and ye wold wochesaff to speke to my master Edmund. **1491** CAXTON *Vitas Patr.* (W. de W. 1495) II. 223 b/2, I prayed hym that he wolde woushesauf to haue me in mynde. **1518** H. WATSON *Hist. Oliver of Castile* (Roxb.) C 4, Wherfore I praye the that thou wouchesauf for to kepe the honour of my fader and me. **1530** PALSGR. 769/1 If he wyll nat wouchesaufe to do it, you lese your payne. *c* **1590** MONTGOMERIE *Sonn.* xxxiv. 2 Melpomene,.. Wouchsaiv to help a wrechit woman weep. **1639** SIR W. MURE *Psalms* cvi. 4 Wowchaife, O Lord, to visite me With thy salvation.

δ[1]. *c* **1425** WYNTOUN *Cron.* VIII. xv. 2332 To pray þis paip Bonyface That he wald witschaif of his grace.. Off þai iniuris to sett remeid. **1455** *Paston Lett.* I. 355 Besechyng you that ye woll weche safe to be her goode mastre. **1462** *Ibid.* II. 119, I beseche yow that ye wole wychesave to send me sume mony. *c* **1500** *Lancelot* 356 Beseiching hyme he wold wichsaif to wende To camelot the Cetee. **1560** ROLLAND *Seven Sages* 8 The caus na way we knaw Quhill y[t] ȝour grace will witchaif for to schaw. **1585** *Sc. Acts Jas. VI* (1814) III. 408/1 That our said souerane lord wald wischeaf.. To appoint [etc.].

δ[2]. **1444** *Aberdeen Reg.* (1844) I. 10 We counsaile.. yhour lordschip.. that.. yhe witsaufe to louse and deliuer frely the said Inglisemen. **1482** *Monk of Evesham* (Arb.) 28 Y blessyd our lorde and thankid him that he wolde white safe to chaste me.. in a fadyrly chastment. **1509** BARCLAY *Shyp of Folys* (1874) II. 228 The Mast nowe meuyth, the taklynge and the sayle, O god wythsaue the wayke shyp to socour. **1523** CROMWELL in Merriman *Life & Lett.* (1902) I. 42 Most humbly beseching.. that he wyll of his haboundaunt goodnes to wytsaufe to take me as I meane. **1549** COVERDALE, etc. *Erasm. Par. Rom.* Prol. **i, Praye God that he wyll witesafe to worke faith in thyne herte. **1589** PUTTENHAM *Eng. Poesie* III. xix. (Arb.) 245 O Phebus,.. Wouldst thou witsafe to slide a downe: And dwell with vs.

†**c.** With omission of the connective *to*. *Obs.*

a **1400** *Prymer* (1891) 26 The makere of mankynde takynge a bode.. fowchede sauf be bore. **1444** *Rolls of Parlt.* V. 73/2 That they wold wochesaf, for the said considerations, pray and beseche our said Soveraigne Lorde the Kyng [etc.]. **1455** *Paston Lett.* I. 357, I besech your gode grace that ye will vouchesafe remember the premissez. **1501** in *Eng. Misc.* (Surtees) 51 We pray.., y[t] thei woll votesave, at our request & prayer, beald, succour, & releffe the said Ric' Hammylton.

†**d.** *intr.* To be pleased to accept *of* something. *Obs. rare.* (Cf. VOUCH *v.* 12.)

1587 GREENE *Penelope's Web* Ep. Ded., I hope your Ladyships wil vouchsafe of Penelopes Web. **1587** —— *Euphues Cens.* Ep. Ded., As Alexander did vouchsafe of Misons rude and vnpolished picture of Mars. **1590** —— *Mourning Garm.* Concl., So I hope.. you will vouchsafe of my Mourning Garment.

†**7.** *ellipt.* To grant; to agree graciously; to condescend. Chiefly in clauses introduced by *as* or *if*. *Obs.*

(*a*) *c* **1308** *Pol. Songs* (Camden) 199 Whan hit is so, ich vouchsave, Ic forȝive the this gilte. *c* **1450** *Mirk's Festial* 234 'Yf þow see hur.. þou most lese þyn een-syght.' Then sayde he: 'Syr, I vouchesaf wele, so þat I may se hur.' **1596** *Edward III*, IV. ii. 27 And if your grace no otherwise vouchsafe, As welcome death is vnto vs as life.

(*b*) **13..** *Northern Passion* (H.) 452 Lat þis paines pas fra me. And noght anly als I will craue Bot, fader, als þou vowchis saue. **1340** HAMPOLE *Pr. Consc.* 3002 Þus sal þe saules, als God vouches save, For sere syns, sere maledys have. **14..** *Tundale's Vis.* 2344 No worldly goode more wold he have, But lyved as longe, as god vowche save.

(*c*) **13..** *Seuyn Sages* (W.) 3030 Gif me a place.. that I may my wonyng haue, At myne ese, if ye vowchesaue. *c* **1380** WYCLIF *Wks.* (1880) 466 And þus ȝif god wolde fouche-saf, hooly chirche shulde be purgid of heresyes in þis mater. *c* **1386** CHAUCER *Frankl. T.* 606, I haue do so as ye comanded me, And if ye vouche sauf ye may go see. **1463** *Bury Wills* (Camden) 17 Item I wyll that Maist' Thomas Harlowe sey the sermon at my interment, if he wochesaft. **1535** COVERDALE *Tobit* xii. 2, I praye the..that thou wilt desyre him, yf happlie he wil voutsafe, to take with him the half of all that we haue brought. **1736** SHERIDAN *Let. to Swift* 15 Sept., If you pleased, or would vouchsafe, or condescend, or think proper, I would rather that you would..charge only five per cent.

†**8.** *impers.* To be pleasing or agreeable to (a person) to do something. *Obs.*⁻¹

1543 GRAFTON *Contn. Harding* 587 Thomas Trencharde ..went to the kyng, desyring hym (yf it would wite salfe hym) to take a lodging at his house.

Hence **vouch'safed** *ppl. a.*, **vouch'safing** *vbl. sb.*

1561 T. NORTON *Calvin's Inst.* III. xxii. (1634) 454 By that vouchsafing, whereof there is found no cause elsewhere than in God. **1601** SHAKS. *Twel. N.* III. i. 100 My matter hath no voice Lady, but to your owne most pregnant and vouchsafed eare. **1649** JER. TAYLOR *Gt. Exemp.* I. Ad Sect. ii. 22 His graces and all other his vouchsafings and descents into our hearts. **1755** JOHNSON, *Deigning*,..a vouchsafing; a thinking worthy.

vouchsafement (vaʊtʃ'seɪfmənt). [f. prec. + -MENT.]

1. An act of condescension, grace, or favour; a boon, benefit, or blessing.

1628 GAULE *Pract. The.* (1629) 135 It was a woundrous vouchsafement, that he who inioyed the highth of Diuinitie, should descend to the bottome of Humanitie. **1652** J. PAWSON *Vind. Free Grace* 22 Christ hath not purchased any such general vouchsafement to all the children of men. **1674** BOYLE *Excell. Theol.* I. i. 59, I am prone to think the early discoveries of such great and important things, to be in God's account no mean vouchsafements. **1726** WODROW *Corr.* (1843) III. 277 To make a judgment how far it will be proper to publish some extraordinary vouchsafements towards them. **1756** AMORY *Buncle* (1770) I. 187 A merciful vouchsafement from God to mankind. *c* **1800** R. CUMBERLAND *John de Lancaster* (1809) III. 231 That indeed ..will be a happiness never to be exceeded, a vouchsafement never to be forgotten. **1822** E. IRVING *Let.* in Oliphant *Life* (1862) I. vi. 135 But these things..delight me not, save as vouchsafements of my Maker's bounty. **1874** PUSEY *Lent. Serm.* 184 But by what giant progress in graces, by what undeviating correspondence to Divine vouchsafements in time, must that soul have been formed.

2. The action of conferring or granting some boon, favour, advantage, etc.

1666 GLANVILL *Serm. Luke xiii. 24* in *Discourses*, etc. (1681) 59 [He] believes..that God is in him of a Truth, in a special way of Manifestation and Vouchsafement. **1668** HOWE *Bless. Righteous* (1825) 22 Reducing them to a.. dispair of relief, otherwise than by his merciful hand and vouchsafement. **1683** J. CORBET *Free Actions* III. xxxiii. 52 God doth ascertain Conversion, by the vouchsafement of such Grace, as doth infallibly produce it. **1721** R. KEITH tr. *T. à Kempis, Solil. Soul* xiii. 203 If thou standest astonished at the Vouchsafement of this Union. **1805** EUGENIA DI ACTON *Nuns of Desert* I. 229 Did he not duly administer pardon, and peace, and indulgence, to every one who applied properly to him, for such portions of Divine Vouchsafement? **1847** R. W. HAMILTON *Rewards & Punishm.* 316 The sovereign vouchsafement of mercy to some.

voud(e, obs. Sc. f. WOOD *sb.* and *a.*

voudoo, voudou, voudoun, varr. VOODOO.

vouge, obs. f. VOGUE.

vought, obs. var. VAULT *sb.*¹

vouȝte, southern ME. var. pa. t. FIGHT *v.*

vougy, var. VOGIE *a.*

vouh, southern ME. var. FAW *a.*

voul, southern ME. var. FOUL *a.*

voulente, var. VOLUNTY *Obs.*

voulf, obs. Sc. f. WOLF.

voult(e, obs. varr. VAULT *sb.*¹ and *v.*¹

voultour, obs. f. VULTURE.

‖**voulu** (vuly), *a.* (*sb.*) [Fr., pa. pple. of *vouloir* to wish, want.] Contrived, deliberate, studied. Also as *sb.* (esp. *collect.*).

1909 E. NESBIT *Daphne in Fitzroy St.* xiii. 207 Perhaps there's something more delicate, less *voulu*, in our little dinner as it is. The poignant beauty of the incomplete. **1938** E. BOWEN *Death of Heart* III. iv. 389 There is a narrowness about fantasy: it figures only the *voulu* part of the self. **1948** F. R. LEAVIS *Great Tradition* ii. 81 There is certainly something of that quality [*sc.* insincerity] in *Daniel Deronda* ..an element of the tacitly *voulu*. **1957** L. DURRELL *Justine* II. 132 The idea is not spontaneous, but *voulue*. **1959** *Encounter* Dec. 64/1 All de Sade's excesses were '*voulus*'. They were a scientific investigation into sex. **1962** *Listener* 17 May 885/3 Here and there the impression of the *voulu* and the freakish cannot be avoided. **1968** *Punch* 3 Apr. 507/1 They simply give an impression of *voulu* oddity, nearer to a harsher, more explicitly sexual A. E. Coppard than to Carson McCullers. **1974** *Times* 2 Feb. 7/6 But her knowledge of people as such? Sometimes profound, sometimes *voulu*.

voun (in Sc. mining): see VEAL *sb.*²

vound, south-w. dial. var. *found* FIND *v.*; obs. Sc. f. WOUND *sb.* and *v.*

†**vounde**, *a. Obs.*⁻¹ (Meaning obscure.)

c **1400** *Rom. Rose* 7063 Nought rought I..Though it were of no vounde stone, Wrought with squyre and scantilone.

vounder, -ir, obs. Sc. ff. WONDER.

vouning (in Sc. mining): see VEALING *vbl. sb.*³

†**vour**, *v. Obs.* (exc. *dial.*). Also 4–5 vowre, 6 vower-. [Aphetic f. DEVOUR *v.*, perh. after L. *vorāre*.] *trans.* To devour, to eat.

c **1330** R. BRUNNE *Chron. Wace* (Rolls) 10318 In þe water ..Are fisches inne foure maners:..Ne þe fisches alle foure, Ne wyþ oþer menge ne voure. **1382** WYCLIF *Exod.* xii. 9 The heed with his feet and entrayls ȝe shulen vowre. **1412–20** LYDG. *Chron. Troy* v. 1644 He hath..made hir bern oute of þe tovnis boundis To be vowrid of bestis & of houndis. [*a* **1881** *Isle of Wight Gloss.* 41.]

Hence †**vourer**, a devourer. *Obs. rare.*

1382 WYCLIF *Luke* vii. 34 Lo! a man deuourere [*v.r.* vourer], ether glotoun. **1533** TINDALE *Supper of Lord* c vj b, I am here compelled to inculpe and iterat it wyth so many wordes, to satisfye..thys carnall fleshe vowerer and fleshly Iewes.

vourd, obs. Sc. f. WORD *sb.*

voure, southern ME. var. FOUR.

vourson, var. VOWSON *Obs.*

vourtaȝte, -tene, -ti, southern ME. varr. FORTIETH, FOURTEEN, FORTY.

†'**voury.** *Obs.*⁻¹ [a. OF. *vowerie*, *vouerie* 'jurisdiction of a civil or ecclesiastical patron' (Godefroy): cf. AVOWRY 1.] (See quot.)

The privilege was obtained by a payment made to the Earl for his 'avowry' or protection.

?*c* **1600** in *Cat. Harl. MS.* (1808) II. 395/2 Of a Sanctuary-Way called the Vouryes, for Dettors: which is such a Priviledge, that a Man my goe all the sayd County of Chester ouer, at Liberty, without any Interruption of the Law.

vous, southern ME. variant of FOUS *a.*

†'**vous**, *int. Obs.* Also **a vous**; and **wous**. [Prob. for *avows* pl. of AVOW *sb.*, by colloquial reduction of the phrase *I make* (*my*) *avows*.] Assuredly, certainly.

The speakers are represented as belonging to Wiltshire.

1674 J. HOWARD *Eng. Mounsieur* IV. i. 40 *Comely*..Is it not very hot to-day? *Will.* 'Vous Elsba. And I have reason to say so. *Ibid.* v. i. 55 *Comely.* But what think you of..finding me your sweet heart instead of him? *Elsba.* No a vous Sir.

†**vousing.** *Obs.*⁻¹ In 5 vowsyng. [f. OF. *vouser*, *vousser* to vault.] Vaulting.

1412–20 LYDG. *Chron. Troy* II. 654 Þe fresche enbowyng, with vergis riȝt as linys, And þe vowsyng ful of babewynes, Þe riche koynyng, þe lusty tablementis.

vouson, obs. form of VOWSON.

‖**voussoir** ('vu:swɔ:(r), -ɑ:(r)). Also 4 vousore, 5 vow-, vau-, **wawcer.** [a. OF. *vausoir* (*wau-*), *vaussoir*, *vossoir*, etc., mod.F. *voussoir*:—pop.L. **volsōrium*, f. **volsum*, pa. pple. of L. *volvĕre* to turn: cf. VOUSING. Found in ME., but in mod. use app. reintroduced in the 18th cent.] One of the stones which form part of an arch or a vault, usually having the sides slightly inclined towards each other.

α. **1359–60** *Ely Sacr. Rolls* (1907) II. 193 In vj^xx ped. de vousores empt. prec. pedis iiij d. 2 *l.* **1411** *Acc. Norwich Cloister* in Parker *Gloss. Archit.* (1850) I. 513 Item, de vowcers xliij ped. pr' ped. vj. d. **1416–7** in Willis & Clark *Cambridge* (1886) II. 442, vj pedum de jambes et j Wawcer xiij^d. *Ibid.*, Pro vij^xx. pedibus vocat' sewlys et vaucers xvij^s.

β. **1728** CHAMBERS *Cycl.* s.v. *Vault*, The several *Voussoirs*, or Vault-Stones whereof it [an arch] consists. **1739** LABELYE *Piers Westm. Bridge* 77 The Coins, or Voussoirs, or Arch-Stones. **1808** *Norfolk Tour, Norwich* 119 The voussoirs of the arch have their joints worked perfectly smooth. **1823** P. NICHOLSON *Pract. Build.* 312 The masonry of domes differs from that of arching, in the figure of each voussoir. **1853** RUSKIN *Stones Ven.* (1874) II. iii. 46 The keystone..is of white marble, the lateral voussoirs of purple. **1886** E. C. ROBINS *Temple of Solomon* (1887) 8 Upon the lowest of these pavements the fallen voussoirs of the arch have been discovered lying.

attrib. and *Comb.* **1875** KNIGHT *Dict. Mech.* 370/2 A brick made voussoir-shaped is known as a *compass*-brick. **1886** G. SCHUMACHER *Across the Jordan* List Illustr. p. xi, Voussoir-stones of Arch. **1905** *Athenæum* 25 Nov. 727/3 The true voussoir arch was extensively used at Pagān.

Hence '**voussoired** *a.*, constructed with voussoirs.

1875 *Encycl. Brit.* II. 388/1 A tomb built up in the centre of the excavation,..covered by three stones as struts, over which was a perfectly formed voussoired arch.

voust (vaʊst), *sb. Sc.* Also 5 **wous**, 6 **voist**, **wost**, **woust.** [Of obscure origin. Cf. next and VOUSTY *a.*] A boast, a brag, a vaunt.

a **1500** *Ratis Raving* 3032 Thai mak gret aithis for lytill thing, Great wous and gret manasing. **1513** DOUGLAS *Æneid* x. vi. 80 And lo, as Pharon cryis and dois rowst With haltand wordis and with mekill woust. **1535** STEWART *Cron. Scot.* (Rolls) III. 454 Sen sua it is that I heir ȝow produce Sic voust and vant of manlines and ruce. **1785** FORBES *Ulysses* in *Poems in Buchan Dial.* 23 Whare then was a' your windy vousts? Ye that is now sae kneef! **1804** COUPER *Poetry* I. 159 Ye dames o' Scotland! sik your voust, And sik your fame sae sair.

voust (vaʊst), *v. Sc.* Also 6 **vost.** [Cf. prec.] *intr.* (and *trans.*). To boast, to brag.

1513 DOUGLAS *Æneid* XII. viii. 84 Hir brothir Turnus in his char, Now brawland in this place, now voustand thar. **1742** FORBES *Ajax* 9 Yet as he did o' slaughter voust I len'd him sik a dird. **1790** SHIRREFS *Poems* p. vii, When e'en th' Apollo o' the class Mith voust upon it. **1794** W. FARQUHAR *Poems Sev. Occas.* 182 For mysel', I sanna voust my kin. There's no ane here, but kens the Merchin' weil.

Hence '**vousting** *vbl. sb.* and *ppl. a.*

1535 STEWART *Cron. Scot.* (Rolls) II. 362 Euerie man hes left of vousting vant. **1580–90** J. STEWART *Poems* (S.T.S.) II. 150 Is it not vousting vaine to say to Men, Mend may all thing by help of guid vemen? **1600** HAMILTON *Facile Traictise* 37 This is..thair auin folische vosting to haue the libertie to reid their saluation in the scriptures. **1813** W. BEATTIE *Poems* 34 For a' your last nights Vousting.

vouster ('vaʊstə(r)). *Sc.* Also 6 **wo(u)stour**, **woistare.** [f. prec.] A braggart or boaster.

1500–20 DUNBAR *Poems* xiv. 41 Sic vant of wostouris with hairtis in sinfull staturis. **1513** DOUGLAS *Æneid* v. vii. 62 Bot war I now..ȝing as ȝone wanton woustour [*v.r.* woistare].. I suld all reddy be. *a* **1568** *Nine Order Knaves* 18 in *Bannatyne MS.* 447 He is als..he and prowd as ane vane woustour. **1670** RAY *Prov.* 276 Of vousters or new upstarts. **1710** RUDDIMAN *Douglas's Æneis* Gloss. s.v. *Woistare*, Scot. *Vouster*, a boaster.

vousty ('vaʊstɪ), *a. Sc.* Also 5 **vowsty**, 6 **voustie**, 7 **vowstie.** [Cf. VOUST *sb.* and *v.*]

†**1.** ? Puffed up, tumid. *Obs.*⁻¹

c **1375** *Sc. Leg. Saints* xliii. (*Cecile*) 536 A bose of wynd þat fillit ware, & with a prene mocht out be latine..and togiddire fal, & tyne þe vowsty blawing al.

2. Boastful, proud.

1596 DALRYMPLE tr. *Leslie's Hist. Scot.* II. 212 Of quhilke victorie..tha war sa vane and voustie, that [etc.]. **1606** BIRNIE *Kirk-Buriall* (1833) 4 Euery Nation seruing it selfe with the owne vowstie deuise. **1789** BEATTIE *To Alex. Ross* xvi, And chiels shall come frae 'yont the Cairn-a-mounth right vousty.

vout(e, obs. variants of VAULT *sb.*¹ and *v.*¹

voute, variant of VULT *Obs.*

†**vouter.** *Obs. rare.* [Aphetic f. *avouter*: see ADULTER.] An adulterer.

c **1386** CHAUCER *Friar's T.* 74 (Lansd. MS.), [Better] þan þis Somenour knewe a lic[h]our Or a vouter [*other MSS.* an avouter] or elles a paramour.

†**voutry.** *Obs. rare.* [Aphetic f. *avoutry*: see ADULTERY.] Adultery.

1382 WYCLIF *Jer.* xiii. 27 Thi shenshepe, thi vouteries, and..the hidous gilte of thi fornycacioun. **14..** *Tundale's Vis.* (1843) 192 Myche thou hast usud voutry. *c* **1450** *St. Cuthbert* (Surtees) 5142 Þai were robbours and vsed voutrys.

Vouvray (vu:'vreɪ). The name of a commune in the department of Indre-et-Loire in N.W. France, used chiefly *absol.* to designate the wines produced in this and neighbouring communes.

1885 H. JAMES *Little Tour in France* vii. 60 She uncorked for us a bottle of Vouvray mousseux. **1920** G. SAINTSBURY *Notes on Cellar Bk.* vi. 97, I have said nothing, in the chapter on Champagne, as to Saumur, Vouvray, and the Swiss imitations... Vouvray..seems to me feeble. **1934** E. WAUGH *Handful of Dust* v. 246 One of them..got drunk for the first time on sparkling Vouvray. **1955** 'W. MOLE' *Hammersmith Maggot* vi. 68 Lunch, properly accompanied by a glass of Vouvray. **1981** 'A. CROSS' *Death in Faculty* xii. 141 I'm going to have a bottle of Vouvray, Clos de Nouys, 1971.

vow (vaʊ), *sb.* Forms: 3–4 vou (uuou, wou, wov), 5 woue (6 *pl.* woues), 6 voue; 4– vow (4, 5–6 *Sc.*, wow), 4–7 vowe (4 wowe, 5 vowhe); 4 *pl.* vouwes, -is, fouwes; 4 voo, 5 voye, *Sc.* woe. [a. AF. *vu(u*, *vou*, *vo*, OF. *vo*, *vou*, *vowe*, *veu* (F. *vœu*):—L. *vōt-um* VOTE *sb.*, neut. of *vōtus*, pa. pple. of *vōvēre* to promise solemnly, to pledge, dedicate, etc. Cf. AVOW *sb.*¹]

1. A solemn promise made to God, or to any deity or saint, to perform some act, or make some gift or sacrifice, in return for some special favour; more generally, a solemn engagement, undertaking, or resolve, to achieve something or to act in a certain way.

1297 R. GLOUC. (Rolls) 9823 Vor þoru a vowe of him þe sone bigan þat strif. **1303** R. BRUNNE *Handl. Synne* 2888 He hys owne doghtyr slowe For a foly and a wykked vowe. **13..** *E.E. Allit. P.* C. 239 Þer was louyng on lofte..on Moyses wyse, With sacrafyse vp-set, & solempne vowes. *c* **1380** WYCLIF *Wks.* (1880) 66 To paie þe pope þe first froytys,.. for assoilyngis of wowes, & many feyned iapis. *c* **1430** LYDG. *Min. Poems* (Percy Soc.) 136 This was his vowhe, with gret humylite, Lik his entent in ful pleyn language. **1502** *Ord. Crysten Men* (W. de W. 1506) IV. vii. 187 To haue knowledge of woues, of testamentes, of cases of symony, useryes and other dyffyculties. **1550** BALE *Apol.* Pref. 12 Such are the rashe vowes of the ydolatrouse and mockynge papystes. **1563** tr. *Musculus' Common-pl.* 508 In a foule vow, alter thy purpose. Do not that which thou haste vnaduisedly vowed. **1617** MORYSON *Itin.* I. 151 The wals are round about hung with Images of men,..which were offered to our Lady upon vow. **1645** QUARLES *Sol. Recant.* v. 66 Make hast to pay what thy vow'd Promise owes; Destruction dwels in unperformed Vowes. **1697** DRYDEN *Virg. Georg.* IV. 775 With Vows and suppliant Pray'rs their Pow'rs appease. **1756–7** tr. *Keysler's Trav.* (1760) IV. 174 It was designed for St. Joseph, in consequence of a vow made by that emperor in the year 1702, on the happy return of his son Joseph.. from Landau. **1822** WORDSW. *Eccl. Sonn.* III. xxi. 13 Shame if the consecrated Vow be found An idle form, the Word an empty sound. **1866** R. W. DALE *Disc. Spec. Occas.* 342 Those vows cannot now be cancelled or recalled. **1869** LECKY *Europ. Mor.* I. 144 The earliest form in which the duty of veracity is enforced is probably the observance of vows.

b. In phrases, as *to make, to hold, keep, pay* (or †*yield*), or *to break, a vow*.

(*a*) *c* **1290** *St. Fides* 51 in *S. Eng. Leg.* I. 84 For ich habbe to him mi vou i-maked. *a* **1300** *Cursor M.* 28286 Ic ha made vous oft vn-right and halden þam efter my might. **1303** R. BRUNNE *Handl. Synne* 2795 3yf þou madest awhere any vowe To wurschyp God for þy prowe. *c* **1340** HAMPOLE *Pr. Consc.* 2942 Þan has þat man grete drede in hert; He mas þan vowes, and cryes on Crist. **1387** TREVISA *Higden* (Rolls) VI. 81 Kyng Oswy made a vow þat 3if he hadde þe victorie in þat bataille he wolde offre his dou3ter Elfleda to God of hevene. *c* **1430** *Syr Gener.* (Roxb.) 1925 To god and you a voye I make, I shal youre seruice neuer forsake. **1473** WARKW. *Chron.* (Camden) 8 He made a woue that the Lorde Willowby schuld lese his hede. **1530** PALSGR. 619/2, I make a vowe to God and to Our Ladye that I shall never slepe one night where I slepe an other, tyll I have sene hym. **1587** *Mirr. Mag., Brennus* ix, I made a vowe to kill the man that causde me flye. **1602** SHAKS. *Ham.* II. ii. 70 He.. Makes Vow before his Vnkle, neuer more To giue th' assay of Armes against your Maiestie. **1700** DRYDEN *Iliad* I. 27 So may the Gods.. accord the vows you make, And give you Troy's imperial town to take. **1718** [see (*b*)]. **1829** SCOTT *Anne of Geierstein* i, He proceeded to recount the vow which was made.. to our Lady of Einsiedlen. **1867** W. FLEMING *Moral Philos.* II. II. ii. 296 We may make a Vow, however, to our fellow-creatures, or even to ourselves.

(*b*) *a* **1300** *Cursor M.* 24907 (Edin.), Do vou, Elis, and hald þi vow It sal te turn til mikel pru. *a* **1340** HAMPOLE *Psalter* cxv. 8 My wowis i sall 3elde till lord in sight of all his folke. **1382** WYCLIF *Job* xxii. 27 Thou shalt pre3en hym.. and thi vouwis thou shalt 3elde. **1526** [see I c]. **1560** BIBLE (Genev.) *Job* xxii. 27 Thou shalt make thy prayer vnto him,.. and thou shalt rendre thy vowes. *c* **1611** CHAPMAN *Iliad* II. 248 Nor would [these men] pay Their own vows to thee. **1651** HOBBES *Leviath.* I. xiv. 69 Being a thing unjust to pay such Vow. **1697** DRYDEN *Æneid* II. 22 They feigned it made For their return, and this the vow they paid. **1718** LADY M. W. MONTAGU *Let. to C'tess of Mar* 10 Mar., She firmly intended to keep the vow she had made. **1819** WORDSW. *Misc. Sonn.* I. xi. 5 How Shall Fancy pay to thee a grateful vow? **1859** TENNYSON *Pelleas & Ettarre* 549 Have any of our Round Table held their vows? **1876** —— *Harold* III. i, He did not mean to keep his vow.

(*c*) *a* **1300** *Cursor M.* 10674 Þe biscop.. Durst noght hir do hir vou to breke. **1362** LANGL. *P. Pl.* A. Prol. 68 Himself mihte a-soylen hem alle Of Falsnesse and Fastinge and of vouwes I-broken. *c* **1450** *Mirk's Festial* 9, I haue avowet chastite. And.. for I wold not breke my vow, pryuely yn a nyght, I stale forþe yn pore wede. **1483** *Cath. Angl.* 404/1 To breke Vowe, *deuotare, deuouere*. **1534** ELYOT *Gov.* III. viii. 179 Only I wyl shewe.. howe terrible a thynge it was amonge them, to breke theyr othes or vowes [*ed.* 1531 avowes]. **1596** *Edward III*, II. i. 335 To breake a lawfull and religious vowe. *a* **1641** SPELMAN *Tythes* xxvii. Wks. 1727 I. 131 So doubtless have we just Cause to fear the Dint of this Curse in breaking this Vow. **1791** COWPER *Iliad* I. 78 That we may learn By what crime we have thus incensed Apollo, What broken vow.. He charges on us. **1889** TENNYSON *Ring* 401 No pliable idiot I to break my vow.

c. Const. *of* (something).

c **1380** WYCLIF *Wks.* (1880) 170 Many prestis vnwisly taken a wow of chastite. *c* **1400** *Apol. Loll.* 38 Bi þe vertu of his degre, he made þe vow of chastite. **1526** *Pilgr. Perf.* (W. de W. 1531) 65 To.. kepe theyr foure essencial vowes the better, that is, the vowe of chastite, the vowe of obedience, the vowe of wylfull pouerte and the vowe of perpetuall inclusyon. **1590** SHAKS. *Mids. N.* I. i. 121 The Law of Athens yeelds you vp.. To death, or to a vow of single life. **1638** BAKER tr. *Balzac's Lett.* (vol. II) 21 Sir, if I had made a vow of humility, you give me here a fair occasion to be proud for not breaking it. **1671** MILTON *Samson A.* 319 Against his vow of strictest purity. **1776** DALRYMPLE *Ann. Scotl.* I. 109 Having made a vow of perpetual virginity. **1859** TENNYSON *Vivien* 545 They bound to holy vows of chastity! Were I not woman, I could tell a tale. **1874** GREEN *Short Hist.* iii. §6. (1882) 144 The vow of Poverty was turned into a stern reality.

†**d.** *to take in vow*, to make a vow. *Obs.*$^{-1}$

1526 *Pilgr. Perf.* (W. de W. 1531) 57 Ye & take it in vowe that thy delectacyon sholde be onely in the passyon & paynes of Jesu Chryst.

2. *Eccl.* A solemn engagement to devote oneself to a religious life of a definite nature, such as that of a monastic or conventual order. Freq. in pl.; *to take the vows*, to enter a religious order.

c **1400** *Apol. Loll.* 101 Þerfor iuge religiouse men in þer consciens, if þei ground hem þus in her vowis. **1560** DAUS tr. *Sleidane's Comm.* 59 Men must be warned that they suffre not them selves to be bounden to Monkish vowes. *a* **1578** LINDESAY (Pitscottie) *Chron. Scot.* (S.T.S.) II. 71 Thow fals heretick hast taught plainlie aganes the wowis of monkes freiris nunes and preistis. **1603** SHAKS. *Meas. for M.* IV. ii. 180 By the vow of mine Order, I warrant you, If my instructions may be your guide. **1651** HOBBES *Leviath.* IV. xlvi. 376 Monks, and Friers, that are bound by Vow to that simple obedience to their Superiour, to which every Subject ought to think himself bound. **1721** STRYPE *Eccl. Mem.* I. xliv. 339 A late proclamation of the king that disallowed of the marriage of priests, and concerning the vows of religious persons, gave them disgust. **1753** CHALLONER *Cath. Chr. Instr.* 171 Those who have chosen the better Part, and consecrated themselves by Vow to God. **1814** SCOTT *Lord of Isles* VI. iii, There Bruce's slow assent allows Fair Isabel the veil and vows. **1845** S. AUSTIN *Ranke's Hist. Ref.* I. 463 On his friends earnestly pressing him to take the vows, he ran away. **1849** JAMES *Woodman* v, [One] who is very dangerous to all ladies not under vows.

3. A solemn promise of fidelity or faithful attachment. Also const. *of* (faith, love, etc.).

1590 SHAKS. *Mids. N.* I. i. 175 By all the vowes that euer men haue broke, (In number more then euer women spoke). **1596** —— *Merch. V.* V. i. 18 In such a night Did young Lorenzo sweare he lou'd her well, Stealing her soule with many vowes of faith. **1601** —— *Jul. C.* II. i. 73 By all your vowes of Loue, and that great Vow Which did incorporate and make vs one. *a* **1762** LADY M. W. MONTAGU *Poems, Epil. to Mary Q. of Scots* 18 Men mock the idol of their former vow. **1797** MRS. RADCLIFFE *Italian* xii, Let me lead you to the first Altar that will confirm our vows. **1813** SHELLEY *Q. Mab* VI. 210 The fair oak, whose leafy dome affords A temple where the vows of happy love Are registered. **1829** LYTTON *Disowned* xxvii, They stood beside the altar, and their vows were exchanged. **1833** TENNYSON *Miller's Daughter* 119 O would she give me vow for vow, Sweet Alice, if I told her all?

4. An earnest wish or desire; a prayer, a supplication. (So F. *vœu*, L. *vōtum*.)

Not always clearly distinct from sense 1.

1563 tr. *Musculus' Common-pl.* 499 A vowe is oftentymes taken for a desyre, and prayer. So whan those thynges whyche we haue desyred, do fall oute accordinge vnto oure mynde, wee saye we haue oure wishe or vowe. *a* **1599** SPENSER *F.Q.* VII. vi. 22 His brow (His black eye-brow, whose doomefull dreaded beck Is wont to wield the world vnto his vow). **1600** O. E. (M. SUTCLIFFE) *Repl. Libel* I. v. 125 They haue nothing more in their vowes, then her Maiesties ruine. **1697** DRYDEN *Æneid* III. 518 When.. priests with holy vows the gods adore. **1742** HUME *Ess., Stoic* I. xvi. (1777) I. 159 Even their own vows, though granted, cannot give them happiness. **1747** HOADLY *Suspicious Husband* Ded., To send up my warmest Vows.. that your Majesty may long enjoy the fruits of [etc.]. **1794** BURKE *Corr.* (1844) IV. 252 You have my most ardent vows for an auspicious beginning. **1820** SHELLEY *Œd. Tyr.* I. 16 Thou to whom Kings and laurelled Emperors.. Offer their secret vows! **1850** TENNYSON *In Mem.* lxxix, At one dear knee we proffer'd vows, One lesson from one book we learn'd.

5. A solemn affirmation or asseveration.

1593 SHAKS. *2 Hen. VI*, III. ii. 159 A dreadfull Oath, sworne with a solemn tongue: What instance giues Lord Warwicke for his vow. **1611** —— *Wint. T.* I. ii. 47 *Her.* Nay, but you will? *Pol.* I may not verely. *Her.* Verely? You put me off with limber Vowes. **1862** R. S. HAWKER in C. E. Byles *Life & Lett.* xvii. (1905) 386 Every Methodist Preacher or Hearer must attest by Vow and Signature his assent to a Paragraph in Wesley's XIth Sermon on the Witness of the Spirit.

†**6.** A votive offering. *Obs. rare.*

1382 WYCLIF *Deut.* xii. 6 (early MSS.), 3ee shul come & offre in þat place brent sacrifises,.. & vouwis & 3iftes. **1535** COVERDALE *Ibid.* **1611** BIBLE *1 Esdras* viii. 58 The vessels are holy, and the golde, and the siluer is a vowe vnto the Lord. **1686** BURNET *Lett.* (1708) 126 The little Vows, that hang without the holy Chapel. *a* **1700** EVELYN *Diary* 21 May 1645, There is belonging to this Church a world of plate,.. and lamps innumerable, besides the costly vowes hung up, some of gold.

7. *Comb.*, as *vow-maker, -making, -pledged, -sanctifier, -sighing*; †**vow-fellow**, one who is bound by the same vow. Also VOW-BREAKER, etc.

1588 SHAKS. *L.L.L.* II. i. 38 Who are the Votaries, my louing Lords, that are vow-fellowes with this vertuous Duke? **1598** FLORIO, *Votario*, a votarie, a vower, a promiser, a vow-maker. **1668** CLARENDON *Ess.* Tracts (1727) 177 That these vow-makers should be thought so necessary, when every one of their three vows is directly against the health.. of the kingdom. **1681** DRYDEN *Span. Friar* II. iii, Love you know, father, is a great vow-maker, but he's a greater vow-breaker. **1743** FRANCIS tr. *Hor., Odes* III. x. 14 Neither presents, nor vow-sighing strain. **1805** WORDSW. *Waggoner* III. 44 What tears of rapture, what vow-making! **1817** LADY MORGAN *France* I. (1818) I. 97 The days of the vow-making Louis XIII. **1832** MOTHERWELL *Poet. Wks.* (1847) 48 So the Vow-pledged One loved another.

vow (vaʊ), *v.*[1] Forms: 4–6 vowe (4 vouw-, 5 vowyn), 4– vow (5–6 *Sc.* wow); 4 vou, wou, 5–7 *Sc.* wou-. [ad. OF. *vouer, vower* (F. *vouer*), f. *vou* VOW *sb.*]

1. *trans.* To promise or undertake solemnly, *spec.* by a vow to a deity or saint; to swear: **a.** With subordinate clause (or equivalent).

The subject of the subordinate clause may be different from that of the verb itself.

a **1300** *Cursor M.* 10603 Þai yald hir to þe temple þan, Als þai voud had be-forn þat sco was of hir moder born. **1338** R. BRUNNE *Chron.* (1810) 182, I vowe to Saynt Michael.. þat for wo ne wele hiþen ne salle I fare.. tille þe castelle be taken. **1390** GOWER *Conf.* I. 144 That veine gloire I schal eschuie, And bowe unto thin heste and suie Humilite, and that I vowe. *c* **1470** HENRY *Wallace* VIII. 47, I wow to God,.. he sall nocht be In to this realme, bot ane off ws sall de. **1535** STEWART *Cron. Scot.* II. 418 Gif tha wald nocht, he vowit tha sould haif Siclike reward as he gaif all the laif. *c* **1570** *Satir. Poems Reform.* xiv. 88, I wow to the.. Thay sall not mys ane riche reward. **1596** SHAKS. *Merch. V.* IV i. 442 She made me vow That I should neither sell, nor giue, nor lose it. **1785** BURNS *Ep. to J. Lapraik* 21 Apr. vi, Quoth I, 'Before I sleep a wink, I vow I'll close it'. **1838** ARNOLD *Hist. Rome* vii. I. 118 Aulus.. vowed that he would raise a temple to Castor and to Pollux,.. if they would aid him to win the battle. **1859** TENNYSON *Enid* 787, I vow'd that could I gain her, our fair Queen.. should make your Enid burst Sunlike from cloud.

b. With infinitive.

1303 R. BRUNNE *Handl. Synne* 2804 3yf þou vowe to do foly.. God wyl nat þou hold yt so þat þou þy vowe yn wykkednes do. **14..** *Langland's P. Pl.* B. v. 388 (Oriel MS.), Þanne gan gloton grete, and greet deel made.., And vowede to faste. **1500–20** DUNBAR *Poems* lxii. 19 To that conditioun ..That 3e had vowit to the Swan, Ane 3eir to be Johne Thomsounis man. **1596** DALRYMPLE tr. *Leslie's Hist. Scot.* II. 13 To God he had vowit, with ane armie to jnvade the Saracenis gif he had lyfe. **1609** DEKKER *Gull's Horn-bk.* Proem. 2, I defie your perfumd scorne: and vow to poyson your Muske cats, if their ciuet excrement doe but once play with my nose. **1641** in *10th Rep. Hist. MSS. Comm.* App. I. 78 Quhilk dyett [of parliament] the Kinge hes woued to keepe except siknesse or deathe previne it. **1653** JER. TAYLOR *Serm. for Year* I. xiv. 189 He that vows never to have an ill thought, never to commit an error, hath taken a course [etc.]. *a* **1768** SECKER *Lect.* xx. (1769) I. 328 Vowing to do what there is no Use in doing, is trifling with our Creator. **1797** MRS. RADCLIFFE *Italian* iii, He secretly vowed to defend her fame and protect her peace at the sacrifice of every other consideration. **1849** JAMES *Woodman* ii, I do not recollect having vowed not to tell any secular persons. **1891** FARRAR *Darkn. & Dawn* xli, Some Greek.. named Hippolytus, who had vowed to live a virgin life for Diana.

c. With direct object.

1303 R. BRUNNE *Handl. Synne* 2825 Eueyl he vowed, and swore hys oþes, þer-for with hym ys now god wroth. *a* **1500** *Ratis Raving*, etc. 575 He.. bydis man kep weill gif he ocht wowis. **1526** *Pilgr. Perf.* (W. de W. 1531) 1 Lyfe.. is as a pilgrymage, whiche we vowe and promesse in our baptym. **1599** WEEVER *Epigr.* IV. xxii. E vj, Their sugred tongues.. Say they are Saints.. For thousands vowes to them subjectiue dutie. **1611** SPEED *Hist. Gt. Brit.* VII. ii. 285/1 Such as hauing vowed their voiage and seruice for Ierusalem, wore.. vpon their backes a red Crosse. **1651** HOBBES *Leviath.* I. xiv. 69 They that Vow any thing contrary to any law of Nature, Vow in vain. **1737** *Gentl. Mag.* VII. 325/1 With solemn Curses and Imprecations upon themselves and Posterities, who should detract any of the Tythes so vowed and granted. **1753** CHALLONER *Cath. Chr. Instr.* 174 He speaks not of such as have vowed Chastity, but of other Christians. **1791** COWPER *Iliad* XXIII. 247 Then, Peleus' son.. two Winds in prayer.. invoked.., to each Vowing large sacrifice. **1819** SCOTT *Noble Moringer* ii, 'Tis I have vow'd a pilgrimage unto a distant shrine. **1828** LYTTON *Pelham* II. xx, I fancied a perfection in her, and vowed an emulation in myself, which it was reserved for Time to ratify or deride. **1848** W. K. KELLY tr. *L. Blanc's Hist. Ten Y.* II. 483 The whole French soul vowed from that moment the capture of Constantina.

d. With cognate object.

a **1340** HAMPOLE *Psalter* cxxxi. 2 Vow he vowed til god of iacob. **1382** WYCLIF *Judges* xi. 30 Passynge to the sones of Amon, he vowede a vowe to the Lorde. **1535** COVERDALE *Num.* vi. 2 To vowe a vowe of abstinence vnto the Lorde. **1601** SHAKS. *All's Well* IV. ii. 22 'Tis not the many oathes that makes the truth But the plaine single vow, that is vow'd true. *a* **1616** BEAUM. & FL. *Wit Without Money* IV. iv, Vow me no vowes, he that dares do this, has bred himself to boldness, to forswear too. *a* **1711** KEN *Div. Love* Wks. (1838) 274 Whenever I voluntarily vow a vow to thee, give me grace to vow with all the due caution I can. **1808** SCOTT *Marmion* v. xxvii, For weal of those they love, To pray the prayer, and vow the vow. **1829** —— *Anne of G.* x, Overwhelming the priests with the wealth which they showered upon them, and, finally, vowing vows, and making pilgrimages. **1867** TENNYSON *Holy Grail* 584 Yet we twain Had never kiss'd a kiss, or vow'd a vow.

2. To dedicate, consecrate, or devote *to* some person or service. (Cf. AVOW *v.*[2] 2.)

1526 *Pilgr. Perf.* (W. de W. 1531) 98 b, [They] hath vowed all theyr lyues to god and to his holy seruyce. **1582** STANYHURST *Æneis* II. (Arb.) 66 A tumb to Troytoune and mouldy templ aneereth Vowed to the godly Ceres. **1596** DANETT tr. *Comines* (1614) 204 He tooke vpon him his voiage to S. Claude, to whom as you haue heard he was vowed. **1613** R. HARCOURT *Voy. to Guiana* 47 Captaine Harueý,.. who hath nobly vowed his time and fortune to bee imployed in the prosecution of this honourable action. **1697** DRYDEN *Æneid* VIII. 796 The first inhabitants, of Grecian blood, That sacred forest to Silvanus vowed. **1725** POPE *Odyss.* XI. 25 The victims, vow'd to each Tartarean pow'r, Eurylochus and Perimedes bore. **1813** SCOTT *Rokeby* IV. xiv, Connanmore, who vowed his race, For ever to the fight and chase. **1843** WORDSW. *Inscr. Mon. Crosthwaite Ch.* 16 He to heaven was vowed Through his industrious life. **1896** A. AUSTIN *Eng. Darling* I. i, Virgins vowed to Heaven, Virgins as white as is the Yule-tide snow.

transf. **1579** E. K. in *Spenser's Sheph. Cal.* June, Argt., This Æglogue is wholly vowed to the complayning of Colins ill successe in his loue.

b. *refl.* Also const. *into*.

c **1500** *Melusine* 292 Vryan & Guyon entred in to the see, & vowed themself to Jherusalem. **1581** G. PETTIE tr. *Guazzo's Civ. Conv.* (1586) I. 8 b, Manie,.. from their statelie pallaces, haue vowed themselues to beggerlie Monasteries. **1592** in J. Morris *Troub. Cath. Forefathers* (1877) 38 Mr. Edward James.. having vowed himself into the Society [*sc.* the Jesuits]. **1602** FULBECKE *1st Pt. Parall.* 95 They have denied Christ and vowed themselues to the diuell. **1623** COCKERAM III, *Decii*, three Roman Captaines,.. who vowed themselues for their countrie. **1630** *R. Johnson's Kingd. & Commw.* 476 Some will lay 20, thirty or forty rubbles into the Caback, vowing themselves to the pot, till the stock be spent. **1826** SCOTT *Talisman* ix, My safety, my lord,.. I cast behind me as a regardless thing when I vowed myself to this enterprise.

†**c.** To dedicate by a ceremony. *Obs.*$^{-1}$

1600 HOLLAND *Livy*, etc. 1355 The temple.. was called Capitolinum; and Tarquinius Priscus vowed it.

3. To make a solemn resolve or threat to inflict (injury), exact (vengeance), harbour (hatred), etc.

1592 KYD *Sp. Trag.* IV. i. 31 May it be that Bel-imperial Vowes such reuenge as she hath daind to say? *a* **1593** MARLOWE & NASHE *Dido* V. ii, Tell him, I never vow'd at Aulis' Gulf The desolation of his native Troy. **1606** SHAKS. *Tr. & Cr.* V. v. 31 Great Achilles Is arming, weeping, cursing, vowing vengeance. **1625** in Foster *Eng. Factories India* (1909) III. 105 Thay both then voued reveng if I cam in their power. **1726** SWIFT *Gulliver* I. v, The Empress.. could not forbear vowing revenge. **1839** tr. *Lamartine's Trav. East* 49/1 In spite of the profound hatred which I had vowed to the pacha, I could not embrace the cause of the French. **1912** A. MCCORMICK *Words fr. Wild-Wood* ii. 43 In vain did he protest and vow vengeance upon his rebellious subjects.

4. *intr.* To make a vow or solemn undertaking; to bind oneself by a vow.

a **1325** *Prose Psalter* lxxv[i]. 11 Voweþ and ȝeldeþ to þe Lord, your God, ȝe alle þat bringe ȝiftes in his cumpas. **1382** WYCLIF *Prov.* xx. 25 Falling is of men ofte to vouwe to seintis, and aftir the vouwis aȝeen drawe. **1560** BIBLE *Eccl.* v. 4 It is better that thou shuldest not vowe, then that thou shuldest vowe and not paye it. **1603** SHAKS. *Meas. for M.* I. iv. 10 You are yet vnsworne: When you haue vowd, you must not speake with men, But in the presence of the Prioresse. **1651** HOBBES *Leviath.* I. xiv. 69 They that Vow any thing contrary to any law of Nature, Vow in vain. **1675** OWEN *Indwelling Sin* xvii. (1732) 237 Knowing no other way to mortifie Sin, but this of vowing against it. *c* **1710** in *Lady M. W. Montagu's Lett.* (1887) II. 3, I had better not vow, for I shall certainly love you, do what you will. **1782** J. BROWN *View Nat. & Rev. Religion* VI. iii. 608 They were capable to vow for themselves. **1812** CRABBE *Tales* vi. 250 She answer'd,..'I have not vow'd against the holy state'. **1867** TENNYSON *Holy Grail* 270 Because the hall was all in tumult—some Vowing, and some protesting.

vow, *v.*² Also 4 vouwe, 4, 6 vowe, 6 *Sc.* wow. [Aphetic f. AVOW *v.*¹ In sense 2 sometimes not clearly distinguishable from VOW *v.*¹]

†**1.** *trans.* To acknowledge, admit. *Obs.*

1338 R. BRUNNE *Chron.* (1810) 180 'If þou to non þat lyues,' said R. 'þou [*read* þi] cheue ne bowe, þi lond men salle gife tille one þat may it vowe'. *c* **1560** A. SCOTT *Poems* vi. 38, I dar not preiss hir to present it, Ffor be scho wreth I will not wow it.

2. To affirm or assert solemnly; to asseverate, to declare. (Cf. AVOW *v.*¹ 4.)

c **1330** *Amis & Amil.* 858 Than dede the douke com forth that may, And the steward withstode alway, And vouwed the dede tho. **1590** in J. Campbell *Balmerino* (1867) 176 Thou nor nane that appertenis to the dar stand up and vow that in my face. **1601** LD. MOUNTJOY *Let.* in Moryson *Itin.* (1617) II. 123 If you haue any authority from the Queene to countermand mine,..it is more then you haue vowed to me to haue. **1642** FULLER *Holy & Prof. St.* III. x. 175 Yet the same party vowed to God, that he knew not that he could do it. *a* **1656** BP. HALL *Rem. Wks.* (1660) 47 These people vow they will watch you. **1833** HT. MARTINEAU *Briery Creek* ii. 41 My wife vowed that a handsome looking-glass was a necessary of life to her. **1848** THACKERAY *Van. Fair* xxix, She vowed that it was a delightful ball. **1865** KINGSLEY *Herew.* xv, The knights of the neighbourhood..had all vowed him the most gallant of warriors.

refl. **1592** *Soliman & Pers.* I. iv, Giue me thy hand, I vowe myselfe thy friend.

absol. **1825** T. HOOK *Sayings* Ser. II. *Sutherl.* (Colburn) 50 Grace protested that it [the performance] was perfection, Mrs. Chatterton exclaimed, and the Colonel vowed.

b. ***I vow***, used to strengthen an assertion.

In later use chiefly U.S., also in the minced forms *van*, VOWNE, and VUM.

1590 SPENSER *F.Q.* II. iv. 18 Our selues in league of vowed loue we knit:..And for my part I vow, dissembled not a whit. **1591** SHAKS. *Two Gentl.* IV. iv. 208 Else by Ioue, I vow, I should haue scratch'd out your vnseeing eyes. **1675** N. LEE *Nero* Prol., A bloody fatal Play you'l see to night, I vow to Gad, 'thas put me in a fright. **1687** T. BROWN *Saints in Uproar* Wks. 1730 I. 80 You'd break a man's sides with laughing, I vow and swear. **1749** FIELDING *Tom Jones* XVII. ii, I vow I am afraid. **1773** GOLDSM. *Stoops to Conq.* III, I vow, child, you are vastly handsome. **1790** R. TYLER *Contrast* II. ii. (1887) 39, I vow I was glad to take to my heels and split home. **1849** LOWELL *Biglow P.* Ser. I. viii. 57, I vow my holl sheer o' the spiles would n't come nigh a V spot. **1865** DICKENS *Mut. Fr.* I. vi, I vow and declare I am half ashamed of myself for taking such an interest in you. **1875** TENNYSON *Q. Mary* III. v. 93 Robin came behind me, Kiss'd me well, I vow.

c. To make solemn assertion of (a feeling or quality).

1742 GRAY *Adversity* 24 To her again they vow their truth, and are again believed. **1816** J. WILSON *City of Plague* III. i. 187 The children of despair and poverty..Do passionately vow their gratitude.

vow (vaʊ), *int. Sc.* [Prob. ellipt. for *I vow*: cf. VOW *v.*² 2 b.] An exclamation used to emphasize a statement. (See also WOW *int.*)

1787 BURNS *What will I do* 4 My only beast, I had nae mae, And vow but I was vogie! **1814** W. NICHOLSON *Poems, Annandale Robin* iii, Hech me! but its lang since I saw you, And vow! ye're grown gaudy and grand. *a* **1870** D. THOMSON *Musings* (1881) 117 When I saw that ye were weel, Vow, man, but I was gled.

voward, obs. form of VAWARD.

†**vow-breach.** *Obs.* [f. VOW *sb.* + BREACH *sb.*] The breaking of a vow.

1647 FANSHAWE tr. *Guarini's Pastor Fido* IV. vii. 150 If I should do That which the Satyr did advise me to, Accusing her of vow-breach. **1647** JER. TAYLOR *Lib. Proph.* xiv. 205 The first was a punishment to Vow-breach and Sacriledge. **1651** —— *Serm. for Year* II. xxxii. 342 Murder on one side, and vow-breach on the other. **1709** MRS. MANLEY *Secret Mem.* (1720) III. 106 Thy early Falsehood; thy, till now, unpractised Sin of Vow-breach!

†**vow-break.** *Obs. rare.* [BREAK *sb.*] = prec.

1646 SHIRLEY *Poems, Curse* 2 Woman, I cannot call thee worse, For thy vow-break, take this curse.

vow-breaker. [BREAKER *sb.*] One who breaks his or her vow.

1532 MORE *Confut. Tindale* Wks. 611/2 Faithful aduoutrers, faithful vowe breakers, faithfull theues. **1565** HARDING *Confut.* I. v. 15 To reuele the truth of his gospell by Apostates, vowebreakers, churchrobbers, and such other. **1681** DRYDEN *Span. Friar* II. ii, Love, you know, Father, is a great Vow-maker; but he's a greater Vow-breaker. **1844** MRS. BROWNING *That Day* iii, I stand by the river—I think of the vow—Oh, calm as the place is, vow-breaker, be thou!

So **vow-breaking** *vbl. sb.* and *ppl. a.*

1533 MORE *Apol.* vi. Wks. 858/1 The vndouted faith of the whole catholike churche full fyftene hundred yeare together agaynste these vowebreakynge brethren. **1599** SANDYS *Europæ Spec.* (1632) 97 A companie of base Rebels and vow-breaking Friers. **1624** BEDELL *Lett.* x. 124 As to his Vow-breaking lastly, if that Vow were foolishly made.., it was iustly broken. **1646** FULLER *Wounded Consc.* (1841) 299 Vow-breaking, though a grievous sin, is pardonable on unfeigned repentance.

vowe, var. VOWEE *Obs.*

vowed (vaʊd), *ppl. a.* [f. VOW *v.*¹ + -ED¹.]

1. Of persons: †**a.** Bound by religious vows. *Obs.*

1532 MORE *Confut. Tindale* II. VI. Wks. 654/2 A man professynge once vowed chastitie, was for all that at hys lawefull lybertie to wedde a vowed professed nunne. **1565** STAPLETON tr. *Bede's Hist. Ch. Eng.* 140 One of those vowed virgins to God..had her departing shewed vnto her the same night in a vision. **1581** ALLEN *Apol.* 60 Incestuous mariages of vowed persons, spoile of Churches. **1631** WEEVER *Anc. Funeral Mon.* 154 One Isola Heton widow.. made sute to King Henry the sixth, that shee might be an Anchoresse, or vowed recluse. *a* **1708** T. WARD *England's Reform.* III. (1710) 55 How Durst you seise Church-Lands, Rob Priests and Poor, And turne the Vow'd Religious out of Door?

absol. **1565** HARDING *Confut.* II. viii. 73 b, The vowed be forbidden mariage by expresse word of God.

b. Devoted to some service or cause.

1560 DAUS tr. *Sleidane's Comm.* 308 Neither hath there chaunced as yet any suche controversie in the Counsell, that I neded any suche addicted and vowed men. **1589** GREENE *Menaphon* (Arb.) 82 Seeing thou hast made a rape of faire Samela, one of her vowed Shepheards is come..to challenge thee to single combate. **1655** LD. NORWICH in *Nicholas Papers* (Camden) III. 227 Your Maties all vowed and most obedient subiect and seruant. **1825** SCOTT *Talism.* i, The Crusader..as a vowed champion of the Cross..might have preferred the latter. **1836** KEBLE in *Lyra Apost.* (1849) 105 The champions vow'd of truth and purity.

†**c.** United by vows; betrothed or wedded. *Obs.*

1577 GRANGE *Golden Aphrod.* L iij b, I craue it not for my selfe but for my vowed wyfe. **1665** MANLEY *Grotius' Low C. Wars* 553 He was absolutely taken with one Gabrielis Estræa, a Noble Woman, but led aside from the Embraces of her vowed Husband.

d. Confirmed (in hostility) by a vow or solemn resolve.

1583 MELBANCKE *Philotimus* T iv, Thy vowed enemie Aurelia. **1590** SPENSER *F.Q.* I. xii. 19 The troubler of my happie peace, And vowed foe of my felicitie. **1633** T. STAFFORD *Pac. Hib.* I. xix. (1821) 204 He was a vowed enemy to the English Government. **1810** SCOTT *Lady of Lake* V. v, Whence the bold boast by which you show Vich-Alpine's vow'd and mortal foe?

†**e.** *transf.* Pertaining to a devotee. *Obs.*⁻¹

1665 T. MANLEY *Grotius' Low C. Wars* 49 Others, after the old manner of Mourning, in a vowed Habit, promise and swear, Never to cut their Hair, untill they had revenged the Blood of those Noble-men.

2. Undertaken or performed in consequence of, or under the sanction of, a vow.

1532 [see 1 a]. **1561** T. NORTON *Calvin's Inst.* I. 25 Why do they wery themselues with vowed pilgrimages to visit those images wherof they haue like at home. **1626** DONNE *Serm., Luke ii. 29–30* (1640) 30 Nothing that countenances a vowed virginity, to the dishonour or undervaluing of marriage. **1712** P. METCALFE *Life S. Winefride* (1917) 7 S. Wenefride offer'd herself a Sacrifice, to preserve her Vow'd Virginity. **1720** WELTON *Suffer. Son of God* I. xi. 280 That the Religious might not over-value themselves on Account of their Vowed Poverty. **1818** SHELLEY *Rosal. & Helen* 342 That mother Whom to outlive, and cheer, and make My wan eyes glitter for her sake, Was my vowed task.

†**b.** Solemnly consecrated or dedicated. *Obs.*

1585 FETHERSTONE tr. *Calvin on Acts* xxiii. 16 Paul shoulde come out on the morrowe to be slaine, as a vowed sacrifice. **1591** SPENSER *Virg. Gnat* 603 Curtius..stifly bent his vowed life to spill. *c* **1630** MILTON *5th Ode Horace* 13 Me in my vow'd Picture the sacred wall declares t'have hung My dank and dropping weeds To the stern God of Sea. **1691** tr. *Emilianne's Frauds Rom. Monks* (ed. 3) 181 These Vow'd Pictures we generally find in all the Churches of Italy.

c. Confirmed by a vow or vows; solemnly promised or guaranteed.

1590 SPENSER *F.Q.* II. iv. 18 Our selues in league of vowed loue we knit. **1603** SHAKS. *Meas. for M.* V. i. 209 This is the hand, which with a vowd contract Was fast belockt in thine. **1625** K. LONG tr. *Barclay's Argenis* II. xv. 111 She would not suffer the memory of their vowed love to be blotted out with absence. **1655** LD. NORWICH in *Nicholas Papers* (Camden) II. 259, I may without danger now present my humblest and all vowed duty to you. **1697** DRYDEN *Æneid* IX. 365 No fate my vow'd affection shall divide From thee, heroick youth! **1704** J. TRAPP *Abra-Mulé* V. i. 2544 Nor Fate, nor you, can my vow'd Faith control.

d. Solemnly sworn or threatened.

1590 SPENSER *F.Q.* II. vi. 8 Of his way he had no souenance, Nor care of vow'd reuenge, and cruell fight. **1697** DRYDEN *Æneid* V. 1063, I sought with joy The vowed destruction of ungrateful Troy. *Ibid.* XII. 1355 If thy vow'd revenge pursue my death. **1808** SCOTT *Marmion* I. xxii, The vow'd revenge of Bughtrig rude, May end in worse than loss of hood.

†**vowee.** *Obs.*⁻¹ Also vowe. [Aphetic form of *avowé* AVOWE.] Advocate, patron.

c **1380** *Sir Ferumbras* 405 Ne were it for repreue, By Mahoun, þat ys my vowee [*v.r.* vowe], of þyn heued y wolde þee reue.

vowel (ˈvaʊəl), *sb.* Also 4 wowel (6 -ell), 5–7 vowell(e. [a. OF. *vouel* (also *vouyel, voy-, voieul*) masc.:—L. *vōcāl-em* or *vōcāle*, masc. and neut. acc. sing. of *vōcālis* VOCAL *a.* The later OF. *voielle*, mod.F. *voyelle*, Prov. and Sp. *vocal*, Pg. *vogal*, It. *vocale* are fem., after the L. sb. *vōcālis*.]

1. a. A sound produced by the vibrations of the vocal cords; a letter or character representing such a sound (as *a, e, i*, etc.).

'A vowel may be defined as voice (voiced breath) modified by some definite configuration of the super-glottal passages, but without audible friction (which would make it into a consonant)' (Sweet *Primer of Phonetics*, ed. 2, §32).

c **1308** *Sat. Kildare* iii. in *E.E.P.* (1862) 153 þis uers is imakid wel of consonans and wowel. *c* **1450** *Mankind* 490 in *Macro Plays* 18 Remembre my brokyn hede in þe worschyppe of þe v. vowellys. **1483** *Cath. Angl.* 404/1 A vowelle, *vocalis*. **1530** PALSGR. Introd. p. xv, They forme certayne of theyr vowelles in theyr brest. *Ibid.* p. xvii, Any of the fyrst thre vowels *A, E* or *O*. **1551** T. WILSON *Logike* G vij b, In these wordes there be foure vowels to be considered, and marked. **1587** GOLDING *De Mornay* xxiv. (1592) 368 They drive their clauses to fall alike, they eschew nycely the meeting together of vowels. **1612** BRINSLEY *Lud. Lit.* 15 More specially to bee carefull, for the right pronouncing the fiue vowels. **1669** HOLDER *Elem. Speech* 29 In all Vowels the passage of the mouth is open and free, without any appulse of an Organ of Speech to another. **1687** DRYDEN *Hind & P.* II. 386 The sense is intricate, 'tis only clear What vowels and what consonants are there. **1751** HARRIS *Hermes* Wks. (1841) 209 It is the variety of configurations in these openings only, which gives birth and origin to the several vowels. **1769** COOK *Voy. round World* I. xix. (1773) 228 Their language is soft and melodious; it abounds with vowels, and we easily learnt to pronounce it. **1816** KEATS *Epist. to C. C. Clarke* 56 Spenserian vowels that elope with ease, And float along like birds o'er summer seas. **1867** ELLIS *E.E. Pronunc.* I. iii. 61 Salesbury does not always discriminate the long vowel, though..he occasionally.. doubles the consonant sign to imply the brevity of the preceding vowel.

b. *transf.* and *fig.*

1576 FLEMING *Panopl. Epist.* 175 This manner of profession is no Vowell in your Alphabet, is no flower in your Garden. **1577** B. GOOGE *Heresbach's Husb.* (1586) 11 Marcus Varro divideth his husbandry necessaries into three parts: vowels, where he puts his owne servants and such as he hireth; halfe vowels, where his working cattell be; and mutes. **1657** TRAPP *Comm. Job* xxxii. 7 We use to say, That at meetings young men should be Mutes, and old men Vowels.

†**2.** A vocable; a word. *Obs.*

1578 T. N. tr. *Conq. West Ind.* (1596) 201 The Temple is called *Teucalli*, that is to say, Gods house, *Teutl* signifieth God, and *Calli* is a house, a vowel very fitte, if that house had bene of the true God. **1614** T. WHITE *Martyrd. St. George* C j, Nor of his Creed one vowell to recant. **1648** GAGE *West Ind.* 47 Mexico is as much as to say a spring or fountain, according to the property of the vowell or speech.

3. *attrib.* and *Comb.*, as ***vowel-alternation, -articulation, -change, -consonant, -ending, -length, -letter, -loveliness, -notation, -phoneme, -rhyme, -sequence, -shade, -sign, -sound, -space, -symbol, -system, triangle***, etc.; ***vowel-initial*** adj.; **vowel colour**, the precise timbre and quality of a vowel sound; so **vowel colouring**; **vowel diagram**, a diagram showing relative degrees of closeness or openness, front-raising or back-raising of the tongue, in the articulation of individual vowels; **vowel-glide** [cf. GLIDE *sb.* 4], the gliding movement from one vowel component to another, as in a diphthong; also, = GLIDE *sb.* 4; **vowel gradation** = ABLAUT; **vowel harmony**, a feature of the Finno-Ugric, Turkish, and other languages, whereby successive syllables of words are limited to a particular class of vowel; **vowel height**, the degree to which the tongue is raised or lowered in the pronunciation of a particular vowel; **vowel-laxing**, the enunciation of a vowel with the speech organs relaxed (cf. LAX *a.* 5 c); **vowel-point**, a sign used to indicate a vowel in certain alphabets (esp. the Hebrew, Syriac, and Arabic); also as *v.*, to supply with points in place of vowels; cf. POINT *sb.*¹ 3 b and *v.*¹ 3 c; **vowel-quality**, the identifying acoustic characteristic of a vowel; **vowel-quantity**, the duration of time needed for the pronunciation of a vowel; **vowel shift**, a phonetic change of vowel or vowels, *spec.* applied to a series of changes between medieval and modern English affecting the long vowels of the standard language; freq. in phr. ***great vowel shift***; cf. SHIFT *sb.* 14 d.

1951 W. K. MATTHEWS *Languages U.S.S.R.* iv. 57 The already noticed Manchu *vowel-alternation to express sex-gender may be paralleled by Evenki examples. **1937** J. R. FIRTH *Tongues of Men* 42 Instead of referring to the *vowel-articulations, we refer to the resulting sounds. **1848** *Bagster's Analyt. Heb. Concordance* 57 The *Vowel-changes of Nouns. **1871** KENNEDY *Public Sch. Lat. Gram.* 9 Syllables may be strengthened by vowel-change. **1948** M. JOOS *Acoustic Phonetics* ii. 59 It seems that a listener can hear a difference of *vowel color [in the [ɛ] of *hotel* spoken by three American speakers] equivalent to a distance of 1 semitone on the formant chart. **1978** *Amer. Speech* LIII. 291 Different arrays of formants constitute different vowel colors. **1939** F. M. FORD *Let.* May (1965) 321 The mere sequence of the *vowel coloring of that phrase will give you acute pleasure.

1979 *Archivum Linguisticum 1978* IX. 156 Pajares notes that the loss of laryngeal and the lengthening (and in some cases vowel coloring) of the preceding vowel can also be considered a monophthongization. **1669** HOLDER *Elem. Speech* 141 This is eminently seen in the *Vowel Consonants, *Y, W*. **1881** W. R. SMITH *Old Test. in Jew. Ch.* ii. Notes 393 This use of the vowel-consonants is found even on the stone of Mesha. **1960** *Amer. Speech* XXXV. 227 Vowel-consonant syllables [are] less intelligible than consonant-vowel syllables. **1977** P. STREVENS *New Orientations Teaching of Eng.* xii. 151 Permissible consonant-clusters and vowel-consonant sequences are similar. **1932** D. JONES *Outl. Eng. Phonetics* (ed. 3) viii. 36 (*caption*) Fig. 23 Diagram illustrating the Tongue-positions of the eight primary Cardinal Vowels. Fig. 24. A more accurate form of *Vowel Diagram. **1976** C. BARBER *Early Mod. Eng.* vi. 299 The long and short pure vowels in StE in the middle of our period are shown on the vowel diagrams in Figure 3 and Figure 4. **1844** *Proc. Philol. Soc.* I. 261 Nouns of the *n* declension often took the nunnation in the nominative in place of the usual *vowel-ending. [**1856** Vocal glide: see GLIDE *sb.* 4.] **1878** H. SWEET *Handbk. Phonetics* 63 (*heading*) Initial and Final *Vowel-Glides. **1932** D. JONES *Outl. Eng. Phonetics* (ed. 3) 25 Such vowel-glides are often called semi-vowels. **1962** A. C. GIMSON *Introd. Pronunc. Eng.* II. vii. 121 Diphthongal Vowel Glides. The sequences of vocalic elements included under the term 'diphthong' are those which form a glide within one syllable. **1973** J. D. O'CONNOR *Phonetics* vii. 220 A diphthong..is phonetically a vowel glide or a sequence of two vowel segments which functions as a single phoneme. *Ibid.* 221 Other vowel glides such as /eu, øu, iu, ɔu/ which also occur [in Danish], must be interpreted as vowel + /v/ since they do not occur freely in the same sorts of context as the remaining vowels and diphthongs. **1887** W. W. SKEAT *Princ. Eng. Etym.* x. 158 To discover the original Teutonic *vowel-gradation..we must compare with one another the oldest known forms of the verbs in the various Teutonic languages. **1938** *Amer. Speech* XIII. 209 The term 'vowel-change' is evidently a new attempt (like 'vowel gradation'..) to avoid the German word *Ablaut*. **1973** A. H. SOMMERSTEIN *Sound Pattern Anc. Greek* ii. 70 As is well known, vowel gradation, or ablaut, was an important feature of proto-Indo-European morphology. [**1893** J. CLARK *Man. Linguistics* vi. 151 The Ural-Altaic languages..which are dominated by a law of vocalic harmony that, to speak generally, requires that one class of vowels..should obtain in the various syllables of a word.] **1900** H. SWEET *Hist. Lang.* vii. 122 In Finnish, the vowels are divided, from the point of view of *vowel-harmony, into the three classes hard, soft and neutral. **1972** *Language* XLVIII. 365 The nature of the rules of vowel harmony is and has been the subject of some discussion... The traditional view is as follows: the vowel harmony rule in Turkish specifies that, for any vowel, the distinctive feature in question is determined by the value of the previous vowel. **1977** *Archivum Linguisticum* VIII. 71 This is obscured by a distinctive feature system which uses a binary classification of [±high] and [±low] to define *vowel height. **1949** E. A. NIDA *Morphology* (ed. 2) ii. 16 Note that *h-* occurs before the consonant-initial stem *k'ab* and *k* before the *vowel-initial stem *akan*. **1978** *Language* LIV. 23 Before apparently vowel-initial nouns like *héros* and *honte*, we find no elision. **1977** *Stud. in Eng. Lit.: Eng. Number* (Tokyo) 155 Rule (24) succeeds in formally expressing a linguistically significant generalization underlying various *vowel-laxing processes. **1980** *English World-Wide* I. 250 The linguistic variables analyzed in the remaining six chapters are: (i) vowel laxing in monosyllabic personal pronouns and a number of non-pronominal forms. **1932** D. JONES *Outl. Eng. Phonetics* (ed. 3) 237 *Vowel-length depends to a considerable extent on the rhythm of the sentence. **1977** P. STREVENS *New Orientations Teaching of Eng.* xii. 151 The relation between stress and vowel-length is of the same general type. **1846**, etc. *Vowel-letter [see MATER LECTIONIS]. **1933** L. BLOOMFIELD *Language* 292 We use the Latin vowel-letters not only in entirely new values..but in inconsistent ways. **1855** tr. *Lepsius' Standard Alphabet* 28 The Indian grammarians, who express the nasalisation..by a *vowel-like sign, namely, by placing a dot over the letter. **1879** SWEET in *Trans. Philol. Soc.* 456 + iv, The unaccented (ə) is dropped in rapid speech between consonants which combine easily, especially between points and vowellikes. **1888** —— *Hist. Eng. Sounds* 9 Those 'vowellike' or 'liquid' voiced consonants which are unaccompanied by buzz are often also syllabic. **1910** D. H. LAWRENCE *Let.* 26 Oct. (1962) I. 67 One can get good Swinburnian consonant music by taking thought, but never Shakespearean *vowel-loveliness. **1860** MARSH *Lect. Eng. Lang.* (1862) 484 In accordance with his general system of *vowel-notation. **1935** G. K. ZIPF *Psycho-Biol. of Lang.* (1936) 316 All the short *vowel-phonemes. **1964** C. BARBER *Present-Day Eng.* iii. 38 There is no pair of English vowel-phonemes which is distinguished solely by length. **1977** D. FRY *Homo Loquens* ii. 13 In English..about twenty are the vowel phonemes, exemplified by the word group *beat, bit, bet, bat*, etc. **1764** *Phil. Trans.* LIV. 419 Nor is it to be wondered at, that, before the invention of the *vowel-points, the quiescent letters should have sometimes been suppressed. **1843** *Proc. Philol. Soc.* I. 138 In fact, with a different notation, nearly all the labour of the vowel-points might be saved. **1845** BROWNING *Lett.* (1899) I. 16, I could not well vowel-point my commonplace letters and syllables with a masoretic *other* sound and sense. **1893** FORBES-MITCHELL *Remin. Gt. Mutiny* 275 The Oordoo in the circular is printed in the Persian character without the vowel-points. **1844** R. GARNETT in *Proc. Philol. Soc.* I. 265 The *vowel-prefix to certain past tenses (Sanscr. *a*, Gr. ε). **1920** W. PERRETT *Peetickay* 23 A notation of *vowel-quality, derived from the 'organic' positions of the tongue, lips, etc., already exists in Alexander Melville Bell's *Visible Speech*. **1965** W. S. ALLEN *Vox Latina* ii. 52 The Latin vowel-quality is vouched for by Italian *borsa*. **1933** L. BLOOMFIELD *Language* 294 For the writers, the *gh* was now a mere silent graph, indicative only of *vowel-quantity. **1977** *Archivum Linguisticum* VIII. 93 According to the Introduction, it has two aims: firstly to examine the various factors involved in the vowel-quantity changes that took place between Middle High German and New High German. **1620** W. FOLKINGHAM *Brachigraphy* iv, In like sort and position are Letters placed apart in *Vowel Regions to imply interceding Vowels. **1838** GUEST *Hist. Eng. Rhythms* I. 316 The *vowel-rhime, or..the assonant rhime, was common in the Romance of Oc. **1873-4** G. M. HOPKINS *Jrnls. & Papers* (1959) 287 Alliteration is initial half-rhyme, 'shothending' is final half-rhyme, assonance is vowel rhyme. **1961** A. CLARKE *Later Poems* 89 In simple patterns, the tonic word at the end of the line is supported by a vowel-rhyme in the middle of the next line. **1939** F. M. FORD *Let.* May (1965) 321 The mere *vowel sequences of certain passages will be sufficient to call back to you all the associations of your youth. **1965** *Language* XLI. 482 It gives a desirable economy of phonemes, which the vowel-sequence solution does not. **1955** J. R. R. TOLKIEN *Return of King* 409 The language that they [*sc.* the Ents] had made was..slow, sonorous..; formed of a multiplicity of *vowel-shades and distinctions of tone and quantity. **1909** O. JESPERSEN *Mod. Eng. Gram.* I. viii. 231 The great *vowel-shift consists in a general raising of all long vowels. **1933** —— *Essentials Eng. Gram.* iii. 34 The greatest revolution that has taken place in the phonetic system of English is the vowel-shift. **1936** *Essays & Studies* XXI. 10 The great vowel-shift of the late Middle Ages was followed by numerous other changes. **1964** C. BARBER *Present-Day Eng.* iii. 51 The great vowel-shift which took place between Middle English and Modern English. **1977** *Canad. Jrnl. Linguistics 1976* XXI. II. 177 After the application of the degemination rule and the vowel shift rule one obtains [eksīd]. **1849** *Jrnl. Amer. Oriental Soc.* I. 523 We begin with the *Vowel-signs, of which there are three in the Persian cuneiform alphabet. **1871** KENNEDY *Public Sch. Lat. Gram.* 9 §12 *E* and *O*, introduced into most other languages as intermediate vowel-signs, exist in Sanscrit only as diphthongs arising from *ai, au*. **1795** *Monthly Rev.* Aug. 410 All the simple sounds, *vowel and consonantal. **1822-7** GOOD *Study Med.* (1829) I. 544 The glottis..forms all the vocal or vowel sounds. **1875** WHITNEY *Life Lang.* iv. 56 The strange names we give to our vowel-sounds. **1965** W. S. ALLEN *Vox Latina* ii. 54 There would have been more *vowel-space to accommodate the new sound. **1979** *Amer. Speech 1978* LIII. 294 Suppose the available 'vowel space' for a community's language were constrained to the relatively small triangular region bounded by the calculated Neanderthal approximations to the three reference vowels. **1932** D. JONES *Outl. Eng. Phonetics* (ed. 3) 5 The naming of *vowel-symbols presents some difficulty. **1957** R. W. ZANDVOORT *Handbk. Eng. Gram.* 337 Words in silent *e* drop it before endings beginning with a vowel-symbol. **1855** tr. *Lepsius' Standard Alphabet* 11 He contended successfully against the English *vowel-system. **1875** WHITNEY *Life Lang.* iv. 55 The consistency of our vowel-system. **1918** D. JONES *Outl. Eng. Phonetics* vi. 16 If we examine the tongue positions of the typical sounds of these five classes [of vowels] we find that the highest points of the tongue lie roughly on the sides of a triangle... This triangle is known as the '*Vowel Triangle'.

vowel ('vaʊəl), *v.* [f. prec.]

†**1. a.** *intr.* To utter the vowels in singing. **b.** *trans.* To sing with vowel-articulation. *Obs.* (Cf. VOWELLING *vbl. sb.* 1 a.)

1597 MORLEY *Introd. Mus.* 179 They ought to studie howe to vowell and sing cleane. **1646** MAYNE *Serm. Unity* (1647) 32 As if they [i.e. the Psalms]..had been tuned through his own loud Cymball, or had more softly been sung and vowell'd to his Harpe.

2. *trans.* To convert into a vowel; to vocalize.

1611 COTGR., *Vocalizé*, vowelled, made a vowell.

3. To supply with vowels or vowel-points.

1681 H. MORE *Exp. Dan.* Pref. 7 They did not know how to point them or vowel them. **1880** *Encycl. Brit.* XI. 797/1 Some syllabics never take a vowel except for an unusual form,—the root and the ordinary derivatives never being vowelled.

†**4.** *slang.* To pay (a creditor) with an IOU.

1709 STEELE *Tatler* No. 12 ¶3 Do not talk to me, I am Voweled by the Count, and cursedly out of humour. **1760** FOOTE *Minor* I. i, They will vowel you, from Father to Son to the twentieth generation. **1796** *Grose's Dict. Vulgar T.* (ed. 3) s.v., A gamester who does not immediately pay his losings, is said to vowel the winner, by repeating the vowels I.O.U. or perhaps from giving his note for the money according to the Irish form.

vowel, southern dial. var. FOUL *a.*, FOWL *sb.*

'**vowelism.** [f. VOWEL *sb.* + -ISM.] A system of vowel-sounds; articulation in respect of vowels.

1842 *Blackw. Mag.* LII. 71 The vowelism of the Scotch is not altogether pure. In some instances it differs, alike from the classic A.-Saxon and from the Icelandic.

'**vowelist.** [f. as prec. + -IST.]

†**1.** One who gives undue study to the vowel-points of the Hebrew scriptures. *Obs.*

1655 SPURSTOWE *Wels of Salvation* 158 Vowalists and Letterists having little or no acquaintance with the deep things of God.

2. One who employs vowels for poetic effect.

1890 in *Athenæum* 6 Sept. 334/2 The *Glasgow Herald* says 'As a repetitionary vowelist Mr. Spratly is virtuous compared with Milton'.

'**vowelize**, *v.* [f. as prec. + -IZE.]

1. *trans.* To modify or produce by means of vowel-sounds. Hence '**vowelized** *ppl. a.*

1816 J. GILCHRIST *Philos. Etym.* 59 The vowelized softness of Greek, Italian, French,..proceeds from the same cause.

2. To render vocalic. In quot. *absol.*

1867 A. M. BELL *Visible Sp.* 87 Then vowelize or expand and tensify the configuration to remove the friction of the breath.

3. To supply with vowel-points or signs representing vowels.

1883 *American* VI. 314 'Tom Brown's School-Days' will be immediately issued in the easy reporting style [of shorthand], fully vowelized.

†'**vowellage.** *Obs.*$^{-1}$ [-AGE.] Vowelling.

1620 W. FOLKINGHAM *Brachigraphy* To Rdr. A 4 b, All coniunctions of Characters will be meere Incorporations sans Implication of Vowellage or intrication of the Lecture.

'**vowelled**, *ppl. a.* [f. VOWEL *sb.* or *v.* + -ED.] Of language or words: Supplied or provided with vowels, esp. to an unusual extent. Also with qualifying term, as *well-vowelled*.

1662 PLAYFORD *Skill Mus.* I. xi. (1674) 56 The Italian Language is more smooth and better vowelled than the English. **1684** DRYDEN *To Earl of Roscommon* 17 Pauses, cadence, and well-vowell'd Words. **1792** ANNA SEWARD *Lett.* (1811) III. 142 My own exquisitely rich and harmonious language; the growing Latinity of which has already..rendered it sufficiently vowelled, sufficiently sweet, copious, and sonorous. **1820** KEATS *Lamia* II. 200 While fluent Greek a vowel'd under-song Kept up. **1860** FARRAR *Orig. Lang.* 67 The soft and vowelled undersong of modern Italian. **1869** MEREDITH *Lett.* 19 Dec. (1912) I. 198 Isn't there a scent of damned hypocrisy in all this lisping and vowelled purity of the Idylls? **1883** *Blackw. Mag.* Oct. 431/2 By melodious juxtaposition, by artful alliteration, by vowelled breathings and consonantal crashes of harmony.

b. Having vowels of a specified kind or quality.

1783 J. BEATTIE *Diss.* 293 The long-vowelled emphatick syllable..and the short-vowelled emphatick syllable. **1868** GEO. ELIOT *Sp. Gipsy* I. 61 As full vowelled words Are new impregnate with the master's thought.

c. *nonce-uses.* (See quots.)

1873-4 G. M. HOPKINS *Jrnls. & Papers* (1959) 287 In Norse poetry..the vowels..seen to be sided or intentionally changed, vowelled off. **1934** DYLAN THOMAS in *Listener* 24 Oct. 691/2 Some let me make you of the vowelled beeches.

'**vowelless**, *a.* [f. VOWEL *sb.* + -LESS.] Having no vowel or vowels.

1870 J. F. SMITH *Ewald's Introd. Hebr. Gram.* 163 A vanishing *o* usually reappears in connexion with the first of the two vowelless consonants which might arise. **1892** BRUCE *Apologetics* II. ix. 304 The Masoretic Hebrew text is thus only an approximately accurate translation by Jewish scholars of the vowelless original.

'**vowelling**, *vbl. sb.* [f. VOWEL *v.* + -ING[1].]

1. †**a.** The articulation of vowels in singing. *Obs.*

c **1500** *Proverbis* in *Antiq. Rep.* IV. 406 Perfite vowellynge of a songe, to the eere is delectable. **1622** MABBE tr. *Aleman's Guzman d'Alf.* II. 284 Shee performed both so sweetely, as well for the ayring of her notes, as the vowelling of her words.

b. The pronunciation of vowels in speech.

1879 G. MACDONALD *Sir Gibbie* xxv, The grand organ roll of it [*Paradise Lost*] losing nothing in the Scotch voweling.

c. *nonce-use.*

1873-4 G. M. HOPKINS *Jrnls. & Papers* (1959) 284 This is given by vowelling, which is either vowelling on (assonance) or vowelling off.

2. The insertion of vowels or vowel-signs.

1627 W. SCLATER *Exp. 2 Thess.* (1629) 95 It is reported of Ioab, that when his Teacher taught him to corrupt the text but in the vowelling, he slew him without ransome. **1870** *Athenæum* 11 June 785/1 Our E. V., following the vowelling assigned to the Hebrew by the Rabbins, renders them 'for ever'. **1880** *Encycl. Brit.* XI. 797/1 The vowelling of Greek and Latin proper names shews that the vagueness of the vowels was not absolute.

'**vowellish**, *a. rare*$^{-1}$. [f. VOWEL *sb.*] Of the nature of a vowel.

1636 B. JONSON *Eng. Gram.* I. iii. (1640) 40 The power [of the letter W] is alwayes Vowellish, even where it leades the Vowell in any Syllabe.

'**vowelly**, *a.* [f. VOWEL *sb.* + -Y[1].] Having many vowels; characterized by vowels.

1712 MRS. CENTLIVRE *Perplexed Lovers* V. i, *Sir Rog.* This Italian is very vowelly, it runs much upon the o methinks. **1841** D'ISRAELI *Amen. Lit.* (1867) 97 The Northmen, in the shock of their hard, redundant consonants, lost the vowelly confluence. **1883** *Advance* (Chicago) 6 Dec., In their soft, vowely tongue.

vower[1] ('vaʊə(r)). [f. VOW *v.* + -ER[1].] One who makes a vow, or has taken vows.

1546 BALE *Eng. Votaries* I. 13 He..called vnto his Apostleship, not wyueless vowers, but marryed men. **1560** DAUS tr. *Sleidane's Comm.* 125 As touching monasticall vowes,..it might be obteined of the byshop, that none should be taken in yong, and before the vowers were of rype yeares. **1599** SANDYS *Europæ Spec.* (1632) 136 From whom also as being too rich for vowers of poverty, he tooke away at one clap above tenne thousand Crownes rent. *a* **1638** MEDE *Wks.* (1672) 179 This extent of the Vow is beyond the intent of the Vower. **1691** tr. *Emilianne's Frauds Rom. Monks* (ed. 3) 407 Of all these Vowers of Chastity there are but a very few, and may be, none at all that observe it. **1848** DICKENS *Dombey* xxix, Youthful vowers of eternal constancy. **1887** H. S. BOWDEN tr. *Hettinger's Dante* 306 *note*, The vower can only change the matter of his vow to some greater offering to God's honour.

†'**vower**[2]. *Obs.*$^{-1}$ In 5 *Sc.* **wowar.** [Cf. VOW *v.*[2] and AVOURE *sb.*[1]] A guardian, patron.

c **1470** HENRY *Wallace* VII. 124 Saynct Androw was, gaiff the that suerd in hand; Off sanctis he is wowar off Scotland.

†**vower**[3]. *Obs.*$^{-1}$ [Aphetic f. *devoure* DEVOIR *sb.*] Devoir, duty.

? *a* **1500** *Chester Pl.* (Shaks. Soc.) II. 145 When the[y] had done their vower [*v.r.* devour] A beaste shoulde come of greate power.

vowerer, variant of VOURER *Obs.*

voweson, variant of VOWSON *Obs.*

vowess ('vaʊɪs). Now *Hist.* or *arch.* Also 6 **voiesse, woys(s)e, vowes, wowes;** 6–7 **vowesse.** [Cf. VOWER[1] and -ESS.]

1. A woman, *esp.* a widow, who has taken a vow of chastity for the remainder of her life.

1506 *Lincoln Wills* (1914) I. 44, I Jane Harby of Lincoln, Wowes, mak my testament, [etc.]. **1512** *Nottingham Rec.* III. 453 Agnes Mellars, wydowe and vowesse. **1546** BALE *Eng. Votaries* I. 13 And at hys departure in the mornynge, he neyther commaunded Peter to breake vp howshold, nor yet to forsake hys wyfe and make her a vowesse. **1865** *Test. Ebor.* (Surtees) III. 312 A lady, after her husband's death, was allowed to take the vow of chastity, and she was then called a vowess. **1875** HENDERSON *Liber Pontificalis Chr. Bainbridge* Pref. p. xl, At the Benedictio Viduæ, the Vowess in a blue dress with white hood..is kneeling before the Bishop.

2. A woman who makes a vow of devotion to a religious life; a nun.

1533 MORE *Answ. Poysoned Bk.* Wks. 1060/1 Some vowesses peraduenture ther are, which as yet neuer intend to breake their vow. **1553** BECON *Reliques Rome* (1563) 37 b, A certayne vowesse or professed nunne. **1587** HOLINSHED *Chron.* III. 1080/2 Vpon which toome there laie a stone image of Edith in the habit of a vowesse holding a hart in hir right hand. **1611** SPEED *Hist. Gt. Brit.* VII. vii. 227 She abandoned her Regencie, and built a house of deuotion in the Ile of Shepey, wherein herselfe became a Vowesse. **1695** KENNETT *Par. Antiq.* ix. 660 A rich Tomb..with her image thereon, in the habit of a Vowess Crown'd.

†**vowgard.** *Obs.*$^{-1}$ (Meaning obscure.)

c **1460** *Towneley Myst.* xxx. 580 Now is all in oureward, youre yeres ar ron, It is commen in vowgard youre dame malison, To bynde it.

vowght, obs. variant of VAULT *sb.*[1]

vowing ('vaʊɪŋ), *vbl. sb.* [f. VOW *v.* + -ING[1].] The action of the verb in various senses.

a **1300** *Cursor M.* 10692 þe biscop..did þam sembled be, O þis vouing [*v.r.* vowing] of chastite For to ask o þaim sum rede. **1550** BALE *Apol.* 136 Where as he calleth geldynge or makynge chast for the kyngdome of heauen, a voweynge of the single lyfe, whych Christ neuer ment. **1594** CAREW *Tasso* (1881) 11 That holy Pilgrims farre from dread of way That great Tombe might adore, and vowings pay. **1782** J. BROWN *View Nat. & Revealed Relig.* VI. iii. §9 (1796) 505 Vowing is the making a solemn promise to God, in which we bind ourselves to do or forbear somewhat for the promoting his glory. **1844** MRS. BROWNING *Man's Requirem.* ii, Love me with thine open youth In its frank surrender; With the vowing of thy mouth With its silence tender. **1886** CORBETT *Fall of Asgard* II. 77 The drinking went forward again, and great was the vowing and boasting as the night went on.

vowis, obs. Sc. pl. of WOLF.

'**vowless,** *a.* [f. VOW *sb.* + -LESS.] Not bound by a vow or vows.

1620 BP. HALL *Hon. Marr. Clergy* I. xvii. Wks. (1628) 757 Hee hath done with their owne vowes, and now descends to vs, Whom hee confesses vowlesse.

†'**vowly,** southern dial. f. FOULLY *adv.* 5.

1633 B. JONSON *Tale Tub* I. ii, And the zame day o' the moneth, as this Zin Valentine, Or I am vowly deceiv'd.

vowne, altered f. VOW *v.*[2] 2 b. *rare*$^{-1}$.

1785 *Mass. Spy* 13 Oct. (Thornton), Ye yanking lads of our town, ye Are brave fellows all, I vowne.

vowre, south-western dial. variant of FOUR.

†'**vowson.** *Obs.* Forms: 3–4 **voweson,** 5–6 **vouson** (5 **vourson, -sone, wouson**), 6 **vowson.** [Aphetic f. *avow(e)son* ADVOWSON.] Advowson, patronage.

1297 R. GLOUC. (Rolls) 9678 Ȝuf bituene tueie lewedemen were eni striuing..As vor voweson of churche weþer ssolde þe churche ȝiue. **1424** *Paston Lett.* I. 18 A sute that he made ageyn the seyd priour of a voweson of the chyrche of Sprouston. **1426** in *E.E. Wills* (1882) 74 þe Maner Enwarle in Deuen, with þe voursone of þe chirche, And..þe maner of Thorncoffyn in Somerset, with þe vourson of þe church. **1464** *Rolls of Parlt.* V. 520/2 Londes, Tenementes, Rentes and Wousons of Chirches. **1550** T. LEVER *Serm.* (Arb.) 115 Not able..to barcke agaynste pluralytyes, improperacions, bying of vousons, nor against anye euyll abuse of the clergies lyuynges. **1560** DAUS tr. *Sleidane's Comm.* 156 An other euill vse is to geue out vousons of benefices, as it were in a reuertion. **1570** ABP. PARKER *Corr.* (Parker Soc.) 361, I was informed that this Rycall was granted in vowson to one Mr. Hamond of Yorkshire.

vowsyng: see VOUSING *Obs.*

vowt, var. VULT *Obs.*

vowt(e, obs. varr. VAULT *sb.*[1] and *v.*[1]

vowtre, obs. f. VULTURE.

†**vowtre.** *Obs. rare.* [Aphetic f. *avowtre*: see ADULTERY.] Adultery. Also †**vowtre** *v. intr.*, to commit adultery. †**vowtriere,** an adulteress. †**vowtry,** adultery. *Obs.*

c **1400** *Apol. Loll.* 21 And al oþer lawis þat semen to sey, þat man how to curse for crime of *vowtre, þeft, & swilk oþer. *Ibid.* 87 þey kepe noiþer clene lif, ne wedding, but ..*vowtrand, or doing a-vowtri. *a* **1400–50** *Alexander* 4532 To Venus þe *vowtriere may noȝt ells a-vaile. *c* **1450** *Mirk's Festial* 72 Synne of lechery and of *vowtrye. *Ibid.* 201, I haue made mony on to sle men, and forto syn yn lechery and yn vowtry.

vowtur, obs. form of VULTURE.

‖**vox** (vɒks). [L. *vox* (pl. *vōcēs*), voice.]

1. ***vox populi,*** the voice of the people; expressed general opinion; common talk or rumour.

The Latin maxim *Vox populi vox Dei* 'the voice of the people is the voice of God', is freq. cited or alluded to in English works from the 15th cent. onwards.

a **1550** in *Skelton's Wks.* (1843) II. 409/1 A wonderfull sorte of selles, That *vox populi* telles, Of those bottomlesse welles. **1570** R. CONSTABLE in *Sadler's St. Papers* (1809) II. 388, I hard *vox populi* that the lord regent would not, for his owne honor,..deliver thearls. **1603** HOLLAND *Plutarch's Mor.* IX. 787 No publicke fame, nor *vox popli* Was ever knowen in vaine to die. **1671** E. HOWARD *Six Days Adventure* Pref. A 4 There being nothing more unstable or erroneous than *vox populi* in point of plays. **1774** (*title*), Vox populi, or Old England's Glory a Destruction in 1774. **1822** GALT *Sir A. Wylie* xcvi, 'O,..—just a wheen havers!' replied Bell—'causey talk—Vox populi!' **1867** E. FITZGERALD *Lett.* (1889) I. 308 Well, but I believe in the Vox Populi of two hundred Years: still more of two thousand.

2. ***vox angelica, vox humana*** (or † ***humane***), varieties of organ-stops imitative of vocal sounds. Also *attrib.*

a **1726** TUDWAY in Burney *Hist. Music* (1776) IV. 355 These [stops] were the Vox-humane,..with some others I may have forgot. **1776** BURNEY *Hist. Music* IV. 147 Of pipes thus constructed are composed the stops called the Vox-humana, Regal,..and many others. **1852** SEIDEL *Organ* 21 In the seventeenth century several registers were..inserted, among which we mention the vox humana, and the vox angelica. **1885** *Vox Humana* 3 The effect of the Vox Humana stop..is to make the organ sound like a choir of human voices.

3. ***vox nihili,*** a worthless or meaningless word, *spec.* one produced by a scribal or printer's error; used *transf.* to denote abstract concepts whose meaning is deemed to be indistinct when analysed.

1892 in *Stanford Dict. Anglicised Words & Phrases.* **1916** H. W. B. JOSEPH *Introd. Logic* (ed. 2) xix. 404 Words like *agency* or *power*, on this view, are *voces nihili*; we think we mean something more by them than habitual sequence, but we do not. **1933** *Mind* XLII. 170 That they [actions] cannot be right *merely* as causes of effects..I have already proved, if I have proved that 'rightness' in this sense is a *vox nihili* or a mere synonym for 'causality'. **1960** *Analysis* XXI. 10 'Inductive *inference*' is a *vox nihili*, unless used—as it is sometimes confusingly used—to denote the concrete factual predictions and retrodictions that the mechanic, the seedsman, the palaeontologist and the astronomer make.

vox, south-western dial. var. FOX *sb.*; obs. Sc. var. VOICE *sb.*; obs. Sc. pa. t. WAX *v.*

vox pop (vɒks pɒp), *sb.* (*a.*) *colloq.* Also voxpop. [Abbrev. of *vox populi* s.v. VOX 1.] **a.** Popular opinion as represented by informal comments from members of the general public, esp. when used for broadcasting; statements or interviews of this kind.

1964 HALL & WHANNEL *Popular Arts* ix. 225 In television ..we could include..the use of the brief survey of popular opinion on any topic by means of the posed question (the so-called 'vox pop'). *Ibid.* 257 The short interview and the occasional 'vox pop' of the local news and sports programmes on radio. **1968** *Listener* 8 Feb. 164/2 A BBC camera crew went round Washington collecting vox pops —close-ups of men in the street saying pithily what they think of things. **1972** D. HURD *Truth Game* 59 Follow him close with the mike and get odds and ends of vox pop. **1975** *Listener* 18 Sept. 377/2 The audience was asked for comments, and very dim the voxpops sounded after the fluency of the two main speakers. **1981** *Times Lit. Suppl.* 25 Dec. 1501/5 There are wonderfully dreadful quotations in these chapters, including paragraphs of vox pop.

b. *attrib.* or as *adj.*

1966 *New Society* 17 Mar. 5/3 A *vox pop* survey I made among 17 housewives of St Ives. **1967** *Punch* 22 Nov. 794/1 Brandish a vox pop microphone in the concrete jungles and the cry..will recur monotonously, interspersed with blank looks. **1973** G. TALBOT *Ten Seconds from Now* iii. 35 'Vox pop' interviews on what the king ought to do. **1983** *Listener* 2 June 20/2 His suitability for the box is being questioned by whipper-snappers who would not have rated a vox-pop appearance..in the Fifties. **1985** *Spectator* 5 Jan. 7/3 A recent sermon included a vox pop poll on who in the congregation, average age 70, was familiar with Michael's song 'Thriller'.

voyage ('vɔɪɪdʒ), *sb.* Forms: *α.* 3–4 **veage,** 6 *Sc.* **weage (wewage, weavage),** 7 *Sc.* **veadge;** 3 **veiage,** 3–4, 6 **veyage** (6 *Sc.* **wey-**); 4–6 **vaiage,** 5, 6 *Sc.*, **vayage,** 5–6 *Sc.* **wayag(e;** 5 (9 *dial.*) **vage,** 5 **vaig,** 8–9 *north.*, 9 *Sc.* **vaige,** 9 *dial.* **vayge,** *Sc.* **vae(d)ge.** *β.* 4–8 (9 *dial.*) **viage** (5 **uiage, viagge,** 6 **viadge, viegde**), 4–6 **vyage** (4 **uyage**); 5 *Sc.* **wiage,** 5–6 **wyage.** *γ.* 5–7 **voiage** (6 **voiadge,** 7 **voige**), 5–**voyage** (6 **voyaige,** 7 **-adge**); *Sc.* 5 **woyage,** 6 **wo(v)age,** 7 **woag.** [a. AF. and OF. *veage, veiage, vayage,* and *voiage, -aige, voage, vouaige* (F. *voyage*), = Prov. *viatge*, Sp. *viage*, Pg. *viagem*, It. *viaggio*:—L. *viāticum* provision for a journey, VIATICUM.]

1. An act of travelling (†or transit), a journey (†or passage), by which one goes from one place to another (esp. at a considerable distance).

a. In the phrases *to take* or *make* (*a, the,* or *one's*) *voyage.* Now *rare.*

In early use including travel by sea as well as by land; for quotations in which the nautical sense is clear see 4 b.

(*a*) **1297** R. GLOUC. (Rolls) 4920 + 85 Cadwal in Yrlonde ys ost ȝarkede vaste & vorþ toward þys lond þe veage nome. **1375** BARBOUR *Bruce* XIV. 117 He his viage soyne has tane, And straucht toward the plas is gane. **1390** GOWER *Conf.* II. 8 He hath himself conformed..To schape and take the viage Homward. *c* **1412** HOCCLEVE *De Reg. Princ.* 1262 Seint Ambroses legende seith, how he Ones to Rome-ward took his viage. *c* **1440** *Generydes* 226 Now to this lady lete vs turne ageyn, Whiche to Surry hath take hir viage. **1564** HAWARD tr. *Eutropius* IV. 41 The consuls toke then their viage to invade Carthage. *a* **1575** tr. *Pol. Verg. Eng. Hist.* (Camden, No. 36) 43 Thei..toke their viage toward Rome, destroying all thinges on everie side. **1584** B. R. tr. *Herodotus* II. 76 b, We must take our voyage on foote the space of forty dayes by the waters side. **1647** HEXHAM I, To take a Viage, *reysen.*

(*b*) **1303** R. BRUNNE *Handl. Synne* 3746 To helle þou makyst þy vyage. *c* **1325** *Metr. Hom.* 54, I mac mi vaiage, Til sain Jam in pilgrimage. *c* **1400** MAUNDEV. (Roxb.) xxxiv. 152 It schuld be a lang tyme are þat vaiage ware made. **1484** CAXTON *Fables of Auian* viii, To make better theyr vyage they were sworne eche one to the other that none of them bothe should leue other. **1550** COVERDALE *Spir. Perle* xxix. (1588) 291 A marchant man maketh far viages and great iourneis..for worldly and transitory gain. **1579** *Poor Knt.'s Pal. Priv. Pleas.* (Roxb.) B iij, This is shee..whom once within the Lake, I shewed vnto Robinson, as our viage wee did make. **1586** WARNER *Alb. Eng.* II. vii. (1592) 27 And Hercules to Calidon a Dismall viage makes. **1860** R. NOEL *Vac. Tour* 467 A voyage I made by a very unfrequented path from Cæsarea to Nazareth.

b. In other contexts. Now *rare.*

α. *c* **1400** *Ywaine & Gaw.* 532 Swith, he sayd, wendes with me, Whoso wil that wonder se... Thar was none so litel page That he ne was fayn of that voyage. **1560** ROLLAND *Seven Sages* 12 To Romes Court the way thay held on richt. Thair seuin Maisters thair veyage passing on [etc.]. *a* **1585** MONTGOMERIE *Cherry & Slae* 625 (Laing MS.), Bot fra we gett our wayage win, thay sall nocht than the cherrie cun. **1875** [W. ALEXANDER] *Sk. Life Ain Folk* 195 Mains of Puddleweal sent his carts on a weekly 'vaege' to the burgh of Innerebrie to fetch his supplies of lime.

β. **1338** R. BRUNNE *Chron.* (1810) 90 He went þat viage To William þe rede kyng, þer he was in Wales. *c* **1386** CHAUCER *Prol.* 792 That ech of yow to shorte with oure weye In this viage shal telle tales tweye. *c* **1400** *Pilgr. Sowle* (Caxton) II. xli. (1859) 46 Theyr journey was fully adetermyned and theyr vyage endyd. *c* **1440** *Gesta Rom.* xxxvi. 140 (Harl. MS.), He thowte to visite þe holy londe,..and he ordeynid þerefore and made al thinge redy for his viage. **1474** CAXTON *Chesse* III. iv. (1883) 108 Hit is a fowle thynge..whan a man is at ende of his Iourney for to lengthe his viage. **1533** BELLENDEN *Livy* (S.T.S.) I. 80 Latumo and his wiffe Tanaquill war passand in ane chariot, with þar gudis tursit with þame in þare viage. **1552** T. BARNABE in Ellis *Orig. Lett.* Ser. II. II. 197 As for the realme of France besyde, I ought to knowe yt, for I have ben xxviij viages in France in poste for the Kings Majestie. **1591** SAVILE *Tacitus, Hist.* I. xxiii. 14 It seemed sore to trot al afoote ouer the Pyrenees and Alpes, and huge long viages at smal ease in their armour. *a* **1672** WOOD *Life* (1848) 85 *note*, I humbly desire your H. to thinke that the ocasion of my stay hear is nott for any dislike of the viage.

γ. **1527** *St. Papers Hen. VIII*, I. 204, I have declared unto Your Grace the successes of al such thinges, as have chaunced in my voyage. **1585** T. WASHINGTON tr. *Nicholay's Voy.* I. i, [It was resolved] that for the more suretie of his voyage, he shoulde returne by Sea. **1601** HOLLAND *Pliny* I. 133 For as much as..the travellers are forced to rest all the day long, therefore twelve daies are set down for the whole voiage betweene Coptus and Berenice. **1611** SPEED *Hist. Gt. Brit.* VII. ii. 285/1 Such as hauing vowed their voiage and seruice for Ierusalem, wore continually vpon their backes a red Crosse. **1649** JER. TAYLOR *Gt. Exemp.* III. xv. 32 Jesus took an Account of the first legation and voyage of his Apostles. **1673** RAY *Journ. Low C.* 147 Upon the mountains we passed over this voyage, we found a great number of plants we had not before met with. **1745** POCOCKE *Descr. East* II. 101 The pasha was lately returned from his voyage towards Mecca. **1808** PIKE *Sources Misciss.* II. 178, I conceive that to be beneath the serious consideration of a man on a voyage of such a nature. **1825** W. COBBETT *Rur. Rides* (1885) II. 50 The utmost extent of her voyages [from home] had been about two and a half miles. **1856** KANE *Arct. Exp.* II. ii. 28, I was just beginning to hope for an easy voyage, when Toodla and the Big Yellow gave way nearly together. **1887–** in dial. glossaries (Chesh., Lancs.).

transf. **1594** CAREW *Huarte's Exam. Wits* iv. (1596) 38 If Galen had considered the demeanure and voiages of the ant ..he would haue taken astonishment to see a beast so little endewed with so great sagenesse.

†**c.** A pilgrimage. *Obs.*

1456 SIR G. HAYE *Law Arms* (S.T.S.) 238 Men that makis vowis of vaigis for the lufe of God. *c* **1489** CAXTON *Sonnes of Aymon* vii. 155 How the kynge Charlemagne made a vyage to saynte Iames in Galice. **1518** H. WATSON *Hist. Oliver of Castile* (Roxb.) P 4 He came towarde ye kynge and sayd to hym that he dyde owe a vyage to Saynt Iames, and that he muste nedes do it withouten ony companye.

†**d.** Without article: Travel, travelling. *Obs.*

1626 BACON *New Atl.* (1650) 11 All Nations have Enter-knowledge of one another, by Voyage into Forraigne Parts, or by Strangers that come to them.

†**2.** A journey or expedition undertaken with a military purpose; a warlike enterprise or undertaking; a march against an enemy. *Obs.*

α. **1297** R. GLOUC. (Rolls) 4509 þo was þe king arþure vol of sorwe & sore..þe veage toward Rome he bileuede vor þis cheance. *Ibid.* 8079 Sulue wimmen ne bileuede þat hii ne wende þuder vaste, Ne ȝong folc þei hii feble were, þe wule þe veage [= crusade] ilaste. **1491–2** *Plumpton Corr.* (Camden) 102 Yt is so that the Kings grace hath appoynted my lord to wayt upon his grace, now at this his noble vage into France. **1533** BELLENDEN *Livy* II. xxi. (S.T.S.) I. 215 þai..bad þame pas fordwart..with gude werde, þat þe end of þare vayage mycht be respondent to þare begynnyng. **1596** DALRYMPLE tr. *Leslie's Hist. Scot.* I. 337 Cardinal Ægedie is sent frome Pape Honorie to Scotland, Legat, to require a gret soume of money..to helpe the veyage to Hierusalem.

β. **13..** *K. Alis.* 5075 (Laud MS.), A morowe þe kyng & his baronage Wenten forþ in her viage. **1338** R. Brunne *Chron.* (1810) 315 To Scotland now he fondes to redy his viage, With þritti þousand Walsh redy at his banere. **1375** Barbour *Bruce* v. 207 His spek discomfort thame all sua, That thai had left haill that viage, Na war a knycht of gret corage. **1422** tr. *Secreta Secret., Priv. Priv.* 204 Al this forsaydyn hostynges, viages, and trauaill done and fufillid weryn in lytill more space than thre Monthes. *a* **1450** *Knt. de la Tour* 51 It happed that..the squier come from a uiage that he hadde ben atte. **1475** *Bk. Noblesse* (Roxb.) 17 [He] had a gret discomfiture at the bataile of Agincourt..at his first viage. *a* **1513** Fabyan *Chron.* vi. clv. (1811) 143 Longe it were to tell all the circumstaunce of this vyage, & victoryes of the same. **1556** *Chron. Grey Friars* (Camden) 23 Thys yere the kynge made a grete army into Scotland by hys brother the duke of Glocester, in the wyche viage he wane Barwike. **1590** L. Lloyd *Dial Daies* Oct. 31 Mar. Scotus saith that he was slaine in his viage against the Parthians.

γ. **1523** Ld. Berners *Froiss.* I. xv. 15 The kyng sent..a great ambassade to syr Iohn of Heynaulte, praying hym..to kepe company with hym in his voiage agaynste the Scottis. **1549** *Compl. Scotl.* Ep. 4 The longinquite of his martial voyaige, ande the grite forse of the oriental pepil. **1584** B. R. tr. *Herodotus* II. 97 b, Sesostris dying,..hys sonne..vndertooke no voyage of warre, but remayned quiet in his kingdome. **1609** Dekker *Gull's Horn-bk.* D 4, If you be a souldier, talke how often you haue beene in action: as the Portingale voyage, Cales voiage, the Iland voiage. **1613–8** Daniel *Coll. Hist. Eng.* Wks. (Grosart) IV. 193 Godfrey of Bouillon..was the first that offered vp himselfe to this Famous Voyage. **1650** Fuller *Pisgah* II. x. 235 The Simeonites second voyage against the Amalekites in Mount Seir.

†**b.** In the phr. *to make* (or *do*) *a voyage. Obs.*

1387 Trevisa *Higden* (Rolls) I. 89 Mithridates..helde þe kyngdom þre and fourty ȝere, in þe whiche tyme he dede many viage, and many faire victories hadde. *c* **1470** Henry *Wallace* III. 118 The knycht Fenweik conwoide the caryage; He had on Scottis maid mony schrewide wiage. **1546** *Supplic. Poore Commons* (E.E.T.S.) 76 Achabe kyng of Israel, when he intended to make a viage, and to take by force the country..of Ramoth Giliade. **1598** Drayton *Heroical Ep.* Notes (1599) 25 In the great voyage Edward the second made against the Scots, at the battell at Striueling [etc.]. **1686** *Voy. Emp. China* in *Misc. Cur.* (1708) III. 179 The Emperour of China made a Voyage into Eastern Tartary, in the beginning of this Year 1682.

†**c.** *voyage royal*, an expedition undertaken by a king in person. *Obs.*

1544 tr. *Littleton's Tenures* (1574) 20 When the king maketh a voyage roial in to Scotland for to subdue yᵉ Scots. *a* **1548** Hall *Chron., Edw. IV*, 248 Euen now his [Edward IV's] Feuer tercian, of the whiche he had languished sore, sithe his voyage royall into Fraunce, was sodainly turned into a vncurable quartain. **1601** R. Johnson *Kingd. & Commw.* (1603) 157 More to be dreaded for their..furious incursions, then..that they are able to raise, or undertake any voiage royal. **1612** Davies *Why Ireland*, etc. 44 For his [*sc.* Richard II's] first voyage in the eighteenth yeare of his raigne (which was indeed a Voyage-Royall) was made vpon another motiue. **1690** (*title*), The Royal Voyage; or, the Irish Expedition.

†**3.** An enterprise, undertaking, or adventure of a private character (in early use implying the making of a journey). *Obs.*

13.. *Gaw. & Gr. Knt.* 535 þen þenkkez Gawan ful sone, Of his anious uyage. *c* **1374** Chaucer *Troylus* III. 732 Ek diane I the biseke That this viagge be nat to the loth. **1390** Gower *Conf.* I. 353 This worthi kniht of his corage Hath undertake the viage. **1412–20** Lydg. *Chron. Troy* I. 2511, I am meved of pite,..þat ȝe of volunte..List take on ȝow þis merveillous viage. *c* **1489** Caxton *Blanchardyn* lii. 198 Madame, yf your wyll be, I shall gladli tak this vyage in hande, and I shall neuer rest noo where tyl that I haue founde blanchardyn. **1567** *Satir. Poems Reform.* iv. 59 Sum vncouth vaiage I purpoisit prepare, Bot not sa vncouth as was preparit for me. **1579** Twyne *Phis. agst. Fortune* II. lxxxiii. 266 b, Takyng in hand an easie viage towardes thine ende. **1598** Shaks. *Merry W.* II. i. 185 If hee should intend this voyage toward my wife, I would turne her loose to him. **1611** Middleton & Dekker *Roaring Girl* III. i, I thinke I fight with a familiar, or the Ghost of a fencer, Sh' has wounded me gallantly, call you this a letcherous viage?

†**b.** In the phr. *to do* (or *make*) *a voyage. Obs.*

c **1374** Chaucer *Troylus* II. 75 He..caste and knew in goode plyte was þe moone To doon viage and take his way ful sone Vnto his neces paleys ther bysyde. *c* **1380** *Sir Ferumb.* 804 Y for-bed hem..fro þenne þay ne scholde go, Or ich hadde sum viage done & til hem come ageyn. **1387–8** T. Usk *Test. Love* I. v. (Skeat) l. 84 If thou drede suche jangleres, thy viage to make, understand wel [etc.]. **1611** Shaks. *Cymb.* I. iv. 169 If you make your voyage vpon her, and giue me directly to vnderstand, you haue preuayl'd, I am no further your Enemy.

4. A journey by sea or water from one place to another (usually to some distant place or country); a course or spell of sailing or navigation, *spec.* one in which a return is made to the starting-point; a cruise.

Arising from contextual uses of senses 1 and 2, and clearly separable from these only after the ME. period. For the phr. †*bon(e, boun, boon voyage* see Boon *a.* 2.

α. *c* **1310** *St. Brendan* 152 in *S. Eng. Leg.* I. 224 'Wendeþ forþ a-godes name: þat þis voyage were idol!' Seint Brendan & his breþeren to schipe wende anon. **1555** *Sc. Acts Mary* (1814) II. 495/1 That nane..cary ony victuallis talloun or flesche..except samekill at salbe thair necessare victualling for thair veyage. *a* **1578** Lindesay (Pitscottie) *Chron. Scot.* (S.T.S.) II. 121 The skipper of the schip..said 'God send ws better handsell and mair forder in our wayage.' **1641** *Sc. Acts Chas. I* (1870) V. 494/2 Ane impost..of tuo shilling scottes to be payed vpoun the tune of all shipes and vesshellis..be Natiues and four shillingis money foir-said to be payed be straingeres for ilke veadge. **1784** *Bishoprick Garl.* (1906) 52 There was a poor little lad that had come a trial vaige to sea. **1887** J. M. E. Saxby *Lads of Lunda* (1888) 123, I don't think there will be much done at the haaf this vaige.

β. *c* **1330** R. Brunne *Chron. Wace* (Rolls) 8840 When he wyste why þat he cam [to Ireland], & so fer viage for stones nam, He scorned þem on his langage. *c* **1400** Maundev. (1839) Prol. 4 It is longe tyme passed, that ther was no generalle Passage ne Vyage over the See. **1442** *Rolls of Parlt.* V. 60/2 [That] noon of the seid vesselles..attendyng to the same viage, be arrested for any viage of oure Souverain Lord ye King. **1492** *Act. Dom. Conc.* (1839) 275 þe proffitis & dewiteis..of þe said auchtane parte of a hale Raiss in zeland ..and als of half a danskin viage. **1506** *Acc. Ld. High Treas. Scot.* III. 206 To Thomas Hathowy to furnis the Kingis schip in the Northland the secund viage, for tymir. **1579** Twyne *Phil. agst. Fortune* I. i. 2 They that fare by Sea, they are caried away in the shypps, and feele not howe, and many tymes are at their viage ende before they be ware. **1587** Fleming *Contn. Holinshed* III. 1369/1 For want of vittels and other necessaries (needful in so long a viage)..[he] was inforced to set saile and returne for England. **1601** R. Johnson *Kingd. & Commw.* 6 The Portugales whose viages beyond the cape of Good Hope..are more true than in reason likely.

γ. **1485** *Naval Acc. Hen. VII* (1896) 25 Paid..to John Cappe..after the said voiage into the parties of Lumbardie ..for the stopping of lekes & castyng Balast. **1599** Hakluyt *Voy.* I. Pref. **2, There they shall read of Godredus the sonne of Olauus his voiage to the king of Norway. **1625** N. Carpenter *Geogr. Delineated* II. vii. (1635) 126 This North-west passage is a long voyage, and hath bin for a long time sought. **1626** Bacon *New Atl.* 12 The Navigation of the World (specially for remote Voiages) was greater then at this day. **1665** Manley *Grotius' Low C. Wars* 923 Where the Spanish Negotiation was short and safe, it enticed Seamen, by their good will, to avoid long Voyages. **1748** *Anson's Voy.* Introd., A Voyage round the World promises a species of information, of all others the most desirable and interesting. **1774** Goldsm. *Nat. Hist.* (1776) I. 346 Those who had set sail five months before, were not in the least farther advanced in their voyage, than those who waited for the favourable wind. **1820** Scoresby *Acc. Arctic Reg.* II. 165 Ships were sent out to different seas, and had prosperous voyages. **1867** Smyth *Sailor's Word-bk.*, *Voyage*, a journey by sea. It usually includes the outward and homeward trips, which are called passages. **1903** F. T. Bullen *Sea Wrack* 310 *note*, The round trip from home back to home again constitutes the 'voyage', all the port to port journeys are 'passages'.

fig. **1864** Browning *Jas. Lee's Wife* II. iv, With whom began Love's voyage full-sail.

b. In the phrases *to take* or *make a voyage*. Cf. 1 a. Also *transf.*

(*a*) *c* **1400** Maundev. (Roxb.) Pref. 2 Wald Godd þat þer werldly lordes ware at gude accorde, and..wald take þis haly viage ouer þe see. **1475** *Bk. Noblesse* (Roxb.) 12 The said king Edward..tooke his vyage to Cane withe xijᶜ shippis. *a* **1578** Lindesay (Pitscottie) *Chron. Scot.* (S.T.S.) II. 10 Thir men of weir tuk vayage and sailled to Scotland. **1596** Dalrymple tr. *Leslie's Hist. Scot.* I. 233 Quhen S. Columba did sayl in Yrland, thay to the Jle of Jon tuik thair vaiage. **1819** Keats *Lamia* II. 180 Fifty wreaths of smoke From fifty censers their light voyage took To the high roof.

(*b*) **14..** *Sir Beues* (O.) 388 Ouer they made gode viage. The sayll they drew, the wynd was good. **1475** *Nottingham Rec.* II. 387 We..purpose..incontinent þeruþon, as winde and weder wol serue, to make our viage into France. **1530** *Hickscorner* 820 For yf I myȝt make iii good vyages to Shoter's Hyl,..Than wolde I never travell the see more. *c* **1580** in *Eng. Hist. Rev.* July (1914) 518 This viadge ys to be made in 3 wekes yf winde and wether sarve. **1584** Powel *Lloyd's Cambria* 87 Cnute king of England about this time made a viage to Denmarke. **1648** J. Beaumont *Psyche* II. 179 It is a full Commission By which he made this voyage. **1669** Sturmy *Mariner's Mag.* IV. i. 139 In five Voyages made before that way, [I] knew by Experience there is a Current.

†**c.** A (single or return) passage or trip on a canal-boat. *Obs.*

1774 *Ann. Reg., Chron.* 145 From Manchester to Warrington..the third cabbin 1*s* for the passage or voyage upon the canal. **1805** Z. Allnutt *Navig. Thames* 15 The Toll of 4*d* per Ton a Voyage on all Barges. A Voyage, is a Trip to London and back again, being two Passages.

d. A flight through the air (or through space); *esp.* a trip in a balloon.

1667 Milton *P.L.* VII. 431 So stears the prudent Crane Her annual Voiage, born on Windes. **1726** Swift *Gulliver* III. ii. It was about ninety leagues distant, and our voyage lasted four days and an half. **1785** V. Lunardi *Five Aerial Voyages* (1786) 30 After a most delightful and glorious voyage of 46 miles, 36 over the water and 10 over land. **1826** *Mechanics' Mag.* VI. 285/2 An aerial voyage, remarkable for its duration, was accomplished at Paris on the 19th of September, 1784. **1860** *Chambers's Encycl.* I. 646/2 Before they [*sc.* fire-balloons] became obsolete, several remarkable voyages were made in them. **1893** Sir R. Ball *Story of Sun* 290 The Earth in its annual voyage round the sun.

e. *spec.* In marine insurance: (see quot.).

1848 Arnould *Marine Insur.* I. xii. I. 333 The voyage insured.., a technical term, which must be carefully distinguished from the actual voyage of the ship,..is a transit at sea from the terminus a quo to the terminus ad quem in a prescribed course of navigation..which is never set out in any policy.

f. *voyage of discovery* (Discovery 3), in fig. use.

1857 Ducange Anglicus *Vulg. Tong.*, *Voyage of discovery*, going out stealing. **1890** 'R. Boldrewood' *Col. Reformer* (1891) 227 After a voyage of discovery round the yard at full speed, [the cattle] return..into the lane.

5. Used *fig.* (in senses 1 or 4) to denote the course of human life (or some part of it), or the fate of persons after death.

1390 Gower *Conf.* III. 326 Fourtiene yer sche was of Age, Whan deth hir tok to his viage. **1423** Jas. I *Kingis Q.* xv, As the schip that sailith stereles,..So standis thou here..And wantis that suld gyde all thy viage. *c* **1430** Lydg. *Min. Poems* (Percy Soc.) 98 Cristallyne water to hym so comfortable. Al his viage bothe in breede and lengthe. **1526** *Pilgr. Perf.* (W. de W. 1531) 12 b, Man receyueth by grace all thynges expedyent and necessary for hym in his vyage and pilgrymage. **1529** Sir T. More *Dyaloge* I. Wks. 175/2 Yᵗ much more special assistence of god with his christen church in their spirituall viage. **1601** Shaks. *Jul. C.* IV. iii. 220 There is a Tide in the affayres of men, Which taken at the Flood, leades on to Fortune: Omitted, all the voyage of their life, Is bound in Shallowes, and in Miseries. **1604** T. Wright *Passions* VI. 345 Blocks and stones our ghostly enemies cast in the narrow way that leadeth to heaven, to hinder our voyage. **1697** Vanbrugh *Prov. Wife* V. v, So, now I am in for Hobbes's voyage; a great leap in the dark. **1705** Hickeringill *Priest-cr.* II. vi. 60 And what I say to Papists I say to all Protestants, if you like to be Priest-ridden, farewel—a good Voyage to you. **1771** Smollett *Humph. Cl.*, *Let. to Sir W. Phillips* 18 July, Among our fellow-lodgers at Berwick, was a couple from London, bound to Edinburgh on the voyage of matrimony. **1779** Cowper *Human Frailty* 17 Bound on a voyage of awful length,..A stranger to superior strength, Man vainly trusts his own. **1813** Shelley *Q. Mab.* IX. 174 Fear not then, Spirit, Death's disrobing hand..'Tis but the voyage of a darksome hour. **1877** Tennyson *Sir J. Franklin* 3 And thou..Art passing on thine happier voyage now Toward no earthly pole.

6. †**a.** The navigation of a particular sea-route; the course or route (to be) taken by a ship. *Obs.*

1581 Marbeck *Bk. of Notes* 1087 Vnder yᵉ name of Tharsis (as some think) is signified some sea yᵗ was farre of, and whose voyage was very long. **1694** W. King *Animadv. Acc. Denmark* i. 7 Any Sea-man, who is acquainted with that Voyage, will tell you that he would ten times rather venture amongst the Rocks of Norway in a Storm, than the Sands of England. **1755** Magens *Insurances* II. 111 The Mate being unacquainted with the Voyage and declaring himself to be so, shall nevertheless be obliged to remain with the Ship, if the Master requires it.

b. A vessel as fitted out for sailing.

1826 Kent *Comm.* (1858) III. xlvii. §209 When the voyage is ready, the master is bound to sail as soon as the wind and tide permit.

c. *Whaling.* (See quot.)

1859 Bartlett *Dict. Amer.* (ed. 2) 497 *Voyage*, among whalers, each man calls his share of the proceeds of the cruize, which he receives instead of wages, his voyage.

d. The quantity of fish taken in one trip or by one boat.

1897 *Clay & Co. Company Prospectus*, The daily arrival of vessels with voyages of live and fresh fish... The Pontoon where the voyages are landed from the vessels and sold.

7. A written account of a voyage, a book describing a voyage (or journey).

From the frequent use of the word in the titles of narratives of voyages.

1587 Hakluyt (*title*), A Notable Historie, containing foure Voyages, made by Certaine French Captaines into Florida. **1699** W. Hacke (*title*), A Collection of Original Voyages. **1704** Churchill (*title*), A Collection of Voyages and Travels, Some now first Printed from Original Manuscripts. **1796** H. Hunter tr. *St.-Pierre's Stud. Nat.* (1799) III. 21 Those of the same kind, which have been collected in the following Voyage, exhibit no regular difference from each other. *Ibid.* 284 The most authentic traditions of Historians, which I found in great numbers in the Voyages of Pausanias into Greece. **1877** Quaritch *Catalogue* 1476 De Bry's Collection of Voyages to the East and West Indies.

8. *attrib.* and *Comb.*, as *voyage-writer*; †**voyage food, provision,** = viaticum 1; **voyage policy** (see quot.).

1610 *Voyage food [see viaticum 1]. **1848** Arnould *Marine Insur.* I. ii. §1. I. 19 A *voyage policy is one in which the limits of the risk are designated in the policy by specifying a certain place at which the voyage is to begin. **1562** *Apol. Priv. Masse* (1850) 11 Their viaticum, as it is termed in the old canons, that is to say, their *voyage-provision. **1564** Harding *Answ. Jewel* ix. 123 So it be reuerently kepte for the viage prouision for the sicke, no catholike man will maineteine strife for the maner and order of keping. **1705** Addison *Italy, Pesaro* 165, I shall say nothing of the *Via Flaminia*, which has been describ'd by all the *Voyage-Writers that have pass'd it. **1717** Lady M. W. Montagu *Let. to C'tess Mar* 1 Apr., The manners of mankind do not differ so widely as our voyage writers would make us believe. **1757** Foote *Author* I. Wks. 1799 I. 137 Except Peter Hasty, the voyage-writer, he was as great a loss to the trade as any within my memory.

voyage (ˈvɔɪɪdʒ), *v.* Also 5 voiage, 5–6 **vyage**, 9 *dial.* **v'yage**, *Sc.* **vaeg.** [ad. F. *voyager*, †*voiager* (15th c.), or f. voyage *sb.*]

1. *intr.* To journey by land; to travel. Now *rare.*

1477 Caxton *Jason* 26 His legges were Royde like a voyager that had alle the day to fore haue voiaged or goon a Iourney. **1490** —— *Eneydos* xv. 57 And in vyagynge thurghe the landes, [fame] hideth her hede bytwyx the clowdes. **1642** Milton *Apol. Smect.* viii. 42 Although my life hath not bin unexpensive in learning, and voyaging about. **1673** Dryden *Marr. à la Mode* II. i, A gentleman, sir,..who has haunted the best conversations, and who, in short, has voyaged. **1778** Foote *Trip to Calais* I. Wks. 1799 II. 344 Nothing can be so vulgar in France, as voyaging about with one's wife. **1898** C. Lee *Paul Carah* ii. 30 Half over the States I've been, an' into Canady—v'yaged thousands o' miles, 'a b'lieve.

†**2.** To carry out an enterprise. *Obs.*⁻¹

c **1500** *Melusine* 171 The maister [of Rhodes] recounted.. all thauentures that had happed to them. 'By my feyth' said the kyng, 'ye haue worthyly vyaged.

3. To go by sea; to sail or cruise; to make a voyage or voyages. Also in fig. context.

1604 E. G[rimstone] *D'Acosta's Hist. Indies* IV. xxxi. 294 All that have voyaged thither, have been curious to carry seedes of all sorts, and all have grown. **1624** Donne *Ess. Div.* (1651) 37 Men which seek God by reason..are like Mariners which voyaged before the invention of the Compass. **1700** Pomfret *Reason* 133 Oh! what an ocean must be voyag'd o'er, To gain a prospect of the shining shore! **1725** Pope *Odyss.* I. 340 Voyaging to learn the direful art To taint with deadly drugs the barbed dart. **1779** Forrest *Voy. N. Guinea* 137 The Dutch ships, voyaging between New Guinea and Aroo, .. frequently see flocks of birds of Paradise. **1819** BYRON *Juan* II. xliii, He was a man of years, And long had voyaged through many a stormy sea. **1846** HAWTHORNE *Mosses* II. viii. (1864) 171 Having voyaged across the Atlantic for that sole purpose. **1875** *Chambers' Jrnl.* 2 Jan. 7 More than seventy merchant-ships, voyaging in almost every ocean.

fig. **1805** WORDSW. *Prelude* III. 63 His .. silent face, The marble index of a mind for ever Voyaging through strange seas of Thought, alone. **1819** SHELLEY *Lett.* Pr. Wks. 1888 II. 305, I have lately been voyaging in a sea without any pilot. *a* **1873** LYTTON *Pausanias* III. i. (1876) 220 Voyagers that never voyaged thither save in song. **1894** H. DRUMMOND *Ascent Man* 300 It is not for food that the plant-world voyages into foreign spheres, but to perfect the supremer labour of life.

b. *transf.* Of things: To move through the water or air. Also *fig.*

1834 H. MILLER *Scenes & Leg.* xvi. (1850) 243 In Britain .. it [the cholera] voyaged along the coasts with the speed of the trading vessels. **1853** KANE *Grinnell Exp.* xliii. (1856) 402 We could see them many fathoms below, voyaging again to the upper world. *a* **1864** HAWTHORNE *Amer. Note-bks.* (1879) I. 42 A log comes floating on, .. having voyaged .. hundreds of miles. **1878** STEVENSON *Inland Voy.* 178 Grand clouds still voyaged in the sky.

4. *trans.* To cross or travel over; to traverse; to sail over or on. Also *fig.*

1667 MILTON *P.L.* x. 471 Long were to tell What I have don, what sufferd, with what paine Voyag'd th' unreal, vast, unbounded deep Of horrible confusion. **1725** POPE *Odyss.* v. 361 Him, thus voyaging the deeps below, From far .. The King of Ocean saw. **1793** COLERIDGE *Lines Autumnal Even.* 44 O heed the spell, and hither wing your way, Like far-off music, voyaging the breeze! **1849** J. WILSON in *Blackw. Mag.* LXVI. 259 Last time we voyaged the Loch you said a few words. **1890** *Century Mag.* Aug. 636/1 The Rhône of to-day must be something like the Rhine of fifty years ago, though much less voyaged now than that was then.

‖**voyagé** (vwajaʒe), *a.* *Ballet.* [Fr., pa. pple. of *voyager* to travel.] Designating a movement in which the pose is held during progression; usu. as ***arabesque(s) voyagée(s)***. Also *absol.* as *sb.*

1931 G. W. BEAUMONT *Dict. Technical Dance Terms* 30 *Voyagé*, .. travelled, travelling. E.g., *arabesque voyagée*. **1957** G. B. L. WILSON *Penguin Dict. Ballet* 278 *Voyagé*, .. a movement across the stage during which the dancer holds a particular pose, usually an arabesque, and progresses in a series of hops or small jumps. **1976** *New Yorker* 26 Jan. 94/3 Tharp several times reinforces the point with moments swiped from the classics: the Wilis' arabesques voyagées.

voyageable (ˈvɔɪɪdʒəb(ə)l), *a.* [f. VOYAGE *v.* + -ABLE.] That can be sailed over; navigable.

1819 SEAGER *Suppl. Johnson*, *Voyageable* .., that may be sailed or travelled over. The existence, or at least the propriety, of this word may be inferred from Milton's use of Unvoyageable. **1882** STEVENSON *Men & B.* 388 There lies between them, instead of the voyageable straits, that great gulf over which no man can pass.

voyager (ˈvɔɪɪdʒə(r)). Also 6 vyager, -eour, 6–7 viager. [ad. OF. *veaigier*, *voi-*, *voyag(i)er* (F. *voyageur*), or f. VOYAGE *v.* + -ER¹.]

1. One who journeys; a traveller by land.

1477 [see VOYAGE *v.* 1]. **1532** MORE *Confut. Tindale* Wks. 616/1 Them coumpte we stylle for vyagers and pylgrimes .. towarde the same place .. that we walke. **1686** BURNET *Trav.* 3 It may look like a presumptuous affectation to be reckoned among Voyagers, if he attempts to say anything upon so short a ramble, and concerning places so much visited, and by consequence so well known. **1833** L. RITCHIE *Wand. by Loire* 20 The Patache is a vehicle that the traveller .. will frequently have recourse to. Its voyagers are a grade lower in society than those of the diligence. **1845** M. PATTISON *Ess.* (1889) I. 11 Such a voyager, if it has ever been his hap to turn his feet to Orleans. **1885** *Sat. Rev.* 23 Oct. 532/2 Let any student of life .. go to a terminus when a train has come in, and watch the faces of the voyagers as they battle for 'their things'.

†**b.** ***knight voyager***, a knight errant. *Obs.*

c **1500** *Melusine* 362 The kyng vnderstod by the report of som knightes vyageours, that there was in the grete Armanye a Castel.

2. One who goes upon, or takes part in, a voyage or voyages by sea; a navigator.

1622 DRAYTON *Poly-olb.* XIX. 298 Fenton next, and Jackman .., Both Voyagers, that were with famous Frobosher. *c* **1645** HOWELL *Lett.* (1650) II. xl. 52 You go on to prefer my Captivity in this Fleet to that of a Voyager at Sea. **1656** COWLEY *Pindar. Odes, Resurrect.* i, Not Winds to Voyagers at Sea, Nor Showers to Earth more necessary be, .. Than Verse to Virtue. **1709** STEELE *Tatler* No. 34 ¶5 It is usual with young Voyagers, as soon as they land upon a Shore, to begin their Accounts of the Nature of the People. **1783** W. F. MARTYN *Geog. Mag.* II. 529 Voyagers .. are much divided in their accounts of the natives. **1812** BYRON *Ch. Har.* II. xci, Long shall the voyager, with th' Ionian blast, Hail the bright clime of battle and of song. **1860** GOSSE *Rom. Nat. Hist.* 1 The Arctic voyagers have seen King Winter on his throne. **1879** E. P. WRIGHT *Anim. Life* 119 The Sea Lion of voyagers in the southern seas.

b. *transf.* and *fig.*, in various applications.

1691 NORRIS *Pract. Disc.* (1707) IV. 189 She prays for the little Infant Voyager, That he may so pass the Waves of this troublesome World as finally to come to the Land of Everlasting Life. **1819** SHELLEY *Lett.* Pr. Wks. 1880 IV. 147 Your boat will be to the ocean of water, what this earth is to the ocean of aether—a prosperous and swift voyager. **1826** *Mechanics' Mag.* VI. 286/2 In this region the voyager [in a balloon] sailed till half-past nine o'clock. **1847** EMERSON *Poems, Humble Bee* 15 Insect lover of the sun, .. sailor of the atmosphere, .. Voyager of light and noon. **1890** *Spectator* 7 June 793/1 This rapid voyager [the dragon-fly] passes over you, proceeds beyond you .., then turns [etc.].

‖**voyageur** (vwajaʒœr). [F.; see prec.] In Canada, a man employed by the fur companies in carrying goods to and from the trading posts on the lakes and rivers; a Canadian boatman.

1793 J. MACDONELL *Diary* 6 June in C. M. Gates *Five Fur-Traders* (1933) 75 Lost the half of this day by rain .. a perfect nuisance to us voyageurs. **1809** A. HENRY *Trav.* 18 In ascending the Longue Sault, a distance of three miles, my canoes were three times unladen, and, together with their freight, carried on the shoulders of the voyageurs. **1842** A. COMBE *Physiol. Digestion* (ed. 4) 90 St Martin returned to Canada .. [and] engaged as a voyageur with the Hudson's Bay Fur Company. **1893** *Nation* (N.Y.) 17 Aug. 121/2 At the nightly bivouac, to the astonishment of the voyageurs, the noises continued.

attrib. **1903** *Daily Mail* 5 Sept. 5/6 The party was put into one of the large voyageur flat-bottomed boats.

voyaging (ˈvɔɪɪdʒɪŋ), *vbl. sb.* [f. VOYAGE *v.* + -ING¹.] The action of the verb (now usually of journeying by sea).

1611 COTGR., *Voyagement*, a voyaging, trauelling, iourneying. **1647** HEXHAM I, A viaging, *een reysinge*. **1706** E. WARD *Wooden World Diss.* (1708) 8 He was Monarch of far more Territories than ever he touch'd at in all his Voyagings. **1823** J. BADCOCK *Dom. Amusem.* 165 Native of a port and given to voyaging. **1856** KANE *Arct. Expl.* II. xvii. 182, I deemed it best to keep up the appearance of ordinary voyaging. **1889** CLARK RUSSELL *Marooned* xiv. (1891) 97 The marine habits of thought I had carried away with me from my early voyagings.

attrib. **1853** LYNCH *Self-Improv.* ii. 25 It is now hurrah! for outset on many a voyaging enterprise. **1891** T. HARDY *Tess* xl, I have separated from my wife for personal, not voyaging, reasons.

b. *transf.* and *fig.*

1837 CARLYLE *Fr. Rev.* III. VII. vii, Our poor Convention, after such voyaging, just entering harbour, so to speak, has struck on the bar. **1842** KINGSLEY *Lett.* (1878) I. 112 We will not listen when men tell us that we can reach Him by weary voyaging on the ocean of intellect. **1862** G. LONG tr. *M. Aurelius' Thoughts* ix. §30. 156 Look down from above on the countless herds of men and their countless solemnities, and the infinitely varied voyagings in storms and calms.

voyal, var. VIOL² *Naut.*

‖**voyant** (vwajɑ̃), *a.* Fem. **voyante** (-ɑ̃t). [Fr.] Showy, gaudy, flashy; *spec.* of clothes, appearance, etc.

1906 *Punch* 18 Apr. 286/3 'Anno Domini' .. whom one would *expect* to be smart and *voyante*, is simply the dowdiest, quietest of mice. **1927** U. M. LYON *Etiquette* x. 113 Anything *voyant* in ties, deplorable always, is doubly so at his wedding. **1937** G. FRANKAU *More of Us* xv. 162 Tactful then mentioned he, maybe the hat—The whole costume indeed—was 'rather voyant'. 'Looks the complete tart if it comes to that', Hissed Innocent.

‖**voyant**, *sb.* [Fr., lit. 'seer'.] A visionary; one gifted with an especial degree of mental perception.

[**1924** E. RICKWORD tr. A. Rimbaud in *Rimbaud: Boy & Poet* 203, I say that one must be a *visionary* (voyant), make oneself a *visionary*. The Poet makes himself a *visionary* by a long immense and reasoned *derangement of all the senses*.] **1938** *Times Lit. Suppl.* 21 May 353/2 The systematic derangement of all the senses that he [*sc.* Rimbaud] envisaged as one of the duties of the *voyant* or visionary poet has been attempted. **1958** *Spectator* 22 Aug. 257/3 The emblem of this evil society is the head of a dead pig .. animated by flies and by the imagination of the *voyant*, Simon. **1972** E. LUCIE-SMITH in Cox & Dyson *20th-Cent. Mind* II. xiv. 483 A way of linking Dada to an older and more specifically French tradition, that of the *voyant*, which could be traced to nineteenth-century writers such as Rimbaud and Lautréamont.

voyd, -ance, -e(e, etc., variants of VOID *a.*, -ANCE, -EE, etc.

†**voye.** *Obs. rare.* [a. OF. *voye*, *voie* (F. *voie*):—L. *via* way.] Way.

1541 *St. Papers Hen. VIII* (1834) III. 329 They can pay no subcedy, for as moch as they be charged other divers voyes. *a* **1578** LINDESAY (Pitscottie) *Chron. Scot.* (S.T.S.) I. 11 Quhan he hes done, fast thy voyes vend To Athoill that most hie cuntrie.

voyed(e, obs. f. VOID *v.*

voyeur (vwɑːˈjɜː(r)). Fem. **-euse** (ɜːz). [a. Fr., f. *voir* to see.] **1.** A person whose sexual desires are stimulated or satisfied by covert observation of the sex organs or sexual activities of others. Cf. *peeping Tom* s.v. PEEPING *ppl. a.*²; *scopophiliac* s.v. SCOPOPHILIA.

1900 H. BLANCHAMP tr. *Féré's Sexual Instinct* vi. 142 The houses of ill-fame have a *clientèle* of 'voyeurs' of both sexes. **1913** E. JONES *Papers on Psycho-Anal.* xv. 341 The patient, who had frequently indulged in pædicatio, was a pronounced *voyeur*. **1937** L. BROMFIELD *Rains Came* I. xlv. 192 A moment after she had disappeared the Major came out, and like a *voyeur* Ransome regarded him sharply to discover .. whether she had made any progress. **1952** S. KAUFFMANN *Philanderer* (1957) xii. 188 The same Jake Simon who later made him a *voyeur* before puberty. **1956** C. P. SNOW *Homecomings* xxxi. 214 Mrs Beauchamp, day-dreaming of a voyeuse's paradise, seeping herself into invisibility. **1972** *Daily Tel.* 7 Jan. 11/4 The hopeful voyeurs were to be disappointed for after this first fine flurry of bosoms and buttocks not a stitch was shed in the rest of the 45 minutes. **1978** C. P. SNOW *Realists* viii. 236 He may have been a bit of a voyeur (he took extravagant pleasure in studying a love-object in bed). **1980** *Times Lit. Suppl.* 10 Oct. 1139/2 The film seems to miss a trick .., in that these two never get it together, but most voyeurs should be satisfied with what is otherwise on offer.

2. *transf.* and *fig.*

1956 C. W. MILLS *Power Elite* vii. 162 The miser .. is an impotent voyeur of the economic system. **1958** *Times* 2 Oct. 3/2 The play .. draws a firm line between those immersed in living and those plaintively watching them at it; and Hauptmann's sympathy goes to the *voyeurs*. **1967** *Spectator* 6 Oct. 404/3 Those films and TV programmes which argue that these are realities only moral cowards would evade seem to me to risk turning us all into *voyeurs* of pain, connoisseurs of private misery. **1978** J. IRVING *World according to Garp* iii. 56, I was brought up to be a spectator... I was raised to be a voyeur.

Hence **voˈyeur** *v. intr.*, to obtain gratification in the manner of a voyeur; usu. as *pres. pple.* or *vbl. sb.*

1959 P. BULL *I know Face* xi. 195 She found herself dressing and undressing between two rows of hanging wardrobes, which involved delightful voyeuring for the gents manipulating the lights on the gantry above. **1970** K. GILES *Murder Pluperfect* iii. 72 'My girl,' said the Inspector, shamelessly voyeuring, lusciously and rashly voyeuring. **1980** M. GILBERT *Death of Favourite Girl* xxv. 240 His conscience wasn't all that clear, if he'd been out doing a spot of voyeuring.

voyeurism (vwɑːˈjɜːrɪz(ə)m). [f. prec. + -ISM.] The state or condition of being a voyeur; scopophilia. Also *transf.* and *fig.*

1924 J. S. VAN TESLAAR tr. *Stekel's Disorders of Instincts & Emotions* II. 341 *Voyeurism*, erotic gratification experienced at looking at another's sexual organs; morbid desire to peep into secrets. **1927** BRYAN & STRACHEY tr. *K. Abraham's Sel. Papers* iii. 83 If sublimation does not take place then a perversion (*voyeurism* and exhibitionism) arises. **1953** E. PODOLSKY *Encycl. Abberrations* 538/1 Voyeurism takes the place of the normal sexual act. **1958** *Oxf. Mag.* 8 May 409/1 Oxford .. seems to appeal to a disagreeable mixture of envy and voyeurism. **1969** *Daily Tel.* 25 Apr. 19/5 There is a feeling that more and more actresses are being asked to take their clothes off at auditions .. as a form of voyeurism. **1976** *Listener* 25 Nov. 682/3 A beggar's expression captured by a camera costing enough to feed, clothe and house him for .. maybe five years. Is this kind of photography good or bad? .. Is it just an obscene form of voyeurism, a record of what one privileged class finds quaint or interesting in another? **1980** *Times Lit. Suppl.* 7 Nov. 1258/3 *Rain on the Roof* is not much more than the averagely good television play featuring voyeurism, adultery and sudden bloody death. **1985** *Times* 21 Jan. 3/3 Many senior politicians have been appalled by the fate of the women, whose sexual activities have been exposed in a bout of national voyeurism.

voyeurist (vwɑːˈjɜːrɪst), *sb.* and *a.* [f. as prec. + -IST.] **A.** *sb.* = VOYEUR 1. **B.** *adj.* = VOYEURISTIC *a.*

1955 J. F. OLIVEN *Sexual Hygiene & Pathol.* xxi. 424 The severe 'compulsive' voyeurist .. is an obsessed .. individual. **1960** *Guardian* 6 Jan. 1/7 One father .. 'yielding to his exhibitionist-voyeurist impulses', regularly went off and joined a nudist colony. **1970** G. GREER *Female Eunuch* 165 Such observers have a vested interest in the detection of love affairs because of the particular voyeurist pleasures they afford. **1980** *Times Lit. Suppl.* 3 Oct. 1112/3 The cool meticulous detail in which these and other depravities are related .. has an obsessive and at times voyeurist tone.

voyeuristic (vwɑːjɜːˈrɪstɪk), *a.* [f. as prec. + -ISTIC.] Of or pertaining to voyeurism. Cf. VOYEURIST *a.*

1929 in Calverton & Schmalhausen *Sex in Civilization* 593 One day when we were stopping at a hotel he made me gratify his voyeuristic tendency. **1960** *Arch. Gen. Psychiatry* III. 317/2 N. T. is interesting because of his unusual voyeuristic habits. **1973** *Daily Tel.* 12 June 14/2 The British censor has made his cutting mark .. so that the camera does not linger with quite the same sort of voyeuristic dedication as it did when the original version was shown at the Berlin Film Festival. **1981** *Times* 14 Sept. 18/8 The dangers of 'voyeuristic' leisure centred on the television set. **1984** *Listener* 26 Apr. 38/3 A certain arrogance in their dealings with the Divis Street tenants, a voyeuristic interest in the more sensational aspects of life in Belfast.

Hence **voyeuˈristically** *adv.*

1967 *Spectator* 14 July 48/1 The sexual autobiography .. of a Victorian gentleman who early in life became voyeuristically obsessed. **1982** *New Musical Express* 30 Oct. 28/1 A slick, flashy, voyeuristically nasty horror movie. **1985** *Times* 6 Mar. 10/1 The fact that the majority of AIDS patients are homosexual dramatizes the illness almost voyeuristically for the population at large.

voymbe, voyme, obs. Sc. varr. WOMB *sb.*

voyol, var. VIOL² *Naut.*

‖**voyou** (vwaju). [Fr.] A street urchin; a lout or hooligan.

1901 *Pall Mall Mag.* Feb. 195 But indeed the Hooligan, under the name of rough, .. *voyou* .. has been with us long, and not in this country alone. **1913** G. DU MAURIER *Martian* 61 'La flotte de Passy', as we called the Passy voyous. **1933** *Times Lit. Suppl.* 4 May 308/3 His curious friendship with a *voyou*. **1980** R. GRAYSON *Monterant Affair* vi. 50 She had fallen in love with one of the 'voyous' of Paris, a brash scoundrel living on his wits.

voys, obs. f. VOICE *sb.*

‖**vozhd** (voʒd). [Russ., lit. = 'chief'.] A leader, one who is in supreme authority: applied esp. to the Russian statesman Joseph Stalin (1879–1953).

1940 E. LYONS *Stalin* xxvii. 247 The 'leader of the world proletariat', the 'greatest representative of creative Marxism', the 'great machinist of locomotive history'... These are typical titles bestowed on the *Vozhd*, the Leader, by officials who owed their jobs and their lease on life to Stalin. **1959** D. W. TREADGOLD *Twentieth Cent. Russia* xviii. 289 Even the top functionaries were subject to Stalin's supreme power, and the word *Vozhd* (Leader) came to be used openly to acknowledge and proclaim that fact. **1978** *Encounter* Feb. 42/1 The *Vozhd* of Moscow made his exit in triumph.

‖**vrac.** *Obs.* Also 7 vrack. [F. dial. (Channel Islands).] The name given in the Channel Islands to a fish resembling a carp. Also *attrib.*

1673 *News from Channel* in *Harl. Misc.* (1809) III. 505 A large fish we call a Vrack-fish. **1694** FALLE *Jersey* ii. 75 But the most common, and to be had at all times, is a Fish we call Vrac, in shape and taste very much like a Carp, and may be called the Sea-carp, with several others. **1742** *De Foe's Tour Gt. Brit.* (1769) III. 341 Here [in Jersey] is the Mullet, red and grey, the Vrac, or Sea-carp, and the Bar.

vrack, Sc. variant of WRACK.

‖**vraic** (vreɪk). [F. dial. (Channel Islands) *vraic*, also *vrec*, *vrac*: see WRACK *sb.* and cf. VAREC.] A seaweed found in the Channel Islands, used for fuel and manure.

1610 W. FOLKINGHAM *Art of Survey* I. x. 30 Vraic or Orewood, (Alga Marina) is diuersly applyed for soyling. **1674** BLOUNT *Glossogr.* (ed. 4), *Vraic*, a kind of Sea-weed, of which they make fuel in the isles of Jersey and Gernsey. **1694** FALLE *Jersey* ii. 67 'Tis a Sea-weed; but a Weed more valuable to Us than the choicest Plant that grows in our Gardens. We call it Vraic;..and it grows on the Rocks about the Island. **1736** [W. R. CHETWOOD] *Voy. Vaughan* vii. II. 203 For Fuel..they make use of a Sea Weed, by the Inhabitants call'd Vraic [*printed* Vraù]. **1742** *De Foe's Tour Gt. Brit.* (ed. 3) III. 269 Their Manure is Sea-weed, call'd Vraic, of which we have taken notice above. *a* **1847** ELIZA COOK *Song Seaweed* xxix, The Vraic! the Vraic! pile it on to the fire. **1862** ANSTED *Channel Isl.* IV. xx. 469 The load of fresh vraic is computed to give three bushels of ashes. **1881** B. WEBBER *In Luck's Way* I. i, Amid this wilderness of rock and vraic and wrinkled sand.

attrib. **1865** MRS. L. L. CLARKE *Common Seaweeds* Concl. 138, I have turned over the *vraic*-heaps as they were carted up from the lowest tide.

Hence '**vraicker**, one who gathers vraic. '**vraicking**, the gathering of vraic. Also *attrib.*

1835 H. D. INGLIS *Channel Isl.* 64 At half tide, or low water multitudes of carts and horses, boats and vraickers, cover the beach. *Ibid.* 63 The vraicking parties consisting of eight, ten, or twelve persons. **1852** LANE CLARKE *Guernsey & Jersey* iii. 57 For a walk or a ride to either of these bays on a vraicing day. **1862** ANSTED *Channel Isl.* I. vi. 123 It is only used..during the vraicking season. *Ibid.* IV. xxii. 515 Vraicking in the Channel Islands is a custom that time has hallowed into an institution.

vraik, obs. Sc. f. WRACK.

vrail, southern dial. f. FRAIL *sb.*[1]

vraini, southern ME. var. FRAYNE *v.*

‖**vrai réseau** (vrɛ rezo). [Fr., = true net.] The fine net ground used in making Brussels lace; also, any net ground for lace made by needle or bobbins as opposed to machine. Cf. RÉSEAU I.

1865 F. B. PALLISER *Hist. Lace* vii. 104 It is the fineness of the thread which renders the real Brussels ground (vrai réseau) so costly. **1900** E. JACKSON *Hist. Hand-Made Lace* vii. 58 The ground was of the *vrai réseau*, or needle-point mesh, now seldom seen. **1953** M. POWYS *Lace & Lace-Making* iv. 29 This specimen has the Fond Rond which was used just before and contemporary with the Vrai Réseau de Valenciennes which is a diamond mesh. **1973** G. POND *Introd. Lace* iii. 28 Old Brussels lace is of fine texture and rich in design..It was often made..in separate sprays sewn on net, which in the earlier days was hand-made and known as 'Vrai réseau' to distinguish it from the machine-made net.

‖**vraisemblable** (vrɛsɑ̃blabl), *a.* (*sb.*) [Fr., f. *vrai* true + *semblable* like.] Believable, likely, plausible. Also *absol.* as *sb.* (esp. *collect.*).

1830 *New Monthly Mag.* XXX. 5/1 How far all this is fact, we have no means of ascertaining, but the vraisemblable is well preserved, and if not true..is bien trouve. **1841** GEO. ELIOT *Let.* 13 Nov. (1954) I. 121, I was amused with your sharp remarks on the advertisement... I immediately perceived them to be vraisemblable. **1876** J. D. HOOKER *Let.* 17 Aug. in L. Huxley *Life & Lett. J. D. Hooker* (1918) II. xlv. 366 The whole of the vraisemblable of the latter falls before the Darwinian Gospel. **1898** E. LYNN LYNTON *Let.* 23 Feb. in G. S. Layard *Mrs. Lynn Linton* (1901) xvii. 228, I have had your sketch... Cleverly done..not very *vraisemblable* in the man's character. **1957** D. PIPER *Eng. Face* ii. 37 The portrait that Sittow painted of Henry VII.. is completely *vraisemblable*. **1969** *Listener* 24 July 99/1 A nobleman..reproved an actor for not holding a scythe as a labourer does: he got a lecture on the elements of the *vraisemblable*. Stage-scything is not like scything. **1978** *Times* 22 Aug. 13/4 Sir John Colville's delightful speculations..on what would have happened if George Washington had lost seemed to be remarkably *vraisemblable*.

‖**vraisemblance** (vrɛsɑ̃blɑ̃s). [F. (16th c.), f. *vrai* true + *semblance* appearance, semblance.]

1. An appearance of truth; verisimilitude.

1802 SCOTT *Let.* 8 Sept. (1932) I. 156 To give to fiction itself the charms of truth or at least of *vraisemblance*. **1831** SCOTT *Quentin D.* Introd., You remove from the mind the vraisemblance, the veracity, of the whole representation. **1841** LADY BLESSINGTON *Idler in France* viii. I. 170 There is a fearful *vraisemblance* in some of the scenes with all that one has read or pictured to oneself, as daily occurring during the terrible days of the Revolution. **1880** *Standard* 10 Dec., He would have given a greater air of fairness and vraisemblance to the story.

2. A representation, picture.

1853 'C. BEDE' *Verdant Green* III. ii, Miss Patty's taper fingers transferred to paper the vraisemblance of a pair of sturdy Bondagers.

vraith, vrak, obs. Sc. ff. WRATH, WRACK.

vrakel, southern var. FRAKEL *a. Obs.*

vram, southern ME. var. FROM.

vrampol, southern var. FRAMPOLD *Obs.*

vran, obs. Sc. var. WREN.

vrang(us, etc., obs. (or dial.) Sc. ff. WRONG(OUS, etc.

†**vray**, *a. Obs. rare.* [a. OF. *vray* (F. *vrai*), reduced form of *verai* VERY *a.*] True.

1460 *Rolls of Parlt.* V. 382/2 His derrest Cousyn Richard, vray and rightfull heire. **1474** CAXTON *Chesse* III. ii. (1883) 89 And none may be vraye and trewe with oute other.

vrayth, obs. Sc. form of WRATH.

vrbaite (vəˈbaːaɪt). *Min.* [ad. Czech *vrbait* (B. Ježek 1912, in *Rozpravy České Akad.* XXI. XXVI. 2), f. the name of K. *Vrba* (1845–1922), Bohemian mineralogist: see -ITE[1].] A sulphide of thallium, mercury, arsenic, and antimony, $Tl_4Hg_3Sb_2As_8S_{20}$, found as dark grey, tabular or prismatic, orthorhombic crystals.

1913 *Mineral Mag.* XVI. 375 Vrbaite... Found.. embedded in realgar and orpiment from Allchar, Macedonia. **1973** *Mineral. Abstr.* XXIV. 22/2 The structure was determined on vrbaite from Allchar, Macedonia, the type locality... Vrbaite is the first structure with mixed (As, Sb) chains.

‖**vṛddhi** (ˈvrɪdhɪ). Also **vriddhi**. [Skr., lit. 'increase'.] In Sanskrit grammar, the strongest grade of an ablaut-series of vowels; also, the process of phonetic change whereby vowels of the middle grade are strengthened to achieve this grade. Cf. GUNA.

1841 [see GUNA sb.]. **1916** A. A. MACDONELL *Vedic Gram. for Students* 5 Beside the Guṇa syllables appear, but much less frequently, the syllables **ai, au, ār** (**āl** does not occur), which are called Vṛddhi by the same authorities [*sc.* the Indian grammarians] and may be regarded as a lengthened variety of the Guṇa syllables. **1965** G. Y. SHEVELOV *Prehist. of Slavic* 116 More important features which led to the rise of length in I[ndo-]E[uropean] were the special kind of morphological analogy called *vṛddhi* (the name used by O[ld] I[ndian] grammarians to denote reflexes of long diphthongs in OI) and the loss of laryngeals. **1979** *Trans. Philol. Soc.* 150 It is time to break away from Herzfeld's notion that fortresses are 'pflanzenbewachsener boden' or 'saatland', and that the vriddhi of initial *u* was *ā*.

vrech, southern ME. var. FRECK *a.*

vrechit, -nese, obs. Sc. ff. WRETCHED, -NESS.

vrecliche, southern var. FRECKLY *adv. Obs.*

vreend, southern dial. var. FRIEND.

vreit, obs. Sc. form of WRITE *v.*

vreo, vret, vridom, southern ME. varr. FREE *a.*, FRET *v.*[1], FREEDOM.

vriesia (ˈvriːzɪə). [mod.L. (J. Lindley 1843, in *Bot. Reg.* XXIX. 10), f. the name of W. H. de *Vriese* (1806–62) Dutch botanist + -IA[1].] A perennial herbaceous plant of the genus *Vriesia* (family Bromeliaceæ), native to South or Central America and bearing rosettes of linear leaves and spikes of yellow, red, or white flowers.

1843 *Bot. Reg.* XXIX. 10 (*heading*) Parrot-flowered Vriesia. **1902** L. H. BAILEY *Cycl. Amer. Hort.* IV. 1957/1 Vriesias are..tropical American stiff-leaved plants. **1979** *Daily Tel.* 17 Nov. 10/1 Another group [of bromeliads], the vriesias, have flowers that at one moment look like tongues of flame, and at others you think they are formed like cuttlefish.

‖**vriester.** *Obs.*[−1] [Du. and Flem. *vrijster*, f. *vrijen* to court, woo.] A girl.

1652 FELTHAM *Low-Countries* (1659) 41 Not a Country Uriester but can handle an oar, steer a boat, raise a mast.

vril. [Invented by Lytton.] A mysterious force imagined as having been discovered by the people described in one of Lytton's novels.

1871 LYTTON *Coming Race* vii. 47 These people consider that in vril they have arrived at the unity in natural energic agencies, which has been conjectured by many philosophers. **1884** *Harper's Mag.* Dec. 154/2 Just as..Tish saw the Ana voyaging in their vril-cars over the mountains and the valleys. **1888** *Pall Mall G.* 27 Dec. 4/1 If so,..we are within hailing distance of the discovery of vril.

‖**vrille** (vril). *Aeronaut.* [Fr., = spin.] A tail-spin; also, a spinning manœuvre engaged in deliberately as part of an aerobatic display.

1918 B. HALL *In the Air* iv. 32 He is trained on the rapid machines and when perfected is sent to the acrobatic school where they are taught all sorts of stunts, such as looping, vrille, tail and wing slips, and all the modern stunts. **1918** W. J. ABBOT *Aircraft & Submarines* 115 The modern airplane is naturally so stable that if *not* interfered with it will always attempt to right itself before the dreaded *vrille* occurs. **1919** [see TAILSPIN *sb.* a]. **1965** *Amer. Speech* XL. 13 /vr-/ can be attested, also in more recent *vrille* and in a proper name.

vrith, southern dial. variant of FRITH *sb.*[2] 3.

vrocht, obs. (or dial.) Sc. pa. t. WORK *v.*

vroefrien, southern var. FROVER *v. Obs.*

vroom (vrʊm). *colloq.* (orig. *U.S.*). Also varoom. [Echoic.] The roaring noise of a motor vehicle accelerating or travelling at speed. Also as *v. intr.*, to make such a noise; to travel or accelerate at speed; as *v. trans.*, to rev (an engine) with such a sound. Also reduplicated and as *int.*

1967 M. J. ARLEN in *New Yorker* 21 Jan. 76 To go varooming all over the desert in a couple of jeeps. **1968** L. DEIGHTON *Only when I Larf* iv. 48, I..shaved off my moustache. Vroom vroom. **1969** *Time* 2 May 33 The foursome would prefer tough scramblers, 'with big drive sprockets, knobby wheels—and more vroom'. **1970** *Atlantic Monthly* Oct. 75 The trooper lies on his back..reading *Hot Rod* magazine, hearing the vroom-vroom of engines. **1971** 'H. CALVIN' *Poison Chasers* vii. 93 The car stood at the red light with the engine making impatient vroom noises. **1971** *Time* 19 July 59/2 Just give me ten showgirls out here, and varoom, the young guys'll come out of Los Angeles in first gear. **1973** J. DI MONA *Last Man at Arlington* (1974) IV. xv. 195 A bullet varoomed over his head. **1974** *Guardian* 21 Mar. 11/2 A score of big bad BSA's vrooming through a sleepy one-pub town. **1975** D. LODGE *Changing Places* 190 Morris pulled out and varoomed down the wrong side of the road. **1976** B. JACKSON *Flameout* iv. 51 A gang of youths sitting astride motorcycles vroomed their engines. **1979** J. HANSEN *Skinflick* x. 77 'How about a sports car?..Let it roll off a cliff and catch fire. Just like TV. Sensational.' 'Varoom!' Spence said. **1984** *New Yorker* 14 May 41/2 It wasn't the *varooms* and the screeching tires that spooked people.

‖**vrouw, vrow** (vraʊ). Also 7 vroa, 20 vrou. [Du. and Flem. *vrouw* (cf. FROW *sb.*) = G. *frau* woman, wife, FRAU.] A (Dutch) woman, matron, goodwife. *spec.* in S. Afr.

α. *c* **1620** [FLETCHER & MASSINGER] *Trag. Barnavelt* IV. iv. in Bullen *Old Pl.* (1883) II. 285 Ten hundred thousand blessings To him and thee, my vroa. *a* **1700** *Songs Lond. Prentices* (Percy Soc.) 34 The Dutchman will go to the sign of the Vrow where each man may drink his flagon. **1701** WOLLEY *Jrnl. New York* (1860) 55 They seized each other's hair with their forefeet, and down they went to the Sod, their Vrows and Families crying out because they could not part them. **1798** A. BARNARD *Jrnl.* 21 May in A. W. C. Lindsay *Lives of Lindsays* (1849) III. 455 We were received by the vrow, the mistress of the house—O house, unworthy such a mistress! **1824** J. PATERSON in *Harp Renfrew.* Ser. II. (1873) 108 Till the riflemen..raised a din..Which nearly deprived the fair vrows of their breath. **1884** *Contemp. Rev.* Oct. 552 The drinking boors of Teniers or the Dutch vrows of Mieris.

β. **1791** NAIRNE *Poems* 129 And Roman dishes, made at Delf, To ornament an old vrouw's shelf. **1827** T. PHILLIPS *Scenes & Occurrences in Albany & Caffer-Land* i. 12 Distance to them is no consideration; the boor put his *vrouw*..into the waggon,..and sets off to travel five hundred miles, with as much ease as we should ten in England. **1829** C. ROSE *Four Yrs. S. Africa* 49 There is the farmer's tall powerful form, his vrouw—in general by no means a tempting lady. **1838** W. C. HARRIS *Narr. Exped. S. Africa* 14 His doating young vrouw received him with overflowing eyes and open arms. **1887** RIDER HAGGARD *Jess* ii, The Boer and his vrouw treated the children fairly well. **1946** *Cape Times Weekend Mag.* 16 Nov. 27 Yesterday your vrou brought to my store a cupboard that she would sell. **1972** A. A. TELFORD *Yesterday's Dress* 79 The 'vrouw' is wearing the thick quilted cap.

vry, southern ME. var. FREE *a.*

†**vrycloth.** *Obs.*[−1] (Meaning obscure.)

1532–3 *Durham Househ. Bk.* (Surtees) 157 Et Lionello Elmedayne 2¼ uln., 5 die Maii, pro le vryclothe.

vryday, southern ME. var. FRIDAY.

vryt(e, vryter, obs. Sc. ff. WRITE *v.*, WRITER.

V-shaped: see V 2 c.

V-sign. Also V sign. [f. *V* = Victory: see V 5 b.] **1. a.** The letter V used as a written symbol of victory during the war of 1939–45. **b.** The Morse Code representation of this letter or the first four notes of Beethoven's Fifth Symphony, which have the same rhythm. Also *transf.*

1941 W. S. CHURCHILL *Unrelenting Struggle* (1942) 198 The V sign is the symbol of the unconquerable will of the occupied territories, and a portent of the fate awaiting the Nazi tyranny. **1959** *Listener* 24 Sept. 489/2 The start of the 'V-sign' by Victor de Lavelaye of the Belgian Section [of the B.B.C.] in July 1941. **1972** *Times* 26 Sept. 4/8 The old V-sign, first used for the Belgian service in 1941, was a low-frequency signal. **1978** L. THOMAS *Ormerod's Landing* v. 95 There came a V-sign knock on the street door.

2. a. = *victory sign* s.v. VICTORY *sb.* 5. **b.** A similar gesture made with the back of the hand outwards as an obscene gesture of contempt (see also quots. 1948, 1973).

a. 1942 H. NICOLSON *Diary* 23 Apr. (1967) 224 Winston.. gives the V-sign to an audience which does not greet him with any tumultuous applause. **1943** A. MOOREHEAD *End in Africa* xiv. 148 They gave the V sign, they shouted and waved flags, the girls kissed the soldiers and the men ran out with bottles of wine and fruit.

b. 1948 PARTRIDGE *Dict. Forces' Slang* 202 *V-sign*, the first and middle fingers uplifted in the form of the letter *V*, for victory. When the hand making the sign was jerked upwards, it was a sign of recognition between two acquaintances passing on a road, or of complete disagreement with the statements or actions of another, adequately replacing a vulgar monosyllable of the same significance. **1959** *Spectator* 4 Sept. 297/2 Congreve's *Double Dealer* is a sex-play... To his immediate predecessors the dirty joke was still a political gesture, a deliberately ambiguous V-sign which semaphored both political and marital freedom. **1973** *Daily Tel.* 29 Nov. 3/8 Two 'louts'..taunted him outside his home by shouting obscenities and making V-signs. **1981** B. HINES *Looks & Smiles* 36 They turned round and gave him the V-sign generously with both hands..the gatekeeper hurried inside his office and slammed the door.

vuagnatite ('vwɑːnjətaɪt). *Min.* [f. the name of M. *Vuagnat* (b. 1922), Swiss petrologist + -ITE¹.] A basic silicate of calcium and aluminium, $CaAl(OH)SiO_4$, found as white, usu. anhedral, orthorhombic crystals.

1976 H. SARP et al. in *Amer. Mineralogist* LXI. 825 Vuagnatite..occurs with prehnite, hydrogrossular, vesuvianite, and chorite in rodingitic dykes from an ophiolitic zone in the Taurus Mountains, southwest Turkey. **1979** *Mineral. Abstr.* XXX. 413/2 Vuagnatite occurs as veinlets less than 5 mm wide or as small lenses less than 15 mm long in pectolite veins cutting serpentinite in the Toba district, central Japan.

†**vue**, perh. an error for *beue* BEVY.

1472 in *Archaeol.* (1836) XXVI. 278 There was a syde table at the whiche satte a greate Vue of ladyes.

‖**vue d'ensemble** (vy dɑ̃sɑ̃bl). [Fr.] A general view; an overall view of matters.

1865 MILL *Auguste Comte* 159 A philosopher's business is with general truths and connected views (vues d'ensemble). **1886** W. JAMES *Let.* 29 Aug. in R. B. Perry *Tht. & Char. W. James* (1935) I. 601, I gained a *vue d'ensemble* of the philosopher. **1975** *Times Lit. Suppl.* 29 Aug. 972/1 The *vue d'ensemble*..shows an enviable mastery of essentials. **1976** *Ibid.* 9 July 843/1 The impetus to crystallize his professional opinions, to create a *vue d'ensemble* of his life's work.

vuel(e, vuemest, vuen, vuere, ME. varr. EVIL, OVEMEST *a.*, OVEN, OVER *a.*

‖**vuelta** ('vwelta). *Bullfighting.* [Sp., lit. 'turn, round'.] The triumphal circuit of the ring awarded to the successful matador.

1932 [see RECORTE]. **1954** H. CASTEEL *Running of Bulls* vii. 134 If the applause continues he [*sc.* the matador] may make another circuit (dos vueltas). **1967** MCCORMICK & MASCAREÑAS *Compl. Aficionado* ii. 62 This is another sort of beauty, and the matador has his full award, of two ears and three vueltas.

vug (vʌg). *Cornish mining.* Also **vugg, vugh,** voog. [ad. Cornish *vooga* (Williams); cf. VOGAL.] A cavity in a rock; a cave, a hollow.

1818 W. PHILLIPS *Geol.* 207 The sound which the miner hears, may reasonably be accounted for by presuming him to be at work in the immediate neighbourhood of a cavity, or as he terms it, a voog. **1838** MRS. BRAY *Tradit. Devon.* III. 256 It is not uncommon in deep mines, where there are what the miners term vugs..to hear loud and frequent explosions. **1855** J. R. LEIFCHILD *Cornwall Mines* 92 Above this mixed mass, and in the level above, a great cavity (called by miners a *vugh*) was found. **1883** *Encycl. Brit.* XVI. 445/2 Dynamite..is very effective even in ground full of 'vughs' or cavities. **1927** in M. Terry *Through Land of Promise* vi. 90 In places there are small 'vugs' containing quartz crystals. **1953** *Amer. Mineralogist* XXXVIII. 7 The vugs are commonly almond-shaped and range in size from 10 cm. down to microscopic dimensions. **1976** *Nature* 29 Apr. 813/1 The eye is captivated by the beautiful scanning electron microscope photographs of iron crystals deposited in vugs.

Hence '**vuggy** (also **vughy**) *a.*, full of cavities.

1864 W. W. SMYTH *Catal. Min. Coll. Museum Pract. Geol.* 12 The lode is full of cavities, or 'vuggy' (as the Cornish miners term it). **1883** GRESLEY *Gloss. Coal-M.* 273 *Vughy rock*, a stratum of cellular structure, or one containing many cavities. **1953** *Amer. Mineralogist* XXXVII. 7 Some of the replaced rock has a very vuggy texture. **1970** [see PYROXFERROITE]. **1971** V. A. FIRSOFF *Gemstones Brit. Isles* iv. 25 Amethyst occurs in druses and 'small vuggy veins' in the former haematite mines of Mwyndy and Garth Ward.

vugular ('vʌgjʊlə(r)), *a. Geol.* [f. VUG + -ULAR.] **a.** Containing vugs. **b.** Of the nature of a vug.

1967 *Trans. Soc. Professional Well Log Analysts* P-1 Non-homogeneous carbonates such as vugular limes or dolomites. **1975** G. ANDERSON *Coring* i. 2 The individual pore may be like a capillary tube or it may be vugular with druzy crystal infilling. **1977** *Géotechnique* XXVII. 435 It is difficult to determine the porosity of a vugular rock sample by conventional techniques because of the problems encountered in measuring the bulk volume of the specimen.

vuhel, southern ME. variant of FOWL *sb.*

vuir, obs. Sc. variant of OVER *a.*

Vuitton (vɥitɔ̃). In full **Louis Vuitton**. A proprietary name for the products of a French firm making high-quality luggage and other personal items.

1975 *Vogue* Sept. 305/4 (Advt.), A Louis Vuitton in the hand. **1976** *Official Gaz.* (U.S. Patent Office) 18 May TM182/2 *Louis Vuitton.* For luggage and ladies' handbags. **1977** C. WOOD *James Bond, Spy who loved Me* vii. 60 His travel-weary Vuitton suitcase. **1978** H. MACINNES *Prelude to Terror* iv. 32 An amazing hodge-podge of luggage..Vuitton combined with cardboard boxes. **1980** *Trade Marks Jrnl.* 6 Feb. 280/2 *Louis Vuitton*...1,081,942. Handbags, suitcases, trunks, umbrellas, pocket wallets, purses..key cases. **1982** C. HOUCK *Fashion Encycl.* 220 Vuitton luggage is the most status-ridden luggage in the world, and some of the cachet has seeped over into Vuitton handbags. **1983** *Time* 1 Aug. 40/2 Louis Vuitton handbags.

vul, southern ME. var. pa. t. FALL *v.*, var. FULL *adv.*

Vulcan ('vʌlkən), *sb.* [ad. L. *Vulcān-us*, the god of fire, son of Jupiter and Juno. Cf. F. *Vulcain*, †*Vulcan.*]

I. 1. *Rom. Mythol.* The god of fire and of metal-working, corresponding to the Greek Hephæstus.

The lameness of Vulcan, and the infidelity of Venus towards him, are occas. the subject of literary allusions.

1513 DOUGLAS *Æneid* VIII. vii. 122 Quhilk forgeis bene Vulcanus duelling call, And eftir Vulcane that cuntre nemyt all. **1579** LODGE *Def. Poetry* 20 Al lame men are not Vulcans, nor hooke nosed men Ciceroes. **1634** MILTON *Comus* 655 Though he and his curst crew Feirce signe of battail make, and menace high, Or like the sons of Vulcan vomit smoak, Yet will they soon retire, if he but shrink. **1725** POPE *Odyss.* VIII. 314 Stung to the soul, indignant through the skies To his black forge vindictive Vulcan flies. **1753** *Chambers' Cycl.* Suppl., *Vulcanalia*, among the Romans, a festival in honour of Vulcan. **1837** CARLYLE *Fr. Rev.* I. III. v, His wig and gown are his Vulcan's panoply, his enchanted cloak of darkness. **1851** BORROW *Lavengro* lxxxiii, I never associate Vulcan and his Cyclops with the idea of a forge.

b. An image or picture of the god.

1638 JUNIUS *Paint. Ancients* 160 There were in old times neere all Chimneys almost some earthen Vulcans set up, seeing that God was the president of these Arts wrought by fire. *a* **1700** EVELYN *Diary* 10 Nov. 1644, In one of the chambers hang two famous pieces of Bassano, the one a *Vulcan*, the other a *Nativity*!

c. *fig.* A lame slow-moving person.

1682 SIR T. BROWNE *Chr. Mor.* III. §20 (1716) 109 Many, who are sinistrous unto Good Actions, are Ambi-dexterous unto bad, and Vulcans in virtuous Paths, Achilleses in vitious motions.

2. a. *transf.* A blacksmith; an iron-worker.

1638 SIR T. HERBERT *Trav.* (ed. 2) 55 Cingis-chan..was at first by profession a Vulcan or Black-smith. **1693** DRYDEN *Juvenal* x. (1697) 255 His Sire, the blear-ey'd Vulcan of a Shop. **1704** R. NORTH *Let.* 20 Aug., in *Lives* (1890) III. App. 252 This bearer is the Vulcan of our village, and one of the eaters of us farmers. **1831** CARLYLE *Sart. Res.* I. vi, Those jingling sheet-iron Aprons, wherein your otherwise half-naked Vulcans hammer and smelt. **1890** W. J. GORDON *Foundry* 15 Here the modern Vulcans, in shirt-sleeves and with unbroken legs, are still casting thunderbolts.

†**b.** A miner. *Obs.*⁻¹

1662 J. BARGRAVE *Pope Alex. VII* (1867) 121 When we came into the vast high vaults, where hundreds and hundreds of men or Vulcans were at work, one of the overseers..would have let us see their art by blowing up a part of the mine by gunpowder.

3. A hypothetical planet supposed to have its orbit between the Sun and Mercury.

1870 PROCTOR *Other Worlds* iii. 58, I would willingly pay some attention here to the story of Vulcan..were it not for the great doubt in which the existence of the planet seems enshrouded. **1879** NEWCOMB & HOLDEN *Astron.* 310 They comprise Venus, Mercury, and, in the opinion of some astronomers, a planet called Vulcan.

II. †**4.** A volcano. *Obs.* (Cf. VOLCAN.)

In Trevisa *Higden* (Rolls) I. 319 and Maundeville (1839) 55 *Vlcane* and *Wlcanes* occur as a name for the Lipari Islands: cf. VULCANIAN *a.* 3.

1578 T. N. tr. *Conq. W. India* 160 Then appeared the vulcan and concavitie which was about halfe a league in compasse. *Ibid.* 161 This vulcan is like unto the vulcan of Cecilia. **1604** E. G[RIMSTONE] *D'Acosta's Hist. Indies* III. ii. 119 Of those which are in the Vulcans or mouths of fire at the Indies..I will speake in their order. **1648** GAGE *West Ind.* xiii. 69 But they were not gone farre, when the Vulcan began to flash out flames of fire. *a* **1691** BOYLE *Hist. Air* xi. (1692) 41 The number of these may..be much increased by those Vulcans, that have open Vents to discharge their Fumes. **1707** FUNNELL *Voy.* v. 111 These Vulcans send out Smoke sometimes.

†**b.** Const. *of* (the matter ejected). *Obs.*

1647 A. ROSS *Mystag. Poet.* iii. (1675) 72 A Hill, on the top whereof were Lions and Vulcans of fire. **1648** GAGE *West Ind.* 179 The Town standeth on the backside of the Vulcan of water. **1680** MORDEN *Geog. Rect., New Spain* (1685) 553 The other Vulcan of Fire is more unpleasant.

5. Fire; a fire. Chiefly *poet.*

1674 JOSSELYN *Voy. New Eng.* 138 They make their *Vulcan* or fire near to a great Tree, upon the snags whereof they hang their kettles. **1708** PHILIPS *Cyder* II. 142 Altho' Devonia much commends the Use Of strengthning Vulcan. **1728** POPE *Dunciad* III. 81 There rival flames with equal glory rise, From shelves to shelves see greedy Vulcan roll.

Hence †**Vulcan** *v. trans.*, to make into a Vulcan; to cuckold. *Obs.*

1623 MASSINGER *Bondman* I. ii, *Corisca.* To me You are a young Adonis. *Gracculo.* Well said, Venus! I am sure she Vulcans him.

†'**Vulcanal.** *Obs.*⁻¹ [f. L. *Vulcān-us* VULCAN *sb.* + -AL¹.] An animal living in fire.

1657 PINNELL *Philos. Reform.* 27 To the Fire or the Firmament doe belong the Vulcanals, Pennats, Salamanders.

Vulca'nalial, *a. rare*⁻¹. [f. L. *Vulcānālia*, neut. pl. of *Vulcānāl-is*, f. *Vulcānus* VULCAN *sb.*] *Vulcanalial festival*, a Roman festival held in honour of Vulcan on Aug. 23. Also **Vulca'nalian** *a.*

1635 LUNDIE *Poems* (Abbotsford Club) 12 Seres glade preists in feisting spent some day's, And pass'd some nichts in Vulcanalian play's. **1654** OGILBY *Virgil, Bucolicks* iii. 17 *note*, The day before and after the Vulcanalial [1684 Vulcanalian] Festivals.

Vulcanian (vʌl'keɪnɪən), *a.* (*sb.*) Also 7 **-ean.** [f. L. *Vulcāni-us*, f. *Vulcān-us* VULCAN *sb.* Cf. F. *vulcanien.*]

1. a. Of or pertaining to, characteristic of, associated with, Vulcan.

1602 F. HERING tr. *Oberndorffer's Anat.* 5 They reiect incomparable Galens learned Commentarie.., hauing found thorow Paracelsus Vulcanian shop a more compendious..way. **1697** DRYDEN *Virg. Georg.* III. 835 Nor could Vulcanian flame The stench abolish, or the savour tame. **1700** —— *Pal. & Arc.* III. 908 With sounding axes to the Grove they go. Fell, split, and lay the fewel on a row, Vulcanian food. **1726** POPE *Odyss.* XX. 154 Meantime the menial train with unctuous wood Heap'd high the genial hearth, Vulcanian food. **1791** COWPER *Iliad* XXIII. 41 Many a saginated boar bright-tusk'd, Amid fierce flames Vulcanian stretch'd to roast. **1854** H. E. J. HOWARD *Rape Proserpine* 15 The ponderous gates, the threshold, and the wall, Cast in Vulcanian mould, were iron all. **1865** RUSKIN *Sesame* i. §45 An armour forged in diviner fire by Vulcanian force.

b. Fashioned or forged by Vulcan. Also *fig.*

1603 J. DAVIES (Heref.) *Microcosmos* Wks. (Grosart) I. 42/1 God's feare, that strong Vulcanian Armor, must Guard such good Soules as doe regard it heere. *a* **1693** *Urquhart's Rabelais* III. xii. 93 The..slinging Casts of the Vulcanian Thunderbolts. **1697** DRYDEN *Æneid* x. 1139 The Trojan Chief..On his Vulcanian Orb sustain'd the War. **1718** J. TRAPP tr. *Virgil* (1735) I. Pref. to Æneis p. xlvii, Ornamental Sculptures upon Homer's Vulcanian Shield. **1762** FALCONER *Shipwr.* III. 287 Thunders, that shook the skies with dire alarms, And, form'd by skill divine, Vulcanian arms. **1792** D. LLOYD *Voy. Life* v. 99 Nor brazen walls, Nor bright Vulcanian shields, can stand before Th' intrepid aim of Resolution. **1849** MACAULAY *Hist. Eng.* xii. III. 166 The Vulcanian panoply which Achilles lent to his feebler friend. **1871** LONSDALE & LEE *Virgil* Gen. Introd. (1903) 8 Criticism is as powerless against the poet as the sword of the mortal hero against the immortal temper of the Vulcanian shield.

2. a. Sprung from, related to, Vulcan.

1630 J. TAYLOR (Water P.) *Gt. Eater Kent* 4 The Vulcanean brood of blacksmiths, fire-men, colliers, gunners, gun-founders, and all sorts of mettle-men. **1697** DRYDEN *Æneid* x. 758 Vulcanian Cæculus renews the fight, And Umbro born upon the mountain's height. **1749** G. WEST tr. *Pindar, 1st Pythian Ode* vi, But he, Vulcanian Monster, to the clouds The fiercest, hottest inundations throws.

†**b.** *sb.* One who resembles Vulcan. *Obs.*⁻¹

1598 MARSTON *Pigmal., Sat.* ii, Yet Muto, like a good Vulcanian, An honest Cuckold, calls the bastard sonne, And brags of that which others for him done.

†**3.** ***Vulcanian Islands***, the Lipari Islands between Sicily and Italy. *Obs.*

1652 HEYLIN *Cosmogr.* I. 72 On the West part of Sicil lie the Æolian or Vulcanian Ilands. **1690** T. BURNET *Theory Earth* II. 57 There are no volcano's in my opinion, that deserve our observation so much, as those that are in and about the Mediterranean Sea; there is a knot of them called the Vulcanian Islands, from their fiery eruptions. **1705** C. PURSHALL *Mech. Macrocosm* 83 The Vulcanian Islands in the Mediterranean Sea, are said to be of this sort.

4. Of, belonging to, or abounding with, volcanoes; volcanic. (Cf. VOLCANIAN *a.*)

1656 [? J. SERGEANT] tr. *T. White's Peripat. Inst.* 126 Aetna, Lipara and Hecla..and especially the Vulcanian Mountains of the new world. **1880** PROCTOR *Poetry Astron.* i. (1881) 18 If no vulcanian forces were at work to prevent submergence. **1883** *Contemp. Rev.* Oct. 575 Only by the action of her vulcanian energies can the earth maintain her position as an abode of life.

5. = PLUTONIAN *a.* 2. (Cf. VULCANIST 3.)

1840 SMART. **1850** OGILVIE s.v. *Vulcanist*, The Vulcanian theory has been expanded and illustrated by Lyell. **1870** BREWER *Dict. Phr. & Fable* 939/2 The Vulcanian or Plutonian theory, which ascribes the changes on earth's surface to the agency of fire.

6. [f. *Vulcano*, name of one the Lipari Islands (cf. quot. 1976).] Of, pertaining to, or designating (the stage of) a volcanic eruption characterized by periodic explosive events.

1912 *Amer. Jrnl. Sci.* CLXXXIV. 412 This hypothesis does not..invalidate the division of the eruption into a 'Strombolian' and a 'Vulcanian' phase—on the contrary, it supplies a cause for the great and continued dynamism of the 'Vulcanian' phase.. It is interesting to note that the 'Vulcanian' phase, as far as actual, external eruption is concerned, is cooler than the 'Strombolian'. **1944** [see PELÉAN *a.*]. **1976** P. FRANCIS *Volcanoes* v. 169 Probably the best known Vulcanian deposit is one produced by an eruption of Vulcano itself in the 1880s. **1985** E. A. K. MIDDLEMOST *Magmas & Magmatic Rocks* i. 28/2 Vulcanian eruptions usually begin with a series of phreatic explosions that eject lithic debris from the volcanic conduit.

vulcanic (vʌl'kænɪk), *a.* [In sense 1 ad. F. *vulcanique*, It. (also Pg.) *vulcanico*, f. It. *vulcano* VOLCANO. In sense 2 f. L. *Vulcān-us* VULCAN *sb.*]

1. = VOLCANIC *a.* 2 b.

1774 *Phil. Trans.* LXV. 24 The vulcanic districts of Auvergne and Velay..afford proofs enough of the truth of this opinion. *Ibid.* 27, I have already observed, that there are many vulcanic mountains of a totally different form from the common volcanos. **1888** DOUGHTY *Arabia Deserta* I. 20 Of such vulcanic breaches there are many in these limestone downs. *Ibid.* 21 The Belka chalk is changed by the vulcanic heat.

2. Of or belonging to, having the character of, Vulcan. (With initial capital.)

1807 *Europ. Mag.* LII. 469/2 What tho' with Vulcanic knocking Thou still may bring forth many a thought. **1866** R. S. HAWKER in C. E. Byles *Life & Lett.* xxiii. (1905) 547

The great majority of Vassals of his own which exists in this Vulcanic [*i.e.* manufacturing] nation.

b. Of or pertaining to fire; fiery.

1866 Lowell *Carlyle* Prose Wks. 1890 II. 83 Even the burning of a meeting-house, in itself a vulcanic rarity, could not..tickle his outworn palate. **1867** J. B. Rose tr. *Virgil's Æneid* 224 Vulcan begot him—in vulcanic lair He breathed forth flame.

vulcanicity (vʌlkəˈnɪsɪtɪ). [f. prec. + -ity, or ad. F. *vulcanicité*.]

1. = volcanicity.

1873 R. Mallet *Palmieri's Eruption Vesuvius* Title-p., An Introductory Sketch of the Present State of Knowledge of Terrestrial Vulcanicity. **1882** E. Hull *Contrib. Phys. Geog. Brit. Isles* 21 Vulcanicity has also played its part in the formation of rock-structures. **1885** *Academy* 3 Oct. 225 He regards the thermal waters as representing a legacy of former vulcanicity.

2. The study of volcanic action.

1879 Rutley *Stud. Rocks* iii. 9 The branches of physical geology known as vulcanicity and seismology.

† **vulcanio,** irreg. var. *vulcano* volcano *sb.*

1676 *Phil. Trans.* XI. 762 This Fire keeping no analogy with other Vulcanio's in any of the particulars mentioned in these three quæries, I thought fit to answer them altogether.

vulcanism (ˈvʌlkənɪz(ə)m). [ad. F. *vulcanisme*, var. of *volcanisme* volcanism.] Volcanic action or condition.

1877 Le Conte *Elem. Geol.* iii. (1879) 93 The sun may be regarded as a globe in an earlier and more active stage of vulcanism. **1883** *Nature* XXVII. 280 The..strata which have been deposited..under the combined influences of internal vulcanism and external atmospherical influences.

vulcanist (ˈvʌlkənɪst). [In early use f. Vulcan *sb.* + -ist. In sense 3 ad. F. *vulcaniste*, var. of *volcaniste* volcanist.]

† **1.** One who works by fire; *spec.* an alchemist, a blacksmith. *Obs.*

1593 Harvey *Pierce's Super.* Wks. (Grosart) II. 177 The Country affordeth sufficient prouision of water, to encounter the terriblest Vulcanist, that brandisheth a burning sword, or a fierie tongue. **1594** Plat *Jewell-ho.* ii. 23, I perswade my selfe, that no philosophicall vulcanist, or perfect paracelsian, will ever finde any true magisterie, tincture, quintessence or Arcanum therein. **1603** Dekker *Wonderf. Yeare* C2b, What Mechanicall hardhanded Vulcanist but perswaded himselfe to bee Maister of the Company.

2. One who is lame, as Vulcan was.

1656 *Artif. Handsom.* 60 Your Lap[s] Charity doth not reprove, but pity those poor Vulcanists, who ballance the inequality of their heels, or badger leggs, by the art and help of the shoemaker.

3. = volcanist 1.

1802 Playfair *Illustr. Huttonian The.* 3 Their followers have of late been distinguished by the fanciful names of Vulcanists and Neptunists. **1830** Lyell *Princ. Geol.* I. 90 In addition to volcanic heat, to which the Vulcanists formerly attributed too much influence, we must allow for the effect of mechanical pressure [etc.]. **1884** Sir L. Playfair in *Gd. Words* Feb. 93/1 Vulcanists of the old school would be equally perplexed, because petroleum is so volatile that..it would be dissipated. **1969** *New Yorker* 19 Apr. 52/2 Baldwin..was the first person to suggest convincingly that meteors might have made many of the moon's craters; previously, almost all selenologists had been vulcanists. **1971** *Nature* 27 Aug. 600/3 Although there is now a vast amount of data on the physics, chemistry and shape of the Moon, the 'vulcanists' and 'impacters' at the symposium on this subject seem to be as widely divided as ever.

vulcanite (ˈvʌlkənaɪt). [f. Vulcan *sb.* + -ite[1]. Hence F. *vulcanite* (in sense 2).]

† **1.** Pyroxene. *Obs.* (Cf. volcanite[1].)

1836 T. Thomson *Min., Geol.*, etc. I. 190 Pyroxene. Augite, baikalite,..vulcanite, asbestus in part. *c* **1840** *Encycl. Metrop.* (1845) VI. 527/2 Vulcanite. Augite.

2. A preparation of india rubber and sulphur hardened by exposure to intense heat; ebonite.

1860 *Ure's Dict. Arts* (ed. 5) I. 602 Indian-rubber and vulcanite, or hard rubber. **1867** Bloxam *Chem.* 482 When a sheet of caoutchouc is..still further heated, [it] is converted into the black horny substance called vulcanite or ebonite, and used for the manufacture of combs, &c. **1889** Welch *Text Bk. Naval Archit.* xii. 135 They..have about four feet of their length made of teak or vulcanite in order to break the continuity of the metal pipe.

b. *attrib.* Made of vulcanite.

1866 *Microscop. Jrnl.* VI. 168 You will oblige me by correcting an error in your report of my remarks on vulcanite cells. **1869** *Eng. Mech.* 3 Dec. 273/1 The same effect may be produced by rubbing a vulcanite comb on the sleeve of a coat. **1879** T. Bryant *Pract. Surg.* II. 34 The vulcanite canula is good for constant use.

vulcaˈnizable, *a.* [f. vulcanize *v.*] That can be vulcanized.

1860 [see partial *a.* 3 g]. **1887** *Sci. Amer.* (N.Y.) 26 Mar. 193/2 Asbestos and India rubber..also other vulcanizable materials enter into its composition.

vulcanizate (ˈvʌlkənaɪzeɪt). [f. vulcanize *v.*, after *filtrate*, *precipitate*, etc.] A material that has been vulcanized.

1942 *Trans. Faraday Soc.* XXXVIII. 345 The vulcanizates. **1959** *Times* 27 Apr. (Rubber Industry Suppl.) p. ii, The general purpose synthetic rubber..does not readily form crystals and so as a gum vulcanizate it is very weak. **1983** *Jrnl. Materials Sci.* XVIII. 515 The abrasion of NR/BR blend vulcanizates has been studied in three different testing machines.

vulcanization (vʌlkənaɪˈzeɪʃən). [f. next. Hence F. *vulcanisation* (also *volc-*).] The method or process of treating crude india-rubber with sulphur and subjecting it to intense heat, by means of which it is rendered more durable and made adaptable for various purposes.

The history of the process is related in detail in *Ure's Dict. Arts*, etc. (ed. 5; 1860) I. 589–92.

1846 Hancock *Patent Specif.* No. 11135. 2 Without the process of vulcanization. **1857** —— *Pers. Narr. India Rubber Manuf.* 107 It appeared desirable to give the material a more definite name..; and whilst discussing the subject amongst my friends, Mr. Brockedon proposed the term 'Vulcanization'. **1869** *Eng. Mech.* 24 Dec. 370/2 The mineral ingredients..are necessarily subject to the action of the sulphur employed to effect the vulcanisation. **1897** *Allbutt's Syst. Med.* II. 949 Carbon bisulphide is used to soften india-rubber so as to allow of its penetration by sulphur in the carrying out of what is known as vulcanisation.

vulcanize (ˈvʌlkənaɪz), *v.* [f. Vulcan *sb.* Hence F. *vulcaniser* (in sense 2).]

1. *trans.* To commit to the flames.

1827 Southey *Lett.* (1856) IV. 41 That great exploit, which..drew upon him so libellous an imputation in certain verses which have long since been vulcanised.

2. To subject (india-rubber, etc.) to the process of vulcanization.

1846 Hancock *Patent Specif.* No. 11135. 2 When cold I remove them from the moulds and afterwards vulcanize them to make their form permanent. **1860** *Ure's Dict. Arts* (ed. 5) I. 591 It appears not to be an easy matter to vulcanise large masses of caoutchouc. **1873** E. Spon *Workshop Receipts* Ser. i. 360/1 The time and heat required to vulcanize or harden the compound.

3. *intr.* To undergo vulcanization.

1890 *Sci. Amer.* 1 March LXII. 140/1 Rubber vulcanizes at 276° Fah.

ˈvulcanized, *ppl. a.* [f. prec. + -ed[1].] Affected or altered by the process of vulcanization.

1845 *Mech. Mag.* Feb. 112 The exhibition by Mr. Brockedon of some specimens of Mr. Thomas Hancock's patent 'vulcanized' india-rubber. **1857** Miller *Elem. Chem., Org.* i. § 1. 16 Gentle suction is then to be effected by means of a tube of vulcanized caoutchouc. **1873** E. Spon *Workshop Receipts* Ser. i. 2/1 Vulcanized rubber is also extremely useful for cleaning off drawings.

transf. **1884** Knight *Dict. Mech.* Suppl. 931/2 *Vulcanized Fiber*, paper, paper pulp, or other vegetable fibrous substance that has been so prepared..as to give it in a measure metallic toughness and strength.

ˈvulcanizer. [f. as prec. + -er[1].] One who or that which vulcanizes; esp., the apparatus used in vulcanizing india-rubber.

1862 *Catal. Internat. Exhib., Brit.* II. No. 3520, Improved gas vulcanizer for dentists. **1862** *Jrnl. Soc. Arts* X. 328/2 An iron frame is then secured round the whole, and it is placed in a small vulcaniser, heated by gas. **1885** C. G. W. Lock *Workshop Receipts* Ser. iv. 2/2 The roll being bound round with a wet cloth bandage, is ready for the 'vulcaniser'.

ˈvulcanizing, *vbl. sb.* [f. as prec. + -ing[1].] The action of the verb. Also *attrib.*

1846 Hancock *Patent Specif.* No. 11135. 2 In all the compounds..I employ sulphur and heat.., which process is now commonly designated vulcanizing. **1855** Goodyear *Gum-elastic* (New Haven) 177 Soon after the discovery of the heating or vulcanizing process. **1884** Knight *Dict. Mech.* Suppl. 931/2 The heating or vulcanizing is conducted in strong cast-iron cylinders.

ˈvulcanizing, *ppl. a.* [-ing[2].] That vulcanizes or is used in the process of vulcanizing.

1862 *Jrnl. Soc. Arts* X. 326 The dough is..put into moulds of the desired form, and exposed in a vulcanising oven to a heat of from 240 to 260 degrees Fahr. **1879** *Cassell's Techn. Educ.* IV. 287/2 The hose is finished by immersing it in a vulcanising solution.

vulcano, obs. variant of volcano.

vulcanoˈlogical, *a.* [See vulcanology and -ical.] Of, pertaining to, or connected with vulcanology.

1888 *Nature* 30 Aug. 410/1 Seismology..is usually treated..as a branch of vulcanological science. **1899** *Ibid.* 11 May 27/2 A..very readable account of the present state of vulcanological science.

vulcaˈnologist. (Also volc-.) [See vulcanology and -ologist.] One who studies or is expert in volcanic phenomena.

1858 Mallet in *Rep. Brit. Assoc.* i. 133 The subject appears to me worthy of more examination at the hands of Vulcanologists and Seismologists. **1881** Judd *Volcanoes* ii. 37 Vulcanologists have only just commenced those series of exact and continuous observations.

vulcaˈnology. (Also volc-). [f. *vulcan-* (cf. vulcanic, etc.) + -ology.] The science or scientific study of volcanoes.

1858 Mallet in *Rep. Brit. Assoc.* i. 117 Books on Earthquakes and Vulcanology in the Gottingen University Library. **1880** *Academy* 17 Jan. 49 The part relating to vulcanology would be considerably improved by a detailed account of some one seismological observatory.

vulgar (ˈvʌlgə(r)), *sb.* Also 5–6 vulgare. [Absolute use of vulgar *a.*, after similar uses of med.L. *vulgaris*, OF. *vulgaire* (also *vulgar*), It. *volgare*.]

† **1.** The common or usual language of a country; the vernacular. *Obs.*

1430–40 Lydg. *Bochas* ix. xxxvi. (MS. Bodl. 263) 441/1 Whos kyngdom hool, as maad is mencioun, In that vulgar.. Of Malliogres pleynli bar þe name. *c* **1450** *Chaucer's Compl. Pite* (Harl. MS.) *heading*, Geffrey Chaucier þe aureat Poete þat euer was fonde in oure vulgare to fore [t]hees dayes. **1501** Douglas *Pal. Hon.* ii. xvii, ȝit saw I thair..Geffray Chaucier, as *a per se* sans peir In his vulgare. **1586** Day *Eng. Secretary* i. (1625) 1 An Epistle therefore is that which vsually we in our vulgar doe tearme a Letter. **1589** Puttenham *Eng. Poesie* ii. iv. (Arb.) 86 Before Sir Thomas Wiats time they were not vsed in our vulgar. **1611** Bible *Transl. Pref.* ¶8 For the behoofe and edifying of the vnlearned..they prouided Translations into the vulgar. **1665** G. Havers *P. della Valle's Trav. E. India* 144 The Canara-Language, which is the vulgar in Ikkeri and all that State.

2. † **a.** *pl.* Persons belonging to the ordinary or common class in the community, esp. the uneducated or ignorant. *Obs.*

1513 Bradshaw *St. Werburge* Prol. 84 Some small treatyse to wryte breuely To the comyn vulgares theyr mynde to satisfy. **1549** Chaloner *Erasm. on Folly* G j, He preferred also the Ideote and simple vulgars, before other learned and reputed persons. **1598** R. Bernard tr. *Terence, Eunuch* ii. ii, I can nothing at all away with these vulgars, wherein there is no excellencie of beautie. **1615** Chapman *Odyss.* vi. 425 For these vile vulgars are extreamly proud, And fouly languag'd. **1678** Butler *Hud.* iii. i. 1129 He therefore sent out all his Senses, To bring him in Intelligences. Which Vulgars out of ignorance Mistake, for falling in a Trance.

b. A person not reckoned as belonging to good society.

pl. **1763** G. Williams in Jesse *Selwyn & Contemp.* (1843) I. 264, I have named you those whom you know; the rest are numerous, but vulgars. **1766** —— *Ibid.* II. 32 Lord Lincoln exhibited his person yesterday on the Stein, to the surprise of all the vulgars. **1796** Wolcot (P. Pindar) *Pindariana, Ode to Sun* viii, The great retire from routs..And cry, ..'Vulgars! that never wax-lights handle!' **1815** *Zeluca* I. 339, I think I told you there was quite nothing but vulgars at the two last balls. **1828** Landor *Imag. Conv.* III. 147 She associated and assimilated with the very worst in the polar circle of both vulgars.

sing. **1767** Lady S. Bunbury in Jesse *Selwyn & Contemp.* (1843) II. 191 A Mr. Brereton (a sad vulgar). **1781** Burgoyne *Ld. of Manor* ii. i, It would be as low to accept the challenge of a vulgar as to refuse it to an equal. **1825** C. Westmacott *Eng. Spy* II. 97 The mobbing a *vulgar*, the hoaxing a *quiz*,..All these were among Jekyl's early peculiarities.

3. ***the vulgar***, the common people. Also with *a.*

1590 Spenser *F.Q.* iii. xii. 4 To the vulgar beckning with his hand, In signe of silence, as to heare a play. **1591** —— *Teares Muses* 194 All places they with follie haue possest, And with vaine toyes the vulgare entertaine But me haue banished. **1614** Gorges *Lucan* ii. 66 The vulgar most to Pompey bends. *Ibid. marg.*, The vulgar do more affect Pompey then Cæsar. **1665** Glanvill *Def. Van. Dogm.* 57 Which saying holds not only in Morals, but in all things else which the Vulgar use to judge in. **1692** Bentley *Boyle Lect.* ii. 46 This is directly levell'd against the gross Idolatry of the Vulgar. **1738** *Gentl. Mag.* VIII. 77/1 Her enlightened Horn is turn'd towards the Horizon, or, as the Vulgar speak, The Moon lies on her Back. **1783** Hailes *Antiq. Chr. Ch.* vi. 182 *note*, The heathen vulgar might have inferred the likelihood of an approaching apotheosis. **1827** Hallam *Const. Hist.* ii. (1876) I. 86 The mysteriousness of an unknown dialect served to impose on the vulgar. **1828** Scott *F.M. Perth* Introd., We talk of a credulous vulgar, without always recollecting [etc.]. **1855** Milman *Lat. Chr.* ix. vii. IV. 126 Nor was this the suspicion of the vulgar alone; it seems to have been shared by the clergy. **1899** *Allbutt's Syst. Med.* VIII. 824 The growths..render the patient a remarkable and hideous object, exhibited for gain to the gaze of the vulgar.

transf. **1697** Dryden *Æneid* i. 266 The Leaders [of the herd] first He laid along, and then the Vulgar pierc'd.

† **b.** A common sort or class (*of* persons). *Obs.*[−1]

1645 Milton *Tetrach.* Wks. 1851 IV. 262 There is a vulgar also of teachers, who are blindly by whom they fancy led, as they lead the people.

† **4.** *pl.* Sentences or passages in English to be translated into Latin as a school-exercise. *Obs.*

1520 Whitinton *Vulg.* (1527) 25 b, Hast thou wryten all the vulgares that our mayster hath given vnto vs this mornynge. **1545–7** in *Archaeologia* (1852) XXXIV. 41 The thrid forme..hath throwgh the weke overnyght a verbe set up to be examyned in the mornyng, and makith vulgares upon yt. **1580** T. M. in *Baret's Alv.* To Rdr. xiv, A booke for such, that can peruse it right, Of profite great, when they their Vulgars write. **1612** Brinsley *Lud. Lit.* 148, I haue giuen them vulgars, or Englishes, such as I haue deuised, to be made in Latine.

† **b.** A vernacular or common expression. *Obs.*

1532 *Gower's Conf.* Ep. Ded. aa ij b, For the plenty of englysshe wordes and vulgars,..whiche olde englysshe wordes and vulgars no wyse man, because of theyr antiquite, wyll throwe asyde.

† **5.** = Vulgate *sb.* 1 b. *Obs.* (Cf. vulgar *a.* 2 b.)

1613 Day *Festivals* v. (1615) 110 So the Vulgar doth read it to, Nisi baptisentur, etc. **1647** Trapp *Comm. Rom.* ix. 25 God calls the Church, the beloved of his soul, or (as the Septuagint and Vulgar reade it) his beloved soul. **1699** T. Baker *Refl. Learn.* xvi. 201, I should be as glad, and would go as far to meet with the Ancient Vulgar of the New Testament, as any Man should do; but [etc.]. *Ibid.* 202 St. Jerome's manner of reforming the Ancient Vulgar was, by comparing and reducing it to the Greek Original. **1711** G. Hickes *Two Treat. Chr. Priesth.* (1847) II. 62 Which expression is also wanting both in the original and in our translation, and in the vulgar.

†**6.** Common or mean character. *Obs.*⁻¹

1655 tr. *Sorel's Com. Hist. Francion* I. 17 The Gentleman told his bed-fellow, that his gallant Garb and Countenance, wherein he perceived nothing of Vulgar, was the charm that had won his affection.

vulgar (ˈvʌlgə(r)), *a.* Also 4–6 **vulgare**, 6 *Sc.* **vlgare, wlgair -ar; vulguar, wulguar, voulger**, 7 **vulger**. [ad. L. *vulgār-is*, f. *vulg-us* the common people. Cf. OF. and F. *vulgaire*, Sp. and Pg. *vulgar*, It. *volgare*.]

I. 1. Employed in common or ordinary reckoning of time, distance, etc.; esp., in later use, ***vulgar era***, the ordinary Christian era.

c **1391** CHAUCER *Astrol.* II. §9 The day vulgare, that is to seyen, from spring of the day vn-to verrey nyht. *Ibid.*, The same manere maistow worke to knowe the quantite of the vulgar nyht. **1617** MORYSON *Itin.* I. 142 The way from Rome to Sienna is thus vulgarly noted.. In all.. ninetie sixe miles. I will follow my Italian consorts.. who doe not much differ from this vulgar number of miles. **1655** STANLEY *Hist. Philos.* I. (1687) 2/2 They.. confound.. the true Epocha of the Olympiads with the vulgar. **1662** STILLINGFL. *Orig. Sacræ* I. iii. §1 The vulgar account of years from the beginning of the world. **1716** PRIDEAUX *Connect. O. & N.T.* I. I. 1 The vulgar era, by which we now compute the years from his incarnation. *a* **1727** NEWTON *Chronol. Amended* i. (1728) 80 Seven hundred forty and seven years before the Vulgar Æra of Christ. **1788** PRIESTLEY *Lect. Hist.* III. xiv. 117 The vulgar Christian Aera answers the same purpose as effectually. **1839** YEOWELL *Anc. Brit. Ch.* (1847) App. I. 169 The fifty-seventh year of the vulgar computation. **1882** *Nature* XXVI. 345 Owing to constant migrations.. throughout the fourth and fifth centuries of the vulgar era.

b. ***vulgar fraction***: see FRACTION *sb.* 5 a.

1674 JEAKE *Arith.* (1696) 279 Simple Cossical Fractions.. are expressed like Vulgar Fractions. **1706** PHILLIPS (ed. Kersey), *Vulgar Fractions*, the ordinary Sort of Fractions, distinguished from Decimal Fractions. **1728** CHAMBERS *Cycl.* s.v. *Fraction*, Vulgar Fractions, called also Simple Fractions, are always express'd by two Numbers, the one wrote over the other, with a Line between them. **1798** HUTTON *Course Math.* (1806) I. 51 Of Vulgar Fractions. **1826** *Encycl. Metrop.* (1845) I. 441/2 Rules are also given for the reduction of vulgar to decimal fractions by a simple proportion. **1873** J. HAMBLIN SMITH *Arith.* (ed. 6) 83 A Vulgar Fraction may be converted into a Decimal Fraction.

†**c.** ***vulgar arithmetic***, ordinary arithmetic as opposed to decimal. *Obs. rare.*

1653 N. BRIDGES (*title*), Vulgar Arithmetique, explayning the Secrets of that Art. **1694** J. SELDEN (*title*), The Tradesman's Help. An Introduction to Arithmetick both Vulgar, Decimal, and Instrumental. *c* **1728** DE FOE *Compl. Eng. Gent.* (1890) 220 How many noble artists have we in the greatest and best branches of the Mathematicks (viz.), in Astronomy, in Geometry, in Arithmetick as well vulgar as decimal.

2. In common or general use; common, customary, or ordinary, as a matter of use or practice.

c **1430** LYDG. *Min. Poems* (Percy Soc.) 87 Isys in Egipt fonde a diversite Of sundry lettres parted in tweyne; First to pristes, and to the comunalte Vulgar lettres he dide also ordeyne. **1552** HULOET, Vulgar, or much vsed, *uulgatus*. **1594** BLUNDEVIL *Exerc.* I. xxvii. (1597) 33 b, As minutes, seconds, thirds, fourthes,.. marked with streekes and vulgare numbers. **1597** HOOKER *Eccl. Pol.* v. lxv. §11 Wee neither omit it.. nor altogether make it so vulgar as the custome heretofore hath bene. **1610** GUILLIM *Heraldry* II. i. 40, I could produce many examples euen to this day; were not the vse heereof so vulgar. **1659** H. THORNDIKE *Wks.* (1846) II. 458 The solemn times.. cannot.. have been settled till Christianity was grown very vulgar. **1693** LOCKE *Educ.* §175 Another thing very ordinary in the vulgar Method of Grammar-Schools there is, of which I see no Use at all. **1729** T. INNES *Anc. Inhab. N. Brit.* I. 18 So the vulgar version of Ziphilin's abridgment of Dio hath it. **1795** BURKE *Th. Scarcity* Wks. 1842 II. 252 Compelling us to diminish the quantity of labour which in the vulgar course we actually employ. **1826** DISRAELI *Viv. Grey* IV. ii, We talk.. as often about our enemies, at least those who have any; which, in my opinion, is the vulgarest of all possessions.

†**b.** Used to designate the Vulgate version of the Bible. *Obs.* (Cf. VULGAR *sb.* 5.)

1535 JOYE *Apol. Tindale* (Arb.) 46 T[indale].. ministreth a shrewd occasion.. by vntrwly translating this sentence *et unicuique seminum dat deus suum* or *proprium corpus* (as hathe the vulgare texte). **1538** COVERDALE *New T.* (title-p.), After the vulgare text communely called S. Jeroms. **1583** FULKE *Def. Tr. Script.* xvii. 447 That S. Hieronyme was author of the vulgar Latine interpretation, of the olde Testament. **1652** NEEDHAM tr. *Selden's Mare Cl.* 31 So they are expressed in the vulgar Edition, out of the Hebrew Original, which is lost. **1674** OWEN *Holy Spirit* I. iv. §6. 71 The Vulgar Latine in this Place renders the Word by *Ornatus eorum*. **1677** —— *Justif.* iv. 185 All which things prefer the Complutensian, Syriack, and Arabick, before the vulgar reading of this place. **1691** tr. *Emilianne's Frauds Rom. Monks* (ed. 3) 51 Contrary to the express words of the Vulgar Translation. **1823** A. SMALL *Rom. Antiq. Fife* v. 102 The vulgar Latin [reads] thus.

3. Of language or speech: Commonly or customarily used by the people of a country; ordinary, vernacular.

In common use *c* 1525–1650; now *arch.*

a **1513** FABYAN *Chron.* I. xvii. 16 Whiche felde or Countre whervpon yᵉ sayd Morgan faughte.. is to this daye called Glanmorgan, whiche is to meane in our vulgare tunge, Morgan hys lande. **1530** PALSGR. 17 Suche as writte farcis & contrefait the vulgare speche. **1585** T. WASHINGTON tr. *Nicholay's Voy.* IV. xix. 133 b, They celebrate their office.. in the Armenian tongue,.. [and] the standers by.. answere them in the same vulgare language. *c* **1610** E. BOLTON *Hypercritica* iv. §2 Mr. Hooker's Preface to his Books of Ecclesiastical Policy is a singular and choice Parcel of our vulgar Language. **1653** W. RAMESEY *Astrol. Restored* 84 To treat.. of this noble Art.. in a plain manner, and our vulgar tongue. **1709** STEELE *Tatler* No. 141 ¶11 To be instructed in their Duties in the known or vulgar Tongue. **1707** J. CHAMBERLAYNE *St. Gt. Brit.* I. III. vii. (1710) 204 There were.. more good, and more bad Books printed and published in the English Tongue, than in all the vulgar Languages in Europe. **1855** MILMAN *Lat. Chr.* IX. viii. IV. 185 They read the Gospels, they preached, and they prayed, in the vulgar tongue. **1873** HALE *In His Name* ii. 8 Bits of Paul or Matthew or Luke which had been translated into the vulgar language.

b. Used to qualify the name of the language.

1483 CAXTON *Knt. de la Tour* Prol., To translate & reduce this said book out of frenssh into our vulgar Englissh. **1613** PURCHAS *Pilgrimage* VI. xii. 530 They are much addicted to Poetrie, and make long Poems of their warres, huntings, and loues,.. in rithme, like the vulgar Italian Sonnets. **1687** A. LOVELL tr. *Thevenot's Trav.* I. 102 Though several of them understand Italian, yet their usual Language is the vulgar Greek, which is for the most part but the literal Greek corrupted. **1699** BENTLEY *Phal.* 404 Which we are sure.. continued to be pure and Vulgar Syriac for 2000 Years. **1717** LADY M. W. MONTAGU *Let. to Pope* 1 Apr., The vulgar Turk is very different from what is spoken at court. **1766** *Compl. Farmer* s.v. *Surveying* 7 E 2/2 This in vulgar English may be called a corner. **1818** HALLAM *Mid. Ages* ix. (1868) 591 We cannot.. ascertain in what degree the vulgar Latin differed from that of Cicero or Seneca. *a* **1873** DEUTSCH *Lit. Rem.* (1874) 358 The Samaritan Dialect, a mixture of vulgar Hebrew and Aramean.

†**c.** In predicative use; also const. *to. Obs.*

1565 JEWEL *Reply Harding* (1611) 383 Hebrew, Greek, and Latine,.. as they were once natiue, and vulgar to those three peoples, so now to none be they natiue, and vulgar. **1612** BREREWOOD *Lang. & Relig.* 2 The Greek tongue.. although it belonged originally to Hellas alone, yet in time it became vulgar to these also. **1668** WILKINS *Real Char.* I. i. §4. 5 After the Captivity the pure Hebrew ceased to be Vulgar, remaining onely amongst learned men. **1699** T. BAKER *Refl. Learn.* ii. 13 The Greek Tongue had the same Fortune with the Latine, tho it continu'd vulgar longer. **1712** SWIFT *Let. Eng. Tongue* Wks. 1755 II. I. 183 Neither was that [*sc.* the Latin] language ever so vulgar in Britain, as it is known to have been in Gaul and Spain.

4. †**a.** Written or spoken in, translated into, the usual language of a country. *Obs.*

1513 DOUGLAS *Æneid* I. Prol. 498 Thair may be na compair Betwixt his versis and my style wlgair. *Ibid.*, *Ane Exclamatioun* 37 Go, wlgar Virgill, to euery churlich wycht Say, I avow thou art translatit rycht. **1556** RECORDE *Cast. Knowl.* Contents, With sundry.. newe demonstrations not Written before in any vulgare woorkes. **1599** G. SANDYS *Europæ Spec.* (1632) 115 They have called all vulgar Bibles streightly in againe. **1617** MORYSON *Itin.* III. 30, I had some skill in that Language, especially for vulgar speeches. **1662** J. DAVIES tr. *Olearius' Voy. Ambass.* 79 Never learning anything but reading and writing, and certain vulgar prayers.

b. Of words or names: Employed in ordinary speech; common, familiar.

1676 HOBBES *Iliad* Pref. (1686) 1 Forein words, till by long use they become vulgar, are un[in]telligible to them. **1776** SIR D. DALRYMPLE *Ann. Scot.* I. 3 *note*, I suspect that Lulach was rather his vulgar sirname, than his name. **1785** MARTYN *Lett. Bot.* Introd. (1794) 2 These plants had a different vulgar name in every province. **1800** BEWICK (*title*), Figures of British Land Birds, to which are added, a few Foreign Birds, with their Vulgar and Scientific Names.

5. Common or customary in respect of the use or understanding of language, words, or ideas.

1553 WILSON *Rhet.* 94, I might tary a longe tyme in declaryng the nature of diuerse Schemes, whiche are woordes or sentencies altered.. contrarie to the vulgare custome of our speache without chaungyng their nature at all. **1612** T. BODLEY in Macray *Ann. Bodleian* (1880) 410, I make request yᵗ all my words be construed directly and in vulgar sense. **1634** *Documents agst. Prynne* (Camden) 48 My expressions too (at least in my intention, opinion, and vulgar acceptacion), are innocent and sincere. **1696** WHISTON *The. Earth* II. (1722) 161 By a Month, in the vulgar way of speaking, is meant 30 Days. **1727** DE FOE *Syst. Magic* I. i. (1840) 25 The people called magicians, in the present vulgar acceptation of the word. **1754** EDWARDS *Freed. Will* I. iii. (1762) 14 The word Necessity, in its vulgar and common Use, is relative. **1798** BAY *Amer. Law Rep.* (1809) I. 85 The vulgar meaning of the words dying without issue. **1862** BURTON *Bk. Hunter* (1863) 5 The vulgar everyday-world way of putting the idea. **1878** STEWART & TAIT *Unseen Univ.* i. §39. 57 The doctrine of the resurrection in its vulgar acceptation could not possibly be true.

6. Commonly current or prevalent, generally or widely disseminated, as a matter of knowledge, assertion, or opinion: **a.** Of sayings, statements, facts, etc.

1549 *Compl. Scot.* Epist. 7 Fra this exempil cummis ane vlgare adagia. **1591** SAVILE *Tacitus, Hist.* II. lxxviii. 99 Neither was there any thing more vulgare in euery mans mouth. **1607** T. ROGERS *39 Art.* Pref. §26 Bookes, and open speeches.. made vulgar within a yeare, and little more after his happy ingresse into this kingdome. **1653** W. RAMESEY *Astrol. Restored* To Rdr. 6 But I shall answer in that vulgar and rustical Proverb, it is a good Horse that never stumbles. **1693** DRYDEN *Persius' Sat.* i. 244 *note*, The Story is vulgar, that Midas King of Phrygia, was made judge betwixt Apollo and Pan, who was the best Musician. **1830** SIR W. HAMILTON *Discuss.* (1852) 72 One vulgar passage from the writings of that philosopher. **1892** *Daily News* 19 Dec. 5/4 It set the seal, however, on his vulgar, as distinct from his professional, fame.

b. Of discourse, rumour, etc.

1590 SHAKS. *Com. Err.* III. i. 100 If by strong hand you offer to breake in,.. A vulgar comment will be made of it. **1595** *Locrine* IV. i. 138 What would the common sort report of me, If I forget my loue, and cleaue to thee? *Loc.* Kings need not feare the vulgar sentences. *c* **1600** SHAKS. *Sonn.* cxii, Your loue and pittie doth th' impression fill, Which vulgar scandall stampt vpon my brow. **1617** MORYSON *Itin.* II. 20 Of late (according to vulgar speech) he had displeased the Earle of Essex. **1691** WOOD *Ath. Oxon.* I. 323 The then vulgar talk was, the Devil came to take away Oliv. Cromwell, who then lay on his death-bed. **1818** SHELLEY *Julian* 362 Believe that I am ever still the same,.. Nor dream that I will join the vulgar cry. **1855** MACAULAY *Hist. Eng.* xix. IV. 302 They did not join in the vulgar cry against the Dutch.

c. Of knowledge, opinions, notions, etc.

a **1548** HALL *Chron., Edw. IV*, 210 b, Notwithstandyng the vulgare opinion.. the wisedome of this world is folishenes before God. **1605** VERSTEGAN *Dec. Intell.* vii. (1628) 199 To giue the reader some knowledge more then is vulger. *c* **1610** SIR J. MELVIL *Mem.* (1683) 125 He was become careless, following in many things the vulgar opinion. **1655** CULPEPPER, etc. *Riverius* XI. iv. 33 That vulgar difficulty which is controverted by almost all Writers. **1701** SWIFT *Contests Nobles & Comm.* v, This is a truth of vulgar knowledge and observation. **1794** HUTTON *Philos. Light*, etc. 127 According to the vulgar notions of things, cold is considered as absolutely subsisting in bodies, in the same manner as heat. **1832** PALMERSTON *Opin. & Pol.* (1852) 219 Taking the merest and vulgarest view of the matter. **1854** MILMAN *Lat. Chr.* IV. i. II. 10 Mohammedanism.. a stern negation.. of the vulgar polytheism which prevailed among the ruder Arab tribes. **1865** M. ARNOLD *Ess. Crit., Spinoza* (1875) 375 This mode of interpreting Scripture is fatal to the vulgar notion of its verbal inspiration.

d. Of errors, prejudices, etc.

1630 *R. Johnson's Kingd. & Commw.* 546 This is but a vulgar errour. **1670** W. PERWICH *Desp.* (Camden) 91 A vulgar mistake of the death of the Duke of Lorraine instead of that of the Great Duke of Florence. **1691** T. H[ALE] *Acc. New Invent.* p. xxiii, The idle conceit of the Fish Remora, which mens sottishness hath made a vulgar one. **1785** REID *Intell. Powers* I. i. 221 May natural judgement not be a vulgar error? **1798** FERRIAR *Illustr. Sterne* vi. 165 Mr. Shandy has passed a similar condemnation on some English names, to which vulgar prejudices are attached. **1845** FORD *Handbk. Spain* I. 5 One of the old vulgar superstitions in Spain. **1856** KANE *Arct. Expl.* I. xxix. 392, I satisfied myself that it was a vulgar prejudice to regard the liver of the bear as poisonous. **1879** MCCARTHY *Own Times* I. v. 104 One of the vulgarest fallacies of statecraft.

†**7.** Of common occurrence; not rare. *Obs.*

1607 TOPSELL *Four-f. Beasts* 111 Other things I omit concerning this beast [the cony], because as it is vulgar, the benefits thereof are commonly known. **1657** S. PURCHAS *Pol. Flying-Ins.* 7 The Chameleon, a vile (and in many Countries a Vulgar) Creature.

8. Of or pertaining to the common people.

1597 SHAKS. *2 Hen. IV*, I. iii. 90 An habitation giddy and vnsure Hath he that buildeth on the vulgar heart. **1605** *1st Pt. Jeronimo* 436, I will buze Andreas landing, Which, once but crept into the vulger mouthes, Is hurryed heer and there, and sworne for troth. **1622** PEACHAM *Compl. Gent.* i. 13 Those [apples] of Hesperides, golden, and out of the vulgar reach. **1646** SIR T. BROWNE *Pseud. Ep.* I. v. 17 Though a weaknesse of the Intellect, and most discoverable in vulgar heads, yet hath it sometime fallen upon wiser braines. **1697** DRYDEN *Æneid* XII. 5 The more he was with vulgar hate oppressed, The more his fury boiled within his breast. **1783** W. THOMSON *Watson's Philip III*, VI. (1793) II. 152 A veil of pomp.. concealed from the vulgar eye the symptoms of its decay. **1796** BP. WATSON *Apol. Bible* 209 You have merely busied yourself in exposing to vulgar contempt a few unsightly shrubs. **1810** SCOTT *Lady of Lake* III. xxvi, Grey Superstition's whisper dread Debarr'd the spot to vulgar tread. *Ibid.* v. xxx, With like acclaim, the vulgar throat Strain'd for King James their morning note. **1855** *Poultry Chron.* II. 561/1 He was in a coop protected from the vulgar gaze, by a covering of green baize. **1870** JEVONS *Elem. Logic* xxvii. 237 All observations.. negative the idea that there can be any such influence as the vulgar mind attributes to the moon.

II. 9. Of persons: Belonging to the ordinary or common class in the community; not distinguished or marked off from this in any way; plebeian: **a.** With collective terms, as *people, sort.*

1530 PALSGR. 369 *Septante, octante*, and *nonante*, be never used of the voulger people. **1551** T. WILSON *Logike* A 3 b, Diuerse learned men.. haue with most earnest trauaile made euery of them familiar to their vulgare people. **1576** FLEMING *Panopl. Epist.* 193 To circumuent the common people, he spared no coloured pretence to allure the vulgar sort. **1609** BIBLE (Douay) *Jer.* xxvi. 23 He cast forth his carcasse in the sepulchers of the base vulgar people. **1632** LITHGOW *Trav.* I. 26 They of the vulgar kind are both ignorant, sluttish and greedy. **1649** MILTON *Eikon.* 13 The last Will of Cæsar being read to the people, and what Legacies he had bequeath'd them, wrought much in that Vulgar audience to the avenging of his death. **1705** STANHOPE *Paraphr.* I. 34 Instead of numerous Guards, and triumphal Chariots, and costly Preparations, we find only the Attendance of a Vulgar and despised Crowd. **1718** PRIOR *Solomon* I. 681 One [elder], in whom an outward Mien appear'd, And Turn superior to the vulgar Herd. **1820** HAZLITT *Lect. Dram. Lit.* 12 He [Shakspeare] was not something sacred and aloof from the vulgar herd of men. **1821** BYRON *Sardanap.* v. i, 'Tis easy to astonish or appal The vulgar mass which moulds a horde of slaves.

b. With individual designations (in *sing.* or *pl.*).

1585 T. WASHINGTON tr. *Nicholay's Voy.* IV. ix. 121 The vulgare Arabians doe cal it Rabach. **1593** SHAKS. *2 Hen. VI*, IV. i. 127 Rather let my head Stoope to the blocke,.. Than stand vncouer'd to the Vulgar Groom. **1634** SIR T. HERBERT *Trav.* 188 If any vulgar fellow meet them, they presently shake and vibrate their swords vpon their Shields, crying aloud Nayroe. *a* **1699** J. BEAUMONT *Psyche* XXI. 11 Thou seest with what exact Obedience all My vulgar Subjects on their shoulders take My heavyest yokes. **1709** STRYPE *Ann. Ref.* I. xxxix. 406 This letter.. may deserve an English translation of it, for the sake of vulgar readers. **1765** H. WALPOLE *Otranto* i, Some of the vulgar spectators had run to the great church which stood near the castle and came back open-mouthed. **1779** JOHNSON *L.P., Milton* Wks. II. 168 The vulgar inhabitants of Pandæmonium, being incorporeal spirits, are at large.. in a limited space. **1798** S.

& Ht. Lee *Canterb. T.* II. 300 Credulity is..the characteristic of the vulgar Italians. 1813 Shelley *Q. Mab* v. 140 How many a vulgar Cato has compelled His energies ..To mould a pin, or fabricate a nail!

transf. 1667 Milton *P.L.* III. 577 Where the great Luminarie Alooff the vulgar Constellations thick.. Dispenses Light from farr.

†**c.** Holding an ordinary place in a certain class; esp. of soldiers. *Obs.*

1607–12 Bacon *Ess., Marr. & Single Life* (Arb.) 268 Despising of Marriage amongest the Turkes, maketh the vulgar Souldiour more base. 1651 Howell *Venice* 129 The greatest prisoners were Achmet and Mahomet..with thirty thousand vulgar soldiers. 1794 Chalmers *Ruddiman* 90 The magistrates [in 1660] steadily prohibited the vulgar schoolmasters from teaching Latin.

†**d.** ***the vulgar world***, the world at large. *Obs.*

1632 Lithgow *Trav.* A 4 My three Voyages, which are now layd open to the Vulgar World.

10. Of the common or usual kind; of an ordinary commonplace character; exhibiting no special or distinguishing quality: †**a.** Of material things.

1555 Eden *Decades* (Arb.) 70 Hauinge .xii. other of their vulgare cotages placed abowte the same. *Ibid.* (Arb.) 159 Of this is made the more vulgar or common breade. 1602 Shaks. *Ham.* I. ii. 99 For, what we know must be, and is as common As any the most vulgar thing to sence, Why should we..Take it to heart? 1617 Moryson *Itin.* III. 63 Copper mettall, adorned with vulgar precious stones. 1656 Beale *Heref. Orchards* (1657) 16 That the setlings might gather root as well in that vulgar ground, as also in the finer mould. 1694 Salmon *Bate's Dispens.* (1713) 42/2 First comes the Flegm, then the volatile Spirit; lastly, the Oil, or vulgar Spirit. 1744 Berkeley *Siris* §10 This vulgar tar, which cheapness and plenty may have rendered contemptible, appears to be an excellent balsam. 1776 *Med. Obs. & Inq.* (1784) VI. i. 14 Punch, made with a maceration of black currants in our vulgar corn spirit, is a liquor that agrees remarkably well with him.

†**b.** Of plants, animals, etc. *Obs.*

c 1586 C'tess Pembroke *Ps.* (1823) civ. vi, The vulgar grasse, whereof the beast is faine, The rarer herb man for him self hath chose. 1607 Topsell *Four-f. Beasts* 731 A vulgar weasell being kept very old and drunke in Wine, to the quantity of two drams, is accounted a present remedy against the venome or stings of serpents. 1610 Holland *Camden's Brit.* (1637) 543, I mean not those vulgar birds which in other places are highly esteemed. 1665–76 Rea *Flora* (ed. 3) 17 The other sorts..you will find..among Greens more vulgar. *a* 1682 Sir T. Browne *Tracts* (1684) 62 Bellonius..observed not the vulgar Oak in those parts. 1782–3 W. F. Martyn *Geog. Mag.* 704 Those of an inferior rank make use of the foliage of some more vulgar tree. 1803 G. Ellis *Let. to Scott* 3 Oct., We possess a vulgar dog (a pointer), to whom it is intended to commit the charge of our house during our absence.

c. Of qualities, actions, etc.

1559 Knox *First Blast* App. (Arb.) 60 Neyther yit wold I that ye should esteam that mercy to be vulgar and commone which ye haue receaued. 1561 Eden *Arte Nauig.* Pref., I thynke that he was a man of no vulgare iudgement. 1596 *Edward III*, II. i. 314 These are the vulgar tenders of false men, That neuer pay the duetie of their words. 1602 *Ld. Cromwell* III. iii. 9 Thou art a man differing from vulgar forme. 1622 Bacon *Hen. VII*, 144 Many Lawes were made, of a more priuate and vulgar nature then ought to detaine the Reader of an Historie. 1649 F. Roberts *Clavis Bibl.* 512 Here are not vulgar but extraordinary Histories. 1716 Gay *Trivia* II. 302 Yet let me not descend to trivial song, Nor vulgar Circumstance my verse prolong. 1754 Gray *Progr. Poesy* 122 Yet shall he mount, and keep his distant way Beyond the limits of a vulgar fate. 1795 Burke *Th. Scarcity* Wks. 1842 II. 248 Philosophical happiness is to want little. Civil or vulgar happiness is to want much, and to enjoy much. 1848 W. K. Kelly tr. *L. Blanc's Hist. Ten Y.* I. 366 That is assuredly a very vulgar policy, and one within the scope of the most ordinary capacities. 1867 Maurice *Patriarchs & Lawg.* v. (1877) 104 A history which exhibits God as an actual personal Being, without whom the vulgarest affairs of men are unintelligible and anomalous.

†**d.** Of persons. *Obs.*

1570 Dee *Math. Pref.* *ij, Vulgar Practisers haue Numbers, otherwise, in sundry Considerations. 1609 Bible (Douay) *1 Chron.* i. *comm.*, We wil present to the vulgar reader, certaine cleare and ordinarie rules, by which the learned Divines doe reconcile such apparent contradictions. 1664 Power *Exp. Philos.* I. 43 We need not so much wonder with the Vulgar Philosophers, how so clear and glorious a body..should be made of so durty..Materials. 1697 Dryden *Virg. Georg.* IV. 653 No vulgar god Pursues thy crimes, nor with a common rod. 1729 T. Innes *Anc. Inhab. N. Brit.* I. Pref. p. vii, These considerations..made me.. resolve to..leave to others the invidious task of reforming our vulgar historians. 1752 Hume *Pol. Disc.* x. 224 The most vulgar slave cou'd yield by his labour an obolus a day, over and above his maintenance. 1794 Burke *Let. to Dk. Portland* (1844) IV. 235 It will not do for you to be vulgar, common-place ministers.

11. Of an ordinary unartificial type; not refined or advanced beyond the common.

1580 G. Harvey *Let. to Spenser* S.'s Wks. (1912) 631/2 It is the vulgare and naturall Mother Prosodye, that alone worketh the feate. 1638 Rawley tr. *Bacon's Life & Death* (1651) 1 Omit for the present, all Astrological Observations ..: Onely insist upon the vulgar and manifest Observations; as whether they were born by Night or by Day. 1671 J. Webster *Metallogr.* i. 1 As also the whole Band of the Chymists, both mystical and vulgar, do sufficiently testifie. 1725 Watts *Logic* I. iii. §4 Ideas are either vulgar or learned. A vulgar Idea represents to us the most obvious and sensible Appearances that are contained in the Object of them. 1748 Hartley *Observ. on Man* I. i. §1. 35 Medicinal Bodies appear, from Observations both philosophical and vulgar, to be endued with more active Properties than common Aliments.

†**b.** Adapted to ordinary minds or comprehensions. *Obs.*

1643 Sir T. Browne *Relig. Med.* I. §45 Unspeakable mysteries in the Scriptures are often delivered in a vulgar and illustrative way. 1651 Hobbes *Govt. & Soc.* Ep. Ded., If it be sound, if it be useful, if it be vulgar; I humbly offer it to your Lordship. *a* 1652 J. Smith *Sel. Disc.* vi. 183 Speaking to the weakest sort of men in the most vulgar sort of dialect.

†**12.** Common in respect of use or association. *Obs. rare.*

1595 Shaks. *John* II. 387 I'de play incessantly vpon these Iades, Euen till vnfenced desolation Leaue them as naked as the vulgar ayre. 1602 —— *Ham.* I. iii. 61 Be thou familiar; but by no meanes vulgar.

13. Having a common and offensively mean character; coarsely commonplace; lacking in refinement or good taste; uncultured, ill-bred.

a. Of actions, manners, features, etc.

1643 J. M. *Sov. Salve* 13 Are not such instances [of time-serving] as vulgar as the spirits that furnish us with them? 1647 Clarendon *Hist. Reb.* II. §86 To Intangle all those.. who were transported with those vulgar and vile Considerations. 1699 Pomfret *Past. Ess.* 134 Nay, all affronts so unconcerned she bore,..As if she thought it vulgar to resent. 1797 Jane Austen *Sense & Sens.* xxi, The vulgar freedom and folly of the eldest left her no recommendation. 1797 *Monthly Mag.* III. 201 So, the word *vulgar* now implies something base and groveling in actions. 1846 Mrs. A. Marsh *Father Darcy* II. i. 17 There is something very coarse and vulgar in their countenances. *Ibid.* II. iv. 90 His features were vulgar, his lips thick and coarse. 1853 Maurice *Proph. & Kings* i. 7 This would be a low, paltry, vulgar way of accounting for his acts. 1875 Jowett *Plato* (ed. 2) V. 315 The vulgar sort of trade which is carried on by lending money.

b. Of persons.

1678 Marvell *Growth Popery* 40 The mean malice of the same Vulgar Scribler, hired by the Conspirators at so much a sheet. 1778 Miss Burney *Evelina* xvii, Miss will think us very vulgar..to live in London and never have been to an Opera. 1809 Malkin *Gil Blas* III. iv. ¶7, I see the vulgar dog in an almshouse. 1835 Willis *Pencillings* I. ii. 18 A vulgar Marseilles shopkeeper. 1865 Ruskin *Sesame* i. §28 It is in the blunt hand and the dead heart, in the diseased habit, in the hardened conscience, that men become vulgar. 1881 'Rita' *My Lady Coquette* iii, How hot and vulgar she looks with all that colour.

c. Of the mind, spirit, etc.

1764 Goldsm. *Trav.* 225 In wild excess the vulgar breast takes fire, Till, buried in debauch, the bliss expire. 1766 [Anstey] *Bath Guide* iii. 4 A Grace, an Air, a Taste refin'd, To vulgar Souls unknown. 1809–10 Coleridge *Friend* (1865) 113 It is so stimulant to the pride of a vulgar mind, to be persuaded that it knows what few others know. 1844 Kinglake *Eothen* v, In all baseness and imposture there is a coarse, vulgar spirit. 1882 Bain *Jas. Mill* vi. 288 Executions and death-scenes are great things for vulgar minds.

d. Of language, etc.

1716 Gay *Trivia* I. 187 Let not such vulgar tales debase thy mind. 1813 *Salem* (Mass.) *Gaz.* 12 Mar. 2/4 To pronounce him a friend to Great-Britain; or, in their language of vulgar abuse, a British Tory. 1865 M. Arnold *Ess. Crit.*, *Joubert* 224 Saugrenu is a rather vulgar French word, but, like many other vulgar words, very expressive. 1891 Farrar *Darkn. & Dawn* x, They said..that—you—were—dare I speak the vulgar word?—a Christian.

e. Of material things.

1812 H. & J. Smith *Rej. Addr.* xii. 75 I've heard our front that faces Drury Lane Much criticised; they say 'tis vulgar brick work. 1817 Chalmers *Astron. Disc.* ii. (1852) 45 While all the vulgar grandeur of other days is now mouldering in forgetfulness. 1905 G. Thorne *Lost Cause* iv, A wilderness of mean little houses and vulgar streets.

14. *Comb.*, as ***vulgar-like***, ***-looking***, ***-reasoning***, ***-sounding***; ***vulgar-minded***, ***-spirited***, ***-viewed*** adjs.; ***vulgar-wise*** adv.; also quasi-*adv.* in †***vulgar plain***.

1563 Foxe *A. & M.* 1050/1 A certayn seuere & graue grace, which I wished oftentymes to haue bene more popular & *uulgarlike in him. 1815 Scott *Guy M.* xxxix, What that *vulgar-looking fellow said after the funeral. 1816 *Remarks Eng. Mann.* 37 Not discriminating between real gentlemen who require no such hint, and *vulgar-minded men who do. 1846 Hare *Mission Comf.* (1850) 398 The vulgarminded in all ages have been incapable of conceiving that a man can be actuated by any but personal feelings. 1869 Geo. Eliot in Cross *Life* III. 100 The most vulgar-minded genius that ever produced a great effect in literature. 1554–9 *Songs & Ball. Phil. & Mary* (Roxb.) 6 Good maners unto all degrese Ys mete for to be *vulgar playne. 1654 Whitlock *Zootomia* 321, I am none of those *vulgar-Reasoning Despisers of that Sex. 1797 Anna Seward *Lett.* (1811) IV. 302 His *vulgar-sounding word, beleaguered, once used in the Paradise Lost, offends us continually in this new epic. 1628 Earle *Microcosm.* (Arb.) 70 A *vulgar-spirited Man Is one of the heard of the World. 1647 Clarendon *Hist. Reb.* VI. §134 The passions, and affections of the Vulgar-spirited. 1852 *Meanderings of Mem.* I. 149 She was not *vulgar-viewed, her thinkings took The selfsame tenor. 1828 P. Cunningham *N.S. Wales* (ed. 3) II. 21 One bird roasting aristocratically upon a wooden spit, and the other, broiling *vulgar-wise, upon the embers.

vulgarian (vʌlˈgɛərɪən), *a.* and *sb.* [f. prec. + -ian.]

A. *adj.* = vulgar *a.* (in later use in sense 13).

c 1650 Denham *To Sir J. Mennis* i, All on a weeping Monday, With a fat vulgarian sloven, Little Admiral John To Boulogne is gone. 1833 *Fraser's Mag.* VIII. 625 Compare this with the vulgarian twaddle of the old Blackingman. 1876 *World* V. No. 114. 3 A position in the scale of popular amusements precisely analogous to the vulgarian paradise known as the music-hall.

B. *sb.* A vulgar person; freq., a well-to-do or rich person of vulgar manners.

1804 Mar. Edgeworth *Ennui* vi, The man is married, to some vulgarian, of course. 1821 L. Hunt *Indicator* No. 66 (1822) II. 106 You are thought little better than a vulgarian. 1853 Lytton *My Novel* v. ix, Did you not marry a low creature—a vulgarian—a tradesman's daughter? 1888 *Athenæum* 21 July 93/1 One of the most repulsive vulgarians we have ever met with out of real life.

Hence **vulˈgarianism**.

1920 D. H. Lawrence *Lost Girl* x. 243 She saw his modern vulgarianism, and decadence. 1963 *New Society* 21 Nov. 22/1 The rising generations of eggheads is notorious for its vulgarianism, admiring Brigitte, canonizing Marilyn.

†**ˈvulgarily**, *adv.* *Obs.*$^{-1}$ [f. vulgar *a.* + -(i)ly².] Commonly.

1655 Fuller *Hist. Camb.* 120 Thomas Lord Audley of Walden..changed Buckingham, into Magdalen, (vulgarily) Maudlin Colledge.

‖**vulgarisateur** (vylgarizatœr). [Fr.] = *vulgarizer* s.v. vulgarize *v.*

1933 D. L. Sayers *Murder must Advertise* xiv. 238, I obtained an introduction to her through what..that incomparable *vulgarisateur*, Charles Dickens—abominably calls a mutual friend. 1948 *Mind* LVII. 383 The introductory chapter..consists of a defence of the philosophical *vulgarisateur*. 1955 J. Wain *Interpretations* p. xiii, The making of large generalizations could safely be left to the *vulgarisateurs*. 1971 Ld. Butler *Art of Possible* viii. 157 The less voluble and extrovert Hall, to act as *vulgarisateur* or publicist for his ideas.

‖**vulgarisation** (vylgarizasjɔ̃). [Fr.] = vulgarization 1. Cf. haute vulgarisation.

1939 *Year's Work Eng. Stud.* 1937 25 J. R. Firth's popular little sketch, *The Tongues of Men*, is an excellent example of that *vulgarisation* by experts which is becoming so fashionable to-day. 1959 *Times Lit. Suppl.* 11 Sept. 520/1 But Porché's later work had to stand up to the essays of.. Sartre and Blanchot, and the propitious moment for his *vulgarisation* had come and gone. 1968 J. A. W. Bennett *Chaucer's Bk. of Fame* ii. 75 Witness his book on the Astrolabe, an admirable piece of *vulgarisation* which we ought not to dissociate severely from his poetry and which may reflect the study of astronomy in the Oxford of his day.

ˈvulgarish, *a.* *rare*$^{-1}$. [f. vulgar *a.* + -ish.] Somewhat vulgar.

1860 Thackeray *Lovel* v, Low, vulgarish sort of man, he was.

vulgarism (ˈvʌlgərɪz(ə)m). [f. vulgar *a.* + -ism. Cf. Sp. and Pg. *vulgarismo*, It. *volgarismo*.]

†**1.** A common or ordinary expression. *Obs.*$^{-1}$

1644 Bulwer *Chirol.* 13 An ineffable latitude of significations: whose vulgarismes, varied through such multiplicity of senses, are of that note and consequence, that [etc.].

2. A vulgar phrase or expression; a colloquialism of a low or unrefined character.

1746 H. Walpole *Let. to Mann* 28 Mar., The Countess.. has entertained the town with an excellent vulgarism. 1758 L. Temple *Sketches* (ed. 2) 43 The Sentiments..cannot be exprest with too much Plainness and Simplicity; provided all Vulgarisms are as much as possible avoided. 1798 *Brit. Critic* XI. 136 It took him, is a grose vulgarism. 1822 Mrs. Shelley in Dowden *Shelley* (1887) II. 381 We hear that she leads him and his mother (to use a vulgarism) a devil of a life. 1874 Green *Short Hist.* viii. (1882) 449 The slipshod vulgarisms of the shopkeeper of to-day.

b. A popular corruption *of* a name. *rare*$^{-1}$.

1852 Miss Yonge *Cameos* (1877) I. xix. 136 This romantic story,..celebrates the Saracen lady by the extraordinary title of Susy Pye, perhaps a vulgarism of her original Eastern name.

3. The quality or character of being vulgar; vulgarity.

1749 Chesterf. *Lett. to Son* 27 Sept., Vulgarism in language is the..distinguishing characteristic of bad company, and a bad education. 1771 Sir J. Reynolds *Disc.* iv. (1876) 345 Familiar and interesting to all Europe without being degraded by the vulgarism of ordinary life in any country. 1788 Mrs. Hughes *Henry & Isabella* I. 168 They were generally written in a style of pretence and sometimes vulgarism. 1819 Keats *Lines to Fanny* 24 Shall I gulp wine? No, that is vulgarism. 1831 *Examiner* 436/2 We are..struck by the absence of vulgarism in the performance.

b. An instance of vulgarity; a vulgar action, practice, habit, etc.

1785 G. A. Bellamy *Apology* (ed. 3) IV. 158 The complaints of having nothing to do, is such a vulgarism, that I wonder any persons..can degrade themselves by the acknowledgement. 1814 Jane Austen *Mansfield Park* xlvi, Visions of good and ill breeding, of old vulgarisms and new gentilities were before her. 1834 *Tait's Mag.* I. 54/1 Since the scent of that flower has been voted a vulgarism!

ˈvulgarist. [f. vulgar *a.* + -ist.] A vulgarian.

1847 *Fraser's Mag.* XXXVI. 53 In the every-day pursuits of the vulgarist there is a link connecting them.

vulgarity (vʌlˈgærɪtɪ). [ad. L. (post-classical) *vulgāritas* the mass or multitude (f. *vulgār-is* vulgar *a.*), or f. vulgar *a.* + -ity. Cf. F. *vulgarité*, It. *volgarità*, Sp. *vulgaridad*, Pg. *-idade*.]

†**1.** The commonalty; the common people. *Obs.*

1579 Northbrooke *Dicing* (1843) 73 The eternall God hath appoynted & diuided his Church militant into four parts: first, into principalitie; seconde, into nobilitie; thirde, into pastoralitie; fourthly, into vulgaritie. 1616 J. Lane *Contn. Sqr.'s T.* VIII. 330 So these condemnd, thence garded weare to dye, lothd, skornd, revild, cursd of th' vulgaritie. 1632 Lithgow *Trav.* IX. 421 A proud Nobility, a familiar and manly Gentry, and a ruvidous vulgarity. 1659 Gauden *Tears Ch.* Pref. 3 The meere vulgarity (like Swine) are prone to cry out more, for a little bite by the eare, than for all the sordidnesse of sin.

†**b.** The ordinary sort or run (*of* a class, etc.).

1646 SIR T. BROWNE *Pseud. Ep.* I. vii. 25 'Tis true by the vulgarity of Philosophers there are many points beleeved without probation. **1681** RYCAUT tr. *Gracian's Critick* 190 His Humour formed of a disagreeing mould and nature to the vulgarity of the World.

†**c.** Used as a mock-title to designate one of the common people. *Obs.*⁻¹

1646 SIR T. BROWNE *Pseud. Ep.* I. iii. 11 For true it is, (and I hope shall not offend their vulgarities) if I say they are daily mocked into errour.

†**2.** General use; common diffusion. *Obs. rare.*

1612 BREREWOOD *Lang. & Relig.* 33 It may well seem that the Roman tongue became not the vulgar language in any of these parts of the empire, which yet are specially instanced, for the large vulgarity of it. *c* **1645** HOWELL *Lett.* (1650) I. 387 The Latin or primitive Roman tongue,.. though living yet in the Schools,.. may be said to be defunct in point of vulgarity, any time these 1000 years passed.

†**3.** The quality of being usual, ordinary, or commonplace; an instance of this. *Obs.*

1646 SIR T. BROWNE *Pseud. Ep.* I. iii. 12 Although their condition and fortunes may place them many Spheres above the multitude, yet are they still within the line of vulgarity. **1656** BLOUNT *Glossogr.*, *Vulgarity*, the common manner or fashion of the vulgar people. **1665–6** *Phil. Trans.* I. 228 In these Vulgarities we may.. trace out the cause and nature of Light, as in Jewels of greatest value. **1716** M. DAVIES *Athen. Brit.* III. 24 He.. was answer'd that he never differ'd any thing to the Morrow, or some such thing to the same learned purpose of Dissenting Sermons, which are often full of such Unscholar-like Vulgarities.

4. The quality of being vulgar, unrefined, or coarse; an instance of this.

a **1774** TUCKER *Lt. Nat.* (1834) II. 681 It seems too narrow a vulgarity in those who value themselves upon being raised above the vulgar, to despise every old woman.. because she does not understand Latin, and has no interest in the county. **1782** V. KNOX *Ess.* xlvii. (1819) I. 257 Verses.. now admired for that artless simplicity, which once obtained the name of coarseness and vulgarity. **1812** H. & J. SMITH *Rej. Addr.* x. (1873) 92 The auditor.. compares incipient grandeur with final vulgarity. **1833** COLERIDGE *Table-t.* 20 Jan., The ignorant zealotry and sordid vulgarity of the leaders of the day! **1860** RUSKIN *Mod. Paint.* V. IX. vii. §23 We may conclude that vulgarity consists in a deadness of the heart and body, resulting from prolonged, and especially from inherited conditions of 'degeneracy'. **1876** LOWELL *Among my Bks.* Ser. II. 260 Our imagination of him has dwelt securely in ideal remoteness from the vulgarities of life.

vulgarization (vʌlgəraɪˈzeɪʃən). [See next and -ATION. So F. *vulgarisation*, Sp. *-izacion*, Pg. *-isação*, It. *volgarizzazione*.]

1. The action of making usual or common; the process of rendering familiar or popular; general dissemination.

1656 BLOUNT *Glossogr.*, *Vulgarization*, a making common or vulgar. **1807** in *Spirit Pub. Jrnls.* XI. 43 She has raised a barrier against the vulgarization of the hump, which cannot be broken down, either by love or money. **1865** *Sat. Rev.* 4 Feb. 148/1 Professional exclusiveness for centuries opposed the vulgarization of such knowledge. **1873** HAMERTON *Intell. Life* III. vi. 104 The vulgarization of rudiments is not the advancement of Knowledge.

2. The action or process of rendering coarse or unrefined.

1819 W. S. ROSE *Lett.* I. 205 From the first appearance of this race.. down to their vulgarization under Leopold,.. we may remark this preponderating feature. **1869** *Pall Mall G.* 8 Oct. 12 George Sand has not only consented to the vulgarization of her thoroughly beautiful novel, she has actually lent a hand to the gentleman who has vulgarized it. **1884** *Contemp. Rev.* Aug. 334 There is no fear that the steam-engine will bring about that hopeless vulgarisation of the country which usually follows in its track.

vulgarize (ˈvʌlgəraɪz), *v.* [f. VULGAR *a.* + -IZE, perh. after med.L. *vulgarizare* (1305), F. *vulgariser* (16th cent. and mod.), Sp. *vulgarizar*, Pg. *-isar*, It. *volgarizzare*.]

1. *intr.* To act in a vulgar manner; to become vulgar.

1605 DANIEL *Epist. Lady Anne Clifford* vi, Honour.. cannot stray and breake abroade Into the priuate wayes of carelesnesse; Nor euer may descend to vulgarize, Or be below the sphere of her abode. **1846** MRS. GORE *Eng. Char.* (1852) 96 A man having too much regard for his complexion to infringe upon the wine-cellar, and too much interest in his slimness to vulgarise on ale.

2. *trans.* To make common or popular; to reduce to the level of something usual or ordinary.

1709 T. ROBINSON *Vind. Mosaick Syst.* Introd. 6 To Vulgarize and to Allegorize the Scripture, are equally of evil Consequence to Religion. **1786** SIR J. REYNOLDS *Disc.* xiii. Wks. 1797 I. 273 To find proper foundations for science is neither to narrow or to vulgarise it. **1839** BAILEY *Festus* 145 The great bards.. Men who have vulgarized sublimity, And bought up truth for the nations. **1870** LOWELL *Among my Bks.* Ser. I. (1873) 154 The invention of printing, without yet vulgarizing letters, had made the thought and history of the entire past contemporaneous. **1872** BROWNING *Fifine* lxxv, Change yourself, dissimulate the thought And vulgarize the word.

3. To make vulgar or commonplace; to debase, degrade.

1756 MRS. F. BROOKE *Old Maid* No. 32. 262 Its being the religion of the whole nation has made it too common, and, if I may be allowed the expression, vulgarized it. *a* **1774** TUCKER *Lt. Nat.* (1834) II. 29 It would vilify, and, I may say, vulgarize the Almighty, to imagine Him.. engaged among the trifling scenes that occupy our notice. **1820** HAZLITT *Table-t.* (1824) II. i. 7 They vulgarise and degrade whatever is interesting or sacred to the mind. *a* **1821** V. KNOX *Winter Even.* xxxviii. Wks. 1824 II. 478 Learning sullied with pedantry, exhortation vulgarized by low wit. *a* **1853** ROBERTSON *Lect.*, *Wordsw.* (1858) 244 It seemed as if all that noise was vulgarizing the poet. **1871** L. STEPHEN *Playgr. Eur.* (1894) ii. 64 Some.. peak, not yet vulgarised by associations with guides and picnics.

b. *absol.* To cause or produce vulgarity.

1849 C. BRONTË *Shirley* vi, Family jarring vulgarizes—family union elevates.

Hence **ˈvulgarized** *ppl. a.*; **ˈvulgarizer**, one who vulgarizes or makes popular; **ˈvulgarizing** *vbl. sb.* and *ppl. a.*

1847 DE QUINCEY in 'H. A. Page' *Life* (1877) I. xv. 349 The absolute realities of *vulgarised life as it exists in plebeian ranks amongst our countrymen. **1884** *Harper's Mag.* Mar. 568/2 The vulgarized phrase, a gentleman. **1899** *Athenæum* 28 Jan. 105/3 He [Albert Smith] was the *vulgarizer of Switzerland. **1831** MRS. HEMANS in Chorley *Mem.* (1836) II. 236 Braham's singing was not equal to the instrumental part, but he did not disfigure it by his customary and *vulgarizing graces. **1871** L. STEPHEN *Playgr. Eur.* (1894) xii. 280 The eternal mountains.. never recall.. the vulgarising association of old days. **1946** J. S. HUXLEY *Unesco* II. 60 They [*sc.* press and radio] have already rendered many disservices—in the *vulgarising of taste, in the debasement of intellectual standards.

vulgarly (ˈvʌlgəlɪ), *adv.* Also 6 vulgarely(e, vulgarlie. [f. VULGAR *a.* + -LY².]

1. In common or everyday speech; vernacularly, colloquially: †**a.** With verbs of speaking, discoursing, etc. *Obs. rare.*

c **1374** CHAUCER *Troylus* IV. 1513 And, vulgarly to speken of Substaunce, Of Tresour may we boþe with vs lede, Y-nowh to lyue in honour and pleasaunce. **1647** TRAPP *Comm. Matt.* xi. 17 And he is the best preacher, saith Luther, that delivereth himself vulgarly, plainly, trivially. **1659** HAMMOND *On Ps.* i. 1 Annot. 6 The Hebrew [word].. vulgarly signifies the result of the consultation.

b. With verbs of naming, esp. in ***vulgarly called, styled***, etc.

1513 *Life Hen. V* (1911) 160 A greate assemblie of estates of Fraunce, vulgarlie called a Parlyament, wherein the three estates of the Realme were present. *a* **1548** HALL *Chron.*, *Hen. VII*, 28 b, The societe of saynct George vulgarely called the order of the garter. **1585** T. WASHINGTON tr. *Nicholay's Voy.* I. i, The mount Rhodope vulgarly called the mountes of siluer. **1632** LITHGOW *Trav.* II. 50 The chiefest .. is called Teucria, but they are vulgarly called the Iles of Diomedes. **1653** H. COGAN tr. *Pinto's Trav.* xxviii. 108 That [river].. enters into the sea in the Empire of Sornaan, vulgarly stiled Siam. **1688** R. HOLME *Armoury* III. 331/2 For the Pitchfork (or Pikel, which we vulgarly call it) it is an Instrument much used in Husbandry for their Loading and Stacking of Hay and Corn. *a* **1718** PENN *Life* Wks. 1726 I. 16 Being the Fourth Instant, vulgarly called Sunday. **1749** FIELDING *Tom Jones* II. iv, The chandler's shop, the known seat of all the news, or as it is vulgarly called, gossiping. **1774** J. HUTCHINS *Dorset* I. 589 The parsonage house, vulgarly called the vicarage house, stood about the middle of the island. **1855** MACAULAY *Hist. Eng.* xiv. III. 406 He was what is vulgarly called a disinterested man. **1861** M. PATTISON *Ess.* (1889) I. 41 This original factory and staple of the German merchants, vulgarly called 'The Steelyard',.. still stands on the banks of the Thames. **1868** *Rep. U.S. Commissioner Agric.* (1869) 95 Many of the species.. are here known as fire-flies, or, more vulgarly, lightning-bugs.

2. Among or by the people generally; commonly or ordinarily: **a.** As a matter of knowledge, belief, etc.

1507 *Justes Moneths May & June* 59 in Hazl. *E.P.P.* II. 123 Hye magesty.. Knowen is in euery realme vulgarely To his honoure. **1593** HARVEY *Pierce's Super.* Wks. (Grosart) II. 275 Which I purposely auoided, as not so vulgarly familiar. **1611** SPEED *Hist. Gt. Brit.* IX. xvii. (1623) 885 Where the Corps is now laide is not vulgarly knowne. **1612** SELDEN *Illustr. Drayton's Poly-olb.* i. 22 What I report thus .. is truth, and differeth much from what vulgarly is receiued. **1632** LITHGOW *Trav.* I. 19 Whose luxurious liues are vulgarly promulgat in this.. prouerbe. *a* **1688** CUDWORTH *Immut. Mor.* (1731) 94 Though they be very different,.. yet they are vulgarly mistaken for one and the same thing. **1712** STEELE *Spect.* No. 462 ¶5 The many good-natured Condescensions of this Prince are vulgarly known. **1793** MARTYN *Lang. Bot.* s.v. *Bulb*, It is vulgarly considered as a root, and was called so by Botanists till Linneus corrected the error. **1865** MOZLEY *Mirac.* ii. 41 The inductive principle is only this unreasoning impulse applied to a scientifically ascertained fact, instead of to a vulgarly ascertained fact.

b. As a matter of use or habit.

1617 MORYSON *Itin.* III. 155 They vulgarly eate harth Cakes of Oates, but in Cities haue also wheaten-bread. **1659** HAMMOND *On Ps.* Annot. 2 Not from any sensual pleasure, such as men vulgarly take in Musick. **1697** BENTLEY *Phal.* (1699) 142 The middle Verse, as it is vulgarly read, is an instance against me. **1806** A. KNOX *Rem.* (1844) I. 61 The dread of Popery and the consequent prejudice against everything vulgarly branded with that stigma. **1841** EMERSON *Ess.*, *Over-Soul* (1876) 233 Our religion vulgarly stands on numbers of believers. **1859** MILL *Liberty* i. 13 The tyranny of the majority was at first, and is still vulgarly, held in dread.

†**c.** With reference to speech: As a vernacular tongue. *Obs.*

1612 BREREWOOD *Lang. & Relig.* 8 These were the places, where the Greek tongue was natively and vulgarly spoken. **1632** LITHGOW *Trav.* III. 116 They speake vulgarly and Maternally here the Hebrew tongue. **1698** HEARNE *Duct. Hist.* (1714) I. 72 The Latin Tongue ceases to be vulgarly spoken in Italy [in] 587.

†**3.** Publicly; in the eyes of the world. *Obs. rare.*

1601 B. JONSON *Poetaster* III. iii, Seeke not to eclipse my reputation thus vulgarly. **1603** SHAKS. *Meas. for M.* V. i. 160 First for this woman, To iustifie this worthy Noble man, So vulgarly and personally accus'd.

†**4. a.** In a commonplace manner. *Obs.*⁻¹

c **1600** *Timon* IV. ii. (1842) 63 *Gelas.* Doth shee loue mee? *Blat.* I knowe shee dothe, and that not vulgarly.

†**b.** By ordinary arithmetic. *Obs. rare.*

1711 *Lond. Gaz.* No. 4825/4 Each Proposition being wrought Vulgarly, Decimally,.. and Instrumentally. **1762** RAMSBOTTOM *Fractions Anat.* 74 Let us now divide 20 Shillings Vulgarly, and then 6*d.* by 6*d.* Decimally, a Pound the Integer.

5. In a vulgar, coarse, or unrefined manner.

1831 SCOTT *Ct. Rob.* vii, The superstition of the Egyptians —vulgarly gross in its literal meaning.. — was disowned by the principles of general toleration. **1847** L. HUNT *Men, Women, & B.* II. x. 232 It is too hard, and bold, and vulgarly pretty. **1881** H. JAMES *Portr. Lady* xxii, He lives on his income, which I suspect of not being vulgarly large.

ˈvulgarness. Now *rare* or *Obs.* [f. VULGAR *a.* + -NESS.]

1. = VULGARITY 2 and 3.

1612 BREREWOOD *Lang. & Relig.* 10 At this day, the Greek tongue is very much decayed, not onely as touching the largness, and vulgarness of it, but also in the pureness and elegancy of the language. **1626** BACON *Sylva* Pref., And for the Vulgarness of them: true Axiomes must be drawne from plain Experience. **1648** HEXHAM II, *Ongemeyntigheydt*, Rarity, not Vulgarnesse, or Commonnesse.

2. = VULGARITY 4.

1642 ROGERS *Naaman* 386 All such indecency and vulgarnesse of carriage. **1721** BAILEY, *Vulgarity*, Vulgarness, the manner of the common People. **1759** *Compl. Lett.-writer* (ed. 6) 226 First come, first serve; I detest such vulgarness. **1796** ANNA SEWARD *Lett.* (1811) IV. 206 Alleging that immorality, vulgarness, bombast, and even obscurity, pervaded all my writings.

Vulgate (ˈvʌlgət), *a.* and *sb.* [ad. L. *vulgāta* (sc. *ēditio* or *lectio*) and *vulgāt-us* (sc. *textus*), fem. and masc. pa. pple. of *vulgāre*: see next. Cf. (in sense B. 1 b) F. *Vulgate*, It., Sp., Pg. *Vulgata*.]

A. *adj.* **1.** In common use as a version of the Bible (or portion of this); employed or occurring in one of these versions.

Ordinarily limited to the versions specified in B 1, and particularly to St. Jerome's. In various contexts the adj. coalesces with attributive uses of the sb.

1609 BIBLE (Douay) To Rdr. p. iii b, So that the old Vulgate Latin Edition hath bene preferred, and vsed for most authentical aboue a thousand and three hundered yeares. **1727** BLACKWALL *Sacred Classics* II. Pref. 16 The Latin vulgate Bible was declar'd authentic and canoniz'd by the council of Trent, A.D. 1546. **1728** CHAMBERS *Cycl.* s.v., M. Simon calls the Greek Version of the Seventy.. The antient Vulgate Greek. **1782** V. KNOX *Lord's Supper* xvii. Wks. 1824 VII. 423 At this hour it stands so translated in the Vulgate Bible, for ages the only Bible of the people. **1818** HALLAM *Mid. Ages* ix. I. (1819) III. 338 The vulgate Latin of the Bible was still more venerable. **1863** W. A. WRIGHT in Smith *Dict. Bible* I. 857/2 The Vulgate rendering of Prov. xxvi. 8. **1872** (*title*), The Vulgate New Testament, with The Douay Version of 1582, in Parallel Columns.

2. Forming (part of) the common or usual version of a literary work.

1861 PALEY *Æschylus* (ed. 2) *Prometh.* 966 *note*, His objection to the vulgate reading and interpretation.. appears quite groundless. **1894** *Athenæum* 26 May 681/2 [The papyri,] as is generally the case with Homer papyri of this period, support the vulgate text.

B. *sb.* **1. a.** The old Italic version of the Bible, preceding that of St. Jerome.

1728 CHAMBERS *Cycl.* s.v., The antient Vulgate of the Old Testament, was translated almost Word for Word, from the Greek of the Seventy. **1855** *Cassell's Pop. Bibl. Educator* II. 39/1 At that time the old Itala was the Vulgate, or Common Version.

b. The Latin version of the Bible made by St. Jerome (completed in 405).

1728 CHAMBERS *Cycl.* s.v. *Septuagint*, The Chronology of the Seventy, is.. very different from what is found in the Hebrew Text, and the Vulgate. **1776** ADAM SMITH *W.N.* v. i. (1869) II. 352 The Latin translation of the Bible, commonly called the Latin Vulgate. **1843** *Penny Cycl.* XXVI. 465 All the Romish translations of the Bible into the modern languages profess to have been made not from the Greek and Hebrew, but from the Vulgate. **1846** MRS. A. MARSH *Father Darcy* II. ii. 65 The answer of the priest.. was to repeat.. the following passage of Scripture from the Vulgate. **1881** WESTCOTT & HORT *Grk. N.T.* Introd. §111 The name Vulgate has long denoted exclusively the Latin Bible as revised by Jerome.

c. The usual or received text or version of the Bible or of some portion of this.

1815 F. NOLAN (*title*), An Enquiry into the Integrity of the Greek Vulgate, or Received Text of the New Testament. **1865** *Smith's Concise Dict. Bible* 992 But both the Greek and the Latin Vulgates have been long neglected. **1883** *Athenæum* 22 Dec. 809/2 This pre-Lutheran Bible version has been fittingly termed by Geffcken the 'German Vulgate'. **1887** *Encycl. Brit.* XXII. 824/1 The so-called Pĕshīṭtā,.. the Syriac vulgate.

d. An edition of the Vulgate.

1865 *Smith's Concise Dict. Bible* 994 The splendid pages of the Mazarin Vulgate. *Ibid.* 995 The Sixtine and Clementine Vulgates.

2. The ordinary reading in a text; the ordinary text of a work or author.

1861 PALEY *Æschylus* (ed. 2) *Supplices* 61 *note*, This is ingenious; but he fails to show that the vulgate is wrong. **1886** LEAF *Iliad* I. Introd. p. xiv, The conclusion is.. that the edition of Antimachos was in the main the same as our present vulgate.

3. Common or colloquial speech.

1855 J. E. Cooke *Virginia Comedians* I. xiii. (Cent.), 'Here's a pretty mess', returned the pompous gentleman, descending to the vulgate; 'you threaten me, forsooth!' **1883** D. H. Wheeler *By-Ways Lit.* ix. 176 There is always 'a free and easy' vulgate for the street, the market, and the fireside.

† **'vulgate**, *ppl. a. Obs.* Also 6 *Sc.* **wlgat.** [ad. L. *vulgāt-us*, pa. pple. of *vulgāre* to make public or common, f. *vulgus* the common people.]

1. (See quot. 1656.)

1513 Douglas *Æneid* I. vii. 69 The famous battellis, wlgat throw the warld or this. **1530** Palsgr. 770/1 This thyng is vulgate nowe howe so ever it happeneth. **1656** Blount *Glossogr.*, *Vulgate*, published abroad, commonly used, set out to the use of all men.

2. Rendered common; vulgarized.

1863 Lytton *Caxtoniana* I. 127 What delicate elegance he can extract from words the most colloquial and vulgate.

'vulgate, *v. rare.* [f. L. *vulgāt-*, ppl. stem of *vulgāre*: see prec.] *trans.* To put into general circulation. Hence **'vulgated** *ppl. a.*

1851 Sir F. Palgrave *Norm. & Eng.* II. 509 Amongst the untruths..few are more detrimental to truth than the epithets vulgated upon Sovereigns. **1857** *Ibid.* III. 90 Amongst the vulgated traditional anecdotes floating about the world.

vulge'rality. *nonce-wd.* = vulgarity 3.

1684 J. Lacy *Sir H. Buffoon* III. i, *Over.* My lord! No, the word lord is too common; it tastes of vulgerality. *Aim.* God's so, there's a fine word! Vulgerality is your own coining, sir? *Over.* Stamped in my own mint, sir.

vulgivagant: see volgivagant.

‖**vulgo** ('vʌlgəʊ), *adv.* [L. *vulgō* adv., abl. of *vulgus* the common people.] Commonly, popularly. Also *Comb.*

a **1623** Buck *Rich. III*, I. (1646) 8 The Signiory of Penrith, vulgò, Perith in Cumberland. **1644** Symonds *Diary* (Camden) 74 Pelynt, *vulgo* Plynt Church, com. Cornub. **1731** P. Miller *Gard. Dict.*, *Siliqua, edulis*, C.B.P. The Carob-Tree, or St. John's-Bread, *vulgò.* [**1753** *Lond. Mag.* Sept. 396/2 Hang a small bugle cap on, as big as a crown, Snout it off with a flow'r, *vulgo dict.* a pompoon.] **1871** *North Oxfordsh. Archæol. Soc., Notes Excurs. to Ducklington*, etc., 28 It is called Yelford, but that is vulgo, it being Eleford, in correct orthography.

‖**'vulgus**[1]. [L.] The common people; the ordinary ruck.

a **1687** Petty *Pol. Arith.* Pref. (1690) a b, The Fire at London, and Disaster at Chatham, have begotten Opinions in the *Vulgus* of the World to our Prejudice. *a* **1734** North *Examen* II. v. §128 (1740) 394 As for the *Vulgus* of the Faction, we know very well what their Employ was.

vulgus[2] ('vʌlgəs). [Prob. an alteration of *vulgars*: see vulgar *sb.* 4.] In some public schools, a short set of Latin verses on a given subject.

1857 Hughes *Tom Brown* II. iii, The three fell to work with Gradus and Dictionary upon the morning's vulgus. **1870** Mansfield *School Life Winchester* 107 We were always excused..Vulgus when the next day was a Saint's-day. **1887** T. A. Trollope *What I remember* I. v. 118 This was independent of a weekly 'verse task' of greater length, and was called a 'vulgus'.

attrib. **1857** Hughes *Tom Brown* II. ii, Tom was the upholder of the traditionary method of vulgus doing. He carefully produced two large vulgus-books, and began diving into them.

vull, southern ME. and dial. var. full *a.*, etc.

vuln (vʌln), *v.* [Irreg. ad. L. *vuln-erāre*, f. *vulner-*, *vulnus* wound.]

†**1.** *trans.* To wound. *Obs.*⁻¹

1583 Melbancke *Philotimus* S iij, The Lion, who being vulned, taketh such heede, that hee knoweth who first smote him.

2. *Her.* (See quots., and cf. next.)

1780 Edmondson *Her.* II, *Vulning*, i.e. wounding, a term applied in Heraldry to the pelican, which is always drawn picking or wounding her breast. **1829** Cassan *Bps. of Bath & Wells* 67 A Pelican in her Nest vulning herself. **1868** Cussans *Her.* (1893) 93 Some writers make a distinction between a Pelican vulning herself, and in her piety.

vulned, *ppl. a.* [f. as prec.]

1. *Her.* Of animals, etc.: Represented as wounded or pierced by a weapon.

1572 Bossewell *Armorie* II. 43 b, N. beareth Gules, a Lyon Rampant d'Or, vulned with a darte d'Argent. **1610** Guillim *Heraldry* III. xxv. (1611) 175 Hee beareth argent, a fesse Gules betweene three Hearts vulned and distilling drops of bloud. **1688** Holme *Armoury* II. 144/1 The sundry ways that Beasts are besides born in Arms... *Vulned*, wounded, when any part is wounded, or made bloody. **1780** Edmondson *Her.* II. s.v., A hind's head couped, pierced through the neck with an arrow, vulned proper. **1850** W. D. Cooper *Hist. Winchelsea* 152 Crest, A halbert erect or. on the point a flying dragon (or wivern) or. without legs, tail nowed sa. bezantée, vulned gu.

†**2.** *fig.* Of conscience: Wounded. *Obs.*⁻¹

1628 Feltham *Resolves* II. [I.] lxiv. 183 Let them that deny the immortality of the Soule, bee immerged in the horrours of a vulned conscience.

vulnerability (vʌlnərə'bɪlɪtɪ). [f. next + -ity.]

a. The quality or state of being vulnerable, in various senses.

1808 Han. More *Cœlebs* ix. I. 108 For fear, however, that your heart of adamant should hold out against all these perilous assaults, its vulnerability was tried in other quarters. **1864** *Reader* 31 Dec. 825/1 Up to the last, however, the self-blinded rulers of China refused to believe in their vulnerability. **1869** Reed *Our Iron-Clad Ship* xi. 253 This report also bears testimony to the vulnerability of the low decks.

b. *spec.* in *Path.* (see quot. 1880).

1880 A. Flint *Princ. Med.* 92 The term *vulnerability* has been, of late, applied to a condition of the system favorable for the morbific operation of any causes, either ordinary or specific. **1898** *Allbutt's Syst. Med.* V. 176 A fact which points to the existence of a special vulnerability of this part of the lung itself.

c. *spec.* in *Contract Bridge*, the quality or state of being vulnerable (see vulnerable *a.* 2 d).

1927 M. C. Work *Contract Bridge* ii. 10 Trick values, the number of points to a game, game and rubber bonuses..are not affected by vulnerability. **1942** E. Culbertson *Official Bk. Contract Bridge* 239 The consequence of vulnerability is exposure to greater penalties and entitlement to greater premiums. **1975** *Times* 15 Nov. 13/5 In May 1925, Mr Vanderbilt..joined in a rubber of the continental game of plafond. He saw possibilities in the game, added the attraction of vulnerability..and..introduced it to the Whist Club under the name of Contract Bridge.

d. *pl.* The weaknesses in a military defence system.

1972 *Science* 19 May 819/1 The purpose of this conference is to define a comprehensive but balanced assessment of the risks, vulnerabilities, capabilities, and intentions for subversive disruption. **1978** *Time* 3 July 36/3 'There is no doubt in my mind,' he said, 'that the U.S. is the most powerful country in the world.' He admitted 'concern' about 'vulnerabilities' in NATO, but said he felt the U.S. could 'outthink, outdesign and outperform the Soviets with the resources we have and the steady increases we are requesting'.

vulnerable ('vʌlnərəb(ə)l), *a.* [ad. late L. *vulnerābilis* wounding, f. *vulnerāre* (see vuln *v.*), but taken passively in accordance with the more usual sense of -able: cf. *invulnerable* and F. *vulnérable*, Sp. *vulnerable*, Pg. *-avel*, It. *-abile.*]

†**1.** Having power to wound; wounding. *Obs.*⁻¹

1609 *Ambassy Sir R. Sherley* 13 The male children practise to ride greate horses, to throw the Vulnerable and Ineuitable darte.

2. a. That may be wounded; susceptible of receiving wounds or physical injury.

1605 Shaks. *Macb.* v. viii. 11 Let fall thy blade on vulnerable Crests, I beare a charmed Life. **1696** Phillips (ed. 5), *Vulnerable*, that may be wounded. **1791** Cowper *Iliad* IV. 606 Turn, turn, ye Trojans! face your Grecian foes. They, like yourselves, are vulnerable flesh, Not adamant or steel. **1796** Morse *Amer. Geog.* I. 217 [Alligators having] plates or scales, said to be impenetrable..except about their heads and just behind their fore legs, where they are vulnerable. **1810** Southey *Kehama* IX. xii, Thrice through the vulnerable shade The Glendoveer impels the griding blade, The wicked Shade flies howling from his foe. **1867** J. B. Rose tr. *Virgil's Æneid* 151 The vulnerable heel Of dread Æacides.

b. *fig.* Open to attack or injury of a non-physical nature; *esp.*, offering an opening to the attacks of raillery, criticism, calumny, etc.

1678 Cudworth *Intell. Syst.* Pref., We had further Observed it, to have been the Method of our Modern Atheists, to make their First Assault against Christianity, as thinking that to be the most Vulnerable. **1769** *Junius Lett.* vii. (1788) 59 Reproaches and inquiries have no power to afflict either the man of unblemished integrity, or the abandoned profligate. It is the middle compound character which alone is vulnerable. **1782** Miss Burney *Cecilia* VII. iii, There, alone, is he vulnerable. **1824** Scott *St. Ronan's* vi, 'How delighted I am,' she said, 'that I have found out where you are vulnerable!' **1863** Mary Howitt tr. *F. Bremer's Greece* II. xvi. 147 His witty tongue was too keen for the easily vulnerable gods of Delphi. **1863** Kinglake *Crimea* (1873) I. i. 5 Modern society, growing more and more vulnerable.., is made to tremble by the mere rumour of an appeal to arms.

c. Similarly with *part, point, portion.*

1776 Gibbon *Decl. & F.* xiii. I. 357 Yet even calumny is sagacious enough to discover and to attack the most vulnerable part. **1789** Belsham *Ess.* II. xxxvi. 290 In this vulnerable part, only, can the shaft of the Satirist find an entrance. **1836** Thirlwall *Greece* III. xviii. 85 His private life presented some vulnerable points, through which his adversaries were able to strike more dangerous blows. **1847** H. Miller *Test. Rocks* ix. (1857) 358 Now this physical department has ever proved the vulnerable portion of false religions. **1872** O. W. Holmes *Poet Breakf.-t.* x. 290 There is a human sub-species..to a certain extent penetrative... It has an instinct which guides it to the vulnerable parts of the victim on which it fastens.

d. *Contract Bridge.* Of or pertaining to the liability of one side to be awarded increased penalties or increased bonuses as result of having won a game.

[**1925** *Work-Whitehead Auction Bridge Bull.* Oct. 5 In circles where high play predominates, there was introduced a variation of the above count, called 'Le Vulnerable'.] **1927** [see *danger-zone* s.v. danger *sb.* c]. **1965** *Listener* 23 Sept. 474/3 Playing the Two Club system, my partner, the dealer, opened a vulnerable No Trump (strong). **1977** M. Kenyon *Rapist* i. 10 Five no trumps! Don't get vulnerable!

3. a. Of places, etc.: Open to attack or assault by armed forces; liable to be taken or entered in this way.

1790 Beatson *Nav. & Mil. Mem.* I. 104 The immense expence the Spaniards have since been at, to fortify the city on that side, shews it to have been vulnerable then. **1797** St. Vincent 16 Aug. in Nicolas *Disp. Nelson* (1845) II. 434 *note*, The Tower of Santa Cruz in the Island of Teneriffe, which, from a variety of intelligence, I conceived was vulnerable. **1809** Wellington in Gurw. *Desp.* (1837) IV. 331 In the action of yesterday, our position was vulnerable only on the right. **1860** Motley *Netherl.* iii. (1868) I. 65 She felt herself vulnerable in Ireland, and on the Scottish border. **1884** *Manch. Exam.* 27 May 5/1 We should find it easier to hold [Russia] in check in the far East if she had vulnerable possessions nearer home.

b. Similarly with *part, point, side.*

1798 Wellington in Gurw. *Desp.* (1837) I. 8 A vulnerable part of the frontiers of the Company's territory. **1800** Colquhoun *Comm. Thames* v. 210 Every vulnerable point was guarded. **1851** Gallenga *Italy* 52 Even within those limits her Lombard subjects had discovered her vulnerable side. **1856** Froude *Hist. Eng.* (1858) II. viii. 277 Charles..was looking for the most vulnerable point at which to strike.

Hence **'vulnerableness; 'vulnerably** *adv.*

1727 Bailey (vol. II), *Vulnerableness*, Capableness of being wounded. **1837** *Foreign Q. Rev.* XIX. 39 We do not think a passage can be quoted to which criticism can be vulnerably attached. **1842** Manning *Serm.* v. (1848) I. 69 There comes over us what I may call a vulnerableness of mind. **1894** Mrs. H. Ward *Marcella* I. 166 The inner vulnerableness, the inner need of her affection and of peace with her.

† **'vulneral**, *a. Obs. rare.* [f. L. *vulner-*, *vulnus* wound.] = vulnerary *a.*

In the first quot. apparently an intentional distortion of *funeral.*

1589 [? Lyly] *Pappe w. Hatchet* E ij, Hee sliues one, has a fling at another, a long tale of his talboothe, of a vulnerall sermon, and of a fooles head in souce. **1657** *Physical Dict.*, *Vulneral*, medicines belonging to wounds, viz., plaisters, salves, &c. and inward potions, diet-drinks, &c.

vulnerary ('vʌlnərərɪ), *a.* and *sb.* Also 6 **-arye**, 7 **-arie.** [ad. L. *vulnerārius* adj. and sb. (Pliny), f. *vulner-*, *vulnus* wound: see -ary. So F. *vulnéraire* (16th c.), Sp., Pg., It. *vulnerario.*]

A. *adj.* **1.** Useful in healing wounds; having curative properties in respect of external injuries: **a.** Of applications or potions.

1599 A. M. tr. *Gabelhouer's Bk. Physicke* 199/2 Applye ther-on a good boneplayster, and let him drinck a vulnerarye potione. **1601** Holland *Pliny* II. 160 The oile..made of the flours of the wild vine serveth in good stead for vulnerarie salves and plastres. **1646** Sir T. Browne *Pseud. Ep.* II. iii. 77 The same method of cure, by ordinary Balsams, or common vulnerary plasters. **1693-4** *Phil. Trans.* XVIII. 43 Which did sufficiently denote this Vulnerary Pouder (as it's called in a late Publick Paper) to be a violent Caustick. **1709** *Ibid.* XXVI. 388 A Compress..dipt in a Mixture of four Ounces of Plantain-water, and two Ounces of a Vulnerary Water. **1754-64** Smellie *Midwif.* I. 385 Large tents or dossils dipped in vulnerary balsams. **1777** G. Forster *Voy. round World* I. 578 A species of night-shade, which is made use of..as a vulnerary remedy. **1818** *Art Preserv. Feet* 229 They may even find some advantage in a lotion called Theden's vulnerary wash. **1846** Gilly in *Proc. Berw. Nat. Club* II. 177 Geranium molle and robertianum are added to vulnerary potions.

b. Of herbs.

1601 Holland *Pliny* XXVII. iv. II. 273 It is..a good vulnerarie hearbe besides, and stancheth the bleeding of wounds. **1661** J. Childrey *Brit. Baconica* 171 To gather vulnerary Plants. **1667** *Phil. Trans.* II. 421 To give a full account of that Vulnerary Root, called *Wichacan.* **1712** tr. *Pomet's Hist. Drugs* I. 154 The Flowers are vulnerary; the Seed pectoral. **1750** Johnson *Rambler* No. 47 ¶2 The wounded stags of Crete are related by Ælian to have recourse to vulnerary herbs. **1788** *Gentl. Mag.* LVIII. I. 103/2 Golden Rod..generally appears among the vulnerary or restorative simples. **1821** Scott *Pirate* xxxiii, So efficacious were the vulnerary plants and salves with which it had been treated. **1830** Lindley *Nat. Syst. Bot.* 60 Another species of the same genus [Lythrum] is accounted in Mexico astringent and vulnerary.

c. Of qualities.

1744 Berkeley *Siris* §61 Turpentines, however famous for their vulnerary and detergent qualities. **1767** Gooch *Treat. Wounds* I. 343 It will be proper to hold medicines, almost continually, in the mouth, of a subastringent and vulnerary nature. **1853** G. Johnston *Nat. Hist. E. Bord.* I. 105 The herb was, in former times, esteemed for its vulnerary virtues. **1880** *Encycl. Brit.* XI. 654/2 The plant is further credited with the possession of vulnerary and astringent properties.

†**2.** Skilled in curing wounds. *Obs.*⁻¹

1601 Holland *Pliny* XXIX. i. II. 345 Called he was (by report) The vulnerarie Physician or Chirurgian.

3. Causing a wound or wounds; wounding. Also *fig.*

1615 H. Crooke *Body of Man* 26, I call it Artificiall, to distinguish it from that which is rash and at aduenture, which Galen calleth Vulnerary Dissection. **1661** Feltham *Resolves* (ed. 8) II. lvi. 301 The aspect of his eye alone, does sometimes become not only vulnerary, but mortal. **1810** Bentham *Packing* (1821) 35 All those who have been either struck, or struck at, by the instrument thus vulnerary to sentimental feelings.

B. *sb.* **1.** Any preparation, plant, or drug used in the cure of wounds.

1601 Holland *Pliny* XXVII. iv. II. 274 Highly commended by Hicesius a Physician of great name and authoritie, also by Aristogiton, for an excellent vulnerarie. **1689** Moyle *Sea Chyrurg.* I. 6 If..you expect wounds and broken Bones, then you must carry more quantity of Vulneraries. **1713** P. Blair *Misc. Observ.* (1718) 109 *Pyrola vulg.* is said to be astringent and a good Vulnerary. **1769** E. Bancroft *Guiana* 88 This is the grand Indian vulnerary, for wounds [etc.]. **1809** *Med. Jrnl.* XXI. 477 Externally, they use the fresh juice to cicatrize wounds. As a vulnerary, I can my-self affirm, it possesses such powers, that [etc.]. **1860** *All Year Round* No. 47. 484 Once upon a time surgeons did not believe that wounds were to be healed properly without vulneraries, balsams, and charpies. **1887** Moloney *Forestry W. Afr.* xx. 279 The yellow resin found at the roots of old [gamboge] trees is used as a vulnerary and diuretic.

†**2.** A curer of wounds. *Obs.*⁻⁰

1656 BLOUNT *Glossogr.*, *Vulnerary*, he that healeth wounds, a Chyrurgeon.

† **'vulnerate**, *v. Obs.* [f. L. *vulnerāt-*, ppl. stem of *vulnerāre* to wound.] *trans.* To wound. Also *Her.* (cf. VULNED *ppl. a.* 1).

1599 A. M. tr. *Gabelhouer's Bk. Physicke* 54/1 If any bodye weare vulneratede in the Eyes, insparge, and strewe this poulder in his Eyes. **1603** DEKKER *Patient Grissill* 1327 He ..inuaded my Rapier hand,..and in that passado vulnerated my hand thus deepe. **1638** T. WHITAKER *Blood of Grape* 60 For the strongest poyson of Animalls or minerals can but vulnerate the flesh. *a* **1692** ASHMOLE *Antiq. Berks.* (1719) I. 145 The Crest is a Stag Couchant, vulnerated through the Neck by a broad Arrow. **1750** *Phil. Trans.* XLVII. 48 So as to blunt the edge of it, and keep it from vulnerating any part of the bladder.
fig. **1612** J. DAVIES (Heref.) *Muse's Sacr.* Wks. (Grosart) II. 10/1 Hedg'd in with cares,..Whose piercing prickes the minde doe vulnerate. *a* **1618** —— *Wittes Pilgr.* lxxxiv, I can proue Where thou thy Chastitie did'st vulnerate. **1652** KIRKMAN *Clerio & Lozia* 124 Without their being vulnerated by the thorns of compassion.

Hence **'vulnerated** *ppl. a.*

1597 A. M. tr. *Guillemeau's Fr. Chirurg.* 44/2 We must allso harder binde on the vulnerated parte then on any of the adioyning partes. **1599** —— tr. *Gabelhouer's Bk. Physicke* 303/1 When you are..sente for to a vulnerated, and wounded Person. **1661** GLANVILL *Van. Dogm.* 208 It is enough for me that *de facto* there is such an entercourse between the Magnetick unguent and the vulnerated body. **1726** C. D'ANVERS *Craftsman* No. 39 (1727) 370 The violent rackings and corrosions of a vulnerated conscience.

† **vulne'ration.** *Obs.* [ad. L. *vulnerātio*, n. of action f. *vulnerāre*: see prec. So F. *vulnération*, Sp. *vulneracion*, Pg. *-ação*.] The action of wounding; the fact of being wounded.

1597 A. M. tr. *Guillemeau's Fr. Chirurg.* c iij b/2 The vulneratione of the bullete, which hath brokene the Legge. **1599** —— tr. *Gabelhouer's Bk. Physicke* 212/2 If in anye vulnerationes, the membre doe chaunce to wither, applye as then theron a Sparadrape, which must in this sorte be made. **1659** PEARSON *Creed* iv. 409 He speaks of the Son of God, which was to be the Son of man, and by our nature liable to vulneration; and withal foretells the piercing of his body. *a* **1688** G. STRADLING *Serm.* (1692) 127 The Son of Man, who alone was liable to Vulneration, and could be pierced.

'vulnerative, *a. rare*⁻¹. [f. as VULNERATE *v.* + -IVE.] Causing a wound or wounds.

1818 W. TAYLOR in *Monthly Rev.* LXXXV. 494 With a sort of hedgehog hostility, which points its vulnerative quills in every direction alike.

vulne'rose, *a. rare*⁻⁰. [f. L. *vulner-*, *vulnus* wound + -OSE.] Full of wounds.

1721 BAILEY. [Hence in later Dicts.]

† **vul'nific**, *a. Obs.*⁻⁰ [ad. L. (poet.) *vulnific-us*, f. *vulnus* wound. Cf. OF. *vulnifique* (15th c.).] (See quot.) Also † **vul'nifical** *a. Obs.*

1656 BLOUNT *Glossogr.*, *Vulnifical*, which woundeth, or makes wounds. **1721** BAILEY, *Vulnifick*, that maketh or causeth Wounds.

vulning *Her.*: see VULN *v.*

vulpanser (vʌl'pænsə(r)). *Ornith.* [mod.L., f. *vulp-ēs* fox + *anser* goose, after Gr. χηναλώπηξ.] The sheldrake (*Anas tadorna*). Also *attrib.*

1706 PHILLIPS (ed. Kersey), *Vulpanser*, the Bergander, or Burrow-duck, a Bird of the kind of Geese. **1753** *Chambers' Cycl.* Suppl., *Vulpanser*, in zoology, a name given by some authors to the shell-drake, or burrow-duck. **1839** W. C. TAYLOR *Anc. Hist.* i. §2 (ed. 2) 24 Wild and tame fowl abounded; the vulpanser goose of the Nile, bustards, partridges, quails, and widgeons, frequented the skirts of the desert, and the valley of the Nile. **1910** THOMPSON tr. *Aristotle's Hist. Anim.* 559 Wind-eggs are laid by a number of birds: as for instance the common hen,..the goose and the vulpanser.

vulpecidal, -cide, -cidism, common varr. of VULPICIDAL, etc.

‖ **Vulpecula** (vʌl'pɛkjʊlə). *Astr.* [L. *vulpēcula*, dim. of *vulpēs* fox.] A small northern constellation lying between Hercules and Pegasus.

More fully called ***Vulpecula et anser*** (fox and goose) or ***cum ansere***.

1866 LOCKYER *Guillemin's Heavens* 407 Another remarkable example of these optical transformations..is furnished by a nebula situated in the constellation Vulpecula.

vul'pecular, *a. rare*⁻⁰. [f. prec. + -AR.] 'Of or pertaining to a fox; vulpine.'

1884 *Imp. Dict.* (hence in later Dicts.).

† **vul'peculated**, *pa. pple. Obs.*⁻¹ [f. as prec. + -ATE.] Robbed by a fox.

1671 T. B. *Let. to T. D.* (1705) 64 The Night before Widdow Wamford was vulpeculated of her brood goose.

'vulpic, *a. Chem.* [f. L. *vulp-īna* (see def.) + -IC.] ***vulpic acid***, an acid occurring in the lichen *Cetraria vulpina*, and extracted from this or obtained artificially. (Also called ***vulpinic acid.***)

1886 MORLEY *Outlines Organic Chem.* 349 Hydric Phenylacetate..obtained..by boiling vulpic acid..with baryta. **1894** MORLEY & MUIR *Watts' Dict. Chem.* IV. 859/2 Vulpic acid is also formed by dissolving pulvic anhydride in a solution of KOH in MeOH.

vulpi'cidal, *a.* Also vulpe-. [f. next + -AL¹.] Committing or taking part in, connected with, of the nature of, vulpicide.

The common spelling of this and the following words with *-e-* is not justified by analogy.

1826 J. COOK *Fox-hunting* 123 A known vulpicidal character. **1844** J. T. HEWLETT *Parsons & W.* liii, You would be astonished at the immense collection I had of brushes, pads, and chops—a perfect museum—a vulpecidal curiosity. **1865** *Pall Mall G.* 22 May 11 If ever the progress of a vulpecidal agriculture should prove fatal to the last of our foxes.

vulpicide¹ ('vʌlpɪsaɪd). Also vulpe-. [f. L. *vulpi-*, *vulpēs* fox + -CIDE 1.] One who kills a fox otherwise than by hunting it with hounds.

1826 *Sporting Mag.* XVII. 367 Would that all the pheasants of all the Vulpecides..were heaped up on one pile. **1828** *Ibid.* XXII. 23, I mean man-kind, always save and excepting vulpecides. **1841** PHILLIPPS-WOLSEY *Sport in Crimea & Caucasus* 43 The absence of fences to make a run interesting, if runs took place in this land of vulpecides. **1887** A. C. SMITH *Birds Wiltshire* 357 Perhaps in the eyes of some as odious an appellation as that of regicide, or even vulpecide.

'vulpicide². Also vulpe-. [f. as prec. + -CIDE 2.] The act of killing a fox otherwise than by hunting with hounds.

1873 H. SPENCER *Stud. Sociol.* x. (1877) 245 Vulpicide, committed in defence of property and condemned neither by religion, nor by equity, nor by any law save that of sportsmen. **1888** *Land & Water* 13 Oct. 427/2 Dandie Dinmont doubtless excelled in sportsmanship,..yet his method would be denominated vulpecide in any of the shires to-day.

'vulpicidism. Also vulpe-. [f. as VULPICIDE¹ or ² + -ISM.] The practice of fox-killing.

1865 *Murray's Handbk. Russia*, etc. 44 Vulpecidism is not here considered a crime, and many is the gallant fox who has fallen before the deadly barrel in a battue. **1880** *Yorkshire Post* 24 May, The discovery of a dastardly act of vulpecidism.

† **'vulpinariness.** *Obs.*⁻⁰ [f. L. *vulpīn-us* VULPINE *a.*] (See quot.) Also † **'vulpinary** *a.*

1656 BLOUNT *Glossogr.*, *Vulpinariness*, craftiness, deceipt. **1721** BAILEY, *Vulpinary*, crafty, subtile, wily. **1820** *Edinb. Mag.* Aug. 129 The name by which this vulpinary veteran of the black art was universally known.

† **'vulpinate**, *v. Obs.*⁻⁰ [f. as prec.] (See quots.)

1623 COCKERAM I, *Vulpinate*, fox-like to deceiue. **1656** BLOUNT *Glossogr.*, *Vulpinate*, to play the Fox; to deceive with crafty wiles or deceits.

vulpine ('vʌlpaɪn), *a.* [ad. L. *vulpīn-us*, f. *vulpēs* fox: see -INE¹. So obs. F. *vulpin* (16th cent.), Sp. *vulpino*, It. *volpino*.]

1. Characteristic of a fox; similar to that of a fox.

1628 FELTHAM *Resolves* II. [I.] xii. 34 There is an innocentiall prouidence, as well as the slynesse of a vulpine craft. **1828** LYTTON *Pelham* lxix, Round those vulpine retreats was a labyrinthean maze of wrinkles, vulgarly called crows feet. **1847** HELPS *Friends in C.* I. i. 12 A very close vulpine nature, all eyes, all ears, may succeed better in deceit. **1865** *Sat. Rev.* 4 Feb. 146/1 Men of business glide about in glossy black cloth, with vulpine features, and hands as brown as a mummy. **1894** J. A. STEUART *In Day of Battle* i, A vulpine calculation and duplicity marked all his doings.

2. Resembling a fox; *spec.* in ***vulpine opossum*** or ***phalanger***.

1789 PHILLIP *Voy. Botany Bay* xv. 150 Vulpine Opossum. This is not unlike the common fox in shape, but considerably inferior to it in respect to size. **1865** *Chambers's Encycl.* VII. 459/2 The Vulpine Phalanger (*P. vulpina*), also called the Vulpine Opossum. *c* **1880** *Cassell's Nat. Hist.* III. 225 The Vulpine Phalanger, an animal with long loose fur, which inhabits New South Wales, Western Australia, and North Australia.

b. *fig.* Cunning, sly.

1830 *Fraser's Mag.* I. 599 How cunningly the vulpine Cantab has shapen his phraseology.

3. Consisting of foxes.

1849 W. S. MAYO *Kaloolah* vi. (1850) 56 Which [food] soon brought numerous lupine and vulpine visitors. **1887** *Field* 19 Feb. 233/2 Sparrow Gorse..seems to offer small inducement to the vulpine fraternity.

4. Of or pertaining to a fox or foxes.

1854 THOREAU *Walden* (1884) 293 Sometimes one came near to my window, attracted by my light, barked a vulpine curse at me, and then retreated. **1885** *Field* 3 Oct. 501/1 A singular instance of vulpine sagacity and daring was witnessed.

Hence **'vulpinism**, foxy character.

1851 CARLYLE *Excurs. Paris* in *Last Words T.C.* (1892) 187 A healthy Human Animal, with due beaverism (high and low), due vulpinism, or more than due. **1858** —— *Fredk. Gt.* IX. v. (1865) II. 457 He was without guile, and had no vulpinism at all.

vulpinite ('vʌlpɪnaɪt). *Min.* [f. *Vulpino* (*Volpino*), near Bergamo in Lombardy + -ITE¹ 2 b. Named by C. F. Ludwig, 1804.] A granular variety of anhydrite.

1823 W. PHILLIPS *Elem. Introd. Min.* 174 Siliciferous Anhydrous Gypsum,..Vulpinite. **1850** ANSTED *Elem. Geol., Min.*, etc. §388 Anhydrite, Muriacite, Vulpinite, Anhydrous sulphate of lime. **1867** *Ure's Dict. Arts* III. 1011 The vulpinite from Vulpino, near Bergamo in Italy, takes a fine polish, and is used for ornamental purposes.

vulpone, -ony: see VOLPONE.

vulsella, obs. form of VOLSELLA.

‖ **vulsellum.** *Surg.* [ad. L. *vulsella* (*volsella*) fem., but taken as neut. pl., f. *vuls-*, ppl. stem of *vellĕre* to pluck.] = VOLSELLUM. Also *attrib.*

1863 WEISS *Catal. Surg. Instr.* Pl. xxix, Spring Forceps with Vulsellum Points. *Ibid.*, Long Vulsellum Forceps. **1872** COHEN *Dis. Throat* 128 A much more satisfactory plan consists in drawing the enlarged gland out from its bed by means of a double vulsellum.

† **'vulsion.** *Obs. rare.* [ad. L. *vulsio*, n. of action f. *vellĕre* to pluck.] (See quots.)

1552 COOPER *Elyot's Dict.*, *Apospasma*, a vulsion. **1656** BLOUNT *Glossogr.*, *Vulsion*, the twinging or pulling of the cramp, or any other thing.

vulsten, southern ME. var. FILST *v.*

† **vult.** *Obs.* Chiefly *Sc.* Also 5–6 **wlt, wult,** 5 **vilt,** 6–7 **volt;** 5 **voute, vowt, wout.** [a. OF. *vult*, *volt*, *voult*, *vout* (= It. *volto*, Sp. and Pg. *vulto*):—L. *vult-us* face, etc.] Face, countenance; esp. expression of the features, cheer or bearing.

c **1375** *Sc. Leg. Saints* v. (*John*) 350 Sancte Iohne..croysit it, & drank al oute but rednes with blith wlte. *Ibid.* xxv. (*Julian*) 705 A laydy..with blyth wlt,..sad to þame þat stud about. ? *a* **1400** *Morte Arth.* 137 Þe voute of thi vesage has woundyde us alle! *Ibid.* 3054 He weres his vesere with a vowt noble. *c* **1425** WYNTOUN *Cron.* v. 3539 Fayr of fasson and of face,..Pert of vult and eloquent. *c* **1470** *Gol. & Gaw.* 1278 To that lordly on loft that lufly can lout,..Salust the bauld berne, with ane blith wout. *c* **1470** HENRY *Wallace* x. 77 Quha couth behald thair awfull lordly wult, So weill beseyn, so forthwart, stern, and stult. **1513** DOUGLAS *Æneid* XII. xi. 93 In the thar wltis, in the thar ene, but faill, The Latyn pepill dressit hes alhaill. **1536** BELLENDEN *Cron. Scot.* (1821) II. 497 He was nathing content of this estate; howbeit, he schew gud vult for the time. **1580** *Well of Woman Hill, Aberdeen* A iij b, This watter, being drunkin, cuirand..prolapsion of the vult, and dolour of the Tonsallis. *c* **1610** SIR J. MELVIL *Mem.* (1683) 70 She welcomed me with a merry volt, and thanked me for the diligence I had used in hasting to give her that intelligence.

† **vultu'osous**, *a. Obs.*⁻⁰ [f. L. *vultuōs-us* having an affected look, f. *vultus* VULT.] (See quot.)

1656 BLOUNT *Glossogr.*, *Vultuosous*, of a grave and solemn countenance, or of a heavy and sad look.

So † **'vultuous** *a. Obs.*⁻¹

1633 T. ADAMS *Exp. 2 Peter* ii. 5 When we delight in discord, our assemblings are dissemblings, our convocations provocations, every man vultuous. **1721** BAILEY.

vulture ('vʌltjʊə(r)), *sb.* Forms: *α.* 4 **volture,** 5 **vowlture,** 4– **vulture** (5 **fulture),** 5 **voultour,** 7 **vultour.** *β.* 4–9 **vultur,** 5 **wltur, fultur, vowtur.** *γ.* 4 **vultre,** 5 **w(u)ltre, vowtre;** 4, 6–7 **vulter,** 6 **voulter, vultar,** 7 **volter.** [a. AF. *vultur* and *voutre*, OF. *voltour*, *voultour*, *voutour* (F. *vautour*), or L. *vultur*, or ad. L. *vulturius*. The OF. forms, like Pr. *voltor*, *voutor*, and It. *avoltore*, *avoltojo*, represent L. *vulturi-us*, while AF. *voutre*, Sp. *buitre*, and Pg. *abutre* are from L. *vultur*.

In Maundeville (1839) xxii. 237 the form *veutour* is prob. inexact for *voutour*.]

1. a. One of a number of large birds of prey of the order *Raptores* which feed almost entirely upon carrion and have the head and neck altogether or almost featherless.

The American vultures belong to different genera from those of the Old World.

α. *c* **1374** CHAUCER *Troylus* I. 788 Ticius yn helle, Whos stomak foughles tiren euere mo, That highte volturis as bokes telle. **1398** TREVISA *Barth. De P.R.* XII. xxxvi. (Bodl. MS.), The vulture haþ þat name of slowe fliȝt. *Ibid.*, Whan manye vultures comeþ and fleeþ togedres hit bodeþ bataille. *c* **1400** MAUNDEV. (Roxb.) xxxiv. 153 Vowltures, egles, rauyns, and oþer fewlez of rauyne. **1456** SIR G. HAYE *Law Arms* (S.T.S.) 41 Grete foulis lyke ernis callit voultouris. **1567** MAPLET *Gr. Forest* 18 Qvandias is a stone..It is found in the Vulture his heade. **1584–7** GREENE *Carde of Fancie* Wks. (Grosart) IV. 115 The Vulture is mortal enimie to the Eele. **1615** CHAPMAN *Odyss.* XI. 784 On his bosome sat Two Vultures, digging through his caule of fat. **1638** SIR T. HERBERT *Trav.* (ed. 2) 11 The destruction of men and women..better contenting them, whose dead carkasses they devoure with a vultures appetite. **1679** COLLIER *Ess.* II. (1703) 129 [Despair] preys upon the vitals, like Prometheus's vulture. **1721** YOUNG *Revenge* IV. i, Give them the vultures, tear them all in pieces! **1774** GOLDSM. *Nat. Hist.* III. 59 The Vulture..is indelicately voracious, and seldom attacks living animals when it can be supplied with dead. **1834** MᶜMURTRIE *Cuvier's Anim. Kingd.* 118 The vultures have eyes flush with the head, and reticulated tarsi, ..an elongated beak,..and a greater or less portion of the head, or even of the neck divested of feathers. **1843** YARRELL *Brit. Birds* I. 2 Vultures are most numerous in warm countries, where a high degree of temperature induces rapid decomposition. **1878** B. TAYLOR *Deukalion* II. v. 84 There wheels a vulture, giving to the blue The shade or sparkle of his slanted wings.

β. **1388** WYCLIF *Job* xxviii. 7 The iȝe of a vultur [*v.r.* vowtur], ethir rauenouse brid, bihelde it not. *c* **1420** *Prose Life Alexander* 71 In þe mornenynge arely þare come many fewlis als grete as wlturs, reed of colour. **1495** *Trevisa's Barth. De P.R.* XII. ii. 410 That egle..dredyth the Fultur. **1580** G. HARVEY *Three Proper Lett.* 36 A Vulturs smelling, Apes tasting, sight of an Eagle. **1638** MAYNE *Lucian* (1664) 282 When the Vultur in his crooked clawes Shall graspe the locust. **1667** MILTON *P.L.* III. 431 As when a Vultur on Imaus bred..flies toward the Springs Of Ganges or Hydaspes. **1695** PRIOR *Ballad on Taking Namur* ii, Too like a Vultur Boileau flies, Where sordid Interest shows the Prey. 1757 W. Wilkie *Epigon.* i. 20 No doves are hatch'd beneath a vultur's wing. 1828–32 Webster s.v., The vultur is one of the largest kinds of fowls.

γ. 1387 Trevisa *Higden* (Rolls) III. 57 Seuen foules schewede hem to Remus, þat beeþ i-cleped vulterus. *Ibid.*, Fourtene vulterus [*v.r.* vultres] schewed hem to Romulus. *a*1400–50 *Alexander* 3945 Þan come a fliȝtir in of fowls.. To vise on as vowtres. 1474 Caxton *Chesse* i. i. (1883) 10 Thre honderd birdes that men calle wultres. 1495 *Trevisa's Barth. De P.R.* xix. cxv. 918 Wltrees egges be grete as Egles egges. 1565 Cooper *Thesaurus*, *Vultur*,.. a rauenous birde called a voulter or geyre. 1579 Lyly *Euphues* (Arb.) 153 Doth not the Lyon for strength.. excell man? Doth not the Eagle see clearer, the Vultur smel better? 1687 *Good Advice* 44 Spurs, Claws and Bills that made her look more like a Vulter then a Dove.

b. With distinguishing terms.

The number of these is very large, and only some of the more important are here recorded. See also auriculated *ppl. a.*, crane *sb.*[1] 7, griffin[1] 4, Maltese *a.* 2, secretary *sb.*[1] 7, sociable *a.* 1 b.

1781 Latham *Gen. Synop. Birds* I. 12 *Alpine Vulture: *Vultur percnopterus.* 1829 Scott *Anne of Geierstein* ii, One of this.. flight chanced to be a lammer-geier, or Alpine vulture. 1896 tr. *Boas' Text Bk. Zool.* 461 The small Alpine Vulture (*Neophron percnopterus*), with naked head and very long, thin beak. 1809 Shaw *Gen. Zool.* VII. 36 *American Vulture. 1781 Latham *Gen. Synop. Birds* I. 8 *Arabian V[ulture]. According to Edwards, the size exceeds that of a common eagle, by one third. 1855 *Orr's Circle Sci., Org. Nat.* III. 374 The *Vultur monachus*, or Arabian Vulture. 1575 Turberv. *Falconrie* 16 The *ashe-coloured Vulture is the most large byrde of praye that is to be founde. 1668 Charleton *Onomast.* 64 *Vultur Cinereus*, the ash-coloured Vultur. 1774 Goldsm. *Nat. Hist.* (1824) II. 252 In this tribe we may range.. the ash-coloured.. vulture. 1750 G. Edwards *Nat. Hist. Birds* III. 106 The *Bearded Vulture. This Bird is of the Bigness of an Eagle. 1809 Shaw *Gen. Zool.* VII. 13 From which circumstance the name of Bearded Vulture is particularly applied to the present species. 1882 *Encycl. Brit.* XIV. 243/2 Lämmergeyer.. or Bearded Vulture,.. one of the grandest birds-of-prey of the Palæarctic Region. 1575 Turberv. *Falconrie* 16 There are two sortes,.. the ashe mayld, or *blacke Vulture, and the browne or whitish Vulture. 1601 Holland *Pliny* x. vi. I. 274 The blacke vultures are the best. 1809 Shaw *Gen. Zool.* VII. 31 Black Vulture.. This bird is described as larger than the Golden Vulture, and of a black colour. 1837 *Partington's Brit. Cycl. Nat. Hist.* III. 825/2 The Black Vulture (*C. atratus*) is a darker and smaller species. 1809 Shaw *Gen. Zool.* VII. 10 *Californian Vulture. 1872 Coues *N. Amer. Birds* 222 Californian Vulture. Brownish-black, lustrous above, paler below. 1888 *Encycl. Brit.* XXIV. 302/1 *Pseudogryphus*, the great Californian Vulture. 1781 Latham *Gen. Synop. Birds* I. 9 *Carrion Vulture. The size of this species is about that of a Turkey. 1849 Tennyson '*You might have won*' 35 For whom the carrion vulture waits—To tear his heart! 1896 tr. *Boas' Text Bk. Zool.* 461 The smaller Carrion Vulture (*Cathartes*). *a*1672 Willughby *Ornith.* (1678) 67 The *cinereous or ash-coloured Vulture. 1781 Latham *Gen. Synop. Birds* I. 14 Cinereous V[ulture].. The size is that of an Eagle, or rather bigger. 1843 *Penny Cycl.* XXVI. 470/1 The Cinereous Vulture is chiefly seen in the plains in winter. 1758 G. Edwards *Glean. Nat. Hist.* 171 The *Crested or Coped Black Vulture.. is a very large bird. 1837 *Partington's Brit. Cycl. Nat. Hist.* III. 824/2 The *Eared Vulture (*V. auricularis*) is an African species of a blackish colour, with a fleshy crest on each side of the head under the openings of the ears. 1781 Latham *Gen. Synop. Birds* I. 13 *Egyptian V[ulture].. is said to be of a rufous ash-colour, spotted with brown. 1837 *Partington's Brit. Cycl. Nat. Hist.* III. 825/2 Egyptian Vulture (*P. leucocephalus*).. also, from its abundance in Egypt, called 'Pharaoh's chicken'. 1888 *Encycl. Brit.* XXIV. 302/1 One of them [sc. *Nephroninæ*] is the so-called Egyptian Vulture or Pharaoh's Hen, *Neophron percnopterus.* *a*1672 Willughby *Ornith.* (1678) 67 *margin*, Our *Fulvous Vulture, like Bellonius his Chesnut one. 1809 Shaw *Gen. Zool.* VII. 27 The Fulvous or Golden Vulture is one of the largest of the genus, exceeding the size of the Golden Eagle. 1840 *Cuvier's Anim. Kingd.* 165 The Fulvous Vulture.. is the most widely-diffused species, inhabiting the mountainous parts of the whole ancient continent. *a*1672 Willughby *Ornith.* (1678) 67 Viewing the skin of the *Golden Vulture, sent me once out of the Alpine Country of the Grisons,.. I thus described it. 1774 Goldsm. *Nat. Hist.* (1824) II. 252 The Golden Vulture seems to be the foremost of the kind. 1809 [see *fulvous vulture*]. 1781 Latham *Gen. Synop. Birds* I. 7 *King V[ulture].. is about the size of an hen Turkey. 1855 *Orr's Circle Sci., Org. Nat.* III. 374 Another species of the genus *Sarcorhamphus*.. is the King Vulture (*S. papa*), which is not uncommon in Brazil and Guiana. 1781 Latham *Gen. Synop. Birds* I. 19 *Tawny Vulture.. inhabits Falkland Islands. 1837 *Partington's Brit. Cycl. Nat. Hist.* III. 824/1 The Tawny Vulture (*V. fulvus*) is a large bird, and has been long known to natural history. *Ibid.* 825/2 The *Turkey Vulture (*C. aura*) is another American species of smaller size. 1855 *Orr's Circle Sci., Org. Nat.* III. 375 The common American Vulture is the Turkey Vulture (*Cathartes aura*), or Turkey Buzzard. 1896 tr. *Boas' Text Bk. Zool.* 461 The large *White-headed Vulture (*Vultur fulvus*).

c. ***king of the vultures***, the king-vulture (*Sarcorhamphus papa*).

1743 G. Edwards *Nat. Hist. Birds* I. 2 The King of the Vultures. This Bird is about the Bigness of a Hen-Turkey. 1774 Goldsm. *Nat. Hist.* (1824) II. 254 There is one of the kind, called the King of the Vultures, which from its extraordinary figure deserves a separate description. 1796 Stedman *Surinam* II. xxvii. 299 The bird called the king of the vultures is very common in Surinam. 1855 *Orr's Circle Sci., Org. Nat.* III. 375 It is from this that he derives his title of the King of the Vultures.

2. *fig.* **a.** Something which preys upon a person, the mind, etc., after the manner of a vulture; *esp.* a consuming or torturing passion.

Commonly in allusion to the punishment inflicted on Tityus (*Odyss.* xi. 576).

1582 T. Watson *Centurie of Love* li, A Vultur worse then his teares all my vaines. 1588 Shaks. *Tit. A.* v. ii. 30, I am Reuenge sent from th' infernall Kingdome, To ease the gnawing Vulture of the mind. *a*1631 Donne *Serm., Ps. xc. 14* (1640) 813 That fearfull Vulture, the Inquisition, hovers over them. 1639 J. Taylor (Water P.) *Summers Trav.* (1873) 33 The Client having Tityus empty maw (His guts tormented with the Vulture Law). 1742 Gray *Eton* 62 These shall the fury Passions tear, The vulturs of the mind, Disdainful Anger, pallid Fear, And Shame. 1816 Byron *Ch. Har.* iii. lix, And could the ceaseless vultures cease to prey On self-condemning bosoms, it were here. 1861 C. Reade *Cloister & Hearth* lxv, The bereaved heart lay still heavy as lead within his bosom; but now the dark vulture Remorse sat upon it rending it. 1883 Macfadyen in *Congregat. Year Bk.* 77 This nation seems preyed upon by vultures of lust and superstition.

b. A person of a vile and rapacious disposition.

1603 B. Jonson *Sejanus* iii. ii, Time shall mature.. what we, with so good vultures, haue begunne. 1613 Beaum. & Fl. *Honest Man's Fort.* ii. i, Ye dregs of baseness, vultures amongst men, That tyre upon the hearts of generous spirits. 1750 Johnson *Rambler* No. 38 ¶ 10 He.. will be at last torn to pieces by the vultures that always hover over fortunes in decay. 1828 Lytton *Pelham* III. ii, Before midnight I was in high fever; they sent for the vultures of physic—I was bled copiously. 1884 *Pall Mall G.* 19 Sept. 4/2 Lord Ripon .. showed that India was not merely the favourite hunting-ground of English vultures.

3. *Astr.* One or other of two northern constellations, distinguished as the ***falling vulture*** = lyra 2, harp *sb.*[1] 3, and ***flying vulture*** = eagle *sb.* 4.

1638 Chilmead tr. *Hues' Treat. Globes* ii. iii. (1889) 53 The ninth is Gallina or Cygnus, the Hen or Swan, and is called in Arabique.. the flying Vulture. 1673 F. Lamb *Acroscopium* 6 The Harp, otherwise called the falling Grype, or Vulture. *Ibid.* 10 The Eagle, by some call'd the flying Grype or Vulture, consisting of 12 stars. 1901 J. F. Hewitt *Mythmaking Age* i. i. 8 When Vega in the Constellation of the Vulture or Lyra became Pole Star.

4. *attrib.* and *Comb.* **a.** Attrib. as ***vulture beak, claw, eye, feather***, etc., denoting either 'of a vulture' or 'like that of a vulture'; also **vulture-feather**, a species of moth.

1834 W. Howitt in *Tait's Mag.* I. 375/2 With a heart free from the *vulture-beak of care. 1867 Morris *Jason* v. 255 Within her filthy *vulture-claws clutched tight. 1593 A. Chute *Beautie Dishonoured* (1908) 110 When coward death .. Lookes on her fayre face, with a *vultar eye. 1820 Scott *Monast.* xxiv, Under the eagle, or rather the vulture eye of the Baron. 1832 J. Rennie *Consp. Butterfl. & M.* 208 The *Vulture Feather (—— *Gryphipennella*) found amongst grass. 1858 Simmonds *Dict. Trade*, *Vulture-feathers*, feathers of species of *Accipitres*, imported from Bombay, and sold for stuffing beds, &c., the larger ones for making artificial flowers, &c. 1883 *Ibid.*, *Vulture feathers*, a commerical name for those of the *Rhea* of South America. 1885 Rider Haggard *King Solomon's Mines* ix, She turned her bald *vulture-head towards us. 1854 *Poultry Chron.* I. 128/2 *Vulture-hocks [in Cochin China cocks] are a matter of taste. 1855 *Ibid.* III. 348/2 The boots, or as Shanghai fanciers would style it, the vulture hock, must be white. 1847 Tennyson *Princ.* iv. 344 Thereat the Lady stretch'd a *vulture throat. 1871 J. Hay *Pike County Ball.* (1880) 86 Cast from the hovering *vulture-wings of one dark thought of woe and doom.

b. Attrib. with nouns of quality or action.

1593 A. Chute *Beautie Dishonoured* (1908) 105 To vultar greedinesse of an easie crowne. 1800 Campbell *Scene in Bavaria* xiii, Who shuns a warring world, nor woos The vulture cover of its wing. 1806 T. Maurice *Fall Mogul* ii. iv, All our treasures His vulture-grasp has seiz'd. 1821 Shelley *Hellas* 940 Victorious Wrong, with vulture scream, Salutes the rising sun.

c. Appositive, also in fig. use (cf. sense 2).

1592 Shaks. *Ven. & Ad.* 551 Whose vultur thought doth pitch the price so hie. *a*1639 T. Carew *Mediocritie in love Rej.* ii, If it prove Disdaine, that torrent will devoure My Vulture-hopes. 1774 Goldsm. *Nat. Hist.* (1776) V. 85 The eagle kind, the hawk kind, the vulture kind. 1809 Shaw *Gen. Zool.* VII. 2 The chief of the Vulture tribe.. is undoubtedly the Condor. *Ibid.* 13 One of the principal distinctions between the Eagle and the Vulture kind. 1818 Keats *Endym.* iii. 620 Cursed, cursed Circe! O vulture-witch, hast never heard of mercy? 1843 T. Edmonston in *Zoologist* I. 38 The vulture-eagle lay in her own nest, bound, gagged, and powerless.

d. In instrumental and similative combs., as ***vulture-gnawn, -hocked*** (see 4 a), ***-like, -rent, -torn, -tortured*** adjs.; ***vulture-wise*** adv.

1598 Sylvester *Du Bartas* ii. ii. *Colonies* 298 The Vultur-rented Prometheus, 'mong the Greeks had fire invented. 1623 G. Daniel *Sonn.* xv, To her that.. laies to view My Vultur-gnawne hart open. 1644 Digby *Nat. Soul* Concl. 456 The ravenous inclemency, and vulturelike cruelty. 1742 Young *Nt. Th.* viii. 418 These rush upon thee; Thy vitals seize, and vultur-like, devour. 1743 Francis tr. *Hor., Odes* ii. xiv. 10 Where vulture-tortured Tityus lies. 1826 *Blackw. Mag.* XIX. 589 To be like poor Prometheus, vulture-torn. 1854 *Poultry Chron.* II. 84/1 They are well booted, or as the Shanghae fanciers style it, 'Vulture-hocked'. 1892 Stevenson & Osbourne *Wrecker* xiii. 206 Towards her the taut *Norah Creina*, vulture-wise, wriggled to windward: come from so far to pick her bones. 1906 W. de la Mare *Poems* 82 This beast in one flat hand clasped vulture-wise A glitt'ring image.

'vulture, *v.* [f. the sb.] *trans.* To tear like a vulture. Also *intr.* with *down*, to descend like a vulture.

1628 Feltham *Resolves* ii. [i.] xxv. 80 Though pleasure merries the Sences for a while: yet horror after vultures the vnconsuming heart. 1922 Joyce *Ulysses* 47 He rooted in the sand.. vulturing the dead. 1948 M. Allingham *More Work for Undertaker* xiii. 164 The tax harpies vultured down for death duties. 1955 *Newsweek* 10 Jan. 49/1 Contestants had vultured the library's reference and guidebooks for the names of the mystery towns. 1977 L. Gordon *Eliot's Early Years* 147 From 'Proteus' came the dog vulturing the dead in part I of *The Waste Land.*

Hence **'vultured** *ppl. a.* (*poet.*).

1946 Dylan Thomas *Deaths & Entrances* 47 O spiral of ascension From the vultured urn Of the morning Of man.

†**vul'turian**, *a.* *Obs.*[−1] [f. vulture *sb.* + -ian.] = next.

1659 T. Pecke *Parnassi Puerp.* 38 A Treasurer, whom Vertue makes to hold, Vulturian Talons, from the Regal Gold.

vulturine ('vʌltjʊəraɪn), *a.* [ad. L. *vulturīn-us*, f. *vultur* vulture *sb.*: see -ine.]

1. Of or belonging to the vulture tribe; resembling a vulture: **a.** In names of birds.

1647 Trapp *Comm. Matt.* xxiv. 28 The vulturine eagles especially.. follow armies, and feed on carcases. *a*1672 Willughby *Ornith.* (1678) 64 The Vulturine Eagle of Aldrovandus, called *Percnopteros.* 1809 Shaw *Gen. Zool.* VII. 58 Vulturine Eagle, *Falco vulturinus.* *Ibid.* 343 Vulturine Raven, *Corvus vulturinus.* 1849 *Sk. Nat. Hist., Mammalia* III. 48 The vulturine eagle.. makes the mountain precipices its abode. 1872 Coues *N. Amer. Birds* 21 A little orbital space is bare in many birds, as the vulturine hawks, and some pigeons. 1880 *Cassell's Nat. Hist.* III. 313 On the coast the chief enemy of the Parrots is the Vulturine Sea-Eagle (*Gypohierax angolensis*).

b. In general use. Also *fig.*

1721 Bailey, *Vulturine*,.. rapacious. 1790 Pennant *Tour Scotl.* i. 58 He.. sells it at five shillings,.. thus happily disappointing the rapacity of the vulturine monopolizer. 1843 Landor *Imag. Conv.* Wks. 1846 II. 229/1 Even the petticoated torch-bearers from rotten Rome, if more blustering,.. were less bitter and vulturine. 1880 Swinburne *Stud. Shaks.* 207 But the virtuous critic, after the alleged nature of the vulturine kind, would appear to have eyes and ears and nose for nothing else. 1886 Guillemard *Cruise Marchesa* II. 219 The rare Pesquet's Parrot,.. half vulturine in appearance and with the face and throat bare.

2. Of or pertaining to a vulture or vultures; characteristic of, like that of, a vulture.

1656 Blount *Glossogr.*, *Vulturine*, pertaining to the ravenous Bird called a Vulture. 1658 Phillips, *Vulturine*, belonging to a Vultur or Geyr. 1852 *Zoologist* X. 3646 It has .. the real vulturine fondness for carrion. 1855 Kingsley *Misc., Raleigh* (1859) I. 31 There is no more to be discovered in the matter, save by the vulturine nose which smells a carrion in every rose-bed. 1882 E. O'Donovan *Merv Oasis* II. 130 An uneasy, vulturine expression of the eye, the pupil being quite surrounded by the white.

vulturish ('vʌltjʊərɪʃ), *a.* [f. vulture *sb.* + -ish.] Somewhat vulture-like.

1826 Syd Smith *Wks.* (1850) 435 That the majority of the flock thought it essentially vulturish to exclude one third of their numbers from the blood and entrails. 1841 [see hawkish *a.*]. 1843 Carlyle *Past & Pr.* ii. xvii, Valiant Wisdom.. escorted by owl-eyed Pedantry, by owlish and vulturish and many other forms of Folly.

'vulturism. *rare.* [f. as prec. + -ism.] Vulturine character or habits.

1843 Carlyle *Past & Pr.* ii. xvii, Lawyers too were poets, were heroes.. Their Owlisms, Vulturisms,.. will disappear.

'vulturizing, *ppl. a.* *rare*[−1]. [f. as prec. + -ize + -ing[2].] Acting like a vulture.

1650 *Descr. Future Hist. Europe* 12 The feet part of Iron and part of Clay, denoted the declining Estate of the Roman Empire.. under the present Papacy and now-vulturizing house of Austria.

vulturous ('vʌltjʊərəs), *a.* Also 7 vulterous. [f. vulture *sb.* + -ous.]

1. Resembling that of a vulture; ravenous.

1623 Webster *Duchess Malfi* ii. ii, There's no question but her techiness and most vulturous eating of the apricocks are apparent signs of breeding. 1647 Hammond *Christ. Oblig.* (1649) 15 And when.. he was shut up alone in the bladder, his vulturous stomack lets loose upon himself, and within few minuits more, one half of him devoures the other. 1672 Penn *Spir. Truth Vind.* 14 [It] is invisible to his vulterous Eye, who so disdainfully writes against it. 1831 Carlyle *Sart. Res.* ii. iv, With such a vulturous hunger for self-indulgence. 1870 Talmage *Crumbs Swept Up* (1871) 278 They watch about the door for new-comers,.. invite him to drink,.. and plunge their vulturous beaks into the vitals of his soul.

2. *fig.* Resembling a vulture in appearance or character.

1843 Carlyle *Past & Pr.* iv. i, The battle, with various weapons, of vulturous Quack and Tyrant against vulturous Tyrant and Quack. 1864 —— *Fredk. Gt.* xvi. i. IV. 243 The Owleries and the vulturous Law-Pedantries. 1885 Tennyson *Dead Prophet* vii, Then glided a vulturous Beldam forth, that on dumb death had thriven.

‖**vulva** ('vʌlvə). [L. *vulva* (*volva*), wrapper, uterus. Cf. It., Sp., Pg. *vulva*, F. *vulve.*]

1. *Anat.* The external organ of generation in the female; *esp.* the opening or orifice of that organ.

1548–77 Vicary *Anat.* ix. (1888) 77 By it goeth forth the vrin, or els it should be shed through out al the Vulua. 1615 Crooke *Body of Man* iv. xvi. (1631) 237 The last dissimilar part of the womb [is called] of some *Vulva.* 1694 Salmon *Bate's Dispens.* (1713) 708/1 Anoint the Vulva and Womb with this Mixture. 1728 Chambers *Cycl.* s.v. 1831 R. Knox *Cloquet's Anat.* 355 It is formed of two planes of fibres, which.. are interlaced, between the anus and vulva. 1841 Ramsbotham *Obstetr. Med.* 53 The whole of the external parts together, as well those that are lined by mucous membrane, as those covered by the common cuticle, are called the vulva. 1877 Huxley *Anat. Inv. Anim.* vi. 274

Anteriorly, each pair of tubes opens into the oviduct of its side, which passes down along the side of the body to terminate at the vulva.

2. *Conch.* The impression behind the umbones of Venus-shells.

1840 *Cuvier's Anim. Kingd.* 379 The ligament often leaves, behind the beaks, an elliptical impression, to which the term *vulva* has been applied.

Hence **'vulval**, **'vulvar** *adjs.*, of or belonging to the vulva.

1859 *Todd's Cycl. Anat.* V. 706/1 From the centre of the vulvar orifice to the end of the fornix. **1866** J. M. SIMS *Uterine Surg.* 328 The whole vulval or outer face of the hymen is sensitive. **1889** *Buck's Handbk. Med. Sci.* VII. 694/1 Such irritation may lead to excoriation of the vulvar mucous membrane.

vulve, obs. form of WOLF *sb.*

vulvectomy (vʌl'vɛktəmɪ). *Surg.* [f. VULV(A + -ECTOMY.] Excision of (part of) the vulva.

1917 *Amer. Jrnl. Obstetr. & Dis. Women* LXXVI. 797 A vulvectomy was done on June 27th and the patient left the hospital August 13th. **1962** *Lancet* 1 Dec. 1171/1 The histological findings of atypical basal-cell hyperplasia in any section can then justify vulvectomy.

'vulviform, *a.* *Bot.* and *Zool.* [f. L. *vulvi-* VULVA + -FORM.] (See quot.)

1849 CRAIG, *Vulviform*, in Botany, like a cleft with projecting edges. **1891** *Cent. Dict.* s.v. *Vulva*, The oval or vulviform conformation presented by certain bivalve shells.

‖**vulvitis** (vʌl'vaɪtɪs). *Path.* [f. VULV-A + -ITIS.] Inflammation of the vulva.

1859 MAYNE *Expos. Lex.* 1338. **1864** BUMSTEAD *Ven. Dis.* (1879) 209 Their effect.. is so slight that they are not to be recommended in vaginitis or vulvitis. **1889** *Buck's Handbk. Med. Sci.* VII. 694/1 In catarrhal vulvitis the pain and redness of the mucous membrane are slight.

vulvo- ('vʌlvəʊ), combining form on Gr. models of L. *vulva* VULVA, occurring in a few anatomical or pathological terms, as ***vulvo-scrotal***, ***-uterine***, ***-vaginal***, ***vaginitis***.

1849 CRAIG s.v. *Vulva*, The vagina or vulvo-uterine canal. **1857** BULLOCK *Cazeaux' Midwif.* 46 The Vulvo-vaginal gland had been completely lost sight of by modern anatomists. **1893** D. J. CUNNINGHAM *Man. Pract. Anat.* I. 380 The two fascial pouches.. are sometimes spoken of as the vulvo-scrotal sacs. **1897** *Trans. Amer. Pediatric Soc.* IX. 113 The urine may be so irritating as to cause a vulvo-vaginitis in the female infant.

vum (vʌm), *v.* *U.S. colloq.* [Alteration of VOW *v.*[2]] *intr.* To vow, swear.

1785 *Mass. Spy* 13 Oct. 2/2 We all must dreadful mindful be That we must fight for liberty And vum we'll 'fend it, if we die. **1845** S. JUDD *Margaret* I. xii, 'I vum,' said he, 'what is the matter?' **1858** O. W. HOLMES *Aut. Breakf.-t.* xi. (1891) 253 But the Deacon swore (as Deacons do, With an 'I dew vum', or an 'I tell yeou').

Hence **vum** *sb.*

1881 *Harper's Mag.* Jan. 249 Darius was piqued, and he said, with a vum, 'I'll pay for the wood, if you'll send it hum'.

†**vumbard.** *Obs.*[−1] [app. a late form of VAMWARD: for the sense cf. VANTGUARD 2.] ? A front guard.

1464 *Mann. & Househ. Exp.* (Roxb.) 195 My mastyr lent hym a payr of smale curas wyth gardys and vumbarde.

vunde, southern ME. pa. t. FIND *v.*

vur, vurness, vurther, southern dial. varr. FAR *adv.*, etc., FARNESS, FURTHER.

vurry ('vɜːrɪ), *a.* *colloq.* Repr. an Amer. pronunciation of VERY *a.* and *adv.*

1889 KIPLING *From Sea to Sea* (1899) I. xii. 306 The tourists.. call to one another: 'Sa-ay, don't you think it's vurry much the same all along?' **1913** E. POUND *Let.* (1971) 14 Have just discovered another Amur'kn [*sc.* Robert Frost]. *Vurry* Amur'k'n. **1943** C. S. CHURCHILL *Let.* 19 Dec. in M. Soames *Clementine Churchill* (1979) xxii. 344 The food, however, is 'vurry' American. **1972** K. BONFIGLIOLI *Don't Point that Thing at Me* vii. 65 [He] wished me a vurry, vurry happy visit to the US of A.

†**vusse.** *Obs. rare.* [? Alteration of FAITH *sb.*] ***by my vusse***, used as an asseveration.

1608 ARMIN *Nest Ninn.* Fijb, But are you my vncle indeed? By my vusse I am sayes the old man. Then vncle by my vusse welcome to Court.

vuste, southern ME. variant of FIST *sb.*[1]

vuz(z, southern dial. variant of FURZE.

vuzeer, variant of VIZIER.

vy, obs. form of VIE *sb.*[3] and *v.*

vyalett, obs. form of VIOLET *sb.*[1]

vyall, obs. form of VIOL *sb.*

vyce, obs. Sc. form of WISE *a.*

vych, vychon, southern ME. varr. EACH (*one*).

vychancellour, obs. f. VICE-CHANCELLOR.

vyche, obs. form of WITCH *sb.*

vycht, obs. Sc. form of WIGHT *sb.* and *a.*

vychtie, obs. Sc. form of WEIGHTY *a.*

vyckyr, obs. form of VICAR.

vycle, southern ME. var. FICKLE *v.*[1]

vycytar, obs. form of VISITER.

vycyte, obs. form of VISIT *v.*

vy'd, vyde, obs. ff. VIED *ppl. a.*

vyd(e, obs. Sc. forms of WIDE *a.*

vydam(e, obs. forms of VIDAME.

vydele, southern ME. variant of FIDDLE.

vydour, obs. Sc. form of VOIDER.

vye, var. VIE *sb.*[1], *sb.*[2], *sb.*[3] *Obs.*; obs. f. VIE *v.*

vyend, southern ME. var. FIEND.

vyer, occas. printed for *vþer* OTHER *a.*

vyf(e, vyff, obs. Sc. ff. WIFE *sb.*

†**vyfnes.** *Obs.*[−1] [f. F. *vif* VIVE *a.* + -NESS.] Liveliness, vivacity.

1475 *Bk. Noblesse* (Roxb.) 4 Therfor.. every man in hym silf let the passions of dolours be turned and empressid into vyfnes of here spiritis.

vyftene, -teoþe, southern ME. varr. FIFTEEN(TH.

vygie ('feɪxɪ). *S. Afr.* [Afrikaans, f. *vy*(*g*), f. Du. *vijg*, *vig* fig + *-ie* diminutive suffix.] Any of several small succulent plants belonging to the genus *Mesembryanthemum* or a closely related genus, or the brightly coloured flower of one of these plants. Also **'vygebosch** [Afrikaans *vyebossie*].

1795 tr. *C. P. Thunberg's Trav. Europe, Afr., & Asia* II. 35 The field was here of the Carrow kind, and the sheep were said to feed on those succulent plants, the Mesembryanthemums (*vygebosches*). **1892** *Jrnl.* (Grahamstown) 11 July 1/2 (Advt.), The Veld consists of much-sought-after Karoo, Vygebosch,.. with Mimosas in the valley. **1931** *Farming in S. Afr.* 393 The mineral and feeding-stuff analyses of a vygie give no clue to its probable palatability. **1950** *Cape Argus* 5 Aug. 7/5 Vygies or sour figs .. blossom in a wide range of colours—scarlet, blue, purple, pink or flaming yellow. **1966** E. PALMER *Plains of Camdeboo* xvii. 271 The little vygies on the flats. **1971** [see GOUSBLOM].

vygne, obs. f. VINE *sb.*

vyhs, obs. form of VICE *sb.*[1]

vyhte, southern ME. var. FIGHT *sb.* and *v.*

vyijs, vyild, obs. Sc. f. WISE *sb.*, WILD *a.*

vying, obs. form of VIEING *vbl. sb.*

vyir, occas. printed for *vþir* OTHER *a.*

vyis(e, vyit, vyl, vyld(e, obs. Sc. ff. WISE *sb.* and *a.*, WITE *sb.* and *v.*, WILL *sb.*, WILD *a.*

vyiss, variant of VISE *v.*[1] *Obs.*

vylarde, variant of VIEILLARD *Obs.*

vylence, -ens, variants of VILLAINS *a.* *Obs.*

vyleny(e, etc., obs. forms of VILLAINY.

vylette, southern ME. variant of FILLET *sb.*

vylie, obs. form of VILELY *adv.*

vylie, vyling, obs. Sc. variant of WILY *a.*, WILING *vbl. sb.*

vylney, obs. form of VILLAINY.

vyloyns, variant of VILLAINS *a.* *Obs.*

vyn, southern ME. var. FIN *sb.*[1]; obs. Sc. f. WIN *v.*, WONE *v.*

vynacre, -eker, obs. variants of VINEGAR.

vynd, obs. form of WYND *sb.* *Sc.*

vyndage, variant of VENDAGE *Obs.*

vynde, southern ME. var. FIND *v.*; obs. f. VINE *sb.*; obs. Sc. f. WIND *sb.*

vyndle, obs. Sc. form of WINDLE *v.*

vyndok, obs. Sc. variant of WINDOW.

vyne, obs. f. VINE; obs. Sc. f. WIN *v.*, WINE.

vynet(t, vyniet, variants of VINET *Obs.*

vynetree, obs. form of VINTRY.

Vynide ('vaɪnaɪd). Also **vynide**. A proprietary name for a plastic used as a substitute for leather in upholstery, clothing, etc.

1943 *Trade Marks Jrnl.* 16 June 257/2 *Vynide*... Leather cloth. Imperial Chemical Industries Limited, Wexham Road, Slough, Buckinghamshire; manufacturers and merchants. **1958** *Archit. Rev.* CXXIV. 395/2 The bookcase shelves and backs, and the wall opposite the window are covered in white vynide. **1960** *Housewife* Feb. 58/2 Thankful I brought good country-looking Vynide jacket ..(looks like leather, won't leak, will sponge clean). **1976** *Lancs. Evening Post* 7 Dec. 12/8 (Advt.), Reupholstery. Your three piece suite made as new in moquette or vynide.

vynk, obs. Sc. form of WINK *v.*

vynne, southern ME. variant of FIN *sb.*[1]

vynnett, variant of VINET *Obs.*

vynour, obs. variant of VINER[2].

vyntre, obs. form of VINE-TREE, VINTRY.

vynued, variant of VINEWED *a.* *Obs.*

vyny, vynye, obs. var. VINE *sb.*, VINNY *v.*

vynyette, variant of VINET *Obs.*

vyral, obs. form of VIRL *sb.*

vyrchippe, obs. form of WORSHIP.

vyre, variant of EURE *sb.* *Obs.*, VIRE *sb.*[1] *Obs.*

vyrelle, -ille, obs. forms of VIRL *sb.*

vyrk, obs. Sc. form of WORK *v.*

vyrne, variant of VERNE *sb.* and *v.* *Obs.*

vyrre, southern ME. variant of FIR.

vysard(e, obs. forms of VIZARD.

vyscele, obs. Sc. form of VESSEL *sb.*

vyse, obs. var. USE *v.*, VICE *sb.*, VISE *v.*[1], VISS, WISE *sb.* and *v.*

vysenamy, obs. form of VISNOMY.

vyseuase, vysiere: see VISEVASE, VISIERE.

vysilie, vysly, obs. forms of WISELY *adv.*

vysotskite (viː'sɒtskaɪt). *Min.* [ad. Russ. *vysotskit* (Genkin & Zvyagintsev 1962, in *Zap. Vsesoyuz. Min. Obshch.* XCI. 718), f. the name of N. K. *Vysotsky* (d. 1932), Russian mineralogist: see -ITE[1].] A sulphide of palladium and often nickel, (Pd,Ni)S, found as minute silvery tetragonal crystals having a metallic lustre.

1963 *Chem. Abstr.* LVIII. 8777 For the genesis of vysotskite is characteristic the assocn. with Pt ores, pentlandite, millerite, and other sulfides, in effusive andesite-diabase in gabbro-diabase intrusions. **1978** *Amer. Mineralogist* LXIII. 832/1 Vysotskite has since been reported.. from the Stillwater Complex of Montana.. and the Lac des Isles deposit, Ontario. *Ibid.* 838/1 We conclude that braggite and vysotskite are simply compositional variants of the same phase, (Pd,Pt,Ni)S... We suggest that the family of minerals be called the braggite series and that all compositions containing less than 10 mole percent PtS be called vysotskite.

vyss, vyssyon, obs. ff. VICE *sb.*[1], VISION.

vyss, vyssare, vysycyon, southern ME. varr. FISH, FISHER[1], PHYSICIAN.

vyt, vytch, vyte, obs. Sc. ff. WIT, WITCH, WITE.

vythulare, vythule, southern ME. variants of FIDDLER, FIDDLE.

vyue, southern ME. var. FIVE; obs. f. VIVE *a.*

vyuer, vyver(e, obs. forms of VIVER[1].

vyveri, obs. variant of IVORY.

vywe(r, obs. forms of VIEW *sb.*, VIEWER.

W

W ('dʌb(ə)lju:), the 23rd letter of the modern English alphabet, is an addition to the ancient Roman alphabet, having originated from a ligatured doubling of the Roman letter represented by the U and V of modern alphabets. When, in the 7th c., the Latin alphabet was first applied to the writing of English, it became necessary to provide a symbol for the sound (w), which did not exist in contemporary Latin. This sound, a gutturally-modified bilabial voiced spirant, is acoustically almost identical with the devocalized (u) or (ʊ), which was the sound originally expressed by the Roman U or V as a consonant-symbol; but before the 7th c. this Latin sound had developed into (v). The single *u* or *v* therefore could not without ambiguity be used to represent (w), though this was occasionally done, and in some Northumbrian texts was the regular practice. The ordinary sign for (w) was at first *uu*, but in the 8th c. this began to be superseded by ƿ, a character borrowed from the Runic alphabet, in which its name was *wyn* (Kentish *wen*). Eventually the use of ƿ became almost universal, but in the mean time the *uu* was carried from England to the continent, being used for the sound (w) in the German dialects, and in French proper names and other words of Teut. and Celtic origin. In the 11th c. the ligatured form was introduced into England by Norman scribes, and gradually took the place of ƿ, which finally went out of use about A.D. 1300. The character W was probably very early regarded as a single letter, although it has never lost its original name of 'double U'.

In OE. the sound (w) occurred initially not only before vowels but also before (l) and (r). The combination *wl* became obsolete in the 15th c. (in Sc. poetry *wlonk*, alliterating with *w*-words, was used in the 16th c.); *wr* is still written, but the *w* is silent in standard English, though in some dialects it is sounded as (w) or as (v). OE. had also the initial combination (hw), written *hu*(*u*, *hƿ*, and subsequently *ph*, *wh*; for the later development of this phonetic combination, and the history of the associated symbols, see WH.

The chief etymological sources of the Eng. (w) are: (1) OE. (w), mainly representing Indogermanic *w*, gh^w, *kw*, or k^w; (2) ON. (w) of the same origin (in cited words expressed by *v*, according to Icelandic usage); (3) OF. (w), retained in north-eastern Fr. dialects, but elsewhere becoming (gw) and ultimately (g), whence in English such doublets as *wage* and *gage*, *warranty* and *guaranty*. The sound also occurs, represented otherwise than by *w*, in words of Latin origin containing the combinations *qu* (kw) and *su* (sw), as *question*, *suavity*, *persuade* (in 16–18th c. often written with *sw*); also in a few Fr. words, as *reservoir* (-vwɑ:(r)).

So far as it remains a consonant-symbol, the letter never denotes any other sound than (w), but in a few words it has ceased to be pronounced, though still written, as in *answer*, *sword*, *two*, and in the combination *wr* referred to above. In the unstressed second element of a compound, (w) tends to be elided in colloquial speech. This contracted pronunciation is in some words a mere vulgarism (marked as such by spellings like *back'ard*, *forrard*, *allus* for *always*); in *Norwich* and some other place-names in *-wich* it is the only one regarded as correct, and the same may be said with regard to the nautical term *gunwale*; in *midwife* the contraction ('mɪdɪf), formerly general, is now rarely heard. The tendency to elision of *w* beginning an unstressed second syllable is shown also in the change of *housewife* into *huzzif*, *huzzy*, where the spelling has followed the pronunciation, though the uncontracted form is now restored exc. in a special disparaging sense.

In some ME. MSS. (northern and north midland), and in many Scottish texts of the 15th and 16th centuries, *w* is written for *v*, and vice versa. In the 16th and 17th c., books printed from continental type often have the letter in the divided form VV, vv.

In ME. a new (w) arose from the development of intervocalic or final (ɣ), inherited from OE., as in *bowe*:—earlier *boȝe*:—OE. *boȝa*. This sound, however, has not survived as a consonant, because every (w) after a stressed vowel became a *u*-glide, the terminal element of a diphthong. From the early ME. period *w* was often substituted for *u* in vowel-digraphs (whether denoting diphthongs or simple vowels). In modern spelling *aw*, *ew*, *ow* are phonetically equivalent to *au*, *eu*, *ou*, though *ow* never stands for (u:), as in the older *yow* = *you* (except in the surname Cowper); the choice between *u* and *w* has been determined to some extent by etymological tradition, but is mainly arbitrary; at the end of a word *w*, not *u*, is used all but invariably. The traditional statement of grammarians that 'W is a vowel as well as a consonant' refers to its use in these digraphs; but in the 14–15th c., and in Sc. also in the 16th c., *w* occasionally represents (u:), as in *trw* = true, *swne* = soon, *swth* = sooth.

In south-eastern dialects (w) is regularly substituted for (v), and many writers of the first half of the 19th c. attribute to the Cockney dialect the habit of misusing (v) for (w) and (w) for (v) on all occasions. No trace of this survives in present-day London speech; and although there is no doubt that the Kentish (w) for (v) at one time extended to London, it is probable that the reverse substitution was merely an occasional (if perhaps rather frequent) result of the endeavour to speak correctly.

1763 FOOTE *Mayor of G.* I. (1764) 21 *Sneak.* Yes, werry like Wenus. **1803** PEGGE *Anecd. Engl. Lang.* (1814) 77 The ..most offensive error in pronunciation among the Londoners..lies in the transpositional use of the letters *W* and *V*, ever to be heard where there is any possibility of inverting them. Thus they always say, *W*eal, instead of *veal*; and *W*inegar, instead of *vinegar*; while, on the other hand, you hear *V*icked, for *wicked*—*V*ig, for *wig*; and a few others. **1805** T. HARRAL *Scenes of Life* III. 26 'Last night thou gavest me to a willain's arms!'—'A villain?'..'Ay, a willain!' **1837** DICKENS *Pickw.* xxxiv, 'Do you spell it [Weller] with a V or a W?'..'I spells it with a V'... 'Quite right too, Samivel... Put it down a we, my lord'. **1844** T. H. KEY *Alphabet* 107 London too is remarkable for the confusion of the sounds, though this confusion does not seem to arise from any inability to pronounce either a *w* or a *v*, each being substituted for the other with a most amusing perversity.

A mispronunciation of (w) for (r), in some persons due to a physical defect, has sometimes been a fashionable affectation.

1837 DICKENS *Pickw.* xxxv, 'Gwacious heavens!' said his lordship. 'I thought evewebody had seen the new mail-cart; it's the neatest, pwettiest, gwacefullest thing that ever wan.' **1844** T. H. KEY *Alphabet* 93 The letter *r* is at times confounded with *w*. Thus it is not a very rare variety of articulation that *rubbish* is pronounced *wubbish*.

II. 1. The letter, its sound or name.

c **1465** in *Pol. Rel. & L. Poems* 2 A Doble W. for Warwike, þat god be his gide. **1552** HULOET Kk ij b, Because there is a diuersitie betwene the single V and the dowble W, therfore the alphabet of them shalbe set diuersly. [The sequence is: *Va*, *Wa*, *Vd*.] **1580** W. BULLOKAR *Bk. at large* 8 W. I account also misnamed to call it double : v : for then shoulde we sounde it : v : v : but his sounde agreeth to the olde name of : y : (which is wy). *c* **1595** R. CAREW in G. G. Smith *Elizab. Crit. Ess.* (1904) II. 286 For letters, wee haue Q. more then the Greekes; K. and Y. more then the Latynes; and W. more then them both, or the French and Italians. **1599** THYNNE *Animadv.* (1875) 65 The latyne, Italiane, frenche, and spanyshe haue no doble W. *a* **1637** B. JONSON *Engl. Gram.* iii. (1640) 40 W, Is but the V. geminated in the full sound, and though it have the seate of a Consonant with us, the power is alwayes Vowellish, even where it leades the Vowell in any Syllabe: as if you marke it, pronounce the two *uu*. like ȣ. quicke in passage and these words: ȣ-ine. ȣ-ant. ȣ-ood. ȣ-ast. ſȣ-ing. ſȣ-am. Will sound wine. want. wood. wast. swing. swam. **1697** DRYDEN *Æneis* Ded. (e) 1, [In the English *Aeneis*] where a Vowel ends a word, the next begins either with a Consonant, or what is its equivalent; for our W and H aspirate..are plainly such. **1704** *Expert Orthographist* in Ellis *E.E. Pron.* I. iii. (1869) 160 All polysyllables ending in obscure *o* have *w* added for ornament's sake as *arrow*, *bellows*, &c. **1796** PEGGE *Anonym.* (1809) 454 One would wonder how the *w* could ever come to be a letter in our language, for it is plainly nothing else but the *u* vowel; for..*uill* spells will, as much as *will*. **1836** CAR. B. SOUTHEY *Birth-day* I. 37 And sprawling W's, and V's, and Y's, Gaped prodigiously. **1869** ELLIS *E.E. Pron.* I. iii. 187 In Europe (w) is thought to be peculiar to England..In Arabic however (w) is quite at home. *a* **1890** W. B. SCOTT *Autob.* (1892) I. ii. 29 He went over the letters, giving them the broad old Scotch pronunciation: A was *awe*, B was *bay*, C was *say*, and so on, ending with U sounded like *oo* in good, W as *duploo*, Z as *izzid*. **1899** *Allbutt's Syst. Med.* VII. 449 *note*, The voiceless *W* and the voiceless *L* have been given above within brackets, the former being now almost confined to Scotland and the latter being peculiar to Wales.

2. The letter considered with regard to its shape. Also *attrib.*

1798 *Hull Advertiser* 28 July 2/1 Chairs in sets..with W, tableau and X backs. **1871** *Cassell's Nat. Hist.* I. 266 The molars show sharp tubercles separated by transverse furrows, generally producing a sort of W-like pattern on each tooth. **1882** FLOYER *Unexpl. Baluchistan* 17 The walls ..are..rendered ornamental by triangular recesses fitting one into another like an endless W, each triangle being filled up with lines of smaller W's.

3. Abbreviations. **W.** = various personal names, as William, Walter, Winifred; **W**, colloq. shortening of W.C.: a lavatory or water-closet; **W** (*Electr.*) = watt; **W.** = West (***W.N.W.*** west-north-west, ***W.S.W.*** west-south-west); †**W.** (*Calendar*) = Whitsunday; **W** (*Chem.*) = tungsten (mod.L. *wolframium*); **W.**, women('s size) (***WX***, extra-large women's size); **W.A.**, Western Australia; **WASP** (*U.S.*), Women's Airforce Service Pilots; **WAT** (*Aeronaut.*), Weight and Temperature; **WATS** (*U.S.*), Wide Area Telephone Service; **W.C.** = water-closet; **W.C.** the West Central postal district of London; **W.C.C.**, World Council of Churches; **WCT**, World Championship Tennis; **W.C.T.U.** (*N. Amer.*), Women's Christian Temperance Union; **W.D.**, War Department; **W.D.C.**, Woman Detective Constable; **W.D.S.**, Woman Detective Sergeant; **W.E.A.**, Workers' Educational Association; **w.e.f.**, with effect from; **W.E.U.**, Western European Union; **wff** (*Logic*) = *well-formed formula* s.v. WELL-FORMED *ppl. a.* c; **WFTU**, World Federation of Trade Unions; **w.h.b.**, wash-hand basin; **W.H.O.**, World Health Organization; **W.I.**, West Indies (also †West India); **W.I.**, Women's Institute; **W.I.Z.O.**, **Wizo** ('wi:tzəʊ), Women's International Zionist Organization; **WKB** (*Physics*) [initials of G. Wentzel, H. A. Kramers, and L. Brillouin, who each published papers on the method in 1926], used *attrib.* with reference to a method for obtaining an approximate solution of the Schrödinger equation based on the expansion of the wave function in powers of Planck's constant, *h*; **W.L.A.**, Women's Land Army; **W.M.O.**, World Meteorological Organization; **W.O.**, War Office; **W.O.**, Warrant Officer; **W.O.C.(S.)**, waiting on cement (to set); **WORM** (wɜ:m) *Computing*, write once read mostly (or many times): used (chiefly *attrib.*) to designate optical memory or an optical storage device on to which data may be written once only by laser, and which is thereafter used as ROM; **W.O.S.B.** (also with pronunc. 'wɒzbɪ), War Office Selection Board; **W.O.W.**, waiting on weather; **w.p.**, weather permitting; **WP**, word processing; **WPA**, (*U.S.*), Works Progress Administration; **W.P.B.**, **w.p.b.** (*slang*), waste-paper basket; **W.P.C.**, Woman Police Constable; **w.p.m.**, words per minute; **W.R.A.N.S.** (rænz) (*Austral.*), Women's Royal Australian Naval Service; hence **WRAN**, **Wran**, a member of this; **W.R.N.S.**, Women's Royal Naval Service; cf. WREN[2]; **w.r.t.**, with respect to; **W.R.V.S.**, Women's Royal Voluntary Service, formerly **W.V.S.**; **W.S.** (*Scotland*) = Writer to the Signet; **W.S.P.U.**, Women's Social and Political Union; **W/T**, **W.T.**, wireless telegraphy; freq. *attrib.*; **w/v** (see quot. 1907); **W.V.S.**, Women's Voluntary Service; **WW (I, II)**, World War (One, Two); **W.W.W.**, World Weather Watch. See also W.A.A.C., W.A.A.F., W.A.C., WASP, W.R.A.C., W.R.A.F., WREN[2].

1953 DYLAN THOMAS *Under Milk Wood* (1954) 11 Talking to the lamp-post..Using language..Singing in the *W. **1954** A. S. C. ROSS in *Neuphilol. Mitteilungen* LV. 41 *W.* either 'the letter W' or 'W.C.' (a frequent non-U expression for 'lavatory'). **1978** E. MALPASS *Wind brings up Rain* x. 105 A small garden of weeds, with a cinder path leading to a W. **1513** SIR E. HOWARD in *Lett. & Papers War France* (1897) 94 The wynd feeryd owt off the *W.N.W. into the E.N.E. **1708** *Lond. Gaz.* No. 4422/7 We came to an Anchor about Noon, the Wind at W. by S. **1778** *Engl. Gazetteer* (ed. 2) s.v. *Fale*, It rises about 2 miles W. of Roche Hills. **1891** W. CLARK RUSSELL *Marriage at Sea* v, The.. compass was about W.S.W. **1926–7**, **1974** W [see *S.W.* s.v. S 4a]. *c* **1565** *Gude & Godlie Ball.* (S.T.S.) Calendar 12b,

Ye shal finde . . at the 29. of April this letter *W where begine for Whitsonday. **1900** *Morning Post* 12 July 9/4 Town Pro. W.A. **1971** *Sunday Australian* 8 Aug. 5/2 The State shipping service in *WA has been made the scapegoat for Government indecision. **1943** *Yank* 24 Sept. 17 *WASP, which stands for 'Womens Air Force Service Pilots' is the new official title of women pilots of the AAF. **1957** *Times* 9 Dec. 12/7 There is an additional requirement governing the maximum take-off and landing weights for the altitude and weight prevailing (known as the '*WAT curve'). **1976** B. LECOMBER *Dead Weight* xi. 136 Those coins weigh 600 lb . . if we pile in three people on top of that we'll be totally WAT-limited... WAT—Weight and Temperature. **1962** *Fleet Owner* Aug. 73/1 With *WATS you pay a monthly fee for a special line over which you can call any telephone number in prescribed States. **1977** *New Yorker* 12 Sept. 68/3 Harry has a WATS line, so Henny called Sadie again, this time for free. **1815** *Corr. W. Fowler* (1907) 330 Apparatus for *W.C. at Normanby, which had to come from London. **1892** EMINSON *Epidemic Pneumonia at Scotter* 11 No W.C. or slaughter-house drains into them. **1857** *Punch* 7 Feb. 51/2 Rowland Hill has just divided London's waste of brick by ten... Lawyers, and good *Coram's* Foundlings, All are found in *W.C. **1935** E. FARJEON *Nursery in Nineties* I. viii. 63 We found the little oblong envelope . . with . . the London W.C. postmark. **1948** *Ecumenical Rev.* Autumn 118 The work of two Conferences convened by the Study Department of the *W.C.C. . . is reported in this book. **1971** K. GRUBB *Crypts of Power* viii. 168 Many Churches of Asia, Africa and Latin America joined the W.C.C. **1969** *N.Y. Times* 19 Feb. 54/5 Robert A. Briner of *W.C.T. said: 'This is a truce.' **1982** *Tennis Today* June 12/3 Dallas had its best field for a few years, which was an effective answer to those who would suggest WCT are on the way out after the split with the Grand Prix. **1888** LINDLEY & WIDNEY *California of South* 109 The *W.C.T.U. was first organized here in 1883. **1956** B. HOLIDAY *Lady sings Blues* (1973) xix. 157 Nobody who has a police record can hold a liquor licence. This was a sop to the WCTU. **1855** *Admiralty Circular* 27 Aug., In future the mark *W.D. (War Department), with the Broad Arrow, shall be used for Stores provided by the Ordnance Department. **1920** *Punch* 7 Jan. 9/1 The orders are dead strict against civilians riding in W.D. vehicles. **1942** E. WAUGH *Put out More Flags* II. 149 Patches of rank land marked on the signposts W.D., marked on the maps as numbered training areas. **1976** 'J. CHARLTON' *Remington Set* xviii. 86, I need something on a three-ton chassis . . ex-WD Bedford would do nicely. **1970** G. F. NEWMAN *Sir, You Bastard* viii. 217 Find two *WDC's to accompany the women. **1972** *Police Rev.* 8 Dec. 1597/1 We in Nottinghamshire have not yet decided whether we have D.P.W.s or W.D.C.s or whether they are *W.D.S.s or D.P.W. Sergts. **1910** S. A. BARNETT *Let.* 10 Mar. in H. Barnett *Canon Barnett* (1918) II. l. 332 The *W.E.A. has life. **1936** A. HUXLEY *Eyeless in Gaza* xxix. 393 W.E.A. lecture-rooms. **1981** D. ROWNTREE *Dict. Educ.* 350 *Workers' Educational Association* (*WEA*), a UK organisation founded in 1903 to stimulate and satisfy the demand for education among working class people... The WEA now arranges adult education classes and courses throughout the UK (no longer primarily for working class people). **1942** PARTRIDGE *Dict. Abbrev.* 101/2 **w.e.f.*, with effect from (a given date). **1954** J. MASTERS *Bhowani Junction* xxxii. 275 It terminated her duty with my battalion w.e.f. June the twelfth. **1978** T. ALLBEURY *Lantern Network* viii. 93 The official notification of his promotion to major w.e.f. 1 Jan. 44. **1954** *Times* 11 Nov. 8/7 The first [of the protocols] modifies the older treaty to allow for the adherence of Italy and the German Federal Republic . . and emphasizes close cooperation with the North Atlantic Treaty Organization, on which *W.E.U. will rely. *a***1974** R. CROSSMAN *Diaries* (1976) II. 401 George [Brown] proposes to go to a meeting of the W.E.U. next Tuesday and wants to make an important declaration there on Europe. **1944** *w.f.f. [see PRENEX *a.*]. **1956** A. CHURCH *Introd. Math. Logic* (rev. ed.) I. i. 70 We shall hereafter use the abbreviations 'wf' for 'well-formed', 'wff' for 'well-formed formula', and 'wffs' for 'well-formed formulas'. **1967** *Encycl. Philos.* V. 2/2 This property will clearly be perceived if a small letter is systematically replaced by any wff. **1971** G. HUNTER *Metalogic* i. 4 What things are to be wffs. **1947** *Times* 17 Nov. 5/6 The International Transport Workers' Federation will meet . . to consider further its decision recently taken in Washington not to affiliate to the *W.F.T.U. **1978** *Statesman's Year-Bk.* I. 39 The WFTU formally came into existence on 3 Oct. 1945. **1975** *Evening Herald* (Dublin) 8 May 10/3 (Advt.), Cloakroom with w.c. and *w.h.b. **1946** *N.Y. Times* 28 July IV. 2/3 Dr Thomas Parran . . described the constitution of the *WHO as a major contribution to world peace. **1960** *New Statesman* 2 Apr. 478/3 The Americans are . . working with the WHO to build hospitals and eliminate malaria. **1977** G. SCOTT *Hot Pursuit* xi. 98 If this was a WHO team . . we could be passing up the one opportunity we had. **1848** *Brit. Army Despatch* 17 Nov. 292/2 Late Captain 2nd *W.I. Regt. **1900** *Naval & Mil. Rev.* July 5 Name of Vessel. Pearl. Present Station. N.A. and W.I. **1973** *Advocate-News* (Barbados) 17 Jan. 2/5 (*heading*) Deep concern over W.I. **1928** *Mid-Sussex Times* 18 Dec. 8/1 A tangible result of the *W.I. trading scheme. **1940** C. MILBURN *Diary* 26 Mar. (1979) 28 A W.I. Produce Meeting . . to hear about sugar for jam and the arrangements about getting it for W.I. members. **1965** *New Society* 7 Jan. 5 At Stony Creek, Ontario, in 1897, the first WI meeting was held... It wasn't until the outbreak of World War I that a Canadian widow named Mrs. Watt introduced the WI to Britain... The first meeting was held in September 1915. **1981** J. SCOTT *Distant View of Death* xii. 158 Jars of home produce to transport to the WI stall set up in the square. **1925** *Zionist Rev.* IX. 50/2 The growing edifice of the *W.I.Z.O. **1940** A. ULITZUR *Two Decades of Keren Hayesod* iii. 47 The Women's International Zionist Organisation (*Wizo*). **1978** *Jewish Chron.* 6 Oct. 14/3 Coventry and Leamington Wizo held a three day nearly new sale and raised £350 for Israel. [**1932** J. L. DUNHAM in *Physical Rev.* XLI. 713 The Wentzel-Brillouin-Kramers method of handling the wave equation (hereinafter referred to as the W.B.K. method) is very well suited to the calculation of energy levels in heavy systems.] **1935** *Ibid.* XLVII. 748/2 The wave function can be represented by the *WKB (Wentzel-Kramers-Brillouin) solution. **1961** POWELL & CRASEMANN *Quantum Mech.* v. 142 The WKB solutions cannot be valid near a classical turning point, where the momentum is zero. **1974** G. REECE tr. *Hund's Hist. Quantum Theory* vii. 97 This was confirmed by later proofs using the Schroedinger equation and the WKB approximation. **1939** *Times* 26 Oct. 11/5 The farmer who is loth to employ one of the *W.L.A. may see his more progressive neighbour very well served. **1942** C. MILBURN *Diary* 17 Oct. (1979) 155, I did a little W.L.A. work, going down to the hostel with some magazines. **1951** *Bull. Amer. Meteorol. Soc.* XXXII. 239/1 The International Meteorological Organization wound up its affairs in Paris on March 15–17, 1951 and handed over its assets, obligations and numerous resolutions to the new World Meteorological Organisation... Sir Nelson Johnson aptly put it when he said . . 'The IMO is dying, long live the *WMO.' **1977** *Whitaker's Almanack 1978* 810/1 World Meteorological Organization (WMO), Geneva... The present membership is 139 States and 8 Territories. **1860** F. NIGHTINGALE *Let.* 8 Dec. in C. Woodham-Smith *Florence Nightingale* (1950) xvi. 358, I do hope you won't have any vain ideas that you can be spared out of the *W.O... You are necessary to the reorganising of the W.O. **1914** R. BROOKE *Let.* 24 Sept. (1968) 619 He may go out as an interpreter... The W.O. has his name. **1931** *N. & Q.* 5 Dec. 408/2 Who was Capt. Robert Holden, of the 130th Regt.? From Army Lists and W.O. Commission Books, it seems that he was commissioned Lieutenant in the 115th Regt., 14 Nov., 1794. **1887** O. L. PERRY *Ranks & Badges H.M. Army & Navy* ix. 102 Such *W.O.'s, N.C.O.'s and men as may be specially placed under their orders. **1977** 'O. JACKS' *Autumn Heroes* iv. 65 He's an ex W.O.II in the Paras. **1949** *Amer. Speech* XXIV. 35 The verbal *wocsing* . . is derived from the initials *W.O.C.S., which stand for *waiting on cement to set* (the written form is often simply *woc* without capitalization or punctuation)... A field worker tells me I must have misspelled the word, as it is always pronounced ['wɒkəsɪŋ] in the field. **1974** D. K. SMITH in P. L. Moore et al. *Drilling Practices Manual* xvi. 400 Improvements in cements, understanding WOC times, and the use of admixes have reduced WOC time to a few hours under present-day practices. **1985** *Electronics* 24 June 85/1 The model 5984 optical disk drive offers 400 megabytes of write-once-read-mostly (*WORM) data-storage space on a 5¼ in. disk. **1985** *Pract. Computing* Oct. 110/1 The Worm (write-once read-many) drive has been around since 1978, when Philips demonstrated a 12 in. optical data disc based on its video-disc technology. **1986** *Guardian* 5 June 13/4 CD-ROM is essentially a publishing medium, but 'write once/read many' (times) or WORM discs enable people to save their own data. **1987** *Financial Times* 6 Jan. I. 20/5 With WORM, personal computer users can write (or scan) new documents onto a disc. **1945** *Jrnl. R. Army Med. Corps* LXXXIV. 75 *W.O.S.B.'s which followed the pattern of the experimental Board. **1978** *Jrnl. R. Soc. Arts* CXXVI. 268/1 The need for skilful selection of officers . . led to the WOSB or War Office Selection Board. **1982** S. RAVEN *Shadows on Grass* (1983) v. 95, I was summoned to a W.O.S.B. . . which would finally determine whether I was fit to be trained for a Commission. **1967** R. DE SOLA *Abbrev. Dict.* (rev. ed.) 277/1 **WOW*, waiting on weather. **1975** *Oil & Gas Industry Gloss. Terms* (Bank of Scotland) 5/2 *W.O.W.*, Waiting on Weather; usually applied to mobile offshore drilling platforms but can also refer to other offshore operations. **1889** E. C. DOWSON *Let.* 2 Mar. (1967) 43, I shall be at Baker St. as you prefer —*w.p. before 3.0, to-morrow. **1931** JOYCE *Let.* 17 Apr. (1966) III. 217, I . . hope to arrive in London . . that evg. (w.p.). **1974** *New Acronyms & Initialisms* (Gale Research Co.), **WP*, word processing. **1980** *City Recorder* 10 Jan. 7/3 In a really small company, the executive who can operate a WP machine can work almost as a one man band. **1936** *N.Y. Herald Tribune* 1 June 8/4 (*heading*) *W.P.A. must increase efficiency, says Ridder. **1943** J. S. HUXLEY *TVA* ix. 69 In the reception room . . the mural by a WPA artist helps the guide to explain the project. **1979** *Listener* 16 Aug. 214/1 The Roosevelt WPA project and other attempts at a social art in the Thirties. **1903** *Photogram* X. 320/1 Anonymous letters are strongly objected to, and . . go into the *W.P.B. **1934** T. E. LAWRENCE *Lett.* (1938) 815 Please dump it in the W.P.B. when it begins to bore you. **1939** *War Illustr.* 16 Dec. p. ii/3 Possessing a very large wastepaper basket, I give short shrift to all anonymous correspondents. A glance at any missive signed with a nom-de-plume and into that w.p.b. it goes. **1974** P. FLOWER *Odd Job* iii. 26 He . . let it fall into the w.p.b. **1984** *Times* 20 Jan. 10/1 So presumably it's someone's job to empty wpbs and clean already clean ashtrays for part of the year. **1963** F. B. FAWCETT *Cycl. Initials & Abbrev.* 158/2 **WPC*, Woman Police Constable. **1966** L. SOUTHWORTH *Felon in Disguise* i. 17 'I'll send in the W.P.C. right away.'.. The Inspector left the room. **1981** 'J. ASHFORD' *Loss of Culion* xiii. 94 Why hadn't she accepted the offer of having a WPC with her? **1936** G. DEWEY *GS Teacher* p. xxiii, Suggested dictation rate: 30 *wpm. **1977** *Belfast Tel.* 17 Jan. 17/1 (Advt.), Applicants should have a typing speed of at least 40 w.p.m. and also 80 w.p.m. shorthand. **1945** BAKER *Austral. Lang.* viii. 159 **W.R.A.N.S.*, Women's Royal Australian Naval Service (called *Wrans* or *Rons*). **1970** M. KELLY *Spinifex* ii. 30 One of the WRANS hurried over, 'Telephone, sir'. 'Thanks, Betty.' **1919** *Daily Mail Year Bk.* 49/2 The Admiralty must feel justly proud of their *W.R.N.S. **1977** *Navy News* Dec. 20/1 Two world wars played a decisive part in the story of the WRNS. The First saw its formation . . The Second swung those doors wide to a tremendous range of opportunities. **1956** W. L. FERRAR *Differential Calculus* iii. 33 Let. $z = f(y)$, $y = \phi(x)$; let z have a finite derivative $f'(y)$ *w.r.t. y. **1979** *Nature* 30 Aug. 845/2 A measure D of the depth of this minimum is defined as the average VAI near days − 2 and + 4 (w.r.t. day 0 as the boundary transit time) minus the average VAI near day 1. **1966** *Care & Distribution of WRVS Processed Clothing* (Women's Royal Voluntary Service) p. iii, The reputation built up by *WRVS in the war years for skilled care . . has been enhanced in post-war years. **1978** *Morecambe Guardian* 14 Mar. 13/1 She holds a long service medal from the WRVS and still retains very strong links with the village of Holme. **1852** THACKERAY *Let.* 24 May in J. Brown *Lett.* (1912) 403 Blackwood the *W.S. I saw in the Park yesterday. *a***1874** R. CHAMBERS in *Casq. Lit.* Ser. II. I. 262/1 Served a regular apprenticeship to a *double-you-ess. **1907** N. A. MARTEL in B. Villiers *Case for Women's Suffrage* 145 A young girl . . came from Huddersfield . . in the care of one of the leaders of the *W.S.P.U. **1967** R. S. CHURCHILL *Winston S. Churchill* II. xi. 402 The WSPU now resorted to stone throwing and later to arson. **1914** W. S. CHURCHILL in M. Gilbert *Winston S. Churchill* (1972) III. Compan. I. 292 A submarine off Sylt report by *W/T (or by pigeons) at night to a waiting destroyer that the weather is favourable. **1923** *Man. Seamanship* (Admiralty) II. 23 Visual and wireless messages . . sent either to the flag deck or the W.T. office for transmission. **1965** 'J. LE CARRÉ' *Looking-Glass War* vii. 84 'He was a trainer in wireless transmission.'.. 'The WT man?' **1978** R. V. JONES *Most Secret War* xlix. 489 Then I saw its astonishing heading: 'Obscene W/T Traffic.' **1907** *Brit. Pharmaceutical Codex* p. ix, '*w/v' represents 'weight in volume', indicating that a weighed quantity of a solid substance is contained in solution in a measured quantity of liquid. **1973** *Nature* 5 Oct. 267/2 Here I report the use of four inhibitors at concentrations of 0·5% w/v which can each stabilize ethanol in blood. **1939** N. LAST *Diary* 4 Sept. in *Nella Last's War* (1983) 11 I've got lots of plans made to spare time so as to work with the *W.V.S. **1976** R. BARNARD *Little Local Murder* iii. 30 The compère talked . . to the head of the town's WVS. **1960** *Acronyms Dict.* (Gale Research Co.) 210 *WWI, World War I. WWII, World War II. **1976** *Greenlist* (J. R. Wrigley Catal.) No. 23. 30 Crascredo—No Joke... (The humour of W.W.I.) **1979** G. F. NEWMAN *List* iii. 25 The bank had been . . incorporated in '41, shortly before America entered WWII. **1963** *Times* 29 Apr. 9/1 It was pointed out during the congress that as ancillary measures must take several years the full realization of plans for a world weather watch (*W.W.W.) was as yet a distant prospect but the interval would enable scientists to ascertain weather potentialities. **1970** *Sci. Jrnl.* Apr. 48 At the time of its inception in 1967 the WWW plan relied entirely on improving and extending existing systems. **1942** A. P. JEPHCOTT *Girls growing Up* i. 33 My biggest tragedy is I am fat & wear *W.X. clothes. **1971** J. THOMSON *Not One of Us* (1972) vii. 79 Cardboard boxes were piled everywhere . . 'Gents' Hose. Assorted Colors.' 'Ladies Knickers. W.X.' **1984** W. BEECHEY *Rich Mrs Robinson* xii. 103 Customers . . [who] thought of themselves as Small Women size when really they were WX.

4. Symbolic uses. **a.** *Genetics.* *W* is used to designate the female-determining sex chromosome in species in which the female rather than the male is the heterogametic sex.

1917 T. H. MORGAN in *Amer. Naturalist* LI. 533 In moths in which the female is the heterogametic sex, the Y chromosome (or the W chromosome to use a different nomenclature) is transmitted only by the female line. **1925** *Amer. Naturalist* LIX. 133 The locus of the F genes is in the W-chromosome that descends from mother to daughter. **1964** R. A. BEATTY in Armstrong & Marshall *Intersexuality* ii. 35 There is one kind of spermatozoon (Z) in animals with the ZW:ZZ mechanism. **1971** [see HETEROGAMETIC *a.*]. **1984** *Nature* 23 Feb. 690/3 Natural populations [of the platyfish, *Xiphophorus maculatus*] are polymorphic for three sex factors (W, X and Y)... The XY and YY genotypes usually develop as males and XX, WX and WY become females; WW genotypes do not in fact occur because male gametes can never bear W factors.

b. *Particle Physics.* [Initial letter of *weak.*] *W* is the symbol for a heavy, charged vector boson that is probably the quantum of the weak interaction.

1960 LEE & YANG in *Physical Rev. Lett.* IV. 310 Possible existence of a weakly coupled boson $W^{\pm}$. *Ibid.*, The question of a neutral W^{0} will not be examined here. **1971** *New Scientist* 2 Sept. 498/3 The experimental results agree with this theory if the W particle has a mass of about 36 proton masses. **1977** *Dædalus* Fall 32 Exchange of the W produces the familiar weak interactions, like nuclear beta decay. **1982** *Nature* 23 Sept. 295/2 The heavy W and Z bosons . . can be produced in $p\bar{p}$ reactions. **1983** *Sci. Amer.* Apr. 62/2 With the discovery of the *W* particle a major goal of experimental elementary-particle physics has been achieved.

w, obs. form of HOW *adv.*

Wa (wɑː), *sb.* (and *a.*) [Native name.] **a.** (Any of) a group of hill-dwelling peoples of eastern Burma and southwestern Yunnan; a member of one of these peoples. **b.** Their (Mon Khmer) language or dialect. Also *attrib.* or as *adj.*

1860 F. MASON *Burmah* (ed. 2) ii. 69 There is a wild tribe called Lawa on the mountains between the Irrawaddy and the Meinan... There is a small settlement of them . . in . . Amherst; there formerly was one in Tavoy, where the Karens called them *Wa*. **1902** *Encycl. Brit.* XXX. 519/2 It [*sc.* the Burmese state Mang Lön] is the chief state of the Vü or Wa tribes. **1911** *Ibid.* XXVIII. 223/2 They are popularly divided into Wild Was and Tame Was. The Wild Was are remarkable as the best authenticated instance of head hunters in the British Empire. **1942** [see PALAUNG *sb.* and *a.*] **1966** D. WILSON *Quarter of Mankind* xvi. 211 They [*sc.* Communist maps] acknowledged the Burmese claim to one piece of territory depicted in Peking as Chinese, but they took an entirely new bite out of the Wa territory shared between the two. **1974** *Encycl. Brit. Micropædia* IV. 272/1 Ethnolinguistic Groups in China . . Wa (Kawa).

wa: see WAW, WAY, WHA *int.*, WOE.

wa', Sc. form of WALL.

waa, north. form of WAY, WHA *int.*, WOE.

W.A.A.C., WAAC, Waac (wæk). Also **wack.** Acronym f. the initial letters of *W*omen's *A*rmy *A*uxiliary *C*orps (1917–19); also *U.S.*, the orig. name of the Women's Army Corps (see W.A.C.), formed in 1942; a member of this. Also *attrib.*

1917 M. MACDONAGH *Diary* 29 Mar. in *In London during Great War* (1935) III. ii. 186 The W.A.A.C.s (Women's Auxiliary Army Corps). *Ibid.*, One of the riddles of the day is: 'Which would you like: a whack on the head or a Waac on your knee?' **1917** W. OWEN *Let.* June (1967) 472 The WAAC's now wait on us. It is rather pleasant. **1918** J. M. GRIDER *Diary* 5 Mar. in *War Birds* (1927) 85 A Waac officer can't walk out with a Tommy any more than an army officer can be seen with a Waac private. **1919** *Times* 31 Dec. 11/4 Queen Mary's Army Auxiliary Corps. To-day the W.A.A.C.'s, to give them the name under which they first earned the gratitude and regard of the Army and the public, cease to have a corporate existence. **1930** A. BENNETT *Imperial Palace* lviii. 456 What do you know of the Western Front, my dear? You aren't old enough to have been a Waac. **1935** A. J. CRONIN *Stars look Down* II. xiii. 379 ''S war work,' Stokes suggested with a ribald leer ''S war work wish [*sic*] a wack.' **1942** *Time* 18 May 62/3 WAAC at last... The Women's Army Auxiliary Corps will provide women for the Army's humbler jobs. **1957** H. H. JENKINS *Diction of 'Yank'* (Univ. Florida thesis) vi. 59 Ordnance announced the addition of the WAAC-Cycle, a light-weight, streamlined bike for the ladies. **1976** 'A. CROSS' *Question of Max* x. 134 Everyone was just WAACs and Tommies together.

W.A.A.F., WAAF, Waaf (wæf). Acronym f. the initial letters of *W*omen's *A*uxiliary *A*ir *F*orce (1939–48, subsequently reorganized as part of the Women's Royal Air Force); a member of this.

1939 *Daily Tel.* 18 Dec. 12/4 (Advt.), Women between the ages of 18 and 43 are required immediately for enrolment in the W.A.A.F. **1942** J. PUDNEY *Dispersal Point* 11 Weather at base closes down for the night: And the ash-blonde Waaf is waiting tea. **1948** W. FORTESCUE *Beauty for Ashes* xxvii. 209 W.A.A.F.s and airmen climbed into a private auto-bus. **1956** R. MACAULAY *Towers of Trebizond* xv. 179 Now the women who go with armies are..called Ats and Wrens and Waafs and Wracs. **1969** G. MACBETH *War Quartet* 42, I had chosen a WAAF, Needing her flesh and heat. **1982** J. AIKEN *Whisper in Night* 25 They wouldn't allow W.A.A.F. girls to fly. **1984** *Sunday Tel.* 16 Sept. 10/3 The contribution by the WAAF to the anti-aircraft defence of this country lay in manning..many of the balloons of Balloon Command.

waaffery, waale, obs. ff. WAFERY, WALE *sb.*[1]

waal (wæl, wɑːl). Also **wal.** Repr. a U.S. colloq. and dial. pronunc. of WELL *adv.* 23.

1863 [see *heater-piece* s.v. HEATER 3]. **1897** KIPLING *Captains Courageous* vi. 129 'D'you suppose we can run her blind?' he shouted. 'Wa-al', *I* can,' Disko retorted. **1978** M. Z. LEWIN *Silent Salesman* xxxvi. 195 Wal, I guess that'll be all right.

waam, var. WAME, north. form of WOMB.

waam(m)le, var. WAMBLE *v.*

waand, var. WONDE *v. Obs.*, to fear, hesitate.

waar, -ness: see WARE, -NESS.

waarnyng, obs. form of WARNING.

waast, obs. form of WAIST, WASTE.

waat, obs. pa. pple. of WET *v.*

wab, north. form of WEB.

wabaïn, wabaio: see OUABAIO.

wabble: see WOBBLE.

wabble, var. WARBLE.

wabe (weɪb). A factitious word introduced by 'Lewis Carroll' (see quot. 1855[2]).

1855 'L. CARROLL' *Rectory Umbrella & Mischmasch* (1932) 139 The slythy toves Did gyre and gymble in the wabe. *Ibid.* 140 *Wabe*, (derived from the verb to *swab* or *soak*). 'The side of a hill' (from its being *soaked* by the rain). **1871** —— *Through Looking-Glass* 24 The slithy toves Did gyre and gimble in the wabe.

Wabenzi (wɑːˈbɛnzɪ). Also **Wabenze, Wa-Benzi.** [Invented to resemble the name of an African people (viz. WATUSI, etc.), with inserted (Mercedes-)*Benz*: see def.] In Africa, 'the Mercedes-Benz tribe': used *joc.* to designate those Black politicians, businessmen, and others whose success is characterized by their ownership or use of a Mercedes-Benz car.

1967 *Economist* 8 Apr. 112/1 Africa is rapidly earning itself the reputation of the world's biggest joke..the 'Wabenze', the new but already well-known African people whose tribal mark is a ministership and a Mercedes. **1972** J. BIGGS-DAVISON *Africa—Hope Deferred* x. 92 The sweeteners of deference and the shining, pennanted cars that have given their name to such new and privileged tribes as the 'Wa-Benzi'. **1978** S. NAIPAUL *North of South* I. i. 42 'Wabenzi' is the pleasantly jocular term used to describe the nouveau-riche black middle-class... They signal their status by the acquisition..of a Mercedes Benz. Hence, the Wabenzi—the Benz tribe. **1980** *Times* 17 July 11/1 The Wa-Benzi are the new tribe of Mercedes-Benz mounted black bureaucrats and politicos.

‖**wabi** (ˈwɑːbi). [Jap.] In Zen Buddhist philosophy, a quality of simple, serene, and solitary beauty of a slightly sombre kind (see also quot. 1962). Cf. SABI.

1934 D. T. SUZUKI *Essays in Zen.* III. vii. 312 This spirit of 'Eternal Loneliness' is something known pre-eminently in Japan. By this spirit..I mean what is popularly known in Japan as 'Sabi' or 'Wabi'. **1962** J. PETRIE tr. *Hasumi's Zen in Japanese Art* iv. 51 The essential features of Higashiyama art, extending into all fields, can be summarized in..the idea of 'Wabi', which is supposed to express the highest beauty and can also be carried over into other fields of art. Fundamentally it means poverty, and at the same time simplicity and calm, but it also implies an inexpressible inner joy hidden in deep modesty. Out of 'Wabi' developed harmony, respect, purity, poverty... That is what the special designation of 'Wabi' amounts to: it was the favourite expression of the Haiku masters. **1965** [see SABI]. **1979** S. COE in I. Webb *Compl. Guide to Flower & Foliage Arrangement* xvii. 227/3 Then comes *wabi*, a recognition of ordinary things but seen in a very clear, almost transparent light.

waboom, var. WAGENBOOM

wabster, north. form of WEBSTER[1].

WAC (wæk). *U.S.* Also **W.A.C., wac.** Acronym f. the initial letters of *W*omen's *A*rmy *C*orps, formed in 1943 (cf. W.A.A.C.); a member of this.

1943 *Yank* 30 July 18 The fellows sent the girls to the WAC barracks to get dressed while they finished the KP jobs. *Ibid.*, When the first bunch of Wacs arrived here recently a group of GIs made dates with the prettiest one night for the Camp movie. **1956** B. HOLIDAY *Lady sings Blues* (1973) xxiii. 198 There was a war on and no damn way for me to get to England except to swim or join the WACs. **1962** E. SNOW *Other Side of River* (1963) xxxix. 290 Women are not recruited for combat training except as parachutists ..but a few are used in auxiliary tasks, like WACs. **1976** 'R. B. DOMINIC' *Murder out of Commission* xiv. 100, I fetched and carried for a WAC from Camp Pendleton.

wac, obs. form of WEAK *a.*

†**wacadash.** *Obs.* Also 7 **wacca-, waka-, wag(g)adash, wakedas(s)h.** [a. Japanese *wakizashi.*] A Japanese short sword.

1613 W. EATON in W. Foster *Lett. recd. E. Ind. Co.* (1897) II. 20 He had given her his wacadash or little cattan. **1613** J. SARIS *Voy. Japan* (Hakl. Soc.) 124 Next those weapons resembling a Welch-hooke called Waggadashes. **1615** R. COCKS *Diary* (1883) I. 81, 10 pike heades, 100 arow heades, and three waccadashes. **1615** W. ADAMS *Log-bk.* (1916) 34 Kattannes wakedasshes and pikes. **1620** *Will of W. Adams* in *Athenæum* (1910) 21 May 610/1, I..bequeath vnto.. Richard Cock..my best Cattane the other of my Cattans and wagadashes I..bequeath vnto my aforesaid sonne Joseph.

wacance, -and: see VACANCE, VACAND.

wacche, -man, obs. forms of WATCH, -MAN.

wace, obs. f. *was*, pa. t. of BE *v.*

c **1380** *Sir Ferumb.* 389, 421.

wace, wach: see WAX *sb.*, WASH *v.*

wach(e, -man, obs. forms of WATCH, -MAN.

wachel, wachle, var. forms of WAUCHLE.

wachet(t, obs. forms of WATCHET.

wacht, obs. f. WAUGHT *sb.* and *v.*, *Sc.* and *north.*

wack[1] (wæk). *slang* (orig. *U.S.*). Also **whack.** [Prob. back-formation f. WACKY *a.*] An eccentric or crazy person; a madman, a crackpot.

1938 'E. QUEEN' *Four of Hearts* (1939) i. 9 All you wacks act this way at first. Them that can take it snaps out of it. **1951** E. PAUL *Springtime in Paris* xi. 198 The show place, the rendezvous of eccentrics, Bohemians, playboys, sightseers and international whacks is the St. Germain des Prés quarter. **1959** R. GRAVES in *Lilliput* Dec. 48/2 'I don't get the joke,' Len grumbled. 'That wack gave me the creeps! One of those 'creative artists' who create chaos'. **1982** G. F. NEWMAN *Men with Guns* xi. 81 The cop shrugged. 'Some wack with a grudge.'

wack[2] (wæk). *dial.* (chiefly *Liverpool*). Also **whack.** [Cf. WACKER.] A familiar term of address; 'pal', 'mate'.

1963 *Beatles* 18 Said Ringo: 'Do you want an anaesthetic, wack?' **1966** P. MOLONEY *Plea for Mersey* 50 I'll get you wack! You must come back! **1972** 'K. ROYCE' *Miniatures Frame* ix. 124 'How's it, whack?' He..eyed me affectionately. **1976** *New Musical Express* 12 Feb. 18/6 Gorra light 'ave yer, wack?

wack: see WAK, WAKE, WALK *v.*[2], WHACK.

wacke (ˈwækə). *Geol.* Also 9 **wacca, wake, wacké.** [a. Ger. *wacke*, dial. *wake* (MHG. *wacke* large stone, OHG. *waggo* pebble), a miners' word, adopted by Werner as a geological term.] A sandstone-like rock, resulting from the decomposition of basaltic rocks *in situ.* Cf. GRAUWACKE, GREYWACKE.

1803 tr. *Pallas' Trav.* II. 115 The calcareous rock above described..sometimes also occurs under the form of Wacca, which is again composed of gritty fragments, caused by the destructive effects of past ages. **1811** PINKERTON *Petral.* I. 171 Two [German] papers..'On argillaceous schistus, hornslate, and on wake'. **1816** P. CLEAVELAND *Min.* 284 Basalt often forms one member of a series, beginning with gravel, sand, and clay; this clay gradually becomes less sandy and harder, till it passes into wacke, and the wacke is by insensible degrees lost in Basalt. **1839** MURCHISON *Silurian Syst.* I. xxxvi. 499 The chief portion of the hill consists of a dull rotten wacke.

†ˈ**wacken.** *Geol. Obs.* [app. a. G. *wacken-*, combining form of *wacke*: see prec.] = WACKE.

1796 KIRWAN *Elem. Min.* (ed. 2) I. 219 [Basaltine] is most found in basalts, wacken, and lava. **1802** PLAYFAIR *Illustr. Hutton. Theory* 67 The wacken, mullen and crag of Kirwan.

b. Comb.: **wacken porphyry.**

1796 KIRWAN *Elem. Min.* (ed. 2) I. 355 Wacken Porphyry. **1807** HEADRICK *Arran* 61 The hills at the head of Glencloy are composed of wacken porphyry.

Hence **wackeˈnitic** *a.*, of the nature or composition of wacke.

1866 LAWRENCE tr. *Cotta's Rocks Classified* (1878) 88 We shall use the adjective 'wackenitic' to designate this [decomposed] state of those rocks.

wacker (ˈwækə(r)), *sb.* (and *a.*) *Liverpool dial.* [Origin unknown.] A Liverpudlian; also = WACK[2]. Also *attrib.* or as *adj.*

1768 T. BOULTON *Sailor's Farewell* III. 32, I was told for certain, that th' king o' th' blacks had as many wenches as would stond i' th' cumpus of seven acres of graund; and, if it be true, he must be a wacker, e'cod! **1966** P. MOLONEY *Plea for Mersey* 21 The typical wacker is descended from a long line his mother listened to. *Ibid.* 22 We will consider the refinements of Wacker figures of speech later. **1970** A. ROSS *Manchester Thing* 122, I can't help you, wacker... Five o'clock shut, on Friday, wack.

wacker, var. WHACKER.

wackerell, var. WAKERELL, Sanctus bell.

wacko (ˈwækəʊ), *a.* and *sb. slang* (orig. and chiefly *U.S.*). Also **whacko.** [f. WACK(Y *a.* + -O.]

A. *adj.* Crazy, mad; eccentric.

1977 J. WAMBAUGH *Black Marble* (1978) ix. 182 What if he doesn't always go whacko when you make him remember the bad old days? **1977** E. LEONARD *Unknown Man* v. 46 You never know, the guy's fucking wacko. **1978** C. BLACK *Asterisk Destiny* iii. 58 Without a sense of balance..and a touch of humor, you could go whacko. **1981** D. UHNAK *False Witness* iv. 39 She's gone slightly wacko politically. **1984** *Miami Herald* 30 Mar. 3E/2 'Anyone in this business relishes the pressure,' Hazzard, 41, said. 'Maybe I'm a little wacko, but I love it.'

B. *sb.* = WACK[1].

1977 *Telegraph* (Brisbane) 24 Mar. 4/1, I am not a weirdo, a wacko or an eccentric for wanting to do good, honest work on a day to day basis. **1980** *Washington Post* 22 Aug. A1 Billy Carter, the president's brother, testified yesterday that he is not 'a buffoon, a boob or a wacko'. **1982** R. LUDLUM *Parsifal Mosaic* xiii. 197 'They catch a whack-o now and then.' 'Whack-o?' 'Someone who's crossed over the mental line, thinks he's someone he's not.'

wacko, var. WHACKO *int.*

wacky (ˈwækɪ), *a. slang* (orig. *U.S.*). Also **whacky.** [f. WHACK *sb.* + -Y[1]: cf. *out of whack* s.v. WHACK *sb.* 4. For earlier uses ('a fool; left-handed') see *Eng. Dial. Dict.*] Crazy, mad; odd, peculiar. **a.** Of persons.

1935 J. HARGAN in *Jrnl. Abnormal Psychol.* XXX. 365 *Wacky*, insane. **1938** J. DIGGES *Bowleg Bill* 28 They all want to know why he done it, and is he gone clean whacky. **1942** *Sun* (Baltimore) 25 July 8/1 Her grandmother, wackier than she is, haunts the place. **1950** 'S. RANSOME' *Deadly Miss Ashley* xv. 172 She might..leave..her kids to that wacky aunt of theirs. **1964** *Economist* 13 June 1242/2 Departed, prostrate or, in former President Eisenhower's recent phrase, 'a little bit whacky'. **1978** J. IRVING *World according to Garp* xix. 420 It did much to drive the Ellen Jamesians even wackier or simply away. **1984** *Observer* (Colour Suppl.) 18 Mar. 7/2 She plays the wacky mother of Debra Winger.

b. Of things or abstract concepts.

1937 *Sun* (Baltimore) 19 Aug. 8/1 This picture is described as 'the wackiest'. **1941** B. SCHULBERG *What makes Sammy Run?* i. 14 The whole office was afraid of him. I know that sounds wacky. Hardened newspapermen being afraid of a..little office-boy? **1959** S. H. COURTIER *Death in Dream Time* x. 141 Your cousin's death was wacky—why go to the trouble of staging an accident? **1969** L. HELLMAN *Unfinished Woman* iv. 37 The office was a wacky joint in a brownstone house on 48th Street. **1975** D. LODGE *Changing Places* v. 191 A characteristically whacky, yet somehow endearing tenderness for individual liberty. **1984** *Listener* 24 May 39/3 In his fear of death Betjeman's hand shook, and lines were created more from wacky fright than profound or energising contemplation.

Hence ˈ**wackiness,** the state or quality of being 'wacky'; craziness, oddness.

1941 *Sun* (Baltimore) 1 Oct. 10/2 Maybe the majority won't think that 'the wonderful bums' [*sc.* the Brooklyn Dodgers] can win, but they will be out by the thousands.. hoping that wackiness will be more than its own reward. **1980** R. L. DUNCAN *Brimstone* iv. 80 For all her wackiness, Annie knew how to live.

wad (wɒd), *sb.*[1] Also 7 **wadd(e, wade.** [Of obscure origin; the identity of the word in all the senses is not quite certain.

With sense 3 cf. mod.Sw. *vadd*, G., Du. *watte*, Fr. *ouate* (whence It. *ovatta*), wadding; the etymology and mutual relation of these words are unknown.]

1. a. A bundle of hay or straw (occas. of hemp, etc.); esp. a small bundle of hay, peas, beans, vetches, etc., made at the time of cutting or reaping; a portion of a sheaf of cereal plants or of reed. Now *dial.*

1573 TWYNE *Æneid* XI. 26 Hereon the lad aloft on wad of cuntrey straw they lay. **1596** SPENSER *Hymn Heav. Love* 226 Where he encradled was In simple cratch, wrapt in a wad of hay. **1601** HOLLAND *Pliny* XVII. ix. I. 508 When it [a crop of lupines] is cut downe, to make it into wads or bottles, and so to burie them at the roots of trees. **1620** MARKHAM *Farew. Husb.* ix. 65 Laying before the Plow long wades or roules of the straw of Lupyns, Pease, or else Fetches,..you shall turne the furrowes..vpon the waddes. **1622** J. TAYLOR (Water-P.) *Arrant Thief* (1625) C 2, A wispe of Rushes, or a clod of land, Or any wadde of Hay that's next to hand They'l steale. **1647** TRAPP *Comm. 1 Cor.* vii. 31 In the Popes inthronization,..a piece of tow, or wad of straw is set on fire before him, and one appointed to say, *Sic transit gloria mundi.* **1693** EVELYN *De la Quint. Compl. Gard.* Dict., To wrap up Plants, or tender Trees with Wads or Wisps of Straw. **1706** ESTCOURT *Fair Example* III. i, You shall find her upon a Wad of Straw, with one Brat at her Breast. **1763** *Museum Rust.* I. 24 The reapers lay it on the land in wads as they call them, or parcels about the quantity of half a sheaf of wheat unbound. **1799** WOLCOT (P. Pindar) *Nil Admirari* III. iii. Wks. 1816 III. 447 At times she finds of hemp a little wad, Begs some young Levite spin it. **1807** SIR R. C. HOARE *Tour Irel.* 302 A wad of straw, or perhaps heath laid on a damp clay floor. **1813** VANCOUVER *Agric. Devon* 123 A cylindrical pearl barley machine, is also used to cleanse the wad of its smut. **1886** *W. Somerset Word-bk.*, *Wad*, a bundle of straw tied up by a thatcher... A bundle of reed less than a full sheaf of 28 lbs. weight is also called a wad.

fig. **1607** HEYWOOD *Fayre Mayde Exch.* I. C 2 b, Yonder bundle of sighes, yonder wad of grones.

b. A heap; also, a swath. *dial.*

1750 ELLIS *Mod. Husb.* IV. iii. 51 [To mow vetches] cock them in little wads as we do the Clover-grass. **1805** R. W. DICKSON *Pract. Agric.* II. 589 It is the usual practice to put them [cut pea crops] up into small heaps, termed wads, which are formed by setting small parcels against each other. **1856** J. C. MORTON *Cycl. Agric.* II. 726 *Wad*, a heap of beans or pease laid out to dry, previous to binding. In the county of Devon, applied to a handful of thatch. **1906** *Times* 25 June 14/4 The wet wads formed by the horse rake are avoided.

2. a. A small bundle of a soft, flexible material; esp. for use as a plug, pad, or rubber.

1580 HOLLYBAND *Treas. Fr. Tong*, *Torche*..a wad of strawe or cloutes that wenches vse to put on their heds when they cary any thing. **1622** MABBE tr. *Aleman's Guzman d'Alf.* II. 355 It was injoyned me..of old ends of Ragges, or of Flax and Tow, to make wads and wisps for those that goe to the Long-house. **1752** SIR H. BEAUMONT *Crito* 17 The vast Wad of Linen that they [women] carry upon their Head. **1781** HAYLEY *Tri. Temper* IV. 85 She on the types her inky wad let fall. **1861** MUSGRAVE *By-Roads* 173 The neck of the flask being closed with only a mere wad of cotton. **1887** *Poor Nellie* (1888) 398 I've to go about with wads of cotton-wool ready in my pocket for my two ears.

b. Something rolled up tightly, as a roll of bank notes. Chiefly *U.S.*

1778 *Exmoor Scolding* Gloss. (E.D.S.) 151 A garment rumbled [*sic*] up to a Wad, with many Plaits and Wrinkles. **1864** SALA in *Daily Tel.* 27 Sept., A little wallet containing one or more dollar bills, or at least a wad of fractional currency. **1888** *Bow-Bells Weekly* 22 June 396 Never roll gloves into each other in a wad, for they will never look as well after. **1890** GUNTER *Miss Nobody* ii. (1891) 24 Handing Everett a wad of greenbacks. **1899** MRS. F. H. BURNETT *De Willoughby Claim* x. 132 He..finally rolled his paper into a hard wad and threw it at the counter. **1899** CROCKETT *Kit Kennedy* lii, MacWalter pulled a thick wad of bank notes out of his pocket. **1908** S. E. WHITE *Riverman* xix, Dabbing at her eyes with a handkerchief dampened into a tiny wad.

transf. **1895** HOWELLS *Impress. & Exp.* (1896) 164 Such a small, dull wad of out-worn womanhood!—her grey old head bent upon her knees, and her withered arms wound in her thin shawl. **1913** *Sat. Rev.* 22 Mar. 365/2 He will find them well padded by wads of extracts from second-hand authorities.

†**3.** A material composed of matted fibres of silk, raw cotton, etc. = WADDING 3. *Obs.*

1540 *Act 32 Hen. VIII* c. 14 Item for every tonne Tolose wadde accompting viij hole bales..for a tonne xx s. **1695** P. MOTTEUX *St. Olon's Morocco* 139 The Traffick of Provence consists in..Velvet, Cottons, Wadds [Fr. *cottonines*], and other Commodities from the Levant. **1706** PHILLIPS (ed. Kersey), *Wad*, a sort of Flocks of Silk, course Flannel, or Cotton. **1761** *Ann. Reg.*, *Chron.* 132/1 The plant known by the name of..*Asclepias*... From the silky wad it affords we [in France] call it *Soyeuse*.

4. a. A plug of tow, cloth, etc., a disk of felt or cardboard, to retain the powder and shot in position in charging a gun or cartridge.

1667 *Phil. Trans.* II. 476 Another [experiment]..is a Wooden Tampion..hollow'd towards the Bullet,..and..hollow likewise towards the Powder, and serving instead of a Wadd. **1669** STURMY *Mariner's Mag.* v. xii. 68 Put the Powder home gently, and after put in a good Wad..; then put in the Shot.., and after him another Wad. **1769** FALCONER *Dict. Marine* (1780), *Wad*, a quantity of old rope-yarns, hay, &c. rolled firmly together into the form of a ball, and used to confine the shot or shell..in the breech of a piece of artillery. **1856** 'STONEHENGE' *Brit. Sports* I. I. ii. §5. 24 After using the powder-flask..drive down..a single piece of wadding; then pour in the charge of shot, drive down another wad, [etc.]. **1862** F. A. GRIFFITHS *Artil. Man.* (ed. 9) 112 No. 5 serves No. 3 with projectiles, wads, if necessary, and traverses. **1879** *Cassell's Techn. Educ.* I. 194/1 The escape of gas was prevented by means of a felt wad attached to the back of the cartridge. **1881** GREENER *Gun* 300 Wads are punched out of sheets of various materials by cutters fixed in a press. Those most commonly used are made of felts, cardboard, or jute. **1890** D. DAVIDSON *Mem. Long Life* ii. 34 We..rowed too closely past the *Victory* as she was firing her royal salute, and one of her wads just cleared our heads.

b. In fig. phr. ***to shoot one's wad***, to do all that one can do. Cf. *to have shot one's bolt* s.v. SHOOT *v.* 21 b. *colloq.* (chiefly *U.S.*).

1914 *Dialect Notes* IV. 112 *Shoot one's wad*, to do or say what one can. **1970** A. CAMERON et al. *Computers & O.E. Concordances* 31 Well, I'm really not an expert on it. I've practically shot my wad. **1971** B. MALAMUD *Tenants* 8, I want to be thought of as a going concern, not a freak who had published a good first novel and shot his wad.

5. a. A lump of a soft or plastic substance. *rare.*

1775 SHERIDAN *Duenna* III. vii, Eyes like two dead beetles in a wad of brown dough! **1838** THACKERAY *Fashnable Fax* Wks. 1900 XIII. 254 The haldermin, who was helpin the tuttle, puts on Biffeter's plate a wad of green fat.

b. A mass, heap, large quantity. *Sc.* and *north.*

1828 *Craven Gloss.*, *Wad*, a large quantity. 'We've a wad o' hay to year.' **1915** *Chamb. Jrnl.* 12 June 442/1 True, we haven't got a great wad of it on hand; but I don't like the idea of that silver being on the premises.

c. A bun, a cake; also, something to eat, a sandwich. *slang* (orig. *Services*').

1919 *War Terms* in *Athenæum* 1 Aug. 695/1 *Wad*, a bun. **1927** T. E. LAWRENCE *Let.* 8 Feb. (1938) 506 No wads, so I'm able to do without money. **1937** D. JONES *In Parenthesis* 4 We've got too many buns—and all those wads. **1942** G. KERSH *Nine Lives Bill Nelson* i. 3 I'm in a caff, getting a tea 'n' a wad. **1960** 'A. BURGESS' *Doctor is Sick* 226 Give us a bob for a cuppa and a wad, guv. **1973** *Guardian* 2 June 13/4 He found himself..in Kashmir sharing a char and wad with Sikh pilots. **1983** *Verbatim* Autumn 8/2 Like a 'pick', a 'wad' is also eaten standing up. A 'wad', however, is a solitary piece of inferior, if not disgusting food. The diner falls upon it with little pleasure, merely to quiet the beast in his belly.

6. *Ceramics.*

1825 J. NICHOLSON *Oper. Mech.* 468 When a sagger is filled with clay ware, on its outer edges are placed thick pieces of coarse clay, called *wads* from their being employed to wedge or closely join the interstice between two saggers. **1891** *Century Dict.*, *Wad*, 3. In *ceram.*, a small piece of finer clay used to cover the body of an inferior material in some varieties of earthenware; especially, the piece doubled over the edge of a vessel.

7. *attrib.* and *Comb.*: (sense 4) as ***wad gauge, punch, room***; **wadcutter** chiefly *U.S.*, a bullet designed to cut a neat hole in a paper range target; **wad hook**, (*a*) a spiral tool for withdrawing wads or charges from guns; (*b*) *Mining* (see quot. 1881).

1957 *Amer. Speech* XXXII. 195 **Wadcutter*, a lead bullet designed to be used on paper targets and having no ogive but abrupt shoulders so that a full caliber hole is punched in a target. **1981** D. BOGGIS *Time to Betray* xi. 61 A potential opportunity to..loose the five rounds of .32 wadcutter from the Walther GSP precision automatic. **1828** SPEARMAN *Brit. Gunner* (ed. 2) 73 *Wad Gauges. **1611** FLORIO, *Cauafieno*, Gunners call it a *wad-hooke. **1766** ENTICK *London* IV. 344 Rammers, hand-spikes, wad-hooks. **1879** *Man. Artill. Exerc.* 199 The shell extractor and wadhook [are placed] outside the pit. **1881** RAYMOND *Mining Gloss.*, *Wad-hook*. A tool with two spiral steel blades for removing fragments from the bottom of deep bore-holes. **1875** KNIGHT *Dict. Mech.*, **Wad-punch*, a tubular steel punch used for cutting gun-wads, etc. **1756** *Gentl. Mag.* XXVI. 426 His gunner concealed 43 barrels of powder in the *wad room, covering them with wads and lumber.

wad (wɒd), *sb.*² In 7 **wadd.** [Perh. cogn. w. ON. *vað-r* masc., measuring line, MSw. *vaþi* wk. masc., boundary-line between properties (cf. sense 2 below), or with OE. *wadan* to go, WADE *v.*]

1. *Surveying.* A straight line taken in measuring from one mark to another. ? *Obs.*

1610 W. FOLKINGHAM *Feudigr.* II. iv. 53 These dimensions are found or performed either *Cominus* or *Eminus*... The first..needes no amplification, but for precise keeping in the Wadd or right line. The Wadd is delineated either to a marke in sight or out of sight. If the First; let the Chaine-leaders Wadd vpon the marke by some intermediall eminence and at the setting down of euery pricke, let each man waue his mate into the right Wadd.

2. *dial.* 'A line, esp. one marked out between two parcels of land' (*Eng. Dial. Dict.*); also see quots.

1869 *Lonsdale Gloss.*, *Wad*, a line or rank. **1886** *S.W. Linc. Gloss.*, *Wad*, a mark set up as a guide to plough straight by. Hence Line, order, position. **1889** *N.W. Linc. Gloss.*, *Wad*, a mark in shooting, ploughing, land measuring, &c.

b. Way or course of travel, track. *lit.* and *fig.*

1854 MISS A. E. BAKER *Northampt. Gloss.*, *Wad.* 3. A way or beaten track, a line of conduct pertinaciously adhered to. 'He goes on in the old wad,' i.e. in the same manner as formerly.

3. *Comb.*: **wad-staff, -stick** (see quots.).

1856 J. C. MORTON *Cycl. Agric.* II. 726 *Wadstaff*, (Notts.), guide staff to plough by. **1889** *N.W. Linc. Gloss.*, *Wad-staff*, *wad-stick*, a tall white wand painted with rims of various colours, used as a mark for ploughmen in setting out furrows.

wad (wɒd), *sb.*³ Also 7 **wadt**, 8 **wadd.** [Of obscure origin.]

1. A local name for plumbago or black lead; also called ***black wad***. Also *dial.* a black-lead pencil (see *Eng. Dial. Dict.*).

1614 in *Mem. Lit. & Philos. Soc. Manch.* Ser. II. (1819) III. 169 Except the wad holes and wad, commonly called black cawke, within the commons of Seatollor, or elsewhere within the commons and wastes of the said manor [of Borrowdale]. **1698** PLOT *Black-lead* in *Phil. Trans.* XX. 183 The Mineral Substance, called, Black Lead..found only at Keswick in Cumberland, and there called, *Wadt*, or *Kellow*. **1836** *Penny Cycl.* V. 225 (Borrowdale) The most remarkable product of the valley is graphite, plumbago, or black-lead (provincially wad). **1872** JENKINSON *Guide Eng. Lakes* (1879) 129 The lead, or plumbago, locally termed 'wad,'..is the best material ever discovered for making lead pencils.

2. An impure earthy ore of manganese.

1783 *Phil. Trans.* LXXIII. 284 Some Experiments upon the Ochra friabilis nigro fusca of Da Costa..; and called by the Miners of Derbyshire, Black Wadd. **1796** KIRWAN *Elem. Min.* (ed. 2) II. 465 Mr. Wedgewood dissolved a quantity of black wadd in a large quantity of nitrous acid heated. **1839** URE *Dict. Arts*, *Wadd*, is the provincial name..of an ore of manganese in Derbyshire, which consists of the peroxide of that metal, associated with nearly its own weight of oxide of iron. **1884** *Athenæum* 16 Aug. 212/3 The not very interesting manganese mineral wad.

3. *Comb.*, as (sense 1) ***wad-hole, -lead, -mine, -pencil.***

1614 *Wad hole [see 1]. **1780** G. JARS *Voy. Metall.* II. 554 (*Philol. Soc. Trans.* 1908, p. 148) Mine de plomb pour les crayons nommés Black-lead or *Wad-Lead. **1747** *Gentl. Mag.* XVII. 583 *Wadd mines in the Cumberland Dialect, signifies the black-lead mines. **1836** *Penny Cycl.* V. 225 (Borrowdale) The wad mine. **1825** BROCKETT *N.C. Gloss.* s.v., A *wad pencil.

†**wad**, *sb.*⁴ *Obs. rare*⁻¹. Origin and sense obscure: only in proverbial phrase, app. meaning 'in that course there is danger'.

1524 WOLSEY in *St. Papers Hen. VIII*, IV. 92 Praying you eftsones, that the ereccion of the yong King be not dilayed by any diet to be kept upon the Bordre or other communicacion; for in that pad there lyeth a wad.

wad (wɒd), *v.*¹ Also 6 **wadde.** [f. WAD *sb.*¹]

I. To form into a wad.

1. *trans.* To lay up (the cut haulm of beans, peas, etc.) in bundles.

1677 PLOT *Oxfordsh.* ix. §101. 256 After the sithe they wad both Beans and Peas. **1733** W. ELLIS *Chiltern & Vale Farm.* 341 They take care to Wad them [*sc.* beans] as soon as Mown, and put them into single small Parcels. **1778** [W. MARSHALL] *Minutes Agric.*, *Observ.* 93 In dry weather, Pease properly wadded with a Prong are much sooner ready to carry than those left in hard bundles by the Foot and Sithe. **1805** R. W. DICKSON *Pract. Agric.* II. 891 When..crops of this sort that have run to seed,..are left..it is the usual practice to cut and wad them in the same manner as for peas. **1813** T. BATCHELOR *View Agric. Bedfordsh.* 108 (E.D.D.) The process of wadding, and gleaning beans..is rather a tedious one.

2. To press (loose or fibrous material) into a small compass or into a close, compact mass; *U.S.* to roll up tightly. Also with *up*.

1675 EVELYN *Terra* (1776) 74 If you lay about them [*sc.* the roots] any fern-brakes or other trash capped with a little Earth..let it not be Wadded too close. **1896** *N.Y. Weekly Witness* 23 Dec. 16/4 A most peculiar cholera-remedy was in use in Persia. It consisted in wadding-up a leaf from the Koran and forcing it down the patient's throat. **1915** MRS. STRATTON-PORTER *M. O'Halloran* viii, 'Can you help me?' 'Sure!' said Mickey, wadding his cap into his back pocket.

3. *transf.* To pack (persons) closely.

1850 THACKERAY *Pendennis* lviii, An honest holiday-maker with his family wadded into a tax-cart.

II. To furnish with or as with a wad or wadding.

4. To put a wad in (a gun, a cartridge).

1579 DIGGES *Stratiot.* 113 His Gunner..to wadde and ramme, to cleanse, scoure, and coole the Peeces. **1881** GREENER *Gun* 301 When loaded with shot, the cartridges are wadded in the Erskine machine. **1894** CROCKETT *Mad Sir Uchtred* 83 He had wadded it [*sc.* a gun] with three leaves of the Bible.

5. To line, fill out, pad, as with wadding; to quilt.

1759 J. G. COOPER *Ver-Vert* IV. 212 His skin with sugar being wadded, With liquid fires his entrails burn'd. **1788** COWPER *Gratitude* 11 This wheel-footed studying chair,..Wide-elbow'd, and wadded with hair. **1842** THACKERAY *Miss Tickletoby's Lect.* iii, Straight the King's great chair was brought him..Languidly he sunk into it, it was comfortably wadded. **1846** —— *Bk. Snobs* xiv, Lord Glenlivat..playfully wadded the insides of the boots with cobbler's wax. **1848** —— *Lett.* 1 Nov., You say your prayers in carved stalls wadded with velvet cushions. **1862** C. A. COLLINS *Cruise upon Wheels* xxiv. (1863) 413 My thick flannel dressing-gown, lined and wadded. **1883** MISS M. BETHAM-EDWARDS *Disarmed* xxiii, She wore a loose gown of crimson satin, wadded after the fashion of the olden time.

fig. **1871** GEO. ELIOT *Middlem.* xx, If we had a keen vision and feeling of all ordinary human life,..we should die of that roar which lies on the other side of silence. As it is, the quickest of us walk about well wadded with stupidity.

†**6.** ? To rub with a wad. *Obs.*

1688 HOLME *Armoury* III. xix. (Roxb.) 184/2 Wad or wash him [*sc.* a horse] round.

7. To plug (the ears) with wads.

1876 'OUIDA' *Winter City* iii, They have wadded their ears and..would not hear.

wad (wɒd), *v.*² In 7 **wadd.** [f. WAD *sb.*²] *intr.* To walk with the chain in a straight line from one mark to another in land-surveying.

1610 W. FOLKINGHAM *Feudigr.* II. iv. 53 Let the Chaine-leaders Wadd vpon the marke by some intermediall eminence. **1688** HOLME *Armoury* III. 139/1 Geometrical Terms used in Surveying and Measuring of Lands... *Wadding*, keeping in a right Line. **1869** *Lonsdale Gloss.*, *Wad*, to set out a line, in land-surveying or engineering, by putting in a series of stakes or stubs.

wad: see WED, WOAD; also WILL *v.*

wadable, wadeable (ˈweɪdəb(ə)l), *a.* Also 7 *Sc.* **weadable.** [f. WADE *v.* + -ABLE.] That can be waded.

1611 FLORIO, *Vadasile*, foardable, wadable. **1611** COTGR., *Gayer*, a Foord, or wadeable passage ouer a riuer. *Ibid.*, *Gueable*, wadeable; fit, likely, or easie, to be waded ouer. **1621** MOLLE *Camerar. Liv. Libr.* IV. xx. 313 Vnderstanding that the Marishes were wadeable. **1693** J. FRASER in *W. Macfarlane's Geogr. Collect.* (S.H.S.) II. 218 Severid by a smal streame weadable sometymes when it is low water. **1823** GALT *R. Gilhaize* xxii, As soon as the fugitives were within wadeable reach of the bank, they jumpit out of the boat. **1864** CARLYLE *Fredk. Gt.* XVII. vi. (1873) VII. 62 Where the Brook withal is of firmer bottom and more wadeable.

[**wadage.** A spurious word, repr. AL. *vadia* 'wages' in the writ appointing a serjeant; the other words represent *feoda* 'fees', *vestura* 'vesture' and *regarda* 'rewards'.

1679 E. CHAMBERLAYNE *Pres. St. Eng.* II. (ed. 12) 262 Out of the Sergeants afore-mentioned, the King by Writ, usually calls some to be his Council at Law, allowing each one Wadage, Feodage, Vesturage, and Regardage.]

wadd, obs. f. WAD; dial. form of WOLD.

wadded ('wɒdɪd), *ppl. a.* Also 6 wadid. [f. WAD *v.*[1] + -ED[1].] Lined with wadding.

1595 *Acc. Bk. W. Wray* in *Antiquary* XXXII. 317, i pece wadded buffinge. *Ibid.* 281 Ite' i pece blacke wadid buffinge. **1710** STEELE *Tatler* No. 245 ¶2 A thick wadded Callico Wrapper, [etc.]. **1835** *Ladies' Cabinet* Jan. 65 Wadded pelisses are expected to be very generally adopted. *Ibid.* Oct. 269 A white *gros de Naples* slip, which..had a deep wadded hem. **1880** 'OUIDA' *Moths* I. 20, I thought Miladi was made ..in Giroux's shop, and was kept in a wadded box when her mechanism was not wound up. **1890** D. DAVIDSON *Mem. Long Life* viii. 196 His costume..consisted of a hunting cap with a white wadded cover.

wadder[1] ('wɒdə(r)). [f. WAD *v.*[1] + -ER[1].]

†**1.** An implement for wadding a gun. *Obs.*

1579 DIGGES *Stratiot.* 115, I mighte here adioyne sundrye Tables..what Bullets, Wadders, Rammers, Ladles,..were conueniente to bee hadde in readinesse.

2. One who lays up (the cut haulm of beans, etc.) in bundles or 'wads'.

1763 *Museum Rust.* (ed. 2) I. 236 This..lays the beans in regular rows, and saves the expense of a wadder.

†'**wadder**[2]. *Land-surveying. Obs.* [f. WAD *v.*[2] + -ER[1].] One who is engaged in determining a 'wad' or line of direction.

1610 W. FOLKINGHAM *Feudigr.* II. iv. 53 If out of sight.. place two Assistants, the one at the marke, and the other at the eminentest Medium, and then your selfe standing at.. the station giuen, and the first Assistant erecting some visible obiect, waft the Wadders into the Wadd.

wadder, obs. Sc. form of WETHER.

waddie, waddin, var. ff. WADDY[1], WALDIN.

wadding ('wɒdɪŋ), *vbl. sb.* [-ING[1].]

1. The action of WAD *v.*[1]

1778 [W. MARSHALL] *Minutes Agric.* 14 Sept. 1776, Whether the crop be thick or thin, Wadding puts it equally out of harm's way.

2. *concr.* Any soft, pliable material from which gun-wads are made; also, a wad.

1627 CAPT. J. SMITH *Sea Gram.* xiv. 66 Waddings is Okum, old clouts, or straw, put after the powder and the Bullet. **1664** PEPYS *Diary* 8 Nov., To the Office of the Ordnance, to discourse about wadding for guns. **1742** *Phil. Trans.* XLII. 175 The Waddings used in all these.. Experiments, were of thick Leather cut round, to fit the Bore of the Piece. **1815** CROKER in *Croker Papers* (1884) I. iii. 73 The whole of the extent..was strewed with the cartridges and waddings of the cannon. **1833** *Reg. Instr. Cavalry* I. 31 The recruit is to be instructed..to ram the paper, as wadding, home. **1853** DICKENS *Bleak Ho.* liv, I found the wadding of the pistol with which the deceased Mr. Tulkinghorn was shot.

3. Any loose, fibrous material for use as a padding, stuffing, quilting, etc. Now chiefly, cotton-wool formed into a fleecy layer.

1734 *Grub St. Jrnl.* 2 May 4/1 Handsome Gowns for Ladies, with Silk Waddings. **1737** DYCHE & PARDON *Dict.*, *Wadding*, a thin, coarse, woollen Manufacture made to line Men's Morning Gowns, the Plaits of their Coats, &c. **1755** JOHNSON, *Wadding*, a kind of soft stuff loosely woven, with which the skirts of coats are stuffed out. **1784** COWPER *Task* I. 31 A generation more refin'd Improv'd the simple plan;.. And o'er the seat, with plenteous wadding stuff'd, Induc'd a splendid cover. **1802** M. CUTLER in *Life, Jrnls. & Corr.* (1888) II. 113, I presented him a specimen of wadding for Ladies' cloaks. **1839** URE *Dict. Arts* s.v., Wadding [for garments] is now made with a lap or fleece of cotton prepared by the carding-engine, which is applied to tissue paper by a coat of size. **1865** *Routledge's Ev. Boy's Ann.* 493 A small ball of cotton wool or wadding enclosed in a piece of linen rag. **1902** HANNAN *Textile Fibres* 54 The raw material ..when beaten out soft is used for wadding in clothing and coverlets. **1904** *Woollen Draper's Terms* in *Tailor & Cutter* 4 Aug. 480/2 Wadding; A loose fibrous material made of cotton waste; one side is finished with paper face; used for padding purposes.

fig. **1846** LANDOR *Imag. Conv.*, *Diogenes & Plato* Wks. I. 455/1 Aristoteles, and all the rest of you, must have the wadding of straw and saw-dust shaken out, and then we shall know pretty nearly your real weight and magnitude.

waddle ('wɒd(ə)l), *sb.* [f. WADDLE *v.*]

1. The action of waddling; a waddling gait. Also, rate of progress by waddling.

1691 SHADWELL *Scowrers* II. i. 15 That must be my sweet Duckling—I know her by her pretty Waddle in her Gate. **1853** READE *Chr. Johnstone* ii. 38 A fisherman's natural waddle is two miles an hour. **1857** KINGSLEY *Two Yrs. Ago* xxv, The lighter woman's step was inaudible to Tom; but the heavy deliberate waddle of the banker was not. **1859** *Todd's Cycl. Anat.* V. 168/2 In the *Natatores*..the great intercotyloid distance gives to their gait its peculiar waddle.

fig. **1827** HOOD *Monkey-Martyr* 50 Striding with a step that seem'd design'd To represent the mighty March of Mind, Instead of that slow waddle Of thought, to which our ancestors inclined.

†**2.** The wane of the moon. *dial. Obs.*

[Perh. a distinct word: cf. OHG., MHG. *wadal*, MLG. *wadel* (:—**waþlo-*) phases or change of the moon.]

1678 *Ray's Prov.* (ed. 2) 343 Sow or set beans in Candlemas waddle, *i.e.* Wane of the Moon. Somerset.

waddle ('wɒd(ə)l), *v.* Forms: 5 wadill, 6–8 wadle, 7– waddle. Also *quaddle*, QUODDLE. [freq. f. WADE *v.*: see -LE.]

†**1.** *intr.* ? To fall heavily or as an inert mass.

*c***1400** *Song of Roland* 991 He rent hym vnredly euyn to the sadill: on ether sid of his horse doun did he wadill.

2. To walk with short steps, swaying alternately from one leg to the other, as is done by a stout short-legged person.

1592 SHAKS. *Rom. & Jul.* I. iii. 37 Then she could stand alone, nay bi' th' roode she could haue runne & wadled all about. **1620** J. TAYLOR (Water P.) *Jack a Lent* B i b, Alwayes before Lent there comes wadling a fat grosse bursten-gutted groome, called Shroue-Tuesday. **1681** T. D['URFEY] *Progr. Honesty* xii. 13 Next a fat Author wadled into view. **1760–2** GOLDSM. *Cit. W.* lxviii, This great man is short of stature, is fat, and waddles as he walks. **1809** MALKIN *Gil Blas* II. vii. ¶20 The old procuress waddled out of sight. *c***1860** B. HARTE *Arctic Vision* 1 Where the short-legged Esquimaux Waddle in the ice and snow. **1893** F. ESPINASSE *Lit. Recoll.* ii. 14 So fat that he waddled rather than walked.

b. said of animals; esp. of ducks or geese.

1611 COTGR., *Caneter*, to waddle, or goe, like a ducke. **1691** *Lond. Gaz.* No. 2686/4 She [a mare] wadles in her Trot. **1728–42** POPE *Dunc.* II. 63 As when a dab-chick waddles through the copse On feet and wings. **1819** CRABBE *Tales of Hall* XIII. 516 And a fat spaniel waddled at his side. **1840** DICKENS *Old C. Shop* xv, Ducks and geese..waddling awkwardly about the edges of the pond. **1845** J. COULTER *Adv. in Pacific* ix. 115, I caught sight of a huge seal waddling up out of the water. **1888** F. HUME *Mme. Midas* II. i, The parrot..waddled clumsily across the table to the inkstand.

c. *transf.* said of things.

1728 POPE *Dunc.* I. 172 Like bias to the bowl, Which, as more pond'rous, made its aim more true, Obliquely wadling to the mark in view. **1858** *Straith's Fortif. & Artillery* (ed. 7) II. 121 The nave need not be more than 12 or 14 inches in length; if too short, the wheel would waddle (or, as it is sometimes called, wabble).

†**d.** *Stock Exchange slang.* To become a 'lame duck' or defaulter (see DUCK *sb.*[1] 9). In full, *to waddle out. Obs.*

1771 GARRICK *Prol. To Foote's Maid of B.* 31 Change-Alley bankrupts waddle out lame ducks! **1799** in *Spirit Publ. Jrnls.* III. 72 A *bear* who pretends to sell what he is not possessed of, and is obliged frequently to *waddle out* at a great loss. **1814** *Stock Exch. Laid Open* 20 A Jobber was never known to waddle (to be a lame duck). **1823** 'JON BEE' *Dict. Turf*, s.v., Jobbers, usually brokers, who cannot make good their engagements for the delivery of stock, or run short in funds to pay for what they have bought,..become lame ducks and waddle out. **1834** MARRYAT *P. Simple* lxv, He's been neither bull nor bear for these three years. He was obliged to *waddle*.

†**3.** *trans.* ? To cause to wallow *in. Obs.*

1569 CROWLEY *Sophistrie Dr. Watson* ii. 26 We, whom you would haue men thinke to be defiled with it, are cleare from it, and you your selfe most filthily wadled in it.

4. Of animals: To trample or tread down (grass). Now *dial.*

1627 DRAYTON *Moon-Calf* Batt. Agincourt, etc. 183 They tread and waddle all the goodly grasse, That in the field there scarse a corner was Left free by them.

†**5.** ? To delude, befool. *Obs.*

1606 N. B[AXTER] *Sydney's Ourania* I 4, Browne Paper, Lute-strings, buckles for a Saddle, Perwigs, Tiffany, Paramours to waddle.

waddle, obs. and dial. f. WATTLE.

waddler ('wɒdlə(r)). [f. WADDLE *v.* + -ER[1].] A person or animal that waddles.

1828 *Lights & Shades* II. 121 A basket containing half a dozen defunct waddlers [ducks]. **1830** J. WILSON in *Blackw. Mag.* XXVIII. 849 A flock of those noisy waddlers [geese]. **1859** *Sporting Mag.* July 3 Many thought Musjid [a race-horse] a 'waddler' with his hind legs. **1893** EARL DUNMORE *Pamirs* I. 143 These waddlers had waddled sufficiently.

†**b.** A defaulter (see WADDLE *v.* 2 d). *Obs.*

1831 *Westm. Rev.* XV. 208 Were he of the Stock Exchange he would rail against waddlers and men of straw.

waddling ('wɒdlɪŋ), *ppl. a.* [-ING[2].] That waddles (see the verb).

1662 GURNALL *Chr. in Arm.* III. verse 17. xii. §5. 90 Thus the little wadling child comes to go strongly, by going often. **1678** OTWAY *Friendship in F.* IV. i, You..Addle-pated, wadling brace of Puppies. **1714** GAY *Sheph. Week* iii. 62 Let the fox..join in wedlock with the waddling goose. **1729** T. COOKE *Tales*, etc. 96 A short squad Figure, with a wadling Pace. **1863** GEO. ELIOT *Romola* lvi, She saw..a little child.. pause from a waddling run and look around him.

Hence '**waddlingly** adv.

1882 O'DONOVAN *Merv Oasis* I. i. 23 Great flocks of wild geese marched waddlingly on either side.

waddy[1] ('wɒdɪ). *Austral.* Also 9 waddie, whaddie. [In use among Australian Aboriginals; perh. a native word, but possibly a corruption of Eng. *wood.*] **a.** An Aboriginal war-club.

[**1788** D. SOUTHWELL in *Hist. Rec. New South Wales* (1893) II. 698 *A stick or club*, wad-di or wad-dty.] **1800** J. HUNTER in *Hist. Rec. Austral.* (1914) I. ii. 406 They had each a Spear and a Warmaraa and a Waddy. **1807** J. SAVAGE *Some Acct. N.Z.* viii. 52 The men..carry a waddy..in figure somewhat resembling a large battledore..usually formed of hard black stone. **1814** FLINDERS *Voy.* II. 189 Something resembling the *waddie*, or wooden sword of the natives of Port Jackson. **1818** OXLEY *Jrnls. Two Exped. N.S. Wales* (1820) 226 After beating their spears and waddies together for about a quarter of an hour,..they went away. **1852** MUNDY *Our Antipodes* iv. (1855) 101 The waddy is a heavy, knobbed club, about two feet long. **1890** 'R. BOLDREWOOD' *Col. Reformer* xviii, Blows from the unerring waddy. **1892** J. FRASER *Aborigines of N.S. Wales* 74 A general name for all Australian clubs is 'waddy', and, although they are really clubs, they are often used as missiles in battle.

attrib. *a***1904** W. CRAIG *Adv. Austral. Goldf.* 283 The waddy blows inflicted..resulted in terrible injuries.

b. *transf.* Any club or stick; *spec.* a walking-stick.

1899 'S. RUDD' *On Our Selection* 19 We each carried a kerosine tin, slung like a kettle-drum, and belted it with a waddy. **1936** M. FRANKLIN *All that Swagger* 88 None of that bad language or I'll take a waddy to you. **1972** *Southerly* XXXII. 200 Freeth had offered him the use of his cane—his 'waddy', as he called it—after the first week. **1974** K. COOK *Bloodhouse* 31 She had seen him..smash his ebony waddy hard down on his neck.

Hence '**waddy** *v. trans.*, to strike, beat, or kill, with a waddy.

1855 LD. SHERBROOKE *Poems* (1885) 100 The black thieves appeared, My shepherds they waddied, my cattle they speared. **1859** HUXLEY *Let.* 25 June in L. Huxley *Life & Lett.* (1903) I. xiii. 252 The fellows who waddied the Amphitherium and speared the Phascolotherium. **1890** *Melbourne Argus* 16 Aug. 4/8 He waddied Kate pretty near to death when he got to camp that night.

waddy[2] ('wɒdɪ). *U.S. slang.* Also **waddie**. [Origin uncertain.] A cattle rustler; a cowboy, esp. a temporary cowhand.

1897 E. HOUGH *Story of Cowboy* 279 A genuine rustler was called a 'waddy', a name difficult to trace to its origin. **1927** J. LOMAX *Cowboy Songs* 374 He rides a fancy horse, he's a favorite man, Can get more credit than a common waddie can. **1931** W. ROGERS in S. K. Gragert *Will Rogers' Weekly Articles* (1982) V. 470 You town waddies know what a Combine is?

†**wade**, *sb.*[1] *Obs.* [= MLG. *wade*, MHG., mod.G. *wate* fem., seine; cf. ON. *vað-r* masc., fishing-line, Sw. *vad* masc., Norw. *vad* neut., Da. *vod* seine.] Some kind of fishing net. Also *wade-net.*

1388–9 *Acc. Obedientiars Abingdon* (Camden) 57, j rete vocatum wade et j flowe, cum alio rete vocato chanenet. **1630** in *Binnell's Descr. Thames* (1758) 75 Nor shall fish.. except with a Wade Net for Bait only.

wade (weɪd), *sb.*[2] *rare.* [f. WADE *v.*] An act of wading.

1665 BRATHWAIT *Comment Two Tales* 166 It is a dear wade, when your Life lies upon the last Stake. **1904** *Daily Chron.* 7 May 5/2 The Japanese..have already begun to erect piers so as to avoid the necessity of that long wade.

wade (weɪd), *v.* Pa. t. and pa. pple. **waded**. Forms: 1 wadan, 4–6 *Sc.* waid, vaid, vayd, 8 *Sc.* wide, 6 waade, 3– wade. *Pa. t.* 1 wód, 3 wode, (4 woude), 4–6 wod, 6 *Sc.* woed, woide, woyd; 6– waded. *Pa. pple.* 4 waad, wad, 8 *Sc.* wid, 7 wade, 6– waded. [A Com. Teut. (orig. strong) verb (not recorded in Gothic): OE. *wadan* (also *ȝewadan*), pa. t. *wód*, pl. **wódon*, pa. pple. **ȝewaden*, corresp. to OFris. *wada* str. vb. (WFris. *wâdzje* wk., NFris. *waar* str., to wade), MDu. *waeden* str., later wk. (Du. *waden* wk.) to wade, MLG. *waden* str. and wk. (LG. *waden*, *waen* wk.) to wade, OHG. *watan* str., to go, press forward, wade (MHG., mod.G. *waten* wk., to wade), ON. *vaða* str., to go through, wade (Norw. *vada*, *vadda*, *vaa* str., Sw. *vada*, Da. *vade* wk., to wade), f. OTeut. **wađ-*: **wōđ-*:—pre-Teut. **wădh-* = L. *vādere* to go, proceed, walk. The root, which occurs only in Teut. and L., is represented also by the sb. OE. *wæd*, ON. *vað*, L. *vadum* neut., ford, shallow water.

The mod.Eng. specific sense, 'to walk in water', though prominent in the other Teut. langs., is not recorded in OE. (unless perhaps in the compound *oferwadan* OVERWADE *v.*). In OE. the vb. is almost confined to poetical use.

The strong inflexion became obsolete in the 16th c.]

1. *intr.* To go (physically). †**a.** Of persons and animals: To go, advance, move onward; *chiefly*, to go *over* or *through* something. *Obs.*

Beowulf 2661 [He] wod þa ðurh ðone wælrec. *a***1000** *Andreas* 1271 (Gr.) Ða com hæleða þreat wadan. *c***1375** *Sc. Leg. Saints* xxviii. (*Margaret*) 250 þi mawmentis..gerris in hel þare makaris wad. *Ibid.* xxix. (*Placidas*) 750 As he towart me cuth wad, a gredy wolf hynt me. *a***1400** *Alexius* (MS. Laud 622) 548 Alexius fer and ner gan wade, For nouȝth wolde he spare. **1581** STYWARD *Mart. Discipl.* I. 85 You maie send certaine rankes of Pikes vnto the Front towards the enimie, which shall wade through to strengthen the battaile. *c***1648–50** BRATHWAIT *Barnabees Jrnl.* IV. (1818) 153 Farewell,..Steepy wayes by which I waded, And those trugs with which I traded.

†**b.** Of inanimate things, esp. of a weapon: To go *through*, to penetrate *into* something. *Obs.*

993 *Battle of Maldon* 157 Ord in ȝewod. *c***1290** *S. Eng. Leg.* 69/51 þe harde scourgene in is tendre flechs deope gonne wade. *c***1300** *Havelok* 2645 He..bi þe shu[l]dre blade þe sharpe swerd let wade þorw the brest unto þe herte. **13..** *Northern Passion* II. 138/1210a þe þornes wode in his flesse. *c***1386** CHAUCER *Monk's T.* 504 Whan myght is ioyned vn-to crueltee Allas to depe wol the venym wade. *c***1400** *Rowland & O.* 478 Thurgh the horse schuldirs the swerde gan wade.

†**2. a.** *fig.* To go (in action, thought, or discourse); to proceed. *Obs.*

Often difficult to distinguish from 3c, in which it ultimately merged.

*c***1374** CHAUCER *Troylus* II. 150 They..gonnen wade In meny an uncouthe glad and depe matere, As freendes don, whan they ben met yfere. **1412–20** LYDG. *Chron. Troy* II. 5762, I holde hym eke vnable To ben acceptid..Whan þat her tonge wadeth on þe lye. *c***1440** CAPGRAVE *St. Kath.* 1624 What wil ȝe ferthere in this mater wade? *c***1535** FISHER *Wks.* (E.E.T.S.) 441 To reherse his reasons, and so waade in this matter with them, it were inough for an holle daye. **1538** BALE *Thre Lawes* 1029 Lucifer I made So hyghly to wade To God he wolde be equall. **1549** LATIMER *1st Serm. bef. Edw. VI* (Arb.) 22, I might seme..to take this parte of scripture because I woulde wade easilye awaye there wyth, and dryue my matter at my pleasure. **1568** GRAFTON *Chron.* II. 877 Which secret Serpent caused their furie to wade farther then reason could retract or restrayne. **1587** GOLDING *De*

Mornay xxv. (1617) 424 Well may mans skill wade into weekes & moneths: but considering the vncertainty of worldly matters, it can neuer wade into yeeres. **1589** R. Robinson *Golden Mirr.* (Chetham Soc.) 60 Thy grace extend to guide my feete Least I should wade awry. **1605** Verstegan *Dec. Intell.* vi. (1628) 156 Martin Luther wadeth further, and will haue England also to be a part of Germany. **1616** Jas. I *Sp. Star-Chamb.* 20 June D 2, That which concernes the mysterie of the Kings power, is not lawfull to be disputed, for that is to wade into the weakenesse of Princes. **1642–7** H. More *Song of Soul* II. iii. IV. xxxiv, If this Out-world continually hath wade Through a long long-spun-time. **1653** R. Sanders *Physiogn.* 279, I have sufficiently waded in this various Doctrine. **1691** Ray *Creation* I. (1704) 64, I will not wade further into this Controversie. **1709** J. Logan in *Pennsylv. Hist. Soc. Mem.* X. 381 Thus far I have waded thro' some parts of his conduct in relation to the Proprietor.

†**b.** To 'go', be (in a certain condition), 'go about' (in certain attire). *Obs.*

1593 Norden *Spec. Brit., Essex* (Camden) Introd. p. xii, Husbandmen.. who wade in the weedes of gentlemen. **1576** Fleming *Panopl. Epist.* 335 In the want of which two thinges you doe not wade, as wise men hould opinion. **1596** Spenser *F.Q.* IV. x. 53 My hart gan throb And wade in doubt what best were to be donne.

†**c.** *to wade out of*: to escape from. *Obs.*

c **1386** Chaucer *Merch. T.* 440 But lat us waden out of this matere. **1525** Berners *Froiss.* II. cxxviii [cxxiv]. 363 Therby shall you wade out of all sclaundre. **1560** Daus tr. *Sleidane's Comm.* 91 Not with standing it waded out of all these daungers at the length [L. *et tamen ex his omnibus malis emersisse tandem*].

†**d.** To continue discussion *with* a person. *Obs.*

1527 Wolsey in *St. Papers Hen. VIII*, I. 203 And thus, wading further with the said Ambassadour, he shewed unto me, that [etc.]. **1539** Cromwell in Merriman *Life & Lett.* (1902) II. 176 Further wading with hym, he hath shewed unto me that [etc.]. **1540** Hen. VIII in *St. Papers* VIII. 362 That you shall likewise wade with the sayde Ambassadour of Portugall, to fynde out the very auctours of his saynges. **1546** Masone in *St. Papers Hen. VIII*, XI. 109 This I tell you.. to thintent that before ywe shall to farre wade wyth him in your instructions, you may [etc.]. **1568** Sir F. Knollys in Ellis *Orig. Lett.* Ser. I. II. 245 Thus farr I waded with hyr Grace to make hyr cawse disputable, but whan I sawe hyr tears, I forbayre to prosequte myn objection.

3. a. To walk through water or any liquid or soft substance which impedes motion. Formerly often, to pass *over* a river, etc., on foot (now *rare*). Phrase, *to wade* (*up*) *to* (the knees, armpits, etc.).

[*c* **893**: see overwade *v.*] *c* **1220** *Bestiary* 357 Oc on swimmeð bi-forn, and alle ðe oðre folezen, weðer so he swimmeð er he wadeð. *c* **1305** *Land Cokaygne* 179 Seuen yearis in swineis dritte He mot wade..up to þe chynne. *c* **1307** *Song on Exec. Sir S. Fraser* 100 in Wright *Pol. Songs* (Camden) 217 He wod into the water his feren him bysyde to adrenche. **1362** Langl. *P. Pl.* A. vi. 58 Wadeþ in þat water, wasscheþ ow wel þere. **1375** Barbour *Bruce* IX. 356 Till at the last he fand a place, That men mycht to thair schulderis vaid. *Ibid.* 388 He weill our woude, Bot till his throt the vattir stude. *c* **1386** Chaucer *Sompn. T.* 376 He [*sc.* Cirus] made that the ryuer was so smal That wommen myghte wade it ouer al. **1390** Gower *Conf.* I. 234 This Geant.. tok this ladi up alofte.. And in the flode began to wade. *c* **1400** *Laud Troy Bk.* 7262 Men myght with-Inne a wyle wade A-mong the hors vp to the hamme. **1470–85** Malory *Arthur* IV. xxvi. 156 He drofe hym in to a water but the gyant was soo hyghe that he myghte not wade after hym. **1513** Douglas *Æneis* x. xiii. 23 The hydduus Oryon Quhen he on fute woyd throu the mekle see. **1530** Palsgr. 770/1 The ryver is nat so depe as you take it, for a man may wade it over. *a* **1533** Berners *Huon* cliv. 587 Huon and the duches waded to the londe. **1624** Capt. J. Smith *Virginia* VI. 230 They were forced to wade a great way vp to the knees in water. **1662** R. Venables *Exper. Angler* x. 99 In small Brooks you may angle upwards, or else in great Rivers you must wade. **1684** W. Hedges *Diary* (Hakl. Soc.) I. 159 The Waters were risen so high that men waded to their middle in most of the Streets. **1727** [Dorrington] *Philip Quarll* (1816) 7 Finding it.. but breast high, we.. waded to the other side. *a* **1728** Ramsay *To W. Starrat* 30 Aft have I wid thro' glens with chorking feet, When neither plaid nor kelt could fend the weet. **1821** Scott *Kenilw.* ix, Through a deep and muddy lane, he at length waded on to the place. **1843** Borrow *Bible in Spain* xxxi, A rill of water, through which we were compelled to wade as high as the knee. **1860** Tyndall *Glac.* I. xxvi. 215 The men wading through the snow appeared as if climbing up a wall. **1884** *Macm. Mag.* Feb. 307 Pilgrims, wading knee deep in the river mud, walk round the holy city in sun-wise circuit. **1894** J. Payn *Gleams of Memory* 99 The gentlemen waded and carried the ladies on their shoulders.

indirect passive **1388** Wyclif *Ezek.* xlvii. 5 The depe watris of the stronde hadden wexe greet, that mai not be waad ouer [1382 be ouer wad]. **1544** Betham *Precepts War* I. cxciii. I v, What is to be done when waters can not be waded ouer. **1672** J. Lacy tr. *Tacquett's Milit. Archit.* 21 It cannot be less than six feet, otherwise a wet Ditch might be waded over.

¶ *transf.* (in nonce-uses).

13.. *Gaw. & Gr. Knt.* 787 Þe walle 'wod in þe water wonderly depe. **1744** M. Bishop *Life & Adv.* 255 The *Edgar*.. was blown up.. after wading through those hazardous Seas that we had just arrived from.

b. in figurative context, esp. *to wade through blood, slaughter,* etc.

c **1400** *Rom. Rose* 5022 To wynne the Ioy that is eterne, Fro which go bakward youthe hir made, In vanite to droune and wade. **1463** Ashby *Poems* ii. 46 For I cannat swym, I stand on the brynk Wadyng no forther, but as crist Iesus Sendith me konnyng. **1591** Harington *Orl. Fur.* Apol. Poetrie ¶ vj b, As one writes very pretily, that children do wade in Virgill, and yet strong men do swim in it. **1597** Hooker *Eccl. Pol.* v. lxvii. §4 They had.. a sea of comfort and ioy to wade in. **1605** Shaks. *Macb.* III. iv. 137, I am in blood Stept in so farre, that should I wade no more, Returning were as tedious as go ore. **1641** J. Jackson *True Evang. T.* I. 21, I will carry you along to wade through that *Acheldama*,.. when the Dogge-star.. of Persecution so raged. **1748** Richardson *Clarissa* (1811) I. 3 To encourage a man who is to wade into her favour (this was his expression) through the blood of her brother. **1750** Gray *Elegy* 67 To wade through slaughter to a throne. **1886** C. E. Pascoe *Lond. To-day* xvi. (ed. 3) 150 When France.. went back for a time to the old form of legitimate monarchy which she had waded through seas of blood to destroy.

c. *fig.* (Now chiefly, to go *through* a tedious task, a long or uninteresting book.)

1398 Trevisa *Barth. De P.R.* I. (1495) 8 It is peryllouse.. to wade depe in thyse materes of dyuynyte. *c* **1530** Frith *Disput. Purgat.* Wks. (1573) 59/1 Me thinketh also that he wadeth to deepe to descende to purgatorye by thys text. **1601** Holland *Pliny* xxv. xi. II. 232 Since we are waded so far into the deepe secrets of Physicke. *c* **1624** Rowley etc. *Witch Edmonton* I. ii. (1658) 12 On every side I am distracted: Am waded deeper into mischief, then vertue can avoid. But on I must. **1756** C. Lucas *Ess. Waters* I. Pref., The griping critic.. wades through massive volumes in search of faults. **1806–7** J. Beresford *Miseries Hum. Life* xvii. ¶ 1 Six-pence a day for the pleasure of wading through 16 columns of dull lies. **1809** Brougham *Contrib. Edin. Rev.* (1856) II. 300 From the large mass of matter through which we have been obliged to wade,.. we have selected the publications mentioned in the title. **1893** Stevenson *Catriona* ii, I warn you that you're wading deep. I wouldn't put myself in your place. **1907** *Verney Mem.* I. 375 Wading through the endless tangle of their accounts.

†**d.** To persevere *under* difficulties. ? *nonce-use.*

1714 in *Jrnl. Friends' Hist. Soc.* (1918) 29 We found the Exercise of the day heavy enough to wade under.

e. *to wade in*: to make a vigorous or concerted attack on one's opponent; to intervene, esp. vocally; *to wade into* (*colloq.*, orig. *U.S.*): to assail or confront energetically.

1863 B. Harte in *U.S. Sanitary Commission Bull.* (1864) I. vii. 201/1 Phrases such as camps may teach... Such as 'Bully!' 'Them's the peach!' 'Wade in, Sanitary! **1893** H. A. Shands *Some Pecularities of Speech in Mississippi* 66 *Wade into*. One man is said to *wade into* another when he attacks him very vigorously with either fist or tongue. This phrase is used by all classes. **1904** J. London *Let.* 17 Nov. (1966) 165 The lawyers.. waded into me good and hard for the cash. **1905** *N.Y. Even. Post* 2 Sept., When a herd of sheep wades in on a patch of bluebells, they stand still and eat all day. **1928** *Daily Express* 30 July 13/6 Though severely punished by Pattenden's lefts to the face he repeatedly waded in. **1935** D. L. Sayers *Gaudy Night* ii. 33, I don't stop to think... I just wade right in and ask for what I want. **1952** E. F. Davies *Illyrian Venture* vi. 104 Luckily the Germans had not known how easily they could have waded into us. **1967** N. Marsh *Death at Dolphin* v. 125 Don't let it give you a moment's pause... Just you wade in to Conducis. **1976** *Sun* 11 Mar. 11/4 Miss Georgina Burton.. waded in with her shopping bag and chased the gang away. **1984** J. Barnes *Flaubert's Parrot* x. 132 The writer must wade into life as into the sea, but only up to the navel.

4. *transf.* Of the sun or moon: To move (apparently) *through* clouds or mist; to be clouded. Chiefly *Sc.* and *north.*

a **1400–50** *Wars Alex.* 4141 Þe son wadis.. & þe wedire gloumes. **1646** Trapp *Comm. John* xviii. 23, 121 We must, when aspersed, labour as the eclipsed Moon, by keeping our motion, to wade out of the shadow. **1677** W. Hubbard *Narrative* 18 After the Moon had waded through the dark shadow of the Earth.. the two Companies marched on. **1725** Ramsay *Gentle Sheph.* I. i, The sun was wading thro' the mist. **1816** Scott *Bl. Dwarf* iii, The moon.. was, in the phrase of that country, wading or struggling with clouds. **1844** H. Stephens *Bk. Farm* I. 293 When the sun is more or less obscured,.. and when he is said to be wading in the cloud, rain may come. **1846** Mrs. A. Marsh *Father Darcy* II. xiv. 247 The pale light of a crescent moon wading among the black and lowering clouds.

5. *trans.* To walk through (water, etc.). †Also *fig.*

a **1300** *Cursor M.* 8964 Sco lift hir skirt.. And barfote wode sco þat burn. **1375** Barbour *Bruce* XIX. 760 The mekill mos.. That wes so hydwis for till waid. *c* **1480** Henryson *Paddock & Mouse* 38 Thocht the brym be perrillous to waid. **1513** Douglas *Æneis* III. x. 31 Nor the deip see Ionium, for all his hycht, Ne mycht he waid equallie ws to arest. *a* **1548** Hall *Chron., Hen. VII*, 18 b, The Englishmen in the forefront waded the dyche. **1563** Foxe *A. & M.* 849 b, Whiche was he sayde, a matter that he hadde diligently waded auncient authors bothe greeke and latine for. **1579** Fenton *Guicciard.* x. (1599) 437 Three thousand footmen.. afterwardes waded the foord of Myncia. **1822** Byron *Juan* VII. xiii, The Danube could not well be waded. **1869** Tozer *Highl. Turkey* I. 291 Our guide.. made a detour into the mountains to avoid wading the stream. **1888** Goode *Amer. Fishes* 20 For wading the bars he uses a much longer rod.

transf. *a* **1891** Morris *Poems by the Way* 122 When we wade the tangled wood.

6. To cause (a horse) to walk through water.

1838 Mrs. Bray *Tradit. Devon.* I. 262 Hence we again waded our horses.

wade, rare spelling of vade *v.*

c **1532** Du Wes *Introd. Fr.* in *Palsgr.* 946 To wade, *flaistrir.*

wade, obs. var. wad *sb.*[1], wed, woad.

wadeable: see wadable.

Wade-Giles (weɪd 'dʒaɪlz). [The names of Sir Thomas Francis *Wade* (1818–95), diplomatist and first Professor of Chinese at the University of Cambridge, and Herbert Allen *Giles* (1845–1935), Wade's successor at Cambridge.] Used *attrib.* and *absol.* to designate a system for the romanization of Chinese script devised by Wade, and subsequently modified by Giles. (Now widely superseded by Pinyin.) Also *ellipt.* as **Wade.**

[**1871** G. C. Stent *Chinese & Eng. Vocab.* p. vi, The tones are also according to Mr. Wade's system.] **1943** Y. R. Chao in *Mathews's Chinese-Eng. Dict.* (1945) p. ix, Now that the standard has come back to the pronunciation of Peiping, we can almost use the unmodified Wade's *Syllabary* or the more widely used Wade-Giles system. *Ibid.*, In Chauncey Goodrich's *Pocket Dictionary*, the syllables *ko k'o, ho* and *o* of Wade-Giles are given as *kê, k'ê, hê*, and *ê*. **1944** Chang & Maxwell *Conc. Eng.-Chinese Dict.* 10 People have become accustomed to the Wade form of spelling. **1947** C. F. Hockett in *Jrnl. Amer. Oriental Soc.* LXVII. 256/2 The numbering /¹/ through /⁴/ is as in Wade-Giles Romanization. **1950** J. De Francis *Nationalism & Lang. Reform in China* xii. 200 Those who have learned Wade as their first transcription of Chinese case are annoyed at the French use of another system. **1961** *Amer. Speech* XXXVI. 190 The Wade-Giles system of romanization of the Peking dialect will be followed. **1966** *Guardian* 29 Nov. 8/2 The Chinese system of romanization will certainly displace Wade-Giles eventually. **1971** R. Newnham *About Chinese* 172 Wade-Giles is the oldest and most widely used of all current romanizations, and its chief merit lies in that wide use. **1979** *Time* 2 Apr. 15/2 The changeover was started by Peking (um, er, Beijing) on Jan. 1, when the government of Zhongguo (otherwise known as China) decreed that in all its foreign-language publications Pinyin would replace the traditional Wade-Giles system of romanization.

wadeite ('weɪdaɪt). *Min.* [f. the name of Arthur *Wade* (1878–1951), British geologist + -ite[1].] A hexagonal silicate of potassium and zirconium, approximately $K_2ZrSi_3O_9$.

1938 Wade & Prider in *Rep. Brit. Assoc. Adv. Sci.* I. 419 Nineteen occurrences of post-Permian volcanic rocks have been found in the West Kimberley area... The rocks are made up.. of leucite, phlogopite,.. wadeite (a new K-Zr silicate), [etc.]. **1980** *Contrib. Mineral. & Petrol.* LXXII. 191/1 The restricted occurrence of wadeite to rocks of West Kimberley, Australia and Leucite Hills, Wyoming is believed to be due to their high K/Al and Zr contents relative to other high potash rocks.

wader ('weɪdə(r)). [f. wade *v.* + -er[1].]

1. One who wades.

1673 [R. Leigh] *Transp. Reh.* 120 So great a wader in discoveries.. might be.. employ'd in groping for the head of Nile. **1855** Tennyson *Brook* 117 James Made toward us, like a wader in the surf, Beyond the brook, waist-deep in meadow-sweet. **1905** J. B. Firth *Highw. Derbysh.* xxv. 372 Muddy channels.. in which a wader would sink to his waist.

b. said of a bird; *esp.* as the distinctive appellation of those long-legged birds (as the heron, plover, snipe, etc., constituting the former order *Grallæ* or *Grallatores*), which wade in shallow water.

1771 Edwards *E. Indian Bird* in *Phil. Trans.* LXI. 55, I judged it to be no wader in the water. **1802** Bingley *Anim. Biog.* (1813) I. 32 *Waders* (*Grallæ*). These have a roundish bill, a fleshy tongue; and the legs of most of the species are long. The principal genera are the Herons, Plovers, Snipes, and Sandpipers. **1851** Richardson *Geol.* (1855) 312, 6th Order.—Grallatores (or Waders). **1860** Emerson *Cond. Life, Fate* Wks. (Bohn) II. 325 Ducks take to the water, eagles to the sky, waders to the sea margin. **1905** *Spectator* 13 May 707/1 Another wader, rather smaller than the redshank,.. which the present writer has not been able to identify.

attrib. **1849** H. Miller *Footpr. Creat.* xi. (1874) 201 Birds of the wader family.

2. *pl.* Waterproof boots reaching above the knee, used by anglers for wading.

1841 J. T. J. Hewlett *Peter Priggins* I. i. 30 Mud-boots, waders, and snow-boots. **1883** *Fisheries Exhib. Catal.* 58 Fishing Waders, very light, requiring no separate Brogues. **1904** Gallichan *Fishing in Spain* 210 Short mackintosh coats to reach the waders will be required.

wadge, obs. f. wage *sb.* and *v.*; dial. f. wedge; var. wodge.

wadger, obs. var. wager.

Wadhamite ('wɒdəmaɪt). [f. the name of *Wadham* College, founded by Nicholas and Dorothy Wadham in 1612 + -ite[1].] A member of Wadham College, Oxford.

1760 J. Woodforde *Diary* 20 May (1924) I. 14 Hooke, Boteler and myself went to Welch's of Wadham College, where we designed to sup and spend the evening, but our entertainment was thus, one Lobster of a Pound, a half-pennyworth of Bread, and the same of Cheese... N.B. A Wadamite. **1976** A. Powell *Infants of Spring* xi. 191 'But', added the young Wadhamite, 'I've heard he's an absolute fish out of water when he's away from the academic world he's accustomed to.'

‖**wadi, wady** ('wɑːdɪ, 'wɒdɪ). Pl. **wadies, wadis, wadys.** [Arab. *wādī*.] In certain Arabic-speaking countries, a ravine or valley which in the rainy season becomes a watercourse; the stream or torrent running through such a ravine. Also *attrib.*

1839 Kinnear *Cairo, Petra & Damascus* iii. (1841) 93 Our route.. continued among narrow rocky wadies of a less desolate appearance. **1843** Whittier *Patucket Falls* Pr. Wks. 1889 I. 360 It resembled.. some Arabian wady, exhausted by a year's drought. **1850** W. Irving *Mahomet* i. (1853) 3 Some of the former occupied the fertile wadies, or valleys, scattered here and there among the mountains. **1856** Stanley *Sinai & Pal.* i. II. 70 A stair of rock brought us into a *wâdy* (Sidri), enclosed between red granite mountains... I cannot too often repeat, that these *wâdys* are exactly like rivers, except in having no water. **1902** D. G. HOGARTH *Nearer East* 139 The palm-lined wadi beds of Jebel Akhdar. *Ibid.* 143 Aromatic scrub and an occasional thorn is all that can be expected in the wadi bottoms. **1912** S. R. DRIVER (transl. of *Judg.* v. 21) in *Expositor* Feb. 121 The wady Kishon swept them away, The on-coming wady. **1980** *Encounter* May 90/2 Off we go, with me stumbling after him over the rough stony ground of the wadi bed.

wading (ˈweɪdɪŋ), *vbl. sb.* [-ING¹.] **a.** The action of the verb WADE.

c **1375** BARBOUR *Bruce* VII. 56 Bot sum men sais, this eschaping Apon ane other maner fell Than throu the vading. **1622** R. HAWKINS *Voy. S. Sea* lii. 124 Wherof more then the one halfe dyed with famine, and continual wading through Rivers and waters. **1813** [LEIGH HUNT] in *Examiner* 19 Apr. 242/2 So many creepings in dust and wadings through mire. **1870** KINGSLEY in *Good Words* 1 June 380/2 We were glad to cool ourselves [in fancy] by talking over..wadings in icy streams beneath the black pine-woods.

b. *attrib.* as in *wading-place*, *pool*; also in names of waterproof articles of attire for wading, as ***wading-boots***, ***-brogues***, ***coats***, ***shoes***, etc.

1598 FLORIO, *Vadetti*, narrow wading places or foards. **1866** J. MACGREGOR *Thousand Miles in Rob Roy Canoe* (ed. 2) i. 10, I took for this tour..canvas wading shoes,..a waterproof overcoat, [etc.]. **1883** *Fisheries Exhib. Catal.* 58 Wading Stockings. Wading Trousers. Wading Brogues. Wading Coats. Wading Boots. **1888** W. E. NORRIS *Chris* vi, Prawning is not bad fun for those who have taken the precaution to put on wading-boots. **1921** Wading pool [see *sand-pile* s.v. SAND *sb.*² 9 a]. **1977** *New Yorker* 15 Aug. 42/3 He inflated and filled a plastic wading pool for the children.

wading (ˈweɪdɪŋ), *ppl. a.* [-ING².] That wades. ***wading bird*** = WADER 1 b.

1597 GERARDE *Herbal* II. cclxxxv. 677 It may be called *Sedum aquatile*, or water Sengreene..in English water Housleeke, Knights Pondwoort, and of some..wading Pondweed. **1867** LYELL *Princ. Geol.* (1875) II. III. xli. 425 Of all families even of wading birds the woodcocks are perhaps the most migratory. **1891** *Hardwicke's Sci.-Gossip* XXVII. 67 A new fossil wading bird has been found in the cretaceous rocks of Sweden, and named *Scaniornis Ludgreni*.

wadle, obs. form of WADDLE.

wadle, wadling, obs. ff. WATTLE, WATTLING.

wadmal (ˈwɒdməl). Forms: α. 4, 6, 7 **wadmoll**, 5, 6 **-male**, 5, 6, 8 **-mole**, (5 **warde-**), 5, 7 **waddemole**, (6 **watmol**, 7 **wadmol**, **-nall**), 6, 7 **wadmell**, 9 **-mel**, 7, 9 **-mall**, 9 **-maal**, **-mail**, 7, 9 *dial.* **-meal**, 8 **-miel**, 9 **-mil**, 5, 8, 9 **wadmal**. β. 5, 6 **wedmole**, 6 **-mell** (**-moll**), (7 **-meill**, **-nel**). γ. 6, 7 **woodmal(e**, 7, 9 *dial.* **woadmell** (7 **-mal**, **woddenell**, 8 **woodmeil**), 9 *dial.* **woodmail**. δ. 8 *corruptly* **wadmus**. Also VADMAL, -MEL. [a. ON. *vaðmál* (Norw. *vadmaal*, with many dial. variants; MSw. *vaþmal*, *-maal*, Sw. *vadmal*, Da. *vadmel*) believed to represent an earlier **váðmál*, f. *váð* cloth (= OE. *wǽd* WEED *sb.*²) + *mál* measure.]

1. A kind of woollen cloth.

a. In England, a coarse woollen material used principally for covering horse-collars, and other rough purposes; also (esp. in the s.-w.) for petticoats, mittens, etc. *Obs.* exc. in *wadmiltilt* (see 2).

In the 16–17th c. mentioned as manufactured in Wales and at Witney (Oxon).

1392 *Earl Derby's Exped.* (Camden) 158 Pro iiij^xx viij vergis wadmoll ad ij d. ob. pro saccis. **1404** *Durham Acc. Rolls* (Surtees) 395 Item j pannus de wadmale pro rebus cariandis. **1423** in *Rolls Parlt.* IV. 241 Item, 111 peces de Wadmole rouge, contenantz xx alnas di., pris. v s. **1425** in Kennett *Par. Antiq.* (1695) 574 In v. virgatis de Waddemole emptis pro coleris equinis..ii sol. i den. **1436** *Libel Eng. Policy* in *Pol. Poems* (Rolls) II. 160 [Imports from Spain] Iren, wolle, wadmole, gotefel, kydefel also. **1485** in *Compotus Rolls Obedient. St. Swithun's, Winch.* (1892) 383 Et in solutis pro le Wedmole ad cooperiendum coleres equorum xvjd. **1502** *Priv. Purse Exp. Eliz. York* (1830) 81 For dyeng of cclxxij yerdes of wardemole blewe and murrey for the Quenes barge. **1525** BERNERS *Froiss.* II. ccxv. 274 b, Many had no armure, but their cootes of wadmoll [Fr. *de gros bureaulx*]. *c* **1580** *Direction for divers trades of marchaundize* in *Eng. Hist. Rev.* (1914) XXIX. 516 Item, for all the partes of Galicia..flaninge and wedmoles of Wales. **1598** STOW *Surv.* (1603) 286 A market house for the sale of Woolen bayes, Watmols Flanels and such like. **1627** CAPT. J. SMITH *Sea Gram.* vi. 27 Which is what you call a Tilt, couered with wadmall in your Wherries. **1662** *Ir. Act 14 & 15 Chas. II*, c. 8 *Bk. Rates*, Mittins of Wadmol the dozen pair, 00 09 00. **1677** PLOT *Oxfordsh.* 279 Of their worst [tail wool] they make Wednel [at Witney] for Collar-makers. **1695** KENNETT *Par. Antiq., Gloss.*, *Waddemole*, now called Woadmel, and in Oxfordshire Woddenell, a course sort of stuff us'd for the covering of the collars of cart-horses. **1710** D. HILMAN *Tusser Rediv.* Sept. (1744) 119 Sedge Collars [for plough-horses] are by much the lightest and coolest, indeed not so comely as those of Wadmus, but will serve a good Team well enough. **1721** C. KING *Brit. Merch.* I. 291 Wadmole *alias* Wadding, 830 Yards. **1750** BLANCKLEY *Nav. Expositor* 189 *Woodmeil*, a hairy coarse Stuff made of Island Wool, and supplied to the Carpenters of Ships..for lining of Ports, &c. *a* **1825** FORBY *Voc. E. Anglia*, *Wadmal*, a very coarse and thick kind of woollen manufacture.

b. In Scotland, a woollen fabric woven in Orkney and Shetland. Now only *Hist.*

Down to the 17th c. the taxes of Orkney and Shetland were paid in wadmal and other commodities.

1572 in *Reg. Mag. Sig. Scot.* 1575, 642/2 (Zetland), 12 den. pro qualibet ulna sive cuttella 24 cuttellarum panni lanei, vulgo wadmell. **1577** in D. Balfour *Oppress. Orkney & Zetland* (1859) 18 Thair clayth, callit Wadmell, quhilk is ane dewitie thai pay to the Kingis Majestie..zeirlie. **1654** *Blaeu's Atlas, Scotia* 148 Pannus quidam ipsis [Hethlandicis] est crassa ex lana confectus, patrio idiomate τὸ Wadmeal dictum. **1774** E. GIFFORD in *G. Low's Orkney*, etc. (1879) 143 Payment to the Crown was called Scatt, which was paid in butter, oil, and a sort of very coarse cloth called Wadmiel. **1821** SCOTT *Pirate* v, Her upper garment.. was of a coarse dark-coloured stuff, called wadmaal, then much used in the Zetland islands, as also in Iceland and Norway. **1884** SHERIFF RAMPINI in *Good Words* Nov. 746/1 All the women..in scarlet petticoats of Shetland 'wadmal'.

c. A woollen fabric worn by country people in Scandinavia and Iceland. Sometimes in mod.Sw. or Da. form: see VADMAL, -MEL.

c **1682** J. COLLINS *Salt & Fishery* 84 The general Employment of the People [in Iceland] is either Fishery or the making of Wadmoll, which is a course sort of woollen Cloth, made of their Sheepes Wool. **1796** MORSE *Amer. Geog.* II. 10 (Iceland) They likewise manufacture a coarse kind of cloth, which they call wadmal. **1845** [C. H. J. ANDERSON] *Swedish Br.* 114 The scarlet kerchiefs, mingling with the bluish-grey of the wad-meal or striped tartan. **1894** *Field* 1 Dec. 838/1 No day is too long..for poor old Niels in his one garment of coarse wadmal.

2. *attrib.* or quasi-*adj.* chiefly in sense 'made of wadmal'; **wadmiltilt** (see quot. 1898 and cf. quot. 1627 in 1 a).

1541 *Will J. Norman* (Som.), My dau. Margerie one wedmole petycote. **1544** *Extracts Aberd. Reg.* (1844) I. 206 Ane schip of fyr..with hir hale salis of wadmale claith. **1598** in *Reg. Mag. Sig. Scot.* 367/1 Malcolme..to have the wedmell dett thairof becaus he wantit the samin at his entrie. *a* **1700** in Alice M. Earle *Costume Colon. Times* (1894) 253 Wadmoll mittens..a woadmell petticoat. **1821** SCOTT *Pirate* x, Her dark wadmaal cloak. **1828** SPEARMAN *Brit. Gunner* (ed. 2) 23 Wadmiltilts. **1898** VISCT. DILLON in *Archæol. Jrnl.* (Inst.) Ser. II. V. 296 *note*, In artillery inventories of to-day will be found wadmiltilts, a kind of tarpaulin covering for stores.

wadna, Sc. pronunciation of *would no* = would not: see WILL *v.*

wadrop, obs. form of WARDROBE.

wadset (ˈwɒdsɛt), *sb.* *Sc.* Now *obsolescent.* Forms: 5–7 **wedset(t**, 6–8 **wodset(t**, 7 **waddset**, 8 **wadsett**, 6– **wadset**. [f. WADSET *v.*]

1. *Sc. Law.* 'The conveyance of land in pledge for, or in satisfaction of, a debt or obligation, with a reserved power to the debtor to recover his lands, on payment or performance' (Bell). Phr. (***to have, lie***) ***in wadset***. Cf. MORTGAGE *sb.*

There are two kinds of *wadset, proper* and *improper* (see quot. 1768).

1449 *Sc. Acts Jas. II* (1814) II. 35/2 Quha sa has tane or takis landes in wedsett. **1520** *Extracts Burgh Rec. Edin.* (1869) I. 196 That the aucht over buthis of thair Tolbuith on the north syde be laid in wodsett vpoun the soume of ix^c and iij^xx frankis vnder ane reuersion. **1527–8** *Ibid.* 233 The commoun buithis quhilk he hes in wedsett of the guid toun. **1536** *Abstr. Protocols Town Clerks Glasgow* (1897) IV. 90 The lowsing and rademyng of his place that lyis in wedset to Jhon Gybson of the xl pwnd of monye. **1609** SKENE *Reg. Maj.* Table 104 b, The saidis profits, and frutes..sall be payed zeirly to him, quha hes the wadset. **1644** *Sc. Acts Chas. I* (1819) VI. 143/2 The Lands, Anual-rents, Wodsets, and others holden by them of the saids forfeited persons. **1708** J. CHAMBERLAYNE *St. Gt. Brit.* II. III. vi. 521 The Scottish Wadsets and Reversions answer to the English Mortgages and Defeazances. *a* **1768** ERSKINE *Inst. Law Scot.* II. viii. §26 A proper wadset is truly of the nature of a redeemable right of property, and not barely of pledge; by which it is covenanted, that the use of the lands possessed by the wadsetter shall, during the not redemption, go for the use or interest of the money lent by him to the reverser... An improper wadset is nothing more than a *pignus*, or right of security; in which the wadsetter is accountable to the reverser for the neat yearly sums which he hath, or might have, received out of the wadset-lands. **1814** SCOTT *Wav.* xlii, There was little time to get the wadset made out. **1873** BURTON *Hist. Scot.* lvii. V. 193 The poor man asked leave to raise money by 'wadset' or mortgage of his estates.

2. A thing pledged.

1796 BURNS '*Wha will buy my troggin?*' Here's a little wadset, Buittle's scrap o' truth, Pawn'd in a gin-shop Quenching holy drouth. *a* **1800** in Cromek *Rem. Nithsdale Song* (1810) 90 Our guidwife coft a snip white coat,..But it's a wadset i' the town.

3. *attrib.* and *Comb.*

1630 in *Inchaffray Reg.* (Bannatyne Club) 106 Christiane Murray..wodsett haver of the landis under written. **1665** *Caldwell Papers* (Maitl. Club) I. 62 Free of any such wadsett ryt. *a* **1728** J. SPOTTISWOODE *Hope's Minor Practicks* (1734) 241 This, for many Years, was the common and ordinary Reason of Reduction of Wadset-rights. *a* **1768** ERSKINE *Inst. Law Scot.* II. viii. §19 This instrument..subjects the wadsetter to account for the rent of the wadsetlands, from the time the order was used. *Ibid.* §28 A back-tack of them [the lands] to the reverser..is made to continue during the not redemption of the wadset, for payment of the interest of the wadset-sum.

ˈwadset, *v.* Chiefly *Sc.* ? *Obs.* Pa. t. and pa. pple. **wadset**, **-setted**. Forms: 4, 5 **wed(de)sette**, 4–7 **wedset(t**, 6, 7 **wodset(t**, 6–8 **wadset**. [Sc. form (with *wad* Sc. var. of WED *sb.*) of ME. *wedset*, f. WED *sb.* + SET *v.*¹; prob. developed from an OE. phrase **tó wedde settan* 'to set to pledge', to pawn, mortgage. (The recorded OE. phrases are *tó wedde lecgan*, *sellan*; cf. 'Mi lond ich wulle sette to wedde', Layamon 25172. OE. and ME. had also *wed settan*, *to sette wed* = to deposit a pledge.)] *trans.* To put (land, clothes, etc.) in pledge; to pawn, mortgage.

c **1330** R. BRUNNE *Chron. Wace* (Rolls) 11796 Al my lond schal y wed-sette ffor gold & seluer. *a* **1400** *Burgh Laws* lxxix. (*Sc. Stat.* I), Of lande þat is wedset wythin burgh. *c* **1440** *York Myst.* xxxii. 346 A place here beside, lorde, wolde I wedde-sette. **1506** *Reg. Privy Seal Scot.* I. 176 A Lettre of Licence..to analy or wedset to quhatsumever person or persons he ples ony xii merkis worth of land. **1508** KENNEDY *Flyting w. Dunbar* 443 Thou drank thy thrift, sald and wedsett thy clais. **1572** *Satir. Poems Reform.* xxxii. 54 All our gay garmentis..We thame wedset, our bodyis to sustene. **1646** Z. BOYD in *Zion's Flowers* (1855) App. 31/1 The said Laird wodset sold and disponed to us..the lands. **1678** [see WADSETTER 2]. **1775** L. SHAW *Hist. Moray* 33 These, and some other possessions, are now wadsetted by William Gordon. **1859** *Bk. Thanes of Cawdor* (Spalding Club) 420 There follows..a list of the wadsets, from which we learn that Budgate was wadset to Mr. William Dallas for 10,000 marks.

fig. **1645** RUTHERFORD *Tryal & Tri. Faith* (1845) 366 Blood, and the blood of God shed, cannot wadset ancient loue.

Hence † **ˈwadsetting** *vbl. sb.*

c **1440** *Promp. Parv.* 520/1 Wedsettynge, *impignoracio*. **1509** *Reg. Priv. Seal Scot.* I. 295/2 The quhilk alienatioun or wedsetting the [King] willis..sal be na hurt..to the biaris. **1654** LAMONT *Diary* (Maitl. Club) 72 No money lent, or bargaine in sailling or wedsetting of land..was to be allowed.

wadsetter (ˈwɒdsɛtə(r)). *Sc.* Also 7 **wodsetter**. [f. WADSET *v.* and *sb.* + -ER¹.]

1. One who puts his land to wadset; a mortgagor. *rare.*

1625 in Ld. Durie *Reports* (1690) 43 He had Comprised the Reversion of the same Lands, which he had in Wodset of before, from the Wodsetter. **1864** LD. DEAS in *Scots Revised Rep.* Ser. III. (1902) III. 330 The right of property in the lands remained with the wadsetter, subject to the burden of the wadset; and when the wadset was subsequently discharged, that burden was effectually wiped off.

2. One who holds by a wadset, a mortgagee.

1678 SIR G. MACKENZIE *Crim. Laws Scot.* I. xxiv. §iv. (1699) 122 The Wadsetter runs all hazard of the Lands Wadset to him. **1758** in *Nairne Peerage Evid.* (1874) 67 James and George Neasmyths wadsetters of a part of Ardblae. **1799** R. BELL *Syst. Forms of Deeds Scot.* II. 23 The purpose of this act was to preserve the right of the reverser, who, by these absolute rights had been exposed to the acts of the wadsetter. **1814** SCOTT *Wav.* xx, The elders of his own tribe, wadsetters and tacksmen, as they were called, who occupied portions of his estate as mortgagers or lessees. **1889** LOCKHART *Ch. Scot. 13th Cent.* 104 *note*, His father.. being a wadsetter at Drumgask.

wadt, wadth: see WAD *sb.*³, WATH.

wady: see WADI.

wadyr, obs. form of WATER.

wae, obs. or dial. form of WOE.

†**wædle**, *sb.*¹ *Obs. rare*⁻¹. In 3 **wælde**. [OE. *wǽdl* str. fem., *wǽdle* wk. fem., related to next.

It is doubtful whether the *wælde* of the Layamon MS. is a scribal error or a genuine metathetic form.]

Poverty.

c **888** ÆLFRED *Boeth.* xxvi. §2 Sio mennisce wædl ðe næfre ȝefylled ne bið wilnað ælce dæȝ hwæs hwuȝu þysses woruldwelan. *c* **1205** LAY. 1002 For al þat god of þisse londe we scule leden mid us & heo bi-læuen wrecches & wælde heom scal fulien.

†**wædle**, *a.* and *sb.*² *Obs.* Also **weaðle**. [OE. *wǽdla*, Mercian *wéðla*.] **a.** *adj.* Poor, needy. **b.** *sb. pl.* The poor.

c **1000** *Ags. Gosp.* Mark x. 46 Timeus sunu bartimeus sæt blind wið þone weȝ wædla. *c* **1000** *Ags. Ps.* (Surtees) cviii. 17, & oehtende wes mon ðearfan & weðlan. *c* **1200** ORMIN 5638 All wrecche & wædle & usell mann. *c* **1205** LAY. 427 Wapmen & wifmen, þa weoleȝen & þa weaðlen, alle he heom sumunde. *Ibid.* 5872 For her scullen þe wædlen alle i-wurðen riche.

wael, obs. form of WALE *sb.*¹

wæl: see WAL (slaughter), WEAL.

wæld, wælden: see WEALD, WIELD *v.*

†**ˈwæling**, *vbl. sb.* *Obs. rare*⁻¹. [? f. ON. *véla*, *væ̍la* to defraud, trick (mod.Norw. *vela* to tempt, flatter, woo) + -ING¹.] In Comb. ***wæling-word*** pl., words of temptation or courtship.

c **1200** ORMIN 2192 Full wel birrþ ure maȝȝdenn ben Forrshamedd, ȝiff mann brinngeþ Biforenn hire unnþæwfull word & wælinng word þurrh scaldess.

wær, obs. form of WARE *a.*

waest, obs. form of WASTE.

waesuck(s (ˈwesʌk, -sʌks), *int.* *Sc.* [f. *wae*, Sc. form of WOE; the ending app. represents *sake(s*: see SAKE *sb.*] Expressing commiseration: Woe is me! Alas!

a **1774** FERGUSSON *Braid Claith* 13 Waesucks for him wha has nae feck o't. **1786** BURNS *Holy Fair* xxv, Waesucks! for him that gets nae lass, Or lasses that hae naething. **1806** [J. BLACK] *Falls of Clyde* 133 Ye trust, waesucks! in works. **1867** J. K. HUNTER *Retrosp. Artist's Life* xxviii. (1912) 291 Waesucks for the back places about London.

waet, obs. Sc. f. WOT *v.*

waf, obs. pa. t. of WEAVE *v.*

Wafd (wɒft). [a. Arab. *wafd* arrival, deputation, in full *al-wafd al-miṣrī* the Egyptian delegation.] The name of an Egyptian nationalist organization formed in 1918 (from 1923, a political party) whose original aims included the establishment of autonomous government in Egypt and the abolition of the monarchy. (The party was dissolved in 1953, but reconstituted as the *New Wafd* in 1978.)

1922 *Times* 24 Jan. 9/1 The Wafd el Masri, or Zaghlul Delegation..has just issued a detailed programme of non-cooperation. *Ibid.* 27 Jan. 11/2 The reconstituted *Wafd.* **1928** E. W. P. NEWMAN *Great Britain in Egypt* x. 239 The Wafd had been constituted in order to lay the case of Egypt before the Peace Conference of Paris. **1932** *Palestine Post* 13 Dec. 7/1 The quarrel between the Wafd and its dissidents continues. **1943** VISCT. WAVELL *Allenby in Egypt* i. 40 Zaghlul Bey..had not, however, been the originator of the Wafd (or Delegation), as his party came to be known. It was the creation of others, notably men like Mohammed Mahmoud. **1962** *Listener* 15 Nov. 795/1 Saad Zaghloul, the founder and leader of the Wafd party. **1974** *Great Soviet Encycl.* IV. 649/2 Some of the Wafd members unsuccessfully fought the government of Nasser in actions of 1954, 1957, and 1961. **1978** *Facts on File World News Digest* 24 Feb. 131/1 The New Wafd had 24 supporters in the 360-seat People's Assembly.

Wafdist (ˈwɒftɪst), *a.* and *sb.* [f. prec. + -IST.] **a.** *adj.* Of or pertaining to the Wafd. **b.** *sb.* A member or supporter of the Wafd; an Egyptian Nationalist.

1926 *Glasgow Herald* 3 June 8 Doubts..were entertained of the prospect of the Wafdist leader taking such a moderate course. **1926** *Spectator* 19 June 1032/2 The Wafdists..are likely to be restrained by the knowledge that any too free indulgence of their characteristic tactics..would quickly make Adly throw up his office in disgust. **1958** J. W. DAY *Lady Houston* xv. 235 That is, indeed, a 'Capitulation', and the worst and most fatal, by Great Britain to the Wafdist mob! **1973** *Times* 29 Oct. 17/7 From being a Liberal Constitutionalist in the days of Sarwat, his protector, he became an active Wafdist under Nahhas Pasha.

wafe, obs. f. WAIF, WAVE; var. WAIVE *v.*² *Obs.*

wafer (ˈweɪfə(r)), *sb.* Forms: 4–6 **wafre**, 4–5 **waffre**, 5–7 **waffer**, 8 *Sc.* **waffor**, **weffer**, 5 **wafier**, **wafir**, **wayfire**, **wafyre**, 6 **wafyrre**, 5–6 **wafur**, 5–7 **waiffur**, (5 -er), 6 **whafer**, 7 **wapher**, 5– **wafer**. [ME. *wafre*, a. AF. *wafre*, ONF. *waufre* (= Central F. *gaufre*, *gofre*, whence GOFER¹), adopted, with change of *l* into *r*, from MLG. *wâfel* (mod.LG. *wâfel*, *wafel*) = early mod.Du. *waefel*, now *wafel* (WFris. *waffel*), whence WAFFLE; the mod.G. *waffel*, Sw. *våffla*, Da. *vaffel* are from LG.

As the F. *gaufre*, wafer, waffle, has also the sense of honeycomb, it is inferred that the Teut. word had originally this meaning, and is cogn. w. OHG. *wabo*, MHG., mod.G. *wabe*, honeycomb; but neither Du. nor LG. seems to have preserved this sense.]

1. a. A very light thin crisp cake, baked between wafer-irons; formerly often eaten with wine, now chiefly with ices; in later use sometimes rolled, sometimes serving as the under part of a macaroon. Cf. WAFRON.

The simile 'thin as a wafer', originally belonging to this sense, is now commonly associated with sense 3.

[**1295** *Will N. Longespee* in *Eng. Hist. Rev.* (1900) July 524 Tria paria ferrea ad wafras, neulas, et galettas faciendas.] **1377** LANGL. *P. Pl.* B. XIII. 264 [A waferer says:] Alle Londoun I leue liketh wel my wafres. *c* **1386** CHAUCER *Miller's T.* 193 He sente hire..wafres pipyng hoot out of the gleede. **1442** in *Bekynton's Corr.* (Rolls) II. 233 Ro. Savage, et Robertus serviens domini Regentis, portaverunt waiffers et poma. *c* **1460** J. RUSSELL *Bk. Nurture* in *Babees Bk.* (1868) 123 For þese may marre many a man changynge his astate, but ȝiff he haue aftur, hard chese, wafurs, with wyne ypocrate. *c* **1500** *For to serve a Lord* ibid. 368 Thenne aftur wafers and frute spended, all maner thinge shalbe take uppe and avoyded. **1530** TINDALE *Exod.* xvi. 31 The taste of it [*sc.* manna] was lyke vnto wafers made with honye [so **1611**]. **1546** WRIOTHESLEY *Chron.* (1875) I. 165 My lord major did electe and chose that daie when he was at waffers and ipocras Mr. Richard Jervis. **1572** HULOET (ed. Higins), Wafre, suche as they geue to younge children, *crustulum.* **1577** GRANGE *Golden Aphrod.* etc. P j b, Yea, yea, she treades so nice, she would not wafers breake. **1608** BONHAM in *Topsell's Serpents* 312 The people of India..doe make of these Wormes diuers iuncats, as we doe Tarts, Marchpanes, Wafers, and Cheese-cakes. **1619** DRAYTON *Idea* viii, Thy Lips, with age, as any Wafer thinne. *a* **1625** FLETCHER *Chances* II. i, A womans oathes are wafers, breake with making. **1671** GREW *Anat. Plants* I. i. (1682) 2 The inner Coat [of the bean]..so far shrinking up, as to seem only the roughness of the outer, somewhat resembling Wafers under Maquaroons. **1769** MRS. RAFFALD *Engl. Housekpr.* (1778) 277 To make Wafers. Take two spoonfuls of cream, two of sugar, the same of flour, and one spoonful of orange flower water, beat them well together for half an hour, then make your wafer tongs hot,..bake them on a stove fire, as they are baked roll them round a stick like a spiggot, as soon as they are cold, they will be very crisp. **1825** T. HOOK *Sayings* Ser. II. *Passion & Princ.* xi. III. 251 The Major having finished the bottle of claret,..together with a large plate of wafers. **1834** ESTHER COPLEY *Housekpr.'s Guide*, Wafers.—Sweeten dried flour with loaf sugar;..make it into a stiff batter with cream. There are irons for the purpose of baking them... They are used for the bottom of maccaroons and some other cakes. **1883** R. HALDANE *Workshop Rec.* Ser. II. 155/2 (Confectionery) Wafers.—Take 4 oz. sugar, 4 oz. butter, 8 oz. flour [etc.]. *Ibid.* 156/1 Close the tongs immediately; put them on the fire, turning them occasionally until the wafer is done.

b. *ellipt.*, a sandwich of ice-cream between wafers.

1936 N. COWARD *Still Life* in *To-night at 8.30* III. i. 48 An old girl..asked if I'd got an ice-cream wafer... What did she think I was, a 'Stop me and buy one?' **1979** *Listener* 6 Sept. 303/2 The vanilla wafer..proved a great healer.

2. The thin disk of unleavened bread used at the Eucharist in the Western Church before the Reformation, and subsequently in the ritual of Roman Catholics, Lutherans, and some Anglicans. Cf. OBLEY.

1559 Q. ELIZ. *Injunct.* D 3 b, The vsuall bread and wafer, heretofore named singing Cakes, which serued for the vse of the priuate Masse. **1570** GILBY in *Part of a Register* (1593) 16 The adoration of the Sacrament, in the Countrey where they knocke and kneele to a Wafer, is a popishe pollicie. **1698** FRYER *Acc. E. India & P.* 94 The Widow..bestows Holway, a kind of Sacramental Wafer. **1719** SWIFT *Abstr. Hist. Eng.*, *Stephen* Wks. 1768 IV. 297 The English, upon a certain engine, raised the mast of a ship, on the top whereof, in a silver box, they put the consecrated wafer. **1853** ROBERTSON *Serm.* Ser. III. xix. 249 To tremble before a consecrated wafer is spurious reverence. **1856** MRS. BROWNING *Aur. Leigh* I. 85 As they went To eat the bishop's wafer at the church. **1862** *Sat. Rev.* 8 Feb. 159 Many of these unbelievers..obtained and outraged consecrated wafers.

3. a. A small disk of flour mixed with gum and non-poisonous colouring matter, or of gelatine or the like similarly coloured, which when moistened is used for sealing letters, attaching papers, or receiving the impression of a seal.

[**1635**: see *wafer-seal* in 7.] **1712** ADDISON *Spect.* No. 305 ¶ 6 Pen and Ink, Wax and Wafers, with the like Necessaries for Politicians. **1749** JOHNSON *Let. to Miss Porter* 12 July, You frighted me with your black wafer, for I was afraid your letter had brought me ill news. **1797** W. JOHNSTON tr. *Beckmann's Hist. Invent.* I. 226 Mr. Speiss [Ger.] has made an observation..that the oldest seal with a red wafer, he has ever yet found, is on a letter written by D. Krapf, at Spires, in the year 1624, to the government at Bayreuth. **1800** MAR. EDGEWORTH *Belinda* xv, Lady Delacour..began..to put wafers into several notes which she had been writing. **1815** J. SMITH *Panorama Sci. & Art* II. 729 In every kind of tracing, the different papers which are employed upon each other, should be fastened together by wafers. **1848** THACKERAY *Van. Fair* liii, Poor men always use messengers instead of the post. Who has not had their letters, with the wafers wet, and the announcement that a person is waiting in the hall? **1883** S. C. HALL *Retrospect* I. 15 To put a wafer on a letter was a thing seldom done.

b. *transf.* Applied to a round spot.

1853 KANE *Grinnell Exp.* xxviii. (1856) 236 Deck covered in with black felt, the frozen condensation patching it with large white wafers of snow. **1897** *Outing* XXIX. 543/1 The Dalmatian, or 'coach dog,' white with black wafers stuck all over him.

4. *Med.* A thin leaf of paste, used to form a cachet for the administration of a powder.

1848 C. BRONTË in C. Shorter *Charlotte Brontë & her Circle* (1896) vi. 173 She has taken no medicine, but.. Locock's cough wafers, of which she has used about 3 per diem. **1887** *Buck's Handbk. Med. Sci.* IV. 699/1 Wafers are of two forms. One style consists of two watch-glass shaped bodies, whose edges, upon moistening, will cohere, leaving a central space for enclosure of the powder... The other style consists of a single large, thin, circular sheet of wafer-material. Such sheet dipped into water, becomes flexible, and..is used as a literal wrap for the dose of powder. **1913** MRS. STRATTON-PORTER *Laddie* iv. (1917) 74 She looked exactly as she does when the wafer bursts and the quinine gets in her mouth.

5. *Gunnery.* A kind of primer.

1867 J. T. HEADLEY *Farragut & Nav. Commanders* 73 Not a gun went off... The gunners had removed the 'wafers' by which they were discharged.

6. *Electronics.* A very thin slice of a semiconductor crystal used as the substrate for solid-state circuitry.

1956 *Bell Syst. Techn. Jrnl.* XXXV. 3 After diffusion the entire surface of the silicon wafer is covered with the diffused n- and p-type layers. **1967** *Electronics* 6 Mar. 25 Litton engineers haven't decided whether to use single or two-layer metalization to interconnect the circuits within the wafers. **1975** D. G. FINK *Electronics Engineers' Handbk.* VIII. 84 After the completion of the test sequence, the probe assembly is automatically lifted up and the probes are indexed over to the next chip to be tested on the wafer. **1979** *Maclean's Mag.* 2 Apr. 37/3 'Wafers' containing hundreds of memory chips (each with 64,000 transistors): dispensing liquor, guiding spaceships. **1984** *QL User* Dec. 18 Currently, chips are manufactured in batches on discs of silicon about four inches in diameter called wafers.

7. *attrib.* and *Comb.*, as (sense 1) ***wafer-baker***, ***-maker***, ***roller***; ***wafer-like***, ***-thin*** adjs.; (sense 3) ***wafer box***, ***-seal***; also ***wafer-sealed***, ***-torn*** adjs.; **wafer-biscuit** = sense 1; **wafer-bread**, unleavened bread to be used at the Eucharist in the form of wafers; **wafer-cachet** (see sense 4); † **wafer-god**, an opprobrious term for the consecrated host; **wafer-iron**, an apparatus for baking wafers, consisting of two iron blades between which the paste is held (also ***pair of wafer-irons***); † **wafer pancake**, a kind of pancake made thin like a wafer; † **wafer-paper**, a preparation of paste in thin sheets, used in cookery and pharmacy (see 4); **wafer stamp**, a hand-stamp for impressing a device on wafers; **wafer-tongs** = *wafer-iron*; † **wafer-wall**, *nonce-wd.*, a wall flimsy as a wafer; † **wafer-woman**, a woman who sold wafers (cf. WAFERER, WAFRESTRE); † **wafer-work**, a kind of ornamental work in which wafers were used to form a pattern. Also WAFER-CAKE.

1580 HOLLYBAND *Treas. Fr. Tong*, *Oublieur*, a *wafer baker. **1848** THACKERAY *Van. Fair* xliv, The hulking fellow carrying the *wafer-biscuits. **1837** DICKENS *Pickw.* liv. 591 Wilkins Flasher, Esquire, was..spearing a *wafer-box with a penknife. **1968** *Canad. Antiques Collector* Nov. 26/1 When envelopes were introduced, the wafer box became a stamp box. **1565** ABP. PARKER *To Sir W. Cecil* 30 Apr., in *Corr.* (Parker Soc.) 240 These were the orders which they must observe; to wear the cap appointed by Injunction,..to communicate kneeling in *wafer-bread. **1637** *Bk. Comm. Prayer Ch. Scot.*, *Commun.* rubric, Though it be lawfull to have wafer bread. *c* **1890** M. CREIGHTON in *Life & Lett.* (1904) II. 57 The use of wafer bread is undesirable and should be discontinued. **1898** *Allbutt's Syst. Med.* V. 992 Chloralamide..may be given in doses of 20 to 50 grains in *wafer cachet. **1609** C. BUTLER *Fem. Mon.* (1634) 17 Certain Thieves having stolen the Silver Box wherein the *Wafer-Gods use to lie. *a* **1743** SAVAGE *Epist. to Walpole* 79 Lo! the priest's hand the wafergod supplies. **1857** PUSEY *Real Presence* iii. (1869) 330 People have profanely spoken of 'wafer-gods'. They might as well have spoken of 'fire-gods', of the manifestation of God in the flaming fire in the bush. **1459** *Paston Lett.* I. 490 Item, ij. payre *wafer irens. **1551** *Will T. Fletcher, Glastonb.*, Oon whafer yron. **1725** *Bradley's Family Dict.* s.v. *Wafer*, The Wafer-Iron is to be heated and rubb'd on both sides..with fresh Butter. **1879** MISS BRADDON *Vixen* III. 302 Coaxing her to eat a *waferlike slice of bread-and-butter. **1906** 'A. HOPE' *Sophy of Kravonia* I. v. 56 Of course the mention of the waferlike mark puts her identity beyond question. **1911** J. WARD *Roman Era Brit.* xii. 220 Wafer-like bone discs..are also of common occurrence. **1530** PALSGR. 286/1 *Wafyrmaker, *gaufrier.* **1694** MOTTEUX *Rabelais* v. *Pantagr. Prognost.* v. 235 Clergy-Taylors, Wafer-makers, Rosary-makers. **1852** BRANDE *Dict. Sci.* etc. Suppl., Wafers are coloured with various materials... The wafer makers are very unwilling to show the process. **1769** MRS. RAFFALD *Engl. Housekpr.* (1778) 165 To make *Wafer Pancakes. **1718** MRS. EALES *Receipts* 70 Then lay 'em in Lumps on *Wafer-Paper, and set 'em on Papers in an Oven. **1773** G. A. STEVENS *Trip to Portsmouth* ii. 17 That ever any school-fellow of mine should play truant from old port, and good roast beef, to live upon whey, and wafer-paper! **1860** R. FOWLER *Med. Vocab.*, *Wafer-paper*, an article of confectionery, now employed for the exhibition of nauseous electuaries, &c. **1889** R. WELLS *Bread & Biscuit Baker* 46 Cover the tins or wires with wafer paper, and lay out the biscuits. **1814** *Gastronomy* (1822) 149 The pastry-bakers, cake-makers, and *wafer-rollers. **1635** *Patent Office* No. 82, Licencing..him and his deputies for the sole makeing of the *wafer seales and he wilbe bound to sell one hundred of them for a penny. **1728** FIELDING *Love in several Masques* III. iii. 33 'Tis but *Wafer-sealed. I'll open it and read it. **1844** DICKENS *Mart. Chuz.* xxxix, He took up the *wafer-stamp, and began stamping capital F's all over his legs. *a* **1911** D. G. PHILLIPS *Susan Lenox* (1917) I. xxi. 371 *Wafer-thin. **1958** *Times* 15 Nov. 11/6 There is dried meat of the Valais cut in wafer-thin slices. **1976** *Times* 1 June 1/1 Pitmen in north Derbyshire are understood to have voted by a wafer-thin majority against continuing wage restraint. **1984** B. FRANCIS *AA Car Duffer's Guide* 63/2 The radiator is made up of a collection of very narrow tubes linked by wafer-thin strips of metal which are exposed to the air-flow. **1763** *Ochtertyre House Bk.* (S.H.S.) 250, 1 pair *weffer tongs. **1769** [see 1]. **1883** R. HALDANE *Workshop Rec.* Ser. II. 156/1 Make the wafer-tongs hot over the hole of a stove or clear fire. **1832** *Boston Herald* 29 May 4/4 The error arose from our letter being *wafer-torn where the figures were written. **1620** QUARLES *Feast for Worms* Introd. B 2 b, Thy *Wafer-walles at dread Iehouahs blast Shall quake. **1607** BEAUMONT *Woman-Hater* II. i, 'Twas no set meeting certainly; for there was no *wafer-woman with her these three days on my knowledge. **1623** FLETCHER, etc. *Maid in Mill* I. iii, Am I not able..to deliver A Letter handsomly! Is that such a hard thing? Why every wafer-woman will undertake it. **1789** CHARLOTTE SMITH *Ethelinde* (1814) II. 169 Miss Ludford's ingenious productions in shell-work, in *wafer-work, in filigree and coloured paper. **1817** MAR. EDGEWORTH *Harrington* vi, She sat at some fashionable kind of work—wafer work, I think it was called, a work which has been long since consigned to the mice.

wafer (ˈweɪfə(r)), *v.* [f. WAFER *sb.*] *trans.* To fasten with a wafer. Also with *on*, *up*.

1748 RICHARDSON *Clarissa* (1811) V. 243 Wafer'd on, as an after-written introduction to the paragraphs which follow. **1775** MME. D'ARBLAY *Early Diary* 4 Mar., My father.. wafered the paragraph upon a sheet of paper, and sent it to his lodgings. **1822** BP. RYDER in Mrs. Crane *Rec. Life W. H. Havergal* (1882) 34, I enclose..a letter which you may read and then wafer or seal. **1835** DICKENS *Sk. Boz*, *Private Theatres*, Such are the written placards wafered up in the gentlemen's dressing-room. **1848** THACKERAY *Roundabout Ride* Wks. 1898 VI. 588 Cards of lodgings wafered into the rickety bow-windows. **1861** SALA *Dutch Pict.* xiii. 202 [He] had wafered the page of the book containing his lesson against the doctor's desk. **1874** SPURGEON *Treas. David* xci. 9, 10, IV. 235 My curiosity led me to read a paper which was wafered up in a shoemaker's window.

† **wafer-cake.** *Obs.*

1. = WAFER *sb.* 1.

1585 HIGINS *Junius' Nomencl.* 84/2 *Crustulum*,..a wafer cake. **1593** *George a Greene* (1599) D 1, You shall haue wafer cakes your fill.

b. *fig.* as a type of fragility.

1599 SHAKS. *Hen. V*, II. iii. 53 Trust none: for Oathes are Strawes, mens faiths are Wafer-Cakes.

2. = WAFER *sb.* 2. Chiefly in hostile use.

c **1560** tr. *Latimer* in Strype *Eccl. Mem.* (1721) III. II. 90 The Papistes..wolde conteyne the natural Body which Christe had (Synne excepted) ageynst all Truthe, into a Wafer Cake. **1584** in Foley *Rec. Eng. Prov. S.J.* (1880) VI. 715 A super-altar, a pyx, a box of wafer cakes. **1594** HOOKER *Eccl. Pol.* IV. vi. §1 The vse of wafer-cakes, the custome of godfathers & godmothers in baptisme, are things not commanded nor forbidden in the scripture. **1630** R. JOHNSON *Kingd. & Commw.* 476 Hee must..conge to the ground with his head, as Priests doe to their Wafer-cakes.

wafered (ˈweɪfəd), *ppl. a.* [f. WAFER *v.* and *sb.* + -ED¹.]

1. Sealed, fastened, or attached with a wafer or wafers.

1829 SCOTT *Jrnl.* 17 Apr., Free from wafered letters,.. notes of hand wanted, and all the worry of an embarrassed man's life. **1859** SALA *Tw. round Clock* (1861) 261 'All the ladies of the ballet at ten.'.. So may run the wafered announcements signed in the fine Roman hand of the.. stage-manager.

2. Of bread: Made into wafers (see WAFER *sb.*²). Also (*nonce-use*), touched by the sacramental wafer.

1837 GEN. P. THOMPSON *Exerc.* (1842) IV. 286 Our ancestors, who saw peril in wafers and in wafered lips. **1889** *Pall Mall Gaz.* 20 Aug. 6/3 The..parishioners..conplained of the following practices:—Using water with wine, using wafered unleavened bread [etc.].

ˈwaferer, *sb. Obs.* exc. *Hist.* Also 5 **waferare, -ere,** 4–7 **wafrer, waffrer.** [a. AF. *wafrer*, f. *wafre* WAFER *sb.* Cf. AL. *waferarius.*] A maker or seller of wafers or thin cakes.

The itinerant wafer-sellers of both sexes had the repute of being ready to act as intermediaries in amatory intrigues. Cf. WAFER-*woman*, WAFRESTRE. In royal and other great households there were one or more 'waferers', whose duties probably included the making of confectionery in general.

1362 LANGL. *P. Pl.* A. VI. 120 'I-wis,' quaþ a waferer, 'wust I þis for soþe, Schulde I neuere forþere a fote for no freres prechinge'. **1393** *Ibid.* C. XVI. 199 Mynstralcie can ich nat muche, bote make men murye, As a waffrer with waffres. *c* **1380** WYCLIF *Wks.* (1880) 12 ȝif þei [the religious] ben made wafreris, ȝeuynge lordes, ladies and riche men a fewe peris, appelis or nottis to haue huge ȝiftis to þe couent, euyl þei coueiten here neȝeboris goodis. *c* **1386** CHAUCER *Pard. T.* 151 Syngeres with harpes, Baudes, wafereres. *a* **1483** *Liber Niger* in *Househ. Ord.* (1790) 72 Offyce of Wafere[r]s, hathe one yoman making wafyrs. *c* **1515** *Cocke Lorell's B.* 9 Yermongers, py-bakers, and waferers. **1514** BARCLAY *Cyt. & Uplondyshm.* (Percy Soc.) 2 Fyrste was he hosteler, and than a wafrer. **1679–88** *Moneys Secr. Serv. Chas. II & Jas. II* (Camden) 107 To William Clopton, in lieu of all fees claimed by him as waferer to his said Majestie on the day of the coronation 30 0 0. **1861** *Our Engl. Home* 70 The brilliancy of a mediaeval feast was chiefly due to the ingenuity of the waferers, or confectioners.

So †**ˈwafrestre** [*-estre*, -STER], a female waferer.

1377 LANGL. *P. Pl.* B. v. 641 'Wite god,' quod a wafrestre [*A text* waferere], 'wist I þis for sothe, Shulde I neuere ferthere a fote, for no freres prechynge.'

waferish (ˈweɪfərɪʃ), *a.* [f. WAFER *sb.* + -ISH.] Like a wafer, very thin.

1866 HOWELLS *Venet. Life* xx. 330 A thin waferish slice of toasted rusk.

†**ˈwafern**, *a. Obs.* [f. WAFER *sb.* + -EN.] Of bread: Having the composition of wafers.

1570 in Gutch *Collect. Cur.* (1781) II. 4 For iiij doz. of waferne bread, for the bottomes of the marche paynes.

wafery (ˈweɪfərɪ), *sb.* Also 5 **waaffery**, 6 **wafrie, waferye, waffrey, wafarie,** 7 **wayfary.** [a. AF. *wafrie*, f. *wafre* WAFER *sb.*]

1. A room or building in which wafers or thin cakes are made; the department of the royal household occupied with the making of wafers. Also †*wafery-house*.

1455 *Househ. Hen. VI* in *Househ. Ord.* (1790) *22 The waaffery—William Overton, Yoman, [etc.]. **1553** in *Archæologia* XII. 362 The Waferye. Adam Alee, yeoman. *a* **1558** in Gutch *Collect. Cur.* (1781) II. 1 Item, flore for the pastre, and wafery, and seller, as nedithe. *a* **1562** G. CAVENDISH *Wolsey* (1893) 24 In the chaundrye, iii persons: in the wafery, ii. **1688** HOLME *Armoury* III. 43/2 Officers and Servants in the Kings Majesties Houshold... The Waffrey-House. Yeoman,..Groom,..[etc.]. *Ibid.* IV. xii. (Roxb.) 499/2 Then followed the Groomes of..The Wafery. **1826** HOR. SMITH *Tor Hill* (1838) II. 271 Not unless you come to him from the wafery, the pantry, the cellerage..or the larder. **1830** NICOLAS in *Priv. Purse Exp. Eliz. York* 229/1 The Wafery..still is one of the offices of the royal household.

†**2.** Wafers collectively, light pastry. *Obs.*

1542 UDALL *Erasm. Apoph.* 170 b, He..bidde theim to kepe a corner of their stomakes for the tartes, wafrie, and iounkettes, that wer to bee serued..after the meate.

ˈwafery, *a. rare.* [f. WAFER *sb.* + -Y.] Like a wafer, extremely thin.

1880 J. P. STRUTHERS *Life & Lett.* v. (1918) 97 A very thin wafery idea. **1891** *Century Dict.* s.v., A wafery thinness.

waff (waf), *sb. Sc.* and *north.* Also 7 **vaiffe, waffe,** 9 **wauf**(f. [f. WAFF *v.*¹ Cf. WAFT *sb.*, WEFF, WAIF *sb.*², WAVE *sb.*²]

1. A waving movement; esp. waving of the hand or something held in the hand: cf. WAFT *sb.* 5, 6.

1678 *Rec. Justiciary Edin.* 13 Sept. in H. Arnot *Hist. Edin.* (1779) 194 *note*, The devil..baptised you upon the face, with an waff of his hand like a dewing. **1712** W. ROGERS *Voy.* (1718) 296 With orders, if they saw 3 sail in the offing, to make 3 waffs with their colours. **1831** J. WILSON *Noct. Ambr.* Wks. 1856 III. 177 Beggars..that wadna understand the repulse..o' a waff o' the haun to be awa wi' theirsels. **1847** HALLIWELL, *Waff*, the movement of a large flame from side to side. **1876** *Whitby Gloss.*, *Waff*, a wave of the hand. The kind of flag or signal used at sea for assistance to the ship from the shore. **1886** 'H. HALIBURTON' *Horace in Homespun* (1900) 93 Wi' ae waff o' my wings I soar A mile abune the city's roar. **1887** P. M'NEILL *Blawearie* 89 These ..youths..first extinguishing his light. This one of them did by a smart 'waff' of his bonnet.

b. *to put out* or *set forth a waff*: to wave something as a signal. Cf. WAFT *sb.*¹ 6 b, WAIF *sb.*² 2.

1600 in Earl Cromarty *Acc. Conspir. Earls Gowry & R. Logan* (1713) 105 And when you are about Half a Mile from Shoar, as it were passing by the House, to gar set forth a Waff. **1685** J. B[ARCLAY] tr. *A. Skene's Surv. Aberd.* 215 And as soon as ye come to the Road, ye can allwayes have a Boat for putting out a Vaiffe at all occasions, for Piloting you into the Harbour.

2. A puff, passing gust, sudden blast (of wind or air). *lit.* and *fig.*

1686 R. FLEMING *Fulfilling Script.* II. ii. (1726) 268 A waffe as it were of the glorious God doth go by to the discerning of others. **1727** P. WALKER *Life R. Cameron, Biogr. Presbyt.* (1827) 294 [He] got a Waff of that murthering East-wind in the 1679. **1818** SCOTT *Hrt. Midl.* xxxix, This increase of profit at Saint Leonard's Crags may be a cauld waff of wind blawing from the frozen land of earthly self. **1822** GALT *Sir A. Wylie* II. xvii. 162 We maun gie something to the young woman and the bairns, that we may get a waff o' their good will likewise. **1836** *Scott. Mag.* July 208 It was not the Highland strength turn'd them that day, But the waff o' the broad-swords that blew them away. **1897** *Northumbld. Gloss.* s.v., 'The waff o' the train'—the rush of air caused by a passing train.

b. A whiff (of perfume), an odour. Cf. WEFF.

1819 W. TENNANT *Papistry Storm'd* (1827) 29 A canny waff o' sweet perfume Was blawn in breezes throu' the room. **1887** SERVICE *Life Dr. Duguid* III. ii. 245 The waff of the wild roses..cam in stoons of sweetness alang the air.

3. A slight blow, esp. one given by something in passing.

a **1754** E. ERSKINE *Serm. Abraham rejoicing* Wks. 1791 II. 536 A very little waff of any thing will do it [*sc.* the eye] hurt. **1808** JAMIESON, *Waff*, 3. A slight stroke from any soft body, especially in passing.

b. A slight attack or 'touch' (of illness, esp. of cold).

1808 JAMIESON, *Waff* 4. A sudden affection, producing a bodily ailment. Thus..it is said that one has *gotten a waff* or *waif of cauld*. **1821** GALT *Steam Boat* vii, I found myself in a very disjasked state..with a waff of cold that had come upon me.

4. A passing view, a glimpse.

1818 SCOTT *Hrt. Midl.* li, I sought every glen and cleuch ..but teil a wauff of his coat-tail could I see. **1819** TENNANT *Papistry Storm'd* (1827) 28 That the bauld-bosom'd clerk mith get A waff o' his face ere aff he set. **1887** SERVICE *Life Dr. Duguid* III. i. 242 It is but seldom,—only at meal times, and aften no' then,—that we get a waff of him ava.

5. An apparition, wraith. = WAFT *sb.*¹ 7.

1777 BRAND *Pop. Antiq.* 99 There is a similar Superstition among the Vulgar in Northumberland: They call it seeing the Waff of the Person whose Death it foretells. **1815** *Dangerous Secr.* II. 163 Your honour forgets I fand my dear maister mysel, an' saw him laid in the cauld grave. It's been his waff. **1884** BESANT *Dorothy Forster* xiii, There is the wauf, or figure of the person about to die seen by another person.

waff (waf), *a. Sc.* Also **waf, wauf.** [var. of WAIF *a.*]

1. Of an animal: Wandering, stray. Also of a person: 'Solitary'; said 'of one who is in a strange place where he has not a single acquaintance' (Jam. 1808).

1720 RAMSAY *Patie & Roger* 127 She..then bade me hound my Dog To weer up three waff Ews were on the Bog. **1776** *Herd's Coll. Sc. Songs* II. Gloss., *Waff*, wandering by itself.

2. Of a person, condition of life: Of no account, worthless.

1788 PICKEN *Poems Scot. Dial.* 248 Gloss., *Waff*, little worth. **1808** JAMIESON, *Waff, Waif, Wayf*, adj... 3. Worthless. *A waff fellow*, one whose conduct is immoral; or whose character is so bad, that those, who regard their own, will not associate with him. **1815** SCOTT *Guy M.* xxxix, Is not it an odd-like thing that ilka wauf carle in the country has a son and heir, and that the house of Ellangowan is without male succession? **1837** LOCKHART *Scott* II. viii. 306, 'I dinna think there's a waufer (shabbier) thing in the world than to be a lassie, to sit boring at a clout'. *a* **1884** J. RUSSELL *Remin. Yarrow* i. (1894) 7 A wauf hand [*i.e.* a bad preacher].

b. Comb.: **waff-like** *a.*, shabby-looking; having a suspicious or disreputable appearance; feeble, of little account.

1808 JAMIESON, *Waff-like*, one [*sic*] who has a very shabby or suspicious appearance. **1823** GALT *R. Gilhaize* lxxix. III. 180 Though the folk afore the house are but a wee waff-like. **1882** J. WALKER *Jaunt to Auld Reekie* 46 A coat o' rusty black The wauflike wretch has on his back. **1893** STEVENSON *Catriona* xxiii, I came upon a lane of lighted houses, the doors and windows thronged with wauf-like painted women.

waff (waf), *v.*¹ Chiefly *north.* Also 5–7 **waffe,** 9 *Sc.* **whaff.** [var. of WAIVE *v.*² or of WAVE *v.*, with onomatopœic modification. Cf. WAFT *v.*²]

†**1.** *trans.* To put *away* with a wave of the hand. *Obs.*

c **1440** *York Myst.* xxxi. 248 *ii Dux...* Youre fauchone hym flaies... *Rex.* Nowe lely I leue þe, And therfore schall y waffe it away.

†**2.** *intr.* To blow (as the wind). *Obs.*

c **1440** *York Myst.* xii. 54 Þir wise wordis ware noght wroght in waste, To waffe and wende away als wynde.

3. *trans.* Of the wind: To cause (something) to move to and fro.

1513 DOUGLAS *Æneis* I. vi. 26 (1553) 16 b, Venus..With wind waffing [*v.r.* waving] hir haris lowsit of trace. *Ibid.* VI. viii. 113 Quhidder waffit vilsum by storm of the se, Or at command of goddis, come thow, quod he?

b. *intr.* To wave to and fro; to flutter in the wind; also *trans.* of a bird, to move (the wings) in flight.

1834 J. WILSON *Noct. Ambr.* Wks. 1856 IV. 97 Rover begins snokin and twinin himsel in a serpentine style,..wi' his fanlike tail whaffin. **1856** J. BALLANTINE *Poems* 59 The rags waffin' round her wad wauken ruth In a mair stieve-breasted chield than me. **1861** R. QUINN *Heather Lintie* (1863) 72 Aff they set on tiptae flicht, Waffin' their wee bit wings wi' micht.

4. *intr.* To produce a current of air by waving something to and fro. Also *trans.*, to direct a current of air against, to fan.

1688 HOLME *Armoury* III. 91/1 [Among goldsmiths and jewellers] Waffing is clearing the Stones from Dust with a Pencill. *a* **1878** H. AINSLIE *Pilgr. Land of Burns* (1892) 190 Waffing her wan face wi' a claith. **1886** J. BARROWMAN *Sc. Mining Terms* 69 To *Waff*, or *Waft*, to fan out. Fire-damp was formerly expelled from the working rooms by *waffing*.

†**waff**, *v.*² *Obs.* [Alteration of WAFT *v.*¹]

1. *trans.* To convey by sea; = WAFT *v.*¹ 2.

1602 WARNER *Alb. Eng.* III. xviii. 84 He waffes an Armie out of France, and Voada pursues. *Ibid.* Epit. 374 He imbarked for Normandie to waffe them into England. **1655** TERRY *Voy. E. India* v. 137 Those huge Vessels [Junks] are ..made exceeding big, on purpose to waff passengers forward and backward.

2. *intr.* To sail. Also *trans.* To sail (the seas).

1611 SPEED *Hist. Gt. Brit.* VI. i. §3. 183 Volusenus returned, hauing waffed vpon the coasts of Britaine so far, as with safety he might. *Ibid.* VII. xxxviii. §6. 364 His nauie waffing along those seas. *Ibid.* VII. xlii. §6. 370 His Nauie roiall..he diuided into three parts, appointing euery of them to a seuerall quarter to waffe the Seas.

waff (waf), *v.*³ Now *dial.* In 7, 8 **waugh.** [Echoic.] *intr.* Of a dog, esp. of a puppy: To yelp.

1610 HOLLAND *Camden's Brit.* II. Irel. 188 Women too throughout the same County barked like big dogges: but the children and little ones waughed as small whelpes. **1787** GROSE *Provinc. Gloss.*, *Waughing*, barking. Probably from the sound. N. **1886** *S.W. Linc. Gloss.*, *Waff*, or *waffle*, to bark, yelp. A dog ran waffing out. **1894** *Northumbld. Gloss.* s.v., A dog 'woughs', but a puppy waffs.

‖**Waffen SS** (ˈvafən ɛsɛs). [ad. G. *Waffen-SS*, in full *Waffen-Schutzstaffel* armed defence squadron: see SCHUTZSTAFFEL and *S.S.* s.v. S 4 a.] In Nazi Germany during the war of 1939–45: the combat units of the S.S.

1943 *Rev. Foreign Press* (F.O. Research Dept.) 18 Oct. 125/1 By a law of the 22nd July, Laval..authorised French citizens to join those units of the Waffen S.S. fighting on the Eastern Front. **1949** 'R. WEST' *Meaning of Treason* I. vii. 164 He wanted to join the Waffen S.S. and fight the Russians. **1957** *Times Lit. Suppl.* 20 Dec. 771/2 A nucleus of the 'commandoes', but also with parachutists, Waffen S.S. **1966** G. STEIN *Waffen SS* p. xxx, At the beginning of World War II the term Waffen SS was unknown. Five years later, prefaced by such adjectives as elite and fanatical, it appeared regularly in Allied war communiqués. By 1940 *Waffen SS* had become the official designation for the combat units of the SS, which had grown from the handful of armed troops maintained by the Reichsführer SS, Heinrich Himmler, for security and ceremonial purposes. *Ibid.* p. xxxi, By 1943, the exigencies of war had forced the Waffen SS to give up some of its exclusiveness. Large numbers of foreigners were recruited or conscripted. **1972** F. FORSYTH *Odessa File* ii. 28 He carried the twin-lightning strikes of the Waffen SS on the right collar lapel.

†**waffer.** *Mining. Sc. Obs.* In 6 **vaffer.** App. an engineering work of some kind; ? a fan (cf. WAFF *v.*¹ 4).

1592 in R. W. Cochran-Patrick *Early Rec. Mining Scot.* (1878) 80 It is noch possible to men to myn cast sinkes vaffers big myls quha never saw ony siclyk.

waffet, obs. form of WAFT *v.*

waffie (ˈwafɪ). *Sc.* Also **waufie.** [f. WAFF *a.* + -IE.] A worthless person, a vagabond.

1808 JAMIESON, *Waffie*, a vagabond. **1818** *Blackw. Mag.* Feb. 524/2 Gypsies have actually among themselves outcasts and vagabonds..by them termed *waffies*. **1896** 'IAN MACLAREN' *Kate Carnegie* xxi. 353 A' the waufies in the countryside come here.

waffinger, var. WAVENGER.

waffle (ˈwɒf(ə)l), *sb.*¹ *U.S.* [a. Du. *wafel*: see WAFER *sb.*] **a.** A kind of batter-cake, baked in a waffle-iron, and eaten hot with butter or molasses.

1744, 1794 [see sense b]. **1809** A. BURR *Jrnl.* 26 Aug. (1903) I. 214 Everywhere, too, you get *wafen*; our wafles, and made and eaten in the same way. **1817** M. BIRKBECK *Notes Journ. Amer.* (1818) 64 Waffles (a soft hot cake of German extraction, covered with butter). **1870** D. MACRAE *Amer. at Home* I. 291 The Americans are all fond of molasses; using them regularly at breakfast and supper to their buckwheat cakes and waffles. **1893** T. N. PAGE *In Ole Virginia* 221 He ordered waffles and hoe-cakes for breakfast.

b. Comb., as *waffle frolic*, *party*; **waffle-iron**, an iron utensil for baking waffles over a fire; **waffle stomper** *U.S. slang*, a boot or shoe with a heavy, ridged sole.

1744 in *Mag. Amer. Hist.* (1878) II. 442 For my own part I was not a little grieved that so luxurious a feast should come under the name of a wafel frolic. **1794** *S. Carolina State Gaz.* 30 Aug. 1/2 (Advt.), Waffle irons. **1808** in *Scribner's Mag.* (1887) II. 183/1 They are going to have a fine *waffle* party on Tuesday. **1882** *Harper's Mag.* Apr. 666/1 She tells him of 'little waffle parties' formed by her intimates. **1888** E. EGGLESTON *Graysons* xxxi. 334 She took down the long-handled waffle-irons. **1899** *Academy* 11 Feb. 183/1 Toasting-forks and waffle-irons had long handles, to make endurable the blazing heat of the great logs. **1974** *Sunday* (Charleston, S. Carolina) 7 Apr. 10-c/8 'Waffle stompers', should anybody be wondering, are hiking shoes.

c. *Textiles.* Used *attrib.* of a style of fine honeycomb weaving (see HONEYCOMB *sb.* 5b). Also applied to the fabric woven and to the effect produced.

[**1948** *Sears, Roebuck Catal.* Fall-Winter 45/2 Cotton Chenille Spread. Sturdy white cotton sheeting tufted with fluffy chenille in regular, even waffle pattern.] **1949** *Good Housek.* Apr. 261/2 Waffle piqué is characterized by a honeycomb weave; it is not a true piqué. **1951** in M. McLuhan *Mech. Bride* (1967) 74 We had it copied faithfully for you in the..white Birdseye waffle pique. **1953** *Sun* (Baltimore) 7 Mar. (B ed.) 3/4 Part of the secret lay in the 'waffle-weave', a..technique which required special machinery... It produces a cloth that looks like a waffle, or a honeycomb. **1961** *Sunday Express* 28 May 14/2 (*caption*) Tops in waffle-knit cotton. **1962** W. SCHIRRA in *Into Orbit* 49 A series of waffle-weave patches on our long john underwear helps to keep the oxygen moving. **1975** G. HOWELL *In Vogue* 242/2 (*caption*) Elements of the mid-fifties—the 'sloppy Joe',..the waffle cotton shorts. **1979** *Men's Wear* 3 May 24 Texture returns with fine seersuckers and waffle cloth.

'waffle, *sb.*² Also **woffle.** [f. the verb.]

1. *dial.* 'The bark of a small dog' (*Eng. Dial. Dict.*).

2. a. *Printers' slang.* 'Twaddle, gossip, or "jaw"' (Jacobi *Printers' Vocab.* 1888). **b.** In *gen.* colloq. use, verbose but inconsequential talk or writing; empty verbiage (see also quot. 1937).

[**1866** J. E. BROGDEN *Provinc. Words Lincs.* 219 *Waffle-bags*, a great talker.] **1937** PARTRIDGE *Dict. Slang* 935/1 *Waffle*, nonsense; gossip(ing); incessant or copious talk. **1953** *Times Lit. Suppl.* 13 Mar. 164/1 A little technical detail and a good deal of emotional waffle. **1957** *Economist* 21 Dec. 1041/2 His ability to distinguish the essence and to cut the waffle in any discussion are exceptional. **1961** C. S. LEWIS *Let.* 9 May (1966) 298 For a good..defence of our position against modern woffle... I know nothing better than G. K. Chesterton's *The Everlasting Man.* **1965** *Spectator* 22 Jan. 96/1 There is a special relationship between Britain and the United States, a special relationship more serious than the waffle we get at banquets. **1973** C. BONINGTON *Next Horizon* i. 20 Cut out the waffle, and let's see your application.

'waffle, *v.* Also **whaffle, woffle, wuffle.** [Freq. of WAFF *v.*³] **1.** *intr.* To yelp. Now *dial.*

1698 *Christ Exalted* §xcv. 77 His branding all that dissent from the Writings of Mr. Williams to be Whaffling Whelps, that can bark and not bite. **1821** CLARE *Vill. Minstr.* II. 23 Waffling curs and shepherd-dogs pursue.

2. a. To waver; to vacillate or equivocate; to 'dither'. orig. *Sc.* and *north. dial.* Now *colloq.* or non-Standard.

1803, etc. [see WAFFLER 1]. **1868** [see WAFFLING *ppl. a.*]. **1893–4** R. O. HESLOP *Northumberland Words* II. 762 *Waffle*, to waft about, to waver, to walk hesitatingly, to act with indecision. **1898** B. KIRKBY *Lakeland Words* 152 Thoo'l waffle aboot an' say owt. **1943** *Horizon* Apr. 234 While I was still waffling I read 'The Mint'. **1961** C. H. D. TODD *Popular Whippet* 51 Have we an ideal or are we just 'waffling around' following this, that and the other. **1976** *Telegraph-Jrnl.* (St. John, New Brunswick) 4 Sept. 17/1 She defends the board against suggestions that it waffled on the issue because of political pressure.

b. To talk (or write) in a verbose but inconsequential manner; to ramble *on*. Also *trans.* with direct speech as obj.

[**1701** J. WHITE *Countryman's Conductor* 128 *Waffling*, all speakers and no hearers.] **1900** FARMER *Public School Word-Bk.* 216 Waffle,..(Durham) to talk nonsense. **1936** R. LEHMANN *Weather in Streets* I. v. 83 Nanny would wuffle on, and make me change my stockings. **1937** G. HEYER *They found him Dead* iv. 83 He woffled a whole lot to me about people bothering his life out. **1949** J. B. PRIESTLEY *Delight* 15 The wise men woffled on about violence and crime, missing the point by miles. **1957** G. SMITH *Friends* 60 'Funny thing is, it seems to improve my game,' waffled Bill amiably. **1960** L. MEYNELL *Bandaberry* i. 8, I under-estimated his shrewdness... I thought he was waffling. **1982** P. DICKINSON *Last House-Party* ii. 22 You can make the correct noises while all the old buffers are woffling on.

Hence **'waffling** *ppl. a.*, and *vbl. sb.*

1698, 1821 [see sense 1]. **1847** J. HALLIDAY *Rustic Bard* 145 'Tis you I punch at, worthless, waffling crood. **1868** J. C. ATKINSON *Gloss. Cleveland Dial.* 554 A windy, *waffling* soort o' chap, wheea nivver kens his ain mind. **1945** J. REITH *Diary* 11 Apr. (1975) vii. 346 A typical silly, waffling letter which Cranborne had written. **1958** J. CANNAN *And be Villain* v. 118 His sharp harsh tones were a joy to hear after the wafflings of the soft voiced Highlander. **1967** *New Yorker* 8 July 67 There will be..a large majority for a waffling resolution..calling for Israel to withdraw from the conquered territories but not passing judgement on the original conquests. **1973** J. WAINWRIGHT *Touch of Malice* 231 Waffling, thoughtless stupidity. **1976** *Sunday Mail* (Brisbane) 23 May 44/6 They should not be regarded as the wafflings of people sounding off in the papers.

waffler ('wɒflə(r)). [f. WAFFLE *v.* + -ER¹.]

1. An unreliable person; an idler or waverer. Chiefly *Sc.* and *north dial.*

1803 R. ANDERSON *Ballads in Cumberland Dial.* (1805) 59 Saint Gworge, the girt champion, o' fame and renown, Was nobbet a waffler to Matthew Macree. **1819** in Carlyle *Early Lett.* (1886) I. 215 The waffler did not get his cart home till Monday. **1927** N. DUNDAS *Castle Adamant* iv. 60 Of course there are wafflers, ye could look or no less in a town of five thousand souls. **1977** B. LANGLEY *Death Stalk* ii. 15 He had an instinctive distrust of all wafflers and ditherers.

2. One who indulges in waffling talk or writing. Cf. WAFFLE *sb.*² 2.

1959 *Viewpoint* July 4 It was a field day for the professional analysts and wafflers. **1968** *Sunday Truth* (Brisbane) 8 Dec. 41 It amazes me that Peter Evans was ever selected to conduct 4QR's Breakfast Show. He must be the original waffler.

waffly ('wɒflı), *a.* [f. WAFFLE *sb.*² and *v.* + -Y¹.] **a.** Wavering, vacillating, imprecise. **b.** Characterized by or indulging in waffling speech or writing.

1890 J. SERVICE *Thir Notandums* xix. 125 Let the waffly body tak ocht I hae written and mak a kirk or a mill o't as pleases himsel'. **1928** A. E. PEASE *Dict. Dial. N. Riding* 149 *Waffly*,..wavering, undecided, shaky, not coherent. **1957** *Economist* 23 Nov. 673/2 The Labour party's attitude to the federation has always been waffly. **1964** *Ibid.* 16 May 691/2 Mr. Duncan Sandys could never be called a waffly man. **1978** *Times* 18 Nov. 11/8, I thought the first part about the World Tree and the Green Man a little thin and waffly.

†**waffore.** *Obs.*⁻¹ ? A drone.

1436 *Libel Eng. Policy* in *Pol. Poems* (Rolls) II. 174 They ..souketh the thryfte awey oute of oure honde, As the waffore [*v.r.* waspe] soukethe the honye fro the bee.

wafrestre: see under WAFERER.

wafrie: see WAFERY.

†**'wafron.** *Obs.* Also 5 **wafrun,** 6 **waffron,** 5–6 **wafroun** (*Sc.* **vafrown**). [a. AF. **wafron*, augm. of *wafre* WAFER *sb.*] = WAFER *sb.* 1.

? *c* **1390** *Form of Cury* (1780) 8 Take obleys other wafrouns in stede of loseyns, and cowche in dyshes. *c* **1420** *Liber Cocorum* (1862) 22 Take obles and wafrons. *c* **1475** *Pict. Voc.* in Wr.-Wülcker 789/1 *Hec nebula, Hec gafra*, a wafrun. **1486** *Engl. Misc.* (Surtees) 57 And y' schall it snaw by craft to be made of waffrons in maner of snaw. **1496** *Acc. Ld. High Treas. Scot.* I. 323 Item,..giffin to a man that brocht wafrounis to the King, ix s. **1572** J. JONES *Bathes Buckstone* 9b, And into diuers formes these graines may be reduced,.. some betwene yrons, as wafrons.

attrib. **1512** *Acc. Ld. High Treas. Scot.* IV. 358 Item, to Disart wafrone sellar, xiiij s. **1538–9** *Ibid.* VII. 140 Item, deliverit to Murdo Striveling, patesser, to by foure vafrown irnis to the quenis grace, vj li.

Hence †**'wafroner** = WAFERER.

1457–8 *Mem. Fountains* (Surtees) III. 59 Ro^to Waf.roner, vj *d.*

waft (wɑːft, -æ-), *sb.*¹ Also β. (senses 1, 5–6), 6–7, 9 *Sc., dial.* and *Naut.* **weft,** (7 **wefte, waift),** 9 **wheft, whift.** [Probably two or more formations: in part certainly a noun of action f. WAFT *v.*¹ and *v.*²; but sense 1 is recorded more than a century earlier than any sense of the verb that could give rise to it; and the β forms of the sb., which do not occur in the verb, seem to indicate a different origin. Cf. WAFF *sb.*, WEFF; also Sw. *vifta*, Da. *vifte*, fan, Sw. *vifta*, Da. *vifte* to fan, Norw. *veift* puff of wind.]

1. a. A taste or flavour, esp. an ill taste, a 'twang'. Now *dial.* Cf. WEFF.

α. **1608** MIDDLETON *Mad World* IV. iii. F 4b, A strumpets loue will haue a waft i' th end, and distast the vessell: I can hardly beare this. **1866** BROGDEN *Provinc. Lincolnsh.*, *Waft*, a disagreeable flavour.

β. **1542** BOORDE *Dyetary* x. (1870) 256 Ale..muste not be ropy nor smoky, nor it must haue no weft nor tayle. **1854** MISS BAKER *Northampt. Gloss.*, *Weft*, a musty taste, generally applied to beer or wine that tastes of the cask. 'The beer has a weft of the barrel.'

fig. **1627** S. WARD *Serm. & Treat.*, *Coal from Altar* 17 Spices and wefts of these evils may be found in the sincerest Christians.

b. A scent or odour passing through the air or carried on the breeze. = WAFF *sb.* 2b, WEFF.

α. **1611** COTGR., *Odeur*, an odor, sent, smell, waft. *Puant*, ..that hath an ill waft, or smell. **1675** EVELYN *Terra* (1776) 70 Aloes and other Sedums..send forth their aromatic Wafts at considerable distance. *a* **1693** *Urquhart's Rabelais* III. xxxii. 273 It is not a sensitive discerning or perception in it of the difference of Wafts and Smells. **1886** *Cheshire Gloss.* s.v., Sitch a waft o' stinkin fish. **1889** AMELIA E. BARR *Feet of Clay* ii. 37 The salt savour..was crossed by a waft of hayfields.

β. **1626** BACON *Sylva* §833 The Strongest Sort of Smells are best in a weft, a farre off. **1640** SHIRLEY *Arcadia* III. ii. E 3b, If this be gold 'tis liquid and yet too thicke to be potable as they say, it has a kinde of weft me thinks if I have not lost a sence upon the sudden, I smell.

2. A current or rush of air, a breath of wind; a blast; the 'wind' of a projectile.

1643 MRS. THORNTON *Autobiog.* (Surtees) 33 A cannon bullett flew soe nigh the place where I stood that..the wafte tooke my breath from me for that present. **1649** G. DANIEL *Trinarch., Hen. IV*, cccv, Chaine-Bulletts of his will Run through all Streets, and in the Waft, they kill. **1650** D. HOTHAM tr. *C. Hotham's Introd. Teut. Philos.* To Author A 3b, Me thought the reading of him was like the standing ..by a Canon shot off, the waft of them lickt up all my brains. **1863** W. THORNBURY *True as Steel* II. 66 A waft of air scattered them [the ashes] apart for ever. **1867** JEAN INGELOW *Gladys* 603 The air was full of voices, and the scent Of mountain blossom loaded all its wafts. **1884** SLADEN *Poetry of Exiles* 55 Reading sweet verse or inhaling a waft of the harbour breeze.

b. *fig.*

1607 WALKINGTON *Opt. Glass* 166 Riot's a barke in th' mindes vnconstant maine, Tost too and fro with wafts of appetite. **1658** G. FOX *Jrnl.* (1852) I. 345, I saw and felt a waft of death go forth against him. **1822** GALT *Sir A. Wylie* II. xxxvi. 321 If I get a favourable waft o' your good will, I can bide a wee for an answer. **1873** GOSSE *On Viol & Flute* 59 Out of grieving at a present blight, Come sweeter wafts of garnered memory. **1880** SHORTHOUSE *John Inglesant* xxxvi, A waft of peace and calm, like a breeze from paradise, fell upon Malvolti's heart.

c. A sound carried by the breeze. Also (*nonce-use*), a transitory gleam (of light).

1697 VANBRUGH *Æsop* v. 67 D'ye hear, Trumpets? When the Bride appears, Salute her with a Melancholy Waft. 'Twill suit her humour. **1845** BAILEY *Festus* 214 Sudden and soft, too, like a waft of light, The beautiful immortals come to me. *a* **1894** STEVENSON *Heathercat* iii. Lay Morals, etc. (1911) 319 The voice of the preacher came to him in wafts, at the wind's will, as by the opening and shutting of a door.

d. A puff (of smoke or vapour).

1896 JANE BARLOW *Mrs. Martin's Comp.* 8 'Twas just the one way wid her as wid the waft of smoke there up in her ould chimney that went fluttherin' out on the width of the air, and sorra another breath anywheres nigh it. **1897** BLACKMORE *Dariel* xii, Clusters of stars..and loose wafts of vapour ever ready to flout them.

3. An act of wafting or carrying off as the wind does.

1727–46 THOMSON *Winter* 271 Oft the whirlwind's wing Sweeps up the burden of whole wintry plains In one wide waft.

4. An act of transporting or carrying over water; a passage across the sea. ? *Obs.*

1654 GAYTON *Pleas. Notes* III. vi. 106 They came to a Bury, which was at that time overflown with water, there Jany and Jocky stood gaping..untill a Traveller passing that way, profer'd the courtesie of a waft successively to them both. **1657** DAVENANT *1st Day's Entertainm. Rutland Ho.* 72 [He] with his long pole gives us a tedious waft, as if he were all the while poching for Eels. **1786** BURNS *Twa Dogs* 156 Or may be in a frolic daft, To Hague or Calais takes a waft.

5. An act of waving (the wings or something held in the hand); a waving movement.

α. **1652** S. PATRICK *Funeral Serm. J. Smith* in *Smith's Sel. Disc.* (1660) 495 He was all in a desire, as if the Angels that fetcht his Father, had lent him a waft of their wings, whereby he strove to fly with him to Heaven. **1865** TENNYSON *Captain* 72 And the lonely seabird crosses With one waft of the wing.

β. **1709** J. JOHNSON *Clergym. Vade M.* II. 103 The *orarium* was a sort of scarf... The use the Deacon had for it..was to give notice to the people and clerks what they were to do or say, by the several wefts or motions that he made with it.

6. *Naut.* A flag (or some substitute) hoisted as a signal; the act of displaying such a signal. (See quot. 1867.) Cf. WAFF *sb.* 1b.

α. **1644** MANWAYRING *Sea-Mans Dict.* s.v., Also wafts are used for signes to have the boate come a-boord (which is Coate, Gowne or the like, hung-up in the shrowdes) also it is a common signe of some extremetie, when a ship doth hang a waft upon the maine-stay, either that it hath sprung a-leake, or is in some distresse. **1719** DE FOE *Crusoe* II. (Globe) 328 We immediately spread our Antient to let them know we saw them, and hung a Waft out as a Signal for them to come on board. **1744** J. PHILIPS *Jrnl. Exped. Anson* 125 This Day the Gloucester made us a Signal by a waft of her Ensign. **1769** FALCONER *Dict. Marine* (1780), *Waft*, a signal displayed from the stern of a ship..by hoisting the ensign, furled up together into a long roll, to the head of it's staff. **1854** G. B. RICHARDSON *Univ. Code* v. (ed. 12) 6394 Hoist a waft.

β. **1613** J. SARIS *Voy. Japan* (Hakl. Soc.) 49 We had sight of a wefte ashoare. **1697** *Admiralty Exam.* (MS.) Bundle 81 fol. 171 A weft hung out for her company to come on board. **1798** COLERIDGE *Anc. Mariner* II. i, The Sun came up upon the right..; And broad as a weft, upon the left, Went down into the Sea. **1836** MARRYAT *Midsh. Easy* xxiii, I have been looking for an English ensign to hoist over the French, but cannot find one; so I will hoist a wheft over it,—that will do. **1840** F. D. BENNETT *Whaling Voy.* I. 266 The wrecked boat ..with two whifts flying as a signal of distress. **1867** SMYTH *Sailor's Word-bk.*, *Waft*, more correctly written *wheft.* It is a flag or ensign, stopped together at the head and middle portions, slightly rolled up lengthwise, and hoisted at different positions at the after-part of a ship. **1894** C. N. ROBINSON *Brit. Fleet* 96 A signal of distress..is accentuated by making it into a 'weft,' which is done by knotting it in the middle.

b. ***to make a waft***; to hang out a flag (or substitute) as a signal.

α. **1673** *Lond. Gaz.* No. 819/4 Being driven near the Shore, they made a waft, and thereupon a Fisherboat went off. **1712** E. COOKE *Voy. S. Sea* 3 He is to make a Waft with his Jack or Ensign. *Ibid.* 455 We made a Waift. **1719** DE FOE *Crusoe* I. (Globe) 264 We..saw her make a Waft with her Antient, as a Signal for the Boat to come on Board.

β. **1653** in J. S. Corbett *Fighting Instr.* (1905) 99 Upon the discovery of a fleet, receiving a sign from the general, which is to be..making a weft, two frigates..are to make sail. **1820** SCOTT *Abbot* xxix, There have already been made two wefts from the warder's turret, to intimate that those in the castle are impatient for your return.

7. An apparition, wraith. Cf. WAFF *sb.* 5.

1897 *Longm. Mag.* July 252 I'm bound to die afore t' year is out... I seed my own waft (wraith) go into the kirk last St. Mark's Eve, and it never cam' out no more.

†**waft,** *sb.*² *Obs.* [? var. WEFT *sb.*] (See quot.)

1688 HOLME *Armoury* III. 99/1 Waft, or Finger Bread [= braid], are kind of Purse strings woven on the Fingers either round or broad.

waft (wɑːft, wæft, wɒft), *v.*[1] Pa. t. and pa. pple. **wafted.** Also 6 ? **waffet, wafftt,** 6–7 **wafte** (7 *pa. pple.* **waft**). [Back-formation from WAFTER.]

†**1.** *trans.* To convoy (a ship or fleet of ships, persons sailing). *Obs.*

1513 W. GONSON in *Lett. & Papers War France* (1897) 130 A letter..in the wyche he comaundyth me thatt..I shall conducte and wafftt hys vytellars to hys grett army in the water of Brest. I..made hys Grace answer..I wolld go my sellfe in the smallist of the 3 Spanyards sentt fforthe wit me ..and leffe John Ysame and Rychiard Barkeley in the other 2 Spanyiarde shyps to wafftt over the Zeland fleett. **1513** ECHYNGHAM *Ibid.* 150 Sir Weston Brown..hath yeven me and Harper in commaundment for to go to Hampton for to wafte the vytlers unto theym. *a* **1548** HALL *Chron., Hen. IV*, 26 Because certain pyrates..were lurkyng at the Temmes mouthe..Thomas Lord Camois with certaine shippes of warre was appointed to wafte over the kyng. **1580** R. HITCHCOCK *Politique Platt* ciiij, That two of her graces Shippes of warre, suche as yeerely be appointed to wafte the Marchants maie contineue vpon her Maiesties Seas..for two yeares: for the defence of these fishing Shippes. **1622** in *Buccleuch MSS.* (Hist. MSS. Comm.) I. 210 Don Faderique de Toledo, who is gone to waft the West India fleet homeward. **1644** MANWAYRING *Sea-Mans Dict.* s.v., To waft, is to guard any ship, or fleete at sea. **1670** J. SMITH *Eng. Improv. Reviv'd* 270 The Fishermen agreed amongst themselves to pay a Dollar upon every last of Herrings, towards the maintenance of certain Ships of Warr, to Waft and secure them in their Fishing.

†**b.** *transf.* To guide or direct the course of (a vessel, a swimmer, a floating object, etc.). *Obs.*

1591 SYLVESTER *Du Bartas* I. v. 360 A little Fish, that swimming still before, Directs him [the Whale]..: Much like a Childe that loving leads about His aged Father when his eyes be out: Still wafting him through every way so right.

2. To convey safely by water; to carry *over* or *across* a river, sea, etc. *Obs.* exc. *poet.*

1593 SHAKS. *2 Hen. VI*, IV. i. 114, I go of Message from the Queene to France: I charge thee waft me safely crosse the Channell. **1593** —— *3 Hen. VI*, III. iii. 253. *Ibid.* v. vii. 41 Away with her, and waft her hence to France. **1618** J. TAYLOR (Water P.) *Penniless Pilgr.* E 2, And as by water I was wafted in, I thought that I in Charons Boate had bin. **1628** BOYLE in *Lismore Papers* (1886) II. 262 We all landed safely..and the next morning I dischardged Capⁿ Jones.. who I hired to wafte me over. **1639** *Act* in *Arch. Maryland* (1883) I. 78 No person..other then the owner of the said ferry boat..shall waft or passe any person over the said River. **1697** DRYDEN *Virg. Georg.* IV. 731 Nor wou'd th' Infernal Ferry-Man once more Be brib'd, to waft him to the farther shore. **1768** *Ann. Reg., Hist. Eur.* 32 Great bodies of the Asiatic troops were continually wafted over to the European side of the Hellespont. **1789** *Massachusetts Spy* 9 Apr. 3/2 An elegant barge is building to waft the great Washington across the Hudson. **1817** MOORE *Lalla Rookh, Fire-worshippers* I. 450 Again she sees his pinnace fly, Wafting him fleetly to his home. **1850** TENNYSON *In Mem.* ix. 4 Fair ship,..Spread thy full wings, and waft him o'er.

fig. **1616** B. JONSON *Ev. Man in Hum.* Prol., Plays..Where neither *Chorus* wafts you ore the seas; Nor creaking throne comes downe, the boyes to please. **1670** MILTON *Hist. Eng.* I. 5 That fond invention that wafted hither the fifty daughters of a strange Dioclesian King of Syria.

refl. **1653** HOLCROFT *Procopius* Pref. A 2 b, He could gain no footing in Italy, but in all that time was forced to waft himself by stealth from one Port-town to another. **1677** W. HUBBARD *Narrative* 27 They, taking the advantage of a low tide, either waded over..or else wafted themselves over upon small Rafts of timber.

b. Of the sea or waves: To carry, transport. *Obs.* exc. *poet.*

1613 DAY *Festivals* v. (1615) 129 Now the Red-Sea of Baptisme..hath conveyed us, and waft us over. **1671** MILTON *P.R.* I. 104 A calmer voyage now Will waft me. **1742** POPE *Dunc.* IV. 310 Where, eas'd of Fleets, the Adriatic main Wafts the smooth Eunuch and enamour'd swain. **1742** YOUNG *Nt. Th.* I. 153 A soul immortal..Thrown into tumult..At aught this scene can threaten..Resembles ocean into tempest wrought, To waft a feather, or to drown a fly. **1878** B. TAYLOR *Deukalion* II. iii. 69 The waves of earth are wafting to and fro The ashes of great lives.

†**c.** *intr.* To sail *about, off, to and fro, up and down*; to cross *over* by water. *Obs.*

a **1562** G. CAVENDISH *Wolsey* (Kelmscott Press) 150 Ther was no lesse than a thousand botts..waffetyng uppe and down in Temmes, expectyng my lord's departyng. **1577–87** HOLINSHED *Chron.* III. 1187/1 Maister William Winter.. made Saile towards Scotland, and wafting along the coast in Januarie came into the Forth. **1579** GOSSON *Sch. Abuse* Ep. Ded., He had not played long in the Sea, wafting too and fro, at his pleasure, but he returned agayne, stroke sayle, [etc.]. **1618** BOLTON *Florus* IV. viii. (1636) 305 And now his Navie wafted up and down in the middle of the Sea. **1631** ANCHORAN *Comenius' Gate Tongues* 92 Where there is no foord or shallow place they passe, or waft ouer with a wherrie or ferrie boat. **1632** J. HAYWARD tr. *Biondi's Eromena* 89 When all these of the Fleete were returned.. fifteene of them wafted off towards Porto di Torre. **1648** GAGE *West Ind.* xxi. 190 We as prisoners were wafting up and down the sea with them. *Ibid.* 200 We that day wafted about for a good wind. **1667** MILTON *P.L.* II. 1042 Satan.. Wafts on the calmer wave by dubious light And like a weather-beaten Vessel holds Gladly the Port. **1700** DRYDEN *Ovid's Met.* I. 432 High on the summit of this dubious Cliff, Deucalion wafting, moor'd his little Skiff. **1774** BEATTIE *Minstrel* II. xlix, He braves The surge and tempest,..And to a happier land wafts merrily away! **1814** CAPT. SCOBELL *Jrnl. of the 'Thais'* in *Tuckey's Narr. Exped. R. Zaire* (1818) Introd. p. xiii, I met several floating islands..which.. wafting to the motion of the sea, rushed far into the ocean.

†**3.** *trans.* To buoy *up*. *Obs. rare.*

1646 SIR T. BROWNE *Pseud. Ep.* IV. vii. 196 Some alledge that spirits are light substances, and naturally ascending do elevate and waft the body upward. **1650** *Ibid.* IV. vi. (1658) 247 Whether Cripples and mutilated persons..who have lost the greatest part of their thighs, will not sink but float, their lungs being abler to waft up their bodies.

4. Of the wind: To propel (a vessel) or convey (a navigator or passenger) safely.

Originally a mere contextual use of sense 2. The frequency of examples in which the verb denotes the action of the wind gave rise in the 18th c. to the notion that the essential meaning of the verb had reference to this agency, and to the identification of the word with the etymologically distinct WAFT *v.*[2] The older sense 2, so far as it survives, is coloured by association with this sense.

a **1707** PRIOR *Song, 'In vain you tell'* 2 In vain you tell your parting Lover You wish fair Winds may waft Him over. **1713** DERHAM *Phys.-Theol.* 18 The Sea, and the Land-Breezes; the one serving to carry the Mariner in long Voyages from East to West; the other serving to waft him to particular Places. **1773** HAWKESW. *Cook's 1st Voy.* III. iii. III. 555 The gale that afterwards wafted us to the shore, would then certainly have beaten us to pieces. **1816** J. WILSON *City of Plague* I. ii. 70 While favouring breezes waft his blessed ship Far from the Plague. **1819** HEBER *Hymn, 'From Greenland's Icy Mountains'* iv, Waft, waft, ye winds, His story. **1842** TENNYSON *'You ask me, why'* 25 Yet waft me from the harbour-mouth, Wild wind!

fig. **1653** JER. TAYLOR *Serm.* I. viii. 98 The sighs of their feares, and the wind of their prayers waft them safely to their port. **1884** *Daily News* 26 May 5/1 The Conservatism of the present is waiting for a wind?.. Will it waft and bear to enterprise and rough seas and daring adventure? **1885** R. BUCHANAN *Annan Water* iii, What wind of utter despair had wafted her to that place of all places.

5. To carry (something) through the air or through space. **a.** with sound, scent, infection, etc. as object: said of the wind. Also with *away, by, round.*

1704 POPE *Pastorals, Summer* 80 Your praise the birds shall chant in ev'ry grove, And winds shall waft it to the pow'rs above. **1781** COWPER *Heroism* 35 The self-same gale that wafts the fragrance round Brings to the distant ear a sullen sound. **1803** *Med. Jrnl.* X. 136 Assuredly, then, this affection [influenza] has been rather wafted on us, than communicated to us in the way of personal intercourse. **1811** SHELLEY *St. Irvyne* I. ii. 4 And low, chilling murmurs, the blast wafted by. **1855** TENNYSON *Maud* I. xxii. 1 And the woodbine spices are wafted abroad. **1887** BOWEN *Æneid* I. 417 Where sweet scents are wafted from garlands ever in bloom.

b. with material object.

1726 SHELVOCKE *Voy. round World* 425 Nitrous and sulphureous particles..are wafted in the air by diverse winds. **1784** COWPER *Task* III. 540 And ev'n the breathing air Wafts the rich prize [pollen] to its appointed use. **1817** J. EVANS *Excurs. Windsor* 457 Our Table Cloth..was in the act of being wafted overboard. **1836** DICKENS *Sk. Boz, Vauxhall-Gardens*, The balloons were wafted gently away. **1878** HUXLEY *Physiogr.* 192 Dense showers of such dust have been wafted by winds for even hundreds of miles.

c. To send (a sound, fragrance, etc.) through the air; to 'blow' (a kiss).

1728 POPE *Dunc.* II. 265 Thames wafts it [the sound] thence to Rufus' roaring hall And Hungerford re-echoes bawl for bawl. **1815** BYRON *Hebr. Mel., 'The harp the monarch'* 12 It [the harp] told the triumphs of our King, It wafted glory to our God. **1837** DICKENS *Pickw.* xi, And many a kiss did Mr. Snodgrass waft in the air, in acknowledgment of something very like a lady's handkerchief. **1855** B'NESS BUNSEN in Hare *Life* (1879) II. iv. 181 At the year's beginning and end, one is peculiarly moved to..waft wishes and kind thoughts to many a far-removed locality. **1871** J. R. MACDUFF *Mem. Patmos* v. 62 This Tree with its perennial fruits, wafting immortal fragrance and distilling immortal balm.

d. To carry in flight: said chiefly of angels.

a **1718** PRIOR *Danistonus' Ad Amicos Imit.* 12 Glad I release it from it's Partner's Cares; And bid good Angels waft it to the Stars. **1791** COWPER *Iliad* v. 925 Swift as her pinions waft the dove away. **1816** J. WILSON *City of Plague* III. ii, O Heaven protect my faithful Isabel, And waft her safe, as on an angel's wing, To that sweet lake. **1817** MOORE *Lalla Rookh, Fire-worshippers* I. 261 Oft..I've wish'd that little isle had wings, And we, within its fairy bow'rs, Were wafted off to seas unknown. **1845** E. FITZBALL *Maritana* II. Aria, Oh! that angels now might waft him To the mansions of the blest!

e. *fig.* To transport instantaneously, as by magic or in imagination.

1781 COWPER *Conversat.* 592 Hopes of heav'n, bright prospects of an hour, That come to waft us out of sorrow's pow'r. **1820** W. IRVING *Sketch Bk.* I. 4 With what longing eyes would I gaze after their lessening sails, and waft myself in imagination to the ends of the earth.

6. *intr.* To pass through the air or through space; to float upon, come or go with the wind or breeze.

1664 POWER *Exp. Philos.* I. 3 Small hairs..which (by blowing upon) you might see waft to and fro. **1676** DRYDEN *Aurengz.* III. i, Those Trumpets his triumphant Entry tell. And now the Shouts waft near the Cittadel. **1690** —— *Amphitryon* II. i, There is an ill savour that offends my Nostrils; and it wafteth this way. **1717** POPE *Eloisa to Abel.* 214 Tears that delight, and sighs that waft to heav'n. **1802** MARIAN MOORE *Lascelles* II. 9, I recognized his charming voice in the delightful strains which wafted on my ear. **1890** *Daily News* 7 July 6/2 Great green boxes [of roses] were being opened with very perceptible whiffs of perfume wafting from them.

†**b.** Of a bird, winged insect: To pass by flying. *Obs.*

1682 N. O. *Boileau's Lutrin* III. 24 Then wafting at one Reach, they proudly Pearch On highest Pinnacle of the fatal Church! **1712–14** POPE *Rape of Lock* II. 60 Some to the sun their insect-wings unfold, Waft on the breeze, or sink in clouds of gold.

c. Of the breeze: To blow softly.

1804 *Something Odd* II. 26 In vain..did the soft breezes of an approaching summer waft around him. **1849** CUPPLES *Green Hand* xvii. (1856) 176 There wasn't a breath of air yet, either, save what seemed now and then to waft out of the thick woods.

7. *trans.* To move, drive, or carry *away* (something) by producing a current of air.

1839 URE *Dict. Arts* 636 A sort of winnowing machine, which wafts away the finer and lighter parts. **1844** KINGLAKE *Eothen* xviii, It seems to you that it is not the donkey, but the donkey-boy who wafts you along with his shouts.

†**waft,** *v.*[2] *Obs.* [App. an alteration of WAFF *v.*[1], perh. due to the pa. t. or pa. pple. *waft.*]

1. *trans.* To wave (the hand or something held in the hand), esp. as a signal.

1604 E. G[RIMSTONE] *D'Acosta's Hist. Ind.* VII. xvi. 540 They were accustomed in their elections to make great feasts and dances, where they wafted many lightes. **1636** HEYWOOD *Loves Mistr.* I. i, Shee now hath climb'd the Rock, And wafts her hand.

absol. *a* **1648** *Ess. Death* in *Bacon's Remaines* 10 These wait upon the shore of death, and waft unto him to draw neer.

b. To signal to (a person, etc.) by waving the hand or something held in the hand. Also, of a flag.

1578 G. BEST in *Hakluyt's Voy.* (1600) III. 63 We espied certaine of the countrey people..with a flag wafting vs backe againe. **1590** SHAKS. *Com. Err.* II. ii. 111 But soft, who wafts vs yonder. **1592** KYD *Sol. & Pers.* I. iii. 116 Hee that will try me, let him waft me with his arme. **1606** CHAPMAN *Gentl. Usher* I. ii. 177 Till you can directly boord him, Waft him aloofe with hats and other favours. **1607** SHAKS. *Timon* I. i. 70 One do I personate of Lord Timons frame, Whom Fortune with her Iuory hand wafts to her. **1608** MIDDLETON *Mad World* III. iii. F 1, The hayre about the hat is as good as a flag vppo' th pole at a common Playhouse to waft company. **1645** STAPYLTON tr. *Musæus* A 4 b, The Tow'r where Sestian Hero lay, And held the Torch, wafting Leander o're. **1670** NARBOROUGH *Jrnl.* in *Acc. Sev. Late Voy.* I. (1694) 49 They saw seven people..making a noise and wafting them to the ship. *a* **1719** GARTH *Ovid's Met.* XIV. Wks. (1790) 134 At length a sail I wafted, and aboard My fortune found an hospitable lord.

c. To move (something) *aside* with a wave of the hand.

1781 COWPER *Hope* 570 Now, truth, perform thine office; waft aside The curtain drawn by prejudice and pride.

2. To turn (the eyes) aside with a disdainful movement. *nonce-use.*

1611 SHAKS. *Wint. T.* I. ii. 372 When hee Wafting his eyes to th' contrary, and falling A Lippe of much contempt, speedes from me.

3. *intr.* To move to and fro, to wave. *Obs.*

1650 JER. TAYLOR *Funeral Serm. C'tess Carbery* 4 The face of the waters wafting in a storm, so wrinkles it self, that it makes upon its forehead furrows.

waftage (ˈwɑːftɪdʒ, ˈwæf-, ˈwɒf-). Also 6 **waiftage.** [f. WAFT *v.*[1] + -AGE.]

I. The action of wafting.

†**1.** The action of convoying merchant-vessels.

1558 Q. ELIZ. in Burgon *Gresham* (1839) I. iii. 197 To advertise the Admirall..that order might be taken for his waftage over with the treasure. **1563** GRESHAM *ibid.* II. 42 Sir Thomas Cotton seant the barck of Bollen with me, for my better waiftage. **1563–4** *Admiralty Exam.* (MS.) Bundle 98, 13 Mar., ij frenche men of warr who then had in their company and under ther waftage ij Flemishe hoyes. **1622** R. HAWKINS *Voy. S. Sea* lviii. 132 Hee had beene many yeares Generall of the south Sea, for the carriage and waftage of the silver from Lyma to Panama.

2. Conveyance across water by ship or boat.

1590 SHAKS. *Com. Err.* IV. i. 95 *An.* What ship of Epidamium staies for me. *S. Dro.* A ship you sent me too, to hier waftage. **1606** G. W[OODCOCK] *Hist. Ivstine* XXII. 84 Agathocles in the same ships that he had waftage ouer out of Sicil, was transported into Syracuse. **1627** DRAYTON *Agincourt* 13 The Ships appointed wherein they should goe, And Boats prepar'd for waftage to and fro. **1655** FULLER *Hist. Cambr.* 3 The Ferrie over the river Grant was a vagrant before (even any where, where passengers could get waftage over). **1673** H. STUBBE *Further Vind. Dutch War* App. 132 There was paid..300000 l. in one year: besides the Tenth fish and Cask, paid for Waftage.

b. Conveyance over the Styx.

Very common in 16–17 c. poetry and drama.

1592 S. DANIEL *Delia, Rosamond* ii. H. 3 Caron denies me waftage with the rest. **1606** SHAKS. *Troylus* III. ii. 11. **1639** G. DANIEL *Vervicensis* 24 Wks. (Grosart) I. 128 The infernall Foorde; Where happie Soules get waftage, with a Worde. **1834** *Fraser's Mag.* X. 26 The crazy bark of old Charon, only fitted for the light waftage of ghosts.

c. *transf.* and *fig.*

1615 CROOKE *Body of Man* VI. vi. 356 The *Pleura*..giueth also to the vessels a safe waftage and a kinde of stability. **1615** T. ADAMS *Spir. Navigator* 9 Praising God..for their safe waftage over the sea of this world. **1662** GURNALL *Chr. in Arm.* III. verse 17. v. §2. 36 Afflictions..are as necessary for our waftage to glory, as water is to carry the Ship to her Port. **1698** FRYER *Acc. E. India & P.* 69 Is this the Elysium after a tedious Waftage?

3. Passage through the air or through space.

a **1658** CLEVELAND *Let.* Wks. (1687) 119 As if their Travel (like Witches in the Air) were nothing but the Waftage of a deluded Phantasie. *a* **1700** KEN *Edmund* Poet. Wks. 1721 II. 132 A Chariot for his Waftage was decreed, With long-wing'd Horses of Cœlestial Breed. **1834** J. WILSON in *Blackw. Mag.* XXXV. 775 Forest flies, ephemerals all like ourselves—but happier far in their airy waftage or watery voyaging, than the vain race of man! **1885** BRIDGES *Eros & Psyche* May ii, The solitary rock where she was left; And thence in dark and airy waftage reft, How on the flowers she had been disburden'd light.

4. The action or power of propulsion which the wind or breeze has; also, conveyance by such propulsion.

1651 SHERBURNE *Salmacis* 327 She..Sent him by the light waftage of the Wind, A sigh, an Ah Mee, Nuncios of her

Mind. **1673** *Phil. Trans.* VIII. 5194 In their [the snow flakes'] continual motion and waftage to and fro touching upon each other. **1861** *Fraser's Mag.* Dec. 758 Then there comes fitfully on the feeble waftage of the awakening night-breeze an uncertain wail of music. **1880** L. Wallace *Ben-Hur* iv. v, Let us give ourselves to waftage of the winds.

II. A means of wafting.

†5. Vessels for the conveyance of merchandise or passengers by water. *Obs.*

1650 T. B[ayley] *Worcester's Apoph.* 107 Passes granted unto him, both by Land and Sea, with carts by Land, and waftage by Sea. **1659** Harrington *Art Lawgiving* iii. iv. 106 For these [men] the Commonwealth in her Sea-guard hath always at hand sufficient waftage.

†6. A means of conveyance through the air. *Obs.*

1636 W. Strode *Floating Isl.* iii. iii, Nothing to carry me but Barges, Coaches? Sedans, and Litters? through the Aire I'd passe By some new waftage.

wafte, pa. t. of waive *v.*^{2} *Obs.*

wafted ('wɑːftɪd, 'wæf-, 'wɒf-), *ppl. a.* [f. waft *v.*^{1} + -ed^1.] Carried or driven by the wind.

1784 Cowper *Task* vi. 68, I again perceive The soothing influence of the wafted strains. **1860** Tyndall *Glac.* i. xxiii. 166, I could see the wafted snow gradually melt away.

†**'wafter**, *sb.*^{1} *Obs.* Also 5 **waughter**, 6 **waghter**, 7 *Sc.* **waughtar**, **-er**. [App. a. Du. or LG. *wachter*, lit. guard, f. *wachten* to guard; but the specific use has not been found in Du. or LG.]

1. An armed vessel employed as a convoy.

1484 in *Lett. & Papers Ric. III & Hen. VII* (Rolls) II. 287 We understande that certain of you entende hastely to departe towardes Island, not purveied of waughters for your suertie. *Ibid.*, That ye gadre and assemble your selff..and..departe alle togider toward Humbre, to attende there upon our shippes of Hull as your waughters, for the suretie of you all. **1524** Wolsey in *St. Papers Hen. VIII*, IV. 89 It appereth that 7 prises and oone wafter of the Island flete be lately taken by 2 shippes of Lethe. **1524** —— *ibid.* VI. 276 Considring what tract of tyme it shalbe, bifore waghters may be put in redynes and sent from hens for your conduytyng. *a* **1548** Hall *Chron., Hen. VIII*, 212 b, Commaundement was geuen to the Haberdashers..that they should prepare a barge..with a wafter and a foyst garnished with banners. *c* **1595** Capt. Wyatt *R. Dudley's Voy. W. Ind.* (Hakl. Soc.) 58 Shee was a man of war and a wafter either to theire Byskin fleet of fishermen for Newfoundlande or bounde to meet theire Indian fleet now comminge home. **1622** R. Whitbourne *Newfoundland* 53 These ships thus sent to guard their [*sc.* the Hollanders'] Fleets, which are called Wafters, doe continually breede many fit seruiceable Seamen. **1623** *Melros Papers* (Abbotsf. Club) II. 489 The lyke charge being execute aganis the captaines of the waughtaris at Abirdeene. **1670** J. Smith *Eng. Improv. Reviv'd* iii. 257 There were about 20 Wafters, as they call'd them, which were Ships carrying about 30 Guns a piece, being the Convoys of the Fleet of Busses.

2. The commander of a convoying vessel.

1482 *Pat. Roll 22 Edw. IV* m. 2 (1802) 326 Certi conductores sive waftores [*printed* wastores] piscatorum Reg' in partibus Norff' et Suff'. **1513** T. Howard in *Lett. & Papers War France* (1897) 163, I shall..send all the vitellers there forth to Hampton warde and with them Antony Poynes, Wisman and Draper for wafters. **1599** Hakluyt *Voy.* II. i. 75 The reuerend lord great master..sent vessels called brigantines, for to cause the wafters of the sea to come into Rhodes for the keeping and fortifying of the towne. *Ibid.* 76 The lord master seeing that the Turkes hoste drew neere, and that he had the most part of the wafters within the towne, he caused generall musters of men of armes to be made. **1622** R. Hawkins *Voy. S. Sea* iv. 9 The Vice-admirall, and other Wafters [*printed* Wasters] that should be the Shepheards to guard and keepe their flocke,..were..the Men who made most hast to flie from the Wolfe.

wafter ('wɑːftə(r), 'wæf-, 'wɒf-), *sb.*^{2} [f. waft *v.*^{1} + -er^1.] One who wafts.

1619 Fletcher *Mad Lover* iv. i. Song, Charon o Charon Thou wafter of the soules to blisse or bane.

†**'wafter**, *v.*^{1} *Obs. rare.* In 5 **waftyr**. [f. the root of wave *v.* Perh. immediately f. a sb. *wafter, formed with suffix as in *laughter*. Cf. wafture.] *intr.* To wave.

c **1450** *Mirk's Festial* 273 When þe bestys þat droghen þe cart seen hys mantell waftyr wyth þe wynde.

†**'wafter**, *v.*^{2} *Obs. rare*$^{-1}$. [f. wafter *sb.*^{1}] *trans.* To convoy (a vessel): = waft *v.*^{1} 1.

1615-6 *Privy Council Reg.* 7 Feb. (MS.), The eastern counties petitioned 'for two of H.M. small shippes to wafter and defend them from the said pirattes'.

wafter: see wafture.

[**wafter**, error for waster foil, singlestick.

The error originated with Meyrick *Ant. Armour* (1824) II. 144. The word occurs in a quot. of 1455; it was not a mere misprint, for Meyrick attempts an etymological explanation from the verb *waft*. Hence in recent Dicts.]

wafting ('wɑːftɪŋ, 'wæf-, 'wɒf-), *vbl. sb.* [-ing^1.]

1. The action of waft *v.*^{1}; esp. †the action of convoying or of transporting by sea (*obs.*).

1559 Gresham in Burgon *Life* (1839) I. 263 [He recommends that Queen Elizabeth should send] three or four of her best ships of war that are out, for the sure waifting of this munition and armour. **1577** Harrison *England* ii. xiii. 87 b/1 in *Holinshed*, [He] employed them [*sc.* his ships] whollye to the waftyng in and out of our marchauntes. **1651** Jer. Taylor *Holy Dying* iii. §4 (1676) 74 So I have seen the rays of the Sun or Moon dash upon a brazen vessel..; but being turned back and sent off with its smooth pretences or rougher waftings, it wandred about the room. **1667** Milton *P.L.* xii. 435 A death like sleep, A gentle wafting to immortal Life.

2. Something wafted or carried by the wind.

1878 Susan Phillips *On Seaboard* 178 And the wild north winds of the winter's day Bring keen fresh waftings from the far-off seas.

'wafting, *ppl. a.* [-ing^2.] That wafts.

1869 Jean Ingelow *Tired* x, She spread her wafting wings, The ship—and weighed her anchor to depart. **1895** Meredith *Amazing Marr.* xxxiii, The countess was not so much a persuasive lady as she was, in her breath and gaze, a sweeping and a wafting power.

wafture ('wɑːftjʊə(r), 'wæf-, 'wɒf-). In 7 **wafter**. [f. waft *v.*^{2} and *v.*^{1} + -ure. Cf. *clefture*, *raisure*; with the spelling *wafter* cf. *jointer* for *jointure*.

It seems most probable that Rowe was right in regarding *wafter* in the former edd. of Shaks. *Jul. C.* as intended for *wafture*. There is, however, a possibility that *wafter* is a word of Shakspere's native dialect, related to wafter *vb.* to wave (Myrc *a* 1450). Since the publication of Rowe's ed. of Shaks., *wafture*, of which no earlier examples are known, has been somewhat common in literary use.]

1. a. The action or an act of waving (the hand or something held in the hand).

1601 Shaks. *Jul. C.* ii. i. 246 You answer'd not, but with an angry wafter [*ed. Rowe* 1709 *and later edd.* wafture] of your hand, Gaue signe to me to leaue you. **1742** Young *Nt. Th.* ii. 545 Caught by the wafture of a golden lure. **1782** Eliz. Blower *Geo. Bateman* I. 52 'Go!' cried she, with an indignant wafture of her hand. **1875** G. Macdonald *Malcolm* II. v. 73 A few mysterious waftures of the hand of his lord set him trembling.

b. The waving (of a wing or wings).

1790 H. Boyd *Shepherds of Lebanon* i. Poetical Reg. (1812) VII. 127 The northern Eagle rous'd, and shook his plumes Tremendous: at the wafture of his wings The clouds disperst. **1845** F. W. Faber *Rosary*, etc. 62 With a murmuring, Soft as the wafture of a stockdove's wing. **1878** C. Stanford *Symb. Christ* viii. 222 Light as the wafture of an insect's wing, that motion might have been.

c. The waving or undulation (of a garment).

1880 A. Smith *Summer in Skye* 209 How we would..note the wafture of your garments!

2. The action of wafting (waft *v.*^{1}); propulsion by air or current.

1755 J. Hervey *Theron & Aspasio* xii. II. 204 Where the Wafture [of the blood] is to be speedy, the Channels either forbear to wind in their Course, or to lessen in their Dimensions. **1821** Lamb *Elia* Ser. i. *Witches*, The gentle Thames, which landed me, in the wafture of a placid wave or two,..somewhere at the foot of Lambeth palace. **1842** Sir H. Taylor *Edwin the Fair* iii. i, The wind..Descended with a wafture and a swoop.

3. Something wafted or carried by the breeze.

1817 *Blackw. Mag.* I. 72 What waftures of incense are filling the air! **1837** *New Monthly Mag.* LI. 197 Gratification seemed to breathe in every wafture of the new-mown fragrance.

wafty ('wɑːftɪ, 'wæf-, 'wɒf-), *a.* [f. waft *sb.*^{1} and *v.*^{1} + -y.]

†1. (See quot.) *Obs.*

1611 Cotgr., *Vapide*, waftie, or wafted; that sends vp an ill fume, that yeelds a stinking vapor.

2. Of the wind: That wafts a perfume.

1863 Dobell *Autumn Mood* Poet. Wks. 1875 II. 333 Oh, old old Minstrelsy, oh, wafty winds of Romaunt, Blow me your harps!

3. That wafts or moves to and fro in the wind. *nonce-use.*

1922 Joyce *Ulysses* 289 The wafty sycamore, the Lebanonian cedar, the exalted planetree.

waful(l(e, obs. forms of woeful *a.*

wag (wæg), *sb.*^{1} Also 6 **wagg(e**. [f. wag *v.*]

1. An act of wagging (the tail, hand, tongue, etc.).

1589 Lodge *Scilla's Met.* Bj, When first with [*printed* which] fingers wagge he gan to still them. **1599** B. Jonson *Cynthia's Rev.* v. iv, *Amo.* You become the simper, well, ladie. *Mer.* And the wag, better. **1823** Scott *Quentin D.* Introd., There was..more..sympathy in the wag of old Trusty's tail, than if [etc.]. **1848** Dickens *Dombey* xi, With..a scarcely perceptible wag of his head. **1870** E. H. Pember *Trag. Lesbos* iii. 68 One wag of thy fool's tongue at her or me, And by the head of Hecate, thou diest! **1885** R. Buchanan *Annan Water* viii, But recognising her, he gave a faint wag of the tail and sank down again to doze. **1891** *Field* 28 Nov. 835/1 The most silent of us are apt to let our tongues wag, or to listen complacently to the wag of others.

b. Power or disposition to wag.

1851 D. Jerrold *St. Giles* xiii. 127 The old house-dog crawled towards him, with no wag in his tail. **1881** *Century Mag.* XXIII. 932/2 [They] stroked his [the dead ass's] long ears out of which the wag had gone forever.

†2. *to hold* (a person) *wag*: to keep at bay, defy. *Obs.*

c **1540** J. Heywood *Wit & Folly* (Percy Soc.) 12, I say, nay!—and wyll so envey, That I wyll hold ye wagg a nother way. **1606** Warner *Alb. Eng.* xvi. cvii. 415 But who against that Ages Mars first Edward might hold-out? Yet twice this Lewlin held him wag.

wag (wæg), *sb.*^{2} Also 6-7 **wagg(e**. [Prob. f. wag *v.*

Possibly (as suggested by Wedgwood) a shortening of waghalter, applied playfully to a child or to a joker. But it may have originated from the verb in other ways.]

†1. A mischievous boy (often as a mother's term of endearment to a baby boy); in wider application, a youth, young man, a 'fellow', 'chap'. *Obs.*

a **1553** Udall *Royster D.* ii. iv. (Arb.) 38, I will rather haue my cote twentie times swinged, Than on the naughtie wag not to be auenged. **1573-80** Tusser *Husb.* (1878) 177 For euerie trifle leaue ianting thy nag, but rather make lackey of Jack boie thy wag. **1584** Lyly *Sappho* v. ii. 55 [Venus says to Cupid:] Vnhappy wag, what hast thou done? **1589** Greene *Menaphon* (Arb.) 27 Mothers wagge, pretie boy. Fathers sorrow, fathers ioy. **1596** Shaks. *1 Hen. IV*, i. ii. 66 But I prythee sweet Wag, shall there be Gallowes standing in England when thou art King? **1601** B. Jonson *Poetaster* iv. iii, But if Cypris once recouer The wag; it shall behoue her to looke better to him. **1607** Heywood *Fair Maid Exch.* H 4, Thou maist..Learne to entice the affable yong wagge. **1672** Marvell *Reh. Transp.* i. 87 Nor was he let down till the Master had planted a Grove of Birch in his back-side, for the Terrour..of all Waggs that divulge the Secrets of Priscian.

2. 'Any one ludicrously mischievous; a merry droll' (J.); a habitual joker. (In early use often combined with sense 1.) Phrase, ***to play the wag***.

1584 R. Scot *Discov. Witchcr.* xiii. xxiii. 324 How to rap a wag vpon the knuckles. *c* **1585** *Fair Em* i. iii. 59 The little boy hath played the wagg with you. **1591** Lyly *Endym.* iii. iii, Heere commeth two wagges. Enter Dares and Samias. **1604** Breton *Grimellos Fort.* (Grosart) 9/2 Hauing wit enough, vpon a litle warning, to plaie the wagge in the right vaine. **1612** Beaum. & Fl. *Coxcomb* v. i, *Just.* Go to, go to, you have a merry meaning, I have found you sir ifaith, you are a wag, away. **1635** *Life Long Meg of Westminster* 37 The little boy, that was a wag, thought to be merry with the miller. **1640** in *11th Rep. Hist. MSS. Comm.* App. vii. 100 Some wagg or other hath sett over the parliament doore pray remember the judges as if they had been too long forgotten. **1744** M. Bishop *Life* 156 We were daily playing the Wag, and as jocular as ever Men were all the time we stayed there. **1745** *Joe Miller's Jests* 61 The same Wagg..said, Taylors were like Woodcocks, for they got their Sustenance by their long Bills. **1779** *Mirror* No. 23 ⁋3 He took in succession the degrees of a wag, a pickle, and a lad of mettle. **1787** Mme. D'Arblay *Diary* June, Colonel Goldsworthy is the wag professed of their community. **1845** Ford *Handbk. Spain* i. 21 The inns of Spain are divided by wags into many classes—the bad, the worse, and the worst. **1849** W. Irving *Goldsmith* i. 29 One Kelley, a notorious wag. **1855** Macaulay *Hist. Eng.* xix. IV. 358 Some wag cried out, 'Burn it; burn it;' and this bad pun..was received with shouts of laughter.

3. ***to play (the) wag***: to play truant. *slang.* Also, ***to hop the wag***: see hop *v.*^{1} 6 a.

1851-61 Mayhew *Lond. Labour* III. 87 Used by school-masters for the correction of boys who neglect their tasks, or play the wag. *Ibid.* 197 They often persuaded me to 'hop the wag,' that is, play truant from school. **1889** Jerome *Three Men in Boat* xvii. 284 A boy, when he plays the wag from school. **1900** 'H. Lawson' *Over Sliprails* 154 Oh! why will you run away from home, Will, and play the wag, and steal, and get us all into such trouble?

wag (wæg), *sb.*^{3} *Archæol.* [ad. Gael. *uamhag*, dim. of *uamh* cave, hollow: cf. weem.] In Caithness, an Iron-age galleried structure set partly below ground-level (see quot. 1963).

[**1776** A. Pope in T. Pennant *Tour in Scotl. 1769* (ed. 4) 338 Figures 2 and 3 are what are styled *forest* or *hunting houses*... They consist of a gallery, with a number of small rooms on the sides..made with the vast flags [stones] this country is famous for... Their length is from fifty to sixty feet. These buildings are only in places where the great flags are plentiful. In Glen-Loch are three, and are called by the country people *Uags*.] **1911** A. O. Curle in *Proc. Soc. Antiquaries Scotl.* 11 Dec. 89 To the galleried structure the name 'wag' in former times was evidently applied and still remains in use, though now transferred from the structure to the place or site, *e.g.* 'Wag-more rig', 'Wag-burn' and 'the Wag'. **1921** *Ibid.* 10 Jan. 93 Interesting as the discovery of these post-holes is in the elucidation of the broch construction, the interest it evokes does not stop here. The arrangement at once recalls the plans of the wags or galleried dwellings in Caithness. **1963** *Field Archaeol.* (Ordnance Survey) (ed. 4) 63 In Caithness there is the local variant structure known as a wag... The dwelling part is represented by a strongly-built hut circle of ordinary plan, but to this is added an oval stone-built chamber about twice as big as the hut with its floor excavated somewhat below the general ground level. **1972** E. M. Mackie in *Dark Ages in Highlands* 16 One site at Forse..could well be a pre-broch defensive structure... This is the so-called 'wag' or 'prehistoric cattlefold' excavated by Alexander Curle.

wag (wæg), *v.* Inflected **wagged**, **wagging**. Forms: 3-7 **wagge**, 4, 6 **wage**, 6-8 **wagg**, 4- **wag**. [ME. *wagge-n*, f. root of OE. *wagian* (ME. *waȝe-n*) to oscillate, shake: see waw *v.*

The verb may be regarded as an iterative or emphatic form of *waȝian* waw *v.*, which is often nearly synonymous; it was used, e.g., of a loose tooth, and (ME.) in the proverb 4 c. Parallel formations from the same root are ON. *vagga* wk. fem., cradle (Sw. *vagga*, Du. *vugge*), (M)Sw. *vagga* to rock a cradle, early mod.G. *waggen* (mod.HG. dial. *wacken*) to waver, totter. Cf. waggle *v.*]

I. Intransitive uses.

1. To be in motion or activity; to stir, move. Now *colloq.* (chiefly in negative context), to stir, move one's limbs.

a **1225** *Ancr. R.* 374 Þis wrastlunge is ful bitter to monie þet beoð ful uorð iðe weie touward heouene; for þe ȝet fondunges..waggeð oðer hwules. *c* **1460** *Towneley Myst.* xxx. 226 Vnethes may I wag, man, for wery in youre stabill Whils I set my stag, man. *c* **1480** Henryson *Test. Cress.* 196 Ane horne he [*sc.* Mars] blew..Quhilk all this warld with weir has maid to wag. *c* **1532** Du Wes *Introd. Fr.* in *Palsgr.* 939 To brawle or to wage, *bransler*. **1582** Fetherstone *Dial. agst. Dancing* A 4 b, The wofull wayling of the widowe doeth not once make him [the rich man] wagge. **1585** —— tr. *Calvin on Acts* i. 4. 6 Warlike discipline requireth this, that no man wagge, vnlesse hee be commanded by the captaine. **1587** Turberv. *Trag. Tales* 52 [He] did feele a thing by happe, Within her wombe to wagge, and beat against her brest. **1593** BILSON *Govt. Christ's Ch.* 289 Binde them fast to their chaires that they shall not wagge. **1631** [MABBE] *Celestina* xix. 189 Our unfortunate Master is falne from the ladder, and neither speakes nor wagges. **1636** FEATLY *Clavis Myst.* xxiii. 297 Driven to fly with her heavie burden with which she is scarce able to wagge. **1650** T. B[AYLEY] *Worcester's Apoph.* Ep. Rdr. 2 Some..field-Chaplains..envying that a loyall pen should wagge, where they [etc.]. **1653** H. COGAN tr. *Pinto's Trav.* xxiv. 91 Which gave us such an alarum, as not daring scarce to wag we got out again with all secrecy. **1692** R. L'ESTRANGE *Josephus, Antiq.* VI. v. (1733) 138 The miserable Distress of their Condition drew Tears and Pity wherever they came, but not a Creature durst so much as wag to help them. **1860** WHYTE MELVILLE *Market Harb.* xii, I've a hack here at Welford... He's short of work, poor devil! and could hardly wag coming up the hill.

†**2.** To totter, stagger, be in danger of falling.

c **1340** *Nominale* (Skeat) 166 M[an] sliduth vp-on hyse, W[oman] waggi[t]h [Fr. *ercule*; error for *croule*] and falluth lowe. **1377** LANGL. *P. Pl.* B. XVIII. 61 Þe wal wagged and clef and al þe worlde quaued. *c* **1440** *Gesta Rom.* (Harl. MS.) 110 Þey [*sc.* two beasts] gnowe at the Rote of the tree..to throwe it downe, in so muche that the wrecchid man felte it wagge. **1470–85** MALORY *Arthur* VII. xvii. 238 And thenne they stode wagyng and scateryng [1529 stakerynge], pontyng, blowynge and bledynge.

3. To oscillate, shake, or sway alternately in opposite directions, as something working on a pivot, fitting loosely in a socket, or the like. Of a boat or ship: To rock.

1377 LANGL. *P. Pl.* B. VIII. 31 Þe wynde and þe water and þe bote waggynge Maketh þe man many a tyme to falle and to stonde. *c* **1386** CHAUCER *Reeve's T.* 119 Yet saugh I neuere, by my fader kyn, How that the hopur wagges til and fra. *c* **1394** *P. Pl. Crede* 226 His chyn wiþ a chol lollede..þat all wagged his flesh as a quyk mire. **1398** TREVISA *Barth. De P.R.* XVII. xlv. (Bodl. MS.) Iuce þerof hette wiþ vynegre fastene[þ] teþe þatt waggen. *c* **1440** *Promp. Parv.* 513/1 Waggon', or waveron', or stere be hyt selfe as a thynge hangynge, *vacillo*. *c* **1520** SKELTON *Magnyf.* 1821, I sawe a wethercocke wagge with the wynde! *a* **1572** KNOX *Hist. Ref.* Wks. 1846 I. 147 Syd gounis mycht have bene sein wantonly wag from the one wall to the other. **1640** WILKINS *New Planet* v. (1707) 196 It could not wag with the least kind of Declination. **1654** WHITELOCKE *Swed. Ambassy* (1772) II. 371 *Mar.* She wagges! she wagges!.. My lord, uppon my life the ship did wag; I saw her move. **1725** *Bradley's Family Dict.* s.v. *Tunnel*, There should be a Stick..to keep up the Head and Tail [of a stalking horse], which last should be at some distance from the Body, that it may wag in moving. **1818** SCOTT *Rob Roy* xviii, Better a finger aff as aye wagging.

†**b.** Of leaves, corn, reeds, etc.: To waver, shake. *Obs.*

1398 TREVISA *Barth. De P.R.* XVII. vii. (1495) 607 A rede ..wagyth wyth the wynde. *c* **1400** *Laud Troy Bk.* 8968 As levis wagges with the wynde. **1423** JAS. I *Kingis Q.* lx, Bot blawe wynd, blawe,..That sum twig may wag, and mak hir to wake. **1568** GRAFTON *Chron.* I. 7 The little boye espying the bush to wag,..imagined that there lay some wilde beast. **1658** tr. *Porta's Nat. Magic* IV. i. 113 Binde [the Vines].. with strings or thongs, that they may be surely stayed from wagging up and down. **1663** PATRICK *Parab. Pilgrim* xxxvi. (1687) 457 If a leaf wagged, it was by the sweet breath of those Musicians which sate among the branches. *a* **1722** LISLE *Husb.* (1757) 243 No grass of any other kind did wag.

Proverbial phrase. **1596** J. MELVILL *Autob. & Diary* (Wodrow Soc.) 362 The King..lyked of nan that wald nocht wag as the bus [= bush] waggit.

†**c.** *fig.* To waver, vacillate. *Obs.*

1387 TREVISA *Higden* (Rolls) VII. 321 Robard, waggynge as a reed, assented anon. **1566** DRANT *Horace, Sat.* I. i. A v, Thy mynde it waues and wagges.

†**d.** To dangle on the gallows, be hanged. *Obs.*

c **1430** *Pilgr. Lyf Manhode* III. xvii. (1869) 144 It is þe hand þat maketh the feet to wagge [Fr. *baller*] and þe eres to be kitte. **1547** BOORDE *Brev. Health* §151 Let them beware of wagging in the Galowes. **15..** *A pore Help* 256 in Hazlitt *E.P.P.* (1866) 261 Your happe may be to wagge Upon a wodden nagge.

4. Of a limb, the head or tail, etc.: To be moved briskly from side to side.

1484 CAXTON *Fables of Æsop* III. xvii, [The ape said to the fox] What auaylleth to the soo long a taylle, hit doth but wagge. **1601** HOLLAND *Pliny* IX. x. I. 241 The Troglodites have among them certaine Tortoises, with broad hornes like the pegges in a Lute or Harpe, and the same will wagge and stirre so, as in swimming they helpe themselves therewith. **1602** SHAKS. *Ham.* V. i. 290 Why I will fight with him vppon this Theme Vntill my eielids will no longer wag. **1693** *Humours Town* 92 Their Elbows wag faster than their Tongues. **1830** SCOTT *Demonol.* i. 15 A humourist, who planted himself..with his eyes riveted on the..bronze lion that graces the front of Northumberland-house.., and having attracted the attention of those who looked at him by muttering 'By Heaven it wags!' [etc.].

b. Of the tongue, †lips: To move briskly in animated talk: often with an implication of foolish or indiscreet speech.

1590 *Tarlton's Newes Purgat.* 24 When her tung could not wagge, she heaued her hands aboue water. **1599** B. JONSON *Cynthia's Rev.* V. iii, For the solemne Addresse, two Lips wagging, and neuer a wise word. **1604** BRETON *Grimellos Fort.* (Grosart) 13/1 Being one that loued to heare a tongue wagge, either her owne, her Gossips, her Maides, or her Pyes. **1828** SCOTT *F.M. Perth* ii, 'Daughter,' said Simon, 'your tongue wags too freely.' **1863** GEO. ELIOT *Romola* x, Boys whose tongues were used to wag in concert at the most brutal street games. **1883** FRANCES M. PEARD *Contrad.* xxvii, I know you will be careful not to set tongues wagging.

c. *Proverb.*

[**13..**: see WAW *v.*] *c* **1550** *Disc. Common Weal Eng.* (1893) 138 It is a common proverbe, it is mery in hall when beardes wagges all. **1562** J. HEYWOOD *Prov. & Epigr.* (1867) 129. **1573–80** TUSSER *Husb.* (1878) 126. **1597** SHAKS. *2 Hen. IV*, V. iii. 37. **1731–8** SWIFT *Pol. Conversat.* 170.

d. To sway the body from side to side; (of a dog) to walk with a swaying movement.

1726 GARRETSON *Sch. Manners* 36 Run not hastily in the street, nor go too slowly: wag not to and fro, nor use any antick or wanton posture either of thy head, hands, feet or body. **1868** JULIA KAVANAGH *Dora* xxi, They all left the inn .., Eva as usual clinging to Dora's side, and Fido wagging slowly behind her.

†**5.** To move about from place to place; to wander. Also, to drift (in water). *Obs.*

c **1325** *Poem Times Edw. II* 190 in *Pol. Songs* (1839) 332 He wole wagge aboute the cloistre and kepen hise fet clene in house. **1382** WYCLIF *Job* xxxviii. 41 Who maketh redi to the crowe his mete, whan his briddis crie to God, hider and thider waggende [Vulg. *vagantes*]. *c* **1400** *Destr. Troy* 13542 Thus I skope fro the skathe with skyrme of my hondes, And with wawes of the water wagget to bonke. *c* **1555** HARPSFIELD *Divorce Hen. VIII* (Camden) 251 The head thus being above, the body beneath in water, wagging and removing to and fro.

†**6.** To move, budge *from* a place. *Obs.*

c **1400** *Laud Troy Bk.* 5875 Thei myght onethes a-wey wagge With siluer and gold. **1585** FETHERSTONE tr. *Calvin on Acts* xvi. 27. 402 Though his bands wer loosed, he did not once wag from his place. **1589** PUTTENHAM *Engl. Poesie* III. xix. (Arb.) 240 It is said by manner of a prouerbiall speach that he who findes himselfe well should not wagge. **1609** C. BUTLER *Fem. Mon.* (1634) 9 As many [bees] as are stricken, within an hour after, will not be able to wag out of the place. **1666** GLANVIL *Consid. Witches* (1667) 20 The separated souls of the wicked..cannot possibly wag from the place of their confinement. **1675** WYCHERLEY *Country-Wife* IV. iv, *Mrs. Pin.* Sir go we'll follow you. *Spar.* I will not wag without you. **1715** HEARNE *Collect.* (O.H.S.) V. 133, I cannot wag out of Oxford till the Term is ended. **1730** FIELDING *Rape upon Rape* III. xi, I'll not wag without you.

7. To go, depart, be off. Now *colloq.*

1594 LYLY *Mother Bombie* II. i. 58 But let mee bee wagging. **1598** SHAKS. *Merry W.* I. iii. 7 Discard (bully Hercules) casheere; let them wag; trot, trot. **1599** —— *Much Ado* V. i. 16 If such a one will smile and stroke his beard, And sorrow, wagge [*read* Bid sorrow waggel], crie hem, when he should grone. **1601** W. PERCY *Cuckqueanes & Cuckolds Errants* IV. i. (Roxb.) 47 My gentleman, let him wagge, whither he please, in the name of Jehoua. **1652** A. ROSS *Hist. World* II. iv. 64 He [Heliogabalus]..never would wag any where without 60 Chariots. **1779** COWPER *Yearly Distr.* 50 Come, neighbours, we must wag.

b. To travel or make one's way; to 'jog *along*'. *lit.* and *fig.*

1684 BUNYAN *Pilgr.* II. 183 They made a pretty good shift to wagg along. **1798** J. JEFFERSON *Let. to Boucher* 23 Feb. (MS.), People in Hampshire not only wag the head or hand, ..but they wag out, when they take a walk.—It always puts me in mind of a Duck. **1840** LONGF. *Sp. Stud.* III. vi, Thus I wag through the world, half the time on foot, and the other half walking. **1903** MCNEILL *Egregious Engl.* 28 So he wagged along and helped to build up the commercial greatness and probity and honour of his country.

c. In proverbial phrases with 'the world' as subject. ***how the world wags***: how affairs are going. ***to let the world wag*** (***as it will***): to regard the course of events with unconcern. (For other expressions analogous to these, see the quots.)

a **1529** SKELTON *Sp. Parrot* 90 In flattryng fables men fynde but lyttyl fayth: But *moveatur terra*, let the world wag. **1538** LATIMER *Let. to Cromwell* Serm. & Rem. (1845) 396 By this bill inclosed your lordship can perceive some-thing, how the world doth wag with Warwick college. **1550** CROWLEY *Epigr.* 361 Let the worlde wagge, we must neades haue drynke. **1575** GASCOIGNE *Glasse Govt.* Wks. 1910 II. 63, I warrant thee wee two will live howe soever the world wagge. **1600** SHAKS. *A.Y.L.* II. vii. 23 Thus may we see (quoth he) how the world wagges. **1611** COTGR. s.v. *Gallere*, *Vogue la gallere*, let the world wag, slide, goe how it will; let goe a Gods name. **1637** SANDERSON *Serm.* (1681) II. 73 Solomons sluggard,..who foldeth his hands together, and letteth the world wag as it will. **1700** T. BROWN *Amusem. Ser. & Com.* 130 Let us then go and see how the World wags in the City Circle. **1702** *Secret Mercury* 2–9 Sept. 2/1, I retir'd to my Lodgings and let the World wagg for that Night. **1790** GOUV. MORRIS in Sparks *Life & Writ.* (1832) II. 105 Let the world wag as it may. **1791** MME. D'ARBLAY *Diary* July, I shall not, I hope, be forgetful, when the world wags ill, [etc.]. **1823** SCOTT *Quentin D.* xxv, 'I will have a rouze with Dunois,' said Crèvecœur, 'wag the world as it will.' *c* **1845** C. BRONTË *Professor* i, But you shall hear.. how the world has wagged with me. **1861** *Congressional Globe* 18 Feb. 967/3 But I believe the world has wagged along about the same after as they did before the resolutions passed. **1877** W. BLACK *Green Past.* xlii, Let the world wag on as it may.

†**d.** To 'get on', associate *with*. *Obs.*

c **1560** A. SCOTT *Poems* (S.T.S.) xxxiv. 89 ȝe wantoun wowaris waggis With thame that hes the cunȝe. **1562** J. HEYWOOD *Prov. & Epigr.* (1867) 90, I with ale, and ale with me wag away.

8. *slang.* To play truant. Also ***to wag it***. Cf. WAG *sb.*[2] 3.

1848 DICKENS *Dombey* xxii, 'My misfortunes all began in wagging, Sir; but what could I do, exceptin' wag?' 'Excepting what?' said Mr. Carker. 'Wag, Sir. Wagging from school.' 'Do you mean pretending to go there, and not going?' said Mr. Carker. 'Yes, Sir, that's wagging, Sir.' **1901** W. S. WALKER *In the Blood* i. 13 They had 'wagged it' from school, as they termed it, which..meant truancy in all its forms.

II. Transitive uses.

†**9.** To set in movement, cause to quiver or oscillate; to shake or stir by force. *Obs.*

1377 LANGL. *P. Pl.* B. XVI. 41 And þanne fondeth þe fende my fruit to destruye, With alle þe wyles þat he can and waggeth þe rote. **1387** TREVISA *Higden* (Rolls) I. 189 Centauri, as it were an hundred wynde waggers: for þey wagged wel þe wynde faste in hir ridynge. **1387–8** T. USK *Test. Love* I. Prol. 90 Ouer that he had power of strength to pull vp the spere, that Alisander the noble might neuer wagge. *c* **1425** *Cast. Persev.* 1943 in *Macro Plays* 135 Þis worthy, wylde werld, I wagge with a wyt. **1471** CAXTON *Recuyell* (Sommer) 212 Than he began a lityll and a lityll to wagge the ston and to seke the Ioyntures that helde hit. **1508** FISHER *7 Penit. Ps.* vi. Wks. (1876) 18 The lefe that with a lytell wynde is wagged and blowen doune. **1582** N. LICHEFIELD tr. *Castanheda's Conq. E. Ind.* I. ix. 25 b, They adiudged that the gabell [*i.e.* cable] had bene wagged or shaken by a kinde of Fish called a Tunnie. **1587** TURBERV. *Trag. Tales* 14 But how much more the louer made his mone,.. The more shee sate vnmoued, like the stone, Whom waues do beat, but wag not from his place. **1609** C. BUTLER *Fem. Mon.* (1634) 51 The Place..must be kept close and quiet; free from noise and noisome cattel, that may either wag or wake them. **1612** SELDEN *Illustr. Drayton's Poly-olb.* i. 16 So great, that many men's vnited strength cannot remoue it, yet with one finger you may wagge it. *a* **1677** BARROW *Serm.* xiv. Wks. 1687 I. 202 A small transient pleasure, a tickling the ears, wagging the lungs, forming the face into a smile [etc.].

†**b.** To nudge. *Obs.*

1377 LANGL. *P. Pl.* B. XIX. 199, I wondred what þat was, & wagged conscience, And was afered of the lyȝte.

10. To brandish (a weapon). Also, to wave (something) defiantly, as a signal, or to attract notice. *Obs.* exc. in jocular use (cf. *flag-wagging*).

c **1300** *Havelok* 89 He was te beste knith at nede, Þat heuere micthe..wepne wagge, or folc vt lede. **1535** COVERDALE *Isa.* x. 24 Be not afrayde for the kinge of the Assirians: He shal wagg his staff at the,.. But [etc.]. **1577–87** HARRISON *England* II. ix. 181/1 in *Holinshed*, The other.. wagging a scroll which he had in his hand before the iudge. **1596** SPENSER *F.Q.* IV. iv. 18 So these two champions..in their hands their idle troncheons held, Which neither able were to wag, or once to weld. **1806** SCOTT *Health Ld. Melville* vii, While there's one Scottish hand that can wag a claymore, sir.

11. To move (a limb or part of the body attached by a joint) to and fro, up and down, or from side to side: usually implying rapid and repeated movement. †Also, to blink repeatedly with, 'bat' (the eyes).

13.. *E.E. Allit. P.* B. 1484 As þay with wynge vpon wynde hade waged her fytheres. **1530** PALSGR. 770/1 Do you nat se hym, he waggeth his hande at you. **1542** BRINKLOW *Lament.* (1874) 111 What a blyndnes is it to thynke my sinnes forgeuen me, when a prest..hath wagged two or thre fyngers ouer my head? **1574** *Withals' Dict.* 67 b/2 *Pætus*, he that waggeth the eyes. **1594** MARLOWE & NASHE *Dido* II. i. 324 Achates, see King Priam wags his hand, He is aliue, Troy is not ouercome. **1597** A. M. tr. *Guillemeau's Fr. Chirurg.* 3/3 When the patient may easylye wagge his lower chawe bone. **1611** COTGR., *Gambayer*, to wag the legs in sitting, as children vse to do. **1611** CORYAT *Crudities* 229 They wagge their hands vp and downe very often. **1768** TUCKER *Lt. Nat.* I. II. xxviii. 202 Nothing can be more harmless than wagging your finger considered in itself, yet if the finger rest against the trigger of a loaded musket and a man stand just before, you cannot do a wronger thing, and why? **1802** SOUTHEY *Ballad St. Antidius* 35 He wagg'd his ears, he twisted his tail, He knew not for joy what to do. **1853** KANE *Grinnell Exp.* xxxvi. (1856) 326 [He] had to wag his leg half an hour by the dial.

transf. **1596** SHAKS. *Merch. V.* IV. i. 76 You may as well forbid the Mountaine Pines To wagge their high tops.

b. (Chiefly in negative context, typifying the minimum of exertion.) To move, stir (a limb, finger, etc.). Now *colloq.*

1596 SPENSER *F.Q.* V. i. 22 He found him selfe, vnwist, so ill bestad, That limb he could not wag. **1660** F. BROOKE tr. *Le Blanc's Trav.* 181 Travelling on the sands his hoof will burn and cleave, so as 'tis impossible to get him wag a foot. **1671** BLAGRAVE *Astrol. Pract. Phys.* 149 For some hours she would be as seemingly dead, and could wagg neither arm or leg. **1697** R. PIERCE *Bath Mem.* I. vi. 125 He told me (with great joy) that he could wagg one of his Toes. **1855** PLANCHÉ tr. *C'tess D'Aulnoy's Fairy Tales* (1858) 16 I'll wager, now, that this idle beauty hasn't wagged one of her ten fingers. **1861** C. READE *Cloister & H.* lxxi. (1896) 207 Had it been any but you, believe me I had obeyed you and not wagged a finger. **1898** F. HARRISON *Autob. Mem.* (1911) II. xxx. 150, I most positively declined to ask him or anyone to wag a finger to get me there.

c. To shake (the head); to move (the head) from side to side.

a **1340** HAMPOLE *Psalter* xxi. 6 Þai spake with lippes and wagid þe heued. **1393** LANGL. *P. Pl.* C. XIII. 19 'Owh! how!' quaþ ich þo and myn hefd waggede. **1470–85** MALORY *Arthur* XIX. ix. 787 And thenne the quene wagged her hede vpon sir Launcelot, as though she wold saye slee hym. *a* **1513** FABYAN *Chron.* ccxxiii. (1533) 147 When Robert had harde that message to the ende, he wagged hys hedde, as he that conceyued some doublenesse in thys reporte. **1526** TINDALE *Matt.* xxvii. 39 They that passed by revyled hym, waggynge [Gr. κινοῦντες] ther heeddes. **1540** PALSGR. *Acolastus* Prol. B iv, Why waggest thou thy heed, as though thou were very angry. **1576** FLEMING *Panopl. Epist.* 277 These extreme passions of mynde,..when Democritus had heard,..he..wagged his head too and fro: wherein he had some meaning. *a* **1618** SYLVESTER *Funeral Elegy* Wks. (Grosart) II. 291 O! Who so constant, but would grieve and grudge (If not a Christian) at th' All-ordering Judge; And wag his head at Heav'n,—weak earthly worm! **1815** SCOTT *Guy M.* ii, The poor parents were encouraged to hope that their bairn, as they expressed it, 'might wag his pow in a pulpit yet.' **1840** THACKERAY *Barber Cox* June, We were introduced instantly..: the little lord wagged his head, my wife bowed very low, and so did Mr. Coddler. **1841** —— *Gt. Hoggarty Diam.* vii, Tidd at this looked very knowing; and, as our host sunk off to sleep again,..wagged his head at the captain. **1863** GEO. ELIOT *Romola* vi, When once a man is obliged to do something besides wagging his head. **1871** LONGF. *Wayside Inn* II. *Cobbler of Hagenau* 92 The cobbler ..wagging his sagacious head, Unto his kneeling housewife said: [etc.].

d. To move (the tongue, †lips) in animated speech: esp. with implication of indiscretion or malignity. Also of the tongue: To utter (words).

1569 J. SANFORD tr. *Agrippa's Van. Artes* lxii. 91 b, They drawe deepe sighes from the harte: and wagging their lippes doo faigne to saie prayers. **1613** SHAKS. *Hen. VIII*, I. i. 33 No Discerner Durst wagge his Tongue in censure. **1657** TRAPP *Comm. Ps.* cix. 2. II. 860 There is nothing more easie, than to wag a wicked tongue. **1820** SCOTT *Monast.* iv, The faithful Tibb and Dame Elspeth, excellent persons both, and as thorough gossips as ever wagged a tongue. **1827** —— *Jrnl.* 10 Mar., It is brave to see how he wags his Scots tongue. **1840** THACKERAY *Paris Sk.-bk.* (1869) 36 Not a tongue was wagged in his praise. **1871** DIXON *Tower* III. xviii. 196 Every one who owed him grudge would eagerly begin to wag his tongue. **1894** J. DAVIDSON *Random Itin.* 160 When they spoke, they simply left their mouths ajar, and allowed their tongues to wag the maimed words of an unknown dialect.

e. Of an animal: To move (its tail) from side to side: in dogs usually an indication of pleasure; in cats often a sign of anger.

c **1410** *Master of Game* (MS. Digby 182) xiii, And whan þei se her maister þei wole make hym chere and wag hir tayles vpon hym. **1545** ELYOT *Dict.*, *Agere caudam*, to wagge his tayle. **1599** MARSTON *Ant. & Mel.* III. (1602) F 2, Tis an old horse can neither wighy, nor wagge his taile. **1620** J. TAYLOR (Water P.) *Jack a Lent* C 2, All the Dogges in the Towne, doe wagge their tailes for ioy. **1661** LOVELL *Hist. Anim. & Min.* 88 They [*sc.* lambs] wagge the taile whilest sucking. **1710** STEELE *Tatler* No. 231 ¶2 The poor Cur looked up and wagged his Tail. **1774** GOLDSM. *Nat. Hist.* V. 245 Pozzo..asserts, that it [a toucan] leaped up and down, wagged the tail, and cried with a voice resembling that of a magpie. **1791** COWPER *Odyss.* x. 264 They..Paw'd them in blandishment, and wagged the tail. **1863** KINGSLEY *Water-Bab.* iv, And there..lay five or six great salmon,..wagging their tails, as if they were very much pleased at it. **1865** H. KINGSLEY *Hillyars & Burtons* lxii, The dog came wagging his tail.

†**f.** To flap (the wings). *Obs.*

1496 *Cov. Leet Bk.* 577 Litell small been, þat al aboute fleen, They waggen their whyng. **1584** R. SCOT *Discov. Witchcr.* XI. vii. 195 Birds..in what sort they wag their wings. **1596** SPENSER *Hymn Heav. Love* 24 Ere flitting Time could wag his eyas wings About that mightie bound.

†**g.** To sway (the body) about. *Obs.*

1665 SIR T. HERBERT *Trav.* (1677) 191 After the Eastern mode they wagg'd their Bodies, bowing their heads [etc.].

III. 12. Combinations: †**wag-feather**, a swaggering coxcomb; †**wag-pasty**, a mischievous rogue; †**wag-string** = WAGHALTER; **wag-tongue**, a malicious chatterer; †**wag-wanton**, a wanton; †**wag-with** [? WITH *sb.*] = WAGHALTER. Also WAG-AT-THE-WALL, WAGHALTER, WAG-LEG, WAGSTART, WAGTAIL.

1611 COTGR., *Coqueplumet*,.. a *wag-feather. *a* **1553** UDALL *Royster D.* III. ii. (Arb.) 40 A little *wagpastie, A deceiuer of folkes, by subtill craft and guile. *c* **1563** *Jack Jugler* (Roxb.) 28 Truelye this wage pastie is either drunken or mad. **1622** MABBE tr. *Aleman's Guzman d'Alf.* II. 278 That souldiers boy, who playd the wagge-pasty with his Masters pasty;..opened the lid of the pastie,..and supt vp all the sirrop. **1578** H. WOTTON *Courtlie Controv.* 30 The boy..bethoughte hym of a knauerye fitte for a *wagstring. *a* **1591** H. SMITH *Serm.* (1637) 223 [We say,] when we see a gracelesse boy, Thou wilt prove a wagstring, if thou live to be elder. **1633** HEYWOOD *Eng. Trav.* IV, Oh thou crafty Wag-string. **1902** C. HEADLAM in *Macm. Mag.* Oct. 466 A chatterbox she is, and worse,—a regular woman *wag-tongue. **1601** DEACON & WALKER *Answ. Darel* 72 Euery little childe that playeth *wag-wanton. **1604** BRETON *Grimellos Fort.* (Grosart) 8/2 Thou wouldest neither carrie a ring, clawe a backe, plaie on both hands, be no wagge-wanton, with thy mistresse, nor Iudas with thy maister. **1611** J. DAVIES (Heref.) *Panegyr. Verses Coryat's Crudities* i 3 b, While he most like a *Wag-with Tooke of his Grapes as much as he could wag-with.

wagadash, wagan: see WACADASH, WAGON.

†**wagand**, var. *vagand*, pr. pple. of VAGUE *Sc. Obs.*; also as *sb.* a vagrant.

1614 in J. Davidson *Inverurie* (1878) 196 Giff ony towne's peopill beis found wagand on the gaitt after the hour of ten, the person fund wagand sall be poyndt as if they wer wagands.

waganga, pl. of MGANGA.

wag-at-the-wall. *Sc.* and *north.* Also **wag-on-the-wall**, etc. [WAG *v.* 3.]

1. A hanging clock with pendulum and weights exposed. Also *attrib.*

1825 JAMIESON Suppl. II. 637/2 *Wag-at-the-Wa'*,..a name given to a clock, which has no case, frequently used in the country. **1825** BROCKETT *N.C. Words*, *Wag-at-the-waw*, *Wagger*, a cheap wooden German clock. Perhaps from the pendulum being exposed; or, provincially, seen wagging against the wall. **1894** J. DAVIDSON *Baptist Lake* 82 'It's nearly half past four,' said he, looking at a wag-at-the-wall that hung behind him. **1904** J. SMITH *Handbk. Old Scottish Clockmakers* 45 The poorer members of the community could not afford the price demanded for the long case clocks and would be content with a 'Wag at the Wa'. **1911** N. H. MOORE *Old Clock Bk.* 59 Many Dutch works were sent to England without their cases... Such clocks went till the dirt and dust clogged their wheels... Such clocks as these are often called in rustic communities by the quaint name of 'wag-on-the-wall'. **1966** P. BOYLE *At Night All Cats are Grey* 221 What was this nagging memory of a wag-o'-the-wall?.. With a bottle of water used as a driving weight.

attrib. **1858** G. ROY *Generalship* 55 To take a fancy to a waggitonawa clock. **1889** BARRIE *Window in Thrums* xix, When I entered, the wag-at-the-wa' clock had again possession of the kitchen.

2. 'A spectre supposed to haunt the kitchen.. wagging backwards and forwards before the death of one of the family' (Jam.).

wage (weɪdʒ), *sb.* Forms: 4 *Sc.* vag, 4 *Sc.*, 6 wag, 6 waige, wayge, *pl.* wagies, *Sc.* vaig(e, vage, 6–7 wadge, 4– wage. [a. AF., OF. (north-eastern) *wage* (AL. *wagium*) = Central OF. *guage*, *gage* (mod.F. *gage*), Prov. *gage-s*, It. *gaggio*:—popular L. **wadium*, of Teut. origin: see WED *sb.*]

†**1. a.** A pledge or security; = GAGE *sb.*[1] 1. Phr. *to hold, lay in wage*. *Obs.*

[**1183** *Pipe Roll 29 Hen. II* (1911) 61 Henricus dec' de Wallebi debet .v. *m.* quia renuit dare wagium et plegium justiciariis.] **1338** R. BRUNNE *Chron.* (1810) 139 He sesed fiue castels, & held þam in his wage. *c* **1375** *Sc. Leg. Saints* xli. (*Agnes*) 400 Here-of in vitnesyng remanis ay þe forsad ryng one þe fyngire of þat ymag of vad of weding in-to vag. **1513** DOUGLAS *Æneis* v. iv. 132 Or thai thar land sul los or vassalage Thai had far levir lay thar lyf in wage. **1530** PALSGR. 286/1 Wage or pledge, *gaige*. **1590** SPENSER *F.Q.* I. iv. 39 But th' Elfin knight, which ought that warlike wage, Disdaind to loose the meed he wonne in fray.

†**b.** A challenge or engagement to fight. In full, *wage of battle*. Cf. GAGE *sb.*[1] 2. *Obs.*

c **1400** *Laud Troy Bk.* 8476 So it was seyde to the Emperoure..How ffight was taken hem be-twene, And no man myȝt here ire a-swage And thei hadde ȝeuen to-gedur wage. **1523** BERNERS *Froiss.* I. ccxvii. 113 And yᵉ same season ther was a wage of batel before the french king, betwene two noble and expert knightes.

2. A payment to a person for service rendered. Formerly used widely, e.g. for the salary or fee paid to persons of official or professional status. Now (exc. in rhetorical language) restricted to mean: The amount paid periodically, esp. by the day or week or month, for the labour or service of an employee, worker, or servant.

Commonly in pl. (after F. *gages*). The sing. is now either *dial.* or has a rhetorical flavour; but it has sometimes a special convenience with reference to a particular instance or amount (see e.g. quot. 1776 in a).

a. *sing.* (For *living wage* see LIVING *vbl. sb.* 7.)

13.. *Coer de L.* 4264 Ther was non so lytyl page, That ne hadde to hys wage, Off gold and sylvyr [etc.]. **1338** R. BRUNNE *Chron.* (1810) 319 Ilk man þou reft his wage. *c* **1440** *Promp. Parv.* 513/1 Wage, or hyre, *stipendium*, *salarium*. **1510** *Sel. Cases Star Chamb.* (Selden Soc.) II. 73 Lewed & evyll disposed persons..to whom..the seid Priour gave wage vjd by the day. **1522** *World & Child* (facs.) A iij, Whan I was seuen yere of age I was sent to the worlde to take wage And this seuen yere I haue ben his page. **1621** SCLATER *Quæst. Tythes* (1623) F 5, Dreames any man hee meant it to the Lord as a Wage for his Worke. **1776** ADAM SMITH *W.N.* I. x. I. 177 When masters combine together in order to reduce the wages of their workmen, they commonly enter into a private bond or agreement, not to give more than a certain wage under a certain penalty. **1855** W. G. CLARK in *Cambr. Ess.* 287 Millions of childen..must needs commence their life of toil in the factory or the field, as soon as their physical strength enables them to get a day's wage for a day's work. **1877** MORLEY *Crit. Misc.* Ser. II. 204 The labourers, having little heart in work for which they had no wage.

b. *pl.*

1377 LANGL. *P. Pl.* B. XI. 283 He þat toke ȝow ȝowre tytle shulde take ȝow ȝowre wages. **1429** *Rolls of Parlt.* IV. 338/2 Ye seide Lord Talbot, servid the Kynges Fader..withoute takyng of any wages. **1444** *Ibid.* V. 110/2 To arreze the wages of the Knyghtes of the shires. *c* **1460** FORTESCUE *Abs. & Lim. Mon.* xv. (1885) 146 It shall not be necessarie, þat the xij spirituell men off this covnsell haue so gret wages as the xij temporall men. **1540** *Test. Ebor.* VI. 107, I will that a prest synge for my fayther..and he to have for his wadges vij markes in the yere. **1588** KYD *Househ. Philos.* Wks. (1901) 265 Gyuing euery one hys sallary or day wages. **1642** J. M[ARSH] *Argt. conc. Militia* 17 By the Law it is enacted, that no Knight Citizen or Burges, absent himself under the paine of the losse of their wages. **1776** ADAM SMITH *W.N.* I. viii. (*init.*) I. 78 The produce of labour constitutes the natural recompence or wages of labour. **1809** KENDALL *Trav.* I. xv. 169 A member would be thought not to earn what are called his wages. These wages amount to two dollars per diem. **1829** CARLYLE *Jrnl.* in Froude *Life* (1882) II. 83 Thus we have private individuals whose wages are equal to the wages of seven or eight thousand other individuals. **1872** RAYMOND *Mines* 282 Wages are still low, $1 per day and board.

¶ The pl. was formerly often construed as sing.

1388 [see 2 e]. **1539** in *Abstr. Protocols Town Clerks Glasgow* (1897) IV. 118 Everilk ane to haif ane lyik waigis. **1551** ROBINSON tr. *More's Utopia* II. ix. (1895) 302 Theire dayly wages is so lytle that it will not suffice for the same daye. **1621** SCLATER *Quæst. Tythes* Introd. (1623) B 1, How easie is it to answer, that Tythes was that inheritance, and Tythes is this wages. **1679** L. ADDISON *1st St. Mahumedism* 23 As for his wages, it amounted to so little, that it would not do him much service. **1731–9** TULL *Horse-hoeing Husb.* Notes on Pref. (1822) 321 As their wages is supposed to be low, their masters find them in tools to work with.

†**c.** *spec.* The pay of a soldier. Chiefly *pl.* *to take wages*: to enlist, take service (*with* or *under* a commander). *Obs.*

1338 R. BRUNNE *Chron.* (1810) 163 A hundreth knyghtes mo..& fiue hundreth o fote, to whilk I salle pay Ilk day þer wages. **1436** *Rolls of Parlt.* IV. 499/1 Wages of Werre for the said Soudeours. *c* **1440** *Generydes* 2441 With the Sowdon he will take no wage. *c* **1489** CAXTON *Sonnes of Aymon* ix. 216 He..wende that it had ben straunge knyghtes that were come vnto hym to take wages. **1535** COVERDALE *1 Macc.* iii. 28 Kynge Antiochus..opened his treasury, and gaue his hoost a yeares wagies in honde. **1560** DAUS tr. *Sleidane's Comm.* 250 b, They also, which..take wages under them in this war. **1651** HOBBES *Leviath.* II. xxx. 181 The Wages, due to them that hold the publique Sword.

†**d.** Phr. *at wage*, *under wages*, *at* or *of* (a person's) *wage* or *wages*, *in* (a person's) *wages*: in the pay or service of another. *to put out of wages*: to discharge, cashier. *Obs.*

? *a* **1400** *Morte Arth.* 302, I salle the forthire..Fifty thowsande mene,..Of my wage for to wende, whare so the lykes. *c* **1400** MAUNDEV. (1839) v. 38 The Soudan may lede out of Egipt mo than 20000 Men of Armes... And alle tho ben at his Wages. **1420** WATERTON in Rymer *Fœdera* (1709) IX. 883 To come ovyr to zowe at zour Wage, Armyd and Arayde, as langys to thaire Estate to do zowe Service. *c* **1470** HENRY *Wallace* v. 909 Xxxᵗʸ with him off nobill men at wage. **1534** BERNERS *Gold. Bk. M. Aurel.* let. v. (1537) 110 And fynally,..ye entre newely into the wages of the worlde. **1542** UDALL *Erasm. Apoph.* 187 When he espyed one of the souldiers..trymmyng a strop or loope to sette on his darte, he putte out of wages, and discharged of his roume. *a* **1548** HALL *Chron.*, *Hen. VI*, 88 b, Many of the Britons.. submitted themselues to the lorde regent..whom he gentely accepted and put them in wages. **1551** ROBINSON tr. *More's Utopia* II. viii. (1895) 253 For them, whomewyth they be in wayges, they fyghte hardelye, fyerslye, and faythefullye. **1553** BRENDE *Q. Curtius* P 1, The Greakes yᵗ were in Darius wagies. **1594** J. MELVILL *Autob. & Diary* (Wodrow Soc.) 318 The King, with companies of horsmen and futtmen under wages. **1665** MANLEY *Grotius' Low C. Warres* 73 A mutiny for want of pay: which was an unavoydable evill in those parts, though in wages under a most wealthy King.

e. *fig.* Reward, recompense.

13.. *Gaw. & Gr. Knt.* 396 þat þou schal seche me þi-self ..& foch þe such wages As þou deles me to day. *c* **1375** *Sc. Leg. Saints* xxii. (*Laurence*) 139 Fere mare Ioyful wictorag þu sal resawe syne to þi wag. **1388** WYCLIF *Rom.* vi. 22 The wagis [1382 hyris] of synne is deth. *c* **1400** *Laud Troy Bk.* 3886 Ne were that ȝe come in message, Veleyns dethe schulde be ȝoure wage. **1513** DOUGLAS *Æneis* XII. xii. 175 Na for small wagis thai debait and stryfe, But apoun Turnus blude schedding and lyfe. **1549** COVERDALE *Erasm. Par. 1 Pet.* i. 3–9 They yᵗ serue the world goe about to haue rewardes yᵗ are transitory & wage that is slyppery. **1605** SHAKS. *Lear* v. iii. 303 All Friends shall Taste the wages of their vertue. *a* **1770** JORTIN *Serm.* (1787) I. vi. 122 Yet we may shew the same temper..by loving our religion and liberties better than the wages of slavery and iniquity. **1864** SWINBURNE *Atalanta* 2205 The gods give thee fair wage and dues of death. **1915** A. SMELLIE *Lift up your Heart* i. 31 He, our Kinsman and Redeemer..bears no relationship to sin any more. He has shaken off its wage and tyranny.

†**3.** A payment for the use or possession of property. *Obs. rare.*

1447 BOKENAM *Seyntys*, *Marg.* 232 If she be bonde and vndyr seruage:..Hyr lord wyl I yeue ryht good wage And to my paramour hyr vndyrfonge. **1562** in Strype *Ann. Ref.* xxvii. (1709) 286 The said incumbents paying to the owners, by the wage of a yearly pension, the yearly rent of all such impropriations. **1592** WEST *1st Pt. Symbol.* I. §25 Letting and hyring..is a Contract by consent of the making or vsing of some thing for a certeine rent, hier or wage. **1628** GAULE *Pract. Theories* (1629) 183 How grossely doth hee [*sc.* Judas] vndervalue him in this sale, and wage, and rate?

4. *attrib.* and *Comb.* **a.** simple attrib., as ***wage(s) bill, board, -book, claim, clerk, contract, cost, cut, demand, dispute, inflation, -labour, labourer, -level, negotiation, packet, payment, policy, push, -rate, restraint, -rigidity, -slave, -slavery, -snatch, spiral, structure, system, -work, -worker***; ***wage-related, -working*** adjs.; **b.** objective, as ***wage-bargainer, -bargaining, control, -earner, -earning*** vbl. sb. and ppl. adj., ***-fixing, -paying, -winner***; †***wages-taking*** ppl. adj.; **c.** appositive, as ***wage-price*** attrib., esp. in phr. ***wage-price spiral***; also **wages council**, any of a number of joint management and employee councils succeeding the trade boards (from 1945), and responsible for determining the conditions of employment in certain trades; **wage differential** = DIFFERENTIAL *sb.* 3 b; **wage drift**, the tendency for wages to rise above national rates through local overtime and other agreements; the extent of this increase; †**wages-fellow**, *contemptuously*, one who receives wages; **wage freeze**, a temporary fixing of wages at a certain level; cf. *pay freeze* s.v. PAY- 4 and FREEZE *sb.*[1] (ii); **wages-fund** *Pol. Econ.* (also ***wage-fund***), that part of the total capital of a community which is available for paying wages; **wage hike** *N. Amer.*, a wage increase (cf. HIKE *sb.* 2); **wages-man** *Austral.*, a man who works for wages; **wage scale**, a graduated scale of wage rates for different levels of work; **wage(s-sheet**, the list of wages paid by an employer of labour; **wage stop** (also ***wages stop***), the limitation of supplementary benefit to the level of the normal wage; hence **wage-stop** *v. trans.*; **wage-stopped** *ppl. a.*; **wage unit** (see quot. 1936).

1968 *Economist* 23 Mar. 16/3 Any *wage bargainer worth his salt should be able to dress up a claim to fit the loose criteria 'justifying' a $3\frac{1}{2}$ per cent increase. **1928** *Britain's Industr. Future* (Liberal Industr. Inquiry) III. xvii. 209 In the boot and shoe trade..it has been thought desirable to keep *wage-bargaining apart from the general discussions carried on by the Joint Industrial Council. **1983** *Times* 24 June 7/6 The fear that mass hunger striking will become a common tool of wage bargaining. **1919** M. BEER *Hist. Brit. Socialism* I. II. v. 169 The total *wage bill of the country diminished. **1923** H. W. B. JOSEPH *Labour Theory of Value in Karl Marx* ii. 49 If all this is true..a capitalist ought not to be indifferent whether he economizes in his wages-bill or in his other expenditure. **1982** T. KENEALLY *Schindler's Ark*

viii. 96 The meeting of his wage bill was the least of Oskar's worries. **1925** *Scribner's Mag.* Oct. 415/2 The regulation of wages has been put in the hands of *wage boards. **1930** *Economist* 22 Mar. 651/1 The success of the Wages Boards ..should be carefully considered. **1970** *Washington Post* 30 Sept. B 11/5 A 6 per cent raise to 850,000 hard-pressed blue-collar (wage board) people. **1864** TROLLOPE *Can you forgive Her?* (1865) II. vii. 54, I don't suppose I've opened the *wages book half a dozen times since last July. **1960** G. E. EVANS *Horse in Furrow* ix. 115 These wages-books.. contained the lists of jobs allocated to people employed on the farm, and the amount of wages due to them. **1971** H. WILSON *Labour Govt.* xxxviii. 787 One of the main groups of printing unions, SOGAT, put in a large *wage-claim. **1921** *Dict. Occup. Terms* (1927) §939 *Wages clerk. **1961** *Evening Standard* 18 July 23/5 Wages clerk to head..wages section. **1921** *Daily Colonist* (Victoria, B.C.) 20 Mar. 1/3 We deny that any *wage contract with the miners has been broken. **1977** P. JOHNSON *Enemies of Society* iii. 39 The medieval manor..yielded to a cash-nexus society based on wage-contracts between freely-negotiating individuals. **1910** *Encycl. Brit.* V. 879/1 This argument, which combined statutory *wage control and statutory poor relief, seems to have been firmly embedded in the English legislative mind ..till after 1600. **1978** *Economist* 18 Feb. 75/1 The [Argentine] government..has relaxed wage controls on private industry. **1985** *Financial Times* 4 Mar. 6/4 The most apparent difference is in their approach to inflation and wage control. **1958** *Spectator* 4 July 33/3 *Wage-cost inflation. **1975** J. DE BRES tr. *Mandel's Late Capitalism* vi. 203 Economies in costs will thus always be accompanied in the long-run by a relative decrease in the share of wage costs in the value of the commodity. **1945** *Wages Councils Act* (8 & 9 *Geo. VI c.* 17) 116 An Act to provide for the establishment of *wages councils. **1971** *Observer* 7 Nov. 16/6 Many trade unionists argue that the very existence of wages councils discourages poorer workers from joining trade unions. **1984** *Listener* 1 Nov. 11/3 The Wages Councils, providing legal minimum wages and conditions for 2·7 million of Britain's lowest-paid workers..are threatened. **1925** *Daily Herald* 30 June 2/4 (*heading*) Folly of *wage-cuts. **1974** J. AIKEN *Midnight is Place* iii. 102 Protests about the wage-cut had been nipped in the bud. **1970** *Guardian* 2 Mar. 1/2 The biggest disagreement is about the effect of *wage demands. **1950** *Wage differential [see DIFFERENTIAL *sb.* 3b]. **1957** *Observer* 6 Oct. 10/2 The pension scheme, by relating superannuation to wages, strengthens the value of wage differentials and hence the incentive to acquire greater skills. **1977** *China Now* Apr.-May 7/1 They were cutting down wage differentials. **1919** in M. Gilbert *Winston S. Churchill* (1977) IV. Compan. I. 498 The moment the revolt advanced over the line of a pure *wage dispute, and the strikers were guilty of a serious breach of the law, then was the moment to act. **1955** W. GADDIS *Recognitions* II. i. 322 Not written to be played by men in worn dinner jackets,..involved in wage disputes. **1963** *Times* 22 Jan. 4/6 This is a comparatively rare phenomenon, '*wage drift' in reverse, and reflects increased short time and lower earnings from bonuses, overtime and so on. *a* **1974** R. CROSSMAN *Diaries* (1976) II. 703 As for the $3\frac{1}{2}$ per cent ceiling, he told me it was quite unrealistic since wage drift by itself probably comes to $3\frac{1}{2}$ per cent. **1885** *Manch. Exam.* 20 Feb. 5/1 Trade will always fluctuate, *wage-earners will always suffer as a consequence. **1865** *Sat. Rev.* 12 Aug. 203 The *wages-earning and beef-eating qualities of the Briton. **1884** *Times* (weekly ed.) 10 Oct. 7/2 To turn their young children into wage-earning machines. **1902** *Edin. Rev.* Oct. 402 Education..may do much to.. raise the power of wage-earning. **1641** BROME *Joviall Crew* IV. i. (1652) I 3b, That she should sleight me, and run away with a *wages-fellow, that is but a petty Cleark and a Serving-man. **1928** *Britain's Industr. Future* (Liberal Industr. Inquiry) II. xvi. 181 The practical considerations which ought to govern the process of wage-fixing. **1942** *Wage freeze [see FREEZE *sb.*^{1} (ii)]. **1967** *Spectator* 1 Sept. 238/2 The wage freeze has been imposed without a murmur of national strike action. **1980** C. MOOREHEAD *Fortune's Hostages* v. 104 The President [of Uruguay]..tried to introduce economic restraint by wage freezes. **1848** MILL *Pol. Econ.* II. xi. §1. I. 402 There is unfortunately no mode of expressing by one familiar term, the aggregate of what may be called the *wages-fund of a country. **1863** FAWCETT *Pol. Econ.* II. viii. 241 The remark has frequently been made that the capital of the country provides its wage-fund. This wage-fund is distributed amongst the whole wage-receiving population, and, therefore, the average of each individual's wages cannot increase unless either the number of those who receive wages is diminished, or the wage-fund, which, in other words, may be described as the capital of the country, is increased. **1976** *Washington Post* 19 Apr. A 23/4 By last spring, some unions were putting in for *wage hikes up to 60 per cent. **1976** *Morecambe Guardian* 7 Dec. 21/7 One woman waving a placard saying '*Wage Inflation' [etc.]. **1871** KINGSLEY *At Last* xvi, Those who cultivate some scrap of ground, or follow some petty occupation, which prevents their depending entirely on *wage-labour. **1957** V. W. TURNER *Schism & Continuity in Afr. Society* v. 135 A man can acquire wealth by working in the White economy as a *wage labourer. **1928** *Britain's Industr. Future* (Liberal Industr. Inquiry) III. 139 A wise wage-policy should aim at the highest practicable *wage-levels. **1965** J. MEUVRET in Glass & Eversley *Population in Hist.* xxi. 517 In normal times wage-levels and price-levels were both very low. **1888** 'R. BOLDREWOOD' *Robbery under Arms* xxvi, They took up a claim... Then they got a *wages-man to help them, and all four used to work like niggers. **1890** —— *Miner's Right* iii. 23 One would think I was a wagesman, the way you three coves bosses it over me. **1928** *Britain's Industr. Future* (Liberal Industr. Inquiry) III. xvi. 188 It is not even enough that the wage-system should be just in itself; it must be visibly and demonstrably just. And this conception ought to inspire the whole system of *wage-negotiation. **1974** *Guardian* 23 Jan. 3/1 Today's wage negotiations were conducted with the Frame group. **1951** R. FIRTH *Elem. Social Organiz.* iv. 140 One point of view is that the size of the *wage-packet remains the most important factor still in the incentive to work. *a* **1974** R. CROSSMAN *Diaries* (1976) II. 638 The trade unionists want to see us spending much less on social services so that there'll be more for wage packets. **1868** RUSKIN *Time & Tide* (1872) 7 This principle of regular *wage-paying. **1923** H. W. B. JOSEPH *Labour Theory of Value in Karl Marx* vii. 154 In the absence of definite agreements or enactments, we can produce no rule of universal application, to which *wage-payments ought to conform. **1928** *Wage-policy [see *wage-level* above]. **1965** *New Statesman* 9 Apr. 576/3 The principles (but not the practice) of a wages policy. **1946** *Sun* (Baltimore) 1 Mar. 1/3 The situation, therefore, presents possibilities of a critical test of the administration's new *wage price line. **1958** *Engineering* 11 Apr. 460/1 There appeared to be no doubt whatever in Lord Cohen's mind that this painful process of breaking the wage-price spiral had to be adopted. **1977** M. EDELMAN *Political Lang.* viii. 147 A wage-price freeze from which major industries quickly won exceptions. **1968** *Manch. Guardian Weekly* 14 Mar. 13 It has become fashionable to say that the British..manage to keep a *wage-push inflation in times of crippling deflation. **1979** *Dædalus* Spring 53 Other things being equal, the greater the wage push, the tougher and more 'lesson-teaching' a policy is necessary to control inflation. **1898** *Edin. Rev.* Apr. 278 *Wage-rates are..the chief cause of trade disputes. **1963** *Punch* 20 Mar. 398/2 There must..be a *wage-related contributory insurance system. **1958** *Listener* 4 Dec. 930/2 Don't think it's a matter of *wage restraint only. **1977** M. EDELMAN *Political Lang.* viii. 153 Employers perceive wage restraint by workers as in the public interest. **1930** W. K. HANCOCK *Australia* ix. 187 It is apparent that *wage-rigidity is less important in its social consequences than in its economic and psychological consequences. **1983** *Economist* 18 June 21/3 Some belief in wage-rigidity is deeply rooted in his work. **1960** F. LYNDE *Quickening* 310 His father was deep in the new *wage scale submitted by the miners' union. **1979** *Gloss. Terms Work Study* (*B.S.I.*) 27 *Wage scale determination*, the construction of a scale of wages reflecting the relative values of jobs. **1903** *Daily Chron.* 9 July 4/4 The cotton spinners..had to diminish their output and the *wage-sheet. **1906** *Westm. Gaz.* 14 Nov. 10/1 Mr. Farrell quoted figures from his wages-sheet to prove that ability and competence..have to be paid for. **1886** MALLOCK *Old Order Changes* II. 29 The hands, as you call them, the poor jaded underfed *wage-slaves. **1886** D. DONOHUE *Let.* 21 Oct. in *N.Y. Times* 24 Oct. 1/5 It is therefore but natural that we should vote for a man who proposes to use his best endeavors to bring about legislation by which *wage slavery and land monopoly shall be abolished. **1903** *Dubl. Rev.* Oct. 243 The attitude taken up by the Pope..in regard to wage-slavery. **1962** *Observer* 25 Feb. 23/3 They were working themselves at the *wage-snatch business, with a bit of smash-and-grab on the side. **1964** J. CREASEY *Look Three Ways at Murder* xx. 183 There's a hold-up... Wages snatch! **1977** L. MEYNELL *Hooky gets Wooden Spoon* xii. 149 She wasn't doing anything for the police in the wages snatch. **1948** *Ann. Reg. 1947* 20 A *wage spiral was only prevented by distortion which would soon become intolerable. **1940** *Economist* 28 Dec. 799/1 The attempt to carry out a *wage stop similar to the price stop had to be abandoned. **1954** E. H. CARR *Interregnum* 73 This quasi-official wages-stop remained in force throughout 1923. **1963** *Guardian* 25 Feb. 11/7 If a man is wage-stopped, he will not get anything at all from the increases. **1971** *Daily Tel.* 16 June 3/3 The wage stop is the system by which men are prevented from drawing more in State benefits than they had earned while in work —even if this means they get less than the commission's official poverty level. **1963** *Times* 18 Feb. 11/6 To suggest.. that all the 15,000 *wage-stopped families were outsize would, on the board's own figures, be plainly absurd. **1955** *Ann. Reg. 1954* 1 The commission..undertook to make a thorough examination..of the whole *wage structure. **1898** *Kansas City* (Missouri) *Star* 18 Dec. 2/1 The ultimate outcome of the labor movement..will be the destruction of the *wage system. **1929** D. H. LAWRENCE *Pansies* 75 Ultimately, we are all busy buying and selling one another. It began with Judas and goes on in the wage-system. **1552** HULOET, *Wages takyng, *stipendiatus*. **1936** J. M. KEYNES *Gen. Theory Employment* iv. 41 The money-wage of a labour-unit we shall call the *wage-unit. **1976** F. ZWEIG *New Acquisitive Society* II. iv. 106 Economic planning which is based primarily on a 'wage unit' determined by the planning authorities as the pivot of economic planning. **1902** J. P. STRUTHERS *Life & Lett.* (1918) 279 They were the chief *wage-winners in the house. **1870** TENNYSON *Coming of Arthur* 417 Dark sayings..echo'd by old folk beside their fires, For comfort after their *wage-work is done. **1888** *Boston* (Mass.) *Jrnl.* 17 July 2/3 Free trade's bitterest foe is the American *wageworker. **1898** G. B. SHAW *Perfect Wagnerite* 29 The starving *wage-working class.

wage (weɪdʒ), *v.* Inflected **waging, waged**. Also 4 **wagge**, 5–7 **wadge** (*pa. t.* **wajed**), (5 *Sc.* **vage**), 7 **waidge**. [ME., a. ONF. *wagier*, *waigier* (Central OF. *guagier*, mod.F. *gager*: see GAGE *v.*):—popular L. type **wadiāre*, f. **wadium* WAGE *sb.*] **I.** To gage, pledge.

†**1.** *trans.* To deposit or give as a pledge or security. Also with *down*. *Obs.*

c **1320** *Sir Tristr.* 1011 He waged him aring, Tristram þe batayl toke. **1393** LANGL. *P. Pl.* C. XIX. 285 þat shal delyuery ous som day out of þe deueles powere, And betere wed for ous wagen þan alle we beon worthi. **1458** *Forman's Monumt. Christ's Hosp., Abingdon* 80 Few folke there were coude that wey wende, But they waged a wed or payed of her purse. **1565** COOPER *Thesaurus* s.v. *Ago, Ex sponso siue ex sponsu agere*,..to sue a man in the action, that is by wagynge downe of a somme of money. *a* **1585** MONTGOMERIE *Cherrie & Slae* 1453 Implaidging and waidging Baith twa thair lyves for myne.

†**b.** To offer as a gage of battle. *Obs.*

c **1430** *Syr Tryam.* 1368 Therfore sche hath takyn a day, Certenly, os y yow say, And waged hur glove for to fyght.

†**2.** *fig.* To offer (one's oath, etc.) as security for the fulfilment of a promise, etc.

c **1430** *Syr Gener.* (Roxb.) 3264 His othe he waged redilie. **1587** GOLDING *De Mornay* xxx. (1592) 476 Or, if he serued not God, how was it possible that the name of God should be waged by a mortall man, against the glory of God?

†**3.** To give pledges or pledge oneself for the fulfilment of (something promised). *Obs.*

1362 LANGL. *P. Pl.* A. IV. 87 For he haþ waget me a-mendes as wisdam him tauhte. *c* **1400** *Laud Troy Bk.* 8026 He sent out his Messanger..Trewes to aske, and trewes to wage. *c* **1400** *Ywaine & Gaw.* 2172, I said, that i sold find a Knyght That sold me mayntene in my right, And feght with tham al thre, Thus the batayl wajed we.

†**b.** with obj. a clause. *Obs.*

1362 LANGL. *P. Pl.* A. IV. 84 For Ichul wage for wrong he wol do so no more. *c* **1400** *Ploughman's Tale* (Skeat) 1208, I trow they do the devell homage In that they weten they do wrong; And thereto I dare well wage, They serven Sathan for all her song.

4. *spec.* in *Law.* Now only *Hist.* **a.** *to wage battle* [= AF. *gager bataille*, Law Latin *vadiare duellum*]: To pledge oneself to judicial combat: = GAGE *v.* 1c.

1568 GRAFTON *Chron.* II. 292 He offered to wage his battayle with the sayde Duke in the court of the French king. **1609** SKENE *Reg. Maj., Quon. Attach.* xxxi. 82b, It is statute, that the defender sall first wage the battell, and thereafter sweare. *a* **1625** SIR H. FINCH *Law* (1636) 25 Brothers or cosins shall not wage battell in a writ of right. *a* **1634** COKE *3rd Inst.* lxxii. (1648) 158 In a Writ of right, if the tenant wage battail by his Champion. **1768** BLACKSTONE *Comm.* III. xxii. 339 When the tenant in a writ of right pleads the general issue,..and offers to prove it by the body of his champion,..the tenant in the first place must produce his champion, who, by throwing down his glove as a gage or pledge, thus *wages* or stipulates battel with the champion of the demandant. **1819** *Act 59 Geo. III*, c. 46 §2 From and after the passing of this Act, in any Writ of Right..the Tenant shall not be received to wage Battel, nor shall Issue be joined nor Trial be had by Battel in any Writ of Right.

b. *to wage one's* (or *the*) *law* (AF. *gager la ley*, Law Latin *vadiare legem*): (*a*) to defend an action by 'wager of law' (see WAGER *sb.*^{2} 5a.). ¶(*b*) In erroneous popular use; to go to law (cf. 10).

(*a*) **1455** *Rolls of Parlt.* V. 326/2 All ye lawes aforesaid so waged and doon. **1456** *Paston Lett.* I. 407 Gunnore hath waged his lawe of that he haade his day to wage it of, &c. **1523** *Act 14 & 15 Hen. VIII*, c. 1 §1 In which sute..the Defendaunt or Defendauntes shall nat be admytted to wage ther Lawe. **1531** tr. *St. German's Doctor & Stud.* I. xviii. 42 Yf the defendaunte wage his lawe in an accyon of dette broughte vpon a trewe dette. **1579** *Expos. Terms Law* 138b, Ley gager. Wager of lawe, is when an action is brought agaynst one without especialtye shewed or other matter of recorde,..then the defendaunt may wage his lawe, that is to say, sweare vppon a booke, and certaine persons with him, that he oweth nothing to the plaintife [etc.]. **1611** COTGR., *Venir à la loy*, to be receiued, or admitted, vnto the waging of his Law. **1716** W. HAWKINS *Pleas Crown* II. x. (1726) 61 The Defendant shall not be suffered to wage his Law in any such Action. **1768** BLACKSTONE *Comm.* III. xxii. 345 It is only in actions of debt upon simple contract, or for an amercement in actions of detinue, and of account, where the debt may have been paid, the goods restored, or the account ballanced, without any evidence of either; it is only in these actions, I say, that the defendant is admitted to wage his law: so that wager of law lieth not, when [etc.]. **1824** BARNEWALL & CRESSWELL *Cases K.B.* II. 538 *marg.*, Where, in debt on simple contract, the defendant waged his law, the Court refused to assign the number of compurgators with whom he should come to perfect his law.

(*b*) **1529** in Mary A. E. Wood *Lett. Roy. & Illustr. Ladies* (1846) II. 51 If so be there be no way..to obtain it, but only by the common law..I am in that poverty I am not able to wage any law with him. **1538** STARKEY *England* (1878) 117 Oft-tymys the vniust cause preuaylyth, in so much as the one party ys not perauentur so abul as the other to wage hys law. **1548** CRANMER *Catech.* 62 And in case that at the lenght we haue sentence on our side, yet..we shal, for the most parte, spende more mony in waginge of the law, than we shall gayne by the sentence. **1579** HAKE *Newes out of Powles* (1872) B ij, Or else to worke their neighbors woe, by waging sutes at Lawe. **1622** MABBE tr. *Aleman's Guzman d'Alf.* II. 325, I wanted money to be able to draw out my thread to it's length, and to wage Law with them. **1625** B. JONSON *Staple of N.* v. i, I am not able to wage Law with him, Yet must maintaine the thing, as my owne right.

†**c.** *to wage deliverance*: = GAGE *v.* 1b. *Obs.*

1607 COWEL *Interpr.* s.v. *Gage*, To wage deliuerance, that is, to giue securitie that a thing shall be deliuered. **1656** BLOUNT *Glossogr.* s.v. *Wage*.

5. To put to hazard, venture or risk the loss of.

? *a* **1400** *Morte Arth.* 2967, I salle wage for that wye alle that I welde. ? *c* **1630** WEBSTER *App. & Virg.* III. i. (1654) 25 If you will needs wage eminence and state, chuse out a weaker opposite. **1825** SCOTT *Talism.* ix, Therefore have you me, and many better Scottishmen, making war against the infidels under your banners... If their numbers are now few, it is because their lives have been freely waged and wasted.

†**b.** *refl.* To throw oneself on the mercy of another. *Obs.*

c **1400** *Pilgr. Sowle* (Caxton 1483) I. xv. 11 Ther nys leon ne cruel leonesse soo fyers..that theyr malyce attempren.. ne wyl..to tho that lowely wyl them seluen wage with meke herte.

†**6.** *esp.* To agree to forfeit in some contingency; to stake, wager, bet. *Obs.*

1483 CAXTON *G. de la Tour* xviii. b vj, Lete laye a wager, that whiche wyf of vs thre that obeyeth best her husbond.. that he wynne the wager: wherupon they waged a jewele. **1598** R. WRAG in *Hakluyt's Voy.* (1599) II. I. 309 And holding them [the wives and children of their poor tenants] in such slauery as though they had beene no better then dogges, would wage them against a grayhound or spaniell. **1607** TOPSELL *Four-f. Beasts* 69 The Indians..make no small reckoning of these beastes (..their..Oxen), for they ..wil runne a race as fast as any horse:..waging both Gold and Siluer vpon their heads. **1633** FORD *Love's Sacrif.* I. ii, I dare Wage a thousand Ducats not a man in France Out-rides Roseilli. **1637** B. JONSON *Sad Sheph.* II. i, They shall rin after yee, and wage the odds, Upo' their owne deceived sights, yee' are her! *c* **1640** J. SMYTH *Lives Berkeleys* (1883) II. 386 And hee..being confident shee went with a son, offered to wage with her ten pound to thirty pound, that soe it was. **1674** *Ch. & Court of Rome* 10 Our Author..wages his reputation in the case. **1704** N. N. tr. *Boccalini's Advts. fr. Parnass.* II. 222 That famous Timotheus Graecus, who having waged his Beard about the Dispute of a Syllable with Francisco Filelfo, upon the loss of the Wager very willingly submitted to have it cut off. **1719** D'URFEY *Pills* II. 60 I'd wage a hundred thousand Pounds. **1742** FIELDING *J. Andrews* III. xii, If I walked alone,.. I would wage a shilling that the pedestrian outstripped the equestrian travellers.

†**II. 7.** To engage or employ for wages; to hire: **a.** for military service. *Obs.*

c **1330** R. BRUNNE *Chron. Wace* (Rolls) 3172 [Brenne] waged souders. **1377** LANGL. *P. Pl.* B. XXI. 258 If þei wage men to werre, þei write hem in noumbre. ? *a* **1400** *Morte Arth.* 333 And I salle wagge to that were of wyrchipfulle knyghtes,.. Twa thosande in tale. **1432–50** tr. *Higden, Harl. Contin.* (Rolls) VIII. 478 Fresche men wagede for men that were sleyne. **1456** SIR G. HAYE *Law Arms* (S.T.S.) 148 A man of armes that is wagit with a lord for all the ȝere. **1563** *Mirr. Mag., Ld. Rivers* liv, For hys defende great store of men I waged, Doubtyng the stormes which at such tymes betyde. **1596** LODGE *Wits Misery* 86 The Turke.. hath alwaies in prest for the war 130 thousand Timariste [*sic*] (who are waged by lands which the Turke hath giuen them ..) he hath beside them 14 thousand Ianisaries, and 36 thousand Spaies, continually waged by mony. **1599** HAYWARD *1st Pt. Life Hen. IV*, 68 Assone as the Duke was come into Brittaine he waged certaine souldiours, and presently departed to Calice. **1623** BINGHAM *Xenophon* I As for the Grecians, he waged them as secretly as he could, to the intent to take his Brother altogether vnprouided. **1652–62** HEYLYN *Cosmogr.* IV. (1682) 63 He wageth mercenary Souldiers of other Nations.

fig. **1607** SHAKS. *Cor.* V. vi. 40 Till at the last I seem'd his Follower, not Partner; and He wadg'd me with his Countenance, as if I had bin Mercenary.

†**b.** *gen. Obs.*

1465 *Paston Lett.* Suppl. (1901) 88 If my servauntis faile I had lever wage some other man, for a jorny or a season, thanne my mater should be on sped. **1468** SIR J. PASTON in *P. Lett.* II. 327, I have wagyd for to helpe yow and Dawbeney to kepe the place at Castr, iiij wel assuryd and trew men. **1593** G. HARVEY *Pierces Super.* Wks. (Grosart) II. 98 He.. waged Zenophantus to enflame and enrage his courage with the furious notes of Battail. **1601** R. JOHNSON *Kingd. & Commonw.* (1603) 234 Mahumetan princes.. to secure their estates doe never trust their home-bred subjects, but wage strangers and slaves, unto whose fidelity they commit their persons. **1608** WILLET *Hexapla Exod.* 497 Such things which a man is waged or hired to keepe.

†**c.** To bribe. *Obs.*

1461 *Rolls of Parlt.* V. 478/1 Convened with the same Scotts, procuryng, desiring and wagyng theym to enter. **1549** LATIMER *3rd Serm. bef. Edw. VI* (Arb.) 88 Thei will be waged by the rich, eyther to geue sentence agaynste the poore, or to put of the poore mannes causes. **1560** DAUS tr. *Sleidane's Comm.* 348 b, The cleargy of Maidenburge.. had waged him with great rewards and promesses. **1563–87** FOXE *A. & M.* (1596) 44/1 Neither could the darke night serue them to that purpose, nor anie intreatie nor waging them with monie, which were appointed for watchmen. **1587** GOLDING *De Mornay* XXV. 442 As though Cyrus had bene bent of set purpose to verifie the Prophesie, or as though hee had bene waged by the Prophet. **1603** FLORIO *Montaigne* I. xxv. 73 The judgement of a man that is waged and bought. *a* **1800** PEGGE *Suppl. Grose, Wag'd*, hired, bribed: They wag'd him to do it. North.

†**d.** *intr.* To make an agreement for wages. *Obs.*

1608 WILLET *Hexapla Exod.* 497 He waged with Iakob to keepe his sheep.

†**8.** *trans.* To put out to hire. *Obs. rare*⁻¹.

1590 SPENSER *F.Q.* II. vii. 18 Thou.. must wage Thy workes for wealth, and life for gold engage.

9. To pay wages to. Now *rare* or *Obs.*

1393 LANGL. *P. Pl.* C. v. 192 And ich dar legge my lyf that Loue wol lene the suluer, To wage thyne, and help wynne that thow wilnest after. *c* **1400** *Sowdone Bab.* 590 Take a thausande pounde of Frankis fyne, To wage wyth the pepul newe. **14..** *Customs of Malton* in *Engl. Misc.* (Surtees) 59 Also in pley of lande and als wele wagyd os be fore. **1460** CAPGRAVE *Chron.* (Rolls) 300 Thei were receyved by the duke of Burgundi ful worchipfully, and waged sufficiently. **1525** BERNERS *Froiss.* II. lxi. [lxiv.] 79 b, The kynge of Aragon sware and sealed.. to sende vnto hym as moche money as sholde wage fyue hundreth speres. **1530** *Test. Ebor.* (Surtees) V. 288, I will that a prest be wadgyd to pray for the helth of my saull.. and to have yerely for his wadges eight marces. **1533–4** *Act 25 Hen. VIII*, c. 21 §6 The charges of obteynyng the seid licences.. and in conductyng of currours and wagyng solicitours.. have be grevous and excessive. *c* **1550** R. BIESTON *Bayte Fortune* A iiij b, Who wageth the seruaunt, who paieth the souldeour. **1552** LATIMER *Serm. Lincs.* v. (1562) 102 At oure tyme, phisike is a remedy prepared only for riche folkes, not for poore: for the poore man is not able to wage the phisicion. **1565** J. HALL *Crt. Vertue* 138 The laboryng man would for his payn, Be wagde with double hyre, Or els would loyter, and not worke At any mans desyre. **1568** GRAFTON *Chron.* II. 726 Knowing his treasurie at home to be so voyde and faynt, that it was not able long to wage his Souldiours. **1585** T. WASHINGTON tr. *Nicholay's Voy.* III. xxii. 112 b, Besides that which is giuen vnto them of almes, they are waged either publikely, or of som in particular. **1640** SIR T. STAFFORD in *Lismore Papers* Ser. II. (1888) IV. 158 There proposition of requiringe 4000li monthlie to wadge there Army. **1823** SCOTT *Quentin D.* v, It is an art this French King of ours has found out,.. to wage his soldiers out of other men's purses. **1833** I. D'ISRAELI in *New Monthly Mag.* XXXVII. 203 The master dresses and wages highly his pampered train.

†**b.** Ironically, to reward (for evil). *Obs.*

1412–20 LYDG. *Troy Bk.* III. 2419 With his swerd.. þoruȝ þe brest, & some þoruȝ þe side He percid haþ, and waged hem for euere. *Ibid.* 3362 To whom Hector bad he shulde goon To þe furies depe doun in helle,.. And þus whan he was wagid for his mede, Anon his broþer.. Swiche sorwe made.. þat pite was for to sen and here.

†**c.** To pay wages for. *Obs.*

1638 HEYWOOD *Wise Woman* II. i, When I receive thee gladly to mine house And wage thy stay, thou shalt have Graciana.

¶**d.** *absol.* (*fig.*) ? To bring reward.

13.. *E.E. Allit. P.* A. 416 My lorde þe lombe.. Corounde me quene in blysse to brede, In lenghe of dayez þat euer schal wage.

III. 10. To carry on (war, a contest).

Developed from sense 3: cf. 4 a.

1456 SIR G. HAYE *Law Arms* (S.T.S.) 255 To vage bataill in lissis.., that is to say in barreris. **1526** *Pilgr. Perf.* (W. de W. 1531) 95 b, How bytter, sharpe, and fearfull is the conflicte to wage batayle & fyght with pryde. **1609** DANIEL *Civ. Wars* II. cxvii. 62 Then hadst not thou, deare Countrie, com'n to wage Warre with thy selfe. **1631** GOUGE *God's Arrows* V. §6. 415 [They] waged many battels valiantly and victoriously. **1667** MILTON *P.L.* I. 121 To wage by force or guile eternal Warr. **1697** PRIOR *A Satire* 118 He should be kept from waging War with Words. **1738** WESLEY *Ps.* LVI. i, My Foes continual Battles wage. *a* **1770** JORTIN *Serm.* (1771) II. 44 It does not follow that Christians may not wage war against their Enemies. **1791** COWPER *Iliad* XVII. 576 Thou, therefore, the resplendent reins receive.. while I, dismounting, wage the fight. **1799** COLERIDGE *Ode to Duchess Devonshire* 33 And some, perchance, might wage an equal strife. **1826** J. F. COOPER *Last of Mohicans* xiii, I had thought the Delawares a pacific people,.. and that they never waged war in person. **1840** DICKENS *Old C. Shop* iv, That lady's mother.. resided with the couple and waged perpetual war with Daniel. **1845–6** TRENCH *Hulsean Lect.* Ser. I. viii. 128 Those.. conflicts, which the Church.. must one day wage with those forms of untruth. **1849** MACAULAY *Hist. Eng.* v. I. 633 As they had been levied for the purpose of waging war on an infidel nation, they bore on their flag.. the Paschal lamb. **1850** TENNYSON *In Mem.* lxxxii, I wage not any feud with Death For changes wrought on form and face. **1861** BUCKLE *Civiliz.* II. iii. 232 How idle, then, is that warfare which reformers are too apt to wage. **1874** GREEN *Short Hist.* ii. §7. 95 In his old age he waged his bitterest war against his son. **1887** BOWEN *Virg. Æneid* VI. 828 Ah! what battles the twain must wage, what legions array.

¶*transf.* (*nonce-use*). *a* **1648** *Ess. on Death* in *Bacon's Remaines* (1648) 12, I.. could wish that like peace to all those with whom I wage love.

b. To contend for (a cause). *rare.*

1839–52 BAILEY *Festus* 65 In Thy name we shall O'ercome, for we will only wage the right.

†**c.** *intr.* in various nonce-uses: To struggle, contend *against*; to struggle *through* difficulties; to contend in rivalry. *Obs.*

1605 SHAKS. *Lear* II. iv. 212 No, rather I abiure all roofes, and chuse To wage against the enmity oth'ayre. **1608** —— *Per.* IV. ii. 34 The commoditie wages not with the daunger. **1656** in *Verney Mem.* (1907) I. 558 My troubles are many, yet.. I indifferently wage through them. **1690** CHILD *Disc. Trade* (1698) 187 If there were no others to wage with us, we might.. make our own Markets; but as the case now stands, that all the World are striving to engross all the Trade they can [etc.].

11. *trans.* To wield (a weapon, etc.). *rare.*

1836 *Lett. fr. Madras* (1843) 17 Mr. Kenrick was mounted on the top of the hay, waging a water-pipe in full play. **1865** SIR J. K. JAMES *Tasso's Jerus. Deliv.* x. lxix. I. 321 Pagans become, and for our kingdom wage 'Gainst impious Godfred, your avenging swords.

wage, obs. form of WEDGE.

†**'wageable,** *a. Obs.* [f. WAGE *v.* + -ABLE.] That may be hired for military service, mercenary.

1614 RALEGH *Hist. World* v. ii. §8. 416 The Gessates, Nations about Rhodanus, wageable as the Switzers in these times.

waged (weɪdʒd), *ppl. a.* [f. WAGE *v.* + -ED¹.] Hired for wages; paid by wages. †Of soldiers: Mercenary (*obs.*).

c **1440** *Engl. Conq. Irel.* (1896) 23 We come not into this londe as wagid men. *c* **1449** PECOCK *Repr.* II. ix. 193 So weel wagid bischopis. **1462** J. PASTON in *P. Lett.* II. 121, I may get leve for to send non of my wagyd men home ageyn. **1535** COVERDALE *Jer.* xlvi. 21 Hir wagid souldyers that be with her, are like fat calues. **1579** MOYSIE *Mem. Affairs Scot.* (Bannatyne Club) 21 For the quhilk effect theare wer iijᶜ waidged men teane vp vpone the Kingis expensse. **1579** TOMSON *Calvin's Serm. Tim.* 123/2 Let us mark.. that we may be watchfull to fight against Sathan, and his waged men. **1590** BARROW & GREENWOOD in *Confer.* 46 You stand a waged Minister vnder them. **1617** MORYSON *Itin.* II. 92 Florence mac Carty.. refused to give his son for pledge, lest his waged souldiers should cast him out of his Countrey. **1829** SCOTT *Anne of G.* xxxv, Wouldst thou aid the enemy of the lord under whose banner thou servest, against his waged soldiers? **1870** *Daily News* 18 June, The continued want of employment among those who live by waged labour.

†**b.** In bad sense: Bribed. *Obs.*

1561 T. NORTON *Calvin's Inst.* III. 290 Yᵉ leud babblers which do let out to hier the seruice of their waged tonge.

'wagedom. [f. WAGE *sb.* + -DOM.] The economic system under which wage-earners live.

1885 *Daily Chron.* 7 Sept. (Cassell), By the substitution of industrial partnership in place of wagedom. **1886** W. DONISTHORPE *Basis Individualism* 19 Such is the modern system of wagedom. The wage-receiver gets just enough to keep himself alive for the use of his employers. **1910** *Dubl. Rev.* Oct. 375 The positive translation of wagedom into partnership.

wagel, waggel ('wægəl). *dial.* Also 7 wagell, 9 waggle. [Perh. Cornish.] A name for the Black-backed Gull, *Larus marinus*, in its immature state, when the plumage is mottled grey and white; formerly supposed to be a distinct species.

a **1672** WILLUGHBY *Ornith.* III. ii. §3 (1676) 266 Wagell *Cornubiensium*,.. The great gray Gull. **1753** *Chambers' Cycl.* Suppl., *Waggel.* **1785** LATHAM *Gen. Synopsis Birds* III. II. 375 Wagel Gull. **1825** SHAW *Gen. Zool.* XIII. 187 Great Black-backed Gull (*Larus Marinus*).. Wagel Gull. **1843** JARDINE *Birds Gt. Brit.* IV. 299 Larus marinus, Linn... Great Black-backed Gull of British authors.—(L. nævius, the Wagel, young). **1880** *W. Cornwall Gloss.*, *Wagel*, a grey gull. **1893–4** *Northumb. Gloss.*, *Waggle-gull*, the young of the greater black-backed gull *Larus Marinus*, L.

wageless ('weɪdʒlɪs), *a.* [f. WAGE *sb.* + -LESS.]

†**1.** That does not pay a wage or recompense.

1615 [see TAXLESS *a.*].

2. That does not earn or receive wages. Also *wagesless* (rare).

1828 LYTTON *Pelham* xlix, Some intrusive, ragamuffin, wagesless lackey. **1843** CARLYLE *Past & Pr.* III. xii. (1858) 232 By unwearied, valiant, and were it wageless effort, in my Parliament, and in my Parish, I would aid [etc.]. **1853** SURTEES *Sponge's Sp. Tour* lxiii. (1893) 335 In came Peter, one of the wageless footmen, with candles. **1889** GISSING *Nether World* II. 18 Employed on piece-work, they might at any moment find themselves wageless.

Hence **'wagelessness.**

1913 *Spectator* 14 June 1004/1 It is impossible.. to make up the amount.. after several weeks of idleness and wagelessness.

†**'wageling.** *Obs. rare.* [f. WAGE *sb.* or *v.* + -LING.] A hireling.

a **1547** BALE *Image Both Ch.* xiii. (1550) e viij, These are the verye false Prophetes,.. wolues, wagelynges, Iudasses, ..[etc.]. **1570** LEVINS *Manip.* 136/32 A Wageling, *mercenarius.*

wagen, obs. form of WAGON.

‖**wagenboom** ('vɑːx(ə)nbʊəm). *S. Afr.* Also 8 wage-boom, waboom. Also anglicized wag(g)on-boom, and corruptly vaboom. [Du., f. *wagen* WAGON + *boom* tree.] (See quots.)

1790 E. HELME tr. *Le Vaillant's Trav. Afr.* I. 255 A few paltry woods.. had some resemblance to that named *Wage-boom.* **1822** BURCHELL *Trav. S. Afr.* I. 123 We passed some large trees of *Wagenboom* (*Protea grandiflora*), so called by the colonists because the wood of it has been found suitable for making the fellies of waggon-wheels. **1873** DAWSON *Earth & Man* xi. 258 Cone-like fruits belonging to the Proteaceæ (..wagenbooms, etc.). **1880** A. H. SWINTON *Insect Variety* 267 The.. Eocene flora.. as evidenced by the London Clay drift beds.. shows fruits of.. Australian banksias, silver-trees, wagonbooms. **1897** DU TOIT *Rhodesia* 126 This region cannot be unhealthy, for the 'sugar-bosch' and 'waggon-boom' grow everywhere. **1907** SIM *Forests Cape Colony* 59 [Used for tanning:] The bark and leaves of various *Proteaceæ* (Sugarbushes, Kreupelbooms, Vabooms, and Amandel). **1946** *Cape Times* 5 Feb. 6/8 He is collecting waboom and kreupelbos seeds above the Camps Bay slopes so that the bare areas.. can be covered with these handsome proteas. **1972** PALMER & PITMAN *Trees S. Afr.* I. 525 The waboom is one of the tallest of the genus *Protea* and is conspicuous in dry rocky areas of the Cape.

Wagener ('vɑːgənə(r)). Also *erron.* Wagner. The name of the Abram *Wagener* (fl. 1796) American farmer, used *absol.* or *attrib.* to designate an apple tree or its fruit belonging to a variety developed on his farm in Penn Yan, New York State (see quot. 1956).

1848 *Trans. N.Y. State Agric. Soc. 1847* VII. 315 The apple for which it is proposed to award the second premium of the society, is called the 'Wagener apple'. **1886** L. H. BAILEY *Field Notes on Apple Culture* iv. 21 For winter:.. Jonathan,.. Northern Spy, Wagener. **1915** A. E. WILKINSON *Apple* ii. 24 The Wagener thus fits in well with the Northern Spy in soil requirements. **1925** E. HEMINGWAY *In our Time* (1930) iv. 45 Nick stopped and picked up a Wagner apple. **1956** *Dict. Gardening* (R. Hort. Soc.) Suppl. 95/2 Wagener.. Medium size, round, flattish, irregular, shining yellowish-green, striped and flushed with bright scarlet. **1969** *Oxf. Bk. Food Plants* 48/2 'Wagener'.. is an example of many good apples raised in the U.S.A. from European stock.

†**'wager,** *sb.*¹ *Sc. Obs.* In 4–6 wageour, vageour, 6 waeger, waigeour, vager. [f. WAGE *sb.* + -ER¹ (spelt *-our* after words from AF.).

While the known instances are exclusively Sc., the surname *Wager* ('Ricardus le Wager' *c* 1275 in *Shropsh. Arch.* I. 126) suggests that the word may at one time have been current in the south.]

A mercenary soldier.

1375 BARBOUR *Bruce* XI. 48 And off tresour so stuffit is he, That he may vageowris haf plente. *c* **1420** WYNTOUN *Cron.* IV. 679 Thre hundyr thousande he had by Off wageouris armyt al at richt. **1456** SIR G. HAYE *Law Arms* (S.T.S.) 87 In the samyn cas, say I of a knycht that is wageour till a king or a lorde. *c* **1470** HENRY *Wallace* x. 755 Thai wageours sone he put to confusion. **1513** DOUGLAS *Æneis* XI. Prol. 71 Gif thou be aganist God,.. Than art thou wageour onto Lucifer. **1532** *Extracts Aberd. Reg.* (1844) I. 144 The furnesing of certane waegeris to conuoy our souerane lordis artailȝery. **1558** *Ibid.* 309 To furneis vageris extranearis to the nummer of ane hundreytht men. **1596** DALRYMPLE tr. *Leslie's Hist. Scot.* (S.T.S.) II. 273 The men of weir waigeours, quhom he commandes to bring the gret gunis.

b. *attrib.* quasi-*adj.* Mercenary, bribed.

1567 *Gude & Godlie B.* (S.T.S.) 182 Thocht wageour Freiris faine wald lie, The treuth will furth.

wager ('weɪdʒə(r)), *sb.*² Forms: 4–5 waiour (= wajour), 5 wayoure, 5–6 wageour (5 -or, -oure, wagour, 7 wadger, 8 waiger), 5– wager. [a. AF. *wageure* (= F. *gageure*), f. *wager* WAGE *v.*¹: see -URE. In the legal use 5, prob. in origin a distinct word, f. WAGE *v.* + -ER⁴; one of the technical nouns of action framed by lawyers in the 16th c. in imitation of Law French infinitives used subst.; the spelling *wageour* in quot. 1533, however, shows that it was already confused with the ordinary word.]

I. †**1.** A solemn pledge or undertaking. *Obs.*

1306 *Exec. Sir S. Fraser* in *Pol. Songs* (1839) 218 A wajour he made, so hit wes y-told, Ys heved of to smhyte ȝef me him brohte in hold wat so bytyde.

2. Something (esp. a sum of money) laid down and hazarded on the issue of an uncertain event; a stake. Now *rare* exc. in phr. ***to lay, win, lose a wager***.

1303 R. BRUNNE *Handl. Synne* 5596 A waiour dar y wyth ȝow ley, þat y shal haue some gode at hym. *c* **1440** *Promp. Parv.* 513/2 Wayoure, *vadium, vadimonium.* *c* **1440** *Jacob's Well* 192 For a waiour I schal gon & askyn almes of Perys tollere,.. þe waiour was leyde. *c* **1450** *Bk. Curtasye* 227 in *Babees Bk.* 306 Ne waiour non with hym þou lay. *a* **1533** BERNERS *Huon* liii. 180 As for the wager that I sholde wyn therby, I am content to relese it quyte. **1596** SHAKS. *Tam. Shr.* v. ii. 69 *Hort.* Content, what's the wager? *Luc.* Twentie Crownes. **1617** MORYSON *Itin.* III. 78 They never play at Dice, seldome at Cardes, and that for small wagers. **1682** O. HEYWOOD *Diaries* (1881) II. 295 Several Lords laid wagers which could out swear one another. **1691** LUTTRELL *Brief Rel.* (1857) II. 207 They being grown so bold and insolent as to offer wagers that Cork will be out of our possession by the last of May. **1702** *Lond. Post* 7–9 Sept. 2/1 Great Wagers are laid in this City, that Cadix is already in our Hands. **1722** N. BLUNDELL *Diary* (1895) 191, I layed a Waiger, and Mr. Jo. Poole held the stakes. **1758** JOHNSON *Idler* No. 6 ¶11 By this performance, she won her wager. **1817** SELWYN *Law Nisi Prius* (ed. 4) II. 1296 It may be proper to state in what cases an action will lie for enforcing the payment of a wager. **1817** BYRON *Beppo* xxvii, Most men.. Will back their own opinions with a wager. **1840** BARHAM *Ingol. Leg.*, *Black Mousquetaire* 284 The Captains and Majors Began to lay wagers How far the Ghost part of the story was true. **1842** DICKENS *Amer. Notes* vi, There was a fire last night, there are two to-night, and you may lay an even wager there will be at least one, to-morrow. **1851–61** MAYHEW *Lond. Labour* III. 116, I won the match, and beat the dog by four minutes. The wager was five shillings, which I had. **1866** G. MACDONALD *Ann. Q. Neighb.* vii. (1878) 118 He would go down the underground stair.. for the wager of a guinea.

†**b.** The prize to be won in a contest. *Obs.*

c **1450** *Brut* ccxliv. 378 For our archers.. schet þat day for a wager. **1513** DOUGLAS *Æneis* v. Prol. 10 At the begynning, the wageouris by and by, And the rewardis, in myddis of the field Befoir thair ene war sett. **1546** LANGLEY tr. *Pol. Verg. de Invent.* II. ix. 53 At the other ende was the wager sette, that they ranne for. **1576** TURBERV. *Venerie* 246 He that giveth most Cotes or most turnes winneth the wager. **1609** DEKKER *Guls Horne-bk.* vii. 36 And let any hooke draw you either to a Fencers supper, or to a Players that acts such a part for a wager. **1667** PEPYS *Diary* 14 Apr., There the girls did run for wagers over the bowling-green.

fig. *a* **1548** HALL *Chron., Hen. VI*, 167 For Kyng Henry.. and Richard duke of Yorke.. wresteled for the game, and strove for the wager.

3. An agreement or contract under which each of the parties promises to give money or its equivalent to the other according to the issue of an uncertain event; a betting transaction.

a **1548** HALL *Chron., Hen. VIII.* 7 Certayn noble men made a wager to runne at the rynge. *a* **1586** SIDNEY *Arcadia* I. xiv. (1912) 93 Love and mischeefe having made a wager, which should have most power in me. **1602** SHAKS. *Ham.* IV. vii. 156 (1604 Qo.) Wee'le make a solemne wager on your cunnings. **1611** —— *Cymb.* I. iv. 181, I will fetch my Gold, and haue our two Wagers recorded. **1641** EVELYN *Diary* 4 Oct., One who, upon divers greate wagers, went to and fro betweene that Citty and Antwerp on foote. **1725** DE FOE *Voy. round World* (1840) 301 Wagers were very rife among us, who should come first to the shore of Patagonia. **1761** BURROW *Cases K.B.* (1766) II. 1171 There are many Conveniences from allowing valued Policies: But where they are used merely as a Cover to a Wager, they would be considered as an Evasion. **1778** MISS BURNEY *Evelina* (1791) II. 118 He was interrupted by a call from the company to discuss the affair of the wager. **1828** SCOTT *F.M. Perth* xvii, I could venture to accept your wager, my lord,.. but there is no time for foolery. **1876** ROGERS *Pol. Econ.* i. 9 If one man makes a wager with another, the occurrence of the event on which the wager depends, does involve loss and gain.

†**b.** ***an equal, even wager***, an even chance. *Obs.*

1638 CHILLINGW. *Relig. Prot.* I. iv. §57. 224 It were an even wager there were none such! **1706** HEARNE *Collect.* 25 Mar. (O.H.S.) I. 209 But 'tis an even Wager whether his Book proves himself or me a schismatick. **1742** HOYLE *Whist* xviii. 84 It being an equal Wager that your Partner has a better Card in that Suit, than the last Player.

†**c.** ***to lie upon the wager***: to be at stake. *Obs.*

1590 SPENSER *F.Q.* I. iii. 12 Full fast she fled, ne euer lookt behind, As if her life vpon the wager lay.

d. An act of putting to hazard, a risk.

1855 MACAULAY *Hist. Eng.* xviii. IV. 220 Nothing could be more natural than that, for the very smallest chance of recovering the three kingdoms.. he should be willing to stake what was not his own, the honour of the French arms ..[etc.]. To a French statesman such a wager might well appear in a different light.

e. A contest for a prize.

1615 MARKHAM *Country Contentm.* I. vii. 102 If you will prepare him [a greyhound] for match and wadger. **1834** *John Bull* 27 July 238/3 Putney Regatta... Twelve pairs of sculls were entered to compete for the prize (a purse of 20 sovereigns). It was what would be termed in the aquatic circles, a double-sculled wager, viz., two pairs in each boat.

4. Something on the issue of which bets are or may be laid; the subject of a bet or bets.

a **1586** SIDNEY *Arcadia* II. vii. (1912) 193 Their ruine was the wager of the others contention. **1625** K. LONG tr. *Barclay's Argenis* v. xvii. 391 But what, thinks she, if they cast Lots for mee, as for a trivial or base wager? **1678** TEMPLE *Let. to Hyde* Wks. 1731 II. 474, I would be glad likewise to know your Conjectures there, whether France will come to the Peace or no, without refusing any longer to evacuate the Towns, which is the present Wager current at Amsterdam. **1865** E. BURRITT *Walk Land's End* iv. 124 Every man and boy of these colored laborers was working as at a wager.

II. 5. *Law* (now *Hist.*). The action of WAGE *v.* (4 a, b).

a. ***wager of law***: an offer to make oath of innocence or non-indebtedness, to be supported by the oaths of eleven compurgators. **b.** ***wager of battle***: a challenge by a defendant to decide his guilt or innocence by single combat.

a. *a.* **1521–2** *Ir. Act 13 Hen. VIII*, c. 2 (1621) 73 The partie or parties defendants shall haue none essoine, protection, ne law wager. **1533** MORE *Debell. Salem* II. xv. 33 Lyke as in the wageour of a lawe, they shall not swere that the defendaunt oweth not the money, but that they byleue that he swereth treuth. **1536** *Ir. Act 28 Hen. VIII*, c. 5 (1621) 102 Wherein no wager of law, essoine ne protection shall lye. **1628** COKE *On Litt.* §514. 293 b, The like oath shall bee made in an Attaint and in battaile, and in wager of Law [Litt. *en Battaile & en ley gager*]. **1696** VENTRIS *Reports* (1701) 261 In this case the Court overruled the Wager of Law. **1768** BLACKSTONE *Comm.* III. xxii. 341 A sixth species of trial is by wager of law, *vadiatio legis.* **1833** *Act 3 & 4 Will. IV*, c. 42 §13 And be it further enacted, That no Wager of Law shall be hereafter allowed.

incorrect use. **1791** BURKE *App. Whigs* Wks. 1808 VI. 142 In this part, his defence will not be made by argument, but by wager of law.

b. *a* **1625** SIR H. FINCH *Law* (1636) The Table, Wager of battell shall not be by Cosins in a writ of right. **1716** W. HAWKINS *Pleas Crown* II. xlv. (1726) 427 He may counterplead the Wager of Battel. **1768** BLACKSTONE *Comm.* III. xxii. 337 The trial by wager of battel. **1819** *Act 59 Geo. III.* c. 46 (*title*) An Act to abolish Appeals of Murder, Treason, Felony or other Offences, and Wager of Battel.

transf. **1824** MISS MITFORD *Village* I. 150 Having accepted the wager of battle, our champion began forthwith to collect his forces. **1869** FREEMAN *Norm. Conq.* (1875) III. xi. 5 When Harold and William met face to face in the great wager of battle.

III. 6. *attrib.* and *Comb.*, in sense 'done for a wager', as ***wager-fight, -shooting, -smoking***; also **wager-boat**, a light racing sculling-boat used in contests between single scullers; **wager-cup**, a 'cup' offered as a prize in a contest; †**wager-hall**, ? the hall of the imaginary guild of betting men; **wager-insurance** = *wager-policy*; †**wager-office**, a place for recording wagers; **wager-policy**, an insurance-policy partaking of the nature of a wager.

1844 ALB. SMITH *Adv. Mr. Ledbury* ix. (1886) 29 [He] began talking about the sweet *wager-boat which his friend ..had bought at Searle's. **1865** DICKENS *Mut. Fr.* IV. i, It was an amateur sculler.. in so light a boat that the Rogue remarked: 'A little less on you, and you'd a'most ha' been a Wagerbut.' **1878** W. J. CRIPPS *Old Engl. Plate* x. 292 The well-known cups, sometimes called '*wager cups', in the form of a woman holding a smaller cup over her head with outstretched arms. **1826** HOR. SMITH *Tor Hill* II. 283 The *wager-fight between the English and Italians was to be a combat of three and three in succession. **1691** DRYDEN *K. Arth.* Prol. 31 Betts.. [are] grown a common Trade for all, And Actions, by the News-Book, Rise and Fall; Wits, Cheats, and Fops, are free of *Wager-Hall. **1824** BENECKE *Mar. Insur.* 142 The statute 19 Geo. II. c. 37, by which *wager insurances have been declared illegal. **1722** DE FOE *Col. Jack* (1840) 54 One Stewart.. kept a *wager-office and insurance. **1761** BURROW *Cases K.B.* (1766) II. 1171 A valued Policy is not to be considered as a *Wager Policy. **1787** J. A. PARK *Law Marine Insur.* 294 Of Wager-Policies. **1913** M. ROBERTS *Salt of Sea* vi. 166 They'll pay premiums reckless and regardless 'ow Lloyd's runs rates up on 'em rapid when they starts wager policies on 'er. **1892** GREENER *Breech-Loader* 235 The 'Red House' at Battersea was.. the favourite metropolitan resort for *wager shooting.

wager (ˈweɪdʒə(r)), *sb.*³ *rare.* [f. WAGE *v.*¹ + -ER¹.] One who wages (war).

1611 SPEED *Hist. Gt. Brit.* IX. v. §46. 481 But the wiser amongst them vnwilling to bee wagers of new warres.. denied his request.

wager (ˈweɪdʒə(r)), *v.* [f. WAGER *sb.*²]

†**1.** *intr.* To contend for a prize. *Obs.*

1574 tr. *Marlorat's Apoc.* 42 None shall bee crowned sauing he that wagereth lawfully.

2. *trans.* To stake or hazard (something of value) on the issue of an uncertain event or on some question to be decided, to bet.

1611 SHAKS. *Cymb.* v. v. 182 Whereat, I.. wager'd with him Peeces of Gold, 'gainst this, which then he wore Vpon his honour'd finger, to attaine In suite the place of's bed, and winne this Ring By hers, and mine Adultery. *a* **1626** BACON *Apophth.* Wks. 1879 I. 326 He would wager twenty shillings with him upon that. **1674** *Govt. Tongue* xi. 201 He that will lay those [his truth and reputation] to stake upon every flying story, may as well wager his estate which way the wind will sit next morning. **1800** WORDSW. *Brothers* 283 I'd wager house and field That, if he is alive, he has it yet. **1828** SCOTT *F.M. Perth* xvii, I will wager a hundred merks with you, that [etc.]. **1849** MACAULAY *Hist. Eng.* vi. II. 137 Everything dear to nations was wagered on both sides. **1887** GUNTER *Mr. Barnes* xii. 85 The stake he plays for is not generally wagered on the tables of the Casino.

b. *fig.* To offer (one's head, etc.) as a pledge, guarantee, or forfeit.

1635 SHIRLEY *Coronation* I. (1640) B 4 b, I beg the honor, for Eubulus cause To be ingag'd, if any for Macarius, Worthy to wager heart with mine, accept it. *a* **1704** T. BROWN *Two Oxf. Scholars* Wks. 1730 I. 3, I'll wager my head against thee. **1832** HT. MARTINEAU *Homes Abr.* iv. 63 Ellen could give no better reason than that she could wager her life upon it.

c. To offer to put to the issue of a contest, to venture.

1819 SCOTT *Ivanhoe* xxv, We hold ye as robbers and traitors, and will wager our bodies against ye in battle, siege, or otherwise. *Ibid.* xxxviii, 'That is but brief space,' answered Rebecca, 'for a stranger.. to find one who will do battle, wagering life and honour for her cause, against a knight who is called an approved soldier.'

3. *intr.* To offer or lay a wager, to make a bet.

1602 SHAKS. *Ham.* IV. vii. 135 Wee'l.. bring you in fine together, And wager on your heads. **1605** B. JONSON *Volpone* IV. i, If I had But one to wager with, I would lay odds now, He tells me instantly. **1722** WODROW *Corr.* (1843) II. 647 It seems certain that an assassination was designed; and I hear the Jacobites.. were wagering on it some weeks ago. **1819** SCOTT *Leg. Montrose* xxi, He hath wagered deeply for a son of Diarmid.

b. With clause or inf.: To make a wager, to bet *that*...

1604 SHAKS. *Oth.* IV. ii. 12, I durst (my Lord) to wager, she is honest; Lay downe my Soule at stake. **1608** —— *Per.* v. i. 43 We haue a maid in Metiline, I durst wager would win some words of him. **1667** *Leathermore: Advice conc. Gaming* (1668) 8, I'le wager the Box shall have 1500*l.* of the Money, and that 18 of the 20 persons shall be losers. **1841** DICKENS *Barn. Rudge* ii, I'll wager that your stopping here to-night would please him better than it would please me. **1848** G. F. RUXTON in *Blackw. Mag.* LXIV. 441 One may safely wager to see a dozen coyotes or prairie wolves loping round.

¶**4.** Misused for WAGE *v.* 7. *Obs. rare*⁻¹.

1592 *Arden of Feversham* I. i. 524 Indaunger not your selfe for such a Churle, But hyre some Cutter for to cut him short, And heer's ten pound to wager them withall.

Hence **ˈwagered** *ppl. a.*; **ˈwagering** *ppl. a.*

1823 'JON BEE' *Dict. Turf* s.v. *Wagers*, These are 'wagering kiddies'—or fellows who lay quirking bets on equivocal subjects. **1876** MORRIS *Æneids* XII. 151, I may not look upon the fight, or see the wagered field. **1902** *Westm. Gaz.* 1 Apr. 6/3 Mr. John Alcock, aged sixty-two, yesterday walked backwards from Macclesfield market-place to the Crescent, Buxton,.. 15 min. 15 sec. under the wagered time.

wager: see WAGGER *v.*

wagerell, variant of WAKERELL.

wagerer (ˈweɪdʒərə(r)). [f. WAGER *v.* + -ER¹.] One who wagers or makes or lays wagers.

1660 INGELO *Bentiv. & Ur.* I. (1682) 166 They made the wagerers part stakes. **1691** LUTTRELL *Brief Rel.* (1857) II. 207 The attorny general hath orders to prosecute some of the late wagerers. **1708** *Brit. Apollo* No. 72. 2/1 We wou'd ..advise the Wagerers to draw Stakes. **1750** H. WALPOLE *Let. to Mann* 1 Sept., When they were going to bleed him, the wagerers for his death interposed, and said it would affect the fairness of the bet. **1854** SURTEES *Handley Cr.* lxxvi. (1901) II. 267 Making a mental bet with himself—for he was a bit of a wagerer—on the double event of [etc.]. **1890** *Harper's Mag.* Nov. 866/2 A silent ring of watchers and wagerers press closely about the table.

b. *Marine Insurance.* The holder of a wagering policy.

1712 *Mod. Reports* I. 78 Surely the law would not put an insurer *non bona fide*, or a wagerer, in a better condition than one that insured *bona fide*.

wagering (ˈweɪdʒərɪŋ), *vbl. sb.* [-ING¹.] The action of the vb. WAGER; an instance of this.

1692 LUTTRELL *Brief Rel.* (1857) II. 473 Sir Henry Fornace, eminently known for wagering, has laid 500£ to 400£ that the seige of Namur by this time is raised. **1697** DE FOE *Ess. Projects* 171 Wagering, as now practis'd by Polities and Contracts, is become a Branch of Assurances; it was before more properly a part of Gaming. **1746** *Act 19 Geo. II*, c. 37 §1 By introducing a mischievous kind of Gaming or Wagering, under the Pretence of assuring the Risque on Shipping, and fair Trade. **1753** RICHARDSON *Grandison* (1781) II. 160 He.. resolved.. to be more cautious in his wagerings than he had hitherto been. **1845** *Act 8 & 9 Vict.* §109 §18 All Contracts or Agreements, whether by Parole or in Writing, by way of gaming or wagering, shall be null and void. **1888** *Daily News* 15 Sept. 3/4 The feature of the wagering on the Cesarewitch was the advance of Kenilworth ..to 8 to 1.

b. *Comb.*: **wagering-policy** = *wager-policy* (see WAGER *sb.*² 6); †**wagering-post**, ? the post at which bets were made.

1758 BURROW *Cases K.B.* (1766) I. 492 The Act of 19 G. 2. c. 37 (made.. for Prevention of *wagering Policies). **1696** *Lond. Gaz.* No. 3215/4 The Horses to be shown at the *Wagering Post the 3d Wednesday in September.

wagery (ˈweɪdʒərɪ). [f. WAGE *sb.* + -ERY, after *slavery*.] The wage system, wage slavery (esp. as opposed by the guild socialists); wage-earners *collect.*

1917 A. S. NEILL *Dominie's Log* xv. 162, I wonder when people will begin to realise what wagery means. When they do begin to realise they will commence the revolution by driving women out of industry. **1917** S. G. HOBSON *Guild Principles in War & Peace* ii. 33 Two generations of wagery were to live their squalid life.. before we find singers.. grasping the true meaning of industrial oppression. **1972** A. M. QUINTON in Cox & Dyson *20th-Cent. Mind* I. iv. 128 Personal fulfilment through work and the production of honest and emotionally satisfying goods could be secured only by the abolition of 'wagery', the wage system in which men sold their labour power unconditionally.

wagesless: see WAGELESS *a.* 2.

waget(t, obs. forms of WATCHET.

Wagga (ˈwɒgə). *Austral. slang.* Also **wagga**. [f. *Wagga Wagga*, the name of a town in New South Wales.] In full, ***Wagga blanket, rug.*** A blanket or covering made by opening out two sacks, chaff bags, etc., and stitching them together along one edge.

1900 H. LAWSON *Darling River* in *Stories* (1964) 1st Ser. 388 The live cinders from the firebox..fell in showers on deck. Every now and again a spark would burn through the Wagga rug of a sleeping shearer. **1938** X. HERBERT *Capricornia* (1939) xxviii. 417 The nap..consisted of two greasy bran-sacks, or, as bushmen call them, Wagga Rugs. **1941** BAKER *Dict. Austral. Slang* 80 *Wagga blanket*, a rough covering used by tramps. **1944** J. DEVANNY *By Tropic Sea & Jungle* 156 When you crawl under your wagga you get in one position and aren't game to move. **1969** L. HADOW *Full Cycle* 248 She went to his camp bed. 'Take your wagga, then.' 'No, it's too heavy.' **1978** *Weekend* (Austral.) 25–26 Nov. 11/4 I'm due to slip under my Wagga blankets.

waggable ('wægəb(ə)l), *a.* [f. WAG *v.* + -ABLE.] That can be wagged.

1854 H. STRICKLAND *Travel Thoughts* 12 By unremitting and persevering agitation of the young caudal shoot, a real waggable tail may be the result.

waggadash: see WACADASH.

wagge, obs. form of WAG, WAGE *v.*[1]

waggel, waggen: see WAGEL, WAGON.

wagger ('wægə(r)), *sb.*[1] [f. WAG *v.* + -ER[1].]

† **1.** One who agitates or stirs. *Obs.*

1387 TREVISA *Higden* (Rolls) I. 189 And so þat name was to hem i-schappe Centauri, as it were an hundred wynde waggers: for þey wagged wel þe wynde faste in hir ridynge.

b. One who wags (his head).

1654 SIR A. JOHNSTON (Ld. Wariston) *Diary* (S.H.S.) II. 249 Thes revylers, waggers of their head, mockers, theives against Christ on the crosse.

2. An animal that wags its tail.

1887 MEREDITH *Poet. Wks.* (1912) 346 Should they once deem our emblem Pard Wagger of tail for all save war. **1911** MAX BEERBOHM *Zuleika Dobson* vi. 89 Corker [a bull-dog] had ever been..effusively grateful for every word or pat, an ever-ready wagger and nuzzler.

3. *pl.* The divining-rod. *dial.* ? *Obs.*

1747 HOOSON *Miner's Dict.* X 3, No one..could affirm that there were this or that particular Mine, that owed its Discovery to his Waggers, (for by that Name they then called them) some Miners told me that by his Waggers he could find out a Vein.

wagger ('wægə(r)), *sb.*[2] *slang* (orig. *Oxford University*). More fully, **wagger-pagger** (**-bagger**). [One of a collection of words jocularly formed by adding *-agger* (see -ER[6]) to the initial consonants of a word or expression, in this case *waste-paper basket.*] A waste-paper basket.

1903 [see -ER[6]]. **1925** O. JESPERSEN *Mankind, Nation & Individual* viii. 162 There is an interesting class of words with an inserted *g*:..*wagger pagger bagger* for *waste paper basket*. **1927** W. E. COLLINSON *Contemp. Eng.* 125 Such playful formations as the Pragger Wagger (the Prince of Wales..) and wagger pagger bagger *waste-paper basket*. **1934** *Neuphilologische Mitteilungen* XXXV. 130 Public-school slang..*wagger* 'waste-paper-basket'. **1961** PARTRIDGE *Dict. Slang* Suppl. 1086/2 *Wagger-pagger*, a waste-paper basket. Short for *wagger-pagger-bagger*.

† '**wagger**, *v.* *Obs.* In 4–5 **wager.** [Frequentative of WAG *v.*: see -ER[5]. Cf. WAGGLE *v.*; also AF. *wa(l)crer* = sense 1.]

1. *intr.* To wander, have no settled abode.

c **1380** WYCLIF *Serm.* Sel. Wks. II. 154 Mannys spirit þat is wageringe aboute desiir of worldli þingis. **1382** —— *Hos.* ix. 17 Thei shulen be wagringe in naciouns [Vulg. *erunt vagi in nationibus*]. *a* **1425** *Cursor M.* 23091 (Trin.) Quen I [Christ] was wagering out of rest godely toke ȝe me to gest.

2. To stagger, totter.

1382 WYCLIF *Eccles.* xii. 3 Whan..the most strong men wageren [Vulg. *nutabunt*]. —— *Ecclus.* xxxvii. 16 Who euere shal wageren in dercnesses, shal not togidere sorewen to thee. —— *Isa.* xxix. 9 Bicometh alle stoneid, and wndreth; flotereth, and wagereth [Vulg. *vacillate*].

Hence † '**waggering** *vbl. sb.* and *ppl. a.*

1382 WYCLIF *Ecclus.* xl. 4 Enuye, noyse, wagering [Vulg. *fluctuatio*], and dred of deth. *c* **1430** *Hymns Virg.* (1867) 89 It is raþir to bileeue þe wageringe wijnde þan þe chaungeable world þat makiþ men so blinde.

waggerell, variant of WAKERELL.

waggery ('wægərı). [f. WAG *sb.*[2] + -ERY.]

1. The action or disposition of a wag; drollery, jocularity; in early use chiefly, mischievous drollery, practical joking.

1594 LYLY *Mother Bombie* II. i. 2 Now, if I could meete with Risio, it were a world of waggery. **1611** COTGR., *Drolerie*, rye, waggerie, good roguerie. **1650** COWLEY *Guardian* I. i, The Colonel's as full of waggery as an egge's full of meat. *c* **1656** SIR H. CHOLMLEY *Mem.* (1787) 35, I, out of folly and waggery, began to kick one of them. **1737** CHESTERF. in *C'tess Suffolk's Lett.* (1824) II. 163 Since which he has contented himself with a little general waggery, as occasion offers, such as snatching the bread and butter out of a girl's hand [etc.]. **1762** FOOTE *Orator* I. Wks. 1799 I. 199 The misapprehension of the second agent, or the ignorance or waggery of the third. **1824** MISS MITFORD *Village* I. 152 He was so good a fellow, so full of fun and waggery! **1832** T. CREEVEY in *C. Papers* (1904) II. x. 243 She has a great deal of natural waggery. **1858** J. BROWN *Horæ Subs.*, *Locke & Sydenham*, etc. 420 Excited by..the waggery of his more intellectual neighbours. **1894** J. KNIGHT *David Garrick* xiii. 252 One friend..perpetrated a harmless piece of waggery on the subject.

2. A waggish action or speech; in early use, a piece of mischievous jesting; a practical joke.

1604 BRETON *Grimellos Fort.* (Grosart) 9/2 If I should tell you the tenth part of the waggeries, that I passed through. *a* **1654** SELDEN *Table Talk* (Arb.) 97 An Ape when he has done some waggery. **1655** tr. *Com. Hist. Francion* III. 69, I must needs passe by severall pretty waggeries, which I committed during this my Non-age. **1691** WOOD *Ath. Oxon.* II. 183 John Birkenhead..pleased the generality of Readers with his waggeries and buffoonries. **1778** S. CRISP *Let.* 8 Dec. in Mme. D'Arblay *Diary* (1891) I. 93 In most of our successful comedies there are frequent lively freedoms (and waggeries that cannot be called licentious, neither). **1850** THACKERAY *Pendennis* liii, In fact they indulged in a hundred sports, jocularities, waggeries, and *petits jeux innocens*. **1865** TROLLOPE *Belton Est.* xxix. 344 Not being a man given to little waggeries.

waggin, rare obs. form of WAGON.

wagging ('wægıŋ), *vbl. sb.* [-ING[1].] **1. a.** The action of the verb WAG in its various senses.

1362 LANGL. *P. Pl.* A. IX. 26 And þe wint and þe watur and þe waggyng of þe Bot Makeþ þe Mon Mony tyme to stomble and to falle. *c* **1440** *Promp. Parv.* 513/2 Waggynge, or wauerynge, *vacillacio*. **1519** HORMAN *Vulg.* 100 Byrdys vse the waggynge of theyr rumpe, to gyde theyr flyght: as doth the sterrne of a shyp to gyde the saylynge. **1530–77** H. RHODES *Bk. Nurture* 331 in *Babees Bk.*, Vse not much wagging with thy head. **1562** J. HEYWOOD *Prov. & Epigr.* (1867) 129 The meanyng herof, differth not twoo pins, Betweene waggyng of mens beardes and womens chins. **1601** HOLLAND *Pliny* XVII. xii. I. 514 As for the white Poplar or Aspen tree..the leaves keepe such a wagging and trembling, and never hang still. **1612** *Two Noble K.* II. ii. 15 The wagging of a wanton leg. **1655** [V. GOOKIN] *Gt. Case Transplantation in Irel.* 25 Can it be imagin'd that a whole Nation will drive like Geese at the wagging of a hat upon a stick? **1848** DICKENS *Dombey* xlviii, Diogenes..had expressed that conflict of feeling by alternate waggings of his tail, and displays of his teeth. **1855** THACKERAY *Newcomes* lxvi, A buzz, a hum,..a meeting of bonnets and wagging of feathers and rustling of silks ensue. **1903** *Times* 9 Mar. 4/5 Did not he..stop the wagging of censorious tongues?

† **b.** *Proverbial phrase. Obs.*

c **1374** CHAUCER *Tr. & Cr.* II. 1745 In titeryng and pursuyte and delayes The folk deuyne at waggynge of a stre. *c* **1520** SKELTON *Magnyf.* 1016 Somtyme I wepe for a gew gaw; Somtyme I laughe at waggynge of a straw. **1525** BERNERS *Froiss.* II. lviii. 80 They murmured & were redy for waggyng of a rysshe to make debate and stryfe. **1558** ABP. SANDYS *Serm.* (1585) 50 As fearfull Hares they flee at the wagging of euerie leafe. **1653** J. TAYLOR (Water P.) *Cert. Trav. of Uncert. Journ.* Wks. 1872 III. 8 They quarrel not for wagging of a straw. **1681** W. ROBERTSON *Phraseol. Gen.* 595/1 He fears the wagging of every straw.

2. Special Comb. **wagging dance** = *waggle dance* s.v. WAGGLE *sb.* 2. Cf. *wag-tail dance* s.v. WAGTAIL *sb.* 6.

1950 [see ROUND *a.* 5 a]. **1967** *Science* 24 Nov. 1072/3 Successful forager bees..inform their hive mates of the location of the feeding place by wagging dances.

wagging ('wægıŋ), *ppl. a.* [f. WAG *v.* + -ING[2].] That wags (in the senses of the verb).

1398 TREVISA *Barth. De P.R.* XVII. cxxxvii. (Bodl. MS.), Poudre þereof..fastneþ wagginge teþe þat beþ in poynte to falle. ? *a* **1400** *Morte Arth.* 3660 Fro þe wagande wynde owte of þe weste rysses, Brethly bessomes with byrre in berynes sailles. **1541** *Bk. Properties Herbs* C iv b, Yf a man haue wagginge tethe and he eate of this herbe, they shall fasten agayne. **1565** COOPER *Thesaurus*, *Pætus*,..he that hath wagginge and stirryng eyes. **1591** SYLVESTER *Du Bartas* II. iii. III. *Law* 1336 So that a wagging leaf,..Yea, the least crack shall make thee turn thy back. **1883** WHITELAW *Sophocles*, *Ajax* 199 Whose scornful wagging tongues to thee Are grievous. **1888** MEREDITH *Poet. Wks.* (1912) 570 There lived with us a wagging humourist [*sc.* a dog]. **1918** *Sunday at Home* June 609/1 A herd of pigs went by or goats with wagging beards.

waggish ('wægıʃ), *a.* [f. WAG *sb.*[2] + -ISH[1].]

1. Of a person: Having the qualities of a wag; playfully mischievous. †Also, wanton, loose.

1590 SHAKS. *Mids. N.* I. i. 240 And therefore is Loue said to be a childe, Because in choise he is often beguil'd, As waggish boyes in game themselues forsweare. **1607** ROWLANDS *Famous Hist.* 13 Fair Hellen was a waggish wench of Greece. **1664** H. MORE *Apology* 562 Certainly some very waggish Master of the Ceremonies has taught you this ill manners. **1716** GAY *Trivia* II. 91 When waggish boys the stunted beesom ply. **1719** LONDON & WISE *Compl. Gard.* VI. ix. 120 If [the tree died] by being shaken or loosen'd at the first spriouting, by waggish People. **1756** TOLDERVY *Hist. Two Orphans* IV. 130 But, O fortune! what a waggish damsel art thou! **1822** SCOTT *Nigel* i, The stranger looked sternly at the waggish apprentice. **1836** HOR. SMITH (*title*), The Tin Trumpet; or, Heads and Tails, for the Wise and the Waggish. **1874** CARPENTER *Ment. Phys.* I. vi. (1879) 307 A long series of ludicrous replies..spelled out..by the direction of waggish questioners. **1904** J. T. FOWLER *Durham Univ.* 65 Certain waggish undergraduates..sowed mustard seed after dark.

2. Pertaining to or characteristic of a wag. Of an act, speech, etc.: Done or made in a spirit of waggery or mischievous fun; prankish.

1589 GREENE *Tullies Love* Wks. (Grosart) VII. 107, I pray you tell me whereof are womens hearts made?.. Venus hearing hir son make such a waggish demaunde, beganne thus to reply. **1594** O. B. *Quest. Profit Concern.* 18 Had I bene complained of for doing shrewdnesses in the time of my waggish youth. **1611** SHAKS. *Cymb.* III. iv. 160 You must forget to be a Woman: change..Feare, and Nicenesse..into a waggish courage. **1616** CHAPMAN tr. *Musæus* Annot. H 5, The word vnhappie in our Language hath diuers Vnderstandings; as waggish or subtle, &c. **1617** R. WHITE *Cupid's Banishm.* in Nichols *Progr. Jas. I* (1828) III. 287 Boye, leave your waggish wit; Putt up your arrowes in your quiver and bee gone. **1659** WOOD *Life* 16 Sept. (O.H.S.) I. 283 Some of the company, who knew the design to be waggish, fell a laughing, and betray'd the matter. **1738** POPE *Epil. Sat.* I. 17 And own, the Spaniard did a waggish thing, Who cropt our Ears, and sent them to the King. **1836** W. IRVING *Astoria* I. 262 The passing..was equivalent among boat-men to the crossing of the line among sailors, and was celebrated with like ceremonials of a rough and waggish nature. **1865** DICKENS *Mut. Fr.* II. i, She..cried, with a waggish shake of her head: 'Aha! Caught you spying, did I?' **1904** *Athenæum* 20 Aug. 234/1 Mr. Tarkington writes in.. a vein of waggish farce.

waggishly ('wægıʃlı), *adv.* [f. prec. + -LY[2].] In a waggish manner.

1609 B. JONSON *Sil. Wom.* V. i, *Cler.* Faith, now we are in priuate, let's wanton it a little, and talke waggishly. **1636** MASSINGER *Bashf. Lover* II. i, I have observ'd him Waggishly witty. **1732** BERKELEY *Alciphr.* VI. §32 One while waggishly smiling, another with a grave mouth and ludicrous eyes. **1781** MME. D'ARBLAY *Diary* May, She.. rather waggishly asked me who wrote to me with such elegant attention? **1831** SCOTT *Jrnl.* 19 Oct., [He] used to say, waggishly, that there was nothing so accommodating as a naval captain on shore. **1854–5** THACKERAY *Newcomes* xxxvi, Other persons in society inquired waggishly why Jack Belsize was not present to give Lady Clara away.

waggishness ('wægıʃnıs). [f. WAGGISH *a.* + -NESS.] The state or character of being waggish; sportive mischief; jocularity of speech or behaviour. Also, †wantonness, licentiousness.

1591 PERCIVALL *Sp. Dict.*, *Travessura*, frowardnesse, wantonnesse, waggishnes. **1625** BACON *Ess.*, *Of Goodness* (Arb.) 201 A Christian Boy in Constantinople, had like to haue been stoned, for gagging, in a waggishnesse, a long Billed Fowle. **1673** *Humours Town* (1693) 67 The Softness of Ovid, the Majesty of Virgil, the Waggishness of Catullus. **1867** TROLLOPE *Chron. Barset* I. xxxiv. 290 Clerical waggishness..generally to be found among minor canons. **1884** *Pall Mall Gaz.* 9 Feb. 3/2 It is only in a spirit of waggishness that this could be said of Sir John Gilbert.

'**waggle**, *sb.* [f. WAGGLE *v.*] **1.** The action or an act of waggling; *spec.* in *Golf* (see quot. 1897).

1885 R. L. & F. STEVENSON *Dynamiter* 199 With a friendly waggle of the hand. **1897** *Encycl. Sport* I. 464 (Golf) In taking aim or addressing the ball, it is the almost invariable practice to pass or flourish the club head a few times backwards and forwards over the top of the ball in the direction of the proposed stroke. This is called the 'waggle'.

2. waggle dance [tr. G. *schwänzeltanz* (K. von Frisch 1923, in *Zool. Jahrb., Abt. f. Allgemeine Zool.* XL. 72)], a movement performed by honey-bees at their hive or nest, believed to indicate to other bees the site of a source of food. Cf. *wagging dance* s.v. WAGGING *vbl. sb.* 2.

1952 [see ROUND *a.* 5 a]. **1961** *Guardian* 15 Sept. 6/6 The waggle dance of the hive bee can convey precise indications as to distance and direction of a food source. **1978** *Sci. Amer.* July 80/3 By means of the 'waggle dance' elucidated by von Frisch the bees inform their hive mates of this source of food.

waggle ('wæg(ə)l), *v.* Also 6–7 **wagle,** 9 *Sc.* **weegle, waigle.** [A frequentative of WAG *v.*; not found before the last decade of the 16th c., but possibly much older. Equivalent formations in Continental Teut. are WFris. *waggelje* to totter, Du. *waggelen* to stagger (early mod.Flem. *waeghelen, wagghelen*; also *trans.* to shake); (M)LG. *waggeln*, G. *wackeln* to stagger, totter (whence prob. Sw. *vakla*, Da. *vakle*); Norw., Sw. *vagla* refl. to rock, sway. Cf. ME. *wagre* WAGGER *v.*; also WIGGLE, WIGGLE-WAGGLE *vbs.*]

1. *trans.* **a.** To move (anything held or fixed at one end) to and fro with short quick motions, or with a rapid undulation; *esp.* to shake (any movable part of the body). In sports or games often (*colloq.* or *humorous*), to wield or manipulate (a bat, oar, etc.).

1594 NASHE *Unfort. Trav.* E 2 b, A third [man] wauerd & wagled his head, like a proud horse playing with his bridle. **1599** —— *Lenten Stuffe* 37 Our moderne phisitions, that to any sicke languishers if they be able to waggle their chaps, propound veale for one of the highest nourishers. **1597** A. M. tr. *Guillemeau's Fr. Chirurg.* 27 If to rigorouslye we waggle the tooth vp or downe. **1819** W. TENNANT *Papistry Storm'd* (1827) 17 And, as she said, She weeglit her wing-wavin' shoon. **1823** in *Spirit Publ. Jrnls.* 316 Thou, Pincher, farewell too! in vain Dost thou waggle thine innocent tail! **1860** THACKERAY *Lovel* iv. (1861) 165 She hinted, she sighed, she waggled her head at me. **1871** C. GIBBON *Lack of Gold* viii, The swarms of geese and milk-white ducks.. would step out to the bank and waggle their tails with satisfaction. **1881** STEVENSON *Virg. Puerisque* (1895) 98 When the old man waggles his head and says, 'Ah, so I thought when I was your age,' he has proved the youth's case.

b. *absol.* Chiefly in *Golf* (cf. WAGGLE *sb.*): To swing the club-head to and fro over the ball in the line of the intended stroke.

1897 *Outing* Aug. 423/1 On the other hand, another player, probably quite as good,..Mr. Horace Hutchinson, waggles, and waggles, as he addresses his ball, before each shot.

c. *U.S. slang.* To get the better of, overcome. In recent Dictionaries.

d. *nonce-use.* To indicate by waggling the head.

1852 READE *Peg Woff.* xiii. 198 They all nodded and waggled assent.

e. *Aeronaut.* To rock (the wings of an aircraft in flight) rapidly from side to side, usu. to convey a signal.

1918 J. M. GRIDER *Diary* 18 June in *War Birds* (1927) 200 Springs waggled his wings and pointed and we waggled back. **1950** *Sun* (Baltimore) 25 Nov. 2/1 The plane waggled its wings in salute to the troops. **1972** *Daily Express* 29 June 1/1 The Nimrod [aircraft] then waggled its wings and started back.

2. *intr.* **a.** With *advs.* or advb. expressions denoting motion: To shake or wobble while in motion; to walk or move shakily; to waddle.

1611 COTGR., *Triballer*, to wagle, or dangle vp and downe; to goe dingle dangle, wig wag. **1625** JACKSON *Creed* v. v. 42 Apt they are not to moue many wayes, either vpward or downeward, but onely to waggle to and fro within a narrow compasse. *Ibid.* x. xxiv. 3080 Like to a Pair of Scales which never came to any Permanent Stay or constant Settling upon the right Center, but have one while wagled this way, another while that way. **1627** MAY *Lucan* v. I. 3, Nor that the crow waggling along the shore Diues downe, and seemes t' anticipate a showre. **1692** R. L'ESTRANGE *Fables* ccii. 194 Why do you go Nodding, and Waggling so like a Fool, as if you were Hipshot? says the Goose to her Gosselin. **1819** W. TENNANT *Papistry Storm'd* (1827) 82 This said, the host wi' richt guid will Begoud to waigle down the hill. *c* **1820** COLMAN *Broad Grins* etc. (1872) 313 A well-fed maggot.. In some deep fruit-plate heaves, from snout to end, And works, and slips, and writhes, and waggles to ascend. **1840** THACKERAY *Shabby-genteel Story* iii, The tall, red, lurid candlewick waggling down, the flame flickering pale upon Miss Caroline's pale face. **1864** M. EYRE *Lady's Walks S. France* xiii. (1865) 160 The little lizards.. waggled off as fast as they could. **1896** BADEN-POWELL *Matabele Campaign* i, The men dance in a circle, stamping the time; the women waggle round and round the circle, outside it.

b. Of things held or fixed at one end: To move backwards and forwards with short quick motions, or with a rapid undulatory movement.

1706 PHILLIPS (ed. Kersey), To *Waggle*, to joggle, or move up and down, to be always in Motion. *c* **1820** COLMAN *Broad Grins* etc. (1872) 162 Harsh creaked the rope in its descent, And waggling down the bucket went. **1837** BARHAM *Ingol. Leg.*, *Jackdaw Rheims* 138 His tail waggled more Even than before; But no longer it wagged with an impudent air. **1862** DARWIN *Orchids* v. 171 When the flowers of this latter species were blown by a breath of wind, the tongue-like labellums all waggled about in a very odd manner. **1881** BESANT & RICE *Chapl. Fleet* I. 129 'Tut, tut,' he replied, shaking his great head till his cheeks waggled.

Hence **'waggling** *vbl. sb.* and *ppl. a.*

a **1586** SIDNEY *Arcadia* II. iv. (1912) 167 A Hearne.. getting up on his wagling winges with paine. **1599** SHAKS. *Much Ado* II. i. 117, I know you by the wagling of your head. **1907** *Westm. Gaz.* 20 Aug. 3/2 That 3lb. bat of his must take a bit of 'waggling'.

waggle, variant of WAGEL.

waggly ('wæglɪ), *a. colloq.* Also **waggley**. [f. WAGGLE *v.* + -Y.] Waggling, unsteady; in quots. *transf.*, having frequent irregular curves.

1894 ELIZ. BANKS *Camp. Curiosity* 135 They keep in the path, even in its most waggly parts. **1915** *Blackw. Mag.* Sept. 303/2 A mud fort it was,.. with a deep waggley narrow trench running all round.

waggon: see WAGON.

wagh: see WAUGH *int.*, WAW.

†**'waghalter.** *Obs.* [f. WAG *v.* + HALTER *sb.*[1] Cf. *wag-string*, *-with* s.v. WAG *v.* 12.] One who is likely to swing in a halter; a 'gallows-bird'.

1570 LEVINS *Manip.* 80/39 A Waghalter, *furcifer, perditus*. *c* **1570** *Misogonus* IV. ii. 6 Stand out of my way waghalter or I will britche the nakte. **1611** COTGR., *Baboin*,.. a crackrope, waghalter, vnhappie rogue. **1620** SHELTON *2nd Pt. Don Quix.* iii. 16 This Bachelour.. was.. a notable Wag-halter. *attrib.* **1546** [see SLIP-STRING 1]. **1638** FORD *Fancies* I. ii, *Nit.* What a terrible sight to a lib'd breech is a sow gelder? *Spa.* Not so terrible as a crosse tree that never growes, to a wag-halter-Page.

waghe: see WAW, WOE.

waghen, -scot, obs. ff. WAGON, WAINSCOT.

waght(e, waghter, obs. ff. WEIGHT, WAFTER *sb.*[1]

waging ('weɪdʒɪŋ), *vbl. sb.* [-ING[1].]

1. The action of WAGE *v.*[1]

1456 SIR G. HAYE *Law Arms* (S.T.S.) 146 Na in his condicioun of feyng was divisioun maid of his wageing. *Ibid.* 258 In how mony syndry casis law tholis vageing of bataill. *a* **1513** FABYAN *Chron.* VII. (1811) 555 Of whome the kynge receyuyd.. iiii. M. li. sterlynge towarde the wagynge of his knyghtis. **1583** STOCKER *Civ. Warres Lowe C.* IV. 36 b, For the leuiyng, dischargyng, entertainyng, and wagyng, of men of Warre. **1591** PERCIVALL *Sp. Dict.*, *Pleytesia*, a sute in law, waging of lawe. *a* **1674** MILTON *Hist. Moscovia* i. Wks. 1851 VIII. 478 By which means the waging of War is to the Emperor little or nothing chargeable. **1826** J. F. COOPER *Last of Mohicans* xiii, Such a scrimmage as was here fou't atween the Mohicans and the Mohawks, in a war of their own waging.

†**2.** The excrement of a fox. *Obs. rare.*

c **1410** *Master of Game* (MS. Digby 182) xxiv, Of hares and of conynges he shall say þei croteth, and of þe fox wagynge.

waging, obs. variant of WEDGING *vbl. sb.*

†**wag-leg.** *Obs.* Also 7 **wagge-legge**. [f. WAG *v.* + LEG *sb.*] A gadfly.

1585, 1611: see LONG-LEG 1. **1607** TOPSELL *Four-f. Beasts* 645 The milk of sheepe being hot, is of force against al poisons, except in those which shal drinke a venemous fly called a Wag-legge, and Libbards bane.

'wagling. *nonce-wd.* [-LING.] A little wag.

1837 T. HOOK *Jack Brag* iii, The sprightly, pert, impudent-looking wagling.

†**wagmoire**, variant of QUAGMIRE.

1579 SPENSER *Sheph. Cal.* Sept. 130 For they bene like foule wagmoires ouergrast.

Wagner ('vɑːgnə(r)). The name of the German operatic composer Richard *Wagner* (see WAGNERIAN *a.* and *sb.*) used *attrib.* in **Wagner tuba**, a valved brass instrument resembling a wide-bore horn devised for Wagner (see quots.).

1938 *Oxf. Compan. Mus.* 963/2 What are sometimes heard to-day under the name of 'Wagner Tubas' represent a considerable modification of the [tenor, bass, and double-bass tubas].., so far as the tenor tuba and bass tuba are concerned, departing more from the French horn model as to bore, and approaching more to that of the saxhorn; they retain.. the funnel-shaped mouthpiece of the horns. **1948** *Penguin Music Mag.* June 132 No one explained that the 'Wagner tubas'.. were assorted saxhorns, with cup-shaped and not funnel-shaped mouth-pieces. **1961** A. BAINES *Mus. Instruments* 315 *Wagner tubas*, 'tuba' here is really a misnomer, the proper name for these instruments being *Wagner-Tuben*... These *Tuben*, conceived by Wagner to bridge certain gaps in the brass tone, are made in two sizes, in B♭ and F, at the same pitches respectively as the B♭ and F horns and using the same part of the harmonic series. In bore they are midway between the horn and the saxhorn... They are fitted with four valves, the purpose of the fourth being to improve the intonation of the lower octave. **1965** *Listener* 3 June 837/3 A platoon of Wagner tubas. **1980** *New Grove Dict. Mus.* XX. 152/1 *Wagner tuba*, a special kind of tuba devised by Wagner for the *Ring* with the object of bridging the gap between the horns and trombones... The main body of the instrument is elliptical, like most German tenor horns, with the bell emerging from the top at a slightly oblique angle, while the lower end almost rests on the player's lap.

Wagnerian (vɑːg'nɪərɪən), *a.* and *sb.* [-IAN.]

a. *adj.* Of or pertaining to the German operatic composer Richard Wagner (1813-83), his music and theories of musical and dramatic composition. **b.** *sb.* An admirer or adherent of Wagner.

1873 *All Year Round* 5 July 225/1 The Wagnerian opera ..presumes that the singer of average ability shall be capable of doing justice to the music. **1882** HIME *Wagnerism* 23 But the marriage of near relations was the custom in primitive times, say the Wagnerians. True, no doubt; that that does not make their customs fit subjects for the representations of Art. **1889** G. B. SHAW in *Engl. Illustr. Mag.* Oct. 49 Richter's great superiority to Herr Levi as a Wagnerian conductor.

Hence **Wag'nerianism**, Wagnerian theories, etc. Also **Wagne'resque** *a.*, resembling the style of Wagner. **Wag'nerianly** *adv.*, in a Wagnerian manner. **'Wagnerism**, Wagner's theory and practice in the composition of music-dramas; the influence or cult of Wagner. **'Wagnerist**, **'Wagnerite** = WAGNERIAN b. **Wagne'ritis** *joc.* [-ITIS], excessive admiration for Wagner, viewed as a morbid condition. **'Wagnerize** *v.*, (*a*) *trans.* to make Wagnerian; (*b*) *intr.* to follow Wagner.

1884 HAWEIS *My Musical Life* 671 Even Verdi had drunk deep, many portions of 'Aida' being quite *Wagneresque. **1887** *Contemp. Rev.* Mar. 448 A number of Wagner caricatures, which really are very valuable documents in the history of *Wagnerianism. **1897** G. B. SHAW in *Sat. Rev.* 13 Nov. 514/1 In 'Hamlet' he is quite enthusiastic about naturalness in the business of the stage, and makes Hamlet hold forth about it quite *Wagnerianly. **1852** *Punch* 19 June 252/2 The infection called *Wagnerism is spreading most rapidly throughout the musical profession. **1869** *Daily News* 20 Dec., Many of us may like to hear of anything, even in the shape of Wagnerism, which can hold its head in Paris by way of opposition to the prevailing taste for Offenbachanalian music. **1889** G. B. SHAW in *Engl. Illustr. Mag.* Oct. 49 Hero-worship of Wagner, or adept Wagnerism. **1891** *Century Dict.*, *Wagnerist. **1855** GEO. ELIOT in *Fraser's Mag.* July 50/2 *Tannhäuser*.. is still the music of men and women, as well as of *Wagnerites. **1883** *Nation* (N.Y.) 22 Feb. 166/3 Nor is there any reason why a Wagnerite should refuse to admire the operettas of Strauss. **1889** G. B. SHAW in *Eng. Illustr. Mag.* Oct. 55 *Wagneritis (a disease not uncommon among persons who have discovered the merits of Wagner's music by reading about it, and among those disciples who know no other music than his). **1977** *N.Y. Rev. Bks.* 26 May 15/3 He recovered from his Wagneritis sooner than most worshippers. **1866** SWINBURNE *Let.* 26 Dec. (1959) I. 215 My art is at a discount here, but yours is idolized; you could Schumannize and *Wagnerize among us to some purpose. **1882** *Standard* 13 Jan., It would, of course, be premature to affirm that the musical mind of England has become completely Wagnerised. **1891** MEREDITH *One of our Conq.* I. xiii. 252 The Italians don't much more than Wagnerize in exchange for the loss of melody.

wagnerite ('wægnəraɪt). *Min.* [Named by Fuchs (*wagnerit*) in 1821, after F. M. von *Wagner*: see -ITE.] A fluophosphate of magnesium and iron, found in yellow crystals.

1825 HAIDINGER tr. *Mohs' Treat. Min.* III. 169. **1836** T. THOMSON *Min., Geol.* etc. I. 182. **1883** *Science* I. 341/2.

wagon, waggon ('wægən), *sb.* Forms: 6 wagan(e, waghen, wagen, 6–7 waggen, 7 waggin, 6– waggon, wagon. [Early mod.E. *wagan*, *waghen*, a. Du. *wagen* (formerly also written *waghen*) = OE. *wæȝn* WAIN.

In Du. (as in Ger.) *wagen* has always been the most general term for a wheeled vehicle; in the 16th c. it was adopted into Eng. in this wide sense (see 2 below) as well as in the specific military application (sense 1) learned in the continental wars.

The Eng. dicts. of the 18th c. have the spelling *waggon*, exc. Johnson, who gives *wagon* without remark, though all his examples have *waggon*. Todd 1818 prefers *wagon* for etymological reasons, but says that *waggon* is the prevailing form. Webster 1828 gives *wagon*, remarking that 'the old orthography, *waggon*, seems to be falling into disuse'. Smart 1836 gives *waggon* as the current form, and *wagon* as 'a disused spelling'. Stormonth 1884 and Cassell 1888 have *waggon, wagon*; later dicts. *wagon* either alone or in the first place. In Great Britain *waggon* is still very commonly used; in the U.S. it is rare.

The Eng. word has been adopted in Fr. as *wagon, vagon* (vagɔ̃) in the sense of 'railway coach or carriage', a meaning which is now obsolete in Eng. (see quot. 1847 in sense 5 b). So also G. *waggon* (pronounced as Fr.).]

1. a. A strong four-wheeled vehicle designed for the transport of heavy goods. In *Mil.* use chiefly with qualifying word, as *ambulance*, *ammunition*, *bread*, *forge wagon* etc., for which see those words.

1523 BERNERS *Froiss.* (1812) I. lxii. 84 And whan these lordes sawe none other remedy, they trussed all their harnes in waganes [Fr. *en voictures*], and retourned to the hoost before Tourney. *a* **1548** HALL *Chron.*, *Hen. VIII*, 46 b, The Flemmynges.. made purviaunce for wagans, vitaile and other thynges. **1570** DEE *Math. Pref.* d j, As, the force which one man hath with the Duche waghen Racke: therwith to set vp agayne, a mighty waghen laden, being ouerthrowne. **1601** HOLLAND *Pliny* VII. lvi. I. 188 The Phrygians invented first the waggon and charriot with foure wheeles [L. *vehiculum cum quatuor rotis*]. **1611** BIBLE *Gen.* xlv. 19 Take you wagons out of the land of Egypt for your little ones, and for your wiues. **1653** HOLCROFT *Procopius*, *Goth. Wars* I. 4 Theodoricus.. went into Italy with all the Goths, putting their Wives and Children in Waggons, and all the Goods they could carry. **1667** MILTON *P.L.* III. 439 The barren plaines Of Sericana, where Chineses drive With Sails and Wind thir caine Waggons light. **1671** —— *P.R.* III. 336 And Waggons fraught with Utensils of war. **1697** DRYDEN *Virg. Georg.* III. 317 Thy well-breath'd Horse.. bred to Belgian Waggons. **1727** DE FOE *Eng. Tradesm.* (1841) II. xlvi. 173 From those barges they [the coals] are loaded into carts and wagons, to be carried to the respective country towns. **1794** MRS. RADCLIFFE *Myst. Udolpho* xv, The numerous waggons that accompanied them contained the rich spoils of the enemy. **1810** WELLINGTON in Gurw. *Desp.* (1838) VI. 302, I shall endeavor to send you some spring and commissariat waggons. **1837** W. IRVING *Capt. Bonneville* I. 75 They [the Indians] had dogged it [Captain Bonneville's party] for a time in secret, astonished at the long train of waggons and oxen. **1850** R. G. CUMMING *Hunter's Life S. Afr.* I. i. 2 The waggons of a trader generally contain every requisite for a farmer's establishment.

b. *transf.* (With capital initial.) The constellation CHARLES'S WAIN.

Quot. *c* 1511 is from a work translated into English by a Fleming, and contains many Flemish words. The quot. therefore does not prove the existence of the word in Eng. at the date of the book.

[*c* **1511** *1st Eng. Bk. Amer.* (Arb.) Introd. 28/1 The northe sayle sterre or pollumarticum, or the waghen called.] **1867** *Chamb. Encycl.* s.v. *Ursa major*, The common names throughout Europe for these seven stars are 'the Plough', 'Charles's Wain', 'the Wagon'. **1889** *N.W. Linc. Gloss.*, Waggon and Horses. *Ursa Major*, the Great Bear.

†**2. a.** A carriage of any kind for the conveyance of persons, their luggage, etc. *Obs.*

1542 UDALL *Erasm. Apoph.* 157 b, Speusippus beeyng ympotente.. was carryed in a wagen [L. *vehiculo*] towarde the schoole called *Academia*. **1555–6** in Ellis *Orig. Lett.* Ser. II. II. 253 One Wagon of tymbre work for Ladies and Gentlewomen of our Prevye Chamber. **1582** in T. Phillips *Hist. & Antiq. Shrewsb.* (1779) 46 This yeare 1582,.. the right honorable Lady Mary Sidney came to thys towne of Salop, in her wagon. **1617** J. TAYLOR (Water P.) *Trav. Lond. to Hamburgh* Wks. (1630) III. 88/1, I appointed a Waggon ouer night to bee ready by three of the Clocke in the morning.

†**b.** A war-chariot; = CHARIOT *sb.* 1 c. *Obs.*

1591 SAVILE *Tacitus*, *Agricola* 244 Some cuntreyes make warre in wagons also [L. *quædam nationes et curru præliantur*]. **1610** HOLLAND *Camden's Brit.* (1637) 30 Their fight is.. with wagons and chariots [L. *bigis et curribus*]. **1614** RALEGH *Hist. World* IV. ii. §20 II. 206 He.. sends his Brother Hagis with.. a hundred armed waggons to entertaine him. Each waggon had in it foure to fight, and two to guide it.

†**c.** *poet.* = CAR *sb.*[1] 1 b, CHARIOT *sb.* 1 b. *Obs.*

1582 STANYHURST *Æneis* III. (Arb.) 118 And two stately lyons this fine dams gilt wagon haled. **1588** SHAKS. *Tit. A.* v. ii. 51 Prouide thee two proper Palfries, as blacke as Iet, To hale thy vengefull Waggon swift away. **1590** SPENSER *F.Q.* I. v. 28 Then to her yron wagon she betakes. *Ibid.* I. v. 44 Whilst Phœbus pure In westerne waues his wearie wagon did recure. *c* **1620** Z. BOYD *Zion's Flowers* (1855) 111 The sunne in wagon makes th'horizon cleare. **1638** JUNIUS *Paint. Ancients* 61 The Poët stepping with Phaëton upon the waggon hath noted [etc.].

3. An open four-wheeled vehicle built for carrying hay, corn, etc., consisting of a long body furnished with 'shelboards'.

(In the 16th c. app. distinguished from *wain*.)

1573–80 TUSSER *Husb.* (1878) 35 Horse, Oxen, plough, tumbrel, cart, waggon, & waine. **1577** B. GOOGE *Heresbach's Husb.* I. 13 There stands my Heybarne, which hath in the vpper roomes my Hey, and beneath, Waynes, Cartes, Carres, Waggons, Coaches, [etc.]. **1600** in W. F. Shaw *Mem. Eastry* (1870) 226 One wagon and waggon harnesse three plowes [etc.]. **1697** DRYDEN *Virg. Georg.* I. 244 The tow'ring height Of Waggons, and the Cart's unweildy weight. **1789** W. MARSHALL *Glouc.* I. 57 The Glocestershire waggon is..the best farm-waggon I have seen in the kingdom... The wheels run six inches wider than those of the Yorkshire waggon. **1803** JANE PORTER *Thaddeus* ii. (1831) 16 Concealing their arms in waggons of hay. **1862** J. C. MORTON *Farmer's Cal.* (ed. 2) 415 The carrying of our grain crops..is done differently in different districts. In the South the use of the two and three horse waggon is almost universal. **1879** JEFFERIES *Wild Life* vi. 115 A waggon..is the pride of the craftsman who builds it, and who is careful to reproduce the exact 'lines' which he learned from his master as an apprentice.

4. A covered vehicle for the regular conveyance of commodities and passengers by road.

See also POST-WAGON (1677–), *stage-wagon* (1761–) s.v. STAGE *sb.* 14.

1615 STOW *Ann.* 867/2 In the yeere 1564 Guylliam Boonen, a dutchman,..brought the vse of Coaches into England... And about that time, began long wagons to come in vse, such as now come to London, from Canterbury, Norwich, Ipswich, Glocester, &c. with Passengers, and commodities. **1641** EVELYN *Diary* 10 Sept., I took waggon for Dort. *Ibid.* 10 Oct., I went by wagon..to Dynkirk. **1660** SIR W. DUGDALE *Diary* 13 Mar., in *Archæologia* XX. 471 My dau. Lettice went towards London in Coventre Waggon. **1776** MRS. P. L. POWYS *Passages fr. Diaries* (1899) 157 The two London waggons came in with sixteen and fourteen horses. **1776** *Pennsylvania Even. Post* 16 July 354/1 A number of Waggons with Teams are wanted for the public service immediately. **1824** BARNEWALL & CRESSWELL *Rep. K.B.* II. 717 The following evidence..was then set out; that defendant was a common carrier, and that his waggon stopped in the parish of Elden. **1859** GEO. ELIOT *A. Bede* v. xxxvi, She heard the rumbling of heavy wheels behind her; a covered waggon was coming, creeping slowly along. **1890** 'R. BOLDREWOOD' *Col. Reformer* xvi, An express waggon with a driving seat. *Ibid.*, He is like to turn back..if he journeys with us in the waggon.

5. a. *Mining.* A truck used to convey minerals along the roadways of a mine, or from the mine to the place of shipment. (See also quot. 1886.)

1649 [W. GREY] *Chorographia* 25 Waggons with one Horse to carry down Coales, from the Pits, to the Stathes, to the River, &c. **1727** DE FOE *Eng. Tradesm.* (1841) II. xlvi. 173 [The coals] are then loaded into a great machine called a wagon; which..goes..to the nearest river or water carriage. **1860** *Eng. & For. Mining Gloss.* (ed. 2) 51 *Chaldron* 53 cwt. The waggons which convey the coals from the pit to the place of shipment carry the above quantity, and are called chaldron waggons. **1867** W. W. SMYTH *Coal & Coal-mining* 148 Certain requirements, in connection with the raising of the mineral in the shafts..necessitate the use of particular kinds of waggon. **1886** J. BARROWMAN *Sc. Mining Terms* 70 *Waggon*, a measure of weight equal to 24 cwt. Coal sold for delivery in carts is usually sold by the waggon of 24 cwt.

b. An open truck or a closed van for the transport of goods on a railway. †Formerly applied also to the open carriages used for conveying passengers at the lowest fares, and as the general term for any kind of railway vehicle.

1756 ABIAH DARBY *Diary* 31 Jan. in *Jrnl. Friends' Hist. Soc.* (1913) X. 83 First Waggon of Pigs [*sc.* of iron] came down the Railway [in Coalbrookdale]. **1825** J. NICHOLSON *Oper. Mech.* 657 The weight of the engine and 16 waggons is equal to 154,560 lbs. **1840** F. WHISHAW *Railw. Gt. Brit. & Irel.* 493 The ordinary train would consist of two wagons, or trucks, of merchandise, &c. placed next to the engine, then the passenger-wagon [3rd class], and lastly the passenger-carriage. **1847** S. C. BREES *Railw. Pract.* 4th Ser. i. 1 The name of wagon is given to vehicles of every description employed on railways. **1872** HELPS *Life T. Brassey* v. (1878) 77 A 'set' is a number of wagons—in fact, a train.

6. *U.S.* A light four-wheeled vehicle used for various business purposes; also, loosely, a similar vehicle used for pleasure. ***dearborn wagon***: see DEARBORN.

1837 HALIBURTON *Clockmaker* Ser. 1. v. 34 People soon began to assemble, some on foot, and others on horseback and in waggons. **1841** [see DEARBORN]. **1868** LOUISA M. ALCOTT *Little Women* xvii, Will you take me out in the trotting waggon with Puck?

7. A covered four-wheeled vehicle used as a living house by gypsies, travelling showmen, travellers, etc.

1851 [see LIVING *vbl. sb.* 7]. **1886** *Cornh. Mag.* Sept. 298 The mess-waggon is always an important feature when an outfit starts on the 'trail'. *Ibid.*, During a halt he never left the waggon, but hung around [etc.].

8. *U.S.* A baby-carriage.

1847: see *wagon-frame* in 12a. **1887** CABOT *Mem. Emerson* II. 282 The whole town assembled, down to the babies in their wagons.

9. a. Short for *dinner-wagon* (see DINNER *sb.* 2). Cf. *wagon-table* in 13.

1906 CHARLOTTE MANSFIELD *Girl & Gods* viii, Margaret proceeded to cut the wire of a bottle, and then fetched glasses from a waggon.

b. Short for *patrol-wagon* s.v. PATROL *sb.* 4. *slang* (orig. and chiefly *U.S.*).

1890 J. P. QUINN *Fools of Fortune* xii. 404 When a raid is made..enough 'pluggers' are captured to fill one or two wagons and are driven to the nearest police station with much clatter and display. **1926** J. BLACK *You can't Win* iv. 31 I'll phone for the wagon. We'll have to take them all to the station. **1953** [see ICE *sb.* 2c].

c. Short for STATION-WAGON 2. Also more *gen.*, a motor car (*colloq.*).

1955 M. ALLINGHAM *Beckoning Lady* vi. 90 'Is this the wagon?' Amanda rose to meet the car. **1968** K. WEATHERLEY *Roo Shooter* 59 When he was ready to go, the wagon wouldn't start. **1975** 'E. LATHEN' *By Hook or by Crook* xviii. 173 'Do you want to take my car, Paul?'..'The wagon or the sports car?'

10. *Bookbinding.* 'A tool having four edges of cane mounted in a frame, and used to trim the edges of gold-leaf to a size for a book'.

1875 KNIGHT *Dict. Mech.*

11. Figurative phrases. **a.** ***to hitch one's wagon to a star***, to set oneself high aspirations; to aspire to another's admirable example.

1870 EMERSON *Society & Solitude* 27 Hitch your wagon to a star. Let us not fag in paltry works... Work..for..justice, love, freedom, knowledge, utility. **1929** D. H. LAWRENCE *Paintings of D.H. Lawrence* 22 What you mentally or 'consciously' desire is nine times out of ten impossible: hitch your wagon to a star, and you'll just stay where you are. **1939** R. BOOTHBY *Let.* 27 May in M. Gilbert *Winston S. Churchill* (1976) V. li. 1072 One of the few things in my life of which I am proud is that in all matters of major policy during the past 5 years I have hitched by waggon to your star. **1953** E. WAUGH *Love among Ruins* i. 10 'The Minister of Welfare and the Minister of Rest and Culture,' continued the Chief Guide. 'The stars to which we have hitched our waggon.' **1978** J. HYAMS *Pool* iv. 44 Overweight and sedentary, he was content to hitch his wagon to David's star.

b. ***on the wagon***, abstaining from alcoholic drink, teetotal. See *water-wagon* (*a*) s.v. WATER *sb.* 29. orig. *U.S.*

1906 B. J. TAYLOR *Extra Dry* 14 It is better to have been on and off the Wagon than never to have been on at all. **1917** J. M. GRIDER *War Birds* (1927) 23 Springs put him on the wagon for a week. **1934** J. T. FARRELL *Young Manhood* xiv. 218 'Was he oiled when the accident happened?' 'No, he was on the wagon again.' **1951** L. HELLMAN *Autumn Garden* III. 138 A few years ago I'd go on the wagon twice a year. Now ..I don't care. **1976** L. DEIGHTON *Twinkle, twinkle, Little Spy* viii. 83 They dug him out of a bar.., stoned out of his mind... He stayed on the wagon for years.

c. ***to fix*** (someone's) ***wagon***, to bring about (a person's) downfall, to spoil (his) chances of success. Cf. FIX *v.* 14c. *U.S. slang.*

1951 T. CAPOTE *Grass Harp* i. 13 She said her brother would fix my wagon, which he did; right here at the corner of my mouth I've still got a scar where he hit me. **1959** J. D. SALINGER in *New Yorker* 6 June 119/1 What ever became of that stalwart bore Fortinbras? Who eventually fixed *his* wagon? **1978** M. PUZO *Fools Die* xxvii. 322 At least he could fix Merlyn's wagon, Ford was beyond his reach. He tried getting her fixed by organizing a campaign of hate mail from fans.

12. *attrib.* and Comb.: **a.** attributive, as ***wagon-cover, -frame, -hire, -horse, -ox, -pole, -rut, -sail, -shed, -spoke, -spoor, -sprag, -tilt, -tongue, -wheel, whip.***

1832 *Boston* (Lincs.) *Her.* 31 July 1 A great Stock of lately-improved *Waggon-Covers. **1847** EMERSON *Poems, Threnody* 49 Awhile to..mend his [a child's] wicker *waggon-frame. **1553** in Burgon *Gresham* (1839) I. iii. 141 And to [be] layd upon every waggon iij dry fatts, for the avoyding of the great charge of *waggon-hyre. **1585** HIGINS *Junius' Nomencl.* 40/2 *Iumentum plaustrarium*,..a cart horse, or *waggon horse. **1829** SCOTT *Anne of G.* xiv, A city-bred burgher of Ghent, Liege, or Ypres, is as distinct an animal from a knight of Hainault, as a Flanders waggon-horse from a Spanish jennet. **1864** KINGSLEY *Roman & T.* i. (1875) 7 The horns of the *waggon-oxen. **1768** E. HOLDSWORTH *Virgil* 154 It is very common at this time, in several parts of Italy, to cover the end of the *waggon-pole with plates of brass. **1660** HEXHAM II, *Een wagen-leese*, a *Wagon-rut. **1848** DICKENS *Dombey* xv, The new streets that had stopped disheartened in the mud and waggon-ruts. **1850** R. G. CUMMING *Hunter's Life S. Afr.* I. vii. 140 These mats are also used instead of *waggon-sails, and are very effectual in resisting both sun and rain. **1896** BADEN-POWELL *Matabele Campaign* xvi, We have put our waterproof sheets ready on going to bed, and sometimes have spread the waggon-sails over the waggons. **1858** SIMMONDS *Dict. Trade*, **Wagon-shed*, a shelter for carts and wagons. **1886** HARDY *Woodlanders* iv, The daylight revealed the whole of Mr. Melbury's homestead, of which the waggon-sheds had been an outlying erection. **1592** SHAKS. *Rom. & Jul.* I. iv. 59 Her *Waggon Spokes made of long Spinners legs. **1940** W. FAULKNER *Hamlet* II. ii. 129 Her companion used the reversed pistol-butt against the wagon-spoke and the brass knuckles of the other two. **1863** W. C. BALDWIN *Afr. Hunting* vi. 174 On reaching the road, I saw fresh *wagon-spoor. **1885** *Times* 31 Oct. 8/3 The railway servants..armed with sticks and *wagon 'spraggs', then advanced upon the criminals' place of concealment. **1832** *Planting* 90 in *Libr. Usef. Knowl., Husb.* III, The lower ends of ash poles cut from six to eighteen feet long... They are cleft for the use of the cooper, *waggon-tilts, &c. **1845** J. PALMER *Jrnl. Trav. Rocky Mts.* (1847) 18 Our pilot notified us that this would be our last opportunity to procure timber for axle trees, *wagon tongues, etc. **1860** MAYNE REID *Hunters' Feast* xvii, The breaking of our waggon-tongue..delayed our journey. **1588** SHAKS. *Tit. A.* v. ii. 54, I will dismount, and by the *Waggon wheele, Trot like a Seruile footeman. **1860** EMERSON *Cond. Life, Considerations* Wks. (Bohn) II. 418 But who dares draw out the linchpin from the wagon-wheel? **1821** SCOTT *Kenilw.* xxv, Their rude drivers..began to debate precedence with their *waggon-whips and quarter-staves.

b. objective and obj. genitive, as ***wagon builder, driver, maker, making.***

1850 R. G. CUMMING *Hunter's Life S. Afr.* I. i. 4 A captent waggon..requires the hand of a skilful *waggon-builder. **1552** HULOET, *Waggon dryuer, *iugarius.* **1850** R. G. CUMMING *Hunter's Life S. Afr.* I. i. 15 A waggon-driver .., a stout active Hottentot. **1558** in Feuillerat *Revels Q. Eliz.* (1908) 51 Skinners Sadlers *waggen makers. **1873** J. RICHARDS *Wood-working Factories* 181 Wagon and carriage makers mainly use parallel iron vices.

c. instrumental, as ***wagon-travelling***; **d.** similative, as ***wagon-shaped*** adj.

1837 HEBERT *Engin. & Mech. Encycl.* II. 742 The kind of boiler attached to this engine is of the waggon-shaped kind. **1863** W. C. BALDWIN *Afr. Hunting* viii. 304 The natural concomitants of wagon-travelling.

13. Special comb.: **wagon-bed**, the body of a wagon; also, the bottom of the body; **wagon-boiler**, a form of engine-boiler (see quot.); †**wagon-borough** [ad. Du. or G. *wagenburg*], a defensive enclosure or barricade formed of baggage-wagons placed close together; **wagon boss** *N. Amer.*, the man in charge of a wagon-train; a wagon-master; **wagon-bow** (see quot.); **wagon box**, (*a*) *U.S.*, the body of a wagon; a wagon-bed; (*b*) a large storage chest, usu. kept under the front seat of a wagon (also used as an article of domestic furniture); **wagon-breast** *U.S.*, a breast or working place in a coal-mine in which the wagons are taken up to the working face; **wagon-ceiling** *Arch.* (see quot.); **wagon chest** = *wagon box* (*b*); †**wagon-coach** = POST WAGON; **wagon-corps** *Mil.* = *Corps of Wagoners* s.v. WAGONER[1] 1; **wagon-coupling** (see quot.); **wagon-drag**, a shoebrake for a wagon; **wagon-drift** *S. Afr.*, a passage for wagons across a river; **wagon-gallery**, a gallery in a mine along which the wagons run; **wagon-hammer** (see quot.); **wagon-house**, a house, shed or shelter for wagons; †**wagon-hunter** *Cant*, an agent of a brothel-keeper who for base purposes visited the inns at which the stage-wagons stopped; **wagon-jack, -lock** (see quots.); **wagon-man**, the driver of a wagon, a wagoner; **wagon-master**, a person who has charge of one or more wagons; spec. *Mil.*, an officer commanding the wagon-train; **wagon-road**, a road for the passage of wagons; spec. in *Coal-mining*, a prepared road or railway for the haulage of wagons; **wagon-roof** = *wagon-vault*; **wagon table** (see quot. and sense 9 above); **wagon-tent** *S. Afr.*, the tent-like canopy of a covered wagon; **wagon-tipper** (see quot.); **wagon-top**, the part of a locomotive-boiler, over the fire-box, which is elevated above the rest of the shell to provide greater steam-room (*Cent. Dict.* 1891); **wagon-track**, the track made by the passage of wagons; **wagon-train** *Mil.*, a train, collection, or service of transport wagons; also, a train of wagons used by colonial settlers; **wagon-tree** = WAGENBOOM; **wagon-vault** (see quot. 1892); hence **wagon-vaulted** *a.*; **wagon-work**, the construction and repair of wagons; **wagon-wright**, a maker or repairer of wagons; a wainwright; **wagon-yard**, a depôt for wagons used on a road or railway. Also WAGON-HEAD, WAGON-LOAD, WAGON-WAY.

1853 A. S. KNIGHT in *Trans. Oregon Pioneer Assoc.* (1933) 40 There is no ferry here and the men will have to make one out of the tightest *wagon-bed. **1885** HOWELLS in *Century Mag.* Sept. 672/1 In the grassy piazza two men had a humble show of figs and cakes for sale in their wagon-beds. **1891** C. ROBERTS *Adrift Amer.* 179 For though the river was fordable with care, the water came over the waggon-bed. **1837** HEBERT *Engin. & Mech. Encycl.* I. 197 Those known by the term of '*waggon boilers', from their shape, formed one of the many improvements of the steam engine introduced by Watt. **1548** W. PATTEN *Exped. Scot.* F 1 b, [Fearing a night attack we] entrenched our cariages and *waggen-boorowe, had good skout without and sure watch within. **1873** J. H. BEADLE *Undeveloped West* 98 Our '*wagon-boss', absolute monarch of a train while on the road, rejoiced in the name of John Monkins. **1973** R. SYMONS *Where Wagon Led* I. vi. 92 The wagon boss is an important man. You don't talk to him, but when he talks *to you*, you keep your ears clean. **1875** KNIGHT *Dict. Mech.*, **Wagon-bow*, an arched-shaped slat with its ends planted in staples on the wagon-bed sides. Used to elevate the tilt or cover. **1810** in *Austin Papers* (1924) I. 168, 13 *Wagon Boxes. **1852** M. B. HUDSON *S. Afr. Frontier Life* I. 206 We come to a door's been off a long while, Near to which stands a wagon-box sacred to books. **1853** V. WILLIAMS in *Trans. Oregon Pioneer Assoc.* (1922) 196 A number of other wagon boxes have been ripped for skiffs and ply singly. **1946** G. FOREMAN *Last Trek* 250 The camp was devastated by a tornado that carried wagon boxes, camp equipage, and some of the people through the air. **1969** N. W. PARSONS *Upon Sagebrush Harp* i. 2 The double wagon box on the stoneboat was our own, and it was full of our household goods. **1881** RAYMOND *Mining Gloss.*, **Wagon-breast.* A breast into which wagons can be taken. **1875** *Encycl. Brit.* II. 475/2 **Waggon-Ceiling*, a boarded roof of the Tudor time, either of semicircular or polygonal section. It is boarded with thin oak, and ornamented with mouldings forming panels, and with loops at the intersections. **1827** G. THOMPSON *Trav. S. Afr.* II. 134 A couple of *waggon-chests. **1968** S. STANDER *Horse* 75 He sat on the wagon-chest. **1675** *Lond. Gaz.* No. 1047/4 Lost..out of the *Waggon-Coach, passing from Hertford to London, a Letter. **1676** LADY ANNE FANSHAWE *Mem.* (1829) 126 We hired a waggon-coach, for there is no other at Calais. **1810** C. JAMES *Milit. Dict.*, Corps of Wagoners, or royal *Wagon corps. **1817** J. SCOTT *Paris Revisit.* (ed. 4) 279 The Austrian waggon corps. **1875** KNIGHT *Dict. Mech.*, **Wagon-coupling*, one for attaching the hind axle to the fore. *Ibid.*, **Wagon-drag*. **1850** R. G. CUMMING *Hunter's Life S. Afr.* II. xxx. 284 We held thither at a sharp trot, holding for the old *waggon drift. **1839** URE *Dict. Arts* 853 The ores are raised in these shafts to the level of the *waggon-gallery (*galerie de roulage*) by the whims provided with ropes and buckets. **1875** KNIGHT *Dict. Mech.*, **Wagon-hammer*, the vertical bolt which connects the double-tree to the tongue, and upon which the double-tree swings. **1660** HEXHAM II, *Een wagen-*

huys, a *wagon-house. **1758** *Ann. Reg.* I. 79/2 He..made him up a bed of straw in the waggon, under the waggon-house. **1886** HARDY *Woodlanders* iii, This erection was the waggon-house of the chief man of business. *c* **1766** *Cheats of Lond. Exposed* 46 *Waggon-hunters. **1875** KNIGHT *Dict. Mech.*, **Wagon-jack*, one for lifting the wheels of a wagon clear of the ground. *Ibid.*, **Wagon-lock*, a device to bring a friction on the wheels of a wagon to retard its motion in descending hills. **1600** HAKLUYT *Voy.* III. 484 The *wagon-man that had charge of me set an Indian carpenter a worke to mend the wheele. **1764** *London Mag.* Mar. 144/2 What the waggon-men call a bye-way, made for the unloaded waggons to be drawn to the pitts. **1645** in *Papers rel. Army Solemn League & Cov.* (S.H.S.) II. 502 *Waggonmrs of the Army. **1688** HOLME *Armoury* III. xix. (Roxb.) 163/2 Wagonmaster generall 10s. per diem. *Ibid.* 164/1 The Waggon maister 5s. Waggoners each 2s. **1757** WASHINGTON *Let.* Writ. 1889 I. 492 The commissary used to act as wagon-master. **1861** Wagon-master [see *forage-master* s.v. FORAGE *sb.* 4]. **1976** *Billings* (Montana) *Gaz.* 17 June 1-c/5 Actor John MacIntire, known as wagonmaster on the television program, 'Wagon Train'. **1774** *Pennsylv. Gaz.* 10 Aug. Suppl. 2/3 To the latter there is a good *waggon road already opened. **1884** JEFFERIES *Life of Fields* 58 A white butterfly follows along the waggon-road. **1893** SELOUS *Trav. S.E. Africa* 371 Assisting the pioneers to make the waggon road. **1866** HOWELLS *Venet. Life* xi. 151 The low *wagon-roofs of the cross-naves. **1899** BARING-GOULD *Bk. of West* I. ii. 35 In a good many cases the waggon roofs are but ceiled cradle roofs. **1844** T. WEBSTER *Encycl. Dom. Econ.* 240 Moving sideboards, or *waggon tables. **1845** *Cape of Good Hope Almanac* (Advt.), Country people can be supplied with..3-inch Canvas for *wagontents. **1926** P. SMITH *Beadle* 59 The women wore stiffly starched plain white sun-bonnets, like miniature wagon-tents. **1955** W. ROBERTSON *Blue Wagon* viii. 72, I was in the wagon-tent when those kaffirs came. **1875** KNIGHT *Dict. Mech.*, **Wagon-tipper*, a device for tilting a wagon in order to dump its load. **1850** R. G. CUMMING *Hunter's Life S. Afr.* II. xx. 76 The larger of these caves is situated on the west side of the *waggon-track. **1884** JEFFERIES *Life of Fields* 57 Leverets play in the waggon-track. **1810** WELLINGTON in Gurw. *Desp.* (1838) VI. 302, I shall endeavor to send you..some horses and drivers belonging to the *wagon train. **1888** J. C. HARRIS *Free Joe*, etc. 181 For years and years before the war it had been noted as the meeting-place of the waggon-trains by means of which the planters transported their produce to market. **1822** BURCHELL *Trav. S. Afr.* I. 123 *heading*, The *Waggon-tree. **1835** R. WILLIS *Archit. Mid. Ages* vii. 72 Amongst the various forms of vaulted apartments..rectangles are of frequent occurrence, and these for the most part are covered with a *waggon vault. **1892** *Dict. Arch.* (Arch. Publ. Soc.), *Waggon roof* or *vault*. A roof, semicircular in section, but somewhat higher than a semicircle or barrel roof, by rising from vertical sides. **1835** R. WILLIS *Archit. Mid. Ages* vii. 68 *Waggon-vaulted apartments. **1850** R. G. CUMMING *Hunter's Life S. Afr.* I. i. 16 *note*, Several coarse chisels for *waggon-work. **1887** MOLONEY *Forestry W. Afr.* 378 Wood tough, used chiefly for wagon-work. **1858** SIMMONDS *Dict. Trade*, **Wagon-wright*, a maker and mender of wagons. **1860** *Eng. & For. Mining Gloss.* (ed. 2) 66 [Newcastle terms.] *Waggonwright*, a man who makes and repairs the chaldron waggons. **1827** E. MACKENZIE *Hist. Newcastle* II. 722 A waggon set out for London from the general *waggon-yard..every day.

wagon, waggon ('wægən), *v.* [f. WAGON *sb.*]

1. *intr.* To travel in a wagon; to transport goods by wagon. Chiefly *U.S.*

1606 N. B[AXTER] *Sydney's Ourania* D 1, She waggoneth to Neptunes Pallace than. **1794** E. DENNY *Jrnl.* 18 Oct. (1860) 403 The French had opened the Indian path..and wagoned considerably upon it. **1828-32** WEBSTER, *Wagon*, v. i. To practice the transportation of goods in a wagon. The man wagons between Philadelphia and Pittsburg. *a* **1904** A. ADAMS *Log Cowboy* ix. 129 It was a hundred miles to wagon from the freight point where we got our supplies. **1907** 'C. E. CRADDOCK' *Windfall* vi. 103, I can't figure out how the lydy managed to stay so stiff and starched these seven miles and more, waggoning down from the mountain.

2. *trans.* To put into a wagon for conveyance.

1649 DAVENANT *Love & Hon.* I. i. 1/2 Is all our pillage waggond? *Ibid.* 3/1 See him well waggond, and provide A surgeon to attend his cure. **1795** *Sporting Mag.* V. 35 Our party..bagged, or rather waggoned 876 hares. **1812** J. FLAXMAN *Let. W. Hayley* 20 Feb. in *Pearson's Catal.* (1886) No. 60 Resignation is at length in, waggoned for Feltham.

3. *U.S.* To transport (goods) in a wagon or by means of a train of wagons. Also with *up*.

1755 WASHINGTON *Let.* Writ. 1889 I. 187 The quantity is too great for the present consumption, and to wagon it up can never answer the expense. **1779** JEFFERSON *Corr.* Wks. 1859 I. 216 They have bought quantities of flour for these troops in Cumberland, have ordered it to be wagoned down to Manchester, and wagoned thence up to the barracks. **1782** —— *Notes State Virginia* (1787) 39 The ore is first waggoned to the river. **1856** OLMSTED *Slave States* v. 321 Sometimes they had had to buy corn at a dollar a bushel, and wagon it home from Raleigh.

wagonage, waggonage ('wægənɪdʒ). [f. WAGON *sb.* or *v.* + -AGE.]

1. Conveyance or transport by wagon.

1609 HOLLAND *Amm. Marcell.* 137 The great losses they had by waggonage and other carriage. **1611** COTGR., *Chariotage*, waggonnage; the riding in, or carrying by, wagons, &c. **1756** WASHINGTON *Let.* Writ. 1889 I. 309 The demands he has had on account of..wagonage of all the flour and stores from Conococheague. **1770** in M. Cutler *Life, Jrnls. & Corr.* (1888) II. 403 In Pennsylvania, where wagonage is cheaper than in any other part of North America.

2. Money paid for conveyance by wagon.

1757 WASHINGTON *Let.* Writ. 1889 I. 491 The amount of waggonage, and other charges of transporting these provisions..will exceed the whole cost of the provisions. **1779** JEFFERSON *Corr.* Wks. 1859 I. 216 Wagonage, indeed, seems to the commissariat an article not worth economising.

3. A collection or train of wagons.

1864 CARLYLE *Fredk. Gt.* XVI. xiv. IV. 479 Wagonage, provender, and a piece or two of cannon.

wagoner, waggoner[1] ('wægənə(r)). Also 6 wagenner, 7 waggonere, -ier, waggouner. [f. WAGON *sb.* + -ER[1]; perh. orig. a. Du. *waghenaer* (now *wagenaar*) of equivalent formation.]

1. One who has charge of a wagon as driver. *Corps of Wagoners* (Mil.); see quots. 1802, 1810.

1544 in Rymer *Foedera* (1719) XV. 57 Dyvers Carts taken ..and Wagenners slain. *a* **1548** HALL *Chron.*, *Hen. V* 47 Thei wer in numbre had .lx. M. horsemen..beside footemen pages and wagoners. **1563** GOLDING *Cæsar* IV. 104b, In the meanewhile the wagoners withdrawe themselues somewhat out of the battell, and set their wagons in such order, that [etc.]. **1645** *Papers rel. Army Solemn League & Cov.* (S.H.S.) II. 502 Williame Rosse waggounr. *Ibid.*, Payed..for the mantanence of the train of waggoniers and horses 0,028 12 00. **1752** *Phil. Trans.* XLVII. 561 Two waggoners were run over by a waggon loaded with stone. **1802** C. JAMES *Milit. Dict.* s.v. *Wagoner, Corps of Wagoners*, a body of men employed in the commissariate, so called. **1810** *Ibid.* (ed. 3), *Corps of Waggoners, or royal Wagon corps*, a body of men originally employed in the train under the board of ordnance. It now forms a part of the regular army, and is subject to the quartermaster general. **1824** BARNEWALL & CRESSWELL *Rep. K.B.* II. 718 It was impossible for the said S. C. Marsh, if his waggoner or book keeper put any thing in the waggon at Thetford or on the road, to know of it. **1849** MACAULAY *Hist. Eng.* v. I. 610 The waggoners drove off at full speed, and never stopped till they were many miles from the field of battle. **1870** *Daily News* 3 Oct., Carters and waggoners of every sort were helping the good work.

attrib. **1898** 'MAXWELL GRAY' *Ribstone Pippins* iii. 79 Oh, the waggoner boy hath a life of joy.

b. *jocular.* The driver of a vehicle.

1841 J. T. J. HEWLETT *Peter Priggins* I. ii. 59 'Now,' said Tom, 'tumble in, old fellow: I'm waggoner—you pay pikes.' **1850** SMEDLEY *F. Fairlegh* xiii, We hired a drag... The first day we went out they elected me waggoner, and a nice job I had of it.

c. Used as the designation of a particular class of farm servant, whose special duties include the driving of a wagon: see quot. 1908. Also called a *carter*.

1790 W. H. MARSHALL *Rur. Econ. Midl.* II. 445 *Waggoner*; an upper man servant; carter. **1804** A. HUNTER *Georgical Ess.* V. 501 (E.D.D.) The waggoner or head ploughman pays an early regard to his horses. **1817** J. BRADBURY *Trav.* 316 The waggoners travel with great economy. **1908** *Daily Mail* 6 Apr. 6/5 The chief duty of the 'waggoner' [Lincs.], despite his name, is to cultivate the arable land... Waggoners also take the threshed corn to the nearest town in wagons (the occupation from which they take their name, though it is one of their least important duties).

d. *Mining.* (See quots.)

1886 J. BARROWMAN *Sc. Mining Terms* 70 *Waggoner*, a man in charge of a horse who arranges railway trucks in pit sidings. **1900** *Daily News* 9 Feb. 3/2 Sometimes the lads and youths who look after the trucks in the main roads are called waggoners.

†**2.** The driver of a chariot, a charioteer. Chiefly with mythological reference. *Obs.*

Frequently applied to Phœbus or to Phaethon as charioteer of the sun.

1588 SHAKS. *Tit. A.* v. ii. 48 And then Ile come and be thy Waggoner, And whirle along with thee about the Globes. **1592** —— *Rom. & Jul.* I. iv. 64 Her Waggoner, a smal gray-coated Gnat. **1603** DEKKER & CHETTLE *Grissil* (Shaks. Soc.) 9 Look how yon one-ey'd waggoner of heaven Hath by his horses' fiery-winged hoofs, Burst ope the melancholy jail of night. **1614** BP. J. KING *Vitis Palatina* 8 Elias, *auriga in aëre*, was a wagoner in the aire, rode in a chariot, through the cloudes. **1636** FITZ-GEFFREY *Holy Transport.* (1881) 169 Now seemes the Sunnes vnwearied Waggonere, Who every day surrounds this earthly sphere, To make a stand. **1638** JUNIUS *Paint. Ancients* 61 The fierce winged beasts..throw the unexperienced waggoner headlong downe with waggon and all.

fig. **1621** T. BEDFORD *Sin unto Death* 29 Spurred..on by two most passionate Waggoners, Feare and Envie.

3. (With capital initial.) **a.** The northern constellation AURIGA. †**b.** Applied to the constellation Boötes, viewed as the driver of 'Charles's Wain'. *Obs.*

a. 1607 TOPSELL *Four-f. Beasts* 248, I might conclude the discourse of Kiddes with a remembraunce of their constellation in the Waggoner, vppon the Bulles Horne. **1771** *Encycl. Brit.* I. 486 The ancient Constellations [include]..Auriga, The Waggoner. **1868** LOCKYER *Guillemin's Heavens* (ed. 3) 382 [The Milky Way] afterwards bears away under the form of a single and narrow branch, which traverses Cassiopea, passes by the Waggoner [etc.].

b. 1590 SPENSER *F.Q.* I. ii. 1 By this the Northerne wagoner had set His seuenfold teme behind the stedfast starre. **1697** DRYDEN *Virg. Georg.* I. 318 Begin when the slow Waggoner descends, Nor cease your sowing till Mid-winter ends.

4. A wagon-horse; in quot. a depreciatory term for a racehorse.

1859 *Sporting Mag.* Oct. 241 Magnum, the Baron's chesnut waggoner, wore huge blinkers.

wagoner, waggoner[2] ('wægənə(r)). *Obs.* exc. *Hist.* Also with capital initial. [Anglicized form of the Dutch surname *Waghenaer*: see below.] Originally, the atlas of charts published by Lucas Janssen Waghenaer in 1584 under the title *Spieghel der Zeevaerdt* (Eng. trans. *The Mariners Mirror*, by Sir A. Ashley, 1588). Hence *gen.* a book of charts for nautical use.

1687 W. HEDGES *Diary* (Hakl. Soc.) I. 246 Ye Shippe *Providence* ran aground, her Commander designing to go between ye Islands Sardinia and Palma de Sol, where ye English Platts and Wagones [*read* Wagoners] make a large passage; but in truth there is none. **1703** DAMPIER *Voy.* III. I. 98 In the East India Waggoner or Pilot-book there is mention made of large Fowls. **1775** ROMANS *Hist. Florida* App. 77 The compilers of the quarter waggoners..have corrupted it into Ponio bay. **1815** *Falconer's Dict. Marine* (ed. Burney), *Waggoner*, is also used for a routier, or book of charts, describing the seas, their coasts, &c. **1916** *Edin. Rev.* July 180 [Sailing directions] have been called by many names—Periploi, Portulane, Rutters, Waggoners [etc.].

†**wagoness.** *Obs. rare.* In 7 **wagonnesse.** [f. WAGONER[1]: see -ESS.] A female charioteer.

c **1611** CHAPMAN *Iliad* v. 348 His chariot (perplext with her late harme) She mounted, and her wagonnesse, was she that paints the aire. *Ibid.* 838.

wagonette, waggonette (wægə'nɛt). Also 9 **waggonet.** [f. WAGON *sb.* + -ETTE.] A four-wheeled carriage, made open or with a removable cover and furnished with a seat or bench at each side facing inwards and with one or two seats arranged crosswise in front.

1858 SIMMONDS *Dict. Trade*, *Waggonette*, a carriage to carry six or eight persons. **1862** MRS. H. FRESHFIELD *Tour Grisons* iv. 58 At half-past five the wagonettes (to give a fashionable name to our primitive vehicles) were in readiness. **1864** J. GILBERT & G. C. CHURCHILL *Excurs. Dolomite Mts.* 95 We..engaged a long-bodied waggonet to Reutte, in Tyrol. **1873** BLACK *Princess Thule* i, There was a large waggonette, of varnished oak, and a pair of small, powerful horses waiting for him there. **1875** S. SIDNEY *Bk. Horse* ii. 23 The wagonette..did not come into general use until some years after the International Exhibition of 1851, although, according to the Report on the Carriage Department of the Exhibition of 1862, 'the first wagonette was built in 1846.'

b. *attrib.* and *Comb.*, as ***wagonette-driver***; **wagonette omnibus**, a motor-omnibus with accommodation resembling that of a wagonette.

1877 'C. BEDE' *Figaro at Hastings* 50 The waggonette-drivers, with uplifted whip-hand, hailing me with 'Now for Fairlight and the Lover's Seat!' **1903** *Motoring Ann.* 244 A waggonette omnibus. A little waggonette 'bus,..capable of seating about a dozen persons, has been plying on the Putney to Piccadilly route for more than a year.

wagonful, waggonful ('wægənfʊl). Also -full. As many persons, or as much baggage, etc. as will fill a wagon.

1846 DICKENS *Pict. Italy* 179 A waggon-full of madmen, screaming and tearing to the life. **1883** STEVENSON *Silverado Squatters* 121 Hanson arrived, with a waggonful of our effects. **1902** OWEN WISTER *Virginian* xviii, The wagonful of guests whom he had evidently been driving upon a day's excursion.

wagon-head, waggon-head. *Arch.* A cylindrical ceiling, roof, or vault.

1823 P. NICHOLSON *Pract. Builder* 430 Ceilings, formed simply of cylindric surfaces, are termed, by mechanics, waggon-heads. **1874** MICKLETHWAITE *Mod. Par. Churches* 215 The best general form is that of a polygonal 'waggon-head' of five or seven sides.

b. *attrib.* or as *adj.*

1842 *Penny Cycl.* XXII. 482/2 Watt adopted a long rectangular form, with a semi-cylindrical top... From this form it is termed the waggon-head boiler. **1870** M. A. LOWER *Hist. Sussex* I. 242 The whole of the building has now a wagon-head ceiling in pannelled oak.

Hence **wagon-headed** *a.*

1823 P. NICHOLSON *Pract. Builder* 114 Lunettes..are made either in waggon-headed ceilings, or through large coves. **1897** F. J. BURGOYNE *Library Constr.* 192 A richly moulded waggon-headed roof.

wagoning, waggoning ('wægənɪŋ), *vbl. sb.* [f. WAGON *v.* + -ING[1].] **a.** The action of travelling or conveying by wagon.

1782 in L. P. Summers *Ann. Southwest Virginia* (1929) 770 He ought to be paid..for one day waggoning. **1837** *Southern Lit. Messenger* III. 87 There never was such a time for waggoning before. **1856** OLMSTED *Slave States* v. 339 More than thirty miles of wagoning is required to bring the spirits of turpentine to a rail-road. **1865** CARLYLE *Fredk. Gt.* XVIII. xiv. (1873) VIII. 59 The greatest activity and wagoning now visible there. **1877** A. DOUAI *Better Times* (1884) 15 Already in the earliest, darkest ages were invented the arts of..navigating and wagoning.

b. *colloq.* Coach-driving.

1875 REYNARDSON *Down the Road* 49 Tom Hennesy, who was always fond of giving me a lesson in 'waggoning', and by whose side I was sitting on the box. **1896** CONAN DOYLE *Rodney Stone* viii, It's a fine day for a little bit of waggoning.

‖**wagon-lit** (vagɔ̃li). [Fr.: *wagon* railway coach (a. Eng. WAGON *sb.*) + *lit* bed.] A sleeping coach on a Continental train.

1884 *Daily News* 4 Feb. 3/4 The wagonlit was abandoned, and our journey was continued in an ordinary carriage. **1904** B'NESS VON HÜTTEN *Pam* 39 The child was quite used to strange quarters and *wagon-lits*.

wagon-load, waggon-load. As much as a wagon can carry. (Often used hyperbolically.)

1721 CIBBER *Refusal* I. i, Well, how goes Mississippi, man? What, do they bring their money by waggon loads to market still? **1728** YOUNG *Love Fame* I. 87 Imperious some a classic fame demand, For heaping up with a laborious hand, A waggon-load of meanings for one word. **1801** *Farmer's Mag.* Nov. 471 A waggon-load [of wheat] is 12 or 14 barrels; each barrel 196 lib. weight. **1837** DICKENS *Pickw.* v, He wouldn't shy if he was to meet a vaggin-load of monkeys with their tails burnt off. **1855** MACAULAY *Hist. Eng.* xvii. IV. 66 He carries with him..a waggonload of plate. **1913** J. G. FRAZER

Golden Bough vii. *Balder* I. iv. 118 The butchers were rewarded with a waggon-load of wine.

‖**wagon-restaurant** (vagɔ̃ rɛstɔrɑ̃). [Fr.: cf. WAGON-LIT and RESTAURANT.] A dining-car on a Continental train.

1910 *Bradshaw's Railway Guide* Jan. 958 Special Wagon Restaurant Corridor Train leaves Paris for Cherbourg on morning of sailing. **1938** H. NICOLSON *Let.* 26 Apr. (1966) 337 This man would be delightful if one met him in a *wagon-restaurant* and got into conversation. **1983** W. BLUNT *Married to Single Life* vii. 199 Seated in the overheated *wagon-restaurant* of the Continental express.

wagonry, waggonry (ˈwægənrɪ). *rare.* [f. WAGON *sb.* + -RY.]

†**1.** ? Chariots collectively. *Obs.*

1595 CHAPMAN *Ovid's Banq. Sence* C 2, Like the fire Stolne from the wheeles of Phœbus waggonrie To lumps of earth, can manly lyfe inspire.

2. Conveyance or transport by wagon.

1641 MILTON *Ch. Govt.* I. i. 5 So long as the Church is mounted upon the Prelaticall Cart..it will but shake and totter, and he that sets to his hand..to hinder the shogging of it, in this unlawfull waggonry wherein it rides, let him beware [etc.]. **1865** CARLYLE *Fredk. Gt.* xx. vi. (1873) IX. 118 Provisions..were not to be had by force of wagonry.

wag-on-the-wall: see WAG-AT-THE-WALL.

wagon-way, waggon-way.

1. An artificial road or a line of rails in a colliery upon which the coal wagons are run.

1727 DE FOE *Eng. Tradesm.* xlvi. (1841) II. 173 [A coal wagon] which by the means of an artificial road, called a wagon-way, goes with the help of but one horse..to the nearest river. **1837** HEBERT *Engin. & Mech. Encycl.* II. 375 The intended rail-road, or 'waggon-way', as it was termed. *attrib.* **1764** *London Mag.* Mar. 145/1 If the waggon-way-rails..be wet sometimes, a man cannot stop the waggon.

2. A road made for the passage of wagons; also a track made by wagons.

1764 *Museum Rust.* II. lii. 148 A Letter..on the Advantages of making good Roads, or Waggon-Ways, in a Farm. **1877** RAYMOND *Statist. Mines & Mining* 213 A wagon-way—not a road—has been made across this divide, by which heavy machinery has been hauled over.

†**ˈwagship.** *Obs.* [f. WAG *sb.*² + -SHIP.]

1. Waggery, waggishness.

1607 MIDDLETON *Fam. Love* II. (1608) B 4 b, No rather lets pierce the Rundlets of our running heads and giue 'hem a neate cuppe of wagshippe, to put downe their Courtship.

2. Used jocularly, with possessive pron., as a title for a wag.

1607 MARSTON *What you will* III. i. E 4, Pleaseth your excellent wagship to bee informed that [etc.]. **1640** BROME *Antipodes* II. ix. E 3 b, You shall to schoole, away with him; and take Their wagships with him.

wagsome (ˈwægsəm), *a. nonce-wd.* [f. WAG *sb.*² + -SOME.] Waggish, addicted to waggery.

1869 W. S. GILBERT *'Bab' Ballads, Peter the Wag* 37 Still humoured he his wagsome turn.

†**ˈwagstart.** *Obs.* Also 5 -sterd, -styrt, 5–6 -stert. [f. WAG *v.* + START *sb.*¹ Cf. MLG. *wage-, wakstert*; also Da. *vip-*, Sw. *vippstjert*, Du. *kwikstaartje*.] = WAGTAIL.

c **1440** *Promp. Parv.* 513/2 Wagstert [*Winch. MS.* Waggestert], byrd, *teda, vel toda.* *c* **1475** *Pict. Voc.* in Wr.-Wülcker 763/2 *Hic tradus*, a wagstyrt. **1570** LEVINS *Manip.* 33/42 A Wagstarte, *motacilla.*

wagtail (ˈwægteɪl), *sb.* [f. WAG *v.* + TAIL *sb.*¹ Cf. prec. and F. *hochequeue.*]

1. a. A small bird belonging to one of the species of the genus *Motacilla* or the family *Motacillidæ*, so called from the continual characteristic wagging motion of the tail. In Great Britain chiefly applied to *M. lugubris*, 'the Pied Wagtail of authors' (Newton), called also *water wagtail.*

1510 STANBRIDGE *Vocabula* (W. de W.) C vj, *Motatula*, a wag tayle. *a* **1529** SKELTON *P. Sparowe* 392 The goldfynche, the wagtayle. *c* **1550** LLOYD *Treas. Health* xxxviii. (Copland) N vij, A special remedy [for the stone] after Auicen, is a wagtayle. **1604** [? CHETTLE] *Wit of Woman* C 2, I..had my spirit as full of life as a wagtayle, but now the case is altered. **1658** ROWLAND tr. *Moufet's Theat. Ins.* 946 All those Birds called Wagtails (if I am not deceived) live upon Flies. **1748** RICHARDSON *Clarissa* (1768) IV. 24, I always illustrated my Eagleship..by disdaining to make a stoop at wrens, phyl-tits, and wag-tails. **1773** G. WHITE *Selborne, To Pennant* 9 Nov., Wagtails, all sorts, remain with us all the winter. **1876** SMILES *Scotch Natur.* xiii. (ed. 4) 260 The melancholy note of the Wagtail.

b. With qualifying words, indicating native country, colour, habits, etc.

Chiefly species of *Motacilla*, or species formerly referred to that genus.

1668 CHARLETON *Onomast.* 90 *Motacilla Flava*, the Yellow wagtail. *a* **1672** WILLUGHBY *Ornith.* II. xvii. (1676) 172 *Motacilla cinerea...* The grey Wagtail. **1678** RAY *Willughby's Ornith.* II. xvii. 237 The white Wagtail. **1783** LATHAM *Gen. Synopsis Birds* II. 396–402 [*Mentions* Collared, Pied, Indian, Yellow, Yellow-headed, Cape or African Wagtail]. **1802** G. MONTAGU *Ornith. Dict.* s.v., Wagtail, Grey... Provincial. Winter Wagtail. *Ibid.*, Wagtail, Yellow... Provincial. Spring, or Summer Wagtail. **1863** BARING-GOULD *Iceland* 332 A coppice of birch, among which darted the redwing and white wagtail. **1884** COUES *Key N. Amer. Birds* (ed. 2) 284 *Motacilla ocularis.* Siberian Wagtail. **1896** NEWTON *Dict. Birds* 1018 The so-called Grey Wagtail of Britain.

2. Applied to other birds. **a.** *U.S.* One of the water-thrushes, *Seiurus nævius* or *S. motacilla* (*Cent. Dict.* 1891).

1868 J. BURROUGHS *Wake-robin* viii. (1884) 296 The two species of water-thrush or wagtails, and the oven-bird or wood-wagtail.

b. *Austral.* The black-and-white fantail, *Rhipidura tricolor*, also called the *wagtail flycatcher* (Morris *Austral English*, 1898). **c.** *dial.* The dunlin (Montagu *Ornith. Dict.*, 1802).

†**3.** *transf.* **a.** A familiar or contemptuous epithet or form of address applied to a man or young woman. *Obs.*

1605 SHAKS. *Lear* II. ii. 73 This ancient Ruffian Sir, whose life I haue spar'd at sute of his gray-beard... Spare my gray-beard, you wagtaile? **1607** MIDDLETON *Mich. Term* III. 211 Wagtail, salute them all; they are friends. **1656** DU GARD tr. *Comenius' Gate Lat. Unl.* 193 A wagtail or busibody desiring to know many things beyond measure, and being unable to bee satisfied with enquiries. **1732** FIELDING *Debauchees* I. i, Good morrow, my little wagtail—my grass-hopper, my butterfly. **1783** O'KEEFFE *Birth-Day* 30 To dangle, frisk, and hop about like an impertinent wag-tail as you are.

†**b.** *esp.* A contemptuous term for a profligate or inconstant woman; hence, a harlot, courtesan.

Common in the 17th c.

1592 LYLY *Midas* I. i, If therefore thou make not thy mistress a goldfinch, thou mayst chance to find her a wagtaile. **1608** MIDDLETON *Trick to Catch Old One* II. i. 84 If men be wags, are there not women wagtails? **1635** SHIRLEY *Traitor* II. i, Join to make her Supple and pliant for the Duke: I hope We are not the first have been advanced by a wagtail. **1694** MOTTEUX *Rabelais* v. Prognost. v. 237 Hedge-whores, Wagtails, Cockatrices, Whipsters. **1710** *Brit. Apollo* III. No. 25. 3/2 Like Paris with his Gleek of Wagtails on Ida.

4. An artificial minnow used in trout-fishing.

1906 *Macm. Mag.* Nov. 26 Shortly after there was a pull at the rod from which the wagtail was fishing.

5. *Joinery.* A parting-strip (see PARTING *vbl. sb.* 7 b) used in the construction of a sash window.

1940 in *Chambers's Techn. Dict.* **1950** M. T. TELLING *Carpentry & Joinery* 43 To prevent this happening a long thin sliver of wood called a parting slip or wagtail is placed between them [*sc.* the weights] inside the box.

6. *Comb.*, as ***wagtail-family, -minnow***; **wagtail dance** = *waggle dance* s.v. WAGGLE *sb.* 2; **wagtail flycatcher** = 2 b; **wagtail kite** *nonce-use*, a toy kite with a wagging or swinging tail; **wagtail-warbler** = 2 a.

1882 *Proc. Berw. Nat. Club* IX. No. iii. 504 Of the Wagtail family, the Pied Wagtail, and the Grey and Yellow Wagtail, visited the Lake. **1884** COUES *Key N. Amer. Birds* (ed. 2) 309 *Siurus nævius.* Wag-tail Warbler. *Ibid.*, *Siurus motacilla.* Large-billed Wagtail Warbler. **1906** *Macm. Mag.* Nov. 25 A green and silver wagtail minnow. **1922** JOYCE *Ulysses* 495 Ragged barefoot newsboys jogging a wagtail kite. **1949** C. G. BUTLER *Honeybee* viii. 120 Von Frisch described two dances, a round-dance and a wag-tail dance. **1973** Wag-tail dance [see ROUND *a.* 5 a].

†**ˈwagtail,** *v. Obs.* [f. WAGTAIL *sb.*] *intr.* To flutter.

1606 SYLVESTER *Du Bartas* II. iv. I. *Tropheis* 137 Even as a paire of busie chattering Pies..feel a chill fear, From bush to bush, wag-tayling here and there. *c* **1620** Z. BOYD *Zion's Flowers* (1855) 118 From bush to bush they in a panick feare, Wagtayling goe.

†**wagtailed,** *a. Obs. rare.* [f. WAGTAIL *sb.* (as if 'wagging tail') + -ED².] Tail-wagging; also *fig.* wanton.

1648 HEXHAM II, *Gewipsteert*, wagg-tailed, or that moves the Taile. **1656** S. HOLLAND *Zara* (1719) 64 You spend your Lives, With wag-tail'd Wives.

wah (wɑː). [Native name.] = PANDA I.

1858 BAIRD *Cycl. Nat. Sci.* s.v. *Ailurus*, *A. fulgens*, the Wah or Panda... It derives its name *Wah* from its cry. **1859** J. G. WOOD *Illustr. Nat. Hist.* I. 420.

wah, early form of WAW *sb.*, wall.

Wahabi, Wahabee, Wahhabi, -bee (wəˈhɑːbiː). Also 9 **Wuhabee, Wahaby, -hebbi.** [a. Ar. *Wahhābī*, f. *Wahhāb* (see below).] A follower of Abd-el-Wahhab (1691–1787), a Muslim reformer and founder of a sect of Muslim puritans who follow strictly the original words of the Koran.

1807 E. S. WARING *Tour to Sheeraz* 119 The founder of the religion of the Wuhabees. **1810** *Naval Chron.* XXIV. 374 The Wahebbis, as we shall, consequently, style the Nedjedis. *a* **1817** BURCKHARDT *Trav. Arabia* (1829) I. 25 During the predominance of the Wahabis, Djidda has been in a declining state. *Ibid.* 354 The Wahabys. **1817** C. MILLS *Hist. Muhammedanism* vii. 375 The tenets of the Wahabees became established all over the peninsula of Arabia. **1865** W. G. PALGRAVE *Journ. Arabia* II. 3 Himself a bitter Wahhabee, and a model of all the orthodox vices of his sect. **1881** W. S. BLUNT in *Lady A. Blunt's Pilgr. to Nejd* II. 257 Abdallah..was acknowledged, without opposition, chief of the Wahhabis.

b. *attrib.* and *adj.*

1807 E. S. WARING *Tour Sheeraz* 119 The Wuhabee Arabs. **1865** W. G. PALGRAVE *Journ. Arabia* I. 445 These differences give Wahhabee worship a peculiar type. **1881** W. S. BLUNT in *Lady A. Blunt's Pilgr. to Nejd* II. 254 Southern Nejd alone seems to have been fanatically Wahhabi.

Hence **Waˈhabiism, -beeism, -bism, Waˈhabite** [see -ISM, -ITE].

1810 *Naval Chron.* XXIV. 298 The attempts of the Wahebites to reduce their theory to practice. *Ibid.* 376 The Wahebite clan. **1826** GEN. P. THOMPSON *Exerc.* (1842) III. 383 Wahabeeism is Arabia marshalled against Turkish domination. **1865** W. G. PALGRAVE *Journ. Arabia* I. 194 If ordinary Islam proved too strait-laced for Arabia, Wahhabeeism is of necessity even more so. **1881** W. S. BLUNT in *Lady A. Blunt's Pilgr. to Nejd* II. 251 The rise and decline of Wahhabism in Arabia. **1884** *Encycl. Brit.* XVII. 773/2 The rise of the Wahhâbite power. *Ibid.*, 'Oneiza sided with the Wahhâbites. **1901** SKRINE *Sir W. W. Hunter* xi. 198 In the darkest days of Wahabiism.

†**wahahowe,** *int. Obs.* Also **wa ha ho, wa'hoh.** = HALLOO.

c **1595** R. CAREW *Excellency Engl. Tongue* in G. G. Smith *Elizab. Crit. Ess.* (1904) II. 287 In detestation wee saye *Phy* ..; in calling, *whowp*; in hallowinge, *wahahowe*: all which (in my eare) seeme to be deriued from the very natures of those seuerall affections. *c* **1600** *Distr. Emperor* II. i. in Bullen *O. Pl.* (1884) III. 194 Wa, ha ho, man! Your buzzard is a kynde of byrde of prey. *a* **1616** BEAUM. & FL. *Little Fr. Lawyer* IV. iv, *La-writ.* So ho? our weapons. *Sam.* Wa, ha, ho, our weapons? **1633** B. JONSON *Tale of Tub* I. i. 23 *Hug.* The Vicar of Pancrace, Squire Tub! wa' hoh! *Tub.* I come, I stoop unto the call; Sir Hugh!

wahine (waˈhine, wɑːˈhiːnɪ). Also 8 **whinie,** 9 **whyenee, wiena, wyeena; wahini.** [Maori, Hawaiian, and other Polynesian languages: cf. VAHINE.]

1. *N.Z.* A Maori woman or wife.

1773 W. BAYLY *Jrnl.* in R. McNab *Hist. Rec. N.Z.* (1914) II. 204 Their Whinies (or women) are not regular featured in general as the men. **1807** J. SAVAGE *Some Acct. N.Z.* xi. 74 *Wyeena*, a woman. **1841** *N.Z. Jrnl.* II. No. 32. 92/2 The chiefs and 'Wienas', or wives, partook. **1845** E. J. WAKEFIELD *Adventure N.Z.* I. ii. 29 Having enquired how many [wives] the Kings of England had, he laughed heartily at finding they were not so well provided, and repeatedly counted 'four *wahine*' (women) on his fingers. **1863** V. LUSH *Jrnl.* 28 Sept. (1971) 253 By noon the following day all the wahines had gone back to the Pah, cockles and all. **1911** W. H. KOEBEL *In Maoriland Bush* viii. 128 Two or three Wahines ply the men lustily with..somewhat broad banter. **1944** *Coast to Coast 1943* 105 You meet te nice girl at te dance. Plenty wahine! **1963** *Times* 7 Feb. 12/3 The warriors and their *wahine* turned away 'towards God', as I was told by an old Maori who sat with me on the grass.

2. In Polynesia: = VAHINE.

1847 H. BINGHAM *Residence 21 Yrs. Sandwich Islands* 188 Give our *aloha* to all the new teachers and their *wahines.* **1865** H. W. BAXLEY *What I saw on West Coast of S. & N. Amer.* 515 The wahine disputes with them the palm of superiority.

3. *Surfing slang.* A girl surfer.

1963 *Surfing Yearbk.* 43/2 *Wahini*, a girl surfer. **1966** *Surfer* VII. 39 There are other things he did on the board, too, especially the full-moon tandem rides with wahines. **1971** *Studies in English* (Univ. Cape Town) II. 26 *Wahine* meaning woman in Hawaiian, a term popular among writers, has never been used in Cape Town.

wahoo¹ (wəˈhuː). Also **waahoo, whahoo.** [Indian name.]

1. The N. American shrub *Euonymus atropurpureus.*

1860 A. GRAY *Man. Bot.* 81 *Euonymus atropurpureus*.. Burning-Bush, Waahoo. **1866** *Treas. Bot.*, Wahoo. **1903** NANCY H. BANKS *Round Anvil Rock* 158 The bright wahoo with its graceful cluster of flame-coloured berries.

2. *U.S.* The winged elm, *Ulmus alata*, or a closely related tree. Also *attrib.*

1770 E. MEASE *Jrnl.* 28 Nov. in *Publ. Mississippi Hist. Soc. Centenary Ser.* (1925) V. 62 The Trees which I remark'd to be the largest were Oaks of different kinds, Wahoos, Button Wood, [etc.]. **1832** D. J. BROWNE *Sylva Amer.* 308 The Wahoo is a stranger to the Middle and Northern States. **1873** *Newton Kansan* 27 Mar. 1/7 One ounce of wahoo (winged-elm) bark, added to a quart of pure whiskey..is very excellent in dyspepsia. **1969** T. H. EVERETT *Living Trees of World* xiv. 130/2 The wahoo elm..is usually characterized by branchlets having two broad corky wings.

wahoo² (wəˈhuː). [Origin unknown.] A large marine fish, *Acanthocybium solandri*, belonging to the family Scombridæ and found in tropical seas.

[**1905** D. S. JORDAN *Guide to Study of Fishes* II. xvi. 266 Still larger is the great guaho, or peto, an immense sharp-nosed, swift-swimming mackerel found in the East and West Indies.] **1909** *Cent. Dict.* Suppl. 1429/2 Wahoo.. A common name of *Acanthocybium solandri*, a scombroid fish of tropical seas. **1920** *Outing* July 248/3 He had fished for —and caught—many a most unheard of species, as well as sharks, sword-fish, wahoo, etc. **1940** *Geogr. Jrnl.* XCV. 130 These fish [*sc.* kingfish] which the Americans call wahoo, are beautifully shaped surface feeders. **1979** *United States 1980/81* (Penguin Travel Guides) 517 The white marlin capital of the world sends fishermen out to the Jackspot..for dolphin, bonita, tuna, and wahoo.

waht, wai, waiche, obs. forms of WHAT, WAY, WOE, WATCH.

wah-wah (ˈwɑːwɑː). Also **wa-wa, wha-wha, wow-wow.** [Echoic.] **1.** *Mus.* (orig. *Jazz*). A musical effect achieved on brass instruments by manipulation of a mute and on an electric guitar by means of a pedal controlling output from the amplifier.

1926 H. O. OSGOOD *So this is Jazz* 98 Then there is the clown of mutes. Leading philologists of the jazz world are at odds over the correct spelling of the name; some favour wow wow, others prefer wha wha, but there is authority for the simplification wa-wa. **1936** *Amer. Mercury* XXXVIII. p. x/2 *Wah-wah*, a brass effect gotten by favoring a bell of a horn with a mute. **1949** R. BLESH *Shining Trumpets* viii. 183

The 'wa-wa', produced by the cupped hand moved in front of the cornet or trumpet bell. **1950** A. Lomax *Mr. Jelly Roll* (1952) 64 There were many other imitations of animal sounds we used—such as the wah-wahs on trumpets and trombones. **1976** *New Musical Express* 12 Feb. 25/2 You can thrill again to.. Clapton playing his insidious wah-wah on 'Get Back Home'. **1977** 'E. Crispin' *Glimpses of Moon* iii. 38 One spends his working life in a perpetual seascape, another writing wah-wahs on trumpet parts for people surfacing in mud-baths into which they have comically fallen.. and so on.

2. The sound of a baby's crying, or a noise resembling this.

1938 D. Runyon *Furthermore* viii. 156 Something goes wa-wa, like a sheep.. because.. Isadore is sitting on John Ignatius Junior's doll, which says 'Mamma' when you squeeze it. **1958** Hayward & Harari tr. *Pasternak's Dr. Zhivago* I. vi. 158 'Wa, wa,' yelled the babies all on one note. .. Only one voice stood out from the others. It was also yelling 'wa, wa',.. but it was deeper.

3. *attrib.*, esp. as (sense 1) ***wah-wah effect, mute, pedal.***

1925 G. Gershwin *Rhapsody in Blue* (music score) (1939) 1 (*direction*) Wha Wha effect. **1926** *Melody Maker* Feb. 23/2 (Advt.), The wow-wow mute is made of spun aluminium. **1926** Whiteman & McBride *Jazz* ix. 200 The first time I ever heard what I call the wawa mutes, used with the cornet. .. The players got that effect by inverting glass tumblers over the bells of the instruments. **1930** R. Paget *Human Speech* 240 The so-called 'wow-wow' mutes for cornets and the like. **1935** *Vanity Fair* (N.Y.) Nov. 71/3 The wah-wah notes of intermittently muted brass. **1943** R. Blesh *This is Jazz* 24 This bad tone.. like dirty tone, growl or wah-wah trumpet work, is expressive and therefore good from the Jazz point of view. **1954** *Grove's Dict. Mus.* (ed. 5) IV. 601/1 The trumpets and trombones very frequently use peculiar mutes, such as the 'wa wa mute', which can make the instrument weep or laugh rather like a human voice. **1969** *It* 13–28 June 13/2 Frank proved quite conclusively that he's a brilliant guitarist, especially with a 'wah-wah' pedal. **1979** R. L. Simon *Peking Duck* xxiii. 175 It's an old song... Now they use a wah-wah pedal and a Moog Synthesizer.

wah-wah, var. wow-wow[1].

waiata ('waiata). *N.Z.* Also 9 **wyata**. [Maori.] A Maori song.

1807 J. Savage *Some Acct. N.Z.* xi. 75 *Wyata*, singing. **1843** E. Dieffenbach *Trav. N.Z.* II. I. iv. 57 E' Waiata is a song of a joyful nature. **1905** W. Baucke *Where White Man Treads* 88 Then Puke.. sang a waiata. **1978** P. Grace *Mutuwhenua* xiv. 104 Singing or chanting the waiata at the conclusion of each speech. **1984** *Metro* (Auckland) Jan. 72/3 Indeed the Maori name for the racecourse is Waiatarua (Two Songs) and tradition suggests it was so named because the sound of the flood waters escaping through the underground caverns closely resembled the singing of waiatas.

waicht, obs. Sc. form of weight.

waid, Sc. form of wade *v.*, woad.

waidge, obs. Sc. form of wage.

waie, obs. form of way, weigh *v.*

waif (weɪf), *sb.*[1] (and *a.*) Pl. **waifs**. Forms: 3–7 **wayf**, 4–9 **waife**, 5 **wayffe**, 5, 7 **weif**, 6 **wayfe**, **wayff**, 6–7 **weife**, 7 **wafe**, **waiefe**, **weyfe**, **wayve**, **waive**, **wave**, 9 **waiff**, 6– **waif**. Also *pl.* 5, 7 **wayves**, 5 **weyves**, 6 **wavys**, 6–7 **waives**. See also weft. [a. AF. *waif*, *wayf* (Sk.), *weif*, *weyf* (Britton), *gwayf* (in Kennett), (Anglo-L. *waivum*, *wayvium*, *weyvium*) = OF. (Norman) *gaif*, *gayf* (fem. *gaive*, *gayve*) sb. and adj.; early mod.F. (Cotgr.) *vuayves* (sb.), and (*choses*) *guesves* or *gayves*; prob. of Scandinavian origin, with the primary sense 'something loose or wandering'; cf. ON. *veif* something flapping or waving (cf. waif *sb.*[2]), related to *veifa* trans. to wave, vibrate. Cf. waive *v.*]

A. *sb.*

1. *Law.* **a.** A piece of property which is found ownerless and which, if unclaimed within a fixed period after due notice given, falls to the lord of the manor; e.g. an article washed up on the seashore, an animal that has strayed. Often ***waif and stray*** or †*straif*: cf. stray *sb.* 1, straif.

Not evidenced as Eng. before 1377; the bracketed quots. represent the AF. use of 13–15th c., in which the word is often collect. sing. meaning lost property collectively or the right of the lord to such property.

[**1223** in Kennett *Par. Antiq.* (1818) II. 275 Recognitum est.. quod ad nos spectat le Gwayf &c in terris nostris. **1228** in *Mem. Ripon* (Surtees) I. 52 Wrek, weyf, stray, merchet. *c* **1290** *Fleta* I. xlvii. (1647) 62 Si quis.. libertatem Weyvii habere clamans, animal vagans in feodo suo invenerit. **1293** *Rolls of Parlt.* I. 115/1 Omnia Animalia que dicuntur Wayf, inventa in predictis terris. **1372** in Kennett *Par. Antiq.* (1818) II. 151 Dicte xix marce sciatis fuerunt ibidem tanquam Wayf in manum prioris. **1400** in *Liber Custum.* (Rolls) 486 Quod prædictus Dux.. haberet.. omnimoda catalla vocata 'Wayf' et 'Stray'.]

1377 Langl. *P. Pl.* B. Prol. 94 Of wardes and wardmotes, weyues and streyues. **1444** *Rolls of Parlt.* V. 126/2 All maner Wayffes and Strayes, and othur godes forfeted. **1447** Shillingford *Lett.* (Camden) 99 He and his predecessours .. have had view of Frank Plegge weif and straif and all other profits longing to a view. **1455** *Rolls of Parlt.* V. 311/2 Wrecke of the Sea, Weyves, Estrayes. **1546** in *Sel. Pleas Crt. Admiralty* (1894) I. 148 The sayde Leonard Sumpter fyndynge the sayde shyppe.. dryvynge with the streamys as a wayff and forsaken of all creatures toke and seased uppon the same as lawfull wayff and thynge forsaken. **1547** in J. H. Glover *Kingsthorpiana* (1883) 93 That all wavys and strays from hense forthe shalbe delyvered to the Baylie by the Thurbarrowes. **1622** Callis *Stat. Sewers* (1647) 22 When an owner cannot be found, the Common Law gives it *Domino Regi*, as Waifs, Strays, Wreck of the Sea. **1765** Blackstone *Comm.* I. viii. 292 Wrecks, treasure trove,.. waifs, and estrays, may be granted by the king to particular subjects, as a royal franchise: and indeed they are for the most part granted out to the lords of manors. **1826** Scott *Woodst.* ii, Sir Henry Lee is keeper of Woodstock Park, with right of waif and stray [etc.]. **1852** Ida Pfeiffer *Journ. Iceland* 85 He has a right to all the waifs, which is a privilege of some importance, on account of the wood drifted from the American continent. **1866** Kingsley *Herew.* vi, The country folk, who were prowling about the shore after the waifs of the storm.

incorrect use. **1871** Ruskin *Fors Clav.* I. iii. 18 Hearing that a considerable treasure of ancient coins and medals has been found in the lands of Vidomar, Viscount of Limoges, King Richard sends forthwith to claim this waif for himself.

†**b.** (See quots.) *Obs.*

1579 *Expos. Terms Law* 186 Wayfe is when a theefe hath feloniously stolne goodes, and beinge neerelye followed with hue, and crye,.. flieth away and leaueth the goods.. behind him, then the queenes officer or the Reeue or Bailife to the Lord of the manour.. may seyse the goodes so wayued to their lordes vse. **1610** W. Folkingham *Feudigr.* III. iv. 71 Waiues, Weifes, or waiued goods, import all goods and chattels, which being stolne, are left or forsaken by the thiefe in his fugacie. **1620** J. Wilkinson *Courts Leet* 125 Waiefes are cattell stolne and weived out of the possession of him that stole them. **1765** Blackstone *Comm.* I. viii. 286 Waifs, *bona waviata*, are goods stolen, and waived or thrown away by the thief in his flight, for fear of being apprehended.

2. *transf.* and *fig.* **a.** In general use.

1624 Donne *Devot.* xiii. (ed. 2) 312 What a Wayue, and Stray is that Man, that hath not thy Marks vpon him? **1676** Marvell *Mr. Smirke, Hist. Ess.* 49 Whensoever a Christian transgresses these bounds once, he is impoundable, or like a wafe and stray whom Christ knows not, he falls to the Lord of the Mannor. **1690** C. Nesse *O. & N. Test.* I. 143 We are faln into our Lords hands.. as wafes and strays; the Lord of the Mannor seizeth on us for not paying our fines. **1785** Burns *Twa Herds* i, Or wha will tent the waifs and crocks, About the dykes? **1823** Scott *Peveril* xxxix, You are here a waif on Cupid's manor, and I must seize on you in name of the deity. **1848** Dickens *Dombey* liii, I had no scruples of conscience in suffering all the waifs and strays of that conversation to float to me as freely as they would. **1855** Tennyson *Brook* 199 Rolling in his mind Old waifs of rhyme. **1877** Symonds *Sk. & Stud. Italy* (1879) 300 A *chiffonnier* of Paris,.. when the night has fallen, goes into the streets.. to rake up the waifs and strays a day of whirling life has left him. **1879** Froude *Cæsar* xxiii. 398 He was now flung as a waif on the shore of a foreign land. **1918** F. Wood-Jones *Probl. Man's Ancestry* 42 The whole fauna of Australia consists (with the exception of a few waifs) of pouched animals.

b. *esp.* A person who is without home or friends; one who lives uncared-for or without guidance; an outcast from society; an unowned or neglected child.

1784 Cowper *Task* III. 80 'Twas hard, perhaps, on here and there a waif, Desirous to return, and not receiv'd. **1830** Galt *Lawrie T.* IV. I. 26 It's no possible.. that such poor waifes could be guilty of any thing like that. **1857** Mrs. Mathews *Tea-Table T.* I. 205 Some blest Alsatia.. wherein to gather up the waifs and strays that abound in the bye-ways. **1862** 'Shirley' (J. Skelton) *Nugæ Crit.* iii. 159 They are the waifs and strays, and cast-aways of society. **1875** *Children reclaimed for Life* 82 Little Jem Jervis was simply a friendless waif. **1916** *Whitaker's Almanack* Advt. 114 Church of England—Waifs and Strays Society needs help for its large family of over 4,600 children... Over 20,000 Children Rescued.

3. *Comb.*, as ***waif-like*** adj.; ***waif-wise*** adv.

1871 Swinburne *Songs bef. Sunrise, Eve of Revol.* 63 Whose multiplying hands Wove the world's web with divers races fair And cast it waif-wise on the stream. **1924** R. Campbell *Flaming Terrapin* ii. 35 Their waif-like corpses on a stormy bed Toss in their deep deliriums. **1962** I. Murdoch *Unofficial Rose* xv. 149 How young she looked, how waif-like.

B. *attrib.* and *adj.*

1. *attrib.* or *appositive* (indicating lost property, a strayed animal, a homeless person, etc.).

1609 Skene *Reg. Maj., Treat.* 155 Ane wafe beast, after zeare and day, is escheit to the King. **1678** Sir G. Mackenzie *Crim. Laws Scot.* I. xix. §iv. (1699) 98 He who finds a waife Beast, which hath strayed from the owner. **1681–2** *Radclyffe Household Bks.* in *Northumb. Gloss.*, Mantayning a wave child in Dilston, 1 l. 8 d. **1754** Erskine *Princ. Sc. Law* (1809) 117 Where one finds strayed cattle, or other moveables, which have been lost by the former owner (waif goods). **1898** F. D. How *Walsham How* xix. 267 A Home for Waif Boys had been established.

2. *adj.* (*Sc.*) **a.** Stray, wandering, homeless: = waff *a.* 1.

c **1730** Ramsay *Vision* i, Mylane I wandert waif and wae. **1806** R. Jamieson *Rosmer Hafmand* iv. *Pop. Ballads* II. 203 And wull and waif for eight lang years They sail'd upon the sea.

b. Applied to a report or saying: Floating, current. *rare.*

1753 *Stewart's Trial* Append. 102 Depones, That he heard a waif report in the country, that [etc.]. **1886** Stevenson *Kidnapped* xvii. 162, I have heard a waif word in the country.. that you were a hard man to drive.

c. Poor or inferior in quality; = waff *a.* 2.

1824 Miss Ferrier *Inher.* III. 164 It will be but a waiff kind of happiness.

Hence '**waifish** *a.*, '**waifishly** *adv.*

1936 S. Smith *Novel on Yellow Paper* 220 Such.. wispish, waifish progeny. **1977** *Time* 31 Jan. 21/3 The waifish face beneath the jaunty white cap never loses its ethereal Pre-Raphaelite look. **1980** *Times Lit. Suppl.* 20 June 703/1 *Hurricane's* Samoan scenery is enticingly picturesque: doesn't art student Charlotte—waifishly played by Mia Farrow—arrive on her vacation exclaiming 'I can't wait to get out my paintbox'?

waif, *sb.*[2] [? a. ON. *veif*, something waving or flapping.]

†**1.** ? A convolution, coil. *Sc. Obs.*

1513 Douglas *Æneis* VII. vii. 25 The grisly serpent semyt sum tyme to be About hir hals a lynkyt goldin cheynȝe; And sum tyme of hir curche, lap with a waif, Becum the selvage or bordoure of hir quayf.

2. A small flag used as a signal: = waff *sb.* 1 b, waft *sb.* 6. Now *Naut. spec.* in whaling. Also *attrib.*, as ***waif-pole***.

1530 *Extracts Aberd. Reg.* (1844) I. 446 And the watch that beis in Sanct Nicholace stepill to pyt on the waiffs that he hes, to the part of the toun he seis thame cumand to. **1839** *Knickerbocker* XIII. 382 Line-tubs, water-kegs, and wafe-poles, were thrown hurriedly into the boats. **1846** T. B. Thorpe *Mysteries of Backwoods* 85 As the waiffe of the whaleman [marks] his victim on the sea. **1850** Scoresby *Cheever's Whalem. Adv.* xiv. (1858) 213 Two waifs, or flags, were immediately set as a signal of distress. **1851** H. Melville *Moby Dick* III. iii. 27 The allusion to the waifs and waif-poles.. necessitates some account of the laws and regulations of the whale fishery. **1874** C. M. Scammon *Marine Mammals* 25 (Cent.) The officer who first discovers it [a whale] sets a waif (a small flag) in his boat, and gives chase.

waif (weɪf), *sb.*[3] [Cf. weff, waff *sb.*] Something borne or driven by the wind; a puff (of smoke), a streak (of cloud).

1854 Patmore *Angel in Ho., Betrothal* 18 The sunny wind that.. shaped the clouds in waifs and zones. **1879** R. H. Elliot *Written on their Foreheads* xxxiii. I. 1 The first waifs of the hot-weather sea-borne breeze had in the evening begun faintly to fan the topmost heights of the border hills. **1886** Parry *Stud. Gt. Composers, Schubert* 232 Nothing but waifs of cloud and howling of wind.

waif (weɪf), *v.* [f. waif *sb.*[1] Cf. waive *v.*[1]] In *passive*: To be thrown up or cast away as a waif.

1848 Lytton *Harold* IX. i. 291 He hath right of life and death over all stranded and waifed on his coast.

waif, obs. form of waive, wave *vbs.*

waifingir, var. wavenger.

waift: see waft, weft *sb.*[2]

waiftage, obs. form of waftage.

waige, waigh: see wage, weigh.

waight, obs. form of wait, weight.

waigle, Sc. form of waggle.

waik: see vake, wake, weak.

waikin, obs. Sc. form of waken *v.*

waikrife, obs. Sc. form of wakerife.

wail (weɪl), *sb.* Also 5–6 **waile**, **wayle**. [Belongs to wail *v.* Cf. ON. *væl* neut.]

1. The action of wailing; expression of pain or grief by prolonged vocal sound.

c **1400** *Destr. Troy* 13979 Miche wepyng & wail, wetyng of lere. **1726–46** Thomson *Spring* 725 Till.. the woods Sigh to her song, and with her [the bereaved nightingale's] wail resound. **1811** W. R. Spencer *Poems* 23 What accents slow, of wail and woe. **1821** Byron *Two Fosc.* I. i, Ah! a voice of wail! **1850** Robertson *Serm.* Ser. II. iii. (1864) 35 He had an ear open for every tone of wail. **1865** Carlyle *Fredk. Gt.* XI. i. (1873) IV. 2 A thousand children.. with shrill unison of wail, sang out: 'Oh, deliver us from slavery!' **1865** Tom Taylor *Ballads & Songs Brittany* (Rtldg.) 55 There was weeping and wail from young and old.

b. *esp.* Sound of lamentation for the dead.

c **1400** *Destr. Troy* 8719 The dole for þat doghty of his dere fryndes Of wepyng & wayle & wryngyng of hondes.. no lettur might tell. **1816** Scott *Antiq.* xxvii, The wives o' the house of Glenallan wailed nae wail for the husband, nor the sister for the brother. **1844** Mrs. Browning *Rom. Page* xx, Wail shook Earl Walter's house; His true wife shed no tear. **1850** Tennyson *In Mem.* xc, The dead, whose dying eyes Were closed with wail. **1862** Stanley *Jew. Ch.* (1877) I. v. 102 'There was a great cry in Egypt,' the loud, frantic, funeral wail, characteristic of the whole nation.

2. A cry of pain or grief, esp. if loud and prolonged.

1863 Geo. Eliot *Romola* vi, Every time we.. directed our eyes towards it, our guide set up a wail. **1881** Besant & Rice *Chapl. Fleet* I. 2 The newborn babe begins his earthly course with a wail. **1900** F. T. Bullen *With Christ at Sea* xii. 223 Six of them died.. and were dropped overboard amid the piercing wails of their companions.

b. *fig.* A bitter lamentation.

1867 Smiles *Huguenots Eng.* ix. (1880) 154 A long wail of anguish was rising from the persecuted all over France. **1871** Freeman *Norm. Conq.* (1876) IV. xviii. 104 The record, or rather the wail of the native writer is more than borne out by [etc.]. **1873** Emma J. Worboise *Our New Home* xv, And still all her wail was, 'Oh, that I had died in Windermere!'

3. *transf.* A sound resembling a cry of pain.

1825 Longf. *Hymn Morav. Nuns* 13 When the battle's distant wail Breaks the sabbath of our vale. **1858** N. J. Gannon *O'Donoghue* I. 10 Varied by fox's bark, the wail Of plover, or the pipe of quail. **1860** Tyndall *Glac.* I. xxv. 185 The storm.. with a melancholy wail,.. bade our rock farewell. **1877** Miss A. B. Edwards *Up Nile* vii. 195 Hark that thin plaintive cry! It is the wail of a night-wandering jackal. **1882** Mrs. A. Edwardes *Ballroom Repent.* I. 219 A cantata.. with a subtle wail of pain underlying the surface joyousness of the centric melody. **1913** M. ROBERTS *Salt of the Sea* xviii. 419 He made the whistle give a melancholy wail.

†**4.** A state of woe. *Obs. rare.*

1682 SIR T. BROWNE *Chr. Mor.* III. xxiii. (1716) 115 Dream not of any kind of *Metempsychosis*.., but into thine own body, and that after a long time, and then also unto wail or bliss, according to thy first and fundamental Life.

wail (weɪl), *v.* Forms: 4–5 **weyle, weile,** 4–7 **wayle,** 5 **waille,** 6 **waill, wale (weale),** 4–7 **waile,** 6– **wail.** [Prob. a. ON. **veila* (cf. *veilan* wailing, Fritzner), f. *vei* int.: see WOE. The recorded ON. word is *vǽla* (whence *vǽl*, *vǽlan* wailing), f. *vǽ* int., synonymous with *vei*. Cf. Sw. dial. *väla*, Norw. *væla* to bleat.]

1. a. *intr.* To express pain or sorrow by prolonged piteous cries. Often with reference to funeral lamentations.

c **1330** *Arth. & Merl.* 2563 Al þat folk he herd waile For þat erl of Cornewaile. **1362** LANGL. *P. Pl.* A. v. 261 A þousent of men þo þrongen to-geders, Weopynd and waylyng for heore wikkede dedes. **1382** WYCLIF *Matt.* xi. 17 We han mourned to ȝou, and ȝe han not weilid. **1393** GOWER *Conf.* II. 383 Anone sche gan to wepe and weile. **1412–20** LYDG. *Troy-bk.* IV. 3625 Þe faire quene Eleyne Wailleth, crieth wiþ a dedly chere. **1513** DOUGLAS *Æneis* III. v. 61 With that word sche brist out mony a teir, And walit so that pietie was to heir. **1577** GRANGE *Golden Aphrod.* G iv b, Then may I wake and wayle the night, my bed wt teares besprent. **1590** SPENSER *F.Q.* I. ii. 7 Then gan she waile and weepe, to see that woefull stowre. **1591** SHAKS. *Two Gent.* II. iii. 7 My Mother weeping: my Father wayling: my Sister crying. **1827** POLLOK *Course T.* x, Where ye shall weep and wail for evermore. **1848** DICKENS *Dombey* xxiii, Alexander Mac Stinger who had stopped in his crying to attend to the conversation, began to wail again. **1875** JOWETT *Plato* (ed. 2) I. 371 To address you, weeping and wailing and lamenting.

b. To cry piteously *for* (something desired).

1573–80 TUSSER *Husb.* (1878) 198 And God the holy Ghost, the soule of man doth winne, By mouuing hir to waile for grace, ashamed of hir sinne. *a* **1771** GRAY *Dante* 45, I heard 'em wail for Bread.

†**c.** *transf.* Of the eyes: To weep. *Obs. rare*$^{-1}$.

1593 SHAKS. *Lucr.* 1508 An humble gate, calme looks, eyes wayling still.

2. *transf.* **a.** Of birds, inanimate things: To give forth mournful sounds.

1595 SPENSER *Col. Clout* 23 Whilest thou wast hence,.. The woods were heard to waile full many a sythe, And all their birds with silence to complaine. *a* **1605** MONTGOMERIE *Cherrie & Slae* (revision) ii, The turtle wails on witherit treis. **1820** KEATS *Hyperion* III. 109 O tell me, lonely Goddess! by thy harp, That waileth every morn and eventide. **1845** DICKENS *Chimes* I. 2 As one not finding what it seeks,.. it [*sc.* the night-wind] wails and howls to issue forth again. **1890** BRIDGES *Shorter Poems* I. iv, A flock of gulls are wheeling And wailing round my seat.

b. Of music, etc.: To sound like a wail.

1852 TENNYSON *Ode Death Wellington* 267 The Dead March wails in the people's ears. **1878** SUSAN PHILLIPS *On Seaboard* 77 While the pibroch wildly wailing tells how all was lost and won.

c. Of a jazz musician: to play very well, with great feeling, etc. (*U.S. slang*). Also *U.S. colloq.*, to perform well.

1955 SHAPIRO & HENTOFF *Hear me talkin' to Ya* 231, I revered the amazing Fats Waller, who had lately made a splash wailing on organ at the Lincoln. **1959** *Encounter* June 43/2 The Beat 'cat' approaches the Beat 'chick' with the ritualistic 'Pad me'..the 'chick's', approach to the male is ..'I'm frigid,' to which he can either reply 'I'll make you wail' (function) or, otherwise, 'Don't bug.' **1962** [see BLOW *v.*[1] 14 e]. **1977** C. MCFADDEN *Serial* (1978) xxxix. 85/2 Despite his back, he was really wailin' when he hung a sharp right into his driveway, pretending Sutton Manor was a picturesque village along the route of the Tour de France.

3. To utter persistent and bitter lamentations or complaints. With clause or quoted words: To say lamentingly.

13.. *K. Alis.* 4653 (Laud MS.) Often he crieþ, and often gynneþ waile, He wolde al Perse habbe yȝiue And he miȝth haue had his lyue. *c* **1388** *On the 25 Articles* in *Wyclif's Sel. Wks.* III. 481 As heþen men skorned þo sabbatis of Jerusalem in þer conquestis..as Jeromy weyleþ. **1555** PHAER *Æneid* I. (1558) A iv b, And therwithin on armour heapes sitts Batail rage, and wailes With brasen cheines a hundred bound his wrastling not auailes. **1865** TROLLOPE *Belton Est.* xii. 138 He went on wailing, complaining of his lot as a child complains. **1894** BARING-GOULD *Kitty Alone* II. 75, 'I wish I was dead,' wailed the poor creature. **1913** *Times* 30 Sept. 10/2 'But I was going with him!' she wails.

4. To grieve bitterly.

c **1374** CHAUCER *Troylus* I. 556 Art now falle in som devocioun And waylest for thy sinne and thyn offence? *c* **1380** WYCLIF *Serm. Matt. v.* Sel. Wks. I. 408 Blessid be þei þat weilen. *c* **1440** *Gesta Rom.* xxxiii. 132 (Add. MS.) There the synner waylithe, or is sory for his synns, he shalle be saf. **1534** MORE *Comf. agst. Trib.* II. Wks. 1176/1 Thei wayled and dydde paynefull penaunce for theyr synne to procure god to pitie them. **1554–9** *Songs & Ballads Phil. & Mary* (Roxb.) 13 For thos that be leale, He makys them to weale, For faute of a meale, And good sustinance. **1601** WEEVER *Mirr. Mart.* E j b, Though foolishnes it be, For treasure lost, to waile, or make great sorrow. *a* **1677** BARROW *Serm.* Wks. 1687 III. xxiii. 208 To fret and wail at that, which, for all we can see, proceedeth from good intention, and tendeth to good issue, is pitifull frowardness. **1865** NEALE *Hymns Parad.* 4 While she wails for her condition. **1879** GEO. ELIOT *Theo. Such* ii. 27 Yet it is held no impiety..for a man to wail that he was not the son of another age and another nation.

5. *trans.* To bewail, lament, deplore. Now *poet.* or *rhetorical.* **a.** To lament, manifest or feel deep sorrow for (sin, misfortune, suffering, whether one's own or that of others).

1362 LANGL. *P. Pl.* A. v. 94 Ac for his wynnynge I wepe and weile þe tyme. *c* **1400** *Rule St. Benet* (E.E.T.S.) 122 Dayly wayling your synnes. *c* **1400** *Pilgr. Sowle* (Caxton) IV. xxxviii. (1859) 65 Yet weyle I more the lesyng of the kynges worship, than of myn awn dysese. **1485** CAXTON *St. Wenefreyde* 3 Wayllyng the deth of their douhter. **1526** *Pilgr. Perf.* (W. de W. 1531) 133 b, O, how they wyll wayle & wepe theyr negligences, & wysshe that they had neuer slepte so longe. **1575** GASCOIGNE *Glasse of Govt.* Wks. 1910 II. 58 We should be greevd, when as wee heare them grone, And wayle their wantes. **1605** SHAKS. *Macb.* III. i. 123 Yet I must not,.. but wayle his fall, Who I my selfe struck downe. **1627** MAY *Lucan* II. C 1, Who now has time to waile Plebeian fates? **1671** MILTON *Samson* 63 Strength.. proves the sourse of all my miseries; So many, and so huge, that each apart Would ask a life to wail. **17..** *Auld Goodman* i. in *Ramsay's Tea-t. Misc.* (1762) 111 Ay she wail'd her wretched life, And cry'd ever, Alake, my auld goodman. **1810** SCOTT *Lady of L.* III. vi, To wood and stream his hap to wail. **1813** —— *Rokeby* III. vi, For never felt his soul the woe, That wails a generous foeman low. **1868** MORRIS *Earthly Par.* I. I. 418 Well then might Psyche wail her wretched fate. **1898** MEREDITH *Napoleon* v. Poet. Wks. (1912) 481 A broken carol of wild notes was heard As when an ailing infant wails a dream.

b. To lament, mourn bitterly for (the dead); to lament the absence or loss of.

1382 WYCLIF *2 Chron.* xxxv. 25 Al Juda and Jerusalem weileden hym [Vulg. *luxerunt eum*], Jeremyas most. **1631** WEEVER *Anc. Funeral Mon.* 309 They neither esteemed him while he was liuing, nor wailed him at all, after that he was dead. **1725** POPE *Odyss.* XI. 216 If no more her absent Lord she wails. **1810** SCOTT *Lady of L.* III. xvi, The voice of the weeper Wails manhood in glory.

†**c.** To deplore the lot of. *Obs.*

a **1400** *Rom. Rose* 6271 If ther be wolves of sich hewe Amonges these apostlis newe, Thou, hooly chirche, thou mayst be wayled!

Hence **wailed** *ppl. a.*, lamented.

1562 A. BROOKE *Romeus & Jul.* 1398 Like as there is no weale, but wastes away somtime, So euery kind of wayled woe will weare away in time. **1568** T. HOWELL *Arb. Amitie* (1879) 51 To bring vnto the wailed graue, this Countesse courteous corse.

wail: see VAIL *v.*[1], VEIL *sb.*[1], WALE *sb.*[1], *v.*[1]

wailaway, obs. form of WELLAWAY.

†**waile**[1]. *Obs. rare*$^{-1}$. [? Alteration (for rhyme) of *welde* rule: see WIELD *sb.*]

13.. *R. Brunne's Chron. Wace* (Rolls) 5334 + 8 (Petyt MS.) Tenuacius..had þe regne all in his waile.

†**waile**[2]. *Sc. Obs. rare*$^{-1}$. ? A willow.

a **1510** DOUGLAS *K. Hart* II. 311 Thocht I be quhylum bowsum as ane waile [*rhymes* begyle, quhyle, oursyle], I sal be cruikit quhill I mak [him fule].

waile, ? obs. var. QUAIL *v.*[1]

1432–50 tr. *Higden* (Rolls) I. 81 There be men also of v. cubites, whiche dye not, neither waile [L. *nec languescunt*].

waile: see VAIL *sb.*[1], VEIL *sb.*[1], WALE *sb.*[1] and *sb.*[2], WEAL.

wailer (ˈweɪlə(r)). [f. WAIL *v.* + -ER[1].] One who wails; *spec.* a professional mourner.

1647 HEXHAM I, A wailer or bewailer, *een kermer*. **1822** SCOTT *Peveril* xlvi, Those dangers from which the poor blushing wailers of my sex shrink. **1851** G. W. CURTIS *Nile Notes* xii. 54 Before us a funeral procession was moving to the tombs, and the shrill melancholy cry of the wailers rang fitfully. **1877** MISS A. B. EDWARDS *Up Nile* xix. 524 A funeral with a train of wailers goes out presently towards the burial-ground. **1915** *19th Cent.* Nov. 1147 These 'howls' have been practised from childhood; they are led in chorus by a professional 'wailer'.

Hence †**'waileress,** a female wailer.

1388 WYCLIF *Jer.* ix. 17 Clepe ȝe wymmen that weilen [*v.r.* weileressis].

waileway, obs. form of WELLAWAY.

wailful (ˈweɪlfʊl), *a.* Chiefly *poet.* [f. WAIL *sb.* + -FUL.]

1. Of cries, complaints, speeches: Having the character of a wail, expressive of grievous pain or sorrow. Of sounds: Resembling a wail, plaintive.

1544 BETHAM *Precepts War* I. clxiii. H vj, Suche owtecryes and waylefull lamentation of women. *a* **1586** SIDNEY *Arcadia* II. Eclog. (1912) 348 Zelmane, whose harte better delighted in wailefull ditties. **1591** SHAKS. *Two Gent.* III. ii. 69 You must lay Lime, to tangle her desires By walefull Sonnets. **1632** J. HAYWARD tr. *Biondi's Eromena* 105 A voice not shreeking or displeasing, but moaning and wailefull. *c* **1750** SHENSTONE *Elegy* iv. 28 Then..Shall..Innocence indulge a wailful cry. **1834** BECKFORD *Italy*, etc. II. 283 Her maids sang tirannas with a wailful monotony that wore my very soul out. **1899** WHITEING *No. 5 John Street* xiv. 140 The wailful sweetness of the violin Floats down the hushed waters of the wind. **1906** *Sat. Rev.* 24 Mar. 361/1 Everyone ..was indulging in the vociferous brogue and wailful Irish melody.

2. Full of lamentation, sorrowful.

1579 SPENSER *Sheph. Cal.* Feb. 82 Thy Ewes..Like wailefull widdowes hangen their crags. *a* **1763** SHENSTONE *Love & Honour* 21 She, she alone, amid the wailful train Of captive maids, assigned to Henry's care. **1855** M. ARNOLD *Balder Dead* I. 176 Then must he not regard the wailful ghosts. **1865** MEREDITH *Farina* 6 A wailful host were the wives of his raftsmen widowed there by her watery music!

b. *transf.* Of animals or inanimate things: Producing plaintive sounds.

1818 KEATS *Endym.* I. 450 A wailful gnat. **1820** —— *To Autumn* 27 Then in a wailful choir the small gnats mourn. **1872** G. MACDONALD *Wilfrid Cumb.* I. xii. 176 A wailful wind made one moaning sweep through the trees. **1885–94** BRIDGES *Eros & Psyche* Sept. 16 Or e'er he join'd his wailful flock. **1887** MEREDITH *Ballads & Poems* 157 The tremulous Ever-wailful trees bemoaning him.

†**3.** Of mournful aspect. *Obs.*

1557 PHAER *Æneid.* VII. (1558) T iv, This dolefull dame vpstertes, with wayful wynges [*fuscis..alis*]. **1577** GRANGE *Golden Aphrod.* E iij, With wailful weeds I clad my corps. **1577–87** HOLINSHED *Chron.* I. *Hist. Eng.* 39/2 They fearing punishment..with wailefull countenance craued mercie.

†**4.** That is to be bewailed, lamentable. *Obs.*

a **1547** SURREY *Eccles.* iv. 10 That neuer felt the waylfull wrongs that mortall folke receue. —— *Æneid* II. 6 The Phrygian wealth, and wailful realm [L. *lamentabile regnum*] of Troy. **1566** GASCOIGNE *Jocasta* I. i. 12, I must to thee recompte The wailefull thing that is alredy spred. **1587** TURBERV. *Trag. Tales* Ep. Ded. to Baynes, Who knew my cares, who wist my wailefull woe. **1590** SPENSER *F.Q.* III. iv. 38 Farre better I it deeme to die with speed, Then waste in woe and waileful miserie. *c* **1620** BRETON *C'tess Pembroke's Passion* (Grosart) 5/2 But if these wept to see his waylefull case: Why dye not I to thinke on his disgrace?

Hence **'wailfully** *adv.*

1611 COTGR., *Douloureusement*, dolourously; heavily, sorrowfully, wailefully, most wofully. **1879** MEREDITH *Egoist* II. 217 The glass did not say so, but the shrunken heart within him did, and wailfully too. **1904** SNAITH *Broke of Cov.* 285 No voice crying in the wilderness can sound more wailfully to human ears.

wailȝe, obs. Sc. form of VAIL *v.*[1]

wailing (ˈweɪlɪŋ), *vbl. sb.* [f. WAIL *v.* + -ING[1].]

a. The action of the verb.

13.. *K. Alis.* 7871 (Laud MS.), Michel spray mychel gradyng Michel weep mychel waylyng. **1382** WYCLIF *Gen.* xxvii. 41 Than Esau..seide in his herte, The dayes of weilyng of my fader shal come, and I shal slee Jacob. *a* **1400** *Prymer* Ps. xxxviii. 8 (1895) 39 Y rorid for þe weilyng of myn herte. *c* **1400** *Destr. Troy* 7155 Myche weping & wo, wayling of teris. **1513** DOUGLAS *Æneis* II. viii. 83 With dulefull scrike and waling all is confoundit. **1532** FRITH *Mirr. to know thyself* iii. Wks. (1573) 90 When he saw the shepheard so sore lamenting, he reynde hys horse, & asked him the cause of his great wayling. *a* **1693** *Urquhart's Rabelais* III. xiii. 107 The..pioling of Pelicanes,..and wailing of Turtles. **1814** BYRON *Lara* II. xxv, Her tears were few, her wailing never loud. **1836** DICKENS *Sk. Boz, Streets—Night*, The child is cold and hungry, and its low wailing adds to the misery of its wretched mother. **1867** LADY HERBERT *Cradle L.* iii. 82 Our travellers proceeded to the 'Place of Wailing' of the Jews, who assemble every Friday to weep and pray for the restoration of their own country.

b. Often *plural.*

13.. *K. Alis.* 2360 (Laud MS.), Michel woo & grete wailynges Was made for þoo ȝongelynges. **1486** CAXTON *Curial* 11 To seche to gete them after wyth grete wayllynges and sorow. **1566** DRANT *Horace, Sat.* title-p., The Wailyngs of the Prophet Hieremiah, done into Englyshe verse. **1695** PRIOR *Ode after Queen's Death* xxiii, To Earth her bended Front she bow'd, And sent her Wailings to the Skies. **1760–72** H. BROOKE *Fool of Qual.* (1809) II. 116 She again set up her wailings. **1801** SCOTT *Glenfinlas* xxiv, I bade my harp's wild wailings flow. **1855** MACAULAY *Hist. Eng.* xi. III. 24 The deposed Laureate..continued to complain piteously ..of the losses which he had not suffered, till at length his wailings drew forth expressions of well merited contempt from brave and honest Jacobites. **1885** *Manch. Exam.* 20 July 6/2 The debate..ended partly in grotesque remedies and partly in wailings of despair.

c. *attrib.* **wailing robes** *nonce-use*, mourning garments; **Wailing Wall,** the remaining part of the wall of the Second Temple of Jerusalem, destroyed in 70 B.C., revered by Jews as a place of prayer (also †*wailing place*); also *transf.* and *fig.*

1591 SHAKS. *1 Hen. VI*, I. i. 86 Away with these disgracefull wayling Robes. **1878** J. FERGUSSON *Temples of Jews* II. xii. 183 The most interesting particular mentioned by the Pilgrim is the 'Lapis Pertusus', which was then the Wailing Place of the Jews. **1919** *Q. Rev.* Apr. 328 To the Jews the principal Holy Place is the Wailing Wall, the fragment of the Wall of the Temple at which the Jews perpetually mourn for their lost glories and pray for the restoration of them. **1922** JOYCE *Ulysses* 532 Darkshawled figures of the circumcised, in sackcloth and ashes, stand by the wailing wall. **1934** C. LAMBERT *Music Ho!* III. 212 Tin Pan Alley has become a commercialized Wailing Wall. **1955** W. GADDIS *Recognitions* III. v. 945 I've just visited the Wailing Wall, and had a good cry. **1963** *Daily Tel.* 23 Dec. 12/2 The dividing wall [in Berlin] becomes a wailing wall at midnight each night. **1980** K. FOLLETT *Key to Rebecca* xxix. 308 Today I went to the Western Wall, which is also called the Wailing Wall.

wailing (ˈweɪlɪŋ), *ppl. a.* [f. WAIL *v.* + -ING[2].]

1. That utters mournful cries.

1382 WYCLIF *Jer.* ix. 17 Beholdeth, and clepeth weilende wymmen [Vulg. *lamentatrices*]. *c* **1425** *Found. St. Bartholomew's* (E.E.T.S.) 45 Whan for defawtynge of his hert the vtteryng of his voice beganne to breke, beholde, aforne the weylyng man seynt Barthilmewe stoid. **1742** COLLINS *Dirge in Cymbeline* 5 No wailing ghost shall dare appear To vex with shrieks this quiet grove. **1821** GALT *Ann. Parish* xviii, A wailing baby, and a widow's heart, was a' he left me. **1891** FARRAR *Darkn. & Dawn* vi, See that every preparation is made for a royal funeral, and that the flute-players, the wailing-women,..be all in readiness.

2. Of cries, words: Expressing lamentation. Of sounds: Resembling a wail.

1576 GASCOIGNE *Kenelworth Castle* Wks. 1910 II. 128 With wailing words and mourning notes. *c* **1586** C'TESS PEMBROKE *Ps.* LXXVIII. xxv, No widow left to use her wailing voice. **1790** BURNS *Elegy Capt. M. H.* 18 Come join, ye Nature's sturdiest bairns, My wailing numbers! **1818** SCOTT *Rob Roy* xxxiii, I only heard..the wailing and prolonged sound of their trumpets. **1860** TYNDALL *Glac.* I. xvi. 112 Through the gaps..the wind rushed with a loud, wild, wailing sound. **1869** Tozer *Highl. Turkey* I. 274 Chanting, as they went, a shrill wailing dirge.

Hence **'wailingly** *adv.*

1836 Lytton *Athens* (1837) II. 37 The wide earth echoes wailingly. **1848** S. Carter *Midnight Effus.* 216 Now tremulous and wailingly Its liquid notes are rushing. **1902** Eliz. Banks *Newspaper Girl* 159 She sang the song of Dixie, sorrowfully, wailingly.

†**'wailish**, *a. Obs.* [f. wail *sb.* or *v.* + -ish[1].] Given to wailing, querulous.

c **1550** *Vertuous Scholehouse* B 7 b, Yf I knewe the not, I shoulde thinke the a waylyshe woman.

waill(e, obs. Sc. forms of vail, vale, wale.

waill(e)ant, obs. forms of valiant.

c **1475** *Partenay* 5354 Thay were good knightes, waillant & worthy.

†**'wailment.** *Obs.* [f. wail *v.* + -ment.] Wailing, lamentation.

1593 Nashe *Christ's T.* 12 b, If thou hadst neuer seene the light, thy walking in darknes would haue brought thee no waylement. **1594** R. C[arew] *Tasso* (1881) 47 That Asias waylments so take breath at last. *a* **1670** Hacket *Abp. Williams* II. (1693) 224 O day of wailment to all that are yet unborn!

wailoway, obs. form of wellaway.

wailsome ('weɪlsəm), *a. rare.* [f. wail *sb.* or *v.* + -some.] †**a.** That is to be bewailed. *Obs.* **b.** Having a wailing sound.

1566 Studley *Seneca's Medea* v. (1581) T 5, And this with wailesome murther like shall lose her tender life. **1891** Kipling *City Dreadf. Nt.* vi. (1892) 36 Another wilderness of shut-up houses, wherein it seems that people do continually and feebly strum stringed instruments of a plaintive and wailsome nature.

†**'wailster.** *Obs. rare*$^{-1}$. [f. wail *v.* + -ster.] A female wailer.

1388 Wyclif *Jer.* ix. 17 Biholde ȝe, and clepe ȝe wymmen that weilen [*MS. I* weilsteris].

waily ('weɪlɪ), *a. rare.* [f. wail *v.* + -y.]

1906 Kipling *Puck of Pook's Hill* 286 He had a voice that changed its tone..sometimes deep and thundery, sometimes thin and waily, but always it made you listen.

wailzeant, obs. Sc. form of valiant.

waim: see whom *pron.*, wame *north.*, belly.

waiment, var. wayment *sb.* and *v. Obs.*

†**waiming.** *Obs.* Also 4 **wamming**, 5 **waymynge**. [Perh. a corruption of wayment *sb.* or waymenting *vbl. sb.*, perh. an alteration of *waining*, woning *vbl. sb.*] Lamentation.

a **1300** *Cursor M.* 5721 He herd þair waiming and vnquert. *Ibid.* 14314 Iesus þair wamming [*Gött.* waining] vnderstod. *c* **1420** *Anturs of Arth.* 87 (Douce MS.), Hit ȝaules, hit ȝameres, with waymynges wete.

waimto, obs. form of wame-tow.

wain (weɪn), *sb.*[1] Forms: 1 **wæᵹn**, (**weᵹn**), **wæᵹen**, **wǽn**, 2–3 *Orm.* **waȝȝn**, 3–7 **wayne, waine**, 4–7 **wayn**, (5 **wayen**, 6 **waayne**, 4 *Sc.* **vayn**), 4–5 **weyne**, (5 **wene**, 6 **weene**, **weane**, 7 **wean**, **whene**), 5–7 **wane**, 3– **wain**. [OE. *wæᵹen*, *wǽn*, str. masc. = OFris. *wein* str. masc. (mod.WFris. *wein*, *woin*, *wīn*, NFris. *wein*, *wā(i)nj*), OLow Frankish *reidi-wagan* (MDu. *waeghen*, Du. *wagen*), MLG., LG. *wagen*, OHG. *wagan* str. masc. (MHG., G. *wagen*), ON. *vagn* str. masc. cart, barrow (Norw. *vagn* the Great Bear, *vogn* cart, Da. *vogn*, Sw. *vagn* cart):—OTeut. **waᵹno-z* :—pre-Teut. **woghno-s* f. Indogermanic root **wegh-*, **wogh-* to carry, etc.: cf. weigh, waw *vbs.*, way *sb.* Outside Teut. cognate words of similar meaning are Irish *fén* (:—pre-Celtic **weghno-s*) wagon, Gr. ὄχος (ϝόχος:—**wogho-s*), chariot, Skr. *vahana* neut., *vāhana* neut., chariot.

The pre-Teut. form may possibly have been **weghno-s*, corresponding with the pre-Celtic form; there is some evidence of an OTeut. change of *we-* to *wa-* before consonant groups.]

1. A large open vehicle, drawn by horses or oxen, for carrying heavy loads, esp. of agricultural produce; usually four-wheeled (but see 1 b); a wagon.

The word does not occur in the Bible of 1611, though Wyclif and the 16th c. translators use it. As a colloquial word it survives only in dialects, but in poetry it is commonly used instead of *wagon*.

Beowulf 3134 Þær wæs wunden gold on wæn hladen. *c* **725** *Corpus Gl.* (Hessels) U 143 *Ueniculum* [read *Uehiculum*], wæᵹn. *c* **1250** *Gen. & Ex.* 2362 He bad cartes and waines nimen, And fechen wiues, and childre, and men, And gaf hem ðor al lond gersen. **1297** R. Glouc. (Rolls) 8596 Þat þer nas non so heuy charge of wayn ne of oþer þinge þat me ne miȝte ouer grete wateres boþe lede & bringe. *a* **1300** *Cursor M.* 5229 His suns all and þair flitting,..In weynis war þai don to lede. **1375** Barbour *Bruce* x. 164 That apon his cowyn gat he Men that mycht [ane] enbuschement ma, Quhill that he vith his vayn suld ga Till lede thaim hay into the peill. *Ibid.* xi. 24 A litill stane oft, as men sayis, May ger weltir ane mekill wane. **1398** Trevisa *Barth. De P.R.* xvii. lxxii. (1495) 646 And at the laste heye is led home in cartes and in waynes and broughte in to bernes for dyuers vse and nedes. **1432–50** tr. *Higden* (Rolls) I. 137 Thei haue noo howses, caryenge theire wyfes and children in waynes [L. *in plaustris*]. **1449** *Yatton Churchw. Acc.* (Somerset Rec. Soc.) 92 For custom for our wene to Bristowe warde comyng and goyng, iiij d. **1473** *Rental Bk. Cupar-Angus* (1879) I. 182 The said tenandis..sal led to the abbay viii score of fuderis of petis the abbai fyndand wanis meit and drink to the ledaris. **1521** *Lincoln Wills* (1914) I. 88 To William my son my bonden wane, ij oxen that cam from Hornecastell, [etc.]. **1523–34** Fitzherb. *Husb.* §5 And or he shall lode his corne, he muste haue a wayne, a copyoke, [etc.]. **1576** *Act 18 Eliz.* c. 10 §1 Everye person..shalbe charged to finde..one Carte Wayne Tumbrell..Carres or Dragges furnished for thamendment..of the Highe wayes within the severall Parishes. **1588** in *Archæologia* LXIV. 366 For viij weanes of Pilleseley which ladd Timber from Penttridge, xvj d. **1617** Moryson *Itin.* iii. 19 Alexander the great set on fier with his owne hands the wanes of carriage taken from Darius. **1627** May *Lucan* v. I i, The horses trample ore Safely where ships haue saild; the Bessians Furrow Mæotis frozen backe with waines. **1641** Best *Farm. Bks.* (Surtees) 46 Wee leade in our winter corne usually with three waines. **1688** W. Scot *Hist. Name Scot* i. (1894) 35 According to the old Proverb, They but fell from the Wains tail. **1731** T. Boston *Mem.* vii. (1899) 106 On Thursday..came the wains with the household-furniture from Dunse. **1784** Cowper *Task* i. 296 From the sun-burnt hay-field, homeward creeps The loaded wain. **1805** Wordsw. *Waggoner* i. 29 That far-off tinkling's drowsy cheer,..The Wain announces. **1821** Scott *Kenilw.* xxv, The highways..were choked with loaded wains, whose axle-trees cracked under their burdens. **1827** O. W. Roberts *Voy. Centr. Amer.* 210 A few large wains or waggons. **1849** Macaulay *Hist. Eng.* v. I. 608 The wains which carried the ammunition remained at the entrance of the moor. **1850** Tennyson *In Mem.* cxxi, The team is loosen'd from the wain, The boat is drawn upon the shore. **1872** Schele de Vere *Americanisms* 565 *Wain*, the obsolete form of wagon, is still in daily use in some parts of the United States, e.g. in the peninsula east of the Chesapeake. **1874** Green *Short Hist.* iv. §5. 197 To the lesser nobles..the long wain of goods as it passed along the highway, was a tempting prey. **1889** *Anthony's Photogr. Bull.* II. 32 Some of the Avon villages are full of interest. Here you may see the great four-horse wain, common on the roads in the days of our grandfathers.

b. In local uses, applied to some particular kind of wagon or cart.

1534 in *Lett. & Papers Hen. VIII*, VII. 208 One weene with two whyles. **1726** *Dict. Rust.* (ed. 3) s.v. *Cart*, It is a Cart when drawn by Horses, having two sides called Trills; but a Wain when drawn by Oxen, and having a Wain-Cope. **1796** W. Marshall *West Eng.* II. 7 A singular kind of two-wheel carriage, for Horses or Oxen, is here [*sc.* Cornwall] in common use;..it is called a 'wain'; and it is a hay cart, or wain, without sides, having only two arches bending over the wheels, to keep the load from bearing upon them! with a wince behind. **1832** *Scoreby Farm Rep.* 4 in *Libr. Usef. Knowl., Husb.* III, The wain, a large cart upon broad wheels, with a pole, and drawn by a pair of oxen, is much used at Scoreby. **1868** Atkinson *Cleveland Gloss.* s.v., The veritable Wain, now never seen, was a narrow, long-bodied vehicle, with two wheels only, and these at the hinder end. The front or foremost end trailed along the ground.

c. *poet.* A car or chariot. Chiefly *fig.* or in mythological use. In ME. often applied to the Four Gospels, symbolized as a four-horsed chariot (= L. *quadriga*).

c **1200** Ormin Pref. 21 Þatt waȝȝn iss nemmnedd quaþþrigan þatt hafeþþ fowwre wheless. *a* **1300** *Cursor M.* 21264 Four ar þai tald, þe wangelistes þat draues þe wain þat es cristes. *c* **1380** Wyclif *Wks.* (1880) 258 See now þe secunde wheel in þis deuelis wayn. **1412–20** Lydg. *Chron. Troy* i. 630 Wher halved is þe standyng estyval Of fresche Appollo with his golden Wayn. **1579** Spenser *Sheph. Cal.* Jan. 74 Phœbus gan auaile, His weary waine. **1590** —— *F.Q.* i. iv. 19 May seeme the wayne was very euill led When such an one had guiding of the way, That knew not, whether right he went, or else astray. **1638** R. Baker tr. *Balzac's Lett.* (vol. III) 86 Not when the moon accomplishing her way Upon her silver wayne..presents the day. **1706** De Foe *Jure Divino* ii. 239 [They] jointly drive the Wain of Government. **1714** *Steele's Poet. Misc.* 112 He..charm'd the Wain of Night along, With his soft harmonious Song. **1885–94** Bridges *Eros & Psyche* April xx, They set on high upon the bridal wain Her bed for bier, and yet no corpse thereon.

Proverb. **13..** *All too Late* 7 in *Pol. Rel. & L. Poems* (1903) 250 Al to late. al to late. þen is te wayn atte yate. *c* **1420** Wyntoun *Cron.* i. 640 Than to cry mercy is to lait, The wane þan standis at þe ȝate.

d. A wain-load, wagon-load.

1613 Purchas *Pilgrimage* iv. x. (1614) 395 Thither they bring euery yeare an hundred and fiftie waines of twigges.

†**e.** *poet.* **winged wain**, a ship. *Obs.*

1598 Sylvester *Du Bartas* ii. i. iii. *Furies* 194 The Masters skilfull most, With gentle gales driv'n to the wished Coast, Not with lesse labour guide there winged wayns On th'azure fore-head of the liquid plains.

2. (Now with capital initial.) The group of seven bright stars in the constellation called the Great Bear: more fully Charles's Wain. *Lesser Wain*: the similarly shaped group of seven stars in the Little Bear.

OE. had *wǽnes þísl* or *þísla*, 'pole or poles of the wain'. With Scott's 'Arthur's slow wain' cf. 'Arthouris Plowe', Lydg. *Chron. Troy* i. 682; Arthur here represents Arcturus, regarded as the teamster or wagoner of the plough or wain.

c **888** Ælfred *Boeth.* xxxix. §3 Swa swa tunglu..þe we hatað wænes ðisla. *c* **1374** Chaucer *Boeth.* iv. met. v. 5 Who so þat.. wot nat why þe sterre Bootes passeþ or gadereþ his weynes. **1555** Eden *Decades* (Arb.) 280 We iudged them to bee the chariotte or wayne of the south. **1601** Holland *Pliny* vi. xxii. I. 130 The starres about the North pole, called Septentriones, the Waines or Beares. **1669** Sturmy *Mariner's Mag.* vi. 95 The..two Bears..Whose hinder parts and Tails contain The lesser and the greater Wain. **1703** Pope *Thebais* 521 When clouds conceal Boötes golden wain. **1805** Scott *Last Minstr.* i. xvii, Arthur's slow wain his course doth roll In utter darkness round the pole. **1812** Cary *Dante, Parad.* xiii. 7 The wain, that, in the bosom of our sky, Spins ever on its axle night and day. **1850** Tennyson *In Mem.* ci, At noon or when the lesser wain Is twisting round the polar star. **1879** Miss Jackson *Shropsh. Word-bk.* 437 *The-wain-and-horses*, sb., Ursa Major. **1887** Bowen *Æneid* i. 744 Bright Arcturus, the showery Hyads, the Bear, and the Wain.

¶ **3.** A rendering of L. *plaustrum* (lit. 'wagon') used in the Vulgate for a kind of thrashing instrument with wheels.

1382 Wyclif *Isa.* xli. 15, I haue set thee as a newe wayn [**1609** *Douay*, a newe threshing wayne] thresshende. **1778** Lowth *Isa.* xxviii. 27–28 Nor is the wheel of the wain made to turn upon the cummin: But the dill is beaten out with the staff; And the cummin with the flail: but the bread-corn with the threshing-wain.

4. *attrib.* and *Comb.* **a.** Obvious combinations, as †***wain-axtree***, ***-blade*** (blade *sb.* 10 b), ***-body***, †***-cart***, ***-driver***, ***-felloe***, †***-folk***, ***-gear***, ***-head*** (also attrib.), ***-horse***, ***-load***, ***-wheel***.

1559 *Richmond Wills* (Surtees) 136 One pare of newe car wheles, both *wane ashe tres [etc.]. **1557** *Ibid.* 101 A pare of *wayne blayds. **1390–91** *Durham Acc. Rolls* (Surtees) 392 In factura unius *waynbody, 6 d. *a* **1566** R. Edwards *Damon & P.* (facs.) F ij, One preached of late not farre hence, in no Pulpet, but in *Waayne carte, That spake enough of this. **1552** Huloet, *Wayne dryuer, *iugarius.* **1360** *Priory of Finchale* (Surtees) p. liii, j gange de *waine-felies de fraxino. **1558** *Wills Northern C.* (Surtees) I. 162 Twoo gang of wayne fellowes wth heades and moldeburdes. **1641** Best *Farm. Bks.* (Surtees) 53 It is a greate furtherance to have one to teame the waines whiles that the *wainefolkes are att breakefast. **1538** *Test. Ebor.* VI. 75 All maner of..*wayne geir. **1557** *Lanc. Wills* (Chetham Soc.) II. 128 Waynes and wayne geare. **1551** *Knaresb. Wills* (Surtees) I. 59 One *waynehedeyoke, one bolt and one shakill. **1557** *Richmond Wills* (Surtees) 101 One yron bound wayne..with wayne hed, [etc.]. **1562–3** *Durham Wills* (Surtees) III. 28 An yrone bounde wayne with a turne teame and a waine head shakle. **1727** E. Laurence *Duty of Steward* 71 The Steward should see that the *Wain-Horses and Oxen be muzzled, to prevent their cropping the young Springs. **1800** Hurdis *Favourite Village* 57 The stout wain-horse of encumbrance stript. **1577** B. Googe *Heresbach's Husb.* ii. 101 b, An other [oak] in an other place, that being cutte out, made a hundred *Wayne lode. **1700** O. Heywood *Diaries* (1885) IV. 238 A wainload of timber, 8 oxen and an horse. **1559** *Richmond Wills* (Surtees) 136 One pare of newe *waine wheles.

b. Special comb.: †**wain-beam**, the pole of a wagon (used to translate L. *temo*); †**wain-clout**, the iron covering for the axle-tree of a wagon (see clout *sb.*[2] 2); †**wain-cope** (see quot. and cope, cop *sb.*[4]); **wain-flakes** *dial.* [= MLG. *wagenvleke*], the movable side-boards of a wagon, used to increase its carrying capacity; †**wain-fork**, a fork used in the loading of a wagon; †**wain-gate**[1] [gate *sb.*[1]], a gate for wains to pass through; †**wain-gate**[2] [gate *sb.*[2]], a cart-track, wagon-road; **wain-house** (*obs.* exc. *dial.*), a wagon-house, cart-shed; †**wain-money**, ? tolls collected from wains (*E.D.D.*); †**wain-rake**, a rake used in the loading of a wagon with hay, etc.; †**wain-shackle**, ? a coupling for a wagon (see shackle 6 a); **wain-stang** *dial.*, the projecting pole of a cart on either side of which oxen or horses may be yoked; †**wain-string**, ? = wain-rope; †**wain-stroke**, a curved segment forming part of the iron rim or tire of a wagon wheel (cf. stroke *sb.*[4]); **wain-trees** *dial.*, the axle-beams supporting the wagon; †**wain-way**, a wagon-road; †**wain-weight**, ? a wagon-load.

1589 Fleming *Virg. Georg.* iii. 42 Let it creake afterwards, and let the brasen *wainebeame strong Draw both the wheels together ioind. **1650** Horn & Rob. tr. *Comenius' Gate Lang. Unl.* Foundat. T 9 One overcom with wine guid's the wain-beam [L. *temonem*] rashly. **1454** *Durham Acc. Rolls* (Surtees) 149, ij *wayneclowtez. **1523–34** Fitzherb. *Husb.* §5 The wheles..must haue an axiltre, clout with .viii. waincloutes of yren. **1596** *Durham Wills* (Surtees) II. 259, v teames, ij horse-teames.., vij wayne cloutes [etc.]. **1688** Holme *Armoury* iii. 339/2 The *waine Cop, that part which the hinder Oxen are yoked unto to draw the Waine. **1726** *Dict. Rust.* (ed. 3) s.v. *Cart*, The Wain-Cope, is a long piece that comes out from the Wain-body, to which Oxen are fasten'd. **1570** *Richmond Wills* (1853) 101 In the yard and parke..a pare of *wayne fleaks. **1876** *Whitby Gloss.*, *Wainfleeaks*, the moveable side-boards of the waggon, adapted to heighten it. **1641** Best *Farm. Bks.* (Surtees) 46 Allowinge to each waine two folkes, viz., a forker and a loader; and theire implements which they are to carry to field with them is a *waine-forke and a waine-rake; theire waineforke should bee in length aboute two yardes and a quarter. *c* **1680** in *Sussex Archæol. Collect.* (1849) II. 108 Richard Butcher..took out of ye highway well nigh an acre of land, and made an enclosure of it, and set up a *wean gate and horse gate. **1596** in *Reg. Mag. Sig. Scot.* 1601, 414/1 Cum lie cairt and wane gait ad easdem [moras]. **1661** *Reg. Gt. Seal Scot.* 18/2 Therefra alongst ane old waingate till you come to the Seggiesyke. **1569** *Lanc. Wills* (Chetham Soc.) I. 34 With other out howses as followith..the furmost barne..the *wayn howse [etc.]. **1791** *Gentl. Mag.* LXI. i. 116/1 After supper, the company all attend the bailiff (or head of the oxen) to the Wain-house. **1828** Carr *Craven Gloss.*, *Wain-house*, wagon house or cart house. **1626** *Gateshead Church Bks.* (E.D.D.) Recaved of the hie ward ffor *wane money, 16s. **1641** Best *Farm. Bks.* (Surtees) 46 Theire *wainerakes haue (for the most parte) theire shaftes made of saugh, theire heade of seasoned ashe, and theire teeth of iron. **1559** *Richmond Wills* (1853) 136, iij *waine shackles. **1876** *Whitby Gloss.*, **Wainstang*, the pole projecting in front of the wagon for carrying stone blocks. **1464** *Inv.* in *Feodar. Priorat. Dunelm.* (Surtees) 120, 1 cowpe-wayne cum *waynstrynges, precium iij.s. **1596** *Durham Wills* (Surtees) II. 259, vij wayne cloutes, ij hay spades,..a *wayne stroke [etc.]. **1876** *Whitby Gloss.*, *Waintrees, the axle-beams supporting the wagon. **1579** *Nottingham Rec.* IV. 189 The *whene waye goinge vpp they hill. **1641** Best *Farm. Bks.* (Surtees) 38 The waine-way into this close is aboute the middle of Pinder lane, wheare yow are to pull downe a gappe. **15..** *Burgh Rec. Edin.* (1869) I. 241 Item of a *wayne weicht of leid, that is to say xxiiij futemellis, iiij d.

†**wain**, *sb.*^{2} *Obs.* Forms: 3-4 **wayne**, 4 **wayn.** [a. OF. *wain* masc., *waaigne* fem., dial. varr. of *gain*, *gaaigne*: see gain *sb.*^{2}]

1. Profit, advantage.

c **1315** Shoreham *Poems* I. 2207 Þe fyfte, þat hys Elyynge, Cryst onleke to oure wayne. **1340** *Ayenb.* 43 Him ne dret naȝt to done..grat harm to oþren uor a lite wayn oþer uor ureme to him.

2. Conquest, possession gained by conquest; also, booty, spoil.

c **1330** R. Brunne *Chron. Wace* (Rolls) 1481 Þeyr fflote wyþ al þer wayne Turnede fro þe lond of Spaigne. *Ibid.* 1857 Albion was Brutes wayne, Þerfore he dide hit calle Brutayne. **1338** —— *Chron.* (1810) 257 We rede ȝe sende to þe kyng of Almayn, & ȝour londes to defende, & reue Philip his wayn. *Ibid.* 297 Þe Scottis bare þam wele, Þe Waleis had þe wayn, als maistere of þat eschele.

†**wain**, *sb.*^{3} *Obs.* In 5 **wayn(e, wayyn.** [Of obscure origin.] A hem, border.

c **1440** *Promp. Parv.* 513/2 Wayne, of a garlement [*v.r.* wayn, wayyn, *Pynson* of a garment], *lacinia*.

†**wain**, *v.* *Obs.* Forms: 2-3 *Orm.* **waȝȝnenn**, 4 **vayne**, 4-6 **wayne**, 6 **waine**, 7 **wein.** [f. wain *sb.*^{1}]

1. *trans.* To transport in a wain or carriage.

c **1200** Ormin Pref. 37 Goddspell forr þatt illke þing Iss Currus Salomoniss, For þatt itt..Waȝȝneþþ soþ Crist fra land to land. *Ibid.* 5909 Þær iss þe Laferrd Crist himm sellf, & tiderr iss he waȝȝnedd Uppo þatt hallȝhe waȝȝn. **1531-2** *Durham Househ. Bk.* (Surtees) 62 Pro navigacione ultra aquam cum le waynnyng 1 but malvaseti, 6 d. **1606** Birnie *Kirk-Buriall* (1833) 10 Before that by the Libitinarian cure the dead was weind, the Pollinctors inbalmed the corps of the great.

2. To carry, bring, convey.

13.. *Gaw. & Gr. Knt.* 2459 Ho wayned me þis wonder, your wyttez to reue. **13..** *E.E. Allit. P.* A. 249 What wyrde has hyder my iuel vayned. **1540** Palsgr. *Acolastus* III. ii. O ij, Pamphagus wold wayne or bring no geste to Sannios howse, but he were riche. **1573-80** Tusser *Husb.* (1878) 107 Then neighbour..if any you see, good servant for dairie house, waine her to mee.

b. ? To bring a report of.

c **1400** *Destr. Troy* 11520 He couet at the kyng,..Eneas eftsones þat erend for to wend..All þere wille for to wete & wayne at þe last.

3. *intr.* To go, rush. [Perh. a different word: cf. ON. *vegna* to proceed, go on.]

c **1400** *Destr. Troy* 7621 A thondir with a thicke Rayn thrublit in þe skewes,..As neuer water fro the welkyn hade waynit before. *Ibid.* 7655 Ector, wrathed at his wordis, waynit at the kyng, þat he gird to þe ground and the gost yald. *Ibid.* 13796 [Ho] Waynyt vp to the welkyn, as a wan clowde.

wain: see vain *a.*, wane *sb.*^{1}, *v.*, wean *v.*

†'**wainable**, *a.* *Law.* *Obs.* [AF. dial. var. of *gaignable* gainable.] = gainable.

1706 Phillips (ed. Kersey), *Wainable*, (in old Deeds) that may be Manured, or Ploughed; Tillable.

wainage ('weɪnɪdʒ). *Hist.* Also 6 **waynage.** [ad. Anglo-L. *wainnagium*: see gainage.]

1. = gainage 3 (q.v. with regard to erroneous interpretations).

c **1500** tr. *Gt. Charter* in *Arnolde's Chron.* (1811) 217 A villayne other than ours the same wise shalbe amercyed, sauyng his waynage yf he falle into our handis. *a* **1632** Coke *Inst.* II. xiv. (1642) 28 It was great reason to save his wainage, for otherwise the miserable creature, was to carry it on his back. **1700** J. Tyrrell *Hist. Eng.* II. 814 His Wainage (i.e. his Carts and Implements) to Till his Land.

2. Land under cultivation.

1810 G. Chalmers *Caledonia* II. ii. 134 The *waynage*, or cultivable lands, and meadows of each district or manor, were possessed, and laboured, in separate portions, by the individuals of the manor. **1875** Stubbs *Const. Hist.* I. xii. 510 That they would..declare how many carucates, or what wainage for ploughs, there were in each township. **1898** W. Farrer *Cartul. Cockersand Abbey* II. I. 362 With acquittance of multure at the grantor's mill of his house and wainage.

†**wainbote.** *Law.* *Obs.* Also **wesne-boot.** [f. wain *sb.*^{1} + *bote*, boot *sb.*^{2} Cf. MLG. (13th c.) *wagenbote*.] The allowance of timber which a tenant had the right to cut for the repair of his wains.

1772 in *Sussex Archæol. Collect.* VI. 61 (Customs of Manor of Batell) Plough-boot and wesne-boot. **1828-32** Webster.

waincot, obs. form of wainscot.

waine: see vain *a.*, wane *sb.*^{1}, *v.*, wean *v.*

wainer ('weɪnə(r)). *rare.* In 5 **wenyher**, 6 **weyner.** [f. wain *sb.*^{1} + -er^1 (in 15th c. -yer).] The driver of a wain, a wagoner.

a **1500** *Tretyce* in *Walter of Henley's Husb.* (1890) 50 Se þat yor wenyheris haue no poketes betwene þer legges to stelle withe. **1566** *S'hampton Crt. Leet Rec.* (1905) I. I. 35 Weyners. **1840** Galt *Demon of Destiny* 77 Aghast the wainers stood.

wainescot, obs. form of wainscot.

'**wainful.** *rare.* [f. wain *sb.*^{1} + -ful.] As much as a wain will hold, a wain-load.

1713 Lady G. Baillie *Househ. Bk.* (S.H.S.) 246 For a wainfull Dails bringing from Berwick, 0 6 10.

†'**waining**, *vbl. sb.* *Obs.*$^{-0}$ [Of obscure origin.] (See quots.)

1585 Higins *Junius' Nomencl.* 385/2 *Versura*,..the waining or turning at y^e lands end, where one furrow endeth and another beginneth. **1611** Cotgr. s.v. *Reversure*.

waining, obs. f. waning; var. woning *Obs.*

wainman ('weɪnmən). Also 4 **waynesman.** [f. wain *sb.*^{1} + man.]

1. = wainer. *Obs.* exc. *Hist.*

1392 *Earl Derby's Exped.* (Camden) 180 Duobus waynemen de Dansk pro eodem viagio, iiij marcz. pr. Cuidam waynesman de Dansk pro eodem viagio, ij. marcz. pr. *c* **1450** *St. Cuthbert* (Surtees) 5833 Þe wayne men wer noȝt ware. **1580** H. F. *Pelegrom. Syn. Sylva* 42 A Carter, a Waine man. *Auriga* [etc.]. **1609** *Churchw. Acc. Pittington*, etc. (Surtees) 154 Item paid to the wainmen that brought the lyme and sand for there drinkes, ix d. **1627** *Act 3 Chas. I*, c. 2 §1 No Carrier with any Horse or Horses..nor Waynemen with anie Wayne or Waynes..shall..travell upon the said Day. **1756** P. Browne *Jamaica* 193 The leaves..yield a strong thready substance..which is commonly used in ropes and whips by the wainmen in that part of the world. **1880** F. G. Lee *Ch. under Q. Eliz.* I. 15 At Canterbury..a holy-oil stock was emptied of its sacred contents, in order to grease the creaking wheels of a wainman's cart.

†**2.** (With capital initial.) The constellation Boötes, regarded as the teamster of 'Charles's Wain'. *Obs.*

1588 A. Ashley *Mariners Mirr.* A 6 b, A catalogue of the more famous fixed starres... The Wainmans right shoulder. **1594** Kyd *Cornelia* III. i. 69 And now the sleepie Waineman softly droue His slow-pac'd Teeme. **1598** Sylvester *Du Bartas* I. iv. 290 Besides these Twelve, toward the Artick side, A flaming Dragon doth Two-Bears divide; After, the Wainman comes, the Crown, the Spear [etc.].

wainny, obs. form of waney *a.*

wain-rope. *Obs.* or *arch.* **a.** A rope used as a trace for drawing a wain. (Cf. *cart-rope.*) **b.** A rope used for binding or securing a load on a wain.

1371 *Durham Acc. Rolls* (Surtees) 129, ij waynraps novi. **1441-2** *Ibid.* 79 Item in 2 Waynrapes et 4 helteres empt., 12 *d.* **1523-34** Fitzherb. *Husb.* §5 And or he shall lode his corne, he muste haue a wayne, a copyoke, a payre of sleues, a wayne rope, and a pykforke. **1581** *Inv.* in *Trans. Cumb. & Westm. Arch. Soc.* X. 40 Item Waine Ropes, xvj *d.* **1601** Shaks. *Twel. N.* III. ii. 64, I thinke Oxen and waine-ropes cannot hale them together.

wainscot ('weɪnskɒt, -skət), *sb.* Forms: α. 4-5 **waynescot**, (4 **-scote**), 4-7 **waynscot**, 5-6 **wayn(e)scotte, wayneskote, weynscott,** (5 **-scotte**, 6 **-skot**), 5-7 **waynscote, -scott,** (5 **wenscote, wansqwatte, waneskott, waynskote, waynscowttez** (*pl.*), *Sc.* **wanskoth**), 6 **wayn(e)skott, wenskot(te, weinscot, wainescot,** (**weanscott, wainscoate, wanskot(t, wenskett,** *Sc.* **wynscott**), 6-7 **wa(i)nscote, wainskot, wanescot,** (6 **-skot**, 7 **-scott**), 6-8 **wainscott, wanscot,** (7 **vain-**, *Sc.* **vandscott, weanscot, waynskot, waynscote, waincot**), 7-9 **wainscoat,** (8 **wanscoate**), 6- **wainscot.** β. 4 *north.* **vayneschote, wandschoth,** 5 **weynshet,** 6 **wa(y)ne-, weyneschot.** [ad. MLG. *wagenschot* (1389 in Schiller and Lübben), app. f. *wagen* carriage, wagon + *schot* (of uncertain meaning; cf. *bokenschot*, mod.LG. *bökenschot*, beechwood of superior quality). Cf. 16th c. Flemish *waegheschot*, *waeghenschot* (Kilian), WFlemish *wageschot* (De Bo), Du. *wagenschot*, WFris. *wagenskot*. The synonymous Flem. or Du. *wandschot* (Kilian), which may be the source of some of the Eng. forms, is either an etymologizing perversion of *wagenschot* or an independent formation on *wand* wall of a room. The Eng. examples of the word are earlier than those given in the MLG. and MDu. dicts., and the first element appears already in the earliest instances assimilated to the Eng. wain *sb.*^{1}

The etymology as above stated does not clearly account for the meaning, and there have been attempts to explain the first element differently. Kilian (1598) identifies it with Flem. *waeghe* wave, taking it to refer to the undulation in the grain of the wood. Some modern scholars regard it as an alteration of MDu. *weeg* wall (= OFris. *wâch*, OE. *wāh*, wough). These suggestions are however open to strong objection, and the probability is that the first element is really *wagen*, though the original meaning of the compound remains for the present obscure.]

1. a. A superior quality of foreign oak imported from Russia, Germany, and Holland, chiefly used for fine panel-work; logs or planks of this oak; oak boarding for panel-work. Now only *technical.*

1352-3 *Ely Sacr. Rolls* (1907) II. 153 Item solut. pro cc et dimid. de Waynscot empt. ad Lenne prec. de cent. xvs. xd. I^l. 19^s. 7^d. **1391-2** *Norwich Sacrist's Roll* (MS.), Pro tabulis de Waynscot. **1404** in *Royal & Hist. Lett. Hen. IV* (Rolls) I. 262 Nova navis cum tritico, braseo, farina..et lignis voaghenschot [? *read* waghen-] onustata. [**1407** in Hakluyt *Voy.* (1599) I. 173 The said marchants [of the Hans of Almaine] doe alleage, that the customers & bailifs of the town of Southhampton doe compel them to pay..for ech hundreth of bowstaues & boords called *Waghenscot*, 2. d.] *a* **1419** *Liber Albus* (Rolls) 238 De chescun c du bord appelle 'weynscotte' obole. **1426-7** *Rec. St. Mary at Hill* (1904) 66 Also for wayneskote, vj d. **1483** *Churchw. Acc. S. Mary Virg., Oxford* in *MS. Wood D. 3* fol. 260 De 4 s solut pro 4 asseribus vocat: weynshet. **1495** *Naval Acc. Hen. VII* (1896) 270 Chayres of waynscotte. **1496** *Acc. Ld. High Treas. Scot.* I. 290 Item, for xxiij burdis callit wanskoth, xvj s. viij d. **1522** *Bury Wills* (Camden) 117 A brode cheste of wayneskott. *a* **1548** Hall *Chron., Hen. VIII*, 60 The Dutchemen bryng ouer Iron, Tymber, lether and Weynskot ready wrought. **1550** *Reg. Mag. Sig. Scot.* 104/2 Exceptis..300 asseribus querneis *lie waneschot* nuncupatis. **1583** *Rates of Customs* D vij b, Playing tables Flaunders making of wainscot the dosen xvs. **1589** [? Nashe] *Almond for Parrat* 1 A brother in Christ of his..kept his wainscot from waste, and his linnen from wearing; sufficeth he tombled his wife naked into the earth at high noone. **1611** Coryat *Crudities* 231 In the midst of the Synagogue they haue a round seat made of Wainscot. **1652** Urquhart *Jewel* 252 Seeing a wedge of Wainscot is fittest and most proper for cleaving of an oaken tree. **1670** Eachard *Cont. Clergy* 108 An unlearned rout of contemptible people..who perhaps shall understand very little more than a hollow pipe made of tin or wainscot. **1732** M. Green *Grotto* 161 As spiders Irish wainscot flee. **1842** Gwilt *Encycl. Archit.* §1686 The wood [of *Quercus robur*] is tolerably straight-grained and pretty free from knots, in many instances resembling the German species called wainscot. *Ibid.* 1689 There is a species of oak ..imported from Holland, known under the name of Dutch wainscot, though grown in Germany, whence it is floated down the Rhine for exportation.

†**b.** A piece or a board of wainscot oak. *Obs.*

1388 in Nicolas *Hist. Royal Navy* (1847) II. 476 Parcels in the store-house..'xxiii. barrell de tarre,..cc. waynscots'. **1396** *Mem. Ripon* (Surtees) III. 123 Et in iij vayneschotes emp. pro j selour et j reredos..18 d. **1486-7** *Priory of Finchale* (Surtees) p. cccIxxvi, Pro xvj waynscowttez ad vjd., viij s. **1532** *Lett. & Papers Hen. VIII*, V. 448 To John de Garnathoo of the Company of the Easterlings, for 100 wainscots, 66*s.* 8*d.* **1603** *Reg. Mag. Sig. Scot.* 515/2 Ilk geist, corball and waynescott..ane penny. **1641** S. Smith *Royal Fishings* 4 Waynskots, Clapboards, Deale.

†**c.** Furniture made of wainscot. *Obs.*

1589 *Wills & Inv. N.C.* (Surtees) 144, I will my wainscott, as well chamberes and parleres, all wainscot beddes covered with wainescott. **1597** *Lanc. Wills* (Chetham Soc.) II. 227, I give to my sonne..all the waynescott glasse painted clothes borders above the waynscott tables.

2. Panel-work of oak or other wood, used to line the walls of an apartment.

1548 in Glasscock *Rec. St. Michael's, Bp.'s Stortford* (1882) 131 Item the weyneschot of the rode loft that was taken downe. **1555** Eden *Decades* (Arb.) 194 Chambers boarded after the maner of owre waynscotte. **1584** *Leycesters Commw.* (1641) 154 The greedy Burglarer is lesse patient of stay..when he..perceiveth only some partition of wane-skot or the like, betwixt his fingers and the cofers or money bags. **1600** Shaks. *A. Y. L.* III. i. 88 This fellow wil but ioyne you together, as they ioyne Wainscot, then one of you wil proue a shrunke pannell. **1611** Coryat *Crudities* 244 In the Quire the whole history of S^t. Bennet is very curiously made in Wainscot. *a* **1667** Cowley *Ess.*, *Greatness* (1906) 432 A convenient brick house, with decent Wainscot, and pretty Forest-work hangings. *a* **1701** Maundrell *Journ. Jerus.* (1732) 77 It was carv'd in such a manner, as to resemble a piece of wainscot. **1711** Addison *Spect.* No. 235 ¶2 A certain Person..who when he is pleased with any Thing that is acted upon the Stage, expresses his Approbation by a loud Knock upon the Benches or the Wainscot. **1715** —— *Drummer* I. i, Like a rat behind a wainscot. **1730** W. Warren *Collectanea* in Willis & Clark *Cambridge* (1886) I. 225 The Stair-case new lin'd with Deal wainscot painted. **1768-74** Tucker *Lt. Nat.* (1852) I. 290 When we look upon the wainscot of a room where the panels are painted of a different colour from the stiles and mouldings. **1781** Cowper *Conversat.* 116, I twirl my thumbs, fall back into my chair, Fix on the wainscot a distressful stare. **1815** Scott *Guy M.* xlii, The great oak-parlour, a long room, panelled with well-varnished wainscot. **1830** Tennyson *Mariana* vi, The mouse Behind the mouldering wainscot shriek'd. **1855** Macaulay *Hist. Eng.* xv. III. 613 The Jacobite country gentlemen..burned their commissions signed by James, and hid their arms behind wainscots or in haystacks. **1875** Miss Braddon *Strange World* II. i. 3 The wainscot was almost black with age.

†**3.** *transf.* and *fig.* (Cf. 5 b.) *Obs.*

1588 *Marprel. Epist.* (Arb.) 31 His face is made of seasoned wainscot, and wil lie as fast as a dog can trot. **1607** Middleton *Fam. Love* III. iii, Cedars to make good wainscot in the House of Sincerity. **1611** Beaum. & Fl. *King & No King* v. i, This Rascal fears neither God nor man, he has been so beaten: sufferance has made him Wainscot. **1630** D. Dyke *Myst. Selfe-Deceiuing* 374 Howsoeuer sometimes this kind of men haue faces of wainscote. *a* **1659** Osborn *Charac. &c.* (1673) 640 How a few years hath changed Alabaster into Wainscot, and ruffled her Neck like a walking Buskin.

4. A book-name for several moths. (See 5 c.)

1819 Samouelle *Entomol. Compend.* 399. *Ibid.* 419. **1832** J. Rennie *Butterfl. & Moths* 87.

5. *attrib.* passing into *adj.* **a.** Made of wainscot. Of a room, lined with wainscot panelling.

1575 in *Archæologia* XXX. 8 Item..ij waynscot chaires viij^e. *Ibid.* 14 Item a waynscott cheste, v^s. **1580** *Ibid.* LXIV. 357 To mak..tow dores on for the portall and on other for the lytle wayneschot chambre. **1585** Higins *Junius' Nomencl.* 229/2 *Mensa vndulata vndatim crispa*,..a wainscot table. **1593** Drayton *Ecl.* iv. 91 The loftie Pines were presently hew'd downe, And Men, Sea-Monsters, swam the bracky Flood, In Wainscote Tubs to seeke out Worlds vnknowne. **1594** Nashe *Terrors Nt.* Wks. (Grosart) III. 265 Through him my tender wainscot doore is deliuered from much assault and battrie. **1649** Davenant *Love & Hon.* III.

iii. 124 Look for one of my cheek teeth That dropt under the wanscote bed. **1702** *Post Man* 6–8 Jan. 2/1 Advt., At Stanmore..is a fair House to be let, 4 Wainscot rooms on a floor, with a Kitchin, [etc.]. **1711** in G. Lorimer *Leaves fr. Bk. West Kirke* vii. (1885) 64 Item,..a green pulpit cloath with silk fringes, six wanscot stools for the Collections. **1748** RICHARDSON *Clarissa* (1811) II. 205 They all remained in the next parlour, a wainscot partition only parting the two. **1796** J. OWEN *Trav. Europe 1791–2* I. 85 Those sculptural vagaries, in which a human figure is often made..the support of a wainscot pulpit. **1833** HT. MARTINEAU *Vanderput & S.* i. 6, I am in the wainscoat parlour to-day. **1848** DICKENS *Dombey* liii, My room..was divided from the Manager's room by a wainscot partition. **1851** W. LAXTON *Builder's Price Bk.* (ed. 28) 58 Wainscot floors. **1862** *Catal. Internat. Exhib., Brit.* II. No. 5719, A wainscot sideboard. **1913** *Blackw. Mag.* July 14/2 The room..had..a wainscot table, rosewood chairs [etc.].

†**b.** Resembling wainscot, hardened or coloured like old wainscot. *Obs.*

1577 GRANGE *Golden Aphrod.* K ij b, Your waynscot face and brasen countenaunce. **1586** A. DAY *Eng. Secretorie* I. (1595) 91 b, Audacious and wainscot impudencie on the other side returneth the greatest impediment in anie thing to bee obtained. **1593** G. HARVEY *Pierce's Super.* Wks. (Grosart) II. 117 But it is not the wainscot forhead of a Rudhuddibras, that can arreare such an huge opinion. **1599** NASHE *Lenten Stuffe* 47 If you marke it, mustard looks of the tanned wainscot hue, of such a withered wrinklefaced beldam as she was, that was altred thereinto. **1626** MIDDLETON *Quiet Life* IV. ii, How does thy Mistriss that sits in a Wainscot Gown, like a Citizens Lure to draw the Customers? **1707** J. STEVENS tr. *Quevedo's Com. Wks.* (1709) 469 They are Wainscot Faces compair'd with white men. *a* **1745** SWIFT *Dick, a Maggot* 11 'Tis beyond the pow'r of meal The gypsey visage to conceal; For, as he shakes his wainscot chops, Down ev'ry mealy atom drops.

c. In book-names of certain moths: see 4.

1832 J. RENNIE *Butterfl. & Moths* 187.

6. *attrib.* and *Comb.*: **a.** simple attrib., as ***wainscot board, colour, log, oak, rafter, timber, work***; **wainscot chair**, a panel-back chair (see PANEL *sb.*[1] 21). **b.** parasynthetic, as †***wainscot-faced*** adj.; **c.** similative, as ***wainscot joined*** adj.

1420 in *For. Acc. 3 Hen. VI*, G/2 In diuersis peciis maeremii *Waynescotbordes. **1594** BLUNDEVIL *Exerc., Navig.* xxiv. (1597) 331 Another square boxe of thinne wainscot boorde. **1663** in *Farm & Cottage Inventories of Mid-Essex 1633–1749* (Essex Record Office) (1950) 95 One *Wainsscott Chair. **1891** I. W. LYON *Colonial Furnit. New Eng.* v. 145 The wainscot chairs which figure in the early records were doubtless those made up—back, seats, and all—of wood, the wood being most invariably oak. *Ibid.* 146 Wainscot chairs were quite common in England and Scotland in the seventeenth century. **1925** [see *panel-back* adj. s.v. PANEL *sb.*[1] 21]. **1978** P. VAN GREENAWAY *Man called Scavener* i. 11 A long passage lined with Pembrokes, a Wainscot chair, a rare Caquetoire. **1741** *Compl. Fam.-Piece* III. 525 Most Rooms are now Painted *Wainscot Colour. **1588** *Marprel. Epist.* (Arb.) 30 Our impudent, shameless, and *wainscote faced bishops. **1640** HOWELL *Dodona's Gr.* 22 But now mee thinkes I spie againe a Sunn burnt wainscot-fac'd Satyr. **1554** in Feuillerat *Revels Q. Mary* (1914) 164, viij targettes of tree shelboard of *waynscot ioyned fair worke for the said maskers. **1812** J. SMYTH *Pract. Customs* 249 *Wainscot logs, 8 inches square or upwards, are charged by the load of 50 cubic feet. **1832** *Planting* 130 in *Libr. Usef. Knowl., Husb.* III, That which is brought down the Rhine from the forests of southern Germany, and imported into this country by the name of *wainscoat oak. *c* **1560** *Aberd. Reg.* (MS.) XXVI. (Jam.) *Wynscott rauchter. **1875** T. LASLETT *Timber* xvi. 96 Riga *wainscot timber passes through the process of bracking prior to its being shipped. **1585** HIGINS *Junius' Nomencl.* 198/2 *Wainscot or seeling worke. **1609** *Acc. Balliol Coll., Oxford* (MS.), Item, for 2 seates, and wainscot worke, in the librarie, 5 *li.*

wainscot (ˈweɪnskɒt, -skət), *v.* Inflected **wainscot(t)ed, -ing.** Forms: see the sb. [f. prec. Cf. Flemish †*waeghenschotten* (Kilian).]

1. *trans.* To line (a wall, roof, etc.) with panel-work of wood.

1570 LEVINS *Manip.* 177 To Waynscotte, *contabulare.* **1599** *Rutland MSS.* (Hist. MSS. Comm. 1905) IV. 415 For waynscotting the roofes of his chamber, xxs. *a* **1650** BOATE *Ireland's Nat. Hist.* (1860) 121 To mend this inconvenience the English did wainscot those walls with oak or other boards. **1676** GLANVILL *Ess. Philos. & Relig.* VII. 3 He led me into an handsome square Chamber wainscotted with Cedar. **1678** MOXON *Mech. Exerc.* vi. 105 Of Wainscoting Rooms. *Ibid.* 106 In Wainscoting of Rooms there is, for the most part, but two heights of Pannels used; unless the Room to be Wainscoted be above ten foot high. **1730** W. WARREN *Collect.* in Willis & Clark *Cambridge* (1886) I. 232 The Treasury..is wainscotted with Deal. **1821** SCOTT *Kenilw.* vi, This apartment..was now beautifully wainscoted with dark foreign wood. **1839** LONGF. *Hyperion* III. iii. Pr. Wks. 1886 II. 162 It was a large room..wainscoted with pine. **1883** G. MOORE *Mod. Lover* xiv, [The room] was wainscotted in light oak.

in fig. context. *a* **1704** T. BROWN *Quakers Grace* Wks. 1730 I. 107 That we..may live to be saw'd out into deal-boards, to wainscoat thy New Jerusalem.

b. To grain in imitation of oak.

1835 DICKENS *Sk. Boz, Parish* iii, The house..was fresh painted and papered from top to bottom; the paint inside was all wainscoted.

2. *transf.* To line (the walls of an apartment) with marble, tiles, or the like; to panel (a wall) with mirrors or pictures.

1613–39 I. JONES in Leoni *Palladio's Archit.* (1742) II. 50 To wainscot their Buildings with rich Stones. **1620** DONNE *Serm.* 2 Apr. (1661) III. 138 The Scriptures are as a room wainscotted with looking-glass, we see all at once. *a* **1668** LASSELS *Italy* (1698) I. 93 Witness those chambers..wainscoted with great Looking-glasses and rich gilding. **1718** LADY M. W. MONTAGU *Let. to C'tess Mar* 10 Mar., The winter apartment was wainscoted with inlaid work of mother of pearl. **1745** POCOCKE *Descr. East* II. II. i. 5 The east side of it within is wainscotted with jasper and beautiful marbles. **1775** JOHNSON in *Boswell* 14 Oct., The ladies' closet wainscotted with large squares of glass over painted paper. **1806–7** J. BERESFORD *Miseries Hum. Life* XVIII. viii. (1826) 154 But enough..of Portraits; though, in truth, the walls are wainscotted with them.

Hence **ˈwainscot(t)ed** *ppl. a.*

1605 ERONDELLE *Fr. Gard.* N 2 b, God grant me alwaies the key of the fieldes, I would like it better, then to be in bondage in the fayrest wainscotted or tapistred Chamber. **1694** WESTMACOT *Script. Herb.* 40 Solomon and others..did build their Magnificent Houses,..and Wain-scotted Rooms therewith [Cedar]. **1814** SCOTT *Wav.* lv, The apartment of Colonel Talbot..was divided from his own by a wainscotted partition. **1848** DICKENS *Dombey* iv, The little wainscoted back parlour. **1866** MRS. GASKELL *Wives & Dau.* xiii, They were taken..into a wainscoted parlour.

transf. and *fig.* **1602** F. H[ERING] tr. *Oberndoerffer's Anat. True Physit.* I, This lost Companion [a quack], hauing a Foxes Head and an whorish and wainscotted Face.

†**wainscotage.** *Obs. rare*$^{-1}$. [f. WAINSCOT *v.* + -AGE.] Wainscot-work, wainscoting.

1677 tr. *Tavernier's Gr. Seignor's Seraglio* xv. 73 Yet is there a delicate piece of Wainscotage, of about the height of a man's waste, carried quite round the Room.

wainscot(t)ing (ˈweɪnskɒtɪŋ), *vbl. sb.* [f. WAINSCOT *v.* + -ING[1].] The action or process of lining a room, its walls, etc. with wainscot; also *concr.*, panelling of wainscot; also, wainscots collectively.

1580 HOLLYBAND *Treas. Fr. Tong, Lambris*, a seeling, wanscotting. **1611** COTGR., *Lambrissage*, a wainscotting, or seeling; also, an embowing, or frettizing in wainscot. **1631** WEEVER *Anc. Funeral Mon.* 870 He..bestowed 100. markes vpon wainscotting of the Library there. **1682** BURNET *Life Hale* 39 He laid by all his Collections..., and that they might not fall into ill hands, he hid them behind the Wainscotting of his Study. **1727** DE FOE *Eng. Tradesm.* xxii. (1841) I. 206 He must sink perhaps a third part, nay, half his stock, in painting and gilding, wainscoting and glazing. **1764** HARMER *Observ.* iii. §8. 97 Their carved wainscottings of wood heightened with painting and gilting. **1836** DICKENS *Sk. Boz, Doctor's Commons*, An old quaint-looking apartment, with sunken windows, and black carved wainscotting. **1859** GEO. ELIOT *Adam Bede* i, The afternoon sun was warm on the five workmen there, busy upon doors and window frames and wainscoting. **1869** 'LEWIS CARROLL' *Phantasmag.* 37 But after twenty years or so The wainscotings begin to go.

waint, obs. Sc. form of VAUNT *v.*

1563 WINȜET tr. *Vincent. Lirin.* xvi. Wks. (S.T.S.) II. 37 Bot Apollinaris in a manere crakis and waintis that he consentis in deid to the vnitie of the Trinitie.

wainwright (ˈweɪnraɪt). [f. WAIN *sb.*[1] + WRIGHT. In OE. *wæȝn-wyrhta.* Not found in ME., but its existence is attested by the surname *Wainwright.*] A wagon-builder.

c **1000** ÆLFRIC *Gloss.* in Wr.-Wülcker 112 *Carpentarius*, wænwyrhta. **1855** HYDE CLARKE *Dict., Wainwright*, wagon-wright. **1891** MEREDITH *One of our Conq.* xix, A rill, that was lured a little further down through scoops, ducts, and scaffolded channels to serve a wainwright.

wainy, variant of WANEY *a.*

‖**waipiro** (ˈwaipirɔ). *N.Z.* Also **waipera, waipero, waipirau.** [Maori, f. *wai* water + *piro* putrid.] Alcoholic liquor, spirits.

1845 W. BROWN *N.Z.* I. iii. 132 Another native..keeps a grog-shop, and sells his *Waipero*..to *Hourangi* (drunken) pakehas. **1847** S. C. BREES *Pictorial Illustr. N.Z.* 13 The natives..say, it is '*all the same as te waipe-ra*', or spirits. **1863** F. E. MANING *Old N.Z.* xi. 152 He *would* go on shore..to get some water to mix with his *waipiro*, and was not his canoe found next day floating about with his paddle and two empty case-bottles in it? **1881** J. L. CAMPBELL *Poenamo* xi. 341 We had the inevitable percentage of indulgers in 'waipirau'. **1933** *Bulletin* (Sydney) 20 Dec. 20/3 Under the influence of waipiro a Rotorua Maori pinched a sedan car. **1972** P. NEWTON *Sheep Thief* xx. 169 She had no time for the waipera... 'Charles,' she said... 'You can decide right now. Me or the drink.'

waipone, waippin, obs. Sc. ff. WEAPON.

†**wair**, *sb. Obs. rare*$^{-1}$. A piece of timber two yards long and one foot broad.

1664 EVELYN *Sylva* xxix. 85 A Tree [an oak]..which yielded of sawn Wair fourteen hundred, and, by estimation, twenty Chords of wood. A Wair is two yards long, and one foot broad, sixscore to the hundred: so that, in the said Tree was 10080 foot of Boards. Hence **1674** BLOUNT *Glossogr.* (ed. 4), and in later Dicts.

†**wair**, *a. Sc. Obs. rare*$^{-1}$. ? Wild, stormy.

c **1480** HENRYSON *Preach. Swallow* xii, Bewis bene are laiht bair of blis, Be wickit windis of the winter wair.

wair, obs. form of *were*, pa. ind. pl. of BE *v.*

wair(e, waird, wairding, wairdour, wairdrope, Sc. or north. ff. WARE, WEIR, WARD, WARDING, WARDER, WARDROBE.

wairakite (ˈwaɪərəkaɪt). *Min.* [f. *Wairakei*, name of a place in New Zealand + -ITE[1].] A hydrous silicate of calcium and aluminium, $CaAl_2Si_4O_{12}.2H_2O$, the calcium analogue of analcime, that occurs as colourless to white monoclinic crystals and is common in low-grade metamorphic rocks.

1955 A. STEINER in *Mineral Mag.* XXX. 691 During the study of hydrothermal alteration of cores recovered from holes drilled at Wairakei..an unusual zeolite mineral was found... The name wairakite is given to the new mineral. **1979** *Amer. Mineralogist* LXIV. 993/1 A marked feature of wairakite crystals is the presence of complex, fine lamellar twinnings.

wairn, obs. Sc. form of WARN.

wairsche, wairsh, var. ff. WERSH *a.*

wairstall, -staw, var. ff. WARESTALL *Sc.*

wais: see WALL, WASE, WAVE, WAY.

waisall, waissel, var. ff. WASSAIL.

waische, waisshe, obs. forms of WASH *v.*

waiscot, obs. form of WAISTCOAT.

waist (weɪst). Forms: 4–6 **waast**, 4–7 **wast**, 4–8 **waste**, 6 *Sc.* **west**, 7 **wayst**, 5, 7– **waist.** [14th c. *wast*, believed to represent an OE. **wæst*, **weahst*, corresp. to ON. **vahstu-r* (Icel. *vǫxt-r*, Sw. *växt*, Da. *væxt*), Goth. *wahstu-s*, growth, size, f. Teut. root **waχs-*: see WAX *v.*[1] With regard to the form cf. OE. *wæstm*, growth, fruit:—OTeut. type **waχstmo-z* from the same root. With regard to the meaning cf. F. *taille*, where the sense 'waist' appears to be developed from the sense 'size (of body)'. The word (in the form *wacste*, which may be either native or Scandinavian) app. occurs with the sense 'greatness' in the following quot.

c **1175** *Lamb. Hom.* 77 þe fader is ine þe sune on þre wise. On wacste [*Trin. Hom.* iv. on westme], for he is muchel and mihti ouer alle þing.

The spelling *waist* was rare until it was adopted in Johnson's Dict. 1755.]

1. a. The portion of the trunk of the human body that is between the ribs and the hip-bones; the middle section of the body, normally slender in comparison with the parts above and below it.

In quot. *c* 1480 humorously misused.

13.. *Gaw. & Gr. Knt.* 144 Bot his wombe & his wast were worthily smale. *c* **1386** CHAUCER *Sir Thopas* Prol. 10 He in the waast is shape as wel as I. **1390** GOWER *Conf.* II. 373 When I beclippe hire on the wast. *c* **1400** *Destr. Troy* 9902 Dyomede..Halfe-lyueles..felle, With a wicked wound thurgh the wast euyn. *c* **1420** *Anturs of Arth.* 578 (Douce MS.) He bronched him yne withe his bronde..þorghe þe waast of þe body. *c* **1440** *Promp. Parv.* 517/2 Waste, of a mannys myddyl.., *vastitas*, Cath. **1470–85** MALORY *Arthur* XI. xii. 589 There he fond a knyght that was bounden with a chayne faste aboute the wast vnto a pyller of stone. *c* **1480** HENRYSON *Fox, Wolf & Husbandman* 192 The tod lap on land..And left the wolf in watter to the waist. **1500–20** DUNBAR *Poems* xxxii. 29 He grippit hir abowt the west. **1509** HAWES *Past. Pleasure* xxix. (Percy Soc.) 135 His necke shorte,..His breste fatte and bolne in the wast. **1571** R. BANNATYNE *Memor.* (Bannatyne Club) 170 Culan and his men..waide to their westis befoir thei come to dry land. **1579** SPENSER *Sheph. Cal.* Apr. 134 Gird in your waste..with a tawdrie lace. **1605** SHAKS. *Lear* IV. vi. 127 Downe from the waste they are Centaures, though Women all aboue. **1650** BULWER *Anthropomet.* xx. (1653) 338 Young Virgins..who thinking a slender waste a great beauty, strive all that they possibly can by streight-lacing them-selves, to attaine unto a wand-like smalnesse of waste. **1667** MILTON *P.L.* IX. 1113 Those Leaves They gathered..And..together sowd, To gird thir waste. **1687** A. LOVELL tr. *Thevenot's Trav.* I. 29 Over the Doliman, they gird themselves about the small of the waste with a Sash. **1774** GOLDSM. *Nat. Hist.* II. 260 He was so tall, that the Spaniards only reached his waist. **1839** LANE *Arab. Nts.* I. 105 And, lo! half of him, from his waist to the soles of his feet, was stone. **1860** TYNDALL *Glac.* I. xviii. 131 Hitherto my guides in dangerous places had tied the ropes round their waists also. **1871** *Figure Training* 17 It is not to be wondered at that ten years ago a waist of sixteen inches in circumference, for a lady of average height, should be regarded as a..much-to-be-admired achievement. **1880** 'OUIDA' *Moths* I. 5 She made her waist fifteen inches round.

? *Proverbial phrase.* **1611** CHAPMAN *May-day* v. Wks. 1873 II. 401 Hauing chaster and simpler thoughts then Leonoro imagines because he measures my wast by his owne.

b. Applied to the corresponding part in an insect.

1713 J. WARDER *True Amazons* 3 The Bee is..very slender in the Waste [1741 p. 15 Waist] or middle part. **1871** STAVELEY *Brit. Insects* xiii. 155 The insects belonging to these two subsections can at once be distinguished from each other by their waists being large or small.

c. *transf.* The middle narrower part (of something compared in shape to the human body). Cf. 4.

1612 DRAYTON *Poly-olb.* VI. 194 That part of Wales,..Which (as her very waste) in breadth from East to West In length from North to South, her midst is every way. **1817** BYRON *Manfred* I. i, Mont Blanc is the monarch of mountains,..Around his waist are forests braced. **1862** MERIVALE *Rom. Emp.* lxi. (1865) VII. 325 He had quitted the waist and had here reached the neck of Britain.

2. †**a.** A girdle. *Obs.*

1550 CROWLEY *Epigr.* 1315 Hyr mydle braced in as smal as a wande; And some by wastes of wyre at the paste wyfes hande. **1588** PARKE tr. *Mendoza's Hist. China* 77 They do weare wastes or girdels imbossed with gold. **1595** SHAKS. *John* II. i. 217 Those sleeping stones, That as a waste doth girdle you about By the compulsion of their Ordinance. **1599** PEELE *David & Bethsabe* G iij b, I might haue giuen thee for thy paines Tenne siluer sickles and a golden wast. **1611** CHAPMAN *Iliad* VII. 264 A faire well glossed purple waste [ζωστῆρα.. φοίνικι φαεινόν].

transf. and *fig.* **1579** FENTON *Guicciard.* IX. 478 The enemies abandoned suddeinly the towne wherein the french being bestowed, planted their artillerie against the first wast [It. *contro al primo procinto*]. **1591** SHAKS. *1 Hen. VI*, IV. iii. 20 Spurre to the rescue of the Noble Talbot, Who now is girdled with a waste of Iron. **1599** MARSTON *Ant. & Mel.* I. Wks. 1856 I. 12 Weele girt them with an ample waste of love.

b. The part of a garment that covers the waist; the narrowed part of a garment corresponding to the narrowing of the body at the waist (but sometimes, in accordance with fashion, worn higher or lower than the position of this); the place in a woman's dress where the bodice and skirt meet.

1650 BULWER *Anthropomet.* App. (1653) 539 The waste (as one notes) is now come to the knee; for, the Points that were used to be about the middle, are now dangling there. **1711** STEELE *Spect.* No. 109 ¶4 The Modern [petticoat] is gather'd at the Waste. **1836** MARRYAT *Midsh. Easy* xix, They loaded the pistols, took a pair each and put them in their waists. **1871** *Figure Training* 25 Ladies of fashion in England might be said to have at that period [*c* 1806] abandoned waists altogether. **1885** *Fairholt's Costume Engl.* I. 405 In 1794 short waists became fashionable. *Ibid.* 408 Open gowns were discarded, and waists about 1798 became longer, until at the end of the century they regained their proper shape.

c. The part of a garment between the shoulders and the 'waist' or narrowed part (see 2 b).

1607 DEKKER & WEBSTER *Northw. Hoe* III. i, What fashion will make a woman haue the best bodie Taylor? *Tay.* A short dutch wast with a round cathern-wheele fardingale. **1837** DICKENS *Pickw.* ii, 'Rather short in the waist, an't it?' said the stranger, screwing himself round to catch a glimpse in the glass of the waist buttons which were half way up his back. **1853** —— *Bleak Ho.* vi, Ladies haymaking, in short waists, and large hats tied under the chin.

fig. **1590** NASHE *1st Pt. Pasquil's Apol.* C iij, These places are too short in the waste to serue hys turne.

d. A bodice, blouse. Chiefly *U.S.*

1816 *Sporting Mag.* XLVIII. 189 A lady observing her neighbour in a public room, dressed very tawdrily in a satin waist, drily remarked, it was a waste of satin. **1878** H. JAMES *Europeans* II. ii. 44 She wore a white muslin waist with an embroidered border. **1893** MRS. CUSTER *Tenting on Plains* 85, I had exchanged the waist for a jacket, and left it under a tree. **1908** W. CHURCHILL *Mr. Crewe's Career* xix. 317 Mrs. Fitch.. had run from the wash-tub to get into her Sunday waist.

e. *U.S.* 'An undergarment worn specially by children, to which petticoats and drawers are buttoned' (*Cent. Dict.*).

1893 HELEN CAMPBELL in *Arena* 435 Two and a half cents each is paid for the making of boys' gingham waists.

3. a. *Naut.* The middle part of the upper deck of a ship, between the quarter-deck and the forecastle.

1495 *Naval Acc. Hen. VII* (1896) 194 Stone gonnes of yron in the Wast of the seid Shipp. **15..** *Batayll of Egyngecourte* 90 A ij, These goodly shyppes lay there at rode .. The wastes decked with serpentynes stronge. **1530** PALSGR. 287/1 Waste of a shyppe, *cors de nauire.* *a* **1586** SIDNEY *Arcadia* II. xxiv. §5 Already it [the fire] did embrace and deuoure from the sterne, to the wast of the ship. **1610** SHAKS. *Temp.* I. ii. 197. *c* **1618** MORYSON *Itin.* IV. viii. (1903) 136 Being built large in the Wast and Keele for Capacitye of Marchandize, they are vnfitt to fight at Sea. **1748** *Anson's Voy.* I. iii. (ed. 4) 41 The waste of the ship was filled with live cattle. **1816** 'QUIZ' *Grand Master* I. 18 Neptune will presently be here, And as his godship is in haste, Muster the people in the waste. **1883** *Man. Seamanship Boys* 9 *Q.* Which is the waist? *A.* That portion of the upper deck contained between the fore and main hatchways. **1915** BADEN-POWELL *Ind. Mem.* i. 5 The heavy seas had.. carried away the ladders leading from the upper deck into the waist.

b. *Naut.* In occasional uses: (*a*) *pl.* = *waist-rails*; (*b*) each of the two sides of the waist.

1667 *Lond. Gaz.* No. 127/4 She has been 52. dayes beating at Sea in fowl weather, in which she spent her Main-Top-Mast and her Wasts. **1679** A. LOVELL *Indic. Univ.* 199 The waste, or defences of the sides of a 'Ship'. **1820** W. SCORESBY *Acc. Arctic Reg.* II. 196 A ship having seven boats carried one at each waist.., two at each quarter.., and one across the stern.

c. *Aeronaut.* The middle section of the fuselage of an aeroplane, esp. a bomber. *U.S.*

1942 [see *waist gunner* in sense 7 below]. **1956** *U.S.A.F. Dict.* 560/2 *Waist*, the middle section of an airplane's fuselage. Applied esp. to the middle section of a bomber.

4. Applied to the narrowest or slenderest part of an object which is smaller in breadth or girth near the middle than at the extremities; esp. of a bell, a violin or similar instrument, a boot or shoe.

1612 S. RID *Art of Jugling* E 2, A peece of lether.. which being thrust vp hard to the middle or waste of the said bell, will sticke fast. **1676** MOXON *Print Letters* 26 Describe the outer Arch under the Waste of g on the left hand. **1791** SMEATON *Edystone L.* (1793) §80 It also seemed equally desirable, not to increase the size of the present building in its Waist; by which I mean that part of the building between the top of the rock, and the top of the solid. **1862** *Catal. Internat. Exhib.* II. xxvii. 51 The 'Cremerian boot', with elastic spring in waist or arch of foot. **1872** ELLACOMBE *Bells of Ch.* viii. in *Ch. Bells Devon* 407 The waist of the bell is studded with stars. **1874** J. D. HEATH *Croquet Player* 26 The amount of spring or elasticity in the handle varies according to the thickness of the waist or thinnest part of it. **1895** HASLUCK *Boot Making* viii. 132 To make a square waist, an iron similar to a double iron is used; for other waists, irons are used according to the shape required.

¶**5.** Affectedly used for: Middle (of day or night). *Obs.*

1602 SHAKS. *Ham.* I. ii. 198 In the dead wast [Qq. 1, 5, 6 vast] and middle of the night. **1604** MARSTON *Malcontent* II. v. D 3 b, Tis now about the immodest waste of night. **1622** J. TAYLOR (Water-P.) *Merrie-Wherrie-Ferrie Voy.* Wks. 1630 II. 7/1 About the waste or Nauell of the Day [*note*, Noone if you'l take it so]. **1644** —— *Crop-eare Curried* 1 About the Waste or Navel of the night, Drowsie Somnus came stealing to me. **1651** *Loves of Hero & Leander* (1653) 2 This was about the wast of day: The middle, as the vulgar say.

6. *attrib.* and *Comb.* **a.** Simple attrib., as ***waist height, size***; ***waist-length*** adj.; with sense 'intended to be placed, or worn, on or round the waist', as ***waist-belt, -buckle, -clout,*** †***-doublet, -girdle, -piece, -plate, -pocket, -scarf***; with sense 'worn from the waist', as ***waist petticoat, slip***; objective, as ***waist-gripping, -hold, -pressing, -tightening***; with adjs., as ***waist-deep, high.***

1672 DRYDEN *1st Pt. Conq. Granada* Prol. 10 I'll write a Play, sayes one, for I have got A broad-brim'd hat, and *wastbelt tow'rds a Plot. **1868** *Queen's Regul.* §1128 Both straps of the havresack are to be worn outside the waist belt, so that the havresack may be easily shifted. **1805** *Ann. Reg., Chron.* 394/2 Her Majesty has recovered a diamond *waist-buckle which she had lost, and for which 10 guineas reward had been offered for the recovery. **1864** LOWELL *Fireside Trav.* 4 The merest *waist-clout of modesty. **1763** SCRAFTON *Indostan* (1770) 117 There was no way of approaching it [*sc.* the place], but through a morass *waist-deep. **1814** SCOTT *Ld. of Isles* v. xiv, The eager Knight leap'd in the sea Waist-deep. **1855** TENNYSON *Brook* 118 Waist-deep in meadow-sweet. **1553** in J. C. Jeaffreson *Middlesex County Rec.* (1886) I. 14 Unum diploidem vocatum a *wast-dublett. *Ibid.* Duos velvet *wast gyrdles. **1908** SIR H. JOHNSTON *Geo. Grenfell & Congo* II. xxiii. 589 A waist-cloth is worn all round the body from below a waist-girdle, down to the knees. **1953** E. SIMON *Past Masters* I. i. 21 The tops of the bookshelves which at *waist-height ran along the walls. **1600** FAIRFAX *Tasso* XI. xxvii, *Wast high Argantes shew'd himselfe withall. **1875** MEREDITH *Beauchamp's Career* xii. (1897) 95 A fence waist-high enclosed its plot of meadow and garden. **1904** *Daily Chron.* 12 Jan. 8/4 Two minutes passed before the men sought the mat, and then Cherpillod got a *waist hold, but failed to turn the American over. **1944** R. LEHMANN *Ballad & Source* I. ii. 14 She wore a *waist-length cape called a dolman. **1977** 'L. EGAN' *Blind Search* i. 1 Her waist-length brown hair [was] untidily braided. **1930–40** *Army & Navy Stores Catal.* 642/2 **Waist petticoats*.. Moiré poplin. **1870** C. C. BLACK tr. *Demmin's Weapons of War* 228 *Waist-piece, or great brayette (Vorderschurz) belonging to a Gothic suit of the fifteenth century. **1902** *New Reg. War Office* 58 *Waist-plate. Frosted Gilt Rectangular Plate with Burnished Edges. On the Plate the Royal Cypher and Crown in Silver within an Oak-leaf Wreath. On the lower part of the Wreath a Scroll inscribed 'Dieu et mon droit'. **1858–61** E. B. RAMSAY *Remin.* v. (1870) 129 His snuff he kept.. in a leathern *waist-pocket. **1841** LEVER *C. O'Malley* xxxv, And the free and easy chuck under the chin, cherishing, *waist-pressing kind of a way we get with the ladies. **1853** KANE *Grinnell Exped.* xxx. (1856) 264 A long *waist-scarf, worn like the kummerbund of the Hindoos, is a fine protection while walking, to keep the cold from intruding at the pockets and waist. **1918** *T. Eaton & Co. Catal.* Spring & Summer 188/1 Women's overalls, made of fine khaki drill... *Waist sizes 24 to 38. **1974** *Country Life* 12 Dec. 1903/1 Tartan skirts.. in waist sizes 24–30 in. **1955** M. HALL *Let's make some Undies* (Let's Make It Ser.) 44 (*heading*) Straight placket for *waist slips and knickers. **1976** T. STOPPARD *Dirty Linen* 9 Maddie is.. wearing.. a waist-slip which is also pretty, silk and lace, with a slit. **1882** BESANT *All Sorts* xxi, The Professor was already come to the period of *waist-tightening.

7. Special comb.: **waist-anchor** *Naut.*, an anchor stowed in the waist of a vessel, a sheet-anchor; **waist-board** *Naut.* (see quots.); **waist-boat** *Naut.*, a boat carried in the waist of a ship, *esp.* of a whaling-vessel; hence **waistboater**, the officer in charge of such a boat; **waist-gun**, a gun set in the waist of an aircraft; also **waist-gunner**; **waist-hammer, -iron**, shoemakers' tools (see 6); **waistline**, (*a*) a line outlining or following the contour of the waist; (*b*) a person's waist, esp. with reference to its size; (*c*) = sense 1 c; (*d*) a notional line running round the body of a motor vehicle at the level of the bottom of the window frames; **waist-nettings** *Naut.* (see quots.); **waist-panel** *Carriage-building* (see quot.); **waist-torque** (see quot.). See also WAISTBAND, -CLOTH, -COAT, etc.

1846 A. YOUNG *Naut. Dict.*, **Waist-Anchor*, a spare bower anchor in a ship of war. **1891** H. PATTERSON *Naut. Dict.* 160 Sheet Anchor, the anchor carried in the waist on board men-o'-war. It is the same in weight as the bowers; sometimes called the waist anchor. **1627** CAPT. J. SMITH *Sea Gram.* ii. 9 The *Waist boords are set vp in the Ships waist, betwixt the Gun-waile and the waist trees, but they are most vsed in Boats, set up alongst their sides to keepe the Sea from breaking in. **1725** DE FOE *Voy. round World* (1840) 326 A kind of waste board, about two feet high, built up on the sides, without any calking or pitching, or anything to keep out the water. **1867** SMYTH *Sailor's Word-bk.*, *Waist-boards*, the berthing made to fit into a vessel's gangway on either side. **1891** *Century Dict.*, **Waist-boat*, a boat carried in the waist of a vessel; specifically, in whaling, the second mate's boat, carried in the waist on the port side. *Ibid.*, *Waistboater*, the officer of the boat carried in the waist of a whaler; the second mate. **1942** *Yank* 23 Dec. 4 From his *waist-gun position he interphoned the appearance of two Jap nightfighters off to the right. **1978** J. IRVING *World according to Garp* 16 Technical Sergeant Garp, at his waist gun position. **1942** *Yank* 7 Oct. 3 The *waist gunner sits patiently in the waist of the fuselage. **1978** J. IRVING *World according to Garp* i. 15 Sergeant Garp had experience as.. a waist gunner in the B-17E. **1895** HASLUCK *Boot Making* vi. 89 The waist.. should be treated with a *waist- or cramp-hammer. *Ibid.* viii. 130 The *waist-iron. **1896** *Woman's Life* 15 Feb. 448/1 Your velvet vest should end in a narrow V at the *waist line. **1897** *Westm. Gaz.* 2 Sept. 3/2 The most critical place in the shirt and skirt costume is the waist-line. .. One rule is universal in every well-made French gown —that the waist-line slopes downward to the front. **1928** *Daily Mail* 25 July 8/5 Even if you are one of the fortunate few who need not keep a watchful eye on their waistline, you'll eat Vita-Wheat for pleasure and health. **1930** R. CAMPBELL *Adamastor* 25 Our Drakensberg's most lofty scalps Would scarcely reach the waist-line of the Alps. **1941** *Ann. Reg.* *1940* 254 The Russians.. attacked the 'waist-line' [of Finland] from further north. **1959** *Times* 2 Oct. 9/1 These cars.. have an entirely new top from the waistline upwards. **1970** J. PHILIPS *Nightmare at Dawn* (1971) I. 41, I don't have to worry about my waistline. **1974** *Country Life* 28 Feb. 446/1 This latest Capri.. has a much bigger window area with a lower waistline. **1849** TER REEHORST *Mariner's Friend* 198 *Waistnetting. **1867** SMYTH *Sailor's Word-bk.*, *Waist-nettings*, the hammock-nettings between the quarter-deck and forecastle. **1884** FORNEY *Car-Builder's Dict.* (Cent.), **Waist-panel*, the panel immediately above the lowest panel on the outside of a carriage-body. **1891** *Century Dict.*, **Waist-torque*, a girdle, properly one of twisted or spiral bars, worn by the northern nations in the early middle ages.

waist, obs. form of WASTE.

'waistband. Also 6–7 **wastband, wastebande.** [f. WAIST + BAND *sb.*[2]]

1. Anything in the fashion of a girdle intended to go round the waist.

1584 B. R. tr. *Herodotus* I. 14 Herewith also were offered the chaynes of the Queene his wyfe, not sparing so much her girdles & wastbands, al which he caused to be dedicated at Delphos. **1884** *Pall Mall Gaz.* 6 Feb. 5/2 The.. messages from Gordon.. were.. concealed in a quill thrust into the hair or sewn on the waistband of the natives employed.

2. *esp.* A band fitting about the waist that forms the upper part of a lower garment (skirt, pair of trousers or drawers, or the like) and serves to stiffen or maintain it; sometimes used as a receptacle for money, etc.

1686 PLOT *Staffordsh.* 294 He only took him up by the wastband of his breeches, and hung him upon one of the hooks in the shambles. **1722** DE FOE *Col. Jack* (1840) 134, I pulled it out of the waistband of my drawers. **1859** DICKENS *T. Two Cities* II. v, For the most part reclining with his hands in his waistband, looking at the fire. **1882** 'OUIDA' *In Maremma* I. 43 A labourer that had got his wages in his waistband.

waist-cloth.

†**1.** *Naut. pl.* Coloured cloths hung about the upper works of a ship as an adornment on occasions of ceremony, or on going into action, when they also served to screen the men aboard. *Obs.*

1615 R. COCKS *Diary* (Hakl. Soc.) I. 31 The China Capt. being ready to goe for Goto, I lent hym our boate and wastclothes, and delivered hym back 120 Rs. of 8. **1627** CAPT. J. SMITH *Sea Gram.* xiii. 59 Out goes his flag and pendants, also his waste clothes and top armings, which is a long red cloth.. that goeth round about the ship on the out sides of all her vpper workes fore and aft, [etc.].. as well for the.. grace of the ship, as to couer the men for being seene. **1660** PEPYS *Diary* 16 May, We.. had our guns ready to fire, and our scarlet waist-cloathes out and silk pendants. **1840** HOR. SMITH *O. Cromwell* I. 284 Hundreds of lighters, pinnaces, and longboats, dressed up with waist-cloths and with streamers.

2. *Naut.* A hammock-cloth stowed in the waist of a vessel.

1815 *Falconer's Dict. Marine* (ed. Burney), *Waist-cloths*, coverings of canvas or tarpauling for the hammocks, which are stowed on the gang-ways, between the quarter-deck and fore-castle. **1867** SMYTH *Sailor's Word-bk.*, *Waist-cloths*, the painted canvas coverings of the hammocks which are stowed in the waist-nettings.

3. A loin-cloth that the native inhabitants of hot climates wear round the waist, either hanging down in front or passed between the thighs.

1810 T. WILLIAMSON *E. Ind. Vade Mecum* I. 247 The dress of the *doby* is generally very plain, consisting of a turban, a *dotee*, (or waist-cloth,) and a *chuddar*, (or sheet). **1835** *Court Mag.* VI. 65/2 Sometimes black glazed jackets formed part of their attire; but generally it consisted of nothing more than a blue checquered dotee, or waistcloth. **1882** DE WINDT *Equator* 81 The deceased is then brought up attired in his waistcloth and ornaments.

waistcoat ('weɪs(t)kəʊt; *colloq.* or *vulgar* 'wɛskət). For forms see WAIST and COAT *sb.*; also 6 **wascoat**, 7 **waiscot, wasecoat, -cote, wascoate, -cot, -cote, -cott.** In representations of vulgar pronunciation written **weskit, veskit,** etc.

A garment covering the upper part of the body down to the waist.

1. a. A garment forming part of ordinary male attire, worn under an outer garment (a doublet, later a coat, jacket, or the like), and intended to be partly exposed to view when in wear.

The earliest waistcoats, intended to show through the slashings and other openings of the doublet, were often extremely elaborate and costly. They were sometimes provided with sleeves, and appear to have reached to or below the hips. The waistcoat now has armholes, but not sleeves; it may be made of the same material as the coat, or of different materials, and is sometimes embroidered or otherwise ornamented. The back is now of inferior or thinner material.

1519 *Nottingham Rec.* III. 354 For makyng of a waste cotte. **1599** B. JONSON *Cynthia's Rev.* II. i, Hee has a rich wrought wast-coat to entertaine his visitants in. **1649** *K. Chas'. Sp. Scaffold* 7 The King..being in his Wastcoat, put his Cloak on again. **1666** PEPYS *Diary* 20 June, I have of late taken too much cold by washing my feet and going in a thin silke waistcoate, without any other coate over it, and open-breasted. **1711** SWIFT *Jrnl. to Stella* 28 Nov., Domville saw Savage in Italy, and says he is a coxcomb, and half mad: he goes in red, and with yellow waistcoats. **1791** BOSWELL *Johnson* an. 1781, 1 Apr., Sir Philip Jennings Clerk..wore.. an embroidered waistcoat, and very rich laced ruffles. **1837** DICKENS *Pickw.* x, He was habited in a coarse-striped waistcoat, with black calico sleeves, and blue glass buttons. **1869** 'LEWIS CARROLL' *Phantasmagoria* 71 He would keep his right-hand buried (Like Napoleon) in his waistcoat.

†**b.** Applied to a plainer and less costly garment, usually of knitted wool, worn chiefly for additional warmth. *Obs.*

1585 HIGINS *Junius' Nomencl.* 163/2 *Indusium*,..a waste coate, or wollen peticoate. **1591** FLORIO *2nd Fruites* 5 *T.* Giue me my wastecote. *R.* Which will you haue, that of flannel? *T.* No, giue me that which is knit. **1617** MORYSON *Itin.* I. 68, I hauing for the cold at Dantzke, in the beginning of September, put on a wollen wasecoat, was forced now at the entring of Italy, for the great heat in the end of October, to put off the same. **1698** *Ogilby's Brit., Itin.* 4/1 Doncaster. .. Enjoys a good Trade for Stockings and Knit Wastcoats, &c. **1711** SWIFT *Jrnl. to Stella* 5 Oct., It grows bloody cold, and I have no waistcoat here.

c. phr. † *in one's waistcoat*; *esp.* as the typical undress of exercise implying the casting aside of an upper garment (cf. mod. *in one's shirt-sleeves*) (obs.). ***under one's waistcoat***: in one's breast.

1607 B. BARNES *Divils Charter* IV. v. I 2 b, Enter Astor and Philippo in their wast-cotes with rackets. **1859** H. KINGSLEY *G. Hamlyn* xxxix, With all our vanity and absurdity, we Irish have good warm hearts under our waistcoats.

†**d.** Applied to a child's first garment. *Obs.*

1538 ELYOT *Dict.*, *Crepundia*..the fyrst apparayle of chyldren, as swathels, wastcotes, and such lyke.

e. *transf.* Applied to the plumage of birds, or the coat of animals, about the breast or stomach, *esp.* where this is strikingly different in colour or marking from that of the rest of the body.

1898 J. D. REES in *19th Cent.* June 1024 A woodpecker with black wings, a white waistcoat, and a crimson crest.

†**2.** A short outer coat or jacket; a 'jersey'.

a **1628** F. GREVIL *Life Sidney* (1652) 24 His wast-coat.. not unlike the best sort of those woollen knit ones, which our ordinary watermen row us in. **1765** in *Sixth Rep. Dep. Kpr. Publ. Rec.* App. II. 134 Floats made of cork in the form of seamen's waistcoats..to prevent drowning.

3. A short (woollen) garment worn next the skin.

1606 HOLLAND *Sueton.* 75 In winter time clad he went against the colde with foure coates, together with a good thick gowne, and his Wastcoate or Peticoate bodie of woollen. **1789** W. BUCHAN *Dom. Med.* (1790) 347 A flannel waistcoat worn next the skin has often a very good effect in the dysentery. **1806–7** J. BERESFORD *Miseries Hum. Life* xx. §32 Putting on a cold shirt, for the first time after throwing off the under flannel waistcoat.

4. As an article of feminine attire.

†**a.** A short garment, often elaborate and costly, worn by women about the upper part of the body (usually beneath an outer gown, but so as to be seen). *Obs.*

In the 16th and early 17th c. the waistcoat was one of the normal garments of women, having superseded the *placard* and *stomacher*. Later in the 17th c. (when going out of fashion), *esp.* if worn without an upper gown, it appears to have been considered a mark of a low-class woman of ill-repute (see WAISTCOATEER 1).

1547 BOORDE *Brev. Health* cxxxviii. (1557) 51, I cause a man to lye in his doublet, and a woman in her waste cote. **1603** DEKKER *Batch. Banq.* iii. C 2 b, Then comes downe mistresse Nurse, as fine as a farthing fiddle, in her petticoate and kertle, hauing on a white wastcoate, with a flaunting cambricke ruffe about her neck. **1688** HOLME *Armoury* III. 95/1 Wastcoat or Waistcoat..is an Habit or Garment generally worn by the middle and lower sort of Women. **1711** ADDISON *Spect.* No. 15 ¶4 A Furbelow of precious Stones, an Hat buttoned with a Diamond, a Brocade Waistcoat or Petticoat, are standing Topicks.

†**b.** Applied to garments of foreign women that resembled the contemporary feminine waistcoat. *Obs.*

1600 HAKLUYT *Voy.* III. 369 The [Indian] women weare of the sayd Turquesses at their nostrils and eares, and very good wast-coats and other garments. **1648** GAGE *West. Ind.* xii. 56 Their Wascoats made like bodies, with skirts, laced likewise with gold or silver. **1653** GREAVES *Seraglio* 130 They [the women] likewise sleep as the men do, in their linnen breeches, and quilted waste-coats. **1707** FUNNELL *Dampier's Voy.* ix. 254 [The Malayan women] wear a Linnen Waste-coat, which reaches no lower than the lower part of their Breasts.

†**c.** A short (sleeveless) undergarment worn about the upper part of the body; a camisole. *Obs.*

1580 HOLLYBAND *Treas. Fr. Tong*, *Vne Chemise de drap*, or *chemiselle*, a wastcoat. **1747** LADY M. W. MONTAGU *Town Ecl.*, *St. James's Coffee-house* 75 Her night-cloaths tumbled with resistless grace, And her bright hair play'd careless round her face; Reaching the kettle, made her gown unpin, She wore no waistcoat, and her shift was thin. **1785** MISS FIELDING *Ophelia* I. vii, I [a woman] had never worn any thing round my waist but thin waistcoats.

d. A garment or a bodice-front designed in imitation of the masculine waistcoat.

1711 TICKELL *Spectator* No. 104 ¶3. **1824** SCOTT *Redgauntlet* ch. xvii, Trolloping things our mothers must have looked [in riding dress of the 18th c.], with long square-cut coats,..and with waistcoats plentifully supplied with a length of pocket, which [etc.]. **1883** *Truth* 31 May 768/2 The bodice had a sweet little waistcoat, over which the edges of the embroidered linen almost met. **1913** *Play Pictorial* No. 134 p. ii./1 Waistcoats [for ladies] are growing more and more in popularity, and the waistcoat blouse is one of the latest novelties.

5. *attrib.* and *Comb.*, as ***waistcoat button***, ***-piece***, ***-pocket*** (hence ***-pocketful***), ***-string***.

1787 in *Sixth Rep. Dep. Kpr. Publ. Rec.* App. II. 178 Of a new method of making..Coat and *Waistcoat Buttons. **1859** *Habits of Gd. Society* iii. 142 Elaborate studs, waist-coat-buttons, and wrist-links, are all abominable. **1789** J. WOODFORDE *Diary* 19 Sept. (1927) III. 193 Gave my Servant Man Ben a *Waistcoat Piece. **1832** HT. MARTINEAU *Hill & Valley* i. (ed. 4) 12 There is not a shop within twenty miles that would furnish me with such a waistcoat-piece as I should choose to wear. **1760** JOHNSON *Idler* No. 95 ¶12 He now openly declares his Resolution to become a Gentleman; ..carries Silver, for Readiness, in his *Waistcoat pocket. **1887** RUSKIN *Præterita* II. 153 The portress receiving a sort of dirty flattened sixpence..and returning me a waistcoat-pocketful of the loveliest clean-struck centimes. **1835** DICKENS *Sk. Boz*, *Mr. Watkins Tottle* ii, Watkins falling bump on his knees, and breaking two brace-buttons and a *waistcoat-string in the act.

Hence **'waistcoatful** *nonce-wd.*, as much (of anything) as would fill, or cover, the waistcoat. **'waistcoating**, a textile fabric made esp. for men's waistcoats. **'waistcoatless**, *a.*, wearing no waistcoat.

1824 LANDOR *Imag. Conv.*, *Cav. Puntomichino & Mr. Talcranagh* Wks. 1853 I. 171/2 The people..would have added new decorations to his *waistcoatful of orders. **1809** MAR. EDGEWORTH *Tales Fash. Life* II. *Dun* 315 Mrs. Carver bespoke from him two pieces of *waistcoating. **1862** *Catal. Internat. Exhib.*, *Brit.* II. No. 4071, Fancy waistcoatings and skirtings. *a* **1876** M. COLLINS *Pen Sk.* (1879) I. 10, I sat in his courtyard, coatless and *waistcoatless.

waistcoated ('weɪs(t)kəʊtɪd), *a.* [f. WAISTCOAT + -ED[2].] Provided with a waistcoat.

1798 CHARLOTTE SMITH *Yng. Philos.* I. 27 He..was pantalooned and waistcoated after the very newest fashion. **1897** MARIE CORELLI *Ziska* i, His paunch..a kind of waistcoated air balloon.

b. with defining word prefixed.

1838 DICKENS *O. Twist* ii, As I purpose to show in the sequel whether the white-waistcoated gentleman was right or not. **1896** R. B. MANSFIELD *Chips* 224 Magpies..the black-coated and white-waistcoated gentry.

,waistcoa'teer. Also 7 wastecoateer, -coater, wastcoateer, -coatier, westecoateer, 8 wastecateer, 9 waistcoatteer. [f. WAISTCOAT + -EER[1].]

†**1.** A low-class prostitute. *Obs.* exc. *Hist.*

a **1616** BEAUM. & FL. *Wit without Money* IV. iv, *Luce.* Doe you thinke you are here sir amongst your wastcoateers, your base Wenches that scratch at such occasions? **1675** *Char. Town-Gallant* 3 Every thing with him is an Incentive to Lust, and every Woman Devil enough to tempt him, Covent-Garden, Silk-gowns, and Wapping Wastcoatiers, are equally his Game. **1822** SCOTT *Nigel* xvii, 'I know the face of yonder waistcoateer', continued the guide. **1916** JOYCE *Portrait of Artist* (1969) v. 176 The grave and mocking music of the lutenists or the frank laughter of waistcoateers. **1922** [see FLAT-CAP 2].

2. *nonce-use.* A person wearing a waistcoat of a specified fashion.

1825 T. L. BEDDOES *Let.* 11 Jan. (1894) 49 Here followed a long Brutus & Cassius discourse between a shilling-buttoned waist-coatteer of a porter and myself.

waisted ('weɪstɪd), *a.* [f. WAIST + -ED[2].] Having a waist (usu. of specified size or form). (For parasynthetic formations, as ***deep-***, ***fair-***, ***long-***, ***short-waisted***, see the first element.)

1582 STANYHURST *Æneis* etc. (Arb.) 141 Shee limps in the going,..And as a cow wasted plods on, with an head like a lutecase. **1824** *New Monthly Mag.* XI. 124 Beautiful as youth; Waisted like Hebe; and with Dian's step. **1913** E. T. LEEDS *Archæol. Anglo-Sax. Settlements* vii. 132 A peculiar waisted beaker with rounded base often terminating in an excrescent knob.

waister ('weɪstə(r)). *Naut.* [f. WAIST + -ER[1].] (See quots.)

1815 *Falconer's Dict. Marine* (ed. Burney), *Waisters*, a name given, to the men stationed in the waist in working the ship. **1846** A. YOUNG *Naut. Dict.*, *Waisters*, 'green hands, or broken-down seamen', placed in the waist of a ship of war, to do duty not requiring a knowledge of seamanship. **1850** H. MELVILLE *White Jacket* I. iii. 12 Then, there are the Waisters, always stationed on the gun-deck. These haul aft the fore and main-sheets, besides being subject to ignoble duties; attending to the drainage [etc.]. **1854** J. HANNAY *Sand & Shells* 13 Mr. Crabb relieved his feelings by pegging into an idle 'waister' with his 'colt'.

waistless ('weɪstlɪs), *a.* [f. WAIST + -LESS.] Having no waist; having the appearance of being without a waist.

1500–20 DUNBAR *Poems* xxvi. 97 Full mony a waistless wallydrag With wamiss vnweildable, did furth wag, In creische that did incress. **1796** *Sporting Mag.* VIII. 185 To conform to fashion's sway, Betsey is become waistless. **1870** MISS BROUGHTON *Red as Rose* I. 122 Their little, bustless, waistless, hipless figures. **1910** SUFFLING *Eng. Ch. Brasses* 128 It is a life size figure, habited in a long flowing gown, waistless and without ornament of any kind.

waist-rail.

1. *Naut.* (See quot. 1867.)

1804 DUNCAN *Mariner's Chron.* Pref. p. xix, Drift-rails, fife-rails, sheer-rails, waist-rails, &c. **1867** SMYTH *Sailor's Word-bk.*, *Waist-rail*, the channel-rail or moulding of the ship's side.

2. *Carriage-building.* (See quot.)

1884 FORNEY *Car-builder's Dict.* (Cent.), *Waist-rail*, a horizontal piece in the framing of the side of a passenger-carriage.

waist-tree. *Naut.* (See quot. 1846.)

1485 *Nav. Acc. Hen. VII* (1896) 50 Wast trees..ij. **1627** CAPT. J. SMITH *Sea Gram.* ii. 9 The Waist boords are set vp in the Ships waist, betwixt the Gun-waile and the waist trees. **1704** J. HARRIS *Lex. Techn.* I, *Wast-Trees*, are those Timbers of a Ship which lie in the Waste. **1846** A. YOUNG *Naut. Dict.*, *Waist-Tree* or *Rough-Tree*, a spare spar placed along the side of a ship's waist where there happens to be no bulwark, in order to protect persons from falling overboard.

wait (weɪt), *sb.* Forms: 3–7 wayte, waite, (5 wayet, whayte), 4–7 wayt, 4, 7 weyte, (6 weytte, wette), 5–6 wate, (5 watte), 6 waytte (waitte, wayght, weyght, wyethe, whet), 7 waight, (weight), 4– wait. [Partly a. ONF. **wait*, *wet* masc. (= OF. *guait*, *gait*, *guet*, mod.F. *guet*, Pr. *gach*, *gait*), vbl. noun f. *waitier* (see WAIT *v.*) and ONF. *waite* fem. (OF. *guaite*, *gaite*, mod.F. *guette*, *guète*, Pr. *gacha*, *gaita*); it is uncertain whether the fem. sb. is f. the vb., or a direct adoption from Teut. (cf. OHG. *wahta*, Goth. *wahtwō*): see WAIT *v.* The word adopted from Fr. has coalesced with an Eng. formation on WAIT *v.* Cf. AWAIT *sb.*

Many apparent examples of this word in texts of 14–16th c. really belong to the synonymous AWAIT *sb.*, which, like other words beginning with a prefix, was often written as two words. It is possible that the *a* was in the 16th c. sometimes apprehended by writers and readers as the indefinite article, but distinct evidence of this is wanting.]

I. The action of WAIT *v.*[1]

1. In various phrases with the general sense: To take up a concealed position in order to make an unforeseen attack, or to be in readiness to intercept one's enemy or intended prey in passing; to lurk in ambush.

†**a.** ***to sit in wait(s.*** *Obs. rare.* (cf. AWAIT *sb.*)

a **1300** *E.E. Psalter* ix. 29 He sites in waites [Vulg. *in insidiis*] with riche of land In derne, to sla þe vnderand. **1667** MILTON *P.L.* IV. 825 Why satst thou like an enemie in waite Here watching at the head of these that sleep?

b. ***to lie*** (or †***lay***) ***in wait.*** †Also, ***to lie at*** (***the***) ***wait***, ***to lie on wait.***

c **1440** *Pallad. on Husb.* IV. 157 For moldywarpes cattes is to kepe To ligge in wayte to touche hem with her cle. *c* **1449** PECOCK *Repr.* I. xix. 113 As if perauenture in oon of thilk weies a man liggith in wait for to sle my seid seruaunt. **1450–1530** *Myrr. our Ladye* 311 The faythful saynge of the crede chaseth away fendes whiche lye on wayte to hynder men. **1503–4** *Act 19 Hen. VII*, c. 36 Preamb., Stanhop..lay in wayte uppon the seid sir William and hym grevously wouneded. **1530** PALSGR. 605/2, I ley in wayte of one to do him a displeasure. *a* **1578** LINDESAY (Pitscottie) *Chron. Scot.* (S.T.S.) I. 31 Or evir he cuild persawe the chancellaris folkis lyand in the wait for him he was invironit and circuatt round about with thame. **1611** BIBLE *Ps.* x. 9 He lieth in waite secretly as a lyon on his denne, he lieth in wait to catch the poore. **1668** H. ROLLE *Abridgm.*, *Action sur Case* 50 Si home dit dun auter, que il lay in wait at shooters hill to rob him, action sur le case gist. *a* **1672** WOOD *Life* Sept. (O.H.S.) I. 123 Some of their partie were upon London road neare Thame to lay in wait for provision or wine that came from London towards Aylesbury. **1709** STEELE *Tatler* No. 34 ¶5 The five Fields where the Robbers lie in wait. **1794** MRS. RADCLIFFE *Myst. Udolpho* xxviii, His friend advised that they should lie in wait for the enemy. **1879** *Cassell's Techn. Educ.* IV. 95/2 Full of rage, he lay in wait for Rosen, and as the latter left the Senate, he rushed upon his sword in hand. **1904** LADY M. VERNEY *Verney Mem.* II. 341 Lying in wait for dowagers' coaches in tortuous lanes.

fig. **1500–20** DUNBAR *Poems* xxi. 34 May no man lang in welth indure, For wo that evir lyis at the wait. **1553** GRESHAM in Burgon *Life* (1839) I. 118 To the intent to prevent the marchaunts, bothe strangers and Englishe, who allwayes lay in wayte to prevent my devisses. *a* **1613** OVERBURY *Characters*, *Meere Fellow* Wks. (1856) 129 His religion lies in wait for the inclination of his patron. **1704** SWIFT *T. Tub* ii, A ring of disciples, who lie in wait to catch up their droppings. **1784** COWPER *Task* III. 553 Ten thousand dangers lie in wait to thwart The process. **1785** T. BALGUY *Disc.* 47 He is constantly lying at wait to correct them. **1791** CHARLOTTE SMITH *Celestina* III. 212 He..had indeed no other design than to lay in wait for traces of that involved mystery. **1865** DICKENS *Mut. Fr.* II. i, The habit.. had given him a suspicious manner, or a manner that would be better described as one of lying in wait.

†**c.** ***to lie wait.*** *Obs. rare.*

1445 in *Anglia* XXVIII. 269 Ambicion..which evir lyeth waite at chambir dorys. *a* **1578** LINDESAY (Pitscottie) *Chron. Scot.* (S.T.S.) I. 55 Thair followit na thing bot slaughter.., ilk ane lyand wait for wther as they had ben settand tinchellis for the murther of wyld beistes.

d. ***to lay wait***, † ***lay one's wait.***

1577 HANMER *Anc. Eccl. Hist.*, *Euseb.* X. viii. 206 But God being the friend..of Constantinus brought to light the wayte layde for him in secret. **1586** THYNNE *Contn. Ann. Scot.* 457/1 in *Holinshed*, But, hauing wait laid for him by an ambush of his enimies, he was in his iorneie towards his castell intercepted. **1597** BEARD *Theatre God's Judgem.* (1612) 333 Wherefore they layed wait for him as hee came one day from hunting, and murdered him. **1653** J. MAYER *Expos. Ps.* xxxi. 4 When wait was layd for him to kill him in his house. **1665** MANLEY *Grotius' Low-C. Wars* 169 Although they could escape all the wait laid for them by

Pirates. **1841** James *Brigand* iii, They were known to lay wait in all the principal passes, both of Piedmont and Savoy. *transf.* and *fig.* **1535** Coverdale *Acts* xx. 19, I haue.. serued ye Lorde.. with many teares and tentacions, which happened vnto me by ye layenges of wayte of the Iewes. **1599** T. Storer *Life & D. Wolsey* G 2b, Those vnbaptised sacrilegious hands, That onely for Gods vestrie laide their waite. **1611** Bible *Jer.* ix. 8 One speaketh peaceably to his neighbour with his mouth, but in heart he layeth his waite. **1755** *Monitor* I. 27 Can a free constitution be out of danger, where one part of it lays wait to destroy the energy of another? **1799** E. Du Bois *Piece Family Biog.* II. 42 By laying wait for a favourable moment, she might ultimately obtain the enjoyment of her criminal passion. **1891** *Sat. Rev.* 14 Nov. 563/2 Their.. followers laid perpetual wait to steal.

†**e.** ***to take under wait***: to capture or surprise by an ambush. *Obs.*

1533 Bellenden *Livy* (S.T.S.) I. 180 Þai war na less astonist þan þai had bene tane vnder wait [*haud secus quam si in insidias incidissent*].

†**f.** The sb. used without the phrasal context: Ambush. *Obs. rare.*

1533 Bellenden *Livy* (S.T.S.) I. 149 Als sone as hermyneus herde the noyis of Valerius cumpany, he Ischit with his buschement haistely fra þe wate [*concurrit ex insidiis*]. **1788** Burns *Written in Friars-Carse Hermitage* 20 Check thy climbing step, elate, Evils lurk in felon wait. **1796** Mme. D'Arblay *Camilla* IV. 375 He was.. always in wait to converse with her when she was seated.

†**2.** The action of watching. *Obs.*

a. In phrases. ***at (the) wait***, on the watch. ***to do, make wait***, to keep watch. ***to have in wait***, to have under observation. Also, ***to lie in great wait, lay good wait*** (cf. 1), to be carefully on the watch.

c **1440** *Partenope* 6745 (B. M. MS.) His ffrendes had hym so in watte.. That his purpose myght not be Atte Bleys parfouremed. *c* **1460** in *Archæologia* XXIX. 339 Þe Fisshe drewe nere vnto þe bayte; Nede haþe no lawe,.. þe Egle þerto euer layde goode wayte. *c* **1470** Henry *Wallace* x. 379 A suttell knycht tharat had gret despyt, Folowyt at wait. **1500–20** Dunbar *Poems* xlii. 21 And in thir termis can thai say, Do wait, and lat him nocht away. **1509** Fisher *Funeral Serm. C'tess Richmond* Wks. (1876) 293 Her sobre temperaunce.. wherin she lay in as grete wayte of herself as ony persone myght. **1513** Douglas *Æneis* xi. xiv. 83 Quhen as ane Aruns, by hys mortal fait Onto myschewos deid predestinate, Circulis at the wayt. *c* **1520** *Everyman* (facs.) Bj, I haue a great enemy that hath me in wayte Whiche intendeth me for to hyndre. **1523** Berners *Froiss.* I. ccxli. 144/2 The moost parte of the state of the prince.. was well knowen with the kynges there about.. for they layed great wayte to knowe it. **1535** Hen. VIII in Strype *Eccl. Mem.* 1721 I. App. liv. 141 That they.. do make & cause to be made diligent search, wait & espyal, whether the said Bps. & Clergy do.. execute.. their said charge.

b. Watchfulness.

1575 Laneham *Let.* (1871) 18 It waz a sport very pleazaunt.. to see.. the nimblness and wayt of the dog too take hiz auauntage.

3. a. ***(day's) wait***: the duty of keeping guard by day performed by the warders of the Tower.

1694 E. Chamberlayne *Pres. St. Eng.* iii. 608 The Yeoman Warders of the Tower are 40 in number... Ten of them are usually upon the Days-wait. **1738–47** in Pegge *Curialia* iii. (1791) 103 When the Man waiting for another hath performed such Wait, he shall not be permitted to wait again, so as to continue his Wait for divers Men one after another.

b. The period of attendance at court of a lord- or lady-in-waiting.

1884 *World* 20 Aug. 10/1 The Queen always likes the yearly rota of waits to be arranged so that her favourite ladies shall be with her at Balmoral. **1893** *Westm. Gaz.* 7 July 1/2 He will have no duties.. as his appointed 'wait' is from October 3 to 17, when the Queen will be at Balmoral, where the attendance of a Lord-in-Waiting is always dispensed with.

4. The state or condition of waiting or remaining expectant. ***at wait***: in an expectant attitude. ***in wait***: waiting, remaining in a place in expectation of some one coming. *rare.*

1873 Longf. *Wayside Inn* iii. *Mother's Ghost* xviii, When she came to the castle gate, There stood her eldest daughter in wait. **1875** Swinburne *Ess. & Stud.* 344 Next to this we find a sudden sunny bank in the dim depth of a wood, with a wolf at watch and a rabbit at wait.

5. A period of waiting; spec. *Theatr.*, the time of an audience's waiting between the acts, or of an actor's waiting between his appearances in the piece.

1855–6 Dickens in Forster *Life* (1874) III. v. 107 The waits between the acts being very much longer than the acts themselves. **1863** Le Fanu *House by Churchyard* III. ix. 93 This was said after a wait of nearly ten minutes. **1876** *Daily News* 27 Oct. 5/6 What a long, tedious wait it was up there on the edge of the wood while we listened.. for some sign of Graf Keller's approach. **1884** *Manch. Exam.* 16 Oct. 5/4 The audience.. passed a long wait pleasantly in singing a number of political songs. **1886** C. E. Pascoe *London To-day* iii. (ed. 3) 50 The Criterion has a chorus of glee singers to wile away waits through the courses.

II. A person who watches or waits.

†**6.** A watchman; a scout, spy. *Obs.*

a. A military watchman, sentinel, or look-out; also a scout, spy; esp. a watchman in a camp, castle, or fortified place who was furnished with a horn or trumpet to sound an alarm or to make a signal.

a **1300** *Cursor M.* 11541 He [Herod] sett his waites bi þe stret, If þai moght wit þaa kinges mett, He commandid son þai suld be slan. **13..** *K. Alis.* 4312 Theo knyghtis heore body dubbeth; The wayte bleow, the belle ryngeth. *c* **1325** *Coer de L.* 2281 The wayts of that host that did espie, And ful loud began to crie: We are betrayd and y-nome! **1340** *Ayenb.* 121 Þet is þe wayte of þe castele þet neure ne slepþ. *c* **1380** Wyclif *Wks.* (1880) 395 Þe holy prophete Ezechiel saiþ: 'If þe wayte or þe wacche-man se ennemys cum [etc.].' **1387** Trevisa *Higden* (Rolls) II. 191 A knyghte þat highte Strabo stode in a weytes place. **1398** —— *Barth. De P.R.* v. v. (1495) 108 And for the eye is in stede of a wayte, kynde settyth hym in the hyghest place of the body. *c* **1400** *Laud Troy Bk.* 7222 Euery man to his In owe, The wayte be-gan nyght to blowe. *c* **1435** *Torr. Portugal* 1065 Waytes on the walle gan blowe, Knyghtis assemled on a rowe. *c* **1440** *Promp. Parv.* 513/2 Wayte, *speculator* (v.r. *explorator*). **1450–80** tr. *Secreta Secret.* lxi. 37 Loke thou haue good waytes and aspies in thyn oste. **1470–85** Malory *Arthur* vii. xxxi. 263 At the last by fortune he came to a Castel and there he herd the waytes vpon the wallys. **1513** Douglas *Æneis* iii. iv. 60 Mysenus, the wait, on the hie garret seyis, And, with his trumpet, thame a takin maid.

transf. **1398** Trevisa *Barth. De P.R.* xvii. clxxx. (1495) 721 A vynyerde is ofte vysyted and ouerseen of the erthe tylthers and kepers of vynes and a wayte is there set in an hyghe place.

b. A watchman attached to the royal household who sounded the watch, etc., by the blowing of a pipe, trumpet, or other wind-instrument.

13.. *K. Alis.* 7769 When theo table was y-drawe, Theo wayte gan a pipe blawe. *c* **1430** *Pilgr. Lyf Manhode* iv. xlvii. (1869) 198 The ladi that thou hast herd pleye with instrumentes and bereth an horn that is the waite that awaketh the king alle times that he slepeth bi hire blowinge. *a* **1440** *Sir Eglam.* 1097 Grete lordys were at the assent; Waytys blewe, to mete they wente. *a* **1483** *Liber Niger* in *Househ. Ord.* (1790) 48 A Wayte, that nyghtly, from Mighelmasse till Shere-Thursday, pipeth the watche within this courte fower tymes,.. and he to make bon gayte, and [? *read* at] everey chambre door and office, as well for fyre as for other pikers or perelles... And under this yoman, a groome wayte. **1802** Mrs. Radcliffe *Gaston de Blondeville* (1826) I. 185 And thus it kept, until the wayte piped his second watch in all the courts.

c. A municipal watchman.

1418 *Maldon* (Essex) *Court-Rolls* Bundle 11, no. 3, [Ordered, by consent] ballivorum et magnatum ville, in defectu ministrorum alias dictorum waytes, quod quedam campana ecclesie Omnium Sanctorum et alia campana ecclesie Sancti Petri congruis horis noctis pulsentur, viz., in mane Daybell, et in vespere Curfewe. **1419** *Liber Albus* (Rolls) 646 Quod quælibet Porta custodiatur per diem per duos homines bene armatos, et de nocte claudetur per Servientem eam inhabitantem; et quod quilibet Serviens habeat unum Wayte, sumptibus suis propriis.

†**7.** *collect.* A body of guards. *Obs.*

1704 in Pegge *Curialia* iii. (1791) 81 Which Twelve Men [of the Guard] are to be chosen by the Six Waits then out of Waiting. **1747** *Ibid.* 104 Upon Forfeiture of his or their share of such Bounty-Money among the rest of the Wait then and there in waiting.

8. †**a.** *pl.* A small body of wind instrumentalists maintained by a city or town at the public charge. Also *sing.*, a member of this body. *Obs.*

They played for the daily diversion of the councillors, on ceremonial and festive occasions, and as a town or city band they entertained the citizens, perambulating the streets, often by night or in the early morning.

1298 [see *waitmeat*]. **1438** in *Cov. Leet Bk.* 189 Hyt is ordeyned that they [*sic*] Trumpet schall haue the rule off the whaytes, and off hem be Cheffe. **1467** *Ibid.* 335 Also þat þe Waytis of þis Cite.. shall not passe þis Cite, but to abbottis & priours within x miles of þis Cite. **1499** in W. Kelly *Notices illustr. Drama* (1865) 189 Thomas Wylkyns Wayte. **1541** *Ibid.* 192 Item paed to Thomas Goldsmyth ffor mendyng of the Towne Waytes Collars iij^{s}. iiij^{d}. **1548** *Ibid.* 193 Item p^{d} to Mr. Gyllott for the Waughts gownes xxxvj^{s} vj^{d}. **1553** Machyn *Diary* (Camden) 47 [The new Lord Mayor went] toward Westmynter [attended by the] craftes of London.. with trumpettes blohyng and the whets playing. **1571** in Picton *L'pool Munic. Rec.* (1883) I. 118 Lewis Lockwood, Bag-piper was admitted Wayte of this town. **1587** Fleming *Contn. Holinshed* III. 289/2 The waits of the citie were placed with lowd musicke, who cheerefullie & melodiouslie welcomed hir maiestie into the citie, this song being soong by the best voices in the same. **1589** [? Nashe] *Almond for Parrat* 2 Who hearing the waites play vnder his window very early, insulted.. that [etc.]. *a* **1596** *Sir T. More* (Malone Soc.) 944 Where are the waytes? goe, bid them play, to spend the time awhile. **1609** B. Jonson *Silent Wom.* i. i, *Trv.* A Trumpet should fright him terribly, or the Hau'-boyes? *Cle.* Out of his senses. The Waights of the citie haue a pension of him, not to come neere that ward. **1617** Moryson *Itin.* iv. iv. i. (1903) 301 In like sorte many Cittyes mantayne at publike charge Musitians, vsing Sagbutts, Hoboyes, and such loude Instruments, which wee call the waytes of Cyttyes, and these play at the publicke house of the Citty each day at Noone, when the Senatours goe to dinner, and at all publike Feasts. *a* **1625** Fletcher *Captain* ii. ii, *Jac.* Hark, are the Waits abroad? *Fab.* Be softer prethee, 'Tis private musick.. *Jac.* Well I will hear, or sleep, I care not whether. **1667** *Lond. Gaz.* No. 189/1 The Mayor, Aldermen and Common Council of this Town, after a Sermon Preached to them, went to the Market-Cross in their Formalities, the Waytes playing before them. **1670** *Moral State Eng.* 132 The Weights of the Town who played upon Cornets and Haut-bois. **1687** Wood *Life* 3 Sept. (O.H.S.) III. 230 When he came to Quartervois he was entertaind with the wind musick or waits belonging to the city and Universitie. **1731** Fielding *Letter Writers* ii. ii, You are a couple of wretched Scrapers, and play ten Degrees worse than the University Waits. **1736** F. Drake *Eboracum* i. vi. 197 [The sheriffs] are preceeded by the city's waites, or musicians, in their scarlet liveries and silver badges playing all the way through the streets. **1762** Goldsm. *Nash* (Globe) 524/1 Upon a stranger's arrival at Bath he is welcomed by.. the voice and music of the city waits. **1764** in Picton *L'pool Munic. Rec.* (1886) II. 202 Ordered that John Bolton and John Langhorn be appointed two publick Waites of this town.

b. *pl.* A band of musicians and singers who perambulate the streets by night at the approach of Christmas and the New Year playing and singing carols and other seasonable music for gratuities.

1773 *Archæologia* II. 66 What we at present call the Waits, or the music on the nights of the Christmas holydays. **1801** Busby *Dict. Mus.* s.v. *Wayghtes*, Those persons who annually, at the approach of Christmas, salute us with their nocturnal concerts, were, and are to this day, called *Wayghtes.* **1820** Irving *Sketch Bk.* II. 37 The sound of the Waits,.. breaks upon the mid-watches of a winter night. **1889** *Grove's Dict. Mus.* IV. 375 *Waits, The.* A name given, from time immemorial, to the little bands of rustic Musicians who sing and play Carols, by night, in country places, at Christmas-time.

†**c.** *gen.* A player on the flute, hautboy, trumpet, etc. *Obs.*

1510 Stanbridge *Vocabula* (W. de W.) Div, *Tibicen*, a wayte. **1585** Higins *Junius' Nomencl.* 501/1 *Spondiales vel spondiauli*,.. such as plaied vpon long pipes at diuine seruice, they may be called the waytes. **1600** Holland *Livy* xvii. Brev. 390 That.. as he returned home to his owne house, the waits should sound the hautboies all the way [*tibicine canente*]. **1648** Gage *West Ind.* 12 Whom travelling, Indian Waites and Trumpets should accompany.

†**9.** One who waits in service, an attendant. *Obs.*

1652 Benlowes *Theoph.* xi. xxx, Still to have toting Waits unseel thine Eyes, In Bed, at Board, when sit, when rise: Such, Card'nal-like, their Paris prize 'bove Paradise.

†**III. 10.** [Originally a transferred use of 8 c.] *pl.* Wind instruments, either hautboys, shawms, or flutes. Also *sing.* (rare). *Obs.*

[Cf. Sp., Pg. *gaita*, a kind of oboe; the word seems to have been adopted from OF., though no examples of the sense have been found in French of any period.]

1530 Palsgr. 286/1 Wayte an instrument, *hauboys.* **1556** Withals *Dict.* (1562) 68/2 The trumpet or waytes, *tuba.* **1592** *Doctor Faustus* in Thoms *E. Eng. Prose Rom.* (1858) III. 178 Lutes, viols, citterns waits.. and all manner of other instruments. **1620** Shelton *2nd Pt. Quixote* xxvi. 173 For amongst Moores you haue.. a kinde of Shaulmes that bee like our Waytes. [**1703** Motteux, like our Waits or Hautboys.] **1636** C. Butler *Princ. Mus.* ii. i. 93 [Wind-instruments, as] Waits or Hobois. **1683** Tryon *Way to Health* 654 Waits are under the dominion of Jupiter, in the Sign Libra; the Sounds and harmonious Consorts of this Instrument are great, noble and pleasing to Nature.

IV. 11. *attrib.* and *Comb.*, as ***wait-pipe, player, -song***; † **wait captain**, the chief of the municipal waits; † **wait fee** (see quot. 1706); † **wait-layer**, one who lies in wait; † **waitmeat**, food supplied to the municipal waits.

1565 in Picton *L'pool Munic. Rec.* (1888) II. 35 Mr. Mayor called James Atherby then being *Waite Captain. **1563** in Spelman *Gloss.* s.v., Per redditum 14*s.* pro *Wayte fee, and Castle garde. **1706** Phillips (ed. Kersey), *Wayt-fee*, (old Law-word) Ward-penny, or a Fee anciently paid for keeping Watch and Ward. **1600** Holland *Livy* xl. xii. 1067 He.. will.. have the world beleeve that I play the part not onely of a secret and cunning *wait-laier, but of an open theefe. **1632** —— *Cyrupædia* 30 Who ever shall effect this, had need be a waitlayer, a deepe dissembler. **1298** *Yorks. Inquisit.* (Yorks. Rec. Soc. 1902) III. 84, 2*s.* for *Waytemete and Schirrefstuthe. **14..** *Nom.* in Wr.-Wülcker 694/40 *Hec colomaula*,.. *waytepype. **1610** in T. Sharp *Cov. Myst.* (1825) 210 Every Maior shall pay to the *waite players iiij d. **1872** Whittier *Penn. Pilgrim* 501 On frosty Christmas eves.. he.. closed his eyes, and listened to the sweet Old *wait-songs sounding down his native street.

wait (weɪt), *v.*[1] Pa. t. and pa. pple. **waited.** Forms: 2–7 **waite**, 3–8 **wayte**, 4–7 **wayt**, (4 *erron.* **whaite, whayte**), 3–4, 6 *Sc.* **waitte**, 4–6 *Sc.* **vaitte**, 5 **waytte**, 6–7 **waight**, 4–6 *Sc.* **watte**, 8 *dial.* **watt**, 3–4 **weite**, 4–6 **weyte**, 7 **weight**, 3–6, 8 *dial.* **wate**, 4 **vate**, 4– **wait.** [Early ME. *waite-n*, a. ONF. *waitier* (Central OF. *guaitier, gaiter*, mod.F. *guetter*) = Prov. *gaitar*, It. *guatare*, to watch, lie in wait for; a. OHG. *wahtên* (mod.G. *wachten*) to watch, guard, f. *wahta* fem. (mod.G. *wacht*) watch, f. OTeut. **wak-*: see wake *v.*]

I. The simple verb.

†**1. a.** *trans.* To watch with hostile intent; to spy upon; to lie in wait for. *Obs.*

c **1200** *Vices & Virtues* 103 Ðat bið ðo werewede gostes ðe waitið ðo soules hier buuen on ðe wolkne. *c* **1200** *Trin. Coll. Hom.* 43 For ure gult god man bicom and ure eldre waiteden him to deaðe. *Ibid.* 87 Þanne ferde þe fule gost, and seuene oðre gostes mid him forcuðere þen him self were, and bitrumede þat child, and waiteden hit on eche wise. *a* **1300** *Cursor M.* 23731 Euer he wates vs þat fede, es nathing certainur þan dede. *c* **1300** *Havelok* 512 He may [me] waiten for to slo. **1340** Hampole *Pr. C.* 1186 His despisers he waytes ay, Als shadow to tak to his pray. *c* **1375** *Sc. Leg. Saints* ii. (*Peter*) 22 In Jerusalem he wes bofte, spyit, waitit, and bundyn ofte. *c* **1420** Wyntoun *Cron.* v. xi. 3062 (MS. Cott.) Ane erl of his companny Waytit Traen sa besely þat wiþe a buschement he has [slayn] Traen. *a* **1450** *Le Morte Arth.* 74 Sir agravayne at home is he, nyght & day he waytes vs two. **1530** Palsgr. 770/2, I wayte, I lye awayte for one to hurte hym, or to spye what he dothe. *Je guette.* I wyll wayte him here tyll to morowe but I wyll have him. **1596** Dalrymple tr. *Leslie's Hist. Scot.* (S.T.S.) II. 22 He thairfor appoynted certan cutthrots to wayt thame as fra the Banquet thay return. **1597** J. Melvill *Autob. & Diary* (Wodrow Soc.) 421 They steir upe and incitats four deboshit young limmers, and wattes.. James Smithe, as he was coming ham at night from the cost syde.

†**b.** *intr.* To keep hostile watch; to lie in wait. *Obs.*

a **1225** *Ancr. R.* 196 Iðe wildernesse heo aspieden [*MS. C.* in þe wildene weiteden] us to slean. *a* **1300** *E.E. Psalter* ix. 30 He waites [Vulg. *insidiatur*] in hidel als lioun in den. *a* **1300** *Cursor M.* 899 Þou sal waite womman for to sting, And sco sal yiet þi hede þring. **1362** LANGL. *P. Pl.* A. VII. 149 To kepen him..From wastors þat wayten winners to schende. ?**1404-8** *Wyt & Wille* 30 in *26 Pol. Poems* 23 Echon wayte oþer for to kille. **1535** COVERDALE *Obad.* i. 14 Nether shalt thou stonde waytinge enymore at yᵉ corners of the stretes, to murthur soch as are fled. **1573-80** TUSSER *Husb.* (1878) 125 Lay pease vpon stacke,..And couer it straight, from doues that waight.

†**2.** *trans.* To be on the watch to inflict (injury): = AWAIT *v.* 2. *Obs.*

The sense is app. due to the confusion of this vb. with WAIT *v.*²

c **1400** *Destr. Troy* 13012 Noght warre of the weghes, þat waited his harme, [He] past furth thurgh the pase with his proude knightes.

†**3. a.** To watch, keep one's eye upon, observe constantly; to look out for, watch for. *Obs.*

a **1300** *Cursor M.* 13285 At see sant Iohn and Iam he fand, Quils þai þair lines war waitand. *c* **1300** *Havelok* 1754 And bad him..Hauelok wel yemen..And wel do wayten al þe nith. **13..** *E.E. Allit. P.* B. 99 Fechez mo gestez, Waytez gorstez & greuez, if ani gomez lyggez,..fechez hem hider. *c* **1386** CHAUCER *Sqr.'s T.* 121 He wayted many a constellacion Er he had doon this operacion. *c* **1400** *Destr. Troy* 2888 Wemen waited hym well, hade wondur of hym one, That of shap for to shew was shene to beholde. *c* **1400** *Rule St. Benet* 863 And when so we ȝern ony thing þat may fall vnto flesch likyng, Thinke we god waites vs weterly. *c* **1450** *St. Cuthbert* (Surtees) 1698 Whethir þou wayted our nyght wayes? *Ibid.* 3761 A monk to wayte þis taken stode.

†**b.** To watch mentally, observe, consider attentively. *Obs.*

1382 WYCLIF *Phil.* iii. 17 Britheren,..wayte ȝe [Vulg. *observate*] hem that walken so as ȝe han oure foorme. **1399** LANGL. *Rich. Redeles* Prol. 45 Ther nys no gouernour on þe grounde ne sholde gye him þe better..ȝif he waite well þe wordis, and so werche þerafter. *c* **1430** *God's Complaint* 57 in *Pol. Rel. & L. Poems* (1866) 165 Waite what y dide to marie maudeleyne, And what y seide to thomas of ynde.

†**c.** To watch over, take charge of, care for (a person's interests). *Obs.*

13.. *Cursor M.* 5416 (Gött.) Þus coude ihoseph, i said ȝou, waite his lauerd þe kinges prou. **1362** LANGL. *P. Pl.* A. VI. 37, I haue ben his felawe þis fiftene wynter..With-Innen and withouten I-wayted his profyt. ?*a* **1400** *Morte Arth.* 164 If thou my wyrchipe wayte..Thou salle haue gersoms fulle grett. *c* **1400** *Rule St. Benet* 2471 Þeir awn winyng þai sal not wayt, þat oþer win þai sal couayt.

†**d.** To search for. *Obs.*

1340-70 *Alisaunder* 808 Hee wendes too a wildernes & waites him erbes. *c* **1400** *Beryn* 424 Þe Pardonere, þat drewe apart, & weytid hym a trest ffor to hyde hym selff.

†**4. a.** *intr.* To keep watch; to look intently. Also with adv. or phrase, ***to wait about, about one, on every side***, etc. *Obs.*

1338 R. BRUNNE *Chron.* (1725) 120 Hir frendes fulle fast waited aboute & woke, & Mald at þe last kyng Steuen scho toke. **13..** *Gaw. & Gr. Knt.* 2163 Þenne he wayted hym aboute. **13..** *E.E. Allit. P.* B. 1423 He waytez onwyde, his wenches he byholdes. **1362** LANGL. *P. Pl.* A. VIII. 128 And þorw heore wordes I awok and waitide [*MS. V.* lokede] aboute, And sauh [etc.]. **1377** *Ibid.* B. XIII. 343, I wayted wisloker, and thanne was it soiled With lykyng of lecherye, as by lokyng of his eye. *c* **1400** *Destr. Troy* 876 He waites vmbe hym wightly, & was ware sone Of þe orible oxin. *c* **1400** *Ywaine & Gaw.* 1815 Sho..waited obout fer and ner. *a* **1400-50** *Wars Alex.* 1585 And as he waytis in a wra, þan was he ware sone Of þe maister of þat meneyhe. **1470-85** MALORY *Arthur* VI. xvi. 209 Ther with he wayted aboue hym and vnder hym, and ouer his hede he sawe a rownsepyk. *c* **1480** HENRYSON *Fox & Wolf* 150 On euerilk syde full warlie couth he wait. *a* **1500** *Flower & Leaf* 106 Wherfore about I waited busily On every syde, if I her mighte see.

†**b.** To act as a watchman. *Obs.*

1436 *Siege of Calais* in *Polit. Poems* (Rolls) II. 153 The porters kept the gattes full manly,..To wate they wer not irk. *c* **1470** HARDING *Chron.* CXXXVIII. xii, To castell Pilgrym ..there was no waye but one full straite, On a cawsey.. Strongly walled, with towres on to wayte. **1591** SHAKS. *1 Hen. VI*, I. iii. 3, I am come to suruey the Tower this day; ..Where be these Warders, that they wait not here? **1605** VERSTEGAN *Dec. Intell.* x. (1628) 327 Wee call him that waiteth at the Towre one of the ward, or a warder.

†**c.** To observe carefully. *Obs.*

1399 LANGL. *Rich. Redeles* III. 128 Ȝit swiche ffresshe ffoodis beth..ffor her dignesse endauntid of dullisshe nollis, And, if þou well waite, of no wight ellis.

†**d.** With indirect question: To watch, observe carefully *what, when, how*, etc. *Obs.*

c **1275** LAY. 23077 Þis ileueþ Bruttus þat he wole come þus and lokeþ and waiteþ wane he come to londe. *c* **1290** *S. Eng. Leg.* 268 Euere he waytede, ȝif ore louerd ani grace him wolde sende. *c* **1330** R. BRUNNE *Chron. Wace* (Rolls) 1495 He sente knyghtes & squiers To waite who made on hym pres. *c* **1350** *Will. Palerne* 1821, I wol..waite ȝif any weiȝh comes wending alone. *c* **1391** CHAUCER *Astrol.* II. §25 Now yif so be þat the semith to long a tarienge.., thanne whaite whan the sonne is in any other degree of the zodiak. *c* **1470** HENRY *Wallace* v. 902 A suerd he drew, rych manlik him to wer, Ay wayttand fast gyff he can get a sper. **1598** R. BERNARD tr. *Terence* (1607) *Andria* I. i, *Observes illum quid agat: quid captet consilii.* Watch him what hee doth, wait what he intendeth.

†**e.** To take precautions, be watchful or cautious. In imperative: Take care, see to it that.

13.. *E.E. Allit. P.* B. 292, I schal wayte to be war her wrenchez to kepe. *c* **1386** CHAUCER *Prol.* 571 Algate he wayted so in his achat That he was ay biforn and in good stat. *c* **1460** J. RUSSELL *Bk. Nurture* 436 in *Babees Bk.*, Euer of a sharpe knyff wayte þat ye be sure. **1470-85** MALORY *Arthur* I. ii. 37 But wayte ye make not many questions with her nor her men, but saye ye are diseased, and soo hye yow to bedde. **1522** *World & Child* (facs.) A iv, Wayte well that thou suffre no shame.

5. a. *trans.* To look forward (esp. with desire or apprehension) to (some future event or contingency); to continue in expectation of. Now somewhat *rare*: usually superseded by AWAIT *v.*

a **1400** *Minor Poems fr. Vernon MS.* 527/80 Ȝif þou waxe pore he wol skorne þe—Wayte of him neuere oþer bounte. *c* **1400** *Destr. Troy* 3322, I wot, sir, witterly, will I or noght, Your wille I moste wirke, waite I non other. *c* **1586** C'TESS PEMBROKE *Ps.* LXIX. i, Waiting aid, with ernest eying. **1634** MASSINGER *Very Wom.* IV. i, *Ped.* I thank ye, And soon I'll wait your promise. **1671-2** SIR C. LYTTELTON in *Hatton Corr.* (Camden) 75 Wee waite much wʰᵗ yᵉ Spaniards will returne to yᵉ King of France message. **1746** FRANCIS tr. *Hor., Epist.* I. xviii. 21 Admitted as an humble Guest, Where Men of Money break their Jest, He waits the Nod, with Awe profound, And catches, ere it reach the Ground, The falling Joke. **1802** H. MARTIN *Helen of Glenross* II. 57 If Harry really loves me.., bid him wait futurity with composure. **1830** TENNYSON *Adeline* iv, What aileth thee? whom waitest thou? **1837** CARLYLE *Fr. Rev.* I. I. i, Or they that in the Bicêtre Hospital, 'eight to a bed', lie waiting their manumission. **1848** THACKERAY *Van. Fair* xl, She took up her residence with Mr. Bowls..and waited the result of the advertisement. **1885** J. H. DELL *Dawning Grey, Higher Creed* 6 We wait the harps of sounder string, Than [etc.].

b. *intr.* (Chiefly ***to wait for*** = sense 5 a above).

1577 HANMER *Anc. Eccl. Hist., Socr.* I. xix. 245 When the woman perceaued her selfe to be daungerously sicke, and wayted for no other then present death. **1581** *Satir. Poems Reform.* xliv. 266, I knaw thou vaittis Lieutenentis place to haue. *a* **1591** H. SMITH *Serm., Noah's Drunk.* (1602) G 4 b, The ground..wayted for nothing now, but a paynefull labourer to till and dresse it. **1621** T. GRANGER *Expos. Eccles.* xi. 5. 297 And hee that waiteth for olde mens shoes, may happily goe bare foote in the meane time. **1641** MILTON *Reform.* II. 87 These importunate Wolves, that wait and thinke long till they devoure thy tender Flock. **1805** *Med. Jrnl.* XIV. 374 We wait with anxiety but not with impatience for the succeeding numbers. **1833** TENNYSON *Dream Fair Wom.* xxviii, Dimly I could descry The stern black-bearded Kings.., Waiting to see me die.

c. To remain for a time without something expected or promised.

1550 CROWLEY *Last Trumpet* 935 If thou be a mans atturney,..Let him not waite and spende money, If his dispatch do lie in the. **1897** HALL CAINE *Christian* x, That was the only condition on which he would agree to wait for his money.

d. Phr. ***wait for it***, said (often parenthetically) to create an interval of suspense before imparting something remarkable or amusing, in order to heighten its effect. Also *ironically*. *colloq.*

1930 M. ALLINGHAM *Mystery Mile* xviii. 170 'Wait a minute,' said Mr. Knapp. '*Wait* for it... That is just exactly wot I do know.' **1958** S. HYLAND *Who goes Hang?* xvi. 74 'You're hiding something...' 'Wait for it my dear.' **1966** 'H. CALVIN' *Italian Gadget* ii. 21 We can have a shower and ..wait for it, dinner at the Palazzo Capucci. **1979** R. LAIDLAW *Lion is Rampant* xviii. 139 The real attack will come from, wait for it, wait for it—anither direction a'thegither.

6. a. *trans.* To continue stationary or quiescent, in expectation of (a person or thing, an event); to defer departure or action until the arrival or occurrence of. Now *rare*: superseded by ***wait for*** (see 7) and AWAIT *v.*

1375 BARBOUR *Bruce* v. 36 Tharfor thair cummyng vatit he, And met thame at thair ariving. **14..** *Pol. Rel. & L. Poems* (1903) 273 Mary hys moder went þe weye To caluery þer he xuld deye, And waytyd þer here chylde. **1578** in Feuillerat *Revels Q. Eliz.* (1908) 297 To waight my Lord Chamberlaines comyng thither. *a* **1604** HANMER *Chron. Irel.* (1633) 59 From thence he went to a place called Lothra, where he builded another Monasterie, and lyeth there wayting the generall resurrection. **1662** STILLINGFL. *Orig. Sacræ* II. vi. §2 That where there were any other evidences, that the Prophet spake by Divine Revelation, there was no reason to wait the fulfilling of every particular Prophecy before he was believed as a Prophet. **1667** DRYDEN & DK. NEWCASTLE *Sir M. Mar-all* I. i, This Tide will bring them from Gravesend. You had best let your man go, as from me, And wait them at the Stairs in Durham-yard. **1771** MRS. GRIFFITH *Hist. Lady Barton* II. 253 We had before agreed to wait the return of the chancellor's messenger at St. Omers. **1797** HT. LEE *Canterb. T., Frenchm. T.* (1799) I. 293 Without waiting her answer..he would have led her down stairs. **1802** *Noble Wanderers* II. 128 One of the slaves, whom he had commanded to wait his return. **1808** PIKE *Sources Mississ.* II. App. 22 We were requested to halt and wait the arrival of the chief, who was half a mile from us. **1816** SCOTT *Old Mort.* xxxviii, Lady Emily's servant was waiting orders in the kitchen. **1819** —— *Leg. Montrose* xxiii, She now waits you at the altar. **1883** WHITELAW *Sophocles, Philoct.* 123 Now then remain, and wait his coming here, Whilst I go hence. **1899** QUILLER-COUCH *Ship of Stars* xxvi, The Vicar clambered out to wait it [the coffin].

b. *transf.* Of things: To remain in readiness for, to await; to be in store for, to be reserved for. Cf. AWAIT *v.* 8 a.

1745 *Sc. Transl. & Paraphr.* LI. i, But better mansions wait the just, prepar'd above the sky. **1761** CHURCHILL *Rosciad* 512 Public Contempt shall wait the Public Fool. **1850** ROBERTSON *Serm.* Ser. III. xviii. (1853) 233 The same ..calculations wait us when we bend our eyes on that which is to come. **1854** SURTEES *Handley Cr.* xl. (1901) II. 36 'Tea and coffee wait your pleasure in the drawing-room', observed the stiff-necked footman.

c. ***to wait out***: (*a*) *U.S. Baseball*, (of a batter) to force (a pitcher) to throw a maximum number of pitches by refraining from striking at pitches in the hope of getting a base 'on balls', i.e. because they were not pitched over the home-plate; hence (chiefly *U.S. colloq.*), to wait during (a period of time, an event, etc.); to wait for the end of; also, ***to wait it out***, to endure a period of waiting; (*b*) = ***to wait for*** (sense 7).

1909 *Amer. Mag.* Aug. 401 Still Chance commanded: 'Wait—wait him out.' Every batter went to the plate intent on making Donovan pitch as many balls to them as possible. **1936** *Philadelphia Rec.* 31 July 15/1 Alf M. Landon is up there under instructions from the bench to wait 'em out. **1956** H. KURNITZ *Invasion of Privacy* xv. 95 He monopolized the phone in the bedroom, where Shelly and Zorn were waiting it out. **1959** *N.Y. Times Mag.* 11 Oct. 18/1 He is sealed into the container and..lies there in his 'contour couch' and waits out the long countdown. **1966** D. FRANCIS *Flying Finish* x. 131, I retired to the snack bar..to wait out the twenty minutes. **1977** R. PERRY *Dead End* i. 9 Unfortunately, I couldn't afford to wait him out. Daley was already overdue.

7. *intr.* or *absol.*

a. To remain in a place, defer one's departure until something happens. Often ***to wait for*** = sense 6.

c **1386** CHAUCER *Knt.'s T.* 71 And certes lord, to abyden youre presence Heere in the temple of the goddesse clemence We han ben waitynge al this fourtenyght. **1535** COVERDALE *Judith* x. 6 Now whan she came to the porte of the cite, she founde Osias and the elders of the cite waitinge there. **1568** GRAFTON *Chron.* II. 642 But he was espyed by diuerse watermen..which wayted for his foorthcomyng on the Thamys. **1599** SHAKS. *Much Ado* I. iii. 17, I must bee sad when I haue cause, and smile at no mans iests, eat when I haue stomacke, and wait for no mans leisure. **1628** FORD *Lover's Mel.* III. i, At the back dore Tatter-demallians waite, who know not how To get admittance. **1711** STEELE *Spect.* No. 132 ¶1, I..dressed immediately, that I might make no one wait. **1779** *Mirror* No. 57 Allowing ladies to go unattended to a public place, to wait there four hours in expectation of the gentlemen with whom they were to dance. **1835** DICKENS *Sk. Boz, Parish* iii, The old adage, 'time and tide wait for no man'. **1856** RUSKIN *King Golden River* i. (ed. 3) 12 What did you keep us waiting in the rain for? **1860** TYNDALL *Glac.* I. xxii. 152 At the summit of these rocks I again waited for him. **1896** CONAN DOYLE *Rodney Stone* xxii, Sir James Ovington's carriage was waiting without. **1905** R. BAGOT *Passport* xi. 104, I must drive back to Genzano. I told the *vetturino* to wait.

b. colloq. ***to wait about***: to linger expectantly, 'hang about' where something is likely to happen. Also (chiefly *U.S.*) ***to wait around***.

1879 MISS BRADDON *Cloven Foot* xxix. II. 268 'What has become of your brother?' Laura asked, as she and Celia waited about, side by side, watching the assembly of the field. **1886** BESANT *Childr. Gibeon* II. xxx, The street was, however, well enough lighted for Claude to see a figure waiting about on the pavement. **1895** M. HALSTEAD *Hundred Bear Stor.* 57 It grew sort of monotonous waiting around. **1899** J. L. WILLIAMS *Stolen Story* etc. 175, I suppose they're waiting around till it stops raining.

c. To defer action until some event has taken place; also with inf., to delay to do something.

a **1633** G. HERBERT *Outlandish Prov.* (1640) 25 Hee puls with a long rope, that waights for anothers death. **1800** *Med. Jrnl.* III. 460 To wait 'no longer than ten or fifteen minutes for the efforts of nature', is a position which cannot be too strongly reprobated. **1836** J. H. NEWMAN *Par. Serm.* III. xxi. 342 If we wait till all the world are worshippers, we must wait till the world is new made. **1843** CARLYLE *Past & Pr.* III. xv, A whole Eternity I waited to be born. **1852** THACKERAY *Esmond* I. viii, Beatrix..waited even to burst out a-crying until she got to the door. **1874** GREEN *Short Hist.* viii. §6. 519 He had shown he knew how to wait, and when waiting was over he knew how to act. **1875** JOWETT *Plato* (ed. 2) I. 434 A man should wait, and not take his own life until God summons him. **1883** WHITELAW *Sophocles, Philoct.* 837 Thou seest, now is the time. Why should we wait to do this deed?

d. ***to wait on***: (*a*) *Sc.* to linger about a place; (*b*) *Sc.* also, to linger in expectation of death; (*c*) *Hawking* (see quot. 1891); (*d*) *dial.* (esp. *Austral.* and *N.Z.*), to wait for a while, to 'hold on'. Freq. *imp.*

(*a*) **1818** SCOTT *Hrt. Midl.* xii, It's a sair thing to hae to do wi' courts of law, unless it be to improve one's knowledge.. by waiting on as a hearer.

(*b*) **1836** *J. M. Wilson's Tales Borders* II. 377, I did hear tell that his faither was waitin on, but I hope he's no that far gane yet.

(*c*) **1773** J. CAMPBELL *Mod. Faulconry* 158 If your hawk wait well on at her being first entered. **1828** SIR J. S. SEBRIGHT *Hawking* (1828) 17 He [the hawk] may thus be made to follow the falconer wherever he pleases; this is called *waiting on*. **1891** HARTING *Bibl. Accipitr.* 231 A hawk is said to 'wait on' when she soars in circles over the head of the falconer, waiting for the game to be flushed.

(*d*) **1943** N. MARSH *Colour Scheme* xiii. 228 'Wait on, wait on,' Dikon heard Webley mumble, 'You'll get it back all right.' **1946** K. TENNANT *Lost Haven* (1947) x. 138 Wait on, Patsy... Wait on, Patsy. You talk of letting the water out, but what about the fish?—bloody fish'll go too. **1967** 'G. DOUGLAS' *Death went Hunting* xviii. 161 For some reason I can't define, he seems quite willing to accept his present position... As we say in Yorkshire, he appears to be waiting on. **1968** S. L. ELLIOTT *Rusty Bugles* in E. Hanger *Three Austral. Plays* 92 *Andy:* Open the one from Darky. *Gig:* I am blast you... Wait on, can't you?

e. Racing. ***to wait off***: to allow oneself to be distanced by other competitors in order to 'romp in' when their energies are exhausted. Cf. WAITING *vbl. sb.*¹ 2 c.

1856 'DRUID' *Post & Paddock* vi. 91 He patiently waited off, while Sancho forced the running.

f. ***to wait up***: to defer going to bed in expectation of the arrival of some one.

1855 TROLLOPE *Warden* xviii, Dr. Grantly..and Mrs. Grantly..are waiting up for you. **1892** *Temple Bar* Oct. 169 Don't wait up for me.

g. ***to wait and see*** (with indirect question or ellipsis of this): to await the course of events. Also ***wait and see*** sb. phr.

In the early 20th c. often used with allusion to Mr. H. H. Asquith's repeated reply of 'Wait and see' to a succession of questions in parliament.

1719 DE FOE *Crusoe* I. (Globe) 267 However, we had no Remedy, but to wait and see what the Issue of Things might present. **1836** DICKENS *Sk. Boz, Scotland-Yard*, The tailor ..bid them wait and see what happened. **1848** —— *Dombey* xxxv, Mr. Towlinson..says wait and see. **1883** MISS M. BETHAM-EDWARDS *Disarmed* viii, When we have had dinner, we will do something better than have stories. Wait and see. **1910** *Blackw. Mag.* May 747/1 Mr. Asquith has deemed it not incompatible with the gravity of his office to elude the curiosity of his opponents with the absurd formula, 'Wait and see'. **1969** S. HYLAND *Top Bloody Secret* II. 121 The philosophy of wait and see..was getting him nowhere. **1976** *Scottish Daily Express* 23 Dec. 11/2 The rest of the back row is in a similar state of 'wait and see'.

attrib. **1870** L. M. ALCOTT *Old-Fashioned Girl* xiv. 231 She..thought she would 'wait and see.'.. The 'wait-and-see' decision was making her friend unhappy. **1915** F. S. OLIVER *Ordeal by Battle* I. vii. 82 History..shows us at every other crisis of this sort always the same triangle of forces —a War party, a Peace party, and a Wait-and-See party. **1930** [see FLOP *adv.* and *int.*]. **1977** A. J. RUSSELL *Pour Hemlock* xii. 147 His was a wait-and-see posture. **1984** *Times* 8 June 20/1 An understandable wait-and-see management caution.

h. *transf.* Of a thing: To remain in readiness for some purpose. Also, to remain for a while neglected.

1838 LYTTON *Alice* I. iii, 'So you are come for your daily lesson?' 'Yes; but Tasso can wait if [etc.].' **1876** J. PARKER *Paracl.* I. ii. 14 John's gospel is waiting until the Church becomes mature enough to understand it. **1894** HALL CAINE *Manxman* VI. xvii, There was a letter waiting for Philip at home. *Mod.* This letter must be answered at once; the others can wait.

i. quasi-*trans.* To postpone (a meal) in expectation of the arrival of some one. *colloq.*

1788 J. WOODFORDE *Diary* 29 Feb. (1927) III. 8 Mr. Taswell..desired us to send to Mr. Custance that they might not wait dinner for him. **1836** DICKENS *Let.* 17 Sept. (1965) I. 174, I hope and trust you did not wait dinner for me. **1838** DICKENS *O. Twist* li, 'It's a trying thing waiting supper for lovers,' said Mr. Grimwig, waking up. **1862** TROLLOPE *Orley F.* xxi, Who asked you to wait tea till near eleven o'clock?

j. ***to be unable*** (etc.) ***to wait*** (*for* or *to do* something), to be very eager or anxious for or to do it. *colloq.*

1938 D. DU MAURIER *Rebecca* xvi. 232 'Oh, Madam, how exciting,' breathed Clarice. 'I don't know how I am going to wait for the day.' **1958** I. MURDOCH *Bell* xix. 234 We're all so excited, we can hardly wait for tomorrow morning. **1971** J. OSBORNE *West of Suez* II. i. 63 Can't wait! Let's go home *now*. **1972** *National Observer* (U.S.) 27 May 10/3 Now the young musicians can't wait to get at their instruments.

k. (***you***) ***wait till*** (or ***until***).., used to imply a threat, warning, etc., or promise of something interesting or exciting, when the specified event has occurred. Also *ellipt.* as ***you wait!***

1938 G. GREENE *Brighton Rock* III. i. 99 'I dunno who Brewer is,' Ida said, 'but things seem lively.' 'You wait till the races start,' the man said. 'They'll be lively all right then.' **1953** E. SIMON *Past Masters* III. iii. 154 Parents brazened out their children's tantrums with the key-phase of, 'You wait!'. **1960** S. BARSTOW *Kind of Loving* II. ii. 162 Seventy-four guineas, Henry. Seventy-four bloody lovely guineas. Just wait till we tell Mr. Van Huyten about this. **1975** J. GORES *Hammett* xix. 130 She was going over to..tea with the George F. Biltmores! Wait until she wrote her mother about *that!* **1984** *Guardian* 5 Oct. 14/3 Mr Scargill ..will soon, very soon—just you wait—emerge triumphant.

8. Phrases. ***to wait one's*** (or ***the***) ***time, hour, opportunity***, etc. †**a.** (sense 3) To watch, look out for an opportunity (*obs.*). **b.** (sense 6) To defer action until a fitting season or opportunity shall present itself.

a. *a* **1300** *Cursor M.* 19715 Þair redes þar-for can þai run, ..Night and dai to wait þe time Quen þai moght cum to murther him. **1303** R. BRUNNE *Handl. Synne* 825 Weyte þy tyme, and be not þe last To come whan holy watyr ys cast. **1338** —— *Chron.* (1725) 94 To triste was he sette, forto waite þe chance. **1375** BARBOUR *Bruce* v. 523 He hame till his houss is gane, And vatit oportunite For to fulfill his mawite. *c* **1386** CHAUCER *Frankl. T.* 535 Nyght and day he spedde hym þat he kan To wayten a tyme of his conclusion. *c* **1420** WYNTOUN *Cron.* VI. xiii. 1220 (MS. Cott.) Twa men he bade in prewate To wayt ane oportunyte, And stel þat barn. **1526** *Pilgr. Perf.* (W. de W. 1531) 83 Waytynge theyr vauntage whan they may smyte the & slee the.

b. *c* **1375** *Sc. Leg. Saints* iii. (*Andrew*) 999 Þe bischope had gret will his fellone lust to fulfill, waitand bot lasare quhen he mycht purchess oportunite. **1626** B. JONSON *Staple of N.* II. ii, Well, Sir, I'll wait a better season. **1701** W. WOTTON *Hist. Rome, Marcus* iv. 59 Cassius was obliged to wait his opportunity. **1799** DUNDAS in Owen *Wellesley Desp.* (1877) 644 We cannot at present materially meliorate his government, but must wait favourable opportunities. **1813** SCOTT *Rokeby* I. xxix, She comes not—He will wait the hour, When her lamp lightens in the tower.

9. a. To be in readiness to receive orders; hence, to be in attendance as a servant; to attend as a servant does to the requirements of a superior. Chiefly const. *on*: see *wait on*, 14 j.

1526 TINDALE *1 Cor.* ix. 13 They which wayte att the aulter are parttakers with the aultre. **1617** MORYSON *Itin.* II. 49 Yea, his Lordships very Grayhound, likewise vsing to waite at his stirrop, was shot through the body. *c* **1655** MILTON *Sonn.*, '*When I consider*' 14 They also serve who only stand and waite. **1818** SCOTT *Br. Lamm.* xviii, He.. dropped a little behind the lady, at whose bridle-rein he had hitherto waited with such devotion.

b. To serve as an attendant at table; to hand food and drink to persons at a meal. Phr. ***to wait at table*** (cf. 14 j), † ***to wait at a trencher***.

1568 T. HOWELL *Arb. Amitie* 36 b, (*Iacke showes his qualities*) Yee and ich can, if neede be than, waight at the table well. *Ibid.*, Where ich did waite, at euerye baite. **1592** in *Sir J. Harington's Nugæ Antiq.* (1804) I. 106 Item, That no man waite at the table, without a trencher in his hand. **1605** BRETON *I pray you* (Grosart) 8/2 To spend my time.. onely for..waighting at a trencher, looking on a faire house. *c* **1618** MORYSON *Itin.* IV. ii. (1903) 90 These gentlemen servants waite with their hatts on, and sett at their masters table, both at home and abroad where their masters are invited. **1742** FIELDING *J. Andrews* I. ii, Joey was now preferred from the stable to attend on his lady, to..wait at her tea-table [etc.]. **1796–7** JANE AUSTEN *Pride & Prej.* xlvii, She had not prudence enough to hold her tongue before the servants, while they waited at table. **1853** DICKENS *Bleak Ho.* iv, The young woman with the flannel bandage waited, and dropped everything on the table wherever it happened to go. **1905** E. T. THURSTON *Traffic* v. iv, 'Is she a musician then [at the restaurant]?' asked Mr. Puckle. 'No—she waited.'

†**c.** ***to wait up***: to be in attendance at the head of the table. *Obs.*

a **1634** CHAPMAN *Alphonsus* III. i, As for the Chambermaid and my self, we will take our places at the neither end, the Jester is to wait up, and live by the crums that fall from the Emperours trencher.

d. quasi-trans. ***to wait*** (***the***) ***table*** = to wait at table. *Sc.*

1827 CARLYLE tr. L. Tieck in *German Romance* II. 135 Andres waited supper. **1879** STEVENSON *Trav. Cevennes* 152 She waited the table with a heavy placable nonchalance. *a* **1894** —— *St. Ives* xi. (1898) 82 We had a good many pleasant passages as she waited table or warmed my bed for me.

†**e.** quasi-trans. ***to wait attendance***: to remain in attendance. *Obs.*

1590 [see ATTENDANCE 5]. **1607** SHAKS. *Timon* I. i. 161.

†**10. a.** *trans.* To attend or escort, to accompany for the purpose of rendering service or showing respect. *Obs.*

c **1384** CHAUCER *L.G.W.* 1269 This Troyan, that..can so well doon alle his obeisaunces, And waytyn hire at festis & at dauncis. **1598** GREENE *Jas. IV*, v. i, I must to Edenbourg, vnto the King, There to take charge and waight him in his warres. **1633** MASSINGER *Guard.* II. i, *Jol.* Waite me. *Calyph.* As your shadow. *Exeunt Jol. Calyp.* **1687** DRYDEN *Hind. & P.* I. 557 She made a mannerly excuse to stay, Proffering the Hind to wait her half the way. **1697** —— *Æneis* VIII. 734 Steeds are prepar'd to mount the Trojan Band; Who wait their Leader to the Tyrrhene Land. *Ibid.* XI. 92 He..chose a thousand Horse..to wait the Funeral. **1725** POPE *Odyss.* IV. 61 Refresh'd, they wait them to the bow'r of state. **1728** —— *Dunc.* I. 265 She bids him wait her to her sacred Dome: Well pleas'd he enter'd. **1816** L. HUNT *Rimini* I. 242 His shield Borne by the squire that waits him to the field.

†**b.** *absol. Obs.*

1599 B. JONSON *Cynthia's Rev.* II. iii, One, that hath newly entertain'd the begger to follow him, but cannot get him to wait neere enough.

†**11.** To attend as a concomitant or consequence.

1675 TRAHERNE *Chr. Ethics* 330 Prudence consists most in attempting the business, for it will go on, and is ever waited with success when undertaken. *a* **1718** PRIOR *First Hymn Callimachus* 64 Swift Growth and wond'rous Grace, O heav'nly Jove, Waited Thy blooming Years.

II. Special constructions with preps.

†**12. wait after** ——. **a.** To expect, look forward to; to be ambitious or desirous of, seek for. *Obs.*

1393 GOWER *Conf.* III. 323 This Leonin..waiteth after gret beyete; But al for noght. **1393** LANGL. *P. Pl.* C. II. 124 Hewes in þe halyday after hete wayten. *c* **1440** *Generydes* 2440 He is descendid of an high lenage, And..waytith after right grete heritage. *c* **1449** PECOCK *Repr.* II. i. 135 That we waite not aftir to be hoosilid with the sacrament of the auter. *Ibid.* v. ii. 489 Certis he may not waite aftir that the conclusioun of this argument be proued or be trewe. *c* **1489** CAXTON *Sonnes of Aymon* xix. 423 It is not for vs to wayte after pyte of hym, for he is over cruell a kyng vpon us. **1533** tr. *Erasm. Comm. Crede* 52 b, They do wayte after a kynge plentuosly appoynted with ryches, with armies or hostes of men, and with other worldly aydes.

†**b.** To look out for; to watch, keep in observation. *Obs.*

c **1400** *Beryn* 1589 Beryne clepid a Marynere, & bad hym 'sty on lofft, And weyte aftir our four Shippis, [þat] aftir vs doith dryve.' **1450–1530** *Myrr. our Ladye* I. xx. 54 He sawe a fende that..wayted busely after all letters, and syllables, and wordes, and faylynges, that eny made. *c* **1489** CAXTON *Sonnes of Aymon* xxvi. 553 Thenne they set theymselfe doun vpon the fayr grasse, waytynge after theyr adverse party.

wait for ——: see 5 b, 7.

13. wait of ——.

†**a.** To execute the commands of. *Obs.*

a **1586** SIDNEY *Arcadia* I. xi. (1912) 69 He would extol the deeds of Philoxenus, who indeede had but waited of him therin. *Ibid.* v. (1598) 465 A Counseller, who hath..the reasonable excuse of a seruant, that did but wait of his mistresse.

†**b.** To escort, accompany on the way, as a mark of honour: = *wait on*, 14 k. *Obs.*

1563 FOXE *A. & M.* 860/1 This deponent..receyued the kynges maiesties Visitors at Chichester,..and conducted and wayted of them into the dioces of Wynton. **1606** CHAPMAN *Gent. Usher* III. ii. 77 Waite of Master Usher to the doore. **1709** N. BLUNDELL *Diary* (1895) 78, I Wated of yᵉ Duke and Dutches of Norfolk &c. out of Wigan part of their way towards Preston. **1724** *Briton* No. 25. 110 Footmen..return when the Play is done to wait of them home. **1734** ADM. GORDON in *10th Rep. Hist. MSS. Comm.* App. I. 193 At 9 acloake I sent my pinnace to wayte of General Lacy.

†**c.** To pay a respectful visit to: = *wait on*, 14 m. *Obs.*

1555 in Lodge *Illustr. Brit. Hist.* (1791) I. 211 Trustyng shortely to wayte of yoʳ Lordshyppe. *c* **1673** W. MOUNTAGU in *Buccleuch MSS.* (Hist. MSS. Comm.) I. 320 My Lord and his sons have been to see me at my chamber, but I had the misfortune to be abroad; and upon that score..I will wait of them again. **1677** *Ibid.* 324, I..shall acquaint his Lordship myself with it on Saturday, before which I cannot wait of him. **1707** N. BLUNDELL *Diary* (1895) 55, I went to Bold to wate of Mr. Molin[eux] but he was gon a hunting.

d. = *wait for*: see 7 a. Now *dial.*

1712 TYLDESLEY *Diary* (1873) 23 Stayed alday at Dick Jackson's watting of Mr. Blackborne, who came not till affter nine att night. **1828** *Trial Wm. Dyon at York Assizes* 8, I was up waiting of my master until two o'clock.

14. wait on or upon ——.

†**a.** To observe, watch; to fix one's eyes upon, gaze at. *Obs.*

c **1384** CHAUCER *H. Fame* 342 For though your loue laste a seson, Wayte vpon the conclusyon. *c* **1394** *P. Pl. Crede* 361 Þei wilneþ worshipes—but waite on her dedes! *c* **1400** *Rowland & O.* 444 To þᵉ castelle he wendes a pase And appone þᵉ kirnells gase, to wayte appon þat were. *c* **1400** *Destr. Troy* 13055 So Eger were all men Elan to se, For to waite on þat worthy went þai belyue. *c* **1430** *Syr Gener.* (Roxb.) 6344 Anoon Jewel to his ship sent To warn his men to be redie, On his comyng to waite and spie. **1538** ELYOT *Dict.*, *Inspecto*, to behold attentiuely, to wayte on.

†**b.** To lie in wait for. *Obs.*

1390 GOWER *Conf.* I. 349 Of his men a gret partie He made in buisshement abide, To waite on him in such a tide That he ne mihte here hond ascape. **1595** *Locrine* IV. i. 183 Millions of diuels wayt vpon thy soule! **1628** HOBBES *Thucyd.* II. (1629) 128 As they sayled along the shore, Phormio waited on them till they were out of the streight, intending to set vpon them in the open Sea.

†**c.** To secure, protect (oneself). *Obs.*

c **1400** *Destr. Troy* 12722 Þan he counseld Clunestra,..To be war of þat wegh, & wait on hir-seluyn.

†**d.** To attend to (a business, a duty). *Obs.*

1526 TINDALE *Rom.* xii. 7 Let hym that hath an office, wayte on his office. [Similarly in later versions.]

†**e.** With clause as obj.: To take care *that*. *Obs.*

1596 DALRYMPLE tr. *Leslie's Hist. Scot.* (S.T.S.) I. 255 He wayted weill onn, be all meines possible, that nathyng dekayet of Justice in his Realme.

†**f.** To await, expect with desire or anxiety. *Obs.*

c **1400** *Destr. Troy* 7944, I wot the in witte to waite on myn end. **1608** *Yorks. Trag.* viii. 23 Was this the answear I long waited on? **1642** MILTON *Apol. Smect.* 37, I perceave how hopelesse it will be to reach the heigth of their prayses at the accomplishment of that expectation that weights upon their noble deeds.

†**g.** To await the action of; to look to (a person) *for* something. *Obs.*

1682 BUNYAN *Holy War* (1905) 253 That the Prince that lay in the Leaguer without the Wall, waited upon them [the townsfolk] for an answer.

h. In Bible phrase, to place one's hope in (God). Cf. WAITER 4 b.

Very common in the Bible of 1611; rendering several Heb. verbs of identical meaning.

1535 COVERDALE *Ps.* lxi[i]. 1 My soule wayteth only vpon God, for of him commeth my helpe. **1611** BIBLE *Ps.* xxv. 3 Let none that wait on thee be ashamed. **1840** GEO. ELIOT *Let.* 20 July (1954) I. 58 That constant waiting on God for instruction and comfort which [the Quietists]..make the sum total of religion. **1931** J. BUCHAN *Blanket of Dark* xvi. 307 Be still and wait on God. **1979** R. BLYTHE *View in Winter* ix. 300 One of the best things which all these new changes have brought about is this notion of waiting upon God.

i. To remain in one place in expectation of = *wait for* (7 a). Also, more generally, to wait for (5 b).

1694 tr. *Marten's Voy. Spitzbergen* in *Acc. Sev. Late Voy.* II. 7 We were forced to wait on him above half an hour, before he came from underneath the Ice. **1817** W. SEWALL *Diary* 2 May (1930) 14/1, I proceeded to the Academy and agreed to enter there upon condition that the Professor would wait on me until the next winter. **1865** O. L. JACKSON *Colonel's Diary* (1922) 227 We have been waiting on the pay department. **1915** J. BUCHAN *39 Steps* vi. 135 He..raised his placid eyebrows and waited on me to speak. **1931** *Amer. Speech* VII. 20 *Wait on*, wait for, the Biblical sense. 'When I got there, John was waiting on me.' (Widespread.) **1955** F. O'CONNOR *Wise Blood* v. 85 He..darted after Hazel Motes. 'Wait on me!' he shouted. **1960** *Observer* 7 Feb. 13/4 The nation waits on the railwaymen, to see if there will be a strike or not. **1984** P. TURNBULL *Big Money* ix. 153, 'I was just waiting on you two coming back.' He stood and reached for his coat.

j. To attend as or in the manner of a servant to the personal requirements of; to minister to the comfort of. †Also in phrases, ***to wait on the cup, the trencher, the table*** (cf. 9 b).

to wait on (a person) ***hand and foot***: see HAND *sb.* 57.

1509–10 *Act 1 Hen. VIII*, c. 14 §1 No servyng manne waytyng uppon his maister..were eny garded Hose. *c* **1550** CHEKE *Matt.* iv. 11 Then let yᵉ devel him go, and lo angels cam vnto him and waited on him. **1552** HULOET, Wayte on the cup, *ad cyathos stare*. **1575** GASCOIGNE *Glasse of Govt.* Wks. 1910 II. 66 Wee should have beene fayne to wayte on the table, and to be contented with their leavinges after supper. **1602** *Kyd's Sp. Trag.* II. v. (Addit.), His Maiestie the other day did grace him With waiting on his cup. **1615** G. SANDYS *Trav.* 80 When they grow old, they most grow contemptible, being put to do the drudgeries of the house, and many times to waite on their children. **1749** FIELDING *Tom Jones* VII. xv, It is not my business, answered the

Drawer, to wait upon the Chambers. If you come to that, answered the Maid, it is not my business to wait upon Gentlemen. **1847** MARRYAT *Childr. New Forest* iv, You can have no servants to wait upon you. **1866** MRS. H. WOOD *Mildred Arkell* xi, When I was only six years old I had to wait on Mamma and Charlotte. **1901** ALLDRIDGE *Sherbro* xii. 114 He is waited upon hand and foot.

k. To accompany on one's way (as a mark of respect or to render service or assistance); to escort. Now *rare* (? exc. *U.S.*).

1450 W. LOMNER in *Paston Lett.* I. 124 With other shippis waytyng on hym. **1481** *Cov. Leet Bk.* (1908) 486 There shuld be xl sowdyers mo waged for a quarter of þe town wages to make vp a C men to wayte vppon the kyng in þis viage etc. *c* **1530** TINDALE *Jonas Prol.* A vj b, Ande one yᵗ cast out deuels in Christes name they forbade because he wayted not on them. **1585** HIGINS *Junius' Nomencl.* 517/1 *Pronuba*, ..a bridemaid, or she that trimmeth and maketh ready the bride, and waiteth vpon her homeward to her husbands house. **1595** SHAKS. *John* v. vii. 98 Let it be so, and you my noble Prince,.. Shall waite vpon your Fathers Funerall. **1601** LD. MOUNTJOY *Let.* 13 Nov. in *Moryson's Itin.* II. (1617) 155 We entertained them so well, that we waited on them to the walls of the Towne, and made them leave some of their dead bodies behind them. **1628** T. BALL *Life Preston* (1885) 175 His friends at Cambridge, who did highly honour him, and desired nothing more then to have wayted on his dust to his long home. **1654** EVELYN *Diary* 4 July, On a letter from my wife's uncle, Mr. Pretyman, I waited back on her to London. **1713** TYLDESLEY *Diary* (1873) 107 Then went to wate on Judge Dormʳ out off the toun. *Ibid.* 125 He watted on her home. **1807–8** W. IRVING *Salmag.* iii. (1860) 51 On landing we were waited upon to our lodgings..by a vast and respectable escort. **1880** P. LUDLOW *Nick Hardy at College* vi. (1882) 29 Nick complied, and was waited on into the drawing-room.

transf. **1691** TATE *Petty's Pol. Anat.* Ded. to Dk. Ormond, Be pleas'd to permit this useful Treatise to wait on you to the Camp.

l. Hence (?) in Hunting, ***to wait close upon***: to keep close to (the horse immediately in front).

1861 WHYTE-MELVILLE *Market Harb.* xxv, Crasher..and Sawyer take their leaps abreast, and latter riding very quietly and carefully... Luxury is waiting close upon them.

m. To pay a respectful visit to; to call upon with the intention of showing respect, asking a favour, or the like.

1501 *Plumpton Corr.* (Camden) 161 Also I shall wate one you at Nottingham one sunday next, except ye comand me contrary. **1594** O. B. *Quest. Profit. Concern.* 5 God willing he shall one day waight vpon you to better his knowledges. **1638** in *Verney Mem.* (1892) I. 279, I have A greate ambition yᵗ you would please to honour me so farre as..to admitt me to waite upon you. **1664** SIR A. BATEMAN in *Extr. St. P. rel. Friends* III. (1912) 215 It is my Lord Chanselors comaund to mee, that I waite vpon your Honor to deliuer this inclosed letter to you. **1713** ADDISON *Guardian* No. 107 ¶3 She will wait upon any Lady at her own Lodging, and talk by the Clock after the Rate of three Guineas an Hour. **1765** R. GEM in Jesse *Selwyn & Contemp.* (1843) I. 367 The Baron D'Olbach and I intend ourselves the pleasure of waiting on you to dinner to-morrow. **1766** GOLDSM. *Vicar W.* xxx, A person of distinction..sent his respects to the gentleman that was with us, and begged to know when he should think proper to be waited upon. **1848** DICKENS *Dombey* xxvi, I took the liberty of waiting on her..to inquire if she could charge me with any little commission. **1849** MACAULAY *Hist. Eng.* ix. II. 474 The Primate and the few Spiritual Peers who happened to be then in London had orders to wait upon the King. **1885** *Manch. Exam.* 6 July 4/7 A deputation had waited upon Lords Salisbury, Redesdale, and Roxburghe.

†*transf.* **1762** WILKES *Let.* 21 Sept. (1769) I. 15 Sunday's post brought me your lordship's [letter] of the 17th, and by the return of it this waits on your lordship.

n. Of things: To accompany; to be associated with; to attend as a concomitant or consequence.

1579–80 NORTH *Plutarch, Lycurgus* (1595) 52 For no man is so..simple witted, as to bring into so povre and meane houses, bedsteads with siluer feete, imbrodered couerlets.. nor such other like costly furniture and finenesse, as those things require to waite vpon them. **1605** SHAKS. *Macb.* I. vii. 44 Letting I dare not, wait vpon I would, Like the poore Cat i' th' Addage. **1611** —— *Wint. T.* v. i. 142 Infirmitie (Which waits vpon worne times). **1622** J. TAYLOR (Water P.) *Farew. Tower Bottles* A 7, For 'tis a Maxim held in euery Nation, Great men are wayted on by Adulation. **1646** CRASHAW *Steps to Temple* 33 To them shee gave the first and fairest Beame That waited on her Birth. **1657** HEYLIN *Eccles. Vind.* II. iii. §6. 146 Prayer..being an action meerly moral, was notwithstanding to be waited on with such rites and gestures. **1692** PRIOR *Ode Imit. Hor.* xi, Justice and Freedom on his Conquests wait. **1746** HERVEY *Medit.* (1818) 60 Her form was symmetry itself; every elegance breathed in her air; and all the graces waited on her motions. **1842** LOVER *Handy Andy* i, Disappointment waited on all affairs in which he bore a part. **1859** MILL *Liberty* i. (1864) 2/2 Elective and responsible government became subject to the observations and criticisms which wait upon a great existing fact. **1875** JOWETT *Plato* (ed. 2) V. 299 Retribution is the suffering which waits upon injustice.

†**o.** To support the opinion of. *Obs.*

1639 FULLER *Holy War* IV. v. (1640) 175 The Master of the Sentences (waited on herein with other learned men) is of opinion, That [etc.].

†**15. wait over** ——. To watch over. *Obs.*

Cf. OVERWAIT *v.* (= supervise, Pecock).

1659 HAMMOND *Paraphr. Ps.* lxxviii. 52 His..providence ..continually waited over them, and provided supplies for all their wants.

†**16. wait to** ——. To keep watch upon, attend carefully to. *Obs.*

c **1440** *York Myst.* xxxiii. 253 Sirs, waites to þer wightis þat no wiles be wrought. *c* **1449** PECOCK *Repr.* III. xviii. 405 And skile whi al this is trewe may be perceyued weel ynowȝ of a diligent considerer, waiting weel to ech word which is now bifore here seid. **1508–13** *Bk. Keruynge* in *Babees Bk.* (1868) 270 And wayte well to yᵉ sewer how many dysshes be couered.

III. 17. Comb.: †**wait-gleed** [= OF. *gaite-tison*], one who sits lazily watching the fire.

c **1310** in Wright *Lyric P.* xv. 47 Me calleth me fulle flet, ant waynoun wayte-glede.

†**wait**, *v.*² *Obs.* Also 4 **weyte, waite, wayte.** [app. a. ON. *veita* to show or do (kindness, etc.), less frequently to do (an ill turn), = OHG. *weizen*:—OTeut. type ***waitjan**, f. ***wait-** abl.-var. of ***wit-**: see WIT *v.* Confused with WAIT *v.*¹: see AWAIT *v.* 2.]

1. *trans.* **a.** With thing as direct obj. and dative of person: To show (unkindness) to, to put (disgrace, suffering, etc.) on. **b.** In similar sense, but with changed construction: To treat (a person) ***with*** (unkindness, cruelty, etc.), to affect ***with*** (disgrace, suffering, etc.).

a. 1303 R. BRUNNE *Handl. Synne* 5987 þeft he wyl vpon hym wyte, Or ouþer skaþe he wyl hym weyte. *c* **1330** *Arth. & Merl.* (Kölbing) 352 Ac ferst þai sworen him an oþ, þai schuld him neuer waite loþ. *c* **1350** *Will. Palerne* 148 He ..þouȝt..he wold..wayte hire sum wicked torn. *Ibid.* 4051 þat no burn nere so bold..to waite þe werwolf no maner schaþe. *c* **1400** *Rom. Rose* 3938 Therfore close I shall the weie Fro hem that..come to wayte me vilonye. *c* **1450** *Erle Tolous* 296 Certys hyt were a traytory, For to wayte hym velany. **1450** *Rolls of Parlt.* V. 183/2 Ye shall not shewe nor wayte..noo malice..to any persone. **1548** UDALL, etc. *Erasm. Par. Matt.* iv. 23–5 Sum came for malice with a mynde to wayte displeasure. **1601** HOLLAND *Pliny* x. lxxiv. I. 308 The bird Ægithus, (the least in manner of all others) waiteth the Asse a shrewd turne.

b. *a* **1300** *Cursor M.* 4330 Sco waited him wit a werr turn. **1303** R. BRUNNE *Handl. Synne* 4186 Whan þys Iudas.. weytede Ihesu with tresun. *c* **1320** *Sir Tristr.* 2175 Meriadok wiþ ille Waited hem ful neiȝe Of her dede. *c* **1330** R. BRUNNE *Chron. Wace* (Rolls) 7122 For þou art no knyght of armes, þe more þey wayte þis lond wyþ harmes. **1352** MINOT *Poems* i. 64 Ay er þai boune To wait Ingland with sorow and schame. *a* **1400** *Sir Perc.* 99 Was noȝte the rede knyghte so rathe For to wayte hym with skathe. *c* **1430** *Syr Tryam.* 101 Yf ye be so hardy To wayte me wyth velanye. *c* **1470** HENRY *Wallace* VIII. 900 We sall be bundyn yow to,..nocht efftyr to wait yow with na ill. *c* **1475** *Rauf Coilȝear* 913 'Sa thriue I', said the Sarazine, '..Quha waitis the Cristin with cair, my cusingis ar thay'. **15..** *Murning Maiden* 81 in *Maitl. Fol. MS.* (S.T.S.) I, And heir to ȝow my treuth I plycht That I sall nowder day nor nycht No wyld beist wait with wrang. **1581** *Satir. Poems Reform.* xliii. 83 Did sho not wait him with sic foule inuy.

2. Comb. **wait-scathe** (as a nickname or quasi-proper name), a perpetrator of mischief.

1481 CAXTON *Reynard* xxviii. (Arb.) 70 Ther is prentout, wayte scathe, and other of my frendis and alyes. *a* **1500** HENRYSON *Fox & Wolf* 54 Freir Wolf Waitskaith.

wait, obs. and dial. f. WET, WITE, WOT.

'**wait-a-bit.** [tr. Cape Du. *wacht-een-beetje.*] Usually *attrib.* with *thorn, thorn-tree*, etc. **a.** A name given to various S. African plants and shrubs with humorous reference to their hooked and clinging thorns; e.g. various species of *mimosa.*

1785 G. FORSTER tr. *Sparrman's Voy. Cape G.H.* I. 236 A new species of *callophyllum*, which from its catching..fast hold of the traveller with its hooked prickles..is commonly called here *wakt een beetje*, or *wait a bit.* **1850** R. G. CUMMING *Hunter's Life S. Afr.* (ed. 2) I. 152 This variety of mimosa is waggishly termed by the Boers 'vyacht um bige', or wait-a-bit thorns; as they continually solicit the passing traveller not to be in a hurry. **1857** LIVINGSTONE *Trav.* iii. 61 The 'wait-a-bit thorn', or *Acacia detinens.* **1899** BERTRAND *Kingd. Barotsi* 48 Various species of thorn, of which the most formidable is the 'wacht-een-beetje', appropriately interpreted as the 'wait-a-bit', a crooked, steely, regular fish-hook of a thorn, that stops and tears everything that comes in its way. **1913** PETTMAN *Africanderisms*, s.v. *Wacht-en-beetje*, The familiar *Zizyphus mucronata, W.*, is popularly known all through Kaffraria and the Eastern Districts as the 'wait-a-bit thorn tree'.

b. Applied by travellers to different plants of similar character in other parts of the world.

1865 TRISTRAM *Land of Israel* 202 The principal tree was the zizyphus spina-Christi..with long pointed and rather reflex thorns, very strong,—a true wait-a-bit tree. **1894** DENNYS *Dict. Malaya* 415 Wait-a-bit. A name conventionally applied to a species of rattan armed with powerful curved thorns.

'**wait-a-while. 1.** *S. Afr.* = WAIT-A-BIT a.

1863 W. C. BALDWIN *Afr. Hunting* vii. 239 The Kaffirs throw in the pits, most virtulent 'wait-a-while' thorn branches into the pits, to prevent the oxen from trampling.

2. In Australia, any of several plants with prickles or spiny leaves, esp. *Acacia colletioides.*

1889 J. H. MAIDEN *Useful Native Plants Austral.* 306 *Acacia colletioides*..'Wait-a-while' (a delicate allusion to the predicament of a traveller desirous of penetrating a belt of it). **1940** F. D. DAVISON *Woman at Mill* 86 Clumps of prickly wait-a-while gave back the light from millions of small shiny leaves. **1967** [see BATHURST BURR].

waitchfull, obs. Sc. form of WATCHFUL.

waite, obs. form of WITE.

waiter ('weɪtə(r)). Forms: 4 **weyter**, 4–5 **waytar**, 4–7 **wayter**, 5 **waytere**, 5–7 **waitor, waytor**, 6 **waighter, waitour, water, weighter**, (*Sc.* **vyttar**), 6– **waiter.** [Orig. a. AF. ***waitour**, OF. *weitteor, gaiteor*, agent-n. f. *weitier, gaitier* WAIT *v.*¹ In later use f. WAIT *v.*¹ + -ER¹.]

I. †**1.** One who watches, or observes closely; one who is on the look-out. *Obs.*

1382 WYCLIF *2 Sam.* xiii. 34 And the child weyter [Vulg. *puer speculator*] heuede vp his eyen and bihelde. *c* **1420** *Wyclif Bible, Pref. Epist. St. Jerome* 70 Sophonyas the wayter [L. *speculator*] and the knower of the priuetees of the Lord, herith a cry. **1549** COVERDALE etc. *Erasm. Par. 1 John* i. 1–4 Euen the thing which we yᵗ were continual waitours heard with our eares, saw with our eies. **1554** *Aberdeen Reg.* (1844) I. 281 That the saidis baillies suld..apprehend the said John Chalmer, and put him in custodie..with vyttaris and vaychearis to awyt and keip him fra doing of skayth. **1672** SWINNOCK *Life T. Wilson* 21 Accordingly, he thus clad came forth, not knowing but that the Waiter was still at the door. **1687** A. LOVELL tr. *Thevenot's Trav.* I. 285 The Health-boat came, and put Waiters on board of us, to keep the People of the Town from mingling with us.

2. †**a.** A watchman at the city gates. *Sc. Obs.*

1684 in G. Sinclair *Satan's Invis. World* (1685) Postscr. ¶1 b, He had..some charge over the Waiters at the Ports of the City [Edinburgh]. **1737** in *Crim. Trials illustr.* '*Heart of Mid-Lothian*' (1818) 294 William Lindsay, waiter at the Netherbow port of Edinburgh..deponed, That [etc.]. **1818** SCOTT *Hrt. Midl.* vi, During this parley the insurgents had made themselves masters of the West Port, rushing upon the Waiters (so the people were called who had the charge of the gates), and possessing themselves of the keys.

b. A warder of the Tower of London. More fully ***yeoman waiter.***

1551 T. WILSON *Logic* N viij b, Yeomen of the gard, and all other waiters. **1592** in *3rd Rep. Hist. MSS. Comm.* 6/2 [Ralph Smythe] one of your highness ordinary yeomen waiters. *c* **1600** in Peck *Desid. Curiosa* (1732) I. II. 16 The Towre..Yeoman Waighters or Warders.

†**c.** An officer in the employ of the Customs. *Obs.* exc. *Hist.* See COAST-WAITER, TIDE-WAITER.

1473 *Stonor Papers* (Camden) I. 134 For þer be so many waytors and controllers. **1556** *Acts Privy Counc.* (1892) V. 295 They have, nevertheles of late byn troubled and disquieted by diverse Wayters at the portes in London. **1561** CLOUGH in Burgon *Life Gresham* (1839) I. 407 So many Quays crowne-serchers, wayters, and other powlyng offycers. **1612** *Proclam. Transport. Corn* 19 Jan., All our Customers, Comptrollers, Searchers, Waitors, and other the Ministers of our Ports. **1685** *Sc. Proclam.* 28 Apr. in *Lond. Gaz.* No. 2032/3 We hereby Require and Command all Our Collectors, Customers, or Waiters, to make strict and diligent Search and Inquiry in all Ships. **1818** SCOTT *Hrt. Midl.* xvi, Some tuilzies about run goods wi' the gaugers and the waiters.

†**3.** An observer in secret. **a.** A spy, scout. *Obs.*

1471 CAXTON *Recuyell* (Sommer) 133 Diuerse espies and waytars that were sent out..to see and to descouuere the state..of their enemyes.

†**b.** In *Hunting*, one set to watch the movements of the intended game. *Obs. rare.*

c **1400** *Master of Game* (MS. Digby 182) xxxiii, þei shulde goo forthe þider as þe deere is herbowred and sette redy wayters aboute þe quarter, or þe wode þat þe deer is Inne to se what commeth oute.

†**c.** One who lies in wait. *Obs. rare.*

c **1430** *Pilgr. Lyf Manhode* II. xii. (1869) 79 An espyour of weyes, and a waytere [*agueteur*] of pilgrimes.

II. 4. a. One who waits expectant of some event, opportunity, appointed time, etc.

1655 R. CAPEL *Tentations* IV. iii. (ed. 5) 124 The expectation of the waiter shall not fail for ever, that is, never. **1870** R. BUCHANAN *Bk. Orm* II. ii. 50 O Shadow sad, Monitor, haunter, waiter till the end. **1900** F. G. KENYON in *Egypt Explor. Fund, Archaeol. Rep.* 45 Students of papyri will indeed be expectant waiters for gifts from their rich table for a long time to come.

b. *waiter upon God* (see WAIT *v.*¹ 14 h). †***waiter upon time*** (obs.), ***waiter upon Providence***, one who awaits the turn of events when required by duty or honour to come to a personal decision; a temporizer.

1592 BACON *Observ. Libel* Resusc. (1657) 132 The Spaniards are great Waiters upon Time, and ground their Plots deep. **1836** MARQ. LONDONDERRY in Dk. Buckhm. *Mem. Crts. Will. IV & Vict.* (1861) II. 228 Such as are rats, and waiters upon Providence, who have now deserted us. **1907** P. T. FORSYTH *Positive Preaching* vii. 231 It is the waiters on God that renew their strength.

III. †**5. a.** One who waits in the presence of another (of superior rank); one who visits, or pays court to a superior.

1530 PALSGR. 286/1 Wayter, *qui baille attendance.* **1542** UDALL *Erasm. Apoph.* 41 b, Diogenes called Aristippus the kynges hownde, because he was a dayly waiter, and gaue contynuall attendaunce in the Courte of Dionysius. **1591** SAVILE *Tacitus, Agricola* (1622) 200 Being admitted to the princes presence, and receiued with a short salutation and no speech, he sorted himselfe with the rest of the wayters [*turbæ servientium inmixtus est*]. **1611** BIBLE *Judith* xiii. 1 Bagoas shut his tent without, and dismissed the waiters from the presence of his lord.

†**b. *waiter at the table***: a parasite. *Obs. rare.*

1552 HULOET, Wayter at the table as vncommaunded to yᵉ entent to get hys dynner, *parasitaster.*

†**6.** A man (more rarely, a woman) whose office or privilege it is to attend upon a superior.

†**a.** A regular member (often a person of high rank) of the retinue or household of a royal or noble personage. *Obs.*

14.. *15th Cent. Courtesy Bk.* (1914) 14 Then shall be þer redy yemen of the chambre yef it be þer, yemen waytors yef it be in þe hall, to take away stolis and bordes and trestelles. *a* **1548** HALL *Chron., Hen. VIII*, 12 The kyng & his thre felowes entred into the felde their bardes and bases of Crimosyn and blew Veluet..and all the wayters in sylke of the same colour. *a* **1562** G. CAVENDISH *Wolsey* (1893) 45

Whan he came to the gallerye's end, he satt hyme down uppon a forme that stode there for the wayters some tyme to take ther ease. **1594** R. CAREW *Huarte's Exam. Wits* (1616) 228 The sixt thing which honoureth a man, is the seemely ornament of his person, and his going well apparelled, and attended with manie waiters. **1630** *R. Johnson's Kingd. & Commw.* 142 They which were wont to be called Pantlers, Tasters and Carvers, are now called Gentlemen Wayters of the Court. **1678-9** DRYDEN & LEE *Œdipus* II. i, Each trembling Ghost shall rise, And leave their grizly King without a waiter.

b. An attendant upon the bride (or, more recently, the bride or groom) at weddings; a bridesmaid. *Obs.* exc. *U.S. dial.* or *Hist.*

1537 in *Lett. & Papers Hen. VIII*, XII. I. 11, 3 goodly ladies in cloth of gold gorgeously decked following as waiters of the bride. *c* **1680** *Roxb. Ballads* (1891) VII. 458 Then come let us be, blithe, merry and free, Upon my life all the waiters are gone!.. The Bride-Maids that waited are gone. **1830** in N. E. Eliason *Tarheel Talk* (1956) 303 [She] says she hears you are to be married. She wishes to know..when.. as you promised she would be one of the waiters. **1927** *Dialect Notes* V. 470 *Waiter*,..an attendant of the bride or groom at a wedding. **1959** *Daily Progress* (Charlottesville, Va.) 19 Mar. 14/1 Four young men and four young women were appointed to be 'waiters' on the bride and groom.

†**c.** = ACOLYTE. *nonce-use.*

1563 MAN *Musculus' Commonpl.* 275 Thei do reckon up, dore keepers, readers, conjurers, wayters [L. *acolytos*], subdeacons, deacons, and priestes, whiche all thei do call clerkes.

†**d.** One who out of courtesy waits at table on special occasions. (Cf. sense 7 c.) *Obs.*

1605 CAMDEN *Rem., Wise Sp.* 196 The Archebishop of Yorke saide vnto the yoong king..'there is never a Prince in the world that hath this day such a waiter at his Table [viz. K. Henry II] as you have'. *a* **1641** BP. MOUNTAGU *Acts & Mon.* (1642) 434 The waiters are all free men, who willingly proffer attendance at such feasts;..their waiters are clad in long loose garments to distinguish them from servants. *a* **1714** PARNELL in Steele *Poet. Misc.* 65 Each sweet engaging Grace Put on some Cloaths to come abroad, And took a Waiters Place.

†**e.** ***waiter at the altar***: (*a*) *gen.* (after 1 Cor. ix. 13), a priest or other minister of the altar; (*b*) one in minor orders (cf. 6 c).

1648 FANSHAWE *Il Pastor Fido* IV. iii. 137 The waiters at the altar [It. *i ministri minori*]. **1711** G. HICKES *Two Treat. Chr. Priesth.* (1847) II. 70 Ministers about holy things, and waiters at God's altar.

7. A man (rarely a woman) of lower rank employed as a household servant. †**a.** A servitor, groom, footman, etc. *Obs.*

a **1483** *Liber Niger* in *Househ. Ord.* (1790) 41 Dayly iiii other of these groomes, called wayters, to make fyres, to sett up tressyls and bourdes. *c* **1586** C'TESS PEMBROKE *Ps.* CXXIII. i, Right as a waiters eye on a graceful master is holden. **1611** BEAUM. & FL. *Philaster* II. (1620) 24 What sawcy groome knocks at this dead of night, where be our waiters? **1655** E. TERRY *Voy. East India* xiii. 244 Death made many breaches into my Lord Ambassadors family, for of four and twenty wayters, besides his Secretary and my self, there was not above the fourth man returned home. **1788** *Massachusetts Spy* 29 May 3/4 A considerable number of the respectable inhabitants of Princeton, consisting of 37 gunners and their waiters, spent the day past in hunting.

†**b.** A waiting-woman. *Obs. rare.*

1639 MASSINGER *Unnat. Combat* I. i, Bid your wayters [two waiting-women] Stand farther of.

c. *esp.* A servant (in a private house) whose particular duty it is to wait upon those seated at table. *Obs.* (? exc. *U.S.*); cf. sense 8.

1528 ROY *Rede me* (Arb.) 98 Then proll the servynge officers, With their yemen that be wayters, So that their levettis are but thynne. **1609** HOLLAND *Amm. Marcell.* d 4 b, Butlers, carvers, yeomen of the cellar, wayters at the table. *a* **1674** MILTON *Hist. Moscovia* v. Wks. 1851 VIII. 507 In dinner time he twice chang'd his Crown, his Waiters thrice thir Apparel. **1856** MRS. STOWE *Dred* xi, She was in the middle of the saloon again, just as the waiter announced dinner.

d. *Mil.* A soldier, etc., employed as a domestic servant to an officer. *U.S. Obs.*

1828 A. SHERBURNE *Mem.* i. 20, I was waiter to Mr. Charles Roberts the boatswain. *Ibid.* ii. 26 Part of our officers with five or six waiters..occupied an elegant house. **1861** *Army Regulations* 559 Non-commissioned officers not employed as waiters.

8. A man employed, at inns, hotels, eating-houses, or similar places, to wait upon the guests (*esp.* during meals). Also a man hired for a similar purpose on special occasions to supplement the staff of a private household.

This sense probably arose in England about the middle of the 17th c., and superseded the older term *drawer*. From the 18th c. onwards it appears to have been the most usual sense of the word.

a **1663** KILLIGREW *Parson's Wedd.* III. v. (1664) 120 *Drawer*... The sum is six pounds, and be pleased to remember the Waiters. **1712** STEELE *Spect.* No. 508 ¶3 We change our Taverns according as he suspects any Treasonable Practices in the settling the Bill by the Master, or sees any bold Rebellion in point of Attendance by the Waiters. **1779** *Mirror* No. 26 But there is another set of persons still more exposed to be treated roughly than even domestic servants, and these are, the waiters at inns and taverns. **1818** HAZLITT *Table-t., Knowl. Charact.* (1822) II. 351 After a familiar conversation with a waiter at a tavern. **1837** DICKENS *Pickw.* xxxv, The White Hart hotel..where the waiters, from their costume, might be mistaken for Westminster boys. **1874** RUSKIN *Fors Clav.* xlviii. IV. 271 Presently afterwards, an evidently German-importation of waiter brings me up my breakfast.

9. A uniformed attendant on the floor of the Stock Exchange, Lloyd's of London, or other City of London institution.

1887 [see HAMMER *v.* 2 d]. **1904** C. DUGUID *Stock Exchange* ii. 12 We have also noticed the Waiters' Stands, about twenty in number, placed in various parts of the House, pulpit-like..so that the important announcements which emanate from these stands may be well heard in the House. **1934** F. E. ARMSTRONG *Bk. Stock Exchange* xvii. 356 It is known that dealers used to foregather in the coffee houses of Change Alley, Cornhill... Here, probably, it was that 'waiters', plying their trade, and seeking out from the interior fastnesses of these refreshment rooms some particular Stock-jobber wanted by his client, gave the name to the uniformed 'waiter' who calls the Members within the walls of the present Stock Exchange. **1962** A. SAMPSON *Anat. of Britain* xxiii. 380 Merchant bankers work in a formal atmosphere... Mahogany, black-coated waiters and grandfather clocks set the tone of privacy. *Ibid.* xxv. 400 The Room [at Lloyd's]... When a broker is wanted, one of the 'waiters' (who stand round the room in scarlet uniform) writes his name on a special instrument. **1976** *Times* 22 Apr. (Baltic Exchange Suppl.) p. i/9 As in other City institutions, attendants wear livery and are called waiters.

IV. A contrivance to supply the place of a waiter or facilitate waiting.

†**10.** = DUMB-WAITER 2.

1833 LOUDON *Encycl. Archit.* § 1474 In lofty Inns, we have often thought that it might be desirable to have an ascending and descending platform, on the principle of the ascending and descending cupboards or waiters. **1861** *Our Engl. Home* 184 Loriot invented, for the salons of Choisy, tables called waiters, which, on touching a spring, sank through the floor, to reappear laden for a repast.

11. A salver, small tray (cf. *waiting-board*, *-salver*).

1738 *Will of Frances, Lady Colepeper*, I give unto my said niece..my dumb waiter and the rest of my waiters. **1778** MISS BURNEY *Evelina* (1791) II. 205 Just then the servant brought Lady Louisa a note upon a waiter. **1802** MRS. SHERWOOD *Susan Gray* 90 She placed a waiter in my hand, and ordered me to carry the tea to the Captain. **1838** DICKENS *Nich. Nickleby* xvii, A heterogeneous litter of pastrycook's trays, lamps, waiters full of glasses, and piles of rout seats. **1886** G. ALLEN *Maimie's Sake* xxxviii, Hetty took the..missive..from the old massive silver waiter.

†**12.** (See quot.) *Obs. rare.*

1779 INGENHOUSZ *Electricity* in *Phil. Trans.* LXIX. 662, I began first by making use of one of those glass stands, which they call a waiter, and which has a glass support fixed at right angles to its center.

V. 13. *Chess.* = *waiting problem* s.v. WAITING *vbl. sb.*[1] 2 c.

1906 A. C. WHITE *Tours de Force* p. xxxii, If a problem has no threat, it is called a 'waiter', and all the different continuations are variations. **1935** *Encycl. Sports* 150/1 There is no simple waiting move for white. The key is, indeed, a 'waiter', but four of the resulting mates are different from those in the set position. **1963** M. LIPTON et al. *Chess Problems* iv. 72 White can neither retain all the set mates as in a Waiter, nor change some of them while still maintaining zugzwang as in a mutate.

Hence (*nonce-wds.*) **'waiterage**, the performance of a waiter's duties. **'waiterdom**, waiters considered as a class. **'waiterhood**, the state or condition of a waiter. **'waitering**, the occupation of a waiter.

1849 CARLYLE *Remin. Irish Journ.* (1882) 38 All was done for me then that human waiterage in the circumstances could do. **1860** *All Year Round* IV. 79 Enter the dusty travellers;..round whom dance expectant gnats and midges in the shape of fluttering waiterdom. **1862** DICKENS *Somebody's Luggage* i, What is the inference to be drawn respecting true Waitering? You must be bred to it. **1865** —— *Mut. Fr.* IV. iv, An innocent young waiter..as yet unversed in the wiles of waiterhood. **1866** *Lond. Rev.* 7 Apr. 388/1 Waitering admits of variation, and can be accommodated to circumstances.

waitership ('weɪtəʃɪp). [f. WAITER + -SHIP.]

†**1.** The office of warder, or watchman. *Obs. rare.*

1485 *Rolls of Parlt.* VI. 364/2 The Office of Portershipp of the Castle of Knaresboro, with the Waytershipp of the same.

2. A position as a waiter in an inn, etc.

1889 *Catholic Househ.* 4 May 9 Workhouses and waiterships are the prizes in life for those who distinguish themselves.

†**waith**, *sb.*[1] *Sc.* and *north. Obs.* Forms: [? 1 **wáð**], 3–5 **waith, wayth**, 3–6 **waithe**, 4 **wath**, 5 **wathe**, 8 **veth**. [a. ON. *veið-r* fem., hunting, fishing, catch of game or fish = OE. *wáð* fem., hunting (also wandering), OHG. *weida* (MHG., mod.G. *weide*) hunting, fishing, food, pasture (also wandering, roaming):—OTeut. **waiþō*, **waipi-z*, f. root **wai-* perh. cogn. with L. *vēnārī* to hunt. It is possible that the OE. form *wáð* may have coalesced with the Scandinavian word.]

1. The action or practice of hunting or fishing; chiefly, unlawful taking of game; also, the right to hunt game.

[*a* **1000** *Boeth. Metr.* xxvii. 13 Deað..ӡeslic hunta, a bið on waðe.] *c* **1400** *Awntyrs Arth.* xxxiv, We arene here in the wode, walkande one our wathe. *c* **1425** WYNTOUN *Cron.* III. 235 For in his waith son eftyr þat Thre hundyr foxis qwyk he gat. *Ibid.* 533 Qwhar þat he trawalit mony day In waithe [*v.r.* weyth], in ware and in bargan. **15..** *Murning Maiden* 94 in *Maitl. Folio MS.* (S.T.S.) I. 362 ȝour deir may walk quhair euir þai will, I win my meit with na sic waithe. **1707** [see VERT *sb.*[1] 2].

2. Game for or obtained by hunting; spoil of the chase; also *gen.* spoil, booty.

a **1300** *Cursor M.* 3522, 3524 Esau went for till hunt,..Bot þat dai wayth [*Fairf.* waiþe, *Gött.*, *Trin.* gamen] þan gatt he noght, For haf man neuer sa gode graith It es noght ilk dai, dai o waith. **13..** *Gaw. & Gr. Knt.* 1381 Here is wayth fayrest þat I seȝ þis seuen ȝere in sesoun of wynter. ? *a* **1400** *Morte Arth.* 3233 That I ne wiste no waye whedire that I scholde, ffore woluez, and whilde swynne, and wykkyde bestez; walkede in that wasternne, wathes to seche. *c* **1400** *Destr. Troy* 2350 Till mydday and more myght we not fynde, ffor to wyn as for waithe in þat wode brode. *c* **1460** *Towneley Myst.* iii. 486 *Noe.* I will cast out also Dowfys oone or two: Go youre way, go, God send you som wathe! *c* **1470** HENRY *Wallace* I. 386 Waith suld be delt, in all place, with fre hart. *c* **1480** HENRYSON *Two Mice* 7 The vther wynnit Uponland..Quhylis in the corne, and vther mennis skaith, As outlawis dois and leuis on thair waith.

†**waith**, *sb.*[2] *Sc.* (chiefly *Orkney* and *Shetland*). *Obs.* [? Altered form of WAIF *sb.*] = WAIF *sb.*

1478 *Reg. Mag. Sig. Scot.* 281 Terras dominiorum de Orknay et Zetland..unacum *le Wrak, Wattell, Waithe* et *Hasewaith*, et cum consimilibus proficuis [etc.]. **1615** *Acts Sherifs Orkney* § 15 in *Edin. Antiq. Mag.* (1849) 8 No person ..sal hyde nor conseall any kynd of thift,..injurie, robrie, nor opressioun in wraik or waith. [**1897** D. J. ROBERTSON in *Longm. Mag.* Feb. 333 Through the heaped mysteries of waith and wrack, When the long wave from the long beach draws back.]

b. *attrib.* or *adj.* (Cf. WAIF *a.*)

1671 *Shetland Docum.* in *Proc. Soc. Ant. Scot.* (1892) XXVI. 194 To..secure all wrack and waith goods.

fig. **1513** DOUGLAS *Æneis* VI. Prol. 68 Virgilis sawis..aucht nocht be hald wagabound nor waith.

†**waith**, *sb.*[3] *Sc. Obs.* Also 8 **weath.** [? a. ON. *váð* = OE. *wǽd* WEED *sb.*[2]] ? Cloth, clothes: chiefly in phrase ***claith and waith*** (see quot. 1825).

1603 *Philotus* xi. (Bannatyne Club), Philotus is..Ane ground-riche man and full of graith: He wantis na jewels claith nor waith. **1768** ROSS *Helenore* I. 48 Bannocks and kebbocks knit intil a clout She had laid by, an' row'd up in her waith. *Ibid.* II. 74 The worth o't twice, in claith or weath ye's get. *Ibid.* II. 75 Your claith an' waith will never tell wi' me. **1825** JAMIESON *s.v.*, *Claith nor waith* seems to have been a Prov. expression; perhaps q. 'neither cloth in the piece, nor cloth made into garments'.

†**waith**, *a. Obs.* Also 5 ? **waithe**, 7 **weath.** Of a horse: See quot. 1710.

c **1425** WYNTOUN *Cron.* I. 1035 Sa waiche [? *read* waithe] and woid þan ar þa hors þat [etc.]. **1662** in Pitcairn *Crim. Trials* III. 613 The Devill will be with hir and ws all lyk a weath-horse efter mearis. **1710** RUDDIMAN *Gloss. to Douglas's Virg.* s.v., *Scot.* they say, a waith horse, i.e. a horse that wanders in pursuit of mares. *a* **1828** *Blancheflour & Jellyflorice* xviii. in P. Buchan *Ballads* (1828) I. 128 Ye'll take out yon wild waith steed, And bring him to the green.

waithe, obs. form of WEIGHT.

†**'waithing.** *Sc. Obs.* [f. ON. *veiða* to hunt, catch fish (related to *veið-r* WAITH *sb.*[1]) + -ING[1].] Fishing; a catch of fish.

c **1470** HENRY *Wallace* I. 387 He bad his child, 'Gyff thaim of our waithyng'. **1592** in *Reg. Mag. Sig. Scot.* 1610, 117/2 My 3 merkland..with..gers, wair, fischingis, waithing.

†**'waithman.** *Sc. Obs.* [a. ON. *veiðimann-*, *veiðimað-r*, f. *veiði-*, *veið-r* WAITH *sb.*[1]] A hunter; esp. applied to forest outlaws.

c **1425** WYNTOUN *Cron.* I. 1446 Þis Menbrot [*i.e.* Nimrod] stalwart was of pythe And waythe man he was þar wiþ. *Ibid.* VII. 3526 Litil Iohun and Robert Hude Waythmen war commendit gud. **1536** BELLENDEN *Cron. Scot.* (1821) II. 354 The waithman, Robert Hode.

attrib. **1500-20** DUNBAR *Poems* xxxiii. 8 Me thocht a Turk of Tartary..lay forloppin in Lumbardy, ffull lang in waithman weid. **1573** *Satir. Poems Reform.* xxxix. 144 Quhill force did faill, and than I saw thame fane To cry 'Peccaui' with the waithman noit. **15..** *Murning Maiden* 64 in *Maitl. Folio MS.* (S.T.S.) I. 362 In waithman weyd Sen I ȝow find In þis wod walkand ȝour alone.

waiting ('weɪtɪŋ), *vbl. sb.*[1] [-ING[1].]

1. The action of WAIT *v.*[1] in various senses.

†**a.** A lying in wait, ambush. Also ***waiting for***. Also *fig. Obs.*

c **1200** *Trin. Coll. Hom.* 193 Shrudeð eow mid godes wapne, and werieð eow wið defles waitinge. **1340** *Ayenb.* 15 Zuo heþ þe dyeuel diverse maneres of waytinges. *c* **1440** *Promp. Parv.* 513/2 Waytynge to don harme, *insidie.* **1526** TINDALE *Acts* xii. 11 The lorde hath..delyvered me..from all the waytynge fore of the people of the iewes.

†**b.** Watching, observation. *Obs.*

1377 LANGL. *P. Pl.* B. II. 89 Lecherye..As in werkes and in wordes and waitynges with eies. *c* **1430** *Syr Gener.* (Roxb.) 4560 But he perceiued hir noo thing From the toure of hir wayting. **1526** TINDALE *Luke* xvii. 20 The kyngdom of God commeth not with waytingefore.

c. Expectation; remaining stationary or quiescent in expectation of something. ***in waiting*** (predicatively): in a state of expectancy, remaining in one place or condition so as to be ready for some expected event: = *waiting* pres. pple.

1743 T. JONES in *Buccleuch MSS.* (Hist. MSS. Comm.) I. 402 After 24 hours' waiting, the troops were obliged to retire. **1760-72** H. BROOKE *Fool of Qual.* (1809) III. 142 While the coach was in waiting, and they all stood on the hill. **1818** BYRON *Let. to Murray* 17 July, I am still in waiting for Hanson's clerk, but luckily not at Geneva. **1853** DICKENS *Bleak Ho.* xxiii, I thought..I would ask Richard to be in waiting for me at the coach-office, that we might have a little talk together. **1885** PAYN *Talk of Town* II. 147 A closed carriage, well appointed, was at the door, in waiting for her, and they took their seats. **1889** BRIDGES *Growth Love* lxiii, I abide and abide, as if more stout and tall My spirit would grow by waiting like a tree.

d. Attendance *upon* a superior.

c **1560** A. SCOTT *Poems* 79 xxvi. 61 Thay wald haif wating on alway, But gwerdoun, genȝeild, or regaird. **1774** J. BRYANT *Mythol.* I. 102 Camillus had the name of Hermes from the similarity of his office, which was waiting upon the Gods.

e. Official attendance at court; one's period or term of such attendance. ***in waiting***: on duty, in attendance (said e.g. of a maid of honour, a lord- or lady-in-waiting, a court official).

For *groom-in-waiting, lady-in-waiting, lord-in-waiting*, see the first element.

1697 J. LEWIS *Mem. Dk. Glocester* (1789) 24 When the Princess asked him, who taught him so? he said, Lewis; then, said her Highness, Lewis shall be turned out of waiting. **1705** LUTTRELL *Brief Rel.* (1857) V. 620 The dutchesse of St. Albans being made one of the ladies of the bedchamber to the queen..begun her first waiting on Monday. **1726** SWIFT *Gulliver* II. iii, His Majesty sent for three great scholars, who were then in their weekly waiting, according to the custom in that country. **1730** R. GALE in *Mem. W. Stukeley* (Surtees) I. 235 Lady Pembroke is in waiting at Windsor. **1765** EARL COVENTRY in Jesse *Selwyn & Contemp.* (1843) I. 402 The letter I had from Lord March ..offering to take my waiting the first of next month, in exchange of his own, which is not till the 29th. **1849** MACAULAY *Hist. Eng.* iv. I. 433 The prelates who were in waiting had from the first exhorted him to prepare for his end. **1912** MRS. H. WYNDHAM *Corr. Sarah Lady Lyttelton* xi. 285 This is the last letter of interest during Lady Lyttelton's first waiting.

2. *attrib.* **a.** Consisting of, or characterized by, waiting (in various senses of the verb WAIT). Sometimes hyphened to the sb. qualified.

1553 EDEN *Treat. New Ind.* (Arb.) 25 [They] distribute their wayting dayes after this order. **1740** tr. *De Mouhy's Fort. Country Maid* (1741) II. 366, I had hired a Waiting Jobb, by the month. **1903** *Times* 6 May 14/3 Consumers.. contend..that a waiting policy may bring some relaxation in values. **1912** *Ibid.* 19 Oct. 5/2 Rumania will..order the mobilization of these Army Corps, abandoning her waiting attitude.

b. Intended to be used or occupied while waiting, as ***waiting-chamber***, ***-lobby***; also WAITING-ROOM.

a **1562** G. CAVENDISH *Wolsey* (1893) 102 The first *waytyng chamber was hanged with fynne arras. **1912** BODLEY *Card. Manning* 19 For Newman the Oriel Common-room was a home. For Manning the Merton Common-room was an unfamiliar waiting-chamber on the road to a profession. **1837** *Civil Engin. & Arch. Jrnl.* I. 7/1 By suspending them in the *waiting-lobbies, the impatient moments of parties might be close occupied.

c. Special comb.: †**waiting board, salver**, a tray intended to be carried by one waiting at table; **waiting game**, used to describe the tactics of a player who abstains from attempting to secure advantages in the earlier part of the game, with a view to more effective action at a later stage; also *fig.*; **waiting list**, a list of people waiting for appointments, selection for any purpose, or the next chance of obtaining something; **waiting (move) problem** *Chess* (see quots.); **waiting race**, a race in which the superiority of the winner is designedly not displayed till near the end of the course; also *fig.*; †**waiting Sunday**, ? a Sunday on which the town-council publicly attended the mayor to church; **waiting time**, time spent waiting, *spec.* in *Computing* (see quot. 1962) or *Work Study* (see quot. 1979).

1770 LADY MARY COKE *Jrnl.* 19 June (1892) III. 247, I bought tea, fans, japan *waiting board, walking sticks, &c. **1890** *Times* 27 Dec. 9/1 The best policy seems to dictate a *waiting game. **1914** *Eng. Hist. Rev.* Apr. 256 The precarious health of Elizabeth..made it desirable to play a waiting game in the east and to shower blows on Bohemia and Moravia. **1897** *Outing* XXX. 347/2 The Michaux Club is composed of two hundred members, with a large '*waiting list'. **1916** A. HUXLEY *Let.* 5 Feb. (1969) 90 There is a huge waiting list for the better jobs on all the Govt. Depts. **1921** *Tax Clerks' Jrnl.* IV. 387 The right to a place on the 'waiting list' for a permanent post. **1976** *Times* 23 Feb. 13/1 Local councils were able to do little to reduce over-long waiting lists. **1891** J. RAYNER *Chess Problems* 9 *Waiting-move problems—*i.e.*, those in which the first move would not lead to a mate if it were not that Black is forced to reply and thereby weaken his position. **1896** *Chess Monthly* May 280 There is another class of waiting problem which is usually found very interesting... A primary position which has every indication that White has but to linger without discouraging the mates as 'set', but..one of the mates has to be given up in exchange for another to be created. **1907** S. S. BLACKBURNE *Chess Problems* 25 *Block problem*—Otherwise called a 'Waiting Problem' is one in which White's first move leads to mate after every reply of Black, in consequence of such reply. **1962** K. S. HOWARD *One Hundred Years Amer. Two-Move Chess Problem* 5 Another type [of problem]..was the complete block, or waiting-move problem, especially where some of the mating moves apparently set in the initial position were changed by the key, for which Brian Harley..coined the apt name *mutate*. **1868** H. WOODRUFF *Trotting Horse* xxxvi. 297 Tallman made a *waiting-race of it, and pulled Flora back three lengths. **1883** MRS. E. KENNARD *Right Sort* xx, Mrs. Forrester will ride a waiting race throughout. **1885** 'MRS. ALEXANDER' *At Bay* vi, You can do no good,—as they didn't find her within the first week it will just be a waiting race. **1886** EARL SUFFOLK & BERKSH. *Racing* xiv. (Badm. Libr.) 224 The style in which Buckle..particularly shone was in riding a waiting race... 'None of your lying off and winning in the last stride for me', would the owner of Euclid exclaim. **1714** *Lond. Gaz.* No. 5286/4 Two *waiting Salvors. **1767** in Picton *L'pool Munic. Rec.* (1886) II. 197 The future dress.. for the Aldermen..to be by them worn only on the *Waiting Sundays and other public state days. **1962** *Gloss Terms Automatic Data Processing* (*B.S.I.*) 85 **Waiting time*, of a store. The time interval between the instant the control unit calls for a transfer of data to or from the store and the instant the transfer commences. **1976** P. R. WHITE *Planning for Public Transport* v. 115 Waiting time is a function of service frequency and thus is not affected directly by spacing. **1979** *Gloss. Terms Work Study* (*B.S.I.*) 16 *Waiting time*, the period of time for which an operator is available for production but is prevented from working.

†**'waiting**, *vbl. sb.*[2] *Obs.* [Prob. a. ON. *veiting* (not recorded in this sense, but cf. mod.Icel. *veitingar* pl., entertainment, *veitinga-hús* restaurant), f. *veita* to give a feast (a special use of *veita* WAIT *v.*[2]).] Entertainment, feasting.

a **1300** *Cursor M.* 3344 Ilk man gaue he [*sc.* Abraham's servant, *Gen.* xxiv. 53] sumkin thing, And batuel made fair waiting [*Gött.* gestning]. *Ibid.* 12544 Ai quen iosep was wont at weind, Til ani waiting wit sum frend, His suns war ai wit him bun.

waiting ('weɪtɪŋ), *ppl. a.* [WAIT *v.*[1] + -ING[2].]

1. That waits upon, or attends to, another; that acts as an attendant, or waiter. Often hyphened to the qualified sb. as in ***waiting-gentlewoman***, ***-lady***, WAITING-MAID, -MAN, -WOMAN, etc.

1538 *N. Country Wills* (Surtees) 159 To every one of my wayting servauntes vj s. viij d. the pece. **1594** SHAKS. *Rich. III*, II. i. 121 When your Carters, or your wayting Vassalls Haue done a drunken Slaughter. **1599** —— *Much Ado* II. ii. 14, I thinke I told your Lordship..how much I am in the fauour of Margaret, the waiting gentlewoman to Hero. **1598** MARSTON *Sco. Villanie* III. ii, If one should sewe For Lesbias loue, hauing two daies to wooe..and should imploy those twaine The favour of her wayting-wench to gaine, Were he not mad? **1620** tr. *Boccaccio's Decam.* II. vi. I. 47 This Gentleman..one especiall day.., with his wife, seruants, and waiting hounds [It. merely *con suoi cani*], wandred vp into the Iland. **1713** HEARNE *Collect.* (O.H.S.) IV. 76 Her little waiting Dogg was got under her Clothes. **1749** FIELDING *Tom Jones* x. ix, Certain pecuniary civilities, which are by custom due to the waiting-gentlewoman in all love-affairs. **1829** SCOTT *Anne of G.* xxi, That dressing my mistress is the only part of a waiting-lady's life that I have the least fancy for. **1861** MEREDITH *Poems, Patriot Engin.* 35 Why, there's the ale-house bench:..And there's my waiting-wench, As lissome as a hound. **1864** BURTON *Scot Abr.* I. v. 268 It would, after all, have perhaps been more difficult to find waiting-boys who could speak English.

2. That waits for some person or thing; expectant; remaining stationary, or deferring action, expectantly.

1654 *Clarke Papers* (Camden) III. 12 The present effect is startling to all nacions round about, all in a waiteing frame where this cloud will light. **1703** ROWE *Fair Penit.* I. i, Thy waiting Bride ev'n chides thee for delaying. **1720** RAMSAY *Rise & Fall of Stocks* 24 As little bairns frae winnocks high Drap down saip-bells to waiting fry. **1896** *Harper's Mag.* Apr. 671/2 All noise and movement gradually ceased, and a waiting stillness followed which was solemn and impressive.

Hence **'waitingly** *adv.*

1882 C. E. TURNER in *Macm. Mag.* Apr. 478/1 [She] lived waitingly and hopefully 'on the eve' of an active career. **1894** CROCKETT *Lilac Sunbonnet* 26 The Marrow minister.. looked waitingly at the young man.

'waiting-,maid. [WAITING *ppl. a.*] A superior female servant in personal attendance on a lady.

1561 T. NORTON *Calvin's Inst.* II. iii. §7. 20 b, Will dothe accompanie it [*sc.* Grace] and not leade it, as a waytinge maide after it & not a forgoer. *a* **1623** FLETCHER *Love's Cure* II. ii, A Ribbon or a Glove. *Cla.* Nay those are tokens for a waiting-maid To trim the Butler with. **1741** RICHARDSON *Pamela* II. 59 Here is Mr. B——, with such and such an Estate, has married his Mother's Waiting-maid. **1875** W. S. HAYWARD *Love agst. World* 76 'Milady is very generous,' said the waiting-maid.

'waiting-,man. [WAITING *ppl. a.*] A male servant who waits or attends upon his employer or on an official. *Obs.* exc. *U.S.*

1518 *Star Chamber Cases* (Selden Soc.) II. 155 Concernyng the waytyngmen, it is thought that the same fees cannot be mynysshid. **1552** HULOET, Waytyng man, *assecla*. **1585** HIGINS *Junius' Nomencl.* 518/2 *Anteambulo*,.. a waiting man, or he that goeth before his maister and mistresse, or conducteth them. **1776** *Pennsylv. Even. Post* 15 Feb. 82/2 An active young man..wants employment. He has served in the capacities of a waitingman, gardener, and groom. **1839** *Southern Lit. Messenger* V. 752/1 The door of the bachelor's hall was assaulted by a repetition of raps, which quickened the steps of Mr. Singlesides' sedate waiting-man. **1884** G. W. CABLE *Dr. Sevier* I. x. 73 The speaker ceased as the mulatto waiting-man appeared.

'waiting-,room. [WAITING *vbl. sb.*] A room set apart for those who are obliged to wait (usually in a public building, now *esp.* in a railway-station; also at a doctor's or dentist's).

1683 J. REID *Scots Gard'ner* (1907) 3 There are ten steps up to the first story (which is hall or dining-room, withdrawing-room, bed-chamber, and waiting-room). **1834** MARRYAT *P. Simple* lii, I had called to pay my respects at the Admiralty, previous to joining, and was kicking my heels in the waiting-room. **1839** *Bradshaw's Railway Companion*, Sufficient time being allowed at the Birmingham Station, where refreshments are provided, and waiting rooms, with female attendants. **1869** TROLLOPE *He Knew* etc. ix. (1878) 50 A club waiting-room is always a gloomy, unpromising place for a confidential conversation. **1888** *Manch. of To-day* 175 A rich-toned musical box is continually playing in the [dentist's] waiting-room.

attrib. **1883** MISS YONGE *Langley Advent.* 257 They offered to make her a waiting-room woman as soon as there was a vacancy.

'waiting-,woman. Now *arch.* [WAITING *ppl. a.*] A female servant, or personal attendant.

1565 In Burgon *Gresham* (1839) II. 391 Suffring only one waiting wooman to attende upon her. **1606** SHAKS. *Tr. & Cr.* V. ii. 91 By all Dianas waiting women yond: And by her selfe, I will not tell you whose. **1749** FIELDING *Tom Jones* X. v, Being now left alone with her maid, she told her trusty waiting-woman, That she never was more easy than at present. **1831** SCOTT *Chron. Canongate* Introd., Neither the Highland cicerone MacLeish, nor the demure waiting-woman, were drawn from imagination.

wait-list. orig. and chiefly *U.S.* [WAIT *v.*[1]] = *waiting list* s.v. WAITING *vbl. sb.*[1] 2 c.

1960 *Amer. Speech* XXXV. 312 'There's a wait list on that one too,' one is told somberly by steamship agents. **1977** in H. J. Eysenck *You & Neurosis* vi. 185 On a rating scale of overall improvement, 93 per cent of the behaviour therapy patients contrasted to 77 per cent of the psychotherapy and wait-list patients were considered either improved or recovered. **1979** *United States 1980/81* (Penguin Travel Guides) 16 *How to Use an Airline*; it's full of information on how to make reservations, the difference between waitlist and stand-by, [etc.].

Hence as *v. trans.*, to put (a person) on a waiting list; to draw up a waiting list for places on (an aircraft, ship, etc.); **wait-listing** *vbl. sb.*

1960 *Amer. Speech* XXXV. 312 A boat is said to be *wait listed*... What gloomy fate, then, awaits the prospective passenger who is *wait listed*? **1971** *Financial Mail* (Johannesburg) 26 Feb. 656/2 What about his wait-listing for an earlier flight? **1973** *Daily Tel.* 5 Sept. 6/7 On less frequent services..overbooking is not employed. Instead, 'wait-listing' is effected, and passengers who learn that their flight is full wait at the airport on the chance of a seat becoming available.

waitress ('weɪtrɪs). Also 6 **waitresse.** [f. WAITER + -ESS.]

†**1.** A waiting-maid, handmaid. *Obs. rare*[−1].

c **1586** C'TESS PEMBROKE *Ps.* CXXIII. i, Unto thee..lift I my earthy seeing..As the look of waitresse fixed on a lady lieth.

2. a. A woman who waits upon the guests at a hotel, restaurant, etc. Also one hired for a similar purpose on special occasions to supplement the staff of a private household. (Cf. WAITER 8.)

1834 *Drakard's Stamford News* 4 Nov., A waitress who lived at Alconbury hill. **1836** HOOD *Let.* Mem. (1860) I. 234, I boarded at the chateau, and only slept and breakfasted at the inn. I had the prettiest girl in the place for my waitress. **1854** DE QUINCEY *Autob. Sk., Coleridge* Wks. II. 188 *note*, Waiter:—Since this was first written, social changes in London..have introduced a corresponding new word—viz., *waitress*; which word, twenty-five years back, would have been simply ludicrous. **1871** M. COLLINS *Marq. & Merch.* III. i. 27 A buxom waitress from the inn.

b. Chiefly *U.S.* A female servant in a private house whose duty is to wait upon those at table (cf. WAITER 7 c); in extended use, a housemaid.

1875 MRS. STOWE *We & our Neighbors* 323 Maggie was parlor-girl and waitress, and a good one too. **1906** *N.Y. Herald* 5 Mar. 14 A competent girl as waitress and to take charge of parlor floor; private family. **1937** C. DAY *Life with Mother* 215 Each brother had his own sacred place where his own toys were kept, except when the waitress cleaned the room and mixed everything up. **1953** A. CHRISTIE *Pocket Full of Rye* iv. 32 Gladys Martin is the parlourmaid or waitress, as they like to call themselves nowadays.

3. Comb.: **waitress service**, service by waitresses in a restaurant, opp. *self-service*.

1960 C. DALE *Spring of Love* i. 3 The floor with waitress service was always crowded. **1970** E. MCGIRR *Death pays Wages* vii. 150 The main room had tables with white cloths and a waitress service.

Hence **'waitressing**, service as a waitress; hence (as a back-formation) **'waitress** *v. intr.*, to work as a waitress.

1936 J. B. PRIESTLEY *They walk in City* xi. 335 Well, you're a nice-looking girl and you have done some waitressing—so it oughtn't to be hard for you to get a place. **1950** *Landfall* Dec. 308 There were pretty good ones [*sc.* jobs] going now—cooking and waitressing in town. **1974** K. MILLETT *Flying* (1975) III. 311, I was a kid from St. Paul waitressing in Glacier Park. **1984** *Times* 15 Oct. 10/4 The waitress..can..make waitressing into a performing art. **1984** *New Yorker* 29 Oct. 43/1 Jenny was waitressing in Denver.

waivable ('weɪvəbl), *a. Law.* [f. WAIVE *v.*[1] + -ABLE.] That may be waived.

1818 CRUISE *Digest* (ed. 2) I. 238 Her estate was originally waivable.

†**waive**, *sb. Law. Obs.* [a. AF. *waive*, *weyve*; prob. to be read as *weyvé* (= *weyvee*), pa. pple. of *weyver* WAIVE *v.*[1]] See quots.

1544 tr. *Littleton's Tenures* xi. 43 A woman that is outlawed is called a wayue. [Fr. Sicome home que est vtlage est dit vtlage et feme que est vtlage est dit wayue.] **1579** *Expos. Terms Law* 187 Waiue is a woman that is outlawed, and she is called waiue as left out or forsaken of the law, and not an vtlawe as a man is.

waive (weɪv), *v.*[1] Forms: 3–4 **weive**, 4–6 **weyve**, (5 **weyfe**, 6 *pa. pple.* **waifed, weft**), 4–7 **wayve**, (4 **wayvye**), 5–9 **wave**, 5– **waive.** [ME. *weyve-n*, a. AF. *weyve-r* (whence Law-Latin *waiviare*, *waviare*), dial. var. of OF. *gaiver*, *guesver* (early mod.F. in Cotgr. *gayver, guesver, guever*) to allow to become a 'waif', to abandon, f. AF. *weyf* (fem. *weyve*), OF. *gaif* (fem. *gaive, gueive*, etc.) *adj.* and *sb.*: see WAIF *sb.*[1]

Johnson 1755 spells this verb as *wave*, and places it as a sense of WAVE *v.*[1], though (following Skinner) he assigns to it a separate derivation from 'Fr. *guesver*.']

1. *trans. Law.* To deprive (a person) of the benefit and protection of the law as a punishment; to outlaw. Chiefly in *passive*.

In AF. *weyver* had the sense 'to abandon, disclaim ownership of (a serf)': see Britton I. xxxii. §8.

†**a.** *gen.* = OUTLAW *v. Obs.*

1297 R. GLOUC. (Rolls) 10823 He let al so uor is loue delmeri of prison Sir hubert de boru & oþere þat in prison were ido & hom þat iweiued were is pes he ȝef al so.

b. In restricted application: To outlaw (a woman). ? *Obs.*

[The expression 'to be outlawed' (AF. *estre utlagé*) was held to be in strictness not applicable to a woman, for the reason given in the following quot.:

c **1290** BRITTON I. xiii. §3 Femme neqedent ne peut estre utlagé proprement, pur ceo qe ele ne est mie ordeyné a dizeyne, ne a la ley, mes weyvé, qe vaut utlagerie.]

1457 *Cov. Leet Bk.* 303 Þat no shirrif of þis Cite frohensfurth take of eny person..beyng outlawed or weyued, for fyne to be eased for a hole ȝer but xl d. **1543** tr. *Act 7 Hen. IV*, c. 13 Where as many of the kinges liege people be outlawed, and many wayued by erronyous processe. **1625** SIR H. FINCH *Law* (1636) 242 When a woman is outlawed, shee is said to be waued and not outlawed, because shee is neuer sworne to the Law. **1741** T. ROBINSON *Gavelkind* I. vi. 116 The Process continued till the Uncles were outlawed, and the Niece waived. **1818** CRUISE *Digest* (ed. 2) V. 185 Persons outlawed, or waived in personal actions, may alien by fine.

2. *Law.* To abandon (stolen goods). *Obs.* exc. *Hist.*

1531 tr. *St. German's Dial. Doctor & Stud.* II. iii. 8b, Goodes stolen, and seased for the kynge or wayued be forfeite onelesse appele or enditement be sued. **1579** *Expos. Terms Law* 186 b, The queenes officer or the Reeue or Bailife to the Lord of the manour..may seyse the goodes so wayued to their lordes vse. *Ibid.* 187 If a man bee pursued..as a felon, and hee flyeth, and leaueth his owne goodes &c. these shalbe taken as goods wayued, & forfait as if they had bin stolne. **1589** COOPER *Admon.* 51 Vpon notice giuen to the said B. that such like cloth was wayued within his Manor of Fulham, and left in a ditch there, and no owner knowen, hee ..appoynted the same to be watched. **1639** *Nuisance to Private Houses* 16 If any goods be wayued in any manner, and if any man take them, that then it shall bee lawfull for mee to destraine. **1765** BLACKSTONE *Comm.* I. viii. 286 Waifs, *bona waviata*, are goods stolen, and waived or thrown away by the thief in his flight, for fear of being apprehended.

†**3. a.** *gen.* To abandon, leave, desert, forsake (a person, place, thing). *Obs.*

c **1330** R. BRUNNE *Chron. Wace* 10185 Al þe contre gan þey weyue & fledde a-wey vn to Murreyue. **1390** GOWER *Conf.* I. 315 The lond was thanne sone weyved. *a* **1400–50** *Wars Alex.* 297 Þen will he wed anoþire wife, & wayfe me for euer. *Ibid.* 2469 Bot bowis first fra ȝour bargis & blythly þaim wayfe [*MS. Dublin* woydez]. *c* **1450** *St. Cuthbert* (Surtees) 5793 Þe hors wayuand sone, he left, And lokyd how he myght fle eft.

†**b.** To cast aside, relinquish, forsake (the truth, one's faith or god, a state or condition, etc.).

1303 R. BRUNNE *Handl. Synne* 6597 Forsake Iew at alle þy myȝt, But ȝyf þou hope þat he wul weyue Hys lawe, and crystendom receyue. *c* **1386** CHAUCER *Pars. Prol.* 33 For Paul that writeth vn-to Thymothee Repreueth hem that weyueth soothfastnesse. **1390** GOWER *Conf.* I. 180 So that baptesme thei receiven And alle here false goddes weyven. *c* **1394** *P. Pl. Crede* 685 Falshed of freres haþ..maid hem to ..wayuen þe trewþe. *a* **1657** R. LOVEDAY *Lett.* (1663) 235 They wav'd the Kings party, and adher'd to this.

†**c.** To abandon, lay aside, forsake (a habit, custom, sin, etc.). *Obs.*

1340 *Ayenb.* 88 And of hire herte alle zenne to waynye [*read* wayuye]. *c* **1374** CHAUCER *Boeth.* I. met. vii. (1868) 29 Weyue þou ioie, drif fro þe drede. *c* **1394** *P. Pl. Crede* 530 Wycliff..grayþliche hem warned To wayuen her wikednesse. *c* **1412** HOCCLEVE *De Reg. Princ.* 1442 Hem hoghte to be mirours of sadnesse, And wayue iolitee and wantonnesse. *Ibid.* 3385 For to hem longith it, for goddes sake, To wayue cruelte and tyrannye. **1658** SIR T. BROWNE *Hydriot*, i. 8 The Ægyptians were afraid of fire..And from such Ægyptian scruples imbibed by Pythagoras, it may be conjectured that Numa and the Pythagoricall Sect first waved the fiery solution.

†**d.** To abandon, give up (a task); to resign (an office). Also with inf. as obj. *Obs.*

c **1386** CHAUCER *Melib.* ⁋2256, I seye that though..ye weyue to perfourne thilke same emprise by Iuste cause men sholde nat seyn therfore that ye were a lier ne forsworn. *Ibid.* ⁋2406 Lest that the charge oppresse thee so soore that thee bihoueth to weyue thyng that thou hast bigonne. **1390** GOWER *Conf.* I. 258 This innocent, which was deceived, His Papacie anon hath weyved, Renounced and resigned eke. *Ibid.* I. 363 Fro ferst that holi cherche hath weyved To preche, and hath the swerd received. *a* **1661** FULLER *Worthies, Bucks* (1662) 135 Walter Haddon was..chosen Vice-Chancellour of Cambridge 1550. Soon after he was made President of Magdalen-Colledge in Oxford, which place he waved in the reign of Queen Mary.

†**e.** To abandon or withdraw formally (legal proceedings, a motion); also, to defeat (a proposal) on a vote. *Obs.*

1647 CLARENDON *Hist. Reb.* III. §104 Though there might be some reason for their [the bishops'] absence when the trial was, according to law, before and by his peers only, yet when that judgment was waived, and a bill of attainder brought up against him, their votes in that bill were as.. essential as of any other of the lords. **1658–9** *Burton's Diary* (1828) IV. 14, I was before for bounding, but that was not relished. It is not for our honour to recede to what we have waved. *a* **1662** HEYLYN *Laud* II. (1671) 295 Others conceived, that they had very well performed their duty.. by waving all Proceedings against them. **1692–3** WOOD *Life* 24 Jan. (O.H.S.) III. 414 It was then discussed or proposed that Dr. William Lloyd's book..be burnt also: but waved only by eleven votes. **1706** HEARNE *Collect.* 24 Mar. (O.H.S.) I. 208 The Prolocutor of yᵉ Lower House of Convocation.. had a great mind to have propos'd..yᵗ publick thanks should be return'd to Mr. Wall..but this seeming a little unpresidented, 'twas wav'd. **1736** *Gentl. Mag.* VI. 441/2 For this Reason, he hoped, the Hon. Gentleman would..wave the Motion he had made.

f. To abandon, relinquish, give up (an intention). Now *rare* or *Obs.*

c **1450** *Pol. Poems* (Rolls) II. 228 Be no more blynde, but weynyth [*read* weyuyth] youre wille. **1700** in *Pepys' Diary* (1875) VI. 231 He designed to have mounted on horseback at some distance from the town,..but seeing the crowd and dust he had to encounter with, very prudently waved it. **1787** *Mirror* 10 He once entertained a desire of taking a tour to Scythia; but waved it. **1817** JAS. MILL *Brit. India* I. I. i. 7 He waved his intention of landing on that island, and steered for Ternate.

†**4.** *intr. to waive from* = 3 b. *Obs.*

1303 R. BRUNNE *Handl. Synne* 235 Þouȝe he to-day fro hys god weyue, To-morwe hys god wyl hym receyue. *c* **1386** CHAUCER *Merch. T.* 239 But þat ye been so ful of sapience That yow ne liketh for youre heighe prudence To weyuen fro the word of Salomon. *c* **1386** —— *Squire's T.* Prol. 6 From a soeth euere wol they [*sc.* women] weyue.

5. *trans.* **a.** *Law.* To relinquish (a right, claim, or contention) either by express declaration or by doing some intentional act which by law is equivalent to this; to decline to avail oneself of (an advantage); to refuse to accept (some provision made in one's favour).

AF. *weyver* with this sense is very frequent in law-books from Britton (*c* 1290) onwards.

to waive the tort, said in common-law pleading of a plaintiff who, having the choice of framing his action in contract or tort, elected to sue in contract.

c **1469** *Stonor Papers* (Camden) I. 103 Þe title of Jobury is by his owne Counsell wayued and taken for nought. *c* **1570** *Pride & Lowl.* (1841) 70 But that ech partie would have his reason, to prove their issue,..And weyven would no point for them might fal. **1666** H. JACKSON in *Extr. St. P. rel. Friends* III. (1912) 248 They..altogeither waved that for which at first they pretended to commit mee. **1685** KEBLE *Rep.* I. 225 *Nota, per Curiam* after special Issue joyned, the parties cannot waive it, and plead general Issue without motion in Court. **1776** G. WILSON *Coke's Rep.* III. II. 26 If lands be given to husband and wife in tail, or in fee, and the husband dies, there the wife cannot devest the freehold out of her by any verbal waver... As if before any entry made by her, she saith that she utterly waves and disagrees to the said estate,..yet the freehold remains in her. **1818** CRUISE *Digest* (ed. 2) I. 177 In cases of this kind the wife cannot waive the provision thereby made for her, and claim dower at common law. **1826** BELL *Comm. Laws Scot.* (ed. 5) I. 422 The parties may, by anticipation, waive the rules of negociation [of bills]. *Ibid.* II. 96 Lien may be waived by agreement before the possession begins. **1839** J. L. ADOLPHUS *The Circuiteers* in *Law Quart. Rev.* (1885) I. 232 Thoughts much too deep for tears subdue the Court When I *assumpsit* bring, and god-like waive a tort. **1875** K. E. DIGBY *Real Prop.* x. §1. (1876) 381 If however the lessor, after knowledge of the happening of the event, continues in any way to treat the lessee as his tenant,..he is said to waive the forfeiture, and can no longer take advantage of it.

b. To refrain from insisting upon, give up (a privilege, right, claim, etc.); to forbear to claim or demand.

1625 DONNE *80 Serm.* (1640) iii. 22 He takes the name of the Son of a woman, and waives the glorious name of the Son of God. **1633** T. GERARD *Descr. Somerset* (1900) 185 A thing even usuall in those times for a man to wave his own armes and take his mothers. **1660** COKE *Power & Subj.* 243 If the Parliament..did endue the Queen with such plentifull power, as to make her supreme Governor (the title of Head was waved) in all causes. **1708** J. CHAMBERLAYNE *St. Gt. Brit.* I. II. xv. 143 The Jurisdiction of this Lord Chief Justice is very great..the Lords sometimes waving their own Power, have directed him to send his Warrant to seize Persons suspected of Capital Crimes. **1750** JOHNSON *Rambler* No. 24 ⁋13 Congreve waved his title to dramatic reputation and desired to be considered only as a gentleman. **1787** COWPER *Bill Mortality* 12 This annual tribute Death requires, And never waves his claim. **1805** NELSON in Nicolas *Disp.* (1846) VII. 108 Perhaps Lieutenant Hewson would waive his rank to be in a Flag Ship. **1820** W. IRVING *Sketch Bk.* I. 128 He lays aside his distance and reserve, and is glad to wave the distinctions of rank. **1836** MARRYAT *Midsh. Easy* xviii, But you just now asserted that you would waive your rank. **1855** MACAULAY *Hist. Eng.* xvi. III. 679 Marlborough consented to waive part of his rights, and to allow precedence to the Duke on the alternate days. **1886** G. ALLEN *Darwin* vi. 81 The younger [naturalist]..waived his own claim..in favour of the elder. **1912** *Throne* 7 Aug. 240/1 The long outstanding appeal to the Union Government to waive a portion of the 60 per cent. tax was likely to be successful.

c. To forbear persistence in (an action or course of action); to refrain from pressing (an objection, a scruple, an argument).

1681 *Pennsylv. Arch.* I. 38 And of yoʳ regard to yoʳ owne and future good of yoʳ posterity makes mee to wave all objections of yᵉ nature. **1706** *Col. Rec. Pennsylv.* II. 284 He was willing to wave all resentmᵗˢ. **1756** BURKE *Vind. Nat. Soc.* 76, I submit to the Condition, and though I have a notorious Advantage before me, I wave the Pursuit. **1774** J. WALKER *Gen. Idea Pronounc. Dict.* 2 If, therefore, every argument for the improvement of language were waved, but what arises from the superior harmony and beauty of an uniform and well-polished tongue, we might with reason conclude, that [etc.]. **1818** SCOTT *Br. Lamm.* xxix, A contract must be supposed to be given up, when the party waves insisting upon it. **1842** BISCHOFF *Woollen Manuf.* II. 29 We trust that the example of so many of those engaged in the same trade, will induce the manufacturers of Leeds and Norwich to wave their opposition to this measure. **1868** J. H. BLUNT *Ref. Ch. Eng.* I. 54 Yet the king is willing to waive his objection. **1881** BESANT & RICE *Chapl. Fleet* I. vi, As he had eaten nothing for two days, he was induced to waive this scruple, and presently made a hearty meal.

d. To dispense with (formality, ceremony, etiquette).

1781 COWPER *Let.* 7 July, Lady Austen, waving all forms, has paid us the first visit. **1810** S. GREEN *Reformist* I. 20 You, it is true, are my servant; but wave all ceremony, all diffidence. **1821** LAMB *Elia* I. *Grace bef. Meat*, The supplementary or tea-grace was waived altogether. **1833** LYTTON *Godolphin* I. xxii. 266 'A few persons come to me to-morrow evening', said she; '*do* waive ceremony, and join us'. **1851** DIXON *W. Penn* xxviii. (1872) 259 Penn was with the Quakers, who agreed to waive the ceremony of the hat.

†**e.** To forgo, deny to oneself (some advantage). *Obs.*

1669 BOYLE *Cont. New Exp.* I. xxxviii. (1682) 129 To make the Trial more accurate, I wav'd the use of other Bellows. *a* **1680** BUTLER *Rem.* (1759) I. 110 Therefore you wisely scorn your Stile to humble, Or for the Sense's Sake to wave the Rumble. **1772** MACKENZIE *Man World* II. vi. (1823) 473 He had prevailed on himself to waive that pleasure. **1785** *Epitaph to Cath. Clive* in *Pall Mall Gaz.* 12 Oct. (1887) 11/2 Content with Fame, ev'n affluence she wav'd.

f. *refl.* To put aside one's own interests. *rare*⁻¹.

1894 BLACKMORE *Perlycross* xiii, She could not claim the pleasure of having waived herself to please him.

6. †**a.** To shun, avoid; to elude, escape; to dodge (a blow). *Obs.*

1303 R. BRUNNE *Handl. Synne* 2591 Okerers men oght to weyue, ȝeue hem noght, ne of hem receyue. **1390** GOWER *Conf.* I. 58 So that he hath the wordes weyved And thurgh his Ere is noght deceived. **1446** LYDG. *Two Nightingale Poems* i. 306 The fende..Goth fast a-boute..Leying hys lynes and..Wsynge his hokes, on theym you to receyue, The which thus lyghtly ye may eschewe & weyfe. **1590** SPENSER *F.Q.* III. iv. 36 Ne of thy late life memory is left, Ne can thy irreuocable destiny be weft. *a* **1656** USSHER *Ann.* (1658) 458 In the fight Jonathan reached forth his arme to strick Bacchides, but he warily waved the blow.

b. To decline (combat). ? *Obs.*

1664 BUTLER *Hud.* II. ii. 578 Both thought it was their wisest course To wave the Fight, and mount to Horse. **1697** DRYDEN *Æneis* XII. 95 Refuse me not this one, this only Pray'r, To wave the Combat, and pursue the War. **1718** POPE *Iliad* XXIII. 689 Not but (my Friend) 'tis still the wiser way To wave Contention with superior Sway.

c. To evade (doing something). †Also with *inf.* as obj.

c **1440** *Pallad. on Husb.* IV. 866 Folis with hond to touche a corser weyueth. **1646** E. WINSLOW *Hypocr. Unmasked* 101 Furthermore in the Government of Plimouth, to our great griefe, not onely the Pastor of a Congregation waveth the administration of baptisme to Infants, but divers of his Congregation are fallen with him. **1657** J. SERGEANT *Schism Dispatch't* 548 They..confess themselves to seek in those points, as wee have seen lately, and as Mʳ Fuller tacitly grants by waving to patronize it. **1665** BOYLE *Occas. Refl.* Introd. Pref. *a* b, That I may have the greater Opportunity to hear other mens Opinions..and the less Temptation to wave the complying with those that shall seem Reasonable. **1768** BOSWELL *Corsica* ii. (ed. 2) 82 The judge could wave the pursuit of justice by saying, 'Non procedatur'. **1793** MME. D'ARBLAY *Lett.* 22 Feb., I have waived and waived acceptance almost from the moment of Madame de Staël's arrival. **1823** SCOTT *Peveril* ix, He calmly waved receiving the paper which Sir Jasper offered to him. **1858** HAWTHORNE *Fr. & It. Note-bks.* (1871) I. 334 There appears to be no concealment on the part of the officers in thus waiving the exercise of their duty.

d. To put aside, avoid (a subject, a discussion).

1746 HERVEY *Medit.* (1818) 71 [My mind] has studiously waved the fearful subject, and seems unwilling to pursue it even now. **1748** RICHARDSON *Clarissa* (1811) II. xxx. 186 To my surprise, he waved everything that would have led to the subject. **1778** MISS BURNEY *Evelina* I. xxvi. 144, I would fain have waved the subject. **1816** SCOTT *Old Mort.* xxxi, Which..they considered as the most effectual mode of solving all difficulties and waiving all discussions. **1847** DISRAELI *Tancred* II. ii, Tancred..waived the subject.

†**7. a.** To refuse, reject (something offered). Also with *clause* as obj. *Obs.*

c **1386** CHAUCER *Melib.* ⁋2398 Thou shalt chese the beste and weyue all othere thynges. **1390** GOWER *Conf.* I. 276 [Constantine proclaimed] Up peine of deth that noman weyve That he baptesme ne receive. **14..** HOCCLEVE *Minor Poems* xxi. 105 Many a man this day, but they gold wey, of men not wole it take ne receyve, and yf it lake his peis, they woll it weive. *c* **1440** CAPGRAVE *St. Kath.* 510 If it [*sc.* a proposed statue] myght kepe my flesh in swiche degree It shulde not rote, I wolde it neuere weyue.

b. To put aside, avoid acceptance of (an offer, something offered); to decline (an honour), deprecate (praise). ? *Obs.*

1642 FULLER *Holy & Prof. St.* II. xviii. 118 The neighbour gentry court him for his acquaintance, which he either modestly waveth, or thankfully accepteth. *c* **1645** HOWELL *Lett.* (1655) I. II. iv. 73 They offer'd the Crown to the Duke of Saxony, and he waving it, they sent Ambassadors to the Palsgrave. **1734** tr. *Rollin's Anc. Hist.* III. VII. 449 He for some time desired leave to wave the honour they offered him. **1753** RICHARDSON *Grandison* III. xii. (1781) 90 The Doctor very modestly received the compliment, and, to wave our praises, gave us [etc.].

8. †**a.** To treat with neglect, ignore, disregard, overlook; to let pass (an opportunity). *Obs.*

c **1400** *Laud Troy Bk.* 17320 The kyng answered..For ȝe wot wele..That I haue done ȝoure consayl here, In al my lyff I wayved hit neuere. **1586** in Motley *Netherl.* (1860) II. i. 43 [Lord Burgh] in a most vehement passion, waived the countermand [and his insubordination was very generally imitated]. **1646** M. HOPKINS *Let.* in Gaule *Cases Consc.* To

Rdr., I would certainely know afore whether your Town ..[is] willing to give..us good welcome.., else I shall wave your Shire. **1652** NEDHAM tr. *Selden's Mare Cl.* 169 It is no hard matter in like manner to wave the Autoritie of those of later time, that oppose a Dominion. **1657** WOOD *Life* (O.H.S.) I. 228 This perswasion of that unfortunate lord occasion'd his majesty to wave the advice of Lilly and others, &c. **1662** MARVELL *Corr.* Wks. (Grosart) II. 82 But there are strange reasons and junctures at Court in all businesses, which must be catched or waived. **1671** E. CHAMBERLAYNE *Pres. St. Eng.* II. 77 The Courts of the Archbishop of Canterbury, where any Ecclesiastical Sutes between any persons may (waving all inferior Courts) be decided. **1675** tr. *Machiavelli's Prince* xix. (1883) 129 The Soldan..being wholly in the power of the soldiers, it is convenient that he also waive the people and insinuate with the army. *a* **1677** BARROW *Serm.* Wks. 1686 III. xxiii. 264 God,..respecteth not onely the good of this or that person,..but often (in some degree waving that, or taking care for it in a less remarkable way) hath a provident regard to the more extensive good of a whole people. **1713** C'TESS WINCHILSEA *Misc. Poems* 263 Receive it then, t'expel these mortal Cares, Nor wave a Med'cine, which thy God prepares.

b. To put aside, refuse to defer to (another's scruples). *rare.*

1833 HT. MARTINEAU *Fr. Wines & Pol.* iv. 53 Being under promise, however, to purchase such and such quantities of wine, he must waive their polite scruples.

9. a. To refrain from applying or enforcing (a rule, law), to make an exception to.

a **1665** J. GOODWIN *Filled w. the Spirit* ii. (1670) 32 And (doubtless) it was the very intention, of the Law-makers themselves, that their Law, calculated for the regulating ordinary cases only, in such cases as these (I mean extraordinaries) should be waved. **1669** STURMY *Mariner's Mag.* VI. iii. 127 So with reason wave the Rule, as occasion requireth. **1849** MISS MULOCK *Ogilvies* xix, But in the present case we will waive the aforesaid excellent rule.

b. *N. Amer.* Of a sports club: to waive its right to buy (a player from another club in the same league). Also *intr.* Cf. WAIVER 1 d.

1908 *Evening Star* (Washington, D.C.) 26 Feb. 13/2 The Giants have given Mike Lynch his unconditional release, as all clubs have waived. **1970** *Globe & Mail* (Toronto) 26 Sept. 36/2 John Schneider..finally was cut and..waived through the Canadian Football League. **1979** *Tucson* (Arizona) *Citizen* 20 Sept. 2D/4 Atlanta Hawks—Waived Tim Claxton, guard, and Rickey Brown, forward.

10. a. To abstain from entering upon (an action, inquiry, a discussion, subject of consideration). Often with some notion of reserving for a future opportunity: To allow to stand over, put aside for the present, defer.

In the 17th c. very often with vbl. sb. as obj.

1650 BULWER *Anthropomet.* xxiii. (1653) 452 Upon which a Quære might be raised... But this, as being not properly appertaining to our Designe, we shall wave it for the present. **1694** F. BRAGGE *Disc. Parables* III. 100, I shall wave the enquiry how far religion is conducive to these things. **1696** WHISTON *Theory Earth* II. 154 Now verbal Descriptions.. being of small advantage..I shall wave more words about it. **1712** ADDISON *Spect.* No. 267 ¶1 For this Reason I shall wave the Discussion of that Point. *a* **1716** BLACKALL *Wks.* (1723) I. 110 A Reason why he wav'd concerning himself to decide this Difference, might be, because the Man came to him..as to a Person invested with secular Power. **1759** DILWORTH *Pope* 76 For our part we shall wave entering into a disquisition about the English translation of the *Iliad.* **1774** MITFORD *Ess. Harmony Lang.* 207, I shall wave all farther remarks. **1797** HT. LEE *Canterb. T., Poet's T.* (1799) I. 74 Let us wave further conversation. **1870** RUSKIN *Lect. Art* i. 22, I waive discussion of this to-day. **1873** BROWNING *Red Cott. Nt.-Cap* 1529 Well now, waive nonsense, you and I are boys No longer.

†**b.** To refrain from dealing with in statement or narrative; to omit, leave out. *Obs.*

1651 DAVENANT *Gondibert* I. xxiii, In pity thus, her beauty's just renown I wave for publique Peace. **1665** BUNYAN *Holy Citie* (1669) 130 John tells us this Wall is an hundred forty four Cubits, (and waves the manner of the measure of Ezekiel). **1684** J. MORRISON tr. *Struys' Voy.* Pref. 1 A Person, whose sufferings (waving other discouraging circumstances) might have very well excused from observing. **1703** POPE *Thebais* 19 But wave whate'er to Cadmus may belong, And fix, O Muse! the barrier of thy song At Oedipus. **1709** STRYPE *Ann. Ref.* I. xxxv. 354 Then followeth his Answer... Which being very long I was in some suspense about inserting it, inclining to abreviate or wave it wholly. **1742** FIELDING *J. Andrews* I. ii, To wave there-fore a circumstance, which..is not greatly material.

¶**11.** [Confused with WAVE *v.*] To put (a person or thing) *aside*, *away*, *off* with or as with a wave of the hand.

1832 HT. MARTINEAU *Ella of Garv.* vi. 80 You should have seen him waive us off with his cane. **1871** FARRAR *Witn. Hist.* ii. 50 Both of whom [St. Peter and St. Paul], having given their clear testimony to facts..are now..contemptuously waived aside as idle dreamers. **1877** —— *Marlb. Serm.* xxii. 210 And pure Faith..will here take you by the hand and waive off each baser temptation. **1897** BP. M. CREIGHTON in *Life & Lett.* (1904) II. vii. 258, I cannot waive away all the teaching of history.

†**waive**, *v.*² *Obs.* Forms: 4–5 **wayfe, weyve, wave,** (4 **weive**), 4–6 **wayve,** 4 *north.*, 5–6 *Sc.* **waif,** 5 **waive,** (**wafe**); *pa. t.* 4–5 **wayved, weyved,** (4 *Sc.* **wavit**), 4 **wafte,** 5 **waivet.** [a. ON. *veifa* (Norw. *veiva*) to wave, swing (trans. with obj. in dat.; also rarely refl.), corresponding to MDu. *weiven* to wave, swing, also (= mod.Du. *wuiven*) to beckon, signal (? whence WEAVE *v.*² *Naut.*), and OHG. *-weiben* (in *ziweiben* to destroy, disperse, *ungeweibet* unbroken):—OTeut. **waiƀjan*. A parallel formation, OTeut. **waiƀōjan*, is represented by OHG. *weibôn*, MHG. *weiben*, to move hither and thither, wander, waver; these senses (cf. branch II below) may, though not recorded, have belonged to the ON. word. The root, OTeut. **wīƀ-*:—Indo-Eur. **weip-*, is a variant of OTeut. **wīp-*:—Indo-Eur. **weib-* as in L. *vibrāre* (see VIBRATE *v.*). Both these roots are represented, with the general sense to wave or swing, to shake, both in Teut. and other langs., and each of them has a variant with prefixed *s*: see SWEEP *v.*, SWIFT *a.* (The Indo-Eur. **weip-*, **weib-*, to wind, represented, e.g. by OE. *wǽfan*, Goth. *biwaibjan* to wrap, clothe, are probably unconnected.)

Cf. ME. *wēve-n*, WEVE *v.*, which is of cognate if not identical origin, and has most of the senses below. In some contexts it is difficult to distinguish between *waive* v.¹ and v.², and probably some shades of meaning may have originated from confusion between the two. See also WAVE *v.*, the relations of which to this verb are to some extent uncertain.]

I. *trans.* **1.** To move to and fro or from side to side (the beard, hand, or something held in the hand); to wave, wag.

1338 R. BRUNNE *Chron.* (1725) 242 Þer pencels þei weyued. **13..** *Gaw. & Gr. Knt.* 306 [He] Wayued his berde for to wayte quo-so wolde ryse. *c* **1450** *St. Cuthbert* (Surtees) 2367 Cuthbert wayued his hand on þaim. **1570** LEVINS *Manip.* 204/15 To Wayue, wag, *agitare.*

2. *to waive up*: to throw open (a window, a wicket, etc.). Cf. *to weve up*, WEVE *v.*

13.. *E.E. Allit. P.* B. 453 Þenne wafte he [Noah] vpon [? *read* vp] his wyndowe, & wysed þer-oute. *c* **1375** *Sc. Leg. Saints* xxv. (*Julian*) 315 With þat þe curtyng vpe he wauit. **1377** LANGL. *P. Pl.* B. v. 611 Biddeth amende-ȝow meke him til his maistre ones, To wayne [? *read* wayue] vp þe wiket þat þe womman shette. *a* **1400–50** *Wars Alex.* 945 (Dubl. MS.) Than passyd forth þe prouude whene into a prevay chamer, Wayfez vp a wyndow & waytes þar-owt. *c* **1400** *Destr. Troy* 676 Medea..Waynet [? *read* wayuet] up a window, the welkyn beheld. *c* **1420** *Anturs of Arth.* 408 (Douce MS.) He wayned [? *read* wayued] vp his viser fro his ventalle.

3. To remove, put away, banish. (Cf. WAIVE *v.*¹ 1 a, of which some of the quots. here may be fig. examples.)

1377 LANGL. *P. Pl.* B. xx. 167 And elde hent good hope and hastilich he shifte hym, And wayued awey wanhope and with lyf he fyȝteth. *c* **1386** CHAUCER *Man of Law's T.* 210 Thou knyttest thee, ther thou art nat receyued; Ther thou were weel, fro thennes artow weyued. *c* **1400** *Destr. Troy* 9783 Hit is wit soche wildnes wayne [? *read* wayue] out of mynd. **14..** HOCCLEVE *Minor Poems* i. 192 [The Virgin says] O Iohn,..an heuy sone Haue I of thee; deeth hath myn othir weyued! *Ibid.* vii. 79 Thy might, I woot wel, is my gilt to weyue. **1426** LYDG. *De Guil. Pilgr.* 5321 Thy .iiij. wyttys thow hast lost. Ther myght, ther force, ar fro the weyved. *c* **1440** *Towneley Myst.* xvi. 247 A-way let ye wafe all sich langage. ? *a* **1500** *Chester Pl., Christ's Entry Jerus.* 52 Though I be wretched and vnworthy, wayve me not from thy wonne! *Ibid., Magi's Obl.* 111 By Myrre, that waues Corruption.

4. a. To cast off (a garment): cf. WEVE *v.* **b.** To cast *away* (money).

c **1400** *Laud Troy Bk.* 15388 Fro his necke his mantel he wayued. *c* **1440** *York Myst.* xxxii. 318 Þis money..Þat Judas in a wreth has wauyd away.

5. To send or dispatch.

a **1400–50** *Wars Alex.* 1175 Him moneste as a maister him ..all þe trouage þare to him tittly to wayne [*read* wayue; *MS. Dubl.* wayfe]. *Ibid.* 1716 (Dubl. MS.) Suche presandez owt of perse he to þe prince wayfez. *Ibid.* 1728 For it is wayved to vs to wete þat wickidly þou haues,.. Puruayd þe pletours oure partis to ride. *Ibid.* 2316 And slike a word he þaim wayues be writ fra him-self. *Ibid.* 2695 Sire, we haue wayued to ȝow writtis.

6. To cause to pass; to divert. *to waive* (*one's*) *wit*: to change one's mind.

1390 GOWER *Conf.* I. 225 Be whom he was deceived Of love, and from his pourpos weyved. *a* **1400–50** *Bk. Curtasye* 322 in *Babees Bk.*, Be stabulle of chere and sumwhat lyȝt, Ne ouer alle wayue þou not thy syȝt. *c* **1400** *Destr. Troy* 9950 Oft ho waivet hir wit & hir wille chaunget. And meuyt hir mynd, as maydons done yet. **1419** in *26 Pol. Poems* xvi. 100 Þat freek may wel be holden a fool, Þat wayueþ wit, and worcheþ by wille.

II. *intr.*

7. To wave, move to and fro in the wind; to be tossed about; to totter.

a **1300** *Cursor M.* 13121 Wend yee þar þe rede to find þat heildes waifand wit þe wind? **1338** R. BRUNNE *Chron.* (1725) 159 R. was perceyued, þei were renged redie, & how þer pencels weyued. **13..** *E.E. Allit. P.* B. 422 Wheder-warde so þe water wafte, hit [the ark] rebounde. *c* **1400** *Gamelyn* 880 The Iustice and the scherreve bothe honged hye, To weyven with the ropes, and with the winde drye. *c* **1400** *Laud Troy Bk.* 14682 Til thei se Gregeis oute comande With brode baneres a-boute wayvande. *c* **1400** *Destr. Troy* 9513 For the smorther, & the smoke of þe smert loghys, Þat waivet in the welkyn..All the Citie might se the sercle aboute. *c* **1430** *Syr Tryam.* 246 And the knyght be there assente Schulde wayue wyth the wynde. *c* **1440** CAPGRAVE *Life St. Kath.* IV. 1377 Looke on your goddis how þei toumble and waue Right whan men swepe hem—so litil is her myght! *c* **1450** *St. Cuthbert* (Surtees) 4702 Þe schip weyued hidir and þidir. *c* **1450** *Gol. & Gaw.* 440 Wourthy to be Hingit heigh on ane tre,..To waif with the wynd. **1513** DOUGLAS *Æneis* VI. v. 124 The south wind Nothus thre dayis me draif Throwout the see, with violent wallis waif. *Ibid.* X. ii. 102 Lyke as first, or wyndis blast be persave, The swouch is hard wythin the woddis waif. *Ibid.* XI. xv. 66 Bot for the tother part, suyth to say, He leit do waif with the swift wynd away. **1535** LYNDESAY *Sat.* 3973 To hunt cattell ȝe war ay speidie, Thairfoir ye sall weaue [*Bann. MS.* waif] in a widdy.

8. To wander, stray.

c **1350** *Will. Palerne* 2386 Many a bold burn after þat best prike,..þat noiþer burde ne barn bi-laft at þe quarrer, but went after þe werwolf & wayned [? *read* wayued] from þe beres. **1390** GOWER *Conf.* I. 338 Here lieges wolde hem noght receive, So that thei mote algates weyve To seche lond in other place. ? *a* **1400** *Morte Arth.* 960 Weryd worthe the wyghte ay, that the thy wytt refede, That mase the to wayfe here in thise wylde lakes! *c* **1440** CAPGRAVE *St. Kath.* III. 593 Ye wolde be with hym euere and neuere fro hym waue. *c* **1460** *Towneley Myst.* ii. 430 The kyng will that thay be safe... At thare awne will let tham wafe. *Ibid.* xxi. 103 If he abowte waue Any langere, his warkys may we ban.

b. *fig.* To stray, wander in purpose.

c **1425** *Cast. Persev.* 380 in *Macro Plays* 88 Whom to folwe, wetyn I ne may:..as wynde in watyr I wave. *c* **1440** CAPGRAVE *St. Kath.* III. 199, I wyl the telle pleynly, I wil not waue, I wil not varye. *Ibid.* v. 390 Fro this decree shal I neuere-more waue.

9. To go by, pass.

1390 GOWER *Conf.* III. 318 And whan the presse of poeple is weived, He takth his hoste unto him tho, And seith, [etc.]. *c* **1400** *Rule St. Benet* 444 And sone when þat scho mai persaiue þair syn, lat noght þe tym ouer wayue, Bot chaistese þam & tery noght.

waive, obs. form of WAIF *sb.*¹

waived (weɪvd), *ppl. a.* [f. WAIVE *v.*¹ + -ED¹.] In senses of the vb.: see quots.

1577 GRANGE *Golden Aphrod.* C ij b, I..persuaded my selfe it was some wayued [*printed* wayned] Bucke, whiche of late had strayed from the lodge of my forest. **1589** COOPER *Admon.* 53 And so is it for waiued goods, as was this cloth. *c* **1640** J. SMYTH *Lives Berkeleys* (1883) II. 435 Wayved goods, Estrayes, Treasure trove. **1706** PHILLIPS (ed. Kersey), *Waived Goods*, are such as a Thief..leaves behind him in his Flight; which are forfeited to the Lord of the Manour, unless [etc.].

waiver (ˈweɪvə(r)). Also 8 **waivure,** 9 **waver.** [a. AF. *weyver* (Britton, 13th c.), subst. use of the inf. *weyver* WAIVE *v.*¹: see -ER⁴.]

1. a. *Law.* The action or an act of waiving; dispensing with a requirement, an express or implicit declining to avail oneself of a known right or to assert a claim.

1628 COKE *On Litt.* §660. 348 b, It appeareth, that the right of the Estate taile discending to him either within age, or of full age, shall worke a Remitter in him, for that the waiuer of the state should haue bin to his losse and preiudice. **1675** SHEPPARD *Grand Abridgm.* IV. 192 This word Waiver is sometimes applyed to an Estate, or something that is made or conveyed to a man, and so it signifieth nothing else but the Refusal to accept of the thing so made and conveyed. And sometimes it is applyed to a plea, and then signifieth a Refusal to stand to a former Plea pleaded, and the pleading a new. **1741** T. ROBINSON *Gavelkind* vi. 116 But the Court held, that the Parol ought not to demur, for that the Infant is out of Court, and by the Waivure the Original is determined against her. **1812** BROUGHAM *Sp. Orders in Council* Wks. 1873 X. 50 That a conduct like this would..throw a single obstacle in the way of exerting on the morrow the very same rights, of which next Saturday's Gazette should contain the waiver. **1817** SELWYN *Law Nisi Prius* (ed. 4) II. 677 Where rent is usually paid at a banker's, if the banker, without any special authority, receives rent accruing after expiration of notice to quit, it will not operate as a waver. **1818** CRUISE *Digest* (ed. 2) III. 335 The taking such subsequent estate was his own folly, and shall be looked upon as a waiver of his prior right. **1838** W. BELL *Dict. Law Scot.* 849 That in this instance the express consent of the tenant amounted to a waiver of the statutory warning. **1846** LD. CAMPBELL *Chancellors* cviii. IV. 127 *note*, Hallam is of opinion that the first two Georges, by their frequent visits to Hanover, made a bad return for the waiver of the condition on which they were invited to the throne. *a* **1850** J. C. CALHOUN *Wks.* (1874) IV. 480 It is well understood that a compromise involves not a surrender, but simply a waiver of the right or power. **1874** GREEN *Short Hist.* ix. §9. 685 It was necessary to bribe the two rival claimants to a waiver of their claims. **1908** *Times* 27 Aug. 11/5 As to the point as to waiver, it had long been decided that every trifling breach of a covenant was not to be taken as a waiver.

b. Comb.: **waiver clause**, a clause in the prospectus of a joint-stock company, by which the subscribers are made to contract themselves out of the provision of the Companies Act requiring that the prospectus shall contain certain particulars respecting the contracts made with the promoters.

1894 *Pall Mall Gaz.* 5 Dec. 5/3. **1899** *Westm. Gaz.* 16 Oct. 10/2 It is becoming quite refreshing to find a prospectus without the objectionable waiver clause.

¶**c.** The alleged use of the word as synonymous with WAIVERY appears to be unauthenticated.

1850 OGILVIE, whence in later Dicts.

d. *spec.* The formal relinquishment by a club in a professional sports (esp. baseball) league of its right to buy the contract of a player from another club in the same league, before he is offered to a club in another league. Freq. *on waivers*. *N. Amer.*

1907 HERRMANN & PULLIAM in *4th Ann. Rep. Nat. Commission* (1908) 99 The Club never had any intention to let the player go;..they only asked for waivers as a bluff. **1946** *Encycl. Brit.* III. 167/1 There is a fixed price in each league that must be paid by the club obtaining a player by this waiver method. The player is said to be sent by club A to club B on waivers. **1951** *Britannica Bk. of Year* 88/2 The Giants claimed pitcher Jim Hearn from the Cardinals on waivers in mid-season. **1972** J. MOSEDALE *Football* v. 75 He was put on waivers at the end of the season. **1978** *N.Y. Times* 29 Mar. B4/4 Oakland..put Dick Allen, first baseman, on waivers for purpose of giving him unconditional release.

2. In non-technical use: An act of waiving or dismissing from consideration. *rare.*

1883 E. C. STEDMAN in *Century Mag.* XXVI. 940 There is something exasperating to serious minds in his placid waiver of things grievous or distasteful.

waiver: see WAVER *sb.*

'**waivery.** *Law. Obs.* exc. *Hist.* [a. AF. *weiverie* (14th c. in *Liber Albus*, p. 190), f. *weive* (fem. of *weif* adj.: see WAIF *sb.*[1]): see WAIVE *sb.*, WAIVE *v.*[1], and -ERY. (In Law Latin *waivaria*.)] (See quot.)

1903 *Cal. Lond. Let.-Bk. E.* p. xxix, Proceedings of outlawry, or 'waivery' (the technical term in the case of women), had been taken against Agnes Westhalle.

waiving ('weɪvɪŋ), *vbl. sb.* [f. WAIVE *v.*[1] + -ING[1].] The action of WAIVE *v.*[1]

1596 BACON *Use Com. Law* (1630) 76 A Thiefe hauing stolne goods, being pursued flyeth away and leaueth the goods. This leauing is called Wayuing. **1654** BRAMHALL *Just Vind.* iv. (1661) 62 This was not a conquest, but a plain waving of his sentences from Rome and a yielding of the question. **1826** BELL *Comm. Laws Scot.* (ed. 5) I. 422 If the drawer say to the holder before the bill falls due,..that he will call and see whether the bill has been paid by the acceptor, it is a waiving of notice. **1914** B. H. STREETER *Restatem. & Reunion* iv. 191 In the minds of a minority, any waiving of the Rubric seems to involve a point of principle.

waivling, var. WAVELING *a. Sc.*

waivode, waiwode: see WAYWODE.

†**wak**, *a.* and *sb. Sc. Obs.* Also 6–7 **wack**, 6 **vak**. [a. ON. **vakw-* (Icel. *vǫk-r*) moist, damp = (M)Du. *wak*:—OTeut. **wakwo-*, cogn. w. Gr. ὑγρός, L. *ūvidus* (:—**ugvidus*) moist.]

A. *adj.* Moist, damp.

1513 DOUGLAS *Æneis* III. ix. 2 Quhen Aurora the wak nycht did arest, And chais fra hevin with hir dym skyis donk. **1528** LYNDESAY *Dreme* 388 First, to the Mone,..Quene of the see,..Off nature wak and cauld, and no thyng clere. **1533** BELLENDEN *Livy* v. xxii. (S.T.S.) II. 224 þai ar nurist with wak humouris and Caldnes. **1572** *Satir. Poems Reform.* xxxiii. 1 ȝe vapurs wak, and watters in the air! *c* **1590** J. STEWART *Poems* (S.T.S.) II. 215 And till eschew nocturnall vapor vak. **1609** SKENE *Reg. Maj., Chalm. Air* xxv. 153 b, They make the claith wak and donke. **1666** *Despauterii Gram. Instit., Lib. VII*, E 7 b (Jam.), *Madeo*, to be wack or drunk. *Permadeo*, to be very wack. **1776** *Herd's Coll. Sc. Songs* II. Gloss., *Wak*, moist, wet.

Hence '**wakness**, moisture.

c **1520** NISBET *N.T. Scots* Luke viii. 6 Ane vthir fell on staan; and it sprang vp and dryit, for it had nocht moistour (or wacnes). **1528** LYNDSAY *Dreme* 460 Than past we vp quhare Jupiter the kyng Satt in his speir,..Complexionate with waknes and with heit. **1563** KNOX *Ressoning betw. Abbot Crosraguell & K.* (1812) Prol. ij b, The earth bringeth forth the tree, it groweth by moistour, and natural wacknes. **1595** DUNCAN *App. Etymol., Mador, humor*, waknesse. **1808** JAMIESON, *Waknes*, humidity.

B. *sb.* Moisture.

1456 SIR G. HAYE *Law Arms* (S.T.S.) 76 Quhen it [the moon] is full, all thingis..that ar governyt be wak or moystnes, ar mare forssy and vigorous na quhen it is wane.

wak, wakande: see WEAK *a.*, VACAND.

‖**waka**[1] ('waka). *N.Z.* Also 9 **walker, wauka**. [Maori.] A Maori canoe (see quots.).

1807 J. SAVAGE *Some Acct. N.Z.* xi. 77 *Wauka*, a canoe. **1834** E. MARKHAM *N.Z. or Recoll. of It* (MS.) 3 Canoes, or in the Native Mourie Tongue, Walker Mouries, or Native boats. **1841** J. C. BIDWILL *Rambles in N.Z.* (1952) 61 Those [Canoes] with topsides..are called Wa-kaw, or in common pronunciation 'Walkers'. **1845** R. TAYLOR *Jrnl.* 19 June (MS.) III. 222 We had a large waka which just held our large party. **1874** W. M. BAINES *Narr. E. Crewe* 81 'Whaka' is the native name, or rather the native generic term, for all canoes, of which there are many different kinds, as tete, pekatu, kapapa and others. **1921** H. GUTHRIE-SMITH *Tutira* x. 73 A miniature *waka* or canoe..was moved..from place to place. **1936** *Discovery* Jan. 13/2 A Moriori Waka or fishing boat. **1949** P. BUCK *Coming of Maori* (1950) II. vii. 203 River canoes (*waka tiwai*), also used on inland lakes, consisted merely of the dug-out hull. Seagoing canoes (*waka tete*).. were larger.

‖**waka**[2] ('waka). [Jap.] **1.** A form of classic Japanese poetry, lyrical in nature and developed from the ancient traditional ballads.

[**1880** B. H. CHAMBERLAIN *Classical Poetry of Japanese* p. vi, *Kokiñ Wa-Ka Shifu Uchi-Giki* ('Memoranda Concerning the Collection of Japanese Odes Ancient and Modern'), by Kamo-no-Mabuchi.] **1932** B. L. SUZUKI *Nōgaku* 24 The forms sung in the Nō are the *shidai*,..*rongi*, *waka*, and *kiri*. **1948** *Introd. Class Jap. Lit.* p. iv, In the sphere of *waka* poetry also, the *Kokinshū* anthology..shows the transition from 'sincerity' to 'sentimentality'. **1968** *Encycl. Brit.* XII. 953/2 The poetic form used—the *waka*, deriving from the earlier folk songs consists of an alternation of five- and seven-syllable lines, without rhyme, stress, metrical pattern or other technical device.

2. A Japanese poem of thirty-one syllables, a *tanka*.

1938 D. T. SUZUKI *Zen Buddhism* I. iv. 95 The secret documents also contain a number of *waka*, versified epigrams, in regard to the mastery of swordsmanship. **1956** D. KEENE *Anthol. Jap. Lit.* 25 His *waka*—thirty-one syllabled poems—are among the most beautiful and melancholy in the language. **1977** *Times Lit. Suppl.* 15 Apr. 448/4 The most striking qualities of the haiku and the waka.

Wakamba (wɑ'kæmbə). [Bantu.] = KAMBA.

1888 *Encycl. Brit.* XXIV. 828/1 [Bantu tongues of eastern group] Wa-Kamba, Wa-Nika, Wa-Pokomo. **1935** [see SIMBA]. **1937** K. BLIXEN *Out of Afr.* II. 138 The immigrant Somalis..have a moral code... But the unprejudiced Kikuyu, Wakambas, or Kavirondos..judge you not. **1955** *Times* 13 July 6/5 Many Nyanza and Wakamba tribesmen in the Nairobi area had taken Mau Mau oaths in the last 18 months. **1977** H. INNES *Big Footprints* I. i. 24 'A Masai?' I asked... 'No, no. He's of the Kamba people—the Wakamba.'

wake (weɪk), *sb.*[1] Forms: 4 **wak, woke**, *Sc.* **walk**, 6 **wacke**, also *pl.* (sense 4) **waakes, wakesses, waks**, 2– **wake**. [In form the word corresponds to OE. **wacu* str. fem., occurring once in *nihtwaco* night-watch. Compare also the wk. fem. forms, MDu. *wake* (Du. *waak*), MLG. *wake*, OHG. *wacha* (MHG., modG. *wache*), wakefulness, watching, watch, ON. *vaka* (MSw., Sw. *vaka*, Norw. *voka*) watch, vigil, eve of a feast; related to WAKE *v.* In the sense 'state of wakefulness', the sb. is prob. in part a new formation in ME. on the stem of WAKE *v.*, on the analogy of *sleep* vb. and sb. In sense 4 adoption from ON. is possible; the sense 'merry-making' is found in ON. and Norw.; cf. ON. *Jónsvaka*, Norw. *Jóns(v)oka* St. John's Eve, Midsummer festivities.]

1. The state of wakefulness *esp.* during normal hours of sleep. *Obs.* exc. in ***sleep and* (*or*) *wake, wake and dream***.

a **1250** *Owl & Night.* 1590 Al for hire louerdes sake Haueþ daies kare and niȝtes wake. **1596** SHAKS. *1 Hen. IV*, III. i. 219 Making such difference betwixt Wake and Sleepe, As is the difference betwixt Day and Night. **1823** 'JON BEE' *Dict. Turf.* s.v., At Bristol one eye is ever upon the wake while the other nappeth. **1844** MRS. BROWNING *Brown Rosary* II, Repeat the vow—declare its cause and kind Which, not to break, in sleep or wake, thou bearest on thy mind. **1898** J. B. CROZIER *My Inner Life* I. iv. 33 In that half-conscious state between sleep and wake. **1913** *Edin. Rev.* Jan. 194 Their beauty is the beauty of a kind of mirage that haunts the borders between wake and dream.

†**b.** A state or period of wakefulness. *Obs.*

1611 BEAUM. & FL. *Philaster* II. (1620) 22 What thinke you of a pleasing dreame to last till morning? *Gal.* I shall chose my Lord a pleasing wake before it. **1626** B. JONSON *Staple of N.* II. v, That youth, and shape, which in my dreames and wakes, I haue so oft contemplated.

†**c.** The act of awaking. *Obs.*

1678 DRYDEN *All for Love* v. i, Who follow'd me, but as the Swallow Summer, Hatching her young ones in my kindly Beams, Singing her flatt'ries to my morning wake.

†**2.** Abstinence from sleep, watching, practised as a religious observance: often coupled with *fasting*. Also, an instance of this; a night spent in devout watching (on the eve of a festival, of the reception of knighthood, etc.); a watch, vigil.

c **1200** *Vices & Vertues* 125 Mid fasten, oðður mid wake. *a* **1300** *Cursor M.* 10302 O-mang þir hirdes duelland þare, In praier, wak, and weping sare. *c* **1375** *Sc. Leg. Saints* xl. (*Ninian*) 59 & hyme abondonit ythanly in prayere, fastyng, & in wake, hyme-selfe seruand to god to mak. **1559** in Strype *Ann. Ref.* (1709) I. App. xvi. 48 Moreover, the Common Watchings, or Wakes, of Men and Women at the Martyrs Graves..was afterwards abrogated and rejected. **1591** G. FLETCHER *Russe Commw.* xxv. 105 b, They haue also 3 Vigils, or Wakes in their great Lent, which they cal *Stoiania*. **1610** HOLLAND *Camden's Brit.* I. 175 As many as the place would receive watched and praied in the said Temple, But the Prince of Wales, held his wake..within the Church of Westminster. *a* **1641** BP. MOUNTAGU *Acts & Mon.* (1642) 434 After this Supper ended followes [among the Essenes] a sacred wake, or vigill, kept in this manner.

3. The watching (*esp.* by night) of relatives and friends beside the body of a dead person from death to burial, or during a part of that time; the drinking, feasting, and other observances incidental to this. Now chiefly *Anglo-Irish* or with reference to Irish custom. Also applied to similar funeral customs in other times or among non-Christian peoples.

1412–20 LYDG. *Chron. Troy* IV. 3261 What shulde I now any lenger dwelle..for to telle..of þe pleies called palestral, Nor þe wrastelyng þat was at þe wake? *a* **1529** SKELTON *P. Sparowe* 437 The gose and the gander, The ducke and the drake, Shall watche at this wake. **1572** *Inv. Ketshange* (Somerset Ho.), Her wacke and buriall xiiij[d]. **1700** DRYDEN *Pal. & Arc.* III. 998 The warlike Wakes continu'd all the Night, and Fun'ral Games were played at new-returning Light. **1724** SWIFT *Acc. Wood's Exec.* Misc. (1735) V. 317 When he was cut down, the Body was carried through the whole City to gather Contributions for his Wake. **1726–31** WALDRON *Descr. Isle of Man* (1865) 60 When a person dies, several of his acquaintance come to sit up with him, which they call the Wake. **1778** *Phil. Surv. S. Irel.* 210 The series of ceremonies used on the night,..that the corpse remains unburied, is what they call a wake. **1814** W. S. MASON *Statist. Acc. Irel.* I. 596 The Presbyterian wake is conducted with profound silence and great decorum... The wakes of the members of the established church differ little from those in other parts of Ireland. **1857** LIVINGSTONE *Trav.* xxiii. 468 A poor man and his wife were accused of having bewitched the man, whose wake was now held in the village. **1874** C. E. NORTON *Lett.* (1913) II. 42 Sumner is dead. We have had a great wake over him, and the echoes of it have scarcely yet died away. **1894** GLADSTONE *Odes Hor.* II. xviii. 18 New contracts for new marbles thou dost make, But thou art near thy wake.

4. The vigil of a festival (and senses thence derived).

In this use *wake* is a translation of Eccl. L. *vigilia*, primarily referring to the rule of the early church that certain feast-days should be preceded by services lasting through the night. When this rule had ceased to exist, the vigil continued to be a pretext for nocturnal festivity, and the use of the word *wake* was extended to denote not only the eve but also the feast-day itself, and the whole period during which festivities continued.

a. The vigil or eve of a festival, and the observances belonging to this. Also, a festival. *Obs.* exc. *dial.*

15.. *Part of a Register* (1593) 64 Their Saints dayes and their prescript seruice. Their waakes, and idolatrous bankets. **1523** BERNERS *Froiss.* (1812) I. clxix. 207 Great solemnytes were made in all churches, and great fyers and wakes, throughout all Englande. **1600** SURFLET *Country Farm* II. xliii. 276, I knowe well that the common sort doe verily thinke and auerre, that this seede cannot be gathered but on the night of the wakes of S. Iohn in sommer. *a* **1629** HINDE *J. Bruen* xxix. (1641) 89 Their Wakes and Vigils, in all riot and excesse of eating and drinking. *a* **1806** H. K. WHITE *Poems* (1837) 136 Such is the jocund wake of Whitsuntide. **1876** *Mid-Yorks. Gloss.*, *Wake*, casually employed in Mid-Yorks. and the north, for vigils, or the superstitious rites performed on the eves of St. Agnes and St. Mark.

b. The local annual festival of an English (now chiefly rural) parish, observed (originally on the feast of the patron saint of the church, but now usually on some particular Sunday and the two or three days following) as an occasion for making holiday, entertainment of friends, and often for village sports, dancing, and other amusements.

In modern rustic use chiefly *pl.* in sing. sense and often with sing. construction (cf. the double pl. *wakeses*, in 16th c. *wakesses*). The word is now current only in certain districts, mainly northern and west midland; elsewhere the equivalent term is *feast* or *revels*.

a **1225** *Ancr. R.* 314 Heo hefde ileaned one wummone to one wake on of hore weaden. *c* **1290** *S. Eng. Leg.* 413/381 Formest he gan haunti wakes: and for compaygnie he wax a syutor of tauernes. *a* **1300** *Cursor M.* 28526 At wrestelyng, at wake, rengd haf i and folud wit lust all luchery. **1562** *Child-Marriages* (1897) 116 She had lent the crosse to a younge woman callid Anne Barker, to go to a weddinge or a wake. **1583** STUBBES *Anat. Abus.* I. M 6, The maner of keeping of Wakesses, and feasts in Ailgna. **1611** SHAKS. *Wint. T.* IV. iii. 109 He haunts Wakes, Faires, and Beare-baitings. **1621** BURTON *Anat. Mel.* III. ii. IV. i. (1624) 424 The very rusticks..Insteed of..Tilts, Turnaments, &c. they haue their Wakes, Whitson-ales, Shepherds feasts. **1633** CHAS. I. *Decl. Lawful Sports* 16 Wee finde..there hath been a generall forbidding..of the Feasts of the Dedication of the Churches, commonly called Wakes. **1690** LOCKE *Hum. Und.* III. xi. §10 Vulgar Notions suit vulgar Discourses, and both..serve pretty well the Market and the Wake. **1695** KENNETT *Par. Antiq.* ix. 610 The institution of these Church Encænia or Wakes, was no question on good and laudable designs. **1711** BUDGELL *Spect.* No. 161 ¶2 Had you stayed there a few Days longer you would have seen a Country Wake, which you know in most Parts of England is the Eve-Feast of the Dedication of our Churches. **1778** *Eng. Gazetteer* (ed. 2) s.v. *Stretton*, Here used to be a wake on the Sunday after All-Saints-day. **1801** STRUTT *Sports & Past.* II. ii. 75 Wrestling, at present is seldom seen except at wakes and fairs. **1861** THACKERAY *Four Georges* ii. (1862) 97 Every town had its fair, every village its wake. **1879** 'OUIDA' *Cecil Castlemaine* 9 Neither could she consort with gentry who seemed to her little better than the boors of a country wake. **1884** *Manch. Exam.* 2 Sept. 5/2 The wakes in more than one place in the district had closed the workshops. **1893** H. VIZETELLY *Glances Back* I. x. 190 It chanced to be the annual wake or holiday at Castleton.

†**c.** *transf.* Applied to similar periodic festivals or revels of other countries or periods. Also occas. in *pl.*, nocturnal revels. *Obs.*

1577 HANMER *Anc. Eccl. Hist., Euseb.* VIII. xxix. 171 About the thirde Nones of March, when the citizens of Cæsarea celebrated their wakes, vpon the day of reuells, Adrianus was throwen at the feete of a fierce lion. **1588** FRAUNCE *Lawiers Logike* I. xix. 66 b, Those men, saith Plato in Protagoras, that use the authoritie of others instead of argumente, of their owne, are like to seely soules of the country, when they keepe their wakes. **1634** MILTON *Comus* 121 By dimpled Brook, and Fountain brim, The Wood-Nymphs..Their merry wakes and pastimes keep. **1638** BAKER tr. *Balzac's Lett.* (vol. II) 89 And most honourable commemoration hath been made of you in all our innocent disorderly wakes [*en toutes nos innocentes débauches*].

¶**5.** Used by Hogg for: A serenade, nocturnal song.

(App. associated with WAIT *sb.* 8 b.)

1813 HOGG *Queen's Wake* Introd. (1814) 5 Those wakes now played by minstrels poor, At midnight's darkest, chillest hour, Those humble wakes, now scorned by all, Were first begun in courtly hall. *Ibid.* ii. 139 The lake-fowl's wake was heard no more; The wave forgot to brush the shore. *Ibid.* 336 So low has the characters of the minstrels descended, that the performers of the Christmas wakes are wholly unknown to the most part of those whom they serenade.

6. *attrib.* and *Comb.* (senses 3 and 4), as ***wake-feast, -game, -light,* †*-meat,* †*-play, Sunday, -week***; also with plural, ***wakes time, week***.

1886 W. J. TUCKER *E. Europe* 207 The wine bottles were replenished, and the company gathered round to partake in eagerness of the first *wake-feast, a goodly number of which would follow the decease of the thus honoured and lamented individual. **1912** K. TYNAN *P'cess Kath.* ii. 28 It was enough to bring Tom Duncan out of his grave,..to see the class of people who played *wake-games in his dining-room, and drank his whisky. **1813** HOGG *Queen's Wake* ii. (1814) 147 Her sail was the web of the gossamer's loom, The glow-worm her *wakelight. **1849** WHITTIER *Kathleen* 57 Get up, old man! the wake-lights shine! *a* **1400** *Gloss* in *Rel. Ant.* I. 6 *Obsonium*, a *wakemete. *c* **1386** CHAUCER *Knt.'s T.* 2102 Ne how that liche-wake was yholde Al thilke night, ne how the Grekes pleye The *wake pleyes, ne kepe I nat to seye. **1884** *St. James's Gaz.* 20 June 6/1 The farmers..also keep an annual holiday which they call *Wake Sunday..on the first Sunday in August. **1863** BRIERLEY *Waverlow, Trevor Hall* i. 17 They were the Waverlow church bells that were ringing, for it was '*wakes time'. **1870** 'OUIDA' *Puck* I. vi. 105 It was '*wake-week' at a little town some twelve miles away. **1886** *Cheshire Gloss.* s.v. *Wake*, It is customary for friends from a distance to visit each other during '*wakes week'.

7. Special comb.: †**wake-day**, the day on which a wake (senses 2, 4) was held; †**wake-fire**, a (? ceremonial) fire by which a night-watch was kept; **wake-house**, †(*a*) ? a house of vigil, or prayer; (*b*) *Anglo-Irish* (see quot. 1814); †**wake-word** = WATCH-WORD.

1538 ELYOT *Dict.*, *Esuriales feriæ*, *wake dayes. **1573–80** TUSSER *Husb.* (1878) 181 To morow thy father his wake day will keepe. Then euerie wanton may daunce at hir will. **1598** BP. HALL *Sat.* v. ii. 107 Except the twelue-daies, or the wakeday-feast. **1681** W. ROBERTSON *Phraseol. Gen.* (1693) 596 Amongst Christians, the consecration, or wake-days of our churches. *c* **1450** *Mirk's Festial* 182 Anoþer ys of clene wod and no bonys, and ys callyd a *wakefyre, for men syttyth and wakyth by hyt. **1575–6** *Durham Depos.* (Surtees) 235 Beinge the awaike night, the said Percivall and Margarett the wyfe went to the waike fyere. **1677** in *Verney Mem.* (1907) II. 308 This Church or *Wake House stands upon Ground Given to yᵉ Church. **1814** W. S. MASON *Statist. Acc. Irel.* I. 318 Whenever a person of any respectability dies, two wake houses are laid out, in one of which is placed the deceased,..in the other are assembled all the young people..who entertain themselves with every species of frolic and amusement. **1856** P. KENNEDY *Banks Boro* xiv. (1867) 66 The wake-house drama of *Old Dowd and his Daughters*. **1510** STANBRIDGE *Vocabula* (W. de W.) Diij b, *Symbolum*, a *wake worde.

wake (weɪk), *sb.*² Also 6 ? **walk**, 7 **wack**. [Not found before the 16th c., but possibly much older; either directly or mediately a. ON. (**vaku*) *vǫk* str. fem., *vaka* wk. fem., hole or opening in ice. The ON. word was probably applied to the path made for itself by a vessel through ice, and from this use the sense 'trace or track of a vessel in the water' may have been developed by Scandinavian navigators in British seas. Sense 5, 'line of hay', if it really belongs to the same word, may be a transferred use of the nautical sense.

The word is represented in all the Scandinavian dialects, and has been adopted in Du., Fris., and Ger. The sense 'track of a vessel' is found, outside Eng., only in Norw. *vok* (dial. *vaak*), NFris. (Sylt) *waak*; the older sense, 'hole or channel in ice' (sometimes, 'a piece of water kept unfrozen by wind or current') belongs to MSw. *vaak*, *vak*, Sw. *vak* (cf. Sw. *väcka* to cut a hole in ice), Norw. *vok*, Da. *vaage*, WFris. *wek*, *wjek(ke*, Du. *wak* neut., MLG., LG. (whence mod.G.) *wake* fem.

The word is commonly supposed to be connected with ON. *vǫk-r*, Du. *wak*, moist, damp: see WAK *a.* This view involves some difficulty, as the ON. adj. has the stem *vǫkv-*, while the sb. has genit. *vakar*, pl. *vakar*, *-ir*. Connexion with WAKE *a.* and *v.* seems not impossible: the freeing of the water from ice may have been regarded as an awakening.]

I. 1. The track left on the water's surface by a ship (in the sea often marked by a smooth appearance).

[*a* **1547**: see 4 a.] **1627** CAPT. J. SMITH *Sea Gram.* ix. 42 The wake of a ship is the smooth water a sterne shewing the way shee hath gone in the sea. **1703** DAMPIER *Voy.* III. I. 97 In the Wake of the Ship (as 'tis call'd) or the Smoothness which the Ship's passing has made on the Sea. **1768–74** TUCKER *Lt. Nat.* (1834) I. 412 The wake of a ship, (by which, I think, the sailors understand the stream drawn after the stern by its motion,) follows the ship throughout her voyage. **1820** W. SCORESBY *Acc. Arctic Regions* II. 240 An 'eddy' having somewhat the resemblance of the 'wake' or track of a ship. **1852** CLOUGH *Poems*, '*Where lies the land*' 8 Or, o'er the stern reclining, watch below The foaming wake far widening as we go. **1861** DICKENS *Gt. Expect.* liv, Both steamers were drifting away from us, and we were rising and falling in a troubled wake of water. **1882** W. H. WHITE *Naval Archit.* (ed. 2) 553 The actual wake of a ship combines the stream line motions with those due to the frictional drag of the skin upon the water. **1913** *Engl. Rev.* Nov. 506 Her wake was without foam and closed sluggishly behind her.

attrib. **1866** MACGREGOR '*Rob Roy*' *Baltic* 229 A canoe was pulled at a rapid pace in the two wake waves astern of this great smack. **1909** BRIDGES *Paraphr. Virg. Æn. VI* 342 What God..Pluckt you away and drown'd i' the swift wake-water abandon'd?

†**b.** Phrases. ***to fetch*** (***get, get into, have***) ***the wake of*** (a pursued vessel): to get so close to her as to be able to see, and steer by, her wake. ***to stay a weather of a wake***: see quot. 1706.

1644 MANWAYRING *Sea-mans Dict.* 113 In chaseing they say, we have got her wake, that is, we are got as far into the wind as she, and so goe right after her as she goes. **1669** STURMY *Mariner's Mag.* I. ii. 19 The Chase is about, come fetch her wack, and we will be about after her. We sail far better than she; we have her Wack. **1706** PHILLIPS (ed. Kersey) s.v., A Ship is said *To stay a Weather of a Wake*, when in her Staying she does it so speedily, that she don't fall to the Leeward, but that when she is tacked, her Wake is to the Leeward; which is a sure Sign that she feels her Helm well, and is nimble of Steerage. When a Ship being in Chace of another, has got as far into the Wind as she, and sails directly after her; the usual Saying is, *That she has got into her Wake*. **1748** *Anson's Voy.* III. viii. 377 About noon the Commodore was little more than a league from the galeon, and could fetch her wake, so that she could not now escape.

2. *transf.* Anything compared to the wake of a vessel. **a.** The disturbance caused by a body swimming, or moved, in water.

1753 FRANKLIN *Let.* Wks. 1840 V. 338 There were numbers of visible animalcules; but I was sure there were likewise some which I could not see; for the wake they made in swimming to and fro was very visible. **1818** *Ann. Reg.*, *Chron.* 561 He [*sc.* the whale] swims with an astonishing swiftness..leaving a track in the sea, like a great ship; and this is called his wake. **1845** DARWIN *Voy. Nat.* iii. (1879) 39 The tracks of the penguins were marked by a fiery wake. **1891** A. LANG *Angling Sk.* 68 The dry fly is difficult to use on a loch, as there is no stream to move it; and however gently you draw it, it makes a 'wake'—a trail behind it.

b. The air-currents behind a body in flight.

1851 ROSSETTI *Sister Helen* viii, Outside it's merry in the wind's wake,..In the shaken trees the chill stars shake. **1870** N. F. HELE *Aldeburgh* vii. 71 The only chance of safety for the rook appeared to be his getting directly in the 'wake' of the falcon, and by this means the bird escaped for a long time. **1891** *Spectator* 28 Feb., The probable object of the wedge-formation when advancing against the wind is, that each bird avoids the 'wake' of its neighbour.

c. A trail of light behind a luminous object (in motion), or its broken reflection in water. Also *fig.*

a **1711** KEN *Prepar.* Poet. Wks. 1721 IV. 74 Fly up, my Soul, along the Wake, Which down from Fontal Love they make, No Lover led by Love's sweet Ray 'Ere lost his Way. **1819** MONTGOMERY *Greenland* I. 14 The pageant glides through loneliness and night, And leaves behind a rippling wake of light. **1847** TENNYSON *Princess* III. 1 Morn in the white wake of the morning star Came furrowing all the orient into gold. **1889** STEVENSON *In South Seas* II. ii. (1900) 152 The harbour lantern and two of the greater planets drew vari-coloured wakes on the lagoon. **1906** E. A. ABBOTT *Silanus* xxv. 237 They depart. There is a momentary wake of light. It disappears. Then we have to wait for a new torchbearer.

d. A track or trail on land. *rare.*

1851 HAWTHORNE *Ho. Sev. Gables* xi, Twice or thrice..a water-cart went along by the Pyncheon-house, leaving a broad wake of moistened earth. **1888** STEVENSON *Black Arrow* v. iv, Thus they had left a wide, discoloured wake upon the snow.

3. A course, or general line of direction, that a ship has taken, or is to take.

c **1595** CAPT. WYATT *R. Dudley's Voy. W. Ind.* (Hakl. Soc.) 52 Wee..altered that course and bare for the coste of Florida..to lie in the wake of the fleet of the West Indies bounde for Spaine. **1722** DE FOE *Col. Jack* (1840) 190 They were..quite out of the wake of the Bermudas. **1871** B. TAYLOR *Faust* (1875) II. v. 279 And from the shore to swifter wakes The willing sea the vessels takes.

4. in the wake of.

a. *Naut.* or quasi-nautical. ***in the wake of*** (***a vessel***); ***in her*** (***its***) ***wake***, etc.: immediately behind, and (properly) in the actual track made by, a vessel; immediately backward and along the track made. Also used of any person or persons aboard, as ***in his, our***, etc., ***wake***; behind his, our, etc., vessel.

a **1547** *MS. Harl.* 309 f. 4 No ship to ride in another's walk. **1769** FALCONER *Dict. Marine* (1780) s.v., A ship is said to be in the wake of another, when she follows her on the same track. **1839** tr. *Lamartine's Trav.* 22/1 The frigate, which has us in tow, hollows out ahead of us a level and murmuring path, along which we glide in her wake. **1847** PRESCOTT *Peru* (1850) II. 323 [They] fell on his little troop whenever he attempted to land, and followed in his wake for miles in their canoes. **1898** F. T. BULLEN *Cruise of 'Cachalot'* 193 The *Mysticetus*' best point of view is right behind, or 'in his wake', as we say.

b. *Naut.* in transferred uses: (*a*) In the direct line aft from (any object on board ship, or any specified part of her). Usually ***in wake of***. (*b*) In the line of sight of (an observed object). (*c*) In the line of recoil of (a gun).

(*a*) **1711** W. SUTHERLAND *Shipbuild. Assist.* 44 The Timbers to be equally scarfed, the Middle of one Timber being in the Wake of the Head and Heels of the others. **1745** P. THOMAS *Jrnl. Anson's Voy.* 138 We found our own Main-top-mast sprung in the Wake of the Cap. **1869** E. J. REED *Shipbuild.* i. 5 The bottom was strengthened by doubling the whole of the inner plates up to the turn of the bilge for 50 feet in wake of the engines. **1879** W. H. WHITE *Ship-Build.* in *Cassell's Techn. Educ.* IV. 61/1 These longitudinal tie-plates form excellent strengthenings to the deck in wake of the principal hatchways. **1896** *Daily News* 4 Nov. 2/4 The deck, which was also found to be started in the wake of the mast.

(*b*) **1769** FALCONER *Dict. Marine* (1780) s.v., Two distant objects observed at sea are called in the wake of each other, when the view of the furthest is intercepted by the nearest.

(*c*) *c* **1860** H. STUART *Seaman's Catech.* 69 They give..support to the beams in the wake of the guns. **1874** THEARLE *Naval Archit.* xviii. §288. 303 In the wake of the explosion of the heavy guns, as at the embrasures, etc., the whole of the frames are of the larger size.

c. *transf.* and *fig.* (*a*) With nautical metaphor (often jocular): Following close behind (a person compared to a ship). (*b*) In wider use (cf. 2): In the train or track of, behind (a moving person or object); in imitation of; following as a result or consequence.

(*a*) **1806** CUMBERLAND *Mem.* 114 A great man in office is like a great whale in the ocean; there will be a sword-fish and a thresher, a Junius and a John Wilkes, ever in his wake and arming to attack him. **1822** W. IRVING *Braceb. Hall* ii. 19 He was swept off in the vortex that followed in the wake of this lady. **1849** MISS MULOCK *Ogilvies* ii, She found herself..following in the wake of her stately parents. **1901** MEREDITH *Reading of Life* I Each claims worship undivided In her wake would have us wallow.

(*b*) **1840** DICKENS *Old C. Shop* xlv, Night, when carts came rumbling by, filled with rude coffins..; when orphans cried, and distracted women shrieked and followed in their wake. **1866** MRS. H. WOOD *St. Martin's Eve* v, Such love does not bring peace in its wake. **1875** MERIVALE *Gen. Hist. Rome* lxxx. (1877) 683 Wealth followed in the wake of traffic. **1877** BLACK *Green Past.* xxxii. 256 Brown dust that came rolling in the wake of our carriage. **1894** H. DRUMMOND *Ascent of Man* 214 [A man], when he talks of the hum of machinery or the boom of the cannon,..is following in the wake of the inventors of Language. **1911** G. MACDONALD *Roman Wall Scot.* x. 351 A proof that Eastern traders had found their way as far north as the Caledonian frontier in the wake of the Roman army.

II. 5. A line of hay prepared for carting. *dial.*

1847 HALLIWELL *Wake*, hay placed in large rolls for the convenience of being carried. *West. Ibid.*, *Wakes*, rows of green damp grass. **1872–4** JEFFERIES *Toilers of Field* (1892) 259 The waggon safely jolted over the furrow, and on between the wakes of light-brown hay. **1879** —— *Wild Life in S. Co.* vii. 143 Watching that the 'wallows' may be turned over properly, and the 'wakes' made at a just distance from each other.

III. 6. An open hole, or unfrozen place in the ice. *dial.* (East Anglia.)

1895 P. H. EMERSON *Birds* etc. *Norf. Broadland* II. xiii. 379, I passed a 'wake'—or open space in the ice—where the swans were swimming like sentries on duty.

†**wake**, *sb.*³ *Obs. rare*⁻¹. [Possibly a. some native African word, but evidently regarded by Jobson as onomatopœic.] A North African bird.

1623 JOBSON *Golden Trade* 155 The next [bird] in greatnesse, is called a Wake, in regard of the great noyse hee makes when hee flyeth, which resembleth what he is called by:..[it] is a bird of great stature, hauing the vpper part of his head carrying a beautiful shew, with a pleasing tuft on his Crowne, which I haue seene worne by great personages here at home.

wake, *a.* *Obs.* exc. *dial.* [? Aphetic var. of AWAKE.] Not sleeping, awake. (Only *predicative.*)

1414 BRAMPTON *Penit. Ps.* (Percy Soc.) 16 Er ryghtwysnesse be fully wake. **1579** SPENSER *Sheph. Cal.* June 87 Well couth he..tell vs mery tales, to keepe vs wake. **1745** W. THOMPSON *Sickness* III. 295 [IV. 288] What guilt is mine, that I alone am wake, Ev'n tho' my eyes are seal'd, am wake alone?

wake (weɪk), *v.* Forms: Inf. and Present stem. α. (? 1 wæcnan: see WAKEN *v.*) β. 1–2 **wacian**, 1 **waciȝan**, **waciȝean**, **wæcian**, 1–2 **wacyan**, 2 **wacyȝan**, 2–3 **wakian**, **wakien**, **wakeȝen**, 3 **wakenn** (*Orm.*), 3–5 **waken**, 4 **waki**, **waky**, 4–5 **wakke**, **waake**, 3– **wake**. *north.* and *Sc.* 4 **wack**, **vak** (*pr. pple.* **vakand**, **wacand**, **quakand**), 4–5 **wak**, 4–6 **waik**, **valk**, 4–8 **walk**, 5 **waulk**, 6 **vaik(e**, **walke**, 8 **wauk**, **wawk**. Pa. t. α. 1 **wóc**, 3–4 **woc**, 3–5 **wok**, 4–6 **wook(e**, 7 **wake**, 9 **'woke**, 3– **woke**; *pl.* 3 **wokenn** (*Orm.*), 4–5 **woken**, **-yn**, 5 **waken**. *north.* and *Sc.* 4 **wock**, 4–6 **wouk(e**, **woik(e**. β. 1 **wæcade**, **wacode**, *pl.* **wacedon**, **-odon**, 2–4 **wakede**, 4–5 **wakid**, **walkid(e**, etc., 4–6 *Sc.* **walkyt**, **-it**, 6 **wakt(e**, 6–7 **wak't**, 7–8 **wak'd**, 4– **waked**. Pa. pple. α. 4, 6 **waken**, 5 **wakyn** (?), 7, 9– **woken**, 8– **woke**. β. 4 **i-waked**, *Sc.* **walkit**, 4–6 **wakid**, **-yd**, 6 *dial.* **wayket**, *Sc.* **walked**, 6–7 **wakt**, 7 **wak't**, 7–8 **wak'd** 3– **waked**. [Two distinct but synonymous verbs from the same root coalesced in early ME.:

(i) The strong verb OE. (? *wæcnan*), *wóc*, *wócon*, **wacen*. (The present-stem is wanting, unless it be presented by *wæcnan*: see WAKEN *v.*) The strong pa. t. is found only in English; the strong pa. pple., not recorded in OE., but found in later periods, occurs in ON. *vakenn*, and as adj. ('awake') in MSw. *vakin*, Sw., Norw. *vaken*, Da. *vaagen*; N.Fris. *vaaken* is prob. from Scandinavian.

(ii) The weak verb OE. *wacian*, corresponding to OFris. *wakia*, *waka* (mod. WFris. *weitsje*, NFris. *waake*), OHG. *wahhên*, *wachên*, *-ân* (MHG., mod.G. *wachen*), ON. *vaka*, pa. t. *vakða* (Norw., MSw., Sw. *vaka*, Da. *vaage*), Goth. *wakan*:—OTeut. **wakǣjan* (whence also the OE. doublet *wæccan* WATCH *v.*), or to OS., OLow Frankish *wakon* (MDu., Du., MLG., LG. *waken*), OHG. *wachôn*:—OTeut. **wakōjan*.

The Teut. root **wak-* (:—**wōk-* in Goth. *wōkains* wakefulness, and, with different sense, in Goth. *wōkr-s*, OE. *wócor*, ON. *ókr* growth, increase, usury: see OCKER *sb.*¹) represents a pre-Teut. **wag-*: **weg-*; cf. L. *vegēre* to rouse, excite, also intr. to be lively or active, *vigēre* to be vigorous, *vigil* wakeful, Skr. *vājas* neut. vigour; perh. to be referred to the Indo-Eur. root **aweg-*, represented by L. *augēre*, Goth. *aukan* to increase, OE. *éacan* to grow (see EKE *v.*), and with *-s* extension by Gr. *αὐξάνειν* to increase, OTeut. **waχs-* to grow (see WAX *v.*).

In OE. the strong verb had probably the sense 'to become awake', though this is evidenced only in the compound *on-wæcnan*, the simple verb being found only in the sense 'to come into being', which may either be a figurative use of the sense 'to awake', or represent a different application of the original wider sense of the root. The weak verb had the static sense 'to be or remain awake'. In ME. the strong and weak forms came to be used indiscriminately in both senses. Out of the sense 'to become awake' there was developed a causative sense, 'to rouse from sleep', in which the word superseded WECCHE (OE. *węccan*:—OTeut. **wakjan*). The sense 'to remain awake, watch' gave rise to a transitive use = 'to watch (over)'; but in the modern Eng. period the static sense, both intr. and trans., has become almost obsolete, the usual meanings of the word being 'to become or cause to become awake'.

The mod. pa. t. *woke* (wəʊk) does not regularly represent the OE. *wóc*, which would have yielded *wook* (wʊk). Apparently the mod. *woke* is a new formation or modification on the analogy of *broke*, *spoke* (for the irregularity in the vowel cf. *stove* pa. t. of STAVE *v.*). When this came in is uncertain, for in ME. and prob. in early mod.E. the spelling *woke* represents the regular phonetic descendant of the OE. *wóc*. The pa. pple *waken* has always been rare, and now survives only in dialects in adjectival use. From the 17th c. onwards the forms *woke*, *woken* (after *broke*, *broken*, *spoke*, *spoken*, etc.) have been more or less current for the pa. pple.; *woke* seems obsolescent, but *woken* is at least as frequent as *waked*. No strong forms either of pa. t. or pa. pple. are found in Shaks., the Bible of 1611, or Milton's verse.]

I. To remain awake.

1. a. *intr.* To be or remain awake; to keep oneself, or be kept, awake. Also, to be still up and about (at night). Now *rare* exc. in *waking* (pr. pple. and ppl. a.).

α. *c* **1290** *Beket* 687 in *S. Eng. Leg.* 126 On of its seriaunz sat a niȝt, þe ȝwile þat men woke, In his chaumbre at caunterburi. *a* **1300** *Cursor M.* 20127 Scho wok wil mar þan scho slepp. *c* **1375** *Sc. Leg. Saints* xxx. (*Theodera*) 448 To þat worde gud tent he tuk, & þat nycht mekyl woike. **1387** TREVISA *Higden* IV. 303 Whanne Cinna his tresoun was i-knowe Cesar wook al þat nyȝt [*MS.* β wakid, γ wakede]. *c* **1450** *Mirk's Festial* 223 þay madyn her bed, and dydyn hur þeryn, .. and waken tyll hyt was mydnyght; then all fellyn on slepe saue þe apostols. **1500–20** DUNBAR *Poems* xlii. 34 Langour .. That nevir sleipit bot evir wouke. **1535** STEWART *Cron. Scot.* II. 558 So greit displesour in the tyme he tuik, But meit or sleip rycht lang fastit and woik. **1848** THACKERAY *Van. Fair* lxii, Whether he woke or slept his friends did not very much miss him.

β. *c* **900** *Beda's Hist.* II. xii. (1890) 128 Ða frægn he hine, hwæt þæs to him lumpe, hwæðer he wacode þe slepe. *c* **1000** *Sax. Leechd.* III. 6 þonne sceal se man wacyan ealle þa niht þe ðone drenc drincan wille. *a* **1225** *Ancr. R.* 4 þet techeð al hu me schal .. eten, drincken, werien, liggen, slepen, wakien [*sic MS.*; *printed* walkien]. *c* **1381** CHAUCER *Parl. Foules* 482, I wol ben hirs whethir I wake or wynke. *c* **1400** *26 Pol. Poems* xv. 88 To slepe, quod þe eyȝe, we may not wynne, þe wrecched wombe so doþ vs wake. *c* **1450** *St. Cuthbert* (Surtees) 2791 þe seke man to slepe lyse; he had lang waked beforne. *c* **1500** *Melusine* 7 He .. knew nat yf it was day-light or nyght, ne yf he slept or wakked. **1508** DUNBAR *Tua Mariit Wemen* 213 Than ly I walkand for wa, and walteris about. **1611** TOURNEUR *Ath. Trag.* II. vi, I cannot force myselfe to wake. (*sleepes*). **1640** tr. *Verdere's Rom. of Rom.* II. 23 The extream desire that he had to see her, made him to wake when others tooke their rest. **17..** *Auld Man's best Argt.* in *Ramsay's Tea-t. Misc.* (1762) 154 O Wha's that at my chamber door? 'Fair widow, are ye wawking?' **1784** R. BAGE *Barham Downs* I. 32, I .. threw myself dressed upon the bed, and—waked all night. **1790** BURNS *Ay waukin O*, When I sleep I dream, When I wauk I'm eerie. **1840** DICKENS *Old C. Shop* lxx, They cannot .. be waking at this late hour. **1855** MACAULAY *Hist. Eng.* xviii. IV. 217 In all places, at all hours, whether he waked or slept. **1902** 'VIOLET JACOB' *Sheep Stealers* ix, Waking and sleeping she had pictured his arrest.

fig. **1697** CONGREVE *Mourn. Bride* III. i, Reason, .. the twinkling Lamp Of wand'ring Life, that winks and wakes by turns.

b. with advb. obj. *the night*, *a night* (poet.). Also, *to wake it*.

α. *c* **1480** HENRYSON *Test. Cresseid* 471 Weping, scho woik the nicht fra end to end.

β. *a* **1547** SURREY in *Tottel's Misc.* (Arb.) 221 To waile the day and wake the night continually in paine. **1760–72** H. BROOKE *Fool of Qual.* (1809) I. 58 These have nothing to do but to sleep it, to wake it. **1787** BURNS '*My heart is sair*' i, I could wake a winter night For the sake o' somebody. **1820** KEATS *Isabella* vii, So once more he had wak'd and anguished A dreary night of love and misery.

c. quasi-*trans.* with complement.

In the first quot. the omission of some such word as Theobald's 'blind' seems certain.

1611 SHAKS. *Cymb.* III. iv. 104 Ile wake mine eye-balles [blind] first. **1766** C. BEATTY *Tour* (1768) 37 Sleeped and waked the night away as well as we could.

†**d.** With unfavourable implication: To sit up late for pleasure or revelry; to turn night into day. *Obs.*

α. **13..** *Gaw. & Gr. Knt.* 1025 For-þy wonderly þay woke, & þe wyn dronken.

β. **1340** *Ayenb.* 52 þet uolk þet late louieþ to soupi and to waki be niȝte. **1387–8** T. USK *Test. Love* II. ii. (Skeat) l. 54 Suche there ben .. that til midnight and more wol playe and wake, but in the churche at matins he is behynde. *a* **1529** SKELTON *Bowge of Courte* 382 Thou muste .. wake all nyghte, and slepe tyll it be none. **1602** SHAKS. *Ham.* I. iv. 8 The King doth wake to night, and takes his rouse.

2. a. To stay awake for the purpose of watching or tending; to keep watch while others sleep, be on guard at night. Const. *on*, *upon*, *over*, *for*, *against*; also *to* (do something). Also with cognate obj., *to wake watch*. Now only *dial.*, to sit up at night *with* a person, esp. one who is sick.

In 16th c. Sc. use ***wake and ward*** (see WARD *v.*) = 'to keep watch and ward,' as a duty incumbent on the freeman of a burgh.

α. *c* **1200** ORMIN 3752 Hirdess wokenn o þatt nahht þatt Crist wass borenn onne. *c* **1400** *Rowland & Otuel* 1187 Grete lordes riste toke, & nyghte wache full worthily wooke. **1430–40** LYDG. *Bochas* III. vii. (1554) 79 b, And lyke a mother to bryng thee aslepe, I woke ful oft. **1471** CAXTON *Recuyell* (Sommer) 284 By this gardyn is vnderstonde the yle. By the serpent wakyng, the subtyll geant commysid to kepe hit that allway wook at the paas.

β. *Beowulf* 660 Waca wið wraþum. *c* **825** *Vesp. Psalter* cxxvi. 1 *In vanum vigilant qui custodiunt eam*, in idelnisse wæciað ða haldað hie. *c* **1200** *Trin. Coll. Hom.* 31 þe herdes þe wakeden ouer here oref. *c* **1350** *Leg. Rood* 76/525 And seker men he sett to wake, So þat þai suld no harmes take. *c* **1465** *Eng. Chron.* (Camden 1856) 62 Alle the weycz about the said toun off Bury .. were kept with gret multitude of peple of the cuntre, wakyng day and nyghte. **1521** in Marwick *Edin. Guilds* (1909) 65 The communitie of the wobstaris walkis, wardis, extentis, and beris all other commoun chargis within this toune. **1533** BELLENDEN *Livy* III. ix. (S.T.S.) I. 282 Na thing was done in þe nycht following Except onelie þe pepill walkit in all partis of þe ciete. **1565** J. HALL *Crt. Vertue* 32 Watchmen, whiche wake al ye night. **1580** in *Rec. Convent. Burghs Scot.* (1870) I. 99 All .. to cum duell .. within the burgh quhair they ar frie, hald stob and staik within the samyn, scatt, loitt, watche, walk and waird with the inhabitantis thairof. **1667** MILTON *P.L.* XI. 368 Let Eve .. Here sleep below while thou to foresight wak'st. **1699** R. L'ESTRANGE *Erasm. Colloq.* (1725) 195 Only let one wake with me, to read to me. **1754** SHEBBEARE *Matrimony* (1766) I. 22 She determined to wake by his Bed-side all Night. **1811** WILLAN *West Riding Words* in *Archæologia* XVII. 162 *Waite*, and *Wake*, v. to sit up with a person all night, or to watch by a corpse. **1847** C. BRONTË *Jane Eyre* xxv, You promised to wake with me the night before my wedding. **1865** *N. & Q.* Ser. III. VII. 84/1 'They have waked with him for several nights', is a common expression in Lancashire. **1883** *Almondbury Gloss.*, *Wake*, to watch with a sick person; to work by candlelight.

†**b.** *fig.*

c **1000** *Ags. Gosp.* Matt. xxiv. 42 Waciȝeað [*v.rr.* Waciað, Waciȝað] witodlice, forþam þe ȝe nyton on hwylcyre tide eower Hlaford cuman wyle. *c* **1200** *Trin. Coll. Hom.* 41 Ðus aȝen alle gode herdes to wakeȝen gostliche. *c* **1200** ORMIN 3792 To frofrenn þa þatt wakenn wel Onnȝæness láþe gastess. **13..** *E.E. Allit. P.* C. 130 þe welder of wyt .. þat ay wakes & waytes. *c* **1380** WYCLIF *Sel. Wks.* III. 142 þo fende is a theff to wake on mon bothe day and nyȝt. *c* **1480** HENRYSON *Swallow & other Birds* 304 Exhortand folk to walk and ay be wair Fra nettis of oure wickit enemie. **1562** WINȜET *Wks.* (S.T.S.) I. 6 War ȝe commandit in vaine of God .. to walk attentlie and continualie vpon ȝour flok?

†**c.** said of the eyes, the brain. *Obs.*

1601 SIR J. OGLE in Sir F. Vere *Comm.* 152 He had his head and his hands full; ours had not aked now, had not his waked then .. for our safeties. **1601** B. JONSON *Poetaster*, *Envie* 4 This is it, That our sunke eyes haue wak't for, all this while. **1639** DU VERGER tr. *Camus' Admir. Events* 122 The power of heaven, whose eies are ever waking on miserable creatures. **1667** MILTON *P.L.* v. 44 Heav'n wakes with all his eyes, Whom to behold but thee, Natures desire.

3. To stay awake or pass the night in prayer; to stay up during the night as an exercise of devotion; to keep vigil (in church, by a corpse, etc.). Const. *in*, *on*. *Obs.* exc. *dial.*

α. **1303** R. BRUNNE *Handl. Synne* 8043 þe toþer nyȝt þat þe chyldryn woke, At þe mydnyȝt þe bere quoke. *c* **1330** *Assump. Virg.* (Add. MS.) 761 Thei leide þe bodi in a stone .. And woke þer al þat nyȝt With many torches & candle lyȝt. **1387** TREVISA *Higden* V. 191 He .. wook al þat nyȝt in his prayers. **1483** CAXTON *Golden Leg.* 87/3 He woke in prayers and made hys prayer lene.

β. *c* **1000** ÆLFRIC *Saints' Lives* xxi. 290 Hwilon wacodon menn swa swa hit ȝewunelic is ofer an dead lic. *a* **1225** *Ancr. R.* 276 Bihold, holie men þet weren sumehwules, hwu heo uesten, & hwu heo wakeden. *c* **1290** *St. Scholastica* 8 in *S. Eng. Leg.* 198 He .. teiȝte hire penaunce forto don, to faste and to wake. **1377** LANGL. *P. Pl.* B. xx. 368 Tyl contricioun hadde clene forȝeten to crye & to wepe And wake for his wykked werkes as he was wont to done. *c* **1450** *Mirk's Festial* 182 Men and woymen .. wakyd in þe chyrch al þe nyht yn hor deuocions. **1900** H. SUTCLIFFE *Shameless Wayne* xxvi. (1905) 333 Soon as he is dead, you are to come with your folk to wake beside the body.

†**4. a.** To stay awake for any work or active occupation; to pass the night in work, study, etc. Const. *in*, *for*, *on* or *upon*, *to*. *Obs.*

α. **1471** RIPLEY *Comp. Alch.* I. ix. in Ashm. (1652) 131 For thys I woke: Many a nyght or I hyt wyst. **1481** CAXTON *Godfrey* clxxix. 264 They woke al the nyght as wel they as theyr peple, in such wyse that theyr engyns were alle ioyned and reysed vp byfore day. **1517** *Acc. Ld. High Treas. Scot.* V. 157 Item, to the franche talbanaris and menstralis that woik and playit all that nycht, in aile, viij s.

β. *c* **900** *Bæda's Hist.* IV. xxv. (1890) 354 Alle .. oððe hefiȝe slæpe syndon, oððe to synnum wacedon. *c* **1300** *Havelok* 2999 þat ilke of you .. Seye a pater-noster stille For him þat haueth þe rym maked, And þer-fore fele nihtes waked. **1352** MINOT *Poems* i. 51 Many nightes als haue þai waked To dere all Ingland with þaire dede. *c* **1386** CHAUCER *Miller's T.* 168 Absolon his gyterne hath ytake, For paramours he thoghte for to wake. **1480** CAXTON *Myrr.* I. v. 17 They waked & studyed many nyghtes and many dayes. *a* **1593** MARLOWE *Massacre at Paris* 105 (Brooke) For this, I wake, when others think I sleepe. **1593** SHAKS. *2 Hen. VI*, I. i. 249 Watch thou, and wake when others be asleepe, To prie into the secrets of the State.

†**b.** *fig.* To be active, alert, stirring, vigilant. *Const.* as above; also, to be diligent, exert oneself *to* (do something). ***to wake over***, to occupy one's mind with. *Obs.*

α. **1352** MINOT *Poems* ix. 33 Wele haue þai waken, For syr Dauid þe Bruse was in þat tyme taken. *c* **1375** *Sc. Leg. Saints* xxvii. (*Machor*) 1468, & fra þat he sic charge tuk, he trawalyt besyly & wok till his discipulis for to preche, & als þe puple besyly teche.

β. *c* **897** ÆLFRED *Gregory's Past. C.* lxiv. 461 Se kok .. hefð up his fiðru, & wecð hine selfne, ðæt he wacie on ðære ȝeornfulnesse godra weorca. *c* **1380** WYCLIF *Sel. Wks.* III. 142 Myche more in state of synne schulde mon wake in Gods servise. *c* **1383** in *Eng. Hist. Rev.* (1911) Oct. 749 Prelatis & seculer lordis shulden wake diligentli [*diligenter vigilarent*] to ordeyne able prelatis & curatis. *c* **1470** HENRY *Wallace* v. 655 On other thing he maid his witt to walk. **1501** DOUGLAS *Pal. Hon.* III. xviii, All thir on Venus seruice vaikis. **1771** GOLDSM. *Hist. Eng.* IV. 77 He incessantly waked over the schemes of contending kings and nations. **1866** KINGSLEY *Herew.* v, I have other things to wake over than making love to you.

†**c.** With clause: To take care *that* (something be done). *Obs.*

a **1425** tr. *Arderne's Treat. Fistula*, etc. 38 þerfore wake ȝe þat ȝe putte noȝt ȝoure hand to þis but in giffyng clisteries.

†**d.** quasi-*trans.* To give diligent heed to, be active in (a matter). *Obs.* (Cf. SLEEP *v.* 7.)

1525 BERNERS *Froiss.* (1812) II. cxiii [cix]. 326 The emperour .. slept nat his busynes, but waked the mater, as ye shall here.

5. Phr. ***to †hold*** or ***keep waking***; earlier, † ***to hold waken***: To prevent from sleeping; to keep watchful or on the alert. †Formerly: To keep (a person, esp. an enemy) occupied, 'give (him) plenty to do', allow (him) no rest; to trouble, harass; also *refl.* to be on the alert.

c **1330** R. BRUNNE *Chron. Wace* (Rolls) 9196 When þe Bretons þe hil had taken, Wyþ sege þe Payens held þem waken. *Ibid.* 9914 No scaþe ȝit þe toun had taken, For þey wyþynne held þem wel waken. **1352** MINOT *Poems* ix. 50 He wakkind þe were þat held him self waken. *c* **1410** *Lantern of Light* 52 þei .. holden waken her ynward iȝe. **1533** BELLENDEN *Livy* II. xxvi. (S.T.S.) I. 238 [He] causit horsmen with swasche and taberne to play all nycht about þe trynchis, to hald þare Inemyis walkand to þe morow. **1535** COVERDALE *Ps.* lxxvi[i]. 4 Thou heldest myne eyes wakynge. **1549** *Compl. Scot.* 6 Ȝour nobil fadir held the grit armye of enemeis valkand on ther tothir syde, throucht the grit assaltis ande escarmuschis that he maid contrar them. **1568** GRAFTON *Chron.* I. 366 Then to followe the Frenche men, but not immediately to fight with them, and to harry them and keepe them waking. **1593** SHAKS. *Lucr.* 1136 Whiles against a thorne thou bear'st thy part, To keepe they sharpe woes waking. **1624** FLETCHER *Rule a Wife* v. iii. 67 Have I not kept thee waking like a hawk? And watch'd thee with delights to satisfy thee. *a* **1670** SPALDING *Troub. Chas. I* (Bannatyne Club) I. 2 Thus they lived as outlaws, oppressing the countrie, .. and openly avowed they had tane this course to gett their own possessions again, or then hold the country walking. **1719** DE FOE *Crusoe* I. (Globe) 162 This confusion of my Thoughts kept me waking all Night. **1793** *Minstrel* I. 87 She was heard by the person who lodged in a room adjoining the closet, and who had been kept waking by ill health.

6. a. *trans.* To watch or guard (one who sleeps); to watch or guard (a person or thing) at night or while others sleep; to keep watch upon or over. *Obs.* exc. *dial.*

α *c* **1200** ORMIN 3773 þa wakemenn þatt wokenn heore faldess. *c* **1375** *Sc. Leg. Saints* ii. (*Paulus*) 355 He set it vpe beside his falde, quhare þat he wok his fe one nycht. *c* **1400** MAUNDEV. (1839) xiii. 145 O tyme befelle, that a Kyng of Ermonye .. woke that Hauk sum tyme. *c* **1440** *Jacob's Well* 53 On a nyȝt as he wooke his dyche of colys. *c* **1480** HENRYSON *Fox, Wolf & Husb.* 144 He chaippit frome thair ill, And on his feit wouke [*v.r.* woke] the dure quhill day. **1504** *Acc. Ld. High Treas. Scot.* II. 424 Item, to the man that woke the fald all ȝeir quhair the deir was tane, xiiijs.

β. *a* **1300** *Cursor M.* 18660 Ne iesus .. Moght neuer dei .. Ne slepe, þat has to wak us all. **13..** *E.E. Allit. P.* B. 85 þen þay cayred & com þat þe cost waked. **1375** BARBOUR *Bruce* VII. 179 May I trast the me to valk, Till I a litill slepyng tak? *a* **1450** *Le Morte Arth.* 2591 Lordyngis, a whyle I rede we lende And oure worthy wallys wake. *a* **1529** SKELTON *P. Sparowe* 668 How Scipion dyd wake The cytye of Cartage. **1543–4** *Acc. Ld. High Treas. Scot.* VIII. 250 Item, to thre men quhilk be the space of tua nychtis walkit the saidis boittis. **1596** DALRYMPLE tr. *Leslie's Hist. Scot.* II. 389 The peiple was compelit to wake the barnes. **1790** BURNS *Tam Glen* vii, The last Halloween I was waukin My droukit sark-sleeve, as ye ken.

b. To keep watch or vigil over (a dead body) until burial; to hold a wake over (see WAKE *sb.*[1] 3). Now only *dial.*, chiefly *Anglo-Irish*.

α. *c* **1300** *Beket* 2215 In a bere faire hi hit leide and tofore an auter hit woke. *c* **1440** *Jacob's Well* 187 Hyre sone, a munke, & here dowȝter, a nunne, wokyn here body iij. nyȝtes in cherche.

β. *c* **1250** *Gen. & Ex.* 2516 Hise liche was spice-like maked, And longe egipte-like waked. **1303** R. BRUNNE *Handl. Synne* 8034 To wake here body were þey set: þe fyrst nyght þat þey shulde here wake, At mydnyȝt þe bere gan to quake. **1375** BARBOUR *Bruce* XIII. 513 Than till a kirk he gert hym be Brocht, and walkit all that nycht. *a* **1500** *Chaucer's Dreme* 1906 The corses, which with torche light, They waked hadde there all that night. **1548** *Lancs. Wills* (1860) II. 199 My dettes taykyne vppe and payde and my bodye extyneguseshed honestly wayket broghfurth and buryd. **1819** W. S. ROSE *Lett. N. Italy* I. 250 They wake their dead the night before interment, performing certain games about the bier. **1824** SCOTT *Redgauntlet* Let. xi, Naebody cared to wake Sir Robert Redgauntlet like another corpse. **1829** M. EDGEWORTH *Garry Owen* (1832) vii. 46 You were right, dear, from first to last concerning the poor cratur's dead child; she did not want to have it *waked* at all, for she is not that way —not an Irishwoman at all. **1834** MARRYAT *P. Simple* li, May you die of a good old age .. and be waked handsomely. **1898** F. P. DUNNE *Mr. Dooley in Peace & War* 188 They waked th' oldest son in small beer, an' was little thought of. **1959** T. H. WHITE *Godstone & Blackymor* 168 Everybody was trying to amuse Charlie Plunkett. Otherwise, why 'wake' him? **1974** D. SEARS *Lark in Clear Air* ix. 117 They waked Holly Dallan in the parlour of the log house where she had been born and reared.

†**c.** ? To pass the night by (a well) as a superstitious observance. *Obs.*

c **1430** in *Rel. Antiq.* I. 1, I have forsworne hit whil I life, to wake the well. The last tyme I the wel woke, Sir John caght me with a croke.

†**d.** To be confined in (prison). *Obs.*

1338 R. BRUNNE *Chron.* (1725) 160 If he of his mot take ouþer erle or baroun, His prison suld he wake, þat wer deppest donjoun.

II. To become awake.

7. a. *intr.* To come out of the state of sleep or unconsciousness; to be roused from sleep, cease to sleep. Const. †*of* (obs.), *from, out of* (sleep, etc.); *to* (a condition or state), *to* (do something). Cf. AWAKE *v.* 1.

α. *c* **1250** *Gen. & Ex.* 2111 Ðe king abraid and woc in ðhogt. *c* **1275** LAY. 25566 Þo he woc [*c* 1205 awoc] of sleape. *c* **1300** *Havelok* 2093 Aboute þe middel of þe nith Wok Ubbe, and saw a mikel lith. **1387** TREVISA *Higden* VII. 411 He..wook of his sleep, and heet brynge liȝt. *c* **1435** *Torr. Portugal* 280 Ye, seyd Torrent, ore he be wakyn, I schall the tell soche a tokyn. *c* **1480** HENRYSON *Lion & Mouse* 97 Till at the last the noble lyoun woke [*v.r.* wouk]. **1523** BERNERS *Froiss.* (1812) I. cccxxii. 501 The watchmen were halfe aslepe, and herde the noyse and woke. **1603** HARSNET *Popish Impost.* 196 This exam[inant] confesseth, that diuers of them were such toyes, as came into her head being woken. **1669** P. HENRY *Diaries & Lett.* (1882) 214 About two or three o'clock in yᵉ morning hee wake. **1833** J. H. NEWMAN *Let.* 23 Jan. (1891) I. 334, I..have almost ever since woke at that hour and fancied it morning. **1869** THIRLWALL *Rem.* (1878) III. 400 He woke, we trust, from that ghastly nightmare to find himself in the light of a Father's countenance. **1901** RIDER HAGGARD *Lysbeth* xxv. 404 He had woken in the night and seen it standing at his bedside.

β. *c* **1275** LAY. 28082 Þo gan ich to wakie [*c* 1205 iwakien]. *a* **1300** *K. Horn* 444 Rymenhild..Wakede of hire swoȝning. **1362** LANGL. *P. Pl.* A. v. 3 Þenne wakede I of my wink. **1560** ROLLAND *Seven Sages* 54 This gud hound rais, and of his sleip did walk. **1565** STAPLETON tr. *Bede's Hist. Ch. Eng.* 158 When I waked, as it were oute of a greate slumber. **1611** CHAPMAN *May-day* v. 76 Imagining when shee wak't shee had something to say to me. **1719** DE FOE *Crusoe* I. (Globe) 202, I wak'd with this Thought. **1787** BURNS '*Again rejoicing Nature*' iii, A dream of ane that never wauks. **1860** GEO. ELIOT in Cross *Life* (1885) II. 232, I waked to find the six horses resolutely refusing..to move the diligence. **1919** J. D. BERESFORD *Jervaise Comedy* xv. 268, I came down from my clouds with..a sense of waking from perfect dreams to the realisation of a hard, inimical world.

b. with *up*.

a **1837** DICKENS *Pickw.* xxviii, 'Oh, you've woke up at last, have you?' said Sam. **1864** DASENT *Jest & Earnest* (1873) II. 288 Next morning Bard woke up to find Haldor busy packing up his baggage.

β. **1533** GAU *Richt Vay* (S.T.S.) 68 Thair sal mony vaik wp of thayme quhilk slepis in the ȝeird. **1535** COVERDALE *Joel* i. 5 Wake vp ye dronckardes, & wepe. **1850** SUSAN WARNER *Wide World* xxii, Ellen barely waked up to feel herself lifted from the floor. **1879** *Leisure Hour* 742/1 He had been asleep and had waked up. **1901** F. HARRISON *Autob. Mem.* (1911) II. 203 Ah! when the dream is over—and I wake up to find myself an average magazine writer.

c. *transf.* and *fig.*, esp. of inanimate things. Of persons (usually with *up*): To become animated, alert, or lively, to throw off lethargy.

It may be noted here that the only recorded sense of OE. *wæcnan* is 'to come into being, be born'.

α. *a* **1814** *Gonzanga* I. ii. in *New Brit. Theat.* III. 104 The sleeping zephyrs woke to fan her bosom. **1844** S. WILBERFORCE *Hist. Prot. Episc. Ch. Amer.* (1846) 46 Whenever this [*sc.* conscience] awoke, the struggle followed between him in whom it woke, and those who sought to keep it sleeping. **1859** FITZGERALD *Omar* viii, A thousand Blossoms with the Day Woke. **1898** *Daily News* 22 Oct. 2/1 Even little Tasmania has woken up.

β. **1523** BERNERS *Froiss.* (1812) I. ccclxviii. 556 Johan Lyon was well aduertysed of all these matters: than he began a lytell to wake. **1535** COVERDALE *Isa.* li. 9 Wake vp, wake vp, & be stronge: O thou arme of the Lorde. **1646** CRASHAW *Steps to Temple* 43 Newly they Peep't from their buds, shew'd like the Gardens eyes Scarce wak't. **1849** M. ARNOLD *In utrumque paratus* ii, O waking on a world which thus-wise springs! Whether it needs thee count Betwixt thy waking and the birth of things Ages or hours: O waking on Life's stream! **1905** R. BAGOT *Passport* xvii. 153 The landscape..waking up to a new day.

d. *to wake to*: to become conscious or aware of; to become 'alive' to. Cf. AWAKE *v.* 3.

α. **1836** LYTTON *Athens* (1837) II. 129 When the Greeks first woke to the certainty, that the vast preparations of Xerxes menaced Greece as the earliest victim. **1862** J. F. STEPHEN *Ess. Barrister* 108 The great standing controversies which have exercised the intellect of mankind ever since it first woke to consciousness of its powers. **1863** S. WILBERFORCE *Ess.* (1874) I. 312 The Church..had woke up to the sense of her true position.

β. **1895** W. R. W. STEPHENS *Life & Lett. E. A. Freeman* I. 120 Men's minds, however, had at last waked to the fact that Greece and Rome did not exhaust the world's stock of wisdom and greatness.

e. *fig.* Of things, conditions, etc.: To be stirred up or aroused; to be put in motion or action. Also with *up*.

α. **1513** DOUGLAS *Æneis* II. i. 9 The voce thus wise throw out the ciete woik. **1863** S. WILBERFORCE *Ess.* (1874) I. 325 The troubles in his diocese which woke up under the subsequent development of ritualistic fervour. **1864** *Ibid.* 363 The loud clamour woke up that he was treacherously [etc.].

β. *a* **1450** MYRC *Par. Pr.* 1542 Leste for þe penaunce sake Wo & wraþþe by-twene hem wake. **1667** MILTON *P.L.* x. 94 Gentle Aires due at thir hour To fan the Earth now wak'd. **1807** WORDSW. *Ode, Intim. Immortality* 159 Truths that wake, To perish never. **1820** KEATS *Eve St. Agnes* xxviii, Porphyro..listen'd to her breathing, if it chanced To wake into a slumberous tenderness. **1885** MRS. ALEXANDER *At Bay* viii, You are looking better, as if some life was waking up within you.

III. Causative uses.

8. a. *trans.* To rouse from sleep or unconsciousness. Also with *up*. Cf. AWAKE *v.* 5.

α. *c* **1400** LOVE *Bonavent. Mirr.* xl. (1908) 221 After this prayer oure lorde Jesu tornede aȝeyn to his disciples, and woke ham. **1523** BERNERS *Froiss.* (1812) I. ccclxx. 608 Whan the englysshmen parceyued howe they of Nantes woke them so often, than they tooke counsayle to kepe better watche. **1763** [H. KELLY] *Babler* (1767) I. 126 My woman woke me in the morning with the following letter. **1778** SUSAN BURNEY in *Fr. Burney's Early Diary* (1889) II. 238 This morning..I was woke by a noise in the next room. **1822** MILMAN *Belshazzar* 83 Sleep that shall be sweetly broken When the God his bride hath woken. **1882** 'OUIDA' *In Maremma* I. ii. 40 She was woke by neighbours' voices. **1915** *Blackw. Mag.* May 608/1, I was woken up to take a message.

β. *a* **1300** *Cursor M.* 7990 Þou slepes dauid, now I þe wak. *c* **1369** CHAUCER *Bk. Duchesse* 294, I was waked With smale foules a grete hepe That had affrayed me out of my slepe. *c* **1380** WYCLIF *Sel. Wks.* I. 92 Þe disciplis comen and wakiden him. *c* **1450** *Mirk's Festial* 290 Þan wakud God Adam, and sette þe womman before hym. **1535** COVERDALE *Luke* viii. 24 Then wente they vnto him, and waked him vp. **1560** *Maitl. Club Misc.* III. 227 Sche rais beand walked be Margaret. **1599** SHAKS. *Much Ado* II. i. 361 She hath often dreamt of vnhappinesse, and wakt her selfe with laughing. **1715** WATTS *Div. Songs, Sluggard* 2 You have wak'd me too soon, I must slumber again. **1759** GOLDSM. *Bee* No. 1. 15 Every morning waked him to a renewal of famine or toil. **1856** MISS YONGE *Daisy Chain* I. viii, It's enough to startle any one to be waked up with such a noise. **1860** TYNDALL *Glac.* I. xvi. 107, I had not the heart to wake him.

b. *transf.* and *fig.* in obvious uses. Also, to disturb (silence), make (a place) re-echo with noise.

α. **1848** THACKERAY *Van. Fair* v, Shrill cries..woke up his pleasant reverie. **1855** M. PATTISON in *Oxford Ess.* 308 The system that woke us to life. **1864** KINGSLEY *Rom. & Teut.* 120 What woke him from his dream? The cry of his starving people. **1919** *Times Lit. Suppl.* 6 Nov. 627/2 Far from falling asleep over her pages..we feel that we have been completely woken up and set gossiping.

β. **1593** SHAKS. *Rich. II*, I. iii. 132 To wake our peace, which in our Countries cradle Drawes the sweet infant breath of gentle sleepe. **1742** YOUNG *Nt. Th.* I. 437 The sprightly lark's shrill Mattin wakes the Morn. **1810** SCOTT *Lady of L.* III. xxvi, No murmur waked the solemn still. **1853** DICKENS *Bleak Ho.* xxxix, The [law-]suit does not sleep; we wake it up, we air it, we walk it about. **1854** PATMORE *Angel in Ho., Betrothal* 146 No wind waked the wood. **1912** MACALISTER *Hist. & Civiliz. Palestine* iii. 31 Those great civilizations of Crete and the Aegean, that have slumbered forgotten till waked to life again in our own days.

c. *to wake snakes* (U.S. slang): 'To cause trouble or disturbance' (Thornton): see also SNAKE *sb.* 2 d.

1848 LOWELL *Biglow P.* I. ii. 104 An' ef it worn't fer wakin' snakes, I'd home agin short meter. **1872** *Punch* 20 Jan. 25/2 The archbishops of the Roman obedience appear to be waking snakes.

9. a. To rouse to action, activity, alertness, or liveliness. Const. *to, into*. Also with *up*.

α. **1851** E. FITZGERALD *Euphranor* 66 Clearly as the trumpet that woke the Greeks to battle.

β. **1398** TREVISA *Barth. De P.R.* II. xix. (1495) 46 The fende taketh a body of the ayre, that the lyf of men be haunted and wakid to besynesse by his dooynge. **1430–40** LYDG. *Bochas* III. xxvi. (1554) 97 Cyrus than, furious as Lion, His aduersaries gan mortally to wake. **1535** COVERDALE *Joel* iii. 9 Proclame warre, wake vp the giauntes, let them drawe nye. **1605** SHAKS. *Macb.* III. vi. 31 Thither Macduffe Is gone, to pray the Holy King, vpon his ayd To wake Northumberland, and warlike Seyward. **1750** GRAY *Elegy* 48 Hands, that the rod of empire might have sway'd, Or wak'd to extasy the living lyre. **1884** H. CHOLMONDELEY-PENNELL *From Grave to Gay* 85 As when waked to sudden speed Darts from the throng the flying steed. **1901** R. GARNETT *Ess.* iii. 72 The highest criticism is..unoriginal in this, that it must be waked into activity by another mind. **1901** W. R. H. TROWBRIDGE *Lett. her Mother to Eliz.* xxiii. 111 We are so terribly dull, and anything will serve to wake us up a bit.

b. *to wake (up) to*: to arouse to the consciousness or enjoyment of. Cf. 7 d.

1868–70 MORRIS *Earthly Par.* II. III. 234 He felt as one who, waked up suddenly To life's delight, knows not of grief or care.

10. To bring into being, raise, stir up (war, strife, woe, etc.); to arouse, excite (an activity, feeling, emotion); to evoke (a sound, echo, etc.). Also with *up*.

α. **1793** *Minstrel* III. 136 A voice whose well known tunings thrilled through my soul, and woke every dormant passion. **1798** SOUTHEY *Lett.* (1856) I. 59 Your account of poor B. woke in me the recollections, and almost the feelings, of old friendship. **1862** S. WILBERFORCE *Ess.* (1874) I. 205 The controversy, which the publication of 'Essays and Reviews' woke up. **1879** GREEN *Read. Eng. Hist.* I. viii. 34 This woke rivalry and dissension among the other nobles. **1903** W. A. ELLIS *Glasenapp's Life Wagner* III. 67 [It] has woken an ambition in me.

β. *c* **1250** *Gen. & Ex.* 360 Ðu haues ðe sorȝes sigðhe waked. *c* **1330** R. BRUNNE *Chron. Wace* (Rolls) 8294 [The Britons] þretten Hengist to wake hys wough. *c* **1400** *26 Pol. Poems* xvi. 29 He is a fool, þat werre wole wake, þat may not maynten it wiþ mede. **1604** SHAKS. *Oth.* I. iii. 30 To wake and wage a danger profitlesse. **1655** tr. *Com. Hist. Francion* I. 10 This waked the Curates curiosity to descend. **1667** MILTON *P.L.* IX. 739 Meanwhile the hour of Noon drew on, and wak'd An eager appetite, rais'd by the smell So savorie of that Fruit. **1741–2** GRAY *Agrippina* 103 And a call, Like mine, might serve belike to wake pretensions Drowsier than theirs. **1808** SCOTT *Marmion* VI. vi, But far more needful was his care, When sense return'd to wake despair. **1889** JESSOPP *Coming of Friars* iii. 164 In every melody that wakes the echoes. **1896** *McClure's Mag.* VI. 423/1 Never a creak did I wake out of that staircase till I was almost at the first landing.

Hence **'waked** *ppl. a.*

1581 A. HALL *Iliad* IX. 165 They keepe the watche, they stand with waked sprites. **1604** SHAKS. *Oth.* III. iii. 363 Thou had'st bin better haue bin borne a Dog Then answer my wak'd wrath. **16..** ? CHAPMAN *Revenge for Honour* III. i. (1659) 34 And on this vicious Prince like a fierce Sea-breach my just wak'd rage shall riot. **1646** BROWNE *Pseud. Ep.* I. x. 40 The discovery of things to come, in sleepe above the prescience of our waked senses.

wake, variant of WACKE *Geol.*

wake: see VAKE *v.*, WALK *v.*[2], WEAK *a.*

wakeaday, wake-a-day ('weɪkədeɪ). ? *nonce-wd.* [f. WAKE *v.* + DAY *sb.*, after WORKADAY.] Of life, etc.: such as one wakes up to each day; that is experienced by ordinary people; regular.

1893 G. B. SHAW *Let.* 21 Aug. (1965) I. 401 All these terrible combats..on behalf of Wilde, Pinero, [Frank] Harris &c. &c. &c. belong to Piona and not to the wake-a-day world. **1951** M. MCLUHAN *Mech. Bride* (1967) 97/2 Synthetic gods and goddesses (stars) appear to assume the roles of our wakeaday existence. **1962** —— *Gutenberg Galaxy* 269 The electric puts the mythic or collective dimension of human experience fully into the conscious wake-a-day world.

‖**wakeel** (wə'kiːl). *Anglo-Ind.* Also **wakil**. [See VAKEEL. (Properly the spelling with *v* should represent the Persian and Indian forms, and that with *w* the Arabic; but this is not observed in our examples).] = VAKEEL 1, 2.

1803 SIR J. MALCOLM in Kaye *Life* (1856) I. 242 The Wakeels of Scindiah had yesterday a long audience. **1834** *Baboo* I. xvii. 296 (Stanf.) Even those who plead my cause; my wakeels, my agents. **1913** *Daily News* 14 Feb. 6 Those among the students [Cairo] who have pursued the laical side of their studies become 'Wakils' (lawyers) or 'Katibs' (public or private accountants and writers).

wakee-wakee, var. of WAKEY-WAKEY.

wakeful ('weɪkfʊl), *a.* [f. WAKE *v.* + -FUL.]

1. Keeping awake, esp. while others sleep, not yielding to sleep.

1549 COVERDALE, etc. *Erasm. Par. Col.* iv. 2–4 Continue in prayer, not as dull & heauy people by reason of any surfetyng, but as sober & wakefull. **1590** SPENSER *F.Q.* I. v. 30. **1598** SYLVESTER *Du Bartas* I. ii. 736 As wakefull Students, in the Winter's night Against the steel,..Strike sudden sparks into their Tinder-box. **1667** MILTON *P.L.* III. 38 The wakeful Bird Sings darkling, and in shadiest Covert hid Tunes her nocturnal Note. **1710** STEELE *Tatler* No. 201 ¶ 10 One of the most wakeful of the Soporifick Assembly. **1729** T. COOKE *Tales*, etc. 44 If the Soul..Still bids the wakeful Eye of Sorrow flow. **1820** BYRON *Mar. Fal.* III. ii. 389 Saint Mark's great bell at dawn shall find me wakeful!

2. Habitually keeping awake; *fig.* keeping on the alert, vigilant, watchful.

15.. in Puttenham *Engl. Poesie* III. xix. (Arb.) 232 When Prince for his people is wakefull and wise. **1611** SPEED *Hist. Gt. Brit.* IX. xx. (1623) 959 These dangers..did worthily make the King wakefull euen ouer smaller accidents. **1823** 'JON BEE' *Dict. Turf* s.v. *Wake*, The Scot considers no man awake or wakeful, who is not alive to his own interests. **1865** KINGSLEY *Herew.* vi, He..had in all things shown himself a daring and wakeful captain.

b. of dispositions or actions.

1561 NORTON & SACKV. *Gorboduc* I. ii. 193 The brother, that shoulde be the brothers aide, And haue a wakefull care for his defence, Gapes for his death. *a* **1639** W. WHATELEY *Prototypes* II. xxvi. (1640) 91 God..hath disposed of things so by his wakefull providence. **1741–2** GRAY *Agrippina* 192 We could not have beguil'd With more elusive speed the dazzled sight Of wakeful jealousy. *c* **1800** H. K. WHITE *Sonn. Dermody*, The pale pilot,..as he plies His wakeful task. **1817** CHALMERS *Astron. Disc.* v. (1852) 116 Bending a wakeful regard over the men of this sinful world. **1871** J. R. MACDUFF *Mem. Patmos* v. 57 His unresting, wakeful vigilance.

c. *transf.* Of inanimate agencies: Continually active, never ceasing or resting.

1697 DRYDEN *Æneis* IV. 289 A hundred Altars fed with wakeful Fire.

3. Unable to sleep, restless.

1675 DRYDEN *Aurengz.* II. (1676) 23, I shrink far off—Dissembling sleep, but wakeful with the fright. The day takes off the pleasure of the night. **1794** MRS. RADCLIFFE *Myst. Udolpho* xxix, Her spirits were wakeful and agitated; and finding it impossible to sleep, she determined [etc.]. **1853** M. ARNOLD *Sohrab & Rustum* 6 All night long He had lain wakeful, tossing on his bed. **1860** THACKERAY *Lovel* vi. (1861) 220 Tick—tock! Moment after moment I heard on the clock the clinking footsteps of wakeful grief.

4. Marked by absence or want of sleep.

1628 PEMBLE *Worthy Rec. Lord's Supper* 48 Sometimes a wakefull bed calls upon us to examine our hearts. **1697** DRYDEN *Æneis* IX. 210 They..pass the wakeful Night in Feasts and Play. **1870** R. S. HAWKER *Footpr. Far Cornw.* 208 That night an inspiration visited me in my wakeful bed.

5. Said of dreams, or what is normally characteristic of sleep: Waking.

1638 JUNIUS *Paint. Ancients* 22 Among our idle hopes and wakefull dreames, these Images do follow us so close. **1641** DENHAM *Sophy* I. ii, All thy feares, Thy wakefull terrors, and affrighting dreames,..have now Their full rewards. **1820** KEATS *Eve St. Agnes* xxvii, In sort of wakeful swoon, perplex'd she lay. **1855** TENNYSON *Maud* II. IV. v, In a wakeful doze I sorrow For the hand, the lips, the eyes, For the meeting of the morrow. **1886** W. J. TUCKER *E. Europe* 316 Following the wayward turn of wakeful fancies.

†**6.** Rousing (one) from sleep, awakening. *Obs.*

1629 MILTON *Christ's Nativity* xvi, Yet first to those ychain'd in sleep, The wakefull trump of doom must thunder through the deep.

Hence **'wakefully** *adv.*, **'wakefulness.**

a **1586** SIDNEY *Arcadia* III. iv. (1912) 374 Making the cowardly Clinias to have care of the watch, which he knew his own feare would make him very wakefully performe. **1626** BACON *Sylva* §925 There be other Perfumes, that.. are fit to be vsed in Burning Agues,..and too much Wakefulnesse. **1753** *Adventurer* No. 39 ⁋11 So, perhaps, to each individual of the human species, nature has ordained the same quantity of wakefulness and sleep. **1776** JOHNSON in *Boswell* (1904) I. 654 He should have a lamp constantly burning.. and if wakefully disturbed, take a book, and read. **1830** COLERIDGE *Table-t.* 1 May, If he had relaxed the stern wakefulness of his reason for a single moment. **1847** EVANSON & MAUNSELL *Managem. & Dis. Childr.* (ed. 5) 352 Wakefulness is a very prominent character of nervous irritation in the child, and should always arrest attention. **1884** *Leeds Mercury* 15 Nov. 6/6 England stands firmly and wakefully on guard behind the line up to which the Russians have seen fit to advance.

† **wake-goose.** *Obs. rare*⁻¹. [? Corrupt form of WAYZGOOSE.] = WAYZGOOSE.

1759 *Brit. Chron.* 17 Sept. 267 The Season comes, in black to dress the year, But with it brings the Wake-Goose, and good Cheer.

wakeless ('weɪklɪs), *a.* [f. WAKE *v.* + -LESS.] Without awakening, unbroken, undisturbed.

1824 MOIR in *Blackw. Mag.* XVI. 279 There is no prospect, save a wakeless sleep. **1854** H. MILLER *Sch. & Schm.* (1858) 364 Though sights and sounds like these circled my bed, Wakeless and heavy would my slumbers be.

'wakeman. *Obs.* exc. *arch.* Also 5 wak-, wayk-, walkman. [f. WAKE *sb.*¹ + MAN. Cf. ON. *vǫkumaðr* (-mann).]

1. A watchman.

c **1200** ORMIN 3812 All all swa summ þa wakemenn.. offdrede wærenn.. off þatt enngless sihhþe. *a* **1225** *Ancr. R.* 14 þe fif wittes, þet witeð þe heorte alse wakemen hwarse heo beoð treowe. **1398** TREVISA *Barth. De P.R.* II. v. (1495) 32 Angels ben called walkmen and wardeyns for they warne men of perylles that maye falle. *c* **1425** *Seven Sag.* (P.) 1443 As thay spoken lowde togyder, The wakmen herde and come thydyr. **1461** in *10th Rep. Hist. MSS. Comm.* App. v. 301 The gaylere and the wakman of the saide citie.. shal have the mesuring of salte and corne. **1483** *Cath. Angl.* 406/2 A Waykman, *noctivagus, pervigill, pernox, vigil* (A.). **1552** *Inv. Ch. Goods York* etc. (Surtees) 59 Churchewardens ..wakmene and inhabitantes of the same parishe [Beverley, St. Nicholas]. **1905** W. WATSON *Ballad Semmerwater* Poems I. 193 King's tower and queen's bower, And the wakeman on the wall.

2. In the borough of Ripon: **a.** In the 15–16th c. the designation of a class of municipal officers, whose duties included attendance on the shrine of St. Wilfrid. (Cf. quot. 1552 in 1, relating to one of the parishes of Beverley.) **b.** The title of the chief magistrate of the borough until 1604, when it was exchanged for the title of mayor.

Lists of the 'wakemen' of the borough from 1400 to 1604 are extant, giving as a rule one name for each year, and ending with Hugh Ripplaye (see quot. *c* 1605). It is commonly assumed that the 'wakeman' who was chief magistrate was the head of the body of 'wakemen' referred to in quots. 1478 and 1511, but there is no evidence of this.

1478 *Mem. Ripon* (Surtees) III. 259 Et in denariis sol[utis]. ministris villæ Ripon vocatis Wakemen, deservientibus feretro in festo Ascensionis Domini et per iij dies præcedentes, cap. per diem 4*d.*, 16*d.* **1511** *Ibid.* 177 De 56*s.* 1*d.* similiter per ipsum receptis de diversis personis electis in officium lez Wakeman. *c* **1605** *Acct. Bk. W. Wray* in *Antiquary* XXXII. 213, 1604. Heughe Ripplaye. The laste wakeman and first maior [of Ripon]. **1733** GENT *Hist. Rippon* 139 A List of the Wakemen of Rippon, from the year 1400 (the rest of the Corporation were then called Elders) 'till King James I alter'd their Government, Anno Dom. 1604. **1875** STUBBS *Const. Hist.* III. xxi. 583 The jurisdiction was exercised [at Ripon] by the bailiffs.., and the elective wakeman.

waken ('weɪk(ə)n), *v.* Pa. t. and pa. pple. **wakened.** Forms: 1 wæcnan, wæcnian, 3 wakenen, -in, *Orm.* waccn-enn, 3–4, 6 *Sc.* wakne, 3–5 wakin, wakken, wacken, 4 wakan, wakkin, *Sc.* vakyn, 4–5 wakyn, -on, wackyn, -on, *Sc.* valkyn, 4–6 *Sc.* walkyn, 5 waykyn, wokyn (?), 5–6 *Sc.* walkin, 6 *Sc.* walkne, valkin, 6–7 *Sc.* walken, waikin, 8–9 *Sc.* wauken, *dial.* wacken, wakken, 3– waken. [OE. *wæcnan* (also *-wæcnian*, ? once *wacnian*) = ON. *vakna* (Norw., Sw. *vakna*, Da. *vaagne*), Goth. *ga-waknan* (found only in pr. pple.), f. root **wak-* (see WAKE *v.*) + *-n-* suffix of inchoative verbs of state.

The suffix in Teut. verbs of this class was originally confined to the present stem; cf. Goth. *fraihnan, frah, frēhum*, also *keinan*, pa. pple. *kijans*. The original conjugation in OE. may have been *wæcnan, wóc, wócon*, **wacen*, but the conjugation of *wæcnan* as a regular weak verb goes back to the earliest known period of the language; in ON. *vakna* is weak, the strong pa. t. being wanting.]

I. Intransitive senses.

1. To cease to sleep; to become awake. Const. †*of* (obs.), *from, out of* (sleep, etc.), *to* (a state of things, etc.). Also with *up*. Cf. WAKE *v.* 7.

c **1300** *Havelok* 2164 So þat he bigan to wakne, And wit hem ful sore to blakne. **1375** BARBOUR *Bruce* VII. 210 He valknyt, and rais all desaly. *c* **1400** *Melayne* 133 When Charls wakenede of his dreme. *c* **1420** WYNTOUN *Cron.* IV. 1167 þan þe Romanys suddandly wayknyt qwhar þai slepande lay. **1500–20** DUNBAR *Poems* xxvii. 103 Quhairthrow I walknit of my trance. **1581** RICH *Farew.* (Shaks. Soc.) 166 He bidde her goe againe, and shake her till she did waken. **1616** S. S. *Honest Lawyer* IV. G 3, Whilst thou wakendst with the chimes, Because thou wentst to bed betimes. **1618** FLETCHER *Mad Lover* V. iv, Looke with the eyes of heaven that nightlie waken, To view the wonders of my glorious Maker. **1760** *Impostors Detected* IV. vi. II. 211 At that very instant Don Vulpez wakened from his trance. **1787** BURNS *'Again rejoicing Nature'* vi, When the lark, 'tween light and dark, Blythe waukens by the daisy's side. **1815** SCOTT *Antiq.* xxi, An he sleeps in this damp hole, he'll maybe waken nae mair. **1856** MISS YONGE *Daisy Chain* II. x, Etheldred's dream was over. She had wakened to the inside of a Great Western carriage. *a* **1874** R. BUCHANAN *Dead Mother* 5, I waken'd up in the dead of night.

b. *transf.* and *fig.*, of inanimate things, etc. †Of a condition, state of things: To come into existence, become manifest or active, be stirred up or aroused; also with *up*. Of wind: To begin to blow or rage. Cf. WAKE *v.* 7 c, e.

Beowulf 85 Ne wæs hit lenge þa ʒen þæt se ecghete.. æfter wælniðe wæcnan scolde. *c* **1200** ORMIN 12223 All þe flæshess fule lusst Waccneþþ þurrh gluterrnesse. *a* **1225** *St. Marher.* 11 þu art walle of waisdom, ant euch wunne wakeneð ant waxeð of þe. *a* **1327** *Pol. Songs* (Camden) 152 Ther wakeneth in the world wondred ant wee. **13..** *E.E. Allit. P.* C. 132 þay [*sc.* winds] wakened wel þe wroþeloker, for wroþely he cleped. *a* **1352** MINOT *Poems* vi. 10 When all yowre wele es went ʒowre wo wakkins ful wide. *c* **1400** *Destr. Troy* 2046 Now wackons vp werre as ye shall note after. *c* **1425** *Seven Sag.* (P.) 1803 Than bygan to wakken wo. **1597** BEARD *Theatre God's Judgem.* (1612) 245 And so though vengeance slept a while, yet at length it wakened. **1634** BRERETON *Trav.* (Chetham Soc.) 4 It was then a great calm, about an hour, and afterwards the wind wakened. **1839** T. T. STODDART *Songs & P.* 21 O waken, winds, waken! **1852** THACKERAY *Esmond* III. vii, We forget nothing. The memory sleeps, but wakens again. **1898** A. AUSTIN *Lamia's Winter Quarters* p. viii, When.. the fig-tree cressets have flamed to green, And windflower wakened, and tulip blown.

c. Of a person: To become lively, animated, or stirring; usually with *up*. Also, to become 'alive' *to* (a situation, etc.). Cf. WAKE *v.* 7 c.

1825 JAMIESON, *Wauken*,.. 2. To become animated..; as, 'He wauken't on his sermon'. **1891** 'R. BOLDREWOOD' *Sydney-side Sax.* xii, The rider going pretty patient like myself, but beginning to waken up. **1899** *Westm. Gaz.* 27 Dec. 2/1 Mr. Collins is wakening to the necessity of a more refined type of Christmas entertainment.

†**2.** To remain awake, refrain from sleeping, keep watch or vigil; to remain alive. *Obs. rare.*

1682 BUNYAN *Holy War* (1905) 430 And dost thou know why I.. do still suffer Diabolonians to dwell in thy walls, O Mansoul? it is to keep thee wakening, to try thy love, to make thee watchful.

II. Transitive senses.

3. To rouse (a person or animal) from sleep or unconsciousness. Also with *up*. Const. †*of* (obs.), *from, out of* (sleep). Cf. WAKE *v.* 8.

c **1200** ORMIN 5843, 5845 & o þe þridde daʒʒ itt [the lion's whelp] iss Waccnedd off slæp & reʒʒsedd, þurrh þatt te faderr gaþ þærto & stireþþ itt & waccneþþ. *a* **1300** *Cursor M.* 14201 þat i til him weind it es time For to wacken him of his suime. **1375** BARBOUR *Bruce* VI. 104 Than his twa men in hy send he To warne & walkyn his menʒe. *c* **1400** *Destr. Troy* 681 [She] Waknet vp a wydow, þat hir with dwellit. *c* **1510** DOUGLAS *K. Hart* I. 381 The Quene is walknit with ane felloun fray. **1601** WEEVER *Mirr. Mart.* B iij b, At length, well wakened from that pleasing slumber. **1611** BIBLE *Zech.* iv. 1 As a man that is wakened out of his sleepe. **1673** *Vinegar & Mustard* (1873) 23 The paltry cur wakened me last Sunday of a good nap. **1818** SCOTT *Hrt. Midl.* xxix, May ye a' sleep till the hangman wauken ye. **1853** MRS. GASKELL *Ruth* xxii, Her dream.. was one of undefined terror.. so great that it wakened her up. **1872** TENNYSON *Gareth & Lynette* 1034 O Sun, that wakenest all to bliss or pain.

b. *fig.*

c **1380** WYCLIF *Sel. Wks.* III. 167 Lord, where slepis þis gode lawe, and when schal hit be wakened? **1594** SHAKS. *Rich. III*, III. vii. 124 Your sleepie thoughts, Which here we waken to our Countries good. **1639** MAYNE *City Match* I. v, Fresh as Pygmalions Mistresse newly wakened Out of her Alabaster. **1820** SHELLEY *Ode West Wind* 29 Thou who didst waken from his summer dreams The blue Mediterranean. **1842** DICKENS *Amer. Notes* xi, A loud high-pressure blast; enough, one would think, to waken up the host of Indians who lie buried in a great mound yonder.

4. To rouse to activity, alertness, or liveliness; to stir up, excite. Const. *to*, †*into*; *to* (do something). Also with *up*. Cf. WAKE *v.* 9.

c **1400** *Destr. Troy* 3610 þerfore wackon þi wille into wight dedis. *c* **1400** *Rule St. Benet* (Prose) xxii. 20 Man sal wakin þaim faire til godis seruise. **1456** SIR G. HAYE *Law Arms* (S.T.S.) 166 The men that I led with me to wakyn ʒow to do me resoun. **1549** *Compl. Scot.* xi. 92 God almychty valknit vitht his grace the hartis of ʒour predecessours. **1577** *St. Augustine's Man.* Pref., That when we bee shrunke away, we may bee wakened to run backe agayne to our true God. **1604** JAS. I *Counterbl.* To Rdr. (Arb.) 97 It is the Kings part.. to waken them vp againe, to be more diligent in their Offices. **1759** JOHNSON *Idler* No. 43 ⁋3 It was therefore necessary that this universal reluctance should be counter-acted, and the drowsiness of hesitation wakened into resolve. **1851** G. BRIMLEY *Ess., Wordsw.* (1858) 110 Where the vanity of social distinction.. wakens the harp of the poet. **1877** R. H. HUTTON *Ess.* (ed. 2) I. Pref. 6 It has been the one purpose of all.. divine revelation.. to waken us up out of this perpetually recurring tendency to fall back into ourselves.

5. To summon into existence, raise, stir up (war, woe, wind, etc.); to kindle (fire, flame); to arouse, excite (an activity, emotion); to evoke (music, sound). Also with *up*. Cf. WAKE *v.* 10.

c **1330** R. BRUNNE *Chron. Wace* (Rolls) 8558 Now hauy take oure moste fo, þat haþ vs wakned many wo! **13..** *E.E. Allit. P.* B. 323 For I schal waken vp a water to wasch alle þe worlde. *c* **1400** *Destr. Troy* 2274 Yff we wackon vp werre with weghes so fele. **1596** DALRYMPLE tr. *Leslie's Hist. Scot.* II. 460 Scho feired that he.. suld in Scotland agane be the raiser of a newe bleise, and wakne vp a new flame. *a* **1616** BEAUM. & FL. *Little Fr. Lawyer* v. ii. 16 Speake to that Lion Lord, waken his anger. **1667** MILTON *P.L.* III. 369 They introduce Thir sacred Song, and waken raptures high. **1786** BURNS *Holy Fair* xix, It kindles Wit, it waukens Lear. **1838** DICKENS *O. Twist* li, What a crowd of emotions were wakened up in his breast. **1863** GEO. ELIOT *Romola* I. Proem 16 The sunlight and shadows bring their old beauty and waken the old heart-strains at morning, noon, and even-tide.

6. *Scots Law.* To revive (a process) which, after calling a summons, has been allowed to 'sleep' for a year and a day.

1560 *Maitl. Club Misc.* III. 234 The cause.. suscitate and newlie walkynnet. **1569** *Reg. Privy Council Scot.* I. 680 The mater being walkynnit of new, and all the partiis comperand personalie. **1609** SKENE *Reg. Maj., Quoniam Attach.* c. 55 And then the principall pley (betwix the persewer and the defender) sall be walkned. **1711** J. SPOTTISWOODE *Forms of Process* (1718) 20 In case Protestation has not been sought within Year and Day,.. no Protestation can be granted, till the Advocation; which on that Account, is said to be sleeping, be wakened. **1790** *Collect. Styles* III. 195. **1838** W. BELL *Dict. Law Scot.* s.v. *Wakening*.

7. To watch, watch over, keep an eye upon. *Sc.*

1535 STEWART *Cron. Scot.* III. 12 This ilk Angus in Quhiterne than tuke girth, Quhair he wes walknit all tyme round about, That be no way that tyme he mycht wyn out. **1865** TESTER *Poems* 156 (E.D.D.) On summer nichts, wauken the claes Wi' maidens fair.

Hence **'wakened, 'wakening** *ppl. adjs.*

c **1600** SHAKS. *Sonn.* cxvii. 12 But shoote not at me in your wakened hate. **1635** D. DICKSON *Hebr.* xii. 24. 304 The wakened Conscience, lying in.. feare of the offended Iudge. **1670** MILTON *Hist. Eng.* II. 95 He therefore with a wak'n'd spirit, to the extent of his Fortune dilating his mind. **1813** SCOTT *Rokeby* II. i, And the rich dale, that eastward lay, Waited the wakening touch of day. **1817** MOORE *Lalla Rookh, Veiled Proph.* I. 166 Ere Peace can visit them, or Truth let in Her wakening day-light on a world of sin! **1892** MEREDITH *Poems, Ode Comic Spirit* 71 Thou, soul of wakened heads, art armed to warn.

waken, obs. form of WEAKEN.

wakener ('weɪk(ə)nə(r)). Also 6 *Sc.* walk(y)nar, wakenar. [f. WAKEN *v.* + -ER¹.]

1. A person or thing that wakens or arouses. Also with *up*.

1513 DOUGLAS *Æneis* VIII. Prol. 109 Quhay ar wirkaris of this weir, quha walkynaris of wa. **1597** JAS. VI *Dæmonol.* III. iii. 67 The procurer & wakener vp of these two natural qualities. *a* **1653** Z. BOYD in *Zion's Flowers* (1855) Introd. 52 A verse, which.. served for a wakener for to rouse me from ..sleep. **1684** tr. *Bonet's Merc. Compit.* XIX. 689 These are the genuine wakeners or exciters of the Ferment of the Stomach. **1878** C. STANFORD *Symb. Christ* xii. 335 The soul's wakener is always Christ. **1887** SMILES *Life & Labour* 269 Tea is another wakener-up. **1895** MEREDITH *Amazing Marr.* I. xvi. 185 Delivering a wakener [*i.e.* a rousing blow] in unexpected quarters.

†**b.** *spec.* An alarm attached to a clock.

1564 *Reg. Privy Council Scot.* I. 308 Ane lytill knok, with ane walknar ouregilt.

2. One who awakes. *rare.*

1857 MRS. GASKELL *C. Bronte* vi. (1860) 78 She remembered the times when watchers or wakeners in the night heard the distant word of command.

† **'wakeness.** *Obs.* [f. WAKE *a.* + -NESS.] The state of being awake; (one's) waking hours.

1585–92 LYLY *Gallathea* III. i. 48 (Bond) My sleepes broken and full of dreames, my wakenesse sad and full of sighes.

wakening ('weɪk(ə)nɪŋ), *vbl. sb.* [-ING¹.] The action of the verb WAKEN; a rousing or being roused from sleep, torpor, etc.

c **1400** *Destr. Troy* 8431 At hir wakonyng. *c* **1440** *Bone Flor.* 1660 A sorowfull wakenyng had sche thore. **1677** *Reg. Privy Council Scot.* Ser. III. V. 263 Threatenings.. to give the petitioner and his familie ane hott walkening. *a* **1796** BURNS *'Jockey's ta'en the parting kiss'* iii, Sweetly blithe his waukening be! **1827** KEBLE *Chr. Y., Morning* vi, New every morning is the love Our wakening and uprising prove. **1856** MISS YONGE *Daisy Chain* II. xxv, Her first wakening to the knowledge that Margaret was gone. **1913** J. H. MORRISON *On Trail of Pioneers* xxiii. 112 The wakening of China was quickened by a generation.

b. *Scots Law.* (See WAKEN *v.* 6.)

1584 in Littlejohn *Aberd. Sheriff Crt.* (1904) Introd. 44 This day being assignit be ane walkining to pronunce Interloquitor in the said caus. **1608** *Melrose Regality Rec.* (S.H.S.) I. 62 Lawrence Scott.. producit ane precept of wakning aganis the haill persons, fewaris, [etc.]. **1765–8** ERSKINE *Inst. Law Scot.* IV. i. §62 Consequently the decree may be extracted, after the year is elapsed, without the necessity of a wakening. **1868** *Act 31 & 32 Vict.* c. 100 §95 It shall be competent for any of the parties.. to lodge a minute craving a wakening of the cause.

waker ('weɪkə(r)), *sb.*¹ [f. WAKE *v.* + -ER¹.]

†**1.** One who 'wakes' or abstains from sleep.

c **1290** *St. Michael* 691 in *S. Eng. Leg.* 319 Hardi and liʒt and stalewarde and wakiare wel guod. **1581** MULCASTER *Positions* xxx. (1887) 113 The spare feeder or great waker, needeth not any such kinde of physicke.

2. One who awakes (early, etc.).

1633 B. JONSON *Tale Tub* I. vi, Late Watchers are no early Wakers, Madam. **1851** MRS. BROWNING *Casa Guidi Wind.* I. 159 Men who will not fear The baptism of the holy morning dew (And many of such wakers now are here). **1893** A. MACKENZIE in *Independent* (N.Y.) 19 Oct., The early waker.

†**3. a.** One who watches; a watcher, watchman. *Obs.*

1382 WYCLIF *Dan.* iv. 10 [13] And loo! the waker, and holy came doun from heuen. **1388** —— *Song Sol.* iii. 3 Wakeris, that kepen the citee, founden me. **1398** TREVISA *Barth. De P.R.* XII. xvi. (1495) 424 Cranes ordeyne watches and the waker stondyth vpon oo fote. *c* **1400** LANGL. *P. Pl.* A. v. 223 (Harl. MS.) Til he woke & wept water wiþ his iȝen, & *vigilate* þe wakere warned him þo. *c* **1440** *Jacob's Well* 187 Sche ros opynly, in syȝt of alle here wakerys, & roryng went out at þe cherche-dore. **1808** JAMIESON, *Wauker*, a watchman, one who watches clothes during night.

b. *dial.* One who sits up with a sick person.

1798 W. HUTTON *Life* 68, I had left her as usual with the waker and my daughter, and had slept two hours.

4. One who rouses another from sleep; *fig.* one who excites or stirs up (some feeling, etc.).

1390 GOWER *Conf.* II. 107 That is for I se hire noght, Which is the wakere of mi thoght. **1591** SOUTHWELL *Marie Magd. Funerall Teares* Ded. (1594) A 3 b, Sorrowe is the sister of mercie, and a waker of compassion. **1722** in W. Andrews *Curios. Ch.* (1890) 181 Paid to sluggard waker, o 10 o. **1903** *Daily Chron.* 15 Dec. 5/2 In the districts where London working men live..sixpence a week from each client is the usual 'waker's' wage. **1913** DITCHFIELD *Parish Clerk* (ed. 2) 264 One Sunday the 'waker' sighted his prey.

5. One who wakes (a corpse).

1808 MOORE *Corrupt.* 172 Nay, when the Constitution has expir'd, I'll have such men, like Irish wakers, hir'd To chant old 'Habeas Corpus' by its side. **1974** D. SEARS *Lark in Clear Air* xi. 139 But to hear the wakers at their trade you would think the deceased was Giant MacCaskill.

Also **waker-upper** *colloq.* (*a*) (with qualifying adj.) in sense 2 of WAKER *sb.*[1]; (*b*) = sense 4 of WAKER *sb.*[1] (cf. sense 8 a of the vb.). *colloq.*

1935 *Morgantown* (W.Va.) *Post* 7 Jan. 5/1 Henderson.. serves as..waker-upper, and general handy man. **1966** 'D. SHANNON' *With a Vengeance* x. 132 He slept so heavily as to need an 'arrangement' with a waker-upper. **1971** 'E. FENWICK' *Impeccable People* vi. 35 Louise..stood quiet, blinking... 'Sorry,..I'm a slow waker-upper. Let's go and have the coffee.'

†**'waker**, *a.* *Obs.* Also 1 **wacor**, **wæcer**, 4–5 **wakir(e**, **wakyr** (5 *Sc.* **walkyr**), (5 **wakare**). [OE. *wacor* = WFris. *wakker* wakeful (also as adv. very), MDu., (M)LG. *wacker* (Du. *wakker*), OHG. *wacchar*, *wahhar* (MHG. *wacher*, *wacker*, mod.G. *wacker* valiant), ON. *vakr* wakeful, alert (Da. *vakker*, MSw. *vakar* watchful, Sw. *vakker* handsome):—OTeut. **wakro-* f. **wak-*: see WAKE *v.*] Unsleeping, watchful, vigilant. Also *fig.*

c **1000** *Laws Cnut* I. xxvi, Þonne moton þa hyrdas beon swyde wacore. *c* **1200** *Trin. Coll. Hom.* 13 Ðe ðridde [werke of brihtnesse] is þat man be waker and liht and snel and seli and erliche rise. *a* **1225** *Ancr. R.* 164 Ant Seint Peter..bit us te beon wakere & bisie ine holi beoden. *a* **1272** *Luue Ron* 150 in *O.E. Misc.* 97 Wyþ þeoues,..þu most beo waker and snel. *c* **1381** CHAUCER *Parl. Foules* 358 The wakyr goos, the cokkow most onkynde. *c* **1410** *Lantern of Light* 25 Wel auȝt suche a man to be waker & wise þat haþ þe greet God Lord of Israel dwelling in hise soule. **1456** SIR G. HAYE *Law Arms* (S.T.S.) 301 Thai war better, mare wakir, and hable to the weris..throu hardness of lyfing. *c* **1530** *Prov.* in *Pol., Rel. & L. Poems* (1903) 60 Waker howndes been profitable. **1560** tr. *Æn. Sylvius' Lucres & Eurialus* F viii b, The waker dragon dyd neuer keepe so well the golden fleece.

waker, obs. Sc. form of WALKER[2].

†**'wakerell.** *Obs.* Forms: 5 **wakerrell**, 6 **wag(g)erell**, **wak(e)rell(e**, (**wakeryng**), 7 **wackerell**. [App. f. WAKER *sb.* + -EL.] The name given in Kent to a church bell (? the sanctus bell). Also ***wakerell bell***, ***rope***.

1485 *Churchw. Acc. St. Dunstan's, Canterb.* in *Archæol. Cant.* XVI. 292 Item for a rope for the wakerrell, iij d. **1545** *Ibid.* XVII. 107 Item payde for ye wakerell rope, v d. **1552** *Ibid.* VIII. 115 Item iij bells in the Steple & a waggerell bell. **1602** *Church-w. Presentm.* in *N. & Q.* Ser. IX. VIII. 405/2 We want one bell and a wackerell, which were sold away [etc.].

wakerife ('weɪkraɪf, -rɪf), *a.* *Sc.* and *north. dial.* Forms: 6 **wacryff**, **walkrife** (**waikryfe**, **walcryif**), 5–7 **walkryf(e**, 6–7 **wakryff**, 8 **wakryfe**, 9 **-rife**, 8, 9 **waukrife**, 6– **wakerife**. [f. WAKE *sb.* + RIFE *a.*: cf. CAULDRIFE.] Indisposed to sleep, wakeful, vigilant. Also *fig.*

c **1480** HENRYSON *Cock & Fox* 103 Oure walkryfe watche, vs for to warne and tell, Quhen that Aurora,..Put vp hir heid betuix the nicht and day. **1513** DOUGLAS *Æneis* IV. v. 17 Mony walkrife ene lurkis ther ondir. **1594** J. MELVILL *Autob. & Diary* (Wodrow Soc.) 315 Acknawlaging thairin the speciall benefeit of God's providence in steiring up the spreits of his servants to be wacryff, cearfull, and curagius. **1622** HANNAY *Nightingale*, etc. 25 When pleasing Prognes longing love For Philomelas sight Grew wake-rife. *c* **1730** RAMSAY *Cordial* v, When thou waukrife art or dry. **1786** BURNS *Epist. Major Logan* x, The witching, curs'd, delicious blinkers Hae..gart me weet my waukrife winkers Wi' girnin spite. **1875** W. ALEXANDER *Sk. Ain Folk* 184 Eh, ye waukrife mannie: arena ye sleepin' yet? **1896** CROCKETT *Grey Man* ii. 14 Being an old man, he was somewhat wakerife in the morning.

Hence **'wakerifely** *adv.*, **'wakerifeness**.

1606 tr. *Rollock's 1 Thess.* 126 (Jam.) So long as the diuell is in the world, so long there is necessity required of walkryfeness. **1633** SIR A. JOHNSTON (Ld. Wariston) *Diary* (S.H.S.) I. 99 Therby I sau God recalling me from impænitence to repentance..from securitie unto wakraifnes. **1825** JAMIESON, *Walkrifelie, waukrifelie, adv.*, wakefully. S. **1891** H. JOHNSTON *Kilmallie* II. 19 During this period of wakerifeness he had longed for action of some sort, but could not well get up in the dark.

†**'wakerly**, *a.* *Obs.* [f. WAKER *a.* + -LY[1].] Wakeful, watchful.

c **1400** LOVE *Bonavent. Mirr.* xl. (1908) 224 Sothely he, as a good herde, was ful wakkerly and besy vppon the kepynge of that litell flok, his byloued disciples. *Ibid.* lxii. 285, I wole that thou be wakerly and quikke in thy soule. **1549** CHALONER *Erasm. on Folly* O iv, If he wiste..how his crosiers staffe admonished him of the wakery [? *read* wakerly] charg he shoulde take ouer his flocke.

†**'wakerly**, *adv.* *Obs.* In 4 **wekyrly**. [f. WAKER *a.* + -LY[2].] Nimbly.

[? *a* **1400** *Morte Arth.* 2104 Qwarelles qwayntly swappez thorowe knyghtez With iryne so wekyrly, that wynche they never.

'wake-,robin. [App. f. WAKE *v.* + ROBIN.]

1. The plant *Arum maculatum*, also commonly called cuckoo-pint, lords-and-ladies, etc.

1530 PALSGR. 286/1 Wakerobyn an herbe. **1538** ELYOT *Dict.*, Addit., *Aros*, an herbe callyd wake Robyn. **1597** GERARDE *Herbal* II. ccxc. 684 There be diuers sorts of wake Robin or Cockow pint. **1601** LYLY *Love's Metam.* I. ii, They haue eaten so much wake-Robin, that they cannot sleepe for loue. **1725** *Bradley's Family Dict.*, *Wake-robin* or *Calvesfoot*, in Latin *Arum*... The Root of this plant is purgative and penetrating; they prepare a powder of it that is used in Astma's, Dropsy, and Hypocondriac Melancholy. **1837** M. DONOVAN *Dom. Econ.* II. 255 The root of the *arum maculatum*, or wake-robin.

b. *dial.* The purple orchis, *Orchis maculata*. **c.** The red campion, *Lychnis diurna*.

1905 *Eng. Dial. Dict.*

2. In *U.S.* applied (*a*) to certain araceous plants, esp. *Peltandra undulata* (or *virginica*, formerly called *Arum virginicum*), arrow-arum, TUCKAHOE; (*b*) to liliaceous plants of the genus *Trillium* (*esp.* the white-flowered species).

c **1711** PETIVER *Gazophyl.* I. i, In South Carolina..it Flowers in June and July, and is called by them Wake-Robin. *Ibid.* VI. lx, A whitish flowred Arum or Wake Robin, with cordated narrow pointed Leaves. **1770** J. R. FORSTER tr. *Kalm's Trav. N. Amer.* I. 125 The Virginian Wake robin, or Arum Virginicum, grows in wet places. **1871** BURROUGHS *Wake-Robin* Pref. (1884) p. vi, Wake-Robin—the common name of the white Trillium. **1884** W. MILLER *Plant-n.* 143 Wake-Robin, American, *Arum dracontium*, *Trillium grandiflorum*, and *T. cernuum*. **1915** MRS. STRATTON-PORTER *M. O'Halloran* ii. 32 So long as I could find a scrap of arbutus, a violet or a wake-robin from the woods.

3. In the West Indies and tropical America, applied to certain araceous plants of either of the genera *Anthurium* (tail-flower) and *Philodendron*.

1864 GRISEBACH *Flora W. Ind. Isl.* 788 Wake-robin, *Anthurium* and *Philodendron*.

wakesses, obs. pl. of WAKE *sb.*[1]

'wake-up, *a.* and *sb.* [f. vbl. phr. *to wake up*: see WAKE *v.* 8 a.] **A.** *adj.* †**1.** ***wake-up kittle***: prob. the Pacific kittiwake. *Obs.*

1832 B. MORRELL *Narr. Four Voyages Chinese Seas* iii. 216 Whale-birds, wake-up-kittles, man-of-war birds, gulls, and tropic-birds.

2. Special collocations: ***wake-up call***, a telephone alarm call for awaking a sleeper, usu. in the morning; ***wake-up pill*** (slang), a pep-pill; ***wake-up service***, a telephone service specializing in wake-up calls.

1976 P. HENISSART *Winter Quarry* xxii. 219 He obtained his key from the night desk clerk and..left a wake-up call for eight a.m. **1979** *Listener* 30 Aug. 274/1 Her addiction to the sleeping pills and the wake-up pills had, on more than one occasion, led to an overdose. **1946** *Birmingham* (Ala.) *News-Age-Herald* 3 Feb. 9A/3 Because his wakeup service requires that he arise early in the morning, Harvey has acquired the habit of remaining up all night. **1969** *New Yorker* 14 June 31/1 A number of young bachelors use us simply as a wake-up service—we're cheaper than Western Union.

B. *sb.* **1.** = ***pigeon-woodpecker*** s.v. PIGEON *sb.* 6.

1844 [see *pigeon-woodpecker* s.v. PIGEON *sb.* 6]. **1897** *Scribner's Mag.* June 773/2 The flicker has a long array of names,..like flicker, clape, wake-up,..derived from his notes.

2. [perh. orig. belonging to AWAKE *a.*] ***to be a (full) wake-up*** (also, of several persons, ***to be wake-ups***): to be alert or wide awake (*lit.* and *fig.*). Often const. *to*. *Austral.* and *N.Z. slang.*

1930 *Bulletin* (Sydney) 16 Apr. 58/2 'Cripes, you're a full wake-up to that at last, are you?' Snow exclaimed. [**1934** W. S. HOWARD *You're telling Me!* i. 12 Well, I'm awake-up; they don't get nothing out of *me!*] **1943** F. SARGESON in *Penguin New Writing* XVIII. 68 Now I was a wake-up to what was in Maggie's mind. *Ibid.* 69 The pair of us were wake-ups when we heard somebody coming up the stairs. **1946** M. TRIST in Hadgraft & Wilson *Century of Austral. Short Stories* (1963) 214 'Don't you think we ought to have a cow?'.. 'No, I'm a wake-up to cows', said Dan. 'Saw enough of them when I was a kid.' **1955** D. NILAND *Shiralee* 19 A man should have hauled the cap off his head and chucked ninepence into it just to show him who was a wake-up to who. **1960** N. HILLIARD *Maori Girl* III. x. 248, I never knew till now! Well, I'm a wake-up! **1977** C. MCCULLOUGH *Thorn Birds* ii. 46 When he saw the army lads were a wakeup he was off like a shot.

3. *ellipt.* for *wake-up pill* above. *slang.*

1969 in Howe & Loraine *Environmental Med.* (1973) xvii. 227 Wake-ups and stay-awakes. **1972** *Sunday Sun* (Brisbane) 2 July 14/3 He calls the pep-pills he swallows wake-ups, truck drivers, [etc.].

4. The act of waking a person from sleep, or of being woken from sleep.

1975 *Globe & Mail* (Toronto) 2 June 27/5 Out of that $609 she could easily hire someone to do all the dirty work, such as housekeeping, and leave the easy work such as cooking and wakeups to herself. **1977** M. HERR *Dispatches* (1978) 80 All of my stuff was..ready for the five-o'clock wake-up.

†**wake-wort.** *Obs.* *rare*⁻¹. Some plant.

1530 PALSGR. 286/1 Wakeworte an herbe.

'wakey-'wakey, *sb.*, (*a.*), and *vbl. phr.* *colloq.* and *slang* (orig. *Services'*). Also **wakee-wakee**, **waky-waky**. [Reduplicated arbitrary or childish extension of WAKE *v.* 7 a, b.] **A.** *sb.* = REVEILLE.

1941 C. GRAVES *Thin Blue Line* iii. 46 At the moment all I want to do is to sleep, sleep, sleep. The thought of 'Wakey, wakey' in the morning terrifies me. *a* **1963** J. LUSBY in B. James *Austral. Short Stories* (1963) 221 Three to a tent, chums, wakey-wakey 0430 hours.

2. *attrib.* or as *adj.* That awakens or induces wakefulness, esp. as ***wakey-wakey pill***.

1946 V. TEMPEST *Near Sun* iii. 29 When the 'wakey-wakey', as the caffeine tablets are called..have been doled out, the crews climb into the W.A.A.F.-driven air-crew buses. **1952** M. TRIPP *Faith is Windsock* xi. 172 Bergen swallowed a couple of wakey-wakey tablets, and Flute did likewise. **1977** *Milestones* Spring 15/2 Rally drivers thought they had found the ideal wakey-wakey pill in amphetamines to help them combat fatigue during marathons. **1979** *Guardian* 4 Aug. 22/9 The last ever Butlin's 'wakey-wakey' call goes out to the snoring chalets.

B. *vbl. phr.* used *imp.* Also **wakey, wakey.** 'Wake up', formerly esp. as a command to soldiers at reveille. Often comb. with phr. *rise and shine* (see RISE *v.* 3 c). Now freq. *joc.*

1945 *Gen* 30 June 51/2 The sarnt came round yelling wakey-wakey. **1948** PARTRIDGE *Dict. Forces' Slang* 203 *Wakee, wakee!*, orderly Corporal's cry at reveille. 'Wakee, wakee! Rise and shine!' **1953** E. SIMON *Past Masters* I. iii. 32 With a start I woke up... 'Waky-waky,' said Gabrielle. **1968** M. WOODHOUSE *Rock Baby* xxi. 199 'Wakey-wakey,' he said. 'Stand by your beds.' **1973** T. HEALD *Unbecoming Habits* v. 149 'Wakey Wakey, rise and shine,' said Brother Barnabas in an unconvincing demonstration of joviality.

‖**wakf, waqf** (wɑkf). [Arab. *waqf*.] In Islamic countries, the custom of giving a piece of land, etc., to a religious institution, so that the revenue can be used for pious or charitable purposes; also, the property given in this way.

1836 E. W. LANE *Acct. Manners & Customs of Mod. Egyptians* I. 159 He first imposed a tax (of nearly half the amount of the regular land-tax) upon all land which had become a *wuckf* (or legacy unalienable by law) to any mosque, fountain, public school, &c. **1877** *Encycl. Brit.* VII. 113/2 The regular dervishes live in..khanakahs, or convents, which are endowed with lands or wakf. **1911** *Ibid.* XVII. 413/1 The law and usage of religious foundations in perpetuity (*waqf*, mortmain) became as important in Islam as monastic endowments in mediaeval Europe... It was the only safe way of providing for posterity. **1917** *Chambers's Jrnl.* July 477/1 The partisans are, on the one side, the clergy, who control the *wakfs* (religious endowments). **1976** M. S. HOQUE *Hunger* I. iv. 27 Yes, the Karaitali plot I shall give to Judge by wakf. **1976** S. R. SIMPSON *Land Law & Registration* i. 11 The inalienability of *waqf* land in Islamic countries similarly holds up development.

wakien, obs. form of WEAKEN *v.*

waking ('weɪkɪŋ), *vbl. sb.* [-ING[1].] The action of the verb WAKE.

1. a. The action of remaining awake or of sitting up at night.

1340 *Ayenb.* 52 Efterward ine zuyche wakinges me deþ manye kueades, ase playe ate ches oþer ate tables. *c* **1386** CHAUCER *Man of Law's Prol.* 22 The tyme..steleth from vs, what pryuely slepynge And what thurgh necligence in oure wakynge. **1422** YONGE tr. *Secreta Secret.* 247 Myche wakynge makyth the body lene. **1477** EARL RIVERS (Caxton) *Dictes* 33 Of thought cometh the wakyngis and unrestis. **1611** SHAKS. *Wint. T.* III. iii. 19 Ne're was dreame So like a waking. **1638** FORD *Fancies* III. iii, I am not So weary of th' authority I hold Over mine owne contents in sleepes and wakings. **1651** HOBBES *Leviath.* III. xxxii. 196 To say he hath seen a Vision..is to say, that he dreamed between sleeping and waking. **1810** SCOTT *Lady of L.* I. xxxi, Days of danger, nights of waking. **1840** DICKENS *Old C. Shop* lxiv. Her eyes were..red with waking and crying.

b. *spec.* Keeping vigil as an act of devotion.

c **1175** *Lamb. Hom.* 69 Vre rihte leue, god, cume to þe þurh festing and þurh wacunge. **1340** *Ayenb.* 232 Him behoueþ wel wysliche his uless ouercome..be uestinges, be wakiinges and be benes. *c* **1386** CHAUCER *Parson's T.* ¶ 1038 Bodily peyne..stant in preyeres, in wakynges, in fastynges. *c* **1400** LOVE *Bonavent. Mirr.* xxvii. (1908) 141 He..doth his tendre body to penaunce, and waketh long wakynges. *c* **1460** *Wisdom* 1030 in *Macro Plays* 69 Lo, wakynge ys a holy thynge! **1710** HILMAN *Tusser Rediv.* June (1744) 81 Waking in the Church was left off because of some Abuses.

2. a. The action of watching, or keeping watch and ward; *dial.* a keeping watch or holding a 'wake' over a corpse.

c **1440** *Promp. Parv.* 514/1 Wakynge, or wetche, *vigilia*. *c* **1440** *York Myst.* xxxviii. 357 Oure wakyng, lorde, withouten wene Is worthed to noȝt. **1529** *Reg. Privy Seal Scot.* 30 Exemand hir fra all walking, warding, and paying of stent within the burgh of Edinburgh or outwith. **1572** *Inv. Ketshange* (Somerset Ho.), For kepinge of her and wackinge of her iij[d]. **1725** RAMSAY *Gentle Sheph.* I. i, Sang 1. *Tune*, The wawking of the faulds. **1823** 'JON BEE' *Dict. Turf* s.v. *Wake*, In England the body is sometimes placed in a coffin; in Ireland, seldom so, the waking being usually called for the purpose of procuring one. **1891** STEVENSON *In South Seas*

IV. v. (1900) 311 Of home life we had but the one view: the waking of a corpse.

†**b.** One of the 'watches' or divisions of the night (L. *vigilia*). *Obs.*

1382 WYCLIF *Matt.* xiv. 25 In the fourthe wakyng of the niȝt [Vulg. *quarta vigilia noctis*]. *c* **1400** LOVE *Bonavent. Mirr.* xxvii. (1908) 143 At the ferthe wakynge of the nyȝt.

3. The action of becoming awake or conscious, of ceasing to sleep. Also with *up*.

1377 LANGL. *P. Pl.* B. xv. 1 Ac after my wakyng it was wonder longe Ar I couth kyndely knowe what was dowel. **1530** PALSGR. 286/1 Wakyng after slepe, *reueil.* **1553** BRADFORD *Serm. Repent.* (1574) G ij, In this his syn, though a great while he lay a sleepe (as many do nowe adayes, God geue them good waking). **1592** SHAKS. *Rom. & Jul.* IV. i. 116 (3rd Qo.) He and I Will watch thy waking. **1709** ADDISON *Tatler* No. 97 Their slumbers are sound, and their wakings chearful. **1860** MRS. CARLYLE *Lett.* III. 63 My own wakings up some twenty or thirty times every night. **1864** G. A. LAWRENCE *M. Dering* II. 119 But, if Dering rested well, his waking was not so enviable.

4. The action of rousing (a person or animal) from sleep; †a night-attack. Also *fig.*

1525 BERNERS *Froiss.* (1812) II. xlix. 168 To close in theyr felde, to lodge therin more at theyr ease, without waking or skries. **1546** J. HEYWOOD *Prov.* I. x. (1867) 24 It is euyll wakyng of a sleepyng dog. **1654** SIR A. JOHNSTON (Ld. Wariston) *Diary* (S.H.S.) II. 238, I took this as a warning and waking and alarum from the Lord to me.

5. *Comb.*: †**waking-silver**, ? a payment in lieu of keeping watch and ward; **waking-time**, the time when one is awake; the moment at which one wakes up.

1390–91 *Durham Acc. Rolls* (Surtees) 597 Item Will'o Patonson pro Argent. sibi dato, et sociis suis pro Wakyng silvyr, vij s. **1546** *Yorks. Chantry Surv.* (Surtees) I. 172 To the Kynges Majestie for waykyng sylver payd..to Pontfret Castell. **1959** T. S. ELIOT *Elder Statesman* 5 To my wife, To whom I owe the leaping delight That quickens my senses in our wakingtime. **1971** H. WILSON *Labour Govt.* xv. 263, I asked for a sleeping pill, in case I came to at English waking-time, 4.00 a.m. in Washington.

waking ('weɪkɪŋ), *ppl. a.* [f. WAKE *v.* + -ING^2.]

1. That remains awake; that keeps watch; *fig.* that continues on the alert, vigilant, watchful.

c **1175** *Lamb. Hom.* 39 Drihten bi-hat þon wakiende ane crune. *c* **1400** *Destr. Troy* 649 Bes wakond and warly. *a* **1475** ASHBY *Dicta Philos.* 715 In your counsail be quick and ay wakyng. **1577** B. GOOGE *Heresbach's Husb.* III. 154 The Mastie that keepeth the house..must..be..very waking. **1601** in Foley *Rec. Eng. Prov. S. J.* (1880) VI. 735 He was thought negligent, and therefore they sent a wakinger spirit. **1620** T. MAY *Heir* II. (1622) C 3, Were there a thousand waking Dragons set To keepe that golden fruit. **1690** LOCKE *Hum. Und.* II. i. §11 The Soul in a waking Man is never without thought, because it is the condition of being awake. **1826** DISRAELI *Viv. Grey* v. xv, The screech of the waking owl.

2. That ceases to sleep, that becomes awake.

1794 MRS. RADCLIFFE *Myst. Udolpho* vii, The breeze that ..swells the melody of waking birds.

3. 'Rousing from sleep; exciting into motion or action'.

1828–32 WEBSTER; and in later Dicts.

4. *transf.* Belonging to, characteristic of, one who wakes or is awake.

1567 TURBERV. *Epit.*, etc. 66 b, And if in dawning chaunce some drouping sleepe to light Upon the carefull Corse that thus hath spent the waking night. **1624** DONNE *Devot.* Med. xv. (ed. 2) 350 Hee may bee ashamed of his waking dreames. **1634** MILTON *Comus* 263 Such sober certainty of waking bliss I never heard till now. **1697** DRYDEN *Æneis* x. 908 Thus haunting Ghosts appear to waking Sight. **1762–71** H. WALPOLE *Vertue's Anecd. Paint.* (1786) V. 261 Realizing to his eyes the scenes of many a waking vision. **1833** L. RITCHIE *Wand. by Loire* 198 Our waking existence is made up almost entirely of anticipations and regrets. **1848** DICKENS *Dombey* xxxix, Captain Cuttle could hardly believe it..though he saw it done with his waking eyes. *a* **1859** MACAULAY *Hist. Eng.* xxiii. V. 94 The subject..was never, during two waking hours together, out of his thoughts.

Hence '**wakingly** *adv.*

1388 WYCLIF *Ecclus.* xiii. 17 And thou schalt wake. [*Gloss*] And in this thou schalt haue thee wakingli and diligently. *c* **1482** *Monk of Evesham* (Arb.) 54 Hys father had apperyd .iij. nyghtis to gedyr to hys moeder wakyngly as sche was yn her prayers at home yn her chambyr. **1552** HULOET, Wakyngly, *uigilanter.*

waking take, rare var. WAPENTAKE.

wakiup, var. WICKYUP, an Indian hut.

wakke, obs. form of WAKE *v.*

‖**wakon** ('weɪkən). [Dakota *wakaŋ* 'a spirit, something consecrated; *taku wakaŋ* and *wakaŋ tanka*, the Great Spirit'; subst. use of *wakaŋ* adj., 'spiritual, sacred, consecrated' (Riggs *Gram. & Dict. Dakota Lang.*). J. F. Cooper (*Prairie* xxviii) has the form *wahcondah.*] Among some American Indians, a spiritual being that is the object of religious reverence; also, a fetish: = MANITOU.

1778 J. CARVER *Trav. N. Amer.* xiii. 381 The Chipéways call this being Manitou or Kitchi-Manitou; the Nadowessies, Wakon or Tongo-Wakon, that is, the Great Spirit. **1809** A. HENRY *Trav.* 299 They believe..in the spirits, gods, or manitos, whom they denominate wakons. **1841** CATLIN *N. Amer. Ind.* II. liv. 166 On the surface of the rocks [are seen] their sculptured hieroglyphics—their wakons, totems, and medicines.

b. *Comb.*: **wakon-bird**, a fabulous bird venerated by the Indians.

1778 J. CARVER *Trav. N. Amer.* xviii. 473 The name they have given it is expressive of its superior excellence, and the veneration they have for it; the wakon bird being in their language the bird of the Great Spirit. **1806** MOORE *To Lady Charl. Rawdon* 75 Swift upon the purple plume Of my Wakon-Bird I fly Where [etc.].

wakrell(e, variant ff. of WAKERELL.

wakrife, -ryfe, variant ff. of WAKERIFE.

†'**wakrong**, *a. Obs. rare*$^{-1}$. [? f. WAKE *sb.*^{1} + *rong*, RANK *a.*] Wakeful.

1340–70 *Alex. & Dind.* 537 Þat þou..mihtest..maken to sclepe Tricerberus þe helle-hound þat holden is kene Boþe wakrong & wikke & wardain of paine.

waks, obs. form of WAX.

†'**waky**, *a. Obs.* [f. WAKE *v.*^{1} or *sb.*^{1} + -Y.] Wakeful.

a **1542** WYATT *Poems*, 'Myne olde Enmye' 58 And eke, the waky nyghte the bannysshed slepe may no wyse recouer. **1597** MIDDLETON *Wisd. Sol.* xviij. 17 Keeping their waky and their sleepy places.

waky-waky, var. WAKEY-WAKEY *sb.*, (*a.*,) and *vbl. phr.*

†**wal.** *poet. Obs.* Forms: 1 **wæl**, 3 **wæl(e, wal(e, wel.** [OE. *wæl* neut. = OS. *wal-* in *waldâd* murderous deed, OHG. *wal* neut., *walu-* (MHG. *wal* neut., masc., *wale* ? masc.), ON. *val-r* masc. (whence *valkyrja* VALKYRIE) :—OTeut. **walo-* (? **walu-*), perh. cogn. w. L. *volnus, vulnus* wound.] Death, slaughter. (In OE. also *collect.* the slain; *rarely* a slain person.)

c **900** *Bæda's Hist.* IV. xv. (1890) 306 Mid grimme wæle & heriȝe. *c* **1205** LAY. 404 Þar aros wale & win. *Ibid.* 4111 Þat wæl wes þe more.

b. *Comb.*: **wal-kemp**, a warrior; **wal-slaught**, deadly battle; **wal-spear**, a battle-spear.

c **1205** LAY. 565 Antigonus..mid his *wæl-kempen swenden toward Brutun. ? *a* **900** *O.E. Chron.* (Parker MS.) an. 839 Her wæs micel *wælsliht on Lundenne, and on Cwantawic, and on Hrofesceastre. *c* **1205** LAY. 1369 Þa Grickes hit biwnnan mid heora wæl slahte. *a* **1000** *Byrhtnoth* 322 (Gr.) Oft he gar forlet, *wælspere windan on þa wicingas. *c* **1205** LAY. 28577 Arður [wes] forwunded mid wal-spere brade.

wal: see WALE, WALL, WAW, WELL.

wala, obs. Sc. form of VALLEY.

Walach, Wallach ('wɒlək). Also 8 Wolock, 9 Wallack. [See VLACH.]

1. a. A former name for a member of a Romanic-speaking race widely disseminated in south-eastern Europe, principally in Romania, and now normally known as ROMANIAN. = VLACH.

1786 tr. *J. R. Forster's Hist. Voy. North* 101 *note*, The Walachs, or Wolocks. **1845** *Encycl. Metrop.* XXV. 730/1 The Wallacks [are] scattered over the whole province [of Transylvania]. **1869** TOZER *Highl. Turkey* I. 146 A few Wallachs, Armenians, and Franks. **1886** W. J. TUCKER *E. Europe* 179 It was he (being a Wallack, just as Jano is), who instigated the Wallacks on our estate when they robbed and devastated the country in the Rebellion.

b. *attrib.*

1864 *Chamb. Encycl.* VI. 513 A petty Walach chief of Transylvania. **1869** TOZER *Highl. Turkey* II. 16 A Wallach shepherd was tending his flock of goats. **1905** *Westm. Gaz.* 24 May 8/2 Full liberty is granted for the use of the Wallach language in schools and churches.

2. The language of the Walachs. *rare*$^{-1}$.

1794 J. B. S. MORRITT *Let.* 24 June (1914) iii. 51 The languages spoken here are Hungarian, Wallach, Sclavonian and a little German. **1895** *Funk's Stand. Dict.*

Walachian, Wallachian (wɒ'leɪkɪən, və'lækɪən), *sb.* and *a.* Also 7 **Valachian**, 9 **Vallakhian.** [f. *Walachia* (in med.L. the country of the Walachs or Vlachs; in mod. use with narrower application, one of the two principalities which united to form the kingdom of Rumania, and subsequently the People's Republic of Romania) + -AN.] **A.** *sb.*

1. a. = WALACH 1. Also, a native of Walachia.

1603 KNOLLES *Hist. Turkes* (1621) 204 Baiazet thus at once inuaded..Europe,..conuerting his forces against the Valachians. **1729** CONSETT *Pres. State Russia* 446 To leave his Allies the Walachians and Moldavians to the Resentment of the Turks for their intended Revolt to the Tsar. **1776** GIBBON *Decl. & F.* xi. (1782) I. 357 *note*, The Walachians still preserve many traces of the Latin language. **1838** *Encycl. Metrop.* XXIV. 154/1 The neighbouring mountains are inhabited by Servians and Vallakhians. **1888** EMILY GERARD *Land beyond Forest* II. 30 This Wallachian was a still greater sorcerer in weather-making than the Wermesch peasant.

b. A Walachian sheep.

1837 YOUATT *Sheep* v. 138 The Wallachians are about the size of the Dorset sheep, but not so tall.

2. The language spoken by the Walachians.

1718 M. W. MONTAGU *Let.* 16 Mar. (1965) I. 390 In Pera they speak Turkish, Greek,..Sclavonian, Walachian, German. **1846** BORROW *Zincali* (ed. 4) III 257 The Hungarian Gypsy tongue..contains many words borrowed from the Wallachian. **1864** MAX MULLER *Sci. Lang.* Ser. II. iv. 182 Their language still lives in the modern Wallachian. **1877** *Quaritch's Catal.* Suppl. 227 Rouman or Wallachian.

B. *adj.* Of or pertaining to Walachia or the Walachians.

c **1791** *Encycl. Brit.* (ed. 3) VIII. 712/1 There are four languages spoken..the German, Sclavonian, Wallachian, and Latin. **1804** E. JONES *Lyric Airs* Introd. 2 Matràki, or, The Wallachian Dance. **1843** *Penny Cycl.* XXVII. 34 According to Thunman, one half of all the Wallachian words are Latin. *a* **1901** W. BRIGHT *Age of Fathers* (1903) I. xxv. 503 The Gothic king..had flung St. Sabas into the waters of a Wallachian stream for refusing to taste idol-meats.

waladay, obs. form of WELLADAY.

walageous, variant of VOLAGEOUS.

walap, obs. form of WALLOP *v.*

walaway, obs. form of WELLAWAY.

walcar, Sc. variant of WALKER (fuller).

Walcheren ('valxərən). [The name of a Dutch island at the mouth of the Schelde.] Used in comb., as ***Walcheren ague, fever.***

1810 DAWSON (*title*) The Walcheren Fever. **1848** THACKERAY *Van. Fair* xxvii, The hottest suns of India never heated his temper; and the Walcheren ague never shook it. **1889** *Mayne's Med. Voc.* (ed. 6) 473 *Walcheren Fever*... An endemic remittent fever.

walchowite ('wælkəʊaɪt). *Min.* [Named by Haidinger 1845 from *Walchow* in Moravia where it was found: see -ITE.] A honey-yellow resin similar to amber.

1849 J. NICOL *Man. Min.* 520. **1852** H. J. BROOKE & MILLER *Phillips' Introd. Min.* 629.

walcryif, obs. form of WAKERIFE.

†**wald**, *conj. Obs. rare.* [OE. *weald*, perh. derived from a use of *weald* imper. of *wealdan* to govern (see WIELD *v.*).

A transitional use is seen in *weald hú = lóca hú* 'however' (*Andreas* 1355): see LOOK *v.* 4 b.]

Followed by or with ellipsis of *if*: In case that. (In OE. chiefly with *þéah* or indef. pronoun.)

c **1000** ÆLFRIC *Hom.* I. 316 Namon ða to ræde, þæt him wærlicor wære, þæt hi sumne dæl heora landes wurðes æthæfdon, weald [? hwæt *omitted*] him ȝetimode. *Ibid.* II. 340 Nyte ȝe ða micclan deopnysse Godes ȝerynu? weald þeah him beo alyfed ȝyt behreowsung. *c* **1315** SHOREHAM *Poems* i. 930–1 To schryue hym wanne he seneȝed heþ Wel syker þing hyt were.. Wald ȝef he sodeynlyche deiþ And wald he hyt forȝete.

wald, obs. f. WEALD, WELD, WIELD *v.*, WOLD.

wald, obs. form of *would*: see WILL *v.*

'**waldemar.** ? *U.S.* 'A variety of velveteen, or cotton velvet, apparently a superior quality of fustian' (*Cent. Dict.*, 1891).

†'**waldend.** *Obs.* Forms: 1 **waldend, wealdend,** 2 **weldende,** 2–3 **wealdende,** 3 **walden(de), wealdent, weldent.** [OE. *waldend, wealdend*, subst. form of pres. pple. of *waldan, wealdan*, to control (see WIELD *v.*).] A ruler, governor (rare except in periphrases for God).

Beowulf 17 Him þæs lif-frea, wuldres wealdend, woroldare forȝeaf. *c* **888** ÆLFRED *Boeth.* xvi. 2 Þa sint eowere hlafordas & eowere waldendas, næs ȝe heora. *c* **1175** *Lamb. Hom.* 75 Scuppende and weldende of heouene and of orðe and of alle iscefte. *c* **1205** LAY. 5059 Nu þu eært londes weldent. *Ibid.* 25569 Lauerd drihten crist, domes waldende, midelarde mund..walden ænglen, let þu mi sweuen to selþen iturnen. *a* **1225** *Leg. Kath.* 1235 Ah þe witti weldent ant te rihtwise bireadde hit swa swiðe wel, þ he þ ouercom mon, were akast þurh mon. *Ibid.* 2065 Hwerto wultu wreastlin wið þe worldes wealdent?

†**waldeneie.** *Obs. rare*$^{-1}$. [app. an alteration of *wald-eye*, WALL-EYE, influenced by **walden* repr. OE. *ȝewealden* small. Cf. WOLDEN-EȜED *a.*] An alleged name of the hare.

13.. *Names of Hare* in *MS. Digby* 86, fol. 168 b, Þe purblinde..þe waldeneie, þe sidlokere.

Walden inversion: see INVERSION 5 b.

Wal'dense. *rare.* [Singular f. next, taken as Eng. plural.] A Waldensian. *rare.*

1888 J. KER *Lect. Hist. Preaching* vii. 126 *note*, Tauler.. was strongly influenced by Nicolas von Basel, a Waldense.

Waldenses (wɒl'dɛnsiːz), *sb. pl. Eccl. Hist.* Also (6 Waldensses), 7–9 **Valdenses.** [a. med.L. *Waldensēs* (*Valdensēs*), app. f. *Waldensis*, a variant form of the cognomen of Peter Waldo: see below. Cf. the Fr. form VAUDOIS.] The adherents of a religious sect which originated in the south of France about 1170 through the preaching of Peter Waldo, a rich merchant of Lyons. They were excommunicated in 1184, and eventually became a separately organized church, which associated itself with the Protestant Reformation of the 16th c., and still exists, chiefly in Northern Italy and the adjacent regions.

[*c* **1449** PECOCK *Repr.* v. iii. 501 Also the sect of Waldensis.] **1537** *Orig. & Sprynge of Sectes* Contents, Waldenses secte. *Ibid.* 48 The order of Waldenses or Picardes. **1579** FULKE *Confut. Sanders* 594 He adioyneth Anno Do. 1160. the Waldensses, whome hee calleth beggers of Lyons. **1579** —— *Heskins's Parl.* 29 Valdo..caused Bookes of scripture to be translated, and so beganne the sect of Valdenses, or Pauperes de Lugduno. **1649** MILTON *Eikon.* xvii. 159 If we may beleeve what the Papists themselves have writt'n of these Churches, which they call Waldenses. **1774** FLETCHER *Hist. Ess.* Wks. 1795 IV. 13 The true Quakers..made as firm a stand against the Antinomians, as the Valdenses did against the Papists. **1888** *Encycl. Brit.* XXIV. 323 The Waldenses, under their more modern name of the Vaudois, have survived to the present day in the valleys of Piedmont.

Waldensian (wɒl'dɛnsɪən), *a.* and *sb.* Also 7–9 **Valdensian.** [f. WALDENS-ES + -IAN.]

A. *adj.* Of or pertaining to the Waldenses.

c **1645** HOWELL *Lett.* (1650) II. 23 Ther are divers sorts of these Polonian Protestants, som embracing the Waldensian ..and som the Helvetian Confession. **1827** (*title*) Authentic Details of the Valdenses..with..The Ancient Valdensian Catechism. **1831** W. S. GILLY (*title*), Waldensian Researches..With an Introductory Inquiry into the Antiquity and Purity of the Waldensian Church. **1888** *Athenæum* 7 Apr. 430/1 Only after Luther's declaration in favour of clerical marriage did the ascetic life cease to be a part of the Waldensian doctrine.

B. *sb.* A member of the sect of the WALDENSES.

1604, **1832** [see *Albigensian* adj. and sb.]. **1847** J. T. MULLOCK tr. *St. Alphonsus's Hist. Heresies* I. x. 260 Rainer ..for seventeen years was a Waldensian. **1885** *Athenæum* 7 Feb. 177/2 The contents of this part are..the Διδαχή and the Waldensians, [etc.]. **1888** *Ibid.* 7 Apr. 429/3 The Waldensians were far more likely to adopt an existing Catholic translation than to originate one for themselves.

Waldenström ('vældənstrɜːm). *Path.* The name of Jan *Waldenström* (b. 1906), Swedish biochemist, used in the possessive to designate a disease described by him in 1944 (see MACROGLOBULINÆMIA).

1961, **1971** [see *macroglobulinæmia*]. **1980** *Daily Tel.* 3 Jan. 1/3 The deposed Shah of Iran is suffering from Waldenstrom's Disease, a rare blood disease which killed President Boumedienne of Algeria a year ago.

walder ('wɔːldə(r)). *dial.* ? *Obs.* [Of obscure origin; perh. some error.] Some weed found abundantly in cornfields.

1764 *Museum Rust.* II. 306 One particular piece of the sandy ground..vastly subject to what we call walder, and buddle, bodle, or gould, as some call it. **1765** *Ibid.* IV. 144, I had great plenty of straw, and it was clear from walder and buddle.

waldflute ('wɔːldfluːt). Also in Ger. form. [ad. G. *waldflöte*, lit. forest flute.] (See quots.)

1852 SEIDEL *Organ* 110 Wald flute..is an open flue-register. **1876** STAINER & BARRETT *Dict. Mus. Terms*, *Waldflute, Waldflöte, Waldpfeife* (*Ger.*)..An organ stop of 4 ft. pitch. **1878** J. HILES *Catech. Organ* (ed. 2) 62 *Waldflöte*, Forest-flute. In Germany this is a 2 feet stop, formerly also of 8 and 4 feet... The English *Waldflöte*..is always of open wood 4 feet pipes..full toned and powerful.

waldgrave ('wɔːldgreɪv). *Hist.* [ad. G. *waldgraf*, f. *wald* forest (see WEALD, WOLD) + *graf* count: see GRAF, GRAVE *sb.*[4]] In mediæval Germany, an officer having jurisdiction over a royal forest. (On the lower Rhine, the title was hereditary in certain families of the higher nobility.) Hence **'waldgravine**, the wife of a waldgrave.

In recent Dicts.

‖**waldhorn** ('valthɔrn). [G. *waldhorn*, forest or hunting horn, French horn.] (See quot.)

1852 SEIDEL *Organ* 110 Wald horn. **1889** GROVE *Dict. Mus.* IV. 375 *Waldhorn* (that is, Forest horn), *Corno di caccia*. The old 'French horn,' without valves, for which Beethoven wrote. The valve horn..is fast superseding it.

†**'waldin**, *a. Sc. Obs.* Forms: 5–6 **waldin**, (5 **waldyne**, **waddin**). [Pa. pple. of *wald*, WIELD *v.*, used in the sense '(easily) controlled'. (In OE. the ppl. adj. *ȝewealden* had the senses 'subject, under control', 'moderate in amount or size').] Easy to manage. Chiefly of the body or limbs: Pliant, supple; freq. in phr. ***waldin and wicht.*** Also *fig.*, yielding or tractable in bearing or disposition.

c **1425** WYNTOUN *Cron.* III. 23 The quhilk sa waldin wes in fecht That baith þe left hand and the rycht He evinlike vsit. **1456** SIR G. HAYE *Gov. Princes* (S.T.S.) 121 And thus sall all thy body be mare waldin, and esy to dispone the till all thyne operaciounis. *c* **1480** HENRYSON *Age & Youth* 19 This ȝowng [man] lap apone þe land ful lycht,..'waldyne [*v.rr.* waldin, waddin] I am,' quod he '& wondir wycht.' **1535** STEWART *Cron. Scot.* I. 55 For twentie ȝeir and foure he wes of age; Waldin and wicht. *Ibid.* 499 Waldin thai war, and wicht as ony hors. *Ibid.* II. 195 Als ferce & waldin than as ane eill. *Ibid.* III. 163 He maid thame all als waldin as ane wand, For to obey and byde at his command. **1536** BELLENDEN *Cron. Scot., Descr. Alb.* xvi. (1821) I. p. lvi, Thair hois war maid of smal lynt or woll, and yeid nevir above thair kne, to make thaim the mair waldin and sowpyll.

walding, Sc. form of WELDING, WIELDING.

Waldism ('wɔːldɪz(ə)m). *rare.* [f. *Waldo* (see WALDENSES) + -ISM.] The doctrine or tenets of the Waldenses. Cf. VAUDISM.

1888 *Athenæum* 7 Apr. 429/2.

waldo, Waldo ('wɔːldəʊ). Pl. **waldos, waldoes**. [f. the name of *Waldo* F. Jones, the inventor of such gadgets in a science-fiction story by Robert Heinlein (see quot. 1942).] A device for handling or manipulating objects by remote control.

1942 'A. MACDONALD' (R. A. Heinlein) in *Astounding Sci. Fiction* 9 Aug. 16 Even the..humanoid gadgets known universally as 'waldoes'..passed through several generations of development..in Waldo's machine shop before he redesigned them for mass production. The first of them..had been designed to enable Waldo to operate a metal lathe. **1966** I. ASIMOV *Fantastic Voyage* vii. 75 A handling device (a gigantic 'waldo'—so named by the earlier nuclear technicians from a character in a science fiction story of the 1940s). **1978** D. A. STANWOOD *Memory of Eva Ryker* iii. 30 The bathyscaphs are both equipped with remote manipulators—the experts call them 'Waldos'—for working under the extreme pressure.

Waldorf salad ('wɔːldɔːf). [Named after the *Waldorf*-Astoria Hotel in New York, where it was first served.] A salad made from apples, walnuts, lettuce and/or celery, dressed with mayonnaise.

1911 LEITER & VAN BERGH *Flower City Cook Bk.* 103 Waldorf salad [recipe follows]. **1930** E. FERBER *Cimarron* 300 She was the first to electrify the ladies of the Twentieth Century Culture Club by serving them Waldorf salad—that abominable mixture of apple cubes, chopped nuts, whipped cream, and mayonnaise. **1979** A. HAILEY *Overload* III. iii. 206 A Waldorf salad, followed by a chicken casserole.

waldrapp ('wɔːldræp). [a. Ger., f. *wald* wood, forest + *rapp* (var. *rappe, rabe*) crow: cf. RAVEN *sb.*[1]] The hermit ibis, *Geronticus eremita*, found in parts of North Africa and the Middle East.

1924 W. L. SCLATER *Systema Avium Ethiopicarum* 35 Waldrapp..Morocco, Tunis, and Asia Minor; formerly in Switzerland and other parts of southern Europe. **1964** A. L. THOMSON *New Dict. Birds* 390/1 The Hermit Ibis (or Waldrapp)..is a bird of dry country, feeding largely on beetles and nesting in colonies on cliffs. **1970** *New Scientist* 3 Sept. 457/1 The waldrapp..has a strong, unpleasant odour. **1976** G. DURRELL *Stationary Ark* iv. 81 The Waldrapp..is a medium-sized ibis, with a long curved beak, sombre black plumage.., a bare reddish-coloured face and a strange crest of long feathers on the back of its head.

wale (weɪl), *sb.*[1] Forms: 1 **walu**, 5–6 *Sc.* **waill**, 6–7 **waile**, 7 **wayle**, (**waale, wael, weale**), 6 *Sc.*, 8–9 **wail**, (6 *Sc.* **vale**), 8–9 **whale**; 5 **walle**, 6–8 **wall**; 4– **wale**. [OE. *walu* str. fem. (also wk. pl. *walan*), mark of a lash, weal; also, in charters, used as a topographical term, perh. ridge, bank (of stone or earth). A sense 'stripe' appears to be implied by the derivative *waled* (tr. L. *histriatus*, app. mistaken for *striatus* striped).

Cf. LG. *wale* (*wale, wâl*, Doornkaat-Koolman), Du. dial. *woal*, mark of a lash, weal (= sense 2). The other senses below are peculiar to Eng. The identity of the word in its various senses is not quite certain, but the assumption of 'raised line or strip' as the primary sense plausibly accounts for all the recorded applications. The relation of the word to OTeut. **walu-z* rod, wand (Goth. *walu-s*, ON. *vǫl-r*, MSw. *val*, OFris. *walu*, NFris. *waale*) is uncertain.]

†**1.** A ridge (of earth or stone). Only OE.

1024 in Kemble *Cod. Dipl.* IV. 31 Of ðam beorȝe suþ on ða ealdan wale, swa on corf ȝetes westran cotan of ðam cotan suþ be wale on ðære dice hyrnan. **1045** *Ibid.* IV. 98 Ofer ðone hæðfeld in stanwale; andlang ðære wale on ðone portweȝ. *Ibid.* V. 334 On ða eastlangan dicwale.

2. a. The mark or ridge raised on the flesh by the blow of a rod, lash, or the like. = WEAL *sb.*[2]

The form *weal*, now more usual, is due to confusion with WHEAL a pustule, swelling, which is often misused for *wale*.

a **1100** *Aldh. Glosses* in Napier *OE. Gl.* 3466 *Uibices.* i. *uerbera*, walan. *Ibid.* 4487 *Uibices*, wala. *Ibid.* 4759 *Uibice*, wale. *Ibid.* 5365 *Asperæ inuectionis*, stiþra wala. *c* **1430** *Pilgr. Lyf Manhode* II. lxxiv. (1869) 103, I keepe him that he haue no peyne and that ther be no wales in the hondes. *c* **1450** *Mirk's Festial* 113 Saynt Barnard yn Cristys person..sayth þus:..I haue my body for thy loue full of gret walus. **1521** WHITINDON *Gramm.* (1523) C iij, *Vibex*, a wale of a rodde. **1530** PALSGR. 286/1 Wall of a strype, *enfleure*. **1598** BP. HALL *Sat.* IV. i, Shall then that foule infamous Cyneds hide Laugh at the purple wales of others side? **1609** BIBLE (Douay) *Isa.* liii. 5 With the waile of his stripe [Vulg. *livore ejus*] we are healed. *c* **1611** CHAPMAN *Iliad* II. 232 He.. strooke, his backe and shoulders so, That bloody wales rose. **1706** E. WARD *Wooden World Diss.* (1708) 101 Ye shall have him as proud of the Wales on his Back, as a Holy Land Pilgrim is of a Jerusalem Print. **1797** UNDERWOOD *Dis. Childhood* I. 106 The..lower limbs..are found covered with large wales, resembling those arising from the sting of nettles. **1867** PUSEY *Eleven Addresses* vi. (1908) 65 The traces of the Crown of thorns,..the wales of the scourges. **1868** J. H. BLUNT *Ref. Ch. Eng.* I. 384 His back was striped with the wales of such frequent scourging.

fig. **1603** HOLLAND *Plutarch's Mor.* 558 The wales, marks, scarres and cicatrices of sinne and vice remaine to be seene.

†**b.** Misused for WHEAL. *Obs. rare*[−1].

1589 [R. HARVEY] *Pl. Perc.* 5 What, what, latine in the mouth of a plaine fellow? Nay I wot neere, but it hath left behind it a wale in my throate like a strange bodylouse in an vnknowne pasture. **1847** HALLIWELL, *Wale*, (9) A tumour or large swelling. *Kent.* **1887** in *Kentish Gloss.*

3. a. *Textile-manuf.* A ridge or raised line (consisting of a thread or threads) in a textile fabric; also *collect.* with epithet, as indicating the texture of a particular fabric. Cf. WALED *a.* and *waling glass* s.v. WALE *v.*[1]

1583 STUBBES *Anat. Abus.* II. 24 To lay down the wooll so close, as you can hardly see any wale. **1604** W. TERILO *Friar Bacon's Prophesie* xxxiv. C 2 b, A Hose with a good wailc. **1607** MIDDLETON *Mich. Term* II. iii. D 2 b, By my troth exceeding good cloath, a good wale t'as. **1662** EVELYN *Chalcogr.* 120 It does not at all concern the tissue, Tenor or range of the Threads, and *Wales* (as they call them) which is easily imitated. **1668** T. ROKEBY *Let.* 28 Sept. in *Mem.* (Surtees Soc.) 16 My wife desires to fix you either to a farandine or a mohaire with a small weale [for a gown]. **1675** *Let. fr. E.I. Co. to Factors Fort St. George* Dec. (MS.), Theis Musters You now Sent Us appeare to be all Taffety Wale. **1684** *Patent Office* No. 241 Lines or creases resembling the Wale of Tabby or Mohaire. **1696** J. F. *Merch. Ware-ho. laid open* 13 A sort of Callico-Dimetty..Wove with a Wale like a plain Dimetty. **1755** JOHNSON, *Wale*, a rising part in the surface of cloth. **1828–32** WEBSTER, *Wale*, in cloth, a ridge or streak rising above the rest. We say, cloth is wove with a wale. **1886** BECK *Draper's Dict.*, *Wale*, a ridge on the surface of cloth.

fig. **1587** GASCOIGNE *Herbs* Posies (1907) 329 The feeble thred which Lachesis hath sponne, To drawe my dayes in short abode with thee, Hath wrought a webbe which now (welneare) is donne, That wale is worne. **1611** BEAUMONT & FL. *Four Plays* (1647) 271 Thou art rougher far, and of a courser wale, fuller of pride.

b. *transf.* A stripe (of colour).

1891 HARDY *Tess* xlvi, The wide acreage of blank agricultural brownness..was beginning to be striped in wales of darker brown, gradually broadening to ribands.

4. *Naut.* **a.** A piece of timber extending horizontally round the top of the sides of a boat; the gunwale.

c **1330** R. BRUNNE *Chron. Wace* (Rolls) 12062 Cordes, kyuiles, atached þe wale. ? *a* **1400** *Morte Arth.* 740 Wyghtly one the wale thay wye vp thaire ankers. *c* **1440** CAPGRAVE *St. Kath.* 642 As with-inne the wale Of a stronge ship a man is bore a-loft. *c* **1440** *Promp. Parv.* 514/1 Wale, of a schyppe, *ratis.* *c* **1470** HENRY *Wallace* IX. 134 Her on the waill ner by the I sall stand. **1513** DOUGLAS *Æneis* V. iv. 76 With sa strang rowthis apon athir waill, The mychty kervell schudderit at euery straik. **1530** PALSGR. 286/1 Wall of a shyppe. *a* **1578** LINDESAY (Pitscottie) *Chron. Scot.* (S.T.S.) I. 251 Scho was ten fute thik in the waill. **1709** *Lond. Gaz.* No. 4510/7 The Hoy Burthen 9 or 10 Tun,..with a clean Tail, a rounding Wale. **1716** B. CHURCH *Hist. Philip's War* (1867) II. 131 That..upon the Wail of each [Whale-]Boat five pieces of strong Leather be fastened on each side. **1797** *Encycl. Brit.* (ed. 3) XVII. 405/1 Describe the curve TMS to represent the sheer or extreme height of the side [of a long boat], which in a ship would be called the..upper edge of the wale. **1857** [COLQUHOUN] *Comp. Oarsman's Guide* 28 The narrow piece of wood running round the sax-board outside, but now generally disused, is called a wale.

b. *pl.* The horizontal planks or timbers, broader and thicker than the rest, which extend along a ship's sides, at different heights, from stem to stem; also called *bends* (see BEND *sb.*[4] 6); also *sing.*, each of such timbers.

For *chain, channel, main, sheer wales*, see CHAIN-WALE, CHANNEL *sb.*[2] 2, MAIN *a.* 11, SHEER *sb.*[2] 3.

1295 *Acc. Exch. K.R.* 5/8 m. 8 Empcio meremii..Et x. d. in ij Wales emptis de Anselmo Carpentario. **1336–7** *Ibid.* 19/31 m. 5 Et in vj. lignis emptis ad eandem pro Wales et bindes inde faciendis..vj. s. **1497** *Naval Acc. Hen. VII* (1896) 292 Tymbre for bemys walys & other Necessaries in the seid Ship. **1534** *Acc. Ld. High Treas. Scot.* V. 233 For valis to cover abone the boit, viij d. **1536** in R. G. Marsden *Sel. Pleas Crt. Adm.* I. (1894) 58 The sterne of the same cock bote was faste under on of the wales of the said catche. **1627** CAPT. SMITH *Sea Gram.* ii. 6 From bend to bend, or waile to waile, which are the outmost timbers on the ship sides. **1664** E. BUSHNELL *Shipwright* 7 The next Waale parallel to the lower Waale. *a* **1693** *Urquhart's Rabelais* III. lii. 429 Bends and Walls [Fr. *rambades*] of his Carricks. **1748** *Anson's Voy.* II. iv. 158 They found her wales and out-side planks extremely defective. **1824** J. F. COOPER *Pilot* xxiv. II. 303 Such a point-blanker would have torn off a streak of our wales. **1881** HARDY *Trumpet Major* xxvi, Boats built of wood which was greenly growing..three days before it was bent as wales to their sides. **1883** *Man. Seamanship for Boys* 11 Q. What are bends? A. The thickest and strongest planks on the outward part of a ship's side,..They are more properly called wails.

5. Each of the horizontal timbers connecting and bracing the piles of a dam, etc. Also, = WALING 1.

1754 T. GARDNER *Hist. Acc. Dunwich* 179 Except Plank upon the Head of the Key, and under the upper Wale, and Plank to join the piles. **1837** *Civil Engin. & Arch. Jrnl.* I. 33/1 The wales are to be in two thicknesses, of half-timbers, ..bolted to the gauge piles. **1879** *Cassell's Techn. Educ.* I. 80 These are called guide piles, and to these horizontal timbers are attached, called wales. **1886** H. C. SEDDON *Builder's Work* i. 7 When the ground is firm enough to admit of it, deep and narrow trenches..may be secured by horizontal planks or wales, placed opposite each other..and kept apart by struts. **1926** A. E. WYNN *Design & Construction of Formwork* viii. 84 Above 6 ft. high there is always danger of the form twisting..from the impact of the concrete if wales are not used. **1964** R. L. PEURIFOY *Formwork for Concrete Structures* ix. 158 The bottom wale should be placed not more than 8 in. above the bottom of the form.

6. *Basket-making.* Each of the horizontal bands round the body of a basket composed of rods intertwined as a finishing-off course.

1907 T. OKEY in *Jrnl. Soc. Arts* 11 Jan. 190/2 A wale is three or more rods woven one after and over the other to form a binding or string course. *Ibid.*, I was interested to find [in an old Egyptian basket] the same strokes—the fitch, the pair, the border, slath, and wale—I had been using yesterday.

7. A ridge on a horse's collar: see quot. 1794.

1794 W. FELTON *Carriages* (1801) II. 139 The Neck Collar is a padded collar made to fit and sit easy round the horse's neck—it has 2 wales or risings on the outside, called the fore and back wales. **1847** HALLIWELL. **1895** *E. Angl. Gloss.* **1908** *N. & Q.* 10th Ser. X. 146/2, I was told by one of the workmen that the rolls or ridges of a horse-collar between which the hames lie are called respectively the fore-wale and the afterwale.

8. Comb.: **wale-piece**, †(*a*) a piece of timber to serve as the gunwale of a boat; (*b*) a horizontal timber connecting and binding the piles or posts of a bridge, dam, etc.; †**wale-reared** *a.* = WALL-*sided*; †**wale-stock, -tree**, ? a piece of timber to serve as a gunwale; **wale-streak**, the gunwale of a boat.

1350 *Acc. Exch. K.R.* 25/32 (P.R.O.) En xxxvij piec' de mesrime achat' pour *wale piecen, wale stockez et fotwalen. **1739** LABELYE *Piers Westm. Bridge* 20 The Plates, Whale-Pieces, Ties and Braces that had been contrived to keep them steady. **1839** *Civil Engin. & Arch. Jrnl.* II. 432/1 Allowing a space of not less than 12 inches wide between the wale pieces, for the piles to fill up the bays between the wale pieces. *c* **1635** CAPT. N. BOTELER *Dial. Sea Services* (1685), *Wale reared. **1644** MANWAYRING *Sea-mans Dict.* 113 *Wale-reared*, that is, when a ship is built right up, after she comes to her bearing. **1769** FALCONER *Dict. Marine* (1780), *Wale-reared*, an obsolete phrase, implying *wall sided*. **1350** *Wale stockez [see *wale piece* above]. **1856** 'STONEHENGE' *Brit. Sports* II. VIII. iii. 474/2 Here he [the coxswain] must sit cross-legged..with a hand on each gun-wale or *wale-streak. **1485** *Naval Acc. Hen. VII* (1896) 72 *Wale trees.. ij, Hausers..ij. **1488** *Acc. & Inv.* 72 (P.R.O.) Waletrees.

wale (weɪl), *sb.*² *Sc.* and *north.* Forms: 3 **wal**, 4 **wall**, 5 **wail**, 5-6 **waill**, 6 **waylle**, 8-9 **wile**, 9 **waile**, 3- **wale**. [a. ON. *val* neut., corresponding to OHG. *wala* (MHG. *wal*, mod.G. *wahl*) str. fem., f. Teut. root **wal-*, **wel-*: see WILL *v.*]

1. The action or an act of choosing; choice. Also, scope for choice, plurality of things to choose from.

Before the 17th c. recorded only *poet.*, chiefly in certain set phrases: *at, to wale*, at one's choice, in abundance; *men of wale*, men of high merit; *worthy in* or *to wale*, of approved valour. (By some writers of the 15-16th c. *to wale* in the last phrase seems to have been taken as the inf. of WALE *v.*¹)

a **1300** *Cursor M.* 4353 If..þat þou mi lefe wald be; O werldes welth to wale and wan Sal þou haf mare þan mai be gan. *Ibid.* 5375. *Ibid.* 7629 And of a thusand men o wal, He made him ledder and marscal. *a* **1352** MINOT *Poems* v. 77 Sir Edward, oure gude King wurthi in wall. *a* **1400** *Sir Perc.* 1587 When he had tolde this tale..He hade wordis at wale To thame ilkane. *c* **1400** *Destr. Troy* 11952 He russhit vp full radly, raght to his clothes, Soche as happit hym to hent, hade he no wale. *c* **1440** *York Myst.* ii. 55 Als ye I haue honours in alkyn welth to wale. *c* **1450** HOLLAND *Houlate* 447 With lordis of Scotland, lerit, and the laif As worthy, wysest to waile, in worschipe allowit. *c* **1470** *Golagros & Gaw.* 211 Wynis went within that wane, maist wourthy to vaill. **1513** DOUGLAS *Æneis* v. xii. 37 Thar wes na strenth of valeant men to waill. **1637** RUTHERFORD *Let. to Lady Kenmure* (1664) 29, I will have no other tutor, suppose I could have waile & choise of ten thousand beside. **1808** JAMIESON s.v., *He gaif me the wale*, he allowed me to choose. **1847** DE QUINCEY *Notes on Landor* Wks. 1859 IX. 297 Our Arab friend, however, is no connoisseur in courts of law: small wale of courts in the desert. **1858-61** RAMSAY *Remin.* (1867) 167 There's nae waile o' wigs on Monrimmon Moor. **1894** CROCKETT *Raiders* xxxiii, She's a wonderfu' woman, the mistress; no the like o' her in the three counties. She micht hae had the wale o' the men.

b. Coupled with *will*.

c **1420** *Anturs of Arth.* xxvii, With alle welthis to wille, and wynus to wale. **1456** SIR G. HAYE *Law Arms* (S.T.S.) 147 [He] mycht in the time that he feit him have had otheris at will and wale. **1742** R. FORBES *Ajax* (1755) 11 Lat him than now tak will an' wile. **1836** J. AFFLECK *Poet. Wks.* 81 (E.D.D.), I've sheets and blankets, will and wale, I'm nae deaf nit.

2. That which is chosen or selected as the best; the choicest individual, kind, specimen, etc.

1513 DOUGLAS *Æneis* VII. vi. 188 The King Latyne, but faill, Gart cheis of all his steidis furth the waill. *a* **1578** LINDESAY (Pitscottie) *Chron. Scot.* (S.T.S.) I. 399 Ane great airme..to the number of lᵐ men the waill of all Ingland. **1717** RAMSAY *Elegy on Lucky Wood* xi, She was the wale of a' her kin. **1786** BURNS *Ordination* vi, For lapfu's large o' gospel kail Shall fill thy crib in plenty, An' runts o' grace the pick an' wale. **1815** SCOTT *Guy M.* lv, The Bertrams were aye the wale o' the country side! **1842** J. AITON *Dom. Econ.* (1857) 262 The best way to get one, and the wale of them, is to intercept one of the packs which are driven from the northern markets. **1887** STEVENSON *Merry Men* v. Wks. 1895 VIII. 166 It's the pride of the eye, and it's the lust o' life, an' it's the wale o' pleesures.

†**wale**, *sb.*³ *Obs. rare.* [? var. of WEEL *sb.*:—OE. *wǣl.*] ? A wave, current.

1565 GOLDING *Ovid's Met.* II. 16 And Doris with hir daughters all: of which some cut the wales [1587 wals; *rhyme* whales] With splaied armes. **1636** JAMES *Iter Lanc.* 323 (1845) 11 Threescore miles from wale Of sea at Conyngton was found a whale Vppon a high downes.

†**wale**, *a. Obs.* Also 3 **wal**, 4 **walle**. [f. WALE *sb.*²] Used as a general laudatory expression: Chosen; choice, select; excellent, noble, goodly.

a. of a person, his attributes, actions, etc.

c **1250** *Gen. & Ex.* 888 Sodomes king in kinge dale, Mette abram wið feres wale. **13..** *Gaw. & Gr. Knt.* 1010 Bot ȝet I wot þat Wawen & þe wale burde Such comfort of her compaynye caȝten to-geder. *a* **1400-50** *Wars Alex.* 294 'Þan will I,' quod þe wale qwene. *c* **1400** *Destr. Troy* 1329 The Troiens..blody beronyn, Wyde woundes & wete of hor wale dyntes. *a* **1500** *Bernard. de cura rei fam.* etc. (E.E.T.S.) iii. 149 And wander in A winter tyme wyth full wale knychtis. **1515** *Scottish Field* 385 in *Chetham Misc.* (1856), It is a losse to the lande,..For his witte and his wisedome, And his wale deedes. **1790** J. FISHER *Poems* 102 Ae simmer e'en baith wale an' trig,..doun the rig A lad cam' to the Fitman-brig.

absol. *a* **1310** in Wright *Lyric P.* xi. 38 A wayle whyt as whalles bon.

b. of a thing.

c **1250** *Gen. & Ex.* 3635 Bokes he wrot of lore wal, Hu ðis folc hem riȝt leden sal. **13..** *E.E. Allit. P.* B. 1716 Bifore þe barounz has hom broȝt, & byrled þerinne [*sc.* the holy vessels] Wale wyne to þy wenches. ? *a* **1400** *Morte Arth.* 741 By wytt of the watyre-mene of the wale ythez, ffrekes one the forestayne fakene theire coblez. *a* **1400-50** *Wars Alex.* 75 Þan was a wardan ware oute in þe wale stremys Of all þe naue & þe note. *c* **1400** *Destr. Troy* 694 She went from þat worthy into a wale chambur. *Ibid.* 1943 He..wound vp full wightly all his wale Ancres.

wale (weɪl), *v.*¹ *Sc.* and *north.* Forms: 4-6 **walle**, 4-5 **weyle**, 5-8 **waill**, 5-9 **wail**, 6 **vale**, **vaile**, **weale**, 7 **wayl**, **weil**, **wehl**, **weal(l**, 6-9 **wyle**, 8-9 **wile**, 9 **wyell**, 4- **wale**. [f. WALE *sb.*² Cf. WELE *v.* (The form *wehl* was prob. due to G. *wählen*, †*wehlen*.)]

1. *trans.* To choose, select, pick out, sort. Also with *out, through*.

a **1310** in Wright *Lyric P.* ix. 33 Mosti ryden by Rybbesdale, Wilde wymmen forte wale, ant welde wuch ich wolde. **13..** *E.E. Allit. P.* A. 999 Iasper hyȝt þe fyrst gemme, þat I on þe fyrst basse con wale. *c* **1400** *Destr. Troy* 105 That worthy hade a wyfe walit hym-sceluon. *a* **1400-50** *Wars Alex.* 1014 Wale ȝow oþer werriouris þat wiȝt ere & ȝonger. *c* **1470** HENRY *Wallace* v. 895 In gret ire he apon thaim sadly socht, Wailland a place quhar he mycht bargane mak. **1496** *Acc. Ld. High Treas. Scot.* I. 319 Item..giffin to Johne Maware, to pas to Clidisdale, to the woddis, to wale tymmyr for the artailȝeri, ix s. **1508** DUNBAR *Tua Mariit Wemen* 530 Of ther thre wantoun wiffis, that I haif writtin heir, Quhilk wad ȝe wail to ȝour wif? **1513** DOUGLAS *Æneis* II. i. 10 Of chost men syne, walit by cutt, thai tuik Ane greit nwmir. **1537** in *Exch. Rolls Scot.* XVII. 741 That ye cause ..Patrik Tennent waill our sa[i]d woll, sort, and pak the samin. **1625** A. GIL *Sacr. Philos.* xii. 192 The Poet gives you an example of a Gardiner, wehling his seeds being mingled together. **1637** RUTHERFORD *Let. to Lady Kenmure* (1664) 30 But more I can neither wish, nor pray, nor desire for to your La: then Christ singled and wailed out, from all created good things. **1674** in *Scott. Hist. Rev.* (1907) Jan. 232 Buy me a good handsom Caudibeck hatt..pray sie that it be good and weall wyled. **1737** RAMSAY *Sc. Prov.* ii. 35 (1750) 7 A lass that has mony wooers aft wales the warst. **1785** BURNS *Cotter's Saturday Nt.* xii, Those strains that once did sweet in Zion glide, He wales a portion with judicious care. **1821** CARLYLE *Let.* 17 Nov., *Early Lett.* (1886) II. 4 To beg that you will accept the brown pair of spectacles which I have *waled* for you. **1832** SCOTT *Redgauntlet* let. xii, Come away, chap—come away, gentle chap—nae time to be picking and waling your steps. **1873** C. GIBBON *Lack of Gold* xi, I said I would wail a man for you myself. **1888** D. GRANT *Sc. Stories* 30 A bodie canna aye wyle his words. **1894** *Northumbld. Gloss* s.v., Wale me an orange... To wale one's way.

b. *to wale by*, to choose and put by.

1789 ROSS *Helenore* I. (ed. 3) 53 Bannocks and kebbocks knit up in a claith, She had wiled by, and row'd up in her waith.

c. *Coal-mining.* (See quot. 1881.)

1860 *Eng. & For. Mining Gloss.*, *Waling*, cleaning the coals. **1881** RAYMOND *Mining Gloss.*, *Wale*, Newc. To clean coal by picking out the refuse by hand.

2. *intr.* To make choice.

13.. *Gaw. & Gr. Knt.* 1276 'I-wysse, worþy,' quoth þe wyȝe, 'ȝe haf waled wel better'. **1786** BURNS *Halloween* iv, They steek their een, an' graip an' wale For muckle anes, an' straught anes. **1826-30** T. WILSON *Pitman's Pay* III. cxvi, Through and through the bowl they wyell—For raisins, how they stritch and strive!

†**3.** *trans.* ? To seek. *Obs. rare*⁻¹.

13.. *Gaw. & Gr. Knt.* 398 Where schulde I wale þe, quod Gauan, where is þy place?

Hence '**waling** *vbl. sb.*; also *attrib.* as ***waling glass*** (see quot. 1880).

1625 A. GIL *Sacr. Philos.* i. 12 Every seed encreaseth by the earth and moisture thereof, which cannot be but with a wehling out, or choice of things that are homogeneous, or of parts like thereto. **1634** RUTHERFORD *Let. to Lady Kenmure* 29 Apr., It should be of your wailing and not of his. **1880** *Antrim & Down Gloss.*, *Waling glass*, a weaver's counting glass, which magnifies a small portion of the surface of linen, and thus enables the set or count to be ascertained.

wale (weɪl), *v.*² Also **whale**. [f. WALE *sb.*¹]

1. *trans.* To mark (the flesh) with wales or weals.

14.. in *Pol. Rel. & L. Poems* (1903) 245 A wycked wound hath me walled [*rimes* called, halt, salt], And traveyld me from topp to too. **1634** BP. HALL *Contempl. N.T.*, *Christ bef. Pilate* 263 O my blessed Saviour, was it not enough that thy sacred body was stripped of thy garments, and waled with bloudy stripes? **1661** FELTHAM *Resolves* II. lxxxv. (ed. 8) 375 Would the Horse..suffer his lazy Rider to bestride his patient back, with his hands and whip to wale his flesh?

2. 'To fasten, secure, or protect with a wale or wale piece' (Webster 1911).

1909 *E. Essex Advertiser* Aug., Suppl. 4/3 The wharf..is ..built with piles and strongly whaled.

3. a. *Mil.* To weave or wattle (a gabion, hurdle). **b.** *Basket-making.* To intertwine (rods) in making a wale (see WALE *sb.*¹ 6); also 'to furnish (a basket) with a wale or wales' (Webster 1911).

1842 BURN *Nav. & Mil. Techn. Dict.*, *Clayonner*, to wattle, wale. **1892** FOX IRWIN *Notes Fortif.* (ed. 2) 60 To make a Wickerwork Gabion... Wale the web by passing each rod in succession over the other two..till the waling is 2-ft. 6-in. high. **1907** *Jrnl. Soc. Arts* 11 Jan. 190/2 The foot rods are waled and then laid down as in a border.

Hence **waled** *ppl. a.*, marked with weals. '**waling** *vbl. sb. Mil.*, the process of making a gabion or hurdle; also, the basket-work thus made; also *attrib.* as ***waling rod***.

1842 BURN *Nav. & Mil. Techn. Dict.*, *Clayon*, a..waling-rod. *Clayonnage*, wattling;..waling. **1885** *Pall Mall Gaz.* 31 Mar. 6/2 A horrible vision of a waled back would come before my eyes and the swish of that terrible whip would sound in my ears. **1892** G. PHILIPS *Text-bk. Fortif.* III. iii. (ed. 5) 88 In brushwood gabions the basket work is called the web, and the process of making it is termed waling. **1892** [see 3 above].

†**wale**. *int. Obs.* [repr. OE. *wá lá*: see WO, LO, and WELLAWAY *intr.*] Alas! woe is me!

c **1205** LAY. 12952 Ah wale þat hit nusten Costantines cnihtes. *Ibid.* 25859 Wale [*c* **1275** wola] þat ich wes iboren.

wale: see VALE *sb.*¹, VEIL *sb.*¹, WAIL *v.*, WALL *sb.*¹, WELL *sb.*, WHALE.

†**waled**, *a. Obs.* [f. WALE *sb.*¹ + -ED².] Striped. ***open-waled***, having an open texture.

c **1050** *Voc.* in Wr.-Wülcker 416/23 *Histriatarum* [understood as = *striatarum* (1 Kings vii. 24)], waledra. **1602** *Inv.* in *Collect. Archæol.* (1863) II. 95 One waled matterice vj *s.* viij *d.* **1611** COTGR., *Linomple*, a fine, thinne, or open-waled linnen, much vsed in Picardie..for womens kerchers. **1665** HOOKE *Microgr.* 6 Fine waled Silk, or Taffety.

waled (weɪld), *ppl. a.*¹ *Sc.* and *north.* [f. WALE *v.*¹ + -ED¹.] Chosen, selected, picked. Cf. HAND-WALED.

c **1400** *Destr. Troy* 386 Walid wyne for to wete wantid þai none. *c* **1470** HENRY *Wallace* VIII. 1219 Fyfty ladyis was in hyr cumpany, Wallyt off wit. *c* **1550** ROLLAND *Crt. Venus* I. 64 Thair waillit weid, and stature to descriue, I can not gif perfite affirmatiue. ? *c* **1640** R. SEMPILL *Piper Kilbarchan* 43 He counted was a weil'd Wight-man. **1649** RUTHERFORD *Let. to Mrs. Gillespie* 14 Aug., Let not your heart say, it is an ill wailed dispensation. **1681** R. FLEMING *Fulfilling Script.* III. iii. (1726) 376 What choice and wailed instruments such were, who were thus called forth. **1818** SCOTT *Hrt. Midl.* xviii, Gude and waled Christians they were too. **1828** *Craven Gloss.*, *Wealed*, picked, chosen.

waled, *ppl. a.*²: see WALE *v.*²

walee, wale-knot: see WALI, WALL-KNOT.

Walentyne, obs. Sc. form of VALENTINE.

walenut, obs. form of WALNUT.

waler¹ ('weɪlə(r)). [f. WALE *v.*¹ + -ER¹.]

1. *Coal-mining.* (See quots.)

1825 E. MACKENZIE *View Northumbld.* (ed. 2) I. 91 Wailers are boys employed to pick out slate, pyrites, and other foul admixtures from the coal. **1860** *Eng. & For. Mining Gloss.* (ed. 2) [Newcastle Terms], *Waler*, boys who pick the refuse from the good coals.

†**2.** 'A handloom silk-weaving term: a man employed to determine the number of "picks" in a piece and to see that uniformity is maintained' (*Eng. Dial. Dict.*). *Obs.*

Waler² ('weɪlə(r)). Also **waler**. [f. *Wale-s* (for New South Wales) + -ER¹.] **1.** *Anglo-Indian.* A horse imported from Australia, esp. from New South Wales. Also, a type of light Australian horse.

1849 *New South Wales* vii. 65 The colonial-bred horses or Walers, as they are called in India. **1888** KIPLING *Plain T.*, *Rout of White Hussars* (ed. 3) 215 The Drum-Horse..is nearly always a big piebald Waler. **1897** 'R. BOLDREWOOD' *My Run Home* xxxiv. 330, 'I can't imagine any thing but the English thoroughbred worthy to be named in the same day with a high-caste Arab.'..'I'll show you a Waler to-morrow that may convert you.' **1900** H. LAWSON *Ballad of Cornstalk* in *Coll. Verse* (1967) I. 380 He mounted his waler and rode to the sea (He was sick of the Bush and he longed for a spree). **1945** BAKER *Austral. Lang.* iii. 71 *Waler*, originally a horse exported from New South Wales to India (in modern times, a light type of army horse used in Australia). **1963** *Weekly News* (Auckland, N.Z.) 8 May 38/4 The farm hack is a multi-breed horse—a dash of cob, a little thoroughbred, maybe a touch of the Australian 'waler' whose ancestry lies with Dutch and Spanish strains. **1968** J. KIDDELL *Euloowirree Walkabout* (1970) xiii. 123 Lord, he exulted, but he's a fast horse. A Waler. One of the descendants of the bush-bred stock, the thoroughbreds of the Outback.

attrib. **1873** *Madras Mail* 25 June (Yule), For sale, a brown Waler gelding. **1888** KIPLING *Plain T.*, *Rout of White Hussars* (ed. 3) 217 Yale had a big, old, white Waler trap-horse.

2. (With capital initial.) A native of New South Wales (or of Australia generally). *slang.*

1880 J. INGLIS *Our Austral. Cousins* xiii. 159 In the matter of awnings and verandahs the 'Walers' had a grand chance for a bright, cheerful..display. **1924** G. H. A. WILLIS *Royal Navy as I saw It* 270 We left the *Oceana*, which continued her voyage to Australia with the 'Walers' (as the Australian passengers were called). **1949** *Geogr. Mag.* Feb. 373 *Sydneysider* or *Waler*, a resident of New South Wales.

†'**Walesman**. *Obs.* [f. *Wales* + MAN *sb.*] = WELSHMAN.

1591 *Canterb. Marriage Licences* Ser. I. (1892) 363 Hugh Evans of Lambeth, Walesman.

walet(t, walew, obs. ff. WALLET, VALUE.

waleway, var. WELLAWAY *int.*

walewe, obs. ff. VALUE *sb.*, WALLOW *v.*

Waleys, obs.: see WELSH.

walfair, obs. form of WALLFLOWER.

Walhalla, var. VALHALLA.

walhwe, obs. form of WALLOW *a.*

‖**wali** (ˈwɑːliː). Also **wálee, waly.** [Arab. *wālī* (classical Arab. *wālin*), subst. use of pres. pple. of *wala* to be foremost.] The governor of a province: = VALI.
1811 tr. *Niebuhr's Trav. Arab.* lxxxiv. in J. Pinkerton *Coll. Voy.* X. 107 Every petty district.. has its governor. If not a prince, or one of the higher nobility, this governor is called Wali and Dola. **1839** E. W. LANE *Arab. Nts.* (1859) I. v. 350 The Wálee inflicted upon him a hundred lashes, and banished him from the city. **1857** W. K. TWEEDIE *Rivers & Lakes of Script.* 24 And how comes it to pass that a Mohammedan Wali disfigures the scene? **1883** SCHAFF-HERZOG *Encycl. Relig. Knowl.* II. 1164 (Stanf.) Jerusalem is the seat of a *mutasarrif* under the *waly* of Syria.

walia (ˈwɑːlɪə). [a. Amharic.] The Ethiopian ibex, *Capra walie.* Also ***walia ibex.***
1932 *Nat. Hist.* XXXII. 69/2 The walia lives in a much worse place. **1965** L. BROWN *Ethiopian Episode* II. 45 The Walia Ibex were.. the principal object of my expedition to Semien. **1971** *Observer* (Colour Suppl.) 31 Oct. 19/2 In the rugged Simien Mountains, where the few remaining walia dwell, farmers continue to destroy the animal's habitat. *Ibid.* 20/1 (*caption*) Fewer than 150 walia ibexes remain on earth.

Walian (ˈweɪlɪən), *sb.* and *a.* [f. *Wale-s* + -IAN.] ***South*** (or ***North***) ***Walian.*** **A.** *sb.* A native or inhabitant of South (or North) Wales. **B.** *adj.* (Characteristic) of or pertaining to this region.
1894 *Wales* Aug. 170/1 He was a Methodist preacher, though he was a South Walian. **1924** J. O. FRANCIS *Legend of Welsh* 63 The best story I have heard of Welsh-speaking Englishmen was told me.. by a South Walian. **1936** *Antiquity* X. 461 Richards was a South Walian. **1968** D. E. ALLEN *British Tastes* iv. 100 The stern Protestant ethos, originally adopted by.. a people that then became the stern North Walian. **1977** D. JONES *My Friend Dylan Thomas* viii. 98, I thought this was a particularly South Walian expression until I read.. *The Lore and Language of Schoolchildren.*

walidrag, variant of WALLYDRAG *Sc.*

walie, var. WALLY *a.*^{2} *Sc.*, WALY *int. Sc.*

waling (ˈweɪlɪŋ). Also *erron.* **whaling.** [f. WALE *sb.*^{1} + -ING^1.]
1. The wales or horizontal timbers with which piles are braced; also, one of such timbers, a wale; a long horizontal member used to brace the lining of an excavation or the walls of a form. (Cf. WALE *sb.*^{1} 5; also FOOT-*waling.*)
1837 *Civil Engin. & Arch. Jrnl.* I. 12/1 To these piles will be fixed three tiers of waling of whole timbers. **1878** F. S. WILLIAMS *Midl. Railw.* 592 After the timbers are fixed, they are braced by what are called 'walings'. **1893** J. P. ALLEN *Practical Building Construction* xxii. 349 Where the ground is looser the poling boards must be placed closer together, perpendicularly, with walings, which are placed horizontally inside them. **1932** [see SOLDIER *sb.* 7 c]. **1966** C. K. AUSTIN *Formwork to Concrete* (ed. 2) 282 The principle on which this system works, is that of a single form consisting of standard steel panels supported by steel channel walings sliding between soldiers against the concrete face. **1972** V. C. LAUNDER *Foundations* x. 132 Vertical planks or baulks are driven into the ground at the sides of the excavation as it proceeds and held vertical by horizontal timbers called walings, strutted across the trench width.
Comb. **1837** WHITTOCK *Bk. Trades* (1842) 202 Oaken piles driven down close to the embankments, with their upper ends crossed by strong 'whaling-boards' of oak. **1891** T. POTTER *Concrete* (ed. 2) I. v. 157 If the sides are loose it is better to stand some boards against them, lifting or removing the latter.. as the concrete is being filled in. This is assuming they are not planked or waled, and stretchers are employed to keep the waling planks in position. **1916** *Chamb. Jrnl.* 1 Jan. 68/2 He worked his way along.. till he reached the edge of the wharf and found footing on the walling [*sic*] strips against which the ship's hull rested.
2. *Naut.* The timbers forming the wale of a boat; in comb. ***waling-piece,*** ? = *wale-piece* (*a*).
1909 *Westm. Gaz.* 6 Jan. 7/4 Some of the survivors saved themselves by seizing the collier's whaling-piece.
3. *Basket-making.* (The process of weaving) a band of rods which forms a wale (see WALE *sb.*^{1} 6); the wales of a basket.
1912 T. OKEY *Art of Basket-Making* vii. 80 The butts of the waling being pieced in at the front. *Ibid.* xi. 135 The waling of the upsett will be begun at each side. **1949** K. S. WOODS *Rural Crafts of England* III. x. 164 The uprights must now be set very firmly in position by several strong rows of waling. **1964** H. HODGES *Artifacts* x. 146 Where three rods were used simultaneously with a crossing.. the weave is referred to as waling. **1983** *Daily Tel.* 20 Sept. 15/5 There is a border of 'waling' at the base of the basket.

Walisc, Walische, obs. forms of WELSH.

walise, Sc. form of VALISE.

walk (wɔːk), *sb.*^{1} Also 4–7 **walke**, 6 **walck, whalke.** [f. WALK *v.*^{1}]
I. Action or manner of walking.
1. a. An act or spell of walking or going on foot from place to place; *esp.* a short journey on foot taken for exercise or pleasure. Phrase, ***to take a walk,*** (*a*) also †***fetch,*** rarely ***make a walk,*** and (somewhat *arch.*) ***to take one's walk***(*s* to make such a journey; (*b*) to 'receive one's marching orders', to be dismissed; freq. *imp.* in formulas of impatient dismissal, sometimes in extended form; sometimes *transf.*; also, to 'walk out' in a labour dispute (WALK *v.*^{1} 13 b). *U.S. slang.*
c **1386** CHAUCER *Man of Law's T.* 461 And in hir walk this blynde man they mette. **1576** FLEMING *Panopl. Epist.* 410 You haue your fine walkes, in places of pleasure, and therewithall communication seasoned with the leuen of learning. **1581** A. HALL *Iliad* II. 23 When as yᵉ green eyed Goddesse thus had heard dame Iunoes talk, To finde the wilie Vlysses straight downe she tooke hir walke. **1638** BAKER tr. *Balzac's Lett.* (vol. II) 48 See here the decree of a country Phylosopher, and Matter of Meditation for one of your walkes at Yssy. **1660** F. BROOKE tr. *Le Blanc's Trav.* 79 The unfortunate Lady Agarida took a walk by a little Rivers side. **1686** tr. *Chardin's Coronat. Solyman* 130 His most usual walks being upon Giulfa side. **1694** MOTTEUX *Rabelais* IV. xxi, Some kind Wave will throw it [my will] ashoar,.. and some King's Daughter, going to fetch a Walk in the fresco on the Evening, will find it. *a* **1700** EVELYN *Diary* 19 Sept. 1683, In my walkes I stepp'd into a goldbeaters work-house. **1737** *Common Sense* I. 205, I am not absurd enough, even to hint the usual rural Recreations, of fetching a Walk. **1753** [see WALK *v.* 5 d]. **1774** GOLDSM. *Nat. Hist.* I. Pref. p. iii, If .. a man should, in his walks, meet with an animal, the name .. of which he desires to know. **1825** T. HOOK *Sayings* Ser. II. *Passion & Princ.* xiv. III. 338 She delighted in little dances, and *walks home* after them, and what are called walks out in the morning, to be met somewhere and joined by her beloved. **1834** SIR H. TAYLOR *Artevelde* I. I. vii. 61 My mistress, Sir, so please you, takes her walk Along the garden terrace, and desires [etc.]. **1837** DICKENS *Pickw.* xxviii, At dinner they met again, after a five-and-twenty mile walk. **1865** E. BURRITT *Walk Land's End* i. 32, I shouldered my knapsack again and made an evening walk to Kingston. **1885** 'MRS. ALEXANDER' *Valerie's Fate* i, We have only ten minutes left for our walk back. **1910** A. LANG in *Encycl. Brit.* X. 135/1 A man, in fun, called to a goat to escort his wife on a walk.
(*b*) **1871** 'MARK TWAIN' *Sketches New & Old* (1875) 248 The first time he opened his mouth and was just going to spread himself, his breath took a walk. **1881** —— in *Century Mag.* Nov. 37 They ring out, 'Oh, dry up!' 'Give us a rest!' .. 'Oh, take a walk!' **1888** in Farmer *Americanisms* (1889) 550/2 The cash returns were so out of proportion to the sales, that Mr. Berry concluded to make a change and Tascott took a walk. **1937** *Amer. Speech* XII. 4 The so-called Jeffersonian Democrats took a walk from their party allegiance. **1946** *Sun* (Baltimore) 19 Nov. 2 (*caption*) Miners 'take a walk'—Black Diamond mine workers at Monongahela, Pa., are shown waiting for a car after quitting their jobs. **1961** *Lebende Sprachen* VI. 99/2 Go take a long walk off a short pier... Go jump in the lake.
†**b.** In wider sense: Travel, wandering. *Obs.*
c **1470** *Gol. & Gaw.* 494 The warliest wane.. That euer I vist in my walk, in all this warld wyde. **1697** DRYDEN *Æneis* VII. 773 For not the Gods, nor angry Jove will bear Thy lawless wand'ring walks in upper Air.
†**c.** Line of march or movement (in quots., of an army, a chess-man). *Obs.*
a **1400–50** *Wars Alex.* 3799 Þai droȝe furth be dissert & drinkles þai spill, Was nouthire waldis in þar walke ne watir to fynde. *a* **1548** HALL *Chron., Hen. VIII,* 258 And so returned home by land,.. burnyng and destroiyng euery pile, fortresse and village that was in their walke. **1589** *Pappe w. Hatchet* in *Lyly's Wks.* (1902) III. 395 He shall knowe what it is for a scaddle pawne, to crosse a Bishop in his owne walke.
d. *fig.* in various uses: †Expatiation, extended discourse (*obs. rare*); an act or a practice of walking, in any metaphorical sense of the verb.
1553 T. WILSON *Rhet.* 16 b, Now in speakyng of honestie, I may by deuision of the vertues make a large walke. **1592** BRETON *Pilgr. Parad.* (Grosart) 19/1 From care, and cost, fancy, and wisedomes folly, He tooke his walke vnto a waie more holly. **1771–2** COWPER *Olney Hymns* I. iii. 1 Oh! for a closer walk with God. **1802** WORDSW. *Sonn. Liberty* I. iv, And the talk Man holds with week-day man in the hourly walk Of the mind's business. **1825** LAMB *Elia* Ser. II. *Barbara S——,* Perhaps from the pure infelicity which accompanies some people in their walk through life. **1862** MRS. BROWNING *Little Mattie* 2 Short and narrow her life's walk.
e. *Baseball.* = *base on balls* s.v. BASE *sb.*^{1} 15 c. Cf. WALK *v.*^{1} 5 q.
1905 *Sporting Life* (Philadelphia) 16 Sept. 2/1 Taking the totals, or hits and walks, and such a famine in tallies would seem impossible, but there are the figures. **1948** *Daily Ardmoreite* (Ardmore, Okla.) 21 Mar. 4/6 Rice, on second from a walk and a sacrifice, crossed the home plate on a fly which Charley Gilbert misjudged. **1967** *Boston Sunday Herald* 7 May (TV Mag.) 14/2 Even the worst of ballplayers can still reach first base on a walk and even get to second should the pitcher throw wild. **1979** *Arizona Daily Star* 5 Aug. C 2/3 Dwight Evans, who had been behind 0–2 in the count, drew a two-out walk.
f. = *sponsored walk* s.v. SPONSORED *ppl. a.* 2.
1971 M. LEE *Dying for Fun* xliv. 213 You ought to get one of the newspapers to sponsor it. Walks and demonstrations and things. **1971** *Guardian* 24 May 11/6 From 1965–69, Oxfam depended on walks for up to £175,000 of its year's £2½ millions budget.
2. a. A procession, ceremonial perambulation.
1563 *Homilies* II. *Rogation-wk.* IV. 248 b, Yet haue we occasion secondarylye geuen vs in our walkes on these dayes, to consider the old auncient boundes & limittes belongyng to our owne Township. *a* **1610** BP. HALL *Epist.* VI. v. 45 You may as well challenge the Trumpets of Rammeshornes, and seauen dayes walke vnto euery siedge. **1888** BARRIE *Auld Licht Idylls* (1892) 23 It is nearly twenty years since the gardeners had their last 'walk' in Thrums.
†**b.** An official perambulation. Cf. sense 10.
1626 BRETON *Fantasticks* (Grosart) 13/1 The Forresters now be about their walkes, and yet stealers sometimes cozen the Keepers.
†**3.** *pl.* Ability to walk. *Obs. rare*$^{-1}$.
1593 R. HARVEY *Philad.* 103 That God which giueth eyes to the blind, and walkes to the lame.
4. An act of walking as distinguished from other more rapid modes of locomotion on foot (see WALK *v.*^{1} 7); the slowest gait of a land animal; a rate of progression which belongs to this gait, a walking pace.
a. of a horse or other quadruped (opposed to *trot, amble, gallop,* etc.).
1688 HOLME *Armoury* II. 150/1 Walk, is the sloest pace a Horse doth go; it is used to cool a Horse after hard Riding. **1788** MRS. HUGHES *Henry & Isabella* I. 50 If the road was in the smallest degree rough.. the horses were never suffered to go off a walk. **1804** A. HUNTER *Georg. Ess.* VI. 187 If the distance is above a mile, they will suffer, unless it is walk all the way. **1832** *Prop. Reg. Instr. Cavalry* II. 15 The rate of walk not to exceed four miles an hour. **1848** DICKENS *Dombey* xlvi, He rode near Mr. Dombey's house; and falling into a walk as he approached it, looked up at the windows. **1902** 'VIOLET JACOB' *Sheep-Stealers* xiv, He did not once let his horse go out of a sober walk.
b. of a human being (opposed to *run*).
1601 SHAKS. *Twel. N.* I. iii. 138 My verie walke should be a Iigge. **1838** DICKENS *O. Twist* xiii, Exchanging her faltering walk for a good, swift, steady run. **1854** SURTEES *Handley Cr.* lxxiii. (1901) II. 255 He.. rounded the corner into Red Lion Street at something between a walk and a run.
c. Applied *spec.* to a firm and regular gait. *nonce-use.*
1784 COWPER *Task* IV. 639 He stands erect; his slouch becomes a walk; He steps right onward, martial in his air.
d. A walking race; a pedestrian contest in which running is not allowed.
1887 *Sporting Life* 2 July 3/5 Clarke should win the Walk, with Lange second, and Ockelford third.
e. ***to win in a walk:*** to win easily and without effort. *U.S. colloq.*
1896 ADE *Artie* xii. 106 'Does he stand a good chance of being elected?' 'That's what keeps me guessin'. Two years ago he win in a walk [etc.].' **1903** A. H. LEWIS *Boss* 138 He won in a walk. **1936** E. S. GARDNER *Case of Sleepwalker's Niece* xiv. 130 The whole thing.. gets back to Duncan. If I can break down Duncan's identification I can win the case in a walk.
f. Any dance modelled on or resembling a walk; chiefly as second element of a Comb., as CAKE-WALK *sb.* 1, *camel-walk* s.v. CAMEL *sb.* 5, *Lambeth walk* s.v. LAMBETH 3.
1937 [see *Big Apple* s.v. BIG *a.* B. 2]. **1975** G. HOWELL *In Vogue* 9/2 In return we get syncopated music, and what to do to it—the Baleta.. the Twinkle.. the Missouri Walk. **1975** *N.Y. Post* 27 Dec. 23 The new Walk.. is an anathema to all this talk of returning romanticism, because you do it alone, without touching.
5. a. A manner of walking; *esp.* the distinctive manner of walking of an individual, as recognizable by visible appearance.
a **1656** R. COX *Actæon & Diana* 35 Who's this..? the clothes and walk of my dear husband. **1697** DRYDEN *Æneis* I. 561 In length of Train descends her sweeping Gown, And by her graceful Walk, the Queen of Love is known. **1705** tr. *Cowley's Plants* Wks. 1711 III. 382 The Mandrake only imitates our Walk And on two legs erect is seen to stalk. **1774** *Pennsylv. Gaz.* 28 Sept. Suppl. 1/1 Run away.. an Irish servant man,.. slender made, long visage, small legs, and hath a clumsy walk. **1863** GEO. ELIOT *Romola* xiii, It was impossible to mistake her figure and her walk. **1878** BOSW. SMITH *Carthage* 438 Who has a walk that can be named with that of the Arab?
†**b.** ***to diminish one's walks:*** ? to walk mincingly. *Obs.*
1609 DEKKER *Gull's Hornbk.* iv. 17 That true humorous Gallant that desires to powre himselfe into all fashions.. must as well practise to diminish his walkes, as to bee various in his sallets, curious in his Tobacco, [etc.].
6. *fig.* **a.** In religious language (cf. WALK *v.*^{1} 6 a): Manner of behaviour, conduct of life.
c **1586** C'TESS PEMBROKE *Ps.* CXIX. ii, Whom in walk Gods way directeth, Sure them no sinnfull blott infecteth Of deed or word. **1760** T. HUTCHINSON *Hist. Mass. Bay* iv. (1765) 421 The irregular walk or demeanor of any one church. **1818** SCOTT *Hrt. Midl.* x, In this proposal there was much that pleased old David,.. the lassie would be under Mrs. Saddletree's eye, who had an upright walk. **1831** CARLYLE *Ess., Early Ger. Lit.* (1840) III. 186 Tauler.. a man of antique Christian walk. **1845–6** TRENCH *Huls. Lect.* Ser. II. vii. 263 What do they require of us but a walk corresponding? **1871** MORLEY *Carlyle* in *Crit. Misc.* Ser. I. 237 The most important question that we can ask of any great teacher, as of the walk and conversation of any commonest person, remains this, how far has he [etc.].
†**b.** A course of conduct. *Obs.*
1772 BURKE *Let.* 17 Nov. *Corr.* (1844) I. 378 None of our friends are to blame for this rejection of that idea... It was impossible at that time to take a separate walk from them. **1786** MME. D'ARBLAY *Diary* 10 Dec., I was ashamed to appear the leader in a walk so new as that of leaving the Lodge in an evening.
†**7.** *Theat.* ? The course of action assigned to one person of a drama. *Obs.*
Davenant speaks of 'the underwalks (or lesser intrigues) of persons'.
1651 DAVENANT *Gondibert,* Pref., To these Meanders of the English Stage I have cut out the Walks of my Poems. **1673** BP. S. PARKER *Reproof Reh. Transp.* 10 You summ up your Charge in Six Heads, which you sometimes entitle Playes, sometimes Hypotheses, sometimes Aphorisms; and why not Plots, and Scenes, and Walks, and under-walks, &c.?

II. Place or path for walking.

†**8. a.** The usual place of walking, the haunt or resort (of a person or animal). *Obs.*

c **1386** CHAUCER *Knt.'s T.* 211 The gardyn.. Ther as this fresshe Emelye.. Was in hire walk, and romed vp and doun. *c* **1400** *Rom. Rose* 2505 Thus shalt thou.. gete enchesoun to goon ageyn Unto thy walk, or to thy place, Where thou biheld hir fleshly face [Fr. *d'aler Derechief encore en la rue Ou* etc.]. *a* **1450** *Mirk's Festial* 55 But þus he [*sc.* the hunter] wole spye wher hys [*sc.* the unicorn's] walk ys, and þer he settyþe a woman þat ys clene mayden. **1488–9** *Plumpton Corr.* (Camden) 59 Sir, I wold advise your mastership cause William Scargell to take good regard to himselfe & not to use his old walkes; for & he doe, he wylbe taken. **1530** PALSGR. 436/2 Beware, come nat in his walke lest he arrest the: *gardes toy de te trouuer la ou il hante.* **1593** MARLOWE *Edw. II* (Brooke) 1804 Edmund away.. Proud Mortimer pries neare into thy walkes. **1607** TOPSELL *Four-f. Beasts* 300 If any male or other stone Horsse come within their walke, then presently they make force at him. **1634** PEACHAM *Compl. Gentl.* x. (1906) 88 For with the weeds there are delicate flowers in those walkes of Venus [Ovid's *Amores*, etc.]. **1702** ROWE *Ambit. Step-Mother* I. i, With heedless steps they unawares Tread on the Lyons walk.

†**b.** *transf.* The region within which something moves. Also *fig. Obs.*

1545 ASCHAM *Toxoph.* I. (Arb.) 75 Meanynge therby, that no man.. came in their [*sc.* the arrows] walke, that escaped without death. **1597** HOOKER *Eccl. Pol.* v. lxxxi. §16 Those coulorable and suttle crimes that seldome are taken within the walke of humaine iustice. **1656** COWLEY *Pindar. Odes, Praise Pindar* iv, Lo, how th' obsequious Wind, and swelling Ayr The Theban Swan does upwards bear Into the walks of Clouds, where he does play. **1692** RAY *Disc.* II. ii. (1732) 101 The middle region of the Air where the Walk of the Clouds is. **1732** POPE *Ess. Man* i. 102 Far as the solar walk or milky way.

9. A place prepared or set apart for walking.

a. In a church or other public building: An ambulatory; a place where people can walk, a cloister, aisle, portico, or the like; *esp.* in the Royal Exchange, each of the portions of the ambulatory formerly allotted to different classes of merchants; designated by special names, as *East India, Virginia, Jamaica, Spanish* etc. *walk* (see Entick *London* ed. 1766, IV. 102).

1530 PALSGR. 286/2 Walke to walke up and downe in, *paruis.* **1556** WITHALS *Dict.* (1562) 42 A walke, galery, or porche to walke in, *porticus.* **1579** HAKE *Newes out of Powles* (1872) F iij, Here, in this Church a walck there is where Papistes doe frequent To talke of newes among themselues. **1593** NORDEN *Spec. Brit.* I. *Mdsx.* 35 Royall exchange... The form of the building is quadrate, with walks round the mayne building supported with pillers of marble. **1595** STOW *Surv.* (1603) 404 They resort all to the said Temple Church, in the round walke whereof [etc.]. *c* **1630** RISDON *Surv. Devon* §42 (1810) 48 In one of the walks of the church there is a stone. **1661** in M. Sellers *Eastland Co.* (Camden) Introd. 75 Our deputies.. will meet theirs at London upon the Exchange Munday and Tusday come senett at noone in the Eastlande Walke. **1710** *Lond. Gaz.* No. 4708/4 Inquire at the.. Royal Exchange East Country-Walk in Exchange Time. **1715** *Ibid.* No. 5341/4 The Spanish Walk in the Royal Exchange. **1858** HAWTHORNE *Fr. & It. Note-Bks.* (1871) II. 101 The great cloister.. has a walk of intersecting arches round its four sides. **1884** *19th Cent.* Jan. 104 The cloister arcade was said to have four walks.

b. An avenue bordered by trees.

1596 SPENSER *F.Q.* IV. x. 25 And all without were walkes and alleyes dight With diuers trees, enrang'd in euen rankes. **1600** J. PORY tr. *Leo's Africa* II. 93 Quinces here are of an incredible bignes. Their vines dispersing themselves vpon the boughes of trees doe make most pleasant bowers and walkes. **1623** J. TAYLOR (Water P.) *New Discov. by Sea* C 2 b, There hath he made Walkes, hedges, and Arbours, of all manner of most delicate fruit Trees. **1626** *Toke* (Kent) *Estate Acc.* (MS.) fol. 98 Quicksett for the further end of the wake in the new orchard. **1693** MOTTEUX *St Olon's Morocco* 8 A fiery Horse, that ran away with him.. as he wheel'd about under a Walk of Orange Trees. **1711** ADDISON *Spect.* No. 110 ¶1 There is a long Walk of aged Elms. **1853** DICKENS *Bleak Ho.* xviii, The old lime-tree walk was like green cloisters.

c. A broad path in a garden or pleasure-ground. Also, a way set apart for foot-passengers at the side of a street or road; a footwalk, sidewalk.

1533 *MS. Rawl.* 776 lf. 171 b, For that Chylderne shall not cast Rubbysh vnto the Kynges new Whalke. **1601** SHAKS. *Twel. N.* II. v. 19 Get ye all three into the box tree: Maluolio's comming downe this walke. **1667** PRIMATT *City & C. Builder* 153 It is decent to have fine gravel Walks in the Garden. **1688** HOLME *Armoury* II. 118/2 Allies, or Walks well Gravelled. **1693** EVELYN *De la Quint. Compl. Gard.* I. 44 A Walk must be broad enough for two Persons to walk a-breast at least,.. without which it would no longer be a real Walk, but a large Path. **1784** COWPER *Task* I. 351 We tread the wilderness, whose well-roll'd walks.. give ample space To narrow bounds. **1848** THACKERAY *Van Fair* xxxix, The library looked out on the front walk and park. **1854** SURTEES *Handley Cr.* xli. (1901) II. 38 That's one of the few pulls we magistrates have—I keep my avenue in repair and my walks weeded by the vagrants. **1913** MRS. STRATTON-PORTER *Laddie* xviii. (1917) 366 Mr. Pryor lay all twisted on the walk.

collect. **1874** *Englishman's Guide Bk. U.S.* 23 There are in it [the Central Park, New York] about 9 miles of carriage drive, 4 of bridle road, and about 25 miles of walk.

d. A public promenade in or near a town.

1840 DICKENS *Old C. Shop* xliv, In the public walks and lounges of a town, people go to see and to be seen. **1842** LOUISA S. COSTELLO *Pilgr. Auvergne* II. iii. 43 This public walk is prettily arranged on the site of a Roman amphitheatre.

e. The circular pavement on which the mill-horse walks in driving the mill.

1734 *Phil. Trans.* XXXVIII. 403 Their Muscles and Tendons.. are unequally strain'd, as the Duty is hardest on one Side, even tho' their Walk is large. **1744** DESAGULIERS *Course Exper. Philos.* II. 536 Those plain and simple Instruments used at the Coal-pits, call'd Barrel-Gins, where an Horse going round in a sufficiently large Walk draws round an *Axis in Peritrochio.* **1834–6** BARLOW in *Encycl. Metrop.* (1845) VIII. 91/1 The diameter of a walk for a horse mill ought to be at least 25 to 30 feet.

f. = ROPE-WALK.

1794 *Rigging & Seamanship* I. 54 *A Capstern..* is fixed in the ground at the lower-end of the walk. *Ibid.* 56 *Ropehouse-ground*, or *Walk*, should be four-hundred yards long. **1839** URE *Dict. Arts* 1070 (*Rope-making.*) As soon as he has reached the termination of the walk, a second spinner takes the yarn off the whirl, and gives it to another person to put upon a reel.

10. a. A tract of forest land comprised in the circuit regularly perambulated by a superintending officer (cf. 3); a division of a forest placed in the charge of a forester, ranger, or keeper.

1541 *N. Country Wills* (Surtees 1908) 190 To poor hous-holders and other honest people within my walkes within the forest of Wyndesore. **1593** SHAKS. *3 Hen. VI*, v. ii. 24 My Parkes, my Walkes, my Mannors that I had, Euen now forsake me. **1642** *Docq. Lett. Pat. at Oxf.* (1837) 330 The Office of Keeper of the lower walke of the great Parke of Windsor. *Ibid.* 338 The Offices of the foure Bayliwickes or eight walkes, and of Ranger and Launderer of the Forrest of Whichwood. **1679–88** *Moneys Secr. Serv. Chas. II & Jas. II* (Camden) 125 To Sr Eliab Harvey, Lieut. of Waltham forest,.. for the repayres of Low-Layton Lodge, wherein he lives, being under-keeper of that walk. *a* **1700** EVELYN *Diary* 23 Oct. 1686, Went with the Countesse of Sunderland to Cranbourn, a lodge and walke of my Lord Godolphin's in Windsor Parke. **1778** *Engl. Gazetteer* (ed. 2) s.v. *New Forest*, There are 9 walks in it; and to every one a keeper, under a lord-warden, besides 2 rangers, and a bow-bearer. **1810** J. EVANS & BRITTON *Beauties Eng. & Wales* XI. Northampt. 31 The Forest of Whittlewood... The whole is divided into five walks, viz. Hazleborough, Sholbrook, Wakefield, Hanger, and Shrobb. **1819** SCOTT *Ivanhoe* xxxii, If the Normans drive ye from these walks, Rowena has forests of her own, where her gallant deliverers may range at full freedom.

†**b.** *Agric.* A tract of land used for corn-growing.

1797 in A. Young *Agric. Suffolk* 39 A walk that is laid down with plenty of seeds for two years, never grows so much corn as when first broke up again.

c. *West Indian.* A plantation.

1793 *Ann. Reg., Nat. Hist.* 310 The usual method of forming a new piemento plantation (in Jamaica it is called a walk) is nothing more than to appropriate a piece of wood-land, [etc.]. **1901** *Westm. Gaz.* 13 June 2/3 Many sugar estates in the West Indies have of late years been converted into banana walks.

11. a. An enclosure in which poultry or other birds are allowed to run freely; a fowl-run. Also (cf. sense 13), a place to which fowls are sent in order that they may have more space to run about than can be allowed them where they are bred: in phrase *at walk.*

1538 ELYOT *Dict.*, *Viuarium*, a place, where wylde beastes, byrdes, or fyshes be kepte. It may be callyd as welle a ponde, as a parke, a counnyngar, a walke for byrdes. **1600** SURFLET *Country Farm* I. xvi. 107 Likewise you must not let them [geese] lay out of their walke or fold. **1880** JESSOPP *Arcady* i. (1887) 10 He eats the eggs for breakfast and the chickens for dinner, goes in for fancy breeds [of fowl], and runs up an ornamental 'walk' for them.

¶**b.** *a walk of snipes* (†*snites*). In the early lists of 'proper terms' the meaning is uncertain; later writers interpret it as a 'company term' (cf. 'congregation of plovers' in the same lists).

c **1450** *MS. Egerton* 1995 fol. 19 A Walke of Snytys. **1801** STRUTT *Sports & Past.* I. ii. 33. **1859** FOLKARD *Wild Fowler* i. 6 A walk of snipes.

c. The place in which a game-cock is kept. *cock of the walk* (*fig.*): a person whose supremacy in his own circle is undisputed (see COCK *sb.*¹ 7).

1615 T. SAVILE in J. J. Cartwright *Chapters Hist. Yorks.* (1872) 350, I have.. borowed my father's cocks... I go.. to get walkes for them. **1688** HOLME *Armoury* II. 251/2 The Cocks Walk is the place where he is bred, which usually is a place that no other Cock comes to. *c* **1770** T. FAIRFAX *Compl. Sportsm.* 4 Let the cock chickens go with their hens, till they begin to fight one with another; but then separate them into several walks, and that walk is the best, that is freest from the resort of others. **1823** *Grose's Dict. Vulgar T.* (ed. Egan), Cock, or Chief Cock of the Walk. The leading man in any Society or body; the best boxer in a village or district. **1823** 'JON BEE' *Dict. Turf*, *Walk* (in cocking)—the ground for keeping them. **1857** TROLLOPE *Barchester T.* xvii. heading, Who shall be cock of the walk? **1875** WHYTE MELVILLE *Katerfelto* i, Mr. Gale, to use his own phraseology, was accustomed to consider himself Cock of the Walk in every society he frequented.

12. Land, or a tract of land, used for the pasture of animals, esp. sheep. *Obs.* exc. in SHEEPWALK.

1549 LATIMER *1st Serm. bef. Edw. VI* (Arb.) 40 He had walke for a hundred shepe, and my mother mylked .xxx. kyne. **1573–80** TUSSER *Husb.* (1878) 62 The housing of cattel while winter doth hold.. spareth the pasture for walke of thy sheepe. *a* **1647** HABINGTON *Surv. Worcs.* (Worcs. Hist. Soc.) I. 254 A large walke for sauage beastes, but nowe more commodiously chaunged to the civill habitations of many gentellmen. **1808** JAMIESON, *Gang*,.. a pasture or walk for cattle.

13. A farm or cottage to which a young hound is sent in order to get accustomed to a variety of surroundings. Phrases, *at walk, to put to walk.*

1735 SOMERVILLE *Chase* IV. Argt., Of the litter of whelps ..of setting them out to their several walks. **1781** P. BECKFORD *Thoughts Hunting* v. 60 The distemper makes dreadful havoc with whelps at their walks. **1840** BLAINE *Encycl. Rur. Sports* IV. v. §3. 474 Hounds are usually named at the time they are sent out to their walks. **1845** YOUATT *Dog* ii. 36 There is a difference of opinion whether the [greyhound] whelp should be kept in the kennel and subjected to its regular discipline, or placed at walk in some farm-house. **1854** SURTEES *Handley Cr.* (1901) I. i. 4 The hounds were still kept at walks during the summer. **1856** 'STONEHENGE' *Brit. Sports* II. iv. §340 The Walks for the Young Hounds should be chosen in such situations as that they shall be accustomed to all sorts of company from children to horses. **1881** E. D. BRICKWOOD *Hound* in *Encycl. Brit.* XII. 315/2 When about ten or twelve weeks old [foxhound] puppies are sent out to walk.

14. The 'beat', round, or circuit of an itinerating official, workman, tradesman, beggar, etc.; the district within which a person is accustomed to practise his occupation without interference from a rival. Now usu., a postman's round.

1703 *Lond. Gaz.* No. 3910/4 Making use of the Company's Pavior of that Walk to Dig the same. **1705** tr. *Bosman's Guinea* 98 The last and most contemptible Office is that of Under-Fiscal, commonly called by us, Auditor, though in his Walks, Informer, as he really is no better. **1824** SCOTT *Redgauntlet* let. xii, The old man [the blind fiddler] struck the earth with his staff... 'The whoreson fisher rabble! They have brought another violer upon my walk!' **1825** HONE *Every-day Bk.* I. 571 Milk people of less profitable walks. **1848** *Sinks of Lond.* 97 Beat, a watchman's walk. **1851** MAYHEW *Lond. Labour* I. 435/2 'My father had a milk-walk', he said. *Ibid.* (1861) II. 8/2 He had thoughts at one time of trying to establish himself in a cats'-meat walk. **1908** *Chambers's Jrnl.* Jan. 102/2 On arriving at the office of delivery letters are at once stamped and sorted to the 'walks' of the postmen. **1977** *Times* 12 July 8/4 A complaint by a postwoman.. that she had been prevented from.. obtaining a particular postal 'walk'.

15. a. A distance or length of way to be walked; esp. such a distance as defined by a specified length of time spent in walking. (Often in phrases used *advb.*)

1562 J. HEYWOOD *Prov. & Epigr.* (1867) 79 Dwellyng a good walke from hir at the townes eende. *a* **1700** EVELYN *Diary* 15 Sept. 1685, Her house being a walke in the forest, within a little of a quarter mile from Bagshot towne. **1808** SCOTT in *Lockhart* I. i. 59, I agreed to go every morning to his house, which, being at the extremity of Prince's Street, New Town, was a walk of two miles. **1834** DICKENS *Sk. Boz, Boarding-ho.* i, 'A cheerful musical home in a select private family, residing within ten minutes' walk of'—everywhere. **1859** MRS. CARLYLE *Lett.* III. 4 Within a quarter of an hour's walk of it. **1875** RUSKIN *Morn. Florence* i. 5 A few hundred yards west of you, within ten minutes' walk, is the Baptistery of Florence. **1883** C. HOWARD *Roads Eng. & Wales* (ed. 3) 123 Beginning with a ½ *m.* walk out of the town, it is an almost continual ascent for 7 *m. Ibid.*, There is a mile run down to the railway, followed by a mile walk up into Stow.

b. *U.S.* (See quot.)

1901 P. FOUNTAIN *Deserts N. Amer.* vii. 118 The Indians had a singular custom in parting with their land. They sold it by the 'walk'. *Ibid.* 119 The duration of a walk was always a day in time, no matter what the distance.

16. A course or circuit, in the country or in a town, which may be chosen for walking.

1617 MORYSON *Itin.* I. 32 In the valley under this Mountaine of Goates, towards the City, is a pleasant walk, of the sweetnes called the Phylosophicall way. **1687** A. LOVELL tr. *Thevenot's Trav.* I. 28 Though the Countrey about Constantinople be not so delightful, nor so well peopled, as in France; yet it is not without pleasant Walks. **1693** DRYDEN *Ovid's Metam.* XIII. *Acis* etc. 51 A Promontory ..over-looks the Seas: On either side, below, the water flows: This airy walk the Giant Lover chose. **1757** MRS. P. L. POWYS *Passages fr. Diaries* (1899) 32, I.. thought myself most happy when I got into the grove, one of the sweetest walks in Matlock. **1786** COWPER *Let. to J. Hill* 9 Dec., Weston is one of the prettiest villages in England, and the walks about it at all seasons of the year delightful. **1850** J. MARTINEAU in J. Drummond *Life* (1902) I. 337 We can find walks that will vie with the Thiergarten even in this desolate country. **1860** TYNDALL *Glac.* I. xv. 100 This walk was full of instruction and delight.

III. Department of action.

17. A department of action; a particular branch or variety of some specified activity, e.g. trade, literature, science, etc.; a special line of work.

1759 FRANKLIN *Ess.* Wks. 1840 III. 145 Two thirds were to be a quorum in the upper walk of business, and one third in the lower. **1762** H. WALPOLE *Vertue's Anecd. Paint.* (1786) I. Pref. p. vii, It would be difficult.. to assign a physical reason, why a nation that produced Shakespear, should owe its glory in another walk of genius to Holbein and Vandyck. **1776** MICKLE tr. *Camoens' Lusiad* Dissert. 167/1 However superior Voltaire may be in the other walks of poetry, certain it is, no originality, no strength of colouring, shines in the Henriade. **1806** BERESFORD *Miseries Hum. Life* vi. Introd., As you appear to have a peculiar kindness for Inns, I will treat you with a choice sample of satisfactions in that walk of enjoyment. **1809** MALKIN *Gil Blas* VII. xiii. ¶9 He had.. taken upon himself to eclipse the best writers each in their own favourite walk. **1815** W. H. IRELAND *Scribbleomania* 147 Three sisters.. displayed much talent in pursuing this walk of literature. **1823** DE QUINCEY *Lett. Educ.* i. (1860) 12 He seeks to renew that elevated walk of study at all opportunities. **1833** CHALMERS *Const. Man* (1835) I. ii. 137 Each affection has its peculiar walk of enjoyment. **1838** PRESCOTT *Ferd. & Is.* I. xix. II. 293 A similar impulse was felt in the other walks of science. **1856** MASSON *Ess.* iv. 112 Butler had shewn the more original vein of talent in one particular walk. **1857** DICKENS *Dorrit* II. vi, 'Does Mr. Henry Gowan paint—ha—Portraits?' inquired Mr. Dorrit. Mr. Sparkler opined that he painted anything, if he could get the job. 'He has no particular walk?'.. 'No speciality?' said Mr. Dorrit. **1866** CRUMP *Banking* ii. 48 It is one of the most singular peculiarities in connection with men who have had much experience in other walks of trade, as merchants, &c. **1888** BRYCE *Amer. Commw.* xcviii. III. 370 When he [a lawyer] has attained real eminence he may confine himself entirely to the higher walks.

18. ***walk of life*** (more rarely ***walk in life***): **a.** A social grade, station of life, rank. Also ***walk of society***. **b.** A trade, profession, or occupation.

a. 1752 FIELDING *Covent-Garden Jrnl.* No. 56 ¶9 Both of these [*sc.* characters of humour] will be almost infinitely diversified according to the different.. natural dispositions of each individual; and according to their different walks in life. **1766** FORDYCE *Serm. Young Women* (1767) II. xiii. 247 Those who are placed in the higher walks of life. **1768** GOLDSM. *Goodn. Man* Pref., The term 'genteel comedy' was then unknown amongst us, and little more was desired by an audience than nature and humour, in whatever walks of life they were most conspicuous. **1800** *Asiatic Ann. Reg.* II. 97/2 The walk of life from which writers are to come should be duly weighed as they are in future, perhaps, to become directors, and probably legislators of India. **1832** *P. Egan's Bk. Sports* No. 5. 66/2 Nature, enriched by art, had rendered the late Mr. Emery a man not often to be met with in the walks of society. **1899** *Ch. Times* 13 Oct. 415/2 But according to the fashion of dress of to-day, it is not easy to tell from what walk in life women may come.

b. 1848 *Sinks of Lond.* 3 In what is termed the 'walks of life'. **1849** MACAULAY *Hist. Eng.* viii. II. 307 They found every walk of life towards which men of their habits could look for a subsistence closed against them with malignant care. **1861** BRIGHT *Sp. India* 19 Mar. *Sp.* (1868) I. 119 Of course there are men of genius in very objectionable walks of life. **1888** BRYCE *Amer. Commw.* xcviii. III. 378 The lawyers outnumber the persons belonging to other walks of life. **1912** *Sat. Rev.* 18 May 615/1 Emolument far greater than what was possible for them in any other walk of life.

19. (= *walk of life*, 18 a and b). **a.** Social grade or station; **b.** trade or profession. *rare.*

a. 1847 MILLER *First Impr. Eng.* xiii. 251, I met a funeral, the first I had seen in England. It was apparently that of a person in the middle walks. **1854** —— *Sch. & Schm.* (1858) 246 To those who move in the upper walks, the superiority in status of the village shop-keeper over the journeyman mason may not be very perceptible.

b. 1836 DICKENS *Sk. Boz, First of May*, Certain dark insinuations.. to the effect that children in the lower ranks of life were beginning to choose chimney-sweeping as their particular walk.

IV. 20. ***attrib.*** and ***Comb.*** (sense 1) as ***walk-companion***, ***shorts***; (sense 9 c), as ***walk making***, ***-side***; (sense 14) as ***walk-rotation***; (sense 12) as ***walk-land***; also **walk-clerk**, a banker's clerk whose duty it is to collect payment of cheques in a particular district; **walksman**, an officer charged with the care of a certain length of the banks of a river or canal; **walkway** *U.S.* = sense 9 c.

1890 H. PRICE *Lond. Bankers* 35 *note*, The following misfortune that befell a *walk-clerk. **1833** LAMB *Let. to Wordsw.* May, I am about to lose my old and only *walk-companion, whose mirthful spirits were the 'youth of our house'. **1797** A. YOUNG *Agric. Suffolk* 108 Ten loads.. an acre upon good land, a middling crop; but upon *walk-land (poor sheep-walks ploughed up) less. **1849** J. FORBES *Physic. Holiday* i. (1850) 1 They.. indulge in farming, gardening, tree-felling, *walk-making, or [etc.]. **1901** *Daily Chron.* 8 June 7/7 The alleged attempts of the [Post Office] department to reduce the value of Christmas boxes by the introduction of a system of '*walk-rotation'. **1965** *Punch* 17 Nov. 745 Then we equipped ourselves for our new surroundings [*sc.* Australia]. My wife.. insisted on polished cotton *walk shorts for a reluctant me. **1976** *National Observer* (U.S.) 6 Mar. 11/6 (Advt.), Authentic lederhosen style classic walk shorts for men and women. **1984** *Gainesville* (Florida) *Sun* 30 Mar. 8A (Advt.), Choose from white tennis shorts or solid and patterned walk shorts in polyester and cotton blends. **1893** STEVENSON *Catriona* iii, A pleasant gabled house set by the *walkside among some brave young woods. **1794** *Ann. Reg., Nat. Hist.* 311 For the care of the banks [of the New River], a *walksman is appointed to every two miles. **1903** *Daily Chron.* 17 Mar. 9/5 A 'walksman' in the service of the New River Company. **1911** H. S. HARRISON *Queed* xvi, He went down the broad steps of the Capitol, and out the winding white *walkway through the park.

†**walk**, *sb.*² *Sc. Obs.* [repr. OE. *wolc*, var. of *wolcn*, *wolcen*: see WELKIN.] A cloud or clouds.

1513 DOUGLAS *Æneis* III. viii. 155 The mone wes vndir walk, and gaif na lycht. *c* **1560** ROLLAND *Seven Sages* 73 Sa as thir twa togidder was at talk, The Mone wox dark, and hid was vnder walk.

walk (wɔːk), *v.*¹ Pa. t. and pa. pple. **walked** (wɔːkt). Forms: *Inf.* and *pres. stem*: 1 **wealcan**, **wealcian**, 2, 3 **walki-en**, 4 **walc**, 2–7 **walke**, 6 **walck(e**, *Sc.* **valk**, 8–9 *Sc.* **wauk**, 4– **walk**. *Pa. t.* α. *strong* 1 **wéolc**, 3–5 **welk(e**, 5 **walke**, **wilke**; β. *weak* 1 **wealcede**, 4 **welkide**, **walkit**, 5 **walkude**, **walkyd**, 6 **walckt(e**, (6 *Sc.* **valkit**), 4– **walked**. *Pa. pple.* α. *strong* 3 **i-walken**, **walke**; β. *weak* 5 **walkude**, 3– **walked**. [OE. had two forms: (1) *wealcan* redupl. str. vb. (pa. t. *wéolc*, pa. pple. *ȝewealcen*), to roll, toss (trans. and intr.); (2) *wealcian* weak vb., occurring only twice, in the senses 'to muffle up' (gl. *obvolvere*), to curl (hair: gl. *calamistrare*). One or both of these vbs. may have had also the sense 'to full (cloth)': see WALK *v.*² The corresponding forms in the other Teut. langs. are: OHG. *walchan* str. vb., recorded only in pa. pple. *giwalchen*, *firwalchen*, felted, matted (said of hair: gl. *concretus*); MHG. *walken* (pa. t. *wielc*, pa. pple. *walken*; later conjugated weak), to knead, to roll (paste) into balls in the palms of the hands; *rarely*, to move about (trans. and intr.), to turn into something; *usually*, to full (cloth), whence to cudgel, drub; mod.G. *walken* wk. vb., to full, to cudgel; (M)LG., (M)Du. *walken* wk. vb., to full, to work (felt), to cudgel; ON. *valka* (Icel. *válka*, mod. *volka*) wk. vb., to drag about, to torment, refl. to wallow; MSw. *valka* wk. vb., to roll (a morsel) about in the mouth, Norw. *valka* wk. vb. to crumple in the hand, MDa. *valke* wk. vb. to torment; the mod.Sw. *valka*, Da. *valke* (wk.), to full, prob. take their sense from LG.

The strong pa. t. survived into the 15th c.; the weak conjugation, recorded from the 13th c. onwards, may perh. not be a survival of the rare OE. *wealcian* but an instance of the frequent change of inflexion from strong to weak. The corresponding weak vb. in continental Teut. is prob. to be explained in this way.

It is remarkable that to the end of the OE. period the sense of the str. vb. was 'to roll', and that from the beginning of the ME. period it was 'to move about, travel'. The explanation of this apparently sudden change may be that the ME. sense had arisen in OE. as a colloquial (perhaps jocular) use, and that when the literary tradition was interrupted after the Conquest, and people wrote as they spoke, the original meaning of the verb was no longer current.

The OTeut. root **walk-* has no certain affinities in any other branch of the Indogermanic family; phonologically the Skr. *valg-* to leap, dance, and the L. *valgus* bow-legged, might be related, but there is no clear similarity of meaning.]

†**I. 1.** *intr.* **a.** In OE. (str. vb.). Of the waves: To roll, toss. **b.** In early ME. of persons: To toss about restlessly. *Obs.*

In OE. also *trans.* (str. vb.) to turn over, roll; also *fig.* to turn over in one's mind, consider; (wk. verb) to curl (hair); to press together (cf. WALK *v.*²). For examples see Bosworth-Toller.

a **1100** *Aldh. Glosses* in Napier *OE. Gl.* i. 2474 *Feruentis oceani*, wealcendre sæ. *a* **1200** *Moral Ode* 240 Ho [*sc.* souls in hell] secheð reste þer nis nan.. walkeð weri up and dun, se water deþ mid winde. ? *a* **1200** *Body & Soul* (Phillips) 5 He walkeþ & wendeþ & woneþ.. þes, he sæiþ on his bedde, wome þæt ic libbe, þæt æffre [etc.]. **1398** W. PARIS *Cristine* (Horstm.) 394 Fyve daies.. Sche welkide þerin [an oven] to & froo. *c* **1400** *Pety Job* 329 in *26 Pol. Poems* 131 Allas, I walke in a lake Of dedly synne that doth me tene.

II. *intr.* To journey, move about, esp. on foot.

†**2.** To go from place to place; to journey, wander. Also with cogn. obj., to go (one's way).

In quot. *a* 1000 the sense appears to be 'to pass over'; if so, the gloss is the only example within the OE. period of any anticipation of the ME. development of the meaning of the word; but it may be significant that the reference is to motion on the sea.

a **1000** *Prudentius Glosses* in *Germania* XI. 400 *Emensus*, ȝewealcon ['*Emensus et multum freti*' Prud. *Peristeph.* v. 471]. *c* **1200** *Trin. Coll. Hom.* 51 Þat israelisshe folc was walkende toward ierusalem on swinche and on drede and on wanrede. *c* **1205** LAY. 112 Heuede Eneas þe duc mid his driht folcke widen iwalken. *c* **1250** *Meid. Maregrete* xlix, Muchel ic habbe iwalken bi water ant bi londe. *a* **1300** *Cursor M.* 6359 Queder-sum he welk her or þare, Þis wandes euer he wit him bare. *Ibid.* 21685 Quen þe nedders.. þe folk stanged of israel, Quen þai welk in þe wilderness. **13..** *Ibid.* 22063 (Gött.) Þe angel.. in þe pitt [þe deuil] sperd fast.. for to be laised at þe last quen þat thousand ȝere war past, to walk his wai [*Edinb. MS.* to walc his waiis forthe] fra þat quile. **1340–70** *Alex. & Dind.* 498 Vs is likful and lef in landus to walke, þere won walleþ of water in þe welle-springus. **1377** LANGL. *P. Pl.* B. VIII. 14 Þei ben men on þis molde þat moste wyde walken. *c* **1400** *Rule St. Benet* 1893 Þai þat sal walk bi way, or wirk, And may not cum to haly kirk,.. Þeir seruyse sal þai not for-gete. **1513** DOUGLAS *Æneis* v. x. 29 And for ilk menȝe A capitane walkis rewland all his rowt.

3. Of things.

†**a.** Of time: To pass, elapse. *Obs.*

c **1250** *Gen. & Ex.* 568 An hundred winter.. welken or it was ended wel.

†**b.** Of reports, fame, also of letters, money: To circulate, pass from one to another; also with *about*. Also said of the person whose fame is spread abroad. *Obs.*

13.. *Gaw. & Gr. Knt.* 1521 Your worde & your worchip walkez ay quere. *a* **1352** MINOT *Poems* viii. 29 Þe word of him walkes ful wide. **1387** T. USK *Test. Love* I. vii. (Sk.) 95 Loke now what people has thou served; whiche of them al in tyme of thyne exile ever the refresshed, by the value of the leste coyned plate that walketh in mony? *c* **1470** HENRY *Wallace* III. 252 The worde of him walkit baith fer and ner. **1533** MORE *Let. to Cromwell* Wks. 1422/1 An vnknowen heretike which hath sent ouer a worke that walketh in ouer many mens handes named the Souper of the lord. **1549** LATIMER *4th Serm bef. Edw. VI* (Arb.) 111 Ther was brybes walking, money makynge, makynge of handes. *a* **1566** R. EDWARDS *Damon & P.* (facs.) B iv, And I vp and downe, Go seekyng to learne what Newes here are walkyng. **1583** STUBBES *Anat. Abus.* II. 13 If any man that hath freends and money.. chance to haue committed neuer so.. flagicious a deed,.. then letters walke, freends bestir them, and mony carrieth all away. **1601** B. JONSON *Poetaster* III. v. 77 For he shall weepe, and walke with euery tongue Throughout the citie, infamously song. *a* **1626** BACON *War with Spain* (1629) 42 A wonderfull erroneous obseruation that walketh about. **1640** tr. *Verdere's Rom. of Rom.* II. 120 This Prince.. never left praying and importuning; every day she had a Page, letters were continually walking [Fr. *les lettres marchoient à toutes heures*]. **1671** MILTON *Samson* 1089, I.. now am come to see of whom such noise Hath walk'd about. **1687** R. L'ESTRANGE *Answ. Dissenter* 22 There may be Mony Walking on the One Side as well as on the Other.

†**c.** Of crime, vice, or virtue: To be rife, spread abroad. *Obs.*

1377 LANGL. *P. Pl.* B. VII. 79 In hym þat taketh is þe treccherye, if any tresoun wawe [*read* walke (*with* 5 *MSS.*)]. **1387** TREVISA *Higden* (Rolls) II. 169 Þese men.. beeþ i-woned to haue the victorie.. in euerich fiȝt wher no treson is walkynge [L. *ubi fraus abfuerit*]. *c* **1450** in Kingsford *Chron. Lond.* (1905) 140 Ther whas so moch treson walkyng that men wist not what to do. **1567** *Gude & Godlie B.* (S.T.S.) 101 Thair violence and wrang walkis full wyde. **1573** L. LLOYD *Pilgr. Princes* 53 Then luste knew no way to the pallace of Cæsars, then abstinence walked in the market place, then all Rome was chast. **1626** BRETON *Pasquils Mad-cap* (Grosart) 8/2 Wealth is a witch that hath a wicked charme, That in the mindes of wicked men doth walke.

†**d.** Of drink, etc.: To be handed round, pass, circulate. *Obs.*

1555 R. SMITH in Foxe *A. & M.* (1563) 1254/1 My Lorde mayre being set with the bishop and one of the shriues, wine was walking on euery syde, I standing before them as an outcast. **1567** HARMAN *Caveat* (Shaks. Soc.) 32 How the pottes walke about! their talking tounges talke at large. **1594** GREENE & LODGE *Looking Gl.* 1858 G.'s Wks. 1905 I. 201 Frolicke, my Lord[s]; let all the standerds walke; Ply it till euery man hath tane his load. **1596** RALEGH *Guiana* 85 Wee found them all as drunke as beggers, and the pottes walking from one to another without rest. **1622** R. HAWKINS *Voy. S. Sea* (1847) 216 The pott continually walking, infused desperate and foolish hardinesse in many. **1691** WOOD *Ath. Oxon.* II. 157 This Hicks.. was also Author.. of other little trivial matters meerly to get bread, and make the pot walk.

†**e.** Of various material things, e.g. a pen, a weapon, an instrument, a heavenly body: To move, be in motion. Of leaves: To come out. *Obs.*

a **1400** *Stockh. Med. MS.* ii. 753 in *Anglia* XVIII. 325 At euery knot ij lewys owt walke. *a* **1530** J. HEYWOOD *Wether* (1903) 686 Whan the wynde doth blow the uttermost Our wyndmylles walk a-mayne in every cost. **1549** LATIMER *Ploughers* (Arb.) 25 And then bothe ploughes not walkyng, nothyng shoulde be in the common weale but honger. **1550** —— *Serm. Stamford* (1562) 103, I hearde a penne walkynge in the chimney behynde the cloth. They hadde appoynted one there to wryte al myne aunsweres. **1565** J. HALL *Crt. Vertue* 150 The great Beare.. Whych wyth the small Beare euermore Doth walke the pole about. **1575** GASCOIGNE *Making of Verse* §1, I would.. finde some supernaturall cause whereby my penne might walke in the superlatiue degree. **1580** BLUNDEVIL *Curing Horses Dis.* xi. 6 Of the Feuer which commeth of rawe digestion... The Horse will blowe at the nose.. you shall see his flankes walke and his backe to beate. **1590** SPENSER *F.Q.* I. vii. 45 From euery coast that heauen walks about, Haue thither come the noble Martiall crew. **1622** DRAYTON *Poly-olb.* xxii. 663 Now English Bowes, and Bills, and Battle-axes walke, Death vp and downe the field in gastly sort doth stalke. **1686** tr. *Chardin's Trav. Persia* 115 They did not like working, so that the Cudgel was forc'd to walk now and then to quick'n their Laziness. **1815** SCOTT *Guy M.* xxiv, [They] got me down, and knevelled me sair aneuch, or I could gar my whip walk about their lugs.

†**f.** Of a vehicle: To make regular journeys.

c **1450** *Godstow Reg.* 671, ij. cartis the which they had every day walkyng to busshyng in his wode of Shottore.

†**g.** Of the tongue, the jaws: To move briskly.

1550 CROWLEY *Epigr.* 908 No man shal fynde a tyme to speake, so faste theyr tonges shal walke. **1590** SPENSER *F.Q.* II. iv. 5 And, ever as she went, her toung did walke In foule reproch and termes of vile despight. **1609** DEKKER *Guls Horne-bk.* v. 24 It will adde much to your fame to let your tongue walke faster then your teeth. **1609** —— *Lanth. & Candle-light* x. Wks. (Grosart) III. 277 If then.. his chappes begin to walke as if he were chewing downe a Horse-loafe. **1673** KIRKMAN *Unlucky Citizen* 231 He could make but little defence with his hands; but his tongue walked, he stormed, raged and threatened.

h. *Naut.* Of a ship: To make progress.

1884 'H. COLLINGWOOD' *Under Meteor Flag* 159 Seeing us walking ahead, he hailed us to keep back in line with him. **1891** W. C. RUSSELL *Marriage at Sea* iii, If.. it lies in my power to keep this here Spitfire [the ship's name] awalking.

†**i.** *fig.* (*a*) ? To be successful. (*b*) To be a substitute, 'pass', 'go' *for*. *Obs.*

(*a*) *a* **1553** UDALL *Royster D.* III. iii. (Arb.) 48, I doubt not but this geare shall on my side walke.

(*b*) **1557** PHAER *Æneid* v. (1558) O iv, One only man shall be, whome lost in depe seas he shall seke, One poll shall walke for all [L. *unum pro multis dabitur caput*]. **1627** W. SCLATER *Exp. 2 Thess.* (1629) 299 That now, writtes walk for words.

†**4. a.** To go about in public, live, move (in a place or region). Also of animals: To range, be found (in a place). *Obs.*

a **1300** *Cursor M.* 17800 In mi cite of aramathi Þar ar þai [*sc.* the risen dead] walkand witerli. **13..** *Propr. Sanct.* (Vernon MS.) in *Archiv Stud. neu. Spr.* LXXXI. 302/310 Þer is a ffisch.. Þat in þe see is walkynge; Euere he slumbreþ and eke slepeþ. *c* **1330** R. BRUNNE *Chron. Wace* (Rolls) 4734 Þys feste day.. Were offred.. þre þousand hyndes, Wylde walkande by wode lyndes. *a* **1350** *S. Lucy* 121 in Horstm. *Altengl. Leg.* (1881) 18 Whils he welk in þis werld here, He said to his appostels in-fere. —— *S. Thomas* 2 (ibid. 19) Saint Thomas, þe apostill trew, Þat welk in werld here with Jhesu. **1456** SIR G. HAYE *Law Arms* (S.T.S.) 244 Men suld nocht lichtly traist in na sauf conditis, and namely in the warld that walkis now. *c* **1470** HENRY *Wallace* IV. 329 He sawe full feill bestis abide, Off wylde and tayme walkand haboundandlye. **1513** MORE *Rich. III*, Wks. 40/1 Robbers and riuers walking at libertie vncorrected. **1559** BP. SCOT in Strype *Ann. Ref.* (1709) I. App. x. 32 Upon the which Place St. Augustine wryteth thus, Christe tooke Fleshe of the blessed Virgin his Mother, and in the same he did walke. [**1856** AYTOUN *Bothwell* I. v, And yet—he bandies texts with Knox, And walks a pious man!]

†**b.** To be, live *in* a cerain condition. *Obs.*

a **1300** *Cursor M.* 755 Adam ȝode walkand in þat welth þat halden was in micul elth. **1493** *Will E. Bonde* (Somerset Ho.), I Edward Bonde in hole mynde walking & some what syke.

†**c.** To busy oneself, be active *about* something. *Obs.* (Cf. WAKE *v.* 4 b.)

a **1300** *Cursor M.* 7530 Dauid..toke bot a staf and a sling þat he was wont to bere in hand Abute his flocke o scep walcand. *c* **1450** *Mirk's Festial* 84 And þi[l]ke folke þat han ben bysy erly and late to walke aboute worldely good, now schuld be bysy, alsoo, to vyset pore and seke.

d. With complementary adj. or phrase: = GO *v.* 6. Now *rare* or *obs.*

1604 JAS. I *Counterbl. Tobacco* (Arb.) 100 Why doe we not as well imitate them [the Indians] in walking naked as they doe? *a* **1625** FLETCHER *Custom Country* II. (1647) 8/1 How long might I have walkt without a cloake, Before I should have met with such a fortune?

5. a. To travel or move about on foot. Also with advs. *about, on,* etc.

to walk about: also *spec.* of an Aboriginal: cf. WALKABOUT 1. ***to walk with*** (a stick): to use it as a partial support in walking. ***to walk on crutches***: to support oneself by crutches in walking.

a **1300** *K. Horn* 953 Ich habbe walke [*other texts* walked] wide Bi þe se side; Nis he nowar ifunde. *a* **1300** *Cursor M.* 17288 + 127 þese thre maries come þiderward, for drede þai stynted oft For ferd of þe Jews, and sithen welk ful soft. *c* **1403** LYDG. *Temple of Glas* 550, I saugh a man, þat welke al solitarie. *a* **1535** *Frere & Boy* (Ritson) 63 An olde man came hym tyll, Walkynge by the waye. **1557** NORTH *Guevara's Diall Pr.* III. xlii. (1568) 71 Thow walkest by the thornes: and wylt not that thy gown bee torne. **1697** COLLIER *Ess.* II. (1703) 99 To walk always upon crutches, is the way to lose the use of our limbs. **1835** DICKENS *Sk. Boz, Miss Evans & Eagle,* They all walked on together, talking, and laughing. **1836** *Ibid., Vauxhall-Gardens,* We walked about, and met with a disappointment at every turn. **1902** 'VIOLET JACOB' *Sheep-Stealers* viii, He carried a stick, but he did not use it to walk with. **1907** 'C. E. CRADDOCK' *Windfall* iv. 75 Why, I'll feel so old whenst I'm twenty that I reckon I'll hev ter walk with a stick by then. **1908** E. J. BANFIELD *Confessions of Beachcomber* II. i. 265 This for Johnny Tritton, before alonga Cooktown; now walk about somewhere down here. Might be catch 'em alonga mainland.

†**b.** with *refl. pron.*

c **1450** *Godstow Reg.* 16, I wil now me walke from sege to sege, And pray to help me now euery saynt. **1509** HAWES *Past. Pleas.* xxvii. (1845) 119 As I went walkyng my selfe to and fro, Full sodaynly Venus wrought me such wo.

¶**c.** conjugated with *to be*. Also *pa. pple.* in intr. sense.

1770 C. JENNER *Placid Man* VI. v. II. 202 Mrs. Stapleton inquired after Lady Clayton; Miss Clayton said she was walked out. **1818** SCOTT *Br. Lamm.* xxxii, I shall never forget how frightened I was when I took him for the picture of old Sir Malise walked out of the canvass.

d. with cognate obj.; also, with advb. accusative of distance. Phrase, ***to walk a turn***, to walk once up and once down.

c **1460** *Towneley Myst.* xxviii. 261 With lucas and with cleophas he welke a day Iurnee. **1548** [see f]. **1610** SHAKS. *Temp.* IV. i. 162 A turne or two Ile walke To still my beating minde. **1653** HOLCROFT *Procopius, Pers. Wars* I. 6 They prayed the King to walk some turns with Arsaces in their presence, to be witnesses of what passed. **1753** JANE COLLIER *Art Torment.* II. iv. 177 Strange disorders in her head, for which she is advised to walk long walks. **1819** SCOTT *Ivanhoe* xxxiv, They walked a turn through the hall. **1833** DICKENS *Sk. Boz, Mr. Minns,* I've walked all the way from Stamford-hill this morning. **1836** *Ibid., Criminal Courts,* They walked a few paces, and paused. **1895** J. WINSOR *Mississ. Basin* 239 A scandalous act of Thomas Penn some years back (1737) had asserted inordinate claims by virtue of what was known as the 'Walking Purchase'. The extent of the concession was dependent on the distance a man could walk in a day and a half by an honest tramp.
Proverb. **1605** ERONDELLE *Fr. Gard.* M 6 b, After Dinner sit a while: After Supper walke a mile.

e. In express or implied contrast with *ride*. Also colloq. *to walk it.*

1668 PEPYS *Diary* 16 Sept., Walking it to the Temple; and in my way observe that the Stockes are now pulled quite down. **1712** STEELE *Spectator* No. 454 ¶6 When I resolved to walk it out of Cheapness. **1766** GOLDSM. *Vicar W.* x, I therefore walked back by the horse-way. **1805** T. HOLCROFT *Bryan Perdue* III. 185, I was obliged to walk the journey. **1853** DICKENS *Bleak Ho.* vi, We alighted and walked up all the hills. **1883** C. HOWARD *Roads Eng. & Wales* (ed. 3) 84 A dangerous descent, best walked down into Banwell. *Ibid.* 139 A long stiff ascent..which most tourists will walk up. **1915** *Blackw. Mag.* Apr. 466 He had ridden and I had walked before him.

f. More explicitly, ***to walk on foot***, also (now rarely) ***afoot***. †Also *transf.* of a stream: To flow slowly (*obs.*).

1362 LANGL. *P. Pl.* A. VI. 1 (MS. H.) Now riden þis folk & walken on fote to seche þat seint in selcouþe londis. *c* **1375** *Cursor M.* 18548 (Fairf.) þa iewes sagh þis ilk man..a pon þe see wiþ-outen wete dry to walke a-pon his fete [*Cott.* and *Gött.* Gangand als apon a strete]. **1548** UDALL, etc. *Erasm. Par. John* xii. 12–16 Where as before he was wunte to walke his iourneyes on foote. **1565** STAPLETON tr. *Bede's Hist. Ch. Eng.* 114 The said..bishop Chadde was wonte alwaies to..doo the worke of the ghospell more walking a fote wher he went, than on horsebacke. **1621** H. KING *Serm.* 37 But Kings haue walkt afoote whilest the Pope hath rode. **1747** W. HORSLEY *Fool* (1748) II. 252 When it [the blood] walks a Foot, in an even, regular Peace, every Faculty coincides. **1749** FIELDING *Tom Jones* IX. vi, How comes it..that such a great Gentleman walks about the Country afoot? *a* **1774** GOLDSM. *Hist. Greece* II. 221 The King walked on foot among the infantry. **1810** S. GREEN *Reformist* II. 37 When he quitted Ellingford, he resolved always to walk on foot. **1849** MACAULAY *Hist. Eng.* v. I. 561 The prisoner..walked on foot, bareheaded, up the whole length of that stately street which..leads from Holyrood House to the Castle.

g. With advs. *in, up,* †*forth,* and const. *into,* the use of this vb. instead of the indefinite *come* or *go* sometimes implies an additional notion of absence of pausing or hesitation. So, 'in the ceremonious language of invitation' (J.), ***walk in*** = 'come in' (now chiefly in rustic use). Similarly in the showman's 'Walk up! walk up!' when the show is on a raised platform. ***to walk in*** (sometimes const. *on*; cf. sense 13 c below): *spec.* to arrive unexpectedly; to enter premises, etc., with unwonted ease; to succeed against all expectations.

In general, the tendency to substitute 'come' or 'go' for this verb has become much more prevalent since the 16–17th c.

a **1300** *Cursor M.* 19737 Paulus þan welk forth her and þar, And spelled fast wit-vten spar. **1450** *Paston Lett.* I. 111 Than we welk forthe, and desyryd an answer of hem. **1598** SHAKS. *Merry W.* I. i. 291, I pray you Sir walke in. **1614** J. COOKE *Greene's Tu Quoque* B 2, Pre thee, walke in, what you bargaine for, Ile discharge. **1696** VANBRUGH *Relapse* IV. v, If your Lordship please to walk in, we'll help you to some Brown Sugar-Candy. **1797** JANE AUSTEN *Sense & Sensib.* xxx, Mrs. Jennings..opened the door and walked in with a look of real concern. **1804** J. TOBIN *Honey Moon* I. i. (1805) 12 Of as tried a courage As ever walk'd up to the roaring throats Of a deep-rang'd artillery. **1834** MARY HOWITT *Spider & Fly* 1 'Will you walk into my parlour?' said the Spider to the Fly. **1836** DICKENS *Sk. Boz, Tuggs's at Ramsgate,* 'Won't you walk in, sir?' said the servant. **1838** —— *Nickleby* iii, The voice replied that the gentleman was to walk up. **1840** —— *Old C. Shop* xlviii, Close here, sir, if you please to walk this way. **1847** HELPS *Friends in C.* I. viii. 149 Men walk up composedly to the most perilous enterprises. **1867** H. LATHAM *Black & White* Pref. p. vi, Every American's house cannot be walked into, like the President's; but [etc.]. **1907** J. H. PATTERSON *Man-Eaters of Tsavo* ix. 101 Rather foolishly, I at once scrambled down from the tree and walked up towards him [the lion]. **1909** in I. G. Sieveking *Francis W. Newman* vi. 126 The door opened and the Professor walked in. **1930** N. COWARD *Private Lives* II. 53 What shall we do if they suddenly walk in on us? **1975** COWIE & MACKIN *Oxf. Dict. Current Idiomatic Eng.* I. 356/2 The security is so bad here that anyone could simply walk in and take what he wanted. **1977** P. HILL *Fanatics* 125 If the Christian Democrats put enough candidates up at the next election they'll walk in. **1978** M. DUKE *Death of Dandy Dinmont* iv. 39, I couldn't think of anything else to do. I was almost relieved when Hamilton walked in on me.

h. To move about or go from place to place on foot for the sake of exercise, pleasure, or pastime; to take a walk or walks. †Also with *abroad.* ***to walk out***: of a soldier off duty, to go into town on pass.

a **1300** *Cursor M.* 4778 Jacob yode walcand be þe nile. **1362** LANG. *P. Pl.* A. IX. 54 And as I wente bi a wode walkyng myn one, Blisse of þe Briddes made me to Abyde. *c* **1381** CHAUCER *Parl. Foules* 297 Forth welk I tho mi seluyn to solace. *c* **1400** *Parce Mihi* 1 in *26 Pol. Poems* 143 By a forest syde, walkyng as I went, Disporte to take. **1569** SPENSER *Vis. Petrarch* 73 On hearbs and flowres she walked pensiuely. **1573–80** TUSSER *Husb.* (1878) 42 Saue sawe dust, and brick dust, and ashes as fine, for alley to walke in, with neighbour of thine. **1617** S. H. *Engl. Mans Doctor* II. (1624) 41 When you arise in the morning..remember to powre foorth your prayers vnto God..Then walke ye gently. *a* **1626** BACON *Med. Rem.* Baconiana (1679) 161 Stir up the Pouder when you drink, and walk upon it. **1640** tr. *Verdere's Rom. of Rom.* II. 120 Carinda said he, being gone out to walk in the garden. **1653** W. RAMESEY *Astrol. Restored* 192 And as touching walking abroad, some of the Ancients have been large. **1685** *Caldwell Papers* (Maitl. Club) I. 153 [At Spa] There is a pleasant garden of the Capuciners, where drinkers of the waters generallie walk. **1718** LADY M. W. MONTAGU *Let. to C'tess Mar* 10 Mar., She asked me to walk in her garden. **1745** ELIZA HAYWOOD *Female Spect.* XII. (1748) II. 309 That monarch being walking in the Mall one day, was infinitely charmed with the beauty of a young lady who happened to be there. **1830** *Portugal; or Yng. Travellers* 239 As he spoke, Mr. Grey rose from table and invited them to walk. **1867** AUGUSTA WILSON *Vashti* xxi, 'Stay, Salome! Where are you going?' 'To walk.' **1911** [implied in *walking-out order* s.v. WALKING *vbl. sb.* 1 b]. **1955** *Times* 27 July 5/1 In Western Command..young soldiers are now forbidden to 'walk out' when off duty in plain clothes of unorthodox pattern.

†**i.** *transf.* To take air and exercise (on horseback). *Obs.*

1541 WYATT *Def.* in H. Walpole *Misc. Antiq.* II. (1772) 49 There be maynie men in the towne and most of them gentlemen, w[ch] walke upon there horses, and here and there tawlke with those ladies.

j. ***to walk*** (***out***) ***with, to walk together***: in rustic use said of a young man and young woman 'keeping company' with a view to marriage.

1827 A. MOORE *Let.* in N. E. Eliason *Tarheel Talk* (1956) 303 [He] has requested to let him have the supreme pleasure of walking out with her. I fear the poor little fellow is pretty far gone, if I may judge from the frequency of his visits. **1849** DICKENS *Dav. Copp.* (1850) v. 47 No sweethearts, I b'lieve?..No person walks with her. **1876** MISS YONGE *Womankind* xxiii. 195 There is a semi-engaged state of 'walking' with a man on trial. **1886** HARDY *Mayor Casterbr.* xx, She..no longer said of young men and women that they 'walked together' but that they were 'engaged'. **1896** HOUSMAN *Shropsh. Lad* xxv, Rose Harland on her Sundays out Walked with the better man. *Ibid.,* When Rose and I walk out together. **1902** W. W. JACOBS *Lady of Barge* (1908) 5 A certain young woman I'm walking out with. **1905** JEROME *Idle Ideas* xx,'You are not engaged, I 'ope?' 'Walking out, ma'am, do you mean?' says Emma. **1906** *Times* 26 Nov. 3/6 Her sister knew him in the way of business, but had never walked out with him.

†**k.** Followed by *a* (= *on*) and vbl. sb.: = GO *v.* 32 e. *Obs.*

1533 MORE *Answ. Poysoned Bk.* Wks. 1076/2 Like as if a ryght great man woulde wantonly walke a mumming, and disguise hymself.

l. In various phrases. †***to walk at rovers***: to have no settled abode (cf. ROVER[1] 2). ***to walk Spanish***: see SPANISH C. ***to walk upon air***: to be in an exultant state of mind. †***to walk will of one's way*** (*Sc.*): to go astray, lose oneself.

c **1475** *Rauf Coilȝear* 73 Or ony vther gude fallow that I heir fand Walkand will of his way. *Ibid.* 106 In wickit wedderis and weit walkand full will. **1528** MORE *Dial. Heresyes* III. Wks. 228/1 The order is rebuked by priestes begging and lewde liuing, which either is fayne to walke at rouers and liue upon trentalles or worse or els [etc.]. **1887** STEVENSON *Mem. & Portr.* iv. 72, I went home that morning walking upon air.

m. *Racing.* Of a jockey: To weigh (so much) when going on foot.

1856 'DRUID' *Post & Paddock* v. 83 He was about 5 ft. 5 in. in height, walked about 9 st. 5 lbs. in the winter months, and could ride, if required for a great race, 7 st. 12 lbs. to the last.

n. quasi-*trans.* with complementary adj., adv., or phrase. ***to walk off***, to get rid of (the effects of liquor, an ailment) by walking exercise. Also in nonce-uses: ***to walk down***, to counteract (poison) by walking; to exhaust (a companion) by walking; ***to walk out a sermon***, to continue walking till it has ended; ***to walk*** (a message or the like) ***through***, to take it in person.

1669 PEPYS *Diary* 2 May, Thence with them to White Hall, and there walked out the sermon with one or other. **1741** RICHARDSON *Pamela* III. xxxvii. 372 'I fear you have sprain'd your Foot—Shall I help you to a Chair?' 'No, no, Sir, I shall walk it off, if I hold by you.' **1823** SCOTT *Quentin D.* iii, I have walked my clothes dry, or nearly so. **1860** SALA *Baddington Peerage* I. vii. 131 Perhaps he wished to walk off the fumes of the punch and tobacco. **1872** BLACK *Adv. Phaeton* xix, He would have liked..to have..walked himself dead with fatigue. **1884** *Harper's Mag.* Jan. 302/2 A walker who gives promise of great things if he doesn't walk his short legs off within the next two or three years. **1884** TENNYSON *Cup* II. 260, I pray you lift me And make me walk awhile. I have heard these poisons May be walk'd down. **1894** FRANCES P. COBBE *Life* I. 341, I do believe I could walk down anybody and perhaps talk down anybody too! **1981** C. POTOK *Bk. of Lights* (1982) v. 144 'How did the major get that memo so quickly, Roger?' 'I walked it through to his desk.'

o. *Naut.* To turn (the capstan) by walking round it; to haul by walking round the capstan or by walking away with a rope. Also, to haul (a balloon) by walking.

1836 MARRYAT *Pirate* viii, The men..walked the anchor up to the bows. **1882** NARES *Seamanship* (ed. 6) 118 Walk the yard up to the derrick head with the hawser. *Ibid.* 203 Walk the anchor up the bow. *Ibid.* 172 Walk back the capstan. **1933** *Sun* (Baltimore) 27 Oct. 7/2 The..passengers disembarked..before the huge dirigible was 'walked' into the hangar. **1938** *Times* 7 Sept. 9/1 He watched a crew 'walk' a balloon out of a shed and connect it to a winch for hoisting.

p. ***to walk*** (***all***) ***over*** —— (*fig.*): to treat (a person) with contempt; also, to defeat (an opponent) decisively. *slang.*

1851 MRS. STOWE in *National Era* 25 Sept. 1/5 St. Clare wouldn't raise his hand if every one of them walked over him. **1884** 'MARK TWAIN' *Huck. Finn* xxii. 219 In the North he lets anybody walk over him that wants to, and goes home and prays for a humble spirit to bear it. **1909** R. E. KNOWLES *Attic Guest* viii. 105 They won't let a pack of negroes walk all over 'em. **1951** N. MITFORD *Blessing* I. vi. 65 A woman who lets her husband do exactly as he likes..lets him walk over her, in fact, would never lose him. **1976** E. DUNPHY *Only a Game?* i. 34 We played QPR in a public practice game at our place today. And won easily. We walked all over them.

q. *Baseball.* Of a batter: to secure a base on balls. Cf. WALK *sb.*[1] 1 e.

1867 *Ball Players' Chron.* 14 Nov. 2/4 Goodrich walked to the first on called balls. **1895** *N.Y. Press* 5 July 6/1 The champions harvested a pair of tallies in the second inning. Clarke did not get them over for Kelly, and Joe 'walked'. **1948** *Chicago Tribune* 7 Mar. II. 1/4 Baker walked, filling the bases. **1979** *Arizona Daily Star* 5 Aug. C-2/5 Alfredo Griffin singled and Bob Bailor walked to start the eighth-inning burst against Rich Wortham, 11–11.

r. ***to walk on***: (of a theatrical performer) to go on stage with few if any lines to say.

1893 H. G. MCCLELLAND *Jack & Beanstalk* 35 She used to walk on in the comic scenes. **1913** *Confessions of Dancing Girl* vii. 127, I obtained an engagement to 'walk on' in a musical comedy... I had no lines and no part. **1920** [see SUPER *v.* 1]. **1959** P. BULL *I know Face* i. 17 He had engaged a lot of art school students to what's known as 'walk-on' in the production.

s. ***walk good*** (*imp.*): farewell, good luck. *Caribbean.*

1929 M. W. BECKWITH *Black Roadways* xiii. 199 'Walk good, me love,' says one to another setting out on a journey. **1953** R. MAIS *Hills were Joyful Together* II. i. 147 You going further, walk good then; walk good, hear? **1979** J. BERRY *Fractured Circles* 58 Walk good, Leela, chile.

t. ***to walk away from*** ——: to leave the scene of (an accident or the like) on one's feet, instead of being carried on a stretcher. Cf. *walking wounded* s.v. WALKING *ppl. a.* 3 d. Also *transf.*

1956 W. A. HEFLIN *U.S. Air Force Dict.* 561/1 *To walk away from an airplane crash or accident,* to survive an accident unhurt or without serious injury. **1966** M. WOODHOUSE *Tree Frog* vi. 50, I had a..cut..but that was all. Walking away from it, they call it. **1980** J. WAINWRIGHT *Eye* *of Beholder* 130 'Anybody walk away from it?'.. 'No. One dead, one smashed up.' 1984 *Times* 19 Apr. 19/6 The provisions for bad and doubtful debts is increased.. and Mr Pattullo stated confidently 'there is no international or domestic loan that we could not walk away from. It might cause us a red face but it would not harm the bank.'

6. *fig.* **a.** Chiefly in religious use, after Bible examples: To conduct oneself, behave (ill or well, wisely or unwisely). Sometimes with reference to a metaphorical 'path' or 'way'. ***to walk with God*** (Gen. v. 22), interpreted to mean 'to lead a godly life' (so rendered by Coverdale, after Luther; later versions retain the Heb. phrase), or to have intimate communion with God.

Cf. Heb. *hālak*, Gr. περιπατεῖν, Vulg. *ambulare*.

1526 *Pilgr. Perf.* (W. de W. 1531) 213 O man (sayth scripture) walke in yᵉ wayes of thy herte as moche as thou wylte, but [etc.]. 1526 TINDALE *2 Thess.* iii. 6 We requyre you.. that ye withdrawe youre selves from every brother that walketh inordinatly [Vulg. *ambulante inordinate*]. 1550 CROWLEY *Last Trump.* 516 And then, lyke a good Christian, Thou dost walke forth in thy callynge. 1581 J. HAMILTON *Cath. Traict.* Epist. 8 b, To.. trauell to reduce yame to ye treu vay quhairin all yair forbearis valkit yir mony hundreth zeris bygane. *a* 1593 MARLOWE *Ovid's Elegies* III. xiii. [xiv.] 13 Be more aduisde, walke as a puritan, And I shall thinke you chaste, do what you can. *a* 1629 HINDE *J. Bruen* xliv. (1641) 140 It was the desire and delight of his soule to walke with God. 1669 STURMY *Mariner's Mag. Penalties & Forfeit.* c 2 If all.. had but the knowledge of what they should know, thay might prevent this loss and damage, and walk safely. 1681 FLAVEL *Meth. Grace* xxx. 323 When a man walks suitably to his place and calling in the world, we say he acts like himself. 1853 MAURICE *Proph. & Kings* vi. 93 If he walked in God's ways he would establish a sure house. 1872 MORLEY *Voltaire* (1886) 11 Those do best who walk most warily.

b. To direct one's conduct *by*, *after* a rule, etc.

1581 LAMBARDE *Eiren.* II. ii. (1588) 113 Many other wayes there bee, after which the Iustice of Peace may walke in taking of this kind of Recognusance. 1706 E. WARD *Wooden World Diss.* (1708) 39 He is the great Exempler they walk by. 1711 ADDISON *Spect.* No. 25 ⁋4 Give me more certain Rules to walk by than those I have already observed. 1821 SCOTT *Kenilw.* xxv, I give thee way, good imp, and will walk by thy counsel. 1884 W. C. SMITH *Kildrostan* 46 We judge a stranger by our home-bred ways, Who, may be, walks by other rule of right.

†**c.** To be associated, act harmoniously *with*. Also ***to walk together***. *Obs.*

1620 J. TAYLOR (Water P.) *Jack a Lent* Ep. A 3 b, And though it be written in a mery stile, yet I dare presume that mirth and truth walke together in it. 1650 H. ELLIS *Pseudochristus* 7 After this, he walked sometime in fellowship with that Congregation. 1657 *Docum. S. Paul's* (Camden) 155 The congregation yᵗ wallke wᵗʰ Mʳ John Symson. *a* 1709 J. LISTER *Autobiog.* (1842) 50 My wife and myself, were admitted into the church at Kipping, with which we walked satisfyingly many years. *Ibid.* 51 Some of his hearers left him [the pastor], and others walked with him till new matters of dissatisfaction broke out. *Ibid.*, After he was gone, the church at Kipping was again united, and walked sweetly together, but could not get a pastor. 1841 S. S. ARNOLD *Diary* 5 Jan. in *Proc. Vermont Hist. Soc.* (1940) VIII. 149 It was a friendly interview; but she said that she could not walk with the Ch[urc]h, and wished to be out.

†**d.** ***to walk wide in words***: to argue at cross purposes. *Obs.*

1529 MORE *Dyaloge* I. xviii. 23 Wythout whych we were lyke to walke wyde in wordys.

†**e.** To proceed, 'go' *upon* (grounds). *Obs.*

1828 *Life Planter Jamaica* 252 What grounds of probability have we to walk upon that the present negroes.. would act otherwise.

7. To go on foot at a walk: see WALK *sb.*¹ 5.

a. Of human beings or other bipeds: To progress by alternate movements of the legs, so that one of the feet is always on the ground: contrasted with *run*, *hop*, etc. ***to walk through*** (a dance) = 7 e; similarly of an actor, ***to walk through his part*** (cf. quot. 1824); also simply ***to walk through***, and *fig.*

1762 FOOTE *Orator* I. Wks. 1799 I. 193 Soft and fair; we must walk before we can run. 1815 STEPHENS in *Shaw's Gen. Zool.* IX. I. 65 The progressive motion of this bird is not by walking but hopping. 1824 SCOTT *Redgauntlet* ch. xix, That caprice which so often tempts painters and musicians and great actors, in the phrase of the latter, to *walk through* their part, instead of exerting themselves with the energy which acquired their fame. 1857 C. M. YONGE *Dynevor Terrace* I. xii. 195 Her grave, pensive character only attained to walking through her part [in society]. 1859 *Habits of Gd. Society* v. 206 'Steps,' as the *chasser* of the quadrille is called, belong to a past age, and even ladies are now content to walk through a quadrille. 1861 WHYTE MELVILLE *Mkt. Harb.* v, It must have been a fine run; but slow... It's labour and sorrow, walking after hounds, to my mind. 1868 J. BURROUGHS *Wake-robin* viii. (1884) 295 Among the land-birds, the grouse, pigeon, quails, larks, and various blackbirds, walk. 1894 *Daily News* 10 Aug. 5/3 A bluejacket never walks, when an order is given, but does everything at the double. 1899 C. SCOTT *Drama of Yesterday & To-Day* II. xiv. 442 Often when she is tired to death,.. her strength fails her. She walks through the part, as it is called. 1922 MRS. P. CAMPBELL *Let.* 11 June in *B. Shaw & Mrs. Campbell* (1952) 256, I would like you to come and see *Hedda Gabler*—it would be nice to hear all the abominable things you might say. Some say I 'walk through'.

b. Of a horse, dog, or other quadruped: To advance by a gait in which there are always two feet on the ground, and during a part of the step three or (in slow walking) four feet: opposed to *amble*, *trot*, *gallop*, etc. Also said of a rider.

1681 *Lond. Gaz.* No. 1639/4 Lost.., a bright Bay Gelding, 14 hands high,.. Walks, Trots, and Gallops, something dull in going, but will leap very well. 1818 SCOTT *Br. Lamm.* xxxiii, Ravenswood walked on with equal deliberation until he reached the head of the avenue... When he had passed the upper gate, he turned his horse. 1863 W. C. BALDWIN *Afr. Hunting* vii. 252 It was only the dogs walking among the dead leaves.

c. ***to walk over*** (***the course***): of a horse, *literally*, to go over the course at a walking pace, so as to be accounted the winner of a race in which there is no opposition; *transf.* and *fig.* to win a race or other contest with little or no effort; also ***to walk over*** (an opponent), to be declared the winner of a contest because of the opponent's failure to compete; ***to walk away from***, to outdistance easily in a race (in quot. *fig.*). Also ***to walk away with***, to win (a prize), steal (a show), with ease; ***to walk home***, to win a contest with ease; ***to walk round*** (an opponent) (*U.S. colloq.*): to beat easily.

1779 WARNER in Jesse *Selwyn & Contemp.* (1844) IV. 245 A little on this side the park is Sir John Thorold's, who, you see by the papers, is walking over the course for the county. 1823 'JON BEE' *Dict. Turf* s.v., 'To walk over' another, is.. to set him at naught, as a racer which is so vastly superior to other cattle that none dare start, and he walks over the course. 1832 *P. Egan's Bk. Sports* 117/2 At Knutsford.. he won the Gold Cup..; and walked over for the Pengwern Stakes at Holywell. 1862 *Cornh. Mag.* V. 26, I was promptly assured that.. I should be elected without opposition..; in short I should walk over the course. 1883 MISS BROUGHTON *Belinda* IV. iii, 'Beaten by a banjo!' says she tragically; 'if it had not been for the banjo I should have *walked* away from her.' 1890 *Rules of Racing* §142 in *Encycl. Sport* (1898) II. 227 When one horse pays forfeit for a match the other need not walk over. 1901 *Westm. Gaz.* 29 June 9/3 To use a colloquial expression, they 'walked round' Gamble and Davies. 1903 WODEHOUSE *Prefect's Uncle* ix. 136 If you'd been there to bowl we should have walked over. 1932 *Sun* (Baltimore) 21 Dec. 12/1 Jack Biener 'Walks' Home... Jack Biener, favorite at $5 for $2, simply spreadeagled the field and won in a common canter by eight lengths. 1951 N. COWARD *Star Quality* 139 It had been the.. play's provincial try-out.. and.. Leonora had unquestionably walked away with the show. 1958 *Times* 11 Aug. 2/7 Treorchy—a magnificent choir—walked away with the prize for big choirs. 1973 *Times* 31 July 9/8 Major J. D. E. Edwards beat Driver D. A. Beck, 6–1, 7–5; Major P. K. Sharp walked over Captain J. B. Merritt.

¶**d.** *transf.* Of a vehicle, a ship, a stream: To go very slowly. *nonce-uses.*

1827 POLLOK *Course T.* I. 346 Round his sacred hill, a streamlet walked, Warbling the holy melodies of heaven. 1852 MUNDY *Antipodes* (1857) 200 Our steamer ran, or rather walked—for she could make no running—plump upon a rock off Bradley's Head. 1865 EMERSON *Let.* in *Harper's Mag.* (1884) Feb. 464/1 The train *walked* all the way.

e. *trans.* To go through (a dance, esp. a minuet) at a walk.

1810 [see MINUET *sb.* 1]. 1827 LYTTON *Pelham* xl, They just walk a quadrille or spin a waltz,.. hang dancing, 'tis so vulgar. 1859 *Habits of Gd. Society* v. 207, I do not attempt to deny that the quadrille, as now walked, is ridiculous. 1863 COWDEN CLARKE *Shaks. Char.* xiv. 362 He walked his minuet in life, and he danced out of it with a caper.

f. Proverbial phrase: ***to walk before one can run*** (and varr.), to understand elementary points before proceeding to anything more difficult; cf. CREEP *v.* 1 b. Also ***to run before one can walk***.

1762 [see sense 7 a]. 1794 G. WASHINGTON *Let.* 20 July in *Writings* (1940) XXXIII. 438 We must walk as other countries have done before we can run. 1876 J. PLATT *Business* 124 We must learn and be strong enough to walk before we can run. 1927 *Melody Maker* Sept. 923/1 Beginners.. commence on their instruments to dabble in so-called 'hot' choruses... They run before they can walk, for, jumping on to what they believe to be 'hot' style, they attempt to cut out all the essential months of study. 1973 *Times* 17 Apr. (Liberia Suppl.) p. ii/5 He does not want Liberia to run before she can walk. 1980 K. AMIS *Russian Hide & Seek* iv. 49 At the moment we can't leave it to the English to do anything. We must learn to walk before we can run. 1984 *New Yorker* 11 June 31/1 'We can't turn you into an actor, but don't turn your back on what we have to offer.' What they meant, of course, was that you've got to learn to walk before you try to run.

g. *Jazz.* Of a bass player: to play a walking bass (see WALKING *ppl. a.* 9). Also said of the beat.

1951 L. HUGHES *Montage of Dream Deferred* 12 Down in the bass That steady beat Walking walking walking Like marching feet. 1952 *Mademoiselle* Dec. 118 And that's the basic jazz beat, that walking beat. Up here in the north all the jazzmen are playing too fast or too slow—nobody walks. 1956 [see *string bass* s.v. STRING *sb.* 32]. 1970 *New Yorker* 23 May 88/2 Then Hall soloed, while Gomez 'walked' behind him.

8. To go away. **a.** *simply* or †with *away*, *forth*. Formerly often in imperative = 'begone', with a vocative of some term of opprobrium (sometimes retained in indirect narration). Now only *colloq.*, to go away perforce, be turned out; also *slang*, to die. Also, of a batsman in *Cricket*, to walk towards the pavilion without waiting for the umpire to give him out; also with *out*.

c 1460 *Towneley Myst.* ii. 106 Leif brother, let vs be walkand. 1526 *Pilgr. Perf.* (W. de W. 1531) 140 b, Yf than the porter wold come forth sodeynly & all to beet vs, & bydde vs walke forth vnthryftes with sorowe. *a* 1529 SKELTON *Agst. Garnesche* iv. 60 Sche praiid yow walke, on Goddes halfe! 1529 MORE *Dyaloge* I. xiv. 18 b, He bad hym walk faytoure. And made hym be sett openly in yᵉ stokkys. 1530 PALSGR. 770/2 Walke, pyke you hence: *tire auant*. 1530 TINDALE *Pract. Prelates* G v b, The Cardinall bad him walcke a vilayne. 1546 J. HEYWOOD *Prov.* II. iv. (1867) 52 Walke drab walke. Nay (quoth she) walke knaue walke. 1605 CHAPMAN *All Fooles* I. B 4 b, I like his learning well, make him your heire, And let your other walke. 1607 MIDDLETON *Mich. Term* II. iii. 169 It stands upon the loss of my credit to-night, if I walk without money. 1712 SWIFT *Jrnl. to Stella* 26 Dec., Lord Bolingbroke told me I must walk away to-day after dinner, because lord treasurer and he and another were to enter upon business. 1858 TROLLOPE *Dr. Thorne* iv, If the governor were to walk, I think Porlock would content himself with the thirty thousand a-year. 1902 S. E. WHITE *Blazed Trail* xxviii, If I want to discharge a man, he walks without any question. 1960 J. FINGLETON *Four Chukkas to Australia* v. 48 Three runs later.. Graveney should have walked but O'Neill dropped him at third slip. 1964 D. SHEPPARD *Parson's Pitch* vi. 107, I never saw him not walk out immediately he was caught at the wicket. He never waited for the umpire's decision. 1973 *Advocate-News* (Barbados) 11 Dec. 14/2 Brian Close, captain of the Robins XI, said: 'A batsman who knows he is out should walk. That is the way we play the game.'

b. *transf.* † Of animals: To be stolen (*Obs.*). Of a thing: To be got rid of; to be carried off. In mod. *colloq.* use said of objects presumed borrowed or stolen. † ***to let*** (something) ***walk***: to dismiss from attention. (*Obs.*)

c 1440 CAPGRAVE *Life St. Kath.* 672 Lete argumentys walk, þei ar not to our be-houe. 1573–80 TUSSER *Husb.* (1878) 141 There horse being tide on a balke, is readie with theefe for to walke. 1596 SPENSER *State Irel.* Wks. (Globe) 619/2 When he comes foorth, he will make theyr cowes and garrans to walke, yf he doe noe other mischeif to theyr persons. 1611 CHAPMAN *May-Day* I. ii, Nay, they [*sc.* houses] shall walke, thats certaine, Ile turne 'em into money. 1898 J. D. BRAYSHAW *Slum Silhouettes* 125 A sack o' taters, or a sieve o' cherries sometimes goes awalkin' if yer don't keep yer eyes skinned. 1978 A. MELVILLE-ROSS *Blindfold* xiv. 87 'Get much theft?' 'Lord yes, but only the sort of stuff you'd expect to "walk" anyway.'

c. With *off*: To depart suddenly or abruptly. ***to walk off with***: to carry away as a prize or plunder.

1604 MARSTON *Malcontent* III. v. E 4 b, I am heauie, walke of, I shall talke in my sleepe, walke of. *Exeunt Pages.* 1705 VANBRUGH *Mistake* IV. i, *Jacin.* Have a care he don't rally, and beat you yet tho'; pray walk off. 1727 M. W. MONTAGU *Let.* 23 June (1966) II. 78 All the little money they had.. they put into the hands of a rogueish Broker who has fairly walk'd off with it. 1836 HAWKER *Diary* (1893) II. 107 A green sub... had walked off with my portmanteau. 1840 THACKERAY *Barber Cox* Apr., I gave Master Baron that day a precious good beating, and walked off with no less than fifteen shillings of his money. 1848 DICKENS *Dombey* ii, Mr. Chick.. said no more, and walked off. *c* 1850 *Arab. Nts.* (Rtldg.) 147 Why dost thou not depart with the rest? Walk off. 1888 'J. S. WINTER' *Bootle's Childr.* ix, And then she gave another sniff and walked off to the drawing-room again. 1889 CONAN DOYLE *Sign of Four* ix, Wait a bit, my friend, .. You have important information, and you must not walk off. We shall keep you, whether you like or not, until our friend returns.

d. ***to walk away from***: to fail to deal with (something); to refuse to become involved with; also ***to walk away*** simply.

1963 *Life* 8 Feb. 4/1 The Kennedy proposals walk away from most of the tax reform problems. 1973 P. O'DONNELL *Silver Mistress* iii. 48 'Why look for trouble?'.. Something comes along, and you just can't turn round and walk away from it.' 1978 S. SHELDON *Bloodline* xx. 237 Roffe and Sons needs an experienced president, Elizabeth... For your own sake, as well as everyone else's, I would like to see you walk away from this. 1981 *Times* 7 Dec. 13/3 Libya and Nigeria started the year trying to maintain prices at a wide premium over the marker, but instead saw buyers walk away. 1983 *Times* 6 May 15/4 No parent which itself took deposits.. could expect to walk away from a subsidiary in trouble without risking a loss of confidence on the part of its own depositors.

e. = sense 13 b below.

1976 *National Observer* (U.S.) 14 Aug. 16/3 Our baby sitter founded the Sitters' Union. They get TV, cookies, and root beer, or they walk. *Ibid.* 28 Aug. 16/1 The sentry in the lobby was a representative of Universal Pictures. His mission: to keep an anxious eye out for 'walkers' and try, if he could, to find out why they walked, since there was still time to do some patching on the film. 1978 S. BRILL *Teamsters* v. 180 Carey called a strike, and all four thousand of his UPS members walked. 1983 W. F. NOLAN *Hammett, Life at Edge* i. 6 He would not lie to keep a job. And he walked.

9. Of a ghost, spectre, fiend: To be seen walking, to appear. Of a dead person: To 'come back' as a ghost. Also † ***to walk out***.

For *the ghost walks* (Theat. Slang), see GHOST *sb.* 8 b.

a 1300 *Cursor M.* 22611 Quen sal scine [= chine] þe heuennes open, þaa warlaus all sal walk þan vte. *c* 1440 *Gesta Rom.* 408 (Add. MS.) All the chambres were take vp, safe oon, in the which was a sperite walkyng. *a* 1513 *Fabyan's Chron.* clxxix. (1533) 105 He also for that the munkes of wynchester sayd that his father Alurede walkyd, caused hym to be remoued vnto the new abbay. 1542 UDALL *Erasm. Apoph.* 111 b, Sore subiecte to the terrours of buggues, and spyrytes, or goblyns, that walken by night and in places solitarie. 1573 L. LLOYD *Pilgr. Princes* 101 We reade in Lucan how that the soules of Silla and Marius.. were alwayes walking and appearing vnto men before they were purged by sacrifice. 1602 SHAKS. *Ham.* I. v. 10, I am thy Father's Spirit Doom'd for a certaine terme to walke the night. 1611 TOURNEUR *Ath. Trag.* IV. iii, There's a talke, thou know'st, that the Ghoast of olde Montfarers walks. *a* 1625 FLETCHER *Hum. Lieut.* III. v, I make your Grace my Executor, and I beseech ye See my poor Will fulfill'd: sure I shall walk else. 1727 DE FOE *Hist. Appar.* x. 201 Such a courage.. would.. lay all the devils that ever walked. 1801

SCOTT *Glenfinlas* xlvi, Alone, I dare not venture there, Where walks, they say, the shrieking ghost. **1882** A. JESSOPP in *19th Cent.* Nov. 737 Everybody knows that it's an awful thing for a dead man to *walk*. **1888** STEVENSON *Black Arrow* Prol. 12 Would ye rob the man before his body? Nay, he would walk!

10. 'To act in sleep' (J.); to walk about or perform other actions as a somnambulist. *rare* exc. in the full phrase ***to walk in one's sleep***.

1605 SHAKS. *Macb.* v. i. 3 When was it shee [Lady Macbeth] last walk'd? *Ibid.* 66 Yet I haue knowne those which haue walkt in their sleep, who haue dyed holily in their beds. **1607** DEKKER & WEBSTER *Northw. Hoe* III. E i b, My mistris makes her husband beleeue that shee walkes in her sleepe. **1728** *Chambers' Cycl.*, *Somnambuli*, an Appellation given to People, who walk in their Sleep. **1848** DICKENS *Dombey* xxxix, Some uneasy ideas that he must be walking in his sleep, or that he had been troubled with phantoms,..beset the Captain at first.

11. a. To go on foot in procession; also, to go in a regular circuit or to and fro over a prescribed track in the course of official duty. Also with cognate accus., as in ***to walk one's round(s, the round, a round, to walk guard***, said esp. of a sentinel.

1594–1600 *Min. Archdeaconry Colchester* (MS.) 99 b, 19 Apr. 1596. Our perambulacion was not walked through the defalte of our vicar. **1596** SPENSER *State Irel.* Wks. (Globe) 679/1 The sheriff of the shire, whose peculiar office it is to walke continuallye up and downe his baly-wick,..to snatch up all those runnagates [etc.]. *Ibid.*, The sherriff may doe therin what he can, and yet the marshall may walke his course besides. **1639** DU VERGER tr. *Camus' Admir. Events* 102 Octavian coms accompanyed with his friend Leobell to walke his accustomed round. *a* **1700** EVELYN *Diary* 12 Sept. 1641, I was permitted to walk the round and view the workes. **1831** SCOTT *Ct. Robt.* xviii, If the lovers have agreed, Agelastes, it is probable, walks his round, to prevent intrusion. **1863** GEO. ELIOT *Romola* xxii, He..was to walk in procession as Latin secretary. **1930** F. A. POTTLE *Stretchers* 51 In France we always wore large automatics when we walked guard.

transf. and *fig.* **1629** MASSINGER *Picture* II. i, Dreames and phantasticke visions walke the round About my widdowed bed. **1834** H. MILLER *Scenes & Leg.* xxiv. (1857) 351 He continued to walk the round of his duties.

†**b.** *Oxford University.* (*a*) Of a proctor or pro-proctor: To perambulate the streets at night, in the exercise of his function. (*b*) Of the proctors: To march to and fro in the Convocation House, as part of the ceremony of conferring degrees.

1530 in W. H. Turner *Select. Rec. Oxford* (1880) 77 It was proved that the ij Proctors servaunts walkyd wᵗ other persons as plesyd them, and theyr maisters walkyd not nor noe other for them. **1677** WOOD *Life* (O.H.S.) II. 384, I [a Pro-proctor] walk by the authoritie of the vice-chancellour. *Ibid.* 391 Dr. Nicholas..verie active in walking and hauling taverns. **1906** J. WELLS *Oxf. Degree Cerem.* 8 Within living memory it was necessary for each 'grace' to be taken separately, and the Proctors 'walked' for each candidate. *Ibid.* 9 It is currently believed that the Proctors walk in order to give any Oxford tradesman the opportunity of 'plucking' their gown and protesting against the degree of a defaulting candidate.

12. walk into——. (*Colloquial* or *slang*.) **a.** In phrase ***to walk into*** (a person's) ***affections***, to win the love of (a person) at once and without effort. Sometimes used jocularly for b or c.

1858 in K. Young *Delhi 1857*, App. 328 Major Erskine was fearful that the jolly 50th would have walked into the affections of the Madrassees, and then all would have gone a regular smash.

b. To make a vigorous attack upon.

1794 LD. HOOD 14 July in Nicolas *Disp. & Lett. Nelson* (1845) I. 438 *note*, From your rapid firing last night I flattered myself it was intended to walk into the Mozelle as this night. **1852** C. B. MANSFIELD *Paraguay* etc. (1856) 20 Some small spermaceti whales, which came in for a lark (luckily for them, after the American and French vessels had left, who would assuredly have walked into them). **1853** 'C. BEDE' *Verdant Green* I. xi, His claret had been repeatedly tapped, his bread-basket walked into, his day-lights darkened.

transf. **1840** COCKTON *Val. Vox* xiii, The carver walked into the pie and bounteously helped each man, woman, and child, to a share. **1846** DE QUINCEY *Syst. Heavens* (1862) III. 185 A call was heard for Lord Rosse! and immediately his telescope walked into Orion; destroyed the supposed matter of stars; but, in return, created immeasurable worlds.

c. To assail with invective or reproof.

1859 LANG. *Wand. India* 399 His Excellency 'walked into' the President, and recommended him to study some catechism of the Law of Courts Martial. **1861** HUGHES *Tom Brown at Oxf.* ix, He walks into us all as if it were our faults.

d. To eat or drink heartily of, to 'make a hole in'.

1837 DICKENS *Pickw.* xxii, I wish you could ha' seen the shepherd walkin' into the ham and muffins. **1849** ALB. SMITH *Pottleton Legacy* xxvi. 280 Look at that little fellow—how he is walking into the raised pie, and how ill he will be to-morrow! **1850** SMEDLEY *F. Fairlegh* xiv, I must walk into old Coleman's champagne before I make a fresh start. **1871** M. COLLINS *Marq. & Merch.* III. iii. 78 He..with most voracious swallow Walks into my mutton chops.

e. To make large inroads on (one's stock of money).

1859 H. KINGSLEY *G. Hamlyn* xv, 'And you've got her money?' 'Yes,' he said; 'but I've been walking into it.'

f. To get *into* an awkward situation as a result of one's own unwariness.

1911 G. B. SHAW *Doctor's Dilemma* III. 60 *Ridgeon*: I don't so much mind your borrowing £10 from one of my guests and £20 from the other—*Walpole*: I walked into it, you know. I offered it. **1942** J. SWEENEY in Murdoch & Drake-Brockman *Austral. Short Stories* (1951) 384 No sooner does the gong go for the third than Irish walks into a haymaker. **1978** M. BIRMINGHAM *Sleep in Ditch* 188, I had walked into this with my eyes wide open. No one could taunt me with being always right.

13. walk out. a. To leave a gathering or place without warning, esp. in protest or disapproval; also *fig.* Const. *on.* orig. *Theat.*

1840 W. C. MACREADY *Diary* 19 Feb. (1912) II. 45 Very much disgusted and irritated by Mʳ Elton walking out in the last scene. **1897** *Daily Tel.* 24 Feb. 10/3 New York did not take kindly to his new play... I am delighted to find, on the assurance of the author, that though New York 'walked out', Washington 'walked in' and received it warmly. **1936** H. G. WELLS *Anat. of Frustration* vi. 55 Suicide..may be represented very attractively as a proud and passionate refusal to drink the cup to the dregs. You 'walk out' as they say in the film world. **1937** M. LEVIN in A. Cooke *Garbo & Night Watchmen* 124, I rarely walk out on a picture, and never want to walk out on a simple programme picture. **1948** W. CHARVAT in R. Spiller et al. *Lit. Hist. U.S.* I. xxxi. 525 When a 'stout Illinoian' walked out on his lectures, he reflected that 'the people are always right'. **1969** H. PERKIN *Key Profession* iii. 103 The A.U.T. delegates to the International Conference walked out the day before Hitler arrived.

b. *spec.* Of an employee: to leave his place of work at short notice, as a form of industrial action. orig. *U.S.*

1894 W. H. CARWARDINE *Pullman Strike* iv. 37 The men passed the word from one to another to 'walk out', which they did orderly and deliberately. **1937** *Irish Press* 11 Feb. 1/2 (*caption*) Photo shows the nursing and boiler house staffs 'walking out'. **1951** E. PAUL *Springtime in Paris* v. 95 Gas workers were about to walk out, and hamstring home cooking to a certain extent. **1979** *Daily Tel.* 27 Nov. 2/2 Last night one of the two lighting and sound engineering crews on BBC-1's 'Nationwide' walked out shortly before the programme was due to go on the air.

c. To desert a partner, esp. a spouse; to withdraw from an agreed arrangement. Const. *on* (cf. sense 5 g above). orig. *U.S.*

1896 *Typographical Jrnl.* (Indianapolis) IX. 232 The Review, Republican daily, 'walked out' on the St. Louis platform. **1921** WODEHOUSE *Indiscretions of Archie* xii. 127 'Has she walked out on you?' 'Left us flat!' **1937** *Sunday Times* 2 May 7/4 Father Donelly..is a fairy godfather to her after she has walked out on her guardians. **1953** *Sun* (Baltimore) (B ed.) 31 Aug. 14/3 The Southern Conference digs in Tuesday for its first football practice since seven of its greatest powers walked out to form a league of their own. **1962** *New Statesman* 7 Dec. 829/1 What surprises is the famous malleability of the two women: did neither one dream of walking out? **1973** 'E. PETERS' *City of Gold & Shadows* i. 6 My father walked out on my mother when I was seven.

III. *trans.* To perambulate, traverse: = *walk over*, *upon*, etc.

†**14.** To travel over (a country, etc.). Cf. 2. *Obs.*

a **1400–50** *Wars Alex.* 519 Sire, þer sall borne be a barne of þi blithe lady, þat driȝtyn efter þi day has destaned to regne, þe quilke sall walke all þe werd & wyn it him selfe.

15. Of fame, etc.: To pervade (a country). Cf. 3 b. *Obs.* exc. as transferred use of 18.

c **1350** *St. John* 43 in Horstm. *Altengl. Leg.* (1881) 35 Þe word of him welk al þe land. **1806** WORDSW. *Char. Happy Warrior* 77 Whether praise of him must walk the earth For ever, and to noble deeds give birth, Or he must fall, to sleep without his fame.

16. a. To go over or traverse on foot.

a **1300** *Cursor M.* 3155 He welk þat fell ner dais thre To sek þe sted quar he wald be. **1576** GASCOIGNE *Kenelworth Castle* Wks. 1910 II. 108 Beware (I say) least whiles we walke these woods... Some harmfull hart entrap your harmlesse moodes. **1748** JOHNSON *Van. Hum. Wishes* 38 The needy traveller..Walks the wild heath. **1763** P. COLLINSON in Darlington *Memorials* (1849) 257 They [Indians] were notoriously..cheated out of their land in your province [Penn.], by a man's walking a tract of ground in one day, that was to be purchased of them. **1871** SIMPSON *Recit.* 9 Hundreds of diggers daily then were walking Melbourne town with their pockets filled with gold. **1868** BROWNING *Ring & Bk.* x. 360 When man walks the garden of this world For his own solace.

b. in contrast with *ride*.

1864 *Good Words* 516/2 Devonshire, to be properly seen, should be walked.

c. Of a stallion: To travel over (a tract of country) serving mares.

1898 *Daily News* 9 Mar. 4/4 The judging yesterday began with stallions that are to walk the Eastern and Midland counties.

17. a. To walk on or along (a road). ***to walk the street(s***: see STREET *sb.* 2 f.

1530 PALSGR. 770/2 In dede you walke the stretes. **1577** GRANGE *Golden Aphrod.* etc. Pj, They onely walke the streates, to see and to be seene. **1590** SPENSER *F.Q.* I. x. 10 All..take delight With many rather for to go astray..Than with a few to walke the narrow way.

b. in contrast with *ride*.

1883 C. HOWARD *Roads Eng. & Wales* (ed. 3) 3 The very steep ascent of Chatham Hill, which most riders will walk. *Ibid.* 134 A very bad hill leading down into Rickmansworth, which is best walked.

18. To walk about upon (a surface, the ground, the sea, etc.). So *Naut.*, of an officer, ***to walk the deck, the quarter-deck***.

to walk the plank: see PLANK *sb.* 6.

1634 MILTON *Lycidas* 173 Through the dear might of him, that walk'd the waves. **1667** —— *P.L.* v. 200 Yee that in Waters glide, and yee that walk The Earth, and stately tread, or lowly creep. *Ibid.* VII. 503 Aire, Water, Earth, By Fowl, Fish, Beast, was flown, was swum, was walkt. **1706** E. WARD *Wooden World Diss.* (1708) 7 It must be a great Change of Weather indeed, when he deigns to walk the Quarter-Deck. **1814** SCOTT *Lord of Isles* IV. xvi, Edward, who walk'd the deck apart. **1840** MARRYAT *Poor Jack* vi, He was..walking the deck. **1849** AYTOUN *Poems, Heart of Bruce* v, The good Lord Douglas walk'd the deck. **1872** M. COLLINS *Two Plunges for Pearl* III. 71 He walked the moorland as if it were his native earth. **1885** R. L. & F. STEVENSON *Dynamiter* xiii. 197 He continued to walk the pavements.

transf. **1813** BYRON *Corsair* I. iii, She [the ship] walks the waters like a thing of life. *a* **1861** T. WINTHROP *Life in Open Air* (1863) 3 At five P.M. we found ourselves..on board the Isaac Newton, a great, ugly, three-tiered box that walks the North River.

19. To walk along (a line); to perambulate (a boundary). Cf. 11.

to walk the chalk (slang): to walk along a chalked line (as a proof of being sober). ***to walk one's chalks*** (slang): see CHALK *sb.* 6 b.

1602–5 *Min. Archdeaconry Colchester* (MS.) 104, 1604. They did not walke the bounds of ther parishe. **1823** 'JON BEE' *Dict. Turf* s.v., 'To walk the chalk'—a military manœuvre to discover which is drunkest. **1842** *Punch* II. 20 Ere death her charms should fix, Gladly I'd walk my chalks or cut my sticks. **1876** FARRAR *Marlb. Serm.* xxiii. 226 You cannot walk the dim borderland between vice and virtue without knowing it.

†**20. a.** To attend, frequent (the exchange, a market). *Obs.*

1634 PEACHAM *Compl. Gentl.* i. (1906) 15 In Venice likewise, every Mechanique is a *Magnifico*, though his magnificence walketh the Market but with a *Chequin*. **1649** W. BULLOCK *Virginia* 43 Let him then enquire of the principallest straights and Spanish Merchants, walking the Exchange. **1750** JOHNSON *Rambler* No. 182 ¶6 To walk the exchange with a face of importance.

b. ***to walk the hospitals*** or ***a hospital***: to receive regular clinical instruction and assist in surgical work.

1781 G. WHITE *Let. to S. Barker* 26 Nov., I have not yet heard—whether he will walk the hospitals in town. **1807** *Picture of Lond.* (ed. 8) 235 The combined method of walking the hospitals and attending lectures. **1823** *Ibid.* (ed. 22) 211 A number of young men, who *walk the hospital*, as it is termed. **1887** RUSKIN *Præterita* II. 333 He became..a ..medical student, came up to London to walk the hospitals.

21. *Shooting.* To start (game-birds) by beating up the ground with pointers or setters. Usually ***to walk up***.

1873 G. S. BADEN-POWELL *New Homes* 255 A good dog for putting them [*sc.* quail] up would be very valuable, but [etc.]... Walking up quail, even with the help of a chain, is equally unsatisfactory. **1900** G. C. BRODRICK *Mem. & Impressions* 8 Year in and year out they lived at home,..walking up their own game with the aid of pointers. **1913** *Times* 12 Sept. 12/6 Now voices are raised in favour of a return..to the use of pointers and setters, in conjunction with the system of walking-up the birds. *Ibid.*, Walked or driven, moreover, the partridge gives more enjoyment to many keen shots than all the pheasants in a beat.

22. To win easily. Cf. sense 7 c *slang.*

1937 PARTRIDGE *Dict. Slang* 935/2 *Walk*, to win easily: Public Schools' coll.: from ca. 1895. [*Refers to quot. 1903 in sense 7 c above.*] **1976** *Times* 12 Feb. 10/2, I went to the British [championship] thinking I'd walk it... This was a mistake... It was a close shave.

IV. Causative uses.

23. To lead, drive, or ride (a horse) at a walk; to exercise (a horse, a dog) by causing it to walk. Also with *out.* Also ***to walk hots*** (see quots.).

1470–85 MALORY *Arthur* v. ix. 176 A man armed walkynge his hors easyly by a wodes syde. **1562** *Child-Marriages* (1897) 82 This deponent scarslie rested walkinge the horses at the doore, half or quarter of an howre, when one callid hym in to his Mistris. **1601** W. PERCY *Cuckqueanes & Cuckolds Errants* IV. ii. (Roxb.) 48 Sirrha Rooke, take my Nagge, and see you walk him faire and soft to Colchester. **1615** G. MARKHAM *Country Contentm.* I. vii. 103 Touching ayring or walking of grey-hounds,..it must dewlie be done euerie morning before sunne-rise, [etc.]. **1681** T. FLATMAN *Heraclitus Ridens* No. 32 (1713) I. 206 Let's walk them a little; for they have run Heats, and must be rubb'd down well. **1833** T. HOOK *Parson's Dau.* I. vii, As he walked his cob [he was riding] back from the fields. **1835** H. HAREWOOD *Dict. Sports* s.v. *Training*, Taking care that he [the horse] is walked for some time afterward, that he may become rather cool before he returns to the stable. **1866** KINGSLEY *Herew.* xvii, You may walk your bloodhound over his grave to-morrow without finding him. **1872** BLACK *Adv. Phaeton* vi, We had walked the horses nearly to the end of the pleasant stretch of beechwood. **1902** A. E. T. WATSON *Hunting* in *Encycl. Brit.* XXIX. 365/2 The kennel huntsman is generally called the 'feeder'. It is his business to look after the pack which is not hunting, to walk them out, to prepare the food for the hunting pack. **1958** *Washington Post* 25 Sept. D-4/1 Each got his start walking hots (leading horses to cool them out following a race or a workout). **1976** *New Yorker* 29 Mar. 109/2 He got an after-school job at a ranch, mucking out stalls and 'walking hots', as the chore of cooling out horses who have just worked or raced is called.

transf. **1583** MELBANCKE *Philotimus* S j, If you be chafed you shal be walked, if you be hot you may be cooled.

24. a. To cause or induce (a person) to walk; to conduct on a walk. Also with advs., *off*, *out*, etc. †***walk your body*** (*Sc.*) = take yourself off, begone (*obs.*).

1630 J. TAYLOR (Water P.) *Gt. Eater of Kent* Wks. I. 144 Now Gentlemen, as I haue walked you amongst the Trees, and thorow the Wood, I pray set downe, and take a taste or two more of this Banquet. **1667** PEPYS *Diary* 14 July, Then I carried them to see my cozen Pepys's house..; and then I walked them to the wood hard by. **1717** BERKELEY in Fraser *Life* (1871) 547 He walked us round the town. *c* **1730** RAMSAY *To Æolus* 11 Pray wauk your body, if you please, Gae gowl and tooly on the seas. **1818** T. JEFFERSON *Writ.* (1830) IV. 448 He walked me backwards and forwards before the President's door for half an hour. **1848**

THACKERAY *Van. Fair* lvii, She slaved, toiled..for old Sedley, walked him out sedulously into Kensington Gardens. **1883** MISS YONGE *Armourer's Prent.* ii, Stephen and Ambrose found themselves walked out of the cloister of St. Grimbald, and the gates shut behind them. **1912** J. S. FLETCHER in *Throne* 7 Aug. 224/2 He soon drew me out of the office to walk me off in the direction of Gray's Inn Road.

b. To force to walk (by holding the arms or pushing before one). Also, to help to walk.

to walk (a person) *Spanish*: see SPANISH C.

1809 R. K. PORTER *Russ. & Swed.* (1813) II. 21 The poor wretch, attended by the police, had been walked through the streets; in order to shew him to the populace. **1848** DICKENS *Dombey* xii, Mr. Feeder himself held a glass of water to his [the boy's] lips, and the butler walked him up and down several times between his own chair and the sideboard. **1853** —— *Bleak Ho.* xxii, Thirdly, Mr. Bucket has to take Jo by the arm a little above the elbow, and walk him on before him. **1918** F. HACKETT *Ireland* viii. 230 Good bewildered people who never knew they were deemed blameworthy until they were walked out to the guillotine.

c. *Baseball.* Of a pitcher: to give (a batter) a base on balls.

1913 *Chicago Record-Herald* 20 Mar. 10/5 Lange walked Kores in the hostile part, then disposed of the next pair on easy infield flies. **1938** *Chicago Tribune* 5 Apr. 19/2 Dobernic walked three batsmen in a row. **1952** B. MALAMUD *Natural* 78 With two out Schultz weakened, walking one man and handing the next a good enough throw to hit for a sharp single. **1976** *National Observer* (U.S.) 16 Oct., Our Pitcher had walked three men in a row and I was invited to take the mound.

25. a. To take charge of (a puppy) 'at walk' (see WALK *sb.* 13). **b.** To keep (a game-cock) in a 'walk'.

a. 1845 YOUATT *Dog* iii. 75 Whelps *walked*, or taken care of, at butchers' houses..are apt to be heavy-shouldered and throaty. **1887** *Field* 19 Feb. 229/1 The practice of walking puppies is not quite so prevalent as it used to be. **1907** *Times* 3 Oct. 4/4 Defendant said he had walked puppies for the Southwold Hunt for 25 years.

b. 1854 *Poultry Chron.* I. 474 Formerly when cock-fighting was more practised, every farm-yard walked a game cock or two. **1889** *Archæol. Æliana* N.S. XIII. 314 'Walking a cock' was the feeding and tending of a game cock.

26. With a thing as obj. †**a.** To send round (drink). Cf. 3 d. *Obs.*

1581 A. HALL *Iliad* I. 14 A seemely sight it was to see the seamen plye their teeth, Wherewith the Cups apace they walke.

b. *Cribbage.* (See quots.)

1803 *Sporting Mag.* XXI. 326 Walking the pegs—at cribbage, means either your adversary putting his own pegs forward, or those of your's back. **1865** *Hotten's Slang Dict.*, '*Walking the pegs*,' a method of cheating at the game of cribbage by a species of legerdemain, the sharper either moving his own pegs forward, or those of his antagonist backward, according to the state of the game.

c. *Bell-ringing.* (See quot.)

1671 [STEDMAN] *Tintinalogia* 53 All changes are to be Rang either by *walking* them (as the term is) or else Whole-pulls, or Half-pulls. By *walking* them, is meant, that the bells go round, four, six, eight times or more, in one change, which is commonly used by young Practisers.

d. To swing (a gun) so as to describe a straight line on the target with successive hits.

1944 *Sun* (Baltimore) 15 June 2/5, I..aimed for his groin and walked my tommy gun right up his middle and blew him 90 feet away. **1969** I. KEMP *Brit. G.I. in Vietnam* xi. 187 'Charlie' really seemed to be walking that mortar up behind me; he was right on target with his shots.

V. 27. The verb-stem in combination: **walk-around**, (*a*) *Colonial*, a kind of rotary mill turned by oxen; (*b*) *U.S.*, among Negroes, a dance in which the performers go round in a large circle; a song or piece of music to accompany such a dance; **walk-away**, a race in which the winner 'walks away' from his competitors, i.e. leaves them far behind; also *transf.* and as *adj.*; **walk-back** *U.S. slang*, a rear apartment; **walk-march** *v.*, to march at a walking pace; of cavalry, to proceed at the walk; also as *sb.* †**walk-street**, one who walks the streets. Also WALK-ON, WALK-OUT, WALK-OVER.

1886 *Official Catal. Colonial & Ind. Exhib.* (ed. 2) 462 Their sugar plots are confined to one or two small green pieces in Tortola, worked by a '*walk-around' or cattle-mill. **1888** B. MATTHEWS *Pen & Ink* 153 'Dixie' was composed in 1859, by Mr. Dan D. Emmett, as a 'walk-around' for Bryant's minstrels. **1888** *Daily News* 16 July 3/6 The final heat was of course a *walk away for Thames, who won by three lengths. **1926** *Amer. Mercury* Dec. 465/2 It [*sc. Variety*] has developed..the following new terms for a [Broadway] success: 'zowied 'em',..'walk-away hit' and 'clicked heavy'. **1958** *Time* (Atlantic ed.) 6 Oct. 16 Turning from a Democratic walkaway into a neck-and-neck sprint. **1978** *Detroit Free Press* 5 Mar. C4/1 For UCLA, the walkaway winner of the Pac-8 title, the game against U-M will be a final tuneup before going into the NCAA tournament. **1945** L. SHELLY *Jive Talk Dict.* 35 **Walk back*, rear apartment. **1973** 'H. HOWARD' *Highway to Murder* vii. 80 One-o-four Platt Street was a rooming house... The Royales lived in a walk-back at the rear of the lobby. [**1851** *Regulations for Cavalry* 190 Commanding Officer, repeated by Squadron Leaders, '*Walk, Trot*, or *Gallop March*.'] **1904** *Mounted Infantry Training* (Provisional, H.M. Army) iv. 36 The word 'Walk' or 'Trot' will in every case precede the word 'March' when the men are mounted... The word on which they move should be drawn out and rolled thus:—'*Walk—M-a-r-r-c-h', and when the pace is to be increased to a trot—'T-r-r-o-t'. **1909** *Mounted Infantry Training* (War Office) iii. 36 On the command, '*Walk—March*'..the whole company moves off..general alignment and cohesion..being secured by the section leaders riding on the same alignment, and at the proper intervals. **1926** T. E. LAWRENCE *Seven Pillars* (1935) IX. ci. 553 Buxton a moment later called 'Walk-March!' to his men, and the four-hundred camels..started off for Jefer. **1942** C. BARRETT *On Wallaby* iv. 88 We flushed many birds as we walk-marched among rocks and stones. *a* **1977** D. WHEATLEY *Officer & Temp. Gentleman* (1978) xiii. 157 We had to move at a sedate walk-march. **1611** COTGR., *Bateur de pavez*, an idle or continuall *walke-street..a lasciuious, or vnthrifty, night-walker.

walk (wɔːk), *v.*[2] Now only *dial.* and *Hist.* Pa. t. and pa. pple. **walked.** Forms: 5 **walke**, 6 **woke**, 7 **wak, wack**, 8 **wawk**, 9 **waulk** (*dial.* **wauk, wack, wake**: see *Eng. Dial. Dict.*). [Orig. identical with WALK *v.*[1]; here separated from that vb. because the sense 'to full (cloth)' is not recorded in Eng. before the 14th c. (see WALK-MILL[1]), though prominent in other Teut. langs.

OE. had the agent-n. *wealcere* WALKER[2] (a Com. WGer. formation), but it is possible that the corresponding sense of the Teut. vb. had not survived into OE., and that the late ME. *walke* is either a back-formation from the agent-n. or an adoption from MLG. or MDu. *walken*.

The Teut. vb. in the sense 'to full' is the source of It. *gualcare* and OF. **gaucher* (inferred from med.L. *gauchatorium* fulling-mill).]

1. *trans.* To subject (woollen cloth) to the operation of beating or pressing (together with other processes, as moistening and heating), in order to cause felting of the fibres and consequent shrinkage and thickening: = FULL *v.* 1.

14.. *Langland's P. Pl.* B. xv. 447 (MS. C) Y walked [*other MSS.* Ytouked]. **1437** *Cov. Leet Bk.* 187 That euery walker withe-in this Cite ffro this tyme fforwarde walke no Cloth & wete hym, but yeff [etc.]. **1467** in *Engl. Gilds* (1870) 383 To dye, carde, or spynne, weve, or cloth-walke, withyn the seid cyte. **1511–12** *Act 3 Hen. VIII*, c. 6 §1 The Walker and Fuller shall truely walke fulle thikke and werke every webbe of wollen yerne. **1568** *Satir. Poems Reform.* xlviii. 41 It is weill walkit, cairdit, and calkit. **1596** *Shuttleworths' Acc.* (Chetham Soc.) 107 For wokinge and ditchinge [i.e. dighting or dressing] of the saide clothe iiij[s] x[d]. **1669** in Cramond *Ann. Banff* (1891) I. 150 The Magistratis ordaines the thesaurer to by thrie scoir elnes of plaiding and caus wack and lit the samen reid to be coittis to the sojoris. **1773** BOSWELL *Tour Hebrides* 11 Sept. (1785) 205 Last night Lady Rasay shewed him the operation of *wawking* cloth, that is, thickening it in the same manner as is done by a mill. Here it is performed by women, who kneel upon the ground, and rub it with both their hands. **1797** W. JOHNSTON tr. *Beckmann's Invent.* III. 266 The fullers received the cloth as it came from the loom, in order that it might be scoured, walked, and smoothed. **1814** SCOTT *Diary* 24 Aug. in *Lockhart*, In a cottage..we heard the women singing as they *waulked* the cloth by rubbing it with their hands and feet.

absol. **1608** in *N. & Q.* 8th Ser. XI. 202/1 That none of the inhabitants..doe washe anie clothes or walk at the well.

b. To mat together, felt. Also *Sc.* 'to render hard and callous, as the skin of the hand by hard work' (*Eng. Dial. Dict.*).

1641 BEST *Farming Bks.* (Surtees) 20 When woll is well risen from the skinne, the fleece is as it weare walked togeather on the toppe.

†**2.** *transf.* To beat, drub (a person). Also, *to walk* (a person's) *coat*. *Obs.* [So G. *walken*.]

a **1530** HEYWOOD *Johan & Tyb* (Brandl) 40 Than I thynke he wyll say by and by, Walke her cote, Johan Johan, and bete her hardely. *Ibid.* 667, I thank god I haue walkyd them well And dryuen them hens. **1556** J. OLDE tr. *Walther's Antichrist* 151 b, The rebellious stubburne fleshe must nedes be walked with a good cudgell. **1562** J. HEYWOOD *Prov. & Epigr.* (1867) 117 Thou wilt foole by walkt with a waster. *c* **1563** *Jack Juggler* (facs.) C iv b, Thou..drunken sote Yt were an almes dyde to walke thy cote. **17..** in R. Chambers *Scott. Songs* (1829) II. 279 We'll wauk their hides, and fyle their fuds.

3. *Comb.*: **walk-apron** *Hat-making* (see quot. 1886); **walk-pin** *Hat-making* (see quot. 1831–3); †**walk-stock** [cf. G. *walkstock*] = FULLING-*stock*. Also WALK-MILL.

1886 *Cheshire Gloss.*, **Walk apron*, hatting term, the apron used by workmen to keep them dry while working at the kettles. **1831–3** *Encycl. Metrop.* VIII. 761/2 The felt is worked and squeezed by means of a rolling pin, called a *walk pin. **1434–5** *Durham Acc. Rolls* (Surtees) 232 In cariacione de le *walkstoke. **1460–1** *Ibid.* 242 Pro factura unius walkestocke pro molendino ibidem [fulling-mill at Rilly] vjs.

walk, obs. form of WAKE.

walkable ('wɔːkəb(ə)l), *a.* [f. WALK *v.*[1] + -ABLE.] **a.** Of a road, country, etc.: Suitable or fit for walking on. **b.** Of a distance: That may be walked. **c.** Of a person (*rare*): Capable of walking.

a. 1736 SHERIDAN *Let. to Swift* 12 May, Our country is now in high beauty, and every inch of it walkable. **1736** SWIFT *Let. to Sheridan* 15 May, We were much disappointed that..your now walkable roads had not roused your spirits. **1822** *Blackw. Mag.* XII. 727 The square of St. Mark's..is the only walkable spot in Venice. **1887** *Taken-in* 58 The deck was not walkable, being wet and slushy.

b. 1799 SOUTHEY *Lett.* (1856) I. 81 Eleven miles is a very walkable distance.

c. 1887 BLACKMORE *Springhaven* xx, Mrs. Stubbard came quite alone, for her walkable children—as she called them—were all up at the battery. **1943** G. G. COULTON *Fourscore Years* ii. 10 For about two years..I was the youngest walkable child.

walkabout ('wɔːkəbaʊt). [Pidgin Eng., f. WALK *v.*[1] + ABOUT *adv.*] **1.** *Austral.* A periodic migration by a westernized Aboriginal into the bush. Often quasi-*advb.* in phr. *to go walkabout*. Also *transf.*

[**1828** *Sydney Gaz.* 2 Jan. 3 When the executioner had adjusted the rope, and was about to pull the cap over his eyes..he said, in a tone of deep feeling,..'Bail more walk about,' meaning that his wanderings were all over.] **1908** MRS. A. GUNN *We of Never-Never* 218 The day after that was filled in with preparations for a walk-about, and the next again found us camped at Bitter Springs. **1918** C. S. STOW (*title*) The walkabouts of Wurrun-Nah. **1927** M. M. BENNETT *Christison* xxv. 227 The manager would give them [*sc.* blackfellows] rations and let them..go off for a month's 'walkabout', picnicking, and fishing at favourite waterholes. **1933** *Bulletin* (Sydney) 9 Aug. 35/3 An old bush abo., then on the 'walk-about'. **1938** X. HERBERT *Capricornia* (1939) xxii. 330 Wha' name—you go walkabout? **1940** F. D. DAVISON in 'B. James' *Austral. Short Stories* (1963) 63 [Heifers] standing motionless..at the end of one of those walk-abouts that cattle running in wild country periodically make. **1950** 'N. SHUTE' *Town like Alice* iii. 82 These bloody boongs, they're always going walkabout. **1958** L. VAN DER POST *Lost World Kalahari* ix. 203 Even the Bushman born on these few remote European farms..rediscovers the need for a long 'walk-about' in the vast desert around him. **1973** P. O'DONNELL *Silver Mistress* i. 15, I like to revert to my childhood ways now and again. Like an aborigine going walk-about. **1984** *Times* 8 Oct. 10/6 First of all the players go walkabout. Then they all return to the stage and sit down. **1985** *Truck & Driver* June 38/2 (*caption*) The crowds get up close to the racing trucks during the Supergrid walkabout.

2. a. A protracted walk or journey, or one that takes in a number of places.

1946 'M. INNES' *From London Far* I. vii. 58, I proposed a walkabout. We were to stroll through Auld Reekie's dusk together. **1956** *Richmond* (Va.) *Times-Dispatch* 17 May 22 (*heading*) End of a six month walk-about [*sc.* a global tour]. **1974** 'G. BLACK' *Golden Cockatrice* i. 9, I've been doing a year's exchange teaching in Hong Kong... These academic walkabouts fascinate me.

b. *spec.* An informal stroll through the crowd by a member of the Royal Family or other public figure.

1970 *Daily Tel.* 31 Mar. 15/3 The Queen realised she was on to a winner with her New Zealand 'walkabouts'. **1974** *Listener* 28 Feb. 263/1 Mr Heath's..electioneering by set speech and walkabout tour. **1980** *Church Times* 25 Apr. 2/5 On Saturday the Bishop met local people during a walkabout in the market. **1984** *Listener* 15 Mar. 20/1, I was engaged in a walkabout during last year's Darlington by-election.

walkathon ('wɔːkəθɒn). *colloq.* (orig. and chiefly *U.S.*). [f. WALK(ING *vbl. sb.*[1] + -ATHON.] A long-distance or protracted walk; orig. a competitive one, now esp. one undertaken to raise money for charity.

1932 *Kansas City* (Missouri) *Times* 20 Feb. 26 Sure a hick town is a place where they have enough superhicks to put on a walkathon. **1933** *Sun* (Baltimore) 4 Nov. 6/6 Next Thursday a number of Hagerstowners will enter upon an endurance contest different from any ever tried here before—a walking marathon, or a 'walkathon', as the promoters insist on calling it. The contestants walk forty-five minutes and rest fifteen for as long as they hold out. **1951** M. KENNEDY *Lucy Carmichael* v. i. 239 If I had that hall I'd put on a Walkathon... In California..after two or three weeks, when there's only a few couples left in, they chain them, see? So if the girl faints, the feller can't push her under the ropes. **1957** *Daily Mail* 27 Dec. 4/3 If Barber gets to the bottom of the world by plane, why on earth are the other boys—the Hillary-Fuchs expeditions—walking?.. I gather that the walkathon idea is the British contribution to the Geophysical Year. **1963** *Weekly News* (Auckland) 31 July 3/4 (*caption*) Representatives of harriers, scouts, bible classes and old soldiers taking part in the recent 50-mile 'walkathon' in aid of the Murray Halberg Trust for Crippled Children. **1976** *Indian Express* 8 June, Walkathon. Indian athlete Harbans Singh, 28, walked non-stop for 144 hours in the town of Jalalabad. **1979** *Honolulu Advertiser* 8 Jan. B-2/2 Manned booths for various charitable walk-a-thons or walked themselves.

walked (wɔːkt), *ppl. a.* Now *dial.* and *Hist.* [f. WALK *v.*[2] + -ED[1].] **a.** Of cloth, etc.: Fulled. **b.** Felted, matted. Also *Sc.* thickened, rendered callous by hard work.

1651 *Rec. Elgin* (New Spalding Club) I. 289 Walter Hay, merchand, ordanit to buye 16 elnes of whyte walked cloath. **1681** in *New Mills Cloth Manuf.* (S.H.S.) Introd. 86, 33 ells raw will yeeld of waked or drest cloath 23 or 23½ ells. *c* **1750** in Smiles *Lives Engin.* II. 97 Cloth made of waulked plaiding. **1786** BURNS *Vision* I. 32, I..heav'd on high my waukit loof, To swear by a' yon starry roof.

Comb. **1829** HOGG *Sheph. Cal.* I. ii. 45 A waukit-woo'd wedder.

walken, obs. Sc. form of WAKEN *v.*

walker ('wɔːkə(r)), *sb.*[1] [f. WALK *v.*[1] + -ER[1].]

I. One who walks.

1. With the construction of the verb in various senses, e.g. One who walks *in* (a place), *on* (a surface), one who walks *about*.

†*walker on ropes*, a rope-walker, funambulist.

1362 LANGL. *P. Pl.* A. x. 102 And Riht so walkers þat walken A-bouten From Religion to Religion Recheles ben þei euere. *c* **1394** *P. Pl. Crede* 89 He [Paul. *Phil.* iii. 18] seyde..Wepyng, y warne ȝow of walkers aboute. *c* **1530** *Hickescorner* 373 Walkers by nyght. **1545** ELYOT *Dict.*, *Neurobatæ*, walkers on cordes or ropes. **1587** GOLDING *De Mornay* iii. (1592) 39 Calling him the euerlasting Father, the Walker vpon the Heauen of Heauens. *c* **1618** MORYSON *Itin.* IV. v. iii. (1903) 476 Not to speak of frequent spectacles in London exhibited to the people by Fencers, by walkers on Ropes, and like men of actiuity. **1642** SIR E. DERING *Sp. on*

Relig. i. 2 So said one of the usuall blacke walkers in Westminster Hall. Another of our Parliament-pressing Ministers.. told me plainely, That my conscience was not so good as in the beginning of the Parliament. **1866** R. S. Candlish *1st Epist. John* viii. 80 He was no privileged walker amid earth's dark scenes of misery and sin.

b. In transitive senses of the vb.: const. *of*.

1611 Bible *Judg.* v. 6 The traueilers [*marg.* walkers of paths] walked thorow by-wayes. **1834** Dickens *Sk. Boz, Boarding-ho.* i, A poetical walker of the hospitals.

c. ***walker-on***: = walk-on *sb.* 1 b.

1897 G. B. Shaw *Our Theatres in Nineties* (1932) III. 217 A good deal of the technique acquired by American actors no doubt makes one almost long for the fatuous complacency of the British 'walker-on'. **1936** N. Streatfeild *Ballet Shoes* xiv. 212 Pauline and Petrova were, of course, principals, and as such separated from the ballet and walkers-on. **1948** [see stand-in 2 a].

d. A person who takes dogs for walks as an occupation; also, one who rears puppies at home for a time before they are returned to kennels.

1930 C. Frederick et al. *Foxhunting* v. 61 The training of .. 'morale' begins from the day when the puppy returns to kennels from its walker. **1967** C. G. E. Wimhurst *Bk. Working Dogs* vii. 45 The day will come when the walker will have to return his charge to the Kennel. **1977** Hooker & Butterworth *M*A*S*H goes to Moscow* (1979) vii. 80 A dog walker.. is a person.. who earns his living by collecting a dozen or so dogs and taking them all for a walk at once. **1984** *Leicester Mercury* 28 June 25/2 Until they are 12 months old, the hound puppies are in the charge of the walkers who keep them at their homes.

†**2.** A traveller. In quot. *fig. Obs.*

c **1430** *Pilgr. Lyf Manhode* i. xiv. (1869) 9 Ther of certeyn hauen gret neede alle pilgrimes and alle walkers that passen bi this eerthe.

3. A person (or animal) that journeys or goes about on foot; one who takes walking exercise. Often with an epithet, as *good*, *quick*, *slow* etc. *walker*.

1578 H. Wotton *Courtlie Controv.* 300 Hee.. conducted them vnto the place where the collation was prepared for the walkers. **1596** Spenser *F.Q.* iv. x. 25 And shadie seates, and sundry flowring bankes, To sit and rest the walkers wearie shankes. **1653** Ramesey *Astrol. Restored* 193 If the walker go to visit any one,.. he shall meet the party. **1713** Steele *Guardian* No. 6 ¶ 5 He gives Plates for the best performing Horse.. for him that trots best,.. for the best Walker, [etc.]. **1786** Reynolds *Disc. R. Acad.* xiii. Wks. 1797 I. 287 The forms and turnings of the streets.. are produced by accident, without any original plan or design: but they are not always the less pleasant to the walker or spectator, on that account. **1815** Scott *Guy M.* lii, The cool breeze served only to freshen, not to chill, the fair walkers. **1858** Mrs. Paul *Maiden Sisters* xxiii. 210, I am the worst walker of the three, and I am not the least tired. **1880** Miss Braddon *Just as I am* xxiii, She was an excellent walker.

b. One who takes part in walking-matches or walks for a wager.

1778 *Ann. Reg.* 210 Mr. Powell, the noted walker, started from Lee-Bridge, to run two miles in ten minutes. **1866** *Athlete* 120 The long distances being of too serious a character for the ambition of the amateur walkers of the present day.

c. A colporteur or tract-distributor.

1846 James *Step-mother* xl. II. 122 'A walker of the Tract Society', said Mr. Prior to himself, as he eyed him.

d. *dial.* An itinerant beggar or vagrant.

1850 Denham *Pop. Rhymes* etc. *I. of Man* Tracts (1892) I. 193 It is customary for these walkers, as they are called, to enter a house without knocking, and take a seat by the fire. .. Some still retain the good old custom of keeping up a bed for the walker.

4. One who acts in a particular manner or pursues a certain line of conduct: with adj. corresponding to the advb. qualification of the verb (see walk *v.*[1] 6 a). Now *rare* or *Obs.*

1680 Manton *Serm. Ps. cxix.* 56 (1725) 300 But a close walker, that waits upon God in an humble and constant Obedience, shall have sufficient encouragement even in this Life. **1683** H. Compton *Episcopalia* (1686) 66 There is another sort of disorderly Walkers who still keep amongst us. *a* **1716** Blackall *Wks.* (1723) I. 8 They would be cast out of the.. Communion of the Faithful as disorderly Walkers.

†**5.** A keeper or ranger who had a specified 'walk' in the forest, a gamekeeper. *Obs.*

1481–90 *Howard Househ. Bks.* (Roxb.) 225 Item, to the parker of Neylond xx.d. Item, to the walkeres, viij.d. **1535** *Act 27 Hen. VIII*, c. 7 §1 Any of the said foresters rulers walkers or fermers. **1647** Haward *Crown Revenue* 42 Walker about the pales of the Chace: Fee 6. 1. 8. **1706** Phillips (ed. Kersey).

†**6.** An officer of the New River Company, having the charge of a 'walk' or section of the bank. *Obs.* (Cf. *walksman*, walk *sb.*[1] 20.)

1613 Middleton *Manner Entert.* (Opening of New River) 3 First here's the Ouer-seer,.. [then various workmen] The Labourers next, Keeper of Amwell-head, The Walkers last.

7. *Sport.* One who 'walks up' partridges.

1913 *Times* 12 Sept. 12/6 The walkers then will soon be manœuvring to keep their coveys in hand.

8. †**a.** (See quot. 1658). *Obs.* **b.** A bird, insect, etc. characterized by walking, as distinguished from other modes of progression. Also a stick-insect (Cent. Dict. 1891).

1658 Rowland tr. *Moufet's Theat. Insects* 1035 Now we proceed to walkers about. We call those walkers, who have no certain houses or food: wherefore they do something superstitiously wander like pilgrims,.. wherefore the English call them Palmer-worms, namely for their wandring life, for they dwell no where. **1817** Kirby & Sp. *Entomol.* xxii. II. 277 The next order of walkers amongst apodous larvæ are those that [etc.]. **1872** Coues *N. Amer. Birds* 44 It is among the Cursores, or walkers, and especially wading birds, that the crus is most naked. **1894** R. B. Sharpe *Birds Gt. Brit.* I. 4 Nearly all the Crows are 'Ambulatores' or 'Walkers', that is to say, they do not hop.

†**9. a.** *pl.* (A person's) legs or feet. **b.** *slang.* The feet. *Obs.*

c **1611** Chapman *Iliad* xx. 36 And with them halted downe .. lame Mulciber; his walkers quite misgrowne, But made him tread exceeding sure. **1832** *P. Egan's Bk. Sports* 130/2 *note*, But her owner,.. the Colonel, from his 'upper crust' down to his 'walker', is a match for all England against any thing.

10. a. Short for *baby-walker* s.v. baby *sb.* B. 2.

1934 in Webster. **1971** *E. Afr. Standard* (Nairobi) 13 Apr. 14/1 (Advt.), Children's bicycles, walkers, car-seats and play-pens at Cycle Mart and Exchange Ltd.

b. = *walking frame* s.v. walking *vbl. sb.* 4 b.

1941 F. H. Krusen *Physical Medicine* xvi. 648 Various types of walkers.. will give the patient firm support through the arms and axillae when he is taking his first hesitant steps. **1971** *Catholic Worker* May 2/3 She is living at Loretto Home for the Aged.. and must use a walker since she broke her hip some time ago. **1980** U. Curtiss *Poisoned Orchard* ii. 12 She's in her seventies *and* in a walker.

Hence †'**walkership**, the office of a walker of the forest.

1647 Haward *Crown Rev.* 47 Com. Leicester. Keeper of the Walke, *alias* Walkership: Fee, 2. 0. 0. **1721** Strype *Eccl. Mem.* (1822) II. i. 481 The King.. gave to.. Sir John Gates the keepership and walkership of two good walks in Waltham forest.

walker ('wɔːkə(r)), *sb.*[2] ? *Obs.* Also 4 **walkere**, 5 **-ar**, 5–6 **walkar(e**, *Sc.* **walcar**, 7–8 *Sc.* **wakar**, **-er**, **wau(l)ker**. [OE. *wealcere* (once, gl. *fullo*) = (M)LG., (M)Du. *walker*, OHG. *walkari* (MHG., mod.G. *walker*), agent-n. f. OTeut. **walkan* walk *v.*[2] The Teut. word is the source of It. *gualchiere* fuller.] One who fulls cloth, a fuller.

c **1050** *Voc.* in Wr.-Wülcker 407/29 Fullones, wealceres. *c* **1300** *Beket* 1135 To Lincolne he com. At a walkeres house his in he nom there. **1379** *Poll-tax W. Riding* in *Yorks. Archæol. Jrnl.* V. 25 Johannes Louot' & Alicia vx[r] ejus, Walkere, xij*d.* **1387** Trevisa *Higden* (Rolls) IV. 409 þey smyte out his brayn wiþ a walkere his perche [L. *pertica fullonis*]. **1435** *Coventry Leet Bk.* 172 No walker off the Cite of Couentre.. Shall Rakke no Clothe on the Tey[n]tur that schall be solde ffor wette-clothe. **1511–12** *Act 3 Hen. VIII*, c. 6 §1 The Walker and Fuller shall truely walke fulle thikke and werke every webbe of wollen yerne. **1560** *Maitl. Club Misc.* III. 227 Williame Cowpar ane walcar dwelland in Edinburgh. **16..** *Boy & Mantle* 53 She curst the weaver and the walker, That clothe that had wrought. *a* **1779** D. Graham *Writ.* (1883) II. 149 They.. scour'd their din skins as a wauker does worsted blankets. **1871** J. H. Thomson in *Cloud of Witnesses* 566 *note*, John Parker was a waulker in East Kilbride. **1876** *Mid-Yorks. Gloss.*

b. *attrib.* (and later, in possessive compounds), in names of implements, materials, etc. used in fulling cloth. ***walker('s earth, clay*** (now *dial.*) = fuller's *earth*.

13.. *Cursor M.* 21144 (Gött), A wicked iuu.. Smate him wid a walker stang. *c* **1375** *Sc. Leg. Saints* vii. (*James Minor*) 215 þane ane, a walkare perk, hynt & gafe sancte Iamis sic a dynte þat he þe harne-pane brak in twyn. **1403** *Nottingham Rec.* II. 20 Unum stryk de walkerherth. *a* **1425** *Cursor M.* 21144 (Trin.) þei.. Siþen smoot him with a walker staue. *c* **1450** *Mirk's Festial* 140 þerwyth a curset man of hom wyth a walkerys staf smot hym on þe hed. **1497** in *N. Riding Rec.* N.S. (1894) I. 188 A payer Sheres, called Walkar Sheres. **1583** L. M[ascall] *Profit. Bk.* A ij b, Then take a quantity of walkars claye, called Fullars earth. **1600** Surflet *Country Farm* ii. lvii. 393 Walkers earth, or other scouring earth. **1703** Thoresby *Let. to Ray* (E.D.S.), Walker's earth for scowring the cloth. **1847** *Archæol. Jrnl.* IV. 147 A species of fuller's earth called 'walker's clay'.

Walker ('wɔːkə(r)), *sb.*[3] The name of John W. *Walker* (b. 1802) used *absol.* and *attrib.* to designate an American fox-hound, usually black, white, and tan, belonging to a strain originally developed by the Walker family.

1904 J. A. Graham *Sporting Dogs* ix. 134 The Walkers are chiefly bred by men in Kentucky of that name and have been shipped to nearly every part of America where foxes are found. *Ibid.* 135 The Walker hounds are fast. **1940** W. Faulkner *Hamlet* 58 A man named Houston, heeled by a magnificent grave blue-ticked Walker hound, led a horse up to the blacksmith shop. **1964** J. Griffen *Hunting Dogs Amer.* v. 195 The Walker Hound is the most popular strain of Foxhound in America today. **1980** *Hunting Ann. 1981* 17/1 Caswell has his two best strike hounds in place: Dan is a registered Walker and a fighter; his white-brown-and-black coat is creased here and there with old scars left by the claws and teeth of a bear.

Walker ('wɔːkə(r)), *int.* More fully **Hookey Walker**. [Always written with initial capital; prob. a use of the surname *Walker*.

It is not unlikely that *Hookey Walker* may originally have referred to some hook-nosed person named Walker; but the various stories told to account for the origin of the expression have probably no foundation.]

An exclamation expressive of incredulity. Also occas. as sb. (= 'humbug'), as in 'That is all Walker'.

1811 *Lex. Balatronicum*, *Hookee Walker*, an expression signifying that the story is not true, or that the thing will not occur. **1812** J. H. Vaux *Flash Dict.*, *Walker*, an ironical expression synonymous with *bender* and used in the same manner. **1838** *Bentley's Misc.* IV. 227 Professor Ketch suddenly interrupted the proceedings by exclaiming, with great excitement of manner, 'Walker!' **1841** Barham *Ingol. Leg.*, *Old Woman in Grey*, For mere unmeaning talk her Parched lips babbled now—such as 'Hookey!'—and 'Walker!' **1887** *Pall Mall Gaz.* 18 Oct. 1/1 To which assurance.. one may best reply 'Walker'.

Walkerite[1] ('wɔːkəraɪt). [f. the proper name *Walker* (see below) + -ite.] A member of an extreme Calvinistic sect founded in Ireland by John Walker (1768–1833). Also *attrib.*

1830 Coleridge *Table-t.* (1917) 88 The Walkerite creed, or doctrine of the New Church, as it is called, appears to be a miscellany of Calvinism and Quakerism.

walkerite[2] ('wɔːkəraɪt). *Min.* [Named by Heddle 1880, after Prof. John *Walker* (1731–1803) who discovered it + -ite.] = pectolite.

1880 Heddle in *Min. Mag.* IV. 122.

walkie-lookie (ˌwɔːkɪˈlʊkɪ). *colloq.* [f. look *v.*, after *walkie-talkie*.] = peepie-creepie.

1946 *Sci. News Let.* 30 Mar. 195 'Walkie-lookie', the picture equivalent to the small remote voice instrument known as 'walkie-talkie', will come from the 'block' system's light-weight, easily portable television camera. **1952**, etc. [see peepie-creepie].

walkies ('wɔːkɪz), *sb. pl. colloq.* [f. walk *sb.*[1] + -ie.] A childish or jocular form of *walk* used chiefly with reference to dogs. Also as quasi-*advb.* in phr. ***to go walkies***.

[**1932** *Amer. Speech* VII. 242 [Jazz jargon.] Thus, we have the line 'I Prefer the Walkies', with its last word coined to rhyme with 'talkies'. **1938** A. Woollcott *Let.* 28 Jan. (1946) 163 There are now—God help me!—four black dogs to go walkee with you.] **1939** A. Thirkell *Before Lunch* iv. 93 'Master's stick for walkies,' said Mr. Middleton. 'Fetch stick for walkies.' **1960** J. Stroud *Shorn Lamb* x. 119, I bring Gorm along here sometimes, for his walkies. **1979** T. Barling *Olympic Sleeper* x. 118 That's one stray piece of information... It's gone walkies some-damned-where. **1981** *Sunday Express* (Colour Suppl.) 26 Apr. 13/1 Before long the subject of walkies comes up. People are obsessed, Mrs Woodhouse says, with taking dogs out for walks.

walkie-talkie (ˌwɔːkɪˈtɔːkɪ). Also **walky-talky**. [f. walk *v.*[1] + talk *v.* + -ie.] **1.** A small radio transmitter and receiver that can be carried on the person to provide two-way communication as one walks.

1939 *Sun* (Baltimore) 4 Oct. 24/3 'Walkie-talkie' is the Army Signal Corps' way of speaking of unit S.C.R. 195—a recently developed radio sending and receiving set so small it is carried on the back and one talks while one walks. **1944** *Life* 3 July 12/1 Above the noise of hundreds of bombs.. his voice barked through the walkie-talkie. **1945** *China at War* May 38/2 Walkie-talkie sets also are used. **1955** G. Band *Road to Rakaposhi* xvi. 178 If we had taken portable 'walky-talky' sets there would have been no problem. **1970** *Timber Traders Jrnl.* 21 Mar. 53/3 Senior members of the yard staff have walkie-talkie radio sets with which they maintain communication with the sideloader operators. **1973** C. Bonington *Next Horizon* xii. 175 We talked over the problem, on the walky-talky. **1979** *Arizona Daily Star* 5 Aug. A 12/1 Secret Service agents with walkie-talkies paced the auditorium's mezzanine and surrounding grounds.

2. A doll that can be made to walk and talk. Freq. *attrib.* or as *adj.*

1952 *Landfall* VI. 82 Everything he does simply runs true to type like the tricks of a walkie-talkie doll. **1957** J. Frame *Owls do Cry* ii. xxviii. 137, I shall buy her.. a sleeping doll, a walkie-talkie that cries and walks. **1958** N. Marsh *Singing in Shrouds* (1959) vi. 107 Las Palmas is known to tourists for its walkie-talkie dolls. **1961** J. Wayne *Day Ceiling fell Down* vii. 72, I thought it was a proper big doll you'd lost... Like one of them walkie-talkies.

walk-in ('wɔːkɪn), *a.* and *sb.* [f. walk *v.*[1] + in *adv.*] **A.** *adj.* **1.** Pertaining to or designating a person who walks into premises casually or without an appointment; *spec.* applied to (*a*) a thief who walks in rather than breaks in; (*b*) a person who offers his services to a foreign power unsolicited, as by walking into its embassy or consulate.

1928 *Daily Express* 6 Oct. 11/2 A criminal of the type described by the police as the 'walk-in-thief', who, if he encounters anyone, slides gently from the house, with a plausible excuse. **1962** *John o' London's* 25 Jan. 82/3 A housebreaker by day is a walk-in man. **1976** *Billings* (Montana) *Gaz.* 1 July, They will be on duty for walk-in and other services from 10.00 a.m. to midnight daily.. said the executive director of the hospital. **1978** D. Bloodworth *Crosstalk* x. 84 In March we got ourselves a walk-in defector from China. **1979** *United States 1980/81* (Penguin Travel Guides) 45 In larger cities, many hospitals have walk-in clinics designed to serve people who do not really need an emergency service, but who have no place to go for immediate medical attention.

2. a. Of a storage area: large enough to walk into.

1943 *Pioneering in Food Preservation* (New Dominion Ser. No. 37), A small walk-in refrigeration plant for curing meat. **1960** *Farmer & Stockbreeder* 19 Jan. 118/1 (Advt.), Makers of walk-in incubators. **1966** T. Pynchon *Crying of Lot 49* ii. 36 Oedipa skipped into the bathroom, which happened also to have a walk-in closet. **1976** *Evening Post* (Nottingham) 15 Dec. 17/1 (Advt.), Large fitted kitchen, walk-in larder. **1982** A. Mather *Impetuous Masquerade* vii. 105 A matching chest and fitted walk-in closets.

b. Of a cinema, etc.: entered on foot, in contrast to a drive-in. *N. Amer.*

1968 *Amer. Speech* XLIII. 157 He recognized.. a desire for something more than the ubiquitous.. drive-in and directed me to a walk-in restaurant a few blocks away. **1973** *Daily Colonist* (Victoria, B.C.) 3 Nov. 2/1 We can't even go to a walk-in movie because he falls asleep and snores so loud it is embarrassing. So we usually go to drive-ins where he can sleep peacefully.

c. Of a room: entered directly from a specified area rather than through an intervening passage.

1967 *Coast to Coast 1965–6* 160 Back left of the bar was a row of walk-in walk-out bedrooms surrounded by a veranda. **1971** D. E. Westlake *I gave at Office* (1972) 75 A narrow walk-in kitchen was off the living room through a doorway in the short wall opposite the window.

B. *sb.* **1.** A walk-in closet or cold-storage room (see sense A. 2a above).

1946 *Daily Progress* (Charlottesville, Va.) 21 Mar. 15/2 Deep Freeze and Frozen Food Storage Walk-In Refrigerators.. Down payment required as all walk-ins are custom built to customers' own specifications. **1970** 'E. Queen' *Last Woman* III. 160 His wardrobe closet was a roomy walk-in.

2. A walk-in defector (see sense A. 1 above).

1975 P. Agee *Inside Company* I. 59 The first type is known as the 'walk-in'. The walk-in is a member of the party who ..decides to offer his services to the U.S. government. He makes his initial contact..by walking into the U.S. Embassy or Consulate. **1980** E. Behr *Getting Even* ii. 23 The only really satisfactory defectors were walk-ins, as they were known in the trade.

walkin, obs. Sc. form of WAKEN *v.*

walking ('wɔːkɪŋ), *vbl. sb.*^{1} [-ING^1.]

1. The action or an act of the vb. WALK^1.

a. The action of moving on the feet at any pace short of breaking into a run or trot; the action of taking pedestrian exercise. Phrase, ***to go a-walking***. Also the manner or style in which a person walks.

c **1400** *Rule St. Benet* lxiv. 42 If I sulde make my herdis to labur to mikil in walkyng, þai sal alle die on one day. *c* **1430** *Dietarium* 18 in *Babees Bk.* 54 Cleer eir and walking makiþ good digestioun. **1585** Higins *Junius' Nomencl.* 188/1 *Hypæthra ambulatio*,..a walking in an open gallerie. **1601** Shaks. *Jul. C.* I. iii. 127 There is no sturre, or walking in the streetes. **1725** Ramsay *Gentle Sheph.* v. iii. Sang xxi, He's comely in his wauking. **1743** Stukeley *Abury* II. 57 The ancients conceiv'd it [*sc.* the motion of a serpent] to be like the walking of the gods. **1817** Kirby & Sp. *Entomol.* xxiii. II. 306 The mode of their walking depends upon the number and kind of their legs. **1821** Clare *Village Minstr.* I. 195 As thou goest a walking. **1853** Dickens *Bleak Ho.* xlix, They must have devoted the greater part of their long and arduous lives to pedestrian exercises, and the walking of matches. **1883** C. Howard *Roads Eng. & Wales* (ed. 3) 115 The surface is very rough and scarcely rideable and much walking will be necessary.

(*b*) ***walking on*** (or ***with***) ***two legs***: in modern China, the use of small-scale, local methods in production and education, as well as large-scale or capital-intensive ones; also *attrib.*

1962 E. Snow *Other Side of River* (1963) xxviii. 209 'Walking on two legs' in 1958 meant starting tens of thousands of small brick blast furnaces or 'back-yard' hearths. **1964** Kang Chao in D. J. Dwyer *China Now* (1974) xiii. 252 Another salient feature of the Great Leap movement was a greater emphasis on indigenous methods of production and labour-intensive investment projects. This policy, officially called 'walking with two legs', represented a sharp departure from previous development strategy which had stressed only modern production techniques and large-scale investment projects. **1971** G. P. Jan in S. E. Fraser *Educ. & Communism in China* I. 141 Technical training for adults in the commune schools, a mixture of modern and native methods, was referred to as the policy of 'walking on two legs'. **1977** *China Now* June 4/1 Agricultural machinery for production (walking-on-two-legs tractors, tractors, bulldozers, pumps, harvesters, etc.).

b. With advs. as ***walking about***, ***in***, ***-on*** (in quots. *attrib.*), ***-out***, ***together***, ***-up***, nouns of action corresponding to verbal phrases.

c **1440** *Promp. Parv.* 514/2 Walkynge abowte, or goynge, *deambulacio, spaciatus.* **1857** C. M. Yonge *Dynevor Terrace* I. xix. 309 Their 'walking together' was recognised. **1893** A. J. Stuart-Wortley *Partridge* 150 Walking up, or shooting partridges over dogs, is..the finest training of all for a young shooter. **1931** E. O'Neill *Homecoming* I, in *Mourning becomes Electra* (1932) 40 Hope you don't mind my walking in on you without ceremony.

attrib. **1905** Wells *Kipps* I. ii. §5 It is considered..as savouring of the 'walking-out' habits of the servant girls. **1911** *Encycl. Brit.* XXVII. 586/2 Undress Uniforms.—In 'walking-out' order most troops wear the tunic. **1948** *Sporting Mirror* 21 May 5/2 At one time he wanted to be an actor and was offered a walking-on part for 'Cavalcade'. **1968** *Jrnl. R. United Service Inst.* XCIII. 470 To encourage recruiting and to make Army service more popular it would certainly seem very necessary to have a smart Walking-out dress. **1982** P. D. James *Skull beneath Skin* vii. 67 She would have had at least a walking-on part in all the plays.

c. *fig.* Manner of conducting or behaving oneself. Also †with *a* and *pl.*

c **1407** Lydg. *Reson. & Sens.* 2994 For this skylle in my walkyng, As she that hath most maistry, I bere thys bowe of yvory. **1550** Bale *Apol.* 35 If chastyte be a perfeccyon, and a walkynge in the lawes and ordynaunces of God wyth-out reproue. **1613** Day *Festiv.* ix. (1615) 257 The Apostle to the Philippians makes speciall mention of both these Walkings. **1675** J. Owen *Indwelling Sin* xv. (1732) 211 The Observation of the Ways and Walkings of others. **1854** H. Rogers *Ess.* (1855) II. 14 That wary walking which all his early life required.

†**d.** Passing (of money) from hand to hand. Cf. WALK *v.*^{1} 3b. *Obs.*

1549 Latimer *5th Serm. bef. Edw. VI* (Arb.) 143 Ther was walkynge of angelles betwene them.

e. The action of a somnambulist.

1605 Shaks. *Macb.* v. i. 13 In this slumbry agitation, besides her walking, and other actual performances, what (at any time) haue you heard her say? **1607** Dekker & Webster *Northw. Hoe* III. E 2, I will finde a remedy for this walking [*sc.* in sleep] if all the Doctors in towne can sell it.

f. The action of appearing as a ghost.

1727 De Foe *Hist. Appar.* x. 200 Spirits who visit people, as well by night as by day, this we call walking and apparition.

g. A going in procession.

The later examples may be *dial.*

1706 tr. *Dupin's Eccl. Hist. 16th C.* II. iv. xviii. 268 They shall banish also out of their Churches all sorts of Musick:.. all Walkings, Noises and Clamours. **1892** C. M. Yonge *Old Woman's Outlook* 100 The attraction of 'walking' and the gala day were lacking. **1939** F. Thompson *Lark Rise* xv. 269 At the club walkings there were brass bands and processions of all the club members.

2. A walk or journey on foot, the distance covered at or in a certain time.

1542 Udall *Erasm. Apoph.* 7 Yf thou stretch yͤ walkynges that thou vsest at home, & laye theim on length by the space of fiue or sixe dayes together, yᵘ shalt easyly reach to Olympia. **1617** Moryson *Itin.* I. 30 The circuit of the City is three houres walking. **1863** W. C. Baldwin *Afr. Hunting* vi. 217 We were about four hours' hard walking on foot from the wagons. **1899** *Westm. Gaz.* 14 Nov. 9/2 His walkings exceed nine times the globe's circumference.

3. The condition of a path or road for walking on.

1631 Anchoran *Comenius' Gate Tongues* 127 Lest the walkings should be all myrie and dirtie. **1766** *Complete Farmer* s.v. *Walk*, From this there may be a communication with the side walks, whereby there may be dry walking all round the garden. **1896** Housman *Shropsh. Lad* xlix, Empty heads and tongues a-talking Make the rough road easy walking.

4. *attrib.* and *Comb.*, as ***walking*** †***alley***, †***camp***, ***distance***, ***exercise***, ***ground***, ***match*** (hence ***walking-matching*** vbl. sb.), ***pace***, ***powers*** pl., ***race***, ***tour***; also with sense 'adapted for or used in walking', as ***walking boot***, ***cane***, ***dress***, ***shorts***, ***suit***, ***weather***, etc.; also used to designate farm implements which are operated by someone walking behind or alongside, as ***walking cultivator***, ***plough***.

1552 Huloet, *Walkinge aley, or place of pleasure in a gardayne with quycke settes, *topiarium.* **1854** M. S. Cummins *Lamplighter* xxx. 217 To change her slippers for thick *walking-boots occupied a few minutes only. **1885** D. Webster *Angler & Loop-rod* 14 The boots are..a size or two larger than ordinary walking-boots. **1608** Willet *Hexapla Exod.* 784 The measure and distance of their ambulatorie, and *walking campe. **1699** Dampier *Voy.* Suppl. ix. 178 Rattans and *Walking-Canes. **1829** Lytton *Devereux* II. v, Did I not give the last guinea I had about me for a walking-cane yesterday? **1869** *Rep. Comm. Agric. 1868* (U.S. Dept. Agric.) 417 Field No. 3..[was] cultivated but once, when about a foot high, with a five-toothed *walking cultivator. **1817** Lady Morgan *France* I. (1818) I. 30 The chateau.. was but at a *walking distance. **1753** G. Washington *Diary* 23 Dec. (1925) I. 63, I put myself in an Indian *walking dress. *c* **1792** Jane Austen *Catharine* in *Minor Wks.* (1954) 211 She sends me a long account of the new Regency walking dress Lady Susan has given her. **1822** *Repos. Arts* etc. 1 Nov. 297 Walking Dress. **1909** H. G. Wells *Ann Veronica* iii. 72 She was in one of her old walking-dresses. **1835** H. Harewood *Dict. Sports* s.v. *Training*, A horse.. requires a great deal of *walking exercise and careful feeding. **1818** Scott *Rob Roy* xxv, I wandered.. to the College-yards, or *walking ground. **1806** Surr *Winter in Lond.* II. 83 For *walking-hats, and hunting-hats, there was not a superior shop in London. **1832** *P. Egan's Bk. Sports* 133/2 In a *walking match..he went four miles in thirty-two minutes and half a second. **1848** Dickens *Dombey* xxii, Ever since I took to bird-catching and *walking-matching. **1817** Kirby & Sp. *Entomol.* xxiii. II. 309 Insects vary much in their *walking paces. **1830** James *Darnley* xxxviii. III. 253 Thus marched on the procession at a walking pace. **1868** *Rep. Iowa State Agric. Soc. 1867* 161 [The] ground [is] plowed and harrowed,..and cultivated with riding and *walking-plows. **1965** E. L. Myles *Emperor of Peace River* I. xi. 114 Hitched to a small walking-plow, the team plodded back and forth. **1856** Kane *Arctic Expl.* I. ix. 100 We.. carried nothing except..a *walking-pole. **1866** *Athlete* 8 *Walking Race, Seven Miles. *c* **1750** *Heir of Linne* xxii. in Child *Ballads* V. 17/1 Wi *walking rod intill his hand, He walked the castle roun. **1859** Dickens *T. Two Cities* I. vi, It is a young lady's *walking-shoe. **1963** *Walking shorts [see *easy-care* s.v. EASY *a.* and *adv.* C.d.]. **1880** 'Mark Twain' *Tramp Abr.* xi. 102 The knapsacks, the rough *walking suits, and the stout walking shoes which we had ordered. **1864** Miss A. B. Edwards *Barbara's Hist.* xx, Mrs. Churchill and Hilda made an elaborate *walking-toilette. **1854** C. M. Yonge *Heartsease* II. II. xviii. 48 He was going to take a *walking tour in Ireland. *a* **1881** Barratt *Phys. Metempiric* (1883) Pref. p. xix, They..frequently went abroad and on walking-tours together. *c* **1825** Lamb *Let. to B. W. Proctor*, We will expect finer *walking weather.

b. Special comb.: as **walking-beam** = BEAM *sb.*^{1} 11; **walking-day**, a day on which schoolchildren walk in procession; **walking frame**, a free-standing metal frame for use as a walking aid by a person who holds or leans on the top; = WALKER *sb.*^{1} 10a, b; **walking-go** *colloq.* a walking-match; †**walking hymn**, a processional hymn; **walking-leg**, in certain arthropods, esp. crustaceans, a limb used for walking; **walking-machine**, a mechanical or robotic device attached to a person to enable him to perform duties beyond his normal capacity or strength; †**walking-mate**, one's companion in walking; **walking-orders** (*U.S. slang*), **-papers** (*colloq.*) *pl.*, a notice of dismissal; **walking party**, a party formed for an excursion on foot; †**walking-path** = FOOT-WAY 1; †**walking-place**, a place for walking in, a walk, an ambulatory; **walking-possession**, a nominal form of distraint in which the man in possession may go away but with right of re-entry; **walking-rapier**, **-sword** (now *Hist.*) a rapier or sword such as was worn by gentlemen in civil life; **walking-ticket** *U.S.* = *walking-orders* (above). Also WALKING-STAFF, -STICK.

1845 *Knickerbocker* XXV. 63 Some rushed to the upper deck, and climbed up the chain and up the machinery to the *walking beam. *a* **1864** Gesner *Coal, Petrol.* etc. (1865) 27 The crank giving motion to a walking-beam, at the end of which boring tools or pump rods are attached. **1932** *Amer. Speech* VII. 263 The walking-beam, a bar, pivoted in the center, which rocks up and down, actuating the tools in cable-tool drilling or the pumping rods in a well being pumped. **1960** [see SAMSON'S POST 2b]. **1973** [see STEM *sb.*^{1} 4j]. **1974** *Petroleum Rev.* XXVIII. 558/1 Each pile handling unit has its own walking beam system for moving from one pile driving position to the next. **1976** M. Machlin *Pipeline* xlii. 461 Lester, he'd been sitting out on the walking beam trying to stab the control head with a joint of pipe screwed in on the casing. **1827** Hone *Every-day Bk.* II. 784 That particular Thursday in this month [June], which is known all over the world of charity-schools by the name of '*walking day'. **1906** *Church Family Newsp.* 29 June 458/2 Warrington to-day observes its old-time festival known as 'Walking Day'. All the principal streets of the town..will be given over entirely to the children attending the Sunday-schools. **1961** J. O. Wale *Tidy's Massage & Remedial Exercises* (ed. 10) x. 202 The patient may begin with *walking frames or rails. **1966** *Physiotherapy* LII. 146/2 Problems to be overcome are: (1) uneven ground; (ii) steep ground; (iii) stairs. Most walking frames can cope with (i) and (ii). **1979** D. Cook *Winter Doves* II. ii. 49 Her child.. was bouncing up and down in a walking frame. **1983** S. Radley *Blood on Happy Highway* v. 39 Osteo-arthritis in her hips made it difficult for May to get about now, even with a walking frame. **1802** *Sporting Mag.* XIX. 199 Your provincial news must take in all the bye races, cock matches, *walking-goes, and every thing that's worth knowing. **1599** Sandys *Europæ Spec.* (1632) 179 Their *walking hymns at solemne Matins and Vespers. **1909** W. T. Calman in E. R. Lankester *Treat. Zool.* VII. xv. 271 The first pair of legs.. are commonly referred to as the chelipeds, and the following four pairs are distinguished as *walking-legs. **1932** J. S. Huxley *Probl. Relative Growth* iv. 123 The pereiopod which was enlarged as the male chela being the first of the walking-leg series. **1977** G. F. Warner *Biol. Crabs* v. 75 They burrow by tilting backwards and digging down into the sand with their walking legs. **1971** *Sci. News* 21 Aug. 118/2 Manipulators, *walking machines, artificial limbs and man amplifiers—cybernetic machines that perform as appendages of man. **1973** *Britannica Yearbk. Sci. & Future 1972* 102 A four-legged 'walking machine' mimics and amplifies the movements of its human operator. The right front leg of the machine is controlled by the operator's right arm, the left front by his left arm, [etc.]. **1978** D. Murphy *Place Apart* vi. 110 Now he is 'out of work' and has to use a complicated walking-machine provided by the NHS. **1596** Nashe *Saffron-Walden* L 4, Not the poorest *walking-mate, or thred-bare cut-purse in a countrey, that can well be with-out them [*sc.* almanacks], be it but to know the Faires and Markets when they fall. **1600** Rowlands *Lett. Humours Blood* v. 70 Rashnesse is his continuall walking mate. **1835** *Col. Crockett's Tour* 170 (Thornton) He got his *walking orders, and Taney was taken into his place. **1825** S. Woodworth *Forest Rose* I. iv. 18 As for the bumpkin, her lover, he must take his *walking papers. **1835** *Col. Crockett's Tour* 80 The first course he took was to give walking papers to every man in office who had dared [to oppose him]. **1916** Joyce *Portrait of Artist* 23 You'll get your walking papers [*sc.* discharge from a school infirmary] in the morning when the doctor comes. **1978** L. Pryor *Viper* viii. 141 Hassan gave me my walking papers last night. **1800** Mrs. P. L. Powys *Passages fr. Diaries* (1899) 337 After our repast the ladies made *walking parties to different places in the forest. **1791** Smeaton *Edystone L.* §77 The stone where-with the *walking paths of Westminster Bridge were laid. *c* **1440** *Promp. Parv.* 514/2 *Walkynge place, *deambulatorium.* **1598** R. Bernard tr. *Terence, Adelphi* IV. ii, Come backe againe into the walking place I told you of [*in porticum rursum redi*]. **1682** Wheler *Journ. Greece* v. 367 The chief Walking-place in the whole Town: whither they went not only to take the Air, but to converse with Men of Learning, to hear the News [etc.]. **1703** T. N. *City and C. Purchaser* 12 A long kind of Galleries, or Walking-places. **1897** *Daily News* 10 Dec. 3/2 Defendant's man was in what was called '*walking possession' of the furniture. **1613** Rowlands *Paire of Spy-Knaues* (1872) 8 Bid him trim vp my *walking Rapier neat. **1821** Scott *Kenilw.* xvi, Soldiers..get out of fashion in peace time, and satin sleeves and walking rapiers bear the bell. **1677** *Lond. Gaz.* No. 1198/4 A small Coûteau *walking Sword. **1910** *Encycl. Brit.* X. 250/2 The walking-sword, fit for a gentleman's side, was..the small-sword of Versailles pattern. **1829** in N. E. Eliason *Tarheel Talk* (1956) 124, I heard..she had given Henry a *walking ticket. **1835** *Col. Crockett's Tour* 162 (Thornton) He received his walking ticket. His services were no longer required. **1888** 'R. Boldrewood' *Robbery under Arms* I. x. 124 Every soul about the place..seemed to have got a cheque and a walking-ticket at the same time. **1970** *Islander* (Victoria, B.C.) 24 May 7/2 If a man spat on the floor, he'd get warned. If he did it again he'd get his walking ticket.

walking ('wɔːkɪŋ), *vbl. sb.*^{2} [-ING^1.] The action of WALK *v.*^{2}; fulling.

1582 Hakluyt *Voy.* (1599) II. 162 The faults in Walking, Rowing, and Burling,..are to be known to the merchant. **1688** [See b.]

b. Comb.: †**walking-mill** = WALK-MILL^1; †**walking-pin**, in hat-manuf. (see quot.); †**walking-staff**, a fuller's staff.

1677 Moxon *Mech. Exerc.* iii. 54 Case Hardning..is used for Tobacco Boxes, Cod-peece Buttons, Heads for walking staves, &c. **1688** Holme *Armoury* III. 291/1 The Walking-pin is a four square Iron,..with pointed ends; upon this the Workman rowls his Hat often times, and makes use of it as a rowling-pin, to lay his stuff close together in the walking of the Hat. **1839** *Whistle-Binkie* Ser. II. 118 Like the thud o' a waukin mill beetle.

walking ('wɔːkɪŋ), *ppl. a.* [f. WALK *v.*[1] + -ING[2].] That walks, in senses of the verb.

1. a. Moving about from place to place, travelling, itinerant. Now only with implication of sense 3.

a **1425** *Cursor M.* 17478 (Trin.) In þat tyme out of Iude Of walkynge men were comen þre To þat folke tolde þei al bidene þat þei had wiþ her eȝen sene. *c* **1430** *Pilgr. Lyf Manhode* I. vi. (1869) 4 For it is thing wel sittinge to eche walkinge pilgrime. **1567** HARMAN *Caveat* (1869) 67 A Walking Mort. **1613** PURCHAS *Pilgrimage* IV. xv. (1614) 421 Townes they [the Tartars] plant none nor standing villages, but haue walking houses built vpon wheeles, like a Shepheards Cottage. **1653** WALTON *Angler* vii. 149, I call that [bait] a ledger which is fix'd, or made to rest in one certaine place..and..I call that a walking bait, which you take with you, and have ever in motion. **1720** C. SHADWELL *Hasty Wedding* III. i, I am what they call a Walking-Merchant, one that gets my Living by the Sweat of my Brows.

†**b.** Leading a wandering life, vagrant, strolling. *Obs.*

149. *Anc. Deed* A. 7494 (P.R.O.) The seid Robert ordend ther j. bedd for poor walkyng pepull to be harborowed therin. **1592** *Goudhurst Parish Reg.* (M.S.), Buried a poore old walking man. **1602** CAREW *Cornwall* II. 131 b, Wideslades sonne led a walking life with his harpe, to Gentlemens houses. **1628** *Lydd Parish Reg.* (MS.), John, the sonne of a walkinge woman, christened. **1641** BROME *Joviall Crew* II. (1652) G 1, See in their rags, then, dauncing for your sports, Our Clapper Dugeons and their walking Morts.

c. Having a roving commission, going about from place to place. *walking delegate*, a trades-union official who visits sick members, interviews employers, etc.

1663 GERBIER *Counsel* 59 The King told him he would have no walking Master Workman. **1889** *Lippincott's Monthly Mag.* Feb. 227, I had no experience of strikes, and 'the walking delegate' was not yet stepping westward. **1892** HOWELLS *Mercy* 131 She decided that he must be a walking-delegate, and that he had probably come on mischief from some of the workpeople in her father's employ. **1897** *Encycl. Soc. Reform* 1381 *Walking delegate.* **1902** S. E. WHITE *Blazed Trail* iii, I think M. & D. is rather full up just now. .. I'm walkin'-boss there.

†**2.** Of a disease: Migratory. *Obs.*

c **1400** *Lanfranc's Cirurg.* 79 A walkynge vlcus [marg. [*vlcus ambulatiuum*] is þat walkiþ hidirward & þidirward, & neþeles he profoundiþ nouȝt depe into þe ground.

3. a. That travels or goes about on foot by moving the legs alternately without running. *walking doll*, a mechanically operated doll that can be made to move its legs; *walking funeral*, one in which the coffin is wheeled by hand.

1697 DRYDEN *Æneis* III. 852 Oft from the Rocks a dreadful Prospect [I] see Of the huge Cyclops, like a walking Tree. **1832** BREWSTER *Nat. Magic* i. 5 The walking statues at Antium. **1841** DICKENS *Barnaby Rudge* ix, in *Master Humphrey's Clock* II. 285, I wish I may only have a walking funeral, and never be buried decent with a mourning-coach and feathers. **1848** MRS. GASKELL *Mary Barton* vi, It was a simple walking funeral. **1859** JEPHSON *Brittany* iv. 42 A walking Englishman was, no doubt, a curiosity. *a* **1870** in *Country Life* (1973) 29 Nov. 1833/2 The patent Autoperipatetikos or walking-doll. **1886** C. M. YONGE *Chantry House* II. xvi. 158 A Chinese walking doll was sent..for the amusement of Miss Winslow's school children. **1968** *Canad. Antiques Collector* Dec. 14/2 In the 1820's the first walking dolls were introduced. These opened and shut their eyes and said 'mama' and 'papa'. **1983** L. TAYLOR *Mourning Dress* i. 40 Even amongst the poor there were grades of funerals. The grandest involved the use of a horse-drawn hearse, but much more common was a 'walking funeral' where the coffin was wheeled on its hearse.

†**b.** Funambulatory. *Obs.*

1730 A. GORDON *Maffei's Amphith.* 321 The walking Elephants on Ropes.

c. *walking sickness*, an illness in which the person is still able to get about and is not confined to bed.

1846 MCCULLOCH *Acc. Brit. Empire* II. 571 In other chronic diseases, slow inflammations of internal organs, reduced dislocations, rheumatisms, ulcerations, the patient can attend partially to his business: he is in possession of half his faculties... This is walking sickness.

d. Of a casualty: able to walk despite his injuries, not in need of a stretcher; chiefly in phr. *walking wounded*, such casualties collectively; also *fig.*

1917 P. GIBBS *Battles of Somme* 265 The long trails of the walking wounded, marvellously brave, wonderfully full of spirits. **1948** G. GREENE *Heart of Matter* II. I. i. 117 We were told to prepare for nine stretcher cases and four walking ones. **1965** *Economist* 4 Dec. 1072/2 Governor Rockefeller.. has been one of the political walking-wounded since his unpopular remarriage in 1963. **1972** *Guardian* 23 Dec. 8/1 There are many less conspicuous casualties, the walking wounded of the affluent society.

4. Theat. *walking gentleman*: an actor playing a part requiring gentlemanlike appearance, but with little or nothing to say. Similarly *walking lady.*

1794 C. MATHEWS *Let.* 14 June in A. Mathews *Mem. Charles Mathews* (1838) I. v. 86 And asked me if I would like to play walking gentleman. **1831** T. L. PEACOCK *Crotchet C.* iii, A sort of serious comedy walking gentleman's face. **1835** *Colburn's New Monthly Mag.* XLIII. 360 The respectably-dressed and well-looking young fellows in comedies are called walking gentlemen, and this is the probationary line of business usually assigned to young actors. **1860** G. VANDENHOFF *Leaves from Actor's Note-bk.* xii. 196 Susan.. was the best walking-lady on the American Stage. **1865** W. DONALDSON *Recoll. Actor* 176 Miss Smithson..was neither more nor less than the 'walking lady'. **1885** JEROME *On the Stage* 132 R——, our walking Gent., got his eye cut out. *fig.* **1815** SCOTT *Guy M.* xvi, A d——d cake-house, the resort of walking gentlemen of all descriptions—poets, players, painters, musicians, who come to rave..about this picturesque land of ours. **1827** BARRINGTON *Pers. Sk.* I. iv. 62 Nothing..could induce me to remain a walking gentleman: and so, every occupation that I could think of having its peculiar disqualification, I remained [etc.]. **1867** GOLDW. SMITH *Three Eng. Statesmen* (1882) 130 George III. tried unconstitutional monarchy, first by Lord Bute, a walking-gentleman, and failed.

5. That goes about in the semblance of a human being. Often in figurative or similative expressions; e.g. *walking corpse*, applied to a person hardly distinguishable from a corpse save by the power of movement; also *walking dead*; *walking dictionary*, *encyclopædia*, *library*, etc., said of a person who has great stores of information at command.

Cf. Eunapius *Vitæ Soph.*, Λογγῖνος βιβλιοθήκη τις ἦν ἔμψυχος καὶ περιπατοῦν μουσεῖον.

1605 SHAKS. *Macb.* v. v. 24 Life's but a walking Shadow, a poore Player, That struts and frets his houre vpon the Stage, And then is heard no more. **1611** BEAUM. & FL. *Maid's Trag.* III. i, Alas! I am nothing but a multitude of walking griefes. *a* **1625** FLETCHER *Captain* II. ii, [His body is] a Trunk-seller, to send wines down in, Or a long walking-bottle. **1691** WOOD *Ath. Oxon.* I. 337 Mathew Slade..was ..a stiff Enemy to the Socinians, and a walking Library. **1693** J. EDWARDS *Author. O. & N. Test.* I. 401 Wherever these walking Corpes, (these Carkases) were to be seen. **1775** SHERIDAN *Duenna* III. vii, Dare such a thing as you pretend to talk of beauty? A walking rouleau! a body that seems to owe all its consequence to the dropsy! **1818** SCOTT *Hrt. Midl.* ii, Looking like a moving and walking corpse, while yet an inhabitant of this world. **1835** LYTTON *Gipsy* v, Heaven deliver me from the proximity of a walking dictionary of technical terms! **1868** L. M. ALCOTT *Little Women* I. xii. 181 Meg..considered him a walking encyclopaedia of useful knowledge. **1912** T. DREISER *Financier* vi. 60 There were many, many wildcat banks, and they were sufficient in number to make the average exchange-counter broker a walking encyclopedia of solvent and insolvent institutions. **1978** *Rugby World* Apr. 28/3 He could..enlist the aid of some other members of the Irish [rugby] squad like Mike Gibson, or Johnny Robbie, or Mick Quinn, who are walking encyclopaedias on English soccer in particular. **1980** J. GARDNER *Garden of Weapons* III. iii. 247 You look terrible. Like the walking dead.

6. Of a spectre: That 'walks' or appears.

1607 DEKKER & WEBSTER *Northw. Hoe* III. E 1, Was there euer any walking spirit, like to my wife? **1709** PENN in *Pennsylv. Hist. Soc. Mem.* X. 354, I have my old order of.. 1685..ratified and confirmed, which has laid those walking ghosts.

7. a. Of a bird: That walks, as distinguished from one that hops. *walking tyrant*: a South American tyrant-flycatcher, *Machetornis rixosa.*

1837 W. SWAINSON *Nat. Hist. & Classif. Birds* II. 225 *Chrysolophus*, Sw. Walking Tyrants.

b. *walking catfish*: a freshwater catfish, *Clarias batrachus*, native to south-east Asia and Africa, and able to use its fins to crawl over land.

1968 *Orlando* (Florida) *Sentinel* 20 Nov. 8-C/1 The state of Florida surrendered Tuesday in its war with the weird 'walking catfish' and said the ambulating invader..is here to stay. **1984** *USA Today* 6 Apr. 3B/1 Walking catfish were imported from Thailand to Florida in 1960 by a fish farmer who sold them to aquarium owners to keep their tanks clean. They since have multiplied rapidly in the wild. Some people are working on recipes to make walking catfish a more palatable dish.

8. *walking fern*: (*a*) a club-moss (see quot. 1829); (*b*) a small tufted evergreen fern, *Camptosorus rhizophyllus*, native of eastern North America (*Cent. Dict.* 1891): = WALKING-LEAF 1 b. *walking orchid*: see quot.

1829 LOUDON *Encycl. Plants* (1836) 892 Lycopodium alopecuroides. Walking Fern. **1910** *Friar Park, Henley, Guide* (ed. 3) 244 *Orchis maculata*. The Walking Orchid. This Orchid, like several other species, seeks new pastures every year.

9. Jazz. *walking bass*: a bass part, often consisting of broken octaves, that goes up and down the scale in 4/4 time in steps or small intervals; so *walking beat.*

1939 L. HOBSON *Amer. Jazz Music* 51 *String bass*, more often plucked or slapped than bowed, usually playing two or four notes per bar on a 'walking' (melodic) bass. **1947** W. RUSSELL in R. de Toledano *Frontiers of Jazz* iv. 61 A rhythmic and a melodic germ motive are developed over a 'walking bass' figure. **1950** [see STRIDE *sb.* 8 b]. **1952** Walking beat [see WALK *v.*[1] 7 g]. **1952** B. ULANOV *Hist. Jazz in Amer.* (1958) iv. 29 If you listen carefully to the Ellington recording of 'C Jam Blues', you will hear a definitive example of the walking bass—1234/1234/1234, over and over again. *Ibid.* iv. 67 He was reliable, he put down a good walking beat, he had learned to read music. **1967** *Crescendo* May 18/2 The way he [*sc.* James Moody] wrote led to the invention of what's called the 'walking' bass, which the Americans took up later. **1980** *New Grove Dict. Mus.* III. 39/1 George Thomas, whose *New Orleans Hop Scop Blues* (1911; published 1916) included a walking bass, used the same device.

10. Mining. *walking dragline*, a large dragline supported on movable feet.

1959 *Times Rev. Industry* June 75/1 A..walking dragline ..will carry a 10 cu. yd bucket at 184 ft. radius and will strip 15 tons at each bite. **1977** *Bulletin* (Sydney) 22 Jan. 39/1 (Advt.), Queensland is rich in coal, but it has to be wrested from the ground, and it's here where the huge Marion walking dragline is in its element.

walking-fish ('wɔːkɪŋfɪʃ). [WALKING *ppl. a.*]

1. A name given to various fishes (see quots.).

1863 J. G. WOOD *Illustr. Nat. Hist.* III. 289 Walking-fish.—*Antennarius hispidus.* **1883** F. DAY *Ind. Fish* 36 A walking-fish (*Ophiocephalus*). **1885** E. BALFOUR *Cycl. India* (ed. 3) III. 1041 Walking Fishes of India are species of Ophiocephalidæ. The hissar, or walking fish of S. America, is a species of Callichthys.

2. = SILVER-FISH 2 (Cent. Dict. 1891).

'walking-leaf. [WALKING *ppl. a.*]

1. †**a.** Some unidentified plant. **b.** An American evergreen fern, *Camptosorus rhizophyllus.*

1659 LOVELL *Herball* 525 Walking leaves, *Arbor foliis ambulantibus*, it seemeth to creep on the ground, and being touched it will presently move it selfe. **1856** A. GRAY *Man. Bot.* (1860) 593 *Camptosorus*, Link. Walking-Leaf.

2. A phasmid insect belonging to the genus *Phyllium* or some related genus. Also *walking-leaf-insect.*

1826 SAMOUELLE *Direct. Collect. Insects & Crust.* 32 This order [*Orthoptera*] contains the Grasshopper, Locust, Mantis, Walking-leaf, and the Cricket. **1892** *Pall Mall Gaz.* 10 Feb. 6/1 A large specimen of the walking-leaf insect.

'walking-staff. Now *rare.* [WALKING *vbl. sb.*[1]] A staff or long stick which one carries in the hand for support or aid in walking. Also *fig.*

1546 J. HEYWOOD *Prov.* I. x. (1867) 21 Now I well understand The walkyng staffe hath caught warmth in your hand. **1593** SHAKS. *Rich. II*, III. iii. 151 Ile giue..My Scepter, for a Palmers walking Staffe. **1694** LUTTRELL *Brief Rel.* (1857) III. 365 A person was taken in St. James Park with 2 pistolls laden in his pocket, his walking staffe being a gunn. **1726** SWIFT *Gulliver* II. i, The farmer..took a piece of a small straw, about the size of a walking-staff. **1784** BLAKE *Poet. Sk.*, *Song Old Sheph.*, Virtue is our walking-staff. **1846** KEIGHTLEY *Notes Virg.*, Flora 383 It [*Ferula communis*] is common in Apulia, where the shepherds make walking-staffs of it. **1876** ROCK *Textile Fabrics* 9 Returning, they brought with them a number of eggs [of silkworms] hidden in their walking-staves.

'walking-stick. [WALKING *vbl. sb.*[1]]

1. A stick or short staff carried in the hand when walking.

1580 HOLLYBAND *Treas. Fr. Tong*, *Baguette*, a white rodde, a walking sticke. **1622** FLETCHER *Beggar's Bush* v. i, You may take me in with a walking sticke, Even when you please, and hold me with a pack-threed. **1788** BARKER *Growth of Trees* in *Phil. Trans.* LXXVIII. 413 No. 21. was about as thick as a walking-stick in 1730. **1836** DICKENS *Sk. Boz*, *Shops & Tenants*, A tobacconist, who also dealt in walking-sticks and Sunday newspapers. **1915** W. P. LIVINGSTONE *Mary Slessor* IV. vi. 216 One man..was dressed in a hat, a loin-cloth, and a walking-stick.

b. The name of a plant (see quot.).

1910 *Friar Park, Henley, Guide* (ed. 3) 184 Walking-stick or Elk-horn (*Opuntia arborescens*), the woody stems are made into walking-sticks.

2. Any insect of the family *Phasmidæ* (see quots.). Also *walking-stick insect.*

1760 G. EDWARDS *Glean. Nat. Hist.* II. 168 Fig. 4.. represents..the Walking-stick. It is so much like a dry stick, that it is supposed to deceive birds and other animals, that prey upon insects. **1872** DARWIN *Orig. Species* (ed. 6) vii. 182 As in the case..of a walking-stick insect (Ceroxylus laceratus). **1885** C. F. HOLDER *Marvels Anim. Life* 146 The walking-sticks..resembling the twig upon which they rest.

3. *attrib.* and *Comb.*, chiefly with the sense 'made to resemble a walking-stick', as *walking-stick gun, stand, stool.* Also **walking-stick palm**, an Australian palm, *Bacularia monostachya*, the stem of which is used for making walking-sticks.

1884 MILLER *Plant-n.*, *Kentia* (*Areca*) *monostachya*, Whip-stick, or Walking-stick, Palm. **1892** GREENER *Breech-Loader* 45 Such weapons as walking-stick guns. **1892** *Photogr. Ann.* II. 387 Walking Stick Stand. **1907** *Gentl. Mag.* July 38 Young gentlemen seated at their ease on patent collapsible walking-stick stools.

'walking-wheel. [WALKING *vbl. sb.*[1] and *ppl. a.*]

a. = PEDOMETER. †**b.** (See quot. 1744.)

1706 PHILLIPS (ed. Kersey), *Perambulator*, a walking-wheel, a rolling Wheel made of Wood or Iron, with a Movement, a Face divided like a Clock and Indexes, to shew how many Yards, Poles, Furlongs and Miles one goes in driving it before him. **1744** DESAGULIERS *Course Exper. Philos.* II. 417 Then the Wheel being also a walking Wheel, the same Men get into it, in which case they have Power sufficient to raise the small Goods 5 or 6 times faster than the heaviest. **1875** KNIGHT *Dict. Mech.*, *Walking-wheel*, a pedometer.

walkist ('wɔːkɪst). *Sporting slang.* [f. WALK *sb.*[1] or *v.*[1]: see -IST 4 b.] An athlete who takes part in walking-matches, a pedestrian.

1879 H. C. POWELL *Amateur Athletic Ann.* 17 The reappearance on the path of J. Gomersall, at one time the champion walkist of the 'north countree'. **1880** L. J. JENNINGS *Rambles among Hills* 172 A professional 'walkist' who goes along seeing nothing.

walklet ('wɔːklɪt). *nonce-wd.* [f. WALK *sb.*[1] + -LET.] A short walk.

1832 J. ROMILLY *Diary* 21 Feb. (1967) 4 Peter Ouvry & I had a walklet. **1896** A. BEARDSLEY *Let.* *c* 12 Dec. (1970) 225 Yesterday I ventured out for a walklet in Winter Gardens.

Walkman ('wɔːkmən). A proprietary name for small battery-operated cassette players and headphones capable of being worn by a person who is on foot.

1981 *Trade Marks Jrnl.* 25 Mar. 623/2 *Walkman*... Electrical and electronic apparatus and instruments.. for transmitting, receiving, tuning, recording and reproducing audio and visual signals.. batteries; aerials; loudspeakers; headphones; earphones.. cassettes.. Sony Kabushiki Kaisha (Sony Corporation).. Tokyo 141, Japan; manufacturers and merchants. **1981** *Japan Times* 31 Dec. 10/1 Sony Walkmans, easy-driving Honda scooters and aluminum household Buddhist altars sold like hotcakes during 1981. **1983** *Chicago Sun-Times* 22 May 9 I'll wear a Walkman in line [for the film] so I won't hear any smart alecks spill the story. **1983** *Sci. Amer.* June 130/1 The smaller zippers would be for products that reflect the current trend toward miniaturization, such as for carrying cases to fit the Walkman type of portable radio. **1983** *Official Gaz.* (U.S. Patent Office) 20 Dec. TM 288/1 Sony Corporation... *Walkman*... For audio tape player, audio tape recorders, radios and headphones. **1984** S. Townsend *Growing Pains A. Mole* 54 They wear red satin side vent running shorts, sleeveless satin vests, white knee socks, Sony Walkman earphones and one gold earring.

'walk-mill^1. Now *rare*. [f. WALK *v.*^{2} + MILL *sb.* Cf. G. *walkmühle*.] A fulling-mill.

1359 *Mem. Ripon* (Surtees) I. 282 Juxta aquam quæ currit usque le Walkemilne. **1473** in *Rental Bk. Cupar-Angus* (1879) I. 188 The tendis of the corn mil and walkmyl remenand fre to the abbay. *a* **1578** Lindesay (Pitscottie) *Chron. Scot.* (S.T.S.) II. 312 [The flood] buir away the walkmylnes. **1601** Holland *Pliny* xxxv. xi. II. 550 Simus took pleasure in painting a yong man lying asleepe in a waulke mill or Fullers worke-house. **1710** in *Nairne Peerage Evid.* (1874) 153 With multures walkmiln and pertinents therof. **1894** R. S. Ferguson *Hist. Westmorld.* 165 The 'steads' or sites of many disused 'walk mills' or fulling mills upon the Kent.

b. *Comb.*

1344 *Mem. Ripon* (Surtees) I. 141 Jacens in le Walkmylnbanke. *c* **1460** *Towneley Myst.* xxx. 314 His luddokkys thai lowke like walk-mylne cloggys.

Hence **'walk-miller**.

1752 in *Scots Mag.* (1753) July 338/1 Angus Macdonald waulk-miller in Anchofragan.

'walk-mill^2. [WALK *v.*^{1} or *sb.*] A mechanical contrivance or machine, the driving power of which is furnished by the walking of a horse, etc.

1773 W. Emerson *Princ. Mech.* (ed. 3) 286 List of Machines &c... Walk-mill. **1892** *Daily News* 15 Nov. 3/1 If there is no wind to supply the necessary power, the leader hopes that twelve men will be able to furnish it by means of a walk-mill, arranged on deck.

walkne, obs. form of WAKEN *v.*, WELKIN.

'walk-off. [f. vbl. phr. *to walk off*: WALK *v.*^{1} 8 c.] An act of walking off: **a.** From a stage.

1936 N. Coward *Red Peppers* in *To-night at 8.30* I. 85 Their exit consists of a neat walk off together, one behind the other, with their telescopes under their arms. **1970** *Time* 5 Jan. 51 The walk-off is the bittersweet image by which.. Chaplin wishes to be remembered.

b. From a ship, sports field, etc. Cf. WALK-OUT *sb.* 1.

1951 *Daily Progress* (Charlottesville, Va.) 13 June 5/1 (*heading*) Walkoff grows at new atomic plant. **1960** *Daily Tel.* 28 July 1/8, 2 liner crews return after walk-off. **1971** *Guardian Weekly* 10 Apr. 6 The 22 Springbok cricketers who held a walk-off at Newlands Ground here yesterday in protest against apartheid in cricket.

'walk-on, *sb.* and *a.* [f. vbl. phr. *to walk on*: see WALK *v.*^{1} 5] **A.** *sb.*

1. *Theat.* **a.** A part in which the performer merely comes on and goes off the stage with little or no speaking.

1902 *Daily Chron.* 1 Sept. 3/7 The actress, too, frequently is glad to accept 12s. a week for a walk-on with half a dozen words. **1907** H. Wyndham *Flare of Footlights* v, The part just now is a walk-on, with an understudy of one of the principals. **1936** R. Lehmann *Weather in Streets* iv. i. 361 Or I might get a walk-on in a film. **1950** *Sun* (Baltimore) 19 May 16/2 It has the all-starriest cast of all time, with all the great ones doing walk-ons and bits. **1971** R. A. Carter *Manhattan Primitive* (1972) xv. 142 She never got another speaking part: a few walk-ons, then she was an extra again.

b. An actor, etc., who has a walk-on part; = *walker-on* s.v. WALKER *sb.*^{1} 1 c.

1946 *Sun* (Baltimore) 20 May 6/1 It can dispense with the star system.. by concentrating on teamwork in which lead actors one night become walk-ons the next. **1964** M. Drabble *Garrick Year* xii. 193 A square, worried-looking girl, who was married to one of the walk-ons. **1980** *Times Lit. Suppl.* 31 Oct. 1228/5 There are several blandly handsome walk-ons, most of them recently out of drama school.

2. *Sport.* A team member without any regular status. *U.S.*

1974 *Plain Dealer* (Cleveland, Ohio) 19 Oct. 2-D/1 East Tech's Mike Lucas, a 6-4 junior college transfer from Arizona, is one of three 'walk-ons' on Ohio State's basketball team. **1980** *New Yorker* 3 Mar. 80 This year.. the Highlands team looks a bit too much like the rest of the students for Martinez's taste... One player.. did not even come to Highlands on a basketball scholarship—a category of athlete known in the trade as 'walk-ons'. **1981** *Washington Post* 4 Sept. D-1 He was beaten by Marty Davis, 22, who made the University of California tennis team as a walk-on.

B. *adj.* **1.** Pertaining to or designating an airline service for which prior booking is not required. orig. *U.S.*

1961 *Flight* LXXX. 488/2 The airline.. earlier this year introduced 'walk-on' services to Chittagong. **1967** J. Gardner *Madrigal* viii. 220 He.. asked if there were any direct flights from Manchester to Zurich... At this time of year there should be no difficulty in getting a walk-on booking. **1977** *Times* 29 July 4/3 British Airways intends to compete with Laker Airways' walk on Skytrain air service between London and New York. **1983** *Flight Internat.* 10 Sept. 680/2 Shuttle's walk-on option with guaranteed backup aircraft.

2. Theat. ***walk-on part***, etc. = sense A. 1 a above. Also *transf.* and *fig.*

1963 *Times* 25 Feb. 4/1 Before luncheon the New Zealanders were so vigorous, accurate and hostile that Illingworth, Sheppard, and even Dexter could play only walk-on parts. **1973** J. Leasor *Host of Extras* viii. 141 If he heard of any jobs going—walk-on parts, crowd scenes, the odd TV commercial—he passed them on to me. **1976** *Private Eye* 24 Dec. 17/3 The Bank of England is determined it shall be in a supporting, if not walk-on, capacity rather than a starring role. **1977** *Time* 8 Aug. 21/1 Her striking good looks eventually won her some small walk-on parts in German films. **1983** J. Juxon *Lewis & Lewis* xxi. 223 Few.. of Parnell's biographers have given Lewis more than a walk-on part in the drama. **1985** *Listener* 24 Jan. 11/3 Salman Rushdie complained that Indians were for the most part given walk-on roles.

'walk-out, *sb.* and *a.* [f. vbl. phr. *to walk out*: see WALK *v.*^{1} 5j, 13.] **A.** *sb.* **1. a.** A strike, esp. one called at short notice. Also *transf.*

1888 in Farmer *Americanisms* (1889) 550/2 The walk out of brewery employés, decided upon at last night's meeting of the union, was considerable of a fizzle. Less than thirty men left their work. **1894** *Evening Sun* (N.Y.) 10 July 1/6 Some of the big firms have already closed their works in anticipation of a walkout. **1919** *New Solidarity* (Chicago) 18 Jan. 1/1 The date.. contemplated as the day for a general strike, or walk-out. **1957** *Economist* 12 Oct. 129/1 An attempt to organise a walkout by the white pupils failed when less than one in thirty left the school. **1982** *Daily Tel.* 22 July 5/1 Porters, cooks, cleaners and other ancillary staff staged an almost complete walk-out. **1985** *Times* 7 Mar. 11/3 The planners speak of lightning strikes and walkouts.

b. An act of leaving a meeting, etc., as a gesture of protest or disapproval.

1927 *Observer* 1 May 13/4 He has fulfilled the assurance he gave on taking the Chair that he would observe strict impartiality in the conduct of business... It may be that on one or two occasions Mr. Patel's judgement has been at fault, as, for instance, in the dramatic episode of the Swarajist walk-out. **1946** *Richmond* (Va.) *Times-Dispatch* 2 Apr. 1/1 Ala presented Iran's side to the council last week after Russia's dramatic walkout. **1958** *Times* 2 Sept. 7/4 The opening film [*sc.* at a festival].. saw a rather considerable number of walk-outs. **1973** H. Trevelyan *Diplomatic Channels* viii. 125 The pointed absence or walk out on official occasions can be overdone, but is necessary if a speech by the host is directly insulting to the ambassador's country.

2. A love affair.

1934 E. Waugh *Handful of Dust* ii. 46 He's having a terrific walk out with a girl called Sheila Shrub. **1983** P. Devlin *All of us There* v. 57 Ellen has been having a walk-out with his brother Joe for years.

B. *adj.* Of a room or basement: with its own exit door, i.e. not dependent on stairs to another floor. *N. Amer.*

1958 *Washington Post* 16 Aug. B6/5 This home.. has.. full walkout basement and a Hotpoint kitchen. **1968** *Globe & Mail* (Toronto) 13 Jan. 42/1 (Advt.), Lower level features striking walk-out family room and sauna. **1978** *Detroit Free Press* 16 Apr. F-10/8 (Advt.), Full finished walkout basement with fireplace.

walk-over. [f. vbl. phrase *walk over*: see WALK *v.*^{1} 7 c.] **a.** A race in which through absence of competitors the winner has merely to 'walk over'; also in extended sense, a contest in which through the inferiority of his competitors the winner has practically no opposition.

1838 *Times* 29 June 8/3 [Election at Cashel] I think it not unlikely that Mr. Richard Moore may have a walk over. **1861** *Sporting Rev.* Oct. 249 Kettledrum's walk-over was quite a little tit-bit for the Yorkshiremen. **1889** *Century Mag.* July 403/1 That's the bay stallion there,.. and he's never been beaten. It's his walk-over.

b. *transf.* Anything accomplished with great ease.

1902 G. H. Lorimer *Lett. Self-Made Merchant* xv. 216 It wasn't any walk-over to hold the belt in those days. **1931** *Daily Tel.* 21 Jan. 8/4 This makes its acquisition by an American crook a walk-over. **1975** P. Fussell *Gt. War & Mod. Memory* (1977) i. 27 His little sporting contest did have the effect of persuading his men that the attack was going to be.. a walkover.

c. *attrib.* or as *adj.*

1936 *Sunday Times* 14 June 4/2 When the law gets them in its clutches, a shady lawyer is allowed to get a walkover verdict of 'Not Guilty'. **1974** *Times* 5 Oct. 14/7 Lauda seemed set for almost a walkover trip to the title (he proved himself the fastest driver.. nine times this year).

walkrife, -ryf(e, obs. forms of WAKERIFE.

†**'walkripe**, *a. Obs. rare*$^{-1}$. [f. WALK *v.*^{1} + RIPE *a.*] Of an ulcer: see quot.

1585 Banister *Chyrurg.* III. xxv. Wks. (1633) 273 Of the filthie and putrified Vlcer... If the malice of this ulcer, grow walkeripe, that is, fall a creeping, it turneth to *Sphacelus*, and so to the death of the partie.

'walk-round, *sb.* and *a.* [f. vbl. phr. *to walk round*: WALK *v.*^{1} 5 a.]

A. *sb.* = *walk-around* (*b*) s.v. WALK *v.*^{1} 27. *U.S.*

1861 *Temple Bar* May 199 The 'Jim Crow dance'.. soon gave place to better tunes.. and 'walk rounds'. **1895** *Century Mag.* Oct. 958/1 His work with the caravan was to sing songs, chiefly darky songs, accompanied by 'hoe-downs' and 'walk rounds'. **1943** *Life* 5 July 80 After the 'walk-round', which served as an entrance for the black-faced showmen, they stood before a semicircle of chairs and waited for the interlocutor's: 'Gentlemen, be seated.'

B. *adj.* Round which one can walk: applied to a self-service shop with goods so arranged.

1974 P. Wright *Lang. Brit. Industry* xiii. 120 Walk-round store (where the goods are so accessible that you may be tempted to buy far more than you need). **1979** *This England* Winter 19/3 Miss Corrie's dim, prim little shop in the market place had survived the competition of walk-round stores and boutiques.

†**'walkster.** *Sc. Obs.* [f. WALK *v.*^{2} + -STER.] A walker or fuller.

1599 in Cramond *Rec. Elgin* (1908) II. 71 Johne Stewart, walkster, accusit for playing at the bowallis on the calsaye the tyme of the evenyng prayeris. **1721** in J. F. S. Gordon *Chron. Keith* (1880) 97 David Clerk, walkster at Keith.

'walk-through, *sb.* and *a.* [f. vbl. phr. *to walk through*: WALK *v.*^{1}] **A.** *sb.* **1.** *Theat.* **a.** A part not requiring the performer to exert himself, one that he may 'walk through' (WALK *v.*^{1} 7 a); *transf.*, an undemanding task.

1944 *Sun* (Baltimore) 15 July 6/1 The principal roles offer no difficulties, permitting Miss Powell to be herself, as always, and giving her leading man a walk-through. **1950** *Ibid.* 13 Oct. 12/2 For Mr. Milland, an actor with 58 photo-plays to his credit, this is a walk-through. **1980** J. Ball *Then came Violence* (1981) iv. 36 We've just had a homicide and this one isn't a domestic walk-through. **1984** *New Yorker* 30 Jan. 82/2 Most skilled politicians take the measure of a crowd and find ways to relate to it specifically. It is as if Glenn were doing a walk-through.

b. A perfunctory or lacklustre performance.

1970 *Globe & Mail* (Toronto) 26 Sept. 23/1 Richard Burton in Hamlet.. giving us only an insulting, offhand walk-through.

2. (See quots.)

1959 W. S. Sharps *Dict. Cinematogr.* 91/2 *Dry run*, otherwise walk-through, a full rehearsal for a production, but without cameras. **1974** *Some Technical Terms & Slang* (Granada Television), *Walkthrough*, one stage after the tech run of a drama, but before moving into the studio proper. The cast and certain technicians will meet for a rough rehearsal in the studio set without cameras. **1977** K. T. Orr *Structured Syst. Devel.* i. 5 Today we see discussions of structured walkthroughs, structured design, and structured analysis. **1983** *Dict. Computing* 388/1 *Walk through*, a product review performed by a formal team... There is a clear statement of the contribution that each member of the review team is required to make, and a step-by-step procedure for carrying out the review... The product is.. openly debated with a view to uncovering problems or identifying desirable improvements.

B. *adj.* Of a building, etc.: permitting access from either end.

In quot. 1950, for the cows to enter and leave.

1950 *N.Z. Jrnl. Agric.* May 477/3 The walk-through [milking] shed with doors at the rear of the shed in the conventional manner. **1967** *Economist* 8 July p. viii, He [*sc.* the driver] will want to reach back to his load without dismounting and walking round to open the back doors—hence the spate of 'walk-through' vans in Britain. **1981** M. C. Smith *Gorky Park* III. i. 295 A remarkable walk-through tube that attached the plane directly to the terminal. **1984** *Buses* Nov. 488/3 A sliding door in the fixed section giving a walkthru' layout for the van.

'walk-up, *a.* and *sb.* [f. vbl. phr. *to walk up*: WALK *v.*^{1}]

A. *adj.* **1.** Of an apartment, etc.: that has to be reached by stairs rather than by a lift. Also applied to a building consisting of such apartments. *U.S.*

1919 Mencken *Amr. Lang.* iv. 110 The term *flat* 'is usually in the United States restricted to apartments in houses having no elevator or hall service'. In New York such apartments are commonly called *walk-up apartments*. **1927** E. Glyn *It* iv. 40 Mary had a tiny two-room apartment in a walk-up building in Brooklyn. **1942** *N.Y. Times* 13 Feb. (late City ed.) 13/4 Six five-story walk-up apartment houses. **1946** Mezzrow & Wolfe *Really Blues* (1957) xiii. 235 Some crummy walk-up tenement flat. **1979** H. Kissinger *White House Years* xxi. 906 Huang Hua and I met around six o'clock in the CIA's walk-up apartment in the East Seventies. **1984** *Business Rev. Weekly* (Austral.) 4–10 Feb. 42/3 The Myer development is a three-storey walk-up affair that has appealed to a lower age group than usual for Gold Coast units.

2. That may be approached on the street, without having to go into a building.

1963 C. J. McCall in A. Dundes *Mother Wit* (1973) 421 The colorful window-signs of innumerable 'readers'.. cry out from their store-front or walk-up locations. **1972** *Sunday Sun* (Brisbane) 8 Oct. 16/1 The same bandit had approached Miss Avery at her outside walkup window post on Tuesday and demanded $3000.

B. *sb.* **1.** A walk-up apartment or apartment block. *U.S.*

1925 *Scribner's Mag.* Oct. 6/2 Vacation heaves into sight over the horizon.. the swirling dust turned into clean sand; the only walk-up a dune; and the total night life two movie theatres. **1942** R. Chandler *High Window* xxv. 149 The kind of dentists who have shabby offices on second-floor walk-ups over stores. **1954** F. P. Keyes *Royal Box* xiii. 165 The friends he had all lived in the identical kind of six-flat walk-up. **1966** R. Stout *Death of Doxy* (1967) i. 6 The person to ask lived on the second floor of a walkup on 52nd Street. **1976** *National Observer* (U.S.) 4 Sept. 1/2 The blue-jeaned couples climbing the stairs to their walk-ups together are most usually the children of affluence. **1980** J. Krantz *Princess Daisy* xxv. 438 Daisy herself lived in a low-rent SoHo walk-up and held down a full-time job.

2. *U.S. Horse-Racing.* The walk of racehorses to a starting line or tape (as opposed to starting gates). Freq. *attrib.*

1938 *Sun* (Baltimore) 1 Nov. 12/1 The only change in the usual order will be a walkup start instead of a start from a gate. **1946** *Richmond* (Va.) *Times-Dispatch* 8 Mar. 23/3 The field might have to be started from a walkup to an old-fashioned web barrier. **1959** *Washington Post* 15 Nov. c 1 The starter who had trouble.. at Laurel in the ragged walk-up, says the foreign entries could be taught in five days to break from the stall gates. **1974** *Encycl. Brit. Macropædia* VIII. 1100/2 Some starts are still effected from a barrier that springs upward when actuated by the starter, or in the 'walk-up' fashion, whereby the starter gives a verbal order when the horses are reasonably well aligned.

3. *Shooting.* The act of walking up gamebirds (WALK *v.*^{1} 21); also *transf.* of clay pigeons; a piece of land kept for this purpose.

1972 *Shooting Times & Country Mag.* 27 May 10/3 There are numerous Bowman traps, designed to simulate varying driven game birds and there is a walk-up with 15 traps. **1975** *Times* 1 Sept. 14/6 An increasing number of landowners.. let walked-up shoots... On the Speyside walk-up the other day was a Marseille dentist.

'walkway. orig. *U.S.* Also **walk-way.** [f. WALK *sb.*^{1} or *v.*^{1} + WAY *sb.*^{1}] **1.** = WALK *sb.*^{1} 9 c.

1792 in *Essex Inst. Hist. Coll.* (1865) VII. 37/2 John Sanders.. agrees to pave the walk way in front of his Father's Estate. **1816** W. BENTLEY *Diary* (1914) IV. 405 A walkway for the first time has been raised in the principal streets in the eastern part of the Town. **1904** *N.Y. Evening Post* 14 May 5 A space.. sufficient to provide each house with a walkway to the rear. **1976** *Outdoor Living* (N.Z.) I. II. 42 (*caption*) Quarry tiled walkway and meandering plants leading through a painted brick archway give a pleasant first impression to this home. **1980** *Daily Tel.* 16 June 2/1 Paths affected by housing development should be retained as 'walkways' through the new estate.

2. A pedestrian passageway linking different parts of a building or structure or complex of buildings, esp. one raised above ground-level and separating the users from machinery, traffic, etc. Also, a specially built path taking sightseers through an area of natural beauty or the like.

1928 R. H. LANSBURGH *Industr. Management* (ed. 2) xv. 175 Accident prevention by making floors and walk-ways safe is a big factor in the industrial accident toll. **1933** *Meccano Mag.* Feb. 109/1 There is perfect communication between all members of the crew, a walk-way from end to end of the aeroplane being provided to enable members to change places quickly. **1953** *Archit. Rev.* CXIII. 83 (*caption*) The walkway.. passes under the three classroom blocks and links the two main courts. **1959** *Daily Tel.* 13 Mar. 18/4 The lay-out [of London Zoo] will include all-weather covered elevated walkways from the main gate. **1960** *Guardian* 20 May 7/2 First-floor shops, walkways and bridges for pedestrians. **1960** 'N. SHUTE' *Trustee from Toolroom* i. 13 The long wooden walkways above the tidal mud, the yachts moored bows-on in tiers. **1968** *New Scientist* 26 Sept. 640/2 There will be.. a moving walkway along the pier to the two terminals [at Heathrow Airport]. **1973** *Times* 18 Oct. (Brazil Suppl.) p. vii/4 Tourists.. will have 'walkways' through special jungle reserves which will remain undisturbed. **1979** *United States 1980/81* (Penguin Travel Guide) 250 The newly restored North Beach with landscaped dunes and oceanfront walkway. **1981** *Sci. Amer.* Nov. 32/1 This environment, the home of the most diverse swarm of species,.. is currently studied from walkways hung high among the treetops, steel towers rising into the leafy canopy. **1984** *Daily Tel.* 3 July 1/7 Outside there will be Tivoli-style gardens with a walkway along the Thames.

walkyn, obs. Sc. spelling of WAKEN.

walkyne, obs. form of WELKIN.

Walkyrie (wɒl'kɪrɪ). [repr. OE. *wælcyrie, -cyrʒe* wk. fem., lit. 'chooser of the slain', f. *wæl* WALE *sb.*^{1} + **cur-* ablaut-root of *céosan* CHOOSE *v.* Cf. VALKYRIE.]

1. *OE. Mythol.* The designation of a class of goddesses or female dæmons supposed to hover in or ride through the air over battle-fields and decide who should be slain: corresponding to the Scandinavian VALKYRIE.

The OE. word (apart from the transferred sense 2) is found only as the rendering of L. *Bellona*, the goddess of war, or of names of the Furies and Gorgons of classical mythology. Possibly the conception may have been less definite in Old English heathendom than in the Scandinavian belief of later times, according to which these 'war-maidens' were twelve in number. (The Ger. *Walküre*, widely known from Wagner's dramas, is from ON., not from OE.).

c **725** *Corpus Gloss.* (Hessels) E 351 *Eurynis*, walcyrʒe. *Ibid.* H 87 *Herinis*, walcriʒʒe. *Ibid.* T 159 *Tisifone*, uualcyrʒe. *c* **1000** in Cockayne *Narratiunculæ* (1861) 34 þa deor habbaþ eahta fet and walkyrian eaʒan [L. *oculos Gorgoneos*]. *c* **1050** *Voc.* in Wr.-Wülcker 360/3 *Bellona*, wælcyrʒe. *Ibid.* 533/26 *Allecto*, wælcyrʒe.

attrib. **1915** *Q. Rev.* Oct. 379 It [Napoleon's overrunning Europe] was a romantic, almost Walkyric dash.

†**2.** Used for: A witch, sorceress. *Obs.*

a **1023** WULFSTAN *Hom.* (1883) 298/18 Wyccan and wælcyrjan and unlybwyrhtan. **13..** *E.E. Allit. P.* B. 1577 Wychez & walkyries wonnen to þat sale.

Hence **Wal'kyric** *a.* [-IC], of or pertaining to the Walkyries.

1913 A. HARRISON in *Engl. Rev.* Aug. 110 Thompson's odes read like Walkyric word-battles.

walkys, obs. pl. of WHELK.

wall (wɔːl), *sb.*^{1} Forms: 1 **weall, weal, wall,** 3–7 **wal, walle,** 4–7 **wale,** 4–6 *Sc.* **vall,** 6 *Sc.* **val(e,** (5 **whalle,**) 6 **waule, (wawle),** 8–9 *Sc.* **wa',** 3– **wall.** [OE. *wall* (WS. *weall*), corresp. to OFris. *wal*, OS. *wal(l*, (M)LG., (M)Du. *wal*, MHG. *wal* from MLG. (mod.G. *wall*), a Saxon and Anglo-Frisian adoption of L. *vallum*. The Sw. *vall*, Da. *val*, are from LG.]

I. 1. a. A rampart of earth, stone, or other material constructed for defensive purposes. [= L. *vallum*.]

In OE. frequently used with the meaning 'a natural rampart, hill, cliff': see Bosw.-Toller.

c **900** *Bæda's Hist.* I. ix [xii]. (1890) 46 þæt hi ʒemænelice fæsten ʒeworhten him to ʒescyldnesse, stænene weal rihtre stiʒe fram eastsæ oð westsæ. *c* **1000** ÆLFRIC *Exod.* xiv. 22 And þæt water stod an twa healfa þære stræte swilce twe3en hcʒe weallas. *a* **1122** *O.E. Chron.* (Laud MS.) an. 189 þa ʒe wrohte he weall mid turfum & bred weall ðær on ufon fram sæ to sæ Britwalum to ʒebeorʒe. **1297** R. GLOUC. (Rolls) 2184 þat folc þo of þis lond.. Bigonne to rere þon stronge wal. *c* **1450** *Mirk's Festial* 2 þe watyr schall be hear then ayny hyll, by xl^{ti} cubytys, stondyng styll yn her styd, as hit wer a wall. **1581** J. HAMILTON *Cath. Traict.* 34 Moyses.. causit the valter stand vp als ferme as ane vall quhil the Israelites past throu. **1601** R. JOHNSON *Kingd. & Commw.* (1603) 26 Their carriages were so many, that therewith they intrenched their campe, like a wal. **1643** R. BAKER *Chron.* 2 The Emperor Adrian,.. who made a great wall of earth between England and Scotland. **1699** TEMPLE *Hist. Eng.* (ed. 2) 38 Agricola began.. a Wall or Vallum, upon that narrow space of Land that lies between the two Fryths. **1728** POPE *Dunc.* III. 76 He, whose long wall the wand'ring Tartar bounds. **1791** BOSWELL *Johnson* an. 1778 (1904) II. 203 He expressed a particular enthusiasm with respect to visiting the wall of China. **1850** *Smith's Class. Dict.* s.v. *Serica*, The Great Wall of China is mentioned by Ammianus Marcellinus under the name of Aggeres Serium.

transf. **1599** SHAKS. *Hen. V*, I. ii. 141 They of those Marches.. Shall be a Wall sufficient to defend Our in-land from the pilfering Borderers.

b. An embankment to hold back the water of a river or the sea. Cf. SEA-WALL.

1330 *Rolls of Parlt.* II. 36/2 De faire & de garder les Walles contre l'ewe de Tamys. *a* **1548** HALL *Chron., Hen. VIII*, 209 b, At whiche season was suche a spryng tide, that it brake the walles of Hollande and Zelande. **1593** NORDEN *Spec. Brit., M'sex* I. 17 Blackwall... The place taketh name of the blackenes or darkenes of the water bankes, or wall at that place. **1697** DE FOE *Ess. Projects* 121 In our Marshes and Fens.. where great Quantities of Land being.. recovered out of the Seas and Rivers, and maintain'd with Banks (which they call Walls). **1713** *Lond. Gaz.* No. 5122/11 Two Pieces of Thames Wall, with the Ozier Ground and Foreland thereto belonging,.. are to be Sold. **1888** FENN *Dick o' the Fens* iv. 49 *foot-note*, 'Wall,' in fen lands, the artificial bank or ridge of clay raised to keep back river, drain, or sea. **1898** P. H. EMERSON *Marsh Leaves* lix. 179 He stopped, and looked along the rosy dike, uttered a hasty exclamation, and ran down the wall.

2. a. A defensive structure enclosing a city, castle, etc. Chiefly *pl.*, fortifications. [= L. *murus*.]

c **825** *Vesp. Psalter* xvii. 30 In gode minum ic ofergaa wall. *c* **1000** *Ags. Ps.* (Th.) lix. 8 Hwylc ʒelædeð me leofran on ceastre, weallum beworhte? *a* **1200** *Moral Ode* 41 in *O.E. Hom.* I. 163 þes riche Men weneð bon siker þurh walle & þurh diche. **1297** R. GLOUC. (Rolls) 11433 A3en alle halwe churche þe verste dich hii nome & brake þe otemoste wal. *a* **1300** *K. Horn* (Hall) 1042 In strong halle, Bi inne castel walle. **1338** R. BRUNNE *Chron.* (1810) 326 The engyns with oute, to kast were þei sette, Wallis & kirnels stoute, þe stones doun bette. **1375** BARBOUR *Bruce* VI. 445 Thai sparit the ȝettis hastely, And in hy to the vallis ran. **1393** LANGL. *P. Pl.* C. XXI. 292 Brynston boilaunt brennyng out-casteþ hit Al hot [on] here heuedes þat entren ny þe walles. *c* **1470** HENRY *Wallace* v. 1136 Tre wark thai brynt.. Wallis brak doun that stalwart war off stanys. **1490** *Cal. Anc. Rec. Dublin* (1889) 371 For the kepyng of every yate of the walleys of this citte. **1586** WHITNEY *Choice Emblems* 110 Then Scipio comes, that Carthage waules did race. **1591** SHAKS. *1 Hen. VI*, IV. ii. 2 Go to the Gates of Burdeaux Trumpeter, Summon their Generall vnto the Wall. *Ibid.* V. iii. 129 At your Fathers Castle walles, Wee'l craue a parley. **1667** MILTON *P.L.* XI. 657 Others from the Wall defend With Dart and Jav'lin, Stones and sulfurous Fire. **1697** DRYDEN *Æneis* II. 456 To ..rush undaunted to defend the Walls. **1791** MRS. RADCLIFFE *Rom. Forest* i, Madame de la Motte gave a last look to the walls of Paris. **1823** LAMB *Elia* II. *Poor Relations*, He was among the first who perished before the walls of St. Sebastian. **1837** *Penny Cycl.* IX. 468/1 Towards the east the external wall [of Ephesus] crosses a hill, called Lepre... Other internal walls extend further south. **1847** GROTE *Greece* (1862) II. xix. 470 Babylon.. was surrounded by walls three hundred feet in height.

fig. **1592** *Arden of Feversham* I. i. 47 Sweete words are fittest engines To race the flint walles of a womans breast.

b. ***within the walls***: within the ancient boundaries (of a city) as distinguished from the suburbs; hence *fig.* within the limits (of the Church, †Europe, †Christendom, etc.)

1599 B. JONSON *Ev. Man out of Hum.* IV. iii. (1600) L 4 b, I think him the tallest man liuing within the walls of Europe. **1627** J. TAYLOR (Water-P.) *Navy of Land Ships* D 3, In a place which I could name within the Walles of Christendome. **1667** *Observ. Burning Lond.* 15 The City of London within the Walls was seated upon about 460 Acres of Ground. **1722** DE FOE *Plague* (1754) 6 To the great Affliction of the City, one died within the Walls, in the Parish of St. Mary-Wool-Church. **1860** WARTER *Sea-board* II. 468 The devout on earth will ever be found within the Church's walls.

c. *Her.* A representation of an embattled wall used as a bearing.

1688 HOLME *Armoury* III. 400/1 He beareth Argent.. a Wall corniced, with two Towers upon it. **1889** ELVIN *Dict. Her.* 131 Wall embattled in bend sinister.

3. *fig.* **a.** Applied to a person or thing that serves as a defence.

1412–20 LYDG. *Troy-bk.* IV. 1958 For he of Troye is þe my3ti wal And diffence, now Hector is [a-]goon. **1500–20** DUNBAR *Poems* lxxxv. 73 Imperiall wall, place palestrall,.. Aue Maria, gratia plena! **1565** ALLEN *Defence Purg.* xvii. 281 One common engine they haue.. for the sore shakinge of the weake waules of the simples faithe. **1581** A. HALL *Iliad* III. 52 It is Aiax the strong, Who is best hope, defence and wall, that to the Greeks belong. **1611** SHAKS. *Cymb.* II. i. 68 The Heauens hold firme The walls of thy deere Honour. **1838** LYTTON *Leila* v. i, We will leave our homes unguarded—our hearts shall be their wall!

b. Applied to the sea, the navy or shipping (as Britain's external defence); also to an army (as the safeguard of a country).

wooden walls (applied to ships): see WOODEN *a.*

1436 *Libel Eng. Policy* in *Pol. Poems* (Rolls) II. 203 Kepte [*v.r.* kepe] than the see abought in speciall, Whiche of England is the rounde walle; As thoughe England were lykened to a cite. **1642** *Declar. Lords & Comm.* 12–13 July 3 The ships which are the wals of the Kingdome. **1643** R. BAKER *Chron.* 2 At which time [of Julius Cæsar] the Island was yet but in manner of a Village, being without Wals, as having no shipping, (which are indeed the true Wals of an Island). **1657** TRAPP *Comm. Ezra* ix. 9 'To give us a wall' —Protection and safeguard, as the Walles of Sparta was their Militia, and the Walles of England, is our Navy. **1697** SIR M. BECKMAN in *Sydney Papers* I. 171 The Army by Land, and the Fleet, was accounted the Walls of England.

4. An enclosing structure composed of bricks, stones, or similar materials laid in courses.

hollow wall, a wall built with an interior cavity or composed of hollow bricks. For *blind, boulder, cob, dead, hot, list, rubble wall*, etc., see those words; also BRICK WALL *sb.*^{1}, MUD WALL, PARTY-WALL, STONE WALL.

a. Each of the sides and vertical divisions of a building.

to stand to the wall (*Sc.*): of a door, to be wide open. ***walls have ears*** (*Prov.*): see EAR *sb.*^{1} 3.

c **900** *Bæda's Hist.* II. xi [xiv]. (1890) 138 Ærþon heo seo heannis þæs wealles [*sc.* of a church] ʒefylled wære & ʒeendad. *a* **1300** *Cursor M.* 19313 We find ur prisuns all a-wai, þe dors sperd, þe walles hale. **1377** LANGL. *P. Pl.* B. XVIII. 61 þe wal wagged and clef and al þe worlde quaued. *c* **1435** *Torr. Portugal* 244 Sone hard he within a whalle The syghyng of a lady smalle, Sche weppte, as sche were wod. **1526** *Pilgr. Perf.* (W. de W. 1531) 142 Of the whiche buyldynge.. the foure walles be the foure cardinall vertues. **1591** SHAKS. *1 Hen. VI*, I. iv. 49 In Iron Walls they deem'd me not secure. **1596** —— *Merch. V.*, II. ix. 29 Which.. like the Martlet Builds in the weather on the outward wall. **1638** JUNIUS *Paint. Ancients* Ep. Ded., To make use of that, which in your service, and within the walls of your own house, I had produced. **1649** LOVELACE *To Althea fr. Prison* iv, Stone Walls do not a Prison make. **1728** RAMSAY *Fables, Monk & Miller's Wife* 256 Wauk forth, the door stands to the wa'. **1732** POPE *Ep. Bathurst* 188 Like some lone Chartreux stands the good old Hall, Silence without, and Fasts within the wall. **1816** SCOTT *Bl. Dwarf* vii, Look at the burnt wa's of our kinsman's house. **1823** P. NICHOLSON *Pract. Builder* 307 Walls of stone may be made one-fifth thinner than those of brick. **1837** DICKENS *Pickw.* xl, Mr. Pickwick found himself, for the first time in his life, within the walls of a debtor's prison. **1876** *Encycl. Brit.* IV. 447/2 The inclined roof of a building, spanning from wall to wall, tends to thrust out the walls.

In figurative context (after Acts xxiii. 3). **1593** G. HARVEY *Pierces Super.* Wks. (Grosart) II. 173 If Percase I happen to touch some painted walles, and godly hypocrites.

b. An enclosing structure built round a garden, field, yard, or other property; also, each of the portions between the angles of such an enclosure.

a **1300** *Cursor M.* 8233 A wall a-bote dide for to rais, And planted tres þat war to prais. **1587** MASCALL *Govt. Cattle, Hogges* (1596) 263 It were good to make the walles or hedges of your sties of foure foote hie. **1592** SHAKS. *Rom. & Jul.* II. i. 5 He ran this way and leapt this Orchard wall. **1698** FRYER *Acc. E. India & P.* 7 A most stately Grove of Cocoes and Oranges.. surrounded by a Wall. **1796** WITHERING *Brit. Plants* (ed. 3) III. 865 On dry banks, trunks of trees, and walls. **1833** TENNYSON *Lady of Shalott* I. ii, Four gray walls, and four gray towers, Overlook a space of flowers.

†**c.** ***wall of timber***: a wooden partition, a fence.

1463 *Bury Wills* (Camden) 20, I will y^t my newe hous.. be deseverid.. with a walle of tymbyr fro the hefd place.

†**d.** As a place or means of torture. *Obs.*

1528 TINDALE *Obed. Chr. Man* 149 And when they crye furiously hold the heretikes vnto the wall and if they will not revoke burne them. **1590** in *Cath. Rec. Soc. Publ.* (1908) V. 179 Another warrant.. to commytte them.. unto such torture upon the wawle as is usuall.

e. The inner side of a sidewalk or pavement; the side next the wall. (Cf. the phrases *to give, take the wall* in 16.)

1606 *Choice, Chance*, etc. (1881) 70 Snuffes vp the Nose, and swaggers for the wall. **1620** I. C. *Two Merry Milk-maids* II. ii. F 2, But now I will giue no man place at Wall or Kennell. **1710** ADDISON *Tatler* No. 250 ¶ 11 All such as have been defrauded of their Right to the Wall. **1732** POPE *Ep. Cobham* 234 Behold a rev'rend sire.. Shov'd from the wall perhaps, or rudely press'd By his own son.

f. (*a*) In the phrase ***at the wall***, designating a species of football peculiar to Eton played against a wall, as distinguished from that played 'in the field'. (*b*) Applied to each of the players who form the 'bully' or scrimmage against the wall.

1864 [B. HEMYNG] *Eton School Days* xxiii. 254 But give me, for real enjoyment.. a good game of football at Eton, either at the wall or in the open field. **1883** *Sat. Rev.* 1 Dec. 696/1 Football 'at the Wall' takes its name from being played against the brick wall which divides the Slough Road from the Lower Playing Fields. *Ibid.*, Three of the players on either side, known as 'walls', form a line against the rough bricks. **1887** SHEARMAN *Athletics & Football* (Badm.) 280 The game is begun by a 'bully' in the centre of the wall. The 'wall' whose turn it is to 'go in', forms down with his shoulder against the wall,..the two other 'walls' back him up... The ball is placed against the wall between the feet of the two first opposing 'walls', and the game begins.

g. ***The Wall***: *ellipt.* for *Wailing Wall* s.v. WAILING *vbl. sb.* c.

1895 J. SMITH *Pilgrimage to Palestine* xvi. 219 The 'Wailing Place of the Jews'..is situated a little to the north... High overhead towered the..stones of the Temple Wall ..with the Wall itself..rising to a height of 60 feet... There, with their faces to the wall—kissing the stones,..or joining in a loud chorus of lamentation..stood a long row of Jews. **1928** *Western or Wailing Wall in Jerusalem* 6 in *Parl. Papers 1928–9* (Cmd. 3229) XV. 105 His Majesty's Government regard it as their duty..to maintain the established Jewish right of access to the pavement in front of the Wall for the purposes of their devotions. **1967** C. POTOK *Chosen* xii. 198 He died while praying at the Wall for the Messiah to come and redeem his people. **1973** *Guardian* 21 June 2/7 The present intention is to link the Wall with the historic 'upper city' (now the Jewish Quarter).

h. ***The Wall***: *ellipt.* for *Berlin Wall*, the wall surrounding West Berlin and separating it from communist East Berlin and the rest of East Germany (erected in 1961).

1961 *Daily Progress* (Charlottesville, Va.) 20 Oct. 1/1 Here in Berlin communism has created one of the ugliest and most depressing sights on the face of the globe. It is The Wall—the wall of death, the new concrete curtain of communism. **1964** *Ann. Reg. 1963* 225 It was stated that 1,283,918 had crossed the Wall by the time it closed on 5 January 1964. **1977** G. MARKSTEIN *Chance Awakening* lxxviii. 243 My father had his legs blown off..when he tried to flee over the Wall.

5. *fig.* Something which is a barrier or impediment to intellectual, moral, spiritual, or social union or intercourse; also more definitely ***wall of partition***.

a **1225** *Ancr. R.* 262 And ȝet, ȝe habbeð þet ilke blod, & tet ilke blisfule bodi..niht & dei bi on. Nis þer buten a wal bitweonen. *a* **1240** *Ureisun* in *O.E. Hom.* I. 187 Mine sunnen beoþ wal bi-tweone me & þe. ? *a* **1500** *Chester Pl., Fall Lucifer* 153 Alas! that pride is the wall of lewtye. **1562** WINȜET *Cert. Tractatis* Wks. (S.T.S.) I. 27/4 To attempt sic proude misordour sall..big vp ane wal betuix vs and ȝou in religioun. **1766, 1872** Wall of partition [see PARTITION *sb.* 2]. **1843** RUSKIN *Arrows of Chace* (1880) I. 17 A wall of tradition, which may not be broken through. **1900** ST. BARBE *Mod. Spain* 16 He..barricades himself behind an unassailable wall of self-sufficiency.

6. A wall considered with regard to its surface. **a.** The interior wall of an apartment.

the writing on the wall (after Dan. v.): see WRITING *vbl. sb.*

Beowulf 326 Setton sæmeþe side scyldas, rondas regn-hearde, wið þæs recedes weal. *c* **1290** *St. Dunstan* 142 in *S. Eng. Leg.* 23 Þe harpe song al bi hire-self as heo heng bi þe walle. *c* **1430** in *Babees Bk.* 27 Aȝen þe post lete not þi bak abide, neiþer make þi myrrour also of þe wal. *c* **1535** DU WES *Introd. Fr.* in *Palsgr.* 949 To sile a wale, *lambroisser*. **1562** A. BROOKE *Romeus & Jul.* 2410 She thinkes to speake to Iuliet, but speaketh to the walles. **1603** SHAKS. *Meas. for M.* I. ii. 171 All the inrolled penalties Which haue (like vn-scowr'd Armor) hung by th' wall So long. **1607** —— *Cor.* I. iii. 12. *a* **1629** HINDE *J. Bruen* xxvi. (1641) 82 They..who have sought for Christ and his Apostles, not in the holy Booke of God, but in painted wales and windows. **1639** J. TAYLOR (Water P.) *Part of Summers Trav.* Wks. III. (1872) 43 In the mean time, the Preacher speaks to the bare walls. **1735** POPE *Prol. Sat.* 20 Is there, who, lock'd from ink and paper, scrawls With desp'rate charcoal round his darken'd walls? **1781** COWPER *Charity* 552 Guns, halberts, swords, and pistols, great and small, In starry forms dispos'd upon the wall. **1781** —— *Hope* 346 From stucco'd walls smart arguments rebound. **1859** LEVER *Dav. Dunn* xix, The walls were decorated with coloured prints and drawings. **1891** *Law Times* XCII. 79/1 This almanack has been familiar for many years on the walls of barristers, solicitors, and public offices.

b. A garden- or house-wall upon which fruit-trees and flowering trees are trained.

1699– Fruit wall [see FRUIT *sb.* 9]. **1707** MORTIMER *Husb.* 527 Having occasion to find fault with the common sort of Walls for Fruits, it gives me an opportunity of recommending..sloping Walls. **1734** POPE *Hor. Sat.* II. ii. 146 And grapes, long ling'ring on my only wall. **1781** COWPER *Retirem.* 494 Like bottled wasps upon a southern wall. **1784** —— *Task* III. 408 Proud of his well-spread walls, he views his trees. **1864** TENNYSON *En. Arden* 336 Yet he sent..garden-herbs and fruit, The late and early roses from his wall.

in fig. context. **1857** TROLLOPE *Barchester T.* I. xix. 287 They habitually looked on the sunny side of the wall. **1858** —— *Dr. Thorne* I. vi. 141 Women grow on the sunny side of the wall.

†**7.** Walling. *Obs. rare*$^{-1}$.

1603 G. OWEN *Pembrokeshire* (1892) 70 This lymestone.. is putt into a kill made of wall.

II. Transferred uses.

8. a. Something that resembles a wall in appearance; a perpendicular surface forming an enclosure or barrier.

1697 DRYDEN *Virg. Georg.* III. 567 Huge Oxen stand inclos'd in wint'ry Walls Of Snow congeal'd. **1736** GRAY *Statius* II. 14 The theatre's green height and woody wall. **1820** SHELLEY *Prometh. Unb.* I. 20 Nailed to this wall of eagle-baffling mountain. **1842** TENNYSON *Day-Dream* 65 A wall of green Closed-matted, bur and brake and briar. **1859** H. KINGSLEY *G. Hamlyn* xlvi, The black wall of forest beyond. *Ibid.* xlviii, A wall of water, looming high above her main-yard, came rushing and booming along. **1860** TYNDALL *Glac.* I. xx. 143 Midway down the spur I lighted upon a transverse wall of rock. **1903** KIPLING *Five Nations* 2 The in-rolling walls of the fog.

†**b.** *Mil.* ***in wall***: of battalions, extended in one continuous line like a wall. *Obs.*

1797 *Encycl. Brit.* (ed. 3) XVIII. 741/1 The enemy's army ..is in two lines, the first of which is formed in wall..; the second is formed with large intervals.

c. In the game of Mah Jong, the arrangement of tiles from which hands are drawn. Cf. TILE *sb.*[1] 4 b.

1922 *Lit. Digest* 30 Dec. 38 One studies the unfolding of Ma Jung, one detects Eastern cunning to whet the skill, first the building of the 'wall', undoubtedly meaning the great wall of China, one of the seven wonders of the world. **1950** E. CULBERTSON *Culbertson's Hoyle* 415 *Wall game*, void game by exhaustion of the wall without any declaration of a complete hand. **1974** *Encycl. Brit. Micropædia* VI. 503/3 Thereafter, the other players, in counterclockwise rotation, each draw one tile, which may be the last discarded tile or a loose tile from the 'wall'.

d. *Baseball.* The barrier marking the outer perimeter of the outfield.

1928 G. H. RUTH *Babe Ruth's Own Bk. Baseball* 25 The boys began smacking the fences with long drives, outfielders began playing with their backs to the wall and infielders had to move back on the grass or have their legs torn off with hot drives. *Ibid.* 117 The ball was hit far over his head to the center field wall. **1973** *Internat. Herald Tribune* 15 June 15/3 The closest the Reds had come to a hit was Pete Rose's long drive to left-center in the third that Jim Dwyer caught at the wall.

e. *Football.* A line of defence players who defend their team's goal during a free kick.

1948 HANKINSON & CHADDER *Soccer for Schools* Plate 29 (*caption*) The usual procedure for the defence to adopt is for a 'wall' of players to block the line of a direct shot for goal. **1965** D. BACUZZI *How to play Association Football* xv. 56 (*caption*) Notice how the 'wall' of defenders allows the goalkeeper space to see. **1976** E. DUNPHY *Only a Game?* v. 149, I scored direct from a free kick. Curled it round the wall into the top corner from just outside the box.

f. *Surfing.* The steep face of a wave before it breaks.

1962 T. MASTERS *Surfing made Easy* 66 *Wall*, the steep portion of a wave almost ready to break. **1965** J. POLLARD *Surfrider* ii. 20 The steep face of that wave is called its 'wall'. **1968** *Surfer Mag.* Jan. 17/1 'Just Ken' probably doesn't know what it is like to ride a well-shaped wall while hanging ten except when he is smoking grass.

9. a. Something that confines or encloses like the wall of a house, prison, etc.; chiefly *pl.*, the containing sides of a vessel, the vertical sides of a tent, and the like.

1594 *Selimus* D 1 You thinke it strange..To see me low laie off effeminate robes, And arme my bodie in an iron wall. **1595** SHAKS. *John* III. iii. 20 Within this wall of flesh There is a soule counts thee her Creditor. **1615** R. COCKS *Diary* (Hakl. Soc.) I. 57 The walle or neting the king caused to be made to fish was borne downe in the night with the force of the tide. **1650** BULWER *Anthropomet.* xx. (1653) 327 The walls..of the Breasts [of infants], are..depraved by Nurses, while they..do overstrictly bind them. **1790** W. H. MARSHALL *Rur. Econ. Midl.* II. 445 Wall; the stem of a rick is called the walls. **1878** HUXLEY *Physiogr.* vi. 89 The walls of a closed vessel containing air are pressed outwards by the elastic force of the confined air. **1879** *Encycl. Brit.* IX. 251/1 The drift-net..forms a long wall or barrier of netting hanging for a few fathoms perpendicularly in the water. **1897** *Outing* XXX. 375/1 [A tent] which has walls at least three feet high, should answer.

b. The pastry forming the sides of a pie.

1747 H. GLASSE *Art of Cookery* viii. 73 Make a good Standing Crust, let the Wall and Bottom be very thick. **1894** L. HERITAGE *Cassell's New Universal Cookery Bk.* 785/1 Form the walls of the pie with the left hand. The sides should be smooth and of equal thickness. **1959** *Listener* 22 Jan. 191/2 Lid the flan with pastry, having egged the top of the 'wall'.

10. *Mining.* **a.** The coating or crust of a lode or vein; also, the side of a mine next to this.

For *foot-wall, hanging-wall* see FOOT *sb.* 35, HANGING *ppl. a.* 6.

1728 *Phil. Trans.* XXXV. 404 Sometimes,..the Mine is lined with an intermediate Substance between the Load and it self. This is (properly speaking) the Wall of the Load: Though, in the Common Acceptation of that Term, it signifies either such intermediate Substance, or the Side of the Mine, where the Load immediately unites it self to it. **1797** *Encycl. Brit.* (ed. 3) XII. 39/1 The capels or walls of the lode. **1818** W. PHILLIPS *Geol.* 210 A..crust occasionally covers one or both sides of the vein, technically called the walls of the load. **1881** RAYMOND *Mining Gloss., Wall.* 1. The side of a level or drift. 2. The country-rock bounding a vein laterally.

b. *Coal-mining.* (See quot. 1883.)

long wall: see LONG *a.*[1] 18. ***stenting wall***: see STENTING *sb.*

1750 in *6th Rep. Dep. Kpr. Rec.* App. II. 124 Carrying Coals from the Coal Walls where they are dug to the bottom of the Pit or Shaft. **1839** URE *Dict. Arts*, etc. 979 The first set [of workmen] curves or pools the coal along the whole line of walls. **1883** GRESLEY *Gloss. Coal-mining, Wall.* 1. The face of a long-wall working or stall, commonly called the coal-wall. 2. (North of Eng.) A rib of solid coal between two boards. *Ibid., Walls* (Scotl.) Short working faces or stalls (also headings 6 ft. in width) from 12 to 20 yards wide.

c. ***to the wall***: see quot.

1883 GRESLEY *Gloss. Coal-mining, Wall* ('To the Wall') (North of Eng.). A term signifying breadth, in reference to the size of pillars in the system of working known as Pillar and Stall.

11. *Engraving.* (See quots.)

1797 *Encycl. Brit.* VI. 742/2 (*Etching*), A border of soft wax..must be fastened round the plate about an inch high, in the form of a little wall or rampart, to contain the aquafortis. **1815** J. SMITH *Panorama Sci. & Art* II. 767 The plate is surrounded with a border or wall, about an inch high, composed of bees' wax. **1839** CHATTO & JACKSON *Wood Engraving* 715 The plate is surrounded with a wall, as it is technically termed, and aquafortis being poured upon it, all the unprotected parts are corroded, and the drawing left in relief.

12. *Anat.* and *Zool.* The membranous investment or lining tissue (of any organ or cavity of the body, of a vesicle, tumour, and the like). Also *Bot.*, the cellulose membrane (of a cell).

1677 GREW *Anat. Fruits* iv. §5 As by Refraction, Objects of all Sizes are represented on the Walls of the Eye. **1830** R. KNOX *Béclard's Anat.* 85 These [adipose] vesicles are so thin that it is impossible to distinguish their walls. **1876** BRISTOWE *Th. & Pract. Med.* (1878) 889 The walls of ovarian tumours consist mainly of connective tissue. **1897** MARY KINGSLEY *W. Africa* 469 He then cut diagonally across, and actually lifted the wall of the chest, and groped about among the vitals for the bullet.

b. The outer horny covering of the foot of a horse.

1830 J. HINDS *Osmer's Treat. Horse* (ed. 5) 7 *note*, This is the earliest mention we can find of the crust or hoof proper, being denominated the wall of the foot, a term which has now become general among us. [The passage referred to (Osmer, ? 1756) reads 'like a wall']. **1831** YOUATT *Horse* xv. 280 The crust or wall of the hoof..is that portion which is seen when the foot is placed on the ground.

III. Phrases.

13. ***to go to the wall*** (or †***walls***): **a.** to give way, succumb in a conflict or struggle.

1589 *Pasquil's Ret.* A iiij, They neuer went to the wall, till they grewe to be factious. **1601** J. WHEELER *Treat. Comm.* 111 Wee should go to the walles, be wronged and exacted vpon euery where. **1859** H. KINGSLEY *G. Hamlyn* xxix, Sam and Mayford are both desperately in love with her, and one must go to the wall. **1861** LD. BROUGHAM *Brit. Const.* xx. 385 It is easy to see which power will go to the wall if a conflict occurs. **1867** TROLLOPE *Chron. Barset* xliii, In all these struggles Crosbie had had the best of it, and Butterwell had gone to the wall.

Proverb. [**1535**: see WAW]. **1549** CHEKE *Hurt Sedit.* (1641) 53 When brethren agree not in a house, goeth not the weakest to the walls? **1579** LYLY *Euphues* (Arb.) 53 The weakest must still to the wall. **1592** SHAKS. *Rom. & Jul.* I. i. 18. **1651** CULPEPPER *Astrol. Judgem. Dis.* (1658) 80 You know the old proverb, The weakest goes to the Walls.

b. Of a business, matter, etc.: To give way or give precedence (to something else).

1858 GLADSTONE *Homer* III. 519 Here is another case of metre against history, and in all such cases history must go (as is said) to the wall. **1890** M'CARTHY *Four Georges* II. 45 Where political interests interfered family arrangements went to the wall.

c. To fail in business.

1842 THACKERAY *Miss Tickletoby's Lect.* vi. Wks. 1886 XXIV. 37 It was better for all parties that poor Shortlegs should go to the wall. **1854** SURTEES *Handley Cr.* lxxii. (1901) II. 253 He had been the property of some East-end Bowker, who, in classical language, had 'gone to the wall'. **1879** SPENCER *Data of Ethics* xv. §103. 266 Others of his [a merchant's] debtors by going to the wall may put him in further difficulties. **1891** *19th Cent.* Dec. 861 In Berlin a newspaper would very soon go to the wall if it did not present its subscribers with light entertainment.

14. ***to †set, †thrust,*** or ***send to the wall***: to thrust aside into a position of neglect.

1583 BABINGTON *Commandm.* 334 God knowes..how often they are wrecked and wronged and set to the wal by cruell..and hard hearted men. **1592** SHAKS. *Rom. & Jul.* I. i. 20 Women being the weaker Vessels, are euer thrust to the wall. **1881** E. W. HAMILTON *Diary* 13 Mar. (1972) I. 115 Lord Bath..is much exercised in his mind as to the Greek question sending to the wall the interests of Servia. **1901** *N. & Q.* 9th Ser. VIII. 411/1 During the later fifties he was sent to the wall by the superior talents of the late Robert Prowse.

15. ***to drive*** (or ***push***) ***to the wall***: to drive to the last extremity.

with or ***having one's back to the wall***: see BACK *sb.*[1] 25.

1546 J. HEYWOOD *Prov.* II. v. (1867) 58 That deede without woords shall driue him to the wall. And further than the wall he can not go. **1644** PRYNNE & WALKER *Fiennes's Trial* 34 The Colonell thus driven to the wall and worsted on every hand, used two pleas more for his last reserve. **1818** SCOTT *Rob Roy* xxxii, I see what you are driving me to the wa' about. **1828** NAPIER *Penins. War* III. iii. I. 336 The commissaries pushed to the wall by the delay, offered an exorbitant remuneration. **1860** L. HARCOURT *Diaries G. Rose* II. 30 Being..driven to the wall, Addington complied.

16. a. ***to give a person the wall***: to allow a person the right or privilege of walking next the wall as the cleaner and safer side of a pavement, sidewalk, etc. Similarly, ***to have, take the wall*** (***of*** a person), to have, take the inside position.

? **1537** *Thersytes* 150 Yes, yes, god wote they geve me the wall, Or elles with my clubbe I make them to fall. **1592** *Arden of Feversham* v. i, I haue made some go vppon wodden legges for taking the wall on me. **1621** T. WILLIAMSON tr. *Goulart's Wise Vieillard* 95 The Persians had a law enioyning all men..to giue him [an elder] the wall when they mett him in the streetes. **1703** *Rules Civility* 11 Giving ..the Right-hand or Wall in the Street. **1773** JOHNSON in Boswell *Tour Hebrides* 20 Sept., In the last age..there were two sets of people, those who gave the wall, and those who took it; the peaceable and the quarrelsome... Now, it is fixed that every man keeps to the right; or, if one is taking the wall, another yields it, and it is never a dispute. **1869** A. J. MUNBY *Diary* 24 Dec. in D. Hudson *Munby* (1972) vii. 278 'If a nigger didn't give me the wall, I'd knock him down as soon as look at him!' Here we have the British Philistine.

1581 PETTIE *Guazzo's Civ. Conv.* II. (1586) 76 b, I weigh it little, that my equall, hauing the wall of me, should goe from it to giue me place. **1605** HEYWOOD *If you know not Me* E 1 b, *Enter the Englishman, and Spaniard. Spa.* The wall, the wall. *Eng.* Sblood Spaniard you get no wall here,..but since you will needs Haue the wall, Ile take the paynes to thrust You into the kennell. **1855** KINGSLEY *Westw. Ho!* xxv, The Spaniards..had..no room, in that narrow path, to use their pikes. The English had the wall of them; and to have the wall there, was to have the foe's life at their mercy. **1587** GREENE *Penelopes Web* Wks. (Grosart) V. 201 The wife of a poore Smith meeting the Empresse Faustina, tooke the wall of her in the streetes. **1617** MORYSON *Itin.* III. 28 Nothing was more common with them then to fight about taking the right or left hand, or the wall. **1757** FOOTE *Author* I. Wks. 1799 I. 135 He wou'd take the wall of a Prince of the Blood. **1821** SCOTT *Kenilw.* iv, To..quarrel in her cause with any flat-capp'd thread-maker that would take the wall of her. **1840** DICKENS *Old C. Shop* xxxiii, The parlour window..is so close upon the foot-way that the passenger who takes the wall brushes the dim glass with his coat sleeve.

b. *fig.* (In early use sometimes without article, *to give, take wall.*)

1591 NASHE *Wonderf. Prognost.* Wks. (Grosart) II. 157 The Bakers Basket shall giue wall vnto the Brewers Barrell. **1608** BP. HALL *Serm. Pharasaism* Wks. (1625) 413 Some Traditions must haue place in euery Church; but, Their place: they may not take wall of Scripture. **1652** —— *Invis. World* III. §1 If a supposed and self respective good be suffered to take the wall of the best and absolute good. **1679** R. W. *Cromwell's Ghost* 2 Though old in Artful Wickedness I be, Yet Rome, I now Resign the Wall to thee. **1758** L. TEMPLE *Sketches* (ed. 2) 59 According to nice Herald-like Ceremony, the Son, as the better Gentleman, ought to take the Wall of the Father.

†**17.** ***to lie by the wall*** (or ***walls***), to lie on one side, remain idle or unused; of a ship, to lie up (in dock or harbour); also ***to lay by the walls.*** *Obs.*

1579 TOMSON *Calvin's Serm. Tim.* 46/2 And the law in the meane time must lye by the walles [Fr. *demeure là*]. **1656** *Burton's Diary* (1828) I. 82, I am glad the mariners are so sensible of the laying of our English ships by the walls. **1658–9** *Ibid.* III. 462 Our ships lie by the walls, and theirs ride. **1672** WALLIS in Rigaud *Corr. Sci. Men* (1841) II. 529 To put forth what France is not willing to venture upon, provided that it do not hinder the printing those of our own nation,..which lie by the wall for want of publishing. **1725** DE FOE *Voy. round World* (1840) 66 He walked towards that part of the Creek, where..three of their largest ships lay by the walls. **1787** GROSE *Provinc. Gloss.* s.v. *Wall*, He lies by the wall. Spoken of a person dead but not buried. Norf. and Suf.

18. (To be able) ***to see***, etc. ***through*** or ***into a*** (***brick, mud, stone***) ***wall***: to be endowed with great keenness of perception or understanding.

1598 MARSTON *Pygmal., Sat.* ii, Thou know'st I am sure, for thou canst cast thine eie Through nine mud walls, or els old Poets lie. **1885** *Illustr. Lond. News* 7 Feb. 136/4 Lord Sherbrooke..can see as far as most people into a stone wall.

19. ***to turn one's face to the wall***: said of a person on his deathbed conscious of the approach of the end (? after 2 Kings xx. 2, Isa. xxxviii. 2).

1579 in *Narratives Reform.* (Camden) 35 He turned his face to the walle in the sayd belfry; and so after his prayers sleapte swheetly in the Lorde. **16..** *Barbara Allen's Cruelty* ix. in Child *Ballads* II. 277 He turnd his face unto the wall, And death came creeping to him. **1856** KNIGHT *Pop. Hist. Eng.* I. xxi. 304 He [Henry II] turned his face to the wall, and exclaimed, 'Let every thing go as it will'. [Cf. Girald. Cambrens. (Rolls) VIII. 295 *iterum se lecto reclinans faciemque suam ad parietem vertens.*] **1876** 'MARK TWAIN' *Tom Sawyer* iii, He would turn his face to the wall, and die with that word unsaid.

20. ***to go over the wall*** and varr.: (*a*) to go to prison; (*b*) to escape from prison; (*c*) to leave a religious order; (*d*) to defect (to another country). Hence (*e*) ***over the wall*** adv. phr., escaped from prison; in prison. *slang.*

a. 1917 W. MUIR *Observations of Orderly* xiv. 228 He would be observed 'going over the wall' or 'going to stir' (going to detention prison).

b. 1933 *Amer. Speech* VIII. III. 27/1 *Go over the wall*, escape. **1936** L. DUNCAN (*title*) Over the wall. *Ibid.* vi. 95 Us guys..pull wires to get jobs as guards, and you convicts go over the wall whenever you can. **1963** *Times* 5 June 16/1 He knew it was an unwritten law that an escape extinguished such a debt, and so he decided to 'go over the wall'. He gave himself up at Clacton-on-Sea. **1974** P. B. YUILL *Hazell plays Solomon* vi. 66 You really think Mancini would've tried to go over the wall?

c. 1949 M. BALDWIN (*title*) I leap over the wall. A return to the world after twenty-eight years in a convent. **1970** *Harper's Mag.* Apr. 110 Mr. Vizzard was a Jesuit seminarian who yearned for the world, leapt over the wall, and found what he was looking for in Hollywood. **1979** 'E. ANTHONY' *Grave of Truth* vii. 190 A bride of Christ, eh? What happens if she jumps over the wall..decides she's had enough of convent life..?

d. 1976 M. BUTTERWORTH *Remains to be Seen* v. 84 The bloody place [*sc.* the Foreign Office]..has never been the same since Kim [Philby] went over the wall.

e. 1935 A. J. POLLOCK *Underworld Speaks* 85/2 *Over the wall*, escaped from prison. **1973** G. BEARE *Snake on Grave* xxiii. 141 He's out. Over the wall.

21. ***up the wall***: angry, furious; distraught, mad, crazy; esp. in phrs. ***to climb, run up the wall***: to become very angry or distraught; ***to drive, send*** (someone) ***up the wall***: to infuriate or put into a frenzy. *colloq.*

1951 S. KAYE-SMITH *Mrs. Gailey* 160 Your mother's running up the wall because he came to dinner. **1953** H. CLEVELY *Public Enemy* xvii. 101 Old Marks 'll climb up the wall if he hears I closed early. **1956** A. WILSON *Anglo-Saxon Att.* II. ii. 307 You drive me up the wall. What sort of a mess have you got poor Dad into? **1959** *Observer* 21 June 8/8 When they found out he was a Catholic, they were up the wall. **1961** *New Left Rev.* Mar./Apr. 30/1 She was right up the wall, and poor Aunt Ada isn't in any state to help. **1966** 'L. LANE' *ABZ of Scouse* 40 Sends me up ther bloody wall. **1970** *New Yorker* 3 Oct. 105/1 Success or failure hardly entered into the picture. It was this kind of argument that drove some..executives up the wall. **1975** 'E. LATHEN' *By Hook or by Crook* xiv. 138 The American wife, the sweetie-pie who sends Everett up the wall. **1977** *Chicago Tribune* 2 Oct. VI. 15/2 The prejudice is so acute; that country is up the wall.

22. ***off the wall*** (also with hyphens used *attrib.*): unorthodox, unconventional; instinctive, intuitive, off the cuff. (See also quot. 1966.) Also used advb. *U.S. slang.*

1966 *Current Slang* (Univ. S. Dakota) Summer 3 *Off the wall*, unimpressive... I have a lit. professor who's *off the wall.* **1968–70** *Ibid.* III–IV. 88 *Off the wall*, adj. Unusual; unorthodox; 'crazy'. **1974** *National Rev.* (U.S.) 4 Jan. 47/2 Brian knows how to startle the over-interviewed with off-the-wall questions that get surprising answers: Ever see a ghost? **1975** *San Francisco Chron.* 11 Jan. 12/3 He became suspicious when Dickenson answered extremely complex questions 'off the wall'. **1976** *Time* 5 Apr. 74, 'I just thought it was off-the-wall funny', says Lear. **1977** C. MCFADDEN *Serial* (1978) iv. 14/1 She had decided to play the whole scene off the wall, to just go with the flow... The really authentic thing to do was to act on your impulses. **1977** *Listener* 20 Oct. 498/2 Among the many new sources of cash—it's called 'off the wall' fundraising—I have heard about a tribe of Apaches which..invested $2 million in the making of..a western. **1982** *Penthouse* Dec. 84 He started talking off the wall about how he should go to El Salvador.

IV. 23. Short for **a.** *wall-tree.* **b.** WALLFLOWER, **c.** *wall butterfly.*

a. 1707 MORTIMER *Husb.* 522 Your Trees being grafted.. the next thing to be consider'd, is which are to be for Dwarfs, Walls and Standards.

b. 1825 R. P. WARD *Tremaine* I. xvi. 100 There was a regular return of the same flowers..such as walls, and provence roses, convolvolus, and sweet-william.

c. 1832 J. RENNIE *Butterfl. & Moths* 12 The Wall (*Hipparchia Megæra*, Leach). The Brown Wall (*H. Phædra*, Stephens).

V. *attrib.* and *Comb.*

24. a. simple attrib., as ***wall arch, -coping, -decoration, -front, -mosaic, -nook, -tiling, -top***; with the meaning 'set or fixed against a wall', as ***wall candlestick, -case, -clock, -cupboard, light, -map, mirror, -panel, -panelling, phone, picture, -press, safe, sconce, socket, switch, telephone***; with the meaning 'growing upon or against a wall', as ***wall-berry, -plant, -plum.***

1886 C. E. PASCOE *Lond. To-day* xxx. (ed. 3) 268 On the wall of Westminster Hall..there are plainly visible the traces of *wall arches erected by Richard II. **1908** [MISS E. FOWLER] *Betw. Trent & Ancholme* 313 Perhaps it had earlier been busy upon the *wall-berries. **1688** HOLME *Armoury* III. 381/2 *Wall or Hanging Candlesticks. **1886** WILLIS & CLARK *Cambridge* III. 181 *Wall-cases were provided, and the collections were removed from the Old Museum. **1891** *Century Dict.*, **Wall clock.* **1887** J. G. ANDREW *Mem. W. Graham* vii. 153 Above the *wall-coping..appeared an endless row of peering sorrow-stricken faces. **1961** *Times* 16 Jan. 13/4 It is furnished throughout with tables, chairs, *wall-cupboards. **1976** 'W. TREVOR' *Children of Dynmouth* ii. 51 The commodious wall-cupboards, the scrubbed wooden table. **1867** D. G. ROSSETTI *Let.* ? 12 Nov. (1965) II. 643 There are sufficient slight representatives of it [*sc.* the severed head] on vases and in *wall-decoration of classic times. **1935** *Burlington Mag.* June 272/2 The question of the connexion between the carpet patterns and the wall-decoration remains difficult enough. **1964** *Listener* 3 Dec. 883/1 This is a rare opportunity to see an important High Renaissance wall-decoration. **1923** D. H. LAWRENCE *Birds, Beasts & Flowers* 115 The black hole, the earth-lipped fissure in the *wall-front. **1869** *Bradshaw's Railway Man.* XXI. p. xvi (Advt.), *Wall Lights and Mantle Piece Lustres. **1905** E. WHARTON *House of Mirth* I. iii. 42 She turned out the wall-lights. **1972** Wall light [see PENLIGHT, PEN-LIGHT]. **1907** T. C. MIDDLETON *Geogr. Knowl. Discov. Amer.* 20 The *wall-map of the world, painted in his banquet-hall at the Lateran. **1934** WEBSTER, *Wall mirror. **1940** M. SADLEIR *Fanny by Gaslight* I. ix. 241 She studied herself in a long wall mirror. **1981** 'J. MELVILLE' *Murder has Pretty Face* i. 20 She could see her reflection in a wall mirror. **1913** EDEN *Ancient Glass* 26 Glass *wall-mosaics for interior decoration. **1847** C. BRONTE *Jane Eyre* iii, The ground-ivy mantling old *wall-nooks. **1880** L. HIGGIN *Handbk. Embroidery* 62 Design for *wall-panel. By Mr. E. Burne-Jones. **1933** *Burlington Mag.* July 22/1 The absence of graining on the wall panels. **1962** A. NISBETT *Technique Sound Studio* 245 Marked acoustic colouration in a studio may be due to the coincidence of dimensional resonances, to wall-panel resonances, or to frequency-selective excessive absorption of sound. **1880** L. HIGGIN *Handbk. Embroidery* 62 Design for *wall-panelling or curtains. **1962** L. DEIGHTON *Ipcress File* xxx. 194 The *wall phone rang. **1975** 'R. BUTLER' *Where all Girls are Sweeter* vi. 70, I..went over to the wall-phone and dialled. **1895** *Wall-picture [see *Japanese lantern* s.v. JAPANESE *a.* and *sb.* b]. **1966** J. DERRICK *Teaching Eng. to Immigrants* v. 195 Wall pictures to match those in the book, with suitable captions printed by the teacher..can be put up in the classroom. **1880** *Archæol. Cant.* XIII. 26 The singular thickness of the *wall-piers causes the central body of the crypt to be narrower. **1873** MARY SOMERVILLE *Recoll.* xviii. 372 The Trachelium cœruleum, a pretty *wall-plant. **1676** SHADWELL *Virtuoso* IV. 72, I have observ'd upon a *Wall-plum..at first beginning to turn blue [etc.]. **1844** H. STEPHENS *Bk. Farm* II. 285 A *wall-press..is necessary in a corn-barn. **1931** W. FAULKNER *Sanctuary* xxiii. 254 The room contained..three over-stuffed chairs, a *wall safe. **1978** A. NEAVE *Nuremburg* iii. 36 Two wall-safes had been found, one in Bertha's bedroom and one in Gustav's dressing-room. **1954** *Wall sconce [see OSCAR^2 b]. **1974** J. AIKEN *Midnight is Place* i. 11 A few candles..burned flickeringly in the wall sconces. **1890** SLINGO & BROOKER *Electr. Engin.* xvii. 608 A *wall socket..is useful in cases where it is required to place a movable lamp in circuit at one or other of a number of positions. **1977** Wall socket [see *start button* s.v. START *sb.*^{2} 12]. **1935** D. L. SAYERS *Gaudy Night* vi. 114 She found the *wall-switch and went down the central corridor of the Annexe. **1981** C. DEXTER *Dead of Jericho* xxv. 142 He..turned on the wall switch... But clearly the electricity had been disconnected. **1914** *Wall telephone [see EXTENSION 9 h]. **1977** *Rolling Stone* 30 June 73/2 Her kitchen is very white—walls, doors, floors, white appliances... And a white wall telephone. **1884** *Health Exhib. Catal.* 83/2 Decorative *wall-tiling. **1849** *Proc. Berw. Nat. Club* II. 371 It is found under..lichens on *wall-tops.

b. objective, and objective genitive, as ***wall-builder, -building, -peeler; wall-like, -loving*** adjs.; instrumental, as ***wall-bound, -fed, -girdled, -girt, -hung, -mounted*** adjs.

1812 E. WEETON *Let.* 15 June in *Jrnl. of Governess* (1969) II. 22, 7d a yard is the price now usually paid to *wall-builders. **1878** BOSW. SMITH *Carthage* 375 Hannibal.. taking his place..among the wall-builders and wonder-workers of Eastern history and legend. **1823** COBBETT *Rur. Rides* (1885) I. 221 Paving and *wall-building. **1862** W. BARNES *Dorset Dial.* II. 78 There, in the geärden's *wall bound square. **1898** *Athenæum* 23 July 137/3 The clinging *wall-fed ivy. *a* **1930** D. H. LAWRENCE *Etruscan Places* (1932) 50 Nowhere is far off, in these small *wall-girdled cities. **1883** *Harper's Mag.* Nov. 876 Gray *wall-girt stillness. **1876** W. MORRIS *Sigurd* 2 The least of its *wall-hung shields. **1970** Wall-hung [see MODULAR *a.* 1 b]. **1878** HUXLEY *Physiogr.* 168 *Wall-like masses are partially detached from the cliffs. **1865** GOSSE *Land & Sea* (1874) 120 Walls..of loose, dry stones, affording in the crevices root-space for many *wall-loving plants. **1964** R. F. FICCHI *Electr. Interference* v. 67 The installation, however, is quite important:..it must be located within the shielding or '*wall-mounted' through the shield. **1980** *Sunday Times* (Colour Suppl.) 21 Sept. 50 (Advt.), Toilets and bidets can be floor standing or wall mounted. **1712** STEELE *Spect.* No. 431 ¶3 These craving Damsels, whether..Coal-Scranchers, *Wall-peelers, or Gravel-diggers.

25. Special comb.: **wall-arcade** *Arch.*, an arcade (see ARCADE *sb.* 3) used as a decoration of a wall; hence **wall-arcading**, the stonework composing a wall-arcade; **wall bar**, one of a set of parallel bars, attached to the wall of a gymnasium, usu. running from floor to ceiling, on which various exercises are performed; **wall-bearing** (see quot.); **wall bed**, a bed which can be folded up against a wall when not in use; **wallboard**, (a piece of) board, made from wood pulp, fibre, and other materials, used for surfacing walls and ceilings, etc.; **wall-border**, a garden-border at the foot of a wall; **wall-box**, (*a*) an aperture made in or through a wall to accommodate a wall-bearing; (*b*) a postal collecting box affixed to a wall as distinguished from a pillar-box; **wall bracket**, a bracket (BRACKET *sb.* 1 a) which is attached to a wall as a stand or support for a lamp, ornaments, shelves, etc.; †**wall-break** *a.*, that breaks down walls; **wall-casing**, the lining or superficial exterior covering of a wall; †**wall-chalker** (see quot. 1823); hence **wall-chalking**; **wall chart**, a chart or poster giving information, often in pictures or diagrams, and designed for display on a wall, esp. in a classroom; **wall-clamp, -coal** (see quots.); **wallcovering**, material used to cover and decorate the inside walls of a building (cf. WALLPAPER 1); **wall-crook** *dial.*, ? a wooden hook for driving into cob walls; **wall-cutting, dock** (see quots.); **wall-dormer** *Arch.*, a dormer whose front is part of the main wall of the building carried up to the required height; **wall-earth** (see quot.); **wall-engine**, a small vertical steam engine bolted to a wall; **wall-face**, (*a*) the working face in a coal mine; (*b*) the surface of a wall; †**wall-fast** *a.*, secure within walls; **wall-fight**, a siege; **wall fish** *dial.*, the edible snail, *Helix pomatia*; **wall-fruit**, the fruit of trees grown against a wall; also a fruit tree so grown; also *attrib.*, as *wall-fruit tree*; **wall-game**, the Eton game of football played 'at the wall' (see 4 f); **wall garden**, a garden surrounded by a wall, or a border planted beside a sheltering wall; **wall-grenade**, a bombshell thrown from the walls by hand or by means of a small mortar called a hand-mortar (*Cent. Dict.* 1891); **wall-gun**, a large hand-gun supported on a tripod or crutch, for firing over a rampart; **wall-hangings**, tapestry hangings for walls; also, embroidered, woven or other decorative drapery for display on walls; occas. *sing.*; **wall-head** *Sc.*, the top of a wall, esp. of a house-wall; also the space on the top of a wall between the roof-beams, used as a receptacle or shelf; also *attrib.*; **wall-hold**, the end (of a beam, etc.) which is inserted in a wall as a bearing; **wall-hook**, †(*a*) a grappling-hook (*obs.*); (*b*) a hook-shaped holdfast for fastening wire, piping, etc. to a wall; †**wall lecture** *Oxford Univ.*, a lecture delivered, according to statute, by a regent-master (to empty benches); **wall-lining**, a covering for the interior surface of a wall; **wall-nail**, a kind of nail made for driving into walls; **wall-net**, a vertical fishing-net forming the wall of an inclosed space (*Cent. Dict.*); **wall**

newspaper, (*a*) a newspaper produced by an educational institution or place of work, typed or hand-written, and displayed on the wall; (*b*) (esp. in Communist countries) an official newspaper displayed on the wall in public places, esp. in the street; †**wall-observer**, one who is addicted to reading placards; **Wall of Death**, a fairground sideshow in which a motor-cyclist uses gravitational force to ride his motor-cycle around the inside walls of a vertical cylinder; **wall-painting**, a mural, a fresco; **wall pass** *Football* = *one-two* (*c*) s.v. ONE 33; **wall plug**: see PLUG *sb.* 1 c (cf. *wall socket*, sense 24 above); **wall-pocket**, (*a*) a receptacle for small household items, designed to hang on a wall; (*b*) = *wall vase* below; **wall-post** *Arch.* = PENDANT *sb.* 6 a; **wall-poster**, a poster affixed to a public wall; *spec.* = TA TZU-PAO; †**wall-rase** *Sc.* [cf. RASEN, RAISING-PIECE, -*plate*] = WALL PLATE; †**wall-reared** *a.* = *wall-sided*; †**wall-reeve**, an official charged with keeping embankments in repair; **wall-rib** *Arch.* (see quots. 1835–50); also *attrib.*; **wall-rock** *Mining*, the rock forming the walls of a vein; **wall-saltpetre** (see quot.); **wall-shaft** *Arch.*, in *engaged wall-shaft*, a shaft or column partly let into the wall (cf. ENGAGED *column*); **wall-side**, (*a*) the side of a wall; (*b*) the side of a pavement, etc., where there is a wall (also *attrib.*); **wall-sided** *a.*, having perpendicular sides like a wall; **wall space**, an expanse of unbroken wall surface, esp. one regarded as an area for displaying pictures, etc.; **wall-strap** (see quot.); **wall-string**, the string-board of a staircase which is next the wall; **wall system** *U.S.*, 'a set of shelves often with cabinets or bureaus that can be variously arranged along a wall' (*Webster's 9,000 Words*); **wall-tent**, a tent with perpendicular sides; **wall-tie**, each of the pieces of iron, slate, or other material used to bind together the two parts of a hollow wall; **wall-tile**, (*a*) a tile used for lining a wall; †(*b*) *north.*, a brick as distinguished from a roofing tile; †**wall-tooth**, a cheek-tooth, grinder; **wall-tower**, a tower forming part of a fortified wall (*Cent. Dict.*); †**wall-town** *Sc.*, a walled or fortified town; **wall-tree**, a fruit-tree planted against and trained upon a wall; also *attrib.*; **wall unit**, a piece of furniture consisting of various sections and compartments such as shelves and cupboards, and designed to stand against a wall; **wall vase**, a vase with one flat side allowing it to be hung on a wall; **wall-wash**, liquid distemper applied to the surface of a wall; **wallwasher**, a type of lighting fixture designed to 'wash' a wall with light (see quot. 1983); **wall-wise** *adv.*, after the manner of a wall; **wall-work**, †(*a*) work done in building a wall (*obs.*); (*b*) a defensive work consisting of walls. Also WALLPAPER, WALL-PIECE, WALL-PLAT, WALL-PLATE, WALL-STONE.

1860 G. E. STREET in *Archæol. Cant.* III. 133 The *wall-arcades in the two churches. **1863** SIR G. SCOTT *Glean. Westm. Abb.* (ed. 2) 33 The spandrels over the *wall-arcading are exquisitely beautiful. *a* **1878** —— *Lect. Archit.* I. 97. **1903** *Handbk. Physical Training* (Admiralty) I. 53 The men are placed with one side towards, and at one pace from the *Wall Bars. **1973** M. RUSSELL *Double Hit* ii. 18 I'll be getting back to the wallbars. **1875** KNIGHT *Dict. Mech.*, **Wall-bearing*, a bearing for receiving a shaft when entering or passing through a wall. **1913** *Maclean's Mag.* Oct. 78/1 The Pacific *Wall Bed is sanitary in every respect. **1974** Wall bed [see MURPHY[3]]. **1925** (*title*) U.S. Government master specification for gypsum *wall board. (U.S. Bureau of Standards.) **1933** *Archit. Rev.* LXXIII. p. lviii, The group of materials commonly known as wallboards, but more correctly termed building-boards, may..be classified in five categories:—(1) fibre boards..(2) laminated boards ..(3) wood pulp boards..(4) plaster boards..(5) composite boards. **1942** [see *storyboard* s.v. STORY *sb.*[1] 9]. **1962** A. LURIE *Love & Friendship* iv. 59 Burned, sodden chunks of wallboard lay about. **1978** *Cornish Guardian* 27 Apr. 34/6 (Advt.), Carpet Tiles. Tools. Wallboards. **1707** MORTIMER *Husb.* 461 They are..transplanted into some *Wall border towards the South and East. **1851** in *Beck's Florist* 128 A shrubbery or wall-border some four or five feet broad. **1875** KNIGHT *Dict. Mech.*, *Wall-box. **1887** D. A. LOW *Machine Draw.* (1892) 34 A neat appearance is given to the opening ..by building into the wall a wall box. **1909** WEBSTER, *Wall bracket. **1926** L. ELMHIRST *Notebk.* in M. Young *Elmhirsts of Dartington* (1982) xii. 295 We eliminated the wall brackets and agreed upon..ceiling lights. **1939** [see STANDARD *sb.* 16 c]. **1951** W. FAULKNER *Requiem for Nun* I. ii. 53 Floor-lamp, wall-bracket lamps, a door left enters from the hall. **1976** *Gramophone* Sept. 516/2 The small size can be easily accommodated particularly if the speakers are mounted on wall brackets. **1598** SYLVESTER *Du Bartas* II. iv. III. *Schism* 727 Fell, *wall-break (all break) Famine..Howls hideously. **1858** HAWTHORNE *Fr. & It. Note-bks.* (1871) I. 28 *Wall-casings of rich, polished marble. **1823** 'JON BEE' *Dict. Turf*, **Wall-chalkers*—fellows who..scrawl balderdash upon garden walls... Others chalk up their trades—as 'try Warren's blacking' [etc.]. **1829** T. HOOK *Bank to Barnes* 95 The Bill-Sticker's Assistant and Wall-Chalker's Vade-Mecum. ? **1932** DYLAN THOMAS *Sel. Lett.* (1966) 5 We're over-ripe, we night-walkers, cunt-stalkers, wall-chalkers. **1853** DICKENS *Bleak Ho.* xli. 409 Lady Dedlock, the *wall-chalking and the street-crying would come on directly. **1958** S. HYLAND *Who goes Hang?* xl. 189 He was..examining a *wall-chart which depicted..the working..of a bicycle. **1980** Wall chart [see SNAKE *sb.* 4 f]. **1875** KNIGHT *Dict. Mech.*, **Wall-clamp*, a brace or tie to hold walls together, or the two parts of a double-wall, to prevent spreading. **1886** J. BARROWMAN *Sc. Mining Terms* 70 **Wall-coal*, breast coal; the middle division of three in a seam, the other two being termed top coal and ground coal. **1970** *Times* 11 Dec. 16/4 The *wallcovering on three walls is glossy yellow p.v.c. **1979** *Tucson Mag.* Apr. 73/2 (Advt.), We offer a multitude of wall coverings and coordinating fabrics. **1869** BLACKMORE *Lorna D.* xxxviii, I worked..in the copse of young ash,..making spars to keep for thatching, *wall-crooks to drive into the cob, [etc.]. **1886** J. BARROWMAN *Sc. Mining Terms* 70 **Wall cutting*, side cutting or shearing the solid coal in opening out working places; trimming the sides of a sinking pit. **1833** LOUDON *Encycl. Archit.* §925 The *wall docks (plugs of wood) are not to be more than 16 inches apart. **1886** WILLIS & CLARK *Cambridge* III. 551 The roof dormers very soon became *wall-dormers, rising in a line with the main walls of the buildings. **1723** *Phil. Trans.* XXXII. 420 The lower half of the Layers of Fullers-Earth, they call the *Wall-Earth. **1839** URE *Dict. Arts*, etc. 982 The instant each corve arrives, from the *wall face,..it is lifted from the tram by a crane. *a* **1878** SIR G. SCOTT *Lect. Archit.* (1879) II. 141 In some of the Byzantine remains..they have architecturalised by mouldings and enrichments only just so much of the arch-stones as was needful for beauty, and left the rest to go as mere wall-face. **1593** *Rites & Mon. Durham* (Surtees) 53 She..laid those two without the doore that before was maid *wall-fast within her house. **1850** GROTE *Greece* II. lxiii. (1862) V. 457 Alkibiadês warned the assembled seamen that they must prepare for a sea-fight, a land-fight, and a *wall-fight, all at once. **1950** O. BLAKESTON *Pink Ribbon* v. 59 They ate snails..in Gloucester, and they called them '*wall fish'. **1980** *Times* 2 Oct. 13/3 The taste of an open mushroom grilled with garlic, parsley and butter is so splendid, and superior to snails given the same treatment, that I would never now dream of bothering to cook that delicacy known in the Mendips as *wallfish*. **1669** WORLIDGE *Syst. Agric.* (1681) 266 Nail and trim *Wall-fruits. **1690** *Lond. Gaz.* No. 2550/4 Good Gardens and Orchards planted with all sorts of choice Wall-fruit. *a* **1700** EVELYN *Diary* 24 Mar. 1688, The wall fruit trees are most exquisitely nail'd and train'd. **1842** LOUDON *Suburban Hort.* 582 The wall-fruits of Britain include all those which in the central districts of England require the aid of a wall to bring them to perfection. **1883** *Sat. Rev.* 1 Dec. 695/2 The *Wall Game [at Eton]. **1780** J. WOODFORDE Diary 26 Apr. (1924) I. 280 Busy in painting some boarding in my *Wall Garden. **1936** *Discovery* Mar. 86/2 Wall Garden, 385 feet long, first planted in 1935 [at the Brooklyn Botanic Garden]. **1812** COL. HAWKER *Diary* (1893) I. 63 We then fired with slugs (Colonel Douglas with a Spanish barrel, and I with a huge *wall gun). **1819** SCOTT *Leg. Montrose* x, They found themselves..exposed to a fire both of musketry and wall-guns. **1865** CARLYLE *Fredk. Gt.* XIX. iv. V. 473 Wall-guns brought from Cüstrin. **1896** LINA ECKENSTEIN *Woman under Monasticism* 233 The great work of her life was the manufacture of *wall-hangings. **1967** E. SHORT *Embroidery & Fabric Collage* i. 9 If the finished piece of embroidery is to be seen from a distance, as for instance a wall hanging. **1979** *Arizona Daily Star* 5 Aug. J 5/7 (Advt.), They've just had a new shipment of Oaxacan Rugs and Wallhangings. **1983** *Listener* 30 June 17/1 By 1972 I needed a small pantechnicon to convey all my books on macrobiotic cookery, my plants, wall-hangings and floor cushions. *a* **1578** LINDESAY (Pitscottie) *Chron. Scot.* (S.T.S.) II. 83 [They] laid him on the *wall heid, that all might sie him deid. **1636** in *Scottish Jrnl. Topogr.* (1848) II. 11/1 Item, for ten hondreth of diffeit [= divot] riggine and wae-heid towrs [= turfs]. **1898** LD. E. HAMILTON *Mawkin of Flow* xvii. 226 Here, Rob, rax me that bit rope that's lying in the wall-head yonder. **1833** LOUDON *Encycl. Archit.* §919 The inside lintels..are..to have at least 12 inches of bond (or *wall-hold) on each end. **1844** H. STEPHENS *Bk. Farm* I. 170 The steps should be droved 3 feet 6 inches clear of the wall, with 6 inches of wall hold. **1681** W. ROBERTSON *Phraseol. Gen.* (1693) 739 A *wall-hook or drag; *Lupus, harpago*. **1823** P. NICHOLSON *Pract. Build.* 408 Fastening the pipes to the wall by means of wall-hooks of iron. **1882** CHRISTY *Joints* 194 A strip of 5 lb. lead,..secured along one edge to the wall with wall hooks. **1662** WOOD *Life* 22 Dec. (O.H.S.) I. 464 Wheras they were left of after the king was restored and *wall lectures onlie read in their places, declamations were now setled and wall lectures too. **1691** —— *Ath. Oxon.* (1721) II. 796 He did also sometimes repair to the Ordinaries (commonly called Wall Lectures from the paucity of Auditors). **1767** J. PENN *By Way of Prevention* To Clergy p. i, Dry Morals and musty Doctrines have turned Sermons into Wall Lectures. **1860** G. E. STREET in *Archæol. Cant.* III. 132 A great deal of chalk is used for *wall lining. **1892** *Dict. Archit.* (Archit. Publ. Soc.), *Wall-lining*, a thin internal wall of brick for keeping dry the interior surface of a house in exposed places. **1344–5** *Exch. Acc. K.R.* 492. 24 (MS.), In M[r] de *Walnail empt. vjd. ob. **1864** ATKINSON *Stanton Grange* 224 Next stood a box of shreds and wall-nails. **1935** N. MITCHISON *We have been Warned* III. 295 She had been shown the *wall newspapers of factories and schools. **1937** E. SNOW *Red Star over China* VIII. v. 293 There was also a wall newspaper in every club, and a committee of soldiers was responsible for keeping it up to date. **1966** J. DERRICK *Teaching Eng. to Immigrants* vi. 213 Project work involving the use of aids and apparatus..such as preparing a broadcast or TV programme or involving the class or group in the production of a wall newspaper should be considered. **1978** *China Now* Mar./Apr. 19/3 They keenly contested for the miserable prizes offered in competitions between groups and individuals in sport, literacy, public health, wall newspapers, and 'factory efficiency'. **1979** *N.Y. Rev. Bks.* 25 Oct. 40/3 The hero stands in Yuryatin reading the wall-newspapers. **1673** [R. LEIGH] *Transp. Reh.* 76 The avenue-readers, the *wall-observers, and those that are acquainted with stall-learning. **1946** G. TYRWHITT-DRAKE *Eng. Circus & Fair Ground* xviii. 210 Undoubtedly the most thrilling side-show was the '*Wall of Death', first seen here..in 1928. **1959** *Listener* 26 Feb. 371/2 It might..spin quickly round the steep hollow like a rider on the Wall of Death. **1976** 'W. TREVOR' *Children of Dynmouth* i. 13 The Hall of a Million Mirrors and the Tunnel of Love and Alfonso's and Annabella's Wall of Death were in the process of erection. **1688** *Wall painting [see FRESCO *sb.* 2]. **1849** *Jrnl. Brit. Archaeol. Assoc.* IV. 92 Church decoration of this kind is..not unfrequently brought to light; but specimens of domestic internal wall-painting are of much greater rarity. **1898** A. BEARDSLEY *Let.* 14 Jan. (1970) 424 I'm afraid good books on the wall paintings of Pompeii are costly and beyond my balance. **1933** *Burlington Mag.* Oct. 146/2 These..portraits.. brought Holbein immediate fame and the order to decorate the King's Privy Chamber in Whitehall Palace with wall-paintings. **1964** W. L. GOODMAN *Hist. Woodworking Tools* 132 A wall-painting from Pompeii. **1958** *Mod. Soccer* (Football Assoc.) v. 41 In Fig. 38 the LB [Left Back], sensing the possibility of a '*wall-pass', quickly backs away. **1973** *Times* 6 Jan. 7/5 The 'wall pass', 'one-two', touch play, 'push and run', call it what you will, we developed it at Tottenham. **1888** *Wall plug [see PLUG *sb.* 1 c]. **1914** BATSTONE *Electr.-Light Fitting* 122 Wall Plugs. **1962** L. DEIGHTON *Ipcress File* xxv. 166 There was a big two kilowatt electric fire plugged into a wall point... It was the work of a minute to switch on the wall plug. **1880** *Scribner's Monthly* Apr. 921/1 The family comb..occupied a convenient *wall-pocket at one side of the small kitchen mirror. **1947** E. BISHOP in *Nation* (N.Y.) 22 Feb. 215/1 The eighty watt bulb..Lighting as well on heads Of tacks in the wall paper, On a paper wall-pocket, Violet-embossed, glistening With mica flakes. **1957** MANKOWITZ & HAGGAR *Conc. Encycl. Eng. Pott. & Porc.* 125/1 Articles for domestic use..included..punch-bowls, wall-pockets and plaques. **1971** L. A. BOGER *Dict. World Pott. & Porc.* 365/1 *Wall Pocket*, in ceramics; a decorative object made of faïence, porcelain or pottery, having the shape of a vase, with one side being flat so that it can be hung on a wall. It is also called a wall vase. **1871** T. MORRIS *Brit. Carpentry* 85 The situation of the *wall posts would seem to indicate a purpose of concentrating the weight. **1962** E. CLEAVER in A. Dundes *Mother Wit* (1973) 14/2 The mass media..television,.. illustrated *wall posters [etc.]. **1966** *China Q.* Oct.–Dec. 3 Within a week or two..20,000 'sightseers' were visiting Peking University each day, partly to read the wall-posters, partly to watch and abuse the 'criminals'. **1977** 'S. LEYS' *Chinese Shadows* (1978) ii. 70 Huge wall posters placed at random throughout the city. ('Increase our Vigilance and Protect our Fatherland!') **1979** 'J. LE CARRÉ' *Smiley's People* xxvii. 322 Wall posters offering cheap ski holidays. **1523** *Acc. Ld. High Treas. Scot.* V. 220 Item, for ij *wall rasis put undre the cuppill feit,..Item, for v corbalis of stane..for bering to the tua wall rasis. **1627** CAPT. J. SMITH *Sea Gram.* xi. 53 We say a Ship is..*wall reared when she is right built vp, after shee comes to her bearing. **1316** *Placitorum Abbrev.* (1811) 352 Et dicunt qđ idem dñs & curia sua de Stebenhethe..ordinavit..duos homines qui vocantur *Walreves ad supervidendum wallias fossata seweras & gutteras praedicta. **1835** R. WILLIS *Archit. Mid. Ages* vii. 82 If the compartment be bounded by a wall as in the case of the clerestory, the rib which is placed at the intersection of the vault with the wall may be called the *Wall Rib. **1850** INKERSLEY *Inquir. Archit. France* 309 The union of the wall-rib-shaft..with the spring of the window-archway. **1877** RAYMOND *Statist. Mines & Mining* 349 On it a shaft has been sunk..showing a continuous vein with well-defined *wall-rock. **1911** *Encycl. Brit.* XXIV. 94/2 *Wall-saltpetre or lime saltpetre, calcium nitrate, $Ca(NO_3)_2$, is found as an efflorescence on the walls of stables; it is now manufactured in large quantities. **1865** G. E. STREET *Gothic Archit. Spain* ix. 191 There are three-quarter engaged *wall-shafts between the windows. *c* **1400** *Destr. Troy* 861 Sho went vp wightly by a *walle syde To the toppe of a toure. **1887** P. M'NEILL *Blawearie* 176 Many alterations on the roof and wall-sides would have to be made. **1933** AUDEN *Poems* (ed. 2) 80 Climbing over to wall-side of bed. **1959** I. & P. OPIE *Lore & Lang. Schoolch.* xii. 266 The old custom of making grottoes at the wall-side edge of the pavement. **1711** W. SUTHERLAND *Shipbuild. Assist.* 165 *Wall-sided. **1769** FALCONER *Dict. Marine* (1780). **1830** LYELL *Princ. Geol.* I. 180 A deep wall-sided valley. **1840** R. H. DANA *Bef. Mast* xxix, She was a good, substantial ship,..wall-sided and kettle-bottomed. **1866** HUXLEY *Prehist. Rem. Caithn.* 88 The transverse contour of the skull inclines to be pentagonal and wall-sided. **1889** in *Cent. Dict.*, *Wall space. **1898** G. B. SHAW *Arms & Man* III. 47 The rest of the wall space being occupied by trophies of war and the chase. **1978** *Lancashire Life* Sept. 101/1 True, a new library is being built in Stanley Road, where wall-space for pictures will be made available, but there will be no gallery proper, and no museum whatsoever. **1833** LOUDON *Encycl. Archit.* §925 The *wall-straps (battens, or pieces of quartering on which to nail the laths) are to be 1 inch and a quarter thick. **1849** *Wall string [see STRING *sb.* 26]. **1978** *Detroit Free Press* 2 Apr. 7B/1 (Advt.), Westwood *wall system from Southern is a handsome backdrop for any room and provides invaluable storage. **1980** *Christian Sci. Monitor* (Midwestern ed.) 4 Dec. 17/3 Wall systems are the fastest-growing category of furnishings. **1862** T. W. HIGGINSON *Army Life* (1870) 19 Two *wall-tents being placed end to end, for office and bedroom. **1894** *Outing* XXIV. 86/1 We had a single wall-tent, ten by twelve. **1884** *Health Exhib. Catal.* 81/2 Section of Hollow Brick Wall, showing our patent cast and wrought *wall-ties. **1358** *York Mercers* etc. (Surtees) 15 Pro xx mille de *Walteghill, vj *li.* **1465** in *Paston Lett.* II. 224 A thousand waltyle that his fadir had fro ye seide Williams wyfes place. **1790** GROSE *Provinc. Gloss.* Suppl., *Wall-tiles*, bricks; opposed to tiles, called Thack-tiles. North. **1882** CHRISTY *Joints* 68 Wall tiles are sometimes bedded in fine plaster. *c* **1475** *Pict. Voc.* in Wr.-Wülcker 748/7 *Hoc maxillare*, a *walthothe. (? Hence) **1847** HALLIWELL, *Wall-tooth*, a large double-tooth. *c* **1470** HENRY *Wallace* VIII. 699 This war the best of all, To kepe our strynth off castell and off *wall toun. *c* **1480** HENRYSON *Death & Man* 7 Wal-townis, castellis, towiris, neuir so wicht, may nocht resist quhill it be at his hert. **1657** AUSTEN *Fruit Trees* I. 66 As concerning the distance of *Wal-trees. **1786** ABERCROMBIE *Gard. Assist.* 42 For wall-tree cherries, plums, pears, etc. allot a portion of the earliest..varieties for south walls. **1844** *Zoologist* II. 493 Another [nest] was completed in an adjoining wall-tree. **1962** *Listener* 11 Jan. 65/1 Making the best use of up-to-date methods, such as the prefabrication of large *wall units, which are being successfully used already in half the European countries. **1979** A. B. EMARY *Woodworking* xxiv. 104 Many of the units purchased from stores are made from melamine-covered chipboard and since it is easy to obtain the home woodworker will find this material useful when making objects such as wall units and shelving. **1889** in *Cent. Dict.*, *Wall vase. **1937** *Burlington Mag.* Dec. p. xx/1,

The book contains many valuable hints..such as..the advantages of wall-vases. **1979** I. Webb *Compl. Guide Flower & Foliage Arrangement* vii. 96/2 (*caption*) Two wall vases hold flowers which suit their differing qualities and appearance. **1898** *Allbutt's Syst. Med.* V. 511 We discovered arsenic in large quantity in the green unsized *wall-wash of her own sitting-room. **1966** D. Phillips *Lighting* 36 The principal lighting method is by *wall washer fittings recessed into the suspended ceiling. **1983** *Homes & Gardens* Nov. 138 Wall-washers have half the aperture closed off and their function is to give an even illumination of one wall surface from skirting to ceiling without lighting the floor. **1596** S. Finche *Let.* 26 Feb., in Ducarel *Hist. Croydon* (1783) App. 155 We have made up that angle..*wall-wyse with stone and morter. *c* **1000** Ælfric *Hom.* (Thorpe) II. 166 Þa ȝebroðra eodon to ðam *weall-weorce. **1581** J. Bell *Haddon's Answ. Osor.* A vj b, Our dutie hadd bene to direct the buildyng of our Religion by this lyne and leuell, and to ramme fast the wallworkes hereof with this cemente and morter. **1837** *Penny Cycl.* IX. 468/1 Other internal walls..communicate with wall-works running east and west.

b. In the names of animals frequenting or living in walls, as **wall-bee** (see quot.); **wall-bird**, a dial. name of the Spotted Flycatcher, *Muscicapa grisola*; **wall-brown**, a common British butterfly, *Satyrus megæra* = *brown wall* (see 19 c); **wall-butterfly** (see quot.); **wall-carpet**, a variety of the carpet-moth (see CARPET *sb.* 5); **wall-creeper** (see quot. 1888); **wall-fly** (see quot.); **wall-gecko** (see quot.); **wall-lizard**, a lizard of the species *Lacerta muralis*; **wall-louse**, †(*a*) the bed-bug, *Cimex lectularius*; (*b*) *dial.* the woodlouse; †**wall-newt**, ? = *wall-lizard*; **wall-usher**, a variety of moth (see quot.); **wall-wasp** (see quot.).

1774 Goldsm. *Nat. Hist.* (1776) VIII. 94 The *Wall Bees are so called, because they make their nests in walls. **1848** *Zoologist* VI. 2186 The spotted flycatcher is the '*wall-bird'. **1846** *Proc. Berw. Nat. Club* II. 171 Not a single specimen has been observed of the..*Wall Brown, or the Dark Green Aglaia. **1860** W. S. Coleman *Brit. Butterfl.* 98 The *Wall Butterfly (*Lasiommata Megæra*). *Ibid.* 99 It is called the Wall Butterfly from its frequent habit of choosing a roadside wall for a perch. **1832** J. Rennie *Butterfl. & Moths* 111 The *Wall Carpet (*Alcis muraria* Curtis). **1667** C. Merrett *Pinax* 177 *Picus murarius*, the Creeper, or *Wall-Creeper. **1678** [see SPIDER-CATCHER 2]. **1764** G. Edwards *Glean. Nat. Hist.* III. 284 The Wall-creeper of Surinam. **1888** Newton in *Encycl. Brit.* XXIII. 534/2 Allied to the Tree-Creeper [*Certhia*]..is the genus *Tichodroma*, the single member of which is the Wall-Creeper (*T. muraria*) of the Alps and some other mountainous parts of Europe and Asia. **1653** Walton *Angler* ii. 54 Nay, sometimes a worm, or any kind of fly; as the Ant-fly, the Flesh-fly, or *Wall-fly [cf. ed. 3 (1661) 63, the black Bee that breeds in clay walls]. **1886** *Cassell's Dict.* s.v. *Platydactylus*, *P. fascicularis* or *muralis* is the *Wall Gecko. *c* **1880** *Cassell's Nat. Hist.* IV. 274 The lively little *Wall Lizard, *Lacerta muralis*. **1540** *Septem Ling. Dict.* D vj, Cimices..*wallyse. **1598–1657** Wall louse [see PUNAISE]. **1673** [see CHINCH *sb.*[1]]. **1693** S. Dale *Pharmacol.* 531 Cimex..The Wall-Louse or Bugg. **1899** *Cumbld. Gloss.*, s.v. *Kirk louse*, *Wall louse*, *Slater*, woodlouse, millipede. *Oniscidæ*. **1605** Shaks. *Lear* III. iv. 135 Poore Tom, that eates..the Tod-pole, the *wall-Neut, and the water. **1708** *Brit. Apollo* No. 88. 2/1 Like the Body of a Red *Wall-Spider. **1832** J. Rennie *Butterfl. & Moths* 102 The *Wall Usher (*Anisopteryx Æscularia*, Stephens) appears on palings and trunks of trees the middle of March. **1881** *Cassell's Nat. Hist.* V. 372 The *Wall Wasp (*Odynerus parietum*)..may be almost constantly seen haunting sunny walls during the months of June and July.

c. In the names of plants growing on or by walls and in dry or stony places, as **wall barley**, the wild barley, *Hordeum murinum*; also **rye-grass**, *Lolium perenne*; **wall bugloss**, a plant of the genus *Lycopsis*; **wall cabbage** (see quot.); **wall-cress**, the genus *Arabis*; also (see quot. 1796); **wall fern**, the common evergreen fern, *Polypodium vulgare*; **wall gillyflower**, the WALLFLOWER; **wall grass**, the stonecrop, *Sedum acre*; **wall hawkweed**, *Hieracium murorum*; **wall moss**, (*a*) the yellow lichen, *Parmelia parietaria* (Cent. Dict.); (*b*) *Sedum acre*; (*c*) see quot. 1855; **wall mustard** = *wall-rocket*; **wall pellitory** = PELLITORY 2; †**wall penny grass**, **wall pennywort** = PENNYWORT 1; **wall pepper**, *Sedum acre*; **wall pie** = *wall rue*; **wall-rocket**, *Diplotaxis tenuifolia*; **wall rue**, a small fern, *Asplenium Ruta-muraria*; **wall sage**, †(*a*) a species of *Sideritis*; cf. GLIDEWORT, IRONWORT; (*b*) = PELLITORY 2 (*Eng. Dial. Dict.*); **wall speedwell**, *Veronica arvensis*; **wall spleenwort** = *wall rue*; **wall weed**, ? mother-of-thousands, *Linaria Cymbalaria*. Also WALLFLOWER, WALLWORT.

1548 Turner *Names Herbes* (E.D.S.) 43 Phenicea or Hordeum murinum of Plinie, is the *wal Barley, whiche groweth on mud walles. **1597** Gerarde *Herbal* I. li. 71 Red Darnell is called..in Latin *Lolium rubrum*: and *Lolium Murinum*: in English Wall Barley. **1763** Mills *Pract. Husb.* III. 333 The Wall barley, or way bennet, as some people improperly term it. **1866** *Treas. Bot.* I. 597/1 We all remember how in our youth we put inverted spikes of the Wall Barley up our sleeves and found them travel to our shoulders. **1650** [W. Howe] *Phytol. Brit.* 36 Echium alterum, *Dod.* Lycopsis Anglica, *Lob.* in agris siccioribus & muris. *Wall Buglosse. **1860** Mayne *Expos. Lex.*, Wall-Bugloss. Common name for the *Lycopsis*. **1796** Withering *Brit. Plants* (ed. 3) III. 593 [Brassica muralis] Sisymbrium *murale*. Linn... *Wall Cabbage. Old walls and rubbish. *Ibid.* 589 *Turritis hirsuta*..*Wall Cress. **1866** *Treas. Bot.* 83/2 Wall-cress, the English name [of *Arabis*] has similar reference to the usual place of growth. **1525** *Grete Herbal* cccxlix. (1529) Tv, De polytryco. *Walfarne. **1639** O. Wood *Alph. Bk. Secrets* 214 Walferne. **1548** Turner *Names Herbes* (E.D.S.) 80 Viola alba... There are diuerse sortes... One is called in english Cheiry, Hertes ease or *wal Gele-floure, it groweth vpon the walles, and..hath yealowe floures. **1796** H. Hunter tr. *St.-Pierre's Stud. Nat.* (1799) II. 94 The butter-flower of the meadow, and the wall gilly-flower. **1882** H. Friend *Devonsh. Plant-n.*, *Wall Grass. *Sedum acre*, L. **1829** Loudon *Encycl. Plants* (1836) 674 *Wall hawkweed. **1855** Anne Pratt *Flowering Pl.* II. 324 *Wall-moss (Dicranum murale). **1886** Britten & Holland *Plant-n.*, Wall Moss. *Sedum acre* L.—N. and E. Yks. **1904** *Wall-mustard [see *wall-rocket*]. **1562** Turner *Herbal* II. 169, I knowe no English name for it [*Vmbilicus veneris*]: but lest it should be wythout a name I call it *wall penny grasse. **1578** Lyte *Dodoens* I. xxv. 37 *Cotyledon vera*. *Wall Pennywurte. **1579**, **1756** [see PENNYWORT 1]. **1855** Anne Pratt *Flowering Pl.* II. 320 *Cotyledon Umbilicus* (Wall Pennywort). **1578** Lyte *Dodoens* I. lxxvii. 115 Of Houselyke and Sengreene... The fourth is called..in English Stone Crop,..& of some it is called *Wall Pepper. **1861** S. Thomson *Wild Flowers* III. (ed. 4) 238 We find the *Sedum acre*, or yellow stone-crop, often called wall-pepper. **1855** Anne Pratt *Flowering Pl.* I. 152 *Sinapis tenuifolia* (*Wall-rocket). **1904** *Westm. Gaz.* 13 Oct. 10/1 This is the wall-rocket or narrow-leaved wall-mustard (*Diplotaxis tenuifolia*), a glaucous plant, one to one and a half feet high, with pale lemon-yellow flowers. **1548** Turner *Names Herbes* (E.D.S.) 86 Saluia vita or Ruta muralis..maye be called in english Stone Rue, or *wal Rue. **1741** *Compl. Fam.-Piece* I. iv. 243 Leaves of Wall-Rue 4 Ounces. **1906** J. Vaughan *Wild-Fl. Selborne* 92 The little wall-rue fern. **1548** Turner *Names Herbes* (E.D.S.) 73 Sideritis prima..may be called in englishe *walsage or stonisage. **1651** J. F[reake] *Agrippa's Occ. Philos.* I. xvii. 40 Geese, Ducks, and such like watery fowle, cure themselves with the Hearb called wall-sage [L. *herba sideritide*]. **1796** Withering *Brit. Plants* (ed. 3) II. 13 *Veronica arvensis*..*Wall Speedwell. **1866** Swinburne *St. Dorothy* Poems & Ballads 288 Green blossom cleaves To the green chinks, and lesser *wall-weed sweet, Kissing the crannies that are split with heat.

†**wall**, *sb.*[2] *Sc. Obs.* Also 6 **vall**, **wal**. [var. spelling (with silent *ll*) of WAW *sb.*] A wave (of the sea).

c **1480** *Wyntoun's Cron.* I. vii. 399 (MS. E.) Of wellis wawerit wallis wid. *c* **1480** Henryson *Paddock & Mouse* 180 The watter is the warld, ay welterand With mony wall of trubulatioun. *c* **1500** *Lancelot* 1316 Thi schip, that goth apone the stormy vall. **1513** Douglas *Æneis* III. viii. 60 Within the havin goith loune, but wind or wall. **1549** *Compl. Scot.* 39 The suelland vallis of the brym seye. **1599** Alex. Hume *Hymns* vii. 89 The waltering wals, and raging windie blast.

†**wall**, *sb.*[3] *Obs.* Also 7 **whall**. [Back-formation from WALL-EYE.] ***eyes of wall*** (nonce-phrase) = 'wall eyes': see WALL EYE. Also *attrib.* or *adj.*, as in ***wall speck***; ***wall-coloured*** adj.

1611 Cotgr. s.v. *Oeil*, *Oeil de chevre*, a whall, or ouer-white eye. **1653** R. Sanders *Physiogn.* 27 The apple [of the eye] is half blew, and all about wall-coloured. **1663** Butler *Hud.* I. i. 424 The Beast was sturdy large and tall, With Mouth of Meal and Eyes of Wall. **1706** *Lond. Gaz.* No. 4285/8 Stolen.., a white Horse, with..a wall Speck in one of his Eyes.

wall (wɔːl), *sb.*[4] *Naut.* Short for WALL-KNOT.

1834 Marryat *P. Simple* vi, 'How is this to be finished off sir?' inquired a sailor of the boatswain. 'Why,..it must be with a double wall.' *c* **1860** H. Stuart *Seaman's Catech.* 30 Make a single wall. *Ibid.* 56 A 'double wall' or deck stopper-knot is made..close up to the wall. **1884** Knight *Dict. Mech.* Suppl., *Wall and Crown*. This knot should be finished with a crown.

wall (wɔːl), *sb.*[5] = LABLAB.

1884 *De Candolle's Orig. Cultiv. Plants* 346 Lablab, or Wall..*Dolichos Lablab*, Linnæus. This species is much cultivated in India and tropical Africa. **1887** Moloney *Forestry W. Afr.* 322 'Wall' of India (*Dolichos Lablab*, L.) A climbing perennial largely cultivated in the Tropics for its unpalatable seeds.

wall, *v.*[1] *Obs.* exc. *dial.* Forms: 1 **weallan**, 2–5 **walle-n**, 7– **wall**. *Pa. t.* 1 **wéol(l**, 3 **weol**, **wul**, 4 **wel**; *weak* 4 **wallede**, 7– **walled**. [OE. *weallan* redupl. str. vb. (pa. t. *wéoll*, pa. pple. *ȝeweallen*) corresp. to OFris. *walla* to well up (WFris. *walle* to boil), MFlem. *wallen* (Kilian) to well up (mod.Flem. to boil), OS. *wallan* str. vb., to boil up, gush forth (MLG. *wallen*), OHG. *wallan* str. vb., to boil, gush forth (MHG. *wallen* str., mod.G. wk., to boil, be agitated, swarm, etc.).

The transitive uses do not occur in OE., and as they are found only with the weak conjugation, it is possible that they descend not from OE. *weallan*, but from *wællan* var. of *wiellan*, *wellan* WELL *v.*; cf. mod. Sc. *wall* (WELL *sb.*) repr. OE. *wælla* var. of *wiella*. The transitive senses below are closely paralleled by those of WELL *v.* and its equivalents in other Teut. langs.

The Teut. **wallan* (:—**waln-*) redupl. vb. with the sense 'to boil, bubble up' is confined to WGer.; but a cogn. and synonymous **wellan* str. vb. exists in ON. *vella* (*vall*, *ollenn*), MSw. *välla* str. vb. (Sw. *välla*, Da. *vælde* wk. vbs.), and a causative type **walljan* wk. vb. in ON. *vella* (Sw. *välla*) to boil (trans.), to weld = MHG. *wellen*, OE. *wiellan*: see WELL, WELD vbs. For other Teut. derivatives of the root in the same specific sense see WALM, WELL sb.; cf. also Goth. *wulan* to be fervent. It is probable that the sense 'to boil, bubble, well up' is developed from the sense 'to roll', which belongs to the root **wel-* in Teut. and Indogermanic (see WALLOW *v.*); for the form **well-* cf. OHG. *wella* roller, axle (MHG., mod.G. *welle*), *wellan* str. vb. trans. to roll.]

†**1.** *intr.* Of a liquid: To boil. Also of a person: To be in boiling liquid. *Obs.*

c **1000** *Sax. Leechd.* II. 358 Do ofer fyr, awyl; þonne hit wealle, sing iii. pater noster. *c* **1200** *Moral Ode* 249 (Trin. MS.) Þar is pich þat afre walleð [*MS. Egerton* wealð]. *c* **1200** Ormin 10507 To bærnnenn & to wallenn Wiþþ deofless dun in hellegrund. *c* **1250** *Song Passion* 45 in *O.E. Misc.* 198 Wallen in helle dep nere neuere so swet wit alle.

†**b.** *fig.* To 'boil' with passion. (Cf. WALLING *ppl. a.*) *Obs.*

Beowulf 2113 Hreðer inne weoll, þonne he wintrum frod worn ȝemunde. *a* **1225** *Leg. Kath.* 1926 Þe king weol al inwið of wreððe. *a* **1225** *Ancr. R.* 118 Þeo hwule þet te heorte walleð wiðinnen of wreððe, nis þer no riht dom.

†**2.** Of liquids: To bubble up; to well up, flow abundantly. Of the sea, waves: To boil up, rage.

c **893** Ælfred *Oros.* IV. iii, Mon ȝeseah weallan blod of eorþan. *c* **1200** *Trin. Coll. Hom.* 167 At eche wunde wul ut atter. **1297** R. Glouc. (Rolls) 662 As þe water deþ vp walle. *c* **1315** Shoreham *Poems* III. 28 Syker þou myȝt be of þat lond þar melke and hony walleþ. *c* **1330** *King of Tars* 1087 Þe blod out of his wounde wel. **1362** Langl. *P. Pl.* A. v. 71 Venim or vernisch or vinegre, I trouwe, Walleþ in my wombe or waxeþ, ich wene. *c* **1450** *Mirk's Festial* 9 Out of þe whech tombe manna and oyle walleþ out yfere.

fig. **1449** Pecock *Repr.* IV. iii. 432 Thes..causis, out of whiche wallen the seid yuelis.

†**b.** To swarm (with vermin). *Obs.*

c **1000** Ælfric *Saint's Lives* iv. 212 On blindum cwearterne..þær manna lic laȝon, þe wæran ær acwealde..þa weollon eall maðon. *c* **1050** *Voc.* in Wr.-Wülcker 531/22 *Scatens*, weallende [gl. Aldh. *Laud. Virg.* (poet.) lxxxix, *scatens vermibus*]. **1387** Trevisa *Higden* (Rolls) V. 235 He wallede ful of wormes [L. *vermibus scatens*].

3. *trans.* To boil. Cf. WELL *v.*

See *pot-walling*, quot. 1456 s.v. POT-WALLOPING.

c **1310** *S. Margaret* 287 in Horstm. *Altengl. Leg.* (1881) 232 Takeþ and walleþ oyle and lete opon hir renne.

b. *absol.* To boil brine in salt-making.

1600 [Implied in WALLER[2]]. **1669** *Phil. Trans.* IV. 1063 They seldom Wall, that is, make Salt, in above 6 Houses at a time.

4. *intr.* To weld, become welded; *fig.* to blend. Cf. WELL, WELD *vbs.*

1629 Sir W. Mure *True Crucifixe* 2692 Pleasure in Him and fleshlie pleasure fall So foull at strife, they can, nor mixe, nor wall.

wall (wɔːl), *v.*[2] Pa. t. and pa. pple. **walled** (wɔːld). [OE. **weallian* (only in pa. pple. *ȝeweallod*), f. *weall* WALL *sb.*[1] Cf. LG. *wallen.*]

1. *trans.* To furnish with a wall.

a. To enclose, surround, or divide with a wall or walls; to provide (a town, etc.) with fortified walls.

[*c* **1000** Ælfric *Num.* xiii. 29 Micele burȝa þær sind and mærlice ȝeweallode.] *c* **1250** *Gen. & Ex.* 435 He ches a stede toward eden, And..Wallede a burȝ, e-no bi name. ? *a* **1366** Chaucer *Rom. Rose* 138, I saugh a Gardin.., Enclos it was, and walled wel, With hye walles enbatailled. **1387** Trevisa *Higden* (Rolls) VI. 339 Þe citee of Ȝork, þat was not ful i-walled. **1471** Caxton *Recuyell* (Sommer) 271 Laomedon the kynge of Troye was besy to walle and mure his cyte with mures and towres. **1589** Bigges *Summarie Drake's W. Ind. Voy.* 39 The same [Priorie] being walled with a wall of stone. **1611** Shaks. *Cymb.* v. iii. 14 Close by the battell, ditch'd, & wall'd with turph. **1643** R. Baker *Chron.* 13 King Athelstan..new walled and beautifyed the City of Exceter. **1794** *Trans. Soc. Arts* XII. 201 The expence of walling the forty-two acres was seventy-eight pounds. **1842** Dickens *Amer. Notes* iii, The House of Correction..is not walled, like other prisons, but is palisaded round about with..stakes. **1849** Lyell *2nd Visit U.S.* II. 295 Some lands near the river..have risen immensely in value, being now trenched and walled. **1881** *Proc. R. Geog. Soc.* (N.S.) III. 31 The town of Shonga..is walled and ditched.

b. with *about*, *round about*, *round*. ***to wall in***, to enclose with a wall. ***to wall off***, ***out***, to shut off or out with a wall.

1297 R. Glouc. (Rolls) 1169 Þe vif tounes of þe vif pors he let walli aboute. **1375** Barbour *Bruce* II. 220 Till Perth then went thai..That then wes wallyt all about. *c* **1420** Wyntoun *Cron.* v. 1303 (Cott.) He gert wal in al þat stede Qwhar Criste his passion tholit of dede. **1481** Caxton *Reynard* v. (Arb.) 10 They..wente in a yerde whiche was walled round a boute. *c* **1530** Tindale *Jonas* Prol. B vij, Enuironed it and walled it aboute on euery syde with yᵉ feare of god. **1600** Surflet *Country Farm* VII. xix. 834 Their parkes therefore must bee walled about. **1633** *Stow's Surv.* 761 He round walled the Church-yard. **1691** J. Gibson in *Archæologia* XII. 189 The garden not being walled about they have less summer fruit. **1719** De Foe *Crusoe* II. (Globe) 564 It was a low marshy Ground, wall'd round with a Stone-wall. **1760–72** H. Brooke *Fool of Qual.* (1809) IV. 58 A gravel-walk that was walled in on the left hand. **1799** Wellington *Let. Lieut. Col. Close* 21 Dec., in Gurwood *Disp.* (1844) I. 47 What I should propose would be to wall off that part occupied by him. **1848** Dickens *Dombey* vii, Traffic was walled out. **1860** Tyndall *Glac.* I. ii. 19 A space for cooking walled off from the sleeping-room. **1865** W. G. Palgrave *Journ. Central & E. Arabia* II. 301 The town is walled in, but not strongly, on the land side.

c. To furnish (a building) with side and partition walls; to build the wall or walls of. Also with *up*.

1377 Langl. *P. Pl.* B. XIX. 323 And þere-with grace bigan to make a good foundement, And watteled it and walled it with his peynes & his passioun. *c* **1394** *P. Pl. Crede* 164 And all was walled þat wone. **1523** Berners *Froiss.* I. ccix. 102 b/2 Therein was a square toure thick walled. **1691** Dryden *K. Arthur* II. 19 That Castle, were it wall'd with Adamant, Can hide thy Head, but till to Morrow's Dawn. **1726** Leoni *Alberti's Archit.* I. 78 The Towers..ought not to be open on the inside, but walled up quite round. **1799** A.

YOUNG *View Agric. Lincoln.* 34 The old buildings are of timber, walled with clay. **1911** G. MACDONALD *Roman Wall Scot.* xii. 401 Perhaps it was now that Castlecary was walled with stone.

d. To line (a well, cistern) with a wall. Also with *round*.

1707 MORTIMER *Husb.* 229 A Cistern of Clay walled within with Bricks. **1833** JAS. DAVIDSON *Brit. & Rom. Rem. Axminster* 84 A hole in the natural soil..walled round in a circular form with flint stones.

2. *transf.* and *fig.* To enclose, defend, bound, or divide as with a wall, or as a wall does.

c **1386** CHAUCER *Manciple's T.* 219 My sone, god.. Walled a tonge with teeth and lippes eke ffor man sholde hym auyse what he speeke. **1558** A. JENKINSON in Hakluyt *Voy.* (1599) I. 331 We feared nothing being walled with the said riuer. **1591** SHAKS. *1 Hen. VI*, IV. ii. 24 On either hand thee, there are squadrons pitcht, To wall thee from the liberty of Flight. **1595** *Polimanteia* in Brydges *Brit. Bibl.* I. 278 Yet both of you [Oxford and Cambridge] so deare to me,..so walled with priuiledges, so crowned with all kinde of honor. **1603–4** SHAKS. *Ham.* IV. v. 122 (QQ 1, 2) There's such diuinitie doth wall [*Fol.* hedge] a king, That treason dares not looke on. *c* **1620** FLETCHER *False One* v. iv. 26 My free mind, Like to the palm-tree walling fruitful Nile, Shall grow up straighter. **1638** SIR T. HERBERT *Trav.* (ed. 2) 165 Either side is wall'd with an amazing hill. **1639** FULLER *Holy War* IV. vii. 179 They..onely spoiled poore villages, which counted themselves walled with the truce as yet in force. **1667** MILTON *P.L.* III. 721 Each [star] had his place appointed, each his course, The rest in circuit walles this Universe. **1818** L. HUNT *Hero & Leander* II. 7 The struggling flare Seem'd out; but then he knew his Hero's care, And that she only wall'd it with her cloak. **1834** LD. HOUGHTON *Mem. Tour Greece* 23 The tall white rock, Walled the far waste of silent sea. **1879** *Daily News* 18 Sept. 6/1 The enclosures were walled with Union Jacks. **1883** BRIDGES *Prometheus* 14 Where the path Is walled with corn I am found. **1913** *Engl. Rev.* Dec. 59 On the right hand, walling the street, [is] the great monastery to the Passion of Christ.

b. with *about*, *across*, *along*, *in*, *round*.

c **1430** *Pilgr. Lyf Manhode* I. xx. (1869) 15 This closure that closeth yow and walleth yow in, disseueringe yow from the world. **1588** SHAKS. *L.L.L.* v. ii. 3 A Lady wal'd about with Diamonds. **1593** —— *Rich. II*, III. ii. 167 As if this Flesh, which walls about our Life, Were Brasse impregnable. *a* **1626** BACON *War with Spain* (1629) 45 The Spaniards..casting themselues continually into Roundels, (their strongest Ships walling in the rest). **1642** DENHAM *Sophy* I. 1 'Tis his single vertue And terror of his name, that walls us in From danger. **1690** C. NESSE *O. & N. Test.* I. 38 A weekly sabbath walls in our wild natures. **1795** SOUTHEY *Joan of Arc* I. 475 At length I heard of Orleans, by the foe Wall'd in from human succour. **1837** W. IRVING *Capt. Bonneville* II. 207 The high precipices which had hitherto walled in the channel of Snake river. **1845** J. COULTER *Adv. in Pacific* xi. 132 The..upper part of the clearing, which was walled along for several hundred yards by solid rock. **1878** BROWNING *Poets Croisic* Prol. 3 World —— how it walled about Life with disgrace. **1883** STEVENSON *Silverado Sq.* (1886) 39 A canyon..was here walled across by a dump of rolling stones. **1890** 'R. BOLDREWOOD' *Col. Reformer* xiv, The..landlocked bay, with..a grand sand-stone bluff guarding and walling-in the farther point like a grim jealous giant.

c. To form the sides of (a room) like walls; to line the walls of (an apartment).

1832 LYTTON *Eugene Aram* I. iii. 20 The rest of the room was walled from the floor to the roof with books. **1846** G. B. CHEEVER *Lect. Pilgr. Progr.* x. 126 It does not take long in such employment to make the room seem walled with retributive flames. **1910** G. W. E. RUSSELL *15 Chapters Autob.* (1914) vii. 149 The great gallery, walled with the canvases of Rubens.

3. To shut up (a person or thing) within walls, to build up or entomb in a wall, to immure. Chiefly with *up*.

1530 PALSGR. 770/2, I wall, I shyt up, or close up, within walles. *Je mure*... It is a harde relygyon to be an anchre, for they be shytte up within walles and can go no farther. **1600** E. BLOUNT tr. *Conestaggio* 243 They were walled vp within their monasterie. *a* **1618** FLETCHER *Mad Lover* I. i, In three [battles] he beat the Thunder-bolt his Brother, Forc'd him to wall himself up. **1621** LADY M. WROTH *Urania* 133 After the sight of one dead, the other wall'd to certaine death,.. what could they say? **1647** in *Verney Mem.* (1892) II. xii. 285 The feather bedds that were waled up are much eaten with Ratts. **1719** D'URFEY *Pills* (1872) VI. 87 But if ne'er so close you wall him,..Blind Love..Will find out the way. **1737** W. COWPER in F. Peck *Mem. O. Cromwell* etc. II. (1740) 88, I am apt to think the person found in the vault was betrayed and walled up alive by the person he trusted. **1845** POE *Black Cat* (end), I had walled the monster up within the tomb!

transf. **1867** G. MACDONALD *Poems* 87, I will be a knight Walled up in armour black.

¶ **b.** An alleged synonym of GATE *v.*[1]

1860 C. BENSON *Mr. Bedlow, Remin. Amer. Coll. Life* in *Macm. Mag.* II. 222/1 To 'gate' or 'wall' a refractory student would be simply impossible, for want of the material masonry. **1871** HOPPE s.v. *Gate* gives the prec. quot.; hence the sense appears (as 'Oxford university slang') in BARRÈRE & LELAND *Slang*, in FARMER, and in recent Dicts.

4. To close (a gate or other aperture) with or as with a wall. Chiefly with *up*.

1503 *Engl. Misc.* (Surtees 1890) 30 John Mitteley & his heires frome now forthe shall wall up..the utter west syde of his swynstye. **1535** COVERDALE *1 Macc.* v. 47 They that were in the cite, wolde not let them go thorow, but walled vp the portes with stones. **1605** *Shuttleworths' Acc.* (Chetham Soc.) 168 A waller, one day wallinge uppe the dower..iiij[d]. **1667** *Observ. Burning Lond.* 23 [They] were talking of walling the Gates to prevent the coming in of the Tartarians. **1707–21** MORTIMER *Husb.* (ed. 5) II. 192 Wall up the sides with Brick. **1848** H. GREVILLE *Leaves fr. Diary* 1 July (1883) 280 The door has been walled to prevent surprise. **1861** DICKENS *Gt. Expect.* viii, Some of the windows had been walled up. **1886** WILLIS & CLARK *Cambridge* II. 125 Bishop Alcock..walled up the arches and inserted in each of them a window.

5. To build (stone) into a wall. Also of stone, to make (a specified length) of walling.

1621 *Shuttleworths' Acc.* (Chetham Soc.) 251 P'd for soe many stones as walled nyne y'des, ij[s] iij[d]. **1791** SMEATON *Edystone L.* (1793) §209 When it [Bath Free Stone] is walled with this kind of mortar,..the joints are more permanent. **1848–9** *L'pool. Archit. Soc.* (1852) II. 190 It [the rubble] may be walled with or without mortar.

6. *absol.* or *intr.* To construct a wall or walls; to build walling.

1588 *Shuttleworths' Acc.* (Chetham Soc.) 44 Towe mene for wallynge towe days, ij[s] ij[d]. **1598** *Ibid.* 112 Towe workemen, for waullynge and daubynge in the bru howse..xvj[d]. **1726** LEONI *Alberti's Archit.* I. 47 We may be said rather to wall than only to fill up.

7. *trans.* To chalk up (a score) on the wall. *slang.*

1848 *Sinks of Lond.* 129 *Wall it*, chalking a reckoning up at a public house.

†**wall**, *v.*[3] *Obs.* [OE. *weallian* = OHG., (M)LG., MDu. *wallen*, OHG. *wallōn* (MHG., mod.G. *wallen*):—WGer. **wallōjan*.

By some scholars referred to the root of WALL *v.*[1]; others regard it as a contraction of **waþlōjan* (cf. OHG. *wadalôn* to roam about).]

intr. To go on pilgrimage.

a **1000** *Canons Edgar, Of Penitents* §10 in Thorpe *Ags. Laws* II. 280 Deoplic dæd-bot bið þæt læwede man his wæpna alecȝe & wealliȝe bær-fot wide. *c* **1485** *Digby Myst.* III. 1848 With me xall ȝe wall to have more eloquens & goo vesyte þe stacyons by and by.

wall (wɔːl), *v.*[4] Now only *U.S.* Also 5–9 *Sc.* **waul(e**, **wawl(e**, 5–6 *Sc.* (? *erron.*) **waill.** [MSc. *wawle*:—**waȝle*, related to *waȝl-* in WALL-EYED *a.*] *trans.* To roll (the eyes). Also *absol.*, and *intr.* of the eyes. Hence **'walling** *ppl. a.* (Sc. *waulen*').

c **1480** HENRYSON *Cock & Fox* 469 The Cok..Vnwarlie winkand, wawland vp and doun. *c* **1500** in *Makculloch MS.* (S.T.S.) iv. 27 Cuttis for þi cot þai kest..out throw þi harnis þe pykis of thorne apliit, wawland [*MS. Arundel* wailland] þi ene. **1513** DOUGLAS *Æneis* VIII. vii. 154 In the breist of the goddes graif thai Gorgones heid,..Wyth ene wauland [L. *vertentem lumina*]. **1818** *Edin. Mag.* Oct. 328/2 The sicht forhow't her waulen' een, Sho lay in the deadthraws. **1821** SCOTT *Pirate* xxx, But presently recovering himself, he wawls on me with his gray een, like a wild-cat. **1817** HOGG *Gude Greye Katt* xxvii. in *Poetic Mirror* (1817) 196 Quhill ilken bosome byrnit with lufe, And waulit ilken ee. **1876** 'MARK TWAIN' *Tom Sawyer* v, The ladies would lift up their hands,..and 'wall' their eyes, and shake their heads. **1883** *Trans. Amer. Philol. Soc.* 55 *Wall the eyes*, that is, 'to roll the eyes so as to show the white.' I can remember this as a very common way among the little negroes in South Carolina of showing displeasure.

wall (wɔːl), *v.*[5] *Naut.* [f. WALL *sb.*[4]] *trans.* To make a wall-knot on (a rope).

1883 *Man. Seamanship for Boys* 112 The end [of the rose-lashing] is finished off by crowning and walling the end close to the crossing turns.

wall: see WALE *sb.*[1] and *sb.*[2], WAW, WELL.

walla, variant form of WALLAH.

wallaba ('wɒləbə). [? a. native name.] A large South American timber-tree (*Eperua falcata*). Also *attrib.*, as ***wallaba oil, tree***.

1825 WATERTON *Wand. S. Amer.* I. (1903) 17 Here the.. wallaba, purple-heart,..and mora, are met with in vast abundance. **1845** LINDLEY *Veg. Kingd.* (1846) 550 Eperua falcata is the Wallaba-tree of Guiana. **1862** *List Contrib. fr. B. Guiana to Lond. Exhib.* in Veness *El Dorado* (1866) App. 122 Wallaba Oil. *Ibid.* 137 Wallaba... Used for house-frames, shingles, staves, palings, and posts. Yields an oil and gum resin having medicinal properties. **1871** KINGSLEY *At Last* vii, I passed the great Australian Blue-Gum which overhangs the road, and the Wallaba-tree.

wallaby ('wɒləbɪ). Also **-bi(e**, **-bee**, **walloby**, **whallabee**. Pl. **wallabies**, †**-bys**. [Native Australian: spelt *wal-li-bah* by D. Collins *Acc. Eng. Colony N.S. Wales* 614, 1798. Morris suggests derivation from *walla* to leap.]

1. a. A kangaroo belonging to any of the small species of the genus *Macropus*, formerly grouped as the sub-genus *Halmaturus*, or of the genera *Onychogale* ('Nail-tailed Wallaby'), *Petrogale* ('Rock Wallaby'), *Lagorchestes* ('Hare Wallaby'), *Lagostrophus* ('Banded Wallaby'), *Wallabia* or *Thylogale*. All the species are confined to Australia and the neighbouring islands.

The sing. form is used in sporting language as collective plural.

1826 J. ATKINSON *Agric. & Grazing N.S.W.* ii. 24 The wallabee and padgy mellon..inhabit brushes, and afford good sport in the chase. **1828** P. CUNNINGHAM *N.S. Wales* (ed. 3) I. 289 The wallabee and paddymalla grow to about sixty pounds each. **1830** R. DAWSON *Pres. State Australia* iii. (1831) 111 A species of small kangaroo..which the natives call the 'Walloby'. **1832** BISCHOFF *Van Diemen's Land* II. 28 The wallabee is not very common. **1843** J. E. GRAY *List Specim. Mammalia Brit. Mus.* 89 The Whallabee. *Halmaturus Ualabatus* [etc.]. **1845** J. O. BALFOUR *Sk. N.S. Wales* 25 The wallaby, or rock kangaroo, is of a dark-grey colour [etc.]. *Ibid.*, The wallabys are to be seen only on the hottest days. **1846** J. L. STOKES *Discov. in Australia* I. ix. 267 The Wallaby are numerous on this part of the island [Tasmania]. **1860** G. BENNETT *Gather. Naturalist* xiv. 286 A species of Wallaby Kangaroo was found about the rocky ranges at the Nepean. **1867** W. RICHARDSON *Tasmanian Poems* 18 Go to the country a week to shoot wallaby. **1884** 'R. BOLDREWOOD' *Melbourne Mem.* iii. 24 Violet was so fast that she could catch the brush kangaroo (the wallaby) within sight. **1893** MRS. C. PRAED *Outlaw & Lawmaker* II. 35 The scared rock wallabies darted out of their holes.

b. *pl.* (With capital initial.) The name of the Australian international rugby football team.

1908 *Daily Chron.* 28 Sept. 4/6 The 'Wallabies', as the Australian football players..have christened themselves. **1945** BAKER *Austral. Lang.* ix. 178 Just as New Zealand football representatives acquired the names *All Blacks*, *Fernleaves*, and *Kiwis*, so did Australian representatives become known as *Kangaroos*, *Wallabies* and *Waratahs*. **1975** *Country Life* 4 Dec. 1528/1 The Wallabies are about to play the first international of their tour against Scotland.

2. ***on the wallaby track***, hence shortened ***on the wallaby***: on tramp; wandering about on foot, whether in search of work or aimlessly as a vagrant.

1865 E. J. OVERBURY *Wallaby Track* in Stewart & Keesing *Old Bush Songs* (1957) 233 There are others who stick during sheaving, Then shoulder their swags on their back; For the rest of the year they'll be steering On their well-beloved Wallaby Track. **1869** MARCUS CLARKE *Peripatetic Philosopher* 41 (Morris) An old bush ditty, which I have heard sung when I was on the 'Wallaby'. **1890** 'R. BOLDREWOOD' *Col. Reformer* ix, What is the meaning of 'out on the wallaby'?..It's bush slang, sir, for men just as you or I might be now, looking for work or something to eat. *Ibid.* xxvii, He wanted a summer on the wallaby track to open his mind. **1896** KIPLING *Seven Seas, Lost Legion* ii, And some of us hunt on the Oil Coast, And some on—the Wallaby track.

3. *attrib.*, as in ***wallaby skin, tail***; **wallaby (-proof) fence**, a fence intended to keep out wallabies; **wallaby-grass**, an Australian grass, *Danthonia penicillata*.

1852 MUNDY *Antipodes* ii. 43, I found myself.. swallowing with relish, a plate of wallabi-tail soup. **1881** *Gentl. Mag.* Jan. 56 A portion of this station was fenced with wallaby-proof fence—a high, close paling, reminding one of an English park. **1890** *Melbourne Argus* 13 June 6/2 A wallaby-skin rug. **1897** *Outing* XXX. 138/2 Down the wallaby fence..the emus turned at a hurricane gait.

Wallace ('wɒləs). The name of Alfred Russel *Wallace* (1823–1913), British naturalist, used *attrib.* or in the possessive to designate concepts originated by him or related to his work, as ***Wallace effect***, the evolution of reproductive isolation between sympatric species; ***Wallace('s) line***, a hypothetical boundary proposed by Wallace in 1858 as separating the Oriental and the Australasian biogeographical regions.

1966 V. GRANT in *Amer. Naturalist* C. 99 It seems fitting and desirable to designate the process of selection for reproductive isolation as the Wallace effect. **1981** *Amer. Jrnl. Bot.* LXVIII. 1247/2 The sympatric origin of isolating mechanisms, the Wallace effect, postulates that those individuals in sympatric populations of the incipient species when crossed with members of the other species waste gametes in so doing, due to sterility or inviability of their progeny. **1868** T. H. HUXLEY in *Proc. Zool. Soc.* 313 Passing south of India and Indo-Malaisia [*sic*], but north of the Nicobar islands, the boundary in question would coincide with what may be called 'Wallace's line', between the Indian and the Papuan divisions of the Malay archipelago. **1911** *Rep. Brit. Assoc. Adv. Sci.* 435 For fresh-water fishes Wallace's Line is..of fundamental importance. **1957** P. J. DARLINGTON *Zoogeography* vii. 469 A small fraction of the Oriental mammal fauna extends for a considerable distance across Wallace's Line. **1958** A. J. TOYNBEE *East to West* xv. 44 Nor am I talking here of 'the Wallace line' between the gum trees and marsupial mammals of Australasia and the standard flora and fauna of the rest of the world. **1982** *New Scientist* 3 June 653/1 Examination of the fauna..on Bali and the adjacent islands led him to define the 'Wallace Line'—the division between the Oriental fauna to the west and the Australasian forms to the east and north.

wallace, variant of WALLIS.

Wallach, Wallachian: see WALACH, -IAN.

walladay, obs. form of WELLADAY.

wallah ('wɒlə). *Anglo-Indian.* Also **wal(l)a**, **wollah.** [a. Hindī *-wālā*, a suffix, forming adjs. with the sense 'pertaining to or connected with' what is denoted by the sb.; hence forming sbs., as in *nāo-wālā* boatman, *Dillī-wālā* inhabitant of Delhi. The suffix in this function may be compared to -ER[1]; Europeans have commonly apprehended it as a sb. equivalent to 'man', 'fellow'.]

a. In certain Hindī or Hindustānī words adopted in Anglo-Indian use or cited in popular Anglo-Indian spelling, as ***Agra wallah***, native of Agra, ***banghy-wallah***, a porter who carries loads with a *banghy* or shoulder-yoke, ***howdah-wallah***, an elephant accustomed to carry a howdah, ***jungle-wallah***, man of the jungle. See also LOOTIE-WALLAH, PUNKAH-*wallah*, TOPI-WALLAH.

Mrs. Sherwood's *purdah-walla* (see PURDAH 3), applied to a woman, is a misuse.

1776 *Trial Nundocomar* 25/1 They were both Agra Walla's..by Agra, I mean the place he came from. **1810** T. WILLIAMSON *E. India Vade-M.* I. 325 The bangy-wollah, that is, the bearer who carries the bangy. **1826** GALT *Last of*

Lairds xvi. 146 The murderous old decoit and his Junglewallah of a servant. **1863** TREVELYAN *Compet. Wallah* v. (1864) 113 My suite comprised sixteen bearers,..and four banghy wallahs. *Ibid.* vi. 176 Strange stories these old howdah-wallahs could tell us, if they had the gift of speech!

b. Used as sb. with Eng. word prefixed attrib., in imitation of native derivatives with the suffix, as in ***box-wallah*** (BOX *sb.*^{2} 24), ***competition wallah*** (COMPETITION 3). Now extended beyond Anglo-Indian contexts.

1785 in Seton-Karr *Sel. Calcutta Gaz.* (1864) I. 93 A band of good Patriot-wallahs. **1834** [A. PRINSEP] *Baboo* II. iii. 55 (Stanf.) These chits of 90, 50, and 200 rupees to box-walas from Mrs. Title. **1853** W. D. ARNOLD *Oakfield* I. 66 'Were you ever in the Lakes?' 'No, I'm a Suffolk walla.' **1894** MRS. DYAN *Man's Keeping* (1899) 195 'The Inseparables'..came in to superintend his toilet, accompanied by a ready-made clothes wallah and a barber. **1917** *Blackw. Mag.* Sept. 299/1 Now, those fellows..those big-ship wallahs—they're only just beginning to take Us seriously. **1940** E. POUND *Cantos* lx. 90 The European church wallahs wonder if this can be reconciled. **1955** *Times* 15 June 3/5 Thousands of the lorries were being worked for 12, 14, 16, and 18 hours a night, with tragic results. The term used on the roads to describe these drivers was 'night-and-day wallahs'. **1977** J. I. M. STEWART *Madonna of Astrolabe* xvii. 248 It's marvellous what these ambulance wallas can do at a pinch. **1982** B. TRAPIDO *Brother of more Famous Jack* xxxvi. 124, I thought briefly of Roger who, being a music wallah, had always made a thing of St. Cecilia's Day.

c. Short for *competition-wallah.*

1863 TREVELYAN *Compet. Wallah* i. (1864) 9 Stories against the Competition Wallahs,..are told... For instance: *Story showing the Pride of Wallahs.*—A Wallah being invited to dinner by a Member of Council, went out before the whole company. **1872** 'ALIPH CHEEM' (Yeldham) *Lays of Ind* (1876) 142 Each unemployed wallah so surely applies To be kindly allowed in that Station to stay, Doing his nothing, and drawing his pay. **1911** SIR W. F. BUTLER *Autob.* iii. 45 M. sleeps. Enter the wallahs and servants.

d. One carrying out a routine administrative job; a civil servant, a bureaucrat. *colloq.*

1965 A. NICOL *Truly Married Woman* 32 There's no end to what you wallahs in the administration would do to show your damned official broadmindedness. **1974** *Courier-Mail* (Brisbane) 7 June 7/3 Some wallahs in Canberra are sitting in air-conditioned offices telling us what has been flooded and what hasn't.

wallah-wallah, walla-walla ('wɒlə 'wɒlə). [Origin unknown.] In Hong Kong, a small boat used as a ferry for casual traffic.

1957 R. MASON *World of Suzie Wong* I. iii. 33 Ships of every shape and size..tramps, junks, sampans, walla-wallas. **1967** E. HUNT *Danger Game* viii. 152 They rode in a rickshaw, a sampan and a walla walla boat. **1969** J. BENNETT *Dragon* i. 5 Back and forth, ply ferry-boats..and hydrofoils ..off to Macao; walla-wallas; scavenger-boats. **1970** D. DODGE *Hatchetman* 8 Sampans, junks, and *wallah-wallahs* caught in the open water were doomed when Tai Fung blew. **1976** W. MARSHALL *Hatchet Man* i. 2 A wallah-wallah boat transporting a sailor late back from leave worked its way to alongside..a moored destroyer.

†**'walland,** *a. dial. Obs.* [Of obscure origin.

The E. Anglian glossary is prob. correct in reading *walland* as one word, not *wall and* as printed in Bloomfield's poem. Cf. the Yorkshire *wallband whip*, 'a whip of plaited leather thongs' (*Eng. Dial. Dict.*).]

(See quot. 1895.)

1802 BLOOMFIELD *Rur. Tales, Richard & Kate* 29 She straight slipp'd off the Wall and Band. **1895** *E. Angl. Gloss.* (citing Rev. E. S. Taylor), *Walland band*, the leather used in spinning.

wallaroo ('wɒləruː). Also 9 wallooroo, wolloroo (see Morris *Austral Engl.*), walluru. [Native Australian *wolarū*: cf. WALLABY.] A large species of kangaroo, *Macropus robustus*; in Queensland and New South Wales applied chiefly to the black variety. Also ***wallaroo kangaroo.***

1826 J. ATKINSON *Agric. & Grazing N.S.W.* ii. 24 There is also found far in the interior another variety [of kangaroo], called wallaroos; they are much larger than any of the others. **1827** P. CUNNINGHAM *Two Years N.S.W.* I. xvii. 309 The wallaroo, of a blackish colour, with coarse shaggy fur, inhabiting the hills. **1845** J. O. BALFOUR *Sk. N.S. Wales* 25 The wallaroo kangaroo is of a darkish red colour, and weighs about 60 lbs. **1847** LEICHHARDT *Jrnl.* xiii. 458 He had been guided by a beaten track of Wallurus. **1890** 'R. BOLDREWOOD' *Miner's Right* v, The southern forest where.. the forester kangaroo and the wallaroo alone run.

wallat, obs. variant of WALLET.

wallaway, obs. form of WELLAWAY.

wallbanger ('wɔːlbæŋə(r)). *U.S.* Also W-. [App. f. WALL *sb.*^{1} + BANGER^1.] In full ***Harvey Wallbanger.*** A cocktail made from vodka or gin and orange juice.

1970 *Gourmet* Nov. 9 (Advt.), Harvey Wallbanger. Fill tall glass with ice cubes. Fill ¾ full with orange juice. Add 1 oz. Vodka. **1972** *New Yorker* 30 Sept. 41/2 A wallbanger is a vodka or gin or whatever you please with orange juice. **1981** T. HEALD *Murder at Moose Jaw* xi. 130 The Mounties ..ordered a brace of Harvey Wallbangers. *Ibid.* 131 Smith took a draught of Wallbanger.

[**wall-can:** perh. a misprint for ****walk-can***: cf. ***walk-pin***, WALK *v.*^{2} 3.

1688 HOLME *Armoury* III. 386/1 An Hatters Wall-Can,.. a Can by which the Felt-maker bears his Liquor from the Furnace to the Bench.]

walle: see WALE *sb.*^{1}, *a.*, *v.*^{1}, WELL.

walle, obs. Sc. variant of VALLEY.

c **1420** WYNTOUN *Cron.* I. 73 In þe feild of Damask faire.. Or in a walle of Ebron.

†**walled,** *a. Obs.* [f. WALL *sb.*^{3} + -ED^2. Cf. WALL *v.*^{4}] Of a horse's eye: Affected with 'wall-eye'.

1577-8 in W. H. Turner *Select. Rec. Oxford* (1880) 396 One grey trotting curtoll mare, crapped on the further yeare, and the neare ie walled. **1672** *Lond. Gaz.* No. 713/4 A dapple gray Gelding, near 15 hands high, both eies walled. **1705** *Ibid.* No. 4182/4 A brown bay Mare,..one walled Eye, the other about half walled.

walled (wɔːld), *ppl. a.* [f. WALL *v.*^{2} + -ED^1.]

1. a. Furnished with or as with a wall, enclosed with a wall. Of a town, etc.: Surrounded or protected with fortifications. Of a well, cistern, pond, the sides of a cavity, etc.: Lined or faced with masonry.

c **1000** *Ags. Ps.* (Spelm.) xxx. 27 [22] On ceastre ȝewealledre [Vulg. *in civitate munita*]. **13..** *K. Alis.* 6068 They haden wallid cite townes, In dalis, and eke in downes. **1450-1530** *Myrr. our Ladye* II. 72 Cytyes and Castelles and walled townes. **1591** SHAKS. *1 Hen. VI*, III. iv. 7 Twelue Cities, and seuen walled Townes of strength. **1605** —— *Lear* v. iii. 18 And wee'l weare out In a wall'd prison, packs and sects of great ones. **1671** MILTON *P.R.* II. 22 Each Town or City wall'd On this side the broad lake Genezaret. **1756-7** tr. *Keysler's Trav.* (1760) I. 191 On one side of this cathedral is a walled terrass. **1789** *Ir. Act 29 Geo. III*, c. 33 §25 Walled deer-parks, and planted avenues excepted. **1819** W. S. ROSE *Lett. N. Italy* II. 85 *note*, Oblong pieces of walled ground, planted with fruit-trees. **1839** URE *Dict. Arts*, etc. 820 [These] have led to the contrivance of surrounding the area on which the roasting takes place with three little walls or with four... This is what is called a walled area. **1869** TOZER *Highl. Turkey* I. 376 A walled Bulgarian village. **1880** C. R. MARKHAM *Peruv. Bark* 130 A succession of..terraced gardens... Their walled sides are thickly clothed with Calceolarias, Celsias [etc.]. **1895** *Outing* XXVII. 237/2 Neptune's Grotto is an enchanting, walled fish-pond.

fig. **1907** RALEIGH *Shakespeare* 201 Bereavement or crime breaking in upon the walled serenity of daily life.

b. with qualifying word prefixed.

c **1400** MAUNDEV. (Roxb.) vi. 24 þe whilk es a strang citee and a wele walled. **1871** W. MORRIS in Mackail *Life* (1899) I. 267 A great double-walled dyke. **1901** C. HOLLAND *Mousmé* 18 Our little fragile-walled house on the hillside at Nagasaki.

2. With advs. **a.** ***walled-up***, closed or blocked up with masonry. ***walled-in***, enclosed by walls.

1777 P. THICKNESSE *Year's Journey* II. xlix. 132 *Bonne* is a good town, well walled-in, pleasantly situated. **1826** COBBETT *Rur. Rides* (1885) II. 118 A..large walled-in garden. **1886** WILLIS & CLARK *Cambridge* I. 219 The third chamber has another old walled-up window. **1903** F. W. H. MYERS *Human Personality* 103 Like wine found in a walled up cellar. **1906** C. BIGG *Wayside Sk. Eccl. Hist.* i. 12 In front of the church was a walled-in court.

b. ***walled-in, -up***, entombed in a wall.

1837 CARLYLE *Fr. Rev.* I. v. ix, Crowds..gaze on the skeletons found walled-up. **1903** *Daily Chron.* 11 Feb. 3/6 The remains of a walled-in nun were discovered.

3. *Anat.* and *Zool.* Furnished with a 'wall' or investing structure: chiefly in parasynthetic formations. Also ***walled-off***, separated by a 'wall'.

1875 HUXLEY & MARTIN *Elem. Biol.* (1877) 201 The atrium: thin-walled, rounded, lies on the dorsal aspect of the truncus and ventricle. **1890** *Retrospect Med.* CII. 362 It was a smooth walled cavity,..about the size of a small marble. **1906** *Brit. Med. Jrnl.* 13 Jan. 70 A small walled-off pocket of pus.

4. Of the nature of a wall, made of stone-work.

1805 R. W. DICKSON *Pract. Agric.* I. 115 Where stones can be easily procured,..walled fences may be preferable.

waller^1 ('wɔːlə(r)). [f. WALL *v.*^{2} + -ER^1.] One who builds walls (see quot. 1908).

c **1440** *Promp. Parv.* 514/1 Wallare, *murator, machio.* Wallare, þat werkythe wythe stone and morter, *cementarius.* **1513** DOUGLAS *Æneis* I. i. 12 Fra quhame..Come..the valleris of greit Rome. *c* **1565** in *14th Rep. Hist. MSS. Comm.* App. III. 30 Four masones and viij wallaris: viij quariouris. **1612** *N. Riding Rec.* (1884) I. 253 Oswald Collyson waller or rough mason. **1683** *Churchw. Acc. Pittington*, etc. (Surtees) 341 To the wallers for work and plastering, 1 l. 2 s. **1890** *Lincoln Gaz.* 30 Aug. 4/1 Choppers, Wallers, and Masons for Ancaster Stone Wanted. **1908** *Remin. Stonemason* 89 He himself was what is called a 'waller'—that is, he did not dress stones, but set them on the walls when dressed, or else built walls of rough, unhewn stone.

waller^2 ('wɔːlə(r)). [f. WALL *v.*^{1} + -ER^1.] In the Cheshire salt-works, a brine-boiler, a worker who attends to the salt-pans. Also ***lead-waller*** (cf. *lead-walling*, LEAD *sb.*^{1} 12).

1600 CAMDEN *Brit.* (ed. 5) 543 Et muliercule (Wallers vocant) rastellis ligneis é fundo salem educunt. **1886** *Cheshire Gloss.*, *Lead-wallers*, commonly abbreviated to *Wallers. Waller*, a salt-maker or boiler. At present the men call *boilers* those who make *stoved* and *butter-salt*, and the others *wallers.* **1892** *Labour Commission* Gloss., *Waller*, a local term, applied to salt boilers, i.e., those who look after the boiling of the salt. It is applied to the men who look after the making of any white salt, whether the pan is required to boil or not.

waller^3 ('wɔːlə(r)). [f. WALL *sb.*^{1} + -ER^1.]

1. A wall-tree.

1688 HOLME *Armoury* II. 87/1 Wall-Trees, called Wallers, are such as are planted at Wall sides, and are pinned up to the Wall.

†**2.** A 'keeper of the walls'. Hence **wallership.** *Obs.*

1578 in *Househ. Ord.* (1790) 264 Keeper of the Walles, alias wallership; fee 2. 5. 4.

3. (See quots.)

1904 *Daily Chron.* 15 Apr. 8/2 'Wallers'..are men who find casual employment as law-writers, and have been facetiously christened 'wallers', because they are generally to be found lounging against a wall in Cursitor-street waiting on an engagement. **1908** *Ibid.* 3 July 6/7 'Waller,' as applied to a man who does law writing... They were called 'wallers', as a term of contempt, by the regular writers.

Wallerian (wɒ'lɪərɪən), *a. Phys.* [f. the name of A. V. *Waller* (1816-70) + -IAN.] Of or pertaining to Waller, or to the kind of degeneration of tissue discovered by him.

1877 M. FOSTER *Physiol.* III. i. (1878) 392 This method of diagnosis is often spoken of as the Wallerian method, after A. Waller. **1897** *Allbutt's Syst. Med.* II. 863 The part of the nerve-fibre between the rupture and the muscle now undergoes Wallerian degeneration. **1899** *Ibid.* VI. 492 The more active or Wallerian degeneration ensues. *Ibid.* 495 The operation of the Wallerian law.

wallet ('wɒlɪt). Also 4-6 walet, 5 wallett(e, 6 walett, wallyt, 6, 7, 9 *dial.* wallat. [Of obscure origin; the stress *wa'let* (beside *'walet*) in Chaucer is unfavourable to the current theory that the word is a metathesis of *watel* WATTLE *sb.*

Possibly a. OF. or AF. **walet*, which might be derived from Teut. **wall-* to go on pilgrimage (WALL *v.*^{3}) or **wall-* to roll up (see under WALL *v.*^{1})]

1. a. A bag for holding provisions, clothing, books, etc., esp. on a journey either on foot or on horseback; a pilgrim's scrip, a knapsack, a pedlar's pack, or the like.

c **1386** CHAUCER *Prol.* 681 But hood, for Iolitee, wered he noon, For it was trussed vp in his walet [*rhyme* Iet]. *Ibid.* 686 His walet [lay] biforn hym in his lappe, Bret ful of pardon comen from Rome al hoot. **1387-8** T. USK *Test. Love* I. i. (Skeat) 106 Yet have I ensample to gadere the smale crommes, and fullen my walet of tho that fallen from the borde among the smale houndes. *c* **1440** *Promp. Parv.* 514/1 Walette, seek, or poke, *sistarcia.* **1506-7** *Acc. Ld. High Treas. Scot.* III. 372 Item, for ane wallat to John of Bute xij d. **1514** A. BARCLAY *Eglogue* iv. 9 Within his wallet were meates good and fine. **1523-34** FITZHERB. *Husb.* §141 Take hede..what maner of people resorte and comme to thy house..and specially if they brynge with them..bottelles, bagges, wallettes, or busshell-pokes. *a* **1529** SKELTON *E. Rummyng* 461 Another brought two goslynges..She brought them in a wallet. **1535** COVERDALE *Judith* xiii. 10 She..delyuered the head of Holofernes vnto hir mayden, and bad hir put it in hir walett [Gr. εἰς τὴν πήραν τῶν βρωμάτων αὐτῆς, Vulg. *in peram suam*]. **1577** B. GOOGE *Heresbach's Husb.* I. 11 b, Husbandry necessaries..the smaller sort be these..Sacks, Wallets, Bottels, [etc.]. **1609** DEKKER *Guls Horne-bk.* i. 7 Neither..the Switzers blistred Cod-peece, nor the Danish sleeue, sagging downe like a Welsh wallet. **1617** *Churchw. Acc. Pittington* etc. (Surtees) 292 For makinge of a wallet to put the challenc and a bottle in, 1 d. **1622** R. HAWKINS *Voy. S. Seas* xxvii. 62 Their Childe they carry in a Wallet about their necke, ordinarily vnder one arme, because it may sucke when it will. *c* **1670** in *10th Rep. Hist. MSS. Comm.* App. I. 39 A wallet to cari books. **1712** *Spectator* No. 289 ¶9 Having looked about him for some time, he [a Dervise] enter'd into a long Gallery, where he laid down his Wallet, and spread his Carpet, in order to repose himself upon it. *a* **1721** PRIOR *Cupid turned Plowman* 2 A rustic wallet o'er his shoulders ty'd. **1760-2** GOLDSM. *Cit. W.* lxii, With her scanty wardrobe packed up in a wallet, she set out on her journey on foot. **1791** A. WILSON *Pack* Poet. Wks. 1876 II. 30 My pond'rous Pack apo' the ground I carelessly had flung; A wallet green, wi straps fast bound. **1840** DICKENS *Old C. Shop* xii, The old man had forgotten a kind of wallet which contained the light burden he had to carry. **1859** THACKERAY *Virgin.* lxii, I have heard he came up to London himself as a young man with only his tragedy in his wallet. **1904** BRIDGES *Demeter* 592 Approach him with a gift: this little wallet. (Giving a little bag of seeds.) **1914** *Miss. Rec. U.F. Ch.* Jan. 3/2 The Highlands, where there is no more welcome visitor than the colporteur with his wallet of healthy and inspiring literature.

Proverb, ***to brew in a bottle and bake in a wallet***: ? to attempt enterprises beyond one's means.

c **1540** BOORDE *Bk. for to Lerne* B iv, These men the whiche doo brewe in a botell and bake in a walet.

b. *spec.* A bag having the opening in the middle and a receptacle at each end.

Some of the instances above may belong to this specific sense. The wallet 'with two pouches in it' was prob. originally slung across the horse, or over the shoulder of the pedestrian.

1528, 1638 [see 1 c]. **1674** *Jackson's Recant.* A 4 b, Being thus early up, I timely met with a long Purse lying neglected in the Street, whose entrance was on the middle like a Wallat. **1706** PHILLIPS (ed. Kersey), *Wallet*, a kind of Bag with two Pouches to it. **1880** JEFFERIES *Gt. Estate* 141 The wallet is almost unknown even in farmsteads now: it is a kind of long bag closed at each end, but with a slit in the centre for the insertion of things. **1886** *Cheshire Gloss.*, *Wallet* or *Wally*,..As a hatting term it is a workbag with the entrance in the centre and made up at each end.

c. *fig.*

The fable here alluded to (Phædrus IV. x) says that Jupiter gave to every man two bags, one of which, containing his own faults, hangs at his back, and the other, containing those of his fellows, hangs at his breast.

1528 MORE *Dyaloge* III. Wks. 233/1 If we wold once tourne oure wallette..and the bagge with other folkes faultes cast at oure backe, and caste the bagge that bereth our own faultes..before vs at our brest. **1570** B. GOOGE *Popish Kingd.* IV. 60 But sure the wallet them beguiles, that hanges behinde their backe, And better others faultes they see, than what themselues doe lacke. **1589** COOPER *Admonit.* (Arb.) 18 They looke not into their owne doings: they cast that end of the wallet behinde them, wherein their owne faultes are wrapped. **1638** SANDERSON *Serm.* (1681) II. 118 Neither of both.. were willing enough to look into the other end of the wallet, and to examine throughly their own spirits.

d. A beggar's bag. †Phrases, *to bear the wallet*, to be a beggar. [= Fr. *porter la besace.*]

1546 *Supplic. Poore Commons* (E.E.T.S.) 19 Bringing them vp other to bear wallettes, other els, if thei be sturdy, to stuffe prisons. **1561** B. GOOGE tr. *Palingenius' Zodiac* v. Nvj, And se thy goodes they not decrease but may augmented be, Least in thy age the wallet come. **1608** DEKKER *Belman Lond.* Wks. (Grosart) III. 85 Thou art likewise to Giue way to any of vs that haue borne all the Offices of the Wallet before thee. **1612** T. TAYLOR *Comm. Titus* ii. 6 (1619) 405 Needs must he beare a wallet, and die a beggar. **1622** BACON *To King* Wks. 1874 XIX. 386 Pity me so far, as I that have borne a bag be not now in my age forced in effect to bear a wallet. **1654** GATAKER *Disc. Apol.* 30 Without House or Land, or so much as a Wallet to go a begging with. **1665** *Surv. Affaires of Netherlands* 33 They coyned Meddals with the Kings Picture, on the one hand a Wallet, and a Dish on the other, with this Inscription, Faithful to God and the King, even to bear the Wallet. **1790** COWPER *Odyss.* XVII. 237 So saying, his tatter'd wallet o'er his back He cast. **1832** HT. MARTINEAU *Hill & Valley* ix. 135 Without a crust in my wallet, as beggars usually have. **1836** [HOOTON] *Bilberry Thurland* I. vi. 124 Their appetites were now recovered, and the contributions of their collected wallets were found insufficient for the whole. **1879** MACLEAR *Celts* viii. 125 Itinerant beggars, who went about with wallets, were not regarded with favour.

fig. **1606** SHAKS. *Tr. & Cr.* III. iii. 145 Time hath (my lorde) a wallet at his backe Wherein he puts almes for obliuion.

e. A lawyer's bag. ? *Obs.*

1645 MILTON *Colast.* 17 A meer and arrant petti-fogger, who lately was so hardy, as to lay aside his buckram wallet, and make himself a fool in Print.

f. *Her.* (See quot.)

c **1828** BERRY *Encycl. Herald.* I. Gloss., *Wallet*, a scrip, or pilgrim's pouch.

†**2.** *transf.* Something (in an animal's body) protuberant and swagging. Cf. WATTLE *sb.*[2] *Obs.*

1610 SHAKS. *Temp.* III. iii. 46 Who would believe that there were Mountayneeres, Dew-lapt, like Buls, whose throats had hanging at 'em Wallets of flesh? **1698** *Phil. Trans.* XX. 137 Since the great Bulk or Wallet of these Intestines must incline and swag towards the Diaphragm.

3. A flat bag, usually of leather, closed by a flap fastened with a button or clasp, or secured by a band. Orig. *U.S.*

a. A pocket-book for holding paper money without folding, or documents.

1845 N. P. WILLIS *Dashes at Life* II. 245 Our several borrowings were thrust into a wallet which was sometimes in his pocket, and sometimes in mine, as each took the turn to be paymaster. **1854** WEBSTER, *Wallet*,.. also, a pocket-book or place for keeping money about one's person. **1884** *Advt.*, Thin Pocket Diary, for Wallet. **1888** CASSELL [as 'American']. **1913** *Daily News* 1 Nov. 7 The plaintiff, a diamond merchant, was carrying a wallet containing £370 in bank-notes, brilliants value £320, two necklaces.., a diamond pendant cluster, [etc.]. **1914** *Ibid.* 29 Jan. 2 He put his hand in his pocket and pulled out a leather dollar wallet and examined its contents.

b. A cyclist's tool-bag.

1887 VISCT. BURY & HILLIER *Cycling* 432 The wallet, or tool-bag, is generally supplied with the machine.

c. 'A small kit carried by anglers,' containing 'thread and needles, awl, waxed ends,.. a pair of small pliers, a file, etc.' (*Cent. Dict.*). ? *U.S.*

4. *attrib.* and *Comb.* as ***wallet-bearer, book***; ***wallet-carrying*** adj.; †***wallet-ways*** adv.; **wallet envelope**, an envelope with a broad flap like that of a wallet.

1611 COTGR., *Besacier*, the bag-bearer, or wallet-bearer of a begging, or beggarly companie. **1654** GAYTON *Pleas. Notes* III. i. 69 You may perchance thinke it improper to behold me upon thy asse hanging Wallet-wayes. **1823** GILLIES *Aristotle's Rhet.* III. ii. 372 In this way Iphicrates insulted Callias, by calling him the wallet-bearer of the goddess, instead of her torch-bearer. **1863** J. C. BRUCE (*title*), The Wallet-book of the Roman Wall. **1929** D. H. LAWRENCE *Pansies* 76 Men in bowler hats, hurrying And a mingling of wallet-carrying women.

walleteer (wɒlɪˈtɪə(r)). *rare*⁻¹. [f. WALLET + -EER[1].] One who carries a wallet.

1778 TOLLET in *Shaks. Wks.* V. 428 At his girdle hangs a wallet for the reception of provision, the only revenue of the mendicant orders of religious; who were named Walleteers or budget-bearers.

walletful (ˈwɒlɪtfʊl). Also **wallet-full**. [f. WALLET + -FUL.] As much as a wallet (sense 3 a) will hold.

1909 in WEBSTER. **1966** *Guardian* 9 Dec. 8/6 He has a walletful of notes. **1968** L. DURRELL *Tunc* ii. 48 'I began to carry around a wallet-full of children... Look.' He tipped out of a wallet a series of grotesque pictures of nude children.

wallett, obs. Sc. form of VALET.

walley, var. WALLY *sb.*[2] (and *a.*[3]).

wall eye, wall-eye (ˈwɔːlˈaɪ, ˈwɔːlaɪ). Also 6 **walowe yee, whal eie**, 7 **whall, waled eye**, 20 **walleye**. [Back-formation from WALL-EYED *a.* In sense 1 pronounced with level stress, the first element being apprehended as an adj.]

1. An eye the iris of which is whitish, streaked, particoloured, or different in hue from the other eye, or which has a divergent squint. (See WALL-EYED *a.* 1.) **a.** in human beings.

1526 *Hundred Merry Tales* (1866) 91, I haue a wall eye in my hed, for I neuer loke ouer my sholder this wyse but I lyghtly espye a knaue. **1599** B. JONSON *Cynthia's Rev.* v. ii, Two Wall-eyes, in a face forced. **1694** *Lond. Gaz.* No. 2965/4 He had.. one Eye bigger than the other, and divers in colour, being a Hazel or Wall Eye. **1815** SCOTT *Guy M.* xxxv, Whose gaunt visage and wall-eyes assumed a most hostile aspect. **1826** —— *Woodst.* xi, Desborough was a stout bull-necked man, of middle size, with.. bushy eyebrows, and wall-eyes. **1828** *Craven Gloss.*, *Wall-een*, white or grey eyes. **1850** R. G. CUMMING *Hunter's Life S. Afr.* (ed. 2) I. 239 A jolly-looking old warrior with a wall eye. **1893** SELOUS *Trav. S.E. Africa* 61 He was deeply pitted with smallpox, and had, too, a wall eye. **1899** BARING-GOULD *Bk. of West* I. vii. 110 She was an ill-favoured person, with a wall-eye.

b. in horses, etc.

1523 *Will of Burton* (Somerset Ho.) A blak mare with one walowe yee. **1577** B. GOOGE *Heresbach's Husb.* III. 115 A wall eye is very good, such as they say Alexanders Bucephalus had. **1607** MARKHAM *Cavel.* I. 16 They are for the most part pied, with white legges, and wall eyes. **1616** *Maldon* (Essex) *Borough Deeds* Bundle 147, no. 6 A hewen [= hue and] cry sent out from Colchester [for] two randed geldings one of them with a waled eye. **1667** *Lond. Gaz.* No. 207/4 Lost.. a Yorkshire Buck-hound, having black spots upon his back, red ears and a wall-eye. **1702** *Post Man* 6–8 Jan. 2/2 Stoln out of a Stable,.. a black Gelding,.. a white face, Wall Eyes, and 4 white Feet. **1787** 'G. GAMBADO' *Acad. Horsem.* (1809) 23 A bald face, wall eyes, and white legs (if your horse is not a grey one) is to be perferr'd. **1822–9** GOOD *Study Med.* IV. 202 In horses, this want of pigment constitutes what is called a wall-eye. **1849** LEVER *Con Cregan* xx, 'I know your mark.' 'My roan, with the wall-eye. You don't mind a wall-eye?'

¶**c.** App. misused for 'blind eye'.

1866 *Sat. Rev.* 25 Aug. 229/2 Honour.. never goes about apparently without one wall-eye, and it is a chance and an accident on which side of the road the wall-eye may be fixed.

2. The condition of being wall-eyed.

1585 HIGINS *Junius' Nomencl.* 428/1 *Glaucoma*,.. a disease in the eye,.. some think it to be a whal eie.

3. An animal that is wall-eyed. In N. Amer. a name for various fishes, esp. the wall-eyed pike, *Stizostedion vitreum*: see WALL-EYED 3.

[**13**..: see WALDENEIE.] **1876** *Fur, Fin & Feather* Sept. 163/1 All along the Minnesota Division are numerous clear lakes and ponds, teeming with.. 'wall-eyes' or pike-perch. **1888** GOODE *Amer. Fishes* 17 The Wall-eye does not often exceed ten pounds in weight. **1968** [see MUSKY *sb.*[2]]. **1982** *Nature* 16 Sept. 202/2 Walleye fish, *Stizostedion*, eat each other 'tail first', and chains of up to four fish engaged in simultaneous cannibalism have been seen.

wall-eyed (ˈwɔːlˌaɪd), *a.* Forms: α. 5 **wawil-, waugle-**, 6 **whaule-**, 7 **whale-**, 6– **wall-eyed**; β. 5 **wald-eȝed**. [The surviving form descends from ME. *wawil-eȝed*, a. ON. *vagl-eyg-r*, occurring only once, and explained in the context to mean 'having speckled eyes'. The second element, *-eygr*, is regularly f. *auga* EYE *sb.* The first element, *vagl*, is of obscure origin; it coincides in form with *vagl* beam of wood, roost, perch (Da., Norw. *vagl*, Sw. *vagel*) which is used in the Icel. New Testament of 1540 for the 'beam' in the eye spoken of in Matt. vii. 3–4; it is, however, prob. a distinct word, not recorded separately in ON., but surviving in mod. Icel. *vagl* film over the eye, Sw. *vagel* sty in the eye.

Beside *wawil-eȝed* ME. had a synonymous *wald-eȝed*. This is commonly believed to be a. ON. *vald-eygð-r*; but that word is only a conjectural reading for *valldœgðr*, occurring in a series of adjs. designating certain defects that a horse may have; the context does not show whether a physcial blemish or a fault of temper is referred to, and if *-œgðr* be correct it must app. mean '-scared'. A strong point in favour of the correction to *valdeygðr* is the coincidence with the ME. form; but the meaning of *vald-* remains obscure. Cf. mod. Slesvig dial. *valdøiet* having a running from the eyes (quoted by Molbech from Outzen's MS. collections), which Outzen would derive from *valde* dial. var. of Da. *valle* whey.

The rare ME. WOLDENEȜED seems to be synonymous with *wawil-eȝed, wald-eȝed*, and if so is prob. an alteration of the latter form due to the influence of ME. **walden*, OE. *ȝewealden* small (preserved, with different sense, in Sc. WALDIN *a.*). See also WALNYED *a.* Cf. WALDENEIE, prob. a similar variant of WALL-EYE.]

1. Having one or both eyes of an excessively light colour, so that the iris is hardly distinguishable from the white. In ME. and in modern dialects (see *Eng. Dial. Dict.*), also in other senses: Having eyes of differing colour; having eyes or an eye streaked or particoloured. Also, having a divergent squint, which exposes an excessive proportion of the white of the eye.

In many examples the sense cannot be determined.

a. of human beings.

[**13**.. see WOLDEN-EȜED.] *a* **1400–50** *Wars Alex.* 608 And he [Alexander] wald-eȝed was, as þe writt schewys, ȝit ..[Lines 606–7 say that one eye was black and the other yellow]. *Ibid.* 1706 A wawil-eȝed [*Dubl.* waugle-eghed] shrewe. **1552** HULOET, Whaule eyed, *glauciolus.* **1588** SHAKS. *Tit. A.* v. i. 44 Say wall-ey'd slaue, whether would'st thou conuay This growing Image of thy fiend-like face? **1601** HOLLAND *Pliny* XI. xxxvii. I. 334 Augustus.. had red eies like to some horses: and indeed wall eied he was, for the white thereof was much bigger than in other men. **1806–7** J. BERESFORD *Miseries Hum. Life* xx. § 25 Wall-eyed portraits in mildewed crayons. **1833** M. SCOTT *Tom Cringle* iii, Captain Deadeye was a staid, stiff-rumped, wall-eyed.. veteran. **1866** LIVINGSTONE *Last Jrnls.* (1873) I. i. 25 A wall-eyed ill-looking fellow.

b. of horses. (See quot. 1831.)

1590 *Durham Wills* (Surtees) II. 184 To.. my brother-in-law, one baie stagge, wall-eyed. **1607** MARKHAM *Cavel.* II. 6 The Horse that is whale-eyde, or white eyed, is for the most part shrewd, craftie, full of toyes, and dim sighted. **1702** *Lond. Gaz.* No. 3857/4 A small black Gelding,.. Wall or Silver-Ey'd. **1714** J. WALKER *Suffer. Clergy* II. 281/2 He had called those Wall ey'd Horses that would not come to the Rails to receive the Communion. **1726** LEONI *Alberti's Archit.* I. 96 The moon's beams.. are very apt to make him wall-eyed and to give him grievous coughs. **1766** GOLDSM. *Vicar W.* x, I objected that walking would be twenty times more genteel than such a paltry conveyance, as Blackberry was wall-eyed, and the colt wanted a tail. **1831** YOUATT *Horse* vi. 93 Horses perfectly white, or cream-coloured, have the iris white, and the pupil red. When horses of other colours.. have a white iris and a black pupil, they are said to be wall-eyed. Vulgar opinion has decided that a wall-eyed horse is never subject to blindness, but this we believe to be erroneous. **1836** HALIBURTON *Clockm.* Ser. I. xvii, He shewed the whites of his eyes like a wall-eyed horse. **1845** DISRAELI *Sybil* VI. vi, Mounted on a white mule, wall-eyed and of hideous form. **1871** M. COLLINS *Marq. & Merch.* III. iv. 107 He was a wall-eyed horse.

c. *transf.*

1852 DICKENS *Bleak Ho.* xxxix, A little, pale, wall-eyed, woe-begone, inn. **1865** —— *Mut. Fr.* III. xvi, The counting-house was a wall-eyed ground-floor by a dark gateway. **1876** GEO. ELIOT *Deronda* ix, Diplow Hall.. which had for a couple of years turned its white window-shutters in a painfully wall-eyed manner on its fine elms and beeches,.. was being prepared for a tenant.

¶**d.** Used for: Dim-sighted, purblind.

1873 *Punch* 3 May 182/1 Wall-eyed people who stick their noses to each picture as though they wished to smell it.

e. *slang.* (See quot.)

1847 HALLIWELL s.v., Any work irregularly or ill done, is called a wall-eyed job. It is applied also to any very irregular action.

†**2.** ? Having glaring eyes (indicative of rage or jealousy).

Quot. 1613 may be an echo of Spenser *F.Q.* I. iv. 24, '[His] whally eyes (the signe of gelosy).'

1595 SHAKS. *John* IV. iii. 49 The vildest stroke That euer wall-ey'd wrath, or staring rage Presented to the teares of soft remorse. **1613** ? MARSTON *Insat. C'tess* I. A 2 b, Hee.. mued mee vp like Cretan Dedalus, And with wall-ey'd Ielousie kept me from hope Of any waxen wings to flye to pleasure.

3. *U.S.* Of fishes: Having large prominent eyes. ***wall-eyed pike***: see quots.

1868 *Rep. U.S. Commissioner Agric.* (1869) 330 The wall-eyed pike, (*Lucio perca*). **1883** GOODE *Fish. Industr. U.S.* (Fish. Exhib. Publ.) 71 Many millions of eggs of the whitefish, lake-trout, and wall-eyed pike are obtained in the waters of Lake Erie. **1888** —— *Amer. Fishes* 13 The largest and most important form is *Stizostedion vitreum*, generally referred to by recent writers upon fishes as the Wall-eyed Pike.

†**wall-fair.** *Obs.*⁻¹. In 5 walfair. [f. WALL *sb.*[1] + FAIR *a.*] = WALLFLOWER.

c **1450** *Alphita* (Anecd. Oxon.) 191 Violaria habet florem aurosum, an[glice] walfair.

wallflower (ˈwɔːlflaʊə(r)). [f. WALL *sb.*[1] Cf. G. *mauerblume.*]

1. a. A plant of the genus *Cheiranthus* (N.O. *Cruciferæ*), esp. *C. Cheiri*, growing wild on old walls, on rocks, in quarries, etc., and cultivated in gardens for its fragrant flowers (normally yellow or orange, though other colours are produced by cultivation). Also called GILLIFLOWER.

1578 LYTE *Dodoens* II. iii. 150 In English Yellow Gillofers, Wall floures.. in French Violes iaunes,.. in high Douche Geel veiel. **1597** GERARDE *Herbal* II. cxiii. 370 The stalkes of the Wall flower are full of greene branches. **1615** W. LAWSON *New Orchard* (1623) 12 Dry wall of earth.. whereon at Mighill-tide it will be good to sow Wall-flowers. **1650** T. BAYLY *Herba Parietis* Ded. 1 The Wall-flower hath been called (as the most sacred Compellation) by the Herbalists, Dames-Violets, Damasen or Matron-Violets, or Queenes Gillyflowers. **1657** S. PURCHAS *Pol. Flying-Insects* I. xv. 93 Double.. Wall-flowers. **1707–21** MORTIMER *Husb.* (ed. 5) II. 245 Wall Flowers are of several sorts, as the common Ones, the great single Ones, the great double Ones, the single White, the double White, the double Red, and the pale Yellow. **1728–46** THOMSON *Spring* 532 The yellow wall-flower, stain'd with iron brown. **1779** SHERIDAN *Critic* II. ii, The vulgar wallflower, and smart gillyflower. **1814** SCOTT *Lord of Isles* III. i, The wall-flower waves not on the ruin'd hold. **1818** BYRON *Ch. Har.* IV. cvii, Cypress and ivy, weed and wall-flower grown Matted and mass'd together. **1838** DICKENS *Nickleby* xl, There is a double-wallflower at No. 6 in the court, is there? **1856** DELAMER *Fl. Gard.* (1861) 158 *Wall-flower*.. The single varieties, which are the most odoriferous, are raised from seed. There are yellow, brown, and purple Double Wallflowers, propagated by cuttings. **1858** GLENNY *Everyday Bk.* 266/1 Wallflowers and Sweetwilliams may be planted out in beds. **1880** 'OUIDA' *Moths* I. 83 There were lavender and a few homely stocks and wallflowers growing in the poor soil about the fences of the houses.

b. *German wallflower.*

1882 *Garden* 25 Feb. 135/1 Double German Wallflowers .. are now useful pot plants.

c. Applied to plants of other genera. ***native wallflower***, the Tasmanian plant *Pultenæa subumbrosa* (N.O. *Leguminosæ*); also, in Australia, one of the Poison-bushes, *Gastrolobium grandiflorum* (Morris *Austral Engl.*, 1898). ***western wallflower***, a name for certain American species of *Erysimum* (Treas. Bot., 1866; *Cent. Dict.*, 1891).

d. A perfume derived from the flowers of this plant.

1907 *Yesterday's Shopping* (1969) 521/1 Perfumes... Verbena. Wallflower. White Carnation. *c* **1938** *Fortnum & Mason Price List* 55/2 Wallflower..Wild Rose..Assorted Bath Ovals. **1972** [see MIGNONETTE 1 d].

2. *slang.* (See quots.) ? *Obs.*

1804 *Sporting Mag.* XXIII. 220 A coat suspended on a peg in Monmouth-street is called a wall flower. **1848** *Sinks of Lond.* 129 *Wall flowers*, old clothes exposed for sale.

3. *colloq.* A lady who keeps her seat at the side of a room during dancing, whether because she cannot find a partner or by her own choice.

1820 PRAED *County Ball* 148 The maiden wall-flowers of the room. **1840** *New Monthly Mag.* LIX. 340 He..dances quadrilles with every wall-flower in the room. **1881** H. JAMES *Portr. Lady* xliii, 'Are you not dancing?' 'As you see, I'm a wall-flower.' **1888** F. HUME *Mme. Midas* II. ix, She has not your capability at playing wallflower.

4. *attrib.* in designations of colour, as ***wallflower brown, red***; also separately as a colour-name. Also Comb. ***wallflower-leaved*** adj.

1786 ABERCROMBIE *Gard. Assist.* Arrangem. 19 Hardy Annuals... Stock gilliflower,..White wallflower leaved. **1883** *Daily News* 17 May 6/1 Lined with silk..in some decided colour, such as old gold, wallflower red, French grey, or pale blue. *Ibid.* 22 Sept. 3/3 A wide bias band of wallflower velvet. **1913** *Daily Graphic* 24 Mar. 13/1 The most notable colours in the crowd included the following:.. Wallflower and café au lait browns.

wallful ('wɔːlfʊl). [f. WALL *sb.*^{1} + -FUL.] As much as the surface of a wall will hold; the area of an entire side of a wall.

1959 *Times* 3 Jan. 2/6 This very personal little miscellany, with its notable Bacon and wallfuls of Keith Vaughan and Burra. **1973** *Art Internat.* Mar. 52/2 The traces in question consisted of a few wallfuls of photo collages and a couple of films. **1975** 'D. RUTHERFORD' *Mystery Tour* vii. 173 A wallful of luggage lockers.

†**wall-hot**, *a.* *Obs.* [f. WALL *v.*^{1} + HOT *a.*] Boiling hot. Also *fig.* fervent. Cf. WALM-HOT.

c **1000** *Sax. Leechd.* II. 256 Acele ðu wealhat isen ðonne hit furðum sie of fyre atoȝen on wine oþþe on ecede. *c* **1200** ORMIN 14196 Wiþþ wallhat herrtess lufe. *a* **1225** *Juliana* (Bodl. MS.) 31 Eleusius..bed biliue bringen forð brune wallinde bres, & healden hit se wal hat hehe up on hire heaued, þat [etc.].

wallicoat, variant of WYLIECOAT *Sc. Obs.*

wallidrag, var. WALLYDRAG *Sc.*

wallie, var. WALLY.

'**walling**, *vbl. sb.*^{1} Now *dial.* [f. WALL *v.*^{1} + -ING^1.] The action of boiling brine in salt-making. (See also quot. 1674.) Also *attrib.*, as ***walling-house, shed***; **walling-lead**, a salt-pan.

1556 *B.N.C.* (Oxon.) *Munim.* 20 No. 47 (MS.) Houses, cottages, saltehouses, wallingehouses, places where any saltehouse or wichehouse hath heretofore been [Middlewich]. **1611** *Inventory* in *Chesh. Local Gleanings* (E.D.D.), ii. Walling Leads. **1669** DR. W. JACKSON in *Phil. Trans.* IV. 1061 The bank..[is] accidentally raised by rubbish of long making Salt, or Walling, as they call it. **1674** RAY *Coll. Words, Making of Salt* 142 A Lead-walling is the Brine of twenty four hours boiling for one house... They have four sworn Officers chosen yearly, which they call Occupiers of Walling, whose duty it is to see equal dealing between Lord and Tenant, and all persons concerned. **1894** BARING-GOULD *Queen of Love* II. 15 The white cloud filled the walling (boiling) house. *Ibid.* 16 The coils of steam turned and rolled and clung in the walling shed.

'**walling**, *vbl. sb.*^{2} [f. WALL *v.*^{2} + -ING^1.]

1. a. The action of the verb; the making of walls, furnishing or fortifying with a wall.

1480 *Cov. Leet Bk.* 463 Yf part of eny olde wall or yate sodenly fall, hit of reason owe first to be made and to be preferred a-fore oþer wallying. **1531** *Maldon* (Essex) *Liber B.* fol. 108 b, ii$^{\circ}$ rodds wallynge marisci vocati pontmermershe. **1610** HOLLAND *Camden's Brit.* II. 194 He gaue fiue hundred pounds to the walling of that towne. **1726** LEONI *Alberti's Archit.* I. 66 The same method for walling of Towns will not serve in all places. **1825** J. NICHOLSON *Oper. Mech.* 547 In walling,..when the work is required to be firm, the best mortar must be used. **1909** *Daily Chron.* 20 Sept. 1/3 When a suitable building plot had been prepared the walling of a structure was a very simple process.

b. with advs. *in, out, up.*

1450 *Rolls of Parlt.* V. 199/1 The somme of xx li., which we have graunte yerely unto the wallyng oute of oure foreside Towne. **1732** SIR W. FOWNES in *Swift's Lett.* (1766) II. 169 The walling-in of the piece of ground..may go on as the fund will bear. **1913** M. BARRETT *Scott. Monasteries* IV. i. 203 They manage to convert it into an inhuman walling-up alive of the wretched monk.

2. *concr.* Wall-work; also, walls collectively; also, the materials of which a wall is made.

1382 WYCLIF *Ezek.* xxxvi. 4 These thingis saith the Lord God..to desert wallingus [Vulg. *parietinis*], and to forsaken citees. **1393** LANGL. *P. Pl.* C. VIII. 234 So shalt þow come to a court as cleer so þe sonne,..Al þe wallynge ys of wit. **1518** *Cov. Leet Bk.* 664 He & his assignes schall kepe the seid yate-house clene, & with ffloryng & wallyng. **1688** HOLME *Armoury* III. 343/1 The Plumb Rule sheweth him whether his Walling doth both range straight, and stand upright. **1791** SMEATON *Edystone L.* (1793) §212, I found the mortar joints of the brick walling very compleat. **1851** *Jrnl. R. Agric. Soc.* XII. II. 352 This plaster..having straw well chopped up amongst it..makes a hard and cheap walling for light buildings. **1870** F. R. WILSON *Ch. Lindisf.* 119 A length of walling, four feet thick, was discovered. **1886** J. BARROWMAN *Sc. Mining Terms* 70 *Walling*, the built sides of a shaft.

transf. **1880** GEO. ELIOT in Cross *Life* (1885) III. 416 Not to the exclusion of old things, which we must carry and stow, especially wallings of books.

3. *attrib.* and *Comb.*, as ***walling material, stone.*** **walling hammer**, a hammer used for dressing stones in a dry wall.

1796 W. H. MARSHALL *W. Eng.* II. 130 Beside being burnt into Lime, it is used as a walling material. **1840** *Civil Engin. & Arch. Jrnl.* III. 2/1 The remaining fronts are to be faced with neat hammer dressed walling stones. **1841** S. BAMFORD *Life of Radical* (ed. 2) I. 84 This person had..threatened to beat in their brains with a walling hammer which he had in his hand. **1846** *Jrnl. R. Agric. Soc.* VII. I. 40 The rest of this district consists of..some very thin-skinned, hungry gravel, and sand, on a dry, thirsty, walling-stone. **1881** W. WESTALL *Old Factory* I. x. 136 Them as has walling hammers comes next and next again them wi' stone-breakers' hammers and hand-hammers. **1964** H. HODGES *Artifacts* vii. 109 In dressing, the usual process was to hack away first the worst of the protruding lumps with a walling hammer. **1971** *Country Life* 9 Sept. 618/1 Prizes include..a walling hammer for the competitor who has travelled the longest distance in order to take part.

†'**walling**, *ppl. a.*^{1} *Obs.* [f. WALL *v.*^{1} + -ING^2.]

1. Boiling: said of liquids, molten metal, etc. In OE. often *fig.*, fervent. Also in phr. ***wallinde hot***, boiling hot, ***walling wood***, raging mad.

c **1000** ÆLFRIC *On N.T.* (Gr.) 16 Se het ȝenyman þone halȝan apostol and on weallendum ele he het hine baðian. **12..** *Moral Ode* (Egerton MS.) 218 His bæþ sceal beo wealliende pich his bed burnende glede. *a* **1225** *Ancr. R.* 246 þu hauest forschalded, he seið, þe drake heaued mid wallinde watere, þet is, mid hote teares. *a* **1225** *Juliana* (Royal MS.) 30 Elewsius..bed..wallinde breas..healden on hire heauet þat hit urne endelong hire leofliche bodi. *Ibid.* 70 Hit [the boiling pitch] colede anan..ant leop wallinde hat up aȝein þeo ilke þat hit hefden iȝarket. *c* **1275** *xi Pains of Hell* 75 in *O.E. Misc.* 149 Fvrþer þer is a water wallinde hot. **13..** *K. Alis.* 1622 (W.) With hot water and wallyng metal They defendid heore wal. **13..** *Gaw. & Gr. Knt.* 1762 Wiȝt wallande Ioye warmed his hert. **13..** *Minor Poems fr. Vernon MS.* xxxvii. 945 Aȝeyn o drauȝt þei drinke ouer-muche þei schul han þre or two Of hot led and walled [? *read* wallend] bras. *c* **1450** *Mirk's Festial* 147/21 þer was a tonne of bras, full of wallyng oyle. **16..** *Eger & Grine* 1057 in *Percy Fol. MS.* I. 387 Gray-Steele went walling woode.

2. Of the sea, waves: Boiling up, raging. Of water: Welling up, flowing abundantly.

Beowulf 546 (Gr.) Oþ þæt unc flod todraf wado weallende, wedera cealdost. **13..** *E.E. Allit. P.* A. 365 My herte was al with mysse remorde, As wallande water gos out of welle.

b. Abundant.

a **1400** *Destr. Troy* 13120 Of all his wallond wele walt he no gode.

'**walling**, *ppl. a.*^{2} [f. WALL *v.*^{2} + -ING^2.] That forms a wall.

1853 M. ARNOLD *Balder Dead* ii. 89 In the strait passage, ..Where the road issues between walling rocks.

walling, *ppl. a.*^{3}: see WALL *v.*^{4}

wallink, variant of WELLINK.

wallis ('wɒlɪs). Now *dial.* Also **wallace.** [Of obscure origin: cf. WARRIDGE.] The withers of a horse.

1686 *Lond. Gaz.* No. 2181/4 The 6th Instant a proper Gentleman..rode away with a black brown Gelding,..bare of flesh, hath had a hurt on the Wallis. **1787** W. H. MARSHALL *Norf.* (1795) II. 391 *Wallace*, the withers of a horse. *a* **1825** FORBY *Voc. E. Anglia*, *Wallis*, the withers of a horse.

wallise, Sc. form of VALISE.

Wallish-bill, variant of WELSH BILL *Obs.*

wall-knot ('wɔːlnɒt), **wale-knot** ('weɪlnɒt). Also 8 (? *erron.*) **walled knot.** [The first element is of obscure origin. The word is found in mod. Scandinavian langs.: Sw., Norw. *valknut*, Da. *valknude*, double knot, secure knot (not confined to nautical use); in Norw. also the gammadion or swastika. Cf. Ger. *waldknoten* (as if 'wood-knot', prob. a popular etymology), in hunting language, a double knot.] A secure knot made on the end of a rope by unlaying and intertwining the strands.

1627 CAPT. J. SMITH *Sea Gram.* v. 27 The Wall knot..is a round knot, so made with the strouds [*read* stronds] or layes of a rope, it cannot slip. **1644** MANWAYRING *Sea-mans Dict.* 70 *Nippers* are small roapes..with a little Truck at one end (or some have only a wale-knot). **1769** FALCONER *Dict. Marine* (1780), *Wale-knot*, or *Wall-knot*, a particular sort of large knot raised upon the end of a rope, by untwisting the strands. **1773** EMERSON *Princ. Mech.* (ed. 3) 166 A wale knot is made with the three strands of a rope, so that it cannot slip. **1788** CLARKSON *Impolicy of Slave Trade* 46 A rope.. with nine tails at one end of it, and a double walled knot of nearly eight inches in circumference at the other. **1867** SMYTH *Sailor's Word-bk.*, *Double Wall-knot*, with or without a crown, or a double crown, is made by intertwisting the unlaid ends of a rope in a peculiar manner. **1883** *Man. Seamanship* (1886) 121 A single-wall knot... A double-wall. .. A double-wall, double-crowned.

wall-less ('wɔːllɪs), *a.* [f. WALL *sb.*^{1} + -LESS.] Having no wall.

1849 LYTTON *K. Arthur* VII. lxii, And wall-less towns secure, Rise from the donjon sites of antique days. **1863** *Life in South* II. 156 We were roasted by the stove on one side, and frozen through our wall-less tenement on the other. **1912** MACALISTER *Hist. & Civiliz. Palestine* viii. 97 The walled cities are being deserted, and people are settling instead in wall-less villages.

walloby, var. WALLABY.

Walloon (wɒ'luːn), *sb.* and *a.* Also 6 **Vallon**, 8 **Waloon**, 6– **Wallon.** [a. F. *Wallon* (fem. *Wallonne*), *sb.* and *a.*:—med.L. *Wallōn-em*, f. Teut. **walah, walh*, foreigner (OE. *wealh*): see WELSH *a.* The name represents the appellation given by the Teut. Flemings and Franks to their Romanic-speaking neighbours.]

A. *sb.* **1.** A man or woman of the race, of Gaulish origin and speaking a French dialect, which forms the chief portion of the population of the south-eastern provinces of Belgium.

1567 GRESHAM in Burgon *Life* (1839) II. 208, I sawe never men so desperate, willing to fight: and speciallie the Vallons. **1577–87** HOLINSHED *Chron.* III. 1145/1 A rumor..that the Lantgraues capteine should be slaine by some Wallons. **1591** SHAKS. *1 Hen. VI*, I. i. 137 A base Wallon..Thrust Talbot with a Speare into the Back. **1665** MANLEY *Grotius' Low C. Wars* 41 The Regent, beside the German Souldiers, ..commanded another Regiment of Walloons to be forthwith raised; for by that name, the people in that part of the Netherlands, which borders upon France, are called, and are distinguished from the others, by the use of the French Tongue, and beside, are more valiant, and not so dull-witted as the rest. **1650** STAPYLTON *Strada's Low C. Wars* IX. 54 Some companies of Wallons were also ordered to bring scaling-ladders. **1777** WATSON *Philip II* (1839) 209 Fifty companies of Spaniards, and one hundred and fifty of Walloons, and other natives of the Netherlands. **1888** *Encycl. Brit.* XXIV. 332/2 The Wallons..are thus Romanized Gauls. **1916** *19th Century* Oct. 717 In the defence of their national territory Flemings and Walloons have alway been so closely united that it would be impossible to distinguish them.

2. The language or dialect of the Walloons.

1642 HOWELL *Instr. For. Trav.* x. (Arb.) 48 The French have three dialects, the Wallon (vulgarly called among themselves Romand), the Provensall,..and the speech of Languedoc. **1815** R. B. BERNARD *Tour France* etc. 292 The lower orders in this city speak a jargon called Walloon, which is completely unintelligible to the higher classes. **1914** E. GOSSE in *Edin. Rev.* Oct. 314 The less known..new school of authors, composing ardently in Flemish and even to some extent in Walloon.

Comb. **1918** *19th Century* Nov. 833 A few Walloon-speaking villages along the German frontier.

B. *adj.* Pertaining to the Walloons.

1530 PALSGR. 35 The kynde of speche nowe called Vallon or Romant. *Ibid.* 286/2 Wallon tonge, *Romant.* *a* **1600** *Hist. Fryer Bacon* in Thoms *E.E. Pr. Rom.* (1858) I. 226 He hyred a Walloon souldier. **1709** STEELE *Tatler* No. 13 ¶2 Monsieur Bosnage, Minister of the Walloon Church at Rotterdam. **1842** BORROW *Bible in Spain* xiii. 97 One of my comrades of the Walloon Guard. **1888** *Encycl. Brit.* XXIV. 332/2 The Wallon domain comprises the four provinces of Hainault, Namur, Liége, and Luxemburg. **1911** G. P. GOOCH *Hist. Our Time* x. 236 Where the Walloon miners and factory-workers of the South confront the Catholic Flemings of the North.

wallooroo, variant of WALLAROO.

wallop ('wɒləp), *sb.* Also 5 **valop, walop**, 6 **wallope**, 9 **wallup, w(h)ollop**, etc. [a. ONF. *walop* (found in 13th c. in pl. *walos*) = F. *galop*, related to *galoper* to gallop: see WALLOP *v.* There is nothing to show whether the verb or the sb. is the earlier formation in OF. Both were introduced together into ME. in sense 1, appearing first in the 14th c.; but in later use in all senses the sb. is more often to be regarded as newly formed from the verb in its later applications, and with its onomatopœic and humorous connotation. The form GALLOP appears first in the 16th c. and replaces *wallop* sb. in the original and more elevated sense, in which, however, WALLOP *v.* continues to be evidenced.]

†**1. a.** A horse's gallop. Only advb. phr. (tr. or imitations of French) (*to ride, go*, etc.) †***a wallop***, at the gallop; †***a*** (or ***the***) ***great wallop***, in full gallop. *Obs.*

c **1350** *Will. Palerne* 1770 þei went a-wai a wallop as þei wod semed. *c* **1450** *Merlin* viii. 127 And than he rode a walop after Vlfyn, gripynge his spere. **1470–85** MALORY *Arthur* I. xxii. 69 So he rode a grete wallop tyll he cam to the fontayne. *c* **1489** CAXTON *Sonnes of Aymon* ix. 229 Foulques of morillon cam afore all the other, well horsed..the grete valop agenste Reynawde.

b. A ride at this pace. *rare*$^{-1}$. (? *Jocular.*)

1896 E. CRAWFORD *Jo of Auchendorass* 201 Famous place this for your morning wallop.

†**2. a.** The series of noisy bubbling motions made by water, etc. rapidly boiling, or approaching boiling point. Usually in phr. †***to boil*** (***seethe***) ***a wallop, a full wallop***: to boil with a rapid noisy bubbling, to 'gallop'. *Obs.* Cf. WALM *sb.*^{1} 3.

1565 GOLDING *Ovid's Met.* VII. (1593) 160 The medcine seething all the while a wallop in a pan Of brasse, to spirt and leape aloft and gather froth began. **1576** TURBERV. *Venerie* lxxix. 230 Put a glasse full of white wine to them, and let them boyle therein, a whalme or a wallop in a pewter pot. **1591** A. W. *Bk. Cookrye* 17 When it seetheth a full wallop, put in your Shrimpes faire washed.

†**b.** One such bubbling motion (as a vague measure, in cooking, of the time anything is

allowed to boil). Only in phr. *to boil* (or *seethe*, trans. or intr.), *to have, so many wallops*. *Obs.*

1577 B. GOOGE *Heresbach's Husb.* III. 130 b, Seethe them [herbs] togeather three or foure wallops, and geue it him bludwarme. **1611** COTGR., s.v. *Onde, Bouillir vne onde*, to boyle a whyle, or but for one bubble, or a wallop or two. **1682** HARTMAN *True Preserver Health* 11 Let it only boil five or six wallops. **1743** *Lond. & Country Brewer* IV. (ed. 2) 267 Put as much Salt, and Nothing else, as will lie on a Crown-Piece, into a Copper.. and as it heats and the Scum rises, take it off before it boils in; then, when it has had a Wallop or two, lade two Pailfuls. **1750** ELLIS *Mod. Husb.* III. I. 128 (E.D.S.) Boil the cream a wallop or two to preserve it.

3. *dial.* (esp. *Sc.*) and *colloq.* A violent, heavy, clumsy, noisy movement of the body; a plunging, floundering, lurching, etc.

1820 SCOTT *Abbot* xv, Some caprioles of the hobby-horse, and some wallops of the dragon. **1834** M. SCOTT *Cruise Midge* xviii, He made the most laughable wallop imaginable, intended for a bow, but more like the gambol of a porpoise. **1842** J. WILSON *Recr. Chr. North* (1857) I. 4 The yellow trout forsakes his fastness beneath the bog-wood; and with a lazy wallop, and then a sudden plunge [etc.]. **1890** D. DAVIDSON *Mem. Long Life* xi. 269, I put a bullet in the centre of his head, when he [the shark] gave a tremendous wallop and sank.

b. Used onomatopœically and quasi-adverbially with verbs of motion to represent the noise of such movements. *to go (down) wallop*: to fall noisily.

1540 PALSGR. *Acolastus* III. i. N iv b, Nowe hath this gredy gutte meat inough to swalow down, by his wide throte, with a choppe and a wallop. **1885** TOWERS *Poems* 182 (E.D.D.) Souple Tam Gaed wallop ower the stile. **1896** *Warwick. Word-bk., He went wallop* = he fell down all of a heap. **1915** *Scot at Hame & Abr.* 1 July 2/1 Then gallop, gallop, gallop, wallop, wallop, wallop. Though I fall at the high jump, an' onlookers quiver, McGregor, the jockey, will ride on for ever.

4. a. *colloq.* A heavy resounding blow; a whack. Also (in boxing slang) the capacity to deliver such a blow. Also *fig.*

1823 'JON BEE' *Dict. Turf, Wallup*, a random hit, any where. **1827** HARDMAN *Battle Waterloo* 10 Be ready, when the 10th retire, to give the French a wallop. **1836** [HOOTON] *Bilberry Thurland* II. viii. 146, I took up a walking-stick, and says to her, 'Here, Kitty; lay hold of this, and fetch me a great whollop on this soft head of mine.' **1838** *Bentley's Misc.* III. 459 To each blow of the brass weapon, Sam returned a wallop of a pewter vessel. **1884** D. GRANT *Lays & Leg. North* (1908) 103 Thus Davie cud the kelpie guide, Wi' mony a wallop on his hide. **1914** *Varsity* 24 Feb. 15/2 (Boxing) His opponent.. has a prodigious 'wallop', but no great amount of skill. **1925** T. DREISER *Amer. Trag.* I. II. iii. 171 What a wallop, eh? An' us leavin' him and that girl in the car. **1936** 'J. CURTIS' *Gilt Kid* v. 57 The brandy went down good and packed a real wallop. **1943** E. B. WHITE *Let.* 4 June (1976) 242 K and I got a big wallop out of hearing from you. **1976** *National Observer* (U.S.) 23 Oct. 22/1 Now it assumes a vertical position on the upper half of the page. Better visibility, more wallop. So we think. **1978** S. BRILL *Teamsters* x. 390 Life for Harold Gibbons didn't pack much of a wallop anymore.

b. *dial.* (*Sc.*) A (violent) beat of the heart or of the pulse.

1787 BURNS *Addr. Unco Guid* iv, Think, when your castigated pulse Gies now and then a wallop, What ragings must his veins convulse, That still eternal gallop. **1824** MACTAGGART *Gallov. Encycl.* 484, I thought it [my heart] wad hae jumped clean out o' my brisket; lord! what wallops it gaed.

c. *colloq.* Alcohol, esp. beer; alcoholic drink.

1933 *Bulletin* (Sydney) 11 Jan. 20/2 This time the wallop was met 40 miles away. **1945** J. B. PRIESTLEY *Three Men in New Suits* viii. 133 It's drink... Booze or wollop... Nine times out of ten.. you wake up in the morning.. with the usual hangover. **1949** 'G. ORWELL' *Nineteen Eighty-Four* I. viii. 90 When I was a young man, mild beer—wallop we used to call it—was fourpence a pint. **1962** N. MARSH *Hand in Glove* ii. 40 'May Leonard fix mine?.. He knows my kind of wallop.'.. Leonard adroitly mixed two treble Martinis. **1972** L. LAMB *Picture Frame* vi. 56 Mrs Tyler could do nothing to improve the wallop she served at the Hurdlemakers [Inn].

5. A flapping or fluttering rag. *Sc.*

1776 C. KEITH *Farmer's Ha'* xxxiv, Beggars they come in gelore, Wi' wallops flapping in great store. **1866** GREGOR *Banffsh. Gloss., Wallop*, a rag hanging loose and fluttering.

wallop ('wɒləp), *v.* Inflected **walloped** ('wɒləpt), **walloping**. Forms: 4-5 **walop(e**, 5 **walloppe**, 5-6 **walap, wallope**, 5-7 **walopp(e**, 9 **wallup, whallup, wollup**, 6- **wallop**. [a. ONF. **waloper* = F. *galoper* (see GALLOP *v.*[1]). The existence of this form is evidenced in addition to the English forms by OF. *walos* sb. pl. and the adopted form Flem. *walop(pe*, MHG. *walop, -ap* sb. MHG. *walopiren* vb., and probably by mod. Walloon (Sigart) *waloper* to rinse linen in water. Cf. Norw. (Aasen) *val(l)hoppa* vb., app. an etymologizing alteration, after Norw. *hoppa* to leap, dance.

A satisfactory origin for this word in French has not been suggested. It is probably purely echoic, or an echoic alteration of some Teut. element or elements. The Provençal form *galaupar* has suggested Teut. **ga-hlaupan* (OE. *ȝehléapan*, f. *ȝe-* Y- prefix + *hléapan* to LEAP), but the evidence for original *w-* precludes the comparison of the initial element.

In English the onomatopœic suggestion of the word has lent itself to varied extension of meanings and to a vague (usually colloq. and humorous) application to violent noisy movements, more especially since the form GALLOP ousted it from the more elevated uses (in the course of the 16th c.).

The sense 'to boil rapidly' is probably derived directly by transference from sense 1 (cf. GALLOP *v.*[2] to boil) in spite of the close resemblance of the word to WALL *v.*[1] + UP (cf. *well up*, and Du. *opwallen*). The relation of POTWALLOPER to POTWALLER indicates that some such association was active.

The sense 'to beat' may be ultimately due to the causative use (sense 2, and cf. F. *galoper* trans.), or may be entirely due to onomatopœic extension.]

†I. 1. *intr.* To gallop. *Obs.*

a. of horses.

a **1400** [see WALLOPING *ppl. a.*]. *c* **1430** *Syr Gener.* (Roxb.) 3642 Al this folk of mych price in feire armes, and helmes shene,.. withe feire stedes walopand. *c* **1440** *Promp. Parv.* 514/2 Waloppon, as horse, *volopto*. *c* **1489** CAXTON *Sonnes of Aymon* xiv. 346 Cam there kyng charlemagn, as fast as his horse myghte walop. **1513** DOUGLAS *Æneis* XI. x. 23 (1710), He [the courser] sprentis furth, and ful proude waloppis he, Hie strekand vp his hede with mony ane ne. **1570** LEVINS *Manip.* 169/34 To gallop, *fundere gradus*, to Wallop, *idem, cursitare*.

b. of a rider.

1375 BARBOUR *Bruce* II. 440 To this word thai assentyt all, And fra thaim walopyt owyr mar. *c* **1420** WYNTOUN *Cron.* IV. 234 (Cott.) Þe cursoure he straik wiþe þe spuris, And walapande our floyis and furis Al befor þe ost he rade. *c* **1440** *Generydes* 3325 He founde anon The kyng of kynggez vppe and down rideng, And he anon to hym com waloping. *c* **1500** *Melusine* xxi. 130 And thenne the Knight broched hys hors, and waloped toward hys felawes. **1529** LYNDESAY *Compl.* 179 And sum, to schaw thare courtlie corsis, Wald ryid to leith, and ryn thare horssis, And wychtlie wallope ouer the sandis. **1721** RAMSAY *Up in Air* i, And witches wallop o'er to France, Up in the air On my bony grey mare.

†2. *trans.* To let gallop, put to the gallop. *Obs. rare.* (Cf. GALLOP *v.*[1] 3.)

c **1489** CAXTON *Blanchardyn* xi. 42 Blanchardyn wyth a glad chere waloped his courser as bruyauntly as he coude. **1490** —— *Eneydos* lxi. 161 A knyghte.. came ayenste hym as faste as he myghte spore and waloppe his horse.

II. 3. *intr.* To boil violently and with a noisy bubbling. Also *fig.*

1579 TOMSON *Calvin's Serm. Tim.* 191/2 Oure affections boyle within vs, & wallop, frothing as a seething potte. **1617** J. MOORE *Mappe Mans Mortalitie* I. iii. 25 This corruption ..sendeth out the filthy scum of all vncleannesse, which continually broyleth and walloppeth in our nature. *a* **1649** S. CROOKE *Div. Charact.* I. xxxiii. (1658) 499 There is little to choose between a boyling pot unscummed, and the pot that, for want of heate, hath no scumme raised.. that wallops as the Sea about Leviathan; and this, paves it with stone. **1716** M. DAVIES *Athen. Brit.* III. 24 We do not measure Milk when it Wallops and Seeths, but when it is Cold. **1787** JOEL BARLOW *Hasty Pudding*, The yellow flour.. thickens to a paste, Then puffs and wallops, rises to the brim, Drinks the dry knobs that on the surface swim. [**1845**: see WALLOPING *ppl. a.* 1]. **1863** HAWTHORNE *Our Old Home* II. 233 We beheld an immense pot over the fire, surging and walloping with some kind of a savory stew.

III. 4. a. To make violent, heavy movements (accompanied by noise); to move clumsily or convulsively; to flounder, plunge. *colloq.* and *dial.*

1715 RAMSAY *Christ's Kirk Gr.* II. x, The lasses babb'd about the reel, Gar'd a' their hurdies wallop. **1820** SCOTT *Abbot* xiv, The dragon walloped and hissed, and the hobby-horse neighed. *a* **1825** FORBY *Voc. E. Anglia, Wallop*, (1) To move as fast as possible, but not without much effort and agitation... The gallop of a cow or a cart-horse is a good specimen of wallopping. **1840** THACKERAY *Barber Cox* Mar., Trumpeter gone clean from under me, and walloping and floundering in the ditch underneath. **1846** LANDOR *Pentam.* iii. Wks. 1853 II. 334/2 They should not waddle and wallop in every hollow lane, nor loll out their watery tongues at every wash-pool in the parish. *c* **1854** FERRIER *Let.* in E. S. Haldane *Life* (1899) 82, I take it that I have caught you in my net, and that wallop about as you will I shall land you at last. **1889** W. C. RUSSELL *Marooned* xxxii, All was now bustle; the negroes walloped about, tumbling into the boat, bawling out like school-boys at play. **1897** *Outing* XXIX. 544/1 In a moment he [a pup] caught sight of his mother and walloped over to her. **1906** HELEN MATHERS *Tally Ho!* I. i, Sir George Freeling came walloping up on his big iron-grey horse. **1916** *Blackw. Mag.* Nov. 650/1 The puppy.. wallops clumsily round trying to get a bit out of every one else's share.

b. Of the heart, the blood: To pulsate (violently). *Sc.* Cf. WALLOP *sb.* 4 b.

1766 A. NICOL *Poems* 21 (E.D.D.) My heart will.. wallop. **1807** TANNAHILL *Soldier's Return* I. i, Odsaffs! my heart did never wallop cadger, Than when the Laird took Harry for a sodger. **1813** PICKEN *Poems* I. 97 (E.D.D.) Whan the tide o' youthful' bluid Thro' a' yer heartstrings wallops.

5. To dangle, flap, 'flop about', wobble. *colloq.* and *dial.* (esp. *Sc.*).

1822 HOGG *Siege Roxb.* xiii. Tales & Sk. VI. 238 Saluting the far loin of his mare.. with an energy that made all his accoutrements wallop. **1843** *Commissioner: or De Lunatico Inq.* 218 His fat sides shook and walloped. **1887** P. MCNEILL *Blawearie* 15 Wee Connie Rogan, the ingenuity of whose parents it altogether surpasses to know how to keep his nether garments from walloping behind him. **1890** 'H. HALIBURTON' *In Scottish Fields* 32 His West-of-England frock-coat so rent.. that the loose half walloped in the dust or mud all the way behind him.

b. Phr. *to wallop in a tow* (or *tether*): to be hanged. *Sc.*

1785 BURNS *To W. Simpson* xvii, Now let us lay our heads thegither, In love fraternal; May Envy wallop in a tether, Black fiend, infernal. **1792** —— *Weary Pund o' Tow* iv, And 'or I wad anither jad, I'll wallop in a tow. *a* **1835** W. ROBERTSON in W. Walker *Bards of Bon-Accord* (1887) 607 I'd rather wallop in a tether Than lightly thee.

IV. 6. *trans. colloq.* To beat soundly, belabour, thrash; also occas. used as humorously for BEAT *v.* in fig. senses, e.g. to get the better of, surpass.

1825 JENNINGS *Observ. Dial. W. Eng.*, To *Wallup*, to beat. **1837** LOVER *Rory O'More* I. ii. 46 'Then what does he [the priest] want the heavy stick for?' 'For wallopin' his flock, to be sure,' said Rory. **1849** W. S. MAYO *Kaloolah* vi. (1850) 52, I wollopped the hoop around him. **1865** MEREDITH *Rhoda Fleming* xxiv, Walloping men is poor work, if you come to compare it with walloping Nature. **1882** BESANT *All Sorts* xxx, He's always up to tricks; and if you wallop him, likely as not, next night, he'll take and spoil your best trick out of revenge. **1886** STEVENSON *Kidnapped* v, I have a rope's end of my own to wollop 'em. **1916** E. PHILLPOTTS *Faith Tresilion* xiii, If I've got to go about walloping the fear of God into everybody who offered for Faith, I shall be busier than I want to be.

walloper ('wɒləpə(r)). *colloq.* or *jocular*. [f. WALLOP *v.* + -ER[1].]

1. a. One who thrashes. **b.** Anything with which one administers a thrashing; a stick.

1832 BARRINGTON *Personal Sk.* III. xviii. 256 Armed with his 'walloper' (as they called their cudgel).

2. *dial.* Anything strikingly large or big; a 'thumper', 'whopper'; e.g. an astounding lie. (See *Eng. Dial. Dict.*)

3. As second element in compounds. ***cod-walloper***, a cod-fishing vessel (Cent. Dict.); ***dock-walloper***, see DOCK *sb.*[3] 7. Also POT-WALLOPER.

4. *Austral. slang.* A policeman.

1945 BAKER *Austral. Lang.* vii. 137 We also call a policeman a.. walloper. **1954** *Coast to Coast 1953–4* 175 A showman he was. Knock-around man. Always two jumps ahead of the wallopers. **1968** D. O'GRADY *Bottle of Sandwiches* 54 Roebourne boasted one pub, one police station with two wallopers in it,.. and a hospital. **1981** *Bulletin* (Sydney) 13 Jan. 391, I could quite happily call them my friends. I could never think of them as wallopers.

walloping ('wɒləpɪŋ), *vbl. sb.* [-ING[1].] The action of the verb WALLOP (in various senses).

c **1440** *Promp. Parv.* 514/2 Waloppynge, of horse, *voloptacio*. **1686** G. STUART *Joco-ser. Disc.* 48 Oh—! Wae betide this galloping! I've got my fill of wallopping! **1837** LOVER *Rory O'More* I. ii. 47 'And what is all this walloping for?' 'Why, sir, whin we have a bit of a fight, for fun,.. his reverence sometimes hears of it, and comes av coorse.' **1833** M. SCOTT *Tom Cringle* xvi. (1859) 391 The water in the immediate neighbourhood seemed quite alive, from the rushing and walloping of numberless fishes. **1871** C. GIBBON *Lack of Gold* ii, Your father gied you a walloping for telling a lie.

walloping ('wɒləpɪŋ), *ppl. a.* [-ING[2].]

1. That wallops. Now chiefly (*colloq.* or *dial.*), that moves with a clumsy irregular gait.

? *a* **1400** *Morte Arth.* 2147 Sweltand knyghtez Lyes wyde opyne welterande one walopande stedez. **1837** HT. MARTINEAU *Soc. Amer.* (1839) I. 305 There were black women ploughing in the field, with.. their wolloping gait and vacant countenance. **1845** S. JUDD *Margaret* II. i, She graduates the walloping syrup when it is likely to overflow.

2. *dial.* Strikingly large, powerful, etc.; 'thumping', 'whopping'. Often reinforced with *big, great.* (See *Eng. Dial. Dict.*)

1847 HALLIWELL, *Walloping*, great. *var. dial.* **1959** F. ASTAIRE *Steps in Time* (1960) xxviii. 317 *Funny Face* proved a walloping success in the main big-city first runs and particularly at the Music Hall, where it broke several records. **1980** M. RICHLER *Joshua Then & Now* I. ii. 55 Joshua slid behind the bar, which was unattended, and poured himself a walloping cognac.

wallow ('wɒləʊ), *sb.* In 6 **walow**. [f. WALLOW *v.*]

1. a. The act of wallowing or rolling in mud or filth; also *fig.* Also *concr.*, the filth in which swine wallow.

a **1591** H. SMITH *Serm., Jacob's Ladder* (1601) 545 Let the dog turne to the vomit, and the swine to the walow. **1896** G. S. OGILVIE *Sin of St. Hulda* II. 40 Thou'st called me from the filthy byre of swine, The wallow of indulgence and gross deeds. **1898** *Advance* (Chicago) 3 Mar. 284/1 Poor wretches who are converted a dozen times in a winter only to return to their wallow and cups. **1913** SIR H. CLIFFORD in *Blackw. Mag.* Oct. 479/2 After a heart-breaking attempt to cleanse the sweat of travel by a wallow in a mud-hole. **1969** J. GROSS *Rise & Fall Man of Lett.* iii. 89 Nor was he at all averse himself, as a reader, to a nice old-fashioned romantic wallow, with wedding-bells ringing out in Chapter the Last. **1975** *Listener* 4 Dec. 746/2 While we are having a wallow, let me suggest that reviewers discussing 'X' films.. should be more explicit.

b. A mud-hole or dust-hole formed by the wallowing of a buffalo, elephant, or rhinoceros. Also *transf.*

1841 CATLIN *N. Amer. Ind.* xxxi. I. 249 'A bull in his wallow'.. has a very significant meaning with those who have ever seen a buffalo bull.. endeavouring to cool his heated sides, by tumbling about in a mud puddle. **1882** *Contemp. Rev.* Aug. 229 The wallows are saucer-like depressions in the ground, made by the buffaloes rubbing themselves. **1900** POLLOK & THOM *Sports Burma* v. 167 One rhinoceros may have two or three wallows, or mud-holes, which he visits in turn. **1963** A. SMITH *Throw out Two Hands* xi. 114 Every so often came a glutinous wallow where some lorry had spent time not only in extricating itself but in deforming the track still further.

c. *fig.* A state of depression or stagnation.

1934 in WEBSTER. **1938** *Times* 19 Jan. 13/5 Cannot some effort be made to rescue from the wallow into which in the provinces it is falling that fine old British institution the Christmas pantomime? **1969** J. GASKELL *Sweet Sweet Summer* 77 And you know how inter-holed and jig-saw-slotted intricate incestuous old showbis is—*one* despairs, they're all down in the black wallow. **1975** *Bookseller* 3 May 2380/2 Lifting the *Sunday Times* novel reviews out of the terrible wallows they have been in for the last few years.

2. †a. A rolling walk or gait. *Obs.*

1676 DRYDEN *Etheredge's Man of Mode* Epil. 22 His various Modes from various Fathers follow; One taught the Toss, and one the new French Wallow.

b. The roll or swell of the sea. *poet.*

1868 MORRIS *Earthly Par.* I. Prol. 31 And much ado had we To ride unspilt the wallow of the sea.

3. *dial.* The line into which hay is raked before being carted or cocked.

1874 JEFFERIES *Toilers of Field* (1892) 119 Twenty women ..turning a 'wallow', or shaking up the green swathes left by the mowers.

wallow ('wɒləʊ), *a.* Now *dial.* (see Eng. Dial. Dict.) Forms: 1 **wealȝ**, 3 **walh**, 5 **walhwe, walow**, 6 **walowe**, 9 **wallow**. See also WAUGH *a.* [OE. *wealȝ* (**walȝ*) = LG. *walg*, insipid (cf. MDu. *walghe* 'nausea, fastidium'), Norw. *valg* tasteless:—OTeut. **walwo-*:—pre-Teut. **wolqwo-*.

The disyllabic *wallow* represents the inflected form *wealȝ-*; in the uninflected form the final (ɣ) became (x), yielding the mod. northern WAUGH.]

Tasteless, insipid; sickly.

c **897** ÆLFRED *Gregory's Past. C.* lviii. 447 Se wearma welð on godum cræftum, ðylæs he sie wealȝ for wlæcnesse, & forðæm weorðe utaspiwen. *c* **1230** *Hali Meid.* 35 þi muð is bitter, & walh al þat tu cheowest. **1825** BROCKETT *N.C. Words, Wallow*, insipid. **1886** *S.W. Linc. Gloss.* s.v., Oh, mother, how wallow this here bread is!—Why, bairn, I'd gotten no salt to put in it; it makes it a bit wallowish.

b. *Comb.*: † **wallow-sweet** *a.*, ?cloyingly sweet.

c **1440** *Promp. Parv.* 515/1 Walhwe swete [*Winch.* walowswete], *supra in* bytter swete. **1532** MORE *Confut. Tindale* Pref. E eiij b, The olde holsome wyne..[doth] offend theyr dronken taste, bycause yt is not so walow swete but drynketh more of yᵉ verder. **1534** —— *Treat. Passion* Wks. 1274/1 But the walowe sweete pleasure of that fruite, soone tourned to displeasure and payne.

wallow ('wɒləʊ), *v.*[1] Forms: 1 **wealwian, weal(o)wiȝan**, 3 **weolewe**, 3–5 **walewe, walwe**, 4 *Sc.* **valou-**, 4–5 **wolow, walu-**, 4–7 **walow(e**, 5 **walo-**, 5, 7 **wallo-**, 5–7 **wallowe**, 6– **wallow**. Also 3–4 **welu**, 5 **welwyn, welowyn**. [OE. *wealwian* :—OTeut. **walwōjan*; a parallel OTeut. **walwjan* occurs in Goth. (*af-, at-, faur-*) *walwjan*, OE. *wielwan*, to roll (trans.); cf. Goth. *walwisōn* to roll (intr.).

The Teut. **welw-*: **walw-* represents Pre-Teut. **welw-*, **welu-*, whence Gr. ἐλυσθείς rolled, wrapped, ἔλυτρον wrapper, case, L. *volvĕre* to roll.]

I. Intransitive senses.

† **1.** Of a round object (a stone, a wheel): To roll (along the ground); to move by revolving or rotating. Only in OE. Hence *fig.* of a thought: To revolve or be turned over in the mind. *Obs.*

c **888** ÆLFRED *Boeth.* vi, Ðonne þær micel stan wealwiende of þam heohan munte oninnan fealð. *Ibid.* xxxix. §7 þa felȝa þeah hongiað on þæm spacan, þeah hi eallunga wealowiȝen on þære eorðan. **1387** TREVISA *Higden* (Rolls) VI. 301, I praye þat it greve ȝow nouȝt..þeyȝ I telle ȝow openliche what haþ longe tyme i-halowed [*v.rr.* walwed, ywalwed] in myn herte [L. *quod animus meus diu volutavit*].

2. a. Of a person or animal: To roll about, toss or tumble from side to side, while lying down or stretched out. Now *rare* exc. as in 3.

c **900** *Bæda's Hist.* III. ix. (1890) 178 [Ðæt hors] ongon wealwian & on æȝhwæðre siidan hit ȝelomlice oferwearp. *c* **1386** CHAUCER *Wife's T.* 229 Whan he was with his wyf abedde ybroght, He walweth and he turneth to and fro. **1388** WYCLIF *Mark* ix. 19 [20] He was throw doun to grounde, and walewide, and fomede. **1480** CAXTON *Myrr.* II. xv. (1913) 102 The hyrchon, whan he fyndeth apples beten or blowen doun of a tree, he woloweth on them tyll he be.. laden wyth the fruyt stykyng on his pryckes. **1530** PALSGR. 771/1, I wallowe, I tourne to and fro. *Je me voystre.* What wylte thou gyve me, an I wyll walowe from this hyll toppe down to the grounde. **1538** ELYOT *Dict., Voluto*, to tourne tylinge, to walow. **1555** EDEN *Decades* (Arb.) 231 The fysshe ..waloweth on euery syde and about the shyppe. **1602** CAREW *Cornwall* I. 3b, Where the Horse walloweth, some haires will still remaine. **1720** DE FOE *Capt. Singleton* v. (1840) 94 Some that were wounded and lame, who lay wallowing and screaming..upon the ground. **1881** JOWETT *Thucyd.* I. 127 The dead lay as they had died, one upon another, while others hardly alive wallowed [ἐκαλινδοῦντο] in the streets.

† **b.** said of persons wrestling together. *Obs.*

c **1386** CHAUCER *Reeve's T.* 358 And in the floor, with nose and mouth to-broke, They walwe, as doon two pigges in a poke. ? *a* **1400** *Morte Arth.* 1142 Wrothely thai wrythyn and wrystill to-gederz, Welters and walowes ouer with-in thase buskez. **1470–85** MALORY *Arthur* v. v. 168 Thenne Arthur weltred and wrong, that he was other whyle vnder and another tyme aboue, And so weltryng and walowynge they rolled doune the hylle.

c. To move about heavily or clumsily; to go along with a rolling or floundering gait.

1570 DRANT *Serm.* B viij b, Pope Leo that was so forgrowen with fatte, that he coulde not wallowe vp two staires in the Capitall. **1576** TURBERV. *Venerie* lxxvii. 216 They [*i.e.* bears] go somtimes a galloppe, & somtimes an amble: but when they wallow then they go at moste ease. **1599** MARSTON *Ant. & Mel.* v. (1602) I 1, When I see.. another wallowe in a greate sloppe, I mistrust the proportion of his thigh. **1603** DEKKER *Wonderf. Yr.* F 2, My gorbelly Host..out of the house he wallowed presentlie. **1609** W. M. *Man in Moone, Glutton* E 2, Now he approacheth wallowing like a woman with childe. **1845** S. JUDD *Margaret* II. i, Toads ..shrugged and wallowed up from their torpid beds. **1864** LOWELL *Fireside Trav.* 232 In a moment you [in the diligence] are rattling and rumbling and wallowing down into the valley. **1876** J. WEISS *Wit, Hum. & Shaks.* iv. 130 This rotund earth that goes wallowing eastward in an aboriginal Falstaff.

† **d.** To flounder in speech. *Obs.*

14.. *Bk. Curtasye* 63 in *Babees Bk.* 301 Yf any man speke þat tyme [*i.e.* when thy mouth is over-full] to the, And þou schalle onsware, hit wille not be But waloande, and a-byde þou most.

3. To roll about, or lie prostrate and relaxed in or upon some liquid, viscous, or yielding substance (e.g. mire, blood, water, dust, sand). Often implying sensual enjoyment or indifference to defilement. Usu. with *in.*

c **897** ÆLFRED *Gregory's Past. C.* liv. 421 He wealwode on ðæm ȝedrofum wætere. *c* **1200** *Trin. Coll. Hom.* 37 þan hie [swine] fulle beð, hie secheð to þe fule floddri and þaron waleweð. *a* **1225** *Juliana* 41 Ich hit am þe reafde þe riche Job his ahte, swa þat he weolewede of wontreðe iþe mixne. *c* **1380** *Sir Ferumb.* 2328 þe Amyral..walwede þanne on þe dyche. **1398** TREVISA *Barth. De P.R.* XVIII. lxxxvii. (1495) 836 Whan swyne ben syke they walowe in fenne and in puddels. *c* **1450** *Mirk's Festial* 226 Loþe had he byn forto haue seen wormes and grubbes walewe yn þat blessyd full wombe. **1577** B. GOOGE *Heresbach's Husb.* III. 149 A marrishe is to be preferred before a dry ground, that they [swine] may.. wallowe in the myre, and toomble in the puddels of water. **1593** SHAKS. *Rich. II*, I. iii. 298 Or Wallow naked in December snow. **1611** BIBLE *2 Sam.* xx. 12 Amasa wallowed in blood in the mids of the high way. **1667** MILTON *P.L.* vii. 411 Part huge of bulk Wallowing unweildie, enormous in thir Gate Tempest the Ocean. **1699** DAMPIER *Voy.* II. III. v. 48 'Tis reported the Commanders do keep Bathing-Troughs full of Water to lye and wallow in. **1791** COWPER *Odyss.* x. 391 Hence—seek the sty. There wallow with thy friends. **1819** STEPHENS in *Shaw's Gen. Zool.* XI. I. 139 They [Gallinaceæ] are fond of wallowing in the dust. **1838** DICKENS *O. Twist* viii, Little knots of houses, where drunken men and women were positively wallowing in filth. **1878** H. S. WILSON *Alpine Ascents* ii. 53 We wallow in soft rotten snow above our knees.

4. Of a ship: To roll from side to side; to sail with a rolling motion; to roll helplessly in the trough of the waves. †Of a floating object: To be tossed about.

c **1300** *St. Gregory* 371 in *Archiv. Stud. neu. Spr.* LVII. 63 Hij seien a bat come walwynge. *c* **1350** *Northern Passion* II. 128 (MS. Rawl.) þar nettes walweþ þat ssolde hem fede. *c* **1590** in Hakluyt *Voy.* (1599) II. II. 163 Which caused our ship to rowle and wallow. **1633** T. JAMES *Voy.* 79 Which made her swag and wallow in her Docke. **1670** MILTON *Hist. Eng.* VI. 247 It were an endless work to relate how they [the Danish ships] wallow'd up and down to every particular place. **1720** DE FOE *Capt. Singleton* ii. (1840) 33 She wallowed so in the sea, that we..thought she would at last wallow herself bottom up. **1914** *Blackw. Mag.* Jan. 23/2 The *Bussorah* was not a good boat, and she pitched and rolled and wallowed all through the Bay.

5. Of the sea, waves: To roll, surge, heave, toss. Of wind: To whirl, blow gustily. Of a liquid: To spout, gush; to spring or well *up.* Of flame, smoke, vapour: To surge *up.*

1362 LANGL. *P. Pl.* A. v. 71 Venim or vernisch or vinegre, I trouwe, Walleþ [*v.rr.* walewiþ, walweþ] in my wombe. *Ibid.* IX. 36 þe goodes in þis world ben lyk þis grete wawes, Riht as wyndes and watres waleweþ aboute. *c* **1374** CHAUCER *Boeth.* II. pr. vi. (1886) 40 They don as grete damages and destrucciouns as doth the flaumbe of the mountaigne ethna whan the flawmbe walweth vp. *c* **1386** —— *Miller's T.* 430 Hym thynketh verraily that he may see Noees flood come walwynge [*v.r.* walkyng] as the see. **1529** MORE *Dyaloge* I. x. 17 To se that great water cum walowynge vp agaynst the wynde. *a* **1593** MARLOWE *Lucan* I. 614 No vaine sprung out, but from the yawning gash In steed of red bloud wallowed venemous gore. **1611** SPEED *Theat. Gt. Brit.* (1614) 105/2 At the ebbe and fall of tide it [the well] walloweth up amaine. **1848** LOWELL *Sir Launfal* II. Pref. 43 Through the deep gulf of the chimney wide Wallows the Yule-log's roaring tide. **1913** *Eng. Rev.* Nov. 514 The smoke-funnel tottered, then fell thundering upon the deck... Enormous clouds of steam wallowed up from below.

6. *fig.* (cf. sense 3). **a.** To remain plunged in the mire of sensuality, degraded habits, or the like; 'to live in any state of filth or gross vice' (J.); to take delight in gross pleasures or a demoralizing way of life. Usu. with *in.*

c **1230** *Hali Meid.* 13 þa ilke sari wrecches, þat i þat ilke fule wurðinge, unweddede, walewið. **1340** *Ayenb.* 126 We waleweþ ase zuyn hyer beneþe ine þise wose of þise wordle. *c* **1380** WYCLIF *Wks.* (1880) 217 To walwe in glotonye & drounkenesse as swyn in þe feen. *a* **1513** FABYAN *Chron.* VI. cxcviii. (1811) 204 He walowed in lechery. **1577** WOLTON *Cast. Christians* H j, Some of them..do wallowe and tumble in al kinde of wickednesse. **1611** BIBLE *Ecclus.* xxiii. 12 The godly..shall not wallow in their sinnes. **1641** MILTON *Animadv.* Wks. 1851 III. 149 To purifie and renew his Church that lay wallowing in Idolatrous pollutions. **1722** DE FOE *Col. Jack* (1840) 180, I wallowed in sloth and voluptuous ease. **1875** JOWETT *Plato* (ed. 2) II. 81 The corrupted nature would fain wallow like a quadruped in sensual pleasures.

† **b.** To be involved *in* (error, self-will); to be immersed or engrossed *in* (some occupation, activity, etc.); to go in and out, be busy *among* (a body of persons). *Obs.*

c **1380** WYCLIF *Wks.* (1880) 261 þerfore sathanas ordeyned þes newe sectis..to walwe among þe peple & stire hem bi word & ensaumple to be vnstable in þe feiþ. **1399** LANGL. *Rich. Redeles* I. 27 Graceles gostis..That..walwed in her willis, ffor-weyned in here youthe. **1415** HOCCLEVE *To Sir J. Oldcastle* 318 þat yee aryse out of your errour soone, þat there-in walwid han goon is ful yore. **1632** G. HERBERT *Priest to Temple* xiv. (1671) 49 There he shall find his flock most naturally as they are, wallowing in the midst of their affairs.

c. To abound or 'roll' *in* (wealth, possessions). Chiefly with contemptuous implication. ? *Obs.*

a **1425** *Cursor M.* 4503 (Trin.) Mon þat waleweþ al in ȝeles [*Cott.* weltres in his weles.]. **1564–78** BULLEYN *Dial. agst. Pest.* (1888) 83 This fellow walloweth in benefices, as the Hedgehog doeth with apples upon his prickles. **1610** HOLLAND *Camden's Brit.* (1637) 742 Egelricke..found such a mighty masse of money buried within the ground..that, wallowing now in wealth, he gave over his Bishopricke. **1679** SHADWELL *True Widow* III. 37 My Lady wallows in money, she knows not what to do with it. **1765** WESLEY *Wks.* (1872) III. 238 A man that wallows in gold and silver.

d. *jocular.* To give oneself up unrestrainedly to enjoyment; to revel *in.*

1876 'MARK TWAIN' *Tom Sawyer* x. 97 But if ever I get off this time, I lay I'll just *waller* in Sunday-schools! **1881** —— *Lett. to Publishers* (1967) 136 The Earl's literary excrement charmed me like Fanny Hill. I just wallowed in it. **1887** MISS BRADDON *Like & Unlike* xxiii, I mean to wallow in strawberries and cream for the rest of the evening. **1905** VACHELL *The Hill* v. 121, I used to buy the *Police News* when I was a kid, and simply wallow in it.

II. Transitive senses (chiefly causative).

† **7.** To cause (a rounded object) to roll on the ground; to trundle. Also with adv., as *away, to.* Also, to carry *forth*, transport. *Obs.*

a **1380** *St. Augustine* 1331 in Horstm. *Altengl. Leg.* (1878) 84 þis messagers gret ȝiftus ȝauen Seint Austines bodi forte hauen, And forþ wiþ hem þei gonne it walwe, Til þei come to þe toun of Janwe. **1382** WYCLIF *Matt.* xxvii. 60 He walowid to a grete stoon at the dore of the biriel. —— *Mark* xvi. 4 And thei biholdinge syȝen the stoon walewid awey. *c* **1440** *Promp. Parv.* 521/2 Welwyn', or rollyn' al thyngys þat may not be borne, *volvo.* **1662** J. CHANDLER *Van Helmont's Oriat.* 18, I clearly beheld, that Reason is wallowed up and down, among thick darknesses.

† **8.** To cause (a person or animal) to roll or toss about; to cause to lie prostrate or immersed (*in* some liquid or sticky substance). Chiefly *refl.* and *pass.* Also *fig. Obs.*

c **1375** *Sc. Leg. Saints* xviii. (*Egipciane*) 467 Ay valouand me in þat syne, as sow a medynge dois vithine. **1382** WYCLIF *Mark* ix. 19 [20] And he cast doun in to the erthe, was walewid frothinge [Vulg. *Et elisus in terram volutabatur spumans*]. *a* **1400** CHAUCER *To Rosemounde* 17–18 Nas neuer pyk walwed in galauntyne As I in loue am walwed and Iwounde. **1553** WILSON *Rhet.* 116, I was merye here upon this bancke wyth an other prieste, and wallowynge me downe upon the grasse, I said these wordes. **1577** B. GOOGE *Heresbach's Husb.* III. 122 A horse that is weery..wylbe woonderfully refreasshed..yf he may wallow him selfe eyther in the stable, or other dry place. **1611** BIBLE *Jer.* vi. 26 Gird thee with sackcloth, and wallowe thy selfe in ashes. **1618** BOLTON *Florus* IV. ii. (1636) 281 The yong Kings body was found as it lay wallowed under mud. **1673** *Lady's Call.* Pref. 3 How can a soul that remembers its celestial extraction, wallow itself in the mire.

† **9.** To cause (the sea) to roll or toss. *Obs.*

c **1374** CHAUCER *Boeth.* I. met. vii. (1886) 19 Yif the trowble wynde þat hyht Auster, turnyng and waluynge the see medleth the hete.

† **10.** With complement: ? To make (dirty) by wallowing. *Obs.*

1573–80 TUSSER *Husb.* (1878) 191 All dirt and mire some wallow bed, as spanniels vse to doo.

Hence '**wallowing** *vbl. sb.* and *ppl. a.* '**wallowingly** *adv.*

a **1225** *Ancr. R.* 294 þet, of þe walewing, rug & side & wombe orn al o grure blode. **1297** R. GLOUC. (Rolls) 517 þe wrastlinge [*v.rr.* walewinge, wallowynge] bitvene hom was somdel toȝt. **1382** WYCLIF *2 Pet.* ii. 22 A sowe waschun in the walewinge of cley [Vulg. *in volutabro luti*]. *a* **1400–50** *Wars Alex.* 4064 Wele seldom is þe see with him-selfe turbild Bot with þir walowand windis. *c* **1440** *Promp. Parv.* 521/2 Welwynge, *volutacio.* **1552** HULOET, Wallowyngelye, *volutatim.* **1553** EDEN *Treat. New Ind.* (Arb.) 16 Their pase in goyng is somewhat slowe & walowinge. **1555** WATREMAN *Fardle Facions* Pref. 18 To cutte through the wallowyng seas. **1592** NASHE *Strange Newes* G 3, Master Stannyhurst ..trod a foule lumbring boystrous wallowing measures [*sic*] in his translation of Virgil. **1606** CHAPMAN *Mons. D'Olive* II. i. D 1 b, There saw I our great Galliasses tost Vpon the wallowing waues. **1642** MILTON *Apol. Smect.* Wks. 1851 III. 317 We cry out Sacriledge and misdevotion against those who in zeale have demolish't the dens and cages of her uncleane wallowings. **1680** R. L'ESTRANGE *Sel. Colloq. Erasm.* 8 The wallowing of the great Ship overturn'd it. **1684** *Lond. Gaz.* No. 1906/4 She [a mare] hath a wallowing pace. **1887** MORRIS *Odyss.* XII. 219 Drive thou thy ship aloof through the reek and the wallowing sea. **1888** BRYCE *Amer. Commw.* II. lxviii. 532 The ringsters of both parties return to their wallowing in the mire. [Echoing *2 Pet.* ii. 22.] **1903** H. CLIFFORD *Free Lance* x. 81 She rose and plunged and rolled wallowingly.

wallow ('wɒləʊ), *v.*[2] *Obs.* exc. *dial.* Forms: 1 **wealwian, wealowian, -uwian, -owiȝan**, 3–4 **weolewe(n, welyhe,** *pa. pple.* **welud, walud**, 3–5 **welewe(n, welwe(n**, 4–5 **welowe, walow(e, welwye, wolwe**, 5 **wellow, walwyn,** *pa. pple.* **walluid, waleyt**, 5– **wallow**. [OE. *wealwian*, f. Teut. root **walχw-*, **walγʷ-*, whence *wealȝ* WALLOW *a.* The ME. *we(o)lewe*, etc. may represent a different ablaut-grade. Cf. WELK *v.*, which may be remotely connected.] *intr.* To wither, fade; to waste *away. lit.* and *fig.* Often conjugated with *be.*

c **888** ÆLFRED *Boeth.* xxi, On lencten hit grewð, & on hærfest hit wealwað. *a* **1300** *Cursor M.* 1326 O þe steppes vmthoght he þan þat welud war for sin of man. *a* **1310** in Wright *Lyric P.* xv. 50 Such serewe hath myn sides thurhsoht, That al y weolewe a-way to noht. **1382** WYCLIF *Isa.* xix. 6 The reed and the resshe shal welewen. **1387** TREVISA *Higden* VII. 477 þis land wiþ his kyng..welwes away. *c* **1420** WYNTOUN *Cron.* I. Prol. 123 To þis my wit is wallowit dry, But fleure or froyte. **1450–1530** *Myrr. our Ladye* 216 The fayrenesse of the worlde was welwed wyth brennyng of thre fyres. **1513** DOUGLAS *Æneis* VII. Prol. 64 Herbis, flouris, and gersis wallowit away. **1535** STEWART *Cron. Scot.* I. 20 Now is he wallowit and waik as ony wand. **1570** *Satir. Poems Reform.* xv. 24 In earth, ȝe sweit flouris, tak na rute, But wallow altogidder! *a* **1699** KIRKTON *Hist. Ch. Scot.* VII. (1817) 269 Indeed after that day his flower begane to wallow. *a* **1792** *Geordie* iii. in Child *Ballads* IV. 127/1 When first she lookd the letter on, She was baith red and rosy; But she had na read a word but twa, Till she wallowt like a lily.

Hence **'wallowed** *ppl. a.*, withered, faded, discoloured. **'wallowing** *vbl. sb.* and *ppl. a.*

c **1230** *Hali Meid.* 35 Al is, wið a welewunge [*v.r.* weolewunge], þi wlite ouer warpen. *a* **1300** *Cursor M.* 11213 He þat þe walud wand moght ger In a night leif and fruit ber. *a* **1437** JAS. I *Good Counsel* 11 Of grene gress sone cumis wallowit hay. *c* **1450** *Mirk's Festial* 256 Roses and flowres wythout welewyng. **1483** *Cath. Angl.* 413/2 Wellowynge, *flactor, flactencia, Marcor; Marcessibilis, Marcibilis.* **1513** DOUGLAS *Æneis* VII. viii. 11 With wallowit wyngis [L. *fuscis alis*]. *c* **1560** A. SCOTT *Poems* xiv. 16 How far þe rosy gowlis Passis the wallowit weidis in þe vaill. **1719** *Hardyknute* I. 297 in Pinkerton *Sel. Sc. Ballads* (1783) I. 13 In thrauis of dethe, wi wallow'd cheik,.. The bleiding corps of warriours lay. **1843** *Whistle-binkie* Ser. v. 117 Our dochters.. Can thow the icy tags that hing About our wallow't hearts.

wallow, obs. Sc. form of VALUE *v.*

wallowae, -way, obs. Sc. ff. WELLAWAY.

wallower ('wɒləʊə(r)). [f. WALLOW *v.*[1] + -ER[1].]

1. A person or animal that wallows.

1611 COTGR., *Veautreur*, a wallower, or tumbler in the mire. **1748** RICHARDSON *Clarissa* (1768) VIII. 61 What miry wallowers the generality of men of our class are in themselves. **1767** T. NEVILE *Imit. Juvenal* xiii. 154 Lust's Votaries who live and die, Eternal Wall'wers in Circean sty. **1823** SCOTT *Quentin D.* xxii, Ye porkers of Liege! ye wallowers in the mud of the Maes! **1876** MORRIS *Sigurd* II. (1877) 112, I knew that the Worm was Fafnir, the Wallower on the Gold. **1898** MEREDITH *Odes Fr. Hist.* 15 He knew.. what raised This wallower in old slime to noblest heights.

2. *Mech.* A trundle, lantern-wheel. Also *wallower-wheel.*

1548 in *Rep. MSS. Ld. Middleton* (1911) 493 Paid to Smaley for a newe waloer, iiij[d]. **1734** *Phil. Trans.* XXXVIII. 404 By enlarging or diminishing the fix'd Wallower, you obtain a Stroke of any required Height. **1773** W. EMERSON *Princ. Mech.* (ed. 3) 284 *Wallower*, a trundle upon a horizontal axis. **1825** J. NICHOLSON *Operat. Mechanic* 97 The vertical shaft FE carries the two equal wallower-wheels E and F. **1866** C. W. HATFIELD *Hist. Notices Doncaster* I. 203 The usual face wheel.. gears into a main pinion or 'wallower'.

wallowish ('wɒləʊɪʃ), *a.* Now *dial.* Also 6 **walowyshe, -(e)ish,** 7 **wallouish.** See also WALSH *a.* [f. WALLOW *a.* + -ISH.] Insipid, tasteless, flat; also, ill-tasting, nauseous, esp. through being over-sweet.

1548 UDALL *Erasm. Par.* Pref. to King a vj, Honey is waloweishe and ouercasteth the stomake. *a* **1586** SIDNEY *Arcadia* II. xvi. (Sommer) 172 b, Like the sicke man, to whom the Phisition sweares, the ill-tasting wallowish medicine he profers, is of a good taste. **1598** FLORIO, *Disapito*, vnsauorie, tasting of nothing, wallowish. **1601** HOLLAND *Pliny* XXIV. i. II. 176 Salt giveth a good rellish to any meat that is over sweet, and tempereth those that have a lushious and wallowish tast. **1657** R. LIGON *Barbadoes* 80 This fruit [the water-melon] is.. waterish, and wallowish. **1686** W. HARRIS tr. *Lemery's Course Chym.* (ed. 3) 557 The wallowish sweetness of Muste. **1691** RAY *N.C. Words* 78 In the South we say *wallouish*, meaning somewhat nauseous. **1886** [see WALLOW *a.*].

b. *transf.* and *fig.*

1549 COVERDALE, etc. *Erasm. Par. Jas.* iv. 7–17 Therfore who so euer backbiteth his neighbour, he either condemneth the lawe,.. or backbiteth it as though it were to muche myngle mangled, and walowyshe, the office wherof the backbytour taketh vpon hym. **1603** FLORIO *Montaigne* I. xlii. 142 He is a foole, his taste is wallowish and distracted. *Ibid.* III. x. 610 My maners are mustie, rather wallowish then sharpe. **1609** G. BENSON *Serm.* 7 May 13 Though those sixe petitions deliuered by our hearts and tongues (by reason of the mixture of our vainty) bee full of water, weake, wallowish.

c. *Comb.*: † **wallowish-sweet** *a.*, so sweet as to cloy, sickly.

1576 TURBERV. *Venerie* lxviii. 189 Few hounds will eate of a Foxes fleshe, but a Badgerdes is wallowish sweet & rammish. **1577** EDEN *Hist. Trav. W. & E. Indies* 328 b, Theyr milk is walowish sweete.

Hence **'wallowishly** *adv.*, **'wallowishness.**

1603 FLORIO *Montaigne* II. xii. 349 The distasted impute wallowishnesse vnto Wine. *Ibid.* III. xii. 631 There are some beauties,.. pleasing-sweete and yet wallowishly tastelesse. **1611** COTGR., *Affadissement*, wallowishnesse, vnsauorinesse, tastlesnesse.

'wall-paper. Also **wallpaper. 1.** Paper, usually printed in ornamental designs, used for covering the interior walls of buildings; paper-hangings. Now also made of other materials, such as vinyl. Cf. *wallcovering* s.v. WALL *sb.*[1] 25.

1827 DRAKE & MANSFIELD *Cincinnati in 1826* viii. 65 Two Wall Paper Factories, 9 hands. **1847** F. A. KEMBLE *Let.* 12 Dec. in *Rec. Later Life* (1882) III. 300 You know how subject I am even to such an influence as that of a ridiculous wall-paper. **1858** SIMMONDS *Dict. Trade, Wall-paper.* See *Paper-hangings.* **1862** *Catal. Internat. Exhib., Brit.* II. xxx. 13 Block-printed chintz furniture and wall paper. [Elsewhere usually called 'paper hangings'.] **1879** BLACK *Macleod of Dare* xli, That was the guide she turned to—the woman-man, the dabbler in paint-boxes, the critic of carpets and wall-papers. **1883** *Harper's Mag.* Mar. 578/1 Should the new wall-paper be plain or gilded? **1904** LOUISE CREIGHTON *Life & Lett. M. Creighton* I. 83 He is spoken of as being the first to.. introduce the inhabitants of Falmouth to Morris's wall-papers. **1905** H. G. WELLS *Kipps* II. viii. §3 Revel came last,.. politely admiring in a flute-like cultivated voice the mellow wall-paper of the staircase.

2. *fig.* An unobtrusive background; esp. with reference (chiefly *derog.*) to sound, music, etc. Freq. with preceding *adj.* or in *attrib.* use.

1919 'C. DANE' *Legend* 28 They wearied me... They faded into a mere wall-paper of sound, and I forgot that they were there. **1934** C. LAMBERT *Music Ho!* III. 228 It is a matter of indifference whether jazz is a stimulant.. or a piece of mental wallpaper. **1959** A. BAILEY *Making Progress* 157 Cool jazz formed a background, like aural wallpaper. **1966** *Guardian* 4 June 6/4 Of course, we have to have wallpaper talk, in a week's broadcasting, just as some people have to have wallpaper music all the week. **1969** *Listener* 24 Apr. 588/1 The cultural wallpaper of his own childhood was the Australian commercial radio stations. **1977** *Zigzag* June 40/1 The best track, for me, is.. 'Living in The Band', but most of this is just so much wallpaper. **1980** *Jrnl. R. Soc. Arts* Mar. 223/2 Possibly television is becoming visual wallpaper in much the same way as radio has become audible wallpaper.

Hence **wall-papering** *vbl. sb.*, wall-papers collectively; **'wallpaper** *v. trans.* and *intr.*, to cover a wall with wallpaper; also *transf.* and *fig.*; **'wallpapered** *ppl. a.*

1865 DICKENS *Mut. Fr.* II. ix, A young lady.. who was better worth staring at, it occurred to Sloppy, than the best of wall-papering. **1934** WEBSTER, Wallpaper *v.t.* & *i.* **1956** *Family Handyman Magazine's Painting & Redecorating Bk.* 34/1 If you want to paint formerly wallpapered walls: 1. Use check system just described. **1962** A. NISBETT *Technique Sound Studio* xi. 198 If this technique.. does not quite come off it may be possible to wallpaper over the cracks by adding a new overall backing. **1973** *Listener* 29 Nov. 733/1 You could wallpaper St. Paul's with the free brochures. **1975** P. DICKINSON *Lively Dead* xxi. 122 She had planned to wallpaper the back room. **1977** M. FRENCH *Women's Room* (1978) ii. 108 She painted and wallpapered, refinished furniture. **1977** *Listener* 28 Apr. 537/1 Into the Cambridge Union, through the amazingly wallpapered lobby. **1978** R. MILLS *Comprehensive Educ.* 80 We did the paintwork and wallpapered the ceiling. **1979** 'P. O'CONNOR' *Into Strong City* xii. 39 The room is wallpapered with.. a section of Soho dressed as artists as distinct from the criminal section who dress in another fashion.

'wall-piece.

1. *Mil.* (See quot. 1876.)

1755 R. ROGERS *Jrnls.* (1769) 5, I embarked.. with a party of thirty men, in four battoes, mounted with two wall-pieces each. **1774** *Ann. Reg.* 244 We.. at proper intervals kept firing our wall-pieces, as signals to the cutter. **1798** *Hull Advertiser* 29 Sept. 1/4 The vessel.. mounting twelve eighteen pounders.. twelve long wall-pieces, and four swivels. **1804** *Naval Chron.* XII. 381 On the taffrel were two large wall-pieces,.. loaded.. with musket balls. **1826** SCOTT *Woodst.* xvii, The malignants shooting their wall-pieces at us, had so much the advantage, that [etc.]. **1860** J. HEWITT *Anc. Armour* III. 748 The various fire-arms in use at the close of this [17th] century are enumerated.. by St.-Remy. There were wall-pieces (*mousquets de rempart*), both match and flint lock:.. the match-lock musquet [etc.]. **1876** VOYLE & STEVENSON *Milit. Dict.* (ed. 3), *Wall-piece*, an enlarged firelock or firearm mounted on a swivel, and placed on the walls of a fort or other fortified place. It may be said to be obsolete, though sometimes issued in India to an expedition proceeding on service. **1884** *Milit. Engin.* I. II. 115 Machine guns and wall-pieces (the latter being of great advantage when the besieger has to resort to sapping) should also form part of the armament.

2. *Arch.* A pendant or pendant-post.

1860 R. & J. A. BRANDON *Open Timber Roofs* 26 The wall-piece is tenoned into the underside of the principal rafter. **1880** *Archæol. Cant.* XIII. 435 The stone corbels which support the wall-pieces.

'wall-plat. *dial.* Also **-plot, -plit.** [f. WALL *sb.*[1] + PLAT *sb.*[2] 3; app. an alteration of WALL-PLATE.]

1. = WALL-PLATE 1.

1420 *Searchers' Verdicts* in *Surtees Misc.* (1890) 17 That William Selby hafe abouen the same walle, space to ryst his walleplat apon. **1617** in Willis & Clark *Cambridge* (1886) I. 205 The roofe.. to stand on wall platts of oake. **1879** MISS JACKSON *Shropsh. Word-bk.* 468 *Wall-plit*, the piece of timber which is placed on the top of a wall for the purpose of fastening roof-rafters to,—the wall-plate.

b. A shelf fixed in the wall.

1841 HARTSHORNE *Salopia Antiq.* 608.

2. The spotted fly-catcher: = RAFTER *sb.*[1] 2, RAFTER-*bird.*

1841 HARTSHORNE *Salopia Antiq.* 608 *Wall-plat* 1. The Flycatcher: *Muscicapa.* Linn.

'wall-plate. Also 4–6 **wal-,** 5 **walle-,** 6 **wail-, wayl-.** [f. WALL *sb.*[1] + PLATE *sb.* 7.]

1. *Building.* A timber placed horizontally on or in a wall, to form a support for joists or rafters.

1394 *Acc. Manor of the Savoy* in *Archæologia* XXIV. 307 Et in stipendio ij sarratorum sarrantium meremium pro walplates et bemes, et plauncheborde et plegges. **1505–6** *Durham Acc. Rolls* (Surtees) 103 Imposicionem unius wailplate. **1669** STURMY *Mariner's Mag.* VII. xxix. 45 If the Plane of the Cieling of the Wall is interrupted, and made irregular by Beams, Wall-plates, Cornishes, [etc.]. **1782** *Phil. Trans.* LXXII. 368 Just beneath the abovementioned hole at the end of the angle-tie, is the extremity of the wallplate which lies upon the eastern wall of the east flank. **1833** LOUDON *Encycl. Archit.* §380 The wooden caps always give, or seem to give, a more secure bearing for the wall-plate or architrave. **1890** 'R. BOLDREWOOD' *Robbery under Arms* i, He.. cut every post and wallplate and rafter himself.

2. *Mining.* (See quots.)

1881 RAYMOND *Mining Gloss., Wall-plates,* Corn. The two side-pieces of a timber frame in a shaft, parallel to the strike of the lode when the shaft is sunk on the lode. The other two pieces are the end-pieces. **1886** J. BARROWMAN *Sc. Mining Terms* 70 *Wall-plate*, vertical strips of wood supporting the ends of the buntons in a wood-lined shaft.

Hence **wall-plating,** wall plates collectively.

1833 LOUDON *Encycl. Archit.* §1804 The wall-plating and bond to be dovetailed and halved at their angles.

Wallsend ('wɔːlzɛnd, ˌwɔːlz'ɛnd). The name of a town in Northumberland, so called from its situation at the end of the Roman wall. Used *attrib.* (and *ellipt.* as sb.), originally as the designation of coal obtained from a local seam now exhausted; subsequently as the trade name for coal of a certain quality, and in pieces too large to pass through a sieve with meshes ⅝ inch in diameter.

1821 *Times* 23 Jan. 1/4 Coals 46s.. warranted Wallsend, 50s. superior. **1827** HONE *Every-day Bk.* II. 24 Wallsends are rising in price. **1835** DICKENS *Sk. Boz, Mr. Watkins Tottle* i, Three tons of the best Walls-end. **1897** AINGER in Edith Sichel *Life & Lett.* (1906) 289, I have a pound or two of best Walls-end wandering about in my Bronchial cavities.

Wallsman, obs. form of WELSHMAN.

'wall-stone. A stone for building; a stone forming part of a wall. Also, in generalized sense, masonry; stone suitable for building; *spec.* see quot. 1870. Also *fig.*

a **1000** *Crist* 2 (Gr.) Ðu eart se weallstan, þe ða wyrhtan in wiðwurpon to weorce. *a* **1000** *Ruin* 1 (Gr.) Wrætlic is þæs weal stan. **1610** R. VAUGHAN *Water-Workes* K 2 b, Hauing.. Wall-stone, Tyle, Lime, and Bricke, as necessary as any man liuing. **1639** *Burgh Rec. Glasgow* (1876) I. 403 Thair is licence grantit to Sir Robert Dowglas to gett ane hundrethe kairtis of wall stones out of the townes quarrell. **1818** SCOTT *Hrt. Midl.* xvii, For a' the folk I see here are as hard as the wa' stanes. **1837** *Civil Engin. & Arch. Jrnl.* I. 72/1 Below the rag is the block stone, [used] for common walls, and usually called wall stone. **1870** GREENWELL in *Jrnl. Ethnol. Soc.* (N.S.) II. 423 This [stratum of flint] is called by the present flint-workers the 'wall-stone', from its being used for building purposes.

attrib. **1837** *Civil Engin. & Arch. Jrnl.* I. 72/1 The block, or wall-stone seam, is in this quarry about 10 or 11 feet thick. *Ibid.*, In Yorkshire the workmen calculate all wall-stone work by the rod of 7 yards.

Wall Street (wɔːl striːt). orig. *U.S.* The name of a street in New York City where some of the most important American financial institutions are centred, used: **1.** *absol.* Denoting the American financial world or money-market. Also *transf.*

[**1806** *Balance* (Hudson, N.Y.) V. 228/1 Walking thro' Wall street yesterday morning, I saw a large crowd.] **1841** *Week in Wall St.* p. ix, In the expressive language of Wall-street, he has himself been 'flunked'. **1871** L. M. ALCOTT *Little Men* xiv. 244 The firm [was] broken up... The barn, which was the boys' Wall Street, knew him no more. **1872** B. JERROLD *London* xii. 104 The New York gossip of yesterday, is ours upon our breakfast table. We can almost hear the hum of Wall Street. **1905** G. B. SHAW *Let.* 3 Jan. (1972) II. 497 Finding Capel Court (our Wall St) against his conscience, he became a carpenter. **1949** *Chicago Daily News* 31 May 1/6 Wall Street traced liquidation to the many new uncertainties created by declining production. **1975** *Times* 25 Sept. 8/7 The banking and business quarter—known as Beirut's 'Wall Street'.

2. a. *attrib.*, as ***Wall Street broker, method, price,*** etc.

1836 *Jamestown* (N.Y.) *Jrnl.* 16 Mar. 1/2 A company—Wall street brokers and speculators—are the applicants for the loan to the New York and Erie Railroad. **1861** in L. C. Baker *Hist. U.S. Secret Service* (1867) v. 100 Such.. is the windy stuff which—uses to draw money out of the Wall Street kings. **1892** A. C. GUNTER *Miss Dividends* 188 All the rest.. [had] fallen victims to his imported Wall Street methods. **1935** G. GREENE *England made Me* II. 47 'Put through any long-distance calls.' 'The Wall Street prices?' **1940** W. FAULKNER *Hamlet* III. ii. 240 He figured if we named him Wallstreet Panic it might make him get rich like the folks that run that Wallstreet panic. **1972** R. PERRY *Fall Guy* iv. 78 His immaculate suit would have put many a Wall Street executive to shame. **1981** A. LURIE *Lang. of Costume* iv. 114 In the urban centers of the West.. bankers.. sometimes adopt an Eastern manner of speech and a Wall Street appearance.

b. Special Comb. **Wall Street crash, crisis,** the collapse of the American stock-market which took place in October 1929.

1929 *N.Y. Times* 26 Oct. 2/8 Commenting on the Wall Street crash of yesterday, the German press unanimously agrees that Germany has no reason to mourn. **1933** R. G. HAWTREY *Trade Depression* iii. 31 The Federal Reserve Banks can hardly be blamed for their policy of credit restriction up to the moment of the Wall Street crisis. **1981** E. LONGFORD *Queen Mother* ii. 38 The slump or depression of the 1930s began with the Wall Street crash of 1929 in America.

Wall Streeter ('wɔːlˌstriːtə(r)). orig. *U.S.* [f. prec. + -ER[1].] A Wall Street financier, esp. of the New York stock-market.

1885 *Weekly New Mexican Rev.* 15 Jan. 2/2 The Wall streeters and money changers want less money that they may have a better chance to grind the borrowers. **1937** [see STEM *v.*[4] 5 b]. **1943** *Sun* (Baltimore) 2 July 17/1 Many Wall Streeters trimmed accounts to be on the safe side. **1967** *Economist* 2 Sept. 788/3 Mr Haack may also have to do something to dampen a speculative attitude which is reminding some Wall Streeters of 1929. **1979** *Listener* 1 Nov. 579/1 Wall Streeters will tell you that, since its [*sc.* the market's] high of 1968, there has been a crash of sorts.

†**wall-tiding,** *a. Obs.* [f. WALL *v.*[1] + TIDE *sb.* + -ING[2].] Welling up with the tide: said of the reputed 'ebbing and flowing well' at Tideswell.
1636 R. JAMES *Iter Lancastr.* (Chetham Soc.) 371 [Wonders of the Peak] The leadmens grooues.. The loftie Winyates, and wall-tiding springe.

wall-to-wall (stress variable), *a.* (*sb.*, *adv.*) [WALL *sb.*[1]] **1.** Of carpeting: covering the whole floor of a room; fitted. Also *absol.* as *sb.*
1953 A. UPFIELD *Murder must Wait* ii. 12, I detest wall-to-wall carpets. **1962** A. LURIE *Love & Friendship* vi. 97 Genuine hooked rugs scattered over the wall-to-wall carpet. **1965** G. MCINNES *Road to Gundagai* iii. 39 The room fascinated me because it had two carpets on the floor, a 'wall-to-wall' covered by an Axminster. **1977** C. MCFADDEN *Serial* (1978) xxxvi. 78/2 Harvey hated crawling around on the wall-to-wall looking for contact lenses. **1977** *New Yorker* 15 Aug. 33/1 What impressed me most about that house was the carpeting, which was mercilessly wall-to-wall. **1978** *Meridian Poetry Mag.* Autumn 10 He bestrides the wall-to-wall carpeting Like a colossus.
2. a. Of objects, etc., other than carpeting: extending from one wall to another; providing coverage of an entire space. Also as quasi-*adv.*
1959 *Observer* 12 Apr. 14/5 Underpinned with warmth—a wall-to-wall convection heater. **1977** *Washington Post* 27 Nov. M3/1 Wall-to-wall art—framed prints, posters or one enormous canvas—can cover a whole wall. *Ibid.* 3/2 I designed everything wall-to-wall... The bed,..being 75 inches long, the distance between two of the walls, is an instant wall-to-wall component.
b. *fig.* Extending from one end or extreme to the other; allowing no unfilled space; ubiquitous.
1967 *New Yorker* 25 Nov. 222 He made a highly successful series of wall-to-wall mood-music recordings. **1973** *Listener* 19 Apr. 522/2 A respite from wall-to-wall Mozart on Radios 3 and 4. **1976** *Patriot-Ledger* (Quincy, Mass.) 10 July 3/1 The state police said it was just wall-to-wall people and wall-to-wall cars. **1977** *Time* 19 Sept. 9/3 When we kick down doors looking for these people at home, we find almost always tons of literature—wall-to-wall Marx and Marcuse. **1982** S. PARETSKY *Indemnity Only* vi. 74 Why would he agree to see me? He'd never heard of me, he has wall-to-wall appointments. **1984** *Listener* 15 Mar. 19/1 Is there any good reason why we should have news bulletins, local and national, every hour on the hour, chat shows..and wall-to-wall discussion programmes? **1984** *New Statesman* 16 Nov. 16/2 Their sponsors include the IBA..and the BBC (in whose Reithian corridors the epithet 'wall-to-wall *Dallas*' was reputedly coined).

wallum ('wɒlʌm). *Austral.* [Aboriginal.] **a.** A tall evergreen shrub, *Banksia æmula*, common in parts of Australia. **b.** The heathland along the Queensland coast where this is common.
1889 J. H. MAIDEN *Useful Native Plants Austral.* 383 *Banksia marginata, Cav.*,.. 'Honeysuckle'. The 'Wallum' of the aboriginals of Wide Bay (Queensland). **1890** F. M. BAILEY *Catal. Indigenous & Naturalised Plants Queensland* 103/2 Wallum, Banksia *æmula.* **1965** *Austral. Encycl.* IX. 310/1 In Queensland, the Wallum coastal formation stretching north of Brisbane has a varied heathland type of flora. **1970** W. W. BRYAN in R. M. Moore *Austral. Grasslands* vii. 107 North of Maryborough rainfall in the Wallum is only 40–45 in. **1979** *Sunday Sun* (Brisbane) 24 June 9/6 CSIRO projects on similar tracts of coastal wallum have shown it can be transformed relatively inexpensively by the aerial application of trace elements. **1979** *Sunday Mail Mag.* (Brisbane) 29 July 18/3 The wallum banksia dominates the dune scrub with its magnificent large flowers atop the serrated leaves.

wallup, variant of WALLOP.

†**wallure.** *Obs. rare.* [f. WALL *sb.*[1] + -URE.] Walls collectively.
c **1475** *Partenay* 1152 Wel was A-cheued this castel beuteuous, Al A-boute reised wonder by wallure. *Ibid.* 5504 Thys chambre well depeynted was fro foote of wallure the ouise vnto.

walluru, variant of WALLAROO.

wallwort ('wɔːlwɜːt). Forms: 1 walh-, weal-, wal-, wælwyrt, vealvyrt, 3, 6 walwurt, 4–7 walwort (5 -wourte), 6 walworte, -woort, (wolworte, walworth), 5 welleuort, wallewort, 6 wallwurte, 6– wallwort. [OE. *wealhwyrt*, f. *wealh*, a (Celtic or Roman) foreigner, a 'Welshman' (see WELSH *a.*) + *wyrt* herb, plant, WORT *sb.*[1]
It is very unlikely that *wealh* in this word has the same import as in *wealh-hnutu* WALNUT, where it is equivalent to 'exotic'; no reason can be shown why the Dwarf Elder should have been called 'the foreign herb'. More probably the name, like its later synonyms DANEWORT, DANES'-BLOOD, DANEWEED, expresses the popular belief that this plant was a product of soil fertilized by the carnage of battle. When the 'Welshman' was succeeded by the Dane as the foe on English soil, the plant supposed to be a native of battlefields recieved a new name. It is possible, though not certain, that the occasional OE. form *wælwyrt* is not a variant of *wealhwyrt*, but a separate word, f. *wæl* slaughter, the slain in battle (see WAL). Cf. LICH-*wort* (literally 'corpse-plant'), which in the earliest known example (*c* 1450) denotes the Dwarf Elder, though it was soon afterwards misapplied (through misinterpretation of its synonym *wallwort*: cf. 2 below) to the Pellitory of the Wall. It is very remarkable that in Swedish the Dwarf Elder is locally called *Danskablod* (Danes' blood), *mannablod* (men's blood), *mannaört* (*ört* = WORT *sb.*[1]) and *valört*; in the last name the first element may correspond either to OE. *wealh* 'Welshman' or to OE. *wæl* slaughter; the latter is the more probable supposition, as the early battles of the Swedes were not fought against Celts or Romans. Kilian's alleged obsolete Flemish *waleworte* is suspicious, because Kilian cites the English word.]
1. The caprifoliaceous plant *Sambucus Ebulus*, also called Dwarf Elder, Ground Elder, Danewort, Danes' Blood, and Daneweed. It has a nauseous taste and an offensive odour, and was formerly valued as a styptic.
c **725** *Corpus Gloss.* (Hessels) E 11 *Ebulum* walhwyrt. *Ibid.* I. 184 *Intula*, uualhwyrt. *c* **1000** *Sax. Leechd.* III. 30 Wið ðeore, ealhtre, wælwyrt, weoduweaxe [etc.]. *Ibid.* 302 *Ebule* vel *eobulum*, Veal vyrt *vel* ellenvyrt. *c* **1265** *Voc. Plants* in Wr.-Wülcker 555/10 *Ebulum*, *i.* eble, i. walwurt. *a* **1400–50** *Stockh. Med. MS.* 185 Lesse walwourt (*ebullus minor*). *Ibid.* i. 304 in *Anglia* XVIII. 302 Take..jws of walwort & of morele. *Ibid.* 321, 303 Take walwort-rotys, styf & starke. *c* **1425** tr. *Arderne's Treat. Fistula* etc. (1910) 31 þer is a naturel vertu in walwort þat moste wele restreyneþ blode of woundes. *c* **1450** *Alphita* (Anecd. Oxon.) 51/2 *Ebulus uel Ebula*, gall. eble, angl. welleuort. *a* **1491** J. ROUS *Hist. Reg. Angl.* (1716) 104 Videre etiam possumus..in villagiis juxta Warwicum, ubi circa maneria populi erant trucidati [by the Danes in 1016], ex sanguine hominum ibi interfectorum herbam ebuli, id est, Walwort, habundanter crescere, quæ ex ebullitione sanguinis humani naturaliter originem trahit. **1541** *Bk. Properties Herbs* C vij, Ebulus minor. Thys is the less Wolworte. It is somewhat like to Walworte. **1650** [W. HOWE] *Phytol. Brit.* 35 Ebulus Chamæacte, sive Sambucus humilis, in agris & cœmeteriis. Wallwort, Dwarfe Elder, or Daneweed. **1778** G. WHITE *Selborne, To Barrington* 3 July, *Sambucus ebulus*, dwarf elder, walwort, or dane-wort.
¶ **2.** *Erroneous uses.* Through misunderstanding of the first element (as if WALL *sb.*[1]) the name has been applied in Herbals, Dictionaries, etc. to the Pellitory of the Wall, and other plants growing on walls. As the word PELLITORY has a double origin, partly repr. L. *parietāria* (f. *pariēs* wall) and partly repr. L. *pyrethrum*, the mistaken identification of *wallwort* with the Pellitory of the Wall led to the further error of applying the name to the Pellitory of Spain (*Anacletus Pyrethrum*). The application of the name to the Comfrey (*Symphyton*) in quot. 1567 is due to confusion with G. *wallwurz* (said to be from *wallen* to heal wounds), whence Du. *waalwortel*, Sw. *vallört*, *wallgras*.
1561 HOLLYBUSH *Hom. Apoth.* 43 Let hym take the roote of Piretrum, that is Walworte in hys mouth, and chawe it. **1567** MAPLET *Gr. Forest* 63 Walwort the Greekes cal Symphyton..It helpeth and putteth away bloud spitting. **1857** ANNE PRATT *Flower Pl.* V. 33 Common Pellitory..The herb was formerly called Wall-wort.

†'**wally,** *a.*[1] *Sc. Obs.* In 6 wallie. [f. WALL *sb.*[2] + -Y.] Of the sea: Tempestuous.
1501 DOUGLAS *Pal. Hon.* II. xxxv, Throw countreis seir, hottis and roches hie, Ouir vailis, planis, woddis, wallie sey. **1721** RAMSAY *Poet's Wish* ii, Wha to the Indian plain Successfu' ploughs the wally sea.

wally, waly ('wɔːlɪ), *a.*[2], *adv.*, and *sb.*[1] *Sc.* Also walie, wallie, waulie, wawlie. [Of obscure origin.] **A.** *adj.* Used as an indefinite term of admiration: Handsome, fine; large, ample.
If quot. 1637–50 is correctly placed here the use is ironical.
1500–20 DUNBAR *Poems* lxxv. 45 Quod he..My kyd..My tendir gyrle, my wallie gowdye. **1637–50** ROW *Hist. Kirk* (Wodrow Soc.) 431 In the beginning of March 1618, he said to his wife, 'Spouse, this wallie March will make an end of all thir things:' and so it was, for he deceased March 31. **1722** RAMSAY *Three Bonnets* i. 83 She was a winsome Wench and waly, And cou'd put on her Claiths fu' brawly. **1739** ALEX. NICOL *Nature without Art* 22 Ilk merry Look and wally Taste Gies Health unto the gamesome Jest. **1786** BURNS *To a Haggis* vii, Clap in his walie nieve a blade, He'll mak it whissle. **1791** —— *Tam o' Shanter* 164 [echoes quot. 1722]. **1839** *Whistle-binkie* Ser. II. 50 Auld Souter Rabby, that dresses sae brawly; Auld Barber Watty, sae smirky an' waly. **1896** LUMSDEN *Poems* 142 Our Wee Toun's wally offspring.
†**b.** *Comb.* **walliman** (*Orkney*): see quot.
1629 *Orkney Witch Trial* in *County Folk-Lore* (1903) III. 103 The devill appeirit to you, Quhom ye called Walliman, claid in quhyt cloathis with ane quhyt head [etc.].
B. *adv.* Finely. †With impersonal vb. used optatively, ***wally fall***, fair fall, good luck to.
1535 LYNDESAY *Satyre* 2434 Iohne to the King. Gude day, gud day! Grit God saif baith ȝour graces! Wallie, wallie fall they twa weill-fairde faces! **1847** H. S. RIDDELL *Poems* 193 For a' gangs wally wi' them, Wha thus live in their native land, Wi' them that's dearest to them.
C. *sb.* 'A toy, a gewgaw' (Jam.).
1722 RAMSAY *Twa Cut-purses* 4 Baith Lads and Lasses busked brawly, To glowr at ilka Bonny-waly. **1728** —— *Poems* II. 404 Gloss., *Bonywalys*, Toys, Gu-gaws. *a* **1774** FERGUSSON *Hallowfair* 29 Here chapman billies tak their stand, An' shaw their bonny wallies [*rhyme* fallows]. **1811** A. SCOTT *Poems* 96 What bonny lassies flock to Boswell's fair, To see their joes, an' shaw their wallies there! **1816** SCOTT *Antiq.* xxix, Glenallan House, wi' a' the pictures and black velvet and silver bonny-wawlies belanging to it. **1821** —— *Pirate* xviii, Bonny-wallies baith of silver and gowd.

wally ('wɒlɪ), *sb.*[2] (and *a.*[3]) *slang.* Also Wally. [Origin uncertain: perh. the same word as WOLLY. Said by some to be the dim. of the personal name *Walter*: cf. CHARLEY, CHARLIE 6. Cf. also WALLYDRAG, WALLYDRAIGLE.] An unfashionable person; one who is foolish, inept, or ineffectual. Also as a mild term of abuse. Also *attrib.* or as *adj.*
1969 *Daily Mirror* 10 Oct. 19/1 *Wally*, out of fashion. **1974** *Times* 8 Aug. 2/4 The successors to the flat-earthers..are at present encamped on the perimeter of the great concentric stone circles... They choose to be known as the Wallies of Wessex, Wally being a conveniently anonymous umbrella for vulnerable individuals. **1976** *Telegraph* (Brisbane) 8 Oct. 10/4 The Arnolds call anybody who wears conventional clothes, such as jeans or skirts, a Wally. **1979** *Listener* 20 & 27 Dec. 861/1 Cuban heel boots..are..like a Wally uniform... John Travolta, the Bee-Gees and Boney M are considered Wally acts. **1983** *Evening Star* (Ipswich) 20 June 7/1 He shrugged off Ms. Ford's throw as temperamental but I bet he felt a right wally. **1983** P. INCHBALD *Short Break in Venice* xviii. 177 Keith cracked a joke over the radio and got called a bleeding wally. **1984** *Daily Tel.* 14 June 1/4 'They looked a right load of wallies,' said an eye-witness. **1985** M. STOTT *Before I Go* iv. 77, I shall seem more of a 'wally' to them than ever because I don't know half the leading telly presenters.

wally, var. WALY *int.*

'**wallydrag,** '**wally'draigle.** *Sc.* Also wal(l)idrag, -draggle, -dragle, -tragle, warydraggel, -draggle, etc. (see *Eng. Dial. Dict.*). [Cf. DRAG, DRAGGLE *vbs.*]
1. 'A feeble, ill-grown person or animal; a worthless, slovenly person, esp. a woman' (*Eng. Dial. Dict.*).
1508 KENNEDY *Flyting w. Dunbar* 43 Waik walidrag, and werlot of the cairtis. **1500–20** DUNBAR *Poems* xxvi. 97 Full mony a waistless wallydrag, With wamiss vnweildable, did furth wag, In creische that did incress. *a* **1508** —— *Tua Mariit Wemen* 89, I haue ane wallidrag, ane worme, ane auld wobat carle. **1817** SCOTT *Rob Roy* xxxiv, That canna be said o' king's soldiers, if they let themselves be beaten wi' a wheen auld carles that are past fighting,..and wives wi' their rocks and distaffs, the very wally-draigles o' the country-side. **1818** —— *Hrt. Midl.* xviii, We think mair about the warst wally-draigle in our ain byre, than about the blessing which the angel of the covenant gave to the Patriarch. **1871** W. ALEXANDER *Johnny Gibb* (1873) 142 Yon bit pernicketty wallydraggle! He'll dee some service, or than no.
2. (See quot. 1808.)
1808 JAMIESON, *Wallidrag*... It appears primarily to signify the youngest of a family, who is often the feeblest. It is sometimes used to denote the youngest bird in a nest. **1826** GALT *Last of Lairds* xxxvii, It's just like a cuckoo dabbing a wallydraigle out o' the nest.

wally-dye, Sc. form of WELLADAY.

wallyt, obs. form of WALLET.

wally-wae, Sc. form of WELLAWAY.

†**walm,** *sb.*[1] *Obs.* Forms: *α.* 1 wælm, 2– walm, 6 (? qualme), wawlme, wawme, whalme, 6–7 walme, waulm(e, waume, 8 waum. *β.* 1 welm, (wi(e)lm, wylm), 4 welm(e. [OE. *wælm* (*wielm*, etc.; also in *ǽ-wielm* spring), str. masc. a gushing, swirling of (boiling) liquids; boiling; heat, etc. = mod. WFris. *wâlm*(*e* smoke, vapour, mod.Flem. (dial.) *walm*, *wolm*, wave bubble, a gushing, etc., Du. *walm*, LG. *walm* smoke, OHG., MHG. *walm*, str. masc. heat, passion, G. (dial.) *walm* ebullition, boiling, whirlpool, MDan. *valm*, *volm* heat:—OTeut. **walmi-z*, a derivative of **wel-* (cf. ON. *olmr* raging:—**walmo-*, *ylja* to warm:—**wuljan*, *ylr* warmth, affection:—**wuli-z*, Goth. *wulan* to be fervent), the radical sense of which is doubtful.
In the sequence of senses here adopted it is assumed that the notion of surging motion was the original, from which, through the idea of boiling, was developed the idea of heat. In this case **wel-* is perh. related to Pre-Teut. **wel*(*ŭ*) to roll, see WALLOW, etc. It is possible that two originally distinct radical elements became confused in Teut. See WALL *v.*[1], to which this word serves as a noun of action.]
1. a. (In OE. only.) Surging or heaving movement (of waves). Chiefly in phrases like *wæteres*, *ýða wielm*, often used poet, for 'sea' or 'waves'. Hence **b.** A wave, billow.
c **900** *Bæda's Hist.* III. xv. (1890) 200 Ðestilde seo sæ fram ðam wylme. *a* **1000** *Andreas* 452 He yðum stilde, wæteres wælmum. *c* **1325** *Songs on Learning Music* in *Rel. Ant.* I. 292 Me is wo so is þe be þat belles in þe walmes. **1558** PHAER *Æneid* VIII. (1562) Aa ij, Ye liuelong night did Tiber flood his streames down couch & calme..yᵗ nether mouing made of waue nor walme. **1581** STUDLEY *Seneca's Hercules Œtæus* II. 195 b, I smoothed haue the wrastling waues, and layde downe euery walme. **1592** WYRLEY *Armorie, Ld. Chandos* 84 The wanton Dolphin dallieth on ech walme.
2. A gushing forth, or upwelling of water; a spring, fountain, water-source; the water of such.
Beowulf 2546 Wæs ðære burnan wælm heaðofyrum hat. *a* **897** ÆLFRED *Gregory's Past. C.* (1871) 373 He drincð of ðæm wielme his agnes pyttes. *c* **1175** *Lamb. Hom.* 141 þe stan to-chan and fouwer walmes of watere sprungen ut þer of. **13..** *Guy Warw.* 3592 Al to-hewe was his helme, þe blod ran out als a welme. **1387** TREVISA *Higden* (Rolls) I. 429 In þe welmes ofter þan ones Is y-founde reed splekked stones; In tokene of [þe] blood reed, þat þe mayde Wynefrede Schadde at þat putte.
3. a. The bubbling and heaving of water, etc. in process of boiling (melting, etc.). Also, one such motion; a 'wallop', a bubble.
a **1000** CYNEWULF *Juliana* 583 In ðæs leades wylm scufan. *c* **1425** *Seven Sages* (P.) 2363 Thys sevene walmes sygnyfye Seven devels in thy Companye, That ben thy seven clerkys. *a* **1450** LOVELICH *Grail* lvi. 397 That water that Cold was before, Anon brenneng hot it be-Cam thore, and with grete walmes it boyllede so faste, that the dewkes hondis it brende.

1594 T. B. *La Primaud. Fr. Acad.* II. lix. 333 Euen as fire causeth water to swell and to send forth great waumes. *a* **1648** DIGBY *Closet Opened* (1677) 28 Let it have a little walm of heat after it. **1688** HOLME *Armoury* III. 85/2 Walm, a little seething or boiling up of Liquor in a Pot.

b. In advb. phrase, (*to be, set*) *a walm*: in a boiling condition. Also used *fig.*

1609 J. DAVIES (Heref.) *Humours Heav.* (Grosart) 46/2 He was a walme, he could not stay impeaching, Who smoakt with heat; and chokt all with the smother. *c* **1612** —— *Wits Pilgr.* (Grosart) 28 The Seas vnfit to saile on, if too calme: As it is when it is too turbulent: Then, the meane motion sets it so a walme As doth the Sailors Eare, and Eye content.

c. A spell of boiling: = WALLOP *sb.* 2 b.

1558 WARDE tr. *Alexis' Secr.* (1568) 63 b, Let them boile at eche time but onelye one wawme. **1575** TURBERV. *Venerie* lxxix. 230 Let them boyle two or three whalmes vpon the fire. *Ibid.*, Let them boyle therein, a whalme or a wallop in a pewter pot. **1579** LANGHAM *Gard. Health* 15 Put in good store of Sugar, & seethe it a walme or two. **1599** A. M. tr. *Gabelhouer's Bk. Physicke* 4/1 Let it seeth on the fyer one qualme or two. **1601** HOLLAND *Pliny* XXIII. ii. II. 157 These togither in a kettle they did set to boile, and let them have ten walms over the fire. **1653** T. BRUGIS *Vade Mecum* (ed. 2) 170 Boyle them a walm or two. **1675** HANNAH WOOLLEY *Gentlew. Comp.* 145 Stir them together, and give them a walm. *a* **1691** BOYLE *Medicin. Exp.* vii. (1693) 62 Stop the Bottle, and keep it in boiling Water, till the Water has made three or four walms. *c* **1720** W. GIBSON *Farrier's Dispens.* x. (1734) 245 Boil..in fiue Pints of Whey made of Cow's Milk, and after two or three brisk Waums, remove..from the fire. **1728** E. SMITH *Compl. Housew.* (1750) 88 Put them in the pot when the water boils, and let them have four or five walms.

4. *Salt-making.* 'A certain measure of salt after boiling' (Leigh *Chesh. Gloss.*, 1877); in quots. a vessel of some kind holding this quantity.

The identity of the word, and the correctness of Leigh's interpretation, are somewhat doubtful.

1634 BRERETON *Trav.* (Chetham Soc.) 16 The salt made is not disposed into sacks, walms, or any other measures, but lieth in huge great heaps. **1693** *Act 5 Will. & Mary* c. 7 §23 Salt made..in the County Palatine of Chester when taken from the Pans is put into Walms Baskettes or Vessells.

5. Comb.: *walm-hot* adj. blazing-hot, boiling-hot. (Cf. *walming hot.*)

a **1000** *Cædmon's Gen.* 2584 Him breȝo engla wylmhatne liȝ to wræce sende. *a* **1225** *Juliana* 68 He het fecchen a ueat and wið pich fullen, and wallen hit walmhat.

†**walm**, *sb.*² Var. of QUALM *sb.*¹, killing, execution.

c **1205** LAY. 22124 And wulc mon swa wurs dude þene þe king hafde iboden he wolde hine ifusen to ane bare walme, and ȝit hit weore læð mon he sculde hongie for þon.

†**walm**, *v. Obs.* Forms: *α.* 4–7 **walm(e**, 6 ?**qualm**, 7 **waulm**. *β.* 4 **welm-**, 7 **welm**, **whelm**. [f. WALM *sb.*¹, possibly repr. an unrecorded OE. derivative **wælman* (**wielman*, etc.). Cf. mod.Flem. (dial.) *walmen* to boil, bubble, Du. *walmen* to smoke, G. (dial.) *walmen* to boil, *welmen* to undulate, well up, flame up.

This verb appears to have become confused (*esp.* in the *β* forms) with WHELM *v.* (*q.v.*). The relationship of WAMBLE *v.* is obscure but may depend upon a transposition of the *l*. Cf. *wamble, whammel, whemmel* etc. = WHELM *v.*]

1. *intr.* **a.** Of water: To well up, gush or spout forth. Usually const. advs. *forth, out, up*, etc.

a **1300** *Floriz & Bl.* (Hausknecht) 719 [Þe wal] He welmeþ up so he were wod And chaungeþ fram water in to blod. ?*a* **1366** CHAUCER *Rom. Rose* 1561 The water is evere fresh & newe, That welmeth up with wawis bright. **1398** TREVISA *Barth. De P.R.* II. viii. (1495) b v, As a thynge yᵗ boyllyth by strengthe welmyth & lepyth, and throwyth & shedyth itself all abowte. **1582** BATMAN *Barth. De P.R.* XIII. i. 190 Other waters spring and walme out of the inner parts of the earth, as well water and pit water. **1606** HOLLAND *Suetonius* 75 He lay with his bed chamber dores open, and oftentimes within a cloisture supported with pillers, hauing water walming out of a spring, or running from a spout in a conduit. **1610** —— *Camden's Brit.* (1637) 505 A place..out of which there walme Springs in great plenty. *c* **1630** RISDON *Surv. Devon* (1714) II. 83 Here is a Pond..maintained by Springs, which continually welm and boil up. *Ibid.* 340 But of certain Pits, in the Moors of this Parish, brackish Water whelmeth forth. **1681** CHETHAM *Angler's Vade-m.* x. (1689) 100 On the very top of Cadier Arthur Hill in Brecknockshire, there walmeth forth a spring of water.

b. *fig.* To abound; be plentiful.

1399 LANGL. *Rich. Redeles* III. 114 Þe wikkid werchinge þat walmed in her daies, And ȝit woll here-after.

c. Of smoke, vapour, etc.: To swirl, billow; to issue forth in such a manner. *rare.*

1601 HOLLAND *Pliny* II. xliii. I. 21 A smokie fume walmeth up with many turnings like waves. **1609** —— *Amm. Marcell.* XVII. i. 80 They saw afarre off a mightie deale of smoke waulming up into the aire. **1908** HARDY *Dynasts* III. III. iii. 387 Throats shout 'advance' And forms walm, wallow, and slack suddenly.

2. To swell, bubble, as in boiling; to boil.

[**1599**: see QUALM *v.*²] **1610** HOLLAND *Camden's Brit.* (1637) 235 The waters boile, and walme to our desire.

Hence '**walming** *vbl. sb.*¹ '**walming** *ppl. a.*, glowing, seething; also in phr. *walming hot.*

c **1530** *Judic. Urines* II. ii. 12 By reason of rollyng and walmyng of the blode about in the veynes of yᵉ body. **1601** HOLLAND *Pliny* II. ciii. I. 46 At the very foot of Ætna..for ..an hundred miles, the waulming round bals and flakes of fire cast out sand and ashes. **1610** —— *Camden's Brit.* I. 681 The Stuples did send away a waulming hote vapor.

†'**walming**, *vbl. sb.*² *Obs.* [Perh. merely a variant of *wamlyng* (see WAMBLE *v.*), which also occurs in the Promp. Parv. Cf. QUALM *sb.*³] Turning (of the stomach), nausea.

c **1440** *Promp. Parv.* 514/2 Walmynge, of the stomake ..*nausea.*

walnut¹ ('wɔːlnʌt). Forms: 1 **walhhnutu**, 4–6 **walnotte**, 5 **wallnott**, 5, 6 **walnutt(e**, 6–8 **wall-nutt**, 7 **walenotte**, 7–8 **wallnut**, 6– **walnut**. See also WALSH-NUT. [OE. *walhhnutu* str. fem. = WFris. *walnút* (NFris. *walnödd* from Da.), MDu. *walnote* (Kilian *walnot*), Du. *walnoot*, MLG. *wallnot*, *-nut*, LG. (Bremisch. Wörterb. *wallnutt*) *walnut*, G. *walnuss* (earlier *wallnuss*), ON. *valhnot* str. fem. (Norw. *valnot*, Sw. *valnöt*, Da. *valnød*). The first element is OTeut. **walχo-z* (OE. *wealh*, OHG. *walah*) 'Welshman', i.e. Celtic or Roman foreigner; see WELSH *a.*

The solitary OE. example (in a glossary *c* 1050) is the earliest known appearance of the word in any language. The word must, however, have come to England from the Continent, but there is no evidence to show whether it belonged to the primitive OE. vocabulary, or was introduced at a relatively late date. It seems to have belonged originally to the LG.-speaking district; etymologically it meant the nut of the Roman lands (Gaul and Italy) as distinguished from the native hazel. It is noteworthy that in the languages of these countries the word descending from L. *nux*, when used without qualification, denotes the walnut. In HG. the word appears first in the 16th c. (adapted from LG.); but MHG. had the equivalent *wälhisch nuz* (mod.G. dial. *wälsche nuss, wälschnuss*): see WALSH-NUT.

The ONF. *noix gauge, gaugue*, walnut (which survives in mod. Picard and Norman dialects) app. represents a popular L. **nux gallica*, a translation of the Teut. word.]

1. a. The nut of the common walnut-tree, *Juglans regia*, consisting of a two-lobed seed (the edible kernel) enclosed in a spheroidal shell covered with a green fleshy husk.

The seed of the mature fruit is eaten like any other nut, and the soft unripe fruit is used entire for pickling.

French walnut: the nut (much larger than the ordinary kind) of a variety of the common walnut tree, *Juglans regia maxima*.

c **1050** *Voc.* in Wr.-Wülcker 452/34 *Nux*, hnutbeam oððe walhhnutu. **1358–9** *Durham Acc. Rolls* (Surtees) 124 Et ij M. de walnottes, prec. millene 15*d.* **1377** LANGL. *P. Pl.* B. XI. 251 As on a walnot with-oute is a bitter barke, And after þat bitter barke..Is a kirnelle of conforte kynde to restore. *c* **1430** *Two Cookery-bks.* 109 (Ashm. MS.) Take curnylles of walnotys. **1580** BLUNDEVIL *Curing Horses Dis.* xcix. 46 Me thinkes that the quantitie of a Walnut were too little for so much wine. **1598** SHAKS. *Merry W.* IV. ii. 171 Let them say of me, as iealous as Ford, that search'd a hollow Wall-nut for his wiues Lemman. **1639** T. DE GREY *Compl. Horsem.* 276 Make it up into pils somewhat bigger than a French Walnut. **1661** J. CHILDREY *Brit. Baconica* 6 Their quantity if from a Pease to a Wall-nut. **1712** STEELE *Spect.* No. 498 ¶3, I was diverting my self with a pennyworth of Walnuts. **1769** MRS. RAFFALD *Engl. Housekpr.* (1778) 223 To preserve Walnuts white. Take the large French walnuts full grown, but not shelled, pare them till you see the white appear, [etc.]. **1870** YEATS *Nat. Hist. Comm.* 187 Walnuts will not bear a long voyage without being kiln-dried.

b. Often referred to as eaten with wine after dinner.

1824 PYNE (*title*), Wine and Walnuts. **1833** TENNYSON *Miller's Dau.* 32 In after-dinner talk Across the walnuts and the wine.

c. Used for *walnut-juice.*

1709 PRIOR *Henry & Emma* 501 Black Soot, or yellow Walnut shall disgrace This little Red and White of Emma's Face.

d. *oil of walnuts*: the essential oil expressed from the kernels of walnuts.

1634 PEACHAM *Compl. Gentl.* xiii. (1906) 130 Then use the oyle of Walnuts. **1800** tr. *Lagrange's Chem.* II. 227 Olive-oil, oil of wallnuts, oil of colsa..are all used in the arts for making soap.

¶**e.** Applied to the cow-nut.

1553 EDEN *New India, 1st Three Bks. on Amer.* (Arb.) 19 This tree..beareth a kynde of walnuttes [L. *iuglandes*] most delicate to be eaten.

2. a. The nut-bearing tree *Juglans regia* (N.O. *Juglandaceæ*). Also applied to other species of *Juglans* and related genera: see 2 b. In the U.S. the word often denotes the Hickory (*Carya*).

1600 FAIRFAX *Tasso* III. lxxvi, The broad-leau'd Sicamore, The barraine Platane, and the Wall-nut sound. **1600** J. PORY tr. *Leo's Africa* IV. 228 Vpon this mountaine are many springs, and woods abounding with walnuts. *a* **1700** EVELYN *Diary* 12 Oct. 1677, Innumerable are the plantations of trees, especially wallnuts. **1869** TOZER *Highl. Turkey* I. 266 There are but few trees, only a few poplars, and a walnut or two.

b. With defining adj. **common walnut** (in British use), *Juglans regia*, called in the *U.S.* **English walnut**. **black walnut**, the American species, *Juglans nigra*; **grey** or **white walnut**, the Butternut of the U.S., *Juglans cinerea*.

1612 R. JOHNSON *New Life Virginea* sig. B3, They cut downe wood for wanscot, blacke walnut tree, Spruce, Cedar & Deale. **1714** J. LAWSON *Hist. Carolina* 99 The Walnut Tree of America is call'd Black Walnut. **1743** J. CLAYTON *Flora Virginica* 190 *Juglans alba*..White Walnuts. **1754** CATESBY *Nat. Hist. Carolina* etc. I. 67 The Black Walnut. Most parts of the Northern Continent of America, abound with these Trees, particularly Virginia and Maryland. **1760** J. LEE *Introd. Bot.* App. 331 Walnut, Jamaica, *Hura*. **1772** C. CARROLL *Let.* 9 June in *Maryland Hist. Mag.* (1919) XIV. 149 It froze Here last Thursday night.., it bit the Leaves of the English Walnut tree. **1785** MARTYN *Lett. Bot.* xxviii. (1794) 439 Common Walnut is distinguished by having the component leaves oval, smooth, sometimes a little toothed, and almost equal. **1822** White walnut [see *creek-bottom* s.v. CREEK *sb.*¹ 8]. **1857** A. GRAY *First Less. Bot.* (1866) 153 Heart-wood..is generally of a different color,..brown in Black-Walnut, black in Ebony, etc. **1864** GRISEBACH *Flora W. Ind. Isl.* 788 Walnut, Jamaica, *Picrodendron Juglans*. Walnut, Otaheite, *Aleurites triloba*. **1876** 'MARK TWAIN' *Tom Sawyer* xvi. 134 Perfectly round white things a trifle smaller than an English walnut. **1882** *Garden* 7 Jan. 1/2 Besides these there are already fruiting..English Walnuts, Persian Walnuts (Kaghazi), Almonds, American Black Walnuts, &c. *Ibid.* 16 Sept. 251/1 The Grey Walnut or Butternut..is smaller in growth and more spreading in habit [than the Black Walnut]. **1912** White walnut [see OIL-NUT b, c].

3. a. The wood of the walnut-tree.

a **1585** in *Eng. Hist. Rev.* (1914) XXIX. 517 The comodities thence ar..Boordes of chestnuttes and walnuttes. **1624** CAPT. J. SMITH *Virginia* II. 25 The wood that is most common is Oke and Walnut. **1853** DICKENS *Bleak Ho.* xviii, How pleasant then, to be bound to no particular chairs and tables, but..to flit from rosewood to mahogany, and from mahogany to walnut,..as the humour took one. **1868** *Rep. U.S. Commissioner Agric.* (1869) 15 The museum has been partly filled with absolutely dust-proof cases of solid walnut shaped in the best style of the art. **1892** *Joseph Gardner & Sons' Monthly Circular* 1 Oct., Walnut —American.—Imports: 394 Logs into Liverpool. *Ibid.*, Walnut—Circassian—No Imports.

†**b.** As material for gun-stocks. Hence colloq. *to shoulder walnut*: to enlist as a soldier. *Obs.*

1838 D. JERROLD *Men of Character* (1851) 10, 'I tell ye, Cuttles, it's no use. I'll shoulder walnut first.' 'Walnut!' 'Ay, go for a soldier.'

4. *attrib.* and *Comb.* **a.** obvious combinations, as (sense 1) ***walnut-cake***, ***-kernel***, ***-ketchup***, ***-oil***, ***-peel***, ***-trade***, ***-wine***; ***walnut-stained*** adj.; (sense 2) ***walnut avenue***, ***garden***, ***leaf***, ***-wood***; (sense 3, quasi-adj. 'made of walnut') ***walnut bed***, ***sideboard***; ***walnut-framed***, ***-panelled*** adjs. **b.** special comb.: **walnut-brown**, the brown colour produced by the application of walnut-juice to the skin; **walnut-juice**, the juice expressed from the green husk of the walnut; used by gipsies as a brown stain for the skin; † **walnut-water** (see quot.).

1898 MISS YONGE *Keble's Parishes* iii. 44 There were two *walnut avenues planted about this time. **1840** THACKERAY *Catherine* xi, This amiable pair were lying in a large *walnut bed. **1865** KINGSLEY *Herew.* xxx, If William's French grooms got hold of you, Torfrida, it would not be a little *walnut-brown which would hide you. **1889** H. A. DE SALIS *Cakes & Confections* 28 *Walnut Cake. Rub four ounces of peeled walnuts..with the whites of three eggs, [etc.]. **1936** *New Yorker* 29 Feb. 21/1 His favourite *Linzertorte*, a walnut cake. **1977** F. PARRISH *Fire in Barley* iv. 39 Some ginger biscuits and a slice of walnut cake. **1908** S. E. WHITE *Riverman* xiv, The *walnut-framed photograph. **1873** KINGSBURY *Comm. Song of Sol., Speaker's Comm.* IV. 671/2 She relates to the chorus how in early spring she had first met the King in a *walnut-garden in her own country. **1912** E. THOMAS *Geo. Borrow* v. 44 They colour his face with *walnut juice so that he looks a 'true son of an Egyptian'. **1908** [MISS E. FOWLER] *Betw. Trent & Ancholme* 9 A string of *walnut kernels. **1796** MRS. RAFFALD *Engl. Housekpr.* (1778) 32 One meat spoonful of *walnut catchup. **1855** DELAMER *Kitchen Gard.* (1861) 166 Walnut ketchup, is obtained from the outer husk of the ripe fruit. **1728** CHAMBERS *Cycl.* s.v. *Ulcer*, A Decoction of *Walnut Leaves in Water, with a little Sugar. **1842** LOUDON *Suburban Hort.* 629 Slugs and earth-worms may be effectually destroyed by ..a decoction of..walnut leaves. **1612** W. STRACHEY *Trav. Virginia* (1953) I. v. 73 A lock of an ell long, which they annoynt often with *walnut oyle. **1649** W. BULLOCK *Virginia* 12 Pot-ashes, Rape, and Walnut Oyle, and other Staples. **1963** *Times* 9 Feb. 11/3 The vegetables are luscious and the salads delicately dressed with walnut oil. **1984** M. BABSON *Death Swap* xii. 90 A large tin of truffles..and the inevitable walnut oil. **1934** WEBSTER, *Walnut-paneled. **1961** M. BEADLE *These Ruins are Inhabited* (1963) ii. 24 We ducked through a narrow passageway and into the chapel, a walnut-panelled room. **1981** P. NIESEWAND *Word of Gentleman* xxv. 162 Macgregor's office was walnut-panelled. **1815** J. SMITH *Panorama Sci. & Art* II. 543 *Walnut-peels managed as for wool, form a cheap and durable brown for silk. **1833** *Veget. Subs. Materials of Manuf.* xxiii. 404 Fawn colours. Sumach—Walnut-peels—Henna. **1862** *Catal. Internat. Exhib., Brit.* II. No. 5731, A *walnut sideboard, Renaissance style. **1906** T. WATTS-DUNTON *Thoreau's Walden* Introd. p. xi, One of those masquerading 'children of the Tent'..who think it fine to play the Man of the Woods, in order that they may..write books with *walnut-stained fingers. **1712** STEELE *Spect.* No. 509 ¶3, I must repeat the Abomination, that the *Walnut Trade is carry'd on by old Women within the Walks. **1747** MRS. GLASSE *Cookery* xx. 158 To distill *Walnut-water. Take a Peck of fine green Walnuts, bruise them well.., put two Quarts of good French Brandy to them, [etc.]. **1769** MRS. RAFFALD *Engl. Housekpr.* (1778) 325 To make *Walnut Wine. **1865** DICKENS *Mut. Fr.* I. vi, An old corner cupboard of *walnut-wood.

walnut². *Naut.* Corrupt form of WALL-KNOT, associated with WALNUT¹ 1. Also ***walnut-knot***.

1769 FALCONER *Dict. Marine* (1780) s.v. *Knot*, There are several sorts of knots..: the principal of these are the diamond-knot, the rose-knot, the wall-knot or walnut. **1794** *Rigging & Seamanship* I. 213 A double-walnut-knot,.. called a button-and-loop.

'**walnut-shell.**

1. The hard shell enclosing the seed of the walnut; also, either of the boat-shaped halves of this.

[*c* **1384**: see WALSH-NUT.] **1523–34** FITZHERB. *Husb.* §93 There wyll ryse pymples as moche as halfe a walnutshell.

1596 Shaks. *Tam. Shr.* IV. iii. 66 Heere is the cap your Worship did bespeake... Why 'tis a cockle or a walnut-shell. **1647** Stapylton *Juvenal* 30 Spiders..at this day are worne in baggs or walnut-shells against a tertian ague. **1842** Dickens *Amer. Notes* ii, In the gale of last night the life-boat had been crushed by one blow of the sea like a walnut-shell. **1885** Sir W. Harcourt in S. Gwynn *Life Dilke* (1917) II. 187, I therefore spoke like a cat in walnut shells.

†**b.** Applied to the outer husk of the walnut.

1552 Huloet, Walnut shele, *gulioca.* **1769** *Ann. Reg.* 128 They were a gang of gypsies..rubbing or dyeing a fine young girl, about seventeen, with walnut-shell.

c. In phrases implying extreme calmness of the sea. (Cf. 2.)

1791 Smeaton *Edystone L.* §6 The sea breaks upon them [*sc.* the Edystone rocks] in a frightful manner..when, figuratively speaking, you might go to sea in a Walnut-shell.

2. *transf.* Applied to a boat, as a hyperbolical expression for extreme lightness and fragility. (†In the 17th c. app. used as the actual name of some fragile kind of boat.)

1614 Gentleman *Eng. Way to Wealth* 27 The Fleet of Hollanders..that go in the Swoard-pinks,..Walnut-shels, and great and small Yeuers, 100. and 200. Saile at one time together. **1836** E. Howard *R. Reefer* xxxiv, Our little walnut-shell got on the top of one [wave]. **1903** E. Childers *Riddle of Sands* xii. 125 Davies nursed our walnut-shell tenderly over their crests.

3. *slang.* A very light carriage.

1810 *Sporting Mag.* XXXVI. 232 Drawing a walnut-shell over a level road.

4. *attrib.*

1460–70 *Bk. Quinte Essence* 20 Of þis watir ȝeue to þe pacient, morowe and euen, a walnot-schelle ful at oonys. **1793–4** [Aikin & Mrs. Barbauld] *Even. at Home* (1805) II. 36 The pond where I used to sail my walnut-shell boats.

'walnut-tree.

1. The tree that bears walnuts.

a **1400** *Nominale* (Skeat) 657 *Tremuler nuger et grosiler*, Aspe walnotetre and theuthorne. **1483** *Cath. Angl.* 407/1 Walnott tree, *auellanus.* **1579** Spenser *Sheph. Cal.* Dec. 34 How haue I wearied with many a stroke, The stately Walnut tree, the while the rest Vnder the tree fell all for nuts at strife. **1697** Dampier *Voy.* I. xiv. 392 The Wild Nutmeg-tree is as big as a Walnut-tree; but it does not spread so much. **1774** Goldsm. *Nat. Hist.* (1776) I. 282 Under it is found a soft oozy earth, made up of vegetables; and at twenty-six feet depth, large trees entire, such as walnut-trees. **1890** *Hardwicke's Sci.-Gossip* XXVI. 115 At the last meeting of the Entomological Society, Mr. W. L. Distant exhibited..a branch of a walnut-tree on which was a mass of eggs laid by a butterfly belonging to the Lycænidæ.

Proverb. **1550** Coverdale *Spir. Perle* xii. 102 A walnut tree yᵉ more it is beaten, the better it is, & not the worsse. Euen so man thorow many stripes and much aduersity turneth from il and waxeth good.

b. *attrib.*

1536 *MS. Rawl. D.* 780 lf. 66, xxiiijᵗⁱ loodes of walnottry and hasshen tymbre. *Ibid.* lf. 69b, Wallnottry Tymbre haysshen tymbre and ellym tymbre. **1705** *Lond. Gaz.* No. 4097/4, 10 Dozen of Walnut-Tree Planks. **1738** Chambers *Cycl.* s.v. *Ulcer*, This is no more than a decoction of walnut-tree-leaves in water, with a little sugar. **1800** *Asiatic Ann. Reg.* 74 *note*, The *Salmoni*, or *Salemoeli* tree,..affords a most beautiful wood; it resembles walnut-tree wood in colour. **1886** C. E. Pascoe *Lond. To-day* (ed. 3) 16 The pleasant walnut-tree walks..of his [Addison's] time.

†**2.** The wood of this tree. = walnut¹ 3. *Obs.*

1587 *B.N.C.* (Oxf.) *Docum., Inventory* A². 31 A bedsteed of wallnuttrye, in Ladies' chamber. **1617** Moryson *Itin.* I. 162 The seates of the Chauncell are of Walnut-tree curiously carved. **1756** Mrs. P. L. Powys *Passages fr. Diaries* (1899) 8 The chimney-pieces, tables, &c. are of green marble from Sweden; all the doors solid walnut-tree, off the estate. **1816** Scott *Old Mort.* xl, A grey doublet and cloak..which Mrs. Wilson produced from a chest of walnut-tree.

†**b.** *attrib.* or *adj.* Made of walnut.

1687 *Lond. Gaz.* No. 2231/4 A drawing Walnut-Tree Box, with two Drawers in it,..to put Mathematical Instruments in. **1702** *Ibid.* No. 3806/8 A Large Parcel of French Walnutt-Tree Venears will be exposed to Sale..on Thursday. **1716** *Ibid.* No. 5402/4 A Fowling-Piece with a Walnut-tree Stock. **1725** *Bradley's Family Dict.* s.v. *Candle*, Roll them upon a Wallnut-tree Table. *a* **1841** T. Hook *Ned Musgrave* i, Sitting in a walnut-tree arm-chair. **1907** *Verney Mem.* I. 11 Chairs with walnut-tree frames.

†**walnyed**, *a.* *Obs.* [? var. of wolden-eȝed, wall-eyed.] Of a horse: ? Light grey.

The meaning is obscure as, the colours are not enumerated in the same order in the original and the translation. A note in the MSS. of the translation has *glaucus*, which does not occur here in Palladius.

c **1440** *Pallad. on Husb.* IV. 827 The walnyed is good, also the blake Is fyn colour, the falow and herthued.

Walon, walop: see Walloon, wallop *v.*

walour(e, obs. Sc. forms of valour.

walow, obs. form of value, wallow.

waloway: see wellaway.

walowe yee, obs. f. wall eye.

Walpolian (wɔːl'pəʊlɪən), *a.* and *sb.* Also **-ean.** [f. the name of Robert *Walpole* (1676–1745), politician, and of his son Horace *Walpole* (1717–97), writer and politician + -ian.] **A.** *adj.*

1. Of, pertaining to, or characteristic of Horace Walpole or his writings. Also applied to neo-Gothic architecture of a type popularized by Horace Walpole.

1867 H. E. H. Jerningham *Life in French Château* vi. 165 She had seen through the empty-heartedness and true Walpolian sense of gratitude of those she had befriended. **1876** Hardy *Hand of Ethelberta* II. xl. 146 A tendency to talk Walpolean scandal about foreign courts was particularly manifest. **1944** J. Lees-Milne *Jrnl.* 2 June in *Prophesying Peace* (1977) 71, I was fascinated by the Walpolian Gothic chapel. **1973** *Country Life* 14 June 1726/1 The greatest Walpolian scholar, W. S. Lewis, remarked in 1934 that Strawberry Hill was 'assembled rather than built'.

2. Of, pertaining to, or characteristic of Robert Walpole or his political career.

1909 J. M. Rigg in *Cambr. Mod. Hist.* VI. xiii. 424 He adhered to the Walpolean tradition of an *entente cordiale* with France. **1979** *N. & Q.* Feb. 76/1 His appeal..to 'custom and reason', 'the practice of former times', and 'the original principles of government' could be used equally against American radicals and Walpolian oligarchs. **1983** *Ibid.* Feb. 23/1 More substance still is given to his role as a Walpolean hack.

B. *sb.* An admirer of Horace Walpole.

1927 *Observer* 24 Apr. 6/2 No Walpolian can be satisfied with anything less than the complete Toynbee edition of the Letters.

So **Walpoli'ana, -e'ana** (see ana *suff.*).

1799 (*title*) Walpoliana. **1875** *Encycl. Brit.* I. 785/2 Of the examples England has produced of this species of composition, perhaps the most interesting is the *Walpoliana*, a transcript of the literary conversation of Horace Walpole, Earl of Orford. **1938** *Times Lit. Suppl.* 26 Feb. 136/4 If General Conway's house, grounds, and.. views..are over-praised, they are only the more authentic as Walpoliana. **1959** *Times* 16 May 8/5 There will be many on this side of the Atlantic who will be deeply grieved by the news of the death of Annie Burr, wife of Wilmarth Sheldon ('Lefty') Lewis, the eminent collector and editor of Walpoliana. **1980** *Jrnl. R. Soc. Arts* Feb. 161/2 Dr. Lewis's collector's flair and comfortable means enabled him to build up an unrivalled assemblage of Walpoleana—original Walpole letters and manuscripts, and books from Walpole's own library.

Walpurgis (væl'pɜːgɪs). The name (St. Walpurga or Walburga) of an 8th-c. Anglo-Saxon saint and missionary in Heidenheim, Germany, used: **a.** in **Walpurgis night** [tr. G. *Walpurgisnacht*], in German folklore and esp. Goethe's *Faust* a feast of the powers of darkness or witches' sabbath (cf. Sabbath 3) celebrated on the Brocken, a peak in the Harz mountains, on 30 April. Also *transf.*, an orgiastic celebration or party.

1823 F. L. Gower tr. *Goethe's Faust* 233 Walpurgis Night. The Hartz Mountain. Wild and desolate country. **1900** J. Frazer *Golden Bough* (ed. 2) I. i. 36 The special season for thus promoting the growth of flax..in some places is Candlemas or Walpurgis Night (the eve of May Day). **1933** J. Cary *Amer. Visitor* xvi. 213 A fire which illuminated a kind of Walpurgis night of ragamuffins, soldiers, doxies from the town. **1964** L. Deighton *Funeral in Berlin* xlv. 286, I sank into a vortex of imaginings in which Walpurgis Night and..the smell of petrol..were indissolubly linked. **1980** *Amer. Scholar* Autumn 456 Walpurgis Night on the eve of Mayday is an excuse for bacchanalia.

b. In other *attrib.* uses with reference to this festival.

1857 C. Kingsley *Two Years Ago* III. i. 33 That Walpurgis-dance of the witches and the fiends, which will.. whirl unbidden through a mortal brain. **1899** R. Whiteing *No. 5 John St.* xxix. 300 The Bosses..have come to keep Walpurgis revel. **1979** J. Tate tr. *K. A. Blom's Limits of Pain* xx. 164 The last day of April..he could mix in the crowds,..warming himself by the Walpurgis bonfires.

‖**Walpurgisnacht** (val'pʊrgɪsnaxt). [Ger.] = prec. a. Also *transf.*

1822 Shelley *Let.* 10 Apr. (1964) II. 407, I have only attempted the scenes omitted in this translation, & would send you that of the *Walpurgisnacht.* **1898** W. James *Let.* 9 July (1920) II. 76 The influences of Nature, [etc.]..all fermented within me till it became a regular Walpurgis Nacht. **1909** —— *Pluralistic Universe* i. 21 Nature can have little unity for savages. It is a Walpurgis-nacht procession, a checkered play of light and shadow, a medley of impish and elfish friendly and inimical powers. **1947** *Partisan Rev.* XIV. 102/2 The *Walpurgisnacht* which is Hollywood. **1965** *Guardian* 10 Dec. 6/5, I might still avoid the woods on Walpurgisnacht. **1977** *Time* 3 Jan. 65/2 *Who's Afraid of Virginia Woolf?* An admirable revival..verifies that after 14 years this marital Walpurgisnacht has become part of the permanent canon of U.S. drama.

walpurgite ('vælpəgaɪt). *Min.* [ad. G. *walpurgin* (A. Weisbach 1871, in *Neues Jahrb. f. Mineral.*, etc. 870), f. *Walpurgis*, name of the vein in a mine near Schneeberg in Germany where the first specimen was found: see -ite¹.] A hydrous arsenate of bismuth and uranium found as yellow, translucent or transparent triclinic crystals.

1872 G. J. Brush in J. D. Dana *Syst. Min.* (ed. 5) App. I. 16 Walpurgite. **1958** *Bull. U.S. Geol. Survey* No. 1064. 242 Walpurgite is a secondary mineral, found in the oxidized zone of a vein carrying uraninite, cobalt and nickel arsenides, and native bismuth from which the U, Bi, and As content of the mineral has been derived.

Walras ('vælrɑː). The name of Marie Esprit Léon *Walras* (1834–1910), French economist, used in the possessive in ***Walras' law*** to denote the mathematical theory of general economic equilibrium devised by him. So **Walrasian** (væl'reɪsɪən) *a.*, of or pertaining to this theory.

1942 O. Lange in O. Lange et al. *Stud. Math. Econ.* 50, I propose to call this identity *Walras' law* because Walras was the first to recognize its fundamental importance in the formulation of the mathematical theory of prices. **1942** W. Jaffé in *Ibid.* 37 The affinities..between these older Walrasian theories and their independently discovered Keynesian counterparts. **1963** *Canad. Jrnl. Economics & Pol. Sci.* XXIX. 535 (*heading*) A note on Marshallian *versus* Walrasian stability conditions. **1964** *Q. Jrnl. Econ.* LXXVIII. 485 Walras' Law..states that the value of all goods demanded, including money, is equal to the value of all goods supplied. **1972** T. Sowell *Say's Law* i. 34 *Walras' Law* states that the sum of the respective values (quantities times money prices) of goods supplied plus money supplied equals the sum of the respective values (quantities times money prices) of goods demanded plus money demanded. **1972** *Times* 26 Oct. 8/6 Sir John [Hicks]..moved away from the partial equilibrium approach of Alfred Marshall back towards the older Continental Walrasian 'general equilibrium' approach. **1983** *Economics Lett.* XIII. 49 The possibility of transfer paradoxes in Walrasian stable markets.

walrus ('wɒlrəs). Also 8 **walrous, wallross,** *pl.* **walrosses,** 9 **-russes.** [probably a. Du. *walrus* (*walros*). Compare (i) LG. *walross*, G. *walross* (earlier also *walruss*, *walrusch*), Sw. *hvalross*, *valross* (*valruss*), Da. *hvalros* (earlier also *hvalrusk*), walrus; (ii) OE. *horschwæl*, early mod.G. *rosswal*, *russwal*, Norw. *russhval*, walrus, ? OFr. *rohal*, *rohart*, *rochal* (whence med.L. *rohanlum*, *-allum*) walrus-ivory; see ruel.

The forms under (i) appear to be later than those under (ii) from which they perh. arose (? in Du.) by metathesis on some analogy such as that of Du. *walvisch* whale.

The interpretation of formation (ii) as 'horse-whale' (zoologically improbable) appears to be only one of the various popular etymologies that have influenced the forms of the word. Ultimately a confusion, either within or outside the Scandinavian languages, has perhaps taken place between ON. *hrosshvalr* a kind of whale, and *rosmhvalr* walrus. The latter is related obscurely to ON. *rosmall*, Norw. *rosmaal*, *rosmaar*, Da. *rosmær*, *-er*, *-ar* walrus, whence the scientific specific name *rosmarus.* See rosmarine². Some scholars have connected *rosm-* with ON., Icel. *rostungr* walrus, and assumed relationship of both with ON. *rauðr* red. (Cf. rorqual and OHG. *ros(a)mo* redness.) This is zoologically possible, but it seems more likely that *rosm-* is a corruption of some non-Teut. word: cf. morse.]

1. The sea-horse, or morse (*Trichechus rosmarus*), a carnivorous pinniped marine mammal allied to the *Phocidae* (seals), and *Otariidae* (sea-lions), and chiefly distinguished by two tusks (exserted upper canine teeth). It inhabits the Arctic seas. A variety found in the N. Pacific has sometimes received the distinct specific name *obesus.*

[*c* **893** Ælfred *Oros.* I. i. §15 For þæm horschwælum, for ðæm hie habbað swiþe æþele ban on hiora toþum. **1655** O. Worm *Mus.* III. xv. 289 Animal..quod Anglis & Russis Walrus, aliis Mors, Danis & Islandis Rosmarus vocatur. **1693** Ray *Syn. Anim. Quadr.* etc. 191 Anglis Mors à Russis mutuato nomine. Belgis Walrus... The Morse or Sea-Horse.] **1728** J. Woodward *Catal. Fossils* II. *Foreign* II. 22 A Tusk of the Morse, or Walrous, call'd by some the Sea-Horse. **1752** Hill *Hist. Anim.* 555 The Phoca, with the canine teeth exerted. The Walrus. **1796** Morse *Amer. Geog.* II. 75 The seals, walrosses, and cod, caught in the Russian seas, are likewise very important articles. **1833** Sir C. Bell *Hand* (1834) 109 The bones of the morse or walrus..are remarkably complete, if we consider the peculiar appearance of the feet in the living animal. **1856** Kane *Arctic Expl.* I. xiii. 140 The last remnant of walrus did not leave us until..the temperature had sunk below zero. **1888** *Encycl. Brit.* XXIV. 337/2 The tusks are formidable weapons of defence, but their principal use seems to be digging..for the molluscs and crustaceans on which the walrus feeds.

†**2.** ***Indian walrus***: the dugong. *Obs.*

1771 Pennant *Syn. Quadr.* 338 Indian Walrus.

3. *attrib.* and *Comb.* as ***walrus-beef, -boat, calf, -fishing, -hide, -ivory.*** **walrus moustache**, a large moustache which overhangs the lips (thus resembling the whiskers of a walrus); similarly **walrus whiskers.**

1856 Kane *Arctic Expl.* I. xxviii. 366 Laden with..as much *walrus-beef..as would pay for their board. **1884** *Pall Mall Gaz.* 15 Aug. 6/1 Each *walrus-boat carried six men. **1896** *Cosmopolitan* XX. 356/2 Old Ickwa put his hand on me, at the same time pointing to the *walrus calf, and said 'pee-yuk!' **1820** W. Scoresby *Acc. Arctic Reg.* II. 5 *Walrus-fishing in succeeding years in high northern latitudes. **1862** *Catal. Internat. Exhib., Brit.* II. No. 4638, Patent *walrus-hide belting. **1875** Maskell *Ivories* 2 In quality and beauty of appearance *walrus ivory scarcely yield to that of the elephant. **1918** W. Owen 31 Oct. (1967) 591 An old soldier with a *walrus moustache. **1982** T. Fitzgibbon *With Love* I. xii. 88, I remember Conan Doyle as a large man with sad thoughtful eyes and a walrus moustache. **1930** J. Dos Passos *42nd Parallel* I. 100 A big man with *walrus whiskers.

Wals, Walsch(e, Walse, obs. ff. Welsh.

Walschaerts ('væl-, 'wælʃɜːts, -ʃɑːts). *Mech.* Also **Walschaert.** The name of Egide *Walschaerts* (1820–1901), Belgian mechanic, used *attrib.* and in the possessive to designate a kind of valve-gear he invented that was used on some steam locomotives (see quot. 1911).

1880 *Proc. Inst. Mech. Engineers* 435 His arrangement.. was simply a modification of the Walschaert gear. **1911** *Encycl. Brit.* XXV. 834/1 A form of radial gear very largely used in locomotives, especially on the continent of Europe, is the Walschaert or Heusinger-Waldegg gear, in which the valve receives its motion in part from the piston cross-head .., and in part from a single eccentric set at right angles to the crank. **1975** B. Reed *150 Yrs. Steam Locomotives* vi. 47/1 Other Group three-cylinder classes..had three separate sets of Walschaerts motion with eccentric drive for the inside set.

walse, var. WALTZ *sb.* and *v.*

walsh, *a. Sc.* and *north.* Also 6 **welsche**, 7, 9 **welsh.** [? contracted f. WALLOWISH *a.* Cf. WASH *a.*, WERSH *a.*] Insipid, tasteless, ill-tasting; having a sickly taste, nauseous.

1513 Douglas *Æneis* vi. vii. 79 To pas.. By gousty placis, welsche savorit, mist, and hair. *c* **1687** in C. K. Sharpe *Witchcraft in Scot.* viii. (1884), It was not bloud, but red as bloud,..it had a welsh taste. **1691** Ray *N.C. Words* 78 *Walsh*, insipid, fresh, waterish. **1825** Brockett *N.C. Words, Welsh*, insipid... Broth and water, and pottage without salt, are *wallow* or *welsh*. **1876** *Whitby Gloss., Walsh*, tasteless. 'As walsh as the white of an egg'.

Hence **'walshness**, insipidity.

1808 Jamieson. **1876** *Whitby Gloss., Walshness*, want of flavour; insipidity.

Walsh(e, obs. forms of Welsh.

†**walsh-nut.** *Obs.* In 4 **walsnote, walsh(e)note, welshnote,** 6 **walshe nutte,** 7 **walsh-nut.** [Corresponds to MHG. *wälhisch nuz* (mod.G. dial. *wälsche nuss, wälschnuss*), early mod. Flemish (Kilian 16th c.) *walsche not*, 'Welsh' (i.e. Italian or Gaulish) nut: see WALNUT. The word was prob. adopted in ME. from MDu. or MLG., though documentary evidence of its existence in those dialects is wanting.]

= WALNUT[1] 1. Also *attrib.*

1368–9 *Durham Acc. Rolls* (Surtees) 574, 2000 de Walsnotes in precio 2*s.* 6*d.* *c* **1384** Chaucer *H. Fame* 1281 (Fairf. MS.) Y saugh him carien a wyndmelle Vnder a walsh note [*MS. Bodley* welshnote] shale. *a* **1400** *Pistill of Susan* 99 With wardons winlich and walshe notes newe. **1502** Arnolde *Chron.* 165 Yf thou wylt plante an almaunde tree or a walsh nott tree or a chery tree. **1578** Lyte *Dodoens* vi. lvi. 731 The fruite is called..in Englishe, Walnuttes, Walshe Nuttes, and of some Frenche Nuttes. **1620** Venner *Via Recta* vii. 132 The dry Walnuts, or Walsh nuts, are hot and dry in the second degree. **1633** Hart *Diet of Diseased* i. xvii. 68 Amongst all these [Nuts], the Wall-nut, or Walsh-nut, beareth away the bell.

Walsingham ('wɔːlsɪŋəm). The name of a town in Norfolk, used *attrib.* in ***Walsingham Way***, a designation of the Milky Way supposed formerly to have been used as a guide by pilgrims travelling to the shrine of Our Lady of Walsingham.

c **1878** G. M. Hopkins *Loss of Eurydice* in *Poems* (1967) 75 A starlight-wender of ours would say The marvellous Milk was Walsingham Way. **1922** Joyce *Ulysses* 685 The waggoner's star: Walsingham way: the chariot of David: the annular cinctures of Saturn. **1973** M. J. Petry *Herne the Hunter* vi. 71 In certain parts of England, and especially in East Anglia, the Milky Way was also known as the *Walsingham Way*, on account of the hosts of *pilgrims* who passed along the roads..to the shrine of Our Lady at Walsingham in Norfolk.

Walsman, obs. form of Welshman.

Walsse, Walsshe, obs. forms of Welsh.

†**walt**, *sb. Sc. Obs. rare*[−1]. ? Beaten clay.

1488 *Rec. Burgh Lanark* (1893) 2 Item, to Jok Inglis for makyn of walt and claying of the flur, iij days, ijs. iijd.

†**walt**, *a. Naut. Obs.* Also 6–7 **walte.** [OE. **wealt*, found only in *unwealt* steady; related to WALT *v.*] Of a ship: Unsteady, crank.

1539 *Adm. Ct. Exam.* 4, 7 Dec., The said boate was very walte & very evyll made. **1627** Capt. J. Smith *Sea Gram.* xi. 53 We say a Ship is walt when shee is not stiffe, and hath not Ballast enough in her to keepe her stiffe. **1656** Bradford *Plymouth Plant.* ii. (1856) 291 For covetousnes sake [they] did so over lade her,..as she was walte, and could not bear sayle. **1694** Motteux *Rabelais* iv. lxiii, That our humane Vessels might not heeld, or be walt, but well trimm'd and stiff. **1769** Falconer *Dict. Marine* (1780), *Walt*, an obsolete or spurious term signifying *crank.*

walt (wɒlt), *v. Obs.* exc. *dial.* Also 3–5 **walte,** 6–8 **wolt,** 9 *dial.* **waut.** Contracted pa. t. and pple. 4–5 **walt.** [early ME. *walten* = OHG. *walzan*, MHG. *walzen* (strong) to roll, revolve (intr. and trans.); the OTeut. root **walt*- appears to be an extension of **wal*- (**wel*-) to roll: see WALLOW *v.* Cf. WELT *v.*]

1. *trans.* (with obj. clause). To revolve in the mind, consider. [So OHG. *walzan.*]

c **1200** *Trin. Coll. Hom.* 29 Witte wel hwat þu hauest walte hwat þe tide.

2. To throw, cast, toss *out, over, up,* etc.; to fling to the ground; to overturn, upset.

Cf. ROOT-WALT *v.* (1532–).

13.. *E.E. Allit. P.* B. 1734 [Tekel] To teche þe of techal, þat terme þus menes, þy wale rengne is walt in weȝtes to heng, & is funde ful fewe of hit fayth dedes. **13..** *Gaw. & Gr. Knt.* 1336 Þay..grayþely departed þe wesaunt fro þe wynt-hole, & walt out þe guttez. *c* **1400** *Destr. Troy* 4633 The storme..walt vp the wilde se vppon wan hilles. *Ibid.* 5888 [Thai] woundit hom wikkedly, walt hom to ground. *c* **1400** *Sege Jerus.* 351 Or y to þe walles schal wende & walten alle ouere. **1513** Douglas *Æneis* i. vii. 13 Ane part haistis to beild the wallis wicht, And sum to..wolt wp stanes to the werk on hie. **1674** Ray *N.C. Words* 51 To *Walt*,..to overthrow. **1703** Thoresby *Let. to Ray*, To *Welt*, or *Wolt*, overturn Cart or Wain. **1875** *Lancs. Gloss., Waut*, to upset; to turn completely over. **1883** *Almondbury Gloss. Walt*, to turn over... 'Nay, lad; it ud walt ma table ovver'.

3. *intr.* To be thrown down, fall over, be upset or overturned; to totter; to lean to one side.

c **1400** *Destr. Troy* 909 As þe welkyn shold walt, a wonderfull noyse Skremyt vp to the skrow. *c* **1400** *Sege Jerus.* 69 Ouer wilde wawes he wende, as alle walte scholde. ? *a* **1500** *Chester Pl., Ador. Sheph.* 268 Ware lest thou walt here by the wall. **1674** Ray *N.C. Words* 51 To *Walt*, to totter, or lean one way. **1875** *Lancs. Gloss., Waut*,..to fall on one side. **1883** *Almondbury Gloss., Walt*, to totter, or fall over.

b. With *open*: To be opened; to gape wide.

13.. *E.E. Allit. P.* B. 501 Þen went þay to þe wykket, hit walt vpon sone. *c* **1400** *Melayne* 1145 So depe wondes þat day þay dalt, þat many on wyde opyn walt, þat wikkidly wondede was.

c. *fig.* To fall, *into* (anger, madness).

c **1400** *Destr. Troy* 1956 Nestor anone noyet þere with, And walt at his wordes into wode yre. *Ibid.* 8685 Sum walt into wodenes, & of wit past.

4. To gush *out*, pour, flow.

13.. *E.E. Allit. P.* B. 364 Waltes out vch walle-heued, in full wode stremez. *Ibid.* 1037 Þer waltez of þat water in waxlokes grete, þe spumande aspaltoun þat spyserez sellen.

walt(e, obs. forms of Welt.

Walt Disney (wɔːlt 'dɪznɪ). The name of *Walt*er Elias *Disney* (1901–66), American pioneer of cartoon films, used *attrib.* to denote the style of his films or their characters. Cf. DISNEYESQUE *a.*

1946 R. Lehmann *Gipsy's Baby* 12 He was a total failure with rabbits, and if he blundered on one in the course of one of his Walt Disney gallops over the fields, he winced. **1962** A. Lurie *Love & Friendship* vi. 107 Bright, cheap, sentimental in a Walt Disney style, it [*sc.* a Christmas card] depicted a group of cherubs carrying packages. **1966** 'K. A. Saddler' *Gilt Edge* x. 144 The ancient home of the Meldmays..glistened in the moonlight like a Walt Disney castle. **1974** C. Hampton *Savages* (1976) ii. 26 Three young men enter. They are all wearing rubber Walt Disney masks.

walte, var. VULT *Sc. Obs.*

1524 Arran in *St. Papers Hen. VIII*, IV. 157 [His] Gracis maist noble jocund walte,..manlye and ferme contenance.

†**'walter**, *sb. Obs.* Also *Sc.* 6 **volter, woltir,** 6–7 **wolter.** [f. WALTER *v.*[1] Cf. WELTER *sb.*]

1. The rolling of the sea in a storm.

c **1400** *Destr. Troy* 3699 So þe bre and the brethe burbelit to gedur, þat hit spirit vp spitiously fyue speire lenght With walter and wawes.

2. The act of wallowing (in mire); in quot. *concr.*, a wallowing-place.

1577 Knewstub *Confut.* (1579) To Rdr. **1 The Lord.. reuengeth the shameful contempt and neglect of his truth: by sending numbers to their stie or walter agaíne.

3. An upset, upheaval, overthrow. *lit.* and *fig.*

1563 Winȝet *Wks.* (S.T.S.) I. 49, I began nocht litill to merwel at sa haisty and sa subdane a wolter of this warlde in sa mony grete materis. **1563** Randolph *Let. to Cecil* 10 Apr. in *Cal. Scott. Papers* II. 5 Yf ther come such a volter in thys realme, that ever that man come agayne into credyt. **1596** Dalrymple *Leslie's Hist. Scot.* II. 221 He spak mekle of the Woltir of the religioune [L. *de religione apud nos evertenda*]. **1678** Ray *Prov.* (ed. 2) 379 (Scott. Prov.) If I can get his cart at a wolter [1670, p. 282 at a whelming], I shall lend it a put.

walter ('wɒltə(r)), *v.*[1] *Obs.* exc. *dial.* Forms: 4–6 **waltre,** 4–7, 9 *dial.* **walter,** 5 **waltyr,** 6 **waulter, -tre,** *Sc.* **woltre, valter,** 6 *Sc.*, 8–9 *dial.* **wolter.** [Freq. of WALT *v.*: see -ER[5]. Cf. WELTER *v.*]

I. Intransitive senses.

1. To roll to and fro, move from side to side; to tumble or toss about; to lie sprawling on the ground, *in* mire, etc.

c **1400** tr. *Higden* (Rolls) VII. 203 He feled a þing þat was myȝti and þicke waltre and turne atwixe hym and his wif. *c* **1400** *Sege Jerus.* 735 Litel he slepiþ, Bot walwyþ & wyndiþ & waltreþ a-boute. *c* **1460** *Towneley Myst.* xiii. 236 [She] lyys walteryng..by the fyere. **1529** [see TOLTER *v.*]. **1530** Palsgr. 771/1, I walter, I tumble. *Je me voystre.* Hye you, your horse is walterynge yonder, he wyll breake his saddell but more happe be. **1535** Stewart *Cron. Scot.* II. 565 So greit terrour in his mynd he tuke, That all that nycht he wolterit and he woik. **1568** Withals *Dict.* 10 b/2 *Voluto*, to turne or walter in myre as hogges doe. **1580** Blundevil *Curing Horses Dis.* xcii. 41 b, The horse will forsake his meate, and lie downe and wallow, and walter vpon the ground. **1603** Holland *Plutarch's Mor.* 1276 Sardanapalus ..tumbling and lying along, waltring among a sort of concubines. **1692** Ray *Disc.* ii. ii. (1693) 87 The Globe cannot walter or reel towards any side. *a* **1825** Forby *Voc. E. Anglia, Walter, wolter*, to roll and twist about on the ground; as corn laid by the wind and rain; or as one who is rolled in the mire. **1880** *Antrim & Down Gloss.* s.v., 'The potatoes lie down and walter on the ground', *i.e.* they remain lying.

b. Of a ship: To roll or be tossed on the waves.

13.. *E.E. Allit. P.* B. 415 Hit waltered on þe wylde flod, went as hit lyste. **1560** Rolland *Seven Sages* 18 Upon the sey thay sufferit great perrell,..Walterand with wind out throw þe mudy wawis.

c. Of the stomach: To be upset or disturbed.

1540 J. Heywood *Four PP.* 600 It..maketh your stomake sore to walter.

2. *fig.* To wallow or revel *in* (prosperity, pleasure, sin).

c **1375** *Cursor M.* 4503 (Fairf.) Man þat walteres [*Cott.* weltres] in his welis. **1528** Roy *Rede me* (Arb.) 62 They are ..lyke to brut beastes and swyne, Waltrynge in synfull wretchednes. **1553** Bradford *Serm. Repent.* (1574) Hij b, Trow you that such a one..wyl willingly walter & wallow in his wylful lusts, pleasure, and fantasies? *a* **1568** Ascham *Scholem.* i. (Arb.) 76 If a man..walter in filthines like a Swyne. *a* **1598** Rollock *Serm.* xi. (1616) 208 The naturall man waltering and wallowing in sinne.

3. To swing or float to and fro. Also *fig.*

c **1350** *Will. Palerne* 947 Þou waltres al in a weih & wel y vnderstande whider þe belaunce bremliest bouwes al-gate. *c* **1425** *Cast. Persev.* 2663 in *Macro Plays* 156 Nedys, my loue must on hym lende, With Coueytyse to walter & wave. *c* **1520** Skelton *Magnyf.* 1936 And some I make in a rope to totter and walter. *c* **1555** ? Coverdale *Carrying Christ's Cross* iii. 29 The aungels gatheryng together y[e] wicked wretches (which now walter and walowe as the worlde and wynde bloweth) to be tyed in bondels, and cast into the fier. **1560** Rolland *Seven Sages* 44 He signifyis a mannis persoun, That walteris betuix wynde and waw Into this warld ay vp and doun.

4. To move or go unsteadily; to totter, stumble. Also, to go with a rolling gait, to waddle.

1399 Langl. *Rich. Redeles* ii 189 So lymed leues were leyde all aboute,..þat where so þey walkid, þey waltrid dounwardis. **1480** Caxton *Ovid's Met.* xi. ii, He [Silenus] was, att that tyme, in Frygye, waltrynge and swaruyng what of wyn and of age. **1577** Dee *Relat. Spir.* i. (1659) 186 [An adder and her young] She..suffereth them to hang upon her back, and so waltereth to her hole. **1703** Thoresby *Let. to Ray, Wolter*, as welter ['to goe aside, or heavily, as Women with Child, or Fat People' (Ray 1691)].

5. Of waves: To surge or roll high. Of water, etc.: To flow, gush. Of a humour: To wander or ooze about the body.

13.. *E.E. Allit. P.* C. 142 Þe wawes ful wode waltered so hiȝe. **13..** *Gaw. & Gr. Knt.* 684 Wel much was þe warme water þat waltered of yȝen. **1555** Phaer *Æneid* ii. (1558) E ij, The fomy floud..waltring down the vales. **1561** Hollybush *Hom. Apoth.* 23 The unnaturall or evell sweate is it that..waltereth only about the harte. *Ibid.* 36 Somtyme growe apostemes in the loynes of humors that are waltering and straying in the body. **1577** J. Bishop *Beautif. Blossoms* xvii. 84 Streames of teares waltering downe his cheekes.

II. Transitive senses.

6. To roll about, toss to and fro. Also *fig.* Also *refl.*, to sprawl or wallow (on the ground, in the mire, etc.).

c **1375** *Cursor M.* 21113 Quik þai haue his bodi flaine & waltered him in barli chaf. *c* **1380** Wyclif *Sel. Wks.* II. 204 And he [*sc.* the demoniac], cast doun in þe erþe, was waltrid and froþid [Vulg. Mark ix. 19 *volutabatur spumans*]. *c* **1400** *Master of Game* (MS. Digby 182) ii, þei smyteth þe grounde with the foote and walters hem as an horse. *c* **1450** *Cov. Myst.* 342 The fete..ar ful wete, Walterid in blood. **1508** Fisher *Penit. Ps.* Wks. (1876) 204 Euen as an hors the softer myre or claye he waltreth hymselfe in the more easely he lyeth. *Ibid.* 358 The Sowe..waultering hir self in the myerie puddle. *a* **1578** Lindesay (Pitscottie) *Chron. Scot.* (S.T.S.) I. 23 Quhill the cuntrie was walterit to and fra in this maner. **1582** Stanyhurst *Æneis* iii. (Arb.) 92 In seas far waltred, he groyleth.

7. To overturn, overthrow.

1571 Sir J. Maitland in *Satir. Poems. Reform.* xxvii. 71 Bewar! we may be walteritt [*v.rr.* weltred, wolterit] or we witt, And lykwayis Loss our land and libertie.

8. *dial. uses* (see quots.).

a **1825** Forby *Voc. E. Anglia, Walter, Wolter*, to cause extreme fatigue... 'I am right-on woltered out, by my day's work'. **1880** *Antrim & Down Gloss., Walthered*, mired or stuck in a boggy road, or swampy place. 'Whiles in the mornin' I find the branches of the trees all walthered and smashed', broken down into the mire.

Hence **'waltering** *vbl. sb.* and *ppl. a.*

13.. *E.E. Allit. P.* C. 247 A wylde walterande whal..bi þat bot flotte. **1501** Douglas *Pal. Hon.* iii. viii, Innumerabill folk I saw flotterand in feir, Quhilk pereist on the walterand wallis weir. **1528** Lyndesay *Dreme* 128 Quhare I mycht se The woltryng [*v.r.* waltreyng] of the wallis vp and doun. *a* **1547** Surrey *Æneid* ii. 267 Whoes waltring tongs did lick their hissing mouthes. **1552** Huloet, Waltrynge or full of wallowynge, *volutabundus*. *c* **1557** Abp. Parker *Ps.* xxxvi. 99 So pride hath hym puft by his waltering wealth. **1578** H. Wotton *Courtlie Controv.* 44 As a man dizzie with the waltering of a vessel, tossed by the hollowe waues of raging seas. **1588** T. Hughes *Misfort. Arthur* iii. Chor. 42 The windes, that sweepe the waltering waues.

†**'walter**, *v.*[2] *Sc. Obs. rare*[−1]. *trans.* To be without, lack.

1463 *Burgh Rec. Edin.* (1869) I. 21 The said Johne [sall remane] at the hous of the said myln and vesy thame daylie at thai walter nocht na behuifull thing to thame that he aucht to find, and gif at thai walter acht in his default, sa that thairthrow the myle be ydill [etc.].

walter, obs. form of Water.

†**'walterer.** *Obs.* In 6 *Sc.* **-ar.** [f. WALTER *v.*[1] + -ER.] One who overthrows.

1572 *Satir. Poems Reform.* xxxiii. 230 Behald now how ȝe do the mater gyde, To caus my Sisters France and England scorne ȝow, That walterars of Courts ȝe lat suborne ȝow. **1581** in *R. Bannatyne's Jrnl.* etc. (1806) 500 Sindrie..that war the kingis enemeis, walteraris of his kingdome, and enemeis of religione.

Walter Mitty: see MITTY[2].

walterot, walth: see WALTROT, WEALTH.

†**ˈWaltham.** *Obs.* [The name of *Waltham* Chase, Hants.] Used *attrib.* in allusion to the disguise adopted by the poachers called 'Waltham Blacks': see BLACK *sb.* 6 b.

1748 RICHARDSON *Clarissa* (1811) V. 191 Such mean devices, such artful, such worse than Waltham disguises put on, to obtrude himself into my company.

Walther (ˈwɒltə(r), ‖ˈva-). The name of a German firm of firearm manufacturers, used *attrib.* and *absol.* to designate pistols and rifles made by them.

1920 H. B. C. POLLARD *Automatic Pistols* v. 49 The *Walther Selbstlade* pistol is a pocket automatic of 6·355 mm., six shots, German manufacture. **1934** G. BURRARD *Identification of Firearms & Forensic Ballistics* ix. 203, I was informed that the defendant was using a Walther rifle at the time of the accident. **1965** I. FLEMING *Man with Golden Gun* v. 76 The Walther PPK inside the waist-band of his trousers. **1968** A. DIMENT *Great Spy Race* vii. 100 He..took a gun, a baby Walther, from its hiding place. **1971** *Guardian* 28 Sept. 24/1 As a point of historical interest, this is the first time that the Walther pistol, a shoulder-holstered gun introduced into the Royal Ulster Constabulary last year.. has been fired in action. **1975** [see LUGER]. **1981** J. B. HILTON *Playground of Death* i. 7 Bielby had been discovered ..with a warm-barrelled pistol in his hand..a Walther 7.65 wartime German police model.

waltir, obs. Sc. form of WATER.

Waltonian (wɒlˈtəʊnɪən), *a.* and *sb.* [f. the name of Izaak *Walton*, author of *The Compleat Angler* (1653): see -IAN.]

A. *adj.* Of or pertaining to Izaak Walton. **B.** *sb.* A disciple of Walton, an angler.

a **1828** T. BEWICK *My Life* (1981) xvii. 165 Some regulations should be laid down as a guide to the fair anglers ..I think Waltonian societies would be all-sufficient to do this. **1832** *P. Egan's Bk. Sports* 314/2 The Waltonians, the Cottonians, and the Saltonians (for Walton, Cotton, and Salter, are their feat-books). **1837** LOCKHART *Scott* xlix. (1845) 432/2 This little group of Waltonians, bound for Lord Somerville's preserve. **1845** J. COULTER *Adv. Pacific* ii. 12 Exhibiting a sized fish that any Waltonian might well stare at. **1866** (*title*) Rules of the true Waltonian Society held at the Crown Tavern, Pentonville Hill. Established 1830. **1908** *Westm. Gaz.* 2 Jan. 12/1 He..is an ardent devotee of the Waltonian art.

So **ˈWaltonizing** *vbl. sb.*, angling.

1841 J. T. J. HEWLETT *Peter Priggins* I. i. 25 A landing-net, minnow-can, casting-net, and half a hundred more requisites for Waltonizing. **1882** H. S. LEIGH *Strains fr. Strand* 1 No sign was near of pebbly brook,..Where patient swains with rod and hook In Waltonising dabble.

[**waltron,** a misreading in Johnson's Dict. for *walrous*: see quot. 1728 s.v. WALRUS 1.]

†**waltrot, walterot.** *Obs. rare*$^{-1}$. [Of obscure origin.] ***a tale of waltrot***, an idle tale, a piece of absurdity.

1377 LANGL. *P. Pl.* B. XVIII. 142 'þat þow tellest' quod treuth 'is but a tale of waltrot' [C. XXI. 146 walterot, *v.rr.* walter, walteret].

waltsom(e, erron. forms of WLATSOME *a. Obs.*

1398 TREVISA *Barth. De P.R.* IV. x. (1495) f v, There is.. waltsomnes wᵗ coleryk, spewynge, dryenes of tongue. *c* **1492** *Chaucer's Nun's Priest's T.* 233 (Pynson), Murdre is so waltsom [Thynne 1532, Stowe 1561 waltsome] and abhomynable. **1563** *Mirr. Mag., Hastings* xxx, O waltsome murther, that attaynteth our fame.

waltt, ? obs. Sc. form of VAULT *v.*[2]

1712 in E. D. Dunbar *Soc. Life* (1865) 43, I am also rejoysed to hear that you are clever and can voltige and waltt a litle as to your former way.

walty (ˈwɒltɪ), *a. Naut.* [f. WALT *a.* + -Y.] = WALT *a.*

Prob. *Obs.*, the knowledge of the word being derived, through Longfellow, from quot. 1702.

1702 C. MATHER *Magn. Christi* I. vi. 25 A New Ship, built at Rhode-Island, of about 150 Tuns; but so walty, that the Master..often said she would prove their Grave. [**1850** LONGF. *Birds of Passage, Phantom Ship* iv, This ship is so crank and walty, I fear our grave she will be!] **1896** KIPLING *Seven Seas, Merchantmen* iv, By sport of bitter weather, We're walty, strained, and scarred. **1904** F. T. BULLEN *Creat. Sea* xxiv. 362 In spite of the walty state of the almost worn-out vessel.

waltz (wɔːlts, wɔːls), *sb.* Also 8 **valze, waltze,** 9 *pl.* **waltses,** 8–9 **valtz, walse.** See also VALSE. [ad. G. *walzer*, f. *walzen* to roll, revolve, dance the waltz.]

1. A dance performed to music in triple time by couples who, almost embracing each other, swing round and round in the same direction with smooth and even steps, moving on as they gyrate.

1781 TWINING in *Select. Papers T. Family* (1887) 74, I found on inquiry that this was a favourite German dance called a waltz. **1796** *Campaigns* 1793–4, II. i. 6 All these fair Flammandes gain force, In the Valtz, as they spin in their whirligig course. **1798** HELEN M. WILLIAMS *Tour Switzerland* I. 34 The walse, which is now never forgotten at a Paris ball. **1812** BYRON (*title*) The Waltz. **1825** W. HAMILTON *Hand-bk. Terms Arts* etc., *Waltz*, in Music, the name of a riotous and indecent German dance. **1872** E. BRADDON *Life in India* iv. 145 She will be able to reward the virtuous youth who is fast and smooth in the *valtz*. **1881** 'RITA' *My Lady Coquette* i, The very memory of those waltzes makes my arms ache.

fig. **1802** COLERIDGE *Lett.* (1895) 403 The ghosts of his departed guineas dance an ugly waltz round my idea.

attrib. **1826** [SHERER] *Notes & Refl. Ramble in Germany* 37 My steps were arrested..by the sound of soft waltz music.

2. A piece of music to accompany this dance, in the same time and rhythm.

1816 JANE AUSTEN *Emma* xxvi, Mrs. Weston..was seated, and beginning an irresistible waltz. **1837** MARRYAT *Dog-Fiend* ix, The band..played a waltz.

†**3.** A party or soirée for waltzing. *Obs.*

1802 *Spirit Publ. Jrnls.* VI. 192 If men and women of fashion will come forward, and..give balls, waltses, and suppers.

4. Something accomplished with ease. *slang.*

1968 *Time* 5 July 38 Though Dancer eased him up at the end, Nevele Pride won in a waltz. **1970** G. F. NEWMAN *Sir, You Bastard* vi. 179 The qualifying examinations conducted through the Civil Service Commission were a waltz.

5. *attrib.* and *Comb.*, as **waltz king** [G. *Walzerkönig*], an epithet applied to the Viennese composer Johann Strauss (1825–99), famous for his waltzes; **waltz-length** *a.*, (of a garment) calf-length.

1908 *Busy Man's Mag.* Feb. 51/2 Johann Strauss, 'the waltz king'. **1938** *Oxf. Compan. Mus.* 1013/1 It seems as likely that such a waltz as the *Blue Danube*, by Johann Strauss the younger, the 'Waltz King', will last for ever as that Beethoven's Fifth Symphony will do so. **1958** *Vogue* Nov. 40 Nightgowns with lace, or ribbons and bows, in waltz length or swirling to the ankles. **1975** *New Yorker* 17 Nov. 134/2 A waltz-length, front-fastened Edwardian robe of snowy cotton, with textured scrolls of guipure on its yokes, is $75.

waltz (wɔːlts, wɔːls), *v.* Also 9 **valtz, walze, walse.** [f. WALTZ *sb.* or directly ad. G. *walz-en.*]

a. *intr.* To dance a waltz. Also, to be addicted to, or practised in, the waltz; to dance the waltz in a specified manner.

c **1794** *Search after Perfect.* III. i. in *New Brit. Theatre* (1814) III. 56 The sight of a lady waltzing. **1812** BYRON *Waltz* To Publ., 'Lord! Mr. Hornem, Can't you see they're valtzing?' or waltzing (I forget which). **1841** MOTLEY *Corr.* (1889) I. iv. 93, I waltzed one waltz. **1870** FURNIVALL *Borde's Introd. Knowl.* Forewords 110 Oh fair-haired Alice, how well you waltz!

b. *transf.* To move lightly, trippingly, or nimbly. Also, to move unconcernedly or boldly, as to waltz *into*, *off*, *up* (*to*), etc. *colloq.*

1862 CARLYLE *Fredk. Gt.* XIV. vii. (1872) V. 237 Big war-clouds waltzing hither and thither, occasionally clashing into bloody conflict. **1887** in *Amer. Speech* (1950) XXV. 39/2 Out on the Mississippi Valley road when his girl waltzed up. **1891** C. ROBERTS *Adrift Amer.* 205 All you have to do is to put a good 'front on', and waltz in with the crowd. **1900** *Century Mag.* Feb. 600/1 With a fair wind she waltzed beautifully round the coast. **1935** G. HEYER *Death in Stocks* v. 63 Tony seemed to have waltzed off for the night, so I wandered out on my own. **1951** J. FLEMING *Man who looked Back* i. 10 Here she was waltzing off with this nurse and leaving Ray..alone. **1974** F. NOLAN *Oshawa Project* ii. 12 He'll walk any nomination..and waltz into the White House without even having to put up a fight. **1978** N. MARSH *Grave Mistake* viii. 240 P'raps..he'll come waltzing back with a silly grin on his face having been to stay with his auntie. **1979** C. MACLEOD *Luck runs Out* v. 50 If any student or students had..got mixed up in a mess like this, they'd hardly come waltzing up to the President in open assembly and say so. **1980** 'R. B. DOMINIC' *Attending Physician* xxiv. 218 He waltzed off to be the first one in the lounge. **1984** B. FRANCIS *AA Car Duffer's Guide* 6/1 That same afternoon.. the vicar's lady waltzes in.

c. quasi-*trans.* (with advb. extension): To move (a person, oneself) as in a waltz.

1853 DICKENS *Bleak Ho.* viii, We are always..revolving about the Lord Chancellor and all his satellites, and equitably waltzing ourselves off to dusty death, about Costs. **1881** MARY C. HAY *Missing* II. 237 How Edgar laughed as he waltzed me through the hall! **1883** *Harper's Mag.* Mar. 600/2 He seized me and waltzed me around the little dining-room.

d. *trans.* To transport or convey (something). *U.S. joc.*

1884 'MARK TWAIN' *Huck. Finn* iii. 22 They've got to waltz that palace around over the country wherever you want it. **1901** MERWIN & WEBSTER *Calumet 'K'* xi. 197 He'd call the men off just the same, and leave us to waltz the timbers around all by ourselves.

e. ***to waltz Matilda***: see MATILDA.

Hence **ˈwaltzing** *vbl. sb.* and *ppl. a.*

waltzing mouse = WALTZER b.

1811 LADY GRANVILLE *Lett.* (1894) I. 22 Her waltzing is the prettiest thing that can be seen. **1811** LD. GLENBERVIE *Jrnl.* (1910) 143 Mr. And Mrs. Johnstone, whose splendid dinners and walzing balls we partook of at Brighton. **1819** *Metropolis* I. 223, I suppose she is disappointed of her waltzing partner. **1848** THACKERAY *Van. Fair* xlvii, The Lord George Gaunt was desired to return from Vienna, where he was engaged in waltzing and diplomacy. **1882** O'DONOVAN *Merv Oasis* I. iv. 75 They commenced sliding round the ring with a peculiar waltzing step. **1896** *Fancy Mice* (ed. 4) 45 Waltzing Mice. **1904** *Biometrika* Jan. 4 Japanese waltzing mice.

waltzer (ˈwɔːltsə(r)). [f. WALTZ *v.* + -ER[1].]

a. One who dances the waltz.

1811 *Sporting Mag.* XXXVIII. 220 The music at first is slow, but, as the Waltzers get animated, it rises to a jig. **1811** LD. GLENBERVIE *Jrnls.* (1910) 139 Both great walzers, and insufferable coxcombs. **1848** THACKERAY *Van. Fair* xlvii, My Lord George Gaunt..was one of the finest waltzers in Europe. **1912** *Times* 28 Sept. 11/5 Special prizes are given this season for the best waltzers.

b. A name for a breed of domesticated mice which have the habit of spinning round rapidly; = *waltzing mouse.*

1904 *Biometrika* Jan. 6 All the waltzers used were of pure strain. *Ibid.*, The offspring produced by crossing a Japanese waltzer with an albino.

c. A fairground ride (see quots. 1961[1], 1968).

1961 F. C. ROOPE *Come to Fair* iii. 71 *The Waltzer*, an appropriate name for an ingenious machine. The motion of the cars..is both round and round the undulating track, and also a spinning one on their own axis. *Ibid.*, The Waltzer is completely safe for everyone except the most foolhardy riders. **1965** [see NOAH'S ARK 7]. **1968** D. BRAITHWAITE *Fairground Archit.* 176 *Waltzer*, a member of the switchback family having freely-pivoted tub-shaped cars mounted on the undulating platform. **1975** *Sunday People* 6 July 11/5 As he lurches about on the waltzer or is shoved away in a dodgem car, it's easy to give him a folded bottom note in place of two. **1980** R. HILL *Killing Kindness* vi. 50 He could be on the dodgems, or the waltzer. He helps around when they're busy.

walue, obs. form of VALUE.

walx, obs. Sc. form of WAX *sb.*[1]

waly (ˈwɔːlɪ), *int. Sc.* and *north.* Also **wally, walie.** [Of obscure formation; ? cognate with WOE, WELLAWAY.] An exclamation of sorrow.

a **1724** '*O waly, waly*' in *Ramsay's Tea-t. Misc.* (1775) I. 186 O waly, waly up the bank, And waly, waly down the brae. **1883** *Gateshead Alm.* (E.D.D.), Wally! Wally! it's a' ower noo! **1894** J. W. M'LAREN *Tibbie & Tam* 41 (E.D.D.) But walie! the sight gar'd even puir Baudrons..jump nearly four feet wi' fricht.

Hence **waly-walying,** lamentation.

1821 GALT *Ann. Parish* xvii. 161 Such a wally wallying as the news of this caused at every door.

waly, variant of WALI, WALLY *a.*[2]

walycoat, var. WYLIECOAT *Sc.*

Walysshe, walywe, obs. ff. WELSH, VALUE.

walz, -er, -ing: see WALTZ, etc.

†**wam.** *Sc. Obs.* In 6 **wam(me, vam.** [App. repr. OE. *wam(m*, *wǫm(m*, masc. and neut., spot, blemish (chiefly *fig.*) = OFris., OS., OHG. *wamm*, ON. *vamm*, Goth. *wamm*. But cf. WAN *sb.*[1]] A scar. Cf. WEM *sb.*

Beowulf 3073 Wommum ȝewitnad. *a* **1000** *Kentish Gl.* in Wr.-Wülcker 64 *Maculam*, wam.

a **1585** POLWART *Flyting w. Montgomerie* 570 (Tullibardine MS.) His peild pallat The fowsome flokis of flaeis dois overflow With vamis [*MS. Harl.* wames; ed. 1639 wams] and wondis. **1595** DUNCAN *App. Etymol.* (E.D.S.), *Cicatrix*, a wamme.

wam, obs. form of WHOM, WOMB.

wamara (wəˈmɑːrə). [Native name.] The brown ebony of Guyana.

1840 SCHOMBURGK *Descr. Brit. Guiana* 33 Wamara..is hard and cross-grained, consequently not apt to split. **1862** *List Contrib. fr. Br. Guiana to Lond. Exhib.* in Veness *El Dorado* (1866) App. 136 Wamara, or Brown Ebony. Used for ship-building and furniture. **1866** *Treas. Bot.*

wamb, obs. form of WAME, WOMB.

wambais. *Obs.* exc. *Hist.* Also **wambas, -us.** [a. OF. *wambais*: see GAMBESON. Cf. WAMUS.] = GAMBESON.

[**1181** *Assize of Arms* in Bened. Peterb. *Chron.* (Rolls) I. 278 Omnes burgenses..habeant wambais et capellet ferri et lanceam.] **1761** HUME *Hist. Eng.* I. ix. 196 All burgesses were to have..a wambais; that is, a coat quilted with wool, tow, or such-like materials. **1792** H. H. BRACKENRIDGE *Mod. Chivalry* (1846) 189 It will be best to present him just as he is in his brogues and wambus. **1821** MEYRICK & C. H. SMITH *Costume Orig. Inhab.* 58 The [Danish] king is habited in a corslet of leather (wambas) passing over his rock or tunic. This wambas was of painted elk or stag-skin, and was a kind of half armour. **1874** STUBBS *Const. Hist.* (1897) I. xiii. 633 The Assize of Arms in 1181..directed that..all burghers..[must possess] a wambais, head-piece, and lance.

wambe, obs. form of WAME, WOMB.

wambetowe, obs. form of WAME-TOW.

wamble (ˈwɒmb(ə)l), *sb.* Also 8– **womble.** Now only *colloq.* or *dial.* [f. WAMBLE *v.*]

1. A rolling or uneasiness in the stomach; a feeling of nausea; spec. see quot. 1899.

1603 HOLLAND *Plutarch's Mor.* IV. 701 Our meat going downe into the stomacke merily, and with pleasure, dissolveth incontinently all wambles. **1865** J. SLEIGH *Derbysh. Gloss.* (E.D.D.), *Wamble*, faintness. **1899** *Syd. Soc. Lex.*, *Wambles*, an old popular term for Milk fever. **1902** C. N. & A. M. WILLIAMSON *Lightning Conductor* 48 There's another thing which gives me the 'wombles'.

†**2.** An act of seething or bubbling up when brought to boiling-point. *Obs.* Cf. WALM *sb.*

1620 VENNER *Via Recta* ii. 44 If you also boyle in it a quantity of ginger, three or foure wambles about,.. it will be much the better. **1681** *Sober Dial. betw. Stafford & the Lords* 2/2 [*Stafford*, as a ghost from Hell *loq.*] Here is a parcel of cold Comfort, but I fear me not enough to mitigate one wamble of the great Lake. **1730** W. BURDON *Gentl. Pocket-Farrier* 16 Set it on [the fire] again, and give it two or three Wambles.

3. An unsteady movement (of a person or thing); a roll of the body; a rolling or staggering gait. ***on*** or ***upon the wamble***, staggering, wobbling.

1825 J. WILSON *Noct. Ambr.* Wks. 1855 I. 7 When Knight's *Quarterly Magazine* took a pain in its head, and gied a wamle ower the counter in the dead-thraws. **1881** BLACKMORE *Christowell* ii, The jump of the horse gave a jerk to the shaft, and this..gave a lollop to the near wheel, already on the wamble. **1887** [see SNAIL *sb.*²].

4. Comb.: **wamble-cropped** (now *U.S.*), † **-stomached** *adjs.*, affected with nausea, sick (*lit.* and *fig.*).

1552 HULOET, *Wamble cropped, *stomachichus*. *a* **1610** HEALEY *Theophrastus* (1616) 14 And yesterday, hee sayth, I was wamble-cropt, and (sauing your presence) parbrak't. **1798** *Massachusetts Spy* 5 Sept. 1/1, I feel a good deal womblecropped about dropping her acquaintance. **1836** HALIBURTON *Clockm.* I. xxiii, It makes me so kinder wamble-cropt, when I think on it, that I'm afeared to venture on matrimony at all. **1844** 'JON. SLICK' *High Life N. York* I. 44, I got back to the sloop and turned in awfully womble-cropped. **1552** HULOET, *Wamble stomaked to be, *nauseo*.

wamble ('wɒmb(ə)l), *v.* Now *dial.* Forms: 4–5 **wamel, wamle,** (4 **wemel,** 5 **wam(m)il, wamylle**), 6 **wambel,** 5, 9 **womble,** 8 **waumle,** 9 **wam(m)le, wammel, wamell, wemble, wommle,** 4– **wamble.** [Prob. two or more verbs have coalesced. In sense 1 the word may correspond to Da. *vamle* to feel nausea, a frequentative formation on the Teut. root **wem-*: **wam-* (:—Indogermanic **wem-*: **wom-*; cf. L. *vomĕre*, Gr. *ϝεμ-, ἐμεῖν* to vomit), whence MSw. *vami* nausea, *vomul* nauseous, Sw. *vämja* refl. to feel sick. A distinct root of identical form seems to be represented in senses 2–4, with which cf. Norw. *vamla, vamra*, to stagger, OHG. *wimidôn, wamezzen* to move, stir, mod.G. *wimmeln* swarm. In sense 5 there may be mixture of a metathetic form of WALM *v.*; on the other hand in some uses *walm* may be a metathesis of *wamble.*]

I. 1. *intr.* To be qualmish, feel nausea.

13.. *E.E. Allit. P.* C. 300 For þat mote in his mawe [Jonah in the whale's belly] mad hym, I trowe, þaȝ hit lyttel were, hym wyth to wamel at his hert. **13..** *W. de Bibbesworth* in *Rel. Ant.* II. 84/2 Wamblez, *laumber*. *a* **1400** *Nominale* (Skeat) 268 Homme lambeie pur ordure. M. wemelith for fulthe. *c* **1440** *Promp. Parv.* 515/1 Wamelon', yn the stomake (wamlyn, P.), *naus(e)o*. **1456** SIR G. HAY *Gov. Princes* Wks. (S.T.S.) II. 119 He that has a wayke calde stomak..oft tymis gantis and wambleis, bolkis, with hevy suollyn eyne. *c* **1480** HENRYSON *Cock & Jasp* xii, His hart wammillis wyse argument to heir. **1483** *Cath. Angl.* 407/2 To Wamylle, *iliacare, navsiare*. **1500** *Ortus Vocab.* (W. de W.) B b v, *Nauseo*..to wamble.

b. Of the stomach or its contents: To be felt to roll about (in nausea).

c **1518** SKELTON *Magnyf.* 1617 A, howe my stomake wambleth! I am all in a swete. **1533** MORE *Answ. Poisoned Bk.* I. xii. 43 Theyr fore fathers murmured in desert agaynst Moyses for manna, and sayed that theyr stomake wambled agaynst that lyght meate. **1534** —— *Treat. Passion* Wks. (1557) 1274/1 Scant was the fruite passed downe both theyr throtes, when it so began to wamble in their stomakes. **1611** COTGR., *Allecter*, to wamble, as a queasie stomacke doth. *c* **1618** FLETCHER *Mad Lover* I. i, When..your cold sallets without salt or vineger Be wambling in your stomachs. **1690** DRYDEN *Amphitryon* III. i, I was never good at swallowing Physick: and my Stomach wambles at the very thought of it. **1738** SWIFT *Love Poem fr. Phys.* 12 My Bowels wambling make me spew. **1781** C. JOHNSTON *Hist. J. Juniper* I. 148 This word..completely turned his stomach that had already begun to wamble at the sight. **1834** LANDOR *Exam. Shaks.* Wks. 1853 II. 266/1 No wonder, Master Ephraim, thy entrails are moved and wamble.

c. *transf.* and *fig.* (Cf. 5.)

1591 LYLY *Endym.* IV. ii, He is resolued to weep some three or foure payle-fuls, to auoyde the rume of loue that wambleth in his stomacke. **1624** MIDDLETON *Game at Chess* IV. ii, [My soul] can digest a Monster, without cruditie, A Sin as weightie as an Elephant, And neuer wamble for 't. **1667** DRYDEN, etc. *Sir M. Mar-all* V. ii, I have such a Plot; ..Shall I speak, dear Warner? let me now; it does so wamble within me, just like a Clyster. **1686** GOAD *Celest. Bodies* II. i. 144 Vast Fires Subterranean..work and wamble in the Bowels of the Earth. **1828** MOIR *Mansie Wauch* xxiii. [xxvi.] 350, I still saw the unleavened pride of womankind wambling within her. **1898** J. M. COBBAN *Angel of Covt.* xv. 168 The pains o' love 'll work and wommle in the inside of ye like a knot o' adders!

II. 2. To turn and twist the body about, roll or wriggle about, roll over and over. Also with *about, over, through.* Also *fig.*

c **1420** *Chron. Vilod.* 3213 When þat litull chylde was leyde a-doune byfore þe tombe..He womblede & tomblede on bak & wombe. **1755** R. FORBES *Ajax* 20, I len'd him sik a dird, As laid him arselins on his back, To wamble o' the yerd. **1819** [see WAME *sb.* 1]. **1854** J. WILSON *Let.* in Mem. viii. (1859) 305 The cod-fish..laid their heads over each other's shoulders, and wambled about like a set of puppy dogs. **1861** *Fraser's Mag.* Dec. 756, I made an experiment on the log and found I could not get my chin six inches above the water level without wembling over. **1866** BLACKMORE *Cradock Nowell* xliii, He have left off talking now for two days only to moan and to wamble.

3. To roll about in walking; to go with an unsteady gait. Also *fig.*

1611 J. DAVIES (Heref.) *Sco. Folly* (Grosart) 43/1 'Neede makes the olde wife trot:' Nay she but wambles. **1676–7** MARVELL *Corr.* Wks. 1875 II. 500, I can not but wonder that ..you should so soon begin to wamble, which is enough to discourage or turne giddy one of so weak a braine and experience. Surely, Brother, it is the best to steere steddy. **1822** GALT *Provost* xxxii, The abominable and irreverent creature was so drunk, that he wamblet to and fro over the drum, as if there had not been a bane in his body. **1862** G. H. KINGSLEY *Sp. & Trav.* (1900) 362 A long row of unfortunates are drawn up on each side of the quarter-deck, wombling and shambling and sniggering. **1893** W. S. PASMORE *Stories Devon & Cornw.* (1900) 36 As us was gwain down awver Bodmin 'ill I zimmed tha 'oss begin to wommle 'bout a bet. **1894** *Northumbld. Gloss.* s.v., He wammelt up the stairs wi' the seck o' floor on iv his back, onyhoo.

b. Of things: To totter, waver; to move unsteadily, stagger, reel.

1589 RIDER *Bibl. Scholast.* I. 1614 To wamble, or wag to and fro, as a crooked arrow wil doe, being shot out of a bowe, *vacillo, sinuo*. *c* **1620** Z. BOYD *Zion's Flowers* (1855) 20 Like to a tower wambling on the sea. **1788** PICKEN *Poems* 161 How the warl',..Hing's waumlan at a tether I' the air. **1825** J. JENNINGS *Observ. Dial. W. Eng.*, To *Wammel*, To *Wamble*, to move to and fro in an irregular and awkward manner; to move out of a regular course or motion. Applied chiefly to mechanical operations. **1896** CROCKETT *Grey Man* i. 7 His feet wambling one over the other like those of a mummer's bear.

4. *trans.* To twist or turn (something) over and over; to turn (a thing) round or upside down.

1561 HOLLYBUSH *Hom. Apoth.* 13 Let him hold it awaye a litle in the mouth, and wambel it round about in the mouth. **1599** NASHE *Lenten Stuffe* 23 Take..a farthing worth of flower to white him ouer and wamble him in. **1828** [W. CARR] *Craven Gloss.*, *Wamble*, to roll the meat in the mouth, when too large to swallow. **1847** HALLIWELL, *Wemble*, to turn a cup upside down in token of having had enough tea. *North.* **1894** *Northumbld. Gloss.* s.v., He wammelt his shillin.

III. † **5.** *intr.* Of water, the blood: To seethe, boil. = WALM *v.* 2, WALL *v.*¹ 2.

1636 DAVENANT *Wits* II. i, Now does my blood wamble. You, Sucket-eater! (*Offers to follow her.*) **1677** COLES *Dict. Eng.-Lat.*, To Wamble [as a pot] *bullio*. **1706** PHILLIPS (ed. Kersey), To *Wamble*, to rise up as seething Water does.

† **6.** To swarm (with vermin): = WALL *v.*¹ 2 b. *Obs. rare.*

1485 *Trevisa's Higden* (Rolls) V. 235 (Caxton) He wambled [*earlier texts* wallede, wellede] ful of wormes [L. *uermibus scatens*].

Hence **'wambling** *vbl. sb.* and *ppl. a.* Also **'wamblingly** *adv.*

1398 TREVISA *Barth. de P.R.* VI. xx. (1495) 207 To moche meete encreasyth humours and postumes and makith wamlynges and spuynges. **1456** SIR G. HAY *Gov. Princes* Wks. (S.T.S.) II. 124 Gif it hapnis the ony hert wamblyng, egirly tak a vomyt of water and vinager. *c* **1518** SKELTON *Magnyf.* 1620 Ofte tymes suche a wamblynge goth ouer my harte; Yet I am not harte seke. **1564–78** BULLEIN *Dial. agst. Pest.* (1888) 45 Noisome and lothesomenesse of stomacke, wambelyng of the harte, pulse not equall. **1566** DRANT *Horace, Sat.* I. i. A v b, Confections sweete or tarte Theylle minge for the, such as beste lykes thy quasye wamblynge hearte. **1581** STUDLEY *Seneca's Herc. Œtæus* II. 193 For my sake Acheloe Did let his streaming bloud amid his wambling waues to floe. **1615** S. WARD *Coal fr. Altar* 78 If wee should make good their resemblances, how then should we please the stomacke of God? who hath indeede brooked and borne vs a long time, I doubt but wamblingly. **1649** J. TAYLOR (Water P.) *Wand. Wonders West* 18 If any one be queasie, or doe feele a wambling in the Gizzard. **1680** BETTERTON *Revenge* V. ii, Yes faith have I [been in love], and have felt your Flames and Fires, and Inclinations, and Wamblings. **1686** GOAD *Celest. Bodies* II. ix. 283 Warmth..cast into a boyling Pot,..allayes the wambling of the Liquor. **1745** BAKER *Don Quix.* I. I. iv. 24, I perceive by the many and powerful wamblings of my Brain, that I shall soon fall a-sleep. **1748** RICHARDSON *Clarissa* (1768) IV. 124, I am amazed at the repetition of thy wambling nonsense. **1756** MRS. CALDERWOOD in *Coltness Collect.* (Maitland Club) 128 We were obliged to cast anchor; which was no sooner done than every one fell a wameling as the ship did. **1859** H. KINGSLEY *G. Hamlyn* xlvii, I feel the queerest wambling in my innards, as we used to say in Devon, at the sight of so many old faces. **1893** 'Q.' (Quiller Couch) *Delect. Duchy* 217 Her reckoned you'd veel a wamblin' in the stommick. **1908** HARDY *Dynasts* III. III. iii, The retreating-way, Along which wambling waggons since the noon Have crept in closening file.

wambly ('wɒmblɪ), *a.* *dial.* Also **wambley, wombly.** [f. WAMBLE *sb.* or *v.* + -Y¹.]

1. Affected with nausea.

1872 *Hartley's Yorksh. Ditties* Ser. I. 104 He wor takken varry wamley for want ov a bit ov a bitin on. **1892** MRS. S. BATSON *Dark* I. iv. 75 If they went without their meal they would be 'wombly' all the morning.

2. Causing nausea.

1899 'ZACK' *On Trail* xxiii. 220 He lies that heavy on the gorge o' me I'd a deal liefer spue the wambly gawkin out and be done wi' un.

3. Shaky, tottering, unsteady.

1857 E. WAUGH *Lanc. Life* 106 Eh! he used to be as limber as a treawt when he're young; but neaw he's as wambley an' slamp as a barrow full o' warp sizin'. **1893** STEVENSON *Catriona* xi, I was still so wambly on my legs that I cowped upon the top of him.

Hence **'wambliness.**

1900 E. PHILLPOTTS *Sons of Morning* I. ix. 90 It do bring him a wambliness of the innards to do or say ought as may draw the public eye upon un.

wambrace, -braiss, -bras: see VAMBRACE.

1416 in Meyrick *Ant. Armour* (1824) II. 109, i par de wambras.

wambtoue, -tow(e, obs. ff. WAME-TOW.

wambus, variant of WAMBAIS.

wamclowte, variant of WOMBCLOUT *Obs.*

wame (weɪm). *Sc.* and *north.* Forms: 5–6 **wayme,** 6 **weyme,** 6–7 **weame,** 6 **waymb, wamb(e,** 7 **weamb,** 7–8 **wem, wemb,** 8 **weme, weem, wyme,** 9 **waim,** 7– **weam,** 4– **wame.** For mod. dial. forms see *Eng. Dial. Dict.* [Northern form of WOMB.]

1. The belly, abdomen: = WOMB in obsolete senses. Cf. BELLY *sb.* 1–3.

c **1425** WYNTOUN *Cron.* III. 45 þan Ayot tit out smertly His suerde..And put it in his wayme sa fast Qwhil hilt and plumat bath in past. **14..** *Nom.* in Wr.-Wülcker 677/14 *Hic venter, Hic alvuus*, a wame. **1500–20** DUNBAR *Poems* xxvi. 92 The fowll monstir Glutteny, Off wame vnsasiable and gredy. **1513** DOUGLAS *Æneis* VIII. Prol. 138 Sum wald haue welth at thair will, and sum thare wame fow. *Ibid.* XI. xv. 105 His taill, that on hys ryg befor tymes lay, Vnder hys waymb [he] lattis fall abasitly. **15..** *Sir Andrew Barton* lvi. in Child *Ballads* IV. 505/2 Then Horsley with a broode-headed arrowe, Stroke then Gírdon throughe the weame. **1533** BELLENDEN *Livy* II. xiv. (S.T.S.) I. 184 þare hail sollicitude ..was direkkit to na vthir fyne, bot alanerlie for the plesere of þe wame. **1566** *Burgh Rec. Edin.* (1875) III. 226 The saidis flescheouris pullis the haill [sheep] skyn fra the hals doun to the taill throw al the wambe thairof. **1785** BURNS *Scotch Drink* v, Food fills the wame, an' keeps us livin. **1817** SCOTT *Rob Roy* xxxi, It would be a daft-like thing to see me wi' my fat wame in a short Hieland coat. **1819** W. TENNANT *Papistry Storm'd* (1827) 63 At Diston's feet he lichtet fair, Wayme uppermost, and wamblit there. *a* **1894** STEVENSON *St. Ives* xxxvi. (1898) 310 He's in bed this hour past with a spoonful of peppermint in his little wame.

phrase. **1824** SCOTT *Redgauntlet* let. xi, But when he tauld his story, he got but the worst word in his wame—thief, beggar, and dyvour, were the saftest terms.

b. The womb, uterus; = BELLY *sb.* 7. † ***great wame*** pred. phr. = great (with child).

c **1425** WYNTOUN *Cron.* v. 1878 Gret wayme wiþe barne þe lady was. **1456** SIR G. HAYE *Law Arms* (S.T.S.) 40 [He] was in his moderis wame quhen his fader deid. **1508** DUNBAR *Tua mariit wemen* 131 Quhen that caribald carll wald clym on my wambe. **1787** W. TAYLOR *Sc. Poems* 35 (E.D.D.) Man naked comes frae Minnie's wyme.

c. (See quot.)

1847 STODDART *Angler's Comp.* 161 Salmon-roe as a bait for angling with..is either cured entire, that is, as it is taken from the fish in the form of what is provincially termed the *waim*; or..reduced to a paste.

† **2.** In the 17th c. the dial. word seems to have been adopted (in the forms *wem, wemb, weamb*) in southern use as a jocular substitute for 'belly'.

1611 L. BARRY *Ram Alley* v. i. H 3 b, I will home,..and drinke some Aquauita To sweeten breath, and keepe my weame from wambling. **1651** H. MORE *Enthus. Tri.* (1656) L 2, Agrippa's Cur sure kennels in thy weamb, Thou yelpest so and barkest in a dream. **1691** *Long Vacation* 6 If not their Purse, their Wems they fill. **1700** T. BROWN tr. *Fresny's Amusem., Lond.* 37 Stuffing their Wembs at Churchings. **1710** ADDISON *Whig Examiner* No. 4 ¶ 12 He clapped his hand to his sword, and told him, were he a man..he would have run him through the wemb. **1719** OZELL tr. *Misson's Trav. Eng.* 105 For two and thirty Days they satisfy'd the Decree of the Oracle, without being oblig'd to expose any human Creature to the Monster's Wem. **1720** SWIFT *Descr. Irish Feast* Misc. 1735 V. 17 A Blow on the Weam. **1764** T. BRYDGES *Homer Travest.* (1797) II. 417 And in his weem he felt a motion As if he'd ta'en a purging potion.

3. *transf.* The cavity, or the protuberant part of a thing: = BELLY *sb.* 11, 12.

a **1765** *Northumberland betrayed by Douglas* xxi. in Child *Ballads* III. 412/2 Shee let him see thorrow the weme of her ring. **1816** SCOTT *Antiq.* vii, And here or yonder—at the back o' a dyke, in a wreath o' snaw, or in the wame o' a wave, what signifies how the auld gaberlunzie dies?

† **4.** The belly-piece of a fur-skin. *Obs. rare.* Cf. WOMB.

1374 *Exch. Rolls Scot.* II. 466 In empcione de xlij wamys de menyvaire.

5. Comb.: **wame-ill** † (*a*) an epidemic disease affecting the stomach; (*b*) = STOMACH-ACHE.

c **1500** *Auchinleck Chron.* (1819) 4 þe wame Ill was so violent, þ^t^ thar deit ma þ^t^ ȝere þan euir thar deit ouder euir that deit ouder in pestilens. *a* **1585** MONTGOMERIE *Flyting* 318 The weam-eill, the wild-fire, the vomit and the vees. **1829** BROCKETT *N.C. Gloss.*, *Wame-ill*, an ache or pain in the intestines.

wamed (weɪmd), *a.* *Sc.* [f. WAME + -ED²: see WOMBED.] Having a belly (of a specified kind); in combs. ***great-wamed, yellow-wamed.***

c **1420** WYNTOUN *Cron.* v. lxxxvi. 1906 Gret wamyt wiþ child þis lady wes. **1513** DOUGLAS *Æneis* II. iv. 68 The fatale monstour..Greit wamit, and stuffit full of armyt men. **1838** *Wilson's Tales of Borders* IV. 176 He can..lurk in the green moss like the yellow-wamed ask.

wameful ('weɪmfʊl). *Sc.* [f. WAME + -FUL. Cf. *wombful* (Trevisa).] = BELLY-FUL.

[**1513**: see WAME 1.] **1722** RAMSAY *Three Bonnets* IV. 39 To drink his wamefu' o' the sea. **1786** BURNS *Ded. G. Hamilton* 12 This may do..wi' them wha Maun please the Great-folk for a wamefou. **1824** SCOTT *St. Roman's* x, A wame-fu' is a wame-fu',..whether it be of the barleymeal or the bran. **1864** LATTO *Tam. Bodkin* xviii. 176 He..had gotten his wamefu' o' guid whey-whullions.

wamel(l, wament: see WAMBLE, WAYMENT.

wame-tow. *north.* Forms: 4 **wambtoue,** 5 **-tow,** 4 **wamb(e)towe, waimto, wamtow, wametoue,** 6 **wayme-,** 5– **wametow.** [f. WAME + TOW *sb.*²] A girth or belly-band for a horse.

c **1310** *Durham Acc. Rolls* (Surtees) 511 Empt...8 Wambtoues et Rigtoues. **1337–38** *Ibid.* 34 In emendacione.. Wambtowes, vidz. 2 webbs pro cingulis. **1411** *Priory of Finchale* (Surtees) p. clvii, ij wametowes. **1663** *Depos. Cast. York* (Surtees) 100 Another..did theareupon cutt the wame-tow and tooke off the pack cloaths. **1846** BROCKETT *N.C. Gloss.* (ed. 3), Wame-towe. **1894** *Northumbld. Gloss*, *Wame-tow*, a belly-band or girth.

attrib. **1395** *Cartul. Abb. de Whiteby* (Surtees) 614 Pro iiij pese de Waimto webs, xx.d. Item pro ij dosan wamtow schafts, ij.s. **1536–37** *Durham Acc. Rolls* (Surtees) 697 Pro.. 1 dd. wametowshaftes ad 2*d.*, 2*s.*

'wamfle, *v. Sc.* [? Phonetically symbolic: of WAMPISH *v.* and WAMBLE *v.* 3 b.] *intr.* To go about with flapping garments. Of garments, etc., to flap, flutter (in the wind).

1808 JAMIESON, To *wamfle*, to move like a tatterdemallion; conveying the idea of one moving about, so as to make his rags flap. Fife. **1825–82** *Ibid.*, It is also said of a vessel at sea; 'Her sails were wamflin i' the wind'. Fife. **1864** LATTO *Tam. Bodkin* ix. 87 Had she gotten a glisk o' my solitary swallow-tail, wamflin' in the wind. **1890** SERVICE *Notandums* iv. 20 The labies o' his sark were wamflin' in the win'.

wamfler ('wɒmflə(r)). *Sc.* ? *Obs.* Also 6 **wanfler, -ar.** [? f. prec. + -ER[1].] ? A beau, gallant.

15.. R. SEMPLE in *Bannatyne MS.* (Hunterian Club) 352 Catitois [= Cotytto's] clerkis quhois college ye frequentit, Quhen ye wor wanfleris of hir wantoun band. **1580** HAY *Demandes* in *Cath. Tract.* (S.T.S.) 62 Quhether it becomes ecclesiasticall men..to have ane certain apparell quhairbe thai may be knawin be the laical people, or to be cled as wanflars. **1583** *Philotus* xvi. (Bannatyne Club), With him mair treitment on ane day, And get mair making off ȝe may, Nor with ane Wamfler, suith to say, Quhen twentie ȝeiris ar spent. **1836** J. STRUTHERS *Dychmont* IV. 412 We joy to see Thee from such wicked wamflers free.

wamle, var. WAMBLE.

wam-lock. *dial.* Also 5 **wamloke,** 6 **wemlocke,** 9 **wamloke, wemlock.** [f. WAME + LOCK *sb.*[1]] A twisted or tangled lock of wool from under the belly of a sheep.

1483 *Cath. Angl.* 407/2 Wamloke, *succida.* **1580** HOLLYBAND *Treas. Fr. Tong*, *Vne touffe de cheveux retors les vns entre les autres*, a wem-locke or locke of haire. **1847** HALLIWELL, *Wamlokes*, unwashed wool. **1876** *Whitby Gloss.*, *Wemlocks*, the loose locks of wool under the sheep's belly.

wammel, obs. form of WAMBLE.

wammera, var. WOOMERA.

wammil, -mle, obs. forms of WAMBLE.

wammus, var. WAMUS.

wampam, wampe, obs. ff. WAMPUM, VAMP.

Wampanoag (wɑːmpə'nəʊəg), *sb.* and *a.* Also †**Wampanong, -noug.** [a. Narragansett, lit. 'easterners'.] **A.** *sb.* (A member of) an Indian people of south-eastern Massachusetts and the eastern shore of Narragansett Bay. **B.** *adj.* Of, pertaining to, or designating this people.

1676 R. WILLIAMS *Let.* 1 Apr. in B. F. Swan *Copy of Let. of R. Williams* (1971) 11 God has prospered us so that wee had had driven the Wampanoogs with Phillip out of his Countrie. **1782** 'J. H. ST. JOHN DE CRÈVECŒUR' *Lett. from Amer. Farmer* iv. 144 Those powerful tribes..the.. Massachusets, Wamponougs, Nipnets, Tarranteens, &c. **1820** EASTBURN & SANDS *Yamoydan* (1834) I. 16 The Wampanoag from the height Of Haup, who strained his anxious sight [etc.]. **1871** C. M. YONGE *Pioneers & Founders* i. 25 The Sachem nearest to Plymouth had been at the first arrival of the Pilgrim Fathers, Massasoiet, chief of the Wampanongs. **1910** F. W. HODGE *Handbk. Amer. Indians* II. 903/2 Wampanoag... One of the principal tribes of New England. Their proper territory appears to have been the peninsula on the E. shore of Narragansett bay now included in Bristol co., R.I., and the adjacent parts in Bristol co., Mass. **1948** *Sat. Even. Post* 26 June 23/3 The township of Dartmouth had been purchased from Chief Massasoit, of the Wampanoag tribe. **1979** *United States 1980/81* (Penguin Travel Guides) 642 There's also the Wampanoag Indian Museum. **1980** *Smithsonian* Aug. 22 Red Wing's museum has some nice relics from early days when the Wampanoags & Narragansets..& Mohegans & Nipmucs ranged around southern New England. **1983** *Times* 3 Oct. 3/4 (*caption*) Slow Turtle, of the Wampanoag Nation, Massachusetts, at a ceremony on Hounslow Heath yesterday.

wampee (wɒm'piː). Also **whampee.** [a. Chinese *hwang-pī* (*hwang* yellow, *pī* skin).]

1. The fruit of an Asiatic tree *Clausena Wampi*, also the tree itself.

1830 LINDLEY *Nat. Syst. Bot.* 124 The Wampee, a fruit highly esteemed in China and the Indian archipelago, is the produce of Cookia punctata. **1887** *Standard* 16 Sept. 5/3 To how many is the wampee familiar?

2. In the southern U.S. = PICKEREL-WEED 2. [? A different word.]

1891 *Century Dict.* s.v. *Pontederia.*

'wampish, *v. Sc.* [Cf. WAMFLE *v.*] **a.** *intr.* To wave to and fro. **b.** *trans.* To wave or toss (one's arms) about. **c.** *intr.* To make waving movements (with the arms).

a. 1818 SCOTT *Hrt. Midl.* xlix, Put by the siller, and dinna keep the notes wampishing in your hand that gate.

b. 1816 SCOTT *Antiq.* xxxix, It's fearsome baith to see and hear her when she wampishes about her arms, and gets to her English, and speaks as if she were a prent book.

c. 1895 MACEWEN *Life Cairns* 214 'Oor John', said his anxious mother, 'wull aye be wampishin' wi' his airms.'

†**'wamplate.** *Sc. Obs.* [f. WAME + PLATE *sb.*] ? An ornamental plate on harness to be put below the belly of a horse.

1508 *Acc. Ld. High Treas. Scot.* IV. 129 Item, for purphaling for wamplates, taggis for harnes, j Birge spounge, ij handis to renȝeis [etc.].

wampum ('wɒmpəm). Chiefly *Hist.* Also 7 **wompam,** 7–8 **wampam, wampom,** 8 **wompom.** [See WAMPUMPEAG. Cf. F. *wampoum* (Littré Suppl.).]

1. Cylindrical beads made from the ends of shells rubbed down, polished, and threaded on strings, which were often combined to form bracelets, belts, collars, etc. See PEAG, ROANOKE, SEAWAN.

a. Serving as currency for the N. Amer. Indians both among themselves and in dealings with Europeans; also, in early colonial times, between Europeans for the payment of small amounts. See quot. 1643, and further quots. under WAMPUMPEAG.

1636 WINTHROP *New-Eng.* (1825) I. 193 The trade of beaver and wampom was to be farmed, and all others restrained from trading. **1643** R. WILLIAMS *Key Lang. Amer.* xxiv. 144 Their owne [money] is of two sorts: one white, which they make of the stem or stocke of the Periwinkle,..and of this sort six of their small Beads..are currant with the English for a peny. The second is black, inclining to blew, which is made of the shell of a fish, which some English call Hens, Poquauhock, and of this sort three make an English peny. *Ibid.* 147 Their white [money] they call Wompam (which signifies white), their black suckauhock (*sucki* signifying blacke). **1648** T. SHEPARD *Clear Sun-shine of Gosp.* 2 They..would..take away..your Wampam from you. **1753** S. HOPKINS *Hist. Mem. Housatunnuk Indians* (1911) 18 *note*, A Wompum is a small cylinder of about one-third of an inch long... A number of these, strung upon small threads and knit together in the form of a belt, are called a Belt of Wompum. **1786** *Phil. Trans.* LXXVI. 234 It is incumbent on the survivor to replace him, by presenting to his family either a scalp, a prisoner, or a belt consisting of some thousands of wampum. **1841–4** EMERSON *Ess., Poet* Wks. (Bohn) I. 161 Life, which can dwarf any and every circumstance, and to which the belt of wampum, and the commerce of America, are alike. **1876** BANCROFT *Hist. U.S.* II. xxvii. 183 The farmers and seamen of Massachusetts nourished its college with coin and strings of wampum, and in every village built the free school.

b. Worn as ornamental garments or jewellery.

1716 B. CHURCH *Philip's War* (1829) 141 He pulled out Philip's belt, curiously wrought with wompom, being nine inches broad, wrought with black and white wompom, in various figures, and flowers and pictures of many birds and beasts. **1771** SMOLLETT *Humphry Cl.* 13 July (1815) 234 Her arms and legs were adorned with bracelets of wampum. **1778** J. CARVER *Trav. N. Amer.* xi. 362 These belts are made of shells found on the coasts of New England and Virginia, which are sawed out into beads of an oblong form... Being strung on leather strings, and several of them sewed neatly together,..with fine sinewy threads, they then compose the same, what is termed a Belt of Wampum. **1855** LONGF. *Hiaw.* ix. 188 The shafts of Hiawatha Harmless hit the shirt of wampum.

c. Serving (as a substitute for writing) a mnemonic or symbolic purpose according to the arrangement of the beads, and so used in intertribal messages, treaty-records, etc. among the N. Amer. Indians.

1751 C. GIST *Jrnls.* (1893) 43 The Speaker with four Strings of Wampum in his Hand stood up. **1761** *Brit. Mag.* II. 480 This declaration they confirmed with belts of wampum. **1772** JOHNSON *N. Amer. Indians* in *Phil. Trans.* LXIII. 145 This chief of a whole nation has the custody of the belts of wampum, &c. which are as records of public transactions. **1823** [G. PROCTOR] *Lucubr. H. Ravelin* 354 Tecumthé..holding in his hands a belt of wampum, or beads, which by their colours and arrangement, form the Indian record for past events. **1865** LUBBOCK *Preh. Times* 227 The art of picture-writing..was supplemented among the North American Indians by the 'wampum'.

†**2.** *Conch.* Used as the name of a particular kind of shell. *Obs.*

1815 S. BROOKES *Introd. Conchol.* 157 Wampum, *Venus mercenaria.*

3. *transf.* (jocular). **a.** (After 1 a) Money. **b.** (after 1 b) *wampum and warpaint*, evening dress.

a. 1897 *Outing* XXX. 367/2, I laid some of their own miserable, smelly, garlicky, paper-wampum upon their official..desk, saying, as I did this: 'You can keep the change'.

b. 1890 'R. BOLDREWOOD' *Col. Reformer* xv, He arrayed himself in the wampum and warpaint proper for such engagements as manufactured by Mr. Poole, of Saville Row.

4. Short for *wampum-snake* (see 5). *striped wampum*, the N. American snake *Abastor erythrogrammus* (Cent. Dict.).

5. *attrib.* and *Comb.*, as *wampum-beads, belt, collar, record*; also **wampum-snake**, a name applied to certain colubrids of the southern U.S.; † (*a*) a blue-and-white snake (*obs.*); (*b*) the red-bellied snake, *Farancia abacura* (Cent. Dict.); **wampum-wise** *adv.*, (threaded) after the manner of wampum.

1766 C. BEATTY *Tour* (1768) 88 A string of *wampum beads. **1910** A. J. CHAMBERLAIN in *Encycl. Brit.* XIV. 470/1 European-made wampum-beads affected native art in the 17th century. **1761** FOOTE *Liar* I. Wks. 1799 I. 286 He shall present you with the *wampum belt, and a scalping knife. **1831** CARLYLE *Sartor Res.* I. v, Sheepskin cloaks and wampum belts. **1865** PARKMAN *Champlain* (1875) 178 Copper bracelets and *wampum collars, lynx-skins. **1895** HOFFMAN *Begin. Writing* 24 *Wampum records are purely mnemonic. **1736** MORTIMER *Nat. Hist. Carolina* in *Phil. Trans.* XXXIX. 258 The *Wampam Snake; so called from the Resemblance it hath in its Colours to the Wampam, or Indian Money, made of Pieces of Shells blue and white, strung together. **1802** SHAW *Gen. Zool.* III. 463 Wampum Snake. Coluber Fasciatus. **1790** *Proc. African Assoc.* 36 The beads are worked *wampum-wise.

wampumpeag ('wɒmpəm,piːg). Now *rare.* Forms: *α.* 7 **wampampeag, -peage, -peague, -peak(e, wampam pieg, wampanpeage, -peak, wampompeag(e, -peke, wampumpeage, -peak, wauompeg, wompampeag, wompompeag,** 7–8 **wampompeak,** 8 **wampomeag, wampompag, wampumpeg,** 9 **wampumpeag.** *β.* 7 **wampompeal.** [Adopted (in 16–17th c.) from the northerly dials. of the Algonkin language. At the time of the earliest colonization these were spoken in the East of the continent from Nova Scotia to Virginia. The ultimate forms indicated are **wampampiak*, **wampampial*, signifying 'string of (white) beads'. Cf. Rasles, *Abnaki Dict.* (1691), *wambambi*, pl. *-ak*, 'grain blan de porcelaine', *wambambiar* 'chapelet'; Delaware (Zeisberger) *wapapi* white wampum (*woapaschapiall* white beads).

The word is in form a compound of two elements meaning respectively 'white' and (probably) 'bead' with the ordinary Algonkin plural endings *-ak* (*-ag*), or *-al* (*-ar*) added. For the first element cf. Natick *wompi*, Delaware *wapi*, Abnaki *wambi-*, etc. white. An ending *-ampi* occurs in Rasles' *Abnaki Dict.* in a large number of words descriptive of strings, etc. See Rasles s.v. *chaîne, collier, corde, tresse.*

The variations between *-k*, *-g*, and between *womp-*, *wamp-*, are probably due to native dialectal differences, but the remaining variations are due to fluctuating orthography and pronunciation after the word had been adopted into English.

The division into WAMPUM and PEAG appears to be a false analysis due to Europeans.

The specific words for 'black bead-money' were never adopted into English, and perh. the tendency to generalize the name of the commoner white variety was already present in the native languages.]

= WAMPUM.

1631 WINTHROP *New-Eng.* (1825) I. 61 Mr. Shurd..sent home James Sagamore's wife, who..writ that the Indiands demanded [blank] fathom of wampampeague..for her ransom. **1635** *Relat. Maryland* v. 36 The Indian money of those parts..is of two sorts, Wompompeag and Roanoke.. Wompompeag is of the greater sort, and Roanoake of the lesser, and the Wompompeag is three times the value of Roanoake; and these serue as Gold and Siluer doe heere. **1643** in *Gen. Laws Massachusetts* (1672) 154 Wampampeag shall pass currant in the payment of Debts, to the payment of forty shillings, the white at eight a penny, the black at four, so as they be entire without breaches or deforming spots. **1683** POYNTZ *Pres. Prosp. Tobago* 22 The Cunck is a Shell Fish..; whose Shell has the tincture of Pearl colour, flame colour, and white, some part thereof being taken out, the Indians make of it their Wampam Pieg; which Shell is a staple Commodity. **1695** LOCKE *Further Consid. Value Money* 27 Among the Indians, when it [*sc.* Corn] will sell for more yards of Wampompeal, which is their Money. **1705** T. M. *Bacon's Rebellion* (1835) 14 The Queen of Pamunky.. having round her head a plat of black and white wampum peage three inches broad in imitation of a crown. **1760** T. HUTCHINSON *Hist. Col. Mass. Bay* v. (ed. 2) 472 Good store of wampompag to purchase some peculiar favors or privileges. **1875** JEVONS *Money* iv. 24 The wampumpeag of the North American Indians is a case in point, as it certainly served as jewellery.

wamtow, wamtye, obs. ff. WAME-TOW, WANTY.

wamus ('wæmʌs). *U.S.* Also **waumus, wammus.** [a. Du. *wammes*, contracted f. *wambuis*, a. OF. *wambois, -eis*: see WAMBAIS, GAMBESON. Cf. G. *wams, wamms*, woollen jacket (MHG. *wambes, -eis*, jacket worn under the armour).] In southern and western U.S., a warm knitted jacket resembling a cardigan.

1805 in Thornton *Amer. Gloss.* 934, I got up, and found that my waumus was bloody. **1854** H. H. RILEY *Puddleford* 14 (Thornton) He was attired with a red flannel 'wamus'. **1887** *Philadelphia Telegraph* 6 July 6/6 His attire was characterized by a long linsey 'wamus'. **1888** E. EGGLESTON *Graysons* xxviii. 309 This [wagon-spoke] he put into the baggy part of his 'wamus', or hunting-jacket.

wamylle, obs. form of WAMBLE.

†**wan**, *sb.*[1] *Sc. Obs.* 6 *pl.* **wannis, wannys.** [Perh. a subst. use of WAN *a.*[1] But cf. WEN.] A dark or livid mark produced by a blow; a bruise.

1533 BELLENDEN *Livy* (S.T.S.) I. 167 He..had done grete vassalege baith for þe honoure & defence of þe ciete, as weil apperit be sindri wannys & markis in his face and vther partis of his body. **1560** ROLLAND *Seven Sages* 59 The knicht ..fand his sone withouttin wan or wound. **1567** *Gude & Godlie Ballads* (S.T.S.) 32 He it is, quhilk geuis wan and wound, And suddanlie he will mak haill and sound.

†**wan**, *sb.*[2] *Obs.* Also 7 **wanne,** 8–9 *erron.* **wand.** [? a. Du. *wanne* (now *wan*): see VAN *sb.*[1]]

1. A winnowing fan: = VAN *sb.*[1] 1.

1615 CHAPMAN *Odyss.* XI. 163 What dost thou with that wanne [Gr. ἀθηρηλοιγόν, winnowing fan], vpon thy necke?

2. The sail of a windmill: = VAN *sb.*[1] 5.

Commonly spelt *wand*, the word being wrongly supposed to be a corruption of WAND *sb.*

1766 *Ann. Reg.* 77 The sails or wands of the mill.. struck her so violently on the head, as to fracture her skull. **1825** BROCKETT *N.C. Gloss.*, *Wan*, a corruption of wand. 'A *yardwan*.'—'A *mill-wan*.' **1846** M. A. RICHARDSON *Borderer's Table-bk.* V. 97 The wands of the.. wind mill.. were forced round with such velocity, that by the friction of the machinery, the mill was set on fire. **1876** *Whitby Gloss.*, *Wands* pl., long flexible rods. The sail frames of a windmill.

wan (wɒn), *a.* Forms: 1 **wan(n, won(n,** 3– **wan,** 3–4 **won,** 4–5 **wane, wonn,** 4–6 **wann(e,** 5 **wonne.** [OE. *wann* (*wǫnn*), dark, gloomy, black. Not found in any of the other Teut. languages. Its original sense appears to have been 'dark in hue', with especially frequent application to things of gloomy unpleasant associations.

Relationships to WIN *v.* (OTeut. **winnan* to strive, toil, suffer, etc.), or to WOUND *sb.*, or WEN, present difficulties of sense-development or form. Relationship to WANE etc. is possible (cf. Celtic **wanno-*, OIr. *fann*, Welsh *gwan* faint, weak, feeble), but association of the two words in later (ME. and ModE.) periods is more probable than ultimate connexion.

In addition to this association the application to heavenly bodies, when obscured, or when compared to others more bright, possibly aided the general application to pale things. The application to the human face etc., when of unwholesome or unusual colour (through various emotions, disease, or death), also provided a possible occasion of sense-change. The senses 'livid,' 'sallow', and 'pale, sickly' are often indistinguishable.]

†**1. a.** Lacking light, or lustre; dark-hued, dusky, gloomy, dark. *Obs.* Chiefly *poet.*

Beowulf 702 Com on wanre niht scriðan sceadugenga. *a* **1000** *Boeth. Metr.* xi. 61 Hwæt, þa wonnan niht mona onlihteð. *c* **1230** *Hali Meid.* 43 Ant tah is betere a briht iacinct þen a charbucle won. *a* **1300** *Signs bef. Judgm.* 43 in *E.E.P.* (1862) 8 As fair and briȝte as þou seest ham hi worþ be-com as blak as cole and be of hiwe durke and wan for man-is sin þat hi sul þole. *c* **1400** *Destr. Troy* 303 So dang he þat dog with dynt of his wappon, þat þe warlag was wete of his wan atter. *Ibid.* 6000 Mony chivalrous Achilles choppit to dethe: All his wedis were wete of þaire wan blode. *c* **1470** HENRY *Wallace* VII. 488 In the furd weill, that was bath wan and depe, Feyll off thaim fell. *c* **1480** HENRYSON *Cock & Fox* 62 In froist, in snaw, in wedder wan and weit. *a* **1529** SKELTON *P. Sparowe* 910 With vysage wan As swarte as tan. **1591** SAVILE *Tacitus, Agricola* 244 The Ocean bringeth forth pearle also, not orient, but duskish and wanne.

b. *esp.* in conventional application in poetry to the sea (waves, etc.) or other waters.

The original significance was perh. that of 'dark-hued', but the sense often approaches, or is blended with, the next. In more recent poetry the word is probably (exc. by conscious archaism) to be understood rather as 'grey, pale', but the gloomy connotation remains.

Beowulf 1374 þonon yðȝeblond up astigeð won to wolcnum. *c* **1386** CHAUCER *Knt.'s T.* 1598 Myn is the drenchyng in the see so wan. ? *a* **1400** *Morte Arth.* 492 Wery to the wane see they went alle att ones. *c* **1400** *Destr. Troy* 4633 The storme.. walt vp the wilde se vppon wan hilles. *c* **1470** HENRY *Wallace* VII. 814 Her is na gait to fle yone peple can, Bot rochis heich, and wattir depe and wan. **1501** DOUGLAS *Pal. Hon.* II. liii, Ouir waters wan, throw worthie woddis grene. **1535** STEWART *Cron. Scot.* I. 9 Quhair that tyme almost tha had all bene lost, Throw wan tydis so stark ran by the land. *a* **1780** *Johnie Cock* xvii. in Child *Ballads* III. 4/1 She'd ha wet her foot ith wan water, And sprinkled it oer my brae. **1865** SWINBURNE *Chastelard* I. ii. 33 Do you yet mind at landing how the quay Looked like a blind wet face in waste of wind And washing of wan waves? **1865** KINGSLEY *Herew.* xviii, Looking outside across the wan water for the sails which never came.

†**c.** Applied to lead, or things compared to it (in colour). *Obs.*

1398 TREVISA *Barth. De P.R.* XIX. xx. (1495) 876 Leed is whyte by kynde though it be wan wythout. **1477** NORTON *Ord. Alch.* v. in Ashmole (1652) 56 Colour wan as Lead. **1520** WHITINTON *Vulg.* (1527) 2 His lyppes be as wanne as lede. **1653** R. SANDERS *Physiogn.* 183 A wan leadish colour.

†**2.** *transf.* or *fig.* Sad, dismal; also awful, fearful, deadly, cruel, wicked, etc. (Cf. uses of *dark*, *gloomy*.) *Obs. poet.*

c **1400** *Destr. Troy* 3602 There is no worship in weping, ne in wan teres! *c* **1440** *York Myst.* vii. 38 Me for to were fro warkes wanne. **1535** STEWART *Cron. Scot.* II. 407 Gratius God that hes all thing in erd, At his weilding to weill or ȝit wan werd.

†**3.** Of an unhealthy, unwholesome colour; livid, leaden-hued. Applied *esp.* to wounds, to the human face discoloured by disease, and to corpses. *Obs.*

c **700** *Epinal Gloss.* 576 *Livida toxica*: tha uuannan aetrinan. *c* **1375** *Cursor M.* 24470 (Fairf.) þi bodi is wanne as þou ware dede. **1388** WYCLIF *1 Pet.* ii. 24 And he hym silf bar oure synnes in his bodi on a tre, that we be deed to synnes, and lyue to riȝtwisnesse, bi whos wan wounde ȝe ben heelid. **1398** TREVISA *Barth. De P.R.* XVII. xxxviii. (1495) 625 Powder of comyn wel medlyd wyth wexe dooth away wanne colour that comyth of smytynge. *Ibid.* XIX. xxi. 876 Wanne colour betokenyth angwysshe and passion of the herte whyche drawyth inwarde the hete of blood. **1483** *Cath. Angl.* 408/1 Wann.., *cerulus, ceruleus, pallidus, liuidus.* **15..** DUNBAR *Poems* lxxxvi. 35 Thy sone Jhesu, with his woundis wan, Quhilk deinȝeit him for our trespass to de. **1526** *Pilgr. Perf.* (W. de W. 1531) 257 And those moost beautyfull & fayre chekes, all bloo & wanne, with buffettes & beatynges. *c* **1560** A. SCOTT *Poems* xxxiii. 16 Evill lyfe, and langour but releif Off woundis wan. **1570** LEVINS *Manip.* 20/21 Wan,.. *liuidus.* **1615** SYLVESTER tr. *H. Smith's Micro-cosm.* 71 The Nobler states with Enuy wan, Without end are torne and tost. **1655** CULPEPPER etc. *Riverius* ix. ix. 273 If.. the wan and deadly color of the Face.. be restored, there is hope of Health.

4. a. Pallid, faded, sickly; unusually or unhealthily pale. Most frequently applied to the human face (or to things with conscious metaphor from this application).

a **1300** *Cursor M.* 4547 For lene he was, and wan þe face. *Ibid.* 24471 þi face es wan as ros vnrede. *a* **1310** in Wright *Lyric P.* vi. 28 Nihtes when y wende ant wake, for-thi myn wonges waxeth won. **1393** LANGL. *P. Pl.* C. VII. 419 Thenne awakyde he wel wan and wolde haue ydronke. *c* **1400** *Destr. Troy* 8034 All wan was the weghe for his wete teres. *c* **1450** in *Retrosp. Rev.* (1853) Nov. 104 On a greene hylle he sawe a tree,.. Pale hyt was and wanne of blee. **1530** PALSGR. 328/2 Wanne of colour, *palle, yndeux, blesme.* **1542** UDALL *Erasm. Apoph.* 120 One.. opposed Diogenes with this question, for what cause golde looked to the yie somewhat pale and wanne of coloure? **1561** T. HOBY tr. *Castiglione's Courtyer* III. (1577) O j, In like manner where shee is somewhat fatter or leaner than reasonable sise, or wanner, or browner, to helpe it with garmentes. **1582** STANYHURST *Æneis* III. (Arb.) 77 Theire face wan withred in hunger. **1599** MARSTON *Antonio's Rev.* Prol. 3 The wan bleak cheek of the numd earth. **1628** GAULE *Pract. Th.* (1629) 360 His Body was now cold, and wanne, stiffe, and still. **1697** DRYDEN *Æneis* III. 773 So thin, so ghastly meagre, and so wan, So bare of flesh, he scarce resembled Man. **1748** *Anson's Voy.* II. xiii. 275 The wan and meager countenances of the crew. **1800** COLERIDGE *Christabel* II. 621 Why is thy cheek so wan and wild, Sir Leoline? **1803** SCOTT *Cadyow Castle* xxiii, There, wan from her maternal throes, His Margaret, beautiful and mild, Sate in her bower, a pallid rose. **1829** LYTTON *Devereux* II. v, The hangings were wan and colourless. **1837** DICKENS *Pickw.* xlvii, The crowd of wan, emaciated faces. **1863** BARING-GOULD *Iceland* 120 Dawn broke at last, wan and blear in the south. **1897** *Allbutt's Syst. Med.* III. 329 The thickening of the blood in cholera is sufficient to account for the fall of arterial pressure, the diminished size of the pulse,.. and the wan appearance of the patient.

fig. **1742** GRAY *Eton* 68 Envy wan, and faded care. **1747** COLLINS *Passions* 25 With woful Measures wan Despair Low sullen Sounds his Grief beguil'd. **1883** R. W. DIXON *Mano* I. viii. 23 Why failed his thoughts to pierce the wan regret Of love within that look?

b. *esp.* in phr. ***pale and wan*** (***wan and pale***).

c **1374** CHAUCER *Troylus* II. 551 He for wo was pale and wan. **1447** BOKENAM *Seyntys, St. Faith* 375 Bryht of ble He was & of colour neþir pale ne wan. **1513** DOUGLAS *Æneis* IX. xiii. 4 Thar feris fleand pail and wan haue thai sene, And thar cheif ennemy closyt in thar wallis. **1588** SHAKS. *Tit. A.* II. iii. 90 Why doth your Highnes looke so pale and wan? **1590** SPENSER *F.Q.* II. xi. 22 As pale and wan as ashes was his looke. **1601** HOLLAND *Pliny* XXVIII. ix. II. 321 Drusus sometimes a Tribune of the Commons in Rome, dranke (as it is reported) Goats bloud, to make himselfe look pale and wan in the face. **1679** in *Verney Mem.* (1907) II. 333 He was grown pale, wan, lean and long-visaged. **1736** AINSWORTH *Eng.-Lat. Dict.*, Blank (pale and wan), *pallens, pallidus.* **1812** J. WILSON *Isle of Palms* i. 675 Yea, many a visage wan and pale, Will hang at midnight o'er my tale. **1867** MISS BRADDON *Rupert Godwin* i, Clara Westford's noble face is pale and wan this sunny morning.

c. ***a wan smile***, a faint or forced smile (as of one sick or unhappy).

1877 MRS. FORRESTER *Mignon* I. 217 With a wan smile as she sees her friend's grieved face. **1896** CONAN DOYLE *Exploits Gerard* v. (1903) 190 'But,' he added, with a wan smile, 'my Lenten fare is always somewhat meagre'.

d. Applied to the (light of) heavenly bodies, etc.: Faint, sickly, partially obscured. Also, of white objects, etc.: Dull, lustreless.

1601 HOLLAND *Pliny* II. xxx. I. 17 In the warres of Antonie, the Sunne continued almost a yeere long with a pale and wan colour. **1633** P. FLETCHER *Purple Isl.* XI. i, The Moon grows wanne, and starres flie all away, Whom Lucifer locks up in wonted folds. **1667** MILTON *P.L.* x. 412 The blasted Starrs lookt wan. **1771** BEATTIE *Minstr.* I. xxv, Ye mildews wan. **1798** WORDSW. *Night-piece* 3 The sky is overcast.. Heavy and wan, all whitened by the Moon. **1861** J. THOMSON *Ladies of Death* xxii, Moonless nights when stars are few and wan. **1873** W. BLACK *Pr. Thule* xxv, There were wan glimmerings of sunshine across the sea. **1889** BRIDGES *Sonn.* lvii, In autumn moonlight, when the white air wan Is fragrant in the wake of summer.

†**e.** Of colour: ? Pale, light. *Obs.*

1567 MAPLET *Gr. Forest* 3 b, Whose interchanged greene colour resembleth almost the wan and yellow colour of Golde.

5. *absol.* (quasi-*sb.*) Wan hue, wanness. *poet.*

1821 JOANNA BAILLIE *Metr. Leg., Lady G. Baillie* iv, She saw a faint glow tinge the sickly wan. **1847** TENNYSON *Princess* III. 9 Melissa, tinged with wan from lack of sleep.

6. *Comb.*: chiefly parasynthetic, as ***wan-coloured***, ***-faced***, ***visaged***; also complementary and advb., with pples., as ***wan-looking***, ***-silvering***, ***-worn***; rarely qualifying other adjs. descriptive of colour, as ***wan-sallow***, †***-white***; ***wanwood***, faded or decaying woodland (*nonce-wd.*).

1820 WODARCH *Introd. Conchol.* 12 Which.. seldom exhibits any other appearance than that of a livid or *wan-colored surface. **1881** 'RITA' *My Lady Coquette* x, It is a sorrowful, *wan-faced girl. **1913** *Blackw. Mag.* Aug. 281/1 Wan-faced men and towsel-haired women. **1882** 'OUIDA' *Maremma* I. 58 Wasted and *wan-looking folks. **1872** TENNYSON *Gareth & Lynette* 443 A man of mien *Wan-sallow as the plant that feels itself Root-bitten by white lichen. **1849** LYTTON *K. Arthur* v. i, *Wan-silvering through the hush, the cresset shone O'er the arch seer. **1508** DUNBAR *Flyting* 101 *Wan wisaged widdefow, out of thy wit gane wyld. *c* **1530** *Judic. Urines* III. xix. 61 And sume Auctours saye that *wan-whyte colour in vryn.. sheweth begynnyng of digestyon. *c* **1880** *Wanwood [see *leafmeal* s.v. LEAF *sb.*^{1} 18]. **1609** W. BARLOW *Answ. Nameless Cath.* 141 To haue her painting wiped from her riueld browes and *wan-worn cheeks.

wan (wɒn, wan), *numeral a., pron.*, etc. [See ONE *numeral a., pron.*, etc.] Repr. dial. pronunc. of *one*.

1651 [see ONE *numeral a., pron.*, etc. A. *γ*]. **1802** in G. Fraser *Lowland Lore* (1880) 70, I ame to Give to him.. wan half of Corn. **1880** L. PARR *Adam & Eve* II. ix. 191 'Twas past wan. **1907** G. B. SHAW *John Bull's Other Island* IV. 81 Larry cleared six yards backwards at wan jump. **1920** F. P. DUNNE *Mr. Dooley on making a Will* 4 'Twud grieve me if some wan broke into song at th' news. *a* **1966** 'M. NA GOPALEEN' *Best of Myles* (1968) 47 If wan is up, all has to be up. **1973** *Black World* Sept. 64 Di ripes juices fruit is di wan Dat stan longer in di sun. **1973** 'J. PATRICK' *Glasgow Gang Observed* vii. 70 He's the wan they're really efter. **1979** *Bull. Yorks. Dial. Soc.* Summer 14 Wan mornin t schooilmaister wor ill.

wan (wɒn), *v.* Inflected **wanned, wanning.** Also 3 **wonne.** [OE. *wannian*, f. WAN *a.*]

†**1.** *intr.* To become dark, discoloured, or livid.

c **1000** *Vercelli MS.* 23 b/7 þonne wannað he & doxaþ; oðre hwile he bið blæc & æhiwe. *c* **1230** *Hali Meid.* 35 þine ehnen schulen doskin & under þon wonnen. *a* **1400–50** *Wars Alex.* 4142 þe son wadis, þe werd wannes at a wap & þe wedire gloumes. *Ibid.* 4627 Quen it [gold] walows & wannes all oure thestres, ȝet ere we toghid to & fra be turnyng of eldris.

2. To grow pale. *poet.*

1582 STANYHURST *Æneis* IV. (Arb.) 118 Al her visage waning with murder aproching [L. *pallida morte futura*]. **1599** MARSTON *Ant. & Mel.* III. (1602) E 4, I haue a good head of haire, a cheeke Not as yet wan'd. **1602** SHAKS. *Ham.* II. ii. 580 (Q 1604) Is it not monstrous that this player heere.. Could force his soule so to his owne conceit That from her working all the visage wand [*Folio* warm'd]. **1847** TENNYSON *Princess* IV. 142 Psyche flush'd and wann'd and shook. **1855** —— *Maud* I. I. iii, And ever he mutter'd and madden'd, and ever wann'd with despair. **1866** CONINGTON *Æneid* IV. p. 128 The queen,.. wanning o'er with death foreseen. **1901** HENLEY *Hawthorn & Lavender* xlvi. 62 And by and by The wide-winged sunset wanned and waned. **1906** F. THOMPSON *To English Martyrs* 18 The troubled heavens do wan with care.

3. *trans.* To make pale.

1889 in *Cent. Dict.* **1903** HARDY *Dynasts* I. I. iii. 16 The grey glooms of a ghost-eyed despondency Wanned as with winter the national mind. **1938** W. DE LA MARE *Memory* 96 Miracle.. That starry flake Can of its myriads Such wide pastures make, For sun to colour, And for moon to wan.

Hence **wanned** *ppl. a.*, **'wanning** *vbl. sb.*

a **1513** FABYAN *Chron.* VII. 683 Whoom deth soo stern wyth his wannyd hewe Hath now pursuyd. **1606** SHAKS. *Ant. & Cl.* II. i. 21 All the charmes of Loue, Salt Cleopatra soften thy wand lip. [**1818**: see WANED *ppl. a.*] **1888** *Longman's Mag.* Feb. 392 Many [actors] assert that the 'wanning' of the visage is a common.. accompaniment of imagined terror.

wan: see WAND *sb.*, WHEN, WHENNE, WHOM, WIN *v.*, WONE *sb.*

wan- (wɒn), a prefix expressing privation or negation (approximately equivalent to UN-^{1} or MIS-), repr. OE. *wan-*, *wǫn-*, corresponding to OFris. *wan-*, *won-*, OS. *wan-* (only in *wanskefti* misfortune = OE. *wansceaft*), MLG., MDu. *wan-* (mod.Du. in many new formations, esp. in the sense 'wrong', 'mis-', as in *wanbestuur* misgovernment, *wanluid* discordant sound), OHG. *wan-*, *wana* (only in *wanwâfan* unarmed, *wanaheil* unhealthy, infirm, *wanawizzi* lacking wit, insane), MHG. *wan-* (only in *wanwitze* inherited from OHG.), mod.G. *wahn-* (in *wahnwitz*, *wahnsinn* insanity, commonly apprehended as compounds of *wahn* sb., delusion; also in some dialect words, chiefly adopted from LG.); ON., Sw., Da. *van-* (in many old formations, to which mod.Sw. and Da. have added many more, chiefly adopted from LG.). The prefix is in origin identical with WANE *a.*

In OE. the number of words formed with the prefix is considerable, but none of them has survived into modern English, and only one (*wanspêd*, ill-success) into ME. Of the many new formations that arose in ME., only *wantoȝen*, undisciplined, WANTON, still survives in use (with no consciousness of its etymological meaning); *wanhope* and *wantrust* may have been suggested by the equivalent MDu. forms. It was in the north that the prefix was most prolific, and it probably continued to be productive far into the modern period. The following words, peculiar to the Scottish and northern dialects, are recorded in the *Eng. Dial. Dict.*, mostly with examples (or references to glossaries etc.) from the 18th c., but few if any of them are now in current use:—***wancanny*** adj., WANCHANCY *a.*, ***wancheer*** grief, sadness, ***wancouth*** adj. = uncouth, ***wandeidy*** adj., mischievous, WANDOUGHT *a.* and *sb.*, ***wanearthly*** adj., WANEASE, WANFORTUNE, ***wanfortunate***, adj. WANHAP, WANLIESUM, ***wanlit*** adj., ***wanluck***, ***wanown't*** adj. = unowned, ***wanreck*** 'mischance, ruin', WANREST, WANTHRIVEN *a.*, ***wanuse*** misuse, waste, WANWEIRD, WANWORTH adj. and sb.

wana, obs. form of IGUANA.

wanacoe, obs. var. GUANACO.

1796 STEDMAN *Surinam* II. xvi. 12 Another monkey.. which is in Surinam called the *wanacoe*.

†**'wanal,** *a. Obs. rare*$^{-1}$. In 7 wainal. [f. WANE *sb.* + -AL^1.] Of the moon: Waning.

1693 EVELYN *De la Quint. Compl. Gard.* I. 14 Blockheads, who cannot speak three words of their own Trade, without intermixing the Full and Wainal-Moon.

‖**wananchi** (wəˈnæntʃɪ), *sb. pl.* [Swahili, pl. of *mwananchi* inhabitant, citizen.] The indigenous workers in Kenya and Tanzania; the labouring masses.

1969 *Busara* (Nairobi) II. ii. 55 The problem was how to unite and propel a nation *into a prosperous future and not into the African past.* The distinction between these two threads of thought has yet to be clarified to millions of expectant *Wananchi.* **1970** *E. Afr. Standard* 2 Jan. 6/7 Musical concerts..for the entertainment of the *wananchi.* **1974** *Sunday Tel.* 8 Dec. 5/6 For it was only a few weeks ago..that President Nyerere was going about giving the *wananchi* (labouring masses) the good word about how Socialist Tanzania was doing very nicely, thank you. **1980** *Standard* (Nairobi) 2 June 7/2 The Machakos District Commissioner ..called on *wananchi* and leaders in the district to maintain peace.

‖**wanax** (ˈwænæks). Also **Wanax.** [ad. Gr. ϝάναξ, early and dial. form of ἄναξ lord.] A Mycenæan or Minoan king or ruler.

ϝάναξ is the word for 'king' or 'ruler' in the Linear B tablets; in the Homeric poems ἄναξ and βασιλεύς are both found.

[**1955** L. R. PALMER in *Trans. Philol. Soc. 1954* 37 ϝάναξ is used in Greek of the human lord..and of the divine protectors... The Tacitean passage inclines me to the view that the *wa na ka* is a priest-king (*rex*), who stands at the apex of the social hierarchy above the military leader (*dux*).] **1956** VENTRIS & CHADWICK *Documents in Mycenaean Greek* v. 120 A monarchical system of government is proved for both Knossos and Pylos by references to the king (*wanax*); the absence of any further qualification shows that the state knew one king only. **1958** *Listener* 11 Dec. 1004/1 The.. more varied documents..have perhaps tempted Professor Webster to assume too easily that the Mycenean *Wanax* was likewise a divine King. **1960** S. DOW *Greeks in Bronze Age* 25 When the destruction of the Twelfth Century took place, the chief of state, the *Wanax,* was evidently completely abolished. **1961** C. G. STARR *Origins Greek Civilization* (1962) ii. 48 The class struggle rose through serfs or slaves ..to the retainers and agents of the great king, the *wanax.* **1978** *Antiquaries Jrnl.* LVIII. 22 At the summit [of an Achaean state] was the wanax, the head of the state, chief administrator, high judge, leader of the armed forces, and absolute controller of all economic activity.

†**wanbeleve.** *Obs.* [f. WAN- + *beleve,* BELIEF.] Unbelief. Also **wanbeleveness.** So **wanbeliever,** an unbeliever; **wanbelieving** *sb.*

c **1440** *Promp. Parv.* 515/1 Wanbeleue, or wanbeleuenesse (*v.rr.* wanbeleuynge, wanbeleve), *perfidia, diffidencia. Ibid.,* Wanbeleuare, *perfidus, perfida.* *a* **1470** *Dives & Pauper* (W. de W. 1496) I. xl. 80/2 Make hym soo afered that he sholde lese his wytte & falle in wanbyleue.

†**wanbode.** *Obs.*⁻⁰ [f. WAN- + OE. *boda* agent-n. to *bēodan* to BID (recorded only in sense 'messenger', etc.: see BODE *sb.*¹).] (See quot.)

c **1440** *Promp. Parv.* 515/1 Wanbode [*v.r.* wambode], he þat byddyth lytylle for a thynge [*v.rr.* he that bedyt nowt to þe worthe,..þat bydyt nowt to wurth or valv], *invalidus licitator.*

†**wanbody.** *Obs. rare*⁻¹. [f. WAN- + ? BODY *sb.* (But the rhyme suggests that the word may be a scribal error for prec., in some obscure use).] ? A 'miscreant', infidel.

1303 R. BRUNNE *Handl. Synne* 6159 Þe sarazyns and ouþer wanbodyes, Þer-of [*sc.* of gold and silver] þey make þat are here goddes.

wance(t): see ONCE *adv.* A. δ.

†**wanchance.** *Sc. Obs.* [f. WAN- + CHANCE *sb.*] Ill-luck, misfortune.

1599 ALEX. HUME *Poems* (S.T.S.) *Hymn* iv. 78 For after death na mischiefe may befall, Bot wo, wan-chance, and perrels all are past.

wanchancy (wɑnˈtʃansɪ), *a. Sc.* (now *literary*). Also **-cie.** [f. prec. + -Y. Cf. UNCHANCY *a.*] Unlucky, dangerous; also, eerie, uncanny.

1768 ROSS *Helenore* etc. *Rock & wee pickle Tow* 60 A mutchkin of linseed I'd in the yerd fling, For a' the wan chansie [1789 wanchansy] beginning o't. *a* **1774** FERGUSSON *Mutual Compl.* 34 My travellers are fley'd to deid Wi' creels wanchancy, heap'd wi' bread, Frae whilk hing down uncanny nicksticks, That [etc.]. **1786** BURNS *Puir Mailie* 38 Wae worth that man wha first did shape That vile, wanchancie thing—a raep! **1814** SCOTT *Wav.* lxiv, Some wanchancy person..fired a shot at him. **1827** —— *Two Drovers* ii, [A dirk] is a wanchancy weapon in a Highlandman's hand. **1893** STEVENSON *Catriona* xv, The tither [boat] lay whaur it was and watched the wanchancy thing on the brae-side.

wanclen: early ME. pl. of WENCHEL.

†**wancraunt,** *a. Obs. rare*⁻¹. [Perh. to be read *waucraunt,* a. AF. *wakerant, walkerant*: see VAGRANT.] Given to wandering.

1422 YONGE tr. *Secreta Secr.* xlix. 212 Precious and dere as an oliphaunt, lytill worth and dull as an asse, Prophitable as a bee, wancraunt and dyssolute as a goote.

wand (wɒnd), *sb.* Forms: 3–5 **wond,** 4–5 **wonde, wende,** 5 **won,** 4 **waande,** 4–6 **wande** 4 **vande,** 6 **vand,** 8–9 *dial.* **wan,** 9 *Sc.* **whand,** 3– **wand.** [a. ON. (**vandu-r*) *vǫnd-r* (MSw. *vand-er,* Sw. *vand,* Da. *vaand,* Norw. *vona*) = Goth. *wandu-s*:—OTeut. **wandu-z* (not found in WGer.), prob. f. the root **wend-*: **wand-* (to turn, wind (see WIND *v.*), so that the etymological connotation is that of suppleness or flexibility).] A stick or rod. The word has little colloquial currency exc. in Sc. and northern dialects, in which it suggests the notion of suppleness; as a literary word it is usually apprehended (by southern readers) as denoting something rigid. In the Bible of 1611 it occurs only once (Ecclus. xxxiii. 24); the Revised Version (1894) substitutes *stick.*

1. a. A straight slender stick. Now Sc. and *dial.* In Scottish use, chiefly a slender pliant stick cut from a stem or branch of a shrub or young tree.

The early examples occur chiefly in biblical references, where mod. usage follows the Bible of 1611 in substituting *rod*; applied, e.g., to the 'rod' carried by Moses, to Aaron's 'rod' that budded, etc.

c **1200** ORMIN 16178 Þatt he swa swiþe mikell follc Draf all ut off þe temmple, All att hiss wille wiþþ an wand. *c* **1250** *Gen. & Ex.* 2923 And worpen he ðor wondes dun, fro euerilc ðor crep a dragun. *c* **1400** MAUNDEV. (Roxb.) xi. 43 In þat ark ware Moyses tables,..and Aaron wand, and þe ȝerde of Moyses. *c* **1460** *Towneley Myst.* viii. 247 *Moyses...* My Wand he bad, in thi present, I shuld lay downe, and the avyse how it shuld turne to oone serpent. **1587** HARRISON *England* I. xviii. 109/2 in *Holinshed,* If it..be accompted good soile, on which a man may laie a wand ouer night, and on the morrow find it..ouergrowen with grasse. **1601** HOLLAND *Pliny* xxxiv. vi. II. 492 [He] made no more adoe, but with a wand or rod that he had in his hand, drew a circle about the king, and compelled him perforce to give him his answere before he stirred his foot without that compasse. **1603** *Reg. Mag. Sig. Scot.* 487/2 Reddendo unam virgam agrifolii (ane grene holene wand) nomine albe firme. **1616** R. C. *Times' Whistle* (1871) 35 He that desires to breake a bunch of wandes, Must not take all at once into his handes. **1624** GATAKER *Transubst.* 49 Moses holding a wand in his hand, did cast it from him, and it became a serpent. **1670** MILTON *Hist. Brit.* IV. 157 Sigebert..they..carried by force out of the Monastery into the Camp; where acting the Monk rather then the Captain, with a single wand in his hand, he was slain with Egric.

fig. *c* **1450** HOLLAND *Houlate* 752 Thow seker trone of Salamon, Thow worthy wand of Aaron.

b. As a type of slenderness or straightness.

1508 DUNBAR *Gold. Targe* 63 Ane hundreth ladyes..With ..mydlis small as wandis. **1591** SHAKS. *Two Gent.* II. iii. 23 Now sir, this staffe is my sister: for, looke you, she is as white as a lilly, and as small as a wand. [1608: see *wand-like* in 15.]

†**c.** A light walking-stick, cane. *Obs.*

1548 UDALL etc. *Erasm. Par. Mark* vi. 6–9 For he geueth them leaue to vse eche one a wande, and a payre of sandals. **1576** FLEMING *Panopl. Epist.* 202 Bringing him into the corne field, and smyting off, with a wand that I helde in my hande, the eares of wheate. **1607** *Peele's Jests* (*c* 1620) 4, I thank you sir, quoth the barber, so on goes George with him in his green Jerkin, a wand in his hand very pretty. **1667** MILTON *P.L.* I. 294 His spear, to equal which the tallest Pine Hewn on Norwegian hills, to be the Mast Of some great Ammiral, were but a wand, He walkt with. **1760–2** GOLDSM. *Cit. W.* xiii, From hence our conductor led us through several dark walks.., talking to himself, and flourishing a wand which he held in his hand.

d. A stick used as a pointer.

1589 [see WANT *sb.*² 5 b]. **1840** DICKENS *Old C. Shop* xxviii, Mrs. Jarley..formally invested Nell with a willow wand, long used by herself for pointing out the characters.

2. a. A young shoot, a slender stem of a shrub or tree, a sapling; a slender branch or twig. *Obs.* exc. *poet.* (*rare*) and *dial.* † *under the wand*: in the greenwood.

a **1300** *Cursor M.* 1418 Þe pipins war don vnder his [Adam's] tung, Þar ras o þam thre wandes yong. **13..** *Gaw. & Gr. Knt.* 1161 At vche wende vnder wande wapped a flone. *c* **1400** *Melayne* 1213 Þᵉ Messangere bare a wande Of ane Olefe in his hande. *c* **1400** *26 Pol. Poems* xv. 60 For al þe body beren þay [*sc.* man's legs], As a tre þat bereþ wandes. *c* **1440** *York Myst.* xii. 78 Vpponne þat wande sall springe a floure. *c* **1440** *Pallad. on Husb.* IV. 537 A toppe of hit [the fig] to sette other a wonde Is holdon best right in Aprilis ende. **1457** HARDYNG *Chron.* in *Eng. Hist. Rev.* (1912) Oct. 746 Men chastyse ofte grete courours by hakenayse, And writhe the wande while it is yonge and grene. *c* **1480** HENRYSON *Town & C. Mouse* iii, Scho tuik in mynde hir sister vponland, And langit..To se quhat lyfe scho had vnder the wand. **1559** in *Reg. Mag. Sig. Scot. 1565* 390/1 Rungis and wandis of hissill and sauch. **1592** GREENE *Disput.* 26 They.. bent the tree while it was a wand. **1596** SPENSER *F.Q.* v. ix. 17 Into a bird it chaung'd, and from him past, Flying from tree to tree, from wand to wand. **1596** *Edw. III,* v. 143 A Hasle wand amidst a wood of Pynes. **1850** ALLINGHAM *Poems, Music-Master* I. xxiv, The heart is new As the green wand fresh budded on a fir. **1919** *Blackw. Mag.* Nov. 645/1 The stem bends like a hazel wand.

b. as a type of suppleness.

1412–20 LYDG. *Chron. Troy* II. 2472 And with hym brouȝt ..His slepy ȝerde as plyaunt as a wonde. *c* **1480** HENRYSON *Age & Youth* 13 His eyne wes hol, his woce wes hace hostand, walowit & wane, waik as ane wand. **1535** STEWART *Cron. Scot.* (Rolls) I. 381 Leicht as ane leif, and waldin as ane wand.

3. A young shoot of willow cut to be used in basket-making, wattled buildings, or the like. Also *collect.* Now *Sc.* and *dial.*

a **1300** *Cursor M.* 1672 First bind it wele wit balk and band, And wind it siþen well wit wand. *c* **1450** *St. Cuthbert* (Surtees) 6900 A litil chapell of wandes þai made. **1457** *Nottingham Rec.* II. 365 Peid to a man for bondyll wandus jd. **1572** *Wills & Inv. N.C.* (Surtees) I. 375 Cowpe waynes of wandes. **1615** MARKHAM *Country Contentm.* I. i. 14 Which seats would bee either boorded, or watled with stakes and small wands on the sides to hold vp the earth from falling. **1724** RAMSAY *Tea-T. Misc.* (1733) I. 29 Ane auld kist made of wands. **1770** *J. Coates's Coll. Poems* 21 The light machine [the cradle] with decent neatness stands, The jetting sides compos'd of slender wands. **1796** W. MARSHALL *Planting* I. 187 In Yorkshire, the 'wands' are sold by the bundle; but in Glocestershire, where Ozier grounds abound.., the grounds are let..to basket makers. *a* **1803** *Lord William* ix. in Scott *Minstr. Scott. Bord.* III. 267 Your cage shall be of wiry goud, Whar now it's but the wand. *a* **1825** FORBY *Voc. E. Anglia, Wan,* a long rod to wave into a wattled hedge.

†**4. a.** A rod, stick, or switch for chastisement; also *fig.* (in religious use) *Obs.* Also *dial.* a 'rod' or bundle of twigs for flogging.

1297 R. GLOUC. (Rolls) 5888 Ȝerd ne vond heo preste non þat child uorto bete. *a* **1300** *Cursor M.* 2612 Abram said ..þou chasti hir sco [*read* þou] has þe wand. **1340** HAMPOLE *Pr. Consc.* 5878 'Þe wande', he says, 'of disciplyne smart, Sal chace foly out of þe childes hert'. *c* **1400** *26 Pol. Poems* xxiv. 48 To ȝerde of loue y moste me boun; Lord, me chastice wiþ þat wande. *c* **1400** *Cursor M.* 29093 (Cotton Galba MS.) þe first [discipline es]..Als wering of haire and oþer thing..þat oþer point to vnderstand, Es kneling and beteing with wand. **1549** *Compl. Scot.* i. 23 Quhiddir that this dolorus afflictione be ane vand of the fadir to correct & chestie the sone be mercy, or [etc.]. **1633** SIR A. JOHNSTON (Ld. Wariston) *Diary* (S.H.S.) I. 46 If I..had humbled myselth unto the Lord whil the wand was above my head, the Lord would haive spaired. **1828** *Craven Gloss., Wand,* a rod, a collection of twigs, used for correction.

†**b.** ***under the wand***: liable to corporal correction. Hence (with influence of sense 6), subject to (the) rule (*of* a person): = med.L. *sub virga.* Cf. YARD *sb.* 4. *Sc. Obs.*

c **1400** *Rule St. Benet* ii. 6 Wide summe sal tu faire speke, and summe gete wid chastiment & haue þam under wand. **1456** SIR G. HAYE *Law Arms* (S.T.S.) 106 The Emperour has mony syndry kynde of peple under his wand. **1575** in *Maitl. Cl. Misc.* I. 125 Thair is sum brether quhilk ar nocht under the vand of the prouest and bailyeis of the burgh. **1609** SKENE *Reg. Maj., Quon. Attach.* xx, Sa lang as her husband was livand, she was vnder his wand and power.

5. A stick or switch for urging on a horse. *Obs.* exc. *dial.*

c **1400** MAUNDEV. (Roxb.) xxvi. 122 Þai hase owþer in þaire hand a whippe or a wand. **1529** LYNDESAY *Compl.* 180 [Thay] nother sparit spurris nor wandis. **1587** MASCALL *Govt. Cattle, Of Horses* (1596) 189 If your horse chance to tyre on the way, if spurre, and wande will not profit, ye shall put three or foure rounde peble stones into one of his eares. **1607** *Puritan* III. v. 81 Ile haue an Hackney-mans wand siluerd ore a purpose for you. **1609** BIBLE (Douay) *Ecclus.* xxxiii. 25 Fodder, and wande [so **1611**; Coverdale 1535, Geneva 1560 whippe; 1894 R.V. stick; Gr. ῥάβδος. Vulg. *virga*], and burden for an asse.

†**6.** A sceptre. *Obs.*

a **1300** [see KING *sb.* 14]. *c* **1320** *Sir Tristr.* 909 Rohand he ȝaf þe wand And bad him sitt him bi. *c* **1440** *Alphabet of Tales* lxxx. 62 He had in his hand a golden wand of þe kynges. *a* **1500** *Lancelot* 1891 For he [God] forsuth haith ifyne hyme the wond To Iustefy and Reull in pece his lond.

7. a. A rod or staff borne as a sign of office; esp. a tall slender rod of white wood, sometimes of ebony or silver, carried erect by an officer of the royal household or of a court of justice, by a verger or beadle, or by an official whose duty it is to walk before a judge or other high dignitary on occasions of ceremony.

c **1430** *Syr Gener.* (Roxb.) 1327 That day in stede of a white wonde A staf he bare thoo in his honde. *c* **1472** *B.N.C.* (Oxf.) *Munim., Coldenorton* Bdl. G. 18 A won of the bullard of the place. **14..** *Sir Beues* 3243 (Pynson) Delyuer me thy wande, For Guy, his fader, was my marchal, And so syr Beuys, hys son, shall! **1573** in Feuillerat *Revels Q. Eliz.* (1908) 200 Poles and Wandes for the Lictors. **1593** SHAKS. *2 Hen. VI,* I. ii. 28 Me thought this staffe mine Office-badge in Court Was broke in twaine And on the peeces of the broken Wand Were plac'd [etc.]. **1598** DRAYTON *Heroical Ep.* xiii. (*Elinor Cobham to Dk. Humfrey*) 62 Do shamefull penance,..Rong with a bell, a Taper in my hand, Bare-foot to trudge, before a Beedles wand. **1610** in J. Davidson *Inverurie* vi. (1878) 194 Comperit Patrick Leslie, John Johnston,..bailzies, and freely dischargit thame of their offices of bailzies, and jurisdiction thereof, be deliverance of the wand in the hands of the clerk and consall. *a* **1618** RALEGH *Prerog. Parl.* 19 What say you to the Parliaments of the White Wands in the three and thirtieth yeere of the King? **1713** SWIFT *Faggot* Wks. 1755 IV. I. 8 Stewards.. who in solemn sort Appear with slender wands at court. **1728** YOUNG *Love Fame* I. 207 Some lords it bids admire their wands so white, Which bloom, like Aaron's, to their ravish'd sight. **1776** *Pennsylvania Even. Post* 9 Apr. 178/2 His Excellency General Washington, the other General Officers and their sutes,..met in the Council Chamber, from whence, preceded by the Sheriff with his Wand, they repaired to the Old Brick Meeting House. **1789** BELSHAM *Ess.* I. xiv. 259 A ribband, a title, or a white wand, have been as eagerly pursued..as knowledge, virtue, and everlasting happiness. **1805** SOUTHEY *Madoc* I. xiii. 97 On either hand Three Monks uphold above, on silver wands, The purple pall. **1835** DICKENS *Sk. Boz, Publ. Dinners,* Up rise the visitors, in march fourteen stewards, each with a long wand in his hand, like the evil genius in a pantomime. **1853** —— *Bleak Ho.* xix, There is only one Judge in town... If the country folks of those assize towns on his circuit could see him now! No full-bottomed wig, no red petticoats, no fur, no javelin-men, no white wands. **1868** MORRIS *Earthly Par.* (1870) I. I. 5 And in their hands Long carven silver-banded ebony wands.

fig. *a* **1894** STEVENSON *In South Seas* I. vi. (1900) 46 Our chief..was always called..Taipi-kikino; and yet that was not his name, but only the wand of his false position.

b. Applied to the *caduceus* of Hermes or Mercury.

c **1407** LYDG. *Reson & Sens.* 1736 He [Mercury] helde a yerde in his ryght honde, That so mervelous a wonde was neuer sen. **1645** STAPYLTON tr. *Musæus* B 3 b, Brought to your service by his golden dart, As rough Alcides by the golden wand Of Hermes, to the Lydian Maid's command. **1697** DRYDEN *Æneis* IV. 355 But first he [Hermes] grasps within his awful Hand The mark of Sov'raign Pow'r, his Magick Wand. **1790** COWPER *Odyss.* x. 337 A God Met me, the bearer of the golden wand, Hermes.

8. a. A staff or baton serving as a symbol in certain legal transactions.

c **1420** WYNTOUN *Cron.* VIII. xii. 1963 Þis Iohun þan tuk vp a qwyt wande, And gaf vp in þis Edwardis hande Off þis Kynrik al þe richt þat he had. **1875** MAINE *Hist. Inst.* ix. 254 The wand which the claimant held in his hand is stated by Gaius to have represented a spear.

†**b.** Scots Law. ***wand of peace***: a silver-tipped baton delivered to an outlaw in token of his restoration to the king's peace; also carried by a king's messenger as the symbol of his office, and broken by him (by way of protest) if he was resisted in the execution of his duty.

1511 *Reg. Privy Seal Scot.* I. 355/2 With power to the schireffis..to relesch him fra the horne and deliver him the wand of pece, etc. **1564–5** *Reg. Privy Council Scot.* I. 311 Restoir him to oure Soverane Ladiis peace, and gif to him the wand thairof. **1672** *Rec. Justiciary Court Edinb.* (S.H.S.) II. 76 He and other persons lybelled, beat and wounded the Messenger after he had laid hold upon the said Hary and touched him with his wand of peace several times. **1678** SIR G. MACKENZIE *Crim. Laws Scot.* I. xxvi. §iii. (1699) 130 The Wand of Peace is that whereby they touch a Rebel, and declares him to be their Prisoner, and when they are deforced, they use to break the wand of Peace. **1815** SCOTT *Antiq.* xlii. **1815** —— *Guy M.* xlvi.

†**9. a.** A measuring rod. (Cf. METEWAND, YARD-WAND, ELL-WAND.) Also *Mining*, a measure of 8 feet. *Obs.*

a **1637** B. JONSON *Underwoods* xlii. (1640) 193 Guided by experience, whose straite wand Doth meet, whose lyne doth sound the depth of things. **1670** PETTUS *Fodinæ Reg.* 86 And a Meer shall contain in length 10 wands and 7 feet, that is to say 87 feet. *c* **1730** RAMSAY *Maltman* ii. (1877) II. 204 Maltmen come for siller, And gaugers with wands o'er soon. **1829** SCOTT *Anne of G.* iii, Your..sentiments..rather belong to the sword than the measuring wand.

†**b.** A measure of land; ? a VIRGATE. *Obs.*

1596 *Yorksh. Deeds* (Yorksh. Arch. Soc., Rec. Ser.) II. 191 [Two] wandes [of meadow] in the Northe Inges. **1684** *Rector's Bk., Clayworth* (1910) 67 Meadow in Easting 5 Wands, Arable 1½ Ac.

†**10.** *Anat.* The smaller bone of the forearm, the radius: = ELL-WAND 2. *Obs.*

1634 T. JOHNSON *Parey's Wks.* VI. xxvi. (1678) 147 The cubit is composed of two bones, the one of which we call the Radius, or Wand.

11. a. A magic rod; the staff used in enchantments by a fairy or a magician. Now the most prominent sense. Cf. F. *baguette*. Also *fig.*

a **1400–50** *Wars Alex.* 57 On hiȝt in his a hand haldis a wand And kenely be coniurisons callis to him spritis. *c* **1480** HENRYSON *Test. Cresseid* 311 This dulefule sentence Saturne tuik on hand,..And on hir heid he laid ane frostie wand. **1610** G. FLETCHER *Christ's Vict.* II. lviii, A Silver wande the sorceresse did sway. **1634** MILTON *Comus* 659 *Comus.* Nay Lady sit; if I but wave this wand, Your nerves are all chain'd up in Alabaster. **1667** DRYDEN *Ind. Emp.* II. i, *High-Priest*..Once, twice, and thrice, I wave my Sacred Wand, Ascend, ascend, ascend at my command. [*An earthly Spirit rises.*] **1742** YOUNG *Nt. Th.* IX. 2174 Sleep's dewy wand Has strok'd my drooping lids, and promises My long arrear of rest. **1794** MRS. RADCLIFFE *Myst. Udolpho* i, If I creep near yonder oak she will wave her fairy wand. **1798** WORDSW. *P. Bell* Prol. 146 A potent wand doth Sorrow wield. **1849** W. IRVING *Goldsmith* xlv. (1850) 422 His pen is a wand of power in his hand. **1853** DICKENS *Bleak Ho.* xxxvi, If a good fairy had built the house for me with a wave of her wand, I could not have been more considered in it. **1914** *19th Cent.* Feb. 262 Such a view, attributing as it does magical powers to the wand of the legislator, is in absolute contradiction with facts.

b. transf. ***electric wand***: see quot.

1898 SLOANE *Electr. Dict.* (ed. 2) 627 *Torch, Electric Gas Lighting*, a portable apparatus for producing a spark for gas lighting... *Synonym*—Electric Wand.

12. A fishing-rod. Now chiefly *Sc.*

1565 SIR W. CECIL in Ellis *Orig. Lett.* Ser. II. II. 296, I dowt not but though yow shall be farr off, yow will use a long anglyng wand to catch some knoledg. **1839** T. T. STODDART *Songs & P.* 13 To all wights of the wand Welcome are ye! **1895** 'COTSWOLD ISYS' *Lyra Piscat.* 102 And under the shade of the beechen boughs, I deftly ply my wand. **1913** N. MUNRO *New Road* xx, He made a fire, and cut a wand, and dropped a maggot in a pool and caught two little fishes.

13. The straight rigid pipe linking the cleaning head to the hose of a vacuum cleaner.

1940 E. HEMINGWAY *For whom Bell Tolls* xi. 149 The round opening at the end of the wand of a vacuum cleaner. **1967** *Boston Sunday Herald* 9 Apr. (Advt.), Attachments include braided hose, two wands and rug-bare floor tool. **1978** *Choice* (Austral. Consumers' Assoc.) Nov. 378 Most vacuum cleaners these days have moulded plastic bodies. Hoses are plastic or cloth covered, and some are of the 'stretch' variety. Wands and cleaning heads tend to be either plastic, steel or aluminium or a combination of these.

14. A hand-held electronic device which can be passed over a bar code to read the data it represents and convert them into a computer-compatible form.

1978 *Bookseller* 17 June 3196/1 The light pen, or 'wand', that could read machine-readable codes on books. **1980** *Sci. Amer.* Apr. 111/1 (Advt.), As part of a portable data entry system, the wand can be used to read shelf tags for inventory control and order entry. **1982** *What's New in Computing* Nov. 62/1 Intermec designs and manufactures..scanning wands for the printing and computer reading of tickets, tags and labels.

15. *attrib.* and *Comb.*, as ***wandlike*** adj. and adv.; with the sense 'made of wicker-work' (*Sc.*) as in ***wand-basket, -bed, -cage, -chair***; in sense 10, as ***wand-smitten, -stricken***. Also **wand-bearer**, one who carries a wand in a procession or otherwise as a sign of office; *spec.* as the title of certain honorary lay officials of St. Paul's Cathedral, London; †**wand-bone** (*wan beyn*) *Sc.* = sense 9; †**wand-church** (*-kirk*), cf. WANDED *a.* 1 b; †**wandclot** *dial.* (meaning obscure); †**wand-hand** *Sc.*, the hand that holds the wand or whip; **wand-weaver** *dial.*, a basket-maker.

1694 SIR J. FOULIS *Acc. Bk.* (S.H.S.) 165 For 2 *wand baskits, 1 1 0. **1840** COCKTON *Val. Vox* xv, Two *wand-bearers started off immediately for the men who were elsewhere engaged in the museum. **1872** H. P. LIDDON in J. O. Johnston *Life & Lett.* (1904) vii. 168 Thanksgiving Day. .. Mr. Foster, John and Mr. G. A. Spottiswoode, as wand-bearers, were present. We all got into church at 9.30. **1875** JOWETT *Plato* (ed. 2) I. 422 He has been a true mystic and not a mere routineer or wand-bearer. *a* **1670** SPALDING *Troub. Chas. I* (Bannatyne Club) II. 297 The young laird lying sore seik also..was transportit in ane *wandbed..fra the tolbuith to the castell. *c* **1470** HENRY *Wallace* XI. 123 On the *wan bayn with gret ire can him ta, Cleyffyt the cost rycht cruelly in twa. **1828** MOIR *Mansie Wauch* i. 10 A blackbird..hung above his head in a *whand-cage of my faither's making. **1680** SIR J. FOULIS *Acc. Bk.* (S.H.S.) 40 To mrs urqrt to buy a bairns *wand-chair, 2 18 0. **1685** G. SINCLAIR *Satan's Invis. World* 98 The Maid did start up out of a Wand-Chair, where she sat. **1898** N. MUNRO *John Splendid* xv, 'It's your welcome, Argile,' said I, putting a wand chair to the front for him. *c* **1450** *St. Cuthbert* (Surtees) 6125 A kirke..*wand kirke was called beforne. **1397** *Priory of Finchale* (Surtees) p. cxviii, Item ij *wand-clots et j stapyll. **1637** RUTHERFORD *Let. to R. Stuart* 17 June, The devil and temptations now have the advantage of the brae of you, and are upon your *wand-hand and your working hand. **1684** J. RENWICK *Serm.* (1776) 54 There is no land or church that is likely to get the wand-hand, so to speak, of Scotland. **1608** SHAKS. *Per.* v. i. 110 Such a one my daughter might haue beene: My Queenes square browes; her stature to an inch, as *wandlike-straight. **1793** MARTYN *Lang. Bot.*, *Virgatus*..*caulis*, a rod-like or wand-like stem or branch. **1834** M. SCOTT *Cruise Midge* ii, The wand-like tops of the polacre's tall masts. **1847** DARLINGTON *Amer. Weeds*, etc. (1860) 433 *Virgate*, wand-like; long, slender, and straight. **1859** MEREDITH *R. Feverel* xxii, Know you those wand-like touches of I know not what, before which our grosser being melts. **1897** H. N. HOWARD *Footsteps Proserpine* 41 As from the nebulous elemental sea, *Wand-smitten by the Eternal Mind, Earth rose. **1847** MARY HOWITT *Ballads* 267 Like that old mystery Of the *wand-stricken rock. **1896** *Leeds Mercury Suppl.* 12 Sept. (E.D.D.), His two uncles, by trade *wand-weavers.

wand (wɒnd), *v.* [f. WAND *sb.*]

1. *trans.* To wattle, interweave, plait. ***to wand in***, to enclose with wattle-work. *Sc.* and *dial.*

c **1475** *Rauf Coilȝear* 368 He kest twa Creillis on ane Capill, with Coillis anew, Wandit thame with widdeis, to wend on that wane. **1573–80** TUSSER *Husb.* (1878) 74 Now make and wand in trim bower to stand in. Leaue wadling about, till arbor be out. **1593** [cf. WANDED *ppl. a.* 1 b]. **1894** *Northumbld. Gloss.* s.v., 'The gate's wanded wi' thorns, so nowt can get in.

2. To beat with a wand or switch. *Sc.* and *dial.*

a **1585** POLWART *Flyting w. Montgomerie* 755 Tait mow, wilde sow! soone bow, or I wand thee. **1657** *Attest. Innocency Z. Crofton* 10 The Father..bad him if shee offended to take a wand and wand his daughter. **1887** *S. Chesh. Gloss.* s.v. *Wan*, Bran yo, I'll wan yo'r hide fo' yō.

3. *trans.* To scan the bar code on (an article) using a wand (WAND *sb.* 14).

1979 *Bookseller* 22 & 29 Dec. 2693/2 Books could be 'wanded' at the point of sale and the information stored on cassettes. **1982** *Fortune* 27 Dec. 100/1 Go to Section X, Jack, and wand all the woofers.

Hence '**wanding** *vbl. sb.*

1585–6 *Reg. Privy Council Scot.* IV. 44 Thay have compellit thame, be onlaying of foull hands and feirfull kynd of wanddingis, to satisfie thair..impostis.

wand, obs. pa. t. WIND *v.*

wand, var. WANNED *ppl. a. Obs.*

†**wandale**[1]. *north. Obs.* Also 4 **wandayle**, 7 **-dill.** [Of obscure formation; the second element is DALE *sb.*[2], the first element possibly WAND *sb.* 8 b.] A division of land (? of the breadth of a 'wand' or perch).

c **1150** *Charter of W. de Percy* in *Whitby Chartulary* (Surtees) II. 526 Totam terram meam de Midethet, a balco qui est inter vandelas demenii mei et vandelas hominum meorum. *c* **1285** *Deed* (Snainton near Scarborough) *Ibid.* I. 114 *note*, Unam wandaylam retro molendinum de Weldale. **1396** *Chron. de Melsa* (Rolls) II. 173 Concessit idem abbas ..Thomæ Walrano, pro 2 solidis annuis et pro homagio, unam wandayle et unam placeam terræ in Hotona. **1479** in *Hexham Priory* (Surtees) II. 81 Super lez Wandales iij rodæ. *Ibid.*, In le Wandale di. acra. **1641** BEST *Farm. Bks.* (Surtees) 127 Exchainged with Alse Edwards..the other of the Fower oxegange landes which lyeth next her landes in the pasture, for her wandill on the north side of the West-beckes.

†'**Wandale**[2]. *Obs.* Also **-dal, -dele.** [a. med.L. *Wandalī* pl. = *Vandalī* Vandals. The form with *W* was adopted by Higden from Paulus Diaconus, his authority in the chapter first quoted.] = VANDAL. Hence †**Wandalyng** [-ING[3]], a Vandal. †**Wan'dalical** *a.* [med.L. *Vandalicus*], pertaining to the Vandals.

1387 TREVISA *Higden* (Rolls) I. 205 Out þereof [Scandinavia] went Winuli and werred in Scorunga and ouer com þe Wandales. *Ibid.* V. 231 Þat tyme was sent an oost out of Rome into Spayne aȝenst þe wandales. **1432–50** tr. *Higden* (Rolls) V. 237 Þer were a c. yere from the begynnenge of the Wandalicalle persecucion begunne by Gisericus un to the goenge owte of theyme from Affrike. **1490** BRADSHAW *St. Werburge* II. 175 Our lorde..Suffred cruell people to entre this region..Danes, Gotes..Pictes and the wandeles, [etc.]. **1908** W. G. COLLINGWOOD *Scandinavian Brit.* ii. 16 The tribal confederacies of the Baltic shores—Danes, Swedes, Wandals, Burgunds, Bards, Goths.

wande, var. WONDE *Obs.*, to fear.

wanded ('wɒndɪd), *a. Obs.* (? exc. *dial.*) Also 7 **wainded.** [f. WAND *sb.* + -ED[2].]

1. Made of wicker-work. Of a bottle: Cased in wicker-work, wickered.

1567 *Richmond Wills* (Surtees) 197 In the lawe buttrye —barrells, aile potts, wanded bottles. **1574** *Ibid.* 251, I will and gyve to my lord Scroope and my laydye his wife..one wanded skeppe to put breade in. **1575** *Ibid.* 255 In the lawe chambre..j wandyt creile. **1652** *Depos. Cast. York* (Surtees) 56 She did there give him a drinke out of a wainded botle. **1653** *Knaresb. Wills* (Surtees) II. 204 In the West Parlour.. 1 wanded chaire. **1677** COLES *Dict. Eng.-Lat.*, A Wanded chair, *cathedra viminea semicircularis*. **1770** *J. Coates's Coll. Poems* 19 She, plac'd in wanded chair, all pale appear'd.

b. Of a building: Wattled. (Cf. *wand-church*, WAND *sb.* 12.)

1593 *Rites & Mon. Ch. Durh.* (Surtees) 57 From the wandyd kirke or chapell they brought the body of that holie man Sancte Cuthbert and translayted him into an other White Kirke.

2. Of cattle: ? Brindled.

1713 *Lond. Gaz.* No. 5126/12 Stoln..4 red Oxen,..one is more wanded than the others.

†**wandelard.** *Obs. rare*$^{-1}$. [a. AF. *wandelard* (13th c. in Chardry *Petit Plet* 979 and 14th c. in Bozon *Contes* lxiii); latinized ('vir valde *wandelardus*') in Wright's *Pol. Songs* (Camden Soc.) p. 49.

In these three instances the word would seem to mean 'extortioner', but this sense may be merely contextual. Doubtless of Teut. origin; possibly from the G. personal name *Wandalhart*; cf., however, MHG. *wandel*, crime.]

? A criminal, traitor.

1338 R. BRUNNE *Chron.* (1810) 115 Þise men lift þer standard..Ageyn Dauid wandelard, & disconfite him.

wander ('wɒndə(r)), *sb.* [f. the verb.]

1. An act of wandering.

1843 J. C. SHAIRP *Let.* 3 Aug., in E. H. Coleridge *Life & Corr. Ld. Coleridge* (1894) I. vi. 134, I should like, so, to have one day's wander with you amongst these hills. **1872** C. KINGSLEY *Poems, Delectable Day* iii, The afternoon's wander to windward, To meet the dear boy coming back. **1899** H. WRIGHT *Depopulation* xii. 66 You and Allan will go away on a world-wide wander all by yourselves. **1910** ELIZ. A. SHARP *William Sharp* vii. 121 One sunset I remember specially. We had gone for a wander westward.

2. A gradual change in the orientation of a gyroscope or other spinning body, esp. the earth.

1930 [see WANDER *v.* 2 g]. **1963** C. A. WILLIAMS *Aircraft Instrument Control Syst.* ii. 23 In moving a gyroscope from the North Pole to the South Pole the apparent wander would change from clockwise to anti-clockwise. **1971** *Q. Jrnl. R. Astron. Soc.* XII. 61 (*heading*) Polar wander and/or plate tectonics in the Palaeozoic. **1980** *Nature* 28 Feb. 845/1 The ~1,100 Myr Grenville mobile belt of the Laurentian (North American) Shield yields a record of uplift magnetisations defining a closed apparent polar wander (APW) loop.

wander ('wɒndə(r)), *v.* Inflected **wandered** (-dəd), **wandering.** Forms: 1 **wandrian**, 2–3 **wandrie-n, wondrie-n, (wuandre)**, 3–5 **wandri-n**, 3 **wondri, wundre**, 3–6 **wandir, -yr**, 4 **wandur**, 4–5 **wandre-n, wandere-n**, 5 **wandery-n, wandry-n**, 4– **wander.** [OE. *wandrian* = OFris. *wondria* (WFris. *wanderje*, NFris. *wāneri*), MDu. *wanderen*, Flemish (Kilian) *wanderen*, MLG. *wanderen* (LG. *wandern*), MHG., G. *wandern*, Norw., Sw. *vandra*, Da. *vandre*:—OTeut. **wandrōjan*.

Not recorded in ON. or OHG. The mod. Scandinavian forms are prob. from LG., and possibly also the MHG. and mod.G. forms.

A similar formation with an *l*- element occurs with somewhat wider distribution; mod. WFris. *wandelje, wannelje, wānlje* to wander, MDu. *wandelen* to change, to wander about (Du. *wandelen* to walk), OS. *wandlon* to change (MLG. *wandelen* to change, LG. *wandeln* to change), OHG. *wantalôn, wantilôn* to change, *intr.* (MHG. *wantelen, wandeln*, G. *wandeln*). The form occurs (once) in OE. in *wandlung* sb. change. Both forms are further related to OTeut. **wend-* turn, see WIND *v.*, WEND *v.* Compare also OE. *wandian* WONDE *v.*, to deviate, flinch, hesitate etc.]

I. Intransitive senses. Formerly often conjugated with *to be*.

1. a. Of persons or animals: To move hither and thither without fixed course or certain aim; to be (in motion) without control or direction; to roam, ramble, go idly or restlessly about; to have no fixed abode or station.

Fight at Finnesburg (Gr.) 36 Hræfen wandrode sweart and sealobrun. *c* **1000** *Ags. Laws, Instit. Polity* xiv. (Thorpe) II. 322 [Hi] maciað eall te luste..woriað & wandriað, & ealne dæg fleardiað. *c* **1200** *Trin. Coll. Hom.* 35 Vre fo þat is þe deuel wuandreð abuten us. *c* **1275** LAY. 7241 And Cesar wende in Flandres lond, wandrenge bi see strond. *c* **1290** *Beket* 69 in *S. Eng. Leg.* 108 In Manie stretes heo hadde i-wandret. **1362** LANGL. *P. Pl.* A. x. 207 Bote wandren as wolues and wasten ȝif þei mouwen. *c* **1475** *Rauf Coilȝear* 330 With thame ane thousand, and ma, of fensabill men War wanderand all the nicht ouir. *a* **1548** HALL *Chron., Hen. IV*,

28 b, Having knowledge that diverse pirates wer wanderyng on the cost of Englande. **1593** SHAKS. *Rich. II*, v. vi. 43 With Caine go wander through the shade of night. **1667** MILTON *P.L.* VII. 20 On th' Aleian Field I fall Erroneous there to wander and forlorne. **1697** DRYDEN *Virg. Georg.* III. 529 Oft the Flocks, without a Leader stray;..Whole Months they wander, grazing as they go. **1711** ADDISON *Spect.* No. 90 ¶3 If one did believe that the departed Souls of Men and Women wandered up and down these lower Regions. **1750** GRAY *Elegy* 11 The mopeing owl does to the moon complain Of such, as wand'ring near her secret bow'r, Molest her ancient solitary reign. **1849** MACAULAY *Hist. Eng.* v. I. 596 Hitherto he seems to have wandered from place to place with no other object than that of collecting troops. **1864** BRYCE *Holy Rom. Emp.* xv. (1875) 263 Frederick the Third, chased from his capital by the Hungarians, is wandering from convent to convent, an imperial beggar. **1891** E. PEACOCK *N. Brendon* II. 15 The ladies were wandering in the garden.

b. *fig.* and in fig. context.

a **1175** *Cott. Hom.* 243 Þas þri fihteð agen elcen ileafful man alse longe se we iðese westen of þesser woruld wandrið. **1357** *Lay Folks' Catech.* 317 And so þis chirche has þre statys be processe of tyme. Fyrst he wandrys here in erthe, and sethen he slepys in purgatory. *c* **1400** *Pety Job* 297 in *26 Pol. Poems* 130 And ofte hym wanteth goddys lore,..And thus he wandreth in a were, As a man blynde, and may nat se. **1555** EDEN *Decades* (Arb.) 99 The people of the Ilande.. wandered in the ignorance and blyndenes of humane nature. **1653** J. TAYLOR (Water P.) *Cert. Trav. Uncert. Journey* 8 Some few do travell in the wayes Divine, Some wander wildly with the Muses nine. **1735** POPE *Prol. Sat.* 340 That not in Fancy's maze he wander'd long, But stoop'd to Truth, and moraliz'd his song. **1875** JOWETT *Plato* (ed. 2) IV. 245 [He] can have his talk out, and wander at will from one subject to another.

c. with adv., as *about, up and down*.

1393 LANGL. *P. Pl.* C. IX. 326 Tho wolde wastour nat worche bote wandrede aboute. *c* **1440** *Promp. Parv.* 515/1 Wandryn a-bowte, *vagor, girovagor.* **1530** PALSGR. 771/1 How sayest thou, is this a good lyfe to wander up and downe on this maner. **1560** DAUS tr. *Sleidane's Comm.* 316 b, The pore wretch wandred vp and downe with .vi. children. **1598** *Mucedorus* IV. ii. 88 Doubtlesse she hath lost her selfe within these woods, And wandring too and fro she seekes the well, Which yet she cannot finde. **1750** JOHNSON *Rambler* No. 33 ¶11 Multitudes wandering about they knew not whither, in quest they knew not of what. **1866** G. MACDONALD *Ann. Q. Neighb.* xiii. (1878) 245, I used now to wander about in the fields and woods. **1875** JOWETT *Plato* (ed. 2) II. 439, I wander up and down, and being in perplexity am always changing my opinion.

d. quasi-*trans.* with cognate object. *poet.*

a **1300** *Cursor M.* 17232 Foluand þat flexs þat es mi fa, Mi wai i wander in-to wa. **1788** BURNS *Auld lang syne* iii, We've wander'd mony a weary fit. **1819** SCOTT *Noble Moringer* xxv, I've wander'd many a weary step, my strength is well-nigh done.

e. To go or take one's way casually or without predetermined route; to go *to* a place by a devious and leisurely course; to stroll, saunter. Also with *forth, out*.

1596 SHAKS. *Tam. Shr.* IV. v. 69 Let me imbrace with old Vincentio, And wander we to see thy honest sonne, Who will of thy arriuall be full ioyous. **1650** EVELYN *Diary* 4 Aug., I heard a sermon at the Rolls; and in the afternoone wander'd to divers churches. **1667** MILTON *P.L.* I. 501 And when Night Darkens the Streets, then wander forth the Sons of Belial. **1715** DE FOE *Fam. Instruct.* Introd. (1841) I. 5 The father, walking in a field behind his garden, finds one of his children wandering out. **1840** DICKENS *Old C. Shop* xxvi, And now there remained but to take leave of the poor schoolmaster and wander forth once more. *a* **1873** R. BUCHANAN *Ballad of Persephone* xxxiv. Poet. Wks. 1874 I. 56 Till, sweet with greenness, moonlight-kiss'd, she wanders home again. **1888** F. HUME *Mme. Midas* I. iii, Here and there could be seen the cattle wandering idly homeward.

¶ **f.** The earlier Wycliffite version of the Bible, and Wyclif himself in his sermons, frequently use *wander* to render the *ambulare* of the Vulgate both in lit. and fig. use; in the later version this is rare, *walke* or *go* being used instead.

c **1380** WYCLIF *Sel. Wks.* I. 301 And so seiþ Mathew þat Crist wandride [1382 walkyng] bi þe water of Galile. *Ibid.* II. 348 þus Poul biddiþ men, Waundre [*so* **1382**; **1388** walke ȝe] in spirit, and do not fulle desires of þe fleishe. **1382** —— *John* v. 8 Jhesu seith to him, Ryse vp, taak thi bed, and wandre [1388 go]. And a non the man is maad hool, and took vp his bed, and wandride [1388 wente forth].

2. a. Of an inanimate thing: To travel, move, or be carried about in an uncertain course; to stray. *lit.* and *fig.* Also *spec.* in *Path.* and *Phys.* (cf. WANDERING *ppl. a.*).

c **888** ÆLFRED *Boeth.* xxxvi. §3 Se [*sc.* Saturnes steorra] wandraþ ofer oðrum steorrum ufor þonne æniȝ oðer tungol. *a* **1300** *Cursor M.* 24857 Þai lete it wandir vp and dun, þair scip ai redi for to drun. **1638** BAKER tr. *Balzac's Lett.* (vol. II) 58 Sir, your letter hath runne great hazarde before it arrived here; It wandred about seven months together. **1764** WHYTT *Observ. Nervous Disorders* (1767) 151 In some, the gout wanders through the whole body. **1855** MACAULAY *Hist. Eng.* xix. IV. 301 It seems that, in this Committee, which continued to sit many days, the debates wandered over a vast space. **1868** MILMAN *St. Paul's* xix. 480 Thomas Newton's monument wandered to another Church. **1899** *Allbutt's Syst. Med.* VIII. 487 W. C. Brown of Penang has described (with others) a very peculiar phase in which the œdema beginning in the feet or hands 'wandered' up the limb. **1904** *Brit. Med. Jrnl.* 10 Sep. 597 The great number of cells which are found wandering far and wide in the submucosa. **1909** J. W. JENKINSON *Experim. Embryol.* iv. 185 In the next stage the clear vegetative cells derived (presumably) from the micromeres wander in to form the primary mesenchyme.

indirect passive. **1851** MRS. BROWNING *Casa Guidi Wind.* II. 19 We poets, wandered round by dreams.

b. Of persons, with reference to movement of part of the body only.

1726 POPE *Odyss.* XXIV. 374 He seiz'd him with a strict embrace, With thousand kisses wander'd o'er his face. **1831** JAMES *Phil. Augustus* xix, The hand which held the letter before his eyes dropped to his side; and with the fingers of the other he wandered thoughtfully over his brow.

c. Of rumours, current opinions, etc.: To be in circulation (on uncertain evidence or authority). Also † *to wander it.*

a **1547** SURREY *Æneid* II. 25 The fame wherof so wandred it at point. *a* **1548** HALL *Chron., Edw. IV*, 241 b, And this immaginacion in especiall, wandred through the heddes of all men. **1831** W. L. BOWLES *Thomas Ken* II. Introd. 7, I am informed by..the Bishop of Hereford,..that there wandered, in his early days, another report of this story. **1849** MACAULAY *Hist. Eng.* ix. II. 515 There was no evidence which could be laid before a jury or a court martial: but strange whispers wandered about the camp.

d. Of the eyes: To turn this way and that; to rove. Hence, of the vision: To pass (idly or restlessly) from one point to another; to traverse a field of view (erratically or vaguely).

1574 HELLOWES *Gueuara's Fam. Ep.* (1584) 344 After the manner of a drunkard, that venteth for the best wine: so doe mine eyes stare and wander to finde out some olde Sepulture. **1663** GERBIER *Counsel* 25 His eyes must wander about every workmans hands. **1704** J. PITTS *Relig. & Mann. Mahommetans* vi. 42 Fixing their Eyes on the Ground just before them, not in the least gadding or wandring with their Eyes. **1794** MRS. RADCLIFFE *Myst. Udolpho* i, Their eyes wandered over the glorious scene. **1848** DICKENS *Dombey* xlii, Mr. Dombey..looked round at the pictures on the walls. Cursorily as his cold eye wandered over them, Carker's keen glance accompanied his. **1863** P. BARRY *Dockyard Econ.* 251 As the eye of the visitor wanders curiously over its ample dimensions.

e. Of the mind, thoughts, desires, etc. (usually personified, and conceived as moving without the direction of reason or will towards, or about, the objects of their consideration): To move (hither and thither) uncontrolled.

c **1400** *Pety Job* 471 in *26 Pol. Poems* 136 My thoughtes wandre wyde whare, For they ben, lorde, full variaunte. **1526** *Pilgr. Perf.* (W. de W. 1531) 167 They wyll not let theyr myndes..wauer or wander abrode. **1577** GRANGE *Golden Aphrod.* etc. Rij b, Where are thy wittes..? If so they wandring be abrode, then call them home againe. **1634** SIR T. HERBERT *Trav.* 2 If my thoughts haue wandred, I must intreat the wel-bred Reader to remember, I haue wandred through many deserts. **1667** MILTON *P.L.* II. 148 Those thoughts that wander through Eternity, To perish rather. **1742** YOUNG *Nt. Th.* I. 107 Why wanders wretched thought their tombs around, In infidel distress? **1837** DICKENS *Pickw.* xxii, Then his mind reverted to Mrs. Martha Bardell; and from that lady it wandered, by a natural process, to the dingy counting-house of Dodson and Fogg. **1884** W. C. SMITH *Kildrostan* 55 The mind was wandering, as it often does On the dim verge of life. **1888** 'J. S. WINTER' *Bootle's Childr.* iv, Her poor, anxious, distraught mind wandering hither and thither in the bewildering mazes of delirium.

f. Of rivers, roads, etc.: To pursue a devious or circuitous course; to wind, meander.

1742 GRAY *Eton* 9 Wanders the hoary Thames along His silver-winding way. **1831** JAMES *Philip Augustus* xxxiii, The hills which confine the course of the Seine fall back..and leave it to wander through a wide rich valley. **1858** KINGSLEY *Misc.* (1859) I. 144 You will find..'deep glooms and sudden glories', in every foot-broad rill which wanders through the turf. **1883** R. W. DIXON *Mano* I. vi. 16 There fountains sprang, and runnels wandered clean.

g. Of a gyroscope or other spinning body: to undergo a gradual change in orientation.

1930 *Engineering* 7 Mar. 323/2 The static gyro-compass did not wander during a week's trials more than about 1 deg ..per day. The wandering was always in the same direction, ..but the rate of wander varied slightly with alterations of the course. **1958** *Listener* 13 Nov. 779/2 The gyroscope will wander at the slightest hint of imperfection in its manufacture or assembly.

3. a. Of persons (or things completely, or in part, personified): To deviate from a given path, or determined course; to turn aside from a mark or object proposed; to stray from one's home or company, or from protection or control.

1500–20 DUNBAR *Poems* v. 8 And sa to hevin the hieway dreidless scho wend, ȝit scho wanderit, and ȝeid by to ane elriche well. **1538** ELYOT *Dict., Aberro*, to erre or wander very moche. **1594** HOOKER *Eccl. Pol.* I. iii. §2 If the Moone should wander from her beaten way. **1606** SHAKS. *Tr. & Cr.* I. iii. 95 When the Planets In euill mixture to disorder wander. **1611** BIBLE *Deut.* xxvii. 18 Cursed be hee that maketh the blinde to wander out of the way. **1617** MORYSON *Itin.* I. 205 One day..he hunted and wandring from his company lost himselfe. *a* **1761** LAW *Comf. Weary Pilgr.* (1809) 123 For every son of Adam has everything in him that is said of that prodigal, he has lost his first state and condition, as he did, is wandered as far from his heavenly father and country. **1875** SCRIVENER *Lect. Text N.T.* 5 His eye may have wandered from one line to another. **1888** STEVENSON *Black Arrow* I. vii, It became difficult to choose a path, and the lads somewhat wandered. **1905** *Times Lit. Suppl.* 15 Sept. 292/1 It is impossible to wander in an avenue.

b. *fig.* or in fig. context: Of persons (also of the mind, thoughts, desires, etc. personified): To turn aside from a purpose, from a determined course of conduct, or train of thought; to digress; to pass out of the control of reason or conscience; to fall into error (moral or intellectual), etc. Often with *away, off,* etc.

c **897** ÆLFRED *Gregory's Past. C.* liii. 415 Ðonne hwelces monnes mod..færð swa wandriende from his hade & of his endebyrdnesse [L. *extra ordinem proprium vagatur*]. **1450–1530** *Myrr. our Ladye* II. 249 And many of them wrongly wandrynge from the ryghtnes of faythe. **1565** J. HALL *Crt. Vertue* 29 b, That each estate May vnderstande howe farre awrye They wandred be from righteousnes, The lyuing God that doe denye. **1596** SHAKS. *1 Hen. IV*, III. ii. 27, I may, for some things true, wherein my youth Hath faultie wandred, and irregular, Finde pardon on my true submission. **1613** —— *Hen. VIII*, III. i. 138 Madam, you wander from the good We ayme at. **1638** JUNIUS *Paint. Ancients* 11 It is then expedient that we should not wander, but rather follow a setled short way, easie both for learners and teachers. **1675** J. OWEN *Indwelling Sin* v. (1732) 38 Look to thy self, take care of thy Affections, they will be gadding and wandring, and that from their Aversation to what thou hast in hand. **1716** LADY M. W. MONTAGU *Let. Pope* 14 Sept., I have..so far wandered from the discipline of the church of England as to have been last Sunday at the opera. **1737** WHISTON *Josephus, Antiq.* Diss. I. §18 So far was his mind wander'd from the right way, that even he was not a believer, as to what he himself said. **1771** *Junius Lett.* 30 Jan., Having travelled thus far in the high road of matter of fact, I may now be permitted to wander a little into the field of imagination. **1879** MISS BRADDON *Cloven Foot* x, John Treverton, smoking his cigar, and letting his thoughts wander away at a tangent every now and then. **1898** FLOR. MONTGOMERY *Tony* i. 21 She could not read her novel with any peace of mind; and she found her attention wandering from it. **1911** MARETT *Anthropol.* 173 But we must not wander off into questions of origin. It is enough..to have noted the fact that, [etc.].

4. Of persons: To be unsettled, or incoherent, in mind, purpose, etc. Hence, later, to be temporarily disordered in mind, as from illness or exhaustion affecting the brain; to be delirious, or (with especial reference to the resulting incoherence of speech) to ramble, rave, talk wildly.

c **1400** *Destr. Troy* 8885 Oft [I] wandrit, & woke, & in my wit caste; And my person enpayret, pynet me sore, For thes lordes þat I lede, and the ledis all. *Ibid.* 10097 The buerne to his bed buskit anon,..And lay in his loge, litill he sleppit, But wandrit & woke for woo of his buernes. **1718** S. SEWALL *Diary* 6 Feb., This morning wandering [*but perh. read* wondering] in my mind whether to live a Single or a Married Life. **1833** T. HOOK *Parson's Dau.* II. iv, She must have wandered—she must have been dreaming. **1840** DICKENS *Old C. Shop* xxiv, They said he was wandering in his head yesterday. **1843** R. J. GRAVES *Syst. Clin. Med.* xiv. 166 On awaking about eleven o'clock, he was wandering. **1876** BLACK *Madcap Violet* xxxvii, He wanders a little, you know, as a feverish person will, when he speaks to you. **1898** P. MANSON *Trop. Diseases* xvii. 273 The patient may wander or pass into a comatose state.

II. Transitive senses.

5. To roam over, in, through (a place); to traverse in wandering.

1573 L. LLOYD *Pilgr. Princes* 104 b, For in the night before Cicero dreamed, being banished from Rome, that he wandred diuers straunge countries. **1590** SPENSER *F.Q.* I. vii. 28 High ouer hils, and low adowne the dale, She wandred many a wood, and measurd many a vale. **1671** MILTON *P.R.* I. 354 Forty days Eliah without food Wandred this barren waste. **1682** LUTTRELL *Brief Rel.* (1857) I. 246 Chusing rather to wander the wide world then under-goe (as they call it) such persecution. **1798** BLOOMFIELD *Farmer's Boy, Winter* 390 Seedtime and Harvest let me see again; Wander the leaf-strewn wood, the frozen plain. **1892** YEATS *Countess Cathleen* v. (1912) 108, I gaze upon them as the swallow gazes Upon the nest under the eave, before She wander the loud waters. **1970** *Globe & Mail* (Toronto) 26 Sept. 29/5 (Advt.), When you are wandering the attractive shops..you can pause for luncheon. **1976** *Times Higher Educ. Suppl.* 12 Nov. 9/2 Born into a London Jewish family in October, 1936, he remembers the excitement of wandering the bomb sites of postwar London. **1981** E. WARD *Baltic Emerald* x. 71 First you wander this place for me, find Suite A.

6. To cause to wander, lead astray; also *fig.* to confuse in mind, bewilder. Chiefly *colloq.* or *humorous.*

1897 FLANDRAU *Harvard Episodes* 319 He meant to ..'wander' her like a cat in a strange wood. **1899** W. E. H[ENLEY] in *Pall Mall Mag.* Aug. 579 Nay, it wanders him to worse purpose yet; for it even makes him say that, if [etc.]. **1899** CROCKETT *Kit Kennedy* xlviii, Mary was conscious that she was not doing herself justice... So she smiled. That smile 'wandered' the assistant. He promptly lost grip. **1914** N. MUNRO *New Road* xxx, 'Ye've knocked the feet from me!' he said in a voice depressed. 'I'm fairly wandered.'

7. *Comb.*, as **wander-bird** = WANDERVOGEL; **wander-plug**, a plug which can be fitted into any of a number of sockets in a dry battery; **wander-spirit** = WANDERLUST; **wander-witted** = WANDERY (cf. *wandrynge-wytted* s.v. WANDERING *ppl. a.* 2 b).

1924 A. HUXLEY *Little Mexican* 184 Parties of ruck-sacked *Wander-Birds. **1926** —— *Essays New & Old* 157 Of northern Germany it is enough to say that it is the home of the wander-birds. **1923** *Daily Mail* 5 June 13/5 A few high-tension batteries (50 volts with *wander-plugs). **1968** Wander plug [see *spade terminal* s.v. SPADE *sb.*[1] 5]. **1927** *Observer* 19 June 22/4 There is a drive..which it is the first duty of every motor owner with the *wander-spirit properly developed to explore. **1959** *Listener* 29 Jan. 225/2 A *wander-witted granddad, a sad bore to his family. **1959** P. FLEMING *Siege at Peking* xiv. 220 The sights he had seen had turned his hair and beard prematurely white and made him wander-witted.

wander, Sc. variant of WANDRETH *Obs.*

'wanderable, *a. nonce-word.* [f. WANDER *v.* + -ABLE.] That one can wander *in*.

1906 E. V. LUCAS *Wand. in Lond.* ii. 17 The more I wander in London, the less wanderable in, for a stranger, does it seem to be.

wandered ('wɒndəd), *ppl. a.* [f. WANDER *v.* + -ED[1].] That has wandered (out of the way, or from familiar places, etc.); astray; bewildered.

c **1420** LYDG. *Commend. Our Lady* 60 Of al Christen protectrice and tutele..To wery wandred tent and pavilioun. **1512** *Helyas* in Thoms *Prose Rom.* (1828) III. 32 It greueth me sore for to leve you here in this place as desolate, wandred and habandoned of your blode. *Ibid.* 122 Almighti God..wolde that they should be wandred of theyr way. **1692** DRYDEN *Cleomenes* v. 59 Wrench ope his mouth, While I infuse these Sovereign Drops, whose Pow'r Will soon recal his wander'd sense—He stirs! **1819** KEATS *Fall of Hyperion* I. 43 A cool vessel of transparent juice Sipp'd by the wander'd bee. **1893** J. WATSON *Conf. Poacher* 78 Wandered birds in outlying copses in the evening are apt to roost there.

wanderer ('wɒndərə(r)). Also 5 **wanderare**, 6 *Sc.* **wandirer**, 6 **wandreer**, 6–7 **wandrer**, **wand'rer**. [f. WANDER *v.* + -ER[1].]

1. A person or thing that is wandering, or that has long wandered (in various senses of the verb); one that is of roving habit or nature. Also *fig.* or in fig. context.

c **1440** *Promp. Parv.* 515/1 Wanderare, *vagus, vaga, vacabundus, profugus.* **1540** PALSGR. *Acolastus* III. iii. Pij, Seynge that she [*sc.* Fortune] is but a wandrer, that strayeth from place to place lyke a vacabunde. **1605** SHAKS. *Lear* III. ii. 44 The wrathfull Skies Gallow the very wanderers of the darke And make them keepe their Caues. **1622** FLETCHER *Sea Voy.* IV, Am I for this forsaken? a new love chosen, And my affections, like my fortunes, wanderers? **1712** ADDISON *Spect.* No. 495 ⁋8 Besides, the whole People is now a Race of such Merchants as are Wanderers by Profession. **1794** COLERIDGE *The Sigh* 20 In distant climes to roam, A wanderer from my native home. **1798** WORDSW. *Lines Tintern Abbey* 56 O sylvan Wye! thou wanderer thro' the woods. **1841** MISS MITFORD in L'Estrange *Life* (1870) III. viii. 116 Gipsies and other wanderers pitch their tents around it in the nutting season. **1853** J. H. NEWMAN *Hist. Sk.* (1873) II. I. iii. 114 The Catholic Church was in the first instance a wanderer on the earth, and had nothing to attach her to its soil. **1855** MACAULAY *Hist. Eng.* xvi. III. 709 He had died as he had lived, an exile and a wanderer. **1857** DICKENS *Dorrit* I. xxx, She don't know what she means. She's an idiot, a wanderer in her mind. **1914** A. S. WOODWARD *Guide Fossil Man* (1915) 3 Such characteristic wanderers over the plains as horses, cattle, antelopes, deer and lions.

b. as tr. L. *planēta* or Gr. πλανήτης: A wandering star, planet.

1614 TOMKIS *Albumazar* II. i, Your patron Mercury in his mysterious character, Holds all the markes of th' other wanderers. *a* **1618** SYLVESTER *Little Bartas* 211 The Sun.. Him, just betwixt Six Wand'rers hast thou plac't, Which prance about Him with unequall haste. *a* **1641** BP. MOUNTAGU *Acts & Mon.* (1642) 117 Even Planets or Wanderers keep course, and station. **1848** BAILEY *Festus* 191 The worlds they call wanderers rolling on high, That enlighten the earth and enliven the sky. **1875** JOWETT *Plato* (ed. 2) III. 536 And God made the sun and moon and five other wanderers, as they are called.

†**c.** *Hist.* (See quot. 1903.) *Obs.*

1724 A. SHIELDS *Life Renwick* 65 in *Biogr. Presbyt.* (1827) II, So many Forces, Foot, Horse, and Dragoons, habitually flashed in Blood, being poured into all Parts of the Country, where the Wanderers were most numerous. **1727** P. WALKER *Life Peden* Ibid. I. 115 Foot and Horse of the Enemy being searching for Wanderers, as they were then called. **1816** SCOTT *Old Mort.* vi, The Wanderer (to give Burley a title which was often conferred on his sect) began to make his horse ready. **1903** HARBOTTLE *Dict. Hist. Allusions* 275 *Wanderers,* the Covenanters who left their homes to follow their dispossessed ministers in 1669 were so called.

2. *Zool.* Used as translation of various mod.L. terms of classification; a bird of the group *Vagatores* in Macgillivray's system; one of the wandering spiders (*Vacabundæ*).

1837 MACGILLIVRAY *Brit. Birds* I. 481 That very important tribe of birds to which the name of Vagatores or Wanderers may be applied.

wandering ('wɒndərɪŋ), *vbl. sb.* Also **wandring**, **wandrynge**, etc. [f. WANDER *v.* + -ING[1].] The action of the verb in various senses.

1. Travelling from place to place or from country to country without settled route or destination; roaming. Often in plural, sometimes denoting a protracted period of devious journeying.

1362 LANGL. *P. Pl.* A. Prol. 7, I was weori of wandringe and wente me to reste Vndur a brod banke bi a Bourne syde. *c* **1440** *Promp. Parv.* 515/1 Wanderynge, *vagacio.* **1552** HULOET, Wandrynge, *discursus.* **1664** JER. TAYLOR *Dissuas. Popery* i. §3. 21 The labors of pilgrimages, superstitious and useless wandrings from place to place. **1697** DRYDEN *Æneis* I. 1061 The fatal Issue of so long a War, Your Flight, your Wand'rings, and your Woes declare. **1705** STANHOPE *Paraphr.* I. 24 The Night here will answer to the present Life, a state of Wandring and Weakness. **1797** HT. LEE *Canterb. T., Poet's T.* I. 119 [The letter] had followed him in his wanderings, and reached him at last by mere accident. **1876** MISS BRADDON *J. Haggard's Dau.* I. i. 8 Joshua.. settled down after his wanderings in his native town.

b. Of inanimate things: Devious movement from place to place.

1827 LYTTON *Falkland* I. 61 The air of heaven [is] not purer in its wanderings. **1867** TENNYSON *Holy Grail* 664 Their wise men Were strong in that old magic which can trace The wandering of the stars. **1913** J. W. JENKINSON *Vertebrate Embryol.* i. 11 Amongst movements of single cells are comprised:..the wanderings of the germ-cells in early stages.

c. Of the eyes: Irregular turning this way and that.

1818 SCOTT *Rob Roy* xx, The idle indicated their inattention by the wandering of their eyes. **1859** *Habits of Gd. Society* vii. 251 You should not show that you think so ..by the toss of your head or the wandering of your eyes. **1869** TANNER *Clin. Med.* (ed. 2) 12 Condition of Nervous System... Wandering of eyes, state of pupils, squinting.

d. Of the mind, thoughts, desires, etc.: Aimless passing from object to object.

a **1300** *Cursor M.* 27793 Vnnait talckhing, vnstedfastnes, o will wandring. **1450–1530** *Myrr. our Ladye* I. xvi. 43 Beholdynge therwyth what pareyl he stondeth in yf he contynew rechelessly in suche wandryng of mynde vnto his deth. **1526** *Pilgr. Perf.* (W. de W. 1531) 161 To call in our mynde from vagacyon or wandryng & to apply vs to our duty reuerently. **1611** BIBLE *Eccl.* vi. 9 Better is the sight of the eyes, then the wandering of the desire. **1712** BUDGELL *Spect.* No. 425 ⁋1 A Poem of Milton's, which he entitles *Il Penseroso*, the Ideas of which were exquisitely suited to my present Wanderings of Thought. **1746** FRANCIS tr. *Horace, Epist.* I. i. 90 *note*, It might well seem, that this Inconsistency, this wandering of Spirit, might be the peculiar Folly of the Rich.

2. Deviation from the right or intended path or direction, straying, aberration.

1711 J. GREENWOOD *Eng. Gram.* 80 Beside denotes erring, or Wandring ('as he shoots beside the mark'). **1818** BYRON *Juan* I. 7 The regularity of my design Forbids all wandering as the worst of sinning. **1844** MRS. BROWNING *Lost Bower* l, The next morning, all had vanished, or my wandering missed the place.

3. Disordered action of the mind due to illness or nervous exhaustion; rambling, delirium; in plural, delirious fancies, esp. as expressed in speech; incoherent ramblings.

1837 DICKENS *Pickw.* iii, The theatre and the public-house were the chief themes of the wretched man's wanderings. **1843** R. J. GRAVES *Syst. Clin. Med.* xii. 130 Here there was a very threatening array of symptoms.. illusions of the sense of hearing, a fiery eye, and incessant mental wandering. *a* **1859** MACAULAY *Hist. Eng.* xxiii. V. 104 Every third day..his dejection, his fits of wandering seemed to indicate the approach of dissolution. **1897** *Allbutt's Syst. Med.* IV. 398 Such are many degrees of transient mental failure, to which such terms as 'wandering' and 'rambling' are applied.

4. Gerundially in *to go*, or *to be, a-wandering*. Now *rare* or *arch.*

1700 LOCKE *Hum. Und.* II. xxxiii. §6 (ed. 4) 222 Though his unattentive Thoughts be elsewhere a wandering. **1898** BESANT *Orange Girl* II. xxiii, His wits gone a-wandering!

wandering ('wɒndərɪŋ), *ppl. a.* [-ING[2].]

1. Of persons or animals: That moves from place to place or from country to country without readily apparent purpose; travelling to a vague (or distant) destination, or by uncertain and devious routes; roving; vagrant; having no fixed abode or station.

c **1000** *Prudentius Glosses* in *Germania* N.S. XI. 388/37 *Uagantes demonas* wandrigende pucan. **1450–1530** *Myrr. our Ladye* II. 157 The darkenesses of dethe whiche the envyous ennemye is wonte to brynge in to wandrynge sowlles. **1538** ELYOT *Dict.*, *Fluctivagus*, wandring in rivers or waters. *Ibid.*, *Vagus*, wandrynge and abydynge in noo place. **1589** NASHE *Anat. Absurd.* B4, The sillie Sheephearde committing his wandering sheepe to the custodie of his wappe. **1607** *Extracts Aberd. Reg.* (1848) II. 293 To sie that thair be no wandering persones efter the hour of ten. **1642** J. TAYLOR (Water P.) *Henry Walker* A2, At least 500. Vagrants..were all suddainely Metamorphis'd and Transform'd into wandring Booke sellers. **1715** POPE *Iliad* II. 553 Thick as Insects play, The wandring Nation of a Summer's Day. **1845** A. POLSON *Law Nations* in *Encycl. Metrop.* II. 802/1 In an age of defective police, wandering labourers and 'valiant beggars' were objects of terror. **1855** MACAULAY *Hist. Eng.* xvii. IV. 95 The wandering adventurer [Baldearg O'Donnel] at first demanded nothing less than an earldom. **1878** J. DAVIDSON *Inverurie* vii. 244 It is of the kind made at that period for the use of wandering priests.

b. Of primitive peoples, or animals: Nomadic, roving, migratory. Frequently tr. scientific L. *errans*, *vagus*, etc.

c **1400** *Prymer* (1895) 10 Alle kynde of bestis & wandrynge [L. *omnes bestiae et pecora*], blesse ȝe to þe lord! **1544** in Hakluyt *Voy.* (1599) II. II. 19 From Mauritania or Barbary toward the South is Getulia, a rough and sauage region, whose inhabitants are wilde and wandering people. **1785** PENNANT *Arctic Zool.* II. 506 Albatross. Wandering. *Diomedea Exulans.* **1801** SHAW *Gen. Zool.* II. 66 Wandering Mouse. *Mus Vagus*... This..is frequent throughout the whole Tartarian desert, and is of a migrating nature. **1802** BINGLEY *Anim. Biog.* (1813) III. 362 The Wandering Spider. This Spider..does not lie in wait for its prey, like several others; it is a lively and active hunter. **1836** [P. B. DUNCAN] *Cat. Ashm. Mus.* 75 Head of the..Wandering Albatross.—*Diomedea exulans. Linn.* **1844** KINGLAKE *Eothen* xii, I was but too glad to set my horse's hoofs upon the land of the wandering tribes. **1854** A. ADAMS etc. *Man. Nat. Hist.* 275 Wandering-Spiders (*Errantia*). **1863** W. C. BALDWIN *Afr. Hunting* viii. 338 The Masaras, or wandering Bushmen.

c. the Wandering Jew. A legendary personage who (according to a popular belief first mentioned in the 13th c., and widely current at least until the 16th century), for having insulted Our Lord on his way to the Cross, was condemned to wander over the earth without rest until the Day of Judgement. Often referred to as the proverbial type of restless and profitless travelling from place to place. Cf. Fr. *le juif errant*, G. *der ewige Jude*. For the application to trailing plants see sense 2e.

In the earliest form of the legend the Wandering Jew is called Cartaphilus; in the best-known modern version his name appears as Ahasuerus, but other names also occur.

1632 LITHGOW *Trav.* VIII. 345 Tradition, as their wandring Jew, the Shoomaker of Jerusalem is, of whom in Rome, they have wrot ten thousand fables. **1646** J. HALL *Satyre* 202 Poems I. 10 Which [might] if..stitch't into a web, supply anew With annuary cloakes the wandring Jew. **1680** V. ALSOP *Mischief Imposit.* viii. 83 Would he have us, like the wandering Jew, ramble up and down for satisfaction, and never accept it? **1837** DICKENS *Pickw.* xxxix, And here am I a-walkin' about like the wanderin' Jew—a sporting character you have perhaps heerd on, Mary, my dear, as wos alvays doin' a match agin time, and never vent to sleep.

2. Of things: Travelling (or carried) along in an uncertain, or frequently changing direction; moved, or moving, (idly) to and fro.

1590 SPENSER *F.Q.* III. ix. 7 It is not yron bandes, nor hundred eyes, Nor brasen walls, nor many wakefull spyes. That can withhold her wilfull wandring feet. ? *a* **1600** *Hist. Tom Thumb* in Hazl. *E.P.P.* II. 195 His shape it being such, That men should hear him speak, but not His wandering shadow touch. **1667** MILTON *P.L.* XII. 648 They hand in hand with wandring steps and slow, Through Eden took thir solitarie way. *a* **1668** DAVENANT *Love & Hon.* II. i. Wks. (1673) II. 234 Lost like A blossom which the wandring wind Blows from the bosom of the Spring, to mix With Summer's dust. **1802** WORDSW. *To the Cuckoo* 4 Shall I call thee Bird, Or but a wandering Voice? **1814** SCOTT *Lord of Isles* III. xiii, A scene so rude, so wild as this,..Ne'er did my wandering footsteps press, Where'er I happ'd to roam. **1850** TENNYSON *In Mem.* xxiv, The very source and fount of Day Is dash'd with wandering isles of night. **1853** DICKENS *Bleak Ho.* lv, The old housekeeper looks at him, and those wandering hands of hers are quite enough for Mrs. Bagnet's confirmation. [Cf. below: Only her fluttering hands give utterance to her emotions.] **1855** MACAULAY *Hist. Eng.* xxii. IV. 719 He had..had in his hands proofs of much that Fenwick had only gathered from wandering reports.

b. Of the mind, thoughts, affections, etc.: Moving vaguely (towards, or about, their object); not directed by reason or fixed purpose; random; restless; wanton.

1450–1530 *Myrr. our Ladye* I. xvi. 42 So the frayle & wretched soulle..can not sturre vp yt selfe from wandryng and vagant thoughtes. **1530** PALSGR. 698/1 The mans mind is so wandringe that he can sattell hym upon nothynge. **1581** PETTIE *Guazzo's Civ. Conv.* I. (1586) 17b, You, cleering altogether my minde, haue now driuen awaie the mistes which dimmed it & made it so wandering & running. **1648** MILTON *Psalm lxxxi.* 50 Then did I leave them to their will And to their wandring mind. **1688** PRIOR *On Exod. iii. 14* vii, Levelling at God his wand'ring Guess,..Laws to his Maker the learn'd Wretch can give. **1705** tr. *Bosman's Guinea* Pref., I had some wandring Reflections upon the Reasons alledged in my first Letter. **1746** FRANCIS tr. *Horace, Art of Poetry* 33 Then learn this wandering Humour to controul. **1797** MRS. RADCLIFFE *Italian* xvii, A deep sigh from Vivaldi recalled his wandering imagination. **1818** SCOTT *Rob Roy* xx, My father had often checked me for this wandering mood of mind.

Comb. **1552** HULOET, Wandrynge-wytted, *vacillans.*

c. Of the eyes: Roving, restless, turning this way and that.

1578 H. WOTTON *Courtlie Controv.* 278 Wherevnto he answered with a wandering eye [Fr. *d'vn œil inconstant*], Ha Mistresse, if I [etc.]. **1746** FRANCIS tr. *Horace, Epist.* II. i. 256 Pageant Shows, that charm the wandering Eye. **1899** *Allbutt's Syst. Med.* VIII. 217 The teacher may observe slow action, wandering eyes, twitchings.

d. Of the moon or stars (*esp.* tr. L. *planēta*, or Gr. πλανήτης): Not fixed, having a separate individual motion.

1526 TINDALE *Jude* 13 They are wandrynge starres to whom is reserved the myst of darcknes for ever. **1585** HIGINS *Junius' Nomencl.* 361/1 *Sidera errantia*,..the planets: the wandering starres. **1590** SHAKS. *Mids. N.* IV. i. 103 We the Globe can compasse soone, Swifter then the wandring Moone. **1632** MILTON *Penseroso* 67 To behold the wandring Moon, Riding neer her highest noon. **1667** — *P.L.* v. 177 And yee five other wandring Fires that move In mystic Dance. **1697** DRYDEN *Virg. Georg.* I. 209 Then Sailers quarter'd Heav'n, and found a Name For ev'ry fix'd and ev'ry wandring Star. **1829** *Chapters Phys. Sci.* 365 Pythagoras..contended that..the comets were a kind of wandering stars.

e. Of plants: Trailing; sending out long tendrils, runners, or adventitious roots. Also in ***Wandering Jew*** (after 1c), ***Sailor(s***, ***Jenny***, ***Willie***, popular names of certain plants: see quots.

1590 SPENSER *F.Q.* II. ix. 24 Of hewen stone the porch was fairely wrought..; Ouer the which was cast a wandring vine. **1878** *Cumbld. Gloss.* Introd. 20 *Lysimachia nummularia.* Wandering Jenny. **1881** *Rep. & Trans. Devonsh. Assoc.* XIII. 96 Wandering Sailors..*Linaria Cymbalaria.* **1882** FRIEND *Dev. Plant-n.*, Wandering Sailor... (2) *Lysimachia Nummularia.* **1882** *Garden* 28 Jan. 53/1 The creeping Saxifrage, or our old friend the 'Wandering Jew'. **1886** BRITTEN & HOLLAND *Plant-n.*, Wandering Jew, *Linaria Cymbalaria*, Mill. *Suss.* **1889** *Hardwicke's Science-Gossip* XXV. 47 The creeping plant known locally as 'Wandering Jew'..is found in the North-West Provinces, particularly, I believe, in Manitoba. **1913** PETTMAN *Africanderisms* 544 *Wandering Jew*, or *Wandering Willie.*—The Eastern Province name of a creeping plant—a sort of periwinkle.

f. ***wandering fire*** or ***light***: Will-o'-the-wisp. (Now often *fig.* after Tennyson's use.)

1667 MILTON *P.L.* IX. 634 A wandring Fire Compact of unctuous vapor, which the Night Condenses, [etc.]. **1789–94** BLAKE *Songs Innoc., Little Boy Found* i, The little boy lost in the lonely fen, Led by the wand'ring light. **1869** TENNYSON *Holy Grail* 319 How often, O my knights,..This chance of noble deeds will come and go Unchallenged, while ye follow wandering fires Lost in the quagmire!

g. *Phys.* and *Path.* Of diseases, pains, etc.: Moving from one part of the body to another (without clearly ascertained cause). Also (in recent use), ***wandering cells***: amœboid cells.

1585 HIGINS *Junius' Nomencl.* 422/1 *Morbus palabundus*, ..a wandering disease, or a sickenesse spread here and there. **1693** tr. *Blancard's Phys. Dict.* (ed. 2), *Arthritis vaga*, or *Planetica*, a Wandring Gout, is a Disease in the Joynts that creates pain, sometimes in one Limb, sometimes in another. **1706** BAYNARD *Cold Baths* II. 320 Aches and wandering Pains. **1725** N. ROBINSON *Th. Physick* 149 As the Scene of all acute continual Fevers is acted in the Blood, so those erratic, wandering Fevers..are deriv'd from the same Original. **1896** *Allbutt's Syst. Med.* I. 92 Here in the immediate neighbourhood of the wandering cells, the short, curved bacillary forms could be seen to have undergone the transformation. **1897** *Ibid.* IV. 442 Uric acid in excess and oxalic acid in the urine are often attended by..wandering.. pains in the back, thigh, calf of leg, and sole of foot. **1899** *Ibid.* VII. 81 Fürster also held that wandering leucocytes might become transformed into glia cells. **1899** *Syd. Soc. Lex.*, *Wandering abscess*, an abscess that tracks along so as to point at a distance from its original seat. *Wandering cells*, a synonym for *Amœboid cells*.

h. Of roads, rivers, etc.: Lying in an irregularly bending line, winding, meandering; also *fig.* Also *transf.* (*Phys.*) as the distinctive epithet of a particular pair of nerves (after mod.L. *par vagum*, *nervi vagi*).

1667 MILTON *P.L.* II. 561 Others apart sat on a Hill retir'd, In thoughts more elevate,..And found no end, in wandring mazes lost. **1718** J. CHAMBERLAYNE *Relig. Philos.* (1730) I. ix. §8 The Parvagum, or Wandering-Nerve. **1764** GOLDSM. *Trav.* 2 Or by the lazy Scheld or wandering Po. **1872** HOWELLS *Wedd. Journ.* (1892) 257 The wandering corridors. **1886** STEVENSON *Kidnapped* xv, A wandering, country by-track. **1899** *Allbutt's Syst. Med.* VI. 812 The term 'accessory' was applied by this anatomist [Willis] to the special nerve which is accessory to the *vagi* or 'wandering pair'.

†**i.** ***wandering name***: a term that may be applied indifferently to various objects. *Obs.*

a **1555** RIDLEY *Treat. agst. Transubst.* (1556) 52 If in the wordes This is my bodye, the woorde (this) be as Dunse calleth it a wanderynge name, to appointe and shewe furthe anye one thinge whereof the name or nature it doeth not tell: so muste it bee lykewyse [etc.]. **1659** SOMNER *Dict.*, *Wudumerce*, Ambrosia, Nectar, a wandring name given unto many severall herbes.

j. Having no fixed arrangement, scattered irregularly.

1785 MARTYN *Lett. Bot.* xiii. (1794) 132 The flowers are irregularly disposed, or wandering, as Linnæus calls them.

3. †**a.** Of persons, etc.: Deviating from the proper or determined course; *fig.* erring, disloyal. *Obs.*

1606 BP. W. BARLOW *Serm.* 21 Sept. B ij, To heale the infected, to splint the spreined, to reduce the wandering. **1628** FELTHAM *Resolves* II. xxix. 90 Wee dare not doe those things that are lawfull, lest the wandring World mis-construe them. **1634** MILTON *Comus* 39 The nodding horror of whose shady brows Threats the forlorn and wandring Passinger. **1667** —— *P.L.* II. 404 Who shall tempt with wandring feet The dark unbottom'd infinite Abyss. **1697** DRYDEN *Æneis* XII. 219 Long hast thou known, nor need I to record The wanton sallies of my wand'ring Lord.

b. Of inanimate things: Straying from the right path.

1600 SHAKS. *Sonn.* cxvi, O no, it is an euer fixed marke That lookes on tempests and is neuer shaken; It is the star to euery wandring barke. **1697** DRYDEN *Æneis* IX. 1008 Imperial Juno turn'd the Course before; And fix'd the wand'ring Weapon in the door. **1812** J. WILSON *Isle of Palms* III. 8 Some wandering Ship who hath lost her way. **1899** J. MILNE *Rom. Pro-Consul* x. (1911) 150 A wandering bullet plunged through the roof of the wooden cottage.

†**c.** Of places: Out-of-the-way, inaccessible, remote. *Obs. rare.*

1600 SURFLET *Countrie Farme* I. xvii. 110 Swans haunt and loue to resort to some particular places onely, as in watrie, wandring and solitarie places [orig. *lieux aquatiques, esgarez & solitaires*].

d. Path. ***wandering spleen***, ***kidney***, ***liver***: see quots.

1897 *Allbutt's Syst. Med.* III. 584 The so-called 'wandering spleen' in which the viscus is found in the lower abdomen. *Ibid.* IV. 518 A case of wandering spleen. **1899** *Syd. Soc. Lex.*, *Wandering*, moving from place to place. *Wandering kidney*, a synonym for floating kidney. *Wandering liver.*

e. *Mining.* (See quot.) Cf. STRAY *a.*

1886 J. BARROWMAN *Sc. Mining Terms* 70 *Wandering coal*, a coal seam that exists only over a small area; an irregular seam of coal.

4. Characterized by wandering.

1582 STANYHURST *Æneis* III. (Arb.) 88 To soyl of Cyclops with wandring iournye we roamed. **1603** DANIEL *Def. Ryme* H 6 b, There is no right in these things that are continually in a wandring motion, carried with the violence of our vncertaine likings. **1697** DRYDEN *Æneis* III. 943 Thus to the listning Queen, the Royal Guest His wand'ring Course, and all his Toils express'd. **1719** DE FOE *Crusoe* I. (Globe) 112 This little wandering Journey, without settled Place of Abode, had been so unpleasant to me, that my own House ..was a perfect Settlement to me. **1781** GIBBON *Decl. & F.* xxxi. (1787) III. 227 He experienced the adventures of an obscure and wandering life. **1814** SCOTT *Lord of Isles* III. xxxi, A landless prince, whose wandering life Is but one scene of blood and strife. **1872** HOWELLS *Wedd. Journ.* (1892) 315 The river..whose wandering loveliness the road follows. **1885** 'MRS. ALEXANDER' *At Bay* iii, Paris is not a bad place to anchor in after a wandering life.

Hence **'wanderingly** *adv.*; **'wanderingness**.

1552 HULOET, Wandrynglye, *palatim, passim.* **1565** GOLDING *Ovid's Met.* To Rdr. A j b, And Pilgrims such as wandringly theyr tyme in trauell waste. **1608** SHAKS. *Per.* III. iii. 7 Your shakes of fortune, though they hant [1609 haunt] you mortally Yet glaunce full wondringly on vs. **1653** JER. TAYLOR *Serm. for Year* I. iii. 32 Were thy prayers made in feare and holinesse, with passion and desire? Were they not made unwillingly, weakly, and wandringly. **1687** MIEGE *Gt. Fr. Dict.* II, Wanderingness, *distraction, egarement, d'Esprit.* **1825** *Blackw. Mag.* XVIII. 437 His eyes Gleam'd wanderingly with brine unbidden. **1867** TENNYSON *Holy Grail* 148 For when was Lancelot wanderingly lewd?

‖**Wanderjahr** ('vandərja:r). Pl. -jahre. [Ger.: see WANDER-YEAR.] = WANDER-YEAR.

1893 YONGE & COLERIDGE *Strolling Players* xiv. 117, I had my 'Wanderjahr' once; but I think I want one about every seven years—a metaphorical spree, anyhow. *a* **1910** 'SAKI' *Coll. Short Stories* (1930) 105 The mouse..seemed to be trying to crowd a Wanderjahr into a few strenuous minutes. **1911** J. WARD *Realm of Ends* xviii. 402 Memories that are revived after death or when all the soul's *Wanderjahre* are over. **1922** 'K. MANSFIELD' *Let.* Nov. (1977) 282, I should like very much to know what he intends to do—how he intends to live now his *Wanderjahre* are over. **1952** G. SARTON *Hist. Sci.* I. xvi. 397 When Plato completed his *Wanderjahre*, he felt in him the vocation of teaching. **1982** *Listener* 7 Jan. 9/3 Wilde..in his American *Wanderjahr*.

wanderlust ('wɒndəlʌst, ‖'vandərlʊst). Also **Wanderlust.** [Ger.] An eager desire or fondness for wandering or travelling.

1902 *Athenæum* 4 Jan. 15 If the present reviewer knows anything of the wanderlust and the wallaby [etc.]. **1902** D. G. BRINTON *Basis Social Relations* iv. 113 The goading restlessness which has driven single tribes or groups of tribes into aimless roving. This *Wanderlust* arises as an emotional epidemic. **1928** *Daily Mail* 7 Aug. 12/5 For people who have the wanderlust there are some nice tours around these parts. **1948** *Rep. Native Laws Commission 1946–48* (Dept. Native Affairs, S. Afr.) 43/1 If..conditions are such that, when their little interval of *wanderlust* is over, they can pass into settled family life, [etc.]. **1969** G. GREENE *Trav. with my Aunt* I. vii. 71 He would get a little restless with the wanderlust. **1981** J. B. HILTON *Surrender Value* xv. 113 The literally thousands of children to whom he had offered their first experience of wanderlust.

Hence **'wanderluster**; **'wanderlusting** *a.*

1927 *Sunday Express* 24 Apr. 3/4 The young wanderluster next turned up in Samoa, and went to Bombay to live in a harem. **1936** MENCKEN *Amer. Lang.* (ed. 4) 219 *Wanderlust*..is used much more frequently in the United States along with its derivatives, wanderluster (Eng. *rambler*), *wanderlusting* and *wanderlust-club*. **1952** S. SPENDER *Learning Laughter* 31 The wander-lusting young Israelis. **1985** A. MCCANDLESS *Burke Foundation* ix. 66 Senior NCOs felt a compulsive urge to track down wanderlusting junior officers.

†**'wanderment.** *Obs. rare.* [f. WANDER *v.* + -MENT.] The action or state of wandering.

1597 BP. HALL *Sat.* II. iii. 20 Genus and Species long since barefoote went, Vpon their ten-toes in wilde wanderment. **1598** SYLVESTER *Du Bartas* II. ii. IV. *Columnes* 614 Rupture to remove, Which would be caused, through their wanderment, In th' Heau'ns inclos'd within the Firmament.

Wanderobo (wɒndə'rəʊbəʊ). Also **Wandorobo, Wandrobo,** etc. [Native name.] The name of a nomadic hunting tribe of Kenya. Also *attrib.* or as *adj.*

1902 *Encycl. Brit.* XXVII. 611/2 Primitive hunting tribes are the Wandorobo in Masailand and scattered tribes of small stature in various parts. **1935** E. HEMINGWAY *Green Hills Afr.* I. i. 2 We were sitting in the blind that Wanderobo hunters had built. **1937** [see NANDI *a.* b]. **1967** M. J. COE *Ecol. Alpine Zone Mt. Kenya* 3 The expedition met men of the wandering nomadic Wanderobo tribe at an altitude of 12,000 ft. **1977** H. INNES *Big Footprints* II. ii. 158 He was attacked by the men of the rain forest, the Wandrobo.

wanderoo (ˌwɒndə'ru:). Also 7–9 **wanderow,** 9 **wandaru.** [a. Sinhalese *wandurō*, monkey, cognate with Hindī *bandar*, repr. Skr. *vānara* monkey, believed to mean literally 'forest-dweller', f. *vanar-* (*vanas*, *vana*) forest. The Fr. form *ouanderou* (Buffon) is a re-spelling of the word as given by Knox.] A name properly belonging to the langur monkeys (genus *Semnopithecus*), inhabiting Sri Lanka, but until recently almost always misapplied, after Buffon's example, to the Lion-tailed Macaque (*Macacus silenus*) of Malabar.

1681 R. KNOX *Hist. Rel. Ceylon & E.-Ind.* I. vi. 26 Monkeys... Some so large as our English Spaniel Dogs, of a darkish gray colour, and black faces, with great white beards... There is another sort just of the same bigness, but ..milk white both in body and face... This sort they call in their Language, *Wanderows*. **1774** GOLDSM. *Nat. Hist.* IV. vii. 215 The Wanderow is a baboon rather less than the former [i.e. the Mandril]... What particularly distinguishes it is a large long white head of hair, together with a monstrous white beard. It..is chiefly seen in the woods of Ceylon and Malabar. **1785** W. SMELLIE tr. *Buffon's Nat. Hist.* (1791) VIII. 133 The Ouanderou and the Lowando. [*Footnote*, Ouanderou, wanderu, the names of this animal in Ceylon.] **1812** MAR. GRAHAM *Jrnl. Resid. India* (1813) 97, I saw one of the large baboons, called here Wanderows, on the top of a coco-nut tree. **1874** F. BUCKLAND in *Life* xii. (1885) 289 One is a Macaque... Another is the Wanderoo... This monkey..comes from Malabar. **1907** *Times* 21 Aug. 2/4 A lion-tailed macaque (*Macacus silenus*) often miscalled the wanderoo, a name which of right belongs to the purple-faced langur (*Semnopithecus cephalopterus*) of Ceylon.

attrib. **1885** HORNADAY *2 Yrs. in Jungle* xxiii. 274 We started a lot of wanderoo monkeys. **1894** *Outing* XXIV. 292/1 Descriptions of the fauna of Ceylon, notably of the wandaru monkeys.

‖**Wandervogel** ('vandərfo:gəl). Pl. **-vögel** (¶**-vogel -vogeln**). [G., lit. 'bird of passage'.] A member of the German youth organization founded by H. Hoffmann at the end of the 19th century for the promotion of out-of-door activities, esp. hiking, and folk culture, as a reaction against the materialistic values of middle-class city life. Also *transf.*, a rambler or hiker. Occas. as *v. intr.* So **ˌwander'vogeling** *vbl. sb.*

1924 D. H. LAWRENCE *Let.* 9 Aug. (1932) 606 If it's going to be Youth, then let it be Youth on the warpath, not wandervogeling and piping imitation nature tunes to the taste of milk and chocolate. **1928** —— *Lady Chatterley* i. 3 They sang the wandervogel songs. **1935** J. BUCHAN *House of Four Winds* ii. 49 They were remarkable young men..not in the least like the Wandervögel whom he had met on many German roads, comfortable sunburnt folk out for a holiday. **1944** M. SAMUEL *Harvest in Desert* xviii. 185 In Germany the *Wandervogel*, youthful rebels against the stodginess of middle-class life. **1958** *Listener* 31 July 149/2 The *wandervogel* student of 1912 with his guitar. **1962** P. PURSER *Peregrinnation 22* xlviii. 223 A couple of the young mid-century *wandervogeln* you find in any youth hostel in Europe. **1967** *Listener* 30 Nov. 705/3 Around 1930, alienated and disaffected youth was being manufactured mainly in Germany, where the First War had produced the biggest earthquake. Some of them called themselves the *Wandervögel*, and wandered around Europe with their guitars and their interchangeable girlfriends, living on what they could get wherever sympathisers would accept them. **1978** J. I. M. STEWART *Full Term* xxi. 241 A bunch of juvenile *Wandervögel.*

wandery ('wɒndərɪ), *a.* [f. WANDER *v.* + -Y[1].] Wandering in thought or speech; vague, distant, 'scatty'.

1912 R. BROOKE *Let.* Feb. (1968) 357, I was being frightfully dim and wandery and solilocutory. **1953** W. DE LA MARE *Private View* p. xi, This vanished creature..was not only more assured, less wandery, more securely based, and more confident. **1976** P. DICKINSON *King & Joker* x. 134 She seemed so tired and wandery.

wander-year. [f. WANDER *v.*, after G. WANDERJAHR, the year, or one of the years, spent in travel for the purpose of perfecting one's skill and knowledge between the completion of apprenticeship and settling down to the practice of a trade.] A year of wandering or travel (usually with more or less direct reference to German usage).

1880 T. W. ALLIES *Life's Decision* i. 6 At Oxford and in my wander-years it was the one subject for which..I not only had no taste, but the most marked repugnance. **1895** *Outing* XXVI. 331/1 Traveling afoot like any poor student or mere *Bursch* of an artisan serving his wander-year. **1906** *Daily Chron.* 26 Oct. 3/3 Off to Philadelphia went Leland, when his wander-years were over, and the necessity of choosing a profession and making a living faced him. **1912** L. TRACY *Mirabel's Isl.* vii. (1915) 109 David had seen a good deal during his wander years, and he had never before secured such an auditor. **1914** H. M. VAUGHAN (*title*), An Australasian Wander-Year.

†**wandis,** *v. Sc. Obs.* In 4–5 **vayndis, wandys.** [a. OF. *wandiss-*, lengthened stem of *wandir*, *gandir*, f. Germanic root **wand-*: see WEND *v.* and -ISH[2].] *intr.* To recoil, retreat, give way. Cf. WOND *v.*

1375 BARBOUR *Bruce* XII. 109 The Ynglis men that war fechtand, Quhen thai the Douglas saw at hand, Thai vayndist [*MS. E.* wandyst] and maid ane opnyng. *Ibid.* XIII. 217 Thai vayndist [*MS. E.* wandyst] a litell we. *Ibid.* XVI. 629.

wandle ('wɒnd(ə)l), *a. Sc.* and *north.* Also **wannel, wanle.** [App. related to WAND *sb.*] Of a thing: Flexible, supple. Of a person: Lithe, agile, nimble.

1803 HOGG *Donald MacDonald* vi, The Stuart is sturdy and wannel. **1816** SCOTT *Antiq.* xxiv, The bairn was sent awa, and bred up near the Highlands, and grew up to be a fine wanle fallow. **1829** BROCKETT *N.C. Gloss.* (ed. 2), *Wandle*, supple, pliant—when spoken of a person, agile, nimble. **1899** *Cumbld. Gloss.*, *Wannel*, lithe, agile, flexible.

wandle ('wɒnd(ə)l), *v. dial.* Also **wannel.** [Perh. f. *wan*, WANE *a.*] *intr.* 'To walk unsteadily or wearily; to move with a slow, trembling step' (*Eng. Dial. Dict.*).

1686 G. STUART *Joco-serious Disc.* 48 Her Stilts [*note*, Crutches] she was not able to handle, But e'en as weak as she cou'd wandle. **1894** *Northumbld. Gloss.*, *Wandle*, *wannel*, to walk with weariness or painful effort. Aa can hardlies wannel hyem.

wandlessour, var. WANLASOUR *Obs.*

wandness, obs. form of WANNESS.

wandoand, var. *wyndowand*, obs. Sc. pres. pple. of WINNOW *v.*

‖**wandoo** (wɒn'du:). [Native Australian.] The White Gum-tree (*Eucalyptus redunca*) of Western Australia, from which is obtained a hard durable wood.

1884 F. VON MUELLER *Eucalyptogr.* x, *Eucalyptus redunca.* .. The 'Wandoo' or principal 'White Gum-tree' of West-

Australia. **1901** *Daily Chron.* 3 Sept. 7/4 Wandoo piles used in bridge construction.

wandought (ˈwandoxt), *sb.* and *a. Sc.* Also wandocht, -dout, -dough. [f. WAN- + DOUGHT *sb.* and *a.* Cf. UNDOUGHT *sb.*, UNDOUGHTY *a.*]

A. *sb.* A feeble or puny person.

a **1728** W. STARRAT *Epistle* 53 in *Ramsay's Poems* (1728) II. 109 And when thou bids the paughty Czar stand yon, The Wandought seems beneath thee on his Throne. **1768** Ross *Helenore* I. 9 Lindy is..Nae bursen bailch, nae wandought [1796, 1812, wandough] or misgrown, But plump an' swack an' like an apple round. **1850** J. STRUTHERS *Poet. Wks.* I. My Life 10 Mrs. Baillie..out of pure compassion for the *wandought*, had him frequently brought in to her.

B. *adj.* Feeble, ineffective, worthless.

1788 PICKEN *Poems* 160 My wandocht, rustic Muse, Gane hafflens daiz't an' doitet, Begins to glunch. **1819** A. BALFOUR *Campbell* I. xviii. 334 That wandought ne'er-do-weel o' a dominie. **1836** MARG. MACKINTOSH *Cottager's Dau.* 62 She was nane o your wandought menseless folk.

† **ˈwandrel.** *Obs. rare*⁻¹. [f. WANDER *v.*: see -LE.] A vagabond.

c **1557** ABP. PARKER *Ps.* cix. 10 As wandrels make: his childrens stray: to beg & seeke their bread.

† **wandreme.** *Obs. rare*⁻¹. [Of uncertain etymology.

Perh. f. WAN- + DREAM *sb.*¹, though this supposition offers some difficulties. The word may be an alteration, for the sake of rhyme, of WANDRETH, with which it seems to be synonymous. Another possibility is that it represents OE. *wódendréam*, used to render *furor animi*, but surviving with difference of meaning in Sc. WIDDENDREAM (varr. *windream*, *widdrim*, etc.) confusion, bewilderment; for the phonology cf. *Wansdyke* repr. OE. *Wódnesdíc*.]

Distress, grief: ? = WANDRETH.

c **1450** *Erle Toulous* 989 The abbot was the ladyes eme, For hur he was in grete wandreme, And moche mornyng he mase.

† **ˈwandreth.** *Obs.* Forms: α. 2 **wandrede, wondrede,** 3 **wandreðe, wondraðe, -reaðe, red(e), -reðe, wontreaðe, -rede, -reðe,** 3–4 **wandret,** 3–7 **wandreth,** 4 **wandred, wandreht, wandretht, wanderet, wanedrethe,** 4–5 **wandrethe,** 6 *Sc.* **wandrecht.** β. 2–3 **wanred(e,** 4 **wonryde.** γ. 6 *Sc.* **wander.** [a. ON. *vandrǽði* neut., difficulty, trouble, f. *vand-r*, difficult + *rǽði* management, related to *ráð* neut. = OE. *rǽd* counsel, REDE *sb.* With this use of *rǽði* cf. the cognate OE. *rǽden*, *-rǽden*, -RED, though the ON. word did not lose its meaning and become a mere suffix.

The β forms seem to be merely phonetic variants due to the dropping of *d* between *n* and *r*; that *wanrede* is an etymologizing perversion (as if f. WAN- + REDE) is less probable. The 16th c. Sc. *wander* is similarly of phonetic origin, though confusion with WANDER *sb.* may have assisted the development.]

Misery, distress, hardship; adversity, poverty.

Often alliteratively coupled with *woe* or contrasted with *weal*.

α. *c* **1175** *Lamb. Hom.* 157 Þe halie Men scedden hate teres ..hwenne ho iseȝen hore emcristene wandrede þolie oðer in seknesse bifalle. *c* **1200** ORMIN 4846 He shall þe gifenn eche blisse, Onngæn all þatt wanndraþ & wa. *c* **1205** LAY. 12511 We beoð ofte hider ifaren mid wandreðe & mid fare. *a* **1225** *Ancr. R.* 156 Godes þreatunge is wondreðe & weane ine licome & ine soule, world a buten ende! *c* **1230** *Hali Meid.* 9 Worldliche wunne þat tu wendes to biȝeten, & hauest ifunden weane þrin, & wondraðe [*v.r.* wontreðe] riue. *a* **1240** *Lofsong* in *O.E. Hom.* I. 213 Louerd ich..wulle luuien þe more..þurh þis wondred þen er in al mine weole. *a* **1300** *Cursor M.* 5787 Þai ar in wandret and in waa. *c* **1325** *Metr. Hom.* 23 For it [hali kirk] and pouer men hauis bathe Of wer and wandreht al the schathe. *Ibid.* 73 Fore worldes wandretht and pouerte Haldes meknes in many mans herte. **1357** *Lay Folks Catech.* (T.) 433 Euenly to sofir the wele and the wa, Welthe or wandreth, whethir so betides. ? *a* **1400** *Morte Arth.* 384 Now he wylnez the were, hys wanedrethe begynnys. *c* **1400** *Destr. Troy* 11514 For bettur is a buerne by hym sum pes, þan in wandreth & woo to wepe all his lyue. *c* **1460** *Towneley Myst.* xv. 127 Greatt god, as he well may, That shope both nyght and day, ffrom wandreth he vs were, And shame. **1500–20** DUNBAR *Poems* lxxi. 33 Grit wer and wandrecht hes bene ws amang, Sin thy depairting. **1570** *Satir. Poems Reform.* xxii. 41 Bludie tirranie, Wandreth, wanrest, feirfull ambitioun. **1680** in *Proc. Soc. Antiq. Scot.* XLV. 242 That..reproacht party..which can hardly get leave to live on earth for a pack of ministers and professers, mickle wo and wandreth com on them.

β. *c* **1200** *Trin. Coll. Hom.* 43 Woreldes richeise wecheð orgel on mannes heorte..wanrede wecheð on mannes heorte ortruwe. ? *a* **1400** *Morte Arth.* 707 Thy wonrydez and thy wepynge woundez myne herte.

γ. **1535** STEWART *Chron. Scot.* (Rolls) III. 334 And all hir cair scho hes maid to him kend; How scho wes put to sic wander and wo. Hir lord wes slane, hir self seigit also. **1535** LYNDESAY *Satyre* 2068 (*Bannatyne MS.*) Ilk man hes me now at dispyte, That reidis the New Testment: Wander be to thame [*ed.* 1602 Duill to thame] that it wrocht. **1557** *Satir. Poems Reform.* xxv. 41 God..Provydet and guyded Hir to ane vncouth land, Whair wander & sclander With enemeis none sho fand.

wands, *sb. pl.* ? *Obs.* Also 5 **waynys,** 6 **wanes, wannes, wandes.** [Of obscure origin; the conjecture in some Dicts. that the word is a. Da. *vand* (:—ON. *vatn*) is inadmissible.

In view of the alternative designations quoted below, it seems not impossible that the word may represent OE. *wagiend, agent-n. from *wagian* to shake, toss.]

Only in ***Orwell wands***, 'the roadstead off Harwich harbour, now known as the Rolling Grounds and Pitching Grounds' (R. G. Marsden in *Eng. Hist. Rev.* XXI. 96).

14.. *Sailing Directions* (Hakl. Soc.) 12 Fro Orfordnesse to Orwell waynys the course is southwest. **1544** *State Papers Hen. VIII*, I. 772 Where we lay in Orwell-wanes. *a* **1554** SIR H. WILLOUGHBY in Hakluyt *Voy.* (1589) 268 The 15 day being at Harewell..we wayed our ankers and went foorth into the wands about two miles from the towne.

wandschott, obs. north. f. WAINSCOT.

wandsman (ˈwɒndsmən). [f. genit. of WAND *sb.* + MAN *sb.*¹] An official who carries a wand or rod; a verger (VERGER² 1) of a cathedral. Cf. WAND-*bearer*.

1865 W. G. PALGRAVE *Arabia* I. iii. 109 After passing between files of wandsmen and swordsmen, Arabs and negroes, we entered on a small court. **1906** *Times* 10 May 3/6 The wandsmen of St. Paul's Cathedral. **1912** JEROME *John Ingerfield* v. 210 Seizing the robe of a passing wandsman, he ..inquired if the Bishop had yet left the Cathedral.

† **ˈwandsomely,** *adv. Obs. rare*⁻¹. In 4 **wandsomdly.** [f. *wand*, WONDE *v.* + -SOME + -LY².] Reluctantly, falteringly.

? *a* **1400** *Morte Arth.* 4012 The waye unto Wynchestre þay wente at the gayneste, Wery and wandsomdly, with wondide knyghtes.

wandy (ˈwɒndɪ), *a.* [f. WAND *sb.* + -Y.]

† **1.** (See quot.) *Obs.*

1611 COTGR., *Baguetteux*, wandie, full of rods, wands, or switches.

2. Resembling a wand; long and flexible. *rare.*

1825 BROCKETT *N.C. Gloss.*, *Wandy*, long and flexible; like a wand. **1880** LANIER *Poems, On a Palmetto* 3 To where expands His wandy circlet with his bladed bands Dividing every wind.

3. *dial.* (See quots.) [Possibly a different word, directly f. *wand-* to turn: see WEND *v.*]

1824 CARR *Craven Dial.* 9 He wor a mortal nice viewly wandy beast. **1876** *Mid-Yorksh. Gloss.* s.v., 'A wandy body,' is a person one would consider stout, but who is well-made and active.

wane (weɪn), *sb.*¹ Forms: 1 **wana (wona,** also **won),** 2– **wane,** 2–5 (? 6) **wone,** 3–8 **wain,** 3–5 **wan,** 5 **woone,** 5–7 **wayne, waine.** [OE. *wana* (*wǫna*) wk. masc. (also *wan* str. neut.) want, lack, deficiency, derived from the adj. *wana* (*wan*, etc.), see WANE *a.* Compare Du. *wan* leakage, also the slack or unfilled part of a sack, Goth. *wan* str. neut. lack.

The development of meaning in branch II is due to the influence of the related verb WANE, with which the existing noun became associated as a noun of action. In some applications actual new formation from the stem of the verb may have taken place.]

I. † **1.** Want, lack, shortage, absence *of. Obs.*

c **888** ÆLFRED *Boeth.* xxxiv. §9 Hit nan mon ne mæȝ eall habban, þæt him ne sie sumes þinges wana. *c* **1000** ÆLFRIC *Hom.* II. 400 Anes ðinges ðe is wana [Mark x. 21: cf. *Ags. Gosp.* an þing þe is wana (*where* wana *is adj.*)]. *c* **1175** *Lamb. Hom.* 145 *Defectio omnis mali. Habundancia omnis boni.* wone of alle uuele; wole and alle gode. *c* **1225** *Ancr. R.* 68 Þe treowe is misleued, & te sakelease ofte bilowen, uor wone of witnesse. *a* **1310** in Wright *Lyric P.* viii. 30 Weping haveth myn wonges wet, for wikked werk ant wone of wyt. **13..** *Sir Beues* (A.) 3478 Of no ioie nas þer wane. *c* **1330** *Arth. & Merl.* 3121 Of fesaunce, pertris & of crane þer was plente & no wane. *a* **1400** *Sqr. lowe Degre* 322 The Cocke, the Corlewe, and the Crane, With Fesauntes fayre, theyr were no wane. *c* **1425** *Cursor M.* 5387 (Trin.) Faute of breed þat ilka tide was ouer al þe world so wide But in no londe so mychel wan As in egipte and canaan.

† **b.** Lack, fault, defect. *Obs. rare.*

a **1000** *Ags. Gloss.* in Wr.-Wülcker 223/1 *Dispendium*,.. wonung, wom, wana *uel* henþa. *c* **1320** *Cast. Love* 229 God ne wrouhte neuer þat þing þat out les þorw his wonyng, ffor nis no wone on him I-long. *c* **1375** *Sc. Leg. Saints* ii. (*Paul*) 867 Blowmand bewte but wane or smyt of sawle and body togiddir knyt. **1390** GOWER *Conf.* II. 307 Thilke suete, Whos beaute was withoute wane, This faire Maiden Adriane.

† **c.** Omission, shortening. *Obs.* (Cf. sense 4.)

c **1315** SHOREHAM *Poems* i. 254 Þe wordes scholle be ised Wiþe-oute wane and eche.

† **2.** Need, want, poverty. *Obs.*

a **1100** in Napier *O.E Glosses* I. 3865 *Inopiam*, wanan. *a* **1225** *Ancr. R.* 192 God hit wot, moni oðer wot lutel of þisse eise, auh beoð ful ofte iderued mid wone, & mid scheome, & mid teone. *c* **1230** *Hali Meid.* 29 And tah þu wone hefdest, oðer drehdest ani derf for his deorewurðe luue. *c* **1250** *Moral Ode* 357 in *E.E.P.* (1862) 33 Ne mai non vuel ne non wane beon inne godes riche.

3. The amount by which a plank (*esp.* one sawn from an unsquared trunk), or a roughly squared log, falls short of a correctly squared shape. Hence, the bevelled edge left on a plank (by reason of one face being narrower than the other), or the imperfect angles of a rough-hewn log (the section of which is thus octagonal, and, according to the size and depth of the 'wanes', approaches more or less nearly, a regular octagon).

1662 ATWELL *Faithf. Surveyour* 132 When they do hew any timber, they..allow nothing for the wanes. *Ibid.* They seldome hew nigher to square in this Countrey, then that the four wanes are as broad as the four flats, all which are equal to a square piece of the breadth of one of those wanes; & although those wanes be less in some places then in other, yet will they be of no service so deep as the deepest wane goes. **1711** W. SUTHERLAND *Shipbuild. Assist.* 9, I shall describe the General Strike in measuring Timber,..which is to see that the 4 Wanes are but equal to two Squares. **1833** LOUDON *Encycl. Archit.* §852 The whole of the materials to be provided and sawed out square free from wane, of the several scantlings and thicknesses herein specified. **1875** LASLETT *Timber* xii. 75 All the thick-stuff and plank to be cut straight, or nearly so, and of parallel thickness, and to be measured for breadth at the middle, or half the length, taking in half the wanes. *Ibid.* xxxiii. 272 The trees..are hewn into a square form, and have a small amount of wane left upon each angle.

† **b.** *Comb.*

1662 ATWELL *Faithf. Surveyour* 133 Hath not he that buyeth wane-timber, that the wanes run not streight, as much need, and as much reason to have allowance for the wanes. **1710** HILMAN *Tusser Rediv.* Apr. (1744) 44 The Seller of the Timber loses all the Gain of the Wane-edges; which Gain in short is a Cheat, altho' a very customary one.

II. Action of waning.

† **4.** Decrease in size. *Obs.*

a **1300** *Cursor M.* 1430 Euer stod þai [þe þre wandis] still in an, Wit-outen wax, wit-outen wain [*Gött.*, *Fairfax*, wane, *Trin.* woone]. **1390** GOWER *Conf.* III. 104 Bot thilke See which hath no wane Is cleped the gret Occeane.

5. The waning, or gradual decrease of the visible illuminated area on the moon. Now *rare* exc. in phrases, ***on, upon*** the ***wane***, ***in*** (***the, her, its***) ***wane***.

1548 *Elyot's Dict.* s.v. *Seneo*, *Luna senescens*, the moone whan it is in the wane. **1561** EDEN *Art of Navig.* II. i. 29 b, The decreasyng or wane of the Moone. **1595** MARKHAM *Sir R. Grinvile* (Arb.) 70 The siluer Moone,..That with the floods fills vp her horned head And by her waine the wayning ebbs doth keepe. **1608** [TOFTE] *Ariosto's Sat.* III. (1611) 38 They easly might espy..How she [the moon] grew in the full, how in the waine. **1613** HEYWOOD *Brazen Age* II. ii. E 4, When the Moone, by which the Seas are gouern'd, Retir'd his waters by her powerfull wane. **1720** SWIFT *Poems, Progr. Beauty* 72 Each Night, a Bit drops off her Face, When Mortals say she's in her Wane. **1726** POPE *Odyss.* XIX. 352 When the pale Empress of yon' starry train In the next month renews her faded wane. **1820** KEATS *Lamia* I. 136 She, like a moon in wane, Faded before him. **1838** WORDSW. *Sonn. 'Tis He'* 8 Yon Moon Doubly depressed, setting, and in her wane. **1850** S. DOBELL *Roman* vii. Poet. Wks. 1875 I. 118 The old moon began to sink (Long, like her, upon the wane).

b. *transf.* and *fig.*

1633 P. FLETCHER *Purple Isl.* VI. lxxi, Can..One onely blot so great a light empair, That never could he hope his waning to repair? Ah! never could he hope once to repair So great a wane, should not that new-born Sun Adopt him [etc.]. **1639** DU VERGER tr. *Camus' Admir. Events* 211 Now is our Berard in the third quarter of the wayne of his liberty. **1678** BUNYAN *Pilgr.* I. 119 Like the Moon That's past the full, into the wain he goes. **1859** FITZGERALD *Omar* lxxiv, Ah, Moon of my delight who know'st no wane.

c. The period characterized by the waning of the moon, *esp.* regarded as a favourable, or unfavourable, time for various (usually agricultural) operations. Usually in phr. ***in*** (***at***, etc.) ***the wane of the moon***, rarely unqualified, ***in the wane***.

1563 HYLL *Art Garden.* (1593) 101 And certaine will, that the root be digged vp in the waine of the Moone, she then being vnder the earth. **1573–80** TUSSER *Husb.* (1878) 88 Sowe peason and beanes in the wane of the Moone. **1577** B. GOOGE *Heresbach's Husb.* II. 60 b, Yet there are that holde opinion, that yf you sowe them in the wane they wyll be the smaller. **1631** WIDDOWES *Nat. Philos.* 13 In part before & after the 8 day, called the encrease and the waine of the Moone. **1651** CULPEPPER *Astrol. Judgem. Dis.* (1658) 4 Seed sown at the wain of the Moon, grows either not at all, or to no purpose. **1669** STURMY *Mariner's Mag.* I. ii. 14 To cut Hair..in the Wane, causeth baldness. **1707** MORTIMER *Husb.* 445 As for Garden-Beans, they are usually set betwixt November and February, at the Wain of the Moon. **1866** A. STEINMETZ *Weathercasts* 41 In Suffolk it is considered unlucky to kill a pig in the wane of the moon.

6. Gradual decrease or decline in splendour, power, importance, intensity, or the like, esp. as following on the culmination of a process of gradual increase; the declining period (of a person's life, an institution, etc.); the latter part (of a period of time). Phrases as in 5.

Quot. *c* 1375 perh. belongs rather to 1 b.

c **1375** *Cursor M.* 3584 (Fairf.) Quen alle wittes ys him gane þen ys alle his wille in wane. **1546** HEYWOOD *Prov.* (1867) 67 Who seeth nought herein, his wit is in the wane. **1579** LYLY *Euphues* (Arb.) 184 Thou which art euen in the wane of thy life,..maist wel know what griefes [etc.]. **1597** HOOKER *Eccl. Pol.* v. lxii. §2 In the waine and declination of Christian pietie. **1601** F. GODWIN *Bps. of Eng.* 431 The Church by them planted had many notable wanes, and intermissions. **1612** W. TRUMBALL *Let.* in *10th Rep. Hist. MSS. Comm.* App. I. 612 His creditt is on the wayne. **1647** LILLY *Chr. Astrol.* clxxxv. 821 Doubtlesse it will be a yeer of some unseasonable unquietnesse, one mischiefe arising in the waine of another. **1657** HEYLIN *Ecclesia Vind.* I. i. 33 The authority of the Church was then in the wane. **1660** R. COKE *Power & Subj.* 91 Christianity it self is in the very wayne here among us. **1680** MORDEN *Geog. Rect., Scot.* (1685) 31 Towards the wain of the Roman Empire. **1762** GOLDSM. *Nash* 54 Mr. Nash's affairs being in the wane, he demanded the money of his lordship's heirs. **1793** MRS. INCHBALD *Ev. one has his Fault* II. i. (1794) 24, I should have lost my eye-sight, and have been blind to the wane of her charms. **1809** MALKIN *Gil Blas* VIII. xii. 306 Signora Mencia ..was still in fashion, though a little on the wane. **1823** T. JEFFERSON *Writ.* (1830) IV. 371 Age, and the wane of mind consequent on it. **1831** JAMES *Phil. Augustus* xxv, In the wane of September, when days are hot and evenings are chilly. **1848** DICKENS *Dombey* xlix, The day was in its prime, the day was in its wane, and still..she slept on. *a* **1859** MACAULAY *Hist. Eng.* xxiii. V. 121 A sign that the influence of Portland was on the wane and that the influence of Albemarle was growing. **1885** *Manch. Exam.* 6 Apr. 4/7 It is quite possible that his power may be on the wane. **1899** *Allbutt's Syst. Med.* VIII. 98 It's [*sc.* anæsthesia's] persistence or disappearance has been used to measure the persistence or the wane of the disease [*sc.* hysteria]. **1904** *Sat. Rev.* 13 Feb. 195/1 This feeling is perhaps somewhat on the wane.

†**wane**, *sb.*² *Obs.* Also *pl.* 4 **wans**, *Sc.* **vanis**, 5–6 *Sc.* **waynys**. See also WONE *sb.*² [Early ME. *wāne*, also *wōne* (with open *o*), whence the synonymous WONE *sb.*² The word belongs to the Teut. root **wan-*: **wun-*, which expresses the two-fold notion 'custom' and 'dwelling'; the precise source is uncertain.

The form **wan-* of the root is otherwise known only in the sense 'custom' (ON. *vane* wk. masc., custom, OE. *wenian* WEAN *v.*:—**wanjan*), while the weak grade **wun-* has both senses (OE. *ʒewuna* wk. masc., custom, WONE *sb.*¹; ON. *una*, OE. *wunian* to dwell, WONE *v.*). There may have been an OE. **wana* (or *-e*) with the sense 'dwelling', or the word may be a. ON. *vane* in an unrecorded sense, or with change of sense due to the influence of WONE *v.*, which meant both 'to be accustomed' (cf. WONT) and 'to dwell'.

After the 14th c. the form *wane* is exclusively Sc. and northern; WONE *sb.*², which in the north was rare, was common in midland and southern use, and survived as a poetic archaism until the 17th c.]

A dwelling-place, residence, house (freq. of religious communities, etc.). Often *pl.* with reference to one building, or group of buildings.

a **1225** *St. Marher.* 21 Ant ne schal nan unwiht wunien iþe wanes þer þi martirdom is iwriten inne. *a* **1300** *Cursor M.* 8667 In wanes war we stad vn-wide, And laid vr barns be vr side. *c* **1330** R. BRUNNE *Chron. Wace* (Rolls) 14554 Þe Saxons ledde þe Aufrykans, & destruyed þe Cristen wans [*v.r.* wanes]. *c* **1375** *Sc. Leg. Saints* vi. (*Thomas*) 277 & schawyt me þe welful stede quhare he þe fare palace has mad ..& set oure all is þat vanis with brycht & schenand preciuse stanys. *a* **1400** *Sir Perc.* 1347 The mene that were with-in the wane, The comone belle gunne knylle. *c* **1400** *Contin. Brut* ccxxxii. (MS. C.C.C.) 317 Þe Danes..turned homwardes aȝen levyng behind hem in her ynnes, pryvyly ywriten, in scrowes and on walles, 'ȝet shull Danos [*Caxton* danes wast] þes Wanes.' *c* **1450** *St. Cuthbert* (Surtees) 2028 A bischope, ane abbot, all vndir ane, Monkes wonand in a wane. *c* **1475** *Rauf Coilȝear* 7 All thay went with the King to his worthy wane. *c* **1470** HENRY *Wallace* VII. 337 Then he gert cry about thai waynys wide, Na Scottis born amang thaim thur suld bid. **1513** DOUGLAS *Æneis* x. iii. 94 Ida forest, to fugytyve Troianis Thayr best belouit wod and natyve wanys. *a* **1568** *Bannatyne MS.* (Hunter. Club) 662 Bot sone within a wane scho went, Most hevinly to behold. [**1820** *Marmaiden of Clyde* xvii. in *Edin. Mag.* VI. 423 A dowie sheen frae his austrous een Gae licht to the dismal wane.]

b. In the obscure alliterative phrase ***worthy*** (***worshipful, wise***) ***in wane***. Cf. WONE *sb.*²

The sense may have originally been 'in the dwellings of men, among men'. Cf. similar uses of TOWN.

a **1400** *Sir Degrev.* 433 Thane spekes that wis in-with wane, 'Ye have well good mene y-slayne.' *c* **1400** *Anturs of Arth.* xiii, 'Welecome, Waynour!' scho says, 'þou worthye in wane!' *c* **1450** *St. Cuthbert* (Surtees) 2514 Slyke monkes haue I knawen and sene, þat..had mare grace of prophecy þan euer hider to had I; Amang þe whilk boysil was ane, þe maste wirschipful man in wane. *a* **1650** *Eger & Grine* 729 in *Percy Fol. MS.* I. 377 It is a lord most worthyest in waine, Erle Gares is his name.

†**wane**, *sb.*³ *Obs.* Forms: 2 **wene**, 2–3 **wane**, **weane**, 3 **wæne**, **wone**, 4 **wan**, **woon**. [perh. an extension (? starting from the inflected forms) of OE. *wéa* wk. masc. misery. The vowel of OE. *wá* *adv.* and *int.* ill, WOE, or of OE. *wáwa* wk. masc. misery, may have influenced the forms, but cf. *fone*, etc. extended forms of FEW *a.* which are phonologically very similar.] Misery, woe.

a **1200** *Moral Ode* 151 in *O.E. Hom.* I. 169 Eure he walde her inne wawe and ine wene [*v.r.* wane] wunien, Wið þet he mihte helle pine bi-flien. *c* **1205** LAY. 2198 Heo stureden heora wepnan wane wes on folke. *Ibid.* 2203 & him seolf mid wæne [*c* 1275 onneþe] ferde into ane watere. *Ibid.* 5655 Þeo cnihtes weoren vnwepned þa þe wæne heo wes ȝeueðe. *c* **1225** *Ancr. R.* 114 Al þet flesch þunccheð sur oðer bitter; þet is, pine & weane, & teone, & alle meseise. *c* **1230** *Hali Meid.* 9 Worldliche wunne þat tu wendes to biȝeten, ant hauest ifunden weane þrin, & wondraðe riue. *c* **1330** *King of Tars* 66 Jhesu,..Let me nevere that day isee A tiraunt for to take. For Marie love,..Arst yif him wan and wrake. **1387** TREVISA *Higden* (Rolls) I. 419 Kyng Fortigern sat on þe water side, and was wel ful of woon [L. *Vortiger sedit anxius*].

b. *Comb.* †**wan-**, †**wen-sið**, misery; †**wæn-slaht**, slaughter.

1205 LAY. 539 Þa Grickes neoren noht warre of heore wen-siðe [*c* 1275 mochele harme]. *Ibid.* 3088 & þu scalt worðen warchen, & wonien in wandiðe [*c* 1275 ine wowe]. *Ibid.* 9520 Faren wit swullen to-somne, & mid fehten hit to-dælen; makien wæn-slahtes.

Hence †'**wanliche** *a.* [*-lich*, -LY¹], miserable, wretched.

1205 LAY. 25990 Þa six swin he gon æten alle... Al biwaled on axen, wanliche weoren þa sonden. *Ibid.* 30288 Nu we maȝen wepen and wanliche i-beren.

†**wane**, *a.* *Obs.* Forms: 1 **wana**, **wona** (also **wan**, **won**), 2–3, 5 **wone**, 3–4 **won**, 4–5 **woon**, 2–7 **wane**, 5 **vane**, 4–6 (9 *dial.*) **wan**. [OE. *wana*, *wǫna*, usually indeclinable, rarely weak (also *wan*, *wǫn*, str. adj.) = OS., MLG., MDu., Flemish *wan*, ON. *van-r* (cf. WANT *sb.* and WAN-), Goth. *wan-s*:—OTeut. **wano-*, prob. f. Indogermanic root **wā̆-* as in L. *vānus* VAIN *a.*]

1. Lacking, absent, deficient.

c **825** *Vesp. Ps.* xxii[i]. 1 Nowiht me wonu bið [Vulg. *nihil mihi deerit*]. **971** *Blickl. Hom.* 131 Ærþon þe he [*sc.* Drihten] on heofenas astiȝe, þonon he næfre won wæs þurh his godcundnesse miht. *c* **1000** *Ags. Gosp.* Matt. xix. 20 Eall þis ic ȝeheold; hwæt is me ȝyt wana? *c* **1175** *Lamb. Hom.* 75 Þe Mon þet haueð þis ilke fif þing mid him he is leful Mon, and, if him is eni þer of wane, he nis nawiht alse leful alse him bihouede. *a* **1225** *Ancr. R.* 26 Nis no god wone [*v.r.* wane] þer ase þreos þreo beoð, mihte & wisdom & luue iveied togederes. *c* **1250** *Gen. & Ex.* 3353 Tidlike hem was ðat water wane. *a* **1300** *Cursor M.* 20056 Qua hertili hers or redis hit Of ur leuedi and sant iohn þair beniscun þan bes not wan [*Gött.*, *Trin.* won]. *Ibid.* 22846 For al welth sal þam be wan [*Gött.*, *Fairf.* wane, *Trin.* wone]. *a* **1325** *Maudelain* 299 in Horstm. *Altengl. Leg.* (1878) 299 When it no milk gete miȝt, þe fader..seyd, 'allas, hir fode is wane'. *c* **1330** R. BRUNNE *Chron. Wace* (Rolls) 8329 Let now no god wille be wane, Bot help to venge my fader bane! **13..** *Gaw. & Gr. Knt.* 493 For he ȝerned ȝelpyng to here, Thaȝ hym wordez were wane, when þay to sete wenten. **1389** in *Engl. Gilds* (1870) 30 And qwo-so be wane, schal paye a pound of wax. *c* **1400** *26 Pol. Poems* ii. 61 Me thenkeþ þere wit is wane To stroiȝe the hony. *c* **1440** *Promp. Parv.* 515/1 Wane, or wantynge, *absens, deessens.* *c* **1475** *Mankind* 412 in *Macro Plays* 16 He [Mercy] hath taught Mankynde, wyll I [Myscheff] haue be vane, To fyght manly a-geyn hys fon. *c* **1522** SKELTON *Why nat to Courte?* 917 Ye must weare bukram, Or canuas of Cane, For sylkes are wane.

2. Destitute *of*.

a **800** *Christ* 270 Þæt we tires wone a butan ende sculon ermþu dreoȝan. **971** *Blickl. Hom.* 17 He bið wana þæs ecan leohtes. *c* **1175** *Lamb. Hom.* 73 He nis noht fulliche cristene mon þet is awiht wone of þisse þreo þing. *c* **1430** *Christ's own Complaint* 427 in *Pol. Rel. & L. Poems* (1903) 217 Alle bestes ..In kindeli worchinge ben durable Saaf oonly I, of wittis wan.

3. With numerals, etc.: Short *of*. Used to express numbers (one or two) less than a complete decade.

c **900** tr. *Bæda's Hist.* III. xxiv. (Schipper) 311 Oþ þæt hyræ daȝa rim ȝefylled wæs, þæt is anes ȝeares wana [*v.rr.* won(a) þe] syxtiȝra wintra. *a* **1122** *O.E. Chron.* (Laud MS.) an. 972 He wæs þa ana wana .xxx. wintra. *a* **1225** *Leg. Kath.* 67 A meiden swiðe ȝung of ȝeres twa wone of twenti. **13..** *Evang. Nicod.* 419 in *Archiv Stud. neu. Spr.* LIII. 399 Ane wane of fourty strakes with yherd he sall be smyten. *c* **1400** *Rule St. Benet* (prose) 22 Þe gude herde, þat lefte in þe munte ane wane of a hundrez sep and yede at seke þis ane þᵗ was want. *a* **1500** in *Bernardus de Cura* etc. 32 Be the yheris of cryst comyn and gone, Fully nynty ande nyne, nocht one wone.

4. Incomplete; not fully formed, or properly shaped. Of the moon: Not full.

1456 SIR G. HAYE *Law Arms* (S.T.S.) 76 Quhen it [the moon] is full, all thingis..ar mare forssy..na quhen it is wane. **1508** DUNBAR *Flyting* 195 Wan wraiglane wasp. **1825** JAMIESON, *A wan tree* is a tree that has not 'grown in a circular form', or that is not filled up on one side... Berwicks.

5. Insufficient, (too) small. *rare*.

c **1400** *Destr. Troy* 3046 Hir nose for the nonest was nobly shapyn,..Nawther to wyde ne to wan, but as hom well semyt. **1624** in *Rec. Convent. Burghs Scot.* (1878) III. 164 [They] buye thair staiple guids quhen the samin does come to the staiple port at ane wane mercatt.

wane (weɪn), *v.* Inflected **waned**, **waning**. Forms: α. 1 **wanian**, 2–3 **wanie-n**, 3–4 **wanye**, 5 ? **wanȝe**, 4–7 **wayne**, 5 **wan**, 6–7 **waine**, 6–9 **wain**, 7 **wean**, 3– **wane**. β. 1 **wonian**, 3–4 **wone**. Also with prefix, 1 **ȝe-**, 2–4 **i-**. [OE. *wanian* (*wǫnian*) wk. vb. to lessen (*trans.* and *intr.*) = OFris. *wonia*, MDu. *waenen*, *wanen*, OS. *wanon*, OHG. *wanôn*, *wanên* (MHG. *wanen*), intr., ON. *vana* trans., *vana-sk* to grow less (Norw. *vana* to spoil, waste), Goth. **wanan* (cf. *wanains* loss, ἥττημα, Rom. xi. 12):—OTeut. **wanōjan*, **wanæian*, f. **wano-* lacking, WANE *a.*]

I. *intr.* To grow less, decrease. (Opposed to *wax*.)

1. To decrease in size or extent; to dwindle. Now *rare*. †Also with pleonastic complement, ***to wane less, too little***.

Beowulf 1607 Þa þæt sweord ongan æfter heaþoswate hilde-ȝicelum, wiȝbil wanian. *c* **1290** *St. Brendan* 332 in *S. Eng. Leg.* 229 Ich wondri houȝ þis taperes bernez þus: and ne waniez nouȝt. *a* **1400–50** *Wars Alex.* 4772 Þis was a wondirfull werk..þat þai [two trees] suld wax soo & wane within a wale time. **14..** *26 Pol. Poems* xix. 44 Þy vices waxen moo, And þy vertues wanen lesse. **1584–7** GREENE *Card of Fancie* (1593) O 4 b, The tree forthwith waineth and withereth. **1647** FULLER *Gd. Th. Worse T.* III. ix. 141 [A disease] Wherein the Head waxeth too great, whil'st the Legges and lower parts waine too Little. **1837** WHEWELL *Hist. Induct. Sci.* (1857) I. 228 Fruits and animals wax and wane. **1875** JOWETT *Plato* (ed. 2) I. 444 That which grows is said to wax, and that which decays to wane. **1896** *Black Horse Gaz.* Jan. 8/2 When the width of an Empire may wax and enlarge Or shrivel and wane with the fate of a charge.

†**b.** To decrease in number. *Obs.*

1297 R. GLOUC. (Rolls) 982 Þat hii hom ssolde vnder stonde & lene hom wimmen þat hii miȝte hor ospring eche so. Vor þing þat woneþ & noþing wexþ sone it worþ ido. *c* **1380** *Sir Ferumb.* 1645 Now haue y lost kyng Moradas.. And othre kynges manye..Now my folkes doþ þus wanye, y-lost ys myn honour.

†**c.** To grow less in quantity or volume. Of the sea, water: To subside, ebb. *Obs.*

c **1290** *St. Laurence* 84 in *S. Eng. Leg.* 342 Þis tresour..ne schal neuere wanie, ake euere wexe faste. **13..** *E.E. Allit. P.* B. 496 How þat watterez wern woned & þe worlde dryed. **1398** TREVISA *Barth. de P.R.* III. xviii. (Tollemache MS.), Physiciens telleþ þat blood waneþ by age [L. *sanguinem minui per ætatem*]. *Ibid.* XIII. xxiii, Whan þe mone is in þe lower corse water begynneþ to wanye. *c* **1440** *York Myst.* ix. 204 It [*sc.* the flood] is wanand, þis wate I wele. **1456** SIR G. HAYE *Law Arms* (S.T.S.) 76 The mannis harnis is full in the full mone and at the full see, and wanis as the see. *c* **1710** CELIA FIENNES *Diary* (1888) 160 This great water seemes to flow and wane with ye wind but it does not Ebb and flow Like the sea with the tyde. **1815** SCOTT *Guy M.* xl, The snow, which had been for some time waning, had given way entirely under the fresh gale of the preceding night. The more distant hills, indeed, retained their snowy mantle, but all the open country was cleared.

2. Of the moon: To undergo the periodical decrease in the extent of its visible illuminated portion, characteristic of the second half of the lunation.

971 *Blickl. Hom.* 17 Þonne se mona wanað, þonne tacnað he ure deaþlicnesse. *a* **1225** *Ancr. R.* 166 Þe mone waxeð & woneð, & nis neuer studeuest. *c* **1386** CHAUCER *Knt.'s T.* 2077 And vndernethe hir feet she hadde a moone, Wexyng it was, and sholde wanye soone. *c* **1440** *Astron. Cal.* (MS. Ashm. 391), Wᵗyn it is an hoole which shewᵗ by similitude how þe moone wexeþ and wanȝeþ [? *read* wanzeþ: *see* WANZE v. 2]. **1590** SHAKS. *Mids. N.* I. i. 4 But oh, methinkes, how slow This old Moon wanes. **1601** *Song of Mary* in Farr *S. P. Eliz.* (1845) II. 428 Her sunne doth neuer clipse nor cloude; Her moone doth neuer wax nor wane. **1762** J. KENNEDY *Compl. Syst. Astron. Chron.* 728 The validity of the sacred writings never can be denied, while the moon shall encrease and wane. **1868** LOCKYER *Elem. Astron.* §232 From New Moon the illuminated portion of our satellite waxes, or increases in size, till Full Moon, and then wanes, or diminishes, to the next New Moon.

3. Of light, colour, luminous or coloured objects: To decrease in brilliance or splendour; to become faint or dim. Also (*nonce-uses*) with pleonastic complement, ***to wane faint, grey***.

c **1000** *Rule of Chrodegang* xix, Æfter þissum tidum sona cymð se æfensang..& þæs dæȝes leoht þonne eac wanoð. *a* **1122** *O.E. Chron.* (Laud MS.) an. 1107 Maneȝe sædon þet hi on þam monan..mistlice tacna ȝesawon, & onȝean cynde his leoman wexende & waniende. **1832** TENNYSON *Lady of Shalott* iv, The pale yellow woods were waning. **1837** CARLYLE *Fr. Rev.* II. v. vi, It has waned faint and again waxed bright. **1840** DICKENS *Barn. Rudge* x, The light waned without, it grew dusk, became quite dark. **1850** KINGSLEY *A. Locke* xxxiii, The candles waned grey, and the great light streamed in through every crack and cranny. **1888** MEREDITH *Reading of Earth* etc. 118 Remote they [*sc.* the stars] wane to gaze intense.

fig. **1843** LYTTON *Last Bar.* I. i, The royal tournaments which were however waning from their ancient lustre. **1874** GREEN *Short Hist.* vii. §8. 445 The old splendour of her Court waned and disappeared.

4. Of a person, nation, institution: To decline in power, importance, prosperity, or renown.

c **1000** *Ags. Gosp.* John iii. 30 Hit ȝebyraþ þæt he weaxe, and þæt ic waniȝe. *c* **1205** LAY. 26991 Þat heore uolc gon waxen and Bruttes gunnen wonien. *a* **1300** *Cursor M.* 924 Iurselem was struid an [tan] þan can þair kingrik for to wan. *c* **1330** R. BRUNNE *Chron. Wace* (Rolls) 1255 Þey wil waxe & we schal wanye. *a* **1628** LD. BROOKE (F. Grevil) *Hum. Learn.* lxviii, And as by artlesse Guides, States euer waine: So doe they where these vselesse dreamers reigne. *a* **1633** T. TAYLOR *God's Judgem.* I. I. xvi. (1642) 51 This was the first shake that ever this kingdome received..whereby it began to waine and decline. **1678** DRYDEN *All for Love* III. 31 *Ven.* I'm waining in his favor, yet I love him. **1690** CHILD *Disc. Trade* Pref. (B 2) b, The inseparable affinity that is..at all times between Land and Trade, which are Twins, and have always, and ever will wax and wane together. **1850** MᶜCOSH *Div. Govt.* I. ii. (1874) 51 When Popery was waning in France, in the days of Louis XIV. **1860** HAWTHORNE *Transform.* xxxii, A people are waning to decay and ruin. **1868** PEARD *Water-farm.* i. 7 Pisciculture began to wane. **1875** JOWETT *Plato* (ed. 2) V. 122 Plato..had seen the Athenian empire..wax and wane. **1876** FREEMAN *Norm. Conq.* V. xxiv. 489 The ban took effect, because the institution was already waning.

b. To decline in vigour, to age. *rare*.

1821 GALT *Ann. Parish* xxix. 252 Even Miss Sabrina Hookie,..though now waned from her meridian,..set herself to learn and to teach tambouring. **1899** J. MILNE *Romance of Pro-consul* xix. 208 Sir George Grey, as he waned under the growing load, realised that he and Greater Britain would be no more together.

5. Of qualities, conditions, activities, feelings, power, etc.: To become gradually less in degree, to decline in intensity, abate.

1297 R. GLOUC. (Rolls) 8488 Þat wiþinne was sorwe inou hor poer wanede vaste. *a* **1340** HAMPOLE *Psalter* Prol., All gladnes & delite of erth wanys & at þe last wytes til noght. **1377** LANGL. *P. Pl.* B. xv. 3 And so my witte wex and wanyed til I a fole were. *c* **1480** HENRYSON *Age & Youth* 46 Thy wittis fyve sall wane, thocht thow nocht wald. **1599** HAYWARD *1st Pt. Life Hen. IV* 140 Whilest the one Kings power was waining, and the other not yet fullye wexen. **1649** C. WASE *Sophocles, Electra* 10 Nor waynes my grief, but still encreases more. **1655** GURNALL *Chr. in Armour* verse 12. x. §2 (1656) 290 But let it [*sc.* our obedience] seem to wain in any service or duty, then the Jordan of our faith flies back. **1742** YOUNG *Nt. Th.* I. 217 How wanes my borrow'd bliss! **1825** LAMB *Elia* Ser. II. *Wedding*, The infinity of full satisfaction..began to wane into something of misgiving. **1833** CHALMERS *Const. Man* (1835) I. i. 92 This sense of a universal law..never waned into total extinction among the tribes of ferocious and untamed wanderers. **1878** LECKY *Eng. in 18th C.* I. i. 161 The influence which his good private character..once gave him had been rapidly waning. **1903** MARY L. BRUCE *Anna Swanwick* v. 184 The precious hours passed, and the still more precious physical strength waned. **1909** E. H. BURTON *Bp. Challoner* xxxiv. II. 270 Gradually his enthusiasm for the Protestant cause waned.

6. Of a period of time: To draw to its close.

Usually with some notion of sense 3 or 5.

1590 in Segar *Honor Milit. & Civ.* (1602) 198 But spurnd in vaine, youth waineth by encreasing. **1766** GOLDSM. *Vicar W.* xxii, As I walked but slowly, the night waned apace. **1795** SOUTHEY *Joan of Arc* x. 186 But soon the night wain'd on, And the loud trumpets' blare from broken sleep Roused them. **1851** MANTELL *Petrifactions* iv. §5. 405 A solitary genus of Australia..whose term of existence seems fast waning to its close. **1853** DICKENS *Bleak Ho.* xxxvi, The day waned into a gloomy evening, overcast and sad. **1865** MISS BRADDON *Sir Jasper's Tenant* iii, The summer waned slowly, very slowly for that quiet dweller in Scarsdale Hermitage. **1903** 'S. G. TALLENTYRE' *Voltaire* vii. (1905) 80 The year waned in such studies.

II. *trans.* To cause to decrease.

†**7.** To lessen, diminish, abridge (a privilege, right, etc.). *Obs.*

a **889** *Charter of Ælfred* in Sweet *O.E. Texts* 452 Ond swa hwylc mon swa hio wonie & breoce, ȝewonie him god almahtiȝ his weorldare ond ea[c] swa his sawle are. *a* **1000** *Riddles* xx[i]. 33 Oft ic wirum dol wife abelȝe, wonie hyre willan. *c* **1200** *Trin. Coll. Hom.* 177 þe oreguil and þe wraððe of kinges and of barones..wurreð uppe chirches oðer wanieð hire rihtes. *c* **1470** *Gol. & Gaw.* 1208, I aught as prynce him to prise for his prouese, That wanyt noght my wourschip, as he that al wan. *a* **1628** LD. BROOKE (F. Grevil) *Hum. Learn.* cxviii, And of these Arts it may be said againe, That since their Theoricke is infinite; Of infinite there can no Artes remaine... Their Theoricke then must not waine their vse.

†**8.** To empty, render vacant. *Obs.*

c **1200** *Trin. Coll. Hom.* 33 Ðos word sede þe angel for þat man sholde fuluullen englene sete þe was er iwaned þo þe lucifer and his ferreden fellen ut þarof.

†**9.** To come short of, lack. *Obs.*

a **1300** *Cursor M.* 4291 Quen hert has þat it will wiss þe bodi mai haue namar bliss, Ne namar wa þan will to wan. *Ibid.* 12196 Bot þai are..Als a chim or brasin bell, þat noþer can vnderstand ne tell Wat takens þair aun sune, þat witt bath wanis and resune.

10. *to wane away*: to cause to wane away, to diminish gradually. Also *refl.* of the moon (*nonce-use*), to wane away.

1601 HOLLAND *Pliny* xxiv. xv. II. 198 Speciall remedie for ruptures, convulsions, and pleurisies: it waneth away the overgrowne splene. **1797** ANNA SEWARD *Lett.* (1811) V. 4 Proud once and princely was the mansion, ere a succession of spendthrifts waned away its splendour. **1867** JEAN INGELOW *Tired* iv, And let that moon of April wane itself away.

b. *nonce-use.* To cause (the moon) to wane.

1904 *Edin. Rev.* Jan. 46 The hidden hand which wanes the moon and ebbs the tide.

wane, obs. f. VAIN *a.*, WAN *a.*, WAIN *sb.*[1], WEAN *v.* and *sb.*, WHEN; north. f. WONE *sb. Obs.*; obs. pa. t. of WIN *v.*

waneand, var. WANIAND *Obs.*

†**wanease**, *sb. Sc. Obs.* Also waneis(e. [f. WAN- + EASE *sb.* Cf. UNEASE.] Uneasiness, vexation. Hence **waneise** *v. refl.*, to put oneself to trouble (Jam. 1808).

15.. *Dumb Wyff* 116 in Laing *Sel. Rem. Pop. Poetry Scot.* (1882), We deuillis can na wayis latt hir; Giue man tak ȝow the waneis. **1776** *Herd's Scott. Songs* II. 214 O waly fu fa' the cat! For she has bred muckle wanease.

wane-cloud. *Meteorol.* [? f. WANE *sb.*[1] or *v.*

The sense meant to be expressed by the compound was perh. 'a cloud in process of waning or becoming smaller'.]

A cirro-stratus cloud.

1823 T. FORSTER *Res. Atmosph. Phenomena* i. §6 (ed. 3) 17 Of the Cirrostratus or Wanecloud.

waned (weɪnd), *ppl. a.* [f. WANE *v.* + -ED[1].] That has waned; diminished, decreased.

1593 SHAKS. *3 Hen. VI*, IV. vii. 4 Once more I shall enterchange My wained state, for Henries Regall Crowne. **1640** J. GOWER *Ovid's Festiv.* II. 35 Ten times the Moon her waned light did gather. **1810** SCOTT *Lady of Lake* II. xxiii, Not so proud Was I of all that marshall'd crowd, Though the waned crescent own'd my might. **1816** COLERIDGE *Lay Serm.* p. xxii, Like an aged mourner..who is watching the wained moon and sorroweth not. **1818** KEATS *Endym.* II. 482 When our love-sick queen did weep Over his waned corse.

wanehope, var. WANHOPE *Obs.*

wanelasour, var. WANLASOUR *Obs.*

†'**waneless**, *a. Obs.* [f. WANE *sb.*[1] or *v.* + -LESS.] Not liable to waning.

a **1618** SYLVESTER *Little Bartas* 216 She [the Moon], Wax-less, Wane-less, doth both wane and wax.

wanen, -ene, var. WHENNE, *Obs.*, whence.

wanesc(h)ot(t, -skot(t, obs. ff. WAINSCOT.

wanese, var. WANZE *v. Obs.*

wanest, wanet, obs. Sc. ff. VANISHED, VAUNT.

wanetreutht: see WANTROTH.

wanewerd, -wit: see WANWEIRD, WANWIT.

waney ('weɪnɪ), *a.* Also 7, 9 wany, 7 wainny, waynny, 9 wainy. [f. WANE *sb.*[1] + -Y.] Of unsquared or imperfectly squared timber: Having wanes (see WANE *sb.*[1] 3) or natural bevels at the angles. Hence, of an angle or edge: consisting of wane.

1662 ATWELL *Faithf. Surveyour* 132 When they do hew any timber, they leave it so wany, that..they leave it nearer round then square. **1679** MOXON *Mech. Exerc.* viii. 140 The Girders..prove commonly somewhat Wainny upon their upper sides. **1860** *Builder* 21 Jan. 46/2, I have found a difference..of from five to twenty-five per cent., according as timber was squared or wany. **1876** *Act 39 & 40 Vict.* c. 80 §24 Any square, round, waney, or other timber. **1878** *Encycl. Brit.* IV. 773/2 The pine prepared for exportation is made into squared timber..; or into waney timber (as it is called when only partially squared or flatted). **1888** BURT *Stand. Timber Meas.* 237 The chord of the defective angle, or waney edge.

In fig. context. **1837** HALIBURTON *Clockm.* Ser. I. v. 34 As hard at the heart as a log of elm; howsomever, said a third, I hope it wont be long afore he has the wainy edge scored off of him, any how.

Hence '**waneyness.**

1679 MOXON *Mech. Exerc.* viii. 140 The Joysts.. strengthen their Bearing by so much as they project over the Roundness or Waynniness of the upper side of the Girder.

wanflar, -er, var. ff. WAMFLER. *Sc.*

†**wanfortune.** *Sc. Obs.* [f. WAN- + FORTUNE *sb.*] Misfortune.

a **1500** *Bernard. de cura rei fam.* (E.E.T.S.) 345 Seldyne.. besy diligence Folowis with wanfortonys violence: Bot seldinar wanfourtowne þu dessewyr Sale fra swernes. **1535** LYNDESAY *Satyre* 4022, I trow wan-fortune brocht me heir. **1711** [DE FOE] *Sp. for D——sse of Arnistoun* 10 Geen I have had the Wanfortune to believe also, That the Pretender is the Q——'s Brother. *Ibid.* 14 If I have been sa wanfortunate as to believe the Pretender to be legitimate.

wang[1] (wɒŋ). *Obs.* exc. *dial.* Forms: 1 **wange, wænge, wenge, wonge,** 3–5 **wong(e,** 4–6 **wang(e,** (4 **woong,** 5 **wangge, wayngе, vange,** 7 **wongge,** 9 *dial.* **whang),** 7– *dial.* **wang.** [OE. *wang*, str. masc., *wange*, wk. neut., corresp. to OS. *wanga* fem., MDu. *wange* (mod.Du. *wang* fem.), MLG. *wange* neut., fem., OHG. *wanga* neut. (MHG. *wange* neut., mod.G. *wange* fem.), ON. *vange* wk. masc. (Norw. *vange*; Da. *vanger* pl. 'cheeks' of a press), Goth. **waggō*, ? fem. or neut. (whence *waggareis* pillow = OE. *wangere*):—OTeut. **waŋgon-, -ōn-*. The further etymology is obscure; some regard the word as cogn. w. OE. *wang* field, WONG.]

†**1.** The cheek. *Obs.*

c **975** *Rushw. Gosp.* Matt. v. 39 ȝif hwa ðec slae on ðæt swiðran wonge *vel* ceke þin. *c* **1000** ÆLFRIC *Saints' Lives* xxiii. B. 556 Þonne astrehte ic me sylfe on eorðan and þa wangas mid tearum oferȝeat. *c* **1000** *Sax. Leechd.* II. 20 Smyre mid þy pæt wenge. *c* **1300** *Cursor M.* 18308 Adam fell dun for-wit his fete And spak til him, wit wonges wete. *a* **1310** in Wright *Lyric P.* vi. 28 Nihtes when y wende ant wake, for-thi myn wonges waxeth won. *c* **1320** *Sir Tristr.* 732 Þe king biheld þat old, Hou his wonges were wete. *c* **1425** WYNTOUN *Cron.* v. ix. 1968 Quhill wepyt, quhill scho wongys wete. *c* **1440** *York Myst.* x. 275 Thy wordis makis me my wangges to wete.

2. A molar tooth: = WANG-TOOTH.

c **1386** CHAUCER *Reeve's T.* 110 Swa werkes ay the wanges in his heed. **1901** F. E. TAYLOR *Folk Sp. S. Lanc.* (E.D.D.), *Wang*, a tooth; *gen.* a back tooth.

wang[2], **weng.** *s.w. dial.* [Of uncertain origin; possibly a var. of WING *sb.*, which in some dialects denotes a part of a ploughshare.] (See quots.)

1813 VANCOUVER *Agric. Devon* 117 The [plough-]beam.. is seven feet long, furnished at the head with an horizontal and vertical graduated wang of rack-work. **1886** W. *Somerset Word-bk.*, *Wang*, or *Weng*. 1. A strong iron fixed to the front end of the beam [of a plough], having notches by which the end of the foot-chain..is adjusted,..as may be needful, according to the width of furrow desired... 2. Of a cart—the iron loop or staple upon each shaft, to which is hooked on the chain of the vore-horse.

wang, var. WONG *dial.*, field.

wang, var. WHANG.

wanga ('wæŋgə). [ad. Haitian Creole *ouanga* witchcraft, perh. ad. Kimbundu *wanga* witchcraft, or Tshiluba *bwanga* charm, fetish.] Witchcraft, sorcery; a charm or spell; a magical object. Freq. *attrib.*

1851 *Picayune* (New Orleans) 20 July 2/6 The Voudous also threw 'Wanga' or spells into the complainant's yard. **1882** J. W. BUEL *Metropolitan Life Unveiled* 532, I will make a wanga-charm to charm him with; I will make him a phantom, a ghost. **1934** B. A. BOTKIN in W. T. Couch *Culture in South* 585 Fragments of hoodoo and conjuration, whose spells,..grigris, wangas, luck balls, conjure bottles, and conjure, tricken, or goofer bags are the special province of the Negro 'root doctor' or 'hoodoo man'. **1946** R. TALLANT *Voodoo in New Orleans* (1947) 91 Another sort held gunpowder and red pepper; these were *wangas* to be thrown into somebody's path to cause them to get into fights. **1964** 'R. SEVERN' *Blood & Gold* x. 102 It's a *Wanga* dance... Black magic... She must be a *Mambo*..a *Voodoo* priestess. **1978** W. HJORTSBERG *Falling Angel* (1979) xxxiii. 158 Sounds like some boko's put a powerful wanga on you. .. A boko is a hungan [*sc.* Obeah priest] who is evil... Wanga's what you'd call an evil curse...a hex, a spell.

wangala, variant of VANGLO.

1862 in Veness *El Dorado* (1866) App. 124 Wangala (*Sesamum orientale*, Linn.), seeds of. Yield a fine bland oil. Used in soups.

wangan, variant of WANIGUN.

†**wangel**, aphetic f. of EVANGEL. *Sc.* and *north.*

c **1375** *Sc. Leg. Saints* xxvii. (*Machar*) 1401 Þe buk of þe wangele. **1389** in Sir W. Fraser *Wemyss of W.* (1888) II. 24 in *N. & Q.* 9th Ser. IV. 438/2 Bath the partys fornemmyt, the haly wangelis twechyt, the gret ath has sworn. *c* **1450** *St. Cuthbert* (Surtees) 6800 Þe text of wangels fell in þe water. **1456** SIR G. HAYE *Law Arms* (S.T.S.) 128 Be law of nature and of the wangel. *a* **1568** in *Bannatyne MS.* (Hunter. Club) 118 So said Sanct Johine in his wangell. **1819** W. TENNANT *Papistry Storm'd* (1827) 6 John Knox..Past like a lion round the land, And wi' the wangyle in his hand.

wangelist(e, -yst: see EVANGELIST.

†'**wanger.** *Obs.* Forms: 1 wongere, wangere, 4 wonger(e, wanger(e. [OE. *wangere* = OHG. *wangâri* (MHG. *wanger*), Goth. *waggareis* :—OTeut. type **waŋgārjo-z*, f. **waŋgō-* cheek, WANG[1].] A pillow.

Speght (1602) explains the word (in Chaucer) as 'a male, or bouget', and this explanation appears in Kersey 1708 and later Dicts. and glossaries.

c **900** tr. *Bæda's Hist.* IV. xiv. [xi.] (1890) 296 To þon þætte from dæle þæs heafdes eac swylce meahte wongere betweoh ȝeseted beon. *c* **1000** ÆLFRIC *Gloss.* in Wr.-Wülcker 124 *Ceruical*, wangere. *c* **1386** CHAUCER *Sir Thopas* 201 His brighte helm was his wonger [*v.rr.* wanger, wongere, wangere.].

wanghee: see WHANGEE.

wangle ('wæŋg(ə)l), *v.*[1] *dial.* [Perh. an altered form of WAGGLE *v.*, due to the influence of the dial. *wankle* to totter (app. rare) or of its source WANKLE *a.* (OE. *wancol*) unsteady, tottering. Cf. Norw. *vangla* to roam about, (of weather) to be unsteady.] *intr.* Of a thing: To move loosely or shakily on its base or in its place of attachment. Of a person: To go unsteadily.

1820 WILBRAHAM *Chesh. Gloss.*, *Wangle*, to totter or vibrate. See Junius in voce, wanckle. **1841** HARTSHORNE *Salop. Ant.* Gloss., *Wangle*, to be unsteady, totter. **1868** ATKINSON *Cleveland Gloss.*, *Wangle*, to totter, or shake to its fall; of a wall, building, &c. **1869** *Lonsdale Gloss.*, *Wangle*, to totter, to walk feebly. **1876** *Mid-Yorksh. Gloss.*, *Wangle*, to rock, or shake, noisily. **1892** M. C. F. MORRIS *Yorksh. Folk-Talk* Gloss., *Wangle*, to shake, to totter, to waver; to be in a sensitive state... Ex.—Thoo mun put it varry wangling (in setting a trap).

Hence '**wangling** *ppl. a.* (in quot. app. 'rambling'). Also '**wangler.**

1869 G. J. CHESTER *Transatl. Sk.* 325 The old gentleman in the pulpit meanwhile drawling out a long, wangling, extempore prayer. **1876** *Whitby Gloss.*, *Wangler*, an unstable person.

wangle ('wæŋg(ə)l), *v.*[2] *slang* and *colloq.* [Of uncertain origin.

First recorded, as printers' slang, in 1888; current among soldiers in the war of 1914–1918, and hence in general colloquial use. There is no evidence of any connexion with the northerly dialect word WANGLE *v.*[1] Probably, like many other slang words, it was formed involuntarily, under the influence of an obscure sense of phonetic symbolism; the suggestion may have come from WAGGLE *v.*]

1. *trans.* To accomplish (something) in an irregular way by scheming or contrivance; to bring about or obtain by indirect or insidious means (something not obtainable openly); to manipulate, 'fake' (an account, report, prices). Also *refl.* and const. advb. phr.

1888 JACOBI *Printers' Vocab.*, *Wangle*, a slang term used by printers to express arranging or 'faking' matters to one's own satisfaction or convenience. **1917** *Edin. Rev.* July 45 No market is ever 'free': probe it deep enough, and.. monopolies will..be found, in many cases deliberately 'wangling' prices and limiting production to sustain them. **1917** *Bulletin* 28 Dec. 3/2 He had come in from the North Atlantic Cruiser Patrol, and when in home waters had 'wangled' a few days' leave. **1918** 'B. CABLE' *Air Men o' War* xi. 143 He had been..planning..how to apply and how to get quickly through his training, and ways of wangling it to get to this Squadron. **1922** *Sat. Rev.* 22 Dec. 953 President Wilson had to 'wangle' through Congress an act to restore the British treaty rights. **1942** 'WYNDHAM LEWIS' *Let.* ? 26 June (1963) 324 In the last war like yourself I joined the army, instead of wangling myself into some safe job in London. **1961** C. V. WEDGWOOD *Thomas Wentworth, 1st Earl of Strafford* 186 In fact, he would bribe and wangle himself back into the possession of his illicit gains.

2. *intr.* To obtain something or get somewhere by irregular means, scheming, etc.; to use irregular means to accomplish a purpose. *rare.*

1918 *Sat. Even. Post* 19 Oct. 93/1 And wet—always, always wet, unless the weather is clear and the sea is calm—but good sea boats. They [*sc.* submarine chasers] wangle through somehow. They weather it out. **1919** W. DEEPING *Second Youth* xxii. 190 He agitated for a transfer..and to his joy he wangled back to the Cockneys. *Ibid.* xxvi. 222 He also knew that a man who has 'wangled'..may find himself.. thrust rudely into the trenches. **1921** *Glasgow Herald* 16 June 9 We wangled in, an' we'll wangle oot.

3. *trans.* To influence or induce (a person) to do something. *rare.*

1926 G. D. H. & M. COLE *Blatchington Tangle* xxi. 147 He was always on at me just lately to get Lady Blatchington to sell him the rubies. He said I could wangle her. **1928** *Daily Express* 27 Dec. 5/4 Aren't you glad..you wangled the old lady to relinquish the key.

Hence '**wangler**, one who 'wangles'. '**wangling** *vbl. sb.*

1911 *Standard* 12 July 10 He denied that he had ever been asked by a driver to 'fake' a meter although he had heard banter in the garage about the 'wangling' of meters. **1912** E. WALLACE *Private Selby* xxxi. 281 You're a bloomin' wangler, Short. **1915** *John Bull* 27 Mar. 16/2 We regret to see them reduced to the level of vulgar weight wanglers, and so far as the bread business is concerned, we are quite prepared to believe that it was all the fault of a..machine. **1920** *Blackw. Mag.* June 790/1 We took it in turns to stay in the garden against the return of the motor wanglers.

wangle ('wæŋg(ə)l), *sb. colloq.* [f. WANGLE *v.*[2]] An act of wangling; an irregular or indirect method of working; something dishonestly contrived or manipulated.

1915 *N. & Q.* 23 Jan. 66 The explanation given was: 'It's a wangle between this Office and the Inland Revenue.' **1923** *Westm. Gaz.* 21 Feb. 11/1 Mr. Justice Sargant: You can't expect the Royal Commission to be bound to what might be called a 'wangle' of this sort. **1927** *Observer* 27 Mar. 16/5 Men who sought to achieve nothing by wangle or intrigue. **1943** H. A. SMITH *Life in Putty Knife Factory* xii. 183 They [*sc.* people of New York City] have made a precise science out of the wangle. **1959** E. POUND *Thrones* xcvii. 29 But by that time they found some other wangle. **1977** P. DICKINSON *Walking Dead* II. ii. 114, I worked a wangle. I got a line on the Minister of Tourism.

† **wangrace**[1]. *Sc. Obs.* [f. WAN- + GRACE *sb.*] Lack of grace, want of propriety.

1513 DOUGLAS *Æneis, Exclam. agst. Detractouris* 13 Sum beyn sa frawart in malice and wangrace, Quhat is weill said thai love nocht worth ane ace.

wangrace[2]. *Sc.* and *Anglo-Irish.* Also **-grease.** A kind of gruel.

a **1733** in C. K. Sharpe *Ballad Bk.* (1823) 113, I gave him wangrace in his bed, And row'd the blankets round him. **1829** *Acc. Persons remark. Health & Longev.* 225 The sweat which he took..was what they call a wangrease in that country. It is made of oatmeal, flummery made very thin, sweetened with honey, and a lump of fresh butter. **1899** *Century Mag.* Oct. 959/1 'Aye, an' a bowl i' wan-grace,' Rosie, the maid, said—'that's what'll put the sthren'th intil yer bones again.'

wang-tooth. *Obs.* exc. *dial.* (see Eng. Dial. Dict.). [WANG[1].] A cheek-tooth, molar.

a **1000** *Laws Ælfred* xlix. 1 ʒif hit sie wongtoð, ʒeselle IIII scill. to bote. *c* **1000** ÆLFRIC *Gloss.* in Wr.-Wülcker 157 *Molares, uel genuini,* wangteð. *c* **1325** *Gloss. W. de Bibbesw.* (MS. Arundel) in Wright *Voc.* 146 *Les messeleres,* wange-teȝ [*read* -teþ; *MS. Cambr.* wangeteth]. **1382** WYCLIF *Judg.* xv. 19 And so the Lord opnede a woong tooth [1388 wang tooth; Vulg. *molarem dentem*] in the cheek boon of the asse. *c* **1386** CHAUCER *Monk's T.* 54 And of this asses cheke, that was dreye, Out of a wang tooth sprang anon a welle. **1393** LANGL. *P. Pl.* C. XXIII. 191 He..bete oute my wang-teþ. **1483** *Cath. Angl.* 406/1 A Waynge tothe [*v.r.* Vange tothe], *genuinus, maxillaris.* **1576** TURBERV. *Venerie* 182 Take them and cut away their nether Iawe wherein there wang teeth be set. **1607** MARKHAM *Cavel.* I. (1617) 79 His two tushes of his nether chappe, and the two wongge teeth of the same next to the tushes. **1659** SOMNER *Dict.* s.v. *Wang,* That old rime: And in witness that this is sooth, I bite the wax with my wang tooth. **1674** RAY *N.C. Words* s.v., The *Wang-tooth;* the Jaw-tooth.

wangun, var. WANIGAN.

† **wanhap.** *Sc. Obs.* Also 6 **van-**. [f. WAN- + HAP *sb.*[1]] Misfortune.

1513 DOUGLAS *Æneis* V. iv. 89 Scho..on the scherp skelleis, to her wanhap Smat with sic fard the airis in flenderis lap. **1549** *Compl. Scot.* viii. 72 O quhat vanhap, quhat dyabolic temptatione. **1571** *Satir. Poems Reform.* xxvii. 102 Gif þatt itt be in bondage brocht be the, Then warreitt war thy weirdis and wanhap. **1819** W. TENNANT *Papistry Storm'd* (1827) 194 Backlins he stagger't wi' a rair to Gamyl's tomb, and hid him thair Frae onie mair wanhap.

So † **wanhappy** *a. Sc.*, unfortunate.

c **1590** J. BUREL *Passage of Pilgr.* I. vii. in *J. Watson's Coll. Sc. Poems* II. (1709) 19 The wildbair that wanhappie beist, Quhois tusks of length war at the leist Ane quarter lang and mair. **1808** JAMIESON, *Wanhappie. c* **1830** in Child *Ballads* IV. 386/1 They hae fawn a wagering them atween At a wanhappy time.

'wanhope, *sb.* and *a. Obs.* exc. *arch.* Also 3–4 **wane-**, 4 **won-**, *Sc.* **van-**, 4–5 **whan-**, 5 **wann-**, 6–7 **wanne-**; 4 **-hop**, 5 **-hoppe**. [f. WAN- + HOPE *sb.*[1] Cf. MLG., MDu. *wanhope* (mod.Du. *-hoop*), whence MSw. *vanhop,* MDa. *vanhob.* Cf. UNHOPE.]

A. *sb.* **1.** Hopelessness, despair.

In early use chiefly, despair of salvation. Hence often in amatory compositions which imitate religious language.

1297 R. GLOUC. (Rolls) 6832 Is men as in wanhope wende hom aȝen bliue. *a* **1300** *Cursor M.* 25769 þou sinful, be þan war wit-all In wreche wanhop þat þou ne fall. *Ibid.* 28345 þat has don me for to fall in wane-hope. **1303** R. BRUNNE *Handl. Synne* 5170 Sloghenes, hyt wyl þe grope To brynge þe yn-to whanhope. *c* **1320** *Cast. Love* 951 Ne beo þou in wonhope non. *c* **1366** CHAUCER *Rom. Rose* 981 Fiue arowis were of other gise..The thridde of hem was clepe Shame. The fourthe, Wanhope cleped is. **139.** —— *Pars. T.* ¶693 (Egerton MS.) Wanhope, þat is, dispeire of the mercy of god. *c* **1425** *Eng. Conq. Irel.* 32 Her of come the Englysshe hope & comfort; & to the Iresshe, dred & wanhope. *c* **1450** *Mirour Saluacioun* (Roxb.) 28 Y[t] wedded folk of wanhope shuld noght be Trowing the stat sauvable of onely virginitee. **1471** CAXTON *Recuyell* (Sommer) 21 He wente out of the oracle..al bare of gladnes and al oppressyd and enuironed wyth wanhope cam to his folk. *c* **1518** SKELTON *Magnyf.* 2337 There is no man may synne more mortally Than of Wanhope thrughe the vnhappy wayes, By Myschefe to breuyate and shorten his dayes. *a* **1542** WYATT in *Tottel's Misc.* (Arb.) 59 Renewyng with my sute my payne, My wanhope with your stedfastnesse. **1570–6** LAMBARDE *Peramb. Kent* 68 They..were driuen in the end, to giue ouer in the plain field, for very dispaire, wanhope, and weerinesse. **1861** *Temple Bar* Dec. 151 Wan-hope had weighed my spirit to the dust. **1870** MORRIS *Earthly Par.* III. III. 279 And [ed. 1903 But] creeping wanhope did he still withstand. **1894** —— *Wood beyond World* 221 Two days he battled thus with storm & blindness, & wanhope of his life.

¶ **2.** Erroneous uses. † **a.** = Vain hope.

There is an apparent instance in the edd. of Douglas *Æn.* I. vi. 82, but the Camb. MS. has *with vaynhope* [L. *vana spe*].

1422 YONGE tr. *Secreta Secret.* 145 Hoppe is a ryghtfull tryste for a ryghtfull Werke, i-put be-twen wanhoppe and dysspayre, or presompsion of goodis to come afftyr to be hadde, And of illis to come afftyr to be Enchued. *a* **1548** HALL *Chron., Rich. III,* 48 That they should brynge her yf yt were possible into some wanhope, or as men saie into a fooles paradise. **1549** CHALONER *Erasm. on Folly* H ij, A few yeres haue they spente yet, in great wanhope, and pleasure [L. *summa cum voluptate*]. *a* **1565** —— tr. *Boeth.* I. met. vii. 22 in Q. Eliz. *Englishings* 158 Wan hope forbere [L. *spem fugato*]. **1570** LEVINS *Manip.* 170/4 Wanhope, *falsa spes.* **1583** STOCKER *Civ. Warres Lowe C.* III. 114b, Suffer not your selues to be abused by fables and trifling toyes, neither be you carried away with a Wanhope. **1593** G. HARVEY *New Let.* B, A wan, or windy Hope, is a notable breake-necke vnto itselfe.

† **b.** In late 16th c. and early 17th c. writers *wan hope* (two words) seems to be used for 'faint hope', as if containing WAN *a. Obs.*

1558 in Froude *Hist. Eng.* (1870) VI. 80 [There was but] a wan hope of recovering Calais. **1586** A. DAY *Eng. Secretorie* I. (1625) 93 The intollerable woes wherein I lived ..might have kindled in me some wan hope one day to have found an hour so happy wherein by a right conceit..our natural care might in some sort or other have been renued. **1589** LODGE *Scillaes Metam.* B3b, I curse fond Loue and Fortune durelesse, Wan hope my weale, my trust but bad aduenture. **1590** SIDNEY *Arcadia* II. iii. (1912) 164 My sheepe are thoughts,..My sheepehooke is wanne hope, which all upholdes. **1607** R. C[AREW] tr. *Estienne's World Wond.* I. xxvi. 213 At last he remembered that the king had often shewed mercy on malefactors, and thereupon conceiuing some wanne hope, he was euer harping vpon that string. **1610** FOLKINGHAM *Feudigr.* I. x. 28 And though the small show of winter verdure giues wanne hope, yet his faire May-florish reuiues the drooping spirits of the doubtful and wauering experimenter, with ful assurance of a rich vesture for haruest. **1612** J. DAVIES (Heref.) *Muse's Sacrif.* (Grosart) 12/1 My Soule dismai'd, not knowing where to flee, With hands of Hope (wan Hope) at thee doth graspe. **1648** G. DANIEL *Eclog* iv. 169 This, his last Refuge, a wan hope, to bring Himselfe to former Glories of a King.

† **B.** *adj.* [Cf. MSw. *vanhopa* adj.] That has no hope, despairing. *Obs.*

1549 COVERDALE, etc. *Erasm. Par. Rom.* xii. 4–16 Suffer it, not with heauye heartes, as men that are wanhope [*later edd.* in wanhope, in dispaire], but [etc.].

Hence † **'wanhope** *v.* [= MLG. *wanhopen,* MSw. *vanhopa,* MDa. *vanhobe*] to despair. † **wanhoping** *vbl. sb.* † **wanhopefully** *adv.*, despairingly. † **wanhopely** *a.*, hopeless.

a **1300** *Cursor M.* 25820 þai..wines for þair mikel sin neuer to merci for to win, and suagat for þair wanhopping þai fall wit-vten vp-couering. *c* **1425** *Eng. Conq. Irel.* 16 He was neuer whan-hopefully argh, ne aferd, ne amayed of hert. *Ibid.* 88 In the man of blode, the blode shall aryse, & wan-hoply shal hys pynsynge be. **13..** *Celestin* 22 in *Anglia* I. 68 Hadde a man neuere so myche mys wroughte, To godes mercy wanhope he nought.

† **wanhue,** *v. Sc. Obs.* In 5 **wanhew.** [f. WAN- + HUE *v.*[2]] *trans.* To stain.

c **1420** WYNTOUN *Cron.* V. XII. 3696 (Cott. MS.) Quhar of sacles blude droppande ȝhit wanhewis [*v.r.* vnhewis] bathe sleyf and hande?

wanian, obs. form of WANION.

† **'waniand.** *Obs.* Also 5 **waneand, wanyende, wenyand(e,** 5–6 **wanyand,** 6 **waniant, wanniaunt, weniand, -ya(u)nt.** [ME. *waniand,* north. pres. pple. of *wanien,* WANE *v.* See the definition.] In the phrase ***in the waniand,*** prob. with ellipsis of *mone* (cf. 'on waniȝendum monan' *Sax. Leechd.* I. 320) = at the time of the waning moon, i.e. in an unlucky hour; hence used as a vague imprecation or as an exclamation of anger, impatience, etc. = 'with a vengeance', 'with a plague'. Also ***in the wild waniand.*** See WANION; also WANING *vbl. sb.* 2 b, WANING *ppl. a.* 1 b.

a **1352** MINOT *Poems* v. 30 In þe wilde waniand was þaire hertes light. *Ibid.* ix. 25 It was in þe waniand þat þai furth went. *c* **1430** *Brut* 441 But þe moste vengeance fell vpon þe proude Scottes, for thei went to Dog-wash the same day..; So that they may say wele 'In the croke of þe mone went thei thidre warde, And in the wilde wanyende come þei homewarde.' *c* **1440** *York Myst.* vii. 45 We! Whythir now in wilde waneand. *Ibid.* xxxiii. 485 Furth in þe wylde wanyand be walkand. *c* **1460** *Towneley Myst.* xx. 748 Step furth, in the wenyande! **1529** MORE *Suppl. Soules* 16b, He wold of lyklyhod bynde them to cartes and bete them, and make them wed in the wanyand. **1540** PALSGR. *Acolastus* II. i. I ij b, Go hens in to yl crosse .i. walke or pycke the hens in the galowes name, or in the weniand, or in the .xx. deuyll waye. **1570** LEVINS *Manip.* 25/23 Y[e] Wenyant, *in malam crucem.*

b. ***with a wanyand:*** cf. WANION.

1563–70 FOXE *A. & M.* II. 1311/1 The Pope..sent into Fraunce Hildebrand, hys Cardinall Chapleine.., and made him with a wanyand to come agayne *coram nobis.*

wanigan ('wænɪgən). *N. Amer.* Also **wammikin, wangan, wangun, wannegan, wannigan, wongen.** [Shortened from Montagnais Indian *atawangan,* f. *atawan* to buy or sell. Cf. Cree and Odjibwa *atawâgan,* 'ce dont on se sert pour acheter ou pour vendre' (Lacombe).]

1. A receptacle for small supplies or a reserve stock; esp., a boat or a chest containing outfit supplies for a lumber camp.

1848 BARTLETT *Dict. Amer., Wangan.* (Indian.) In Maine, a boat for carrying provisions. **1854** *Americans at Home* (ed. Haliburton) III. 254 The boats appropriated for the removal of the whole company, apparatus, and provisions [of river-drivers], when loaded, are called 'wanguns', an Indian word... Among the dangers to be incurred..is that of 'running the wangun'..which..means the act of taking these loaded bateaux down river from station to station. **1860** *Harper's Mag.* XX. 451 Behind each regiment of logs follows the wangan—a small boat or barge with a canvass awning stretched over it, and the cook and supplies. **1864** LOWELL *Fireside Trav.* 132 We..took possession of a deserted *wongen,* in which to cook and eat our dinner. **1878** *Scribner's Mag.* XV. 150 The drive is accompanied by what is called a wammikin, consisting of a raft of square timber or long logs on which is built a comfortable shanty. **1902** S. E. WHITE *Blazed Trail* 323 Outside the cook and cookee were stowing articles in the already loaded wanigan. **1911** —— *Rules of Game* I. xiii. [Log-driving.] Ordinarily on drive we have a wanigan... A wanigan's a big scow. It carries the camp and supplies to follow the drive. **1945** F. J. FUGINA *Lore & Lure of Upper Mississippi* 221 Wanigans were small flatboats, built of natural crook knees and planked lengthwise. **1957** *Bush News* (Port Arthur, Ontario) 1 June 1/1 Three wanegans, a floating mess hall and cook shack, and six drive camps are maintained to keep the wood moving.

b. Stores, provisions.

1907 *Scribner's Mag.* Jan. 2/1 Now load up with the bundles and boxes, the tent,..the provisions—all that stuff that is known as 'duffel' in New York, and '*butins*' in French Canada and '*wangan*' in Maine.

c. *attrib.*

1907 *Black Cat* June 19 An ancient Wangan-chest, relic of his father's river-days. **1908** S. E. WHITE *River Man* xv. 131 The ground had now hardened so that a wanigan boat was unnecessary. Instead, the camp outfit was transported in wagons.

2. A cabin, usu. wooden, mounted on runners; = CABOOSE 3 b.

1949 in *Dict. Canadianisms* (1967) 834/1 The Wannegan has a sled mounted house type body made of light gauge metal, and heavily insulated for use in sub zero temperatures. **1949** *Survey* June 303/2 The industry is based no longer in isolated logging camps, with lonely men living in 'wannigans' dragged through the forests on sled-like runners. **1958** L. CRISLER *Arctic Wild* 133 At Barrow, Cris chained the wolves in front of our wanigan, one of a row of four or five empty wanigans beside the airstrip. They had made up a cat train. A wanigan is a narrow shack on runners: it can be drawn by tractor across snow or tundra. **1966** *Islander* (Victoria, B.C.) 20 Feb. 7/3 While sleeping in a wanigan, a hut on sleds, I was awakened..by native children shouting. **1979** C. KILIAN *Icequake* xii. 211 We'll have to build some wanigans that'll fit on the sledges. Otherwise we'll never be able to shelter everybody.

waning ('weɪnɪŋ), *vbl. sb.* [f. WANE *v.* + -ING[1].] The action of the verb.

1. *gen.* Decrease or diminution in magnitude, importance, brilliancy, intensity, etc.

As OE. *wanian* (WANE *v.*) had the trans. sense 'to make less' as well as the intr. sense 'to become less', the vbl. sb. had the two corresponding meanings, but (as often occurs with nouns of action) the two are often practically coincident, and cannot be distinguished with certainty.

c **900** tr. *Bæda's Hist.* II. ii. (Schipper) 121 Nalæs butan micelre wonunge his weorodes [L. *non sine magno exercitus sui damno*]. *c* **1375** *Sc. Leg. Saints* xxxvi. (*John Baptist*) 224 þat tyme of þe ȝere borne wes he, quhene þat þe dais takis linthynge; & Iohne, quhen þai tak wanynge. **1398** TREVISA *Barth. De P.R.* VIII. xl. (Tollemache MS.), This lyȝte with oute wanynge of it selfe scheweþ and schedeþ by-schinynge. **1593** SHAKS. *2 Hen. VI,* IV. x. 22, I seeke not to waxe great by others waining [*so Rowe conj.: Folio* warning]. **1633** P. FLETCHER *Purple Isl.* VI. lxx, Can.. One onely blot so great a light empair, That never could he hope his waning to repair? **1884** *Harper's Mag.* July 260/1 The Gunnings' beauty was at the waning.

†*Phrase.* **1583** BABINGTON *Commandm.* (1590) 429 Will not the dread of dolefull day strike such a filthy fault into the waning, and by little and little cut quite the throte of it, and make it bleede to death in vs?

† **b.** Damage inflicted by a person. *Obs.*

c **1175** *Pater Noster* 278 in *Lamb. Hom.* 71 Kep us from his waning, þat laþe gast.

† **c.** Default, shortcoming. *Obs.*

c **1320** *Cast. Love* 228 in *Minor Poems fr. Vernon MS.* 361 God ne wrouhte neuer þat þing þat out les þorw his wonyng, ffor nis no wone on him I-long.

2. Of the moon: Periodical decrease in apparent size (see WANE *v.* 2); the half of the lunar month in which this takes place.

c **1000** *Sax. Leechd.* III. 268/13 Æfre hi [*sc.* seo sæ & se mona] beoð ʒeferan on wæstme & on wanunge. **1398** TREVISA *Barth. De P.R.* VIII. xvii. (1495) 326 The mone encreasyth all humours, and in her wanynge the..humours of the body ben made lesse. **14..** *Lat.-Eng. Voc.* in Wr.-Wülcker 593/48 *Lucubrax* [*sic*], wonynge of monythe. *c* **1440** *Pallad. on Husb.* I. 826 To graffe and sowe in growynge of the mone, And kitte or mowe in wanyng, is to done. **1657** J. WATTS *Scribe, Pharisee,* etc. 87 Their light was as the light of the Moon, mingled with some spots, subject to wainings, decreases, and eclipses. **1683** *Digby's Chym. Secr.* II. 198 The best time to gather the Misletoe of the Oak..is in the.. Waning of the Moon. **1822** IMISON *Sci. & Art* I. 437 The waning or decreasing of the moon takes place in the same manner, but in a contrary order.

fig. **1642** FULLER *Holy & Prof. St.* II. xxi. 138 He with many others helped to the waining of that half Moon, which sought to govern all the motion of our Sea.

† **b.** with the epithet *wild:* cf. WANIAND.

c **1435** in Kingsford *Chron. London* (1905) 75 In the croke off the mone went they thedirward, and in the wilde wanynge kom they homward.

† **3.** Decline (of life); concluding part (of a day, or period of time). *Obs.*

1561 T. NORTON *Calvin's Inst.* III. 269 Them, whom..the tendre kindnes of the Lord hath rewarded at the waining of the daye, and at the ending of their life. **1579** LYLY *Euphues* (Arb.) 159 In the wayning of the world, wherein so many false Christs are come. **1592** GREENE *Disput. Conny-catchers* Wks. (Grosart) X. 238 Beeing gotten in the wayning of my parents age, they doted on me aboue the rest [of their children]. **1594** NASHE *Unfort. Trav.* C 2, Let mee quietly descend to the waining of my youthful daies, and tell a little of the sweating sicknes.

4. Comb.: ***waning time.***

a **1639** WOTTON *Life & D. Buckingham* (1642) 3 There is nothing..more jealous, then a favorite, especially towards the wayning time and suspect of saciety. **1680** C. NESSE *Church Hist.* 154 The moon..is the embleme of the church ..as having her filling and weaning times.

ˈ**waning,** *ppl. a.* [f. WANE *v.* + -ING².] That wanes or is on the wane.

1. Decreasing or declining in importance, power, influence, etc. (See the senses of the vb.)

1596 SHAKS. *Tam. Shr.* Induct. ii. 65 Thou hast a Ladie farre more Beautifull, Then any woman in this waining age. **1622** FLETCHER *Sea Voy.* IV. (1647) 14/2 Am I because I am in bonds and miserable,..My fortune like my wayning selfe, for this despis'd? **1831** LAMB *Elia* Ser. II. *Ellistoniana*, The last retreat, and recess, of his every-day waning grandeur. **1856** FROUDE *Hist. Eng.* (1858) I. ii. 90 The clergy sunk under the influence of a waning religion. **1882** GEIKIE *Text-bk. Geol.* III. I. i. §2. 209 The dormant or waning condition of a volcano. **1896** CONAN DOYLE *Exploits Gerard* ix, I hurried wildly onward through the waning darkness.

¶ **b.** ***in the wild waning world***: perversion of *in the wild waniand*: see WANIAND, WANION, and cf. quot. *c* 1435 in WANING *vbl. sb.* 2 b.

c **1485** *Digby Myst.* (1882) III. 140 In þe wyld wanyng word, pes all at onys!

c. Ageing, growing old. *rare.*

1895 *Season* Mar., Suppl. 45/3, I do not, as a rule, approve of black for waning people..but in this case, as the wearer was rather florid, the garment was a success.

2. Of the moon.

c **1000** *Sax. Leechd.* I. 320 Þas wyrte þu scealt niman on waniȝendum monan. **1705** ADDISON *Italy, Ferrara* 115 Waining Moons their settled Periods keep To swell the Billows. **1755** B. MARTIN *Mag. Arts & Sci.* 123 When God appoints, the horned Moon renews Her waining Light. **1797** COLERIDGE *Kubla Khan* 15 Beneath a waning moon. **1814** BYRON *Lara* II. xxiv, When Cynthia's light almost gave way to morn, And nearly veil'd in mist her waning horn. **1837** WHEWELL *Hist. Induct. Sci.* (1857) I. 100 The waning, and the re-appearing moon.

3. Of light, or a luminary: Declining in lustre, tending towards extinction.

1700 BLACKMORE *Song of Moses* (Exod. xv.) 45 Let him.. lift on high his Adamantine Shield, Whose brighter Lustre drowns the waining Sun. **1802** MARIA EDGEWORTH *Moral T., Forrester* xiv, His waning candle sunk in the socket. **1840** DICKENS *Old C. Shop* xxxi, At last the day turned her waning candle pale, and she fell asleep. **1846** KEBLE *Lyra Innoc., Fine Clothes*, Around where late the waning sun Sank in his evening cloud. **1873** E. E. HALE *In His Name* ix. 77 The waning embers of the fire.

b. Of the day: Drawing to a close.

1767 JAGO *Edge-hill* IV. 156 But of the waining Day Mindful, and many a Theme as yet unsung, To future Bards she leaves your copious Praise.

4. Becoming scanty, running short. Now *rare.*

1632 LITHGOW *Trav.* VIII. 375 Our victuals and water done, we were forced to relye vpon Tobacco, and to drinke our owne wayning pisse. **1810** MISS MITFORD in L'Estrange *Life* (1870) I. iv. 111 It is well for you that my waning paper ..brings this tiresome letter to an end. **1900** CONAN DOYLE *Green Flag* etc. 77 Behind him stood the watchful steward, for ever filling up his waning glass.

wanion, wannion (ˈwɒnjən). *Obs.* exc. *arch.* Forms: 6 **wanian, wenyon,** 6–7 **wennion,** 7 **wannian, wenian, -on,** 6– **wanion, wannion.** An altered form of WANIAND used in certain formulas of asseveration or imprecation. **a.** ***in a wanion,*** later ***with a wanion,*** with a plague, with a vengeance. Also ***with a wild wanion.***

1549 LATIMER *2nd Serm. bef. Edw. VI* (Arb.) 63 Was not this a good prelate? he should haue bene at home a preachynge in hys Dioces in a wanian. **1583** STUBBES *Anat. Abus.* P vj, We must have these goodly pageants played upon the sabaoth day (in a wanion) because there are no mo daies in a week. **1607** R. C[AREW] tr. *Estienne's World Wond.* I. xxxix. 341 He..cryed aloud, Come downe in a wannian. **1567** HARMAN *Caveat* 62 Hee went with a wannion to his mothers chamber. *a* **1568** *Jacob & Esau* I. i. A ij, Up with a wilde wenyon, how long wilt thou lie? **1596** NASHE *Saffron Walden* H 4 b, Take it, with a wennion, altogether, if you will have it. **1607** SHAKS. *Per.* II. i. 17 Come away, or Ile fetch'th with a wanion. **1663** COWLEY *Cutter Coleman St.* IV. iv, Boys must not have their meanings, Colonel: Let him mean what I mean with a Wennion. **1694** MOTTEUX *Rabelais* IV. xlvii, Come out with a vengeance, come out with a wannion. **1826** SCOTT *Woodst.* iv, He would have battered the presbyterian spirit out of him with a wanion. **1861** READE *Cloister & H.* xxxvii, Let him go with a wanion.

b. ***a* (*wild*) *wanion on, with a wanion to,*** may a curse or plague light on (a person, etc.)!

? *c* **1570** *Buggbears* IV. iv. 11 Now a wild wannion on it. **1605** CHAPMAN, etc. *Eastw. Hoe* III. ii. D 2, Marie hang you: Westward with a wanion te 'yee. **1624** DAVENPORT *City Nightcap* IV. (1661) 36 Is here any work for Grace, with a wannion to her? **1663** DRYDEN *Wild Gallant* III. i, I'll teach you to take place of Tradesmens Wives with a wannion to you. **1822** SCOTT *Peveril* vi, A d——d Presbyterian scoundrel,..whom I hope to fetch down from his perch presently, with a wannion to him!

wanish, obs. f. VANISH *v.*, WANNISH *a.*

wanite, obs. Sc. f. VANITY.

wank (wæŋk), *sb.* (*a.*) *slang.* Also †**whank.** [Origin unknown.]

1. Of a male: (an act of) masturbation.

This word and its derivatives are not in polite use.

1948 PARTRIDGE *Dict. Forces' Slang* 203 *Wank-pit*,..a bed. (Air Force.) **1951** —— *Dict. Slang* (ed. 4) 1220/1 *Whank*, (male) self-abuse: low: from ca. 1870. Perhaps echoic. **1966** P. WILLMOTT *Adolescent Boys* iii. 49 When I was 13, my friends at school asked me if I'd ever had a wank. **1970** T. LEWIS *Jack's Return Home* 18 Valerie Marshbanks showed everybody her knickers and charged a penny a wank, in the bushes, one at a time. **1971** B. W. ALDISS *Soldier Erect* 83 Oh, Christ! And there wasn't even anywhere in this wilderness where you could enjoy a decent sensuous wank—certainly not in the tent or the latrine. Nowhere. **1977** *Sniffin' Glue* July 15 Behind that bog door are you thinkin' readin' or just havin' a wank?

2. An objectionable or contemptible person or thing. Cf. WANKER 2.

1970 P. LAURIE *Scotland Yard* vi. 158 Fred's counsel is a fat wank. **1973** *Nation Rev.* (Melbourne) 31 Aug. 1434/5 Kenneth S. Jaffrey, that naturopathic scientific wank. **1977** *Time Out* 17–23 June 14/1 Why did Aldrich direct this lengthy wank for Sinatra and Martin just after he'd made a film as interesting as 'Baby Jane'? **1977** *Maledicta* I. 11 He may be called a *jerk*, a *jerkoff* or a *jackoff*; a *wank* (Brit.), or a *whack*.

3. *attrib.* or as *adj.* Likely to induce masturbation.

1976 J. I. M. STEWART *Memorial Service* viii. 122 'He has an enormous great wank picture in his room. Makes the place like a porn shop.' 'I know that picture too... It's wanky all right.' **1981** P. PORTER *Coll. Poems* (1983) 277 But you are talking about love, you'll say. Yes, and I know the difference, Taking down a wank magazine.

wank (wæŋk), *v. slang.* Also †**whank.** [Origin unknown: see prec.]

1. *intr.* Of a male: to masturbate. Freq. with *off.*

1950 P. TEMPEST *Lag's Lexicon* 229 *Whank, to*, to masturbate. **1951** PARTRIDGE *Dict. Slang* (ed. 4) 1220/1 *Whank*, loosely *wank*, v.i., to masturbate: low: late C. 19–20. Also *whank off*. **1966** P. WILLMOTT *Adolescent Boys* iii. 49 Some boys..think, 'I'm not going to tell anyone in case they think I'm dirty, wanking myself off.' But me and my mates, we tell everybody we wank off. **1969** F. NORMAN *Banana Boy* 108, I am certain that he could have wanked for Britain in the Olympics and won a gold medal with ease. **1977** W. MCILVANNEY *Laidlaw* xli. 192 You've been wankin'... That's no' nice in public places.

2. *trans.* To masturbate (a man). Freq. with *off.*

1966 [see sense 1 above]. **1975** O. SELA *Bengali Inheritance* xi. 94 'You like for me to wank you?'.. 'No... My wife would not like it.' **1980** 'D. KAVANAGH' *Duffy* v. 93 Lots of punters wanted you to wank them off... You'd think that was the one thing they could do for themselves. **1984** J. BARNES *Flaubert's Parrot* iv. 56, I saw a monkey in the street jump on a donkey and try to wank him off.

Hence **wanked-out** *a.*, exhausted (by masturbation).

1973 W. H. CANAWAY *Harry doing Good* ii. 23 A wanked-out shivering wreck. **1976** M. HARTMANN *Leap for Sun* i. 14 I worked on a wanked-out farming magazine.

wankapin, -kopin (ˈwɒnkəpɪn). *U.S.* Also **yoncopin** (*Cent. Dict.*). [prob. N.Amer. Indian.] The water-chinkapin, *Nelumbo lutea.*

1832 J. P. KENNEDY *Swallow B.* xxiii. (1860) 199 This fine garden of wankopins and snake-collards.

Wankel (ˈwæ-, ˈvæŋkəl). The name of Felix *Wankel* (1902–88), German engineer, used *attrib.* and *absol.* to designate a kind of rotary internal-combustion engine that he invented in which an approximately triangular, eccentrically pivoted shaft rotates continuously in a chamber with its corners touching the walls, so forming three combustion spaces that vary in volume as it turns. Also *Comb.*

1961 *Engineering* 19 May 682/1 Many other people have felt that something to replace the conventional engine is needed and a promising design to rear its head has been the Wankel engine. **1966** E. RUDINGER *Consumer's Car Gloss.* 120 The Wankel engine is much smaller than a conventional engine with a similar power output, and runs more smoothly. **1967** *Economist* 2 Sept. 811/1 The motor industry has waited a long time for the first car in production to use the wankel rotary engine. Now the small German manufacturer, NSU, has got there with the Ro 80. *Ibid.* 811/2 Will the wankel be enough to sustain NSU as an independent motor company, or will NSU one day have to close ranks further with Citroen? **1970** *Guardian* 10 Nov. 11/5 Citroën..has built and sold 500 Wankel engined cars. **1972** *Sci. Amer.* Aug. 17/3 Since the Wankel has no valves, it does not need a camshaft, valve lifters and so on, and it requires no more than two spark plugs per rotor. **1979** *Motorcycling Manual* (Motorcycling Monthly) 6/1 Apart from the few Wankel-engined bikes..all current machines have either two-stroke or four-stroke piston engines.

wanker (ˈwæŋkə(r)). *slang.* Also †**whanker.** [f. WANK *v.* + -ER¹.]

1. One who masturbates; ***wanker's doom,*** disability caused by excessive masturbation.

1950 P. TEMPEST *Lag's Lexicon* 229 A man suspected of excessive masturbation is said to be suffering from 'whanker's doom'. **1961** H. S. TURNER *Something Extraordinary* ix. 158 Because Willy always has big black circles round his eyes he is classified as 'pocket billiard player' or 'wanker'. **1971** B. W. ALDISS *Soldier Erect* 86 Failed fucker, failed wanker was an inglorious double billing. **1972** K. BONFIGLIOLI *Don't point that Thing at Me* xiii. 111 Mortdecai Minor, the likeliest candidate for wanker's doom. **1977** *Maledicta* I. 11 He is *whacky*, or *whacked to the gills*; he is *wonked goggle-eyed*, or is suffering from *Wanker's Doom*. The last refer to the old idea or threat that masturbation will make a person go blind or deaf or crazy.

2. An objectionable or contemptible person. Cf. WANK *sb.* 2.

1972 A. DRAPER *Death Penalty* v. 36 'Get out, you fucker,' screamed a youth... Another said, 'You wanker,' and indulged in a masturbatory gesture. **1976** U. HOLDEN *String Horses* vi. 69 Her kiddies..rarely spoke except to mutter 'Wanker' or something crude. **1978** K. AMIS *Jake's Thing* xii. 123 'Damon, what's a wanker?'.. 'These days a waster, a shirker, someone who's fixed himself a soft job or an exalted position by means of an undeserved reputation on which he now coasts.' 'Oh. Nothing to do with tossing off then?' 'Well, connected with it, yes, but more metaphorical than literal.' **1981** P. NIESEWAND *Word of Gentleman* xxxii. 222 They're such a bunch of wankers... You can't trust them to do anything properly.

wanking (ˈwæŋkɪŋ), *vbl. sb. slang.* Also †**whanking.** [f. WANK *v.* + -ING¹.] Masturbation. Also with *off.* So ***wanking couch, -pit,*** a bed.

1951 PARTRIDGE *Dict. Slang* (ed. 4) 1220/1 *Whanking(-)pit*, the Army's form of *whank-pit*: since early 1920's. But used also by R.A.F. **1966** D. HOLBROOK *Flesh Wounds* 39 Wakey, wakey old mate. You want to get smartly outa that wanking pit! **1969** M. PUGH *Last Place Left* xxvi. 192 You rooting goat. Why can't you take them to your own wanking couch? **1971** P. L. CAVE *Chopper* xi. 106 He'd have so many women he could say goodbye to wanking for life. **1977** *Sounds* 9 July 23/3, I don't think the cutting was any more extreme than hanging from the rafters or wanking off on stage or vomiting.

wankle (ˈwæŋk(ə)l), *a. Obs.* exc. *dial.* Forms: 1 **wancol,** 3 **wankel,** 4 **-kyll,** 4–5 **-kill(e,** 7, 9 **wancle, wankle.** [OE. *wancol* = OS. *wankol*, MDu., Du. *wankel*, OHG. *wanchal*, MHG., G. (obs.) *wankel*; cf. OHG. *wankôn* (MHG., mod.G. *wanken*), to waver, totter.] Unsteady, insecure; changeable, unsettled, precarious; inconstant, wavering. Also, weak in health, delicate, sickly.

c **888** ÆLFRED *Boeth.* vii. §2 Nu ðu hæfst onȝiten ða wanclan truwa þæs blindan lustes. *Ibid.* xx, Hio hit ȝecyð self mid hire hwurfulnesse þæt hio bið swiðe wancol. *c* **1220** *Bestiary* 566 in *O.E. Misc.* 18 Ðis wunder wuneð in wankel stede, ðer ðe water sinkeð. **13..** *Gosp. Nicod.* 340 (Addit. MS.) If my kyngdome..Within þis wankill worlde nowe were. **14..** *Thomas of Erceldonne* 494 (Camb. MS.) þe worlde is wondur wankill. **1674** RAY *N.C. Words, Wankle*, limber, flaccid, ticklish, fickle, wavering. **1683** *Yorke-sh. Dial.* 7 Here's wancle weather for gittinge of our Hay. **1686** G. STUART *Joco-ser. Discourse* 50 Your Wankle Leggs canno' support ye. **1790** GROSE *Provinc. Gloss.* (ed. 2), *Wankle*, weak, unstable, not to be depended on; as a wankle seat; wankle weather. N. *a* **1825** FORBY *Voc. E. Anglia, Wancle, wanky*, weak; pliant. **1869** J. P. MORRIS *Furness Gloss.* 107 That barne's terble wankle on its legs. **1888** FENN *Dick o' the Fens* 381 He don't wear as I should like to see un. He's wankle.

wanky (ˈwæŋkɪ), *a. slang.* [f. WANK *sb.* or *v.* + -Y¹.] Objectionable, contemptible; masturbatory.

1972 K. BONFIGLIOLI *Don't point that Thing at Me* xix. 173, I was now quite calm, the wanky old avenger preparing to kill his man. **1973** M. AMIS *Rachel Papers* 78 No, man, don't get too wanky with her. And cut out all this intellectual shit. **1976** [see WANK *sb.* (*a.*) 3]. **1977** *Zigzag* Aug. 15/3 We loved that, 'cos it's such a wanky plastic paper and they thought by slagging us early they'd be in first. **1983** W. MCILVANNEY *Papers of Tony Veitch* xxx. 188 I'm not interested in his wanky theories about why he did it—just that he did it, the bastard.

†**wanlace.** *Obs.* Also 5 **wanlas(e, wenlace,** 5–6 **wanles(s:** and see WINDLASS *sb.*¹ [a. AF. *wanelace, wenelaz* (12–13th c.), recorded in the fig. sense 'deception, fraudulent device'. As the word does not occur in continental Fr., it is not unlikely that it may be a Norman mispronunciation of some native English word. In the 16th c. *wanlace* was superseded by WINDLASS *sb.*², but it is not clear whether this was a survival of the native form or an etymologizing alteration of the AF. word. Latinized forms of the word, in the original hunting sense, are *wenelacia* and *wanlassum* (in Du Cange erroneously *waulassus*). The phrase *fugare wanlassum* was used for 'to drive back the game'.]

1. *Hunting.* A circuit made by a portion of a hunting party for the purpose of intercepting and heading back the game. Hence, an appointed station in hunting, = TRIST *sb.*², TRISTRE, med.L. *stabulum.*

c **1400** *Master of Game* (MS. Digby 182) xvii, Neuerthelesse þer beth somme þat falleth to be berselettes, and also to brynge wele and faste a wanlas aboute. *c* **1420** WYNTOUN *Cron.* III. iii. 520 (MS. W.) Quhen he wes xv ȝeris of cass He slew his fader at þe wanless. *Ibid.* VII. iv. 446 (MS. Cott.) A knycht hym [*sc.* William Rufus] slew þar at wanles.

2. *transf.* An intercepting movement; an ambush. Phrase, ***at the wanlace.***

c **1330** R. BRUNNE *Chron. Wace* (Rolls) 12860 Bytwyxt þem [*sc.* the opposing armies] were many chaces, ffele turnynges & fele wanlaces. **1456** SIR G. HAYE *Law Arms*

(S.T.S.) 164 Men may..barate thair inymyes..and se quhen thay ar in disaray, and wate thame at the wanlas. **1596** DALRYMPLE tr. *Leslie's Hist. Scot.* (S.T.S.) II. 192 Quhen we war gatherit, we waytet thame at the wanles.

3. *fig.* A crafty device, a plot.

1303 R. BRUNNE *Handl. Synne* 4375 Where þat he [a taxgatherer] myght make a wanlace, And any þyng to þe kyng purchace, He ne lette for no fals othe. *Ibid.* 12008 Þat he [*sc.* God] wulde..brynge þe aȝen to his grace þat þou lostest with þy wanlace. *c* **1400** *Beryn* 2874 By þat tyme I have I-made al my wanlase. **1481** BOTONER *Tulle of Old Age* (Caxton), And all such corrupt untrue werkis which ben nevir mevid not undirtakyn but by the insolence and wantonness and wenlacys of flesshely delectacyon.

† **wanlasour.** *Obs.* In 5 **wanelasour, wandlessour.** [Prob. AF.; f. *wanelace* (see prec.) + *-our* -OR. Cf. WINDLASS *v.*[1]] A hunting servant whose duty is to intercept and turn back the game; a driver.

14.. *Lat.-Eng. Voc.* in Wr.-Wülcker 562/31 *Alator*, a wanelasour. *c* **1440** *Ipomydon* 387 The wandlessours went þrow þe forest And to þe lady brought many a best.

wanle, var. WANDLE.

† **wanless, waneless**, *a. Obs.* [f. *wan(e*, WONE, hope + -LESS.] Hopeless.

a **1300** *Cursor M.* 23998 Bot quen i sagh þaa juus snell, Rise again mi sun sua fell, ful wanles [*Fairfax* waneles] wex i þan.

Wan-Li (wænliː). Also **Wan Li.** The royal name of Shen Zong, emperor of China 1573–1620, used *attrib.* and *absol.* with reference to pottery and porcelain made during his reign.

1876 HOOPER & PHILLIPS *Man. Marks on Pott. & Porc.* 186 The dark rich blue of the *Kea-tching* and the white granulated surface of the *Wan-leïh*, are very choice. **1885** *Jrnl. Peking Oriental Soc.* I. 98 Plain white cups of *Wan li* porcelain were several taels of silver each. **1902** C. MONKHOUSE *Chinese Porc.* i. 36 Some of the blue is fine in colour, as in some pieces which were lent by Mr. William Agnew to the Burlington Fine Arts Club in 1895. One of them has the Wan-li mark. **1915** R. L. HOBSON *Chinese Pott. & Porc.* II. v. 66 Another group of marked Wan Li ware, comprising bowls and dishes with trim neat finish..has a soft-looking glaze. **1960** H. HAYWARD *Antique Coll.* 313/2 *Wu ts'ai (five-colour) wares.* This generally implies the characteristic Wan Li period Chinese porcelain wares, painted in underglaze blue and enamel colours (red, green, yellow and purple). **1978** K. BONFIGLIOLI *All Tea in China* i. 12 In London today they are crazy for blue-and-white wares and cannot tell Wan-Li from *De Metalen Pot.*

† **wanlich**, *a. Obs. rare*⁻¹. [? f. *wan* WANE *sb.*[2] + *-lich*, -LY[1].] Baleful, fraught with evil.

c **1205** LAY. 25990 Wanliche weoren þa sonden.

† **wan'liesum**, *a. Sc. Obs.* [f. WAN- + LEESOME *a.*[1]] Unlovely.

1815 G. BEATTIE *John o' Arnha'* (1826) 36 A waesum, wild, wanliesum sight.

wanluck. *Sc.* Now *rare.* [f. WAN- + LUCK. Cf. MSw. *vanlykka*, MDa. *vanlykke*, Norw. *vanlukka.*] Unhappy fate. Cf. UNLUCK.

1571 SIR J. MAITLAND *Admon. to Regent* 30 Wanlukis quhair by thow may be lost. **1730** RAMSAY *Horse's Compl.* 7 Up frae my bed..I'm rais'd to draw the sled, Or cart, as haps to my wanluck.

wanly ('wɒnlɪ), *adv.* [f. WAN *a.* + -LY[2].] With a wan look or appearance; palely, pallidly; *fig.* with a dejected air, sorrowfully.

c **1205** LAY. 25828 Þa iherde he wepen wunder ane swiðen. wepen and weinen and wanliche iberen. *Ibid.* 30288 Nu we maȝen wepen and wanliche iberen. **1591** SYLVESTER *Du Bartas* v. i. 1028 An extream Fever..wanly did displace The Rose-mixt Lillies in her louely face. **1849** LYTTON *K. Arthur* I. xxxi, Save where the thin clouds wanly, slowly roll O'er the mute darkenss of the forest mountain. **1897** FLANDRAU *Harvard Episodes* 177 McGaw, looking ill at ease, but smiling wanly.

† **wanmol**, *a. Obs.* [f. WAN- + MOAL, speech, language.] Destitute of eloquence.

c **1250** *Gen. & Ex.* 2817 Louerd, ic am wanmol, un-reken Of wurdes, and may ic Iuel speken.

wanna ('wɒnə), repr. colloq. pronunc. of *want to* or *want a.* Cf. WANT *v.* 4, 5 and WANTA.

1896 S. CRANE *Maggie* v. 42, I see he had a still on, an' I didn' wanna give 'im no stuff. **1926–7** *T. Eaton & Co. Catal.* Fall & Winter 305/1 (*song-title*), I 'wanna' go where you go. **1941** B. SCHULBERG. *What makes Sammy Run?* vi. 121 Look, do you wanna be smart? **1962** J. D. MACDONALD *Girl* (1974) x. 140, I don't wanna be no nuisance woman. **1971** *Frendz* 21 May 2/1 Right on, Paul! Wanna job? **1980** G. V. HIGGINS *Kennedy for Defence* x. 104 'That's fine by me,' I said, 'if you wanna leave.'

wanne, obs. f. WAN, WHEN, WHENNE, WHOM.

wanne, obs. pa. t. WIN *v.*

wannegan, wannigan, varr. WANIGAN.

wannel, var. WANDLE.

wannen, wannes: see WHENNE, WHENCE.

wanness ('wɒnnɪs). Also 7 **wand-**. [f. WAN *a.* + -NESS.] The state or condition of being wan; †lividity (*obs.*): a pale, dead, or sickly colour (of the face), pallidness.

1382 WYCLIF *Gen.* iv. 23, I slowe a man into my wound, and a litle waxen man into my wannesse [Vulg. *in livorem meum*]. **1398** TREVISA *Barth. De P.R.* VII. liv. (1495) 268 Wyth to grete holdynge of emeroides comyth..palenesse of face and wannesse and heuynesse of loynes. **1530** PALSGR. 286/2 Wannes of colour, *indeur.* **1611** COTGR., *Blaimeur* palenesse, wannesse, bleakenesse; a dead, or whitish colour. *Ibid.*, *Lividité*, liuiditie, lewnesse, wannesse,..blewishnesse; the colour appearing vpon a stroake, blacke and blew. **1615** CROOKE *Body of Man* 40 The heat of the heart being drawne inward, there appeareth a pale wannesse in the face. **1643** A. TUCKNEY *Balm of Gilead* 22 The wannesse of his dead look upon the Crosse. **1653** R. SANDERS *Physiogn.* 180 A pale wandness in the face, as in the Flegmatique. **1771** MRS. GRIFFITH *Hist. Lady Barton* III. 275 My wanness was the effect of ill health. **1840** DICKENS *Old C. Shop* xliii, In the pale moonlight, which lent a wanness of its own to the delicate face. **1879** MISS BRADDON *Vixen* III. iii. 108 There was a faded look about her complexion, too,..a wanness, a yellowness.

wannion: see WANION.

wannish ('wɒnɪʃ), *a.* Also 5–6 **wannyssh(e, 6 -yshe, wanishe, 7 -ish.** [f. WAN *a.* + -ISH.] Somewhat wan; somewhat pale, dull, lustreless, or livid.

?*a* **1412** LYDG. *Two Merchants* 326 His vryne..was ful thynne and wannyssh for to see. **1545** RAYNALDE *Byrth Mankynde* 122 The which causethe..the eye sight to waxe wannysshe or tawnye. *a* **1547** SURREY *Poems*. '*This name*' 13 And eke the wanishe moone whiche sheenes by night also. **1585** HIGINS *Junius' Nomencl.* 438/2 With blacke wannish spots. **1594** R. C[AREW] *Tasso* (1881) 73 He that graund foe was aie to human kind, His wannish eyes [*i lividi occhi*] doth on the Christians cast. **1601** HOLLAND *Pliny* XXI. xxi. II. 108 The day Lillie Hemerocalles, hath leaves of a pale and wannish greene colour. **1630** MILTON *Passion* 35 The leaves should all be black wheron I write, And letters where my tears have washt a wannish white. **1784** COWPER *Task* I. 309 Paler some, And of a wannish gray. **1820** KEATS *Lamia* I. 57 Upon her crest she wore a wannish fire. **1855** TENNYSON *Maud* I. VI. i, No sun, but a wannish glare In fold upon fold of hueless cloud.

wannock, anglicized form of GUANACO.

1724 *Postmaster* 2 Oct. 4 On Tuesday Night a Wannock was carried from on board the said Ship..He hath a Body like that of a Deer.

† **wannowe**, *int. Obs. rare*⁻¹. [? f. *wa* WOE *int.* + NOW.] Alas.

c **1450** *Northern Passion* (MS. Addit.) 147/59* Wannow sayde kayme her es Envy My smoke gose down & thyne gose hye.

† '**wanny**, *a. Obs.* Also 6 **wannye, wannie.** [f. WAN *a.* + -Y[1].] Wan, pallid.

1555 EDEN *Decades* (Arb.) 311 With flatte visagies, pale and wannye coloure. **1566** STUDLEY *Medea* IV. (1581) 136 b, In faynting Face, with pale and wanny whyght The sanguyne hewe exyled thence is fled. **1594** WILLOBIE *Avisa* xvi. (1880) 48 Your wannie cheekes, your shaggie lockes. **1602** MUNDAY *Palmerin* I. xvii. (1639) F 3 b, A pale and wanny face.

† **wanpa**, Sc. var. VAMPEY. *Obs.*

1541 *Extracts Aberd. Reg.* (1844) I. 176 Item, solis exemplis over ledderis exemplis, with a wanpa for a buytt.

wanred(e: see WANDRETH *Obs.* (β).

† **wanrest.** *Sc. Obs.* [f. WAN- + REST *sb.*]

1. A state of inquietude or trouble: = UNREST.

c **1550** ROLLAND *Crt. Venus* II. 456 For my wanrest I wald thow saw remeid. **1570** *Satir. Poems Reform.* xxii. 41 This birdis counsall confoundit hes yis land,..That mouit hes..Wandreth, wanrest, feirfull ambitioun. **1584** J. MELVILL *Autob. & Diary* (Wodrow Soc.) 205 Sall nocht this sillie ease be turned in sorrowfull wanrest? **1603** *Proph. of T. Rymour* (Bannatyne Cl.) 22 The Ratches workes them great wanrest. **1768** ROSS *Helenore* I. 33 Quo' she, I wiss I could your wanrest ken. **1874** R. BUCHANAN *Poet. Wks.* I. 196 And Effie ..Turn'd from the happy shining of the sun, In wanrest and in tears.

2. The pendulum of a clock.

1794 [W. ANDERSON] *Piper of Peebles* 13 (Jam.) The house from top to bottom shook, An' as a wanrest wagg'd the crook. **1808** JAMIESON s.v., 'The wanrest of a clock gaes as far the tae gate, as it gede the tither;' S. Prov. signifying, that an unstable person generally goes from one extreme to another.

Hence **wan'restful** *a. Sc.*, restless.

1783 BURNS *Death Poor Mailie* 36 An' may they never learn the gaets Of ither vile, wanrestfu' Pets! **1887** SERVICE *Dr. Duguid* III. iii. 255 Wanrestfu' and troubled, she couldna sit still.

† **wanrufe.** *Sc. Obs. rare*⁻¹. [f. WAN- + *rufe* var. RO *sb.*] Disquiet, unrest.

c **1480** HENRYSON *Robene & Makyne* 28 Bot I haif mervell incertane Quhat makis the this wanrufe.

wanruly, *a. Sc.* [f. WAN- + RULY *a.*[2]] Unruly.

a **1774** FERGUSSON *Hallow-Fair* xii, Frae their wanruly fellin paw Mair cause ye hae to fear Your death that day. **1867** G. W. DONALD *Poems* (1879) 56 When..Big bars o' airn, wanruly an' strang, Are broken in flinders.

wanschon, var. WANZE *v. Obs.*

wanscoate, -scot(e, obs. ff. WAINSCOT.

wanse, var. WANZE *v.*, to wane.

† **wanshapen**, *a. Obs.* Also 4 **wanshape.** [f. WAN- + SHAPEN. Cf. (M)Du., (M)LG. *wanschapen*, whence G. *wahnschaffen.*] Misshapen, deformed.

13.. *Celestin* 561 in *Anglia* I. 81 A wanshape best forþ þei broughte, wiþ wenges, forto fleon on lofte. *a* **1585** MONTGOMERIE *Flyting* 268 Wanshapen woubet.

wanshon, var. WANZE *v. Obs.*

wanskot(t, -skoth, obs. forms of WAINSCOT.

† '**wansome**, *a. Obs.* Also 3–4 **wansum.** [f. *wan*, WANE *sb.*[3] + -SOME[1].] Miserable, unhappy.

c **1250** *Gen. & Ex.* 1099 Loth was wansum, and ðugte long vp to ðo dunes ðe weie hard and strong. *a* **1300** *Cursor M.* 24853 Ful wansum war þai þan o rede, for drerili þai dred þe ded. *a* **1400** *Sir Perc.* 1065 His wo es wansome to wreke, His hert es bownne for to breke.

wansonsy, *a. Sc.* [f. WAN- + SONSY *a.* Cf. UNSONSY.] Mischievous.

1819 HOGG *Jacobite Relics* I. 70 We'll learn ye to be douce, Ye auld wansonsy b——h.

† **wanspeed.** *Obs.* [OE. *wanspéd*: see WAN- and SPEED *sb.*] Ill-success; adversity, poverty.

c **893** ÆLFRED *Oros.* III. vii. §6 On þæm ȝefeohte wæs ærest anfunden Sciþþia wanspeda [L. *inopiæ Scythicæ*]. *a* **1050** *Liber Scintill.* (1889) 226 Wer feohtende ateoriȝende þurh wanspede [L. *per inopiam*]. *a* **1300** *Cursor M.* 23708 Yee cristen men, yow vmbilok,..O yur lijf þat yee her lede Yee turn it noght into wan-spede! *Ibid.* 28175 O strif oft haue i sauun þe sede To bring my brother to wan-spede. *c* **1400** *Destr. Troy* 9327 What whylenes, or wanspede, wryxles our mynd?

† **wanspeedy**, *a. Obs.* [OE. *wanspédiȝ*: see prec. and -Y.] Unfortunate, unprosperous.

c **1000** ÆLFRIC *Lev.* xxv. 25 Ȝif þin wanspediȝa mæȝ beo mid þe. *c* **1200** *Trin. Coll. Hom.* 177 Ðanne hauen wanspedie men on heorte wowe.

wansqwatte, rare obs. form of WAINSCOT.

wanst (wɒnst, wanst), dial. (chiefly *Anglo-Ir.*) var. of ONCE *adv.* (*conj.*). Cf. ONCE *adv.* A. δ.

1838 W. CARLETON *Fardorougha* (1839) iv. 81 Repeat the words at wanst. **1889** T. E. BROWN *Manx Witch* 80 Jack.. bore it wanst, and bore it twicet. **1890** [see ONCE *adv.* A. δ]. **1936** M. FRANKLIN *All that Swagger* xvi. 153 The young Delacys were all for the police at the end, but Danny said no. 'Wanst you begin law, it never ends.'

wanston, var. FONT-STONE *Obs.*

1297 R. GLOUC. (Rolls) 5898 Vor þat child fuled in is hond þat water & þe vantston [MS. *a* wanston].

wansum var. WANTSUM *a. Obs.*

want (wɒnt), *sb.*[1] Now *dial.* Forms: 1 **wand, wond;** 4–6 **wonte,** 7 **wounte,** 5– **wont;** 6 **wante,** (**vant**), 6– **want;** 9 *dial.* **waunt, wunt, woont,** (**h**)**unt,** (**h**)**oont,** etc. (see *Eng. Dial. Dict.*). [OE. *wand, wǫnd* = Sw. dial. *vand* (cited by Aasen), Norw. *vand, vaand, vond, vønd*, mole, also shrew (also in comb. *moldvond* 'earth-mole', in contradistinction to *vatsvond* water-rat, and in *vandskjer* shrew, synonymous with *musskjer*, where the first element is *mus* mouse). The word is possibly a shortened form of the synonymous compound OE. *wandeweorpe*, MLG. *wandworp, windeworp, wannewörpe*, mod.LG. *winneworp* (Doornkaat Koolman), in which the second element (f. Teut. **werp-* to throw) corresponds to that of MOULDWARP. The root seems clearly to be the Teut. **wend-*: **wand-* to turn (see WIND, WEND *vbs.*); prob. the word has reference to the winding passages made by the animal.

The word is found in the 8th c. glossaries, but does not again appear till near the end of the 14th c. All the ME. and mod. Eng. forms agree in the unexplained substitution of *t* for the final *d* of the OE. form. The word is unknown to the dialects of the northern and north-east midland counties, but is elsewhere in common use.]

A mole.

c **725** *Corpus Gloss.* (Hessels) T 16 *Talpa*, wond [*Epinal* wand, *Erfurt* uuond, *Leiden* uoond.] **1387** TREVISA *Higden* (Rolls) I. 339 Þere [*sc.* in Ireland] lakkeþ..wontes, and oþere venemous bestes [L. *talpis et cæteris venenosis*]. **14..** *Metr. Voc.* in Wr.-Wülcker 625/9 Wont, *talpa.* **1509** BARCLAY *Shyp of Folys* 206 b, A slouthfull creature is..as a molle, or vant mete and able For to do profyte within a garden grene. **1530** PALSGR. 286/2 Want beest a molle, *taulpe.* **1566** *Act 8 Eliz.* c. 15 §2 For the Heades of everie Moldwarpe or Wante one halfpenny. **1581** J. BELL *Haddon's Answ. Osorius* 113 b, By this Argument you may playnely perceave unlesse you wilbe wilfully blind like a want. **1607** TOPSELL *Four-f. Beasts* 498, I do vtterly dissent from all them that holde opinion that the Mole or Want is of the kinde of Myse. **1610** R. VAUGHAN *Water-Workes* E 2 b, As Wountes or Moles, hunt after wormes. **1660** *Guillim's Displ. Heraldry* III. xvii. (ed. 4) 207 He beareth, Argent, a Cheuron between three Moles or Wants, Sable. **1686** PLOT *Staffordsh.* 196 Part of a stone..that prettily represented a Mole or Want. *a* **1800** PEGGE *Suppl. Grose, Want*, a mole. Herefordshire; where it is pronounced *Wunt.* **1829** J. L. KNAPP *Jrnl. Nat.* 146 The mole, want, mouldwarper, or mould-turner (talpa Europæa) is common with us. **1884** *Blackw. Mag.* Dec. 785/2 Not much bigger than a mouse or small want.

b. *Comb.*, as ***want-catcher, -killer, -taker; want-hill***, a molehill.

1598 T. BASTARD *Chrestoleros* (1880) 21 Walking the fieldes a *wantcatcher I spide. **1905** *Athenæum* 16 Sept. 371/1, I can..remember..sitting..in the chimney corner of the house at Luccombe of..the parish want-catcher. **14..**

Lat.-Eng. Voc. in Wr.-Wülcker 615/10 *Talpefodium*, a *wonthylle. **1585** HIGINS *Junius' Nomencl.* 380/1 *Grumus*,.. an hop hil, mole-hill, or want hill. **1610** R. VAUGHAN *Water-Workes* R 2, Were it not for my brauing-trench and my stankes, I should neuer need the vse of a *Want-killer. **1533** in *Lett. & Papers Henry VIII*, VI. No. 914. 392 [Deposition] of John Shubrocke, of Northover, *wanttaker.

want (wɒnt), *sb.*[2] Also 2–3 **wannt**, 4–5 **wont**, 4–6 **wante**, 6 **wannte**. [a. ON. *vant* neut. of *van-r* adj. lacking, missing (see WANE *a.*), also quasi-sb. in such expressions as *var þeim vettugis vant*, they were in want of nothing; *var vant kýr*, a cow was missing. Mod. NFris. *waant* lack, fault (Sylt), need, lack, necessity, starvation (Amrum), is perhaps derived from the vb. of identical form (see WANT *v.*), and ultimately of Scandinavian origin. In English also, in later usage, the sb. is often a direct derivative from the vb. (q.v.). Cf. also QUART *a.* and *sb.*[1], SCANT *a.* etc.]

†**1.** *predicatively*, or quasi-*adj.* (Something that is) wanting, missing. In Ormin const. with dative. *Obs. rare.*

c **1200** ORMIN 14398 Acc hemm wass wannt gastlic innsihht I þeȝȝre gode lare. *c* **1330** R. BRUNNE *Chron. Wace* (Rolls) 1914 Troye newe ys Trenouant, Two wordes in one, & non ys want. *c* **1400** *Rule St. Benet* xxvii. 22 þe gude herde, þat lefte in þe munte ane wane of a hundrez sep, and yede at seke þis ane þat was want.

2. a. Deficiency, shortage, lack (*of* something desirable or necessary, *esp.* a quality or attribute).

no want (*of*): no lack, abundance (of). ***without want***: without deficiency in any point (*obs.*).

a **1300** *Cursor M.* 10406 þai þat stad er in þair blis, Witvten want has alle þair wis. **13..** *Gaw. & Gr. Knt.* 131 Now wyl I of hor seruise say yow no more, For vch wyȝe may well wit no wont þat þer were. **1530** PALSGR. 286/2 Want of beauty, *laideur*. **1587** MASCALL *Bk. Cattle, Hogs* (1596) 261 The forrests and commons are most conuenient for them to feede on.. where there is want of such trees ye must haue them to other feeding ground. **1611** BIBLE *Judg.* xix. 19 There is both straw and prouender for our asses, and there is bread and wine also for me and for thy handmaid..: there is no want of any thing. **1651** HOBBES *Leviath.* I. viii. 34 'Tis the want of Discretion that makes the difference. **1684** ROSCOMMON *Ess. Transl. Verse* 114 Immodest words admit of no defence, For want of Decency is want of Sense. **1775** FRANKLIN *Let. to M. Dumas* 9 Dec., Their total want of English is at present an obstruction to their getting any employment among us. **1825** SCOTT *Talism.* x, He retained also a general sense of respect for his own reputation, which sometimes supplies the want of the better principles by which reputation is to be maintained. **1844** H. H. WILSON *Brit. India* III. 97 The want of cattle for the conveyance of stores and baggage was one of the most serious obstacles of the march of the army. **1859** H. KINGSLEY *G. Hamlyn* xxxiv, A miserable faction..have assumed the reins of government, and, in spite of three votes of want of confidence, persist in retaining the seals of office. **1870** *Pall Mall Gaz.* 23 Sept. 10/1 Owing to the confusion incident to this arrangement, or want of arrangement, the duties proper to each institution are inefficiently discharged. **1884** *Law Times Rep.* LXXIII. 616/2 note, The deceased was also guilty of negligence or of want of reasonable care contributing to the accident.

†**b.** *pl.* Instances of shortage. *Obs.*

1660 in J. Simon *Ess. Irish Coins* (1749) 127 And so proportionable for greater or less wants of weight in the said pieces [coins]. *a* **1700** EVELYN *Diary* 23 June 1689, An extraordinary drowth, to the threatening of great wants as to the fruits of the earth. **1751** LABELYE *Westm. Bridge* 75 Difficulties occasioned by.. frequent Wants of Stone, which was kept from us by long easterly Winds.

c. ***for*** (occas. ***by, from, in, through***) ***want of***: for lack of; because of the absence or deficiency of.

c **1400** *Destr. Troy* 12085 Antenor.. denyet hym onon, þat noqwere he knew þat commly be keppet, ne in cloese haldyn. þen wrathid þo worthi [Agamemnon] for wont of þe burde. **1556** *Rec. Inverness* (New Spalding Club) I. 2 That day.. assingit to James Paterson.. to preif quhat skayth he had sustenit in want of his boyt quhilkis Necoll Kar intromettit with. **1573–80** TUSSER *Husb.* (1878) 31 For want of seede, land yeeldeth weede. **1591** SHAKS. *Two Gent.* II. i. 172 For often haue you writ to her: and she in modesty, Or else for want of idle time, could not againe reply. **1608** *Pennyless Parl. Threadbare Poets* in *Harl. Misc.* (1744) I. 180 Many, for Want of Wit, shall sell their Freehold for Tobacco-pipes and red Petticoats. *a* **1633** G. HERBERT *Outlandish Prov.* (1640) 499 For want of a naile the shoe is lost, for want of a shoe the horse is lost, for want of a horse the rider is lost. **1697** DRYDEN *Virg. Georg.* III. 796 'Twas then that Buffalo's, ill pair'd, were seen To draw the Carr of Jove's Imperial Queen For want of Oxen. **1742** KAMES *Decis. Crt. Sess. 1730–52* (1799) 55 When a man is pinched for want of money, he will submit to any conditions, however hard, to come at it. **1808** E. S. BARRETT *Miss-led General* 136 They could not pursue them for want of cavalry. **1848** DICKENS *Dombey* xlv, I have deferred doing so, for want of opportunity. **1872** BRYANT *Pract. Surg.* (1884) I. 778 Umbilical Hernia.. is common in children from want of closure of the umbilicus. **1889** 'J. S. WINTER' *Mrs. Bob* x. (1891) 125 He..had no notion of losing anything for the want of asking for it. **1891** *Law Times* XCII. 125/1 An agreement in writing which they cannot produce in the County Court for want of a stamp.

†**d.** ***in*** (rarely ***in the***) ***want of***: failing; in the absence of (something needed or desired). *Obs.*

1655 CULPEPPER etc. *Riverius* x. vi. 298 In want of Milk, you may give Almond Milk, or Barley Cream, or Rice Milk. **1729** BUTLER *Serm.* Wks. 1874 II. 186 There is just the same reason for quiet resignation in the want of every thing equally unattainable.

3. a. The state of lacking the necessaries of life; penury; destitution. Also, the condition of lacking food; famine; starvation. ***to come to want***: to be reduced to penury.

1340–70 *Alex. & Dind.* 857 For-þi bi-houus ȝou, haþel, harde to libbe & wo drie in þis word for wante & for nede! *Ibid.* 867 Swich hungur as ȝe han by-houus ȝou þolie, &, be ȝou lef oþur loþ libben in wante. **1597** *Extracts Munic. Acc. Newcastle* (1848) 44 Paide for the charges of buringe 9 poore folkes who died for wante in the streetes, for their graves making, 3*s.* **1610** SHAKS. *Temp.* IV. i. 116 Scarcity and want shall shun you, Ceres' blessing so is on you. **1633** P. FLETCHER *Purple Isl.* VII. xix, And with him [Porneius] Wastefulnesse, that all expended, And Want, that still in theft and prison ended. **1653** RAMESEY *Astrol. Restored* 241 The People generally shall be driven to want. *a* **1718** PRIOR *Knowledge* 622 Whilst We struggle in this Vale beneath, With Want and Sorrow. **1766** GOLDSM. *Hermit* 13 Here to the houseless child of want My door is open still. **1782** MISS BURNEY *Cecilia* IV. x, Who could have thought of his living so among the great folks, and then coming to want! **1840** DICKENS *Old C. Shop* lxxiii, Through the same kind agency, his mother was secured from want, and made quite happy. **1866** MACDONALD *Ann. Q. Neighb.* ix. (1878) 162 Many was the time that want had come in at her door. **1888** BRYCE *Amer. Commw.* cxii. III. 607 In Europe.. he will perceive that by far the greater number lead very laborious lives, and are.. liable to fall into want. **1900** R. S. BARBOUR *Thoughts* (1909) 46 Want is a mighty leveller.

Prov. **1736** BAILEY (fol.) s.v. *Waste*, Wilful Waste makes woful Want.

†**b.** *pl.* Straits; circumstances (or times) of want, hardship, suffering, etc. *Obs.*

1588 PENRY (*title*) A viewe of some part of such publike wants and disorders as are in the seruice of God, within.. Wales. **1614** RALEGH *Hist. World* III. x. §13. 124 Hitherto the danger of enemies and miseries of weather and wants, had kept the companie in firme unitie. **1653** HOLCROFT *Procopius, Vandal Wars* II. 47 In the mean time Jabdas leaving a sufficient guard for the Castle was gone up to the top of Aurasium, fearing to be blockt up in the Castle, and reduced to wants. **1697** DRYDEN *Æneis* VII. 1009 Rough Saticulans, inur'd to Wants. **1731** in *Buccleuch MSS.* (Hist. MSS. Comm.) I. 380 Ere long I shall be reduced to great wants.

†**4.** The fact that a person (*rarely* a thing) is not present; absence. *Obs.*

c **1480** HENRYSON *Want of Wyse Men* 8 Now sele is sorow, this is a wofull werde, Sen want of wyse men makis fulis to sit on binkis. **1581** A. HALL *Iliad* I. 4 Sith I needes muste yeelde hir vp,.. (Ah) take hir then.. hir want I rather craue, Than that this people here, should not their health and safety haue. **1590** SPENSER *F.Q.* I. viii. 11 As when.. An heard of Bulles.. Do for the milkie mothers want complaine. **1591** *2nd Pt. Troub. Raigne K. John* (1611) 73 The King entreats your soonest speed To visit him, who on your present want, Did ban and curse his birth, himselfe and me. **1610** B. JONSON *Sp. Pr. Henry's Barriers* 114 For being deprest a while, Want makes vs know the price of what we auile. **1611** TOURNEUR *Ath. Trag.* V. ii, The price of things is best known in their want. *a* **1625** FLETCHER *Women Pleas'd* III. iii. (1647) 34/2 *Lord*... No roome in all the Court but we search'd through it Her women found her want first and they cry'd to us. **1633** SHIRLEY *Witty Fair One* I. i, I leaue her to your trust, And in my absence doubt not you will be Both Vncle and Father. *Wor.* Willingly... I know she is your study, in your want I will put on your jealousie. **1831** JAMES *Phil. Augustus* ii, The want of his gauntlets and brassards showed his arms covered with a quilted jacket of crimson silk.

5. a. A condition marked by the lack of some necessary thing, or requiring some extraneous aid or addition; need; also, an instance of this, and so freq. *pl.* (passing into the quasi-*concr.* sense 'requirement', 5 b). Phrase, ***a*** (***long-***)***felt want*** (also in sense 5 b). ***to supply*** (***anticipate, consult, provide for,*** etc.) ***one's wants***: to satisfy (provide for, etc.) one's needs.

1578 H. WOTTON *Courtlie Controv.* 251 The Grecian Prince.. caried a bagge full of winde to supply his want at all times. **1596** SHAKS. *Merch. V.* I. iii. 141, I would.. Supplie your present wants. **1611** BIBLE *Judg.* xix. 20 Let all thy wants lie vpon me; only lodge not in the street. **1617** MORYSON *Itin.* I. 62 The Citizens lay up corne brought out of Poland, and according to the wants of Europe, carry it into many kingdomes. **1648** GAGE *West Ind.* 127 The Fryers.. upon a sudden want or occasion take out from thence as much fish as will give the whole Cloister a dinner. **1790** BURKE *Fr. Rev.* 88 Government is a contrivance of human wisdom to provide for human wants. Men have a right that these wants should be provided for by this wisdom. Among these wants is to be reckoned the want, out of civil society, of a sufficient restraint upon their passions. **1819** SHELLEY *Cenci* II. ii. 12 The eldest son of a rich nobleman.. has wide wants, and narrow powers. **1840** DICKENS *Old C. Shop* xi, Day after day, and night after night, found her still by the pillow of the unconscious sufferer, still anticipating his every want. **1876** MOZLEY *Univ. Serm.* xv. 258 As soon as one great want is satisfied another arises, and then another.

b. quasi-*concr.* Something needed or required; a requirement, desideratum. Freq. *pl.* Also, something that one wishes to have (as opposed to what one needs or requires).

1579 in *10th Rep. Hist. MSS. Comm.* App. v. 430 That no.. tymber be ladden or transported oute of this towne.. salfe onely fuell of wood for fyre and the presente wannte of repayringe of the shippis. **1589** HAKLUYT *Voy.* Ep. Ded. ⁋1 He pointed with his wand to all the knowen.. Empires, Kingdomes, Dukedomes, and Territories of ech part, with declaration also of their speciall commmodities, & particular wants. *c* **1645** HOWELL *Lett.* (1650) I. 169 For the soil of Spain, the fruitfulness of their vallies recompences the sterility of their hills; corn is their greatest want. **1785** PALEY *Mor. Philos.* VI. xi. (1786) 593 Habitual superfluities become real wants. **1850** CARLYLE *Latter-day Pamph.* i. (1872) 37 Your want of wants, I say, is that you be commanded in this world. **1861** FLOR. NIGHTINGALE *Nursing* 5 The remedies are just as well known; and among them is certainly not the establishment of a Child's Hospital. This may be a want. **1872** *Bookseller* 2 Apr. 341 Advt., Wants and Vacancies. A Medium for the Selection of Servants and Situations. Price One Penny [bi-monthly]. **1875** J. H. BENNET *Winter Medit.* (ed. 5) 408 Vividness in colour probably becomes an actual want to southerners. **1881** JOWETT *Thucyd.* I. 177 You will gain the alliance of a great naval power, and a navy is your chief want. **1946** G. M. TREVELYAN *English Social History* (ed. 2) xii. 388 Tea, porcelain and woven cotton goods were now being imported.. in such quantities that they came within reach of the mass of the population. They created new wants and.. demand was so great that home-manufacturers took to making cotton goods and china ware. **1950** *Sport* 24–30 Mar. 19/4 (Advt.), Clubs.. can use our national net-work of experts to provide grounds, fixtures, insurance, fund-raisers and all club wants. **1955** W. J. BATE *Achievement of Samuel Johnson* (1978) ii. 70 General wishes have to localize themselves into definite wants. **1977** *Chicago Tribune* 2 Oct. XII. 1/4 The first-floor laundry room is definitely more a 'need' than a 'want' item nowadays. **1983** J. BARZUN *Stroll with W. James* 280 He did not fall into the trap of supposing that a child's needs are the same as his wants.

c. ***in want of***: in need of; not having, or having in insufficient measure. ***in no want of***: having abundantly.

1694 STANHOPE *Epictetus* etc. i. 28 Inanimate Creatures.. are oftentimes in great want of some Quality or other; Heat, or Cold, or Drought, or Moisture. **1710** STEELE *Tatler* No. 5 ⁋5 Their Troops were in Want of all Manner of Necessaries. **1769** BLACKSTONE *Comm.* IV. ii. 31 A man in extreme want of food or clothing. **1837** W. IRVING *Capt. Bonneville* II. 269 You are more in want of horses than I am: keep him. **1853** DICKENS *Bleak Ho.* xii, She is in no want of words to shower upon Rosa.

d. Proverbial phrase, ***then want must be your master***, etc., used in refusing a demand expressed by 'I want ——'.

1731–8 SWIFT *Pol. Conversat.* i. 59, I want that Diamond-Ring of yours. Why, then, Want's like to be your Master. **1828** [J. P. COLLIER] *Punch & Judy* 80 *Punch.* Come up stairs: I want you. *Judy.* Then want must be your master. I'm busy.

e. ? A sense of need. *rare.*

1820 SHELLEY *Sensit. Pl.* I. 11 Like a doe in the noontide with love's sweet want. **1894** 'G. EGERTON' *Discords* 179 The band.. strike up.. a weird witching thing with a want in it.

6. †**a.** A defect, failing, fault; a shortcoming; *rarely* a natural blemish. *Obs.*, and apparently almost confined to the 17th c.

1592 BABINGTON *Notes Genesis* ix. 38 Greater men then wee haue had theyr wants. **1599** T. M[OUFET] *Silkwormes* 18 So perfit loue in mortals is not found Some little warts or wants in all we spie. **1603** BRETON *Post Packet Mad Lett.* (Grosart) 14/1 Touching my husband, though his wants were grieuous, yet to want him is my greatest sorrow. **1611** BEAUM. & FL. *King & No K.* I. (1619) 6 Were shee So perfect, that no one of her owne sex Could finde a want. **1635** *Maldon* (Essex) *Borough Deeds* Bundle 80 No. 2 b, For repairinge and amendinge of the wants and present decayes of the bridges. **1677** SEDLEY *Ant. & Cl.* Wks. 1722 I. 122 A Sceptre may for pers'nal wants attone. **1728** YOUNG *Love Fame* ii. (1757) 95 Wants of all kinds are made to fame a plea; One learns to lisp; another, not to see.

b. Sc. ***to have a want***, to be mentally deficient.

1825 JAMIESON, Suppl. s.v., *To Hae a want*, to be under mental imbecility. **1826** GALT *Last of Lairds* vii. 62 The whutch maid her jeer me as if I had a want, and been daft likewyse. **1879** 'S. TYTLER' in *Good Wds.* 349 He has a 'want', you know, and is not fit for much.

7. A gap, hole, hollow. *Obs.* exc. *dial. rare.*

1663 BAXTER *Div. Life* I. x. (1664) 82 The wants in the wheels of your watch are as useful to the motion as the nucks or solid parts. **1725** *Bradley's Family Dict.* s.v. *Saddle*, The Saddle should be placed exactly on the middle of the Back, the Fore-bow just at the Want of the Shoulders. **1828** CARR *Craven Gloss.*, *Want*, a deficiency or hollow place in a piece of timber, or the edge of a board.

8. *Coal-mining.* = NIP *sb.*[1]

1867 W. W. SMYTH *Coal & Coal-mining* 26 [See NIP *sb.*[1]].

9. *Comb.* as ***want-begotten, -creating*** ppl. adjs.; ***want column*** (sense 5; cf. also ellipt. use of *wanted* pa. pple. in advertisements); see WANT *v.* 4; similarly ***want ad***(***vertisement***).

1897 *Chicago Record* 1 Mar. 10/4 Record '*want ads' bring results. **1919** MENCKEN *Amer. Lang.* 160 *Ad-writer*, *want-ad*,.. and *ad-man*, are already accepted in technical terminology. **1940** R. CHANDLER *Farewell, my Lovely* vii. 43 The Montgomery killing hadn't even made the want-ad section. **1977** C. MCFADDEN *Serial* (1978) xlv. 96/1 The want ads.. no longer solicited secondhand Hide A Beds. **1887** *Courier-Jrnl.* (Louisville, Kentucky) 12 Jan. 5/3 The *World* is treating Mr. Conkling as it treats its circulation and its '*want' advertisements upon occasion. **1919** F. HURST *Humoresque* 116 She took to.. scanning want-advertisements as she stood at the news-stand. **1850** TENNYSON *In Mem.* xxvii. 12, I envy not in any moods.. The heart that never plighted troth But stagnates in the weeds of sloth; Nor any *want-begotten rest. **1884** E. W. NYE *Baled Hay* 239 The *want column of the Chicago *News*.. has the following: 'Twelve "frightful examples" wanted.' **1901** W. R. H. TROWBRIDGE *Lett. her Mother to Eliz.* iv. 14 Lady Beatrice found her [her cook] in the Want column of the *Standard*. **1897** MARY KINGSLEY *W. Africa* 651 The manifold, *want-creating culture of modern European civilisation and education.

want (wɒnt), *v.* Also 2–3 (*Ormin*) **wannte**, 3 **wonti(e**, 3–5 **wont(e**, 3–7 **wante**, 4–5 **wantt(e**, *Sc.* 4–6 **vant**, 5 **whante**, 6 **waunt**. [prob. a. ON. *vanta* wk. vb. impers. = MSwed. *vanta*, also *vantas* refl., Swed. dial. *vanta* to be wanting, Norw. (Aasen) *vanta* to be lacking, absent, also trans. to lack, Da. (Jutland dial.) *vante* trans. to lack. From Scandinavian also is prob. mod. NFris.

waant to need, fail, lack, do without (*pers.* and *impers.*). ON. *vanta* perh. represents an earlier **wanatōn* with a derivative *-t* suffix not connected with the neut. adj. ending seen in the sb.]

1. a. *intr.* To be lacking or missing; not to exist; not to be forthcoming; to be deficient in quantity or degree. In early use const. with dative or *to*. *rare* since the 17th c., and now *arch.* (*to be wanting* is current; see WANTING *ppl. a.*)

a **1225** *Ancr. R.* 194 Hwonne ou ne wonteð nowiht, þeonne ueineð he mid ou. *Ibid.* 406 Ne þunche hire neuer wunder þauh hire wontie þe Holi Gostes froure. *c* **1250** *Gen. & Ex.* 2155 Ðan coren wantede in oðer lond, Ðo ynug [was] vnder his hond. *a* **1300** *Cursor M.* 3053 Þam wanted brede, þeir water es gan, Hope of lijf ne had þai nan. **13..** *Northern Passion* 156/440* So it bifell þe folk had care ffor þat þam wanted water þare. **1340** HAMPOLE *Pr. Consc.* 593 Bot proud man of þis tas na hede For hym wantes skille, þat hym suld lede. **1375** BARBOUR *Bruce* v. 422 And it is to perelouss thing In castell till assegit be, Quhar that ane vantis of this thre, Vittale, or men with thair armyng. *c* **1460** SIR R. ROS *La Belle Dame* 449 To give the good where it wanteth, trewly, That were resoun and a curteys maner. **1484** CAXTON *Fables of Æsop* II. ix, They whiche ben on lyue haue some whiche drede them but theyr drede wantith and faylleth whan they ben dede. **1488** *Acc. Ld. High Treas. Scot.* I. 89 To a sclatar for the poyntin of al the place of Stirling, and for sclaytis that wantit and lyme, xij li. **1526** *Pilgr. Perf.* (W. de W. 1531) 81 Where obedyence wanteth (sayth saynt Austyn) there is no goodnes. **1546** J. HEYWOOD *Prov. & Epigr.* (1867) 42 Diners can not be long, where deinties want. **1579** SPENSER *Sheph. Cal.* June 3 Tell me, what wants me here, to worke delyte? *a* **1592** GREENE *Jas. IV*, IV. iv, O wearie life, where wanteth no distresse. **1598** GRENEWEY *Tacitus, Ann.* IV. ii. (1622) 90 The armies were to be supplied with a new muster. For voluntarie men now wanted: or if there were any; they were not of so vertuous and modest a cariage. **1630** EARL MANCH. in *Buccleuch MSS.* (Hist. MSS. Comm.) I. 273 If your help be in this business, as I know it shall not want, it is no matter though your hand wanted to the certificate. *a* **1648** LD. HERBERT *Hen. VIII* (1683) 17 Besides, that in France there neuer wanted discontented Persons, who would joyn with his Forces. **1827** HALLAM *Const. Hist.* I. viii. 465 There wanted not reasons in the cabinet of Charles for placing the navy at this time on a respectable footing. **1830** GEN. P. THOMPSON *Exerc.* (1842) I. 245 There wants a collection of dying speeches of nefarious governments.

†**b.** To fall short *of* a certain amount. *Obs.*

1472-3 *Rolls of Parlt.* VI. 56/2 All such sommes of money, as shall want or lak of the forseid sommes.

†**c.** To be lacking to complete a certain total or achieve a result. Const. *of* or negative clause. Also impers., in absolute uses of 2d: ***hem wantiþ***, they are not fully qualified; ***there wants***, something is lacking (const. *to* with inf.); ***it wants of six*** (o'clock), it is not quite six. *Obs.*

a **1300** *Cursor M.* 14667 Littel wantid þat þam [? *read* þai ne *with Gött.*] war wode. **13..** *Gaw. & Gr. Knt.* 1062 & of þat ilk nwȝere bot neked now wantez. **13..** *E.E. Allit. P.* B. 739 'And fyne wont of fyfty,' quod god, 'I schal forȝete alle & wyth-halde my honde for hortyng on lede. *c* **1380** WYCLIF *Sel. Wks.* III. 434 Þei feynen falsliche þat þei ben vikeris of Crist; for likliche hem wantiþ to be þe leeste membre þat Crist haþ ordeyned to be of his Chirche. **1618** J. WILKINSON *Treat., Of a Court Leet* 79 b, The steward may impanell any stranger, if there want to make xii. of yᵉ Iury. **1639** DU VERGER tr. *Camus' Admir. Events* 164 He..abusing him with injurious words, & threats, (& as he was surly & apt to strike) little wanted of blows. **1697** DRYDEN *Æneis* XII. 937 Then, shall I see Laurentum in a flame, Which only wanted to compleat my shame. **1709** MRS. MANLEY *Secret Mem.* (1720) IV. 136 The Prince was true to his Letter. It wanted of Six, when in my Man's Apparel I got to the Grotto, but found Endymion in possession of it. **1768** WILKES *Hist. Eng.* I. Introd. 13 The fire had been long laid, and there only wanted such a spark to force a blaze.

†**d.** To fail (const. with dative or *to*); to give out; to be insufficient *for* (a purpose, etc.). *Obs.*

c **1400** *Rom. Rose* 2530 But word and wit, with chere ful pale, Shul wante for to telle thy tale. *a* **1400-50** *Wars Alex.* 5480 Or els þai tillid þaim to þe trees as þe buke tellis, And gert þaim laike with þaim so lange till þaim þe life wantis. **1553** EDEN *Treat. Newe Ind.* Ded. (Arb.) 6 One whose good will hath not wanted to gratifie your grace with a better thing if mine abilitie were greater. **1598** HAKLUYT *Voy.* I. 58 But they of the citie fought manfully against them, with engines, dartes, and arrowes, and when stones wanted they threw siluer, and especially melted siluer.

†**e.** To fail *to do* something; to be wanting (*in* one's endeavours). *Obs.*

In quot. 1576 perh. 'to lack the wherewithal', to be too poor.

1426 LYDG. *De Guil. Pilgr.* 16733 For thow, lady, ffayllest neuere, nor thow wantest nat to do socour and helpe to alle that deuoutly besechyn and prayen vn-to the. **1576** *Common Conditions* 216 (Brooke) Like beggers wee liue and want to pay rent. **1643** BURROUGHES *Exp. 1st 3 ch. Hosea* xviii. 455 So far as you want in your endeavours after this, so far there is an evil.

†**f.** To be a defaulter; to be absent, missing. *Obs.*

1435 MISYN *Fire of Love* II. iv. 76 Saluum me fac deus, quoniam defecit sanctus, þat is to say: 'lorde, make me sayffe, for þe sayntis wantys.' *c* **1440** *Alphabet of Tales* 169 In þe kurk of Palernens was þer a certan dean þat sent a servand of his to seke a palfray of his þat hym wantid. *c* **1475** *Rauf Coilȝear* 290 Ane man that office suld beir be tyme at this tyde, He will be found in his fault, that wantis foroutin weir. *c* **1480** HENRYSON *Wolf & Wether* 45 In all thingis he [the wether] counterfait the Dog; For all the nicht he stude and tuke na sleip, Swa that weill lang thair wantit not ane Hog. **1600** E. BLOUNT tr. *Conestaggio* 153 For there wanted aboue sixe thousand souldiers of them which had been leuied.

2. a. *trans.* Not to have; to be without, to lack; to have too little of; to be destitute of, or deficient in; to fail to have, or get. Now *rare*, exc. with object a desirable quality or attribute; in *Palæography* and *Bibliography*, to lack (a leaf or a page).

c **1200** ORMIN 13380 All þatt wanntedd Cristess hald All sinnkeþþ inntill helle. *a* **1352** MINOT *Poems* vii. 103 Sir Philip wanted all his will, þat was wele on his sembland sene. *c* **1375** *Sc. Leg. Saints* xxxiv. (*Pelagia*) 23 Wantande nathing of bewte, þat in a woman suld fundyn be. *c* **1460** *Towneley Myst.* xiii. 421 Full wofull is the householde That wantys a woman. *c* **1470** HENRY *Wallace* VI. 340 Thre thousand haill off likly men in wer, And feill on fute quhilk wantyt hors and ger. *c* **1480** HENRYSON *Cock & Fox* 2 Thocht brutall beistis be Irrationall, That is to say, wantand discretioun. *a* **1533** FRITH *Disput. Purgat.* Wks. (1573) 22 We haue all sinned and want the glory whiche before God is allowed. **1560** *Peebles Burgh Rec.* (1872) 262 Tua beddis wantand the sydis nixt the wall. **1577** in W. H. Turner *Select. Rec. Oxford* (1880) 395 Everye one that shall wante his gowne shall lose his place. **1625** BURGES *Pers. Tithes* 67 It is a thousand pitties they should want blowes who will doe nothing without them. **1684** tr. *Bonet's Merc. Compit.* I. 16 If you want Peaches, you may use Juice of soure Apples. **1700** DRYDEN *Monum. Fair Maiden Lady* 2 Below this Marble Monument is laid All that Heav'n wants of this Celestial Maid. **1710** HEARNE *Collect.* (O.H.S.) III. 80 He has sent 3 Lectures to be printed at Oxford (they wanting Arabick Types at Cambridge). **1728** T. SHERIDAN tr. *Persius* iii. (1739) 48 It is very natural that Sciences should be ridiculed by those who want them. ? **1793** BURNS *Selkirk Grace* 2 Some hae meat, and canna eat, And some wad eat that want it. **1836** [J. GRANT] *Random Recoll. Ho. Lords* xvi. 402 His matter wants vigour and depth, and his manner is deficient in energy. **1849** MACAULAY *Hist. Eng.* iii. I. 302 Mulgrave, though he wanted experience, wanted neither parts nor courage. **1852** R. A. WILLMOTT *Pleas. Lit.* (ed. 2) vi. 37 The Library of Petrarch wanted the *Divine Comedy*, until Boccaccio sent it decorated with gold. **1876** L. STEPHEN *Eng. Th. 18th C.* I. 170 A purely optimistic creed always wants any real stamina. **1895** M. R. JAMES *Catal. MSS. Sidney Sussex Coll.* 114 Vellum... Cent. xiv, xv... *Collation*: a⁸ (wants 1, 2) b⁸-ff⁸. **1976** *Anglo-Saxon England* V. 150, i⁸ wants 1.

†**b.** To be free from (something undesirable).

1631 MAY tr. *Barclay's Mirr. Mindes* I. 206 The English which want somewhat of the pompous shew of the French humanity, doe want much more of their barbourous cruelty. **1787** [BEATTIE] *Scoticisms* 105 We wanted the plague in Scotland, when they had it in England. *a* **1791** GROSE *Olio* (1792) 110 [Scotsman *loq.*] I am much better indeed; I have wanted the gout these three months.

†**c.** To spare (labour). *Obs.* (? *nonce-use.*)

1573-80 TUSSER *Husb.* (1878) 10. I haue no labour wanted to prune this tree thus planted, whose fruite to none is scanted, in house or yet in feeld.

d. To come short by (so much) of completing a certain total or attaining a certain result. Now chiefly *impers.* in telling the time of day: ***it wants*** (so many minutes) ***of*** (now more commonly *to*) such an hour. †Formerly often ***to want little, nothing***, etc. used personally and impers., const. *of* with vbl. sb., *to* with *inf.*, or negative clause, to indicate a close approach to the attainment of a certain result.

In referring to the time of day this form of expression is now becoming less usual: the ordinary phrase is *it is* (so many minutes) *to* (such an hour).

c **1420** *Anturs of Arth.* 584 (Douce MS.) He wanted noȝte to be slayne þe brede of ane hare. **1530** PALSGR. 771/1 It wanted but a lytell that I was nat taken. **1617** MORYSON *Itin.* I. 217 We had now some two miles to Ierusalem, yet in the very Hauen, we wanted little of perishing. **1638** tr. *Bacon's Hist. Life & Death* 135 Eight Men, whose Age computed together, made up eight hundred yeares; In so much, that what some of them wanted of an hundred, others exceeded as much. **1653** *Clarke Papers* (Camden) III. 6 Lettres came from the Generalls that they wanted a dayes sayle from the Dutch fleete, but were in great hopes to overtake them. **1665** HOOKE *Microgr.* 201 If it chanced to want anything of being perfectly opposite. **1699** BENTLEY *Phalaris* Addenda 541 They wanted two years of Man's Age. **1727** SWIFT *Let. to Sheridan* 29 Aug., I now want only three months of sixty. **1748** *Anson's Voy.* I. i. 7 His squadron wanted three hundred seamen of their complement. **1749** FIELDING *Tom Jones* XI. v, Of my fortune not one farthing could be touched till I was of age, of which I wanted now more than two years. **1784** HENLEY *Note on Beckford's Vathek* (1868) 126 It wanted little but that the genii had pressed on him in crowds. **1830** JAMES *Step-mother* lxxix. III. 326 You vagabond, you said it was ten o'clock, and it wants twenty minutes. **1834** *Tracts for Times* No. 22. 5 It still wanted a considerable time to school. **1848** DICKENS *Dombey* lv, 'How goes the time? My watch is unwound.' 'Wants a few minutes of five o'clock, sir.' **1865** TROLLOPE *Belton Est.* vi. 59 It only wants five minutes to dinner. **1891** W. C. RUSSELL *Marriage at Sea* xi, It wanted but twenty minutes to eight. **1905** R. BAGOT *Passport* iii. 25 Although it wanted yet twenty minutes to midnight the church was nearly full.

†**e.** To be deprived of, to lose. *Obs.*

c **1480** HENRYSON *Wolf & Wether* 35, I [*sc.* the wether] sall not spair To follow him [*sc.* the wolf] als fast as did ȝour Doig, Swa that, I warrand, ȝe sall not want ane hoig. **1500-20** DUNBAR *Poems* xxxiii. 42 He cowth gif cure for laxatyve, To gar a wicht horss want his lyve. **1535** COVERDALE *Isa.* xxxviii. 10, I thought I shulde haue gone to the gates of hell in my best age, and haue wanted the residue of my yeares. **1536** BELLENDEN *Cron. Scot.* (1821) II. 89 He maid mony lawis for the liberte of haly kirke; He that dang ane preist suld want his hand. **1596** DALRYMPLE tr. *Leslie's Hist. Scot.* I. 121 Lat him want his sword, and thair eftir avoyd his cumpanie. **1695** A. TELFAIR *New Confut. Sadd.* (1696) 4 The Pot-hooks and Hanger were carried out of the Chimney, and being wanted four days, they found them at last in a Cockloft. **1724** *Ramsay's Tea-t. Misc.* (1733) I. 14, I neither wanted ew nor lamb While his flock near me lay.

†**f.** To feel the loss of, to miss. *Obs.*

1623 WEBSTER *Duchess Malfi* III. ii, You shall want him, For know an honest states-man to a Prince, Is like a Cedar, planted by a Spring. **1626** B. JONSON *Staple of N.* I. vi, I must needes say, I lost an Officer of him, a good Bayliffe, And I shall want him; but all peace be with him. **1749** CHESTERF. *Let. to Son* 14 Nov., You should be *alerte, adroit, vif*; be wanted, talked of, impatiently expected, and unwillingly parted with in company.

†**g.** To fail to recollect. *Obs. rare.*

c **1381** CHAUCER *Parl. Foules* 287 And manye a mayde of whiche the name I wante. *a* **1500** *Flower & Leaf* 150 Diamondes fyne and rubies rede, And many another stoon, of which I want The names now.

¶**h.** (Confused use.) ***who cannot want the thought?*** who can help thinking?

1605 SHAKS. *Macb.* III. vi. 8 Who cannot want the thought, how monstrous It was for Malcolme, and for Donalbane To kill their gracious Father?

i. ***wanting*** (pres. pple.), not having, deprived of, without; (in definitions of a smaller quantity by its difference from a larger) lacking, less, minus. *Obs.* exc. *Sc.*

1536 in [Ledwich] *Antiq. Sarisb.* (1771) 192 A cross, with Abraham offering up Isaac, and a lamb behind him, with an Angel wanting one wing. **1570** BILLINGSLEY *Euclid* I. def. ii. 2 A lyne is..length wantyng breadth and thicknes. **1593** SHAKS. *Rich. II*, II. iii. 10 What a wearie way From Rauenspurgh to Cottshold will be found, In Rosse and Willoughby, wanting your companie. **1629** HOBBES *Thucydides* II. 89, 10000 Talents wanting 300. *a* **1700** EVELYN *Diary* 27 Feb. 1645, Three chips of the real Crosse; one of the nailes, wanting a point. **1726** SWIFT *Gulliver* II. i, I measured the Tail of the dead Rat, and found it to be two Yards long wanting an Inch. **1777** ABIGAIL ADAMS in *Fam. Let.* (1876) 268 'Tis four months wanting three days since we parted. **1809** BAWDWEN *Domesday Bk. York* etc. 246 In Scireburne (Sherborn) with the Berewicks, the archbishop has 100 carucates of land, wanting four. **1886** STEVENSON *Kidnapped* xviii, I would not go wanting sword and gun, and with a long fishing-rod. *Ibid.* xx, I have come wanting a water-bottle.

j. To go or do without. Usually in negative expressions, *esp.* with *cannot*, etc. *Obs.* exc. *dial.*

1562 BULLEYN *Bulwark, Bk. Simples* (1579) 27 The fysher and Fouler must haue hempe to make their nettes. And no Archer can want his Bowstring. *a* **1572** KNOX *Hist. Ref.* Wks. 1846 I. 287, I can nott weall want him, or some preachar. I can nott put away sic ane man. **1592** KYD *Sol. & Pers.* v. i. 37 And sweete Perseda, I will stay with you, From Brusor my beloued; and Ile want him Till he bring backe Erastus vnto you. **1606** CHAPMAN *Mons. d'Olive* II. i, Tabacco, that excellent plant, the vse whereof (as of fift Element) the world cannot want. **1637** RUTHERFORD *Let. to Ld. Craighall* 10 Aug., Ye have a fair occasion to gratifie Christ now, if ye will..want the night's sleep with your suffering Saviour one hour. **1644** MILTON *Areop.* (Arb.) 48 Such books are..usefull drugs.., wherewith to temper and compose effective and strong med'cins, which mans life cannot want. **1667** —— *P.L.* v. 365 By descending from the Thrones above, Those happie places thou hast deignd a while To want, and honour these. **1705** STANHOPE *Paraphr.* III. 568 Servants, in those Countries where long and loose Garments are worn, could not, without great inconvenience, want a part of Cloathing so necessary for Expedition. **1772** COWPER *Let. to J. Hill* 27 June, I had rather want many things, any thing, indeed, that this world could afford me, than abuse the affection of a friend. **1814** JANE AUSTEN *Mansf. Park* I. vi. 119 To want a horse and cart in the country seemed impossible. **1818** SCOTT *Br. Lamm.* xxix, A worthless old play-fellow of mine, whose company I would rather want than have. **1880** *Antrim & Down Gloss.* s.v., We can't want the pony the day.

†**k.** ***to want*** (gerundial inf.): to seek, not forthcoming. *Obs. rare*⁻¹.

1563 *Homilies* II, *Rogation Wk.* III. 243 b, Remember I say once againe your duetie of thankes, let them be neuer to want.

3. *intr.* (partly *absol.* of sense 2). †**a.** *simply.* To be in want of something implied by the context, or of the necessaries of life. *Obs.*

13.. *Lay-Folks Mass-Bk.* App. IV. 311 He wrot so faste til þat he want, For his parchemyn skin was so scant. **1579** HAKE *Newes out of Powles* (1872) E v b, Though their bellies want: Their backs must brauely clothed be. **1618** J. TAYLOR (Water P.) *Penniless Pilgr.* F 4 b, Master James Acmootye comming for England, said, that if I would ride with him, that neither I nor my horse should want betwixt that place and London. **1620** *Westward for Smelts* (Percy Soc.) 31 He [*sc.* the King] being moved to see one so well featur'd (as she was) to want, entertained her for one of his pages. *a* **1626** BACON *Use of Law* (1630) 84 *marg.*, If the Executors doe want they may sell any Legacie to pay Debts. **1679** [T. KIRKE] *Mod. Acc. Scot.* 13 In the Highlands,..if one Man has two Cows, and another wants, he shall soon supply himself from his Neighbour. **1684** *Contempl. St. Man* II. iii. (1699) 147 It was a Position of the Stoicks, that he was not Poor who wanted, but he who was necessitated.

†**b.** ***to want of***: to lack, not to have, or to have in insufficient measure: = the trans. sense 2.

a **1400-50** *Wars Alex.* 4586 Þe same wyse does a wolfe þat wantis of his pray. *c* **1500** *Melusine* 147 He demanded of them what they ayled, and yf they wanted of eny thing. **1600** F. L. *Ovid's Remedie of Love* I. D 1 b, Are her teeth blacke or wants shee of the best? Relate some merry iest that shee may grinne. **1672** MARVELL *Reh. Transp.* I. 69 Though you may discover the same fury, yet it wants of the same vigour. **1658** *Whole Duty Man* xvii. §8 We want of the due compassion, if we can be content our poor brother should have one hour of unnecessary suffering, when we [etc.]. **1730** SAVERY in *Phil. Trans.* XXXVI. 301 And if ever it is found otherwise, I cannot but think that Load-stone wants of Perfection. **1760-72** H. BROOKE *Fool of Qual.* (1809) II. 52 However brilliant a diamond may be..it wants of its value and lustre till suitably set. **1799** G. SMITH *Laboratory* I. 89 Unwrought gold and silver want considerably of that lustre and brightness they appear in at goldsmiths' shops.

c. *to want for*: (chiefly in negative context) to suffer from the want of; to be ill-provided with; in later use also, to be lacking in (some quality). ***to want for nothing***: to have no lack of any of the necessaries or comforts of life.

1607 SHAKS. *Timon* III. ii. 10 Fye no, doe not beleeue it: hee cannot want for money. **1652** in *Verney Mem.* (1907) I. 519 Let her want for nothing. **1652** WADSWORTH tr. *Sandoval's Civ. Wars Spain* 325 Though it was Lent, their Bishop gave them leav to eat flesh, so they wanted for no good cheer. **1679** DRYDEN & LEE *Œdipus* I. 12 While Argos is a People, think your Thebes Can never want for Subjects. **1714** MRS. MANLEY *Adv. Rivella* 54 The Ambassador did not want either for Friends in England, nor in Hilaria's own Family. **1733** POPE *Let. to Swift* 28 May, It will not want for Satire. **1747** E. POSTON *Pratler* I. 74, I hope thou art well, and dost not want for the common Necessaries of Life. **1786** MRS. A. M. BENNETT *Juvenile Indiscr.* III. 153 But that was his misfortune, as he wanted not for perseverance, cunning, or cold blood, the three grand characteristics of a Scotchman. **1838** DICKENS *O. Twist* xxxviii, Mrs. Bumble.. did not want for spirit, as her yoke-fellow could abundantly testify. **1858** CARLYLE *Fredk. Gt.* VII. v. (1873) II. 295 Frederika did not want for temper, as the Hohenzollerns seldom do. **1882** P. FITZGERALD *Recreat. Lit. Man* (1883) 227 But she did not want for pluck or courage, as every streetboy knew. **1885** 'OUIDA' *Rainy June* (1901) 90 He was happy and wanted for nothing.

4. a. *trans.* To suffer the want of; to have occasion for, need, require; to stand in need of (something salutary, but often not desired. Hence *colloq.* senses 4 and 5 are often humorously contrasted.)

In advertisements the pa. pple. ***wanted*** is used elliptically (= F. *on demande*, G. *wird gesucht*), prefixed or appended to the designation of the kind of person or thing sought for; e.g. 'Wanted, a governess'; 'Experienced bookkeepers wanted'; 'Wanted, any early books on America.' Similarly, ***wanted to purchase***.

c **1470** HENRY *Wallace* I. 446 Deyr cusyng, pray I the, Quhen thow wantts gud, cum fech ynewch fra me. **1530** PALSGR. 771/1, I wante monaye, *argent me fault.* **1593** SHAKS. *3 Hen. VI*, v. i. 66 Oh welcome Oxford, for we want thy helpe. **1630** WINTHROP *Let.* in *New Eng.* (1825) I. 379 Though we have not beef and mutton, &c. yet (God be praised) we want them not; our Indian corn answers for all. **1694** MOTTEUX *Rabelais* v. Epist. Pantagruel's Lymosin 251 Incluse with Sylves behind, and Lakes before us, Our outward man wants something that's calorous. **1737** WESLEY *Jrnl.* 18 Dec., I was seized with a violent Flux, which I felt came not before I wanted it. **1766** GOLDSM. *Hermit* viii, Man wants but little here below, Nor wants that little long. **1770** LANGHORNE *Plutarch, Solon* (1879) I. 97/2 The soothsayers declared, that there were certain abominable crimes which wanted expiation. ? **1791** *Jrnls. Ho. Comm.* XLVII. 373/2 Throwing the Timber, fresh cut, into Salt Water, and letting it lie there till wanted. **1827** FARADAY *Chem. Manip.* xv. (1842) 367 A tube is wanted for the conveyance of fluids. **1836** DICKENS *Sk. Boz, Streets —Night*, He must want his tea, poor man, after his dirty walk from the Docks. **1853** LYTTON *My Novel* VI. xiv, She wants some one to read to her, and tend on her—she is old, and has no children. She wants a companion, and prefers a girl of your age to one older. Will this suit you? **1884** 'MARK RUTHERFORD' *Deliverance* v. (ed. 9) 74 He had got a notion in his head that his mind wanted rest and reinvigoration. **1898** 'H. S. MERRIMAN' *Roden's Corner* viii. 85 The nurse whose services had not hitherto been wanted, had.. spent some pleasant weeks at a pension at Scheveningen.

b. With *vbl. sb.* or *inf.* (esp. *passive*) as object (now chiefly *colloq.*). ***it wants doing*** (***it wants to be done***): it needs doing, should be done. ***one wants to do it*** (***this way***): one's best, or proper course is to do it; one should do it, etc.

The idiom (common *colloq.* in North and North-midlands) by which the verb apparently takes two objects, a sb. or pron. and a vbl. sb. that in sense governs it (as, ***I want that doing*** is perhaps a blend of *it wants doing*, and *I want it done*.

1563–83 FOXE *A. & M.* 2123/1 For we may in no wise betray the case of God, nor will not doe, but susteine it to the vttermost of our powers... But hereunto we want presently indifferent vsing [? = 'we need to be impartially treated']. **1587** *Nottingham Rec.* IV. 216 We present the Bull Ringe to want raylinge. **1697** VANBRUGH *Prov. Wife* II. ii, *Madam.* Inteed Matam, to say de trute, he wanted leetel good breeding. *Lady Fan.* Good breeding! He wants to be can'd, Madamoiselle. **1719** DE FOE *Crusoe* I. (Globe) 160 My goats wanted to be milked. **1724** R. FIDDES *Morality* Pref., p. cxix, A train of accusations which, severally, want to be proved themselves. **1741** MIDDLETON *Cicero* II. viii. 359 The merit of this speech is too well known, to want to be enlarged upon here. **1791** R. MYLNE *2nd Rep. Thames Navig.* 13 The Banks of the [Lock] Chamber want to be laid down properly, and some Trees cut down. **1865** 'L. CARROLL' *Alice in Wonderland* vii. (1866) 96 'Your hair wants cutting', said the Hatter. **1868** E. BECKETT DENISON *Life Bp. Lonsdale* 172 Those who wanted a church consecrating, or a meeting to be held. **1898** 'H. S. MERRIMAN' *Roden's Corner* xiv. 146 'That loose-shouldered chap Roden is a scoundrel,' he said bluntly,.. 'and wants thumping.'

5. a. To desire, wish for. Often with *inf.* as object.

1706 E. WARD *Wooden World Diss.* (1708) 2 All such as want to ride in Post-haste from one World to the other. **1727** A. HAMILTON *New Acc. E. Ind.* I. v. 52 If either want to be separated during the term limited, there must be a Commutation of Money paid by the separating Party to the other, according as they can agree. **1751** LAVINGTON *Enthus. Meth. & Papists* III. (1754) 127 Cheats mingle the Flower or Seed among the Food of those whom they want to defraud. **1840** DICKENS *Old C. Shop* xxxiii, If every one of your clients is to force us to keep a clerk, whether we want to or not, you had better leave off business. **1871** MOZLEY in Liddon *Pusey* (1897) IV. 221 What you mention about persons actually not *wanting* an hereafter is a horrible feature of the day. **1885** 'MRS. ALEXANDER' *At Bay* iv, Now *I* have got over my first foolish fear of him, he is so gentle and polite, and seems to want to be friends with my father. **1895** *Law Times Rep.* LXXIII. 650/1 If the under-writers had wanted to know they could have asked at once. **1902** J. F. RUSLING *European Days & Ways* 299 Blücher wanted to hang or shoot Napoleon as an outlaw and monster. **1902** R. BAGOT *Donna Diana* x. 116 She came repeatedly to the Castelnuovo gardens, generally accompanied by Frau von Raben, but occasionally, when the latter was wanted to drive with her cousins, by Princess San Rocco's maid.

b. To desire (a person) *to* (do something). Also, *U.S.*, with clause as object.

1845 S. JUDD *Margaret* I. ix, I want you to be a good boy. **1852** H. C. KIMBALL in *Brigham Young's Jrnl. Discourses* (1859) VI. 256 If this is your determination, I want you should manifest it by raising your right hands. **1903** C. L. BURNHAM *Jewel* ii, Mr. Evringham wants you should saddle his horse and bring her round. **1918** *Oxford Mag.* 21 June 343/1 Most of them do not make it quite plain what they want the teacher [of the Classics] to do.

c. To wish to see, or speak to (a person); to desire the presence or assistance of one (for a specified purpose). Frequently *passive.*

wanted! sometimes used ellipt. (for 'you are wanted'). Cf. *shop!*

c **1760** CHALLONER in E. Burton *Life* (1909) II. xxiv. 28 We will spend our evenings, as much as possible, at our own lodgings, so that we may be found by those who shall want us for the sick. **1794** MRS. RADCLIFFE *Myst. Udolpho* xxv, 'Retire!' said Barnardine sternly: 'you are not wanted:' and as Emily said nothing, Annette obeyed. **1825** T. HOOK *Sayings* Ser. II. *Passion & Princ.* vi, When from a side and smaller door a female enquired 'whom he pleased to want'. **1837** DICKENS *Pickw.* ii, 'Winkle—Winkle!' shouted Mr. Tupman, calling into the inner room.'.. 'You're wanted —some one at the door.' **1842** TENNYSON *Locksley Hall* 2 Leave me here, and when you want me, sound upon the bugle horn. **1866** TROLLOPE *Claverings* v, 'She is not likely to press herself where she is not wanted'.

d. ***wanted*** (pa. pple.): *colloq.* or humorous ellipsis for ***wanted by the police***, said of persons whose apprehension is required for some offence.

1812 J. H. VAUX *Flash Dict., Wanted*, when any of the traps or runners have a private information against a family person [*sc.* a thief] and are using means to apprehend the party, they say, such a one is wanted. **1838** DICKENS *O. Twist* xliii, 'Yes, he was wanted.' 'Very particular?' inquired Mr. Bolter. 'No,' replied the Jew, 'not very. He was charged with attempting to pick a pocket,' [etc.]. **1905** *Times* 5 Sept. 5/5 The prisoner.. said he wished to give himself up, having heard that he was 'wanted'.

e. ***what does he want with*** (such or such a person or thing)? = 'What is his object in dealing with (the person)?' or 'Why should he care to possess (the thing)'. Also (chiefly *U.S.*) const. *of*.

1828 W. TAYLOR *Hist. Surv. Germ. Poetry* I. 309 (tr.) Death, what can you want of Fanny? With your lipless teeth and sockets, How should you contrive to kiss her? **1831** SCOTT *Ct. Robt.* vii, Once more, what dost thou want with me? and why hast thou the boldness to watch me? **1855** *Knickerbocker* XLV. 136 Salt, Miss? What do you want of salt? **1862** MRS. H. WOOD *Channings* xxiv, It is an incredible mystery. What could he want with the money? The tale told, about his having debts, has no foundation. **1868** BROWNING *Ring & Bk.* VI. 105 Men, for the last time, what do you want with me? **1884** 'MARK TWAIN' *Huck. Finn* xxxv. 357 What do we want of a saw? **1897** MCCARTHY *Own Times* V. xxi. 489 What does the Irishman want with tobacco, or wine, or spirits? it might perhaps fairly be asked. But then comes the other question, 'What does the Englishman want of wine, or spirits, or cigars?' **1914** G. ATHERTON *Perch of Devil* II. 246 But what does he want of two cottages?

f. With ellipsis of a verb of motion, ***to want out*** (***in***, etc.): to wish to go out (in, etc.). *colloq.* (Orig. *Sc.*, *north. Ir.*, and *U.S. colloq.*).

1836 J. D. DAVIDSON *Diary* 29 Oct. in *Jrnl. Southern Hist.* (1935) I. 354 He still called out in a plaintive, infant tone, '*I want in*'—'*I want in*'. **1844** W. JAMIE *Muse of Mearns* 86 (E.D.D.) A sturdy chap.. Cam to the door and wanted in. **1870** J. NICHOLSON *Idylls o' Hame* 10 Jenny, are ye wantin' oot 'Mang the knowes to frisk aboot? **1887** *Columbus* (Ohio) *Dispatch* 3 Sept., The turnkey says if the prisoner had informed him he wanted out, he would have been released. **1888** *Advance* (Chicago) 6 Dec. 798 Just then he heard a knock at the door, and told me that some one wanted in. **1893** *Columbus* (Ohio) *Dispatch* 19 Sept., An old gentleman who was drawn to serve on the grand jury.. wanted off, and when the court asked for excuses he said [etc.]. **1897** CROCKETT *Lad's Love* xxiii. 236 It was cold and he wanted back to the inn fire-side. **1925** *Amer. Speech* I. 149/2, I want out at the bank because this sack of silver is too heavy to pack around with me. **1959** E. AMBLER *Passage of Arms* viii. 219 They can keep everything... We just want out. **1973** *Time Out* 2–8 Mar. 14/1 One of the kids who had paid his money .. wanted out. **1973** *Nature* 28 Sept. 173/2 Britain may just be weary of industrial growth and may be saying in quite a sophisticated way that it wants out regardless of the cost. **1977** *Zigzag* Mar. 24/1, I had no regrets about leaving... I just wanted out. **1979** A. HAILEY *Overload* III. i. 194 Well, I'm not afraid, or proud, or anything any more. I just want out. **1984** *Guardian* 5 Nov. 17/4 In recent weeks the Federal Reserve chairman Mr Paul Volcker has reportedly told friends that he wants out and would be interested in the presidency of the World Bank. **1985** *Times Lit. Suppl.* 25 Jan. 102/2 If you want out, it is just about possible to live, if only internally, a better life.

6. *Comb.*: † **want-grace**, one who lacks grace, a reprobate: cf. *lack-grace, scapegrace*. See also WANT-WIT.

1603 J. DAVIES (Heref.) *Microcosm.* (Grosart) 57/2 And rather then they should not die by force, Or want a Want-grace to performe the Deede, Their Vncle and Protector must perforce Their Crowne from Head, and Head from Life divorce. **1621** BRATHWAIT *Nat. Embassie* 31 Thus may adulterous want-graces looke into Tereus fall.

want, obs. pa. t. of WEEN *v.*

wa'n't (wɑːnt). Now *dial.* (chiefly *U.S.*). A contracted form of *was not* (cf. *wasn't*). Now only used, in literature, in representations of dialectal or vulgar speech. Cf. *ain't, don't*, etc.

1702 VANBRUGH *False Friend* v. i, Who did you let in then? it wan't your Master, sure? **1757** FOOTE *Author* Epilogue Wks. 1799 I. 129 Says Lady Bell.. There wa'n't a creature there. **1893** H. A. SHANDS *Some Peculiarities of Speech in Mississippi* 67 *Want*, Negro and illiterate white for *was not* or *were not.* **1929** H. W. ODUM in A. Dundes *Mother Wit* (1973) 194/1 Wan't no hero, wan't no coward. **1942** W. FAULKNER *Go down, Moses* 144 Ah went to yo house last night, but you want dar.

wanta ('wɒntə), repr. U.S. colloq. pronunc. of *want to*. See WANNA.

1894 S. CRANE in *Arena* Oct. 666 Let up, will yeh? Do yeh wanta kill somebody? **1925** T. DREISER *Amer. Trag.* (1926) I. I. i. 7 That oldest boy don't wanta be here. **1946** E. O'NEILL *Iceman Cometh* II. 98 Don't let Hickey put no ideas in your nuts if you wanta stay healthy! **1977** *New Yorker* 12 Sept. 54/3 Do fast lines and play lousy—one phrase of 'Smoke Gets in Your Eyes' and then: 'Folks, you wanta drive somebody crazy?'

'wantable, *a.* [f. WANT *v.* + -ABLE.] Desirable, of a kind likely to become sought after.

1970 *Times* 21 July 7 This collection [of clothes].. is extremely pretty, wantable and smart in a personal private way. **1979** *Daily Tel.* 22 Jan. 11/2 Most wantable garment in the Paris collections, a Fifties' style soft leather dress cinched with an ultra-wide cummerbund in the Claude Montana collection.

wantag, obs. Sc. form of VANTAGE *sb.*

'Wantage[1]. In 7 **Wantige**. The name of a town in Oxfordshire (formerly in Berkshire) (OE. *Wanating*), the birthplace of King Alfred. Used *attrib.* in † ***Wantage cap***.

1609 ROWLEY *Search for Money* (Percy Soc.) 31 Monmouth caps, Wantige caps, round caps.

wantage[2] ('wɒntɪdʒ). *U.S. Comm.* [f. WANT *v.* + -AGE.] Deficiency, shortage.

1828–32 WEBSTER, *Wantage*, deficiency; that which is wanting. **1888–9** *New York Produce Exchange Report* 256 (Cent.) Inspectors and Gaugers shall make a detailed return .. of each lot inspected, showing.. the gauge, wantage, proof, and number of proof gallons.

wantage, obs. Sc. form of VANTAGE.

wan tan, var. WON TON.

wante, wanteau, obs. forms of WANTY.

wanted ('wɒntɪd), *ppl. a.* [f. WANT *v.* + -ED[1].]

1. In the senses of the verb: **a.** Lacking, missing; desired, needed.

1697 DRYDEN *Æneis* IX. 346 Make me but happy in his safe Return, Whose wanted Presence I can only mourn. **1718** POPE *Iliad* XIII. 338 To whom the Cretan: Enter, and receive The wanted weapons. **1801** SOUTHEY *Lett.* (1856) I. 167 They will not pay him for executing a wanted work.

b. *dial.* Dispensed with.

1821 CLARE *Vill. Minstr.* I. 84 And locks would be a wanted thing, To keep out thieves at night.

c. Of a person: Sought for by the police.

1903 G. R. SIMS *Living London* III. 18/2 Down the long lines of beds the uniformed figures go,.. till they reach the bedside of the two 'wanted' men, who awake to find themselves in the grip of the law. **1912** *Sphere* 28 Dec. 338/3 A periodical called *The Detective*, in which portraits of wanted persons are given.

2. *absol.* as *sb.* Chiefly in *plural.* Persons or things that are 'wanted' (i.e. advertised for, sought by the police, etc.). Chiefly *colloq.*

1793 W. ROBERTS *Looker-on* No. 51 ¶5, I design to publish a list of Wanteds, wholly for the use of your Paper. **1903** *Daily Chron.* 25 Mar. 3/4 A policeman arresting a 'wanted' in a common lodging-house. **1907** *Shrewsbury Chron.* 27 Dec., *heading of Advt. column*, Wanteds. **1910** *Sat. Rev.* 22 Jan. 98/2 Two 'wanteds' figured conspicuously in a crowd.. in Shoreditch.

3. Special collocations: ***wanted list***, a list of persons sought by the police or by a similar agency; also ***wanted file***; ***wanted poster***, a poster displaying details of a wanted person or persons, usu. under the headline 'Wanted'.

1967 'E. PETERS' *Black is Colour* i. 20 Just take a look at 'em!.. Every one of 'em straight out of the *wanted file. **1964** I. FLEMING *You only live Twice* xix. 228 The C.I.A. on whose *WANTED list I certainly feature. **1968** P. DURST *Badge of Infamy* v. 50, I checked with the International War Crimes commission to see if Von Friede was on the wanted list. **1970** T. LILLEY *Projects Section* xiv. 177 There would always be those in the crowd who would recognise the corpse—either from '*Wanted' posters or from personal acquaintance. **1982** A. PRICE *Old Vengeful* 12 Oh dear! A good likeness... It looks like a prison picture.. or maybe a 'Wanted' poster.

† **wantel.** *Obs.* [Of obscure origin: perh. some error.] A bundle, burden, pack.

1599 MINSHEU, *Garróte*, a cudgell to winde a cord as carriers do to packe their wantels with [Cf. Percyuall (1591), *Garote*, Fustis quo funem torquent in ligandis sarcinis.]

wanter[1] ('wɒntə(r)). [f. WANT *v.* + -ER[1].]

1. One who is deficient in something. ? *Obs.*

1611 J. DAVIES (Heref.) *Sco. Folly* (Grosart) 21/2 What should I think of courage? if it wants, The wanters are despis'd of God and men. **1886** *Spectator* 13 Feb. 209/2 The wanters were many and the wealthy few.

2. One who is in need or desirous of something.

1727 SWIFT *Let. to Mrs. Howard* 9 July, But you know too well already how very injudicious the general tribe of wanters are. **1748** RICHARDSON *Clarissa* VIII. 144 Suppose *B*, in such great want of this treasure, as to be unable to live without it. And suppose *A*, the Miser, has such an opinion of *B*, the Wanter, that he would rather lend it to him, than to any mortal living. **1867** *Chamb. Jrnl.* 21 Dec. 801 An exchange..in which the wanters and the wanted may meet.

b. One who seeks a husband or wife. *dial.*

1723 RAMSAY *Fair Assembly* viii, Then, ilka wanter wale a wife, Ere eild and humdrums seize ye. **1804** R. ANDERSON *Cumbld. Ball.* 82 There's lads but few in our town, And lasses wanters plenty. **1818** SCOTT *Hrt. Midl.* xxviii, And dinna sneeze at Joe, if he should be for drawing up wi' you, ..he's a handy boy, and a wanter. **1871** C. GIBBON *Lack of Gold* xxii, He did not belong to the set of lively 'wanters' —as the bachelors were designated.

wanter[2] ('wɒntə(r)), *dial.* [f. WANT *sb.*[1] + -ER[1].] A mole-catcher.

1903 *Daily Chron.* 8 July 3/5 John Perry, the old 'wanter', or mole-catcher of Luccombe.

wantey, -teye, obs. forms of WANTY.

wantful ('wɒntfʊl), *a.* [f. WANT *sb.*[2] + -FUL.] Full of wants, exacting.

1889 *Harper's Mag.* Jan. 180/1 My Caesar's whims, which, day and night More wantful, do but grow with surfeiting.

wantgard, obs. Sc. form of VANGUARD.

wanthrift ('wɒnθrɪft). *Sc.* [f. WAN- + THRIFT *sb.*[1]] **a.** Lack of thrift or economy; prodigality. **b.** A thriftless person; also *collect.*

a. 1513 DOUGLAS *Æneis* VIII. Prol. 79 Quhat wickitness, quhat wanthrift now in warld walkis! **1903** W. CHRYSTAL *Kingdom of Kippen* 100 Never to wanthrift may ony deil drive ye Is the wish o' wee Wattie the bard o' Bucklyvie.

b. *a* **1585** MONTGOMERIE *Flyting* 438 Let no vice in this warld in this wanthrift be wanted. *a* **1586** R. MAITLAND in *Maitland MS.* (S.T.S.) I. 39 Off our wanthrift sum wytis playis.

Hence **'wanthrifty** *a. Sc.*, unthrifty.

a **1585** MONTGOMERIE *Flyting* 261 Vyle venemous viper, wanthriftiest [*Tullibard.* wanthreivinest] of things.

wan-thriven, *a. Sc.* [f. WAN- + THRIVEN *a.* Cf. Da. *vantreven.*] Ill-developed, stunted in growth.

1508 KENNEDY *Flyting w. Dunbar* 493 Evill schryvin, wan-thryvin, not clene na curius. *a* **1585** MONTGOMERIE *Flyting* 327 Threed-bare bee their thrift as thou art wan-threivin [*v.rr.* vanthrewin, wanthriuen]! **1818** SCOTT *Hrt. Midl.* xx, And what am I but a poor wasted, wan-thriven tree? **1825** JAMIESON Suppl., *Lingit*, thin, lean, wanthriven.

wantie, wantige, obs. ff. WANTY, WANTAGE.[1]

wanting ('wɒntɪŋ), *vbl. sb.* [f. WANT *v.* + -ING[1].] The condition of being without, or lacking, something; the absence or deficiency of something.

a **1300** *Cursor M.* 11676 We o water has nu wanting, Vr water purueance es gan. *c* **1380** WYCLIF *De Apostasia Cleri* i. Sel. Wks. III. 431 Bodyliche abyte, or wantyng þerof, makiþ not men religiose neyþer apostataes. *a* **1395** HYLTON *Scala Perf.* (W. de W. 1494) I. lxxxi, What is synne but a wanting or a forberyng of good. **1423** JAS. I *Kingis Q.* lxxxvi, Sum [died] sorowfully, for wanting of thare makis. *c* **1500** *Melusine* xxiv. 179 Woo were to me yf for wantyng of a preu & valyaunt man it shuld retourne in to the pay-nemes handes. **1600** SHAKS. *A.Y.L.* II. vii. 126 And take vpon command, what helpe we haue That to your wanting may be ministred. **1637** SANDERSON *Serm.* (1681) II. 92 If we would ..exercise our selves sometimes to fastings and wantings and other hardnesses and austerities. **1680** *W. Allen's Persuas. Peace & Unity* Pref. p. lxxxvi, The Printers wanting of Copy to fill up this sheet, is the only occasion of this Postscript. **1682** OTWAY *Venice Preserv'd* IV. i. Why was such happiness not given me pure? Why dash'd with cruel wrongs, and bitter wantings? **1883** WHITELAW *Sophocles, Electra* 265 They rule me, and from them comes all I have —My having and my wanting, both are theirs.

wanting ('wɒntɪŋ), *pres. pple.* and *ppl. a.* [f. WANT *v.* + -ING[2].]

I. As *pres. pple.* (only predicatively).

1. a. That is absent or lacking; not forthcoming, not supplied or provided.

c **1400** *Rule St. Benet* (Verse) 1505 So þat, if oght wantand be, In whom defaut es, may men se. *c* **1440** *Alphabet of Tales* 54 So þai lukid aboute þaim, & one of þaim sayd þat þe chamberlayn was wantand. **1577** B. GOOGE *Heresbach's Husb.* I. 36 If doung be wantyng to mende the ground withall. **1671** MILTON *P.R.* II. 450 And what in me seems wanting, but that I May also in this poverty as soon Accomplish what they did? **1707** *Curios. in Husb. & Gard.* 168 When the Saltseller was wanting, the Table was look'd on as Profane. **1837** DICKENS *Pickw.* ii, Mr. Winkle eagerly watched his opportunity; it was not long wanting. **1883** *Manch. Guard.* 22 Oct. 5/2 There are not wanting indications that the calm is more apparent than real. **1886** C. SCHOLL *Phraseol. Dict.* II. 830 Nothing will be wanting on my part to render your stay in our city as agreeable as possible.

b. Const. *to* (†formerly also simple dative)

13.. *Cursor M.* 6499 Quen manna sal vs wantand be, He sal send vs wid plente. **1591** SHAKS. *1 Hen. VI*, I. i. 82 Were our Tears wanting to this Funerall. **1640** tr. *Verdere's Rom. of Rom.* II. xlv. 174 As for my parents,..I may say without vanity, that Crownes are unjustly wanting to their worth. [Fr. *que les couronnes manquent iniustement à leurs merites.*] **1849** MACAULAY *Hist. Eng.* iv. I. 430 No gift of nature or of fortune seemed to be wanting to her. **1861** PALEY *Aeschylus* (ed. 2) *Choeph.* 817 *note*, By this slight and happy change.. an imperative, hitherto wanting to the sentence, is obtained.

c. fig. ***to be wanting to***: to fail to help or satisfy (a person or need); to prove unequal to, fall below (a claim, expectation, duty, opportunity). ***to be wanting to oneself***: to fail to do justice to oneself; to fall below the standard imposed by one's character and abilities (now *rare* or *arch*).

1640 tr. *Verdere's Rom. of Rom.* I. xliii. 176 When they had all promised rather to dye then be wanting to the duty of a good Knight [Fr. *plustost que manquer au deuoir d'vn bon cheualier*]. **1642** D. ROGERS *Naaman* 11 Some alledge God will not be wanting to any who are not wanting to themselves. **1667** MILTON *P.L.* x. 271 Nor shall I to the work thou enterprisest Be wanting, but afford thee equal aid. **1701** W. WOTTON *Hist. Rome* 343 He was mightily wanting also to himself in the choice of his Officers. **1762** HUME *Hist. Eng. to Hen. VII*, I. i. 17 Cerdic was not wanting to his good fortune. **1785** COWPER *Let. to Unwin* 31 Dec., You observe therefore that I am not wanting to myself; he that is so, has no just claim on the assistance of others. **1794** *Ann. Reg., Hist.* 89 The Vendéans were not wanting to themselves in so terrible a crisis. **1868** FREEMAN *Norm. Conq.* (1877) II. vii. 140 The Earl was not a man to be wanting to his country at such a moment. **1872** J. H. NEWMAN *Hist. Sk.* II. Ded. p. vi, You have never been wanting to me..when I had occasion in any difficulty to seek your guidance.

†2. Needful, requisite, necessary. *Obs.*

1756 WASHINGTON *Writ.* (1889) I. 261 To carry on all these works, a number of tools..will be absolutely wanting. **1797** MRS. A. M. BENNETT *Beggar Girl* (1813) II. 98 Mrs. Buchanan's first plan was to take such a number of servants with her as would be wanting to attend on her husband. **1802** MAR. EDGEWORTH *Moral T., Prussian Vase* Wks. 1816 I. 248 She added, that the count had written all that was wanting for her.

3. a. That lacks, or is without, something. Usu. with a defining prepositional phrase: see b, c, d.

1611 BIBLE *Dan.* v. 27 Thou art weighed in the balances, and art found wanting. **1849** MACAULAY *Hist. Eng.* ix. II. 453 His rectitude and piety, tried by strong temptations and never found wanting.

†b. const. *of. Obs.*

1592 SHAKS. *Rom. & Jul.* II. ii. 78 My life were better ended by their hate, Then death proroged wanting of thy Loue. **1654–66** EARL ORRERY *Parthen.* (1676) 788, I give those Kingdoms to you and your Heirs for ever..and wanting of Heirs, to revert unto my Successors again. **1709** MRS. MANLEY *Secret Mem.* I. 2 Her Limbs enervated and supine, wanting of that Energy that should bear her [etc.]. **1721** BRADLEY *Philos. Acc. Wks. Nat.* 23 It is wanting of Leaves.

c. const. *in.*

1697 DRYDEN *Virg. Past.* Ded. to Ld. Clifford, Though England is not wanting in a Learned Nobility. **1724** POPE *Let.* 1 Aug. in *10th Rep. Hist. MSS. Comm.* App. I. 153 And hope..he will not be found wanting in the knowledge of his profession. **1869** TOZER *Highl. Turkey* II. 257 No one.. would suspect them of being wanting in fun. **1896** *Law Times* C. 393/1 The Doctor's reply to Junius was not wanting in incisiveness.

d. const. *for. rare.*

1874 DASENT *Half a Life* I. 115 As I was wanting for a nickname,..I was called 'the Companion of the Bath'.

†4. That is short *of* (a certain age). *Obs.*

1709 MRS. MANLEY *Secret Mem.* (1736) I. 189, I was then wanting of Fourteen.

†5. With inf. Slow or backward *to* (do something). *Obs.*

1691 *d'Emiliane's Frauds Rom. Monks* (ed. 3) 286 The Monk was extraordinarily applauded for this his curious Thought, and he was not wanting to make good use of it. **1738** *Wesley's Hymns*, '*When to the Temple*' ii, Should we be wanting to rejoice Thro' Deadness or Delays The Stones themselves would find a Voice To celebrate his Praise. **1755** MAGENS *Insurances* II. 119 All those that are wanting to do their Duty in this Respect, shall be obliged to make Satisfaction.

6. Mentally defective, weak-minded. *dial.* or *colloq.*

1839 DICKENS *Nickleby* xxxiv. 331 'He was a little wanting here,' touching his forehead. **1877** *Holderness Gloss.* s.v., You moant tak nooatis o' what he says; he's a bit wantin. **1911** *Times* 12 July 11/3 Making him seem to be what village-people call 'wanting'. **1924** J. BUCHAN *Three Hostages* vi. 85 Had something given in my brain last night ..so that now I was what people call 'wanting'? **1976** 'J. BELL' *Trouble in Hunter Ward* xvii. 180 Maisie, poor mite, wanting from birth, she was.

II. As *ppl. a.* (in attrib. use).

7. Absent, lacking, missing.

1573 *Aldeburgh Rec.* in *N. & Q.* 12th Ser. VII. 226/2 To Jeaffrye Freman for a wanton [*sic*] Box that barker loste, xii[d]. **1683** MOXON *Mech. Exerc., Printing* xxv. ¶ 5 He Sets out.. a Quire..to make good the wanting Sheets. *a* **1700** EVELYN *Diary* 16 Sept. 1685, Then they spake of the boy who was pretended to have a wanting leg restor'd him. **1851** SYLVESTER in *Lond.* etc. *Phil. Mag.* Sept. 229 It is difficult to see how the wanting factor escapes detection. **1854** H. MILLER *Sch. & Schm.* 302 Many a wanting feature had to be supplied. **1915** *Blackw. Mag.* Aug. 232/1 By no searching in his girdle..could he produce the wanting money.

8. Deficient, lacking (in something expressed or implied by the context); esp. lacking in money or necessaries of life, needy, necessitous. Also *absol.* Now *rare* or *Obs.*

a **1616** BEAUM. & FL. *Wit without Money* II. iv, I have not seene a Gentleman so backward, a wanting Gentleman. **1657** S. PURCHAS *Pol. Flying-Ins.* 338 Bees though..they have sufficiently stored and replenished their hives..; yet will they not give over working; nay some, not leave robbing and that from the weaker and wanting hives. **1683** MOXON *Mech. Exerc., Printing* xxiv. ¶ 10 He thrusts the Wooll from the bunching-out side, towards the wanting side. **1685** SIR W. PETTY *Will* in *Trans. R. Ir. Acad.* XXIV. III. 114, I give twenty pounds to the most wanting of the parish wherein I dye. **1727** SWIFT *Let. to Mrs. Howard* 9 July, Thus wanting people are like drowning people, who lay hold of every reed or bulrush in their way. **1747** *Will* in J. O. Payne *Rec. Engl. Catholics* (1889) 23 £50 to the two bishops..to give to the most pious and wanting of their clergy to pray for me.

Hence **'wantingly** *adv.*, **'wantingness.**

1643 HERLE *Answ. Ferne* 14 The maine ends..are.. supply of wantingnesse, allay of wilfulnesse. **1865** J. GROTE *Mor. Ideals* ii. (1876) 24 The wantingness which is the call to action. **1894** 'EHA' *Naturalist on Prowl* 54 Gaunt frames of..cows and calves with..lustrous eyes staring wantingly.

wantless ('wɒntlɪs), *a. rare.* [f. WANT *sb.*[2] + -LESS.] Having no want or lack. Hence **'wantlessness.**

1586 WARNER *Alb. Eng.* III. xiv. (1589) 56 The want-les Counties Essex, Kent, Surrie, and wealthie Glayde Of Hertfordshire. **1591** SYLVESTER *Du Bartas* I. iii. 393 All Winter-long, Thou [the Lambourn stream] never shows't a drop, Nor send'st a doit of need-less Subsidie, To Cramm the Kennet's Want-lesse Treasurie, Before her Store be spent, and springs be staid. **1890** C. MONKHOUSE *Corn & Poppies* 81 No faith in giving To wantless dead the crumbs that feed the living. **1896** *Contemp. Rev.* Apr. 498 A German thinker has denounced the 'accursed wantlessness of the masses as the great inner obstacle of social progress.

†want-louse. *Obs. rare.* [a. Du. *wandluis* or LG., G. *wandlaus* (cf. MLG., OHG., MHG. *wantlus*), a 'wall-louse', bug.] A bed-bug, bug (*Cimex lectularius*).

1655 MOUFET & BENNET *Health's Improv.* (1746) 83 The Smell of a Wantlouse may kill a Child in the Mother's Womb. **1706** PHILLIPS (ed. Kersey), *Want-Louse*, a sort of Insect. Hence in later Dicts.

wantoe, obs. north. f. WANTY.

wanton ('wɒntən), *a.* and *sb.* Forms: 4 **wantowen,** 4–5 **-towne,** 5 **wantowe, wantton,** 4–6 **wantoun,** (6 **wantount**), 4 *Sc.* **vanton,** 4–5 **wantun,** 5–6 **vantoun,** 4– **wanton.** [ME. *wantowen*, f. WAN- + *towen*:—OE. *togen* pa. pple. of *téon* TEE *v.*[1] to discipline, train. The word thus literally means 'undisciplined'; cf. UNTOWEN *a.*, and the equivalent G. *ungezogen*; also ME. *welitowen* well-brought-up.]

A. *adj.*

†1. a. Of persons: Undisciplined, ungoverned; not amenable to control, unmanageable, rebellious. Of children: Naughty, unruly. *Obs.*

wanton of word: violent or insolent in speech.

a **1300** *Cursor M.* 11952 Yur sun þat wantun [*Gött.* wantoun] and þat wild, Wit his banning has slan vr child. **1362** LANGL. *P. Pl.* A. x. 57 For whonne Blod is Bremore þen Brayn þen is Inwit I-bounde, And eke wantoun and wylde withouten eny Resoun. **14..** *26 Pol. Poems* xii. 113 The fadir, þe wanton child wole kenne, Chastyse wiþ ȝerde, and bete hit sore. *c* **1420** ? LYDG. *Assembly of Gods* 1230 'A' seyde Reason, 'then I know well that felawe. Wylde he ys & wanton, of me stant hym noon awe.' *c* **1440** *Promp. Parv.* 515/2 Wantowe..*insolens, dissolutus.* *c* **1470** HENRY *Wallace* I. 211 A hely schrew, wanton in his entent. *c* **1475** *Rauf Coilȝear* 100 The Carll was wantoun of word, and wox wonder wraith. *c* **1491** *Chast. Goddes Chyld.* 15 Yf the childe wexe wonton the moder beteth hym fyrst with a litell rodde and the strenger he wexeth the gretter rodde she taketh. *a* **1513** FABYAN *Chron.* cxxvii. (1533) 62 Dagobert.. associated vnto hym certayne wanton persones and bete his mayster. **1568** GRAFTON *Chron.* II. 183 He with Piers of Gauestone and other wanton and wilde persons, had broken the Parke of the sayde bishop. **1612** T. TAYLOR *Titus* i. 7 (1619) 127 Thus he shal make such wanton who should rather be kept vnder, by speaking peace to whom it belongeth not. **1697** J. LEWIS *Mem. Dk. Glocester* (1789) 72 The Dutchess of Northumberland came with several ladies of fashion to the Duke [a little boy] at Windsor, when unfortunately he was a little wanton, suffering some improper expressions to escape him.

†b. Of an animal: Skittish, refractory. Of a hawk: Out of hand, unmanageable. *Obs.*

1535 COVERDALE *Hos.* iv. 16 For Israel is gone backe, like a wanton cowe. *c* **1575** *Perf. Bk. Kepinge Sparhawkes* (1886) 26 Sugarcandy and butter will make her lustye, moyste, and proude, and being ofte used will make her wanton and to sore away. **1760–72** H. BROOKE *Fool of Qual.* (1809) II. 115 The cow kicked up her heels, and proved wanton and refractory.

†c. Of actions: Lawless, violent; in weaker sense, rude, ill-mannered. *Obs.* Cf. 5 b.

a **1400–50** *Wars Alex.* 12 Sum [couettis to lestyn] of wirschip I-wis slike as þam wyse lattis, And sum of wanton werkis þa þat ere wild-hedid. *c* **1430** *Bk. Curteisie* 20 in *Babees Bk.*, And take good hede bi wisdom & resoun þat bi no wantowne lauȝinge þou do noon offence.

d. Said of boys, with mixture of sense 4; often (after Shakespeare's use) with reference to childish cruelty.

1605 SHAKS. *Lear* IV. i. 38 As Flies to wanton Boyes are we to th' Gods, They kill vs for their sport. **1692** E. WALKER tr. *Epictetus' Mor.* xxxiv, Else you'll desist, and jade like wanton Boys. **1741–2** GRAY *Agrippina* 189 Had her wanton son Lent us his wings, we could not have beguil'd With more elusive speed the dazzled sight Of wakeful jealousy. **1822** SCOTT *Peveril* xliii, You make me feel like the poor bird, around whose wing some wanton boy has fixed a line, to pull the struggling wretch to earth at his pleasure.

2. Lascivious, unchaste, lewd. †Also, in milder sense, given to amorous dalliance.

a. of persons (in early use only of women).

1393 LANGL. *P. Pl.* C. IV. 143 That alle wommen wantowen shulleþ be war by þe one, And biterliche banne þe. *Ibid.* VIII. 300 Ich haue ywedded a wyf, quaþ he, wel wantowen [*v.rr.* wantoun, wanton] of maners. *c* **1420** WYNTOUN *Cron.* IV. vi. 464 A woman occupyit þat steid Twa ȝeris as paip.. Bot scho wes wantoun of hire waire. **1514** BARCLAY *Cyt. & Uplondyshm.* (Percy Soc.) 26 Her name was wanton Besse, Who leest with her delt he thryved not the lesse! *c* **1515** *Cocke Lorell's B.* 14 And many whyte nonnes with whyte vayles, That was full wanton of theyr tayles. **1569** UNDERDOWN *Ovid's Invect. Ibis* D vj, Tyresias ..gaue sentence of Iupiters syde, and concluded that women were the wantoner. Wherefore Iuno moued to anger put out hys eyes. **1591** SHAKS. *1 Hen. VI*, III. i. 19 Thou art a most pernitious Vsurer,.. Lasciuious, wanton, more then well beseemes A man of thy Profession, and Degree. **1592** KYD *Sp. Trag.* I. i, My soule Did liue imprisond in my wanton flesh. *a* **1661** FULLER *Worthies, Yorks.* (1662) 190 Henry [I].. was very wanton, as appeareth by his numerous natural issue. **1712** ARBUTHNOT *John Bull* II. i, As for his personal Reflexions, I would gladly know who are those Wanton Wives he speaks of? **1766** FORDYCE *Serm. Yng. Women* (1767) I. i. 16 A daughter.. turns out unruly, foolish, wanton.

b. *transf.* and *fig.*

1590 SHAKS. *Mids. N.* II. i. 129 When we haue laught to see the sailes conceiue, And grow big bellied with the wanton winde. **1606** —— *Tr. & Cr.* IV. v. 220 Yond Towers, whose wanton tops do busse the clouds, Must kisse their owne feet. **1679** *The Confinement: a Poem* 55 Curst be those Mountains, wanton with the Sun, From whose first hot embraces, Tagus run.

c. of dispositions, thoughts, speech, action, or appearance.

c **1386** CHAUCER *Merch. T.* 602 And after that he sang ful loude and cleere, And kiste his wyf, and made wantowne cheere. *c* **1400** *Destr. Troy* 10824 Oft in wanton werkes wex þai with childe. *c* **1420** ? LYDG. *Assembly of Gods* 378 But aboue all other she [Venus] had a wonton ey. **1568** GRAFTON *Chron.* II. 760 She thought him secretly familiar with the king in wanton company. **1577** *Bk. Nurture* in *Babees Bk.* 64 But especyally keepe them from reading of fayned fables, vayne fantasyes, and wanton stories. **1651** C. CARTWRIGHT *Cert. Relig.* I. 175 But consider this Commandment in the full extent of it, as forbidding all wanton lookes. *a* **1672** WOOD *Life* etc. (O.H.S.) I. 366 A wanton (in plaine terms, a baudy) expression. **1782** JOHNSON *Let. to Mrs. Thrale* 12 June, I should have cared little about a wanton expression. **1789–96** MORSE *Amer. Geog.* II. 546 By the continuation of wanton attitudes, they acquire.. a frantic lasciviousness. **1843** LYTTON *Last Bar.* I. ii, And dancing round him, with wanton looks and bare arms. **1846** KEBLE *Lyra Innoc.*, *Gleaners*, Those evil powers,.. rude gaze and wanton word.

d. of writers.

1820 HAZLITT *Lect. Dram. Lit.* 144 They are always abusing 'wanton poets'.

3. Sportive, unrestrained in merriment.

†**a.** Of persons: Jovial, given to broad jesting, waggish. Also, free from care. *Obs.*

c **1386** CHAUCER *Prol.* 208 A frere ther was, a wantowne and a merye, A lymytour, a ful solempne man. *c* **1560** A. SCOTT *Poems* xv. 3 Art thow nocht wantoun, haill, and in gud howp... Bathing in bliss, and sett in hie curaige? *Ibid.* xxvii. 7 Wantone in weill but wo, Glaid withowt grief also.

b. Of young animals: Frisky, frolicsome. Chiefly *poet.*

1565 COOPER *Thesaurus* s.v. *Lasciuus*, Wantoner then a yonge kidde. **1593** DRAYTON *Ecl.* vi. 81 The early wanton Lambs, That 'mongst the Hillocks wont to skip and play. **1694** ADDISON *Poems, Hor. Ode* III. iii. 74 Let the wanton flocks unguarded stray. **1733** POPE *Ess. Man* III. 29 Who for thy table feeds the wanton fawn. **1746** SMOLLETT *Tears of Scot.* 14 Thy swains are famish'd on the rocks, Where once they fed their wanton flocks.

c. Said *poet.* of moving objects, viewed as if endowed with life: Sportive, impelled by caprice or fancy, free, unrestrained.

1601 WEEVER *Mirr. Mart.* E ij b, Tide for the ship, and ship was for the tide.. For Neptune men, and Neptune them to guide, Thames wanton currant stealing on behind. **1667** MILTON *P.L.* IX. 517 So varied hee, and of his tortuous Traine Curld many a wanton wreath in sight of Eve. **1742** COLLINS *Or. Ecl.* i. 15 When wanton gales along the valleys play. **1743** FRANCIS tr. *Hor.*, *Odes* v. xv. 9 While Phœbus' locks float wanton in the wind. **1777** SIR W. JONES *Poems, Seven Fountains* 33 A wanton bark was floating o'er the main.

†**d.** Of colour, music: Gay, lively. *Obs.*

1583 STUBBES *Anat. Abuses* I. M 2, Then euerie one of these his men, he [the Lord of Misrule] inuesteth with his liueries, of green, yellow or some other light wanton colour. **1597** MORLEY *Introd. Mus.* 150 Though he were a priest he would rather choose to excell in that wanton and pleasing musick then in that which [etc.]. **1743** COLLINS *Epist. to Hanmer* 41 With graceful ease the wanton lyre he strung.

†**4. a.** 'Spoiled', petulant (of children); hence, self-indulgent, effeminate, luxurious. *Obs.*

1538 ELYOT *Dict.*, *Mollio*,.. to make wanton or tender. *Ibid.*, *Sibariticus*, wanton or delycate. **1597** SHAKS. *2 Hen. IV*, IV. i. 55 Wee are all diseas'd, And with our surfetting, and wanton howres, Haue brought our selues into a burning Feuer. **1601** I. R. *World or Kingd. & Commw.* 169 The inhabitants [of China] partly by their effeminate and wanton kinde of life, partly by their forme of gouernment,.. haue little valour or manhood left them. **1712** STEELE *Spect.* No. 438 ¶4 Your Temper is Wanton, and incapable of the least Pain. **1746** FRANCIS tr. *Hor.*, *Epist.* II. i. 128 When Greece beheld her Wars in Triumph cease, She soon grew wanton in the Arms of Peace. **1835** THIRLWALL *Greece* I. ii. 59 Hence the name and the legend of Piasus, who reigned over the Pelasgians in the valley of the Hermus, and grew wanton from the exuberant increase of the land.

†**b.** Fastidious or dainty in appetite. *Obs.*

1530 PALSGR. 328/2 Wanton of condycions.. *friant; friande.* **1693** LOCKE *Educ.* §14 If he be hungry more than wanton, bread alone will down. **1727** ARBUTHNOT etc. *John Bull* IV. Postscr. ch. ix, How John pamper'd Esquire South with Tit-bits, till he grew wanton.

†**c.** Of clothing, diet: Luxurious. *Obs.*

1489 CAXTON *Faytes of A.* I. ix. B iij b, The auncient noble men.. made not theyre children to be norisshed in the kyngis & prynces courts for to lerne pryde, lechrey nor to were wanton clothing. **1562** TURNER *Baths* 6 It commeth by evell and wanton diet. **1825** JAMIESON, *Wanton-meat*, the entertainment of spirits, sweetmeats, etc., given to those in a house at the birth of a child, Teviotd[ale]; elsewhere called *Blithe-meat.*

†**d.** Said of money or wealth, as tempting to extravagance or luxury. *Obs.*

1529 MORE *Dyaloge* (1531) 76 b, And hauyng a lytell wanton money, which hym thought brenned out the botom of his purs.. he toke his wyfe.. to see Flaunders and Fraunce, [etc.]. **1568** GRAFTON *Chron.* II. 783 The hope of gaye apparell, ease, pleasure, and other wanton welth was able soon to pierce a soft tender hart. *a* **1700** EVELYN *Diary* (1819) I. 2 Wotton.. most tempting for a great person and a wanton purse to render it conspicuous. **1770** GOLDSM. *Des. Vill.* 260 The midnight masquerade, With all the freaks of wanton wealth arrayed.

†**5. a.** Of person: Insolent in triumph or prosperity; reckless of justice and humanity; merciless. *Obs.*

1513 DOUGLAS *Æneis* XI. xiv. 149 O, quod the maid, thou fals Liguriane, Our wantoun in thy proud mynd, all in vane [L. *frustraque animis elate superbis*]. **1624** CAPT. J. SMITH *Virginia* IV. 129 They now began to shrinke, and giue vs leaue to be wanton with our aduantage. **1643** BURROUGHES *Exp. 1st 3 ch. Hosea* vi. 266 When men get abundance, they soon grow wanton. *a* **1683** SIDNEY *Disc. Govt.* II. xv. (1704) 114 When that proud City [Rome] found no more resistance, it grew wanton. **1722** STEELE *Consc. Lovers* III. i, You took no Delight, when you immediately grew wanton, in your Conquest. **1764** GOLDSM. *Trav.* 385 When I behold .. Each wanton judge new penal statutes draw.

b. Of cruelty, injury, insult, or neglect: Unprovoked and reckless of justice or compassion; arbitrary, gratuitous.

1651 HOBBES *Leviath.* IV. xliv. 342 Which is not arguing from Scripture, but a wanton insulting over Princes. **1729** BUTLER *Serm.* Wks. 1874 II. 29 Profane swearing.. implies wanton disregard and irreverence towards an infinite Being. **1750** JOHNSON *Rambler* No. 75 ¶12 Some of them revenged the neglect.. by wanton and superfluous insults. **1769** BURKE *Late St. Nat.* Wks. 1842 I. 109 The wanton and indiscriminate seizure of papers, even in cases where the safety of the State was not pretended in justification of so harsh a proceeding. **1841** DICKENS *Barn. Rudge* lxxxi, You see the destruction that has been wanton here. **1849** MACAULAY *Hist. Eng.* ii. I. 161 The feeling which has.. induced the legislature to interfere for the purpose of protecting beasts against the wanton cruelty of men. **1868** J. H. BLUNT *Ref. Ch. Eng.* I. 222 *note*, It is impossible to pass by the wanton manner in which this is perverted by Mr. Froude. **1888** BRYCE *Amer. Commw.* lxxxv. III. 133 Tyranny consists in the wanton and improper use of strength by the stronger.

†**c.** In weaker sense: Reckless of decorum. *Obs.*

1663 GERBIER *Counsel* 20 Some wanton persons, who.. affect low leanings, to make use either to sit on, and break the glasse-windowes, or to shew themselves in Quirpo to passengers.

†**d.** Of natural occurrences: Abnormal, extraordinary. *Obs. rare.*

a **1754** FIELDING *Ess. Conv.* Wks. 1784 IX. 364 These men .. are no less monsters than the most wanton abortions, or extravagant births.

†**6. a.** Capricious, frivolous, giddy. *Obs.*

1538 STARKEY *England* (1878) 137 They were no thyng mete to kendyl.. Chrystyan hertys to deuotyon.. but rather to ster wanton myndys to vayn plesure. *c* **1560** A. SCOTT *Poems* xx. 40 Thy wantoun, folich mynd! **1602** CHURCHYARD *Wond. Air* in Farr *S.P. Eliz.* (1845) II. 404 The bedstocke and the tycke, And all belongs to bed, Is but vaine pleasures that we like To please a wanton head.

†**b.** Of a material substance: Changeable. *Obs.* (? *nonce-use.*)

1681 GREW *Musæum* III. §ii. i. 323 Gold hath the least variety of regular figure, in the Ore, of any Metal. Because, more solid, and therefore, less wanton, than the rest.

7. a. Profuse in growth, luxuriant, rank. *poet.*

1590 SHAKS. *Mids. N.* II. i. 99 The queint Mazes in the wanton green For lack of tread are vndistinguishable. **1596** —— *1 Hen. IV*, III. i. 214 She bids you, On the wanton Rushes lay you downe. **1704** POPE *Spring* 35 Where wanton Ivy twines. **1876** BLACKIE *Songs Relig.* 217 Wanton weeds my garden cumbered.

†**b.** Robust, overflowing with health. *Obs.*

1674 R. GODFREY *Inj. & Ab. Physick* 78, I have examined the Bloods of two hundred wanton Country healthy people.

†**8.** Unrestrained. **a.** Of speech or imagination: Extravagant. **b.** Of physical movement: Headlong, impetuous. *Obs.*

a. **1680** OTWAY *Orphan* I. i, I have heard him wanton in his Praise Speak things of him might charm the ears of Envy. **1713** ADDISON *Cato* I. iv, How does your Tongue grow wanton in her Praise! **1759** HUME *Hist. Eng.*, *Ho. Tudor* II. Eliz. iv. 589 Sir Philip Sidney.. is described.. as the most perfect model of an accomplished gentleman which was ever formed even by the wanton imagination of poetry or fiction.

b. **1753** HOGARTH *Anal. Beauty* xvii. 223 A fine Arabian war-horse, unbacked, and at liberty, and in a wanton trot.

9. Comb.: ***wanton-eyed, -headed, -winged*** adjs.; †**wanton mad, sick** *adjs.*, made with the insolence of prosperity.

1603 BRETON *Mad World* (Grosart) 8/1 A.. sharpe-witted, *wanton-eyed, and faire-handed.. gentlewoman. **1918** D. H. LAWRENCE *New Poems* 22 By-paths where the *wanton-headed flowers doff their hood. *a* **1700** EVELYN *Diary* 15 July 1683, In a word, we were *wanton madd, and surfeiting with prosperity. **1599** MARSTON *Antonio's Rev.* II. iii, That griefe is *wanton sick Whose stomacke can digest and brooke the dyet Of stale ill relisht counsell. **1608** ARMIN *Nest Ninn.* (1880) 47 The world wanton sick, as one surfetting on sinne. **1777** POTTER *Æschylus* 128 Each insect, and each *wanton-winged bird.

B. *sb.*

†**1.** A person, esp. a child, spoiled by over-indulgence and excessive leniency; a spoilt child, a pampered pet. *Obs.*

1526 *Pilgr. Perf.* (W. de W. 1531) 41 b, Our lorde knoweth well that we be wantons.. and.. farre from the holy lyfe of perfeccyon. **1530** PALSGR. 286/2 Wanton[.] cockeney, *mignot, mignotte.* Wanton of condicyons, *saffre.* **1548** UDALL etc. *Erasm. Par. Luke* Pref. ¶ ij, A Queene.. if she would become fortunes wanton, she might without coumptrollemente swimme in the delices of all suche prosperitee. **1580** LYLY *Euphues* (Arb.) 36, I am enforced to thinke.. that thy parents made thee a wanton with too much cockering. **1595** SHAKS. *John* V. i. 70 Shall a beardlesse boy, A cockred-silken wanton braue our fields. **1623** ROWLANDSON *God's Bless.* 8 So mothers deale with their little wantons, by taking the bread from them, which they tread under foot. **1656** SANDERSON *Serm.* (1689) 103 A Father may love a child too fondly and make him a Wanton.

†**2. a.** A person, esp. a child, of playful, roguish, or sportive conduct. (Sometimes used as a term of endearment.) *Obs.*

1589 GREENE *Menaphon* (Arb.) 27 Sephestias Song to her Childe. Wepe not my wanton! smile vpon my knee! **1616** B. JONSON *Masque Oberon* 977 *Silenus* [to the Satyrs] Peace my wantons.

†**b.** A sportive or roguish animal, bird, etc. *Obs.*

1605 SHAKS. *Lear* II. iv. 126 As the Cockney did to the Eeles, when she put 'em i' th' Paste aliue, she knapt 'em o' th' coxcombs with a sticke, and cryed downe wantons, downe. **1697** DRYDEN *Æneis* VII. 678 Their Sister Silvia cherish'd with her Care The little Wanton [a young stag]. **1791** *Lochmaben Harper* iv. in Child *Ballads* IV. 17 And tak a halter.. And.. wap it oer the Wanton's nose, And tie her to the gray mare's tail. **1805** WORDSW. *Waggoner* III. 118 Yon screech-owl,.. I know that Wanton's noisy station. **1812** CARY *Dante, Parad.* v. 83 The lamb, That, fickle wanton, leaves its mother's milk, To dally with itself in idle play.

3. A lascivious or lewd person. (The current use.)

† ***his wanton*** = his mistress. *Obs. rare.*

1540 PALSGR. *Acolastus* III. i, N iv b, He.. playeth his parte stoutely or lyke a man, whyle the swete man .i. the plesantly disposed wanton leadeth wenches. **1599** SHAKS. *Much Ado* IV. i. 45 *Leonato.* What doe you meane, my Lord? *Clau.* Not to be married, Not to knit my soule to an approued wanton. **1604** —— *Oth.* IV. i. 72 Oh, 'tis the spight of hell,.. To lip a wanton in a secure Cowch And to suppose her chast. **1611** BIBLE *Prov.* vii. Argt. 22 Solomon.. sheweth the cunning of an whore, And the desperate simplicitie of a yong wanton. *a* **1661** FULLER *Worthies, Northampt.* (1662) 281 She confessed her self too worthless to be his wife, yet pleaded too worthy to be his wanton. *a* **1693** SOUTH *Serm.* (1697) II. 215 An old Wanton will be doating upon Women, when he can scarce see without Spectacles. **1751** JOHNSON *Rambler* No. 171 ¶1 Nothing would more powerfully.. guard inexperience from seduction, than a just description of the condition into which the wanton plunges herself. **1858** MERIVALE *Rom. Emp.* l. (1865) VI. 176 The hot blood of the wanton smoked on the pavement of his gardens. **1887** MISS BRADDON *Like & Unlike* xxvii, You are a wanton by nature; but you have reckoned without your host, you fair, false devil. You shall not live to dishonour me.

4. Phrase. ***to play the wanton*** (or †***the wantons***), to dally, trifle; also, †to behave lewdly or lasciviously (*obs.*). Similarly, ***to play the wanton's part.***

1529 MORE *Suppl. Souls* 16 b, Yf the wench be nyce and play the wanton and make the mater strange, then wyll he bete her to bed to. **1593** SHAKS. *Rich. II*, III. iii. 164 Or shall we play the Wantons with our Woes, And make some pretty Match, with shedding Teares? *a* **1677** T. MANTON *Serm. Ps. cxix.* (1681) 290 The word of God was appointed.. to increase our reverence of God; Not that we may play the wantons with Promises, and feed our Lusts with them. **1712** STEELE *Spect.* No. 266 ¶4 [Asking] Whether she was well educated, could forbear playing the Wanton with Servants and idle Fellows. *a* **1718** PRIOR *Henry & Emma* 540 Did e'er my Tongue speak my unguarded Heart The least inclin'd to play the Wanton's Part? **1852** D. G. MITCHELL *Dream Life* 120 It has very likely occurred to you, my reader, that I am playing the wanton in these sketches.

†**5.** ***the wantons***: wanton fits, lascivious desires, wantonness. *Obs. rare.*

1727 [E. DORRINGTON] *Philip Quarll* 53 'Tis to be hop'd you won't be troubled with the Wantons, and play the Trick your sister Juno did.

6. Comb., as ***wanton-like*** adj.

1617 T. CAMPION *3rd Bk. Ayres* xxii. Wks. (1909) 171 Though she be wilde and wanton-like in shew, Those little staines in youth I will not see.

wanton ('wɒntən), *v.* [f. WANTON *a.* and *sb.*]

1. *intr.* To sport amorously, to play lasciviously or lewdly. Also, *to wanton it.*

1588 SHAKS. *Tit. A.* II. i. 21, I will be bright and shine in Pearle and Gold, To waite vpon this new made Empresse. To waite said I? To wanton with this Queene. **1589** GREENE *Menaphon* (Arb.) 44 As if Venus in a countrey peticoate had thought to wanton it with her louely Adonis. **1665** R. BRATHWAIT *Comm. 2 Tales* 54 He who even now, so lasciviously wantonned,.. see how he is scarrified! **1670** MILTON *Hist. Eng.* v. Wks. 1851 V. 231 On the very day of his Coronation, he abruptly withdrew himself from the Company of his Peers,.. to sit wantoning in the Chamber with this Algiva. **1728** YOUNG *Love Fame* VI. 384 Who marry to be free, to range the more, And wed one man, to wanton with a score.

b. To play sportively, heedlessly, or idly, to frolic unrestrainedly, to gambol. Also *to wanton it.* (Said esp. of a child or young animal.)

1582 STANYHURST *Æneis* IV. (Arb.) 106 Yf a.. Prittye lad Æneas in my court wantoned [*L. luderet*] ere thow Took'st this filthye fleing. **1611** SHAKS. *Wint. T.* II. i. 18 We shall Present our seruices to a fine new Prince One of these dayes, and then youl'd wanton with her, If we would haue you. **1657** G. THORNLEY *Daphnis & Chloe* 53 A boy appear'd in the.. grove. Naked he was, alone he was; he play'd and wantoned it about. **1725** POPE *Odyss.* XI. 554 Thy infant son her fragrant bosom prest, Hung at her knee, or wanton'd at her breast. **1762** FALCONER *Shipwr.* I. 332 In curling wreathes, they [porpoises] wanton on the tide, Now sport aloft, now downward swiftly glide. **1818** BYRON *Ch. Har.* IV. clxxxiv, And I have loved thee, Ocean!.. from a boy I wanton'd with thy breakers. **1820** LAMB *Elia, Christ's Hosp.*, How merrily we would sally forth.. and strip under the first warmth of the sun; and wanton like young dace in the streams. **1827** KEBLE *Chr. Y., All Saints' Day*, As bloodhounds hush their baying wild To wanton with some fearless child.

c. To go idly or heedlessly *up and down, over, through* (a place); also, to spend one's time carelessly.

1682 KIRCHEVALL tr. *Nepos, Elysander* 46 They left their ships to the mercy of the winds and waves and carelessly wanton'd up and down the fields [L. *dispalati in agris*]. **1786** tr. *Beckford's Vathek* (1883) 130 The horses, camels, and guards wantoned over their tulips and other flowers, and made a terrible havoc. **1807** J. BARLOW *Columb.* VIII. 490 Steeds, herds and flocks o'er northern regions rove, Embrown the hill and wanton thro the grove. **1847** TENNYSON *Princess* IV. 91 O tell her, Swallow, that thy brood is flown: Say to her, I do but wanton in the South, But in the North long since my nest is made. **1916** L. P. JACKS *From Human End* i. 3 Like guests in a hospitable mansion where we may eat and drink, work and wanton, as we please.

d. *transf.* of inanimate things.

1596 SHAKS. *Tam. Shr.* Induct. ii. 54 Citherea all in sedges hid, Which seeme to moue and wanton with her breath. **1612** DRAYTON *Poly-olb.* ii. 174 When, like some childish wench, she [*sc.* the river Stour] loosely wantoning, With tricks and giddy turns seems to in-isle the shore. **1697** DRYDEN *Æneis* VI. 302 And dancing Leaves, that wanton'd in the Wind. **1748** RICHARDSON *Clarissa* (1811) III. iii. 29 The wavy ringlets of her shining hair,.. wantoning in and about a neck that is beautiful beyond description. **1759** JOHNSON *Rasselas* xx. A rivulet, that wantoned along the side of a winding path. **1786** BURNS *Lasso' Ballochmyle* 3 The zephyr wanton'd round the bean, And bore its fragrant sweets alang. **1796** SOUTHEY *Joan of Arc* VI. 124 When afar they.. mark the distant towers Of Orleans, and.. many a streamer wantoning in air. **1838** LYTTON *Alice* V. i, The sea-breeze wantoned amongst the quivering leaves of the chestnut-tree that overhung their seat.

e. To trifle (*with* something). Also quasi-*trans.* with *out*.

1589 T. BRABINE in *Greene's Menaphon* (Arb.) 20 Whose warbling tunes might wanton out my woes. *a* **1797** H. WALPOLE *George II* (1847) II. viii. 249 He found it was no longer a season for wantoning with the resentment of his successor.

2. To run into excesses or extravagances of conduct or living; to revel (*in* a course of action). Also with *it*.

1631 MAY tr. *Barclay's Mirr. Mindes* I. 5 Soe that both the awe of their parents may not too sensibly decrease in them, and they not wanton it, through a suddaine, and vnexpected encrease of liberty. **1750** JOHNSON *Rambler* No. 148 ¶2 The power [parental authority] which we are taught to honour from the first moments of reason;.. and which therefore may wanton in cruelty without control. **1752** *Ibid.* No. 190 ¶10 His house was soon crowded with poets, sculptors, painters, and designers, who wantoned in unexperienced plenty. **1850** KINGSLEY *A. Locke* iv, Because he would not sit and starve.. while those who fattened on the sweat of his brow.. were wantoning on venison and champagne.

b. To indulge in extravagances of language or thought.

1640 FULLER *Joseph's Coat* 50 The witty extravagances, and Rhetoricall phrases of these Fathers, were afterward interpreted to be their distilled doctrinall positions: so dangerous it is for any to wanton it with their wits in mysteries of Religion. **1750** JOHNSON *Rambler* No. 2 ¶2 The pleasure of wantoning in common topicks is so tempting to a writer, that he cannot easily resign it. **1789** BURKE *Sp. agst. W. Hastings* Wks. 1813 XV. 86 We are not persons of an age,—of a disposition.. to *wanton* as these counsel call it; that is to invent fables concerning Indian antiquity. **1838** MACAULAY *Ess., Temple* (near end), For once he [Bentley] ran no risks;.. he wantoned in no paradoxes.

c. *transf.* Of a garden, plant: To flourish profusely or extravagantly; to grow or ramble at will.

1800 *Asiatic Ann. Reg., Misc. Tracts* 296/1 On the latter [garden] no decoration of art has been spared; the former wantons in all the luxuriance of nature. **1890** CONAN DOYLE *White Company* xviii, As though some great ivy-plant of stone had curled and wantoned over the walls. **1907** E. GOSSE *Father & Son* v. 113 [A] wilderness, in which loose furze-bushes and untrimmed brambles wantoned into the likeness of trees.

d. *fig.* or of things (esp. Nature) personified.

1667 MILTON *P.L.* v. 295 A Wilderness of sweets; for Nature here Wantoned as in her prime, and plaid at will Her Virgin Fancies. **1769** BLACKSTONE *Comm.* IV. xxxiii. 409 From this root has sprung a bastard slip, known by the name of the game law, now arrived to and wantoning in it's highest vigour. **1833** CHALMERS *Const. Man* II. x. 114 All nature smiles in beauty, or wantons in bounteousness for our enjoyment. **1866** B. TAYLOR *Poems, Mondamin*, Where nature wantoned wild.

3. To deal carelessly or wastefully (*with* property, resources). Also *trans.* with *away*, to spend carelessly or wastefully, to dissipate (life, time, resources).

1646 J. HALL *Horæ Vac.* iv. 39 [Of Preaching] Humane learning being a good Hand-maide and an ill companion to divinity, who though she carry away the Jewels and Eare-rings of the Ægyptians she desires to use them and not wanton with them. *a* **1656** BP. HALL *Serm. Ps. lxviii. 30* Wks. 1837 V. 232 He wantons away his life foolishly, that, when he is well, will take physic to make him sick. **1669** PEPYS *Diary* 28 Apr., With this money the King shall wanton away his time in pleasures. **1775** JOHNSON *Tax. no Tyr.* 47 It is urged that the Americans have not the same security, and that a British Legislature may wanton with their property. **1811** J. PRATT in *R. Cecil's Wks.* (1827) I. 121 A minister has no right to wanton away the support of his family.

†**4.** *trans.* To make wanton; to lead into extravagances of conduct, living, etc. *Obs.*

c **1600** CHALKHILL *Thealma & Cl.* (1683) 88 For he reign'd More like a Beast than Man;.. weak'ning his strength By wantoning his people, without Law Or Exercise to keep their minds in awe. **1628** FELTHAM *Resolves* II. xxvi. 83 If wee sleepe, hee [the Devil] comes in dreames, and wantonneth the ill-inclining soule.

Hence **'wantoning** *vbl. sb.* and *ppl. a.*

1596 WARNER *Alb. Eng.* XII. lxxiii. (1612) 304 Full fortie thousand Curtizans there, Ladies-like, do liue, That to the Pope for wantoning no small Reuenew giue. **1597** BP. HALL *Sat.* I. ii. 34 But since, I saw it painted on Fames wings, The Muses to be woxen Wantonings. **1624** HEYWOOD *Gunaik.* I. 5 Her embracings and wantonnings. **1701** W. NICHOLS *Consol. Parents* 40 The innocent Wantonings of a beloved Child. **1883** E. GOSSE *17th Cent. Stud.* 134 Chance melodies that seem like mere wantonings of the air upon a wind-harp. **1901** T. R. GLOVER *Life & Lett. Fourth Cent.* viii. 184 The story of the wantoning Dido.

wanton: see WANTY (*β*).

wantoner ('wɒntənə(r)). *rare.* Also 9 -onner. [f. WANTON *v.* + -ER[1].] A person who acts wantonly or is given to wanton behaviour.

1812 *Examiner* 28 Dec. 831/2 Was this the action of a penitent wantonner in libel? **1820** *Blackw. Mag.* VII. 372 Falsely, alas! poor wantoner! **1865** ANNA SWANWICK *Æschylus, Agamem.* 742 In human ill Wild wantoner for aye. **1912** 'R. DEHAN' *Betw. Two Thieves* xxiv. 191 There is a hell for chamberers and wantoners!

† **'wantonhede.** *Obs.* Also 5 wantow(n)hede, wantoned. [f. WANTON *a.* + *-hede*, -HEAD.] Wantonness.

c **1400** *Destr. Troy* 2911 Wemen are wount in Wantonhede yet, With a likyng full light in loue for to falle. **1435** MISYN *Fire of Love* 4 Wharefor þe ioy of clerenes þat sall not rote, þai chaunge to wantoned of beute þat sal noȝt last. *c* **1440** *Promp. Parv.* 515/2 Wantowhede [*v.rr.* wantown-, wanton-], or wantownesse, *insolencia, dissolucio.*

wantonize ('wɒntənaɪz), *v. arch.* Also 6–7 wantonnize. [f. WANTON *a.* and *sb.* + -IZE.]

1. *intr.* To play the wanton; to dally, sport, frolic; to indulge in lasciviousness.

1592 DANIEL *Rosamond* K 3 b, Sweetly it fits the fair to wantonise. **1603** FLORIO *Montaigne* I. xxix. 98 It is women communicate their partes as much as a man list to wantonize with them. **1613** W. BROWNE *Brit. Past.* I. iv. (1616) 79 When the prettie Rill a place espies, Where with the Pibbles she would wantonize. **1661–98** SOUTH *12 Serm.* III. 279 The mind of Man.. would, if let alone, lash out, and Wantonize in a boundless enjoyment and Gratification of all its Appetites, and Inclinations. **1826** LAMB *Elia, Sanity of True Genius*, The judgment might with some plea be pardoned if it ran riot, and a little wantonized.

†**b.** with *it.*

1611 COTGR., *Rager*, lasciuiously to toy, dallie, or wantonize it. **1652** EARL MONM. tr. *Bentivoglio's Hist. Relat.* 55 The Spring for many moneths together doth wantonnize it there.

†**c.** quasi-*trans.* with *away.*

1673 HICKERINGILL *Gregory, Father-Greyb.* 43 Wantonizing away their time and opportunities to do good.

2. *trans.* To make wanton. *rare.*

1598 SYLVESTER *Du Bartas* II. iii. I. *Vocation* 236 Their Wealth so growes, that, wantoniz'd withall, Their envious Shepheards broach a civill Brawl. **1652** BENLOWES *Theoph.* XI. xxxi. 197 Prosperitie's a gin If wantoniz'd breeds storms within. **1908** *Smart Set* June 49 Pure are your lips and eyes; Must years onpressing Teach you to wantonize Them in caressing?

Hence **'wantonizing** *vbl. sb.* and *ppl. a.*

1599 NASHE *Lenten Stuffe* To Rdrs. A 4 b, Wherin I follow the trace of the famousest schollers of all ages, whom a wantonizing humour once in their life time hath possesst to play with strawes. **1612** W. PARKES *Curtaine-Dr.* (1876) 29 The coyest wantonizing Citty-dame. **1633** EARL MANCH. *Al Mondo* (1636) 153 Pride.. must be counted State,.. Wantonising, a tricke of youth. **1640** tr. *Verdere's Rom. of Rom.* II. xxxix. 148 A thousand amorous wantonizing[s].

wantonly ('wɒntənlɪ), *adv.* [-LY[2].] In a wanton manner. **a.** Lewdly, lasciviously; voluptuously, luxuriously; lavishly.

c **1375** *Sc. Leg. Saints* vi. (*Thomas*) 466 þe flesche þat we fed here maste vantonly in daynttis sere. *c* **1386** CHAUCER *Shipman's T.* 381 And wantownely agayn with hym she pleyde. *c* **1430** *Pilgr. Lyf Manhode* II. xxxii. (1869) 87 Wantounliche thou wilt hose him, and take him noble robes. *c* **1489** CAXTON *Blanchardyn* xxii. 72 The smylynges and fayre shewes of their eyen, which wauntonly they caste full often vpon that yonge knyght. **1538** ELYOT *Dict.*, *Delicatus*, delycate, wantonlye broughte vppe. **1568** GRAFTON *Chron.* II. 531 The bishop saw.. that vittailes were not wantonly consumed, nor vainely spent. **1662** J. DAVIES tr. *Olearius' Voy. Ambass.* 89 Some of our young men.. would talk wantonly with them [the women]. **1712** STEELE *Spect.* No. 466 ¶3 The flippant insipidly Gay and wantonly Forward, whom you behold among Dancers.

b. Frolicsomely, sportively, playfully, light-heartedly.

1426 LYDG. *De Guil. Pilgr.* 11249 She held a gloue vantounly, And tournyd yt ffful ffetysly Aboute hyr ffyngres vp & doun. **1549** *Compl. Scot.* vi. 37, I beheld the pretty fische vantounly stertland vitht there rede vermeil fynnis. **1612** DRAYTON *Poly-olb.* viii. 448 She.. oft in-Isles the shore, as wantonly she flowes. **1621** FLETCHER *Pilgrim* v. iv. 1 How wantonly The wind blows through the leaves, and courts, and playes with 'em! **1663** COWLEY *Country Mouse* 9 A Mouse of high degree, which lost his way, Wantonly walking forth to take the Air. **1777** SIR W. JONES *Seven Fountains* 37 Some wantonly were tripping in a ring.

c. Recklessly, unadvisedly; without proper excuse or motive; without regard for right or consequences; in a way that betrays delight in wrong-doing or mischief, wilfully.

1390 GOWER *Conf.* II. 35 For he the hors withoute lawe The carte let aboute drawe Wher as hem liketh wantounly. *c* **1400** *Destr. Troy* 3496 Why wrought ye so wantonly in your wilde yre? **1566** STAPLETON *Ret. Untruths to Jewel* iii. 90 He denieth Christ wantonly. **1675** DRYDEN *Aurengz.* IV. (1676) 58 But do not wantonly my passion movc. **1749** FIELDING *Tom Jones* II. vi, To pardon great criminals wantonly, without any reason whatever. **1781** GIBBON *Decl. & F.* xxxi. III. 229 The Goth.. expressed.. his lively sense of the insult so wantonly offered to his person. **1801** HELEN M. WILLIAMS *St. Mann. Fr. Republic* II. 217 The [Spartan] tribunal which condemned a boy to death for wantonly plucking out the eyes of a bird. **1883** *Law Times* 20 Oct. 407/2 Preventing a litigant without a case from wantonly harassing his opponent. **1888** A. H. SMITH *Catal. Engr. Gems Brit. Mus.* 228 The [Portland] vase was wantonly broken on February 7, 1845, by a scene-painter, named William Lloyd.

wantonness ('wɒntənnɪs). Forms: see WANTON *a.* [f. WANTON *a.* + -NESS.]

1. The quality of being wanton, in various senses.

a. Lasciviousness, unchastity.

c **1340** HAMPOLE *Prose Tr.* 4, I rane [be] the wanntonnes of flesche and I fand noghte Ihesu. **1362** LANGL. *P. Pl.* A. III. 120 Wyues and widewes wantounesse heo techeþ. *c* **1386** CHAUCER *Man of Law's Prol.* 31 It wol nat come agayn,.. Namoore than wole Malkynes maydenhede, Whan she hath lost it in hir wantownesse. *c* **1430** *Christ's Compl.* 238 in *Pol. Rel. & L. Poems* (1866) 175, I haue myspendid my ȝong age In synne, & wantownesse also. **1513** MORE *Rich. III* Wks. 36/1 Hee [Edw. IV] was of youthe greately geuen to fleshlye wantonnesse. **1526** TINDALE *Jude* 4 They are vngodly and turne the grace of oure lorde God vnto wantonnes. **1589** NASHE *Anat. Absurd.* A 2, The riotous wantonnesse of Pasiphae. **1634** PEACHAM *Compl. Gentl.* x. (1906) 88 Concerning his [Ovid's] bookes, *Amorum* and *de arte amandi*, the wit.. will beare out the wantonnesse. **1709** STEELE *Tatler* No. 49 ¶8 That Scene of Wantonness, Messalina's Bed-chamber! **1835** THIRLWALL *Greece* xi. (1839) II. 50 To protect the state from the.. pollution of wantonness and profaneness.

†**b.** Effeminacy, foppish affectation. *Obs.*

c **1386** CHAUCER *Prol.* 264 Somwhat he lipsed for his wantownesse To make his englissh swete vp on his tonge.

†**c.** Excessive appetite. *Obs.*

a **1400** in Hearne *Robt. of Glouc.* 482 *note*, His flesshe wolde haue charged him with fatnesse, but that the wantonesse of his wombe with trauaile and fastyng he adaunteth.

†**d.** Unbridled luxury, extravagance in expenditure. *Obs.*

c **1400** *Pilgr. Sowle* (Caxton 1483) IV. xxxvi. 84 The honour.. of this maner of peple oweth not to ben acounted .. of clothynge of syluer harneys ne wantonesse of his owne persone. **1500–20** DUNBAR *Poems* xxxix. 5 All weilfair, welth and wantones Ar chengit in-to wretchitnes. *a* **1571** CAMPION *Hist. Irel.* vi. (1633) 18 Linnen shirts the rich doe weare for wantonnes and bravery. **1601** R. JOHNSON *Kingd. & Commw.* (1603) 200 In India and Cambaia they vse it at the burial of great Lords, in bathes and in other wantonnes. **1713** STEELE *Guardian* No. 6 ¶3 The servants below them seem to live in Plenty, but not in Wantonness.

e. Arrogance, insolence of triumph or prosperity. Now *rare.*

c **1480** HENRYSON *Test. Cress.* 549 Sa eleuait I was in wantones, And clam vpon the fickill quheill sa hie. *c* **1518** SKELTON *Magnyf.* 2504 With sad Cyrcumspeccyon correcte my Vantonnesse. *a* **1665** GOODWIN *Filled w. the Spirit* (1867) 23 Others [of the devils].. may be employed to stir up and cherish a spirit of pride and wantonness. **1779** J. MOORE *View Soc. Fr.* (1789) I. xliv. 372 Nothing can be a greater check to the wantonness of power. **1796** MME. D'ARBLAY *Camilla* III. 83 He has therefore turned fop from mere wantonness of time and of talents. **1815** JANE AUSTEN *Emma* I. v. 75 Weston may grow cross from the wantonness of comfort. **1868** M. PATTISON *Academ. Organ.* v. 148 Some check on knowledge is highly necessary to prevent it from running riot in the wantonness of its own wealth.

†*plural.* **1712** STEELE *Spect.* No. 426 ¶7 The Heir.. could not forbear, in the Wantonnesses of his Heart, to measure the Length and Breadth of his beloved Father.

†**f.** Unruliness, naughtiness (of a child); restiveness (of a horse). *Obs.*

1533 MORE *Apol.* xlvii. Wks. 922/2 As doeth the tender mother which when she hath beaten her chylde for hys wantones, wypeth his yien and kisseth hym. **1611** SPEED *Hist. Gt. Brit.* IX. v. §48 William.. was through the wantonnesse of his horse cast to the ground.

†**g.** Caprice, whim. *Obs.*

1595 SHAKS. *John* IV. i. 16 Yet I remember, when I was in France, Yong Gentlemen would be as sad as night Onely for wantonnesse. *a* **1631** DONNE *Serm., Ps.* vi. 2 (1640) 516 David.. comes not to take physick upon wantonnesse; but because the disease is violent. **1736** BUTLER *Anal.* II. i. Wks. 1874 I. 158 It is mere idle wantonness, to insist upon knowing the reasons. **1835** SIR J. ROSS *Narr. 2nd Voy.* xxi. 310 Man alone eats from pure wantonness; that he may gratify his taste, not satisfy his hunger.

h. Lawless extravagance, unrestrained license.

1712 ADDISON *Spect.* No. 315 ¶12 His Flight.. with the particular Description of the Sun, are set forth in all the Wantonness of a luxuriant Imagination. **1774** J. BRYANT *Mythol.* I. 129 Many in the wantonness of their fancy have yielded to the most idle surmises. **1830** D'ISRAELI *Chas. I*,

III. 28 Charles cannot be reproached for exacting monies.. from any wantonness of prodigality.

i. Reckless and unprovoked ill-doing.

1775 ADAIR *Amer. Ind.* 153 When an Indian sheds human blood, it does not proceed from wantonness, or the view of doing evil, but solely [etc.]. **1789–96** MORSE *Amer. Geog.* I. 356 The whole [of the stalactites] have since, by the wantonness of visitors, been broken down. **1823** LAMB *Elia* Ser. II. *Sonn. Sydney*, I have been hurt by the wantonness (I wish I could treat it by a gentler name) with which W. H. takes every occasion of insulting the memory of Sir Philip Sydney. **1828** SCOTT *F.M. Perth* ii, He would be as loath, in wantonness, to kill a spider, as if he were a kinsman to King Robert. **1845** MISS MITFORD in L'Estrange *Life* (1870) III. xi. 201 We have had here four incendiary fires! I don't know for what—mere wantonness. **1870** DISRAELI *Lothair* lviii, A Zouave, in wantonness firing his weapon before he threw it away, sent a random shot which struck Theodora. **1875** JOWETT *Plato* (ed. 2) V. 433 A man may.. commit some of these crimes.. in a fit of childish wantonness. **1914** KIPLING '*For all we have*' i, Our world has passed away In wantonness o'erthrown.

2. An instance of wantonness; a caprice, whim; a reckless and unjustifiable act. ? *Obs.*

1630 BP. HALL *Occas. Medit.* lxxi. (1633) 174 It is a wantonnesse to complaine of choyse; No Law bindes us to read all. **1664** DRYDEN *Rival Ladies* Ep. Ded. A 3 b, I wish we might at length leave to borrow Words from other Nations, which is now a Wantonness in us, not a Necessity. **1768** JOHNSON *Let. to F. A. Barnard* 28 May, Things.. which are prized at a high rate by a wantonness rather than by use. **1795–1814** WORDSW. *Excurs.* I. 626 It were a wantonness, and would demand Severe reproof, if we were men whose hearts Could hold vain dalliance with the misery Even of the dead.

†**3.** As the name of an allegorical personage in a morality play. *Obs.*

1506–7 *Acc. Ld. High Treas. Scot.* III. 369 Item, that nycht, to Wantonnes that sang to the King, xiiij s.

†**b.** *transf.*

1596 *Edw. III*, III. iii. 156 For whats this Edward but a belly god, A tender and lasciuious wantonnes, That thother daie was almost dead for loue? *Ibid.* III. v. 101 Now, Iohn of Fraunce, I hope, Thou knowest King Edward for no wantonesse, No loue sicke cocknev.

wantoun, obs. form of WANTON, WANTY.

wantow, obs. form of WANTY.

wantowe(n, -towne, obs. forms of WANTON.

†**wantrokie**, *v. Obs.* [ME. (*Kentish*) f. WAN-; the second element is obscure, as TROKE *v.* yields no good sense.] *intr.* To despair; in quot. *impers.*, with dative of person and *of*. Hence †**wantroking** *vbl. sb.* despair; false or mistaken expectation.

c **1315** SHOREHAM I. 919 Ac þat ne schalt þou neuere do, Bote þe wantrokye of lyue. *Ibid.* VII. 759 Loke that thou ne go nauȝt onder Thorȝ wantrokynge. **1340** *Ayenb.* 265 Þer ne is non hope of guode, non wantrokiynge of kueade.

†**wantroth, -truth.** *Obs. rare.* Forms: 3 (*Orm.*) wanntrowwþ, 4 vantrauth, wanetreutht. [ME. f. WAN- + TROTH *sb.*, TRUTH *sb.* Cf. next.] Unbelief.

c **1200** ORMIN 3148 Forr þatt wass þurrh wanntrowwþess slæp, Þatt he wass off hiss macche All orrraþ whatt he mihhte don, Of þatt ȝho wass wiþþ childe. *c* **1325** *Metr. Hom.* 120 Bale sal I bete Wit mirakel, that I sal schaw, And mikel folc fra vantrauth draw. *c* **1375** *Sc. Leg. Saints* xxvii. (*Machor*) 674 To pas into fere land, & preche godis word alquhare to þame at in wane-treutht are.

†**wantrowing**, *vbl. sb. Obs. rare*⁻¹. [ME. f. WAN- + TROWING *vbl. sb.*] Mistrust, faint belief.

c **1440** *York Myst.* xliii. 83 In grete wanne-trowing haue ȝe bene, And wondir harde of hartis ar ȝe.

†**wantrust.** *Obs.* Also 4 -trost, trest, 4–5 -truste, 5 -triste. [ME. f. WAN- + TRUST *sb.* Cf. MDu. *wantroost*.] Mistrust, lack of confidence.

c **1374** CHAUCER *Troylus* I. 794 But ones nyltow for þi coward herte,.. For wantrust tellen of þi sorwes smerte. **1387** T. USK *Test. Love* I. viii. 19, I saye nat these thinges for no wantrust that I have in supposinge of thee otherwyse than I shulde. **1412–20** LYDG. *Chron. Troy* IV. 81 For now victorie is redy to oure hond,.. And excludid,.. Boþe of wantrust & of foreyn drede. *c* **1450** —— *Life Our Lady* xli. (1484) f vj, For wantriste of her felow salome. *c* **1450** *Cov. Myst.* 225 Many a man With his wantruste hymsylf hathe slayn.

wantruth: see WANTROTH.

†'**wantsum**, *a. Obs.* Also 4 wansum. [ME. f. WANT *sb.*² + *-sum* -SOME.] Indigent, poor; devoid *of*.

c **1200** ORMIN 14824 To gengenn att te nede Whammse þu sest tatt wanntsumm iss & wiþþ wanndraþ biþrungenn. *a* **1300** *Cursor M.* 24853 Ful wansum [*Edinb.* wantsum] war þai þan o rede.

wantt-, obs. Sc. form of VAUNT *v.*

wantum ('wɒntəm). *nonce-wd.* [Blend of WANT *sb.*² + QUANTUM.] Deficiency or desire, considered as something quantifiable.

The quot. alludes to Prov. xxx. 15 The horse-leach hath two daughters, crying, Giue, giue. There are three things that are neuer satisfied, *yea* foure things say not.

1938 S. BECKETT *Murphy* 57 The horse leech's daughter is a closed system. Her quantum of wantum cannot vary.

'**want-wit.** [f. WANT *v.* + WIT *sb.* Cf. *lack-wit* (LACK *v.*¹ 7).] One who lacks wit or sense.

1448–9 METHAM *Amoryus & Cl.* 1459 But alle to late now, as wantewyttys we make owre mone. **1579** W. WILKINSON *Confut. Fam. Love* 41 Shall we thinke.. that he would be such a want witte as to take all kynde of coine.. and neuer examine it? **1596** SHAKS. *Merch. V*, I. i. 6 And such a Want-wit sadnesse makes of mee, That I haue much ado to know my selfe. **1610** *Chester's Triumph* (Chetham Soc.) C 3, Because I hate to heare a want-wit preach Beyond wits bounds. [**1684** BUNYAN *Pilgr.* II. (1900) 266 They saw one Fool, and one Want-wit, washing of an Ethiopian with intention to make him white.] **1900** H. SUTCLIFFE *Shameless Wayne* iii. (1905) 42 She trembled now to think that they had turned a want-wit.. into the heart of the pathless and bog-riddled heath.

b. *attrib.* or *adj.* Witless, senseless.

1894 'G. EGERTON' *Keynotes* 44, I laugh at myself for my want-wit agitation. **1900** H. SUTCLIFFE *Shameless Wayne* iii. (1905) 47 To pick a quarrel with the want-wit fellow.

wanty ('wɒntɪ). Forms: α. (4 waynte), 5 wanteye, 6–8 **wantey** (6 **wantie, wante,** 7 **wantyghe, waunty**), 7–9 **wantye,** (8 **wamtye**), 6– **wanty**; β. *Sc.* and *north.* 6 **wantow,** 6–7 **wanton** (6 **wantoun, wyanton**), 7 **wantoe,** (9 **wanteau**). For mod. dial. forms see *Eng. Dial. Dict.* [Apparently two synonymous words (ultimately identical in etymology) have been confused. The β forms represent the later phonetic development of WAME-TOW. The α forms seem to presuppose an original **wametie*, in which TOW *sb.*² (a. ON. *taug*) has been replaced by the etymologically equivalent TIE *sb.* (:—OE. *téaȝ*). But since in some dialects the unstressed *-tow* would regularly become *-ty*, the two words cannot be distinguished with certainty.]

†**1.** A rope or band used to fasten the pack on a pack-saddle or a load on the back of a horse. *Obs.*

α. **1390** *Earl Derby's Exped.* (Camden) 48 Pro ij girthes ij wayntes et ij hokes pro les paniers pro pullis, ij s. j d. st. **1434** *Maldon* (Essex) *Court Rolls* Bundle 20, No. 2 Per I equum nigrum cum paksadel et wanteye. **1573–80** TUSSER *Husb.* (1878) 36 A panel and wantey, packsaddle and ped. **1587** MASCALL *Govt. Cattle, Horses* (1596) 119 Harnaises.. and all things belonging thereunto: as haltars,.. wanties, packsaddels, backwanties and belly wanties. **1607** TOPSELL *Four-f. Beasts* 58 They carry also great burthens or loads tyed to their backs with ropes and wantyghtes [? *read* wantyghes]. **1618–19** *Maldon* (Essex) *Deeds* Bundle 477 (MS.), At severall tymes hath gone ouer Fulbridge with his horse and pack and refuseth to paye the duty for his wantye. **1713** *Lond. Gaz.* No. 5140/4 Lost.. a.. Gelding, with Hair-cloth and Wanty. **1793** *Jrnls. Ho. Comm.* 28 Mar. 535/2 Toll.. for every Horse tied with a Wantye or Wamtye, 2d. that shall pass through Stratford Langthorn. **1813** A. YOUNG *Agric. Essex* I. 108, 3 belly wanties, at 2*s.* 6*d.* **1886** *W. Somerset Work-bk., Wantye*, the belt or strap of raw hide which used to pass over the pack-saddle and round the belly of the horse.

β. **1503** *Acc. Ld. High Treas. Scot.* II. 404 Item, for ane collair to him and ane wantoun for the weschale, xiiij d. **1545–6** *Ibid.* VIII. 441 Item, for ane bridill with the bit,.. ane collar with bellis, and ane wanton. **1549** *Inv. Brisse* (Somerset Ho.), Hackney saddill, stirropes, & garthes and other wantowes. **1577** *Inv. Airaie* (Somerset Ho.), Wanton sadle and girth. **1828** [CARR] *Craven Gloss.* s.v., A wanteau was generally made of hemp, to which was attached an iron hoop, to fasten sacks on pack-saddles. **1837** THORNBER *Blackpool* 310 Grain.. was conveyed to Preston on the back of pack-horses, the load being tied on a wooden saddle, with a girth named a 'wantah'.

2. The belly-band of a shaft-horse. *dial.*

1854 MISS A. E. BAKER *Northampt. Gloss., Wanty*,.. the name is still preserved in the hempen cord or leather strap which passes under the horse, and is secured to both shafts, to prevent the cart rising up when heavily laden.

3. *attrib.*, as †*wanty bottom*, †*rope*, †*shaft*.

1583 *Shuttleworth's Acc.* (Chetham Soc.) 6 Fyve *wyantones boddomes, xij*d*. **1612** *Ibid.* 204 Wanton bothomes, x*d*. **1569** *Bury Wills* (Camden) 155 Item I gyue to my brother.. my best pack sadell withe a newe wante and *wantyrop withe the best girt. **1624** *Toke* (Kent) *Estate Acc.* (MS.) fol. 66, 2 wanty rops. **1611–12** *Shuttleworths' Acc.* (Chetham Soc.) 199 Foure *wanton shaffes and a paire of tresses, xviij*d*. **1617** *Ibid.* 226, 4 wantoe shaftes, xij*d*.

†**wanweird.** *Sc. Obs.* In 6 wan-, wanewerd. [f. WAN- + WEIRD *sb.*] Hard lot, ill fate, misfortune. (In quot. 1631 personified.)

1513 DOUGLAS *Æneis* I. v. 24, I tuik comfort heirof, thinkand but baid That hard wanwerd suld follow fortun glaid. **1535** STEWART *Cron. Scot.* II. 407 Sen gratius [God] that hes all thing in erd At his weil[d]ing to weill or ȝit wan werd. ? *a* **1550** '*Doun by ane rever*' 76 in *Dunbar's Poems* (S.T.S.) 307 Sen for no wisdome, nor no strenth, Nor for no richess in this erd, That ony man his lyf may lenth, Naythir for freyndschip agane wanewerd. *a* **1580** *Murning Maiden* 19 in *Maitland Fol. MS.* 360 Wanweird, sche said, quhat haue I wrocht That on me kythit hes all this cair? **1631** A. CRAIGE *Pilgr. & Heremite* 9 Perchance before that thou her againe see, By vote of the Wan-weirds, that buried shee bee. **1802** JAMIESON *Water Kelpie* xvi, Nor wit nor pow'r put aff the hour, For his wanweird decreed.

†**wanwit.** *Obs.* (Chiefly *Sc.*) Also 4 uanwite, 4–5 **wane-wit, -wyt.** [ME. f. WAN- + WIT *sb.* Cf. G. *wahnwitz*, Sw. *vanvett*, Da. *vanvid*, Norw. *vanvit*.] Lack of wit, foolishness.

a **1400** *Symb. Passion* 72 in *Leg. Rood* 180 Schild me from þein of helle pit þat i haue deseruud þorow uan-wite. *c* **1425** WYNTOUN *Cron.* VI. Prol. 48 Giff it war wilfully forȝhet, It walde be repute vnkyndnes, Wanwit, or þan reklessnes. **1456** SIR G. HAYE *Law Arms* (S.T.S.) 300 Prodigalitee.. cummys of grete foly and wan witt. *a* **1500** *Ratis Raving*, etc. 565 It is better a pur wys barne na an auld fule kinge, quhilk fore wane-wyt may perys a realme. *a* **1500** *Bernard. de cura rei fam.* I. 400 Thar moderis þan desyris mariage Quhilk is wanwyt and foly in þar age.

Hence †**wanwitty** *a. Obs.*, foolish.

a **1500** *Ratis Raving*, etc. 454 Fulys and wanwitty men.

'**wanwordy**, *a. Sc.* ? *Obs.* [f. WAN- + *wordy*, WORTHY *a.*] Worthless.

a **1774** FERGUSSON *To Tron-kirk Bell* I Wanwordy, crazy, dinsome thing, As e'er was fram'd to jow or ring. —— *Drink Eclogue* 308 Wanwordy gowk! did I sae aften shine [etc.].

'**wanworth**, *a.* and *sb. Sc.* (See Eng. Dial. Dict.) [f. WAN- + WORTH *a.* and *sb.*] **a.** *adj.* Worthless. **b.** *sb.* 'An undervalue' (Jam.).

17.. RAMSAY *Dunbar's Flyting* in *Evergreen* II. 57 Worlin wanworth [*the original has* Forworthin wirling]. *a* **1774** FERGUSSON *Poems* (1789) II. 88 The Council winna lack sae meikle grace As lat our heritage at wanworth gang.

wany, variant of WANEY *a.*

Wanyamwezi (wənjæm'weɪzɪ). Also **Wanyamwesi.** [Native name, lit. 'people of the moon', hence (prob.) 'people of the West'.] The name of a Bantu people of Tanzania.

1860 R. F. BURTON *Lake Regions Central Afr.* II. xii. 4 The correct designation of the inhabitants of Unyamwezi is, therefore, Mnyamwezi in the singular, and Wanyamwezi in the plural: Kinyamwezi is the adjectival form. *Ibid.*, According to the people.. in the days of the grandfathers of their grandfathers the last of the Wanyamwezi emperors died. **1911** J. FRAZER *Golden Bough: Magic Art* (ed. 3) I. v. 268 The Wanyamwesi, a large tribe of Central Africa, to the south of the Victoria Nyanza. **1947** *E. Afr. Ann. 1946–7* 93/1 The Wanyamwezi have been one of the better known tribes of Tanganyika from the time when Arab slave raiders first set up their centre at Tabora. **1955** HILL & MOFFETT *Tanganyika* 515 The Wanyamwezi are one of the more virile and hard-working tribes of the Territory, and also one of the largest.

wanyand, -ende, var. ff. WANIAND. *Obs.*

wanys(e, obs. forms of VANISH *v.*

wanyte, obs. Sc. form of VANITY.

†**wanze**, *v. Obs.* Forms: 1 **wansian**, 3 *Ormin* **wannsenn**, 4 **wanese**, 5 **wanyse**, **whanse**, 4–5 **wanse**, (5 *inf.* **wansyn**, **wanson**, **wanshon**, **wanschon**, 6–7, 9 *dial.* **wanze**. [OE. *wansian* (also *áwansian*) trans., to diminish, f. *wan*, WANE *a.* Cf. ON. *vanse* wk. masc. (Mid.Sw., Norw. *vanse*) want, defect.]

1. *trans.* To diminish, waste; in later use, to render lean.

a **1121** *O.E. Chron.* (Laud MS.) an. 656 Swa hwa swa ure ȝife ouþer oðre godene manne ȝyfe wansiað wansie him seo heofenlice iateward on heofenrice. *c* **1200** ORMIN 1904 Crist ras upp off dæþess slap, Forr dæþess nahht to wannsenn. *Ibid.* 7157 To wannsenn himm hiss riche. *Ibid.* 12238. **1647** TRAPP *Comm. Matt.* vi. 16. 215 They doe so disfigure their faces, so wanze and wither their countenances, that [etc.]. **1657** —— *Job* xvi. 8. 152 That with fasting and paines taking he had so wanzed and macerated himself, that at past thirty, he was looked upon as one towards fifty.

2. *intr.* To decrease, grow less (*lit.* and *fig.*); of the moon, to wane.

c **1200** ORMIN 1901 Marrchess nahhtess wannsenn aȝȝ, & Marrchess daȝhess waxenn. *Ibid.* 17969 Ned iss.. þatt he nu forrþwarrd waxe, & ec iss ned.. þatt I nu forrþwarrd wannse. *c* **1380** WYCLIF *Sel. Eng. Wks.* II. 148 He mut wex and Y mut wanese. *a* **1400** *Pol. Rel. & L. Poems* (1903) 263 Worldes catel passet sone. þat wacset & wansit rit as te mone. *c* **1407** LYDG. *Reson & Sens.* 6187 They be nat lyche the hornyd moon That kan encrese and wanse ageyn. *c* **1440** *Promp. Parv.* 515/2 Wanschon' [*Winch. MS.* wanshon], *idem quod* wanson'. *Ibid.*, Wanson', *evaneo*, Cath., *evanesco*. Wanson', or wanyn', as þe mone, *decresco*. *c* **1440** CAPGRAVE *Life St. Kath.* I. 487 Peyntyng & wrytyng & grauyng in entayle It wyll wanyse [*MS. Arund.* whanse] & wast, roten & be brent. **1447** BOKENAM *Seyntys, 11,000 Virgins* 207 Thys was here feer þat.. Eche day shuld growen & encrese Crystyn relygyoun.. And paynymry wansyn & discrese. **14..** *MS. Ashm.* 191, fol. 199 b, Wiþ ynne it is an hole, ye whiche schewiþ bi symylitude howe þe moone wexiþ & wansiþ.

b. To wither, fade, waste away; to become emaciated.

1567 GOLDING *Ovid's Met.* III. 618 And all that things that lyked him did wanze away at length. *Ibid.* VI. 58 A ruddynesse besprent Hir cheekes which wanzed away againe. **1593** NASHE *Christ's T.* T 1 b, Decke our selues how we will,.. wee cannot equalize one of the Lillies of the fielde; as they wither, so shall we wanze and decay. **1614** D. DYKE *Myst. Self-Deceiv.* ii. 30 Doth Timothie weaken his constitution by abstinence? The Pharisee will neuer giue ouer till his complexion be wholly withered and wanzed. **1623** COCKERAM I, *Wanze*, to perish, to decay. **1633** D. R[OGERS] *Treat. Sacram.* ii. 46 Recover thy losse, quicken that hath wanzed, strengthen the feeble knees or hands. **1642** —— *Naaman* 118 In a short time have bewraied themselves to be time-servers, and wanzed away to nothing. *Ibid.* 111, 153. *a* **1825** FORBY *Voc. E. Anglia, Wanze*, to waste, pine, wither. **1917** HARDY *Moments of Vision* 171 Not as one wanzing weak From life's roar and reek, His rest still to seek.

Hence '**wanzing** *ppl. a.*, evanescent; '**wanzingness**.

1571 GOLDING *Calvin on Ps.* iii. 8 b, So did he not rashly thrust oute wanzing woordes [L. *voces evanidas*] into the aire as vnbeleuers are woont to do. **1633** D. R[OGERS] *Treat.*

Sacram. ii. 22 The life of faith..is very poore and wanzing in us. *Ibid.* 48 Each wanzing motion and Pang after faith. **1642** —— *Naaman* 143 That pleasingnesse of it..doth bewitch them so, that they rest in wanzing hope of it. *Ibid.* 268 Shewes them the vanity and wanzingnesse of their own principle.

wap, *sb.*[1] *Obs.* exc. *dial.* Also 4–5 **wappe.** [Belongs to WAP *v.*[1]]

1. A blow, knock, thump.

c **1400** *Destr. Troy* 6405 Ector for þat od dynt, ournyt in hert, Wode for the wap, as a wild lyon. *c* **1400** *Laud Troy Bk.* 9338 On smytes his felawe thorow the pap, And he ȝeues him a sori wap. **15..** *Christ's Kirk* xi, in *Bannatyne MS.* (Hunter. Club) 285 He hit him on the wame a wap, It buft lyk ony bleddir. **1810** *Splendid Follies* II. 138, I had such a plumper off the old mare the first time I went out! What a wap of the head I had surely. **1818** SCOTT *Br. Lamm.* xxv, A wap wi' a corner-stane o' Wolf's Crag wad defy the doctor! **1823** 'J. BEE' *Dict. Turf, Wap,* a species of slap, resounding, as if imparted by a wet dishclout. **1914** C. C. MURRAY in *Aberd. Univ. Rev.* Nov. 45 An' fat was a wap wi' a spainyie or tag To hands that were hard as a steen.

b. *at a wap*: at one blow, suddenly.

13.. *E.E. Allit. P.* C. 499 Þou..trauayledez neuer to tent hit þe tyme of an howre, Bot at a wap hit here wax & away at an oþer. *a* **1400** *Wars Alex.* 3040 Alexander allþire first on þaim all he settis And aithire ward at a wapp wiȝtly inIoynes. *Ibid.* 4142, 5318. *c* **1400** *Sege Jerus.* 515 (E.E.T.S.), & wel wenen at a wap alle þe wo[r]ld quelle. *c* **1460** *Towneley Myst.* xxiv. 314 As I wold at a wap wyn all at ones.

2. *Sc.* A sudden storm (of snow).

1818 SCOTT *Let.* in *Lockhart* (1837) IV. vi. 204 You will find it [a plaid] a good bosom friend..when your country avocations lead you to face a dry wap of snow.

3. A shake, flap; a sweeping or tossing movement.

a **1663** D. DICKSON *Serm.* Pract. Writ. (1845) I. 99 Preaching is like the wap of a fan, to tell the one that they are chaff [etc.]. *c* **1800** *'Leesome Brand'* vii. in Child *Ballads* I. 182 Ye do you to my father's stable, Where steeds do stand baith wight and able... Strike ane o them upo the back, The swiftest will gie his head a wap. **1820** SCOTT *Abbot* xvii, Pomp and pleasure pass away as speedily as the wap of a falcon's wing.

4. A pugilistic fight. Also, a quarrel. *Sc.*

1887 P. McNEILL *Blawearie* 24 It not unfrequently happened, if a well matched pair or two met and had not had their 'wap' out, both pits would be thrown idle on the Monday that all who wished might see the affair wound up. **1887** SERVICE *Life Duguid* xi. 68 It happened ae day that a neebor woman..and Bessie had a terr'ble wap.

†**wap**, *sb.*[2] *Obs.* In 5 **wapp**, 6 **wappe.** [f. WAP *v.*[3]] A kind of mongrel formerly used as a house-dog.

Owing to a mistake of his translator Fleming (1576), Caius has commonly been said to have identified the 'wappe' with the 'turnspit', and to have given *waupe* as an actual variant form. His Latin for *Wappe* is *Admonitor* (rendered 'Warner' by Fleming); for *Turnespete* he gives *Versator*.

1464 *Plumpton Corr.* (Camden) 14 Sir Henry Vavasor was gone hence or I wist, so that I might not speak to him for the wapp. **1570** CAIUS *De Canibus Brit.* 12 b, Ad postremum, degeneres, Wappe and Turnespete nominari dicebamus: hunc à verbo nostrati turne,..& spete..; illud à naturali canis voce Wau, quàm in latratu ædit admonendo. Vnde, originaliter Waupe dicendum fuit. Sed euphoniæ bonæque consonantiæ gratia, vocali in consonantem mutata, Wappe à nostris vocitatur. **1589** NASHE *Anat. Absurd.* B 4, The sillie Sheephearde committing his wandering sheepe to the custodie of his wappe.

†**wap**, *sb.*[3] *Obs. rare.* [? f. WAP *v.*[2]]

1. A turn of a string wrapped round something.

1545 ASCHAM *Toxoph.* II. (Arb.) 111 You must looke that youre bowe be well nocked for fere the sharpnesse of the horne shere a sunder the strynge. And that chaunceth ofte when in bending, the string hath but one wap to strengthe it wyth all. *Ibid.* 111 *below,* 119.

2. *Naut.* A shroud-stopper. [Perh. another word: cf. WARP *sb.*]

1704 J. HARRIS *Lex. Techn.* I, *Wapp,* is that Rope in a Ship, wherewith the Shrouds are set taught with Wale-knots; one end is made fast to the Shrouds, and to the other are brought the Laniards. **1867** SMYTH *Sailor's Word-bk.*, Wapp, or Whap.

3. (See quot.) *dial.*

1828 [CARR] *Craven Gloss., Wap,* a bundle of straw, called also a loggin.

wap (wɒp), *v.*[1] Now *dial.* Also 5 **quappe,** 9 *Sc.* **waup.** [Of obscure origin; cf. SWAP *v.* and *whap,* WHOP *v.*]

1. a. *trans.* To throw quickly or with violence. Often with adv. or phrase, *down, to the ground,* etc. †*to wap off*: to pull off roughly; †*to wap sindry* (see SUNDRY *adv.*), to scatter, disperse; *to wap wide,* to throw wide open.

c **1400** *Destr. Troy* 7297 Mony doughty þat day deghit in the fild, Mony [were] wofully woundit, & wappid to ground! *c* **1440** *York Myst.* xxxiii. 343 Do wappe of his wedis þat are worne. *c* **1470** *Gol. & Gaw.* 127 The yettis wappit war wyde. *c* **1480** HENRYSON *Paddock & Mouse* 171 (Bann.) Now on þe quheill, now wappit [*Harl.* wrappit] to þe ground. **1513** DOUGLAS *Æneis* VIII. iv. 150 Wyth branchis rent of treis, and quarrell stanis Of huge wecht doun wappand all at anis. **1562** WINȜET *Cert. Tract.* Wks. (S.T.S.) I. 94 Quhy hef ȝe wappit doun al the affixit tabellis of the Lord? **1563** —— tr. *Vincent Lirin.* v. II. 22 Than wes..monasteriis destroyit, clerkis wappit sindry [L. *clerici disturbati*], the ministeris of the Kirkis strikin [etc.]. *Ibid.* vi. II. 23 That be them he wald raiss vp his Kirkis afoir wappit doun. **1572** *Satir. Poems Reform.* xxxviii. 30 Be war with the wand syne he wapis in the fyre. **1596** DALRYMPLE tr. *Leslie's Hist. Scot.* (S.T.S.) I. 25 Gif thay sie ony fishe mair diligate..the pray quhilke..thay brocht far aff, with speid thay wap out of thair mouth. *Ibid.* II. 29 At last, the Jnglisman wappit fra his horse, the Scot winnis the Victorie. *c* **1730** RAMSAY *O Mither dear!* v, Get Johny's hand in haly band, Syne wap ye'r wealth together. **1828** [CARR] *Craven Gloss., Whap,* to shut or close with violence, as, 'twind waps door tull'. **1912** A. McCORMICK *Words fr. Wild-Wood* vi. 82, I had.. mechanically 'wapped' my line once or twice in the glassy pool above.

†**b.** In figurative expressions like *wapped in woe,* there is some doubt whether *wapped* belongs to this verb with the sense 'thrown', or to WAP *v.*[2] with the sense 'wrapped'. Cf. the similar use of WARP *v.* The word may have been variously apprehended by those who used the proverbial expression. *Obs.*

c **1375** *Sc. Leg. Saints* xliii. (*Cecilia*) 239 Ve sal be wappyt in til yre, percace in erde in brynnand fyre [L. *incurremus furorem exurentem in terris*]. *c* **1440** *York Myst.* xxxi. 12 In wrathe when we writhe, or in wrathenesse ar wapped. *c* **1440** *Ibid.* xlvi. 1 In waylyng and wepyng, in woo am I wapped. *c* **1450** HOLLAND *Houlate* 748 For ws, wappit in wo in this warld wyde, To thi son mak thi mane. *c* **1480** HENRYSON *Paddock & Mouse* 166 Now in fredome, now wappit in distres. *c* **1550** ROLLAND *Crt. Venus* Prol. 107 Syne the xij Signes, and of thair conuersatioun, How thay ar wapt to diuers variatioun. *Ibid.* II. 619, I se this warld wappit with variance. *Ibid.* 641 To Ilk man geuis in warld his fatall weir[d], Quhidder it be to weill wappit, or wo. *c* **1560** A. SCOTT *Poems* xx. 3 Oppressit hairt, indure..Wappit without recure In wo remidiless.

c. intr. *slang.* To copulate. *Obs.*

[**1567** T. HARMAN *Caveat* sig. G4v, He tooke his Iockam in his famble, and a wapping he went.] **1611** MIDDLETON & DEKKER *Roaring Girl* sig. K4v, Wee'l couch a hogshead vnder the Ruffemans, and there you [*sc.* Moll Cutpurse] shall wap with me, & Ile niggle with you. **1699** B. E. *New Dict. Canting Crew, Wap,* c. to Lie with a Man. *If she won't wap for a Winne, let her trine for a Make,* c. If she won't Lie with a Man for a Penny, let her Hang for a Half-penny. *Mort wap-apace,* c. a Woman of Experience, or very expert at the Sport. **1725** in Farmer & Henley *Slang* (1903) VII. 293/1 This doxy dell can cut been whids, And wap well for a win.

†**2.** To shake. *Obs.*—0

1570 LEVINS *Manip.* 27/24 To wappe, *motare, agitare.*

3. *intr.* To strike, knock *upon*; to strike *through.*

13.. *E.E. Allit. P.* B. 882 Þe ȝonge men..Wapped vpon þe wyket & wonnen hem tylle. *a* **1400–50** *Wars Alex.* 2226 Othire athils of armes Albastis bendis, Quirys out quarrels, quappid [*Dubl. MS.* wappyd] thurȝe mayles. **1889** H. JOHNSTON *Glenbuckie* 99 Yer cannon balls, well they wud just wap through them [spirits] and no do them wan bit o' hairm.

†**4.** Of the wind: To blow in gusts. Of a cloth: To flap in the wind. Of wings: To flap, beat. *Obs.*

13.. *Gaw. & Gr. Knt.* 2004 Þe werbelande wynde wapped fro þe hyȝe. *c* **1400** *Destr. Troy* 9513 The smorther, & the smoke of þe smert loghys..waivet in the welkyn, wappond full hote. *c* **1400** *Isumbras* 632 A rede clothe therinne he seghe Owte-wappande with the wynde. *a* **1600** *Flodden F.* i. (1664) 5 When flickering fame that monstrous wight With hundred wings wapping was blown.

5. Used to express the intermittent sound of shallow water over stones: cf. PLAP, PLOP *vbs.*

1910 J. MASEFIELD *Ballads & P., Fragments* 12 Simois babbles over stone And waps and gurgles to the sky.

Hence **wapping** *vbl. sb.* and *ppl. a.*

1398 TREVISA *Barth. De P.R.* v. xxxi. (1495) 142 Grete wappynge and lepynge in any of the rybbes betokeneth woo and sorowe other rauynge. **1610** S. RID *Martin Mark-All* sig. E3, *Nigling,* company keeping with a woman: this word is not vsed now, but *wapping,* and thereof comes the name *wapping morts* Whoores. **1612** DEKKER *O Per Se O* sig. O1v, And wapping Dell, that niggles well, And takes loure for her hire. **1629** GAULE *Holy Madn.* 296 The wapping of a Towell will urge a Beare. **1707** J. SHIRLEY *Triumph of Wit* (ed. 5) III. 198 Wapping thou I know do's love.

†**wap**, *v.*[2] *Obs.* Also 5 *inf.* **whappyn,** 4–6 **wappe.** [Of obscure origin; possibly an altered form of WARP *v.*; cf. WRAP *v.* and *wlappe* LAP *v.*[2]] *trans.* To wrap, envelop; also, to wrap (a covering) *about* something.

c **1375** *Sc. Leg. Saints* xvi. (*Magdalen*) 524 Þai lad þat body, þat ded was,..wappyt in a furrit mantele. *c* **1420** WYNTOUN *Cron.* cxlv. 1989 A mantill wappit him about. *c* **1425** *Cast. Persev.* 1212 in *Macro Plays,* Whanne ȝe be in bedde browth boþe, wappyd wel in worthy wede. *c* **1440** *Promp. Parv.* 287/1 Lappyn, or whappyn in cloþys, *involvo. Ibid.* 515/2 Wappon', or hyllyn' wythe clothys or oþer lyke, *tego, contego. Ibid.*, Wappyn', or wyndyn' abowte yn clothys, *involvo.* *c* **1440** *York Myst.* xlvi. 274 It [Mary's girdle] was wonte for to wappe þat worthy virgine. *c* **1440** *Alphabet of Tales* 211 Þat womman..had a little chylde syttand on hur kne wappid in a clothe. *c* **1460** *Towneley Myst.* xx. 593 Kythe youre strengthe, And wap you wightly in youre wede. **1501** DOUGLAS *Pal. Hon.* Prol. 40 The vmbrate treis that Tytan about wappit. **1542** *Acc. Ld. High Treas. Scot.* VIII. 131 Item, for ix stane merling cord deliverit to George Halyburtoun to wap and mak the lowpes of the somes and thetis, v li. viij s.

Hence †**wapping** *vbl. sb.*

c **1440** *Promp. Parv.* 515/2 Wappynge, happynge or hyllynge (*v.rr.* lappynge, lappinge), *coopertura, coopericio* (*involucio*).

†**wap**, *v.*[3] *Obs.* Also 7 **whap.** [Echoic.] *intr.* To bark. Hence †'**wapping** *vbl. sb.* and *ppl. a.*

c **1440** *Promp. Parv.* 515/2 Wappyn', or baffyn' as howndys, *nicto,* Cath. *Ibid.*, Wappon' or berkyn', *idem quod* berkyn, *supra. Ibid.* 516/1 Wappynge, of howndys, whan þey folow here pray or that they wolde harme to..*nicticio, nictacio. Ibid.*, Wappynge (of howndys, MS. *K.*) or berkynge, *bajulatus, latratus.* **1642** FULLER *Holy & Prof. St.* v. iii. 366 As the harmlesse wapping of a curs'd curre may stir up a fierce mastiffe to the worrying of sheep. **1650** —— *Pisgah* III. i. 409 Solomon was an absolute Prince,..in his peaceable Countrey, where no dog durst bark against him (save two or three whapping curs toward the end of his reign).

wap, occas. spelling of WHOP *v.*

‖**wapacut** (ˈwɒpəkʌt). Also 8–9 **wapacuthu.** [American Indian; Watkins *Cree Dict.* 1865 has the form *wapikunee*; the Montagnais form is given as *wapikulu.*] 'A large white spotted owl, believed to be the common snowy owl, *Nyctea scandiaca*' (*Cent. Dict.*).

1785 PENNANT *Arct. Zool.* II. 231 Red, Mottled, and Wapacuthu Owl. *Ibid.* 232 Called by the Indians, Wapacuthu, or the Spotted Owl. **1828–32,** WEBSTER *Wapacut,* the spotted owl of Hudson's Bay.

wapato(o: see WAPPATOO.

waped, var. WHAPED *pa. pple.*, amazed, bewildered.

wapen(e, obs. forms of WEAPON.

wapens(c)haw, variant of WAPPENS(C)HAW.

wapentake (ˈwɒp(ə)nteɪk). Now *Hist.* Forms: 1 **wǽpenȝetæc** (*dat.* **-tace**), **wǽpentake, wapentac,** 3 **-tak,** 4 **wapne-, wepentake,** 5 **wapyntak,** 5–7 **wapentache** (5 **-tage,** 7 **weapontack, -tage**), 6–7 **wapentack,** (8 **-tac**), 6–8 **wappentake,** (6 **wapintake,** 8 **waking take**), 4– **wapentake**; (5 **wepyntale, -taille**). [a. ON. *vápnatak,* f. *vápna* genit. pl. of *vápn* WEAPON + *tak* act of taking (related to *taka* to TAKE). The late OE. *wǽpenȝetæc* shows assimilation of form to native compounds like *wǽpenȝewrixle* exchange of blows.

The recorded senses of the word in ON. are: (1) a vote of consent expressed by waving or brandishing weapons; (2) a vote or resolution of a deliberative assembly; (3) in Iceland, the breaking up of the session of the Althingi, when the members resumed their weapons that had been laid aside during the sittings. In English there is no trace of these senses, and the development of the actual sense can only be explained conjecturally. It is noteworthy that 'wapentakes', like 'hundreds', often received their names from some natural or artificial object (e.g. a barrow or a tree) which afforded a suitable rallying-place for open-air meetings. Assuming that in England *wapentake* originally meant the act of signifying assent at a public assembly, it seems not improbable that the men of the district whose place of meeting was (e.g.) at Osgod's Cross might be said to belong to 'the wapentake of Osgod's Cross (Osgoldcross)'; the use of the word to denote a territorial division would thus be sufficiently accounted for.]

A subdivision of certain English shires, corresponding to the 'hundred' (HUNDRED 5) of other counties.

The shires which had divisions so termed were Yorkshire, Derbyshire, Notts, Lincolnshire, Northamptonshire, and Leicestershire; in all of which the Danish element in the population was large. In Derbyshire there was latterly only one wapentake (that of Wirksworth), the other divisions of the shire being termed 'hundreds'. In Lincolnshire most of the county divisions were 'wapentakes', but a few were called 'hundreds' and 'sokes'. Traces of the existence of the term remained in popular use in other counties, as Cheshire and Cumberland into the 20th cent.

c **1000** *Laws of Edgar* IV. c. vi. (Lieberm.), & ælc mon mid heora ȝewitnysse bigcge & sylle ælc þara ceapa, þe he bigcge oððe sylle aþer oððe burȝe oððe on wæpenȝetace. *c* **1000** *Laws of Ethelred* III. c. i. §2 (Lieberm.) On wæpentake. **1086** *Domesday Bk.* (1783) I. 272 Derbyscire... Scarvedele Wapentac... Hammenstan Wapent. *Ibid.* 290 Snotinghamscire... Brocolvestov Wapent. Bernesedelav Wap. *Ibid.* 315 Evrvicscire... Siraches Wapentac. *a* **1325** *MS. Rawl. B.* 520 lf. 46 On Þusse manere sullen þe enquerours gon fram wapnetake to wapnet[ake]. **1326** *Rolls of Parlt.* II. 10/1 Et qe nule Baillie, ne Hundred, ne Wapentake, ne soit lesse a plus haut ferme qe les auncienes fermes. **1338** R. BRUNNE *Chron.* (1725) 145 Þe bisshop of Durham bouht Saberg, with þe wapentake. **1387** TREVISA *Higden* (Rolls) II. 97 Wepentake and an hondred is al oon, for þe contray of an hondred townes were i-woned to ȝilde vppe wepene in þe comynge of þe lord. *c* **1400** *Brut* I. 235 Kyng Edward [*sc.* Edw. II]..by his lettres ordeynede, þat euery hundred & wapentake of Engeland [etc.]. **1444** *Rolls of Parlt.* V. 110/1 That no Shirref lete to ferme..his Counte, ne noon of his Baillywykes, Hundreth' ne Wapentakes. ? **1556** in Pettus *Fodinæ Reg.* (1670) 95 The custom of the Mines within the Wappentake of Wricksworth. **1599** NASHE *Lenten Stuffe* 6 All the hundreds and wapentakes nine miles compasse, fetch the best of their viands and mangery from her market. **1641** BEST *Farm. Bks.* (Surtees) 90 There is in every shiere soe many ridinges, in everie ridinge soe many weapontackes. **1665** J. NORTH in *Extr. S.P. rel. Friends* III. (1912) 234 To ympannell a Jury out of that weapontage out of such Townes, as are not within Doncaster liberty. *c* **1710** CELIA FIENNES *Diary* (1888) 183 Richmondshire has in it 5 waking takes as they call them. **1717** GAY *Ep. to Lowndes* 12 Great L—— his praise should swell the trump of fame And Rapes and Wapentakes resound his name. **1769** *Ann. Reg.* 66/2 One of the high constables of Osgoldcross was indicted for extorting..1250*l.* from twenty-five townships belonging to his wapentake. **1797** BRYDGES *Homer Trav.* I. 119 As for these various ragged packs Of rogues from different wapentakes. **1836** *Penny Cycl.* V. 238 The petty sessions for the wapentakes of Kirton and Skirbeck are held every Wednesday. **1846** McCULLOCH *Acc. Brit. Empire* (1854) I. 161 Nottinghamshire is divided into 6 wapentakes or hundreds. **1914** *Victoria Hist. County York* I. 36 The Wapentake of Gilling West containing the parishes of [etc.]. .. This wapentake was held by the successive lords of Richmondshire, which it followed in descent.

b. The judicial court of such a subdivision.

14.. *Customs of Malton* in *Engl. Misc.* (Surtees) 59 Yffe any man..be sommonyd..to the wapyntak. **1611** SPEED *Theat. Gt. Brit.* I. xxx. §4. 57 Aboue this, and held 12 times a yeare, was our Hundred or Wapentake. **1676** *Lond. Gaz.* No. 1095/4 If any person or persons shall apprehend..the said Robbers, and give notice thereof to the Wapentack of Aslaccoe in the County of Lincoln..they shall have 50 *l.* reward. **1809** BAWDWEN *Domesday Bk., York* etc. 473 This belonged to St. Benedict of Ramsey, according to the testimony of the jurors of the wapentake [L. *testimonium hominum de Wapentac*]. **1898** B. KIRKBY *Lakeland Wds.* s.v., 'If he doesn't pay up Ah'll set t' wapen-tack on tull him.' This officer is reported to have existed in the town of Kendal till as late as 1836.

c. *attrib.*: ***wapentake court, fine.***

1543 *Fountains Abbey* (Surtees) I. 407 Paid to the exchetor ..for Wapin take fyne callyd castle worke, iij[s]. iiij[d]. **1658** HUBBERTHORN *Sufferings for Tythes* 13 William Iackson for tythes of ten shillings value, had sixteen shillings taken by a judgment in the Weapontage-Court. **1874** STUBBS *Const. Hist.* v. §46 This court, the hundred-gemot or wapentake court, was held every month.

wapher, obs. form of WAFER.

wapin, obs. form of WEAPON.

wapins(c)haw: see WAPPENS(C)HAW.

Wapishana (wæpɪˈʃɑːnə), *sb.* and *a.* Also **Wapishiana, Wapisiana;** 9 **Wapiana, Wapisiano.**

A. *sb.* **a.** A member of an Arawakan people of Guyana and Brazil; also this people collectively. **b.** Their language. **B.** *adj.* Of, pertaining to, or designating this people or their language.

1855 H. G. DALTON *Hist. Brit. Guiana* I. ii. 77 The Acosi, Awake, Wapishiana..are also the names of several other tribes which have been met with by late travellers. *Ibid.* (*caption facing* p. 80) The 'Belle' of the Wapisianas. **1868** W. H. BRETT *Indian Tribes of Guiana* II. v. 280 Southward of Roraima the great range of the Pacaraima Mountains extends... Beyond it are the savannahs of the Rupununi, inhabited by the *Wabean* or *Wapisiana* nation. **1883** E. F. IM THURN *Among Indians of Guiana* vi. 165 The languages of the four branches, Warrau, Arawak, Wapiana, and Carib, will be found to be quite distinct from each other. **1924** 15 see LAP *sb.*[1] 4 c]. **1949** *Caribbean Q.* I. III. 41 Of the two tribes likely to be displaced, one, the Wapisiana, is not likely to be demoralised. **1959** P. CAPON *Amongst those Missing* 167 'An Indian, isn't he?' asked Judith. 'I think so. He has the look of a Wapishana.' **1972** S. E. BROCK *Jungle Cowboy* xii. 135 *Wai-Wai* is the Wapishana for tapioca.

wapiti (ˈwɒpɪtɪ). Also ? *erron.* **wipiti.** [a. Cree *wapitik* (Shawnee *wahpetee*) lit. 'white deer'.] The North American stag or elk, *Cervus canadensis*, allied to but larger than the European Red Deer. Also attrib., ***wapiti deer, stag.***

1817 *Thomson's Ann. Philos.* IX. 325 At the same meeting [of the Linnæan Society] was read a description, by Dr. Leach, of the Wapiti deer, a species of animal from the banks of the Missouri. **1829** SIR J. RICHARDSON *Fauna Bor. Amer.* I. 251 *Cervus strongyloceros.* (Schreber.) The Wapiti. *Ibid.* 252 The trivial name of 'wapiti' has been only recently adopted in scientific works. **1890** S. W. BAKER *Wild Beasts* II. 200 If a wapiti stag were placed in a line with a fine German, and a Scotch red-deer, there would be an immense difference in size. **1901** P. FOUNTAIN *Deserts N. Amer.* ix. 179 The wapiti deer (which the American trappers and people always call the elk). **1904** —— *Gt. North-West* v. 49 The wipiti is 'the elk' of Americans. *Ibid.* xi. 119 The wipiti. *Comb.* **1880** *19th Cent.* Oct. 593 (*title*), Wapiti-running on the plains.

b. The flesh of this animal.

1884 *Pall Mall Gaz.* 3 May 3/2 Second course: Californian salmon, roast wapiti.

wapito, variant of WAPPATO(O.

†**Wap-John.** *slang. Obs.* (See quot.)

1826 *Sporting Mag.* XVIII. 278 *note*, A gentleman's coachman, or what we call 'a Wap-John'.

†ˈ**wapman.** *Obs.* Forms: 1–2 **wǣpman, wǣpnman, wǣpen-, wēpenmon,** 3 **wepman,** (*Ormin* **weppmann**), **weopmonne, wepmon(ne, wapmon, -man.** [OE. *wǣpnman*, f. *wǣpn* WEAPON (= *membrum virile*) + *man* MAN *sb.* Cf. OE. *wǣpned* adj., male.] A man as distinguished from a woman, a male human being.

c **950** *Lindisf. Gosp.* Luke ii. 23 Eȝhuelc he *vel* woepenmon to-untynes hrif [Vulg. *omne masculinum adaperiens uuluam*]. *c* **1000** ÆLFRIC *Deut.* xxii. 5 Ne scride nan wif hiȝ mid wæpmannes reafe, ne wæpman mid wifmannes reafe. **1123** *O.E. Chron.* (Laud. MS.), Forbearn eall meast se burh of Lincolne & micel ungerime folces wæpmen & wimmen forburnon. *c* **1200** ORMIN 7998 Þær comenn forrþ to lofenn himm An weppmann & an widdwe. *c* **1205** LAY. 1119 Leode nere þar nane ne wapmen [*c* **1275** wepmen] ne wifmen. *a* **1225** *Ancr. R.* 316 Forði mi sunne is more þen of one weopmonne. *a* **1250** *Owl & Night.* 1379 Luue..Bitweone wepmon & wimmane [*Jesus MS.* þe mon & wymmone]. *c* **1250** *Gen. & Ex.* 1001 And of is hird euerilc wapman wurð circumcis. *c* **1275** *XI Pains of Hell* 145 in *O.E. Misc.* 151 Uvrþer þer beoþ wimmen and wepmen.

b. Comb.: **wapman-kin,** persons of the male sex.

c **1200** ORMIN 4092 All þatt weppmannkinn þatt wass inn hise walde. *c* **1205** LAY. 498 Al þæt wapmon-cun [*c* 1295 monkun] þa mihte beren wapen.

wapnetake, obs. form of WAPENTAKE.

wapnis, obs. pl. form of WEAPON.

waponschawing, var. WAPPENS(C)HAWING.

wapour, obs. form of VAPOUR.

wappato(o (ˈwɒpətəʊ, -uː). *U.S.* Also **whapto, wapto, wapito, wapato(o, wapata.** [a. Cree *wapatowa* white mushroom.] The tubers of the plant *Sagittaria variabilis*, used for food by N. Amer. Indians.

1807 P. GASS *Jrnl.* 160 We got some dogs and roots from the natives. The roots..are called whapto; resemble a potatoe when cooked, and are about as big as a hen egg. *Ibid.* 170 We..procured a few roots, called Wapto. **1814** *Lewis & Clark's Exped.* (1893) 693 Here he treated us with a root.. which they call wappatoo. **1838** PARKER *Exploring Tour beyond Rocky Mts.* 223 The wappatoo is the *sagittaria*, or arrow-head... The root is bulbous, and becomes soft by roasting, forming a nourishing and agreeable food. **1841** CATLIN *N. Amer. Ind.* (1844) II. xlviii. 113 The wapito, a bulbous root much like a turnip. **1893** E. COUES in *Lewis & Clark's Exped.* 824 *note*, The wappatoo is the root of *Sagittaria variabilis*,..the common arrowhead.

wappen, obs. form of WEAPON.

†ˈ**wappened,** *a. Obs. rare*$^{-1}$. Of obscure origin and meaning, perh. corrupt. Cf. WAPPERED *a.*, which Singer proposed as a conjectural reading.

1607 SHAKS. *Timon* IV. iii. 38 This is it That makes the wappen'd Widdow wed againe.

wappens(c)haw (ˈwapnʃɑ). *Sc.* Forms: α. 6–7, 9 **wap(p)ins(c)haw,** 7 **waponeschawe,** 9 **wap(p)ens(c)haw;** β. *semi-modernized* **weapons(c)haw.** [f. *wapin* WEAPON + *schaw* SHOW *sb.* Prob. orig. a shortening of the older WAPPENSCHAWING.

Both words are used *Hist.* by Scott; the official edition of the Statutes of Scotland (1814) has only *wapinschaw* in the index, though the actual text of the Acts has *wapinschawing* exc. in 1503 (see below).

Cf. G. *waffenschau*, given by Adelung as an obsolete HG. word, but prob. a mere 18th c. adaptation of Du. *wappenschouwing* = next.]

1. *Hist.* = WAPPENS(C)HAWING.

a **1503** *Sc. Acts Jas. IV* (1814) II. 243/2 Item þ[t] all scotland mak ȝerely þair wapinschawis apon thursday in wit-sonday wolk. *Ibid.* 251/2 þ[t] all scotland mak þair wappin-schawis [etc.]. **1609** SKENE *Reg. Maj., Stat. Will.* c. xxiii. §6 It is statute, that wapinschaw sal be keiped & haldin. **1627** in Cramond *Ann. Banff* (1891) I. 56 To the effect they may be the better prepared agane the xxiij of this instant qlk is the principall waponeschawe day. **1816** SCOTT *Old Mort.* ii, [The Calvinists] discouraged, as far as lay in their power, even the ancient wappen-schaws, as they were termed, when the feudal array of the county was called out, and each crown-vassal was required to appear with such muster of men and armour as he was bound to make by his fief. **1905** G. WILSON *Ann. Glover Incorporat. Perth* 13 Other and more rational forms of amusements became popular with our Craft..such as wappenschaws, foot-ball, quoits, golf, archery, etc.

β. **1776** *Herd's Sc. Songs* II. 122 When we went to the field of war, And to the Weaponshaw, Willie. **1805** SCOTT *Last Minstr.* IV. xxviii, Already on dark Ruberslaw The Douglas holds his weapon-schaw. **1830** —— *Doom of Devorgoil* I. i, Godden, good yeoman. Come you from the Weapon-shaw? **1830** —— *Demonol.* i. 14 The majority..had considered the heavenly phenomenon as a supernatural weapon-schaw for the purpose of a sign and warning of civil wars to come.

2. A volunteer rifle-meeting.

1868 *Morning Star* 9 Jan., At Edinburgh, on New Year's Day, the Wappinschaw was celebrated. Years ago this, we believe, was a gathering at which the country side shot, with homely smooth-bore pieces, for hams and cheeses, but until revived in 1866 the custom had long fallen into disuse. In that year the Wappinschaw was rehabilitated by the local volunteers. **1869** *Pall Mall Gaz.* 2 July 6 The Aberdeen Volunteer wapinschaw was held yesterday. The chief prize ..was won by Ensign Niven.

b. *South Africa.* Used to render Du. *wappenschouwing* (see next), applied by the Boers to a rifle-shooting competition.

1899 *Daily News* 23 June 5/4 The Boers never drill, and it is thought that the scene witnessed was probably an ordinary season's wapenshaw. *Ibid.* 13 Oct. 5/5 The local Dutch have decided to postpone their wappenschaw (rifle meeting) at the request of the magistrate.

wappens(c)hawing (ˈwapnʃɑɪŋ). *Sc. Hist.* Forms: α. 5 **wapinschawin, wapynschawing,** 5–6 **wap(p)inschawing, -schewing,** 6 **waping-, vapin-, wapo(u)nschawing, vaupynschauyng,** 9 **wappenschawing;** β. *semi-modernized* 6 **weapon-showing,** 9 **weapon-shawing.** [f. *wapen* WEAPON + *schawing* SHOWING *vbl. sb.*; = Du. *wapenschouwing*. Cf. prec.] A periodical muster or review of the men under arms within a particular lordship or district.

1424 *Sc. Acts Jas. I* (1814) II. 8/2 It is ordanyt þan in ilk scheredome of þe realme þere be maid wapynschawing four tymis in þe ȝer. **1512** *Reg. Privy Seal Scot.* I. 366/2 The kingis hienes..has ordanit him to resave the musteris and wapinschewingis of all his folkis. **1541** in *15th Rep. Hist. MSS. Comm.* App. VIII. 66 The Wapinschawing off Annerdale tane be my Lord Maxwell wppon Burniswerkhill. **1549** *Compl. Scot.* xi. (1872) 96 Kyng eduard..ordand thre vaupynschauyngis to be maid al on ane day in scotland be scottis men.., and at thay vaupynschauyngis, al the vaupynis and armour of scotland to be delyuerit to the inglismen. **1560** in Calderwood *Hist. Kirk* (1843) II. 3 That frome hencefurth they be not compelled to tak on credite, they sall be everie moneth satisfeid of their wages, so that two Scotish lords, chosin by the counsell, may present it at weapon-showing and musters of the said men of warre. *a* **1578** LINDESAY (Pitscottie) *Chron. Scot.* (S.T.S.) II. 321 Thair vas vapin-schawing throch all Scotland. **1633** in *Reg. Mag. Sig. Scot.* 1634, 45/2 At all generall musteris and wapounschawingis within the said schirrefdome. **1828** SCOTT *F.M. Perth* iii, The best wrestler,..the king of the weapon-shawing—the breaker of mad horses. **1830** —— *Doom of Devorgoil* I. i, Hark! they have broken up the weapon-shawing. **1905** G. WILSON *Ann. Glover Incorporat. Perth* 13 On one of these occasions of wappenschawing a serious riot took place.

wappentake, obs. form of WAPENTAKE.

†ˈ**wapper,** *sb. Obs. rare*$^{-1}$. [a. Du. *wapper*, cogn. with *wapperen* to swing: see next.] ? A (leaden) ball attached to a strap used as a striking weapon. So †ˈ**wapper** *v.*[1] *trans.*, to strike (a person) with this weapon.

1481 CAXTON *Reynard* (Arb.) 16 That one had an leden malle and that other a grete leden wapper therwyth they wappred and al for slyngred hym.

wapper (ˈwɒpə(r)), *a.* Now *dial.* [Back-formation from *wapper-eyed, -jawed*: see WAPPER *v.*[2]] †**a.** Of the eyes: Blinking, unsteady. *Obs.* **b.** Of a jaw (see quots.). *dial.* and *U.S.*

1581 J. BELL *Haddon's Answ. Osor.* 280 What if he will geve no credite to your opinions? no nor yet to your wapper eyes that are bleared and dimme with rancour and malice? **1608** ARMIN *Nest Ninn.* (1842) 6 But such was his, who thus busied, was tooke napping by the weale publike, who smiles upon him with a wapper eye, a iealous countenance, and bids him all haile. *a* **1825** FORBY *Voc. E. Anglia, Wapper-jaws*, a wry mouth; a warped jaw. **1891** *Century Dict.*, *Wapper-jaw.* 2. A projecting under-jaw. (Colloq., U.S.)

wapper, *v.*[1]: see WAPPER *sb.*

wapper (ˈwɒpə(r)), *v.*[2] *Obs.* exc. *dial.* [Perh. cogn. w. WAVE *v.*; cf. Du. *wapperen* to swing, oscillate, waver.]

1. *intr.* To blink the eyes. Also, 'to move tremulously' (Halliwell 1847, as a Somerset word).

1575 *Mirr. Mag.* I, *Nennius* 75 b, But still he stode his face to set awrye, And wappering turnid vp his white of eye. **1622** MABBE tr. *Aleman's Guzman d'Alf.* I. 40 She was toothlesse, chap-falne, hollow-eyed, and wappering withall.

2. *passive.* To be tired *out*.

1898 J. A. GIBBS *Cotswold Village* xii. 258 [Period 1592] Thou'll not see Stratford to-night, sir, thy horse is wappered out. *Foot-note.* Wappered = tired. A Cotswold word.

3. Comb.: **wapper-eyed** *a. dial.*, blinking, blear-eyed (see quots.); **wapper-jawed** *a. U.S.*

1604 T. M. *Black Bk.* D 2 b, I..changed my shape into a little wapper-eid Constable, to winke and blinke at small faults. *a* **1700** B. E. *Dict. Cant. Crew, Wapper-eyed*, that has Sore or running Eyes. **1746** *Exmoor Scolding* (E.D.S.) Gloss., *Wapper-eyed*, goggle-eyed, having full rolling Eyes; or looking like one scared; or squinting like a Person overtaken with Liquor. **1848** LOWELL *Fable for Critics* Prelim. note, Fancy an heir that a father had seen born well featured and fair, turning suddenly..squint-eyed, hair-lipped, wapper-jawed. **1849** 'N. HOGG' *Poet. Lett.* (1850) Gloss., *Wapper-hy'd*, sleepy, groggy. **1886** *W. Somerset Word-bk., Wapper-eyed*, having quick-moving restless eyes —constantly rolling from side to side, as is seen in very nervous persons.

wapper, variant of WHOPPER.

ˈ**wappered,** *a.* Now *dial.* Also **woppered.** [f. WAPPER *v.* + -ED.] Fatigued, wearied.

[**1612**: implied in UNWAPPERED.] **1868** R. W. HUNTLEY *Cotswold Dial., Wappered*, fatigued; beaten. **1890** *Gloucestersh. Gloss., Woppered*, restless, fatigued. (Hund. of Berk.)

wappet: see WHAPPET *Obs.*, kind of dog.

wappie (ˈwɒpɪ). *West Indies.* Also **wap(p)ee, wappy.** [perh. f. WAP *sb.*[1] + -IE.] A gambling game played with cards.

1943 in Cassidy & Le Page *Dict. Jamaican Eng.* (1967) 462/2 *Wappie*, a game of cards. **1952** S. SELVON *Brighter Sun* ii. 26 The older boys and men play wapee, a gambling game with cards. *Ibid.* vii. 123 Ah play cards—Ah was a rummy test in me days, and don't talk 'bout wappee! Yuh cud play cards? **1952** *Evening News* (Port of Spain) 22 Jan. 12/3 Tom ..happens to back the right cards at wappie. **1959** V. S. NAIPAUL *Miguel St.* i. 12 They played *wappee* and drank rum. **1968** K. S. LA FORTUNE *Legend of T-Marie* xii. 51 Cab-men sat on benches or on boxes talking politics or playing wappie.

wappin, obs. Sc. form of WEAPON.

†**Wappi'neer.** *Obs.* [f. the place-name *Wapping*, a part of London close to the Docks + -EER[1].] An inhabitant of Wapping. Also *attrib.* Cf. WAPPINGER.

1690 D'URFEY *Collin's Walk* II. 72 In kennel sowc'd o're Head and Ears Amongst the crowding Wappineers. **1710** SHADWELL *Fair Quaker of Deal* Dram. Pers., *Flip*, The Commadore, a most illiterate Wappineer-Tar. *a* **1792** HORNE in *Olla Podrida* (1820) I. 135 Whilst a Wappineer, a Mile-ender, and a Boroughman, are terms proverbially used, about the Exchange.., to express an inferior order of beings.

wappin(g): see WHOPPING *ppl. a.*

Wappinger (ˈwɒpɪŋə(r)). [f. *Wapping* + -ER[1].] An inhabitant of Wapping. Cf. WAPPINEER.

a **1734** NORTH *Exam.* III. viii. (1740) 585 Rous..was a thorough paced Traitor, and looked upon to be Paymaster of the Mob; a Wappinger, and good at mustering Seamen. **1898** BESANT *Orange Girl* I. vi, The girls..stared with more rudeness than one would expect even from a Wappinger.

waps, obs. or dial. form of WASP.

wapto, variant of WAPPATO(O.

wapure, wapyn(e, obs. ff. VAPOUR, WEAPON.

wapynschawing: see WAPPENS(C)HAWING.

wapyntak, obs. form of WAPENTAKE.

waqf, var. WAKF.

war (wɔː(r)), *sb.*[1] Forms: 2 uuerre, werre, wyrre, 3 weorre, worre, 3–5 werre, (4 *pl.* werren), 4–6 werr, 5 guerre, gwerre, 4, 5–6 *Sc.* wer, 4–5, 6–7 *Sc.* were, 4 *Sc.* vere, 4, 7 *Sc.* weer, 4–6 *Sc.* veyr, 5 *Sc.* veir, 5–6 *Sc.* weire, weyr(e, 4–9 *Sc.* weir, 6 *Sc.* wair, wiar, weare, veare, 7 *Sc.* ware, 8 *Sc.* wear, 5 waar, 5–7 warr(e, 6– war. [Late OE. (*c* 1050) *wyrre, werre*, a. North-eastern OF. *werre* = Central OF. and mod.F. *guerre*, Pr. *guerra, gerra*, Sp., Pg., It. *guerra* (med.L. *werra, guerra*) a. OHG. *werra* (MHG. *werre*) confusion, discord, strife, related to the OHG., OS. *werran* str. vb., to bring into confusion or discord (whence mod.G. *wirren* wk. vb. to confuse, perplex; the earlier vb. survives in *verworren* ppl. a., confused), f. Teut. root **werz-, *wers-*, whence also WORSE *a.*

It is a curious fact that no Germanic nation in early historic times had in living use any word properly meaning 'war', though several words with that meaning survived in poetry, in proverbial phrases, and in compound personal names. The Romanic-speaking peoples, who were obliged to avoid the L. *bellum* on account of its formal coincidence with *bello-* beautiful, found no nearer equivalent in Teut. than *werra*. In OE. the usual translation of *bellum* was *ȝewin*, struggle, strife. The continental Teut. langs. later developed separate words for 'war': G. *krieg* (whence Sw., Da. *krig*), Du. *oorlog*; Icelandic uses *ófriðr* 'un-peace'.]

I. 1. a. Hostile contention by means of armed forces, carried on between nations, states, or rulers, or between parties in the same nation or state; the employment of armed forces against a foreign power, or against an opposing party in the state.

For *civil, intestine*, etc. *war*, see the adjs. ***war to the knife*** [after Sp. *guerra al cuchillo*], see KNIFE *sb.* 1 b; ***war to the death***, see DEATH *sb.* 12 c.

1154 *O.E. Chron.* (Laud MS.) an. 1140, Þer efter wæx suythe micel uuerre betuyx þe king & Randolf eorl of Cæstre. *a* **1225** *Leg. Kath.* 20 Ah se wide him weox weorre on euch halue [L. *bellis undique consurgentibus*]. *c* **1290** *Holy Rood* 336 in *S. Eng. Leg.* 11 Sethþe þare cam an Aumperour þat hiet costantin; In weorre and bataylle he was so muche þat þare-of nas no fin. **1297** R. GLOUC. (Rolls) 1321 Þe.. king nis to preisi noȝt þat in time of worre as a lomb is boþe mek & milde, & in time of pes as leon boþe cruel & wilde. *c* **1375** *Sc. Leg. Saints* vii. (*James Minor*) 462 Iosaphus, prince wes & als ledare of þat towne, bath in pese & vere. **1377** LANGL. *P. Pl.* B. XVIII. 226 Wote no wighte what werre is þere þat pees regneth. **1421** LYDG. *Horse, Goose, Sheep* 425 in *Pol. Rel. & L. Poems* (1903) trs. 33 Thou Causist werre and seist thu louest pees. *c* **1449** PECOCK *Repr.* v. x. 537 Whanne therupon hangith ceesing of greet werre and making of greet pees. **1462** in *Eng. Hist. Rev.* (1914) Oct. 720 The said Erle shal haue the iij[rds] of all wynnyngs of werre won or gotten by the said Cristofre. *c* **1480** HENRYSON *Test. Cres.* 196 Ane horn he blew..Quhilk all this warld with weir hes maid to wag. **1513** MORE *Rich. III* Wks. 36/2 Richarde Duke of Yorke..beganne not by warre, but by lawe, to challenge the crown. **1573** *Reg. Privy Council Scot.* II. 218 Except sic change and fortoun of weare as salbe commoun and alike to bayth. **1593** SHAKS. *3 Hen. VI*, IV. vii. 36 These Gates must not be shut, But in the Night, or in the time of Warre. **1613** J. SARIS *Voy. Japan* (Hakl. Soc.) 54 The prince of Tidore, whoe had beene out in warr, and was retorned with 100 Ternatans heades. **1648** MILTON *Sonn. to Fairfax* 10 For what can Warr, but endless warr still breed, Till Truth, and Right from Violence be freed. **1690** LOCKE *Govt.* II. iii. §16 The State of War is a State of Enmity and Destruction. **1697** DRYDEN *Virg. Georg.* IV. 810 Mighty Cæsar, thund'ring from afar, Seeks on Euphrates' Banks the Spoils of War. **1728** RAMSAY *Lochaber* i, The dangers attending on wear. **1759** B. PORTEUS *Death* 179 War its thousands slays, Peace its ten thousands. **1765** BLACKSTONE *Comm.* I. vii. 250 In order to make war completely effectual, it is necessary with us in England that it be publicly declared and duly proclaimed by the king's authority. **1846** *Congressional Globe* 14 May 808/1 It puts it in the power of any military squad..to put this nation in a state of war. The killing of people is not war. In order to constitute war between nations, that killing must be sanctioned by the war-making power. **1857** BUCKLE *Civiliz.* I. viii. 551 Formerly religion had been the cause of war, and had also been the pretext under which it was conducted. **1871** MOZLEY *Univ. Serm.* v. (1876) 101 War is one of these rights, because under the division of mankind into distinct nations it becomes a necessity.

Personified. **1563** SACKVILLE *Induct. Mirr. Mag.* lvi, Lastly stoode Warre in glitteryng armes yclad, With visage grym. *c* **1614** SIR W. MURE *Dido & Æneas* I. 37 Bloody warre, the mistres of debait. **1803** WORDSW. *Addr. Kilchurn Castle* 1 Child of loud-throated War!

b. *transf.* and *fig.* Applied *poet.* or rhetorically to any kind of active hostility or contention between living beings, or of conflict between opposing forces or principles.

a **1200** *Moral Ode* 246 in *O.E. Hom.* I. 175 Þa þe ledden here lif in werre and in winne. *c* **1275** *On Serving Christ* 37 in *O.E. Misc.* 91 Bi-leueþ oure weorre, warlawes wode. *a* **1300** *Cursor M.* 9666 Þes mai nourquar abide þar hate wons, or werr, or pride. **1303** R. BRUNNE *Handl. Synne* 10570 Þarfore þat tyme was mykyl þro, And ofte was boþe werre and wo. *c* **1374** CHAUCER *Troylus* v. 234 Who kan conforten now youre hertes werre? *c* **1386** —— *Frankl. T.* 29 Ne wolde neuere God bitwixe vs tweyne, As in my gilt, were outher werre or stryf. **1456** SIR G. HAYE *Law Arms* (S.T.S.) 5 Amang the quhilkis is grete discorde discensioun and were. **1624** QUARLES *Job Milit.* xviii. 30 Know'st thou the cause of Snow, or Haile, which are My fierce Artill'ry, in my time of warre? **1774** GOLDSM. *Nat. Hist.* V. 306 Whatever be the motives that thus arrest a flock of birds in their flight, whether they be of gallantry or of war, it is certain that [etc.]. **1817** BYRON *Manfred* II. ii. 135, I have affronted death—but in the war Of elements the waters shrunk from me. **1912** L. TRACY *Mirabel's Isl.* ii. (1915) 32 His keen hearing was of no avail in that war of wind and wave.

c. The *plural* (esp. with def. art.) was formerly often used in the same sense as the sing.

to have been in the wars (colloq.), to show marks of injury or traces of rough usage.

c **1374** CHAUCER *Anel. & Arc.* 22 Whan Theseus with werres longe and grete The aspre folke of Cithe had ouercome. *a* **1400** R. GLOUC. (Rolls) App. Z. 19 Wel fale ȝer þer after þo worres aslakede. **1448–9** METHAM *Amoryus & Cl.* 218 And for yowre labour in werris that with vs ye haue be, We þanke yow. **1470–85** MALORY *Arthur* VI. x. 198 For knyghtes that ben..lecherous shal not be..fortunate vnto the werrys. **1538** STARKEY *England* (1878) 47 So dothe the multytude of pepul..sone, by warrys and iniury of ennemys, wyth-out strenghth, lose hys welth. **1549** CHEKE *Hurt Sedit.* (1569) H iij, After warres it is commonly seene, that a great number of those that went out honest, returne home againe like roisters. **1581** HAMILTON in *Cath. Tractates* (S.T.S.) 74 The miserable estait of your maiesties cuntrie oppressit be famine and intestine vearis. **1599** SHAKS. *Much Ado* I. i. 31 Is Signior Mountanto return'd from the warres, or no? **1601** —— *All's Well* II. iii. 308 Warres is no strife To the darke house, and the detected wife. **1606** G. W[OODCOCKE] *Justine* IV. 23 Hereupon, the warres by Sea was againe renued. **1644** DIGBY *Nat. Bodies* xxvii. §7. 247 When he was a little boy, there being warres in the country. **1721** RAMSAY *Richy & Sandy* 37 His fame shall last: last shall his sang of weirs. **1850** SCORESBY *Cheever's Whalem. Adv.* x. (1858) 133 Sundry other marks upon his body, that showed him to have been in the wars.

d. ***open war***: avowed active hostility.

c **1380** WYCLIF *Wks.* (1880) 16 Ȝif þei..conseilen men more to taken vengeaunce bi open werre of here breþren þan to suffren paciently wrongys. **1450** *Paston Lett.* I. 100 To leve, reise, and make open werr ayenst you. **1487** *Cely Papers* (Camden) 165 Hytt ys open warre betwyxte Gaunte & the Kynge of Romayns. **1609** DEKKER *Work for Armourers* C ij, That open warre should presently be proclaimed against that arrogant, haughty, ambitious Tyrant Money. **1623** COCKERAM II, *Open Warre*, Hostilitie. **1667** MILTON *P.L.* II. 41 By what best way, Whether of open Warr or covert guile, We now debate.

†**e.** ***abstinence, prorogation of war***: suspension of hostilities. *Obs.*

1517 in *Acts Parlt. Scot.* (1875) XII. 38/1 The foresaid prorogacioun of were past concludit and approbate as said is. **1521** *Ibid.* 39/2 Þat..We may have abstinence of Weire for ane tyme quhill an Ambaxat may be maid Reddy. **1548** HALL *Chron., Edw. IV*, 245 b, That an especial abstinence of warre should be kept..betwixte the Realmes of England and Scotland.

2. In various phrases. (For *declare, levy, wage war*, see the vbs.)

a. ***(to be) at war, † at wars, † in war, † in wars***: engaged in war. *lit.* and *fig.* So ***at open war, † wars.***

1377 LANGL. *P. Pl.* B. XIV. 222 Buxomenesse and boste aren euer-more at werre, And ayther hateth other in alle manere werkes. *c* **1400** MAUNDEV. (Roxb.) xiii. 58 When twa rewmes er at were and owþer party ensegez citee, toune or castell. *c* **1407** LYDG. *Reson & Sens.* 1936 For to sette hem al at werre. *c* **1450** *Mirk's Festial* 22 Kyndomes and prouynces wern at werre. **1456** SIR G. HAYE *Law Arms* (S.T.S.) 3 Men kennyis almaist na realme in cristyndom bot it is in were. **1565** STAPLETON tr. *Bede's Hist. Ch. Eng.* 29 The Britannes being free from all foraine warres, fell at warres with in them selues and to all other myscheifes. **1567** *Gude & Godlie B.* (S.T.S.) 26 All Christin men tak tent and leir, How saull and body ar at weir. **1573** L. LLOYD *Pilgr. Princes* 12 When Turnus and Aeneas were in wars for the mariage of Lauinia. **1600** W. WATSON *Decacordon* (1602) 235 The Iesuits doe mightily disagree, and are often at open warres. **1614** R. WILKINSON *Paire of Serm.* etc. 30 So wee are, indeed, at warres with God, and at warres with one another. **1630** *R. Johnson's Kingd. & Commw.* 215 King Gustavus Adolphus..hath taken Elbing..from the Polander, with whom he is still in warres. **1637** J. BATTIERE in *Ussher's Lett.* (1686) 489 This Kingdom being now in Wars on all sides, doth not afford any great Design for the advancement of Learning. **1677** *Govt. Venice* 91 Nine times have they been at Wars together. **1698** FRYER *Acc. E. India & P.* 352 When England was at Wars with Portugal. **1780** *Mirror* No. 82 We have been two years at war with France. **1792** BURKE *Corr.* (1844) III. 387 Sentiments of liberty which were not at war with order, virtue, religion, and good government. **1816** BYRON *Stanzas to Augusta* II. ii, And when winds are at war with the ocean. **1860** PUSEY *Min. Proph.* 171 Man, in his powerlessness, at war with Omnipotence! **1862** MRS. H. WOOD *Mrs. Hallib.* II. xiv, In that moment..Cyril felt at war with everybody and everything. **1884** *Graphic* 23 Aug. 186/3 Teetotallers and moderate drinkers will probably be at war on this point..as long as the world lasts.

b. ***to go to war*** or †***wars***: to enter on hostilities. ***to go to the war(s)*** (arch.): to go abroad as a soldier.

c **1450** CAPGRAVE *St. Aug.* xxxix. 50 Þat he schuld neuer councell man to go to werre. **1597** SHAKS. *2 Hen. IV* III. ii. 196 Come, thou shalt go to the Warres in a Gowne. **1606** —— *Ant. & Cl.* II. ii. 66 Would we had all such wiues, that the men might go to Warres with the women. **1807** MOORE *Minstrel Boy* 1 The Minstrel Boy to the war is gone. **1871** MOZLEY *Univ. Serm.* v. (1876) 117 The aim of the nation in going to war is exactly the same as that of the individual in entering a court; it wants its rights, or what it alleges to be its rights.

†**c.** ***to have war***: to be at war (*with, to*). ***to hold, keep war*** or ***wars***: to be continuously at war.

a **1122** *O.E. Chron.* (Laud MS.) an. 1116, Se cyng Henri fylste his nefan..þe þa wyrre hæfde toȝeanes his hlaforde þam cynge of France. *c* **1275** LAY. 4347 To holde werre [*c* 1205 To halden comp] and eke fiht. **13..** *Northern Passion* 154/218* Agaynes kynge pharoo he helde werre. *c* **1400** MAUNDEV. (1839) vi. 64 Thei han often tyme werre with the Soudan. **1456** SIR G. HAYE *Law Arms* (S.T.S.) 167 Thai.. nouthir had were to him, na he to thame. *c* **1540** tr. *Pol. Verg. Eng. Hist.* (Camden No. 29) 32 [They] beganne to keepe warre against their neighbours. **1553** EDEN *Treat. New Ind.* (Arb.) 37 They kepe warre against their borderers. **1560** J. DAUS tr. *Sleidane's Chron.* 310 b, Englande hath oftentymes kepte warre with Scotlande. **1588** PARKE tr. *Mendoza's Hist. China* 342 These Ilandes were wont to haue warre the one with the other.

d. ***to make war***: to carry on hostilities. *lit.* and *fig.* Const. *on, upon, with*; also *against*, and †*to, unto*, or dative.

c **1205** LAY. 170 Weorre makede Turnus. **1297** R. GLOUC. (Rolls) 6095 His folc made euere uaste worre ȝut after is deþe. **1439** *Rolls of Parlt.* V. 17/2 The seide Phelip..hath contynuelly..made werre unto the seide John. **1515** in *Archæologia* XLVII. 302 In caace the duke or any other lordes wol make garriable werr ayeinst the castell. *c* **1532** BERNERS *Huon* lvii. 193 When yuoryn herd this he made me warre & was here before my cete with all his pusance. *a* **1548** HALL *Chron., Hen. IV*, 7 Item he assembled certain Lancashire and Cheshire men to the entent to make warre on the foresaid Lordes. *c* **1560** A. SCOTT *Poems* i. 126 As werrie waspis aganis Goddis word makis weir. **1577–87** HOLINSHED *Chron., John* (1807) II. 320 That if the king would not confirme the same, they would not cease to make him warre, till he should satisfie their requests in that behalfe. *a* **1586** SIDNEY *Ps.* XXXVII. xiii, Bad folkes shall fall, ..Who to make warre with God presumed. **1590** SHAKS. *Com. Err.* III. i. 86 *Dro.* In her forhead, arm'd and reuerted, making warre against her heire. **1600** J. PORY tr. *Leo's Africa* IV. 216 He leuied a puissant armie, and made warre against Barbarossa. **1606** G. W[OODCOCKE] *Hist. Justine* XXVI. 94 He made warre to the Athenians. **1615** G. SANDYS *Trav.* 73 His valour rests yet untried, having made no warre but by disputation. **1626** COCKERAM II, s.v. *War*, To make warre, Belligerate. **1774** GOLDSM. *Nat. Hist.* III. 331 As the fox makes war upon all animals so all others seem to make war upon him. **1794** PALEY *Evid.* (1825) II. 255 Aristotle maintained the general right of making war upon barbarians. **1885** *Scribner's Monthly* XXX. 396/1 The.. colonists were accustomed..to make war on the creatures of the forest. **1918** *Nation* (N.Y.) 7 Feb. 129/2 To get more beef the Government is making war on the cattle tick.

†**e.** ***(to win, etc.) of, on, with war***: by warfare.

c **1374** CHAUCER *Troylus* I. 134 The thinges fellen as they don of were Bytwixen hem of Troye and Grekes ofte. ?*a* **1400** *Morte Arth.* 22 How they whanne wyth were wyrchippis many. *Ibid.* 33 And Wales of were he wane at hys wille. *Ibid.* 516, 621. *c* **1420** *Avow. Arth.* xxii, Thus hase he wonun Kay on werre. *c* **1425** WYNTOUN *Cron.* II. 1562 Þar wiþe hir ost scho coyme of weyre. *Ibid.* v. 4458 (Royal MS.) A tyrawnd, Odonater, Held all that land tyll hym off were [*v.rr.* of weyre, of weire, awere] Agayne the mycht of the empyre.

3. a. In particularized sense: A contest between armed forces carried on in a campaign or series of campaigns.

Freq. used with def. art. to designate a particular war, esp. one in progress or recently ended. Hence ***between the wars***, between the war of 1914–18 and that of 1939–45 (cf. INTER-WAR *a.*).

Often with identifying word or phrase, as in ***the Trojan war, the Punic Wars, the Wars of the Roses, the Thirty Years' War. holy war***: a war waged in a religious cause: applied, e.g. to the Crusades, and to the JIHAD among Muslims. ***Sacred War*** [= Gr. ἱερὸς πόλεμος]: in *Gr. Hist.*, the designation of two wars (B.C. 595 and 357–346) waged by the Amphictyonic Council against Phocis in punishment of alleged sacrilege. ***War Between the States*** (esp. in the use of Southerners), the American Civil War. For *servile, social war*, see the adjs.

a **1300** *Cursor M.* 2491 Þare had a were ben in þat land, þat had lasted sumdel lang. *c* **1320** *Sir Tristr.* 29 Þe wer lasted so long Til morgan asked pes Þurch pine. *c* **1330** R. BRUNNE *Chron. Wace* (Rolls) 437 Þat werre..lasted two & twenty ȝer. *c* **1350** *Will. Palerne* 2613 A gret warre, þat was wonderli hard in þe next londe. **1375** BARBOUR *Bruce* I. 522 Wes nocht all troy with tresoune tane, Quhen x ȝeris of the wer wes gane? **1377** *Death Edw. III* in *Pol. Poems* (Rolls) I. 217 This gode comunes..That with heore catel and with heore goode Mayntened the werre both furst and last. **1485** *Cal. Patent Rolls* (1914) 46 [The war called] le Barons' werre. *c* **1550** LYNDESAY *Trag.* 113 Duryng this weir war takin presoneris, ..Mony one Lorde, Barrone, and Bachileris. **1595** SHAKS. *John* II. i. 36 The peace of heauen is theirs y[t] lift their swords In such a iust and charitable warre. *a* **1631** DONNE *Songs & Son., Canonization* 16 Soldiers find warres, and Lawyers find out still Litigeous men. **1659** B. HARRIS *Parival's Iron Age* 245 This fatall War is like the Hydra; the more heads are cut off, the more grow up. **1754** SHEBBEARE *Matrimony* (1766) I. 103 The French Cannon which took some of the Towns defended by the Dutch, last War in Flanders. **1774** Sacred war [see PHOCIAN *sb.*]. **1814** *Columbian Centinel* 18 June 2/3 The southern war-hirelings say the Administration will continue the War. **1840** *Penny Cycl.* XVIII. 99/2 The celebrated Phocian or Sacred War, in which all the great states of Greece were more or less concerned. **1841** ELPHINSTONE *Hist. India* I. 583 His conduct of the war evinced more activity than skill. **1861** *Chicago Tribune* 26 May 1/9, I, Samuel M. Fassett, photographist,..will continue to take those fine plain photographs for the low sum of one dollar, during the war. **1867** A. H. STEPHENS (*title*) A constitutional view of the late War between the

States. **1882** Freeman *Impress. U.S.* (1883) 21 Still the War of Independence must be, on the American side, a formidable historic barrier in the way of perfect brotherhood. **1911**, etc. Sacred war [see Phocian *a.*]. **1934** *Sun* (Baltimore) 5 June 14/7 There was a time when it was almost worth one's life in the city of Richmond to refer to the Civil War as the Civil War. The Richmonder who held the memories of the sixties close to his heart always called it the War Between the States. **1936** *Punch* 2 Dec. 640/1 Our telephone system is partly British and partly German and Turkish, and all of it served through the War with varying degrees of distinction. **1942** C. S. Lewis *Screwtape Lett.* xv. 76, I had noticed, of course, that the humans were having a lull in their European war—what they naïvely call '*The War*'! **1958** 'N. Shute' *Rainbow & Rose* i. 3 He lived and worked in England and the Far East all the time between the wars. **1973** R. Thomas *If You can't be Good* vi. 46 The Maurys..had supplied the South with two generals during the War Between the States.

b. *transf.* and *fig.* A contest, struggle (between living beings or opposing forces). Cf. 1 b. Also ***war of nerves***: see nerve *sb.* 8 f; ***war of words*** (Journalese), a sustained conflict conducted by means of the spoken or printed word; a propaganda war.

a **1300** *Cursor M.* 3458 O suilk a wer was neuer herd, Ne suilk a strijf o childir tuin. *c* **1400** *Anturs of Arth.* iii, Thayre werre on the wild squyne wurchis hom wo. **1602** *2nd Pt. Return fr. Parnass.* i. ii. 160, I thinke there be neuer an Ale-house in England..but sets forth some poets petternels or demilances to the paper warres in Paules Church-yard. **1607** Shaks. *Cor.* ii. i. 232 Our veyl'd Dames Commit the Warre of White and Damaske In their nicely gawded Cheekes, to th' wanton spoyle Of Phoebus burning Kisses. **1620** J. Taylor (Water P.) *Jack a Lent* A 4, Blacke Iacks..Whose liquor oftentimes breedes houshold wars. **1697** Dryden *Virg. Georg.* iii. 415, I pass the Wars the spotted Linx's make With their fierce Rivals, for the Female's sake. **1711** Steele *Spect.* No. 78 ¶5 What a learned War will there be among future Criticks about the Original of that Club. **1718** Prior *Solomon* i. 706 My Prophets, and my Sophists finish'd here Their Civil Efforts of the Verbal War. **1725** Pope *Odyss.* ii. 96 O insolence of youth! whose tongue affords Such railing eloquence and war of words. **1744** J. Love *Cricket* (1770) 16 Scarce any Youth wou'd dare At single Wicket, try the doubtful War. **1821** Byron *Cain* iii. i, For what should I be gentle? for a war With all the elements ere they will yield The bread we eat? **1855** Brewster *Newton* II. xxii. 295 That deadly war, which, to the disgrace of mathematical science, has raged for three years between the geometers of Britain and Germany. **1864** Lowell *Fireside Trav.* 108 The war between the white man and the forest was still fierce. **1885** *Manch. Exam.* 16 May 5/1 There is already a talk of..a war of tariffs being declared. **1981** *Times* 10 Oct. 1/7 As the war of words continued in the Tory party Mrs Thatcher arrived back from the Commonwealth Conference. **1984** *Guardian* 8 Mar. 9/1 (*heading*) Vietnamese intensify war of words on Peking.

c. ***to carry the war into the enemy's camp*** (***into Africa***, etc.): see carry *v.* 19 b.

d. ***war to end war(s)***: a war which is intended to make subsequent wars impossible; usu. *spec.* the war of 1914–18.

[**1914** H. G. Wells (*title*) The war that will end war.] **1921** G. B. Shaw *Back to Methuselah* iv. 187 There was a war called the War to End War. In the war which followed it about ten years later, none of the soldiers were killed; but seven of the capital cities of Europe were wiped out of existence. **1932** P. Quennell *Let. to Mrs. V. Woolf* (1933) 17 He can recall barely five or six summers; then the War to End Wars and so good-bye. **1949** E. Benn *Happier Days* vi. 71 If..war debts between nations had been wiped off the slate, and reparations in money never attempted, the 'war to end war' might have achieved its high purpose. **1953** Earl Winterton *Orders of Day* xxiv. 345 The Government of that day and the then leaders of opinion in general had assured us and the nation at large that it was 'a war to end war'. **1967** W. Lippman in W. Safire *New Lang. Politics* (1968) 480/2 Each of the wars to end wars has set the stage for the next war. **1978** E. Malpass *Wind brings up Rain* ix. 99 Now..the War To End War was over.

e. ***to have a good war***: to achieve success, satisfaction, or enjoyment during a war. Also with other adjs. Often ironic.

1969 P. Dickinson *Pride of Heroes* i. 49 Harvey Singleton..had a good war. A very good war indeed. After the Raid he was parachuted into France three times. **1970** —— *Seals* ii. 35 He had a very bad war. **1972** P. D. James *Unsuitable Job for Woman* iv. 124 He had what the men call a good war; we'd call it a bad war I dare say, a lot of killing and fighting. **1974** 'J. le Carré' *Tinker, Tailor, Soldier, Spy* xviii. 153 He had a dazzling war... The comparison with Lawrence was inevitable.

†**4. a.** Actual fighting, battle; a battle, engagement. *Obs.* (chiefly *poet.*)

c **1320** *Sir Tristr.* 752 Rohand told anon..How þe batayle bi gan, Þe werres hadden y ben. *c* **1330** R. Brunne *Chron. Wace* (Rolls) 5464 Ȝyf we were bold, now be we baldere, & y schal vndertake þys were. **1398** Trevisa *Barth. De P.R.* xviii. xlii. (1495) 804 Elephauntys drede not the sharpnesse of werre and dredyth and fleeth the voys of the leest sowe or swyne. *a* **1400** *Octovian* 1621 Tho began greet werre awake, Scheldes cleuede and speres brake. ? *a* **1400** *Morte Arth.* 257 Now wakkenyse the were! wyrchipe be Cryste! **1422** Yonge tr. *Secreta Secret.* 185 The croncyles makyth no mencion of no chyualry ne werre done by the kynge al the tyme that he in Irland was. **1697** Dryden *Æneis* v. 569 Their Heads from aiming Blows they bear a far, With dashing Gauntlets then provoke the War. *Ibid.* vii. 742 First, Almon falls,..Pierc'd with an Arrow from the distant War. **1750** Gray *Long Story* 76 Where, safe and laughing in his sleeve, He heard the distant din of war. **1805** Scott *Last Minstr.* iv. xiii, The boy is ripe to look on war. **1827** Pollok *Course T.* vi. 479 War brayed to war.

†**b.** A hostile attack, invasion, assault. *Obs.*

c **1386** Chaucer *Knt.'s T.* 429 Thou mayst..make a werre so sharpe on this Citee. **1387** Trevisa *Higden* (Rolls) VI. 285 Þe werre of þe Danes þat assaillede first Norþhumberlond and þanne Lyndeseie. *c* **1400** *Beryn* 1599 Wee have no nede to dout werr, ne molestacioun. **1603** Knolles *Turks* (1621) 589 Now the Turkes began to make faire warres, their terrible batteries began to grow calme.

5. a. The kind of operations by which the contention of armed forces is carried on; fighting as a department of activity, as a profession, or as an art. Cf. man-of-war, ship-of-war.

c **1350** *Will. Palerne* 2349 But god for his grete grace gof i hadde now here horse & alle harneys þat be-houes to werre. **1375** Barbour *Bruce* xvi. 492 This poynt of weir..Wes vndirtane so apertly, And eschevit richt hardely. *c* **1400** *Destr. Troy* 1038 Nestor, A noble man naitest in werre. *Ibid.* 10037 The Mirmydons were..Wise men in werr. **1513** More *Rich. III* Wks. 37/2 None euill captaine was hee in the warre, as to whiche his dispocion was more metely then for peace. **1579** Tomson *Calvin's Serm. Tim.* 908/2 Saint Paules meaning is, to shew to Timothie, that it is more then time, he were throughly trained, and made to warre, (as we say). **1759** Robertson *Hist. Scot.* I. ii. 111 War was the sole profession of the nobles. **1781** Logan *Hymn*, '*Behold the Mountain*' 24 They hang the trumpet in the hall, and study war no more. **1841** J. F. Cooper *Deerslayer* vii, I'm young in war, but not so young as to stand on an open beach to be shot down like an owl by daylight.

b. In titles of office, ***captain of the war***, ***treasurer of the king's wars***, ***treasurer at wars***. *Obs.* exc. as ***minister of*** (or ***for***) ***war***, ***secretary at war***, ***secretary of*** (***state for***) ***war***.

c **1450** *Brut* 450 Þe Lord Wylloghby was made Capten of hys werris. **1474** Caxton *Chesse* ii. v. (1883) 66 Ioab the sone of Saryre that was captayn of the warre of the kynge Dauid [Cf. *Vulg.* 2 Sam. viii. 16 *Joab..erat super exercitum*]. **1495** *Naval Acc. Hen. VII* (1896) 139 Sir Reignold Bray Knyght late Tresorer of Our Soueraigne Lorde the Kynges werres. **1617** Moryson *Itin.* ii. 53 The Treasurer at Warres *per diem* thirtie five shillings. **1693**, etc. [see secretary *sb.*[1] 3 a]. **1802** C. Wilmot *Let.* 15 Nov. in *Irish Peer* (1920) 115 The six Ministers of the Interior, of the Police, of Justice, of Finance, of War, and of foreign affairs. **1867** Crown Princess of Prussia *Let.* 27 Apr. in R. Fulford *Your Dear Letter* (1971) 133 The King wishes for peace..so does the Minister for War. **1877** J. Blackwood *Let.* 21 Dec. in *Geo. Eliot Lett.* (1956) VI. 434, I am happy to say that our Minister of War is I think a man who may be trusted at the helm. **1903** *Ceremonies at Laying Corner Stone of Army War College Building* (U.S. Army Corps of Engineers) 9 The master of ceremonies then introduced the honorable Secretary of War. **1964** *Act Eliz. II* c. 58 §1 There shall be transferred to a Secretary of State the functions conferred by any enactment on the Minister of Defence, or on the Secretary of State for War or for Air (however styled). **1980** A. Marwick *Illustr. Dict. Brit. Hist.* 64/2 He [*sc.* Churchill] served the coalition subsequently as secretary of state for war and air (1918–21).

c. in phrasal combinations designating things pertaining to warfare, as ***munitions***, † ***weeds of war***. † ***castle, house, place, town of war*** (obs.), a fortified building or place. † ***line of war*** Naut., the flotation-line of a ship when fully armed, ammunitioned, and victualled for three months.

For *articles, contraband, council, honours of war*, see those words.

1375 Barbour *Bruce* xiii. 405 Bothwell..That than at Ynglis mennys fay Wes, and haldin as place of wer. *Ibid.* xvii. 243 Till mak aparale For till defend and till assale Castell of wer or than cite. *c* **1375** *Sc. Leg. Saints* vii. (*James Minor*) 465 With alkyne Instrument of were, as gyne, slonge, darte & spere. **1441** in *Plumpton Corr.* (Camden) p. liv, The Archbishop' officers by his commaundement kept the said towne of Ripon like a towne of warr. *c* **1470** *Gol. & Gaw.* 549 That wy walit, I vis, all wedis of veir That nedit hym to note. **1474** *Acc. Ld. High Treas. Scot.* I. 50 Passande to Sanctandros with lettres vndir the signete for cartis of were. **1581** *Reg. Privy Council Scot.* III. 382 To fortefie and detene the samin [*sc.* house] as ane hous of weir. **1605** Camden *Rem.* 1 Prouided with all complete provisions of Warre. **1691** T. H[ale] *Acc. New Invent.* 125 The line of War..is to be discovered by computing the weight..of the Ordnance..and..the weight of Men with three months Victuals.

†**d.** Manner of fighting. *Obs.*

14.. *Sir Beues* 169/3323 (Pynson) For no catel Wolde I let sle Arundel, For he is gode in euery were. **1456** Sir G. Haye *Law Arms* (S.T.S.) 84 Usage makis him..expert, be oft hanting of the were that he is wont till.

6. *concr.* Used *poet.* for: **a.** Instruments of war, munitions. ? *Obs.*

1667 Milton *P.L.* vi. 712 Go then thou Mightiest..Ascend my Chariot,..bring forth all my Warr, My Bow and Thunder, my Almightie Arms Gird on. **1697** Dryden *Æneis* viii. 572 Inferior Ministers, for Mars repair His broken Axeltrees, and blunted War. *Ibid.* xi. 901 Shields, Arms, and Spears, flash horrible from far; And the Fields glitter with a waving War. **1713** Addison *Cato* i. iv, Th' embattled elephant, Loaden with war.

b. Soldiers in fighting array. ? *Obs.*

1667 Milton *P.L.* xii. 214 On thir imbattelld ranks the Waves return, And overwhelm thir Warr. **1677** Oldham *David's Lament. Saul & Jon.* v, Seneh..Where he, him-self an Host, o'ercame a War alone. **1700** Dryden *Pal. & Arc.* iii. 101 In this Array the War of either side Through Athens pass'd with Military Pride. **1726** Pope *Odyss.* xxiv. 578 The opening gates at once their war display. **1814** Scott *Lord of Isles* vi. xxx, To arms they flew,..And mimic ensigns high they rear, And..Beardown on England's wearied war. **1816** L. Hunt *Rimini* i. 141 It seems as if the harnessed war were near. **1822** W. Tennant *Thane of Fife* i. i, On the plain Of Fife debark'd his proud invasive war.

†**7.** ***course, jousts, tournament of war***: a tournament, joust. Similarly, ***to joust of war***. *Obs.*

1375 Barbour *Bruce* xix. 787 And thai, that worthy war and wicht, At that metyng iustit of wer. *c* **1400** *Rowland & Otuel* 812 Kyng askuardyn in his gere Rydes owte a course of were. *c* **1420** *Avow. Arth.* xxiv, Take thi schild and thi spere And ride to him a course on werre. *a* **1440** *Sir Degrev.* 379 To the castelle he rad..And axed yef ther eny were, That wold hyme delyvere him ther Off thre corses of wer, Hym and xij. knythus. *Ibid.* 393 He axit justes of were, And prays the of answere. *c* **1450** *Brut* 366 Þe Erle of Marre..come ynto Engelond for to chalange Ser Edmunde, þe Erle of Kent, of certeyn cours of warre on hors-bak. **1796** H. Macneill *Links o' Forth* xxxii, Or break the lance, and couch the spear At tilts and tournaments o' weir.

II. *attrib.* and *Comb.*

8. In simple attributive use, with the senses 'of or belonging to war', 'used or occurring in war', 'suited or adapted for war', etc. **a.** *gen.* as ***War Department, war aim, base, camp, casualty, -code***, † ***-feat, footing, hospital, -law, measure, neurosis*** (hence ***-neurotic***), ***news, period***, † ***point, production, profiteer, propaganda, -psychosis, ration, record, restriction, scare, -service, situation, strain, surplus*** (chiefly attrib.), ***victim, -weariness, widow, -word, wound, years, zone***, etc. (In this and the senses that follow the use of the hyphen follows no regular pattern.)

1918 A. Bennett *Pretty Lady* xxviii. 193 The Germans were discussing their *war aims. **1972** *New Yorker* 22 July 66/3 In the My Lai massacre the soldiers abandoned the unrealistic war aims of Dean Rusk and drew their illogical but understandable conclusion..all Vietnamese have to be killed. **1947** *Daily Tel.* 19 Apr. 4/2 Its virtual disappearance yesterday..is probably the only answer to the fear of its use as a *war-base once more. **1977** *South China Morning Post* (Hong Kong) 14 Apr. 5/3 Militarist forces clutch at the blocs and war bases they established in Asia. **1832** A. Earle *Narr. Residence N.Z.* (1966) 176 Mr. Hobbs, the Wesleyan missionary,..had visited the *war-camp of the assembled chiefs. **1969** G. Macbeth *War Quartet* 25 In our minds A dream of war-camps festered. **1921** G. B. Shaw *Back to Methuselah* ii. 88 It was the *war casualty lists and the starvation afterwards that finished me up with politics and the Church and everything else except you. **1974** A. Price *Other Paths to Glory* ii. ix. 225 The late Turcos... Another war casualty? **1853** Grote *Greece* ii. lxxxvi. XI. 286 To inquire whether Thebes had exceeded the measure of rigour warranted by the *war-code of the time. **1797** *Rep. Committees Ho. of Comm.* XII. 301 The Office of Secretary of State for the *War Department was first established on the 11th July 1794. **1819** D. B. Warden *Acc. U.S.* III. 395 Chapter xliv. Of the War Department. *Ibid.* 405 The original proceedings of all courts-martial, ordered by the war department, are transmitted to that department by the judge advocate of the court. **1866** G. B. McLellan *Let.* 26 Dec. in *McLellan's Own Story* (1887) xii. 221 The entire establishment..was removed to the War Department building, without my knowledge. **1944** *Time* 2 Oct. 19/1 This was strictly a military document drafted by the War Department. **1656** Earl Monm. tr. *Boccalini's Advts. fr. Parnass.* ii. xxxviii. (1674) 190 They had very exactly considered his *War-Enterprises. **1582** Stanyhurst *Æneis* iv. (Arb.) 97 Thee coompanye youthful Surcease from *warfeats. **1847** Thackeray *Van. Fair* (1848) xxviii. 242 The armies of the allied powers were all providentially on a *war-footing, and ready. **1872** 'Mark Twain' *Roughing It* ii. 22 We were reduced to a war-footing. **1894** *Times* (weekly ed.) 9 Feb. 118/3 The army has been placed on a war footing. **1860** F. Nightingale *Notes on Nursing* iii. 23, I by no means refer only to..*war hospitals, but..to..military hospitals at home, in time of peace. **1982** P. Quennell *Customs & Characters* ii. 33 The French Ambassadress..had promised she would visit a nearby war-hospital. **1855** Milman *Lat. Chr.* (1864) II. iv. i. 197 Towards them [*sc.* Christian priests] the [Mohammedan] *war-law speaks in a sterner tone. **1808** W. Eaton in R. C. Prentiss *Life W. Eaton* (1813) 414 The Embargo was contemplated as a *war measure. **1948** *Rep. Native Laws Comm. 1946–48* (Dept. Native Affairs, S. Afr.) 32/1 A War Measure has been promulgated as a temporary attempt to relieve the situation. **1975** *Toronto Star* 1 Nov. B4/4 Pierre Trudeau invoked the War Measures Act and plunged Canada into a time of arrest without warrant and detention without charge. **1920** *Internat. Jrnl. Psycho-Anal.* I. 283 Freud's introduction gives some of the chief points of view for the psycho-analytical consideration of the *war neuroses. **1944** *Yank* 31 Mar. 8 For this reason there is actually no such thing as 'war neurosis', any more than there is 'war malaria' or 'war pneumonia'. **1955** J. Strachey tr. *Freud's Psycho-Anal. & War Neuroses* in *Compl. Wks.* XVII. 215 With the end of the war the *war neurotics, too, disappeared—a final but impressive proof of the psychical causation of their illness. **1857** C. Kingsley *Two Years Ago* II. v. 200, I cannot sit here quietly, listening to the *war-news. It makes me mad to be up and doing. **1915** F. H. Burnett *Lost Prince* xiii. 96 [They] sat down to read the morning paper. The war news was bad to read. **1967** C. Potok *Chosen* iii. 59 There was war news all the time, but no one got this excited unless something very special was happening. **1918** H. Crane *Let.* 12 Aug. (1965) 11 All minors,..if drafted at all, will be apprenticed in machine shops, etc., during the *war period. **1939** *Ann. Reg. 1938* 260 The declared policy of Senor Negrin to look beyond the war-period to a Spain in which one day the Spaniards on both sides would have to live together. *a* **1586** Sidney *Ps.* xviii. ix, He me *warre points did show. **1965** A. J. P. Taylor *Eng. Hist. 1914–45* xiv. 517 Bomber command claimed the largest share of Great Britain's *war-production. **1918, 1975** *War-profiteer [see profiteer *sb.*]. **1918** W. Owen *Let.* 25 Oct. (1967) 588 He had no qualifications for *War Propaganda. **1974** *Guardian* 31 Jan. 1/5 War propaganda on both sides was, of course, bad and distorted. **1927** W. E. Collinson *Contemp. Eng.* 103 Symptoms of that *war-psychosis, which afflicted us in common with the other belligerent nations. **1953** H. S. Whitman tr. *Janetschek's Emperor Franz Joseph* 302 Don't worry so much, and you will soon be free of your war-psychosis. **1766** *Mansfield's Sp. agst. Suspending & Dispensing Prerog.* in *Parl. Hist.* (1813) XVI. 261 As that would have been using the war power of embargoes indirectly for another end than a *war purpose, such an evasion of the law was not judged wise or fit. **1924** D. H.

LAWRENCE in M. Magnus Mem. Foreign Legion 16 He yelled for more bread—bread being *war-rations and very limited in supply. **1890** E. CUSTER Following Guidon 2 They longed individually and as a regiment for a *war 'record'. **1978** F. MACLEAN Take Nine Spies iv. 126 The men were impressed by his war record. **1922** W. J. LOCKE Tale of Triona xxvi. 292 England..awoke to find *war restrictions removed,..and petrol to be had. **1938** J. CHARLESWORTH Law of Negligence vii. 133 Where a refuge was erected in the middle of the street, and inadequately lighted, so that a taxi-cab collided with it in the dark because..owing to war restrictions, no lights were maintained,..the local authority were held liable. **1894** W. LE QUEUX Gt. War in Eng. in 1897 i. 15 *War-scares had been plentiful. **1977** Listener 10 Feb. 177/2 The war scare in 1938. **1601** HOLLAND Pliny VIII. xlii. I. 222 The Scythians chuse rather to use their mares in *warre-service than their stone-horses. **1916** J. BAILEY Let. 8 Oct. (1935) 168 It was a great joy to see you both and King's Weston again, and to admire your wonderful 'war service' and feel that all the beauties of the house and place are being put to such splendid use [as a War Hospital]. **1979** A. PRICE Tomorrow's Ghost iv. 47 They both looked old enough to have seen war service. **1614** R. TAILOR Hog hath lost Pearl II. D 3, With what pleasing passions he did suffer Loues gentle *war-siege. **1936** C. DAY LEWIS We're not going to do Nothing 29 In an actual *war-situation the trade unions are in the key-position. **1775** ADAIR Amer. Ind. 380 Each gets a small bag of parched corn-flour, for his *war-stores. **1914** T. A. BAGGS Back from Front xx. 94 It is there that human nature, exuberant or impassive under the *war-strain, reveals its own true colours once again. **1952** H. INNES Campbell's Kingdom I. v. 110 They wore *war surplus clothing relieved by bright scarves. **1968** P. GEDDES High Game viii. 97 When the big round of war surplus prosecutions started, none of the dirt ever stuck to him. **1982** D. WILLIAMS Copper, Gold & Treasure 16 I'll let you know if he asks me to buy him any war surplus. **1599** SHAKS. Much Ado I. i. 303 But now I am return'd, and that *warre-thoughts Haue left their places vacant: in their roomes Come thronging soft and delicate desires. **1969** Guardian 28 Aug. 11/5 The starving *war victims. **1917** 'CONTACT' Airman's Outings p. xviii, What, then, would be the effect on German *war-weariness if giant raids on fortified towns by a hundred or so allied machines were of weekly occurrence? **1976** Classical Q. XXVI. 294 Sinon begins the first section of his lying speech with a reference to the death of Palamedes.., the second by describing the war-weariness of the Greeks. **1866** Ann. Rep. Commissioner Indian Affairs (U.S.) 164 These last came from Laramie during the winter, and claim to be *war-widows. **1922** F. H. BURNETT Robin v. 44 Slim young war-widows were to be seen in black dresses and veiled small hats with bits of white crape inside their brims. **1978** R. BARNARD Unruly Son xvii. 186 We moved to London, where she passed as a war widow. **1932** E. WEEKLEY Words & Names 21 We have the *war-word Minnie for the German minenwerfer. **1938** E. AMBLER Cause for Alarm iii. 47 The limp? Probably a *war wound. **1981** C. MILLER Childhood in Scotland 68 He was in continual pain from his war-wound. **1920** W. J. LOCKE House of Baltazar i. 9 The strain of the *war years began to tell. **1977** D. BENNETT Jigsaw Man xiii. 231 They had hidden the microfilm in the same cache they had used during the war years for passing messages. **1914** Wells Fargo Messenger Oct. 27/1 A late report from the *war zone states that Mr. Gaston has returned to London. **1918** Nation (N.Y.) 7 Feb. p. xii/1 The Government..compel all ships plying to ports in the war zone to insure their men. **1939** Daily Tel. 18 Dec. 6/5 The danger of 'rupture' has been vastly reduced by Congress's prohibition of American ships from entering the war zone. **1971** D. E. WESTLAKE I gave at Office 142 The bar ..had temporary plywood over its glassless windows, making it look like a correspondents' hangout in a war zone.

b. With words that denote arms, accoutrement, implements, etc.; as ***war-axe, -belt, -bow, -club, -dress, material, saddle, souvenir, †weeds; war-balloon, -beacon, -cart, -chariot, -pony, -tower; war-boat, -canoe, -steamer.***

1825 SCOTT Talisman ii, Take my *war-axe, and dash the stone into twenty shivers. **1843** Practical Mechanic 16 Dec. 114/1 (heading) *War balloon. **1884** St. James's Gaz. 8 Feb. 5/1 An ordinary war-balloon..may either contain an officer in charge or be dispatched unattended. **1954** J. R. R. TOLKIEN Fellowship of Ring II. ii. 277 Such light and flame cannot have been seen on Weathertop since the *war-beacons of old. **1754** P. WRAXALL Abridgement Indian Affairs (1915) 242 He calls upon them now to..join us in our Defence & Revenge & presents the Large *War Belt to them. **1798** LANDOR Gebir VII. 28 Whirling headlong in his war-belts fold. **1847** C. LANMAN Summer in Wilderness 17 Captain James Clarke,..when about to be murdered by a council of Indians.., threw the war-belt in the midst of the savages, with a defying shout. **1965** Canad. Historical Rev. June 109 In December [1775] the Iroquois delegation told Philip Schuyler that Johnson after offering them a war belt and hatchet had invited them to 'feast on a Bostonian and drink his blood'. **1836** MARRYAT Olla Podr. xxv, The Burmah *war-boats are very splendid craft, pulling from eighty to one hundred oars. **1934** WEBSTER, *War bow. **1958** 'W. HENRY' Seven Men at Mimbres Springs iv. 48 Nothing so guaranteed a safe passage through Apacheland as a coach that would not tip or leave the road when the warbows were bending and the Springfields blasting back at them. **1789** Loiterer 18 July 5 A large *War Canoe and some small fishing Proas had been forced out to Sea. **1882** DE WINDT Equator 77 We now came in sight of a fleet of some 100 huge war-canoes. **1513** DOUGLAS Æneis VIII. vii. 144 Ane vther sort full byssely to Mart The rynnand quhelis forgeis, and *weir cart. **1911** FLETCHER & KIPLING School Hist. England i. 15 They [sc. the Celts] rode on war-ponies, and, like the Assyrians in the Bible, they drove war-chariots. **1778** J. CARVER Trav. N. Amer. 269 He gives a violent blow with his *war-club against a post that is fixed in the ground. **1907** J. W. SCHULTZ My Life as Indian xvii. 198 The fleeing men.. were overtaken and shot, or brained with war clubs. **1943** R. PEATTIE Great Smokies & Blue Ridge 24 The Cherokee weapons were the ballheaded war club, spears and bows and arrows. **1984** Listener 4 Oct. 13/3 They were attacked by Kukukuku..with stone war-clubs. **1695** J. E. EDWARDS Perfect. Script. 214 Great commanders..fought in open chariots or *war-coaches. **1724** H. JONES Present State Virginia 5 The Seneca Indians in their *War Dress may appear as terrible as any of the Sons of Anak. **1825** J. NEAL Bro. Jonathan II. 16 A command for Eagle to put on his war-dress. **1826** J. HOWELL (title) An Essay on the *War-galleys of the Ancients. **1807** P. GASS Jrnl. 215 The *war-mallet is a club with a large head of wood or stone. **1881** W. D. HAY 300 Years Hence iv. 67 The progress of The Final Wars was marked by a whole series of inventions in *war material. **1939** Ann. Reg. 1938 265 Meanwhile war material from Germany and Italy continued to pour in. **1865** J. PIKE Scout & Ranger xi. 123 Many had friends..who came after them with wagons; refusing to let them ride their *war ponies. **1929** D. H. LAWRENCE Pansies 128 Prancing their knees under their tiny skirts Like war-horses; or war-ponies at least! **1838** Civil Engin. & Arch. Jrnl. I. 328/1 Improvements in *War Rockets. **1688** HOLME Armoury III. 345/2 The Great Saddle or *War Saddle, which is accounted the chief of Saddles. **1819** SCOTT Leg. Montrose ii, His rider occupied his demipique, or war-saddle, with an air that shewed it was his familiar seat. **1963** L. DEIGHTON Horse under Water xliv. 180 An old *war-souvenir pistol. **1852** LONGF. Warden of Cinque Ports iii, To see the French *war-steamers speeding over. **1839** CARLYLE Chartism viii. 158 Or was the smith idle, hammering only *wartools? **1909** G. M. TREVELYAN Garibaldi & the Thousand xii. 213 A high hill, on the spur of which Talamone and its old *war-tower projected into the sea. c **1470** Gol. & Gaw. 198 *Were wedis.

c. With words that denote a commander, officer, army, etc., as ***war-captain, -chief, -leader; war-array, -company, -force, -tribe.***

1610 HOLLAND Camden's Brit. (1637) 77 The Generall of all the warre-forces throughout Britaine. **1757** [BURKE] Europ. Settlem. Amer. I. II. iv. 182 When..the fury of the nation is raised to the greatest height,..the war captain prepares the feast, which consists of dogs flesh. **1800** COLERIDGE Piccolomini I. iii. 18 We had not seen the War-Chief, the Commander. **1814** SCOTT Ld. of Isles VI. xii, The rest of Scotland's war-array With Edward Bruce to westward lay. **1825** P. S. OGDEN Jrnl. 18 Feb. (1950) 23 The War tribes appear determined that we Shall not want for their Company this year it cannot be otherwise as we are following the main War track. **1906** C. SQUIRE Mythol. Anc. Brit. v. 48 The traditions which make him [Arthur] a supreme war-leader of the Britons. **1909** 'MARK TWAIN' Is Shakes. Dead? v. 53 It could have gone soldiering with a war-tribe..and learned soldier-wiles and soldier-ways. **1913** J. A. CRAMB Germany & England i. (1914) 35, I seem to hear again the thunder of the footsteps of a great host... It is the war-bands of Alaric!

d. With words denoting cries, songs, musical instruments, etc., as ***war-chant, -cheer, -horn, -march, -music, -pipe, -shout, -tramp, -trumpet, -whistle, -yell.***

1775 ADAIR Amer. Ind. 388 Taking from him his drum, war-whistle, and martial titles. **1793** BLAKE America 76 Sound! sound! my loud war-trumpets. **1808** SCOTT Marmion v. v, And varying notes the war-pipes bray'd, To every varying clan. **1809** CAMPBELL Gert. Wyom. III. xxvi, And for the business of destruction done Its requiem the war-horn seemed to blow. **1810** SCOTT Lady of Lake II. ix, What marvel, then, At times, unbidden notes should rise, Confusedly bound in memory's ties, Entangling, as they rush along, The war-march with the funeral song? **1831** TRELAWNY Adv. Younger Son II. 43 Thus I stopped his triumphant war-yells. **1843** LYTTON Last Bar. II. ii, The first blast of the war-trump will scatter their greenness to the winds. **1847** TENNYSON Princess v. 256 When first I heard War-music. **1866** LYTTON Lost Tales Miletus, Secret Way 41 The huge walls Shook with the war-shout of ten thousand voices. **1892** RIDER HAGGARD Nada xxvii. 228 As they went they sang the Ingomo, the war-chant of the Zulu. **1970** R. LOWELL Notebk. 191 Frederick the Great of Prussia's war-cheer, 'Move, you bastards, do you want to live forever?'

e. With words that refer to finance, as ***war bond, debt, expenditure, -fund, gratuity, -insurance, -loan, -price, relief, savings, -tax.***

1918 Daily Mirror 12 Nov. 6/4 It bore a poem, titled 'A Message from Mars', eulogising the airmen and urging them to buy *War Bonds. **1981** B. LANGLEY Autumn Tiger v. 67 A gigantic billboard..urged him to 'Buy War Bonds'. **1865** Nation (N.Y.) I. 386 The Reconstructing State Convention of Alabama has pronounced against the repudiation of the *war debt of the state. **1924** Lit. Digest 9 Feb. 20/2 The whole subject of war debts should undergo a new process of accountancy. **1931** Keesing's Archives 76/2 The oppressive problem of war-debts and reparations. **1983** T. POCOCK 1945 vii. 241 The British owed their dominions, colonies, and the rest, a war debt of £4,000,000,000. **1931** *War expenditure [see INCONSEQUENTIALNESS]. **1853** GROTE Greece II. lxxxviii. XI. 495 It is true that the Athenians might have laid up that surplus annually in the acropolis, to form an accumulating *war-fund. **1945** Ann. Reg. 1944 80 All those returning to civil life would receive *war gratuities as a reward for their service. **1978** D. DUNLOP in D. Abse My Medical School 31 Besides ordinary freshmen like myself staight from school, many came up on their war gratuities. **1898** Amer. Rev. of Reviews Sept. 322/2 Newspapers were required to bear the..expense of fire, marine, accident, and *war insurance. **1848** MILL Pol. Econ. II. III. xxiii. 185 The only instance of the kind in recent history on a scale comparable to that of the *war loans, is the absorption of capital in the construction of railways. **1974** Daily Tel. 24 June 17/1 'War Loan is a buy when the price equals the yield' was the joke on everyone's lips in Throgmorton Street a couple of years ago. Today it is no longer a joke—almost a reality. On Friday $3\frac{1}{2}$ p.c. War Loan dropped to an all time low of £$23\frac{1}{2}$. **1824** Cobbett's Weekly Reg. 7 Feb. 354/2 Corn has not reached half the *war-price yet. **1854** Tait's Mag. I. 599/1 Gentlemen farmers formed another exception during the era of war-prices and yeomanry cavalry. **1940** G. MARX Let. 5 Sept. (1967) 25 The proceeds are given to British *War Relief and the actors all donate their services. **1815** in Orders of Council Naval Service (1866) I. 16 To direct that the salaries established as *war salaries, by the said Order in Council,..should be the permanent salaries, both in war and peace of the several persons. **1919** Maclean's Mag. Jan. 55/3 Every man, woman and child in Canada should invest in *War-Savings Stamps all the money that he or she can save. **1799** Times 1 June 2/3 The Directory have converted his accusation into a *War Tax of three per cent. upon all capital. **1817** COLERIDGE Lay Serm. 'Blessed are ye' 32 The Revenue was diminished by the abandonment of the war-taxes. **1875** JOWETT Plato (ed. 2) III. 107 War-taxes depress the poor and keep them at work. **1901** Daily Tel. 9 Mar. 10/4 He had to ask for a *war vote amounting to close upon eighty-eight millions sterling.

f. With words that denote works of art, etc., of which the subject is war, as ***war-ballad, book, history, -impression, novel, play, poem*** (also ***poetry***), ***sonnet, story, verse; war film, movie, photograph*** (also ***photography***); also their authors, as ***war novelist, photographer, poet.*** Cf. also ***war artist, picture*** in sense 11 below.

1854 'C. BEDE' Further Adventures Verdant Green ii. 9 What internal evidence does the Odyssey afford, that Homer sold his Trojan *war-ballad at three yards an obolus? **1916** W. OWEN Let. 23 Nov. (1967) 416, I have suddenly seen what I wanted to do with that War Ballad. **1809** M. L. WEEMS Life Gen. Francis Marion (1814) 3, I never dreampt of such a thing as writing a book; and least of all a *war book. **1904** J. LONDON Let. 4 June (1966) 159 There won't be any war-book so far as I am concerned. **1978** A. WAUGH Best Wine Last xviii. 235 Starting with Journey's End..there had been a spate of war books. **1897** C. M. HEPWORTH Animated Photogr. p. vii (Advt.), *War films. **1930** P. ROTHA Film till Now I. v. 124 Like all war films manufactured in Hollywood, The Big Parade carried little of the real spirit of war. **1972** J. MANN Mrs Knox's Profession ii. 14 She looked like an amateur vamp in a war film. **1929** E. LINKLATER Poet's Pub ii. 31 He had been offered a knighthood for his official *War History of the submarines. **1966** 'G. BLACK' You want to die, Johnny? xi. 198 Split-second timing..isn't achieved as often as the writers of popular war histories tend to suggest. **1917** W. OWEN Let. 11 Mar. (1967) 442 Do you think, now, that I am going to read the *war-impressions of home-editors? **1914** N.Y. Times 14 Jan. 9/6 Real *war 'movies' shown... Moving pictures of real warfare were exhibited in the Seventy-first Regiment Armory last night. **1981** J. VAN DE WETERING Mind-Murders I. iv. 43 An old war movie that ended well when the bad enemies surrendered. **1923** W. J. LOCKE Moordius & Co. viii. 99 He had not read the marvellous *war novel to which he alluded. **1975** D. LODGE Changing Places v. 178 Stephen Crane wrote his great war-novel first and experienced war afterwards. **1966** J. FREDERICS Ready to Die (1968) iv. 20 He made *war novelist sound like something not discussed in polite company. **1977** M. HERR Dispatches (1978) ii. 18, I can remember..when I was a kid looking at *war photographs in Life. **1978** R. GIBSON Catal. 20th. Cent. Portraits (Natl. Portrait Gallery) 36/1 Lee Miller (1907–77), well known as a *war photographer. **1908** J. DANZIGER Beaton 46/2 The naïve approach of his *war photography. **1896** Godey's Mag. Feb. 182/1 The instrument..imitates horses' hoofs with.. untiring fidelity in all *war-plays. **1915** Sphere 26 June 322/2 The production of a war play is a perilous business at the present time. **1972** P. BLACK Biggest Aspidistra I. iv. 41 Brigade Exchange, a war play..created by the pre-Nazi German radio. **1857** J. A. SYMONDS Let. May (1967) I. 105 He chiefly talked about..[Tennyson's] Maud which he considers a true *war poem & praises highly. **1917** W. OWEN Let. 25 Sept. (1967) 496, I send you my two best war Poems. **1978** Listener 23 Mar. 378/3 There was a fine slim anthology of war poems read [aloud]. **1857** C. KINGSLEY Two Years Ago III. vi. 177 The true *war poets..have been warriors themselves. Körner and Alcæus fought as well as sang. **1939** E. BLUNDEN in W. Owen Poems 39 He [sc. Owen] was, apart from Mr. Sassoon, the greatest of the English *war poets. But the term 'war poets' is rather convenient than accurate. **1962** Listener 8 Feb. 259/3 By 'war poet' we now automatically assume anti-war poet. This was no tacit assumption in 1916. **1865** Atlantic Monthly May 589/1 We have no such *war-poetry. **1917** W. OWEN Let. 27 Nov. (1967) 513, I knew he valued War Poetry before he told me so! **1973** D. AARON Unwritten War IV. x. 152 Their best war poetry tended to be philosophical and personal. **1915** W. S. CHURCHILL in Times 26 Apr. 5/5 The very few incomparable *war sonnets which he [sc. Rupert Brooke] has left behind. **1864** M. B. CHESNUT Diary 1 Jan. in C. V. Woodward M. Chesnut's Civil War (1981) 524, I mapped out a story of the war. Johnny is the hero... It is to be a *war story. **1982** G. LYALL Conduct of Major Maxim xv. 145 They weren't interested in her war story, they'd heard a million war stories. **1918** G. FRANKAU Judgement of Valhalla 41 The other Side Being a letter from Major Average.. acknowledging a presentation copy of a book of *war-verse. **1952** E. WILSON Shores of Light 780, I refrained from mentioning her war-verse.

9. Objective, etc., as ***war-breeder, -chronicler, -jobber, -maker, -winner, -writer; †war-keeping, -making, preparation, †-thirst, -winning*** (also ppl. adj.); ***war-bearing, -breathing, -denouncing, -loving, †-parting, -stirring*** ppl. adjs.; ***war-hungry*** adj.

1456 SIR G. HAYE Law Arms (S.T.S.) 123 Defence of the kingis persoun..is fer mare privilegit na is ony..were making till his awin legis. **1542** UDALL Erasm. Apoph. 160 Capitaines..apte and meete..for warrekepyng. **1598** SYLVESTER Du Bartas II. i. III. Furies 806 But if (brave Lands-men) your war-thirst be such. **1598** BARRET Theor. Warres 5 This is my opinion of the diuersitie of warrewriters. **1610** HEALEY St. Aug. Citie of God VII. xv. Vives 274 Mars is violent, a war-breeder. **1611** SPEED Theat. Gt. Brit. xxi. (1614) 41/1 The Cattieuchlani, a stout and warre-stirring people. **1747** COLLINS Passions 43 The war-denouncing trumpet. **1791** BLAKE Fr. Revol. 253 Then the King will disband This war-breathing army. **1833** Niles' Reg. XLIV. 148/1 Very few persons questioned the right of congress to lay an embargo, under the war-making power. **1848** THACKERAY Van. Fair xxxi, The war-chroniclers who write brilliant stories of fight and triumph. **1860** GEN. P. THOMPSON Audi Alt. Part. III. 53 The war-jobbers have plainly won. **1908** Westm. Gaz. 2 Mar. 2/2 Raids by war-loving hill tribes on our Indian frontiers. **1931** W. S. CHURCHILL World Crisis VI. vi. 97 Neglect in the war-preparations. **1934** V. M. YEATES Winged Victory I. xx. 159 Tom was afraid Miller might be feeling his responsibility and want to do an undue amount of war-winning. **1936** DYLAN THOMAS Twenty-Five Poems 10 Dumbly and divinely stumbling Over the warbearing line. **1947** CROWTHER & WHIDDINGTON *Science at War* I. 49 Manufacturers found it very difficult to give up mass production, in order to make the 200 or so sets 'off', which were often the war-winners. **1956** *Nature* 11 Feb. 251/1 This was largely due to the efforts of..Sir Henry Tizard, whose foresight resulted in such war-winning devices as radar. **1962** E. SNOW *Other Side of River* (1963) lx. 456 The Western caricature of the mad-dog war-hungry Chinese. **1974** P. GORE-BOOTH *With Great Truth & Respect* 123 Their object was to go hell-bent for victory with all the stupendous war-winning momentum which the United States developed. **1978** LD. DROGHEDA *Double Harness* xix. 230 He was indeed one of the real war-winners, having done more than anyone to lighten Churchill's load. **1982** WARNER & SANDILANDS *Women beyond Wire* v. 69 The Japanese.. could be lethal..their business in the islands was that of professional war-making.

10. Instrumental and locative, as ***war-battered, -bitten, -bleached, -blinded, -bright, -broken, -brutalized, -devastated, -famed, -made, -marked, -mazed, -orphaned, -ravaged, -scarred, -shaken, -shattered, -torn, -tossed, -triumphant, -wasted, -wearied, -wounded*** (freq. *absol.*), ***-wracked*** adjs. Also with sense 'for war', as ***war-apparelled, -dight, -laden*** adjs.

1591 SHAKS. *1 Hen. VI*, IV. iv. 18 Whiles the honourable Captaine there Drops bloody swet from his warre-wearied limbes. **1606** —— *Ant. & Cl.* III. vii. 45 Your Armie, which doth most consist Of Warre-markt-footmen. **1624** DAVENPORT *City Night-cap* III. (1661) 26 The hoofs Of war-apparell'd horses. **1649** G. DANIEL *Trinarch., Hen. IV*, ccxlii, Warr-famed Douglas. *Ibid., Hen. V*, xcix, Our Warre-tost Realme. **1652** J. TAYLOR (Water P.) *Short Rel. Journ. Wales* (1859) 12 An old ruined winde and war-shaken castle. **1660** *Speech to Gen. Monk* 1/1 Her War-made breaches now are cur'd again. **1725** POPE *Odyss.* III. 486 Pallas herself, the War-triumphant Maid. **1777** POTTER *Æschylus, Sev. agst. Thebes* 150 Nor the war-wasted town betray. **1804** CAMPBELL *Soldier's Dream* 22 Fain was their war-broken soldier to stay. **1821** JOANNA BAILLIE *Metr. Leg., Wallace* xcv, From war-dight youth, to barefoot child. **1827** G. DARLEY *Sylvia* 149 The wild, war-blasted marches. **1857** J. G. WHITTIER in *National Era* 11 June 94/5 When each war-scarred Continental,.. Waved his rusted sword in welcome. **1900** W. B. YEATS *Shadowy Waters* 33 War-laden galleys, and armies on white roads. **1902** J. H. ROSE *Napoleon I* (ed. 2) II. xxv. 101 Duroc, a short, stern, war-hardened man. **1909** M. B. SAUNDERS *Litany Lane* iv. 43 Women of prayer who had raised just as many waxen palms to altars, in nunnery and in palace, for many a war-wracked generation. **1915** A. READE *Poems of Love & War* 52 Joan, the Mystic Maiden, rides Through the war-swept countrysides. **1931** W. S. CHURCHILL *World Crisis* VI. xxi. 323 A hundred and twenty-five thousand ragged, war-bitten men. **1937** *Daily Tel.* 19 Oct. 15/3 (*heading*) War-shattered shrine restored. **1938** *Times* 24 Aug. 12/1 The removal of import duties on mining, agricultural, and other machinery, ostensibly designed to facilitate the rehabilitation of war-devastated areas. **1938** W. B. YEATS *Herne's Egg* ii. 12 A weather-stained, war-battered Old campaigner such as I. **1939** C. DAY LEWIS *Child of Misfortune* 144 For one of our war-brutalized soldiery, you have considerable perception. **1939** L. JACOBS *Rise of Amer. Film* v. xix. 386 Griffith revealed his superficial understanding of the war by remarking his sets for *Intolerance* had been more impressive than anything he saw in war-torn France and Belgium. **1940** C. DAY LEWIS *Poems in Wartime* 10 Along this war-mazed valley. **1941** L. B. LYON *Tomorrow is a Revealing* 28 Eyes, and the ploughshare, baulk at the recovery Of skeletons war-bleached a grave ago. **1942** W. S. CHURCHILL *End of Beginning* (1943) 220 We recreated and revivified our war-battered Army. **1950** War-wounded [see TEAM *v.* 1 b]. **1954** W. FAULKNER *Fable* 46 A wealthy American expatriate.. who was supporting near Paris an asylum for war-orphaned children. **1960** *Farmer & Stockbreeder* 15 Mar. 99 It is made by Garden Machinery, Ltd., of Slough. Director of the firm,..extreme right, is a war-blinded South African. **1968** *Guardian* 23 Feb. 10/6 Few, other than surgical cases (including occasional war-wounded) were brought to the hospital. **1970** R. LOWELL *Notebk.* 108 Regret those jousting aristocracies, War-bright. **1975** 'E. LATHEN' *By Hook or by Crook* xxiii. 209 It was imperative to get the children out of their war-torn background. **1976** *Billings* (Montana) *Gaz.* 17 June 1-A/3 The driver took 'the route normally taken' by anyone wishing to cross from the Christian to the Moslem sides of war-wracked Beirut. **1978** *Poland* May 48/3, In the Fifties, twice as many children were born in Poland than was thought appropriate to the poverty of the war-ravaged country. **1980** J. LEES-MILNE *Harold Nicolson* vii. 114 Harold Nicolson..considered the choice of war-scarred Paris for the site of a peace-seeking meeting a psychological mistake.

11. Special comb.: **War Ag.**, colloq. abbrev. of 'War Agricultural Committee'; **war-arrow** (= ON. *her-ǫr*), an arrow split into segments which are sent out by a chief as a call to arms; **war artist**, an artist employed to provide paintings or drawings of a war; **war baby**, (*a*) one born during a war, esp. an (illegitimate) child of a man on active service; (*b*) *slang*, a young or inexperienced officer; (*c*) *U.S. slang*, a bond or the like which is sold during a war, or which increases in value because of a war; **war bag** *U.S.*, †(*a*) = *war budget* (*a*); (*b*) a bag containing money, clothing, or other supplies; **war-bird** *U.S.*, (*a*) = *war-eagle*; (*b*) *fig.*, a fighting aircraft or airman; **war bonnet**, a head-dress decorated with eagle feathers, worn by American Indians; **War Box** *slang*, the War Office; **war-boy**, in Africa, a Black fighting man or soldier; **war bride**, a woman who marries a man who is on active service or a man (esp. a foreigner) whom she met while he was on active service; **war bridle** *Canad.*, a harsh bridle made by placing a loop of rope round the lower jaw of a horse; **war budget**, (*a*) *U.S.*, a packet carried by American Indians, containing amulets and military trophies; (*b*) a budget to raise funds for a war; **War Cabinet**, a Cabinet with responsibility for the political decisions of a country during a war; **war cemetery**, a cemetery composed of war graves; **war chest**, (a chest or strong box for) funds used in waging war; freq. used *fig.*, esp. of funds used by a political party to finance an election campaign; **war-cloud**, a cloud of dust and smoke rising from a battle-field (cf. πολέμοιο νέφος *Iliad* xvii. 243); *fig.* something that threatens war; **war college** chiefly *U.S.*, a college providing advanced instruction for senior officers of the armed services; **war communism**, an economic policy, based on strict centralized control of the economy, adopted by the Bolsheviks during the Russian Civil War (1917–21); **war-correspondent**, a journalist engaged by a newspaper to send home first-hand descriptions of the fighting; **war crime**, an offence against the rules of war, formerly excluding, but since the 1939–45 war including, any such act performed on the orders of a higher authority; **war criminal**, one who has committed a war crime; **war damage**, damage caused by action taken by or against an enemy during a war; hence **war-damaged** *a.*; **war dead** *pl.*, servicemen who have died on active service; **war diary**, (*a*) a diary recording the experiences of an individual during a war; (*b*) (see quot. 1918); **war dream**, a dream about war; **war-eagle**, the golden eagle, so called because the N. American Indians decorate themselves with its feathers; **war economy**, (*a*) a measure taken in order to save money or other resources because of a war; (*b*) an economy, characteristic of wartime, in which a large part of the labour force is engaged in arms production, etc., rather than in the production of goods for export or for civilian use; **war effort**, the effort of a nation to win a war, or of an individual group to contribute to that end; **war-fain** *a. pseudo-arch.*, eager to fight; **war fever**, an enthusiasm for war; **war-fighting**, the fighting of wars; also *attrib.*; **warfront**, the foremost part of the field of operations of opposing armies; **war-game** = KRIEGSPIEL; also *attrib.* and *fig.*; also used of any game simulating war, esp. an elaborate game played with model soldiers, or of any exercise by which a military strategy is examined or tested; **war-game** *v. trans.*, to examine or test (a strategy or the like); **war-gamer**, one who plays a war-game; **war-gaming**, the playing of war-games; the use of such games to examine or test strategies; **war gas**, a gas or other chemical agent used in war to produce irritant or poisonous effects; **war generation** a generation which has experienced a war; **war grave**, the grave of a serviceman who died from wounds inflicted, accident occurring, or disease contracted on active service; **war-guilt**, the responsibility for having caused a war; freq. with reference to the claim that Germany had caused the war of 1914–18, which was embodied in an article of the Treaty of Versailles (1919); †**war-hable** *a.*, [*hable* = ABLE *a.*; cf. HABILE *a.*], fit for war, of military age; **war-hatchet**, a hatchet used by the N. American Indians to symbolize the declaration or cessation of hostilities (see quots. and cf. HATCHET *sb.* 2); **war-hawk** *U.S.*, one who is eager for the fray, a 'brave'; **warhead** (of a torpedo: see quot. 1898); also, that of any missile, esp. one deriving its destructive power from the release of nuclear energy; †**war-headling**, a military chieftain or commander; **war hero**, a man who has acted heroically in a war; also **war heroine**; **war-hound** *fig.* (cf. WAR-DOG); **War House** *slang*, the War Office; **war hysteria**, unhealthy emotion or excitement caused by war; an enthusiasm for war; **war machine**, (*a*) an instrument or weapon of war; (*b*) *transf.*, the military resources of a country organized for waging war; **war marriage**, a marriage taking place in wartime, esp. one in which the bridegroom is on active service; **war medicine** *N. Amer.*, (a form of) magic formerly used by North American Indians to ensure success in war; also *fig.*; **war memorial**, a monument, etc., commemorating those (esp. from a particular locality) killed in a war, and freq. inscribed with their names; **war-mind**, a mind attuned to or desirous of war; hence **war-minded** *a.*, having such a mind; **war-mindedness**; **war-minister**, the person who directs the war-affairs of a state; the Secretary of State for War; **war museum**, a museum of the history of warfare in general, or of warfare during a particular period; **war orphan**, a child orphaned by war; **war pension**, a pension paid to someone disabled or widowed by war; **war picture**, (*a*) a painting of which the theme is war; (*b*) a photograph of a scene from the theatre of war; also, a documentary film of action from a war, and *transf.* a written account of this; (*c*) a cinematographic film with war as its subject or background (the usual sense); cf. *war film, movie* (sense 8 f above); **warplane**, an aeroplane equipped for fighting, bombing, etc., in war-time; **war-post**, a post into which N. American Indians strike the war-hatchet; **war refugee**, one who seeks refuge in another country, etc., from the effects of war; a displaced person; **war reporter** = *war-correspondent*; hence **war-reporting**; **war resistance**, opposition to war, pacifism; hence **war resister**, an opponent of war or of a particular war; **war risk** *Insurance* (chiefly *Marine*), a risk of loss, etc., during war-time; freq. in *pl.* and *attrib.*; **war road** *N. Amer.* = WAR-PATH a (*concr.*); **war room**, a room from which a war or part of a war is directed; **war-substantive** *a.* [SUBSTANTIVE *a.* 1 e], confirmed (in a rank) for the duration of a war; **war-talk**, (*a*) a formal discussion among N. American Indian chiefs about war; also *fig.*; (*b*) talk about war in general; **war toy**, a toy with which a child can play war-games; **war-trail** = WAR-PATH; **war trial**, the trial of a person for a war crime or crimes; cf. *Nuremberg trial(s)* s.v. NUREMBERG 2; **war veteran** orig. *U.S.* = VETERAN *sb.* 1 b; **war-weary** *a.*, (*a*) weary of war; (*b*) *U.S.*, *spec.* applied to aircraft badly damaged in war-time, and which are withdrawn from service for repair, conversion, or scrapping; also *ellipt.* as *sb.*; **war wedding** = *war marriage*; **war-woman** (see quot.); **war work**, special work occasioned by war, and which is intended to advance the war effort; **war-worker**, a person undertaking war work; also *transf.*; **war-worthy** *a.*, suitable for or befitting war; so **war-worthiness**. Also WAR-CRY, WAR-DANCE, WAR-DOG, WAR-DRUM, WAR-GOD, WAR-HORSE, WAR-KETTLE, WAR-LOCK *v.*[2], WAR-LORD, WAR-MAN, WAR-NOTE, WAR OFFICE, etc.

1949 E. COXHEAD *Wind in West* vi. 152 The farmer I stay with there is a member of the *War Ag. **1970** G. E. EVANS *Where Beards wag All* ix. 106 When the *War Ag.* (Agricultural Committee) took over I asked 'em would they send the gyro-tiller. **1866** KINGSLEY *Herew.* xx, Split up the *war-arrow, and send it round. **1890** KIPLING *Light that Failed* (1891) xii. 237 Some man unknown who would be employed as *war artist by the Central Southern Syndicate. **1981** S. CHITTY *Gwen John* ix. 148 Augustus..was in France as a war artist. **1901** E. W. B. MORRISON *With Guns in S.A.* xxxiv. 239 (*caption*) Mrs. Jourdain's '*war baby'. **1917** 'CONTACT' *Airman's Outings* 35 Even these war babies (three of them died very gallantly before we re-assembled for breakfast next day) had bottled most of their exuberance. **1917** R. W. LARDNER *Gullible's Travels* 83 'You forgot somethin',' she says, 'You forgot them war babies.' Did I tell you about that? Last fall I done a little dabblin' in Crucial Steel. **1935** I. MILLER *School Tie* xv. 286 It was possible to join a Junior Training Battalion—commonly known as the War Babies' Brigade—at the age of seventeen and a half. **1948** *Green Bay* (Wisconsin) *Press-Gaz.* 13 July 4/2 The idle rich of Europe..clamored for war while they invested great amounts in American war babies and reaped superlative profits. **1974** G. BUTLER *Coffin for Canary* ix. 105 Born Belfast, 1944, so she was just a war baby. **1820** *Western Rev.* II. 48 After the action is over, each person returns his *war bag to the commander of the party. **1897** A. H. LEWIS *Wolfville* 33 S'pose you-alls gropes about in your war-bags an' sees. I'm needin' of a drink mighty bad. **1933** J. V. ALLEN *Cowboy Lore* I. 6 What's known as the 'war bag' is carried by many of the boys in their beds to protect their wardrobe, tobacco, etc., and may be anything from a flour sack to a rather pretentious container. **1972** F. VAN W. MASON *Roads to Liberty* 241 Higsby fumbled in his war bag. **1836** [MRS. C. P. TRAILL] *Backw. Canada* 289 [An Indian squaw] adorned with the wings of the American *War-bird. **1855** LONGF. *Hiaw.* IX. 184 Then began the greatest battle That the war-birds ever witnessed. **1917** G. FRANKAU *City of Fear* 3 Above, The wrr-birds beat And whistle. **1936** 'R. HYDE' *Passport to Hell* 206 German and British warbirds were mixing it in an aerial free-for-all. **1981** *Pilot* Jan. 23/2 Some of the war-birds flying today are quite bent, cracked, patched up. **1845** J. C. FRÉMONT *Rep. Exploring Exped.* 134 Indians..with the long red streamers of their *war bonnets reaching nearly to the ground. **1928** 'BRENT OF BIN BIN' *Up Country* xxii. 356 Adjusting her widow's cap like a war-bonnet, she arose to her full height of five-feet-one-and-a-half. **1973** A. H. WHITEFORD *N. Amer. Indian Arts* 151 The flowing war bonnet of the Plains has become the symbol of the American Indian. **1952** M. ALLINGHAM *Tiger in Smoke* i. 12 The *War Box cited him 'Missing believed killed'. **1969** M. PUGH *Last Place Left* xxix. 213, I flit between Downing Street and the War Box and the Ministry of Defence. **1889** *Daily News* 23 Jan. 6/6 An encounter took place recently just outside the Sulymah district, between a small British force and a party of *war-boys. 1901 ALLDRIDGE *Sherbro* xxvii. 314 They began to be chased by war-boys in canoes. 1918 A. BENNETT *Pretty Lady* xi. 61 She was becoming hysterical: the special liability of the *war-bride. 1939 *Daily Tel.* 18 Dec. 9/5 Silver tea and coffee sets are being bought..as gifts to the many war brides unable to set up homes. 1978 J. KRANTZ *Scruples* i. 10 She was as alert as a vixen, as humorous as the song by Maurice Chevalier after which her homesick war-bride mother had named her. 1962 J. ONSLOW *Bowler-hatted Cowboy* xviii. 175 One summer day, they [*sc.* two horses] came home, gaunt, their heads bloody and scarred from '*war bridles' with which someone had tried to halter-break them. 1813 R. STUART *Jrnl.* 14 Apr. in *Discovery Oregon Trail* (1935) x. 236 A Pole surpassing in height any put in the roof, is put out at the chimney where are suspended their Medicine Bags and *War Budgets carefully concealed in innumerable wrappers. 1887 J. C. MORISON *Serv. Man* p. xv, The removal of all fear of war would be even a greater gain than the suppression of war-budgets. 1916 *Times* 9 Dec. 9/2 It is an immense gain to have the Prime Minister definitely and irrevocably committed to the creation of a small *War Cabinet, constantly..devoted to the prosecution of the war. 1940 J. REITH *Diary* 5 Jan. (1975) v. 237, I asked if the job carried War Cabinet rank and he said no. 1980 P. FITZGERALD *Human Voices* ii. 38, I don't know who authorised him to speak. I understand it was the War Cabinet. 1922 *Encycl. Brit.* XXXII. 953/1 It is possible that the conspicuous success with which Arlington Cemetery has been designed had a share in influencing the Imperial War Graves Commission in the construction of the British *war cemeteries on somewhat similar lines. 1982 'J. GASH' *Firefly Gadroon* xv. 145 There's a turning through the woods where the American War Cemetery stands. 1901 CORVO *Ho. Borgia* 34 The papal jewels were pawned, and their price added to the *war-chest. 1912 W. DEEPING *Sincerity* xvi. 124 He had about forty pounds left, no great sum to start a war-chest with. 1932 *Sun* (Baltimore) 30 Aug. 1/6 (*heading*) War chests practically empty, parties curtail on campaign. 1973 R. L. SIMON *Big Fix* iv. 34 All the guilt-stricken celebrities contributing to their war chest. 1827 MRS. HEMANS *Last Constantine* lxxxv, *War-clouds have wrapt the city. 1908 C. W. WALLACE *Childr. Chapel, Blackfriars* 172 Absence of reference in these two plays is negative proof that the personal war-cloud had passed, by 1602. 1894 *Abstract of Courses* (Naval War. Coll.) 3 The summer course at the Naval *War College began on the 13th of June. 1913 R. MEINERTZHAGEN *Diary* 1 Nov. (1960) 56 A joint war college for all branches of Government Services [in India] would be a God-send. 1978 H. WOUK *War & Remembrance* i. 11 Talking in a calm War College vein. 1928 M. DOBB *Russian Econ. Devel. since Revolution* iii. 64 '*War communism', accordingly, sprang into life in the 'forcing-house' of a mortal struggle of the new régime—a struggle in which all things were subordinated to military necessity, and the problems of industry were simply regarded as..the problem of military supplies. 1965 B. PEARCE tr. *Preobrazhensky's New Economics* 32 The economics of War Communism were those of a state economy of the war-consumption type, when we were not accumulating but were forced to *spend* our resources. 1844 *War-correspondent [see CORRESPONDENT *sb.* 4b]. 1870 A. MAVERICK *Henry J. Raymond & N.Y. Press* 256 The 'war correspondents' who had been sent out to the battle-fields to represent the newspapers of New York throve and grew famous. 1891 KIPLING *Light that Failed* ii. 25 Dick was made free of the New and Honourable Fraternity of war-correspondents. 1906 L. OPPENHEIM *Internat. Law* 264 Violations of rules regarding warfare are *war crimes only when committed without an order of the belligerent government concerned. If members of the armed forces commit violations by *order* of their government, they are not war criminals and may not be punished by the enemy; the latter can, however, resort to reprisals. 1945 *Daily Express* 16 May 1/1 The United Nations War Crimes Commission announced last night: Hermann Goering's name was placed ..on the first list of persons charged with war crimes. 1980 *Oxf. Compan. Law* 1288/2 After World War II, three classes of offences against international law came to be regarded as war crimes, crimes against peace, as by planning or waging a war of aggression, conventional war crimes, or violations of the accepted laws or customs of warfare and crimes against humanity, including extermination, enslavement, deportation and other inhumane acts. 1906 *War criminal [see *war crime*]. 1929 W. S. CHURCHILL *World Crisis* V. viii. 158 An article of the Peace Treaty obliged the Germans to stigmatize all their greatest men and potentates as War Criminals. 1943 *Ann. Reg. 1942* 190 The question of the trial of war criminals ruffled..the ever-growing friendliness between Britain and America. 1981 J. WAINWRIGHT *Urge for Justice* 121 An organisation devoted to tracking down war criminals. 1939 *Act 2 & 3 Geo. VI* c. 72 §4 Where the land comprised in a lease is unfit by reason of *war damage, the following provisions..shall have effect. *Ibid.* §24 'War damage' means damage caused by, or in repelling, enemy action, or by measures taken to avoid the spreading of the consequences of damage caused by, or in repelling, enemy action. 1950 E. HYAMS *From Waste Land* 10 Sharp and hopeful landlords claimed war-damage compensation. 1975 J. CLEARY *Safe House* iv. 177 The walls were spattered with bullet and shrapnel marks..all war damage. 1946 *Mind* LV. 380 The Secretary reported appeals from *war-damaged libraries in Europe. 1978 *Times* 8 May 9/8 Volunteers.. shivering in war-damaged, makeshift offices. 1969 J. BURMEISTER *Hot & Copper Sky* i. 17 They're French *war dead. From the Indo-China campaign. 1917 W. J. LOCKE *Red Planet* i. 4 To fill in my time, I first started..a sort of *War Diary. 1918 E. S. FARROW *Dict. Mil. Terms* 657 *War diary*, a record of events kept in campaign by each battalion and higher organization, each ammunition, supply, engineer, and sanitary train. 1937 KIPLING *Something of Myself* iii. 49 An accursed Muscovite paper..published the war diaries of Alikhanoff, a Russian General. 1955 E. WAUGH *Officers & Gentlemen* 142 Guy chalked the nightly wanderings of the Commandos on..his map and recorded them next day in the War Diary. 1981 J. BARNETT *Firing Squad* ii. 105 The War Diary of Sergeant Michael Lugard. 1918 W. OWEN *Let.* 18 Feb. (1967) 534, I confess I *bring on* what few *war dreams I now have, entirely by *willingly* considering war of an evening. 1855 LONGF. *Hiaw.* iv. 188 From his eyrie screamed..The Keneu, the great *war-eagle. 1919 W. B. YEATS *Cutting of Agate* 16 The Print Room of the British Museum is now closed as a *war-economy. 1940 *Economist* 3 Feb. 189/1 The problem of war economy is to man and equip the Forces, to raise output for war and export needs to the utmost and to cut down civilian consumption. 1948 [see *peace economy* s.v. PEACE *sb.* 17d]. 1972 M. J. BOSSE *Incident at Naha* 56 Like any girl caught up in a war economy. She had a pimp. 1919 *Maclean's Mag.* Jan. 49 (*heading*) Britain's wonderful *war effort. 1934 W. S. CHURCHILL *Marlborough* II. v. 101 Whigs and Tories alike wished the fleet to be used as a part of the main war-effort. 1954 N. COWARD *Future Indefinite* iv. vii. 194 A job which ..would be of real value to the war effort. 1977 A. WILSON *Strange Ride Rudyard Kipling* vii. 299 He would never have repeated the story lest it weakened our war effort. 1876 MORRIS *Sigurd* III. (1877) 217 Guttorm the young and the *war-fain. 1812 J. STEELE *Papers* (1924) II. 668 The late report of the Secty. of the Treasy. will cool the *war fever in some. 1908 H. G. WELLS *War in Air* vi. 180 To the normal high-strung energy of New York streets was added a touch of war-fever. 1978 N. GOSLING *Paris 1900–1914* 187 In 1912 the slowly developing war fever..began to show itself in sinister local symptoms. 1965 H. KAHN *On Escalation* 284 Deterrence-only is the opposite of '*war-fighting'. 1983 *Listener* 10 Feb. 7/1 They are war-fighting weapons with a first-strike capability. 1950 *Sun* (Baltimore) 29 June 1 General MacArthur left for the South Korean *warfront today. 1976 *Billings* (Montana) *Gaz.* 11 July 1-A/2 Lebanon's three major warfronts resounded to artillery, rocket and mortar fire. 1828 A. B. GRANVILLE *St. Petersburgh* II. 75 The '*war-game' table, on which the present Emperor, when Grand-duke, used to play. 1891 *Tablet* 17 Oct. 613 A struggle more serious than that of any mere clerical war-game. 1910 H. G. WELLS *New Machiavelli* (1911) i. iii. 84 The spectacle of volunteer officers fighting the war game in Caxton Hall. 1951 D. KNIGHT *In Deep* (1964) 92 The cadets..carrying out one of the prescribed war games under the direction of student squad leaders. 1966 *Punch* 6 July 26/2 Entertaining incidental scenes (the children's war games, the husband's home movies, haggling over the junk) keep interest always alive. 1967 *Guardian* 16 Oct. 8/5 The National Wargame Championships organised by the British Model Soldier Society. 1970 *Time* 5 Oct. 13 At one point Nixon told Kissinger: 'Let's you and me war-game this,' and they worked the plans over to see, as Nixon put it, 'where the weak points might be.' 1975 *Times* 2 June 13/1 Politicians of all parties cooped up in..Westminster have become so absorbed in their own war-games that they have lost touch with the wider world. 1981 *Washington Post* 8 Nov. L1/6 'Well,' Wakko said, 'I've got to go back to work. We're war-gaming an LNW in Monaco.' 1967 *Guardian* 16 Oct. 8/5 One thing only is causing the *wargamers concern. There are so many different societies in the field. 1982 M. LEAPMAN *Yankee Doodles* IV. 208 War-gamers are not the only people undertaking such simulations. 1954 MCCLOSKEY & TREFETHEN *Operations Research for Management* I. 15 They used the technique of *war-gaming to develop models of possible operations, then 'tested' various tactics and weapons. 1970 *Daily Tel.* (Colour Suppl.) 30 Oct. 43/2 Today war-gaming has reached a point of sophistication where one almost needs a computer to play. 1980 J. MCNEIL *Spy Game* ix. 96 War gaming is like that, dashed unpredictable. 1934 WEBSTER, *War gas. 1939 L. W. MARRISON tr. *M. Sartori's War Gases* p. viii, The most efficient war gases are organic compounds, the inorganic compounds which have great toxicity being unsuitable for use owing to their physical and chemical properties. 1974 M. C. GERALD *Pharmacol.* vii. 134 In 1968, 6000 sheep were accidentally killed in Utah, allegedly as a result of exposure to the war gas VX that was being tested by the Army about 17 miles away. 1930 W. S. MAUGHAM *Bread-Winner* i. 18 They were a dreary lot that *war generation. 1978 CADOGAN & CRAIG *Women & Children First* ii. 47 The sense of isolation that characterized the war generation. 1917 *Imperial War. Conf.* 5 in *Parl. Papers* (Cd. 8566) XXIII. 323 The Conference..humbly prays His Majesty to constitute by Royal Charter an Imperial *War Graves Commission. 1945 J. REITH *Let.* 11 June in *Diaries* (1975) vii. 350, I should have thought..you would have welcomed the establishment of an imperial corporation—the first to be achieved (except War Graves). 1981 J. BARNETT *Firing Squad* xii. 175 Search all names against..war casualty lists, ditto War Graves Commission. 1922 *Nation* 9 Sept. 758/1 (*heading*) The myth of *war-guilt. 1940 W. TEMPLE *Thoughts in Wartime* ii. i. 60 The war-guilt clause, against which many of us have protested. 1971 *Guardian* 5 Aug. 12/3 Concepts of war 'guilt' derived from the Second World War have encouraged some elements of the Left to identify the war in Vietnam with an emerging American fascism. 1981 J. B. HILTON *Surrender Value* xi. 88 And she had been intense: about war-guilt, about Borchert and Kafka. 1590 SPENSER *F.Q.* II. x. 62 The weary Britons, whose *war-hable youth Was by Maximian lately led away. 1760 G. GROGHAN *Jrnl.* 4 Dec. in R. G. Thwaites *Early Western Trav.* (1904) I. 116 That you [*sc.* chiefs and warriors]..may..bury the *War Hatchet in the Bottomless Pitt. *a*1818 B. HAWKINS *Sk. Creek Country* (1848) 72 He lifts the war hatchet against the nation which has injured them. 1841 J. F. COOPER *Deerslayer* xxx, Our great fathers across the Salt Lake have sent each other the war-hatchet. 1881 TYLOR *Anthropol.* ix. 224 The bundle of arrows wrapped in a rattlesnake's skin, or the blood-red war-hatchet struck into the war-post. 1798 T. JEFFERSON *Let. to J. Madison* 26 Apr., Writ. 1854 IV. 238 At present, the war hawks talk of septembrizing, [etc.]. 1815 in M. Cutler *Life, Jrnls. & Corr.* (1888) II. 332 Our war-hawks..affect to speak of it as a glorious war and an honorable peace. 1865 F. PARKMAN *Champlain* ix. (1875) 308 The Indian tribes, war-hawks of the wilderness. 1898 F. T. JANE *Torpedo* 19 The parts of a torpedo are as follows:—(a) The explosive head (*war head). This is only fitted when the torpedo is to be used in earnest: for practice, a collapsible head is fitted. 1944 *Sun* (Baltimore) 20 June 3/3 Explosive carried in a warhead [of a German robot plane] is equal to a 2,200 pound German bomb. 1955 *Bull. Atomic Sci.* Apr. 168/3 In the not too distant future we can foresee the dominance of intercontinental guided missiles with hydrogen war heads. 1978 R. V. JONES *Most Secret War* xlv. 447, I was now prepared to call everyone else's bluff, and declare for a rocket of 12 tons all-up weight with a 1 ton warhead. 13.. *Coer de L.* 2011 Sir, thus thou shalt lere To mis-say thy *werhedlynge. 1898 *Kansas City Star* 19 Dec. 1/5 Following are the names of the members of the entertainment committee who received the *war heroes. 1953 L. P. HARTLEY *Go-Between* iv. 59, I already felt violently jealous of Trimingham, and the fact that he was a war-hero did not recommend him to me. 1982 T. ALLBEURY *Shadow of Shadows* v. 44 Your father was a war hero. He was awarded..the Legion of Honour. 1932 *New Yorker* 9 Jan. 34/1 On the sidewalks are..a few *war heroines with nothing to sell. 1979 'D. KYLE' *Green River High* viii. 106 We..read: *War heroine returns to Sarawak.* 1812 BYRON *Ch. Har.* I. xl, What gallant *war-hounds rouse them from their lair, And gnash their fangs, loud yelling for the prey! 1848 LYTTON *K. Arthur* II. civ, Unleash the warhounds—stay us those who can! 1925 FRASER & GIBBONS *Soldier & Sailor Words* 300 **War House, the*, General Staff slang for the War Office. 1926 'SAPPER' *Final Count* xii. 302 They thought I was mad at the War House. 1978 D. WHEATLEY *Officer & Temporary Gentleman* iii. 29 A man in control at the War House who had an enormous hold upon the popular imagination. 1940 'G. ORWELL' *Inside Whale* 172 The very people who..had sniggered over their own superiority to *war hysteria were the ones who rushed..into the mental slum of 1915. 1968 O. WYND *Sumatra Seven Zero* ii. 20 Birgid is the child of my war hysteria. Her father was a blond Norwegian. 1881 W. D. HAY *300 Years Hence* iv. 70 The last inventions in *war-machines. 1914 W. J. BRYAN *Mem.* (1925) 390 The allies see peace only in a success so signal as to crush the German war machine. 1979 *Sci. Amer.* Mar. 123/1 With the introduction of catapults, together with other war machines just coming into use in the West, sieges became more effective. 1981 B. LANGLEY *Autumn Tiger* xv. 244 Stalin..was wary of the German war machine. 1921 'C. DANE' *Bill of Divorcement* II. 54 If it hadn't been for the war—and the *war marriages. 1805 W. CLARK *Jrnl.* 11 Jan. in *Lewis & Clark Exped.* (1904) I. vi. 247 Some of our Men go to See a *War Medeson made at the Village on the opposite Side of the river. 1893 *Chicago Tribune* 28 Apr. 4/1 Gov. Altgeld..proceeded to administer a dose of war medicine he had been making for some time. 1962 E. E. EVANS-PRITCHARD in *Ess. Social Anthropol.* v. 95 He used some of these forms of magic himself, getting old commoners to bring the medicines and perform the rites, except in the case of the war-medicines, which he administered himself, from the large bongo horn in which they were kept. 1912 *War memorial [see LATE *a.*[1] 3]. 1930 KIPLING *Limits & Renewals* (1932) 324 The little cast-iron *poilu*, which seemed to be standard pattern for War memorials in that region. 1980 P. LIVELY *Judgement Day* v. 55 The starling flew across the nave, crashed into the War Memorial window..and thumped to the ground. 1928 BLUNDEN *Undertones of War* iii. 27 The joyful path away from the line..was full of pictures for my infant *war-mind. 1932 H. CRANE *Let.* 13 Apr. (1965) 409 Dos Passos has written a very important record of the war and the 'war mind' in 1919. 1936 *Mind* XLV. 289 A society which prefers war to peace and organises itself for success in war, may be rational in the above sense, if (a) the majority of its members are genuinely *war-minded, and (b) the small minority of pacifists in its ranks is allowed to express..its dissenting opinion. 1948 W. FORTESCUE *Beauty for Ashes* xxii. 172 At intervals it stopped..to allow warminded little boys to finger the ugly noses of guns. 1936 H. READ *Surrealism* 36 Motives no less irrational than those which promote *war-mindedness. 1790 BURKE *Fr. Rev.* Sel. Wks. II. 255 From my heart I pity the condition of a respectable servant of the publick, like this *war minister. 1917 *Times* 20 Feb. 11/3 At No. 6, Avenue de Malakoff..in two spacious first-floor *appartements*..is housed the *War Museum which, when complete, will be presented to the French nation. 1967 O. WYND *Walk Softly, Men Praying* x. 165 An inspirational experience in a war museum. 1979 E. BERCOVICI *Wolf Trap* 161 The War Museum on the upper fortress fascinated him. 1915 W. OWEN *Let.* 29 June (1967) 342 All France is collecting for its *War Orphans. 1971 H. MCCLOY *Question of Time* i. 14 The nuns kept on trying to trace the families of war orphans left in their care. 1930 E. H. YOUNG *Miss Mole* xxv. 224 The little poultry farm which was to supplement..the hero's *war pension. 1980 *Daily Tel.* 24 Apr. 14/5 His mother brought him up alone on a war pension plus what she could make by smocking children's clothes. 1883 B. POTTER *Jrnl.* 28 Apr. (1966) 39 First we went to the Fine Arts Gallery..to see..the Egyptian *war pictures. 1900 (*title*) War pictures. 1914 R. GRAU *Theatre of Science* ii. 40 The war pictures released by this company reflected the high aims of a man. 1915 V. WOOLF *Diary* 25 Jan. (1977) I. 28 The Picture Palace was a little disappointing—as we never got to the War pictures, after waiting 1 hour & a half. 1946 J. B. PRIESTLEY *Bright Day* viii. 246 Honest war pictures, made on the spot here by people who know what it's like. 1978 *Listener* 30 Mar. 410/1 *In Which We Serve* I remember as the best war picture that I have ever seen. 1911 *Flight* 16 Dec. 1078/2 No one has any very definite ideas of what the future type of *war-plane will be like. 1938 C. DAY LEWIS *Overtures to Death* 17 Oh, look at the warplanes! Screaming hysteric treble In the long power-dive, like gannets they fall steep. 1967 A. MACLEAN *Where Eagles Dare* xi. 230 The Mosquito bomber, all engines and plywood, was, he was well aware, the fastest warplane in the world. 1978 *Guardian Weekly* 4 June 16/1 Categories so politically volatile as warplanes. 1826 J. F. COOPER *Last of Mohicans* xxiii, None of my young men strike the tomahawk deeper into the *war-post. 1881 War-post [see *war-hatchet* above]. 1942 D. POWELL *Time to be Born* vii. 163 Amanda was nobly..adopting a *war refugee. 1973 'B. MATHER' *Snowline* iii. 33 There are three million war refugees from Bangladesh in West Bengal. 1950 E. H. GOMBRICH *Story of Art* 118 The final result is possibly more impressive than the accounts of our own *war reporters and newsreel men. 1976 S. HYNES *Auden Generation* x. 342 Compared to *war-reporting of the Spanish war..*Journey to a War* is superficial and uninformative. 1932 *Week-End Rev.* 19 Nov. 611/2 We appeal to those who wish to take part in a truly practical and effective effort at *war resistance to send us a donation. 1935 J. BELL in *We did not Fight* p. xviii, The most active and ardent *war resisters..are more likely to take the line of revolutionary action than conscientious objection. 1976 *Pacifist* Jan. 10/1 We remain an organisation of war-resisters. 1920 *Lloyd's List Law Rep.* 22 July 288/2, I am perfectly clear this is a case that is not brought within the *War Risks Policy. 1934 WEBSTER, *War risk insurance*, term insurance written by the United States Government for members of the military and naval forces. 1939 *Country Life* 11 Feb. 133/2 An insurance against war risks should be attached to Schedule 'A'. 1974 E. R. H. IVAMY *Marine Insurance* (ed. 2) xv. 219 The term 'war risk' in a marine policy has been held to include a civil war. 1782 in V. W.

Howard *Bryan Station Heroes & Heroines* (1932) xii. 144 On the Southward side below where the *War road crosses the said fork. **1968** E. Russenholt *Heart of Continent* II. iii. 41 Canadians and Indians follow the old Indian war road. **1914** A. Wilson *Let.* 29 Oct. in M. Gilbert *Winston S. Churchill* (1972) III. Compan. I. 233, I should like to have a room set apart for me near the *War room. **1976** J. Lee *Ninth Man* I. 82 The War Room occupied the southwest corner of the main floor of the White House. *a* **1944** K. Douglas *Alamein to Zem Zem* (1946) ii. 13 He had..returned to his *war-substantive rank of captain. **1965** *New Statesman* 10 Dec. 919/1 How could a poor war-substantive captain hope to hold his own against someone like Colonel Passy. **1831** Trelawny *Adv. Younger Son* II. 38 Then they call a *war-talk, and say they would speak with these white men. **1834** *Sk. & Eccentr. David Crockett* xiv. 185 His public harangues, or his war talks, as electioneering speeches are called in the west. **1861** M. B. Chesnut *Diary* 23 Apr. in C. V. Woodward *M. Chesnut's Civil War* (1981) 53, Maria—are you crying because all this war talk scares you? **1939** C. Day Lewis *Child of Misfortune* III. i. 264 You're not letting this war-talk throw a scare into you? **1973** M. Kaye *Toy is Born* xv. 114 It is interesting to note that the hue and cry against *war toys a few years ago had little effect on Avalon Hill. **1851** Mayne Reid *Scalp Hunters* xxvi. II. 41 Over the western section of this great prairie passes the Apache *war-trail. **1949** R. Chandler *Let.* 25 Feb. (1981) 149 There is an element of hypocrisy in these *war trials. **1971** P. D. James *Shroud for Nightingale* vii. 242 He'd seen her before... In Germany. She was in the dock. It was a war trial. **1906** *N.Y. Even. Post* 29 Jan. 1 A guard of honor selected from the ranks of the Spanish *war veterans here. **1980** J. McClure *Blood of Englishman* x. 92 War veterans... It'd all gone a bit to their heads. **1895** W. B. Yeats *Poems* 7, I have not yet, *war-weary king, Been spoken of with any man. **1902** *Edin. Rev.* July 39 Campbell's 'Soldier's Dream' is the most beautiful rendering in English verse of the war-weary mood. **1945** *Sat. Even. Post* 17 Mar. 20 Thousands of once precious B-17's are now 'war-wearies'. Not worth salvaging, they clutter up foreign and domestic airfields. **1945** *Fortune* Aug. 208 Five war-weary Liberators, described with horrors by their pilots as 'clunkers'. **1915** *Truth* 4 Aug. 181/2 What do we hear from London about *war-weddings? **1786** Ferriar in *Mem. Lit. & Philos. Soc. Manch.* (1790) III. 28 In every Indian village, the *war-woman..is a kind of oracle; by dreams and presages, she directs the hunters to their prey, and the warriors to the enemy. **1890** Kipling *Light that Failed* (1891) ii. 24 Do you want me to do *war-work? *Ibid.* iv. 64 He has thrown up war work. **1916** A. Huxley *Let.* 2 Mar. (1969) 92 A friend of mine at Magdalen, a Quaker..objected to war-work of any kind, combatant or non-. **1954** W. K. Hancock *Country & Calling* vii. 189 The answer to that difficulty was for my wife to take up paid war work in place of the voluntary work she had been doing in Birmingham. **1977** *Belfast Tel.* 14 Feb. 9/6 Rene, who was in Mackie's on war work, lived with her widowed father and looked after her young brothers. **1915** *Political Q.* May 108 It is not clear whether or no the special..*war-workers.. will be permanently shut out of the trades. **1930** Blunden *De Bello Germanico* iv. 41 War-workers varying from whizzbangs to woolly bears. **1978** Cadogan & Craig *Women & Children First* ii. 48 The experiences of the war workers had been thoroughly documented. **1909** *Q. Rev.* Oct. 578 The aim must now be..to seize every opportunity to improve its *war-worthiness. **1908** Hardy *Dynasts* III. VII. viii. 510 Ney holds indignantly that such a feint Is not *war-worthy.

‖**war**, *sb.*² *Obs.*⁻¹ [Thevenot's rendering of a dial. var. of Hindī *baḍ*.] The Banyan-tree.

1687 A. Lovell tr. *Thevenot's Trav.* III. 25 Trees of several kinds; as Manguiers, Palms, Mirabolans, Wars, Maisa-trees. *Ibid.*, We saw the War-tree in its full extent. It is likewise called Ber, and the Tree of Banians.

war, waur (wɑr, wɔr), *a.* and *adv. Sc.* and *north.* Forms: 3–5 werre, 4 *Sc.* ver, 4–6 wer, 4–5 were, werr, worre, 6 wor, *Sc.* woir, 4–5 ware, 5–6 warre, 5–8 warr, 6 *Sc.* var, (uar), 4–9 war, 8– *Sc.* waur. See also werrar *a.* [a. ON. *verre* adj., *verr* adv.: see worse *a.* and *adv.* The spelling *waur*, which first appears in the 18th c., was adopted by Burns and Scott, and is now general in Scottish use.]

A. *adj.* = worse *a.* in all senses.

c **1250** *Gen. & Ex.* 3951 To madian lond wente he [*sc.* Balaam] his ride, And wente is herte on werre ðhogt. *a* **1300** *Cursor M.* 454 Qua herd euer a warr [*Gött. MS.* werr] auntour. *c* **1375** *Ibid.* 13411 (Fairf.) þe gode wine sulde þou first dispende & siþen drink þe worre [*earlier texts* wers] at hende. **1375** Barbour *Bruce* I. 269 Thryldome is weill wer than deid. *c* **1400** *Apol. Loll.* 55 Are þei not..werr, and abhominabler þan carnal sodomits? *c* **1440** *Alphabet of Tales* 50 Sho said þatt sho sulde sende hym a war question þan owther off þe tother was. **1549** *Compl. Scot.* vi. 57 Thai schel fische dimuneuis and grouis les, and of ane var qualite. *a* **1578** Lindesay (Pitscottie) *Chron. Scot.* (S.T.S.) I. 178 They pairtit war freindis nor they mett. **1578** Moysie *Mem.* (Bannatyne Club) 15 They ran togither; the said Willie wes strickin to the grund and died, the vther throw the thie and litle war. **1579** Spenser *Sheph. Cal.* Sept. 108 They sayne the world is much war then it wont. **1584** J. Melvill *Autob. & Diary* (Wodrow Soc.) 187 Quhilk is maist sacrilegius and war nor Papisticall. **1654** Z. Coke *Logick* 77 World so called of War-old, because the older it is, the War or worse it is. **1786** Burns *A Dream* iii, There's mony waur been o' the race, And aiblins ane been better Than you this day. **1815** Scott *Guy M.* v, 'Vanity and waur!' said the Dominie; 'it is a trafficking with the Evil One'. **1849** C. Brontë *Shirley* xx, We're no war nor some 'at is aboon us; are we? **1883** *Longman's Mag.* Nov. 72 Losh me! it's just waur than useless the day whativer.

†**b.** ***father war***, worse than one's father, degenerate. *Obs.* Cf. ON. *fǫður-verringr* sb.

1535 Stewart *Cron. Scot.* (Rolls) I. 206 And lat ws nocht be cawit fader war, Thocht we be hapnit now fra thame so far.

c. *absol.* (quasi-*sb.*) as in ***to get the war***, to get the worst of it.

a **1300** *Cursor M.* 7579 Fle þat wynnes to haue þe warr, For ar i fle i sal cum nerr. **13..** *Gaw. & Gr. Knt.* 1588 Lest felle hym þe worre. *Ibid.* 1591 þe worre hade þat oþer. *c* **1375** Barbour *Bruce* IX. 159 Bot thar bowmen the wer had ay. *a* **1568** *Wyf Auchtermuchty* xv. in *Bannatyne MS.* (Hunter. Club) 345 For and we fecht I ill gett the woir. **1824** Scott *Redgauntlet* Let. x, If ye expect to be ranting among the queans o' lasses.., ye will come by the waur.

B. *adv.* = worse *adv.* in all senses.

c **1200** Ormin 4898 And swa þu tellesst werre off þe, Swa telleþþ Drihhtin bettre. *a* **1300** *Cursor M.* 11900 þai..drund him [*sc.* Herod] in pike and terr, And send him quar he faris werr, werr þan he fard euer ar. *c* **1375** *Sc. Leg. Saints* xl. (*Ninian*) 1324 þu sal wyt I ame of mycht ver þane þu wes þe to dycht. *c* **1440** *York Myst.* xxii. 54 þer was neuere dede þat euere he dide, þat greued hym warre. *c* **1440** *Alphabet of Tales* 73 Other patt er hongry suld com & pryk me war þan þai did. *c* **1520** Skelton *Magnyf.* 923 All is out of harre, And out of trace, Ay warre and warre In euery place. *a* **1585** Montgomerie *Flyting* 280 They fand ane monstour on the morne, War facit nor ane cat. **17..** *South-sea Song* 7 in *Ramsay's Tea-Table Miscellany* (1775) I. 34 The lave will fare the war in trouth For our lang biding here. **1816** Scott *Old Mort.* vi, A' the warld kens that they maun either marry or do waur. **1828** [Carr] *Craven Gloss.*, *War and war*, worse and worse.

war (wɔː(r)), *v.*¹ Inflected **warred** (wɔːd), **warring** (ˈwɔːrɪŋ). Forms: 2 uuerrien, 3 wurre, weorre, weorri, 3–4 worri, worry, 3–5 worre, werri, werry, 3–6 werre, 4 werr, 4–5 wer, were, 4–7 warre, 6 warr, *dial.* var, *Sc.* weir(e, 4, 6– war. [f. war *sb.*¹ Cf. the equivalent OF. *guerrer*, *werrer; also *werreier* warray *v.*]

†**1.** *trans.* To make war upon. *Obs.*

1154 *O.E. Chron.* (Laud MS.) an. 1135, Dauid king of Scotland toc to uuerrien him. **1297** R. Glouc. (Rolls) 4636 þe kunde men of þis lond recetted were þere [*sc.* in Wales] Euere wanne of straunge men yworred hii were. *Ibid.* 4987 Ac penda þe heþene duc adde euere god wille To worry him [Oswy] & don him ssame. *c* **1383** in *Eng. Hist. Rev.* (1911) Oct. 744 þough it be leful in caas to werre & sleen euele cristene men..whanne riȝtfulnesse..shulde perisshen elles. **1390** Gower *Conf.* I. 363 To passe over the grete See To werre and sle the Sarazin. *a* **1400** *Prymer* (1891) 49 *Sepe expugnauerunt.* Oft they werreden me fro my ȝouthe sey now israel. *c* **1470** Harding *Chron.* cxxvi. vi. (1812) 244 Kyng Henry warred Robert Estenuyle. **1534** *St. Papers Hen. VIII* (1834) II. 186 The traison, rebellion, extorcion, and wilfull ware of your forsaid Erles,..the one varing, burning, and distroing the other. **1609** Daniel *Civ. Wars* IV. xxx, To warre the Scot, and Borders to defend.

fig. *a* **1225** *Ancr. R.* 246 Kastel; þet is eueriche god mon þet te ueond weorreð. *c* **1275** *Five Joys of the Virgin* 26 in *O.E. Misc.* 89 Al hire weorreþ þat wuneþ ine londe. **1340** *Ayenb.* 57 þe tauerne is..þe dyeules castel uor to werri god an his halȝen. *c* **1366** Chaucer *A.B.C.* 116 He not to werre us swich a wonder wroughte [Fr. *ne cuit pas que fust pour guerre*], But for to save us that he sithen boughte. **1422** Yonge tr. *Secreta Secret.* 156 Al the day of oure lyfe in grete Perill we byth, for thre enemys ws werryth. **1609** Daniel *Civ. Wars* VIII. lxxv. 222 Loue and Ambition..tyranniz'd on his diuided hart, Warring each other with a powerfull part.

†**b.** To ravage (a city, land, etc.) by warlike operations; to harry. *Obs.*

1297 R. Glouc. (Rolls) 43 Engelond haþ ibe inome & iwerred ilome [*v.rr.* iworred, werred]. *Ibid.* 7648 Hii worrede al norþhomberlond, & uorþ euere as hii come. **1523** Berners *Froiss.* I. cxci. 93 Thus in euery parte was the realme of Fraunce warrede in the tytell of the kynge of Nauer.

†**c.** To harass, persecute. *Obs.*

a **1225** *Ancr. R.* 186 Doð god, ȝif ȝe muwen, to þeo þet ou weorreð. *c* **1290** *Holy Rood* 324 in *S. Eng. Leg.* 10 Sethþe þare cam An Aumperur þat hiet Adrian, heþene he was and swiþe luþur and werrede [*v.r.* worrede] ech cristine man. **1297** R. Glouc. (Rolls) 1587 Vaspasyan..after nero com, þat betere man was þan he & ne worrede noȝt cristendom. **1523** Berners *Froiss.* I. ccclix. 235 b, Whan the gauntoyse sawe them selfe thus mocked and warred by the gentlemen of Flaunders [etc.].

2. *intr.* To make or carry on war; to fight. Now only *literary*.

a. with const. ***against, on,*** †***toward, upon, with.***

c **1205** Lay. 20191 Arður..bi-læi Colgrim þe weorrede aȝæin him. *c* **1230** *Hali Meid.* 5 Babilones folc..þe deoueles here of helle..weorreð & warpeð eauer toward tis tur for to kasten hit adun. **1297** R. Glouc. (Rolls) 1755 He bigan to worri anon vpe þe king basian. **1303** R. Brunne *Handl. Synne* 4970 He lete þe fals Phylystyens, þe folk of Isrel to werre aȝens. *a* **1300–1400** *Cursor M.* 2493 (Gött.) Four kinges werrid [*Cott. MS.* werraud (? *for* werraiid)] apon fijf. *c* **1330** R. Brunne *Chron. Wace* (Rolls) 4786 He [Cassibolan] swor he scholde on hym [Androcheus] were; & þat he had, he scholde hym reue. *c* **1380** Wyclif *Sel. Wks.* III. 298 þis proude worldly prest..priuely meyntenеþ oure enemyes to weren aȝenst us wiþ oure owene gold. *c* **1450** Lovelich *Merlin* 12153 So whanne this Galachim gan to vndirstonde ..how his fadir kyng Newtris with Arthour gan werre, to his Modyr he wente, [etc.]. **1486** *Bk. St. Albans, Coat-arm.* a v b, And the cursed peple of Sem wered ayenys them. *a* **1513** Fabyan *Chron.* an. 1263 (1533) 36 They drew to them great power, and warred vppon the landes and castellys of syr Roger Mortymer. **1530** Palsgr. 772/1 The turke hath warred with Christendome all my dayes. **1565** Peend *Hermaphr.* C j, Helena..For whom the Grecians warred ten yeares space with the Troyans. **1629** Hobbes *Thucyd.* I. 42 The Athenians had done vniustly, and ought speedily to be warred on. *c* **1643** Ld. Herbert *Autobiog.* (1824) 209 Monsieur de Luynes continuing still the [French] King's favourite, advised him to war against his subjects of the reformed religion in France. **1678** Wanley *Wonders* v. ii. §82. 472/2 Solyman..War'd upon the Venetians and invaded the Islands of Corfu and Malta. **1726** *Shelvocke's Voy. round World* Pref. p. xx, Capt. George Shelvocke may make use of this Imperial Commission in warring against the Spaniards. **1806** *Gazetteer Scot.* (ed. 2) 207 Fergus,..after having warred unsuccessfully with his sovereign,..retired in the habit of a monk to the abbey of Holyroodhouse. **1827** Pollok *Course T.* VII. 451 The fated crew that warred Against the chosen saints. **1879** Green *Readings Engl. Hist.* i. 3 Tribe warred with tribe.

transf. **13..** *Gaw. & Gr. Knt.* 720 Sumwhyle wyth wormez he werrez, & with wolues als. **1603** Holland *Plutarch's Mor.* 234 In this wise doe eagles warre with dragons. **1814** Scott *Lord of Isles* IV. iii, What make ye here, Warring upon the mountain-deer, When Scotland wants her King?

b. *simply.*

1297 R. Glouc. (Rolls) 7887 & vor roberd was eldore & eir, gret folc he sende al so Fram normandie to worry & is fader biquide vndo. *a* **1352** Minot *Poems* i. 12 Of Ingland had my hert grete care When Edward founded first to were. **1387** Trevisa *Higden* (Rolls) V. 237 Oon Gylomaurus þe tyraunt, þat hadde i-werred in Irlond and in Bretayne. *c* **1400** Maundev. (1839) xxiii. 251 And whan thei werren, thei werren fulle wisely. *c* **1400** *Brut* II. 322 In whiche tyme rayned and werred thilk orpid kniȝt Sere Iohn Hawkwode. **1471** Caxton *Recuyell* (Sommer) 645 And they were enduced to warre and to fyght. **1593** Shaks. *Rich. II*, II. i. 252 Wars hath not wasted it, for war'd he hath not, But basely yeelded vpon compromize That which his Ancestors atchieu'd with blowes. **1621** Bp. Mountagu *Diatribæ* 499 All the time hee warred in Asia, and had the spoile of yᵗ wealthy Country. *a* **1727** Newton *Chronol. Amended* ii. (1728) 214 Sesostris..warred first under his father. **1764** H. Walpole *Otranto* iv, He received the agreeable news that the confederate princes, who were warring in Palestine, had paid his ransom. **1816** Byron *Ch. Har.* III. xxxv, Here, where the sword united nations drew, Our countrymen were warring on that day! **1887** Mahaffy & Gilman *Alexander's Empire* xxii. (1890) 213 The murder of the young king Seleucus Soter (III.), who was warring in Asia Minor.

c. Of peoples, sovereigns, etc.: To carry on war against each other; to be (mutually) at war.

1297 R. Glouc. (Rolls) 9568 Hii nadde iworred bote a lute þat hii acorded were. **1338** R. Brunne *Chron.* (1725) 25 Whan Alfrid & Gunter had werred long in ille, þorgh þe grace of God, Gunter turned his wille. *c* **1375** *Cursor M.* 21872 (Fairf.) Folk þai salle gaine oþer rise to were [*earlier texts* werrai] samin in mani wise. **1607** Rowlands *Famous Hist.* 34 As we are Christians, let us War no more, But fight 'gainst such as will not God adore. **1832** R. & J. Lander *Exped. Niger* I. 88 We were told that the natives of Cape La Hoo and Jack-a-Jack had been warring for three years previously.

d. To serve as a soldier.

1535 Coverdale *2 Tim.* ii. 4 No man that warreth [Gr. στρατευόμενος] tangleth him selfe with wordly busynesses. (Similarly **1611.**) **1594** *Selimus* 669 Ile follow Mars, and warre another while, And die my shield in dolorous vermeil. **1631** Gouge *God's Arrows* III. xxxvii. 248 A righteous man ..may rightly warre at his command. **1841** James *Brigand* xv, The young gentleman we speak of has been long warring with the armies in Italy.

3. *fig.* Of persons: To contend, fight with immaterial weapons; to carry on a metaphorical warfare. Of things, forces, principles: To be in strong opposition.

a. with const. as in 2 a.

c **1200** *Trin. Coll. Hom.* 177 þe wraðđe of kinges..þe.. wurreð uppe chirches, oþer wanieð hire rihtes. *Ibid.* 195 ief [he hadde] werred wið god alse þe deuel him to eggede. *a* **1225** *Ancr. R.* 348 Vlesliche lustes, þet weorreð aȝean þe soule [= 1 Pet. ii. 11]. **1390** Gower *Conf.* I. 366 Homicide ..Which werreth ayein charite. **1484** Caxton *Chivalry* 77 Chastyte and strengthe warren and fyghten ageynste lecherye and surmounte hit. **1512** Colet *Serm. Convoc.* B vij, Lette the lawes be rehersed that warreth agaynst the spotte of Symonie. **1582** Bible (Rheims) *1 Pet.* ii. 11, I beseche you..to refraine your selues from carnal desires which warre against the soule. (Similarly **1611**). **1595** Daniel *Civ. Wars* I. civ, But was by tempests, windes, and seas debarr'd; As if they like-wise had against him warr'd. **1611** Bible *Rom.* vii. 23, I see another Lawe in my members, warring against the Lawe of my minde. **1765** *Museum Rust.* IV. 443 This writer is so determined to war with common opinion, that, in the eighth paragraph, he tells us, that [etc.]. **1780** Madan *Thelyph.* I. 242 How this learned man's prejudices warred against his judgment [etc.]. **1792** Rogers *Pleas. Mem.* I. 314 When..on the scathed oak warred the winter-wind. **1831** James *Phil. Augustus* xxiii, Such were the thoughts..that warred against each other in his breast. **1842** Newman *Par. Serm.* VI. 36 It is our duty to war against the flesh as they warred against it. **1866** W. R. Alger *Solit. Nat. & Man* IV. 412 Whoso follows these directions,..however warred on, will never be desolately alone. **1871** Freeman *Norm. Conq.* (1876) IV. xvii. 12 William, at this stage of his reign, warred rather against the memory of the dead than against the lives or fortunes of the living.

b. *simply.*

c **1400** *Beryn* 1990 Litil vailith wisdom..Ther fortune evir werrith, & eke hap & chaunce. **1582** Bible (Rheims) *James* iv. 1 Your concupiscences which warre in your membris. (Similarly **1611**). **1797** Coleridge *Christabel* I. 271 But vainly thou warrest.

c. To be in mutual opposition. Cf. warring *ppl. a.*

1845 James *Arrah Neil* i, Antagonist principles are ever warring within us.

4. *trans.* with cognate object: To carry on, wage (a warfare, etc.). *rare.*

1390 Gower *Conf.* II. 62 For this a man mai finde write, Whan that knyhthode schal be werred, Lust mai noght thanne be preferred. *c* **1425** *Eng. Conq. Ireland* iv. 10 Robert ..sette the bowmen for to wer [*MS. Rawl.* were] the fight of the kernels. **1530** Tindale *Lev.* Prol. ¶9 Circumcysion was vnto them a comen bagge sygnifienge that they were all sodiars off God to warre his warre. **1582** Bible (Rheims) *1 Tim.* i. 18 That thou warre in them a good war-fare. (Similarly **1611.**)

war (wɑr, wɔr), *v.*² *Sc.* Also 5 werre, warre, 8 warr, 8–9 waur. [f. WAR, WAUR *a.*] *trans.* To 'worst', defeat in a contest or competition; to surpass, excel.

1483 *Cath. Angl.* 408/1 To Warre, *depremere, deterere,.. deteriorare, peiorare* (A.). ? *a* **1500** in *Hardyng's Chron.* cxiii. *note,* The which [a feat of strength] He perfourmed.. that neuer mai be werde. **1513** DOUGLAS *Æneis* v. iii. 100 And now hes Pristis the fordaill, and syne, in hy, The big Centaur hir warris, and slippis by [L. *nunc victam præterit ingens*]. **1570** *Satir. Poems Reform.* xii. 53 Fecht weill and war yame and wyn the ryches yair, And gif ȝe de, in deid ȝe neid na mair. *a* **1578** LINDESAY (Pitscottie) *Chron. Scot.* (S.T.S.) I. 157 Thay debeitit manfullie and wareit edwartis wangard. *a* **1585** POLWART *Flyting w. Montgomerie* 710 Grant, guiss, þat my Inventioun waris the than, with out þe quhilk þow micht haue barkit waist. **1596** DALRYMPLE tr. *Leslie's Hist. Scot.* (S.T.S.) I. 13 Wigtoune waris the vthir 2 baith in citizenis and riches. *a* **1614** J. MELVILL *Autob. & Diary* (Wodrow Soc.) 154 And, on the uther part, Mr. Andro, wha warred him far in credit without the contrey.. wrot unto the Kirks at lainthe. **1721** J. KELLY *Sc. Prov.* 304 The Water will never warr the Widdie [= 'He that's born to be hang'd will never be drown'd']. **1785** BURNS *Death & Dr. Hornbook* xiii, And mony a scheme in vain's been laid, To stap or scaur me; Till ane Hornbook's taen up the trade, And faith he'll waur me. **1816** SCOTT *Antiq.* ix, It was a paper of great significance to the plea, and we were to be waured for want o't.

†**war**, *v.*³ *Obs. rare*⁻¹. [Of obscure origin. Possibly a misprint for *roar.*] (See quot.) Hence *Comb.* **war-back**, a trough used in salting herrings. Cf. ROWER-BACK.

1682 J. COLLINS *Salt & Fishery* 106 The manner of Salting. The Nets are haled on Board, and the Herrings are taken out of them, and put into the Warbacks, which stand on the side of the Vessel and resemble Chests. *Ibid.* 107 It is common to allow 2 barrels of Salt in a Last, of 14 barrels to War withall, that is to rowle the Herrings in the Salt before they are Packt.

war: see BE *v.*, WARE, WARRE, WEAR *v.*, WHERE, WHETHER.

waragi ('wærəgɪ). [ad. Swahili *wargi.*] In Uganda, a potent alcoholic drink made from bananas or cassava.

1916 in C. Griffin *Laws Uganda Protectorate* (1924) II. 1031 'Native liquor' means any liquor prepared or manufactured in accordance with native custom and includes.. Waragi. **1935** THOMAS & SCOTT *Uganda* xix. 295 It is forbidden by the Liquor Ordinance, 1916, that any person shall supply natives with any liquor other than.. beer ..and the Rules promulgated under the Ordinance make it an offence.. to distil or even to possess the raw cassava spirit known locally as *waragi.* **1973** *Guardian* 13 Jan. 13/3 The ferocious Ugandan spirit Waragi. **1976** *Listener* 19 Aug. 195/3 He had had three tots of Waragi (a highly potent Ugandan gin made from bananas). **1977** *Time* 7 Mar. 18/3 They [*sc.* Ugandans] would rather have scarce butter or a slab of meat or a bottle of *waragi,* a potent, banana-based liquor.

waran, obs. form of WARRANT *sb.*¹

warancie: see WARRANCY.

warand, obs. form of WARRANT.

warandare, obs. form of WARRENER.

warande, obs. form of WARRANT, WARREN.

warander, obs. form of WARRENER.

warandice, -dise, obs. forms of WARRANTISE.

warant(e, -ie, obs. forms of WARRANT, -Y.

warantise, -ize, obs. forms of WARRANTISE.

warantte, obs. form of WARRANT.

Warao (wə'raʊ). Also 9 Warow, Worrow; Warrau, Warraw. [Native name.] (A member of) an American Indian people inhabiting Guyana, Surinam, and Venezuela; also, the language of this people. Also *attrib.*

The spelling *Warao* has recently emerged as the usual spelling for the language and the people.

1807 H. BOLINGBROKE *Voy. to Demerary* vii. 151 The Worrows principally inhabit the sea coast lying between the Demerary and Surinam. **1834** W. HILHOUSE in *Jrnl. R. Geogr. Soc.* IV. 321 (*heading*) Memoir on the Warow Land of British Guiana. *Ibid.* 324 On these reefs are situated many Indian villages—Warows, Arawacks, [etc.]. **1883** E. F. IM THURN *Among Indians of Guiana* vi. 167 The Warraus are the shortest. **1891** D. G. BRINTON *Amer. Race* 354 The Guaraouna or Warrau was, and continues to be, spoken by the tribes of the [Orinoco] delta. **1910** *Encycl. Brit.* XII. 676/2 [British Guiana] The aborigines—Arawaks, Caribs, Wapisianas, Warraws, &c.—.. are now estimated at about 6500. **1948** P. KIRCHHOFF in J. H. Steward *Handbk. S. Amer. Indians* III. 870 The Warrau language constitutes an independent family. *Ibid.* 869 The Warrau live in the intricate Delta of the Orinoco. **1950** J. A. MASON in *Ibid.* VI. 252 The independence of the Warrau linguistic family has been admitted by all authorities. **1965** *Internat. Jrnl. Amer. Linguistics* XXXI. 106 Warao appears to have a large number of compounds. *Ibid.,* The Warao text is divided into numbered sentences without any other punctuation. **1973** *Advocate-News* (Barbados) 18 Dec. 9/5 Several cuckoos have befouled the nests of the Arawaks, Caribs, Wapisianas, Warraws and what-nots. **1978** *Amer. Poetry Rev.* Sept./Oct. 13/3 Roth.. gave the title 'The Adventures of Kororomanna' to a long Warao story. **1979** J. HALIFAX *Shamanic Voices* (1980) i. 28 The Warao shaman also believes the rattle to be the world axis.

‖**Warasdin.** *Hist.* [ad. G. *Warasdiner,* f. *Warasdin* (Magyar *Varasd*) the name of a town and county in Croatia.]

1802 C. JAMES *Milit. Dict., Warasdins,* a kind of Sclavonian soldiers, clothed like the Turks, with a sugar-loaf bonnet instead of a hat. Their arms are a fuzee and pistols. **1864** [see TOLPATCH].

waratah ('wɔːrətɑː). Also **war-ra-taw, warrataw, warratah.** [Native Australian name.]

1. A name for Australian shrubs of the genus *Telopea* (N.O. *Proteaceæ*), esp. *T. speciosissima* and *T. oreades,* which bear crimson or scarlet flowers in terminal clusters; also, the flower.

1793 J. E. SMITH *Bot. New Holland* 19 (Morris) The most magnificent plant which the prolific soil of New Holland affords is, by common consent both of Europeans and natives, the Waratàh. **1801** P. G. KING *Let. Sir J. Banks* 25 Aug. in *Hist. Rec. N.S.W.* (1896) IV. 514, I have also sent ..a box of waratahs. **1802** D. COLLINS *Acc. N.S. Wales* II. 66 Ben-nil-long assisted at the ceremony, placing the head of the corpse, by which he stuck a beautiful war-ra-taw. **1830** *Hobart Town Almanack* 66 That magnificent shrub called Warrataw or tulip tree and its beautiful scarlet flowers. **1885** 'WANDERER' *Beauteous Terrorist* etc. 62 And the waratahs in state, With.. their flamy blood-red crowns.

2. A variety of the camellia. In full ***waratah camellia.***

1824 LOUDON *Encycl. Gard.* §6613 Camellia.. double white waratah. **1866** *Treas. Bot.* II. 207/2 The anemone-flowered or Waratah Camellia.

waraunt(e, -tyse: see WARRANT, -TISE.

warawnt, obs. form of WARRANT.

warb (wɔːb). *Austral. slang.* [Perh. f. WARB(LE *sb.*²] A lazy, unkempt, or contemptible person (see also quot. 1959).

1933 L. ROBINSON in Murdoch & Drake-Brockman *Austral. Short Stories* (1951) 215 We were both of us what, in the back country, are called 'warbs', meaning confirmed and irredeemable loafers. **1959** BAKER *Drum* (1960) II. 155 *Warb,* a low-paid manual worker. 2. A dirty or untidy person. 3. A simpleton or fool. **1967** K. TENNANT *Tell Morning This* 201 But it's a no-hoper's jail—a lot of old warbs and kids mixed up with coves like Amos the Cannibal and chaps that razors bounce off.

warback: see WAR *v.*³ *Obs.*

warble ('wɔːb(ə)l), *sb.*¹ Forms: 4 warbele, -bul, 5 -bell, varble, 4–6 werble, 4 -bele, -bul, 5 wherble, 6 *Sc.* verbille, -ble; 4– warble. [a. OF. *werble:* see WARBLE *v.*¹] **1. a.** In early use, a tune or melody (perh. of some special kind) performed on an instrument or sung. Subsequently (influenced by WARBLE *v.*¹), the action or an act of warbling; gentle and melodious singing, esp. of birds.

13.. *Gaw. & Gr. Knt.* 119 Nwe nakryn noyse with þe noble pipes, Wylde werbles & wyȝt wakned lote. *c* **1374** CHAUCER *Troylus* II. 1033 þough þe beste harpour vpon lyue Wolde.. Touche ay o streng or ay o werbul [*v.rr.* warbul, -bele, -ble, werble, -bul] harpe. **1387** TREVISA *Higden* (Rolls) I. 355 In þe whiche instrumentis.. þey makeþ wel mery armonye and melody wiþ wel þicke tunes, werbeles, and notes. *c* **1400** LYDG. *Chorle & Bird* xi. in *Min. Poems* (Percy Soc.) 182 [Harl. MS. 116] The soote sugred armonye Of uncouthe varblys and tunys drawen on longe. *c* **1407** —— *Reson & Sens.* 1249 So as the Swan.. Syngeth to forn his fatal day, With werbles ful of melodye. **1501** DOUGLAS *Pal. Hon.* I. xlv, Na mair I will thir verbillis sweit define. *c* **1590** J. STEWART *Poems* (S.T.S.) II. 76 Quhair birds outbirstit doulcest verblis rair. **1628** FELTHAM *Resolves* II. xxv. 80 Damned Sathan! that with Orphean ayres, and dextrous warbles, lead'st vs to the Flames of Hell. **1742** GRAY *Let. to West* Apr., I give you thanks for your warble, and wish you could sing yourself to rest. **1757** DYER *Fleece* I. 614 With ev'ry murmur of the sliding wave, And ev'ry warble of the feather'd choir. **1818** SCOTT *Hrt. Midl.* xl, The strain was solemn and affecting, sustained as it was by the pathetic warble of a voice which had naturally been a fine one. **1834** WORDSW. *Even. Volunt.* v. I The linnet's warble, sinking towards a close, Hints to the thrush 'tis time for their repose. **1868** LOUISA M. ALCOTT *Little Women* ii, Hagar puts back the cup which holds the poison meant for Roderigo. Hugo, getting thirsty after a long warble, drinks it, loses his wits, [etc.].

transf. **1871** TENNYSON *Last Tourn.* 254 Quiet as any water-sodden log Stay'd in the wandering warble of a brook.

b. Manner of warbling.

a **1547** SURREY in *Tottel's Misc.* (Arb.) 7 There shalt thou here and se all kindes of birdes ywrought, Well tune their voice with warble smal, as nature hath them tought. **1776** BURNEY *Hist. Mus.* I. 191 A sound so much the more agreeable, as it is not monotonous, which is the case in the warble of most other birds. **1776–83** JUSTAMOND tr. *Raynal's Hist. Indies* I. 307 Birds have a warble that is peculiar to them. *a* **1900** DK. ARGYLL *Autob. & Mem.* (1906) I. 202 The song of the willow-wren is too low a warble to attract general attention.

c. *collect.* The united sound of bird-songs.

1776 PENNANT *Brit. Zool.* (ed. 4) I. 314 Its notes are part of that time drowned in the general warble of the season. **1794** MRS. PIOZZI *Synon.* I. 200 Whose destructive temper and disposition help to disturb the peace of the forest and the warble of the grove.

2. Special combination. **warble tone** *Physics,* a constant amplitude tone whose frequency is cyclically varied between certain limits, used in acoustic measurement to avoid irregularities associated with the use of single frequencies.

1933 *Proc. IRE* XXI. 1183 The introduction of a 'warble tone' into the technique of acoustical measurements.. has also supplied a growing interest in this kind of oscillation. **1958** H. J. GRAY *Dict. Physics* 527/1 A warble tone can be produced from an oscillator by rotating a small variable condenser in the tuned circuit at a constant speed. **1971** B. J. SMITH *Acoustics* v. 96 To attempt to eliminate the variations due to room modes for each frequency a band of noise is used, either in the form of white noise or in warble tones.

warble ('wɔːb(ə)l), *sb.*² Also 9 **wabble, worble, wurble.** [Of uncertain origin; cf. MSw. *varbulde* boil, f. *var* pus (see WARE *sb.*⁶) + *bulde* tumour; also WARBOT, WARIBREED, and the dial, names for the warble-maggot, *warback* (Orkney), *warbeetle* (Norf.), *warbie* (Sc.), *warblet* (Suff.); and *worbitten* (Suff.), pierced by the larvæ of beetles (said of growing timber).]

1. A small hard tumour, caused by the pressure of the saddle on a horse's back. Usually *pl.*

1607 MARKHAM *Cavel.* III. (1617) 78 You shall bathe his backe where the Saddle stood, which will keepe him from warbles. **1705** *Lond. Gaz.* No. 4178/4 A.. Gelding near 14 hands high,.. a Warble newly broke on the off side of his Back. **1737** BRACKEN *Farriery Impr.* (1757) II. 161 The first [Horse] will fret, gall, and be full of Warbles, with even the least Journey. **1831** YOUATT *Horse* ix. 169 The little tumours resulting from the pressure of the saddle are called *warbles,* and when they ulcerate they frequently become *sitfasts.*

2. A small tumour or swelling on the back of cattle, deer, etc. produced by the larva of a gad-fly (see 3).

a **1585** MONTGOMERIE *Flyting* 314 þe mair, the migram,.. the warbillis, þe wood-worme. **1808** JAMIESON, *Warble,*.. a swelling on the back of a cow or ox, A. Bor. [i.e. North of England]. **1834** YOUATT *Cattle* xix. 574 A great many of the cattle in the same pasture will have only a few warbles on their backs, while others will, in a manner, be covered with them. **1857** GOSSE *Omphalos* xi. 309 The Worble of the Ox. **1880** *Times* 27 Sept. 12/6 Then, graziers are appealed to in order to prevent the hides of the living animals being injured by 'warbles', produced by parasitic insects.

3. The gadfly or its larva which produces 'warbles'. Cf. *warble-fly* in 4.

1808 JAMIESON, *Warble,* a sort of worm that breeds betwixt the outer and inner skin of beasts, S. **1810** *Encycl. Brit.* (ed. 4) VIII. 495/1 The larvæ of the *Oestrus bovis* are commonly known to the country people by the names of *wormils,* or *wormuls,* or *warbles.* **1814** *Illustr. North. Antiq.* 404 The hole.. (which has probably been made by a warble) in the skin of a beast that has been elf-shot. **1886** *Daily News* 5 May 3/5 The warble, or bot fly.. strikes the cattle in the summer months, depositing its eggs upon the skin, or hair. **1889** *Rep. U.S. Dept. Agric.* I. 215 (Cent.) A very large percentage [of fifty chipmunks].. were infested with wabbles.

4. *attrib.* and *Comb.,* as ***warble-hole, -lump, -maggot, tumour;*** **warble-fly** (see 3).

1877 J. G. WOOD *Nat. Teaching, Usef. Arts* vii. 396 The *Wurble-fly of the ox, scientifically known as *Œstrus bovis.* **1851–4** TOMLINSON *Arts & Manuf.* II. 30/1 Those [hides] which contain *warble or wurmal holes. **1886** *Daily News* 5 May 3/5 The two familiar *warble-lumps which may be felt on the back and loins of the.. beasts affected. *Ibid.,* The results of the presence of the *warble-maggots.. is a general derangement of health. **1805** R. W. DICKSON *Pract. Agric.* II. 1188 *Warble tumours arising upon the backs or sides of horses.

†**'warble,** *sb.*³ *Obs.* In 7 **werble.** [var. **whervel* WHORL *sb.*] The part of the spindle that receives the thread: = WHORL *sb.*

1561 [Implied in WARBLED *a.*¹] **1611** COTGR. s.v. *Fusée, Fusée avec ses pesons;* as *Astragale;* because commonly the worke on it resembles many spooles and werbles threaded, or ioyned together.

warble ('wɔːb(ə)l), *v.*¹ Forms: ? 4 **werbel,** ? 5 **-il,** 6 **warbell,** 6– **warble.** [a. north-eastern OF. *werbler, werbloier* (Central OF. *guerbler, guerbloier;* 16th c. in corrupt forms *verbloier, verboier, verbier*), f. *werble* WARBLE *sb.*¹, a. OHG. *werbel,* recorded only as glossing L. *plectrum* and *sistrum,* but prob. used in many other applications of the general sense 'something that revoles' (MHG. *werbel, wirbel,* mod.G. *wirbel,* whirlpool, whirlwind, spinning-top, vertex of the head, etc.); cogn. w. (M)Du. *wervel* harp, ON. *hvirfill* circle, ring, crown of the head, f. OTeut. root **hwerƀ-* to revolve: see WHIRL *sb.* and *v.,* WHORL.

The Fr. vb. seems to have primarily referred to the manipulation of the strings of a musical instrument (cf. 5 a below), but was also used for the production of delicate varieties of tone in singing. The sb. *werble* has only one example in Godefr., where it may mean 'modulation' or 'melody'. It is not possible to determine with certainty in which of its senses the Ger. sb. was adopted in OF.; perh. in that of 'plectrum': perh. in that of 'tuning-peg' (so MHG. *werbel*). Mod.G. has a verb *wirbeln* to warble.

In Eng. the existence of the vb. before the 16th c. is doubtful (see the remark under 1 below), though there are several examples of the sb. in the 14th c.]

†**1. a.** *intr.* ? To resound. **b.** *trans.* ? To proclaim by flourish of trumpets; ? to sound (a trumpet). *Obs.*

The identity of the word in quot. 13.. is uncertain; the sense may be 'whirling'. In quot. *a* 1400–50 the reading and construction are doubtful.

13.. *Gaw. & Gr. Knt.* 2004 Þe werbelande wynde wapped fro þe hyȝe, & drof vche dale ful of dryftes ful grete. ***a* 1400–50** *Wars Alex.* 2222 Now ere his seggis all sett & þe saute neȝis, Were wakens be-twene, werbild in trompis. [*Dubl. MS.* Were wakned be-twene; werblet trompez.]

2. a. *intr.* To modulate the voice in singing; to sing with trills and quavers. In later use (influenced by sense 4), to sing softly and sweetly, in a birdlike manner; often merely a jocose substitute for *sing*.

1530 PALSGR. 771/2, I warbell with the voyce, as connyng syngers do, *Je verbie*. It is a worlde to here hym synge, whan he is disposed to warbell. **1594** CAREW *Huarte's Exam.* viii. (1596) 114 Children.. who haue a good voice, and warble in the throat, are most vntoward for all sciences. **1600** SHAKS. *A.Y.L.* II. v. 38 Come, warble, come. **1611** COTGR., *Fredonner*, to shake, diuide, warble, quauer in singing. **1811** BUSBY *Dict. Mus.* (ed. 3) s.v., To warble is to sing in a mode, or manner, imitative of birds. Those soprano performers, whose voices are of a clear, fluted, and shrill tone, and who run divisions with a close and liquid sweetness, are said to warble. **1884** MRS. PRAED *Zero* xiv, Patti warbled in the theatre.

quasi-*trans.* with complement (jocular).

1850 THACKERAY *Pendennis* xliv, She'd sit down and sing to you, and gaze at you, until she warbled your soul out of your body a'most.

b. Of music: To sound in quavering, flexible melody; to be produced with free, smooth, and rapid modulations of pitch. ? *Obs.*

1714 GAY *Sheph. Wk.* Wed. 3 Such Strains ne'er warble in the Linnet's Throat. ***a* 1751** DODDRIDGE *Hymns*, '*Lord of the Sabbath*' iii, No Groans to mingle with the Songs, Which warble from immortal Tongues. **1813** *Sketches of Character* (ed. 2) i, At the same instant, Emily's sweetest notes warbled in his ear.

c. *poet.* Of a small stream: To make melody as it flows. Also of the wind.

1579 [see WARBLING *ppl. a.*[1] 1]. **1667** MILTON *P.L.* III. 31 The flowrie Brooks beneath That wash thy hallowd feet, and warbling flow. **1706** PHILLIPS (ed. Kersey), To *Warble*.. to gargle or purl, as a Brook or Stream. **1728–46** THOMSON *Spring* 399 High to their fount,.. amid the hills And woodlands warbling round, trace up the brooks. **1783** CRABBE *Village* II. 201 As old Thames.. Sees his young streams run warbling at his side. **1814** SOUTHEY *Roderick* XVIII. 207 The quiet voice Of waters warbling near.

d. *U.S.* To yodel. (In recent American Dicts.)

1880 [see WARBLING *vbl. sb.* c.]

3. *trans.* **a.** To sing with quavering trills and runs, to utter melodiously, to carol. Also to ***warble forth, out, over.***

1576 GASCOIGNE *Philomene* (Arb.) 89 And many a note, she warbled wondrous wel. ***a* 1593** MARLOWE *Ovid's Elegies* I. i. 33 Elegian Muse, that warblest amorous laies. **1634** SIR T. HERBERT *Trav.* 207 The lookers on incessantly warble out soft trembling Musique. **1693** DRYDEN *Juvenal* VI. 98 Softly She Warbles over all she hears. **1754** GRAY *Pleasure* 13 The Sky-lark warbles high His trembling thrilling ecstacy. **1848** THACKERAY *Van. Fair* xxv, Emmy.. began to warble that stanza from the favourite song of 'Wapping Old Stairs'. **1854** *Poultry Chron.* II. 118/1 Again, we have that pretty songster.. warbling forth its melodious song, the Canary. **1868** LOUISA M. ALCOTT *Little Women* xii, Ned, getting sentimental, warbled a serenade.

b. To express or celebrate in song or verse. Also with *forth*, †*out*.

1591 SYLVESTER *Du Bartas* I. i. 18 O Father, grant I sweetly warble forth Vnto our seed the World's renowned Birth. **1623** MILTON *Ps. cxxxvi.* 89 Let us therfore warble forth His mighty Majesty and worth. **1634** SIR. T. HERBERT *Trav.* 7 The Riuer Læthe so warbled out by Poets. **1725** POPE *Odyss.* I. 446 Warbling the Grecian woes with harp and voice. **1750** JOHNSON *Rambler* No. 109 ¶2 You.. warble out your groans with uncommon elegance. **1868** LOUISA M. ALCOTT *Little Women* ii, Having warbled his thanks.. Hugo departed. **1875** TENNYSON *Q. Mary* III. vi, Or would you have me turn a sonneteer, And warble those brief-sighted eyes of hers?

4. *intr.* †**a.** To twitter, as a young bird; to make uncertain attempts at singing. Also *fig.* *Obs.*

1605 BP. ANDREWES *Serm.* (Heb. ii. 16) (1629) 8 It brought forth a Benedictus, and a Magnificat, from the true seed of Abraham; If it do not the like, from us, certainely it but flotes in our braines; we but warble about it. **1611** COTGR., *Gazouiller*,.. to warble, as a young bird when it first begins, or learnes, to sing.

b. Of birds: To sing clearly and sweetly.

1606 WARNER *Alb. Eng.* XIV. lxxxii. (1612) 343 No birds were heard to warble. **1667** MILTON *P.L.* VIII. 265 Birds on the branches warbling. **1732** POPE *Ess. Man* I. 216 The life .. which warbles thro' the vernal wood. **1750** GRAY *Elegy* (Pembroke text) 119 The Red-breast loves to build, & warble there. **1859** CAPERN *Ballads & Songs* 138 When thrushes warble in the elm tree's crown.

c. Of telephones (*spec.* Trimphones): to make a distinctive trilling sound.

1965, 1969 [see TRIMPHONE]. **1973** G. MOFFAT *Deviant Death* v. 68 The telephone was warbling softly. **1981** T. BARLING *Bikini Red North* x. 206 The telephone warbled... 'You must answer it.'

5. †**a.** *trans.* To manipulate (the strings of a musical instrument) in playing. *Obs.*

1578 H. WOTTON *Courtlie Controv.* 285 Then hee tooke his Lute, and warbling the strings with tenne thousand delicate diuisions, hee beganne to saye [etc.]. **1638** JUNIUS *Paint. Ancients* 297 The left [hand].. did with divided fingers warble the strings.

†**b.** *intr.* Of a stringed instrument: To give forth melodious sounds. *Obs.*

1620 T. GRANGER *Div. Logike* 66 The Harpe warbleth. **1794** MRS. RADCLIFFE *Myst. Udolpho* xv, The while we chant our ditties sweet To some soft shell that warbles near.

†**c.** To play *upon* as upon strings. *Obs.*

***c* 1640** J. SMYTH *Lives Berkeleys* (1883) I. 371 Upon which stringe I have already warbled in the ill harmony of the six last lords lives. ***a* 1677** BARROW *Serm.* Wks. 1686 III. 107 New objects with a gentle and gratefull touch warble upon the corporeal organs, or excite the spirits into a pleasant frisk of motion.

d. *Sc.* 'To play the quicker measures of a piece of bagpipe music, in which there are a large number of grace-notes' (*Eng. Dial. Dict.*)

warble ('wɔːb(ə)l), *v.*[2] *Falconry.* Also 5 **warb(b)el(l, warbul,** 6 **warbile.** [Of obscure origin; perh. a. Du. *wervelen* to turn round (= OE. **hwierflian*, whence *hwierflung* vbl. sb. For the change of consonant cf. *nable* obs. and dial. var. NAVEL.] *trans.* To cross (the wings) together over the back after 'rousing' and 'mantling'. Also *absol.* Hence **'warbling** *vbl. sb.*

1486 *Bk. St. Albans, Hawking* a vj b, Whan she hath mantilled hir and bryngith booth her wynges to geider ouer hir backe ye shall say yowre hawke warbelleth hir wynges. *Ibid.* c viii b, She warbbelyth when she drawith booth her wyngys ouer the myddys of her backe. **1575** TURBERV. *Falconrie* 134 Stroke on hir wings that shee [your Sparhawke] may mantle and warble. ***c* 1575** *Perf. Bk. Kepinge Sparhawkes* (1886) 10 Yf good, let her styre, rouse, mantle, or warbile a while. **1632** *Guillim's Displ. Heraldry* III. xx. (ed. 2) 228 Which action you shall terme, the warbling of her wings. **1852** R. F. BURTON *Falconry Valley Indus* vi. 65 *foot-n.*, Rousing themselves, 'mantling' and 'warbling' (crossing the wings over the back, after stretching the legs), as though they had escaped a prison.

†**'warble,** *v.*[3] *Obs.* [Perh. a. Du. *wervelen*: see prec. Cf. WOBBLE *v.*]

1. *trans.* To shake or cause to vibrate, to brandish.

1510 STANBRIDGE *Vocabula* (W. de W.) D iv, *Vibro*, to warble. **1548** THOMAS *Ital. Dict.* (1567), *Vibrare*, to shake or warble, as to shake a sword against the sunne.

†**2.** *intr.* To vibrate, quiver; to wobble. *Obs.*

1549, 1573, 1632 [see WARBLING *ppl. a.*[2]]. ***?a* 1560** *Jack Jugler* 231 She quauerith, and wardelith [? *read* warbelith], like one in a galiard Euerye ioynt in her bodye and euerie part. **1604** T. WRIGHT *Passions* v. §2. 221 The heartes of men without thee their last end and eternall quietnesse, are ever ranging, warbling, and never out of motion. **1688** HOLME *Armoury* II. 17/1 Stars.. seem to have resplendent Rays waving or warbling forth. *Ibid.* IV. ix. (Roxb.) 402/1 The English shipps haue.. ouer the sterne, a Red square ensigne as large as the ship will giue liberty to Warble about without touching of the mizen mast.

†**'warble,** *v.*[4] *Obs. rare*⁻¹. [Of obscure origin.] *intr.* ? To quarrel, wrangle. ? Hence **'warbling** *vbl. sb.* and *ppl. a.*

1600 HOLLAND *Livy* x. xl. 382 There arose some warbling [*altercatio*] amongst the chicken-maisters touching the auspice.. of that day. **1632** LITHGOW *Trav.* i. 2 [He] can crowd and chawe from his warbling waspishnes, this stinging censure of absurd vntrueth. **1647** TRAPP *Comm. Gen.* xvi. 5 (1650) 130 These couples that are ever warbling, can neither be at peace within themselves,.. nor pray as they should do to God,.. which if they did often.. they could not disagree.

†**'warbled,** *a.*[1] *Obs.* [f. WARBLE *sb.*[3] + -ED[2].] Of a spindle: Fitted with a whorl.

***?a* 1561** ? CAVENDISH in *Life Wolsey*, etc. (1825) II. 92 That the warbled spindle were no more abought shold ronne.

warbled ('wɔːb(ə)ld), *a.*[2] [f. WARBLE *sb.*[2]] Of hides: Injured by warbles.

1885 *Athenæum* 11 July 52 The cattle producer.. receives .. almost the same amount for the warbled hide of the animal as he would obtain if it were uninjured by the bot fly. **1886** *Daily News* 5 May 3/5 No less than 1,906 [hides] were 'warbled'—that is to say more or less riddled or scarred from warble attacks.

warbled ('wɔːb(ə)ld), *ppl. a.* [f. WARBLE *v.*[1] + -ED[1].] In senses of the verb.

1. Melodiously sung or sounded. Also, celebrated in song.

1634 MILTON *Comus* 854 If she be right invok't in warbled Song. **1725** POPE *Odyss.* I. 420 Hush'd in attention to the warbled song. **1742** COLLINS *Ode to Simplicity* 21 By old Cephisus deep, Who spreads his wavy sweep In warbl'd wanderings round thy cool retreat. **1794** COLERIDGE *Sonn.*, *La Fayette*, As when far off the warbled strains are heard.

†**2.** Of a musical string (see WARBLE *v.*[1] 5 a).

***a* 1645** MILTON *Arcades* 87 As I.. touch the warbled string.

warbler ('wɔːblə(r)). [f. WARBLE *v.*[1] + -ER[1].]

1. a. One who, or something which, warbles or sings; a singer, songster.

1611 COTGR., *Gasouilleur*, a warbler, chirper. **1633** MASSINGER *Guardian* IV. ii, And you Warbler, Keep your Windpipe moist, that you may not spit and hem, When you should make division. **1673** M. STEVENSON *Norf. Drollery* 19 At her call, Comes Blackbird, Linit, Alph, Thrush, Nightingal, Melodious warblers. ***c* 1750** SHENSTONE *Elegy* xiv. 20 Nor for the worthless bird of brighter plumes Would change the meanest warbler of my grove. **1818** BYRON *Juan* Ded. iii, Your wish To supersede all warblers here below. **1833** TENNYSON *Dream Fair Wom.* 5 Dan Chaucer, the first warbler. **1850** 'SYLVANUS' *Bye-lanes & Downs* ii. 23 The sun had not yet risen, and all, save the warblers of the woods, was still.

b. *slang.*

1823 'JON BEE' *Dict. Turf*, *Warblers*, singers who go about to 'free and easy' meetings, to chaunt for pay, for grog, or for the purpose of putting off benefit-tickets.

c. *slang.* A female singer.

1946 B. TREADWELL *Big Bk. Swing* 125/2 *Warbler*, girl singer. **1961** *Times* 21 Nov. 13/2 Barbara Holt, making her stage debut, displayed the promise of an uncommon warbler. **1981** *TV Picture Life* Mar. 16/1 (*caption*) Regardless of where her love life leads, the warbler is very much in demand for films these days.

d. *colloq.* A telephone which warbles. Cf. WARBLE *v.*[1] 4 c.

1973 G. MOFFAT *Deviant Death* vii. 106 'I didn't hear a telephone, did you?' 'It's one of the new warblers.'

2. a. In the Old World: Any one of the numerous small plain-coloured singing-birds of the family *Sylviinae*, including the blackcap, white-throat, and others having names in which *warbler* is the second element, as ***garden-w., grasshopper-w.,*** REED-WARBLER, ***sedge-w., willow-w., wood-w.***

1773 PENNANT *Genera of Birds* 35 Warblers. **1776** —— *Brit. Zool.* (ed. 4) I. 329 Dartford Warbler. **1802** BINGLEY *Anim. Biog.* (1813) II. 183 Of the warblers in general. **1835** JENYNS *Man. Brit. Vertebr.* 104 *Sylvia Suecica*, Lath. (Blue-throated Warbler). *Ibid.* 108 *Sylvia Atricapilla*, Lath. (Black-cap Warbler). **1890** C. DIXON *Ann. Bird Life* 41 Of the five species of Warbler that stray here in the spring, three of them, the Aquatic Warbler, the Great Reed Warbler, and the Icterine Warbler, are regular visitors to France.

b. In America: One of the small, usually bright-coloured, birds, with little power of song, of the family *Mniotiltidae*.

1783 LATHAM *Gen. Synopsis Birds* II. II. 482 Spotted Yellow Warbler, *Le Figuier brun de Canada*. **1808–14** A. WILSON *Amer. Ornith.* (1831) II. 162 *Sylvia autumnalis*, Wilson.—Autumnal Warbler. **1871** BURROUGHS *Wake-Robin* viii. (1895) 207 Audubon figures and describes over forty different warblers. *Ibid.*, The cerulean warbler, said to be abundant about Niagara; and the mourning ground warbler, which I have found breeding about the head-waters of the Delaware. **1872** COUES *Key N. Amer. Birds* 93 *Helmitherus vermivorus*. Worm-eating Warbler.

c. In Australia and New Zealand: A bird of the genera *Gerygone*, *Malurus*, and others.

1790 *J. White's Jrnl. Voy. N.S. Wales* App. 256 Superb Warblers. **1889** PARKER *Catal. N.Z. Exhib.* 119 (Morris) Grey Warbler (*Gerygone flaviventris*) also belongs to an Australian genus. **1896** AFLALO *Nat. Hist. Australia* 136 The Wrens and Warblers—chiefly *Maluri*, with the allied *Amytis* and *Stipiturus*—are purely Australian.

3. *Sc.* A group of grace-notes on the bagpipe.

1875 *Encycl. Brit.* III. 235/2 The players introduce among the simple notes of the tune a kind of appoggiatura, consisting of a great number of rapid notes of peculiar embellishment, which they term warblers. **1886** STEVENSON *Kidnapped* xxv. **1894** J. A. STEUART *In Day of Battle* viii, He owned I was no hand at the warblers.

4. ***Little Warbler***: app. the title of a song-book.

'The Little Warbler. Scotch Songs' is the title of a chap-book of about 1820. There may have been other books with the same title; the British Museum has three collections of songs called 'The Warbler', 1760 (?), 1772, and 1840 (?).

1840 THACKERAY *Barber Cox* Sept., A vast number of things.. such as a ball of string, a piece of candle, a comb, a whip-lash, a little warbler. **1848** —— *Van. Fair* v, He.. bought him.. presents of knives,.. toffee, Little Warblers, and romantic books.

5. *attrib.* and *Comb.*, as ***warbler tribe; warbler-like*** adj.; †**warbler thrush**, a North American olive-brown thrush.

1817 STEPHENS in *Shaw's Gen. Zool.* X. 197 Warbler Thrush (Turdus motacilla). **1894** R. B. SHARPE *Hand-bk. Birds Gt. Brit.* I. 102 The mottled Warbler-like eggs which are often found. **1907** *Westm. Gaz.* 9 Dec. 10/1 With.. all the lesser warbler tribe to bear them company.

warbling ('wɔːblɪŋ), *vbl. sb.*[1] [f. WARBLE *v.*[1] + -ING[1].] The action of the verb in various senses, *esp.* soft and melodious singing.

1587 M. GROVE *Pelops & Hipp.* (1878) 68 With shrillish notes I would ne stay nor stent of warbuling. **1608** WILLET *Hexapla Exod.* 231 Running catches and curious warbling. **1707** *Curios. Husb. & Gard.* 24 The Air.. resounds with the Warbling of Birds. **1825** SCOTT *Jrnl.* 21 Nov. (1890) I. 6 Tom Moore's is the most exquisite warbling I ever heard.

pl. **1757** GRAY *Bard* III. iii, And distant warblings lessen on my ear. **1781** COWPER *Retirem.* 569 The warblings of the blackbird, clear and strong. **1830** COBBETT *Rur. Rides* (1885) II. 319 The groves.. are echoing with the warblings of thousands upon thousands of birds.

b. *Sc.* Playing grace-notes on the bagpipe.

1896 N. MUNRO *Lost Pibroch*, etc. 251, I heard him fill the night-fall with the 'Bhoilich' of Morar, with the brag of a whole clan in his warbling.

c. *U.S.* = YODELING *vbl. sb.*

1880 'MARK TWAIN' *Tramp Abr.* xxviii. 257 We recognised, also, that it was that sort of quaint commingling of baritone and falsetto which at home we call 'Tyrolese warbling'.

†**'warbling,** *vbl. sb.*[2] *Obs.* [f. WARBLE *v.*[3] + -ING[1].] A vibration or quivering.

1621 T. GRANGER *Expos. Eccles.* xii. 5. 323 The.. spirit of life is feeble, and is little quickened with the warbling of melodious ayre. **1688** HOLME *Armoury* I. 21/1 It hath a resemblance to the Rays of the Sun, which shooteth out like the warbling of a Flame of Fire.

warbling ('wɔːblɪŋ), *ppl. a.*[1] [f. WARBLE *v.*[1] + -ING[2].]

1. That warbles; *esp.* singing or making tuneful melody with sweet quavering notes.

1549–62 STERNHOLD & H. *Ps.* cxxxvii. 5 Then let my fingers quite forget, The warbling harpe to guide. **1576** PETTIE *Petite Pallace* 14 b, The bird..heares his felowes sing, and is not able to vtter one warbling note out of his mourneful voice. **1579** SPENSER *Sheph. Cal.* June 4 The gentle warbling wynde. **1610** TOFTE *Honours Acad.* III. 119 Hauing a warbling Lute in her hand. **1697** DRYDEN *Virg. Past.* VI. 114 The warbling Nightingale in Woods complains. **1757** DYER *Fleece* II. 32 Alternate songs shall sooth your care, and warbling music break from ev'ry spray. **1765** J. BROWN *Chr. Jrnl.* I. 42 O hast thou tuned these birds to sing forth thy honour in their warbling notes? **1883** D. C. MURRAY *Hearts* xiv. (1885) 115 The soaring soprano and the high warbling tenor.

†**b.** Of discourse: ? Ineffectual. (Cf. WARBLE *v.*[1] 4 a *fig.*). *Obs.*

1621 T. GRANGER *Expos. Eccles.* xii. 12. 334 He..may iustly retract the Reader from other warbling, erroneous, imperfect discourses, and treatises of men.

2. In names of birds, as the Warbling Flycatcher or Vireo, *Vireo gilvus.*

1783 LATHAM *Gen. Synopsis Birds* II. I. 157 Warbling Grosbeak. **1808–14** A. WILSON *Amer. Ornith.* (1831) II. 76 *Vireo gilvus*,..Warbling Flycatcher. **1888** SCLATER & HUDSON *Argentine Ornith.* I. 51 Ringed Warbling Finch.

†'**warbling**, *ppl. a.*[2] *Obs.* [f. WARBLE *v.*[3] + -ING[2].] In continual motion, quivering.

1549 COVERDALE, etc. *Erasm. Par. Jas.* i. 13–21 He..that letteth his tongue runne at large, which is a warblyng membre and a slippery. **1573** BARET *Alv.* F. 300 *Tremula in pileo pluma*, a warbling or quavering feather, &c. **1604** T. WRIGHT *Passions* v. §2. 170 When wee cast a stone into a calme water, we may perceiue diuers warbling naturall circles. **1632** LITHGOW *Trav.* VIII. 376 Whilst I cut, and crush their [*sc.* the serpents'] warbling wombe.

†**warbot.** *Obs.* [? Alteration of WARBLE *sb.*[2], after SCARBOT.] = WARBLE *sb.*[2] 3.

c **1440** *Promp. Parv.* 516/1 Warbote, wyrme, *emigran(e)us.* **1530** PALSGR. 286/2 Warbot a worme, *escarbot.*

warbrace: see WARDEBRACE *Obs.*

Warburg ('wɔːbɜːg). *Biochem.* The name of Otto *Warburg* (1883–1970), German biochemist, used *attrib.* and in the possessive to denote apparatus for the study of the metabolism of small pieces of tissue by the manometric measurement of the rate of oxygen consumption and carbon dioxide production, a technique he pioneered.

1930 *Biol. Abstr.* IV. 2745/1 By use of suitable suspensions of *B. coli* in Warburg's apparatus a biological, direct (manometric) method of measuring the hexoses is described. **1946** *Nature* 3 Aug. 155/2 The kinetics of these reductions may be followed manometrically in the Warburg apparatus by carrying out the reactions in an atmosphere of carbon dioxide. **1975** K. WILSON in Williams & Wilson *Biologist's Guide to Princ. & Techniques Pract. Biochem.* viii. 233 (*caption*) Diagrammatic representation of a Warburg manometer.

Warburgian (ˌwɔː'bɜːgiən), *a.* [f. the name of Aby *Warburg* (1866–1929), German-Jewish cultural historian + -IAN.] Of, pertaining to, or characteristic of Warburg or his work, or the Warburg Institute, founded (1904) by him in Hamburg as Kulturwissenschaftliche Bibliothek Warburg but subsequently (1933) transferred to London. Hence **War'burgianism.**

1956 A. WILSON *Anglo-Saxon Attitudes* II. ii. 273, I have neither an aesthetic inclination towards it [*sc.* Renaissance paganism] nor a Warburgian interest in the development of myth. **1958** *Times Lit. Suppl.* 23 May 277/1 It is true that when people ask the staff of the Institute what the 'Warburgian Method' really is they sometimes receive the answer that the whole point of 'The Warburg' is that it has no method. **1974** K. CLARK *Another Part of Wood* v. 190 The parts of my writing that have given me most satisfaction, for example, the chapter in *The Nude* called 'Pathos', are entirely Warburgian. **1977** *N.Y. Rev. Bks.* 24 Nov. 36/3 In nearly all his studies Gombrich follows the Warburgian practice of studying subject rather than form; but it is a humanized Warburgianism.

warby ('wɔːbɪ), *a. Austral. slang.* [f. WARB + -Y[1].] Unprepossessing in appearance or disposition; unkempt; disreputable, contemptible, decrepit.

1941 K. TENNANT *Battlers* xviii. 207 'Of all the warby ideas,' he said.., 'the warbiest is you going on your own.' **1949** R. PARK *Poor Man's Orange* 181 Yeah, there she was, in a warby kind of blue dress, and low-heeled shoes. **1959** D. NILAND *Big Smoke* 183 A warby unshaven young man in working clothes walked through and right up to him at the back. **1965** E. LAMBERT *Long White Night* 135 That was one of the funniest sights the main street ever saw—my old man's warby old Model A towing Foran's dirty big gleaming new Packard! **1973** J. MCNEIL *Old Familiar Juice* 74 He's down there whackin' up bumpers with a couple of 'is warby mates.

warch(e: see WARISH *v.*, WARK, WRETCH.

warck, dial. form of WORK.

†**warcodling.** *Obs.* [See CODLING[1]; the first element is uncertain.] Some kind of sea-fish.

1525 in *Excerpta e libris dom. Jacobi Quinti* (Bannatyne Club) 9, iij girlsis,..v warcodlingis.

warcraft ('wɔːkrɑːft, -æ-). [f. WAR *sb.*[1] + CRAFT *sb.*]

1. Cunning and skill in warfare; the art of conducting a war.

a **1661** FULLER *Worthies, Lancs.* (1662) 124 Duke Hambleton..had Officers who did Ken the War-craft, as well as any of our Age. **1846** *Eclectic Rev.* XIX. 177 The leading secret of Napoleon's war-craft, consisted in an inversion of the current rules of warfare. **1863** KINGLAKE *Crimea* (1877) V. ii. 370 Sir De Lacy Evans, a veteran well skilled in that part of the war-craft which belongs to the hour of combat. **1897** E. CONYBEARE *Hist. Cambridgesh.* 98 The king plainly felt the matter one of extreme urgency, needing his own presence, with all his warcraft and statecraft, to deal with it.

2. War-vessels collectively; also, a warship.

1898 *Daily News* 6 Aug. 5/6 Claiming the right to lock the Bosphorean gates of the Euxine against the fleets of the other Powers after passing our superfluous warcraft outwards. **1918** *Chambers's Jrnl.* May 318/1 With a whisk of her stern, the warcraft stood off. **1927** *Daily Tel.* 1 Mar. 11/3 It is believed here that the British and Japanese acceptances will pave the way for a conference of these Powers with the United States to consider the limitation of warcraft other than capital ships in line with the principles of the Washington Conference. **1930** *Tablet* 16 Aug. 202/2 These scribblers..would have us..cease building war craft.

'**war-cry.** [Cf. F. *cri de guerre.*] **a.** A cry (whether a shout or a significant name or phrase) uttered by a body of fighters to encourage each other in charging the enemy or in rallying to the fray.

1748 *Anson's Voy.* I. iii. 30 Orellana placed his hands hollow to his mouth, and bellowed out the war-cry used by those savages. **1757** [BURKE] *Europ. Settlem. Amer.* I. II. iv. 187 Setting up a most tremendous shout, which they call the war cry, they pour a storm of musquet bullets upon the enemy. **1808** JAMIESON, *Slogan*, the war-cry, or gathering word, of a clan. **1815** ELPHINSTONE *Acc. Caubul* II. v. 216 Proclaiming the Selaut (or war-cry of the Mussulmans). **1836** THIRLWALL *Greece* III. xxiii. 290 The army followed with an appalling war-cry.

b. *fig.*

1836 S. HOUSTON *Let.* 25 Apr. in W. B. Dewees *Lett. from Early Settler Texas* (1852) XIX. 198 Col. Sherman, with his regiment,..rung the war cry, '*Remember the Alamo*'. **1837** DICKENS *Let.* 24 Sept. (1965) I. 312 Of course we refused it—a new agreement and copyright, being the War Cry. **1848** SIR J. GRAHAM in C. S. Parker *Life & Lett.* (1907) II. 69 A further reform of the representation will be the stalking-horse of the ambitious, and the war-cry of their dupes. **1880** (*title*) The War-Cry and Official Gazette of the Salvation Army. **1902** L. STEPHEN *Stud. Biog.* IV. ii. 72 He was content with any general principle which would serve for a war-cry.

†**ward,** *sb.*[1] *Obs.* Forms: 1 weard, 4–5 warde, 5– ward. [OE. *weard* masc. = OS. *ward*, OHG. (MHG., mod.G.) *wart*, ON. *vǫrð-r*, Goth. *daurawar-s* doorkeeper:—OTeut. **warđu-z*, **warđo-z*; synonymous words differing in declension are OE. *wearda*, OHG. *warto* (MHG. *warte*):—OTeut. **warđon-*, and Goth. *wardja*:—OTeut. **warđjon-*; f. Teut. **warđ-*, an extended form of **war-* to watch, guard: see WARE *sb.*[2] and *a.*] A watchman, guard, keeper, warden.

Common in OE. (often applied to God, as in *rodora weard*, keeper of the skies). Later, chiefly as the second element in compounds, as *bear-, gate-, hay-, mill-, woodward.*

Beowulf 229 Weard Scildinga, se þe holmclifu healdan scolde. *a* **680** CÆDMON *Hymn* 1 Nu scylun herȝan hefaenricaes uard. **971** *Blickl. Hom.* 11 Salomones reste wæs mid weardum ymbseted. **1377** LANGL. *P. Pl.* B. XVIII. 320 For any wye or warde wide opene the ȝatis. **1471** CAXTON *Recuyell* (Sommer) 213 Thou hast slayn the wardes of the serpentes and the portyers of the lions [Fr. (1510) *les soursers des serpens & les portiers des lyons*] that kepte this contre Inhabitable.

ward (wɔːd), *sb.*[2] Forms: 1 weard, 3–7 warde, 4 *Sc.* vard, 5 waard, *north.* wayrd, 5–8 *Sc.* waird, 6–7 (*rare*) word(e, 7 *Sc.* wairde, 4– ward. [OE. *weard* str. fem. = MLG. *warde*, OHG. *warta* (MHG. *warte, wart*, guard, watch, observation, mod.G. *warte* watch-tower):—OTeut. **warđō*, f. **warđ-* (see prec.), whence also ON. *varðe* wk. masc., *varða* wk. fem., cairn, heap of stones. The Teut. word was adopted in Rom.: OF. *warde* (north-eastern), *guarde, garde* (whence GUARD *sb.*), mod.F. *garde*, Pr., Sp. *guarda.*

Some of the senses below are derived from the Law French *warde* (whence AL. *warda*), which appears to be in part an adoption of the Eng. word, and in part the north-eastern OF. form. In Law French, from the 13th c. onward, the word has regularly the form *garde.*]

I. Action of watching or guarding.

1. The action or function of a watchman, sentinel, or the like; observation for the purpose of discovering the approach of danger; look-out, watch, guard; also, surveillance. Phrases, *to hold, keep ward.* Also in the alliterative formula *watch and ward* (orig. a law phrase): see WATCH *sb.* Now *arch.*

Beowulf 319 Ic to sæ wille wið wrað werod wearde healdan. *c* **1350** *Will. Palerne* 2202 But ward was þer set wide wher aboute of bold burnes of armes þe beres for to seche. **1393** LANGL. *P. Pl.* C. VI. 186 Let no kynne consail ne couetyse ȝow departe, That on wit and on wil alle ȝoure wardes kepe. **1502** *Ord. Crysten Men* (W. de W. 1506) III. iii. 158 And therefore watche they upon theyr warde. **1546** *Reg. Privy Council Scot.* I. 52 Rise with the said Eirle and pay ward and watch with him during the tyme of were. **1563** P. WHITEHORNE *Onosandro Platon.* 47 Those, whiche shalbe appointed to make the ward, let them go before the Campe, ..and make fyres after suche sorte, that they may see those farre of. **1585** T. WASHINGTON tr. *Nicholay's Voy.* I. xx. 26 [We] gaue to vnderstand too him that had the warde, that the Ambassadour was there. **1649** C. WASE *Sophocles, Electra* 50 Had not I light in the house to keep A faithfull ward. **1697** DRYDEN *Æneis* VI. 750 And dire Tisiphone there keeps the Ward. **1765** BLACKSTONE *Comm.* I. ix. 345 Ward, guard, or *custodia*, is chiefly intended of the day time... Watch is properly applicable to the night only. **1778** BP. LOWTH *Transl. Isaiah* xxi. 8. 51 O my Lord, I keep my station all the day long; And on my ward have I continued every night. **1813** SCOTT *Trierm.* III. x, Sounds were heard, as when a guard, Of some proud castle, holding ward, Pace forth their nightly round. **1835** TRENCH *Poems, Gibraltar*, I ..saw thy gallant children to and fro Pace, keeping ward at one of those huge gates.

2. a. *gen.* Guardianship, keeping, control. Now *rare.* † *out of ward*: beyond control, out of hand (*obs.*).

c **1205** LAY. 19402 He bitahten him þa warde of alle þissen ærde. *a* **1225** *Ancr. R.* 430 Almihti God, he wite ou in his warde. *c* **1290** *St. Francis* 66 in *S. Eng. Leg.* 55 Seint Fraunceys nam þat tresor..and in ore louerdes warde it tok. *a* **1300** *Cursor M.* 10342 Ioseph..of egypti was hei stiward, And al þat land had in his ward. *c* **1305** *St. Swithin* 26 in *E.E.P.* (1862) 44 Wel him wiste þis holi man and god warde to him nom. *c* **1386** CHAUCER *Parson's T.* ¶880 My lord hath take to me vnder my warde al that he hath in this world. *c* **1400** *Destr. Troy* 3709 The two brether were abidyng bothe in a shippe, þat was stird with the storme streght out of warde. *c* **1425** WYNTOUN *Cron.* II. 340 Bot he [Joseph] refoysitt þat curtassy, For þe worschep of his larde, þat al his gud put in his warde. **1459** *Paston Lett.* I. 495 That fyrst an inventorie be made holye of hys godes and catell..and thayt they be leyd yn sure waard. **1485** CAXTON *Paris & V.* (1868) 57 That he kepe you in hys holy warde. **1530** TINDALE *Exod.* xii. 6 And ye shall kepe him [*sc.* the paschal lamb] in warde vntyll the .xiiii. daye of the same moneth. **1756** C. LUCAS *Ess. Waters* III. 144 The infant from his birth is overfed.. till he is put into his own ward. **1827** J. F. COOPER *Prairie* xiv, Such events as occurred during the ward of Ellen Wade. [A person left in charge of the camp and children.] **1873** J. G. HOLLAND *A. Bonnicastle* xi. 175 Under the conduct and ward of a Shepherd who would lead me only through green pastures.

b. *spec.* Guardianship of a child, a minor, or other person legally incapable of conducting his affairs. Also, the condition of being subject to a guardian.

c **1290** *Beket* 267 in *S. Eng. Leg.* 114 So muche he caste is heorte on him þat in his warde he let do his eldeste sone sire henri. **1297** R. GLOUC. (Rolls) 6426 King edmond biqueþ Is kinedom & al is lond king knout biuore is deþ, & þe warde of is tueye sones vor te hii of elde were. **1390** GOWER *Conf.* I. 345 He..tok this child into his warde. **1444** *Maldon* (Essex) *Liber A* 32 b, If the children be with in xiiii ȝere age, the moder shall haue the warde of hem tyl thei come to the seide age. **1538** STARKEY *England* 186 The faute of bryngyng vp of the nobylyte, wych, for the most parte, are nuryschyd wyt[h]out cure, bothe of theyr parentys being alyfe, and much wers of them in whose ward commynly they dow fal aftur theyr deth. **1709** STEELE *Tatler* No. 40 ¶4 The Law certainly gives these Persons [*sc.* idiots] into the Ward and Care of the Crown. **1849** JAMES *Woodman* xxxvi, You are in ward to me, and not Lord Calverly. *a* **1901** W. BRIGHT *Age of Fathers* (1903) I. 365 Ecclesiastics were to abstain from visiting widows and heiresses under ward.

c. *Feudal Law.* The control and use of the lands of a deceased tenant by knight-service, and the guardianship of the infant heir, which belonged to the superior until the heir attained his majority.

1338 R. BRUNNE *Chron.* (1810) 214 Of wardes & relefe þat barons of him held, þer ne was ore of chefe, tille him no þing suld ȝeld. **1375** BARBOUR *Bruce* XII. 320 Gif ony deis in this battaill, His air, but ward, releif, or taill, On the first day his land sall weild. **1422** *Rolls of Parlt.* IV. 176/1 All maner Wardes, Mariages, Fermes, and other casueltees. **1461** *Ibid.* V. 473/1 Any Graunte made..of the Warde of Lond and of the body, with the mariage of John Kenne. **1507** *Reg. Privy Seal Scot.* I. 205/2 Pertenyn to the King be reson of ward throw the said Patrikkis deceis. *a* **1513** FABYAN *Chron.* VII. (1533) 20 A parlyament was holden..where..the lordes and baronye of the lande graunted vnto the kynge and to his heyres kynges, the warde and mariage of theyr heyres. **1601** SHAKS. *All's Well* I. i. 5, I must attend his maiesties command, to whom I am now in Ward. **1616** A. RATHBORNE *Surveyor* 192 The Lord..shall haue the Ward, that is, the custodie and keeping of those lands so holden of him, to his owne vse and behoofe, without account, vntill the heire come to the full age of one and twentie yeares. *a* **1646** SIR T. HOPE *Minor Practicks* iv. (1734) 180 The Donatar during the Time of the Ward is in Place of the Master. **1765** BLACKSTONE *Comm.* I. viii. 293 [The statute 17 Edw. II, c. 9] directs..that the king shall have ward of the lands of natural fools, taking the profits without waste or destruction. **1810** SCOTT *Lady of Lake* II. xxxvii, My sovereign holds in ward my land. **1878** J. DAVIDSON *Inverurie* ii. 73 Norman de Leslie..held the ward of the estate of Kemnay in 1348.

d. *Court of Wards*: a court established by Hen. VIII for the trial of causes relating to wardships; subsequently called ***Court of Wards and Liveries***; abolished by Stat. 12 Car. II. cap. 24 (1660). Also, in British India, the title of a court which dealt with cases pertaining to the property of minors. ***Master of the Wards*** (***and Liveries***), the presiding judge of the Court of Wards (1541–1660).

1560 B. GOOGE tr. *Palingenius' Zodiac* Ep. Ded. (1561), To..Sir William Cecill, Knight,..Master of the Wardes, and Liueries. 1591 LAMBARDE *Archeion* (1635) 233 The Court of Wards began in our memorie, about 32. yeare of the Raigne of K.H. 8. who also in the next yeare after added thereunto the office of the Master of the Liveries, .. ordayning that it should bee called the Court of Wards and Liveries. 1647 CLARENDON *Hist. Reb.* III. §86 The Lord Say was to be Master of the Wards. 1914 *Contemp. Rev.* Mar. 397 Legal Adviser to Purdanashins under the guardianship of the Court of Wards of Bengal.

3. Care or charge of a prisoner; the condition of being a prisoner; custody, imprisonment. Now *rare*.

free ward: the condition of being a prisoner with permission to go anywhere within prescribed limits.

The phrase *to ward* was sometimes written as one word.

c 1290 *St. Katherine* 63 in *S. Eng. Leg.* 94 Maide, he seide, þou schalt abide In warde here mid me. 1297 R. GLOUC. (Rolls) 6619 Gentil men þat he vond in prison ek ydo, Oþer in warde mid vnriȝt, he boȝte hom out al so. c 1400 *Rom. Rose* 5856 The olde wyf that [kepeth] so harde Fair-Welcoming within her warde. 1423 JAS. I *Kingis Q.* xxv, In strayte ward and in strong prisoun. 1429 *Rolls of Parlt.* IV. 346/1 That the Keper and Wardeyn of the same Prisone .. savely kepe every persone to his warde so commytted. c 1460 *Towneley Myst.* xxv. 238 Here haue they soriornyd, noght as thyne, bot in thi wayrd. 1474 *Acc. Ld. High Treas. Scot.* I. 53 Item gevin to Skrymgeour masare to convoye James Hering to warde, vs. 1546 *Reg. Privy Council Scot.* I. 36 Remane in fre waird within ony place the Eirle of Huntlie forsaid pleissis to assign. 1564 *Ibid.* 293 He sall remane in fre ward within the burgh of Edinburgh, and on na wayis depart furth of the samyn. 1565 *Ibid.* 414 He brak his ward furth of oure castell of Edinburgh. 1568 GRAFTON *Chron.* II. 408 He was attached by the Erle Marshall, and committed toward in the Abbey of Saint Albones. 1578–9 *Reg. Privy Council Scot.* III. 66 That Hob Ellot .. sould remane and keip his ward with Williame Portarfeild of Duchall, and on nawayis eschaip. 1599 in T. Stafford *Pac. Hib.* I. i. (1633) 11 To bee committed to ward, there to remaine in safe custodie, untill [etc.]. 1611 BIBLE *Gen.* xl. 3 And he put them in ward in the house of the captaine of the guard, into the prison. a 1614 J. MELVILL *Autob. & Diary* (Wodrow Soc.) 267 It was thought best that the first sort sould be chargit to warde; the second apprehendit at unawars and punished. 1637 RUTHERFORD *Let. to Ld. Craighall* 10 Aug., It is easie for you to cast your light into prison, .. But that prisoner will break ward to your incomparable torture. 1828 SCOTT *F.M. Perth* xxx, I trust your Grace remembers that you are under ward. *Ibid.*, I have already said your Highness lies in ward here. 1869 FREEMAN *Norm. Conq.* (1876) III. xii. 193 He .. kept him in ward two years till he agreed to the hard conditions. 1871 BLACKIE *Four Phases* i. 148 He remained in ward thirty days, till the sacred ship should return from the Delian festival.

†**4.** Charge, duty entrusted to one; office. *Obs.*

1338 R. BRUNNE *Chron.* (1810) 149 We þre haf þe ward of God & our ladie, þe schippes of kyng Richard to kepe & ȝow þam bie. c 1460 J. RUSSELL *Bk. Nurture* 1193 þerto let hym take good hede, and his warde wayte wisely.

†**5.** Care, regard. In phrases, ***to have no ward of***, not to regard, not to fear; ***no ward***, no matter (*if, how*). *Obs.*

a 1300 *Cursor M.* 11637 Moder, he said, haf þou na ward, Noþer o leon ne o lepard. *Ibid.* 20705 Ne has na ward of na juu For i self ai wel be wit ȝow. c 1330 R. BRUNNE *Chron. Wace* (Rolls) 5011 He wende of þeym haue hed no warde, Bot hym fel þer a chek ful harde. c 1380 WYCLIF *Wks.* (1880) 24 For haue þei here myrþe and iolite, no warde to hem hou faste þe woluys of helle wirien cristen soulis & beren hem to helle. *Ibid.* 72 ȝif mennus soulis gon to helle bi brekynge of goddis comaundementis no warde, so þat þe peny come faste to fille here hondis & coffris.

II. A person who is 'in ward' (see 2).

6. a. A minor under the control of a guardian. Also *Sc.* †***ward-minor***.

In Feudal Law the term (AF. *garde*) was applied *spec.* to an heir or heiress whose person and lands after the father's death were held 'in ward' (see 2 c) by the superior during his or her minority.

ward in Chancery, ward of court: a minor for whom a guardian has been appointed by the Court of Chancery, or who has become directly subject to the authority of that Court.

1433 *Rolls of Parlt.* IV. 441/2 To the Kyng .. louly compleynes .. your Warde John Duc of Norffolk. c 1440 *Alphabet of Tales* 285 He .. servid a wurthi prince: & he made hym a knyght and gaff hym a warde, a grete gentylwomman, vnto his wyfe. 1470–85 MALORY *Arthur* v. xi. 180 In that stoure was syr Chestelayne a chyld and ward of syre Gawayne slayne. 1553 T. WILSON *Rhet.* 66 In lamentyng the miserye of wardeshyppes I might saie it is not for noughte so communely said, I wil handle you like a warde. 1560 DAUS tr. *Sleidane's Comm.* 103 This cause did not concerne the Marques George only, but also his nephewe Albert, whiche was his warde [L. *cuius erat tutor*]. 1604 T. WRIGHT *Passions* IV. ii. 126, I thinke the punishment meetest for them, should be, that it were lawfull to beg them for Wardes, and giue them tutors, because they lacke discretion to vse their money. a 1656 BP. HALL *Rem. Wks.* (1660) 30 Sr Walter Leveson .. leaves his young Orphan Ward to the King. 1731 KAMES *Decis. Crt. Sess. 1730–52* (1799) 5 It was objected .. that .. the aliment of her infant-children was a proper burden upon herself, as being their mother, and liferentrix of their whole estate, which is provided by act of parliament in case of ward-minors, and extended by practice and analogy to other fiars. 1741 RICHARDSON *Pamela* (1824) I. 84 Here, .. said she, here is your pretty ward and mine; let us try to make her time with us easy. 1790 *Stevens v. Savage* in *Eng. Rep.* (1903) XXX. 277 Stevens having been committed for a contempt, by having married Miss Jeffry, a ward of the Court. 1810 SCOTT *Lady of Lake* II. xxvi, This youth, though still a royal ward, Risqued life and land to be my guard. 1814 —— *Lord of Isles* VI. ix, Then, 'twas her Liege's strict command, And she, beneath his royal hand, A ward in person and in land. 1815 H. MADDOCK *Treat. Princ. & Pract. High Court of Chancery* I. ii. 264 If a Child, a Ward of Court, would not be safe, the Chancellor would not permit it to go to *Scotland*. 1837 DICKENS *Pickw.* lvii, Mr. Snodgrass .. had been in his minority a ward of Mr. Pickwick's. 1837 C. SELBY (*title*) The Irish Dragoon; or, Wards in Chancery. 1842 TENNYSON *Locksley Hall* 156, I was left a trampled orphan, and a selfish uncle's ward. 1853 DICKENS *Bleak Ho.* viii, He is a ward in Chancery, my dear. 1870 H. SMART *Race for Wife* ii, Grenville Rose had been brought up a great deal with his cousin Maud, being, indeed, a ward of Denison's. 1875 A. H. SIMPSON *Treat. Law & Pract. Infants* viii. 145 The general rule of the Court is that a ward of Court may not be removed out of the jurisdiction. 1928 A. BICKNELL *Law & Pract. Infants* iv. 89 To remove a ward of Court from the jurisdiction without proper leave is contempt of Court. 1977 *Jersey Even. Post* 26 July 13/4 If the children were allowed to leave, they could be made wards of Court and could find themselves in a position similar to that of the recent 'tug of love' children.

b. *transf.* One who is under the protection or control of another.

a 1435 *Torr. Portugal* 1351 Than said the kyng: 'I vnderstond, Thou hast fought for my doughter & my lond, And art my ward, i-wys. 1560 DAUS tr. *Sleidane's Comm.* 116 b, The Prince and his heires males, shall holde the Dukedome of Wirtemberge of kyng Ferdinando as Archeduke of Austriche, and so tobe his wardes and clientes. 1593 NASHE *Christ's T.* I 3 b, [Mother to her infant son] Nere shall the Romains haue thee for theyr Warde. 1600 MARSTON, etc. *Jack Drums Entert.* I. (1601) B 3, When being maried to a wise man (O the Lord) You are made a foole, a Ward, curbd and controlld. 1653 MILTON *Hirelings* Wks. 1851 V. 373 For the Magistrate in Person of a nursing Father to make the Church is meer Ward, as always in Minority, .. is neither just nor pious. 1659 F. OSBORN *Miscell. Ess.* etc. 166 So that, instead of being a Ward, .. you shall be Guardian of the Person and Estate of your Husband. 1848 DICKENS *Dombey* iii, With these words, Susan Nipper .. made a charge at her young ward, and swept her out of the room.

†**7.** An orphan under age. *Obs.*

1559 *Mirr. Mag., Dk. York* iii, When her brother Edmund died a warde, She was sole hayer by due discent of line. a 1577 SIR T. SMITH *Commw. Eng.* (1609) 109 A Ward or Infant is taken for a child in base age, whose Father is dead. 1577 tr. *Bullinger's Decades* II. v. (1592) 156 In the same sort also there are here commanded vnto vs, widdowes, Orphans, wardes, poore men. 1592 SHAKS. *Rom. & Jul.* I. v. 42 His Sonne was but a Ward two yeares agoe.

III. Defence.

8. a. *Fencing.* A defensive posture or movement; a mode of parrying. Cf. GUARD *sb.* 3.

a 1586 SIDNEY *Arcadia* III. xi. §8 He .. strake so thicke vpon Amphialus, as if euery blow would faine haue bene foremost. But Amphialus .. let passe the storme with strong wardes, and nimble auoidings. 1589 [see PORR *sb.* 2]. c 1590 GREENE *Fr. Bacon* IV. iii. 1812, *1 Scholler.* Ah, well thrust! *2 Scholler.* But marke the ward. 1595 *Saviolo's Practise* I. F 2, With this readinesse must hee strike this reuerso, but withall, his lefte hand must bee vppon the warde of his teacher. *Ibid.* K 1, When you lie in this warde, and make vppon your enemie towardes his right side. 1596 SHAKS. *1 Hen. IV*, II. iv. 215 (Q. 1598) Thou knowest my olde warde: here I lay, and thus I bore my poynt. 1599 G. SILVER *Paradoxes of Def.* Wks. (1898) 26 All single weapons haue foure wardes, and all double weapons haue eight wardes. The single sword hath two with the point vp, and two with the point downe. *Ibid.* 34 The Dagger is an imperfect ward, although borne out straight. 1640 *Wits Recreat.* E 1, On a Souldier. The souldier fights well, and with good regard, But when hee's lame, he lies at an ill ward. 1652 URQUHART *Jewel* 88 He alters his wards from Tierce to Quart. 1810 SCOTT *Lady of Lake* V. xv, Fitz-James's blade was sword and shield. He practised every pass and ward.

b. *fig.* Now *arch.*

1581 PETTIE tr. *Guazzo's Civ. Conv.* III. (1586) 135 b, So these poore women .. come to the amourous incounter with one, and with an other: but at length being driuen from their warde, they ly so open that they are soone venued. 1604 T. WRIGHT *Passions* VI. 337 Will not so many warnings of death, iudgment, .. sufficiently stirre vs vp to stand vpon our warde? 1619 in *Eng. & Germany* (Camden) 197 Otherwise they would long ere this have brought the deciding of their case to the greate assise of a day of battell, which hath bene their ancient and ever happy ward against their oppressors. 1622 MASSINGER & DEKKER *Virg. Mart.* II. i. D 1 b, I lay at my old ward of lechery. 1643 SIR T. BROWNE *Relig. Med.* I. §55. 124 To perfect vertue .. there is required a .. compleat armour, that whilst we lye at close ward against one vice we lye [not] open to the vennie of another. 1647 MAY *Hist. Parl.* Pref. 2 For against the unexpected stroke of partiall history the ward is not so ready, as against that Polemike writing where [etc.]. 1863 WHYTE MELVILLE *Gladiators* xxii, Duplicity was no new effort for the Tribune. He had often, ere now, betaken himself to this mode of defence when driven to his last ward. 1892 STEVENSON *In South Seas* III. v. (1900) 248 He hastily returned to his old ward. 'I don't deny I could if I wanted,' said he.

†**c.** Defence, protection, shelter. *Obs.*

1582 T. WATSON *Centurie of Love* xxiv, The beames, which then proceeded from her face Were such, as for the same I found no warde. 1697 DRYDEN *Æneis* I. 691 In their right Hands a pointed Dart they wield; The left, for Ward, sustains the Lunar Shield.

†**d.** *Chess.* ? The protection afforded by a specified piece or pawn. *Obs. rare*$^{-1}$.

c 1450 *Treat. Chess* (MS. Ashm. 344) lf. 3 b, Chek wt thy Roke in thy Pon Ward. *Ibid.* 17 b, Then check wt thy Roke in thy knyghts warde.

9. *Scots Law.* Tenure by military service, WARD-HOLDING: sometimes quasi-*adv.* in ***to hold ward*** = 'to hold in ward' (see HOLD *v.* 6, 19 b). Also, a payment in commutation of military service; more explicitly ***taxed ward*** (see TAXED *ppl. a.* 2 c), in contradistinction to ***simple*** or ***black ward***. Now only *Hist.* Cf. CASTLE-GUARD 2, 3, CASTLE-WARD 2.

The lawyers connected this sense with sense 2 c, as if 'to hold land in ward' meant to hold it subject to the lord's right to 'ward' when the heir was a minor.

1508 *Reg. Privy Seal Scot.* I. 271/1 Landis .. haldin of the kingis hienes be service of ward and releyf. 1530 *Ibid.* II. 66/1 His landis within our realme that wer haldin of us be service of ward and releiff to Archibald Douglas. 1578 *Reg. Privy Council Scot.* II. 693 All altering of haldingis blanche quhilk of befoir wees haldin ward. 1642 SIR T. HOPE *Diary* (Bannatyne Club) 176 A neu commissioun, for changing of ward in few, both of lands haldin off the King and Prince. 1684 SIR G. MACKENZIE *Inst. Laws Scot.* II. iv. (1694) 71 Some Lands hold Ward, some Feu, some Blench, and some Burgage. 1892 J. A. HENDERSON *Ann. Lower Deeside* 59 The king [c 1680] in changing the holding of the lands from simple ward to taxed ward took occasion [etc.].

†**10.** Sc. ***ward and warsel***: security, pledge.

a 1600 *Aberdeen Reg.* (MS.) XXIV. (Jam.), To remane wpoun his ward and warsall. *Ibid.*, He tuik nothyr ward nor wersell of the said claith. 1768 ROSS *Helenore* 25 E'en sit you still, an' rest you here wi' me, An' I shall ward an' warsel for you be.

IV. A body of guards.

11. A company of watchmen or guards. Cf. GUARD *sb.* 9. Now *rare*.

c 1000 ÆLFRIC *Judg.* Epil., þa Iudeiscan .. besetton his [*sc.* Christ's] birgene sona mid wearde. 13.. *K. Alis.* 1976 (Laud MS.), þer þai telden her pauyloune þat niȝth & hem resteþ þare Mid warde þat was good & war. [*Lincoln's Inn MS.* With wardes, bothe gode and warre.] c 1330 R. BRUNNE *Chron. Wace* (Rolls) 5085 He dide sette in wardes seers, Knyghte to wachem, & squiers. 1382 WYCLIF *Jer.* li. 12 Vp on the wallis of Babilon rereth a tocne, eecheth the warde [Vulg. *augete custodiam*]. 1585 HIGINS *Junius' Nomencl.* 483/2 *Miles stationarius*, .. one of the watch or ward. 1605 *Famous Hist. Stukeley* E ij, Bid the Seriant Maior shut the gates, And see them guarded with a double ward. 1805 SCOTT *Last Minstrel* III. xxx, Was frequent heard the changing guard, And watch-word from the sleepless ward. 1870 J. R. MACDUFF *Mem. Patmos* xx. 276 Twenty-four wards or companies were appointed night by night to guard the various entrances to the sacred courts.

†**12.** A garrison. *Obs.*

c 1500 *Melusine* xxiv. 170 Thenne þey recouered there six of theire galeyes, .. and lefte in it good wardes [Fr. *gardes*] for to kepe them. 1586 HOOKER *Chron. Irel.* 160/2 in *Holinshed*, This house of Asketten is a verie strong castell, .. and the chiefest house of the earles, wherein he had a strong ward. 1590 SPENSER *F.Q.* II. xi. 15 On th' other side, th' assieged Castles ward Their stedfast stonds did mightily maintaine. 1596 —— *State Irel.* Wks. (Globe) 664/2, I will have .. some of them be putt in wardes, upon all the straytes thereaboutes. 1610 HOLLAND *Camden's Brit.* II. 97 There were planted little forts with wardes .. to restraine the inroades of prey taking robbers. a 1660 *Contemp. Hist. Irel.* (Ir. Archæol. Soc.) II. 102 Carrige beinge betrayed by the Protestant warde there.

†**13.** One of the three main divisions of an army, the van, the rear, and the middle or 'main battle'. Also sometimes applied *gen.* to any division led by a subordinate commander. *Obs.*

[Orig. a use of the second element in the compounds *avantward* (*vanward, vaward*) and *arrearward* (*rearward*) adopted from OF. In these compounds the OF. *warde* meant 'guard', and so was applicable only to the bodies placed in the front and rear. In English, on the analogy of *vanward* (also *first ward, foreward*) and *rearward* (also *hinder ward*), the term *middle ward*, MIDDLEWARD, came to be used for the 'main battle', and thus *ward* acquired the sense above defined.]

13.. *K. Alis.* 1995 (Laud MS.), Sendeþ ymagu wyt ȝoure standard And Archillaus in þe first ward. 1412–20 LYDG. *Chron. Troy* I. 4046, 4050 Nestor þe duke schal in þe firste ward Metyn with hym... þe bridde warde Pelleus schal lede. *Ibid.* III. 3401 þer cam with hem þe kyng Machaoun, And alderlaste þe grete Agamenoun, With alle her wardis, & fel in sodeynly Vp-on Troyens. c 1430 *Syr Generides* (Roxb.) 3771 Now wendeth this ost in wardes ten Ful wel araied with noble men. c 1450 *Merlin* xviii. 286 Than com Gaheries with his warde of iijMl goode men. 1450–1530 *Myrr. our Ladye* 119 And eche pryncehode ys departed in thre orders, as in thre wardes. [Cf. *ante.* As an hooste in batayle ys departed in thre, that ys to saye, the forwarde, the mydel warde, and the rerewarde.] 1513 DOUGLAS *Æneis* XII. ix. 113 Apon this wys the ostis and wardis haill On athir part returnyt in bataill. 1523 BERNERS *Froiss.* I. xxxix. 22 b, Thus they went forthe in thre great batayls: the marshalles and the Almaygnes had the first, the kynge of Englande in the myddle warde, & the duke of Brabant in the rerewarde. *Ibid.* xlv. 25 b, In the mornyng they aproched in thre wardes. 1524 PACE *Let. to Hen. VIII* 5 Aug. in Strype *Eccl. Mem.* (1721) I. II. 21 Four & twenty great peaces of Artillerie .. dayly foloing us in the hinder ward. 1563 P. WHITEHORNE *Onosandro Platon.* 126 b, And after the first warde, cause the seconde, to succeede, and the thyrde next the same, and the fourth, and the fifte also, if so many shall nede. c 1585 *Fair Em* v. i. 6 See all our men be martialed for the fight. Dispose the Wardes as lately was deuised. 1587 HOLINSHED *Chron.* III. 980/2 The fore-ward foremost, the battell in the middest, the rere-ward hindermost, ech ward hauing his troope of horssemen and gard of ordinance. 1656 HARRINGTON *Oceana* Wks. (1700) 171 But as to the peculiar Policy, of twelve Manipuls or Wards, divided into three Cohorts, each Cohort containing four Wards.

V. Place for guarding.

14. In a fortress: †**a.** The portion of the defences entrusted to a particular officer or division of the garrison. *Obs.* †**b.** A guarded entrance. *Obs.* **c.** The (*inner* or *outer*) circuit of the walls of a castle; the ground between two encircling walls. *Obs.* exc. *arch.*

1297 R. GLOUC. (Rolls) 8301 A maister þat was wiþinne sende to þe erl beumond To ȝelde vp is warde to ben hol & sound. Ar his felawes were iwar he ȝeld him vp þere þre toures of þe cite þat in is warde were. 1340 HAMPOLE *Pr. C.* 9087 Bot þa wardes of þe ceté of heven, Er mare crafty and strang þan any kan neven. 1375 BARBOUR *Bruce* XVII. 349 Till thar wardis thai went in hy, That war stuffit richt stalwardly With stanys, schot, and other thing. c 1400 *Rom. Rose* 3191 The lady of the high warde [Fr. *la dame de la haute garde*] Which from hir tour lokide thiderward. c 1400 *Beryn*

238 The knyȝt [tho] with his meyne went to se the wall, And þe wardes of the town, as to a knyȝt be-fall. c1400 Sowdone Bab. 332 He entred to the maister Toure. The firste warde thus thay wonne. 1423 Rolls of Parlt. IV. 199/1 [He] made assaute to the said Castell, and wan the said warde. c1425 Cursor M. 9894 (Trin. MS.) Bailyes haþ þis castel þre Wiþ feire wardes [Cott. & Gött. walles] semely to se. c1440 Jacob's Well 222 As þou hast v. watyrgatys in þe vttere-warde, owtward in þe pytt of þi body... Ryȝt, so, þou hast v. watyrgatys in þe indere-warde of þi soule. 1485 Rolls of Parlt. VI. 384/1 The Offices of Keping of the Keys of th' ynerward of oure Castell of Wyndesore. c1500 Melusine xix. 62 Soone was the Fortres made up not only with one warde but two strong wardes. 1509 HAWES Past. Pleas. xxvi. (Percy Soc.) 116 And therwith all he ledde me to his warde, Me to repose in pleasaunt due saufgard. 1530 PALSGR. 234/1 Inderwarde of a castell, cengle de chastel. Ibid. 250/1 Outterwarde of a castell, courtbasse. 1584 SIR R. SADLER St. Papers (1809) III. 171 The strength of this howse, having two wards, the gentleman porter ever at the one with 4 or 5 in his company, and dyvers soldyers at the other. 1649 G. DANIEL Trinarch. To Rdr. 209 Euery hand Of accident doth wth a Picker stand, To scale the wards of Life. 1808 SCOTT Marmion I. iv, Then to the Castle's lower ward Sped forty yeomen tall. 1813 —— Rokeby III. xxvii, Then, vain were battlement and ward! 1843 AINSWORTH Windsor Castle IV. iii, Just as they entered the lower ward. Ibid., The party directed their course towards the middle ward.

transf. 1513 DOUGLAS Æneis VI. vii. 7 In the first circil, or the vtir ward, ȝoung babbeis saulis weping sor thai hard. Ibid. viii. 4 And sone thai wer in cumin to the plane And lattir wardis, quhairin dois remane Vailȝeant folkis in feild and chevalry.

†15. An appointed station, post (for a body of soldiers). Obs.

1375 BARBOUR Bruce XVII. 349 Quhen that thai saw That menȝe raynge thame swa on raw, Till thar wardis thai went in hy. Ibid. 627 Engynys alsua for till cast Thai ordanit and maid redy fast, And set ilk man syne till his ward. c1489 CAXTON Sonnes of Aymon xxi. 463 They wente to their warde to defende the towne.

†16. within one's ward: within the region in which one is safe: in quot. fig. Also, within (another's) ward: in the region controlled by (another). Obs.

1490 CAXTON Eneydos xvii. 66 The fyne louer that alwayes kepeth hym selfe wythin his warde, and fyndeth noo thynge soo sure but that he putteth it in adoubte, can not be lyghtely deceyued. 1556 PHAER Æneid IV. (1558) Kj, What meanes he? why remaines he thus within his enemies ward?

17. †a. A prison (cf. sense 3). Obs. b. Each of the divisions or separate departments of a prison.

1338 R. BRUNNE Chron. (1810) 278 Opon þe toþer dai Edward þider cam, þe prisons.. Were brouht him bifore, þre erles þre barons, & mo be fiue score kynghtes & lordes of touns, þise were in his wardes, & auht & tuenti mo. 1535 COVERDALE Isa. xxiv. 22 These shalbe coupled together as prisoners be, and shalbe shut in one warde and punished innumerable daies. 1577 HANMER Anc. Eccl. Hist., Euseb. II. xii. 15 Thus Iohn, because of Herods suspicion, was sent bounde to Machærous the warde..and there beheaded. 1591 SYLVESTER Du Bartas I. ii. 710 Thus Fire, desirous to break forth again From's cloudy Ward, cannot itself refrain. 1602 SHAKS. Ham. II. ii. 252 A goodly [prison], in which there are many Confines, Wards, and Dungeons. 1614 J. COOKE Greene's Tu Quoque I i b, Be plaine with him, and turne him out o' th Ward. Ibid., Hold. If you haue no monie, You'd best remoue into some cheaper Ward. Spend. What Ward should I remoue in? Hold. Why to the Two-pennie Ward. 1675 BURTHOGGE Causa Dei 68 Nor is Hell a Sheriffs Ward, in which the Debtor is Imprisoned till he pay his Debt. 1780 J. HOWARD State of Prisons App. 125 The new gaol has separate wards and courts for debtors. 1821 SCOTT Kenilw. xxxiii, 'What the devil's noise is this in the ward?' he said—'What! man and woman together in the same cell?' 1825 MACAULAY Ess., Milton, Once more, compare the lazar-house in the eleventh book of the Paradise Lost with the last ward of Malebolge in Dante. 1836 DICKENS Sk. Boz, Visit to Newgate, The buildings in the prison, or in other words the different wards, form a square. 1894 LADY M. VERNEY Verney Mem. III. 150 Tom..could not face the horrors of the common wards [of the Fleet prison].

18. a. An apartment or division in a hospital or lunatic asylum, containing a certain number of beds, or allocated to a particular class of patients.

1749 SMOLLETT Gil Blas XI. vii. (1782) IV. 171, I walked through two or three wards full of sick people a-bed. 1758 J. S. tr. Le Dran's Observ. Surg. (1771) 207 He was lodged in the Fever Ward. 1842 DICKENS Amer. Notes vi, The different wards [of the lunatic asylum] might have been cleaner and better ordered. 1850 L. HUNT Autobiog. I. iii. 102 The wards, or sleeping-rooms [in Christ's Hospital], are twelve. 1881 Encycl. Brit. XII. 305/2 No cooking should be done in the wards. 1961 R. SHAW Sun Doctor I. i. 47 She looked at the two main wards of the hospital—long low rooms divided into cubicles like an old dormitory in an English public school. 1975 I. ILLICH Medical Nemesis vi. 111 Ailments had to be turned into objective diseases. Species had to be clinically defined..so that officials could fit them into wards. 1982 B. TRAPIDO Brother of More Famous Jack xlvii. 193, I was required, during the first three months, to spend occasional week-long spells in hospital in a special ward for the observation of problem pregnancies.

b. The patients in a ward, collectively.

1768 FOOTE Devil III. Wks. 1799 II. 277 Yesterday..we bled the west ward, and jalloped the north.

19. a. An administrative division of a borough or city; originally, a district under the jurisdiction of an alderman; now usually, a district which elects its own councillors to represent it on the City or Town Council. Also, the people of such a district collectively.

In Anglo-L. documents the wards (wardæ) of London are mentioned by that name from the 12th c., sometimes designated by the name of the alderman and sometimes by their locality. An occasional synonym was custodia.

[c1130 in 9th Rep. Hist. MSS. Comm. (1883) 66 In warda Osberti Drinkepinne, terra quam tenuit Wulwinus juvenis. 1226-7 in Madox Hist. Exch. (1711) 489 note, Tallagium Wardarum Londoniæ, quod colligi debet per Aldermannos subscriptos: Willelmus filius Benedicti re de L l., de Custodia fori. 1229-30 Ibid. 490 note, Willelmus filius Benedicti re de xxxv marcis, de Warda fori. 1275 in Rotuli Hundred. (1812) I. 403 Warda de Bassingeshol. Ibid. 418 Warda Symonis de Hadestok.]

1377 LANGL. P. Pl. B. Prol. 94 Somme seruen þe kyng and his siluer tellen, In cheker and in chancerye chalengen his dettes Of wardes and wardmotes, weyues and streyues. 1427 in Heath Grocers' Comp. (1869) 4 Conyhoope-lane in the Warde of Chepe. 1433 Rolls of Parlt. IV. 425/2 Every Parisshe or Warde, desolate, wastud, [etc.]. a1513 FABYAN Chron. VII. (1533) 28 b, The sayde Iohn Mansell chargyd the mayre, that euery Alderman in hys warde shulde vppon the morowe folowyng assemble hys wardemote, [etc.]. 1518 Sel. Cases Star Chamb. (Selden Soc.) II. 127 Within v wardes of the same Towne..ther hath byn v Cunstables that is to say in euery ward oon. 1588 W. SMITH Brief Descr. Lond. (MS. Harl. 6363) lf. 13 There is also The Wardmote Enquest, Chosen euery St. Thomas day, in euery ward a quest. c1590 Sir T. More II. iv. 226 We meete at the Guildehall and there determine That thorow euery warde the watche be clad In armour. 1598-1603 STOW Surv. (1908) I. 117 The Auncient diuision of this Cittie was into Wardes or Aldermanries. 1603 SHAKS. Meas. for M. II. i. 281 They do you wrong to put you so oft vpon 't [sc. the office of constable]. Are there not men in your Ward sufficient to serue it? 1631 GOUGE God's Arrows V. xix. 432 London should have as many Artillery Gardens, as it hath Wards. a1700 EVELYN Diary 6 May 1645, Rome..is divided into 14 Regions or Wards. 1715 LEONI Palladio's Archit. (1742) II. 72 In the Ward [It. regione] of the Temple of Peace, stood a Colossus. 1733 SWIFT On Poetry 286 In ev'ry Street a City-bard Rules, like an Alderman his Ward. 1751 Engl. Gazetteer I. s.v. St. Albans, There are four wards here, in each of which are a constable, and two church-wardens. 1824 G. CHALMERS Caledonia III. vi. 569 By an act of Parliament, in 1800, for regulating the police of Glasgow, that city was divided into wards. 1854 LOWELL Camb. 30 Yrs. Ago Pr. Wks. 1890 I. 94, I would rather have had that slow, conscientious vote of P.'s alone, than to have been chosen Alderman of the Ward! 1863 COX Instit. III. ix. 730 Large boroughs are divided into wards, which elect their councillors severally.

b. An administrative division of the Mormon Church (the Church of Jesus Christ of Latter-Day Saints).

1859 Mountaineer (Salt Lake City) 27 Aug. 2/4 If the water-masters of our district or ward will see that we have a double portion of water during the ensuing week for our garden, we will now agree not to mention them again. 1925 M. R. WERNER Brigham Young xii. 422 The bishop was in charge of all the families of his ward. 1979 M. P. LEONE Roots Mod. Mormonism ii. 36 Wards average about seven hundred people.

20. In Cumberland, Northumberland, and some Scottish counties: One of the administrative districts into which these counties were formerly divided.

1431 Reg. Mag. Sig. Scot. 43/2 Alex. of Cragy serjand of fee wythin the Myddyll Ward of Edynburgh. 1495 Acc. Ld. High Treas. Scot. I. 216 Johne Hepburne of the Est Ward of Edinburgh. 1496 Ibid. 312 The Upper Ward of Clydesdale. 15.. Peblis to the Play 185 (Maitland Fol.) Iohne niksoun of ye nether warde. 1832 Act 2 & 3 Will. IV c. 64 §15 Such Northern Division shall include..the several wards of Bamborough, Coquetdale, Glendale, and Morpeth. 1864 G. V. IRVING & A. MURRAY (title) The Upper Ward of Lanarkshire described and delineated. 1872 E. W. ROBERTSON Hist. Ess. 120 The Ward or Quarter still represents the highest subdivision of the county. 1882 JAMIESON, Ward 3. Lanarkshire is divided into Upper, Middle and Lower Wards.

†21. a. 'A part or division of a Forrest' (Phillips 1671). App. only Sc. Obs.

1425 Reg. Mag. Sig. Scot. 1426, 11/1 The offyce off maistrischip off our ward of Yarrow lyand wythin our saide forest. [1485: see OVER-WARD sb.] 1509 Reg. Privy Seal Scot. I. 285/1 The forest stedis of Cawdanle [etc.] liand within the forest of Ettrik and warde of Twede. a1884 J. RUSSELL Remin. Yarrow ix. (1894) 233 About the same time the Forest was divided into three 'wards,' that of Tweed, Yarrow, and Ettrick. Each ward had a ranger, who collected the rents [etc.].

b. Sc. 'A small piece of pasture ground, inclosed on all sides, generally appropriated to young quadrupeds' (Jam.).

1473 Rental Bk. Cupar-Angus (1879) I. 173 The sade tenandis sal kepe thar self..out of hanyngis, treys, stankis, parkis, medows and wardis. 1657 Melrose Regality Rec. (S.H.S.) I. 146 Cutting and destroying of thair riges of brome that is growand in the wairds and aikers of Melrois. a1670 SPALDING Troub. Chas. I (Bannatyne Club) I. 139 The countrie lords..sent out their horses and destroyed both grass and corn, fed where they pleased in the bishop's waird. a1673 Mare of Collingtoun in Watson's Coll. I. (1706) 49 Within the Ward I might have clos'd thee, Where well thou mightest have repos'd thee, Amang the Laird's best Fillies. 1785 Calf-ward [see CALF[1] 7 b]. 1799 Rec. Elgin (New Spalding Club) I. 210 A piece of ground full of sandbanks and covered with whins..as a common for the several proprietors taking sand to make up their wairds and cattails.

†22. ? A store-cupboard or wardrobe. Obs.

a1529 SKELTON Agst. Garnesche iii. 53 Your drapry ȝe ded wante, The warde with yow was skante. c1550 Disc. Common Weal Eng. (1893) 75 Nature semeth to haue layd them [sc. gold and silver] vpp in a farder warde then her other guyftes.

VI. An appliance for guarding.

†23. The part of the hilt of a sword that protects the hand: = GUARD sb. 16 b. Obs.

1634 SIR T. HERBERT Trav. 147 The hilts [of Persian swords] are without ward.

24. a. Each of the ridges projecting from the inside plate of a lock, serving to prevent the passage of any key the bit of which is not provided with incisions of corresponding form and size. b. Each of the incisions in the bit of a key, corresponding to the 'wards' of the lock. Cf. step-ward, STEP sb.[1] 18.

In untechnical (literary and popular) use these applications are sometimes reversed, the word being taken to denote the cavities of the lock or the solid parts of the key.

a. c1440 Promp. Parv. 516/1 Warde, of a lokke, tricatura. 1530 PALSGR. 286/2 Warde of a locke, garde. 1536 MS. Rawl. D. 780 lf. 59 Mending of a lock and makyng new wardes for the gentlemen hushers chambre. 1593 SHAKS. Lucr. 303 The lockes betweene her chamber and his will, Ech one by him inforst retires his ward. 1615 R. COCKS Diary (Hakl. Soc.) I. 10 He thought to have pickt the lock of my money chist the other day, and had so wrong the wardes that I could not open the lock with my key. 1644 SIR E. DERING Prop. Sacr., c iiij b, As if it were a false ward against the key. 1667 MILTON P.L. II. 877 Thus saying, from her side the fatal Key..she took;..then in the key-hole turns Th' intricate wards. 1677 MOXON Mech. Exerc. ii. 21 There are several Inventions in Locks..in the making and contriving their Wards, or Guards. 1725 POPE Odyss. XXI. 49 The wards respondent to the key turn round. 1818 SCOTT Hrt. Midl. vi, Withdrawing from the wards a ponderous key of about two feet in length. 1893 PATMORE Relig. Poetæ 47 The key is not the less a key because it will not open a lock the wards of which are filled with stones. 1911 J. WARD Roman Era Brit. xiii. 237 To render this difficult or impossible, obstructions or wards were introduced into the case [of the lock], which could not be passed by the bitt unless it had corresponding slits or openings.

fig. 1647 TRAPP Comm. Rom. xiv. 1 (1656) 650 Wring not mens consciences: you may hap to break the wards, if you do. 1840 LANDOR Fra Rupert II. vi, My hand at last [may] Turn in their golden wards the keys of heaven. 1851 MRS. BROWNING Casa Guidi Wind. II. 319 The key, O Tuscans, too well fits the wards! Ye asked for mimes,—these bring you tragedies. 1920 MASEFIELD Enslaved, etc. 118 The wards of life slipt back and set him free From cares of meat and dress.

b. 1390 GOWER Conf. II. 189 The wardes of the cherche keie Thurgh mishadlinge ben myswreynt. 1655 MARQ. WORCESTER Cent. Inv. §44 A Key of a Chamber-door, which ..hath its Wards and Rose-pipe but Paper-thick. 1677 MOXON Mech. Exerc. ii. 26 File the wards or slits in the Bit with thin files. 1688 R. HOLME Armoury III. 301/2 The Wards are all the nicks in the Bite [of the Key]. c1705 POPE Jan. & May 510 She took the wards in wax before the fire, And gave th' impression to the trusty squire. 1828 SCOTT F.M. Perth xxiv, The incidents of a narrative of this kind must be adapted to each other, as the wards of a key must tally accurately with those of the lock to which it belongs. 1853 DICKENS Bleak Ho. xlii, 'Oh! I knew that, did I?' says Mr. Tulkinghorn, examining the wards of the key. 1864 BOUTELL Her. Hist. & Pop. xxi. (ed. 3) 359 Two keys, in saltire, wards towards the base, or.

c. transf. Applied to mechanical contrivances resembling the wards of a lock or key.

1599 T. M[OUFET] Silkwormes 35 [To an 'artificial flea':] Thy cogs, thy wardes, thy laths, how didst thou lay. 1852 SEIDEL Organ 40 Whilst the upper part is sinking the wards open and let the wind pass from the bellows into the principal trunk.

VII. 25. attrib. and Comb.: a. Simple attrib. (sense 19 a), ward-alderman, boss (U.S.), committee, committeeman, meeting, politics, politician, pump, school, statesman, system; (sense 18), ward clerk, -keeper, matron, nurse, sister, table, work; (sense 19 b), ward teacher; (sense 24) ward-hole, -plate.

1899 Athenæum 21 Oct. 548/3 London, however, was destined to be ruled..by a council of mayor and *ward-aldermen. 1890 T. ROOSEVELT Wks. (1926) XIV. 110 Many forces..combine to produce the *ward boss, the district heeler, the boodle alderman. 1908 Sat. Rev. 8 Feb. 163/2 The blackmailing ward-boss. 1964 G. L. COHEN What's Wrong with Hospitals? iii. 52 *Ward clerks will relieve Sisters of paper work. 1807 Salmagundi 2 June 212 The secretaries of the *ward committees strut about looking like wooden oracles. 1922 C. E. MERRIAM Amer. Party System 71 Each of the forty-eight Ward Committees [in Philadelphia]..chooses two members of the City Committee. Ibid. 70 Each of the thirty-five wards [in Chicago] elects by direct vote of the party in a primary a *ward committeeman for a term of four years. 1976 Honolulu Star-Bull. 21 Dec. A-11/3 He knew the workings of the ward committeemen, who directed the precinct captains and stood ready to see that the garbage of the faithful voters was picked up and the potholes in their streets were filled. 1911 J. WARD Roman Era Brit. 237 Many of these keys have 'island' *ward-holes. 1836 J. M. GULLY Magendie's Formul. (ed. 2) 127 Each *ward-keeper of hospitals should be provided with a bottle of chlorine water. 1886 Daily News 26 Mar. 5/2 Family prayers are conducted by the *ward-matron, sister, or nurse. 1813 JEFFERSON Writ. (1830) IV. 229 A general call of *ward-meetings by their wardens on the same day through the State. 1899 Allbutt's Syst. Med. VIII. 414 The others [i.e. patients] were easily controlled by the *ward nurses. 1883 PITT-RIVERS Primitive Locks & Keys 24 A modern English latch-key..furnished with a *ward-plate. [1807 Salmagundi 24 Feb. 68 He however maintained as mysterious a countenance as a seventh ward politician.] 1860 Harper's Mag. June 94/2 'A house-breaker or a *ward politician,' thought I. 1976 National Observer (U.S.) 1 May B5/1 In the emerging big cities, ward politicians held control of school systems for a time in the late Nineteenth Century. 1883 Century Mag. Aug. 581/2 He had been a little alarmed at the sudden irruption of such men as Farnham and his associates into the field of *ward politics. 1957 Ward politics [see poker-game s.v. POKER sb.[4] b]. 1844 DISRAELI Coningsby V. iv, Two of the Rigbyites met in the market-place... 'Well, how goes it?' said one. 'I have been the rounds. The blunts going like the *ward-pump.' 1818 Niles' Reg. XIV. 174/1 Neither the people, nor their representatives, would agree to the plan of assessment on the wards for the expenses of the *ward schools. **1904** G. Stratton-Porter *Freckles* 15 They sent me out to the nearest ward school as long as the law would let them. **1918** H. Matthews in Murdoch & Drake-Brockman *Austral. Short Stories* (1951) 244 'She be a pretty one—the *ward sister,' a Tommy patient said to him one evening. **1980** J. O'Faolain *No Country for Young Men* iv. 94 'Good night now, Aunt Judith.' Grainne summoned a ward sister's authoritative manner. **1885** *Atlantic Monthly* Apr. 467/1 These roadways..the *ward statesman regards with tender solicitude as furnishing a large..field of operations in the line of contracts. **1857** J. T. Smith *Parish* ii. (ed. 2) 61 It is the adoption of Townships, or the adaptation of the *Ward system, that is really needed in such cases. **1878** J. H. Beadle *Western Wilds* xxi. 332 The *ward teachers had reported every case of real or supposed heresy. **1888** Hon. Morten *Hospital Life* 2 *Ward work commences at seven with sweeping, dusting, making beds.

b. Special comb.: **ward aide**, a person employed to do non-medical work in a hospital ward; **ward-book**, a register of admissions to a hospital; **ward-dyke**, a wall enclosing or bounding a ward (sense 21 b); also, a defensive dyke against water; **ward-fire** *Orkney and Shetland*, a beacon-fire [ON. *varða* cairn: cf. ward-hill]; †**ward-guard** *Sc.*, a protective covering or receptacle for clothes; **ward-heeler** *U.S.* (see quot. 1890; cf. heeler[1] 5); **ward-heeling** *a. U.S.*, pertaining to, engaged in, or designating, the activities of a ward-heeler; **ward-land** *Sc.*, land held 'in ward' (see ward-holding); **ward-like** *adv.*, after the manner of a ward; **ward(s)maid**, a maidservant who performs the menial offices of a hospital ward; †**ward marriage** (see marriage 5), in Scots feudal law, the right in wardholding arising to the ward superior on the marriage of the vassal's heir or on his becoming marriageable; **wardmaster**, (*a*) *Dutch Hist.* (rendering Du. *wijkmeester*), an alderman or administrator of a city ward; (*b*) the master or superintendent of a hospital ward; **ward orderly**, a person employed to assist nurses in a hospital ward; **ward round**, a visit paid by a doctor, or by a group of doctors and medical students, to each of the in-patients in a ward or wards, or under the care of a particular doctor; cf. round *sb.*[1] 15; †**ward-silver**, a payment to the lord in commutation of military service; †**ward-staff** (see quot. 1610); **ward-vassal**, in Scots feudal law, a vassal holding land 'in ward' (see ward-holding); †**ward-ware**, ? 'wardrobe stuff', articles of clothing; **ward-woman** *arch.*, a tirewoman, a woman in charge of her mistress's wardrobe; †**ward-word**, a 'word' of defence; a reply to an attack or 'watch-word' of an opponent. Also ward-corn, ward-fee, ward-hill, etc.

1965 *Nursing Times* 5 Feb. 172/2 Ten hospitals in the Manchester region have been authorized by the RHB to employ *ward aides. **1976** *Billings* (Montana) *Gaz.* 20 June 2-c/1 She is employed as a ward aide at Billings Deaconess Hospital. **1557** *Order of Hospitalls* G ij b, That no Child be receved by them, before the name of the same childe be entred into the *Ward-booke. **1836** J. Paget *Let.* 10 Jan. in *Mem. & Lett. Sir James Paget* (1901) i. iv. 66 The active new apothecary..cures the patients. The ward-books hardly know themselves, the *Mistura Cascarillæ* bottle stopper sticks from disuse, and *Emplastrum Lyttæ* is never mentioned. **1977** *Lancet* 7 May 975/2 The allocation of the patients was done automatically by the ward nurse (by reference to the ward book). **1561** in *Reg. Mag. Sig. Scot.* 1585, 256/2 Fra the said croft north..to the brig of Balgonie, ewin to the *ward-dyk of the Brig-feildis now pertening to Alex. Paip. **1602** *Ibid.* 474/1 Ane merchestane infixit in the waird-dyke standand beneth the place of Kirktounhill. **1854** *Jrnl. R. Agric. Soc.* XV. i. 19 Crests, cradges, and ward-dykes constructed to hold off fen-waters from inned grounds. **1859** D. Balfour *Oppress. Orkney & Zetl.* Introd. 31 Nothing short of actual invasion entitled the Jarl to call them to arms by the *Ward-fire. **1551** *Acc. Ld. High Treas. Scot.* X. 29 Item, for ane *wardegard to hir, iij li. x s. **1552** *Ibid.* 70 Item, vj elnis bukcrame to be wardegardis to hir and to hir kepar Effame..xxiiij s. **1890** *Q. Rev.* July 265 The lowest grade [of politician] is the '*ward-heeler', or hanger-on of the political head of the city ward in which he resides. **1907** *Times* 23 Jan. 6/2 [San Francisco] Bar-room politicians, roughs, ward-heelers, bullies. **1972** R. Thomas *Porkchoppers* (1974) xxiv. 208 Practical politics, the *ward-heeling kind. **1976** *Billings* (Montana) *Gaz.* 1 July, But neither ward-heeling councilmen nor grandstanding mayors can provide the kind of leadership that gets things done. **1980** N. Freeling *Castang's City* xv. 100 Why the hell would there be any integrity in these ward-heeling affairs? **1502** *Reg. Privy Seal Scot.* I. 115/1 The proffitt of the said *warde landis quhil the are recover sesing thairof. **1581** *Sc. Acts Jas. VI* (1814) III. 230/1 Anent the taxatioun of wardlandis. *a* **1659** Bp. Brownrig *Serm.* (1674) I. i. 11 He that purchases but one foot of Ward-land, makes all his Estate lyable to the King. **1684** Sir G. Mackenzie *Inst. Laws Scot.* ii. v. (1694) 76 If the Vassal sells or dispones the half of his Ward-Lands to any except his appearand Heir. **1689** E. Howard *Caroloiades* 197 O're which [army], tho Fairfax, Generall we finde, His Power to Cromwell *ward-like was design'd. **1888** Hon. Morten *Hospital Life* 68 The *ward-maid was out. **1901** *Daily Chron.* 1 May 1/7 Hartley Wintney Union. Wanted a wardsmaid. **1909** *Englishwoman* Apr. 240 In the smaller infirmaries, there are often wardmaids, with no training, who are expected to do nurses' work. **1473** *Rolls of Parlt.* VI. 72/2 With the Londes and Tenementes and other Profittes, and Mariage, or *Ward mariage of the same heire or heires. **1747** *Act 20 Geo. II*, c. 50 §1 That the Tenure of Lands..in Scotland by Ward Holding..and the Casualties consequent upon the same by Ward Marriage and Recognition, be taken away. **1855** Motley *Dutch Rep.* ii. vii. I. 560 John Van Immerzeel, Margrave of Antwerp, was then holding communication with the senate, and awaiting the arrival of the *ward-masters. **1883** *Fortn. Rev.* July 126 The ward-masters, nurses, and attendants in the hospitals. **1946** *Nature* 13 July 54/1 The Government and the hospital authorities have agreed upon..the training of more male nurses and the formation of a grade of '*ward orderlies' to assist the nurses. **1971** P. D. James *Shroud for Nightingale* viii. 275 She went ..as ward orderly. **1938** *Amer. Speech* XIII. 228/2 Doctors regularly visit the patients under their care and for some reason their visits are called **ward rounds* or *ward walks*. **1963** *Oxford Med. School Gaz.* XV. 81 At some stage during the ward-round he would lead his flock down to the P.M. room. **1977** *Lancet* 5 Feb. 317/1 His ward-rounds were very popular and were attended by a large number of undergraduates and postgraduates. **1314–15** *Rolls of Parlt.* I. 318/1 De diversis redditibus annuatim Regi debitis, qui vocantur Hydag' et *Wardselfur'. ? **1418** in *Essex Rev.* (1904) XIII. 133 [Paying yearly 18s. as] 'ward-silver' [in lieu of all services]. **1610** Holland *Camden's Brit.* i. 440 Lambourn Manour, which is held by service of the Wardstaffe, vz. to carrie a load of strawe in a Carte with sixe horses, two ropes, two men in harnesse to watch the said *Ward-staffe when it is brought to the towne of Aibridg, &c. **1681** Stair *Instit.* i. 422 Recognition was found not excluded or burdened by Inhibition against the *Ward-vassal. *a* **1768** [see ward-fee]. **1598** Marston *Sco. Villanie* i. ii. C 2, Tail'd and retail'd, till to the pedlers packe, The fourth-hand *ward-ware comes, alack, alack. **1831** Scott *Ct. Robt.* i. iv, How long she had passed that critical period, was a secret to all but the trusted *ward-women of the purple chamber. **1599** N. D. [R. Parsons] (*title*), A Temperate *Ward-Word, to the Turbulent and Seditious Wach-word of Sir Francis Hastinges knight. **1603** Harsnet *Popish Impost.* 53 The priests had their ward-word ready. **1716** M. Davies *Athen. Brit.* III. 51 And disperse once more from another Babel of one another's Catchpoling Watch-words without any precautionary Ward-words.

†**ward**, *sb.*[3] Also 7 *Sc.* **waird.** Aphetic form of award.

c **1400** *Beryn* 3568 They made Syrophanes,..plegg[e] fynd..To byde þe ward & Iugement of þat he had mys-do. **1464** in *10th Rep. Hist. MSS. Comm.* App. v. 332 All thes wardes and ordenances forsaide. **1477** *Stoner Papers* (Camden) II. 27, I have done my dewte in every ponte accordyng to your warde. **1531** *Abstr. Protocols Town Clerks Glasgow* (1897) iv. 30 As air fwnd be ane ward of þe court. **1534** *Ibid.* 68 Efter ane ward and dome of court gevin in the tolbwtht of Glasgw. **1609** Skene *Reg. Maj., Quon. Attach.* xxxvi. §3 Ilk soytour..sould be examinat in thrie courts, gif he can make recorde of the court (of ane proces deduced in court) or report ane sufficient warde (interloquutour) or dome, anent wardes, or exceptions asked in the court. *Ibid.* ii. Table 101 They [the suitors] sould trye, advise, and pronunce the wardes (interloquutors) of court.

ward, *sb.*[4] *dial.* [? var. of wart *sb.* or of warre (OE. *wearr* callosity). Cf. warded *a.*[2]] (See quot.)

a **1825** Forby *Voc. E. Anglia*, *Ward*, callosity of the skin; on the hands, from hard labour, and on the feet from much walking.

ward (wɔːd), *v.*[1] Forms: 1 **weardian, -iȝan,** 2 **wærdien,** 3 **wardie,** 3–4 **wardi, wardy(e,** 6 *Sc.* **vard(e, vayrd,** 6–7 *Sc.* **waird,** 3–7 **warde,** 4– **ward.** Also 7 pa. t. **ward** (*rare*). [OE. *weardian* = OFris. *wardia*, OS. *wardon* (MDu. *waerden*, MLG. *warden*), OHG. *wartên* (MHG., mod.G. *warten*), ON. *varða*:—OTeut. **warðōjan, -ǣjan*, f.**warðō*: see ward *sb.*[2] The Eng. verb may in some of its uses have been influenced by OF. *warder* (north-eastern) = Central OF. *guarder* (mod.F. *garder*), Pr. *gardar*, Sp., Pg. *guardar*, It. *guardare*, a Com. Rom. adoption of the Teut. word.]

1. *trans.* To guard, stand guard over; to keep in safety, take care of; to defend, protect. (For *to watch and ward*, see watch *v.*) *Obsolescent* or *arch.*

In OE. sometimes *const.* genitive.

? *a* **1035** *Cnut's Secular Laws* lxxvi. (Liebermann) Ac þære cæȝean heo sceal weardian. *a* **1122** *O.E. Chron.* (Laud) an. 1087, Þa Englisce men þe wærdedon þære sæ. **13..** *K. Alis.* 7324 (Laud MS.), [They] ben so warded al aboute þat hem ne stondeþ none doute. **13..** *Leg. Gregory* (Schulz) 980 To help and ward Cristendom. **1382** Wyclif *Matt.* xxvii. 66 Thei goynge forth kepten, [*gloss*] or wardiden, the sepulcre. **1475** *Bk. Noblesse* (Roxb.) 27 For golde,..conquerithe not ennemies, nother in time of pease wardithe the peple to be in rest. **1592** Kyd *Sp. Trag.* ii. iv. 40 *Hor.* But first my lookes shall combat against thine. *Bel.* Then ward thy selfe: I dart this kisse at thee. **1594** Shaks. *Rich. III* v. iii. 254 Then if you fight against Gods Enemy, God will in iustice ward you as his Soldiers. *c* **1613** Middleton *No wit like Woman's* v. i. 145, I found the door Warded suspiciously. **1631** Weever *Anc. Funeral Mon.* 704 On the farther side..the Britaines warded the bankes. **1893** Stevenson *Catriona* viii. 87 Hope Park, a beautiful pleasance,..warded by a keeper. **1913** *Blackw. Mag.* Dec. 787/1 Your wits must ward your head.

b. To defend, protect *from*. Now *arch.*

a **1225** *Ancr. R.* 174 Bisecheð ȝeorne God..þet he wite & wardie ou urom alle þeo þet ou awaiteð. **1297** R. Glouc. (Rolls) 970 Hii wolde..Wardi hom fram alle men, þat hom ne tidde no drede. **13..** *Sir Beues* 2946 Min em, þe bischop Florentin,..Schel þe warde fro damage. **1475** *Bk. Noblesse* (Roxb.) 77 Youre roiaume forto warde, kepe, And defende frome youre adversaries. **1565** Stapleton tr. *Bede's Hist.* iii. xix. 95 The other two [angels] warding him on eche side from the danger of the fire also. **1588** Shaks. *Tit. A.* iii. i. 195 Tell him, it was a hand that warded him From thousand dangers. **1604** T. Wright *Passions* vi. 318 Abraham..was constrayned to warde his offring from the molestfull crowes. *a* **1677** Barrow *Serm.* vii. Wks. 1687 I. 90 No better can any man ward himself from blame, by imputing the neglect of devotion to some indisposition within him thereto. **1850** Blackie *Æschylus* I. 185 Loxias himself will ward His holiest shrine from lawless outrage.

c. *fig.* To guard, keep carefully (a secret). *rare.*

1881 Duffield *Don Quixote* II. 442 'My profession,' answered the priest, '..obliges me to ward a secret.'

†**d.** *intr.* (*absol.*) To keep guard. Often with *watch*. (For *to watch and ward*, see watch *v.*) *Obs.*

1390 Gower *Conf.* II. 304 And in this hous to loke and warde Was Minotaurus put in warde. *c* **1450** Holland *Houlate* 619 Baith to walk and to ward, as watchis in weir. **1569** J. Hawkins in *Hakluyt's Voy.* (1589) 555 Our men which warded a shore being stricken with soden feare, gaue place, fled, [etc.]. **1579–80** North *Plutarch, Romulus* (1595) 24 The Kings souldiers which warded at the gates of the city. **1610** Holland *Camden's Brit.* i. 107 A garrison.. which warding there day and night became lazie with doing nothing. **1722** De Foe *Plague* (1884) 74 The Family..left the..Fellows warding, and watching.

†**2.** *trans.* To rule, govern (a land, people); to administer (an estate); to act as guardian to (a child). *Obs.*

a **1000** *Cædmon's Dan.* 665 Nabochodonossor..weardode wide rice. **1297** R. Glouc. (Rolls) 643 þulke time þat samuel þe prophete wardede þat folc of israhel. *Ibid.* 6453 To þe king of hongri þis seli children tueie He sende uor to norisi, þat he wardede hom wel beye. **13..** *Guy Warw.* (1891) 510 Þemperour haþ made him his steward, To wardi his lond about. *c* **1350** *Will. Palerne* 101 Þanne was þe best bliþe i-nov for þe barnes sake, For he wist it schold be warded wel Þanne at þe best. **1390** Gower *Conf.* I. 345 He..tok this child into his warde, And seide he wolde him kepe and warde.

†**3.** To man *with* a garrison; to protect or shield *with* some work or contrivance; to fortify (a castle). *Obs.*

1340–70 *Alisaunder* 265 Grim thei were, To warden þeir walles with weies ynow. **1398** Trevisa *Barth. De P.R.* v. viii. (1495) 114 The lyddes ben warded and kept wyth rowes of heer. *c* **1400** *Parce michi* 194 in *26 Pol. Poems* 148 Castelles and toures, Withoute y-warded with stronge dyches. **1544** Betham *Precepts War* ii. liv. L iij b, Cytis warded with all kyndes of defences. **1633** T. Stafford *Pac. Hib.* iii. ix. 321 The Castle of Leam-con neere Crooke haven which the rebels warded, was recovered from them.

†**b.** said of the defending work. *Obs.*

a **1000** *Ags. Ps.* (Th.) ciii. 3 Heofon..þone weardiað ufan wætra ðryðe. **1398** Trevisa *Barth. De P.R.* v. xxvi. (Bodl. MS.), þe yȝen defendeþ and wardeþ alle þe forþer parties of þe body. **1555** Eden *Decades* (Arb.) 177 Towarde the west on the Northe syde, great Cuba..wardeth owre Tethys [*i.e.* Hayti] on the backe halfe. **1579** Spenser *Sheph. Cal.* July 42 S. Michels Mount who does not know, That wardes the Westerne coste? **1596** —— *F.Q.* iv. x. 7 And for defence thereof, on th' other end There reared was a castle faire and strong, That warded all which in or out did wend.

†**4.** To keep in close custody or confinement; to put in ward, imprison. Chiefly *Sc. Obs.*

1390 Gower *Conf.* II. 354 A Maiden, which was warded streyte Withinne chambre and kept so clos, That [etc.]. ? *a* **1400** *Morte Arth.* 1614 That they be weisely wachede and in warde holdene, Wardede of warantizez with wyrchipfulle knyghttez. *c* **1480** Henryson *Paddock & Mouse* 166 (Bannatyne MS.) Now in fredome, now wardit in distress. **1508** *Reg. Privy Seal Scot.* I. 247/1 Dome [was] gevin apoun thair personis to be wardit thairfor. **1581** N. Burne in *Cath. Tractates* (S.T.S.) 116, I..vas vayrdit in the Tolbuith of Edinburgh. **1597** in *Maitl. Club Misc.* I. 129 The kirk desyris the bailleis to waird him quhill the nixt Sonday, his fude to be bread and wattir allanerlie. *a* **1670** Spalding *Troub. Chas. I* (Bannatyne Club) I. 220 He was shortly wairded for these words.

†**b.** *fig.* To keep in close check or control. *Obs.*

1390 Gower *Conf.* I. 53 Thin yhe forto kepe and warde, So that it passe noght his warde. *Ibid.* I. 60 If thou..wisly cowthest warde and kepe Thin yhe and Ere. **1555** Hooper in Coverdale *Lett. Martyrs* (1564) 158 True confession is warded on euery side, with many daungers.

5. With *in*, *off*, *up*: To enclose, hem in, seclude, shut off (esp. for safety or protection). *rare.*

a **1586** *Satir. Poems Reform.* xxxvii. 37 Wakde ȝe ward ȝow vpe betwne tua ways, ȝit so ȝe sall not frome þair sayingis save ȝou. *c* **1590** Greene *Fr. Bacon* ii. i. 446 (Collins) The Pyren mounts..That ward the welthie Castile in with walles. **1842** Dickens *Amer. Notes* xi, The machinery not warded off or guarded in any way, but doing its work in the midst of the crowd of idlers..who throng the lower deck.

6. To parry, repel, fend off, turn aside (a stroke or thrust, blow, attack, weapon, missile). Now almost always with *off*.

1571 Golding *Calvin on Ps.* lv. 13. 214 Too put backe a stroke by striking it upward, according as wee say in English I had warded his blowe. **1590** Spenser *F.Q.* i. ix. 10 Their God himselfe..Shot many a dart at me with fiers intent, But I them warded all with wary gouernment. *c* **1643** Ld. Herbert *Autobiog.* (1824) 126 All I could well do to those two which remained, was to ward their thrusts. **1652** Urquhart *Jewel* 137 He for twenty several bouts, did but ward their blows, and pary with the fort of his sword. **1697** Dryden *Æneis* v. 584 Entellus..with his warping Body wards the Wound. **1732** Lediard *Sethos* II. ix. 277 He employ'd one part..to ward off the flights of arrows. **1830** Praed *Poems* (1864) I. 352 And now he wards a Roundhead's pike, and now he hums a stave. **1844** Mrs. Browning *Romaunt of Page* ii, Once in the tent, and twice in the fight, [thou] Didst ward me a mortal blow. **1845** Darwin *Voy. Nat.* ii. (1879) 25 Seeing a great powerful man afraid even to ward off a blow, directed, as he thought, at his face. **1851** Mayne Reid *Scalp Hunters* lv, Before El Sol could ward it off, the thrust was given, and the weapon appeared to pass through his body.

fig. **1638** FEATLEY *Sir H. Lynde's Case for Spect.* Ep. Ded. A 6, Your Lordship in your last..unanswerable masterpiece, held up your buckler over the Knight then living,..and ward off the Iesuits blowes. *a* **1734** NORTH *Life Ld. Kpr. Guilford* (1742) 224 He met sometimes with a Reprimand, which he would wittily ward off.

b. *absol.* or *intr.* To parry blows; to stand on the defensive in a combat. *arch.*

1393 LANGL. *P. Pl.* C. XXII. 218 And wepne to fight [*v.r.* warde] with þat wol neuere faille. **1567** MAPLET *Gr. Forest* III. 101 [The unicorn] in his fight wardeth and foyneth at the Elephant his bellye. *a* **1586** SIDNEY *Arcadia* I. xi. §13 As soone as he spied Palladius, he drew his sword, and..let flie at him. But Palladius..sought rather to retire, and warde. **1591** HARINGTON *Orl. Fur.* Pref. ¶ ij b, As good fensers vse to ward and strike at once. **1592** LYLY *Midas* IV. ii, A Nation ..so valiant, that are redier to strike than ward. **1653** HOLCROFT *Procopius, Vandal Wars* II. 38 Solomon.. commanded the rest..to stand still, warding with their shields, against the enemies Javelins. **1697** DRYDEN *Æneis* V. 575 Yet equal in Success, they ward, they strike. **1820** PRAED *Poems* (1864) II. 15 Life is won by ready sword, By strength to strike and skill to ward.

7. *trans.* To avert, keep off (harm, danger, etc.).

a. *simply.*

a **1586** SIDNEY *Arcadia* I. Eclogue (1598) 85 While they did ward sun-beames with shadie bay. **1673** *Lady's Call.* I. iii. §18 It concerns them therefore to ward those beginnings whose end may be so fatal. **1710** PHILIPS *Pastorals* ii. 125 Fold Thy Flock with mine, to ward th'injurious Cold. *c* **1750** SHENSTONE *Elegy* iii. 13 He little knew to ward the secret wound. **1810** SCOTT *Lady of Lake* V. xx, I, only I, can ward their fate. **1850** BLACKIE *Æschylus* II. 240 Theirs it is to ward fulfilment of all evil-omened sights. **1882** LD. ACTON *Lett. to Mary Gladstone* 21 Mar. (1904) 132 Images would probably impress him as a danger to be warded, rather, I think, than Transubstantiation.

b. with *off.* Also (rarely) *aside.*

1759 GOLDSM. *Bee* No. 3 If, then, you would ward off the gripe of poverty, pretend to be a stranger to her. **1774** —— *Nat. Hist.* (1776) V. 322 Covering their heads at the same time to ward off any danger of the falling of pebbles or stones from above. **1798** JEFFERSON *Writ.* (1859) IV. 241 If we can ward off actual war till the crisis in England is over. **1803** *Edwin* II. xiv. 214 To ward aside the threatened tempest. **1854** SURTEES *Handley Cr.* lviii. (1901) II. 129 Rising hills ward off the wintry winds. **1865** DICKENS *Mut. Fr.* I. vi, To keep out weather, to ward off cold,..or what not. **1881** W. H. DAY *Dis. Childr.* 593 Which may obviate the tendency to congestion, and so ward off the paroxysms.

†**8.** *intr.* To take up a position of defence, take precautions *against.* Also, to be careful *that* (something be done). *Obs.*

a **1225** *Ancr. R.* 182 Sicnesse þet God sent..wascheð þeo sunnen þet weren er iwrouhte: wardeð to ȝein þeo þet weren touwardes. *c* **1475** *Partenay* 805 Warde that ye be a monday in thys place. **1709** PRIOR *Paulo Purganti* 100 Our Don, who knew this Tittle Tattle Did, sure as Trumpet, call to Battel; Thought it extreamly *à propos*, To ward against the coming Blow. **17..** ? SWIFT *S.'s Wks.* (1841) II. 850/2 In England, this pusillanimity is more to be warded against than in most other countries. **1726** LEONI *Alberti's Archit.* I. 99 Regard must be had..in cold Countries to ward against the bleak Northwind. **1755** *Mem. Capt. P. Drake* Ded., But where is the Necessity of warding against the Imputation of Flattery, when I dedicate to Your Lordship?

9. *trans.* To place (a patient) in a particular ward in a hospital; to lodge (a vagrant) in a 'casual ward'. (A new formation on the sb.)

1879 *St. George's Hosp. Rep.* IX. 62 Warded at 2 P.M. next day with the same symptoms. **1889** SIR D. DUCKWORTH in *Lancet* 5 Jan., She appeared there [*sc.* at the Hospital] and being very ill..was warded. **1909** *Westm. Gaz.* 23 Feb. 12/1 The question as it seemed to these Town Councillors was how to get the vagrants warded, not how to keep them out of the Casual Ward.

10. Of a dog: To line or cover (a bitch).

1781 P. BECKFORD *Th. Hunting* v. 59 When you breed from a very favourite sort, and can have another bitch warded at the same time, it will be of great service, as you may then save all the puppies. **1826** J. COOK *Fox-hunting* 11 It is therefore not very probable that one Stallion-hound can ward many bitches besides those of the owner.

†**ward,** *v.*² *Obs.* Aphetic f. AWARD *v.* Hence '**warding** *vbl. sb.* or *ppl. a.*

1442 *Rolls of Parlt.* V. 43/2 If..Processe theropon be wardet. **1475** *Ibid.* VI. 141/1 That the Juges of the said Bench.., have auctorite..to ward that the said James have ayein his said Goodes,..and theruppon to ward Writtes of execution in that behalve. **1487** *Cely Papers* (Camden) 160 A sarpler..poyntyd be the lefftenaunte to be casten owte to wardd the sortt bye as the ordenaunce ys now made that the lefftenaunte schall poynt the warddyng sarplers of every mans wull. **1555** in Strype *Eccl. Mem.* App. No. 47 (1721) III. 145 Which shalbe proved, yf a commission might be warded to that purpose.

ward, Sc. contr. f. *were it.*

c **1580** MONTGOMERIE *Misc. P.* xl. 8 Weill ward thou weep, O ouer audacious ee!

ward, obs. pa. t. of WARE *v.*², WORTH *v.*

-ward, *suffix*, OE. *-weard*, primarily forming adjs., with the sense 'having a specified direction', corresponds to OFris. *-ward*, OS. *-ward, -werd*, OHG., MHG. *-wart* (as in *heimwart* adj., homeward):—OTeut. **-warđo-*, f. **warđ-* abl.-var. of **werþ-*:—pre-Teut. **wert-* to turn (= L. *vertĕre*); in the suffix the primary sense of the root is preserved, though the strong verb **werþan* has only the derived sense 'to become' (see WORTH *v.*); cf. the L. *-versus* (a ppl. formation from the same root), which in sense coincides with OTeut. **-warđo-*. Two other suffixes precisely identical in function with **-warđo-*, but representing different grades of the root, are: OTeut. **-werþo-*, in Goth. *-wairþ-s*, ON. *-verð-r*, OHG. *-wert* (MHG. and mod.G. only in the adverbial *-wärts*: cf. -WARDS), OFris. *-wirth*; and OTeut. **-urđo-* in ON. *-urð-r*, OHG. *-ort*; neither of these types is found in OE.

The pronunciation of the suffix when attached to a monosyllable is (wəd); for the occasional colloquial shortening see W (the letter). Following one or more unstressed syllables it is usually sounded (wɔːd).

Down to the 16th c. the suffix occasionally appears with irregular spellings, as *warde, -werd, -word, -whard*; the form *-wart* in Sc. and northern dialects represents a pronunciation still heard.

1. The suffix was originally appended only to local advs., and in OE. was still confined to this use. The adjs. in *-weard* usually denoted direction of movement, but many of them could also be used to designate aspect or relative position; in this function they often occur in partitive concord: e.g. *foreweard* must often be translated 'front or first part of'. (With regard to the adjs. originating in mod.E. from advs. in *-ward*, see 5 below.)

2. The OE. adjs. in *-weard*, like the corresponding words in the other Teut. langs., admitted of being used adverbially in the accus. (OE. *-weard*) or in the genitive (OE. *-weardes*) of the neut. sing. (For the history of the genitival advs. see -WARDS.) The advs. in *-weard* found in OE. are all (exc. *hámweard* homeward) advb. forms of adjs. actually recorded in the language, and the first element is always a local adv. (*hámweard* being not really an exception). On the analogy of the older advs. with this suffix, there were formed in ME. several compounds in which *-weard* was added to advs., esp. to compound advs. of phrasal origin, as in *abackward, adownward, awayward, aboutward, againward, aforeward*; the first three of these were soon displaced by the aphetic forms *backward, downward, wayward.*

3. In OE. the adv. *tóweard* was used also as a prep., with the sense 'in the direction leading to'. In early ME. †*fromward* acquired a similar prepositional use, and later there are isolated examples of this development of function in some other advs. in *-ward* (e.g. *inward, onward*) of which the first element is an adverb-preposition expressing movement.

4. The type of expression represented by the (now obsolete or archaic) forms 'to heavenward(s', 'to the city ward(s', 'to us-ward', and the (wholly obsolete) forms 'from..ward(s', is commonly spoken of as a 'tmesis' of the preps. *toward(s*, †*fromward(s*. This is convenient as a description of its function, but is not historically correct.

In reality, the practice of attaching the suffix (which thereby assumes more or less the character of a separate adv.) to a phrase consisting of a sb. or pronoun governed by a prep. must be older than the development of the advs. *toward(s* and *fromward(s* into preps. In OE., though no prep. **wiðweard* is known to have existed (cf. *wiðerweard* adj., adverse), there are many examples in which *wið..weard* is virtually a prep. governing the interposed word in the genitive (this being the case governed by *wið*). Although in OE. *tó* and *wið* are the only preps. that are recorded in this use, it is significant that in MHG. and in early mod.Ger., while no compound preps. with *-wart, -wärts* existed, these suffixes were added to phrases consisting of a sb. or pronoun governed by a prep. (chiefly *zu, nach, gegen*; also *von* corresponding to ME. *from* in *from..ward*). In this use, however, they wre commonly treated not as suffixes but as advs., and written as separate words. In English also *ward* in this construction (which is now archaic) is sometimes apprehended as a separate adv., and so written. But it is usually felt as forming a compound with the governed sb. When the sb. is qualified by the definite article, as in 'to the heavenward', there is a tendency to interpret the compound as a sb. or an adj. used absol., because of the apparent analogy of expressions like 'to the eastward'. Where the definite article was absent, the compound came to be regarded as an adv.; the prefixed *to* therefore became otiose, and therefore went out of use.

5. On the analogy of the advb. compounds originating from the omission of *to* (e.g. *heavenward* adv. from *to heaven ward*), the suffix has in the mod.Eng. period been added freely to sbs. (including proper names) to form advs. expressing direction, aspect, or tendency. From the 16th c. onwards there has been a growing disposition to use the advs. in *-ward* as adjs.; in the 19th c. or the last years of the 18th c. several new adjs. of this formation appear for the first time: e.g. *earthward, heavenward, Godward, manward, skyward*; these, however, have been confined to literary use.

6. Examples of *to..ward, till..ward* (north. dial.), *into..ward, unto..ward.*

a. with proper name, or sb. without determining word. For other instances see BEDWARD, CHURCHWARD, DEATHWARD, EARTHWARD, GODWARD, HEAVENWARD, HELLWARD, MANWARD.

c **1000** ÆLFRIC *Hom.* (Thorpe) I. 336 He..hine..bær to mynstreweard. *a* **1122** *O.E. Chron.* (Laud MS.) an. 1052 ʒewendon heom þa to Norðmuðan, & swa to Lundene weard. *a* **1300** *K. Horn* 1180 Ifond horn child stonde To schupeward in londe. **13..** *Coer de L.* 2452 King Richard Came sailing to Acres-ward. **1377** LANGL. *P. Pl.* B. XIV. 308 He tempreth þe tonge to treuthe ward. **1387** TREVISA *Higden* (Rolls) V. 175 Julianus wente into Perseward. **1448** SHILLINGFORD *Lett.* (Camden) 37 Y mette with my lorde atte high table ende comyng to meteward. **1482** *Cely Papers* (Camden) 91 And the xj day I wndyrstond ȝe pwrpose to Bregyswhard. *a* **1500** *Nutbrowne Maide* xix. in *Arnolde's Chron.* (1502) O j b, To wood ward wyl I flee. **1523** BERNERS *Froiss.* I. lxxxvi. 108 Dyuers lordes and knyghtes of France were goyng into Spayne warde. **1526** TINDALE *2 Cor.* i. 16 To have bene ledde forth to Jewry warde of you. **1549** COVERDALE etc. *Erasm. Par. Rom.* vii. 13–18 The one..is wholly gyuen to synne, the other..laboureth to honestie-warde. **1571** GOLDING *Calvin on Ps.* iv. 2. 10 As to David-ward, the solution is casye. **1601** W. PARRY *Trav. Sir A. Sherley* 30 The Emperor of Rusciaes country to Persia ward. **1647** TRAPP *Marrow Gd. Authors* in *Comm. Ep.* 619 The despensation of the grace of God is given us to others-ward. **1889** *N.W. Linc. Gloss.* (ed. 2) *Toward.* The word is often divided thus: He lives to Grimsby ward noo. She's goän to Lunnun ward.

b. with sb. determined by article or otherwise.

¶ In quot. 1523, *on* is used instead of *to* or *into* (after a verb of motion).

c **1000** ÆLFRIC *Saints' Lives* xxxi. 78 [He] het þæt he biheolde to his drihtne werd. *a* **1122** *O.E. Chron.* (Laud MS.) an. 1048, Ða..wendon him þa up to þære burȝe weard. *c* **1340** HAMPOLE *Pr. Consc.* 1407 Til our contre-warde. *c* **1375** *Sc. Leg. Saints* xxx. (*Theodera*) 462 Scho with camelis and cart held on to þe merkat wart. *c* **1386** CHAUCER *Miller's T.* 386 Unto the gardynward. *c* **1400** *Lanfranc's Cirurg.* 161 Þe herte..hangiþ sum-what to the liftsideward. **1412–20** LYDG. *Chron. Troy* I. 4045 Whan he cometh to-our-schippisward. **1480** CAXTON *Chron. Eng.* cxlix. 1 1 b, When the tydynge come to the pope,..tho was he to the kyngward ful wroth. **1523** BERNERS *Froiss.* I. cxxxiv. 66 Assone as the skirmyssh was begon, he toke his horse with the spurres & came on the skirmysshe warde. **1526** TINDALE *Mark* xiv. 8 She cam afore honde to anoynt my boddy to his buryinge warde. *a* **1547** SURREY *Æneis* II. 303 Thus slided through our town The subtil tree, to Pallas temple ward. **1609** DOWLAND *Ornith. Microl.* 40 A Quauer is a figure like a Crochet, having a dash to the right hand-ward. **1644** MANWAYRING *Sea-mans Dict.* 71 If her sterne lie towards the sea, we say her sterne lies to the off-ward, and her head to the shore-ward. **1653** H. COGAN tr. *Pinto's Trav.* v. 195 This Pilot desiring to avoid certain sands that were to the Prow-ward of him, put forth to sea. **1884** W. BLACK *Jud. Shakespeare* xxxi, Casting his eyes to the isleward.

c. with pronoun, *me, thee,* etc. Now only *arch.*

c **1250** *Owl & Night.* 375 ȝif hundes urneþ to him ward. *c* **1250** *Gen. & Ex.* 2726 To hemward swide he lep. **1338** R. BRUNNE *Chron.* (1810) 170 Bi tyme turne to me ward, for I wille speke with þe. *c* **1374** CHAUCER *Troylus* IV. 1666, I shal so doon..That ay honour to me-ward shal rebounde. **1387** TREVISA *Higden* (Rolls) VI. 413 Elfleda..regnede in al Mercia, outtake Londoun and Oxenforde, þe whiche þe kynge hylde to hymselfward. **1441** *Plumpton Corr.* (Camden) p. lvi, He, with officers of the said forest, rode to themward in all that they might pricke. **1448** *Paston Lett.* Suppl. (1901) 19 His master was at Causton to yow ward. *a* **1533** BERNERS *Huon* lxxxii. 254 He tournyd his face to her warde. **1540** PALSGR. *Acolastus* III. ii. O ij, She..seketh out the way to vs warde. **1571** GOLDING *Calvin on Ps.* lxiv. 12. 240 God wilbe the same to themward, that he shewed himself to be towards his servant David. **1576** FLEMING *Panopl. Epist.* 16 Of whiche your bountie to him warde I am a witnesse. **1593** R. HARVEY *Philad.* 71 Coil..brought the peoples goodwill into such a wheele, and so turned it to himselfeward, that [etc.]. **1611** BIBLE *2 Cor.* xiii. 3 Since ye seeke a proofe of Christ speaking in me, which to you-ward is not weake, but is mightie in you. **1632** J. HAYWARD tr. *Biondi's Eromena* 14 The subtile Lady Admirall (who was long before aware of the Prince's love to her-ward). **1674** N. FAIRFAX *Bulk & Selv.* 180 Then I think he will have set before us such a Hoghen moghen Leviathan, that that of Holy Job would be but a kind of Spratkin to it ward. **1738** WESLEY *Hymns, 'Dear Lord, my thankful Heart receives'* iii, Thine Eyes to me-ward ever turn. **1830** COLERIDGE *Let. to Mrs. Gillman* Lett. (1895) II. 754 An anxious friend and tender sister to me-ward! **1848** LOWELL *Biglow P.* iii. Let. 4 Nov. 1847, When rumor pointed to himward. **1901** HARDY *Poem, To an Unborn Pauper Child*, No hint of mine may hence To theeward fly.

†**7.** Examples of *from..ward, fro..ward. Obs.*

See also FROMWARD C 1 b.

c **1220** [see FROWARD C b.] *c* **1340** HAMPOLE *Pr. Consc.* 7281 Þe ded..Salle ay þan fle fra þam-ward. *c* **1386** CHAUCER *Prol.* 397 Ful many a draughte of wyn had he ydrawe Fro Burdeuxward whil that the chapman sleepe. *c* **1440** *Alphabet of Tales* 285 He mett his wife fro þe kurkward. **1495** *Act 11 Hen. VII* c. 9 §2 Leasses..for the which noe such suertie shalbe hadde..[shall] stand from thensforth ward voide and of noon effecte. **1607** T. ROGERS *39 Articles* xxxviii. (1625) 216 No man..can desire to appropriate..any thing to himselfe, eyther yet to make any priuate vse to himselfe from the rest ward. *a* **1608** DEE *Relat. Spir.* I. (1659) 56 His face is (now) from meward. **1621** LADY M. WROTH *Urania* 108 Amphilanthus..was then looking from herward, carelesse of her. **1683** MOXON *Mech. Exerc., Printing* xxiv. ¶ 7 With the nail of his Right Hand Thumb, sloaping from his Thumbward, he draws or slides forward the upper Sheet.

8. Examples of nonce-wds. (advs.) f. sb. or proper name (rarely pron.) + *-ward.*

1623 L. ANDREWES *Serm.* I. xvi. (1629) 154 In Man, there was onward [= oneward] an abridgement of all the rest. Gather God and him into one, and so you have all. **1728**

SWIFT *Let. to Pope* 26 July ¶ 3 You are the most temperate man Godward, and the most intemperate yourselfward of most I have known. **1752** H. WALPOLE *Let. to Mann* 27 July, Our beauties are travelling Paris-ward. **1793** COWPER *Let. to Lady Hesketh* 29 Aug., I will therefore.. refer the time of your journey Weston-ward entirely to your own election. *a* **1849** POE *Marginalia* Wks. 1864 III. 499 The whole tendency of the age is Magazine-ward. **1851** CARLYLE *Sterling* II. iii, In the afternoon we went on the Thames Putney-ward together. **1865** E. BURRITT *Walk to Land's End* 241 The waif breezes.. convey but a little way youward the breath of thyme they take up from these rough hills and valleys. **1893** *Tablet* 4 Nov. 742 Its eyes turned eastward and past-ward. **1899** 'G. F. MONKSHOOD' *Kipling* 69 Mr. Kipling thoughtfully points out to him that men do not float Simla-ward in paper ships upon a stream of ink.

wardable (ˈwɔːdəb(ə)l), *a. Hist.* [f. WARD *sb.*[2] + -ABLE.] Liable to pay castle-guard or castle-ward.

c **1620** in *Sussex Archæol. Collect.* VI. 226 The Parsonadge .. wth too akers of the Mannor land, called the Wren Wish, is Wardable as the Mannor is. **1888** *Archæol. Rev.* Mar. 58 In Pevensey Rape much of the land round the Castle was wardable, i.e., paid Castle-guard, or Castle-ward.

† **ˈwardage**[1]. *Obs.*[−0] [ad. AL. *wardāgium*, f. *warda*: see WARD *sb.*[2] and -AGE.] = WARDPENNY.

[**1294** in *Cal. Charter Rolls* (1906) II. 437 Lastage, stallage, hidage, wardage, [etc.].] **1672** *Cowel's Interpr.* (ed. Manley), *Wardage*.. seems to be the same with the wardpeny. **1706** PHILLIPS (ed. Kersey). **1721**– in BAILEY. **1864**– in WEBSTER. In recent Dicts.

wardage[2] (ˈwɔːdɪdʒ). *rare.* [f. WARD *sb.*[2] + -AGE.] The function of a sentinel or guardian.

1878 SUSAN PHILLIPS *On Seaboard* 170 The old square tower in the churchyard kept A solemn wardage.

wardain(e, obs. forms of WARDEN[1].

wardan: see WARDEN[2].

ˈwar-dance. A dance performed before a warlike excursion or in celebration of a victory. Also, a mimetic dance representing warfare. Also *transf.*

1757 [BURKE] *Europ. Settlem. Amer.* I. II. iv. 183 The captain.. strikes his club against the stakes of his cottage, and begins the war dance. **1775** J. TRUMBULL *M' Fingal* I. 1 The true war-dance of Yanky-reels. **1778** J. CARVER *Trav. N. Amer.* 269 The War Dance, which they use both before they set out on their war parties, and on their return from them. **1814** SCOTT *Diary* 7 Aug. in J. G. Lockhart *Life Scott* (1837) III. 163 In a stall pamphlet, called the history of Buckshaven [Fifeshire], it is said those fishers sprung from Danes, and brought with them their *war-dance* or *sword-dance*, and a rude wooden cut of it is given. **1851** *San Francisco Picayune* 24 Oct. 2/2 Having thus satisfied his taste for hat smashing, the tiles were kicked into a heap, and the six joining hands around them went through an extemporary war dance. **1883** G. C. DAVIES *Norfolk Broads* iv. (1884) 33 The boiling liquid.. is rapidly covered with sawdust, which is trodden down by a war-dance on the part of the men. **1886** J. G. WOOD *Man & Handiwork* v. 69 In their terrific war-dances, the Maoris put out their tongues to a wonderful extent.

† **wardatar(e.** *Sc. Obs.* Also 6 -atair, -atour. [f. med.L. type **wardatārius*, f. med.L. *warda*: see WARD *sb.*[2] Cf. *feudatary*.] In Scots feudal law, the person who has the wardship of lands while the heir is a minor.

1535 *Sc. Acts Jas. V* (1814) II. 344/2 Gif þe wardatouris of sik landis Refusis to find souirtie. **1579–80** *Reg. Privy Council Scot.* III. 263 George Dowglas, wardatare of Carthorall. **1580** *Exchequer Rolls Scot.* XXI. 547 John Leslie of Buchquhane, schireff wardatour of Abirdene. **1584** *Reg. Privy Council Scot.* III. 705 Williame Douglas of Lochlevin, principall schireff, wardatar thairof. **1765–8** ERSKINE *Inst. Law Scot.* II. ix. §62 The former part of the statute [of 1491] had enacted, that both wardatars and liferenters should give security to uphold, in good condition, the subject of the ward or liferent.

warday. *dial.* Also in many corrupt forms, ware-, wartday, warder, warter, wharter, etc.: see *Eng. Dial. Dict.* [Of Scandinavian origin: cf. Sw. *hvardag*, Da. *hverdag*, lit. 'every day' (ON. *hver-r* every, *dag-r* day).] A week-day, as opposed to Sunday: = EVERYDAY *sb.* b. Also *attrib.*

1598 *Knaresb. Wills* (Surtees) I. 214 To Anne Atkinson my warday gowne. **1788** MARSHALL *Rur. Econ. Yorks.* II. 363 *Wark-day* (pron. warday); week-day; in contradistinction to Sunday: 'Sunday and war-day.' [For later examples see *Eng. Dial. Dict.*]

† **ˈwardcorn.** *Feudal Law. Obs.* [f. WARD *sb.*[2] + CORN *sb.*[1]] A periodical payment in corn to the superior in commutation of military service. Cf. WARDPENNY.

1415 *Foundation Charter, Shene, Surrey* in Dugdale *Monast.* (1830) VI. I. 33/1 Et quod omnia bona.. hominum .. prædictorum quorumcunque, sint.. quieta de omnimodo pavagio, passagio,.. &c. et de omni scotto et geldo,.. et wardepeny, wardecorne, averpeny, hundredpeny, et borthalpeny, [etc.]. **1441** *Court Rolls* (P.R.O.) 1/3 Decennarius.. presentat.. j quarterium drageti vocati Wardecorne.

¶ Du Cange wrongly identified *wardcorn* with *cornagium*, to which he gave an erroneous explanation: see CORNAGE ¶. His error has been adopted in many Eng. Dicts.

1701 *Cowel's Interpr.* (ed. Kennett), *Wardecorn*, the Duty of keeping Watch and Ward with a Horn to blow, upon any occasion of surprize. **1706** PHILLIPS (ed. Kersey). **1721–1800** in BAILEY. In recent Dicts.

warddrope, obs. form of WARDROBE.

† **wardebrace.** *Obs. rare.* Also 5 **warbrace.** [a. OF. (north-eastern) **wardebras*, dial. var. of *gardebras*.] = GARDE-BRAS.

c **1440** *Promp. Parv.* 516/1 Warbrace, or bracere, *brachiale*. **14..** *Voc.* in Wr.-Wülcker 568/36 *Brachiale*, a wardebrace.

† **wardecorps.** *Obs.* Forms: 4 **wardecors, -corps,** 5 **ward(e) corce, wardcors(e, (wardecose, wardcorpse).** [a. AF. *wardecors* (recorded in sense 2; also latinized *wardecosia, wordecorsum*, etc.) = OF. *gardecorps*; f. OF. *warde*, f. *warde-r* = *garder* to guard (see GUARD, WARD *vbs.*) + *corps* body.]

1. A body-guard; an armed personal attendant. Cf. GARDE-DU-CORPS.

a **1330** *Otuel* 1409 His wardecors a non he fond, & tok a spere out of his hond. *c* **1386** CHAUCER *Wife's Prol.* 359 Thogh thou preye Argus with hise hundred eyen To be my wardecors. **1387** TREVISA *Higden* (Rolls) III. 389 Þerfore whan Phelip sat in þe feste of spousaille withoute wardecorses [L. *sine custodibus*: 1485 *Caxton* wardcorpses] Pausania, a noble ȝong man, slowȝ him riȝt þere. *a* **1450** *Mirk's Festial* 287 Kyng Darius made a questyon to þre of hys wardcorsis.

2. An over-garment for out-door use.

c **1440** *Promp. Parv.* 516/1 Warde corce, clothe (*v. rr.* wardecose, ward corscloth, wardcorce), *tunica, tunicella*. **1483** *Cath. Angl.* 408/1 Wardcorse, *reno*.

warded (ˈwɔːdɪd), *a.*[1] [f. WARD *sb.*[2] + -ED[2].] Of a key, lock: Constructed with wards. (Usually with defining word prefixed.)

1572 BOSSEWELL *Armorie* II. 94 b, This Crosse ought to be figured as a double warded key. **1591** GREENE *Conny Catch.* II. 25 He.. can picke a lock if it be not too crosse warded. **1628** FELTHAM *Resolves* II. xxxiii. 105 Attendants are like to .. lockes... If they be such as a stranger may picke.. it is very fit to change them instantly. But if they be well warded, they are then good guards of our fame. **1850** CHUBB *Locks & Keys* 8 There was also another lock constructed on the warded principle, but with the addition of a single tumbler. **1853** HOBBS & TOMLINSON *Locks* v. 58 Complex warded locks.

ˈwarded, *a.*[2] *Obs.* exc. *dial.* [f. WARD *sb.*[4] + -ED[2].] ? Affected with callosity.

1658 GURNALL *Chr. in Arm.* II. verse 16 xix. 650 Acts of mercy and forgivenesse are with so much difficulty drawn.. from those that are Saints, even like milk out of a warded breast. *a* **1825** FORBY *Voc. E. Anglia* s.v. *Ward* v., The hands of hard working people are said to be warded.

ˈwarded (ˈwɔːdɪd), *ppl. a.*[1] [f. WARD *v.*[1] + -ED[1].]

† **1.** Detained 'in ward', imprisoned. *Sc. Obs.*

c **1610** J. FORBES *Certain Rec.* (Wodrow Soc.) II. viii. 455 The guard came.. with a warrand to receive the warded ministers, and convoy them to the Councell.

2. Furnished with a protective padding; guarded.

1853 DICKENS *Bleak Ho.* i, Running their goat-hair and horse-hair warded heads against walls of words.

warded (ˈwɔːdɪd), *ppl. a.*[2] [f. WARD *v.*[2], aphetic form of 'award' + -ED[1].] (See quot.)

1894 *Northumbld. Gloss.*, 768 *Warded*, assigned, set out, awarded by commissioners appointed to carry out the division of common lands. *Warded roads*, the roads thus set out.

wardee (wɔːˈdiː). *nonce-wd.* [f. WARD *sb.*[2] + -EE[1].] An inmate of a hospital ward.

1938 S. BECKETT *Murphy* xi. 240 No sound reached him from the adjacent female wards but the infinite variety of those made by the female wardees.

wardein(e, obs. forms of WARDEN.

wardel, obs. Sc. form of WORLD.

warden (ˈwɔːd(ə)n), *sb.*[1] Forms: 3–6 **wardein,** 6 **wardeine,** 4–6 **wardeyn(e,** 4–5 **wardain(e, -ayn(e,** 4 *Sc.* **vardane,** 4–6 *north.* and *Sc.* **wardan(e,** 5 **werdein, werdeyn,** *Sc.* **wardand,** 5–6 **wardyn,** 6 *Sc.* **varden, -an, vordan, wairdan(e,** 4– **warden.** [a. OF. *wardein*, north-eastern var. of *guarden*, *-ene*: see GUARDIAN.

The word is current as a traditional designation of office; in other uses it is *poet.* or *arch.* In the legal uses the AF. form is *gardein*, and in many of them *guardian* is the preferred form in Eng. In Anglo-Latin rendered by *custos*.]

† **1. a.** One who guards, protects, or defends; occas. a guardian angel: = GUARDIAN 1. *Obs.*

a **1225** *Ancr. R.* 312 Wat Crist ure euerichon to so gentil wardein bereð to lutel menske. *c* **1290** *John* 31 in *S.E. Leg.* 403 Þere in ●eint Iohanes warde is ●wete moder he tok,.. hire wardein he was aftur also þat he to heouene i-wende. *a* **1340** HAMPOLE *Psalter* xxxiii. 7 Þat he be wardayn of þaim þat dredis him purly. *c* **1400** *Pylgr. Sowle* (Caxton) I. vii. (1859) 6 There is none so caitif pilgrym that he ne hath assigned hym a wardeyne the hour of his byrthe. *c* **1412** HOCCLEVE *De Reg. Princ.* 2441 Silence of tunge is wardein of good fame. **1513** DOUGLAS *Æneis* XI. xv. 43 O brycht Apollo.. Of haly mont Soractis the wardane.

† **b.** *Astr.* = GUARD *sb.* 12. Cf. GUARDIAN 5.

1555 EDEN *Decades* (Arb.) 218 The starres which are cauled the wardens of the north starre. *Ibid.* 270.

2. a. One who has the care of something specified; a keeper. *Obs.* exc. *poet.*

a **1290** *S. Eustace* 230 in Horstm. *Altengl. Leg.* (1881) 216 Þe hayward nom and bleu his horn, For he wes wardein of þat corn. *a* **1300** *Cursor M.* 4691 [Ioseph] Garners and granges fild wit sede, In ilk sted a sere wardain. **1362** LANGL. *P. Pl.* A. I. 53 For Rihtfoliche Resoun schulde rulen ou alle, And kuynde wit be wardeyn oure weolþe to kepe. **1387** TREVISA *Higden* (Rolls) I. 393 One of þe wardeynes þat kepte þe body of Seint Andrewe in Constantinople. *Ibid.* II. 425 þe wardeyn [L. *custos*] of þe asse folowede after. *Ibid.* IV. 33 Demetrius þat was wardeyn of his bookes. **1422** HOCCLEVE *Jonathas* 223 Let me been of it [*sc.* the ring] wardeyn; ffor as my lyf, keepe it wole y certeyn. **1871** ROSSETTI *Poems, Eden Bower* xxi, Of all this wealth I have made thee warden.

† **b.** One in charge of a division of an army. *Obs.*

1297 R. GLOUC. (Rolls) 9003 Þe king henri is ost a þre delde þere.. him sulf in þe oþer was.. & þanne is tueie sones were wardeins of þe þridde.

c. ***Warden of the Peace*** = 'Guardian of the Peace': see GUARDIAN 1 b.

1543 tr. *Act 4 Edw. III* c. 2 The iustices assigned.. shall haue power to delyuer the same iayles of those that shalbe endited before the wardeins of the peace [orig. *les gardeins de la pees*]. **1854** J. T. SMITH *Parish* ii. 38 The Sheriffs and other Wardens of the peace.. are required [etc.].

d. A gatekeeper, porter, sentinel. Now *rare.*

a **1225** *Ancr. R.* 272 He sette one wummon uorto beon ȝeteward, þet is, feble wardein. *c* **1374** CHAUCER *Troylus* v. 1177 The wardeyn of þe yates gan to calle The folk, which þat with-oute the yates were, And bad hym dryuen In here bestes alle. **1801** SOUTHEY *Thalaba* XII. xix, At the threshold of the rocky door,.. Fit warden of the sorcery-gate, A rebel Afreet lay. **1815** *Falconer's Dict. Marine* (ed. Burney), *Wardens of His Majesty's Dock-Yards*, are generally old lieutenants in the royal navy, appointed.. to see that no person whatever be admitted without an order from the commissioner. **1838** PRESCOTT *Ferd. & Is.* I. x. II. 21 The man was apprehended by the warden of the frontier of Jaen. *a* **1839** PRAED *Poems* (1864) II. 376 I've won from the warden The key,—the key; And the steed's in the garden For me, —for me. **1892** STEVENSON *In South Seas* IV. iii, Female wardens made a fit outpost for this palace of many women.

† **3.** The person invested with the control of the person and lands of an orphan heir during his minority; also, in wider sense, one who has the charge and oversight of young persons: = GUARDIAN 2. *Obs.*

c **1290** *Beket* 269 in *S.E. Leg.* 114 In his warde he let do his eldeste sone sire henri.. þat he were is wardein and al is ordeinour. **1297** R. GLOUC. (Rolls) 6418 Þo bed he þe court segge soþ.. wan edmond made is eir of is lond wiþoute striue, & wan of is ȝonge sones wardein ek ydo. *c* **1305** *St. Kenelm* 105 in *E.E.P.* (1862) 50 Þis ȝunge child a maister hadde: þat his wardeyn was. *c* **1350** *Will. Palerne* 1104 Þemperour.. made him kniȝt on the morwe & mo for his sake of proude princes sones douȝti men toward,.. & made william here wardeyn as he wel miȝt, to gye & to gouerne þe gay yong kniȝtes. *c* **1385** CHAUCER *L.G.W.* 753 Thus here wardeynys wolde they disceyue. **1387** TREVISA *Higden* (Rolls) III. 85 [Ancus] made hym wardeyn of his heyres. **1543** tr. *Act 3 Edw. I*, c. 21 The wardeyns shall kepe and susteyne the landes without makynge dystruction of any thynge. **1579** *Expos. Terms Law* 97 b, Wardeine most properly is he that hath the wardship or keeping of an heire, & of lande holden by knightes seruice, or of one of them to his owne vse during yͤ nonage of the heire, [etc.]. **1700** TYRRELL *Hist. Eng.* II. 811 The Warden, or Guardian of the Land of such Heir, who shall be under Age.

4. a. A regent or viceroy appointed to rule a country in the king's absence or minority. *Obs.* exc. *Hist.*

a **1300** *Cursor M.* 4651 Al þat barunage,.. To þis ioseph an ath þai suare, Til him als wardan for to tent. **1375** BARBOUR *Bruce* XVI. 33 The tane the steward walter was, The tothir Iames of dowglas, Vardanis in [his] absens maid he. ? *a* **1400** *Morte Arthur* 650, I make the kepare.. of kyngrykes manye, Wardayne wyrchipfulle, to weilde al my landes. *c* **1420** WYNTOUN *Cron.* cxxxii. 2175 Throu Schir Andro Murrayis renovne, Quhen he wes wardane of Scotland. *c* **1470** HENRY *Wallace* VI. 768 Thai chesd Wallace Scottis wardand to be. **1509** *Reg. Privy Seal Scot.* I. 262/2 Ony proclamatioun.. made generaly be the king or his wardanis anent the intercommonyn and sitting apoun the Inglismenis assouerans. **1640** YORKE *Union Hon.* 27 Edward.. the eldest sonne of king Edward [II] in the.. absence of his Father.. was made Lord Warden of England, by a common decree. **1651** N. BACON *Disc. Govt. Eng.* II. xv. 134 Vicegerents... Sometimes they are called Lord Warden, or Lord Keeper of the Kingdome, and have therewith the generall power of a King. **1878** J. DAVIDSON *Inverurie* ii. 69 Randolph, Earl of Moray, who was Warden of Scotland in the minority of David, having died in 1331. **1912** E. RUSSELL *Maitland of Lethington* i. 33 The *finesse* with which Maitland contrived to get the necessary co-operation of Bothwell, the Scottish Warden.

† **b.** The governor of a town, province or district; the commander of a fortress. *Obs.* exc. *Hist.* in the title ***Warden of the Marches.***

1297 R. GLOUC. (Rolls) 2078 Þritti þousend kniȝtes hor wardeins hii sette & delde among hom al þe lond. **1338** R. BRUNNE *Chron.* (1725) 72 To London com William,.. His barons with him nam, knyghtes þat wer bold. Wardeyns of tour & toun. *a* **1352** MINOT *Poems* viii. 83 He was wardaine of þe toune. *c* **1400** *Brut* ccviii. 237 Kyng Edward.. sent maistre Walter of Stapleton, his Tresorer, forto bene wardein and keper of þe citee of London wiþ þe Mair. *c* **1450** *Ibid.* ccxl. 346 Þe King.. made hym warden and gouernour of þe cite. **1470–85** MALORY *Arthur* I. viii. 44 And sire Brastias was maade wardeyn to wayte vpon the northe fro Trent forwardes. **1517** *Acc. Ld. High Treas. Scot.* V. 123 The vordan of the Myddil Marche. **1557** NORTH *Gueuara's Diall Pr.* (1568) 2 Pretor of the Rhodian Armies, and also wardein in other frontiers. **1563** in Rymer *Foedera* (1719) XV. 631 Schir Johne Maxwell of Terreglie Knycht Wardane of the West Mercheis of Scotland. **1917** *Eng. Hist. Rev.* Oct. 480 The notable feature of these proceedings [Nov. 1248] is that in them there is no mention of a Warden of the Marches. *Ibid.* 493 The little Duke of York.. Warden-general of the Marches.

5. In certain guilds, esp. in the Livery Companies of the City of London: A member of the governing body under the authority of the Master or the Prime Warden (the title varies in different companies).

[**1261** in *Liber Custum.* (Rolls) 79 Les Wardeyns [of the Lorimers] le moustrent au Meire qe donqe serra]. **1389** in *Eng. Gilds* (1870) 3 þe forsaide bretherhede wil þæt þer be wardeins þerof. **1454** *Cal. Anc. Rec. Dublin* (1889) 283 The wardyns of the Trinite Yelde. **1547** in Rymer *Foedera* (1719) XV. 134 The Maisters Wardeyns Governours Rulers and Overseers of all and singuler the Hospitals Guylders Fraternyties and Houses for poor People. **1566** *Act 8 Eliz.* c. 13 §1 The Mayster Wardens and Assistauntes of the Trinytie House of Deptforde Stronde. **1624** MASSINGER *Parlt. Love* IV. iii, Next year we will have him warden of our society. **1637** *Decree Star Chamb.* §13 in Milton *Areop.* (Arb.) 15 He..shall first giue notice to the said Master and Wardens of the Company of Stationers. **1848** DICKENS *Dombey* lvii, The inscription about what the Master and Wardens of the Worshipful Company did in one thousand six hundred and ninety-four. **1886** C. E. PASCOE *London Today* vii. (ed. 3) 84 Interest with the Prime Warden, Master, or Clerk of a Company might possibly procure an invitation to one of these [banquets].

†**6. a.** The person having the direction or oversight of some work or enterprise. *Obs.*

1398 TREVISA *Barth. De P.R.* XII. v. (Bodl. MS), 3if hem lakkeþ honye to eete þanne þe warden schalle feede hem [*sc.* the bees] with figes and oþur swete mete leste þey schulde deye. *c* **1400** *Gamelyn* 279 Tho that wardeynes were of that wrasteling Come and broughte Gamelyn the ram and the ring. **1423** *Rolls of Parlt.* IV. 255/1 The serche of the wardens of Brauderie. **1543** tr. *Act 18 Hen. VI*, c. 16 A warden of the aulnage of cloth. **1552–3** in Feuillerat *Revels Edw. VI* (1914) 132 Robert Trunkewell Joyner being theyre warden and setting owte y^re^ woorkes. **1601** HOLLAND *Pliny* XXIII. vii. II. 167 Pythagoras, a great maister and warden of these exercises.

b. *Freemasonry.* Either of two officers (called ***Senior*** and ***Junior Warden***) in a symbolic lodge whose duty it is to assist the Worshipful Master.

a **1723** WREN *Parentalia* (1750) 307 A Surveyor govern'd in chief; every tenth Man was called a Warden, and overlooked each nine. **1797** *Encycl. Brit.* (ed. 3) X. 622/1 The king [Hen. VII] presided as grand-master; and having appointed John Islip, abbot of Westminster, and Sir Reginald Bray, knight of the garter, his wardens for the occasion, proceeded in great state to..Westminster Abbey. *Ibid.* 623/2 On the 27th of December 1663, a general assembly was held, where Henry Jennyn earl of St. Alban's was elected grand-master; who appointed Sir John Denham his deputy, and Mr. Christopher Wren..and John Webb, his wardens.

7. a. The superintendent of a harbour, market, or the like.

1538 ELYOT *Dict.*, *Limenarcha*, the wardeyn of the portes. **1543** tr. *Act 9 Edw. III* Stat. II. c. 7 That the tables of exchange shalbe at Douer,..And that the wardeyns of suche tables shall make suche exchaunges by the testymony of controllers whiche we shall put to them. **1543** tr. *Act. 5 Rich. II*, c. 2 Any serchours or wardeyn of the portes and passages through the sayd realme. **1546** *Yorks. Chantry Surv.* (Surtees) 245 To the burgh balyff of Skipton and the warden of the market ther. **1835** *App. Munic. Corpor. Rep.* II. 1043 [Officers of Sandwich corporation] Wardens of the Flesh Market 2, Wardens of the Fish Market 2.

b. Forming the second element in the designation of certain officials, as ***barrack-warden. fire-warden***, U.S.: see FIRE *sb.* 5. ***fish-warden***, U.S., an official in charge of fisheries. ***game-warden***, an officer having the superintendence of the game of a particular locality.

1835 *App. Munic. Corpor. Rep.* IV. 2295 [Officers of Ipswich corporation] Two Fleshwardens. Ale Conner. **1883** G. B. GOODE *Fish Industr. U.S.A.* (Fisheries Exhib.) 66 To enforce these laws would, however, render necessary a large force of fish-wardens. **1894** *Daily News* 7 Feb. 6/4 The duties hitherto carried out by barrack-masters are in future to be performed by pensioned non-commissioned officers of the army, who, on appointment, will be termed 'barrack wardens'. **1898** *Westm. Gaz.* 30 Sept. 3/1 The State 'game-wardens'. **1912** *Nature* 26 Dec. 468/2 Major J. Stevenson-Hamilton, Game Warden of the Transvaal.

c. An air-raid warden.

1936 [see AIR-RAID]. **1937** *Lancet* 13 Mar. 669/2 The wardens would probably also be used in connexion with the distribution of civilian respirators. **1951** N. MARSH *Opening Night* vi. 139 'Anyone here done respiration for gassed cases?'.. 'I can,' said the A.S.M. 'I was a warden.' **1978** E. MALPASS *Wind Brings up Rain* xxvi. 232 A tin-hatted Air Raid Warden was hurrying along the street... The Warden hurried on.

†**8. a.** A custodian of a building, esp. a temple or church. *Obs.*

c **1290** *Brendan* 626 in *S.E. Leg.* 237 In þe Abbeye of seint paterich, Monek ich was, i-wis And of is churche a wardein. **1303** R. BRUNNE *Handl. Synne* 1566 Of þe cherche þe wardeynys alle were waked oute of here slepe. **1483** CAXTON *Golden Leg.* 265/1 A wardeyn of the hows of god. **1642** FULLER *Holy & Prof. St.* II. xxii. 141 The good Herald..is a Warden of the temple of Honour.

†**b.** The dean of a cathedral or collegiate church, or of a royal chapel. *Obs.*

1429 *Rolls of Parlt.* IV. 346 John Arundell, Dean or Wardein of the Chapelle Roiall of Seint George,..Windsor. *Ibid.*, The saide Wardein is named and wretyn Dean; also.. Wardeins therof have usually be called Deans. **1538** FITZHERB. *Just. Peas* 121 b, Al..wardens of cathedrall and collegiate Churches.

9. a. = CHURCHWARDEN 1. There are regularly two, the ***rector's*** (or ***vicar's***) ***warden*** and the ***parish*** (or ***people's***) ***warden***.

1439 *E.E. Wills* (1882) 114 The wardeyns of Seynt Austyns chirch. **1461** *Rolls of Parlt.* V. 475/1 Late Wardeyns of the goodes of the seid Chirch. **1547** EDW. VI *Injunct.* §13 b ij b, The Wardeynes of euery paryshe churche or Chapel. **1589** R. HARVEY *Pl. Perc.* Ded. p. iv, I will present you at the law day for a ryot, though I be neither side man for this Meridian, nor Warden. **1853** MARSDEN *Early Puritans* 105 The minister and wardens undertook to go from house to house to take the names of the communicants. **1914** *Contemp. Rev.* Mar. 352 Rival candidates for the office of the people's warden.

b. *transf.* Applied to an official with similar functions of a Jewish synagogue.

1879 F. HITCHMAN *Public Life Earl of Beaconsfield* I. i. 15 The quarrel with the Wardens of the Synagogue was a more serious matter. **1910** MONYPENNY *Life B. Disraeli* I. iii. 22 In 1813 he was for some pedantic reason elected Parnass or Warden of the Congregation of Bevis Marks.

10. In the titles of officers holding positions of trust under the Crown.

†**a.** ***Warden of the Forest***: see quot. 1706. *Obs.*

1598 MANWOOD *Laws of Forest* viii. 43 Hereupon the Lord chiefe Iustice of the Forrest..will cause a writ of *Ad quod dampnum* to be directed to the chiefe warden of the Forrest. *c* **1600** *Rolls of Parlt.* II. 376/2 Wardens of Forrests shall be commanded to keep their Officers from extorting. **1706** PHILLIPS (ed. Kersey), *Keeper of the Forest*, otherwise called Chief Warden of the Forest, is he that has the principal Government of all things belonging to the Forest, and the Check of all the other Officers. **1797** H. ROOKE *Descr. Gt. Oak Salcey Forest* 5 The Forest is under the Government of the following Officers:—A Warden, or Master Forester,..Lieut. or Deputy Warden [etc.].

b. (***Lord***) ***Warden of the Cinque Ports***: see CINQUE PORTS.

1435 *Rolls of Parlt.* IV. 489/2 Constable of the Castell of Dovorr, and Wardeyn of fyve Portz. **1544** in Rymer *Foedera* (1719) XV. 55 The Lorde Warden of the Fyve Ports. **1617** MORYSON *Itin.* III. 138 William the Norman Conquerour.. instituted a Warden of the five Ports, Hastings, Dover, Hith, Rumney and Sandwiche. **1643** *Proc. late Treaty of Peace* 56 Such a Noble Person as your Majesty shall appoint to be Warden of the Cinque-Ports. **1844** *Queen's Regul. Army* 46 The Lord-Warden of the Cinque Ports is to be saluted by the forts within his jurisdiction with the number of guns specified.

fig. (*allusively.*) **1616** T. SCOT *Philomythie* B 3, Supposing Ibis their trustie warden, had beene closing The lands strong Ports. *Ibid.* B 3 b, Make not your will warden of your Cinque Ports [*i.e.* the five senses].

c. ***Warden of the Mint***: until 1823 the title of the chief officer of the Mint.

1463 *Irish Act 3 Edw. IV*, c. 32 We..have Ordeyned and made..Germyn lynche..Wardeyne and Maister worker of oure moneis and coignes. **1587** *Reg. Privy Council Scot.* IV. 220 The generall, wardane, countare wardane, sinkare and assayare,..of his Majesteis cunyiehous. **1670** PETTUS *Fodinæ Reg.* 41 The Warden [of the mint]..is by his Office to receive the Silver from the Goldsmiths. **1688** *Lond. Gaz.* No. 2368/4 Owen wynne Esq; Warden of the Mint.

d. (***Lord***) ***Warden of the Stannaries***: an officer appointed by the Duke of Cornwall to preside over the mining parliaments of Cornwall.

1485 [see STANNARY 1]. **1761** *Brit. Mag.* II. 10 He served the king in the different offices of lord warden of the Stannaries, lord admiral of England and Ireland. **1812** *Morn. Chron.* in *Examiner* 28 Sept. 623/1 The new Lord Warden [of the Stannaries] has not been idle. **1814** MOORE *Hor. Ode* II. xi. 19 Then, why, my Lord Warden! oh! why should you fidget Your mind about matters you don't understand? **1896** *Law Times* CI. 534/2 By the Judicature Acts the jurisdiction of the Lord Warden was transferred to the Court of Appeal.

†**e.** In the titles of various offices of the royal household or the courts of law. (Mainly as the rendering of AF. *gardein.*) *Obs.*

1543 tr. *Act. 51 Hen. III*, Stat. Excheq., The wardeyne of the kynges wardrobe. **1543** tr. *Act. 1 Edw. IV*, c. 1 Warden of the rolles of his chauncerie. *Ibid.*, The..warden of his armour in the towre of London. *Ibid.*, In thoffice of his priue seale, clerke or warden of his hamper of his sayde chauncery. *Ibid.*, The..warden of the kynges wryttes..of his common benche. **1601** TATE *Househ. Ord. Edw. II* (1876) 9 The clarke which shalbe warden or keper of the privy seale. *Ibid.* 18 The kinge shal have a squier surveiour and warden of the viandes for his mouth. *Ibid.* 39 And a serjant herberjour, warden of the kinges palfreis. [**1892** STEVENSON *In South Seas* IV. iii. (1908) 294 These were keybearers, treasurers, wardens of the armoury, the napery and the stores.]

†**f.** ***Warden of the Standards***: an officer of the Board of Trade having the custody of the standards of weight and measure. *Obs.*

1878 *Act 41 & 42 Vict.* c. 49 §1.

11. a. The title given to the head or presiding officer of certain colleges and schools, hospitals, etc.

Usually = L. *custos.*

1575–6 *Act 18 Eliz.* c. 6 §1 No Provoste Warden or other Hed Officer of the saide Colledges of Winchester or Eaton. **1587** LADY F. COBHAM in *Collect.* (O.H.S.) I. 193 Warden of Al Soules Colledge. **1632** MARMION *Hollands Leaguer* I. ii. B 4 b, I'll..talke as superciliously, and walke As stately, as the Warden of a colledge. **1763** *Brit. Mag.* IV. 612 Dr. Golding, Warden of Winchester College. **1782** PENNANT *Journ. Chester to Lond.* 305 St Thomas's hospital [Northampton]..Originally it maintained twelve poor people... It is governed by a warden, who is one of the aldermen. **1845** *New Statist. Acc. Scot.* XII. 988 An hospital or alms-house..founded in 1272..for maintaining a warden, six chaplains, and thirteen poor husbandmen of Buchan. **1855** A. TROLLOPE *Warden* i, John Hiram..also appointed that an almshouse should be built for their abode, with a fitting residence for a warden. **1908** *Act 8 Edw. VII*, c. 20 Sched. §2 From the time at which..a chancellor shall be appointed, the office of warden of the University [of Durham] shall cease.

†**b.** The superior of a Franciscan convent. Cf. GUARDIAN 4. *Obs.*

1420 *E.E. Wills* (1882) 47 þe wardeyn and þe Couente. **1455** *Linc. Diocese Docum.* (1914) 76 The Wardeyn and the Covent of the gray frerys of Oxford. **1588** *Exchequer Rolls Scot.* XXI. 407 To Freir Charles Home, sumtym varden of the cordeleris of Drumfreis.

12. An officer to whose custody prisoners are committed; the governor of a prison, esp. in the old title ***Warden of the Fleet*** (Prison).

13.. *Sir Beues* (A.) 3708 þo Ascopard wiþ outen dwelling In to þat castel gan hire bring,..And half a ȝer a was hire wardaine. *c* **1330** R. BRUNNE *Chron. Wace* (Rolls) 13112 þe kyng dide his prisons loke Wiþ wardeyns þat hem vndertoke. *c* **1400** *Destr. Troy* 13847 Thus he keppit hym full cloise, & in care held, þat no whe to hym wan but wardens full sure. **1429** *Rolls of Parlt.* IV. 346/1 The Keper and Wardeyn of the same Prisone. **1535** LYNDESAY *Satyre* 3986 The widdifow wairdanis tuke my geir. **1543** tr. *Act 1 Rich. II*, c. 12 From hensforth no wardeyn of the Flete shall suffre any prysoner there..to goo out of prysone by maynpryse, bayle, [etc.]. **1751** SMOLLETT *Per. Pickle* xcviii. (1779) IV. 281 He intreated the warden to accomodate him with a lodging. **1827** *Statutes of Connecticut* (1854) 726 The warden shall have the entire control and management of said prison. **1828** SCOTT *F.M. Perth* xxiii, My Lord High Constable,..Since I am to lie in ward, I could not have desired a kinder or more courteous warden. **1837** DICKENS *Pickw.* xli, The room where you're a-going to sleep to-night is the warden's room. **1889** *Century Mag.* Feb. 506/1 As we entered the main corridor [of a prison] the officer of the day sprung hastily to the door, saluted the warden [etc.].

13. A member of a committee (of two or more persons) appointed to take charge of the repair and make regulations for the use of a bridge, a highway, etc. Cf. WAYWARDEN.

1486 *Rec. St. Mary at Hill* (1905) 13 To haue & to hold to the wardeyns of the said Brigge [*sc.* London Bridge]. **1575–6** *Act 18 Eliz.* c. 17 §1 To make an Election of Twoo persons of the same Comminaltie to be the Wardens of the saide Rochester Bridge. **1876** FREEMAN *Norm. Conq.* V. xxv. 550 A later reform has entrusted the care of the highways..to Boards of Wardens.

†**14.** At Coventry, the title of two officers, chosen annually, charged with the collection of municipal rents. *Obs.*

1422–1507 *Cov. Leet. Bk.* 22, 58, etc.

15. *U.S.* (and earlier in colonial use). **a.** The officer who presides at ward-meetings or elections.

1763 J. ADAMS *Diary* Feb., Wks. 1850 II. 144 Boston.. The Caucus Club meets, at certain times... There they choose a moderator..and selectmen, assessors, collectors, wardens, fire-wards, and representatives, are regularly chosen before they are chosen in the town. **1796** MORSE *Amer. Geog.* I. 678 Charleston was..divided into 13 wards, which choose as many wardens, from among whom the citizens elect an Intendant of the city. The Intendant and wardens form the city council. **1813** T. JEFFERSON *Writ.* (1830) IV. 229 A general call of ward-meetings by their wardens on the same day through the State. **1822** *Charter of Boston, Mass.* §3 It shall be the duty of such warden to preside at all meetings of the citizens of such ward.

b. 'In Connecticut boroughs, the chief executive officer of the municipal government; in a few Rhode Island towns, a judicial officer. In colonial times the name was sometimes used instead of *fire-warden* or *fire-ward*' (*Century Dict.*).

1842 *Statutes of Connecticut* (1854) 87 All persons who shall be engineers or wardens of any fire department.

16. *Canada.* The head of a county council.

1873 *Rev. Statutes Ontario* (1877) II. 1606 The Council of every County shall consist of the Reeves and Deputy Reeves of the Townships and Villages within the County..and one of the Reeves or Deputy Reeves shall be the Warden. **1886** BOURNIOT *Local Govt. Canada* 73[In the province of Quebec] The county council is composed of the mayors of the several local municipalities of the county... The warden is chosen by the county council.

17. *Australia.* The government official, with magisterial powers, in charge of a goldfield.

1855 R. CARBONI *Eureka Stockade* 120 A Public Meeting was held... The Resident Warden in the Chair. **1860** S. DAVISON *Discovery & Geognosy Gold Deposits Austral.* XI. 332 A number of new offices had been created for the gold fields, under the name of 'wardens'. **1861** MRS. MEREDITH *Over the Straits* iv. 141 The chief official in a digging settlement..is entitled the Warden.

18. *attrib.* and *Comb.*, as ***warden-angel*** (rare); also 'of or pertaining to the warden-courts', as †***warden-book***, †***-clerk***, †***-fee***; **warden-raid**, *nonce-use*, a raid commanded by the Warden of the Marches in person. Also WARDEN-COURT.

1839 BAILEY *Festus* xx. (1848) 246 The sweet offices Of *warden-angel. **1583** *Reg. Privy Council Scot.* III. 584 He findand..souirties actit in the *warden buikis to be answerable for all attemptatis. **1584** *Ibid.* 726 Robert Menteith, sumtyme his *wardane clerk. **1531** *Acc. Ld. High Treas. Scot.* VI. 47 Item, to the lord Huym, wardane off the eist marchis, for his *wardane fee, de anno, etc. xxxj^o^, j^c^li. **1564** *Reg. Privy Council Scot.* I. 278 That the said Lord Home, wardane foirsaid, have payment of his wardane fee. **1805** SCOTT *Last Minstrel* IV. iv, 'And by my faith,' the gate-ward said, 'I think 'twill prove a *Warden-Raid.'

warden ('wɔːd(ə)n), *sb.*[2] Forms: 5 wardun, -one, -oun, -ane, 5–6 wardyn (6 -in), 5–7 wardon, 6

wardayne, -eine, -eyne, 5– warden. [Of obscure origin.

Perh. a. AF. **wardon* f. *ward-er* = F. *garder* to keep. Palsgrave 1530 renders *wardon* by *poire de garde* (= keeping pear). As the arms of Wardon or Warden Abbey (Beds) were 'Argent, three warden pears or', it has been conjectured that the pear derived its name from the abbey. There can be little doubt, however, that the arms were devised with punning intention.]

An old variety of baking pear. Also ***pear warden*** (see PEAR *sb.* 5).

a **1400** *Pistill of Susan* 99 With wardons winlich and walshe notes newe. *c* **1430** LYDG. *Min. Poems* (Percy Soc.) 15 The frutis wiche more comon be, Quenyngez, pechis, costardes, *etiam* wardons. **1481–90** *Howard Househ. Bks.* (Roxb.) 464 My Lord paid to a woman that browght wardones xij.d. **1523–34** FITZHERB. *Husb.* §137 After saynt Valentynes daye; it is tyme to graffe bothe peares and wardens. **1542** BORDE *Dyetary* xxvii. (1870) 291 Vse to eate stued or baken wardens, yf they can be goten. **1612** BEAUM. & FL. *Cupid's Rev.* II, *Dori.* Faith I would have had him rosted like a warden in brown paper, and no more talk on't. **1653** W. J. *True Gentlew. Delight* 84 To make a Tart of Wardens. You must first Bake your Wardens in a pot, then [etc.]. **1687** SEDLEY *Bellamira* III. i. 24 She looks like a Warden Roasted in the Embers. **1764** *Museum Rust.* II. 56 Pears..Perkinson Wardens. **1802** FORSYTH *Fruit-Trees* 93 Pears..Spanish Red Warden. **1860** HOGG *Fruit Man.* 170 Black Worcester (Parkinson's Warden; Pound Pear).

b. *attrib.* and *Comb.*, as ***warden-pear, -pie, -tree.***

138. *Anc. Deed* A. 9011 (P.R.O.), *Wardon peryz. **1635** MARKHAM *Eng. Husbandm.* I. II. i. 122 Your stone-Peare, Warden-Peare, and Choake-Peare [are] those which endure longest. **1579** in *Narratives Reform.* (Camden) 34 He sayd his stomache was gonne from all meate excepte it wer a *warden pye. **1611** SHAKS. *Wint. T.* IV. iii. 48, I must haue Saffron to colour the Warden Pies. **1841** BARHAM *Ingol. Leg., Nelly Cook* 88 And a Warden-pie's a dainty dish to mortify withal. **14..** *Metr. Voc.* in Wr.-Wülcker 629/7 *Wardentre, *uolemus.* **1523–34** FITZHERB. *Husb.* §137 The sappe commeth sooner..in-to the peare-tree and warden-tree, thanne in-to the apple tree. **1630** DEKKER *2nd Pt. Honest Wh.* F 3b, The 4th man I hold my life, is grafting your Warden tree.

'warden, *v.* [f. WARDEN *sb.*¹] *trans.* To watch over or guard as a warden; *spec.* to watch over or patrol (a nature reserve, etc.) by or as a warden; also *intr.*, to act as a wildlife warden.

1906 T. HARDY *Dynasts* II. I. vi, To warden the waves was his further bent. **1971** *Times* 7 May 17/7 Having wardened at the Royal Society for the Protection of Birds reserve at Loch Garten, may I enlarge upon the letter from M. S. M. Burns? **1974** *Oxford Times* 4 Jan. 7/6 It would be wardened and visited regularly to prevent vandalism and litter. **1977** *Birds* Spring 40 Philip Coxon has wardened the RSPB Balranald reserve for the last four summers. **1982** *Lakeland Echo* 18 Mar. 5 The eyres are well wardened against egg collectors. **1984** *Natural World* Summer 14/1 Several orchids on a number of sites were wardened, efforts being concentrated on lizard, early spider, military and monkey orchids.

Hence **'wardened** *ppl. a.*, **'wardening** *vbl. sb.*

1962 *Listener* 1 Mar. 375/2 There is as yet no system of wardening for the valleys... Wardening is limited by statute to places where the Board has access-agreements or owns property. **1971** *Guardian Weekly* 3 July 15 The wardening of Exmoor, for example, with its wide acres of moorland under rising pressure of visitors, is described as rudimentary. **1980** *Birds* Autumn p. v/1 Although the most obviously efficient form of protection is to establish adequately wardened reserves, this is not possible in many cases. **1980** R. MABEY *Common Ground* I. 32 A wardening system was established for the more vulnerable eyries.

Warden-court. *Hist.* [WARDEN *sb.*¹ + COURT *sb.*¹] A court held by the Warden of the Marches.

1434 *Proc. Privy Council* (1835) IV. 271 Alle þe bookes of þe wardein courtes and of þe marches. **1549** *Compl. Scot.* xii. (1872) 103 The vardan of the vest marchis of ingland cam to hald ane vardan court on the vest marchis of scotland. **1556** LD. WHARTON in Lodge *Illustr. Brit. Hist.* (1791) I. 220, I have called a Warden Courte, whiche dyd begynne, at.. Alnewyk, the iii^d of this instaunt. **1583** *Reg. Privy Council Scot.* III. 621 A persoun fylit bakbilland and cravand a warden court to be sett upoun his perrell. **1863** SARAH S. JONES *Northumbld.* 162 The days of Trews, or Warden Courts, had to be held frequently, and not by deputies, but by the Lords Wardens themselves.

wardency ('wɔːdənsɪ). [f. WARDEN *sb.*¹ + -CY.] The position of warden; also the sphere or district in which a warden exercises his functions.

1845 *New Statist. Acc. Scot.* XII. 988 In 1412, Bishop Greenlaw erected the wardancy [*sic*] here into a prebend. **1867** W. MCDOWALL *Hist. Dumfries* xiv. 160 Douglas.. accordingly called a meeting of the whole lords, freeholders [etc.]..within his wardency. **1892** *Sat. Rev.* 30 Apr. 496/2 Heir-looms to go with the Wardency [of the Cinque Ports].

wardenry ('wɔːdənrɪ). [f. WARDEN *sb.*¹ + -RY.]

1. The office or position of warden.

1375 BARBOUR *Bruce* VIII. 362 He gaf vp thar his vardanry. *c* **1420** WYNTOUN *Cron.* VIII. xxx. 5036 Mony dedis worthi, þat he did in his wardanry. **1434** *Proc. Privy Council* (1835) IV. 270 Commissions to be maade to þerle of Sarum of boþe wardeneryes. **1546** *Reg. Privy Council Scot.* I. 28 The office of wardannre of the West Marchis. *a* **1637** SPOTTISWOOD *Hist. Ch. Scot.* v. (1677) 279 The first had been lately dispatched from his office of Wardenry in the West Marches. **1828** SCOTT *Tales Grandfather* Ser. I. II. 272 He ..during his absence, committed the wardenry of the Scottish frontiers to a brave French knight.

2. The jurisdiction of, or district under the care of, a Warden of the Marches.

1462–3 *Script. tres* (Surtees) App. p. ccclxvii, Every place within our wardenry. **1569** HUNSDON in E. Lodge *Illustr. Brit. Hist.* (1791) II. 32 She must sende a good companie, more then either her Wardenries or the garrison of this towne will yelde. **1587** *Sc. Acts Jas. VI* (1814) III. 459/1 Quhilkis iustices..salbe ressauit..be þe wardanis within þe wardanries. **1590** HUNSDON *Let. to Marshal of Berwick* in *Archæologia* XXX. 172 Least they, hearing of it, being within the wardonrie [*printed* wardourie] should fly upon it. **1805** SCOTT *Last Minstrel* IV. xxiv, They may not tamely see, All through the Western Wardenry, Your law-contemning kinsmen ride.

3. The official residence of a warden. *rare.*

1859 [J. PAYN] *Foster Brothers* vi. 75 The Wardenry was a fine stone building occupying the entire side of a huge square court.

4. Guardianship. *nonce-uses.*

1903 HARDY *Dynasts* I. VI. viii, He wills the wardenry of his affairs To his old friend. **1906** *Ibid.* II. I. iii, Still professing our safe wardenry, To fatten other kingdoms at our cost.

'wardenship. [f. WARDEN *sb.*¹ + -SHIP.]

1. Guardianship, safe-keeping. *rare.*

a **1300** *Cursor M.* 4253 þe wardein-scipp of al his aght Has putifar ioseph bi-taght. *Ibid.* 4643, I wil him do at vndertak þe wardanscipp of al mi land. **1890** H. FREDERIC *Lawton Girl* 63 All the nameless feminine yearnings for wardenship and shelter from life's battle took voice and pleaded in her heart.

2. The office or position of a warden, in various uses of that word.

1464 *Rolls of Parlt.* V. 520/2 Any Graunte..made..to Maister William Say..of the custodie or Wardenship of the Hous or Hospitall of Seint Antony in oure Cite of London. **1481** in *Engl. Gilds* (1870) 332 If any of the Jornaymen refuse to take the office of Wardynschippe. **1536** *Act 28 Hen. VIII*, c. 11 Euery..hospitall, wardenshyppe, prouostshyppe, or other spiritual promocion. **1628** EARL MANCH. in *Buccleuch MSS.* (Hist. MSS. Comm.) I. 267 Your wardenship when I found undispatched I would not let longer to stick. **1651** N. BACON *Disc. Govt. Eng.* II. xv. 136 The power and place of the Wardenship of the Kingdome doth utterly vanish by the personall accesse of the King. **1691** A. WOOD *Ath. Oxon.* I. 398 In the Wardenship of Mert. coll. succeeded Nath. Brent. **1791** *Ann. Reg., St. Papers* 153* There is no longer wardenships, or corporations of professions, arts, and crafts. **1804** G. ROSE *Diaries* (1860) II. 191 *note*, The Wardenship of the Cinque Ports. **1870** *Daily News* 12 Nov., The Wardenship of St. Peter's College, Radley, has been filled by the selection of [etc.].

3. *nonce-use.* The funds in the hands of or set apart for a warden or wardens.

1424 *Cov. Leet Bk.* 83 þe wich xl s. com oute of the wardenship and thei owen to haue hit agayn.

warder ('wɔːdə(r)), *sb.*¹ Also 7 wardour, *Sc.* wairdour. [a. AF. *wardere, wardour*, agent-n. f. *warder*, north-eastern dial. var. of OF. *garder* to GUARD.]

I. One who wards or guards.

1. A soldier or other person set to guard an entrance; also, a watchman on a tower.

c **1400** *Destr. Troy* XI. 4690 Comyn to the castell,..the Grekes Ingird, gripped the warders, And all the fonnet folke fell to the dethe. **1560** DAUS tr. *Sleidane's Comm.* 90 So were the warders [L. *stationes*] remoued from the gates the same daye. **1577** tr. *Bullinger's Decades* III. v. (1592) 338 When the temple was builded, there were porters and warders of the temple appointed among the Leuits. **1605** SHAKS. *Macb.* IV. i. 56 Though Castles topple on their Warders heads. **1605** VERSTEGAN *Dec. Intell.* x. (1628) 327 Wee call him that waiteth at the Towre one of the ward or a warder. **1679–88** *Moneys Secr. Serv. Chas. II & Jas. II* (Camden) 93 Wages due to their respective husbands as late wardours in the Tower of London. **1697** DRYDEN *Æneis* II. 453 The Warders of the Gate but scarce maintain Th'unequal Combat. **1802** MRS. RADCLIFFE *Gaston de Blondeville* Posth. Wks. (1826) III. 4 Amongst these, were the wardours of a postern, near the north walls. **1813** SCOTT *Trierm.* I. xiii, Upon the watch-tower's airy round No warder stood his horn to sound. **1831** WORDSW. *Yarrow Revisited* 6 Once more, by Newark's Castle-gate Long left without a warder, I stood. **1853** DICKENS *Bleak Ho.* xxxii, The gates [of Lincoln's Inn] are shut; and the night-porter, a solemn warder with a mighty power of sleep, keeps guard in his lodge.

b. *transf.* and *fig.*

1605 SHAKS. *Macb.* I. vii. 65 Memorie, the Warder of the Braine, Shall be a Fume, and the Receit of Reason A Lymbeck onely. **1818** SCOTT *Br. Lamm.* xxvi, There mounted guard on the other side of the mirror two stout warders of Scottish lineage; a jug,..and a quegh, or bicker. **1849** LYTTON *K. Arthur* VI. vi, Hill after hill the land's grey warders rose. **1880** W. WATSON *Prince's Quest* III, A fair-built seaport, warder of the land And watcher of the wave.

†**2.** The title of an English official in Ireland.

1617 MORYSON *Itin.* II. 97 Warders in Leinster per annum one thousand three hundred ten li nineteene s. two pence.

3. An official in charge of prisoners in a jail.

1855 MACAULAY *Hist. Eng.* xvii. IV. 22 The prisoner's confinement was not strict... He was permitted to go into the country under the care of a warder. **1863** P. BARRY *Dockyard Econ.* 152 The convicts and warders in Milbank Prison. **1904** A. GRIFFITHS *50 Yrs. Publ. Service* xvii. 241 The Chief Warder..had been promoted to his office from Dartmoor.

4. *attrib.* and *Comb.*

1831 JAMES *Phil. Augustus* xix, De Coucy hastened to demand of the squire wherefore he had sounded the great warder horn, which hung in the watch-tower. **1864** SWINBURNE *Atalanta* 1213 Where the dawn Cheers first these warder gods that face the sun. **1904** A. GRIFFITHS *50 Yrs. Publ. Service* xii. 163 The warder officers arraigned before him all those whom they desired to report for offences.

†**II. 5.** *Sc.* A person in ward, a prisoner. *Obs. rare.*

1584 *Acts Jas. VI* (1814) III. 352/1 The gard and keping of prissoneris and wardours. **1629** *Reg. Privy Council Scot.* Ser. II. III. 12 Who under pretext and cullour of freindship unto the wairdours sould crave accesse unto them... Who.. sould stryke the jaylour and so give way to the wairdours and escape.

warder ('wɔːdə(r)), *sb.*² Also 9 (? erron.) wardour. [See WARDERER.] In early use: A staff or wand. Later, the baton or truncheon carried as a symbol of office, command, or authority; esp. as used to give the signal for the commencement or cessation of hostilities in a battle or tournament.

c **1440** *Promp. Parv.* 516/2 Warder, staffe..*bacillus*.. *perticulus.* **1500** *Maldon* (Essex) *Court Rolls* Bundle 59, No. 3b, Super quo dictus constabularius eum percussit cum predicto warder. *a* **1548** HALL *Chron., Hen. V*, 49b, Before whom there went..syr Thomas of Herpingham..with a warder in his hand, and when he cast up his warder al the army shouted. **1568** GRAFTON *Chron.* II. 396 The king cast downe his warder and commaunded them to stay. **1643** R. BAKER *Chron., Rich. I* (1653) 88 [At the coronation] William de Patricke, Earl of Salisbury.. bare the Warder or Rod, having on the top thereof a Dove. **1765** H. WALPOLE *Castle of Otranto* iii, So saying, the herald cast down his warder. **1813** SCOTT *Trierm.* II. xx, When the strife grows warm,.. thy king commands, Thou drop the warder from thy hands. **1824** MEYRICK *Ant. Armour* II. 32 At this King Edward threw down his warder, the marshal cried 'Ho!' and the combat ceased. **1898** S. J. WEYMAN *Shrewsbury* xxxii. (1917) 253 The portrait of a man in armour, with a warder in his mailed hand, frowned down on me.

†**warder,** *sb.*³ *Obs. rare.* [? Corruption of Norw. *varde* (cf. ON. *varða, varð-r* of the same meaning).] A beacon or sea-mark. *Obs.*

1584 R. NORMAN tr. *Safegard of Sailers* 50b, When you are a little within, there [Norway coast] stands a little Warder which is a beacon or marke before the entrie. *Ibid.* 53b, Then as far from that lies another little rocke in sight aboue water, and there stands a warder or marke vpon it. **1588** ASHLEY *Wagenar's Mariners Mirr.* II. Plot VII, On the North side stande two warders [Du. *twee warderen*] vpon a high hill.

warder ('wɔːdə(r)), *sb.*⁴ *rare.* [f. WARD *v.*¹ + -ER¹.] †**a.** *Fencing.* One who parries. **b.** One who wards off (something). Also ***warder-off.***

1599 G. SILVER *Paradoxes of Def.* Wks. (1898) 7 It is a great question, and especially amongst the Rapier-men, who hath the vantage of the thruster, or of the warder. *Ibid.* 13 [He] hath the aduantage, whether he be striker, thruster or warder. **1871** R. ELLIS *Catullus* lxviii. 63 Mallius e'en such help brought me, a warder of harm. **1873** SYMONDS *Grk. Poets* ii. 41 Empedocles..received in consequence the title of κωλυσανέμας, or warder-off of winds.

warder ('wɔːdə(r)), *v.* [f. WARDER *sb.*¹] *trans.* To provide with a warder or sentinel.

1849 RUSKIN *On the old Road* (1905) I. 218 *Samuel Prout*, Its countless churches wardered by saintly groups of solemn statuary. **1850** S. DOBELL *Roman* vi. Poet. Wks. (1875) 92 Heavenly calm Warders the room. **1901** J. H. MCCARTHY *If I were King* vi, The Lord of Montcorbier was, indeed, wardered..by very different stars from the fellow of the Fircone.

warder: see WARDAY.

'warderer. *Obs.* exc. *Hist.* Also ward(e)rere. [Identical with WARDER *sb.*²; if the longer form be the original, it may have been a jocular use of WARDERERE *int.*] A warder or truncheon.

a **1400–50** *Wars Alex.* 838 þan Alexander at þis knyȝt angirs vnfaire, Wynnes him vp a wardrere [*v.r.* wardrerd] he walt in his handis, So hard him hittis on þe hede, his hernes out weltid. *c* **1420** *Prose Life Alex.* (1913) 110 Alexander smate Iobas on þe heued wit a warderere for na trespasse. **14..** *Lat.-Eng. Voc.* in Wr.-Wülcker 567/14 *Bacillus*, a warderere. *a* **1513** FABYAN *Chron.* VII. (1811) 656 þe Kyng.. caste downe a warderer whiche he then helde in his hande. **1523** BERNERS *Froiss.* I. ccclii. 229 Iohan Lyon helde in his hande a whyte warderere. **1843** LYTTON *Last Bar.* IV. vii, By the laws, the combat may go on at thine asking—I retract my warderer.

†**warderere,** *int. Obs. rare.* [a. AF. **ware derere* (*ware* = mod.F. *gare*, look out; *derere* = mod.F. *derrière* behind).] ? Look out behind!

c **1386** CHAUCER *Reeve's T.* 181 Thise sely clerkes rennen vp and doun With keepe, keepe, stand, stand, Iossa, warderere [*v.rr.* ware þe rere, ware derere].

wardering ('wɔːdərɪŋ), *vbl. sb.* [f. WARDER *sb.*¹ + -ING¹.] The business of a warder.

1928 *Daily Express* 23 Nov. 10/3 He has also been a prison warder, and told me that wardering is by no means to be despised.

warderob(e, -rop(p(e, obs. ff. WARDROBE.

wardership ('wɔːdəʃɪp). [f. WARDER *sb.*¹]

1. The office or position of warder.

1867 DE ROS *Memor. Tower Lond.* 301 The Duke [of Wellington] at once stopped the purchase of Warderships.

2. The carrying out of the duties of a warder.

1897 *Edin. Rev.* Jan. 16 To an active and energetic soldier the wardership of these [Trans-Indus] marches offered a tempting field for military distinction. **1907** J. OXENHAM *Carette of Sark* xxv. 238 There was no sound, nor sign of wardership.

wardeyn(e, obs. forms of WARDEN.

ward-fee. [f. WARD *sb.*² + FEE *sb.*¹]

†**1.** In feudal law, a sum of money paid by a vassal to a superior lord in lieu of military service.

1202 in *Cal. Charter Rolls* (1903) I. 257 Sint liberi et quieti ..de hundredfeh, wardfeh, et fisteh, et de operatione castellorum. **1765–8** ERSKINE *Inst. Law Scot.* II. iv. §4 Ward vassals found it their interest to charge the ward fee with a determinate sum, to be paid yearly to the superior.

2. A fee charged in a hospital ward.

1789 J. HOWARD *Lazarettos* 136 Here are *no* ward-fees taken.

'ward-hill. *Orkney* and *Shetland.* Also **wart-hill, wardill.** [f. WARD *sb.*² (after ON. *varða, varð-r* beacon) + HILL *sb.*] A beacon hill.

?*a* **1680** in W. Macfarlane *Geogr. Coll.* (S.H.S.) III. 252 Fabrics..from the top of which when there was any imminent danger, they made a sign by fire one to another. The like they did from Promontories or Wart Hills. **1797** *Encycl. Brit.* (ed. 3) XIII. 499/2 The alarm was given by the beacons lighted on the tops of the rocks and highest mountains. These beacons, known by the name of ward-hills, are still to be seen in every island. **1822** J. LAING *Voy. Spitzbergen* 20 Along the shores are a great many ancient towers, originally known by the name of Burrows or Duns; but by the inhabitants they are now called Wart or Wardhills.

ward-holding. *Sc. Hist.* [f. WARD *sb.*² + HOLDING.] In feudal law, a tenure of lands in ward (see WARD *sb.*² 9), i.e. by military service.

1681 STAIR *Instit.* I. xiii. §31. 252 The main importance of a Ward-holding was indefinite service to be performed by the Vassal to his Superiour, and especially in War. **1684** SIR G. MACKENZIE *Inst. Law Scot.* II. iv. (1694) 71 Ward-holding, which is the properest holding, is called *servitium militare*; and all Lands are therefore presumed to hold Ward, except another holding be express'd. *a* **1712** in W. Macfarlane *Geneal. Coll.* (S.H.S.) II. 154 He got his Ward Holding changed into Taxt Ward. **1747** *Act 20 Geo. II*, c. 50 (*title*) An Act for taking away the Tenure of Ward Holding in Scotland. **1897** J. C. LEES *Hist. Inverness* xii. 204 The right of ward-holding, by which landlords commanded the military services of their tenants, was also done away with.

attrib. **1758** J. DALRYMPLE *Ess. Feudal Property* (ed. 2) 246 The ward-holding act and the jurisdiction act were the ideas of..lord Bacon.

†**'wardhouse.** *Obs.* Also 7 *Sc.* **waird-.** [f. WARD *sb.*² + HOUSE *sb.*]

1. (*the*) *Wardhouse*: used to render Norw. *Vardøhuus*, the name of a fortress situated on the island of Vardö, off the NE. coast of Norway.

1555 in Hakluyt *Voy.* (1589) 295 Articles..determined for the Commission of the Merchants of this company resiant in Russia, and at the Wardhouse, for the second voiage. **1557** A. JENKINSON ibid. 334 Being at this North Cape the 2. day of July, we had [etc.].. The 3. day we came to Wardhouse. **1615** I. R. *Trades Increase* 4 Whereas the Hollander..betweene the Warde-house and the Eastward, at Tippenie, Kilden, Olena,..and at Saint Nicholas in Russia, had aboue thirty fiue sailes of their shippes the last yeare.

2. A guard-house for prisoners. *Sc.*

1590 *Reg. Privy Council Scot.* IV. 538 Ane sufficient wardhous for prisonaris. **1611** *Burgh Rec. Stirling* (1887) I. 127 The lettres..concerning prissones and wairdhoussis. **1618** *Extracts Aberd. Reg.* (1848) II. 357 Thomas Watsoune, maister measone to the bigging of the wardhous.

3. ? A post or station of a military guard.

1633 SIR J. BURROUGHS *Sov. Brit. Seas* (1651) 83 The King of Denmarke at his Wardhouse in the Sound, hath for a Licence a Doller.

Wardian ('wɔːdɪən), *a.* [f. the name of the inventor, N. B. *Ward* + -IAN.] In *Wardian case*, a close-fitting case with glass sides and top for growing small ferns and other moisture-loving plants.

1842 D. MOORE *Let. N. B. Ward* 1 Feb., in Ward *Growth of Plants in Gl. Cases* App. 91, I find all the species of ferns ..to grow well either in glazed Wardian cases, under hand-lights, or in close frames. **1845** *Florist's Jrnl.* (1846) VI. 230 Many of the Alpines may also be successfully grown in Wardian cases. **1877** *Encycl. Brit.* VI. 642/1 The writer has kept the *Cenobita Diogenes* from the Antilles, tenanting an *Achatina* shell, alive in a Wardian case for three months.

wardill, obs. Sc. form of WARD-HILL, WORLD.

‖**wardin.** *Obs. rare.* Also **vardin.** [Du. *waardinn*, fem. of *waard* (= G. *wirt*) landlord.] A landlady, hostess.

1493 HALYBURTON *Ledger* (1867) 5 Paid to our vardin of Bery 4s. that scho lent hym. *Ibid.*, Paid for a gon [= gown] that I causit our wardin frist hym.

wardin, obs. form of WARDEN.

warding ('wɔːdɪŋ), *vbl. sb.*¹ [f. WARD *v.*¹ + -ING¹.]

1. The action of guarding (a place) or furnishing it with a guard.

c **1425** tr. *Vegetius' De Re Milit.* (MS. Digby 233) lf. 222 b/2 More necligent of here wardynge of here walles. **1595** *Locrine* III. ii. 54 What strange accidents Makes you to leaue the warding of the campe.

b. The action or duty of keeping guard. Chiefly in ***watching and warding***: see WATCHING *vbl. sb.*

1633 P. FLETCHER *Purple Isl.* VI. xxxi, And while his weary kingdome safely sleeps, All restlesse night he watch and warding keeps. **1724** in Temple & Sheldon *Hist. Northfield, Mass.* (1875) 202, 1 day's work with his oxen..and 1 day's warding for a soldier which did work at the mount.

†**2.** *concr.* **a.** A defensive force or work. **b.** The body of watchmen. *Obs.*

a. 13.. *K. Alis.* 7114 (Laud MS.), Þer he dude his meignee alle Abouten þe diches maken walle And holde hem wiþinne wiþ grete wardynges. **1382** WYCLIF *Ezek.* iv. 2 And thou shalt ordeyne aȝens it a bisegynge; and thou shalt bilde waardingis [1388 strengthis; Vulg. *munitiones*].

b. 1549 WRIOTHESLEY *Chron.* (Camden) II. 25 And this day the wardinge of the gates beganne their watch in harnis.

3. Imprisonment. *Sc.*

1497 *Acta Dom. Conc.* II. 48 Andro..was chargit to compere under the pane of warding of his person. **1524** *Diurn. Occurr.* (Bannatyne Club) 9 All the kirkis of thar dyocies wer interdyted induring their [*sc.* the two bishops'] wairding. **1563–4** *Reg. Privy Council Scot.* I. 259 The said Alexander is be hir Hienes fred of his said warding. **1601** P. OGLEBY in *Buccleuch MSS.* (Hist. MSS. Comm.) 33 What satisfaction can my warding be to England. **1689** in *Acts Parlt. Scot.* (1875) XII. 75/2 Executione Be poynding and wardeing against the deficients in payment of the town revenue. **1825** SCOTT *Talism.* xvi, He was put under warding for a time. **1826** G. J. BELL *Comm. Laws Scot.* (ed. 5) II. 538 The warrant for imprisonment for debt in Scotland, analogous to that under the English statute-merchant, is called an Act of Warding. **1912** E. RUSSELL *Maitland of Lethington* vii. 237 By wholesale warding of all who were thought dangerous..she..kept them from joining Moray.

4. Guardianship, keeping.

1548 UDALL, etc. *Erasm. Par. Luke* xi. 1–4 That thei maie vnder the tuicion and wardyng of their heauenly father, bee safely defended against Satans ingiens. **1893** STEVENSON *Catriona* xv, They began to crack about the Bass and which o' them twa was to get the warding o't.

5. The fashioning of the wards of keys, in ***warding file*** (see quots.).

1846 HOLTZAPFFEL *Turning* II. 824 Sometimes, as in the warding files for locksmiths, the two broad surfaces are left uncut or safe. **1881** YOUNG *Every Man his own Mechanic* §1495. 676 If a key will not exactly fit a little filing of the nicks with a thin flat file called a 'warding file' may have the desired effect.

6. Comb.: †**warding-place**, (*a*) a place where guard is kept; (*b*) *Sc.*, a place of confinement for prisoners.

1571 GOLDING *Calvin on Ps.* lv. 15 Like as one warding-place maketh souldyers felowelike in a camp. **1573** *Reg. Privy Council Scot.* II. 232 Thay intendit to have biggit..a warding place and a place of pressoun for keping of malefactouris. **1752** J. LOUTHIAN *Form of Process* 78 All Persons in whose Custody the said C.D. is detained, furthwith to set him at Liberty, out of their Tolbooths, and others their warding Places.

†**'warding**, *vbl. sb.*² [Aphetic form of *awarding.*] Judicial award.

1485 *Rolls of Parlt.* VI. 274/2 The said Actes of Atteindre and Forfeiture, Disableing, Inditements, Warding of Exegent, [etc.].

'warding ('wɔːdɪŋ), *ppl. a.* [f. WARD *v.*¹ + -ING².] That wards or guards; protecting.

1697 DRYDEN *Æneis* VII. 1013 Short crooked Swords in closer Fight they wear, And on their warding Arm light Bucklers bear. **1916** A. G. MITCHELL *War Songs* 13 Thy guiding, warding Arm we own.

wardite ('wɔːdaɪt). *Min.* [f. the name of Henry A. *Ward* (1834–1906), U.S. naturalist and dealer + -ITE¹.] A hydrated basic phosphate of sodium and aluminium, $NaAl_3(PO_4)_2(OH)_4.2H_2O$, found as transparent tetragonal crystals.

1896 J. M. DAVISON in *Amer. Jrnl. Sci.* CLII. 154 A considerable quantity of this mineral has been received by Ward's Natural Science Establishment, of Rochester, N.Y. It is in the form of nodules and shows the mineral in several shades of green, and one specimen of pure milk-white... I would give [it] the name of Wardite, in honor of Prof. Henry A. Ward, of Rochester. **1942** [see MILLISITE]. **1952** *Amer. Mineralogist* XXXVII. 849 Wardite in well-formed, white to colorless crystals has been found in a pegmatite at Beryl Mountain near West Andover, New Hampshire.

wardle, obs. Sc. form of WORLD.

Ward-Leonard (wɔːd'lɛnəd). *Electr. Engin.* Also **Ward Leonard.** The name of Harry *Ward Leonard* (1861–1915), U.S. electrical engineer and inventor, used *attrib.* to designate a method of controlling a direct-current motor in which its armature current is supplied by an auxiliary d.c. generator (driven by an a.c. motor), the field current of which is varied to vary the speed of the motor.

1902 H. A. FOSTER *Electr. Engineer's Pocket-bk.* 737 The motors are controlled by the Ward-Leonard system. **1969** *Jane's Freight Containers 1968–69* 541/1 All three designs have the following features: rack operated traversing gear driven by a motor through Ward Leonard control [etc.]. **1981** CARLSON & GISSER *Electr. Engin.* xix. 745 This arrangement, known as the Ward-Leonard system, also provides regenerative braking.

wardless ('wɔːdlɪs), *a.*¹ [f. WARD *v.* + -LESS.] That cannot be parried.

1693 S. HARVEY *Juvenal's Sat.* IX. (1697) 236 He gives like Destiny a wardless Blow.

wardless ('wɔːdlɪs), *a.*² *rare.* [f. WARD *sb.*² 24 a + -LESS.] Of a key: having no wards.

1927 R. A. FREEMAN *A Certain Dr. Thorndyke* xv. 220 These wardless pin-keys are more subtle than they look.

wardlie, wardly, obs. Sc. ff. WORLDLY.

†**'wardman.** *Obs.* [f. WARD *sb.*¹ + MAN *sb.*¹ Cf. WARDSMAN².]

1. In certain boroughs, a member of a select body of burgesses, representing the several wards, and empowered to choose municipal officers.

1444 *Maldon* (Essex) *Liber A* lf. 32 b, The xviii wardemen that day shall chese the newe baylees and other officers of the moste worthi men. **1467** *Maldon* (Essex) *Court-Rolls* Bundle 43 no. 6ᵛ, All the wardemen ben acorded that John Parll the elder is put owt of yᵉ ward.

2. In certain boroughs, the designation of an officer employed by the corporation.

1792 BOYS *Coll. Hist. Sandwich* 403 When the mayor goes in form to the court-hall,..he is preceded by the common wardman [L. *communis serviens*] and the two sergeants at mace. **1835** *App. Munic. Corpor. Rep.* II. 1043 [Officers of the corporation of Sandwich]. Town Clerk. Common Wardman. Serjeants at Mace. *Ibid.* IV. 2527 The other Officers of the corporation [of Stamford] are a Gaoler... Collector of Stallage. Beadle and Wardman.

wardmote ('wɔːdməʊt). Also 4–7 **wardemote,** (7 **vordimote, wardmoot**); (6 *in combinations corruptly* **warmoll, warnmall, wardmol**). [f. WARD *sb.*² + *mote*, MOOT *sb.*¹] A meeting of the citizens of a ward; esp. in the City of London, a meeting of the liverymen of a ward under the presidency of the alderman.

1377 LANGL. *P. Pl.* B. Prol. 94 Somme seruen þe kyng and his siluer tellen, In cheker and in chancerye chalengen his dettes Of wardes and wardmotes [*v.r.* wardemotes] weyues and streyues. *a* **1513** FABYAN *Chron.* VII. (1811) 340 That euery aldreman in his warde, shulde vpon the morowe folowynge, assemble his wardemote, and that all those wardemootys shuld assemble in one place. **1603** STOW *Surv. Lond.* 268 The said crosse hauing beene presented by diuers Iuries (or quests of Wardmote) to stand in the high way to the let of cariages (as they alledged). **1682** *Lond. Gaz.* No. 1730/3 Sir Thomas Bludworth Alderman for the Ward of Aldersgate, being lately dead, the Wardmoot met this day in order to the supplying the Vacancy. **1758** *Payne's Universal Chron.* 21–28 Oct. 237/1 Yesterday Mr. Alderman Alsop held a Wardmote at Armourer's-hall, for the election of a Common Council-man for Coleman-street Ward. **1861** *Daily Tel.* 24 Oct., Yesterday a wardmote was held at the King's Arms Hotel, Newgate St., before Mr. Alderman Phillips, for the election of a representative of the ward in Common Council. **1897** *Daily News* 22 Dec. 4 The various wards into which the City is divided assembled yesterday in wardmote.

b. *attrib.* and *Comb.*, as ***wardmote court, man***; **wardmote horn**, a horn formerly blown before the houses of the members of a wardmote court to call them to a meeting; **wardmote inquest, quest**, (*a*) a judicial inquiry made by a wardmote; (*b*) the body of men composing a wardmote; also *attrib.*, as ***wardmote inquest man***.

1607 COWELL *Interpr.* s.v., Wardmote, is a court kept in euery ward in London..ordinarily called among them, the *Wardmote Court. **1899** A. C. BENSON *Life Abp. Benson* II. i. 5 He then drove to the Guildhall [at Canterbury] where he was greeted with loud blasts upon the *Wardmote horn. **1529** S. FISH *Supplic. Beggers* (1871) 9 Your grace may se whate a worke there is in London, howe the bisshoppe rageth for endyting of certayn curates of extorcion and incontinency the last yere in the *warmoll quest. **1540** *Act 32 Hen. VIII* c. 17 §3 To enquire bothe in their Quarter cessions, and all wardemote enquestis to be kept within the Citie of London. **1545** BRINKLOW *Lament.* 91 There is a custome in the Cytie, ones a yeare to haue a quest called the warnmall queste, to redresse vices. **1603** STOW *Surv. Lond.* 225 Candlewicke street warde..hath now..Wardmote inquest men 12. **1606** DEKKER *Sev. Sinnes* 33 In whose Ship [of Fools] whilest they all are sayling, let vs obserue what other abuses the vordimotes Inquest doe present on the lande, albeit they bee neuer reformed, till a second Chaos is to bee refined. **1632** B. JONSON *Magnetic Lady* I. ii, For of the Wardmote Quest, he better can, The mysterie, then the Levitick Law. **1603** STOW *Surv. Lond.* 139 This ward [Tower street] hath..*Wardmote men thirteene. *Ibid.* 152 Aldgate-warde..hath..Wardmote men for inquest eighteene.

†**wardnape, -napp.** *Obs.*⁻¹ [a. OF. **wardenappe*, dial. var. of *gardenappe.*] = GARDNAP.

c **1475** *Cath. Angl.* 408/1 A Wardnapp [**1483** a Wardnape], *limas, limus.*

'war-dog. A dog trained for use in war (formerly, to attack the foe; latterly, for carrying messages, sentry-work, etc.). Also *fig.*, a fierce warrior (cf. *sea-dog*); *U.S.* one whose voice is for war, a 'war-hawk'.

1813 *Columbian Centinel* 23 Oct. 2/1 in A. Matthews *Uncle Sam* (1908) 28 War-dogs. **1846** *Congressional Globe* 18 Apr. 687/1 The gentleman regarded 54° 40′ men as 'war-hawks' and 'war-dogs!' **1852** THACKERAY *Esmond* II. ix, In the hour of battle..the Prince..shrieked curses and encouragement, yelling and harking his bloody war-dogs on, and himself always at the first of the hunt. **1856** EMERSON *Eng. Traits, Race* Wks. (Bohn) II. 30 But they know where their war-dogs lie. Cromwell, Blake, Marlborough, Chatham, Nelson, and Wellington, are not to be trifled with. **1877** *Encycl. Brit.* VII. 325/2 Corinth was said to have been saved by 50 war dogs, which attacked the enemy that had landed while the garrison slept. **1894** *Daily News* 1 June 6/7 A type-writing cyclist, who sends despatches back from the front by a war-dog. **1900** *United Service Mag.* Jan. 425 The umpires decided that the carrying of despatches was the first and indispensable qualification for a 'war-dog'. **1920** E. H. RICHARDSON (*title*) British War Dogs.

†**wardon.** *Sc. Obs.* Also **werdoune.** [a. OF. **werdon*, dial. var. *guerredon*.] = GUERDON *sb.*

c **1375** *Sc. Leg. Saints* xxvii. (*Machor*) 1358 Quhill god of richtwisnes þi full far crowne þe giff in hewine to þi werdoune. *Ibid.* xliii. (*Cecilia*) 164 Of martirdome þe fare crone to bruk in hewine as ȝoure wardone.

wardon(e, obs. forms of WARDEN².

wardor, -our(e: see VERDOUR¹, WARDER.

Wardour Street ('wɔːdəstriːt).

1. The name of a street in London, formerly occupied mainly by dealers in antique and imitation-antique furniture. Used *attrib.* in ***Wardour-street English***, applied to the pseudo-archaic diction affected by some modern writers, esp. of historical novels. Also in other attrib. phrases.

1888 A. BALLANTYNE in *Longm. Mag.* Oct. 585 (*title*) Wardour-Street English. *Ibid.* 589 This is not literary English of any date; this is Wardour-Street Early English—a perfectly modern article with a sham appearance of the real antique about it. **1896** *Sat. Rev.* 8 Feb. 154/2 Our Wardour Street romancers and whimpering Scotch humourists. **1918** *Spectator* 20 Apr. 422/1 What we are obliged by our sincerity to describe as thoroughly bad, Wardour Street English. *Ibid.* 422/2 There are obvious reminiscences of..*Ivanhoe* in this piece of most unblushing but rather vivid Wardour Street. **1958** L. FORSTER in *Aspects of Translation* 20 The peculiar Wardour Street language which some classical scholars used for English a generation or so ago. **1976** *New Yorker* 19 Apr. 118/3 To the difficulty of following Borgese's Wardour Street diction ('Bread and wine needs a man to fight and die'; 'Us enchants he, but eke frightens') Sessions adds that of hearing the words.

2. Used *attrib.* and *absol.* with reference to Wardour Street as a centre of the British film industry.

1920 *Stage Year Bk.* 51 A still more ambitious 'ten million pound' company died even before it became more than a Wardour Street fairy tale. **1927** *Melody Maker* Aug. 818/3 A 'phone message, or note perhaps, from Wardour-street. **1948** *Daily Mail* 7 Feb. 2/5 This has caused a few long faces in Wardour-street. **1958** *Punch* 17 Sept. 360/1 Any Wardour Street film-distributor knows that the public wants a boy-girl story, a happy ending..and sensational spectacle. **1975** *Times* 20 Dec. 9/7 It amazes me how few films we manage to make in a year here: Wardour Street seems to have accepted defeat.

'**wardpenny.** *Obs.* exc. *Hist.* Also **war-.** [f. WARD *sb.*² + PENNY.] In feudal law: A rent paid to the superior in commutation of military service.

? **1087** *Charter* in G. F. Warner & Ellis *Facsimiles* (1903) ii, Cum Omnibus Rebus & Regalibus Consuetudinibus sibi adiacentibus. Scilicet Cum Saca & Socna & Tol..& Warpenig [*sic*] & Murdrum. **1161-2** *Pipe Roll 8 Hen. II* (1885) 62 Et Monachis de Sancto Edmundo..xvj.d. in Warpeni [*printed* Warpent]. **1177** *Charter of Hen. II* in Gervase of Canterb. *Chron.* (Rolls) I. 262 Wardpeni [*v.r.* warpini]. **1253-1378** [see AVER- 3]. **1398** *Cockersand Chartul.* (Chetham) 1083 Quite of amerciament..of the helpes of worke of any Castells, houses,..warpenye, withdrawpeny. **1415** [see WARDCORN]. *c* **1450** *Godstow Reg.* 665 Quyte..of summage and cariage, of warde peny, and aver-peny, [etc.].

wardraipper, -rape: see WARDROBER, -ROBE.

wardress ('wɔːdrɪs). Also **warderess.** [f. WARDER *sb.* + -ESS.] A female warder in a prison.

1878 E. C. GRENVILLE-MURRAY *Russians To-day* 87 A servant girl, who is committed for trial on a charge of thieving, often gets a smart flagellation or two at the hands of a stout-armed wardress. **1885** *Standard* 28 Aug. 6/3 A Wardress of Millbank proved two previous convictions.

wardrobe ('wɔːdrəʊb). Forms: 4-7 **wardrop, -ropp,** 5-6 **-roppe,** (4-5 **wadrop,** 5 **warderop,** 6 **warderoppe),** 4-5 **warderope,** 4-8 **wardrope, warderobe,** (5 **warddrope,** 6 **warderob,** *Sc.* **wardroippe, -rape, wairdrope,** 7 **waredrop),** 4- **wardrobe.** [a. OF. *warderobe*, north-eastern var. of *garderobe*: see GARDEROBE.]

†**1. a.** A room in which wearing apparel (sometimes armour) was kept; esp. a room adjoining the 'chamber' or sleeping apartment; hence, a dressing-room. *Obs.*

In the 16-18th c. often applied (after the contemporary F. *garderobe*) to a room for keeping costly objects generally, not merely articles of clothing.

1387-8 T. USK *Test. Love* II. ix. (Skeat) l. 140 Jupiter hath in his warderobe bothe garmentes of joye and of sorowe. ? *a* **1400** *Morte Arth.* 901 Aftyre euesange, sir Arthure hyme selfene Wente to hys wardrope, and warpe of hys wedez, Armede hym in a actone [etc.]. *Ibid.* 2622 A knafe of his chambyre Has wroghte in his wardrope wynters and ȝeres, One his longe armour. *Ibid.* 4217 He braydes owte a brande ..That..In the wardrop of Walyngfordhe was wonte to be kepede. *a* **1400-50** *Bk. Curtasye* 429 in *Babees Bk.*, The marshalle shalle herber alle men in fere, That ben of court of any mestere; Saue þe lordys chambur, þo wadrop to, þo vssher of chambur schalle tent þo two. *c* **1460** J. RUSSELL *Bk. Nurture* 939 In þe warderobe ye must muche entende besily the robes to kepe well & also to brusche þem clenly. **1519** *Registr. Aberdon.* (Maitl. Club) II. 174 The chawmer abun þe wardrape with Item ane standing bed of aik wiþouit lofting. **1574** in Gage *Hengrave* (1822) 202 To young John Dawson for xvij days work sewing in the wardrope, *vs.* viijd. **1590** SPENSER *F.Q.* I. x. 39 The third had of their wardrobe custodie, In which were not rich tyres, nor garments gay,.. But clothes meet to keepe keene could away. **1596** RALEGH *Discov. Guiana* 11 He had in his wardroppe hollow statues of golde. **1599** SHAKS. *Hen. V*, II. Chorus 2 Now..silken Dalliance in the Wardrobe lyes: Now thriue the Armorers. **1631** MAY tr. *Barclay's Mirr. Mindes* I. 170 His Lord laughing heartily, commanded a furrd gowne to bee brought out of his wardrope, and put vpon him. **1683** J. REID *Scots Gard'ner* (1907) 4 Above the dining-room story may be bed-chambers,..and above these you may have garrets for wardrops. *a* **1700** EVELYN *Diary* 25 Jan. 1645, In the wardrobe above they shew'd us fine wrought plate, porcelan, [etc.]. **1717** PRIOR *Dove* xxv, Her Keys He takes; her Doors unlocks; Thro' Wardrobe, and thro' Closet bounces. **1756-7** *Keysler's Trav.* (1760) I. 37 In the royal wardrobe at Paris, they shew you the whole suit of armour which Francis wore on that memorable day. **1831** SCOTT *Kenilw.* VI, With this enviable sleeping apartment.. corresponded two wardrobes, or dressing-rooms as they are now termed. **1847** HALLIWELL, *Wardrope*, a dressing-room. *Yorksh.* **1859** ROSE PIDDINGTON *Last of Cavaliers* I. xvii. 230 The general scene of their conversations..was Lady Flora's dressing-room, or wardrobe as it was then called. This apartment was divided on the inside from her sleeping-chamber by three or four steps.

b. A room in which theatrical costumes and properties are kept.

1711 ADDISON *Spect.* No. 44 ⁋5 It is indeed very odd..to observe in the Wardrobe of the Play-house several Daggers, Poniards, Wheels, Bowls for Poison. **1867** *Chamb. Encycl.* IX. 390/1 There are also numerous apartments required in connection with the stage..—such as..the wardrobe, in which the costumes are kept; furniture stores, scene stores.

c. A movable closed cupboard, fitted with hooks or pegs, or with shelves or movable trays and drawers, in which wearing apparel is kept; esp. as a piece of bedroom furniture.

1794 A. HEPPLEWHITE *Cabinet-Maker* (ed. 3) *title-p.*, Displaying a great variety of patterns for Chairs,..Basin Stands, Wardrobes, [etc.]. **1833** LOUDON *Encycl. Archit.* §626 Wardrobes are as essential in a bed-room, as a dresser is in a cottager's kitchen. **1842** DICKENS *Amer. Notes* iii, Our bedroom..had one unusual luxury, however, in the shape of a wardrobe of painted wood. **1864** MISS BRADDON *Doctor's Wife* I. x. 256 A lumbering old wardrobe—or press, as it was called—of painted wood. **1883** D. C. MURRAY *Hearts* xi. (1885) 82 A great old-fashioned wardrobe of black oak.

d. *transf.* and *fig.*

1605 *1st Pt. Jeronimo* III. ii. 17 Now death..crams his store house to the top with bloud; Might I now and Andrea in one fight Make vp thy wardroope richer by a Knight. **1624** DONNE *Devot.* vi. (ed. 2) 136 Whether it bee thy pleasure, to dispose of this body, this garment so, as to put it to a farther wearing in this world, or to lay it vp in the common wardrope, the graue, for the next. **1630** *R. Johnson's Kingd. & Commw.* 543 In this Countrie that false Prophet [Mahomet] first opened his superstitious Wardrobe. **1656** COWLEY *Pindar. Odes, To Mr. Hobs* v, I little thought..That all the Wardrobe of rich Eloquence, Could have afforded half enuff, Of bright, of new, and lasting stuff, To cloath the mighty Limbs of thy Gigantique Sence. **1754** *Connoisseur* No. 36 ⁋7 France appears to be the wardrobe of the world. **1821** LAMB *Elia* I. *Imperf. Sympathies*, Their intellectual wardrobe (to confess fairly) has few whole pieces in it. **1866** G. MACDONALD *Ann. Q. Neighb.* xxxi. (1878) 539 The dead bodies were laid aside in the ancient wardrobe of the tomb.

2. The office or department of a royal or noble household charged with the care of the wearing apparel. Also, the building in which the officers of this department conduct their business.

removing wardrobe, that which moves with the Court, as distinguished from ***standing wardrobe***, one that is permanently attached to a royal residence.

1433 *Rolls of Parlt.* IV. 439/1 The which Warantes yf I shuld paye hem, youre Household, Chambre, and Warderope, and youre Werkes, shuld be unservid and unpaide. **1450** *Ibid.* V. 193/2 Oure servaunt Richard Wadnyng, Grome of oure Warderobe of Bedds. **1500-20** DUNBAR *Poems* lii. 10 ȝour Hienes can nocht gett ane meter, To keip your wardope, nor discreter, To rule ȝour robbis, and dress the sam. **1524** *Reg. Privy Seal Scot.* I. 496/2 Ane Lettre to James Dog..makand him ȝeman of the Kingis wardrop. **1553** *Rec. St. Mary at Hill* (1905) 55 These parselles of ornamenttes..were Receued of Arthur Stovrton at ye Qvenes wardroppe at westminster. **1601** SHAKS. *Twel. N.* II. v. 45 The Lady of the Strachy, married the yeoman of the wardrob. **1642** *Docq. Lett. Pat. at Oxf.* (1837) 334 Clement Kinnersley yeoman of his Majesties removinge wardrobe of Beddes. **1642** Standinge Wardrobe [see STANDING *ppl. a.* 11]. **1668** PRYNNE *Aurum Reg.* 127 The Queen [has] the Tayle, to make Whale-bones for her Royal Vestments, Dresses, and other uses in her Wardrobe. **1755** H. WALPOLE *Let. to Mann* 29 Sept., Sir Thomas Robinson is to return to the Great Wardrobe, with an additional pension on Ireland of 2000 *l.* a year. **1886** *Encycl. Brit.* XXI. 37/1 The bedchamber, privy chamber, and presence chamber, the wardrobe, the housekeeper's room,..are in the lord chamberlain's department. **1909** *Whitaker's Almanack* 102 His Majesty's Household... Superintendent of the Wardrobe.

3. a. A person's stock of wearing apparel.

a **1400-50** *Bk. Curtasye* 565 in *Babees Bk.*, The chaunceler answeres for hor clothyng, For ȝomen, faukeners, and hor horsyng, For his wardrop and wages also. **1599** B. JONSON *Cynthia's Rev.* II. i, If he be furnish'd with supplies for the retyring of his old ward-robe from pawne. **1610** SHAKS. *Temp.* IV. 222. **1632** LITHGOW *Trav.* VII. 332 It often hapneth; that a toule and deformed carkasse hath a faire and rich wardrope. **1672** MARVELL *Reh. Transp.* I. 111 This onely troubles me, how his majesty would look in all..the Pontifical Wardrobe. *a* **1727** NEWTON *Chronol. Amended* v. (1728) 339 Officers who took care of the Perfume, the Veil, and the Wardrobe of the Priests. **1760-2** GOLDSM. *Cit. World* lxii, With her scanty wardrobe packed up in a wallet, she set out on her journey on foot. **1834** MRS. CARLYLE *Let. to Mrs. Carlyle, Sen.* 21 Nov., Lett. & Mem. 1883 I. 10 The weather is grown horribly cold, and I am chiefly intent, at present, on getting my winter wardrobe into order. **1870** MISS BRIDGMAN *R. Lynne* II. iii. 55 He insisted on his wife re-marking the whole of the infantile wardrobe.

b. *transf.* and *fig.*

1592 BRETON *Pilgr. Parad.* (Grosart) 8/1 Came Flora forth ..Laying abroad the wardrope of her wealth, Her fairest flowers. **1613** JACKSON *Creed* I. 78 Vsually the Græcian Poets haue borrowed their best Stage-attire from the glorious wardrope of Israel. **1633** MARMION *Fine Companion* III. iii, A soule..Wherein is lockt the wardrope of all vertues. **1637** MILTON *Lycidas* 47 As killing as..Frost to Flowers, that their gay wardrop wear, When first the White thorn blows. **1856** EMERSON *Eng. Traits, Literature* Wks. (Bohn) II. 109 New and gigantic thoughts which cannot dress themselves out of any old wardrobe of the past.

†**4.** A private chamber; esp. a sleeping apartment. *Obs.*

a **1300** *Cursor M.* 1686 [In the Ark] A hous als in to drink and ete And wardropp þat þou noght for-get. *a* **1450** *Knt. de la Tour* vi. 8 As sone as she had herde a litell masse..she come into the warderobe to ete browesse or som other mete. *c* **1450** *Merlin* xxvii. 507 Gyomar..a-bode spekynge with Morgain..in a wardrope vnder the paleys, where she wrought with silke and golde. *a* **1548** HALL *Chron., Edw. IV*, 227 b, Kyng Lewes..withdrew himself into hys warderobe, and sending for the English Herault sayd to hym [etc.]. **1570** BUCHANAN *Admonit.* Wks. (S.T.S.) 32 This is nowther dreamit in ane wardrob nor hard throw ane boir bot ane trew narrative. **1670** COTTON *Espernon* II. VI. 254 The King without any motion was carried up in a Cloak, and laid upon the Bed in his Wardrobe.

†**5.** A privy. *Obs.* [So F. *garderobe*.]

1382 WYCLIF *2 Kings* x. 27 Thei distroyeden the hous of Baal, and thei maaden for it wardropis [1388 priuyes, Vulg. *latrinas*] vnto this day. *c* **1386** CHAUCER *Prioress' T.* 120, I seye that in a wardrobe they hym threwe Where as thise Iewes purgen hire entraille. *c* **1450** *Nominale* (Harl. MS. 1002) lf. 145 *Cloaca*, a pryvaye or wardrope. **1847** HALLIWELL, *Wardrope*, a house of office.

†**6.** The excrement of the badger. *Obs.*

c **1400** *Master of Game* (MS. Digby 182) xxiv, Of hares and of conynges he shall say þei croteth, and of þe fox wagynge, of þe grey þe warderobe. **1847** HALLIWELL, *Warderebe* [sic], the dung of the badger.

7. *attrib.* and *Comb.*, as ***wardrobe account, -keeper, -maid, -man, -woman***; also **wardrobe bedstead**, a bedstead adapted to fold up into a wardrobe; **wardrobe book**, a book in which the accounts of a wardrobe were kept; **wardrobe dealer**, a dealer in second-hand clothes; **wardrobe master, mistress**, one who has charge of the professional wardrobe of an actor or actress, or of a theatrical company; **wardrobe-room**, the room, at a theatre, in which the stage-costumes are stored; †**wardrobe-stuff**, household necessaries and supplies; **wardrobe trunk**, a travelling trunk which can be used as a wardrobe.

1770 *Archæologia* I. 361 Observation on the *Wardrobe Account for the Year 1483. **1830** N. H. NICOLAS (*title*), Privy Purse Expenses of Elizabeth of York: Wardrobe Accounts of Edward the Fourth. **1806-7** J. BERESFORD *Miseries Hum. Life* xx. xxviii. (ed. 3) II. 249 Starting out of your sleep on a *wardrobe bedstead, at the sudden desertion of the temporary posts at the bottom. **1557** *Order of the Hospitalls* G viij, You shall also kepe the *Wardrobe-booke, wherein shalbe written..the remainder of all thinges at euery Michaelmass [etc.]. **1896** *Daily News* 8 Apr. 3/6 *Wardrobe dealer. **1763** *Crt. & City Kalendar* 81 *Wardrobe-keeper and Keeper of the Royal Apartments at Somerset House. Mrs. Brietzcke, 100l. **1782** D. E. BAKER *Biogr. Dram.* I. 25/2 This gentleman..had been wardrobe-keeper to the Theatre in Black-Friars. **1821** SCOTT *Kenilw.* xv, The wardrobe keeper,..shall have orders to supply the suit which you have cast away in our service. **1865** QUEEN VICTORIA *Jrnl.* 9 Oct. (1980) 121 The Duchess took me to my room..next to which was one for my *wardrobe maid, Mary Andrews. **1899** *Allbutt's Syst. Med.* VIII. 425 The patient..became wardrobe maid at the Salpêtrière. **1583** *Leg. Bp. St. Androis* 1021 in *Satir. Poems Reform.* xlv, The Bischop..Send for his *wardrop man fre hand. **1667** PEPYS *Diary* 2 Sept., He swore..that the king his father would have hanged his Wardrobeman, should he have been served so. **1833** HT. MARTINEAU *Three Ages* ii. 50 His wardrobeman had this morning lamented that the King had no handkerchiefs. **1897** EMILY SOLDENE *Theatr. & Mus. Recoll.* xxix. 249, I.. made over the whole of my wardrobe, both personal and professional, to my *wardrobe master. *Ibid.* xvi. 137 Mrs. Quinton, my *wardrobe mistress, whose husband was super-master. **1885** JEROME *On the Stage* iv. 31 A little lower down was the *wardrobe room. There was not much in it though. Dresses are borrowed as they are wanted, now, from the costumiers. **1537** *Rutland MSS.* (Hist. MSS. Comm.) IV. 286 Item paid to Peter Barret for his dyner, when he helpe to cary my Lorde's *wardrope stuffe to Grynwyche, ijd. **1890** B. HALL *Turnover Club* 221 In Matt's *wardrobe trunks there are very many suits. **1928** S. LEWIS *Man who knew Coolidge* I. 39 She pointed out I'd have to get my dress-suit in New York and it wouldn't get wrinkled in a wardrobe trunk. **1979** *Country Life* 16 Aug. 490/3 The murderee..had in his Louis Vuitton wardrobe trunk, full white-tie evening dress. **1853** DICKENS, etc. *Househ. Words* Christm. No. 2/2 Jane was a sort of *wardrobe-woman to our fellows [at school], and took care of the boxes. **1892** W. S. GILBERT *Foggerty's Fairy* 213 She obtained a little employment as dresser and wardrobe-woman at a provincial theatre. **1897** *Westm. Gaz.* 6 July 6/3 Mrs. M'Donald..had been for forty years in the Queen's service, thirty-one of which as wardrobewoman.

wardrober ('wɔːdrəʊbə(r)). *Obs.* exc. *Hist.* Forms: 5 **ward(e)ropere,** *Sc.* **wardropar,** 5-7 **wardroper,** (6 **werdroper),** 6 *Sc.* **wardraipper, -raipair,** 5 **warderober,** 5- **wardrober.** [ad. OF. *warderobier*, dial. var. of *garderobier*, *-rober*, f. *warde-*, *garderobe*: see prec.]

1. An officer of a royal household who had charge of the robes, wearing apparel, etc.

a **1400–50** *Bk. Curtasye* 481 in *Babees Bk.*, þo vsshere schalle bydde þo wardropere Make redy for alle nyȝt be-fore þe fere. *c* **1420** WYNTOUN *Cron.* VIII. xviii. 2867 Prewaly his wardropere He gert to þis Robert ber. *Ibid.* 2877 þe siluir to þe wardropar He gaf. **1430–40** LYDG. *Bochas* IX. xxxiv. (1554) 214 By processe he was made wardropere. *c* **1475** *Rauf Coilȝear* 276 The King buskit him sone, with scant of Squyary. Wachis and Wardroparis all war away. **1500–20** DUNBAR *Poems* li, Of James Dog, kepar of the Quenis wardrop.. The Wardraipper of Wenus boure, To giff a doublett he is als doure, As it war off ane futt syd frog. **1642** FULLER *Holy & Prof. St.* IV. viii. 275 One who had well licked his fingers under Queen Margaret (whose Wardroper he was). **1878** J. GAIRDNER *Rich. III*, iv. 129 An indenture dated the 27th of June in the first year of Richard III, in which Peter Curteys, the king's wardrober, undertakes to furnish..the articles specified for the coronation.

†**2.** The tailor attached to a religious house. *Obs.*

1526 *Visit. Dioc. Norwich* (Camden) 200 Uxor scissoris videlicet the wardroper's wiff.

ward-room. [WARD *sb.*²]

1. The mess-cabin of naval commissioned officers above the rank of sub-lieutenant; hence, the commissioned officers as a body.

Since 1948 ward-rooms have been used by warrant officers as well as commissioned officers.

1758 in *Ann. Reg. 1758* (1791) 306/1 On Thursday the 13th inst. at half an hour past one in the afternoon, word was passed into the ward room, by the centry, that the fore part of our ship, the Prince George, was on fire. The lieutenants ran immediately forward. **1801** NELSON in Nicolas *Disp.* (1846) VII. p. ccxxx*, The Wardrooms will prate, I believe, none of us can doubt. **1815** *Falconer's Dict. Marine* (ed. Burney), *Ward-room*, in ships of war, a room over the gun-room, where the lieutenants, and other principal officers, sleep and mess. **1850** H. MELVILLE *White Jacket* I. vi. 35 In a [U.S.] frigate it comprises the after-part of the berth-deck. Sometimes it goes by the name of the Gun-room, but oftener is called the Ward-room. **1902** *Monthly Rev.* Aug. 103 The engineer is received into the ward-room on his own merits. **1948** *Admiralty Order* in *London Gaz.* 25 June 3719/1 We are of the opinion that all officers of the Warrant Officer classes should be regarded as Wardroom Officers for messing purposes and the Warrant Officers Mess as such be abolished.

2. A military GUARD-ROOM.

1853 JAMES *Agnes Sorel* II. iv. 53 A page ran into the ward-room of the gate-tower. **1902** *Lond. Mag.* VIII. 444/2 Closing the ward-room door behind him he then shut the gate, thrusting the bolts into their places.

3. A room or hall used for the meetings of a city ward. *U.S. rare.*

1895 *Funk's Stand. Dict.* **1911** WEBSTER.

4. *attrib.*, as ***ward-room mess***, ***officer***, ***rank***.

1887 GUNTER *Mr. Barnes* xix. 138 Danella was soon *en rapport* with the *ward-room messes of half the British squadron. **1850** H. MELVILLE *White Jacket* I. vi. 36 Besides the First Lieutenant, the *Ward-room officers include the junior lieutenants, in a [U.S.] frigate six or seven in number, the Sailing-master [etc.]. **1867** SMYTH *Sailor's Word-bk.*, *Ward-room officers*, those who mess in the wardroom, namely: the commander, lieutenants, master, chaplain, surgeon, paymaster, marine-officers, and assistant-surgeons. **1850** HUXLEY in L. Huxley *Life* (1900) I. iv. 46 He is a great advocate for the claims of assistant surgeons to *ward-room rank.

†'**wardrope.** *Obs.* In 4 warderape. [? f. WARD *v.*¹ + ROPE *sb.* But cf. WARROPE.] A rope for some mechanical purpose.

1338 *Durham Acc. Rolls* (Surtees) 376 Item ij warderapes quarum utraque de xiiij fadomes.

wardrope, -roper: see WARDROBE, -ROBER.

'**war-drum.** A drum beaten as a summons to war or an accompaniment to the fray. Also *fig.*

1593 PEELE *Edw. I*, A 3 b, Welcome, manly followers, That..on your war drums carry crownes as kings. **1809** CAMPBELL *Gert. Wyom.* III. xx, But hark! what nearer war-drum shakes the glade? **1842** TENNYSON *Locksley Hall* 127 Till the war-drum throbb'd no longer, and the battle-flags were furl'd. **1880** MCCARTHY *Own Times* IV. lvii. 245 He beat the war-drum this time with tremendous energy.

-wards, *suffix*, OE. *-weardes*, corresponds to OS., MLG. *-wardes*, Du. *-waarts*, OHG., MHG. *-wartes*, early mod.G. *-warts*, the ending of the neut. genit. sing. (used adverbially) of adjs. in OTeut. **-warđo-*: see -WARD. A parallel formation of identical function, the adverbial neut. genit. sing. of adjs. in OTeut. **-werþo-* (ablaut var. of **-warđo-*), is represented by Goth. *-wairþis*, OHG. *-wertes*, early mod.G. *-werts*, now written *-wärts*. The adverbial genitives of adjs. in **-warđo-*, **-werþo-* appear to have in early Teut. differed little if at all in sense from the advb. accusatives.

1. In English the history of *-wards* as an advb. suffix is identical with that of *-ward* (see -WARD 3 and 4); beside every adv. in *-ward* there has always existed (at least potentially) a parallel formation in *-wards*, and vice versa. The two forms are so nearly synonymous (the general sense of the advs. being 'in the direction indicated by the first element of the compound') that the choice between them is mostly determined by some notion of euphony in the particular context; some persons, apparently, have a fixed preference for the one or the other form. Sometimes, however, the difference in the form of the suffix corresponds to a difference in the shade of meaning conveyed, though it would not be possible to give any general rule that would be universally accepted. Where the meaning to be expressed includes the notion of manner as well as direction of movement, *-wards* is required, as in 'to walk backwards', 'to write backwards'. In other instances the distinction seems to be that *-wards* is used when the adv. is meant to express a definite direction in contrast with other directions: thus we say 'it is moving *forwards* if it is moving at all', but 'to come forward', not 'forwards' (see further the note on FORWARD *adv.*); so 'to travel eastward' expresses generally the notion of travelling in the direction of an eastern goal, 'to travel eastwards' implies that the direction is thought of as contrasted with other possible directions. Hence *-wards* seems to have an air of precision which has caused it to be avoided in poetical use.

There appears to be no appreciable difference in meaning between the prepositions TOWARD and TOWARDS; the latter is now, at least in British use, more common colloquially. The now obsolete prepositions FROMWARD and FROMWARDS appear to have been perfectly synonymous.

2. In OE. the suffix *-weardes*, like *-weard*, was added to phrases containing the preps. *tó* and *wiđ* (see -WARD 5). In the locutions *to..ward(s*, *from..ward(s* (the so-called tmesis of the prep.), the two forms of the suffix were formerly equally common, but *-wards* now survives only in dialects.

3. Examples of ***to..wards***.

a. with proper name or sb. without article or other defining word.

c **1374** CHAUCER *Troylus* I. 59 Yt is wel wist how þat Grekes stronge In armes with a þousand shippes went To Troye-wardes. *c* **1430** *Contin. Brut* 430 And tho the Kynge disposid hym to Godwardis. **1560**, *c* **1645** [see GODWARDS]. **1622** R. HAWKINS *Voy. S. Sea* xxii. 53 Our other Shippes.. having kept their direct course, and far to windwards and Sea-wards, could not heare the report. **1650** W. BROUGH *Sacr. Princ.* (1659) To Rdr. A 3, Using them [*sc.* Books]..as ..Guides and Helps to Heaven-wards. **1892** M. C. F. MORRIS *Yorksh. Folk-Talk* 260 The addition of 'wards' to nouns as a suffix denoting direction is frequent in our folk-talk—as 'ti Newton-wards' or 'fra Newton-wards'.

b. with sb. determined by definite article or otherwise.

1415 EARL CAMBRIDGE in *43rd Rep. Dep. Kpr. Rec.* 589 My wyttys arne not to ye world wardys so redy as yey werne. **1565** SPARKE in Hakluyt *Voy.* (1589) 532 He marched to the townewards.

c. with pers. pron.

1387–8 T. USK *Test. Love* I. x. (Skeat) l. 121 If that Margarite denyeth now nat to suffre her vertues shyne to thee-wardes with spredinge bemes. *Ibid.* III. viii. (Skeat) l. 148 Aungels blisse that to-him-wardes was coming. **1399** LANGL. *Rich. Redeles* III. 76 þe nedy nestlingis..burnisched her beekis and bent to-him-wardis. *c* **1400** MAUNDEV. (Roxb.) xxviii. 128 And, when þe Cristen men sawe þam com to þam wardes, þai ware riȝt ferde. **1442** T. BECKINGTON *Corr.* (Rolls) II. 216 The continuancis of true obeissaunce unto us wardes of our subgetts. **1472** SIR J. PASTON in *P. Lett.* III. 58 Also I praye yow feele my Lady off Norfolks dysposicion to me wards. **1574** W. BOURNE *Regiment for Sea* xiv. (1577) 42 If you remoue the transitory but a quarter the length of the transitory to youwards. **1583** GOLDING *Calvin on Deut.* cxx. 738 When God gathereth vs to him by death, wee cease not to liue still to himwardes. *a* **1586** SIDNEY *Arcadia* II. v. §3 Ever concluding ech thing he did with his face to me-wards. **1635** J. HAYWARD tr. *Biondi's Banish'd Virg.* 20 Behaving my selfe unmanerly to-you-wards. *Ibid.* 169 The courteous inclination to me-wards, which to my good hap I discover in you. **1648** HERRICK *Hesper.*, *Love me little* 55 You say, to me-wards, your affection's strong; Pray love me little, so you love me long.

4. Examples of ***from..wards***.

1548 VICARY *Anat.* viii. (1888) 63 Two Latitudinales comming from the backe-wardes to the wombe. **1574**, **1669** [see SUNWARDS 1]. **1612** R. CH. *Olde Thrift newly revived* 76 The degrees of a Quadrant are likewise 90, from the Centre towards your right hand, hauing the Sines vpmost, & holding the Centre from you wards. **1644** DIGBY *Nat. Bodies* xxx. (1658) 322 The objects comming into the glasse by a superficies not parallel..but slooping, from the objectwards. **1665** [see TAILWARDS]. **1678** MOXON *Mech. Exerc.* iv. 64 Not letting the Plain [= plane] totter to, or from you-wards.

5. Examples of nonce-words (advs.) f. sb., proper name, or pers. pron. + *-wards*.

1670 T. BROOKS *London's Lament.* 124 Yet the bent of their hearts will still be God-wards, Christ-wards, Heaven-wards, and Holiness-wards. **1842** THACKERAY *Fitz-Boodle's Prof.* i, The nobles come peoplewards as the people..rise and mingle with the nobles. **1842** BROWNING *Let.* 13 July in F. G. Kenyon *Robert Browning & Alfred Domett* (1906) 39 Here is a slip just off you-wards and I write at night. **1845** FABER *Lett.* (1869) 229 Seventeen persons strikingly converted..some really being led in extraordinary ways, and perfectionwards. **1850** THACKERAY *Contrib. Punch* Wks. 1898 VI. 683 A third darling, with..eyes of hazel, lifts them up ceiling-wards. **1866** TROLLOPE *Claverings* iii, Mr. Burton was not..an ambitious man. He had never soared Parliamentwards. **1866** H. H. FURNESS *Let.* 14 Nov. (1922) I. iii. 156 If you were anyone else than the dear.., kindly fellow that I knew & loved.., I should never dare to write this letter, my manifold sins of omission you-wards would palsy my hand and freeze my ink. **1868** *Rep. Munit. War* 60 The chief feature of the invention..consists in the contrivance adopted for preventing the escape of gas breech-wards. **1878** HUXLEY in *Fortn. Rev.* XXIII. 170 The theory of the motion of the blood returned once more to the strait road which leads truthwards. **1887** *Pall Mall Gaz.* 21 July 4/1 Russiawards the new line may be fire-fringed and fatal. Afghanwards it is no such thing. **1893** K. GRAHAME *Pagan Ess.* 145 Aunt Eliza's fowls—already strolling roostwards. **1893** D. C. MURRAY *Time's Revenges* I. vii. 129 He was growing downwards, brutewards.

wardship ('wɔːdʃɪp). [f. WARD *sb.*² + -SHIP.]

1. The office or position of guardian.

a. The guardianship of a minor; *spec.* in *Feudal law*, the guardianship and custody of the person and lands of a minor with all profits accruing during his minority.

1454 *Paston Lett.* I. 306 Sir, forasmych as the Kyng hathe grauntyd be hese lettres patent the wardship with the profites of the londes of T. Fastolf duryng hese nun age to you and T. H. [etc.]. **1540** *Act 32 Hen. VIII*, c. 46 Personnes, to whom the kinges highnes shall graunt the custodye and wardeship of any of his graces wardes. **1543** tr. *Act 3 Edw. I* c. 47 And yf an other wardeyne than the chiefe lorde do it, he shall lese the wardshyp of all togyther. **1586** T. RANDOLPH in Ellis *Orig. Lett.* Ser. II. III. 123 The Master of Glames and the Secretarye have gotten of the King the wardshippe and marriage of the Erle Mongomeris sonne, being but two yeares of age. **1641** EARL MONM. tr. *Biondi's Civ. Warres* v. 127 He gave him two rich wardships. **1766** BLACKSTONE *Comm.* II. v. 67 The lord was intitled to the wardship of the heir; and was called the guardian in chivalry. This wardship consisted in having the custody of the body and lands of such heir, without any account of the profits, till the age of twenty one in males, and sixteen in females. **1870** FREEMAN *Norm. Conq.* (ed. 2) I. iv. 210 King Lewis may have already begun to entertain some dim notion that wardship over the fief of a minor vassal was a right which of necessity belonged to the Lord. **1884** *Law Times* LXXVII. 309/1 Sect. 35..assigns to the Chancery Division the wardship of infants.

b. *gen.* Guardianship, protection, custody. Chiefly *fig.*

1631 WEEVER *Anc. Funeral Mon.* 456 [He] freed this kingdome from the wardship of the Peeres. **1635** QUARLES *Embl.* II. iii. 5 Thou grand Impostor, how hast thou obtain'd The wardship of the world! **1641** MILTON *Reform.* II. 43 This is the master-piece of a modern politician,..how the puny Law may be brought under the wardship and controul of lust and will. **1647** CLARENDON *Contempl. Ps.* Tracts (1727) 385 Truth itself is so much in the wardship of Almighty God,..that if all other means fail, he will by his own immediate power vindicate it. **1765** BLACKSTONE *Comm.* I. ix. 335 This officer is of equal antiquity with the sheriff; and was ordained together with him to keep the peace, when the earls gave up the wardship of the county. **1825** SCOTT *Betrothed* xxix, I pray you let me have the grace to take first possession of the Garde Doloureuse, and the wardship or forfeiture of the offending lady. **1884** LD. ROSEBERY in *Pall Mall Gaz.* 9 Dec. 7/2 Great Britain could have no wish for selfish annexation. She was already committed to wardship and protection of an empire such as the world had never yet seen. **1887** HALL CAINE *Deemster* xxxvii, I try in these my last days to put my memory under wardship.

2. The state or condition of being a ward; *spec.* in *Feudal law*, the condition of being under guardianship as a minor.

1549 COVERDALE, etc. *Erasm. Par. Gal.* iv. 4–5 Assone as we came out of wardeship, and wer growen vp to a ryper age. **1553** T. WILSON *Rhet.* 66 In lamentyng the miserye of wardeshyppes, I might saie it is not for noughte so communely said, I wil handle you like a warde. *a* **1577** SIR T. SMITH *Commw.* (1609) 111 The man is not out of Wardship by our Lawe till one and twenty yeere olde, from thence hee is reckoned of full age, as well as in the Romaine Lawes at fiue and twenty. **1579–80** NORTH *Plutarch*, *Demosthenes* (1612) 846 When he came out of his wardship, he beganne to put his guardians in suite. **1631** MASSINGER *Emperor East* II. i, *Theod.* Let it suffice My wardships out. If your designe concernes vs As a man, and not a boy, with our allowance You may deliuer it. **1641** BAKER *Chron.*, *Rich. II*, 10 He was somewhat more then one and twenty; Well, then (said he) I am out of Wardship. **1780** BENTHAM *Princ. Legisl.* xvi. §44. 266 *note*, In certain nations, women, whether married or not, have been placed in a state of perpetual wardship. **1874** GREEN *Short Hist.* iii. §5. 140 Three English earls who were in royal wardship were wedded by the King to foreigners.

b. *transf.* and *fig.*

a **1577** SIR T. SMITH *Commw. Eng.* (1609) 7 Lewes the xi. ..was wont to glorie and say, he had brought the crowne of Fraunce, *hors de page*, as one would say, out of wardship. **1648** FAIRFAX, etc. *Remonstr.* 46 To deliver His Crown once for all, from Wardship (as he counts it) to Parliamentary power. **1800** COLERIDGE *Piccolom.* I. iii. 112, I must perforce Leave him in wardship to his innocence. **1876** BANCROFT *Hist. U.S.* II. xxvii. 186 We have written the origin of our country; we are now to pursue the history of its wardship.

†'**wardsman**¹. *Obs.* [f. *ward's* genit. of WARD *sb.*³ (= AWARD) + MAN *sb.*] An arbitrator.

1482 *Cely Papers* (Camden) 107 The warddysman hath sen yowre lyve lodd and entyd hit in her bokes. **1622–3** (28 Feb.) *Essex Archdeaconries, Depositions bk.* (MS.) lf. 27 b, Mr. Sweno and Mr. Knivett should be wardes men to end all matters and controversies betwene them.

wardsman² ('wɔːdsmən). [f. *ward's* genitive of WARD *sb.*² + MAN *sb.* Cf. WARDMAN.]

1. In certain boroughs: A member of the governing body, consisting of representatives elected by the several wards.

1712 SIR R. ATKYNS *Glouc.* 347 Cirencester..hath two High-Constables and fourteen Wardsmen over seven distinct Wards, appointed yearly at the Court-Leet.

2. An inmate appointed to supervise his ward in a prison or workhouse.

1789 J. HOWARD *Lazarettos* 125 To every ward here [Newgate], and at both the Compters, there is an orderly prisoner called a *wardsman*, who should wash, sweep and keep his ward fresh and clean. **1821** SYD. SMITH Wks. 1859 I. 339/1 Wardsmen, selected in each yard among the best of the prisoners, are very serviceable. **1836** DICKENS *Sk. Boz, Visit to Newgate*, The wardsmen and wardswomen are all prisoners, selected for good conduct. **1891** *Daily News* 26 Dec. 5/5 'That man I employ as wardsman,' observed the master [of the workhouse].

3. A watchman who is responsible for prisoners.

1683 T. ELLWOOD *Life* (1885) 126 [The watchman].. went out to seek the constable... He was a young man,.. somewhat better mannered than his wardsman.

So **'wardswoman**.

1836 DICKENS *Sk. Boz, Visit to Newgate*, In every ward on the female side, a wardswoman is appointed to preserve order. **1897** *Daily News* 17 Sept. 7/3 An aged inmate, wearing the workhouse clothes, said she was night wardswoman of the infirm ward.

wardun, wardur: see WARDEN², VERDOUR¹.

†**'wardwite.** *Obs.* [OE. *weardwíte*: see WARD *sb.*² and WITE *sb.*] A fine paid to the lord by a tenant who has failed to provide a man to perform castle-guard.

1066 *Charter Edw. Conf.* in Thorpe *Charters* (1865) 411 Nomina consuetudinum.. mundbryche, burhbryce, miskænninge,.. weardwite, hængewite, hamsokne [etc.]. **1227** in *Cal. Charter Rolls* (1903) I. 6 [Grant to the church of St. Mary, Coventry, and the prior and monks thereof of all their lands and holdings with soc and sac,.. ficht-wite, ward-wite, and mund-briche]. *c* **1250** *Gloss. Law Terms* in *Rel. Ant.* I. 33 Wardwite.. Quite de wardein truver. *c* **1290** *Fleta* I. xlvii. (1647) 63 Wardwyte quietantiam misericordiæ in casu quo non invenerit hominem ad wardam faciendam in castro, vel alibi. **1381** *Cal. Patent Rolls* 1381–5 (1897) 54 Granting them exemption from burghbote, brugbote, wardwyte, horngeld, and scot. *c* **1440** JOHN BROMPTON in Twysden *Hist. Angl. Script. X.* (1652) 957 Wardewithe est sursise de garde. **1579** *Expos. Terms Law* 187 b, Warwite (or wardwite as some copies haue it) that is to bee quite of giuing of money for keeping of watches.

wardyn, obs. form of WARDEN¹ and ².

ware (wɛə(r)), *sb.*¹ *Sc.* and *dial.* Forms: 1 **wár** (waar, uaar, uar), 6 **wayr, vare**, 6–7 **wair**, 7 **war, waar, weir**, 8 **wear**, 8–9 **waur(e**, 5– **ware**; see also *Eng. Dial. Dict.* and ORE⁵. [OE. *wár*, corresp. to NFris. *wier* neut. sea-weed, pond-weed, whence prob. Du. *wier* neut. (first found in Kilian, referred to the 'Holland' dialect), repr. OTeut. **wairo-m*, f. **wai-*: *wī-* to bind: see WIRE *sb.*] Seaweed; esp. large drift seaweed used as manure. In *Scots Law*, the right of gathering seaweed on the shore. Also SEAWARE.

c **725** *Corpus Gloss.* A 434 *Alga*, waar. **1491** *Reg. Mag. Sig. Scot.* 429 Insulam et rupem de Inchgarde.. cum mettagiis, ancoragiis, *le wrak* et *ware*. **1513** DOUGLAS *Æneis* VII. x. 104 Skelleis and fomy cragis thai assay, Routand and rarand, and may nocht empayr, Bot geif thai shed fra his sydis the wayr. **1528** in *Trans. Roy. Hist. Soc.* VI. 374 With fre ingress and regress to the wayr and fra the wayr. **1544** in *Reg. Mag. Sig. Scot.* 1545, 727/1 Cum privilegio lucrandi *lie wair* marium pro terris stercorandis. **1574** R. SCOT *Hop Garden* (1578) 2 If you shall feele a Clod (being dissolued with water) to be very clammy or cleauing like Ware to your fyngers in kneading it, the same to be profitable lande. **1643** *Orkney Trial* in Dalyell *Darker Superst. Scotl.* (1834) 492–3 Ye sall .. be fain to eat grass vnder the stanes and wair vnder the bankis. **1659** SOMNER *Dict.*, *Waar*, Alga marina,.. called.. of the Thanet-men Wore or woore. **1721** in W. Macfarlane *Geogr. Collect.* (S.H.S.) I. 45 The sea being tossed with an East and North Wind, yeelds a great quantity of salt water weeds, which the Countrey [sic] call Ware, it fattens the ground and makes it yeild plentifully. **1727** E. LAURENCE *Duty of Steward* 206 Wear, a Sea-weed growing chiefly on such Rocks as are cover'd only at High-water, is good to be laid on Tillage for one Crop, the drying and burning of which makes Kilp, used in making Glass. **1812** SIR J. SINCLAIR *Husb. Scot.* I. 187 The ware, however, in that part of the frith, is of a weaker sort.

b. *attrib.* and *Comb.*, as *ware-barley*, *-bear* (BEAR *sb.*²), *-goose*, *-hack*, *-strand*.

1806 FORSYTH *Beauties Scot.* IV. 522 Distillers prefer the *ware-barley.. on account of its fairer colour and thinner husk. **1793** *Stat. Acc. Scot.* VI. 17 *note*, When bear or big is manured with sea ware, the crop is very abundant, but the grain is very small, and is known by the name of *Ware-bear. **1852** MACGILLIVRAY *Brit. Birds* IV. 629 *Bernicla Brenta*. The Black-faced Bernicle-goose... *Ware Goose. **1585–6** *Durham Wills* (Surtees) II. 131, iiij pycke forkes,.. iij *ware hackes. **1909** J. GUNN *Orkney Bk.* 230 Each *ware-strand, or beach where drift-weed comes to land, is set apart for a certain number of tenants on the estate to which it belongs.

†**ware**, *sb.*² *Obs.* [OE. *waru* fem. = OFris. *ware*, OS., OHG. *wara* (MHG. *ware*, *war*):—OTeut. **warō*, f. **war-* to guard, watch:—pre-Teut. **wor-*; cf. Gr. ϝορ- in θυρωρός (*θυρā-ϝορός) doorkeeper.] Watchful care, heed; safe-keeping, defence, protection. Phr. ***on ware***, on one's guard, cautious.

c **893** ÆLFRED *Oros.* v. iv. (1883) 224 For þon Antiochus ȝiemde hwæt he hæfde monna ȝerimes, & ne nom nane ware hulice hie wæron. *a* **1000** *Guthlac* 718 Stod se grena wong in godes wære. **1297** R. GLOUC. 2483 Vor wanne ich am dukes sone, it become to me Vor to abbe some gret cite oþer castel me to ware. *c* **1300** in Wright *Lyric P.* 46 Ah feyre levedis be on-war, To late cometh the ȝeyn char, when love ou hath y-bounde. *c* **1400** *Destr. Troy* 7380 Honerable Ector, þat eger was ay, Euer waker and vnwar [= on ware], wightist in armys.

ware (wɛə(r)), *sb.*³ Forms: 1 **waru**, 4–6 **war**, (4 **quare, whare**), 5–6 **warre**, 6 **waar**; 5–6 *Sc.* and *north.* **wayr(e**, 6 **wayere**, 6–7 **wair(e**; 2 **ware**. [OE. *waru* fem. = OFris. *were*, MLG., MDu. *ware* (Du. *waar*), ON. *vara* (Sw. *vara*, Da. *vare*). MHG. *ware*, *war*, G. *ware* (earlier *waare*) are from MLG. or MDu.

Prob. the same word as WARE *sb.*² used in the concrete sense 'object of care'.]

1. A collective term for: Articles of merchandise or manufacture; the things which a merchant, tradesman, or pedlar, has to sell; goods, commodities. **a.** *collect. sing.*

c **1000** ÆLFRIC *Hom.* I. 246 Hi ðа wurpon heora waru oforbord. *a* **1100** *Voc.* in Wr.-Wülcker 311/35 *Merx*, waru. *c* **1205** LAY. 11356 Chæpmen bunden heore ware. *a* **1300** *Cursor M.* 4180 Wit camels þat gret birþin bar, O spice and of oþer ware. *c* **1386** CHAUCER *Wife's Prol.* 522 Greet prees at market maketh deere ware. **1484** CAXTON *Fables of Alfonce* i, The merchaunt of Baldak came in to egypte for to chepe & bye somme ware or marchaundyse. **1542–3** *Act 34 & 35 Hen. VIII*, c. 10 §2 Putting the same naughtie ware to sale secretly. **1614** OVERBURY *Wife* etc. (1638) 126 Its now like Ware miss-laid in a Pedlers pack; a ha 's it but knowes not where it is. **1634** SIR T. HERBERT *Trav.* 61 The windowes of painted glasse (no common ware). **1697** DRYDEN *Virg. Past.* iv. 47 No Keel shall cut the Waves for foreign Ware. **1748** SMOLLETT *Rod. Rand.* viii, He certainly intended to make free with the pedlar's ware. *c* **1820** [see PIEMAN]. **1822** SCOTT *Peveril* xlii, I am always provided with ware which a gentleman may risk his life on. **1844** KINGLAKE *Eothen* xviii, The owners raised various objections to the display of their ware [*sc.* white slave-girls].

b. *pl.*

c **1000** ÆLFRIC *Hom.* II. 120 Ða ȝelamp hit æt sumum sæle .. þæt Englisce cypmenn brohton heora ware to Romana-byriȝ... þaȝeseah he betwux ðam warum cype-cnihtas ȝesette. *c* **1400** *Destr. Troy* 1581 There were stallis by þe strete stondyng for peopull, Werkmen into won, and þaire wares shewe. **1487** *Cely Papers* (Camden) 165 He avysyth yow to bestowe yowre mony in grosse warys now betymys. **1567** HARMAN *Caveat* 62 Consideringe wyth hym selfe that wares woulde bee welcome where money wanted. **1622** BACON *Hen. VII*, 188 With whom ventured also three small Shippes of London-Merchants, fraught with some grosse and sleight Wares, fit for Commerce with barbarous people. *a* **1625** FLETCHER *Woman's Prize* v. i, Give 'em as little light As Drapers doe their wares. **1698** *Acts Massachusetts* (1724) 117 Leather.. wrought into Shoes, Boots, or other Wares. **1776** ADAM SMITH *W.N.* IV. ii. II. 52 A capricious man of fashion might sometimes prefer foreign wares, merely because they were foreign, to cheaper and better goods of the same kind that were made at home. **1834** JAMES *J. Marston Hall* I. xii. 159, I perceived.. a man in the dress of a pedlar, with his box of wares laid down by his side. **1913** G. EDMUNDSON *Ch. Rome 1st C.* v. 123 A fire broke out.. amidst shops containing inflammable wares.

c. An article of merchandise, a saleable commodity. *rare.*

1881 *Contemp. Rev.* Oct. 600 They treated him [*i.e.* the labourer] as a ware, buying him in the cheapest market. **1896** A. E. HOUSMAN *Shropshire Lad* iv, Breath's a ware that will not keep.

2. With defining word, as ***dye-***, ***dyeing-***, †***fell-***, ***grocery-***, †***haberdash(er-***, ***mercery-***, ***peltry-ware***: see quots. and s.v. the first element. Also HARD-WARE, HOLLOW-WARE, IRONWARE, †LENTRINWARE, SMALL-WARE(S, TABLEWARE, and others mentioned in 3.

1398 TREVISA *Barth. De P.R.* XVI. xlv. (Tollemache MS.), It is þe maner to tempre yren ware [L. *ferramenta*] with oyle, leste þey be to muche hardened by coldenesse of water. **1408** *Little Red Bk. Bristol* (1900) 105 La dusseyn de souliers appelez Courseware.. vij d. **1515–18** *Early Chanc. Proc.* 379/29 (*List* p. 5) Pannys named haberdasher ware. **1585** HIGINS *Junius' Nomencl.* 490/2 An habbardasher, or seller of smal wares. **1612** *Sc. Bk. Rates* in *Halyburton's Ledger* (1867) 309 Glasses called looking glasses, halfpenny wair the groce,.. xls., penny wair the groce, iiiili. **1617** MORYSON *Itin.* III. 80 Nurnberg wares (so they call small wares). **1683** *Brit. Spec.* 46 In exchange for Tynne and Lead.. they received Earthen Vessels, Salt and Brazen Ware of the Phænicians. **1838** *Murray's Handbk. N. Germ.* 167 Spa is famous for a peculiar manufactory of wooden toys, somewhat like the Tunbridge ware. **1888** *Encycl. Brit.* XXIII. 607/1 Tunbridge ware.. includes work tables, boxes, toys, &c., made of hard woods.. and inlaid with mosaic.

3. In *spec.* uses. **a.** Vessels, etc., made of baked clay. Chiefly with defining word, as *brown*, *china-* (CHINA¹ 3 a), *Delf-*, *glass-*, *Japan*, *porcelain*, *pottery*, *Queen's*, *Staffordshire*, *Wedgewood ware*: see these words, and EARTHENWARE, STONEWARE.

1741 W. STEPHENS *Jrnl.* 23 July in *Colonial Rec. Georgia* (1908) IV. Suppl. 199 He had lately drawn his Kiln of Ware, which was baking a second Time. **1761** *Brit. Mag.* II. 101 Constant at ev'ry sale, the curious fair, Who longs for Dresden, and old China ware. **1827** FARADAY *Chem. Manip.* v. (1842) 149 If [the pestle is] in two pieces,.. the handle being of wood and the bottom only of ware, the cement by which they are fastened occasionally falls out. **1882** 'OUIDA' *In Maremma* I. 127 Vases and jars in black ware. **1911** G. MACDONALD *Roman Wall in Scot.* xi. 370 Both classes of vessel are of the same coarse ware.

†**b.** Textile fabrics. Hence CODWARE², a pillow-case, for which also *ware* simply is found.

1442 *Rolls of Parlt.* V. 60/2 Persones that maken untrewe ware of all maner Worstedes. **1551–2** *Acc. Ld. High Treas. Scot.* X. 49 Item, for tway coddis.. Item, four elnis bartane claith to be waris to the samyn. **1557** NORTH *Gueuara's Diall Pr.* Prol. (1568) *ij, For euen as by the yard the marchante measureth al his ware: so by the life of the Prince is measured the whole common weale. **1661** *Sc. Acts Chas. II* (1814) VII. 61/1 Item, eightein cods with their wairs worth three merk the peice. **1713** ADDISON *Ct. Tariff* ¶2 Euerything he wore was substantial honest, home-spun ware. **1748** Millinery ware [see MILLINERY 3].

c. Field-produce, crops, vegetables. Now *dial.* and *Trade* (= large potatoes intended for sale). Also in attrib. phr. ***ware potato***.

1398, 1669 [see CODWARE¹ 1]. **1562, 1750** field-ware [see FIELD *sb.* 21]. *a* **1661** FULLER *Worthies, Gen.* (1662) 57 Intimating that she had mingled Ware, Corn, and Tares in those who were descended from her. *Ibid.*, *Somerset* 17 No Shire can shew finer ware,.. being generally fruitful. **1693** EVELYN *De La Quint. Compl. Gard.* I. 32 Their Ware is much finer than that of others who water less. **1707** Garden-ware [see GARDEN *sb.* 6]. **1894** BLACKMORE *Perlycross* viii. 57 He had two large butts to receive the filled sacks—assorted into ware and chats. **1920** *Discovery* Nov. 348/2 (Potatoes.) In the North and in Scotland another riddle is used between the ware and the chats, and by this means 'seed' is obtained. **1961** *Ann. Reg. 1960* 509 Heavy imports of new potatoes early in the year depressed the market for old ware potatoes. **1963** *Times* 10 June 7/1 The trade for old ware potatoes in England and Wales is now largely confined to caterers.

†**d.** Live-stock (cattle, sheep, poultry). *Obs.*

1422 *Coventry Leet Bk.* 43 þer schall noo beestys be pynnyd at the comen pynfold by the comien seriante, but chapmannys warre. **1465** Plough-ware [see PLOUGH *sb.*¹ 8]. **1531–2** Poultry-ware [see POULTRY 4]. **1523–34** FITZHERB. *Husb.* §118 If a horse wante wartes behynde, benethe the spauen-place,.. then he is noo chapmannes ware, if he be wylde. **1535** in W. H. Turner *Select. Rec. Oxford* (1880) 133 The bochers.. shall voyd and kyll noe moe ware. **1538** BALE *God's Promises* IV. (facs.) C ij b, By a Soden plage, all their firstgotten ware, Thu slewest in one nyght. *c* **1550** CHEKE *Matt.* xxii. 4 Mi beves and mi fed waar be killed. **1561** DAUS tr. *Bullinger on Apoc.* (1573) 264 b, And first an allusion is made of such as sley wares and prepare a feast. **1609** BIBLE (Douay) *Ezek.* xxxix. 18 Of buck-goates, and bulles, and of fed wares [Vulg. *altilium*]. **1655** MOUFET & BENNET *Health's Improv.* (1746) 143 The like may be also in all gelded Ware, (and consequently in Muttons). *a* **1732** GAY *Fables* (1738) II. 6 Dame Dobbins with her poultry-ware.

e. The spat of oysters in its third year.

1877 *Q. Rev.* CXLIV. 487 A bushel-measure of brood or ware, that is, oysters of the size of a threepenny-piece. **1879** *Cassell's Techn. Educ.* IV. 154/1 Spat in the second year is denominated 'brood'... In the following year 'brood' becomes 'ware'.

4. *transf.* and *fig.*

Formerly often in distinction from *money*, like 'goods'. Sometimes with depreciatory implication, like 'stuff'.

c **1200** *Moral Ode* 68 in *Trin. Coll. Hom.* 222 þis is þet wunderlukeste war þat ani man funde. *a* **1300** *Cursor M.* 16476 Here i yeld yow yur mone, ges me a-gain mi war. *c* **1450** *Cov. Myst.*, *Christ Disputing* (Shaks. Soc.) 197 Wete ȝe not wele that I muste bene Amonge hem that is my faderes ware, His gostly catel for to ovyrsen? **1549** COVERDALE, etc. *Erasm. Par. Jas.* i. 22–7 Ceremonies.. are pernicious ware, yf a man thinke that he is made religious by meane of them. **1600** *1st Pt. Sir J. Oldcastle* III. iv. 53 If you haue no mony, you shal haue ware: as many sound drie blows as your skin can carrie. **1642** D. ROGERS *Naaman* 547 The obedience of hypocrites is dead ware. **1647** CLARENDON *Hist. Reb.* III. §222 They resolved to shew all their ware and to produce the whole evidence. *a* **1661** FULLER *Worthies, Westmerld.* (1662) 135 This County.. is fruitful by some few exceptions, having some pleasant vales, though such ware be too fine, to have much measure thereof. **1793** MRS. PIOZZI 7 Feb. in *Intim. Lett.* (1913) 80 A mythological play of the dark days, Theseus and Ariadne, and *that* old ware. **1865** J. G. HOLLAND *Plain Talk* ix. 314 There is nothing immodest or otherwise improper in the advertisment of a man's literary wares. **1918** *Oxford Mag.* 21 June 343/1 None of them [*sc.* the essayists] cries his own wares to the exclusion of those of others.

b. Applied jocularly to women. (Cf. 'piece of goods'.)

Sometimes with explicit ref. to sense 3 a; cf. also 3 d.

1558 W. FORREST *Grysilde Seconde* (Roxb.) 55 Hee had in hym a lyttle sensuall luste Whiche withe younge ware hee neadys accomplische muste. **1624** DAVENPORT *City Nightcap* IV. (1661) 37, I keep no common company [of women] I warrant ye; we vent no breath'd ware here. **1687** J. PHILLIPS *Quix.* I. I. i. 5 A young fresh-colour'd smerking Country Wench that went for a Maid, but in truth, was a crackt piece of Ware. **1826** SCOTT *Woodstock* x, I may get a peep of fair Rosamond, and see whether she was that choice and incomparable piece of ware which the world has been told of.

†**c.** The privy parts of either sex. Also ***lady ware***. *Obs.*

1561 B. GOOGE tr. *Palingenius' Zodiac* v. M j b, So hurtes the Bees their honye sweete, so makes the Beuer yell His hoysting ware. **1579** G. GILPIN tr. *Marnix van Sant Aldegonde's Beehive Rom. Ch.* (1580) 299 For the auoiding of such a chaunce, the holy Romishe Churche did ordaine twoo chaires too bee heawen of Porphyr stone, where they vsed to feele from vnder, whether the newe chosen Pope was furnished of all his ware. **1592** *Soliman & Pers.* IV. ii. 49 The Ladies of Rhodes, hearing that you haue lost a capitoll part of your Lady ware. **1608** [TOFTE] *Ariosto's Sat.* IV. (1611) 61 The slie Venetian lockt his Ladies ware, Yet through her wit Acteons badge he bare. **1615–16** *Bk. Depositions 1612–16 Archdeaconry of Colchester* (MS.) lf. 72 The said William Land once so drundke at Sturbridge fayer that he did shewe his ware openly in the fayer. **1656** MENNIS & J. SMITH *Mus. Delic.* (ed. 2) 73 Your Breasts all open bare, So farre, that a man may almost see Unto your Lady-ware. **1693** DRYDEN *Juvenal* VI. 491 Seen from afar, and famous for his Ware, He struts into the Bath, among the Fair. **1721** E. WARD *Merry Trav.* I. (1729) 29 Here [at the Lock-hospital] all are welcome to repair Their aching Limbs or damag'd Ware.

†**d.** ***wormes ware***, food for worms. *Obs.*

c **1400** *Pety Job* 7 in *26 Pol. Poems* 121 Yet shall my fayrenesse fade and fle, And I shalbe wormes ware. *c* **1450**

Songs & Carols (Warton Club) 20 ȝyt am I but wermys ware.

e. ***the hale ware*** (Sc.), also anglicized ***the whole ware***: the whole number, quantity, or amount; the sum-total.

1563 WINȜET *Wks.* (S.T.S.) II. 73 Nocht that the canoun allane may nocht be sufficient to the hail wair. *a* **1578** LINDESAY (Pitscottie) *Chron. Scot.* (S.T.S.) I. 154 Sa the haill wair, being comptit, was threttie thowsand pund sterling. **1591** R. BRUCE *Serm.* v. L 6, He saith in the wholware of these things. The life of my soule standeth. *a* **1689** W. CLELAND *Poems* (1697) 18 (Jam.) Then this will follow, I suppose, She drags the whole-ware by the nose. **1742** R. FORBES *Ajax* (1755) 11 He..gar'd the hale-ware o' us trow That he was gane clean wod. **1824** MACTAGGART *Gallovid. Encycl.* 307 The haleware o't seemed to be gran plowable lan. **1894** CROCKETT *Raiders* x, The verra last shot that was fired..carried awa' the halewar (whole) o' their steerin' gear.

†**f.** In periphrastic use (cf. e). *Obs. rare.*

a **1300** *E.E. Psalter* xvii. 11 He flegh ouer fetheres of windes ware [Vulg. *super pennas ventorum*]. *Ibid.* 16 And schewed welles of watres ware [Vulg. *et apparuerunt fontes aquarum*]. *Ibid.* lxxii. 13 And betwix vnderand ware [Vulg. *inter innocentes*] Mine handes wesche i þare.

5. *attrib.* and *Comb.*, as ***wair almery*** (Sc.), ***ware-barge, chamber, -room, trash***; (sense 3 a) ***ware-basin***; (sense 3 b) ***ware-man***; also †**ware-cloth** [? cf. ON. *vǫruklæði* common cloth] (sense uncertain).

1489 *Acta Dom. Conc.* (1839) 131/1 A met almery,.. a *wayr almery. **1698** FRYER *Acc. E. India & P.* 26 These Boats are as large as one of our *Ware-Barges,..and carry a great Burthen with little trouble. **1849** D. CAMPBELL *Inorg. Chem.* 92 In not very nice experiments, instead of a platinum crucible a small *ware basin may be used. **1533** *Linc. Diocese Docum.* (1914) 163, I bequeyth to herry my sone all the ware in my *ware chamber. **1499** *Will of John Buysshope* in *Somerset Medieval Wills* (1901) 379 Item, I bequeith unto John Busshop of Lyme 2 peaces of *ware-clothes. **1659** W. SHEPPARD *Corporations* 16 The Wardens..and Fellowship of Drapers, Taylors, Mercers, and *Ware-Men, and Coopers in D. **1811** PINKERTON *Petral.* II. 96 The first quantity that was exposed in Edinburgh, was in the year 1790, in a *ware-room on the south bridge. **1841** LYTTON *Night & Morn.* I. viii, Mr. Roger Morton and his family sat in that snug and comfortable retreat which generally backs the ware-rooms of an English tradesman. **1655** FULLER *Hist. Cambr.* v. 71 Provision may be made, that a sufficiency of such *Ware-trash may still be preserved.

†**ware,** *sb.*[4] *Obs. rare.* [Seems to represent OE. *wǣr* pledge; the form may have been assimilated to *warant* WARRANT *sb.*] In the phrase ***to ware*** (tr. L. *ad warantiam, ad warantizandum*); as a surety.

c **1460** *Oseney Reg.* 166 Anoþer tyme þabbot i-callid þereof to ware Richard of lyonns And Emme his wife, Raph the Soone of Ranulph of Astrop and William his wife [etc.], the which nowe come by summornenyng and axe to be schewed to þem by what thyng þey bee holde to ware [*warantizare*]. *Ibid.*, Þe which..Byndeth hym-selfe and his heyres to ware, to þe same Nycoll and to his heyres and to his assynes, þe foresaide tenementes.

ware (wɛə(r)), *sb.*[5] *Sc.* and *north. dial.* Forms: 5 waire, wayr(e, 8 wair, 9 waur, 3– ware. See also VOAR. [a. ON. *vár* (Icel. *vor*, Sw. *vår*, Norw., Da. *vaar*).

By some regarded as cogn. w. L. *vēr*, Gr. ἔαρ (:—**wesr*), but the phonology has not been satisfactorily explained.]

The season of spring.

a **1300** *E.E. Psalter* lxxiii. 18 Somer and ware, þou schope þa. *c* **1375** *Sc. Leg. Saints* xxvii. (*Machor*) 983 It hapnyt a tym in-to ware. *c* **1425** WYNTOUN *Cron.* IV. xv. 1484 Wythtin the fyrst moneth off wayre. **1483** *Cath. Angl.* 408/2 Wayr, *quoddam tempus, ver.* **1684–92** A. SYMSON in W. Macfarlane *Geogr. Collect.* (S.H.S.) II. 120 Hence their common proverb, speaking of the stormes in February; Winter never comes till Ware comes. **1814** W. NICHOLSON *Tales in Verse* 70 Ere the winds o' ware were blawn. **1898** J. MACMANUS *Bend of Road* iii. 40 He'll go to him the throngest day of Ware, an' the warmest day in Harwust, an' work the skin off his bones.

b. *attrib.*, as ***ware day, evening, -time***; **ware-corn**, corn sown in spring; *spec.* barley and oats as distinguished from wheat and rye (so Da. *vaarsæd*).

1426 *Inv. Jarrow & Monk-Wearm.* (Surtees) 196 In frumento et *ware corn emptis. **1593** *Durham Wills* (Surtees) II. 235 All the arrable landes,..as well harde corne lande, as ware corne lande. **1810** J. BAILEY *Agric. Durham* 411 *Ware-corn*, barley or oats. **1861** QUINN *Heather Lintie* (1863) 232 In winter, anent her, The birds resume their *ware day sang. **1721** J. KELLY *Scot. Prov.* 334 The *Ware Evening is long and tough, the Harvest Evening runs soon o'er the Heugh. **1820** HOGG *Bridal of Polmood* vii. Tales & Sk. 1837 II. 35, I..fleechyt Eleesabett noore [= never] to let us torfell in the *waretyme of owir raik. **1824** MACTAGGART *Gallovid. Encycl.* 37 Perhaps till the next waurtime.

†**ware,** *sb.*[6] *Obs.* Forms: 3 war, 4–5 ware, 5 wore. [a. ON. **var* (cf. *vare* serum) = MSw., Norw. *var*, OHG. *warah*:—OTeut. **warχo-z* in the same sense. Cf. WARIBREED.] Pus, matter.

c **1200** ORMIN 4782, I war & wirrsenn toc anan Ut off hiss lic to flowenn. *a* **1300** *Cursor M.* 11835 Ouer-al wrang vte worsum and ware. **13..** *Metr. Hom.* (Vernon MS.) in *Archiv. Stud. neu. Spr.* LVII. 298 Fel aunter þat his fot was sare And wox full of fulþe and ware. *c* **1440** *Alphabet of Tales* 390 His feet wan rotyn vnderneth hym & ware come out of þaim. *a* **1450** *North. Passion* (MS. D) 1479 Þei [his hands] were waxen ful of wore þat were not be forn sore [*other texts rhyme* sare: mare]. *c* **1450** *St. Cuthbert* (Surtees) 3494 Ware oute ran, nede to be heeled.

ware (wɛə(r)), *a.* Forms: 1–2 wær (*inflected* wære, ware), 2–7 war, 2–3 warr, 3 wear, 3–5 wer, 4 were, (5 werre), (4 whar, quar, waare), 4–5 *compar.* warr(e, 5 waar, 5–6 warr(e, *compar.* warrer, -are, 4–6 *Sc.* var, 4– ware. [OE. *wær* = OS. *war*, ON. *var-r* (Da., Sw. *var*), Goth. *war-s* (in *warai sijaima* νηφῶμεν 1 Thess. v. 6) :—OTeut. **waro-*, f. **war-* to observe, take care; see WARE *sb.*[2] Cf. AWARE *a.* (OE. *ȝewær* :—OTeut. **ȝiwaro-*).]

I. In predicative use.

1. Cognizant, informed, conscious; chiefly with *of, how, that*, etc. = AWARE 2. †*be (well) ware*: take note, 'nota bene'. *Obs.* exc. *arch.*

O.E. Chron. (Parker MS.) an. 917, & þa wurdon þa landleode his ware, & him wiþ ȝefuhton. *c* **1000** ÆLFRIC *Saints' Lives* xxii. 230 He eode ða nihtes þæt he his life ȝeburȝe ac ða hæðenan wurdon wære his fare. **1154** *O.E. Chron.* (Laud MS.) an. 1140, & hi wurthen war wid uten & folecheden heom. *c* **1200** ORMIN 5210 & Helyseow hiss mann wass warr þatt teȝȝ þa sholldenn shædenn. *Ibid.* 7286 þatt hæþenn follc, Kalldisskenn follc, Wass war off Cristess come. *a* **1225** *St. Marher.* 16 Ant ichulle makien þe war of alle mine wiheles. *c* **1250** *Gen. & Ex.* 1308 Ðo wurð ðe child [Isaac] witter and war ðat ðor sal offrende ben don. *a* **1300** *Cursor M.* 6549 Quen þai war war o moyses þai fled a-way, als in a res. *c* **1325** *Spec. Gy Warw.* 45 A god man þer was.. Alquin was his rihte name, Off him þe eorl was wel war. *c* **1330** R. BRUNNE *Chron. Wace* (Rolls) 11498 Oure auncestre Iulius Sesar Wan Bretayne (art þou nought war?). *c* **1350** *Will. Palerne* 3382 William was wiȝtly whar of his come. **1377** LANGL. *P. Pl.* B. XIII. 421 Þise ben þe braunches, beþ war, þat bryngeth a man to wanhope. *c* **1386** CHAUCER *Knt.'s T.* 38 He was war, as he caste his eye aside, Where that ther kneled in the hye weye A compaignye of ladyes. **1470–85** MALORY *Arthur* II. xvi. 94 And at the last he came in to a fayr forest in a valey and was ware of a Toure. *Ibid.* IV. xvi. 140 And thenne was syr Gawayne ware how ther henge a whyte shelde on that tree. **1530** TINDALE *Lev.* v. 2 Ether when a man toucheth any vnclene thinge..and is not warre of it, he is also vnclene and hath offended. *Ibid.* 18 And the preast shall make an attonement for him for the ignoraunce which he dyd and was not ware. **1556** OLDE *Antichrist* 16 b, Our most cruel blood thirstye enemies are not ware of this glory of our persecution. **1592** SHAKS. *Rom. & Jul.* I. i. 131 Towards him I made, but he was ware of me, And stole into the couert of the wood. **1600** —— *A. Y. L.* II. iv. 58 Thou speak'st wiser then thou art ware of. **1612** R. FENTON *Usury* 7 Wee shall finde much more in it, then they that make the lightest account of it, are ware of. **1812** CARY *Dante, Parad.* VIII. 15, I was not ware that I was wafted up. **1847** EMERSON *Poems, Saadi* 34 Be thou ware where Saadi dwells. **1886** BURTON *Arab. Nts.* (abr. ed.) I. 111, I was ware of a ship in the offing.

2. Prepared, on one's guard, watchful, vigilant, cautious, alert. Cf. AWARE 1. Now *arch.*

c **1000** *Ags. Gosp.* Luke xii. 40 And be ȝe wære forþam þe mannes sunu cymð þære tide þe ȝe ne wenað. *a* **1023** WULFSTAN *Hom.* xlii. (1883) 191 Us is micel þearf, þæt we wære beon þæs eȝeslican timan, þe nu towærd is. *a* **1225** *Juliana* 35 Make me war & wite me wið his crefti crokes þat ha me ne crechen. *a* **1250** *Owl & Night.* 170 Ne spedestu nouht mid þin vnwrenche For ich am war and can blenche. **1303** R. BRUNNE *Handl. Synne* 8084 Yn a prouerbe, telle men þys 'He wyys ys, þat ware ys'. *c* **1325** *Evil Times Edw. II* 343 in *Pol. Songs* (Camden) 339 Theih wolen bigile the in thin hond, but if thu be the warre. **1375** BARBOUR *Bruce* v. 546 Bot how that euir it fell, perde, I trow he sall the varrar be. *c* **1380** WYCLIF *Wks.* (1880) 20 And þerfore comaundiþ crist þat we be war and flee fro þe ypocrisie of pharisees. *c* **1440** *Promp. Parv.* 516 War, or a-war (*v.r.* aware), *cautus*, Cath. *precavens*. *c* **1450** *Merlin* i. 5 Than this holy man counselled hem to be wele ware, and kepe hem fro euell dedes. *c* **1480** HENRYSON *Swallow & other Birds* 193 His pray full sendill tymis will he mis, Bot gif we birdis all the warrer be. **1561** T. NORTON *Calvin's Inst.* IV. 54 But when he warneth vs of the daunger, he doeth it to this entente to make vs the warer. *a* **1584** MONTGOMERIE *Cherrie & Slae* 687, I wischt them to be war, And rashlie not to ryn ouir far, Without sik gydis as ȝe. **1814** SCOTT *Lord of Isles* v. xv, But evil news the letters bare,—The Clifford's force was strong and ware. **1860** TRENCH *Serm. Westm. Abbey* xxxi. 353 When the world speaks thee fair, and thy very enemies are at peace with thee,—then be thou ware. *a* **1897** H. NEWBOLT *Drake's Drum* 24 They shall find him ware an' wakin,' as they found him long ago!

†**3.** Careful or guarded in action. Const. *of, in, with* and *inf.* *Obs.*

a **1240** *Sawles Warde* in *O.E. Hom.* I. 253 Reade hwet us beo to donne at we beon þe warre ant wakere to witen us on euch half under godes wengen. *a* **1340** HAMPOLE *Ps.* xvi. 9 Kepe me as þe appel of þe eghe: þat is, perfitly and tendirly, for a man has no lym þat he is warere with, þan wiþ his eghe. **1398** TREVISA *Barth. De P.R.* III. xi. (1495) 55 By the vertue estimatiue we ben waar to voyde euyll and folowe that is good. **1450–1530** *Myrr. our Ladye* I. xviii. 48 The goodman droue sleape from hym, and was more ware to kepe hymselfe waker in goddes seruyce alway after. **1538** STARKEY *England* II. i. 170 Thys..schold make the vnder offycerys to be ware and dylygent to dow theyr duty. **1583** GOLDING *Calvin on Deut.* xxxiii. 195 Neuertheless he warneth us therewithal to bee more ware in abstayning from all wicked othes.

4. Careful or cautious in avoiding.

†**a.** Const. *with.* *Obs.*

c **1000** ÆLFRIC *Saints' Lives* xiii. 150 And ða woruld-menn wæron wære wið heora fynd. *c* **1200** *Vices & Virtues* 71 Ðat tu..lierne fastliche ða ȝekyndes of sennes, hwannen and hwanne hie cumen, þat ðu muȝe bien war wið hem. *a* **1300** *Cursor M.* 23827 þe soth þai spar us noght to tell, for to do us be war wit hell. **1357** *Lay Folks' Catech.* T. 425 Prudencia —That wisses us to be war with wathes of the world. *c* **1380** WYCLIF *Serm.* Sel. Wks. I. 19 Þis gospel biddiþ men to be ware wiþ false prophetis þat comen in cloþing of sheep.

†**b.** with *inf.* Cf. BEWARE *v.* 1 c. *Obs.*

c **1375** *Sc. Leg. Saints* xxx. (*Theodera*) 27 Ȝet suld gud wemen ware be to rowne with þaim in priuete. *c* **1380** WYCLIF *Sel. Wks.* III. 184 And þerfore men schulden be war to take of þes foure statis. **1475** *Bk. Noblesse* (Roxb.) 81 The ennemies of youre roiaume..wol doubt and be ware to take any entreprise ayenst your noble mageste. **1560** DAUS tr. *Sleidane's Comm.* 20 But he marueleth at their rashenes that they can not be ware by so many examples to blemishe them selues, and other Universities for euer.

c. with *of.* Cf. BEWARE *v.* 1 b. *Obs.* exc. *arch.*

1382 WYCLIF *Matt.* xvi. 6 Beth war of the sourdowȝ of Pharisees and Saducees. **1390** GOWER *Conf.* I. 231 For who these olde bokes rede Of suche ensamples as were ar, Him oghte be the more war Of alle tho that feigne chiere. *a* **1400** *Hymns Virg.* etc. (1867) 65 Quod Besinesse, 'man! of Slouthe be waare'. **1477** *Rolls of Parlt.* VI. 193/1 In exemple to others to have been ware of suche attempting here-after. **1548** HALL *Chron., Edw. IV*, 211 For suche thynges as wee se before our iyes, we bee well ware of. **1596** DALRYMPLE tr. *Leslie's Hist. Scot.* (S.T.S.) I. 101 *margin*, They ar war of bludscheding. **1865** SWINBURNE *Chastelard* III. i. 98 You would swear now you have used me faithfully; Shall I not make you swear? I am ware of you. **1868** G. MACDONALD *R. Falconer* I. xii. 164 'Laddie,' she said, 'be ye waure o' judgin' the Almichty.' **1885–94** BRIDGES *Eros & Psyche* June x, But Psyche when that wistful speech she heard Was ware of all her spouse had warn'd her of.

†**d.** with negative or interrogative clause. Cf. BEWARE *v.* 1 d. *Obs.*

a **1000** ÆLFRIC *Gen.* xxiv. 6 Beo wær æt þam, þæt þu næfre minne sunu þyder ne læde. *a* **1100** in Napier *Contrib. O.E. Lexicogr.* 58 Preostas synt to myngienne þ hi beon ware þ hi ne wurðon beswicene fram deoflum þurh ȝeþanca smealicnysse. *c* **1325** *Spec. Gy Warw.* 645 Nowe be þou were, þou proude gome, þat þou ne be in pryde enome. **1340** HAMPOLE *Pr. Consc.* 1397 By þis way byhoves us al gang, Bot be we war we ga noght wrang. **1393** LANGL. *P. Pl.* C. XVIII. 39 'A! wyf! be war,' quaþ he [Tobit] 'what ȝe haue here-ynne; Lord leyue,' quaþ þe lede 'no stole þyng be here!' *c* **1400** MAUNDEV. (Roxb.) xvi. 74 It es gude to him þat schall wake þis hawke þat he be wele warre þat he slepe noȝt. *c* **1430** *Two Cookery-bks.* i. 38 Be wyl war þat þey ben nowt Browne. **1475** MARG. PASTON in *P. Lett.* III. 135 Never the less I shall be the warer how I shall dele here aftyr. **1531** tr. *St. German's Doctor & Stud.* II. viii. (1638) 74, I would advise every man to be well ware how hee distraineth in such cases. **1577** B. GOOGE *Heresbach's Husb.* III. 143 Others vse the roote of Mandracke, being wel ware that they suffer them not to tast it. **1596** DALRYMPLE tr. *Leslie's Hist. Scot.* I. 100 Thay ar war with al possible diligens that thay sched nocht thair blude.

5. Prudent, sagacious, cunning, skilled; ? also, rarely, staid. Frequently coupled with *wise*. *Obs.* exc. *arch.*

c **888** ÆLFRED *Boeth.* xxvii. § 2 Wisdom ȝedeð his lufiendas wise & weorðe [*MS. Junius* wære] & ȝemetfæste & ȝeþyldiȝe & rihtwise. *c* **897** —— *Gregory's Past. C.* xxxv. 236 Bio ȝe swæ ware swæ nædran, & swæ bilwite swæ culfran. *c* **1200** ORMIN 18313 Ȝe wenenn wrang Off me; beþ warre & wise, Namm I nohht Godd, acc icc amm mann. *c* **1205** LAY. 2108 þe wes þe wiseste þe wes þe warreste [*c* **1275** he was wis and war]. *Ibid.* 2967 Gornoille was swiðe wær [*c* **1275** war] swa beoð wifmen wel ihwær & seide ane lesinge. *a* **1300** *Cursor M.* 8696 Þe king, þat was sa sli a clerc, Bath warr and wis in all his werc. ? *a* **1366** CHAUCER *Rom. Rose* 1258 She was not nyce, ne outrageous, But wys and war, and vertuous. *c* **1400** *Ywaine & Gaw.* 12 Of al knightes he bare the pryse, In werld was non so war ne wise. **1423** JAS. I *Kingis Q.* clxiv, And they were ware that longe sat In place, So tolter quhilum did sche It to-wrye. *c* **1440** *York Myst.* xxxiii. 137 [*Pilate to Caiaphas*] 3a, butt be wise, witty, and warre. **1526** *Pilgr. Perf.* (W. de W. 1531) 131 We sholde also be wele ware or wyse, as is yᵉ serpent. **1549** LATIMER *3rd Serm. bef. Edw. VI* (Arb.) 76 Sathan..is ware inough, he is wily, and circumspect for stiryng vp any sedicion. **1563** *Mirr. Mag.* II. *Collingbourne* xxi, A poet must be..No flatterer, no bolsterer of vyce, But sound and swete, in all thinges ware and wyse. **1915** R. BROOKE *1914 & other Poems* 29 And, sits there nothing ware and wise Behind the curtains of her eyes.

†**b.** with *in, of* (something specified), *to* (do something). *Obs.*

1307 *Elegy Death Edw. I*, ii, Trewest mon of alle thinge, Ant in werre war ant wys. **13..** *Seuyn Sag.* 410 He.. thought al night,..Hou that he might be wis and wer To overcome the emperice. **1382** WYCLIF *Dan.* i. 4 [Men] lernd in al wisdam, war in science [Vulg. *cautos scientia*], and tauȝt in disciplyne. ? *a* **1400** *Morte Arth.* 1973 Bot owre wyese kyng es warre to wayttene his renkes, And wyesly by the woddez voydez his oste. *c* **1425** *MS. Digby 233* lf. 225 b/2 He þat is a werrur on þe see he mot of ebbynge & of flowyng tyme be boþe wise and waar.

†**II. 6.** Used attributively. Prudent, cautious, cunning. *Obs.*

c **1386** CHAUCER *Prol.* 309 A Sergeant of the Lawe war and wys..Ther was also. *a* **1400–50** *War Alex.* 202 Þare gan þai graithly þam graue in golden lettirs, All þe wordis at he þaim werpid of þaire ware kynge. **1450–1530** *Myrr. our Ladye* 114 Ye saye that she ys prudente and a ware spender and dysposer of goodes. *Ibid.* II. 124 When crysten people a woke in busy prayer and in ware kepynge of themselfe that they myghte be redy to suffer martyrdom. **1555** EDEN *Decades* (Arb.) 386 They are very ware people in theyr bargenynge, and wyl not lose one sparke of golde of any value. *a* **1568** ASCHAM *Scholem.* II. (Arb.) 142 And as for Plautus, except the scholemaster be able to make wise and ware choice..your scholer were better to play. *a* **1614** J. MELVILL *Autob. & Diary* (Wodrow Soc.) 165 Being a slight and war man, and perceaving the esteat of the Kirk deceying, [etc.].

ware (wɛə(r)), *v.*[1] Forms: 1 warian, 3 ware-n, 3–6, 8–9 *dial.* war, 3–4 warr(e, 5 waar, 7–9 'ware, 4– ware. [OE. *warian* = OFris. *waria*, OS. *waron*, OHG. *be-warôn* = BEWARE *v.* (MHG. *waren*), ON. *vara* (Sw. *vara*, Da. *vare*) :—OTeut. **warōjan*, f. **warō* WARE *sb.*[2] In ME. the native word coalesced with *ware* a. OF. (north-eastern) *ware-r* (= Central OF., mod.F. *garer*), of the same meaning, adopted from

Teut. The interjectional imperative *ware!* used in hunting is prob. to be regarded as of Fr. origin.

In OE. the verb had, in addition to the senses illustrated below, certain other meanings ('to guard, defend; to inhabit') which did not survive into ME.]

†**1.** *intr.* To give heed, take care, be on one's guard. Const. *of*, *with*; *to* oneself; *to* and inf. *to do to ware*: to inform, notify (const. *of* or clause). *Obs.*

c **1250** *Gen. & Ex.* 2154 Ðe vii fulsum ȝeres faren, Iosep cuðe him bi-foren waren. *a* **1352** MINOT *Poems* ii. 6 War ȝit with þe Skottes for þai er ful of gile. *c* **1380** *Sir Ferumb.* 1592 War now of me, ich þe diffie. **1382** WYCLIF *Ecclus.* xiii. 16 War to thee [Vulg. *cave tibi*], and tac heed bisili to thin heering. **1390** GOWER *Conf.* III. 123 Bot war whan thei togedre duellen. **1415** HOCCLEVE *To Sir J. Oldcastle* 88 Waar of the swerd of god for it is keene. **1594** CAREW *Huarte's Exam. Wits* xii. 188 And this wil fall out a plain matter when you are done to ware, that in this region, the sunne yeeldeth a feruent heat. *Ibid.* xv. 267 Of all these points were the eies and the eares naturally done to ware. **1598** Q. ELIZ. *Plutarch* ii. 123 That better the [= they] may ware the warnid to correct.

b. *imper.*, as a warning cry, a call to animals, and in hunting. *Obs.* (? exc. *dial.*)

?*c* **1000** *Gloss* in *Germania* (1878) XI. 393 Caue wara. ?*a* **1200** WILLELM. CANTUAR. *Vita S. Thomæ* in *Mat. Hist. Thos. Becket* (Rolls) I. 128 Patria voce exclamavit.. Huge de Morevile, ware, ware, ware, Lithulf heth his swerd adrage. **13..** *Gaw. & Gr. Knt.* 1158 Þe hindez were halden in, with hay & war. *c* **1400** *Master of Game* (MS. Digby 182) xxxiv, War, war, ha, ha, war. *c* **1460** *Towneley Myst.* ii. 25 Io furth, greyn-horne! and war oute, gryme! *Ibid.* 29 War! let me se how down will draw. *c* **1500** *Hyckescorner* 456 *Imagy.* Ware make rome he shall haue a strype I trowe. **1513** DOUGLAS *Æneis* VI. Prol. 168 War at Pluto, I sall hym hunt of sty. **1602** DEKKER *Satirom.* B 3, *Flash.* Ware there, roome for Sir Adam Prickeshaft. **1760** MISS FIELDING *Ophelia* xxxiv, Ware, Hector! ware, Juno! **1825** J. JENNINGS *Observ. Dial. W. Eng.*, *War*, beware! take care! **1825** BROCKETT *N.C. Words*, *War*, beware. '*War below.*'

c. with clause, introduced by *that*, *lest*, or a relative. Also without *that*. *Obs.* or *arch.*

a **1000** *Canons of Edgar* xxxviii. in *Thorpe* II. 252 Warige þæt hit na forealdige. **1398** TREVISA *Barth. De P.R.* VII. xiii. (1495) 232 But ware the pacyent that he put hym not sodenly to grete heete. *a* **1400-50** *Bk. Curtasye* 240 in *Babees Bk.*, Þou that stondys so sure on sete, Ware lest þy hede falle to þy fete. *a* **1460** *Play Sacrament* 596 Here master master ware how ye tugg. **1530** PALSGR. 701/2 Ware you shede nat your potage upon the table cloth. **1559** MORWYNG *Evonymus* Pref. A ij, This sacred to God Pluto (theues) ware that ye touch not. **1616** B. JONSON *Devil an Ass* v. v. [v. iii.], Ware what you do, M. Ambler. **1900** G. E. EVANS *Lion's Whelps* i. 8 Let the hunters 'ware who flout him When he calls his whelps about him.

†**2.** *refl.* To guard oneself, be careful, take care. Const. with clause, *fro*, *from*, *for* (= from), *of*. *Obs.*

a **1000** *Cædmon's Gen.* 236 Forlætað þone ænne beam, wariað inc wið þone wæstm. *a* **1300** *Cursor M.* 17210 Warr þe þou namar thrald be. **13..** *Guy Warw.* 1867 Hennes forward war þe fro me, þi dedliche fo ichil now be. **13..** *E.E. Allit. P.* B. 165 Bot war þe wel, if þou wylt, þy wedez ben clene. **1362** LANGL. *P. Pl.* A. v. 225 War þe for wonhope, þat wol þe bi-traye. **1377** *Ibid.* B. XVIII. 273 Ac war hym of þe periles. **1390** GOWER *Conf.* I. 312 Bot war thee wel that thou ne lieve Al that thou sest tofore thin yhe. *c* **1400** *Cato's Morals* 132 in *Cursor M.* App. iv. 1671 Mare mai þou be agast of anli man vn-wrast, and warre þe for him.

3. *trans.* To beware of, guard against; to avoid, shun, keep clear of. Chiefly in imper. = look out for! (cf. b). *arch.*

a **900** *Kentish Glosses* in Wr.-Wülcker 65/40 Cauet ['*qui cauet laqueos*' Prov. xi. 15], warat. **1388** *Pol. Poems* (Rolls) I. 275 Ware ȝe the prophecye. **1400** in *26 Pol. Poems* i. 71 War wordes of dowble entendement. *c* **1440** *Pallad. on Husb.* I. 213 War arrogaunce in takyng thyng on honde. ?*c* **1520** SKELTON *Col. Cloute* 341 A man myght saye in mocke Ware the wethercocke Of the steple of Paules. **1588** SHAKS. *L.L.L.* v. ii. 43 Ware pensals. How? **1599** NASHE *Lenten Stuffe* G 2, O, ware a naked man; Cithereaes Nunnes haue no power to resiste him. **1622** MABBE tr. *Aleman's Guzman d'Alf.* I. 199 A roguish Boy.. threw downe vpon me a great bucket of scalding water; and when hee saw it had fairely lighted vpon me, he leisurely vtters:.. Ware water. **1624** BP. MOUNTAGU *New Gagg* To Rdr. 3 My desire is to ware heresie, to quit error. **1792** HOLCROFT *Road to Ruin* II. 28 *Harry.* When they do I'll horsewhip them myself. *Goldfinch.* Yourself?—'Ware that! Wrong there! **1833** GEN. P. THOMPSON *Exerc.* (1842) II. 480 To despise rhetoric, and eschew fine writing;.. to ware flippancy and bad jokes. **1839** MRS. KIRKLAND *New Home* xxxvii. 252 My prime and practical favourite among mottoes and maxims, is ''ware snakes!' **1861** THACKERAY *Round. Papers, On two Round. Papers* (1869) 164 We meet each other in public. Ware a fight! **1878** BROWNING *La Saisiaz* 44 Must.. Every sweet warn ''Ware my bitter!'

b. In hunting and in cries to animals, as *ware hawk* (fig.: cf. HAWK *sb.*[1] 3), *ware horse*, etc. Now chiefly in *ware wheat* (= don't ride over it), *ware holes*, *ware wire*. Sometimes pronounced (wɔː(r)).

Similarly, on the Trent, *ware ager*, a warning to boats to beware of the tidal wave.

a **1529** SKELTON (*title*) Ware the Hauke. **1590** COCKAINE *Treat. Hunting* C 4 b, Take him vp in a line, and beating him, say, awe, ware that. **1606** SHAKS. *Tr. & Cr.* v. vii. 12 The bull has the game: ware hornes ho? **1626** B. JONSON *Staple of N.* v. v. [v. ii], See! the whole Couy is scatter'd, 'Ware, 'ware the Hawkes. I loue to see him flye. **1673** *S' too him Bayes* 31 But now ware hawk! **1677** N. COX *Gentl. Recr.* I. (ed. 2) 80 The first Ceremony when the Hunts-men come in to the Death of a Deer, is to cry Ware Haunch, that the Hounds may not break into the Deer. **1705** VANBRUGH *Confederacy* v. i. 62 *Mon.* Your Goodness, Madam, is —— *Flip.* [*Aside to Moneytrap.*] War Horse, No fine Speeches, you'll spoil all. **1793** J. WOLCOT (P. Pindar) *Pair of Odes to the Pope* i. 35 Ware Lark! the Sportsman to his Pointer cries; Designing him for Partridge—nobler Game. **1814** *Sporting Mag.* XLIV. 193 Ware chase! where such daring unpardonable crime has been committed. **1828** *Ibid.* N.S. XXI. 187, I never heard an harangue upon 'ware wheat' given in a more gentlemanlike way. **1823** MOOR *Suffolk Words* 470 *Warr*, an abbreviation probably of beware—'Warr, horse'—a caution to a hound in danger of being trodden on. 'Warr, sheep'—warns him from agression. **1864** E. MAYHEW *Illustr. Horse Managem.* 527 However, walk down the gangway of the two-year old stalls in any trainer's stable, and ''ware horse,' ''ware heels,' is frequently shouted out. **1908** R. BAGOT *A. Cuthbert* v. 48 We have four or five miles to do yet—and a nice bit of open grass country before us—but 'ware holes!

†**4.** To be apprehensive or careful for. *Obs.*

c **1420** WYNTOUN *Cron.* VIII. v. 894 Gif þe Broys þe kynge sulde be Off Scotlande, war ȝoure ryalte, ȝoure marchis, and ȝoure wallit townys.

†**5.** To teach (a person) to beware. *Obs.*

1634 HEYWOOD & BROME *Lancash. Witches* IV. H 4, Let me be honckt up for a show Ile ware them to mel or ma with a woman that [etc.].

ware (wɛə(r)), *v.*[2] Now *Sc.* and *dial.* Forms: 5 **warre, werre** (?), *Sc.* **var(e**, 5-6 *Sc.* **war, wayr,** (6 *pa. t. Sc.* **ward**), 8-9 **wear,** 9 **waur,** 5- *Sc.* **wair,** 4- **ware.** [a. ON. *verja*, pa. t. *varðe*, pa. pple. *varið-r*, 'to invest (money), lay out', a transferred use of the primary sense 'to clothe': cf. the corresponding OE. *werian* to clothe, to wear: see WEAR *v.*] *trans.* To spend, lay out (money, goods). Const. *in*, *on*, *upon*, †*of*.

a **1417** *York Memo. Bk.* (Surtees) I. 222 Ayther of them shall ware xviij *d.* in fyssh or thay passe the market. *c* **1440** *Bone Flor.* 405 Now schall y neuer my golde spare, But faste upon thys warre hyt ware. *c* **1460** *Towneley Myst.* xxx. 252 Had I bot a penny on the wold I warte [*i.e.* ware it]. **15..** *Cokelbie Sow* 75 in *Bannatyne MS.* (Hunter. Club) 1023 And verrely as I hard Thus the money he ward. **1521** *Lincoln Wills* (Linc. Rec. Soc. V.) 103 The residew off the money.. I will it be wared in the reparacions of a new lofte. **1545** ASCHAM *Toxoph.* II. (Arb.) 122 They shall fynde it bothe lesse charge and more pleasure to ware at any tyme a couple of shyllynges of a new bowe. **1600** HEYWOOD *1st Pt. Edw. IV* III. i, I have wared all my money in cow-hides at Coleshill Market. **1634** *Burgh Rec. Stirling* (1889) II. 299 Item, wairit on the beiting and mending of the brig and lang calsey, 220 0 0. **1725** RAMSAY *Gent. Sheph.* IV. ii, Ne'er grudge ilk year to ware some stanes of cheese, To gain these silent friends that ever please. **1729** P. WALKDEN *Diary* (1866) 57 So I signed a bill to Alice Slater for the £3 2s. 6d. I had weared. **1785** BURNS *Ep. Davie* ii, While coofs on countless thousands rant, And ken na how to wair't. **1826** GALT *Last of Lairds* xxviii. 246 He gaed to Widow McPlooky's public, and waur'd the sixpence on gills. **1880** TENNYSON *Northern Cobbler* v, I grabb'd the munny she maäde, and I wear'd it o' liquor, I did. **1893** STEVENSON *Catriona* i, I would hae waired my siller better-gates than that.

b. *fig.* (e.g. one's time, wit, life, love).

13.. *Gaw. & Gr. Knt.* 402, I schal ware alle my wyt to wynne me þeder. *Ibid.* 1235, I schal ware my whyle wel, quyl it lastez. *c* **1480** HENRYSON *Cock & Jewel* 153 Weill war that man ouer all vther, that mocht All his lyfe dayis in perfite studie wair To get science. *a* **1578** LINDESAY (Pitscottie) *Chron. Scot.* (S.T.S.) I. 205 Ready to wair thair lyffis.. in his defence. **1639** SIR A. JOHNSTON (Ld. Wariston) *Diary* (S.H.S.) I. 342 We wil not so mutch as to waire our thoughts upon it. **1725** RAMSAY *Gent. Sheph.* IV. ii, Since we've little time, To ware 't on words, wad border on a crime. **1794** BURNS *On Willie Chalmers* ii, And faith ye'll no be lost a whit, Tho' waired on Willie Chalmers. **1818** SCOTT *Br. Lamm.* xxviii, There would be little love wared on the matter. **1826** —— *Jrnl.* 8 June, The struggle is worth waring a headache upon. **1894** CROCKETT *Raiders* xxxiii. 279 A good honest heart.. that hasna been weared on ither lasses.

c. with *out*. (*lit.* and *fig.*)

1508 DUNBAR *Tua Mariit Wemen* 39 Thay wauchtit at the wicht wyne, and waris out wourdis. **1774** *Petition* in A. McKay *Hist. Kilmarnock* 303 To ware out and expend the haill necessary depursements.

d. Phr. *to be well*, or *ill*, *wared*.

?*a* **1418** *Pol. Poems* (Rolls) II. 244 The wages ben ful yvel wared With suiche a capitayn to abide. *c* **1440** *Alphabet of Tales* 94 Ane of þaim vpbrayed hym.. & said his yong wife was ill warid on hym. **1535** STEWART *Cron. Scot.* I. 449 Ȝour riches thus is waistit and euill waird. *a* **1585** MONTGOMERIE *Flyting* 265 The cuff is weill waired that twa hame brings. *Ibid.* 697 Na maruell though ill won ill waired bee. *a* **1614** J. MELVILL *Autob. & Diary* (Wodrow Soc.) 68, I haiff bein ready to gyff my lyff whar it was nocht halff sa weill wared, at the pleasour of my God. **1686** G. STUART *Joco-ser. Disc.* 33 If aw the rest were right repair'd, I trow our Labour were well wair'd. **1807** TANNAHILL *Soldier's Ret.* II. iii, A glass, to croun a wish, was never better wair'd.

ware, obs. f. WAR *sb.*[1] and *a.*; var. WARY *v. Obs.*; obs. f. WEAR *v.* (and obs. pa. t.); obs. and dial. f. WEIR; var. VAIR *a. Obs.*, WERE *Obs.*; obs. f. *were* (see BE *v.*); obs. f. WHERE.

wareant, Sc. var. VARIANT *a.* (sense 3 b).

1549 *Burgh Rec. Stirling* (1887) 57 Ane gown of wareant champit worset, price four li. xs.

†'**wareband.** *Obs.*[−0] [? f. WARE *v.*[1] (taken in the sense 'guard, secure') + BAND *sb.*[1]] A mill-rind.

1677 COLES *Dict. Eng.-Lat.*, The Wareband of a milstone, *subscus.*

warecorn: see WARE *sb.*[5] b.

wared, *ppl. a. Sc.* [f. WARE *sb.*[1] + -ED.] Manured with seaweed.

1795 *Statist. Acc. Scot.* XVI. 253 In the spring season, after the oats are sown, the farmer gives the wared land one ploughing.

wared, var. WARIED *ppl. a. Obs.*

wareday: see WARDAY *dial.*

waredrop, obs. form of WARDROBE.

'**wareful,** *a.* [f. WARE *sb.*[2], *a.* or *v.*[1] + -FUL.] Watchful, cautious. Now only *poet.*

1548 THOMAS *Ital. Dict.* (1550), *Scalterita*, or *Scaltrito*, he or she that is warefull or forecastyng. **1557** *Tottel's Misc.* (Arb.) 256 Well furnisht brest to bide eche chanses changing chear. In woe hath chearfull hope, in weal hath warefull fear. **1563** P. WHITEHORNE *Onosandro Platon.* 69 Wherby thou shalt make thy souldiers not fearefull, but warefull. **1937** G. FRANKAU *More of Us* xv. 160 Slow went his feet, and wareful As federal agent's in some gangster joint.

Hence †'**warefulness.**

1548 THOMAS *Ital. Dict.* (1567), *Sagacitá*, wisdome or warefulnesse. *a* **1586** SIDNEY *Arcadia* II. 2nd Ecl. (1912) 342 His eyes are curious search, but vailde with warefulnesse.

warehou ('warɛhuː). *N.Z.* Also 9 **wareho.** [Maori.] A large marine food-fish, *Seriolella brama*, found near the South Island of New Zealand.

1848 E. J. WAKEFIELD *Handbk. N.Z.* v. 161 The *Wareho* is a fish somewhat resembling the kawai, but of much better flavour. **1886** R. A. SHERRIN *Fishes N.Z.* 99 The fish known as trevalli in the Dunedin market is a different fish, allied to the warehou. **1949** P. H. BUCK *Coming of Maori* II. viii. 215 *Warehou*.. were caught with a rod. **1966** *Encycl. N.Z.* III. 552/1 Warehou.. resemble trevally in general shape and colouring (blue-green above, silver below, with a dark blotch just behind the head).

warehouse ('wɛəhaʊs), *sb.* [f. WARE *sb.*[3] + HOUSE *sb.* Cf. Du. *warenhuis*, G. *warenhaus*.]

1. a. A building or part of a building used for the storage of merchandise; the building in which a wholesale dealer keeps his stock of goods for sale; a building in which furniture or other property is housed, a charge being made for the accommodation; a government building (more fully BONDED *warehouse*) in which dutiable imported goods are kept in bond until it is convenient to the importer to pay the duty.

1349 *Will of W. Erl* in *Red Register of Lynn* (MS.) fol. 85, j seldam cum.. duobus warehouses. **1453** MARG. PASTON in *P. Lett.* I. 256, I kowd not gette no grawnt of hym to have the warehows. **1522** MORE *De quat. Noviss.* Wks. (1557) 94 Let them here what Christ saith in the ghospell to the ryche couetous gatherer, yt thoughte to make his barnes and his warehouses larger to laye in the more. **1530** PALSGR. 286/2 Warehouse to shewe marchandyse in, *une monstre a marchandise.* **1535** COVERDALE *Jer.* xl. 10 Therfore gather you wyne, corne and oyle, and kepe them in youre ware houses. **1539** T. PERY in Ellis *Orig. Lett.* Ser. II. II. 140, I so beinge in my ware howsse bessy, ther yentrede in a pryste. **1609** DEKKER *Gull's Horn-bk.* i. 6 The first suit of apparell that euer mortall man put on, came neither from the Mercers shop, nor the Merchants ware-house. **1632** MASSINGER *City Madam* I. iii, Their prayers will.. keep your ware-houses From fire, or quench 'em with their tears. **1660** in *Verney Mem.* (1894) III. x. 375 My Mr. was all the while in the Warehouse with him wch brought ye Silke. **1670** MILTON *Hist. Eng.* III. Wks. 1851 III. 95 Some who had bin call'd from shops and warehouses.. fell to huckster the Commonwealth. **1768-74** TUCKER *Lt. Nat.* (1834) II. 416 It is the retailer and petty shop-keeper.. that must supply the demands of the public: importation is not their business, but to resort to the warehouse, and retail out the goods as received from thence. **1799** *Local Act 39 Geo. III*, c. 58 §4 Every Box, Basket, Packet, Parcel [etc.].. brought to any Inn, Ware-house, or other Place, by any Public Stage Coach. **1840** *Act 3 & 4 Vict.* c. 17 §2 Spirits.. in Warehouse under Her Majesty's Locks. **1844** G. DODD *Textile Manuf.* i. 11 We have around us the wholesale 'warehouses' and offices wherein is transacted all the business between the dealers, the manufacturers, the spinners, the bleachers, the calico-printers. **1848** DICKENS *Dombey* xlvi, A packer's warehouse, and a bottle-maker's warehouse. **1918** *Act 8 & 9 Geo. V*, c. 15 §7 Tobacco exported from Great Britain.. or deposited in a bonded or King's warehouse.

b. *transf.* and *fig.*

1610 HEALEY *St. Aug. Citie of God* VI. vii. 246 As Budæus calleth the worke in his Mercuries seller, or Minerua's warehouse [*i.e.* Παλλάδος Ταμεῖον]. **1612** ROWLANDS *Knave of Spades* E 2 b, His richest ware-house is a greasie pocket, And two pence in Tabacco still doth stock it. **1836** DICKENS *Sk. Boz, Streets—Night*, The kidney-pie man has just walked away with his warehouse on his arm.

†**c.** A mason's or carpenter's workshop. *Obs.*[−0]

1530 PALSGR. 286/2 Warehouse for masons or carpentars, *astillier* [= *atelier*].

†**d.** A tradesman's inner or back shop. *Obs.*

1580 HOLLYBAND *Treas. Fr. Tong*, *Magazin*, or *arriére boutique*, a warehouse, an inner shop. **1598** B. JONSON *Ev. Man in Hum.* II. i, *Tho.* Where's the boy? *Piso.* Within sir, in the warehouse. **1605** TIMME *Quersit.* II. vii. 139 Neither did they care for so great confusion of compositions and mixtures which fill a whole ware-house and shoppe.

†**e.** Used as a more dignified synonym for 'shop'. *Obs.*

With defining word, as in *baby-linen warehouse*, *Italian warehouse*, the word was in the early 20th c. still met with on the signboards of London shops.

c **1730** BURT *Lett. N. Scot.* (1818) I. 65 Here and there you may now see an ordinary shop dubbed with the important title of a Warehouse. **1796-7** JANE AUSTEN *Pride & Prej.*

(1813) III. v. 93 She does not know which are the best warehouses. **1798** —— *Northang. Abb.* ix, Mrs. Hughes saw all the clothes after they came from the warehouse. *c* **1852–7** *Katey's Voy.* 13, 'I know him,' said one of the men. 'He lives at Douglas, just off the quay.' 'I know him too. I've bought goods at his warehouse,' observed a lady.

f. In a printing office (see quot.).

1888 JACOBI *Printers' Vocab.*, *Warehouse*, the department responsible for printed work and 'white' paper... *Warehouse-knife*, a large knife used for cutting up by hand small quantities of paper.

g. Phr. ***warehouse to warehouse***, used *attrib.* to designate a clause in a cargo insurance policy which provides that the insurance policy applies throughout all of the normal course of transit. Also applied to the policy itself, etc.

1922 *Lloyd's List Law Rep.* 30 Nov. 270/1, I am not sure that in a warehouse to warehouse policy the word 'theft' ought to be limited to theft by violence in the same way as it is in a purely marine policy. **1924** *Ibid.* 24 Apr. 450/2 The policy..incorporates the 'warehouse to warehouse' Clause No. 6 of the Institute Cargo Clauses. **1932** *Law Times Rep.* 27 Aug. 168/2 In my view, the practice has always been that the rule as to ship's papers applies though there is a warehouse to warehouse clause in the policy. **1974** E. R. H. IVAMY *Marine Insurance* (ed. 2) xiii. 121 The general rule is that the risk attaches when the goods are loaded, but may attach beforehand if the policy contains a 'craft' clause or the 'transit' ('warehouse to warehouse') clause. **1982** J. PHILLIPS *Dict. Trading Terms* 65/2 *Transit clause*,..one of the clauses in a marine insurance policy defining the normal course of transit, and including the warehouse to warehouse cover that many traders require.

h. *U.S. colloq.* A large and impersonal institution providing accommodation for mental patients, old people, or poor people.

1970 *Sat. Rev.* (U.S.) 3 Oct. 25/1 We have too many such 'human warehouses', staffed by underpaid and poorly trained personnel. **1972** *Time* 14 Feb. 67 But for most of Willowbrook's residents, the institution is a warehouse, a place capable of providing only shelter and the barest essentials, for those whose families are either unwilling or unable to care for them. **1974** J. FLETCHER *Ethics of Genetic Control* 157 We ought to protect our families from the emotional and material burden of such diseased individuals, and from the misery of their simply 'existing' (not *living*) in a nearby 'warehouse' or public institution. **1976** *N.Y. Times* 25 Apr. IV. 1 Subsidized public housing has been anathema to the emigres who now live in the suburbs, where the very mention conjures specters of high-rise 'human warehouses' like those that have been erected in ghetto areas.

2. *attrib.*, as ***warehouse-door***, ***-keeper***, ***-rent***; **warehouse-knife** (see 1 f); **warehouse-room**, storage in a warehouse.

1838 DICKENS *O. Twist* xxvi, A salesman..who was smoking a pipe at his *warehouse-door. **1683** W. HEDGES *Diary* (Hakl. Soc.) I. 73 They have been forced to give Mr. Ellis, *ware-house keeper, each of them, a Bribe. **1683** MOXON *Mech. Exerc.*, *Printing* xxv. ¶ 1 The Warehouse-keeper takes the Heap out of the Press-room..into the Warehouse. **1709** *Act 8 Anne* c. 21 §5 The Ware-house-Keeper of the said Company of Stationers. **1821** J. SMYTH *Pract. of Customs* (ed. 2) 392 Delivered the above, 10 November, 1819. A. B. Ware-house-keeper. **1799** *Local Act 39 Geo. III*, c. 58 §6 *marg.*, Parcels..to be delivered..on Payment of Carriage and *Ware-house-Rent. **1615** E. S. *Britain's Buss* in Arber *Eng. Garner* III. 640 For *Warehouse-room there, till the herrings be sold, allow, at most £2 0s. 0d. **1799** *Local Act 39 Geo. III*, c. 58 §6 The additional Sum of Two Pence for the Warehouse-Room thereof [*sc.* of the Parcel]. **1830** GEN. P. THOMPSON *Exerc.* (1842) I. 259 Does the value of this probability pay for the expense of warehouse-room?

Hence **'warehouseful**.

1859 MILL *Liberty* iii. 121 A man cannot get a coat or a pair of boots to fit him, unless they are either made to his measure or he has a whole warehouseful to choose from.

warehouse ('wɛəhaʊs), *v.* [f. WAREHOUSE *sb.*] *trans.* To deposit or secure (goods) in a warehouse; to deposit (furniture) for safe keeping, a charge being made for storage; to place (imported goods) in a bonded warehouse pending the payment of the import duty. Hence **'warehoused** *ppl. a.*

1799 *Hull Advertiser* 9 Nov. 4/2, 16 bales of sugar which have been landed and warehoused. **1819** *Act 59 Geo. III*, c. 52 Table A—Inwards, Warehoused Goods. For a List of those Goods which may be warehoused, or otherwise secured on Importation into Great Britain without Payment of Duty in the First Instance, See Table F. **1874** *Daily News* 16 Feb. 6/5 A building..in which will be found complete accommodation for warehousing the valuables of noble-men and gentlemen in their absence from town. **1886** SCHOLL *Phraseol. Dict.* II. 832 Any cotton you may consign to us will be warehoused pending your further instructions.

b. *transf.* and *fig.*

1824 LANDOR *Imag. Conv.*, *Washington & Franklin* Wks. 1846 I. 124 Their stores of intellect are not squandered in the regions of fancy..but warehoused and kept sound at home. **1835** *Edin. Rev.* LXI. 457 Our coal mines may be regarded as vast magazines of hoarded, or warehoused power. **1855** SMEDLEY *Occult Sciences* 149 Its wondrous fount, from the days of Herodotus to our own, has been warehoused by small poets as part of their stock in trade of sparkling illustrations.

c. *slang.* To put in prison.

1881 *Punch* 12 Feb. 71 D'you want to get us both 'warehoused'?

d. *U.S. colloq.* To place (a person, esp. a mental patient) in a large and impersonal institution.

1972 *Tuscaloosa* (Alabama) *News* 22 Feb. 1 The current federal lawsuit against Partlow State School and Hospital may become a landmark decision in America as the country continues its 'trend away from large custodial institutions where people are warehoused and where they are denied the opportunity to develop their full potential,' Dr. Philip Roos said here Monday. **1979** *Time* 2 Apr. 42/2 Freud's dazzling and complex theory of the mind..came along when American psychiatry was doing little more than warehousing the insane and performing the occasional crude Cuckoo's Nest lobotomy.

e. *Stock Exchange slang.* To buy (shares) as a nominee of another trader, with a view to a take-over. Cf. sense 1 b of the vbl. sb.

1977 *Private Eye* 13 May 17/2 The suggested reward to the Swiss holders for 'warehousing' the ex-Bates shares would be perhaps 10p or more per share profit.

'warehouseage. ? *U.S.* [f. WAREHOUSE *sb.* or *v.* + -AGE.] The cost of warehousing.

1915 W. H. PAGE *Note to Sir E. Grey* 5 Nov. §31 Costs and expenses..such as pilotage,..harbour dues, warehouseage, ..etc., be paid by the claimants.

warehouseman ('wɛəhaʊsmən, 'wɛərəsmən). [f. WAREHOUSE *sb.* + MAN *sb.*]

1. A man employed in or having the charge of a warehouse.

1635 in *Times Lit. Suppl.* (1918) 5 Sept. 416/2 Hee was one that was at the imbayling thereof, for twas his place beeing warehousman alwayes to doo that businesse. **1798** *Bay's Rep.* (1809) I. 45 The custom is for a shop-keeper to send home goods in the care of a trusty servant or warehouse man. **1850** J. H. NEWMAN *Serm. Var. Occ.* xii. (1881) 233 He began..with the poor; then he went among shopmen, warehousemen, clerks in banks. **1872** *Daily News* 15 July, A cricket match at the Kennington Oval in which all the players are warehousemen. **1885** *Law Times Rep.* LII. 648/1 Plowright was..employed as a warehouseman by a firm of general merchants in Manchester.

b. (See quot. and WAREHOUSE *sb.* 1 f.)

1875 SOUTHWARD *Dict. Typogr.*, *Warehouseman*, the person who has charge of the warehouse.

2. A wholesale merchant (esp. a trader in textile materials) who has a warehouse for the storing of merchandise.

1677 *Lond. Gaz.* No. 1208/4 Robert Harper Apprentice to John Briant at the Golden Cross in Cateaton-street, London, Warehouse-man,..Ran away from his said Master on the 15 day of June. **1708** *Ibid.* No. 4427/16 Whereas a Commission of Bankrupt is awarded against Thomas Carey, late of London, Warehouse-man. **1745** *De Foe's Eng. Tradesm.* xxxii. (1841) II. 1 The wholesale tradesman is frequently called a warehouse-man, or factor. **1887** *Brit. Textile Warehouseman* 15 Sept. 463 Mr. Campbell is not merely a warehouseman but a manufacturer of the goods displayed. **1903** *Times* 12 Mar. 11/3 Berlin Textiles... Warehousemen report a pause in the demand.

b. ***Italian warehouseman***: see ITALIAN *a.*

warehousing ('wɛərhaʊzɪŋ), *vbl. sb.* [f. WAREHOUSE *v.* + -ING[1].]

1. The depositing goods, etc., in a warehouse whether under bond or otherwise. Also *concr.*, money paid for the accommodation of a warehouse.

1795 J. PHILLIPS *Inland Navig.* Add. 135 Profits arising from the warehousing and wharfage of goods. **1853** *Act 16 & 17 Vict.* c. 107 §10 To provide Warehouses for the warehousing of Tobacco at the Ports. **1878** LECKY *Eng. in 18th C.* (1883) I. 335 The system of warehousing, or admitting as a temporary deposit, foreign goods, free of duty, to await exportation.

b. *Stock Exchange slang.* (See quot. 1974.) Cf. WAREHOUSE *v.* e.

1971 *Daily Tel.* 23 Jan. 14/6 'Warehousing' is an old City practice. **1973** *Times* 8 June 1/3 The memorandum has proposals designed to stop the practice of 'warehousing'. **1974** *Daily Tel.* (Colour Suppl.) 22 Feb. 22/2 'Warehousing'—the technique of building up in collusion a major shareholding in a company behind the cloak of nominee names with a view to a take-over. **1983** *Observer* 27 Mar. 18/9 Not a little 'warehousing' may have proved the prelude to recent attacks from South of the border.

c. *U.S. colloq.* The placing of mental patients or other disadvantaged people in large and impersonal institutions. Cf. WAREHOUSE *sb.* 1 h.

1973 *National Rev.* (U.S.) 7 Dec. 1259 California's shift from the 'warehousing of the mentally ill' in large state mental institutions has become a model for the nation. **1976** *National Observer* (U.S.) 10 Jan. 2/1 Mental patients have the right to receive community care as an alternative to institutional 'warehousing' or release without care, according to a ruling by a Federal court in Washington, D.C. **1983** *Chicago Sun-Times* 2 Aug. 7 Warehousing became the new 'thing'. Forget about making men better, the theory ran.

2. *Comb.*

1800 *Asiatic Ann. Reg.* II. 41/1 An act passed in the last session, commonly called the 'warehousing act'. **1817** *Evans's Parl. Deb.* I. 1327 Mr. W. Pole said, the warehousing system was not thought of at the time the hon. baronet mentioned (1806). **1844** H. H. WILSON *Brit. India* I. 505 The Ministers would have been pledged to support the sale and warehousing system of the Company.

wareide, variant of WARIED.

wareine, obs. form of WARREN.

wareland, var. WARLAND *Obs.*

'wareless, *a.* ? *Obs.* [f. WARE *sb.*[1] + -LESS.]

Very frequent in Spenser and Daniel.

1. Unwary, incautious, imprudent.

1562 A. BROOKE *Romeus & Jul.* 220 How surely are the wareless wrapt by those that lye in wayte? **1596** SPENSER *F.Q.* v. v. 17 Yet was he iustly damned by the doome Of his owne mouth, that spake so wareless word, To be her thrall. **1595** DANIEL *Civ. Wars* v. v, For warelesse insolence whilst vndebard Of bounding awe, runnes on to such excesse. **1751** MENDEZ *Seasons* xxvi. in Pearch *Coll. Poems* (1770) II. 241 The wareless sheep no longer bite the mead. **1767** MICKLE *Concub.* I. xxvi, Ythrilld with Horrour gapd the wareless Wight. **1813** HOGG *Queen's Wake* Introd. 6 Your blights, your chilling influence shed, On wareless heart and houseless head. **1847** H. S. RIDDELL *Poems* 18 But that's a' true, now that I mind To caution ane sae wareless.

absol. **1563** *Mirr. Mag.*, *Blacke Smyth* iii, Who seemes in sight as simple as a saynt, Hath layd a bayte the wareles to begyle.

2. Unguarded, unconscious (*of* danger).

1562 PHAER *Æneid* IX. Bb 3, And first Euryalus he seeth whom al mens hands had got, Through fraud of night and place of troublous tumult wareles trapt. **1596** SPENSER *F.Q.* IV. ii. 3 Both they vnwise, and warelesse of the euill, That by themselues vnto themselues is wrought. *Ibid.* v. i. 22 That when he wak't out of his warelesse paine, He found him selfe, vnwist, so ill bestad, That lim he could not wag. **1821** *Blackw. Mag.* IX. 540 How bright it burns!—of threatening wreck To warn the wareless mariner.

†'wareliness. *Obs.* [f. WARELY *a.* + -NESS.] Caution, carefulness.

c **1000** *Ags. Hom.* (Assmann) xiii. 263 Us is on ðam micel wærlicnys ʒetacnad and æteowed on ðære onfangennysse ures drihtnes lichaman. *a* **1425** tr. *Arderne's Treat. Fistula* etc. 74 Aftirward..be þe longaon putte into his place, and be it fast bondyn with warlynez [L. *ligetur cum cautela*] þat it go noȝt out.

warelond, variant of WARLAND *Obs.* exc. *Hist.*

†'warely, *a.* *Obs.* Forms: 1 wærlic, 5 warli, waarly, 4–5 warly. [OE. *wærlic*, f. *wær* WARE *sb.*[1]: see -LY[1]. Cf. ON. *varligr.*] Of a person, his actions, etc.: Cautious, circumspect, prudent.

a **900** CYNEWULF *Elene* 544 (Gr.) Wisdomes beðearf, worda wærlicra, & witan snyttro, se ðære æðelan sceal and wyrde aʒifan. *a* **1000** *Gloss.* in Wr.-Wülcker 201/40 *Cauta*, wærlic, *sollicita*. *c* **1000** *Laws of Æthelred* VI. xxxiii. (Lieberm.), Wærlic bið, þæt man æʒhwilce ʒeare sona æfter eastron yrdscipa ʒearwiʒe. *c* **1380** WYCLIF *Sel. Wks.* III. 242 For knowynge of perels makiþ men warlyer to flee hem. *c* **1400** *Destr. Troy* 649, I wull send to you sone by a sure maydon: Bes wakond and warly. *c* **1400** *Rule St. Benet* (Verse) 453 Bot first hir-self,..Sal councel þam,..Bi wordes warli anes or twis. **1491** CAXTON *Vitas Patr.* (W. de W. 1495) II. 178/2 Men ought to thynke dyscretly and by waarly delyberacyon; yf a thynge is lawfull to be doon.

†'warely, *adv.* *Obs.* Forms: 1 wærlíce, 3 wearliche, 3–4 warliche, warli, (3 warlyche), 4–6 warly, *Sc.* varly, 4 waarly, (5 waarli, werly), 5–6 *Sc.* warlie, 6 warelye, 5–6 warely. [OE. *wærlíce*, f. *wær* WARE *a.*: see -LY[2].] Watchfully, cautiously, circumspectly; prudently. Cf. WARILY *adv.*

c **897** ÆLFRED *Gregory's Past. C.* xxviii. 190 Forðæm him is swiðe micel ðearf ðæt he swæ micle wærlicor [L. *tanto cautius*] hiene healde wið scylda. *c* **1000** ÆLFRIC *Jos.* ii. 16 Farað eow nu wærlice and ʒewendað to muntum. *c* **1200** *Trin. Coll. Hom.* 199 Bute we þe warluker us bureȝen. *c* **1205** LAY. 12277 Ah Ælfwald & his broðer al heo þuhten oðer heo uerden swiðe warliche. *Ibid.* 12300 þa cheorles wenden to þan wuden & warliche heom hudden. *a* **1225** *Ancr. R.* 198 Goð, þauh, ful warliche: vor iðisse wildernesse beoð monie vuele bestes. *a* **1240** *Sawles Warde* in *O.E. Hom.* I. 245 We ahen wearliche to biwiten us seoluen wið þe unwiht of helle ant his wrenches. **1388** WYCLIF *1 Sam.* xviii. 14 And Dauid dide warli [1382 wiseli, Vulg. *prudenter*] in alle hise weies. *a* **1425** tr. *Arderne's Treat. Fistula*, etc. 12 Putte it hotte vppon and bynde it warly þat it fal not away. *c* **1440** *Promp. Parv.* 517/1 Warely, or slyly, *caute*. *c* **1449** PECOCK *Repr.* II. ix. 194 The feendis wijlis and deceitis ben forto be waarli considerid and forto be smertli fled. **1540** PALSGR. *Acolastus* IV. iii. T j b, He that ones falleth into the dytche, wyll after loke better or warelyer or he lepe. **1548–9** *Book Com. Prayer*, *Offices* 31 And maye walke more warely in these daungerous dayes. **1574** WHITGIFT *Def. Aunsw.* II. 100 He speaketh also of Ceremonies and traditions, as moderately, as diuinely, and as warely as any man dothe. **1590** SPENSER *F.Q.* I. xii. 36 They..bound him hand and foote with yron chains. And with continuall watch did warely keepe. **1594** PLAT *Jewel-ho.* III. 34 So as the same bee warely distilled with a trew diuision of the partes. **1908** HARDY *Dynasts* III. III. iii, He warely closes up his remnant to the walls.

waren, obs. f. WARN *v.*[1], WARREN, WHEREON.

†warence. *Obs.* [a. OF. *warance* (12th c. in Hatz.-Darm.; also 13th c. in Wr.-Wülcker 556/19, 15th c. in *Alphita* 155) = mod.F. *garance* madder.] = MADDER *sb.*[1]

1525 *Grete Herbal* cccl xvii. (1529) U iv, Rubea the more.. is the herbe that warence or madder is made of. *Ibid.* ccccxvii. Z j b, Spargula..is lyke to warence in leues. **1597** GERARDE *Herbal* Suppl., Warence is Madder. **1665** LOVELL *Herball* (ed. 2) 464 Warence, see Madder.

warener, obs. form of WARRENER.

'wareness. *Obs.* exc. *poet.* Forms: 1 wærnes, -nys, 4–5 warnesse, 4–6 warenes, 5 waarnes(s, 6 wareness(e, 5–6 warnes. [OE. *wærnes*, f. *wær* WARE *a.*: see -NESS.] Cautiousness, vigilance.

971 *Blickl. Hom.* 213 Hæfde he miccle lufan & ealle wærnesse to ælcum men. **1357** *Lay Folks Catech.* (L.) 1273 The v. vertu ys warnesse and sleyȝte. in god to know þe goode fro þe yuyl. *c* **1449** PECOCK *Repr.* I. xvi. 92 He schal.. take greet waarnes that he be not..bigilid. **1526** *Pilgr. Perf.* (W. de W. 1531) 44 b, Discrete cautele or warenes, and diligence, with suche other. **1562** TURNER *Herbal* II. 78, I.. dare not wthout grete warnes geue it in to ye body. **1583** GOLDING *Calvin on Deut.* xxi. 125 Let euerie of vs..rowse vp all our wittis, and gather them about vs applying them earnestly to this care and warenesse which Moses speaketh of here. **1930** AUDEN *Poems* 57 In his day-thinking and in his night-thinking Is wareness and is fear of other.

warent(e, -ise, obs. ff. WARRANT, -ISE.

warenyss, variant of WARNISH *v.*[1] *Obs.*

wareshi (wæˈrɛʃɪ). Also **warishi.** [Origin obscure; variously asserted to be Carib and Arawak.] In Guyana, a type of basket worn on the back and held by a headband round the forehead.

1924 *38th Ann. Rep. U.S. Bureau Amer. Ethnol. 1916–17* xviii. 375 The way soldiers carry their knapsacks..is the general mode which the Indians adopt..for carrying burdens... The names of these articles: waiyari (Arawak), ..and walishi or warishi (Carib.). **1958** J. CAREW *Black Midas* vi. 102 Naked Amerindian families in single file, the men in front with wareshis harnessed to their foreheads and shoulders. **1964** C. HENFREY *Gentle People* v. 103 He was reluctant to use a wareshi, an Indian carrier made from vines. **1975** C. F. GRITZNER *Guyana in Pictures* v. 59 (*caption*) A prospector ready for the trail carries his gear in a 'warishi' (Amerindian basket) capable of carrying weights of up to 200 pounds.

ware so, southern ME. var. WHERESO.

wares(s)che, var. forms of WARISH *v. Obs.*

warest, pa. t. of WARISH *v. Obs.*

†ˈ**warestall.** *Sc. Obs.* Forms: 6 **wairstall, wairstaw, waistaw, vairscall, vairsta, war-, varstay.** [f. WARE *sb.*[3] + STALL *sb.*] A store cupboard.

1508 *Acc. Ld. High Treas. Scot.* IV. 111 Item, for lokkis and bandis to the gret wair stallis in the Kingis wardrob in Edinburgh, vs. **1530** *Burgh Rec. Edin.* (1871) II. 39 Ane waistaw, a schryne, ane chyrater. **1538** *Aberd. Reg.* (MS.) XVI. (Jam.), Ane fysche fat, a geill fat, a vairscall. **1561** *Extracts Aberd. Reg.* (1844) I. 336 Ane almary, ane vairsta, ane maill fatt. **1565** in D. Hay Fleming *Reform. Scot.* (1910) 610 Ane langsadill of aik, with ane greit wairstaw of aik. **1572** *Rec. Elgin* (New Spalding Club) I. 134 Airschip guidis ..ane karr, ane muksled, ane varstay, ane almrie.

waret, variant of WARIED *ppl. a. Obs.,* cursed.

†ˈ**waretack.** *Obs.* [Perh. a use of the nautical WARTAKE (associated with WARE *v.*[1]).] A safeguard.

1542 BRINKLOW *Lament.* (1874) 86 Ye will haue a prest to singe for you also, as it ware for a waretack. *Ibid.* 88 Bycause ye haue not full trust in Christes meretes, ye grope after vayne waretackes.

wareþoru, southern ME. var. WHERETHROUGH.

ware uore, southern ME. var. WHEREFORE.

ware wiþ, ME. var. WHEREWITH.

warewolf, obs. var. WERWOLF.

wareyn(e, obs. forms of WARREN.

warf, obs. form of WHARF *sb.* and *v.*

warfare (ˈwɔːfɛə(r)), *sb.* Forms: see WAR *sb.*[1]; also 6 **-far,** 6–7 *Sc.* **-fair.** [f. WAR *sb.*[1] + FARE *sb.*[1]] A going to war (cf. b); the action of carrying on, or engaging in, war; the act or state of conflict; military life or service.

1456 SIR G. HAYE *Law Arms* (S.T.S.) 114 Out of his lordis land suld pas nouthir hors na men till othir contree in armes na werefare. *c* **1514** BARCLAY *Eglog* iii. (1570) B vj b, For nought is in warfar saue care and misery. **1611** BIBLE *1 Sam.* xxviii. 1 The Philistines gathered their armies together for warfare. **1651** HOBBES *Leviath.* II. xxviii. 166 The most common Souldier, may demand the due wages of his warrefare, as a debt. **1841** J. F. COOPER *Deerslayer* vii, He was as yet unpractised in the ruthless expedients of savage warfare. **1900** *Longman's Mag.* March 440 Having acquired ..a brevet colonelcy in Indian frontier warfare.

†**b.** Phr. *to go (forth) a warfare,* to go to the war; also *to go* (etc.) *on warfare, to pass (forth) in warfare* (Sc.); *to send a warfare.* Also *a warfare,* in the field (= L. *militiae*). *Obs.*

In these phrases *a* is A *prep.*[1], but is often mistaken for the indef. article.

1483 *Cely Papers* (Camden) 144 Richard Awrey..ȝede forthe a warfare in a schypp of hys owne. **1526** TINDALE *1 Cor.* ix. 7 Who goeth a warfare [τίς στρατεύεται] eny tyme att his awne cost? **1533** BELLENDEN *Livy* (S.T.S.) I. 94 Þir ȝoung men war ordanit to be reddy to pas in werefare aganis þare Inemyis. *a* **1533** BERNERS *Golden Bk. M. Aurel.* (1546) K iv, Torquate her housband was in Asie a warre fare. **1542** UDALL *Erasm. Apoph.* 201 b, Alexander hauing taken a viage on warrefare into Asia. **1553** T. WILSON *Rhet.* 24 He whiche had maried a wyfe, the same yeare shoulde not be forced to go on warrefaire. **1560** DAUS tr. *Sleidane's Comm.* 270 b, Not only at home, but in the campe also, and a warfare. **1571** GOLDING *Calvin on Ps.* xliv. 1. 170 Rather yᵗ we should go a warfare under the crosse. **1574** HELLOWES *Gueuara's Fam. Ep.* (1577) 88 What iniurie doth the Prince to the Captaine that sendes him a warrefare, if he makes him sure to haue the victorie?

c. *transf.* and *fig.*

1549 E. ALLEN *Jude's Par. Rev.* vii. 9–12 So long as they remayne in the warrefare of this transitorye lyfe. **1657** *Penit. Conf.* 348 Nor can there in this spiritual warfare be better weapons than prayers and tears. **1735** POPE *Ep. Lady* 118 Who, with herself, or others, from her birth Finds all her life one warfare upon earth. **1807–8** W. IRVING *Salmag.* (1824) 291 All the various artillery of fashionable warfare. **1875** JOWETT *Plato* (ed. 2) I. 194 They are most skilful in legal warfare.

†ˈ**warfare,** *v. Obs.* [f. prec. sb.] *intr.* To wage war; to take part in war; to serve in the field. Also *fig.*

1565 STAPLETON tr. *Bede's Hist.* III. xviii. 94 Wherein having, with much devotion, warfared a longe time to God. **1567** PAINTER *Pal. Pleas.* Concl., Euery sort and sexe that warfare in the fielde of humaine life. **1569** SANFORD tr. *Agrippa's Van. Artes* xxiii. 40 Yet with these shippes we make them muche more daungerous, robbing and warrefairinge in them, no otherwise then we do in the maine lande. **1598** FLORIO, *Militare,* to warrefarre, to follow the warres. **1652** GAULE *Magastrom.* 369 A certaine Germane warfaring in Italy.

Hence †ˈ**warˌfarer,** a warrior. ˈ**warˌfaring** *vbl. sb.*

1591 J. ELIOT tr. *B. de Loque's Disc. Warre* 31 Thus much for the rules of warfarers. **1598** R. BERNARD tr. *Terence, Heaut.* Argt., Menedemus..forced his sonne Clinia..to goe a warrefaring. **1656** EARL MONM. tr. *Boccalini's Advts. fr. Parnass.* I. xxxv. (1674) 44 His indiscreet way of warfaring in Asia. **1840** CARLYLE *Heroes* ii. (1858) 232 During these wild warfarings and strugglings. **1876** MORRIS *Sigurd* III. (1877) 196 The Burg of the Niblung people and the heart of their warfaring.

warfarin (ˈwɔːfərɪn). *Pharm.* Also **Warfarin.** [f. *W*isconsin *A*lumni *R*esearch *F*oundation + *-arin,* after COUMARIN: see -IN[1].] A water-soluble crystalline anticoagulant used as a selective rodenticide, and as a prophylactic against embolism in the treatment of thrombosis; 3-(3-oxo-1-phenylbutyl)-4-hydroxy-coumarin, $C_{19}H_{16}O_4$; (also *warfarin sodium*) the sodium salt of this.

1950 *Chem. Abstr.* XLIV. 7019 *Warfarin,* a coined name for the anticoagulant rodenticidal chemical 3-(α-acetonylbenzyl)-4-hydroxycoumarin. S. A. Rohwer... U.S. Dept. Agr. Interdepartmental Comm. on Pest Control, June 29, 1950, 2 pp. (mimeographed). **1968** *Times* 16 Dec. 7/4 Rats which are immune to warfarin, the most widely used rat poison in the world, are spreading. **1973** *Country Life* 1 Mar. 510/1 The grey squirrel cannot be tolerated... Shortly it will be permissible to use Warfarin in hoppers. **1976** *Lancet* 25 Dec. 1414/2 Anticoagulant therapy with warfarin sodium was started.

ˈ**warˌfaring,** *ppl. a.* [f. WARFARE *v.* + -ING[2].] That wages war; that serves, or takes part, in war; militant. Also *fig.*

1549 E. ALLEN *Jude's Par. Rev.* xxii. 1–4 This militant & warrfarynge churche. **1644** MILTON *Areop.* (Arb.) 45 He is the true warfaring Christian. **1840** CARLYLE *Heroes* iv. (1858) 272 He is the warfaring and battling Priest. **1882** STEVENSON *New Arab. Nts., Sire de Malétroit,* Lads were early formed in that rough, warfaring epoch.

Hence †ˈ**warfaringly** *adv.*

1611 COTGR., *Belliqueusement,* martially, warlikely; warfaringly.

warff, obs. form of WHARF.

warfor(e, obs. forms of WHEREFORE.

†ˈ**warful,** *a. Obs. rare.* [f. WAR *sb.*[1] + -FUL.] Bellicose.

1530 PALSGR. 328/2 Warfull, *batailleux.* **1755** H. WALPOLE *Let. to Chute* 20 Oct., Lord Robert Bertie, with a company of the Guards, has thrown himself into Dover Castle; don't they sound very war-full?

warg (wɑːg). [ad. ON. *vargr* wolf; cf. OE. *wearg* and WARY *sb.*] In the tales of J. R. R. Tolkien: a wolf of a particularly evil kind.

1937 J. R. R. TOLKIEN *Hobbit* vi. 107 Even the wild Wargs (for so the evil wolves over the Edge of the Wild were named) cannot climb trees. **1954** —— *Fellowship of Ring* II. i. 234 There are wargs and werewolves. **1968** *Radio Times* 26 Sept. 48 It [*sc. The Hobbit's* Middle-Earth] is..peopled by dwarves, elves, goblins, giant spiders, trolls, wargs.

war-god, war-goddess. A god or goddess who presides over war. Also *fig.*

c **1611** CHAPMAN *Iliad* v. 30 The War-god..Who raged so on the Ilion side. **1837** CARLYLE *Fr. Rev.* I. v. iii. (*heading*), Broglie the War-God. **1860** GEO. ELIOT *Mill on Fl.* VI. x, Maggie..glared at him like a wounded war-goddess. **1906** W. A. CRAIGIE *Relig. Anc. Scand.* i. 15 Odin..is a war-god, who assigns victory or defeat to men.

ˈ**war-horse. a.** A powerful horse ridden in war by a knight or trooper; a charger.

1653 RAMESEY *Astrol. Restored* 184 In buying of Arms, War-horses, or Instruments of War. **1688** HOLME *Armoury* II. 150/2 Warr Horses, such as are trained and brought up not..to run back at the rattling of Drums, [etc.]. **1709** STEELE *Tatler* No. 61 ¶6 A War-Horse belonging to one of the Colonels of the Artillery, to be Let or Sold. **1814** SCOTT *Lord of Isles* I. xv, So chafes the war-horse in his might, That fieldward bears some valiant knight. **1845** D. JERROLD *St. Giles* xx, The old war-horse pricks his ears at the murderous music of the trumpet. **1883** J. PARKER *Apost. Life* II. 174 The war-horse will paw when he can no longer stand.

b. *fig.* A veteran soldier or politician; a person full of warlike memories. Also used of veterans of other activities, esp. acting.

1837 R. M. BIRD *Nick of Woods* I. 68 Ar'nt thee the Pennsylvanny war-horse, the screamer of the meeting-house? **1867** A. D. RICHARDSON *Beyond Mississippi* 151 That old war horse..threw off the black shaggy bearskin overcoat which he invariably wore. **1884** *American* VIII. 291 Which reminds us of the well-known admission of the party 'war-horse' that he would vote for the enemy of mankind if he got the 'regular' nomination. **1902** *Daily Chron.* 26 Apr. 5/1 That old political war-horse..Sir George Dibbs. **1910** *National Police Gaz.* (U.S.) 16 July 3/1 She mixed with a lot of old war-horses and really thought she was an actress. **1933** S. LEWIS *Ann Vickers* xi. 128 If she had been nervous behind the scenes, this old war-horse, this professional who had played her Lady Macbeth to much worse houses, did not seem nervous now. **1958** *Spectator* 13 June 778/1 Dr. Inge, as an old *Evening Standard* war-horse, has even posthumously some truculent things to say.

c. A tough or determined woman.

1921 R. FRY *Let.* 13 Oct. (1972) II. 514 An old campaigning English lady artist..this excessively repulsive and brick-red old war horse. **1959** A. CHRISTIE *Cat among Pigeons* v. 67 A sharp old war-horse, called Miss Chadwick, keeps a wary eye on me.

d. *fig.* Something which is frequently used or very familiar; *spec.* a work of art, esp. music, which is frequently performed.

1947 A. EINSTEIN *Music in Romantic Era* xv. 209 There is a whole series of operatic transcriptions..all pieces that are great technical war-horses. **1952** *Mind* LXI. 495 These verbs..are important because they include such philosophical war-horses as *know, believe* and *deduce.* **1958** J. FLANNER in *New Yorker* 27 Sept. 96/2 'Ben Hur'—the old theatrical war horse that has had Ben running..since.. 1899. **1969** *Listener* 1 May 594/1 Deliberately constructed secondary films fall into various types. There are the old-style 'visual aids', such as the famous war-horse on medieval castles which has for long been cantering round the primary and secondary schools. **1977** *New Yorker* 10 Oct. 37/2, I turned on the radio, and there was Artur Rubinstein, playing my old war-horse, the Saint-Saëns, G-Minor Concerto, live from Festival Hall.

wari (wɒˈriː, ˈwɒrɪ). Also **awari, warri.** [prob. Ashanti.] A board game, originally West African but now played also in the West Indies and Guyana, a variation of mancala.

1927 G. T. BENNETT in R. S. Rattray *Religion & Art in Ashanti* xxxii. 382 Wari..is a game for two players using.. 48 pebbles and a board hollowed out into two parallel rows of six cups. **1959** *Chambers's Encycl.* VI. 162/2 *Mancala,* a sedentary game with some likeness to chess or draughts... It was carried by slaves to the West Indies (with its Ashanti name of *wari*) and into Dutch Guinea. **1960** R. C. BELL *Board & Table Games* 120 Awari is a masculine pastime though women occasionally play... Making Awari boards involves spiritual danger, and only old men who have lost a wife are allowed to make them. **1975** *Observer* (Colour Suppl.) 30 Nov. 40/2 Groups of men [in Bridgetown] play 'warri', an old game brought to Barbados from Africa.

wari, var. WARY *v. Obs.,* to curse.

†ˈ**wariable,** *a. Obs.* [f. WARY *v.* + -ABLE.] Deserving of cursing; execrable.

1382 WYCLIF *Prov.* xviii. 1 Alle time wariable [Vulg. *exprobabilis*] he shal be. —— *Ecclus.* xxvii. 33 Wrathe and wodnesse, either ben wariable [Vulg. *execrabilia*].

wariable, -ance, -and: see VARIABLE, VARIANCE, VARYING.

†**wariangle.** *Obs.* Forms: 1 ? **wearȝincel,** 4–5 **variangel, were-, weryangle, wayryngle,** 4, 7–8 **waryangle,** 6–9 **wariangle,** 6 **warriangle,** 7 **warwinckle, wierangle, -angel, wirrangle.** [? OE. *wearȝincel* shrike (Sweet: authority not known). Cf. OHG. (MHG.) *warchengil, wargengel, wargingel,* etc. 'cruricula', etc. (Steinmeyer-Sievers, Diefenbach), G. *wargengel, warkengel* (with very many local variants due to different etymologizing alterations; as *würgengel, quasi* 'destroying angel'). Cf. also MLG. *worgel,* OHG. (MHG.) *wargil, warigel, wergil, worgel* (Bavarian dial. *wörgl* shrike, Salzburg *wörgel* greenfinch). All these forms appear to be diminutives of OTeut. **warȝo-z* murderer: see WARY *sb.*

The OE. word, if genuine, perh. preserves most nearly the original form. For the suffix compare OE. *húsincel, túnincel, þéowincel,* etc. (all without umlaut). Cf. OHG. *-inklî(n.* It remains, however, very remarkable that in G. or in later E. there is no trace of *-k* forms with the single exception of *warwinckle* in quot. 1618. As there is no evidence of the word later until Chaucer, the ME. and later forms are perhaps in part due to, or influenced by, some continental form. The prevalent form of the ending, *-angle, -ingle,* is perh. partly due to association with HANG *v.* (owing to the habits of the shrike). In early times the first element would assist this etymology: cf. OE. *wearȝtréo,* WARYTRE gallows. Such an association was apparently present in early G.: cf. such forms as *wurgelhâch, wurgelhâhe, warchengil, warkengel,* etc.]

1. A name formerly given to the Shrike or Butcher-bird, either the (Great or European) Grey Shrike (*Lanius excubitor*) or the smaller red-backed Shrike (*L. collurio*). See SHRIKE *sb.*[2]

Apart from the doubtful OE. form and two obscure passages in ME. the evidence for the existence of the word is almost solely drawn from dictionaries, glossaries, and dialect collections of doubtful value, some of which perh. merely echo quot. 1598.

c **1386** CHAUCER *Friar's T.* 110 This Somonour, that was as ful of Iangles, As ful of venym been thise waryangles. **1598** SPEGHT *Chaucer's Wks.* Annot. Bbbb v, *Warriangles* Be a kind of birdes full of noyse and very rauenous, preying vpon others, which when they haue taken, they vse to hang vpon a thorne or pricke, & teare them in pieces and deuoure them. And the common opinion is, that the thorne wherupon they thus fasten them and eate them, is afterward poysonsome. In Staffordshire and Shropshire the name is common. **1611** COTGR., *Ancrouëlle,* a Shrike, Nin-murder,

Wariangle. **1618** LATHAM *2nd Bk. Falconrie* 144 The Warwinckle which is a pyed bird, and vses most in pasturground, or other champane places whereas growes great and tall bushes. **1674** RAY *Collect., Eng. Birds* 83 The great Butcher-bird called in the Peak of Derbyshire Wirrangle, *Lanius cinereus major.* **1678** —— *Willughby's Ornith.* II. xi. 87 This Bird in the North of England is called a Wierangle, a name, it seems, common to us with the Germans, who (as Gesner witnesseth) about Strasburgh, Franckfort, and elsewhere, call it Werkengel or Warkangel. **1686** PLOT *Staffordsh.* 229 The Butcher-bird or Wierangel, here called the Shriek or French-Pye. **1885** SWAINSON *Prov. Names Birds* 47 *Red-backed shrike*, Butcher bird, Murdering bird, Ninekiller, Weirangle or Wariangle (Yorkshire).

2. Used as a term of contemptuous abuse. *rare*$^{-1}$.

a **1400-50** *Wars Alex.* 1706 A wirlyng, a wayryngle [*Dubl. MS.* warlow], a wawil-ȝid shrewe.

warians, obs. Sc. form of VARIANCE.

† **'waribreed.** *Obs.* Forms: 1 **wearȝ(e)-, wearhbrǽde,** 6 **warrybrede,** 8 **waribreed.** [OE. *wearhbrǽde* wk. fem., f. **wearh-* = WARE *sb.*^{6}, pus, matter + *-brǽde* cogn. w. *brǽd* flesh.] In OE. some kind of ulcer or eruption; in 16–18th c. = WARBLE *sb.*^{2} 2.

c **1000** ÆLFRIC *Voc.* in Wr.-Wülcker 158/23 *Impetigo*, eaȝan wenn, *uel* wearhbræde. *c* **1050** *Voc., ibid.* 457/6 *Neuum*, wearȝebræde. *c* **1000** *Sax. Leechd.* I. 86 Ȝif hwylcum wearȝbræde [*v.r.* wearh-; L. *ulcus*] weaxe on þam nosum oððe on þam hleore. **1523–34** FITZHERB. *Husb.* §63 There be beastes that wyll haue warrybredes in dyuers partes of theyr body and legges. **1725** *Bradley's Family Dict.* s.v. *Warnel-worm*, This Disease in some Cattle runs into divers Parts of their Bodies, called by some the *Wari-breed.*

wariche, variant of WARISH *v. Obs.*

warie, variant of WARY *v. Obs.*, to curse.

† **'waried**, *ppl. a. Obs.* [f. WARY *v.* + -ED^1.] Cursed, accursed.

c **975** *Rushw. Gosp.* Matt. xiii. 19 Cymþ se wærȝad [Vulg. *venit malus*] & ȝeriseð þte sauwen wæs. *a* **1175** *Cott. Hom.* 239 Þe wereȝede gastes. *c* **1250** *Gen. & Ex.* 544 Mis-wiuen hem gunnen seðes sunes, .. And mengten wið waried kin. *a* **1300** *Cursor M.* 2077 Fle me fra, þou wared thing. *Ibid.* 10067 Quar-thoru þe warlaw wirid wight. For-cummen es. **13..** *E.E. Allit. P.* B. 1716 Wale wyne to þy wenches in waryed stoundes. *a* **1340** HAMPOLE *Psalter* i. 1 This is a werid counsaile. **1340** —— *Pr. Consc.* 6186 Yhe weryed wyghtes wende fra my sight. *c* **1375** *Sc. Leg. Saints* xxviii. (*Margaret*) 526 Þis waryt Iug, in stul set, gert margaret son befor hym fet. *c* **1470** HENRY *Wallace* VIII. 1377 In waryit tym that Hesilryg was born! *a* **1585** MONTGOMERIE *Flyting* (Tullibardine MS.) 607 Sua knavishe, canker[d], execrabill, And vareit ane wicht.

Hence † **wariedhed** [-HEAD], cursedness.

1382 WYCLIF *Wisd.* v. 13 In oure wariedhed [Vulg. *malignitate*] forsothe wee ben wastid. *Ibid.* v. 24.

† **'warier.** *Obs.* Also 4 **-ere,** 5 **-ar, waryare,** 6 **weriour.** [f. WARY *v.* + -ER^1.] One who curses.

1382 WYCLIF *Ps.* xxi. 17 The counseil of wariers [Vulg. *concilium malignantium*] besegide me. —— *1 Cor.* v. 11 A .. cursere [*gloss*] or wariere [Vulg. *maledicus*]. *c* **1410** *Lantern of Light* 131 War[i]ars, cursars, schidars, sclaundirars & blasfemars. *c* **1440** *Promp. Parv.* 516/2 Waryare, or bannare, *imprecator, -trix, anathematizator, maledicus.* **1513** DOUGLAS *Æneis*, etc. (1874) IV. 226 That, ȝou to pleys, I set all schame behind, Offeryng me to my weriouris wilfully.

† **'warify,** *v. Obs.* (*nonce-wd.*) [? f. WARY *a.* + -FY.] *trans.* To render wary or timorous.

1614 SYLVESTER *Panaretus* 801 *Parlt. Vertues Roy.* 34 Thou [Andria = Fortitude] art lockt vp in Princes Cabinets; Among the Corselets, which, now wariefied Through loue of Peace, they haue new layd aside.

warily ('wɛərɪlɪ), *adv.* [f. WARY *a.* + -LY^2.] In a wary manner, cautiously, †watchfully.

1552 HULOET, Warilye, *solerter, uigilanter.* **1599** SHAKS. *Hen. V*, III. vii. 61 They that .. ride not warily, fall into foule Boggs. **1605** B. JONSON *Volpone* I. v, Shee's kept as warily, as is your gold: Neuer do's come abroad, neuer takes ayre, But at a windore. **1646** SIR T. BROWNE *Pseud. Ep.* I. viii. 33 More warily are we to receive the relations of Philes, who in Greeke Iambicks delivered the proprieties of Animals. **1658** ROWLAND tr. *Moufet's Theat. Ins.* 914 It [*sc.* honey] is a heavenly gift, and very profitable for men, if they use it well and warily. **1747** WESLEY *Prim. Physick* (1762) 37 Take ripe Puff balls. Break them warily. **1849** MACAULAY *Hist. Eng.* vii. II. 163 Surrounded by snares in which an ordinary youth would have perished, William learned to tread at once warily and firmly. **1875** JOWETT *Plato* (ed. 2) IV. 396 Their adversaries defend themselves warily from an invisible world.

† **'wariment.** *Obs. rare*$^{-1}$. [f. WARY *a.* + -MENT.] Precaution.

1596 SPENSER *F.Q.* IV. iii. 17 Full many strokes .. The whiles were enterchaunged... Yet they were all with so good wariment Or warded, or auoyded .. That [etc.].

warinar, obs. form of WARRENER.

† **warine.** *Obs.* [A rendering of Buffon's *ouarine*, a misreading for **ouarive*, ad. Sp. *guariba* (*b* = *v*).] = GUARIBA.

1774 GOLDSM. *Nat. Hist.* IV. 235 The first of the sapajous is the Warine, or the Brazilian Guariba. [**1785** SMELLIE *Buffon's Nat. Hist.* (1791) VIII. 176 *note*, Ouarine, the name of this animal at Maragnon.]

war-ine, obs. form of WHEREIN.

wariner, obs. form of WARRENER.

wariness ('wɛərɪnɪs). [f. WARY *a.* + -NESS.] The quality of being wary; cautiousness, circumspection.

1552 HULOET, Warines, *solertia, uigilantia.* **1561** HOBY tr. *Castiglione's Courtier* II. (1900) 114 The discretion and warinesse that count Lewis shewed us yesterday. **1666** BOYLE *Orig. Forms & Qual.* 258 And having agen made the former Experiment with more wariness then before, we had the like success in our Distillation. **1774** REYNOLDS *Disc. R. Acad.* vi. (1778) 221 He that is forming himself, must look with great caution and wariness on those peculiarities or prominent parts, which at first force themselves upon view. **1821** LAMB *Elia, All Fools' Day*, Prizing their simplicity beyond the .. somewhat unfeminine wariness of their competitors, I felt a kindliness .. for those five thoughtless virgins. **1871** DARWIN *Desc. Man* I. ii. 50 Our domestic dogs are descended from wolves .. and though they may not have gained in cunning, and may have lost in waryness and suspicion, yet [etc.]. **1893** LYDEKKER *Horns & Hoofs* 106 They are marvellously shy and wary, this wariness being fully confirmed by Messrs. Danford and Buxton.

'waring, *vbl. sb. Obs.* exc. *dial.* Also 4 **varinge,** 5 **waryn(e, varin,** 6 **wayring.** [f. WARE *v.*^{2} + -ING^1.]

1. The action of the verb; spending, investing (of money). † *at the waring of*: at the cost of (one's life).

c **1375** *Sc. Leg. Saints* v. (*Johannes*) 125 [God] þat wald þat men mad sic varinge As for almus to sel þare thinge. **1494** HALYBURTON *Ledger* 37 Som off this waryne of this syd, 119 li. 10 s. 7 g. **1494** *Ibid.* 63 Som of my varin is, 59 li. 13 s. 8 g. **1497** *Ibid.* 59 Item for my seruis sellin and waryn sen my last cont, 10 li. *a* **1572** KNOX *Hist. Ref.* Wks. 1846 I. 273 We shall .. defend thame, the haill congregatioun of Christ .. at our haill poweris and waring of our lyves, against Sathan. **1586–7** *Burgh Rec. Edin.* (1882) IV. 487 Gevis power .. to Jhonn Robertsoun .. to tak the aythis of the merchants vpoun the quantities of thair wayrings and guids schippet. **1752** *Scotland's Glory & Shame* (1786) 65 And sure I am, that never a man had loss by such a wareing.

† **2.** Payment of a price. *Obs.*

c **1315** *E.E. Psalter* xliii. [xliv.] 13 Þou salde þi folk with out waring [Vulg. *sine pretio*].

† **'waring**, *ppl. a. Obs. rare*$^{-1}$. [f. WARE *v.*^{1} + -ING^2.] Aware, cognisant *of*.

1571 in Strype *Eccl. Mem.* (1721) III. App. lix. 200 He .. was not wytting nor waring of that letter.

Waring ('wɛərɪŋ), *sb.*^{1} *Math.* The name of Edward *Waring* (1734–98), English mathematician, used in the possessive to designate a conjecture that he published in 1770 and which was proved by Hilbert in 1909, that every integer is equal to the sum of not more than *g s*th powers, *g* depending on *s* but not on the integer.

1920 G. H. HARDY *Some Famous Probl. Theory of Numbers* 14, I pass on .. to the principal object of my lecture, the very famous problem known .. as Waring's Problem. **1920** L. E. DICKSON *Hist. Theory of Numbers* II. xxv. 721 E. Maillet proved Waring's theorem for eighth powers. **1940** E. T. BELL *Devel. Math.* xiv. 294 Equally prolific of new analysis and far-reaching theorems in arithmetic was the advance beginning in 1909 with Hilbert's solution of Waring's problem. **1962** C. S. OGILVY *Tomorrow's Math* v. 92 Nineteen fourth powers are required to make up 79, and it is conjectured that 19 is the answer to Waring's problem for fourth powers.

Waring ('wɛərɪŋ), *sb.*^{2} *U.S.* In full: **Waring blender** (also **blendor**). A trade name for a make of food processor, manufactured by Waring Products Corporation, of N.Y. (The device is also used as an agitator in scientific experiments, etc.)

1948 *Amer. Home* June 117/1 Waring blendor. **1950** *House Beautiful* May 188/2 In a Waring Blendor, you mix them in less time... Flips, frappés, fizzes .. are easy hot-weather drinks. **1959** [see HOMOGENIZE *v.* d]. **1960** *Times Lit. Suppl.* 1 July 414/2 'Never nothing like it.' The shops were filled with goods and buyers... In the houses washers, dryers, freezers and refrigerators, air conditioners, vacuum cleaners, Mixmasters, Waring-blenders, television and stereophonic high-fi sets, [etc.]. **1967** M. E. HALE *Biol. Lichens* v. 74 The fragmented mycobiont culture was mixed with the algae in a Waring blender so as to form a suspension. **1977** C. MCFADDEN *Serial* (1978) xxv. 57/1 Last year he gave me this Waring blender.

war-inne, obs. form of WHEREIN.

warinstour, variant of WARNESTORE *sb. Obs.*

† **'warish**, *sb. Obs.*$^{-0}$ [Connected with OE. *wearr*, callosity, wart: see WARRE.] A callosity.

1570 LEVINS *Manip.* 144/11 A warish, *callus.*

† **'warish**, *v.*^{1} *Obs.* Forms: 3–6 **waris,** 4–5 **waris(s)che, -ys(s)che, -es(s)che, -isshe, -ysh, -iche, -yche, -isse, -ys(e, warsche, wars(s)he, warche** (*pa. t.* **warest**), 4–6 **warysshe,** 4–9 **warish.** [f. OF. *wariss-*, pres. stem of *warir*, *g(u)arir*: see GUARISH *v.*]

1. *trans.* To heal, cure (a person, etc.) *of*, (*out of*), a sickness or trouble.

c **1250** *Kent. Serm.* in *O.E. Misc.* 31 Al-so raþe he was i-warisd of his maladie. *a* **1300** *Cursor M.* 21690 Quen þe stanged men moght se þe nedder on þe tre þat hang þai war all warist o þair stang. *c* **1350** *St. Peter* 33 in Horstm. *Altengl. Leg.* (1881) 49 Many þat war seke and sore .. prayd him forto be þare belde And warisch þam out of þaire wo. *c* **1369** CHAUCER *Bk. Duchesse* 1104, I was warshed of al my sorwe. *c* **1450** *Merlin* xii. 173 The kynge Alain .. that lith in sekenesse, and shall neuer be warisshed till [etc.]. **1613** R. C. *Table Alph.* (ed. 3), *Warish*, ease, deliuer.

b. To heal, cure (a sickness, ill).

c **1375** *Sc. Leg. Saints* vii. (*James*) 388 For-þi þi crafte þu keth one me, & waryse myn Infyrmyte. *c* **1386** CHAUCER *Melib.* ¶320 And therfore o vengeaunce is nat warisshed by another vengeaunce ne o wroong by another wroong. *a* **1400** *Stockh. Med. MS.* in *Archæologia* XXX. 353 Fastande to vse sponfull thre Till his sekenesse warched be. **1601** HOLLAND *Pliny* VII. ii. I. 154 There be some there who warish and cure the stinging of serpents with their spittle.

c. *intr.* To recover from sickness or trouble.

13.. *Seuyn Sag.* 1097 The child warisscht fair and wel. *c* **1375** *Sc. Leg. Saints* xxxvii. (*Vincent*) 336 And fosteris hyme wele .. til he begyne to waryse. *a* **1386** CHAUCER *Melib.* ¶16 Youre doghter with the grace of god shal warisshe and escape. *c* **1440** *Promp. Parv.* 517/2 Warschyn' or recuryn of sekenesse, *convalesco.* **1530** PALSGR. 771/2, I warysshe, I recover my helth after a sycknesse or daunger (Lydgat). **1828** W. CARR *Craven Gloss.* II. 239 *Warish*, to recover from sickness. *Ibid.* 286 Hees niver warish'd o't' surfeit he gat last Kersmas. *a* **1864** R. B. PEACOCK *Lonsdale Gloss.* s.v., 'He'll never warish on it' = He will not get over it.

2. *trans.* To guard, secure, protect, preserve; to save, rescue.

c **1350** *Will. Palerne* 2622 For burwes & bold tounes al forbrent were, but ȝit were þei wiþ walles warchet a-boute. **13..** *E.E. Allit. P.* B. 921 Nov walle þe a wonnyng þat þe warisch myȝt. *c* **1400** *Rule St. Benet* 1306 How a hird-man A febil schepe warest & wane. *a* **1568** in *Bannatyne MS.* (Hunter. Club) 233 Beir Chrystis croce .. That is to say, .. Help vthir to beir that ourladin be: Sa sall this warld be .. warisid accordinle. **1600** HOLLAND *Livy* XXXII. xxi. 822 The mediteranean parts within the continent, were so secure and warished from the Romane forces, that [etc.]. **1601** —— *Pliny* XVII. x. I. 511 But ever after it [*sc.* the tree] is warished and safe ynough. **1674** RAY *N.C. Words, Warisht*, that hath conquered any disease, or difficulty, and is secure against the future; also, well stored, or furnished.

Hence † **'warishing** *vbl. sb.*

c **1386** CHAUCER *Melib.* ¶49 As to the warisshynge of youre doghter. *c* **1440** *Promp. Parv.* 517/2 Waryschynge, of sekenesse, *convalescencia.*

† **'warish**, *v.*^{2} *Obs.*$^{-0}$ [f. WARISH *sb.*] *intr.* To become hard or callous.

1570 LEVINS *Manip.* 144/41 To warish, *occallescere.*

warish, variant of WERSH *a.*

† **'warisome**, *a. Obs. rare.* [f. WARY *a.* + -SOME.] Cautious or careful (*that*—). Hence † **'warisomeness.**

1607 TOPSELL *Four-f. Beasts, Of Swine* 682 When the beasts do eat the white [Hellebore], they forbeare the blacke with all wearisomenesse [*sic*]. **1628** WITHER *Brit. Rememb.* IV. 2217 That they might .. Amend their courses; and be warisome That they displeas'd not God, in times to come.

† **'warison.** *Obs.* Forms: 4–6 **wary-, wari-, ware-,** (4 **warei-, vari-,** 5 **wery-, warry-**)**; -soun(e, -son(e,** 4 **-sun,** 5 **-sowne, -sonne, summe;** 9 **warrison.** [a. OF. *warison*, northeastern form of *g(u)arison*: see GARRISON *sb.*]

1. Wealth, possessions. *to bring* (a person) *in* or *to* (*his*) *warison*: to enrich.

1297 R. GLOUC. (Rolls) 2463 Hengist þat hor maister was he [Vortigern] ȝef him lindeseye Londes vaire & Rentes & tounes grete & heye Ware þoru him & is men in vair warison he broȝte. *Ibid.* 8878 Mabile is doȝter was eir of al is londe þe king vor ire eritage him gan vnderstonde To bringe roberd is sone abast in is warison þere þoru spousinge of þis mayde. **13..** *Sir Beues* (MS. A.) 2142 Wide whar ichaue iwent And me warisoun ispent. **1390** GOWER *Conf.* I. 64 Bot yet his herte .. Among his bedes most devoute Goth in the worldes cause aboute, How that he myhte his warisoun Encresce. *Ibid.* I. 155 Mi fader hier hath bot a lite Of warison. *c* **1400** *Ywaine & Gaw.* 918 Bot i sal help the fra presowne, And bring the to thi warisowne. *c* **1475** *Rauf Coilȝear* 919 For thy my warysoun is full gude at hame quhair I dwel.

b. (*to give, have*) *to warison*: in full possession. Also, *to give* (a woman) *in warison*: to give in marriage; similarly *to have, in warison, wed to warison.*

c **1330** R. BRUNNE *Chron. Wace* (Rolls) 1284 My moste fo & my feloun Schal haue my doughter to warisoun. **1338** —— *Chron.* (1725) 21 Elfride þorgh heritage toke him þe coroune, & gaf Alfride his broþer Surray to warisoune. *Ibid.* 69 Þe duke wrote to þe kyng .. Bisout him .. þat he wild hold his oth, & ȝeld him þe coroun of Inglond .. Or Marie to warisoun wed hir, & joy it wele. *c* **1400** *Ywaine & Gaw.* 2399, I sal hir gif to warisowne Ane of the foulest quisteroun That ever yit ete any brede. *c* **1430** *Syr Gener.* (Roxb.) 10046 The lordeship of a grete tovn He yafe him to his warison. *c* **1450** *Godstow Reg.* 111 And for this quyte-clayme the forsaid Symond yaf to her ij. shillings of siluer into warison. *c* **1460** *Oseney Reg.* 164 And for this ȝevyng and of this present charter confermyng and warantiȝyng aquite & defendyng, þe foresaide Nycoll ȝafe to me Cl li. of goode & lawfull moneye by-fore handes in weryson.

c. *fig.* Applied to an immaterial 'treasure'; esp. a maiden's honour.

a **1300** *Prov. Hendyng* 21 Wyt & wysdom is god warysoun. *a* **1300** *Marina* 109 in Horstm. *Altengl. Leg.* (1878) 172 Þou ne dudest nout ase hende To bynymen þat may hire wareison. **1303** R. BRUNNE *Handl. Synne* 2190 Ȝyf þou rauysshe a mayden powre, .. Þou hast stole here warysun.

2. A gift bestowed by a superior; a reward.

13.. *K. Alis.* 2507 (Laud MS.), Þer nas knaue ne quystroun þat ne had his warisoun. **1338** R. BRUNNE *Chron.* (1725) 325 Þre hundreth marke he hette vnto his warisoun, Þat with him so mette, or bring his hede to toun. *c* **1375** *Sc. Leg. Saints* xx. (*Blasius*) 270 His wark sal haf warysone & of his master benysone. *c* **1440** *Promp. Parv.* 516/2 Warysone, *donativum, possessio.* c **1440** *Jacob's Well* 254 We arn alle felawys in goddys host, þat yche day fyȝten as his knyȝtes, and alle we abyde on warysoun. c **1460** *Battle of Otterbourne* xliii. in Child *Ballads* III. 297/2 Mynstrells, playe vp for your waryson And well quyt it schall bee. **1470–85** MALORY *Arthur* IX. xxii. 372 And now haue I my waryson. a **1510** DOUGLAS *King Hart* II. 35 My warisoun, .. Lord, pay to me, and gif me leif to ryde. **1572** *Satir. Poems Reform.* xxxi. 66 My ladds of Leith, be wice—ȝe ken ȝour warisoun.

b. In bad sense: 'Reward', due punishment.

? a **1366** CHAUCER *Rom. Rose* 1537 He [*sc.* Narcissus] lost his witte .. And diede withynne a lytel space, And thus his warisoun [F. *guerredon*] he took For the lady that he forsook. c **1440** *York Myst.* xxxvi. 89 For thy presumpcyoune þou haste thy warisoune. **1535** STEWART *Cron. Scot.* (Rolls) III. 562 Robert the Grahame, .. for his waresoun, Vpoun ane flaik wes traillit throw the toun. a **1578** LINDESAY (Pitscottie) *Chron. Scot.* (S.T.S.) I. 8 This cochreine with his companie Within schort tyme gat thair warison, On lather brig wer hanged schamefullie. [**1881** J. SARGISSON *Joe Scoap* 31 (E.D.D.) Thoo's gittn thy warrison, me lad; lig thee theer till sec-like times as ah send for theh.]

¶**3.** tr. med.L. *gersuma*, ad. ME. GERSUM.

c **1450** *Godstow Reg.* 156 And for this yifte .. the forsaid mynchons of Godestowe yaf to hym ix. marke of siluer into waryson. *Ibid.* 222 And for thys graunt .. the foreseyd mynchons yaf to hym xj. marke, ij. shillings, viij. d, in warysumme.

4. ? Preservation, defence.

c **1450** BURGH *Secrees* 2337 With greet rewardys doo them avance .. Which aldayes besy and waking be In thy nedys; for in them stant the warysoun Of thy worshepe, thy lyf or thy destruccion.

¶**5.** Misused by Scott for: A note of assault.

The source of the mistake is prob. the line 'Mynstrells, playe vp for your waryson', in *The Battle of Otterbourne*, which Scott had doubtless read in Percy's *Reliques*.

1805 SCOTT *Last Minstrel* IV. xxiv, Either receive within thy towers Two hundred of my master's powers, Or straight they sound their warison, And storm and spoil thy garrison. **1824** BYRON *Juan* XV. lix, As my friend Scott says, 'I sound my warison.' **1867** *Contemp. Rev.* VI. 342 He thinks of sounding his warrison against what he strikingly calls the army of the Philistines.

warisse, -isshe, var. ff. WARISH *v. Obs.*

waritreo: see WARYTRE *Obs.*, gallows.

warius, obs. form of VERJUICE.

c **1425** *Voc.* in Wr.-Wülcker 662/13 *Hoc ius uiride*, warius [*printed* warins].

wark (wɑːk), **warch** (wɑːtʃ), *sb.*[1] *Obs.* exc. *dial.* Forms: 1 wærc, 3 warche, 5 werk(e, 5–6 warke, 7 warck, 7– warch, 9 wark. [OE. *wærc* masc. = ON. *verk-r* (Sw. *värk* pain, Da. *værk* gout, rheumatism):—OTeut. **warki-z*, from the same root as **werko-m* WORK *sb.*

With the dial. variation between the types *wark* and *warch* cf. the similar variation in ME. between *like* and *liche* (LIKE *a.*). The form *wark* may be partly due to ON. *verkr*.]

A pain, an ache.

c **900** tr. *Bæda's Hist.* IV. xix. (1890) 322 Seo readnis & bryne þæs swiles & wærces. c **1000** *Sax. Leechd.* II. 318 Wiþ maȝan wærce wyl pic on cu meolce. a **1225** *Ancr. R.* 326 Þet he ne mei .. speken ase he schulde, bute gronen uor his eche [*MS. T.* warche]. a **1400–50** *Wars Alex.* 2811 As warysche I my warke [*MS. Dubl.* werk] þat I am in wonden. **14..** *Medical Receipts* in *Rel. Ant.* I. 51 For evel and werke in bledder: take ache, percel [etc.]. c **1440** *Alphabet of Tales* 265 Furth-with a grete warke went þurgh his hand. **1570** LEVINS *Manip.* 32/1 Warke, ache, *dolor.* **1613** POTTS *Discov. Witches* T 3 b, Hee hath beene sore pained with great warch in his bones. **1825** BROCKETT *N.C. Gloss.*, *Wark* .. a pain or ache. 'The belly wark.' **1862** [C. C. ROBINSON] *Dial. Leeds* s.v., Gotten t' back-wark, shoother-wark, leg-wark .. —ne'er wur so done up i' my life.

†**wark**, *sb.*[2] *Obs.* Also 8 werk. [Of obscure origin.] (See quots.)

1707 SLOANE *Jamaica* I. Pref. B 2 b, I know not but that the several Species of new Ferns .. may be discover'd upon some of the Stones or Slates called Werk, which lie in plenty in the Strata over the Cole-pits in many Places of England. **1759** B. MARTIN *Nat. Hist.* I. 68 In several of the Coal Pits of this Country [Somerset], the Veins are covered with a Shell of hard, and stony Substance called Wark, which splits like Slate, but is much more brittle.

wark (wɑːk), **warch** (wɑːtʃ), *v. Obs.* exc. *dial.* Forms: 1 wærcan, 3 warche, 5 werk, 6 warke, 7 warck, 7, 9 warch, 5– wark. [OE. *wærcan* = ON. *verkja, virkja*:—OTeut. **werkjan*, f. **werki-z*: see WARK *sb.*[1]] *intr.* To ache, suffer pain; to throb painfully. (In OE. impers. with accus., like L. *dolet.*)

a **1000** *Sax. Leechd.* II. 272 Ȝif hine innan wærce ȝenim niȝes ealað amber fulne [etc.]. *Ibid.* 318. a **1225** *Ancr. R.* 368 Leste hor heaued ake [*MS. T.* warche]. c **1440** *Promp. Parv.* 523/1 Werkyn', and akyn' as a soore lymme, *doleo, indoleo.* c **1440** *Alphabet of Tales* 100 Yit it was a grete mervayle, for for all þis, nowder warkid hur hevud, nor sho lefte not þe labur of hur handis. c **1460** *Towneley Myst.* iii. 269 My bonys ar so stark, No wonder if thay wark, ffor I am full old. c **1520** SKELTON *Magnyf.* 1581, I wolde hauke whylest my hede dyd warke. **1572** *Satir. Poems Reform.* xxxiii. 77 For laik of quhilks my heid dois wark and ȝaik. **1674–91** RAY *N.C. Words*, *Warch*, or *Wark*, to ake, to work. **1828** CARR *Craven Gloss.* **1841** HARTSHORNE *Salop. Ant. Gloss.* s.v., My corns warchen. **1881** SARGISSON *Joe Scoap's Jurneh* 50 (Cumbld. Gloss.) Me heid warkt as it had niver warkt afooar.

Hence '**warking** *vbl. sb.* and *ppl. a.*

c **1340** HAMPOLE *Ps.* xxxvii. 2 Þin arues ere festid in me: þat is, þi vengaunce, as werkyngis of body and saule. c **1400** *Destr. Troy* 1238 The souerayn .. the kyng with the caupe caste to þe ground, With a warchand wounde thurgh his wedis all. *Ibid.* 10035. c **1440** *Promp. Parv.* 523/1 Werkynge, or heede ake, *cephalia.* c **1460** *Towneley Myst.* vi. 8, I haue maide me, in this strete, sore bonys & warkand feete. c **1470** HENRY *Wallace* VIII. 732 Thai .. Wrocht the Sotheroun mony werkand wound. *Ibid.* 858. **1596** DALRYMPLE tr. *Leslie's Hist. Scot.* (S.T.S.) I. II. 157 Nocht long eftir, throuch the warking woundes that in the battel he receiuet, he dies. *Ibid.* II. x. 397.

wark, obs. and dial. form of WORK *sb.* and *v.*

warkefull, obs. form of WORKFUL.

war-kettle. Among North American Indians, a kettle which was set on the fire as a part of the ceremony of inaugurating a war; also *fig.*

1754 *World* No. 102 ¶ 7 At a meeting of the Sachems it was determined to take up the hatchet, and make the war-kettle boil. **1757** [BURKE] *Europ. Settlem. Amer.* I. II. iv. 181 The principal captain summons the youth of the town to which he belongs; the war kettle is set on the fire; .. the hatchet is sent to all the villages of the same nation, and to all its allies. **1764** MRS. E. CARTER *Let. to Miss Talbot* 3 Feb., The Duke had made a dinner in honor of the wedding, for the Dukes of D. G. P. B. Lord R. and other chiefs of the war-kettle. **1776** MICKLE tr. *Camoens' Lusiad* Introd. p. lxxxviii. *note*, His [the prisoner's] dissevered limbs are boiled in the war-kettle, and devoured by his executioners. **1791** J. LONG *Voy. Ind. Interpr.* 146 They .. brought him to the war-kettle to make his death-feast: which consisted of dog, tyger-cat, and bear's grease, [etc.] .. of which he was compelled to eat. **1861** SPURGEON in *Metrop. Tab. Pulpit* No. 383. 283 They shall empty their war-kettle, and they shall bury their swords.

warkmanly, obs. form of WORKMANLY.

warlag(h: see WARLOCK.

'**warland.** *Obs.* exc. *Hist.* Forms: 3 **warlond**, 4 **warelond**, 5 **warlant, -londe**, 5, 9 *Hist.* **warland**, 7, 9 **wareland.** [f. OE. *waru* defence (see WARE *sb.*[2]) + LAND *sb.*[1]: in AL. *terra de wara.*] Agricultural land held by a villein.

See Vinogradoff *Eng. Soc. in Eleventh Cent.* (1908).

c **1158** *Oseney Latin Register* (Ch. Ch. MS.) fol. 17 Unam hidam terre cum quatuor hominibus de warland. **1290** *Inq. Post Mortem. C. Edw. I* File 56 (18) (P.R.O.) Le warlond ejusdem manerii [*sc.* Norcliffe co. Chester] tenetur pascere servientes domine regine de Maklesfeld de mense in mensem quolibet mense per unum diem. **1331** [see THIGGING]. **1456–7** *MS. Bursar's Bk. of Fountains* 58 In xiiij acr. et ij Rod. de Warland—ix s. viij d. c **1460** *Oseney Reg.* 30 Þere also j. hide of londe with iiij. men of Warlande [tr. quot. c **1158** above] ..; In Weston iij. ȝerdes of londe of Warlant. *Ibid.* 31, j. ȝerde of londe of þe lordship and another of Warlonde. **1811** *Extract Court Rolls Great Oakley, Essex*, [Francis Fisher a tenant of the Manor is described as holding 5 acres of] Wareland.

¶ Erroneously explained.

1688 HOLME *Armoury* III. 137/2 Wareland, is as much Land as containeth three Lands. [See LAND *sb.*[1] 7, LOON *sb.*[3]] **1691** BLOUNT *Law Dict.*, *Warland*, The same with *Warectum.*

warlare: see WRAWLER.

warlau, warlaw(e: see WARLOCK.

warld, warldlie, etc.: see WORLD, -LY, etc.

warless ('wɔːlɪs), *a.* In 5 werreles. [f. WAR *sb.*[1] + -LESS.] Free or exempt from war; not engaging in war.

1436 *Pol. Poems* (Rolls) II. 203 And thus shulde everi lande one with another .. life togedre werreles in unité. **1857** *Chamb. Jrnl.* VIII. 256 The pale, pure crescent in the warless heavens. **1866** NEALE *Sequences & Hymns* 6 So him they lead to warless rest. **1886** TENNYSON *Locksley Hall After* 165 Earth at last a warless world, a single race, a single tongue. *Ibid.* 170 Universal ocean softly washing all her warless Isles. *Ibid.* 172 Who can fancy warless men?

Hence '**warlessly** *adv.*, in a warless manner.

1887 *Harper's Mag.* July 267 Little flags would mark battles all over the map of their country—the country Mademoiselle Couper despised as so hopelessly, warlessly insignificant.

'**warlessness.** [f. WARLESS *a.* + -NESS.] Absence of war.

1928 BLUNDEN *Undertones of War* xiv. 158 The sluggish weather and the general silence and warlessness encouraged us to take life easy. a **1930** D. H. LAWRENCE *Last Poems* (1932) 114 Look at the young men under thirty ... A certain warlessness even moneylessness, A waiting for the proper touch, not for any word or deed.

warli(e, -liche: see WARELY *a.* and *adv. Obs.*

warlike ('wɔːlaɪk), *a.* and *adv.* Forms: 5 *Sc.* **wir-, weirelyk, werlik**, 5–6 *Sc.* **weirlyk(e**, 6 *Sc.* **were-, weirlike, -lic**; 6 **warlycke, warrelike**, 6–7 **warlicke, warrelyke**, 6–8 **warlick**, (7 **warlique**), 6– **warlike.** [f. WAR *sb.*[1] + -LIKE.]

A. *adj.*

1. Of a person, nation, etc.: Naturally disposed to warfare or fighting; skilled in war, martial; courageous in war, valiant; fond of war, bellicose.

† *the warlike god*, the god of war, Mars.

c **1470** HENRY *Wallace* IV. 323 Thir werlik Scottis, all with one assent, Northt so our Ern throuch out the land thai went. **1555** EDEN *Decades* (Arb.) 75 Thinhabitantes [of Jamaica] are .. warrelyke men. **1591** SHAKS. *1 Hen. VI*, III. ii. 118 Warlike and Martiall Talbot, Burgonie Inshrines thee in his heart. **1599** SHAKS. etc. *Pass. Pilgr.* 147 Euen thus (quoth she) the warlike god embrac't me. **1610** HOLLAND *Camden's Brit.* I. 712 Joane wife unto that most warlicke [1637 warlique] Knight Edw. Prince of Wales. **1635–56** COWLEY *Davideis* IV. 557 As when a wrathful Dragons dismal light Strikes suddenly some warlike Eagles sight. **1667** MILTON *P.L.* IV. 902 The warlike Angel mov'd, Disdainfully half smiling thus repli'd. **1777** ROBERTSON *Hist. Amer.* VI. Wks. 1851 V. 584 The warlike tribes in North America. **1837** W. IRVING *Capt. Bonneville* III. 200 Some trifling assistance from government, to protect them from the predatory and warlike tribes. **1837** DICKENS *Pickw.* ii, Mr. Winkle retraced his steps .. with the gloomy and dreadful resolve of accepting the challenge of the warlike Doctor Slammer.

b. Of actions, attributes, etc.: Martial, valiant.

1594 KYD *Cornelia* IV. 188 And so let his warlike browes Still be deckt with Lawrel boughes. **1836** THIRLWALL *Greece* xiii. II. 190 These exercises do not create and are not sufficient to keep alive the warlike spirit of a nation.

c. Of things: Martial in character.

c **1470** HENRY *Wallace* VIII. 1021 Ȝeit thai within on lowd defyit Wallace, And trumpattis blew with mony werlik soun. **1595** SHAKS. *John* II. 242 For this downe-troden equity, we tread In warlike march, these greenes before your Towne. **1602** —— *Ham.* V. ii. 360 What warlike noyse is this? **1667** MILTON *P.L.* I. 531 At the warlike sound Of Trumpets loud and Clarions. **1811** SCOTT *Roderick* lvi, Then peals the warlike thunder of the drum.

d. Favouring or threatening war.

1915 *Nation* (N.Y.) 17 June 671/1 After his own outgivings he [Mr. Bryan] had the effrontery to blame the press for making people think the note would be warlike.

†**e.** *fig.* Of writings: = POLEMIC *a. nonce-use.*

a **1603** T. CARTWRIGHT in *Presbyt. Rev.* (1888) Jan. 121 Ambrose and especially Austin in their warlike writings as they are termed.

†**2.** Equipped for fighting or for war. *Obs.*

c **1420** WYNTOUN *Cron.* IX. xvi. 1704 Schir Henry, qwhat makis ȝow to be Sa wirlyk as now heyr we ȝow se? **1563** in Rymer *Foedera* (1719) XV. 631 With one Shippe .. Marchant-like and not Warlike. **1591** SPENSER *Virg. Gnat* 124 He, that .. No deadly fight of warlick fleete doth feare. **1602** SHAKS. *Ham.* IV. vi. 15 Ere we were two dayes old at Sea, a Pyrate of very Warlicke appointment gaue vs Chace. **1630** *R. Johnson's Kingd. & Commw.* 537 Monasteries, ancient and warlike, so built for feare of theeves and pyrats. **1697** DRYDEN *Virg. Georg.* III. 285 If to the Warlike Steed thy Studies bend. **1711** in *10th Rep. Hist. MSS. Comm.* App. v. 124 They are .. destitute of warlick ships and other vessells.

3. Of or pertaining to war.

1560 DAUS tr. *Sleidane's Comm.* 78 b, The assemblie of the Empire .. was in this warlyke preparation. **1573** *Satir. Poems Reform.* xxxix. 93 For ordinance thay dung at day and nycht By weirlyk volyis. **1585** T. WASHINGTON tr. *Nicholay's Voy.* I. xxi. 26 b, [They] surrendred the same [castle] .. without any warlike reason. **1590** SPENSER *F.Q.* II. ii. 16 They were two knights of perelesse puissance, And famous far abroad for warlike gest. **1591** SHAKS. *1 Hen. VI*, II. i. 44 Since first I follow'd Armes, Nere heard I of a warlike enterprize More venturous .. then this. **1610** HOLLAND *Camden's Brit.* I. 282 Who being brought up in warlike feats .. most manfully defended this Castle against King Stephen. **1675** TRAHERNE *Chr. Ethics* 363 A warlike-field is the seed-plot of great and heroical actions. **1687** A. LOVELL tr. *Thevenot's Trav.* III. xxi. 39 He was upon his return from a Warlike expedition. **1784** COWPER *Task* V. 234 Him they serv'd in war, And him in peace, for sake of warlike deeds Rev'renc'd no less. **1817** BYRON *Manfred* III. i. 141 Mortals .. who .. die ere middle age, Without the violence of warlike death. **1846** GREENER *Sci. Gunnery* 81 All our arrangements in warlike preparations, at present, involve [etc.]. **1847** MRS. A. KERR tr. *Ranke's Hist. Servia* 342 Their former glorious warlike exploits .. led them to entertain very different expectations.

b. of formation, order, etc.

1599 ALEX. HUME *Hymns* vii. 191 Poems (S.T.S.) 57 Euen sik .. Sall armed be that day with spear and sheild, Baith horsse and fute in weirlike maner drest. **1667** MILTON *P.L.* IV. 780 The Cherubim .. stood armd To thir night watches in warlike Parade. **1808** SCOTT *Marmion* I. xx, Were I in warlike wise to ride, A better guard I would not lack. **1870** BRYANT *Iliad* IX. 102 With each A hundred youths in warlike order marched.

c. Of arms, munitions, etc.: For use in war.

1561 DAUS tr. *Bullinger on Apoc.* xliii. 283 We shall learne also howe to fight agaynst Antichrist, and howe he muste be ouercomen not with warlike, but spiritual weapons. **1585** HIGINS *Junius' Nomencl.* 183/1 *Armamentarium*, .. an armourie, or place wherein warlike furniture is kept. **1606** SHAKS. *Tr. & Cr.* Prol. 13 To Tenedos they come, And the deepe-drawing Barke[s] do there disgorge Their warlike fraut-age. **1652** WADSWORTH tr. *Sandoval's Civ. Wars Spain* V. xxx. 312 They were in all six thousand compleat Foot and hors, besides thirtie Carts loaden with Munition, carriages, and other warlike utensils. **1895** J. G. MILLAIS *Breath fr. Veldt* 24 Ample provisions, ammunition, and warlike stores were deposited in the hunting-carts.

d. Of exercises, training, etc.: Of a military character, martial. ? Now *rare.*

1585 T. WASHINGTON tr. *Nicholay's Voy.* II. xviii. 51 b, [They are] exercised .. to shoote, and doe all other warlyke exercises. **1626** GOUGE *Serm. Dignity Chivalry* §7 Were Artillery Gardens, and Military Fields for Martiall discipline and warlike trainings, fostered .. thorow-out this land.

4. Of or belonging to a warrior or soldier.

1551 in Feuillerat *Revels Edw. VI* (1914) 59 Item for our Master of yͤ Ordnaunce a ffayre apparell warlyke. **1591** SHAKS. *1 Hen. VI*, IV. iii. 31, I breake my warlike word. **1621** G. SANDYS *Ovid's Met.* VIII. (1626) 150 For when he wore his fairely plumed cask; She thought him louely in that warlick mask. **1671** MILTON *Samson* 137 He .. In scorn of thir proud arms and warlike tools, Spurn'd them to death by Troops. **1813** SCOTT *Trierm.* I. xvii, Behind him were in triumph borne The warlike arms he late had worn. **1818** SHELLEY *Homer's Hymn to Minerva* 5 From his awful head Whom Jove brought forth, in warlike armour dressed.

†**B.** *adv.* As is usual in war. *Obs. rare.*

1583 A. MELVILL in *J. Melvill's Autob. & Diary* (Wodrow Soc.) 161 The quhilk merciless men .. ar gorgiuslie arrayit, and accompanied warlyke with a sort of limmers and godles suddartes. **1632** LITHGOW *Trav.* VIII. 343 Some warlike maim'd, some lame.

Hence † **'warlikely** *adv.*, in a warlike condition or manner. † **'warlikeness**, warlike disposition.

1548 HALL *Chron., Edw. IV* (1550) 2 When his army by the sea, was thus warlykely set forward. *Ibid.* 37 b, So he hym selfe with his nobilitie warlikely accompaignied, passed ouer betwene Douer and Caleys. **1605** Warlikenesse [see WARLINESS]. **1606** WARNER *Alb. Eng.* XIV. lxxxiii. 345 We shall the warlikenesse compend of those fame-wronged Men. **1615** G. SANDYS *Trav.* I. 51 Many tall ships.. warlikely appointed. **1626** *Sir W. Rawleigh's Ghost* 3 The Cound.. began to repeate many relations.. touching the generall warlikenesse of the British Nation.

warlike, obs. variant of WARLOCK.

† **'warliness.** *Obs. rare*$^{-1}$. [f. WARLY *a.*^{2} + -NESS.] Warlike disposition, valiantness.

1599 SANDYS *Europæ Spec.* (1629) 209 And all to keepe the Father from jealousie of his owne sonne, whose brauenesse of mind and warlinesse [*the pirated ed. of 1605 reads* warlikenesse] is still suspected.

† **'warling.** *Obs.* Forms: 6 **werlyng**, 7 **worling, worldling**, 7- **warling**. [app. formed arbitrarily to rhyme with *darling*. The resemblance to the Sc. WIRLING seems to be accidental.] One who is despised or disliked. Only in the proverb (see quots.) and allusively.

In the proverb *snarling* is sometimes substituted for *warling*; the form *worldling* is an obvious perversion.

1546 J. HEYWOOD *Prov.* II. vii. (1867) 65 It is better to be An olde mans derlyng, than a yong mans werlyng. **1604** [? CHETTLE] *Wit of Woman* F 4, A young mans worldling. **1611** L. BARRY *Ram Alley* II. i, A young mans warling. **1671** T. HUNT *Abeced. Scholast.* 91 A young mans Worling. **1857** SIR F. PALGRAVE *Norm. & Eng.* (1864) III. iii. 162 Fully does King Henry appear self-vindicated from the stigma of inertness, the failing assigned by his vixen Mother as justifying her schemes for aggrandizing her darling at the expence of her warling.

warlock ('wɔːlɒk), *sb.*^{1} Forms: 1 **wǽrloȝa, wêrloȝa**, 3 **werlau, werlaw**, 3-4 **warlou**, 3-5 **warlagh(e, warlau, warlaw(e**, 4-5 **warlag, warlaȝ(e, warloghe, werlaughe**, 4-5 (6-7 *Sc.*) **warlow(e**, 4-6 (? 9) *Sc.* **warlo**, 5 **warlach, warloo, warlowȝ, werlawe**, 6 *Sc.* **warloche, warlok, vairloche, varlo**, 7 ? **warelocke, warlike, warluck**, 8 (*Sc.*), 9 **warlock**. [OE. *wǽr-loga* wk. masc. traitor, enemy, devil, etc. = OS. *wâr-logo* wk. masc. ? deceiver (once, *Hêliand* 3817, in pl. *wârlogon* applied to the Pharisees). The first element is probably OE. *wǽr* str. fem. covenant = OHG. *wâra* truth, ON. *várar* str. fem. pl. solemn promise, vow (cf. *Vǽringi* confederate, Varangian); cf. OSlav. *věra* faith. This is a derivative from the adj. represented by OE. *wǽr* true (once, *Genesis* 681; ? a. OS.) = OS., OHG. *wâr* true:—OTeut. **wǽro*-:—Pre-Teut. **wēro*- = L. *vērus*. The second element (an agent-n. related to OE. *léoȝan* to LIE, belie, deny) occurs also in the similar comps. *áp-loȝa, tréow-loȝa* (OS. *treulogo*), *wed-loȝa* (ME. *wedlowe*), an oath-breaker, etc.

This seems to have been the original sense of the present word, but the special application to the Devil (either as a rebel, or a deceiver) was already in OE. the leading sense. The applications to sorcerers, with especial reference to the power of assuming inhuman shapes, and to monsters (esp. serpents), appear to be developments, partly due to Scriptural language, of the sense 'devil'.

The modern forms with final -*(c)k* are of obscure origin, for they appear first in Sc. of 16th c., and owe their spread to Sc. writers, and so cannot represent, as has been assumed, a Southern sound-substitution of (k) for the -*ch* (x) of some of the rarer North. and Sc. forms. From the first they have been used exclusively in the sense 'wizard'. Some other word, lost or not discovered, has perh. influenced both form and sense. ON. *varðlokkur* wk. fem. pl. (cf. also *urðar lo(k)kur*) ? incantation, suggested already in Johnson, is too rare (? occurring once), with regard to the late appearance of the -*k* forms, to be considered.]

† **1.** An oath-breaker, traitor. *Obs.*

Widsið 9 (Gr.) Hreðcyninges ham.. Eormanrices, wraþes wærloȝan. *a* **1023** WULFSTAN *Hom.* (1883) 266 He sceal wedloȝan and wærloȝan hatian and hynan. ? *a* **1400** *Morte Arth.* 3771 Sir Gawayne i-wysse, he waytes hym wele To wreke hyme on this werlaughe [Modred], that this werre mouede.

† **b.** A wicked person; a scoundrel, reprobate; a general term of reproach or abuse. *Obs.*

a **1000** *Judith* 71 (Gr.) Weras winsade.. ðone wærloȝan [Holofernus], laðne leodhatan læddon to bedde. *c* **1275** *Serving Christ* 37 in *O.E. Misc.* 91 Bi-leueþ oure weorre warlawes wode. Al þes world is bi-heled myd heþene-hode. *c* **1394** *P. Pl. Crede* 783 Wenest þou þer wold so fele swiche warlawes worþen, Ne were worldlyche wele and her welfare. *a* **1400-50** *Wars Alex.* 4425 Þus fra þe rote of riȝtwisnes rauyst ere ȝe clene, And to þe way of wickidnes be warlaȝes gidid. *c* **1440** *York Myst.* xxx. 141 Sir, what warlowe yow wakens With wordis full wilde, þat boy for his brawlyng were better be vn-borne. *Ibid.* xliv. 176 Undo youre dores, and haues no doute, For to ȝone warlowes [the Jews] will we wende. *c* **1450** *St. Cuthbert* 4544 Þan all þe hoste with Elfride To Assendoun þai turne þat tyde, Whare þa warlowes ware. **1500-20** DUNBAR *Poems* xxvi. 60 Catyvis, wrechis and okkeraris, Hud-pykis, hurdaris and gadderaris, All with that warlo [Covetousness] went.

† **c.** A damned soul in hell. *Obs. rare.*

a **900** CYNEWULF *Crist* 1562 Ðonne mansceaða fore meotude forht deorc on þam dome standeð.. bið se wærloȝa fyres afylled feores unwyrðe egsan ȝeþread and-weard gode won & wliteleas. *a* **1300** *Cursor M.* 23250 Þe aghtand pine it es ful grise, to se þaa warlaus in þat wise.

† **2.** The Devil; Satan. *Obs.*

Freq. in *Cursor Mundi*, where *warlau* occurs as a genitive (:—OE. *wǽrloȝan*).

a **1000** *Cædmon's Gen.* 36 (Gr.) [God] sceop ðam werloȝan wræclicne ham weorce to leane. *a* **1300** *Cursor M.* 22275 [Antichrist] þe warlau aun child. *Ibid.* 23747 Vr flexs, þis werld, and þe warlau, We ar bunden vnder þair au. *Ibid.* 27060 For qua witstandes warlau will, he has na might to do him ill. *c* **1375** *Sc. Leg. Saints* xviii. (*Egipciane*) 636 [Christ] þat ws fra þe warlo wane. *c* **1460** *Towneley Myst.* xiii. 640 That warloo to sheynd this nyght is he borne. *a* **1568** in *Bannatyne MS.* (Hunter. Club) 78 Betuix ws, varlo, and thy weris All Chrystis passioun we put compleit.

† **b.** A devil, demon, spirit of hell. *Obs. rare.*

a **900** CYNEWULF *Guthlac* 269 Wid is þes westen, wræcsetla fela, eardas onhæle earmra gæsta; sindon wærloȝan, þe þa wic buȝað. *a* **1300** *Cursor M.* 22611 Þan sal þai þat in helle es cropen Quen sal scine þe heuennes open, Þaa warlaus all sal walk þan vte. *c* **1440** *De mirac. B. Marie* 105 in Horstm. *Altengl. Leg.* (1881) 504 Þe foulle warlawes of helle Vndir þe wallys skrykked schille.

† **3.** A savage or monstrous creature (hostile to men). The word is applied to giants, cannibals, mythic beasts, etc. *Obs.*

a **1000** *Cædmon's Gen.* 1266 (Gr.) Frea wolde on wærloȝan wite settan & on deað slean dædum scyldiȝe ȝiȝantmæcgas, gode unleofe. *a* **1300** *Cursor M.* 7478 Allas! quar sal we find a man þat dar þe fight, for mi sake, Again yon warlau [Goliath] vndertake. **13..** *E.E. Allit. P.* C. 258 Þe hyȝe heuen kyng, þurȝ his honde myȝt, Warded þis wrech man [Jonah] in warlowes guttez. *c* **1400** *Destr. Troy* 303 So dang he þat dog [*sc.* Cerberus] with dynt of his wappon, þat þe warlag was wete of his wan atter. *Ibid.* 7765 The warlagh [the Centaur] with a wicked arowe woundit hym be-hynd. *a* **1400-50** *Wars Alex.* 3795 Þai went be waldis & be wastis.. And armed bud þam all bee for angwischis o bestis, As colwers & for coltris & crabbid snakis, And oþire warlaȝes wild þat in þe wod duelled. *a* **1585** POLWART *Flyting w. Montgomerie* 634 Ane vairloche [*v.rr.* warloch(e], ane woirwolf, ane wowbat of hair.

4. One in league with the Devil and so possessing occult and evil powers; a sorcerer, wizard (sometimes partly imagined as inhuman or demonic, and so approaching sense 2 or 3); the male equivalent of *witch. Sc.* and *north. dial.*

Frequently used by Scott, whence it has obtained some general literary currency. On the form *warlock*, specialized for this sense, see the etymology.

13.. *E.E. Allit. P.* B. 1560 Segges.. þat wer wyse of wych-crafte & warlaȝes oþer. *c* **1460** *Towneley Myst.* viii. 232 *Pharao*... Say, whence is yond warlow [Moyses] with his wand that thus wold wyle oure folk away? *a* **1585** MONTGOMERIE *Misc. Poems* iii. 25 That witch, that warlok [*sc.* Fortune].. Turnis ay the best men tittest on thair bakis. **1685** G. SINCLAIR *Satan's Invis. World* 45 An eminent Warlock whose name was Robert Grieve. **1689** tr. *Buchanan's De Jure Regni apud Scotos* 65 No Thief or Warlike will willingly compear before a Judge to be judged. *c* **1730** BURT *Lett. N. Scot.* (1818) I. 234 He was himself a warlock, or wizard, which they knew by his taking the witch's part. **1795** BURNS *Song, 'Last May a braw wooer'* v, I gaed to the tryste o' Dalgarnock, And wha but my fine fickle lover was there! I glowr'd as I'd seen a warlock, a warlock. **1816** SCOTT *Bl. Dwarf* v, 'But you forget that they say he is a warlock,' said Nancy Ilderton. 'And, if his magic diabolical should fail him,' rejoined her sister, 'I would have him trust to his magic natural'. **1822** S. HIBBERT *Shetl. Isl.* IV. 576 The warlocks and witches of Thule used, by the same means, to raise tempests. **1840** BARHAM *Ingol. Leg., St. Aloys*, The gipsy.. always sneaks out at night with the bats and the owls,—So do Witches and Warlocks, Ghosts, Goblins, and Ghouls. **1860** LONGF. *Wayside Inn* I. *King Olaf* v. x, In their real forms appeared The warlocks weird, Awful as the Witch of Endor. **1865** BARING-GOULD *Werewolves* 29 In like manner the Danish king Harold sent a warlock to Iceland in the form of a whale. **1882** MISS BRADDON *Mt. Royal* I. ii. 51, I am prepared to believe in witches—warlocks.

b. *Sc.* In weaker sense, a magician, conjurer.

1721 RAMSAY *Prospect of Plenty* 75 But gin ye be nae warlock, how d'ye ken? **1828** SCOTT *Aunt Marg. Mirr.* ii, 'That rascally quack would make my fortune were he to stay in Edinburgh,' said the graduate... 'I suppose I must not ask your ladyship anything about this Italian warlock's proceedings?' **1877** A. J. ROSS *Mem. Alex. Ewing* xiv. 197 'The Bishop.. never came to my private room.. without leaving me the impression that he was ——' an auditor, interrupting, said, 'A godly warlock.' 'Yes,' rejoined the speaker, 'that was just it, he was a wizard..'. **1886** STEVENSON *Kidnapped* iii, I'm nae warlock, to find a fortune for you in the bottom of a parritch bowl.

† **5.** By Dryden taken to mean: A warrior magically immune from wounds inflicted by certain metals. *Obs.*

Dryden's spelling perh. indicates that he imagined the word to be f. WAR *sb.* + LUCK.

1697 DRYDEN *Æneis* Ded. (b) 4 b, It seems he [Æneas] was no War-luck, as the Scots commonly call such Men, who, they say, are Iron-free, or Lead-free.

6. *attrib.* and *Comb.* **a.** Appositive or adj. †Malignant, wicked (*obs.*); in later use, That is a warlock or wizard.

c **1375** *Cursor M.* 7489 (Fairf.) Agayne ȝone warlagh hethen þing [*Cotton MS.* wreche haiþen þing] for-soþ I drede me noȝt sir king. *c* **1400** *Destr. Troy* 6425 Nay, warloghe wolfe, in þi wode hongur,.. The tydis not to taste of þis triet meite! **1560** ROLLAND *Seven Sages* 131 This reid Reifar & this rank warlo witche. **1683** G. SINCLAIR *Nat. Philos.* 243 The Devil answered,.. I and my Father will come and fetch you to hell, with Warlock-theeves. **1685** —— *Satan's Invis. World* 123 Saying, You Warlok Cairle, what have you to do here? **1724** RAMSAY *Ever Green* (1761) I. 51 A Bytand Ballat on warlo Wives, That gar thair Men live pinging Lives. **1786** BURNS *Brigs of Ayr* 71 Our warlock Rhymer instantly descry'd the Sprites that owre the Brigs of Ayr preside. (That Bards are second-sighted is nae joke, And ken the lingo of the sp'ritual folk.) **1896** KIPLING *Seven Seas, Rhyme Three Sealers*, A Stralsund man shot blind and large, and a warlock Finn was he.

b. Pertaining to a warlock or warlocks, as in ***warlock claw, fight, knoll***, etc.; **warlock brief**, a charter conveying magical powers; **warlock fecket** *Sc.* (see quot. 1810).

1786 BURNS *To J. Smith* 3 Ye surely hae some warlock-breef Owre human hearts; For ne'er a bosom yet was prief Against your arts. **1793** —— *Song, 'Now rosy May'* Chorus, Meet me on the warlock-knowe, Daintie Davie, daintie Davie. **1803** H. K. WHITE *Lines.. spoken by a Lover* Rem. 1807 II. 47 No wicked elves upon the Warlock-knoll Dare now assemble at their mystic revels. **1807** TANNAHILL *Soldier's Ret.* II. i, A great red dragon, wi a warlock claw, Has come, and wi your dochter flown awa! **1810** CROMEK *Remains Nithsdale Song* 281 Jackets, woven of water snake skins, at a certain time of a March moon, were much in vogue among the crusading servants of Satan; and are yet remembered by the name of warlock feckets. **1819** J. R. DRAKE *Culprit Fay* viii, Yet.. If thy heart be pure and thy spirit right, Thou shalt win the warlock fight! **1905** *Academy* 21 Oct. 1103/1 A warlock voice from the slumber of ages stirred.

† **warlock**, *sb.*^{2} *Obs. rare.* In quots. **warloc, warlok.** [Perh. repr. an OE. **wærloc*, f. OE. *waru* WARE *sb.*^{1} guard, safe-keeping + *loc* LOCK *sb.*^{2} It is, however, possibly an alteration of WARROK *sb.* caused by some such etymological association as that indicated. Cf. the senses in mod. dial. of WARLOCK *v.*^{1} and WARROK *v.*]

1. ? A shackle, fetter.

13.. *E.E. Allit. P.* C. 80 Pynez me in a prysoun, put me in stokkes, Wryþe me in a warlok, wrast out myn yȝen.

2. A fetterlock.

c **1440** *Promp. Parv.* 517/1 Warlok, a fetyr lok.. *sera pedicalis, vel compedicalis.*

'warlock, *sb.*^{3} *Obs.* (? exc. *dial.*) *rare.* Also 5 **warich**, (? **warkecok**), **warlok.** [Of obscure origin. The early forms *warich, warkecok* are perh. nearer to the original than *warlo(c)k*, which may be due to association with CHARLOCK.] Apparently applied like CHARLOCK (q.v.) to various field-weeds of the N.O. *Cruciferæ*, esp. to species of the genus *Sinapis*, Mustard.

c **1425** *Voc.* in Wr.-Wülcker 644/29 *Hoc sinapium*, warkecok. *c* **1440** *Promp. Parv.* 349/1 Mustard, or warlok, or se(n)vyne, herbe.. *sinapis. Ibid.* 517/1 Warlok, herbe, *eruca. c* **1450** *Alphita* (Anecd. Oxon.) 37/1 *Cenapium*, gall. ceneue, angl. warich, uel mostard. **1784-1815** A. YOUNG *Annals Agric.* V. 251 (E.D.S.) Warlock, *Raphanus Raphanistrum* (?) Suff[olk]. *a* **1850** W. A. BROUSFIELD *Flora Vectensis* (1856) 37 *Sinapis nigra*, L. Common or Black Mustard. *Vect.* Warlock.

† **'warlock**, *sb.*^{4} *Obs.* [app. a real or supposed Norw. word: cf. Norw. *varde* (dial. *vale*) cairn.] A cairn, pile of stones (in Scandinavian regions).

1584 R. NORMAN tr. *Safegard of Sailers* 51 Item, if it were so that you would saile into Calfe sound, then you shall hale in by a high land which is called Winge, and there stands fiue Warlocks or Bomes vpon it. *Ibid.*, The fiue Warlocks or Beacons. *Ibid.* 52 b. **1612** GATONBE in *Churchill's Voy.* (1732) VI. 250 We rowed about the cape and came to an island whereon was a warlock. **1614** R. FOTHERBY in Purchas *Pilgrims* (1625) III. 725 Here vpon the mountaine wee set vp a Warelocke, and then came downe againe.

'warlock, *v.*^{1} *Obs.* (exc. *dial.*) *rare.* Also **warloke.** [f. WARLOCK *sb.*^{2}] *trans.* † **a.** ? To secure (a horse) as with a fetterlock. *Obs. rare*$^{-1}$. **b.** *dial.* (See quot.) Cf. WARROK *v.*

a **1400-50** *Wars Alex.* 769* (Dubl. MS.) So carez he in þe castell-ȝarde & commes on a day By a wyndow als þis wild horse [was] warloked in bandez. **1886** *Cheshire Gloss.* s.v. **1905** *Eng. Dial. Dict., Warlock*, to tighten the rope or chain which binds the load upon a waggon.

war-lock, *v.*^{2} *nonce-wd.* [f. WAR *sb.*^{1} + LOCK *v.* (? suggested by WARLOCK *sb.*^{1})] *trans.* ? To bar against hostile invasion.

1800 HURDIS *Fav. Village* 40 The western fort, That.. war-locks imminent the mouth of Ouse.

'warlockry. ? *Obs.* [f. WARLOCK *sb.*^{1} + -RY.] The practice of magic (by men, or male beings); wizardry.

1818 *Blackw. Mag.* II. 527 Hence proceed.. the warlockry and fortune-telling abilities of the shrewd sagacious gypsies. **1822** HOGG *Siege of Roxburgh* i, Sin' the Rhymer's days, the spirit o' true warlockry is gane. **1831** J. WILSON in *Blackw. Mag.* XXIX. 21 The shadows o' a' the eatables and drinkables that his wild warlockry cou'd hae conjured up. **1834** HOGG in *Fraser's Mag.* X. 404 Yes, witchcraft! Wicked warlockrye!

warlogh(e, warloo, obs. ff. WARLOCK *sb.*^{1}

warlonde, obs. form of WARLAND *Hist.*

war-lord. a. A military commander or commander-in-chief. Often used to render *Kriegsherr* as a title of the German Emperor; also *attrib.*

1856 EMERSON *Eng. Traits, Aristocr.* Wks. (Bohn) II. 77 Piracy and war gave place to trade, politics, and letters; the war-lord to the law-lord. **1875** MORRIS *Æneids* IX. 39 Æneas, war-lord wise. **1888** *Boston* (Mass.) *Transcript* 7 July 4/4 The very bristling and 'war-lord' talk of the young Emperor William. **1897** *Edin. Rev.* Oct. 534 The officers of the [German] army, with all their traditional loyalty to their 'war-lord'.

b. [tr. Chinese *jūnfà*.] In China, a military commander who had a regional power base and ruled independently of the central government, esp. in the period 1916–28.

1922 *N.Y. Times* 31 Dec. VIII. 12/3 Each provincial Tuchun, or Military Governor, is a little or a big war lord with his own army and his own laws; and his regard for the Peking Government is proportioned inversely to the size of his army and his distance from the capital. **1926** P. WEALE *Why China sees Red* ii. 43 The whole war-lord system, which is based on the interception of national revenue at the points where it is levied and on nothing else, was about to be rudely tested. *Ibid.* 44 The Manchurian war-lord was just as sly. **1937** V. BARTLETT *This is my Life* xi. 174 Many gentlemen.. at the Shanghai Club became indignant over my pronunciation of the names of Chinese war-lords. **1959** *Listener* 5 Feb. 238/2 Many millions more have died since, because of floods, drought, war lords, and civil war. **1962** E. SNOW *Other Side of River* (1963) xxxv. 264 The local warlord governor, Yang Hu-ch'eng, was also more interested in keeping the Generalissimo's troops out of Shensi than continuing the civil war. **1978** D. BLOODWORTH *Crosstalk* vii. 56 Any Chinese general who decided to play the rebel warlord in those regions.. would.. prove a dangerous and difficult man to suppress.

Hence **'warlordism**, the policies or practices of a war-lord; government by war-lords; **'warlordship**, the status of a war-lord.

1913 C. TOWER *Germany To-day* ii. 36 The Kaisership is the old Presidency of the bund plus the warlordship. **1962** E. SNOW *Other Side of River* (1963) xxxix. 285 Throughout his struggles with provincial warlordism, 'communist-bandits', and finally with the Japanese, Chiang remained essentially an old-fashioned militarist. **1966** *New Statesman* 18 Mar. 366/3 Is Indonesia now in for a spell of regional warlordism? **1971** W. F. DORRILL in T. W. Robinson *Cultural Revolution in China* ii. 42 Individual numbers of this journal.. charge that P'eng Teh-huai.. instituted 'warlordism' (maltreating troops and straining relations between officers and men). **1979** *Guardian* 1 Aug. 5/6 Petty warlordism, protection rackets, the levying of 'taxes'.. have alienated the natural allies of the Palestinians.

† **'warlott.** *local. Obs.* [f. *war-* as in WARLAND + LOT *sb.*] Some kind of waste or common lands.

c **1290** *Register Malton Priory* (MS. Cott. Claudius D.xi) 206 Cum prato que dicitur Warlotes. **1614** *Terrier of Morley of Winterton*, Warlotes, the long; the short. **1794** *Act Inclos. South Kelsey* 3 Commissioners for dividing.. and inclosing the said Open and Common Fields,.. Warlotts, or Whoselotts, Furze Leas, and Waste Grounds, within the Manor or Lordship of South Kelsey.

warlou, -low(e, -luck: see WARLOCK.

† **'warly**, *a.* and *adv. Obs.* Forms: 5 **werly**, *Sc.* **werely**, 5–7 **war(re)ly**, 6 **warely**, **warlye**, *Sc.* **werelie**, **weirlie**, **-ly**, **weyrly**, 6–7 **warlie**. [f. WAR *sb.*[1] + -LY[1] and -LY[2].]

A. *adj.*

1. Skilled in war, martial; fond of war, bellicose; valiant. = WARLIKE *a.* 1.

1423 JAS. I. *Kingis Q.* clv, The werely porpapyne. *c* **1475** *Partenay* 1362 The petyuins tham bare As warly men fre;.. Assautes tha[y] gafe dyuers And sondry. *a* **1513** FABYAN *Chron.* VII. (1533) 77b/1 Y^e^ arche bisshop of yorke.. with great nombre of men and fewe warly or discrete cheuetaynes, yode agayne ye Scottes. **1513** MORE *Rich. III* Wks. (1557) 37/1 Richard the thirde sonne.. was.. hard fauoured of visage, and suche as is in states called warlye [L. *quale bellicosum in purpuratis, ac Martium appellari*], in other menne otherwise. **1594** T. B. *La Primaud. Fr. Acad.* I. 585 If a yoong prince.. be warlie, he will hazard his subjects, his estate, and his person, to make triall of his valure. **1596** DALRYMPLE tr. *Leslie's Hist. Scot.* (S.T.S.) I. 86 Thay war a people baith ciuile and weirlie. **1605** VERSTEGAN *Dec. Intell.* v. (1628) 122 The lacke of Warrely courage in the Britaines.

b. Of actions, things: Martial. = WARLIKE *a.* 1 b, c.

1536 BELLENDEN *Cron. Scot.*, Proheme Cosmogr. 262 Of feirs Achill, the weirlie dedis sprang In Troy and Grece, quhill he in vertew rang. **1599** ALEX. HUME *Hymns* vii. 57 Poems (S.T.S.) 54 Mak shouting shalms and persing phiphers shill,.. Cause mightily the weirly notis breik.

2. Equipped or munitioned for war. Of a horse: Equipped and trained for war. = WARLIKE *a.* 2.

c **1470** *Golagros & Gaw.* 493 Yone is the warliest wane, said the wise king, That euer I vist in my walk. *a* **1513** FABYAN *Chron.* VII. (1533) 123/2 The sayde sowdiours came vnto a castell.. & wan it by strength, & after vytayled & manned it in moste warly wyse. **1591** HARINGTON *Orl. Fur.* XXXIII. lxxxv, This said, he mounted on the steed so warly. **1593** G. HARVEY *Pierces Super.* Wks. (Grosart) II. 104 Could the Warlie Horse speake, as he can runne and fight, he would tell them, they are hoat Knightes.

3. Of or pertaining to war. = WAR-LIKE *a.* 3.

1457 in R. R. Sharpe *Lond. & Kingd.* (1895) III. 382 Ships.. in their most defensible and warrely araye. ? *c* **1507** C. BRANDON [etc.] *Justes May & June, Justes June* 233 in Hazl. *E.P.P.* II. 129 This weerly vsage and martes entreprise These monthes twayne yonge folke dyd exercyse. **1533** BELLENDEN *Livy* I. i. (S.T.S.) I. 13 King latyne of laurence assemblit þe auld Inhabitantis of his realme.. in þare maist werelie ordinance. *Ibid.* I. iv. I. 32. **1544** BETHAM *Precepts War* I. cix. F v, They being practysed in warly knowledge can discerne what is profytable. **1548** HALL *Chron., Hen. V*, 45 b, Kyng Henry.. determined.. to set forward in performyng his intended purpose and warrely enterprise. **1570** FOXE *A. & M.* (ed. 2) II. 1000/2 The Bernates.. renounced the league made before with the French king, refusing.. his warly stipend, whereby they were bound at his call to fede hys warres. *a* **1676** HALE *Prim. Orig. Man.* II. iv. (1677) 161 The Manufacture, during those Warly times, held its course in France, the Netherlands, and the Hans Towns.

4. Belonging to a warrior. = WARLIKE *a.* 4.

1535 STEWART *Cron. Scot.* (Rolls) I. 277 The king of Pechtis, in his weirlie weid, With his power come and met corbreid. **1567** *Gude & Godlie B.* (S.T.S.) 107 His wingis ar thy weirlie weid [*v.r.* weerely weed], His pennis ar thy strang defence. **1609** BIBLE (Douay) *1 Macc.* iii. 3 And he.. girded about him his warlie armour in battels.

B. *adv.* In a warlike manner.

c **1400** *Rowland & O.* 813 Kyng askuardyn in his gere Rydis owte a course of were, Full werly and with ill will. *c* **1475** *Partenay* 1741 Then thes brethren, ech by thaim-self, tho, So ful werrely wrought, can noght be said, lo! **1592** WYRLEY *Armorie, Capitall de Buz* xxiv, And goodly armd beside Him stands the Duke of Orleance warly dight.

warly, -lyche: see WARELY *a.* and *adv. Obs.*

warm (wɔːm), *sb.*[1] [f. WARM *v.*] An act of warming or state of becoming warm. Phr. ***to give, get, have, take a warm.*** Somewhat *colloq.*

In the first quot. *warmes* is a mistake for *walmes*: see WALM *sb.*[1] 3 c.

[**1655** WALTON *Angler* (ed. 2) x. 239 Boil it [*sc.* the malt] in the kettle (one or two warmes is enough).] **1768** ROSS *Helenore* 70 This morning's raw, gin ye've a' night been out, That ye wad thole a warm, I mak na doubt. **1800** in *Spirit Publ. Jrnls.* IV. 6 The dark and dreary night, the dreadful storm Drove me unwillingly to get a warm. **1838** DICKENS *O. Twist* i, The surgeon had been sitting with his face turned towards the fire, giving the palms of his hands a warm and a rub alternately. **1843** —— *Chr. Carol* iii, Sit ye down before the fire, my dear, and have a warm. **1861** —— *Gt. Expect.* ii, When I.. was taking a final warm in the chimney-corner before being sent up to bed. **1861** FLOR. NIGHTINGALE *Nursing* 55 If, after washing a patient, you must put the same night-dress on him again, always give it a warm first, at the fire. **1891** C. ROBERTS *Adrift Amer.* 120, I made a fire, and.. had a good warm.

warm (wɔːm), *a.* (and *sb.*[2]) Forms: 1 **wearm**, 2 **wæarm**, 3 *Orm.* **warrm**, 3–7 **warme**, 3– **warm**. [Com. Teut.: OE. *wearm* = OFris. *warm* (mod.WFris. *waerm*, NFris. *wārəm*), MDu., Du. *warm*, OS. *warm* (MLG. *war(e)m*, LG. *warm*), OHG. *war(a)m* (MHG., G. *warm*), ON. *varmr* (Norw., Sw., Da. *varm*), Goth. *warm-* in *warmjan* to warm, cherish:—OTeut. **warmo-*, also **werm-* (in ON. *verme* wk. masc. warmth, OHG. *wirma*, MHG. *wirm(e)* fem. warmth).

The further relationship of this word is somewhat doubtful. In spite of certain difficulties it is probably to be identified with Indogermanic **g^w^hormo-*, or **g^w^hermo-* found in Skr. *gharmá* heat, Zend *garᵊma-* hot, Gk. θερμός hot, L. *formus* warm, OPrussian *gorme* heat, Albanian *zjarm* heat, Armenian *yerm* warm, derivatives of **g^w^her-* with a radical sense of heat. For another possible example of initial *w* in Teut. from **g^w^h* or **ghw* see WILD *a.* Compare also the similar phonetic phenomena in Latin whereby older *g^w^* gave *g* before *ŭ* and consonants, *v* before other vowels (e.g. *gurgēs*, *vorāre*).

Some scholars have referred the word to a root **wer-* found in Lith. *virti* to cook (trans.), OSl. *vrěti* to boil, cook (intr.), *variti* to cook (trans.), *varŭ* hot. The primary sense of this root, however, seems to be rather 'to well up, bubble' than 'to be hot'; cf. Lith. *versmě* a spring. The root is confined to the Balto-Slav. langs., and in them has no derivative corresponding in sense and suffix to the Teut. adj., which on the other view represents a widespread Indogermanic formation.]

A. *adj.*

1. Having a fairly high temperature; affording or giving out a considerable degree of heat (less than that indicated by *hot*).

a. of natural agencies and things, as the weather, air, climate, soil.

out of God's (Christ's) blessing into the warm sun: see GOD *sb.* 5 c.

c **888** ÆLFRED *Boeth.* xxxiii. §5 Sie lyft.. is ægþer ȝe ceald ȝe wæt ȝe wearm. *a* **1000** *Boeth. Metr.* xi. 61 Sumor æfter cymeð, wearm ȝewideru. *a* **1250** *Owl & Night.* 622 Þar inne ic habbe god ihold A wintre warm a sumere cold. **1377** LANGL. *P. Pl.* B. XVIII. 410 Is no weder warmer þan after watery cloudes. *c* **1440** *Pallad. on Husb.* I. 219 In spryngyne of the mone is best to sowe, In dayis warm. **1540** PALSGR. *Acolastus* II. i. H iij, To leappe out of the halle, into the kytchyn, or out of Chrystis blessynge in to a warme sonne. **1549** *Compl. Scot.* vi. 58 [Rain falls] sum tyme in soft & varme schouris. **1577** B. GOOGE tr. *Heresbach's Husb.* I. 34 Pease.. must be sowen in warme groundes. **1727** E. LAURENCE *Duty of Steward* 75 On a warm soil well shelter'd with Trees and Hills. **1750** GRAY *Elegy* 87 The warm precincts of the chearful day. **1774** GOLDSM. *Nat. Hist.* VI. 347 The prisoners of congelation.. waiting the approach of a warmer sun, to restore them at once to life and liberty. **1833** ARNOTT *Physics* (1853) 35 England is much warmer in winter than central Germany, which lies south of England. **1854** *Poultry Chron.* I. 249 We.. stand much in need of warm weather, and especially, warm nights for the young poultry. **1915** *Blackw. Mag.* Apr. 467 A warm south wind was melting the fall [of snow].

b. of other things, typically with reference to artificial heating.

c **1385** CHAUCER *L.G.W.* 914 His swerd sche tok a-swythe That warm was of hire louys blod & hot. **1577** B. GOOGE tr. *Heresbach's Husb.* III. 119 b, In winter, your stable should rather be warme, then hot. **1606** SHAKS. *Ant. & Cl.* III. i. 6 Whil'st yet with Parthian blood thy Sword is warme. **1697** DRYDEN *Æneis* XI. 323 They rake the yet warm Ashes, from below. *a* **1700** EVELYN *Diary* 11 Mar. 1651, They.. carried him before a warme fire to bring him to himselfe. **1741** M. GRINDAL (*title*) Warm Beer, a Treatise proving.. that Beer so qualify'd, is far more wholesome than that which is drank Cold.. With a full Confutation of all the Objections.. against Drink being used Warm. **1764** WHYTT *Observ. Nervous Disorders* (1767) 434 The warm bath affects the nerves with an agreeable sensation, removes spasms in the small vessels, [etc.]. **1848** DICKENS *Dombey* v, Promise me to take a little something warm before you go to bed. **1849** JAMES *Woodman* vii, Our houses are more warm and air-tight than those of that day. **1871** A. MEADOWS *Midwifery* (ed. 2) 339 Warm poultices should also be kept over the abdomen.

c. *fig.* ***to keep a seat*** or ***place warm***: to occupy it temporarily for another who is not yet qualified to hold it. (Cf. WARMING-PAN 3 c.)

1845 JERROLD *St. Giles* vi. (1851) 55 Of course, the borough will be kept warm for the young gentleman... He may count upon my vote. **1853** MRS. GASKELL *Ruth* xxi, Before the Cranworths had determined who should keep the seat warm till the eldest son came of age.

2. a. Of the body, the blood, etc.: Having the degree of heat natural to the living organism.

a **1000** *Riddles* v. 7 Wearm lim ȝebundenne beaȝ bersteð hwilum. *c* **1200** ORMIN 10146 Forrþi þatt itt [the tunic] iss neh þe lich & haldeþþ warrm þe mare. **1338** R. BRUNNE *Chron.* (1810) 36 Þe blode was boþe warme & fresh, þat of þe schankes lete. *c* **1386** CHAUCER *Sompn. T.* 119 Though I him wrye a-nyght and make hym warm. **1562** J. HEYWOOD *Prov. & Epigr.* (1867) 148 Thou art wyse inough, if thou keepe thee warme. **1603** SHAKS. *Meas. for M.* III. ii. 9 A fur'd gowne to keepe him warme. **1693** DRYDEN *Persius* vi. 13 For me, my warmer Constitution wants More cold, than our Ligurian Winter grants. **1697** —— *Æneis* II. 867 Go you, whose Blood runs warm in ev'ry Vein. **1754** GRAY *Progr. Poesy* 40 O'er her warm cheek, and rising bosom. **1855** *Poultry Chron.* III. 398 New milk, warm from the cow. **1878** BROWNING *La Saisiaz* 21 At the least warm touch of hand. **1919** *Blackw. Mag.* Nov. 644/2, I found the carcase of a hartebeeste still warm.

fig. **1737** POPE *Hor. Ep.* II. i. 147 Then Marble, soften'd into life, grew warm.

b. Of persons: Glowing with exertion or exercise, with eating and drinking, etc.; often with mixture of one of the senses 10–12. Of exercise: Strenuous enough to raise one's temperature.

1606 SHAKS. *Tr. & Cr.* IV. v. 118, I am not warme yet, let vs fight againe. **1665** DRYDEN *Ind. Emp.* III. i, And Fighting gains us but to dye more warm. **1746** FRANCIS tr. *Horace, Art of Poetry* 322 A lawless Croud, with Wine and Feasting warm. **1753** JANE COLLIER *Art Torment.* I. ii. 61 For although it is noble sport to have a girl of sense to work upon, yet 'tis warm exercise. **1769** *Ann. Reg.* 25 There is nothing that an army will not attempt or endure for a general who keeps the soldiers warm in continual action. **1850** TENNYSON *In Mem.* xc. 9 'Twas well, indeed, when warm with wine, To pledge them with a kindly tear. **1900** *Pall Mall Mag.* May 43, I was warm from my company, and was propelled by an abundant flow of vitality.

c. Applied to tears.

1377 LANGL. *P. Pl.* B. XV. 187 And with warme water at his eyghen wasshen hem after. **1483** CAXTON *Golden Leg.* 196/1 Thenne she.. prayed god wyth warme teerys to helpe hyr. **1588** SHAKS. *Tit. A.* III. i. 20 In Winter with warme teares Ile melt the snow. **1648** BP. HALL *Sel. Th.* lxxvi. 221 But if.. we shall suffer our selves to be drawn away into some heinous wickedness, it must cost warm water to recover us.

d. Of a kiss, embrace (combining the literal idea of bodily warmth with that of affection).

1588 SHAKS. *Tit. A.* V. iii. 153 Oh take this warme kisse on thy pale cold lips. *a* **1764** R. LLOYD *Whim* 45 Give me the man.. Who.. Can meet him with a warm embrace. **1822** M. A. KELTY *Osmond* I. 29 Imprinting on it another fond warm kiss. **1866** TROLLOPE *Claverings* iv, With the kiss of the dear, modest, affectionate girl still warm upon his lips.

e. = WARM-BLOODED. *rare.*

1793 T. BEDDOES *Calculus* etc. 242 The ordinary temperature of the blood of warm animals.

3. Of clothing, or the natural integument of animals: Made of material which retains heat in the body.

a **1225** *Ancr. R.* 418 Þet heo [i.e. your clothes] beon unorne & warme & wel i-wrouhte. *a* **1300** *Cursor M.* 23090 (Edinb.) Of nakidhed quen I drow harme, Ye gaf me cleþing þat was warme. *a* **1450** *Mirk's Festial* 39/36 Hit wer almes forto ȝeue ȝondyr pore man warmer cloþes þen he haþe. **1535** COVERDALE *Job* xxxvii. 17 And how thy clothes are warme, when the londe is still thorow the south wynde? **1653** in *Verney Mem.* (1904) I. 547 Here is now some cold snowie weather approaching, which incites mee to putt on warmer cloths. **1774** GOLDSM. *Nat. Hist.* (1776) V. 39 These are generally cloathed with a warmer coat of feathers. **1849** JAMES *Woodman* xi, Would that I had brought warmer garments. **1917** H. GIBSON *Diplom. Diary* 259 Mrs. Whitlock.. is busy getting warm clothing for the poor.

4. Of a drug or edible: Producing a sensation of heat in the body.

1737 J. STEVENSON in *Med. Ess.* IV. 387 Common Practice bids us.. give warm, generous Medicines, Alexipharmicks, and all of that Tribe that heats, stimulates and forces Sweat. **1822–7** GOOD *Study Med.* (1829) I. 251 A pretty free dose of turpentine, or some of the warmer balsams. **1842** LOUDON *Suburban Hort.* 689 Its seed-pods.. make a warm aromatic pickle.

5. Of a scent or trail: Fresh, strong.

1713 GAY *Rural Sports* II. 68 The scent grows warm; he stops; he springs the prey. **1832** *P. Egan's Bk. Sports* 211/2 As the scent grew warmer, the certainty of finding was confirmed.

6. Of the person chosen to seek or guess, in children's games: Being near the object sought; being on the verge of finding or guessing. Also *fig.*

1860 *All Year Round* 4 Feb. 339/2 Here I get 'warm', as children say. **1865** DICKENS *Mut. Fr.* III. vi, He's warm... He's precious warm. He's close. **1893** *Nation* (N.Y.) 24

Aug. 139/3 Showing how the author was 'warm', and passed without seeing it very near to the object of his search.

†7. Comfortable, comfortably settled (*in* a seat, throne, office); securely established *in* (possession of). Also, with converse construction, ***to feel the crown warm upon one's head***. *Obs.*

c 1374 CHAUCER *Troylus* III. 1630 Be not to rakel þough þou sitte warme. c 1430 *How Wise Man taught Son* 114 in *Babees Bk.* 51 If þou be weel at eese, And warme amonge þi neiȝboris sitte. 1601 *Imp. Consid. Sec. Priests* (1675) 55 Her Highness had scarcely felt the Crown warm upon her head, but it was challenged from her. 1610 B. JONSON *Alchemist* II. vi, A Gentleman, newly warme in his land. 1614 RALEGH *Hist. World* II. xvii. §4. 481 The Philistims hearing that Dauid was now anointed king..thought to try him in the beginning, before hee was fully warme in his seat. 1647 N. BACON *Disc. Govt. Eng.* I. xlvii. (1739) 78 The conquering King was scarce warm in his Throne, whenas the Pope demanded Fealty of him for the Crown of England. a 1670 WOOD *Life* (O.H.S.) I. 129 A. W. seemed very sorry at this news, because he was well and warme where he was. 1715 M. DAVIES *Athen. Brit.* I. 47 Before he was quite warm in Winchester, he fell into the King's displeasure. 1809 W. IRVING *Knickerb.* VII. iii. (1900) 258 Scarcely had the worthy Mynheer Beekman got warm in the seat of authority on the South River than enemies began to spring up all around him.

8. Comfortably off, well to do; rich, affluent. Now chiefly *colloq.*

1571 CAMPION *Hist. Irel.* II. ix. (1633) 114 But you are well and warme and so hold you. 1573–80 TUSSER *Husb.* (1878) 8 But I must plaie the farmer, and yet no whit the warmer. a 1624 BP. M. SMITH *Serm.* (1632) 118 All things seeme to fall out alike, to the one and to the other: nay, the wicked seeme to be the warmer, and to haue a greater portion in this life. 1626 MIDDLETON *Anything Quiet Life* I. i, You are warm, and blest with a fair wife. 1699 FARQUHAR *Love & Bottle* I. 2 Your warm fellows are so far above the sense of our Misery, that they can't pitty us. 1712 STEELE *Spect.* No. 450 §2 For who does not know or imagine the Comforts of being warm or living at Ease? 1742 FIELDING *J. Andrews* II. xiv, 'Though I am but a curate,' says Trulliber, 'I believe I am as warm as the vicar himself.' 1766 GOLDSM. *Vicar W.* xvi, They who had warm fortunes were always sure of getting good husbands. 1767 A. YOUNG *Farmer's Lett.* 74 These farmers, and their warm, comfortable families, are of great consequence to the well being of agriculture itself. 1834 MACAULAY in *Life & Lett.* (1880) I. 381 A warm man; a fellow who will cut up well. 1888 RIDER HAGGARD *Col. Quaritch* xxviii, He is about the warmest man in our part of the country. 1908 J. S. FLETCHER *Mothers in Israel* 304 With the serene consciousness of his value as a warm man. 1920 *Guardian* 5 Nov. 1034/4 In 1836 he was presented..to the very snug vicarage of Cheddar, and a year later he took to himself the still warmer benefice of Wiveliscombe.

9. a. Of fighting, conflict, an onset: Vigorously conducted; pressing hard on or harassing the foe; also *fig.* Of a combatant: Dangerous to tackle. Of a locality: Dangerous to live in, inhabited by turbulent spirits. Phr. ***warm work***, hot fighting. ***to make it*** (or ***things***) ***warm for*** (a person): to attack or 'go for' him, to involve in hostilities or broils.

1627 J. TAYLOR (Water P.) *Armado* C 2, The Sweat, a vessell of warme imployment or hot seruice. 1667 *Hatton Corr.* (Camden) 53 You may easily imagine this does give us a warme alarum. 1682 BUNYAN *Holy War* (1905) 235 They had from the Camp of Shaddai such frequent, warm, and terrifying alarms. 1726 SHELVOCKE *Voy. round World* 163, I saw the Mercury standing out of the bay, by which I judged the ship was too warm for her. 1759 R. ROGERS *Jrnls.* (1769) 119 The Canadians and Indians..were soon stopped by a warm fire from the Rangers and Mohocks. 1760 *Cautions & Advices to Officers of Army* 182 If we had [been discovered], they might have made warm Work of it. 1793 WASHINGTON *Let.* Writ. 1891 XII. 380 If he should be detected in any knavish pranks I will make the country too warm for him to remain in. 1813 SOUTHEY *Nelson* II. ix. 255 Nelson then smiled, and said, 'This is too warm work, Hardy, to last long.' 1817 JAS. MILL *Brit. India* II. v. v. 527 The action.. was close, warm, and general. 1840 DICKENS *Old C. Shop* vi, This being warmer work than they had calculated upon, speedily cooled the courage of the belligerents. 1847 YEOWELL *Anc. Brit. Church* iii. 28 In his Second Epistle to Timothy..there are many traces of a warm persecution. 1874 'MAX ADELER' *Out of Hurly-burly* xv. (Rtldg.) 208 The bishop saw clearly enough that if he gave presents to the other children, and not to the late Simpson's, the bride would make things warm for him. 1884 *Good Words* June 399/1 The 'habituals'..are, as a body, congregated together in one particularly warm little street... Outsiders do not care to venture into this warm spot.

b. ***a warm reception***: a vigorous onslaught or resistance; a demonstration of hostile feeling.

The phrase prob. belonged originally to sense 12c, in which it is still current.

1702 [see RECEPTION 5 a]. 1737 [S. BERINGTON] *Mem. G. di Lucca* (1738) 37 We thought, by that warm Reception, they would have given us over. 1841 JAMES *Brigand* xxvi, We must give him [the rival] a warm reception.

10. a. Of persons, party-feeling, controversy, etc.: Ardent, zealous, keen; eager, excited, heated. Const. *for*, *upon.*

Very common in the 17th and 18th c.; now somewhat *rare*.

1390 GOWER *Conf.* III. 230 Yong conseil, which is to warm, Er men be war doth ofte harm. 1668 TEMPLE *Let. to Ld. Keeper* Wks. 1731 II. 99 Which I could not have known, if the Marquis were not a very warm Talker, and sometimes farther than he intended. 1682 BUNYAN *Holy War* (1905) 314 Then said the warm man, and true hearted Mr. Zeal-for-God, Cut them off. 1687 ATTERBURY *Answ. Consid. Spirit Luther* 20 Yet the Pamphlet is very warm with Luther for impiously accusing the Religious of uncleanness. 1705 HEARNE *Collect.* 24 Aug. (O.H.S.) I. 34 He is now very warm for them. 1720 DE FOE *Capt. Singleton* xiii. (1840) 233 So warm were the men upon it, that they grew..clamorous. 1737 WATERLAND *Eucharist* 113 Smalcius, a warm Man, and who seldom knew any Bounds. 1742 E. MONTAGU in *Mrs. Montagu's Corr.* (1906) I. 130 The Debates were very warm, and the Chancellor of the Exchequer was terribly roasted. 1776 *Trial of Nundocomar* 59/2 The Counsel for the Prisoner speaking in a warm and improper manner to the Jury. 1791 BURKE *Th. Fr. Affairs* Wks. 1842 I. 575 Of all men, the most dangerous is a warm, hot-headed, zealous atheist. 1847 DICKENS in Forster *Life* (1872) I. ii. 49, I never can forget, that my mother was warm for my being sent back. 1850 GROTE *Greece* II. lviii. (1862) V. 161 A warm and even angry debate arose upon his present speech. 1874 GEO. ELIOT *Coll. Breakf.-P.* 348 Doting reasoners Who hugged some reasons with a preference As warm Laertes did. 1883 D. C. MURRAY *Hearts* xix. (1885) 163 They..found the young man there in a state of warm indignation at the libellous paragraph.

b. Of the passions or disposition in general: Prone to excitement, ardent, impulsive; apt to disregard the voice of cool reason.

1749 FIELDING *Tom Jones* XII. xiii, As Jones had the vices of a warm disposition, he was entirely free from those of a cold one. a 1768 SECKER *Serm.* (1770) III. 50 They are just entering into the World..with lively Spirits and warm Passions to mislead them.

11. Hot-tempered, angry.

1547 Q. CATHERINE PARR in S. Haynes *St. Papers* (1740) 61 My Lord your Brother hathe thys Afternone a lyttell made me warme. Yt was fortunate we war so muche dystant, for I suppose els I schulde have bytten hym. 1581 A. HALL *Iliad* IX. 168 This warme and bitter wrath it grew of strife. 1712 ADDISON *Spect.* No. 440 ¶4 This insensibly grew into some warm Words. *Ibid.* No. 481 ¶3 They say he's a warm Man, and does not care to be made Mouths at. 1719 DE FOE *Crusoe* II. (Globe) 505, I..begun to be a little warm with him. 1822 GALT *Provost* xxxvii, A fine bold rattling lad, warm in the temper. 1849 MACAULAY *Hist. Eng.* vi. II. 123 He was mortified and irritated by the tidings. He held warm and menacing language. 1855 D. COSTELLO *Stories fr. Screen* 131 'It's an expression of mine when I'm angry.' 'You're warm,' says he.

12. a. Of the heart, feelings, etc.: Full of love, gratitude, approbation, etc.; very cordial or tender.

c 1480 HENRYSON *Cock & Fox* 60 Quhen I behald ȝour fedderis fair and gent,..My hart is warme. 1526 *Pilgr. Perf.* (W. de W. 1531) 150 The soule melteth whan it waxeth warme in deuocyon. 1740 *New Hist. Jamaica* IV. 86 He had a warm Side to the Royal Party, and encouraged the loyal Sufferers. 1749 FIELDING *Tom Jones* v. iii, He was not yet free from doubt of misconstruing compassion, or at best esteem, into a warmer regard. 1822 M. A. KELTY *Osmond* I. 73 Her heart was warm in the cause of her young friend. 1828 MACAULAY *Ess. Hallam* ¶43 The conduct of Hampden in the affair of the ship-money met with the warm approbation of every respectable Royalist in England. 1834 DICKENS *Sk. Boz, Boarding-ho.* ii, A very warm friendship soon sprung up between them. 1864 D. G. MITCHELL *Seven Stories* 57, I was beginning to feel a warm interest in the people over the way. 1904 *Verney Mem.* II. 239 Her warm heart..made her welcome in every household.

b. with agent-noun or equivalent sb., as ***a warm friend, supporter***. Also of persons: Full of tenderness or affection.

1765 *Museum Rust.* IV. 314 A certain noble lord, a warm friend to every improvement in husbandry. 1827 LYTTON *Pelham* ii, Yet to those he loved, no one could be more open and warm. 1838 —— *Alice* III. vii, We should have thought that Lord Vargrave was her warmest admirer. 1842 DICKENS *Amer. Notes* ix, I have frequently heard this admitted, even by those who are its warmest advocates. 1854 PATMORE *Angel in Ho.* I. II. vii. (1879) 205 Others as chaste and warm there are. 1891 E. PEACOCK *N. Brendon* II. 379 They were now warm friends.

c. of utterances or manifestations.

1742 in *10th Rep. Hist. MSS. Comm.* App. I. 277, I beg you would present my warmest thanks to my Lord Carteret. 1766 GOLDSM. *Vicar W.* xxxi, As you once had my warmest vows of constancy, you shall now have them repeated. 1782 COWPER *Let. to J. Hill* Nov., I received a note from old Mr. Small, which was more than civil—it was warm and friendly. 1814 BYRON *Lara* I. vii, Warm was his welcome to the haunts of men. 1855 MACAULAY *Hist. Eng.* xii. III. 206 He concluded by acknowledging in warm terms his obligations to the King of France. 1885 'MRS. ALEXANDER' *At Bay* ix, She dispatched a warm invitation.

13. Characterized by, of the nature of, prone to, sexual desire; amorous.

1592 SHAKS. *Ven. & Ad.* 605 The warme effects which she in him finds missing, She seekes to kindle with continuall kissing. c 1630 MILTON *On May Morning* 6 Hail bounteous May that dost inspire Mirth and youth and warm desire. 1897 FLOR. MARRYAT *Blood Vampire* iv, She's rather a warm customer, and if she takes a fancy to a man, 'e won't well know 'ow to get out of it.

14. a. With reference to fancy and imagination, ideas, expectations, and the like: Ardent, lively, glowing.

1668 EVELYN tr. *Freart's Idea Perf. Paint.* 49 Our Painters Idea was not, it seems, so warm. 1669 T. ALLISON *Voy. Archangel* 52 Notwithstanding it froze extream hard at this time, yet we had warm hopes of getting to Sea. 1702 *Post Man* 23–26 May 2/1 Yesterday there was a warm report that Her Majesty's Ship the Lenox..had attacked a Fleet of French Merchant Ships. 1746 HERVEY *Medit.* (1818) 33 May we learn to renounce our own will, and be ready to make a sacrifice of our warmest wishes. 1838 PRESCOTT *Ferd. & Is.* II. viii. (1846) II. 424 Their imaginations were warm with the beauty and novelty of the scenes which met their eyes in the New World. 1849 RUSKIN *Sev. Lamps* v. §24. 160 There is not one tender touch, not one warm stroke, on the whole façade. 1872 E. W. ROBERTSON *Hist. Ess.* 192 Bridferth has drawn a very warm picture of the scene from which the indignant abbot snatched the king.

b. Of imaginative composition: Indelicate in its appeal to sexual emotion.

1814 JANE AUSTEN *Mansfield Park* xv, I do not know the play; but, as Maria says, if there is anything a little too warm ..it can be easily left out. 1826 DISRAELI *Viv. Grey* III. vii, And then he stumbled on rather a warm scene in an old Château in the South of France. 1831 SCOTT *Ct. Robt.* x, He ..avoided those warm descriptions which had given such offence to the Countess Brenhilda. 1846 *Hints on Husband-catching* 18 The most immoral doctrines, the warmest scenes.

15. a. Of colour: Suggestive of warmth; said esp. of rich red or yellow, and tints mingled with these.

1764 GOLDSM. *Trav.* 137 The canvas glow'd, beyond e'en Nature warm. 1815 J. SMITH *Panorama Sci. & Art* II. 752 Where a richer and warmer effect..is required, strong body colours must be employed. 1820 KEATS *Eve of St. Agnes* xxv, Full on this casement shone the wintry moon, And threw warm gules on Madeline's fair breast. 1858 KINGSLEY *Misc.* (1860) I. iv. 198 The delicate yellow-green..fly, with its warm grey wings. 1860 RUSKIN *Mod. Paint.* V. IX. xi. 320 If the tones of the picture are kept low.., and the reflected lights warm. 1892 *Photogr. Ann.* II. p. lv, Prints can be made either of warm or cold tones. 1897 SARAH GRAND *Beth Bk.* xxxvii, The walls were painted a pale warm pink.

b. qualifying an adjective of colour.

1864 TENNYSON *Aylmer's F.* 155 The warm-blue breathings of a hidden hearth.

16. Of a bill: Exorbitant in its charges. *colloq.*

1892 *Daily News* 20 July 5/4 He had expressed the opinion that a certain bill for stoves was 'a warm one.' 'Excuse my ignorance,' interrupted the Lord Chief Justice, 'but what does "warm" mean?'

17. Comb. and spec. collocations: **a.** parasynthetic, as ***warm-backed, -bosomed, -coloured, -complexioned, -constitutioned, -gloved, -seated, -tempered, -veined*** adjs.; **b. warm bath**, a bath of warm water (often as a medical treatment); also **warm bathing**; **warm boot** *Computers*, a reloading or restart of an operating system, etc., without switching off the computer, esp. when changing programs; also as *v. trans.*, to reload in this way; **warm front** *Meteorol.*, the forward boundary of a mass of advancing warm air; **†warm head**, a warm-headed person; **warm-headed** *a.*, having a heated fancy or excitable temperament; **warm-house**, a kind of hot-house; **warm with** *colloq.*, (spirits) mixed with hot water and sugar (cf. *cold without*).

1847 R. S. SURTEES *Hawbuck Gr.* iii, An atmosphere warranting the *warm-backed waistcoat. 1731 R. PORTER in *Med. Ess.* (1737) III. 371, I resolved therefore to try what might be the Advantage of a *warm Bath, by relaxing the Intestine, and opening the Passage. 1858 J. H. WALSH *Dom. Med.* 370 Action on the skin by means of the warm-bath or the vapour-bath. 1744 J. STEVENSON in *Med. Ess.* V. II. 867 *Warm Bathing, by relaxing and enlarging the Capacities of the Vessels, makes a Derivation of the Fluids into the Parts bathed. 1813 J. THOMSON *Inflammation* 173 Hot fomentations and warm-bathing. 1980 R. ZAKS *CP/M Handbk. with MP/M* i. 22 This combination..produces a 'warm start' (or '*warm boot', or 'system reboot'). A warm start essentially interrupts whatever the computer is doing and starts the operation system over again. *Ibid.* 32 If you are only *reading* from a new diskette..a warm boot is not necessary to introduce the new diskette. 1981 *Your Computer* (Austral.) May–June 100/3 *Warm boot*, to reload the operating system a second or subsequent time. 1983 *Ibid.* May 21/1 After a program has run [on the Commodore 64], CP/M warm-boots—a process that takes about 30 seconds. Once a CP/M program is loaded, it runs just fine. 1983 *Byte* May 28/2 The Model 100..did not need extra time to load the text editor and the document file from the disk and later store the document on disk and reload CP/M (do a warm boot). 1925 BLUNDEN *Eng. Poems* 54 *Warm-bosomed hawthorn stands in fruitful rest. 1818 SCOTT *Br. Lamm.* xxvi, It was comfortably hung with a sort of *warm-coloured worsted. 1761 A. MURPHY *All in Wrong* II. 28 A smooth-faced, fiery eyed, *warm-complexioned, taper young fellow. 1775 ADAIR *Amer. Ind.* 190 The *warm-constitutioned young widows. 1921 BJERKNES & SOLBERG in *Geofysiske Publikationer* II. III. 12 In the first case, the boundary line at the ground will be the front of advancing cold air, or, to introduce a shorter expression, a 'cold front'. In the latter case, the boundary line will be the front of advancing warm air, or simply a '*warm front'. 1969 A. G. FORSDYKE *Weather Guide* 49 The rain belt ahead of a warm front is often 200 to 300 miles wide. 1922 JOYCE *Ulysses* 536 Hobbledehoy, *warmgloved,..stunned with spent snowballs, struggles to rise. 1684 *Def. Resol. Case of Consc. conc. Symbolizing with Ch. Rome* 32 By what figure do you call one Start-up *Warm Head a new Generation? 1690 LOCKE *Hum. Und.* IV. iv. §1 The advantage will be on the *warm-headed Man's side, as having the more Ideas, and the more lively. 1749 LAVINGTON *Enthus. Meth. & Papists* (1820) 95 Our rambling, warm-headed, itinerant preachers. 1843 *Florist's Jrnl.* (1846) IV. 175 They may then be placed in the *warm-house. 1903 *Westm. Gaz.* 8 Oct. 10/2 The tubers..were first planted in a warm-house. 1922 JOYCE *Ulysses* 265 Sprawled, *warmseated, Boylan impatience, ardentbold. 1591 SYLVESTER *Du Bartas* I. ii. 437 *Warm-temp'red show'rs it sendeth in the Spring. 1796 MME. D'ARBLAY *Camilla* III. 244 The Ensign [was] more warm tempered and wrong-headed. 1818 SCOTT *Br. Lamm.* xxii, I know Lady Ashton is a warm-tempered and prejudiced woman. 1943 DYLAN THOMAS *New Poems* 12 A man outside with a billhook,..The *warm-veined double of Time. 1838 *Bentley's Misc.* IV. 575 A second tumbler of brandy and water, '*warm with,' stood exhaling its fragrance at my elbow. 1840 T. A. TROLLOPE *Summer in Brittany* I. 213 They have some other object and enjoyment in life besides the consumption of 'warm with' or 'cold without'.

B. *absol.* and *sb.*[2]

1. a. That which is warm; a state, or sensation, of being warm; warmth. *rare.*

a **1250** *Owl & Night.* 538 Hi beoþ houhful & wel arme And secheþ yorne to þen warme. *c* **1350** *St. Christina* 251 in Horstm. *Altengl. Leg.* (1881) 95 Of al þe fire scho felid no warm. þan come scho furth with-outen harm. **1379** *Glouc. Cath. MS.* 19, No. 1, fol. 9 b, The more nere the sonne ys to vs the more hete or warme. **1513** DOUGLAS *Æneis* VI. xii. 16 A hait fyry power, warme, and dew. *a* **1547** SURREY '*The sonne hath twise*' 7 The winters hurt recouers with the warm. **1839** A. PIKE in *Blackw. Mag.* XLV. 819 A pleasant warm is felt upon the sea.

b. ***in the warm***: (of a solution, etc.) in a warm state.

1903 *Brit. Med. Jrnl.* 21 Mar. 654 The union of toxin and antitoxin occurs in fixed ratios, more rapidly in concentrated solution and in the warm.

c. ***in(to) the warm***: indoors, out of the cold.

1969 F. HURT *Death in Mist* vii. 74 I'll just put the spade away and then we can go into the warm. **1974** J. AIKEN *Midnight is Place* viii. 231, I don't think Mr Oakapple is ready for more news until we have him sitting in the warm.

2. ***British*** (***Service***) ***warm***, a warm short overcoat worn especially by officers of the army. Also without *British* (*Service*), and (*rarely*) *attrib.*, as ***warm-coat.***

1901 *Imp. Yeom., Rep. D.A.G.* 15 May (1902) 123 The coat or jacket known as 'British Service Warm,' which is practically an overcoat made to wear over uniform, thick and warm. **1912** *Blackw. Mag.* June 803/2 In a 'British Warm' and patched breeches. **1928** BLUNDEN *Undertones of War* iii. 26 My warm-coat was not adequate. **1954** W. FAULKNER *Fable* 114 His braces knotted about his waist under his open warm. **1958** *Spectator* 11 July 53/2 A florid gentleman in a military warm.

warm (wɔːm), *adv.* Now only quasi-adv., in predicate-extensions. [OE. *wearme*, f. the adj.] Warmly; so as to be warm.

c **1000** *Sax. Leechd.* II. 116 Bewreoh ðe wearme. ? *a* **1366** CHAUCER *Rom. Rose* 409 Wel had she clad hir silf and warme. *c* **1410** *Lantern of Light* 46 Whanne þe sunne schynneþ warme. **1596** *Edw. III*, III. v. 90 With thy sword, yet reaking warme With blood of those that fought to be thy bane. **1707** MORTIMER *Husb.* (1721) II. 356 When the South or West Winds blow, or the Sun shines warm. **1774** GOLDSM. *Nat. Hist.* (1776) V. 336 They should be put nest and all into a little basket, which should be covered up warm. **1820** KEATS *Lamia* I. 8 Hermes empty left His golden throne, bent warm on amorous theft. **1840** DICKENS *Old C. Shop* xlvi, The women straightway carried her off to bed; and, having covered her up warm, [etc.].

b. *Comb.*, qualifying an adj. or pple., as †***warm-hot***; ***warm-breathed***, ***-contested***, ***-sheltered***; ***-kept***, ***-lying***, ***-reeking***, ***-working***.

c **1430** *Two Cookery-bks.* 8 Set it on þe fyre tyl it be warme hot. **1599** SHAKS. *Hen. V*, v. ii. 335 For Maides well Summer'd, and warme kept, are like Flyes at Bartholomewtyde. **1634** W. WOOD *New Eng. Prosp.* I. ii. 4 The North-east and South winde.. bringing in the warme-working waters of the Sea, loosneth the frozen Bayes. **1740** SOMERVILE *Hobbinol* III. 245 The panting Rivals.. in Conceit Already grasp the warm-contested Prize. **1757** DYER *Fleece* II. 161 The high heath, by trees Warm-shelter'd, may despise the rage of storms. **1775** SHERIDAN *Rivals* II. i, Their quivering, warm-breathed sighs impregnate the very air. **1786** BURNS *To a Haggis* iii, O what a glorious sight, Warm-reekin, rich! **1786** ABERCROMBIE *Gard. Assist.* 294 Plunge plants in pots—in some dry warm-lying ground.

warm (wɔːm), *v.* Pa. t. and pa. pple. **warmed** (wɔːmd). Forms: 1 **werman, wærman, wirman, wyrman; wearmian**; 2–3 *Orm.* **warrmenn**, 3 **werme, wormie**; 3–7 **warme**, 5– **warm.** [Two formations: (i) OE. (*wierman), *wẹrman*, *wirman* trans. = OS. *warmian* (MLG., (M)Du. *warmen*), OHG. *warmen*, *wermen* (MHG. *wermen*, mod.G. *wärmen*), ON. *verma* (Sw. *värma*, Da. *varme*), Goth. *warmjan*:—OTeut. **warmjan*; (ii) OE. *wearmian* intr. = OHG. *war*(*a*)*mên* (MHG., early mod.G. *warmen*) :—OTeut. type **warmǣjan*; both f. OTeut. **warmo-* WARM *a.*]

I. *trans.* To make warm.

1. a. To make (one's body, limbs, etc.) warm by approach to a fire, exposure to the sun's rays, exercise, clothing, etc.; to impart warmth to (a person or animal suffering from cold).

c **900** *Bæda's Hist.* III. xiv. (1890) 196 Se cyning þonne, forðon he of huntað cwom ȝestod æt þam fyre & hine wyrmde. *c* **1000** *Ags. Gosp.* John xviii. 14 Þa þeȝnas stodon æt þam gledon, & wyrmdon hiȝ. *c* **1200** ORMIN 2711 To wasshenn hemm, to warrmenn hemm, To beddenn hemm & frofrenn. *c* **1205** LAY. 12609 Nu þu scalt þe warmen [*c* **1275** wormie] þer. *c* **1275** *Passion of our Lord* 230 in *O.E. Misc.* 43 Peter stod.. and wermede hym at the glede. *a* **1300** *Cursor M.* 23090 O naked-hed quen i drogh arme, Yee gaf me clething me to warme. **1340–70** *Alex. & Dind.* 332 For no cold þat vs comeþ in oure kinde age, We ne faren to no fir our fingrus to warme. *c* **1440** *Alphabet of Tales* 431 Þan he oppynd þe dure & said vnto hym: And þou be a man, þou hase myster to hafe þe dure opynd, and to hafe meatt and warm þe. **1471** CAXTON *Recuyell* (Sommer) 169 Prayng hym that he wold brynge her in to some hous where she myghte warme and chauffe her wyth her chyld for he was nyhe ded for cold. *a* **1548** HALL *Chron., Hen. VIII* 238 b, All the Ladyes entered the tentes and there warmed them a space. **1604** E. G. tr. *Acosta's Hist. Indies* II. ix. 101, I felt so great cold, as I was forced to go into the sunne to warme me. **1642** FULLER *Holy & Prof. St.* II. xix. 121 His hands must be their own fire, and warm themselves with working. **1798** SOPHIA LEE *Canterb. T., Young Lady's T.* II. 74 A group of fishermen sat warming themselves in the sun. **1831** SCOTT *Ct. Robt.* xxvi, Think not I will once more warm in my bosom the household snake which had so nearly stung me to death. **1852** THACKERAY *Esmond* I. xiv, You little serpent, warmed by my fire. **1860** TYNDALL *Glaciers* I. xi. 72 We rose .. renewed the fire and warmed ourselves. **1902** R. BAGOT *Donna Diana* i. 4 Shall we go to Aragno's on our way home and have some coffee to warm us?

absol. **1611** BIBLE *Isa.* xlvii. 14 There shall not be a coale to warm at, nor fire to sit before it.

b. Said of a fire, the sun, etc. Also *absol.*

a **1548** HALL *Chron., Edw. IV*, 216 b, Whiche sight as much pleased the citizens, as a fier paynted on the wall, warmed the olde woman. **1583** BABINGTON *Commandm.* 413 When they are colde, they goe to the fire, and not to the water to warme them; and can they not tell which dooth warme and which dooth coole? **1732** POPE *Ess. Man* i. 271 All are but parts of one stupendous whole.. That.. Warms in the sun, refreshes in the breeze.

c. To increase the animal heat of. In quot. *absol.*

1610 MARKHAM *Masterp.* II. clxxiii. 483 It looseth and scattereth humors, warmeth and moisteneth.

d. Said of the blood.

1759 STERNE *Tr. Shandy* II. xvii, He was as honest a soul, added Trim, (pulling out his handkerchief) as ever blood warmed. **1810** SCOTT *Lady of Lake* v. xiv, For I have sworn this braid to stain In the best blood that warms thy vein. **1896** HOUSMAN *Shropshire Lad* xxxi, The blood that warms an English yeoman.

2. In various figurative uses.

a. To inspire with affection or kindly feelings; to cause to 'glow' with pleasure.

1526 *Pilgr. Perf.* (W. de W. 1531) 266 It calefyeth & warmeth the hert of man or woman with the flame of loue. **1665** BOYLE *Occas. Refl.* Introd. Pref. (1848) p. xxx, Whilst pious Reflections are making, they are proper to Instruct the Mind, and Warm the Affections. **1773** MRS. CHAPONE *Improv. Mind* (1774) I. 78 The effusions of a heart warm'd with the tenderest affection. **1836** J. GRANT *Random Recoll. Ho. Lords* xvi. 391 That eloquence which approves itself to the judgment, though it never warms the heart by appeals to the passions. **1837** DICKENS *Pickw.* lvii, It will warm my heart to witness the happiness of those friends who are dearest to me. **1847** C. BRONTE *Jane Eyre* xi, The charm of adventure sweetens that sensation, the glow of pride warms it. **1864** TENNYSON *Aylmer's F.* 554 Once indeed, Warm'd with his wines, or taking pride in her, She look'd so sweet, he kiss'd her tenderly. **1905** C. G. LANG *Th. Parables Jesus* 16 When the example of a true man or woman warms the heart and fires the will.

absol. **1883** R. W. DIXON *Mano* I. viii. 21 Those lightsome words that warm like summer days.

b. To render eager or zealous; to rouse from indifference, esp. to put (an audience) into a receptive mood. Also *absol.* Now usu. with *up.*

c **1580** HOOKER *Sir P. Carew* (1857) 42 Sir Peter Carew was then present, and one unto whom, as they thought, the speeches were specially directed.. and indeed, he being some-what warmed theirin, deviseth how to compass the matter. **1638** DAVENANT *Madagascar* 10 When honours warmes him, and his blood is young. **1706** *Epistle after Battle Ramillies* 106 Prior's Wks. 1907 II. 372 The rescu'd chief, by the past danger warm'd, Our weaken'd houshold with new fury storm'd. **1712** STEELE *Spect.* No. 521 ⁋2, I had arrived at a particular Skill in warming a Man so far in his Narration, as to make him throw in a little of the Marvelous. **1737** WHISTON *Josephus, Hist.* I. i. §4 When he was warmed by this great success, he made an assault upon the garrison that was in the city. **1764** GOLDSM. *Trav.* 380 Calm is my soul, nor apt to rise in arms, Except when fast approaching danger warms. **1764** CHURCHILL *Gotham* III. 323 The Soul, with great and manly feelings warm'd, Panting for Knowledge, rests not till inform'd. **1765** BURKE *Corr.* (1844) I. 59, I am not used to defend my conduct;.. I have been warmed to it by the imputation you threw on me. **1857** MRS. CARLYLE *Lett.* II. 308 Anne, who is so difficult to warm up to bare satisfaction point. **1892** 'MARK TWAIN' *Amer. Claimant* xxiv. 236 I'll just go over there and warm up that House of Lords. **1923** *N.Y. Times* 14 Oct. VIII. 4 Warming 'em up—Going on early as a sacrifice for the later acts. **1966** *Guardian* 28 Mar. 3/7 Mrs Bessie Braddock warmed up the meeting for him. **1974** *Times* 21 Jan. 12/8 In the studio.. Llew Gardner, the chairman, warmed us up music-hall style and the three panellists appeared. **1982** N. PAINTING *Reluctant Archer* vii. 113 We might have warmed up his audience for him.

†**c.** To exhort to valour. (Often in Dryden and Pope.) *Obs.*

1697 DRYDEN *Æneis* VII. 657 The Gods invok'd, the Rutuli prepare Their Arms, and warm each other to the War. *Ibid.* VIII. 927 The Queen her self,.. With Cymbals toss'd, her fainting Souldiers warms. **1718** POPE *Iliad* XVI. 653 First to the Fight his native Troops he warms.

d. Of drink: To excite, stimulate.

1617 MORYSON *Itin.* I. 3 When the common people are once warmed with drinke, they are apt to doe them injury. **1743** FRANCIS tr. *Hor., Epodes* xi. 12 When the gay Liquor warm'd my opening Soul.

†**e.** To provoke, excite (temper). *Obs.*

1752 CHESTERF. *Let. to Son* 26 Sept., Keep your own temper, and artfully warm other people's.

3. a. To make (a material object or substance) warm; to heat moderately; to 'take the chill off'.

a **1000** *Riddles* xii[i]. 10 Wonfeax Wale.. wæteð in wætre, wyrmeð hwilum fæȝre to fyre. *c* **1000** in Assmann *Ags. Hom.* xi. 84 For ðy he cwæð þe ðam colan wætere, ðæt nan man ne ðorfte hine beladian, ðæt he fæt næfde, on hwy he hit wyrman mihte. *c* **1374** CHAUCER *Troylus* v. 1109 The laurer crowned Phebus with his hete Gan.. To warmen of the est See þe wawes wete. *a* **1425** tr. *Arderne's Treat. Fistula* etc. 40 Þe Iuyse of celidone y-medled wiþ vinegre and warmed at þe fire.. quenchiþ wele þe wickid hete. **1530** PALSGR. 771/2 You must warme your medecyne or you drinke it. *a* **1589** R. WILLES in Hakluyt *Voy.* 611 Before the Sunne hath warmed the ayre and dissolued the ise,.. there can be no sailing. **1617** S. H. *Preserv. Health* (1624) 45 In the Winter time, warme well your garments at the fire, and warm the linings of the same. **17..** WATTS *Hymns & Spir. Songs* II. cxlvii. (1751) 259 E'er there was Rain to bless the Earth, Or Sun to warm the Ground. **1747–96** MRS. GLASSE *Cookery* xv. 269 Skim it, warm it blood warm, and drink it. **1774** GOLDSM. *Nat. Hist.* VI. 168 In summer, they [*sc.* fish] are seen in great numbers in the shallows near the shore, where the sun has power to warm the water to the bottom. **1859** H. KINGSLEY *G. Hamlyn* xix, The tea's cold; put it on the embers and warm it a bit. **1862** MRS. H. WOOD *Mrs. Hallib. Troub.* I. i, You can get my slippers warmed, Jane. **1900** *Jrnl. Soc. Dyers* XVI. 12 Powerful jets with water warmed by steam. **1907** J. A. HODGES *Elem. Photogr.* (ed. 6) 159 The negative should be slightly warmed.

†**b.** Said jocularly for: To occupy (one's bed).

1599 MARSTON *Antonio's Rev.* III. ii, I thinke we shall not warme our beds to day.

c. ***to warm up*** (U.S. ***to warm over***): to make warm again (cooked food that has become cold). Also (*rarely*) without adv.

1848 DICKENS *Dombey* lix, She requests to have that little bit of sweetbread that was left, warmed up for her supper. **1853** SOYER *Pantroph.* 380 Another custom.. was that of warming the remains of a preceding banquet for other guests. **1863** W. C. BALDWIN *Afr. Hunting* iii. 68 We lived for three days on a most recommendable stew,.. which appeared, warmed up fresh, at every meal. **1885** 'MRS. ALEXANDER' *Valerie's Fate* iv, Valerie went.. to the kitchen to warm up an appetizing little dish prepared by the femme de ménage.

fig. **1876** LD. HARTINGTON in Ld. E. Fitzmaurice *Earl Granville* (1905) II. 167 All the old anti-Turk abuse was warmed up again. **1879** O. W. HOLMES *Motley* xxi. 162 [The reply] took up the old exceptions, warmed them over into grievances.

d. To impart warmth of colour to.

1853 KANE *Grinnell Exp.* xxxv. (1856) 321 A peculiar purple, slightly warmed or bronzed at its margins. **1862** MISS BRADDON *Lady Audley* iii, Not one glimmer of gold or auburn warmed the dull flaxen of her hair.

4. To heat (a building, a room) to a moderate temperature.

1858 LARDNER *Hand-bk. Nat. Phil.* 278 Warming buildings by hot water. **1874** MICKLETHWAITE *Modern Par. Churches* 200 A perfect method of warming churches has yet to be invented. **1915** *Blackw. Mag.* Mar. 345/1 The room was warmed by a brazier.

†**5.** To inaugurate (a new house) by a feast or entertainment. *Obs.* Cf. HOUSE-WARMING 2.

1617 in *Crt. & Times Jas. I* (1848) II. 50 On Monday, to warm it [the renovated house], he made a great feast. **1661** HEYLIN *Eccl. Restaur.* (1674) 237 Sir Thomas Tresham.. took possession of his place, which having scarce warmed, he was taken from it by the stroke of death. **1800** *Gentl. Mag.* LXX. II. 786/2 The Prince, it is said, will be present at the first dinner that *warms* this room.

†**6.** ***to be well warmed***: to be settled *in* (a residence, position of dignity or profit). *Obs.* Cf. WARM *a.* 7.

1565 ALLEN *Defence Purg.* (1886) 16 Ere they be well warmed in their benefices. **1711** *Country-Man's Let. Curat* 79 Even before she was well warm'd on the Throne.

7. †**a.** *Mil.* To throw (an enemy) into commotion by a cannonade. ***to warm the field***: to carry on a furious cannonade. *Obs.*

Cf. F. *chauffer un poste*, 'le canonner vivement' (Littré).

1705 *Addr. Blessington* in *Lond. Gaz.* No. 4089/2 The English warm'd the Field to that degree, that Thirty Squadrons.. were forc'd to fly. **1720** DE FOE *Capt. Singleton* xi. (1840) 187 Resolving to give him a broadside that should warm him.

†**b.** Sporting. ***to warm up***: to give (one's competitor) reason to fear defeat. *Obs.*

1868 *Field* 4 July 14/3 First Trinity rowed over for the trial heat, and in the final heat on the second day 'warmed up' University to some tune.

c. ***to warm the bell*** (see quots.). *Naut. slang.*

1924 G. H. A. WILLIS *Royal Navy as I saw It* 116 'To warm the bell', meaning literally to strike the bell a minute or two before the exact time, was applied to circumstances in which to be in good time was meant. **1925** FRASER & GIBBONS *Soldier & Sailor Words* 300 *Warming the bell*, putting on the clock. Advancing the time illegitimately for some particular reason. **1956** H. W. EDWARDS *Their Lawful Occasions* xxiv. 130 'Ah! I see. All ready dressed for the shore,' I said. 'Warming the bell, eh?' **1976** *Oxf. Compan. Ships & Sea* 924/2 *To warm the bell*... On board warships in the days of sail, time was measured by a half-hour sand-glass. Each time the sand ran through the glass was turned .. and the appropriate number of bells struck. It was supposed.. that if the glass was warmed the expansion of the neck would allow the sand to run through a little more quickly. Hence.. eight bells and the return to one's hammock, would come gratifyingly earlier than it should.

8. *dial.* To beat, flog.

1824 CARR *Craven Gloss.*, *Warm*, to beat. 'I'll warm thy jerkin for the.' **1825** BROCKETT *N.C. Words*, *Warm*, to beat. 'Aw'l warm yor hide.' **1828** SCOTT *F.M. Perth* xxix, Old Dorothy, whose hand has warmed my haffits before now. **1853** 'C. BEDE' *Verdant Green* I. i, You take out your strap and warm him! **1862** MRS. H. WOOD *Mrs. Hallib. Troub.* I. xxi, Won't Charlotte warm his back for him! **1892** M. C. F. MORRIS *Yorks. Folk Talk* 95 Every Yorkshireman knows what warming a child means; perhaps not a few.. by bitter experience. **1915** 'Q' (Quiller-Couch) in *Blackw. Mag.* Jan. 102/2 To 'warm' a child in Polpier signifies to beat him with a strap.

II. *intr.* To become warm.

9. a. Of a living body, a material thing or substance: To be raised in temperature.

a **1000** *Phœnix* 213 Wyrta wearmiaþ. *c* **1000** ÆLFRIC *Gram.* xxvi. (Z.) 154 *Caleo*, ic wearmiȝe. *c* **1400** *Destr. Troy* 4035 Wyndis wastid away, warmyt the ayre. *c* **1648–50** BRATHWAIT *Barnabees Jrnl.* III. (1818) 95 Thence to Cambridge where the Muses Haunt the Vine-bush.. Like sparks up a chimney warming. **1827** FARADAY *Chem. Manip.* iv. (1842) 141 A large thermometer.. may from the lapse of time necessary to allow of its proper change, occasion an alteration of temperature, by allowing the body tried to cool or warm. **1868** LOUISA M. ALCOTT *Little Women* i, Beth put a pair of slippers down to warm. **1872** O. W. HOLMES *Poet* i. (1885) 19 A cold day warming up to 32°. **1889** 'R. BOLDREWOOD' *Robbery under Arms* xi, Here's some damper and mutton..while tea warms. **1904** S. E. WHITE *Forest* xiv, The weather had warmed, the sun shone.

b. Of colour: To become 'warmer' or more ruddy.

1831 JAMES *Phil. Augustus* xv, On a bright morning of July, when the grey of the sky was just beginning to warm with the rising day. **1906** *Westm. Gaz.* 8 June 8/1 His head and underparts are of a pearly grey that warms to a pinkish hue on the breast.

c. With *up.* Of a sportsman, etc.: to prepare oneself by light exercise or practice immediately before the start of a contest or other physical exertion.

1883 [see WARMING *vbl. sb.* 1 d]. **1926** *Amer. Speech* I. 369/2 Pitchers 'warm up' on a plot of grass called 'the bull pen'. **1955** R. BANNISTER *First Four Minutes* 16, I was warming up on the uneven grass near the track. **1972** J. MOSEDALE *Football* viii. 118 Ed Neale..used to warm up for the game by breaking beer bottles across his forearm. **1976** J. SNOW *Cricket Rebel* 35 Graeme Pollock again. Warming up with his first half century in 70 minutes and dashing to his century [in]..only 35 minutes.

d. With *up.* Of an engine, electrical appliance, etc.: to reach a temperature high enough for efficient working.

1947 A. RANSOME *Great Northern?* i. 24 There was a whirr from below as the engine started and a steady throbbing as it was warming up. **1955** A. BUDRYS in D. Knight *100 Yrs. Sci. Fiction* (1969) 255 Halsey's familiar figure appeared on the screen as the set warmed up. **1958** 'N. SHUTE' *Rainbow & Rose* i. 18 He went to the transceiver and turned it on to warm up. **1972** *Daily Tel.* 12 Apr. 13/5 The engine warms up rapidly and performs eagerly.

10. Of a person, his heart, feelings, etc.: To become affectionate, kindly, or genial (*to, towards* a person).

c **1400** *Destr. Troy* 3376 And I in longing am Laght & Lappit full sore, With hete of þi hegh loue, þat my hert warmys. **1779** MME. D'ARBLAY *Diary* Feb., Mr. Thrale was ..at first, cold and quiet, but soon..warmed into sociality. **1818** SCOTT *Hrt. Midl.* xxxv, I judged that..your Grace's heart wad warm to the tartan. **1833** L. RITCHIE *Wanderings by Loire* 46 Every heart seemed..to warm towards the little devotee. **1848** DICKENS *Dombey* xx, Mr. Dombey, in his friendlessness, inclined to the Major. It cannot be said that he warmed towards him, but he thawed a little. **1874** L. STEPHEN *Hours in Library* (1892) I. iv. 141 Carlyle..cannot, indeed, but warm to Scott at the end. **1883** D. C. MURRAY *Hearts* i, His heart warmed over Baretti as they walked along together.

11. To become eager, animated, or enthusiastic. Also, with *up. to warm* (*up*) *to*: to become interested in, acquire zest for, to 'put one's back into' (one's work, a contest, etc.).

1749 SMOLLETT *Gil Blas* XI. xiv. (1782) IV. 209, I expected every moment to see them warm, and to go to loggerheads, the usual end of their dissertations. **1835** DICKENS *Sk. Boz, Mr. Watkins Tottle* i, 'I'll tell you,' replied Mr. Gabriel Parsons, warming with the subject, and the brandy-and-water,—'I know a lady [etc.].' **1846** DISRAELI in Moneypenny & Buckle *Life* (1914) III. 11, I have not yet added much to my abortive MSS. of the German Schloss of last year, but am beginning to warm up. **1858** THACKERAY *Virgin.* xxxviii, Papa's first nervousness is over: his noble voice clears, warms to his sermon. **1867** H. LATHAM *Black & White* 5 Congress will by that time have met, and be warming to their work. **1868** E. EDWARDS *Ralegh* I. iv. 72 When he found that his competitor was formidable, he warmed to the race. **1879** MᶜCARTHY *Own Times* II. xxix. 364 He warmed up as he went along. **1885** MARY E. WILKINS in *Harper's Mag.* Mar. 594/1 She warmed up on the subject.

warmable ('wɔːməb(ə)l), *a. rare.* [f. WARM *v.* + -ABLE.] Capable of being warmed.

1839 A. LANGTON *Jrnl.* in *Gentlewoman Upper Canada* (1950) 98, I must tell you then that the drawing-room is as warmable as ever. **1887** W. MORRIS in Mackail *Life* (1899) II. 180 We have had a hard frost for nearly a fortnight..; and our stable-meeting-room is not very warmable under such conditions.

'war-man.

1. A fighting-man, warrior, soldier. In early use chiefly *Sc.*; now *rare.*

In Minot's *Poems* x. 9 Ritson and Hall print 'weremen' as an emendation of the MS. reading 'werkmen'.

1456 SIR G. HAYE *Law Arms* (S.T.S.) 162 And gif innocent folk takis scathe, than, in sik opyn weris, the prince na the were men may nocht..set remede. *c* **1470** HENRY *Wallace* IV. 256 Wallace commaundede thai suld na wermen saiff. **1513** DOUGLAS *Æneis* x. xiv. 151 Syne on that weyrman ruschit he in teyn. **1547** J. HARRISON *Exhort. Scottes* a iij b, How the countrey hath been ouer runne..by our awne warremen. **1588** SHAKS. *L.L.L.* v. ii. 666 The sweet War-man is dead and rotten. **1591** *2nd Pt. Troub. Raigne K. John* (1611) 97 Backe warremen, backe. **1797** T. DIBDIN *Snug Little Island*, A very great war-man, called Billy the Norman. **1831** SCOTT *Cast. Dang.* ix, You will command at least twenty war-men, with bow and spear. **1864** R. F. BURTON *Dahome* I. 48, I detected several warmen privily borrowing from their neighbours. **1911** G. K. CHESTERTON *Ballad of White Horse* 104 Meeting may be of war-men Where the best war-man wins.

b. *U.S.* One whose voice is for war. Cf. WAR-DOG, *war-hawk.*

1814 *Columbian Centinel* 11 June 2/4 in A. Matthews *Uncle Sam* (1908) 28.

†**2.** A man-of-war, warship. *Sc. Obs.*

1546 *Burgh Rec. Edin.* (1871) II. 123 The pryses takin be the Cristopher..to the nummer of sex weirman.

ˌwarm-'blooded, *a.* (Also *'warm-ˌblooded.*) **a.** Having warm blood; *spec.* of mammals and birds, which have a uniform high temperature.

1793 T. BEDDOES *Let. Darwin* 68 At a temperature considerably below that of warm-blooded animals. **1839** T. BEALE *Nat. Hist. Sperm Whale* 41 All the cetacea, as is well known, are warm-blooded animals. **1889** G. ALLEN *Falling in Love*, etc. 80 Even among warm-blooded animals like the bears and dormice, hibernation occurs.

b. *fig.* Ardent, fervent, passionate.

1831 SCOTT *Cast. Dang.* v, Strict discipline,..since the death of that great monarch, had been considerably neglected by the young and warm-blooded valour of England.

Hence **warm-'bloodedness**, the character or condition of being warm-blooded.

1923 J. S. HUXLEY in *Cornh. Mag.* Apr. 427 In the birds as in the mammals,..we see the evolution..of physiological characters like warm-bloodedness or efficiency of circulation. **1946** F. E. ZEUNER *Dating Past* xii. 84 Warm-bloodedness and many other characters of the mammals are probably the consequence of a single important aromorph. **1982** *N.Y. Times Mag.* 7 Feb. 34/4 High metabolisms, a characteristic of the warm-bloodedness of mammals and birds.

warmed (wɔːmd), *ppl. a.* [f. WARM *v.* + -ED[1].] Made warm. Also with *over, up.* **a.** *lit.*

1597 A. M. tr. *Guillemeau's Fr. Chirurg.* 28/1 With a warmed table naptkinne, rubbe the insyde of the arme. **1679** TRAPHAM *Disc. Health Jamaica* 146 Dissolution in Wine or Broth or other warmed Liquids. **1820** KEATS *Eve St. Agnes* xxvi, She..Unclasps her warmed jewels one by one. **1895** S. CRANE *Red Badge* v, He grasped his canteen and took a long swallow of the warmed water. **1897** *Private Life of Queen* xvii. 141 The Queen..made a delightful luncheon off warmed-up broth and potatoes she had helped to boil herself. **1916** B. M. BOWER *Phantom Herd* 246 A midnight supper of warmed-over coffee and cold bean sandwiches. **1977** H. GREENE *FSO-1* vi. 57 Warmed-over moussaka uneaten before him.

b. *fig.*

like death warmed up: see DEATH *sb.* 17 c.

1690 LOCKE *Hum. Und.* IV. xix. §7 This I take to be properly Enthusiasm..rising from the Conceits of a warm'd or over-weening Brain. **1854** PATMORE *Angel in Ho., Betrothal* 141 And all thank God with their warmed wits. **1883** MISS BROUGHTON *Belinda* I. vi, The sense of physical emptiness, that..no warmed passions redeem. **1887** *Nation* (N.Y.) 2 June 465/3 They will be spared the future bitterness of finding..themselves treated to insult and warmed-over excuses. **1950** *New Yorker* 8 Apr. 96/2 *Oggi*.. came out with..a warmed-over photograph taken in the Farfa displaced-persons camp. **1965** *Listener* 9 Sept. 391/1 The comfort given by warmed-up studio audiences. **1978** W. MANKOWITZ *Extraordinary Mr Poe* vi. 186 Verses dedicated *To F*, actually warmed-over lines written for another.

warment, var. VARMENT[1] *dial.*

warmer ('wɔːmə(r)). [f. WARM *v.* + -ER[1].]

1. A person who warms. *poet.*

a **1595** SOUTHWELL *St. Peter's Compl.* 11 Coales were kindled to the warmers cost. **1658** COKAINE *Poems* 249 Tis Loves best musick, all ears charmer, All hearts enthraller, and blouds warmer. **1903** BRIDGES *Ep. Socialist* 413 Unashamed to have outliv'd Your breeders, feeders, warmers and toiling attendants.

2. A contrivance for warming.

Chiefly with defining word prefixed, as *foot-, plate-, vegetable-warmer.*

1812–83: see FOOT *sb.* 35. **1837–75**: see PLATE *sb.* 20 b. **1844** T. WEBSTER *Encycl. Dom. Econ.* 845 The well-known japanned plate warmer for the parlour in small families. *Ibid.*, A lower kind sold in the shops under the name of vegetable warmers, for keeping those dishes of vegetables warm that are not put on the table. **1871** *Daily News* 13 Jan., Covered up till we were nearly suffocated, and with a warmer for our feet. **1894** *Times* 16 Apr. 7/3 The whey is dipped out into large warmers and these placed in the boiler.

3. *warmer-up*, something that warms oneself or another up; *spec.* (*a*) a preliminary item designed to put an audience in a receptive mood; also, one who presents this; (*b*) a stimulating drink. Also *warmer-upper*, esp. in sense (*b*) above.

1960 *House & Garden* Aug. 70/1 A tipple that has been a warmer-upper for British sailors since before Nelson's day. **1962** *Guardian* 22 Dec. 5/2 As so often it is the warmers-up (in this case Gordon and Bunny Jay) who do the hard work. **1972** *Jazz & Blues* Nov. 28/1 *Shaw nuff* is a very fast warmer-up. **1976** *Ulverston* (Cumbria) *News* 3 Dec. 19/2 As a 'warmer-up' the concert began with a rather pedestrian rendering of the Hebrides overture. **1980** *Times* 9 Dec. 2/1 Stone's Ginger Wine. The original warmer-upper. On its own or as a Stone's Whisky Mac.

warme store, variant of WARNESTORE *Obs.*

†**'warmful**, *a. Obs. rare.* [f. WARM *a.* + -FUL.] Full of warmth.

c **1611** CHAPMAN *Iliad* x. 121 A mandilion..Of purple, large, and full of folds; curld with a warmefull nap. **1738** *Gentl. Mag.* VIII. 314/1 Who kindled first his warm-ful, vital ray?

ˌwarm-'hearted, *a.* (Also *'warm-ˌhearted.*) Having a warm heart; of a generous and affectionate disposition. Also, proceeding from, or indicating, such a disposition; hearty, cordial.

1500–20 DUNBAR *Poems* lxxv. 32 Be warme hairtit and nocht ewill-willie. **1808** HAN. MORE *Cœlebs* xlv[i], Flam is naturally an open, warm-hearted man. **1844** *Mem. Babylonian Princess* II. 80 The kind and warm-hearted treatment which I had experienced from the Dryaah tribe. **1859** GEO. ELIOT *Adam Bede* I, He's of a rash, warm-hearted nature, like Esau.

Hence **warm-'heartedly** *adv.*, **warm-'heartedness.**

1808 HAN. MORE *Cœlebs* xi. I. 142 Her extreme naïveté and warm-heartedness. **1840** DICKENS *Old C. Shop* xlii, That's the way I've gone through life. Experience has never put a chill upon my warm-heartedness. **1911** *Concise Oxf. Dict.*, *Warm-heartedly* adv.

warming ('wɔːmɪŋ), *vbl. sb.* [f. WARM *v.* + -ING[1].]

1. a. The action of making warm; the state of becoming warm.

c **1440** *Promp. Parv.* 517/1 Warmynge, *calefactio.* **1597** SHAKS. *2 Hen. IV*, IV. iii. 111 The second propertie of your excellent Sherris, is, the warming of the Blood. *c* **1680** R. FLEMING *Fulfilling Script.* II. iv. (1726) 302 As it is sure our bodies are influenced with the warmings of the sun. **1835** DICKENS *Sk. Boz, Parish* vi, Such a nursing and warming of little legs and feet before the fire. **1883** MISS BROUGHTON *Belinda* II. vii, Whether he will have time for a good warming and breakfasting before setting off.

b. *transf.* and *fig.*

c **1621** in *10th Rep. Hist. MSS. Comm.* App. I. 105 The estates hauing of late made great fiers in the Infanta her country of Brabant, euen to the warminge of her courte at Bruxells. **1681** R. FLEMING *Fulfilling Script.* III. ii. (1726) 359 To unite further those amongst themselves with the more warmings of that ancient love that was wont to be amongst them. **1743** J. GLAS *Lord's Supper* v. v. Wks. 1761 IV. 143 Many warmings and seemingly good motions and wishes, that never carry us out..to do any good work.

†**c.** *warming of the house* = HOUSE-WARMING 2.

1653 GREAVES *Seraglio* 184 The warming of the house, as we call it in England.

d. With *up*: the action or condition of 'warming up' (see WARM *v.* 3, 9, and 11). Freq. *attrib.*

1874 J. G. MCCOY *Hist. Sk. Cattle Trade* 244 This style, ..of wintering cattle, is called 'Roughing', and the feeding of corn in the spring is termed 'Warming up'. **1883** *Chicago Inter-Ocean* 27 June 5 The players..began their practice play. This is called 'warming up'. **1952** *Times* 22 Feb. 6/4 Jet-engined aircraft have two further advantages—no preliminary 'warming up' is necessary, so they can take off in shorter time. **1960** *Practical Wireless* XXXVI. 429/1 The warming up time for this unit is about 30 seconds.

2. A thrashing, trouncing. Also *fig.*

1681 W. ROBERTSON *Phraseol. Gen.* 664/1, I'le give your hide a warming. **1880** S. BUTLER *Let.* 20 May in H. F. Jones *Mem.* (1919) I. 332 My new book..will..give old Darwin the best warming that I can manage to give him.

3. *attrib.*, as *warming-chamber, drawer, -house, oven, -stone* (see quots.).

1791 BENTHAM *Panopt.* I. 201 The *warming chamber, or set of warming-chambers..consists of earthen retorts, open at both ends, and inclosed in iron ones. **1876** in Willis & Clark *Cambridge* (1886) III. 238 The warming chamber..is common to both portions of the building. **1972** J. BURMEISTER *Running Scared* vii. 95 Your breakfast will be in the *warming drawer if I'm not there. **1897** J. W. CLARK *Observ. Barnwell Priory* p. lxiii, The *Warming-House (*calefactorium*). **1950** in M. Cecil *Heroines in Love* (1974) 199 Jocelyn turned out the *warming oven. **1973** J. BURROWS *Like an Evening Gone* iii. 38 There was a square warming oven... 'For keeping tins and dinner plates hot.' **1668** CHARLETON *Onomast.* 243 *Lapis Schistos*..the *Warming stone. **1677** PLOT *Oxfordsh.* 253 If Mault-kills or Oasts made with ordinary stone prove so advantagious, what would one of them do, if the Joists and Laths at least were made of the Cornish warming-stone, that will hold heat well eight or ten hours. **1691** RAY *Creation* I. (1692) 83 To these useful Stones I might add the Warming-stone, digged in Cornwal, which being once well heated at the fire retains its warmth a great while, and hath been found to give ease and relief in several Pains and Diseases, particularly that of the internal Hæmorrhoids.

warming ('wɔːmɪŋ), *ppl. a.* [-ING[2].] That makes warm, or becomes warm; *lit.* and *fig.* Also with *up.*

c **1450** *Mirk's Festial* 160 Lyght fyre, schapon lyke tonges, brennyng and not smertyng, warmyng not harmyng. **1661** FELTHAM *Resolves* liii. (ed. 8) 293 The gentle..rayes of the warming Sun. *c* **1680** R. FLEMING *Fulfilling Script.* II. v. (1726) 309 It is rare to find a warming heat with a large profession, such as can make it convincing to others. **1765** J. BROWN *Chr. Jrnl., Winter Day* 287 With what amazing power do the warming beams of the Sun of righteousness dart into my soul! **1819** SCOTT *Ivanhoe* xxxvii, A warming and spicy-smelling balsam. **1851** MEREDITH *Poems, Pict. Rhine* iii, And now the sun In saffron clothes the warming atmosphere. **1886** HARDY *Woodlanders* ix, Do you think a Christmas party..is a warming-up thing, and likely to be useful in hastening on the matter?

'warming-pan.

1. A long-handled covered pan of metal (usually of brass) to contain live coals, etc., formerly in common use for warming beds.

1573 BARET *Alv.* W 64 A warmyng pan, *thermoclinium.* *c* **1590** MARLOWE *Jew of Malta* 1745 A fellow..with..a Dagger with a hilt like a warming-pan. **1669** PEPYS *Diary* 1 Jan., Presented from Captain Beckford with a noble silver warming-pan, which I am doubtful whether to take or no. **1710** HILMAN *Tusser Rediv.* May (1744) 62 The tinkling after them with a Warming-Pan, Frying-Pan, or Kettle, is of good Use to let the Neighbours know you have a Swarm [of Bees] in the Air. **1840** DICKENS *Old C. Shop* xiv, A nosegay resembling in shape and dimensions a full-sized warming-pan with the handle cut short off.

fig. **1626** BRETON *Fantasticks* (Grosart) 9/2, I thus conclude, I hold it [August] the worlds welfare, and the earths Warming-pan. **1762** *Gentl. Mag.* XXXII. 137/2 For wedlock is the warming-pan, That best can warm the bed.

2. *Hist.* With allusion to the story that James II's son, afterwards called the Old Pretender, was a supposititious child introduced into the Queen's bed in a warming-pan. Also *attrib.*

1689 *Full Answ. Depos. Birth Pr. Wales* 13 Do you think it [the child] was conveyed there in a Warming-pan, or otherwise? 1689 *Muses Farew. Popery* 141 A Warming pan Plot, worse than Celliers Meal-Tub. 1716 *Collect. State Songs, Poems*, etc. 64 Let those Rebels, if they can, Make us forget the Warming Pan, Which first convey'd that pretty Man Into the Chamber Royal. 1818 Scott *Rob Roy* ix, Our immortal deliverer from papists and pretenders, and wooden shoes and warming pans.

3. *slang.* a. A large old-fashioned watch. Cf. turnip *sb.* 3 b. b. A female bed-fellow. *Scotch warming-pan*: a chambermaid who lay in the bed a while to warm it for the intending occupant.

1668 Davenant *Man's the Master* ii. 25 None but a cold Bed-fellow would have two Warming-Pans. 1678 Ray *Prov.* (ed. 2) 83 A Scotch warming-pan, *i.e.* a wench. The story is well known of the Gentleman travelling in Scotland, who desiring to have his bed warmed, the servant-maid doffs her clothes and lays her self down in it for a while. *a* 1700 B. E. *Dict. Cant. Crew, Warming-pan*, an old fashion'd large Watch. *A Scotch Warming-pan*, a She-bed-fellow.

c. A person who temporarily holds a place or employment until the intended occupant is ready to take it.

1846 *Eclectic Rev.* June 662 A *locum tenens* (ecclesiasticè, a warming-pan) was wanted for a Yorkshire living. 1847 Disraeli *Tancred* ii. i, Hungerford is not a warming-pan;.. he never was originally; and if he had been, he has been member for the county too long to be so considered now. 1883 D. C. Murray *Hearts* xiv. (1885) 117, I only serve the place of what in Parliament is called a warming-pan.

attrib. 1875 *Daily News* 2 June 2/2 The Act.. was simply employed for conserving livings for the use of the children of the patron, and was popularly known as the 'warming-pan' Act.

warmint, var. varment[1] *dial.*

warmish ('wɔːmɪʃ), *a.* [f. warm *a.* + -ish.] Somewhat warm.

1597 A. M. tr. *Guillemeau's Fr. Chirurg.* 51/3 A south-west wind, with warmishe showres of rayne. 1647 Trapp *Comm., 1 Thess.* v. 3 As Philosophers say, that before a snow the weather will be warmish. 1826 S. Cooper *Surg.* (ed. 5) 61 The patient is to be kept in a warmish, but well-ventilated apartment. 1895 Meredith *Amaz. Marriage* xxxi. II. 345 Odd movements of a warmish curiosity brushed him when the cynic was not mounting guard.

†'**warmly**, *a. Obs. rare.* [f. warm *a.* or *v.* + -ly[1].] Full of warmth.

c 1470 Harding *Chron.* cix. viii, As they [the Danes] vnto theyr Shyppes agaynwarde flewe, He droue them there vnto a warmely stowe. 1637 Rutherford *Let. to Lady Kilconquhair* 8 Aug., The sweet presence, the long lasting goodwill of our God, the warmely & lovely comforts of our Lord Jesus be with you.

warmly ('wɔːmlɪ), *adv.* [f. warm *a.* + -ly[2].] In a warm manner.

1. So as to be warm (in temperature); so as to impart warmth. †Also Comb. *warmly-wet.*

1591 Sylvester *Du Bartas* i. iii. 836 Our mealy grain.. Rots to revive; and, warmly-wet, puts forth His root beneath, his bud above the Earth. 1623 J. Taylor (Water P.) *Discov. by Sea* B 6 b, Couetousnesse is Embroidered with Extortion, and warmely lined and furred with oppression. 1667 Milton *P.L.* iv. 244 Where the morning Sun first warmly smote The open field. 1725 Pope *Odyss.* xxiv. 262 His habit course, but warmly wrapt around. 1790 Cowper *On Receipt Mother's Picture* 59 Thy nightly visits to my chamber made, That thou might'st know me safe and warmly laid. 1860 Tyndall *Glac.* i. xxvii. 203 The Aiguille .. half of its granite cone was warmly illuminated, and half in shadow. 1914 *Blackw. Mag.* Aug. 176/2 The sun shone warmly upon him.

2. With warmth of feeling.

a. Fervently, earnestly.

1529 More *Suppl. Soulys* Wks. 336/2 Yet heare we sometime our wiues pray for vs more warmely. 1698 O. Heywood *Diaries* (1885) IV. 159 Father and two sons prayd warmly for him. 1766 Goldsm. *Vicar W.* xxxii, My son's bride warmly insisted that Lady Thornhill (that was to be) should take the lead. 1836 Thirlwall *Greece* xx. III. 150 Corinth warmly entered into the views of her colony. 1888 *Poor Nellie* 145 On a matter I have warmly at heart.

b. With warm affection, gratitude, kindness, admiration, etc.

1719 De Foe *Crusoe* ii. (Globe) 433 He spoke this very affectionately and warmly. 1791 Mrs. Radcliffe *Rom. Forest* i, And interested him more warmly in her favour. 1823 Scott *Quentin D.* xxvi, They.. barely thanked him in very cold terms for his courtesy while at his Court, and something more warmly, for having permitted them to retire. 1826 Disraeli *Viv. Grey* v. xv, All applauded him very warmly. 1876 Hardy *Ethelberta* xxx, Neigh.. pressed her fingers more warmly than she thought she had given him warrant for. 1904 *Verney Mem.* I. 146 Sir Edmund Verney was warmly attached to both husband and wife.

c. With controversial ardour, eagerly.

1665 Boyle *Occas. Refl.* vi. iv. (1848) 352 There are not many [controversies] that have been more curiously and warmly disputed, than the Question, Whether [etc.]. 1739 Hardwicke *Let.* in G. Harris *Life* (1847) I. 424 Points, on which our friends may be likely warmly to differ. 1830 D'Israeli *Chas. I*, III. vi. 90 The King and he often warmly disputed on the principles of a good Government.

d. With warmth of temper.

1776 *Trial of J. Fowke* iv. 28/1 The Governor.. reproached me warmly for taking up a business in which he was so immediately concerned. 1799 Ht. Lee *Canterb. T.*, *Frenchm. T.* (ed. 2) I. 200 'Let us not talk of him,' interrupted Dorsain, warmly. 1838 Lytton *Leila* i. ii, The young king spoke warmly and bitterly. 1873 W. Black *Pr. Thule* xvi. 254 'And if he has, whose fault is it?' the girl said, warmly.

3. With reference to attack or defence: Fiercely, vigorously.

1684 *Scanderbeg Rediv.* vi. 149 They came briskly on, and Charged very desperately, but being as warmly received,.. the Infidels were put to Flight. *a* 1700 Evelyn *Diary* 12 Mar. 1672, They so warmly plied our divided fleets, that [etc.]. 1708 *Lond. Gaz.* No. 4493/2 The Germans receiv'd him so warmly, that few of his Men escaped with their Lives. 1755 R. Rogers *Jrnls.* (1769) 7 We warmly pursued the enemy,.. and obliged them to disperse. 1797 in Nicolas *Disp. Nelson* (1845) III. 188 No person has a right to know that the Culloden was not as warmly engaged as any Ship in the Squadron.

warmness ('wɔːmnɪs). Now *rare.* [f. warm *a.* + -ness.] The condition of being warm, warmth.

1. Moderate heat.

c 1000 Ælfric *Saints' Lives* xi. 157 He wolde hine baðian on þam wlacum wætere .. ac he ȝewat sona swa he ðæt wæter hrepode, and wearð seo wearmnys him awend to deaðe. *c* 1386 Chaucer *Melib.* ¶ 2375 It may nat be seith he [Seneca] that where greet fyr hath longe tyme endured, that ther ne dwelleth som vapour of warmnesse. *c* 1440 *Alphabet of Tales* 473 He fand a serpent slayn with hurd-men, & bon vnto a stokk; and he lowsid hur becauce sho was som-what on lyfe, & layd hur þer sho mot fele warmenes of þe son. 1526 Tindale *Jas.* ii. 16 If.. one of you saye vnto them: Departe in peace, God sende you warmnes and fode. 1607 Markham *Cavel.* iii. (1617) 11 Make your horse run the traine with good courage and liuelinesse, and so in his warmnesse trot him home. 1696 J. F. *Merch. Wareho.* 25 Which [*sc.* cotton goods] if any person made trial of, he would scarcely make use of any other by reason of their duration and warmness. 1785 T. Reid *Let.* Wks. (1846) 65/1 A comfortable warmness in the air.

fig. 1589 *Pappe w. Hatchet* D iij b, The heate of some mens braines, and the warmnes of other mens bloud. 1681 D. Abraham in *Jrnl. Friends' Hist. Soc.* (1912) July 141 Love.. the course and motion whereof is in no wise to be stopped; Neither the warmness of Its stream refrigerated.

†2. The state of being well to do. *Obs.*

1399 Langl. *Rich. Redeles* iii. 288 þis warmnesse in welth with wy vppon erthe My3te not longe dure as doctourz us tellith. 1411–12 Hoccleve *De Reg. Princ.* 3059 Al þi bysynesse Is for þi lucre, and þi cofres warmnesse.

†3. Lukewarmness. *Obs. rare.*

1561 Daus tr. *Bullinger on Apoc.* xx. 127 The lothsom[n]es whiche God conceaueth of this newtralitie or warmnes [L. *ex tepiditate*].

4. Warmth of affection or devotion.

1526 *Pilgr. Perf.* (W. de W. 1531) 150 The soule melteth when it waxeth warme in deuocyon, whiche warmenesse,.. is moch swete and pleasaunt. 1631 *Eng. Primer Our Lady* 477 Make the sturdy for to bend, To the cold kind warmenes send. 1725 Ramsay *Gentle Sheph.* iii. iii, I lo'ed your company; And ever had a warmness in my breast, That made ye dearer to me than the rest.

†5. Heat of anger. *Obs.*

1563 Bp. Sandys in Strype *Ann. Ref.* (1709) I. 362 He saith, he is sory for those letters he wrote to me in his Warmeness.

warmoll, obs. form of wardmote.

warmonger ('wɔːˌmʌŋgə(r)). [f. war *sb.*[1] + monger *sb.*] One who traffics in war. Contemptuously applied to: †a. a mercenary soldier (*Obs. rare*$^{-1}$); b. one who seeks to bring about war. So '**war,mongering** *vbl. sb.* and *ppl. a.*

1590 Spenser *F.Q.* iii. x. 29 As much disdeigning to be so misdempt, Or a war-monger to be basely nempt. 1817 Hazlitt *Effects War & Taxes* Wks. 1902 III. 249 This is a singular slip of the pen in so noisy and triumphant a warmonger as the Poet Laureate. 1862 J. Bright *Let.* in Trevelyan *Life* (1913) 316 The war-mongers here are baffled for the time. 1878 E. Jenkins *Haverholme* 76 His bitter scoffs at the Chauvinists and war-mongers. 1934 *Sun* (Baltimore) 5 Mar. 6/3 Dr. Toynbee differs from Mr. McFadden's war mongers in that he makes a suggestion for avoiding such a catastrophe. 1940 N. Coward *Australia Visited* ii. 9 Many of those in high places.. dismissed his [*sc.* Winston Churchill's] eloquent prophetic words as alarmist warmongering. 1940 'G. Orwell' *Inside Whale* 170 The war-mongering to which the English intelligentsia gave themselves up in the period 1935–9. 1944 Mrs. Belloc Lowndes *Let.* 4 June (1971) 249 Algernon Cecil.. regards Churchill as 'a warmonger'. 1955 *Times* 2 Aug. 7/7 They have their war-mongers.. of course, but their fervency on Palestine derives as much from a sense of injustice as from wounded pride. 1981 R. Reagan in *N.Y. Rev. Bks.* 25 June 25 It is not war-mongering to say that some things are worth dying for.

warmot, obs. form of wormwood.

warmouth ('wɔːmaʊθ). A name given to a fresh-water sunfish belonging to the genus *Chænobryttus* found in the eastern U.S.

1888 Goode *Amer. Fishes* 67 The Warmouth, *Chænobryttus gulosus*, is well-known throughout the South. .. The Black Warmouth, *Chænobryttus antistius*, a species also called 'Warmouth', 'Big-mouth', [etc.].. abounds in the tributaries of the Upper Mississippi.

warmstore, variant of warnestore. *Obs.*

warmth (wɔːmθ). In 2 **wermþe**. [OE. **wiermþu*, **wærmþu* = MLG. *wermede*, Du. *warmte*, MHG. *wermede*, *warmede*, *warmte* (early mod.G. *wärmte*):—OTeut. type **warmiþō*, f. **warmo-*: see warm *a.* and -th[1].]

1. A moderately hot or pleasantly heated state of the atmosphere, esp. as an essential of physical comfort and well-being; a temperate heat radiating from the sun, a fire, etc.

c 1175 *Lamb. Hom.* 37 Do þine elmesse of þon þet þu maht ifor ðien.. Wrecche men sceos and claðes.. and wermþe and herburȝe. 1481 Caxton *Reynard* vii. (Arb.) 12 Reynart laye within the gate as he ofte was wonte to doo for the warmth of the sonne. 1548 Udall, etc. *Erasm. Par. Luke* xxiv. 25–9, 188 b, Petur, who.. abiured yͤ Lorde.. whyle being throughly taken wᵗ colde, he taketh warmth & heate by the coles of yͤ wicked Jewes. 1577 B. Googe *Heresbach's Husb.* i. 36 Yet desyreth it [Lupines] the warmth of Autume, that it may be well rooted before Winter come. 1662 R. Venables *Exper. Angler* ix. 91 In March, beginning of April, later end of September, and all winter fish bite best in the warmth of the day. 1671 Milton *P.R.* ii. 74 When scarce a Shed Could be obtain'd to shelter him or me [Mary] From the bleak air; A Stable was our warmth, A Manger his. 1690 Locke *Hum. Und.* ii. viii. §16. 57 The same Fire, that at one distance produces in us the Sensation of Warmth, does at a nearer approach, produce in us the far different Sensation of Pain. 1784 Cowper *Task* iv. 310 How the frost, Raging abroad, and the rough wind, endear The silence and the warmth enjoy'd within! 1819 Shelley *Cenci* ii. i. 187 If there be a sun in heaven She shall not dare to look upon its beams; Nor feel its warmth. 1836 Dickens *Sk. Boz, Doctors' Commons*, He had gathered up his robe behind,.. in order that he might feel the full warmth of the fire. 1864 Tennyson *Aylmer's F.* 185 The girl Nursing a child, and turning to the warmth The tender pink five-beaded baby-soles. 1908 S. E. White *Riverman* iv, A fine sun, tempered with a prophetic warmth of later spring, animated the scene.

b. *fig.*

1653 Jer. Taylor *Serm. for Year* i. xiii. 167 Many persons, from vicious, and dead, and cold, have passed into life and an excellent grace, and a spirituall warmth. 1781 Cowper *Table-T.* 382 Virtue quickens, with a warmth divine, The pow'rs that sin has brought to a decline. 1864 Tennyson *En. Arden* 38 But when the dawn of rosy childhood past, And the new warmth of life's ascending sun Was felt by either, [etc.].

2. The natural heat of a living body; vital heat.

1592 Shaks. *Rom. & Jul.* iv. i. 98 No pulse Shall keepe his natiue progresse.. : No warmth, no breath shall testifie thou liuest. 1606 —— *Ant. & Cl.* v. ii. 294 Come then, and take the last warmth of my Lippes. 1667 Milton *P.L.* vii. 236 But on the watrie calme His brooding wings the Spirit of God outspred, And vital vertue infus'd, and vital warmth Throughout the fluid Mass. 1711 Addison *Spect.* No. 120 ¶ 14 When she has laid her Eggs.. what Care does she take in turning them frequently, that all Parts may partake of the vital Warmth? 1820 Shelley *Prometh. Unb.* ii. i. 104 The warmth Of the life-blood, for loss of which I faint, Quivered between our intertwining arms.

†b. Of herbs: Aphrodisiac quality. *Obs.*

1697 Dryden *Virg. Georg.* iii. 199 When now the Nuptial time Approaches.. Feed him with Herbs, whatever thou canst find, Of generous Warmth.

3. A moderate degree of heat inherent or produced in a substance or liquid.

1748 Gray *Alliance* 3 A niggard Earth, Whose flinty Bosom starves her generous Birth, Nor genial Warmth, nor genial Juice retains. 1765 *Museum Rust.* IV. 122 The extreme coldness of the soil had overcome the warmth of the ashes. 1784 Cowper *Task* iii. 491 Ere the warmth, Slow gathering in the midst [of a hot-bed], through the square mass Diffus'd, attain the surface.

b. Pungency (of seasoning).

1816 Tuckey *Narr. Exped. R. Zaire* iv. (1818) 138 The stews were.. so highly peppered that our gentlemen, not accustomed to such warmth of seasoning, could scarcely swallow them.

4. An excited or fervent state of the feelings; strength or glow of feeling; fervent or vehement character (of an expression, welcome, salute, etc.); ardour, enthusiam; cordiality, heartiness.

1596 Shaks. *Merch. V.* i. ii. 36 But what warmth is there in your affection towards any of these Princely suters that are already come? 1647 Clarendon *Hist. Reb.* i. §44 His majesty sent for them, and with much warmth and passion dissuaded them from appearing further in it. 1677 Sir W. Temple *Ess. Gout* Wks. 1720 I. 134 The same warmth of Head disposes Men to both, though one be commonly esteemed an Honour, and the other a Reproach. 1702 Steele *Funeral* Pref., I know not in what words to thank my Fellow-Soldiers for their Warmth and Zeal in my behalf. 1709 Pope *Ess. Crit.* 678 An ardent Judge, who zealous in his trust, With warmth gives sentence, yet is always just. 1776 *Mirror* No. 6 The singular opinions which have influenced his conduct, I have often heard him attempt, with great warmth, to defend. 1833 Ht. Martineau *Manch. Strike* vii. 81 All with different degrees of warmth declared their readiness to sacrifice or to be sacrificed. 1835 Marryat *J. Faithful* xxxiii, Mr. Drummond.. shook me by the hand with a warmth which made me more ashamed of my conduct towards him. 1856 *N. Brit. Rev.* XXVI. 204 The warmth of his gratitude to Warburton,.. may be taken as the measure of his fears. 1875 Jowett *Plato* (ed. 2) I. 496 The warmth of your professions will be of no avail. 1893 F. Adams *New Egypt* 277 When the Conservatives came in,.. the matter was taken up with unexpected warmth. 1902 'Linesman' *Words of Eyewitness* Pref. 7 The warmth of welcome accorded to my book has surprised no less than it has gratified me.

b. A heated state of the temper approaching anger; the expression or exhibition of this; also, heated language or argument.

1710 Steele *Tatler* No. 150 ¶ 6 As an honest Man ought, (when he sees Two Friends in Warmth with each other) I took the first Opportunity I could to leave them by themselves. 1712 in Maclaurin *Argts. & Decis.* (1774) 53 An apology for the warmth of expression in his former paper, to which he had been.. provoked. 1817 Jas. Mill *Brit. India* II. iv. vii. 243 He expressed warmth, and even resentment, upon the hardness of these arbitrary conditions. 1837 DICKENS *Pickw.* iii, I am ashamed to have been betrayed into this warmth of feeling. 1879 *Cassell's Techn. Educ.* IV. 22/2 The strife was carried on with great warmth.

c. Excitement, exhilaration. *rare.*

1749 FIELDING *Tom Jones* XII. ii, Sportsmen, in the warmth of a chase, are too much engaged to attend to any manner of ceremony.

5. A glowing hue (of colouring in a picture, in nature); *spec.* in *Painting*, a glowing effect produced by the use of warm colours (see WARM *a.* 15).

1717 POPE *Ep. to Mr. Jervas* 38 We..Match Raphael's grace with thy lov'd Guido's air,..Paulo's free stroke, and Titian's warmth divine. 1803 IBBETSON *Accid. Painting* (1828) 9 Warmth, or a tint made of red and yellow,..is the next valuable thing. 1834 W. H. AINSWORTH *Rookwood* I. i, As to complexion, his skin had a truly Spanish warmth and intensity of colouring. 1855 MACAULAY *Hist. Eng.* xii. III. 135 When the sun shines out in all his glory, the landscape has a freshness and a warmth of colouring seldom found in our latitude. 1856 KANE *Arct. Expl.* II. iii. 47 For the past ten days we have been watching the growing warmth of our landscape.

6. *nonce-use.* The state of being prosperous or 'well-off'. (Cf. WARM *a.* 8.)

1888 J. PAYN *Prince of Blood* I. x. 163 What care I for his 'warmth' and reputation for integrity in the city?

7. *attrib.* and *Comb.*

c 1830 COLERIDGE *Marginalia* in *Blackw. Mag.* (1882) Jan. 116 Animal magnetism will be found connected with a warmth sense. 1909 tr. *Hopf's Human Species* 39 A warmth-loving fauna.

warmthless ('wɔːmθlɪs), *a. rare.* [f. WARMTH + -LESS.] Devoid of warmth.

a 1834 COLERIDGE *The Pang More Sharp* 3 Poems 1912 I. 457 He too..Has flitted from me, like the warmthless flame, That makes false promise of a place of rest. 1852 *Meanderings of Mem.* I. 100 Vain and virtueless and warmthless grown.

warm-up. [f. the vbl. phr. *to warm up*: see WARM *v.* 3, 9, and 11.] **1.** = WARM *sb.*[1]

1878 MRS. STOWE *Poganuc People* 156 A knot of the talkers were gathered round the stove, having a final talk and warm-up. 1960 H. PINTER *Room* in *Birthday Party* 112 Thank you for the warm-up, Mrs. Hudd. I feel better now. 1974 J. AIKEN *Midnight is Place* ix. 257 'Tis a poor lad half drownded—can tha..give him a bit of a roob-down an' a warm-oop?

2. Warmth, the quality of exciting or stimulating. *rare.*

1883 'MARK TWAIN' *Life on Mississippi* iii. 52 The song didn't seem to have much warm-up to it, somehow.

3. a. The act or process of 'warming up' for a contest, etc., by light exercise or practice. See sense 9 c of the vb.

1915 *Baseball Mag.* Dec. 116/2 Alex, after a short warm-up, vanished from the foreground. 1949 SHURR & YOCOM *Mod. Dance* iii. 31 The transition is used only when use of next warm-up is desired. 1951 *Publ. Amer. Dial. Soc.* XVI. 68 Some horses run better after a stiff warm up, others just tire. 1975 *New Yorker* 28 Apr. 32/1 Her second serve was good, was well returned by Jill, and then was driven by Sylvia to Jill's backhand in a way that left her frozen, as it had in the warmup. 1984 *Times* 22 Sept. 3/3 Warm-ups should be taken slowly, as sweating does not mean that muscles are sufficiently stretched for exercises.

b. *transf.* and *fig.*

1943 *Daily Progress* (Charlottesville, Va.) 18 Aug. 1/8 Allied guns boomed in a duel with heavy Axis batteries across the Messina Strait today in a warm-up against the European fortress. 1945 *Sun* (Baltimore) 11 July 9-0/6 Polynesian was running in the Shevlin as a 'warm-up' for Saturday's $50,000 Dwyer. 1958 *Times* 17 Oct. 20/1 It was a slow warm-up that Keenan could scarcely afford. 1976 D. HEFFRON *Crusty Crossed* xiv. 101 A party in the afternoon, a kind of warm-up to the night's dark devilry.

c. *attrib.*

1943 *Sun* (Baltimore) 22 May 1/7 The bombing of Nauru, Tarawa and other islands in the central Pacific, were warmup attacks. 1945 *Ibid.* 12 Mar. 7-0/2 One of Mexico's leading matadors..sharpens his skill with a 'warm-up' workout..an hour before a..performance. 1958 [see HOUSE *sb.*[1] 4 h]. 1968 C. DRUMMOND *Death & Leaping Ladies* v. 120 They arrived at Mexico City to play a warm-up match. 1978 L. PRYOR *Viper* (1979) viii. 152 The field of cars was allowed one warm-up lap.

4. The act or process of raising the temperature of an engine, electrical appliance, etc., to a level high enough for efficient working. Also *attrib.* See sense 9 d of the vb.

1945 *Sun* (Baltimore) 18 May 1/6 Massed after on the flight deck, engines roaring for the warmup,..were more planes. 1956 H. KURNITZ *Invasion of Privacy* ii. 17 There was an even, monotonous thud emanating from the machine now—the warm-up period. 1958 *Spectator* 1 Aug. 167/2 That infuriating warm-up time necessary for many TV sets. 1966 P. O'DONNELL *Sabre-Tooth* xx. 270 The Dove began to taxi forward... He wished there had been a few minutes grace for a warm-up before taking off. 1975 *Physics Bull.* Dec. 550/1 The detector has a warm-up time of 10 s. 1978 *Dumfries Courier* 13 Oct. 11/2 Another refinement the picture tube designers have incorporated is a really quick warm-up which..eliminates that infuriating delay when switching on late for an important programme. 1984 B. FRANCIS *AA Car Duffer's Guide* 63/1 Modern water-cooled systems incorporate a thermostat to give a quick warm-up.

5. a. The 'warming up' of an audience into a receptive mood, esp. before a broadcast programme is recorded or transmitted. See sense 2 b of the vb.

1958 *New Statesman* 15 Mar. 333/1 So that spontaneity shall not degenerate into chaos, the programme is preceded by a half-hour closed-circuit 'warm-up', in which those taking part get to know each others' names and voices. 1970 *Guardian* 14 Feb. 8/4 For this particular show there is an audience..and they arrive at 7.30 p.m. and are given a 'warm-up' to get them in the mood for the show. 1983 *Oxford Diocesan Mag.* Aug. 10/2 For pre-service warm-ups, say—a [tape or record of a] full orchestra playing Beethoven's Fifth for Harvest Festival, [etc.].

b. *attrib.*, esp. as ***warm-up man.***

1959 R. G. STERN in N. Mailer *Advts. for Myself* (1961) 319 There was no warm-up session except thirty seconds of irrelevant talk which we used for volume control. 1966 *Observer* 30 Oct. 23/4 The warm-up man (an assistant producer) jumps on to the platform. 1974 P. DE VRIES *Glory of Hummingbird* xii. 159 Falconer regaling..spectators..with some intendedly relaxing 'warmup' chatter. 1979 S. BRETT *Comedian Dies* xvi. 149 The audience..were greeted by..a little-known comedian who had been booked for the occasion as a warm-up man.

6. *U.S.* **a.** A garment designed to keep the wearer warm. **b.** One worn during light exercise or practice; a track suit or track-suit top.

1949 *Sun* (Baltimore) 22 Sept. 7/1 (Advt.), Make a friend of Jack Frost in smart warm-ups! 1969 *Sears Catal.* Spring/Summer 35/1 Sweatshirt warm-ups fit sizes 2 to 6x. 1983 W. SAFIRE in *N.Y. Times Mag.* 12 June 22/2 *Exercise classes* of the 1950's, where one wore *sweat suits*; these are now *workouts* with *warm-ups*.

c. *attrib.* and *Comb.* **warm-up suit**, a track suit. (Cf. also sense 3 c above.)

1945 *Richmond* (Va.) *Times-Dispatch* 9 Jan. 16 When winter comes..it's time for warm-up clothes. 1972 *N.Y. Times* 3 Nov. 44/5 (Advt.), Stretch pants, warm-up pants, skisuits. 1975 *New Yorker* 28 Apr. 31/1 She was wearing a pastel-blue warmup suit over her tennis dress. 1984 *New Yorker* 1 Oct. 30/1 Mr. Sims..wore a Nike cap, a crisp tan warmup suit.

warm water. Water heated to a degree considerably below boiling-point. Also *attrib.* (with hyphen).

c 1460 J. RUSSELL *Bk. Nurture* 902 in *Babees Bk.* 178 And watur warme his handes to wasche. 1577 B. GOOGE *Heresbach's Husb.* I. 34 b, Lyntels..groweth hye..when it is wette in warme water and Saltpeter before it be sowen. *a* 1756 ELIZA HAYWOOD *New Present* (1771) 267 Wet the linen with warm water. 1876 *Clin. Soc. Trans.* IX. 10 A vesicular rash,..which subsided with warm-water dressing. 1896 *Allbutt's Syst. Med.* I. 428 A warm-water pillow may be ordered.

b. The seas of warmer regions as opposed to the Arctic Ocean. Also *attrib.*

1883 WALLEM *Fish Supply Norway* 4 These warm-water basins in the Norwegian Ocean are of the greatest importance for the fauna and flora. 1898 *Westm. Gaz.* 7 Mar. 1/2 Our own Ministers have invited Russia to a warm-water port. *Ibid.* 26 Sept. 1/2 Russia..may fairly desire access to 'the warm water', as the phrase goes.

†**c.** *fig.* Cf. HOT WATER 3. *Obs.*

1813 *Examiner* 29 Mar. 207/2 He lives in eternal warm water.

warn (wɔːn), *sb.* [f. WARN *v.*[1] (The OE. *wearn* refusal, is a different word: see WARN *v.*[2]).]

†**1.** An intimation or notice of something as about to happen. *Obs.*

a 1300 *Cursor M.* 11133 He fand wit-vten oþer warn þat þis leuedi was wit barn. *c* 1400 *Cato's Morals* 264 in *Cursor M.* App. IV. 1672 Hope ay of gode hap to come wiþ a gode clap wiþ-out ani warne.

2. *poet.* Warning.

a 1851 MOIR *Poet. Wks.* II. 283 The moat o'erpassed, at warn of bell, Down thundering the portcullis fell.

†**3.** *Comb.* (perh. f. the stem of WARN *v.*[1]): **warn-word**, a word of warning.

1602 [PARSONS] *title*, The Warn-word to Sir Francis Hastinges Wast-word. 1624 BP. SANDERSON *Serm. ad Pop.* v. (1681) I. 241 The whole Chapter is none other but a warn-word against unthankfulness.

warn (wɔːn), *v.*[1] Pa. t. and pa. pple. **warned.** Forms: 1 **war(e)nian, wearnian, 2 warnian, -en, (wernin), 2–6 werne, 2–3 warnie, warni, 3 wearne, weorne, 3–4 warny(e, 4–5 waren, 4–7** *Sc.* **varn, 5 wern, waarne, waran, 6** *Sc.* **wairn, 3–7 warne, 6** *dial.* **warren, 3– warn.** [OE. *warenian, warnian, wearnian* = MLG. *warnen* to warn, inform, Flem. (Kilian) †*waernen* to warn, put on one's guard, OHG. *warnôn, warnên* to warn, refl. to provide oneself, to take precautions (MHG., mod.G. *warnen* to warn; the Sw. *varna*, Da. *varne* are prob. from German):—OTeut. **waranōjan* (-*ǣjan*), f. **war-* to be cautious: see WARE *a.*

In OE. and in Continental Teut. this verb seems to have been to some extent confused with OTeut. **warnōjan*, cogn. and synonymous with **warnjan* to refuse, forbid, etc. (see WARN *v.*[2]).]

†**I. 1.** *intr.* and *refl.* To take heed, be on one's guard, beware. Only OE.

c 1000 *Ags. Gosp.* Luke xi. 35 Warna þæt þæt leoht þe ðe on is ne syn þystru. *c* 1000 ÆLFRIC in *Lamb. Hom.* 301 Heo [*sc.* þet sidefulle wif] hi warnað [*c* 1175 (*ibid.* 111) wernað] wið druncennysse.

II. To make aware, to put on one's guard.

2. a. *trans.* To give timely notice to (a person) of impending danger or misfortune.

Const. *of, against* (OE. and early ME. *wið*) or subord. clause. *to warn off*: to keep away (from danger) by timely notice.

c 1000 ÆLFRIC *Hom.* II. 166 Ða sende Benedictus swiðe hrædlice and warnode ða ȝebroðra wið þæs deofles to-cyme. *a* 1023 WULFSTAN *Hom.* xii. (1883) 79 þæt hy godes folc warnian ȝelome wið þone eȝesan, þe mannum is towerd. *a* 1122 *O.E. Chron.* (Laud. MS.) an. 992 Ða sende se ealdorman Ælfric & het warnian þone here. *a* 1200 *Moral Ode* 226 in *O.E. Hom.* I. 173 Ich hit wille seggen þan þe hit hom solf nusten Warni hom wið hore unfrome ȝif ho me wulleð lusten. *Ibid.* 228 Ich wulle tellen of helle pin and wernin ow wið herme. *c* 1205 LAY. 7984 For Julius Cesar of his hærme wæs wær a-buten mid-nihte he warnede alle his cnihtes & to scipen ferden & fusden an veste. *c* 1250 *Gen. & Ex.* 1091 Loth hem [his sons-in-law] warnede, wislike and wel, Oc he ne troweden him neure a del. *a* 1300 *Cursor M.* 1731 Þe folk to preche for-gate he [Noe] noght, To warne þam of our lauerds wrake. *c* 1320 *Cast. Love* 390 Milce and merci he haþ for-loren, He was warned þer-of bi-foren. *c* 1385 CHAUCER *L.G.W.* 2658 For In myne dremys it is warnede me How that myn Neuew shal myn bane be. 1387 TREVISA *Higden* (Rolls) VIII. 193 For he hadde i-warnede hym of meny myshappes þat schulde falle hem for his cruelnes... Also he hadde i-warnede hym þat he schulde regne but fourtene ȝere. 1445 in *Anglia* XXVIII. 273 Thaventurous knyȝte by thyn reporte is warnyd of his perellys. *c* 1450 HOLLAND *Houlate* 975 All ȝour welth will away, Thus I warn ȝow. 1470–85 MALORY *Arthur* I. x. 47, I warne yow al, your enemyes are passyng strong for yow. 1526 TINDALE *Matt.* ii. 22 Notwithstondynge after he was warned in hys slepe, he tourned asyde into the parties off galile. 1599 ALEX. HUME *Hymns* v. 96 Poems (S.T.S.) 44 The godly Hezekiah king, was sick in great distres, And be the Prophete wairnd, that he sould neuer conuales. 1667 MILTON *P.L.* IV. 6 O..that now, While time was, our first Parents had bin warnd The coming of thir secret foe, and scap'd..his mortal snare. 1794 MRS. RADCLIFFE *Myst. Udolpho* vi, They say it often comes to warn people of their death. 1859 TENNYSON *Elaine* 274 He learnt and warn'd me of their fierce design Against my house. 1860 —— *Sea Dreams* 128 And then I fear'd Lest the gay navy there should splinter on it, And fearing waved my arm to warn them off.

Proverbs. *c* 1530 R. HILLES *Common-pl. Bk.* (1858) 140 He that ys warnyd beffore ys not begylyd. 1546 J. HEYWOOD *Prov.* (1867) 63 Halfe warnd halfe armde. 1591 HARINGTON *Orl. Fur.* XIII. xlvii, The Proverb saith, one that is warn'd is arm'd. 1700 DRYDEN *Fables, Cock & Fox* 799 Once warn'd is well bewar'd.

b. *absol.*

a 1000 *Sax. Leechd.* III. 196 Swefnu binnon þrim daȝum beoð onwriȝene hwilan to warnienne. *a* 1225 *Ancr. R.* 182 Sicnesse..wardeð [MS. C. weorneð] to ȝein þeo [sins] þet weren touwardes. 1398 TREVISA *Barth. De P.R.* XII. xxxiii. 124 b/2 (Bodl. MS.), [þe] sparowe dredeþ þe wesell and cryeþ and warneþ ȝif awesel come [L. *presentiam ejus prodit*].

3. To put (a person) on his guard, to caution *against* some person or thing as dangerous.

†Formerly const. *of, from.*

a 1225 *Ancr. R.* 54 Al þus þe holi Gost lette writen one boc uor to warnie wummen of hore fol eien. 1399 LANGL. *Rich. Redeles* IV. 77 [They] blamed þe maister, þat knewe not þe kynde cours þat to þe crafte longid, And warned him wisely of þe wedir-side. 1422 YONGE tr. *Secreta Secret.* 195 She was all venym; And yef I had not varnyte the therof at the furste tuching she had shent the. 1577 KENDALL *Flowers Epigr.* 62 Warnde of my foe, I shunne my foe. 1594 SHAKS. *Rich. III*, I. iii. 298 What dost thou scorne me For my gentle counsell? And sooth the diuell that I warne thee from. 1773 *Cook's 1st Voy.* I. iv. in Hawkesw. *Voy.* II. 48 Dr. Solander himself was the first who found the inclination, against which he had warned others, irresistible. 1809 *Med. Jrnl.* XXI. 404 This ..will for ever operate as a friendly beacon to warn.. anatomists and surgeons, against a hasty or superficial dissection of a dead body. 1860 TENNYSON *Sea Dreams* 69 Ah love, there surely lives in man and beast Something divine to warn them of their foes.

4. a. To give (a person) cautionary notice or advice with regard to actions or conduct; to caution against neglect of duty or against wrong or mistaken action or belief.

c 1000 ÆLFRIC *Saints' Lives* xvii. 72 Forðan butan ic eow warniȝe and þone wol eow forbeode ic sceal aȝyldan ȝescead þam soðfæstan deman. *c* 1175 *Lamb. Hom.* 117 Ʒif þu wernast þane unrihtwise mon and he nule icherran from his sunnan þurh þe. *c* 1200 *Vices & Virtues* 11 Ðar ic ðe scal undernemen mid ða ilche wordes ðe ðu ofte hafst ȝeherd for ðe te warnien. *a* 1225 *Ancr. R.* 270 Ine swuche manere tentaciuns nis non so wis ne so war, but ȝif God ham warnie, þet nis bigiled oðer hwules. 1387 TREVISA *Higden* (Rolls) V. 425 He was afterward i-warned by febilnesse of his body, and þo he was i-cristenede. *c* 1400 *Rule St. Benet* xlviii. 33 Þai sal be warnid ane tyme, and a-noþir time. Yef sho wil noht a-mende, Man sal take suilk amendis of hir. 1450–1530 *Myrr. our Ladye* I. xi. 31 Often tymes when other were moste besy in prayer, he wente out and wandryd aboute,.. whan his abbot had often warned hym, and he amendyd not. 1535 COVERDALE *Ps.* ii. 10 Be wyse now therfore (o ye kynges) be warned, ye that are iudges of the earth. 1581 *S'hampton Crt. Leet Rec.* (1905) I. II. 206 Wherof we have thought good to amerse them at 2/6, for that they have byne often tymes warrened and no redresse. 1697 DRYDEN *Virg. Georg.* III. 831 Sheep, Oxen, Horses fall; and..lye. 'Till warn'd by frequent Ills, the way they found, To lodge their loathsom Carrion under Ground. 1780 COWPER *Progr. Err.* 35 Divine authority within his breast..Warns him or prompts, approves him or restrains. 1852 THACKERAY *Esmond* I. ix, [He] marshalled the village boys,.. domineering over them with a fine imperious spirit, that made his father laugh when he beheld it, and his mother fondly warn him.

absol. *c* 1440 *Jacob's Well* 202 Ʒif þou seest thefte be do, ..& wylt noȝt telle, warne, ne speke, whan þou myȝt lette it. 1781 COWPER *Expost.* 441 The priestly brotherhood.. Prompt to persuade, expostulate, and warn. 1804 WORDSW. *'She was a Phantom'* 28 A perfect Woman, nobly planned, To warn, to comfort, and command.

b. Const. *against*; also with inf. or subordinate clause, or †double object.

c 1000 ÆLFRIC *Saints' Lives* xvii. 68 Ʒelome ic eow warnode and..cuðlice manode þat ȝe andsætan wiȝlunge þe unwise men healdað mid ealle forlætan. *c* 1290 *Beket* 1078 in *S. Eng. Leg.* 137 Þo it was to-war[d] eue twei seriaunz þare come, Sore weopinde, and warnede him þat he sum red him nome. 1390 GOWER *Conf.* I. 229, I speke it for no mannes blame, Bot forto warne thee the same. *Ibid.* II. 49 And warneth alle for mi sake, Of love that thei ben noght ydel. *a* **1425** tr. *Arderne's Treat. Fistula*, etc. 26 Bot warne þe lech þe pacient that he dispose hym so þat he remoue noȝt þe medycyne. *a* **1450** *Mirk's Festial* 199 And þagh hit [St. Margaret's Day] be a lyȝt holyday.. I warne you.. þat ȝe wol fast hor evyn. **1450–1530** *Myrr. our Ladye* I. xiii. 37 They warne the riche to knowe themself and not to be prowde. **1540** Palsgr. *Acolastus* I. iii. F iij, My father wyll neuer geue me this money, but he wyll first warne me.. that I shall not waste it prodigallye. **1594** Kyd *Cornelia* v. 95 Caesar.. euery Regiment warn'd with a worde Brauely to fight for honor of the day. **1667** Milton *P.L.* III. 185 The rest shall hear me call, and oft be warnd Thir sinful state, and to appease betimes Th' incensed Deitie while offerd grace Invites. **1687** A. Lovell tr. *Thevenot's Trav.* II. 39, I warn also those that come to Aleppo that they fail not to see the Birds of Grandouilles. **1702** Addison *Dial. Medals* i. Wks. 1721 I. 446, I must only warn you, that you do not charge your Coins with more uses than they can bear. **1718** Prior *Solomon* II. 936 The Father, whilst he warn'd his erring Son, The sad Examples which He ought to shun, Describ'd, and only nam'd not, Solomon. **1781** Cowper *Hope* 355 The screaming nations.. seem to warn him never to repeat His bold intrusion on their dark retreat. **1846** Mrs. A. Marsh *Father Darcy* II. xvii. 295 His page delivered a letter.. It warned him not to attend in his place in parliament. **1852** W. Collins *Basil* III. i. 6 You.. may be tempted to tear up my letter, and throw it from you unread. I warn you not to do so; I warn you to read what I have written. *Ibid.* III. i. 74 Be warned, therefore, against seeking a false hope in the belief that my faculties are shaken. **1856** Froude *Hist. Eng.* (1858) I. iii. 266 The ambassador warned him on peril of his life to deal no further with such things. **1868** Morris *Earthly Par.* (1870) I. I. 33 Yet, fellows, must I warn you not to shout Ere we have left the troublous wood behind.

†*absol.* *c* **1440** *Alphabet of Tales* 22 And he warnyd þat on no wyse no man sulde know þat it wer a womman. **1526** Tindale *Gal.* ii. 10 Then Iames, Cephas and Iohn.. agreed with vs, that we shulde preache amonge the Hethen, and they amonge the Iewes: warnynge only that we shulde remember the poore.

†**c.** Const. *of*. *Obs.*

1303 R. Brunne *Handl. Synne* 6905 And y warne ȝow alle of o þyng, Forþenkeþ nat of ȝoure almess-ȝyuyng. **1362** Langl. *P. Pl.* A. v. 214 His wyf warnede him þo of wikkednesse and of sinne. *c* **1400** *Apol. Loll.* 72 Þe kirk makiþ lawis; and schuld wern men þer of, þat þei offendid not þer in. *a* **1529** Skelton *Bowge of Courte* 106 But of one thynge I werne you er I goo, She that styreth the shyp, make her your frende. **1541** Elyot *Image Gov.* xvi. 29 b, Than sadlye and with a wonderfull grauitie, he wolde admonest or warn him of his lacke in diligence.

†**d.** Const. *from*.

1765 *Museum Rust.* IV. 264 When I began farming, I was warned from expecting profit, by two different sets of people.

5. To inform, notify. Now only in restricted use, to notify of something requiring attention.

a. To inform or notify of something actual.

c **1205** Lay. 30639 And al þat he auunde in þan lufte & bi þan grunde þurh ælches cunnes þing he warnede æure Ædwine king. **1340–70** *Alex. & Dind.* 205 But litil leue we þat lud, i þe warne. **1362** Langl. *P. Pl.* A. v. 30 He warnede watte his wyf was to blame, þat hire hed was worþ a Mark. *c* **1375** *Sc. Leg. Saints* ii. (*Paul*) 729 For is na payne, we wele þe [*sc.* Nero] warne, In life sa gret as to ber barne. *c* **1384** Chaucer *H. Fame* 893 Now see.. yonde adovne Wher that thou knowest any tovne.. And whan thou hast of ought knowynge Looke that thou warne me And y anoon shall telle the How fer that thou art now therfro. **1389** in *Eng. Gilds* 5 ȝif eny of þe brethren.. be chosen wardein in þe bretherhede,.. he shal take þe charge al-sone as he is warned þerof. *c* **1400** Maundev. (Roxb.) xxviii. 128 Þe emperour þat was warned of þaire fleyng lay before þam with his oste. *c* **1480** Henryson *Test. Cress.* 359 Ane Chyld come fra the hall, To warne Cresseid the Supper was reddy. **1530** Palsgr. 772/1, I warne one of a mater in processe, *je intime*. .. No man hath warned me yet. **1836** Dickens *Sk. Boz, Visit to Newgate*, The deathlike stillness of the street without.. warns him that the night is waning fast away. **1871** Freeman *Norm. Conq.* (1876) IV. xviii. 114 Count Eustace (of Boulogne) was warned that the wished for moment was come. **1880** Mrs. Parr *Adam & Eve* II. 25 The clock warned them it was time to get ready. **1886** C. Scholl *Phraseol. Dict.* II. 832 The broker did not warn us of the arrival of the vessel.

†*absol.* **1398** Trevisa *Barth. De P.R.* xvi. viii. (1495) 557 The adamas [the stone adamant] warnyth of venim [L. *dicitur.. venena deprehendere*] as Electrum dooth. **1590** Spenser *F.Q.* I. ii. 1 And chearefull Chaunticlere with his note shrill Had warned once, that Phœbus fiery carre In hast was climbing vp the Easterne hill.

†**b.** To tell (a person) when it is time *to do* something. *Obs.*

c **1325** *Chron. Eng.* 507 When the on condle wes ydo, The aht tiden weren alsuo; The kyng he warnede by thon, Hys purpos ariht to don. **1539–40** in *Devon N. & Q.* (1903) Oct. 238 Payed to a man for his labor to warne the lymers to bryng more lyme when ther lyme was almost don. **1697** Dryden *Virg. Past.* vi. 121 Now the setting Sun had warn'd the Swain To call his counted Cattle from the Plain.

†**c.** *to warn custos*: in school language, to inform the 'custos' or monitor of a misdemeanour: in quot. *indirect passive*. *Obs.*

1558 R. Ramsey *Serm. Child Bishop* (Camden) 28 Yf a scoler in the gramer scole speak false Lattyn or Englysh forbyddyn, he is takyn withall of one or the other and warnyd custos to be beatyn. *Ibid.*, Let them be first warnyd custos, or wrong by the ears for it, and after be correctyd as the custos is usyd.

d. To give previous notice to. More definitely †*to warn before* (obs.). Const. with *of*, subord. clause, or infinitive.

c **1275** Lay. 22059 Leteþ blowe bumes warnie cnihtes .. þat ich faren wolle. **1297** R. Glouc. (Rolls) 1056 We ssolle hom warni of oure þoȝt ar we þanne wende. *a* **1300** *Cursor M.* 10933 Speke we nu of zachari, hu þe angel com him to warn, he suld haue Ion, þat seli barn. *c* **1330** *Otuel* 1691 Otuwel.. warende fore a non þo Rouland & oliuer bo. *c* **1384** Chaucer *H. Fame* 1559, I werne yow hit, quod she anon, Ye gete of me good fame non. **1387** Trevisa *Higden* (Rolls) IV. 385 Oon of his prisoneres þat was konnynge in devyne warned hym þat he schulde sone be delyvered out of prisoun. **1393** Langl. *P. Pl.* C. xviii. 97 Astronomyens al day in here art faillen, That whilom warned men by-fore what shoulde by-falle after. *c* **1440** *York Myst.* xxii. 84 Þi biddyng will I noȝt full-fill, þat warne I þe. **1483** *Acta Audit.* in *Acta Dom. Conc.* II. Introd. 114 The day that he was warnit to ressave the some conteint in his said reversione. **1534** *Abstr. Protocols Town Clerks of Glasgow* (1897) IV. 67 Allane C... hes warnyt Janet Boyd, at hyr awn dwelling place within Glasgow, to rasaef ane hundretht merk.. upon Wytsunday evyn. **1551** *Rental Bk. Cupar-Angus* (1880) II. 71 Our said place at all tymes salbe.. reddy to ws.. als oft as it salhappyn ws.. to cum thairto.. we warnand thame thairto xxiiij houris warnyng of befor. **1848** Thackeray *Van. Fair* xli, The mourning being ready, and Sir Pitt Crawley warned of their arrival, Colonel Crawley and his wife took a couple of places in the.. Highflyer coach. **1866** G. Macdonald *Ann. Q. Neighb.* xxxi. (1878) 533 But I warn you I will call again very soon.

e. *absol.* or *intr.* Of a clock: To make the clicking or whirring noise which indicates that it is about to strike; to 'give warning'. [So G. *warnen.*] *dial.*

1846 M. A. Richardson *Local Historian's Table-bk., Leg. Div.* I. 116 And just as the clock warned for twal' the hin'most game was concludet. **1885** W. Towers *Poems* 189 (E.D.D.) Hark! the clock is warning ten. **1894** Hall Caine *Manxman* III. xviii, Every time the clock warned to strike, she felt one hour nearer her doom.

6. a. To notify of something commanded; to order under penalties.

c **1380** *Sir Ferumb.* 1808 We buþ y-sent to þe, Balan.. to warnye þe by-forn, þe nayles þow scholdest him ȝelde aȝeyn .. & elles þow gest a torn. **1387** Trevisa *Higden* (Rolls) V. 153 He was i-warned by an aungel þat he schulde translate Clement his body. *c* **1400** *Destr. Troy* 1092 Pelleus full prestly the peopull did warne To appere in his presens. *c* **1420** *Chron. Vilod.* 2208 For by a uysione seynt Dunstone was y-warnot of þat cas þat Alphege.. Of Wynchester shulde bysshoppe y-sacrid be. *c* **1450** *Mankind* 516 in *Macro Plays* 20 Com a-gayn, I werne, as sone as I yow call. **1456** Sir G. Haye *Law Arms* (S.T.S.) 53 [He] gert warne all his obeysaunce of Lombardye to mak thame redy to bataill. **1483** *Acta Audit.* in *Acta Dom. Conc.* II. Introd. 115 That he .. profferit the said some.. to the said William the said day that he was warnit to. **1814** Scott *Lord of Isles* vi. v, His royal summons warn'd the land, That all who own'd their King's command Should instant take the spear and brand, To combat at his side.

†**b.** *to warn in*: to order to come in. *Obs.*

1654 Whitelocke *Swed. Ambassy* (1772) I. 176 So many waggons were warned in.. because of the smallenesse of them, and the great quantity of baggage and provision.

c. To notify (a person) to go *from*, *out of* (a place), *away*, *thence*.

1592 *Arden of Feversham* I. 353 To warne him on the sudden from my house Were too confirme the rumour that is growne. **1697** Dryden *Æneis* Ded. (d) 2 He had already chidden the Rebellious Winds..: He had warn'd them from the Seas. *Ibid.* iv. 546 Now Hermes is employed from Jove's abode, To warn him hence. **1847** Tennyson *Princess* v. 328 He batter'd at the doors; none came: the next, An awful voice within had warn'd him thence. **1853** Dickens *Bleak Ho.* lvii, So having warned him out of London, I [Inspector Bucket] made an afternoon of it to warn him to keep out of it now he *was* away. **1868** Louisa M. Alcott *Little Women* vi, She never saw Laurie mount guard in the hall to warn the servants away.

d. *to warn off*: to notify (a person) to keep at a distance. Also *fig.*

1842 Tennyson *Love & Duty* 46 For Love himself took part against himself To warn us off. **1853** Dickens *Bleak Ho.* xxviii, 'Pray, Mr. Rouncewell,' says my Lady, warning Sir Leicester off with the slightest gesture of her pretty hand, as if he were a fly, 'explain to me what you mean.' **1858** Eliz. Sewell *Ursula* I. x. 108 He warned her off admirably, not letting her know anything he chose to keep to himself.

e. To give notice to (a person) to keep *off* (private ground). Also with *off* adv. Also *fig.*

1815 Scott *Guy M.* iii, There's Dunbog has warned the Red Rotten and John Young aff his grunds. **1848** *Athenæum* 10 June 579/3 Can the fact of Mr. Prior's having written a biography of Goldsmith give him the right to warn all others off the ground? **1863** Mrs. Gaskell *Dark Night's Work* x. 176 Miss Monro stole out after the doctor to warn him off the subject for the future. **1872** Yeats *Growth Comm.* 303 All merchants being warned off from Indian commerce as poachers from a preserve. **1892** *Photogr. Ann.* II. 249 'Go for' a building, and not hang around like a tramp to be.. warned off by timid caretakers.

f. Racing. *to warn off the course*: To prohibit (a defaulter against the laws of the Jockey Club) from riding or running horses at meetings under its jurisdiction. Also with *off* adv.

The expression was finally deleted from the Jockey Club's Rules of Racing in 1969 when the Jockey Club and National Hunt Committee amalgamated, and the course and training grounds at Newmarket were transferred to the Newmarket Estates and Property Co. Ltd.

1845 *Racing Calendar 1844* p. lii, Samuel Rogers and John Braham were warned off the Course and exercising ground at Newmarket. **1856** 'Stonehenge' *Brit. Sports* II. I. xiv. §4. 375 [The Stewards of the Jockey Club] have full power to warn off recusants [at Newmarket.].. Other races are held under the same conditions as the Newmarket, but, being on public land, there is not often the power to warn off improper characters, as at Newmarket, Goodwood, and some few others. **1861** *Sporting Rev.* June 474 Mr. Bryan having admitted that he gave orders to his jockey to lose the race, it was resolved, 'That Mr. Bryan be warned off the course at Newmarket, and other places where the Jockey Club have jurisdiction, for the year 1861.' **1900** Quiller-Couch *Old Fires* iii. 55 If I'd been warned off Newmarket Heath.. shouldn't I feel just as you are feeling.

†**g.** *absol.* To notify a requirement, give an order *for*. *Obs.*

1530 in W. H. Turner *Select. Rec. Oxford* (1880) 80 He had.. brewed.. xxx[ti] quarters malt which they had warnyd for, and so they wold not receyve theyr ale at the tyme it was sent to them.

7. a. To summon (a person *to* a duty, place, etc.). In later use chiefly, To summon officially; to command the attendance of. Now only *Mil.*

a **1250** *Owl & Night.* 330 Hwenne ich iseo arise veorre oþer day rewe oþer day steorre Ich do god mid mine þrote & warni men to hore note. *c* **1430** *Chev. Assigne* 190 Lette sommene þy folke... And she wendeth here adown & lette hem a-none warne. **1530** Palsgr. 771/2, I warne a man to apere at a courte in judgement, *je somme*. **1550** Crowley *Epigr.* 253 When he should warne a guest in sessions to appeare. **1574** in *Maitl. Club Misc.* I. 99 M. Symsone being wernit to ansuer the kirk *super inquirendis*. **1594** Shaks. *Rich. III*, I. iii. 39, I Madam he desires to make attonement Betweene the Duke of Glouster, and your Brothers,.. And sent to warne them to his Royall presence. **1595** —— *John* II. i. 201 Who is it that hath warn'd vs to the walles? **1598** B. Jonson *Ev. Man in Hum.* v. i. 319 Sirha goe warne them hether presently before me. **1608** Bp. Hall *Char. Vertues & Vices* II. 122 When he is warned on a Iurie, hee had rather pay the mulct, than appeare. **1610** T. Lorkin in Ellis *Orig. Lett.* Ser. II. III. 221 Which entertains him till twelve of the clock, when the bell warns him to dinner. **1663** (27 Aug.) in *Orders of Council Naval Service* (1866) I. 165 And other officers belonging to His Majestye's yards and Navy, are many times warned to attend His Majestye's service at Assizes and Sessions, [etc.]. **1676** *Office Clerk of Assise* (a viij), The names of such as the Bailiffs shall warn for the great Inquest. **1802** C. James *Milit. Dict.*, *Warned*, admonished of some duty to be performed at a given time or place. Thus officers and soldiers are warned for guard, &c. **1809** Kendall *Trav.* I. v. 29 The constables are required to summon or as it is said to warn all the freemen to meet together yearly. **1860** Whyte Melville *Holmby House* II. xix. 288 [He] commanded that the guard.. should be relieved every four hours, and that the same men should not be warned twice for this duty until after the execution.

absol. *a* **1562** G. Cavendish *Wolsey* (1893) 103 My lord's officers caused the truppetts [*sic*] to blowe to warne to supper. **1814** Scott *Lord of Isles* iv. xxix, Brother, for little space, farewell! To other duties warns the bell.

†**b.** To call, give notice of (a meeting). *Obs.*

1465 Marg. Paston in *P. Lett.* II. 239 On Saterday last was, Jenney ded warne a corte at Calcotte to be holde ther in hys name. **1617** *Eastland Co.* (Camden) 12 If any Courte be warned and for wante of Assistants the same bee not full. **1792** N. Chipman *Rep.* (1871) 10 The Clerk has not inserted (in the record) that the proprietor's meeting was regularly warned.

†**8.** To give (a person) notice to leave his employment or tenancy. Also to ***warn out***. *Obs.* (but see warning *vbl. sb.* 6).

14.. in *Babees Bk.* (1868) 329 And they that wylle not here that ȝe say, effectually be they ywarnyd, and ye shalle prouide other seruantis. **1702** Luttrell *Brief Rel.* V. 208 The duke of Somerset.. has (by her majesties order) turned out 40 grooms of the stables, and warned out others who had lodgings and stables at the Meuse. **1706** Phillips (ed. Kersey), To *Warn*,.. to bid one provide for himself elsewhere. **1713** W. Hawkins *Life Bp. Ken* 8 The Prince.. threatned to turn him from the Service [*sc.* chaplaincy to P'cess of Orange]; which the Doctor resenting.. warn'd himself from the Service, and would not return to the Court. **1850** *Bentley's Misc.* XXVIII. 284 We're teetotally ruined. .. Warned out by the landlady... Where are we to move into, and obtain a lodging!

Hence **warned** *ppl. a.*

1639 J. Clarke *Parœm.* 21 Warn'd folkes may live.

†**warn**, *v.*[2] *Obs.* Forms: α. 1 **wiernan, wirnan, wyrnan, wærnan,** 3 **wearne,** 3–4 **wurne,** 3–5 **wern,** (3 **worne,** 5 **wernne**), **weerne,** 2–6 **werne;** β. 1 **wearnian, war(e)nian,** 3–5 **warn,** 3–4 *Sc.* **varn,** 4–6 **warne.** [Two formations: (1) OE. *wiernan* = OFris. *werna*, ON. *verna* (Da. *værne*):—OTeut. **warnjan*; (2) OE. *wearnian* (also *warnian*, *warenian*, by confusion with warn *v.*[1]) = OFris. *warna*, OS. (Hildebr.) *warnen*, ON. *varna* (Sw. *varna*):—OTeut. **warnōjan*. The two OTeut. types are f. **warnō* fem. (OE. *wearn*) obstacle, refusal, etc., f. the root **wer-*: **war-* to obstruct, defend.

It is possible that the ME. and later form *warn(e* may descend partly from the OE. *wearnian*; influence from ON. *varna* is also possible. But the form would be normal as a dial. variant of *werne*:—OE. *wiernan*; on the other hand the ME. *werne* may partly represent OE. *wearnian*. The α and β types therefore probably do not accurately correspond to the two original formations.]

1. *trans.* To refuse or deny (a thing *to* a person); to refuse to grant (a boon, request, etc.).

In OE. and early ME. const. *dat.* of person and *genit.* of thing; later, the genitive is sometimes represented by the construction with *of*, but more freq. by the accusative.

a. *c* **897** Ælfred *Gregory's Past. C.* xlix. 380 Se þe ne wiernð [*MS. Hatton* wirnð] ðæs wines his larc ða mod mid to oferdrencanne þe hiene ʒehieran willað. *a* **1000** *Riddles* xxi. 11 (Gr.) Cyning mec ʒyrweð since & seolfre & mec on sele weorþað: ne wyrneð word-lofes. *a* **1122** *O.E. Chron.* (Laud. MS.) an. 1048 Þa wyrnde him mann ðera ʒisla. *c* **1205** Lay. 30310 For ne scal he nauere.. kine-helme broken and ȝif he hit wule auon ich hit wulle wernen. *c* **1250** *Song to Virg.* 39 in *O.E. Misc.* 195 He wyl nout werne þe þi bone. **1340** *Ayenb.* 189 Vor þet he him wernde his elmesse, god him wernde ane drope of weter þer he wes ine uere of helle. *c* **1384** Chaucer *H. Fame* 1539 They.. seyde, Graunte vs.. of thy grace a bone. And somme of hem she graunted sone And somme she werned wel and faire, and some she graunted the contraire Of her axyng. **1387** Trevisa *Higden*

(Rolls) I. 275 þe Romaynes asked her tribute: and Sicambri werned it and wolde none paye. **1387–8** T. Usk *Test. Love* I. iv. 47 Yet al thing desyreth ye werne no man of helpe. *c* **1412** Hoccleve *De Reg. Princ.* 1847 But his hert is ful applied To graunte, and nat þe needy werne his grace. **1414** *Rolls of Parlt.* IV. 22/2 To graunte whiche of thoo that you luste, & to wernne the remanent. *c* **1430** *Devils' Parl.* 406 Quod helle 'not wiþ þy [Satan's] poowere I myȝte not werne him [Christ] oon of tho; He took out alle þat were him dere'. *c* **1475** *Partenay* Prol. 126 Hys commaundment wern shal I no-thing. *Ibid.* 86 Take here vnto you which you best do plese, No man shall ther-of you werne ne withsay.

β. *a* **1000** *Guthlac* 1183 [1156] in *Exeter Bk.* 176 Ic me warnade hyre onsyne ealle þraȝe in woruld-life. *c* **1205** Lay. 4719 & Belin him war[n]de [*c* **1275** wornede] al þat he ȝernde. *a* **1300** *Cursor M.* 4939, I receiud þam and warnd ham noght Of alle thing þai me be-soght. *Ibid.* 28889 Be man neuer sua wik of mode men agh noght warn him his liues fode. **1375** Barbour *Bruce* XVIII. 332 And tald thame quhat kyn velcummyng Dowglass thaim maid.. And varnyt thame the playn herbery. **1387** Trevisa *Higden* (Rolls) III. 101 Nabugodonosor byseged Ierusalem for tribute þat was i-warned hym. *a* **1400–50** *Wars Alex.* 1467–8 'For me had leuer', quod þe lede, 'be lethirely forsworn.. þan anys haue greuyd þat gome, or warned him his erand! þat euer I warned him his will, wa is me þat stonde!' *c* **1450** Capgrave *Life St. Aug.* xxxvii. 47 Swech mete and drynk as he had in vse was not warned to no man þat wold ask it. **1456** Sir G. Haye *Law Arms* (S.T.S.) 148 Ȝe suld nocht warne me leve. **1470–85** Malory *Arthur* XVI. xi. 679 And yf thou warne her loue she shalle goo dye anone yf thou haue no pyte on her, that sygnefyeth the grete byrd, the whiche shalle make the to warne her.

b. Of a thing: To prevent (a person) from having (something).

a **1240** *Ureisun* in *O.E. Hom.* I. 187 Mine sunnen beoþ wal bi-tweone me and þe. Mine sunnen werneþ me al þis swotnesse. ? *a* **1400** *Morte Arth.* 700, I may wery the wye, thatt this werre mouede, That warnes me wyrchippe of my wedde lorde.

c. With dat. of person only: To refuse the request of; to deny something to.

α. *c* **1000** *Ags. Gosp.* Matt. v. 42 þam þe wylle æt þe borȝian, ne wyrn þu hym. *c* **1175** *Lamb. Hom.* 137 Mon sulðe his elmesse þenne he heo ȝefeð swulche monne ðe he for scome wernen ne mei. *a* **1225** *Ancr. R.* 330 [She] halseð ure Louerd so & he ne mei uor reouðe wernen hire. *a* **1272** *A Luue Ron* 7 in *O.E. Misc.* 93 A Mayde cristes me bit yorne þat ich hire wurche a luue ron... Ich hire nule nowiht werne. *a* **1300** *K. Horn* (Hall) 1404 Fikenhild gan wende Rymenhild to schende. To woȝe he gan hure ȝerne, þe kyng ne dorste him werne. **1377** Langl. *P. Pl.* B. xx. 12 For thre thynges he taketh his lyf forto saue, That is, mete, whan men hym werneth and he no moneye weldeth, [etc.]. *c* **1400** Love *Bonavent. Mirr.* vi. (Sherard MS.), Whan she.. asked herbergh in diuerse places.. alle they werned [*Gibbs MS.* weerne, *W. de W.* refused] hem and lete hem go. *c* **1420** *Sir Amadace* (Camd.) xiii, Quil he hade any gud to take, He wernut no mon. *a* **1450** *Knt. de la Tour* 31 Her husbonde must nedis ordeine her that she desirithe,.. for thei wol finde so mani resones that thei wille not be werned. *c* **1475** *Partenay* 82 Of thes thre on [*i.e.* one] your plesire do and take,.. Reson is ne right that you werne shold y.

β. *c* **1400** *Rom. Rose* 2604 And who-so askith folily, He moot be warned hastily. *c* **1420** Wyntoun *Cron.* II. iii. 201 Iacob warnyt hym vttraly.

d. To refuse (*to* do something).

α. *a* **1225** *Ancr. R.* 248 þeo ancre þet wernde an oðer a cwaer uorto lenen. *a* **1300** *Cursor M.* 12106 If þou him wenis for to lern, To lere him wel we þe noght wern. *c* **1320** *Sir Tristr.* 1367 Ȝe sigge ich wern mi nem to wiue, For y schuld be ȝour king.

β. *c* **900** *Bæda's Hist.* v. xx. [xxii.] (1890) 474 Ond he blissade in þon, þæt.. he ȝeseah þa his ȝeherend þone Eastordæȝ onfon,.. þone hie simle ær þon warenedon to anfonne [L. *quem semper antea vitabant*]. *a* **1300** *Cursor M.* 3040 Hir bidding do sal þou not warn. *Ibid.* 3261 For quas luue he wild not warn To sacrifise his auen barn. **1398** Trevisa *Barth. De P.R.* XII. Introd. (Tollemache MS.), þat man may be a schamid.. to warne to serue fader and moder, while he knoweþ þat briddes and foules serueþ.. euerichone oþer.

e. *absol.* To make refusal.

α. **1297** R. Glouc. (Rolls) 7553 Of þe heyemen of þe lond.. He esste ostage strong inou & hii ne ssolde noȝt wurne, Ac toke him ostage god. **1390** Gower *Conf.* I. 130 The wylde loves rage.. Hath mad him that he can noght werne, Bot fell al hol to hire assent. **1406** Hoccleve *La Male Regle* 430 For estaat real can nat al day werne.

β. **1456** Sir G. Haye *Law Arms* (S.T.S.) 30 Thai ar.. nocht large of gift, and redily wil tak and wele can warne.

2. To refuse to allow (some action or course of action) *to* a person; to forbid (a person) *to* do something.

α. *c* **893** Ælfred *Oros.* I. vii. §1 Hi ær Moyse & hys folce þæs utfæreldes wyrndon. *c* **1000** *Sax. Leechd.* II. 330 Ƌeorne is to wyrnanne bearneacnum wife þæt hio aht sealtes ete oððe swetes. *c* **1250** *Gen. & Ex.* 2966 Eft he comen to pharaon, And he wernede ðis folc ut-gon. **1303** R. Brunne *Handl. Synne* 1021 Holy chyrche wyl þe werne þe halyday to go to þe tauerne,.. whan goddys seruyse owyþ to be doun. *c* **1386** Chaucer *Wife's Prol.* 333 He is to greet a nygard that wolde werne A man to lighte his candle at his lanterne. **1390** Gower *Conf.* I. 162 Thogh it be noght the houndes kinde To ete chaf, yit wol he werne An Oxe which comth to the berne Therof to taken eny fode. *c* **1449** Pecock *Repr.* II. ii. 146 And therfore thilk processe hath no strengthe forto weerne ymagis of God to be had and vsid in the chirche.

β. **1340** Hampole *Pr. Consc.* 7985 And na thing salle þam warn ne lett, To do þair wille whare-swa it es sett. *c* **1400** *Ywaine & Gaw.* 2261 For nane other enchesowne, Bot for i warned hym to wyve My doghter. **1550** Crowley *Informacion* 142 Whoe shall warne me to do wyth myne owne as me selfe lysteth. **1550** *S'hampton Crt. Leet Rec.* (1905) I. I. 12 And that theye warne none to have Ale for theire money so theye have yt in theire houses. **1591–5** C'tess Pembroke *Lay of Clorinda* 12 in *Spenser's Astrophel*, From them [the heavens] comes good, from them comes also il, That which they made, who can them warne to spill.

b. Of a thing: To forbid, not to allow of (some action or procedure). Also *absol.*

α. *c* **1000** *Sax. Leechd.* II. 255 Ƌif hæto oþþe meht ne wyrne læt him blod. *c* **1440** *Pallad. on Husb.* IX. 19 Yf so benygne And loughly be the vyne hit not to werne.

3. To refuse, forbid, deny (entry, the gate, door, way, one's house). Constr. *dat.* of person or *from*.

α. ? *a* **1366** Chaucer *Rom. Rose* 442 From hir the gate ay [? *read* shal] werned be Of paradys. *c* **1400** *Rom. Rose* 5840 But whan he prayde hir, pore was he, Therfore she warned him the entree. **14..** *St. Alexius* 18 (Cott. MS.) Of all pormen of ylk a gate, there was none þat werned þ[e] yate. *c* **1420** *Avow. Arth.* ix, Quo-so wernes me the waye, Hym to dethe diȝte!

β. **1399** Langl. *Rich. Redeles* III. 233 þe portir with his pikis þo put him vttere, And warned him þe wickett while þe wacche durid. *c* **1400** *Destr. Troy* 5251 All þat warnyt hym þe way he warpet to ground. *c* **1400** *Rom. Rose* 7502 The hous, quod he, such as ye see, Shal nat be warned you for me. *c* **1440** Capgrave *St. Kath.* I. 737 þere was no ȝate warnyd to no-maner wyte, But.. þei were kept opyn both day & nyth. **1456** Sir G. Haye *Law Arms* (S.T.S.) 61 Quhen Julius Cesar was cummyn to Rome, thai durst nocht warne him the portis. *a* **1513** Fabyan *Chron.* VII. ccxxviii. (1811) 257 The Kynge.. warned hym ye entre of his lande. **1611** Middleton & Dekker *Roaring Girl* D 2, *Mist. Open.* Get you from my shop. *Mol.* I come to buy. *Mist. Open.* Ile sell ye nothing, I warne yee my house and shop.

b. To forbid, exclude (a person *from* a place or position, Death *from* a person). Cf. warn *v.*[1] 6 c.

α. ? *a* **1366** Chaucer *Rom. Rose* 636 Fro thilke assemblee, if I may, Shal no man werne me to-day. **1536** *Primer Salisb., Eng. & Lat.* 145 Of sapiens thou art eterne Frome the and thy father who can the werne.

β. **1590** Spenser *F.Q.* II. i. 36 But if that carelesse heauens (quoth she) despise The doome of iust reuenge,.. Yet can they not warne death from wretched wight.

c. To stop the way of.

α. *a* **1225** *Ancr. R.* 60 (MS. T.) Hund wile in at open dure, þer man him ne wernes. *c* **1300** *K. Horn* 725 (Laud MS.) To boure he gan ȝerne Durst hym noman werne.

β. **1375** Barbour *Bruce* II. 137 The Dowglas then his way has tane Rycht to the hors, as he him bad: Bot he, that him in ȝhemsell had, Than warnyt hym dispitously.

4. To prevent, hinder, restrain (a person or thing) from action. Const. with *clause* or *inf.*

α. *c* **888** Ælfred *Boeth.* xli. §4 He.. us ne wernð [*v.r.* wyrnþ] þæt we yfel don. *a* **1225** *Ancr. R.* 408 Ȝif eni luuede þe ariht, he muhte holden þe, & wearnen þe to smiten. *c* **1330** R. Brunne *Chron. Wace* (Rolls) 7063 What he wold do, non durste hym werne. **1382** Wyclif *Gen.* xxiii. 6 In our chosun berielis birye thi deed, and no man shal mow wern [1388 forbede, Vulg. *prohibere*] thee. *a* **1400** *St. Alexius* 516 (Laud MS. 463) So sone so she to him come, vpon þe liche she fel y-lome... On þe liche she lay, & nolde not wond, Mighte noman hire werne. *c* **1502** *Joseph Arim.* 164 To delyuer goddes seruauntes he sayd he wolde; I knowe no maner man that shall me werne.

β. *a* **1300** *Cursor M.* 2726 'And quat thing es,' he said, 'may warn þat godd ne may his will of do?' *Ibid.* 13733 'Vs thinc to lang we duell,' said þai, 'Qua warns yow to wend a-wai?' *c* **1380** Wyclif *Wks.* (1880) 50 Ȝif þei ben his riȝtfully oure kyng may not warne ne lette his hoste to reste in þo places. *c* **1400** *Sege Melayne* 500 Thay stirtt vp on those stedis full steryn, þay fande no man þat þam wolde warne. *c* **1520** Skelton *Magnyf.* 1833 My hawke.. Flewe.. in to an olde barne, To reche at a rat, I coude not her warne.

b. Phrases, ***to warn*** (a person) ***his will*** or ***of his will***; ***to warn*** (a person's) ***thoughts***.

α. **1340–70** *Alisaunder* 905 But all his werk was in waste, þei werned his thoughtes. *c* **1400** *Destr. Troy* 7288 He was tarriet with the Troiens.. And wernit of his wille, þof hym wo thoght.

β. [*a* **1400–50**: cf. 1 *β*.] *c* **1400** *Destr. Troy* 6465 Thay pre-set so the prince with power of knightes, þat þai warnit hym his wille, & away put. *a* **1450** *Le Morte Arth.* 3011 Trowiste thow to warne me of my wille?

c. To resist.

α. *c* **1175** *Lamb. Hom.* 85 In þe deie of liureisun.. he wile ison hwiche boð þo þet muȝe stonden aȝein þes fleisces lust and wernen his aȝene fleisces iwille.

β. *a* **1300** *Cursor M.* 22342 Sal nan ha might þair might to warn.

5. To refuse to take or accept.

α. *c* **1300** *Havelok* 926 Sit now doun and et ful yerne: Daþeit hwo þe mete werne! **13..** *Gaw. & Gr. Knt.* 1824 Ho bede hit hym ful bysily, & he hir bode wernes.

β. *a* **1300** *Cursor M.* 16236 Coth pilate,.. to varn yur consail better it es þan to do mar foli.

b. To deny (a statement).

a **1300** *Cursor M.* 21334 þe stat of ilk ewangelist Bers in him-self vr lauerd crist. He es man and ox, leon, and ern, Mai na skilful man þis wern.

† **warn**, *v.*[3] *Obs. rare.* [a. OF. *warnir* (var. of *garnir* garnish *v.*) a. Teut. **warnjan*: see warn *v.*[2]] *trans.* To fortify; to protect, defend. *lit.* and *fig.*

c **1330** R. Brunne *Chron. Wace* 8836 Ageyn þe Bretons þey cam right ȝerne þe lond ȝyf þey myghte þem werne. **1338** —— *Chron.* (1725) 39 þe toun was warned wele. *Ibid.* 268 Now gos þis Thomas, his treson to purchace, But how Edward was warned þorgh Gode's grace [Fr. *Coment la grace Jhesu Krist Ly gentiz ray Edward de la tresun garnyst*]. *c* **1400** *Rule St. Benet* (Prose) lxix. 45 þat nane defende ne warne oþir for nane achesun. [L. *ne presumat alius alium defendere.*] **1449** Pecock *Repr.* v. vi. 517 For to close and kepe and hegge yn and werne so manye persoones fro so miche gretter synnes.

Hence † **warned** *ppl. a. Obs.*

a **1300** *E.E. Psalter* xxx. 22 He selkouthed to me His mercy in warned cite [Vulg. *in civitate munita*].

warn, obs. pa. t. pl. of be *v.*; obs. f. warrant *sb.*[1]

† ˈ**warnable**, *a. Obs. rare.* In 5 **weernable.** [f. warn *v.*[2] + -able.] That may be forbidden.

c **1449** Pecock *Repr.* IV. ix. 470 He expressith tho gouernauncis.. in the maners and circumstauncis.. in which thei ben forbedable or weernable.

warnage, obs. Sc. var. vernage.

c **1470** Henry *Wallace* III. 17 Bot Inglismen.. Stuffit housis with wyn and gud wernage. *Ibid.* 317 King Eduuardis self could nocht get bettir wyn Than thai had thar, warnage and wenysoune Off bestiall in to full gret fusion.

† **warne**, *conj. Obs.* Also **warn.** [app. a phrase f. *war*, *were*, 3rd sing. pa. t. subj. of be + ne. Cf. Sc. *werena*.] Were it not that, but that, unless.

1340 Hampole *Pr. Consc.* 2342 For warne syn war þai [the devils] had ay bene Bright aungels. **13..** *Cursor M.* 2798 (Gött.) All his praier mith noght help, Warn godes might þar wald ȝelp. *c* **1400** Maundev. (Roxb.) xiv. 65 Warne þe snawe ware, þare schuld na man passe ower þe ysz. *c* **1450** *Mirour Saluacioun* (Roxb.) 51 And warne godde ȝaf to menne the freendful angelic keping Thare shuld neure man eschape the feends crowell temptyng.

warnel (ˈwɔːnəl). Now *dial.* Forms: 1 **wernæȝel**, 7 **warnell, wornel**, 8– **wornil** (9 *corruptly* **wommal, wurmal**), 8– **warnel.** [OE. *wernæȝel*, perh. f. **wearh* pus (see ware *sb.*[6], waribreed) + *næȝel* nail *sb.*]

1. A hard tumour on the back of cattle, produced by the larva of a gadfly: = warble *sb.*[2] 2.

c **1000** Ælfric *Hom.* II. 28 þa lærde hi sum iudeisc man, þæt heo name ænne wernæȝel of sumes oxan hricge [etc.]. **1844** H. Stephens *Bk. Farm* III. 838 *Warbles* or *wommals*, that is, small swelled protuberances along the chine, caused by the larvæ of the *Œstrus bovis* or cattle-bot. **1852** T. W. Harris *Insects Injur. Veget.* 500 Large open boils, sometimes called wornils or wurmals, that is, worm-holes. **1864–5** Wood *Homes without H.* xxvi. (1868) 512 The swellings caused by the Breeze Fly are called Wurbles or Wornils.

b. The maggot producing tumours of this kind: = warble *sb.*[2] 3.

1674 tr. *Scheffer's Lapland* xxviii. 132 About March worms or wornels do begin to breed in their backs. **1713** Derham *Phys.-Theol.* VIII. vi. (1727) 378 In the Backs of Cows.. there are Maggots generated, which in Essex we call Wornils; which are first only a small Knot in the Skin.

c. *Comb.*

1708 Kersey, *Warnel-worms*, certain Worms that stick within the Skin of Cattel on their Backs. Whence in later Dicts.

†**2.** = agnail 1. *Obs.*

1611 Cotgr., *Frouelle*, An agnell, pinne, or warnell in the toe.

† ˈ**warnement.** *Obs. rare*[−1]. [a. OF. *warnement*, *garnement*: see garment.] Equipment, armour, clothing.

13.. *K. Alis.* 7443 (Laud) He ȝiueþ londes, he ȝiueþ rentes, Stedes, tresores, warnementes [*Linc.* warentmentis].

warner[1] (ˈwɔːnə(r)). [f. warn *v.*[1] + -er[1].]

1. One who warns or gives warning to others.

1565 Cooper *Thesaurus*, *Monitor*, a warner. **1572** Huloet (ed. Higins), Warner, or admonisher, *monitor*, *admonitor*. **1637** Rutherford *Let. to Ld. Craighall* 8 July, If ye advise.. with that warner within you that will not fail to speak against you in God's time. **1805** Southey *Madoc* II. xxvi, Again the ominous warner cried, Woe! woe! the Cycle of the Years is full! **1820** T. Erskine *Remarks Internal Evid.* iii. (1827) 66 Must the Almighty Warner demonstrate the evil of sin by undergoing its effects? *a* **1849** Mangan *Poems* (1859) 148 The Wildgrave fiercely spurns his warner.

b. *transf.* esp. a mechanical device for giving warning.

1823 *Mechanic's Mag.* No. 4. 59 The Warner is to give the mariner immediate intelligence when in shoal water. **1841** *Civil Engin. & Arch. Jrnl.* IV. 240/2 The other wheels of the train produce no further effect till the warning has been replied to from D, which at the same time restores the electric circuit of the 'warner' for another signal. **1867** Smyth *Sailor's Word-bk.*, *Warner*,.. Also, beacons, posts, buoys, lights, &c. warning vessels of danger by day as well as by night. **1906** Lockyer *Stonehenge* iii. 24 This star would act as a warner of sunrise at some time of the year.

c. As the second element in ***rent***, ***storm warner***.

1885 *Manch. Exam.* 5 May 6/2 An article by Herr Emmerig.. on German bees as storm warners. **1907** *Times* 2 Oct. 12/5 The owner of the cattle is bailiff and rent warner on several properties near Ennis.

†**2.** One who summons people to attend a gathering. *Obs.*

1572 in W. H. Turner *Select. Rec. Oxford* (1880) 341, 4 bedells or warners. **1813** Shipway *Campanalogia* I. title-p., By William Shipway, Late Warner to the Society of Cumberland Youths.

†**3.** *local.* A man who gives notice of arrival of ships at a port. *Obs.*

1761 *Ann. Reg.* 169 The young man who gives the intelligence of the arrival of ships at that port [Bristol], commonly called the warner. **1867** Smyth *Sailor's Word-bk.*, *Warner*, a sentinel formerly posted on the heights near sea-ports to give notice of the approach of vessels.

†**4.** A mongrel used as a house-dog. *Obs.*

1576 Fleming tr. *Caius' Engl. Dogges* v. (1880) 34 Curres of the mungrell and rascall sort and first of the Dogge called in Latine *Admonitor* and of vs in Englishe Wappe or Warner.

†**5.** *Anc. Cookery.* A table decoration or device, probably similar to the SUBTLETY (sense 5) but preceding it. *Obs.*

1505 *Inthronization Abp. Warham* in Leland *Collect.* (1716) VI. App. II. 21 The first course at my Lordes Table in the great Hall. First, a Warner conveyed upon a rounde boorde, of viii. panes, with viii. Towres, enbatteled and made with flowres, standyng on every towre a Bedil in his habite, with his staffe. *Ibid.* A Warner with three Stages, with vanes and towres enbateled.

† **'warner²**. *Sc. Obs.* In 6 **warnour**. [? f. WARN *v.*² + -ER¹.] ? A miser.

1513 DOUGLAS *Æneis* VIII. Prol. 96 Sum warnour for this warldis wrak wendis by his wyt.

warner(e, obs. forms of WARRENER.

† **'warnership.** *Obs.* [f. WARNER¹ + -SHIP.] ? The district of an official 'warner'.

It is very doubtful whether these quots. do not belong to WARRENERSHIP.

1636 in G. Roberts *Soc. Hist.* (1856) 290 [Precautions against infection of the plague] Thomas Stowell of the warnership of Pymperne,..innkeeper, hath divers times entertained carriers, travellers, and others that came from London. *Ibid.*, The constables or other officers of the warnership of Pymperne.

warnes(se, var. ff. WARENESS *Obs.*

† **'warnestore**, *sb. Obs.* Forms: α. 3-4 **warnest(o)ur(e**, (5 **warusture** ?), 3-4 **warnisto(u)re**, (4 **warinstour**), 5 **warn(e)stor(e**, **warny stoor**. β. 3 **wermestore**, 4-5 **warmstore**, 5, 7 **warme store**. [a. OF. *warnesture*, northeastern var. of *garnesture*, f. *warnir*, *garnir*: see GARNISH *v.* Cf. GARNITURE.]

1. Provisions kept in store, provender.

a **1300** *Cursor M.* 1698 Þou sal alsua mak a boure For to hald in þi wermestore. *Ibid.* 4688 Ma þan a thusand selers Fild he wit wins, neu and fress, And warnistore o salt fless. *c* **1375** *Ibid.* 24788 (Fairf.) He..caried warnestoure on mani wise. *c* **1400** tr. *Secreta Secret., Gov. Lordsh.* 65 Whanne men trowyn wynter þat it is cold, men ordeyns herbergage and cloþing, and warmstores of cole and woode, and of many oþer þynges. **14..** *26 Pol. Poems* xiii. 122 Stuffe ȝoure castels in eche coost, Warnestor and folk þeder sende. *c* **1470** HENRY *Wallace* IX. 1200, I will remayn quhill this warnstor be gane. **1483** *Cath. Angl.* 409/1 Warnstore, *annona*, *entica*, *wernestura*.

2. ? A magazine for provisions, ? a fortified place.

1297 R. GLOUC. (Rolls) 2075 In eche stude hii sette þer strong warnesture & god. **1338** R. BRUNNE *Chron.* (1810) 180 Þe Sarazins kept it þat tym for þer chefe warinstour.

3. *in warnestore*: in safe keeping, in reserve.

c **1440** *Bone Flor.* 878 They were not ordeygned therfore [for the siege], They had golde in warme store, But mete was them full nede. **1615** BRATHWAIT *Strappado* (1878) 182 Nor doth he want for any one of these, A statute in warme store if that he please.

† **'warnestore**, *v. Obs.* Forms: α. 4 **warnestur**, 4-5 **warn(e)sto(o)re**, **warnystor**. β. 4-5 **warmstore**. [f. prec. sb.] *trans.* To furnish with supplies. Also, to fortify, secure.

c **1350** *Will. Palerne* 1121 Wel þei were warnestured of vitayles i-now. *c* **1374** CHAUCER *Boeth.* I. pr. iii. (1886) 7 We þat ben..warnestored and enclosyd in swich a palis whider as chateringe or a-noyenge folye ne may nat atayne. *c* **1386** —— *Melib.* ⁋2487 Ye sholde doon youre diligence to kepen youre persone and to warnestoore youre hous. *Ibid.* ⁋2523 That I shal warnestoore myn hous with toures..and Armure and Artelries. *c* **1400** tr. *Secreta Secret., Gov. Lordsh.* 57 It ys to ȝelde to ilk man þat his ys, ffor so er citeez warmstoryd and rentys gyuen.

Hence † **'warnestoring** *vbl. sb.*

c **1386** CHAUCER *Melib.* ⁋2525 Warnestooryng..of heighe toures and of grete edifices.

† **warnett.** *Obs. rare.* [Of obscure origin.] Alleged name of a variety of building-slate.

1688 HOLME *Armoury* III. 265/2 Names of Slates according to their several Lengths... Chitts. Warnetts. Shorts.

warnice, variant of WARNISH *v.*²

warning ('wɔːnɪŋ), *vbl. sb.*¹ [OE. *war(e)nung*, *wearning*, fem., f. *war(e)nian*, *wearnian*, WARN *v.*¹: see -ING¹. Cf. OHG. *warnunga* (MHG. *warnunge*, mod.G. *warnung*).] The action of WARN *v.*¹

† **1.** Taking heed, precaution. *Obs.*

Spenser's use suggests that the antithesis of 'warning' and 'weird' (fate) may have survived proverbially.

c **1000** *Sal. & Sat.* 427 Full oft ic frode menn fyrn ȝehyrde Secgan..hwæðer wære tweȝra..strengra, wyrd ðe warnung. **1590** SPENSER *F.Q.* III. iv. 27 But ah, who can deceiue his destiny, Or weene by warning to auoyd his fate?

2. a. Previous intimation or threat of impending evil or danger. Phrase, *to give warning* (*to*), to warn. Also Sc. *to make warning*.

† *Scarborough warning*: see SCARBOROUGH.

a **800** CYNEWULF *Crist* 922 Ðæt mæȝ wites to wearninga, þam ðe hafað wisne ȝeþoht. *a* **1300** *Cursor M.* 2993 O þis warning he þam tald, And þai þam dred both yong and ald. **1330** R. BRUNNE *Chron. Wace* (Rolls) 8764 To opene my mouþ y ne dar ne may, Bot hit be a byhouely þyng at nede, þat were warnyng of tokene of dede. **1375** BARBOUR *Bruce* v. 502 Thai maid him mony tyme varnyng, Quhen that thai his tynsale mycht se. *c* **1430** *Syr Gener.* (Roxb.) 2279 Of treason first I gaf him warnyng, Therfor I haue lost my living. **1548** HALL *Chron., Edw. IV* 215 The erle of Warwycke..wrote to the Marques Montacute..geuynge hym warnyng, and aduertesyng him in what perill their whole affayres stode in. **1590** SPENSER *F.Q.* I. xi. 14 As two broad Beacons..Send forth their flames..And warning giue, that enemies conspyre, With fire and sword the region to inuade. *c* **1600** *Timon* I. ii. (1842) 6 Looke to thy selfe; I gyue thee fayre warning. **1656** N. BERNARD *Life Abp. Usher* 91 So great a Prophet..might have at some speciall times more then ordinary motions and impulses in doing the Watch-mans part, of giving warning of Judgements approaching. **1681** PRIDEAUX *Lett.* (Camden) 91 They talk nothing now but of wageing war with yᵉ King... However they thought fit first to give his Majesty some warneing. *c* **1718** PRIOR *Paulo Purg.* 160, I give you warning: You'll die before to-morrow morning. **1759** HUME *Hist. Eng. Hen. VIII*, i. 84 He gave his master warning of the danger [*later edd.* He made warning of the danger to his master]. **1814** SCOTT *Lord of Isles* IV. xxvi, 'In murderous strife,' Said Bruce, 'his warning saved my life'. **1846** MRS. A. MARSH *Father Darcy* II. xvi. 276 [Tresham] insisted vehemently that warning should be given to the Lord Mounteagle, his kinsman. **1855** MACAULAY *Hist. Eng.* xviii. IV. 229 The banished oppressor had at least given Englishmen fair warning.

b. A sign or portent of coming evil.

c **1325** *Yesterday* 55 in *Minor Poems fr. Vernon MS.* 676 Nis non so fresch on fote to fare..Ne non so bold, Beores to bynde þat he naþ warmynges [*read* warnynges] to beo ware. **1601** SHAKS. *Jul. C.* II. ii. 80 And these does she apply, for warnings and portents, And euils imminent. *a* **1700** EVELYN *Diary* 12 Dec. 1680, They [*sc.* comets] may be warnings from God, as they commonly are forerunners of his animadversions. **1794** MRS. RADCLIFFE *Myst. Udolpho* vi, But I have heard it these many years, and outlived the warning. **1899** *Allbutt's Syst. Med.* VII. 767 This is called the 'warning' of the attack, or in medical terminology, the 'aura'.

3. Advice to beware of a person or thing as being dangerous.

a **1225** *Ancr. R.* 62 Al Holi Writ is ful of warningge of eie. Dauid seide, 'Averte oculos meos ne videant vanitatem'. **1842** DICKENS *Amer. Notes* xvi, There we all stood, watching this revolving light upon the rock at Holyhead, and praising it for its brightness and its friendly warning. **1860** TYNDALL *Glac.* I. xi. 83 Urged by the warnings of our..guide, we..began the descent. **1870** A. R. WALLACE *Contrib. Theory Nat. Select.* (1871) 118 Some..perceived signal was therefore necessary to serve as a warning to birds never to touch these uneatable kinds [of caterpillars]. **1888** F. HUME *Mme. Midas* I. i, The result of this blind confidence justified the warnings of her friends.

4. a. Deterrent counsel; cautionary advice against imprudent or vicious action, or neglect of duty.

c **1000** ÆLFRIC *On Old T.* (Gr.) 7 [The Book of Proverbs is] wisdomes biȝspell and warnung wið disiȝ. *c* **1380** WYCLIF *Wks.* (1880) 378 He had many grete warnyngis of hydousnes & perille of þis synne. **1393** LANGL. *P. Pl.* C. IV. 431 The kyng [*sc.* Saul] spared, For-bar hym and hus beste bestes..Otherwise than god wolde by warnyng of the prophete. *c* **1400** *Brut* 116 Þe gode man warnede ham ofte-tymes þat folie to lete; but his warnyng availede litel for þe loue bituene ham was so miche. *c* **1440** *Jacob's Well* 8 þou..awȝtyst gretly to desyre, to heryn his warnyng & his techyng. **1471** CAXTON *Recuyell* (Sommer) 538 O what pyte was hyt, That the Troyans beleuyd not this warnyng and Amonycion. **1535** COVERDALE *Prov.* x. 8 A wyse man wil receaue warnynge, but a foole wil sooner be smytten in the face. **1540** PALSGR. *Acolastus* I. i. D iij b, Surely he were a gaye gyuer of warnynge, yf his aduyse were ought worthe. **1642** J. TAYLOR (Water P.) *Life Walker* A 3, But all these faire warnings could not make M. Walker give over writing, lying and Libelling. **1713** ROWE *Jane Shore* IV. 47 Oh! should'st thou wrong her Just Heav'n shall double all thy Woes upon thee, And make 'em know no End—Remember this As the last Warning of a dying Man. **1855** MACAULAY *Hist. Eng.* xix. IV. 344 'My Lord,' said the King,..'you will live to repent the part which you are taking in this matter.' The warning was disregarded. **1858** FROUDE *Hist. Eng.* II. ix. 322 History is never weary of repeating its warnings against narrow judgements. **1907** *Verney Mem.* II. 54 Abstaining from a single word of reproach for the past or of warning for the future.

b. An experience, sight, etc. that serves as a caution; a deterrent example.

1613 J. SARIS *Voy. Japan* (Hakl. Soc.) 41 They laye a good while aboard of hir, and charged them to take this for a wardning [*sic*], and giue ouer there scoffing of them, or the next time they would teach them better manner. **1684** BUNYAN *Pilgr.* II. (1900) 219 Let Christian's slips before he came hither, and the Battles that he met with in this place, be a warning to those that come after. **1771** *Junius Lett.* No. lxvii. 331 *note*, It deserves to be recorded for the curiosity of the fact, and should be given to the public as a warning to every honest member of society. **1857** MAURICE *Ep. St. John* xi. 170 Such a man is a spectacle and a warning to us all.

c. *to take warning*: to alter one's course of action when warned of its danger. Const. *by* (another's ill-fortune, etc.).

1550 CROWLEY *Epigr.* 784 An example thou shalt be, That all stouburne priestes may take warnyng by the. **1607** SHAKS. *Timon* III. i. 28 He wold embrace no counsell, take no warning by my comming. **1684** BUNYAN *Pilgr.* II. (1900) 198, I think it is well that they hang so near the High-way that others may see and take warning. **1859** TENNYSON *Enid* 1520 Girl, for I see ye scorn my courtesies, Take warning.

d. *the usual warning*: the caution that a police officer making an arrest is bound to give, viz. that anything the suspect says may be taken down and used in evidence against him or her.

[**1919** GREGG & MCGRATH *Police Constable's Guide* (ed. 3) p. xlix, Persons in custody should not be questioned without the usual caution being first administered.] **1931** 'G. TREVOR' *Murder at School* xiii. 255, I gave her the usual warning, of course, but she began to talk, all the same. **1975** 'R. PLAYER' *Let's talk of Graves* v. 181 Holding my warrant in my right hand, I then gave her the usual warning and arrested her.

e. The action or an instance of warning (someone) *off*: see sense 6 of the vb.

1977 K. BENTON *Red Hen Conspiracy* ix. 56 He gets an ambiguous warning-off from the Embassy, but that doesn't stop him. **1980** D. FRANCIS *Reflex* xv. 181 They could have half-killed me... All they were truly delivering was a warning off. **1981** *Times Lit. Suppl.* 30 Jan. 108/5 The warning off of the racing correspondent of the *Morning Post.*

5. a. Previous notice of an event whether good or bad. † *in warning*: by way of warning. Also, time allowed for preparation, interval between the notice and the event (e.g. in *long*, *short warning*, *a day's warning*, etc.).

a **1300** *Cursor M.* 21879 He sends us þis all in warning, For to be warr of his cuming. *c* **1370** *Roberd of Cysille* 464 in Hazl. *E.E.P.* I. 286 The aungelle gaf hym in warnynge Of the tyme of hys levynge. ? **1471** *Stonor Papers* (Camden) I. 117 A pryve seall..was delivered to him on Munday..which as your maystership knoweth well was right shorte warnyng. **1560** F. ALLEN in Lodge *Illustr. Brit. Hist.* (1791) I. 345 The Quene's Maᵗᵉ hathe sworne that the daye and tyme shall be kepte secrete to herself,..so as the very tyme..will be so shorte and sodeyne that men are like to have small warninge of the matter. *c* **1590** MARLOWE *Faustus* 391 Thou art at an houres warning whensoeuer or wheresoeuer the diuell shall fetch thee. **1596** SHAKS. *Tam. Shr.* IV. iv. 60 The worst is this,—that at so slender warning, You are like to haue a thin and slender pittance. **1607** *Statutes* in *Hist. Wakefield Gram. Sch.* (1892) 59 Lawfull warninge of the daye of the election. **1617** MORYSON *Itin.* II. 44 The truce..was then concluded..till the Calends of May, except either of them should give fourteen daies warning of their purpose to breake the same. **1633** FLETCHER & SHIRLEY *Night-Walker* IV. i, But this will be reveng'd in a short warning. *a* **1701** MAUNDRELL *Journ. Jerus.* (1732) 104 Where an Angel gave the Blessed Virgin three days warning of her Death. **1849** MACAULAY *Hist. Eng.* iv. I. 479 At a moment's warning the Sheriff adjourned the poll to Newport Pagnell.

b. In some clocks, the rattling or whirring noise which precedes the striking.

1775 J. BERRIDGE *Wks.* (1864) 388 This, like the warning of a clock, prepares for the stroke. **1843** *Penny Cycl.* XXVII. 107/1 From that time till the hand comes to 60 the clock is on the warning. **1850** DENISON *Clock & Watch-m.* 119 The noise made by this is called giving warning. **1875** KNIGHT *Dict. Mech.* s.v. *Warning-piece*, The warning-piece, by starting the fly, causes a rustling noise, which is the precursor of the striking, and is called the warning.

c. *U.S. local.* (See quot.) ? *Obs.*

1807 JANSON *Stranger in Amer.* 422 On such occasions [*sc.* burial of the dead] what they call 'warnings' is the day before, or early in the morning, given of the funeral.

d. A signal given by means of a siren, etc., to indicate that an air attack is imminent, an air-raid warning. Cf. ALERT *sb.*¹ 1 b.

1917, **1938** [see AIR-RAID]. **1940** H. NICOLSON *Diary* 7 Sept. (1967) 111 The all-clear sounds at 6, but there is another warning at 8 which actually lasts till 5.30 a.m. **1953** R. LEHMANN *Echoing Grove* 284 There are several regulars who bustle along the moment the Warning goes and don't stick their noses out again till the All-clear. **1982** T. FITZGIBBON *With Love* I. viii. 57 The air-raid siren had sounded..but a warning about a week previously had amounted to very little.

6. Notice of the termination of a business relation, given by one of the parties to the other; esp. by a landlord to a tenant, a master to a servant, an employer to an employee, or vice versa.

1432 *Paston Lett.* I. 33 The said Erle desireth that..he may, by warnyng to my Lordes..be and stande freely discharged of the saide occupation..about the Kinges persone. **1562-3** *Act 5 Eliz.* c. 4 §4 That no suche Mʳ Mʳˢ or Dame shall put awaye any suche Servante..without one quarter warning gyven before thende of his sayd terme. **1571-2** *Reg. Privy Council Scot.* II. 125 It salbe leful to ayther of the saidis partiis to use warningis for removing fra landis and heretabill possessioun. **1577** J. DEE *Diary* (Camden) 3, June 26th, Elen Lyne gave me a quarter's warning. *a* **1646** T. HOPE *Minor Pract.* xiii. (1734) 363 The Objections against the Lawfulness of the Warning are, That the Parties are not lawfully warned personally, or at their Dwelling-places, or upon the Ground of the Lands,..or, That the Warning is not stamped, &c. **1666** PEPYS *Diary* 30 Mar., Up and away goes Alce, our cook-maid;..and would go away of her own accord, after having given her mistress warning fickly for a quarter of a year together. **1676** *Office of Clerk of Assize* 112 If any Master hath put away his Servant before the end of his term, without a quarter warning, he shall forfeit forty shillings. **1697** VANBRUGH *Relapse* II. (*fin.*), You shou'd never take a Lease of a House you can hire for a Quarter's Warning. **1715** ADDISON *Drummer* I. i, *Coachman.* I'll give Madam warning, that's flat—I've always liv'd in sober families. **1742** RICHARDSON *Pamela* III. 209, I had talk'd to Mrs. Jervis to induce the Girl (to whom, in hopes of frightening her, I had given Warning..) to desire to stay. **1799** R. BELL *Syst. Forms of Deeds Scot.* II. 389 There is first a precept of warning given by the landlord; it is in this form... I..lawfully premonish, warn, and charge C. D. tenant and possessor of the lands of [blank], to flit and remove himself [etc.] **1837** DICKENS *Pickw.* xxxii, I'll pay her [the landlady] what I owe her, and give her warning to-morrow morning. **1872** *Punch* 6 Apr. 141/2 Mary Dishley gave her mistress warning: no fault to find with her place, but wanted a change. **1884** *Ibid.* 22 Nov. 246 Cook, I give you a Month's Warning from To-day. **1886** J. BARROWMAN *Sc. Mining Terms* 70 *Warning*, notice, given or received, of a workman leaving his employment.

fig. **1828** SCOTT *Aunt Marg. Mirror* Introd., A little group of trees, that still grace the eastern end,..have just received warning to quit, expressed by a daub of white paint.

† **7.** Previous notice of being called upon to perform some duty. *Obs.*

1459 *Rolls of Parlt.* V. 369/2 He had..a commaundement fro youre Highnes, to be redy to come..with his said fel[y]ship, upon a day warning. **1477** *Ibid.* VI. 194/2 To be redy in harnays within an Houre warnyng. **1549** THOMAS *Hist. Italie* 74 b, For there [at the Arsenal of Venice] they haue well neere two hundred galleys in suche an ordre, that vpon a verie small warnyng they maie be furnisshed out vnto the sea. **1554–5** in Feuillerat *Revels Q. Mary* (1914) 170 In a redines to serve vpon further warnynge. **1556** LD. WHARTON in Lodge *Illustr. Brit. Hist.* (1791) I. 220, I called the gentilmen, freholders, and rulers of men, and declared unto them the Quenes Ma[tie's] comaundement for their servyse, and reddynes upon an hower's warnyng. **1759** ROBERTSON *Hist. Scot.* I. III. 256 For this purpose she summoned him to appear before her on a short warning.

†**8. a.** Intimation, notification of a fact or a present occurrence. ***to give warning of***: to call attention to. *Obs.*

c **1386** CHAUCER *Can. Yeom. Prol.* 40 Sires, now in the morwe tyde, Out of youre hostelrie I saugh you ryde And warned heer my lord,.. Which to ryden with yow is ful fayn ..Frend, for thy warnyng god yeue thee chance. **1398** TREVISA *Barth. De P.R.* II. i. (1495) 27 By warnyng of angels men knowe goddis wyl & so angels is a name of offyce & not of kynde. **1449** PECOCK *Repr.* I. xvi. 89 If of this consideracioun no mensioun and waarnyng were bi me or bi sum other in writing bifore mad. *c* **1480** *Robt. Devyll* 787 in Hazl. *E.E.P.* I. 250 And whan thy synnes be cleane forgeuen the, By an Aungell god wyll sende the warnynge. **1611** BIBLE *Transl. Pref.* ¶17 Many other things we might giue thee warning of (gentle Reader) if wee had not exceeded the measure of a Preface alreadie.

†**b.** ***a by warning***: a private hint or prompting to do something. *Obs.*

1542 UDALL *Erasm. Apoph.* 25 When..his familiar coumpaignions gaue hym a by warnynge to auenge suche a naughtie touche..with his tenne comaundementes: gayly saied [etc.].

†**c.** A notice or signal that a certain hour has come, or that it is time to do something. *Obs.*

1389 in *Eng. Gilds* (1870) 7 Alle þe breþeren schulle be redy at here warnynge. *c* **1566** J. ALDAY tr. *Boaystuau's Theat. World* S 3, A Diall, the which..gave warning with a stroke unto him that did weare it of everie houre. **1573** J. SANDFORD *Hours Recr.* (1576) 67 The swallowe agaİne giveth them warning to go away. **1597** SHAKS. *2 Hen. IV*, IV. iii. 117 The sherris..illuminateth the Face, which (as a Beacon) giues warning to all the rest of this little Kingdom (Man) to Arme. **1633** B. JONSON *Tale Tub* I. vi, He sat up at Play, and watch'd the Cock, Till his first warning chid him off to rest. **1687** A. LOVELL tr. *Thevenot's Trav.* I. 162 These Timbrels..serve not only to chear up the Camels..but also to give warning to those that stay behind. **1821** JOANNA BAILLIE *Metr. Leg., Malcolm's Heir* liv, And aye, when the midnight warning sounds, He hastens his beads to tell.

†**9.** A summons, command for attendance. *Obs.*

a **1425** *Cursor M.* 16022 (Trin.) Mony gedered of þe toun bi certeyn warnynge [*otherwise in earlier texts*]. **1461** *Paston Lett.* II. 3 If this Lords above wayte aftyr more pepill in this cuntre, be lyklyness it woll not be easy to get with owt a newe comission and warnyng. *c* **1495** HEN. VII in Ellis *Orig. Lett.* Ser. I. I. 21 We praye you herein ye wol make suche delegens as that ye be redy with your said nombre to come unto us uppon any our sodein warnyng. **1496** *Cov. Leet. Bk.* 573 The Craft shall mete on seynt Anne day..and what persones þat be absent þat day vppon warnyng shall pay xij d. **1509** *Reg. Privy Seal Scot.* I. 271/2 He..durst nocht cum to the said burgh to hald the said court without warnyng, support and supple of his frendis. **1600** *Child-Marriages* 173 That the said Pattrick shalbe ready to appeare within xij howres before the said maior, vppon warninge geuen at any of the houses of the said Roberte Bennett & Randle Ince. **1623** COCKERAM II, A Warning to appeare to a court. Citation. **1784** *Acts & Laws Connecticut* 179 A Copy of this Paragraph of this Act,..published on the Sign-Post in said Town..at least three Days before said second Monday of March next, shall be a legal Warning of the Freemen of said City to attend said first meeting. **1792** N. CHIPMAN *Rep.* (1871) 10 It does not appear that the warning for the proprietor's meeting was published according to law.

†**10.** The action of advertising (lost property).

c **1610** in *Heriot's Mem.* App. VII. (1822) 218 To the goldsmith's officer for warning of her Majestie's diamond, which was lost at Salisburie, 6s. 8d.

†**11.** *Law.* = GARNISHMENT. *Obs.*

1579 *Expos. Terms Law* 98 b, Warninge is when an actyon of detinue of charters is brought against one, & the defendant saieth, y[t] the charters were deliuered to him by the plaintife, and by an other vpon certein conditions and praiethe y[t] the other may be warned to pleade with the plaintife whether the conditions be performed or noe, and therevppon a write of *Scire facias* shall goe forthe against him.

12. *attrib.* and *Comb.*, as ***warning light***; ***warning-giver***; †**warning-arrow** (cf. *warning-gun*); **warning bell,** (*a*) a bell for giving alarm of fire or invasion; (*b*) a bell announcing the imminent departure of a vessel; (*c*) a bell alerting people to prepare for a meal, etc.; (*d*) *fig.*, an alarm-bell sounded 'in the head', giving a presentiment of danger; **warning gong** *rare* = *dressing-gong* s.v. DRESSING *vbl. sb.* 5 a; **warning-gun,** a gun sounded as an alarm or announcement; **warning-lever** *Horology*, the lever that sets in motion the warning-wheel; **warning-pipe,** an overflow pipe serving to show when a cistern is too full; **warning triangle,** a triangular red frame carried by motorists, and set up on the road as a danger signal to warn approaching drivers of the proximity of a broken-down vehicle or other hazard; **warning-wheel** *Horology*, the wheel that produces the 'warning' (see 5 b). Also WARNING-PIECE.

1628 FELTHAM *Resolves* II. xii. 30 The sight of vice in others, is like a *warning-Arrow, shot, for vs to take heed. **1511** *Pilton Churchw. Acc.* (Som. Rec. Soc.) 61 Item for the *warnyng bell and iiij polysse, ii[s]. viii[d]. **1591** SHAKS. *1 Hen. VI*, IV. ii. 39 Harke, harke, the Dolphins drumme, a warning bell, Sings heauy Musicke to thy timorous soule. *a* **1592** LODGE & GREENE *Looking Gl.* (1598) D 4, Foresee in time, the warning bell doth towle. **1606** DAY *Ile of Gulls* I. i. B 1, I heare the warning bell, some strangers are ariued. **1849** DICKENS *Dav. Copp.* (1850) xxi. 212 The warning-bell will ring at nine; the family take breakfast at halfpast nine. **1853** KINGSLEY *Hypatia* xxi, Having disposed his sentinels, [he] took his station on the top of his tower, close by the warning-bell. **1864** G. A. LAWRENCE *Maurice Dering* II. 233 The 'Tigris' was on the point of getting under way, and the first warning-bell had rung. **1951** E. COXHEAD *One Green Bottle* vii. 202 Somewhere, right at the back of her head, there rang a little warning bell. **1951** *Publ. Amer. Dial. Soc.* XVI. 68 *Warning bell*, a signal made to warn that it is time to saddle the horses entered in the next race. **1981** S. BRETT *Situation Tragedy* ii. 26 'I'll join you.' Something rang warning bells for Charles. 'Well, no.' **1984** *Times* 5 June 23 (*heading*) Another warning bell for the secretaries. **1577** B. GOOGE *Heresbach's Husb.* IV. 166 The best watchmen, and also the best *warning geuers in the nyght tyme. **1938** D. SMITH *Dear Octopus* III. i. 116 Ring the *warning gong, will you, dear? **1830** JAMES *Darnley* xxxviii. III. 251 The *warning gun was fired from the castle of Guisnes, giving notice that the King of England was ready to set out. **1884** F. J. BRITTEN *Watch & Clockm.* 219 The rack pulls over the hour *warning lever. **1937** *Motor Catal.* (East London Rubber Co. Ltd.) 131 Ignition replacements..*warning lights. **1962** *Which? Car Suppl.* Oct. 130/2 The Fiat 1500 had a particularly comprehensive array of warning lights, including lights to show when choke, side lights and hand brake were in use. **1972** J. AIKEN *Butterfly Picnic* i. 6 The encircling mountains outlined by small red warning lights. **1974** 'W. HAGGARD' *Kinsmen* xiii. 126 The warning lights were out and flashing. Her mother had some absurd new plan. **1833** LOUDON *Encycl. Archit.* § 1808 To put a half-inch *warning-pipe from the cistern to a convenient place near the pump. **1971** *Good Motoring* Sept. 23/3 It is essential for motorists to carry *warning triangles for use in case of accident or breakdown. **1696** W. DERHAM *Artif. Clock-m.* i. 6 The next is the Third, or Fourth-Wheel, (according as it is distant from the First-Wheel) called also the *Warning-Wheel. **1884** F. J. BRITTEN *Watch & Clockm.* 249 The last wheel of the striking train, called the warning wheel.

†**'warning,** *vbl. sb.*[2] *Obs.* [OE. **wiernung*, *wærnung*, f. *wiernan* WARN *v.*[2] See -ING[1].] Refusal, denial.

c **1000** *Laws of Athelstan* II. iii. (Lieberm.) 152 Be rihtes wærnunge. Se hlaford se rihtes wyrne ond for his yfelan mon licge. *a* **1225** *Ancr. R.* 330 He ne mei uor reouðe wernen hire, ne sweamen hire heorte mid wernunge. *c* **1330** *Arth. & Merl.* 5522 Ac þat þou graunt ous now a þing, & þer of no make werning. **13..** *Gaw. & Gr. Knt.* 2253 Bot styȝtel þe vpon on strok, & I schal stonde stylle, & warp þe no wernyng, to worch as þe lykez, no whare. *a* **1366** CHAUCER *Rom. Rose* 1142 For al his purpos..Was for to make greet dispense, Withouten werning or defence. **1375** BARBOUR *Bruce* XVI. 260 Thai fand nane that thame varnyng maid. *c* **1420** WYNTOUN *Cron.* III. viii. 977 Þar sulde be made hym na warnynge Off qwhat thynge he made askynge. **1449** PECOCK *Repr.* III. xvi. 380 That preestis and othere clerkis mowen weel with-oute weernyng of Holi Scripture..be endewid with temporal and vnmouable godis. *Ibid.* V. v. 506 Summe comaundementis of God ben negatyues, that is to seie, weernyngis or forbodis.

warning ('wɔːnɪŋ), *ppl. a.* [f. WARN *v.*[1] + -ING[2].] That warns, in senses of the verb.

1552 HULOET, Warnynge, or geuynge warnynge, *monitorius.* **1796** SCOTT *Wild Huntsm.* ix, To-day the Warning Spirit hear, To-morrow thou mayst mourn in vain. **1810** —— *Lady of Lake* III. i, The warning note. **1840** DICKENS *Old C. Shop* lxvii, The warning lights and fires upon the river were powerless beneath this pall [of fog]. **1857** LIVINGSTONE *Trav.* xxiv. 476 *note*, A deluging shower, which began without warning-drops. **1891** FARRAR *Darkn. & Dawn* xiii, She raised her hand with a warning gesture.

b. *spec.* in *Biol.* of coloration or other distinctive marks found in caterpillars, etc.

1869 J. J. WEIR in *Trans. Entom. Soc.* I. 21 The birds were deceived into tasting them [*sc.* the larvae] because the characteristic warning hairs were undeveloped. **1877** A. R. WALLACE in *Macm. Mag.* XXXVI. 396 Theory of Protective Colours... Theory of Warning Colours—These differ greatly from the last class, inasmuch as they present us with a variety of brilliant hues, [etc.]. **1887** POULTON in *Proc. Zool. Soc.* 194 Instances of very distasteful species which have no warning colours, but, on the other hand, are well disguised by protective tints and markings.

'warningfully, *adv. rare.* [f. WARNING *vbl. sb.*[1] + -FUL + -LY[2].] = WARNINGLY *adv.*

1922 JOYCE *Ulysses* 197 Quickly, warningfully Buck Mulligan bent down:—The tramper Synge is looking for you, he said, to murder you. **1945** J. STEINBECK *Cannery Row* ix. 53 'I guess everything that comes out of the human mouth is poison,' said Doc warningfully.

'warningly, *adv.* [f. WARNING *ppl. a.* + -LY[2].] In a warning manner, by way of warning.

1840 G. S. FABER *Prim. Doctr. Regen.* IV. iii. 369 Then she speaks warningly and therefore specifically. **1885** *Harper's Mag.* Mar. 628/1, 'I play a wretched game,' said the..lady, warningly.

warning-piece ('wɔːnɪŋpiːs). [f. WARNING *vbl. sb.*[1] and *ppl. a.* + PIECE *sb.*]

1. A signal-gun discharged to give notification of arrival, danger, time, etc.

c **1592** MARLOWE *Jew of Malta* V. 2322 A warning-peece shall be shot off from the Tower, To giue thee knowledge when to cut the cord, And fire the house. **1596** MARBECK in Hakluyt *Voy.* (1598) I. 608 There it pleased the Lords to call a select Councell, which was alwayes done by hanging out of a flagge of the armes of England, and shooting off of a great warning peece. **1607** CHAPMAN *Bussy d'Ambois* I. i. 25 As great Seamen..(comming neere their Hauen) Are glad to giue a warning peece. **1634** SIR T. HERBERT *Trav.* 21 We gaue them a-sterne, two Gunnes as warning peeces of great danger. **1867** SMYTH *Sailor's Word-bk.*, *Evening-gun*, the warning-piece, after the firing of which the sentries challenge.

b. *transf.* and *fig.*

In 17th c. often used in titles of books.

1615 J. H. (*title*) This World's Folly, or a Warning-Peece Discharged upon the Wickednesse thereof. **1650** HUBBERT *Pill Formality* 1 This glorious Apostle..writes unto Timothy..a warning peece to future ages. **1660** BONDE *Scut. Reg.* 379 Oh therefore let our distracted England be a warning-piece to all Nations, that they never attempt to Try and Judge their King, for what cause soever. **1711** STEELE *Spect.* No. 144 ¶1, I shall make this Paper rather a Warning-piece to give notice where the Danger is. **1719** DE FOE *Crusoe* I. (Globe) 140, I am a warning-piece..to all rash.. pilots. **1831** SCOTT *Quentin D.* Introd., The spectacle of his deathbed might of itself be a warning-piece against the seduction of his example.

2. *Clock-making.* The piece that 'warns' that the clock is about to strike.

1875 KNIGHT *Dict. Mech.* **1884** F. J. BRITTEN *Watch & Clockm.* 284 The last wheel..carries a pin which butts on the warning piece during the interval between warning and striking.

warnis, obs. Sc. form of VARNISH *v.*

†**'warnish,** *sb. Obs. rare*[−1]. [f. WARNISH *v.*[1]] The state of being guarded.

1387–8 T. USK *Test. Love* II. vii. 78 And thus warnisshed mot he be, and of warnisshe the hour drede.

†**'warnish,** *v.*[1] *Obs.* Forms: 4 **warnische, -ysch, -issh, -yssh, warenyss, warnise, -yse,** 4, 5 **warnish.** Also *pa. t.* and *pa. pple.* 4–5 **war-, varnist, -yst,** 4 **varnys(i)t.** [a. AF. *warniss-*, *warnir* dial. var. of OF. *garnir*: see GARNISH *v.*]

1. *trans.* To provide or furnish with an ample supply of something; *esp.* to supply (a place) with men and stores.

13.. *K. Alis.* 6052 (Laud MS.) Hij hadden warnysshed Cites & tounes. *c* **1330** *Arth. & Merl.* 6605 Castels, tours, heiȝe & lowe, He dede warnise wiþ store þan. *c* **1340** HAMPOLE *Psalter* lviii. 7 Thai sall warenyss halykirke with lare and vertus. **1375** BARBOUR *Bruce* IV. 102 For thai sa stith saw the casteill, And wist that it wes varnist weill. *c* **1400** *Sc. Trojan War* I. 247 Þai woddys warnist were In-to haboundance of wylde dere. *c* **1470** HENRY *Wallace* IV. 214 On Gargownno was byggyt a small peill, That warnyst was with men and wittaill weill.

b. *refl.* To equip oneself.

13.. *Cursor M.* 24788 (Gött.) He dred him sare þat were suld rise, And warnist him on mani wise. *c* **1400** *Sc. Trojan War* II. 726 One þare best wyse Inne þar armour they thame warnyse.

2. To provide with guards.

1387–8 [see WARNISH *sb.*].

Hence **'warnished** *ppl. a.*; **'warnishing** *vbl. sb.* (esp. in sense 'that with which one is provided').

c **1340** HAMPOLE *Psalter* xvi. 10 Vndire the shadow of thi wengis that is, in the warnysnge of thi charite and of thi mercy. *Ibid.* xxx. 27 He selkouthed his mercy til me in cyte warnyst [L. *in ciuitate munita*]. **1375** BARBOUR *Bruce* VI. 350 It [*sc.* valour] Has so gret varnasyng [*v.r.* warnysing] of vit, That it all peralis weill can se. **1382** WYCLIF *2 Kings* xix. 32 He schal not commen in to this cytee,..and warnyschynge [Vulg. *munitio*] schal not enuyroun it.

'warnish, *v.*[2] *Obs.* exc. *Sc.* Forms: 4 **warnis, wernis,** 9 *Sc.* **warnice, -ise.** [a. AF. *warniss-*, *warnir*, of Teut. origin: related to WARN *v.*[1]] *trans.* To warn or inform beforehand.

a **1300** *Cursor M.* 15611 For-þi godmen, i warnis yow to thinc al of his care. *Ibid.* 19897 Saint petre þar-wit was warnist, Thoru gastili might o iesu crist. *Ibid.* 21674 þar-of was wernist moyses. **13..** *Ibid.* 21884 (Edin.) Bot ai þe ma taknis þat we se, ai þe werre warnisit er we. **1864** LATTO *Tam. Bodkin* ix. 85 They waukened me up frae a maist enchantin' reverie, an' warniced me to prepare belyve to tak' a last fond look o' the slae-black een. **1873** [P. BUCHAN] *Leg. North* 44 Weel was I warnised ere I cam' frae hame.

Hence †**'warnishing** *vbl. sb.* Also **'warnishment,** *Sc.* warning.

a **1300** *Cursor M.* 21927 Thoru warnissing of oþers wrake, Vnnes [we] will ani sample take. **1894** LATTO *Tam. Bodkin* (new ed.) x. 104 Gin I had gotten due warnicement feint a flee wad I hae cared.

†**'warnison.** *Obs.* Also 4 *Sc.* **varnysoun,** 6 *Sc.* **vernysoun.** [a. AF. *warnisoun*, OF. *warnison*, dial. var. of *garnison*: see GARNISON *sb.*] Provision of men, stores, etc. Also a garrison.

1338 R. BRUNNE *Chron.* (1810) 143 Þe pes did he crie, & purueid warnisoun. **1375** BARBOUR *Bruce* x. 325 Quhen thai of his varnysoun Saw the sege set thair stithly, Thai mystrowit hym of tratory. **1570** *Henry's Wallace* VIII. 869 *note*, Thai drede full sar for thair awin vernysoun.

warnisto(u)re, var. ff. WARNESTORE *Obs.*

warnmall, obs. form of WARDMOTE.

war-note. A musical summons to war (*poet.*). Also *fig.*

1805 SCOTT *Last Minstrel* III. xxvi, The Warder..blew his war-note loud and long. **1816** BYRON *Ch. Har.* III. xxvi, Wild and high the 'Cameron's gathering' rose, The war-note of Lochiel. **1897** *Edin. Rev.* Oct. 399 The old war-note of strife for strife's sake has lost something..of its relentless and brutal barbarities.

warnstor(e, var. ff. WARNESTORE *Obs.*

warn't, dial. and vulgar f. *was not, were not.*

warny stoor, -stor, var. ff. WARNESTORE *Obs.*

war of, obs. form of WHEREOF.

War Office. *Hist.* **a.** The former department of the British government, presided over by the Secretary of State for War, which was charged with the entire administration of the Army; the building in which the business of this department was carried on. **b.** *U.S.* The War Department.

The British War Office was incorporated in 1964 into the Ministry of Defence, under the Secretary of State for Defence.

1721 *Constat* in *L.T.R. Particulars of Leases* 4084 (P.R.O.), A passage leading from Whitehall Court to the Warr Office and from thence to Scotland Yard. **1747** *Court & City Reg.* 145 War-office. Secretary at War, Right Hon. Henry Fox, Esq [Then follow names of subordinate officials]. **1818** SCOTT *Hrt. Midl.* l, It should cost Sir George but the asking a pair of colours for one of them at the War-office, since we have always supported government. **1824** in *Nairne Peerage Evid.* (1874) 76 An entry in the books of the war office. **1865** ANGUS *Handbk. Eng. Lit.* 613 The father of M. G. Lewis was deputy-secretary of the war-office. **1870** *Act 33 & 34 Vict.* c. 17 §1 This Act may be cited for all purposes as 'The War Office Act, 1870'. **1899** *Daily News* 21 Dec. 7/1 Lord Roberts spent an hour-and-a-half at the War Office, and then returned to Dover-street with a small War Office staff.

war on, obs. form of WHEREON.

warow, var. WARY *v. Obs.*

warp (wɔːp), *sb.*^{1} Also 1 **wearp,** (4 **werpe, worp**), 4–7 **warpe.** [OE. *wearp* warp in weaving (also used to gloss L. *vīmen* osier-twig), corresponds to OLG. *warp* (MLG. *warp, warpe*), OHG. *warf, warph, waraf* (MHG., early mod.G. *warf*) warp in weaving, ON. *varp* neut., cast of a net, a laying of eggs (Sw. *varp* neut., cast of a net, draught of fish, hauling-rope, masc. warp in weaving, Da. *varp* neut. hauling-rope) :—OTeut. **warpo-*, f. root **werp-*: **warp-* to throw: see WARP *v.* Branch IV is prob. a new formation on the verb.

Sense 6 may possibly represent an unrecorded sense of ON. *varp*: cf. *-warp* in Eng. place-names in Scandinavian districts.]

I. 1. a. *Weaving.* The threads which are extended lengthwise in the loom, usually twisted harder than the weft or woof, with which these threads are crossed to form the web or piece.

c **725** *Corpus Gloss.* (Hessels) S. 563 *Stamen*: wearp. *a* **1000** *Riddles* (Gr.) xxxv[i]. 5 Wundene me ne beoð wefle, ne ic wearp hafu. **1346** *Little Red Bk. Bristol* (1900) II. 2 Item quod nulla trama que dicitur ab sit in loco panni vbi stamen quod dicitur warp poni debet. **1398** TREVISA *Barth. De P.R.* XVIII. xi. (1495) 766 A spinner stretchyth the warpe wyth wonder craft fro the nether syde to the ouer and drawyth and bryngyth out ayen his threde thwarte ouer fro poynt to poynt. *c* **1420** WYNTOUN *Cron.* v. xiii. 5039 þat þar sulde litil leiff behynde Off warpe or weft to mak hir claythe. **1530** PALSGR. 287/1 Warpe of clothe, *chayne de drap.* **1613** J. MAY *Decl. Estate of Cloth* 26 A common thing it is for the weauer to couer a course warpe with a fine woofe, the warpe beeing spon hard and small, and the woofe soft and round to couer the warpe from sight. **1621** G. SANDYS *Ovid's Met.* VI. (1626) 108 Both spread At once their warps, consisting of fine thred, Ty'd to their beames. **1714** *Fr. Bk. Rates* 189 The Weavers shall be obliged to mount the Warps of their Linen with a sufficient Number of Threads. **1831** G. R. PORTER *Silk Manuf.* 219 The warp is now composed of threads of an equal length. **1833** J. HOLLAND *Manuf. Metal* II. 350 Wire loom... C, the beam or wooden roller, which is turned with a succession of deep grooves, into which the warp is wound, each groove receiving a greater or less number of wires, according to the fineness of the fabric. **1867** MORRIS *Jason* XVII. 501 For she herself within her fair-hung room Had set the warp and watched the fine weft glide Up from the roller. **1893** J. T. TAYLOR *Cotton Weaving* 55 By having the shed fully open before the shuttle enters the shed, the warp is spread and a good cover put on the cloth.

b. *fig.* and in fig. context.

1575 GASCOIGNE *Posies, Compl. Gr. Knt.* 28 O weauer, weauer, work no more, thy warp hath done me wrong. **1583** MELBANCKE *Philotimus* Ee j b, Neither had I this clue of care to worke my warpe vpon. **1679** EVERARD *Discourses* 13 By the whole sincere Warp of this History here related, we may see how rash a thing it is to judge of the Actions of a great Prince. **1849** ROBERTSON *Serm.* Ser. I. xxi. (1866) 348 Sorrow is.. the.. woof which is woven into the warp of life. **1875** JOWETT *Plato* (ed. 2) II. 86 He weaves together the frame of his discourse loosely and which is the warp and which is the woof cannot always be determined. **1896** W. WATSON in *Westm. Gaz.* 2 Jan. 2/3 Still, on Life's loom, the internal warp and weft Woven each hour! **1911** E. C. SELWYN *Oracles N.T.* iii. 85 Throughout his narrative there is the underlying warp of the Old Testament.

2. *Naut.* (See quot.)

1794 *Rigging & Seamanship* I. 179 *Warp*, or more properly *Woof*, is the twine.. woven across the knittles in pointing. *Ibid.*, *Warp of Shrouds*, the first given length, taken from the bolster at the mast-head to the foremost dead-eye.

II. 3. *Naut.* A rope or light hawser attached at one end to some fixed object, used in hauling or in moving a ship from one place to another in a harbour, road, or river; a warping hawser. †Also (at Ilfracombe), a certain apparatus for hauling in vessels: cf. *warp-house* (in 10).

1296 [see *warp-rope* in sense 9]. **1342** *Cust. Acc.* 176/3 (MS.), j cord' pro worp. **1420** in *For. Acc. 3 Hen. VI* K/2 (MS.), ij hauusers de filo Burdegalie pro Frapelines et Warpe inde faciendis ponderis ciij quart. ix. lb. **1485** *Naval Acc. Hen. VII* (1896) 36 Smalle Warpes.. j, Hawsers.. xij. **1550** *Acts Privy Council* (1890) II. 370 Cables, hawsers, warpes, pitche, tarre. **1562** BULLEYN *Bulwark, Bk. Simples* (1579) 27 No Shippe can sayle without Hempe, the sayle clothes,.. yearde lines, warps & Cables can not be made without it. **1615** in W. Foster *Lett. recd. E. Ind. Co.* (1899) III. 201 We have been much troubled about the getting up of the ship-pinnace for lack of men and warps. **1630** *Lex Londinensis* (1680) 212 Likewise to have a Warpe of forty fathom to sheer off and give way if any Ship.. shall chance to drive upon them. **1726** SHELVOCKE *Voy. round World* 19, I.. laid warps to haul into shoal water. **1731** *Act 4 Geo. II* c. 19 There shall be paid by the Master or Commander of every Vessel, belonging to the Port of Ilfordcombe, who shall make use of the Warp, the Sum of Six Shillings and eight Pence. **1840** R. H. DANA *Bef. Mast* xxxvi. 139 [We] took the warp ashore, manned the capstan [etc.]. **1841** B. HALL *Patchwork* II. 3 An entering.. ship is drawn along by a rope, or warp, as it is called. **1899** F. T. BULLEN *Log Sea-waif* 254 Our discharging was soon over, the warps cast off.

transf. **1851** *Harper's Mag.* III. 518 Loads are eased down hillsides by the use of.. a strong warp taking a bight round a tree and hitching-to one yoke oxen.

b. *Trawl-fishing.* A rope attached to a net.

1835 J. COUCH in *3rd Rep. R. Cornw. Polytechn. Soc.* 74 When every thing is favourable, a warp from the end of the stop-sean is handed to the *volyer.* **1854** *Putnam's Monthly Mag.* Apr. 362/2 The fishermen beach the boat at the other side of the bay, carry the warp at that end to the further capstan, and prepare to haul. **1883** R. F. WALSH *Ir. Fisheries* 11 Some use stoppers, which extend from the top line downwards to the warps, but these are not so advantageous, as they tend to huddle the net together.

c. *Whaling.* (See quot.)

1897 F. T. BULLEN *Cruise of 'Cachalot'* 226 The second mate had three fish fast.. two on 'short warps', or pieces of whale-line some eight or ten fathoms long fastened to harpoons, with the other ends running on the main line by means of bowlines round it.

†**4.** ? A strand of a fishing-line. *Obs.*

1496 *Fysshynge wyth Angle* 13 Thenne twyne euery warpe one waye and ylyke moche: and fasten theym in thre clyftes ylyke streyghte.

III. 5. a. A tale of four (occas. three or a couple), esp. used of fish and oysters.

1436 *Nottingham Rec.* II. 156 Item in uno warpe de salt-fyssh. **1509** *Market Harb. Rec.* (1890) 230 In salt Fyshe xcvij warpe and half. **1533** in *Archæologia* XXV. 523 For ij warpe off lynge & a warpe of codd, viij d. **1589** R. HARVEY *Plain Perc.* (1590) 14 In euery trade and occupation, there is a better and a worse, as there is in euery warpe of fish, a great and a lesse. **1623** *Althorp MS.* in Simpkinson *Washingtons* (1860) p. lii, M^{dm} That every two fishes of linge, haberdine, & greenfish is one warpe. **1674** JEAKE *Arith. Surv.* (1696) 66 Yet at Yarmouth they sell 33. Warpe to the Hundred. **1796** *Statist. Acc. Scot.* XVII. 69 A hundred [of oysters], as sold by the fishers, contains 33 warp equal to six score and twelve... Four oysters make a warp. **1816** SCOTT *Antiq.* xxxi, His honour Monkbarns should never want sax warp of oysters in the season. **1894** HALL CAINE *Manxman* v. iii, Every man ate his warp of herring.

†**b.** *nonce-use.* ***a warp of weeks,*** four weeks.

1599 NASHE *Lenten Stuffe* C 1, Those embenched shelues .. where cods & dogfishe swomme (not a warp of weeks fore-running).

IV. 6. a. Alluvial sediment deposited by water; silt. Sometimes artificially introduced over low-lying land, and sometimes occurring as a stratum in soil.

1698 DE LA PRYME *Diary* (Surtees) 184 In digging of the well.. they found.. three yard sand, one foot fine warp. *Ibid.* 314 Y^e muddy waters of ye Don and Idle.. deposited so much silt and warp that they made a great deal of high land on both sides of their streams. **1798** *Trans. Soc. Arts* XVI. 179 Greatly improved by a sediment or mud (commonly called warpe) from the river Dun. **1805** R. W. DICKSON *Pract. Agric.* I. 435 The tide is let in at high water to deposit the warp or enriching substance. **1839** STONEHOUSE *Isle of Axholme* 25 At Althorpe, in sinking wells, eight or ten feet of warp have been dug through, then one or two feet of sand, and then warp again. **1865** W. WHITE *East. Eng.* II. 38 Bog .. converted into corn-fields, by spreading over them the warp or muddy deposit dug from an old river-bed. **1894** *Athenæum* 9 June 744/3 The evidence of their antiquity rests, therefore, upon their geological position under the contorted drift otherwise called 'warp and trail'.

b. A bed or layer of this. See also quot. 1867.

1678 PHILLIPS (ed. 4), *Warp*, a Shole, that beginning near the Buoy of Oar-hedge, comes out of the Swin up the River. **1867** SMYTH *Sailor's Word-bk*, *Warp*,.. land between the sea-banks and the sea. **1870** E. PEACOCK *Ralf Skirl.* II. 87 He would gallop like mad down the warps. **1872** A. C. RAMSAY *Phys. Geol.* (ed. 3) 107 Covered.. with an oozy loam like the warps of the Wash and the Humber.

V. 7. A twist or bending, esp. in wood not properly dried; also the state of being warped or twisted.

1679 EVELYN *Sylva* xxvii. (ed. 3) 143 The Wind shock is a bruise, and shiver throughout the Tree, though not constantly visible, yet leading the Warp from smooth renting, caused by over-powerful Winds, when young. **1668** WILKINS *Real Char.* II. ix. §4. 243 Bending, bow, warp, crooke. **1871** M. COLLINS *Marq. & Merch.* I. ix. 295 A warp in the glass made him look as if he had taken poison. **1878** BOSW. SMITH *Carthage* xviii. 329 Those [ships] which were newly built he laid up for the winter in dry docks.. that their unseasoned timbers might warp or leak in a place where a warp or leak would not be fatal to them. **1894** BLACKMORE *Perlycross* iv. 20 Ah! it is a little on the warp, I fear.

8. a. *fig.* A perversion or perverse inclination of the mind; a mental twist; a wrong bias.

1764 *Mem. G. Psalmanazar* 41 An unchristian warp of the will. **1786** HAN. MORE *Florio* 689 A little warp his taste had gain'd. **1830** *Examiner* 615/1 One of the author's warps was against.. Utilitarians. **1848** DICKENS *Dombey* xlv, Mr. Dombey.. is so prone to pervert even facts to his own view, when he is at all opposed, in consequence of the warp in his mind, that he [etc.]. **1875** RUSKIN *Fors Clav.* liii. 121 All the teaching of God.. is not only mysterious, but, if received with any warp of mind, deceptive. *a* **1878** S. BOWLES in Merriam *Life* (1885) II. 337 (Cent.) Somebody in Berkshire, I fancy, had warped his mind against you, and no mind is more capable of warps than his.

b. *Science Fiction.* = *space warp* s.v. SPACE *sb.*^{1} 20.

1936 *Astounding Stories* June 30 AKKA is the symbol for humanity's secret weapon. Its user, with simple instruments, can destroy any object in the universe—by so altering the warp of space that neither matter nor energy can exist. **1954** *Galaxy* Aug. 80/2 Halfway between Earth and Venus there was a sudden shimmer as the Vegan ship slipped out of warp into normal space.

VI. 9. *attrib.* and *Comb.*, as (sense 1) ***warp edging, line, machinery, -mill, -roller, -scouring*** vbl. sb., ***-spinner, -thread, -twist, -yarn***; (sense 3) ***warp-anchor, -rope***; (sense 6) ***warp-bank, land, loam.***

1699 T. ALLISON *Voy. Archangel* 12, I.. carried both the Kedge Anchor and *Warp Anchor ashore. **1799** A. YOUNG *Agric. Lincoln.* 166 Mr. Webster.. has it [lucerne] drilled; and very luxuriant the first year, on a *warp bank. **1888** *Daily News* 9 July 2/7 Irish crochet trimmings and *warp edgings are dull of sale. **1794** LEATHAM *Agric. E. Riding Yorks.* 11 Along the side of the Ouse and Humber we find a considerable quantity of *warp land. **1879** ASHENHURST *Weaving* 110 The *Warp Line. **1799** A. YOUNG *Agric. Lincoln* 9 Beyond this.. is a very rich *warp loam of various description. **1838** *Civil Engin. & Arch. Jrnl.* I. 390/2 Fabrics produced by *Warp Machinery. **1839** URE *Dict. Arts* 1284 One-sixth of that number of bobbins is usually mounted at once in a *warp mill. **1825** J. NICHOLSON *Oper. Mech.* 411 These rods are at different periods moved towards the *warp-roller B. **1296** *Acc. Exch. K.R.* 5/20 m. 4b (MS.), j. Boulyn, j. *Warperape, iij^{es} Cabule. **1497** *Naval Acc. Hen. VII* (1896) 115 Hawser cald warp rope. **1844** G. DODD *Textile Manuf.* iv. 130 A process of '*warp-scouring' in which the warp, after being washed, is squeezed between rollers. **1634** *Canterb. Marriage Licences* (MS.), Robert Wood of Salehurst in Sussex, *warpe spinner. **1831–3** P. BARLOW *Manuf.* in *Encycl. Metrop.* (1845) VIII. 741 The *warp thread proceeding from the lower roller. **1851** *Art Jrnl. Illustr. Catal.* p. vi**, The long threads are called the *warp-twist, or organzine. **1835** URE *Philos. Manuf.* 110 This mill spins *warp yarn by throstles, weft yarn by mules.

10. Special comb.: †**warp-bar,** some kind of appendage to a loom; **warp-beam,** the roller on which the warp is wound and from which it is drawn as the weaving proceeds; **warp-dresser** (*a*) = WARPER 2; (*b*) a machine for sizing yarns for the loom (Knight); †**warp-faced** *a.*, having distorted features; **warp-farmer,** a farmer who uses 'warp' on his land; **warp-frame** = *warp-machine*; †**warp-house,** at Ilfracombe, the building containing the apparatus for hauling vessels; **warp-lace,** a kind of lace having threads so placed as to resemble the warp of a fabric; also *attrib.*; **warp-machine,** a lace-making machine having a thread for each needle employed (Knight); **warp-net frame** = prec.; **warp print** = *shadow print* s.v. SHADOW *sb.* 16; hence **warp-printed** *a.*; **warp-river,** a river depositing 'warp'; **warp-slat** = SLAT *sb.*^{1} 5 a; **warp-stitch** (see quot.); **warp-wire,** one of the lengthwise wires in a wire-loom.

1538 *Nottingham Rec.* III. 200 Unum wollenlome cum ryngrathes, *warpbarres et spoyle whele. **1831–3** P. BARLOW *Manuf.* in *Encycl. Metrop.* (1845) VIII. 734, B is the *warp beam, or that on which the warp is first wound. **1851** in *Inquiry, Yorks. Deaf & Dumb* (1870) 45 William Sutton, *warp-dresser. **1611** CORYAT *Crudities* 232 A weather beaten *warp-faced fellow. **1799** A. YOUNG *Agric. Lincoln* 278 A considerable *warp farmer told me, that the stiffer warp was the best. **1831–3** P. BARLOW *Manuf.* in *Encycl. Metrop.* (1845) VIII. 740 The *warp frame. **1731** *Act 4 Geo. II* c. 19 Preamble, The Warp and *Warp-house by long Usage gone to Decay. **1742** *De Foe's Tour Gt. Brit.* (ed. 3) II. 13 The Warp-house, Light-house, Pilot-boats, and Taw-boats belonging to the Port [Ilfracombe]. **1812** *Ann. Reg., Chron.* 30 Others.. demolished five *warp-lace frames. **1832** BABBAGE *Econ. Manuf.* xv. (ed. 3) 138 Another similar article, called 'warp lace'. **1875** KNIGHT *Dict. Mech., Warp-frame* or **Warp-net Frame.* **1916** *Daily Colonist* (Victoria, B.C.) 23 July 8/7 This offering comprises Fancy Ribbons in *warp-print, Dresden, Pompadour and novelty stripe and plain effects. **1968** J. IRONSIDE *Fashion Alphabet* 246 *Shadow* or *Warp print.* The warp yarns are printed with the design before weaving, giving a shadowy print effect. **1957** *Times* 16 Sept. 11/1 The short dress.. is in white satin with a small *warp-printed design in black. **1799** A. YOUNG *Agric. Lincoln* 277 No floods in the countries washed by the *warp rivers bring it [the muddy water]. **1907** C. HILL-TOUT *Brit. N. Amer., Far West* vi. 115 To give the bottom [of the basket] the ovaloid form, which most have, the *warp-slats are trimmed to the desired shape before the weft strand is woven into them. **1882** CAULFEILD & SAWARD *Dict. Needlework* 195 **Warp Stitch*, an Embroidery Stitch used when threads are drawn away from the material to form the pattern. Warp stitch consists of drawing away the threads that form the weft, or cross the material, and leaving the warp or lengthways threads. **1833** J. HOLLAND *Manuf. Metal* II. 351 The *warp-wires being made to change positions by means of the treadle.

†**warp**, *sb.*[2] *Thieves' Cant. Obs.* (See quots.)
1591 GREENE *2nd Pt. Conny-catching* Wks. (Grosart) X. 86 In blacke Art [picking of lockes]. He that hooks, the Comber [*read* Courber *as on* p. 122] He that watcheth, the Warpe. *Ibid.* 122 When he..spyes any fat snappings worth the Curbing, then streight he [the Courber] sets the Warp to watch, who hath a long cloak to couer whatsoeuer he gets. *Ibid.* 123.

warp (wɔːp), *v.* Pa. t. and pa. pple. **warped** (wɔːpt). Forms: 1 **weorpan, wurpan, wyrpan,** 2–3 **werpen,** (*Orm.* **werrpenn**), 3 **weorpen, wearpe, worpe(n,** 3–4 **warpen,** 3–6 **werp(e,** 5 **warpyn, -on,** 4–6 *Sc.* **varp,** 7 *Sc.* **worp,** 3–7 **warpe,** 4– **warp.** *Pa. t. sing.* 1 **wearp,** 1 *Northumb.*, 2–4 **warp,** (*Orm.* **warrp**), 3 **weorp,** 3–4 **werp,** 4–5 **warpe;** *pl.* 1 **wurpon,** *Northumb.* **worpon, -un,** 3 **wurpen, worpen, weorpen.** *Pa. pple.* 1, 3–5 **worpen,** 3 **(i)worpe,** *Orm.* **worrpenn,** 6 *Sc.* **warp.** Also *pa. t.* and *pa. pple.* 4–6 **war-, werpid, -it, -et,** 4– **warped.** [A Com. Teut. str. vb.: OE. *weorpan* (*wearp, wurpon, worpen*) corresponds to OFris. *werpa* (*worp, wurpon, ewurpen*), OS. *werpan* (*warp, wurpun, worpan*), Du. *werpen* (*wierp, worpen*), OHG. *werfan* (*warf, wurfun, worfen*), MHG., mod.G. *werfen* (*warf, wurfen, geworfen*), ON. *verpa* (*varp, urpu, orpenn*), Sw. *verpa*, Da. *verpe*, Goth. *waírpan* (*warp, waurpum, waurpans*); f. OTeut. root *werp- (*warp-, wurp-*):—pre-Teut. *werb-; the root is not found outside Teut.
The strong conjugation did not survive in Eng. later than the 15th c.]

I. To cast, throw.

†**1. a.** *trans.* To project through space; to cast, throw, fling. *Obs.*
c **888** ÆLFRED *Boeth.* vii. §3 Ða hine mon on þæt fyr wearp þa alysde ic hine mid heofonlicon rene. *c* **1000** *Ags. Gosp.* Matt. vii. 6 Ðe ne wurpen eowre meregrotu toforan eowrum swinum. *c* **1200** ORMIN 10488 & werrpenn all þe chaff anan, Inntill þe fir to bærnenn. *c* **1205** LAY. 17430 Al swa feor swa a mon mihte werpen ænne stan. *a* **1225** *Ancr. R.* 404 Mon worpeð Grickischs fur upon his fomen. *c* **1250** *Owl & N.* 768 Mid liste me may walles felle & werpe [*v.r.* worpe] of horse knyhtes snelle. *c* **1300** *Havelok* 1061 He warp þe ston Ouer þe laddes euerilkon. *c* **1375** *Sc. Leg. Saints* ii. (*Paul*) 344 Sanct paulis hed eftir his discese In a depe vewar warpit was. *c* **1425** WYNTOUN *Cron.* VIII. 4743 Þe wardane gert his wrichtis syne Set vp richt stoutly ane ingyne, And warpit til þe toure a stan. **1513** DOUGLAS *Æneis* I. Prol. 280 And bot my buik be fundin worth sic thre, Quhen it is red, do warp it in the se.

†**b.** with adv., as *down, up, out, away. Obs.*
c **1000** *Ags. Gosp.* Matt. xvii. 27 Gang to þære sæ, and wurp þinne angel ut [Vulg. *mitte hamum*]. *c* **1200** ORMIN 16040 Þurrh þatt he warrp ut i þe flor þe sillferr & te bordess. *c* **1205** LAY. 5083 Awei he warp his gode breond. *c* **1330** R. BRUNNE *Chron. Wace* (Rolls) 15875 His staf ful sleyly vp he warp. **1375** BARBOUR *Bruce* III. 642 He had bene tane but dout, Na war it that he warpyt owt All that he had, him lycht to ma. *c* **1400** *Destr. Troy* 13412 He..warpet ouer-burde Mikill riches & relikes reft fro the toune.

†**c.** To cast (lots). *Obs.*
c **1000** *Ags. Gosp.* Matt. xxvii. 35 Hiȝ todældon hys reaf, and wurpon hlot þær-ofer [Vulg. *sortem mittentes*]. *c* **1205** LAY. 15498 Þe king..bad heom leoten werpen.

†**2.** To sprinkle, scatter (something) *on* (a surface). Also with *out*: To cause to spirt; to emit, shoot forth. *Obs.*
c **1000** *Sax. Leechd.* II. 240 Dweorȝe dwostlan weorp on weallende wæter. *c* **1175** *Lamb. Hom.* 41 Seodðan he him sceaude an ouen on berninde fure he warp ut of him seofe leies. *Ibid.* 129 Þurh þisse tacne Moyses werp ut þet welle weter of þan herda flinte. *c* **1200** *Trin. Coll. Hom.* 161 Hie wenden þe eorðe and wurpen god sed þaronne. *c* **1205** LAY. 4518 Me warp on his nebbe cold welle watere. *a* **1225** *Ancr. R.* 246 Ase ofte ase þe ueond assaileð ouwer castel..worpeð ut uppon him schaldinde teares.

†**3. a.** With *up, open, wide, on brede*: To open (a gate) violently or suddenly, fling open. With *to*: To shut, slam. *Obs.*
c **1000** ÆLFRIC *Saints' Lives* iii. 347 Þa com færlice mycel wynd and wearp upp þa duru. *a* **1400–50** *Wars Alex.* 1526 Þus atired he þe toune & titely þar-eftir On ilka way wid open werped he þe ȝatis. *Ibid.* 2142 Ȝa, werpis þam [the gates] vp..& wide open settis. *c* **1400** *Destr. Troy* 10462 Þai wan in wightly, warpit to þe yates, Barrit hom full bigly with boltes of yerne. *Ibid.* 11924 When the buernes of the burgh were broght vpon slepe, He warpit vp a wicket. **1513** DOUGLAS *Æneis* X. i. 1 On breid, or this, was warp and mayd patent The hevynly hald of God omnipotent. *Ibid.* XII. x. 80 Sum bad..Warp vp the portis, and wide the ȝettis cast To the Troianis.

†**b.** *intr.* Of a door: To open (*wide*, etc.).
a **1375** *Joseph Arim.* 257 He bad him lifte vp and þe lide warpes. **1513** DOUGLAS *Æneis* VI. i. 118 Bot thow do, thir gret durris..sall nevir warp on breid. *Ibid.* VI. ii. 2 The hundreth gret durris..At thair awin willis warpit wyde.

†**4.** *trans.* To put (a garment) *on* or *off* hastily.
13.. *Gaw. & Gr. Knt.* 2025 Whyle þe wlonkest wedes he warp on hym-seluen. ?*a* **1400** *Morte Arth.* 901 Sir Arthure ..Wente to hys wardrope, and warpe of hys wedez. *a* **1400** *Pistill of Susan* 124 Þe wyf werp of hir wedes vn-werde.

†**5. a.** To throw down, overthrow. Usually with adv., as *down, under, to ground. Obs.*
c **1175** *Lamb. Hom.* 7 Þu warpest þene alde feont. *c* **1200** ORMIN 3575 Forr Crist wass strang wiþþ hannd inoh To werrpenn dun þe deofell. *c* **1205** LAY. 25889 Þæs bures dure he warp adun þat heo to-barst a uiuen. *Ibid.* 28729 Mine wiðer-iwinnen, weorpeð heom to grunden. *c* **1250** *Gen. & Ex.* 2640 Ðe child it warp dun to de [*read* ðe] grund. *c* **1400** *Destr. Troy* 1297 The Troiens..Wondid of þe wightist, warpide hom vnder. *c* **1400** *Laud Troy Bk.* 6683 We schal of hem to grounde warpe With swordes bryght and speres scharpe.

†**b.** Of wind: To toss or drive (a ship) violently about. *Obs.*
13.. *E.E. Allit. P.* B. 444 As þat lyftande lome luged aboute, Where þe wynde & þe weder warpen hit wolde.

†**c.** ? To swing round, whirl. *Obs.*
1513 DOUGLAS *Æneis* XI. xi. 103 And oft about hyr hed ..[she] Wald warp the stringis of the stowt staf slyng.

†**6.** *fig.* **a.** To drive out, expel, reject, renounce; usually with *out, away*. Also, to trample (under foot). *Obs.*
c **1000** *Ags. Gosp.* John vi. 37 Ic ne weorpe ut [Vulg. *non eiciam foras*] þone þe to me cymð. *a* **1225** *Ancr. R.* 40 Gif me worpen mid him al þe world under vet. *Ibid.* 230 Þeo deoflen þet ure Louerd werp ut of one monne. *Ibid.* 356 Worp awei urom me alle mine gultes. *a* **1225** *Leg. Kath.* 829 Sone se ich awei warp ower witlese lei. *c* **1230** *Hali Meid.* 5 Þeos þohtes warp ut of þin heorte. *a* **1300** *Cursor M.* 24247 Nu comforth þe..And werp awai þi wepe.

†**b.** To plunge (a person) suddenly or roughly (*into* prison, distress, etc.); to put *to* death. *Obs.*
c **1175** *Lamb. Hom.* 143 Þe sunfulle Men..sculen beon iwarpen ine eche pine. *c* **1200** ORMIN 19608 He let bindenn himm,..& i cwarrterrne werrpenn. *c* **1400** *Destr. Troy* 10973 Mony worthy þai woundit, & warpit to dethe. *c* **1460** *Towneley Myst.* xxiii. 413 Thou art warpyd all in wo. *c* **1590** J. STEWART *Poems* (S.T.S.) II. 17 Dreid of dainger varps hir in ane trans.

†**7. a.** *intr.* To go hastily, fling *away*. Of wind: To rise *up*. *Obs.*
?*a* **1400** *Morte Arth.* 2746, I rede ȝe..warpes wylily awaye. *a* **1400–50** *Wars Alex.* 557 Wild wedirs vp werpe & þe wynd ryse.

b. *Sc.* Of bees: To swarm. Cf. CAST *v.* 22.
a **1824** in Mactaggart *Gallovid. Encycl.* 94 The hive which warped owre the fell.

†**8.** *trans.* With inversion of const.: To strike, hit, assail *with* (a missile). Also, to besprinkle (with a liquid). *Obs.*
Beowulf 2791 He hine eft ongon wæteres weorpan. *c* **888** ÆLFRED *Boeth.* xvi. §2 Þa forceaw he his tungan & wearp hine mid ðære tungan on þæt neb foran. *c* **1205** LAY. 29562 Heo..wurpen hine mid banen. *a* **1250** *Owl & Night.* 1121 Ȝif þu art iworpe oþer ischote.

†**9.** *transf.* and *fig.* In various uses: To thrust (one's hand) *forth*; to lay (hands) *on*; to cast (one's head) *down*; to strike (a stroke). *Obs.*
a **1225** *St. Marher.* 3 As theos cnihtes walden warpen honden on hire ha bigon to cleopien ant callen þus to criste. *a* **1225** *Ancr. R.* 88 [He] Weorpeð adun þet heaueð. *Ibid.* 96 Ȝif eni wurðeð so wod..þet he worpe his hond forð touward þe þurl cloð. *c* **1375** *Sc. Leg. Saints* xxviii. 267 Þat þai suld tak þat maydin schen,..and strakis fel til hyre let warpe.

10. †**a.** To cast, shed (horns). *Obs.*
c **1220** *Bestiary* 325 in *O.E. Misc.* 11 He werpeð er hise hornes in wude er in ðornes.

†**b.** To lose (the natural hue). *Obs.*
c **1200** *Trin. Coll. Hom.* 183 Among þat þe sowle witeð, þe licame worpeð hewe.

†**11. a.** To utter, pronounce (a word, speech); to utter (a cry), heave (a sigh). Also with *out*. Also *absol.*, to talk, speak (*of*). *Obs.*
a **1225** *Ancr. R.* 306 Mid tisse schulen þe uorlorene worpen a swuch ȝeor þet heouene & eorðe muwen beoðe grisliche agrisen. *a* **1225** *Leg. Kath.* 1325 Þet we ne cunnen ..warpen na word aȝein. *a* **1225** *Juliana* 21 He..weorp a sic as a wiht þat sare were iwundet. **13..** *E.E. Allit. P.* A. 879 A note ful nwe I herde hem warpe. **13..** *Gaw. & Gr. Knt.* 2253, I schal stonde stylle, & warp þe no wernyng, to worch as þe lykez. *c* **1400** *Destr. Troy* 2683 Ho..Warpet out wordes wonder to here. *c* **1420** WYNTOUN *Cron.* lxxxiv. 1707 (Wemyss) Quhen þis wif had warpit þus Off this abbot Eugenyus. **1513** DOUGLAS *Æneis* II. xi. 23 Scarslie the auld thir wordis hed warpit out. *Ibid.* V. viii. 116 And he abufe hym werpis sic sawis.

†**b.** To cast (one's eyes) *on* or *upon* (an object).
c **1200** ORMIN 12758 Crist warrp eȝhe upponn Symon. *a* **1225** *Ancr. R.* 52 Hwoso heuede iseid to Eue þeo heo werp hire eien þerone, A! wend te awei; þu worpest eien o þi deað.

12. *dial.* **a.** To lay (eggs). Also *absol.* [So ON. *verpa.*]
a **1340** HAMPOLE *Psalter* xc. 13 Þe snake werpis and þe tade nuryssis þe eg, and þarof is broght forth þe basilyske. **1483** *Cath. Angl.* 409/1 To Warpe as byrdis dose, *jncubare, ponere oua.* **1570** LEVINS *Manip.* 33/6 To warp an egge, *ouum ponere.* **1787** GROSE *Prov. Gloss.*, *Warp*, to lay eggs. A hen warps or warys. N. **1825** BROCKETT *N.C. Words* s.v., A hen is said to warp when she lays.

b. To bring forth (young) naturally. *rare.* (In quot. *absol.*)
1738 G. SMITH *Cur. Relat.* II. 453 They [beavers] don't warp in their Houses, but in Hollows dug under Ground.

c. Of a ewe, cow, etc.: To bring forth (young), prematurely; to cast, slip, drop. Also *absol.*
a **1722** LISLE *Husb.* (1757) 283 A cow, that..warps her calf three months before her time. *Ibid.* 310 If the ewes warped, they turned them out to the rams again. **1813** RUDGE *Agric. Glouc.* 297 Cows are liable to slip or warp their calves. **1903** *Athenæum* 7 Mar. 307/3 Never had so many ewes been known to warp.

II. To bend, twist aside.

13. To bend, curve, or twist (an object) out of shape; *spec.* to curve (timber) by the application of steam; also, to distort, contort (the body or a limb, the features).
a **1400–50** *Wars Alex.* 798 Al to-wraiste þai þar wode & werpis in-sondire. *c* **1440** *Promp. Parv.* 517/1 Warpyn', or make wronge, *curvo.* **1593** NASHE *Christ's T.* P 1 b, Age will ..warpe our backs. **1648** HERRICK *Hesp.*, *Paneg. Sir L. Pemberton* 9 Laden spits, warp't with large Ribbs of Beefe. **1665** MANLEY *Grotius' Low C. Wars* 419 As in some places, the violence of Heat; so in other, the extremity of Cold, hath often warped Nature, and made it become deformed. **1742** JARVIS *2nd Pt. Quixote* III. x. II. 219 If perchance the rod of justice be warped a little. **1799** *Naval Chron.* I. 288 The method was introduced of warping planks to the timbers by the means of steam. **1835** W. IRVING *Tour Prairies* xxvii. 244 Baring his left arm, he showed it warped and contracted by a former attack of rheumatism. **1847** C. BRONTË *Jane Eyre* xx, A singularly marked expression of disgust, horror, hatred, warped his countenance almost to distortion. **1849** MISS MULOCK *Ogilvies* xxi, Trying to bend it straight, as he would a tree which wrong culture had warped aside. **1876** MISS BROUGHTON *Joan* I. i, A book with its back still warm and warped from having been held over the fire. **1896** CONAN DOYLE *Rodney Stone* xxi, Age had warped and cracked the boards.
fig. **1662** PETTY *Taxes & Contrib.* 9, I descend no lower, wishing onely that there might be an universal Reformation of what length of time hath warped awry.

14. a. *intr.* To become bent, twisted, or uneven, by shrinkage or contraction. Said esp. of timber. (Cf. CAST *v.* 53.)
c **1440** *Promp. Parv.* 517/1 Warpyn', or wex wronge or avelonge, as vesselle, *oblongo.* **1530** PALSGR. 772/1, I warpe, as bordes do, whan they croke for want of good seasonnyng. **1577** B. GOOGE *Heresbach's Husb.* II. 106 The Elme..is meete for the cheekes and postes of Gates,..for it wyll not bowe, nor warpe. **1657** TRAPP *Comm. Esther* ii. 2 Green wood is ever shrinking and warping. **1783** JUSTAMOND tr. *Raynal's Hist. Indies* III. 159 If the pieces..are thicker..on one side than another,..they will warp to that side. **1815** J. SMITH *Panorama Sci. & Art* I. 37 Cast iron, when annealed, is less liable to warp by a subsequent partial exposure to moderate degrees of heat. **1826** SCOTT *Woodstock* ii, Old wood seldom warps in the wetting. **1881** YOUNG *Every Man his own Mechanic* §46. 23 Black Ebony..will not warp readily.

b. *fig.*, or in fig. context. (Cf. 19.)
1599 MARSTON *Antonio's Rev.* V. vi, You are well seasond props, And will not warpe, or leane to either part. **1600** SHAKS. *A.Y.L.* III. iii. 90 This fellow wil but ioyne you together, as they ioyne Wainscot, then one of you wil proue a shrunke pannell, and like greene timber, warpe, warpe. **1682** FLAVEL *Fear* 44 It would make them warp and bend under such temptations. **1690** LOCKE *Hum. Und.* I. iii. §20 It being all one, to have no Rule, and one that will warp any way. **1736** LEDIARD *Life Marlborough* I. 58 To set that Law streight again, which he had made to warp to his Prince's Humour. **1874** C. E. NORTON *Lett.* (1913) II. 33, I, too, warp and crack in this dry, clear atmosphere.

15. a. *trans.* To contract, cause to shrink or shrivel, corrugate. *rare.*
1600 SHAKS. *A.Y.L.* II. vii. 187 Freize, freize, thou bitter skie..Though thou the waters warpe, thy sting is not so sharpe, as freind remembred not. **1875** B. TAYLOR *Faust* I. ii. 46 Then from the East they come, to dry and warp Your lungs.

b. *intr.* To shrink or shrivel, become contracted or wrinkled. Also *fig. rare.*
1579 GOSSON *Sch. Abuse* (Arb.) 61 You must keepe your sweete faces from scorching in the sun, chapping in the winde, and warping with the weather. **1611** SHAKS. *Wint. T.* I. ii. 365 Me thinkes My fauor here begins to warpe. **1696** TUTCHIN *Pindarick Ode* ii. 10 The Fames of Shakespear and of Ben Must warp, before my nobler fire To their regardless Tombs retire.

16. *trans.* (*fig.*) To pervert, distort (the mind, judgement, principles, etc.); to give a 'twist' or bias to; to turn (*aside*) from rectitude or the straight path.
1599 B. JONSON *Cynthia's Rev.* IV. i. (1601) G 1 b, Me thinkes thy seruant Hedon is nothing so obsequious to thee, as he was wont to be: I know not how, Hee's growne out of his Garbe a-late, hee's warp't. **1700** DRYDEN *Sigism. & Guisc.* 402 Nor Folly warp'd my Mind, Nor the frail Texture of the Female Kind Betray'd my Vertue. **1710** ADDISON *Whig-Exam.* No. 4 ¶4, I have no private considerations to warp me in this controversy. **1718** DK. BUCKHM. *Let. to Pope* Wks. 1723 II. 289 Suffering their judgments to be a little warped (if I may use that expression) by the heat of their eager inclinations. **1725** WATTS *Logic* II. iv, Watch against every Temptation that might bribe your Judgment, or warp it aside from Truth. **1852** SMEDLEY *L. Arundel* xxvii. 205 These two men, each warped and hardened differently..by the world's evil influence. **1879** M. ARNOLD *Fr. Crit. Milton, Mixed Ess.* 252 Johnson's mind..was at many points bounded, at many points warped. **1884** A. R. PENNINGTON *Wiclif* Pref. p. ix, He often allows his prejudice against Wiclif to warp his judgment. **1919** C. GORING *Eng. Convict* i. 11 The science of criminology..has been..warped by its subjection to all sorts of superstitious and conventional dogmas.

b. Const. *from, out of*; *to, into.*
1650 B. *Discolliminium* 17 He that is warp'd in his Divinity, will never be at rest till he hath wrap'd [? *read* warp'd] his Policy to it. **1685** DRYDEN *Threnod. August.* 322 Not Faction,..Not Foreign or Domestick Treachery, Could Warp thy Soul to their Unjust Decree. *a* **1711** KEN *Poet. Wks.* (1868) 272 My treacherous heart I fear, Warp'd to the world. **1758–65** GOLDSM. *Ess.*, *Taste* (Globe) 315/2 By the present mode of education we are forcibly warped from the bias of nature. **1768–74** TUCKER *Lt. Nat.* (1834) II. 628 There is such perpetual danger from all quarters of having the moral sense warped to a false direction. **1796** BP. WATSON *Apol. Bible* 379 Some men have been warped to infidelity by viciousness of life. **1842** TENNYSON *Locksley Hall* 60 Cursed be the social lies that warp us from the living truth! **1853** DICKENS *Bleak Ho.* xxxv, Jarndyce and Jarndyce has warped him out of himself, and perverted me in his eyes. **1857** RUSKIN *Pol. Econ. Art* ii. §97 The bribe of wealth and honour warps him from his honest labour into efforts to attract attention. **1882** 'OUIDA' *In Maremma* viii, This narrowness of the peasant mind which..demagogues ..warp to their own selfish purpose and profits.

17. a. To distort, wrest, misinterpret, give a false colouring to (a fact, account, etc.). Const. *from, to, into.*
1717 BENTLEY *Serm. bef. K. Geo.* 19 Those that *interpret* all actions of their Governors; that warp the most innocent

Occurrences to Censure and Calumny. **1741** WATTS *Improv. Mind* I. viii, In matters of dispute, take heed of warping the sense of the..writer to your own opinion. **1775** DE LOLME *Const. Eng.* I. x. (1784) 102 Writs, being warped from their actual meaning. **1780** COWPER *Progr. Err.* 437 The worst is—Scripture warp'd from its intent. **1816** SCOTT *Old Mort.* xxvii, While..you, Mr Poundtext, were warping the Scriptures into Erastianism. **1830** D'ISRAELI *Chas. I*, III. x. 218 Probably..both [accounts] are warped by the opposite feelings of the writers. **1857** RUSKIN *Pol. Econ. Art* §8 We have warped the word 'economy' in our English language into a meaning which it has no business whatever to bear. *a* **1872** MAURICE *Friendship Bks.* xiii. (1874) 381 A..spirit which would not suffer us to pervert or warp any documents to suit a purpose of ours.

b. *intr.* Of a statement: To become distorted.
1914 *Blackw. Mag.* July 48/2 Whether all this be true I cannot tell, but as I guess it is an old report that has warped in wandering.

18. a. *trans.* To turn aside or divert (a moving body) from its path or orbit. Also, to deflect, change the direction of (one's journey). *rare.*
1725 POPE *Odyss.* IV. 103 Then [I] warp my voyage on the southern gales. **1814** CARY *Dante, Parad.* I. 130 As from a cloud the fire is seen to fall, From its original impulse warp'd, to earth. **1837** EMERSON *Amer. Schol.* Wks. (Bohn) II. 178, I had better never see a book, than to be warped by its attraction clean out of my own orbit.

b. *intr.* To turn or incline in a (specified) direction. *rare.*
1674 N. FAIRFAX *Bulk & Selv.* 67 There being no more reason why it [an arrow] should warp to the right hand than to the left, why this way rather than that, it must needs stir no way. **1684–94** tr. *Plutarch's Mor.* (1718) III. 16 But as she [the Moon] warps back again to meet her Illustrious Mate, the nearer she makes her approach, the more she is eclipsed until no longer seen.

c. *Science Fiction.* To travel through space by way of a space warp.
1946 F. BROWN in *Astounding Sci. Fiction* May 129/1 The *Ark*..would warp through space to a point a safe distance outside the Argyle I-II system and come in on rocket power. **1957** T. STURGEON *Thunder & Roses* 117 Earth was ready for him when he warped in.

†**19.** *fig.* (Cf. 14b, 16.) To receive a 'twist' or bias, which influences one's judgement or sentiments; to turn from the straight path; to deviate, swerve, go astray. Const. *from. Obs.*
1603 SHAKS. *Meas. for M.* I. i. 15 There is our Commission, From which, we would not haue you warpe. **1642** D. ROGERS *Naaman* 550 If we feele..that our hearts warpe from Gods commands. **1642** MILTON *Apol. Smect.* 34 He fals off again warping and warping till he come to contradict himselfe in diameter. **1681** BAXTER *Apol. Nonconf. Min.* Pref. p. ii, Learned men, when they warp and err. **1738** NEAL *Hist. Purit.* IV. 211 Any single officer that should hereafter warp from his obedience. **1748** HARTLEY *Observ. Man* I. iii. §5. 384 A pleasurable or painful State of the Stomach or Brain, Joy or Grief, will make all the Thoughts warp their own way, little or much. **1791** BURKE *Th. French Aff.* Wks. 1842 I. 574 Amongst them there are no leaders possessed of an influence for any other purpose but that of maintaining the present state of things. The moment they are seen to warp, they are reduced to nothing. *a* **1817** T. DWIGHT *Trav.* (1822) IV. 314 He [Edwards] never warped from the path of common sense.

†**b.** To be biassed, incline, lean, be drawn or attracted (*to, towards*). Also, to bend, submit, yield (*to*); to submit *to do* something. *Obs.*
a **1592** GREENE *Jas. IV*, I. 654, I can no more; my patience will not warpe To see these flatterers how they scorne and Carpe. **1624** GEE *Foot out of Snare* xi. 71 A Gentlewoman..that was well inclining and warping toward the Popish pale. **1643** *Plain English* 17 How miserably will you find the..Clergie wraping [*read* warping] to the prevailing party. *a* **1661** FULLER *Worthies, Lond.* (1662) 222 Others more truly tax him [Chamnee], for warping to the Will of King Henry the eighth, not so much to decline his own death, as to preserve his Covent from destruction. *a* **1677** BARROW *Serm.* Wks. 1716 II. 27 Men generally do sute their opinions to their inclinations; warping to that side where their interest doth lie. **1772** FLETCHER *Logica Genev.* 34 Our Church far from warping to Crispianity strongly inforces St. James's undefiled religion.

III. To weave, twine.

20. *trans.* †**a.** To weave (a web). *Obs.* **b.** To arrange (threads, yarn) so as to form a warp; to wind on a warp-beam. Also *absol.*
c **1220** *Bestiary* 467 in *O.E. Misc.* 15 Ðe spinnere..werpeð ðus hire web, and weueð on hire wise. *c* **1340** *Nominale* (Skeat) 336 *Homme poet teil perer.* M[an] may a webbe warpe. *c* **1430** *Pilgr. Lyf Manhode* II. cxxiii. (1869) 121 It is furred with fox skynnes in lengthe and in brede, al be it with oute wouen maad, and worpen of the wulle of white sheep. *c* **1440** *Promp. Parv.* 517/1 Warpon', as webstarys, *stamino, licio.* **1483** *Cath. Angl.* 409/1 To Warpe A web, *protelare.* **1540** HYRDE tr. *Vives' Instr. Chr. Wom.* I. iii. (1541) 3 b, To spinne, to warpe, or els wynd spindels in a case for to throw wofe of. **1556** PHAER *Æneid* IV. (1558) Kj, Her self the web had wrought, & warpyd fine with wreath of gold. **1598** FLORIO, *Ordire*, to warpe or lay as weauers do their webbs before it be wouen. **1662** *Burgh Rec. Stirling* (1887) 240 The saids proveist, baillies and councill..discharges them..from litting any plaid yairn, and from worping and working any that shall not be of the lenth and breidth abone writtin. **1788** BURNS '*My heart was ance*' ii, My mither sent me to the town, To warp a plaiden wab. **1844** G. DODD *Textile Manuf.* i. 42 The yarn is dressed, beamed, and warped by steam-power. **1879** ASHENHURST *Weaving* 50 The yarn..may be warped direct from the cop or bobbin upon which it has been spun.

†**c.** *fig.* To weave, contrive, devise. Also with *up*, and *absol.*
1387 TREVISA *Higden* (Rolls) V. 365 He answerde..þat he wolde warpe suche a webbe to the emperise [*talem se telam Augustae orditurum*], þat sche schulde nevere have it of to here lyves ende. *c* **1430** *Pilgr. Lyf Manhode* IV. viii. (1869) 179 And alwey he werpeth temptaciouns and breideth þem, and weueth hem. **1549–62** STERNHOLD & HOPKINS *Ps.* lii. 2 Why doth thy minde yet still deuise, such wicked wiles to warpe? **1577** HELLOWES *Gueuara's Chron.* 393, I haue warpt such a webb, as thou neither knowest to vnframe, or mayst cut off when it is finished. **1604** E. HAKE in Farr *S.P. Jas. I* (1847) 256 All these are but the loome That warpeth up my death. **1611** SPEED *Hist. Gt. Brit.* IX. xxiv. §22 Like a wise man, that meant to warpe no more then he could well weaue. **1616** S. S. *Honest Lawyer* III. E 4, We'll trie what mischeefes he can warpe. **1652** URQUHART *Jewel* Wks. (1834) 198 Before the contexture of another universal language [than mine] can be warped. **1785** BURNS *2nd Ep. J. Lapraik* viii, Ne'er mind how Fortune waft an' warp.

21. a. *Rope-making.* To stretch (yarn) into lengths to be tarred.
1815 *Falconer's Dict. Marine* (ed. Burney), To Warp Yarn, in rope-making, is to stretch the yarns, previous to their being tarred, all to one given length. **1846** G. DODD *Brit. Manuf.* Ser. VI. 197 The reels of yarn are first 'warped' into a 'haul', that is, the yarns are unwound from the reel, stretched out straight and parallel, and assembled together.

b. To weave, twine (a willow-basket). *dial.*
1806 J. GRAHAME *Birds Scot.* I. 67 He..warps the skep with willow rind.

c. To lace together (the ends of a seine). *dial.*
1835 J. COUCH in *3rd Rep. R. Cornw. Polytechn. Soc.* 74 While the larger boats are engaged in warping the ends together.

†**22.** To twist, entwine, insert (something *into* something else). Also *fig.*; also, to unite or combine *with. Obs.*
1803 W. TAYLOR in *Ann. Rev.* I. 256 The public papers and fragments of oratory warped into its text, are selected with taste. **1814** SCOTT *Wav.* xvi, A scathed tree, which had warped its twisted roots into the fissures of the rock. **1821** —— *Kenilw.* xxii, I care not for all those strings of pearl, which you fret me by warping into my tresses. **1822** A. RANKEN *Hist. France* IX. 13 With this proposal..was warped..the condition, that the regent, who entertained strong prejudices against the Jesuits, should become their friend and protector.

23. *Angling.* To fasten (the materials of an artificial fly) to the hook. With adv., as *on, in, down, up.*
1676 COTTON *Angler* II. v. 40 Warp them so down, as to stand, and slope towards the bend of the hook, and having warpt up to the end of the shanck [etc.]. *Ibid.* II. viii. 73 When you warp on your dubbing. *Ibid.* II. viii. 78 Some red warpt in for the Tagg of his tail. **1836** RONALDS *Fly-Fisher's Entom.* 29 Warp the remnant round the shank. **1867** F. FRANCIS *Bk. Angling* xiii. (1880) 465 The silk must be warped up from the tail to required spot. *Ibid.* 466 When the body is being warped on.

†**24.** To surround, involve, infold *in, with. Obs.*
But perhaps a metathetic form of WRAP.
14.. *Medical MS.* in *Anglia* XIX. 79 ȝif on hyde hymself in a busch þer-of, or ellys he be warpyd weel in his lewys & his braunchys, no thonder nor leuene schall hym towchyn. **1513** DOUGLAS *Æneis* I. iii. 33 Lyke as ane wall with sand warpit about. *Ibid.* v. xiii. 24 His awin heid warpit with a snod olive.

IV. To tow; to move gradually forward.

25. *Naut.* To move (a ship) along by hauling on a rope or 'warp'. Also with adv., as *out, off, in, round.*
1513 [see WARPING *vbl. sb.* 4]. **1587** T. SANDERS *Voy. Tripoli* B j b, Then went we to warpe out the Ship. **1600** HOLLAND *Livy* XXII. xx. 444 Those [ships] they drew up, and warped into the deepe, with ropes fastened to their poupes. **1624** CAPT. J. SMITH *Virginia* IV. 128 Seeing them warp themselues to windward, we thought it not good to be boorded on both sides at an anchor. **1726** SHELVOCKE *Voy. round World* 189 The water being smooth I soon warp'd her off again. **1791** SMEATON *Edystone Lightho.* §250 We let go an anchor and warped the buss to her proper birth. **1836** MACGILLIVRAY *Trav. Humboldt* xvii. 236 When the current was too strong, the sailors leapt out and warped the boat along. **1870** MORRIS *Earthly Par.* I. I. 292 About the capstan did the shipmen run, Warping the great ship to the harbour mouth. **1881** *Three in Norway* 3 We were warped out of dock about eight o'clock.

b. *absol.* Also *intr.* of a ship: To move by warping.
a **1547** SURREY *Æneis* IV. 791 Out of the rode sone shall the vessell warpe. **1580** H. SMITH in Hakluyt *Voy.* (1589) 470 At 3. in the afternoone we did warpe from one piece of ice to another. **1617** MORYSON *Itin.* II. 158 The Fleete with much difficulty warped in, and recovered the Harbour. **1748** *Anson's Voy.* II. xiii. 272 As there was but little wind,..they were obliged to warp out of the harbour. **1753** HANWAY *Trav.* (1762) I. II. xxi. 94 They warp thirty..miles in a day against the stream. **1842** DICKENS *Amer. Notes* xv, Its width is so contracted at one point, indeed, that they [*sc.* steamboats] are obliged to warp round by means of a rope. **1843** *Civil Engin. & Arch. Jrnl.* VI. 139/1 Two large transporting buoys..for vessels to moor to or warp from. **1858** *Times* 30 Nov. 4/3 The current gets..too strong for sailing ships, which could only warp up. **1913** *World* 25 Feb. 279/1 As she warped slowly from the quay.

c. *to warp one's way.*
1836 *Uncle Philip's Convers. Whale Fishery* 192 Warping their way with great danger from lane to lane of open water. **1853** KANE *Grinnell Exp.* x. (1856) 73 We commenced..to warp our way through the impacted ice.

26. To progress slowly or with effort by using the hands as well as the feet. Also *refl.*, to haul oneself along.
1796 *Hist. Ned Evans* IV. 32 Having fastened another rope round his body for security,..he warped along the first over the chasm. **1849** KINGSLEY *Misc.* (1859) II. 292, I recollect our literally warping ourselves down to the beach, holding on by rocks and posts. **1851** MAYNE REID *Scalp-Hunters* vii. 58 He slowly warped himself through the gay crowd. **1854** H. MILLER *Sch. & Schm.* v. (1857) 88 My rough garments..frayed, at times,..by warping to the tops of great trees, and by feats as a cragsman. **1859** H. KINGSLEY *G. Hamlyn* xlviii, The first mate, coming forward, warping himself from one belaying-pin to another.

27. *intr.* To float or whirl through the air. Chiefly *poet.*
1565 in Picton *L'pool Munic. Rec.* (1883) I. 108 The snow driving and warping to and fro. **1667** MILTON *P.L.* I. 341 A pitchy cloud Of Locusts, warping on the Eastern Wind. **1728–46** THOMSON *Spring* 120 Oft, engender'd by the hazy north, Myriads on myriads, insect armies warp Keen in the poison'd breeze. **1828** *Blackw. Mag.* XXIII. 102 What clouds of ephemeral children are for ever warping away on the wind of death! **1856** BRYANT *Hymn of Sea* 10 A hundred realms Watch its broad shadow warping on the wind.

V. †**28.** *trans.* To run (a ship) aground, fix on a shoal or sand-bank. *Obs.*
1535 STEWART *Cron. Scot.* II. 634 As that the flude come rynnand by the land, Amang tha schippis warpit in the sand. *a* **1661** Sand-warpt: [see SAND *sb.*² 10.]

29. a. To choke *up* (a channel) with alluvial deposit. Also *intr.*, to become choked *up.*
1745 *Beverley Beck Act* ii. 2 The said beck being now in very great danger of being choaked and warped up. **1799** A. YOUNG *Agric. Lincoln* 284 In case the drains should warp up at any time, provision of sluices is made to let water out of the canal into either, to scour them out clean. *Ibid.* 287 The rivers warp up in dry seasons to a great height, with a muddy sand or silt, which the tides deposite. **1876** *Whitby Gloss.*, *Sand-warped*, silted up, or choked with sand. **1878** MILLER & SKERTCHLY *Fenland* vii. 193 A new sluice was erected for the purpose of warping up the old channel.

b. To heap *up* (sand) by gradual deposit from a current. ? *Obs.* Also, to cause (sand) to be heaped up.
1674 MARVELL *Corr.* Wks. 1872–5 II. 422 Our House..desiring you to sound once again whether the Sand do continue as when the Captains last surveyed, or it be warped up higher. **1841** *Civil Engin. & Arch. Jrnl.* IV. 395/1 He has lately been occupied in forming a defence, by warping silt, with whin or gorse kids, laid horizontally.

30. To cover (land), by natural or artificial flooding, with a deposit of alluvial soil. Cf. WARP *sb.* 6.
1799 A. YOUNG *Agric. Lincoln* 278 They are attempting to warp 400 acres in one piece. **1805** R. W. DICKSON *Pract. Agric.* I. 436 The main canal may be cut..so as to warp the lands on each side of it. **1839** STONEHOUSE *Axholme* 37 Drains to flood and warp the land. **1867** *Good Words* 306/1 The mud caught by it soon 'warps' the space within into firm and rich dry land.
absol. **1799** A. YOUNG *Agric. Lincoln* 284 If a landlord warp, it should be deep at once; if a tenant, shallow, and repeat it. **1828** *Trial of W. Dyon* 22 He was warping with his son from four..o'clock.

warpage ('wɔːpɪdʒ). [f. WARP *v.* + -AGE.]

1. App. a charge for 'warping' or hauling ships entering certain harbours.
1863–7 SIMMONDS *Dict. Trade* Suppl., *Warpage*, a charge per ton made on shipping in some harbours.

2. The extent or result of warping (sense 6).
1950 J. OSBORNE *Dental Mechanics* (ed. 3) xi. 195 The celluloid bases of 1870..suffered from warpage in the mouth. **1952** *Shell Aviation News* No. 163. 14 (*caption*) Straight-edge laid along surface of wing leading-edge shows that the earlier warpage has been entirely eliminated. **1969** [see POSTCURE *v.*]. **1970** R. LOWELL *Notebk.* 221 We're warpage in the drift to *fin de siècle.*

'war-paint.

1. Among North American Indians: Paint applied to the face and body before going into battle.
1826 J. F. COOPER *Last of Mohicans* xxiii, The young Huron was in his war-paint. **1837** R. M. BIRD *Nick of the Woods* II. 44 His countenance, grim with war-paint. **1857** *Putnam's Monthly Mag.* May 452/2 He [the Indian] has put on his war-paint, and is prepared for death.

2. *colloq.* **a.** One's best clothes and finery; esp. ceremonial military or official costume, 'full fig'.
1859 H. KINGSLEY *G. Hamlyn* xiv, Old Lady E——..in her war-paint and feathers—pinker than ever. **1879** H. N. MOSELEY *Notes Nat. 'Challenger'* 497 The officers of the ship donned, as in duty bound, full 'war paint' to receive him. **1883** E. PENNELL-ELMHIRST *Cream Leicestersh.* 380 A stiff shower took all the glaze off our war-paint ere the meet was reached.

b. Cosmetics, make-up.
1869 B. HARTE *Luck of Roaring Camp* 84 The stranger..[brightened] through the color which Red Gulch knew facetiously as her 'war paint'. **1945** L. SHELLY *Jive Talk Dict.* 35 *War paint*, cosmetics. **1957** *Landfall* XI. 41 'In a moment,' Sylvia said, clicking open her purse. 'Just a daub of warpaint.' **1970** R. LOWELL *Notebk.* 57 If I look for the unbelievably beautiful In a city, it's mostly women in their war-paint. **1977** J. GARDNER *Werewolf Trace* x. 91 She had a fresh coat of warpaint and was all breathless.

'war-party.

1. A political party that favours war.
1798 T. JEFFERSON *Let. to J. Madison* 26 Apr., Writ. 1854 IV. 237 Parker has completely gone over to the war party. **1835** T. MITCHELL *Acharn. of Aristoph.* 510 *note*, Why Lamachus is thus selected as the representative of the war-party in Athens is pretty evident. **1849** C. BRONTE *Shirley* iii, Moore was a bitter Whig—a Whig, at least, as far as opposition to the war-party was concerned. **1976** *Classical Q.* XXVI. 257 The motives of the Spartan war-party are clearly stated.

2. a. A body of Indian 'braves' banded together for war.
1755 in J. W. Lydekker *Faithful Mohawks* (1938) 84 He had ye care of providing for all ye War-parties of Indians that went thro' that place. *c* **1800** B. HAWKINS *Sk. Creek*

Country (1848) 70 The war parties all march in Indian file, with the leader in front. **1826** J. F. COOPER *Last of Mohicans* xiii, The brothers and family of the Mohican formed our war-party. **1837** R. M. BIRD *Nick of the Woods* III. 108 There is a war-party of fourteen painted Wyandotts sleeping on the Council-square. **1876** BANCROFT *Hist. U.S.* IV. xv. 421 The backwoodsmen, who were hunters like the Indians,.. were forming war-parties along the frontier.

b. *transf.* and *fig.*

1921 C. A. W. MONCKTON *Some Experiences New Guinea Resident Magistrate* xxiv. 293 They had dispatched..a war party..and remorselessly slaughtered the Oobudura. **1946** *Sat. Even. Post* 3 Aug. 81/2 Pass the word back to Mr. Topliff at the gallop! Here's his war party! **1957** V. W. TURNER *Schism & Continuity in Afr. Society* i. 7 He inflicted several defeats on a large war-party of Chokwe. **1969** M. PUGH *Last Place Left* xiv. 99, A solitary raven scout..was summoning the raven war party to the scene.

'war-path. a. Among North American Indians: The path or route taken by a warlike expedition. ***to be*** or ***go on the war-path***: to go to war, seek the foe, be out for scalps.

1775 ADAIR *Hist. Amer. Indians* 396, I often have rode that war path alone. **1841** J. F. COOPER *Deerslayer* xv, The great Serpent of the Mohicans must be worthy to go on the warpath with Hawkeye. *Ibid.* xvii, She sees he is lame, and a poor hunter, and he has never been on a warpath. **1859** MARCY *Prairie Trav.* vi. 185 Their war-path has reached the shores of the Pacific. **1876** BANCROFT *Hist. U.S.* IV. xv. 422 With chosen companions, he went out upon the war-path, and added scalp to scalp.

b. *transf.* and *fig.*

1880 'MARK TWAIN' *Tramp Abr.* xxxii. 345 She was on the war path all the evening. **1888** *Pall Mall Gaz.* 10 Aug. 8/2 The Omagh Controversy. Mr. William O'Brien on the War Path. **1891** MRS. RIDDELL *Mad Tour* 266 A tremendous rapping at my door announced that Bobby was again on the war-path. **1897** *Daily News* 30 Jan. 8/1 It is a safe prophecy that the Cretans will again be on the warpath.

warped (wɔːpt), *ppl. a.* [f. WARP *v.* + -ED[1].]

1. Bent, contorted, or twisted out of shape.

c **1460** *Promp. Parv.* (Winch.) 517/1 Warpyd, or auylonge. *a* **1547** SURREY *Æneis* II. 229 The god that they by sea had brought In warped keles [L. *curvis carinis*]. **1589** [? LYLY] *Pappe w. Hatchet* B iiij, Ile make his braines so hot, that they shall..rattle in his warpt skull, like pepper in a dride bladder. **1604** MARSTON *Malcontent* v. iii. H 2 b, Hauing a red beard and a paire of warpt legges. **1706** E. WARD *Wooden World Diss.* (1708) 72 A warp'd Piece of Plank. **1798** COLERIDGE *Anc. Mar.* VII. iv, The planks look warp'd. **1813** SCOTT *Rokeby* II. xiv, Now to the oak's warped roots he clings. **1876** MISS BROUGHTON *Joan* I. xxx, Under the warped door..comes the iced blast. **1888** JACOBI *Printers' Vocab.*, *Warped cut*, woodcuts twisted through dampness, generally caused by improper cleansing or storing.

fig. **1602** DEKKER *Satirom.* I. 4, Were thy warpt soule put in a new molde, Ide weare thee as a Iewell set in golde. **1771** SMOLLETT *Humphry Cl.*, *To Dr. Lewis* 2 June, A good sort of a man, though most ridiculously warped in his political principles. **1830** D'ISRAELI *Chas. I*, III. iv. 48 The warped suggestions of the writer are perpetually supplying the absence of all real knowledge. **1875** JOWETT *Plato* (ed. 2) IV. 245 He has resorted to..dishonesty and falsehood, and become warped and distorted.

b. *Mining.* (See quot.)

1886 J. BARROWMAN *Sc. Mining Terms* 70 *Warped*, irregularly bedded, or plicated.

2. That has cast its young prematurely.

a **1722** LISLE *Husb.* (1757) 283 The warped cows.

3. Enriched with alluvial warp.

1799 A. YOUNG *Agric. Lincoln.* 284 At Reeveness warped land has sold for £100 an acre. **1842** C. W. JOHNSON *Farmer's Encycl.* 1229 Warped lands are found capable of growing most kinds of crops in great plenty. **1878** RAMSAY *Phys. Geog.* xxxiii. 577 The broad warped meadows.

warpeni(g, -penye: see WARDPENNY *Obs.*

warper ('wɔːpə(r)). [f. WARP *v.* + -ER[1].]

†**1.** One who throws, a thrower. *Obs.*

a **1000** *Riddles* xxviii. 7 (Gr.) Nu ic eom bindere & swingere, sona weorpere. [*a* **1225**: see KNIFE *-warper*.]

2. One who winds yarn in preparation for weaving, one who lays the warp for the weaver.

1611 COTGR., *Ourdisseur*, a warper; a putter of a web of cloth into the loome. **1822** [see CORDING *vbl. sb.*[1] 1]. **1825** *New Monthly Mag.* XIV. 259 Your warpers, your windsters, your weavers..no longer flourish and fatten. **1881** J. BRIGHT in *Daily News* 17 Nov. 2/5 The warpers in those days, as far as my recollection serves me..were all women. **1891** *Labour Commission* Gloss., *Warpers*, those in cotton mills who 'beam the yarn,' *i.e.* take the bobbins from the winders, placing them in a machine, and wind up some four or five hundred of the threads, side by side,..upon what is called a warper's beam... *Warpers*, women employed in reeling warp yarns from bobbins on to reels, before they are taken to the dressing machines.

3. A warping-machine.

1847 [see SPEEDER 3]. **1875** KNIGHT *Dict. Mech.*

4. A local name for the eel. Cf. WRIGGLER.

1901 *Shooting Times* 22 June 21/2 On a certain river where the eel is plentiful, and many rustic anglers go forth to catch him with rod and line.., the name 'eel' is seldom or never heard, but instead he is significantly known as a 'warper.'

†**'warpfat.** *Obs.* [f. WARP *sb.* + FAT *sb.*[1]] ? = *warping-fat, -trough* (WARPING *vbl. sb.* 10 c).

The OE. word glosses *calathus*, which should mean either 'basket' generally (cf. '*Vimen*, wearp,' *Corpus Glossary*) or 'basket for thread.' The rendering *alueolus* in the *Cath. Angl.* app. means a trough.

c **1000** ÆLFRIC *Voc.* in Wr.-Wülcker 152/21 *Calathus*, wearpfæt. **1483** *Cath. Angl.* 409/1 A Warpe fatte, *alueolus.*

'warping, *vbl. sb.*[1] [f. WARP *v.* + -ING[1].]

†**1.** The action of throwing. *Obs.*

a **1150** in *Archiv. Stud. neu. Spr.* CXVII. 27 *Iactura*, werpinge. **14..** *Hist. K. Boccus & Sydracke* (? 1510) Tj b, And whan the fowle is a lofte..With the warpyng of his wynge He doth the ayre a sondre mynge.

2. a. The action of preparing a warp for weaving.

c **1440** *Promp. Parv.* 517/1 Warpynge, of webstarys werkynge, *staminacio.* *c* **1640** J. SMYTH *Lives Berkeleys* (1883) I. 167 The charges in the wholl manufactory soe particularly in..spoolinge, warpinge, quillinge..and the like. **1788** BURNS '*My Heart was ance*' ii, My mither sent me ..To warp a plaiden wab; But the weary, weary warpin' o't Has gart me sigh and sab. **1878** A. BARLOW *Weaving* 68 Warping, therefore, consists in arranging the threads according to number and colour, or in any special manner that may be necessary, and to keep them in their relative places after they have been so laid.

b. *concr.* = WARP *sb.* 1. Also in pl., the threads of a warp. ? *Obs.*

1684 R. WALLER *Nat. Exper.* 97 From the sides of these shoot out other small Threads close together like feathers, or Palm branches; these are as it were the first warping, and.. they proceed shooting and increasing till the Woofe closes all with a total freezing of the Water. *c* **1817** HOGG *Conf. Fanatic* Tales & Sk. (1837) V. 178 My feet had slipped down through the double warpings of a web.

†**3.** *fig.* The action of fabricating or devising, a fabrication. Also gerundial in ***a-warping*** (predicatively). *Obs.*

1583 MELBANCKE *Philotimus* L j, But the Deuill loues al colliers and thou selflike reasons of thine owne warping. **1603** HOLLAND *Plutarch's Mor.* 497 Lampsace..acquainted the Greeks under-hand with this treason, which was a warping against them. **1814** CARY *Dante, Parad.* ix. 50 One Lords it, and bears his head aloft, for whom The web is now a-warping.

4. The action of moving a ship from one place to another by means of warps.

1513 T. HOWARD in *Lett. & Papers War France* (1897) 163, I trust agaynst nyght this W.N.W. wynd will ly, and then we woll forth with warpyng. **1627** CAPT. J. SMITH *Sea Gram.* viii. 35 His Mate [is to haue] the command of the long boat, for..weighing..an anchor, warping, towing, or moring. **1769** FALCONER *Dict. Marine* (1780) R r 4, Warping is generally used when the sails are unbent, or when they cannot be successfully employed. **1820** SCORESBY *Acc. Arctic Reg.* I. 310 During five days we persevered in the most laborious exertions, in towing, boring, warping and mill-dolling. **1883** *Man. Seamanship Boys* 196 Q. What is warping? A. Transporting a ship from one part of a harbour to another by means of hawsers.

5. a. The process of flooding low-lying land near a tidal river so that the muddy alluvium may be deposited when the water is withdrawn. Also ***warping up***, the process of filling up hollows by deposit of alluvium.

1799 A. YOUNG *Agric. Lincoln* 284 It is not by the canal that the warping is done, but by a soakage drain on each side of it. **1830** LYELL *Princ. Geol.* I. 307 By repeating this operation, which is called 'warping,' for two or three years, considerable tracts have been raised, in the estuary of the Humber, to the height of about six feet. **1839** *Civil Engin. & Arch. Jrnl.* II. 450/1 It was found necessary to encourage the warping up of the old floor pits, by introducing fascine jetty work, which greatly accelerated the deposit of the sea warp. **1879** *Cassell's Techn. Educ.* II. 171/2 Warping gives an entirely new surface to soil. It may be best explained as a process by which the suspended mud which occurs in certain rivers is allowed to deposit itself upon a prescribed area of land.

b. *concr.* The silt or alluvial matter deposited by the sea or a tidal river.

c **1440** *Promp. Parv.* 517/2 Warpynge, of the see or oþer water, *alluvium.*

6. a. The action of twisting or bending, or the fact of becoming twisted or bent; an instance of this.

c **1440** *Promp. Parv.* 517/1 Warpynge..of vessel þat wax wronge or avelonge..*oblongacio.* **1656** *Artif. Handsom.* 60 Who fears to set straight or hide the unhandsom warpings of bow leggs? **1683** MOXON *Mech. Exerc., Printing* 27 Letter-Boards are..Clamped..to keep them from Warping. **1756–7** tr. *Keysler's Trav.* (1760) I. 445 This may be no more than the natural warping of dry wood. **1823** P. NICHOLSON *Pract. Builder* 221 Casting or Warping, the bending of the surfaces of a piece of wood from their original position. **1873** B. HARTE *Fiddletown* 16 The multitudinous small noises, and creakings, and warpings of the vacant house. **1892** *Photogr. Ann.* II. 53 See that the hinged backs of your frames are clamped, and then defy warping.

b. *fig.* The action of distorting or perverting from the right course or direction, or the fact of deviating or going astray; an instance of this.

1608 DOD & CLEAVER *Expos. Prov.* xi–xii. 168 For the same causes it will appeare that the warping of sinfull courses wil turn to their hurt that imagine them. **1656** *Artif. Handsom.* 36 The heart is upright, without any sinfull warpings. **1681** MANTON *Serm. Ps. cxix.* 80 (1725) 413 The old Man is not put off, but there will be many warpings and deceitful workings still. **1709** G. STANHOPE *Paraphrase* IV. 271 If these Bents and Warpings of the Will had destroy'd all Freedom in us. **1782** *Burke Corr.* (1844) II. 460 These old warpings of the human heart and understanding. **1838** EMERSON *Addr., Lit. Ethics* Wks. (Bohn) II. 212 This starting, this warping of the best literary works from the adamant of nature, is especially observable in philosophy. **1873** SPENCER *Sociol.* xvi. 388 The warping of opinion which the bias of patriotism causes. **1884** *Contemp. Rev.* XLV. 28 The mischief done by asceticism was the warping of the moral nature of man.

7. *Carpentry.* A strengthening brace.

1833 LOUDON *Encycl. Archit.* § 1070 The trevises..to have angle warpings (braces) 4 inches by 1 inch and a half. *Ibid.* 1212 The trevises..to have angle spars or warpings (diagonal braces) on each side.

8. *Rope-making.* (See quots.)

1688 HOLME *Armoury* III. 113/1 Warping, is the laying of so many Thrids or Rope Yarns together, as will make a Rope. **1794** *Rigging & Seamanship* I. 58 *Warping* is running the yarn off the winches into hauls to be tarred.

9. *Angling.* The wound thread which attaches the artificial fly to the hook.

1676 COTTON *Angler* II. v. 40 Where the warping ends, pinch or nip it with your thumb nail against your finger, and strip away the remainder of your dubbing from the silk. **1836** RONALDS *Fly-Fisher's Entom.* 31 A little of the dubbing may be left out in the warping, or picked out of the body with a needle, after the winding or warping, to serve for legs instead of the hackle feather.

fig. **1867** R. R. BEALEY in *Country Words* 23 Feb. 262 We're nobbut a 'bundle of habits,' Teed round wi' a warpin' o' time.

10. *attrib.* and *Comb.* **a.** In collocations concerned with the 'warping' of land, as ***warping bank, clough, cut, district, drain, gutter, hatch, operation, sluice, works.*** **b.** In names of machines and parts of machines used in the preliminary process of weaving, as ***warping-bar, board, -frame, -jack, -machine, -mill, -wheel, -woof***; also ***warping-room.***

1819 REES *Cycl.*, **Warping-Banks.* **1813** VANCOUVER *Agric. Devon* 395 A stripe that measures 31 inches..should be laid in the *warping-bars full 29 yards, and contain 1440 threads. **1885** 'C. E. CRADDOCK' *Prophet Gt. Smoky Mts.* i. 20 The great frame of the warping-bars on one side of the room. **1910** L. HOOPER *Hand-Loom Weaving* iv. 42 Although the *warping board..is very useful for small warps of moderate length,..it would not be convenient for very long warps, or accurate enough for warping several thousands of fine silk threads. **1960** G. LEWIS *Handbk. Crafts* 99 The warping board and the mill have the same process in common, the main difference being that when using the board you have to walk backwards and forwards to get your length, whereas when using the mill you revolve it the required number of times. **1819** REES *Cycl.*, **Warping Clough, Hatch, or Sluice. Ibid.*, **Warping Cuts, Drains, or Gutters.* **1805** R. W. DICKSON *Pract. Agric.* I. 436 The business being discontinued in the *warping districts during fresh-water floods. **1799** A. YOUNG *Agric. Lincoln* 280 The aforesaid *warping drains to be 18 feet wide at bottom. **1688** HOLME *Armoury* III. xxi. (Roxb.) 251/1 He beareth Sable, a *warping Frame, Argent. **1835** URE *Philos. Manuf.* 112 Apartments for winding the cotton on the large bobbins used for the warping-frame. **1875** KNIGHT *Dict. Mech.*, *Warping-jack. **1819** REES *Cycl.* s.v. *Weaving*, The most improved *warping-machines. **1825** J. NICHOLSON *Oper. Mech.* 399 The silk is now taken to the *warping-mill. **1882** MOZLEY *Remin.* II. 418 The vast '*warping' operations, that is, the reclamation of marshy land irregularly flooded by the Trent. **1871** *Daily News* 27 Jan., The carding, winding, and *warping rooms at the west end were preserved. **1799** A. YOUNG *Agric. Lincoln* 279 We should recommend a *warping sluice to be built. **1788** BURNS '*My Heart was ance*' iv, I sat beside my *warpin' wheel. **1891** *Labour Commission* Gloss., **Warping woof* (or *bars*). **1799** A. YOUNG *Agric. Lincoln* 278 The first *warping works which I viewed were at Morton Ferry.

c. Special comb.: **warping-block**, a block used by rope-makers in warping off yarn; **warping-buoy**, a buoy used in warping a vessel; †**warping-fat** [cf. WARPFAT], ? = *warping-trough*; **warping-hook**, an iron hook for hanging the yarn on when warping into hauls for tarring; **warping-post**, a strong post used in warping rope-yarn; †**warping-stock**, †**-tree**, ? = prec.; †**warping-trough** (see quot.).

1794 *Rigging & Seamanship* I. 157 *Warping-block. **1875** BEDFORD *Sailor's Pocket Bk.* v. (ed. 2) 137 All *warping buoys are coloured white. **14..** *Lat.-Eng. Voc.* in Wr.-Wülcker 577/11 *Cupatorium*, a *worpynfat. **1565** *Burgh Rec. Prestwick* (Maitl. Club) 69 Ane warpene fat, price xij[s]. **1815** *Falconer's Dict. Marine* (ed. Burney), **Warping-Hook.* **1797** *Encycl. Brit.* (ed. 3) XVI. 486/1 The other block..is fixed to a firm post, called the *warping post. **1404** *Nottingham Rec.* II. 22, j. *warpyngstok et *warpyngtree. **1588** in *Aston's Manch. Guide* (1804) 24 A warpinge stocke with ryngs and yarne in yt, 00 02 06. **1688** HOLME *Armoury* III. 346/1 He beareth Sable, a Weavers *Warping Trough, Or;... The Weavers Trough is that in which he puts his Clews of Yarn, when he runs them off for Warping.

warping ('wɔːpɪŋ), *vbl. sb.*[2] *nonce-wd.* [As if f. **warp* vb., evolved from MOULDWARP.] The mole's action of throwing up earth into mole-hills.

1829 J. L. KNAPP *Jrnl. Nat.* 143, I am not aware of any benefit occasioned by their [the moles'] presence; their warpings certainly give our pastures in the spring a very unsightly appearance.

warping ('wɔːpɪŋ), *ppl. a.* [-ING[2].] That warps or is warped, in senses of the verb.

1598 CHAPMAN *Hero & Leander* vi. 20 Who like a fleering slauish Parasite, In warping profit or a traiterous sleight, Hoopes round his rotten bodie with deuotes. **1599** B. JONSON *Ev. Man out of Hum.* III. viii, The warping condition of this greene and foggy multitude. **1631** DEKKER *Match Mee* III. 35 How easie were it, For you to set this warping Kingdome straight? **1653** R. SANDERS *Physiogn.* 101 A crooked warping line from the angle, above the hill of Jupiter. **1700** DRYDEN *Ovid's Met.* XIII. *Acis* etc. 85 More warping than the Willow [*lentior et salicis virgis*]. *a* **1722** LISLE *Husb.* (1757) 230 Warping beasts and barren heifers.. are begun to be fatted with hay from Christmas. **1806** J. GRAHAME *Birds of Scot.* II. 143 The swallow..Skims 'long the brook,..Where dance the midgy clouds in warping maze Confused. **1850** MARSDEN *Early Purit.* (1853) 121 The warping influence of faction. **1875** TENNYSON *Q. Mary* I. v, You see thro' warping glasses.

†**warpiss**, *v. Sc. Obs.* [a. OF. *werpiss-*, lengthened stem of *werpir*, *guerpir* to quit, abandon (now only in comp. *déguerpir*), f. Germanic root *werp-*: see WARP *v.*] *trans.* To cast or throw off, to put aside.

*c*1375 *Sc. Leg. Saints* xxvii. (*Machor*) 473 Bot for þu ȝuthad has warpyst & is parfyt man in cryst, þu sal be callyt machore. 1444 *Extracts Aberd. Reg.* (1844) I. 11 God forbid that yhe suld, for a litil monee that thir Inglismen has promissit yhou, warpiss your gude name.

warple (ˈwɔːp(ə)l), *sb. dial.* Forms: 6 *pl.* **warpelles, warples,** 7 **whaple,** 7– **whapple,** 9 **wapple, waffel, warple, worple, wopple.** [Of obscure origin; perh. repr. an OE. **wyrpel* or **wierpel* f. the root of WARP *v.* Cf. the place-name *Warplesdon* (Surrey).] A green lane, a bridle-road. Chiefly in comb. ***warple-road, -way***; **warple-gate**, a gate on a bridle-road (*Eng. Dial. Dict.*).

1565 *Extr. Crt. Rolls of Manor of Wimbledon* (1866) 128 Ordinacio pro Warpelles. Cum ad ultimam Curiam Generalem hic tentam ordinatum fuit de exponendis, anglice Warples, in Communibus campis de Wimbledon [etc.]. 1658 in *Sussex Archæol. Coll.* (1871) XXIII. 253 One whaple or bridle way sett forth..through the premises leading from Newbridge Mill. 1674 RAY *S. & E.C. Words* 79 A Whapple way, i.e. where a cart and horses cannot pass, but horses only. 1704 R. STAPLEY *Diary* in *Sussex Archæol. Collect.* II. 126 Yᵉ great oake yᵗ stood in yᵉ lane, going yᵉ whapple way to Bolney from Hickstead, was cut down. 1860 J. W. WARTER *Seaboard & Down* II. 34 You ought to have kept to the wopple road. 1868 *Gloss. Sussex Words* in Hurst *Horsham* (1889), *Whapple-way*. A public bridle path, which went through fields, woods, and farms. 1886 *Law Rep. 31 Chanc. Div.* 680 There was an old way or track, formerly known as a warple way, leading from the Uxbridge Road: it was about ten feet wide and was not metalled. 1893 *Times* 21 Mar. 13/3 A..plot of land..bounded on the north and north-west by a cart road or 'warple way'. *Ibid.* 13/4 An old 'warple way' or easement (i.e., a rough, unmade cart track used..for agricultural purposes, as the removal of crops or conveyance of manure).

warple (ˈwɔːp(ə)l), *v. Sc.* Also 8 **wraple.** [Of obscure origin; connexion with WARP *v.* or with WRAP *v.* is possible.]

1. *trans.* To entangle, intertwine. Also *fig.*

1768 ROSS *Helenore* 80 Nory's heart began to cool right fast, Fan she saw things had taken sick a cast, An' sae thro' ither warpl'd [1789, p. 86 wrapl'd] were, that she Began to dread atweesh them, what meith be. 1825 JAMIESON Suppl. *s.v.*, That yarn's sae warplit, that I canna get it redd. *Ibid.*, *Warple v.*,..used in a moral sense, to denote the confusion of any business.

2. *intr.* To move with sinuous movement; also to walk unsteadily.

1768 [See WARPLING *vbl. sb.*]. 1887 SERVICE *Dr. Duguid* III. iii. 254 Her auld guidman..cam warplin' an' fanklin' owre the muirs by himsel.

3. To twist or wind *round*. Also *fig.*

*a*1870 D. THOMSON *Musings among Heather* (1881) 227 Warl's griefs an' cares are unco rife, An' warple roond a body's life. 1890 A. J. ARMSTRONG *Ingleside Musings* 141 They [*sc.* tawse] warpled roun' his lanky shanks Like snakes aroon' 'Laocoon'.

Hence **ˈwarpled**, *ppl. a.*; **ˈwarpling** *vbl. sb.*, the action of the verb; †***warpling o' the green***, a rustic game.

1768 ROSS *Helenore* i. 10 Whan she among the neiper bairns was seen, At greedy-glad or warpling o' the green, She 'clipst them 'a. 1897 'L. KEITH' *Bonny Lady* vii. 71 An old quarrel's like warplit wool that cannot be redd in a minute.

ˈwar-proof, *sb.* and *a.* **a.** *sb.* Valour tried in war. **b.** *adj.* Able to resist a hostile attack.

a. 1599 SHAKS. *Hen. V*, III. i. 18 On, on, you Noblish English, Whose blood is fet from Fathers of Warre-proofe. **b.** 1777 POTTER *Æschylus, Suppliants* 81 A surer refuge Than tow'r or shield war-proof an altar gives. 1819 KEATS *Otho* III. ii. 34 Your knights, found war-proof in the bloody field, Speed to the game.

warr, obs. form of WAR *sb.*¹, *v.*, WARE *a.*, *v.*¹

warra, variant of WARRAY *v.*

†**ˈwarrable**, *a. Obs. rare*⁻⁰. [f. WAR *v.* + -ABLE.] (See quot.)

1611 COTGR., *Guerroyable*, warrable; fit to be warred on.

‖**warraˈcoori.** [Native name.] (See quots.)

1858 SIMMONDS *Dict. Trade, Warracoori*, a native name for the wood of the white cedar, obtained in Demerara from the *Icica altissima*. It is light, easily worked, and very aromatic, and is used for oars and paddles, and for boards for the inside work of houses. 1862 *List Contrib. Br. Guiana to Lond. Exhib.* in Veness *El Dorado* (1866) App. 137 Warracoori, or White Cedar... Used for frame and inside work of houses,..paddles, canoes, &c. 1866 in *Treas. Bot.*

warragal, variant of WARRIGAL.

warrai, var. WARRAY *v. Obs.*; obs. f. VERY.

warraine, -er, obs. ff. WARREN, -ER.

warral, variant of WORRAL.

warran(d, obs. forms of WARRANT.

warrander, obs. form of WARRENER.

warrandice (ˈwɒrəndɪs). Chiefly *Sc.* Also 5 **varandis, -eisse, warandis(s, werrandisse,** 5–6 **warandice, -ise, warrandise,** 7 **warrandize.** See also WARRANTISE. [a. AF. *warandise*, var. of *warantise* (OF. also *garantise*), f. *warantir* (*garantir*): see WARRANT *v.*]

1. a. *gen.* A guarantee, an undertaking to secure another against risk. Chiefly in *Scots Law*; now only as a literary archaism.

1488 *Acta Audit.* (1839) 125/1 For þe werrandis[se] of him of þe said teyndis and froitis. 1495 HALYBURTON *Ledger* (1867) 53 Giffin to Derik Jacopsone of Horne for the forbettryn off 2 sekis of woyll that had his letter of varandis, 24s. 1531 *Abstr. Protocols Town Clerks Glasgow* (1897) IV. 37 [He] oblissis his place in the Gallowgaet Port,..in warrandise of the paement of the xvj s. anwell. 1561 *Reg. Privy Council Scot.* I. 173 It specifiis nocht quhane,..nor yit quhome fra, I ressauit the gudis,.. takand thairthrow away my defencis, baith for warrandice and releif. 1565 COOPER *Thesaurus, Author*..he that selleth on warandice. *A malo authore aliquid emere*, to bie of him, that can make no sufficient warandice. *Ibid.* s.v. *Caueo*, *Ab sese caueat quemadmodum velit*. Cic. Let him take as good suretee and warandise for him selfe as he will. 1592 *Sc. Acts Jas. VI* (1814) III. 547/2 Oblissand him in maist strait forme for warrandice of the said pensioun. 1597 SKENE *De Verb. Sign.*, *Claremethen*,..the Law of Claremethen concernis the warrandice of stollen cattell, or gudes. 1632 LITHGOW *Trav.* III. 116 They lent two millions of money, and for warrandice whereof, they haue this Towne and Prouince made fast to them. 1704 *Gd. Exped.* in *Harl. Misc.* (1746) VIII. 14/2 If the Safety of the Government could be Sufficiently provided for, and obtain any sure Warrandice from Men's Vowing Fealty. 1814 SCOTT *Wav.* lxvi, Never fear, I'se be caution for them—I'se give you my personal warrandice. 1824 —— *Redgauntlet* ch. xi, My warrandice goes no farther. 1893 STEVENSON *Catriona* iii, I have Rankeillour's word for it..and I count that a warrandice against all deadly.

b. *spec.* in *Scots Law.* The obligation to indemnify the grantee or purchaser of land if an evictive or paramount claim should be established against the lands through defect of title.

personal warrandice is that by which the grantor and his heirs are bound personally. ***real warrandice*** is where the grantor or vendor conveys what are called ***warrandice lands*** to be held by the grantee in security of the lands originally granted.

1466 *Acta Audit.* (1839) 4/2 þe actioun..tuiching þe Warrandice of twa merkis worth of land. 1481 *Ibid.* 97/1 þe said Adam allegit to haue a tak of þe saide land, & warandiss of þe samyn. 1562 *Abstr. Protocols Town Clerks Glasgow* (1896) III. 23 Hew Mwre renunceit all warrandice quhilk he had of Allexander Cwnynghame..of the xxvj s. viij d. lande of Westir-blak-law. 1587 *Sc. Acts Jas. VI* (1814) III. 432/1 Incaiss ony of þe saidis prelattis..salbe heireftir callit and persewit at þe instance of qᵗsumeuir personis for warrandice of ony of þe saidis kirklandis set in few or tak be þame. 1681 STAIR *Instit.* I. xiii. 264 But oftimes when Warrandice is not exprest, it is implyed as Rights are to be warranted, which are granted for an Equivalent Cause onerous. 1690 in *Nairne Peerage Evid.* (1874) 27 This clause of warrandice wherin the Marqueis has bound himselfe. *a*1722 FOUNTAINHALL *Decis.* Suppl. (1826) III. 293 Warrandice is only incurred by legal deeds..and not by such a natural fact of unclean heartsomeness. *a*1768 ERSKINE *Inst. Law Scot.* II. vii. §3 All voluntary transmissions in which absolute warrandice is either expressed or implied. 1815 R. BELL *Treat. Conveyance* 30 The warrandice of the sale of land is absolute warrandice; and, accordingly, where no warrandice was expressed, the Court found that absolute warrandice was the natural warrandice of the transaction. 1868 *Act 31 & 32 Vict.* c. 101 §8 The clause..shall be held to imply absolute warrandice as regards the lands and writs and evidents.

Comb. *a*1768 ERSKINE *Inst. Law Scot.* II. iii. §28 Where some lands..which get the name of *warrandice-lands*, are disponed only eventually in security of the principal lands.

†**2.** Security from danger, safety. *Obs.*

1512 *Helyas* in Thoms *Prose Rom.* (1828) III. 84 My mother..is fled for warrandise into a castell of hers. 1553–63 BECON *Reliques of Rome* 239 b, Al thoe that any manner of goods with violence or malice beare out of holy Churche,.. or house of Religion, whiche that therein is layde or done for warrandise or succoure or for to be kepte. 1826 SCOTT *Jrnl.* 12 May, Good apartments..and absolute warrandice against my dreaded enemies, bugs.

warrane, obs. f. WARRANT, WARREN.

warrant (ˈwɒrənt), *sb.*¹ Forms: 3–6 **warant,** 5 **warante, warente,** 3–5 **waraunt,** (5 **warawnt,** 6 **warantte),** 6 **waraunte,** 6–7 **warraunt,** 6 **warraunte,** 6 **warrante,** (7 *Sc.* **quarrente),** 4– **warrant;** *Sc.* and *north.* 4–7 **warand,** 4–5 **warande,** 5 **waronde,** (6 **woran,** 5 **warrane,** 6–8 **warran, waran, warn),** 4 **warrande, varrand,** 5 **werrand,** 4– **warrand.** [a. OF. *warant*, *warand*, dial. var. of *guarant*, *garant* (mod.F. *garant*) = Pr. *garen-s*, *guiren-s*, Sp., Pg. *garante*, It. *guarento*, Frankish L. *warens*, *warentem*, *warandus*, *-um*; the Teut. source is represented by MLG. *warend*, *warent*, warranty, subst. use of pres. pple. of *waren* to warrant (= OFris. *wara*, early mod.Du. *waren*; early mod.G. *wahren* in legal formulas, from LG.), cogn. and synonymous with OHG. *werên* (MHG. *wern*, mod.G. *währen*, *gewähren*); cf. MHG. *wari*, *ware*, MDu. *ware* fem., warranty, and the synonymous MHG. *were* (mod.G. *währe*) fem.

The affinities of the root **wer-*: **war-* in these words are disputed: see K. v. Bahder in the *Deutsches Wörterbuch* (Grimm) s.vv. *Wahre, Währe, Wahren, Währen*.]

I. One who or something which protects or authorizes.

†**1.** A protector, defender. *Obs.*

*a*1225 *St. Marher.* 8 þu art iweddedes weole ant wide-wene warant. *a*1240 *Lofsong* in *O.E. Hom.* I. 211 Beo mi scheld and mi warant on euche halfe aȝein þes feondes flon. *c*1300 *Havelok* 2067 Cum now forth with me,..For nou wile y youre warant be. *c*1330 *King of Tars* 455 Bi Mahoun, and bi Termagaunt, No mon schal be heore waraunt, Emperour ne kyng with croun. 1375 BARBOUR *Bruce* II. 502 In commownys may nane affy, Bot he that may thar warrand be. *c*1400 *Ywaine & Gaw.* 2583 For hir warand mai thou noght be, Bot thou allane fight with us thre. *c*1440 *Promp. Parv.* 516/1 Warant, *protector, defensor*. *c*1450 LOVELICH *Grail* xliv. 455 On Goddis Enemyes now let vs gon In Iesus Name..Oure warawunt and Oure Governour, that vs wele Save In Every stour. *a*1548 HALL *Chron., Hen. IV*, 8 The kyng craftely perswaded the saied byshop to make no answere, for he would be his warrant. 1549–62 STERNHOLD & H. *Ps.* cxxi. 5 The Lord is thy warrant alway, The Lord eke doth thee couer. 1567 *Gude & Godlie B.* (S.T.S.) 111 Had not the Lord bene our warrand,..Thay had us all on liue deuorit. *a*1600 *Capt. Car* xv. in *Trans. New Shaks. Soc.* (1880–6) App. 54† 'Lap him in a shete', he sayth, 'And let him downe to me, And I shall take him in my arme; His waran wyll I be.' 16.. *Rising in North* vii. in Child *Ballads* III. 405/1 But goe to the court yet, good my lord, Take men enowe with thee; If any man will doe you wronge, Your warrant they may be. *a*1828 *Charlie Macpherson* iv. in Buchan *Ballads* I. 86 Jamie McRobbie, likewise Wattie Nairn, All ga'ed wi' Charlie for to be his warran'. 1829 SCOTT *Anne of G.* xi, I swear to thee..by the shoulder of my horse, and the edge of my good sword, I will be thy warrand for a year and a day.

†**2.** A safeguard, protection, defence. *Obs.*

*a*1272 *Luue Ron* 27 in *O.E. Misc.* 94 Nis non so riche ne non so freo þat he ne schal heonne sone away Ne may hit neuer his waraunt beo. 1338 R. BRUNNE *Chron.* (1810) 183 Himself as a Geant þe cheynes in tuo hew, þe targe was his warant, þat non tille him threw. *c*1450 LOVELICH *Grail* xii. 301 From deth thi waraunt this [*sc.* the Cross] schal be, And from Alle presonementis. *c*1450 *Merlin* xxii. 408 Whom that he raught a full stroke was so harde smyten that noo armure was his warante fro deth.

†**3. a.** Security or safety from one's enemies; also a place of refuge, shelter. *Obs.*

13.. *Coer de L.* 5749 Whom that he ovyr-raught that tyde, Off lyff ne was her waraunt non. 1375 BARBOUR *Bruce* VI. 422 Thai that saw sa suddandly That folk sa egirly cum prikand Betuix thame and thair varrand. *Ibid.* VIII. 485 And thai mycht help thaim-self no thing, Bot fled to varrand quhan thai mocht. 1490 CAXTON *Eneydos* xlvii. 139 But elecor, that was ryght swyfte & lyght, fled toward the castel for his waraunt. 1513 DOUGLAS *Æneis* XI. xvii. 9 The chiftanis.. Socht to warrand on horsbak. 1596 DALRYMPLE tr. *Leslie's Hist. Scot.* (S.T.S.) II. 119 Was prouydet, that nane of Jngland entir into Scotland,..without his kingis lettres for his defence and warran.

†**b.** *to draw to warrant* (cf. 5): to resort for protection *to* (a person). ***to hold in*** or ***to warrant***: to keep (subjects) in safety, to protect. *Obs.*

*c*1330 R. BRUNNE *Chron. Wace* (Rolls) 1472 Coryneus.. was a man als a Geaunt, Tyl hym þey drowe alle to waraunt. 1375 BARBOUR *Bruce* XIII. 710 God grant that thai, that cummyne ar Of his ofspring, maynteyme the land, And hald the folk weill to warrand. *Ibid.* XX. 604 The gude erll gouernit the land, And held the pure weill to warand.

†**4. a.** A guarantor, surety, bail. *Sc. Obs.*

1478 *Acta Dom. Conc.* (1839) 6/1 Gife þe said ser Johne has ony vþer to waurand him, he sall haue priuilege to call þat warand. *c*1575 *Balfour's Practicks* (1754) 320 Ane beand callit and persewit for the singil and doubil avail of his mariage, may leasumlie call ony persoun for his warrand, quha is bund and oblist to warrand him thairanent. 1609 SKENE *Reg. Maj.* III. xii. 52 Quhen ane challenges fra the buyer anie thing, as thifteouslie stollen: the buyer sould defend him anent the thift alledged against him: or else to alledge and call ane warand there anent.

†**b.** Assurance given, pledge, guaranty. ***to take warrant on oneself*** (? quasi-*arch.*), to pledge oneself, make oneself responsible. *Obs.*

1460 *Rolls of Parlt.* V. 381/2 Prejudiciall to any.. Ratification Confirmation or Warante. 1591 SHAKS. *Two Gent.* II. iv. 102 His worth is warrant for his welcome hether. 1593 —— *Rich. II*, IV. 235 There should'st thou finde one heynous Article, Contayning the deposing of a King, And cracking the strong Warrant of an Oath. 1604 —— *Oth.* III. iii. 20, I giue thee warrant of thy place. 1611 —— *Cymb.* I. iv. 63 This Gentleman, at that time vouching (and vpon warrant of bloody affirmation) his to be more Faire, Vertuous,..then any, the rarest of our Ladies in France. 1828 SCOTT *F.M. Perth* xxi, I can take warrant upon myself for the innocence of my household and followers.

5. a. One who is answerable for a fact or statement; an authoritative witness. †*to draw, take to warrant*: to appeal to as evidence.

For *to vouch to warrant*, see VOUCH *v.* I.

*a*1300 *Cursor M.* 14651 He þat es fader of heuen king.. Him drau i me to mi warand. 13.. *Guy Warw.* 547 þei ich hir loue, blame me noman; To warant ichil drawe atte frome þat loue doþ me þider come. *c*1320 *Sir Tristr.* 1539 To his waraunt he drouȝ His schippe and al his pride. *c*1330 *Arth. & Merl.* 5229 þe Brut þer of is mi waraunt. ? *a*1366 CHAUCER *Rom. Rose* 6 This may I drawe to warraunte [F. *trere à garant*] An author, that hight Macrobes. *c*1425 WYNTOUN *Cron.* I. Prol. 116 For few wrytis I redye fand That I couth draw to my warrand. *c*1480 HENRYSON *Fox & Wolf* 2148 Wend quhen ȝe will, I dar be warrand now That ȝe sall de na suddan deith this day. 1583 STUBBES *Anat. Abus.* II. 48 A manifest deceite before the Lorde, and one daye shall be answered for, I dare be their warrante. 1873 BROWNING *Red Cott. Nt.-cap* 225 If insufficient faith have done thus much,..More would move mountains, you are warrant.

b. A conclusive proof.

a 1450 *Le Morte Arth.* 1142 Thys lettere there-of [*sc.* of Lancelot's innocence] warannte wolle be. 1860 HAWTHORNE *Transf.* III. ii. 21 Though but a single word, and the first that he had spoken, its tone was a warrant of the sad and tender depth from which it came.

†6. One whose command justifies an action. *Obs.*

a 1300 *Cursor M.* 14968 Gais fotte hir me, if animan Lais apon yow hand To lette yow, ye sai yee haf þe lauerd to your warand. 1579 TOMSON *Calvin's Serm. Tim.* 138/2 You are not here in your own proper names, men shall not be your warrants, it is God that must gouerne aboue al. 1821 SCOTT *Kenilw.* xxii, Janet, alarm the house!—Foster, break open the door—I am detained here by a traitor!—Use axe and lever, Master Foster—I will be your warrant!

7. a. Command or permission of a superior which frees the doer of an act from blame or legal responsibility; authorization, sanction; an act of authorization.

a 1300 *Cursor M.* 18426 And if þe yate-ward þe witstand, Sa him þou has ful gode warand. 1387 TREVISA *Higden* (Rolls) VIII. 135 He bygan rabbilsiche to passe his waraunt [L. *fines creditae sibi potestatis petulanter excedere*] in absens of þe kyng. *c* 1400 *Rule St. Benet* (Prose) ii. 5 He [*sc.* the abbot] ah na þing at cumande bot þat he may haue warant at god. *c* 1440 *York Myst.* xvii. 67 For haue we his wille and his warande þan may we wende with-outen drede. 1453 *Rolls of Parlt.* V. 268/2 That noo Letters Patentes..be made hereafter, but by Warrant of bill, enselid by the Tresorer of Englond. *c* 1480 HENRYSON *Poems* III. 173 Now wrang hes warrane, and law is bot wilfulness. 1547–8 *Ordre Commun.* 8 Where as he hath no warrant of God's worde for thesame. 1563 *Reg. Privy Council Scot.* I. 249 This present ordinance salbe sufficient warrand to thame. 1575 GASCOIGNE *Glasse of Govt.* Wks. 1910 II. 15, I..have by warrant of the same commission brought with me my Brother Phylomusus. 1629 in A. I. Ritchie *Ch. St. Baldred* (1880) 219 The minister..culd not gett sik quarrente to punishe the prophaners of the Sabbothe in tyme of draife. 1635 D. DICKSON *Hebr.* x. 2. 199 Hee that is purged by Vertue of the sacrifice of Christ, hath God's Warrand, to haue a quyet and peaceable Conscience. 1637 *Star Chamb. Decree* §4 in Arber *Milton's Areop.* 11 Euery person and persons, which..shall be appointed or authorized to Licence Bookes, or giue Warrant for imprinting thereof. 1651 HOBBES *Leviath.* III. xxxix, That Assembly, which is without warrant from the Civil Soveraign, is unlawful. 1683 *Col. Rec. Pennsylv.* I. 84 That it was Convenient Warrant should be sent from this board. 1855 PRESCOTT *Philip II*, I. v. (1857) 85 The Spanish monarch determined to ease his conscience, by obtaining, if possible, a warrant for his proceedings from the Church itself.

b. A token or evidence of authorization. (Cf. branch II.)

1390 GOWER *Conf.* I. 201 Thei..have him thilke lettre rad, Which he hem sende for warant. 1595 Q. ELIZ. in Rymer *Foedera* (1705) XVI. 282 And thes our Letters shall be your sufficient Warraunt and Discharge in that behalf. 1611 BEAUM. & FL. *King & no K.* IV. ii, *Bac.* It was your own command, to barr none from him, Besides, the Princess sent her ring Sir, for my warrant. 1614 in Rymer *Foedera* (1705) XVI. 767 To the end sufficient Warrant may remayne here in our Exchequer for the Payment of the said Annuity, our Pleasure is..that you cause a Duplicate of the said Graunt to be sealed with our said Great Seale, and the same..to be sent to our said Exchequer. 1635 D. DICKSON *Hebr.* xi. 8. 255 Fayth is willing to obey, as soone as it seeth a Warrand. 1875 STUBBS *Const. Hist.* II. xiv. 110 He produced an old rusty sword and cried, 'See, my lords, here is my warrant.'

c. *Scots Law.* ***jedge and warrant***, 'the authority given by the Dean of Guild to repair a ruinous tenement' (W. Bell *Dict. Law Scot.*).

1715 *Morison's Dict. Decis.* (1806) XXXIII. 14521 Deacon Brownhill..obtained jedge and warrant from the Dean of Guild, for taking down and rebuilding a ruinous house. 1816 G. J. BELL *Comm. Law Scot.* (1826) I. 750 The judicial process of Jedge and Warrant creates a real burden on a burgage tenement, which will be effectual against creditors and purchasers.

8. a. Justifying reason or ground for an action, belief, or feeling.

1597 HOOKER *Eccl. Pol.* V. xxxv, Sith his promise is our plaine warrant, that in his name what we aske we shall receyue. 1609 ALEX. HUME *Admon.* 365 Wks. (S.T.S.) 176 Ye wer eschamed..to be called Lordis..whiche wes a takin ye had no guid warrand in your conscience for it. ?1622 FLETCHER *Loves Cure* IV. iv, *Gen.* Nay you are rude; pray you forbear, you offer now More than the breeding of a Gentleman Can give you warrant for. *a* 1628 PRESTON *New Covt.* (1634) 413, I have applyed these promises, but upon what warrant, upon what ground have I done it? 1664 BUTLER *Hud.* II. i. 786 But for a Lady no ways Errant To free a Knight, we have no warrant In any Authentical Romance. 1695 WOODWARD *Nat. Hist. Earth* i. 2 Intending..not to offer anything but what hath due warrant from Observations. *a* 1703 BURKITT *On N.T.*, John xviii. 11 Good intentions are no warrant for irregular actions. 1781 COWPER *Charity* 183 Canst thou..Trade in the blood of innocence, and plead Expedience as a warrant for the deed? 1828 SCOTT *F.M. Perth* vii, We relate it as it is given by an ancient and uniform tradition, which carries in it great indications of truth, and is warrant enough, perhaps, for its insertion in graver histories than the present. 1832 HT. MARTINEAU *Demerara* ii. 23 But that they will die out the slave history of Europe is our warrant. 1846 TRENCH *Mirac.* xxi. (1862) 333 Still there is no warrant for ascribing to them such treachery here. 1848 DICKENS *Dombey* xlvii, Florence took her seat..with an uneasiness amounting to dread. She had no other warrant for it than the occasion, the expression of her father's face [etc.]. 1862 SPENCER *First Princ.* II. iv. §53 (1875) 174 This last fact naturally raises the question, whether we have any higher warrant for this fundamental belief than the warrant of conscious induction. 1893 *Daily News* 15 Apr. 3/7 Another painter who repeats himself this year, but with more warrant, is Mr. Herbert Marshall.

†b. Phrases. ***of (good) warrant***: ? held in esteem, important. ***out of warrant***: unlawful. *Obs.*

In quot. *c* 1330 the sense may be 'well-defended': cf. 2.

c 1330 *Arth. & Merl.* 4210 Til þai com to Norhant, A fair cite of gode waraunt. 1576 *Charter at Thirkleby Park* (MS.), Prouyded also that nether the said Henry Procter..shall fell or cutt doune any oke trez eshe trez crabtrez or other wood of warrant. 1602 SHAKS. *Ham.* II. i. 38 Marry Sir, heere's my drift, And I belieue it is a fetch of warrant. 1604 —— *Oth.* I. ii. 79, I therefore..do attach thee, For..a practiser Of Arts inhibited, and out of warrant.

II. A document conveying authority or security.

9. a. A writing issued by the sovereign, an officer of state, or an administrative body, authorizing those to whom it is addressed to perform some act.

†*Premier's warrant* (Cape Colony), an order given by the Premier on his own responsibility, authorizing expenditure for the public service in some sudden emergency. *Obs.*

a 1513 FABYAN *Chron.* VII. (1811) 306 Then this abbot gate a warrant of the kynge, and at London callyd dyuerse offycers before hym, for to yelde to hym theyr accompte. 1551 in Feuillerat *Revels Edw. VI* (1914) 56 A warraunt from kynge Edward ffor ffurnyshyng of A tryeumfe. *a* 1568 ASCHAM *Scholem.* II. (Arb.) 154 Antonius Triumuir,..whan Varros name..was brought in a schedule vnto him, to be noted to death, he tooke his penne and wrote his warrant of sauegard with these most goodlie wordes, *Viuat Varro vir doctissimus.* 1682 FOUNTAINHALL *Hist. Observes* (Bannatyne Club) 73 He had coined a quantity of copper beyond the 3000 stone contained in his Majesties warrands. 1711 SWIFT *Let. to Abp. King* 4 Jan., Mr. secretary St. John..told me from Mr. Harley that I need not to be in pain about the first-fruits, for the warrant was drawn in order toward a patent: but must..take up some time, for the queen designs to make a grant by her letters-patent. 1765 BLACKSTONE *Comm.* I. ii. 171 As soon as the parliament is summoned, the lord chancellor..sends his warrant to the clerk of the crown in chancery; who thereupon issues out writs to the sheriff of every county, for the election of all the members to serve for that county, and for every city and borough therein. 1800 WELLINGTON in Gurwood *Desp.* (1834) I. 150 You will easily perceive the difference in the warrant and in the other papers from those usually given for a General Court Martial. 1842 DICKENS *Amer. Notes* iii, The indigent blind ..from the adjoining state of Connecticut, or from the states of Maine, Vermont, or New Hampshire, are admitted by a warrant from the state to which they respectively belong. 1853 STOCQUELER *Milit. Encycl.*, *Warrant*,..also a document under the sign manual, to authorize the assembling of a general court-martial, &c. 1880 ADYE in *19th Cent.* Apr. 697 The general provisions of the warrant were, that military rank, rising according to length of service, with commensurate pay and pension, should be given to all who entered.

Proverb. 1616 R. C. *Times' Whistle* i. (1871) 12 'A warrant seald with butter!' as we say.

†b. A licence to go abroad. *Obs.*

c 1645 HOWELL *Lett.* (1650) I. iii. 5, I have got a Warrant from the Lords of the Councell to travell for three years any where, Rome and S. Omer excepted.

†c. warrant-dormant: see DORMANT *a.* 2 b.

1423 *Proc. Privy Counc.* (1834) III. 85 That it like to zour grace to graunt letters of warant dormaunt..to the seyd Tresorer commaundyng hym to pay to the seyd Thomas the seyd somme fro tyme to tyme. 1551, 1614 [see DORMANT *a.* 2 b].

fig. 1635 PAGITT *Christianogr.* I. iii. (1636) 208 A man may haue for money a warrant dormant, or dispensation to commit sinnes.

10. a. A writ or order issued by some executive authority, empowering a ministerial officer to make an arrest, a seizure, or a search, to execute a judicial sentence, or to do other acts incident to the administration of justice. In early use, †***letter of warrant***.

See also BENCH-*warrant*, DEATH-WARRANT, PRESS-WARRANT, SEARCH-*warrant*.

a 1450 *Mirk's Festial* 53 He ȝeode to hom þat haden þe lawe of Iewes to kepe, and gete hym lettyrs of warant, forto take and bryng all crysten men and woymen..bonden yn Ierusalem, forto take hor deth þer. 1464 *Mann. & Househ. Exp.* (Roxb.) 185 Iohn Boteler of Herwesche is on of the iij. that was arested at the same towen be Pertones warente. 1538 in *Lett. Suppress. Monasteries* (Camden) 200 My gude lorde, if that ȝe wold..send to me a hunderyd worans for the delyverans of a hunderyd ffreeres that [etc.]. *Ibid.* If ye wold be so gode to sende to me iij. or iiij warenttes with a space for ther namys, I wer bonde to yow. 1595 SHAKS. *John* IV. ii. 70 This is the man should do the bloody deed: He shew'd his warrant to a friend of mine. 1620 ROWLANDS *Nt. Raven* 33 A Warrant to a Constable was sent, Of speciall charge, disorder to preuent. 1621 FLETCHER *Pilgr.* III. vi, The Justice keeps such a stir yonder with his Charges, And such a coil with warrants. 1623 COCKERAM II, A Warrant to commit one, *Mittimus.* *a* 1634 COKE *Inst.* IV. (1648) 176 One or more Iustice or Iustices of Peace cannot make a warrant upon a bare surmise to break any mans house to search for a Felon, or for stoln goods. 1635 *Life Long Meg of Westminster* xv. (1816) 24 Come in, master Constable,..let me see your warrant, what suspected persons you seeke for in my house. 1697 CONGREVE *Mourn. Bride* IV. i, Wherefore a Warrant for his Death is sign'd. 1724 W. HAWKINS *Pleas Crown* II. (ed. 2) 117 The *Habeas Corpus* Act, seems to suppose, That all Persons who are committed to Prison, are there detained by Virtue of some Warrant in Writing. 1726–31 TINDAL *Rapin's Hist. Eng.* (1743) II. XVII. 89 Which made her sign a Warrant to send the Duke of Norfolk to the Tower. 1835 DICKENS *Sk. Boz, Parish* v, This is my warrant of distress, mum. 1836 *Ibid., Visit to Newgate*, When the warrant for a prisoner's execution arrives, he is removed to the cells, [etc.]. 1845 DISRAELI *Sybil* v. ix, There's a warrant from the Secretary of State for your release. 1859 H. KINGSLEY *G. Hamlyn* vi, You see, I'm in trouble, there's a warrant out against me, and I must fly. 1874 'MAX ADELER' *Out of Hurly-burly* xiv, It was a constable with a warrant for her arrest. 1891 *Law Times* XC. 373/1 The magistrate..granted an English warrant on which the prisoner was now under arrest.

b. *general warrant*: a warrant for the apprehension of the persons suspected of an offence, no individual being named or particularly described in special.

According to Blackstone, the practice of issuing general warrants, founded on some clauses in the Acts (of Charles II) for regulating the press, was inadvertently continued after those Acts expired in 1694, and (except during the last four years of Queen Anne) remained down to 1763. In that year the arrest of John Wilkes on a general warrant raised the question of the legality of such warrants. In 1765 the Court of King's Bench decided that they were illegal, and in 1766 this was affirmed by a vote of the House of Commons.

1657 BULSTRODE *Rep.* I. 146 Williams Iustice, this is a most perilous example, to breake a mans house in the night, by force, and by vertue of a generall warrant. 1763 A. B. *Let.* 7 May in *Gentl. Mag.* XXXIII. 246 The question, Whether a Secretary of State can grant a general warrant against authors, printers, and publishers, without naming any names..remains yet to be determined. 1766 *Jrnls. Ho. Comm.* 22 Apr. 753/2 Resolved, That a General Warrant for apprehending the Author, Printer, or Publisher, of a Libel is illegal. 1769 BLACKSTONE *Comm.* IV. xxi. 288. 1843 *Penny Cycl.* XXVII. 380/1.

11. A writing which authorizes one person to pay or deliver, and another to receive, a sum of money.

For *dividend warrant*, *share warrant*, see the first words.

1433 *Rolls of Parlt.* IV. 439/1 Many Warantis come to me of paiementz. ?1470 *Stonor Papers* (Camden) I. 115 He had it [the money] in grete for that his labour, and a warrant made to Harre Dogett to pay yt. 1555 EDEN *Decades* II. VII. (Arb.) 127 A warrant to thofficers of his escheker to delyuer hym money in preste. 1613 in Rymer *Foedera* (1705) XVI. 742 The Somme of Two Thousand Pounds, now by Warrant of our Exchequer appointed to bee delivered unto you. 1794 *Rep. Committees Ho. Comm.* XII. 364 Warrant for the Pay, &c. of the 11th Regiment of Foot, for 365 Days. 1802 C. JAMES *Milit. Dict.*, *Warrant*... Likewise a document with the sign manual attached to it, to authorize the receipt of public monies at the treasury, &c. 1855 MACAULAY *Hist. Eng.* xxi. IV. 551 Sir Thomas Cook..had merely told them in general terms that he had been at a charge of twenty three thousand, of twenty five thousand, of thirty thousand pounds,..and his colleagues had..ordered warrants for these great sums to be instantly made out. 1912 *Times* 19 Oct. 18/5 (Company's report) Third interim dividend of 75 per cent. (actual), less tax, in respect of the year ending December 31. Warrants will be posted on January 14.

†12. A voucher, certificate. *Obs.*

1433 *Rolls of Parlt.* IV. 455/1 Youre Custumers..writen no Warants in discharge of youre said Merchantz. 1598 HAKLUYT *Voy.* I. 172 He..caried a warrant also with him, that he had at Sandwich paid the custome due vnto our lord the king. 1598 SHAKS. *Merry W.* I. i. 10 And a Gentleman borne (Master Parson) who writes himself Armigero, in any Bill, Warrant, Quittance or Obligation, Armigero.

13. A form of receipt given to a person who has deposited goods in a warehouse, by assignment of which the title to the goods is transferred.

1825 *Act 6 Geo. IV*, c. 94 §2 Any Person..in Possession of any Bill of Lading, India Warrant, Dock Warrant,.. Warrant or Order for Delivery of..Merchandize described ..in the said several Documents. 1861 *Times* 10 July, On two occasions in September last he had received warrants for wine of the bankrupt, and had advanced money on them without charging interest. 1864 A. MILLER *Coatbridge* 27 The stock of 'good merchantable brands' [of iron] at present in store, represented by 'warrants' is 280,000 tons. 1870 *Act 33 & 34 Vict.* c. 97 Schedule, [Stamp Duties] Warrant for Goods, 0 0 3. 1875 *Economist* 2 Jan. 6/1 Scotch pig iron (warrants) per ton. 103/. 1894 *Daily News* 19 Mar. 3/7 Makers..have very little stock, the bulk of the iron being in the shape of warrants. 1912 *Pitman's Commerc. Encycl.* III. 876 Iron Warrants, or warrants for iron, differ from warrants for other goods, since by the custom of the iron trade, an indorsee of the warrant obtains the goods free from any vendor's claim for purchase money.

14. *Mil.* and *Naval.* **a.** An official certificate of appointment issued to an officer of lower rank than a commissioned officer. Cf. WARRANT OFFICER.

1786 GROSE *Milit. Antiq.* I. 316 *note*, The commissioned staff officers of a corps of infantry are the chaplain, adjutant, quarter master, and surgeon. The surgeons' mates, though reckoned among the staff, have only warrants from the colonel. 1802 C. JAMES *Milit. Dict.*, *Warrant*, a writ of authority inferior to a commission: thus quartermasters are warrant officers. 1815 *Falconer's Dict. Marine* (ed. Burney), *Warrant*, the name given to a sort of commission or authority to those officers appointed by the Navy-Board, while the authorities granted by the Admiralty are styled commissions. 1858 SIMMONDS *Dict. Trade*, *Warrant*,..a commission from the Admiralty to petty officers of a vessel of war.

b. Short for WARRANT OFFICER.

1706 E. WARD *Wooden World Diss.* (1708) 74 He's marry'd as well as his Brother Warrants. 1904 KIPLING *Traffics & Discov.* 349 She kep' a little hotel for warrants and non-coms close to Auckland.

15. a. *warrant of attorney*: a formal document by which a person appoints another to perform certain acts on his behalf: = *letter*, *power of attorney*. See ATTORNEY².

1512 *Act 4 Hen. VIII*, c. 20 §2 All Warant of Attourney made..by the said Kateryne Agnes and Edward..in the said Appelys [shall] be utterly voyde. 1747 *Gentl. Mag.* XVII. 495/2 The new lord mayor..was sworn at the Exchequer bar, and having recorded warrants of attorney in the proper courts, returned to a magnificent entertainment at Guildhall. 1768 BLACKSTONE *Comm.* III. xxiv. 397 It is very usual, in order to strengthen a bond-creditor's security, for the debtor to execute a warrant of attorney to any one empowering him to confess a judgment..in an action of debt to be brought by the creditor for the specific sum due. 1837 DICKENS *Pickw.* xx, And if he gives us a warrant of attorney, as he must in the end, I know his employers will see it paid. **1870** *Act 33 & 34 Vict.* c. 97 Schedule, [Stamp Duties] Warrant of Attorney to confess and enter up a judgment given as a security for the payment or repayment of money, or for the transfer or retransfer of stock. See Mortgage, &c... Warrant of Attorney of any other kind, 0 10 0.

b. ***warrant of fitness***, a certificate of roadworthiness valid for six months, which must be carried by most classes of motor vehicle in New Zealand. (The equivalent of an M.O.T. test certificate: see M 5.)

1936 *N.Z. Statutory Regulations 1936–37* (1938) 331 Save as provided in clause (3) hereof, the driver of every motor-vehicle used on a road after the 31st day of March, 1937, shall carry in the vehicle a warrant of fitness... The warrant of fitness shall be issued only by a city authority or a person or firm appointed or approved for the purpose by the Minister. **1948** *N.Z. Law Rep.* 1229, I am convinced that a warrant of fitness does not extend to the drag link or steering assembly of a car. **1953** *Road Code* (N.Z.) 1 Jan. 39 There must be carried on a motor vehicle a Warrant of Fitness issued within the past six months. **1961** B. CRUMP *Hang on a Minute* 23 Are you aware of the law regarding warrants of fitness for motor vehicles? **1983** *N.Z. Official Yearbk.* XIII. 371 Most lightweight vehicles are required to have a warrant of fitness which can be issued at approved garages, or at testing stations operated by local authorities or the Ministry of Transport.

III. ? Concrete uses of sense 2.

16. *north.* 'A mill-dam in a stream' (*Eng. Dial. Dict.*). Now written *warren.*

1406–7 *Priory of Finchale* (Surtees) p. cxxxvii, In expensis pro le warand pro defensione molendini et fleme. **1457–8** *Durham Acc. Rolls* (Surtees) 637 Et sol. eisdem operantibus apud le Warraunte Molendini Abbathie. **1531–2** *Durham Househ. Bk.* (Surtees) 82 Ad molendinum de Sheylez,.. super le warrant ibidem. **1901** *Durh. Acc. Rolls* (Surtees) III. Gloss., *Warraunte.* Millers in Durham and North Yorkshire say that the 'Warrant' is the mill-dam, and that it is pronounced War'n'... So Halliwell, '*Warren-head*, a dam across a river in the more northern parts of Northumberland'.

†**17.** *Archery.* (See quot.). *Obs.*

1688 HOLME *Armoury* III. xvii. (Roxb.) 117/1 The Warrants, are Knots in a Bow, which are left strong there for the securing of it.

IV. 18. *attrib.* and *Comb.*, as (sense 9) ***warrant-book***; (sense 13) ***warrant-market, stock***; (sense 14) ***warrant machinist, mechanician, rank***; **warrant card**, a document of authorization and identification carried by police officer; **warrant chief**: in Nigeria, an African local official, esp. (formerly) one appointed by the colonial power; **warrant holder**, a tradesman who has written authority to supply goods to the household of the king or a member of the royal family; †**warrant-man** (see quot. 1746); †**warrant-parol**, a judicial sentence given by word of mouth.

1873 *Nairne Peerage Evid.* (1874) 14 Do you produce from the General Record Office a *Warrant Book for Scotland, containing entries of the date of January 1681? I do. **1920** H. L. ADAM *Police Encycl.* III. iv. 77 All officers in plain clothes are furnished with a '*warrant card', by means of which they can, should they be challenged, at once prove their *bona fides.* **1933** D. L. SAYERS *Murder must Advertise* xvii. 296 Beware of.. the plain-clothes cop without a warrant-card. **1983** R. ALLASON *Branch* xii. 169 He stresses to newcomers to the Branch that they hold the same warrant cards as the rest of the Metropolitan Police. **1922** S. M. GRIER *Rep. Eastern Provinces by Secretary for Native Affairs* 5 The Native Court Clerk.. conveys to the *warrant chiefs instructions sent from the Divisional Officer. **1957** LD. HAILEY *African Survey 1956* viii. 465 The members of these Councils, who came to be known as Warrant Chiefs, were selected from villages within the Council or Court area. **1976** *Daily Times* (Lagos) 12 Oct. 5/2 The role of some warrant chiefs in the selection of the new Owa of Indanre was consistent with the chieftaincy regulations. **1893** *Daily News* 12 June 5/8 The Association of her Majesty's and the Prince and Princess of Wales's *Warrant Holders. **1902** *Monthly Rev.* Aug. 93 Admiral Melville, in his report dealing with the *warrant machinists of the U.S. Navy, says [etc.]. **1746** *Rep. Committees Ho. of Comm.* II. 100 But the real Charge being greater, as there are a Number of fictitious Names allowed upon the Muster Rolls by Warrant, called *Warrant-men. **1896** *Daily News* 28 Dec. 3/7 The Cleveland *warrant market has been stronger, and 40s. 10d. is asked by sellers. **1906** *Daily Chron.* 12 Apr. 6/7 [A stoker] eligible for advancement to the rank of *warrant mechanician. **1609** HOLLAND *Amm. Marcell.* 363 And by this *warrant-parol [L. *hoc elogio*] the eloquent man lost his life. **1903** *Daily Chron.* 9 Nov. 3/2 Boys passing through training ships.. can ultimately reach *warrant rank.

Hence †'**warrantship** = GUARANTEESHIP.

1702 *Anguis in Herba* 63 There is but one way to warrant this Peace; and that is, we must enter into a League of Warrantship with the Emperor, the Empire, the Dutch, and all other Nations.

warrant ('wɒrənt), *sb.*[2] *Mining.* Also warren. [Of obscure origin; perh. a use of prec.] Under-clay.

1847–89 HALLIWELL, *Warrant*, the bottom of a coal-pit. **1871** A. H. GREEN *Coal* (Manch. Sci. Lect., Ser. II) 5, I think in Lancashire that you know it [the under-clay] by the name of 'warrant', or 'seat earth'. **1883** GRESLEY *Gloss. Coal-mining*, Warrant; Warren or Warren Earth.

†'**warrant**, *a. Obs. rare*[−1]. [f. WAR *v.* + -ANT.] Warring, conflicting.

1606 WARNER *Alb. Eng.* XV. c. 396 How many seuerall Lawes at once had Britaine long agoe? The Britons theirs, the Romanes theirs, the Picts and Scots also... But that I know be lawes in force for Sabbaths, feasts of Saints, For Fasts, for Vagrants,.. I should haue thought those too prophane and warrant lawes had bin, So common and so vncontrould is sufferance of such sin.

warrant ('wɒrənt), *v.* Pa. t. and pa. pple. **warranted.** Forms: 3 **warantye, waraunti,** 4 **waranti,** 4–5 **warente,** 5–6 **warent,** 4–5 **warante,** 4–7 **warant,** 4–6 **waraunt,** 5–6 **warraunt,** (6 **-e**), 5 **warawnt,** 6–7 **warrante,** 5– **warrant;** *Sc.* and *north.* 4–5 **warand(e,** 5 **werrand,** 6 **warrande,** (7 *pa. pple.* **warand**), 8 **warran,** 5– **warrand** (*occas.* written **wand** etc.). [early ME. *warant, waranti, warand*, a. OF. *warantir, warandir*, dial. variants of *g(u)arantir, g(u)arandir* (mod.F. *garantir*) = Pr. *garentir, guirentir*, Sp., Pg. *garantir*, It. *guarantire, guarentire*; a Com. Rom. formation on the sb.: see WARRANT *sb.*[1]]

†**1.** *trans.* To keep safe from danger, to protect. Const. *from. Obs.*

c **1275** *Five Joys of the Virg.* 9 in *O.E. Misc.* 89 Bidde we vre louerd crist þat hire warantye. *c* **1290** *Magdalen* 40 in *S. Eng. Leg.* 463 Iesu crist of heouene of heom habbe merci And for is names seouene fram helle heom waraunti! **13..** *K. Alis.* 2131 (Laud MS.), Alisaunder.. bad hem be hardy & noþing drede He wolde hem warant in euery nede. **13..** *Guy Warw.* 4415 Seþþe þou no miȝt nouȝt waranti me, Whar-to schuld y serui þe. **1375** BARBOUR *Bruce* II. 504 For he Thaim fra thar fais mycht nocht warand, Thai turnyt to the tothir hand. *c* **1386** CHAUCER *Pard. T.* Prol. 10 Oure lige lordes seel on my patente That shewe I first my body to warente. *c* **1400** *Master of Game* (MS. Digby 182) ii, If he hath a deere þat be his felawe, he leueth hym to þe houndes in entente, þat he may warrant hymselfe. *c* **1450** LOVELICH *Merlin* 3498 What good Man was he that from the deth warawnted the? *c* **1450** *Merlin* ii. 29 Yef ye will leve me, ye shal warant youre owen lyves. *c* **1470** HENRY *Wallace* VIII. 978 Wictaill as than was nayne left in the land, Bot in houssis quhar it mycht be warrand. *c* **1489** CAXTON *Sonnes of Aymon* i. 19 Hym I beseche to kepe and waraunt thee.. from evyl. **1489** —— *Faytes of A.* I. x. 28 Iulius cesar yᵗ for to waraunt his owne lyf sauf dide swimme in yᵉ see. **1570** *Satir. Poems Reform.* xix. 14 This commoun weill quhat wicht sal now warrand, Sen he is gone, that Gouernd vs befoir. **1589** R. HARVEY *Pl. Perc.* (1590) 8 We shall speake so long of the diuell in iest, that he shall come amongst vs in good earnest: God warrant vs [they crossed themselves on saying this]. **1600** SHAKS. *A.Y.L.* III. iii. 5 *Clo*[*wne*]. Doth my simple feature content you? *Aud.* Your features, Lord warrant vs: what features?

†**b.** Of armour: to protect physically. *Obs.*

c **1450** *Merlin* x. 162 He.. smote a knyght so sore that ther was noon armoure myght hym warante. *c* **1475** *Partenay* 2237 A paynym to smyte went he forth Anon, hym not warented harnes ne helme Aboute. *c* **1500** *Melusine* xxi. 136 For hys harneys coude neuer waraunt hym.

†**c.** With inverted construction: To keep off (enemies) *from* a person. *Obs.*

1586 EARL LEYCESTER *Corr.* (Camden) 431 For who can warrant these villaines from her [Q. Eliz.], if that person [Mary Q. Scots] liue, or shall liue, anie time?

2. *Law.* **a.** To guarantee the security of (land, possessions *to* a person).

1406 in *Reg. Mag. Sig. Scot. 1427* 17/2, I oblis me my ayris to kep and warand and defende tha said landis to the said Jon. **1440** in *Cartul. S. Nicholai Aberdon.* (New Spalding Club) I. 11 And I.. all ye forsaid landes.. againis all dedelik sal warand acquit and defend for evyr. *c* **1450** *Godstow Reg.* 82 The forseyd Dame Margery.. warentyd the fore-seyd ij acris of londe.. to the for-seyd Richard.. a-geynst all pepull. **1495** *Act 11 Hen. VII*, c. 47 §1 You.. be not bounden to warant the seid Manoris.. by reason of any warantye comprised in the same lettres patentes. **1551** *Rental Bk. Cupar Angus* (1880) II. 71 We.. sall warrand, acquiet, and defend this our present assedatioun,.. to the saidis personis. **1564** *Abstr. Protocols Town Clerks Glasgow* (1896) III. 50 Robert sall warrande the saidis reversioune.. fre of all byrwnnyn annuallis. **1570** JEWEL *View Seditious Bull* Wks. 1848 VII. 256 Was not the crown due to her [Elizabeth].. by the laws of this realm? did not her father warrant it to her by will, as his daughter? **1628** in Cramond *Ann. Banff* (1891) I. 58 He to.. warrand the grein yeird and ground thereof to be uncassin up or riwin or away carried. **1642** *Perkins' Prof. Bk.* ii. §176. 78 If this acre bee warranted unto them, this warranty is good.

†**b.** To be surety for. *Obs.*

1478 [see WARRANT *sb.*[1] 4]. **1609** SKENE *Reg. Mag.* 15 Gif anie thing thifteouslie stollen, is challenged be anie man; and he quha is challenged, alledges ane Priest for his warrant; and the Priest will willinglie warant the samine.

c. To give warranty of (title); to give warranty of title to (a person). Also with the land as obj. Cf. *to vouch to warrant*: VOUCH *v.* I.

? **1475** *Stonor Papers* (Camden) I. 159 Yowre masterchyp muste warent hym agaynst al men. **1480** *Acta Dom. Conc.* (1839) 51/2 þe said vmfra sall warand þe said macolme þe said landis of W. **1488** *Acta Dom. Audit.* (1839) 123/2 He haid deliuerit þe said malez to him, and þerfore askit him to Werrand him þerintill. **1544** tr. *Littleton's Tenures* 34 He ought to warrante his tenaunt whan he is impleaded of the landes holden of him. **1579** *Expos. Terms Law* 53 b, Where the tenaunt in hys aunswere and plee, voucheth or calleth for anie manne to warrant his title. **1845** WILLIAMS *Real Property* (1877) 45 The tenant then alleged that this third person had warranted the title.

3. With obj. and complement or inf.: To guarantee (goods, an article sold or made) to be of the quality, quantity, etc. specified.

1387 *Charters* etc. *Edin.* (1871) 36 The qwilke werke the forsaide masounys sal warande watir thicht. **1484** CAXTON *Fables of Alfonce* iii, This Ryche man thenne sold his oylle to the marchaunts and warraunted eche toune al ful. **1530** PALSGR. 771/2, I warant, as a marchaunt, or seller dothe his ware that it is good. *Je pleuuis.* **1602** FULBECKE *1st Pt. Parall.* 4 If a mans seruant sell to one certaine clothe, and warrant it to bee of a certaine length the Action will lye against the Maister onely. **1608** *Pennyless Parl. Threadbare Poets* §23 Bow bell in Cheapside, if it break not, shall be warranted by Letters Pattents to ring well. **1742** FIELDING *J. Andrews* I. xvi, Perhaps you may sell them by advertising the manuscript sermons of a clergyman lately deceased, all warranted originals, and never printed. **1789** W. H. MARSHALL *Glouc.* I. 331 'Will you warrant them siddow [= tender]?' is the ordinary question asked on buying peas for boiling. **1837** DICKENS *Pickw.* v, 'Not the slightest fear, sir,' interposed the hostler. 'Warrant him quiet, sir.' **1848** —— *Dombey* xxix, One French roll rasped, one egg new laid (or warranted to be). **1886** C. SCHOLL *Phraseol. Dict.* II. 832 Warranted free from adulteration. *Ibid.*, The colors of all stuffs warranted fast.

fig. **1809–10** COLERIDGE *Friend* (1866) 131, I could almost venture to warrant our patriot's publications innoxious. **1865** W. G. PALGRAVE *Arabia* II. 176, I would not warrant the numerical precision of this statement.

b. To promise under guarantees.

1849 FREESE *Comm. Class-bk.* 63 Ship warranted to sail on or before 10th August next. **1886** C. SCHOLL *Phraseol. Dict.* II. 832 We warrant the vessel will be loaded by the time specified.

4. To guarantee as true, make oneself answerable for (a statement).

a. with clause as obj. Chiefly in phrase ***I warrant, I will (I'll) warrant***, often used *colloq.* as a mere expression of strong belief = 'I'll be bound'.

13.. *Coer de L.* 3523 Kyng Richard schal waraunt, There is no flesch so noryssaunt,.. As the hed off a Sarezyn. **13..** *Northern Passion* 245/39* þe knightes said: 'we will warand þat ioseph es in his awind land.' *c* **1400** *Ywaine & Gaw.* 1049 Madame, sho said, i dar warand A genteler lord es none lifand. *c* **1440** *York Myst.* xxxiii. 384 He swounes or sweltes, I swarand. *c* **1460** *Towneley Myst.* xxiii. 484 Haue here the draght.. And I shall warand it is not swete. *a* **1533** BERNERS *Huon* li. 172 Or it be halfe a yere past I warraunt thou shalt haue a horse. **1598** SHAKS. *Merry W.* II. i. 76, I warrant he hath a thousand of these Letters. *Ibid.* III. iii. 174 Ile warrant wee'le vnkennell the Fox. *Ibid.* IV. v. 114 And haue not they suffer'd? Yes, I warrant. **1677** LADY CHAWORTH in *12th Rep. Hist. MSS. Comm.* App. v. 37 All from Court say the House will infailibly sit, but none dares warrant how long. **1715** DE FOE *Fam. Instruct.* I. iv. (1841) I. 88, I warrant she kissed thee. **1742** FIELDING *J. Andrews* IV. v, He.. refused, saying he could walk by its side, and he'd warrant he kept up with it. **1786** BURNS *Earnest Cry* xiii, Dempster, a true-blue Scot I'se warran. **1794** MRS. RADCLIFFE *Myst. Udolpho* xxvii, I heard one of the soldiers.. say to his comrade, that he would warrant they'd bring home a rare deal of booty. **1860** DICKENS *Uncomm. Trav.* ix, Some chapel where she comforts herself with brimstone doctrine, I warrant. **1864** TENNYSON *En. Arden* 847, I warrant, man, that we shall bring you round.

b. with obj. and complement, inf., or clause; also with ellipsis of the complement. *arch.*

1377 LANGL. *P. Pl.* B. XVIII. 46 'Crucifige,' quod a cacchepolle 'I warante hym a wicche'. *c* **1440** *York Myst.* xxix. 373, I warande hym wakande. *c* **1520** SKELTON *Magnyf.* 1835 Nay fole, I warant her blode warme. **1532** TINDALE *Expos. v–vii. Matt.* (?1550) 93, I warrante hym synge masse on the next daye after as wel as he dyd before. **1607** SHAKS. *Cor.* V. ii. 115 A Noble Fellow I warrant him. **1684** BUNYAN *Pilgr.* II. (1879) 210, I will warrant her a good Huswife, quoth he to himself. **1751** F. COVENTRY *Pompey the Little* I. xi. 100 Why don't they send out V-rn-n with a strong Fleet..? I warrant him,.. he would not leave a Harbour or a Ship in France. **1884** TENNYSON *Becket* V. ii, *Becket.* Doth he remember me? *Rosamund.* I warrant him.

c. with neut. pronoun as obj. (sometimes pleonastic). Now *dial.*

a **1400** *Sir Perc.* 1843 Here mone I stande, For a faute that he fande, That salle I warande Is my moste mone. *c* **1475** *Rauf Coilȝear* 122 Thow art vncourtes, that sall I warrand. **1603** SHAKS. *Meas. for M.* II. iv. 59 Nay Ile not warrant that: for I can speake Against the thing I say. **1719** DE FOE *Crusoe* II. (Globe) 493 They told me, like Seamen, they'd warrant it they would come off again. **1877** *Holderness Gloss.* s.v. *Wand it*, He'll come tiv a bad end yan o' these days, Ah'll wand it he will.

d. With sb. as obj.: To vouch for the truth of (an opinion).

c **1375** *Sc. Leg. Saints* xxi. (*Clement*) 648 Opunyonys ware sere.. bot I dare nane of þame warand.

†**e.** To promise or predict as certain. Also, of a thing: To be a sure presage of. *Obs.*

1591 SHAKS. *1 Hen. VI*, II. v. 95 True; and thou seest, that I no Issue haue, And that my fainting words doe warrant death. *Ibid.* v. v. 46 Beside, his wealth doth warrant a liberal dower. **1639** in *Verney Mem.* (1907) I. 106 My frenchman.. tells me he will warrant I shall speak it [French] perfectly before we draw into the field! **1662** R. MATHEW *Unl. Alch.* 160 He.. willed me to get good Oyl of Amber, and drink three or four drops in the morning fasting, and he would warrant my recovery. **1821** SCOTT *Kenilw.* xviii, 'My son,' replied the astrologer, 'let me remind you, I warranted not his death'.

†**f.** To undertake, pledge oneself *to do* something. Also with neut. pronoun as obj. *Obs. rare.*

13.. *Souyn Sages* (W.) 111 Bot for to lere him I warand, Als mekil als he mai vnderstand. *c* **1440** *York Myst.* xix. 355 *Cayph.* 3a, and felawes, wayte þat he be ay wakand. ii *Miles.* ȝis lorde, þat warant will wee! **1532** MORE *Confut. Tindale* Wks. 630/1 Yet hys grace and good wyll he hath warraunted neuer to take from them.

5. To give (a person) assurance of a fact. Chiefly in ***I (I'll) warrant you***, used colloq. = 'I warrant' in 4 a.

c **1520** SKELTON *Magnyf.* 506, I shall the warent, As long as I lyue, thou haste an heyre parent. **1529** MORE *Dyal.* xiv. 19/2 There be many such I warrant you yᵗ neuer cum to light. **1599** B. JONSON *Cynthia's Rev.* IV. i, The very marchpane of the court, I warrant you? **1632** LITHGOW

Trav. x. 454, I warrant you (sayd he) I shal lodge him well enough. **1670** EACHARD *Cont. Clergy* 13 A forward boy, (cries the school-master)..he proves a brave clergyman, I'll warrant you. **1689** *Selden's Table-talk* 17, I..warranted him, if he would follow my directions, to Cure him in a short time. **1711** BUDGELL *Spect.* No. 77 ¶6, I warrant you he is now thrusting his short Face into some Coffee-house about 'Change. **1725** DE FOE *Voy. round World* (1840) 25, I warrant him, let us but go up the height of St. Helena, we will soon reach the Rio de la Plata. **1777** JOHNSON *Let. to Mrs. Thrale* 25 Oct., Cicely, I warrant you, will do well enough. **1799** SOUTHEY *To a Spider* iv, I'll warrant thee thou'lt drain His life-blood dry. **1826** SCOTT *Woodst.* xi, Sent him to share with us, I'se warrant ye. **1835** J. POOLE *Sk. & Recoll.* I. 37 'He be vive mile off by now.' 'You are certain of that?' 'I warrant 'ee, zur.' At this assurance I felt a throb of joy. **1860** W. W. READE *Liberty Hall* II. 136 Many's the horn of old Pharoah ale have I mopped up in their brick floor kitchens, I warrant 'ee.

¶ **b.** ***I warrant me*** (originally quasi-*arch.*) = 'I warrant', 'I'll be bound'.

1825 SCOTT *Talism.* xviii, And I warrant me thou wouldst have another—in requital, ha? **1826** DISRAELI *V. Grey* VI. i, No enemy with the girls, I warrant me.

6. To attest the truth or authenticity of; to authenticate.

1598 MARSTON *Sco. Villanie* x. H 4 At least what ere he sayes Is warranted by Curtaine plaudeties. **1599** SHAKS. *Much Ado* IV. i. 168 *Friar*... Trust not..my obseruations, Which with experimental seale doth warrant The tenure of my booke:..If this sweet Ladie lye not guiltlesse heere. **1600** *Chester Pl., Banes* 13 This moonke..In pagentes set fourth..the old and newe testament..Interminglinge therewith..some thinge, not warranted by any writt. **1617** MORYSON *Itin.* II. 8, I purpose to write nothing which is not warranted..by Letters interchanged betweene the States of England and Ireland, or like authenticall writings. *c* **1620** FLETCHER *False One* Prol., New Titles warrant not a Play for new, The Subject being old. **1635** SWAN *Spec. M.* iv. §2 (1643) 66 The truth of it was never questioned, but warranted by all antiquitie. **1649** MILTON *Eikon.* xi. 109 Antiquity that adds or varies from the Scripture is no more warranted to our safe imitation then what was done..at Trent. **1700** LOCKE *Hum. Und.* IV. xix. §15 (ed. 4) 427 Reason warrants it, and we may safely receive it for true. **1769** BLACKSTONE *Comm.* IV. xxiii. 305 Wherever any capital offence is charged, the same law requires that the accusation be warranted by the oath of twelve men, before the party shall be put to answer it. **1855** MACAULAY *Hist. Eng.* xix. IV. 287 That it [his confession] was genuine could not be doubted: for it was warranted by the signatures of some of the most distinguished military men living.

†**b.** with clause as obj. or with obj. and complement. *Obs.*

1591 SHAKS. *Two Gent.* II. vii. 71 A thousand oathes, an Ocean of his teares,..Warrant me welcome to my Protheus. **1605** BACON *Adv. Learn.* I. ii. §2 Experience doth warrant, that bqth in persons and in times, there hath beene a meeting and concurrence in learning and Armes. **1655** MOUFET & BENNET *Health's Improv.* (1746) 189 Experience warranteth them [Martinets] a dainty and good Meat.

†**7.** To furnish (a person) with a guarantee or assurance. Const. *of*, or with subord. clause. *Obs.*

1548 GESTE *Pr. Masse* K ij, The cause why..they sacrifyce and praye for thee dead, was..partly to assure & warrant the suruyuers at the remembraunce of the good & blesful estate of the deceased. **1569** NEWTON *Cicero's Olde Age* 23 Young men also are subject to the same, and cannot warrant themselves of health, no more than old men can. **1590** SHAKS. *Com. Err.* I. i. 140 And happy were I in my timelie death, Could all my trauells warrant me they liue. **1597** HOOKER *Eccl. Pol.* v. lxvii. §4 They being the first that were commaunded to receiue from him, the first which were warranted by his promise that [etc.].

†**b.** With double obj.: To guarantee or ensure (a person something). Also, to promise (a person something) as certain. *Obs.*

a **1548** HALL *Chron., Hen. IV* 8 b, The Duke biddyng him to be of good comfort and out of feare warranted him his lyfe. **1568** GRAFTON *Chron.* II. 488 Warrantyng him a famous victorie. **1574** tr. *Marlorat's Apocalips* 6 For what can a man find in worldly writers too warrant himselfe saluation by? **1582** STANYHURST *Æneis* I. (Arb.) 25 No worldly corner can theym securitye warrant. **1662** *Pagitt's Heresiogr.* Ep. Ded., Your present annual authority cannot warrant your Lordship that effect..which might be expected.

†**c.** To secure (something) *to* a person. *Obs.*

1613 PURCHAS *Pilgrimage* (1614) 163 He had great authority ouer all Congregations of Israelites, warranted to him with the Amirs seale.

8. To guarantee the security or immunity of (a person or thing). Const. *from*, *for* (= from), *against*. Now *rare*. Cf. sense 1.

1530 PALSGR. 772/1, I warrant one to save him harmlesse. *Je garantis*..I wyll gyve hym twenty pounde that dare warrante me. **1560** *J. Fisher's Godly Treatise* D 4 b, For in this lyfe no man ought to warrant and assure hym selfe, and lyue thereby out of feare. **1560** DAUS tr. *Sleidane's Comm.* 268 That the women and maydens are wickedly defloured, [etc.]..Where the Emperour hath warraunted them for Religion, it is but dissimulation. **1586** B. YOUNG *Guazzo's Civ. Conv.* IV. 190 b, I doe not thinke that our Cauallero, could be exempted or warranted from this fault. **1590** SHAKS. *Com. Err.* IV. iv. 3 *An.* [*to jailor*] I will not breake away, Ile giue thee ere I leaue thee so much money To warrant thee as I am rested for. **1610** —— *Temp.* I. i. 49 I'le warrant him for drowning, though the Ship were no stronger then a Nutt-shell. **1627** MAY *Lucan* v. I 3 b, Spread sailes, and if the sky Warrant thee not to goe for Italy, Ile warrant thee. **1642** FULLER *Holy & Prof. St.* v. vii. 385 He had so cunningly contrived his plots, as to warrant himself against all events. **1648** tr. *Senault's Paraphr. Job* 339 Consider that it [Heaven] is so high, that they cannot assault it, that the distance which seperates it from us, warrants it from all our attempts. **1660** INGELO *Bentiv. & Ur.* II. (1682) 213 [They] think they have sufficiently warranted their present Sensuality against all just Reproof. **1683** *Apol. Prot. France* vi. 82 Thus they had only promis'd to warrant Jerome of Prague, from violence, and not from the arrests of Justice. **1821** SCOTT *Kenilw.* xiv, He bore..the higher share in Elizabeth's favour, though..by no means so decidedly expressed as to warrant him against the final preponderance of his rival's pretensions. **1831** JAMES *Phil. Augustus* xxxix, Let him come! I will warrant him from harm or from injustice. **1873** BROWNING *Red Cott. Nt.-cap* 1633 Like some kindly weathercock Which, stuck fast at Set-Fair, Favonian Breeze, Still warrants you from rain.

9. To give (a person) warrant or authority, authorize (*to* do something); to authorize, sanction (a course of action).

1579 LYLY *Euphues* I. (Arb.) 179 Doth his preheminence in the court, warrant him to oppresse the poore by might, and acquit him of punishment? **1581** LAMBARDE *Eiren.* I. ix. (1602) 38 The forme of their commission was enlarged, so as they..were..warranted also to arrest Felons that were indited. **1583** *Exec. for Treason* (1675) 14 All [are] warranted to disobey her and her Laws. **1624** BACON *Apophth.* §242 (1625) 264 Marius did Denison them all, for Citizens of Rome, though there was no Law to warrant it. **1642** D. ROGERS *Naaman* 436 The Lord warrants us to suspect the inconstant. **1649** [LANGBAINE] *Answ. Univ. Oxf.* 16 But onely such just Power as they are by Law..warranted unto. **1678** SIR G. MACKENZIE *Crim. Laws Scot.* I. i. §iii. (1699) 5 Nor can the Council, by their Acts, warrand any to do what would be otherwise a Crime. **1685** *Lond. Gaz.* No. 2031/4 But even in the Business of the Excise and Militia..I am warranted to go the greatest lengths for your ease and conveniency that the nature of these things can bear. **1859** KEBLE in J. O. Johnston *Liddon* (1904) 47 What most perplexes me is some names in the list of those who have warranted this step.

†**b.** ***to warrant out***: to claim licence for (one's action). *Obs.* (? *nonce-use.*)

1599 B. JONSON *Cynthia's Rev.* v. i. 23 Though Mercurie can warrant out His vnder-takings, and make all things good, Out of the powers of his diuinitie.

†**c.** To license for printing. *Obs.*

1628 LAUD *Diary* 12 June, Wks. 1853 III. 207, I was complained of by the House of Commons for warranting Doctor Manwaring's sermons to the press.

d. To authorize (a payment).

1662 PETTY *Taxes* 34 Why might not another take much more than 100*l.* at London for warranting the like sum to be paid at Carlisle on a certain day. **1818** CRUISE *Digest* (ed. 2) IV. 219 The donee of the power may make any lease or grant, provided it does not exceed the utmost extent of interest that the power warrants.

†**10.** To direct (a person) authoritatively; to command. *Obs. rare.*

1631 MASSINGER *Emperor East* Prol. at Blackfriars, But that imperious custome warrants it, Our Author with much willingnes would omit This Preface to his new worke.

11. Of things: To furnish good and sufficient grounds for (a course of action); to render allowable, justify.

1654 BRAMHALL *Just Vind.* i. (1661) 3 Henry the Eighth.. pursued but..a way warranted by the practice of the most Christian Emperors of old. **1675** BAXTER *Cath. Theol.* II. i. 284 They..will know that I have enough to abase me before God and man: But will that warrant a course of lying and backbiting in others? *a* **1716** SOUTH *Serm.* (1744) XI. 302 All which considerations of a danger so..great, are certainly very sufficient to warrant the nicest caution and fearfulness in this case. **1774** tr. *Chesterf. Let. to Son* xv. I. 47 The Rape of the Sabines was more an advantageous than a just measure; yet the utility of it should not warrant its injustice. **1813** LAMB *Reynolds & Leonardo da Vinci* Wks. 1908 I. 191 The hand was by the boldest licence twice as big as the truth of drawing warranted. **1820** W. IRVING *Sketch Bk.* II. 244 It is impossible to say whether this accusation was warranted by facts. **1833** RITCHIE *Wand. by Loire* 3 Every one has a higher opinion of himself than his station warrants. **1853** BRONTE *Villette* xiv, It was not my intention to approach or address him in the garden, our terms of acquaintance not warranting such a step. **1875** GLADSTONE *Glean.* (1879) VI. 238 Our general information..is not sufficient to warrant our giving an immediate opinion on the question. **1883** *Manch. Exam.* 24 Oct. 4/6 Any advance of wages at present is not warranted by the condition of trade.

b. To justify (a person *in* or *to* a course of action).

1671 [R. MACWARD] *True Nonconf.* Contents, Positive grounds from Scripture warranding Subjects to defend Religion by armes. **1765** BLACKSTONE *Comm.* I. i. 2 And in this I am warranted by the example of ancient Rome. **1794** R. J. SULIVAN *View Nat.* II. 79 From the universality of this magnetic influence, we might, in some degree, be warranted in conjecturing, that [etc.]. **1804** ABERNETHY *Surg. Obs.* 210, I said that I did not think a surgeon warranted in tying the external iliac artery. **1843** MILL *Logic* I. iii. §7 We are not warranted in referring our sensations to a cause. **1845** T. W. COIT *Puritanism* 48 These are ample..to well warrant the Dr. in his conclusion. **1883** *League Jrnl.* 20 Oct. 657/3 If we could have more earthly enjoyment by shortening life this would not warrant us to shorten it.

c. Of a person: To countenance by one's action or example. ? *Obs.*

1631 SHIRLEY *Love's Cruelty* I. ii. (1640) B 4 b, Warrant not so much ill by your example To those that live beneath you.

†**d.** To justify by appeal to authority or evidence, to find warrant for. *Obs.*

1612 T. TAYLOR *Comm. Titus* i. 6 It is no lesse then our dutie to warrant out of this place the marriage of Ministers. **1635** D. DICKSON *Hebr.* vii. 13–15. 127 It is not warranded from Scripture; therefore I am not bound to believe it. **1662** HOBBES *Consid.* 33 But seeing there is no such word in the Scripture, how will you warrant it from natural reason?

12. To appoint (an officer) by a warrant.

1746 W. THOMPSON *R.N. Adv.* (1757) 32 All Officers were warranted from the Admiralty Board.

warrant, obs. variant of WARREN.

warrantable ('wɒrəntəb(ə)l), *a.* [f. WARRANT *v.* + -ABLE.] For which warrant may be given.

1. Of actions, sentiments, motives, etc.: That may be authorized, sanctioned, or permitted; justifiable.

1597 HOOKER *Eccl. Pol.* v. lxxiii. §5 Tutors, without whose authoritie there was no act which they did, warrantable. **1617** MORYSON *Itin.* II. 104 Pardon this my digression, not warrantable in a journall. **1691** NORRIS *Pract. Disc.* 49 Tis therefore very Warrantable to pass a Severe Judgment upon a Man, when 'tis plain and out of question that he deserves it. **1774** SIR J. REYNOLDS *Disc.* vi. (1778) 217 It is a necessary and warrantable pride to disdain to walk servilely behind any individual, however elevated his rank. **1834** MARRYAT *P. Simple* viii, Any other expenses which you may consider warrantable or justifiable. **1846** J. KENRICK *Ess. Primæval Hist.* Pref. p. xviii, Since..we can neither deny the fact of a contrariety, nor remove it by any warrantable means. **1875** H. C. WOOD *Therap.* (1879) 482 Only in desperate cases is such heroic use of the remedy warrantable.

b. Const. *by*, *from*, *to*.

1639 MASSINGER *Unnat. Combat* I. i. B 4, Everie minute to me will be a tedious age till our embraces are warrantable to the world. **1656** in *Burton's Diary* (1828) I. 254 They have done nothing but what was warrantable by former precedents. **1659** MILTON *Of Civil Power* 5 Having no other divine rule or autoritie from without us warrantable to one another as a common ground but the holy scripture. **1713** CHALKLEY *Wks.* (1751) II. 57 It is Warrantable from Scripture, that Gospel Ministers be honourably supported and maintained.

†**2.** That may be guaranteed as good, true, genuine, or the like; of good warrant; praiseworthy, acceptable. *Obs.*

1581 J. BELL *Haddon's Answ. Osor.* 471 b, Lett us peruse the Argumentes wherewith this gentle and obedient childe of the Popes good grace doth make his wordes warrantable. **1599** NASHE *Lenten Stuffe* B 4 b, But this is most warrantable, the Alpha of all the Yarmouths it was, and not the Omega correspondently. *c* **1618** E. BOLTON *Hypercritica* iv. §1 The Books..out of which we gather the most warrantable English are not many to my remembrance. **1626** MIDDLETON *Anything for Quiet Life* III. ii, She says you vent ware that is not warrantable, braided ware. **1709** T. ROBINSON *Vind. Mosaick Syst.* Introd. 11 A Man of the highest Political Accomplishments, as well as True and Warrantable Prudence. **1747** tr. *Astruc's Fevers* 108 From what we have said, it evidently appears, that the works in general of Hippocrates are not warrantable. **1821** LAMB *Elia, Imperf. Sympathies*, [I] thought I could not do better than follow the example of such grave and warrantable personages.

3. That can be legally guaranteed.

1876 BLACKMORE *Cripps* liii, Not a pound should be deducted from his warrantable value, simply because he now did what any other young horse in the world would have felt to be right.

4. *Venery.* Applied to a stag which is of an age to be hunted.

1677 PLOT *Oxfordsh.* 190 The Deer themselves were well enough grown, and warrantable. **1847** MARRYAT *Childr. N. Forest* v, A warrantable stag—that is, one old enough to kill and to be good venison. **1856** 'STONEHENGE' *Brit. Sports* 82/1 At six [years], a Warrantable Stag. **1884** JEFFERIES *Red Deer* vi. 104 It must be a runnable stag, or warrantable, a term in its strict meaning indicating a stag of five years.

'warrantableness. [-NESS.] The quality of being warrantable.

a **1586** SIDNEY *Arcadia* II. xx. §3 (1912) 279 That..you may see the noblenes of my desire to you, & the warrantablenes of your favour to me. **1663** BOYLE *Usef. Exp. Nat. Philos.* II. v. xix. 290 The warrantableness of which caution..was confirm'd to me not long since by a skilful Physitian. **1732** E. ERSKINE *Serm.* Wks. 1871 I. 33 We see here the warrantableness of believing in Christ. **1898** T. ADAMSON *Stud. Mind in Christ* viii. 195 The warrantableness of this interpretation is fully borne out.

warrantably ('wɒrəntəblɪ), *adv.* [-LY².] In a warrantable manner; with good warrant.

1628 WITHER *Brit. Rememb.* Pref. 699 It shall be seene, That I have warrantably called beene. **1657** HEYLYN *Eccles. Vind.* Gen. Pref. a 1, A Church so rightly constituted, so warrantably reformed. **1703** J. QUICK *Serious Inquiry* 23 Jacob might warrantably enough have returned Leah back again unto her deceitful Father. **1732** E. ERSKINE *Serm.* Wks. (1791) 641 None can warrantably lay a stone in this building, except he be regularly called. **1856** MRS. BROWNING *Aur. Leigh* VIII. 227 And though the thing displease us, ay, perhaps Displease us warrantably. **1918** *Cornhill Mag.* June 562 From Carlyle's later works chapter and verse for the whole doctrine of force could warrantably be quoted.

†**'warrantage.** *Obs.*⁻⁰ [f. WARRANT *v.* + -AGE, after OF. *garant-*, *garentage.*] Warranty.

1611 COTGR., *Garentage*, warrantie, warrantize, warrantage.

warranted ('wɒrəntɪd), *ppl. a.* [-ED².]

1. Allowed by law or authority; approved, justified, sanctioned.

1600 SHAKS. *All's Well* II. v. 4 You haue it from his owne deliuerance And by other warranted testimonie. **1603** —— *Meas. for M.* III. ii. 151 The very streame of his life, and the businesse he hath helmed, must vppon a warranted neede, giue him a better proclamation. **1605** —— *Macb.* IV. iii. 137 Now wee'l together, and the chance of goodnesse Be like our warranted Quarrell. **1693** NORRIS *Pract. Disc.* (1707) IV. 123 Some..generous spirits have..rescued their understandings from this long-settled, and by use almost warranted usurpation. **1714** STEELE *Lover* No. 32 (1723) 183 The..Delight, which virtuous Minds feel in the Enjoyment of their lawful and warranted Passions. **1831** SCOTT *Cast. Dang.* xviii, I cannot presume to understand what you call prophecies, with or without warranted authority of old painted books [etc.].

2. Furnished with a legal or official warrant.
a. Of an officer: Holding a rank by warrant.
1746 W. THOMPSON *R.N. Adv.* (1757) 47 These warranted Gentlemen in Office might be more circumspect. **1798** NELSON in Nicolas *Disp.* (1845) III. 22 An old and faithful Servant of the Crown, and who has been near thirty years a warranted Carpenter.
b. *U.S.* Granted by a warrant: see LAND-*warrant*.
1774 *Pennsylv. Gaz.* 14 Dec., Suppl. 2/3 To be sold.. One tract of patented land... Four tracts of warranted land.
3. For which a warranty is given; guaranteed. *Mod.* Our goods are all of warranted quality.

warrantee (ˌwɒrən'tiː). [f. WARRANT *v.* + -EE[1].]
1. *Law.* The person to whom a warranty is given.
1706 PHILLIPS (ed. Kersey), s.v. *Exchange*, The Compensation.. which the Warranter must make to the Warrantee, Value for Value, if the Land warranted be recover'd from the Warrantee. **1818** CRUISE *Digest* (ed. 2) IV. 430 It is the same with respect to the person to whom the warranty is made; for if it be not to the warrantee and his heirs,.. it will cease upon the death of the warrantee. **1860** WHARTON *Law Lex.* (ed. 2), *Warrantee*, a person to whom a warrant is made.
¶ **2.** Misused for WARRANTER or GUARANTEE *sb.* 1, and (*U.S.*) for WARRANTY 1.
1668 *Lond. Gaz.* No. 256/2 [tr. of Let. from the Q. of Spain to the States of Holland] You will also joyntly endeavour as Warrantees, to do all that in reason can be expected.. for the.. strengthening of this Peace. **1730** *Phil. Trans.* XXXVI. 400 If some Authors can be quoted for Warrantees of what this *Se ma Tsien* advances, they were modern to the Time when he wrote. **1874** J. WANAMAKER in *Philadelphia Inquirer* 26 Sept. 8/2 (Advt.), A printed guarantee, bearing the signature of the firm, will accompany each garment as a warrantee. This binds us in every sense, and will be honored as quickly as a good draft of the Government of the United States. **1980** *Verbatim* Autumn 17/1 We have three perfectly good words in English, *guarantee*, *warranty*, and *guaranty*, all of the same origin and having the same meaning. Now some people are trying to add a fourth, *warrantee*. A TV salesman says, 'We have a great warrantee on this product.'

warranter ('wɒrəntə(r)). [f. WARRANT *v.* + -ER[1]. Cf. WARRANTOR.] One who warrants.
1. One who assures, authorizes, or guarantees (something).
1583 GOLDING *Calvin on Deut.* i. 5 That oure faithe resteth not upon men.. but that the liuing God is the author and will also be the warranter thereof. **1628** tr. *Mathieu's Powerfull Favorite* 19 Piso.. assuring himselfe that his warranter should be his Iudge, coueted rather to depend on the authoritie of one alone, then on the passion of many. **1642** H. MORE *Song of Soul* To Rdr. 7/1, I would be so understood, as a Representer of the Wisdome of the Ancients rather then a warranter of the same. **1800** COLERIDGE *Piccolomini* I. xii. 182 If I stand warranter of the event, Placing my honour and my head in pledge. **1834** —— *Remorse* I. ii. 133 'Twas little probable, that Don Ordonio, ..Should prove the patron of this infidel! The warranter [*earlier edd.* guarantee] of a Moresco's faith!
†**2.** One who assures (another) of safety; a protector. *Obs. rare.*
1611 COTGR., *Garent*, a Warranter, Protector, Defendor; [etc.]. *c* **1800** *Capt. Car* v. in Child *Ballads* III. 436/1 Come doun and speak to me; I'll kep thee in a feather bed, And thy warraner I will be.
3. *Law.* = WARRANTOR[1].
1706 [see WARRANTEE 1]. **1848** WHARTON *Law Lex.* s.v. *Warrant*, A warrenter may except, that the complainant does not hold the land of which he seeks the warranty.

warranting ('wɒrəntɪŋ), *vbl. sb.* [-ING[1].] The action of the verb.
1303 R. BRUNNE *Handl. Synne* 12404 Hyt were foly, comaunde a þyng þat myȝt nat ȝyue no warantyng. *c* **1450** *Godstow Reg.* 249 The forsaid Richard Robert and Thedulf called the forsaid Iohn to the warantyng. **1565** GOLDING *Cæsar* III. 77 Manye things pricked forward the Galles in this deuice: as.. the warranting of the runagate: [etc.].

'warranting, *ppl. a.* [-ING[2].] That warrants.
1561 DAUS tr. *Bullinger on Apoc.* (1573) 155 Least any man should doubt any whit of these celestiall miseries. Here is added the warranting word, Amen. **1766** BLACKSTONE *Comm.* II. xx. 302 The obligation of the heir.. was only on condition that he had other sufficient lands by descent from the warranting ancestor.

warrantise ('wɒrəntaɪz), *sb. Obs.* exc. *arch.* Forms: 4–5 **warantize**, 4–6 **-ise**, 5 **warentice**, **warantyce**, **-ice**, 5–6 **-yse**, **warauntyse**, **-ise**, 6 **warrauntise**, **warrantyse**, 6–7 **-ize**, **-ice**, 7 **-is**, 6–7, 9 **-ise**. [a. OF. *warentise*, *garantise*, f. *warantir*, *garantir* WARRANT *v.* Cf. WARRANDICE.]
1. *Law.* = WARRANTY 1 a. Phr. ***clause of warrantise*** (also used *fig.*); ***plea of warrantise***.
a **1325** *MS. Rawl.* B. 520, lf. 57 ȝif he habbe þe kinges chartre ware þoru þe king be i holde to warantise. *Ibid.* 62 b, ȝif þe aloinaunce were i mad þoru fin i mad. þanne a sullen boþe ben i cleped to warantise þer of. **1396–7** in *Eng. Hist. Rev.* (1907) XXII. 301 For a busschel of qwete.. he welen selle þe blisse of heuene be chartre of clause of warantise. **14..** *Pol. Rel. & L. Poems* (1866) 24 And yf thou may in any wyse Make thy chartyr on warantyse To thyne heyres & assygnes all-so, This shall a wyse purchasser doo. *c* **1450** *Godstow Reg.* 265 Wherof a ple of warantize was I-take bitwene them in the same courte. **1495** *Act 11 Hen. VII*, c. 42 With a Clause of Warantise accordyng to yᵉ seid dede. **1544** tr. *Littleton's Tenures* 131 Yt tenaunt in the tayle in this case release to the dysseasour & byndeth him and his heyres to warrantyse, &c. **1559** *Boke Presidentes* 40 b, A release made by deede of tenementes before purchased with a clause of warrantise. **1627** J. CARTER *Plain Expos.* 93 A clause of warrantize against all danger.
2. *gen.* The action of warranting, guaranteeing, or giving assurance; the state or fact of being guaranteed. Phr. ***to hold, clepe, bind, call to warrantise***; ***on, with, by warrantise***.
c **1440** *Promp. Parv.* 516/1 Warantyse, *warantizacio*. **1534** MORE *Comf. agst. Trib.* III. xvii. (1553) Q vij b, Withoute anye bolde warrantise of oure selfe, or foolishe truste in oure strength. **1548** UDALL, etc. *Erasm. Par. Luke* iii. 21, 22 A doue.. had.. brought a braunche of an oliue tree.. for.. a caucion or pledge of warauntise yᵗ the floude was at an ende. **1551** ROBINSON tr. *More's Utopia* II. (1895) 171 In so doyng they neuer followe the credence of pryuat men, but the assureaunce or warrauntise of the hole citye. **1565** COOPER *Thesaurus*, *Amphoteroplon*, a double freight or dutie, that is payed, when the shippeman vndertaketh on warantyse to conducte a man salfe foorth, and brynge him salfe home agayne. **1577** B. GOOGE *Heresbach's Husb.* III. 128 The Butchers that bye for slaughter, and such as by for sacryfises, vse no worde of warrantise. **1583** FULKE *Def. Tr. Script.* i. 42 They doe the better proue, that for which I called him to warrantize. *c* **1600** SHAKS. *Sonn.* cl. 7 In the very refuse of thy deeds, There is such strength and warrantise of skill, That in my minde thy worst all best exceeds? **1601** HOLLAND *Pliny* XXXIII. iii. II. 462 All buyings and sellings at this day which passe with warrantise [L. *in his emptionibus, quae mancipii sunt*]. **1608** DOD & CLEAVER *Expos. Prov.* IX–X. 5 He giuing warrantise for their safety. **1862** SIR H. TAYLOR *St. Clement's Eve* III. v. 109 We humbly crave Some warrantise that what we're bid to speak, Spoken, shall bring no jeopardy of life Or liberty or goods.
b. ***to make*** (also ***give***) ***warrantise***: to guarantee, give assurance. Const. *of* or clause.
1534 MORE *Comf. agst. Trib.* III. xvii. (1553) Q vj, I can make no warrantise of my selfe, seing yᵗ S. Peter so sodainly fainted at a womans word. **1542** UDALL *Erasm. Apoph.* 296 Talke that.. maketh ioyly royall warantise of thynges in wordes, but without any effecte or comyng to passe of deedes. **1577–87** HOLINSHED *Chron.* III. 58/1 But whether it were so or not, I am not able to make warrantize. **1601** MUNDAY & CHETTLE *Death Robt. Earl Huntingdon* [IV. ii.] I 3, Againe, the place doth giue thee warrantise.
c. Said predicatively of a thing or person that serves as a guarantee or surety.
a **1300** *Cursor M.* 25604 þat we mai tak þat ilk flexs.. Wit bodi and hert clene: And þat it be vr warantise, On domes-dai quen þou sal rise, Al þis werld to deme. **1591** SHAKS. *1 Hen. VI*, I. iii. 13 Breake vp the Gates, Ile be your warrantize. **1596** EARL OF ESSEX in Ellis *Orig. Lett.* Ser. III. IV. 134 His assent.. shalbe my warrantize.
d. Phr. ***of, on, in warrantise***: of a surety, for certain, without fail, I warrant you.
c **1430** LYDG. *Min. Poems* (Percy Soc.) 137 Of warantise he shal nevir the. *c* **1440** *Generydes* 5938 Ther shall no man do yow harme o warantise. *a* **1500** *E.E. Misc.* (1855) 91 Thanne ȝour crymsons beth y-made in warantyse withowte fayle. *a* **1500** *Assemb. Ladies* 406, I pray you, tel it me in secret wyse; And I shal kepe it close, on warantyse. *c* **1550** LLOYD *Treas. Health* ¶4 Put into thyne eye a verey litle, it is safe and without danger in warrantise and ofte approved. **1592** WYRLEY *Armorie* 29 No mortall man with Gods gaine fauor might Of warrantice to see next mornings light. **1639** O. WOOD *Alph. Bk. Secrets* 29 Then.. anoynt the Griefe with a feather,.. and it will be whole on warrantice.
3. Defence, protection.
?*a* **1400** *Morte Arth.* 1614 That they be weisely wachede and in warde holdene, Wardede of warantizez with wyrchipfulle knyghttez. **1481** CAXTON *Godfrey* xvii. 45 Alle the peple of the contre.. made to hym feaulte for to haue his ayde and warantise in the waye of the sayd pylgremage. **1489** —— *Faytes of A.* II. xxxv. 149 No manere of warantyse can not kepe theym that assaylle yf they be hytte with all, but that they shal be beten doune as the thondre felle upon hem.
4. Authorization, permission, sanction.
1580 GRINDAL *Let. to Ld. Burleigh* Wks. (1843) 366 Dr Howland.. added further, that if error were committed in that, it was no sufficient warrantize for other errors afterwards to be attempted. **1601** HOLLAND *Pliny* XXII. vi. II. 118 Yet we.. are so unhappie, as to commit our selves to other mens tuition, and live under their warrantize and assurance [L. *vivimus aliena fiducia*]. **1602** SHAKS. *Ham.* v. i. 250 Her Obsequies haue bin as farre inlarg'd, As we haue warrantis. **1606** WHETENHALL *Discov. Abuses Ch. Christ* 66 A Bishop ought to doe nothing in the Church, unlesse he be certaine and sure of the warrantise thereof by Gods word. *a* **1624** BP. M. SMITH *Serm.* (1632) 234 Lest the yonger sort take example, nay warrantize from vs to slacke their paines.
5. Assurance, confident statement.
1586 A. DAY *Eng. Secretorie* I. (1625) 78 Too much impertinent were it for me to hale you on with arguments who onely goe about to persuade you with warrantise. **1601** HOLLAND *Pliny* XXVIII. vii. II. 310 Thus they prescribe with great warrantize, To take all the naile parings of toes and fingers of man, [etc.].

†**'warrantise,** *v. Obs.* For forms see the sb. [f. the sb.; in Law-L. *warrantizāre*.]
1. *trans. Law.* To guarantee the possession of (real property) *to* a person.
c **1450** *Godstow Reg.* 346 They warantized to the forsaid Richard and to his heires the forsaid tenement with the pertynentis ayenst all maner of men for ever. *c* **1460** *Oseney Reg.* 53 And I vmfrey and my heyres all þe forsaide thynges to þe forsaide church and Chanons for Euer shall warantize agaynste all men and women.
2. *gen.* To guarantee; to be a guarantee or security for; to secure the possession of (something) to a person; to secure (a person or thing) *from*.
c **1532** DU WES *Introd. Fr.* in *Palsgr.* 952 Pleuir, to warantise. **1593** NASHE *Christ's T.* Q 4, Certaine meanes hee hath assigned vs, which he hath promised to blesse, but without means no blessing hath he warrantizd. **1598** YONG *Diana* 235 Who shall.. this old age from sorrowes warrantize? **1598** HAKLUYT *Voy.* I. 144 In regard whereof you wil vndertake to warrantize, and make good vnto vs those penalties and forfaitures which shal vnto vs appertaine, for all wools [etc.]. **1616** R. C. *Times' Whistle* i. 275 A moste lawfull act,.. For which you will.. warrantize him heaven and happie day. **1628** WITHER *Brit. Rememb.* iii. 461 To warrantize thy health.
b. To warrant, sanction, authorize; to confirm, corroborate.
1600 NASHE *Summer's Last Will* D 4, A sillie fancie, Autumne, hast thou told, Which no Philosophie doth warrantize. **1603** HOLLAND *Plutarch's Mor.* 863 There is nothing else but necessitie alone, doeth warrantize the killing of a man. **1643** S. MARSHALL *Copy of Let.* 8 Like enough some Court-Chaplaine.. might warrantize the kings conscience. **1664** J. WEBB *Stone-Heng* (1725) 125 The Customs of the Romans.. highly warrantize Mʳ. Jones his Discovery of our Antiquity.
3. To protect, defend.
c **1450** *Merlin* xvi. 269 But yef I may haue bailly ouer his body, he shall so be deffouled that ther ne shall nothinge in the worlde hym warantise. *c* **1489** CAXTON *Blanchardyn* xxiv. 88 But what occysion or defence that he made myght not warauntyse hym. *c* **1500** *Melusine* xxiv. 200 Thenne anthony.. smote a knyght by such vertue that the targe nor his cote of stele might not warauntyse hym.
Hence †**'warrantising** *vbl. sb.* and *ppl. a.*
c **1450** *Godstow Reg.* 226 & that hys yft, graunt, & warantizinge shulde be stronge & sure, he put to hyt hys seele. **1628** VENNER *Baths of Bathe* (1650) 360 Their Spaniel-like fawning carriage, and warrantizing promises.

'warrantless, *a.* [f. WARRANT *sb.*[1] + -LESS.]
1. Without justification, unwarrantable. *rare.*
1863 MRS. WHITNEY *Faith Gartney's Girlh.* v, The stinging and warrantless accusation.
2. *U.S.* Without judicial authorization; without a search warrant.
1950 F. FRANKFURTER in *U.S. Reports* CCCXXXIX. 80 To tear 'unreasonable' from the context and history and purpose of the Fourth Amendment.. is to make the arrest an incident to an unwarranted search instead of a warrantless search an incident to an arrest. **1968** *U.S. Rep. Cases Supreme Court* 367 The Amendment deserves.. a liberal construction in order to protect against warrantless searches of buildings. **1978** *Detroit Free Press* 14 Apr. 1A/4 The activities that are alleged in connection with the Weatherman investigation, I would categorize as warrantless activities.

†**'warrantment.** *Obs.* [f. WARRANT *v.* + -MENT.] = WARRANT *sb.*[1] 9.
1599 in T. Stafford *Pac. Hib.* I. i. (1633) 16 Any warrantment signed by the said Lord President.. shall be a sufficient dischardge.

warrant officer.
1. An officer in the armed services who holds office by a warrant, as distinguished from a commissioned officer. (In the Army, the warrant officers are now intermediate in rank between the commissioned and the non-commissioned officers. The rank was abolished in the Royal Navy in 1949.)
1693 *Lond. Gaz.* No. 2848/4 Two or more Commission or Warrant-Officers of Their Majesties Ships. **1704** *Milit. Dict.* (ed. 2) s.v. *Officer*, *Warrant*, or *Staff-Officers*, those who have not the King's Commission, but are appointed by the Colonels and Captains; as the Quarter-Masters, Sergeants, Corporals, and in the same number are included Chaplains and Surgeons. **1725** DE FOE *Voy. round World* (1840) 103, I called all the Warrant officers together. **1815** *Falconer's Dict. Marine* (ed. Burney), *Warrant-Officers*, are persons employed in the royal navy, by warrant from the Commissioners of the navy, to take charge of the stores issued to them from his Majesty's dock-yards. **1836** MARRYAT *Midsh. Easy* x, The boatswain talked over the matter with the other warrant officers. **1850** H. MELVILLE *White Jacket* I. vi. 36 Next in order come the Warrant or Forward officers, consisting of the Boatswain, Gunner, Carpenter, and Sail-maker. **1867** SMYTH *Sailor's Word-bk.*, *Warrant-officer*,.. In the royal navy it was an officer holding a warrant from the navy board, as the master, surgeon, purser, boatswain, gunner, carpenter, &c. In the year 1831, when the commissioners of the navy, or navy board, were abolished, all these powers reverted to the admiralty. **1912** *King's Regul. Army* §284 The position of warrant officers is inferior to that of all commissioned officers, but superior to that of all N.C.Os. **1949** *Order in Council* (Admiralty) No. 30/C-W. 1 Whereas we are of the opinion that the title 'Warrant Officer' and the term 'Warrant List' in use in the Royal Navy and Royal Marines should no longer be used but be replaced by 'Branch Officer' and 'Branch List' respectively.
2. An officer whose duty it is to serve warrants.
1895 *Funk's Stand. Dict.* **1901** *Daily Chron.* 16 Apr. 3/2 The remainder of the staff, consisting of the jailer, the under-jailer, the warrant-sergeant, and various warrant officers, are all policemen, selected for their duties by the police authorities.

warrantor ('wɒrəntə(r)). [f. WARRANT *v.* + -OR. Cf. GUARANTOR.]
1. *Law.* One who gives warranty.
1685 *Les Termes de la Ley* 419 s.v. *Garranty*, It behoves that every Warranty, whereby the Heir shall be barred, discend by course of the Common Law to him who is Heir to the Warrantor. **1741** T. ROBINSON *Gavelkind* I. vi. 123 If Land warranted comes to a younger Brother by Borough-English or Gavelkind, he is without Remedy against the Warrantor. **1766** BLACKSTONE *Comm.* II. xxx. 470 Each indorsor is a warrantor for the payment of the bill. **1863** A. J. HORWOOD *Yearbks.* 30 & 31 *Edw. I* Pref. 32 The liability of a warrantor when the purchaser of land has erected a building on the land warranted. **1875** K. E. DIGBY *Real Prop.* ii. (1876) 78 *note*, Upon the acceptance of the warrantor the suit as to the title to the chattel proceeded

between the claimant and the warrantor. **1911** *Times* 16 Feb. 4/5 The right to appear of ordinary warrantors in cases in which action was taken..did not apply.

2. *gen.* = WARRANTER 1. *rare.*

1850 KINGLAKE *Crimea* (1877) VI. ix. 371 As the warrantor of what an Englishman means when he says he insists on 'fair play'.

warranty ('wɒrəntɪ). Forms: 4–5 **warantie**, 5–6 **-ye**, 5–7 **warrantie**, 6 **-ye**, (6 **warraunty**), 6– **warranty**. [a. AF. (OF.) *warantie*, dial. var. of *guarantie* (whence GUARANTEE *sb.*), *garantie* (mod.F. *garantie*): f. *warant* (*garant*) WARRANT *sb.*]

1. *Law.* An act of warranting: in certain specific applications.

to vouch to (rarely *for*) *warranty*: see VOUCH *v.* 1.

a. A covenant (either expressed by a ***clause of warranty*** or implied) annexed to a conveyance of real estate, by which the vendor warrants the security of the title conveyed. (In modern English practice the term has little or no application. In the U.S. the ***covenant of warranty*** corresponds to the English 'covenant for quiet enjoyment'.)

The early examples below relate to feudal law, under which the 'warranty' given by the grantor of a freehold estate obliged him to yield to the grantee other lands of equal value if the latter should be evicted. For *collateral*, *lineal warranty* see those adjs.

1338 R. BRUNNE *Chron.* (1810) 263 If he had..gyuen þam ..þer wynnyng ilk a dele, þat þei mot reyme & gyue, Holdand in warantie [Fr. *Terre et tenement à tenir par garaunt*], of him & of his heyres. **1439** *Rolls of Parlt.* V. 10/2 And therof have do made astate to you and to youre heires ..with clause of Warantie. **1472–3** *Ibid.* VI. 44/2 To have and to hold to the forseid William, John and Robert, and their heires, with warantie of the said Phelip. **1495** *Act 11 Hen. VII*, c. 47 §1 You..be not bounden to warant the seid Manoris..by reason of any warantye comprised in the same lettres patentes. **1544** tr. *Littleton's Tenures* 147 b, It is comonly sayd that there be thre maner of warrantyes, that is to saye, warrantye lyneall, warranty collaterall, and warranty that begynneth by disseasyn. **1596** BACON *Elem. Com. Law* II. (1630) 31 If a man..do make a warranty of Land binding him and his heyres to warrantie. **1651** G. W. tr. *Cowel's Inst.* 191 Lessor is bound to warranty to the Lessee. **1766** BLACKSTONE *Comm.* II. xx. 300 Next may follow the clause of *warranty*; whereby the grantor doth, for himself and his heirs, warrant and secure to the grantee the estate so granted. **1858** LD. ST. LEONARDS *Handy-Bk. Prop. Law* v. 24 If one sell another's estate, without covenant or warranty for the enjoyment, it is at the peril of the purchaser. **1871** MARKBY *Elem. Law* §236 A warranty, properly speaking, is in form an undertaking that certain events will happen, or will not happen; have happened, or have not happened; but it is in reality a promise to make compensation for the loss occasioned by their happening or not happening.

attrib. **1855** EMERSON *Misc.* i. 16 This is the best part of these men's farms, yet to this their warranty-deeds give no title. **1892** G. OWEN *Pembrokesh.* 176 *Footnote*, The warranty clause..arose out of the old feudal doctrine that the land could not be alienated without the consent of the heir.

b. An undertaking, express or implied, given by one of the parties to a contract to the other, that he will be answerable for the truth of some statement incidental to the contract; esp. an assurance, express or implied, given by the seller of goods, that he will be answerable for their possession of some quality attributed to them.

1543 tr. *Act 28 Edw. III*, c. 13 The warranty of packyng of wolles for dyuers mischieues, which the commens haue therof perceiued, shall holly be out. **1552** HULOET, Bye and sell wyth warantye. **1628** COKE *On Litt.* II. vii. 102 By the Ciuill Law euery man is bound to warrant the thing that he selleth or conueyeth,..but the Common Law bindeth him not, vnlesse there be a warrantie. **1768** BLACKSTONE *Comm.* III. ix. 165 But if the vendor knew the goods to be unsound, and hath used any art to disguise them,..this artifice shall be equivalent to an express warranty,..A general warranty will not extend to guard against defects that are plainly and obviously the object of one's senses. **1812** *Sporting Mag.* XXXIX. 235 An action upon the warranty of a horse. **1846** *J. Baxter's Libr. Pract. Agric.* (ed. 4) I. 467 If the horse should be afterwards discovered to have been unsound at the time of warranty, the buyer may return it.

c. In a contract for insurance, an engagement by the insured that certain statements are true or that certain conditions shall be fulfilled: the breach of this engagement involving the invalidation of the policy.

1817 W. SELWYN *Law Nisi Prius* (ed. 4) II. 977 If there be not any warranty or condition on the part of the insured, the insurer is subject to all risks. **1835** *Tomlin's Law Dict.* (ed. 4) s.v. *Insurance*, I. §3 Warranties in a policy of [marine] assurance are either express or implied... The three cases of warranty, on which most questions have arisen, are, as to the time of sailing, convoy, and neutrality of property. **1866** *Arnould's Marine Insur.* I. II. i. 487 A warranty not implied by law must always be in writing and in every case is inserted on the face of the policy. **1886** C. SCHOLL *Phraseol. Dict.* II. 832 A warranty to that effect is on the margin of the policy. **1913** *Times* 13 Sept. 18/3 The ordinary tramp steamer, tied down by strict warranties, would not have been covered..in that region after October 1.

2. *transf.* A guarantee, an assurance. Now *dial.* (see *Eng. Dial. Dict.*).

1555 EDEN *Decades* I. VII. (Arb.) 92 That he had betrayed his geste whom he tooke into his house with warranties. **1691** LOCKE *Money* Wks. 1727 II. 43 The Stamp [on coinage] was a Warranty of the publick, that under such a denomination they should receive a piece of such a weight, and such a fineness. **1823** SCOTT *Quentin D.* v, 'Think you that I am likely to recommend to you any thing unworthy?' ..'I cannot doubt your warranty, fair uncle,' said the youth.

3. Formal or official sanction (for a course of action, etc.); authorization. = WARRANT *sb.*¹ 7. Now *rare.*

1591 SPENSER *M. Hubberd* 186 We shall ronne Into great daunger..Thus wildly to wander in the worlds eye, Without pasport or good warrantie. **1596** SHAKS. *Merch. V.* I. i. 132 And from your loue I haue a warrantie To vnburthen all my plots and purposes. **1599** B. JONSON *Cynthia's Rev.* v. vi, Nor farther notice (Arete) we craue Then thine approuals soueraigne warrantie. **1604** SHAKS. *Oth.* v. ii. 60, I..neuer lou'd Cassio, But with such generall warrantie of Heauen, As I might loue. **1618** LD. SHEFFIELD in *Fortescue Papers* (Camden) 52, I desire your Lordship that under such warrantie I may bee protected, otherwise I shall not adventure to doe his Majestie service in those places. **1664** JER. TAYLOR *Dissuas. Popery* I. ii. §10. 142 If these things come from God, let them shew their warranty, and their books of Precedents.

4. Justifying reason, ground (*for* an action or belief).

1836 HOR. SMITH *Tin Trumpet* II. 108 It [the doctrine of Purgatory] may not have the clear warranty of Scripture, but [etc.]. **1869** ROGERS *A. Smith's W.N.* Pref. 9, I am not acquainted with any part of his writings which will give any warranty for such an inference. **1877** BLACK *Green Past.* xxix, The smallest civility was sufficient warranty for the opening of an acquaintanceship. **1918** *Q. Rev.* Jan. 210 The Pope was claiming powers, Döllinger urged, for which there was no warranty in the history of the Church.

5. Substantiating evidence or witness.

1561 BRENDE *Q. Curtius* VI. (ed. 2) 117 b, The matter was fyrst shewed me by a light felowe, who coulde not bringe any witnes or warrantie [1553 warant] of hys tale. **1676** J. OWEN *Worship of God* 81 There is sufficient evidence and warranty of this institution. **1866** DICKENS *Mugby Junct.* i, As Barbox Brothers (so to call the traveller on the warranty of his luggage) took his seat [etc.]. **1883** WHITELAW *Sophocles, Trachin.* 744 My son, how say you? By what warranty A deed so hateful say you I have wrought?

†**6.** One who warrants or gives a warrant. *Obs.*

1586 T. B. *La Primaud. Fr. Acad.* I. 394 The prince..is the formal warrantie [Fr. *garend formel*] unto all his subjects, of that fidelity which is amongst themselves.

warratah, -taw: see WARATAH.

Warrau, var. of WARAO.

warraunt(e: see WARRANT, WARREN.

warraunty, obs. form of WARRANTY.

†**warray**, *v. Obs.* Forms: α. 4 **werrai**, **werri(e**, (**werhai**, **werrei**, **weirai**), 4–5 **werray(e**, **werrey(e**, 5 **verray**, (**verrie**, **werrye**), 4–6 **werey**; β. 4 **warrai**, **wary**, *Sc.* **varray**, **varra**, **warra**, 4–5 **warry**, 4–6 **warrey**, 4–6, 8–9 *arch.* **warray**. [ME. *werreye*, a. OF. *werreier*, dial. var. of *guerreier* (mod.F. *guerroyer*) = Pr. *guerreiar*, Sp., Pg. *guerrear*, It. *guerreggiare*; a Com. Rom. formation on **werra* WAR *sb.*¹]

1. *trans.* To make war upon, ravage by war. = WAR *v.* 1.

a **1300** *Cursor M.* 7338 Men werraid þam on ilka side. *a* **1340** HAMPOLE *Psalter* xxxiv. 1 Crist..says..werray [Vulg. *expugna*], that is ouercum, thaim that fightis agaynes me in ded. **1375** BARBOUR *Bruce* IX. 646, I trow he sall nocht mony a day Haue will to warra that cuntre. *c* **1386** CHAUCER *Sqr.'s T.* 2 At Sarray in the land of Tartarye Ther dwelte a kyng that werreyed Russye. *c* **1425** WYNTOUN *Cron.* II. i. 7 Nynus..Tuk vp armys to warray [*v.r.* verray] Seyr landis þat about hym lay. *c* **1450** *Merlin* xx. 320 We go the gladlyer ..to turneyen a-gein these sarazins that this londe do werryen. **1456** SIR G. HAYE *Law Arms* (S.T.S.) 140 Gif a lady..is warraid with a hautane knycht of Gascoyne. *a* **1513** FABYAN *Chron.* VII. (1811) 458 Iohn duke of Normandy.. herynge that his father was thus warreyed wᵗ the Kynge of Englonde, brake vp his syege and came..vnto his father. **1590** SPENSER *F.Q.* I. v. 48 And them long time before, great Nimrod was, That first the world with sword and fire warrayd. *Ibid.* II. x. 50. *Ibid.* II. x. 72. **1594** *Selimus* B 3 b, But after Ninus, warlike Belus sonne; The earth with vnknowne armour did warray. **1600** FAIRFAX *Tasso* I. vi, Sixe yeeres were ronne since first in martiall guize The Christian Lords warraid the eastren land.

b. *transf.* and *fig.*

a **1300** *Cursor M.* 23752 þe flexs.., þe werld.., þe warlau ..,þis werrais vs on ilk side. *c* **1375** *Sc. Leg. Saints* ii. (*Paul*) 541 Saule, saule, quhy werrais þou me? *c* **1386** CHAUCER *Pars. T.* ⁋401 Impacient is he that wol nat been ytaught ne vndernome of his vice and by strif werreieth [*v.r.* werreth] trouthe wityngly. *c* **1400** *Rom. Rose* 3917 Bothe in cloistre and in abbey Chastite is werreyed over-al. *c* **1430** LYDG. *Compl. Bl. Knt.* 665 Jelousye..That hath so longe,.. Werreyed Trouthe with his tirannye. **1456** SIR G. HAYE *Law Arms* (S.T.S.) 17 Sanct Augustyne, sanct Jerome,.. with mony othir quhilkis warrayd the inymyes of the faith. **1595** SPENSER *Amoretti* xliv, This continuall cruell ciuill warre, The which my selfe against my selfe doe make: Whilest my weak powres of passions warreid arre. **1768** DOWNMAN *Land of Muses* xlix, With this she oft hath Villainy warray'd.

2. *intr.* To make war. Const. *on*, *upon*, *against*; also ***to warray forth***. = WAR *v.* 2.

a **1300** *Cursor M.* 2493 Four kinges werraiid a pon fiue. *Ibid.* 21872 Folk þai sal gain oþer rise To werrai samen mani wise. *Ibid.* 24766 A king was hight willam basterd, þat warraid in jngland ful hard. *c* **1374** CHAUCER *Former Age* 25 What sholde it han avayled to werreye [*v.r.* warrey]? Ther lay no profyt ther was no rychesse. **1375** BARBOUR *Bruce* I. 140 [He] That was than in the haly land, On saracenys warrayand. *Ibid.* XII. 363 Bot quha sa varrayis vrangwisly, Thai faynd god all too gretumly. *c* **1400** MAUNDEV. (Roxb.) xxxii. 145 þou schall fynd na thing with vs wharfore þou schuld werray vpon vs. **1430–40** LYDG. *Bochas* VIII. i. (1558) 2 b/2 First agaynste Parthois he cast him to werrey. ? **1436** in *Pol. Poems* (Rolls) II. 167 Oure meny wode Wyth grete poure passed overe the ffloode, And verrie forth into the dukes londe. *c* **1470** HARDYNG *Chron.* (1812) Pref. i At sextene yere, to werray and to wage, To juste and ryde. **1590** SPENSER *F.Q.* II. x. 21 Ebranck..warreyd on Brunchild In Henault. **1600** HOLLAND *Livy* IX. xvii. 325 In case he had fought the Carthaginian were first (for if he had lived he ment to have warried there) and then passed over into Italie.

b. *transf.* and *fig.*

a **1300** *Cursor M.* 32 On charite ai werrais wreth. *Ibid.* 727 Bath þai werhaid on adam, For to bring him in to blam. *Ibid.* 7548 Goddes euer on rightwis side, werraiand again wrangwis pride. *a* **1340** HAMPOLE *Psalter* xvi. 14 The whilk toke my saule to werray with the kyngdome of wickidnes. *c* **1450** LYDG. *Life our Lady* lxiv. (1484) i viij b, It yaue hem myght to make resistence Ageyn synne and knyghtly to wareye. **1456** SIR G. HAYE *Law Arms* (S.T.S.) 110 There suld na subject obey till his soverane to werrey agaynis his God. **1590** SPENSER *F.Q.* III. v. 48 Thus warreid he long time against his will.

Hence '**warraying** *vbl. sb.*, warring; persecution. '**warraying** *ppl. a.* (also *absol.*, a persecutor = WARRIOR 1).

a **1300** *Cursor M.* 19602 Lat we nu þe prechurs stand, For to spek of a warraiand; Saulus soght aiquar and thrett All þe cristen he wit mett. *Ibid.* 27259 Enentes knightes, & mistakyng and namli wrangwis warraing [*v.r.* werraing]. **1375** BARBOUR *Bruce* IV. 650 Bot ȝe wat nocht quhat-kyn forton ȝhe mon dre in ȝour warraying. *Ibid.* v. 140. *c* **1489** CAXTON *Faytes of A.* II. i. 91 With moo than one manere of werreyng. **1513** DOUGLAS *Æneis* XII. x. 33, I sal distroy..the tovn, Quhilk is the caus of all our werying. **1852** *Fraser's Mag.* XLV. 649/2 Those world-warraying heroes that left in every land of Europe the memory of their incredible valour.

warray, obs. Sc. form of VERY.

†**warrayable**, *a. Obs. rare*⁻¹. In 5 **varyable**, **warryable**. [a. OF. *werreiable*, dial. var. of *guerroyable*, f. *werrei-er* (*guerroyer*): see WARRAY *v.* and -ABLE.] Fit for warfare.

14.. *Siege of Rouen* in *Archæologia* XXI. 51 The wallys were fulle warryable And the dykys depe and defensabylle.

warrayn, -aynte, obs. form of WARREN.

†**warre**. *Obs.* Also 5 **werre**, 6 **war**. [repr. OE. *wearr* str. masc., recorded only in the sense 'callosity'; but cf. *wearriht* full of callosities, also of a tree, knotty (see WARRIED *a.*). Cf. Flem. *warre* fem., *weer* masc., callosity, knot in wood.] A knot in a tree or in timber.

[*c* **725** *Corpus Gloss.* (Hessels) C 161 *Callos* weorras *uel* ill. *c* **1000** *Sax. Leechd.* I. 356 Ða wearras and ða swylas ðe beoð on mannes handum oððe on oðrum limum.] *c* **1407** LYDG. *Reson & Sens.* 5428 The tother [bow]..Ful of knottys and of skarrys, The tymber is so ful of warrys. *c* **1440** *Promp. Parv.* 516/2 Warre, or knobbe of a tre, *vertex.* **1483** *Cath. Angl.* 409/1 A Werre [*Addit. MS.* Warre] of a tree, *vertex.* **1513** DOUGLAS *Æneis* XII. xii. 212 Bot festynnit sa is in the war the grip That by na maner fors..Furth of the stok the schaft vp pull he mycht. **1530** PALSGR. 287/1 Warre or knobbe of a tree, *neu.*

Hence †**warred** *a.* having knots. (Cf. WARRIED *a.*)

1398 TREVISA *Barth. De P.R.* v. lvii. (1495) 1iij b/1 The ouer endes of the bones..ben warryd wyth grete knottes. *Ibid.* XVII. xx. O ij/2 Boxe growyth in hote places and stony and is therfore harde and sadly warrid [*Tollemache MS.* warred].

warre, obs. f. WAR and WARE (*sb.*, *a.*, and *v.*).

warree, waree ('wɒriː). Also 7 **warre**, 9 **warrie**. [Of uncertain origin.

The word most probably belongs to one of the langs. of the Isthmus of Panama, but it may possibly be a corruption of the W. Indian synonym *javaris* (Rochefort, 1658), which seems to be a mispronunciation of Sp. *jabalí* wild boar.]

The white-lipped peccary, *Dicotyles labiatus*, native in Central and South America. Cf. TAGNICATI, TAYASSU.

1684 B. SHARP *Voy.* (1729) 48 Our Supper-Entertainment was a very good sort of a Wild Beast, called a Warre, which is much like unto our English Hog. **1697** DAMPIER *Voy.* I. i. 9 When hunger begins to bite, he [the Moskito Indian].. hunts about for Pecary, Warree, each a sort of Wild Hogs, or Deer. **1699** L. WAFER *Voy.* 105 [Isthmus of Darien] The Warree is another kind of Wild-Hog they have. **1769** E. BANCROFT *Guiana* 125 Besides the Hogs..there are two species which are peculiar to those parts of America..the Picary and Warree. **1842** T. YOUNG *Resid. Mosquito Shore* 102 It was favourable weather for hunting, the woods near us being full of warrie. **1885** *Encycl. Brit.* XVIII. 449 The white-lipped peccary or warree..is..about 40 inches in length, of a blackish colour, with the lips and lower jaw white.

warree, variant of WHARE *Austral.*

warren ('wɒrən), *sb.*¹ Forms: 4 **wareine**, 4–5 **wareyne**, 5 **warenne**, **warreyne**, 5–6 **-ayn**, **wareyn**, **war(r)ane**, 6 **warryn**, 6–7 **waren**, **warraine**, 7 **warrin**, 5– **warren**; β. 4–5 **warraynte**, 5 **warand(e**, **-ant**, 5–6 **warraunte**, 6, 8 **warrant**. [a. AF. *warenne*, North-eastern OF. *warenne*, *waresne* (whence AL. *warenna*), corresp. to Central OF., mod.F. *garenne*, game-park, also (now chiefly) rabbit-warren, Pr. *garena*; of Teut. origin, f. root **war-* to protect, guard: cf. OF. *warir* WARE *v.* The suffix is obscure, and it is uncertain whether the word is of Teut. or Rom. formation. The OF. type **warande* (*garande*, *-ende*), whence the (M)Du. *warande* park, may be a mere variant, or it may represent a Teut. pr. pple. OF. had also a form *varene* (perh. due to the med.L. *varenna* of charters) which survives in mod.F. *varenne* moor inhabited by game.

The β forms below may possibly in part represent the OF. **warande*, but cf. the English addition of *t* in tyrant. Caxton's *warande* was adopted from his Du. original.]

1. a. A piece of land enclosed and preserved for breeding game. *Obs.* exc. *Hist.*

α. **1377** LANGL. *P. Pl.* B. Prol. 163 Vncoupled þei wenden Boþe in wareine & in waste where hem leue lyketh. **1429** *Rolls of Parlt.* IV. 344/1 Unlaweful hunters of Forestes, Parkes or Warennes, or any other opyn Mysdoers. *a* **1440** *Sir Degrev.* 422 He made my londes barreyne, My wodes and my warreyne, My wylde ys away. *c* **1500** *Melusine* xix. 99 Thanne they came out of the wareyne [where they had chased a hart]. **1558** in *Phillipps Wills* (*c* 1830) 127 All that part of my Warren of Albourne which lieth within the precincts of Southwood Walke. **1563** in Rymer *Fœdera* (1719) XV. 629 Keeper of Parks Houses Waranes or other Games of Venerye. **1577–87** HARRISON *England* II. xix. 206/1 in *Holinshed*, In parks and warrens we haue nothing else than..the keepers and wareners lodge. **1592** *Expos. Terms Law* 196 b, Warren is a place priuiledged by prescription or graunt of the Queene for the preseruation of hares, conies, partriges and feasantes or anie of them. **1599** SHAKS. *Much Ado* II. i. 222, I found him heere as melancholy as a Lodge in a Warren. *c* **1610** BEAUM. & FL. *Scornf. Lady* v. i, Ile make you take a tree, whore,..and then haue you cast, and hung vp ith warren. *a* **1634** COKE *Inst.* IV. lxxiii. (1648) 298 He that hath a Warren within a free Chase may build upon his own inheritance within his Warren a convenient lodge for preservation of his game. **1683** *Brit. Spec.* 17 The Forests, Parks..Warrens, and Woods stored with wild Beasts only for Recreation and Food. **1698** T. FROGER *Voy.* 9 A sort of wild Apple, or Crab tree, that grow as thick as Broom in a Heath or Warren. **1700** EVELYN *Diary* 13 July, I went to Marden, which was originally a barren warren bought by Sir Robert Clayton. **1769** BLACKSTONE *Comm.* IV. xiii. 175 Being the owner, or keeper, of a forest, park, chase, or warren.

β. **1481** CAXTON *Reynard* xvii. (Arb.) 42 It stondeth in a woode named hulsterlo vpon a warande in the wyldernesse. **1519** *Surtees Misc.* (1890) 32 That no man hawke nor hunte wᵗin my Lord's warraunte. **1583** STUBBES *Anat. Abus.* II. E 3, You shall haue some that..will not sticke to pull downe whole townes..and..make them parkes, chases, warrants and I cannot tell what of the same. **1702** *Phil. Trans.* XXIII. 1051 Therefore when Orders are given to hunt the Elephants, they pitch upon a convenient place for a Warrant or Park.

b. *transf.* and *fig.*

a **1586** SIDNEY *Apol. Poetrie* (Arb.) 25 Hee goeth hand in hand with Nature, not inclosed within the narrow warrant of her guifts, but freely ranging onely within the Zodiack of his owne wit. **1749** FIELDING *Tom Jones* v. iv, He bid him beat abroad, and not poach up the Game in his Warren. **1860** MILL *Repr. Govt.* (1865) 135/2 One people may keep another as a warren or preserve for its own use, a place to make money in.

†**c.** (*free*) ***warren***, a right of keeping or hunting beasts and fowls of warren (see d). *Obs.*

1485 *Rolls of Parlt.* VI. 374/1 The Office of Keping of Woode, in the Lordshipp of Kyrtlyngton, and Keping of Warren of Hares there. **1512** *Act 4 Hen. VIII*, c. 10 §2 The Bailifwike of Toppsam with the Selerage and Cranage and the Waren of Cones within the same. *a* **1513** FABYAN *Chron.* VII. (1533) 20 b, The kynge grauntyd to yᵉ sayd cytesyns of London wareyn, that is to meane that the cytesyns haue free lybertye of huntynge certayne cyrcuyte aboute London. **1596** BACON *Elem. Com. Law* I. (1630) 13 If I haue free warren in mine owne hand, and let my land for life not mentioning the warren, yet the leasee by implication shall haue the warren discharged and extract during his lease. **1603** G. OWEN *Pembrokesh.* (1892) 268 Whosoever hath libertie of free warren, maye haue his speciall action of Trespasse at the comon lawe, against anye that shall hunte or chase therein. **1766** BLACKSTONE *Comm.* II. iii. 38 Free-warren is a similar franchise, erected for preservation or custody (which the word signifies) of beasts and fowls of warren. **1766** PORNY *Heraldry* iv. (1777) 89 Sir John de Chetwynd..had a charter of free-warren through all his demesne. **1810** *Sporting Mag.* XXXVI. 26 Whether the rights of free warren and free chace were conferred. **1875** BLACKMORE *Alice Lorraine* II. xx. 274, I am to have free warren of all Sir Remnant's vast estates. **1913** H. W. C. DAVIS *Regesta Reg. Anglo-Norm.* Introd. 31 Grants of free hunting are few in number; even the right of free warren is sparingly granted.

†**d.** ***beasts, fowls of warren***: see quots. 1598 and 1628.

1539 *Act 31 Hen. VIII*, c. 5 A chase..for nourishyng generacion and feeding of beastes of venery, and of foules of waren. **1598** MANWOOD *Laws of Forest* iv. 22 b, The beasts and foules of Warren are these, the Hare, the Connie, the Phesant, and the Partridge. **1628** COKE *On Litt.* 233 There bee both Beasts and Foules of the Warren, Beasts, as Hares, Conies, and Roes..Fowles..as Partridge, Quaile, Raile,.. Phesant, Woodcocke,..Mallard, Herne.

2. a. *spec.* A piece of land appropriated to the breeding of rabbits (formerly also of hares). More fully ***rabbit-warren*** (see RABBIT *sb.*¹ 3 a), CONY-WARREN, HARE-WARREN.

Now usually a piece of uncultivated ground on which rabbits breed wild in burrows.

c **1400** *Master of Game* (MS. Digby 182) i, Whan hares be ygete with the kynde of a conynge, as somme ben in the warrayntes [*Bodl. MS.* wareynes], the houndes lust nor sentith hem nought so wele. *a* **1513** FABYAN *Chron.* VII. (1533) 50 These chyldren..entred the warrayn of a lord of Fraunce..and there chased and shote at Conyes for theyr disport. **1529** *Supplic. to King* (E.E.T.S.) 48 Warrens swarminge full of conyes. **1538** ELYOT *Dict.*, *Lagotrophia*, a warren or parke of hares. **1566** *Act 8 Eliz.* c. 15 §5 In any Parke Warren or Grounde employed to the mayntenaunce of any game of Conyes. **1600** HAKLUYT *Voy.* III. 442 We found the whole countrey to bee a warren of a strange kinde of Conies. **1607** J. NORDEN *Surv. Dial.* III. 114 Whether hath he any Warren of Conies, or Hares. **1697** VANBRUGH *Relapse* II. i, Like a young Puppy in a Warren, they have a Flirt at all, and catch none. **1773** GOLDSM. *She stoops to Conq.* II, When company comes you are not to pop out and stare, and then run in again, like frighted rabbits in a warren. **1807** CRABBE *Par. Reg.* I. 813 He poach'd the wood, and on the warren snared. **1850** 'SYLVANUS' *Bye-lanes & Downs* iv. 51 After passing..over a warren crenelled like a cullender, and divers stubble fields. **1875** W. MᶜILWRAITH *Guide Wigtownsh.* 81 The land along the coast [of the Bay of Luce] is a vast warren of rabbits.

b. *transf.*

1601 HOLLAND *Pliny* IX. lvi. I. 267 Fulvius Hirpinus was the first inventor of warrens as it were for Winkles [L. *cochlearum vivaria*]. **1845** DARWIN *Voy. Nat.* xvii. (1860) 388 The holes..enter the ground at a small angle; so that when walking over these lizard-warrens, the soil is constantly giving way.

†**c.** *slang.* [Misapprehension of *warren* var. of WARRANT *sb.*] (See quots.)

1609 DEKKER *Lanth. & Candle-light* iv. Wks. (Grosart) III. 231 He vpon whose credit these Rabbet-suckers runne, is called the Warren. *Ibid.* 236 Whilst this faire weather lasteth,..These Rabbet suckers keep to the Warren wherein they fatned. *a* **1700** B. E. *Dict. Cant. Crew*, *Warren*, he that is Security for Goods taken up, on Credit, by Extravagant young Gentlemen.

3. The inhabitants of a warren; *transf.* any collection or assemblage of small animals.

1607 TOPSELL *Four-f. Beasts* 271 In which, three or foure couple of Hares do quickly multiply into a great warren. **1625** FLETCHER *Women Pleas'd* II. iv, He is so hairie, That a tame warren of flyes frisk round about him. **1692** R. L'ESTRANGE *Fables Æsop*, etc. cccxxxiii. 291 The Cony.. Convenes a Whole Warren; Tells her Story, and Advises upon a Revenge. **1856** KANE *Arct. Expl.* I. xxix. 393 It was marvellous..what a perfect warren [of rats] we soon had on board.

4. A building or settlement likened to a rabbit-warren; †a brothel; a building or cluster of dwellings (esp. if partly underground) densely populated by poor tenants. Also, any area of living or office space characterized as a mass of passages and (small) rooms. Cf. *rabbit-warren* s.v. RABBIT *sb.*¹ 3 a.

a **1649** DK. NEWCASTLE *Country Capt.* III. i, And New yeares giftes from soadred virgins and their shee Provincialls whose warren must bee licenc'd from our Office. *a* **1700** B. E. *Dict. Cant. Crew*, *Warren*,..also a Boarding-school and a Bawdy-house. **1884** *Standard* 5 June, The Conservative party has recognized it in the case of the rookeries with which London still swarms. Will it not do something also for the warrens? **1886** TENNYSON *Locksley Hall Sixty Yrs. after* 224 And the crowded couch of incest in the warrens of the poor. **1918** *Blackw. Mag.* Jan. 124/1 The marg..is covered with a warren of huts scattered haphazard. **1919** *Ibid.* Nov. 693/1 A large passenger steamer..is, as every one who has travelled by water knows, an amazing warren of passages. **1922** JOYCE *Ulysses* 423 Figures wander, lurk, peer from warrens. **1954** J. R. R. TOLKIEN *Fellowship of Ring* I. 31 Mr. Frodo left an orphan..brought up anyhow in Brandy Hall. A regular warren, by all accounts. **1977** W. J. WEATHERBY *Home in Dark* xxi. 113 It was a house to hide in: you hardly existed in this anonymous warren. **1980** R. RENDELL *Lake of Darkness* iv. 41 A room smaller than this one divided into *three*... It's a real warren.

†**5.** An old name for the site of Woolwich Arsenal. Hence used *gen.* (see quot. 1769). *Obs.*

1769 FALCONER *Dict. Marine* (1780), *Fr. Terms*, *Arcenal de marine*, a royal dock-yard, together with its warren or gun-wharf. *Ibid.*, *Commissaire*, He keeps a register of all the artillery within the warren where he resides. **1774** *Ambulator* 223 Woolwich..In the warren or park, where they make trial of great guns and mortars, there are several thousand pieces of ordnance for ships and batteries [etc.]. **1805** *Ann. Reg.* (Otridge's ed.) 400 The ordnance board have signified to general Lloyd who commands the Artillery at Woolwich, that the warren at that place is to be from this time denominated the 'Royal Arsenal'.

†**6.** (See quot.) *Obs.*⁻⁰

[A spurious sense; the article is translated from the article *Garenne* in Chomel's Dict. Littré has *garenne à poisson*.]

1725 *Bradley's Family Dict.*, *Warren*, a Term in Fishery, being an easy and cheap way, of preserving and storing Fish, in the midst of a River, by making, as it were a Warren, for the Fish to retreat to.

7. *attrib.* and *Comb.*, as ***warren-hill***, ***-rabbit***, ***-wall***; ***warren-like*** adj.

1700 CHAUNCY *Hertfordsh.* 481 Upon the Warren Hill is an Eccho, which will repeat to a Trumpet twelve times together. *a* **1742** in *Ann. Reg.* 1762, II. 52, I have lived three years in a poor cottage under your warren-wall. **1876** TYNDALL *Ess. Float-Matter Air* (1881) 128 It was the same green hue throughout, though of varying degrees of intensity... In rabbit it was less fine than in hare, and in a tame rabbit less fine than in a warren rabbit. **1889** *Fabian Ess.* 218 A warren-like scuttle of alarmed..Radicals across the floor of the House of Commons. **1890** 'LYTH' *Golden South* 168 We found 'New Old Pipeclay' [diggings] more warren-like than the one we had seen.

Warren ('wɒrən), *sb.*² *Engin.* The name of James *Warren* (fl. 1848), of Middlesex, used *attrib.* and † in the possessive to designate a truss he designed composed of alternately inclined diagonal members joining two horizontal ones, so as to form a series of non-overlapping triangles pointing alternately up and down. [Patented by Warren and Monzani in *Brit. Patent 12,242* (1848).]

[**1852** *Minutes Proc. Inst. Civil Engineers* XI. 12 He had only used the simple triangulation for spans not exceeding 60 feet and generally for shallow girders, but he believed that some girders had been made on Captain Warren's plan for much greater spans.] *Ibid.* 14 Mr. Brunel..said..it was necessary to draw a distinct line of demarcation between the lattice bridge and that kind of construction called Warren's girder. *Ibid.*, The Warren girder was decidedly superior to the lattice bridge. **1866** B. B. STONEY *Theory of Strains in Girders* I. vi. 79 This class of bracing includes girders whose web consists of a simple system of triangles, such as 'Warren's' Girder. **1911** A. SMITH *Stresses in Simple Framed Structures* xiv. 83 The Warren truss has a complete system of web members composed..of diagonals. **1952** *Archit. Rev.* CXI. 159/2 Where the roof over the drug room joins that over the mill room there is a reinforced concrete Warren girder spanning 64 ft. and 13 ft. deep. **1967** *Jane's Surface Skimmer Systems 1967–68* 18/2 The lift fan bay forms part of the plenum chamber, the top skin of which is of Warren girder construction.

†'**warren, -yn**, *a. Sc. Obs. rare*⁻¹. [? f. WARRE + -EN.] ***warren tree***, a hard oak. Cf. WARRIED *a.*, WARRY *a.*¹

1513 DOUGLAS *Æneis* XI. iii. 84 The mekill syllis of the warryn [*ed.* 1710 warren] tre Wyth wedgis and with proppis bene devyd.

warren, obs. form of WARRANT, WARN *v.*¹

†'**warrenage.** *Obs. rare*⁻¹. [f. WARREN *sb.* + -AGE.] ? A payment for the right of free warren.

1610 [see COMMONAGE 1].

warrender, variant of WARRENER.

warrener ('wɒrənə(r)). Forms: α. 3 warener, 4–5 waryner(e, warinar, 5 warenner, 6 warrennar, warryner, -eyner, -ainer, 6–7 war(r)iner, 7 warrenor, 7–8 warrenner, 6– warrener; *Sc.* and *north.* 5 warander, -dare, 6 warrander, varrandar, 9 (*hist.* and *dial.*) warrender; β. 4–6 warner, 5 -ere. [a. North-eastern OF. *warrennier* (= Central OF., mod.F. *garennier*), f. *warenne* (*garenne*) WARREN *sb.*]

1. a. An officer employed to watch over the game in a park or preserve. *Obs.* exc. *Hist.* **b.** A servant who has the charge of a rabbit-warren.

In the earlier quots. the two applications of the word cannot be distinguished with certainty.

α. **1297** *Placita coram Rege* m. 25 b (1897) 165 Thomam le Warener de Fakenham. **1362** LANGL. *P.Pl.* A. v. 159 Sesse þe souters wyf sat on þe Benche, Watte þe warinar [**1377** warner, **1393** warynere] and his wyf boþe. **1467–8** *Rolls of Parlt.* V. 609/2 Th' office of Warenner, or kepyng of the Warenne. **1473** *Rental Bk. Cupar-Angus* (1879) I. 188 Tha sal gife twa akrys of land fre til our warander of our kunynȝare. *c* **1500** tr. *Charter Lond.* in Arnolde *Chron.* (1502) 6/2 Wythin whiche wareyn nether waryner ne forester nor Justice of our forest of her landis and wodes ne huntynge ne of repynge of her cornes entermet hem any thing. **1551–2** *Acc. Ld. High Treas. Scot.* X. 66 Item..to ane warrander send to Arrane to mak clapparttis for cunnynges, xls̄. **1573–80** TUSSER *Husb.* (1878) 72 Get warrener bound to vermin thy ground. **1584** *Churchw. Acc. Pittington* (Surtees) 17 Item given to the warrander for killinge of twoe foxes, xijᵈ. **1598** SHAKS. *Merry W.* I. iv. 28. **1613** MARKHAM *Eng. Husbandman* II. II. iv. (1635) 59 We see Warriners and Poulters sell Rabbets, a fat, and a leane ever coupled together. **1643** PRYNNE *Sov. Power Parl.* III. 17 May a Forrester, Warrener, or Keeper of a Parke, lawfully beate and kill another in defence of his..game? **1680** *Lond. Gaz.* No. 1560/4 William Hooker, Warriner and Servant to George Vernon of Sudbury. **1770** G. WHITE *Selborne*, *To Barrington* 12 Apr., Warreners observe..that their rabbits are never in such good case as in a gentle frost. **1800** *Hull Advertiser* 6 Dec. 1/2 The warren contains an ample breeding stock of rabbits... The warrener upon the premises will shew the same. **1829** T. BROWN *Biogr. Sk. Dogs* 529 Warreners..make use of *nux vomica* as a poison, which is not unfrequently concealed in a piece of raw meat, to entice foumarts and weasels to eat it. **1835** *App. Munic. Corpor. Rep.* III. 1714 [Among officers of Scarborough corporation] Warrener and Gamekeeper. **1877** *N.W. Linc. Gloss.* s.v., My father was warrender at Thorganby when I was born.

attrib. **1591** GREENE *Not. Discov. Coosnage* Wks. (Grosart) X. 32 A cony-catcher..what is he a wariner felow?

β. **1377** [see α]. *c* **1440** *Promp. Parv.* 517/1 Warnere, *warinarius*. **1485** *Rolls of Parlt.* VI. 378/2 The Offices of Bailliff of the Manour and Lordshipp foren of Myche Marlowe,..and Warner, Warlowe. *a* **1500** *Tale K. Edw. & Sheph.* in Hartshorne *Anc. Metr. T.* (1829) 45 The warner is hardy and fell. **1503–4** *Act 19 Hen. VII*, c. 10 §7 The Office of Warner or Warnershipp of oure Waren of Methwolde.

2. One who owns or rents a warren. Also *transf.*

1846 *J. Baxter's Libr. Pract. Agric.* (ed. 4) I. 335 Warreners are sometimes liable to great losses from an epidemical disorder among rabbits. **1856** 'STONEHENGE' *Brit. Sports* I. I. vii. §10 The sport of shooting rabbits is never carried on in the warrens, because the warrener does not wish his property wasted, and prefers trapping them. **1880** *Daily Tel.* 27 Sept., Numerous parcels of ground let out formerly to warreners have been ploughed up. **1929** R. BRIDGES *Testament of Beauty* IV. 114 Poor nomads.. warreners of the waste.

3. A warren rabbit.

1864 *Peter Parley's Ann.* VII. 325 The warrener burrows underground, and has the most valuable fur.

†'**warrenership.** *Obs.* [-SHIP.] The office of warrener.

For some quots. that possibly belong to this word see WARNERSHIP.

1485 *Rolls of Parlt.* VI. 352/2 The Baillishipp and Warrenership of Brayles. *Ibid.* 371/1 The Offices of Warnershipp of Methwold within oure Countie of Norff'. **1503–4** [see WARRENER 1 β].

warrer ('wɔːrə(r)). Forms: 3 weorreur, 3–5 werrour(e, 3–4 werreur, wereur, verreur, 5 werrur, verrour, 5– warrer. [Early ME. *weorreur*, *werrour*, etc., a. AF. *werrour*, agent-n. f. *werrer* to war, f. *werre* WAR *sb.*; coalescing with the later English formation on WAR *v.* + -ER¹.]

†**1.** One who engages in warfare, a soldier, warrior. Also, an antagonist, a persecutor. *Obs.*

a **1225** *Ancr. R.* 246 Þe weorreur of helle mei longe asailen ou. *a* **1300** *Cursor M.* 8306 Wereur art þou ful wight. *Ibid.* 20933 To þaim he [Paul] first was verreur [*Gött.* werreur] And afterward becom prechur. **13..** *Ibid.* 18014 (Gött.) [S]ir sathan þan till hell ansuerd.. Receiue iesu.. vr werreur bath mi and þine. **13..** *Guy Warw.* (1891) 398 Hou he hadde euer ben strong werrour, For Iesu loue. *c* **1400** *Laud Troy Bk.* 3773 Theire Cite Is bothe styff, stalworthe, and strong, ..And ful of men and gode verroures. ? **1436** *Pol. Poems* (1859) II. 199 The merveillouse werrour and victorious prince, Kynge Herry the vᵗʰ. *c* **1440** *Gesta Rom.* iv. 11 (Harl. MS.) Oure lord, þe do3ty werrour, ihesu criste. **1482** WARKW. *Chron.* 2 The best warrer of all that time.

2. One who wars or contends (*against* something).

1836 LANE *Mod. Egypt.* II. xi. 168 On the occasions of all the great religious festivals in Cairo,..these female warrers against modesty [*i.e.* unveiled girls]..are sure to be seen.

warrey, variant of WARRAY *v. Obs.*

warreyne, -er: see WARREN *sb.*, WARRENER.

warreyour, obs. form of WARRIOR.

warriangle, variant of WARIANGLE *Obs.*

warrick, variant of WARROK *dial.*

'warridge, 'warrage. *north.* Also war(r)ish. See also *Eng. Dial. Dict.* [Of obscure origin; cf. WALLIS of the same meaning.] The withers (of a horse).

1790 GROSE *Provinc. Gloss.* (ed. 2), *Warridge*, the withers of a horse. North. **1798** *Hull Advertiser* 9 June 2/2 A dark-brown galloway, has..a barish place upon her warrish. **1899** *Cumbld. Gloss.*, *Warridge*, the withers of a horse. 'A grand-like colt, but a wee bit thick i' t' warrage.'

warrie, obs. f. WARY *a.*; var. WARY *v. Obs.*

†**'warried**, *a. Obs. rare.* [f. WARRE; cf. OE. *wearriht*, knotty, of which this word may be an altered survival.] Of a tree: Full of knots. Cf. WARRED, WARREN *adjs.*, WARRY *a.*¹

1567 GOLDING *Ovid's Met.* XIII. 942 More hard than warryed Oke too twyne [*Durior annosa quercu*].

warrigal ('wɒrɪgəl), *sb.* (and *a.*) *Austral.* Also 9 warragal, -gle. [An Aboriginal word, spelt *warregal*, *wor-re-gal*, *war-ri-gal*, *wor-rikul*, *wa-ri-kul* etc. by various writers on the Aboriginal language; said to have the senses 'dog' and 'savage' (*sb.* and *adj.*). In the former sense it is freq. quoted as a native word from 1793 onwards; the sense 'savage' is given by Bunce *Lang. Aborigines Victoria*, 1859.]

A. *sb.*

1. The wild dog of Australia, the DINGO.

1838 J. HAWDON *Jrnl. Journey N.S.W. to Adelaide* (1952) 25 We could find no traces of the sheep except in two places, where we could perceive they had been pursued by the Warrigals. **1848** H. W. HAYGARTH *Recoll. Bush Life Austral.* v. 44 His 'coolie' dogs will awaken him on the approach of a 'warragle', or native dog. **1852** [see DINGO *sb.*]. **1890** 'R. BOLDREWOOD' *Squatter's Dream* xix. 240 A warrigal will be picking some of your bones before this day six months. **1897** KIPLING *Seven Seas, Song of Dead* 4 Where the warrigal whimpers and bays through the dust of the sere river-courses.

2. An Australian Aboriginal living in a traditional manner (esp. as distinct from one accustomed to, or living amongst, whites), a myall.

1890 'R. BOLDREWOOD' *Col. Reformer* xvii, I swore to shoot the old warrigal at sight. **1890** *Pall Mall Gaz.* 4 Aug. 4/2 A 'warrigal' originally meant a wild Blackfellow.

transf. **1890** *Pall Mall Gaz.* 4 Aug. 4/2 By an easy and natural transition, 'warrigal' has now come to signify a hot-blooded youth who goes the pace and makes things hum when he gets out of his teens.

3. A wild or untamed Australian horse.

1881 *Australasian* 21 May 647/4 (Morris) How we ran in 'The Black Warragal'. **1890** *Melbourne Argus* 14 June 4/2 Mike, he'd fret himself to death in a stable and maybe kill the groom. Mike's a warrigal, he is.

B. *adj.* Wild.

1855 in Stewart & Keesing *Old Bush Songs* (1957) 164 I'm a warragle fellow that long hath dwelt In the wild interior, nor hath felt, Nor heard, nor seen the pleasures of town. **1890** 'R. BOLDREWOOD' *Col. Reformer* viii, A real good wholesome cabbage—warrigal cabbage, the shepherds call it. —— *Squatter's Dream* xx. 249 He's a good shot and these warrigal devils knows it.

warrin, -er: see WARREN *sb.*, WARRENER.

warring ('wɔːrɪŋ), *vbl. sb.* [f. WAR *v.*¹ + -ING¹.] The action of the verb.

13.. *K. Alis.* 6095 Ac, for they weore in the fen Kyng Alisaunder leoseth many men, Ac, allegate, the kynges Losen ten ageyns on in werrynges. *c* **1380** WYCLIF *Wks.* (1880) 147 Þei techen cristen men to sufre..moche wakynge & dispisynge & betynge for to gete worldly honour & a litel drit bi fals werrynge out of charite. *a* **1450** *Le Morte Arth.* 2975 Arthur louyd noght but warynge. *c* **1450** LOVELICH *Merlin* 12,022 To Socouren leodagan the kyng that jn his contre hath gret werryng. *a* **1625** FLETCHER *Hum. Lieut.* II. v, *Leu.* When was the Prince with her? answer me directly. *Gov.* Not since he went a warring.

b. *fig.*

1511 COLET *Serm. Convoc.* A viij b, The warrynge of them is nat carnall but spirituall. For our warrynge is to pray, to rede and study scriptures [etc.]. **1884** *Athenæum* 5 Jan. 15/2 A sense of effort in reading a poem..arises from a warring between the rhythm of nature and the rhythm peculiar to the metrical structure adopted.

warring ('wɔːrɪŋ), *ppl. a.* [f. WAR *v.*¹ + -ING².]

1. a. That makes or carries on war; that contends in warfare. (Now chiefly with plural subject and the implication 'mutually'.)

1702 ROWE *Tamerl.* II. i, Half the warring World upon thy Side. **1706** PRIOR *Ode to Queen* xxiii, Hence..Herbert's and Churchill's Warring Progeny. **1818** BYRON *Ch. Har.* IV. lxiii, Such is the absorbing hate when warring nations meet! **1849** JAMES *Woodman* i, The human vulture, which follows on the track of warring armies to feed upon the spoils of the dead. **1874** GREEN *Short Hist.* vi. §3. 295 The two warring lines were united by his [Henry VII] marriage with Elizabeth. **1907** *Times* 22 May 9/4 Our sword..stands between peace and the chaos of warring races.

b. ***Warring States***, used to designate the last period (475 B.C. onward) of Chinese history prior to the unification of the country in 221 B.C.

1929 J. JOSHUA tr. *R. Wilhelm's Short Hist. Chinese Civilization* iii. 133 The period of 'the Warring States'..is usually regarded as lasting from 403 to 221 B.C. **1935** C. P. FITZGERALD *China* iii. 65 If the story of the period of the Warring States was merely a record of anarchy and violence it would not be worthy of detailed attention in a cultural history. **1937** R. W. SWALLOW *Anc. Chinese Bronze Mirrors* Pl. 3 (*caption*) Warring states type of mirror. **1963** KWANG-CHIH CHANG *Archaeol. Anc. China* vii. 177 For our purposes, round figures are sufficient: 1100 for the conquest ..450 for the beginning of the Warring-States period. **1978** *Nagel's Encycl.-Guide: China* 327 The names of the states of the Warring States period almost all survive as surnames now.

2. *fig.* Engaged in strife, contending; *esp.* with plural subject, mutually contending, discordant.

a. of the elements.

1608 SHAKS. *Lear* IV. vii. 32 (Qtos.) Was this a face To be expösd against the warring [*Fol.* iarring] winds. **1697** DRYDEN *Virg. Georg.* I. 432 Oft have I seen a sudden Storm arise, From all the warring Winds that sweep the Skies. **1697** —— *Æneis* I. 753 When Winds, and ev'ry warring Element, Disturb'd our Course. **1725** POPE *Odyss.* VI. 206 Twice ten tempestuous nights I roll'd, resign'd To roaring billows, and the warring wind. **1845** DARWIN *Voy. Nat.* x. (1879) 217 How delightful was that still night, after having been so long involved in the din of the warring elements! **1912** L. TRACY *Mirabel's Isl.* i. (1915) 10 Ages of warring tides had thrust a deep-water passage..through the opposing barrier.

b. of passions, etc.

1703 ROWE *Fair Penit.* II. i, The warring Passions, and tumultuous Thoughts. **1706** PRIOR *Ode to Queen* vii, Betwixt Despair, and Rage, and Hope, and Pain, Something within his warring Bosom roll'd. **1791** BURNS *'Ae fond kiss'* 4 Warring sighs and groans I'll wage thee!

c. of persons, parties, etc.

1883 WHITELAW *Sophocles, Oedipus King* 634 What means this senseless din of warring tongues? **1908** *Times Lit. Suppl.* 10 Sept. 290/1 It..would inevitably have offended one or other of the warring schools into which their flocks are divided.

Warrington ('wɒrɪŋtən). The name of a town in Cheshire, used chiefly *attrib.* to designate a variety of cross-peen joiner's hammer.

1935 N. R. ROGERS *Technol. Woodwork & Metalwork* ix. 96 There are two patterns of cross-pane hammers, Warrington and London Riveting, or Exeter. The former.. is made in twelve sizes specified by Nos. 00 to 10 consecutively. **1956** A. P. MORGAN *Woodworking Tools* i. 8 The Warrington hammer, and similar types with a tapering 'pene' instead of claws, is more suitable for..joinery and finer work. **1966** A. W. LEWIS *Gloss. Woodworking Terms* 42 The common woodworker's hammer with its cross pane is known as the 'Warrington pattern'... A pin hammer is merely a very small Warrington. **1979** A. B. EMARY *Woodworking* ii. 14 Although joiners use the Warrington-type hammer, the claw hammer is considered the best for someone who will be doing a wide variety of jobs.

warrior ('wɒrɪə(r)). Forms: 3–4 **werreour, worreour,** 4 **weorriour, werraiur, werrayure, werreyoure,** 4–5 **werrayour, werriour, worreor,** 5 **werryour, werryor, weryor, verriour,** 6 *Sc.* **weirreour,** 5 **warreyour, warryour, varioure,** 6 **warreoure, waryer, warryar,** 6–7 **warrier,** 6–9 **warriour,** 6– **warrior.** [Early ME., a. north-eastern OF. *werreieor*, *werrieur*, etc. (= Central OF. *guerreieor*, *guerrieur*, *guerroyeur*, etc., mod.F. *guerroyeur*), agent-n. f. *werreier* (*guerreier*): see WARRAY *v.*

The synonymous F. *guerrier* (= Pr. *guerrier*, Sp. *guerrero*, Pg. *guerreiro*, It. *guerriero*, *-ere*) is a different formation. For the ME. *weorreur*, *werreur*, *werour*, *-eur*, *verrour*, see WARRER.]

†**I. 1.** One who makes war upon; a persecutor. (Cf. WARRAY *v.* 1 b, 2 b.) *Obs.*⁻¹

a **1300** *Cursor M.* 20933 (Edinb.) To þaim he [Paul] firste was werrayur, eftirward bicom prechure.

II. 2. a. One whose occupation is warfare; a fighting man, whether soldier, sailor, or (latterly) airman; in eulogistic sense, a valiant or an experienced man of war. Now chiefly *poet.* and *rhetorical*, exc. as applied to the fighting men of the ages celebrated in epic and romance and of primitive peoples, for whom the designation *soldier* would be inappropriate.

The word found a memorable application in the designation of 'The Unknown Warrior', who on 11 Nov. 1920 was honoured with a stately funeral in Westminster Abbey as the representative of all who had given their lives for England in the great war. To which of the services he belonged was kept a secret, so that the comprehensive word 'warrior' was both necessary and felicitous.

1297 R. GLOUC. (Rolls) 2164 Kni3tes & oþer worreours, þat to þis londe wende. *Ibid.* 2548 Sende we 3ute after mi sones, octo, & ebyse, þat quointe werreours beþ, & stalwarde & wyse. **13..** *K. Alis.* 1458 (Laud MS.) He had of hem al þat he wolde, Steden, armes, siluer & golde, And many stronge wereyoure [*v.r.* weorriour]. *c* **1330** R. BRUNNE *Chron. Wace* (Rolls) 2729 Donewal was wereour god. **1338** —— *Chron.* (1810) 166, I haf kept thi lande, I se that dishonoure Is now the nerhand, thorgh this conquerour, That [is] an Inglis kyng, a wys werreour [Langtoft *sage guerraiour*]. **1375** BARBOUR *Bruce* xx. 416 Than, as gud werriours, and wis, With thame stoutly assemblit he. *c* **1380** WYCLIF *Sel. Wks.* II. 412 Petir was not heed of þe Chirche, but a capteyn of þe Chirche. And certis werriouris wolen scorne þis resoun, þat if a man be capteyn, he is heed. **1388** —— *Ecclus.* xxvi. 28 A man a werriour [Vulg. *vir bellator*] failynge bi nedynesse. **1410** *26 Pol. Poems* ix. 138 Caste þe not to couetys, 3e þat ry3twys werryours be, But loke where ri3t querel lys. **1422** YONGE tr. *Secreta Secret.* 155 Iulyus Cesar the forte werryor. **1448–9** METHAM *Wks.* (1916) 11 O Mars! cheuetyn off nobyl weryouris. **1456** SIR G. HAYE *Law Arms* (S.T.S.) 5 Men that wont was to be werreyouris to defend the kirk rycht. *a* **1513** FABYAN *Chron.* VII. (1533) 111 The duke of Lancastre landed at Caleys with a stronge company of archers and other warryours. **1535** STEWART *Cron. Scot.* (Rolls) I. 384 Thir weirreouris into thair weirlie weid,..He gart thame enter in the thickest thrang. *c* **1538** STARKEY *England* I. ii. 49 To the handys are resemblyd bothe craftysmen and warryarys wych defend the rest of the body from iniury of ennymys vtward. *a* **1548** HALL *Chron.*, *Hen. V*, 48 Kyng Henry..ordred his men for his most aduantage like an expert capitaine and a couragious warirer [*read* warrier]. **1551** T. WILSON *Logic* H vij, Then should al captaines, and men of warre, be tendre ouer there poore warriours and base souldiours. **1570** DRANT *Serm.* E vj b, It should behoue me..to tell a long story what warriers and fire brandes of warre these Popes of Rome haue bene. **1593** SHAKS *3 Hen. VI*, I. iv. 14 And when the hardyest Warriors did retyre, Richard cry'de, Charge, and giue no foot of ground. **1641** EARL MONM. tr. *Biondi's Civil Wars* IV. 28 Hee was rightly ranked in the number of the chiefe warriers of that age. **1732** LEDIARD *Sethos* II. x. 363 He had beforehand gain'd the reputation of a warrior. **1788** J. WHITE *Jrnl. Voy. N.S. Wales* (1790) 118 Many of their warriors, or distinguished men, we observed to be painted in stripes, across the breast and back. **1806** WORDSW. *Happy Warrior* 1 Who is the happy Warrior? Who is he That every man in arms should wish to be? **1814** SCOTT *Lord of Isles* IV. xx, Warriors!—and where are warriors found, If not on martial Britain's ground? **1826** J. F. COOPER *Last of Mohicans* xv, A swarthy band of the native chiefs..with the warriors of their several tribes. **1837** DICKENS *Pickw.* vii, He sprang like an ardent warrior from his tent. **1902** *Times* 15 Apr. 10/6 On April 6 a band of 40 to 50 native warriors made a dash for the camp.

fig. **1581** MARBECK *Bk. of Notes* 1045 Whosoeuer will playe the warrier vnder Christ.

b. occas. applied to a woman. *lit.* and *fig.*

c **1400** MAUNDEV. (Roxb.) xvii. 78 Þir wymmen er noble werrayours and wys. **1595** SPENSER *Amoretti* xi. 3 Dayly when I do seeke and sew for peace,..She, cruell warriour, doth her selfe addresse To battell. *Ibid.* lvii. 1 Sweet warriour when shall I haue peace with you? **1604** SHAKS. *Oth.* II. i. 184 *Oth.* O, my faire Warriour. *Des.* My deere Othello. **1762** GOLDSM. *Ess.* x, Female Warriors.

c. *transf.* Applied to an animal.

1697 DRYDEN *Virg. Georg.* III. 340 The stooping Warriours, aiming Head to Head, Engage their clashing Horns. **1774** GOLDSM. *Nat. Hist.* V. 307 Small birds..are remarkably brave. However contemptible these little warriors are to larger creatures, they are often but too formidable to each other. **1887** W. S. S. TYRWHITT *New Chum in Queensland Bush* vii. 135 'Look out for that old cow again, Jack,' shouts Jim, 'and I think that bullock's a bit of a "warrior".' **1895** J. G. MILLAIS *Breath fr. Veldt* (1899) 161, I had a nice easy shot at the old warrior [a wild pig].

d. ***warrior's belt***: see quot.

1879 W. ROSSITER *Dict. Sci. Terms*, *Warrior's belt*, three bright stars Alnitak, Alnilam, and Mintaka, in the constellation Orion.

3. (***bloody***) ***warrior***: a local name for the wallflower, *Cheiranthus Cheiri*.

1825 JENNINGS *Observ. Dial. W. Eng.*, *Bloody warrior*, the wall-flower. **1873** L. BELCHER *My First Book* 25 Fragrant warriors with bloodred blossoms. **1875** W. CORY *Lett. & Jrnls.* (1897) 381 All wallflowers (which our people call 'bloody warriors') died in the winter. **1883** MISS BROUGHTON *Belinda* I. vi, The little garden-path, where the bloody warriors..grow in the sandy border.

4. A South American humming-bird of the genus *Oxypogon*.

1861 GOULD *Monogr. Trochilidæ* III. Pl. 182 *Oxypogon Guerini*. Guerin's Helmet-crest... *Warrior*, of the dealers in specimens of natural history. *Ibid.* Pl. 183 *Oxypogon Lindeni* ..*Black Warrior*, of the dealers.

5. ***black warrior***: an American bird of prey: see quot.

1884 COUES *Key N. Amer. Birds* (ed. 2) 543 *Buteo harlani*. Harlan's Buzzard. 'Black Warrior'.

6. *attrib.* **a.** quasi-adj., belonging to or characteristic of a warrior, martial [? after F. *guerrier* adj.], as ***warrior-blood***, ***hilt***, ***hymn***, ***laurel***, ***lay***, ***mêlee***, ***plume***, ***sound***, ***spirit***, ***threat***, ***trumpet***, ***wreath***, ***youth***. **b.** appositive, that is a warrior, as ***warrior-angel***, ***ant***, ***bird***, ***chief***,

dame, god, guest, hero, king, love, maid, man, poet, priest, prophet, queen, saint, son, steed, woman; consisting of warriors, as ***warrior-caste, class, file, host, nation, train, tribe***. c. similative, as ***warrior-like*** adj. and adv., ***warrior-wise*** adv.

1667 MILTON *P.L.* IV. 946 To whom the *warriour Angel soon repli'd. **1834** *Penny Cycl.* II. 63/1 There are whole communities of *warrior-ants. **1897** *Outing* XXX. 248/2 It was the advance guard of the warrior ants, and each leaf was carried by an ant! **1830** MRS. HEMANS *Wounded Eagle* 2 *Warrior bird! what seek'st thou here? **1828** —— *Birds of Passage* 10 Proud rivers, whose tide hath roll'd All dark with the *warrior-blood of old. **1842** W. C. TAYLOR *Anc. Hist.* ii. §2 (ed. 3) 50 In the reign of Psammetichus, the entire *warrior-caste of the Egyptians migrated to Ethiopia. **1715** POPE *Iliad* IV. 408 Then give thy *Warrior-Chief a Warrior's Due. **1862** SPENCER *First Princ.* II. xvi. §134 (1867) 372 The *warrior-class attains a perfect separation from classes devoted to the cultivation of the soil. **1697** DRYDEN *Æneis* VII. 1095 A *Warriour Dame. **1817** SCOTT *Harold* VI. xiv, What rage is thine, To quit the worship of thy line, To leave thy *Warrior-God? **1820** KEATS *Eve St. Agnes* xlii, That night the Baron dreamt of many a woe, And all his *warrior-guests.. Were long be-nightmar'd. **1701** J. HUGHES *Praises Heroic Virt.* 10 How glorious 'tis to see The *warrior hero fight for liberty. **1844** MRS. BROWNING *Rom. Page* v, While in Palestine The *warrior-hilt we drave. **1725** POPE *Odyss.* VI. 196 By the Delian coast I voyag'd, leader of a *warrior host. **1887** MEREDITH *Ballads & P.* 98 Fear of silence made them strive Loud in *warrior-hymns. **1725** POPE *Odyss.* XI. 662 With haughty stalk he sought the distant glades Of *warrior Kings. **1851** TENNYSON *To Queen* 4 The warrior kings of old. **1703** PRIOR *Ode to Mem. Col. G. Villiers* 87 Plant the *Warrior Lawrel o'er his Brow. **1815** SCOTT *Troubadour* iii, And still was heard his *warrior-lay. **1552** HULOET, *Warriour lyke, *bellicosus*. *a* **1716** WYCHERLEY *Posth. Wks.* (1728) I. 118 Thou, Warrior-like, do'st scour the dang'rous Field. **1590** SHAKS. *Mids. N.* II. i. 71 Why art thou heere.. But that forsooth.. Your buskin'd Mistresse, and your *Warrior loue To Theseus must be Wedded. **1725** POPE *Odyss.* VI. 25 The *warrior Maid Glides thro' the valves, and hovers round her head. **1812** BYRON *Ch. Har.* II. lv, He heard the busy hum of *warrior-men. **1839** THACKERAY *Knightly Guerdon* iii, Sir Ulric rode first in the *warrior-*mêlée*. **1872** MACDUFF *Comfort Ye* xxvi. 378 The spoil and treasure of *warrior-nations. **1823** MRS. HEMANS *Vespers of Palermo* v. iii, The joyous winds Are tossing *warrior-plumes. **1878** O. WILDE *Ravenna* 9 Her *warrior-poet, first in song and fight. **1958** O. CAROE *Pathans* xv. 241 The warrior-poet whose words still kindle fire in the hearts of his compatriots. **1911** W. W. FOWLER in *Encycl. Brit.* XVII. 760/2 The Salii or dancing *warrior-priests of Mars. **1817** LADY MORGAN *France* (1818) II. 373 To whom Moses gave the most fearful command ever issued by the *warriour-prophet to his obedient legions. **1697** DRYDEN *Æneis* XI. 756 Then with a graceful Meen, Lights from her lofty Steed, the *Warrior Queen. **1780** COWPER *Boadicea* I When the British warrior queen, Bleeding from the Roman rods, Sought [etc.]. **1845** SARAH AUSTIN *Ranke's Hist. Ref.* II. iii. I. 447 The *warrior saints, St. George and St. Martin. **1697** DRYDEN *Æneis* VIII. 140 Hercules, the *Warrior Son of Jove. **1920** *Discovery* May 133/1 A series of striking military successes gained by Mehemet [Ali] and his warrior son. **1803** SCOTT *Cadyow Castle* xiii, The hoarse bugle's *warrior-sound. **1841** MYERS *Cath. Th.* III. §4. 11 We find ..the *warriour spirit of the Judges,..sanctioned rather than rebuked by prophetic communications. **1899** *Engl. Hist. Rev.* Apr. 226 The almost total absence of the warrior-spirit from the poetry of the Far East. **1685** DRYDEN *Thren. Aug.* 474 No neighing of the *Warriour Steeds. **1814** SCOTT *Lord of Isles* IV. ix, The *warrior-threat, the infant's plain,.. were heard in vain! **16..** COWLEY *Wks.* I. 124 (Jod.) The *warrior train Though most were sorely wounded none were slain. **1726** POPE *Odyss.* XX. 96 To seek my lord among the warrior-train. **1812** S. ROGERS *Voy. Columbus* III. 29 Those the wild hunter worships as he roves,.. Or *warrior-tribes with rites of blood implore. **1697** DRYDEN *Æneis* VI. 244 None so renown'd, The *Warrior Trumpet in the Field to sound. **1871** TENNYSON *Last Tourn.* 516 But *warrior-wise thou stridest thro' his halls Who hates thee. **1876** W. H. G. KINGSTON *On Banks of Amazon* 354 The early voyagers ..declared that they met a nation of *warrior-women on the banks of this river. **1810** J. MONTGOMERY *Cast-away Ship* 12 A gay and gallant company,.. For *warriour-wreaths upon the sea, Their joyful brows prepare. **1816** WORDSW. *Fr. Army in Russia* 20 He smote the blossoms of their *warrior youth.

Hence **'warriorhood; 'warriorism; 'warriorship.**

1837 *Tait's Mag.* IV. 726 The stirring and barbarous ages of universal warriorship. **1885** OMAN *Art of War* 30 What wonder then if his contemporaries..glorified him into the normal type of warriorhood. **1892** *Nation* (N.Y.) 24 Mar. 222/2 The secret of warriorism.

warrioress ('wɒrɪərɪs). [f. WARRIOR + -ESS.] A female warrior.

1594 CAREW *Tasso* (1881) 59 Now to the combat had this wariouresse Plighted her selfe. **1596** SPENSER *F.Q.* v. vii. 27 Eftsoones that warriouresse with haughty crest Did forth issue, all ready for the fight. **1652-62** HEYLYN *Cosmogr.* I. (1682) 126 Mathildis, that famous Warrioress, who carried so great a stroke in the state of Italy. **1755** T. H. CROKER *Orl. Fur.* XXII. lxxxviii, He quickly turns, and in his turning view'd, Sight of his warrioress belov'd to gain. **1885** AUBREY DE VERE *Ess.* (1887) I. ii. 58 The virgin warrioress assails the castle.

fig. **1598** J. DICKENSON *Greene in Conc.* (1878) 137 With her tongue she was as tall a warriouresse as any of hir sexe.

†**'warrious,** *a. Obs. rare*⁻¹. [f. WAR *sb.*[1] + -IOUS (the form suggested by WARRIOR).] Warlike.

1581 MULCASTER *Positions* xxxix. 202 Valiancie of courage which is the meane to make a noble and a warrious captaine.

†**'warrish,** *a. Obs.* [f. WAR *sb.*[1] + -ISH.] Warlike.

1747 E. POSTON *Pratler* I. 43 Doubtless a warrish Spirit receives all its Might and Power from Weakness, and false Notions. **1788** WOLCOT (P. Pindar) *Romish Priest* 8 He.. Gave to the Prince of Darkness such hard blows, That Satan was afraid to show his nose..before this priest so warrish! **17..** —— *Ep. to the Pope* 186, I know the rascals have a sin in petto, To rob the holy lady of Loretto; Attack her temple with their guns so warrish.

warrish, variant of WARRIDGE.

warrison: see WARISON.

warrit, obs. Sc. var. of VARIED *ppl. a.*

1578 *Inv.* in W. Hunter *Biggar & Fleming* xxvi. (1862) 332 Ane clok of blak dalmes wᵗ ane collat warrit wᵗ welnot [? *read* weluot].

'warrok, *sb.* Also 9 **warrick.** [f. WARROK *v.*]

†**1.** A girth. *Obs.*

1392-3 *Earl Derby's Exped.* (Camden) 238 Pro horscombes, warrokes, et sagmine emptis ibidem pro equis domini, xxij s. **14..** *Voc.* in Wr.-Wülcker 612/23 *Sirentorium*, a warrok.

2. *dial.* A peculiar tackle used in shipyards, etc. on Tyneside. (*Eng. Dial. Dict.* 1905.)

'warrok, *v.* Also 4 **warroke,** 9 **warrick.** [a. OF. *waroquier, garochier*; perh. of Teut. origin.]

†**1.** *trans.* To girth (a horse); to bind (a person). *Obs.*

1362 LANGL. *P.Pl.* A. IV. 19 Sette my Sadel vppon Soffre-til-I-seo-my-tyme, And loke þou warroke [*v.r.* warrok] him wel wiþ swiþe feole gurþhes. *c* **1440** *York Myst.* xxx. 525 Sir knyghtis.. That warlowe ye warrok and wraste, And loke þat he brymly be braste.

2. *dial.*

1894 *Northumbld. Gloss.*, *Warrick*, to cramp or fasten with ropes or chains... Ropes are warricked by passing one end of a lever through a loop and heaving it tight. The end of the lever is then tied down.

3. Comb.: **warrick-screw, -soam** (see quots.).

1894 *Northumbld. Gloss.*, *Warrick-screw*, the screw used for warricking or tightening the chains passed round a waggon-load of round timber. **1905** *Eng. Dial. Dict.*, *Warrick-sowm*, a chain for girding timber on a wood-wagon.

†**'warrope.** *Obs.* Also **-roape, -ropp.** [Of obscure origin; possibly a misapprehension of ('warəp), northern pronunciation of *warp*: cf. WARP *sb.* 3 and *warp-rope* (WARP *sb.* 9). But cf. also WARDROPE and WARTAKE.] ? = WARP *sb.* 3.

1615 E. S. *Britain's Buss* A 3 b, Fourthly, the particulars of her Herring Nets, and of the Warropes and other Ropes, Cords and lines. *Ibid.* B 3 b, All the said 50 Nets being finished must be hanged al arow vpon a strong large rope called a Warrope:..So each Net taketh vp 15 fathom of Warrope. **1645** *Papers rel. Army Solemn League & Cov.* (S.H.S.) II. 425 To Robert Hooge a war-ropp sould 2. 8. 7½.

†**'warry,** *a.*[1] *Obs. rare.* [f. WARRE + Y. OE. had *wearriȝ* callous.] Of a tree: Full of knots. Cf. WARRIED, WARREN *adjs.*

1567 GOLDING *Ovid's Met.* VIII. 930 There stood in it a warrie Oke [*annoso robore quercus*].

warry ('wɔːrɪ), *a.*[2] *poet.*⁻¹. [f. WAR *sb.*[1] + -Y[1].] Belligerent, warlike.

1901 W. B. YEATS in Lady Gregory *Ideals in Ireland* 96 She looked 'very strong and warry and fierce, but not wicked'.

warry, obs. f. WARY *a.*; variant of WARY *v. Obs.*

warry, -able, var. ff. WARRAY *v.*, -ABLE *Obs.*

warryar, obs. form of WARRIOR.

warrybrede, variant of WARIBREED *Obs.*

warryn: see WARREN *sb.* and *a.*

wars, Sc. and north. form of WORSE.

warsaw[1] ('wɔːsɔː). *U.S.* [An attempt to pronounce the Sp. name GUASA (gwasa).] (See quot.)

1888 GOODE *Amer. Fishes* 49 The Black Grouper..at Pensacola, known by the name 'Warsaw'.

Warsaw[2] ('wɔːsɔː). The name of the capital of Poland, used *attrib.* in ***Warsaw Pact***, to designate a military alliance of the Soviet Union with certain other European nations (see quot. 1978), formed by the Treaty of Warsaw, signed on 14 May 1955. (Principally established as a Communist counterpart to N.A.T.O.)

1955 *N.Y. Times* 14 May 18/1 It would be a mistake to discount the Warsaw pact. **1962** *Listener* 22 Mar. 500/2 The Warsaw Pact countries. **1976** LD. HOME *Way Wind Blows* xii. 167 There was, however, a running argument among the professionals as to whether the line between the Warsaw Pact and the NATO forces should be thinly held (by a trip-wire) or more strongly manned. **1978** *Internat. Relations Dict.* (U.S. Dept. State Library) 46/2 *The Warsaw Pact*, a multilateral military alliance formed by the Treaty of Warsaw, signed May 14, 1955 by the Soviet Union, Bulgaria, Czechoslovakia, East Germany, Hungary, Poland, Romania, and Albania. Like NATO, the Warsaw Pact has military and civilian institutions.

warsch(e: see WARISH *v.*[1] and WERSH *a.*

warse, Sc. and north. form of WORSE *a.*

warse, variant of WRASE *Obs.*, bundle.

†**'warsel.** *Sc. Obs.* [a. ON. *varzla*, watch, security, f. *varða* to watch: see WARD *v.*] Only in phr. ***ward and warsel***: see WARD *sb.*[2] 10.

warsel, variant of WARSLE.

warsen, north. form of WORSEN *v.*

warset, warseth. Corrupt form of *barcelet*: see BERCELET. Wyntoun's *Cron.* VI. 1610 (Royal MS.) has the form *wersslete*.

c **1200** *Leges Forestarum* c. 1, in *Acts Parlt. Scot.* I. 687 Cum custode..canem habente qui warseth appellatur. **14..** (Translation) *ibid.* A hund þe quhilk is callit warset.

warsh(e: see WARISH *v.*[1] and WERSH *a.*

†**'warsheet, 'waresheet.** *Naut. Obs.* [f. *war-* of obscure meaning (cf. WARTAKE) + SHEET *sb.*[2]] Some kind of rope used on a ship.

1420 in *For. Acc. 3 Hen. VI* G/2 In..ij haunsers de eodem filo pro Warschetes et handeropes. *Ibid.* I, De..j. haunser pro Gireropes..j. Cabul[o] pro Wareschetes ponderis iiijᶜ. j. quart. vij lb. **1435** *Exch. Acc.* 53/5 f. 22 d, j pr. corda voc. warshetes.

†**'warship**[1]. *Obs.* Forms: 1 **wærscipe, -scype, werscipe,** 2 **warshipe,** 3 **warscipe, -sipe, -schipe.** [OE. *wærscipe* str. masc., f. *wær* WARE *a.*: see -SHIP.] Caution, prudence, astuteness, sagacity.

c **888** ÆLFRED *Boeth.* xxvii. §2 Wisdom is se hehsta cræft, and se hæfð on him feower oðre cræftas; ðara is an wærscipe, oðer ȝemetȝung. *a* **1124** *O.E. Chron.* (Laud MS.) an. 1086, ðif he [William of Normandy] moste þa ȝyt twa ȝear libban he hæfde Yrlande mid his werscipe ȝewunnon. *c* **1200** *Trin. Coll. Hom.* 193 Biddeð ȝiu to gode þat he ȝiue ȝiu ȝepshipe, and warshipe ȝiu wið to werien. *c* **1205** LAY. 5603 Belin wes swiðe wis & warscipe [*c* **1275** warsipe] him folweden [= folwede]. *c* **1220** *Bestiary* 426 in *O.E. Misc.* 14 Twifold forbisne in ðis der to frame we muȝon finden her, warsipe and wisedom wið deuel and wið iuel man. *a* **1225** *Ancr. R.* 252 Dumbe bestes habbeð þeos warschipe, þet hwon heo beoð asailed of wulue..heo þrungeð alle togederes. *a* **1225** *Hali Meid.* 57 (Titus MS.) As rihtwisnesse & warschipe aȝaines unþeawes.

warship[2], **war-ship** ('wɔːʃɪp). [f. WAR *sb.*[1] + SHIP *sb.*] A ship armed and manned for war.

1533 *Acc. Ld. High Treas. Scot.* VI. 134 To..desist fra all making furth of weir schippis in contrar the Inglismen for weill of peace. **1776** MICKLE tr. *Camoens' Lusiad* VI. 261 Brave Coello's war-ship. **1848** LYTTON *K. Arthur* II. xciv, Send seven tall war-ships to the Cymrian lands. **1864** BURTON *Scot Abr.* I. iii. 114 They dared not attempt, in face of the English war-ships, to land at a southern harbour. **1895** *Review of Rev.* Nov. 383/2 Russian warships were to be authorised to anchor in Port Arthur.

fig. **1645** RUTHERFORD *Tryal & Tri. Faith* xxvi. 321 Satans works of sin and Hell..was a prison house, and a castle of strength, and a strong war-ship.

warsle ('wars(ə)l), *sb. Sc.* and *north.* [f. WARSLE *v.*] A struggle, tussle; a wrestling bout.

1819 [RENNIE] *St. Patrick* I. xi. 166 Though I had got a fell crunt ahint the haffit, I wan up wi' a warsle. **1828** SCOTT *F.M. Perth* xix, They quarrelled, as you saw, on the St. Valentine's Even, and had a warstle. **1864** LATTO *Tam. Bodkin* xix. 191 At length wi' a sair warsel he did get into the bed. **1869** A. MACDONALD *Love, Law & Theol.* iii. 46 He had thrown him doun in a warstle.

b. *fig.*

1792 BURNS *My Wife's a winsome wee Thing* ii, The warld's wrack we share o't, The warstle and the care o't. **1862** in *Hawick Archaeol. Soc. Trans.* (1868) 40 The minister had a weary warsle wi' a wersh discource. **1888** D. GRANT *Sc. Stories* 6, I canna say I'm sorry that the weary warsle o' life is sae nearly owre.

warsle ('wars(ə)l), *v. Sc.* and *north.* Forms: 4-5 **werstil,** (5 **werstle, -ssle, wyrstylle**), 6 **wersil,** (**virsle, worsill**), 5 **warstel,** 6 **warsill,** 4-5, 8- **warstle,** 8- **warsel,** 6- **warsle.** [Metathetic var. of WRESTLE *v.*]

1. *intr.* To wrestle (*together, with* an antagonist), to struggle (*against* an adversary).

13.. *Cursor M.* 3933 (Gött.) In hand he [Jacob] lahut an angel briht, þat in handis werstild [*Cott.* wrestild, *Fairf.* wresteled, *Trin.* wrestleled] þai. *c* **1400** *Brut* 319 Oppon þe sond of the Scottyssh see..þere were sene ij. Eglez,..& cruelly & strongly þey foughten togider & warstled togider. *c* **1425** WYNTOUN *Cron.* II. iii. 224 Wytht hym wyrstyllyde the Angelle. *c* **1440** *Partonope* 2306 And thus they warsteled and stryvid sore. *c* **1450** *St. Cuthbert* (Surtees) 943 Som lappe, som werstild. **1535** STEWART *Cron. Scot.* (Rolls) III. 493 To worsill or cast the stane, In all England that tyme maik had he nane. *a* **1572** KNOX *Hist. Ref.* Wks. 1846 I. 468 To feght with God, and to ovircum him, as Jacob did in warsling with his Angell. *a* **1823** *Twa Brothers* ii. in Sharpe *Ballad Bk.* (1823) 57 They warsled up, they warsled down, Till Sir John fell to the ground.

b. *transf.* and *fig.*

1500-20 DUNBAR *Poems* xxiv. 16 Quha with this warld dois warsill and stryfe, And dois his dayis in dolour dryfe. **1787** BURNS *Brigs of Ayr* 79 He seem'd as he wi' Time had warstl'd lang. **1902** JOANNA E. WOOD *Farden Ha'* xiii. 242 It isna for us tae come tae grups wi' the facts o' oor lives; we must jist tak' them and no' warstle wi' them.

c. *trans.* To wrestle with (an adversary). In quots. chiefly *fig.*

1790 BURNS *Scots Prol.* 44 Ye'll soon hae poets o' the Scottish nation, Will..warsle Time, and lay him on his back. **1804** TANNAHILL *Coggie* iii, The puir man's patron coggie, It warsels care, it fechts life's fauchts. **1820** HOGG *Winter Even. Tales* I. 289 I'm sair cheatit gin some o' your warstlers dinna warstle you out o' ony bit virtue..that ye hae. *a* **1830** *Twa Brothers* ii. in Child *Ballads* I. 439/1 But gin ye come to yonder wood I'll warsle you a fa'.

2. *intr.* To struggle, to move with struggle or effort (*against, through, over, out of, up*); also with advs., as *by, on, out, over, round.*

c **1500** *Lancelot* 3384 The ded hors lyith virslyng with the men. **1553** *Douglas's Æneis* XIII. iv. 82 Or like as that, on the house syde the snale,..Ane lang tyme gan do wersil [*older text* wrassill], and to wrele Thristand fast with thare feit, vnto the wale. **1783** BURNS *Death Poor Mailie* 4 As Mailie..Was ae day nibbling on the tether, Upon her cloot she coost a hitch, An' owre she warsl'd in the ditch. *c* **1790** A. WILSON *Loss o' the Pack*, For aye the mair I warsled round and roun', I fand mysel' aye stick the deeper down. **1891** M. MURIEL DOWIE *Girl in Karp.* 231 Holes over my depth, but none but what I might have warsled out of. **1895** 'IAN MACLAREN' *Dr. of the Old School* i. 34 Neither can you 'warstle' through the peat bogs and snow drifts for forty winters without a touch of rheumatism.

b. *transf.* of an inanimate thing.

1788 PICKEN *Poems Scot. Dial.* 107 An' let him kiss the tear awa', That warsles doun thy charmin face. **1822** GALT *Provost* xxiv, The five poor barks, that were warsling against the strong arm of the elements.

c. *fig.*

a **1600** MONTGOMERIE *Misc. Poems* xlii. 9 Warsill, as it war against ȝour will, Appeiring angrie, thoght ȝe haif no yre. **1821** W. SUTHERLAND *Poems & Songs* 32 Yet happy still, blest wi' content, They warsle through. **1837** R. NICOLL *Poems* (1842) 116 A mickle share o' love we've had The warld as we've warsled through. *a* **1877** W. CHISHOLM *Poems* (1879) 62 Auld Time warsles by wi' slow an' laggin' wing. **1893** STEVENSON *Catriona* xii, It was a driech employ, and praise the Lord that I have warstled through with it! **1895** ANNA M. STODDART *J. S. Blackie* II. 233 He was sent to a tutorial class for a month or two, after which he was allowed to warstle through. **1901** G. DOUGLAS *House with Gr. Shutters* xxii, Lots of young chaps, when they warstle through their Arts, teach the sons of swells.

d. quasi-*trans.* To get (something *out, up, on*) with a struggle.

c **1790** A. WILSON *Loss o' the Pack*, Ay! thae were days indeed, that gar'd me hope, Aiblins, through time, to warsle up a shop. **1887** SERVICE *Dr. Duguid* I. xx, I..warsled on my claes. **1888** D. GRANT *Sc. Stories* 72 That was a question that cost me nae little serious reflection an' prospection; but I warsled it oot in my ain min'.

Hence **'warsling** *vbl. sb.* Also **'warsler**, a wrestler.

c **1425** WYNTOUN *Cron.* I. 340 Coryne..Of Cornewell first, had grete liking To cast þai carllis in werstling. *Ibid.* III. 974 Off turnamentis or of justynge, Menstrailssy or gret wersslynge. **1500–20** DUNBAR *Poems* I. 22 He hes att warslingis beine ane hunder. *a* **1578** LINDESAY (Pitscottie) *Chron. Scot.* (S.T.S.) I. 340 All kynd of games..as..lepping ryding and warsling. **1820** Warstler [see WARSLE *v.* I c.]

war-song. A song inciting to war, or celebrating martial deeds.

1757 [BURKE] *Europ. Settlem. Amer.* I. II. iv. 182 The war songs are heard in all parts. **1775** ADAIR *Amer. Ind.* 159 The leader..singing the war-song, and beating the drum. **1818** KEATS *Endym.* III. 603 Despair sung A war-song of defiance 'gainst all hell. **1840** *C.O. Müller's Hist. Lit. Greece* xiii. §3. 168 His war-songs express a stirring martial spirit. **1897** HENTY *On Irrawaddy* 174 The Burmans..continued chanting a war-song, swaying themselves to its cadence.

warsse, warst, north. ff. WORSE, WORST.

warsshe, var. WARISH *v.*[1] *Obs.*

war-steed. *poet.* = WAR-HORSE.

1776 MICKLE tr. *Camoens' Lusiad* x. 453 Here the proud war-steed glories in his force. **1810** SCOTT *Lady of Lake* I. xxxi, No rude sound shall reach thine ear, Armour's clang, or war-steed champing. **1829** —— *Anne of G.* xxxii, Don your harness..—mount your war-steed—cry, René for Provence! **1870** BRYANT *Iliad* II. 2 Mortal men, Tamers of war-steeds.

fig. **1848** LYTTON *K. Arthur* VIII. xxx, Beorn, the bold son of Sweyn, the Göthland king, Whose ocean war-steeds on the Baltic deeps Range their blue pasture.

warstel, -stle, obs. var. ff. WARSLE *v.*

wart (wɔːt), *sb.* Forms: 1 wearte, 2, 4–6 werte, 4–5 wertte, 3–7 wert, 5–6 warte, 7–8 whart, 4– wart; 4 wrot, 4–5 wret(e, wrett(e, 6 wratte, 7–9 *Sc.* and *dial.* wrat, 9 *dial.* wret, writ. [OE. *wearte* wk. fem. = OFris. *warte, worte* (WFris. *wart*), OS. *warte* (MLG. *warte, wratte,* LG. *wratte, wratt*), Du. *wrat* (dial. *warte*), OHG. *warza* (MHG., mod.G. *warze*), ON. *varta* (Sw. *vårta,* Norw. *vorta,* Da. *vorte*):—OTeut. **wartōn-*.

The OHG. *werza* (MHG. *werze,* mod.G. dial. *wärze*) appear to point to a derivative formation (OTeut. type **wartjōn-*); but the apparently coincident ME. forms *werte, wrette,* etc. are regular dialectal representatives of OE. *wearte.* The existence both in Eng. and continental Teut. of metathetic forms with *wr-* is somewhat noteworthy.]

1. a. A small, round, dry, tough excrescence on the skin; especially common on the hands of young persons.

c **725** *Corpus Gloss.* U 77 Uerruca, wearte. *c* **1000** *Sax. Leechd.* I. 100 Wið swylas & wið weartan. *a* **1300** *Cursor M.* 27088 Bot wald þai seme to mans sight In þair licam bath fair and slight, Wit-vten any wert or weme. *c* **1386** CHAUCER *Prol.* 555 Vp on the cope right of his nose he hade A werte [*Camb. MS.* wrete], and ther on stood a toft of herys. *c* **1440** *Promp. Parv.* 533/2 Wrette, or werte yn a mannys skynne, *veruca.* *a* **1529** SKELTON *P. Sparowe* 1043 Her beautye to augment, Dame Nature hath her lent A warte vpon her cheke. **1562** BULLEYN *Bk. Simples* 48 The juce thereof will ..make smothe the skinne from wrattes. **1601** HOLLAND *Pliny* XXXII. x. II. 448 The liver of the fish Glanus, causeth werts to fall off, if they be rubbed withall. **1614** MARKHAM *Cheap Husb.* I. xxxi. 25 The Wart, Pearle, Pin, or Webbe, which are euils growne in and vpon the Eye [of a horse]. **1629** Z. BOYD *Last Battell* 1051 In such a case his wrats and his wrinkles must be wroght with the pinsell, that the image may bee like unto himselfe. *c* **1645** HOWELL *Lett.* (1650) I. I. xliii. 76 Our mountains in Wales..are Mole-hills in comparison of these [*sc.* the Alps], they are..but blisters compar'd to Impostumes, or Pimples to Werts. **1658** A. FOX tr. *Wurtz' Surg.* II. xiv. 105 There were..found about the Wound Blisters and Wharts, which were caused by the hot dressings. **1718** QUINCY *Compl. Disp.* 112 Ray says, its Juice will wear out Wharts. **1839** DICKENS *Nich. Nick.* viii, An unhealthy-looking boy, with warts all over his hands. **1878** T. BRYANT *Pract. Surg.* I. 343 Warts are not unfrequently met with about the eyelids.

b. = CONDYLOMA. In full ***syphilitic wart.***

1552 HULOET, Wartes in the priuye partes, *mirmeciæ.* **1578** LYTE *Dodoens* VI. lxxiv. 767 The leaues of Sauin..do also cause wartes to fal of, which grow about the yarde and other secrete places of man. **1803** *Med. Jrnl.* X. 322 Syphilitic warts. **1879** *St. George's Hosp. Rep.* IX. 621 Syphilitic mucous tubercles (so-called warts) in the external auditory canal.

c. A normal callosity on the legs of a horse, ass, etc.

1523–34 FITZHERB. *Husb.* §118 If a horse wante wartes behynde, benethe the spauen-place. **1824** J. E. GRAY in *Zool. Jrnl.* I. 243 The Asses and Zebras..have warts only on the arms and none on the hind legs;..the true Horses..are furnished with warts on their arms and legs.

d. Applied to other small excrescences on animate creatures.

1774 GOLDSM. *Nat. Hist.* VII. 109 These [*sc.* frogs'] eggs are buried deep in the skin..and the spaces between them are full of small warts, resembling pearls. **1861** J. R. GREENE *Man. Anim. Kingd., Cœlent.* 149 The general surface of the body..in some Sea-anemones..exhibits a number of clear warts or vesicles.

†**2.** A nipple. *Obs. rare*[−1]. (So G. *warze.*)

c **1440** *Promp. Parv.* 534/1 Wrette, of a pappe or tete, *papilla.*

3. *Bot.* A rounded protuberance or excrescence on the surface of a plant.

[**1677** MIEGE *Eng.-Fr. Dict.* s.v., The wart in the middle of a flower, *le bouton d'une fleur.*] **1793** [see WARTED]. **1832** LINDLEY *Introd. Bot.* 43 *Verrucæ,* or warts, are roundish excrescences, formed of cellular tissue filled with opaque matter. **1862** DARWIN *Orchids* vi. 283 In Calanthe we have a cluster of odd little spherical warts on the labellum. **1884** BOWER & SCOTT *De Bary's Phaner.* 425 Tough prominent warts, as those of Aloe verrucosa. **1895** W. R. LAWRENCE *Kashmir* xiii. 353 There was a demand for the huge warts which grow on the walnut stem,..and a Frenchman obtained from the State the right to saw off these warts.

4. *transf.* and *fig.* (from sense 1). A relatively small, or disfiguring, protuberance. Sometimes with implied reference to next sense.

1602 SHAKS. *Ham.* v. i. 306 Let them throw Millions of Akers on vs; till our ground Sindging his pate against the burning Zone, Make Ossa like a wart. **1611** TOURNEUR *Ath. Trag.* III. iii, I've lost a Signorie That was confin'd within a piece of earth, A wart upon the body of the world. **1650** JER. TAYLOR *Holy Living* ii. §4. 111 His faults are but warts, his vertues are mountainous. **1792** HOLCROFT *Road to Ruin* I. 12 You will not deny you are..A nuisance, a wart, a blot, a stain upon the face of nature! **1838** EMERSON *Addr. Cambridge, Mass.* Wks. (Bohn) II. 195 That which shows God out of me, makes me a wart and a wen. **1865** DICKENS *Mut. Fr.* I. iii, The low building had the look of having once been a mill. There was a rotten wart of wood upon its forehead that seemed to indicate where the sails had been. **1869** F. KOHN *Iron & Steel Manuf.* 88 If it be attempted to strengthen the linings by iron ribs,..the iron undergoing puddling immediately attaches itself to these, and forms great warts and scabs difficult of removal. **1934** J. B. PRIESTLEY *Eng. Journey* vi. 187 You can meet them, a trifle subdued perhaps but there to the last wart, in the solid downright fiction of my friend, Phyllis Bentley. **1961** *Listener* 2 Nov. 738/2 The Catholic revivalists..the author presents as no doubt they would like to be presented... No warts here, perhaps regrettably. **1982** *Times* 1 Dec. 2/5 It was [the television companies']..job to hold up mirrors, some of which showed the warts in society.

b. ***warts and all:*** without concealment of blemishes or unattractive parts (esp. applied to a description or likeness.) Also hyphened as *attrib. phr. colloq.*

[**1763** H. WALPOLE *Anecd. Painting* III. i. 15 Oliver [Cromwell]..said to him, 'Mr Lely, I desire you would use all your skill to paint my picture truly like me, and not flatter me at all; but remark all these roughnesses, pimples, warts and everything as you see me, otherwise I will never pay a farthing for it.'] **1930** W. S. MAUGHAM *Cakes & Ale* xi. 138 Don't you think it would be more interesting if you went the whole hog and drew him warts and all? **1961** *Listener* 21 Sept. 437/1 A convincing warts-and-all likeness of Wingate. **1962** *Sunday Times* 1 Apr. 13/1 The Duke of Edinburgh presents himself warts and all, without blunting the rough edges of efficiency and enthusiasm. **1966** K. GILES *Provenance of Death* iii. 96 In fact you want a run down on Stanisgate, warts and all. Huh? **1974** *Publishers Weekly* 18 Feb. 24 An intimate, in-depth, 'warts-and-all' portrait of our new Vice President. **1976** H. A. WILLIAMS *Tensions* vii. 111 God..accepts us, accepts all men, unconditionally, warts and all. **1980** *Times Lit. Suppl.* 12 Sept. 986/3 This book..may disconcert the pious more than it jolts the sceptic, but it has the story, warts, statistics and all.

5. a. *Mil. colloq.* A very young subaltern.

1894 'J. S. WINTER' *Red Coats* 5 Anything more terrifying for 'a wart' than to have to sit for two hours—or three, if the Colonel is long-winded enough—and make talk, one can hardly imagine. **1914** *Blackw. Mag.* Sept. 309/1 A regimental 'wart', reconnoitring along the river bank with a score of men.

b. *colloq.* An obnoxious or objectionable person.

1896 ADE *Artie* i. 5 There they was, holdin' to this wart. **1925** WODEHOUSE *Carry on, Jeeves* vii. 167 Sippy had described them as England's premier warts, and it looked to me as if he might be about right. **1948** C. DAY LEWIS *Otterbury Incident* i. 6 Everyone called him the Wart because he had a huge wart on his left cheek... And because he was a wart. **1977** C. MCCULLOUGH *Thorn Birds* xvii. 431 Watch your language, you dumb wart! **1984** *N.Y. Times Bk. Rev.* 1 Apr. 33/1 What!..is the old wart going to go on some more about reading?

c. *Naval slang.* A junior midshipman or naval cadet.

1916 [see CRAB *sb.*[1] 12]. **1921** *Blackw. Mag.* July 50/2 They all ignored the six 'warts'. **1962** GRANVILLE *Dict. Sailors' Slang* 129/1 *Wart,* naval cadet or junior midshipman, the 'lowest form of Naval life'; an unseemly excrescence.

6. *attrib.* and *Comb.*, as ***wart-like, -eating,*** †***-ribbed*** adjs.; **wart-biter** [= G. *warzenbeisser, -fresser,* Sw. *vårtbitare*], a grasshopper (*Gryllus verrucivorus*) supposed to destroy warts by biting them; **wart-cress,** the genus *Senebiera*; **wart disease,** a disease of potatoes caused by the fungus *Synchytrium endobioticum* and producing dark pustules on the tubers; †**wart-gowry** [see GOWRIE], a variety of cowrie; **wart-grass,** *Euphorbia Helioscopia* (Britten and Holland); **wart-herb** (see quot.); **wart-hog,** a swine of the African genus *Phacochœrus* (see quot. 1913); **wart-pock, -pox,** a variety of chicken-pox; **wart-shaped** *a.*, verruciform (*Treas. Bot.* 1866); †**wart-shell,** some variety of univalve shell; **wart-snake,** a colubriform snake of the family *Acrochordidæ,* having wart-like scales; **wart-weed,** *Euphorbia Helioscopia, E. Peplus,* and *Chelidonium majus* (the juice of these plants being used to cure warts). Also WARTWORT.

1864–5 WOOD *Homes without H.* viii. (1868) 161 The *Wart-biter. **1880** A. H. SWINTON *Insect Variety* 162 The Great Green Leaf-cricket, or Wart-biter. **1806** J. GALPINE *Brit. Bot.* 298 Coronopus. *Wart-cress. **1866** *Treas. Bot.* 1048 *Senebiera didyma,* the Lesser Wartcress. [**1903** *Jrnl. R. Hort. Soc.* XXVIII. p. clxxviii, Warty Disease of Potatoes.. was introduced from the Continent, and first appeared in Cheshire.] **1915** *Wart disease [see *black scab* s.v. BLACK *a.* 19]. **1948** W. G. BURTON *Potato* v. 103 Potato varieties vary greatly in their susceptibility to attack by wart disease. **1970** H. W. HOWARD *Genetics of Potato* vii. 46 Breeding for resistance..to wart disease..has been very successful. **1822–7** GOOD *Study Med.* (1829) V. 670 In Sweden they [i.e. warts] are destroyed by the *Gryllus verrucivorus,* or *wart-eating grasshopper. *c* **1711** PETIVER *Gazophyl.* x. Tab. 97 Fork-mouth'd *Wart Gowry. **1864** GRISEBACH *Flora W. Ind. Isl.* 788 *Wart-herb, *Rhynchosia minima.* **1840** *Cuvier's Anim. Kingd.* 131 The *Wart-hogs. **1895** J. G. MILLAIS *Breath fr. Veldt* (1899) 127 We came across a fine old wart-hog boar. **1913** PETTMAN *Africanderisms, Wart hog...* The name refers to the fleshy excrescences or warts on its face. **1698** PETIVER in *Phil. Trans.* XX. 329 Small *wart-like Tubercles. **1897** *Allbutt's Syst. Med.* IV. 754 Epithelioma usually appears as a wart-like growth. **1873** F. T. ROBERTS *Handbk. Med.* 186 Horn-pock or *Wart-pock. *c* **1711** PETIVER *Gazophyl.* VIII. Tab. 80 *Wart-rib'd Barbadoes Limpet. *Ibid.* VII. Tab. 70 Jamaica *Wart-shell. *c* **1880** *Cassell's Nat. Hist.* IV. 324 Family Acrochordidæ.—The *Wart Snakes. **1573** *Arte of Limning* A ij b, The like sise maye you make..with the milke of spourge, or of *wartwede. *a* **1825** FORBY *Voc. E. Anglia, Wret-weed,* any wild species of euphorbia. **1857** ANNE PRATT *Flower. Pl.* V. 5 *Euphorbia helioscopia* (Sun Spurge)... Country people call it..Wart-weed.

wart, *v. nonce-wd.* [f. WART *sb.*] *trans.* To form a wart-like excrescence on.

1819 H. BUSK *Vestriad* II. 228 Not one molehill warts the glassy plain.

wart, obs. 2 sing. pa. t. of BE; obs. Sc. pa. t. of WRITE.

†**'wartake.** *Naut. Obs.* Also 5 **warre takke.** See also WARETACK. [f. *war* of uncertain origin (cf. WARROPE, WARSHEET) + TACK *sb.*[1]] Some particular kind of tack or rope.

14.. *Pilgr. Sea-Voy.* 37 in *Stac. Rome* 39 Hale in the wartake! **1485** *Naval Acc. Hen. VII* (1896) 71 Mayne drynges..ij, Warre takkes..ij, Garnettes..ij.

wartday, variant of WARDAY *dial.*

warted ('wɔːtɪd), *ppl. a.* [f. WART *sb.* + -ED[2].]

1. Covered with warts. *rare.*

1615 NICCHOLES *Marr. & Wiving* vi. 17 Lip-bearded, as wiches, with their warted antiquity and age. **1689** N. LEE *Princess Cleve* III. i, She's warted all over like a pumpl'd Orange. **1876** BLACKMORE *Cripps* xlix, That heavy gate.. banged her chubby knees, and it bruised her warted hand.

2. *Bot., Zool.,* etc. Studded with wart-like knobs or excrescences; verrucose.

1681 GREW *Musæum* II. §iii. ii. 230 The Warted Gourd. **1763** MILLS *Syst. Pract. Husb.* IV. 170 The Zatte melon.. its coat is warted like that of the Cantaleupe. **1793** MARTYN *Lang. Bot., Verrucosa capsula,* a warted capsule. *Ibid., Verrucosum folium,* a Warted leaf. **1802** SHAW *Gen. Zool.* III. 296 Warted Newt. **1822** *Hortus Anglicus* II. 339 *Lapsana Zacintha.* Warted Nipple Wort. **1830** LINDLEY *Nat. Syst. Bot.* 153 Seeds very numerous, minute, slightly warted. **1852** DICKENS *Bleak Ho.* xxviii, The gnarled and warted elms. **1885** H. O. FORBES *Nat. Wand. E. Archip.* 469 Blocks of rugged and warted coral-like limestone.

warter, variant of WARDAY *dial.*

wartern, dial. form of QUARTERN *sb.*[2]

warth. *Obs.* exc. *dial.* [OE. *waroð* (*waruð*, *warað*, *wareð*, *wearoð*, *weroð*, *warð*) masc., corresp. to OHG. *warid*, *werid* (MHG. *wert*, *werd-*, mod.G. *werd*, *wert*):—OTeut. **waruþo-z*, **wariþo-z*.] A shore, strand; in mod. use, 'a flat meadow, esp. one close to a stream; a stretch of coast' (*Eng. Dial. Dict.*).

Beowulf 234 Ʒewat him þa to waroðe wicge ridan. *a* **1000** *Boeth. Metr.* viii. 30 Næniȝ cepa ne seah ofer earȝeblond ellendne wearoð [*MS.* wearod]. *c* **1000** *Ags. Ps.* (Th.) cv. 9 þær wæron þa wareðas driȝe. **13..** *E.E. Allit. P.* C. 339 þe whal wendez at his wylle & a warþe fyndez, & þer he brakez vp þe buyrne. **13..** *Gaw. & Gr. Knt.* 715 At vche warþe oþer water þer þe wyȝe passed, He fonde a foo hym byfore. **1372** *Bridgewater Corp. MSS.* No. 462 Septem acras terre cum Wartha versus mare. *c* **1450** *Mirk's Festial* 7 On a day, as he walket on þe see-warth, he segh a drownet man cast vp on þe watyr. *c* **1465** *Warrington in 1465* (Chetham Soc.) 10 Item tenet quandam parcellam terræ arabilis jacentem super le Warthe. *c* **1640** J. SMYTH *Lives Berkeleys* (1883) I. 190 The pasture called the warth in the other side of Seaverne. *Ibid.* 341 Hee..held in severalty divers parcells of Slimbridge Warth..and shortly after inclosed fifty four acres more of the same Warth. **1839** SIR G. C. LEWIS *Gloss. Hereford.* 117 *Warth.* On the banks of the Severn, a flat meadow close to the stream is so called; *e.g.* the Warth opposite Blakeney.

warth, var. WATH, ford; pa. t. of WORTH *v.*

wart-hill, variant of WARD-HILL.

war time. 1. The time when war is being waged.

1387 TREVISA *Higden* VIII. 283 The woodes in Wales.., þat were grete socour to men of þe contray to hyde hem self in werre tyme. **1445** tr. *Claudian* in *Anglia* XXVIII. 271 Whom than thou makist not riche Whan werre tyme is and whan pees is, þou list not hem to knowe. **1545** ASCHAM *Toxoph.* I. Wks. (1904) 59 When he shalbe..compelled in war tyme..to faule to his bowe. **1707** MORTIMER *Husb.* 33 The Seed coming from France, this War-time hath prevented its being so much propagated as otherways it would have been. **1831** SCOTT *Cast. Dang.* i, Above all, it was war-time, and of necessity all circumstances of mere convenience were obliged to give way to a paramount sense of danger. **1849** C. BRONTË *Shirley* ii, These war times were hard, and everything was dear. **1851** KINGSLEY *Yeast* xiii, There was too much filthiness and drunkenness went on in the old war-times, not to leave a taint behind it, for many a generation.

attrib. **1915** H. H. HENSON (*title*), War-time Sermons. **1915** LADY JEPHSON (*title*), A War-time Journal. **1922** C. E. MONTAGUE *Disenchantment* viii. 121 Men's friends at home would have the agonies of false alarms added to their normal wartime miseries. **1935** D. L. SAYERS *Gaudy Night* ii. 30 The present lot are the real War-time generation. **1945** *ABC of Cookery* (Ministry of Food) 1 It is intended to be used with the Ministry of Food Recipe Leaflets although it is not restricted to war-time cookery. **1965** *New Statesman* 7 May 709/3 Without the exigencies of war, he would need to have war-time powers. But he would lack..the simple war-time criterion of the need 'to maintain production'. **1978** CADOGAN & CRAIG *Women & Children First* viii. 179 Tilli is..suffering wartime shortages bitterly.

2. *U.S. Hist.* Daylight-saving time introduced during World War II (see quots.).

1942 *Time* 9 Feb. 12/3 Franklin Roosevelt decided what he will call wartime daylight saving when it starts next week. Official name: War Time. **1979** *Sci. Amer.* May 39/3 Year-round daylight-saving time, or 'war-time', as it was named by President Roosevelt, began on February 9, 1942.

† **ˈwarting,** *vbl. sb. Obs. rare*[−1]. [f. WART *sb.* + -ING[1].] A growth of warts.

1755 *Phil. Trans.* XLIX. 23 During which disorders the warting came off, and his skin appeared white and smooth.

† **ˈwartle.** *Obs.* [Diminutive of WART: see -LE. Cf. OHG. *warzala*, Ger. dial. *warzel*, a wart.]

a. A 'kernel' in the neck or groin. **b.** A small wart. **c.** A hard lump in molten metal.

1598 FLORIO, *Ghiandole*, wartles or kernels that come in the throte; the glanders in a horse. *Ibid.*, *Pallottole*, the kernels or wartles that breede betweene the flesh and the skin, about the neck or groine. **1611** COTGR., *Gangules*, Kernels, or wartles in the throat. **1659** TORRIANO, *Verrúca formicánte*, a wartle black like an ant, and therefore called an ant-wart. *Verrúca pensíle*, a long and hanging wartle. **1725** *Bradley's Family Dict.* s.v. *Antimony*, They put it to be melted..in pots..and strain it through a scummer.., that so you may take away the Kernels or wartles thereof.

ˈwartless, *a.* [-LESS.] That is without a wart or warts; free from warts.

1846 WORCESTER. **1898** BLAKEBOROUGH *Wit, Char.* etc. *N. Riding* 139 In a fortnight's time he was wartless. **1904** *Daily News* 10 June 4 It [Carlyle's *Cromwell*] transformed an ogre into a saint, almost a wartless saint.

ˈwartlet, [-LET.] A small wart.

Proposed as a name for certain sea-anemones.

1856 W. L. LINDSAY *Pop. Hist. Brit. Lichens* 43 In the form of granules or very minute wartlets. **1860** GOSSE *Actinologia Brit.* 206 The Marigold Wartlet. *Tealia digitata. Ibid.* 209 The Dahlia Wartlet. *Tealia crassicornis.*

ˈwartwale. *Obs.* exc. *dial.* In 4–5 wort(e)wale, 6 **warte-, wertwale, wartwayle, water whele**; for mod. dial. forms see *Eng. Dial. Dict.* s.v. *Warty-well.* [App. repr. OE. *wyrtwala* wk. masc., *-walu* str. fem., root, corresp. to OHG. *wurzala* (:—**wurzwala*) mod.G. *wurzel* fem., MDu. *wortele*, mod.Du. *wortel.*

In the sense of 'root' the word did not survive into ME., being superseded by the shorter Scandinavian synonym (see ROOT *sb.*). The sense 'agnail' is not recorded in OE., but is paralleled by the Ger. dial. *neidwurzel*, a synonym of *neidnagel* agnail.]

A growth or loose piece of skin at the base of the finger-nail; an agnail.

In the 3rd quot. app. used for: The root of a cock's spur.

c **1325** *Gloss. W. de Bibbesw.* in Wright *Voc.* (1857) 172 Coupet des cisours des ungles les eles [*glossed* the wortewale (nailes)]. *a* **1400** *Nominale* (Skeat) *Deiez cieles et galeyns* Fyngres wortwales and ȝespons. **14..** *Songs & Carols* (Warton Club) 31, I have a gentil cook crowyt me day,.. His spores arn of sylver qwyt into the wortewale. **1510** STANBRIDGE *Vocabula* (W. de W.) A v b, *Pterigium*, wartewale [1525 ed., a water whele]. **1556** WITHALS *Dict.* (1562) 77 A wertwale, *pterigium.* **1570** LEVINS *Manip.* 199/21 A wartwayle, *pterigium.*

wartwort (ˈwɔːtwɜːt). [f. WART *sb.* + WORT[1].] A name for *Euphorbia Helioscopia*, *E. Peplus*, and *E. Peplis* (Sea Wartwort). Also applied to other plants, as *Chelidonium majus* and *Senebiera Coronopus.* (Cf. *wart-weed*, WART *sb.* 6.)

a **1400** *MS. Arund.* 42 f. 67 þe same erbe [*'Eliotropia'*] is called *verrucaria*, wrotwort, by cause þat it destruyth & fordoth wrottys. *c* **1450** *Alphita* (Anecd. Oxon.) 9 *Anabulla*, ..wartwort. *Ibid.* 185 *Titimallis*,..wertewert. **1548** TURNER *Names of Herbes* 60 Peplis..is very like vnto wartwort but that it is shorter, thicker and spred vpon the grounde. It may be called in english sea wartwurt. **1562** —— *Herbal* II. 154 b, This kinde is called..Wartwurt; it maye also be called son spourge. **1578** LYTE *Dodoens* III. xxxii. 363 Peplos..is called ..Wartwurt,..also Pety Spurge. **1665** LOVELL *Herball* (ed. 2) 464 Sea wart-wort, see Sea spurge. **1725** *Bradley's Family Dict.*, *Petyt-Spurg*, otherwise called *Wartwort.* **1802** G. V. SAMPSON *Statist. Surv. Londonderry* App. 21 Sun-spurge, or wartwort; the juice is white, caustic, and is applied successfully to take off warts. **1842** *Civil Engin. & Arch. Jrnl.* V. 172/2 The spurge or wartwort..yields a milky juice applicable for the purpose [of tempera-painting].

warty (ˈwɔːtɪ), *a.* Also 5 **varty**, 6–7 **wartie**, 8 **wharty**, 9 *Sc.* **wrattie**. [f. WART *sb.* + -Y.]

1. Afflicted with warts on the skin.

1483 *Cath. Angl.* 409/1 Varty, *verucosus.* **1570** LEVINS *Manip.* 111/44 Wartie, *verrucosus.* **1605** CAMDEN *Rem.*, *Names, Dorcas* 78 Freckled, wartie, and wodden-faced wenches. **1655** [J. PHILLIPS] *Sat. agst. Hypocr.* 5 Oh how he's wonder'd at by many an asse That see him shake so fast his warty fist. *c* **1825** BEDDOES *Poems, A Ruffian*, Brown and warty hands. **1898** BLAKEBOROUGH *Wit, Char.* etc. *N. Riding* 138 The charmer..Told the warty one to go home.

2. Chiefly *Zool.*, *Bot.*, etc. Having wart-like excrescences or protuberances.

1693 EVELYN *De La Quint. Compl. Gard.* I. 86 The Leschasserie pears are pretty often..bunch'd and warty. *c* **1711** PETIVER *Gazophyl.* x. Tab. 97 White Warty Gowry. **1768** G. WHITE *Selborne, To Pennant* 8 Oct., A large black warty lizard. **1796** WITHERING *Brit. Plants* (ed. 3) I. 246 Capsules are hairy, warty, or smooth. **1863** WOOD *Illustr. Nat. Hist.* III. 168 The Warty Toad of Fernando Po (*Bufo tuberosus*). **1894** DU MAURIER *Trilby* II. 205 Tall, warty, black-boled trees. **1914** *Q. Jrnl. Microsc. Sci.* LX. I. 69 The head [of the tadpole] is somewhat warty and wrinkled.

3. Of the nature of, or resembling, a wart.

1762 *Gentl. Mag.* XXXII. 82/1 The whole eruption put on a very wharty and palid appearance. **1767** A. CAMPBELL *Lexiph.* (1774) 49 A warty excrescence on the tip of Hymenaeus's little finger. **1796** WITHERING *Brit. Plants* (ed. 3) III. 228 Seeds with many warty angles. **1857** MILLER *Elem. Chem.* III. 59 Glucose crystallizes with difficulty in warty concretions. **1861** HULME tr. *Moquin-Tandon* II. 289 The warty tubercles on the loins. **1897** *Garden* 9 Jan. 20/3 Extravasation of sap occurs, giving rise to..warty growths.

4. *fig.* Rocky, rough.

1648 HERRICK *Hesp.*, *Dean-bourn, a rude River in Devon*, Dean-bourn, farewell; I never look to see Deane, or thy warty [*some copies* wartry] incivility. **1822** *Blackw. Mag.* XI. 163 'An Ode,' rather warty, came to Nap Buonaparte.

5. *Comb.*

c **1711** PETIVER *Gazophyl.* IX. Tab. 85 Warty-rib'd Cape Limpet. **1836** *Todd's Cycl. Anat.* I. 786/2 Covered with little warty-looking enlargements. **1857** ANNE PRATT *Flower. Pl.* III. 152 *Galium saccharatum* (Warty-fruited Bed-straw). *c* **1880** *Cassell's Nat. Hist.* IV. 74 The Warty-faced Honey-eater (*Meliphaga phrygia*).

warve, obs. variant of WHARVE *sb.*

warwayn, obs. form of VERVAIN.

war-whoop (ˈwɔːhuːp, -hwuːp). **a.** The cry or yell of American Indians and other peoples on rushing into battle.

1739 W. STEPHENS *Jrnl.* 21 Dec. in *Colonial Rec. Georgia* (1906) IV. 474 In marching, our Indians set up the war whoop. **1761** FOOTE *Liar* I. Wks. 1799 I. 286 Permit him, Madam, just to give you..a short specimen of their warhoop. **1763** W. ROBERTS *First Discov. Florida* 6 Horrible bellowings and clamours, not unlike the war-hoop of the Indians of the Six Nations. **1775** ADAIR *Amer. Ind.* 250 Their mortal crime consisted in sounding the war-whoop, and [etc.]. *Ibid.* 394 He put up the shrill war whoo whoop, as his last salute. **1791** J. LONG *Voy. Indian Interpr.* 21 The Savages..setting up the war-hoop, fell upon the enemy. **1837** R. M. BIRD *Nick of the Woods* I. 91 'A fight!' replied Captain Stackpole, uttering a war-whoop. **1850** J. B. CLUTTERBUCK *Pt. Phillip in 1849*, 59 When the favorable opportunity for attack has arrived, the war-whoop resounds through hill and dale. **1865** PARKMAN *Pioneers of France* vi. (1876) 76 The war-whoop rose, and a tempest of stone-headed arrows clattered against the breastplates of the French. **1875** HIGGINSON *Hist. United States* xvi. 147 The children lay awake afterwards, listening for the Indian's war-whoop.

b. *transf.* and *fig.*

1798 COLERIDGE *Fears in Solit.* 89 Secure from actual warfare, we have loved To swell the war-whoop, passionate for war! **1807** BYRON *Let. to Miss Pigot* 11 Aug., My nice mamma would..raise the accustomed maternal warwhoop. **1817** MOORE *Lalla Rookh, Fire-worshippers* III. 116 But hark!—that war-whoop on the deck. **1828** D'ISRAELI *Chas. I*, II. 92 In the early speeches..the name of the unhappy favourite no longer served as the war-whoop of a party. **1851** LONGF. *Life* (1891) II. 212 If they are not forthcoming, I shall raise such a war-whoop that it will frighten him. **1876** 'MARK TWAIN' *Tom Sawyer* xv, Then they set up a war-whoop of applause, and said it was 'splendid!'

warwickite (ˈwɒrɪkaɪt). *Min.* [Named from Warwick, New York, where it was found: see -ITE.] A borotitanate of magnesium and iron in dark-brown acicular crystals.

1838 C. U. SHEPARD in *Amer. Jrnl. Sci.* XXXIV. 314 A new species, which I designate Warwickite, from its original locality. **1850** ANSTED *Elem. Geol., Min.* etc. §482 Warwickite, Fluoride of titanium and iron.

warwinckle, variant of WARIANGLE *Obs.*

war-wolf.

1. *Hist.* A kind of siege engine.

A translation of *lupus belli*, occurring in the *Flores Historiarum* ('Matthew of Westminster') in the account of Edw. I's siege of Stirling in 1304, where it is said that the battering-ram (*aries*) proved almost useless, but that the less costly 'war-wolf' was much more effective. In an AF. document relating to this siege (*Cal. Docum. Scot.* II. 405), the same machine is mentioned as 'le lup de guerre'. The med.L. *lupus* is found elsewhere as the name of a military engine, but nothing seems to be known of its nature. The conjecture that *war-wolf* is a perversion of WERWOLF is unfounded.

1610 HOLLAND *Camden's Brit.* I. 400 Of these Mangonells, Patraries, Trabucks, Bricols, Espringolds, and of that which our ancestors termed the Warwolfe, by which ..they discharged volies of mighty huge stones. **1614** CAMDEN *Rem.*, *Artill.* (ed. 2) 239 Some kind of Bricol it seemed which the English & Scots called an Espringold, the shot whereof K. Edward the first escaped faire at the siege of Striuelin; wher he with another Engine, named the *Warwolfe* pierced with one stone,..two vauntmures. **1796** SOUTHEY *Joan of Arc* VIII. 534 The war-wolfs there Hurl'd their huge stones. **1810** JANE PORTER *Sc. Chiefs* liii, The.. war-wolves..sent forth showers of red-hot stones into the midst of the Scottish battalions. *a* **1839** PRAED *Leg. Drachenfels* xi, The mightiest engines that ever the trade Of human homicide hath made, Warwolf, balist, and catapult.

2. Used by Scott for: A fierce warrior.

1810 SCOTT *Lady of Lake* VI. xx, Lightly we'll tame the war-wolf then. **1813** —— *Trierm.* III. xvii, He that would win the war-wolf's skin, May rue him of his boast.

warwolf, obs. form of WERWOLF.

war-worn, *a.* Wasted, ravaged, or battered by war; worn by the toils or privations of war.

1599 SHAKS. *Hen. V*, IV. Chor. 26 Their gesture sad, Inuesting lanke-leane Cheekes, and Warre-worne Coats. **1757** W. WILKIE *Epigoniad* VII. 190 But with a mind unmov'd, I'll meet my doom; Nor stain this war-worn visage with a tear. **1792** R. CUMBERLAND *Calvary* (1803) II. 120 War-worn Sisera. **1825** SCOTT *Betrothed* xvi, His war-worn shamois doublet. **1826** HOR. SMITH *Tor Hill* (1838) I. 33 Through this war-worn region did Sir Giles Hungerford and his party of horsemen press eagerly forward. **1849** W. IRVING *Mahomet & Successors* (1850) II. xvi. 142 Khaled entered with his hundred war-worn veterans. **1868** G. DUFF *Pol. Surv.* 30 The warworn fortress..had added another volume to its history.

† **ˈwary,** *sb. Obs.* In 3 **wari, weri.** [OE. *wearȝ*, *wearh* = OS. *warag*, OHG. *warc*, *warch* criminal, felon (whence Frankish Law Latin *vargus* outlaw), MHG. *warc* monster, ON. *varg-r* outlaw, hence wolf (Sw., Norw. *varg*, wolf, mod.Icel. *vargur* fox), Goth. **warg-s* (attested by the compound *launawargs* unthankful person, and the derivatives *ga-wargjan* to condemn, *wargiþa* condemnation) :—OTeut. **warȝo-z*.

Probable cognates outside Teut. are Lith. *vâ̂rgas* misery, *vargti* to be wretched, OPrussian *wargs* suffering (sb.), evil, bad (adj.), Lettish *wahrgs* ill, OSl. *vragŭ* (Russian *vrag*) enemy.]

A felon, outlaw, villain.

a **1000** *Dream of the Rood* 31 Strange feondas..heton me heora werȝas hebban. *a* **1000** *Gloss.* in Wr.-Wülcker 245/40 *Furcifer*, wearh. *a* **1200** *St. Marher.* 4 þe wari of þeos wordes warð utnumen wrað. *c* **1205** LAY. 28215 Mi seolf ich wulle hine an-hon haxst alre warien. *a* **1225** *Ancr. R.* 352 My Louerd, þuruh hwam þe world is me unwurð, & ich am unwurð to him, as weri [*v.r.* wari] þet is anhonged.

wary (ˈwɛərɪ), *a.* Also 6 **waree, warye**, 6–7 **warie**, 7–8 **warry**, 7 **wairie, warrie.** [First recorded in the 16th c.; f. WARE *a.* + -Y[1].]

1. Given to caution, habitually on one's guard against danger, deception, or mistake; circumspect.

1552 HULOET, Wary or wily, *oculeus, solers, uigilans.* Warye or wyse, *uigilans.* **1563** *Mirr. Mag.*, *Rivers* x, Warne thou the wary, least they hap to stumble. **1575** GASCOIGNE *Posies*, Ep. Yong Gentl. (1907) 13 If you take example by the harmes of others who have eaten it [Hemlocke] before you, then may you chaunce to become so warie, that you will looke advisedly on all the Perceley that you gather, least amongst the same one braunch of Hemlock might anoy you. **1594** HOOKER *Eccl. Pol.* Pref. viii. §13 Vpon which question

..the warier sort of you taking the one part, and the forwarder in zeale the other. **1614** SYLVESTER *Micro-cosm., Parlt. Vertues Roy.* 270 The wisest errs:..The holiest sins: the wariest slips: God is fault-lesse: neuer, Man. **1677** DRYDEN *Apol. Heroic Poetry* b 2, This kind of Genius writes indeed correctly. A wary man he is in Grammar; very nice as to Solæcism or Barbarism. **1718** ECHARD *Hist. Eng.* III. 588 He being a Person of great Vertue and Piety..; besides this, of a very rich, and of a wary, or rather timorous Nature. **1805** WELLINGTON in Gurw. *Desp.* (1835) III. 590 If he had recollected the cautious and wary character of that chief. **1820** BYRON *Mar. Fal.* II. i. 113 The wariest of republics Has lavish'd all its chief employs upon him. **1849** MACAULAY *Hist. Eng.* vi. II. 153, 'I say nothing about consequences,' answered the wary diplomatist. **1868** FREEMAN *Norm. Conq.* (1876) II. vii. 32 Godwine was essentially a wary statesman. **1884** *Law Rep.*, 25 *Chanc. Div.* 319 Mr. Bramley was far too wary to admit of even the suspicion of such a thing.

Comb. **1832** HT. MARTINEAU *Hill & Valley* (1843) 123 A cool, wary-looking man stood by.

b. said of animals.

1614 EARL STIRLING *Domesday* III. lvi, The warie Hare, whose feare oft sport hath made. **1634** SIR T. HERBERT *Trav.* 213 The Goats are wary and haue their centinels. **1670** DRYDEN *Conq. Granada* I. i, Whose wary Gennet shunning still the Harm, Seem'd to attend the Shock, and then leap'd wide. **1858** KINGSLEY *Misc.* (1859) I. 135 How many have you delivered from..wary old alligators? **1865** LIVINGSTONE *Zambesi* xxiii. 465 The animals are wary, from the dread they have of the poisoned arrows. **1884** *Pall Mall Budget* 22 Aug. 27/1 Of all birds the wariest is the curlew. **1912** J. L. MYRES *Dawn of Hist.* ix. 193 The horse, which is as wary as a watch-dog, is defended against strangers by his heels.

c. with agent-noun or its equivalent.

1570 DEE *Math. Pref.* b iiij, The third man..erreth to the discredit of the Wary, and modest Astrologien. **1603** KNOLLES *Hist. Turks* (1621) 110 A warie observer of his delights..and faithfull partaker of his secrets. **1609** HOLLAND *Amm. Marcell.* XIV. x. 22 A warie advertiser and adviser of profitable wayes. **1639** FULLER *Holy War* IV. viii. (1640) 181 All know his Holinesse to be too wary an archer to shoot away his arrows at nothing. **1701** G. STANHOPE *Pious Breath., St. Bernard* VIII. ii. (1704) 363 Even the most wary liver cannot be clear of guilt. **1855** KINGSLEY *Heroes, Theseus* II. 214 Theseus was a wary wrestler.

2. On one's guard, cautious, careful.

1592 SHAKS. *Rom. & Jul.* III. v. 40 The day is broke, be wary, looke about. **1602** —— *Ham.* I. iii. 43 Be wary then, best safety lies in feare. **1659** *Burton's Diary* (1828) IV. 272, I hope the gentlemen will be clear, and that they will be warier hereafter. *a* **1676** HALE *Prim. Orig. Man.* (1677) 315 Men must be wary and considerate before they conclude against the Frame and Order of things as they appear in Nature. **1797** MRS. RADCLIFFE *Italian* vii, If you can, descend with me in silence, I warn you to be wary. **1822** BYRON *Wern.* I. i, I must be wary; An error would spoil all. **1883** D. C. MURRAY *Hearts* x. (1885) 77 Mark was disposed to be wary after what had happened.

b. const. *of*.

1580 LYLY *Euphues* (Arb.) 226 If Trauailers in this our age were as warye of their conditions, as they be venterous of their bodyes. **1584-7** GREENE *Carde of Fancie* Wks. (Grosart) IV. 102 She which in her virginitie is charie of her chastitie, in her marriage will be as warie of her honestie. *c* **1600** SHAKS. *Sonn.* xxii. 9 O therefore loue be of thy selfe so wary, As I not for my selfe, but for thee will. **1686** in *Verney Mem.* (1907) II. 424 You Hadd Best Bee very wary of all yr words and Actions. **1745** *De Foe's Eng. Tradesman* vi. (1841) I. 37 A tradesman ought to be very wary of taking too much credit. **1822** SCOTT *Peveril* xvii, You have already seen enough of the evils of civil war, to be wary of again awakening its terrors in a peaceful and happy country. **1840** BARHAM *Ingol. Leg., Bagman's Dog,* If ever you travel, like Anthony Blogg, Be wary of strangers!—don't take too much grog.

c. const. *in*. In early examples the sense of *wary in* is that now expressed by *wary of*: 'to be wary in (doing something)' = 'to be wary of', 'to beware of'.

1617 MORYSON *Itin.* II. 55 Aduising his Lordship to be wary in crediting intelligences, which were commonly false. **1640** in *Verney Mem.* (1907) I. 108, I am most wary in giving my father the least distast. **1653** RAMESEY *Astrol. Restored* 290 Ever remember you be wary in pronouncing judgement touching weather and the alteration of the ayr. **1672** SIR T. BROWNE *Let. Friend* §8 A remarkable coincidence, which tho Astrology hath taken witty pains to salve yet hath it been very wary in making predictions of it. *a* **1674** CLARENDON *Surv. Leviath.* (1676) 149 Nor was he more wary in any thing, then..that the people might imagine, that he pretended any other title to the Government, then by the Confessor. *c* **1680** BEVERIDGE *Serm.* (1729) I. 53 It cannot but highly concern us all to be very cautious and wary in the choice of our words. **1754** EARL OF CORKE in J. Duncombe *Lett.* (1773) III. 26, I want instructive companions, and in them I shall be very wary.

d. With indirect question. Now *rare* or *Obs.*

1575 GASCOIGNE *Glasse Govt.* Wks. 1910 II. 39 For surely as it [time] is the greatest treasure which God hath given unto man, so ought he to be verie curious and warie how he bestoweth the same. **1602** W. S. *Thomas Ld. Cromwell* IV. v. 94 Therefore, take heed, be warie what you doe. **1622** GATAKER *Spirit. Watch* (ed. 2) 83 [They] are wont to bee more wary and chary how they carry themselues in their affaires. **1634** SIR T. HERBERT *Trav.* 5 They should be wary, where, and when they wash themselues. *a* **1661** FULLER *Worthies, Lond.* (1662) 208 Thus men cannot be too wary what they inscribe on Tombs. **1740** RICHARDSON *Pamela* (1824) I. i. 18 You ought to be wary what tales you send out of a family. **1812** CARY *Dante, Parad.* xx. 125 O mortal men! be wary how ye judge.

e. With clause or inf. of purpose. ? *Obs.*

1668 EVELYN tr. *Freart's Idea Perf. Paint.* 56 A Painter is here to be wary, that he introduce no other Figures of Men, or any Buildings in the Landskip. *a* **1674** CLARENDON *Surv. Leviath.* (1676) 27 Without being in any degree wary to avoid palpable contradictions.

3. Of action, behaviour, observation, etc.: Proceeding from or characterized by caution.

1557 LD. SHREWSBURY in Lodge *Illustr. Brit. Hist.* (1791) I. 283 The L. Wardeyn who..is..instructyd by good cyrcumspeccion, & waree doing to shewe [blank] to th' enymye, in anoying hym, & defendyng of the countrey. **1579** HAKE *Newes out of Powles* (1872) F viij b, Common Innes they [*sc.* bawds] watch with warie eye If that..they may..espye The country maides that come from far. **1586** A. DAY *Engl. Secretorie* I. (1625) 63 If it bee deemed once fit for you to marry again and that upon the warie and circumspect choice thereof dependeth a manner of necessity. **1587** —— *Daphnis & Chloe* (1890) 6 With so tender & warie touch as yᵗ with her hoofs going in she might no wayes hurte the babe. **1595** DANIEL *Civ. Wars* III. xxxvi, Sober, milde Blunt..warnes a warier cariage in the thing. **1599** MARSTON *Antonio's Rev.* IV. i, When will the Duke..Keepe warie observation in large pay, To dogge a fooles act? **1612** BRINSLEY *Lud. Lit.* xxv. (1627) 270 Yet a wary care must be had, that he be used with respect by the Master. **1646** SIR T. BROWNE *Pseud. Ep.* I. viii. 30 If any man..shall carry a wary eye on Paulus Venetus..and many other, I think his circumspection is laudable. **1653** GATAKER *Vind. Annot. Jer.* 55 No Delphik Oracle..could ever have given a wiser and warier answer. **1660** BOYLE *New Exp. Phys.-Mech.* xxii. 161 The wary letting in the Air upon them. **1690** LOCKE *Hum. Und.* III. v. §9 When they appear, upon a more wary survey, to be nothing else but an Artifice of the Understanding. **1711** STEELE *Spect.* No. 91 ¶2 Crastin professes a wary Observation of the Turns of his Mistress's Mind. *a* **1732** ATTERBURY *2nd Serm. on 2 Pet.* iii. 16 (1734) I. 277 To read that Sacred Volume, with a Wise Jealousy, and a Wary Distrust of our own selves. **1794** MRS. RADCLIFFE *Myst. Udolpho* xlv, I shall keep a wary eye upon all that passes in the chateau. **1821** LAMB *Elia, Old Benchers,* L. who had a wary foresight of his probable hallucinations. **1837** W. IRVING *Capt. Bonneville* III. 111 It was necessary, also, to keep a wary eye upon the land, for they were..continually in reach of any ambush that might be lurking on shore.

†**4.** Careful in expenditure, thrifty, provident.

1605 *Lond. Prodigal* I. ii. 159, I knewe your father, he was a wary husband. *a* **1657** SIR W. MURE *Hist.* 244 Wnless he had been both stout, warrie, and provident in the turbulent times quherin he lived, he could hardlie have maintained quhat his father had recovered. **1708** MRS. CENTLIVRE *Busy Body* I. i, I knew thy father, he was a hearty wary man, and I cannot consent that his son should squander away what he saved to no purpose. **1709** STEELE *Tatler* No. 91 ¶1, I have, by leading a very wary Life, laid up a little Money. **1812** H. & J. SMITH *Rej. Addr., Theatre* 68 Jews from St. Mary Axe, for jobs so wary, That for old cloaths they'd even axe St. Mary.

†**'wary**, *v. Obs.* Forms: 1 **wierȝan, wirȝan, werȝan, wyr(i)ȝan, wiriȝan, wirian,** *north.* **wœrȝa,** *Mercian* **wærȝan,** 2 **wereȝian,** 3-4 **werie,** 4-5 **wery,** 4 **werye, werry,** *Sc.* **very,** 6 **weray;** 3-7 **warie,** 4-5 **wari, warrie,** 4 *Sc.* **vary,** 4-6 **warye,** (5 **warow),** 4-5, 8 **warry,** 5-6 **warre,** 6 **warrye,** 4-7 **wary.** [OE. *wierȝan, wærȝan*:—OTeut. **warȝjan*, f. **warȝo-z*, OE. *wearȝ* felon, WARY *sb.* Cf. Goth. *gawarȝjan* to condemn (= OE. *ȝewierȝan* to curse), OS. *giwaragean*, OHG. *far-wergen* to curse (cf. FOR-WARY *v.*)]

1. *trans.* To invoke a curse upon; to declare accursed; to pour maledictions upon.

c **725** *Corpus Gloss.* D 25 *Deuotaturus*, werȝendi. *c* **897** ÆLFRED *Gregory's Past. C.* xlix. 376 Se þe his hwæte hyt, hiene wierȝð ðæt folc. *c* **1000** *Ags. Gosp.* Matt. v. 11 Eadiȝe synd ȝe þonne hiȝ wyriað eow and ehtað eow. *c* **1000** ÆLFRIC *Gloss.* in Wr.-Wülcker 131/3 *Deuoto*, ic wyrȝe. *c* **1200** *Trin. Coll. Hom.* 183 Iuele wurmes mote þe chewe.., rotie mote þu to time. þus wareð þe sowle þe licame, for þat hit haueð þar after ierned. **1338** R. BRUNNE *Chron.* (1810) 319 þe Inglis men were wone, to wery long trayne. **1340** HAMPOLE *Pr. Consc.* 7422 þai salle wery þe tyme þat þai war wroght. *c* **1374** CHAUCER *Troylus* II. 1619 And Poliphete þey gonnen þus to waryen An-honged be swych on were he my broþer. *Ibid.* v. 1378 My Ioye in wo I kan seye yow naught ellis Bot torned is, for which my lif I warie. *c* **1400** *Pilgr. Sowle* (Caxton 1483) IV. xxxviii. (1859) 65 Thus is the kynge of his people waryed, and cursid. *c* **1440** *Rel. Pieces fr. Thornton MS.* xiv. 195 Than thay wepede and weryede þaire werke and þaire wyll. *c* **1440** *Pallad. on Husb.* I. 530 It is an adversarie To every seed, now everie birdde hem warie! *c* **1440** *Promp. Parv.* 516/2 Waryyn', or cursyn', *imprecor, maledico, execror.* *c* **1450** HOLLAND *Houlate* 954 He waryit the tyde That he was wrocht in this warld wofull in weir. *c* **1460** *Play Sacram.* 479 in *Non-Cycle Myst. Plays* 72 Now alle þe deuyllys of hell hym wari. *c* **1470** HARDING *Chron.* CCIII. iv, The commens all than of all Englande grounde, Warred his gate [*v.r.* cursed his viage] to Wales euery yere. *a* **1500** *Ratis Raving* 1994 For-thi I bles it [this age] nocht as best, Na yit I wary it nocht as verst. **1509** BARCLAY *Ship of Fools* (1874) I. 70 Consyder this prouerbe of antyquyte And your vnkyndnes weray ban and curse. **1513** DOUGLAS *Æneis* III. vi. 188 Thus oft the pepill but ansueir gayis thair wayis, And wariis the sait of Sibyll all thair dayis. **1572** *Satir. Poems Reform.* xxxi. 193 Than sall thay warie, curse, & ban The murtherars yat yir weiris began. *a* **1605** MONTGOMERIE *Misc. P.* xxi. 25 O! waryit be the vhyle That euer we wer acquent! —— *Sonn.* xxxiii. 1 Vhom suld I warie bot my wicked weard. *a* **1667** SKINNER *Etymol.* (1671), To Wary, vox agro Lanc. familiaris quæ significat Maledicere. *c* **1746** J. COLLIER (Tim Bobbin) *View Lanc. Dial.* (1770) 19 Theyr'n warrying, banning, on cawing one onother leawsy Eawls, os thick os leet.

b. To pronounce a formal curse against. (Said of God, the Church, etc.)

a **1352** MINOT *Poems* App. ii. 214 Weried with Goddes mowth mai ȝe warand. *c* **1375** *Sc. Leg. Saints* xv. (*Barnabas*) 157, & þare tempyl waryt he [Barnabas] quhare-in sik men had entre. *c* **1400** *Apol. Loll.* 14 þe kirke..mai not iustli wari him, ne pray iuil to him. *a* **1425** *Cursor M.* 22103 (Trin.) Oure lorde warieþ þese two townes. And thus seiþ..Corozaym euer be þe wo And þe bethsaida eke also. **1562** *Aberd. Kirk Sess. Rec.* (Spalding Club) 7 God commandis fader and moder to be honored..cursing and wareyng all brekaris of this commandment.

absol. *c* **1400** *Apol. Loll.* 13 þo ministris of þe kirke..owe boþe to curse and wari, but neuer for iuil wille ne veniaunce, but for luf of ritwisnes.

2. To speak impiously or profanely against; to blaspheme.

c **1000** ÆLFRIC *Lev.* xxiv. 16 Se man, þe wiriȝð drihtnes naman, swelte he deaðe. *a* **1340** HAMPOLE *Psalter* lxxxviii. 31 *Si iusticias meas prophanauerint*..If thai wery my rightwisnesis. *c* **1375** *Sc. Leg. Saints* iv. (*James*) 226 Bot þu wary þe name of criste Ihesu,..þu sal be vnheidyt. *a* **1500** *Ratis Raving* 3411 Wary nocht god for thi mischans.

3. To afflict with evils or calamities: = CURSE *v.* 5. Chiefly as pa. pple., also in phr. ***waried worth*** (it, them, etc.) = may it, they, be afflicted.

c **1200** *Trin. Coll. Hom.* 181 For þat þu ete þat ich þe forboden hadde, waried wurðe þe eorðe on þine werke. *a* **1300** *Cursor M.* 920 þe werld es werid wit þi sin. *c* **1330** R. BRUNNE *Chron. Wace* (Rolls) 203 Whan God took wreche of Kaymes synne, þe erthe was waryed in his werk. *a* **1340** HAMPOLE *Psalter* ix. 24 The wickid that noyes til his neghtbure es blissid,..thof he ware better worthi to be werid. *a* **1400** *Morte Arth.* 959 Weryd worthe the wyghte ay, that the thy wytt refede. *c* **1400** *Laud Troy Book* 6373 Waried worth hem vs hedir broght! *c* **1400** *Destr. Troy* 12212 Thurgh the craft of þat cursed, knighthode may shame And wary all oure workes to the worldes end. *c* **1420** WYNTOUN *Cron.* I. iv. 15 Adam worthit to wyn his fud Off þe erd þat warite was. **1597** *Guistard & Sismond* B ij, Cursed might he be and waried eternally.

4. *absol.* or *intr.* To utter a curse or curses.

a **1225** *Ancr. R.* 70 ȝe ne schulen uor none þinge ne warien, ne swerien. *Ibid.* 186 Ne wrekie ȝe nout ou suluen,..ne ne warien hwon me agulteð to ou. *a* **1300** *E.E. Psalter* lxi. 5 With þaire mouth þan blissed þai, And with þair hert þai weried ai. **1303** R. BRUNNE *Handl. Synne* 1288 And, ȝe wyuys,..werryþ nat for lytyl trespas. *c* **1380** WYCLIF *Wks.* (1880) 234 þei grucchen aȝen, & cursen & warien nyȝt & day. **1382** —— *Matt.* xxvi. 74 Thanne he began to warye and swere, that he knewe nat the man. *c* **1440** *Jacob's Well* 92 Whanne þou warowyst, chydest, betyst, & faryst as a wood man. **1501** DOUGLAS *Pal. Hon.* III. 816 Thus I remanit..Cursand the feildis with all the fair colouris, That I awolk oft wariand the quhile. *c* **1518** SKELTON *Magnyf.* 2238 What beggar art thou, that thus doth banne and wary. **1535** *Goodly Primer, Passion* IV, Then began he to bann, to wary, & to forswear himself stiffly. *a* **1578** LINDESAY (Pitscottie) *Chron. Scot.* (S.T.S.) I. 30 The peopill began to warie and curs that evir it chanceit theme to leiwe in sick wicked and dangerous tymes. *c* **1746** J. COLLIER (Tim Bobbin) *View Lanc. Dial.* (1770) 20 He glooart awvishly ot Mezzil fease; on Mezzil fease glendurt os wrythenly ot him ogen; bot noather warrit, nor thrapt.

Hence †**'warying** *vbl. sb.*

c **1200** *Trin. Coll. Hom.* 177 þe oreguil and þe wraððe of kinges..þe..bringen on þe folkes heorte grete stormes..of hatienge, and on here muðe curses, and werȝinges. *Ibid.* 179 Ne wrec þu þe mid wussinge, ne mid wariengе, ac heald me þe wrache. *a* **1225** *Ancr. R.* 200 þe Unicorne of Wreððe..haueð six hweolpes.. þe veorðe is Wariunge. *a* **1340** HAMPOLE *Psalter* ix. 29 *Cuius maledictione os plenum est,*..Whas mouth is ful of weriynge & bitternes & treson. *c* **1440** *Promp. Parv.* 516/2 Waryynge, *malediccio, imprecacio.* *c* **1450** *Mirour Saluacioun* (Roxb.) 20 This Balaam thoght to hynder gods folk be werying. **1552** ABP. HAMILTON *Catech.* (1884) 32 It war to lange to reherse here all the malesonis waryingis or cursingis.

attrib. *a* **1660** *Contemp. Hist. Irel.* (Ir. Archæol. Soc.) I. 286 It is verie strange how those abortiue statists,..makes noe scruple of the fearfull sworde of waringe excommunication, too often unsheathed against them.

wary, obs. Sc. f. VARY; var. WARRAY *v. Obs.*

waryacyon, obs. form of VARIATION.

c **1485** *Digby Myst.* III. 1815 To worchep Iesu þey ar behold, nor never a-ȝens hym to make waryacyon.

waryance, -aunce, obs. Sc. ff. VARIANCE.

waryangle, variant of WARIANGLE *Obs.*

waryche, variant of WARISH *v.*[1] *Obs.*

†**'waryeld.** *Sc. Obs.*[−1] [Of uncertain origin: possibly a survival of OE. *werȝield* WERGELD, with altered sense.] A requital, recompense.

c **1375** *Sc. Leg. Saints* xlviii. (*Juliana*) 204 For-þi gyf hir hir warȝeld noo, or mykil mare scho sal hourt ȝou.

waryer, obs. form of WARRIOR.

†**'waryish**, *a. Obs. rare.* [? var. of WERSH *a.*] ? Unwholesome-looking.

1565 GOLDING *Ovid's Met.* II. 968 Hir teeth were furde with filth and drosse, hir gums were waryish blew. **1567** *Ibid.* VII. 446 He lifting up his olde Pale waryish armes.

waryner(e, obs. forms of WARRENER.

warys(e, -ysh, -ys(s)che: see WARISH *v.*[1]

†**'warytre.** *Obs.* Forms: 1 **waritroe,** 3 **waritreo, weritreo, warh treo,** 5 **warytre.** [OE. **wearȝ-*(*weriȝ-*) *tréo*, f. *wearȝ* WARY *sb.*, *wearȝ, weriȝ* wicked + *tréo* TREE.] A gallows, gibbet. Often applied to the Cross.

? *a* **1200** *Charter of Æthelric* A.D. 706 in Kemble *Cod. Dipl.* III. 375 Norð fro Beornedune siðe ðe wowe brondred; siðe to ðe waritroe. *c* **1205** LAY. 5714 And doð up and [an?] waritreo [*c* **1275** and doþ vp a wer-itreo] þer on heo scullen winden. *a* **1225** *Ancr. R.* 122 Me ledde him amorwen uorte hongen o waritreo & driuen þuruh his four limes irene neiles. *Ibid.* 190 þenne dusie worldes men goð bi grene weie, touward te waritreo & to deaðe of helle. *a* **1240** *Wohunge* in *O.E. Hom.* I. 283 A nu raise þai up þe rode. Setis up þe warh treo. *c* **1290** *Beket* 2192 in *S. Eng. Leg.* 169 Heo bi-radden for-to nime þat holi bodi: and with wilde hors to-drawe And seththe hangen it on a waritreo. *c* **1425** *Engl. Conq. Ireland* xiv. 34 Thay ne hadden no wone of warytres.

was (wɒz), *sb.* [The pa. t. sing. of BE.] What was; something past.

1340 *Ayenb.* 104 þanne is he propreliche yclieped: þet art. Vor he is zoþliche..wyþ-oute ende, wyþ-oute heaued, wyþ-oute wes, wyþ-out ssel-by. **1390** GOWER *Conf.* III. 357 The thing is torned into was; That which was whilom grene gras Is welked hey at time now. **1581** SIDNEY *Apol. Poetrie* (Arb.) 37 Where the Historian in his bare *Was*, hath many times that which wee call fortune, to ouer-rule the best wisedome. **1876** MISS BROUGHTON *Joan* I. xxx, But if the 'was' is hard to face, how much harder the 'might have been'. **1884** W. S. GILBERT *Princess Ida* II, I once was Some one—and the Was Will Be.

was (wɒz, w(ə)z), 1st and 3rd pers. sing. pa. t. of BE *v.*

was, obs. form of WHOSE *pron.*

was, obs. form of *woe is*: see WOE *sb.*

wasabi ('wasabi). [Jap.] A Japanese herb, *Eutrema wasabi*, whose thick root is used in Japanese cooking.

1903 *Bull. Bureau of Plant Industry* (U.S. Dept. Agric.) No. 42. 20 There is a fresh sharpness about Japanese wasabi that not even the finest Austrian sorts of horse-radish possess. *Ibid.* 21 For two years, the young wasabi plants are cared for in the field. **1972** Y. LOVELOCK *Vegetable Bk.* 333 The roots of the related toothworts..serve as a horseradish substitute in North America... Wasabi..is a Japanese relation cultivated for the sake of its roots, which are used as a condiment. **1981** J. MELVILLE *Sort of Samurai* xviii. 145 Otani..watched the *sushi* master deftly season the rice-cakes with a dab of tear-jerking *wasabi* paste.

waschael, obs. form of VESSEL.

wascoat(e, -cot(e, -cott, obs. ff. WAISTCOAT.

wase (weɪz). *Obs.* exc. *dial.* Also 6 **wayse,** 6–7, 9 **waze,** 9 **weize, weise, weese, wais, waese,** etc. (see *Eng. Dial. Dict.*). [Found in various Teut. langs.: MSw. *vasi* wk. masc., Sw., Da., Norw. *vase* bundle of straw, fascine, etc., MLG. (whence mod.G. dial. and technical) *wase* faggot, fascine, pad worn on the head for carrying burdens, MDu. *wase* torch, NFris. *waas*, pad inside a horse-collar. It is doubtful whether the Eng. word is adopted from Scandinavian, or represents an OE. **wasa*. See WRASE, which appears to be a variant.]

1. A wisp or bundle of straw or reeds; in early examples with reference to its use as a torch.

c **1375** *Cursor M.* 8878 (Fairf.) Out of þat tree brast a blase þat brinde ham alle as a wase. [*Other texts differently.*] *c* **1400** *Beryn* 2351 He..goith a-bout þe wallis with a brennyng wase. *c* **1400** *Laud Troy Bk.* 18147 Thei bad thanne..of stre gete him a wase And make on the walles ther-of a blase. **14..** *Metr. Voc.* in Wr.-Wülcker 627/23 Wase, *stupa.* **1565** HARDING *Confut. Apol.* IV. xv. 206 b, He geueth him [*sc.* his 'man of straw'] a waze of strawe in his hande. **1602** CAREW *Cornwall* 28 b, One standeth watching..while another maketh a light with a waze of reed. **1888** *Berksh. Gloss.*, *Waze*, a wisp of straw for rubbing down a horse.

2. 'A pad of straw, cloth, etc., worn on the head to relieve the pressure of a burden carried on it' (*Eng. Dial. Dict.*).

1548 *Elyot's Dict.*, *Arculum*, a roll that women do weare on their heades, to beare water or milk easily, a wase. **1556** WITHALS *Dict.* (1562) 43 b/1 A wase or wreath to be layed vnder the vessell, that is borne vpon the head, as women vse, *cesticillus vel arculus.* **1570** LEVINS *Manip.* 36/41 A Wase, *circus. Ibid.* 203/13 A Wayse, *cirrus, i, cesticillus, i.* **1824** CARR *Craven Gloss.*, *Wais, Wase*, a wreath of straw or cloth on the head, to relieve the pressure of burthens. **1825** BROCKETT *N.C. Gloss.*, *Weeze.* **1835** CHATTO *Rambles Northumbld.* 106 *note*, A *weise* is a circular pad, commonly made of an old stocking, but sometimes merely a wreath of straw or grass, to save the head from the pressure of the pail. **1851** *Cumberld. Gloss.*, *Waze.*

3. 'A washer or "packing-ring" for making pipe-joints watertight' (*Eng. Dial. Dict.*).

1851 GREENWELL *Coal-trade Terms Northumb. & Durh.* 26 Before the bolts are put in, weizes, made of rope or spun-yarn, or of lead, are put between the flanches [flanges of the pump].

wase, obs. form of OOZE *sb.*[3]

1483 *Cath. Angl.* 409/2 A Wase (*v.r.* Wayse), *alga.*

wase, obs. form of *was* (see BE *v.*), WHOSO.

wasecoat, -cote, obs. forms of WAISTCOAT.

† '**wasel,** *v. Obs.* [f. OE. *wáse* mud, OOZE *sb.*[2]: see -EL. Cf. mod.dial. *wassle, wozzle*, to beat down, trample.] *intr.* To trample in mud.

c **1394** *P. Pl. Crede* 430 þis wight waselede in þe fen almost to þe ancle.

wash (wɒʃ), *sb.* Forms: 5 **wesche, wesshe,** 5–6 **was(c)he,** 6 **wasch, wasshe, wesch,** *Sc.* **weische,** 7–9 *dial.* **wesh,** 7– **wash.** [f. WASH *v.* in many unconnected applications. OE. had *wæsc* (sense 2) and *ȝewæsc* 'alluvio' (sense 6). Cf. OHG. *wasga* fem. (MHG., early mod.G. *wasche*), *wesga, weska* fem. (MHG. *wesche*, mod.G. *wäsche*); also MHG., mod.G. *wasch* masc., mod.G. *wäsch* neut.]

I. Act of washing.

1. a. *gen.* An act or process of washing or cleansing with water. Also *fig.*

1663 TUKE *Adv. Five Hours* I. 2 The Blemish once received, no Wash is good For stains of Honor, but th' Offenders blood. **1666** SANCROFT *Lex Ignea* 41 A Baptism in Reserve, a Wash for all our Sins. *Mod.* This table needs a wash. I am going to give the dog a wash.

b. An act of washing oneself, esp. of washing one's hands and face. ***wash and brush-up***, a quick wash together with a tidying of one's hair; also *transf.*, and as *v. trans.* and *intr.*

1825 T. HOOK *Sayings* Ser. II. *Doubts & F.* ii, While sleepy lackeys..are crawling down the second staircase to breakfast, before the wash. **1838** DICKENS *Nickleby* vii, Mind you take care, young man, and get first wash. **1852** C. B. MANSFIELD *Paraguay* etc. (1856) 89 Next morning,.. after a wash in a neighbouring rivulet,..we started again. **1872** *Gentl. Mag.* June 722 We must have a wash..and eat some breakfast. **1899** E. W. HORNUNG *Amateur Cracksman* 31 We must have a wash-and-brush-up before we go,—for I'm as black as your boot. **1910** BEET *Rise Papacy* iii. 138 The Patriarch of Antioch appeared on the scene, and.. without waiting for a wash and change of raiment, proceeded to hold a Council of his own. **1912** 'R. ANDOM' *On Tour with Troddles* ix. 62 What we really did want was a wash and a brush up, with a good substantial meal to follow. **1938** G. GREENE *Brighton Rock* III. i. 107, I had to have a wash and brush up. **1941** *Vogue* June 58/2 Wash-and-brush-up your face... Creams are rationed and soap is not. **1956** G. DURRELL *Drunken Forest* v. 98 The cockroach ambled about for a bit and then stopped for a quick wash and brush-up. **1959** G. MITCHELL *Man who grew Tomatoes* i. 10 I'll wash and brush up, as they say, and be down in ten minutes. **1978** R. H. LEWIS *Antiquarian Bks.* viii. 167 Most old books in for rebinding have an automatic 'wash and brush-up'..before getting decked out in their new finery.

2. a. An act, spell, or task of washing clothes or other textile articles; the process of washing undergone by clothes or the like. (***to be lost, damaged,*** etc.) ***in the wash***, in course of being washed. (***to be***) ***at the wash***, of clothes, etc., sent away to be washed.

[*c* **1050** *Glosses on De Consuetudine Monachorum* in *Anglia* XIII. 441 *Vestimentorum ablutio*, reafa wæsc.] **1704** *Lond. Gaz.* No. 3981/4 Stolen..Wearing Linen from the Wash. **1813** WELLINGTON in Gurw. *Desp.* (1838) X. 56 The packet arrived at so late an hour..and our shirts being at the wash as usual, we did not leave Lisbon till the 20th. *a* **1814** *Fam. Politics* IV. i, in *New Brit. Theatre* II. 230, I was going to pull it [a gown] to pieces for the wash. **1832** MARRYAT *N. Forster* iii, It returned from the wash. **1838** DICKENS *O. Twist* viii, Ah, you're a-staring at the pocket-handkerchiefs... We've just looked 'em out, ready for the wash. **1840** —— *Old C. Shop* xli, This objection, and a great many others, founded on certain articles of dress being at the wash,..were overcome by Kit. **1848** THACKERAY *Van. Fair* xi, Mrs. Bute, who knew how many days the sirloin of beef lasted at the Hall; how much linen was got ready at the great wash [etc.]. **1848** MRS. GASKELL *Mary Barton* i. Though she may have done a hard day's wash, there's not [etc.]. **1876** E. JENKINS *Blot Queen's Head* 26 You mark their linen 'Empress's Crown Hotel', and our linen 'Queen's Inn'... What if they get mixed in the wash?

b. *concr.* The quantity of clothes or other textile articles washed (or set apart to be washed) on one occasion.

1789 *New Lond. Mag.* Apr. 224/1 The apprehension of [several people]..for stealing a whole wash of wet linen. **1857** DICKENS *Dorrit* I. xxii, In this yard a wash of sheets and tablecloths tried..to get itself dried on a line or two. **1889** MRS. H. L. CAMERON *Lost Wife* I. i. 7 The family wash.. flutters gracefully in the breeze. **1898** HAMBLEN *Gen. Manager's Story* xvii. 268 The native women having a custom..of taking in the wash before dark. **1914** MARY R. RINEHART *K* iii. (1915) 35 Where her aunt..was hanging out the week's wash of table linen.

¶**c.** *pl.* App. used (after G. *wäsche*) for: Washable articles of apparel, body-linen.

1827 CARLYLE *Germ. Rom.* II. 139 She took special heed to pack up her clothes and washes with her own hands.

d. fig. phr. ***to come out in the wash***: (of the truth) to be revealed, become clear; (of a situation, events, etc.) to be resolved or put right eventually. Cf. WASHING *vbl. sb.* 8 a.

1903 KIPLING *Five Nations* 196 An' it all went into the laundry, But it never came out in the wash. **1917** WODEHOUSE *Man with Two Left Feet* ii. 29 A sort of fate, what?.. Heredity, and so forth. What's bred in the bone will come out in the wash. **1930** 'BRENT OF BIN BIN' *Ten Creeks Run* xxii. 266 That scandal has been such a long time comin' out in the wash that you must have been mistaken. **1943** N. COWARD *This Happy Breed* II. i. 53 Ethel:..I thought everything was going to be all right... Frank: Don't worry, old girl, it'll all come out in the wash. **1947** 'N. BLAKE' *Minute for Murder* vii. 145 'How on earth could Bill know?'.. 'Oh, well, it'll all come out in the wash, no doubt.' **1971** J. R. L. ANDERSON *Reckoning in Ice* vii. 147 When it all comes out in the wash—if it does—I suppose the company will meet our fees. **1978** J. DUNN in Hookway & Pettit *Action & Interpretation* 161 All human scientists..practise in the fond hope that the deficiencies of description or the errors and gaps in the intelligibility of record will all come out in the wash.

3. A washing with some liquid for the purpose of producing a particular effect; a liquid preparation used or intended to be used in this manner.

a. A medicinal lotion. (The word suggests the use of liquid in somewhat larger quantity than is implied by *lotion*.)

black, yellow wash: various liquid preparations of mercury for application to ulcers or to the skin in eruptive diseases. ***white wash***: dilute liquor of subacetate of lead.

1626 BACON *Sylva* §757 [Try] whether Children may not haue some Wash, or Some thing to make their Teeth Better, and Stronger? **1672** WYCHERLEY *Love in Wood* IV. ii, My eyes are none of the best since I have used the last new wash of mercury-water. **1697** TRYON *Way to Health* xviii. (ed. 3) 409 There are many various things..prescribed by Physicians..as Washes, etc., to preserve the Teeth and Gums. **1732** FIELDING *Mock Doctor* iv, The doctor, with a sort of wash, wash'd her tongue 'till he set it agoing. **1808** *Med. Jrnl.* XIX. 572, I tried a variety of ointments and washes, but without deriving any material benefit from their use. **1828** *Lancet* 16 Feb. 717/1 The employment of yellow wash (a solution of oxymuriate of mercury in lime water) was recommended. *Ibid.* 732/2 The calomel and lime water, known by the name of the black wash. **1849** PEREIRA *Elem. Mat. Med.* (ed. 3) I. 838 *Lotio nigra*... Black Wash. *Ibid.* 839 *Lotio flava*... Yellow or Phagedenic Wash. **1850** *Reece's Med. Guide* (ed. 17) 557 Milk, so frequently employed by nurses as a wash in these cases, by turning sour on the part, often excites fresh irritation. **1871** GARROD *Mat. Med.* (ed. 3) 117 Externally, when freely diluted, liquor potassæ may be employed as a wash in some chronic skin disorders.

b. A liquid cosmetic for the complexion.

Very common in the 17–18th c.; now chiefly *Hist.*

1639 MASSINGER *Unnat. Combat* IV. ii, These are perfum'd too, Of the Roman wash. **1649** LOVELACE *Lucasta* 146 No Cabinets with curious Washes, Bladders and perfumed Plashes [are here]. **1676** SHADWELL *Virtuoso* III. 49 All manner of Washes, Almond-water, and Mercury-water for the Complexion. **1693** DRYDEN *Juvenal* vi. 605 Her Cheeks as smooth as Silk; Are polish'd with a Wash of Asses Milk. **1706** FARQUHAR *Recruit. Officer* I. ii, I need..no Harts-horn for my Head, nor Wash for my Complexion. **1735** POPE *Ep. Lady* 54 Narcissa's nature, tolerably mild, To make a wash, would hardly stew a child. **1766** GOLDSM. *Vicar W.* vi, They were making a wash for the face. Washes of all kinds I had a natural antipathy to; for I knew that instead of mending the complexion they spoiled it. **1809** MALKIN *Gil Blas* X. x. (Rtldg.) 364, I know how to make washes and creams for the ladies' faces. **1852** THACKERAY *Esmond* I. vi, The box..contained—not papers regarding the conspiracy—but my lady's wigs, washes, and rouge-pots. **1860** *All Year Round* No. 49. 531 Pure soft water is the truest beauty wash.

fig. *a* **1625** FLETCHER *Nice Valour* III. iii, There is no handsomenesse, But has a wash of Pride and Luxury. *a* **1680** BUTLER *Rem.* (1759) I. 224 Th' artificial Wash of Eloquence Is daub'd in vain upon the clearest Sense. **1689** COLLIER *Ess. Pride* 56 Conceit, when it is Corrected with a mixture of Gravity, is an admirable Wash, and will make one look as Wise, and as Great as you would wish.

c. A liquid applied to the hair to alter its colour, to impart smoothness, or to promote growth. Now chiefly *Hist.*, exc. in ***hair-wash***.

a **1668** LASSELS *Italy* (1698) I. 60 They dry their hair in the sun, after they have washed it in a certain wash. *a* **1700** EVELYN *Diary* June 1645, They weare very long crisped haire, of severall strakes and colours, which they make so by a wash. **1859** *Habits of Gd. Society* ii. 118 Essences, powders, pastes, washes for the hair, washes for the skin, recal the days of one's grandmothers.

d. A liquid preparation used to protect plants against pests or disease.

1921 *Discovery* May 130/1 The providing of suitable sprays and washes, and other material connected with the checking of plant pests. **1951** *Dict. Gardening* (R. Hort. Soc.) IV. 2081/1 Other washes have had to be derived for use against it [*sc.* the red spider mite]. **1984** *Which?* Apr. 166/3 Dirt or discoloration by lichen and algae on a wall.. often isn't harmful... Brush on a sterilising wash.

e. = SHEEP-WASH *sb.* 1, 2.

1933 *Press* (Christchurch, N.Z.) 25 Nov. 15/7 *Wash*, place and plant for washing sheep. **1965** [see *draining-pen* s.v. DRAINING *vbl. sb.* 4].

4. †**a.** Mural painting in water-colour. *Obs.*$^{-0}$.

1598 FLORIO, *Aquazzo*, wash or water colour. **1611** *Ibid.*, *Affrésco*, a Painters worke called wash or water-colours.

b. *Water-colour Painting.* A broad thin layer of colour laid on by a continuous movement of the brush.

1728 CHAMBERS *Cycl.* s.v. *Washing*, These washes are usually given in equal Teints, or Degrees, throughout; which are afterwards brought down and soften'd over the Lights with fair Water. **1882** HAMERTON *Graphic Arts* 84 Line and auxiliary washes are employed together in great variety. *Ibid.* 86 At Florence there are some drawings by Cambiaso, in pen and wash. **1884** *American* VIII. 59 The beauty of the clear, broad wash. **1886** RUSKIN *Præterita* I. xii. 396 To produce dark clouds and rain with twelve or twenty successive washes.

c. *transf.* (Cf. WASH *v.* 10 b.)

1597 GERARDE *Herbal* I. lxvii. 92 In the middle of the leaues there riseth vp a yellow welt,..shadowed all ouer with a wash of thin blew. **1877** BLACK *Green Past.* xliv, The valley was a plain of rich vegetation—long water-colour washes of yellow, and russet, and olive-green. **1879** STEVENSON *Trav. Donkey* (1886) 30 The intervening field of hills had fallen together into one broad wash of shadow. **1887** CONSTANCE C. HARRISON *Bar Harbor Days* xiii. 157 The summer sunshine fell like a wash of gold upon the shores of Mount Desert. **1891** G. E. SHELLEY *Catal. Birds Brit. Mus.* XIX. 456 Abdomen, thighs, and under tail-coverts white, with a very faint pink wash.

d. A thin coat of water-colour or distemper spread over a wall or similar surface; a preparation used for this purpose. Cf. WHITEWASH *sb.*

1698 FRYER *Acc. E. India & P.* 149 The Pillars from top to bottom being overlaid with a Golden Wash. **1826** SHERER *Notes & Refl. Ramble Germany* 127 The white and yellow washes on the walls looked fresh. **1849** MACAULAY *Hist. Eng.* I. iii. 348 The floors of the dining rooms..were coloured brown with a wash made of soot and small beer. **1859** JEPHSON *Brittany* viii. 105 The walls and pillars are all covered with a cold grey wash. **1884** *Macm. Mag.* Oct. 426/1 Syra is almost entirely a white town, relieved now and again by a dash of yellow wash. **1885** *Harper's Mag.* Mar. 547/1 The Pompeiian red..is only 'water wash'.

5. A solution applied to metals for producing a counterfeit appearance of gold or silver.

1697 COLLIER *Ess. Moral Subj.* II. 98 Imagination.. stamps Value and Significancy upon his Face, and tells the People he is to go for so much; who oftentimes, being deceived by the wash, never examin the Metal, but take him upon Content. **1861** *Act 24 & 25 Vict.* c. 99 §3 Whosoever shall gild or silver, or shall, with any Wash or Materials capable of producing the Colour or Appearance of Gold or of Silver,..wash, case over, or colour any Coin whatsoever.

II. Washing movement of water.

6. a. The washing of the waves upon the shore; surging movement of the sea or other water. *Neptune's salt wash* (quot. 1602) a bombastic periphrasis for 'the sea'.

[*c* **1050** *Suppl. Ælfric's Gloss.* in Wr.-Wülcker 179/35 *Aquarum alluuio*, wætera ʒewæsc. *Ibid.* 187/8 *Alluuium*, wæter-ʒewæsc.] **1579** GOSSON *Apol. Sch. Abuse* (Arb.) 65 Truth is..harde, and cannot be broke with washe. **1602** SHAKS. *Ham.* III. ii. 166 Full thirtie times hath Phœbus Cart gon round Neptunes salt Wash, and Tellus Orbed ground. **1698** FRYER *Acc. E. India & P.* 57 At the Entry into the Harbour only a Rock withstands the Washes. **1725** DE FOE *Voy. round World* (1840) 327 Their carpenters..raised their sides as well as they could to keep off the wash of the sea. **1733** W. ELLIS *Chiltern & Vale Farm.* 59 The wash and bash of Rains, and the violence of the Winter Winds, which are all fatal to this Ground. **1778** *Engl. Gazetteer* (ed. 2) s.v. *Watchet*, Great quantities of alabaster, which fall down the cliffs here, by the wash of the sea, are also sent to that city. **1855** TENNYSON *Brook* 194 Katie walks By the long wash of Australasian seas Far off. **1865** GOSSE *Land & Sea* (1874) 5 Here we were..facing the westerly breeze, and pitching and rolling in the wash of the sea. **1872** DANA *Corals* ii. 137 An important protection to the roof against the wash of the waters. **1894** HALL CAINE *Manxman* IV. xviii, The wash of the waves touched his feet.

transf. **1855** BROWNING *Two in Campagna* v, Silence and passion, joy and peace, An everlasting wash of air—Rome's ghost since her decease.

b. (*a*) A surge raised in the sea or other piece of water by the passage of a vessel.

1883 *Harper's Mag.* Feb. 393/1 We were steaming along splendidly now, sending up a fine wash and swash along the banks. **1884** *Ibid.* Feb. 344/2 The steam-launch..sends a 'wash' along the shore. **1890** R. C. LEHMANN *Harry Fludyer* 121 They were standing on the bank close to the water, and our boat raised a wash and wetted their feet.

(*b*) The air current caused by the passage of an aircraft.

1910 R. FERRIS *How it Flies* xx. 474 *Wash*, the air-currents flowing out diagonally from the sides of a moving aeroplane. **1931** *Flight* 9 Oct. 1012/1 Certain modifications have been suggested which are intended to reduce the wash from the tailplane on the rudder during a flat spin. **1972** *Daily Tel.* 9 Aug. 4/8 It was not that the hundreds of [helicopter] pilots just overflew the nudist colony, but some flew so low they knocked over tents with the wash from their rotor blades.

c. The sound of the surge of water.

1845 J. COULTER *Adv. Pacific* ix. 109, I..listened to the wash of the briny element on the beach. **1871** LONGF. *Life* (1891) III. 177 The low wash of the sea very soothing. **1873** BLACK *Pr. Thule* iii. 39 The wash of ripples along the coast could be heard. **1918** *Blackw. Mag.* June 717/2 The wash of the swell on rocks met my ear.

d. Wear or attrition due to the action of waves. Also, the removal or displacement of soil by rain and running water (in quot. 1835, a place where this occurs); freq. in *Comb.* with preceding sb., as in *rain-wash* s.v. RAIN *sb.*[1] 6, *sheet-wash* s.v. SHEET *sb.*[1] 12b, *soil wash* s.v. SOIL *sb.*[1] 10.

1791 SMEATON *Edystone L.* §78 To prevent that wash of the joints, that a very exposed situation might subject it to. **1835** J. H. INGRAHAM *South-West* II. 88 Bermuda grass is used with great success to check the progress of a wash. **1859** *Trans. Illinois Agric. Soc.* III. 412 Land lying in such a position as to protect it from wash..may be kept in constant cultivation. **1872** LOWELL *Dante* Writ. 1890 IV. 224 This three-arched bridge, still firm against the wash and wear of ages. **1913** [see *soil-binding* adj. s.v. SOIL *sb.*[1] 9]. **1959** G. H. DURY *Face of Earth* iii. 17 Rivers, surface-wash, and the downhill movement of solid rock combine to remove the substance of the land. **1972** R. J. SMALL *Study of Landforms* vi. 209 On the upper part of the slope the increased 'erosional' effect of wash away from the crest may tend to produce convexity of profile, and this may be exaggerated.. by soil creep.

7. a. A sandbank or tract of land alternately covered and exposed by the sea; a portion of an estuary admitting of being forded or crossed on foot at low tide. † *the Washes*, applied *spec.* to the fordable portion of the estuary between Lincolnshire and Norfolk; hence used as a name for the estuary itself, now called *the Wash*.

c **1440** *Promp. Parv.* 517/2 Wasche, watur or forde (*v.r.* forth), *vadum*. *a* **1548** HALL *Chron., Edw. VI*, 208b, King Edward..with all hast possible passed the wasshes..& came to the toune of Lynne. **1595** SHAKS. *John* v. vi. 41 Halfe my power this night..are taken by the Tide, These Lincolne-Washes haue deuoured them. **1601** HOLLAND *Pliny* III. xxvi. I. 71 As for the coast of Illyricum, it is pestred with more than a thousand [islands]; such is the nature of the sea, full of shelves and washes, with narrow chanels running betweene. **1611** COTGR. s.v. *Passade*, The swift course of the flowing, and ebbing of the sea, on the Sandes, or Washes. **1617** MORYSON *Itin.* III. 140 Upon the bay which Ptolomy names, *Æstuariam Metaris*, vulgarly called, the Washes, lieth the large Towne of Linne. *a* **1631** DONNE *Serm.* lxiv. (1640) 647 A washing begun in Baptisme,..Not such a washing, as the Washes have, which are those sands that are overflowed with the Sea at every Tide, and then lie dry, but [etc.]. **1641** PRYNNE *Disc. Prel. Tyrr.* ii. 93 Hee departed out of Chester..his friends conducted them over the washes which are dangerous. **1649** G. DANIEL *Trinarch., Rich. II*, ccliii, Mowbray, who had gone all the way along Vpon these Washes..Now to goe further, thought a Quick-sand sprung Might swallow him. **1681** W. ROBERTSON *Phraseol. Gen.* (1693) 1295 The washes, as in Lincolnshire; *Æstuaria*. **1722** DE FOE *Col. Jack* vii, There was no way now left, but that by the washes into Lincolnshire. **1740** *Phil. Trans.* XLI. 689 An Easterly Breeze, which the Borderers on the Coast of Lincolnshire and Norfolk call Tide-weather, and may be occasioned by the Vapours arising from the Tides, which then cover a vast Wash of Sands in their Neighbourhood. **1851** *Jrnl. R. Agric. Soc.* XII. II. 289 The great bay or wash, which forms the sole receptacle for the drainage waters, is so shallow.

†**b.** The portion of the shore washed by the waves. *Obs.*

1614 RALEGH *Hist. World* II. iii. §7. 259 Euen at the very brincke and wash of the Sea. *a* **1618** —— *Apol.* 15 The Towne being scated vpon the very Wash of the Sea. **1698** *Phil. Trans.* XX. 410 Some Vessels have been cast so far on the Shore, that..they have been from Twenty to Thirty Yards dry from the Wash of the Shore.

c. A low-lying tract of ground, often flooded, and interspersed with shallow pools and marshes.

1483 *Cath. Angl.* 414/2 A Wesche, *tesquum, in plurali tesqua*. **1601** HOLLAND *Pliny* III. i. I. 52 Within the washes and downes of Bœtis there is the town Nebrissa. **1794** VANCOUVER *Agric. Cambridge* 174 The crops on the interior commons and washes suffered extremely by these [wire worms, etc.] at first. **1866** KINGSLEY *Herew.* xxviii, Beyond Earith where now run the great washes of the Bedford Level. **1905** *Athenæum* 30 Dec. 902/1 The book records.. the enclosure of commons and washes, and the continuous advance of building operations.

d. *Western U.S.* The dry bed or portion of the bed of a winter torrent.

1894 *Amer. Rev. Reviews* Nov. 508/2 The center of it [Pachango Valley] is occupied with the broad sandy 'wash' characteristic of Southern California streams. **1897** *Outing* XXIX. 582/1 Temescal Wash is a mile wide and composed of sand and prickly pear cactus. **1904** *19th Cent.* Mar. 431 The bed of the wash, or dry valley bed, up which we were driving, was planted with corn.

8. A tract of shallow water, a lagoon. Also, a shallow pool or runnel formed by the overflow of a river, a backwater; a stream running across a road.

1530 PALSGR. 287/1 Wasshe of water, *marre*. **1545-6** LELAND *Itin.* (1745) I. *New Yr.'s Gift* p. xxii, There is almoste nother Cape, nor Bay, Haven, Creeke, or Peere, River or Confluence of Rivers, Breches, Waschis, Lakes, Meres, Fenny Waters, Montaynes, Valleis, Mores, [etc.]. **1592** GREENE *Def. Conny-catching* Wks. (Grosart) XI. 65 Jack..away he rides singing towardes Endfield [from Edmonton]: as he rode, he mette at the washes with the Miller. **1601** HOLLAND *Pliny* XXXI. iv. II. 410 The raine that fell caused all the washes arising from the river Nilus which watered the grounds, to be bitter. **1609** —— *Amm. Marcell.* 248 Conveying themselves over the washes and marishes in flotes and troughes of hollowed trees. **1610** FOLKINGHAM *Feudigr.* I. ii. 3 The other sort is digged vp in Fountaines, Riuers, Washes, Salt-Meeres, Sea-shoares. **1656** EARL MONM. tr. *Boccalini's Advts. fr. Parnass.* I. xxxix. 52 The glorious Venetian Liberty..was planted in those Washes. **1658** —— tr. *Paruta's Wars Cyprus* 109 The Washes, or Moorish grounds, whereon the City of Venice is placed. **1673** *Pleas. Treat. Witches* 53 With whom he travelled, till at last they came to a great wash; where the man profered the Monk..to carry him over on his back. **1695** THORESBY *Diary* (1830) I. 295 We..had some showers, which raised the washes upon the road to that height that passengers from London that were upon the road swam. **1782** COWPER *Gilpin* 135 Till he came unto the Wash Of Edmonton so gay. **1847** L. HUNT *Men, Women, & Bks.* I. iii. 41 The gutters were suddenly a torrent; the pavement a dancing wash. **1848** H. W. HERBERT *Field Sports U.S.* II. 28 The wide extent of salt marshes and meadows, interspersed with shallow land-locked washes and lagoons. **1857** HAWTHORNE *Eng. Note-bks.* (1870) II. 204 Along the base of the castle [Skipton].. flows a stream, but only a 'wash', whatever that may be. **1878** S. H. MILLER & SKERTCHLY *Fenland* vi. 158 Banks were made..enclosing a space called a Wash 'for the waters to bed in' in time of flood. **1884** *Auk* Oct. 356, I came to a wash a few feet wide and a foot or so deep.

III. 9. Waste water discharged after use in washing; liquid refuse. Also *fig.* Now *rare*.

c **1440** *Pallad. on Husb.* I. 1105 And all the wesshe out of thi bathis [L. *balnearum..eluvies*] The gardyn thorgh to go, therto no scathe is. **1797** BURKE *Reg. Peace* III. (1892) 192 If his Majesty had kept aloof from that wash and off-scouring of every thing that is low and barbarous in the world. **1833** HT. MARTINEAU *Brooke Farm* iii. 39 He advised..that the sweepings from the cottage floors,..and the wash and boilings of all sorts, should be thrown into it [the pit].

10. *Sc.* and *north.* Stale urine: used as a detergent and as a mordant.

Perhaps so called from its use in washing.

c **1480** HENRYSON *Sum Practysis of Med.* 48 This vntment is rycht ganand for ȝour awin vss, With reid nettill seid in strang wesche to steip. **1535** LYNDESAY *Satyre* 4146 Ane curtill queine..Of strang wesche scho will tak ane iurdane, And settis in the gyle-fat. **1546** —— *Death Beaton* etc. E ij, Thou false hereticke [Wishart], saydest that holy water is not so good as washe, & such lyke. **1703** THORESBY *Let. to Ray, Wesh*, or *wash*, Urine. **1737** RAMSAY *Sc. Prov.* (1750) 65 Learn your goodame to kirn wash. **1743** in R. Maxwell *Sel. Trans. Agric.* 368 Put into your Copper a little stale Wash, which will make your Wald spend, and raise your Colour. **1882** CROOKES *Dyeing* 19 Stale urine..known in Lancashire as 'lant', and in Yorkshire as 'wash' or 'weeting', owes its action to the carbonate of ammonia formed by the decomposition of urea.

11. a. Kitchen swill or brewery refuse as food for swine: = HOGWASH, PIG'S WASH. (So G. dial. *wäsch*.)

1585 HIGINS *Junius' Nomencl.* 51/1 *Porcus colluuiaris*,..an hogge fed with wash and draffe. **1592** BRETON *Pilgr. Parad.* (Grosart) 22/2 The sweetest wine, is but as swinish wash, Unto the water, of the well of life. **1594** SHAKS. *Rich. III* v. ii. 9 The wretched, bloody, and vsurping Boare,..Swilles your warm blood like wash, and makes his trough In your embowel'd bosomes. **1665** SOUTH *Serm.* (Prov. iii. 17) 18 As different as the silence of an Archimedes in the study of a Problem, and the stillness of a Sow at her wash. **1732** *Acc. Workhouses* 79 They have a pig or two brought in, to live upon their wash, and dregs. **1851-61** MAYHEW *Lond. Labour* II. 132/1 The hogs' food obtained by these street-folk, or, as I most frequently heard it called, the 'wash'. **1869** BLACKMORE *Lorna D.* xxxii, She..pointed to the great bock of wash, and riddlings, and brown hulkage. **1896** BARING-GOULD *Dartmoor Idylls* v. 129 When she carried the sow her pail of wash.

fig. **1655** FULLER *Ch. Hist.* I. 16 Clean Stomacks will be better satisfied with one drop of the Milk of Truth, then foul Feeders..with a Trough of Wash, mingled with the water of Fabulous Inventions.

b. Liquid food for other animals.

1847 W. C. L. MARTIN *Ox* 96/2 The mangers extend along the whole length of each row of cattle; these are for the wash, or fluid food;..The wash..is very nutritious, as it contains the finer particles of the ground malt.

IV. 12. a. Matter washed away by running water; solid particles carried away by a stream and deposited as sediment; alluvial deposit.

1707 MORTIMER *Husb.* 86 The Wash of Pastures, Fields, Commons, Roads [etc.]..where..Rain water hath a long time settled.., [is] of very great advantage to all sorts of Land. **1757** [BURKE] *Europ. Settlem. Amer.* VI. i. II. 60 In these plains, the soil augmented by the wash of the mountains for so many ages, is prodigiously fertile. **1860** MOTLEY *Netherl.* (1868) I. i. 8 A territory, the mere wash of three great rivers. **1865** DICKENS *Mut. Fr.* I. xiii, 'Tastes like the wash of the river.' 'Are you so familiar with the flavour of the wash of the river?' **1883** *Modern Rev.* IV. 682 The land..has been built up out of the wash of ancient rivers and the sands of vanished seas. **1888** J. D. WHITNEY *Names & Places* 125 (Cent.) The debris-piles which stretch along the lower slopes of the ranges in the Cordilleran Region are locally known as washes. **1895** BARING-GOULD *Noémi* x, The course taken by the flood is easily recognisable by this fact—that it has left its wash on the tops of the plateau, where to the present day lies a film of caoline.

b. *Mining.* 'A formation of gravel, etc. over an abraded coal-seam'. (Eng. Dial. Dict.)

1882 [see DRIFTING *vbl. sb.* 2]. **1888** W. E. NICHOLSON *Gloss. Coal Trade Northumb.* (E.D.D.), The Team Wash, which extends from Dunston on the river Tyne and, following the line of the river Team, to Tursdale,..and washes out several seams of coal in its course.

V. 13. a. (See quot. 1728.) ? *Obs.*

1619 DONNE *Serm.* 18 Apr. (1661) III. 270 Of this Gold (this virtue of Repentance) there is no Mine in the Earth; in the books of Philosophers, no doctrine of Repentance; this Gold is for the most part in the washes. **1728** CHAMBERS *Cycl.*, *Washings*, or *Washes*, among Goldsmiths, Coiners, &c. are the Lotions whereby they recover the Particles of Gold and Silver out of the Ashes, Earths, Sweepings, &c.

b. Soil from which gold (or diamonds) can be extracted by washing.

a **1875** HECTOR in *Offic. Handbk. N. Zealand* 171 Gold was obtained on terraces along the sides of the valley, and in the river bed, the wash everywhere resting on water-worn bars and ledges of greenstone, [etc.]. **1879** ATCHERLY *Trip Boërland* 143 We had extracted about a hundred-weight of wash. **1880** FISON & HOWITT *Kamilaroi* 272 The great 'reef washes' of Ballarat are to be referred to the period of depression. **1886** *N.Z. Herald* 28 May 6/7 Last week, after driving about 80 feet, they struck payable wash. The wash is about two feet thick, lying on a slate bottom. **1890** *Goldfields of Victoria* 7 A company has been formed to work the 'first floor' which shows gold and tin in 10 feet of wash. **1897** *Daily News* 30 Nov. 9/5 Inverell Diamond Fields.—.. 101 carats of diamonds from five loads washed. Wash improves as development progresses.

VI. Watery infusion or mixture.

14. Originally, the partially fermented wort remaining after ale or beer has been brewed from it; this wort as subjected to further fermentation in order that ardent spirit may be distilled from it. In later use, malt or other fermentable substance or mixture of substances steeped in water to undergo fermentation preparatory to distillation.

a **1700** B. E. *Dict. Cant. Crew*, *Wash*, After-wort. **1701** LUTTRELL *Brief Rel.* (1857) V. 55 That 2*d.* per gallon be laid on all low wines or spirits drawn from brewers wash. **1709** *Lond. Gaz.* No. 4624/1 An Act to Prohibit the Exportation of..Worts and Wash drawn from Malted Corn. **1753** *Chambers' Cycl.* Suppl., *Wash*, the distillers name for the fermentable liquor, made by dissolving the proper subject for fermentation and distillation in common water. **1815** *Ann. Reg., Chron.* 43 Besides the still, a considerable quantity of wash, and some low wines, were found. **1825** *Gentl. Mag.* XCV. I. 215 The molasses are conveyed by channels into a large vat in the still house, to which a certain quantity of water is added, and in this state the liquor is called 'wash'. **1880** *Act 43 & 44 Vict.* c. 24 §5 (1) No person may, without being licensed..(*b*) Brew or make wort or wash. **1903** *Times* 22 Aug. 8/6, 200 gallons of 'wash'—liquor prepared with sugar, barley, flour, &c. **1908** *Westm. Gaz.* 23 Mar. 2/1 The liquid from which spirit is distilled is termed 'wash', and may be made from almost anything. If the distiller be righteous, it is made from malt, or, in the case of Irish whisky, malt and unmalted grain.

15. a. Washy or vapid liquor. Also *fig.*, vapid discourse or writing.

1548 UDALL etc. *Erasm. Par. Luke* iii. 15-18 My doctrine is but verai washe, if it be compared vnto his doctrine [Erasm. *Mea doctrina diluta est, si ad illius doctrinam conferatur*]. **1819** W. S. ROSE *Lett. N. Italy* I. 108 A remedy ..is thought to have been discovered in coffee; not the vile and vapid wash which is usually made in England,..but [etc.]. **1839** RAYSON *Poems* (1858) 49 Nae mair weaste yer money on ony sec wesh. **1895** J. NICHOLSON *Kilwuddie* 166 (E.D.D.) We kentna the goo' o' the wash we drink noo, That puir, feckless skiddle ca'd tea. **1911** R. BROOKE *Let.* in *Memoir* (1918) p. lxx, To remove it [the sonnet called *Lust*] would be to overbalance the book still more in the direction of unimportant prettiness. There's plenty of that sort of wash in the other pages for the readers who like it.

b. Nonsense, rubbish, 'twaddle'. Cf. senses 11 a *fig.* and 15 a *fig.*, and HOGWASH b.

1913 A. LUNN *Harrovians* xvii. 287 The Housemasters call their Sixth together at intervals and gass 'em... You know the kind of wash. **1933** G. HEYER *Why shoot Butler?* vi. 86 Not strictly the clean potato, is it?.. Guest in the man's house, you know. The Public School Spirit, and Playing for the Side, and all that wash.

VII. 16. The blade of an oar.

1769 FALCONER *Dict. Marine* (1780) D d 4, That part of the oar..which enters into the water, is called the blade, or wash.

VIII. Senses of obscure or doubtful origin.

17. A measure for oysters and whelks.

1481–90 *Howard Househ. Bks.* (Roxb.) 370 Item, for ij. wash and di. of oystres at Wevenho, iiij. d. **1574** in *Rep. MSS. Ld. Middleton* (1911) 444 To Walter Tayler for viij washe of oysters and for charges from Dunesbye, vj s. viij d. **1661** BLOUNT *Glossogr.* (ed. 2), A *Wash of Oysters* is ten Strikes. **1677** *Maldon* (Essex) *Borough Deeds* Bundle 101. no. 2, Paid for a wash of oysters presented to a gent. in London vpon the town's account. **1851** MAYHEW *Lond. Labour* I. 163 The trade in whelks is one of which the costermongers have the undisputed monopoly..this shell-fish is bought by the measure (a double peck or gallon), half measure, or wash. A wash is four measures. **1879** *Encycl. Brit.* IX. 256/2 Each smack takes about 40 wash of whelks with her for the voyage. **1882** *Standard* 26 Sept. 2/2 Whelks are sold by the 'wash', a wash consisting of 21 quarts and one pint,..worth on an average four shillings.

†18. Some part of a horse's eye. *Obs.*

1639 T. DE GREY *Compl. Horsem.* II. viii. (1656) 293, I have oft times seen the French Marishalls take up the wash of the eye, with a Spanish needle, threeded with a double brown threed,..But I cannot commend this manner of curing the Haw, for by that means he cutteth away the wash of the eye, which indeed is the beauty of the eye. **1737** BRACKEN *Farriery Impr.* (1756) I. 141 Farriers taking up the Wash of the Eye with a Needle and Thread.

19. The underground den of a beaver or a bear.

1809 A. HENRY *Trav.* 128 It [the beaver's house] is always entirely surrounded with water; but, in the banks adjacent, the animal provides holes or washes, of which the entrance is below the surface, and to which it retreats on the first alarm. **1877** COUES *Fur-bearing Anim.* ii. 52 They [wolverenes] bring forth in burrows under ground, probably old Bear washes, and have four or five young at a birth.

20. *slang.* **a.** *Printers'.* An act of 'washing' (see WASH *v.* 20 a).

1841 SAVAGE *Dict. Printing* 810.

b. *Stock Exchange.* A fictitious sale of securities by a broker who has a commission from an intending buyer and also from an intending seller, and who instead of effecting the two transactions separately, in the interest of each client, simply transfers from the one account to the other, the difference going to his own profit.

1891 in *Century Dict.*

IX. 21. *attrib.* and *Comb.*, in sense 14, designating various vessels in which the distiller's 'wash' is contained or elaborated, as ***wash-back***, ***-batch***, ***-charger***, ***-cistern***, ***-heater***, ***-warmer***; in sense 11, as ***wash-buyer***. Also **wash-bag**, a small waterproof bag for holding toilet articles; a sponge-bag; **wash-basket**, (*a*) *U.S.* see quot. 1881; (*b*) a basket for clothes sent to the wash; **wash-bill** *U.S.* = *washing-bill*; **wash coat**, an undercoat, esp. one for improving or preparing the surface rather than giving a colour; **wash-day**, the day for the washing of clothes in a household = *washing-day*; **wash-fast** *a.*, that can be washed without losing colour or dye; so **wash-fastness**; **wash-land**, a tract of land periodically overflowed by a river; **wash-linen**, linen sent to the wash; **wash-plain**, a tract of land formed by alluvial deposits; **wash primer**, a wash coat for use on metal; **wash-sale**, see quot. 1891 (cf. sense 20); cf. WASHED *ppl. a.* 1 f; **†wash-tumbler**, ? a glass for holding washes for the complexion or the teeth; **†wash-yard**, ? the yard attached to a wash-house. See also WASH *v.* 21 b.

1839 URE *Dict. Arts* 403 Before the fermented wort goes into the still, a calculation is made of the quantity of wash drawn from the *wash back, and which is first pumped into what is called the *wash charger. **1972** E. THORPE *Night I caught Santa Fé Chief* i. 11, I took the *wash-bag out of the grip; the face-cloth was slightly damp. **1980** G. LORD *Fortress* i. 10 She..picked up her wash-bag. She went..to the bathroom. **1881** E. INGERSOLL *Oyster Industry* 249 **Wash-bàsket*, a rude splint basket, circular, shallow, holding about a peck, and with a high bale-handle (Rhode Island). **1903** *Daily Chron.* 26 June 3/7 The family wash-basket. **1696–7** *Act 8 & 9 Will. III* c. 19 §10 That no common Distiller..shall..erect or sett upp any Tun Cask *Wash-batch Copper Still or other Vessell for the brewing making or keeping of any Worts Wash [etc.]. **1873** B. HARTE *Fiddletown* 26 Finding his *wash-bill made out on the unwritten side of one of these squares, and delivered to him with his weekly clean clothes. **1851** MAYHEW *Lond. Labour* II. 149 There are a number of *wash-buyers in the suburbs, who purchase..their stock..at gentlemen's houses, and retail it..to those who feed pigs. **1839** *Wash charger [see *wash back*]. **1853** URE *Dict. Arts* I. 5 The *wash-cistern.. should be supported on a shelf near the ceiling of the stove-heated apartment. **1951** M. HESS *Paint Film Defects* 385 On wood which has been treated with water-stains the application of *wash coats of a 5 to 8 per cent. shellac solution seem [*sic*] to be popular. **1960** *McGraw-Hill Encycl. Sci. & Technol.* X. 593/1 Primers are always pigmented. In clear finishes, the coat which performs this function is described as a sealer, an undercoater, or a wash coat. **1961** J. G. E. HOLLOWAY *Mod. Painter & Decorator* (ed. 5) I. 152 Often the application of a full coat of plastic paint will be preceded by a wash coat..to produce a ground of uniform colour. **1846** *Southern Lit. Messenger* XII. 598/1 Thursday is *wash-day. **1864** MRS. A. GATTY *Parables Nat.* Ser. IV. 9 He had watered it..with soap-suds on a wash-day. **1963** A. J. HALL *Textile Sci.* iv. 184 This method of dyeing can be used to produce *wash-fast shades. **1977** *Private Eye* 4 Mar. 21/1 (Advt.), T-shirts and sweater shirts printed to your design in wash-fast dyes, permanent whites, gold, silver or velvet flock finishes. **1962** J. T. MARSH *Self-Smoothing Fabrics* xx. 334 The thermosetting resin..gave moderate recovery but some discolouration and great embrittlement, together with a lack of *wash-fastness. **1839** URE *Dict. Arts* 1182 The water..is carried off by the pipe m, through the vessel n, called the *wash-heater. **1794** VANCOUVER *Agric. Cambridge* 191 The *washlands amount to about three thousand acres. **1878** S. H. MILLER & SKERTCHLY *Fenland* i. 6 Along this course..are wash-lands which receive the waters of the river when it overflows. **1883** *Eng. Illustr. Mag.* Nov. 70/2 In some cases the rivers have even inner and outer banks, with washlands between them. **1901** OSLER *Princ. Med.* I. (ed. 4) 5 The infection [of typhoid fever] may be spread by means of clothing and *wash-linen. **1899** *Nature* 13 July 259/1 These '*wash plains' or stream deltas and fans constitute a very important feature in the Pleistocene deposits of the region. **1961** WEBSTER, *Wash primer. **1963** *Times* 22 Apr. 6/5 Zinc tetroxychromate is the most commonly used pigment in the so-called 'wash primers' for metals, which concurrently etch and coat the metal surface before the application of other paint coats to ensure good adhesion. **1973** Wash-primer [see *polyvinyl acetal* s.v. POLYVINYL a]. **1848** W. ARMSTRONG *Stocks* 19 These *wash sales are of course void between parties. They are of very frequent occurrence and very mischievous. **1891** *Century Dict.*, *Wash sales*, in the stock-market, feigned sales, made for the sake of advantage gained by the report of a fictitious price. **1908** *Times* 26 Aug. 5/5 In the words of the *Evening Post*..since 1901 the two terms 'wash sales' and 'matched orders' have become a familiar explanation of the erratic movements of prices on the Exchange. **1774** *Pennsylv. Gaz.* 14 Dec. 1/1 Glass. Cut candlesticks, decanters, *wash tumblers, wine glasses, [etc.]. **1900** SADTLER *Handbk. Industr. Org. Chem.* (ed. 3) 220 Interposing between the still and the refrigerating apparatus a '*wash-warmer', or vessel filled with the liquid ready for distillation. *c* **1625** in W. Robinson *Hackney* (1842) I. 111 [Inventory of Goods] In the Wash-house..In the *Wash-yarde. Item—One great cesterne of leade, [etc.].

†wash, *a. Obs.* [? f. WASH *v.*; perh. in part a corruption of WALSH *a.*] Washy, weak, tender.

1548 UDALL *Erasm. Par. Luke* xii. 49–53 It is no washe doctrine, ne worldely [Erasm. *non est diluta, nec humana doctrina*], that I haue brought down from heauen. **1607** MARSTON *What you Will* I. i, But how long doth this perfume of sweete Madam last? Faith tis but a wash sent. *a* **1616** BEAUM. & FL. *Bonduca* IV. i, Their bodies of so weak and wash a temper, a rough-pac'd bed will shake 'em all to pieces. **1624** FLETCHER *Rule a Wife* III. i, Tis a wash knave, he will not keep his flesh well. **1639** T. DE GREY *Compl. Horsem.* II. iii. (1656) 104 They are naturally slow, dull, heavy, and nesh or wash of their flesh.

wash (wɒʃ), *v.* Pa. t. and pa. pple. **washed** (wɒʃt). Forms: *Inf.* and *present stem*: 1 wæscan, wacsan, waxan, wacxan, waxsan, 2–6 wasche, wasse, 2–7 wasshe, 3 was(s)ce, weasche, 3–4 was(e, waass, 3–5, 6 *Sc.* wass, 3–5 wassche, 3–6 wasch, 4 whasche, 4–5 wach(e, wasch(s)che, wassh, 5 vasshe, whas, 7 *Sc.* vash, 3–7 washe, 3– wash; 4 waysch(e, waiisse, wayss, 4–5 wais(s)che, wais(s)he, wayssh(e, waisse, 4–6 wayshe, waysse, weische, weysshe, weysch, 6 weish; (chiefly *north.* and *Sc.*) 2–6 wesche, 3–5 wess(e, 4–5 wessch(e, 4–6 wessh(e, vesch(e, 4–7 wesch, 5 whess, 5–7 weshe, 9 *dial.* wesh; also 4 wisshe, whosshe, 5 wosche, wosshe, 6 *Sc.* woucht, 6–7 wysch(e. *Pa. t.* α. 1 wósc, 2–4 wosch, 4 woisse, 4–5 wossch(e, wosh(e, wossh(e, 4–5, 6 *Sc.* wosche, 5 woschsse, *Sc.* wousche, 6 *Sc.* woushe, 7 *Sc.* woosh. β. 1 wéox, 2 weosc, 2–3 weis, 2–4 wess(e, 2–5 wesch, wessh, 3 weosch(s, wes, 3–4 wex(s, weiss(e, 3–5, 6 *Sc.* wesche, 4 we(s)chs, weesche, weysche, 4–5 wessch(e, wesh(e, 4–6 wesshe, 5 weeshe, (*pl.* whesshen), 6 *Sc.* weisch(e, 9 *Sc.* weesh, weish; 3–4 wasch, was, 4–5 wasche, wassh(e; 2–3 wuesh, 3 wuchs, (*pl.* wuschschen), 3–5 wusch, 4 wuesch, 6 *Sc.* wus(c)he, 9 *Sc.* wush; 3–4 wis, 4 wysch, 4–5, 6 *Sc.* wisch(e, 4–5 wissch(e, wissh(e, wys(s)che, wysh, wyssh(e, 5 wishe, whisse, (*pl.* wissen), 7 *Sc.* wyshe. *Pa. pple.* 1 -wæscen, -wahsen, -waxen, 2 (i)wasse, 2–3 (i)wasshen, 2–5 waschen, 3 weaschen, 3–4 wassen, 3–5 (i)wasche, 4 wasshin, (i)washe, whasche, wahche, 4–5 wassche(n, -yn, (y)wasshe, wasshun, whasshen, 4–6 wasshen, 5 was(c)hyn, wassh, wasch, whassche, 6 wasz(s)hen, *Sc.* waschin, 7 *Sc.* washine, 3–9 (now *arch.* and *dial.*) washen; 2 (i)wesscen, 2–5, 6 *Sc.* weschen, 3–4 wessen, 4 wesche, (y)wesse, 5 wessch, (y)wesh, wesshe, (y)whess, weshen, 5, 6 *Sc.* weschin, -yn, 6 *Sc.* veschin(e; 4 waysen, 4–5 waische(n, -un, -yn, wayschen, waissche(n, waisshe(n, wayshun, weische(n, weysche, 5 waishe, waisch; 8 *Sc.* wush. *Weak pa. t.* and *pa. pple.* 3–4 wassed, 4–5 wascht, 4–6 wasched, wasshed, wesshed, etc.; 5 wesht, *Sc.* wecht; 4–5 washid, 6 washte, 7 washd, 6–8 washt, 7–9 wash'd, 5– washed. [A Com. Teut. vb. (not recorded in Gothic), originally strong: OE. *wæscan*, *wascan*, also by metathesis *waxan*, pa. t. pl. *wóxon*, *wéocson*, pa. pple. *-wæscen*, corresponds to OFris. **waska* (E. and N.Fris. *waske*, W.Fris. *waskje*), OS., OLow Frankish *wascan* (Du. *wasschen*, pa. t. *wiesch*, pa. pple. *gewasschen*), OHG. *wascan*, pa. t. *wuosc*, pa. pple. *giwascan* (MHG. *waschen*, *weschen*, mod.G. *waschen*, pa. t. *wusch*, pa. pple. *gewaschen*), ON. (rare) *vaska*, conjugated weak (Sw. *vaska*, Da. *vaske*):—OTeut. ***waskan**:— ***watskan** f. root ***wat-** as in WATER *sb.*

It is uncertain whether the original conjugation was of the reduplicating type (OE. pa. t. *wéosc* = Du. *wiesch*) or of the ablaut type (OE. *wósc* = OHG. *wuosc*). In English the weak conjugation appears occasionally in the 14th c., but the strong forms prevailed till the close of the 16th c., after which they seldom occur exc. in dialects.]

I. To cleanse by means of water. Also with compl. adj., ***to wash white, clean.***

1. a. *trans.* To cleanse, remove the dirt from (something) by affusion of or immersion in water.

In OE. the verb was almost confined to the specific use 2 below. For the washing of vessels, and for the washing of the human body, the word used was *þwéan*.

900 in Thorpe *Dipl. Angl. Sax.* (1865) 145 Hi sculan waxan sceap. *c* **1000** ÆLFRIC *Levit.* i. 9 And waxan þæt innewerde and þa fet [of the burnt offering]. *c* **1000** *Ags. Gosp.* Luke v. 2 Ða fisceras eodon, & woxon heora net. *c* **1205** LAY. 10182 Heo..wascen þa waȝes [*c* **1275** wassen þe wowes]. **13..** *St. Alexius* 311 (Laud MS. 108) As he wessch here dissches. **1387** TREVISA *Higden* III. 315 Diogenes wisshe [*v.rr.* wische, wysch] wortes in a tyme. *Ibid.* VI. 403 Sche wolde take þe schoon of here sustres priveliche by nyȝte and wasche [*v.rr.* wasse, wayssche] hem and smere hem. **1412–20** LYDG. *Chron. Troy.* II. 751 It [*sc.* the conduit water] made a ful purgacioun Of al ordure & fylþes in þe toun, Waschyng þe stretis as þei stod a rowe. *c* **1430** *Two Cookery-bks.* 18 Pyke hem clene, & skrape hem, & Wasshem clene. *Ibid.* 114 Nym ye ris, whess hem clene. *c* **1449** PECOCK *Repr.* II. xiv. 230 A good huswijf..now sche sethith, now sche rostith, now sche weischith disschis. **1520** in *Archæologia* XXV. 437 For wayshyng of the flocke at Frynge iij s. iiij d. **1617** MORYSON *Itin.* I. 24 Water..for washing of glasses. *a* **1722** LISLE *Husb.* (1757) 317 In Kent..they wash their sheep in the following manner. **1764** ELIZA MOXON *Engl. Housew.* (ed. 9) 175 Take cockles at a full moon and wash 'em. **1773** J. CAMPBELL *Mod. Faulconry* 199 When you give her casting of flannel or cotton, take care to have them washen as clean as they can be. **1834** DICKENS *Sk. Boz*, *Boarding-ho.* ii, The second-floor front was scrubbed, and washed, and flannelled. **1849** LEVER *Con Cregan* xviii, Carriages, too, were washing, and high-bred horses standing out to be groomed. **1861** FLOR. NIGHTINGALE *Nursing* (ed. 2) 61 In the sick room, the doctor should always be asked..at what hour he chooses the floor to be washed. **1905** R. BAGOT *Passport* xxvii. 295 We could talk afterwards —while Ernana is washing the dishes.

†b. Prov. ***to wash a wall of loam, a brick or tile*** (= L. *laterem lavare*), to labour in vain. Cf. 3 d.

1586 HOOKER *Serm.* ii. §19 But we wash a wall of lome; we labor in vaine. **1612** *Two Noble K.* III. v. 41 We have, As learned Authours utter, washd a Tile. **1779** WARNER in Jesse *Selwyn & Contemp.* (1844) IV. 263, I wish I could make him feel as he ought, but one may as well wash a brick.

c. Naut. ***to wash a ship***: see quot. Also *absol.* ? *Obs.*

1644 MANWAYRING *Sea-mans Dict.* 113 *To Wash a Ship.* That is used at sea, when we cannot come aground, or careene-her: we make her heeled-over with her Ordnance and men, upon the yard-arms to a side, and so wash that side and scrape it (so much as is out of the water, which is commonly some 5, or 6 strakes). **1666**, **1720** [see TALLOW *v.* 1 b]. **1679** *Lond. Gaz.* No. 1445/1 They will Wash and Tallow, and then take their course to the Westward.

†d. Fishing. ***to wash off***: to wash (the net) after a day's work. Also *absol.* *Obs.*

1630 in Binnell *Descr. Thames* (1758) 73 Upon Saturday Sun set, to wash off his Net, hale up and go home. *Ibid.* 77 That no Trawler do fish..upon the Saturday after Sun-rising, but to wash off, hale up, and go home.

e. ***to wash out***: to cleanse the interior of (a vessel).

1827 FARADAY *Chem. Manip.* ii. (1842) 54 It is requisite that it [the bottle] be washed out after every experiment, the last two or three rinsings being made with distilled water. **1899** *Allbutt's Syst. Med.* VIII. 757 A tube of convenient size open at the top or sides so that it can be properly washed-out.

f. ***to wash up***: (i) to wash (table utensils) after a meal. Also *absol.*

1751 F. COVENTRY *Pompey the Little* II. xiii. 241 When he had done sipping his Tea, he used to wash up the Cups with the most orderly Exactness. **1820** J. SEVERN *Let.* 17 Dec. in Keats *Lett.* (1958) II. 363, I am obliged to wash up—cook —& read to Keats all day. **1837** J. MORIER *Abel Allnutt* xx. 116 That Betsy might be allowed to come in and help to 'wash up'. **1853** DICKENS *Bleak Ho.* xlix, Sitting in state to see the room cleared, the hearth swept, and the dinner-service washed up and polished in the back yard. **1905** R. BAGOT *Passport* xxiii. 233 His supper over, and Ernana having retired into the kitchen to wash up.

(ii) *fig.* To bring to a conclusion; to end or finish (something). *U.S. slang.*

1925 *World* (N.Y.) 25 Oct. II. 3/1 'That guy might be all right if he washed up [*sc.* washed, cleaned himself],' commented Buck... Just then the stage manager called out: 'What will I do with this act, Mr. Ziegfeld?' 'Wash up him and the bird,' said Flo [Ziegfeld] and that was the last of the Italian and his trained canary... Hype Igoe, the World's sporting writer, heard of the incident..and in commenting ..upon Frank Moran, heavy weight pugilist, advised that matchmakers 'wash him up'. The phrase caught the sporting fancy..and has become a colloquial fixture..as a meaty synonym for finals and farewell. **1929** *Sat. Even. Post* 2 Nov. 24/3 'I had an idea,' he explained... 'Just came to me, riding back. I think I know how I can wash it up.'.. He would write it now tonight! **1940** J. O'HARA *Pal Joey* (1952) 65 They said act of God and fire etc. wash up a contract automatically. **1972** D. DELMAN *Sudden Death* iv. 98 That man washed himself up with me because he couldn't keep his big, fat, fairy's mouth shut.

g. ***to wash down***: to wash from top to bottom or from end to end.

1877 STABLES *Pract. Kennel Guide* 129 A portion of carbolic acid should be used with the water you wash down the yard with. **1898** *Jrnl. Sch. Geog.* (U.S.) Oct. 300 The waters of the bay are so foul that..ships which visit Rio..do not wash down their decks..during their stay in port. **1901** G. DOUGLAS *House with Green Shutters* 14 Gilmour..was washing down the legs of a horse.

h. *fig.* In the game of mah-jong, to shuffle (the tiles).

1926 A. CHRISTIE *Murder of Roger Ackroyd* xvi. 196 Caroline got out the Mah Jong box and poured out the tiles upon the table. 'Washing the tiles,' said the colonel. **1929** *Encycl. Brit.* XIV. 677/1 All the tiles are..put face downward on the table and thoroughly shuffled or 'washed'. **1977** 'J. LE CARRÉ' *Hon. Schoolboy* xiv. 319 Jerry heard a ritual clicking as the habitual mah-jong party washed the pieces before distributing them.

i. *absol.* To wash table utensils as opposed to drying them. Cf. DRY *v.* 1 c, WIPE *v.* 1 c.

1943 L. I. WILDER *Those Happy Golden Years* xxi. 192 Neither of you need worry about the dishes... I'll wash and Grace will wipe. **1958** J. CANNAN *And be a Villain* vii. 150 Evadne..insisted on washing while Laura dried. **1962** M. DUFFY *That's how it Was* xiii. 115 Billy washes, Arthur wipes, you put away. **1978** *Listener* 13 Apr. 483/1 Let's pack away the tea. I'll wash, you dry.

2. a. To cleanse (soiled clothes, wool, etc.) by rubbing in water, with soap or some equivalent. Also *to wash clean, white.* ***to wash through***, to wash (a garment) by hand, often individually and hastily.

c **900** tr. *Bæda's Hist.* I. xxvii. (1890) 84 He þa ærest bebead, þæt heo heora hrægl woosce & clænsode. *c* **1200** *Trin. Coll. Hom.* 57 Sume bereð sole cloð to þe watere forto wasshen it clene. *a* **1225** *Ancr. R.* 324 Wule a weob beon, et one cherre, mid one watere wel ibleched, oðer a sol cloð hwit iwaschen? **1340** *Ayenb.* 236 Ase linene kertel erþan hi by huyte uelezipe him behoueþ þet he by ybeate and ywesse. **1377** LANGL. *P. Pl.* B. XIII. 315 Þi best cote..Hath many moles and spottes, it moste ben ywasshe. *c* **1450** *Two Cookery-bks.* 84 Take hit vppe in a faire lynnen cloth that is clene wasshen. **1497** HALYBURTON *Ledger* (1867) 149 Item ffor iiij men to weysch it [the wool] and dry it,..3 s. **1522** *Burgh Rec. Stirling* (1887) I. 17 That na persoun nor personis woucht ony maner of clais at the toune bouirn.. undir the pain of..brekin of the weschal that tha wous with. **1538** ELYOT *Dict.*, *Radicula*, an herbe, the iuyce whereof is good to wasshe woulle. **15..** *Wyf of Auchtirmwchty* 94 He trailit the fowll scheitis doun the gait, Thocht to haif weschit [*Ramsay* wush] thame on ane stane. **1842** MACAULAY *Ess.*, *Fredk. Gt.* (1897) 814 'See,' exclaimed Voltaire, 'what a quantity of his dirty linen the King has sent me to wash!' **1868** LOUISA M. ALCOTT *Little Women* ii, How nice my handkerchiefs look, don't they? Hannah washed and ironed them for me. **1936** N. STREATFEILD *Ballet Shoes* ix. 136 I'll just wash your jersey through. **1968** M. WOODHOUSE *Rock Baby* xvii. 168 'Isn't that one of my spare shirts?'.. 'Sorry. Yes it is. But I washed it through for you.'

b. *to be (a) washing*: to be getting washed.

1600 ROWLANDS *Lett. Humours Blood* v. 72 Except his Shirt's a washing. *a* **1704** T. BROWN *Pleas. Lett. to Gentl.* Wks. 1709 III. II. 16 Their Commodes and Smocks were *washing* below by the Landlady of the House.

c. ***to wash one's dirty linen at home, in public***: said *fig.* with reference to domestic quarrels or grievances, the discussion of which is best confined to the family circle.

Cf. F. *Il faut laver son linge sale en famille.*

1867 TROLLOPE *Last Chron. Barset* xliv, I do not like to trouble you with my private affairs;—there is nothing, I think, so bad as washing one's dirty linen in public. **1891** *Law Times* XCI. 21/2 It is ridiculous that grave disputes.. should be kept waiting while the dirty linen of high society is..washed in public. **1895** [see LINEN *sb.*].

d. †***to wash up***, ? to wash with vigorous rubbing. ***to wash out***, to rinse so as to remove soap or other substance from the web of the stuff.

1756 F. HOME *Exper. Bleaching* 214 Give it a boil or two at most, and then wash it up while the gross body of the lime is in the substance of the cloth. **1876** *Encycl. Brit.* IV. 688/2 They [dyed calicoes] are treated with a hot solution of soap; they are then washed out, squeezed, and again soaped.

e. *absol.* To wash clothes (as an occupation or as part of one's household duties). Also, to wash the clothes of a household periodically.

1591 SHAKS. *Two Gent.* III. i. 313 Item, she can wash and scoure. **1623** COCKERAM II, She that Washeth. Lauatrix. **1671** H. M. tr. *Erasm. Colloq.* 420 What wilt thou do to the Germans, who wash scarce twice in a year? **1725** *View Lond. & Westminster* 9 They were extraordinary Oeconomists, brew'd their own Beer, wash'd at home. **1828** *Lights & Shades* I. 242 Mrs. Stevens's things hanging out again! I thought she washed last week. **1837** DICKENS *Pickw.* xxxiii, Betsy Martin, widow,..Goes out charing and washing by the day. **1854** SURTEES *Handley Cr.* x. (1901) I. 83 Lucy Sandey would mangle, wash, and clear-starch.

f. *trans.* To wash clothes for (a customer or lodger). *dial.*

1786 J. WOODFORDE *Diary* 31 May (1926) II. 247, I paid her up to this Day and told her I would get another to wash him. **1795** VANCOUVER *Agric. Essex* 82 They cook, wash, lodge, and find them [the workmen] in small beer for 2s. per week. **1886** *S.W. Linc. Gloss.* s.v., She has weshed him ever sin he came. **1895** 'ROSEMARY' *Under Chilterns* ii. 81 That'd be nigh enough for me to wash 'im an' mend 'im.

g. *absol.* To have one's clothes washed; to pay the laundress's charges. *jocular nonce-use.*

1837 DICKENS *Pickw.* lv, It was by very many degrees the best professional job he had ever had, and one on which he boarded, lodged, and washed for six months afterwards.

h. *trans.* Of water or other agent: To have the property of cleansing (clothes) easily and well. Also *absol.*

1697 TRYON *Way to Health* vi. (ed. 3) 101 It [rain-water] Brews and Washes to greater advantage than others.

i. *intr.* Of a fabric, a dye: To bear cleansing with soap and water without damage to colour or texture.

1765 FRANKLIN *Lett.* Wks. III. 402 Mrs. Stevenson bids me tell Sally, that the striped gown I sent her will wash. **1798** JANE AUSTEN *Northang. Abb.* iii, It is very pretty, madam,..but I do not think it will wash well: I am afraid it will fray. **1840** H. BROWNRIGG in K. Meadows *Heads of People* I. 93 'You told me, sir, the print would wash!' she exclaimed, shewing to the unmoved shopman the colourless purchase. **1883** *Harper's Mag.* Nov. 971/1 Only eighteen-pence a yard, ma'am, and warranted to wash.

j. *fig.* (*colloq.*) To bear trial or investigation, stand the test, find acceptance, prove to be genuine, reliable. Chiefly in phr. (*it*) ***won't wash.***

1849 C. BRONTE *Shirley* xviii, That willn't wash, Miss. **1857** HUGHES *Tom Brown* II. ii, He's got pluck somewhere in him. That's the only thing after all that'll wash, ain't it? **1867** TROLLOPE *Last Chron. Barset* xvi, The men—and the women too,—who are so..soft-natured, so kind,..—it so often turns out that they won't wash. **1881** LD. ACTON *Lett. to Mary Gladstone* (1904) 99 The defect of the argument is that it will neither wear nor wash. **1911** *Spectator* 21 Oct. 643/1 He was not to be taken in by plausibilities that 'wouldn't wash'.

k. *Pass.* or *intr.* with *out.* Of a fabric: To lose colour in the wash. Hence *fig.* to lose all vigour or freshness.

1848 DICKENS *Dombey* i, The lady..was a long, lean figure, wearing such a faded air that she seemed not to have been made in what linen-drapers call 'fast-colours' originally and to have, by little and little, washed out. **1868** 'HOLME LEE' *B. Godfrey* l. 282 That claptrap won't wash any longer,..it is quite washed out. **1886** G. ALLEN *Maimie's Sake* xxii, A reaction has set in, and I'm quite washed out and unfit for anything.

3. a. To cleanse (the body or part of it) with water. Also to ***wash clean, white.***

c **1160** *Hatton Gosp.* Matt. xxvii. 24 Pilatus..weosc [*c* 1000 *Ags. Gosp.* þwoh] hys hande beforan þam folke. *c* **1200** ORMIN 15122 To wasshenn offte þe33re lic Wiþþ waterr all wiþþutenn. *a* **1225** *Ancr. R.* 324 Þu waschest þine honden in one elpi deie twies oðer þries. *c* **1250** *Gen. & Ex.* 2289 After ðat grot, he weis is wliten. *a* **1300** *Marina* 172 in Horstm. *Altengl. Leg.* (1878) 173 Go we whosshen vr dede broþer. **1340–70** *Alex. & Dind.* 423 Oure bodies ne ben in no baþ wahche. **1382** WYCLIF *Judith* x. 3 She wesh [**1388** waischide] hir bodi. *c* **1470** HENRY *Wallace* II. 267 Scho warmyt wattir, and hir serwandis fast His body wousche. *c* **1489** CAXTON *Sonnes of Aymon* ii. 61 They..asked after water for to wasse their handes. **1535** COVERDALE *Gen.* xix. 2 Let your fete be waszshen. **15..** *Christ's Kirk on Gr.* 6 in *Bannatyne MS.* (Hunter. Club) 282 Thair come our kitteis weschin clene. **1622** J. TAYLOR (Water P.) *Farew. Tower-Bottles* A 8, Many times you haue beene fild with trash, Scarce good enough your dirty skins to wash. **1709** STEELE *Tatler* No. 73 ⁋3 Keep your Temper, wash your Face, and go to Bed. **1848** THACKERAY *Van. Fair* xxxviii, To wash and dress this young gentleman. **1862** MRS. H. WOOD *Mrs. Hallib.* I. i, Here's Francis coming down-stairs. He went up to wash his hands. **1899** *Allbutt's Syst. Med.* VIII. 610 The patient may be washed with sulphur soap.

b. const. *of. rare.*

1398 TREVISA *Barth. De P.R.* VI. v. (1495) 193 Whan chyldren ben wasshe of fylthe anone they defoyle themself ayen. **1897** O. WISTER in *Harper's Mag.* Mar. 520/2 Both were aware that when shaved and washed of their round-up grime they could look very engaging.

c. said of the water as agent.

1398 TREVISA *Barth. De P.R.* XIII. ix. (1495) 445 The ryuer Jordan wisshe and clensyd Naaman of Syria of his lepre. **1562** J. HEYWOOD *Prov. & Epigr.* (1867) 100 Saue water, which dooth wash thy handis.

d. Proverbs. † ***one hand washeth another*** (see quots. 1593, 1596). ***to wash an Ethiop, a blackamoor*** (***white***); ***to wash an ass's head*** (or ***ears***): to labour in vain (cf. 1 b).

1581 PETTIE *Guazzo's Civ. Conv.* III. (1586) 165 As one hand washeth another, and both of them the face, so one brother ought to support another. **1592** LODGE *Euphues Shadow* (1882) 53 Who washeth the Asses eares, looseth both his Sope and his labour. **1593** G. HARVEY *New Let. Notable Cont.* Wks. (Grosart) I. 269 One hand washeth an other: and it apperteineth vnto him, that taketh something, to giue some-thing. **1596** J. MELVILL *Autob. & Diary* (Wodrow Soc.) 375 We mein nocht to tyne tyme in wassing of sic Moores. **1604** MARSTON *Malcontent* IV. iii. F 3, I washt an Ethiop, who for recompence Sullyde my name. **1624** MASSINGER *Parlt. Love* II. ii, For, being censured, Or to extenuate, or excuse my guilt, Were but to wash an Ethiop. **1635** L. FOXE *N. W. Fox* 268, I have now washt the Blackmoore these five yeares, having yet received neither Sallery, wages or reward. *marg.* Laboured in vaine. **1639** J. CLARKE *Paræm.* 155 He that washeth an asses head loseth both his lye and his labour. *a* **1791** [see ETHIOP A]. **1845** R. FORD *Handbk. Spain* I. 65 It is loss of time and soap to wash an ass's head.

e. Phrase, ***to wash one's hands of***: to disown responsibility for; to refuse to have any further connexion with.

So in Fr. and other mod. langs.; orig. an allusion to Pilate's washing his hands (Matt. xxvii. 24).

1554 LADY JANE GREY *Epistle* B vij, I wil wash my hands giltles thereof. **1570** BUCHANAN *Chamæleon* Wks. (1892) 53 Pilat wesching his handis of ye deid of Chryst. **1642** in Clarendon *Hist. Reb.* IV. §346 He said, 'he should wash his hands before all the world from the least imputation of slackness.' *c* **1645** HOWELL *Lett.* II. xix. (1892) 411, I intend to spend my breath no longer upon them, but to wash my hands quite of the business. **1693** CONGREVE *Old Bach.* II. i, Mony is but Dirt Sir Joseph—Mere Dirt. *Sir Jo.* But I profess, 'tis a Dirt I have wash'd my Hands of at present. **1749** FIELDING *Tom Jones* VIII. iii, 'Then I wash my hands of you,' cries the doctor. **1766** H. WALPOLE *Let. to Lady M. Coke* 3 Mar., Politics, of which I washed my hands for ever when I came away. **1853** DICKENS *Bleak Ho.* vi, He had entirely washed his hands of the difficulty, and it had become ours. **1887** 'EDNA LYALL' *Knt.-Errant* (1889) 29 You are incorrigible. I wash my hands of you.

¶ **f.** The expression 'I will wash my hands in innocency' (Ps. xxvi. 6) is echoed in the following passage, where the meaning is 'to lead a life of heedless ease'.

1630 *R. Johnson's Kingd. & Commw.* 324 Who of all men living wash their hands most in carelesnesse, being never disturbed with worldly cares or incumbrances.

g. ***to wash one's hands***: to rub the hands alternately one over the other, in imitation of the action of washing them. (Cf. Shaks. *Macb.* v. i. 33).

1563–83 FOXE *A. & M.* 1493/2 Rogers..was burned into ashes, washing his handes in the flame as he was in burning. **1840** HOOD *Miss Kilmansegg* 315 (*Christening*) He..Seem'd washing his hands with invisible soap, In imperceptible water.

h. Of a cat, etc.: To cleanse (itself, its face) by licking and rubbing with its paw.

1661 M. STEVENSON *Twelve Moneths* 27 The Hare in a Furrow sits washing her face. **1792** BURNS *Sic a Wife as Willie had* 26 Auld baudrons by the ingle sits, An' wi' her loof her face a-washin'. **1858** H. W. DULCKEN *Picture Fables* 89 Why do you wash yourself, Pussy?

i. *refl.* To cleanse one's body, or (often) merely one's face and hands, with water.

c **1175** *Lamb. Hom.* 73 Wascheð ou and wonieð clene. *a* **1225** *Ancr. R.* 56 Ase heo weoschs hire. *c* **1250** *Kent. Serm.* in *O.E. Misc.* 29, vi. Ydres of stone þet ware i-clepede baþieres wer þo gius hem wesse for clenesse. **1340** *Ayenb.* 202 Elyseu þe profete het to naaman þet wes mezel þet he him wesse ine þe flom Jordan zeuezipe. **1390** GOWER *Conf.* II. 254 Into his bath he wente anon And wyssh him clene as eny bon. *c* **1449** PECOCK *Repr.* IV. viii. 468 That no man schulde take mete, but that he anoon bifore waischid him. **1596** in *Spalding Club Misc.* I. 86 Eftir thei hed anes waschin tham selffis and dryit agane. **1632** LITHGOW *Trav.* IV. 142 They wash themselues in a *Lauotoio.* **1643** TRAPP *Comm., Gen.* xxxv. 2 We wash us every day; but, when to dine with great ones, we wash us with balls, and put on our best. **1711** ADDISON *Spect.* No. 94 ⁋8 He threw off his Clothes with a Design to wash himself. **1887** BOWEN *Virg. Æn.* II. 719 Until I wash me again Clean in the running fountain.

j. *intr.* for *refl.* (= to wash oneself, one's hands, etc.).

c **1175** *Lamb. Hom.* 159 Þos fure kunnes teres boð þe fuwer wateres þa þe beoð ihaten us on to weschen. *c* **1320** *Sir Tristr.* 541 Þe king no seyd no more, But wesche and 3ede to mete. *c* **1350** *Will. Palerne* 2997 Whan þei samen hade souped & seþþe whasche after. **1377** LANGL. *P. Pl.* B. XIII. 28 Þei wesshen [*v.r.* wasscheden] and wypeden and wenten to þe dyner. **1470–85** MALORY *Arthur* I. x. 49 Anon as they had wasshen & rysen. *a* **1562** G. CAVENDISH *Wolsey* (1893) 174, I woll not presume to wassche with yow & therfore I pray you hold me excused. Than was my lord Cardynall constrayned to wasshe alone, and my lord of Norfolke alone also. **1596** SHAKS. *Tam. Shrew* IV. i. 157 Come Kate and wash, and welcome heartily. **1605** ERONDELLE *Fr. Gard.* L 4 b, Come, wash with my Lady and me, We may wash well foure in a Basen. **1694** E. CHAMBERLAYNE *Pres. St. Eng.* I. III. (ed. 18) 410 No Earl is to wash with a Duke without the Dukes Permission. **1718** LADY M. W. MONTAGU *Let. to C'tess* [*Mar*] 10 Mar., These served her coffee, kneeling; brought water when she washed, [etc.]. **1770** G. WHITE *Selborne, To Barrington* 8 Oct., As far as I can observe, many birds that dust themselves never wash. **1823** SCOTT *Quentin D.* xi, And now wash speedily..and follow me. **1854** *Poultry Chron.* I. 49 Here the birds can wash.

k. To cleanse, rinse, drench (the mouth, etc.) with a douche or medicinal application. Also with *out.*

1538 ELYOT *Dict.*, *Gargarisso*, to gargaryshe or washe the mouthe and throte of a man. *c* **1550** H. LLOYD *Treas. Health* vi. C vj, Then let yᵉ pacyent fastyng hold this bage in his mouth & chaw it betwixt hys teeth, & after washe his mouth wyth warme wyne and Hony. **1825** T. HOOK *Sayings* Ser. II. *Sutherl.* (Colburn) 43 The Colonel..began to wash out his mouth. **1899** *Allbutt's Syst. Med.* VII. 583 Antral and other cavities washed out with strong antiseptic solution. *Ibid.* VIII. 300 It is a good thing to keep washing out the vagina by antiseptic douches.

l. Said with reference to baptism.

⁋Used by Cheke to translate βαπτίζειν to baptize.

a **1300** *Cursor M.* 23686 Waters þat wete þan cristes flexs, and in batism his santes wexs. **1303** R. BRUNNE *Handl. Synne* 9508 Adams synne was so grefe, Þat þyr was to God none so lefe, þyt he ne shulde to helle gone But he were wasshe yn þe fonte stone. *c* **1380** WYCLIF *Sel. Wks.* I. 72 Joon hadde office of God to se Crist, and waishe him. **1450–1530** *Myrr. our Ladye* 123 All that ar wasshed in the floude of baptym. **1483** CAXTON *Golden Leg.* 188b/2 He baptysed our lord and wysshe hym where he had neuer fylthe. *c* **1550** CHEKE *Matt.* xx. 22 Can ie..be wasched with yt wasching yt I schal be wasched withal. **1623** COCKERAM II, To Wash. Belaue, Baptize. **1653** R. CARPENTER (*title*) The Anabaptist washt and washt, and shrunk in the washing.

m. *fig.* To cleanse from the stain of sin. Const. *from*, †*of*.

c **1175** *Lamb. Hom.* 157 Swiche teres scedde M. Magdalene þa heo wosch ure drihtenes fet and heo werð hire solf waschen of hire fule sunnen. *a* **1310** in Wright *Lyric P.* xxv. 70 Of blod ant water the stremes be, Us to whosshe from oure fon thre. **1340** *Ayenb.* 112 þe herte þet is..yclensed and ywesse be zoþe ssrifte. **1382** WYCLIF *Rev.* i. 5 The which..waschide [*v.r.* wesh] us fro oure synnes in his blood. **1430–40** LYDG. *Bochas* VIII. xiii. (1558) 8 As man most sinful I come vnto the well..For to be washen of mine iniquity. *a* **1572** KNOX *Hist. Ref.* Wks. 1846 I. 23 Christ woushe us with his blood. *c* **1650** BINNING *Serm.* Wks. (1735) 566 We are washen from the Guilt of our Sins. **1707** WATTS *Hymn*, '*Not the Malicious*' iii, But we are wash'd in Jesus' blood, We're pardon'd thro' his name. **1874** *Sankey's Sacred Songs* (1878) 45 Washed in the blood of the Lamb.

†**n.** To clear, free from blame or aspersion.

1659 *Burton's Diary* (1828) IV. 405 Major-general Kelsey laboured to wash him.

o. ***to wash up***: = sense 3j. *U.S.*

1934 in WEBSTER. **1935** MARSH & JELLETT *Nursing-Home Murder* iii. 42 Thoms came into the [operating] theatre. 'We ought to get washed up, sir,' he said. **1947** J. STEINBECK *Wayward Bus* 214 A neatness of a mechanic who has just washed up. **1967** L. BLOCK *Deadly Honeymoon* ii. 26 Wash up and change your clothes. **1979** R. JAFFE *Class Reunion* (1980) I. xi. 145 She was glad when he came out of the bathroom and she could go in and wash up.

p. ***to wash one's hands***: euphemistic expression for 'to go to the lavatory'.

1938 I. GOLDBERG *Wonder of Words* vi. 108 We are invited to wash our hands, or, if we wear dresses, to powder our noses. **1953** R. WARNER *Escapade* 119 She pointed to a large oak tree... 'Stupid woman,' said Lady Average. 'If she wants to wash her hands, why doesn't she go to the house?' **1966** G. GREENE *Comedians* I. iii. 84 He was out 'washing his hands', as he put it in polite English. **1974** J. GARDNER *Return of Moriarty* 291, I wonder if Rosie could, perhaps, take Miss Malloney to, er, to wash her hands.

4. a. To flush or drench (a substance) with water or other liquid, in order to remove impurities or to dissolve out some component.

a **1650** E. NORGATE *Miniatura* (1919) 17 Then take the remayning grounds and wash them as before. **1651** FRENCH *Distill.* iii. 71 This Oil must be washed in good store of water. **1815** J. SMITH *Panorama Sci. & Art* II. 407 By washing the residuum, a portion of it dissolves in the water. **1849** D. CAMPBELL *Inorg. Chem.* 303 This crust, washed with anhydrous alcohol, breaks up into small crystals. **1853** S. HUGHES *Gas-works* 42 The process of washing the gas is adopted for the purpose of separating ammonia, and consists of passing the gas through a simple sheet of water 6 or 8 inches in depth. **1857** MILLER *Elem. Chem., Org.* 56 By washing the distilled liquid with water, the acetone may, therefore, be removed. **1874** F. CLOWES *Pract. Chem.* 44 A precipitate which has been filtered from the liquid in which it is suspended has often to be washed until perfectly free from the liquid adhering to it.

b. Of running water, rain, etc.: To pass over (a surface) so as to carry off adherent matter; to waste, abrade, or erode in its flow. Also with *out*.

1523–34 FITZHERB. *Husb.* §16 All the rayne that commeth shal washe the lande, and dryue away the dounge and the good moulde. **1801** *Farmer's Mag.* Apr. 125 In cases where the stream is not rapid, and where there is little risk of the banks being washed or hurt during the summer months. **1805** R. W. DICKSON *Pract. Agric.* I. 399 Taking the water off without washing the land. **1817** BYRON *Manfred* I. ii. 124 A pathway, which the torrent Hath wash'd since winter. **1860** TYNDALL *Glac.* II. viii. 263 The glacier..is flanked by mountains which are washed by rain. **1894** CROCKETT *Raiders* 13 The moon..of early April, clean washen by the rains. **1897** J. L. ALLEN *Choir Invisible* v. 65 This stream flows unseen beneath the streets of the city now with scarce current enough to wash out its grimy channel.

II. To subject to the action of water or other liquid.

5. a. To bathe, lave (the body, limbs, wounds, etc.) with water or other liquid.

Where the reference is to wounds, there is sometimes the additional notion of cleansing from blood, pus, etc.: cf. sense 3.

c **1175** *Lamb. Hom.* 83 He weis his wunde mid wine. **1387** TREVISA *Higden* VIII. 235 þan he wesche [*v.rr.* weesche, wuesch] þe woundes of þe ymage of the crucifixe. *c* **1400** *Lanfranc's Cirurg.* 199 þanne waische þe lyme wiþ a decoccioun of malowis & violet & rotis of bismalue in watir. *c* **1470** HENRY *Wallace* VIII. 787 The wery ost..Wysche woundis with wyn, off thaim that was wnsound. **1481** CAXTON *Reynard* xliii. (Arb.) 116 Wyse Maistres and Surgyens,..bonde them, and weeshe hem [*sc.* the wounds]. **1622** MABBE tr. *Aleman's Guzman d'Alf.* II. 354 After this my rubbing and being washt with Salt and Vineger. **1626** BACON *Sylva* §998 The Wound must be at first Washed cleane, with White Wine. **1686–7** in *Spalding Club Misc.* V. 237 He saw Alex. Chalmer, his hand blooding, after it was washen, being hurt. **1809** *Med. Jrnl.* XXI. 37 A solution of the muriat of mercury in alcohol, to wash the affected parts with twice a day.

b. To bathe (the eyes). Also, ***to wash clean, clear***. †Also *transf.* (jocularly), to clear or sharpen the sight of (the eyes) with strong drink (cf. next).

c **1200** *Vices & Virtues* 125 Wassce and wipe wol clane ða eiȝene, for ðan soð is ðat hie ðe siggen. *a* **1300** *Cursor M.* 13571 Ga wasse þin eien þar. *c* **1420** *Chron. Vilod.* 2826 þis bysone mon to þat water he ladde And wosshe þere-wt his ynon two. **16..** CHALKHILL in Walton *Angler* xvi. 210 We..Drink a cup to wash our eyes, Leave the sluggard sleeping. **1826** SCOTT *Woodst.* xxxviii, His eyes washed with only a single cup of canary. **1831** —— *Cast. Dang.* ii, Thou shalt have no cause to complain that thine eyes..have been damaged by a Scottish mist, while we can find an English coin to pay for the good liquor which should wash them clear.

c. To moisten (the throat) with wine. †Hence ***to wash one's brain, head***, etc., as jocular expressions for wine-drinking.

1390 GOWER *Conf.* II. 176 For Bachus was a glotoun eke, Him for the throte thei beseke, That he it wolde waisshen ofte With swote drinkes and with softe. **1540** PALSGR. *Acolastus* II. i. H ij b, My teth be al to furrid with flakes of skurfe (sticking vpon them syns I washed them with any merye go downe). **1589** NASHE *Anat. Absurd.* D 4, He that washeth his braines with diuers kinds of wines, is the next doore to a drunken man. **1590** LODGE *Rosalynde* (1592) F 3, Washing their heades well with wine. **1599** B. JONSON *Ev. Man out of Hum.* v. iv, I'le wash my temples with some on't presently. **1606** SHAKS. *Ant. & Cl.* II. vii. 105. **1618** FLETCHER *Loyal Subj.* IV. v. *init.*, Beleeve me fellow here will be lusty drinking. Many a washt pate in wine I warrant thee.

†**d.** *intr.* for *refl.* To use cosmetic washes. *Obs.*

1676 ETHEREGE *Man of Mode* II. i. 22 Young Ladies, Who notoriously wash, and paint, though they Have naturally good Complexions. **1693** SOUTHERNE *Maid's Last Prayer* II. i, I may Wash, and Patch, and please my self.

6. a. To plunge, bathe (a person) in a river or lake.

1398 TREVISA *Barth. De P.R.* XIII. xii. (1495) 446 In Ethiopia is a lake and yf a body be wassh therin he shinyth as though he were anoynted wyth oyle. **1660** F. BROOKE tr. *Le Blanc's Trav.* 129 Having washed him in a lake..they cloath him in a white gown.

†**b.** *refl.* Used for: To bathe. *Obs.* (? In later use *jocular*.)

1388 [see 6c.]. **1483** CAXTON *Golden Leg.* 414b/1 The emperour frederyk vysyted the holy londe and wysshe hym in a ryuer. **1511** *Guylforde's Pilgr.* (Camden) 42 There we wesshe us, and bayned us all nakyd in the water of Iordan. **1600** SHAKS. *A. Y.L.* IV. i. 103 He went but forth to wash him in the Hellespont, and being taken with the crampe, was droun'd. **1711** HEARNE *Collect.* (O.H.S.) III. 195 One Mr. Reynalds..was drown'd by Ferry Hinksey, he being washing himself, but not able to swim. **1775** BURKE *Corr.* (1844) II. 38 My brother is washing himself at Brighthelmstone.

c. *intr.* for *refl.* To bathe. *Obs.* exc. of animals.

1382 WYCLIF *2 Kings* v. 14 He wente doun, and wasche [1388 waischide hym] in Jordane seuen sithis. **1621** J. TAYLOR (Water P.) *Motto* E 2, Old Chaucer, Sidney, Spencer, Daniel, Nash, I dipt my finger where they vs'd to wash. **1908** [MISS E. FOWLER] *Betw. Trent & Ancholme* 12 The 'Wire Pond', where the horses came to wash.

†**d.** *trans.* To dip, plunge, immerse (a thing) *in* water. *Obs.*

c **1374** CHAUCER *Boeth.* IV. met. vi. (1886) 111 Ne the same sterre vrsa nis neuer mo wasshen in the depe westrene see [L. *nunquam occiduo lota profundo*]. *c* **1386** —— *Pard. T.* 25 If that this boon be wasshe in any welle.

e. ***to wash one's spears*** (sc. in blood): a phrase attributed to South African chiefs as expressing their motive for going to war.

1892 RIDER HAGGARD *Nada* v, With every moon a fresh impi started to wash its spears, and came back few and thin. **1903** BRYCE *Stud. Contemp. Biogr.* 221 In one thing the young men [Sir Stafford Northcote's followers], who, like Zulu warriors, wished to wash their spears, were right and he was wrong.

7. a. To wet or moisten thoroughly; to inundate or saturate with water (esp. rain) or other liquid; to sprinkle or pour water upon.

c **1205** LAY. 17188 Heo wasceð [*c* **1275** wasseþ] þene stan, & þer mide baðieð heore ban. *a* **1300** *Cursor M.* 1997 Now es ..þe erth waiker þan it was þan, Thoru þe watur þat it sua wex, þer-for behoues now man ete flesse. *c* **1386** CHAUCER *Monk's T.* 766 Reyn shal thee wasshe, and sonne shal thee drye. **1390** GOWER *Conf.* I. 138 Til that the water of the hevene Have waisshen him be times sevene. *c* **1400** *Laud Troy Bk.* 18570 Pirrus.. hewe to gobetis al hir flesch, And with hir blod the tombe wesch. **1535** COVERDALE *Isa.* xxxiv. 7 Their londe shalbe washed [1611 soaked] with bloude. **1538** ELYOT *Dict.*, *Roresco*, to be washed with dewe. **1577** KENDALL *Flowers Epigr.*, *Trifles* 13 A powryng shower that ..well the kyng did washe. **1590** SHAKS. *Mids. N.* II. i. 104 Therefore the Moone (the gouernesse of floods)..washes all the aire. **1596** —— *Tam. Shr.* II. i. 174 She lookes as cleere As morning Roses newly washt with dew. **1596** *Edw. III*, III. ii. 23 He, that no sooner will prouide a Cloake, Then when he sees it doth begin to raigne, May, peraduenture, for his negligence, Be thoroughly washed, when he suspects it not. **1662** J. DAVIES tr. *Olearius' Voy. Ambass.* 35 Ever and anon our Sails were wash'd by the Waves. **1724** RAMSAY *Vision* xxviii, Flora..New washen with a showir of May. **1783** COWPER *Rose* 1 The rose had been wash'd, just wash'd in a shower. **1810** SCOTT *Lady of Lake* IV. i, The rose is sweetest wash'd with morning dew.

b. To wet copiously (with tears).

Chiefly in religious use, after Ps. vi. 6 Vulgate, *lavabo lectum meum*, and with reference to Luke vii. 38.

c **1200** *Trin. Coll. Hom.* 65 Swo ich wile biwepe mine synnes þat mi bed bie iwasshen mid mine teares. *Ibid.* 151 He wasseð his neb mid teares. *c* **1300** *Judas* 125 in *E.E.P.* (1862) 110 His fet heo wosch wiþ hire teres. **1340** *Ayenb.* 171 He ssel grat zorȝe habbe..and ofte mid his teares his bed wesse. *c* **1400** LOVE *Bonavent. Mirr.* xlvii, And þer wyth of þe habundaunce of teres sche woschsse muche bettere hys heuede. **1450** *Paston Lett.* I. 124, I..have soo wesshe this litel bille with sorwfulle terys, that [etc.]. **1603** SHAKS. *Meas. for M.* III. i. 239 He, a marble to her teares, is washed with them, but relents not.

c. With predicative extension: To form *in* (holes) by the action of dropping or running water. Similarly, to form a hole or depression in (a surface) by erosion.

1766 *Complete Farmer* s.v. *Walk*, The dripping of the water from their branches in hard rains, is apt to wash the gravel in holes, and where the walks very unsightly. **1911** *Concise Oxford Dict.* s.v., Water had washed a channel.

†**8.** To sweat (gold or silver coin) by the application of acids. *Obs.*

Distinct from the 'washing' of coin forbidden in 19th-c. statutes: see 9c.

1421–2 HOCCLEVE *Min. P.* xxi. 106 How may it [gold coin] holde his peise when it is waishe so that it lackethe somewhat in thiknese? **1543** tr. *Act 3 Hen. V*, c. 6 They that so do clyp, wasshe, and fyle the money of the lande, shalbe iudged traytours to the kynge and to the realme. *a* **1547** in J. R. Boyle *Hedon* (1875) App. 88 Of them that countrefetes, clypis, washes, or fylis the Kinges coyne. **1597** HOOKER *Eccl. Pol.* v. lxxix. §12 To wash or clip that coyne which hath on it the marke of God. **1643** *Docq. Lett. Patent at Oxf.* (1837) 45 Pardon..for counterfeiting forging clipping washing or falsefying Money of Gold or silver.

9. a. To cover or smear (a surface) with a liquid substance lightly applied. Also with *over*.

1755 *Art of Drawing in Perspective* 91 When these are dry, wash all over with the white Varnish before the Fire. **1854** MARIA CHARLESWORTH *Minist. Children* v. 60 [She] washed over the tops of the loaves with a feather dipped in beer.

b. To cover (a wall, etc.) with pigment mixed with water or watery liquid; to whitewash or colour-wash.

1604 *Shuttleworths' Acc.* (Chetham Soc.) 157 A plasterer, ..v days plasteringe and wasshinge in the chambers on the soth syed, ijs jd. **1606** *Ibid.* 172 A plasterer, v days wasshinge the halle and dyninge chamber, ijs vjd. **1722** *Lond. Gaz.* No. 6103/3 The Walls of the Houses were washed with Water in which Lime had been slaked. **1826** COBBETT *Rur. Rides* (1885) II. 296 The windmills..are all painted or washed white.

c. To cover *with* a film of metal deposited from a solution.

1792 *Gentl. Mag.* LXII. I. 19/1 A chain and medal..is silver washed over with gold. **1853** HUMPHREYS *Coin Coll. Man.* xxvi. 381 The ten-centime piece of Napoleon..being of copper washed with silver. **1861** *Act 24 & 25 Vict.* c. 99 §1 Any of the current Coin which shall have been gilt, silvered, washed, coloured, or cased over..so as to resemble ..any of the Queen's current Coin of a higher Denomination.

10. a. *Water-colour Painting.* To cover with a broad layer of colour by a continuous movement of the brush; to depict (a coloured surface) by this means; to lay (colour) in washes. ***to wash in***: to depict (a portion of a subject) with a wash of colour. Also with *over*.

1622 PEACHAM *Comp. Gentl.* xii. 110 Beginne first to wash ouer some plaine printes. *a* **1650** E. NORGATE *Miniatura* (1919) 30 In your dead colourings, you must wash over and colour your ground and complexion, with this red. *Ibid.* 32 Washing the colour with a bold hand. *Ibid.* 50 When you have..sleigtly washt in your skie. **1662** ATWELL *Faithf. Surveyor* 53 Arable for corn you may wash with pale straw-colour made of yellow-ocre and white-lead. **1675** A. BROWNE *Appendix Art Paint.* 13, 14 That manner I do approve of better, for Washing or Drawing any Design with Indian Ink, and indeed ought not be called Limning but Washing. **1755** *Art of Drawing in Perspective* 9 Sometimes the Design is washed, that is, the Shadows are done with a Pencil in Indian Ink, or some other Liquor. **1807** J. LANDSEER *Lect. Engraving* iii. 132 A drawing washed with bistre or Indian ink. **1843** RUSKIN *Arrows of Chace* (1880) I. 5 Gaspar..washes his sky half blue and half yellow. **1860** SMILES *Self Help* v. 125 He [Turner] was glad to hire himself out at half-a-crown a night to wash in skies in Indian ink upon other people's drawings. **1860** J. D. HOOKER *Flora Tasmania* II. 372 The scape should be washed over with a pale brown, leaving hardly a trace of green. **1871** *Routledge's Ev. Boy's Ann.* 1872, 406 The bushes..may be washed in with Indian yellow. **1886** RUSKIN *Præterita* I. xii. 396 Copley Fielding taught me to wash colour smoothly in successive tints.

fig. **1861** J. BROWN *Horæ Subs.* Ser. II. 249 Such a man as I have sketched, or washed faintly in, as the painters say.

b. *transf.* in *passive.* Said in Natural History of surfaces that appear to have a superficial layer of colour spread over them.

1844 BLYTH in *Jrnl. Asiatic Soc. Bengal* XIII. I. 466 The legs and feet..are pale; the hands are washed with blackish. **1888** P. L. SCLATER *Argentine Ornith.* I. 25 Tail-feathers black, washed with blue. **1894** R. B. SHARPE *Handbk. Birds Gt. Brit.* I. 25 The intermediate form..differs from the typical bird in having the head and throat washed with purple.

11. *Mining.* To agitate in water, or to pass a stream of water through (metalliferous earth) in order to separate the metallic particles.

1543 *Mem. Fountains Abbey* (Surtees) I. 403 For washinge the leade ure at Grenehow morr. **1555** EDEN *Decades* (Arb.) 212 Then they washe all the earthe... And if herein they fynde any golde, they folowe it. **1619** S. ATKINSON *Gold Mynes Scot.* (Bannatyne Club) 1 The buddle where the same earth must be readled or washed. **1853** C. R. READ *Austral. Gold Fields* 34 In many cases men used to pay other £20 a-week to be allowed to wash their tailings. **1863** B. A. HEYWOOD *Vac. Tour Antipodes* 48 The Chinese..have been known to wash over again the deserted washings of the Europeans, and to find gold in paying quantities.

b. *absol.*

1604 G. BOWES in Cochran-Patrick *Early Rec. Mining Scot.* (1878) 107, I bestowed my workemen to washe for golde in Whites meadowe. **18..** C. A. GOODRICH *Child's Hist. U.S.* (1882) 122 Men..were found gathered there.. washing for gold.

c. ***to wash up***: to retrieve (gold) from the riffles, sluices, etc., in which it has collected during washing. Also *absol.*

1869 J. ANDERSON *Sawney's Lett.* (ed. 2) 27 Now say, what have you 'wash'd up'? Small wages. **1874** A. BATHGATE *Colonial Experiences* xi. 142 After some months' hard work, we would wash up, and my mate would go off to sell the gold. **1900** B. HARTE *From Sand Hill to Pine* 103 To dig for three or four hours in the morning, smoke their pipes.. for an hour at noon, take up their labors again until sunset, when they 'washed up' and gathered sufficient gold to pay for their daily wants, was.. the realization of a charming socialist ideal.

III. Of flowing water: To flow past or over land.

12. a. Of a sea or river: To flow over or past (the sand, shore, coast); to beat upon (walls, cliffs, etc.); to touch, adjoin (a town, country, etc.). Also of a river: To pass through, 'water' (a country).

c **1205** LAY. 123, I þere Tyure he eode alond þer þa sea wasceð þat sond. **1538** ELYOT *Dict.*, *Subluere*, to vnderwashe, as water, whyche runneth lowe vnder a banke or hylle, and washeth the foote thereof. **1585** T. WASHINGTON tr. *Nicholay's Voy.* II. xii. 47 The two sides are washed by the sea. **1591** SPENSER *Vis. Bellay* 158 The golden grayle That bright Pactolus washeth with his streames. **1697** DRYDEN *Æneis* VIII. 90 In Times to come My Waves shall wash the Walls of mighty Rome. **1698** FRYER *Acc. E. India & P.* 329 They seldom stretch into Rivers at length, but stagnate in the Low Grounds, which they wash. **1700** CHAUNCY *Hertfordsh.* 3 The Bulborne.. washing the North East side of Barkhamsted. **1814** CARY *Dante, Parad.* viii. 69 The crown, Which gave me sovereignty over the land By Danube wash'd. **1839** THIRLWALL *Greece* VI. xlix. 168 The waves washed the foot of the cliffs. **1842** BORROW *Bible in Spain* xxiv, A small village, washed by the brook. **1877** HUXLEY *Physiogr.* 45 The British Isles, washed by warm water on their western shores, are peculiarly subject to fogs.

transf. **1902** KIPLING *Five Nations* (1903) 64 The granite of the ancient North—Great spaces washed with sun.

b. *intr.* Of waves: To sweep *over* a surface; to break or surge *against* (the shore, etc.); to break *in*.

1774 GOLDSM. *Nat. Hist.*, *Hist. Earth* xvii. (1824) I. 122 The tides,.. constantly washing over them, have always left some part of their substance behind. **1831** JAMES *Phil. Augustus* xxxi, Nothing was.. heard but the rippling of the waters of the Seine, then at high tide, washing against the very foundations of the tower. **1873** BLACK *Pr. Thule* viii. 119 The tiny waves that washed in on the white shore. **1885** FROUDE *Oceana* xvi. 243 The lightest ripple washed over the gunwale.

transf. **1920** *In the Mountains* 132 It is a very good practice.. to lean out of one's window.. before going to bed and let the cool darkness wash over one.

c. Used by onomatopœia to suggest the sound of moving water, or of objects moving in water.

1842 TENNYSON *Morte d'Arthur* 70, I heard the ripple washing in the reeds. **18..** JEAN INGELOW *Days without Alloy* iii. (Funk), Then I hear the water washing, never golden waves were brighter. **1891** *Century Dict.*, *Wash*, to make a swish, swash, or swirl of the water; as, the shad are washing.

IV. To remove, or carry away, by the action of water or other liquid.

13. a. *trans.* To remove (dirt, a stain, colouring, etc.) by the application of water or other liquid. Chiefly with adv., as *away*, *out*, *off*.

c **1400** *Beryn* 661 Yet, or he cam in company, he wissh awey the blood. *c* **1450** *Mirk's Festial* 90 Then was þys woman agrysed of þe blod, and wold haue weschyn hit away. **1513** DOUGLAS *Æneis* IX. (last line), All blude and slauchtyr away was weschyn clene. **1562** TURNER *Herbal* II. 32 Bay berries.. weish out frekles. **1581** A. HALL *Iliad* IV. 66 After he had beheld the stroke, and washte away the bloud. **1605** SHAKS. *Macb.* II. ii. 60 Will all great Neptunes Ocean wash this blood Cleane from my Hand? **1663** PATRICK *Parab. Pilgr.* xxxv. (1687) 437 Would you not have us pull off the Mask or wash off the paint, that we may shew things in their proper colours? **1681** tr. *Belon's Myst. Physick* Introd. 45 The Volatil Salt.. is to be washed off with the said Water. **1755** *Art of Drawing in Perspective* 91 Then wash off the Tripoli with a soft Sponge and Water. **1827** FARADAY *Chem. Manip.* xxiv. (1842) 629 Agitate it [the gas] with water to wash out the sulphurous acid. **1831** JAMES *Phil. Augustus* xxxiv, Though the blood of his nephew was scarce washed from his hands. **1899** *Allbutt's Syst. Med.* VIII. 868 Washing discharge away with sublimate solution.

b. *fig.*

Very common in reference to sin, etc. regarded as a stain or defilement. In early use often without adv.

a **1225** *Ancr. R.* 324 Euerich god word, & euerich god werc wascheð smele sunnen. *a* **1240** *Ureisun* in *O.E. Hom.* I. 189 As wis ase drope of þi deorwurþe blod mahte waschen a-wai alle folkes fulþe. *a* **1300** *Cursor M.* 1594 God.. thoght a neu wengaunce to sent,.. And waass þat wrang, þat was sa rijf. **1303** R. BRUNNE *Handl. Synne* 9544 Whan Ihesu was baptysed þer-ynne [*sc.* in Jordan] For to wasshe awey þat synne. **14..** *Pol., Rel. & L. Poems* 142 That.. thy .v. woundis.. May wach in vs all surfetis reproueable. *c* **1586** C'TESS PEMBROKE *Ps.* LI. i, O clense, O wash my foule iniquitie. **1664** MARVELL *Corr.* Wks. (Grosart) II. 121 His subjects.. have with their ancient loyalty washed out the staines of the late Rebellion. **1709** PRIOR *Henry & Emma* 313 Nor Tears, that wash out Sin, can wash out Shame. **1781** GIBBON *Decl. & F.* xxxi. III. 238 The ignominious lashes, which they had formerly received, were washed away in the blood of the guilty, or obnoxious, families. **1855** MACAULAY *Hist. Eng.* xii. III. 130 This merit was thought sufficient to wash out even the stain of his Saxon extraction. **1880** LD. ACTON *Lett. to Mary Gladstone* (1904) 38 The Republican party.. had a good deal of dirty work to wash off.

c. *transf.* and *fig.* To blot out, obliterate, cancel.

c **1380** WYCLIF *Wks.* (1880) 289 ȝif chartris of men ben contrarie to goddis lawe, þes chartres schulde be wayschen and goddis lawe schulde stonde. **1568** GRAFTON *Chron.* II. 703 The brotherly loue betwene them washed away and diminished all suspicion. **1584** R. SCOT *Discov. Witchcr.* v. ii. (1886) 74 Bodin washeth away all our arguments with one word. **1603** HOLLAND *Plutarch's Mor.* 236 Now of these three causes before specified, the first doth not wash away envie.

d. *intr.* with *out*. Of colouring matter: To disappear from a fabric when washed.

1755 in *6th Rep. Dep. Kpr. Rec.* App. II. 128 A certain Liquid Composition.. which.. will neither Wash Out, Fade, or Tarnish. **1972** J. WILSON *Hide & Seek* vii. 122, I am making a purse.. but I pricked my finger and got a bit of blood on it, but.. it will wash out.

e. *to wash out* (trans.): (i) to obliterate, cancel, remove.

1580 H. F. *Pelegrom. Syn. Sylva* 70 To Crosse or Cancell out, or to wash out writinges. **1616** *Withals' Dict.* 563 *Lutum luto purgare.* To wash out incke with incke. **1763** SPENS *Plato's Repub.* IV. 151 Such wool as is not managed in this manner, you know what sort it proves; whether one is dying other colours, or this one, without the due preparation beforehand. I know, said he, that they are easily washen out. **1850** SMEDLEY *F. Fairlegh* xxvi, This Wilford is a noted duellist, and no doubt thirsts to wash out the insult he has received in blood. **1859** FITZGERALD *Omar* li, Nor [shall] all thy Tears wash out a Word of it. **1932** R. NIEBUHR *Moral Man & Immoral Society* (1933) iii. 81 It will prevent the idea of justice, which is a politico-ethical ideal, from becoming a purely political one, with the ethical element washed out. **1983** *Sci. Amer.* Feb. 86/3 Coronal structure hinted at in ordinary photographs is largely washed out by overexposure of the bright inner corona.

(ii) *colloq.* To call off (an event), esp. because of bad weather; to eliminate (a possible course of action). Usu. *pass.*

1917 A. G. LEE *Let.* 25 May in *No Parachute* (1968) 24 Today I have two patrols, one this morning.. but after an hour it was washed out through bad weather. **1933** P. MACDONALD *Mystery of Dead Police* vii. 49 I'll get that murder charge washed out altogether. **1953** 'N. SHUTE' *In Wet* v. 149 If there's an awful lot of work before we go, I might have to wash it out. **1964** MRS. L. B. JOHNSON *White House Diary* 8 Apr. (1970) 104 When the commentator inquired about the possibility of McNamara [being Vice-President] and pointed out that he had been a registered Republican at one time, Lippman rather washed that one out. **1977** *Belfast Tel.* 14 Feb. 22/4 Bangor's first ever mid-week racing fixture.. was washed out today when stewards inspected the course and found it waterlogged.

(iii) *Air Force slang.* To kill (an airman) in a crash; to crash (an aircraft); also (const. *of* or *from*), to withdraw (a person) from a course. Usu. *pass.*

1918 J. M. GRIDER *War Birds* (1926) 87 Wholesale funerals... Six American Naval pilots.. thought that Camels were as easy to fly as the Hanriots they had been flying in France and they wouldn't listen to any advice from the instructors here. Three of them were washed out one week. **1927** C. A. LINDBERGH *We* v. 73 Coupled with this was the anxiety of waiting for the returns from our examination papers, the failure of any two of which would be sufficient cause for their owner to be washed out from the courses. **1928** *Pop. Sci. Monthly* May 72 That Kiwi washed out the only peppy crate in the outfit. **1942** F. H. JOSEPH *Lett. home from Brit. at War* 16 Three planes were washed out completely, others damaged. **1943** *Yank* 30 July 18 The air cadet needed only 20 flying hours for his commission when he was suddenly washed out of advanced training and shipped. **1979** M. HASTINGS *Bomber Command* vi. 145 Owen was washed out of pilot training within a fortnight, and posted to learn to be a navigator.

14. trans. *to wash down*: to swallow liquor along with or after (solid food), in order to assist deglutition or digestion. Also with *fig.* object. Also rarely *to wash over*.

1600 *1st Pt. Sir J. Oldcastle* v. viii. 41 In this one draught I wash my sorrow downe. **1649** LOVELACE *Being treated, To Ellinda* 4 Flutes of Canary That well did wash downe pasties-mary. **1744** M. BISHOP *Life & Adv.* 193, I had three plentiful Meals, and some good Liquors to wash it down. **1848** DICKENS *Dombey* xxxviii, This profound reflection Mr. Toodle washed down with a pint mug of tea. **1854** SURTEES *Handley Cr.* ii. (1901) I. 13 Then a good cut out of the middle of a well-browned saddle of mutton, wash it over with a few glasses of iced champagne. **1859** JEPHSON *Brittany* ix. 151 This we washed down with a.. 'bowl' of mulled Bordeaux.

15. a. Of waves, running water, rain, etc.: To remove, dislodge, carry away; to carry or transport in a specified direction. With advs. *away*, *down*, *off*, *out*, *up*, etc., or const. *from*, *into*, *out of*, etc. Also *fig.*

1362 LANGL. *P. Pl.* A. x. 163 Til Fourti dawes ben folfuld þat þe flod haue I-wassche Clene awey þe cursede blod þat Caym haþ I-maket. *a* **1500** *Bernardus*, etc. III. 82 He walde þat A watter, or a well, hayd wecht it away. **1555** EDEN *Decades* (Arb.) 212 The water wassheth the earth.. owte of the trais. **1592** SHAKS. *Rom. & Jul.* III. v. 71 What wilt thou wash him from his graue with teares? **1593** —— *3 Hen. VI*, v. iv. 31 Bestride the Rock, the Tyde will wash you off. **1622** J. TAYLOR (Water P.) *Merry-Wherry-Ferry Voy.* Wks. 1630 II. 10/2 The raging Sea.. euery day.. eateth further in, Still.. wasting, washing downe the sand doth win. *a* **1670** SPALDING *Troub. Chas. I* (1829) 44 Waters and burns flowed over bank and brae, corn mills and mill-houses washen down, [etc.]. **1674** *Jackson's Recant.* A2, A Clod of Earth, which.. the least shower of Rheums [can] wash away to nothing. **1709** T. ROBINSON *Nat. Hist. Westmorld. & Cumbld.* xiv. 81 Violent Currents of Water wash off the outer Coat of the Earth, and leave the Vein naked. **1745** P. THOMAS *Jrnl. Anson's Voy.* 180 That the Rain-water may spread equally, and not wash down the Ground. **1748** *Anson's Voy.* II. iii. 152 Several pieces of beef.. had been washed out of the ship. **1842** DICKENS *Amer. Notes* xi, The river has washed away its banks. **1858** TRELAWNY *Recoll. Shelley* etc. 120 The other body was washed on shore three miles distant from Shelley's. **1883** *Manch. Guard.* 18 Oct. 4/7 The bodies of five seamen have been washed ashore. **1929** *Times* 30 Oct. 14/1 Trans-America, which closed last night at 6¼, opened today at 20¼,.. —$840,000,000.. nominally washed away over-night.

b. To separate (metallic particles) by treating the containing earth with water. Also *to wash out*.

1555 EDEN *Decades* (Arb.) 212 These mynes.. owght euer to bee soughte nere to sum ryuer.. to thende that the golde may be wassbed. **1665** *Phil. Trans.* I. 117 A peculiar way of washing out very small Dust-gold. **1748** *Anson's Voy.* I. v. 50 The washing the gold.. from the sand and dirt, with which it is always mixed. **1920** *Conquest* May 324/1 Potassium and sodium cyanides are employed.. for the purpose of washing out the gold from the quartz.

c. Of a hard surface: To beat *off* waves and flotsam as they are borne against it.

1697 DRYDEN *Æneis* VII. 812 His solid sides Wash off the Sea-weeds, and the sounding Tides.

d. *intr.* To be carried away or detached by moving water. Chiefly of soil, etc.: To be eroded or abraded, wear away by inundation. Chiefly with *adv.*, as *away*, *down*.

c **1590** MARLOWE *Jew of Malta* I. ii. 451 Who.. Thinke me to be a senselesse lumpe of clay That will with euery water wash to dirt. **1653** WALTON *Angler* viii. 171 You must work or pound it [*sc.* your paste] so long in the Mortar, as to make it so tough as to hang upon your hook without washing from it. **1709** T. ROBINSON *Nat. Hist. Westmorld. & Cumbld.* vii. 47 Whose Soil, by great Rains and Floods, washeth down into the Vallies. **1789** W. JESSOP in *Rep. Engin. Thames-Isis Navig.* (1791) 23 If the Stones are set in moss and wrecked full of Gravel to prevent the Earth from Washing from behind thro' the Joints. **1822** COBBETT *Rur. Rides* (1885) I. 13 It [the soil] has great tenacity; does not wash away like sand or light loam.

16. To be tossed about, to be carried or driven along, by waves or stream. Also with *up*, *ashore*, etc. Also *fig.*

1623 J. TAYLOR (Water P.) *New Discov. by Sea* A 5, These sands so shallow In which thou seest our ship thus wash and wallow. **1745** P. THOMAS *Jrnl. Anson's Voy.* 22 Four or five dead Bodies at a time.. washing about the Decks. *Ibid.* 154 Our Bedding was.. left washing in the Break of The Sea. **1815** *Ann. Reg.*, *Chron.* 83 The vessel struck on the ground.. and afterwards washed up against the piles on the west side. **1837** CARLYLE *Fr. Rev.* II. v. ix, War-Minister Narbonne is washed away by the Time-flood; poor Chevalier de Grave, chosen by the Court, is fast washing away. **1880** *Times* 17 Dec. 5/6 The Adolph.. is reported.. to be total wreck. Cargo washing ashore. **1907** *Daily Chron.* 26 Sept. 6/5, I was glad to lay hold of a spar that washed by me. **1947** G. GREENE *Nineteen Stories* 74 And so he'd washed up here, under my eyes, sitting all day under the band-stand.

17. *Rowing.* **a.** *trans.* To steer so as to impede (a competitor) by the 'wash' of one's own boat.

1865 *Field* 26 Aug. 152/2 His next step, when half a length ahead, was to edge in as much as he dare in front of Kelley, notwithstanding the admonition of the umpire, for the purpose of washing him. **1872** *Field Q. Mag.* III. 107/1 [Cambridge] passed under the Middlesex arch of Barnes Bridge.. a length and a half ahead of the Oxonians, who, to escape being washed, elected to pass under the centre span.

b. *intr.* in phrase *to wash out*, to fail to lift out the blade of the oar squarely at the finish of the stroke.

1884 *St. James's Gaz.* 28 Mar. 6/2 Stroke and No. 4 were washing out and rowing light in the finish of the stroke.

18. *slang.* To murder. Also with *away*.

1941 in B. A. Botkin *Treas. Amer. Folklore* (1944) I. 124 So Stack, with his gun handle filled with notches, knowed there was a reward out for him for men he had washed away. **1960** 'E. MCBAIN' *See them Die* (1963) v. 48 'This Alfredo kid, he not sush a bad guy.' 'He's getting washed and that's it.' **1979** P. HILL *Washermen* xxiv. 54 They had broken the code... The Washermen must be washed.

V. 19. *Mech.* (trans.) *to wash off*, to cut to a slope or bevel. *to wash down* (see quot. 1911).

1833 LOUDON *Encycl. Archit.* §1117 The sole for the [window-] frame.. to be washed off (sloped) on the outside to carry off the rain. **1911** WEBSTER, *To wash down*, to work to a thin edge or featheredge. *Scot.*

VI. 20. *slang.* **a.** *Printing.* To punish or 'rag' (a fellow-workman for telling falsehoods) by hammering on his desk. Cf. WASHING *vbl. sb.* 5.

1841 SAVAGE *Dict. Printing* 810.

b. *Stockbroking.* To subject (stock) to a 'wash': see WASH *sb.* 20. [Perh. orig. with allusion to the phrase 'one hand washes the other' (see 3 d).]

1895 *Funk's Stand. Dict.* **1903** S. S. PRATT *Work of Wall St.* 146 The syndicate may be washing sales by matched orders through curb brokers in order to market watered stock.

c. = LAUNDER *v.* 1 b.

1973 *Black Panther* 30 June 2/2 The money had been 'washed' through the Mexican bank passing off as a legal fee to the Mexican lawyer in order to conceal the source of the donation. **1977** B. FREEMANTLE *Charlie Muffin* xii. 127 We *must* wash the money... If that money isn't broken down, Kalenin.. just won't cross. **1981** R. THOMAS *Mordida Man* xxvii. 237 What was their payoff for washing the money?

VII. 21. The verb-stem in combination.

a. Combinations of *wash-* + object, '(some one or something) that washes', as WASH-DISH 1, WASH-HAND *a.*, WASHMOUTH.

b. (Not all clearly distinguishable from the Combs. listed in sense 21 of the *sb.* above.) Attributive combinations of *wash-* (often synonymous with parallel combs. of WASHING *vbl. sb.*), denoting things or places used for washing, or persons employed in washing clothes, as *wash-boy, -cloth, -jug, -place, -rag* (now *U.S.*), *-solution, -tray, -vessel*; **wash-and-wear** orig. *U.S.*, the property of a garment or fabric of being easily washed, drying readily, and needing no ironing; usu. *attrib.*; **wash-beetle**, a wooden mallet for beating clothes as part of the process of washing; **wash-bench** *U.S.*, a bench on which washing is done; **wash-boiler** (see quot. 1875); **wash-bottle** *Chem.* (*a*) a bottle containing liquid through which gases may be passed for purification; (*b*) a bottle with a mouthpiece and issue tube, for directing a stream of liquid on a substance or utensil to be washed; **wash-brush**, a large brush for 'washing' or laying on washes of colour; **wash-cloth** *U.S.*, a facecloth; **wash-deck** *attrib. Naut.*, used in, or pertaining to, the washing of the deck of a ship; ***wash-deck tub*** (slang), a small boat, with decks easily washed by the sea; **wash-dyke** *dial.* = WASH-POOL; **wash-gourd**, the loofah (Webster Suppl. 1902), also called *washing-*, *towel-gourd*; **wash-kettle** *U.S.*, a kettle in which water is heated for washing; **wash-kitchen** [= G. *waschküche*], a kitchen used for washing clothes; **wash-line** chiefly *U.S.* = *washing-line* s.v. WASHING *vbl. sb.* 9a; **wash-pan** *U.S.*, a metal wash bowl; a pan for washing ore; **wash-pen** *Austral.* and *N.Z.*, the pen into which sheep are driven to await their turn to be washed; **wash-pitcher** *U.S.*, a ewer for the toilet; **wash sink** *U.S.*, a sink for washing oneself; **wash-table**, a table for holding a wash-hand basin and ewer. Also in combs. denoting machinery used for washing in various industrial processes, as *wash-drill, -stocks, -wheel.*

1959 *Sears, Roebuck Catal.* Spring/Summer 493/1 *Wash and wear suits... Launder by hand or washing machine... Machine-dry or drip-dry. **1966** *Wall St. Jrnl.* 11 Feb. 1/1 Permanent press differs from wash-and-wear... Wash-and-wear doesn't involve baking, but rather depends on the blending of synthetic and natural fibers for wrinkle resistance. Also, wash-and-wear has no permanent crease. **1981** CLARK & SWAINE *Home Managem.* x. 251 The more sophisticated American machines may have a choice of programmes, e.g...synthetics with pre-wash, wash and wear and cold wash. **1981** M. C. SMITH *Gorky Park* I. xii. 164 Parties the Film-Makers Union gave for foreign guests, where the civilized appreciation of a bottle of French perfume or a wash-and-wear skirt was routine. *c* **1555** HARPSFIELD *Divorce Henry VIII* (Camden) 276 One in Kent ..all to beat her yokemate with a *washbeetle or battledore. **1843** *Wash-bench [see *ironing board* s.v. IRONING *vbl. sb.* 1]. **1884** G. W. CABLE *Dr. Sevier* I. xxi. 157 She had reached down and taken from the wash-bench the lump of yellow soap. **1969** N. W. PARSONS *Upon Sagebrush Harp* xxiv. 132 The man was wiping his neck on the roller towel hung above the outdoor washbench. **1875** KNIGHT *Dict. Mech.* 2726 *Wash boiler*, a domestic boiler for clothes. **1913** MRS. STRATTON-PORTER *Laddie* vii. (1917) 124 While Sarah Hood cooked other things, and made a wash-boiler of coffee. **1849** D. CAMPBELL *Inorg. Chem.* 40 This gas..is partially purified by passing through a *wash-bottle containing caustic potash or soda. **1912** *Nature* 19 Dec. 437/2 The experiment succeeds about equally well even when distilled water from a wash-bottle is substituted for powerful reagents. **1900** *Wide World Mag.* Oct. 97/2 We asked of one of the Celestials (our own *wash-boy for the past seven years) permission to take a photograph of the queer scene. **1873** SPON *Workshop Rec.* Ser. I. 6/2 To tint large surfaces, a large camel-hair brush is used, termed a *Wash-brush. **1901** *Macm. Mag.* Apr. 470/1 She produced from her pocket my wash-brush. .. 'What in the world is a brush of that size used for?' she went on. **1915** MRS. STRATTON-PORTER *M. O'Halloran* i. 20 The pieces he saved for *washcloths. **1949** M. MEAD *Male & Female* xii. 262 A baby's face gently washed with a supersoft wash-cloth. **1978** *Detroit Free Press* 5 Mar. (Parade Suppl.) 14E/1 (Advt.), Bath towel, hand towel & washcloth—all cuddly cotton terry. **1878** E. WAKEMAN *Log of Ancient Mariner* ii. 41 Him I had lowered from the bow one dark night, into the *wash-deck tub, in which he paddled to a little schooner close to. **1884** *Naval Encycl.* 835/1 *Wash-deck Gear*, the brooms, squilgees, holy-stones, buckets, etc., used in washing decks. **1901** F. T. BULLEN *Sack of Shakings* 98 One morning, at wash-deck time, when I was prowling around forrard [etc.]. *Ibid.* 115 The wash-deck tub was hauled forrard. **1938** C. S. FORESTER *Ship of Line* i. 22 His captain's admission that he, too, had baths under the washdeck pump. **1907** *Contrib. Econ. Geol., U.S. Geol. Surv., Bulletin* 648 (Cent.) The borings through the alluvium were made by the '*wash drill' or 'water jet'. **1765** *Local Act, Road Barton-Riseham, Lincs.* 9 Sheep going to or returning from any *Wash-dyke. **1927** W. DE LA MARE *Stuff & Nonsense* 54 It galloped up bolsters and *wash-jugs and chairs. **1946** S. SPENDER *European Witness* ii. 18 A large enamel wash-jug. **1787** *Kentucky Gaz.* 24 Nov. 2/3 Samuel Blair, Has for sale..a Quantity of excellent..copper and brass *wash kettles. **1882–3** W. WHITMAN *Specimen Days* 23 They put wash-kettles on the fire for soup, for coffee. **1973** A. DUNDES *Mother Wit* p. xiii, The custom of placing an inverted wash kettle in the center of the floor during a prayer meeting so that the sounds of the singing might go into the pot and thereby not disturb the white folks. **1838** C. GILMAN *Recoll. Southern Matron* xxix. 206 Preparations were made for the wedding which she chose to have performed in the *wash-kitchen instead of our parlour. **1909** 'Q' (Quiller-Couch) *True Tilda* xx, One for Tilda in the wash-kitchen itself, the other for Arthur Miles in a small outhouse adjoining. **1922** JOYCE *Ulysses* 601 It was the daughter of the mother in the washkitchen that was fostersister to the heir of the house. **1890** K. D. WIGGIN *Timothy's Quest* 48 There's lots of baby-clothes hanging on the *wash-lines. **1952** J. STEINBECK *East of Eden* vii. 56 They stole..garments from a wash line. **1969** E. H. PINTO *Treen* 157 Wash line winders are usually strictly utilitarian objects, without any collector interest. **1851** *Washpan [see STUFF *sb.*[1] 4 d]. **1857** J. D. BORTHWICK *Three Yrs. in Calif.* 124 A 'prospecter' goes with a pick and shovel, and a wash-pan. **1884** 'MARK TWAIN' *Huck. Finn* xxxvii. 375 We..scratched around and found an old tin washpan. **1946** G. WILSON *Fidelity Folks* 175 The tin washpan or the creek was good enough for that. **1855** H. PHILLIPS *Rockwood Jrnl.* (typescript) 20 John went with him to *Wash-pen in afternoon. **1890** 'R. BOLDREWOOD' *Col. Reformer* xii, Shearers' huts, wash-pens, machinery, and woolshed. **1852** MRS. STOWE *Uncle Tom's C.* i, Eliza had upset the *wash-pitcher. **1774** J. WOODFORDE *Diary* 15 Oct. (1924) I. 141, I caught a remarkable large Spider in my *Wash Place. **1889** WELCH *Text-bk. Naval Archit.* xi. 130 The lift and force pumps draw from the sea-suctions of the various 9-inch Downton's, to supply the baths, wash places, galleys, etc. **1890** E. L. BYNNER *Begum's Dau.* iv, She employed the interval while her guests were at their luncheon in plying the *wash-rag and comb. **1899** B. C. HIRST *Text-bk. Obstet.* v. ii. 677 Scrubbing the genital region most thoroughly with soap, hot water, and a soft bristle brush or a wash-rag. **1925** F. SCOTT FITZGERALD *Great Gatsby* ii. 27 'It's more of an Airedale.' He passed his hand over the brown washrag of a back. **1964** S. BELLOW *Herzog* 257 He got into her ears with the washrag as she screamed, cleaned off her face, the nostrils, wiped her mouth. **1978** J. UPDIKE *Coup* (1979) v. 192 Her momma's a washrag and her daddy's a redneck. **1857** *Lawrence* (Kansas) *Republ.* 2 July 4 'Here are all the conveniences for washing,' said the landlord, stepping to a mahogany *wash sink and raising the lid. **1873** 'MARK TWAIN' & WARNER *Gilded Age* xxix. 270 It was a small room ..with a wash-sink in one corner. **1849** D. CAMPBELL *Inorg. Chem.* 18 The solution to wash the gas... The small tube passes down into the *wash solution. **1875** *Encycl. Brit.* III. 813/2 (*Bleaching*) The *wash-stocks..consists of a trough or box for holding the goods to be washed, through which a constant stream of water is passing. **1908** *Daily Rep.* 28 Aug. 8/2 Although late in the Empire period the square variety of *wash-table was sometimes used, it is clear that [etc.]. **1909** 'Q' (Quiller-Couch) *True Tilda* xx, Two long *wash-trays stood ready and steaming. **1841** S. CLEGG *Treat. Coal-Gas* 110 If after condensation 'dry lime' is used for purifying, the gas must pass through a *wash-vessel. **1839** URE *Dict. Arts* 417 (*Dyeing*) The hydraulic relations refer to the *wash-wheels and other similar apparatus. **1897** C. T. DAVIS *Manuf. Leather* (ed. 2) 331 Fig. 94 shows a view of the lime-vats,..while in the background is shown the 'wash-wheel'.

c. In certain mining terms, denoting material from which metal is to be obtained by washing: ***wash-gravel, -stuff*** = WASH-DIRT; † **wash-ore** *Lead-mining*, ore ready for washing.

1653 MANLOVE *Lead-Mines* 270 (E.D.S.) Stringes of oar, Wash-oar, and Pumps. **1860** in *Occas. Papers Univ. Sydney Austral. Lang. Res. Centre* (1966) No. 9. 27 The runs of gold and lower deposits are not traceable to reefs but to made hills, composed principally of water-worn quartz nodules and debris, often cemented together with ferruginous matter, the wash-gravel resting on whitish or yellow felspathic schist. **1891** *Century Dict.*, Wash-gravel. Wash-stuff.

d. In recent use (originally *U.S.*), the verb-stem is often prefixed to names of garments and fabrics, with the sense 'washable': e.g. in ***wash-chamois, -foulard, -glacé kid, -glove, -gown, -pants, -ribbon, -silk, -waist.***

In these combinations *wash* is often written as if a separate adj. Cf. WASHING *ppl. a.*

1888 *Boston* (Mass.) *Jrnl.* 23 June 6/3 Rural retreats where she can sleep ten hours out of the twenty-four, wear wash-gowns, and live out of doors all day long. **1902** ELIZ. BANKS *Newspaper Girl* 168 He wore neckties of wash-ribbon—which, though it cost more per yard than the ordinary ribbon, I found the most inexpensive in the end—without a bark of dissatisfaction. **1914** 'AMÉLIE RIVES' *World's-End* xii, A soft gown of white wash-silk fell in straight folds to her feet. **1941** *Daily Progress* (Charlottesville, Va.) 3 July 10/7 (Advt.), Mens & boys swim trunks, wash pants, slack suits, sport shirts, etc. **1972** J. MARYLAND in T. Kochman *Rappin' & Stylin' Out* 210 Red and grown out of wash pants and levis to Oleg Cassini imported mohair suits.

washa'bility. [f. WASHABLE: see -ITY.] The quality of being washable.

1896 H. G. WELLS *Wheels of Chance* ii, Else they [*sc.* drapers] could never have the faith they show in the ..washability..of the goods they sell you. **1958** *Times* 20 Oct. 13/2 This tweed has been woven for the school..and tested for washability. **1970** *Cabinet Maker & Retail Furnisher* 23 Oct. 173/1 Acrylic fibre is nearest to wool in its characteristics with the additional benefit of washability and recovery. **1985** *New Yorker* 20 May 7 (Advt.), The polyester-and-cotton poplin has the convenience of washability.

washable ('wɒʃəb(ə)l), *a.* (*sb.*) [f. WASH *v.* + -ABLE.]

† **1.** That can be used for washing, with which one can wash. *Obs. rare*$^{-1}$.

1623 WODROEPHE *Spared Hours of Soldier* 247 *On dit..que l'eau est nauigable, beuuable & lauable*... Men say..that Water is both nauigable, drinkable & washable.

2. a. That can be washed without damage to texture or colour.

1821 *Blackw. Mag.* X. 562 Pocket-handkerchiefs were quite abandoned,..yea, most things washable. **1838** DICKENS *O. Twist* xxxvii, Like washable beaver hats that improve with rain, his nerves were rendered stouter and more vigorous by showers of tears. **1839** *Civil Engin. & Arch. Jrnl.* II. 141/2 Washable paper hangings. **1887** *Eng. Illustr. Mag.* May 546 Everything was planned so as to be readily washable and brushable.

b. ***washable distemper.***

1894 *Country Gentlemen's Catal.* p. v (Advt.), Taylor's Washable Distemper, in all tints. **1926** F. M. FORD *Man could stand Up* I. ii. 27 Washable distemper was not like the poor—always with you. **1939** *Archit. Rev.* LXXXV. 158 (*caption*) Washable distempers.

c. *sb. pl.* Articles of clothing that may be washed without being damaged.

1951 in M. McLuhan *Mech. Bride* (1967) 95 Colors perk up—brighten up—when you suds your washables in Ivory Flakes. **1973** *Philadelphia Inquirer* 7 Oct. 6 (Advt.), Our lovable washables in Arnel triacetate/nylon pretty with satin piping and bow.

3. Exposed to the washing of the waves.

1878 SMILES *Robt. Dick* v. 44 The sea dashes in through the washable rocks, and drives up in clouds of vapour far inland.

was-hael, washail(e, -hayl: see WASSAIL.

washamouth: see WASH-MOUTH.

washateria, var. WASHETERIA.

'washaway. [f. verbal phr. *to wash away*: see WASH *v.* 15.] The removal by flood of a portion of a hillside; the destruction of a portion of railway or road track by flood; a hole or breach produced by the washing away of soil.

1893 *Westm. Gaz.* 7 Mar. 8/3 The new railway also suffered severely, and traffic has been interfered with owing to several washaways. **1896** *Daily News* 18 July 8/5 In several parts of the mountain where the washaways appear, the lode can be seen right down to the present surface. **1906** *Times* 18 Dec. 5/2 A number of washaways have taken place, and a mail-train was derailed.

washayl, obs. form of WASSAIL.

wash-ball. Now chiefly *Hist.* [f. WASH *v.*] A ball of soap (sometimes perfumed or medicated) used for washing the hands and face, and for shaving.

1601 HOLLAND *Pliny* xxiv. vii. II. 184 This Mastich..is used in sope, and wash-bals. **1672** NEWTON in *Phil. Trans.* VII. 5102 Let some Water, in which a convenient quantity of Soap or wash-ball is dissolv'd, be agitated into Froth. **1683** *Lond. Gaz.* No. 1800/4 James Norcock..sells..the true and large Bolognia Wash-balls. *a* **1700** EVELYN *Diary* (1879) May 1645, We furnish'd ourselves with wash-balls, the best being made here [Bologna]. **1714** [BLANCH] *Beaux Merchant* I. 6 Have you brought my Riding-Whig, Mr. Barber, and your best Scented Wash-balls? **1758** JOHNSON *Idler* No. 40 ⁋4, I remember a wash-ball that had a quality truly wonderful. **1805** [S. WESTON] *Werneria* 39 Some clays are marbled, and look like wash-balls ready made. **1806–7** J. BERESFORD *Miseries Hum. Life* xx. xlii, Dropping a wash-ball out of your frozen fingers. **1842** BORROW *Bible in Spain* xiii, He..forthwith produced two scented wash-balls which he offered for sale. **1936** *Burlington Mag.* Mar. 123/2 A plain globular soap-box (called a washball box in England some fifty years earlier). **1966** T. H. RADDALL *Hangman's Beach* II. x. 150 And now came the grey attendant with wash-ball and towel, and a small wooden tub of steaming water. **1970** *Canad. Antiques Collector* Nov. 16/1 Out of the..cupboard came a silver plated shaving bowl and ewer, while from one small drawer appeared a pair of silver soap or wash ball boxes. **1980** E. JONG *Fanny* II. xii. 280 The true Royal Chymical Wash-Ball for the beautifying of the Hands and Face.

wash-basin. [f. WASH *v.*] A wash-hand basin.

1812 *Examiner* 23 Nov. 739/2 The wash-bason [was] almost filled. **1855** J. SCOFFERN in *Orr's Circ. Sci., Elem. Chem.* 431 The..negro princes obtain English wash-basins. **1860** O. W. HOLMES *Professor* iv, A new nursery,..with Lake Superior, and Huron..for wash-basins! **1904** S. E. WHITE *Forest* ii, Dishes, pails, wash-basins, and other receptacles. **1928** GALSWORTHY *Swan Song* I. v. 35 We must get some more wash-basins in. **1980** *Sunday Times* (Colour Suppl.) 21 Sept. 50 (Advt.), This soft, subtle shade..reveals the potential..of the range of wash basins. **1984** WORTHINGTON & KNIGHT *Home Plumbing* 103/2 The normal height for a wash-basin is 800 mm..from the rim to the floor.

wash-bear. ? *U.S.* [f. WASH *v.* In Ger. *waschbär*, a transl. of the zoological name *Ursus lotor* (Linn.); cf. WASHER 4 b, *washing bear*, WASHING *ppl. a.* 3.] The racoon.

1891 *Century Dict.*

washboard, *sb.* (*adj.*) [f. WASH *sb.*; cf. G. *waschbrett.*]

I. 1. *Naut.* A board on the side of a boat to prevent the sea breaking over; also, a board on the sill of a lower-deck port, for the same purpose.

1742 WOODROOFE in *Hanway's Trav.* (1762) I. II. xvii. 78 The largest boat was towed a-stern, being raised with washboards for that purpose. **1825** T. HOOK *Sayings* Ser. II. *Passion & Princ.* xv. III. 399 She shipped a heavy sea, which washed away all the starboard bulwarks and washboards. **1888** T. T. WILDRIDGE *Northumbria* 134 The structural points of interest in this [ancient] boat are the 'washboards' and the wooden pegs.

2. A board round the walls of a room with its edge resting on the floor; a skirting-board. *dial.*

1828–32 WEBSTER, *Wash-board*. 2. a board in a room, next to the floor. **1860** GEO. ELIOT *Mill on Fl.* II. iii, To stand looking out of the study window at the rain, and kicking his foot against the washboard in solitude. **1862** [C. C. ROBINSON] *Dialect of Leeds*, Gloss., *Washboard* (pron. *weshboard*), the wainscot.

3. † **a.** A flat piece of wood fixed on an axis within the barrel of a washing-machine, and made to revolve so as to agitate the clothes in the water. *Obs.* **b.** *U.S.* A hardwood board, with a fluted surface or covered with corrugated zinc, on which clothes are rubbed in washing.

1799 *Hull Advertiser* 29 June 2/2 Washing machines which move with a pendulum or upright wash-board in the inside. **1845** J. W. Norris *Business Adviser & Gen. Directory Chicago* 95 Manufacturer of the improved zinc wash-boards. **1882** Howells in *Longman's Mag.* I. 56 Wherever the piano-forte penetrates, lovely woman lifts her fingers from the needle, the broom-handle, and the washboard. **1902** Eliz. Banks *Newspaper Girl* 158 Clothes washed by her own hands on an American washboard in a big wooden tub.

c. A washboard (sense 3 b) used as a percussion instrument; hence, the kind of music produced by bands using this instrument. Freq. *attrib.*

1925 J. Taylor (*title of musical composition*) Wash-board blues. **1933** *Gramophone* June 26/1 Washboard bands are the red-nosed comedians of dance music... They usually play about with delightfully inconsequent tunes. *Ibid.*, There is a good deal to be said for Yes Suh..by the Washboard Rhythm Kings... The gent on the washboard is a dexterous performer. **1946**, etc. [see JUG *sb.*[2] 1 c]. **1947** R. de Toledano *Frontiers of Jazz* 107 The first washboard was recorded by me. **1961** W. Sansom *Last Hours Sandra Lee* vii. 173 There came a machine slamming of washboard music and wailing voices that sounded as if they were lost in a large, echoing cave. **1973** J. Marks *Mick Jagger* (1974) 56 Washboard was also fair enough, if you wanted that sort of sound... You know..more or less a primitive sort of Chicago sound. **1973** J. Wainwright *Pride of Pigs* 174 Instead of a drummer there was a young kid with a washboard and thimbles.

4. *fig.* A corrugated surface, esp. of a road.

1934 in Webster. **1950** J. Dempsey *Championship Fighting* 186 Bending exercises are best to develop the stomach muscles into a protective 'washboard' against body blows. **1968** G. Jones *Hist. Vikings* III. i. 156 Not only a 'washboard' of wide furrows is visible, but even the wheel-tracks of the viking farmer's last carting. **1976** [see REG[2]]. **1979** *Tucson Mag.* Apr. 51/1 The long gravel drive to its shore..tends to turn into a washboard in the drier summer months.

II. 5. *attrib.* as *adj.* Corrugated, furrowed, esp. as a result of weather and usage.

1913 *Bull. Geol. Soc. Amer.* XXIV. 145 The till sheet over large areas has been rubbed into a fluted or wash-board form on a large scale, but with low relief. **1936** *Trans. R. Soc. Canada* XXX. IV. 10 In the general area where these wash-board moraines were noted there are extensive sand plains. **1949** *Consumer Rep.* Jan. 8/1 Pick out a hubbly surface or a 'washboard' gravel road. **1953** W. Moore *Bring Jubilee* (1955) i. 6 The morasses or wash-board roads which were the only highways. **1968** R. W. Fairbridge *Encycl. Geomorphol.* 989/2 Steep valley slopes [in a rain forest] typically have a washboard topography, a simple parallel consequent drainage system. **1976** *New Motorcycling Monthly* Oct. 6/3 Washboard surfaces would set the rear wheel pattering.

wash bough. *dial.* [? WASH *a.* Cf. WATER-BOUGH.] (See quot. 1823.)

1612 T. Taylor *Comm. Titus* i. 16. 321 Their care is but to cut off the wash boughs of sin, but they leaue the bole, and stumpe standing. **1823** Moor *Suffolk Words*, *Wash-boughs*, the lower straggling branches of trees.

wash-bowl. [f. WASH *v.*]

†**1.** A wash-tub. *Obs.*

a **1529** Skelton *Sp. Parrot* 155 Our Grekys ye walow in the washbol *Argolicorum*. **1585** Higins *Junius' Nomencl.* 231/1 *Labrum*,..a washing tub or washbooll. **1620** Gataker *Mariage Praier* 19 It is no shame for thee, though thou beest wealthy, to seeke her [a wife] at the wash-boule. **1673** Bp. S. Parker *Reproof Reh. Transp.* 11 So that methinks according to your notion, there is nothing so patly emblematical of Soveraign Princes, as Dufoy in his Tub, or a Pig under a wash-bole. **1698** Collier *Immor. Stage* v. § 3. 222 So that if he was resolv'd to have shown her thus unpolish'd, he should have made her keep Sheep, or brought her up at the Wash-Boul.

2. a. A wash-hand basin.

1816 U. Brown *Jrnl.* in *Maryland Hist. Mag.* (1915) X. 369 His wash-bowl [is] the knot of a tree. **1883** C. D. Warner *Roundabout Journ.* 183 The guest is allowed a wash-bowl, but no pitcher. **1888** *Q. Rev.* Jan. 132 Emerson alone took no part in this 'storm in a wash-bowl'. **1904** E. Nesbit *Phœnix & Carpet* viii. 157 Jane fetched the wash-bowl from the sink.

b. *spec.* A vessel in which gold is washed.

1848 in *Essex Inst. Hist. Coll.* (1874) XII. 106, I came from Salem City, With my wash bowl on my knee. **1850** E. Christman *Jrnl.* 3 Apr. in *One Man's Gold* (1930) 131, I am standing in a hole to the depth of my knees, with my pick raised high in the air; my spade and washbowl are lying upon the ground by my side. **1925** E. O'Neill *Desire under Elms* I. iv. 66 Their voices..take up the song of the gold-seekers to the old tune of 'Oh Susannah'... 'I'm off to Californi-a! With my wash bowl on my knee.'

'washbrew. *dial.* [f. WASH *sb.* or *v.*] Oatmeal boiled to a stiff jelly.

1620 Markham *Farew. Husb.* xv. 134 Of Oatemeale is made that meate which is called in the West, Washbrew. **1623** —— *Eng. Housew.* vi. 222 You shall not heare of any that euer did surfeite of this Wash-brew or Flammerie. **1837** J. F. Palmer *Mrs. Palmer's Dial. Devon. Dialect* Gloss. 95 *Wash-brew*, flummery; oatmeal boiled in water till it acquires a gelatinous consistence.

wash-coloured, *a.* [f. WASH *sb.*] Having the appearance of a 'wash' or transparent layer of colour.

1879 E. P. Wright *Animal Life* 195 The fur [of chinchilla] is long, thick, close, woolly, somewhat crisped,..greyish wash-coloured above and paler beneath.

wash-dirt. *Mining.* [WASH *sb.* or *v.*] Auriferous soil or gravel to be submitted to washing.

1862 *Otago: Goldfields & Resources* 20 All the wash-dirt is auriferous. **1864** Eliz. Murray *Ella Norman* III. 58 Under the wash-dirt or stuff..there is always pipeclay. **1864** J. Rogers *New Rush* II. 30 A bucket-full of wash-dirt tried —the best—Is of its value a sufficient test. **1877** Raymond *Statist. Mines & Mining* 43 Large piles of wash-dirt are accumulated to be washed in the winter. **1890** *Goldfields of Victoria* 28 Good tin can be obtained, mixed with a fair percentage of gold in the dish of washdirt.

'wash-dish. [f. WASH *v.*]

1. *dial.* = DISH-WASHER 3. [Cf. F. *lavandière* (Cotgr.).]

1825 Jennings *Observ. Dial. W. Eng.*, *Wash-dish*, the bird called wagtail. **1862** Johns *Brit. Birds* 625 Wash-dish and Washerwoman, the Pied Wagtail. **1867** Rock *Jim an' Nell* cxxv, 'Twas a wash-dish.

2. A wash-hand basin. *U.S.*

1805 *Austin Papers* (1924) I. 140, 1 Wash dish. **1839** Mrs. Kirkland *New Home* iv. 26 After the 'wash dish' had been used in turn, and various handkerchiefs had performed.. the part of towels. **1857** *Quinland* I. II. i. 275 An iron kettle, which I and all the family used as a common wash-dish before breakfast. **1876** *Rep. Vermont Board Agric.* III. 628 The farmer..was able to furnish a large maple block to set the wash-dish on. **1891** M. E. Freeman *New England Nun & Other Stories* 271 I've got my tin wash-dish there on the bench.

'washdown. [f. vbl. phr. *to wash down*: see WASH *v.* 1 g.] **1.** The, or an, act of washing down; *spec.* an act of washing oneself from top to bottom at a wash-basin as distinct from in a bath or under a shower.

1949 *Amer. Speech* XXIV. 35 Another characteristic of oil-field language is the predominance of compound words. .. The conversion of some verb-adverb combinations into nouns and adjectives are *back-up*, *clean-out*..and *washdown*. **1972** *Bottlers' Year Bk. 1972–73* 40 Taking washdown first —obvious waste can be reduced from running hoses left unattended. **1972** J. Wilson *Hide & Seek* vii. 132, I have a washdown every day and a bath on Sundays. **1979** *Nature* 29 Mar. p. xxx/1 The instrument eliminates bumping and smearing of the sides of the tubes thus eliminating the necessity for washdowns.

2. *attrib.* Of a lavatory: (see quot. 1967). Also *absol.*

1967 *Gloss. Sanitation Terms* (*B.S.I.*) 64 *Washdown W.C. pan*, a W.C. pan in which the excrement falls into the water in the trap and is subsequently removed by the momentum of the flushing water. **1976** *Evening Advertiser* (Swindon) 31 Dec. 4/2 (Advt.), Bathroom suite: consisting of..low level washdown toilet. **1984** Worthington & Knight *Home Plumbing* 96/2 There is a choice of pan styles... The most common is the washdown.

wash-drawing. [f. WASH *sb.* or *v.*] The method of water-colour drawing in which washes of colour are extensively used; a picture produced by this method.

1889 J. Pennell *Pen Drawing* 305, I have heard from them more expressions of pleasure in a pen drawing..than I have ever heard given to a pencil or a wash drawing. **1892** *Photogr. Ann.* III. p. ccliii, Photographs from Nature, Wash Drawings, Paintings, &c. **1894** C. G. Harper *Handbk. Drawing* 121 Wash drawings for reproduction by half-tone process should be made upon smooth or finely grained cardboards. **1905** *Athenæum* 9 Dec. 806/3 In this..Ludlow Castle..the real science of wash-drawing is shown.

washe, obs. form of WATCH.

washeall, rare obs. f. WASSAIL.

washed (wɒʃt), *ppl. a.* [f. WASH *v.* + -ED[1].]

1. a. Cleansed by rubbing in water or other liquid; also, moistened or drenched with water.

1557 North *Guevara's Diall Pr.* IV. vii. (1568) 125 b, A paire of washed or perfume gloues. **1586** Whitney *Choice Emblems* 136 With Towell faire, to wipe theire washed hands. **1605** Shaks. *Lear* I. i. 271 The Iewels of our Father, with wash'd eies Cordelia leaues you. **1620** Markham *Farew. Husb.* xiii. 104 Now it is not amisse that I speake here a word or two of washt corne, or the washing of corne. **1705** *Lond. Gaz.* No. 4184/4, 302 Bags of Cloth wash'd and unwash'd Spanish Felt Wooll. **1812** Byron *Ch. Har.* I. lxix, Then thy spruce citizen, wash'd artisan, And smug apprentice gulp their weekly air. **1864** T. S. Williams & Simmonds *Engl. Commerc. Corresp.* 239, 1s. 6d. pr. lb. for washed Merino free from burr.

b. Treated with water or other liquid so as to remove impurities or soluble matter, to separate heavier from lighter parts, etc.

c **1575** *Perf. Bk. Kepinge Sparhawkes* (1886) 9 This..will make more synues then all the scourings or washed meates that are used. **1600** Surflet *Country Farm* v. xxi. 721 Washed bread is a meate very profitable for the health.. bicause the washing of it doth wholie take away the heauines and clammines belonging vnto the earthie parts thereof. **1729** Woodward *Fossils* I. I. 169 This last the People who gather it here, call Wash'd-Amber. ? **1785** Imison *Sch. Arts* (1796) II. 68 Adding about one part of washed whiting to three parts of carmine. **1810** J. Bailey *Agric. Durham* 40 *note*, This is not clean or washed ore; but ore mixed with other substances that could not be separated in washing. **1849** Pereira *Elem. Mat. Med.* (ed. 3) I. 344 When thus purified, it is called washed sulphur (*sulphur lotum vel depuratum*). **1884** F. J. Britten *Watch & Clockm.* 101 Washed or double-washed Emery.

†**c.** Of coin: Sweated. *Obs.*

1711 J. Tonson *Waller's Poems* A 3, Clipt and washt money goes about, when the entire and weighty lies hoarded up.

d. Covered with a coating of precious metal.

1772 *Lond. Chron.* 21–24 Mar. 288/3 It appeared there was but four shillings out of the guinea and half [of silver] good, the rest being only a washed metal. **1776** *Pennsylv. Even. Post* 25 May 264/2 An olive coloured short fustian coat, with..silver washed buttons.

e. Of a water-colour or monochrome drawing: Having the tints produced by colour laid on in 'washes'.

1770 *Exhib. R. Acad.* 19 The Resurrection,..a washed drawing. **1784** J. Barry *Lect. Art* iii. (1848) 133 Raphael's washed drawing of the Calumny of Apelles. **1884** Linton *Wood-Engraving* 50 A 'washed drawing' is one in which shadows, broad tints,..(indeed all masses of colour,) are washed in broadly with a brush in sepia or India ink.

f. Of stock, or sale of stock: see quot. and WASH *v.* 20 b.

1886 *Harper's Mag.* July 205/1 Washed or fictitious sales, or false reports of sales, are also penal offences. **1888–9** *New York Produce Exch. Rep.* 265 (Cent.) Washed or fictitious sales are positively forbidden.

†**g.** *fig.* Of language: ? Refined, elegant. (? after L. *lautus*.) *Obs.*

1628 Feltham *Resolves* I. xx. 67, I know, God hath chosen by weake things, to confound the wise: yet I see not but in all times, a washed Language hath much preuailed.

†**h.** ***washed leather*** = WASH-LEATHER. *Obs.*

1694 Motteux *Rabelais* IV. xxxii, Wash'd-Leather Boots [*botines de cordouan*].

i. Of a carpet: faded, bleached; specially treated so as to soften the colours and impart a sheen.

1911 G. G. Lewis *Pract. Bk. Oriental Rugs* iii. 40 What the trade speaks of as a 'washed' rug is not necessarily a 'doctored' one. There is a legitimate form of washing which is really a finishing process... It merely washes out the surplus color and sets the rest. **1962** C. W. Jacobsen *Oriental Rugs* 121 The danger of your buying both chemically washed and painted rugs today is practically nil. **1969** [see *Peking carpet* s.v. PEKING 3]. **1970** 'D. Halliday' *Dolly & Cookie Bird* ii. 20 My room had..wall-to-wall washed Chinese carpeting in quiet shades of money. **1982** G. F. Newman *Men with Guns* x. 74 Wallechinsky moved agitatedly across the living room..his expensive, imported shoes making a faint squeak on the washed silk Chinese rug.

2. washed out. a. Of a fabric, dye, etc.: That has faded, or lost freshness, in the wash.

1796 Jane Austen *Let.* 1 Sept. (1952) 9 My new coloured gown is very much washed out, though I charged everybody to take great care of it. **1837** J. Morier *Abel Allnutt* xx. 117 The threadbare carpets, the washed-out curtains. **1851** Mayhew *Lond. Labour* I. 342/1 Habited in a washed-out-blue French kind of pinafore. **1875** Jowett *Plato* (ed. 2) III. 51 The shabby washed-out look of any colour which has not been dyed in this way.

b. *fig.* Lacking in colour, animation, etc.

1850 Smedley *F. Fairlegh* i, A complexion and general appearance only to be described by the term 'washed out'. **1862** Trollope *Orley F.* xii, There was..none of that lanky, washed-out appearance which sorrow and trouble so often give to females. **1865** W. Cory *Lett. & Jrnls.* (1897) 166 They are a washed-out lot; but they laugh. **1885** Huxley in *Life* (1900) II. vi. 95, I am better..but curiously weak and washed out.

3. ***(all) washed up***: finished; without prospect of further success or competence; no longer on intimate terms; exhausted, 'washed out'. *slang* (orig. and chiefly *U.S.*).

1923 *N.Y. Times* 9 Sept. VII. 2/1 [Stage slang.] *Washed up*, all through for the night. **1925** *Amer. Speech* I. 36/1 [Stage slang.] How cheery it would be, when family ties begin to irk, to use their honest, 'I'm washed up with you,' to indicate that you hope the breach is permanent. **1933** S. Kingsley *Men in White* (1934) III. i. 109 I'm washed up with the whole business. **1934** W. Saroyan *Daring Young Man* 38 We're washed up as a race, we're through, it's all over. **1935** J. T. Farrell *Judgment Day* (1945) I. xvi. 312 His lips twisted into a sneer at himself, and he thought that he was just a goddam washed-up has-been. **1942** J. B. Priestley *Black-Out in Gretley* viii. 182 You're too careless, Joe..and now you're all washed up. **1958** C. Williams *Man in Motion* (1959) ii. 23 I'm washed up as a writer. **1980** *Newsweek* 17 Nov. 7/1 Once he was the most underestimated man in American politics—a washed-up movie star, it was said, who was too old, too simple and too far right to be President.

4. ***to get washed up***: to get the washing up done.

1950 J. Cannan *Murder Included* i. 12 Have to dine early now... We've only got Mrs Witts in the kitchen, and she likes to get washed up and finished.

†**'washel.** *Obs.* In 4 wass(c)hele. [f. WASH *v.*: see -EL.] **a.** A bath. **b.** A vessel for washing.

1303 R. Brunne *Handl. Synne* 11033 Þere besyde, yn a paþ Was a wasshyng, at an hote baþ; 'Termes' men calle þat watyr wasshele, For many one had þerat here hele. *a* **1375** *Joseph Arim.* 288 Þenne comen two Angeles..Oþur Tweyne aftur hem with cruetes sone, and wasscheles wiþ haly water with hem þei brouȝten.

washen ('wɒʃ(ə)n), *ppl. a. arch.* and *dial.* [str. pa. pple. of WASH *v.*] Washed. Also with adv. prefixed, as ***clean-***, ***ill-***, ***new-***, ***well-washen***.

1483 *Cath. Angl.* 415/1 Weschyn, *lotus*. **1525–34** Fitzherb. *Husb.* § 122 Laye a clene washen shete vppon the stole. **1594** A. Hume *Poems* etc. (S.T.S.) 101 Til eit meat with weschen or vnweschen hands. **1617** *Extracts Aberd. Reg.* (1848) II. 350 With goode bedding, weele washine and weele smellit naprie. **1637** Rutherford *Let. to Ld. Craighall* 10 Aug., Some ill-washen and foul distinctions. **1868** H. Law *Beacons of Bible* (1869) 89 The washen swine returning to the mire. **1870** Bryant *Iliad* I. 563 With washen hands They took the salted meal. **1879** Butcher & Lang *Odyss.* VI. 64. 94 These are always eager for new-washen garments wherein to go to the dances.

†**b.** ***washen leather*** = WASH-LEATHER. *Obs.*

Cf. *washed leather*, WASHED 1 h.
*c*1425 *York Memo. Bk.* (Surtees) I. 65 For a dossan wesshyn leddyr.

washer ('wɒʃə(r)), *sb.*[1] Forms: 4 ? **waschere**, 5–6 **wassher**, (5 **wasscher**, 6 **waysher**), 6 *Sc.* **weschear, veschiar**, 7 *Sc.* **wascher**, 6– **washer**. [f. WASH *v.* + -ER[1].

An OE. *wæscere* is given by Sweet *A.S. Dict.*, but no example has been found, though the existence of the word is probable: cf. WASHESTER.]

1. One who washes.

1450–1530 *Myrr. our Ladye* III. 306 Mediatrix, Menesse of men, and wassher of synnes. **1572** HULOET (ed. Higins), Washer, *lotor.* **1706** BAYNARD in Sir J. Floyer *Hot & Cold Bath.* II. 263 No Men live so long and healthful, as the Washers and Dablers in Cold Water. **1760–72** H. BROOKE *Fool of Qual.* (1809) IV. 55 The lowliness of a washer of feet. **1770** G. WHITE *Selborne, To Barrington* 8 Oct., Common house-sparrows..are great washers. **1886** *Daily News* 16 Sept. 8/5 Good Laundrymaid Wanted in a private house. Must be a good washer and ironer. **1909** *Daily Chron.* 24 Mar. 4/6 In these days when washing is made either a fad or a religion, according to the temperament of the washer.

†**2.** One who sweats coin. See WASH *v.* 8. *Obs.*

[**1414** *Rolls of Parlt.* IV. 35/2 Les lavours, tonsours, & contrefaitours del monie de la Terre.] *c*1440 *Jacob's Well* 19 And we denounce acursed alle makeres of fals monye, & clypperes, and wasscherys. **1534** *Act 26 Hen. VIII* c. 6 §6 There to cause all suche counterfaytors, washers, clyppers of money..to be indyted. **1771** *Encycl. Brit.* III. 256/1 Clippers and washers of coin.

3. a. One whose occupation or profession is the cleansing of materials, vessels, etc.

1515 *Acc. Ld. High Treas. Scot.* V. 20 Ane fynour, weschear, and meltar of gold. [*a* **1529**–: see DISH-WASHER 1.] **1621** ELSING *Lords' Deb.* (Camden) 34 Shewes the washing by them [the silk-throwsters], who washed away the gum. Then the dyer was founde out to add that to the weight what the washers had taken away, which the washer coulde not doe. **1807** E. S. WARING *Tour Sheeraz* 21 A Moordu-Sho (a washer of dead bodies). **1844** M. T. ASMAR *Mem. Babyl. P'cess* II. 176 'Wherefore,' said the washer of skins, 'thou seest, a marvellous change was wrought in me'.

†**b.** A person employed to wash and 'get up' household linen, a launderer or laundress. *Obs.*

1530 PALSGR. 287/1 Wassher of gownes, *relaueur.* **1557** *Order of Hospitalls* G ij, Yow shall geue diligent heede that the said Washers and Nurses of this Howse be alwaies well occupied. **1598** SHAKS. *Merry W.* I. ii. 5 One Mistris Quickly; which is in the manner of his Nurse;..or his Laundry; his Washer, and his Ringer. **1620** MIDDLETON *Chaste Maid* II. ii, Two of my wife's foul smocks going to the washers. **1642** *St. Mary le Bow* (Durham) *Par. Reg.*, Margarett the washer bur. 15 May. **1732** FIELDING *Covent Gard. Trag.* I. ix, Thus burning from the fire, the washer lifts The red-hot iron to make smooth her shifts. **1775** S. J. PRATT *Liberal Opin.* lxxii. (1783) III. 34 A girl in Hodge-lane, who owed some three or four pound to her washer.

c. One who washes sheep before shearing.

1520 in *Archæologia* XXV. 437 Item p[d] to Barnaby Bryse ..for castyng inne y[e] shepe to y[e] wayshers viij d. **1612** *Shuttleworths' Acc.* (Chetham Soc.) 200 To the washers of the sheepe, vj[d]. **1641** BEST *Farm. Bks.* (Surtees) 18 One good washer will..wash sixe score or sixe score and tenne [sheep] in a day. **1827** HONE *Every-day Bk.* II. 788 The rude grasp of the relentless washer.

d. One who washes (ore, alluvial soil, etc.) as a mining operation.

1531–2 [see BUDDLE *sb.*[2]]. **1555** EDEN *Decades* (Arb.) 212 These wasshers [at the gold mines] for the moste parte, are the Indian women. **1609** in Cochran-Patrick *Early Rec. Mining Scot.* (1878) 143 Waschers with the seiff. *Ibid.*, Dressaris and wascheris with the buddill, wascheris with the canves. **1747** HOOSON *Miner's Dict.* N 3 b, And the washer always keeps a Lay of this over the Bottom of the Seive. **1849** LEVER *Con Cregan* xxii, Others rarely rise above the rank of mere 'washers'—men employed to sift the..deposits of the rivers in which the chief product is gold-dust. **1870** J. O. TUCKER *Mute* 40 A thousand washers in their rude array Bend to a toil and none superior knew.

e. One who is employed in a stable-yard, cab or omnibus depôt, etc., to wash down the vehicles after use.

1868 *Daily News* 8 Sept., Besides the yard money..we must give the horsekeeper at least 3d., the washer 2d. **1884** *Bath Jrnl.* 26 July 7/3 On returning to the yard at night he has to stump up..a tip..of three pence to the washer.

f. with advs.

1859 K. CORNWALLIS *Panorama New World* I. 323 Wanted, a Washer-up.—Victoria Dining-rooms. **1881** M. REYNOLDS *Engine Driving Life* 132 Another gang of men known as *washers-out*, set to and clean the boiler out. **1906** A. B. TODD *Poet. Wks.* etc., Remin. vii. 68 My duties were to be what is called a 'washer-off' to a tile-moulder.

4. a. A popular name of the Wagtail, *Motacilla lugubris.* Cf. WASH-DISH 1, DISH-WASHER 3, and WASHERWOMAN 2.

*c*1325 *Gloss. W. de Bibbesw.* in Wright *Voc.* 165 La vanele e le pounzot (*glossed* a wype and wasthere [? *read* waschere]). **1556** WITHALS *Dict.* (1562) 5/1 A wagtaile, wassher ..*motacilla.* [**1575**–: see DISH-WASHER 3.] **1668** CHARLETON *Onomast.* 90 *Motacilla*..the washer, or water-wagtail. **1797** BEWICK *Brit. Birds* I. 187 *note*, They are sometimes called Washers, from their peculiar motion. **1885** SWAINSON *Prov. Names Birds* 44 Pied Wagtail..Moll washer.

b. A name of the Racoon. Cf. WASH-BEAR, *washing-bear* (WASHING *ppl. a.* 3).

[**1858** BAIRD *Cycl. Nat. Sci.* (1860) 569/2 The racoon, *Procyon lotor*, is a native of America... Its specific name, *lotor* (washer), is derived from its habit of plunging its dry food into water before eating it.] **1891** *Century Dict.*; and in other recent Dicts.

5. a. An apparatus for washing; a washing-machine used in various industries.

1808 I. C. CURWEN *Econ. Feeding Stock* 33 The washer being removed by the crane, to the place where the dirty potatoes are laid. **1860** R. HUNT *Ure's Dict. Arts* (ed. 5) III. 977 The small coal resulting from the washer..is delivered into a common pit placed under the washers. **1875** *Encycl. Brit.* III. 816/2 (Bleaching) The continuous washer.. patented in 1852, is deserving of notice as a simple and efficient washing-machine. **1877** RAYMOND *Statist. Mines & Mining* 389 The cement silver is washed in a washer invented by Professor Pearce.

b. A machine in which the rags used in paper-making are worked to wash and open their fibres.

1825 J. NICHOLSON *Oper. Mech.* 366 The paper-mill consists of a water-wheel,..connected with..wheels, so arranged as to cause the cylinder in the washer, and the one in the beating engine,..to make from 120 to 150 revolutions per minute. **1839** URE *Dict. Arts* 926 There is another [engine],..called the washer, in which the rags are first worked coarsely with a stream of water.

c. An apparatus for cleansing coal-gas.

1853 S. HUGHES *Gas-works* 134 Of the washer and condenser for separating the tar and ammoniacal liquor. **1883** *Chamb. Jrnl.* 267 The resulting gas is led off to a washer, and thence to a gasholder.

d. A machine for washing domestic linen.

1884 *Health Exhib. Catal.* 116/2 Seven of Greenall's Steam Washers, different sizes, for domestic use. Clothes are washed by steam. **1894** ELIZ. BANKS *Camp. Curiosity* 190 She carefully measured the amount of soda that was put into the washers. **1908** *Daily Chron.* 19 Feb. 9/6 Washer (40-shirt hand) by Whitaker.

e. An apparatus for washing photographic plates or prints.

1891 *Anthony's Photogr. Bull.* IV. 97 The prints on being taken out of the washer are well sponged..before drying.

f. A machine for washing dishes; a dish-washer.

1958 I. ASIMOV *Whiff of Death* xvii. 170 Just let me put the dishes in the washer and then we'll go to bed. **1976** H. MACINNES *Agent in Place* xx. 215 She stacked dishes into the washer.

†**6.** An instrument or tool used for sprinkling or cleansing. **a.** A smith's tool: see quots. **b.** ? A sponge for cleansing the bore of a gun. *Obs.*

a. 1677 MOXON *Mech. Exerc.* i. 10 With your Washer dipt in Water damp the outside of the Fire to keep the Heat in. **1688** HOLME *Armoury* III. 321/1 Smiths Tools... The Washer, is a Bundle of Rushes..with an Iron Stail to it; with this Water is sprinkled out of the Trough into the Fire to make it burn the hotter.
b. 1708 [see SCOURER[2] 5].

7. a. A cock or outlet valve of a water-supplying pipe. **b.** The outlet valve of a basin, cistern, etc. to which the waste-pipe is attached.

1596 HARINGTON *Anat. Metam. Ajax* L iij b, To which pype you must haue a Cocke or a washer to yeeld water with some pretie strength, when you would let it in. **1712** J. JAMES tr. *Le Blond's Gardening* 199 If it be a Four-inch Pipe, you should give it a Washer and Opening of six Inches at the Bottom of the Reserver. *Ibid.* 211 To empty the Bason entirely.., which is done by means of a Washer, and a Waste-Pipe at the Bottom of it. **1716** *Lond. Gaz.* No. 5493/3 Brass Cocks, Washers, &c. of all Sizes. **1859** GWILT *Archit.* (ed. 4) Add. to Gloss., *Washer*,..the perforated metal plate of a sink or drain, which can be removed for letting off the waste water. **1875** KNIGHT *Dict. Mech.* s.v., *Washer* 3. b. A street-washer or pavement-plug, where a hose may be attached to water the street, pavement, or urban garden.

†**8.** Some kind of cloth. *Obs.*

1613 J. MAY *Decl. Estate Clothing* v. 32 There haue some merchants caused counterfeit Deuonshire kersies to bee made in Yorkshire out of washers or halfethicks. **1627** *Treasurer's Almanacke* (ed. 2) B 8 b, [List of Woollen cloths.] Washers of Lancashire.

9. A face-flannel. *Austral.*

1951 D. CUSACK *Say No to Death* xxxi. 194 Doreen had given her a washer and a drop of warm water to wash the sleep out of her eyes. **1970** P. WHITE *Vivisector* iv. 236 He was reminded of an old face-washer, often grubby, one of the maids had crocheted for him, in wide mesh.

10. *Comb.*, as (sense 3 b) ***washer-girl, -maiden***; (sense 5) ***washer-cloth***; **washer-drier**, a machine that both washes clothes and dries them; also WASHERMAN, WASHERWOMAN.

1876 HENLEY *Life & Death* xxx. *Bk. Verses* (1888) 92 The pretty washer-maiden, She washes on always! **1887** *Manch. Exhib. Catal.* 63 Cotton Manufacturers' Roller, Clearer, Washer, and Sizing Cloth. *Ibid.*, Washer Cloth for Mill Furnishing. **1907** JEAN WEBSTER *Jerry Junior* ii. 22 The washer-girls were dressed in the gayest of peasant clothes. **1968** *Listener* 1 Aug. 130/1 The unappealing image of America as a country..whose highest aspirations were another car in the garage or a bigger washer-dryer. **1971** *Which?* Mar. 72/2 Contracts for automatics cost about £9, for a washer-drier (like a Bendix) about £12. **1983** *The Mag.* Dec. 59/4 Built-in kitchen equipment, including dishwashers and washer-dryers.

washer ('wɒʃə(r)), *sb.*[2] Also 4 **whasher**, 6 **wassher**, 8 **wisher**. [Of doubtful origin; usually assumed to be a use of prec., but the development of meaning has not been accounted for.] A perforated annular disc or flattened ring of metal, leather, or other material placed between two surfaces subject to rotative friction, to relieve friction and prevent lateral motion and unsteadiness.

1346 *Acc. Exch. K.R.* 470/17 m. 2 De..v Cheynes pro barr[a] continentibus L. Linches, v. paribus tenellarum, ij. Whashers [etc.]. **1544** in *Lett. & Papers Hen. VIII*, XIX. I. 148 Spare wheles for small ordynaunce 12 pair, lyncepynnes, wasshers, [etc.]. **1611** FLORIO, *Cérchio di ferro*, an iron hoope, amongst gunners called a washer, which serues to keepe the iron pin at the end of the axeltree from wearing the naue. **1682** [see LINCH-PIN]. **1704–26** *Dict. Rust.* s.v. *Cart*, The *Washers*, being the Rings on the ends of the Axle-tree. **1705** tr. *Guillet's Gentl. Dict.* II. s.v. *Nave*, It has likewise in each end of the hole, through which the end of the Axletree goes, a ring of iron called the wisher, which saves the hole of the nave from wearing too big. **1795** HERSCHEL in *Phil. Trans.* LXXXV. 371 It is keyed fast at C; with proper washers between the joints to allow of a very smooth motion. **1805** R. W. DICKSON *Pract. Agric.* I. Plate xii, Every tooth screws through a double frame separated by iron washers for greater steadiness. **1847** BRANDON *Anal. Goth. Archit.* 102 The closing ring or door latch..[consists of] the flat plate or washer, fixed to the outer surface of the door; the handle or ring; and the spindle. **1872** O. W. HOLMES *Poet* i, A washer..makes a loose screw fit. **1876** BLACKMORE *Cripps* xxvi, The vast diversity of wheels, as well as their many caprices of wagging, according to the state of their washers.

b. An annular disc of leather, rubber, or other material placed between the flanges of abutting water-pipes, beneath the plunger of a screw-down water-tap, etc. to prevent leakage.

1850 OGILVIE s.v., Washers of leather or pasteboard are also used to render screw and other junctions air-tight or water-tight. **1908** *Cassell's Handyman's Enquire Within* (ed. P. N. Hasluck) 492/2 In the case of ordinary household water taps..they should be taken to pieces and new leather washers..fitted and fixed on to the jumpers.

c. A bearing-plate of iron placed under the nut of a bolt or tie-rod.

1821 R. STEVENSON in *Edin. Philos. Jrnl.* V. 246 The under ends of these perpendicular rods..are attached..with screw-nuts, resting upon corresponding washers, or plates of iron. **1839** [see *tie-rod*, TIE- 3]. **1859** GWILT *Archit.* (ed. 4) Add. to Gloss., *Washer*, a flat piece of iron, or other metal, pierced with a hole for the passage of a screw, between whose nut and the timber it is placed. **1875** KNIGHT *Dict. Mech.*, *Wall-washer*, a large plate at the end of a tie-rod to extend the external bearing.

d. *Comb.*

1839 URE *Dict. Arts* etc. 1027 Its other face..receives the flat ring *x*..in four notches corresponding to the four projections of the washer-ring. **1849** J. GLYNN *Constr. Cranes* 108 The strong cast-iron cross..lays hold of the masonry by means of the holding-down bolts and washer-plates.

Hence '**washerless** *a.*, without a washer.

1908 *Cassell's Handyman's Enquire Within* (ed. P. N. Hasluck) 493/1 Washerless Water-tap (Lord Kelvin's).

'**washer**, *v.* [f. WASHER *sb.*[2]] *trans.* To furnish with a washer. Hence '**washered** *ppl. a.*

1869 BLACKMORE *Lorna D.* lxx, I had worked myself up,.. growing hot like an ill-washered wheel revolving, though I start with a cool axle. **1873** ELIZ. PHELPS *Trotty's Wedding Tour* 215, I must have the buggy washered. **1886** *Sci. Amer.* 11 Sept. 160/3 He washered the knobs of the doors that had a rattling play whenever handled.

'**washeress.** *rare*$^{-0}$. [f. WASHER *sb.*[1] + -ESS.] A female washer.

1648 HEXHAM II, *Een Wasschersse uyt de looge*, a Washeresse out of the lees.

washerette (wɒʃə'rɛt). [f. WASHER *sb.*[1] + -ETTE.] = LAUNDERETTE.

1968 *Punch* 10 Apr. 521/3 The Mariner he beats his brow; But the Guest is well away. 'She runs a mobile washerette Down here, or so they say.' **1974** *State* (Columbia, S. Carolina) 1 Apr. B-9/6 (Advt.), Philco-Bendix Quality. For the best in washerette profits. **1976** *Honolulu Star-Bull.* 21 Dec. F-3/8 (Advt.), Washerette in prime location. 10 washers & 5 dryers. Good lease.

'**washerman.** [f. WASHER *sb.*[1] + MAN *sb.*] A man whose occupation is the washing of clothes.

'Chiefly designating the Chinese laundryman of the U.S. and the Asiatic native washer of clothes.'—*N.E.D.*

1715 J. STEVENS *Hist. Persia* 77 His Beauty and Wealth made the Washerman sensible that the Parents must be great. **1743** BULKELEY & CUMMINS *Voy. S. Seas* 126 William Callicutt, Washerman. **1810** T. WILLIAMSON *E. Ind. Vade Mecum* I. 244 The *Doby*, or washerman, is also exclusively a domestic, washing for only one family. **1874** L. J. TROTTER *Hist. India* Introd. 10 Each village kept..its own.. schoolmaster, washerman, goldsmith, [etc.]. **1888** BRYCE *Amer. Commw.* III. IV. lxxxi. 71 One trade, however, the Chinese are permitted to follow, and have now almost monopolized, that of washermen.

washer-up (wɒʃər'ʌp). Pl. **washers-up**. [f. vbl. phr. *to wash up* (WASH *v.* 1 f) + -ER[1].] One who washes up dishes.

1907 *Daily Chron.* 19 Apr. 12 (Advt.), Woman (young) wanted as washer-up. **1933** D. C. PEEL *Life's Enchanted Cup* xiv. 173 An experienced washer-up in canteens. **1960** *House & Garden* Oct. 165/3 Washers-up who seem to spend one third of their life at the kitchen sink. **1978** L. DAVIDSON *Chelsea Murders* viii. 42 They always had the meal together: the patron..the chef, the under-chef, the washer-up.

So **washer-'upper** *colloq.*

1961 *John o' London's* 21 Sept. 318/3 But Dunham was more than a washer-upper. **1968** C. DRUMMOND *Death & Leaping Ladies* v. 127 The usual two washer-uppers..who also prepare vegetables. **1977** *New Society* 25 Aug. 381/1 Rubbish-collector, tea boy, washer-upper and so on.

washer-wife. *Sc.* [f. WASHER *sb.*[1] + WIFE. Cf. G. *wäscherweib.*] A washerwoman.

1800 *Monthly Mag.* Apr. 238/2 In Scotland, the word linens is often used for linen. For example, 'carry my linens to the washer-wife'. **1910** N. MUNRO *Fancy Farm* xi, The word itself [*sc.* gossip] is noble in its origin, for all its washer-wife associations.

'washerwoman. [f. WASHER *sb.*[1] + WOMAN. Cf. G. *wäscherfrau.*]

1. a. A woman whose occupation is the washing of dirty linen; one who takes in washing.

1632 SHERWOOD, A washer woman, *lauandiere, buandiere.* **1674** R. GODFREY *Inj. & Ab. Physick* 151 A Poor Washer-woman. **1757** FOOTE *Author* I. Wks. 1799 I. 133 Mrs. Suds, your washer-woman. **1799** SOUTHEY *Love Elegies* i. 25 No washerwoman's filthy hand shall e'er, Sweet pocket-handkerchief! thy worth profane. **1811** *Regul. & Orders Army* 169 Servants..and Washer-women for each Troop. **1837** DICKENS *Pickw.* xxxiv, Mrs. Bardell..looked out his linen for the washerwoman when it went abroad. **1848** THACKERAY *Van. Fair* xxxvii, The pertinacity with which the washer-woman..brought..her bills week after week. **1877** TENNYSON *Harold* IV. iii, *First Thane.* Down with William! *Third Thane.* The washerwoman's brat!

b. ***washerwoman's fingers, hand,*** a condition of the hands, characteristic of cholera, resembling the wrinkling of the skin produced in the hands of washerwomen by the action of soap and soda. ***washerwoman's itch, scall,*** a form of eczema incident to the hands of washerwomen; ***washerwoman's skin,*** skin that is much wrinkled as a result of immersion in water.

1844 HOBLYN *Dict. Med.*, Washerwoman's Scall, *Psoriasis lotorum.* **1894** GOULD *Illustr. Dict. Med.*, *Washerwoman's Hand*: See Cholera-hand. *Washerwoman's Itch* or *Scall.* **1898** P. MANSON *Trop. Diseases* ii. 60 As in cholera, the serous drain may lead to..pinched features, washerwoman's fingers. **1981** C. A. MCLAREN *Twister over Thames* iv. 65 In the light of my discoveries, notably from the wrinkled nature of the skin—washerwoman's skin, it is called..Master Thacker had been immersed for about twelve hours before..discovery. **1985** 'E. MCBAIN' *Snow White & Rose Red* v. 73 When a body hadn't been submerged too long..the so-called washerwoman's skin wasn't too bad.

2. = WASHER *sb.*[1] 4 a.

1817 STEPHENS in *Shaw's Gen. Zool.* X. II. 546 The Water-wagtail, or as it is called in many parts Dish-washer, or Washerwoman. **1832** [see DISH-WASHER]. **1862** JOHNS *Brit. Birds Haunts* 171 The popular name Washerwoman belongs to the whole family [of wagtails].

washery ('wɒʃərɪ). [f. WASH *v.* + -ERY.] A place at which the washing of coal, ore, wool, etc. is carried on. Also, a laundry or wash-house.

1875 TROLLOPE *Prime Minister* (1876) I. xix. 305 We've got the steam-washery put up. **1895** *Columbus* (Ohio) *Dispatch* 6 May 7/6 A most disastrous fire broke out..at the Coke plant. The destruction of the washery and machinery was complete. **1898** *Daily News* 2 Dec. 2/2 Quantities of fish are caught, and sent to the gold washeries. **1907** CLAPHAM *Woollen & Worsted Ind.* vi. 246 Some washing of both combing and carding wools is done in separate 'washeries'.

† **'washester.** *Obs.* [f. WASH *v.* + -STER.] A female washer (of linen), a washerwoman: in OE. also applied to a man.

c **900** WÆRFERTH *Gregory's Dial.* III. viii. 191 Iobinus, se wæs min wæscestre [L. *fullo*]. *Ibid.* IV. xii. 276 Se mæssepreost..wæs lufigende his wæscestran [L. *presbyteram*] swa swa his agne swuster. *c* **1200** *Trin. Coll. Hom.* 57 *Quod melius patefacit exemplar lotricum*, and þis us doð to understonden þe forbisne of þe wasshestren.

washeteria (wɒʃə'tɪərɪə). orig. and chiefly *U.S.* Also **washateria.** [f. WASH *v.* + -ETERIA.]

a. = LAUNDERETTE.

1959 [see -TERIA *suffix*]. **1966** *Sunday Times* 17 July 30 Now that we have grown accustomed to the blandishments of..something called Washeterias, the next step may be drive-in laundries. **1971** L. GRIBBLE *Alias the Victim* i. 17 She wore a skirt and jumper that had the nondescript shapeless look that derives from too many visits to a washeteria. **1976** *San Antonio* (Texas) *Express-News* 27 Nov. 1B/1 T's Washhouse—the only washeteria for 75 miles in any direction. **1982** P. D. JAMES *Skull beneath Skin* xlii. 339 She'll be at the Washateria... She always does her washing on Monday afternoons.

b. ***car washeteria***: a self-service car-washing establishment.

1965 *Daily Tel.* 14 May 20/2 (Advt.), The demand from motorists for simple-to-operate inexpensive car washing facilities will go on growing. Here's how the Car Washeteria answers these requirements. **1970** *Times* 24 Dec. 9, I have long grown accustomed to a cafeteria but I now clean my car at a car washeteria.

† **wash ground.** *Obs.* [WASH *sb.* or *v.*] ? A drying-ground.

1714 *Lond. Gaz.* No. 5272/8 One Acre and a half of Wash ground in Crucifix-lane in Southwark. **1724** *Ibid.* No. 6247/2 An Estate, consisting of Garden-Grounds, Wash-Grounds,..and Houses.

'wash-hand, *a.* In 8 **wash-hands.** [f. WASH *v.* Cf. F. †*lavemain(s* sb., wash-hand stand, wash-hand basin.] Intended for use in washing the hands. Only in certain combinations (sometimes hyphened or written continuously as single words). **a.** ***wash-hand basin,*** a basin for washing the hands. **b.** ***wash-hand stand,*** a piece of furniture for holding the wash-hand basin, ewer, soap-dish, etc. **c.** ***wash-hand table,*** a table serving the purpose of a wash-hand stand.

a. 1759 *Phil. Trans.* LI. 284 There was a small stand with a wash-hands basin on it. **1815** SCOTT *Guy M.* xxxvi, He..ordered lights and a wash-hand basin and towel. **1878** BROWNING *Poets Croisic* cxi, Reach The washhand-basin for admirers!

Comb. **1871** A. MEADOWS *Man. Midwifery* (ed. 2) 89 A large wash-hand basinfull of this hydatidiform mass.

b. 1789 J. WOODFORDE *Diary* 17 Nov. (1927) III. 153 Ben returned home about 5 o'clock with..a wash-hand Stand. **1820** G. COLMAN *XYZ* I. 10 Overset my wash-hand stand;—grop'd to bed in the dark. **1836** DICKENS *Sk. Boz, Brokers' Shops*, Rosewood chiffoniers and mahogany wash-hand-stands. **1839** W. CHAMBERS *Tour Holland* 43/1 Wash-hand stand. **1854** SURTEES *Handley Cr.* xxvii. (1901) I. 204 Having deposited a can of hot water on the washhandstand. **1894** 'R. ANDOM' *We Three & Troddles* xx. 115 He bounced over to the wash-hand-stand.

attrib. **1848** CLOUGH *Bothie* ii. 291 We return to the shop and the wash-hand-stand-bason. **1854** SURTEES *Handley Cr.* xii. (1901) I. 90 'Tother night it was raining perfect wash-handstandbasins full. **1881** OLIVE SCHREINER *Story African Farm* II. iii, I left them in the wash-hand-stand drawer.

c. 1863 GLADSTONE *Glean.* (1879) II. 204 Again, take such a jug as he would construct for the washhand-table of a garret.

wash-house ('wɒʃhaʊs). Also 6–7 **washouse,** 9 *vulgar* **washus, wash'us.** [f. WASH *v.* + HOUSE *sb.* Cf. Du. *waschhuis*, G. *waschhaus.*]

† **1.** A bath-house. *Obs. rare.*

c **1000** *O.E. Glosses* in *Ztschr. f. deutsches Altertum* XXXI. 13 *Colimbum*, wæschus. **1704** PITTS *Acc. Moham.* 47 They have many *Hammams*, or Wash-houses to bath themselves in.

2. a. An outbuilding or apartment used for washing clothes.

1577 B. GOOGE *Heresbach's Husb.* I. 13 There is also a thirde stie, not farre from the washouse, for the fatting of my Porkes. **1580** in *Archæologia* LXIV. 358 To set upp the gat at the washouse. **1671** T. LACY in *Extr. St. Papers rel. Friends* IV. (1913) 350, I..saw a little shedd or washouse all on fire. **1753** MISS COLLIER *Art Torment.* I. i. (1811) 36 In the wash-house or the scullery. **1835** DICKENS *Sk. Boz, Mistaken Milliner*, Four beautiful rooms, and a delightful little washhouse at the end of the passage. **1837** —— *Pickw.* xxv, We keep a boy to do the dirty work, and a gal besides, but they dine in the washus. **1848** THACKERAY *Van. Fair* lvi, The Rev. Mr. Veal had..a theatre (in the wash-house). **1916** *Blackw. Mag.* Aug. 191/1 A large shed—that had at one time been used as a wash house—still contained some broken wash-tubs.

b. A building in which goods are washed in the process of bleaching, or calico printing.

1701 *Lond. Gaz.* No. 3760/4 A House, and Ground fit for a Whitster, or Callico-Printer, is to be Let, with several Sheds and Wash-houses.

c. *U.S.* An establishment at which clothes are washed; a laundry.

1856 *Democratic State Jrnl.* (Sacramento, Calif.) 4 Aug. 3/2 There is a washhouse on Font street which seems to imbue its occupants with a desire to quarrel. **1873** B. HARTE *Fiddletown* 28 The next day he entered the wash-house of Chy Fook as an assistant.

d. A building, provided with suitable accommodation, at which the public may wash clothes.

c **1806** D. WORDSWORTH *Jrnl.* (1941) I. IV. 236 In the middle of the field is a wash-house, whither the inhabitants of this large town [*sc.* Glasgow], rich and poor, send or carry their linen to be washed. **1846** *Act 9 & 10 Vict.* c. 74 §1 To encourage the Establishment therein of public Baths and Wash-houses. **1859** JEPHSON *Brittany* v. 49 Public washhouses have been established in many places. **1912** *Throne* 7 Aug. 206/2 A local borough councillor..who points with pride to the new borough wash-houses.

3. *attrib.*

1835 DICKENS *Sk. Boz, Parish* v, I felt as lonesome as a kitten in a wash-house copper with the lid on. **1838** —— *O. Twist* l, Charley and I made our lucky up the wash'us chimney. **1901** *Daily Chron.* 4 Dec. 9/2 Engineer and Washhouse-man required [in a steam laundry]. **1909** 'Q' (Quiller-Couch) *True Tilda* xx, Run, Hepsy, and fill the wash-house boiler.

† **washical.** *Obs. rare*[−1]. App. a corruption of *what shall I call (it)* or *what do you call it.*

See other forms under WHAT-D'YE-CALL-'EM.

1575 *Gammer Gurton* v. ii. 116 Geue my Gammer again her washical thou stole away in thy lap.

'wash-in. *Aeronaut.* Also **washin.** [After WASH-OUT 5.] An increase in the angle of incidence of an aeroplane wing towards the tip.

1916 H. BARBER *Aeroplane Speaks* 82 The advantages of the wash-in must, of course, be paid for. **1943** *Jrnl. R. Aeronaut. Soc.* XLVII. (Abstr. Section) 70 As the wing tips approach the tunnel wall, both the induced drag corrections and the angles of apparent washin or of apparent twist increase rapidly. **1979** BERTIN & SMITH *Aerodynamics for Engineers* iii. 83 If the angle of incidence increases toward the tip, the wing has 'washin'.

washiness ('wɒʃɪnɪs). [f. WASHY *a.* + -NESS.] The quality or state of being washy.

1. Diluted condition, wateriness, weakness (of a liquid); *fig.* feebleness, lack of solidity (of thoughts, etc.).

1631 R. BYFIELD *Doctr. Sabb.* 72, I proceed to examine your solution, as you call it; the phlegmaticall washinesse whereof hath over-spread many pages. **1763** in *Owen's Weekly Chron.* (1767) 7 May 55 Humanity..is nothing more than a childish washiness of nature. *a* **1806** J. BARRY *Lect. Art* vi. (1848) 232 In Lely..we sometimes meet with the other extreme of too little solidity, too much flickering and washiness. **1814** *Q. Rev.* XI. 96 The washiness of the following line is only surpassed by that of the two which succeed it.

2. Chronic looseness of the bowels (in animals).

1844 [see WASHY *a.* 5].

washing ('wɒʃɪŋ), *vbl. sb.* [-ING[1].

In OE. recorded only in the compound *weascingweᵹ* 'washing-way', ? 'a road leading to a sheep-wash'.]

I. The action of WASH *v.*

1. a. The action or an act of cleansing by water, or of laving or bathing with water or other liquid. Also *fig.* with reference to spiritual or moral purification.

a **1225** *Ancr. R.* 332 þe wassunke ine fuluhte wiðuten bitocneð þe wasschunge of þe soule wiðinnen. *c* **1305** *Land Cokaygne* 48 Watir seruiþ þer to no þing Bot to siȝt and to waiissing. **1340** *Ayenb.* 178 Ase þet line cloþ þet is y-huyted be ofte wessinge. *a* **1425** tr. *Arderne's Treat. Fistula* etc. 53 Wasche wele þat legge..with hote watre... And so after þe waschyng lat it lye by a naturel day. ? **1466** *Stonor Papers* (Camden) I. 92 For wosshyng of yowyr shertys and M. Wyllyams. **1508** FISHER *Penit. Ps.* li. I. (1509) ii vj, If a table be foule and fylthy..fyrst we rase it, after whan it is rased we wasshe it, and laste after the wasshynge we wype and make it clene. **1523–34** FITZHERB. *Husb.* §51 Beware, that thou put not to many shepe in a penne at one tyme, neyther at the washyng, nor at the sheryng. **1587** D. FENNER *Song of Songs* vi. 3 Thy teeth are like a flocke of sheepe which comme vp from washing. **1603** in *10th Rep. Hist. MSS. Comm.* App. I. 31 For the wysching of my chlos, xii d. **1636** SANDERSON *Serm.* (1681) II. 53 Stains of a deep dye will not out of the cloth, with such ordinary washings, as will fetch out lighter spots. *c* **1650** BINNING *Serm.* Wks. (1735) 567 The Blood and Water might be joined, the justifying Saviour, and the sanctifying Spirit; for both these are in this Gospel Washing. **1765** *Museum Rust.* IV. 234 Both these gentlemen depend on the clean washing of the seed, and the trials of both met with the wished-for success. **1829** J. L. KNAPP *Jrnl. Nat.* 149 It taints the fingers, which have touched it, with its peculiar odour, so that one washing does not remove it. **1857** MILLER *Elem. Chem., Org.* 77 The tubers are first freed from adhering earth by a thorough washing. **1869–71** *Cassell's Househ. Guide* II. 50/2 The white things will require two washings. **1899** *Allbutt's Syst. Med.* VIII. 611 Every other evening a washing with naphthol and sulphur soap may be given in a bath.

† **b.** ***to give one's head*** (or ***beard***) ***for the washing***: to submit tamely to indignities (see HEAD *sb.* 65). *Obs.*

c **1583** [see HEAD *sb.* 65]. **1596** NASHE *Saffron Walden* L 4, But the time was, when he would not haue giuen his head for the washing. **1613** BEAUM. & FL. *Cupid's Revenge* IV. i, And so am I [*sc.* resolved], and forty more good fellows, That will not give their heads for the washing, I take it. *a* **1616** —— *Bonduca* II. iii, *Car.* And to morrow night say to him, His Head is mine. *Jud.* I can assure ye Captain, He will not give it for this washing. **1663** [see HEAD *sb.* 65].

c. In reflexive sense.

1896 CONAN DOYLE *Rodney Stone* vii, It was his custom to go through a whole series of washings and changings after even the shortest journey. **1911** A. PLUMMER *Ch. Brit. bef. A.D. 1000* I. 121 Abstention from washing was a common form of asceticism.

d. A ceremonial ablution. (By Sir John Cheke used for: Baptism.)

c **1375** *Lay-Folks Mass-Bk.* (MS. B.) 263 Til after wasshing þo preste wil loute þo auter. *c* **1449** PECOCK *Repr.* IV. ix. 468 That the bodili waisching with water schulde clense the soule fro moral vnclennessis. **1526** *Pilgr. Perf.* (W. de W. 1531) 65 These cerimonyes that this doctour calleth but small thynges, I suppose they be be as stacyons, inclynacyons, gestures, turnynges, wesshynge..& suche other. *c* **1550** CHEKE *Matt.* xxi. 25 Joanns waschyng from whens was it. from heaven, or from men. **1606** *Arraignmt. & Exec. Traytors* D i b, Their pilgrimages to Idols, their shauings and their washings. **1644** MILTON *M. Bucer* Wks. 1851 IV. 308 We are not to use Circumcision, Sacrifice, and those bodily Washings prescrib'd to the Jews. **1698–9** OSBORN *Let.* in Maundrell *Journ. Jerus.* (1732) 147 Addressing themselves to their Devotions, with the most solemn and critical Washings. **1772** PRIESTLEY *Inst. Relig.* (1782) II. 340 Washing..accompanied many of the Jewish rites. **1846** S. SHARPE *Hist. Egypt* ix. 303 In their dislike of pork, in their washings, and in other Eastern customs, they [the Jews] were like the Egyptians.

e. *spec.* = 'washing of clothes', esp. as one of the regular requirements of a person or household.

'Meat, drink, washing, and lodging': a proverbial summary expression for the necessaries of life; in rustic use often *fig.* = 'all that one needs'.

1480 *Cov. Leet Bk.* 459 As to þat þat is seid þat the people of þis Citie hurten þe fisshe in Swanneswell pole be þeire weysshyng there þe people vnderstanden þat þe place of the seid weysshyng ys þe soyle of þe hospitall of sent John Baptiste. **1543** *Sel. Cases Star Chamber* (Selden Soc.) II. 274 To the sayd ij prest [*sic*] for brede wyne and washyng for the yere v s. **1610** *Shuttleworths' Acc.* (Chetham Soc.) 187 A quarters washinge, to Roger Isherwood, vj[d]. **1617** MORYSON *Itin.* I. 8 A Dollor for chamber and washing. **1637** in *Verney Mem.* (1907) I. 88 It costs mee two and twenty shillings a week for my diet, lodging and washing. **1643** *Select. Rec. Regality Melrose* (S.H.S.) I. 100 [He is to maintain him] in meatt, drink, bed and board and clothes washing. **1725** RAMSAY *Gent. Sheph.* I. ii, We'll end our washing while the morning's cool. **1745** MRS. E. MONTAGU *Corr.* (1906) I. 225 He is to have livery, and frock every year, and six pounds wages the first year, the second seven. He is to put out his washing. **1765** *Museum Rust.* IV. 357 They usually give ten shillings by the week, with meat, drink, washing, and lodging, to stout men. **1797** JANE AUSTEN *Sense & Sens.* xxxvi, She..was not without hopes of finding out, before they parted, how much her washing cost per week. *c* **1800** *Whole Life & D. Long Meg of Westm.* ii. 4 She had not been bred unto her needle, but to hard labour, such as washing, brewing and baking. **1832** *Athenæum* 9 June 370/1 To whom bargains and bargain-making are the true meat, drink, washing, and lodging of life. **1841** LYTTON *Nt. & Morn.* I. vi, He shall share and share with my own young folks; and Mrs. Morton will take care of his washing and morals. **1856** *Putnam's Monthly Mag.* Oct. 390/2 Only to think, too, of a hundred and fifty dollars, £30 a month—and board, lodging and washing, all free.

†**f.** ***at (the) washing*** = 'at the wash' (see WASH *sb.* 2). *Obs.*

1633 B. JONSON *Tale of Tub* II. ii. 136 *Clay*... I never zaw you avore. *Hil.* You did not? where were your eyes then? out at washing? **1638** BP. MOUNTAGUE *Art. Enq. Norwich* A 4, Have you two faire large Surplices for your Minister to officiate Divine Service in, that the one may be for change, when the other is at washing? **1755** SHEBBEARE *Lydia* (1769) II. 279 The stock of shirts being large, almost every man having one at the washing, and the other on.

g. In chemical and mining operations (see WASH *v.* 4, 11).

1600 HAKLUYT *Voy.* III. 66 Upon this Iland was found good store of the Ore, which in the washing helde gold to our thinking plainly to be seene. *a* **1650** E. NORGATE *Miniatura* (1919) 17 And soe your colour will appeare by reason of soe many washings cleane and faire. **1756** C. LUCAS *Ess. Waters* I. 144 These washings..tended to change sirup of violets to a pale green. **1778** PRYCE *Min. Cornub.* Gloss. s.v. *Jigging*, *Jigging*, is a method of dressing the smaller Copper and Lead Ores by a peculiar motion of a wire sieve in a kieve or vat of water,..In the Lead Mines..they also term this operation, ..'Washing'. **1839** URE *Dict. Arts* 813 The most simple and economical washings are those that certain iron ores..are subjected to. **1853** S. HUGHES *Gas-works* 135 It is also thought..that too much washing has the effect of diminishing the illuminating power of the gas. **1855** *Orr's Circ. Sci., Inorg. Nat.* 252 In Siberia there are but few localities where the gold washings are largely carried on. **1886** *Daily News* 17 July 5/8 Special illustrations of diamond washing, cutting, and polishing were given.

h. With advs. *away*, *off*, *out*, *up* (often hyphened): see quots. and senses of WASH *v.*

1612 SIR D. CARLETON in *10th Rep. Hist. MSS. Comm.* App. I. 587 For ye washing away of wch aspersion the Duke maketh profession [etc.]. **1858** GEO. ELIOT *Scenes Clerical Life* II. viii. 157 The necessary sum of meals and the consequent 'washing up'. **1875** WOOD & LAPHAM *Waiting for Mail* 106 Owing to the want of water for washing-up their funds were low. **1880** D. C. DAVIES *Metallif. Min.* 425 Washing off (Washing up, *Am. & Aus.*), the periodical final cleaning out of all the gutters and appliances used in alluvial and rock gold mining. **1888** JACOBI *Printers' Vocab.*, *Washing up*, the operation of washing up rollers or ink slabs. **1890** 'R. BOLDREWOOD' *Miner's Right* xviii. 177 The washings up were frequent and flourishing. **1890** SIR W. STOKES in *Brit. Med. Jrnl.* 3 May 999/2 Washing-out or irrigation of the stomach is a desirable antiseptic precaution. **1896** *Allbutt's Syst. Med.* I. 330 These waters can be taken in large quantities, and thus exercise a washing-out effect. **1899** W. DE MORGAN in Mackail *W. Morris* II. 17 A story which kept us all quiet and well-behaved till washing-up time.

2. *Painting.* The action of laying on a thin coat of colour. Also ***washing in***. Also *attrib.* in ***washing colour***, ***manner***.

a **1650** NORGATE *Miniatura* (1919) 59 To worke in the apparrell and foldings in a washing manner without a ground. **1758** [DOSSIE] *Handmaid to Arts* 172 Gamboge, Indian ink, sap-green, [etc.]..as they really dissolve and become transparent in water are true washing colours. **1811** *Self Instructor* 522 Technical terms in painting..washing-in. **1823** J. BADCOCK *Dom. Amusem.* 111 Employed in the first washings by house painters, and by them termed a first coat. **1856** KANE *Arctic Expl.* II. iii. 47 It emerged from buried shadow, through all the stages of distinctness of an India-ink washing. **1877** S. REDGRAVE *Descr. Catal. Water-Col. Paintings* 17 The papers..were not sufficiently sized to bear the repeated washings of the artist.

3. Sweating of coin by means of acids.

14.. HOCCLEVE *Min. Poems* xxi. 116 If it be golde and hole that men hym profre..take it yf him lyst..for wasshinge or clyppynge hold hym content. *a* **1513** FABYAN *Chron.* VII. (1533) 177 b, The coyne of golde at those dayes was greatly mynysshed wyth clyppyng & wasshyng. **1543** tr. *Act 3 Hen. V, Stat.* II. c. 6 Great doubte..hath ben whether that clyppynge, wasshynge, and fylynge of the money of the land ought to be iudged treason or not.

4. a. Surging, overflowing (of waves); the action of moving water in carrying off loose matter.

1471 CAXTON *Recuyell* (Sommer) 279 Hercules and exione were all wette of the wasshing and springyng of the wawes. **1610** SHAKS. *Temp.* I. i. 61 Would thou mightst lye drowning the washing of ten Tides. *a* **1701** MAUNDRELL *Journ. Jerus.* (1707) 125 Upon any violent Rain, the whole City [of Damascus] becomes, by the washing of the Houses, as it were a Quagmire. **1719** DE FOE *Crusoe* I. (Globe) 248 The Washing of the Sea having spoil'd all their Powder. **1726** LEONI *Alberti's Archit.* I. 41 Mount Morello..is quite wild and naked; occasioned, as I suppose, by the washing of the Rains. **1778** T. HUTCHINS *Descr. Virginia* etc. 37 Fort Chartres..was abandoned in the year 1772, as it was rendered untenable by the constant washings of the River Missisippi in high floods. **1867** MORRIS *Jason* I. 398 And in their dreamless rest the wind in vain Howled round about, with washing of the rain. **1868** —— *Earthly Par.* I. 257 Hearkening the washing of the watery way. **1888** GOODE *Amer. Fishes* 402 The rapid, vigorous, spasmodic movements which accompany this operation produce a splashing in the water which can be plainly heard from the shore, and which the fishermen characterize as 'washing'.

b. with *adv.*

1873 TRISTRAM *Moab* vii. 124 Unsound ground, rendered more treacherous than usual by the washing in of the burrows of the mole-rat. **1886** J. A. BROWN in *Q. Jrnl. Geol. Soc.* May 200 They [the furrow-gravels] could not have been formed by the washing-in of gravel by running springs.

5. a. *Printers' slang.* (See quots. and WASH *v.* 20 a.)

1825 HANSARD *Typogr.* 308 Washing is had recourse to upon two occasions,—either for rousing a sense of shame in a fellow-workman who had been idling when he might have been at work; or to congratulate an apprentice upon the hour having arrived that brings his emancipation from the shackles of his subordinate station. **1888** JACOBI *Printers' Vocab.*, *Washing*, an old-fashioned term for 'jerrying', or making a noise on an apprentice coming out of his time.

b. *Stockbroking.* (In sense 20 b of the vb.)

1849 *Hunt's Merchant's Mag.* XXI. 118 'Washing' will hardly go down at the board. **1870** J. K. MEDBERY *Men & Mysteries Wall St.* 138 Washing is where one broker arranges with another to buy a certain stock when he offers it for sale. The bargain is fictitious. **1894** S. LEAVITT *Our Money Wars* 287 In 1887..by the process known as 'Washing',—that is, by hiring one set of brokers to buy and another set of brokers to sell,—the price of shares was forced to fifteen times their value.

II. Concrete senses.

6. a. *pl.* (formerly also *sing.*). The liquid that has been used to wash something; matter removed when something is washed. Also ***washing-out***.

c **1330** R. BRUNNE *Chron. Wace* (Rolls) 8816 þo þat were seke..Wasche þe stones, did hit in baþes;..Wasched þem of þe selue waschinges, & warysched wel of al þer pyne. *c* **1375** *Sc. Leg. Saints* xxiv. (*Alexis*) 323 Of þe weschel þe weschyng ful oft one his hed wald fling. *c* **1480** HENRYSON *Two Mice* 249 My dische weschingis is worth ȝour haill expence. **1577** HARRISON *England* III. i. 96/2 in *Holinshed*, [Meade] is nothing else but the washing of the combes, when the hony is wrong out. **1598** *Epulario* B ij b, Wash the flesh well with good white wine mingled with as much water, and straine the washing, and seeth the flesh therin. **1637** J. TAYLOR (Water P.) *Drinke & Welcome* A 4, Small Beere in England, such as is said to be made of the washings of the Brewers legges and aprons. **1775** A. BURNABY *Trav. N. Amer.* 34 Two curious hot springs, one tasting like alum, the other like the washings of a gun. **1805** [S. WESTON] *Werneria* 12 Swine-stone, when rubbed against a hard body, has a fetid odour like Harrowgate water, or rotten eggs, or the washing out of a gun. **1828** SCOTT *F.M. Perth* xxiv, The leech gave him a draught of medicated wine, mixed with water. He rejected it, under the dishonourable epithet of 'kennel-washings.' **1833** LOUDON *Encycl. Archit.* §1324 The must is afterwards again pressed, and about one hogs-head of what is termed washings is obtained from the same quantity that had previously afforded about three hogsheads of cider. **1851** MAYHEW *Lond. Labour* II. 146 It [hogs' wash] is composed of..the washings of cooking utensils. **1890** *Retrospect Med.* CII. 397 The peculiar reddish, watery discharge, 'like the washings of raw meat,' as a German writer has described it.

b. Matter carried away by rain or running water; alluvial soil deposited by a stream.

1707 MORTIMER *Husb.* 225 [Breeding-ponds] A fat Soil with a white fat Water, as the washings of Hills, Commons, Streets, Sinks, &c, is the best to fatten all sorts of Fish. **1739** LABELYE *Westm. Bridge* 5 A Shoal..made up of Sand and of the Washing or Silting of the River. **1816** BRACKENRIDGE *Jrnl.* 181 This limestone constitutes at least one half in the washings which are carried to the Missouri. **1834** *Brit. Husb.* I. 276 Some farmers, indeed, think these washings from the farmyards, though of a brown colour, are yet, in most instances, so diluted with rain, as not to be worth the expense of carriage. **1867** J. HATTON *Tallants* i, Their rivers are black with coal washings.

c. Metal obtained by washing ore or soil.

1604 E. G[RIMSTONE] *D'Acosta's Hist. Indies* IV. xii. 244 There slippes away also some small portion of silver and quicke-silver with the earth and drosse, which they call washings. **1846** McCULLOCH *Acc. Brit. Empire* (1854) I. 614 The produce of the mines..may be taken, inclusive of the washings, at about 5,000 tons a year.

d. Places containing soil from which gold or diamonds are obtained by washing.

1865 LIVINGSTONE *Zambesi* ii. 52 In former times, when traders went with hundreds of slaves to the washings. **1899** *Edin. Rev.* Apr. 317 In Griqualand West diamonds occur in 'washings', as well as in mines.

†**7.** A medical 'wash' or lotion. *Obs.*

1541 COPLAND *Guydon's Form.* Y ij b, The chauffynges..of the gummes are appeased..wt this wasshing made of [etc.]. **1563** T. GALE *Antidot.* II. 23 The patyente..must vse good lotions, or washynges for hys mouth vntyll it be hole.

8. a. Clothes newly washed or set apart to be washed. Phr. ***to come out in the washing***: = *to come out in the wash* s.v. WASH *sb.* 2 d; ***to take in one another's washing***: to help one another by buying one another's goods or services, esp. where no new wealth accrues overall; to render mutual services, to be mutually dependent.

1854 SURTEES *Handley Cr.* xxxviii. (1901) II. 8 Family washings were whisked away [by the wind], or torn to tatters on the drying lines. **1876** TROLLOPE *Prime Minister* IV. xii. 183 The effects which causes will produce,..the manner in which this or that proposition will come out in the washing, do not strike even Cabinet Ministers at a glance. **1889** BARRIE *Window in Thrums* xxi, She got her death..one day of sudden rain, when she had run out to bring in her washing. **1889** G. B. SHAW *How to become Mus. Critic* (1960) 147 The inhabitants either live in villas on independent incomes or else by taking in one another's washing and selling confectionery, scrap books, and photographs. **1901** *C.T.C. Gaz.* Oct. 390 Perambulators used by poor people to carry home washing in the evening. **1905** J. MACKENZIE *Michael Bruce* iii. 34 The box was returned regularly with his washing, so that during the session a constant supply from home was furnished. **1913** R. BROOKE *Let.* 1 Sept. (1968) 501 Most of happiness is because one's friends are happy: so that spiritually—whatever the damned Economists may say—we *do* live by taking in each other's washing. **1937** M. BORDEN *Black Virgin* iii. 63 Quite half the women she knew were [working] in shops of one sort or another. The only drawback to that being..that they took in each other's washing... Mona and Peg bought Cimmie's clothes. Cimmie bought her hats from Mona, her nighties from Peg. **1959** J. L. AUSTIN *Sense & Sensibilia* (1962) i. 4 These two terms, 'sense-data' and 'material things', live by taking in each other's washing. **1967** G. SIMS *Last Best Friend* xviii. 169, I expect you know what dealers are like for selling among themselves, it's rather like taking in each other's washing.

b. ***washing-up***, table utensils awaiting washing up.

1972 J. MCCLURE *Caterpillar Cop* xiii. 211 Lisbet had eaten and stacked the washing up ready for the girl. **1977** P. HILL *Fanatics* 6 He made his bed but left the washing-up in the sink.

III. 9. a. In combinations (often synonymous with parallel formations in WASH-), as ***washing-basin***, ***-blue***, ***-brush***, †***-kit*** (KIT *sb.*[1] 1), ***-room***, ***-soap***, ***-soda***, †***-towel***, ***-trough***, ***-tub***; †**washing-ball** = WASH-BALL; **washing basket**, a basket for holding articles newly washed or waiting to be washed; **washing bat** *Hist.* (see quot. 1898); †**washing-beetle**, a wooden bat used to beat or pound clothes in the process of washing; **washing-bill**, a statement of laundry-charges; **washing-block**, **-board**, a wooden block or board on which clothes are beaten while being washed; **washing-book**, a book in which a person's laundry-charges are entered; **washing-bottle** = WASH-*bottle* a, b; **washing-bowl**, †(*a*) a wash-hand basin; (*b*) a pan or tub for washing clothes, etc. (*obs.* exc. *local*); cf. WASH-BOWL; **washing-crystals**, crystallized soda used for washing clothes, etc.; **washing-day**, the day on which the dirty clothes of a household are washed; **washing-engine**, a machine for washing rags, etc., esp. in paper-making; **washing-green**, a piece of common grass-land on which clothes are spread or hung out to dry after washing; **washing-house** = WASH-HOUSE; **washing-leather** = WASH-LEATHER; **washing-line** = *clothes-line* s.v. CLOTHES *sb. pl.* 4; **washing-machine**, a machine for washing clothes, cloth, etc.; **washing-mill**, †(*a*) a machine used for recovering particles of gold or silver from refuse matter; (*b*) a machine for washing cloth in the process of bleaching; **washing-place**, (*a*) a place where washing is done; a lavatory; a laundry; (*b*) a place where gold is washed out from sand or earth; **washing powder**, a cleansing agent in powder form for adding to the water used for washing household linen; **washing-rod**, a rod used to wash out a gun; **washing-stand** = WASHSTAND 1; †**washing-stock** (see quot. 1879); **washing-stone**, †(*a*) a kitchen-sink; (*b*) a stone on which clothes are beaten while being washed; **washing-stool**, a stool used when washing; **washing-stuff**, a miners' name for auriferous earth; †**washing-temple**, used to tr. L. *delubrum* temple, shrine, as if f. *deluere* to wash thoroughly; †**washing-vessel**, a laver; **washing-water**, water for washing the hands, a chemical substance, etc. (cf. WASH-WATER); **washing-week**, a week devoted to washing the dirty clothes of a household; also *fig.*; †**washing-well**, *fig.* a fount of spiritual cleansing; †**washing-woman** = WASHERWOMAN.

1538 ELYOT *Dict.* s.v. *Magmata*, Pomaundres and *washing balles. **1597** DELONEY *Gentle Craft* I. x. Wks. (1912) 114 Then shalt thou scoure thy pitchy fingers in a bason of hot water, with an ordinary washing Ball. **1612** *Sc. Bk. Rates* in *Halyburton's Ledger* (1867) 288 Ballis called weshing ballis the dozen, xii s. **1538** ELYOT Addit., *Labrum*, a *wasshynge basyn. **1558** *Bury Wills* (Camden) 150 One wasshinge basone of pewter. **1878** TRELAWNY *Rec. Shelley* etc. I. 161, I went to make my toilet, the sea my washing-basin—there was no other. **1947** M. MORRIS in 'B. James' *Austral. Short Stories* (1963) 362 She went down to the lines, walking heavily with her *washing-basket full. **1967** *Listener* 17 Aug. 204/3, I..used to fill a big washing-basket with books and bring it downstairs as often as I wanted to. **1898** *Eng. Dial. Dict.* s.v. *Bat*, The *washing bat was used to beat the dirty clothes after they had been 'put to soak'. **1969** E. H. PINTO *Treen* 149/2 A woman hitting a man with a washing bat is carved on an oak misericord of 1401, in Carlisle Cathedral... It shows that early washing bats were more shovel-shaped, with wider, shorter blades. **1983** *Daily Tel.* 16 Nov. 15/3 These finely decorated washing bats ..were once used to beat the washing. *c* **1440** *Promp. Parv.* 517/2 *Waschynge betyl, or batyldore, *feritorium*. *c* **1566** *Merie Tales of Skelton* in S.'s Wks. (1843) I. p. lxiii, Skelton ..sayd to the wyfe, Geue me a washyng betle. *a* **1625** FLETCHER *Woman's Prize* II. v, Have I liv'd thus long to be knockt o'th head, With halfe a washing beetle? **1798** JANE AUSTEN *Northang. Abb.* xxii, She held a *washing-bill in her hand. **1905** H. G. WELLS *Kipps* II. v. §3 After that the washing-bill of Kipps quadrupled. **1590** in *Archæologia* XL. 333 In the Boulting Howse,..a *washing block. **1676** DURFEY *Mad. Fickle* I. i. (1677) 7 Like a Taylor [vaulting] ore' a Washing-block. **1829** *Sporting Mag.* XXIV. 112 He looked like a frog on a washing-block. **1881** A. WATT *Sci. Industr.* I. 5 Indigo..mixed with starch..forms the '*washing blue' of the laundry. **1810** T. WILLIAMSON *E. Ind. Vade Mecum* I. 247 The *washing-board, its prop, the drying lines [etc.]. **1868** W. COLLINS *Moonstone* I. xiii. 216 Before we begin, I should like..to have the *washing-book. .. I want to be able to account next for all the linen in the house, and for all the linen sent to the wash. **1905** H. G. WELLS *Kipps* I. vi. §1 He..produced a washing-book and two pencils. **1857** MILLER *Elem. Chem., Org.* 169 The vapours which are evolved should be transmitted through a *washing bottle containing water. *c* **1865** J. WYLDE in *Circ. Sci.* I. 406/1 Wash the precipitate by means of the washing-bottle. **14..** *Rules & Const. Nuns Syon* lvi. in Aungier *Syon* (1840) 392 *Waschyng bolles and sope. **1530** PALSGR. 287/1 Wasshyng boll, *jatte*. **1622** MABBE tr. *Aleman's Guzman d'Alf.* II. 54 Like a basket of Buck-cloathes, when they are taken from the washing-Bole. **1884** McLAREN *Spinning* 33 Petrie's washing-bowl [for washing wool]. **1585** HIGINS *Junius' Nomencl.* 304/1 *Penicillus rectorius*,..a *washing or white liming brush. **1626** MIDDLETON *Anything for Quiet Life* v. ii, The day after *washing-day; once a week I see't at home. **1754** in J. COX *Narr. Thief-takers* (1756) 103 It being Washing-day at her Father's, she attended there. **1853** DICKENS *Bleak Ho.* xiv, His scrambling home, from week's-end to week's-end, is like one great washing-day—only nothing's washed! **1825** J. NICHOLSON *Oper. Mech.* 366 This stream of water is kept running through the rags in the *washing-engine. **1844** G. DODD *Textile Manuf.* ii. 49 This enormous piece passes into a washing-engine, to cleanse it from the 'dressing' or mucilage which the weaver had introduced into his warp. **1836** PRICHARD *Phys. Hist. Mankind* (ed. 3) I. 40 He was about to make a *washing-green in the immediate neighbourhood. **1890** D. DAVIDSON *Mem. Long Life* i. 27 One of the posts in the washing green. **14..** *Rules & Const. Nuns Syon* xiv. in Aungier *Syon* (1840) 296 Also silence..is to be kepte..in the *waschyng howse in tyme of waschynge. **1577** GOOGE *Heresbach's Husb.* I. 12b, My maides chamber neere the Kitchin, and the wasshing house. **1705** *Lond. Gaz.* No. 4101/3 A Brew-house, Dairy, Washing-house. **1822** GALT *Provost* xxxviii, The mistress had her big summer washing at the public washing-house on the Green. **1608** in Cochran-Patrick *Early Rec. Mining Scot.* (1878) 148 Money debursit vpoun the dressing of the ore. For ane wesching tub and ane *wesching kitt, xviij[s]. **1799** UNDERWOOD *Dis. Childhood* (ed. 4) II. 103 The heels only may be covered by a piece of *washing-leather. **1939** L. MACNEICE *Autumn Jrnl.* viii. 33 But Life was comfortable, life was fine With two in a bed and patchwork cushions And checks and tassels on the *washing-line. **1961** J. STROUD *Touch & Go* iv. 45 Any idea where I can get a washing-line post? **1978** J. THOMSON *Question of Identity* xii. 115 Betty Lovell was pegging out sheets on a washing-line. *c* **1754** in *Hermathena* (1965) CI. 40 Things to be done... Morning Caps made..Curtains Chairs Carpets for Dublin ..*Washing Machine. *a* **1780** *Rake's Progress* (1977) 9 Enter Porter with a Washing Machine, puts it down—Enter Beat'em, pursued by Washerwomen, who beat him & break his washing machine. **1780** *Brit. Patent 1269* 1 Washing machine. Rogerson's specification... My invention of an entire new machine called a laundry, for the purpose of washing and pressing all sorts of household linen. **1799** *Hull Advertiser* 15 June 2/4 A washing machine. **1875** *Encycl. Brit.* III. 816/2 (*Bleaching*) From the washing-machine the chain of cloth is passed through a pair of squeezers. **1897** *Sears, Roebuck Catal.* 139/2 Washing Machines... The Electric Washers are warranted to be well made. **1944** A. HUXLEY *Let.* 10 Apr. (1969) 503 Fully furnished and equipped down to an electric washing machine. **1975** *Sunday Times* 16 Nov. 44/3, I also kept rushing to the other side of the room trying to empty rubbish into the washing machine. **1728** CHAMBERS *Cycl.* s.v. *Washings*, To get out the finer Parts, gone off with the Earth, they use Quicksilver, and a *Washing Mill. **1756** F. HOME *Exper. Bleaching* 92 Were this to happen on the surface of the cloth, the oil would remain; nor would the washing-mill afterwards be able to carry it off. **1875** *Encycl. Brit.* III. 820/2 (*Bleaching*) Washed at washing-mill or stocks. **1538** LONDON in *Lett. Suppress. Monasteries* (Camden) 223 Ther towne hall..stondith upon the ryver, wher ys the commyn *wassching place of the most partt of the towne, and in the cession dayes..ther ys such betyng with batildores as oon man can nott here another. **1659** BAXTER *Key for Catholicks* I. xxxv. 252 The rest they no more regard then a meeting of women in a workhouse or a washing place. **1748** *Anson's Voy.* I. v. 50 Negroes who have accidentally fallen upon rich washing places. **1851–3** *C. Tomlinson's Cycl. Useful Arts* (1866) I. 3/2 The washing-place [in an abattoir] is fitted up with coppers for boiling water. **1869** J. G. FULLER *Uncle John's Flower-Gatherers* 182 The old Prof..calls salt 'chloride of Sodium' and sets me thinking of *washing powders. **1895** [see BLUEING, BLUING *vbl. sb.* 2]. **1969** I. & P. OPIE *Children's Games* ii. 104 The mother..asks the shopkeeper for household goods, such as ..some washing-powder. **1977** A. WILSON *Strange Ride of R. Kipling* v. 244 Those who find to their surprise that washing powders wash whiter. **1850** R. GORDON CUMMING *S. Africa* I. xvi. 365, I accordingly stowed some ammunition and a *washing-rod in my old game-bag. **1838** F. A. KEMBLE *Let.* in *Rec. Later Life* (1882) I. 175 One towel was considered all that was requisite not even for each individual, but for each *washing-room. **1865** DICKENS *Mut. Fr.* IV. v, The cherub..was accordingly conducted to a little washing-room, where Bella soaped his face. **1720** J. STEUART *Letter-Bk.* (1915) 121 Six barells *washing soap. **1947** *Daily Gleaner* (Kingston, Jamaica) 5 Nov. 3/3 (*heading*) No washing soap this weekend. **1865** *Enquire Within* §1930 *Washing Soda as a Freezing Mixture. **1789** J. WOODFORDE *Diary* 13 Nov. (1927) III. 151 Bought this day..one new Mohogany *Washing-Stand. **1799** *Times* 1 June 4/1 Dressing and washing stands. **1806–7** J. BERESFORD *Miseries Hum. Life* x. ci, Rising, in a bitter frost, and going up to the washing-stand. **1889** GRETTON *Memory's Harkback* 187 If you had a chest of drawers, the top of it was turned to account as the washing stand. **1417–18** *Acc. Obedientiars Abingdon Abbey* (Camden) 88 Et in vno *wasshyngstok de nouo facto ij s. iiij d. **1700–1** R. GOUGH *Hist. Myddle* (1875) 31 The next morning Hopkin was found dead in Oatley Parke, haveinge beene knocked on the head with the foote of a washing stocke which stood at Ellesmeare meare. **1879** MISS JACKSON *Shropsh. Word-bk.*, *Washing-stock*, a bench on which clothes were laid and beaten with a kind of bat. **1585** HIGINS *Junius' Nomencl.* 193/1 *Vrnarium*,..the sinke or *washing stone in a kitchen, where the Scullion makes cleane the dishes. **1813** J. FORSYTH *Excurs. Italy* 288, I observed a group of these nymphs standing up to their knees in a fountain at washing-stones. **1868** DICKENS in *All Year Round* 19 Dec. 62/2, I found a man, his wife, and four children, sitting at a *washing stool by way of table, at their dinner. **1853** J. SHERER *Gold-Finder Australia* 177 The gold..lies upon a sort of pipe-clay, called by the diggers '*washing stuff', which is from two inches to four feet thick. **1382** WYCLIF *Isa.* lxv. 4 In *washing temples of mawmetis [Vulg. *in delubris idolorum*]. —— *Jer.* xliii. 12 In the washing templis of the godus of Egipt. **1404** *Durham Acc. Rolls* (Surtees) 398, 3 *wessyng towell. *c* **1460** *Invent. Sir J. Fastolfe* in *Archæologia* XXI. 275 Item, ij Wasschyng Tewellys of warke, eche of x yerds. **1557** in Pettus *Fodinæ Reg.* (1670) 95 Everie man that hath a *Washing Trough of his own by the custom of the Mine. **1833** LOUDON *Encycl. Archit.* §431 Boiler, washing-trough, and sink. **1560** *Burgh Rec. Stirling* (1887) I. 72 Ane *wesching tub. **1677** HORNECK *Gt. Law Consid.* iii. (1704) 67 He that makes a curious vessel of gold, doth not intend it for a washing-tub. **1842** DICKENS *Amer. Notes* xv, A hoopless washing-tub. **1388** WYCLIF *1 Kings* vii. 23 Also he made a ȝotun see, [*gloss*] that is, a *waisching vessel for preestis. *Ibid.* 31 The mouth of the waischyng vessel [1382 watir vessel; Vulg. *os luteris*]. *c* **1440** *Promp. Parv.* 517/2 Waschynge vessel, *luter*. **1827** FARADAY *Chem. Manip.* ix. (1842) 245 When a precipitate is soft and close in consistency, it is often of use to retain the *washing water on it, so as to penetrate and remove the soluble matter. **1876** TYNDALL *Float. Matter Air* (1881) 70 A portion of this washing-water reaching the infusion was clearly the origin of the life observed. *a* **1631** DONNE *Serm.* lxxxviii. (1649) II. 64 Doe not thinke to put off all to the *washing weeke; all thy sinnes, all thy repentance, to Easter, and the Sacrament then. **1825** T. HOOK *Sayings* Ser. II. *Passion & Princ.* iv, Next week is our washing-week. *c* **1425** *Cast. Persev.* 3146 in *Macro Plays* 170 Whanne man crieth mercy, & wyl not ses, Mercy schal be his *waschynge well. **1782** R. CUMBERLAND *Anecd. Emin. Painters* II. 170 Crowds of *washing-women ..and rows of linen. **1822–7** GOOD *Study Med.* (1829) V. 325 The ganglion..is peculiarly common to the wrists of washing-women.

b. The phr. ***washing up*** (see sense 1 h) in *Comb.*, as ***washing-up bowl, machine, water***; **washing-up cloth**, a square of loose-weave fabric for washing dishes, etc.; **washing-up liquid**, liquid detergent for adding to washing-up water.

1938 N. STREATFEILD *Circus is Coming* vii. 98 They hurried back to the *washing-up bowl. Santa..put a cup in the water. **1983** D. CLARK *Vicious Circle* i. 19 Marian had emptied the washing up bowl and mopped down the draining board. **1973** L. COOPER *Tea on Sunday* xvi. 136, I wouldn't myself trust poor Charlot to sell a row of *washing-up cloths. **1975** G. SEYMOUR *Harry's Game* iii. 49 The publican pushed the washing-up cloth..across the wooden bar. **1971** C. BONINGTON *Annapurna South Face* 254 *Washing-up liquid. **1980** P. HILL *Savages* vii. 135 Found your true occupation then?.. Washin' up... What made you go mad with the washin' up liquid? **1930** *Daily Tel.* 1 Dec. 23/7 (Advt.), Electric *washing-up machines..will be sold by auction. **1972** C. DRUMMOND *Death at Bar* i. 7 He has three helpers in the kitchen, one working the washing-up machine. **1932** S. GIBBONS *Cold Comfort Farm* x. 137 Niver put my liddle pretty [mop] in that gurt old greasy *washin'-up water. **1981** J. WAINWRIGHT *All on Summer's Day* 161 It hasn't a head on it [*sc.* beer]... An' it tastes like washing-up water.

ˈwashing, *ppl. a.* [f. WASH *v.* + -ING².]

1. That washes, in various senses of the verb: **a.** Surging, overflowing; streaming with water; dipping in the waves.

1560 GOOGE tr. *Palingenius' Zodiac* II. (1561) B iij, The washyng winter now is fledde, the hoary snowes be gon. **1653** J. TAYLOR (Water P.) *Cert. Trav.* 22, I was..three and thirty dirty Kentish miles, With washing dashing ways and rain wel sous'd. **1697** DRYDEN *Æneis* IX. 80 The washing Tyde Secures from all approach this weaker side. **1867** MORRIS *Jason* II. 63 For he was dizzy with the washing stream. **1882** *Daily Tel.* 12 Sept. 2/2 The washing heights of foam which swell up as high as the rail of the bulwarks. **1913** MASEFIELD *The River* iii. in *Engl. Rev.* Dec. 1 Till with a stripping crash the tree goes down, Its washing branches founder and are gone.

b. Of a garment, a textile fabric: That will 'wash' or admit of being washed without injury to colour or texture; washable.

a **1733** LD. BINNING in Maidment *New Bk. Old Ballads* (1844) 62, I fain wad wear a camblet skirt,..But camblet's an untasty thing, And it would wear out soon. If I should make a washing thing, It soon would flimsy be. **1750** F. COVENTRY *Pompey the Little* II. xii, A white washing Gown. **1849** LEVER *Con Cregan* xiv, The satin sinner was pardonable, where the 'washing silk' would have been found guilty without a 'recommendation'. **1868** 'HOLME LEE' *B. Godfrey* v, The..material of her dresses was..washing prints. **1901** *Lady's Realm* X. 648/2 Some lovely silk nightgowns are being made with double cape collars of washing-chiffon.

†**2.** Of a blow: = SWASHING *ppl. a.* 2. *Obs.*

1567 GOLDING *Ovid's Met.* v. 252 Astyages..Did with a long sharpe arming sworde a washing blow him giue. **1589** R. HARVEY *Pl. Perc.* (1590) 22 You see my quarter staffe... A washing blow of this is as good as a Laundresse, it will wash for the names sake: it can wipe a fellow ouer the thumbs. **1592** SHAKS. *Rom. & Jul.* I. i. 70 (Qo. 1599) Gregorie, remember thy washing blowe [and so Fo. 1]. **1621** FLETCHER *Wild-Goose Chase* v. iv, 'Tis a lustie wench: now could I spend my forty-pence..to have but one fling at her, To give her but a washing blow. **1625** B. JONSON *Staple of N.* v. v, I doe confesse a washing blow.

3. ***washing bear, racoon*** = WASH-BEAR.

1891 *Century Dict.*, *Washing-bear*, the wash-bear or racoon, *Procyon lotor*. **1896** tr. *Boas Zool.* 516 The Washing Racoon (*Procyon*).

Washington (ˈwɒʃɪŋtən). *U.S.* [Name of George *Washington* (1732–99), first president of the United States of America.]

1. ***Washington lily***: a tall lily, *Lilium washingtonianum*, that grows in the mountains of the Pacific Coast of N. America and bears white flowers.

[**1859** A. KELLOGG in *Hesperian* (San Francisco) III. 340 (*caption*) Lady Washington lily. **1863** *Proc. Calif. Acad. Nat. Sci.* II. 13 Dr. Kellogg also exhibited a drawing and growing specimens of a new species of lily from the Sierra Nevada... *L. washingtonianum* (Kellogg) Lady Washington Lily... Stem erect, glabrous, three to four feet high, two or more flowers on peduncles four to five inches long.] **1869** J. MUIR *My First Summer in Sierra* (1911) 43 Here and there a Washington lily may be seen nodding above its even surface. **1937** [see *Shasta lily* s.v. SHASTA *a.* 2].

2. ***Washington pie***: †(*a*) some kind of pie; (*b*) a light cake made of sponge layers with a jam or jelly (†or cream) filling.

1878 N. A. DONNELLEY *Lakeside Cook Bk.* 33/1 Washington pie. **1904** F. M. FARMER *Boston Cooking-School Cook Bk.* xxxi. 421 Mix and bake Cream Pie. Put raspberry jam or jelly between layers. **1905** J. C. LINCOLN *Partners of Tide* i. 10 Won't you have somethin' to eat? One of them turnovers or some Washington pie, or somethin', hey? **1968** E. R. BUCKLER *Ox Bells & Fireflies* xv. 231 The taste of the Christmas ribbon candy, and the fleeting taste of the good-luck thimble and the birthday wedge of Washington pie.

Washingtonia (wɒʃɪŋˈtəʊnɪə). [mod. L., f. prec. + -IA¹.] Either of two species of fan palm of the genus of this name, *Washingtonia filifera* and *W. robusta*, found in California and Mexico and elsewhere.

1945 J. L. MARSHALL *Santa Fe* 188 There were date palms and New Washingtonia palms from the Colorado desert.., but they were tricks of irrigation. **1949** *Los Angeles Times Home Mag.* 14 Aug. 32/4 There is today an impressive row of Washingtonias..standing like sentinels to direct the way to the ocean's cove park. **1976** *Hortus Third* (L. H. Bailey Hortorium) 1168/1 Washingtonias are extensively grown in Calif., often for street planting, and are common along the Gulf Coast, and in Fla., as well as in other parts of the world, particularly those with Mediterranean type of climate.

Washingtonian (wɒʃɪŋˈtəʊnɪən), *sb.* and *a.* [f. as prec. + -IAN.] **A.** *sb.* †**1.** A supporter or admirer of George Washington and his political standpoint. *Obs.*

1789 *Mass. Centinel* (Boston) 11 Feb. 172/3 The following gentlemen are chosen Electors... All firm federalists—and Washingtonians. **1816** M. B. SMITH *Forty Yrs. Washington Society* (1906) 134 If I was a Washingtonian you might say I worshipped the sun.

2. *Hist.* A member of an American temperance society founded in 1840.

1842 *Joliet* (Illinois) *Courier* 2 Feb. 1/4 A meeting of Washingtonians was held at the methodist church on tuesday evening the 18th inst. **1891** *Cycl. Temperance & Prohibition* 203/1 The 'Washingtonians' originated in the conversion into a temperance society in April, 1840, of a Baltimore drinking club..of six men. **1947** F. D. DOWNEY *Lusty Forefathers* 299 The fervor of the Washingtonians, founded by self-redeemed drunkards, felled thousands of apple trees, the fruits of which might otherwise..have become hard cider.

3. An inhabitant of Washington, D.C., or of the state of Washington.

1852 M. EASTMAN *Aunt Phillis's Cabin* 234 The beautiful prospect, to which Washingtonians are so much accustomed that they are too apt not to notice it. **1892** *Irrigation Age* 1 May 31/3 Washingtonians know a blessing when they see it. **1945** *Maryland Conservationist* Summer-Fall 7/2 The Potomac River..is very heavily fished by Washingtonians. **1972** *Times* 22 Dec. 5/6 Other Washingtonians, who do not have Air Force One to call on to fly them off to a viewing area, have booked motel rooms in York. **1978** G. VIDAL *Kalki* x. 227 'It's my fault,' she apologized. 'I'm the Washingtonian. I should have told you.' **1980** *Blair & Ketchum's Country Jrnl.* Oct. 19/3 Recently a Washingtonian informed us there's real danger that the federal government will collapse.

B. *adj.* **1.** Of, pertaining to, or characteristic of George Washington or his politics.

1812 *Salem Gaz.* 22 May 3/1 The political character of Vermont is really Washingtonian. **1858** A. LINCOLN *Coll. Wks.* (1953) III. 19 Fighting it in the Jeffersonian, Washingtonian, and Madisonian fashion. **1902** 'MARK TWAIN' in *N. Amer. Rev.* May 614 The Washingtonian character would not have been built. **1919** G. B. SHAW *Peace Conference Hints* ii. 21 The United States were still in the Washingtonian phase of non-intervention.

2. Of or pertaining to the Washingtonian Temperance Society or the practice of temperance that it advocated.

1842 *Knickerbocker* XX. 298 The festival was conducted on the Washingtonian principle. **1880** *Harper's Mag.* Jan. 191/2 Its influence is still visible in the Washingtonian homes which usefully supplement the charities of our large cities. **1911** *Encycl. Brit.* XXVI. 579/2 In the United States a flash of enthusiasm of a similar character, but on a smaller scale, known as the Washingtonian movement, had appeared.

3. Of, pertaining to, or characteristic of an inhabitant of Washington, D.C., or the state of Washington.

1961 in WEBSTER. **1977** L. MEYER *Capitol Crime* iv. 26 There was nothing particularly Washingtonian about Reilly... Washington is full of people..who once had.. ideas about changing things.

Washita (ˈwɒʃɪtɔː). The name *Washita* (see below) used *attrib.* and *absol.* to designate: **a.** [Fort *Washita*, Oklahoma.] (The rocks of) a subdivision of the Cretaceous in the central-southern U.S.A. **b.** [Ouachita or *Washita* Mountains, Arkansas.] A porous variety of novaculite used for sharpening cutting tools.

1860 *Trans. Acad. Sci. St. Louis* I. 586 Washita limestone.—This important member of our Cretaceous System is made up of a nearly white, yellow, gray and blue limestone. **1885** [see ARKANSAS¹]. **1963** A. GEIKIE *Text-bk. Geol.* (ed. 4) II. VI. iii. 1212 The Texas Lower Cretaceous deposits.. have been divided into three formations... The highest formation, termed the Washita, consists of four groups. **1938** A. DURST *Wood Carving* 18 The largest stone shown is the Washita oilstone; the others are various slips for the smaller tools. **1958** J. R. Biggs *Woodcuts* 32 The knife should be kept sharp on the India or Washita stone. **1974** *Encycl. Brit. Micropædia* X. 562/2 The Washita Group is the uppermost member of the Comanche Series.

'wash-leather. [f. wash *v.* Cf. G. *waschleder* (perh. from Eng.)

According to some writers the material is so called 'from the fact that it may be easily washed' (*Encycl. Brit.* ed. 9 XIV. 390). But the obsolete synonyms *washen, washed leather* suggest that the original reference may have been to the 'washing' which is an important part of the process of manufacture.]

A soft kind of leather, usually of split sheepskin, dressed to imitate chamois leather.

1681 Chetham *Angler's Vade-m.* iv. §13 (1689) 43 Making the body of yellow wash-leather. **1774** *Phil. Trans.* LXIV. 349 Two or three circles of wash-leather dipt in oil. **1848** Dickens *Dombey* xxxviii, Miss Tox..polished him up with a piece of wash-leather. **1857** Reade *Course of True Love* 8 All one colour, like wash-leather, or an actor by daylight.

b. *attrib.* (quasi-*adj.*) Made of wash-leather. Also *Path.* of eruptions: Resembling wash-leather in appearance.

c **1662** in *Verney Mem.* (1907) II. 262 [For the cold in winter he wants] wash-leather gloves to write in. *a* **1672** Wood *Life* (O.H.S.) II. 51 A paire of wash leather gloves. **1772** Foote *Nabob* II. (1778) 37 Tom Ramskin..had a fifty-pound note for a pair of wash-leather breeches. **1836** Dickens *Sk. Boz, Parish* vii, He wore..wash-leather gloves. **1854** Surtees *Handley Cr.* xli. (1901) II. 36 Wellington boots with wash-leather kneecaps. **1899** *Allbutt's Syst. Med.* VIII. 245 In frosty weather the wearing of wash-leather socks both by night and day is an advantage. **1900** J. Hutchinson *Archives Surg.* XI. 4 Large patches of xanthelasma palpebrarum of the ordinary wash-leather type. **1907** J. A. Hodges *Elem. Photogr.* (ed. 6) 25 The lens being placed in a wash-leather bag.

†**'washlock.** *Obs.* [f. wash *sb.* or *v.* + lock *sb.*[1] (sense 2). Cf. G. *waschlocke.*] A tuft of wool detached in the process of sheep-washing.

1604 *Proclam. Winding Wools* 18 June, Lambes wooll,.. washlocks, cummer, and many other deceiueable things.

†**'washmaid.** *Obs.* [f. wash *v.*] A maid-servant employed in washing clothes.

c **1610** Lady Compton in Grose *Antiq. Rep.* (1808) III. 438 Not pestering my Things with my Womens, nor theirs with Chambermaids, nor theirs with Washmaids. **1673** *Rutland MSS.* (Hist. MSS. Comm. 1905) IV. 550 To my Lady's washmayd, 1 ginny. **1682** Shadwell *Lanc. Witches* II. i. 17 My Woman-Chambermaid, Wash-maid, Cook-Maid, &c.

washman ('wɒʃmən). [f. wash *v.*]

1. A man whose occupation is washing clothes; = washerman.

1868 *Proc. Amer. Phil. Soc.* X. 552 Employing washmen instead of washwomen. **1892** Stevenson *Vailima Lett.* xvi. (1895) 150 Steward's assistant and washman Arrick, a New Hebridee black boy.

2. A workman employed in applying the wash or coating of tin in the manufacture of tinplate.

1851-4 *C. Tomlinson's Cycl. Useful Arts* (1867) II. 746/2 The washman prepares an iron pot,..called the wash-pot. **1881** *Instr. Census Clerks* (1885) 94 Tin Goods Manufacturer... Washman.

†**'washmeat.** *Obs.* [f. wash *sb.* (? and *a.*)]

a. Unsubstantial food. **b.** 'Wash' for swine.

1682 'R. Burton' *Admir. Curios.* 122 Having once eat 60 pound weight of Cherries, he said they were but wash-meat. **1688** Holme *Armoury* II. 181/2 A Trough, or Stone Trough, a hollow place cut in Wood or Stone, in which the Swine have their Wash-meat given them.

'wash-mill. [f. wash *v.*]

†**1.** ? A mill-race in which sheep are washed. *Obs.*

a **1722** Lisle *Husb.* (1757) 317 Being..to wash our sheep on the morrow, I asked my shepherd, what time in the morning he would drive them to the wash-mills.

2. *Brick-making*, etc. A machine for washing clay or materials for cement.

1856 *Builder* 16 Aug. 443/3 The principal machines which have been worked for this purpose [brick-making] are three—1st. The pug-mill. 2nd. The wash-mill. 3rd. The rolling-mill. **1879** *Spons' Dict. Engin.* Suppl. I. 332 These [*sc.* limestone and clay] are mixed in what are known as wash mills.

3. *Leather Manuf.* A machine for washing skins after unhairing by the application of lime.

1897 C. T. Davis *Manuf. Leather* (ed. 2) 377 From the unhairing room the skins pass to the 'wash-mill', where they receive a thorough washing, removing all adhering lime.

'wash-mouth. *s.w. dial.* Also **washamouth.** [f. wash *v.* Cf. G. *waschmaul* of the same meaning.] One who blabs out everything; a babbler.

1746 *Exmoor Scolding* 138 Hold thy Popping, ya gurt Washamouth. **1891** 'Q' (Quiller-Couch) *Noughts & Cr.* iii. 20 Parson Morth wanted to know if he couldn't let his cottage to an invalid lady and her sister without consulting every wash-mouth in the parish.

Washoe ('wɒʃəʊ, -ʃu:). Also **Washo.** [Washoe *'wášiw* Washoe Indian, Washoe Indians.]

1. (A member of) a North American Indian people inhabiting the area around Lake Tahoe on the border of California and Nevada. Also *attrib.*

1846 J. Clyman *Jrnl.* 4 May in C. L. Camp *J. Clyman, Frontiersman* (1960) 206 The tribe we are now passing through call themselves as well as understood Washee. *Ibid.* 8 May 207 But as the tribe of natives inhabiting this stream and the adjacent country call themselves the Washew tribe and nation I think it would [be] correct to call the stream by the same name viz Waushee River. **1860** H. De Groot *Sk. Washoe Silver Mines* 15/2 To this place, on the approach of cold weather, not only the Washoes, whose territory lies adjacent, but also bands of the Pah-Utahs, from a greater distance repair. **1879** H. R. Mighels *Sage Brush Leaves* 225 We saw..a..young Washoe brave escorting his wife and mother-in-law up towards the campoody. **1903** *Out West* Apr. 439 The colors in Washoe baskets are all natural. **1947** *Desert Mag.* Dec. 32/3 The Washoes, of whom less than 1,000 remain, live in valleys along the Sierra Nevada. **1976** *Amer. Speech 1974* XLIX. 287 The Indian nomenclature belongs principally to three major Numic-speaking groups (Shoshone, Northern Paiute, and Southern Paiute) and to two non-Numic tribes, the Washo and the Mohave.

2. The region inhabited by the Washoe Indians; hence, a nickname for Nevada. Also *attrib.*

1856 *San Francisco Bull.* 26 May 3/2 The rumored trouble from the Indians of Carson, Wash-hoe and Walker's valley, is entirely without foundation. **1872** 'Mark Twain' *Roughing It* xxi. 160 Washoe is a pet nickname for Nevada. **1896** C. H. Shinn *Story of Mine* 110 Not merchants these.. but a brave, honest outdoor race whose huge Washoe wagons were the forerunners of the railroads. **1947** *Amer. Weekly* 2 Nov. 21/3 Back in Washoe, later to become the state of Nevada, the Comstock Lode waited—waited to be discovered.

3. The language of the Washoe Indians, one of the Hokan group of languages.

1882 *Mag. Amer. Hist.* Apr. 255 The area of the Washo languages borders to the west on the Maidu. **1921** E. Sapir *Language* iv. 81 Washo..an Indian language of Nevada. **1968** *Language* XLIV. 822, I am thinking of the contrast with the vowel harmony patterns in Washo.

4. Special Combs.: **Washoe canary** *U.S. colloq.*, a burro; **Washoe zephyr**, a strong west wind that blows in Nevada.

1867 *Daily Territorial Enterprise* (Virginia City, Nevada) 8 Mar. 3/1 The discouraged 'Washoe canary' refuses to cheer us with its tuneful warblings. **1877** W. Wright *Hist. Big Bonanza* 114 A queer genius thus described the donkey, called by everybody in that region, 'The Washoe Canary'. **1947** *Sat. Rev.* (U.S.) 10 May 32/2 He is..discoursing on the Washoe zephyr and the Washoe canary. **1865** *Washoe* (Nevada) *Times* 4 Mar. 3/2 We have heard of hail and chain-lightning, etc., but ye gentle Washoe zephyr can discount all and everything in that line. **1872** 'Mark Twain' *Roughing It* xxi. 159 According to custom the daily 'Washoe Zephyr' set in; a soaring dust-drift..came with it, and the capital of the Nevada Territory disappeared from view. **1947** Washoe zephyr [see *Washoe canary* above].

wash-off, *a. Calico-printing.* [f. verbal phr. *to wash off*: see wash *v.* 13.] Of colours: Capable of being washed off; not permanent.

1864 Webster.

'wash-off, *sb.* [f. vbl. phr. *to wash off* (wash *v.* 15a).] **a.** Material that is washed off. **b.** The process or fact of being washed off.

1979 *Nature* 17 May 180/2 The pollutants are the wash-off of fertilisers and pesticides from the surrounding banks, the paddy and orchard fields, and the famous Mughal gardens. **1984** *Gardening from 'Which?'* June 181/1 Surface wash-off..can occur with other chemicals.

washomat ('wɒʃəʊmæt). *colloq.* Also **wash-o-mat.** [f. wash *v.* + -o + -mat; cf. Laundromat.] = launderette.

1959 *Times* 30 Dec. 8/7 Twenty-storey skyscrapers were shooting up..among the Chinese laundries, the wash-o-mats. **1983** W. Garner *Think Big, think Dirty* ix. 135 Suttin used a local washomat, launderette, what you will. **1984** T. Hillerman *Ghostway* (1985) vii. 31 Laundries are magnets. .. The people at the Shiprock Economy Wash-O-Mat would know their customers.

wash-out. [f. verbal phr. *to wash out*: see wash *v.* 13.]

1. a. An act of washing out a cistern, etc.; a pipe or other appliance for doing this. Also *attrib.*

1877 Hellyer *Plumber* ix. 86 This 'water-battery' water-closet is similar in principle and shape to the 'wash-out' closet-basin. **1903** *Architect* 24 Apr. Suppl. 23/2 Valves are provided *en route* to divide the delivery main into sections and control the supply. Wash-outs and air-valves are provided, also hydrants in the villages for fire protection. **1884** *Health Exhib. Catal.* 94/1 Shanks' Patent 'Tubal' Washout Closets with Patent 'Reliable' Syphon Cisterns. **1901** *Feilden's Mag.* IV. 430/1 There was a 6-in. washout pipe which was connected to the 12 in. main.

b. *Biol.* and *Med.* The removal of material, esp. from a physiological system, by means of a fluid; the fluid used for, or matter removed by, this.

1955 in *Shorter Oxf. Eng. Dict.* (ed. 3) Add. **1966** *Jrnl. Lab. & Clinical Med.* LXVI. 856 The rapidity of indicator washout..should yield information regarding fluid flow patterns within the cardiovascular system. **1971** *Nature* 23 July 266/2 With a closed system technique in which a nitrogen-free atmosphere was made with helium-oxygen washout, a substantial increase in the concentration of nitrogen was measured. **1977** *Lancet* 8 Oct. 745/1 In a check of the wash-out from swabs and surgical drapes with measured volumes of blood the maximum error recorded was +2.8% by volume. **1980** *Nature* 17 Jan. 265/1 Spontaneous synaptic activity was detected in most myotubes within 1-2 min of curare washout.

c. *Meteorol.* The removal of particles from the air by falling water droplets. Cf. rain-out 2.

1955 A. C. Chamberlain *Aspects of Trav. & Deposition of Aerosol & Vapour Clouds* (A.E.R.E. Doc. HP/R 1261) 2 Consideration is given to the four mechanisms by which aerosol particles and vapours are removed from the atmosphere, namely: (a) Sedimentation, (b) Impaction, (c) Diffusion.., (d) Wash out by rain. **1974** [see rain-out 2]. **1980** Iribarne & Cho *Atmospheric Physics* ii. 26 The water cycle is important in the cleansing of the atmosphere by two mechanisms: Rainout... Washout—This is the name given to the elimination of gases by dissolution and of aerosol particles through capture by falling water drops.

2. *Mining.* A place where a portion of a coal or ironstone seam has been carried away by a stream, a deposit of sandstone being left in its place.

1876 Cudworth *Rambles Bradford* 56. **1911** *Act 1 & 2 Geo. V*, c. 50 §20 The position, direction, and extent of every known fault of every seam with its vertical throw, and.. every known washout and intrusive dyke.

3. The removal by flood of a portion of a hillside; a hole or breach in a railway or road track caused by flood or erosion. Orig. *U.S.*

1873 *Newton Kansan* 29 May 3/2 Owing to a wash out on the Cottonwood last Sunday night, we had no train from the east until Tuesday afternoon. **1883** *Daily News* 24 Sept. 2/1 The well built Mexican Railway..has had difficulty enough to prevent 'wash-outs'. **1883** *Standard* 25 Dec. 5/4 A train ..ran into a wash-out. **1885** Roosevelt *Hunting Trips* 153 (Cent.) The rains and torrents cutting away the land into channels, which at first are merely wash-outs, and at last grow into deep canyons. **1910** *Times* 5 Mar. 5/6 On the Peking and Hankau Railway..washouts may extend, not for one or two miles, but for fifty or a hundred miles.

4. *slang.* **a.** A disappointing failure, a 'sell'.

1902 *Westm. Gaz.* 1 Nov. 2/1 As Harker remarked, 'Half a guinea for an essay is no wash-out'. **1915** P. MacGill *Amateur Army* 57 What the dickens did you take this here [rifle] for!.. It's a blooming wash-out. *Footn.* 'Wash-out' is a term used by the men when their firing is so wide of the mark that it fails to hit any spot on the card. The men apply it indiscriminately to anything in the nature of a failure.

b. A useless or unsuccessful person; *spec.* in *Air Force slang*, a person who is eliminated from a course of training.

1918 J. M. Grider *War Birds* (1926) 65 Yesterday was washout day so we all went into town and threw a party at the Court. **1925** [see napoo *int., a.,* and *v.*]. **1927** C. A. Lindbergh *We* 115 We waited for the almost weekly list of washouts to be published. **1929** D. H. Lawrence *Pansies* 126 Now it's a country of..young wash-outs pretending to be in love with death. **1936** J. B. Priestley *They walk in City* v. 115 Gregory Porson was no good, a blighter,..a worm, a wash-out. **1950** *Chicago Tribune* 27 Apr. iv. 1/5 But there's a redeeming feature about the washouts, etc. The Wrigley field tenants still have their perfect percentage based on three straight victories. **1973** *Times* 23 Apr. 4/7, I think I'm a washout.

c. *Air Force slang.* A wrecked aeroplane.

1928 *Pop. Sci. Monthly* May 72/1 Damage to a plane is spoken of as a..'crash' and if beyond repair as a 'washout'. **1972** in *Amer. Speech 1972* (1975) XLVII. 114 Wash out —complete wreckage.

5. *Aeronaut.* A decrease in the angle of incidence of an aeroplane wing towards the tip. [Perh. f. wash *sb.* 6 b (*b*), but cf. wash *v.* 2 k, 13 e and quot. 1916[1].]

1913 *Flight* 25 Jan. 87/2 The fact of them [an aeroplane's wing tips] appearing to be negative does not necessarily imply more than a 'wash-out'. **1916** H. Barber *Aeroplane Speaks* 25 The Angle of Incidence..is sometimes decreased or washed-out towards the Wing-tips.] *Ibid.* 81 The wash-out also renders the ailerons..more effective. **1939** *Jrnl. R. Aeronaut. Soc.* XLIII. 792 The designer has available in this connection not only the use of tip slots, but the use of wash-out and of varying aerofoil section along the span. **1979** Bertin & Smith *Aerodynamics for Engineers* iii. 83 The wings of numerous subsonic aircraft have wash out to control the spanwise lift distribution.

'wash-pool. [f. wash *v.*] A pool for washing sheep.

1827 Clare *Sheph. Cal.* 56 He drives the bleating sheep from fallow fold To wash-pools. **1873** Trollope *Australia* I. 471 The Australian wool-grower..will take you to his washpool. **1890** 'R. Boldrewood' *Col. Reformer* xvii, The brush yard at the equally primitive washpool.

'wash-pot. [f. wash *v.*]

†**1.** A servant employed to wash pots; *spec.* the designation of a servant employed at the Inns of Court. *Obs.*

1570 in *Black Bks. Linc. Inn* (1897) I. 373, 10s. to Ralph Richardson, the washpot in the buttery, for 6 months' wages. **1645** *Ibid.* II. 367 The Washpot 20s., the Laundress £4, [etc.]. **1678** Ravenscroft *Engl. Lawyer* II. i. 15, I was an under-Butler, or Wash-pot in the Inns of Court. **1816** *Temple Ch. Reg. Burials*, Thomas Lock Washpot of the honble Society of the Inner Temple.

2. A vessel for washing one's hands. *Obs.* exc. *fig.* in allusion to Ps. lx. 8.

1535 Coverdale *Ps.* lx. 8 Moab is my washpotte, ouer Edom wil I stretch out my shue. **1635-56** Cowley *Davideis* II. 341 Sev'en comely blooming Youths..in their hands sev'en silver washpots bear. **1810** Scott *Let.* in *Lockhart* (1837) II. viii. 285 In an age when every London citizen makes Lochlomond his wash-pot, and throws his shoe over Ben-Nevis. **1839** Carlyle *Chartism* viii. 166 He had to fly, with broken washpots. **1884** *Daily News* 5 Feb. 3/1 French philosophers were using it [China] as a washpot for their satires on institutions nearer home.

3. A vessel containing melted tin, into which iron plates are plunged to be converted into tin-plate.

1839 URE *Dict. Arts* 1253 s.v. *Tin-plate*.

4. A vessel used in separating silver from lead.

1879 G. GLADSTONE *Mining, Silver* in *Cassell's Techn. Educ.* IV. 112/2 It is usual to have small pots, called temper or wash-pots, placed between every second crystallising pot.

5. A vessel in which to wash clothes over a fire; a wash-boiler. *U.S.*

1926 B. ISBELL in J. F. Dobie *Rainbow in Morning* (1965) 105 At a later dance a large wash-pot of coffee, surrounded with ample tin cups, was kept boiling under a live oak tree in the yard. **1940** W. FAULKNER *Hamlet* I. 12 The women surrounded by laden clotheslines and tubs and blackened wash pots. **1944** T. D. CLARK *Pills, Petticoats & Plows* xviii. 330 The devil had him imprisoned under an upturned washpot. **1952** F. O'CONNOR *Wise Blood* iii. 62 His mother was standing by the washpot in the yard.

wash road. = WASH-WAY 2.

1765 *Museum Rust.* IV. 247 That wash roads (however applauded by some) are rarely without notorious exceptions.

washroom ('wɒʃruːm). orig. and chiefly *N. Amer.* [f. WASH *v.* + ROOM *sb.*^{1}] **a.** A room equipped for washing oneself. **b.** A lavatory or W.C.

1806 in *Mass. Hist. Soc. Coll.* (1809) X. 77 They have usually two good rooms in front, bed-rooms, kitchen, wash-room, and other convenient apartments in the rear. **1855** 'P. PAXTON' *Capt. Priest* 160 Finally a long wash-room completed the odd assemblage. **1878** R. T. COOKE *Happy Dodd* 293 He..fairly went down on his knees to her in the wash-room. **1892** GUNTER *Miss Dividends* v, He ejaculates nervously: 'I'll just wash my hands, and be with you in a moment,' and moves hurriedly back to the gentlemen's wash-room at the rear of the car. **1908** S. E. WHITE *Riverman* xi, That evening..Orde returned to the hotel. After freshening up in the marbled and boarded wash-room, he hunted up Newmark. **1941** AUDEN *New Year Let.* III. 54 In Pullman washrooms. **1952** S. SPENDER *Learning Laughter* 140 The indoor separate lavatory and washroom with shower. **1962** A. LURIE *Love & Friendship* iv. 76 The jokes one makes in washrooms. **1978** *Detroit Free Press* 5 Mar. (Parade Suppl.) 12/3 A queasy stomach sends him dashing for the washroom on bumpy plane flights. **1980** *Ottawa Citizen* 16 June 35/2 Washroom sex can mean a hand reaching for a groin underneath toilet cubicles or it can involve two men in the cubicle.

'washstand. [f. WASH *v.*]

1. A wash-hand stand.

1789 J. WOODFORDE *Diary* 13 Nov. (1927) III. 151 For the ..Mohogany Wash-stand 0.10.6. **1808** E. WEETON *Let.* 14 Nov. in *Jrnl. of Governess* (1969) I. 126 A box 7 feet by 9, with a bed, a chest of drawers, two chairs, and a washstand in it. **1839** URE *Dict. Arts* 1149 Such soap is exceedingly pleasant at the wash-stand. **1844** T. WEBSTER *Encycl. Dom. Econ.* 276 A wash stand, to be complete, should have, besides the basin and ewer, a carafe for spring water, vessel for hot water, soap tray, several glasses, [etc.]. **1847** C. BRONTË *Jane Eyre* iv, She hauled me to the washstand, inflicted a merciless, but happily brief, scrub on my face and hands with soap, water, and a coarse towel. **1898** G. B. SHAW *Plays* II. *Arms & Man* 3 The washstand..consists of an enamelled iron basin with a pail beneath it in a painted metal frame, and a single towel on the rail at the side.

attrib. **1902** MABEL BARNES-GRUNDY *Thames Camp* 196, I have made four fascinating washstand mats.

2. *U.S.* (See quot.)

1911 WEBSTER, *Wash stand*, in stables, a place in the floor prepared so that carriages may be washed there and the water run off. *Cant.*

†**'washstart.** *Obs. rare*$^{-1}$. In 4 **waschesterte.** [App. a confused form between WASH-DISH and WAGSTART.] The Water Wagtail.

a **1400** *Nominale* (Skeat) 786 Gryue et croulecowe Feldefare and waschesterte.

wash-strake. *Naut.* Also **-streak.** [? f. WASH *sb.*] = WASHBOARD 1.

1809 *Naval Chron.* XXI. 299 Exclusive of a moveable wash strake. **1834** M. SCOTT *Cruise Midge* iii, A large Eboe canoe,..the bottom hollowed out of one single tree, but there was a washstreak of some kind of hardwood plank, so as to raise the gunwale about a foot above the ledge of the original vessel.

wash-trough. [f. WASH *v.*]

1. *Mining.* A trough in which ore is washed.

1557 in Pettus *Fodinæ Reg.* (1670) 95 Also that no Purchasors shall let or stop any Miners from any Wash-trough at any time. **1756–7** tr. *Keysler's Trav.* (1760) IV. 146 The first sort is reserved for use; the second, or middling sort, is again put into the stamping-mill, and afterwards into the wash-trough, where the parts that contain no cinnabar float in the water.

2. A trough used for washing the hands and face.

1902 O. WISTER *Virginian* ii. 16 It was not much of a toilet that I made in the first wash-trough of my experience, but it had to suffice.

'wash-tub. [f. WASH *v.* Cf. Du. *waschtobbe.*]

1. A tub in which clothes are washed: = WASHING-*tub*.

1602 *Inv.* in *Collect. Archæol.* (1863) II. 111 Fowre boordes, cover of the vate, and a washtubb .xij*d.* **1753** *Scots Mag.* Sept. 469/1 Indicted for drowning in a wash-tub..her son. **1838** DICKENS *O. Twist* xxxvii, Glancing distractedly at a couple of old women at the wash-tub.

2. *Comb.* **wash-tub (bass)**, a wash-tub converted into a musical instrument like a double-bass by stretching a string across it.

1968 *Blues Unlimited* Nov. 8 We recorded Dewey Corley, who..plays kazoo and washtub bass. **1970** *Western Folklore* XXIX. 229 Two kinds of plucked one-stringed instruments are known to Negroes in America today. One is the familiar one-stringed bass, sometimes called a 'washtub bass' or 'gutbucket' from the materials of its construction. **1972** *Time* 17 Apr. 39/3 He played a washtub in a group named the Five Hip Cats.

wash-up. [f. vbl. phr. *to wash up*: see WASH *v.* 1 f.]

1. a. An act of washing table utensils after a meal. In quots. *attrib.*

1884 *Health Exhib. Catal.* 93/2 Butler's Pantry and Wash-up Sinks. **1900** 'H. LAWSON' *On Track* 128 Grease inches deep in great black patches about the fireplace ends of the huts, where wash-up and 'boiling' water is thrown.

b. ? *dial.* A washing-up place, scullery.

1869 BLACKMORE *Lorna D.* xi, He made even mother laugh..and Betty Muxworthy roared in the wash-up.

c. A wash; an act of washing oneself. *N. Amer.*

1887 B. HARTE *Millionaire & Devil's Ford* i. 176 You boys can go there for a general wash-up. **1917** C. MATHEWSON *Second Base Sloan* 64 They..dropped from the car and went back to the station for a wash-up. **1968** *Globe & Mail* (Toronto) 13 Feb. B-12/7 The shutdown of the assembly line for 30 minutes each shift—for rest and wash-up.

2. *Mining.* The washing of a collected quantity of ore; the quantity of gold that has been obtained by washing.

1890 'R. BOLDREWOOD' *Miner's Right* xxiii, As soon as we had finished the next wash-up, I was to go back to Yatala. **1898** *Westm. Gaz.* 16 June 4/3 The gold consisted of about a quarter of a million dollars in dust and three-quarters of a million in drafts. The estimate of the wash-up varies from twelve millions to thirty millions.

3. A dead body washed up by the waves.

a **1903** 'MERRIMAN' *Last Hope* i, Passen thinks it's [*sc.* the grave is] over there by the yew-tree—but he's wrong. That there one was a wash-up found by old Willem the lighthouse keeper one morning early.

'wash-water. [f. WASH *v.*] Water that has been used for washing.

1853 HICKIE tr. *Aristoph.* I. 25 Those who pour out their dirty wash-water of an evening. **1856** G. GORE *Pract. Chem.* in *Orr's Circ. Sci.* 73 The wash-waters should not be thrown away without first being tested for gold. **1877** RAYMOND *Statist. Mines & Mining* 401 The evaporation of the excess of liquid derived from the wash-waters. **1892** *Photogr. Ann.* II. 69 No trace of bromide could be found in the wash water. **1900** *Jrnl. Soc. of Dyers* XVI. 12 When, however, wash waters accumulate.

'wash-way. *dial.* [f. WASH *v.* + WAY *sb.*]

1. A portion of a road crossed by a shallow stream.

a **1631** DONNE *Serm.* civ. (1649) II. 195 He that hath not been accustomed to a sin, but exercised in resisting it, will finde many tentations, but as a wash way that he can trot thorough, and goe forward religiously in his Calling for all them. **1766** *Ann. Reg.* 66 Yesterday morning..the North mail cart, going through Tottenham Washway, was under water. **1804** *Aston's Manch. Guide* 17 The cart road through Hanging-ditch was through a wash-way, so narrow, that only one cart could pass at once.

†**b.** *to make wash-way of, with*: to make light of, make short work of. Cf. WASH-WORK 1.

1642 D. ROGERS *Naaman* 32 But man heares like the Adder with a deafe eare: she makes wash-way with patience, word conscience and all. *Ibid.* 298 A common servant makes wash way of his service; lookes at his Master for his owne ends. *Ibid.* 618 Made wash-way of all sorts of performances, and made them common things.

2. A road deeper in the middle than at the sides.

1790 W. H. MARSHALL *Midl. Co.* I. 44 A 'wash-way road'. **1808** T. BATCHELOR *Agric. Bedford* 588 The form of the roads is generally convex, and the few concave or wash-ways that may be observed, seem [etc.].

'washwoman. Now *U.S.* [f. WASH *v.*] = WASHERWOMAN.

1590 *Dewsbury Parish Ch. Reg.* 28 Sept., Massoley a maid of Mr. Rowland Owans a washwoman buried. **1778** MISS BURNEY *Evelina* (1791) I. xiv. 52 *You* would much sooner be taken for her wash-woman. **1816** W. TAYLOR in *Monthly Rev.* LXXXI. 121 Among the lost plays of Sophocles, are enumerated..Nausicaa, or the Wash-women (πλύντριαι). **1852** C. W. DAY *Five Yrs.' Resid. W. Indies* II. 297 The Spanish flounces of the negro wash-women. **1856** OLMSTED *Slave States* 72 'Is you come from Colonel Gillin's, massa?' asked the wash-woman.

wash-work. [f. WASH *sb.* or *v.*]

†**1.** *to make wash-work with*: app. 'to make short work of'. Cf. the phrase under WASH-WAY 1 b, of which this appears to be an altered form.

1637 J. WILLIAMS *Holy Table* 159 And if this Leader should chance to be overcome,..we shall make wash-work with the rest of his followers.

2. Used for WASH-DRAWING.

1893 A. BEARDSLEY *Let. c*15 Feb. (1970) 44 Nobody gave me credit for caricature and wash-work, but I have blossomed out into both styles. **1900** *Pall Mall Gaz.* 2 Nov. 1/3 Mr. Frank Craig..is scarcely behind Mr. Hatherell in his excellent wash-work.

washy ('wɒʃɪ), *a.* [f. WASH *sb.* or *v.* + -Y^1.]

†**1.** Having too much moisture, water-logged. Of wind or weather: Bringing moisture or rain.

In quot. 1566 the word corresponds to Horace's *plumbeus*, lit. 'leaden', used app. for 'depressing'.

1566 DRANT *Horace, Sat.* II. vi. H 6, Not lewde ambition vexethe here; nor washye southerne wynde. **1661** J. CHILDREY *Brit. Baconica* 133 Under this upper Clay lyes a mouldring washy Clay. **1661** PEPYS *Diary* 24 Sept., We.. found a most sad alteration in the roade by reason of last night's rains; they being now all dirty and washy. **1667** MILTON *P.L.* VII. 303 They..on the washie Oose deep Channels wore. *a* **1722** LISLE *Husb.* (1757) 216 In washy weather all the hay one can give to cattle will not make them thrive. **1726** LEONI *Alberti's Archit.* I. 40/2 Of places..some are..damp and washy, as are those which lie near Seas or Lakes.

2. a. Of food, drink, etc.: Too much diluted, weak, sloppy, thin, watery.

1615 T. ADAMS *England's Sickn.* ii. 72 Meates of a washy and fluid nature. **1763** *Museum Rust.* I. 327 New oats are a washy food, owing to a crude humidity that abounds in them. **1825** E. HEWLETT *Cottage Comforts* viii. 99 Common corn and washy potatoes. **1832–4** DE QUINCEY *Caesars* Wks. 1862 IX. 133 *note*, By comparison with the washy tea breakfasts of most Englishmen. **1883** *Harper's Mag.* July 165/2 Serving pots of washy ale over the counter.

Comb. **1746** W. THOMPSON *R.N. Adv.* (1757) 42 The Flesh of such washy fed Sows is..flabby.

b. *fig.* Of literary style, productions, utterances, etc.: Wanting in force or vigour, feeble, sloppy, thin.

1806–7 J. BERESFORD *Miseries Hum. Life* VII. xl, Being compelled by a deaf person..to repeat some very washy remark three or four times over. **1829** [see SPEWY *a.* 1 b]. **1831** CARLYLE *Ess., Schiller* (1840) III. 21 *note*, Our English translation, one of the washiest, was executed..in Edinburgh by a 'Lord of Session'. **1879** GEO. ELIOT *Theo. Such* v. 113 This mixture of other persons' washy opinions. **1897** MRS. OLIPHANT *W. Blackwood* I. 100 The publication altogether was a weak and washy production.

3. Of the stomach: Having an accumulation of liquid and undigested food, relaxed.

1622 MABBE tr. *Aleman's Guzman d'Alf.* I. 47 But for such washie Tripes as mine then were, I held it no good meate. **1897** *Allbutt's Syst. Med.* III. 491 The physician who neglects the factor of dilatation because the stomach is not as blown out and washy as to force itself on his notice, has an imperfect comprehension of his case.

4. Of colour, painting, etc.: Having too much 'wash', lacking body, weak, pale.

a **1639** WOTTON *Surv. Educ.* Reliq. (1651) 325 A palish Clearnesse, evenly and smoothly spread, not overthin and washie, but of a pretty solid consistence. **1647** TRAPP *Comm. Matt.* xxv. 4 Christ putteth not upon his a washy colour of profession..but he dyeth them in grain, with true grace and holinesse. **1718** OZELL tr. *Tournefort's Voy.* I. 188 Four rows of Scales of a washy purple. **1785** H. WALPOLE *Let. to H. S. Conway* 6 Oct., Sir Joshua's washy Virtues make the Nativity a dark spot from the darkness of the Shepherds. **1811** *Self Instructor* 524 A middling full pencil, not too washy. **1848** MRS. GASKELL *Mary Barton* ii, With a washy, but clean stencilled pattern on the walls. **1884** *19th Cent.* Feb. 355 The colours are washy and unimpressive. **1886** G. ALLEN *Maimie's Sake* xix, Blue eyes like hers..look so mild and gentle and washy.

5. Of a horse or cow: Poor in quality or condition; esp. liable to sweat or scour after slight exertion.

1639 T. DE GREY *Compl. Horsem.* I. iv. (1656) 40 The Horse..is generally weake,..tender, and washy of flesh. *a* **1722** LISLE *Husb.* (1757) 300 Your thin necked and bodied cows, that are washy and flue. **1730** W. BURDON *Gentl. Pocket-Farrier* 61 Some Horses..part with their Food before 'tis well digested, and scour all the Way; which makes 'em so thin and lank, that they are ready to slip through their Girts; they are called washy. **1809** *Sporting Mag.* XXXIII. 138 It was a washy ill constitutioned horse. **1828–32** WEBSTER, *Washy*..liable to sweat profusely with labor; as, a washy horse. **1844** H. STEPHENS *Bk. Farm* II. 163 [This] gives to a beast what is called a washy appearance, and is always attended with a liability to looseness in the bowels. This washiness is generally attended with an inordinate breadth of hooks [i.e. hips]. **1864** E. MAYHEW *Illustr. Horse Managem.* 483 A leggy, a washy, a soft species of creature, which gentlemen find it cheaper to hire than to buy.

6. Of a person: Lacking strength or stamina; weak, feeble, insipid; exhausted, washed-out; poor, mean, worthless. Now *rare* or *Obs.*

a **1631** DONNE *Serm.* xlv. (1640) 448 All the good of man, considered supernaturally, is in grace; but that will not grow in a washy soule, in a liquid, in a watery, and dissolute, and scattered man. **1657** J. WATTS *Scribe, Pharisee*, etc. III. 24 Like as some, who used water instead of wine..were called by the Church ὑδροπαραστάται, or *Aquarii*, watry and washy Hereticks, as Augustine witnesseth. **1682** DRYDEN *Epil. to King & Q.* 37 Alas, our Women are but washy Toys. **1693** LD. FALKLAND *Congreve's Old Bach.* Prol., If the Slave, After his bragging, prove a washy Knave; May he be banish'd to some lonely Den. **1719** D'URFEY *Pills* III. 337 What washy Rogues are here, are these the Sons of Beef, and English Beer? *a* **1721** PRIOR *Daphne & Apollo* 10 One mile has put the fellow out of breath;..Washy he is, perhaps not over sound. **1922** JOYCE *Ulysses* 734, I looked a bit washy.

waskeine, variant of VASQUINE *Obs.*

†**'waskite.** *Obs. rare*$^{-1}$. [Of obscure origin; prob. an erroneous form.

Not for WASP-KITE, as that word (if genuine) denotes a bird of the Old World.]

Given by Izaak Walton as the name of a long-winged hawk, native of Virginia.

1655 WALTON *Angler* i. (1661) 13 [List of long-winged hawks.] The Waskite from Virginia.

waskyne, variant of VASQUINE *Obs.*

waslage, obs. Sc. form of VASSALAGE.

wasn't, colloq. contraction of *was not*.

wasp (wɒsp), *sb.*^{1} Forms: α. 1 **wæfs, wæps**, 2 **weaps**, 5, *dial.* 8–9 **waps**, 7, 9 *dial.* **wapse**, 9- *dial.* or *joc.* **wops**(e. β. 1 **wæsp**, 4–7 **waspe** (7 **whaspe**, 8 **whasp**), 6- **wasp.** *Pl.* α. 5 **wappys.** [OE. *wæfs*, *wæps*, *wæsp* masc. corresponds (with differences of declension) to OS. *uuepsia*, fem. (MLG. *wepse*, *wespe*, *wispe*), MDu. *wespe* fem. (mod.Du. *wesp*), OHG. *wafsa*, *wefsa* fem. (MHG. *wefse*, *webse*, mod.G. *wespe*, dial. *webes*):—OTeut. **waƀiso-z*, *-isō*, **waps-*:—pre-Teut. **wobhes-*, **wops-*: cf. Lith. *vapsà* gadfly, OSl. *vosa* (Russ. *osá*) wasp; L. *vespa* has another ablaut-grade. The root is believed to be **webh-* to weave, the name having reference to the nests which the insect constructs.

The word is not found in Gothic, and in the Scandinavian langs. it exists only as an adoption from Low German: Da. *hveps*, Norw. *kvefs*, *gvefs*, *veps*, *vops*, etc., mod.Icel. *vespa*. The OF. *guespe*, mod.F. *guêpe*, represents the L. *vespa*, but the initial *gu-* (:—*w-*) for *v* seems to be due to the influence of the Teut. word.]

1. In popular language, any insect of the genus *Vespa*; chiefly applied to *V. vulgaris*, the Common Wasp, and such other species as are not readily distinguishable from this; sometimes taken to include the Hornet, *V. crabro*, which resembles the Common Wasp, but is larger and has a more powerful sting. The obvious characteristics of the genus are the alternate rings of black and yellow on the abdomen, the narrow stalk or petiole by which the abdomen is attached to the thorax, the fully developed wings, and the formidable sting (which, however, is peculiar to the females and the workers or imperfect females). In scientific language applied generally to two divisions of hymenopterous insects, the Diploptera or true wasps, and the Fossores or digger wasps.

The true wasps (*Diploptera*) are divided into three families; (1) *Vespidæ*, to which the common wasp belongs; (2) *Eumenidæ*; and (3) *Masaridæ*.

See also DIGGER *sb.* 4, PAPER *sb.* 12, QUEEN *sb.* 14, SAND *sb.*² 10 b, SOCIAL *a.* 6 b, SOLITARY *a.* 4.

*c*725 *Corpus Gloss.* (Hessels) C 902 *Crabro*: waefs *vel* hurnitu. *Ibid.* F 136 *Fespa*, waefs. *c*875 *Erfurt Gloss.* 255 *C[r]abro*: uaeps. *a*1100 *Ags. Voc.* in Wr.-Wülcker 318/36 *Uespa*, weaps. *c*1375 *Sc. Leg. Saints* vii. (*James Minor*) 420 þe waspis þat in his hewid ware, at his nese-thrillis flaw al owt. *c*1394 *P. Pl. Crede* 648 þer is no waspe in þis werlde þat will wilfullok[e]r styngen, For stappyng on a too of a styncande frere! 1400–50 *Wars Alex.* 3011 Full many flees may fell, bot a fewe waspis. *a*1450 *Mirk's Festial* 141 Out of hys nasepurles dropped wormys out lyke waspes. 1496 *Cov. Leet Bk.* 577 Where as they light, The been will byte, And also styng. Be-ware of wappys. 1523–34 FITZHERB. *Husb.* §122 And beware, that no waspes come in-to the hyue, for they wyll kyl the bees, and eate the honny. 1546 J. HEYWOOD *Prov.* I. xi. (1867) 25 Nowe mery as a cricket, and by and by, Angry as a waspe, though in both no cause why. 1593 G. HARVEY *Pierces Super.* 148, I cannot maruell enough, how the nimble Bee should be ingendred of the sluggish Oxe, or the liuely waspe of the dead Horse. *a*1591 H. SMITH *Serm.* (1637) 239 God is not like a Waspe, which when she hath stung cannot sting again. 1653 WALTON *Angler* xii. 226 To take the Roch and Dace, a good bait is the young brood of Wasps or Bees, baked or hardned in their husks in an Oven. 1724 DERHAM in *Phil. Trans.* XXXIII. 54 The Male Wasps are lesser than the Queens, but as much longer and larger than the Common Wasps, as the Queen is longer and larger than these. 1730 YOUNG *Epist.* i. *To Pope* 33 As by depredations whasps proclaim The fairest fruit. 1802 BINGLEY *Anim. Biog.* (1813) III. 263 The nest of the Common Wasp is always formed under the surface of the earth. 1848 ALB. SMITH *Chr. Tadpole* xlix. 421 'Just as if we hadn't enough wapses,' exclaimed the old lady.. 'No, my good Grittles—that's a hornet,—not a "waps" as you wrongly call it.' 1862 CALVERLEY *Verses & Transl.* (ed. 2) 95 As females vanish at the sight Of shorthorns and of wopses. 1893 A. LANG *Prince Ricardo of Pantouflia* vii. 128 'Hang that wops!' said Prince Ricardo.. when it buzzed in his ear. 1905 H. G. WELLS *Kipps* II. iii. §3 'These old Roman chaps ——' he said; and then the wasps arrived. They killed three in the jam alone. 1908 O. SEAMAN *Wearing of Whisker* in *Salvage* 82 Trained like the ampelopsis, That happy haunt of woolly bears and wopses. 1932 E. STEP *Bees, Wasps, Ants* 81 Wopses, what eat up all our fruit. 1937 D. L. SAYERS *Busman's Honeymoon* xv. 308 Out comes me lord, and they wos all on to 'im like wopses round a jam-pot.

2. *fig.* **a.** Applied to persons characterized by irascibility and persistent petty malignity, esp. to a multitude of contemptible but irritating assailants.

1508 DUNBAR *Flyting* 195 Wan wraiglane wasp. 1560 BP. PILKINGTON *Aggeus* Pref. A iij, So.. vnder our gracious late Iosias, crepte oute a swarm of romish waspes, stynging to death all who wold not worshyp theyr gods, nor beleue theyr doctrine. 1596 SHAKS. *Tam. Shrew* II. i. 210 Come, come you Waspe, y'faith you are too angrie. 1611 BEAUM. & FL. *King & no K.* IV. iii, I will not hear you, wasp. *a*1660 *Contemp. Hist. Irel.* (Ir. Archæol. Soc.) I. 169 The Frenche Agent.. promised to joine with the Generall for a publicke redresse from those perfidious whaspes. 1721 AMHERST *Terræ Fil.* No. 5. 23, I had no sooner undertaken this task, but I raised a nest of holy wasps and hornets about my ears. 1775 H. WALPOLE *Let. to W. Cole* 25 Apr., The reviewers and such litterati have called me a learned and ingenious gentleman... These wasps, I suppose, will be very angry at the just contempt Mr. Gray had for them. 1791 D'ISRAELI *Cur. Lit.* I. 97 Sallo, after having published only his third Journal, felt the irritated wasps of literature thronging so thick about him, that he very gladly abdicated the throne of Criticism. 1844 W. CROSS *Disruption* xxxiii. 362 Mr. Bacon, ye ken, is in a pretty pickle wi' this wasp o' a body McCorkle. 1910 LD. ROSEBERY *Chatham* vii. 177 Glover was an ill-conditioned wasp, and his story refutes itself.

b. Something that irritates or offends one.

† *the wasp got him by the nose* (Prov.): he was infuriated.

1588 *Marprel. Epist.* (Arb.) 20 At the hearing of this speeche, the waspe got my brother by the nose, which mad him in his rage to affirme, that [etc.]. 1613 SHAKS. *Hen. VIII*, III. ii. 55. 1781 COWPER *Truth* 160 Of temper as envenom'd as an asp; Censorious, and her ev'ry word a wasp. 1845 JERROLD *St. Giles* iv. (1851) 34 That little head of his is full of wasps as July.

3. An artificial fly for salmon-fishing (made to imitate the appearance of a wasp). Cf. *wasp-fly* in 6 b.

1867 F. FRANCIS *Angling* x. (1880) 352 Some of the Tay flies, particularly the Wasps, dressed small, will kill well in the Tweed.

4. *Conchol.* A variety of cowry (see quot.).

1815 S. BROOKES *Introd. Conchol.* 157 Wasp, *Cypræa Asellus*.

5. (With capital initial.) A kind of flame-thrower developed by the British army during the war of 1939–45.

1944 *Hutchinson's Pict. Hist. War* 12 Apr.–26 Sept. 467 Like that of the Crocodile, the range of the Wasp is upwards of 150 yards. Fitted to the standard bullet-proof carrier, it is a terrorising weapon. 1965 *Listener* 11 Nov. 763/3 There was this Bren gun carrier with the flame thrower, sir, a Wasp I believe they're called, and I thought it was my duty to see how it worked. 1975 *Incendiary Weapons* (Stockholm Internat. Peace Research Inst.) v. 38 British and Canadian engineers developed a lighter mechanized flamethrower, called the Ronson... This was the forerunner of the Wasp (Mark 1) flame gun of which 1000 were ordered and went into production in March 1943.

6. *attrib.* and *Comb.*, as ***wasp-comb***, ***-egg***, ***-grub***, ***-honey***, ***-larva***, ***-maggot***, ***-pupa***, ***-sting***, ***-worm***; ***wasp-barbed***, ***-like***, ***-striped*** adjs.

1887 RUSKIN *Præterita* II. 346 One of the worst, *wasp-barbed, most tingling pangs of my memory is yet of a sunny afternoon at Pisa, when [etc.]. 1877 WOOD *Nature's Teachings* 168 There is.. one curious point of difference between the *Wasp-comb and human architecture. 1870 *Ann. & Mag. Nat. Hist.* Ser. IV. VI. 327 It is.. also a great deal smaller than the *wasp-egg. 1678 *Wasp-grub [see *wasp-maggot* below]. 1760 HAWKINS *Walton's Angler* xi. 197 *note*, There are no better Baits for this fish than.. a Gentle, a young Wasp-grub boiled, or a green Worm. 1919 J. MASEFIELD *Reynard* 61 Brocks eat wasp-grubs. 1904 *Westm. Gaz.* 4 July 2/3 Some *wasp honey. 1870 *Wasp-larva [see *wasp-pupa*]. 1668 WILKINS *Real Char.* 125 *Wasp-like Fly Maggot. 1867 G. MUSGRAVE *Nooks Old France* II. 209 Picturesque and coquette as ever their [mills] wasp-like waists were. 1678 RAY *Willughby's Ornith.* II. v. 72 *marg.* *Wasp-Maggots or Grubs. 1836 JESSE *Angler's Rambles* 197 The chub may be taken with.. gentles, wasp-maggots, and black-snails. 1870 *Ann. & Mag. Nat. Hist.* Ser. IV. VI. 314 Doubtless also their fellow inhabitants, described.. as injured *wasp-pupæ, were in reality the partially devoured wasp-larvæ. 1726 SWIFT *Gulliver* II. viii, Four *Wasp Stings, like Joyners Tacks. 1822 SCOTT *Halidon Hill* I. ii. 339 A cobweb gossamer were guard as good Against a wasp-sting. 1952 P. ATKEY *Juniper Rock* x. 87 *Wasp-striped.. the helicopter reappeared. 1974 E. AMBLER *Dr. Frigo* I. 49 A black butler in a wasp-striped waistcoat. 1804–6 *Wasp-worm [see WASPHOOD].

b. Special comb.: **wasp-bee**, a bee of the genus *Nomada*, a cuckoo-bee; **wasp-beetle**, a beetle of the genus *Clytus*, esp. *C. arietis*; **wasp-cake** *dial.*, the comb in a wasp's nest; **wasp-flower**, a flower frequented by honey-gathering wasps; **wasp-fly**, a syrphid fly somewhat resembling a hornet; also an artificial fly for fishing; **wasp-paper**, the paper-like material, produced by mastication, of which wasps' nests are made; † **wasp-spade**, a spade for digging out wasps' nests; † **wasp-stung** *a.*, irritable (as if stung by a wasp); **wasp-waist**, a very slender waist, *esp.* the characteristic waist of a woman who laces tightly; **wasp-wood** *dial.* (see quot.).

1844 F. SMITH in *Zoologist* II. 587 Descriptions of the British *Wasp-Bees. 1704 PETIVER *Gazophyl.* III. Tab. xxvii, The Maryland *Wasp Beetle. 1863 WOOD *Illustr. Nat. Hist.* III. 476 The common wasp beetle (*Clytus arietis*). 1907 *Westm. Gaz.* 28 Aug. 10/1 Experienced anglers cannot recall a season in which *wasp-cake is so difficult to obtain. 1884 *Cornhill Mag.* Oct. 399 *Wasp-flowers are remarkable for having a helmet-shaped tube, exactly fitted to a wasp's head, with abundant honey filling the bottom of the bell. 1676 COTTON *Angler* II. viii. 77 We have likewise this month [July] a *Wasp-flie, made.. of a dark brown dubbing.. ribb'd about with yellow silk. 1681 GREW *Musæum* I. §vii. i. 156 The Wasp-Fly, *Tabani species altera*. 1854 MARY HOWITT *Pict. Cal. Seasons* 404 The buzz of a wasp-fly, when resting apparently motionless on the window. 1867 F. FRANCIS *Angling* xii. (1880) 456 The Wasp Fly.—Three mauve hackle fibres for tail [etc.]. 1899 D. SHARP *Insects* II. 83 These little habitations consist of masses of cells, wrapped in *wasp-paper, in which there are one or more orifices for ingress and egress. 1609 C. BUTLER *Fem. Mon.* (1634) 126 With a *Wasp-spade, search for the nest. 1596 SHAKS. *1 Hen. IV*, I. iii. 236 (1598 Qo.) Why what a *waspe-stung [later Quos. wasp(e) tongue; Folios wasp(e)-tongu'd] and impatient foole Art thou? 1870 *Illustr. Lond. News* 24 Sept. 330 The fearful displacement of the vital organs which must be effected to procure a *wasp-waist. 1905 *Athenæum* 18 Mar. 344/3 The cylinder.. shows a person tightly cinctured, and with a wasp-waist, resembling the men on Mycenæan monuments. 1887 *N. & Q.* Ser. VII. III. 421 Touchwood, or as it is sometimes called, *wasp-wood, because wasps use it to make their nests.

Wasp (wɒsp), *sb.*² orig. and chiefly *U.S.* Also **WASP.** [Acronym f. the initial letters of *W*hite *A*nglo-*S*axon *P*rotestant.] A member of the American white Protestant middle or upper class descended from early European settlers in the U.S. Freq. *derog.* Also *attrib.* or as *adj.*

1962 E. B. PALMORE in *Amer. Jrnl. Sociol.* LXVII. 442/2 For the sake of brevity we will use the nickname 'Wasp' for this group, from the initial letters of 'White Anglo-Saxon Protestants'. 1963 *Times* 2 May 15/5 There is such a thing as a 'Human Engineering Laboratory'; whether a man is a Wasp (white Anglo-Saxon Protestant) can decide his career. 1963 *New Statesman* 10 May 716/2 This year's executive model will be over six feet tall, clean-shaven, lean, and with large fleshy ears... He should try to be or pretend to be a WASP (White Anglo-Saxon Protestant) and ought to have gone to an Ivy League college, preferably Princeton. 1964 E. D. BALTZELL *Protestant Establishment* (1965) i. 9, I should first like to show how the aristocratic process still worked quite well in the case of the family of Abraham Lincoln, and especially how the WASP establishment authoritatively retained the leadership of American society in the generation of Robert Todd Lincoln. 1968 *Times Lit. Suppl.* 4 Apr. 329/1 The Jew can choose to leave his ghetto by 'passing' or by breaking the more and more flimsy barriers put up by Wasp (and non-Wasp) anti-Semitism, but the Negro cannot. 1971 M. MCCARTHY *Birds of Amer.* 71 He was the only older WASP Peter knew. 1977 *Time* 19 Dec. 66/2 United States Secretary of State Felix John Vandenberg—slim, silver-haired, tallish, Wasp—speaks with 'the lingering trace of a British accent, which had been acquired at Eton and Oxford'. 1978 *Jrnl. R. Soc. Arts* CXXVI. 276/1 Can what one calls a WASP properly and without any discrimination select an Asian? 1979 R. JAFFE *Class Reunion* (1980) I. i. 37 Daphne's father was the senior partner of the leading prestigious Wasp law firm in New York.

wasp (wɒsp), *v.* [f. WASP *sb.*¹]

1. *trans.* To sting as a wasp does. *nonce-wd.*

1846 LANDOR *Imag. Conv., Emp. China & Tsing-Ti* Wks. II. 137/1 That blow upon the cheek-bone! those rotten eggs! .. surely they have wasped thee!

2. *intr.* Const. *around*, *about.* To dart about in the manner of a wasp, in an irritating, noisy, or tenacious fashion.

1967 G. F. FIENNES *I tried to run a Railway* iii. 22 Most nights brought an intruder bumbling overhead with one of our fighters wasping around looking for him. 1981 B. HEALEY *Week of Scorpion* ii. 43 'It must be very unpleasant for her'.. 'No doubt.. But have you conseedered how you'll make it any less so by having the police wasping about your own ears?' 1981 B. FREEMANTLE *Madrigal for Charlie Muffin* (1982) xx. 152 Traffic wasped around the piazza.

wasp, obs. Sc. var. WISP, quantity of fish.

'Waspdom. [f. WASP *sb.*² + -DOM.] The characteristics, beliefs, etc., of American white Protestant 'Wasps'.

1969 *Time* 17 Jan. 21 Thus Roman Catholics like William Buckley, Sargent Shriver and Ted Kennedy are pushed toward Waspdom by their associations, professions and life styles. 1976 *Time* 27 Sept. 39/1 *Noblesse oblige* has yielded to *bourgeoisie oblige*—even at the country club, traditionally the most closely guarded bastion of upper-class Southern Waspdom.

wasper, variant of WAWSPER *Sc.*

wasphood ('wɒsphʊd). [WASP *sb.*¹ + -HOOD.] The condition of a wasp.

1804–6 SYD. SMITH *Mor. Philos.* xvii. (1850) 244 When the wasp-worm is hatched, it finds a store of provisions ready made; and.. the quantity allotted to each is exactly sufficient to support it, till it attains the period of wasphood.

waspie ('wɒspɪ). [f. WASP *sb.*¹ + -IE.] A ladies' corset designed to make the waist appear very small; a belt of similar design. Cf. *wasp-waist* s.v. WASP *sb.*¹ 6 b.

1957 *Housewife* Sept. 89/2 A 'waspie' to whittle your waist. 1962 P. BRACKEN *I hate to housekeep Bk.* (1963) xi. 124 If it's a snug-fitting dress, and you know you'll be wearing your waspie with it, but don't want to be stuck with it or in it while you shop, put it in your big handbag too, and change in the fitting room. 1970 *Daily Tel.* 20 Apr. 15 The belt of the season is undoubtedly the laced-up waspie in suède or leather. 1976 *Times* 27 May 6/4 There were plenty [of women] still to heave a sigh of relief (if their waspies would let them).

waspily ('wɒspɪlɪ), *adv.* [f. WASPY *a.*¹ + -LY².] = WASPISHLY *adv.*

1854 B. P. SHILLABER *Life & Sayings Mrs. Partington* 231 'Because she is a low, vile creature of the town,' said she, waspily. 1928 *Sunday Dispatch* 29 July 2/3 'That's what I'm doing. Turning over a new leaf—and I'm going to do well.' 'Yeah? And what comes after that?' snapped the P.C.M. waspily.

waspish ('wɒspɪʃ), *a.*¹ [f. WASP *sb.*¹ + -ISH.]

1. Pertaining to or resembling a wasp or some characteristic of it.

1596 SHAKS. *Tam. Shr.* II. i. 211 If I be waspish, best beware my sting. 1681 COLVIL *Whigs Supplic.* (1751) 90 Thy waspish tongue will never fail To prat, to scold, revile and rail. 1822 SCOTT *Halidon Hill* I. ii. 354 Let a body of your chosen horse Make execution on yon waspish archers. 1865 TROLLOPE *Belton Est.* iv. 40 Her waist showed none of those waspish proportions. 1915 B. DIGBY in *Travel* July 22/1 In the dock lay a pair of waspish, one-funnelled steamers.

2. *esp.* Quick to resent any trifling injury or affront; irascible, petulantly spiteful.

1566 DRANT *Horace, Sat.* a iv b, Satyre of writhled waspyshe Saturne may be namde. *a*1568 ASCHAM *Scholem.* I. (Arb.) 33 In aige, sone testie, very waspishe. 1673 HICKERINGILL *Gregory F. Greybeard* 222 The leven of whose religion makes them waspish, peevish, touchy, clamorous. 1751 JOHNSON *Rambler* No. 177 ¶11 Their conversation was, therefore, fretful and waspish, their behaviour brutal. **1808** SOUTHEY *Lett.* (1856) II. 112 It is lamentable that that good heart of his should be coupled with so bad a judgement and so waspish a temper. **1838** DISRAELI in *Corr. w. Sister* 23 Jan. (1886) 90 Sharp and waspish, he would have made a good petulant Opposition speech. **1861** HUGHES *Tom Brown at Oxf.* ix, Such a set of waspish, dogmatical, over-bearing fellows. *a* **1901** W. BRIGHT *Age of Fathers* (1903) II. 375 He had been charged by waspish enemies with ascribing a heavenly origin to the holy body of Christ.

Comb. **1610** SHAKS. *Temp.* IV. i. 99 Her waspish headed sonne [*sc.* Cupid], has broke his arrowes, Swears he will shoote no more, but play with Sparrows.

b. Marked or characterized by virulence or petulance, spiteful.

1870 *Even. Standard* 9 Sept. 1 This waspish article created great indignation. **1880** *Scribner's Monthly* May 118 'The Literati'..are a prose Dunciad, waspish and unfair, but [etc.].

quasi-*adv.* **1855** KINGSLEY *Westw. Ho!* ix, We may excuse Raleigh's answering somewhat waspish to some quotation of Spenser's from the three letters of 'Immerito and G. H.'

Hence **'waspishly** *adv.*; **'waspishness.**

1593 BILSON *Govt. Christ's Ch.* 116 That they be not cast out of the church by the weaknes, waspishnes (frowardnes) or rashnes of the bishop. **1653** W. RAMESEY *Astrol. Restored* 334 Where he is pleased now and then..to vent his waspishness. **1684–94** tr. *Plutarch's Morals* (1718) III. 24 To preserve her from being waspishly proud, out of a Conceit of her Fidelity and Vertue. **1797** GODWIN *Enquirer* I. x. 87 A state of continual waspishness. **1827** DE QUINCEY *Murder* Wks. 1862 IV. 24 Berkeley, feeling himself nettled by the waspishness of the old Frenchman, squared at him. **1883** MISS BROUGHTON *Belinda* IV. iv, 'Well, may I go?' 'Why do you ask?' retorts he waspishly.

Waspish ('wɒspɪʃ), *a.*² orig. and chiefly *U.S.* Also **Wasp-ish, WASPish.** [f. WASP *sb.*² + -ISH¹.] Of, pertaining to, or characteristic of American white Protestant 'Wasps'. Cf. WASPY *a.*²

1968 *Listener* 27 June 843/3 Charles Newman, making a most impressive debut, gives in *New Axis* a picture of a community that is diametrically the opposite of Mr Baldwin's Harlem: that of an upper-middle-class WASPish suburb in an Illinois dormitory town. **1974** *Times Lit. Suppl.* 31 May 591/2 Postwar antisemitism in America... Echoes of haughty Waspish outrage..are to be heard in [this] silly novel about the marriage in 1946 of a sexy, clever Jewish girl from the wrong bit of New York to a handsome booby from an aristocratic Long Island family. **1978** E. TIDYMAN *Table Stakes* II. v. 261 His WASPish good looks. **1983** *Times* 8 July 7/5 He is Scorsese's contemporary, but from a different, Wasp-ish social class.

wasp-kite. *rare*⁻⁰. [A translation of the G. name *wespenbussard* or *wespenfalke*: the bird preys on wasps' nests.] The Honey-buzzard, *Pernis apivorus.*

1891 *Century Dict.*

waspling ('wɒsplɪŋ). [f. WASP *sb.*¹ + -LING¹.] A young wasp.

1905 PECKHAM *Wasps Social & Solitary* 90 Startle it ever so slightly and the waspling retreats by way of its web.

wasp's nest, wasp-nest. The nest of a wasp. Also *fig.*

c **1386** CHAUCER *Prioress' T.* 107 Sathanas That hath in Iues herte his waspes nest. *c* **1440** *Promp. Parv.* 517/2 Waspysnest, *vesparium.* **1603** HOLLAND *Plutarch's Mor.* 128 Which..bring foorth a swarme (as it were) of bees, or rather a waspes neast in us. **1611** SHAKS. *Wint. T.* IV. iv. 814 Hee has a Sonne, who shall be..set on the head of a Waspes Nest. **1745** *Phil. Trans.* XLIII. 363 Two Sorts of curious Wasps Nests made with Clay. **1819** SHELLEY *Cyclops* 474 If like a wasp's nest I could scoop the eye out Of the detested Cyclops. **1853** LYTTON *My Novel* III. xxiv, Your policy of half-measures,..which flaps an exasperated wasp-nest with a silk pocket-handkerchief, instead of blowing it up with a match and train, is rarely successful. **1858** CARLYLE *Fredk. Gt.* x. ii. (1873) III. 223 Cannot we get away from this scurvy wasp's-nest of a Paris? **1870** *Ann. & Mag. Nat. Hist.* Ser. IV. VI. 328 The female *Rhipiphorus* lays her eggs before leaving the wasps' nest. **1899** D. SHARP *Insects* II. 82 It would be impossible..to give a satisfactory account of all the forms of wasp-nests. *Ibid.* 86 A wasp's nest.

Hence **wasp-nesting** *vbl. sb.* [-ING¹], the action of searching for wasp's nests.

1872 *Routledge's Ev. Boy's Ann.* 1873, 263/1 Fancy going about wasp-nesting with some one at your heels to take care of you.

wasp-waisted, *a.* Having the waist very slender, esp. as the result of tight-lacing.

1775 MRS. DELANY *Lett.* Ser. II. II. 160, I hope Miss Sparrow will not fall into the absurd fashion of yᵉ wasp-waisted ladies. **1839** DUNCAN in *Congr. Globe* Jan., App. 104/2 A thousand of the wasp-waisted gentry to quell the Democracy of Pennsylvania—monstrous!!! **1892** *Daily News* 7 Sept. 6/4 These young women..are not wasp-waisted.

transf. **1867** G. MUSGRAVE *Nooks & Corners Old France* II. 147, I saw several wasp-waisted windmills.

'waspy, *sb. Obs.* exc. *dial.* Now *dial.* **wapsy.** [f. WASP *sb.*¹ + -Y⁶.] A wasp.

a **1529** SKELTON *E. Rummyng* 330 Angry as a waspy! *a* **1825** FORBY *Voc. E. Anglia, Waps, wapsy,* a wasp.

waspy ('wɒspɪ), *a.*¹ [f. WASP *sb.*¹ + -Y¹.]

1. Resembling a wasp in form, wasp-like.

1658 ROWLAND tr. *Moufet's Theat. Ins.* 921 Whereupon that Greek Comick Poet calls those Maids,..for their slendernesse in the waste σφηκοδεῖς [*sic*], waspy or like Wasps. **1869** T. W. WOOD in *Student* II. 87 The hornet clearwing,..so waspy in appearance. **1870** *Daily News* 19 July 6 A brown horse with a light waspy middle. **1889** *Sportsman* 29 July 2/1 So long as a waspy waist is considered 'a thing of beauty'.

2. Abounding in wasps.

1681 *Rector's Bk. Clayworth* (1910) 53 It was also a very waspy year. **1880** MORRIS in Mackail *Life* (1899) II. 13 Very hot and waspy it was at dinner.

Waspy ('wɒspɪ), *a.*² orig. and chiefly *U.S.* Also **WASPy.** [f. WASP *sb.*² + -Y¹.] = WASPISH *a.*²

1968 *N.Y. Times* 23 July 41/1 Black-power stalwarts suspiciously eying the Waspy surroundings. **1975** *Publishers Weekly* 9 June 61/3 Max Herschel, a high-powered industrialist in his 60s, coarse but with all the trappings of class, has lost his..mistress Bones to Steven Routledge, who is the antithesis of Max, WASPy, idealistic, a failed novelist. **1978** M. PUZO *Fools Die* xxxiii. 383 A slim, Waspy, forty-year-old ex-debutante.

wass, obs. f. *was* (see BE *v.* 3 and WASH *v.*).

wassa: see WHASSA.

wassail ('wɒs(ə)l, 'wæs(ə)l, -eɪl), *sb.* Now only *arch.* and *Hist.* Forms: 3 **wæs hæil, wæshail, washayl, washail, wesseyl,** 3–4, 7 **wassayl,** 3, 6–7, 9 *arch.* **wassaile,** 5 **wassaylle, wessayle,** (**whatsaile, -saill**), 6 **wassaill, -ayle,** 6–7 **wassall,** 7–8 **wassal,** (7 **vassaile,** *Hist.* **was-haile, washeall, waes heal,** 9 **waisall, waissel,** *arch.* **was-hael**), 5–9 **wassel(l,** 3– **wassail.** [ME. *wæs hæil* etc., a. ON. *ves* (= later *ver*) *heill*, corresp. to OE. *wes hál* lit. 'be in good health' or 'be fortunate': see BE *v.* A. 3 and WHOLE *a.*

As an ordinary salutation (= 'hail' or 'farewell') the phrase, or an approximation to it, occurs both in OE. (*hál wes þú*, and in pl. *wesað hále*: see BE *v.* A. 3) and in ON. (pl. *verið heilir*). But neither in OE. nor in ON., nor indeed in any Teut. lang., has any trace been found of the use as drinking formulas, of the phrases represented by *wassail* and *drinkhail.* It seems probable that this use arose among the Danish-speaking inhabitants of England, and became more or less common among the native population; in the 12th c. it was regarded by the Normans as markedly characteristic of Englishmen. The earliest known occurrence of the phrases is in Geoffrey of Monmouth VI. xii. (*c* 1140), in the well-known story of Rowena (*wes heil..drinc heil*: v.r. *was heil*, printed edd. corruptly *wacht heil*). Geoffrey's attribution of the phrases to the 5th century is an anachronism; the original story as told by Nennius contains nothing corresponding to them. In Wace's *Brut* (*c* 1180), which is a metrical version of Geoffrey, various MSS. have *weshel, waisseil, gasel; drinkel, drincheheil, drechehel.* That Wace's acquaintance with the 'English' phrases was not wholly derived from the passage in Geoffrey is shown by his reference to them in the *Roman de Rou*, where it is said that the night before the battle of Hastings was spent by the English in revelry, with cries of *weissel* (v.rr. *wesse heil, welseil, weseil*) and *drincheheil* (v.rr. *drinceseil, drinqueheil, drinkeil*). In the *Speculum Stultorum* of Nigellus Wireker (*c* 1190) the English students at the university of Paris are praised for generosity and other virtues, but are said to be too much addicted to *wessail* and *dringail.* The earliest example of the phrases in an English context is in Layamon's translation of Wace.

In *drinkhail* the second element is, as in *wassail*, the ON. adj. *heill* used as complement. Although the phrase *drekk heill* is not recorded in ON., it has an exact syntactical parallel in *sit heill*, 'sit in health'. Whether the form of the first element in *drinkhail* is due to OE. influence or is archaic Scandinavian is doubtful; the form *drechehel* in one MS. of Wace is noteworthy from its resemblance to the ON. of the literary period.]

1. A salutation used when presenting a cup of wine to a guest, or drinking the health of a person, the reply being DRINK-HAIL.

c **1205** LAY. 14309 Reowen..bar an hir honde ane guldene bolle i-uulled mid wine..& þus ærest sæide in Ænglene londe Lauerd king wæs hæil [*c* **1275** wassayl]. *Ibid.* 14332 [see DRINK-HAIL]. *Ibid.* 14970 Heo fulde hir scale of wine..& þus hailede him on..Lauerd king wæshail [*c* **1275** wassail]. **13..** *E.E. Allit. P.* B. 1508 Weȝe wyn in þis won 'wassayl!' he cryes. *c* **1400** *Brut* 52 Ronewenne..come wiþ a coupe of golde..and knelede bifore þe kyng, and saide to him 'Whatsaile!'..þat was þe ferst tyme þat 'whatsaile' and 'drynkehaile' come vp into þis lande; and fram þat tyme into this tyme it Haþ bene wel vsede. **1568** GRAFTON *Chron.* II. 116, I trust this wassall shall make all England glad. And with that he dranke a great draught, the king pledging him. **1832** MOTHERWELL *Poems, Battle-Flag of Sigurd* i, Then lift the can to bearded lip,..Wassaile! to every dark-ribbed ship, To every battle-field! **1843** LYTTON *Last Bar.* I. v, Fair mistress Sybill, your dainty lips will not, I trow, refuse me the waisall. [*Another ed. reads* waissel.] **1860** LONGF. *Wayside Inn, K. Olaf* XII. xiii, The Berserks drank 'Was-hael! to the Lord!'

†**b.** As a mere salutation. quasi-*arch.*

a **1643** CARTWRIGHT *Ordinary* IV. ii, *Ha.* What? who goes there? *Moth.* Waes heal thou gentle Knight.

¶**c.** *ironically.* A 'salute', smart attack. *Obs.*

c **1400** *Laud Troy-bk.* 9020 Odemoun..Toke Menelaus In that swyng, And him bare ouer his hors tayl: He ȝaff him there suche a wassail, That he lay longe In colde swot.

2. The liquor in which healths were drunk; esp. the spiced ale used in Twelfth-night and Christmas-eve celebrations.

wine and wassail (now *arch.*, echoing Shaks.): *vaguely*, strong drink in abundance (cf. sense 4).

c **1300** *Havelok* 1246 Wyn and ale deden he fete, And made[n] hem glade and bliþe, Wesseyl ledden he fele siþe. **1494** in *Househ. Ord.* (1790) 121 When the steward cometh in at the hall doore with the wassell, he must crie three tymes, Wassell, wassell, wassell. *a* **1548** HALL *Chron., Hen. VIII*, 9 Then was the wassaill or banket brought in, and so brake vp Christmas. **1601** HOLLAND *Pliny* XXV. viii. II. 224 And even at this day [in Spain] in their great feasts..they have a certaine Wassaile or Bragat, which goeth round about the table, made of honied wine or sweet mead, with..hearbes in it. **1605** SHAKS. *Macb.* I. vii. 64 His two Chamberlaines Will I with Wine, and Wassell, so conuince, That Memorie..shall be a Fume. **1616** B. JONSON *Forest* iii, The jolly wassall walkes the often round, And in their cups, their cares are drown'd. **1616** —— *Masque of Christmas* 2 Enter..Wassal, Like a neat Sempster, and Songster; her Page bearing a browne bowle, drest with Ribbands. **1661** *New Carolls for Christmas, For Twelfth-day* iii, The Wassell well spiced, about shall go round. **1742–50** R. O. CAMBRIDGE *Archimage* xiii. Wks. (1803) 39 'Bove all things else he Wassel priz'd and ale. **1808** SCOTT *Marmion* VI. Introd. 64 On Christmas eve..The wassel round, in good brown bowls Garnish'd with ribbons, blithely trowls. **1816** —— *Old Mort.* ix, Women, wine, and wassail, all to be had for little but the asking. **1824** W. IRVING *T. Trav.* I. 7 The wine and the wassail of mine host began to operate upon bodies already a little jaded by the chase. **1836** DICKENS *Pickw.* xxviii, They sat down..to a substantial supper, and a mighty bowl of wassail,..in which the hot apples were hissing and bubbling. **1850** TENNYSON *In Mem.* CV. v, And strangely falls our Christmas-eve... But let no footstep beat the floor, Nor bowl of wassail mantle warm. **1851** LONGF. *Gold. Leg.* I. *Court-yard of Castle* 17 No song, no laugh, no jovial din Of drinking wassail to the pin. **1857** G. A. LAWRENCE *Guy Liv.* iv, Two hundred gownsmen, wild with wrath and wassail, came leaping to the rescue. **1898** J. B. CROZIER *My Inner Life* v. 43 He was much addicted to wine and wassail too, as his blood-red face sufficiently attested.

†**3.** A custom formerly observed on Twelfth-night and New-Year's eve of drinking healths from the wassail-bowl. †Also, ? the person invited to drink from the wassail-bowl. *Obs.*

1598 E. GUILPIN *Skial.* (1878) 25 A wassaile on twelfe night. **1612** SELDEN *Illustr. Drayton's Poly-olb.* IX. 153, I see a custome in some parts among vs,..I meane the yearely washaile in the country on the vigil of the New-yeare. *a* **1654** —— *Table-Talk* (1689) 42 The Pope in sending Rellicks to Princes, does as Wenches do by their Wassels at New-years-tide, they present you with a Cup, and you must drink of a slabby stuff; but the meaning is, you must give them Moneys. **1658** PHILLIPS, *Wassail*,..an ancient Ceremonious custome, still used upon twelf day at night, of going about with a great bowl of Ale, drinking of healths. **1661** *New Carolls for Christmas, For Twelfth-day* ii, For a King of our Wassell this night we must chuse.

4. A carousal; riotous festivity, revelling.

1602 SHAKS. *Ham.* I. iv. 9 The King doth wake to night, and takes his rouse, Keepes wassels. **1606** —— *Ant. & Cl.* I. iv. 56 Anthony, Leaue thy lasciuious Vassailes. **1614** R. TAILOR *Hog hath lost Pearl* G 3, I sweare,..By Cresus name and by his castle, Where winter nights he keepeth wassell. **1805** SCOTT *Last Minstrel* V. viii, The blithesome signs of wassel gay Decay'd not with the dying day. **1820** BYRON *Juan* III. lxi, Meantime the lady and her lover sate At wassail in their beauty and their pride. **1820** W. IRVING *Sketch Bk.* (1849) 148, I at length arrived in merry Eastcheap, that ancient region of wit and wassail. **1848** LYTTON *Harold* IV. ii, A board was spread and a wassail was blithe around me. **1878** H. PHILLIPS Jr. *Poems fr. Sp. & German* 72 Two kings held wassail in Orkadàl. **1903** R. S. HAWKER *Footpr. Far Cornwall* 28 Now there was signal made of banquet in the halls of Stowe, of wassail and dance.

†**5.** A carol or song sung by wassailers; a wassailing or health-drinking song. *Obs.*

In quot. 1607 *ironical* or *jocular.*

1607 BEAUM. & FL. *Woman-Hater* III. i, Have you done your wassayl? 'tis a handsome drowsie dittie I'll assure ye, now I had as leave hear a Cat cry. *c* **1650** *New Christmas Carols, Carrol for Wassel-Bowl* 7 Good Dame here at your Door Our Wassel we begin.

6. *attrib.* and *Comb.*, as (sense 3), *wassail-candle, -day, -singer, -singing*; (sense 4), *wassail-bout, -revelry, -roar, -rout, -season, -song*; also **wassail-cup** = WASSAIL-BOWL.

A spurious compound *wassail-bread*, given in many Dicts., is due to a misinterpretation of *wastell-bread*: see WASTEL. For a similar figment, *wassail-cake*, see quot. 1686–7 s.v. WASSAIL *v.* 2.

1840 LONGF. *Skeleton in Armour* vii, Many a *wassail-bout Wore the long Winter out. **1597** SHAKS. *2 Hen. IV*, I. ii. 179 *Iu.* What? you are as a candle, the better part burnt out. *Fal.* A *Wassell Candle, my Lord; all Tallow. **1634** BRERETON *Trav.* (Chetham Soc.) 6 Such as they met gave them money..to buy a *wassail-cup, a carouse. **1600** HOLLAND *Livy* XXVI. xiii. 593 The same wassaile cup [L. *poculum idem*] that first will be presented to me, shall go round about to you all. **1853** C. BRONTE *Villette* xxv, Let us haue a Christmas wassail-cup and toast Old England here, on the hearth. **1742** SHENSTONE *Schoolmistr.* xiii, O *wassel days! O customs meet and well! **1814** SCOTT *Lord of Isles* VI. xix, But now, from England's host, the cry Thou hear'st of *wassail revelry. **1808** —— *Marmion* I. xxx, This was the sign the feast was o'er; It hush'd the merry *wassel roar. *Ibid.* III. Introd. 187 Of forayers, who,..home returning, fill'd the hall With revel, *wassel-rout, and brawl. **1767** MICKLE *Concub.* I. xxix, Now fly the *wassal Seasons wingd with Glee. *a* **1825** FORBY *Voc. E. Anglia*, *Wassail-singers. **1895** 'Q' [Quiller-Couch] *Wand. Heath* 182 December and January, with..carols and *wassail-singing. **1829** SCOTT *Anne of G.* xxiii, The chorus of a *wassel-song, which some reveller was trolling over in his sleep. **1854** GRACE GREENWOOD *Haps & Mishaps* 88 A hall of the old castle, which had rung to the clang of rude armour, and the wassail songs of Erin's princes and knights.

wassail ('wɒs(ə)l, 'wæs(ə)l, -eɪl), *v.* Forms: 4 **wosseyle, wesseyle,** 7 **wassaile, -ayle,** 6 **wassal,** 8 **wessel,** 8– **wassail.** [f. WASSAIL *sb.*]

1. *intr.* To 'keep wassail'; to sit carousing and health-drinking.

c **1300** *Havelok* 1737 Hwan he.. fele siþes haueden wosseyled, And with gode drinkes seten longe. *Ibid.* 2098 Hwat may þis be? Better is i go miself, and se: Hweþer he sitten nou, and wesseylen. **1686** PLOT *Staffordsh.* 430 A Horn; the ancient vessel in which the Danes use to Wassayle, or drink healths. **1889** F. M. CRAWFORD *Greifenstein* III. xxv. 136 He feasted and wassailed with his warriors.

2. *trans.* To drink to (fruit-trees, cattle) in wassail, in order to ensure their thriving. *local.*

1648 HERRICK *Hesper., Christmasse-Eve*, Wassaile the Trees, that they may beare You many a Plum, and many a Peare. **1686–7** AUBREY *Rem. Gentilism & Judaism* (1881) 9 Mdm. at Twelve-tyde at night they use in the Countrey to wassaile their Oxen and to have Wassaile-Cakes made. **1865** R. HUNT *Pop. Rom. W. Eng.* 2nd Ser. 176 This drink was called *lamb's-wool*, and with it the trees were wassailed. **1878** *Folk-Lore Rec.* I. 13 It is the custom, in the cider districts of Sussex, to worsle (wassail) the apple-trees. **1895** F. T. ELWORTHY *Evil Eye* iii. 105 The old Christmas custom of wassailing the apple-trees.

wassail-bowl. A large bowl or cup in which wassail (sense 2) was made and from which healths were drunk; a loving-cup; also the liquor contained in the bowl.

1606 *Sir G. Goosecappe* II. i. D 3 b, Hee is a most excellent Turner, and will turne you wassel-bowles, and posset Cuppes. **1608–9** *Shuttleworths' Acc.* (Chetham Soc.) 179 Given to the maides which came with the wassell-boule, xij^{d}. **1610** FLETCHER *Faithf. Shepherdess* v. i, Some neere towne,.. Hath drawne them thether, bout some lusty sport; Or spiced wassal Boule. **1648** HERRICK *Hesper., Country Life* 56 Thy Wassaile bowle, That's tost up after Fox i' th' Hole..; thy Christmas revellings. **1661** PEPYS *Diary* 26 Dec., We went into an alehouse and there..a washeall-bowle woman and girle came to us and sung to us. **1686–7** AUBREY *Rem. Gentilism & Judaism* (1881) 40 They goe into the Ox-house to the oxen, with the Wassell-bowle and drink to the ox. **1777** BRAND *Pop. Antiq.* xvi. 195 Young Women went about with a Wassail-bowl, that is, a Bowl of spiced Ale on New Year's Eve. **1808** SCOTT *Marmion* I. xv, A mighty wassail-bowl he took, And crown'd it high in wine. **1820** W. IRVING *Sketch Bk.* (1849) 287 A huge silver vessel of rare and curious workmanship..the Wassail Bowl, so renowned in Christmas festivity. *Ibid.* 288 *note*, The Wassail Bowl was sometimes composed of ale instead of wine; with nutmeg, sugar, toast, ginger, and roasted crabs. **1860** G. P. MORRIS *Poems* (ed. 15) 178 Some love to stroll where the wassail-boul And the wine-cups circle free.

wassailer ('wɒsələ(r), 'wæsələ(r)). [f. WASSAIL *v.* + -ER^{1}.] One who takes part in riotous festivities; a reveller.

1634 MILTON *Comus* 179, I should be loath To meet the rudenesse, and swill'd insolence Of such late Wassailers. **1794** COLERIDGE *Relig. Musings* 284 O pale-eyed form, The victim of seduction,..Who in loathed orgies with lewd wassailers Must gaily laugh, while [etc.]. **1821** BYRON *Sardanap.* II. i, *Sar.* And you will join us at the banquet? *Sal.* Sire, Dispense with me—I am no wassailer. **1844** DISRAELI *Coningsby* v. ii, A rather boisterous party of wassailers who had been celebrating at Buckhurst's rooms the triumph of 'Eton Statesmen'. **1882** *Standard* 18 Feb. 5/2 Christopher North pictures the wassailer of the 'Noctes Ambrosianæ' as revelling in a plenitude of Pandores.

†**b.** One who takes part in Twelfth-night or Christmas-tide 'wassailing'. *Obs.*

1706 PHILLIPS (ed. Kersey), *Wassellers*..such as in the Country go about from House to House, during the Festival of Christmas, and sing Catches for Drink or other small Boon. **1817** N. DRAKE *Shaks. & Times* I. vi. 130 The persons thus accompanying the Wassal bowl, especially those who danced and played, were called Wassailers. **1912** J. B. PARTRIDGE in *Folk-lore* XXIII. 455 Wassailers still go round at Randwick, Woodchester, [etc.].., and probably many other villages [in Gloucestershire].

'wassailing, *vbl. sb.* [f. WASSAIL *v.* + -ING^{1}.]

1. The action of the verb WASSAIL; carousing, riotous festivity.

a **1586** SIDNEY *Arcadia* III. (1598) 390 Spending all the day, and good part of the night, in dauncing, carolling and wassailing. **1641** MILTON *Ch. Discipl.* II. 61 That men should bee..push't forward to gaming, jigging, wassailing, and mixt dancing is a horror to think. **1820** W. IRVING *Sketch Bk.* (1849) 237 Its feudal hospitalities, and lordly wassailings, have passed away. **1913** J. G. FRAZER *Golden Bough* (ed. 3), *Balder* I. ii. 58 Before the wassailing begins, the various fathers perform a curious operation on the arms of their sons.

†**2.** The action (practised in English country districts by the poorer classes, esp. by the children) of going from house to house at Christmas-time, singing a song expressive of good wishes for Christmas and the coming year, usually with the addition of carols or other songs.

1742 *Agreeable Compan.* in Halliwell *Shaks.* (1856) VI. 332 'Twas an ancient custom amongst poor people to go a wesseling at Christmas... Such poor people went about to get money to drink your health, and for which they carried a box..to put their money in. **1889** DOR. E. HURST *Horsham* (ed. 2) Gloss. Sussex Wds., *Wasseling*, a name given to the singing of Christmas carols at the doors of houses, a practice ..which is dying out.

3. *attrib.*, as ***wassailing bowl, song, watch.***

1555 W. WATREMAN *Fardle Facions* II. ix. 194 The maner is, out of one of these Skulles, as out of a wassailing boule, to giue all those the wine that haue slaine an enemie. *a* **1586** SIDNEY *Arcadia* II. xxvii (1912) 321 Meaning to observe a wassailing watch all that night. **1914** *Contemp. Rev.* Jan. 134 The wailing songs and wassailing songs of darker days.

wassailous ('wɒsələs), *a. nonce-wd.* [f. WASSAIL *sb.* or *v.* + -OUS.] Given to revelry.

1893 F. THOMPSON *Poems* 43 The wassailous heart of the Year is thine.

wassailry ('wɒs(ə)lrɪ). *rare.* [f. WASSAIL *sb.* + -RY.] Carousing, revelry.

1814 SOUTHEY *Roderick* xii. 102 No season this for old solemnities, For wassailry and sport. **1860** SIR T. MARTIN *Horace, Odes* II. xiv. 35 A worthier heir..with a lordlier wine, Than at the feasts divine Of pontiffs flows, your floor in wassailry shall stain.

wassal. *local.* Also **wassel.** [Of obscure origin.] The stems of seaweed used as a manure.

1797 J. BAILEY & CULLEY *Agric. Northumbld.* 118 The *fucus digitatus* (wassels) is the great favourite. **1892** J. C. HODGSON in *Hist. Berwicksh. Naturalists' Club* XIV. 115 *note*, The stems..become detached from their rocks about October, and are locally named 'belks' or 'wassal'.

wassal(l, -ale: see VASSAL, WASSAIL.

wassal(l)age, -edge, obs. Sc. ff. VASSALAGE.

wassa matter: see WHASSA.

wassat, repr. *colloq.* pronunc. of *what's that*. Cf. WHAT *pron.* I.

1967 J. WAINWRIGHT *Talent for Murder* 83 'Is that usual? Or, is it unusual?' 'Wassat?' **1976** T. WILDEN *To die Elsewhere* i. 5 'I'll have to be off now,' I said... 'Wassat?' said Heyward. **1981** 'J. Ross' *Dark Blue & Dangerous* xxi. 117 'Wassat, sir?' There was deep incomprehension in his expression.

wassayl(e, -lle, obs. forms of WASSAIL.

wasse, obs. f. *was* (see BE *v.*) and WASH *v.*

wassel, obs. f. WASSAIL; var. WASSAL.

wassell: see VASSAL, WASSAIL, WASTEL.

†**'wasser^{1}.** *Obs. rare.* ? Shortened form of WASSERMAN.

1600 *New Metamorphosis* (Wright *Dict.* 1857 *s.v.*), The horrible huge whales did there appeare: The wasser that makes marryners to feare.

wasser^{2} ('wɒzə(r)). Also **was-ser.** [f. WAS, 1st and 3rd pers. sing. pa. t. of BE *v.* + -*s* + -ER^{1}.] = HAS-BEEN *sb.*

1924 KIPLING *Debits & Credits* 313 Bert was for it, with a few remarks from the patriotic old was-sers on the bench. **1936** F. M. FORD *Let.* 6 Sept. (1965) 259 But I don't want to be harmed by people calling me a lousy old wasser.

†**'wasserman.** *Obs.* [a. G. *wassermann* lit. 'water-man'.] A fabled sea-monster partly in the form of a man, supposed to destroy ships.

1590 SPENSER *F.Q.* II. xii. 24 The griesly Wasserman, that makes his game The flying ships with swiftnesse to pursew. **1593** NASHE *Christ's T.* D 2 b, [The devils] entred and inhabited the Sea-monsters, such as the Whale, the Grampoys, the Wasserman, whom they haue suborned and inspyred to lye in wayte for Shipswrack. **1599** —— *Lenten Stuffe* 50 The greater giants of Russia & Island, as the whale, the sea horse, the Norse, the wasserman, the Dolphin, the Grampoys.

Wassermann (‖'vasərman, 'wɒsəmən). *Med.* Also (*erron.*) **-man.** The name of August Paul *Wassermann* (1866–1925), German bacteriologist, used *attrib.* with reference to a test for syphilis devised by him in 1906, in which antibodies to the causative organism are detected by a complement-fixation test. Also *absol.*, the Wassermann test.

1909 *Jrnl. Exper. Med.* XI. 392 Unless a great simplification of the Wassermann test can be devised, it will never attain the usefulness which it really deserves. *Ibid.* 401 Cases which were negative to the Wassermann and weakly or quite often strongly positive to the present method were met with. **1952** 'N. SHUTE' *Far Country* 214 A Wassermann test would be interesting, and probably positive. **1970** PASSMORE & ROBSON *Compan. Med. Stud.* II. xxii. 16/2 The test system consists of Wassermann antigen mixed with dilutions of the patient's serum in the presence of guinea-pig complement. **1976** H. KEMELMAN *Wednesday Rabbi got Wet* xxiii. 71 When she had last had a checkup, she had asked him to do a Wassermann, too, because 'Joe was out of town on business and you know how it is when men go out of town.'

wassh(e, obs. ff. WASH.

wassilaige, wassolage, obs. Sc. ff. VASSALAGE.

wast (wɒst, wəst), 2nd pers. sing. pa. t. of BE *v.*

wast, obs. form of WAIST, WASTE, WEST.

wastable ('weɪstəb(ə)l), *a.* [f. WASTE *v.* + -ABLE.]

1. Liable to be wasted; subject to wastage. Also, in *Law*, said of things in respect of which a tenant may be chargeable with waste.

1436 *Libel Eng. Policy* 362 in *Pol. Poems* (Rolls) II. 173 For moche of thys chaffare that is wastable Mighte be forborne for dere and dyssevable. *c* **1460** J. RUSSELL *Bk. Nurture* 179 in *Babees Bk.* (1868) 129 For ale þat is newe is wastable with-owten dowt. **1611** COTGR., *Adustible*,.. burneable, wasteable. *a* **1625** HOBART *Reports* (1650) 234 A Lessee..must neither take Timber or other things wastable. **1825** BENTHAM *Offic. Apt. Maximized Indications* Postscr. (1830) 4 After hearing, [from 4 to 6 years are] wasteable in reference to a Master.

†**2.** Of a country: Desolate, waste. *Obs.*

a **1450** LOVELICH *Grail* xlviii. 306 Vpon a day as they forth wente, In a wastable Contre veramente, where that was scars of vyaunde.

wastage ('weɪstɪdʒ). [f. WASTE *v.* + -AGE.]

1. a. Loss or diminution by use, decay, leakage, or the like.

1756 P. BROWNE *Jamaica* (1789) 23 His goods must be shipped on board of some drover, where they seldom fail paying the usual tributes of pilferage and wastage. **1796** *Ann. Reg., Projects* 436 The allowance from a pound to a pound and half for wastage. **1800** *Asiatic Ann. Reg., Misc. Tracts* 203/1 The allowance for the wastage in the drying is rendered perfectly arbitrary. **1852** MORFIT *Tanning & Currying* (1853) 325 The loss and wastage upon hides, from hair, flesh, &c., may be estimated at from 12 to 15 per cent. **1861** SMILES *Engineers* II. 196 The lightermen claimed as their right the perquisites of 'wastage' and 'leakage'. **1904** *Times* 24 Aug. 6/1 The scheme for reinforcement is prepared for a far heavier wastage than has as yet taken place.

b. The action of spending uselessly or using wastefully; loss incurred by wastefulness.

1885 H. C. MCCOOK *Tenants of Old Farm* 118 A noble German lady found..there was a vast wastage in her household. **1889** *Harper's Mag.* Jan. 178/2 There is a subtlety which here in Rome Men look for in blind wastage of their lives, Not knowing where to seek it. **1906** *Daily Chron.* 8 May 6/6 It is doubtful if anywhere in the world there is a greater wastage of coal than in Bombay.

c. The action of laying (land) waste.

1911 WEBSTER. **1954** M. BERESFORD *Lost Villages* v. 165 Rokeby and Mortham on the Tees had not recovered from their wastage by the Scots in the fourteenth century.

d. (*a*) The loss of students through failure to complete a course of study or training; (*b*) the loss of employees by any means other than dismissal, esp. by retirement or resignation. Freq. as ***natural wastage.***

1919 M. GREENWOOD in *Jrnl. R. Stat. Soc.* LXXXII. 187 Our industrial 'death' rate would then merely be the rate at which entrants to a trade pass out of it, or,..with a.. narrower circle, the rates of departure from particular factories. In this sense, 'death' or wastage rates for different factories will be *prima facie* measures of the efficiencies of the respective factories. **1944** *Min. of Fuel & Power Statistics Digest from 1938* 6 in *Parl. Papers 1943–44* (Cmd. 6538) VIII. 151 Net natural wastage... [Note] This is the gross natural wastage *less* the normal juvenile recruitment. **1948** *Ann. Rep. Nat. Coal Board 1947* iv. 45 in *Parl. Papers 1947–8* X. 387 The manpower target set for the Board..was .. 730,000 men... This meant a net increase..of 40,000.. and, since wastage was estimated at 60/65,000 men over the year, a recruitment of 100,000 was needed. **1952** [see FAVOURABLY *adv.* 3]. **1956** *School Sci. Rev.* June 375 The Rector of Imperial College, Dr. R. P. Linstead, in a lecture last October, said (speaking of what he called 'academic wastage'), 'This academic wastage makes itself shown in different universities, but in this College much of the wastage occurs during the first year.' **1958** *Technology* May 66/2 The question of wastage in apprenticeship. **1963** *Higher Educ.: Rep. Comm. under Ld. Robbins 1961–3* 20 in *Parl. Papers 1962–3* (Cmnd. 2154) XI. 639 We discount all those who begin courses but do not successfully complete them. This is commonly described as 'wastage'—a term that we adopt for reasons of conformity but that we regard as carrying misleading implications. Wastage rates in higher education have not varied much in recent years. **1975** *Times* 25 Nov. 1/3 Nursing staff..were liable to 'natural wastage'. **1979** 'J. LE CARRÉ' *Smiley's People* (1980) v. 65 He resigned of his own accord.., part of the wastage rate that gets everyone so worried. **1983** *Financial Times* 23 Apr. I. 34 The savings which the bank is seeking will involve natural wastage, retraining, redeployment and some measure of redundancy.

2. The product of wear or decay, waste.

1898 *Blackw. Mag.* Oct. 538/1 One of eight principal glaciers that bear away the icy wastage of Mount Kazbek.

3. *Sc.* A ruined or deserted place; also, a waste piece of ground.

1823 GALT *Gilhaize* xx, Carsewell's family has gone all to drift, and his house become a wastage. **1830** —— *Lawrie T.* III. x, The settlement..was plainly ordained to be soon a wastage; for the houses received no repair, [etc.]. **1832** *Fraser's Mag.* V. 694 Their grand theatre became a wastage. **1881** *Mem. G. Thomson* ix. 125 A row of houses on either side,—the houses not quite attached to each other, but having a wastage between.

wastayne, var. WASTINE *Obs.*, wilderness.

wast-coat, obs. form of WAISTCOAT.

waste (weɪst), *sb.* Forms: 3–7 **wast,** 4–5 **waast,** 6, 8 **waist,** 6 **wayste,** 4–6 *Sc.* **vast(e,** 3– **waste.** [a. OF. *wast(e*, dial. variant of *guast(e, gast(e*, partly repr. L. *vāstum*, neut. of *vāstus* WASTE *a.* (q.v. for the phonology), partly a verbal noun f. *waster* (*guaster, gaster*) WASTE *v.* Cf. Pr. *gast* ravage, waste, Sp., Pg. *gasto* expense, It. *guasto* ravage, damage, injury.

In early ME. the word adopted from OF. took the place of the cognate native WESTE of the same meaning. In mod.Eng. the sb. in some senses may be f. WASTE *v.*]

I. Waste or desert land.

1. a. Uninhabited (or sparsely inhabited) and uncultivated country; a wild and desolate region, a desert, wilderness. Somewhat *rhetorical.*

c **1200** *Trin. Coll. Hom.* 163 Ac seðen hie henen wenden, atlai þai lond unwend and bicam waste, and was roted oueral and swo bicam wildernesse. *a* **1300** *Cursor M.* 3072 Þe barn sco [*sc.* Hagar] dide drinc o þat wel, In þat wast þan can þai duell. *c* **1375** *Sc. Leg. Saints* xvii. (*Martha*) 21 In þat vaste scho fand a tovne, þat nov is callit Terrascone. *a* **1400–50** *Wars Alex.* 3487 Þare many daies be dissert he dryfes with his ost,.. Be wast & be wildirnes & be watirles bournes. *c* **1450** *Erle of Tolous* 451 From them he wente into a waste. **1704** POPE *Windsor For.* 80 But see, the man who spacious regions gave A waste for beasts, himself deny'd a grave. *a* **1718** PRIOR *Solomon* I. 279 North beyond Tartary's extended Waste. **1807** WORDSW. *White Doe* v. 1164 Among the wastes of Rylstone Fell. **1849** C. BRONTE *Shirley* xxiii,

The shadowless and trackless wastes of Zahara. **1854** J. S. C. ABBOTT *Napoleon* (1855) II. xiii. 221 Napoleon was now.. in an uncultivated country of almost boundless wastes. **1864** TENNYSON *Aylmer's F.* 742 Is there no prophet but the voice that calls Doom upon kings, or in the waste 'Repent'? **1871** BLACKIE *Four Phases* i. 46 Wandering about in a boggy waste. **1885** *Athenæum* 23 May 669/1 A sandy waste, which is scantily clad with herbage.

b. *transf.* Applied, e.g., to the ocean or other vast expanse of water (often ***waste of waters***, ***watery waste***), to land covered with snow, and to empty space or untenanted regions of the air.

1552 in Feuillerat *Revels Edw. VI* (1914) 89 A place caulled *vastum vacuum* .i. the great waste asmoche to saie as a place voyde or emptie withoute the worlde where is neither fier ayre water nor earth. **1655** WALLER *Panegyr. Ld. Protector* 41 Lords of the Worlds great Waste, the Ocean, wee Whole Forrests send to Raigne upon the Sea. **1667** MILTON *P.L.* II. 1045 Satan..in the emptier waste, resembling Air, Weighs his spread wings. **1697** DRYDEN *Æneis* VII. 310 From that dire Deluge, through the wat'ry Waste,..at last escap'd, to Latium we repair. **1712** ADDISON *Spect.* No. 309 ¶21 In Satan's Voyage through the Chaos there are several Imaginary Persons described, as residing in that immense Waste of Matter. **1724** RAMSAY *Vision* xviii, Millions of myles throch the wyld waste. **1727** DE FOE *Syst. Magick* I. vi. 160 The utmost extent of the waste, or expanse of space. **1728** POPE *Dunc.* III. 88 Where Mæotis sleeps, and hardly flows The freezing Tanais thro' a waste of snows. **1757** GRAY *Couplet about Birds* 2 The song-thrush there Scatters his loose notes in the waste of air. **1804** MOORE *To Marchioness Dowager Donegall* 32 Those pure isles..Which bards of old, with kindly fancy, plac'd For happy spirits in th'Atlantic waste? **1804** W. L. BOWLES *Spir. Discov.* 308 Whose volcanic fires A thousand nations view, hung like the moon High in the middle waste of heaven. **1818** SCOTT *Hrt. Midl.* li, As these broad black raindrops mingle with the waste of waters. **1864** D. G. MITCHELL *Sev. Stor.* 257 A raft is floating upon an ocean waste. **1871** L. STEPHEN *Playgr. Eur.* (1894) iii. 82 Showing their bare faces of precipitous rock across the dreary wastes of snow. **1892** M. CREIGHTON *Hist. Ess.* ix. (1902) 266 The waste of waters which spread on the east..was not sea-water. **1892** LADY F. VERNEY *Verney Mem.* I. 198 The 'great level' round the isle of Ely..was..a waste of water in winter.

c. *fig.*

1814 SCOTT *Lord of Isles* III. xvii, His soul a rock, his heart a waste. **1825** T. HOOK *Sayings* Ser. II. *Man of Many Fr.* (Colburn) 86 If she could at any time..have claimed the smallest spot in the 'waste' of George's memory. **1836** J. H. NEWMAN *Par. Serm.* III. xiv. 221 The open inhospitable waste of this world. **1840** DICKENS *Old C. Shop* xxxvi, Miss Brass..opening the safe, brought from it a dreary waste of cold potatoes, looking as eatable as Stonehenge. **1901** *Scotsman* 15 Mar. 7/4 There still stood between the House and its most urgent business a dreary waste of more than a hundred and twenty questions.

2. A piece of land not cultivated or used for any purpose, and producing little or no herbage or wood. In legal use *spec.* a piece of such land not in any man's occupation, but lying common.

In some dialects the ordinary word; otherwise rare in colloquial use.

1377 LANGL. *P. Pl.* B. Prol. 163 Vncoupled þei wenden Boþe in wareine & in waste where hem leue lykeþ. **14..** *Customs of Malton* in *Engl. Misc.* (Surtees) 58 It was graunted to the for sayd Burgeses a wast of ather syde of the town. **1423** *Cov. Leet Bk.* 46 The Prioures wast in Hasillwod. **1580** in *Lancs. & Chesh. Wills* (1884) I. 72 With th' appurtennes of and all and singular the said Mannors.. moores, mosses, wasts [etc.]. **1582** *Durham Wills* (Surtees 1860) II. 54 My house I dwell in,..and the waist adjoyninge upon the same. **1600** *Knaresb. Wills* (Surtees) I. 222 One waist with two cottages thereupon builded. **1662** in Horsfield *Hist. Lewes* (1824) I. 179 Times for the putting the tenants cattle into the common pastures, wastes, and commons of the manor. **1727** E. LAURENCE *Duty of Steward* 59 That they do not encroach upon the Lord's Waste, by digging Stone, Sand, &c. **1786** J. ROBERTS *Life* 60 [He was] permitted to keep six or seven cows upon the waste. **1799** A. YOUNG *View Agric. Lincoln* 147 At Leak and Wrangle there are some wastes, which the cottagers sometimes take in, and cultivate potatoes. **1820** STARKIE *Rep. Cases N.P.* II. 464 It was contended on his part, that the *locus in quo* belonged to Lady Smith in right of her manor, as being part of the wastes of that manor. **1828** BARNEWALL & CRESSWELL *Rep. K.B.* VII. 305 It was contended, that as the adjoining land belonged to Roberts, the primâ facie presumption was that the waste between his land and the high road belonged also to him. **1864** TENNYSON *North. Farmer, Old Style* vii, An' I a' stubb'd Thurnaby waäste. *Ibid.* x, Dubbut looök at the waäste; theer warn't nor feeäd for a cow; Nowt at all but bracken an' fuzz. **1864** —— *Enoch Arden* 729 Behind, With one small gate that open'd on the waste, Flourish'd a little garden.

†3. A devastated region. *Obs.*

1611 BIBLE *Isa.* lxi. 4 They shall build the olde wastes, they shall raise vp the former desolations. **1697** DRYDEN *Æneis* x. 572 All the leafie Nation sinks at last; And Vulcan rides in Triumph o're the Wast.

4. *Coal-mining.* A disused working; a part of a mine from which the coal has been extracted.

1695 *Par. Reg. St. Andrew's, Newc.* in Brand *Hist. Newcastle* (1789) II. 501 *note*, [Two men] were drowned in a coal-pitt..by the breaking in of water from an old waste. **1708** J. C. *Compl. Collier* (1845) 29 There is this and that Invention found out to draw out all great Old Waists, or Drowned Collieries. **1773** *Ann. Reg.* 151 The foul air in an old waste of a colliery..took fire, and breaking down the barrier..between the waste and the working pit, made the most terrible explosions. **1839** URE *Dict. Arts* 990 In collieries which..have goaves, creeps, or crushed wastes, the disengagement of the fire-damp from these recesses is much influenced by the state of atmospheric pressure. **1877** *Encycl. Brit.* VI. 64/2 The space from which the entire quantity of coal has been removed is known in different districts as the 'goaf', 'gob', or 'waste'. **1911** *Act 1 & 2 Geo. V* c. 50 § 52 (2) Props shall not be withdrawn from the waste or goaf..otherwise than by means of a safety contrivance. *transf.* **1812** JOHN WILSON *Agric. Renfrew.* 26 The extent of excavation or waste, in these mines [the alum mines of Hurlet, Renfrews.] is about 1½ mile in length, and the greatest breadth about ¾ of a mile.

II. Action or process of wasting.

5. a. Useless expenditure or consumption, squandering (*of* money, goods, time, effort, etc.).

1297 R. GLOUC. (Rolls) 7725 Þulke festes he wolde holde so nobliche Wiþ so gret prute & wast & so richeliche þat [etc.]. **13..** *Cursor M.* 252 (Gött.) And till þaim speke i alþermast þat ledis þair liues in mekil wast. **1303** R. BRUNNE *Handl. Synne* 7261 Rere sopers yn pryuyte, With glotonye, echone þey be; And þyr ys moche waste ynne, And gadryng of ouþer synne. *c* **1380** WYCLIF *Wks.* (1880) 15 Þouȝ þei hem self han neuere so muche wast of mete and drynk. *Ibid.* 60 For aȝenst cristis wilful pouert þei techen in dede worldly coueitise & moche wast in worldly goodis. *c* **1386** CHAUCER *Pars. T.* ¶813 Men oughten eschue fool largesse that men clepen wast. **1411–12** HOCCLEVE *De Reg. Princ.* 521 Now wold god þe waast of cloth & pryde Y-put were in exyl perpetuel. *c* **1450** CAPGRAVE *Life St. Aug.* xxxvii. 47 Grete wast was not in his hous of sotil metes. **1526** *Pilgr. Perf.* (W. de W. 1531) 174b, They consumeth superfluously & spendeth in waste, in one daye, the goodes that wolde suffyse & serve for theyr necessite many dayes. *c* **1532** DU WES *Introd. Fr.* in *Palsgr.* 905 Waste, *prodigalité*. **1593** SHAKS. *2 Hen IV*, I. ii. 160 Your Meanes is very slender, and your wast great. **1601** —— *Twel. N.* III. i. 141 *Clocke strikes.* The clocke vpbraides me with the waste of time. **1613** PURCHAS *Pilgrimage* (1614) 218 They may not bury the corps in silke or needle-worke..for this were waste, and a worke of the Gentiles. *c* **1645** MILTON *Sonn.* xii. 14 For all this waste of wealth and loss of blood. **1697** DRYDEN *Æneis* x. 1295 Why these insulting Words, this waste of Breath, To Souls undaunted, and secure of Death? **1812** H. & J. SMITH *Rej. Addr.* IV. vi, Your debts mount high—ye plunge in deeper waste. **1852** KINGSLEY *Yeast* xiii, Everywhere waste? Waste of manure, waste of land, waste of muscle, waste of brain, waste of population—and we call ourselves the workshop of the world! **1853** DICKENS *Bleak Ho.* lvii, All this was done with the greatest despatch, and without the waste of a moment. **1879** HUXLEY *Sensation* Sci. & Cult. (1881) 246 The maxim that metaphysical inquiries are barren of result, and that the serious occupation of the mind with them is a mere waste of time and labour.

Proverb. **1546** [see HASTE *sb.* 6]. *a* **1591** H. SMITH *Serm., Reb. Jonah* (1602) E 8, It is good that men looke before they leape, hast makes wast. **1641** SANDERSON *Serm. ad Aulam* xiii. (1689) 550 But haste maketh waste, we say. **1736** [see WANT *sb.*[2] 3 *Prov.*]. **1877** RAYMOND *Statist. Mines & Mining* 347 Since there has been less haste there has been less waste.

b. Phrases, ***to make***, **†** ***do waste***, to be wasteful.

1390 GOWER *Conf.* II. 139, I bidde noght that thou do wast, Bot hold largesce in his mesure. *c* **1480** *Lyt. Childr. Lyt. Bk.* 56 in *Babees Bk.* 20 Loke þou doo noo waste. **1481** CAXTON *Godfrey* xciii. 144 But they made grete waast & more than neded, & so by their oultrage & folye they lacked in short tyme. **1854** PATMORE *Angel in Ho., Betrothal* 138 Long lease of his low mind befall The man who, in his wilful gust, Makes waste for one, to others all Discourteous, frigid, and unjust!

†c. (***words of***) ***waste***: useless talk. *Obs.*

c **1400** *Destr. Troy* 2547 Why fader..are yo so fer troublet At his wordys of waste, & his wit febill? **1432–50** tr. *Higden* (Rolls) VII. 187 The erle perceyvynge that he hade spoken wordes of waste [*se superflua dixisse*]. *c* **1460** *Towneley Myst.* ii. 134 Thou Iangyls waste.

†d. Wasted labour. *Obs.*

c **1400** *Laud Troy Bk.* 2908 Thei armed hem with mochel haste; But sekirly it was but waste, For thei of Troye were mo than thai,..And sclow hem foule, when thei were met. *c* **1430** *Syr Gener.* (Roxb.) 6672 Folow noo ferthir, for it is waste.

†e. ***in waste***, in vain, to no purpose. *Obs.*

1340–70 *Alisaunder* 905 But all his werk was in waste. *c* **1375** *Sc. Leg. Saints* xliv. (*Lucy*) 280 Bot al ves in wast þai wrocht. **1390** GOWER *Conf.* I. 82 He spilleth many a word in wast That schal with such a poeple trete. *c* **1400** *Beryn* 1232 Beryn..axid aftir clothis; but it was al in wast. **1449** PECOCK *Repr.* I. iv. 21 He presupposith tho gouernauncis, vertues, and trouthis to be bifore knowen of tho same men, and ellis in waast he schulde so speke to tho men of hem not bifore knowen. *c* **1470** HENRY *Wallace* VI. 916 Than Wallace said: 'In waist is that trawaill'. **1513** DOUGLAS *Æneis* V. viii. 24 Ther hardy Kempis all in waist let draw, Athir at vthir, mony rowtis gret. *a* **1553** UDALL *Royster D.* IV. v, While my life shall last, For my friende Goodlucks sake ye shall not sende in wast. **1553** BRENDE *Q. Curtius* IX. Cc iij, Meethinkes I..go about in wast to stirre up your unwilling, and unmoveable mindes. **1556** T. HOBY tr. *Castiglione's Courtyer* Transl. Epist. A ij, Whatsoever I shoulde write therein, were but labour in waste. **1568** GRAFTON *Chron.* II. 681 He thought to spende no lenger tyme in waste. **1590** SPENSER *F.Q.* III. x. 13 [She] Laught at his foolish labour spent in waste. [**1725** WATTS *Logic* I. vi. §3 So foolish and lavish are we, that too often we use some words in mere waste, and have no ideas for them.]

f. A profusion, lavish abundance *of* something.

1725 POPE *Odyss.* VI. 356 And there the garden yields a waste of flow'rs. **1831** SCOTT *Ct. Robt.* iii, Cooling the fragrant breeze which breathed from the flowers and shrubs, that were so disposed as to send a waste of sweets around. **1855** TENNYSON *Brook* 191 Poor Philip, of all his lavish waste of words Remains the lean P. W. on his tomb.

g. An instance or example of wasting.

1612 BACON *Ess., Of Dispatch* (Arb.) 246 Prefaces, and passages, and excusations, and other speeches of reference to the person, are great wastes of time. *c* **1650** HIGFORD *Instit.* (1658) 6 Use Parsimony betimes before a wast be made, for Seneca tells you, *Sera est in fundo Parsimonia*. *Ibid.* 9 Riches may be well compared unto Cisternes or Pooles, which a small stream will easily fill, if there be no leaks or wasts, but small wasts and expences continuing, and not prevented, have decieved [sic], and undone many. **1658** *Whole Duty of Man* viii. §12. 187 This is a waste of that which is much more precious, our time. **1780** *Mirror* No. 79 ¶1 But to win them by offices of kindness, or attach them by real services, they consider as a fruitless waste of time. **1867** SIR C. DILKE in *Life* (1917) I. vii. 76 You think it a waste of money for me to contest Chelsea. **1909** *Daily Chron.* 4 Mar. 7/5 The economical woman..keeps a close watch for the small wastes that eat up more principal than the big purchases. **1920** CHESTERTON *Uses of Diversity* 54 He is somewhat anticlerical; which seems a waste of talent in a country where there is no clericalism.

6. a. Destruction or devastation caused by war, floods, conflagrations, etc. Now *rare* or *Obs.*

1560 DAUS tr. *Sleidane's Comm.* 433b, He would doubtlesse haue made an horrible destruction and waste through oute all Germany. **1596** *Edw. III*, I. ii. 159 Like a cloake, doth hide From weathers Waste the vnder garnisht pride. **1599** SHAKS. *Hen. V*, III. iii. 18 What is it then to me, if impious Warre..Doe..all fell feats, Enlynckt to wast and desolation? **1601** HOLLAND *Pliny* VI. xxix. I. 145 It was the Ægyptians warres and not the Romanes that gave the wast to Æthyopia. [L. *Nec tamen arma Romana ibi solitudinem fecerunt.*] **1657** AUSTEN *Fruit Trees* Ep. Ded., There having been so great a wast and destruction of Wood. **1768–74** TUCKER *Lt. Nat.* (1834) II. 304 Were charity..to be the prevailing humour in the world, it would..turn industry into its proper channel, where it would not overflow to make waste and do mischief, nor be lost among the barren sands of whimsy. **1855** MACAULAY *Hist. Eng.* xviii. IV. 223 In three years they had committed such waste on their native land as thirty years of English intelligence and industry would scarcely repair. **1864** TENNYSON *Aylmer's F.* 640 When since had flood, fire, earthquake, thunder, wrought Such waste and havock as the idolatries Which [etc.].

†b. *pl.* Ravages. *Obs.*

1615 G. SANDYS *Trav.* IV. 242 This City doth welnigh ioyne to the skirts of Ætna... The eiected flames haue heretofore committed horrible wasts. **1736** I. H. BROWNE *Pipe of Tobacco* i. 20 While Wastes of War deform the teeming Coast. **1738** WESLEY *Psalms* CIV. vii, Pleas'd with the Work of thy own Hands, Thou dost the Wastes of Time repair.

†c. *concr.* Something wasted or destroyed. *Obs.*

c **1600** SHAKS. *Sonn.* xii. 10 Then of thy beauty do I question make That thou among the wastes of time must goe. **1640** SUCKLING *Discont. Col.* III. (1642) E 4, Shal.. This pretious Lovelinesse, Passe with other common things Among the wasts of time?

7. *Law.* 'Any unauthorized act of a tenant for a freehold estate not of inheritance, or for any lesser interest, which tends to the destruction of the tenement, or otherwise to the injury of the inheritance' (Pollock, *Law of Torts*, 1887, p. 285). ***writ of waste*** (= AF. *bref de wast*), a writ commanding the sheriff to inhibit a tenant from an act of waste. **†** ***year, day, and waste***: see YEAR[1] 7b. ***impeachment of waste***: see IMPEACHMENT 4b.

For examples of AF. *wast* in this use see *Rolls of Parlt.* I. 9/1 (1278), II. 40/1 (1330), II. 170/2 (1347).

1414 *Rolls of Parlt.* IV. 60/2 Moreover, to enqueren what wast was made in the Kynges Maners, fro the tyme of Kyng John..into that day. *c* **1450** *Godstow Reg.* 317 Hit shold not be lawfull to the same sir william..to cast downe ony treys, noþere to make wast, sellyng or distroiyng, with-in the terme abouesaid, but for housebote. *c* **1475–80** in *Oxf. Stud. Soc. & Legal Hist.* (1914) IV. 225 In an accon of waste suyd ..before the kinges Justices..for brennyng of a water Mill. **1503–4** *Act 19 Hen. VII* c. 33 Preamble, The said Dame Cicile shuld not be therof impeched of Wast. **1544** tr. *Littleton's Tenures* vii. 15 In such case yf the lesse make wast, yᵉ lessour shal haue agaynst hym a wryt of Wast. **1628** COKE *On Litt.* I. 53 There be two kinds of Wasts, viz. Voluntarie or actuall, and permissiue. **1651** N. BACON *Disc. Govt. Eng.* II. i. 13 The King..leaves the noble Crown of England in the base condition of a Farme, subject to strip and waste by mean men; and crosses the Irish Seas with an Army. **1651** tr. *Kitchin's Jurisd.* (1653) 331 If a house be uncovered by suddaine tempest, it is not waste, but if the Lessee suffer that to be uncovered, that the Timber rot, it is waste. **1770** *Ann. Reg.* 173 Having caused a man to be apprehended who had committed waste on the estate of the earl of Donnegal. *a* **1845** POLSON *Law* in *Encycl. Metrop.* II. 828/1 The principal incidents to a tenancy in estate tail are, (1) the right of the tenant to commit what is called *waste*. **1863** H. COX *Inst.* II. viii. 500 Such injunctions include those against waste where a person having only a limited interest in an estate in his occupation, threatens to wastefully cut down timber, or otherwise injure the freehold.

fig. **1679** OWEN *Christol.* xvii. Wks. 1851 I. 216 Yet the inheritance is secured for us; and we are preserved from such offences against the supreme Lord, or committing such wastes, as should cast us out of our possession.

8. a. The consumption or using up of material, resources, time, etc. *Obs.* as distinct from 5.

1568 GRAFTON *Chron.* II. 751 He had long maintayned the siege to no small wast and consumyng of his brothers treasure and riches. **1597** HOOKER *Eccl. Pol.* v. lxii. §10 Euill ministers of good things are as torches, a light to others, a wast to none but themselues only. **1605** SHAKS. *Lear* II. i. 102 'Tis they haue put him on the old mans death, To haue th' expence and wast of his Reuenues.

†b. The consumption (of candles, etc.) at a funeral or obit. *Obs.*

1477–9 *Rec. St. Mary at Hill* (1905) 78 For the wast of ij tapres at Caustons obite, iiij d. **1506** in Glasscock *Rec. St. Michael's, Bp.'s Stortford* (1882) 31 Rec. of Thomas Whepyll for the waste of torches at his wife's burieng, iiij*d.* **1555** *Churchw. Acc. St. Helen's, Abingdon* (Nichols 1797) 141 For wast of the paskall and for holye yoyle, 5ˢ 10ᵈ. **1556–7** in *Archæol. Jrnl.* (1886) XLIII. 175 Paide to the chandler for waste of yᵉ waxe, viijᵈ.

9. a. Gradual loss or diminution from use, wear and tear, decay or natural process. Now somewhat *rare.*

1497 *Naval Acc. Hen. VII* (1896) 300 Deliverances employmentes perusynges losse & wast of the Stuff takle Store & other the premisses. **1514–15** *Act 6 Hen. VIII* c. 9 §1 The Carder and Spynner to delyver agayn to the same clothier yerne of the same Wolle by the same..true..weight the wast therof exceptid. **1547** in Sir J. Williams *Accompte* (Abbotsf. Club 1836) 7 Allowaunce..for the waste of souche plate as was..delyuerde..vnto thofficers of his housholde to be daylye vsed. *c* **1600** SHAKS. *Sonn.* ix. 11 But beauties waste hath in the world an end. **1626** BACON *Sylva* §218 Thinne Aire is better pierced; but Thicke Aire preserueth the Sound better from Wast. **1676** W. B. *Touch-st. Gold & Silver Wares* 3 Silver is a Mineral..that will endure melting for a long time in extream heat, with but very little wast. *a* **1767** M. BRUCE *Life & Wks.* (1914) 182 Each would fondly raise Some lasting monument, to save his name Safe from the waste of years. **1791** SMEATON *Edystone L.* §90 Workmen..look upon the stone so coated, as not to be in a state of waste or decay. **1801** *Farmer's Mag.* Nov. 422 An old venerable Cathedral still remains here, in defiance of the waste of time, and the rude hand of reformers. **1815** J. SMITH *Panorama Sci. & Art* I. 272 The odour of all bodies that excite the sensation of smell cannot be given out without a waste of their substance. **1830** LYELL *Princ. Geol.* I. 135 Rounded pebbles derived from the waste of..the older Apennine rocks. **1847** in Aiton *Dom. Econ.* (1857) 339 The repairs now required are not mere ordinary repairs, but ..rebuilding rendered necessary by the waste of time. **1877** HUXLEY *Physiogr.* 168 Abundant evidence of marine waste may be seen on any visit to the seaside.

b. with reference to animal tissues and structures.

1398 TREVISA *Barth. De P.R.* VII. xliv. (1495) 257 Yf abhomynacyon comyth of fastynge and of waste of the body, men shall restore that whyche is wasted with meete and Electuaryes. **1691** RAY *Creation* II. (1692) 39 Which was most providently design'd to repair the wast that is daily made of them by the frequent Attrition in Mastication. **1695** *New Light of Chirurg. put out* 15 Sudden Waste made upon Fat Persons by violent Fevers. **1725** N. ROBINSON *Th. Physick* 45 Thus far we have consider'd, how our Bodies acquire the Reparations for those Wastes, that are daily expended in carrying on the Laws of the Animal Oeconomy. **1796** MME. D'ARBLAY *Camilla* V. 497 To repair the wastes of strength some time yet was necessary. **1814** MRS. J. WEST *Alicia de Lacy* IV. 247 It was that oblivion of thought which best repairs the waste of nature, and gives elasticity to the weary faculties. **1841** DICKENS *Barn. Rudge* vi, Reclining in an easy-chair before the fire, pale and weak from waste of blood, was Edward Chester. **1875** B. STEWART & TAIT *Unseen Univ.* §59 Just as no single action of the body takes place without the waste of some muscular tissue, so, it is believed, no thought takes place without some waste of the brain.

c. A wasting of the body by disease; a consumption or decline. Now only *dial.*

1570 LEVINS *Manip.* 203/25 Wayst of body, *tabes.* **1584** COGAN *Haven Health* lxxii. 71 Clarie..is found by experience verie good for the back, and restoratiue in a wast. **1601** HOLLAND *Pliny* XVII. xxiv. I. 540 In a wast, consumption, or fever hecticke. *c* **1816** MRS. SHERWOOD *Stories Ch. Catech.* xix. 169 His disease was what the country people in England call a waste. **1878** MRS. H. WOOD *Pomeroy Abb.* I. 49 Her mother went off in a waste. **1893** 'L. KEITH' *Lisbeth* vii, Your father's family going off one after the other in a waste, and nobody but me to see to them.

d. *Phys. Geog.* Material derived by mechanical and chemical erosion from the land, carried by streams to the sea. (W. Suppl. 1902.)

10. Phrases. **a.** ***to run to waste*** (rarely † ***to flow at waste***): primarily of liquor, to flow away so as to be wasted; *fig.* of wealth, powers, etc., to be expended uselessly. **b.** ***to go to waste***: to be wasted. **c.** † ***to grow to waste***: Of a period of time, to approach its end. **d.** ***to cut to waste***: lit. to cut (cloth) in a wasteful manner; *fig.* (? *slang*) to apportion (time) wastefully.

a. 1511 *Guylforde's Pilgr.* (Camden) 22 Moche water renneth nowe to waste. **1624** MASSINGER *Parlt. Love* II. iii, Shall this nectar Run useless, then, to waste? **1641** MILTON *Reas. Ch. Govt.* II. 41 Like that which flows at wast from the pen of some vulgar Amorist. **1741** WATTS *Improv. Mind* I. iii, This will secure the workings of your soul from running to waste, and..even your looser moments will turn to happy account. **1803** LAMB *Let. to Coleridge* 20 Mar., You, like me, ..reckon the lapse of time from the waste thereof, as boys let a cock run to waste. **1818** BYRON *Ch. Har.* IV. cxx, Alas! our young affections run to waste, Or water but the desert. **1849** MACAULAY *Hist. Eng.* iii. I. 412 In an age of Scotists and Thomists even his intellect might have run to waste. [**1853** C. BRONTE *Villette* viii, Beside a table, on which flared the remnant of a candle guttering to waste in the socket.] **1856** SIR B. BRODIE *Psychol. Inq.* II. v. 166 The faculties of the mind..run to waste if neglected. **1863** *Jrnl. R. Agric. Soc.* XXIV. II. 437 The sewage..ran to waste on the sea-shore. **1900** *Jrnl. Soc. of Dyers* XVI. 12 The water..is run to waste.

b. *a* **1500** *Hist. K. Boccus & Sydracke* (?1510) Giij b, There goyth of it [*sc.* of the sea] to wast somdele As euery man may wyt wel. **1796** H. HUNTER tr. *St.-Pierre's Stud. Nat.* II. 144 There is not a particle of vapour in the Universe that goes to waste. **1854** *Poultry Chron.* II. 42 We are importing ship-load after ship-load of guano..while hundreds of tons of poultry manure, which is ascertained to be equal in value, is suffered to go to waste in the United States. **1866** T. T. STODDART *Angler's Rambles* 365 Five-sixths at the least of salmon *ova* go directly to waste.

c. 1604 SHAKS. *Oth.* IV. ii. 250 The night growes to wast.

d. *c* **1863** READE *Hard Cash* xxxix, He..said the Firm did not care to send its stuff to ladies not in the business; I might cut it to waste. **1863** *Baily's Mag.* Apr. 153 An hour and a half had been 'cut to waste', as the sporting reporters would say, and no tidings..had been received.

III. Waste matter, refuse.

11. a. Refuse matter; unserviceable material remaining over from any process of manufacture; the useless by-products of any industrial process; material or manufactured articles so damaged as to be useless or unsaleable.

c **1430** *Lybeaus Disc.* (Cott.) 1471 For gore, and fen, and full wast, That was out ykast. **1764** in *Sixth Rep. Dep. Kpr. Rec.* App. II. 133 The Refuse or Waste used in the making of Allom, called Allom Slam. **1812** J. SMYTH *Pract. Customs* (1821) 323 The above Duty on Cotton Wool, or Waste of Cotton Wool,..is to be charged [etc.]. **1827** FARADAY *Chem. Manip.* xix. (1842) 532 The object of the preceding directions is to enable the economical experimenter to cut up into useful forms, old glass, which would otherwise be thrown away as waste. **1851–61** MAYHEW *Lond. Labour* II. 9, I may instance another thing in which the worth of what in many places is valueless refuse is exemplified, in the matter of 'waste', as waste paper is always called in the trade. **1863** *Technologist* III. 358 All the fibre and gluten wastes of the maize plant which are precipitated during the process of extracting the fibres, are used for manufacturing paper. **1864** TENNYSON *Enoch Arden* 16 Three children..play'd Among the waste and lumber of the shore, Hard coils of cordage, swarthy fishing-nets, [etc.]. **1902** JOANNA E. WOOD *Farden Ha'* xviii, The surrounding country (the aspect of which was scarred by pits, and distorted by black heaps of 'waste').

† **b.** *fig.* Offscourings, dregs, worthless people.

1592 NASHE *P. Penilesse* F 3 There is a certaine waste of the people for whome there is no vse, but warre.

c. = COTTON-*waste.*

1864 *Chambers's Jrnl.* 16 July 460/2 Smith the driver.. standing upon the foot-plate of No. 69, leisurely attempting to remove the surplus oil from his black hands with a very suspicious piece of 'waste'. **1886** J. BARROWMAN *Sc. Mining Terms* 70 *Waste*, cotton refuse for cleaning machinery. **1909** *Blackw. Mag.* Sept. 315/2 The old order of Engineer Officer ..was swaddled in 'waste' rather than sail-cloth, and smelt not of pitch but of warm oil.

d. *Printing*, etc. The surplus sheets of a work. See also quot. 1888.

1785 W. TOOKE in *Lett. Lit. Men* (Camden) 430 What is called in typographical language the waste of works printed at the Academy, is seldom or never preserved. **1841** SAVAGE *Dict. Printing* 810. **1888** JACOBI *Printers' Vocab.*, *Waste*, surplus sheets of a book beyond the plus copies. Also spoilt sheets used for running up colour on a machine, etc.

e. *Coal-mining.* (See quot.)

1883 GRESLEY *Gloss. Coal-mining* 278 *Waste.* 2. (North) very small coal or slack.

12. † **a.** An overflow of surplus water. *Obs.* **b.** A pipe, conduit, or other contrivance for carrying off waste matter or surplus water, steam, etc. Cf. *waste-pipe*

1587 FLEMING *Contn. Holinshed* III. 1312/1 Means is made, by a standard with one cocke at Holborne bridge to conueie the wast. *Ibid.* 1348/2 Vp vnto the northwest corner of Leaden hall..where the waste of the first maine pipe ran first this yeare. **1660** F. BROOKE tr. *Le Blanc's Trav.* 262 He went and washed his hands at the waste [Fr. *russeau*] of the well. **1707** MORTIMER *Husb.* 224 If 'tis made very sloaping on each side 'tis the better, leaving a waste to carry off your waste Water in times of Floods or Rains. **1877** S. S. HELLYER *Plumber* v. 47 If more than one basin is fixed upon the same waste, the size should be proportionately increased. **1892** *Photogr. Ann.* II. 48 Have the sink deep, as it can, by plugging the waste with a cock through which the glass tube passes, be utilised for washing purposes.

c. Waste water, effluent; *spec.* that which is free of excrement. Cf. SOIL $sb.^3$ 7.

The distinction between waste and soil is commoner in the combs. with *pipe.*

1886 *Encycl. Brit.* XXI. 715/2 To connect a water-closet soil-pipe with sinks and basins..is to multiply possibilities for the spread of disease within the house, and it is strongly advisable to convey the waste from them by a separate pipe. **1913** E. H. BLAKE *Drainage & Sanitation* vii. 239 We may next consider the kinds of waste pipe... They comprise rain-water pipes.., soil pipes taking the wastes from closets and housemaids' sinks, and pipes taking the wastes from baths, lavatories, and sinks. **1959** GOODIN & DOWNING *Domestic Sanitation* v. 127 Sanitary fitments, may be divided broadly into those intended to receive the wastes of the human body, and those designed for dirty, soapy or greasy water. **1973** [see SOIL $sb.^3$ 7]. **1976** *National Observer* (U.S.) 28 Aug. 12/3 One theory not in the report was that frozen plumbing may have caused a backup of wastes and a contamination of the water system. **1978** T. PETTIT *Home Plumbing* x. 51/2 Waste from WCs is discharged into the soil and vent system of pipework.

IV. Combinations.

13. Obvious combinations, as (sense 1) ***waste-dwelling*** adj.; (sense 5) ***waste-preventing*** adj., ***-preventor***; (sense 11) ***waste-collector***, ***-dealer***, ***-disposal***, ***-pit***, ***-tip*** (TIP $sb.^5$ 4 b).

1851–61 MAYHEW *Lond. Labour* II. 9, 'I don't know how it is, sir,' said one *waste collector,..'but paper gets scarcer or else I am out of luck.' **1876** MRS. G. L. BANKS *Manch. Man* xviii. (1902) 79 Nadin..followed up the clue to a *waste-dealer's who bought at his own price workpeople's 'waste' (*i.e.* warp, weft, silk, &c. remaining after work was completed). **1882** W. WESTALL *Tales & Trad. Switzerland* 289 'A doctor! What for?' interrupted the retired waste-dealer. **1968** E. A. POWDRILL *Vocab. Land Planning* iv. 64 Industrial land does not include..land for..*waste disposal (where this occupies a significant area detached from the industrial process). **1977** P. JOHNSON *Enemies of Society* vii. 91 We now have a good idea of the extensive damage done in the areas of Lake Baikal, the Volga, the Caspian and the Aral seas, and other Soviet areas of industrial waste-disposal. **1900** A. LANG *Hist. Scot.* I. iv. 70 The elder gods may have been degraded to *waste-dwelling demons. **1906** R. A. S. MACALISTER *Bible Sidelights* 135 That it was a temple of some sort was indicated..by a *waste-pit full of sheep-bones, apparently those of sacrificial victims. **1884** MCLAREN *Spinning* 173 With *waste-preventing machines much more progress has been made. **1884** *Health Exhib. Catal.* 94/1 New English Wash-out and noiseless *Waste-preventor Cistern. **1906** *Victoria County Hist. Cornw.* I. 520/2 The rock..is taken.., the useless to the *waste tip, and the good to the deposit floors.

14. Special combinations: **waste-basket** (now chiefly *U.S.*) = WASTE-PAPER *basket*; hence **waste-basket** *v.*, to put in the waste-paper basket; **waste-bin**, a dustbin; **waste-box** *Mining* (see quot.); **waste-cock**, a cock to regulate the discharge of waste water; **waste disposal unit** (see quot. 1967); **waste-disposer** = *waste disposal unit* above; **waste-drain**, a drain for carrying off waste water; **waste-gate**, **-hatch**, (*a*) a gate or hatch for regulating the outflow of waste water; (*b*) *Engin.*, a device in a turbocharger which regulates the pressure at which exhaust gases pass to the turbine by opening or closing a vent to the external atmosphere; **waste-heap**, (*a*) a pile of refuse matter; (*b*) *transf.* in *Cards*, a pile of cards formed from the accumulation during the course of a game of those which cannot be played (cf. *rubbish heap* s.v. RUBBISH *sb.* (and *a.*) 3 b); **waste heat**, heat produced as the by-product of some process; ***waste-heat boiler***, a boiler employing this; **waste-hole**, a hole for the discharge of superfluous water; **waste-inspector**, a water-company's or municipality's official employed to report cases of waste of water; **waste maker** [f. title of book: see quot. 1961], a manufacturer of consumer goods that are intended not to be durable or to be partially wasted so that the demand for new goods is kept high; **waste-man** *Mining*, a man whose duty is to inspect the waste (sense 4), and to secure the proper ventilation of the mine; **waste mould**, in *Sculpture*, a simple negative mould which has to be broken to release the cast inside it; so **waste moulding**; cf. *piece mould* s.v. PIECE *sb.* 23; **waste-pallet** *Organ-building*, see PALLET $sb.^3$ 6; **waste-pipe**, a pipe to carry off waste water or steam; also *spec.* a pipe for the drainage of effluent from sinks, baths, etc., in contrast to a soil-pipe; **waste plug** = PLUG *sb.* 1 b, †2 k; **waste silk**, the inferior silk from the outside of cocoons and from cocoons out of which the moths have been allowed to escape; **waste-sluice**, a sluice for regulating the outflow of waste water; **waste-spout**, a spout for the issue of waste-water; **waste-way** *U.S.*, a channel for the passage of waste water; **waste-weir** (see quots.); **waste-yard** ? *Obs.*, ? a yard for the reception of odds and ends of little value.

1850 LYTTON *My Novel* II. vi, Public men have such odd out-of-the-way letters that their *waste-baskets are never empty. **1868** 'HOLME LEE' *B. Godfrey* lv, Basil tore the paper .., and thrust it into the waste-basket. **1913** JEAN WEBSTER *Daddy-Long-Legs* 35 If my letters bore you you can always toss them into the waste-basket. **1889** 'MARK TWAIN' *Lett.* (1917) II. xxix. 514 Send me the pages with your corrections on them, and *waste-basket the rest. **1900** —— *Man that corrupted* etc. 127 Indefinite testimonies might properly be waste-basketed, since there is evidently no lack of definite ones procurable. **1915** *Daily Tel.* 14 Aug. 10/7 If all the scraps after meals..be carefully kept, instead of..put into the *waste-bin or burned. **1860** *Engl. & For. Mining Gloss.* (ed. 2) 66 (Newcastle) **Waste boxes*, boxes in which the waste water of the pumping-pit is conveyed from the rings. **1844** H. STEPHENS *Bk. Farm* II. 317 He is able..so to adjust the cock that the requisite supply shall go to the boiler, without entirely shutting the *waste-cock. **1967** *Gloss. Sanitation Terms* (*B.S.I.*) 63 **Waste disposal unit*, an electrically operated mechanical device for reducing kitchen garbage into fragments small enough to be flushed into the *drainage system.* **1968** R. V. BESTE *Repeat Instructions* vi. 64 His first conscious memory was of being in the kitchen stuffing the torn pieces into the waste disposal unit. **1977** *Evening Post* (Nottingham) 27 Jan. 14/4 (Advt.), Lounge, hall, fitted cupboards, fully fitted kitchen with waste disposal unit. **1962** *Which?* Mar. 82/1 There are obvious advantages..in being able to get rid of kitchen scraps straight down the drain, with a *waste disposer. **1980** A. N. WILSON *Healing Art* vi. 62 A new sun lounge..a waste-disposer in the sink. **1833** LOUDON *Encycl. Archit.* §32 A large cock in the bottom of the receiving tank, communicating with the *waste drain. **1791** R. MYLNE *2nd Rep. Thames* 11 The *Waste and Buck Gates are quite ruinous. **1948** *Shell Aviation News* No. 115. 19/1 The closed wastegate limitation is the condition where all of the available exhaust gas energy is required to drive the compressor, and all of the exhaust gas is directed through the turbine. **1981** *Pop. Hot Rodding* Feb. 22/1 It will be a relatively simple matter of welding in sections of bent tubing to make the necessary connections (including a waste-gate, should one be required). **1983** *Which?* Dec. 559/1 So a valve is needed—the wastegate—which opens when the pressure is at its maximum safe level to divert some of the exhaust gases away from the turbine. **1705** *Act 4 & 5 Anne* c. 8 (21) §5 One Scuttle or small Hatch of a Foot Square in the *Waste Hatch or Water course in the direct Stream wherein no Water Wheel standeth [etc.]. **1873** B. STEWART *Conserv. Energy* v. 153 Universally diffused heat forms what we may call the great *waste-heap of the universe. **1892** 'L. HOFFMANN' *Illustr. Bk. Patience Games* 4 If its [*sc.* the card's] nature does not allow of its being so played, it is laid face upwards in front of the player, the cards so deposited being known as the 'waste-' or 'rubbish-heap'. **1913** —— *Sel. Patience Games* 5 The cards so dealt with being known as the 'waste-heap' or 'rubbish-heap'. **1915** *Blackw. Mag.* Nov. 702/2 Fosse Eight is a mighty waste-heap. **1975** *Way to Play* 145/3 *Waste pile or heap*, cards from the stock that cannot immediately be played onto the layout are sometimes placed face up in one or more waste piles, to be brought back into the game as appropriate. **1908** A. G. KING *Pract. Steam & Hot Water Heating* xxvii. 343 When no *waste heat is available, an ordinary type of pipe heater may be used. **1930** *Engineering* 8 Aug. 188/3 The utilization of exhaust gases in waste-heat boilers had improved the efficiency of the large gas engine. **1972** R. G. KAZMANN *Mod. Hydrol.* (ed. 2) iv. 130 The remainder of this energy, 'waste heat', must be disposed of into the immediate environment of the power plant. **1982** W. F. OWEN *Energy in Wastewater Treatment* xii. 281 Three basic types of heat recovery equipment are typically used in wastewater heat recovery systems: shell-and-tube exchangers, waste heat boilers, and heat wheels. **1839** *Civil Engin. & Arch. Jrnl.* II. 436/1 The same adjustment may be made by stopping the pump, and letting out the water from the *waste-holes. **1898** *Daily News* 17 June 3/3 A turncock and *waste inspector, in the service of the Vauxhall Waterworks Company. **1961** V. PACKARD *Waste Makers* v. 48 In some cases the consumers have no choice but to be *waste makers because of the way products are sold to them. Many paste pots come with brushes built into the cover, and the brushes fail.. to reach the bottom... Thus millions of 'empty' paste jars are thrown away with a few spoonfuls of paste still in them. **1970** G. JACKSON *Let.* 17 June in *Soledad Brother* (1971) 282 You dig, no waste makers, nor harnesses on production. **1812** J. HODGSON in J. Raine *Mem.* (1857) I. 96 The *waste-men or ventilators of the mine. **1825** E. MACKENZIE *View Northumbld.* (ed. 2) I. 90 *Wastemen*, persons that daily examine the state of the workings, and see that they are properly ventilated. **1891** *Labour Commission* Gloss., *Wastemen*, generally old men who are employed in building pillars for the support of the roof in the waste, *i.e.* old workings and airways; and in keeping the airways open and in good order. **1929** F. J. GLASS *Modelling & Sculpture* viii. 73 You now proceed to chip away the white portion of the *waste mould. **1971** *Daily Tel.* (Colour Suppl.) 5 Mar. 8/2 From this brittle clay an impression—a 'waste-mould'—is taken, from which a plaster cast is made. **1911** A. TOFT *Modelling & Sculpture* vi. 90 The term '*waste moulding' implies that the mould is only made to serve the purpose of taking one cast. **1918** H. H. STANSFIELD *Sculpture* ii. 9 In waste moulding the plaster is chipped away so that the mould is destroyed. **1881** C. A. EDWARDS *Organs* 44 The *waste-pallet is an arrangement corresponding to the safety-valve in the steamboiler. *c* **1512** *Archæologia* LVIII. 301 Boþe þe suspirel and þe *waste pipe awoyde ther water in a gotir of breke. **1585** HIGINS *Junius' Nomencl.* 362/1 *Aqua caduca*,.. water that runneth ouer, or at the waste pipes or spowts of condut heads. **1712** J. JAMES tr. *Le Blond's Gardening* 211 To empty the Bason entirely.., which is done by means of.. a Waste-Pipe at the Bottom of it. **1876**, etc. [see *soil-pipe* s.v. SOIL *sb.*³ 9]. **1877** HUXLEY *Physiogr.* 39 The steam which issues from the waste-pipe being cooled down by contact with the cold air. **1907** J. A. HODGES *Elem. Photogr.* (ed. 6) 35 To connect the waste pipe with nearest drain or gutter. **1946** E. MOLLOY *Plumbing & Gas-Fitting* x. 221/2 For a waste pipe from a bath, sink, bidet, or lavatory basin discharging into a soil pipe from a water-closet, or a waste pipe from a slop sink, the Model By-laws specify 'a suitable trap adequately secured against destruction of the water seal'. **1877** G. E. WARING *Sanitary Condition City & Country Houses* 79 If the *waste plug is operated by a handle rising the slab, there is a considerable length of pipe between it and the bottom of the basin. **1882** S. S. HELLYER *Lect. Sci. & Art Sanitary Plumbing* v. 193 These water-closets were made of marble—A the pan; B the waste-plug; C the service-pipe; D the overflow. **1965** Waste plug [see PLUG *sb.* 1 b]. **1797** *Encycl. Brit.* XVII. 486/1 Before you begin to wind, you must prepare your cocoons.. stripping them of that *waste silk that surrounds them, and which served to fasten them to the twigs. **1875** [see SPUN *ppl. a.* 1 a]. **1921** Waste silk [see SCHAPPE]. **1844** H. STEPHENS *Bk. Farm* II. 327 As a *waste-sluice, the most convenient and simple, in a mill of this kind, is the trap-sluice. **1667** FLAVEL *Saint Indeed* (1754) 19 Few words run then at the *waste spout. **1881** THAYER *Log-cabin to White Ho.* xii. 149 There was a *waste-way just ahead. **1884** *Harper's Mag.* Sept. 621/2 Above these.. is a wasteway.. over which the surplus water can pour. **1793** R. MYLNE *Rep. Thames* 23 There was Seven Inches of Water running over at the *Waste Weir at Boulter's Old Lock. **1840** H. S. TANNER *Canals & Rail Roads U.S.* 264 *Waste weir*, a water guage; a cut at the side of a canal by which the surplus water of canals is carried off. **1868** *Chamb. Encycl.* X. 516/2 There is also the waste-weir, for the purpose of preventing a reservoir embankment being overtopped by floods. *c* **1620** MORYSON *Itin.* IV. v. i. (1903) 460 Theire houses, (which haue no such *wastyardes about them as euery Farmers house hath with vs). **1826** COBBETT *Rur. Rides* (1885) II. 182 And rick-yard, farm-yard, waste-yard, horse-paddock, and all round about, seemed to be swarming with fowls, ducks, and turkeys. **1854** DICKENS *Hard T.* I. xi, In the waste-yard outside [the mill], the steam from the escape pipe, the litter of barrels and old iron, the shining heaps of coals, the ashes everywhere, were shrouded in a veil of mist and rain.

waste (weist), *a.* Also 4-7 wast, 4-5 waast, *Sc.* vast(e, 5-7 (chiefly *Sc.*) waist, 6 waiste, *Sc.* waest. [ME., a. OF. *wast*, dial. var. of *guast, gast* = Pr. *gast*, Pg. *gasto*, It. *guasto*:—Rom. **wasto*, repr. (with influence from the cogn. and synonymous OHG. *wuosti*) L. *vāstus* waste, desert, unoccupied (distinct from *vāstus* VAST *a.*).

The adopted OF. word took the place of the early ME. WESTE *a.* (cogn. w. L. *vāstus*). In mod.E. it seems to have coalesced with the contracted pa. pple. of WASTE *v.* and with the attributive use of WASTE *sb.*]

1. Of land: a. Uncultivated and uninhabited or sparsely inhabited. Sometimes with stronger implication: Incapable of habitation or cultivation; producing little or no vegetation; barren, desert. See also WASTELAND.

c **1290** *S. Eng. Leg.* 205/180 Al-a-boute in a waste londe. *c* **1387** TREVISA *Higden* (Rolls) I. 51 Affryca.. hath more wyldernes and waste londe, for grete brennynge and hete of þe sonne, þan Europa. *c* **1420** WYNTOUN *Cron.* II. ix. 787 He sende wiþe þaim sum of his men Til Irlande, þat was nocht ȝit þen Inhabit, bot was wast haly. *c* **1480** HENRYSON *Test. Cress.* 588 My Spreit I leif to Diane,.. To walk with hir in waist Woddis and Wellis. *c* **1500** *Melusine* i. 18 He began within her land, that was wast & deserte for to byld.. fayre tounes & strong Castels. **1535** COVERDALE *Wisd.* xi. 2 They ..pitched their tentes in yᵉ waist deserte. **1598** HAKLUYT *Voy.* I. 103 We trauailed directly Eastward, hauing a Sea on the South side of vs, and a waste desert on the North. **1635** D. DICKSON *Hebr.* xii. 22. 301 Vagabonds, wandring abroad in a waste Wildernesse. *c* **1639** SIR W. MURE *Ps.* xxix. 8 Yea, at the dreadfull voyce of God, Waist Kadesh desart quaikes. **1653** HOLCROFT *Procopius, Pers. Wars* I. xii. 20 [They] ever neglected the Province beyond the Euphrates, being without water and wast. **1671** MILTON *P.R.* I. 7, I.. now sing.. Recover'd Paradise to all mankind,.. And Eden rais'd in the wast Wilderness. **1819** SCOTT *Leg. Montrose* xi, He therefore plodded patiently on through a waste and savage wilderness. **1843** DE QUINCEY *Ceylon* Wks. 1890 VII. 436 Ceylon has not much of waste ground, in the sense of being irreclaimable—for of waste ground in the sense of being unoccupied she has an infinity.

b. *fig.* Desolate, barren. Cf. 4.

c **1825** W. M. PRAED *Poems, Farewell* iv, And still the shadowy hope was rife That once in this waste weary life My path might cross with thine. **1839** J. H. NEWMAN *Par. Serm.* IV. xii. 215 The world, in which our duties lie, is as waste as the wilderness. **1845** —— *Ess. Developm.* 314 Dreary and waste was the condition of the Church. **1851** CARLYLE *Sterling* III. vi, Our conversation was waste and logical, I forget quite on what, not joyful and harmoniously effusive. **1908** W. M. RAMSAY *Luke* i. 3 Nothing in the whole history of literary criticism has been so waste and dreary as great part of the modern critical study of Luke.

Comb. **1839** CARLYLE *Chartism* v. 133 It is not chaos and a waste-whirling baseless Phantasm. **1851** —— *Sterling* I. v, This waste-weltering epoch. **1871** —— in Mrs. Carlyle *Lett.* (1883) I. 141 On the solitary coach-roof, under the waste-blowing skies.

c. In weaker sense: Not applied to any purpose; not utilized for cultivation or building.

1439 *Charters* etc. *Edin.* (1871) 64 Beside the vaste lande neire byside the house of John of Turyng. **1480** *Cov. Leet Bk.* 445 Be lawe of þis lande, the lorde of þe waste soyle may surcharge and put þerin what nombre [of cattle] hym lykes. *Ibid.* 472 The seid Priour & Couent seyn that þe same grounde is parcell of the Churcheyarde, and was no wast-grounde. **1531** *Abstr. Protocols Town Clerks Glasgow* (1897) IV. 32 Ane waest bornesteyd, lyand into Sant Tenewsgaet. **1538** STARKEY *England* iii. 73 That we haue so much wast ground here in our cuntrey, hyt ys not to be attrybute to the nature of the erthe.. but [etc.]. **1543** tr. *Act 13 Edw. I*, c. 45 Where as in a statute made at Merton it was graunted that lordes of wast woodes and pastures myght improwe the sayde wast woodes and pastures, [etc.]. **1551** CROWLEY *Pleas. & Payne* 479 Caste downe the hedges and stronge mowndes, That you have caused to be made Aboute the waste and tyllage groundes. **1690** LOCKE *Govt.* II. v. §42 Land that is left wholly to Nature, that hath no Improvement of Pasturage, Tillage, or Planting, is called, as indeed it is, Waste. **1725** *Lond. Gaz.* No. 6398/1 A Piece of waste Ground for Building. **1820** STARKIE *Rep. Cases N.P.* II. 464 The lords of the manor of Hampstead had, from time immemorial, exercised the right of granting out parcels of the waste lands within the manor, with the consent of the copy-holders. **1842** DICKENS *Amer. Notes* viii, A melancholy piece of waste ground with frowzy grass. **1858** J. B. NORTON *Topics* 225 The district officers had not had leisure to settle all the contending applications for permission to take up waste lands. **1875** JOWETT *Plato* (ed. 2) V. 109 Let the fowler confine himself to waste places and to the mountains. **1900** W. H. HUDSON *Nat. in Downland* 41 Thistly, and weedy waste lands. **1908** W. M. RAMSAY *Luke* v. 179 The soil originally was waste and valueless.

†**d.** *transf.* ? Uncultured mentally. *Obs.*

? **1541** COVERDALE *Confut. Standish* i j, Yf I shuld saye ye were puft vp, ignoraunt, a waist brayne, et cete... ye wolde happlie be angrie.

†**2.** Of former places of habitation or cultivation, buildings, etc.: Devastated, ruinous. *Obs.*

a **1300** *Cursor M.* 18890 þe psalm sais, thoru þe haligast, His woning stede be wild and wast. **1338** R. BRUNNE *Chron.* (1725) 62 þer þe Inglis had bigged, he mad it wast & bare. **1375** BARBOUR *Bruce* VII. 151 And than the formast cumin weir Till a vast [*v.r.* waist] husbandis hous. *c* **1375** *Sc. Leg. Saints* xxix. (*Placidas*) 326 [Satan] Kist don castellis in hast, & towne & tilth al mad wast. **1390** GOWER *Conf.* I. 32 The toun is wast. **14..** *Polit. Poems* (Rolls) II. 244 An old castel, and not repaired, With wast walles and wowes wide. **1491** *Newminster Cartul.* (1878) 251 Two waste chapellez. **1523** BERNERS *Froiss.* I. cclxix. 163 He.. rested hym in certayne olde wast & broken howses. **1535** COVERDALE *2 Kings* xix. 25 Now haue I caused it for to come, that contencious stronge cities mighte fall in to a waste heape of stones. **1600** J. PORY tr. *Leo's Africa* v. 236 [He] built a strong forte vpon the sea shore, and repaired an other which had lien a long time waste. *a* **1604** HANMER *Chron. Irel.* (1633) 53 The which Abbey.. was afterward destroyed by Pyrates.. and so continued waste unto the time of Malachias, Bishop of Armach. **1823** SCOTT *Quentin D.* Introd., A very large and well-proportioned saloon;.. but so waste and dilapidated, that [etc.].

3. a. *to lie waste*: To remain in an uncultivated or ruinous condition.

1338 R. BRUNNE *Chron.* (1725) 239 It lies now waste & lorn, half may þei not tille. **1535** COVERDALE *Isa.* i. 7 Youre londe lieth waist, youre cities are brent vp. **1557** TUSSER *100 Points Husb.* 94 Thryfallowe betime, for destroing of weede: ..And better thou warte, so to doe for thy hast: then (hardnes) for slougth make thy lande to lie wast. **1653** [see LIE *v.*¹ 8]. **1890** D. DAVIDSON *Mem. Long Life* ix. 214 At the close of the Pindaree war many villages were lying waste in the valley of the Nerbudda for more than thirty years.

b. *to lay waste*: to devastate, ravage (land, buildings).

1535 COVERDALE *Ps.* lxxix. 7 For they haue deuoured Iacob, and layed waiste his dwellinge place. **1560** DAUS tr. *Sleidane's Comm.* 19 All the country aboute layde waste. **1563-4** *Reg. Privy Council Scot.* I. 257 Layand thairthrow waist ane grete part of the cuntre. *c* **1586** C'TESS PEMBROKE *Ps.* LXXIV. vii, Not one house doth stand.. But they by fire have laide it waste. **1610** R. NICCOLS *Winter Nt.'s Vis.*, *Robt. Dk. Norm.* l, There all the host as towards Nice we past, With spoilefull hands laid all the countrie wast. **1611** BIBLE *Ezek.* xxxv. 4, I will lay thy cities waste, and thou shalt be desolate. *c* **1680** BEVERIDGE *Serm.* (1729) II. 549 When Judas Maccabeus had.. repaired the temple at Jerusalem after it had been.. laid waste. **1796** BURKE *Let. Noble Ld.* Wks. 1843 II. 273 Which, like columns of locusts, have laid waste the fairest part of the world. **1824** CAMPBELL *Theodric* 346 For war laid waste his native land once more. **1879** MISS YONGE *Cameos* Ser. IV. 42 Villages were burnt and laid waste. **1890** S. LANE-POOLE *Barbary Corsairs* I. ix. 96 He laid waste the Apulian coast.

fig. **1660** H. MORE *Myst. Godl.* I. v. 14 [This] is a sign they are stark naught, and that Pride has laid wast their Intellectuals. **1680** W. A[LLEN] *Persuas. Peace & Unity* Pref. p. xlviii. Because they laid waste Charity in a great measure by their divisions and contentions. **1845-6** TRENCH *Huls. Lect.* Ser. II. viii. 275 To hinder him from utterly laying waste his moral life.

†**4. a.** Of speech, thought, or action: Profitless, serving no purpose, idle, vain. *Obs.*

1303 R. BRUNNE *Handl. Synne* 1552 þys nunne was of dedys chaste, But þat she spake wurdys waste She made many of here felawys þenke on synne for her sawys. *Ibid.* 1586 Here wurdys were al vyle & waste. *c* **1330** —— *Chron. Wace* (Rolls) 9359 þe kyng sey þe sege was wast. *c* **1340** HAMPOLE *Pr. Consc.* 2184 Haly men thogh[t] þis lyf bot wast, þarfor þair yhernyng til God was mast. **1382** WYCLIF *Gen.* xvii. 14 For he hath maad my couenant wast [Vulg. *irritum fecit*; 1388 he made voide]. *c* **1400** *26 Pol. Poems* iv. 177 Alle þe þouȝtes ben but wast Wiþoute contemplacioun. *c* **1430** in *Pol. Rel. & L. Poems* (1903) 211 My waast expensis y wole with-drawe; Now, certis, 'waast' weel callid þei be, for þei were spent, my boost to blowe. *c* **1440** *York Myst.* xii. 196 Saue þe, dame, from sak of synne, And wisse þe fro all werkis wast! **1465** MARG. PASTON in *P. Lett.* II. 217 For as for any indytementes that we schuld labor a yenst them it is but wast werk. **1583** RICH *Phylotus* (1835) 21 Alas.. suche wishes are but waste, and vnpossible it is, that any suche thing should happen. *a* **1592** GREENE *Alphonsus* IV. iii. 1411 Ile lay my life that, ere this day be past, You shall perceiue these tidings all be waste. **1598** R. BERNARD tr. *Terence, Heautontim.* IV. iv, He shall make but a wast errand [L. *frustra veniet*].

†**b.** quasi-*adv.* In vain, to no purpose. *Obs.*

1418 *26 Pol. Poems* xiv. 76 Spende waste, passyng his rent, For suche a kyngdom haþ ben shent. *c* **1440** *York Myst.* xlii. 87 And spekis now no whare my worde waste. *a* **1585** MONTGOMERIE *Flyting* 690 Gif that my invention wars thine then, Without the whilk thou might haue barked waist.

†**5.** Void, destitute *of. Sc. Obs.*

c **1425** WYNTOUN *Cron.* (Wemyss) lxxxix. 2916 For statut law first ordanit he That.. all ydolis were bot waist Off godheid, and deuillis ware. **1513** DOUGLAS *Æneis* XI. vii. 177 Our large feildis and boundis all betwene Left desolate and waist of induellaris. **1596** DALRYMPLE tr. *Leslie's Hist. Scot.* I. 208 In the meine tyme King Eugenie and the Peychtes Inuadet Britannie wast of men of weir, quhen na campe lay in it.

†**6.** Superfluous, needless. *Obs.*

c **1380** WYCLIF *Wks.* (1880) 5 þei stryuen nyȝt and day who of hem may bilde gaiest wast housis. *Ibid.* 14 þei gederen to hem self many wast and precious cloþes. *Ibid.* 60 Prelatis.. lyue so contrariously aȝenst here [the apostles'] pore lif, in wast seruauntis, in grete fatte hors & nedles. **1382** —— *Eccl.* ii. 26 To the synnere forsothe he ȝaf tormenting and wast bisynesse [Vulg. *curam superfluam*]. *c* **1400** *Apol. Loll.* 75 Sum supprise wiþ seruil chargis our religioun, þat our Lord Ihu Crist wold to be fre, in so wast halowing of sacramentis, so þat þe condicoun of Jewis is more suffurable. **1618** W. LAWSON *Orch. & Gard.* (1623) 34 The waste boughs closely and skilfully taken away, would giue vs store of fences and fewell.

†**7.** Of time, leaves in a book: Spare, unoccupied, unused. Of buildings or rooms: Unoccupied, empty. *Obs.*

1574 *Satir. Poems Reform.* xlii. 140 ȝe se out throw this land How mony waist Kirkis thair dois stand But outher Prayers or Preiching. **1589** GREENE *Orpharion* (1599) 4, I would bestow a little wast time while my Sheepe grase so hard, to holde thee chat. **1615** *Life Death* etc. *Lady Jane Gray* C 2, Offering to close vp the book shee found in the end thereof some few leaues of cleane paper vnwritten;.. shee took penne and inke and in those wast leaues wrote a most Godly and learned exhortation. **1717** BERKELEY *Tour in Italy* Wks. 1901 IV. 253 A large waste inn (i.e. little inhabited for the size, having [been] the country palace of some nobleman). **1725** SLOANE *Jamaica* II. 217 It is frequently to be met with in large waste houses. **1729** LAW *Serious C.* xii. (1732) 200 All the hours that are not devoted either to repose, or nourishment, are look'd upon by Succus as waste or spare time. **1760-72** H. BROOKE *Fool of Qual.* (1809) II. 156, I was locked up and confined in a waste room. *Ibid.* III. 63, I took up my lodging in a waste hut. *Ibid.* 69 We took shelter in a waste barn.

†**8.** Of a person: ? Worthless. *Obs.*

1616 B. JONSON *Epigr.* xlvi, Is this the Sir, who, some wast wife to winne A knight-hood bought, to goe a wooing in?

9. a. Of materials, incidental products, etc.: Eliminated or thrown aside as worthless after the completion of a process; refuse.

1677 MOXON *Mech. Exerc.* Pref. A 3, How waste and useless would many of the Productions of this and other Countries be, were it not for Manufactures? **1842** LOUDON *Suburban Hort.* 389 Temporary manures, such as soot, bone-dust,.. waste yeast.. and liquid manures,.. are most advantageously applied on the surface of the ground. **1857** DICKENS *Dorrit.* I. ix, The waste droppings of the pump. **1868** JOYNSON *Metals* 38 One striking feature of the practical science of the day is the attempts which it has made.. to utilise the waste products of our manufactures. **1900** *Jrnl. Soc. of Dyers* XVI. 5 It is obtained from the waste liquors. **1907** J. A. HODGES *Elem. Photogr.* (ed. 6) 33 To carry off the waste developer and washing water.

b. Said of the excreta of animal bodies.

1836 A. COMBE *Digest.* (1842) 354 Besides the bowels, there are several other channels by which the waste materials of the body pass out. **1908** *Animal Managem.* (War Office) 16 The duty of the kidneys is to filter waste matters from the blood as it circulates through them.

c. ***waste water*** (now freq. written as one word), (*a*) superfluous water, or water that has served its purpose, allowed to run away; (*b*) water that has been used in some industrial process; (*c*) sewage; also *attrib.* as ***waste-water pail, pipe***. ***waste steam***, the superfluous steam discharged from a boiler, or the spent steam discharged from the cylinder of a steam-engine; also *attrib.* in ***waste-steam pipe***.

c **1450** in *Archæologia* LVIII. 301 The goter of breke for þe waste watre. **1712** J. James tr. *Le Blond's Gardening* 212 This Waste-Water is carried away in Drains. **1791** R. Mylne in *Rep. Engin. Thames Navig.* 33 A gauged long weir should be run across the River, at the waste water draw-lock ..and another, upon the Stone tumbling bay. **1839** R. S. Robinson *Naut. Steam Eng.* 122 The waste steam pipe is generally of cast iron or copper, terminating at its upper end in a bell mouth. *Ibid.* 148 The oil, &c., put into the cylinders ..is rapidly carried away through the waste water pipe into the sea. **1846** A. Young *Naut. Dict.* 313 When the steam in the boiler exceeds its proper pressure it raises the valve and escapes by a pipe called the waste-steam-pipe. **1854** Ronalds & Richardson *Chem. Techn.* (ed. 2) I. 100 A current of hot air produced by a fan driven by the waste steam from the apparatus. **1862** *Catal. Internat. Exhib., Brit.* II. No. 6130, Foot bath, hot-water jug, and waste-water pail. **1886** J. Barrowman *Sc. Mining Terms* 70 *Waste-water*, water from old workings. **1976** *Billings* (Montana) *Gaz.* 27 June 6-c/3 The liquifaction process could give off up to 4.8 million gallons of wastewater per day and..there could be another 100 tons of solid waste generated each day by the coal scrubbing process. **1977** *N.Z. Herald* 8 Jan. 2-12/7 (Advt.), C/1073: M. K. Morrison —to discharge wastewater from State Highway No 1 into Alexandra Creek headwaters..in connection with quarrying operations at Cuthill, Albany. **1979** *Arizona Daily Star* 1 Apr. D 3/1 Stephen J. Tencza, former project engineer with the Pima County Department of Wastewater Management, has joined John S. Collins & Associates as a project engineer for the firm's sanitary engineering department.

d. Of manufactured articles: Rejected as defective. Also, (e.g. of sheets of a printed book) produced in excess of what can be used.

1842 *Civil Engin. & Arch. Jrnl.* V. 201/1, 2 per cent. of waste-castings are made. **1888** Jacobi *Printers' Vocab.*, *Waste cards*, defective or rejected cards, usually sold at a cheaper rate than perfect ones. **1892** *Photogr. Ann.* II. p. xxix, Intended for the purpose of using up waste negatives by mounting.

10. As complement in certain phrases. † ***to fly waste***, of a missile, to be discharged uselessly (*obs.*). ***to run waste*** (? rare) = to run to waste (see waste *sb.* 10).

1797 Brydges *Homer Trav.* II. 330 But this good broom-staff ne'er flies waste. **1814** *Q. Rev.* XI. 71 Savages, who suffer the productions of the earth, as well as their own moral and intellectual faculties, to run waste. **1891** M. Muriel Dowie *Girl in Karp.* xx. 274 The talent that was running waste among the village people.

waste (weɪst), *v.* Forms: 3–7 **wast**, 4 **wost(e**, *Sc.* **vast**, 4–5 **waast(e**, 5 **vaast**, 5–6 **wayst(e**, 5–6, 8 **waist**, 6 *Sc.* **vaist**, 3– **waste**. Also 4–5 *pa. t.* and *pple.* **wast(e**. [a. AF., north-eastern OF. *waste-r*, dial. var. of OF. *guaster*, *gaster* (mod.F. *gâter* to spoil) = Pr. *guastar*, *gastar* to devastate, spoil, Sp. *gastar*, Pg. *guastar*, to spend, devastate, It. *guastare* to devastate, damage:—Com. Rom. **wastare*, repr. (with influence from the cognate Teut. synonym **wōstjan*: see weste *v.*) L. *vāstāre*, f. *vāst-us* adj. desert, desolate, whence Com. Rom. **wasto*: see waste *a.* The verb first appears in English in the 13th c., superseding the native synonym weste *v.*, which is etymologically cognate.]

I. Transitive uses.

1. To lay waste, devastate, ravage, ruin (a land or town, its inhabitants, property, etc.).

c **1205** Lay. 22575 [They] scullen þi lond wasten and þine leoden aslan. **1297** R. Glouc. (Rolls) 2880 Þis lond þat was so riche [they] wastede al to noȝte. *a* **1300** *Cursor M.* 19479 Fast þai ras.. Gain hali kirc, it for to wast. **13..** *E.E. Allit. P.* B. 1178 He wast wyth werre þe wones of þorpes. **1463** *Stat. Roll Irel. 3 Edw. IV* p. 185 Brannyng destruyng and wastyng al the said Ormond is lordships. **1535** Coverdale *2 Chron.* xxiv. 7 Athalia & hir sonnes haue waisted the house of God. **1591** Drayton *Harm. Church, Song of Moses & Israelites* v, Euen as the fire doth the stubble wast. **1596** *Edw. III*, III. iii. 21 Some of their strongest cities we haue wonne,..And others wasted. **1631** Gouge *God's Arrows* I. § 70. 117 An Epidemicall plague wasted the whole world for three yeares together. **1667** Milton *P.L.* XI. 567 Where casual fire Had wasted woods on Mountain or in Vale. **1798** Southey *Battle of Blenheim* viii, With fire and sword the country round Was wasted far and wide. **1855** Macaulay *Hist. Eng.* xiii. III. 326 He wasted the lands of the Mackintoshes. **1879** Froude *Cæsar* xvii. 285 He fell suddenly on the Nervii with four legions, seized their cattle, wasted their country.

absol. **1667** Milton *P.L.* XI. 784 For now I see Peace to corrupt no less then Warr to waste. **1849** Aytoun *Lays Scot. Cavaliers* (ed. 2) 73 The Moors have come from Africa To spoil and waste and slay.

2. *Law.* To destroy, injure, impair, damage (property); to cause to deteriorate in value; to suffer to fall into decay. Cf. waste *sb.* 7.

c **1450** *Godstow Reg.* 240 So nathelesse that they shold not hegge, wast, nother turne hit [a wood] into tylthe. **1531** *St.-German's Doctor & Stud.* I. xxiii. 37 To restore the place wasted immedyatlye after the waste done. **1543** tr. *Act 6 Edw. I*, c. 5 And who that is attaynted of wast, shal lese the thing wasted. **1581** Lambarde *Eiren.* II. vii. (1588) 291 If a man command one to set fire on the house of A,..and by kindling the same fire the house of B. is wasted also. **1628** Coke *On Litt.* I. 355 b, In an Action of Wast..the place wasted is the principall. *a* **1676** Hale *Prim. Orig. Man.* II. x. (1677) 236 In the Survey of Gloucester there are reckoned 23 Burgages and Houses; 16 that were demolished for the building of the Castle, 14 that were wasted.

3. To consume, use up, wear away, exhaust, diminish (a thing) by gradual loss; †to reduce in numbers (a family); †to wear out (clothes); †to sell out (an edition); †to evaporate (a liquid). Also with *away*. *Obs.* exc. with mixture of sense 9.

c **1230** *Hali Meid.* 29 Þer as muchel is, eauer se þer mare is, se ma beoð þat hit wasteð. *c* **1350** *Leg. Rood* iii. 746 For so þai trowed þat mens fete.. Suld cum and ga all ouer þat tre So þat it suld wasted be. *c* **1375** *Sc. Leg. Saints* xviii. (*Egipciane*) 1002 Vthyr clathis had I nane þane I brocht oure flume Iordane; bot in few ȝeris clene war þai for grete elde wastit away. *c* **1425** *MS. Sloane 73* lf. 201 Whanne þi colour in þi saflour bagge is al wastid or elles ny by wastid. *c* **1470** Henry *Wallace* IV. 579 Fyfteyn that day he schot to dede of hys hand. Be that his arrous waistyt war and gayne. **1489** Caxton *Faytes of Armes* I. xix. 60 In the meane whyle thy prouysions and stores be wasted awaye. **1513** Douglas *Æneis* x. iv. 28 The ile.. Sa rich of steill it may nocht wastit be. **1559** tr. *T. Geminus Anat.* 4/2 The former impressions bothe are nowe wasted. **1577** Grange *Golden Aphrod.* etc. S iv b, My penne is stubbed, my paper spente, my Inke wasted. **1593** Shaks. *Lucr.* 959 To.. wast huge stones with little water drops. **1604** E. G. tr. *Acosta's Hist. Indies* II. vii. 99 The waxe melts nor droppes not, for that the flame doth waste it by little and little as it riseth. **1617** Moryson *Itin.* II. 3 During the said civill warre..most of the Noble Families were wasted and some destroied. **1639** O. Wood *Alph. Bk. Secrets* 189 Boyle all these [herbs] in white wine till the wine be wasted. *a* **1700** Evelyn *Diary* 12 Dec. 1680, After many daies..the comet was very much wasted. **1708** J. C. *Compl. Collier* (1845) 44 We haue wrought..all the Coal we can, with safety venture to Work or take away; and so by chance haue Wrought, or waisted the Colliery. **1709–29** V. Mandey *Syst. Math., Arith.* 17 Repeat this Process, until all the figures of the Dividend be wasted. **1747** Wesley *Prim. Physick* (1762) 104 It both wastes the Stone and brings it away. **1747** Mrs. Glasse *Cookery* vi. 63 [Gravy Soup.] Let it stew over a slow Fire, till half is wasted. **1799** G. Smith *Laboratory* I. 389 When the vat is wasted, fill it with the lye. **1845** J. Phillips *Geol.* in *Encycl. Metrop.* VI. 702/1 The felspathic portion of the hypersthene rocks of Carrock Fell is so wasted that the crystals of hypersthene and magnetic iron are projected from the surface considerably.

4. a. To consume or destroy (a person or living thing, his body, strength) by decay or disease; to cause to pine, emaciate, enfeeble; to undermine the vitality or strength of. Also with *away*, †*up*.

a **1225** *Ancr. R.* 138 Also wiðuten wisdom, fleschs, ase wurm, uoruret hire, & wasteð hire suluen. *a* **1300** *Cursor M.* 27934 It [lechery] wastes bodi and als catel. *c* **1386** Chaucer *Knt.'s T.* 2162 Loo the ook, þat..hath so long a lif.., Yet at the laste wasted is the tree. *c* **1400** *Laud Troy Bk.* 5787 Menescen myght was almost wast. **14..** *Tundale's Vis.* 882 (Wagner) In stronge fire þai brenned ay, Tille þai were nere wasted away. *c* **1480** Henryson *Cock & Fox* 511 Waistit he wes, of Nature cauld and dry. **1513** More *Rich. III* Wks. 54/1 Ye shal al se in what wise that sorceres and that other witch of her counsel shoris wife..haue by their sorcery & witchcraft wasted my body. **1540** Palsgr. *Acolastus* II. i. H ij, My bely or panche is all wasted quyte vp or shronke to gether (with lankenesse). **1590** Spenser *F.Q.* III. x. 57 But through long anguish, and selfe-murdring thought, He was so wasted and fore-pined quight, That all his substance was consum'd to nought. **1593** Shaks. *3 Hen. VI* III. ii. 125 Would he were wasted, Marrow, Bones, and all. **1628** Ford *Lover's Mel.* IV. iii, The span of time Doth waste vs to our graues. **1686** tr. *Chardin's Coronat. Solyman* 11 A Potion, that should waste him by degrees. **1766** Goldsm. *Vicar W.* xxviii, He feared my daughter's life was already too much wasted to keep me long a prisoner. **1809** *Med. Jrnl.* XXI. 363 These symptoms continued three or four days, and wasted the patients very much. **1815** Scott *Guy M.* iv, He wasted his eyes in observing the stars. **1853** Kane *Grinnell Exp.* xlviii. (1856) 445 We were wasted with ennui. **1861** M. Pattison *Ess.* (1889) I. 33 French wars..which wasted our strength.

†**b.** *refl.* To consume one's strength or faculties.

1630 Bp. Hall *Occas. Medit.* lxxi. (1633) 175 And blessed be the memory of those his faithful Servants, that have left their bloud, their spirits, their lives, in these precious papers; & have willingly wasted themselves into these during Monuments, to give light unto others.

c. To beat up, kill, murder (someone); to devastate a place, to kill its inhabitants. *slang* (orig. and chiefly *U.S.*).

1964 P. Marshall in J. H. Clarke *Harlem* 317 Stomping and wasting our Little People. *Ibid.* 319 You..president.. since Duke got wasted? **1966** J. M. Brewer in A. Dundes *Mother Wit* (1973) 240/2, I wasted (punched) one of the studs. **1971** *Guardian* 2 Apr. 12/2 The intention to 'waste' My Lai. **1975** C. Weston *Susannah Screaming* xxix. 147 They wasted Barrett because he blew their deal. **1977** *Courier-Mail* (Brisbane) 21 Sept. 2/4, I think Simone has been wasted (killed) by the southern heavies. **1981** M. C. Smith *Gorky Park* I. xii. 177 You want to go chasing after the guy who wasted your detective.

†**5. a.** To destroy, annihilate, put an end to (something immaterial, e.g. sin, sorrow). Also with *away*. *Obs.*

c **1325** *Metr. Hom.* 11 He sal wit the haligaste Baptiz you and your sinnes waste. *c* **1340** Hampole *Pr. Treat.* 3 This name Ihesu..wastys discorde, reformes pese. *c* **1400** *Rule St. Benet* (Verse) 844 Befor godes sight I salbe clene, Yf I waste myne euil dedes bedene. *c* **1440** *York Myst.* ii. 52 The more lyght sall be namid þe son, dymnes to wast be downe and be dale. **1477** Earl Rivers (Caxton) *Dictes* 16 Derysion and scornyng putteth away and wastith loue as the fiere doth the bronde. ? *a* **1500** *Chester Pl., Magi's Oblation* 55 Stench of the Stable it [incense] shall wast. **1535** Coverdale *Zech.* xi. 3 The pryde off Iordane is waisted awaye. **1579** Spenser *Sheph. Cal.* Nov. 201 Ceasse now my song, my woe now wasted is. **1591** Savile *Tacitus' Hist.* I. xlii. 24 There is question, whether the present feare wasted his speech, or els that he cried aloude. **1641** J. Jackson *True Evang. T.* III. 173 He doth by his Word and Spirit, waste and take away all hatreds, enmities, and antipathies. **1689** Lady R. Russell *Lett.* II. ci. 42 No time..can ever waste my sorrow.

†**b.** *refl.* To ruin one's prospects. *Obs.*

a **1548** Hall *Chron., Hen. VII* 49 Perkyn, whether it greued him to be kept inwarde, or els..because he woulde wilfully wast & cast away him selfe, studied how to escape & flye away.

†**6.** To spoil, diminish the goodness or virtue of, cause to deteriorate. [Cf. F. *gâter*.] *Obs. rare.*

1572 Huloet (ed. Higins), To waste, or spylle, *conspurco, deprauo, disperdo*. **1669** Sturmy *Mariner's Mag.* v. xii. 66 That time shall not wast it,..mix it with Brandy.

†**7.** To diminish or consume the livelihood of, impoverish (a person). Also *refl.* to spend one's substance, impoverish oneself; also with *out*. *Obs.*

1599 Sandys *Europæ Spec.* (1632) 191 Before they wast out them selves in giving ayde unto him. **1604** Shaks. *Oth.* IV. ii. 187, I haue wasted my selfe out of my meanes. **1655** M. Carter *Honor rediv.* (1660) 54 King Stephen..is said to have wasted the Crown, by the many of them [*sc.* Earls] that he created. **1656** Earl Monm. tr. *Boccalini's Advts. fr. Parnass.* I. lxiv. (1674) 80 Many people having wasted themselves in keeping great Tables. **1727** De Foe *Eng. Tradesm.* I. vi. (1732) 67 He has been oblig'd to trade for less and less, till at last he is wasted and reduc'd.

†**8.** To spend, part with, diminish one's store of (money, property); to spend, pass, occupy (time); to get over (a distance in travelling). *Obs.* (cf. 9.)

c **1381** Chaucer *Parl. Foules* 283 Of maydenys swiche as gunne here tymys waste In hyre seruyse. **1590** Spenser *F.Q.* II. ix. 9 So talked they, the whiles They wasted had much way, and measurd many miles. **1596** Shaks. *Merch. V.* III. iv. 12 Companions That do conuerse and waste the time together. **1600** —— *A.Y.L.* II. iv. 95, I like this place, And willingly could waste my time in it. **1614** Ralegh *Hist. World* II. x. §4. 390 Fourteene Kings of Iuda comming betweene, who wasted three hundred and odde yeares. **1639** Du Verger tr. *Camus' Admir. Events* 321 They related the whole circumstance of their theft, whereof they had wasted a very small matter. *c* **1656** Milton *Sonn. to Lawrence* 4 Where shall we sometimes meet, and by the fire Help wast a sullen day. **1667** —— *P.L.* x. 820 Fair Patrimonie That I must leave ye, Sons; O were I able To waste it all my self, and leave ye none! **1697** Dryden *Æneis* VII. 15 The Goddess wasts her Days In joyous Songs. **1718** Ramsay *Christ's Kirk Gr.* III. xiv, Wasted was baith cash and tick, Sae ill were they to slocken. **1738** Gray *Propertius* iii. 62 Each in his proper Art should waste the Day. **1764** H. Walpole *Otranto* iv, I will withdraw into the neighbouring monastery, and waste the remainder of life in prayers and tears for my child.

9. In unfavourable sense: To spend, consume, employ uselessly or without adequate result. (Now the most prominent use.)

a. To consume, expend, bestow (money, property) uselessly, with needless lavishness or without adequate return; to make prodigal or improvident use of; to squander. Const. *in*, *on*.

1340 *Ayenb.* 19 Me halt ane man wod..þet..þe timliche guodes þet he heþ ine lokinge,..wasteþ and despendeþ ine folyes and ine outrages. **1340–70** *Alex. & Dind.* 292 We holde hit nedful to nime þat nouht may be wastid. *c* **1375** *Sc. Leg. Saints* xii. (*Mathias*) 254 Quhene Iudas saw..þe vngymente wes vastit swa. *c* **1380** Wyclif *Wks.* (1880) 13 Ȝif þei wasten delicat metis and drynkis and ȝeuen nouȝt to pore men. **1382** —— *Luke* xv. 13 And there he wastide his substaunce in lyuynge leccherously. *c* **1450** *Knt. de la Tour* 65 With that that was wasted of her clothes, she might haue clothed .ij. or .iij., the whiche deied for colde. **1596** Shaks. *Merch. V.* II. v. 50 Therefore I..part with him To one that I would haue him helpe to waste His borrowed purse. **1848** Thackeray *Van. Fair* xxxv, His irregularities and his extravagance had already wasted a large part of his mother's little fortune. **1874** Green *Short Hist.* iii. §5. 141 A sixth of the royal revenue was wasted in pensions to foreign favourites. **1884** W. C. Smith *Kildrostan* 78 Your father.. Had wasted his estate with cards and dice.

†**b.** with *away*. *Obs.*

1474 Caxton *Chesse* III. viii. (1883) 147 He that of custome hath had haboundance of moneye and goth and dispendith hit folily and wasteth hit away. *a* **1600** Hooker *Eccl. Pol.* VII. xxii. §5 When Mary to testifie the largeness of her affection, seemed to waste away a gift upon him. **1711** Steele *Spect.* No. 252 ¶2, I have a Sot of a Husband..that wastes away his Body and Fortune in Debaucheries. **1730** A. Gordon *Maffei's Amphith.* 340 Those who had wasted away their Substance.

c. *absol.*

1390 Gower *Conf.* II. 139, I bidde noght that thou do wast, Bot hold largesce in his mesure. **1474** Caxton *Chesse* III. viii. (1883) 147 Yet she doth harme and domage to hym that so wasteth. **1595** Daniel *Civ. Wars* I. lix, Now he exactes of all, wasts in delight, Riots in pleasure. *a* **1641** Mun *England's Treas.* (1664) 218 Let Princes oppress,.. Usurers bite, Prodigals wast. **1855** Bohn *Handbk. Prov.* 551 Waste not, want not.

d. ***to waste words, breath***, † ***wind***: to speak to no purpose; †also *refl.* in the same sense. Similarly ***to waste paper, space*** (i.e. in writing).

c **1400** *Destr. Troy* 9788 But all þaire wordis þai wast, & þaire wynd alse. *c* **1480** Henryson *Cock & Jewel* 159 (Bann.) Of þis mater I do bot waistis wind. **1583** Melbancke *Philotimus* K iv b, Meaning no more at this time to build

Castles in the aire, nor wast my wordes to a deafe man. **1603** SHAKS. *Meas. for M.* II. ii. 72 You but waste your words. *a* **1647** HABINGTON *Surv. Worcs.* I. 91 That I may not heereafter wast my sealfe in tedious repetitions. **1667** DRYDEN *Ind. Emp.* III. iii, In vain complaints you vainly waste your Breath. **1709** BERKELEY *Ess. Vision* §137 As for the idea of motion in abstract, I shall not waste paper about it. **1812** SHELLEY *Address* Prose Wks. 1888 I. 226 A great many words were wasted, and a great deal of blood shed. **1892** *Photogr. Ann.* II. 214 Without wasting any more time and space, I will proceed to describe the drawings. **1905** R. BAGOT *Passport* xxxv. 405 We need not waste words in coming to our point.

e. To spend, pass, occupy (time, one's life, etc.) idly or unprofitably. Const. *in*, *on*, †*to*, and inf. Also with *away*.

a **1300** *Cursor M.* 252 To wast þair liif in trofel and truandis. **1495** *Act 11 Hen. VII* c. 22 §4 Divers artificers.. waste moch part of the day and deserve not their wagis. *a* **1547** SURREY *Æneid* II. 19 The war, Wherin they wasted had so many yeres. **1591** SHAKS. *Two Gent.* I. i. 51 But wherefore waste I time to counsaile thee. **1606** —— *Ant. & Cl.* I. iv. 4 He fishes, drinkes, and wastes The Lampes of night in reuell. **1654** GATAKER *Disc. Apol.* 103 Not to wast pretious time..in dealing with their filth. **1656** COWLEY *Pindar. Odes, Extasie* i, I have no time in Complements to wast. **1725** POPE *Odyss.* VI. 29 Oh indolent! to waste thy hours away! **1741** MIDDLETON *Cicero* I. vi. 418 When Clodius rose afterwards to speak, he endeavoured to wast the time so, as to hinder their coming to any resolution that day. **1837** DICKENS *Pickw.* xv, But I waste your time, sir... I know its value, sir. I will not detain you. **1881** *Temple Bar* LXI. 403, I am afraid mademoiselle allowed you to waste a great deal of time in novel reading. **1884** *Manch. Exam.* 21 May 5/1 The sole aim of the mover..was to waste the time of the House. **1896** HOUSMAN *Shropshire Lad* xi, Lads that waste the light in sighing.

f. To employ, put forth (energy, effort, qualities, talents) uselessly or without adequate return. Also *refl.* Const. *on*, *upon*, *over*.

1340–70 *Alex. & Dind.* 238 Hit wasteþ no wisdam weihes to lere. **1390** GOWER *Conf.* I. 329 And kep that thou thi witt ne waste Upon thi thoght in aventure. **1728** YOUNG *Love of Fame* iii. 71 Not all on books their criticism waste. **1854** MAURICE *Mor. & Met. Philos., Philos. 1st 6 Cent.* 90 It seems to us that in general too many lamentations are wasted over lost books. **1856** *N. Brit. Rev.* XXVI. 258 The temporary character of the subjects on which he wasted himself. **1868** RUSKIN *Pol. Econ. Art* i. 76 We..waste our labour on things that vanish. **1872** MORLEY *Voltaire* i. 10 Good causes lost, and noble effort wasted. **1878** JEVONS *Primer Polit. Econ.* 30 No one is so foolish as to spend his labour in a place where it would be wasted altogether. **1886** 'MAXW. GRAY' *Silence Dean Maitl.* I. x, He did not, however, waste much thought on this trivial incident. **1891** FARRAR *Darkn. & Dawn* lxvi, To..retire to Spain with the memories of talents wasted, for the most part, over things vain and vile.

g. To bestow *on* unappreciative recipients.

1750 GRAY *Elegy* 56 Full many a flower is born to blush unseen, And waste its sweetness on the desert air. **1812** BYRON *Ch. Har.* I. xviii, Why, Nature, waste thy wonders on such men?

h. In *passive* (without distinct reference to an agent). Of something appealing to intelligence or sensibility: To fail to be appreciated; to make no impression *on* a person. Of a person, his qualities or abilities: To have no opportunity for distinction or usefulness.

1898 A. M. BINSTEAD *Pink 'Un & Pelican* 1 Our kindly host..gave it as his unsolicited opinion that two such amusing liars as we were utterly wasted on after-dinner oratory. **1905** 'G. THORNE' *Lost Cause* v. 139 'You ought to have been on the music hall stage, vicar,' Mrs. Stiffe said, 'you're wasted in Hornham.' *Mod.* As I had not read the book, the allusion was wasted on me. He is a profound scholar, but quite wasted as a village schoolmaster.

i. To fail to take advantage of, 'throw away' (an opportunity).

1836 THIRLWALL *Greece* xxvi. III. 455 The secret correspondence..which induced him to waste the irresistible opportunity of a safe retreat. **1856** FROUDE *Hist. Eng.* (1858) I. ii. 111 It was not likely that they would waste an opportunity thrust upon them by Providence.

j. To cause or allow (a substance, physical energy) to be used unprofitably or lost.

1826 *Art of Brewing* (ed. 2) 3 Every particle of matter may be used, and none wasted. **1827** FARADAY *Chem. Manip.* xvii. (1842) 466 If these bridges of communication be small, much power will be wasted. **1860** TYNDALL *Glac.* II. viii. 265 A considerable portion of the heat..is wasted by radiation. **1920** *Conquest* June 400/2 The invaluable by-products are all wasted and escape into the air in the form of smoke.

10. To reduce (paper, books) to 'waste': see WASTE *sb.* 11 d.

1883 *Fortn. Rev.* Apr. 499 Many unsaleable books..are 'wasted', that is, are sent to the mill, ground up, pulped down, and made again into paper.

II. Intransitive uses.

11. a. Of a person or living thing: To lose strength, health, or vitality; to lose flesh or substance, pine, decay; to become gradually weak or enfeebled.

a **1300** *Body & Soul* in *Mapes' Poems* (Camden) 336 In unlust for to lye, waste, wane. **1398** TREVISA *Barth. De P.R.* XVIII. ix. (1495) 762 The adder absteyneth and wastyth many dayes: that his skynne may so the easelyer be departyd fro the flessh. *c* **1400** *Beryn* 1057 A tre without more, That may not bowe, ne bere fruyt, but root & euer wast. *c* **1460** *Wisdom* 437 in *Macro Plays* 50 Wan þey haue wastyde by feyntnes, Than febyll þer wyttis. **1622** WITHER *Faire-Vertue* K4b, Shall I wasting in Dispaire, Dye because a Womans faire? **1630** BP. HALL *Occas. Medit.* lxi. (1633) 144, I had rather waste with worke, then batten with ease. **1635** J. HAYWARD tr. *Biondi's Banish'd Virg.* 210 His griefe augmenting his feaver whilst his spirits hourely wasted. **1775** SHERIDAN *Duenna* III. v, Ye..gormandize, and thrive, while we are wasting in mortification. **1800** *Med. Jrnl.* III. 443 Her appetite declines, her strength and flesh gradually waste. **1840** DICKENS *Old C. Shop* lxiv, In these slow tortures of his dread disease, the unfortunate Richard lay wasting and consuming inch by inch. **1849** C. BRONTE *Shirley* xx, Life wastes fast in such vigils as Caroline had of late but too often kept. **1897** *Allbutt's Syst. Med.* III. 925 The patient is wasting. *Ibid.* VII. 216 Almost simultaneously..the deltoid begins to waste.

b. with *away*.

1387 TREVISA *Higden* (Rolls) II. 371 þe þridde age is elde ..and wasteþ alle away. *c* **1400** *Destr. Troy* 4035 Wyndis wastid away, warmyt the ayre. *c* **1430** *Two Cookery-bks.* i. 25 In cas þe lycoure wast a-way, caste more of þe same wyne þer-to. **1523–34** FITZHERB. *Husb.* §23 If drye wether come, it [the grass] wyll drye and burne vpon the grounde, and waste away. **1611** BIBLE *Job* xiv. 10 But man dyeth, and wasteth away. **1711** ADDISON *Spect.* No. 289 ¶2 Were we not counted out by an intelligent Supervisor, we should sometimes be over-charged with Multitudes, and at others waste away into a Desart. **1747** WESLEY *Prim. Physick* (1762) 96 *note*, Such a degree of Scurvy as causes the Flesh to waste away. **1775** JOHNSON *Tax. no Tyr.* 19 From this time Independence perceptibly wasted away. **1841** J. H. NEWMAN *Corr.* (1917) 163 For centuries she [*sc.* the Church] has been wasting away, because persons have made the best of things and palliated serious faults. **1848** DICKENS *Dombey* xlviii, I know I'm wasting away... Burgess and Co. have altered my measure, I'm in that state of thinness.

c. *Sport.* To reduce one's weight by training. Also *refl.* (with *down*).

1763 COLMAN *Jealous Wife* v. 82, I have waisted three Stone at least. **1832** *P. Egan's Bk. Sports* 186/1 Fitzpatrick [a jockey] caught cold in wasting, and died in the prime of life. **1833** *Q. Rev.* XLIX. 398 Being occasionally called upon to waste, he [a jockey] feels the inconvenience of his disorder. **1856** H. H. DIXON *Post & Paddock* xii. 208 He resumed the sweaters, and wasted himself down to a ghastly 7 st. 3 lb. shadow. **1880** W. DAY *Racehorse in Training* xvii. 167 When my father trained, he often wasted by walking on the Downs.

12. a. Of material things: To be used up or worn away; to lose substance or volume by gradual loss or wear or decay. †Of the moon: To wane (*obs.*).

c **1375** *Sc. Leg. Saints* l. (*Katherine*) 126 All ydolis of stok & stane mone nedling rot, & wast, & wane. *c* **1386** CHAUCER *Knt.'s T.* 2165 Considereth eek how that the harde stoon, Vnder oure feet on which we trede and goon, Yit wasteth it as it lyth by the weye. *c* **1400** MAUNDEV. (1919) 39 And þanne þei schewen the bussch þat brenned & wasted nought. *a* **1548** HALL *Chron., Edw. IV* 232 Promysynge mountaynes of golde, whiche turned into snowe and wasted to water. **1579** LYLY *Euphues* (Arb.) 106 Euphues had rather shrinke in the wetting then wast in the wearing. **1600** SURFLET *Country Farm* I. ix. 42 He shall mowe and cut downe his corne with sythe, the moone wasting. **1618** W. LAWSON *Orch. & Gard.* vi. (1623) 12 Dry wall of earth, and dry Ditches, are the worst fences saue pales or railes, and doe waste the soonest. **1622** J. TAYLOR (Water P.) *Shilling* B5, The whilst a Candle in the Kitchin wasts. **1625** BACON *Ess., Plantations* (Arb.) 533 Cramme not in People, by sending too fast, Company, after Company; But rather hearken how they waste, and send Supplies proportionably. **1747** *Gentl. Mag.* XVII. 28/2 In two months time, the liquor will waste a quart. **1873** GOSSE *On Viol & Flute* 53 Plashing with slow feet The warm and tidal pools that wasted there. *a* **1918** D. W. FORREST in *Mem.* etc. (1919) 160 'The more the marble wastes', said..Michael Angelo, 'the more the statue grows'.

b. Of riches, non-material things: To be consumed or spent; to dwindle or disappear by gradual loss or diminution.

a **1400–50** *Wars Alex.* 3254 (Dubl. MS.) All þe welth of þis werld waystes be þe last To caryon & corrupcion. *c* **1410** LYDG. *Life Our Lady* lxiii. (MS. Ashm. 39) 85 Of parfite riches hit is tresoryeie Whiche may not waste but Iliche abide. *c* **1460** CAPGRAVE *Chron. Eng.* (Rolls) 104 In his tyme that empire wasted and went to nowt. **1530** PALSGR. 772/1 All thyng wasteth but the grace of God. **1598** CHAPMAN *Hero & Leander* iii. 35 Joy grauen in sence, like snow in water wasts. **1656** COWLEY *Mistress, Bathing in River* iii, And with swift current to those joys they haste, That do as swiftly waste. **1657** AUSTEN *Fruit Trees* II. 30 As grace growes, Corruption wasteth or is kept under. **1715** WATTS *Div. Songs, Sluggard* 12 His money still wastes, till he starves or he begs. **1827** KEBLE *Chr. Y., 2 Sund. Lent*, If the treasures of thy wrath could waste. **1834** HT. MARTINEAU *Farrers* iv. 60 Her traffic declined, her wealth wasted, and she knew, at length, the curse of pauperism.

†**13.** To lose quality, deteriorate, spoil. (Cf. 6.)

1669 STURMY *Mariner's Mag.* v. xii. 66 How to make Powder [so that] it shall not wast with time.

14. Of time: To pass away, be spent. (Often conjugated with *be*.) Also const. *away*.

c **1385** CHAUCER *L.G.W.* 2678 The nyght is wastid, and he fyl a slepe. *c* **1400** *Destr. Troy* 4030 Comyn was by course þat the cold wyntur Was wastid & went with his wete shoures. **1540** *Test. Ebor.* (Surtees) VI. 99 The lif of man upon erthe dothe daylie waist and drawith towarde our ende. *a* **1586** SIDNEY *Arcadia* IV. Ecl. (1598) 430 The day was so wasted that onely this riming Sestine..could obtaine fauour to be heard. **1634** FORD *Perk. Warbeck* I. iii, The night doth waste. **1687** DRYDEN *Hind & P.* III. 596 So long they flew with inconsiderate haste, That now their afternoon began to waste. **1759** *Ann. Reg.* 39/1 The season wasted apace. **1767** STERNE *Tr. Shandy* IX. viii, I will not argue the matter: Time wastes too fast. **1834** LANDOR *Exam. Shaks.* Wks. 1846 II. 266 We are losing the day; it wastes toward noon and nothing done. **1847** C. BRONTE *Jane Eyre* xxv, The month of courtship had wasted. **1881** 'MARK TWAIN' *Prince & Pauper* xvii. 187 The afternoon wasted away. **1961** W. VAUGHAN-THOMAS *Anzio* i. 8 The year wasted to an end. **1978** J. A. MICHENER *Chesapeake* 282 The boys were only eight and seven, but already the years were wasting.

waste, obs. form of WAIST.

'waste-book. *Book-keeping.* [WASTE *a.*] A rough account-book (now little used in ordinary business) in which entries are made of all transactions (purchases, sales, receipts, payments, etc.) at the time of their occurrence, to be 'posted' afterwards into the more formal books of the set.

In the simpler forms of book-keeping the DAY-BOOK and the JOURNAL were not distinguished from the waste-book.

1613 J. SARIS *Voy. Japan* (Hakl. Soc.) 115 As apeares in the wast booke. **1615** R. COCKS *Diary* (Hakl. Soc.) I. 45 Broad cloth; measurd, as apereth per perticulers in the wast book. **1673** T. BROWNE (*title*), The absolute Accomptant.. consisting of a memorial (vulgarly called a 'Waste book') and a 'Cash book'. **1689** *Lond. Gaz.* No. 2480/4 With a practical Waste-book, Journal and Ledger. **1706** PHILLIPS s.v. *Post an Account*, To transcribe, or enter what is written in a Merchant's Waste-Book into the Journal. **1818** SCOTT *Rob Roy* ii, This is a kind of waste-book, Owen, in which all the transactions of the day, emptions,..draughts, commissions, and advices, are entered miscellaneously. **1831** *Sutherland Farm Rep.* 84 in *Libr. Usef. Knowl., Husb.* III, The waste-books..are carried on from week to week throughout the year. **1849** FREESE *Comm. Class-bk.* 95 The Waste-Book, called also sometimes the Day-book or Diary.

wasted ('weɪstɪd), *ppl. a.* [f. WASTE *v.* + -ED[1].]

1. Laid waste, devastated, ravaged, ruined.

c **1440** *Promp. Parv.* 517/2 Wastyd, *vastatus*. **1500–20** DUNBAR *Poems* xiv. 29 Sa mony waistit wawis. **1587** in *Border Papers* (1894) I. 259 This ruinose and waysted cuntre. **1588** SHAKS. *Tit. A.* v. i. 23 As I earnestly did fixe mine eye Upon the wasted building. **1671** MILTON *P.R.* III. 102 If young African for fame His wasted Country freed from Punic rage. **1697** DRYDEN *Virg. Georg.* I. 689 Perfidious Mars..o'er the wasted World in Triumph rides. **1813** SCOTT *Trierm.* III. i, Of wasted fields and plundered flocks The Borderers bootless may complain. **1855** MACAULAY *Hist. Eng.* xx. IV. 514 The sufferings of the thrice wasted Palatinate. **1871** FREEMAN *Norm. Conq.* (1876) IV. xviii. 197 Destroyed or wasted houses.

2. a. Diminished or reduced in substance, bulk, strength, health, etc.; worn, decayed.

1508 DUNBAR *Tua Mariit Wemen* 90 A waistit wolroun. **1561** T. NORTON *Calvin's Inst.* II. 112 Neither may we pretend this excuse that we want power, and like wasted detters be not able to pay. **1590** SHAKS. *Mids. N.* v. i. 382 Now the wasted brands doe glow. **1653** WATERHOUSE *Apol. Learn.* 74 No more then it follows that a wasted man must get a child unhail, because he himself is consumptive. **1709** T. ROBINSON *Nat. Hist. Westmorld. & Cumbld.* vii. 47 Laid to Fallow, that it may..recover its wasted Strength. **1785** COWPER *Task* I. 128 Youth repairs His wasted spirits quickly. **1849** C. BRONTE *Shirley* xi, Keeping her pale face and wasted figure as much out of sight as she could. **1867** MORRIS *Jason* I. 372 And the thin, wasted, shining summer rills Grew joyful with the coming of the rain. **1883** D. C. MURRAY *Hearts* xv, 'You are better, Moore?' Tom asked... 'No,' said the farmer in a wasted voice. **1919** *Blackw. Mag.* Aug. 166/2 Ribs and bones showed through their wasted bodies.

†**b.** Morally marred or defiled. *Obs.*

1483 CAXTON *Golden Leg.* 188/b 2 Thou comest..whyche arte pure and clene to be baptysed and wasshen of me that am foule and wasted.

3. Spent, put forth, bestowed, used, unprofitably; squandered; misused; 'thrown away'.

1741 WATTS *Improv. Mind* I. xx. §12 But let them take great care lest they intrench upon more necessary employments, and so fall under the charge and censure of wasted time. **1781** COWPER *Conversation* 357 Our wasted oil unprofitably burns. **1785** —— *Task* IV. 225 A world..most pleas'd when idle most; Whose only happy are their wasted hours. **1883** WHITELAW *Sophocles, Oedipus King* 365 Say what thou wilt: 'twill be but wasted breath. **1894** LADY M. VERNEY *Verney Mem.* III. 352 His blighted hopes and wasted opportunities.

4. Of time: Gone by, elapsed.

c **1600** SHAKS. *Sonn.* cvi, When in the Chronicle of wasted time, I see discriptions of the fairest wights. **1781** COWPER *Retirement* 13 The remnant of his wasted span.

5. Intoxicated (from drink or drugs). Chiefly used outside the U.K.

1968–70 *Current Slang* (Univ. S. Dakota) III–IV. 135 *Wasted, a.* Drunk; unable to function. **1972** J. S. GUNN in G. W. Turner *Good Austral. Eng.* iii. 56 Being under the influence is..*turned on, wasted.*

wasteful ('weɪstfʊl), *a.* Forms: see the sb. and -FUL. [f. WASTE *sb.* + -FUL.]

1. That causes devastation, desolation, or ruin; that destroys or lays waste.

a. of a person or animal, thing personified, personal action or attribute. ? *Obs.*

a **1300–1400** *Cursor M.* 18230 (Gött.) þu prince of tinsel and þu duke Of wastful werk, sir belzabuk. **1576** FLEMING tr. *Caius' Dogs* (1880) 32 What man..with more vehemency of voyce giveth warning eyther of a wastefull beaste, or of a spoiling theefe than this [dog]? **1579** SPENSER *Sheph. Cal.* Jan. 2 When Winters wastful spight was almost spent. **1596** SHAKS. *Hen. V*, I. ii. 283 Wastefull vengeance. **1615** G. SANDYS *Trav.* IV. 218 England..defended by the Sea from wastfull incursions. **1667** MILTON *P.L.* x. 620 Yonder World, which I So fair and good created, and had still Kept in that state, had not the folly of Man Let in these wastful Furies. **1783** BURKE *Sp. Fox's E. India Bill* Wks. 1842 I. 282 The several irruptions of Arabs, Tartars, and Persians into India were, for the greater part, ferocious, bloody, and wasteful in the extreme. **1819** SCOTT *Leg. Montrose* xvii, He collected his scattered forces from the wasteful occupation in which they had been engaged.

quasi-*adv.* **1728–46** THOMSON *Spring* 122 Insect armies.. wasteful eat Through buds and bark into the blackened core Their eager way.

b. of a thing, its action. Now *rare*.

c **1590** MARLOWE *Jew of Malta* III. 287 First will we race the City wals our selues,..And..Open an entrance for the wastfull sea. **1600** FAIRFAX *Tasso* VIII. lxxii, Mongst them Alecto strowed wastefull fire. **1671** MILTON *P.R.* IV. 461 [Storms] being oft times noxious where they light On man, beast, plant, wastful and turbulent. **1712** BLACKMORE *Creation* I. 747 But not impel them o'er their bounds of sand, Nor force the wasteful deluge o'er the land. **1830** LYELL *Princ. Geol.* I. 266 The wasteful action [of water] is very conspicuous at Dimlington Height. **1833** HT. MARTINEAU *Tale of Tyne* ii. 28 These wasteful fires were a terrible nuisance.

2. Useless, worthless; unused.

†**a.** Of desires, words, etc.: Empty, vain, profitless. Of time: Unoccupied, spare. *Obs.*

c **1440** *Jacob's Well* 303 þow3 þou be poore..þou mayst haue þis grauel of wast in þin herte in wastfull & feruent desyris, wyllys, & dely3tes. *Ibid.* 304 þe secunde fote depthe is wast of þi mowth, þat is, wastfull woordys, whann þou spekyst all of þi good, of þi rycches, [etc.]. *a* **1547** SURREY *Paraphr. Eccl.* ii. 32 But when I made my compte with howe great care of mynd..that I had sought, so wastfull frutt to fynde Then was I streken strayte. **1573** ABP. PARKER *Corr.* (Parker Soc.) 426, I was the bolder to take mine occasion thus *equitare in arundine longa*, so spending my wasteful time within mine own walls. **1577** FULKE *Confut. Purg.* I. iii. 216 That I haue alleaged already is sufficient to represse that vaine and vnskilfull insultation, that you vse in so many wastfull wordes against vs.

b. Refuse, waste. *rare.*

1868 LYNCH *Rivulet* (ed. 3) CII. i, For He, the Sower, must return..The wheat to garner, and to burn Of tares the wasteful heap.

3. Of a place: Desolate; unused, unfrequented, uninhabited, void. *Obs.* exc. *arch.* and *poet.*

1572–3 ABP. PARKER *Corr.* (Parker Soc.) 419, I would remove some part of an old, decayed, wasteful, unwholesome, and desolate house at Ford, to enlarge the little house I have at Bekesborne. **1579** SPENSER *Sheph. Cal.* June 50 Thy rymes and roundelayes, Which thou were wont on wastfull hylls to singe. *Ibid.* Dec. 23, I went the wastefull woodes and forest wyde. **1642** H. MORE *Song of Soul* To Rdr., Thus sing I..To wastefull woods, to empty groves. **1667** MILTON *P.L.* II. 961 When strait behold the Throne Of Chaos, and his dark Pavilion spread Wide on the wasteful Deep. **1712** BLACKMORE *Creation* II. 119 A wasteful, cold, untrodden wilderness. **1827** POLLOK *Course of Time* III. 261 At the midnight hour..in wasteful hall,..Thou mightst have seen him bending o'er his heaps, And holding strange communion with his gold. **1883** BRIDGES *Prometheus* 43 When he had taken the throne and chained His foes in wasteful Tartarus. **1890** E. H. BARKER *Wayfaring in France* 313 The Druids of old, who sought these wasteful places as the fittest for the worship of that Mystery.

as *complement*. **1618** AINSWORTH *Ps.* cxxxvii, Daughter of Babel, wastful layd.

4. Of a person, his disposition, etc.: Addicted to waste; given to useless or excessive expenditure; regardless of economy in the management or use of resources; prodigal, extravagant, thriftless.

1538 ELYOT *Dict.*, *Prodigus*, prodigall, wastefull, an outragious expender. **1540** PALSGR. *Acolastus* Prol. B ij b, The gospell reherseth the lyfe of the prodigal son .i. of the wastfull spendyng chylde by a knowen parable. **1570** LEVINS *Manip.* 186/32 Waystfull, *dispendiosus*. **1597** HOOKER *Eccl. Pol.* v. lxxvii. §4 As in the Gospell that wastfull young man which returned home to his Fathers house was with ioy both admitted and honoured. **1604** ROWLANDS *Looke to it* 40 You carelesse wretches of the wastfull vaine, That for your Families will not prouide. **1662** HIBBERT *Body Divinity* I. 186 They that lose time are the greatest losers and wastfullest prodigals. *a* **1768** SECKER *Serm.* (1770) III. vii. 170 For it is hardly to be hoped, but that our Negligence about their Conduct will tempt them, either to be dishonest, or idle, or wastful, in our Service.

b. Of expenditure, style of living, etc.: Characterized by waste or extravagance.

1451 CAPGRAVE *St. Gilbert* 69 In his riding had he no costful hors, no wastful aray, not many hors, ne many seruantis. **1540** PALSGR. *Acolastus* v. iv. Z iij, By prodygalitie or wastfull spendyng. **1595** SHAKS. *John* IV. ii. 16 Or with Taper-light To seeke the beauteous eye of heauen to garnish Is wastefull, and ridiculous excesse. **1849** MACAULAY *Hist. Eng.* iii. I. 289 By plundering the public creditor, it was possible to..support..the wasteful expenditure of the court. **1885** TENNYSON *Anc. Sage* 5 One..richly garb'd, but worn From wasteful living. **1885** *Manch. Exam.* 6 May 5/2 No society..is more free from the drawback of wasteful expense in management.

†**c.** Beneficently extravagant, lavish. *Obs. rare.*

1701 ADDISON *Let. fr. Italy to Ld. Halifax* 106 How has kind Heaven adorned the happy land, And scattered blessings with a wasteful hand!

5. Of a person, an action, process, etc.: That wastes, consumes or expends unprofitably (something specified or implied); not economical. Const. *of*.

1587 MASCALL *Govt. Cattle, Of Oxen* (1596) 72 Some do vse to feede them on the ground without a racke, but that is thought to be..more wastfull of hay. **1825** J. NICHOLSON *Oper. Mech.* 171 A wasteful condensation of the newly introduced steam must take place. **1837** W. IRVING *Capt. Bonneville* III. 263 Rival parties of trappers soon exhaust the streams, especially when competition renders them heedless and wasteful of the beaver. **1874** H. H. COLE *Catal. Ind. Art S. Kens. Mus.* 234 The material..is in itself of such beautiful texture that it seems wasteful of good things to cover it with embroidery. **1892** *Photogr. Ann.* II. 203 It seems to me rather wasteful to spend a lot of extra money on half-plate slides, and then only use them for quarters. **1893** *Bookman* June 85/2 He knows what he can do, and, avoiding any wasteful dissipation of his powers, does that efficiently.

†**b.** of a thing. *Obs.*

1607 SHAKS. *Timon* II. ii. 171 When euery roome Hath blaz'd with Lights,..I haue retyr'd me to a wastefull cocke, And set mine eyes at flow. **1618** W. LAWSON *Orch. & Gard.* xi. (1623) 33 The greater Trees..haue filled and ouerloaden themselues with a number of wastfull boughs and suckers.

6. That causes bodily waste or decay. Now *rare.*

1600 SHAKS. *A.Y.L.* III. ii. 341 The one sleepes easily because he cannot study,..lacking the burthen of leane and wasteful Learnings. **1824** MISS FERRIER *Inher.* xcvi, Using every argument to rouse her from this wasteful excess of grief. **1829** I. TAYLOR *Enthus.* ix. 241 Self-inflicted penances, wasteful abstinences,..and all such like spontaneities.

wastefully (ˈweɪstfʊlɪ), *adv.* [f. WASTEFUL *a.* + -LY².] In a wasteful manner.

1. In a manner involving waste; without regard to economy; prodigally, extravagantly, thriftlessly.

1513 WOLSEY in *Lett. & Papers War France* (1897) 167 That ye wol not out of the havons, but lye ther spendyng wastefully the King's vitaill and money. **1624** DONNE *Serm.* ii. (1640) 14 Never say, God hath given me these and these temporall things, and I have scattered them wastfully, surely he will give me no more. **1675** DRYDEN *Aurengz.* III. (1676) 35 Fortune..to her new-made Favourite, Morat, Her lavish hand is wastefully profuse. **1879** *Cassell's Techn. Educ.* II. 33/2 Formerly the workings were carried on with less system and more wastefully than now. **1885** *Manch. Exam.* 21 Oct. 5/6 The tin clippings are wastefully thrown into the river.

†**2.** Destructively, ruinously. *Obs. rare.*

c **1557** ABP. PARKER *Ps.* cii. 286 Ah God my God to wastefully Cut not my dayes by halfe away Where thy yeares last eternally. **1791** MME. D'ARBLAY *Diary* July, Scarce any misfortune..can so wastefully desolate the very soul of my existence as a banishment..from those I love.

ˈ**wastefulness.** [-NESS.]

1. The quality of being wasteful; prodigality in expenditure; want of economy.

1551 T. WILSON *Logic* II. I viij b, Liberalitie is a vertue. Therfore liberalitie maie not be called wastefulnes. **1603** HOLLAND *Plutarch's Mor.* 212 Even so be these wretches more odious..who by their miserable parsimonie..doe mischiefe, than those who by their riot and wastfulnesse be hurtfull to a common-weale. *a* **1768** SECKER *Serm.* (1770) III. 251 Wastefulness also, and even mere Negligence, approach to the same Sin. **1839** DICKENS *Nickleby* xxxiv, I really cannot afford to encourage him in all his wastefulness. **1884** *Harper's Mag.* Oct. 781/2 A lamentable wastefulness of the public funds.

†**2.** The state of being waste or void. *Obs. rare.*

1674 N. FAIRFAX *Bulk & Selv.* 195 Having taken away altogether that boundless wastfulness beyond the world, we are no whit careful, about the light or darkness of it.

†ˈ**waste-good.** *Obs.* [f. WASTE *v.* + GOOD *sb.* (sense 7). Cf. *scatter-*, *spend-*, *stroy-good*.] A spendthrift.

1585 HIGINS *Junius' Nomencl.* 523/2 *Barathro*,..a spend all: a waste-good. **1592** NASHE *P. Penilesse* B 2 b, If hee haue playde the waste-good at the Innes of the Court. *a* **1639** W. WHATELEY *Prototypes* II. xxvi. (1640) 69 The worldly-minded man, though hee live in better reputation on Earth, hath no better reputation in Heaven than the waste-good. **1681** W. ROBERTSON *Phraseol. Gen.* 1295 A waste-good, or spend-all, *Nepos, decoctor*.

wastel (ˈwɒst(ə)l). *Obs.* exc. *Hist.* Forms: 4–7 **wastell**, (7 **vastell**), 5 **wastelle**, (**wastle**, **wastyl(le**, **wastil**), 9 *Sc.* **wastell**, 4– **wastel**; also, by confusion with *wassail*, 6, 9 **wassell**. [a. OF. *wastel*, north-eastern var. of *guastel*, *gastel* (mod.F. *gâteau*). In Anglo-L. records the word often occurs latinized as *guastellum*, *wastellum*: see examples under SIMNEL and TREAT *sb.*² 2.]

1. Bread made of the finest flour; a cake or loaf of this bread. (See note s.v. TREAT *sb.*² 2.)

[**1194** in Palgrave *Doc. & Rec. Scot.* (1837) I. Illustr. p. xxviii, Habere solebant..singulis diebus..duodecim de dominicis guastellis nostris et totidem de simenellis nostris dominicis et duodecim sextercia vini.] *c* **1300** *Havelok* 878 þe bermen let he alle ligge, And bar þe mete to þe castel, And gat him þere a ferthing wastel. *Ibid.* 779 [see SIMNEL 1]. **1377** LANGL. *P. Pl.* B. v. 293 þow hast no good grounde to gete þe with a wastel. *c* **1420** *Liber Cocorum* (1862) 52 Storve myed wastel with colde ale þen. **1421** *Coventry Leet Bk.* 23 We commaunde 3ou..þat euery Baxster..bake & sell iiij wastels for a peny. *c* **1430** *Two Cookery-bks.* 22 þen take..Roysonys y-hole, or hard Wastel y-dicyd. *c* **1470** *Golagros & Gaw.* 223 Thus refreschit he his folk in grete fusion, With outin wanting in waill, wastell or wyne. **1530** TINDALE *Lev.* xxiv. 5 And thou shalt take fine floure and bake .xii. wastels thereof. *c* **1530** *Assyse of Breade* (Wyer) A iij b, A farthynge Wastell. **1557** R. EDGEWORTH *Serm.* i. 6 b, Like as a Molle if a man would feede her with wine and wastel, she will none thereof. *c* **1638** *Order Priv. Counc.*, in Penkethman *Artachthos* H 3, That no Baker..shall make or bake to bee sold any other..sorts of bread (except Simnell, Wastell, and Horse-bread, allowed by the Lawes..of this Realm).

fig. *c* **1430** *Pilgr. Lyf Manhode* II. iii. (1869) 117, I blowe with thilke belyes the herth to thilke, that of his soule wole make a wastel to the maister devel.

b. *attrib.* as ***wastel bread, cake.***

c **1386** CHAUCER *Prol.* 147 Of smale houndes hadde she þat she fedde With rosted flessh or Milk and *wastel breed. *c* **1430** LYDG. *Min. P.* (Percy Soc.) 184 Thouhe I were fedde with mylke and wastelbrede. **1569** in *N. & Q.* 9th Ser. X. 27/1 Two acres of land called wassell-land, out of which there hath been paid two bushels of wheat yearly, to be made in wassell-bread and given to the poor. **1655** FULLER *Ch. Hist.* VI. ii. §8. 285 The Abbot..had Vastellum, that is, not common bread, but vastell bread, or simnels for his diet. **1820** SCOTT *Monast.* xiii, A skin as white as her father's finest bolted flour, out of which was made the Abbot's own wastel-bread. *Ibid.* xvi, I will send up in secret, not only household stuff, but wine and wassell-bread. **1843** F. E. PAGET *Warden of Berkingholt* 66 Time was, when the wastel-bread, and the mortrel pottage,..were bestowed as a pittance to sixty of the poorest..persons in the neighbourhood. **1820** SCOTT *Monast.* xxvi, Mysie made no answer, but began to knead dough for *wastel-cake. **1912** SIR H. MAXWELL *Early Chron. Scot.* v. 194 From the moment he entered England, the King of Scots [K. Wm.] was to be supplied with twelve royal wastel cakes and twelve royal simnel loaves.

2. *Her.* = TORTEAU I.

1486 *Bk. St. Albans, Coat-arm.* b iv b, Tortlettis be calde in armys wastell. **1562** [see TORTEAU]. *c* **1828** BERRY *Encycl. Her.* I. Gloss.

ˈ**wasteland.** [f. WASTE *sb.* + LAND *sb.*¹; cf. *waste land* under WASTE *a.* This compound is now indistinguishable from collocations of the adjective: see WASTE *a.* I.]

1. a. Land in its natural, uncultivated state. Also *attrib.*

1887 MORRIS *Odyss.* XI. 293 The wasteland neatherds. **1916** *Nature* 12 Oct. 105/1 The most accessible of the wastelands would be selected and the order of planting laid down. **1919** *Contemp. Rev.* Aug. 181 A flock of from thirty to forty meadow-pipits feeding on waste-land.

b. Land (esp. that which is surrounded by developed land) not used or unfit for cultivation or building and allowed to run wild.

1922 W. J. LOCKE *Tale of Triona* x. 116 They walked..through the maze of new and distressingly decorous avenues, some finished, others petering out..into placarded building lots or waste land. **1933** *Archit. Rev.* LXXIV. 166/1 Farm and meadow, hedge and coppice are all part of a system which the urban dweller takes for granted but which agricultural decay can only transform..into wasteland, flood and marsh. **1969** *Daily Tel.* 5 Sept. 18 Within a stone's throw of the Guildhall are wasteland areas created by the bombing of 25 years ago. **1974** A. J. HUXLEY *Plant & Planet* xxix. 359 Land sterilization by building and industrial use, and the subsequent creation of wastelands. **1980** *Daily Tel.* 23 July 2/2 A conference on wasteland, organised in London by Thames Television.

c. *spec.* a waterless or treeless region, a desert. (Not distinguishable from some examples at sense 1 a.)

1966 F. HERBERT *Dune* 399 The stranger might think nothing could live or grow in the open here, that this was the true wasteland that had never been fertile and never would be. **1969** *Daily Tel.* (Colour Suppl.) 3 Oct. 20/4 Horses cannot last long in that pitiless wasteland where no rain has fallen for the last five years. **1979** P. THEROUX *Old Patagonian Express* (1980) vii. 131 We were in a waterless desert: no sign of the river in this parched wasteland.

d. *transf.* and *fig.*, sometimes with allusion to T. S. Eliot's poem *The Waste Land* (1922).

1868 TROLLOPE *Phineas Finn* (1869) I. xxxvi. 310 Young members..who are green from the waste lands and road-sides of private life. **1932** H. NICOLSON *Let.* 15 Apr. (1966) 114 He [*sc.* Sir Oswald Mosley] will be edged gradually into becoming a revolutionary—and to that waste land I cannot follow him. **1934** C. LAMBERT *Music Ho!* v. 281 The composer finds himself in a spiritual waste land. **1964** S. BELLOW *Herzog* 75 The commonplaces of the Wasteland outlook. **1972** *Sat. Rev.* (U.S.) 27 May 7/1 Television's sad wasteland. **1976** *Brit. Jrnl. Sociol.* XXVII. 35 Above all, there is one fundamental chasm which divides this terminological wasteland. **1981** *N.Y. Rev. Bks.* 5 Nov. 34 The once proud and efficient public school system of the United States...has turned into a wasteland.

2. *N.Z.* (See quot. 1875.)

1844 F. MATHEW *Reports* (typescript) II. 18 Any attempt on his part to assert the right of the Crown, without purchase, to what are known as Waste Lands would have immediately been attended with serious results. **1875** J. VOGEL *Official Handbk. N.Z.* 103 Public—or as they are called, 'waste'—lands are sold on several principles. **1930** L. G. D. ACLAND *Early Canterbury Runs* 1st Ser. viii. 205 Godley..was very much against letting the 'waste lands' in large areas.

wasteless (ˈweɪstlɪs), *a.* [f. WASTE *sb.* + -LESS.] Without diminution, unwasting.

1589 GREENE *Tullies Love* Wks. (Grosart) VII. 196 Thou doest wring water out of the flint, fier forth of yᵉ dry sandes,..so that by wastelesse perswasions for thy friende, I am forst to say [etc.]. **1620** MAY *Heir* IV. (1633) G 1 b, Those powers above..That from their wastlesse treasures heape rewards. **1679** in *Roxb. Ball.* (1881) IV. 170 He was become, for England's good, An endless Mine, a wasteless Flood. **1868** A. C. GLYN tr. *Ozanam's Hist. Civiliz.* I. 95 The sun pouring forth a wasteless light. **1886** W. F. WARREN *Serm.* in *Hom. Rev.* Jan. 50 He started those wasteless fires and forces of the sun.

†ˈ**wasteling.** *Obs. rare.* In 8 **wastleing.** [f. WASTE *a.* + -LING.] = WASTER *sb.*¹ 6 a.

1750 R. POCOCKE *Trav.* (Camden) 7 Such of all sorts [of stone ware] as are not perfect are call'd wastleings, and are sold very cheap to hawkers.

wastell(e: see WASTEL.

†ˈ**wastely**, *adv.* *Obs.* *rare*⁻¹. [f. WASTE *a.* + -LY².] Unprofitably.

1382 WYCLIF *Isa.* xxx. 7 Egipt forsothe wastli, and in veyn [Vulg. *frustra et vane*, 1388 in veyn, and idili] shal helpen.

ˈ**wastemaster.** Also Wastemaster. [f. WASTE *sb.* 11 + MASTER *sb.*¹] The name of a type of waste disposal unit. (In quot. 1963 a similar imaginary or futuristic device.)

A proprietary name in the U.S.

1946 *Official Gaz.* (U.S. Patent Office) 5 Nov. 15/1 Wastemaster; Lockley Machine Co. For electrically driven garbage grinders... Claims use since June 14, 1945. **1949**

House Beautiful Feb. 85 Choose from these disposers... Wastemaster—Lockley Machine Co. **1963** *Punch* 16 Oct. 569/1 The wastemasters were able to come into their own and people began buying—..for scrap. **1966** *New Statesman* 13 May 710/4 (Advt.), Mais... 2 beds, k. & b., waste-master. **1973** A. Holden *Girl on Beach* 12, I suppose you've got a washing-machine and a clothes-drier and a wastemaster and a pop-up toaster. **1981** I. A. Gordon in *N.Z. Listener* 27 June 86 You know all about dishmasters and maybe even wastemasters.

'wastements, *sb. pl.*, *rare*. [f. WASTE *a.* + -MENT, after *fragment*.] Waste pieces.

1843 *Peter Parley's Ann.* IV. 95 To carry a few scraps and wastements from the kitchen.

wastene, variant of WASTINE *Obs.*

wasteness ('weɪstnɪs). [-NESS.]

1. The state of being waste.

†**a.** Desolation, destruction, ruin. *lit.* and *fig.* (Chiefly *Biblical.*) *Obs.*

1382 Wyclif *Isa.* xlvii. 11 Ther shal feerli falle vp on thee wastnesse [Vulg. *calamitas*]. —— *Hos.* ix. 6 Thei ben gon fro wastnesse [Vulg. *a vastitate*]. **1535** Coverdale *Isa.* xxiv. 12 Desolacion shal remayne in the cities, and the gates shalbe smytten with waistnesse. **1561** T. Norton *Calvin's Inst.* iv. xii. 74 b, We do now se at hande certaine beginninges of a horrible wastenesse in the Chirch. **1598** Spenser *Wks.* (1882) I. 538 Out of the ashes of disolacon and wastnes of this your wretched Realme of Ireland. **1611** Bible *Zeph.* i. 15 A day of wastenesse and desolation. *a* **1672** Sterry *Freed. Will* (1675) 144 A dark, horrid, and bottomless pit, where all wastness, woe, disorder, deformity..dwell together. **1863** J. G. Murphy *Comm. Lev.* iv. Introd., Trespass is the moral wasteness.

b. The state of lying waste, being wild or uncultivated or barren.

1608 in *Buccleuch MSS. Whitehall* (Hist. MSS. Comm.) I. 76 The present wastenes of that country proveth both the facility and the necessity of the plantation. **1799** S. Robertson *Agric. Perth* 245 Wasteness admits of various degrees. Some land in a state of nature may be worth ten or even fifteen shillings an acre of yearly rent; while other land is not worth so many farthings. **1818** Scott *Rob Roy* xxviii, Under her rays, the ground over which we passed assumed a more interesting appearance than during the broad daylight, which discovered the extent of its wasteness. **1863** J. G. Murphy *Comm. Gen.* i. 14 The wasteness of the land ..has begun to be adorned with the living forms of a new vegetation.

2. An uninhabited or unfrequented region or place. *Obs.* or *dial.*

a **1500** *Hist. K. Boccus & Sydracke* (? 1510) U iv, He shuld fynde wastenes ful great There nethere were drynke ne mete But wylde beastes many one. **1572** Buchanan *Detect. Mary Q. Scottis* (1727) 68 Was not that desolate Waistnes [orig. L. *illa deserta vastitas*], that unhantit Place, abill of itself to put simpill Men in Feir? **1590** Spenser *F.Q.* i. iii. 3 She of nought affrayd, Through woods and wastnesse wide him daily sought. **1600** Fairfax *Tasso* iv. iii, The drearie trumpet blew a dreadfull blast,..Through wastnes wide it roard, and hollowes vast. **1647** Cressy *Exomologesis* 17 Which is able to convert Paradice it selfe into a savage wastnesse. **1876** *Mid-Yorksh. Gloss.*, *Wasteness*, a waste place.

†**'wastening**, *vbl. sb. Obs. rare*$^{-1}$. [f. *wasten v. (f. WASTE *a.* + -EN^{5}) + -ING^{1}.] = WASTING *vbl. sb.*

1604 Abp. York in Lodge *Illustr. Brit. Hist.* (1791) III. 252 As one that honoreth and loveth his most exc^{t} Matie wth all my heart, I wish lesse wastening of the treasor of the realm.

†**'wastening**, *a. Obs. rare*$^{-1}$. In 7 **wastning**. [Formed as prec. + -ING^{2}.] That is undergoing waste or decay.

1647 H. More *Song of Soul* ii. *Infinity of Worlds* lxxxii, Besides that firie flame that was so narre The Planets self, which greedily did eat The wastning mold.

waste-paper.

1. a. Paper cast aside as spoiled, superfluous, or useless for its original purpose. Also *fig.*

1585 Higins *Junius' Nomencl.* 6/2 *Segestria*,..waste paper, or other stuffe, wherein occupiers wrap their seuerall wares. **1589** Nashe *Anat. Absurd.* B ij, [They] pretending forsooth to anatomize abuses,..when as there waste paper beeing wel viewed, seemes fraught with nought els saue dogge daies effects. **1601** Weever *Mirr. Mart.*, To Wm. Couell A 2, This Poem..so long keeping the corner of my studie, wherein I vse to put waste paper. **1682** Dryden *Medal* Ep. Whigs A 4 b, That so much skill in Hebrew Derivations, may not lie for Wast-paper in the Shop. **1730** Swift *Drapier's Hill* 17 His famous Letters [are] made waste paper. **1772** *Hartford Merc.* Suppl. 18 Sept. 4/1 A draft..being laid in the office, as waste-paper, the prisoner Rogers..altered the date, and..carried it to Sir Robert's as a new draft. **1840** *N. Amer. Rev.* L. 317 It was then..he [Botta] sold to an apothecary, at the price of waste paper, the last six hundred copies of his 'History of the American War'. **1853** Mrs. Gaskell *Ruth* xxviii, Will you allow me to send you over my *Times*? I have generally done with it before twelve o'clock, and after that it is really waste-paper in my house. **1869** *Bradshaw's Railway Man.* XXI. 361 The conventions of 1858 and 1862..would thus have been almost rendered mere waste paper. **1905** R. Bagot *Passport* ii. 8 The securities which Monsignor Lelli held..proved to be little better than waste paper.

b. *attrib.*, as ***waste-paper price, trade***; **waste-paper basket**, †**box**, a basket (or box) into which waste paper is thrown; also *fig.*

1859 Geo. Eliot *Adam Bede* xlviii, There was the *waste-paper basket full of scraps. **1880** Miss Broughton *Second Thoughts* ii. x, The almanack..was..angrily torn to shreds, and consigned to the waste-paper basket. **1923** J. S. Huxley *Ess. Biologist* vi. 217 The waste-paper basket of outworn imaginations. *a* **1930** D. H. Lawrence *Last Poems* (1932) 120 All that we know is nothing, we are merely crammed waste-paper baskets Unless we are in touch with that which laughs at all our knowing. **1979** *London Rev. Bks.* 25 Oct. 23/2 Marriage, the Webbs agreed, was the waste-paper basket of the emotions. **1836** F. Mahony *Rel. Father Prout, Songs Horace* v. Wks. (1881) 449 In its October number, just received, and now lying in our *waste-paper box. **1859** *D'Israeli's Cur. Lit.* I. 11 *note*, His noble library was scattered at *waste-paper prices. **1865** Dickens *Mut. Fr.* iii. i, Half the lump will be waste-paper... Can you get it at waste-paper price? That's the question. **1869** W. C. Sandars tr. *Uhland's Poems*, Biog. Mem. 12 The larger portion of the two first editions was eventually disposed of to the *waste-paper trade.

†**2.** Blank or unused paper. *Obs.*

1691 *Lond. Gaz.* No. 2662/4 Lost.., an Affidavit with the Copy thereof, and several Accompts and Memorandums writ in the Wast-Paper thereof.

waster ('weɪstə(r)), *sb.*^{1} Forms: 4 **wastere**, **wastor**, **(waaster)**, 4–5 **wastoure**, **-owre**, **wastur**, 4–6 **wastour**, 5 **wayster**, 5–6 **waister**, *Sc.* **-our**, 6 *Sc.* **westour**, **westar**, 4– **waster**. [Orig. a. AF. *wastere*, *-our*, agent-n. f. *waster* WASTE *v.* This coalesced with the later formation on WASTE *v.* + -ER^{1}. In sense 6 the word may be f. WASTE *a.* or *sb.* + -ER^{1}.]

I. One who or something which wastes.

1. a. One who lives in idleness and extravagance; one who wastefully dissipates or consumes his resources, an extravagant spender, a squanderer, spendthrift. Now chiefly *dial.*, with some notion of sense 6, a worthless person, 'ne'er-do-well'.

1352 *Winner & Waster* 194 'ȝee wynnere', quod wastoure, 'thi wordes are vayne: With oure festes and oure fare we feden the pore.' *Ibid.* 390 Who so wele schal wyn, a wastour moste he fynde, For if it greues one gome it gladdes anoþer. **1362** Langl. *P. Pl.* A. Prol. 22 Summe..In Eringe and in Sowynge swonken ful harde, þat monie of þeos wasturs In Glotonye distruen. *Ibid.* A. v. 24 He bad wastors go worche what þei best couþe, And wynne þat þei wasteden with sum maner craft. **1387** Trevisa *Higden* (Rolls) VII. 445 Þe Kyng was a ravener in gaderynge and a greet wastour in spendynge. **1390** Gower *Conf.* II. 162 Bachus..A wastour was, and al his rente In wyn and bordel he despente. **1470** *Paston Lett.* Suppl. (1901) 137 Which..shuld cause..your frendis to thynk..that ye shuld be a wastour and wuld wast your lyvelod. **1508** Stanbridge *Vulgaria* (W. de W.) C iij b, He is a waster. *Profusus est pecunie.* **1597** in *Spalding Club Misc.* (1841) I. 177 The said Walter did never strik his wyff, nather yit onis fund fault with hir,..althocht scho wes ane westour. **1603** Holland *Plutarch's Mor.* 94 Prodigall ding-thrifts and wasters. **1631** Lenton *Charact.* G 7, A Good Husband... He is the sole happinesse of a good wife, and the torment of a Waster. **1641** D. Ferguson *Sc. Prov.* No. 511 (1785) 20 It is well wairt that wasters want gear. *a* **1697** Aubrey *Lives*, *Hobbes* (1898) I. 347 His lord, who was a waster, sent him up and downe to borrow money. **1741** Richardson *Pamela* IV. 369 This would..instruct him..to avoid being a Squanderer or Waster. **1775** Adair *Amer. Ind.* 407 He who will not work, must..leave the town, as they will not sweat themselves for an healthy idle waster. **1818** Scott *Hrt. Midl.* xxviii, Ye will think I am turned waster, for I wear clean hose and shoon every day. **1877** *N.W. Linc. Gloss.*, *Waster*,..a wasteful person. **1887** J. W. Matthews *Incwadi Yami* ii. 20 The class of wasters which public grumbling bred and fostered. **1896** Baden-Powell *Matabele Campaign* i, A mining population of whites and blacks and 'wasters',..'Wasters?'—oh, it's a South African word, and most expressive; applies to the specious loafer who is so common in this country. **1904** J. Sweeney *At Scotland Yard* viii. 203 Here was a wretched invertebrate fellow, an absolute 'waster'.

quasi-*adj.* **1596** in *Maitl. Club Misc.* (1840) I. 82 The presbiterie findis Johne Graye to have callit sir Bartilmo Simsone, ane wastourfallo, commoun theve, [etc.]. **1728** Ramsay *Last Sp. Miser* xiv, But waster wives, the warst of a'.

b. One who wastefully dissipates or consumes (something specified; in early use money, resources). Const. *of.*

c **1380** Wyclif *Wks.* (1880) 200, & ȝif men..wolden fayn paie, & traueile bisily þerfore in treuþe, & ben not wastouris of here litil good. *c* **1386** Chaucer *Merch. T.* 291 Men moste enquere..Wher she be wys..or wastour of thy good. **1422** Yonge tr. *Secreta Secret.* 131 He is a wastoure of his goodes, and destrueth his roialme whate he may. **1549** Cheke *Hurt Sedit.* (1569) H iij b, But what is a loyteror? A sucker of Honie, a spoyler of corne, a destroyer of fruite, naye a waster of money [etc.]. **1568** Grafton *Chron.* II. 73 A man of an yll lyfe and an inordinate waster of the goodes of the Church. **1611** B. Jonson *Catiline* i. i. B 3, Diuers Roman Knights (The profuse wasters of their patrimonies). **1701** Penn in *Pennsylv. Hist. Soc. Mem.* IX. 72 Learn who have been the wasters of timber. **1815** W. H. Ireland *Scribbleomania* 81 This waster of ink, this defiler of paper. **1842** J. Wilson *Chr. North* (1857) II. 18 No waster was she of her tears, or her smiles. **1883** *American* VII. 6 But the good sense of the majority soon suppressed these wasters of time.

c. An action or habit that causes waste.

a **1633** G. Herbert *Outlandish Prov.* (1640) 11 Building and marrying of Children are great wasters. **1748** Richardson *Clarissa* (1811) I. 75 Gaming, that great waster of time as well as fortune, is not his vice.

2. a. One who lays waste, despoils or plunders; a devastator, ravager, plunderer.

1382 Wyclif *Isa.* xvi. 4 Moab, be thou the lurkyng place of hem fro the face of the wastere [Vulg. *a facie vastatoris*]. *a* **1400–50** *Wars Alex.* 5310 Þe werreour of all þe werd & wastoure of ynde. *c* **1440** *Promp. Parv.* 518/1 Wastowre, of a place, *dilapidator.* **1544** *Supplic. to King* (E.E.T.S.) 42 Truly no lytle wasters, spoylers, and robbers; and that of the most poore. **1575** *Luther's Comm. Gal.* ii. 9 Of a persecuter and waster of the Church, he was made an Apostle. **1583** Babington *Commandm.* viii. (1590) 321 It can not bee, that our heartes should bee right in affections towardes our brethren, and wee spoylers and wasters, or any way harmers of the commodities which they inioy. **1738** Wesley *Ps.* cxxxvii. xi, The Lord shall all thy Pow'r o'erthrow And lay the mighty Waster waste. **1817** Scott *Harold* i. ix, Witikind the Waster. **1868** Morris *Earthly Par.* (1870) I. ii. 649 And press around each new-come man to learn If Harfleur now the pagan wasters burn. **1879** Butcher & Lang *Odyss.* 115 Odysseus..the waster of cities.

†**b.** One who or something which destroys. Const. *of*, *to*. *Obs. rare.*

c **1375** *Sc. Leg. Saints* xviii. (*Egipciane*) 791 þu art..confourt of wrech, waster of syn. *c* **1400** *Cursor M.* 27983 (Cotton Galba) þis licheri es..waster of man-kin. **1646** Hammond *Of Conscience* §67. 35 That only sin continued in for any long time,..was a far greater waster to Conscience.

Prov. **1672** W. Walker *Parœm.* 27 Water is a waster. *Aqua dentes habet.*

3. The designation of a class of thieves mentioned along with 'Roberdesmen' and 'Drawlatches' in a statute of Edw. III. *Obs.* exc. *arch.*

The occurrence of the word in the AF. statute of 1331 is no proof that it was current in English at that date. All subsequent examples merely echo the statute.

1331, **1581** [see Roberdsmen]. **1543** tr. *Act 5 Edw. III*, c. 14 Bycause there hath ben dyuers manslaughters, felonies, and roberies done in tymes past, by people that be called Roberdesmen, wastes [*sic*], and Drawlaches. **1706** Phillips (ed. Kersey), *Wastors*, a kind of Thieves, or Robbers anciently known by that Name. **1890** Conan Doyle *White Company* iv, It shall never be said whilst I am Bailiff of Southampton, that any waster, riever, drawlatch or murtherer came scathless away from me and my posse.

¶ Misused to render AF. **westour** in a statute relating to Wales. *Obs.*$^{-1}$

The AF. word represents Welsh *gwestwr* (f. *gwest* lodging, hospitality + *gwr* man), a vagrant who went about exacting free board and lodging.

1543 tr. *Act 4 Hen. IV*, c. 27 Mischieues, whiche hath happened before this tyme in y^{e} land at wales, by many wasters, rymours, mynstrels, and other vacabondes [orig. *Westours, Rymours, Ministralx & autres vacabondes*].

4. a. An animal that is wasting away or losing flesh, or that will not fatten. Also *attrib.* as †***waster ox.***

14.. in *Walter of Henley's Husb.* (1890) 51 Þe feble ox costithe as moche and more þen þe beste ox for yeff he be a wayster ox he moste be þe more spared. **1614** Markham *Cheap & Good Husb.* ii. [ii.] i. 45 Which [healthfulness of an ox] you shall know by a good taile and a good pyzel, for if the haire..be lost, then hee is a waster and will be long in feeding [for the butcher]. **1681** Chetham *Angler's Vade-m.* xli. §3 (1700) 308 A lean..slender Pike, though he seem to advance in length; yet is commonly a waster, and in a decaying condition;..yet he'll live and be as hungry and greedy as ever. **1895** *E. Angl. Gloss.*, *Waster*, a rabbit or other animal that looks like a dier, wasting away. **1907** *Daily Chron.* 13 Sept. 6/7 In an adjoining shed there was a 'waster' [i.e. a cow affected with tuberculosis], which was so ill that it could not stand up.

b. ***a bad waster***: said of a jockey who has difficulty in 'wasting' (see WASTE *v.* 11 c).

1833 *Q. Rev.* XLIX. 399 He is a bad waster, and is much punished to bring himself to the three-year-old weights. **1849** *Bentley's Misc.* XXVI. 581 Some men are bad wasters, when nothing but very severe exercise, aided by medicine, ..suffices to get off the last twenty-four ounces.

5. a. Something which causes or allows waste or loss of material.

1842 *Penny Cycl.* XXII. 142/1 [Sluices] also act as wasters, to allow the surplus water of a reservoir to escape. **1880** Spurgeon *Ploughm. Pict.* 135 A leaking tap is a great waster.

b. A foreign body in the wick of a candle which causes it to gutter and waste. *dial.*

1788 G. Wilson *Coll. Masonic Songs* 72 (Jam.) Oft on the wick there hangs a waster, Which makes the candle burn the faster. **1877** *Holderness Gloss.*, *Wasther*, a thief in the candle. **1886** *W. Somerset Gloss.*, Waster.

c. *Path.* = COMEDO.

1899 *Allbutt's Syst. Med.* VIII. 752 It is also known as grub, worm, black-head, or 'waster'.

II. 6. Something rejected as waste.

a. An article of faulty or inferior manufacture.

a **1800** Pegge *Suppl. Grose*, *Wasters*, damaged or misshapen goods. North. **1828** [Carr] *Craven Gloss.*, *Waster*, any thing among wares that is damaged or of inferior workmanship. **1829** J. Hunter *Hallamsh. Gloss.*, *Waisters*, articles of cutlery laid aside on account of any imperfection. **1833** J. Holland *Manuf. Metal* II. 360 The former [*i.e.* needles with broken eyes]..are thrown aside as wasters. **1846** Greener *Sci. Gunnery* 135 A great number of barrels declared 'wasters', such as..having holes in the sides, or some other fault sufficient to condemn them in the eyes of a..barrel-maker. **1869** F. Kohn *Iron & Steel Manuf.* 106 If cast in a fireclay mould, the contraction was still irregular, and 10 per cent. of all tyre castings were 'wasters'. **1878** L. Jewitt *Ceramic Art Gt. Brit.* I. iv. 76 A kiln..in and around the remains of which were many vessels —'wasters' as they would be technically called—of various kinds. **1879** *Cassell's Techn. Educ.* II. 177/2 Such lenses, together with those that possess..other defects, are technically called 'wasters'. **1880** P. W. Flower *Hist. Trade in Tin* xiii. 173 Some of the sheets thus thrown out are called menders.., others are called wasters, for which there is always a market at a reduction in price; the worst are called waster waste. **1892** *Athenæum* 30 Apr. 577/1 A pottery, worked at however distant a period, leaves traces of *coccj* and 'wasters'. **1900** *Bath Herald* 15 Sept., Galvanized Corrugated Iron, for Roofing, best quality only, no wasters. **1928** W. B. Honey *Old Eng. Porcelain* i. 15 Nothing short of an undoubted 'waster' can prove conclusively that a particular type was made on the factory site in question. **1950** D. T.-D. Clarke *Roman Pottery Kiln* 4 Pots of similar grey ware have been found at Market Overton..which are undoubtedly wasters. **1961** M. KELLY *Spoilt Kill* II. 81 Pots that were twisted, shrunken and collapsed... Wasters, they called them. **1974** *Canad. Antiques Collector* Sept.-Oct. 27/2 There are remains of many little potteries scattered all over southern Ontario, and mounds of 'wasters' or broken or discarded ware.

b. An animal, bird, etc. which is not good enough to be kept for breeding purposes.

a **1722** LISLE *Husb.* (1757) 405 A young sow,.. having as many as nine pigs, it could not be expected any of them would be so properly fat for wasters, as if she had brought but four or five. **1904** *Nature* 25 Aug. 408/2 But now let him breed from his 'wasters' and he will find that the extracted blacks are pure and give blacks only.

† **'waster**, *sb.*² *Obs.* Also 6 **wayster**. [Of obscure origin.]

1. A wooden sword or a foil used in sword-exercise and fencing.

1455 in Meyrick *Ant. Armour* (1824) II. 144 Furst viij swerds and a long blade of a swerde made in wafters [*read* wasters].. for to lerne the king to play in his tendre age. **1541** *Rutland MSS.* (Hist. MSS. Comm.) IV. 313 For Bryngyng ..of hiltes for the crosse wasters for my Lorde Roose, iiij d. **1561** HOBY tr. *Castiglione's Courtyer* I. (1577) E i b, If going about to cast a dart, or holding in his hande a sworde or any other waster. **1600** HOLLAND *Livy* XL. vi. 1063 Foule worke they made with their wodden wasters and headlesse pikes. **1621** BP. HALL *Heaven upon Earth* §11 Even as with woodden wasters we learne to play at the sharp. *a* **1661** HOLYDAY *Juvenal* (1673) 111 The fencer's staffe or waster.. was call'd *rudis* (as some think) because with such cudgels they practiz'd the rudiments of fencing, before they came in publick to fight at sharp.

2. A cudgel, staff, club.

1533 HEYWOOD *John, Tyb & Sir John* A j b, Nought shulde preuayle me, nother staffe nor waster Within a whyle she wolde be my mayster. **1555** W. WATREMAN *Fardle Facions* App. 327 Let there bee giuen vnto hym by the commune Sergeaunt of the batte .xxxix. stripes with a waster. **1570** FOXE *A. & M.* (ed. 2) I. 92/1 Verianus and Marcellianus.. were beat with wasters or trunshons, after that [they] were hanged.. vpon the gibbet. **1598** STOW *Surv.* (1603) 96 The youthes of this Citie also haue vsed on holy dayes after Euening prayer, at their Maisters doores, to exercise their Wasters and Bucklers. **1611** J. DAVIES (Heref.) *Sco. Folly* (Grosart) 49/2 'A groning horse and grunting wife neuer failes their master': Yes, if the master haue not life to ply them with the waster. ? **1615** LENNARD tr. *Charron's Wisd.* (? 1620) Pref. §10 A 4, A weake arme wanting power and skill well to welde a waster or staffe that is somewhat too heauy for it, wearieth it selfe and fainteth.

3. Fencing with a 'waster'; single-stick, cudgel-play. Also *pl.* esp. in ***to play at wasters***.

1519 HORMAN *Vulg.* 281 Let vs pley at buckeler and at waster in feyre game. This waster [*rudis*] is not laufull. **1594** *Selimus* 1812 in *Greene's Wks.* (Grosart) XIV. 264, I thought my selfe as proper a fellow at wasters, as any in all our village. **1596** NASHE *Saffron-Walden* T 1, To see a Gillian draggell taile.. play at wasters with a quil for the britches. **1630** DEKKER *2nd Pt. Honest Wh.* D 3 b, If o're husbands their wiues will needes be Masters, We men will haue a law to win't at wasters. **1631** GOUGE *God's Arrows* III. §11. 206 Such kind of recreations as.. playing at wasters and foines. **1636** *King & Queen's Entert. Richmond* (Bang) 11 And what can Richard doe, play a little at wasters, and make the blood ..run about his vellowes eares at a Wake.

attrib. **1599–1600** [? G. RUGGLE] *Club Law* IV. i, To night is holy daye, and there will be waster play.

4. *fig.*

? **1615** LENNARD *Charron's Wisd.* (? 1620) §10 A 3 b, Science or Learning is a very good and profitable staffe or waster. **1640** G. ABBOTT *Job Paraphr.* 73 Be perswaded to lay downe the wasters, to give over reasoning the matter. **1646** SIR T. BROWNE *Pseud. Ep.* I. iii. 8 Being unable to weild the intellectual armes of reason, they are faine to betake themselves unto wasters and the blunter weapons of truth.

waster ('weɪstə(r)), *sb.*³ *Sc.* Also 9 **wester**. [Altered form of WAWSPER, influenced by the synonymous LEISTER.] A fishing-spear.

1580, 1634 [implied in WASTERING *vbl. sb.*]. **1815** SCOTT *Guy M.* xxvi, This chase, in which the fish is pursued and struck with barbed spears, or a sort of long-shafted trident, called a waster, is much practised at the mouth of the Esk, and in the other salmon rivers of Scotland. *Ibid.*, Ground the waster weel, man! **1825** JAMIESON, *Waster*, a kind of trident used for striking salmon, Dumfr., Eskdale: the same with *Wester*. *a* **1835** HOGG *Sheph. Wedding* ii. Tales & Sk. 1837 II. 152 My teeth war a' waterin to be in him, but I kend the shank o' my waster wasna half length. **1843** W. SCROPE *Salmon Fish. Tweed* ix. 195, I shall give a description of the clodding, or throwing leister, or waster, as he was used to term it... The spear has five prongs of unequal, but regularly graduated, length.

waster ('weɪstə(r)), *v. Sc.* [f. WASTER *sb.*¹] *trans.* To spend or use extravagantly, to waste.

1821 GALT *Ann. Parish* v. 58 My servant lassies.. wastered every thing at such a rate.. that, long before the end of the year, the year's stipend was all spent. **1823** —— *Entail* II. xix. 184 Since that time he's been neither to bind nor to haud,.. wastring his income in the most thoughtless way.

wasterful ('weɪstəfʊl), *a. Sc.* [f. WASTER *v.* + -FUL.] Wasteful.

1821 GALT *Ayrshire Legatees* i. 5 There's no need, for all the greatness of God's gifts, that we should be wasterful. **1879** MACDONALD *Sir Gibbie* lxii, Hae ye nae sang-thrift, 'At ye scatter't sae heigh, an' lat it a' drift? Wasterfu' laverock! **1894** CROCKETT *Raiders* v. 48 You are michty wasterfu', my laddie! What for are ye wearin' your best claes, I wad like to ken?

Hence **'wasterfully** *adv.*, **'wasterfulness**.

1885 'J. STRATHESK' (J. Tod) *More Bits* xi. 206 She did not quite like some of Bell's remarks about wasterfu'ness and 'thowlessness'. **1891** H. JOHNSTON *Kilmallie* I. x. 178 The shepherd fares sumptuously and spends wasterfully.

wasteriff, var. WASTRIFE.

† **'wastering**, *vbl. sb. Sc. Obs.* Also 6 **vastering**. [f. WASTER *sb.*³ + -ING¹.] The action or process of taking fish with a 'waster'; leistering.

1580 *Reg. Mag. Sig. Scot.* 55/1 Cum omni alia piscatione salmonum.. inter dict. bondas, sive reticulis et modo appellato vastering. **1634** *Ibid.* 70/2 Cum cetera piscatione salmonum.. reticulis aut modo vocato wastering.

† **'wastern**. *Obs.* In 4 **wasternne, -urne**, *Sc.* **wastrone, -ine**. [Altered form (after WASTE *sb.*) of ONorthumb. *wǽstern*, var. of *wésten*: see WESTEN.] A wilderness.

13.. *E.E. Allit. P.* B. 1674 In wasturne walk & wyth þe wylde dowelle. *c* **1375** *Sc. Leg. Saints* xviii. (*Egipciane*) 885 In þis wastrone fra þine haf I dwelt euir contynualy. *Ibid.* 1125,& faste hame syne ȝed.. ewyne throu þe wastrine þat ilke day, þat he come fra þat abbay. ? *a* **1400** *Morte Arth.* 3233 Woluez, and whilde swynne, and wykkyde bestez Walkede in that wasternne.

† **'wastership**. *Obs. rare*⁻¹. [? f. WASTER *sb.*² + -SHIP.] ? Fencing exercise.

1575 *Aldeburgh Rec.* in *N. & Q.* 12th Ser. VII. 227/1 For yᵉ dynners of Jentlemen thᵗ came for wastershippe.. iiiˢ.

wastery: see WASTRY.

'wastethrift. Now *rare*. [f. WASTE *v.* + THRIFT *sb.*¹] A spendthrift.

1608 MIDDLETON *Trick to Catch Old One* I. iii. B 2, Hee's a rioter, a wast-thrift, a brothell-maister. **1611** BEAUM. & FL. *Knt. Burn. Pestle* I. iii. (1613) C 3, Thou art a wast-thrift, and art run away from thy maister. **1868** H. BRANDRETH (*title*) Wastethrifts and Workmen. Of the mode of producing them, and their relative value to the community. **1886** *Pall Mall Gaz.* 5 Feb. 2/1 Let him, as a wholly useless and absolutely dangerous criminal wastethrift, be deprived altogether either of freedom or of life.

† **'waste-time**. *Obs.* [f. WASTE *v.* + TIME *sb.*, after PASTIME.] A means of wasting time; an occupation in which time is passed unprofitably.

1609 ELLESMERE *Sp. Post-nati* 24 Call it either a Passe-time, or Wast-time, as pleaseth you. *a* **1661** FULLER *Worthies, Lincs.* II. (1662) 153 Some think that the Men must be mad as well as the Bull, who can take delight in so dangerous a Wast-Time. **1863** J. C. JEAFFRESON *Sir Everard's Dau.* 166 Busily employed with drawing, or painting, or wool-work, or some other graceful form of feminine waste-time.

wasteyn(e, var. forms of WASTINE *Obs.*

† **'wastie**. *Obs.* [If not an error, prob. f. WAIST *sb.* + *-ie* = -Y.] ? Capacity (of a ship).

1600 HOLLAND *Livy* XXXVII. xxiii. 957 The kings fleet consisted of 37, and those of greater burden and wastie [L. *majoris formae*]. *Ibid.* XXX. 961 The enemies armada consisted of fourescore and nine, all ships of the greatest wastie and making [L. *maximae formae*].

wastil, obs. form of WASTEL.

† **wastine**. *Obs.* Forms: 2–4 **wastine**, 3 **-ene, -in**, 4 **-ayne, -eyn(e, -yne, -en**. [a. OF. *wastine, guastine, gastine*: f. root of *wast* WASTE *a.*] A wild, uncultivated tract of country; a desert region, wilderness.

a **1175** *Lamb. Hom.* 141 Sunnedei smat Moyses þene stan ine þe wastine. *c* **1200** *Trin. Coll. Hom.* 161 Ðis woreldes biwest is efned to wastene, for þat þe hit is ferren atleien holie tilðe. *a* **1300** *Cursor M.* 5801 In wildrin land and in wastin I wil þam bring of þair nocin. **13..** *K. Alis.* 7097 Unicornes they fond in that wasten [*Laud MS.* wastayne]. **1303** R. BRUNNE *Handl. Synne* 6112 An ermyte woned fer ouer a doune, Yn a wasteyne, fer fro þe toune. **1338** —— *Chron.* (1810) 75 Alle mad he [William] wasteyn, pastur, medow & korn. *c* **1375** *Sc. Leg. Saints* ii. (*Paul*) 838 [He] fled allane owt of þe towne, willand in wastine vpe and done.

wasting ('weɪstɪŋ), *vbl. sb.* [f. WASTE *v.* + -ING¹.]

1. The action of laying waste; devastation.

a **1300** *Cursor M.* 27839 [Covetousness causes] manslaghter and suik, wasting and were. **1543–4** *Act 35 Hen. VIII* c. 12 The same Scottes.. make.. burnynges murders wastinges and depopulations in this his realme. **1596** DALRYMPLE tr. *Leslie's Hist. Scot.* II. 83 Except he had left taknes quhair he had beine in Robrie, Spoylzie, and Waisting of the kirkes. **1656** EARL MONM. tr. *Boccalini's Advts. fr. Parnass.* I. iii. (1674) 4 The miserable wasting of their Country.. in.. Civil Wars. **1756** BURKE *Vind. Nat. Soc.* 30 The Horrors that attend the Wasting of Kingdoms, and Sacking of Cities. **1864** SWINBURNE *Atalanta* 164 For wasting of the boar That mars with tooth and tusk and fiery feet Green pasturage [etc.].. I praise her not.

2. The action of using or spending lavishly or to no profit. †Also *concr.*, that which is thus wasted.

a **1300** *Cursor M.* 23850 Ai to spell and noght to spede, wasting it es o godds sede. **1377** LANGL. *P. Pl.* B. v. 25 He bad wastoure go worche what he best couthe, And wynnen his wastyng with somme manere crafte. **1523** in *Acc. Fam. Innes* (1864) 97 His friends tak him and put him in fermance for eschewin of any forther waisting of his saidis landis and gudis. **1867** PUSEY *Eleven Addr.* iii. (1908) 24 He foresaw Adam's wasting of His grace.

3. Gradual diminution or decrease; gradual wear or loss.

a **1425** tr. *Arderne's Treat. Fistula*, etc. 73 Boile þam togidre to þe wastyng of þe iuysez. **1509** in Glasscock *Rec. St. Michael's, Bp.'s Stortford* (1882) 31 Item ressived ffor wastyng of torchis when that jenyns wyfe was beryed and at her monthe mynde, ijd. **1633** P. FLETCHER *Purple Isl.* VIII. xxvi, His clothes all patcht with more then honest thrift, And clouted shoon were nail'd for fear of wasting. **1686** tr. *Chardin's Trav. Persia* 416 Two strong dams.. to prevent the water from wasting. **1770** GOLDSM. *Des. Vill.* 87 To husband out life's taper at the close, And keep the flame from wasting by repose. **1883** D. C. MURRAY *Hearts* xvii, When he remembered how friendly everybody was in his new world, he forgot the rapid wasting of his little fortune.

4. Gradual decay of life or organic tissue; gradual loss of strength and vitality; consumption, atrophy.

1398 TREVISA *Barth. De P.R.* v. lvii. (1495) 174 The bones somtyme ben greuyd of wastynge of humours of the marow. **1538** ELYOT *Dict.*, *Tabo*, a consumption, wastynge, or putrifaction of things. **1567** MAPLET *Gr. Forest* 81 b, So that if he shaketh him not off betimes by suche wasting of bloud as he will make, thereby he is quickly enfeebled. **1628** A. LEIGHTON *Appeal to Parlt.* 143 The groning of the brute and sencelesse creatures amongst us, under murreings and wastings. **1671** MILTON *P.R.* II. 256 Though hunger still remain: so it remain Without this bodies wasting, I content me. **1808** JAMIESON, *Wasting*, a consumption, a decline. **1860** MAYNE *Expos. Lex.*, *Analosis*.. a consumption, wasting, or atrophy. **1893** *Daily News* 9 Jan. 3/4 A baby who is rapidly recovering from 'wasting', a very general malady among the little ones of the poor. **1899** *Allbutt's Syst. Med.* VII. 229 Wasting of the levator palati and of the vocal cord muscles cannot actually be seen.

b. *Sport.* Reduction of weight by 'training down'.

1856 H. H. DIXON *Post & Paddock* xii. 207 With medicine and vigorous wasting, they can come to their weight again.. in three weeks. **1913** GRETTON *Mod. Hist. Eng. People* I. viii. 191 His suicide was attributed to depression of spirits caused by the incessant 'wasting' to keep down his weight.

5. *Mining.* (See quots.)

1831 J. HOLLAND *Manuf. Metal* I. 39 The first operation to which the iron ore is subjected, is wasting; that is exposing the stones to a moderate heat, which volatilises any extraneous mixture of the ores. **1886** J. BARROWMAN *Sc. Mining Terms* 70 *Wastings*, workings.

'wasting, *ppl. a.* [f. WASTE *v.* + -ING².]

1. a. That lays waste, devastates, or destroys.

c **1230** *Hali Meid.* 43 And te oðre.. liueð i godes luue, wiðuten euch heate of þe hali gast, þat bearneð se lihte, wiðute wastinde brune in alle hise icorene. **1535** COVERDALE *Dan.* viii. 13 The waistinge abhominacion. **1591** SHAKS. *1 Hen. VI*, III. iii. 46 And see the Cities and the Townes defac't, By wasting Ruine of the cruell Foe. *a* **1646** BURROUGHES *Exp. Hosea* iii. (1652) 190 Sin is of a wasting nature: Sin layeth wast Countreyes and places that people live in. **1707** ROWE *Success H.M.'s Arms* 14 The dreadful Ravage of the wasting War. **1738** WESLEY *Hymn*, '*To Thee, O Lord, our God and King*' ii, Whate'er is human ebbs and flows As wasting Time prevails. **1812** BYRON *Ch. Har.* II. i, Here thy temple was, And is, despite of war and wasting fire. **1808** SCOTT *Marmion* II. x, The wasting sea-breeze keen Had worn the pillar's carving quaint. **1889** J. B. BURY *Later Rom. Emp.* II. i. I. 66 Stilicho.. departed to Salona, allowing Alaric to proceed on his wasting way into the lands of Hellas.

b. That undermines strength and vitality. Of a disease: Causing atrophy or gradual decay.

a **1600** SIR J. DAVIES *Epigr.* xxxvi. 21 The wasting Hectique, and the Quartain Feuer. *a* **1721** PRIOR *24 Songs* iii. 4 A lingering fever's wasting pain. **1828** SCOTT *F.M. Perth* xi, A haggard paleness, which seemed the effect of care or of dissipation, or of both these wasting causes combined. **1836** DICKENS *Sk. Boz, Shops & Tenants*, A slow, wasting consumption prevented the eldest girl from continuing her exertions. **1838** PRESCOTT *Ferd. & Is.* II. xxi. III. 384 The state of his own health, too infirm to encounter, with safety, the wasting heats of an African summer. **1899** *Allbutt's Syst. Med.* VIII. 564 Wasting diseases, such as cancer, diabetes and phthisis.

2. a. That is being gradually consumed or destroyed; decaying, waning, passing away.

1340–70 *Alex. & Dind.* 980 In þis wastinge word we ne wone nouht euere. **1591** SHAKS. *1 Hen. VI.* II. v. 8 These Eyes, like Lampes, whose wasting Oyle is spent, Waxe dimme. **1665** HOOKE *Microgr.* Pref. e 2 The other Mandril ..has an even neck instead of a taper one, and runs in a Collar, that by the help of a Screw, and a joynt made like M in the Figure, it can be still adjustned to the wearing or wasting neck. **1697** DRYDEN *Æneis* II. 11 And now the latter Watch of wasting Night, And setting Stars, to kindly Rest invite. **1738** WESLEY *Hymn*, '*Thee we adore, Eternal Name*' ii, Our wasting Lives grow shorter still As Months and Days increase. **1830** LYELL *Princ. Geol.* I. 272 The wasting cliff at Pakefield. **1899** *Allbutt's Syst. Med.* VI. 889 For the wasting muscles massage and electrical treatment should be employed.

b. *Sport.* (See WASTE *v.* 11 c.)

1880 W. DAY *Racehorse in Training* xvii. 166 It was once no uncommon sight at Newmarket to see, daily, ten or a dozen wasting jockeys returning from an eight-mile walk, thoroughly exhausted.

c. ***wasting asset*** (see quot. 1974).

1930 *Economist* 26 Apr. 951/2 Dividends to shareholders —representing return of capital, since gold mines are a wasting asset—have shown much less than a corresponding rate of increase. **1953** *Times* 31 Oct. 2/7 The cost will be almost competitive with coal-based electrical power, and it would be contrary to all experience if the cost comparison did not turn steadily in nuclear energy's favour, particularly when coal is a wasting asset and steadily more costly in real terms to extract. **1970** *Guardian* 3 Nov., Dr. Beeching breathed his kiss of death on the Inverness to Kyle [railway line] in 1963; since then it has been regarded as a wasting asset. **1974** *Terminol. Managem. & Financial Accountancy* (Inst. Cost & Managem. Accountants) 65 *Wasting assets*, assets of a fixed nature which are gradually consumed or exhausted in the process of earning income (e.g. mines or quarries).

Hence **'wastingly** *adv.*

1552 HULOET, Wastinglye, or wastfullye, *prodige*. *a* **1637** B. JONSON *Discov.* (1640) 123 Not to cause the trouble of making Breviates by writing too riotous, and wastingly. **1834** H. TAYLOR *Artevelde* I. III. v. 164 No poison works so wastingly amongst them As a low diet.. yea, it brings them down. *a* **1853** WARDLAW *Lect. Jas.* (1869) 241 Thus consuming, and wastingly, and wantonly, and wickedly, abusing the divine bounty.

†**'wastity.** *Obs.* In 4 **wa(a)stete, wastyte.** [f. WASTE *a.* + -(I)TY. Cf. OF. *gasteté* (gl. L. *vastitas*).] Desolation. (Only in Wyclif's rendering of *vastitas* in the Vulgate.)

1382 WYCLIF *Deut.* xxviii. 53 Thow shalt ete the fruyt of thi woombe.. in angwish and wastete [Vulg. *vastitate*; 1388 distriyng], with the which thin enemye shal oppresse thee. *Ibid.* 57 Thei shulen ete hem priuely, for the scaarsnesse of alle thingis in the seege and waastete [Vulg. *vastitate*; 1388 distriyng], bi the which thin enemy shal oppresse thee. *Ibid. Jer.* vi. 7 Wickednesse and wastyte.

†**'wastive,** *a. Obs. rare*⁻¹. [f. WASTE *v.* + -IVE.] Liable to waste.

1756 TOLDERVY *Hist. 2 Orphans* II. 13 Here, no excess decays our vig'rous health, A blessing greater far than wastive wealth.

wastland, obs. Sc. variant of WESTLAND.

wastle, obs. form of WASTEL.

wastme, var. WASTUM *Obs.*

wastor, -our(e, -owre, obs. ff. WASTER *sb.*[1]

wastrel ('weɪstrəl), *sb.* and *a.* Also 9 **wastorel.** [f. WASTE *v.* + -REL.] **A.** *sb.*

1. In Cornwall: A tract of waste land. *Obs.* exc. in narrower sense, a strip of road-side waste.

1589-90 *Anc. Deed* A. 13002 (P.R.O.), [Land in the] towne and feeldes severalls and wastrells of Tregorrock within the parish of St. Austoll. **1602** CAREW *Cornwall* I. 13 Their [tin] workes.. lie either in seuerall, or in wastrell, that is, in enclosed grounds, or in commons. *Ibid.* 13 b, The Wastrel workes are reckoned amongst chattels, and may passe by word or Will. **1899** 'Q' (Quiller-Couch) *Ship of Stars* xi. 99 The Chapel stood.. on a turfed wastrel where two high roads met and crossed. **1902** *C.T.C. Gaz.* Nov. 466/1 [Launceston] The heaps.. were not on the metal portion of the road, and the width of the wastrel where the heaps were was about four feet.

2. = WASTER *sb.*[1] 6.

a. An article of bad or imperfect workmanship, rejected as unserviceable or not saleable at the full price.

1790 MARSHALL *Midl. Co.* II. 445 *Wastrels*; outcasts; as wastrel bricks, &c. **1847** HALLIW., *Wastrels*, imperfect bricks, china, &c. **1858** SIMMONDS *Dict. Trade*, *Wastrels*, waste substances. **1870** *Churchm. Shilling Mag.* VI. 42 The word *wasteril* or *wastril*, in the dialect of Hallamshire, signifies a knife that is made to sell, for show and not for use.

b. An unhealthy, wasted-looking animal.

1819 REES *Cycl.*, *Wastorels*, or *Wastrels*... The young lambs, pigs, and calves, sold to the butchers, which are improper for keeping as stock, are sometimes also called by this name. **1899** 'Q' (Quiller-Couch) *Ship of Stars* vi. 48, I wouldn't ask a bird of mine to break the Sabbath for a wastrel like that.

3. a. A good-for-nothing, idle, worthless, disreputable person.

1847 HALLIW., *Wastrel*, a profligate. *West.* **1857** WAUGH *Lanc. Life* 120 There's ir Jammy; he's as big a wastril as ever stare't up a lone. **1881** *Times* 4 Jan. 3/4 In Glasgow last night a 'Hogmanay supper' was given by some good Samaritans to a company of 2,000 outcasts and wastrels. **1885** D. C. MURRAY *Rainbow Gold* I. ii, I'm not a runaway. I'm not a wastrel. I think if I set myself to do it that I can make a living somehow.

b. A neglected child of the streets, a city arab.

1877 HUXLEY *Techn. Educ.* Sci. & Cult. (1881) 77 The educational method, the intelligence,.. and good temper on the teacher's part, which are now at the disposal of the veriest waifs and wastrels of society. *c* **1880** BARNARDO *Taken out of Gutter* 2 The juvenile 'wastrels' of London streets are, alas! still to be reckoned by their thousands.

4. A wasteful person, a spendthrift.

1887 BARING-GOULD *Red Spider* vi, Young Hillary, who, brought up in his father's improvident ways, was sure to turn out a like wastrel.

transf. **1889** *Q. Rev.* Apr. 390 London is the most conspicuous wastrel of both men and means.

B. *adj.*

1. Of manufactured articles: Waste, rejected as imperfect. Of workmanship: Good for nothing.

1790 MARSHALL *Midl. Co.* II. 445 Wastrel bricks. **1852** J. ALLIES *Brit.* etc. *Antiq. Worc.* (ed. 2) 106 The piles of encaustic tiles which were found.. which were built up in columns with cement, probably were wastrel tiles, which were so used. **1898** H. SUTCLIFFE *Ricroft* ix. 111 Wenches.. all.. full o' wastrel wark sooin as ye let 'em go an inch beyond weshing an' sewing.

2. Of an animal: Feeble, lacking strength or vigour.

1880 *Gardening Illustr.* 7 Aug. 278 At this time the inferior and imperfect or wustrel [*sic*] birds may be killed. **1895** CROCKETT *Bog-myrtle* v. vii. 412 A wastril whalp could hae dung us owre with its tail. We war tha surprised like.

3. Running to waste, spendthrift.

1894 KIPLING *Seven Seas*, *McAndrews' Hymn* 47 Blot out the wastrel hours of mine in sin when I abode. **1896** *Ibid.*, *Last Rhyme of True Thomas* 23 Where, blown before the wastrel wind, The thistle-down she floated by.

Hence **'wastreldom, 'wastrelism,** extravagance, esp. with reference to government spending.

1906 *Westmorland Gaz.* 14 Mar. 3/2 He was, indeed, heard to say that under our present Fiscal system the wine of our manhood was oozing out while the water of wastrelism was oozing in. Sir Wilfrid Lawson was.. somewhat annoyed to think that the best of all drinks should be confounded with wastrelism. **1906** *Daily Mail* 3 Nov. 4/2 All the old strongholds of Wastreldom have been carried. St. Pancras has thrown out its Wastrels; Islington will have none of them. **1919** *Ibid.* 15 Oct. 6/2 Such arguments in the interest of wastrelism have been abundantly refuted. **1931** J. BUCHAN *Blanket of Dark* 102 It was hard to believe that this was a gathering of the kings of wastreldom.

wastrife ('weɪstrɪf), *a.* and *sb. Sc.* Also **wasteriff.** [f. WASTE *a.*: cf. *cauldrife*, *waukrife*.] **a.** *adj.* Wasteful, extravagant. **b.** *sb.* Wastefulness, extravagance.

a. 1822 SCOTT *Nigel* v, Do not slit the quill up too high, it's a wastrife course. **1873** *Routledge's Young Gentl. Mag.* May 365/2 The old housekeeper, who always declared Master Jacob was so *wasteriff* with his goods, that he would certainly come to beggary some day.

b. 1818 SCOTT *Hrt. Midl.* xxviii, She confessed afterwards, that, 'besides the wastrife, it was lang or she could walk sae comfortably with the shoes as without them'.

wastrine, -one: see WASTERN. *Obs.*

wastry, wastery ('weɪstrɪ), *sb. Sc.* and *north.* Also 8-9 **wastrie.** [f. WASTE *v.* + -(E)RY.]

Reckless extravagance, esp. in living; wastefulness; also, an act or case of wastefulness.

1645 RUTHERFORD *Tryal & Tri. Faith* xix. 184 The same very fault and sin of wastry, that is inherent in the broken bankrupt. **1661** R. BAILLIE in *Lauderdale Papers* (Camden) I. 96 Through his wastery, hes left.. in debt. **1786** BURNS *Twa Dogs* 64 Yet ev'n the ha' folk fill their peghan Wi' sauce, ragouts, an' sic like trashtrie, That's little short o' downright wastrie. **1830** *Fraser's Mag.* I. 340 How is a nation to be converted from extravagance to frugality, when the intent and purpose of all men's minds and endeavours is to foster this wonderful wastery. **1863** 'HOLME LEE' *A. Warleigh* III. 247 He was a gentleman born, but he'd ruined himself wi' gambling an' wastry. **1893** STEVENSON *Catriona* xxviii, My disposition has always been opposed to wastery.

b. Waste *of* (what is specified).

1830 GALT *Lawrie T.* III. xiv, I thought with myself.. what a wastrie of time was caused by the inconsiderate talk of uninformed men. **1900** B. KIRKBY *Granite Chips* 41 (E.D.D.) It was fair weastry o' ink an time.

'wastry, *a. Sc.* ? *Obs.* [? f. WASTER *sb.*[1] or *v.* + -Y. Cf. WASTRIFE *a.*] Wasteful, extravagant.

1791 J. LEARMONT *Poems* 364 (E.D.D.) To live wi' sic a wast'ry, braisant jade. **1825** JAMIESON, *Wastrie*, prodigal; a *wastrie* person, one who is extravagant.

†**'wastum.** *Obs.* Forms: 1 **wæstum, -em, -im, wæstm, westom, westm, weastm,** 3 *Orm.* **wasstme, vestme, westum.** [OE. *wæstm* masc. = OS. *wastum*:—OTeut. type **waχstmo-z*, f. root of WAX *v.*]

1. Fruit, crop, produce; abundance of produce.

c **888** ÆLFRED *Boeth.* xxxix. 13 Be þæs cyninges ʒebode brengð eorðe ælcne westm. *c* **1000** *Ags. Gosp.* Matt. vii. 17 Ælc god treow byrþ gode wæstmas. *c* **1175** *Lamb. Hom.* 109 Iliche þan treo þe bereð lef and blosman, and nane westmas ne bereð. *c* **1200** ORMIN 9284 Illc an treo þatt.. Ne bereþþ nohht god wasstme Shall.. beon hæwenn upp. *c* **1205** LAY. 32108 þenne scullen i Bruttene blissen wurðen riue, wastmes and wederes sele after heore i-wille.

b. *transf.* Fruit (of the body, womb), offspring.

971 *Blickl. Hom.* 5 Forþon se wæstm þines innoþes is ʒebletsad. *c* **1200** ORMIN 1937 þær brohhte ȝho þatt wasstme forþ Off all unnwemmedd wambe.

c. *fig.*

971 *Blickl. Hom.* 249 Andreas, for hwan gæst þu swa buton wæstme þines ʒewinnes. *c* **1200** ORMIN 15911, & nesshenn itt [thy heart] & godenn, Swa þatt itt bere þess te bett God wasstme i gode dedess.

2. Growth of body, stature, form. Also (*nonce-use*), greatness.

Beowulf 1352 (Gr.) Oðer earmsceapen on weres wæstmum wræclastas træd. *c* **1000** *Ags. Gosp.* Luke xix. 3 Zacheus.. wæs lytel on wæstmum. *c* **1200** *Trin. Coll. Hom.* 19 þe fader is on þe sune on þrie wise. þat on is on westme, for þat he is muchel and mihti ouer alle þing. *Ibid.* 127 Alse wat se he was þoȝen on wintre and on wastme.. þo nam he ȝeme of mannes liflode. *c* **1205** LAY. 15698 þa iwarð ich on vestme wunder ane fær. *a* **1225** *Leg. Kath.* 69 A meiden.. feier & freolich o wlite & o westum.

Hence †**'wastumless** *a.*, without fruit.

c **975** *Rushw. Gosp.* Matt. xiii. 22 *Sine fructu* westemleas. *c* **1200** ORMIN 13858 All iss itt [the heart] uss bifrorenn swa þurrh hete & nip & irre, þatt all itt liþ uss wasstmelæs Off alle gode dedess.

wastur, obs. form of WASTER *sb.*[1]

†**'wasty,** *a.*[1] and *sb. Obs.* Forms: 3 **wasti,** 4 **wasty,** 6 **vaistie, waisty, wastie.** [Altered form (after WASTE *a.*) of ME. WESTY *a.*] **A.** *adj.*

1. Desolate, desert.

c **1230** *Hali Meid.* 43 (Titus MS.) And hwat ȝif ha beoð þe wone, þat tu.. schalt greni godles inwið wasti wahes [*Bodley MS.* westi wahes]. *c* **1375** *Sc. Leg. Saints* xx. (*Blasius*) 37, & þare in-to [a] wasty stede heremytis lyf wel lang he lede. **15**.. ALEX. HUME *Ep. G. Moncrieff* Poems (S.T.S.) 61 Of barran Syrt, and wastie Scythia.

b. Phr. ***wasty wanes, wones,*** a desolate place of habitation; also, a spacious place.

c **1400** *Sc. Trojan War* II. 2444 It was a fair rowme wasty wones. **1500-20** DUNBAR *Poems* xxvi. 18 First of all in dance wes Pryd, with bair wyld bak and bonet on syd, Lyk to mak vaistie wanis. **1513** DOUGLAS *Æneis* XII. viii. 6 Alhaill the barnage flokkis furth atanis, Left voyd the tovn and strenth with waisty wanis.

2. Extravagant in upkeep.

c **1380** WYCLIF *Wks.* (1880) 129 þei han many grete houses, costlewe & wasty.

B. *sb.* A desert place.

c **1325** *Metr. Hom.* 148 An ermyt.. That woned in wasti bi him an.

wasty ('weɪstɪ), *a.*[2] [f. WASTE *sb.* + -Y.]

1. Liable to waste from deterioration.

1904 *Westm. Gaz.* 26 Sept. 7/2 Pineapples from the Azores are 'wasty', and sell from 6d. to 3s. 6d. each, but they are not of good quality. **1905** *Ibid.* 6 July 12/1 The rain has ruined 50 per cent of the strawberries on the plants... Tons of soft wasty berries have been marketed and sold at any price obtainable.

2. *U.S.* 'Resembling cotton-waste' (*Cent. Dict.*).

1886 *U.S. Consular Reports* No. lxii. 470 (Cent.) The wool becomes impoverished on account of the heat and dust, and is very tender, with a dry, wasty top. **1888** *Ibid.* 389 The wools.. are.. dry and wasty.

wastyl(le, obs. forms of WASTEL.

wastyne, variant of WASTINE *Obs.*

wa-swa, obs. form of WHOSO.

wasyll, obs. Sc. form of WEASEL *sb.*

†**wat**[1]. *Obs.* Also 4-5 **watt.** [Of obscure origin: not connected with WIGHT *sb.*] A person; esp. ***a great wat.***

1399 LANGL. *Rich. Redeles* IV. 49 We beth.. y-sent ffro þe shiris to shewe what hem greueth,.. And to graunte of her gold to þe grett wattis By no manere wronge way. *c* **1412** HOCCLEVE *De Reg. Princ.* 2816 If so be þat oon of þe grete wattes A dede do, which þat a-geyn þe lawe is, No thyng at al he punysshid for þat is. *c* **1450** *Cov. Myst.* (1841) 294 Ye xal fynde hym a strawnge watt. *c* **1460** *Towneley Myst.* xx. 10 Ye wote not wel, I weyn, what wat is commen to the towne. *c* **1500** MEDWALL *Nature* (Brandl) 821 What man ys that; Fathers soule, thys ys some great wat.

wat[2] (wɒt). *Obs.* exc. *dial.* Forms: 5-6 **watte,** 6-7 **watt,** 5-7, 9 *dial.* **wat.** [Prob. a use of *Wat*, short for *Walter* (†*Water*).] A hare.

a **1500** *Mourn. Hare* 26 in *E.E. Misc.* (Warton Club) 44 Lo! he sayth, where syttyt an haare! Aryse upe, Watte, and go forthe blyve! *Ibid.* 60 As doth the sylly Wat. *c* **1500** in *Babees Bk.* (1868) 404, I wold my master were a watt & my boke a wyld Catt, & a brase of grehowndis in his toppe. *c* **1532** DU WES *Introd. Fr.* in *Palsgr.* 913 The watte, *le leurart.* **1556** J. HEYWOOD *Spider & Fly* xxiv. 25 Neuer was there yet, any larke or wat, Before hawke or dog, flatter darde or squat. **1592** SHAKS. *Ven. & Ad.* 697 Poore wat farre off vpon a hill, Stands on his hinder-legs with listning eare. **1622** DRAYTON *Poly-olb.* xxiii. 331 The man whose vacant mind prepares him to the sport, The Finder sendeth out, to seek the nimble Wat. **1692** R. L'ESTRANGE *Fables* ccclxxxvii. 360 Had he not better have born Wat's Nibling of his Plants and Roots now, then the Huntsman's.. Laying of his Garden Wast.

†**wat**[3]. *Obs.* Also **watte.** [a. F. *watte*, a. Du. *watte* = F. *ouate*: see WAD *sb.*[1]] = WAD *sb.*[1] 3.

1662 J. DAVIES tr. *Mandelslo's Trav.* II. 99 He presented him with a noble coverlet of Watte [*Fr.* 1659 *watte*]. **1671** tr. *Palafox's Conq. China* xxxii. 566 Over this Shirt they wear a Vest.. lined with Wat, or Cotton. *Ibid. foot-n.*, Wat is the Down which covers the seeds of the *Apocynum Syriacum*, called in English Silk-grass.

‖**wat**[4] (wat). Also **watt.** [Thai, said to be a. Skr. *vāṭa* enclosure, grove.] A Thai Buddhist temple.

1844 *Chinese Repository* XIII. 204 The Siamese are in the habit of burning their dead, and the place selected for this purpose is near the wats. **1871** ALABASTER *Wheel of Law* 264 We stop for the night at a Wat, or Buddhist monastery. **1886** *Encycl. Brit.* XXI. 853/2 (*Siam*) The temples (*wats*) hold very little landed or house property. **1886** *Pall Mall Gaz.* 3 Aug. 4/1 Almost every 'wat', or temple, in that country [Siam] has in the grounds attached to it a large flat slab of whitewashed masonry. **1897** *Outing* Mar. 586/1 The occasional spire of a '*Watt*' or temple, showing that this canal is one of the streets of the city [the capital of Siam].

wat, obs. f. QUOTH, WHAT; Sc. and north. f. WET *a.* and *sb.*, WOT *v.*; pa. t. of WET, WITE *vbs.*; var. WHATE *sb. Obs.*

wat, obs. Sc. form of WAIT *sb.*

a **1578** LINDESAY (Pitscottie) *Chron. Scot.* (S.T.S.) II. 255 The erle of Mortoun also beand in leith halding wat on him.

watap, wattap ('wɒtæp). Also **watape, watapeh.** [Narragansett Indian *wattap* 'a root of tree' (Roger Williams *Key Lang. Amer.*, 1643).] (See quot. 1789.)

1789 A. MACKENZIE *Voy. fr. Montreal* iii. (1801) 37 The vessels in which they cook their victuals, are in the shape of a gourd,.. and of watape, fabricated in such a manner as to hold water. *Ibid. foot-n.*, Watape is the name given to the divided roots of the spruce-fir, which the natives weave into a degree of compactness that renders it capable of containing a fluid. The different parts of the bark canoes are also sewed together with this kind of filament. **1809** A. HENRY *Trav.* 14 The small roots of the tree afford the wattap, with which the bark is sewed.

watch (wɒtʃ), *sb.* Forms: 1 **wæcce, wæce, -æ, wecce,** 2 **wæcche,** 3-5 **wecche,** 5 **wecch,** 3-6 **weche,** 5 **wetche,** 3-5 **wacche,** 4 **wachche,** 4-6 **wache,** 5-6 **wach,** (6 **wash(e),** 4-6 *Sc.* **vach,** 6 *Sc.*

vatche, wyche, 5 waicche, waiche, waycche, 5–7 watche, (6 wash(e, wattch), 7 wauch, 6– watch. [OE. *wæcce* wk. fem., f. stem of *wæccan* WATCH *v.* Cf. WAKE *sb.*[1]]

I. Wakefulness, vigil.

†**1. a.** The state of being awake; voluntary or involuntary going without sleep; wakefulness. *Obs.*

c **1000** *Sax. Leechd.* I. 350 To slæpe, gate horn under heafod ʒelæd weccan [*v.r.* wæccan] he on slæpe ʒecyrreþ. *Ibid.* II. 152 ðif men sie micel wæce ʒetenge, popiʒ ʒegnid on ele smire [etc.]. *c* **1400** *Rom. Rose* 4132 Long wacche on nightis, and no slepinge. *c* **1440** CAPGRAVE *St. Kath.* 125 My lord youre eem may not wedde yow neyther in wetche [*v.r.* wecch] ne in dreem. **1533** ELYOT *Cast. Helthe* (1539) 48 Sembably immoderate watch drieth to moch the body. **1602** SHAKS. *Ham.* II. ii. 148 He.. Fell into a Sadnesse, then into a Fast, Thence to a Watch, [etc.]. **1611** —— *Cymb.* III. iv. 43 False to his Bed? What is it to be false? To lye in watch there, and to thinke on him? **1631** WIDDOWES *Nat. Philos.* 52 There be certaine appointed courses for watch and sleepe, lest creatures languish with overmuch motion.

¶ **b.** ***watch of nightingales***: in the early lists of 'proper terms', app. intended to designate wakefulness as the distinctive quality of the bird; by late writers misapprehended as the proper term for a flock or company of nightingales. Cf. WATCHING *vbl. sb.*

c **1452** *Egerton MS.* 1995 (Hodgkin) Waycche of Nyghtynggales. **1486** *Bk. St. Albans* f. vi, A wache of Nyghtingalis. **1801** STRUTT *Sports & Past.* I. ii. 33. [**1847** HALLIWELL, *Wache*, a flock of birds.]

2. a. Watching as a devotional exercise or religious observance; an act or instance of this. Now *rare arch.* except in *watch-night* (see 27).

971 *Blickl. Hom.* 37 Mid fæstenne, & mid halʒum wæccum, & mid ælmessum. *c* **1200** *Vices & Virtues* 89 Lieue saule, ic ðe bidde and warni ðat tu none hope ne haue upe ðine fasten, Ne upe ðine wæcche, ne uppe non oðre gode. *c* **1200** ORMIN 1451 Wiþþ fassting, & wiþþ bedesang, Wiþþ cnelinng, & wiþþ wecche. *a* **1225** *Ancr. R.* 138 Vesten, wecchen & oðre swuche ase ich nemde nu beoð mine sacrefises. *c* **1275** *Orison* 21 in *O.E. Misc.* (1872) 139 Wunderliche þurh wacche and fast þi swete lychome þu teonedest. **1421** in *26 Pol. Poems* xviii. 113 Kepe ȝoure wacche and seruyce dewe, And rule of habyte clenely ȝeme. *c* **1450** CAPGRAVE *Life St. Aug.* 27 So for to make hem mor lith in her wecch, þis same bischop ded ordeyn swete songis and delectable. **1526** *Pilgr. Perf.* (W. de W. 1531) 42 With the merytes & werkes of harde penaunce, abstynence, watche, prayer, turmentes and martyrdome. **1877** *Life St. Willibrord* i. 7 There for some years he served God in fast, watch, and prayer, in a little cell.

†**b.** A wake or revel held on St. John the Baptist's (Midsummer) Eve (23 June), sometimes renewed on St. Peter's Eve (28 June). *Obs.*

1445 *Cov. Leet Bk.* 220 Pur le Ridyng on Corpus Christi day and for Watche on Midsomer even. **1511** in *Songs, Carols* etc. (E.E.T.S.) App. 156 On Myd-somer nyght þe Kyng cam prevyly to the Kyngis Hed in Chepe,.. & so departid agayn after þe washe. & on seynt Peters nyght the Kyng & þe Quene cam rydyng to the Kyngis Hed royally; & after þe washe, departid to þe Towr. *a* **1548** HALL *Chron.*, *20 Hen. VIII* (1550) 177 By reason of this plague the watches whiche were wont to be kept yerely in London on saint Ihons euen at Mydsommer & saint Peters euen were.. commaunded to be left for that yere. **1552–3** in Feuillerat *Revels Edw. VI* (1914) 92, vj hobby horses for mydsomer watch. **1592** STOW *Ann.* 1004, 1548.. The watch.. of long time laid downe, was now againe vsed, both on the eeuen of S. Iohn, and of S. Peter, in as comely order as it had beene accustomed, which watch was greatly beautified by the number of more than 300. demilances and light horsmen [etc.].

c. A 'wake' over a dead person.

c **1250** *Gen. & Ex.* 2467 Cristene folc.. don for þe dede chirche-gong elmesse-gifte, and messe-song, And ðat is on ðe weches stede. **1908** *Ch. Times* 13 Mar. 347/2 A watch was kept all night, the Men's Guild making themselves responsible.

3. The action or a continued act of watching; a keeping awake and vigilant for the purpose of attending, guarding, observing, or the like.

c **888** ÆLFRED *Boeth.* xxxi. §1 Hu micele wæccan & hu micle unrotnesse se hæfð þe ðone won willan hæfð on þisse woruIde. **1390** GOWER *Conf.* II. 96 So mot I nedes fro hire wende And of my wachche make an ende. *c* **1450** *Mirk's Festial* 180 He com to þe chyrch and to þe scryne of Saynt Wenefryd, and was þer yn his prayers al a nyght. But on þe morow, what for wach, what for wery, he fylle on slepe. **1541** PAYNELL *Conspir. Catal.* i. 1 He was an experte man of warre: he could suffer and endure labour, watche, colde, thyrste, and hunger, far beyond that any man wolde beleue. **1577** GRANGE *Golden Aphrod.* Ep. Ded. A ij b, Diodorus the Stoike.. thorow his continuall watch and excessiue studie, being blinde of long time. **1592** SHAKS. *Rom. & Jul.* II. iii. 35 Care keepes his watch in euery old mans eye, And where Care lodges, sleepe will neuer lye. **1600** E. BLOUNT tr. *Conestaggio* 317 They were so wearied with the watches of the last night. **1697** DRYDEN *Æneis* IX. 312 The Foe securely drench'd in Sleep and Wine, Neglect their Watch. **1704** ADDISON tr. *Ovid, Phaeton's Sisters* 31 All the long night their mournful watch they keep, And all the day stand round the tomb and weep. **1788** MME. D'ARBLAY *Diary* 25 Nov., These night watches, and this close attendance, disagree with them all. **1847** TENNYSON *Princess* VI. 129 Wan was her cheek With hollow watch. **1859** H. KINGSLEY *G. Hamlyn* xxxix, Sometimes we would think of poor Mary Hawker, at her lonely watch up at the forest station. **1890** STEVENSON *In South Seas* II. vi. (1900) 190 Others had wearied of the watch; and as the sun was setting, he found himself by the grave alone.

4. [tr. L. *vigilia*, Gr. φυλακή, Heb. *ashmōreth.*] Each of the (three, four, or five) periods into which the night was anciently divided. Now often in collective plural, ***the watches of the night***, used rhetorically for 'the night-time'.

The Hebrews divided the night into three watches, the Greeks usually into four (sometimes five), the Romans (followed by the Jews in New Testament times) into four.

c **1000** ÆLFRIC *Hom.* II. 388 Drihten com to his leorning-cnihtum.. on ðære feorðan wæccan. An wæcce hæfð þreo tida; feower wæccan ʒefyllað twelf tida; swa fela tida hæfð seo niht. *c* **1000** *Ags. Gosp.* Luke xii. 38 ðif he cymð on þære æfteran wæccan, oððe on þære þriddan. [So Tindale and all later versions; Wyclif has *wakynge*.] **1526** *Pilgr. Perf.* (W. de W. 1531) 247 b, In iewry.. the nyght was dyuyded into iiii partes whiche they called iiii watches. The fyrst was from the begynnyng of the nyght vnto ix of the clocke. The second from ix to xii. The thyrde from xii to iii and the fourth from iii to vj of the clocke. **1535** COVERDALE *Exod.* xiv. 24 Whan the mornynge watch came, the Lorde loked vpon the armies of the Egipcians. **1597** SHAKS. *2 Hen. IV*, IV. v. 28 As hee whose Brow (with homely Biggen bound) Snores out the Watch of Night. **1604** —— *Oth.* I. i. 124 At this odde Euen and dull watch o' th' night. **1613** PURCHAS *Pilgrimage* (1614) 119 The day was not diuided of the first Hebrewes.. into houres, but was distinguished by *Vigiliæ*, or Watches, of which they had foure. **1706** ESTCOURT *Fair Example* IV. i. 51 *Fan.* Well, my dear, it begins to grow late, and it's time I shou'd leave you. *Mrs. Fan.* It do's indeed, Husband, I believe the first watch is expir'd. **1742** FIELDING *J. Andrews* I. xvi, When the Company had retired the Evening before, the Thief was detained in a Room where the Constable, and one of the young Fellows who took him, were planted as his Guard. About the second Watch a general Complaint of Drowth was made. **1826** SCOTT *Jrnl.* 21 Jan., The watches of the night pass wearily when disturbed by fruitless regrets. **1850** TENNYSON *In Mem.* xci. 13 Come: not in watches of the night, But where the sunbeam broodeth warm. **1883** MISS BROUGHTON *Belinda* I. viii, How *can* she hurry the pace? she asks herself desperately, in the watches of the night.

†**5.** A vicious turning of night into day, 'chambering'. *Obs.*

c **1225** *Leg. Kath.* 1766 For nabbe ich nawt þeos niht i worldliche wecchen, ah habbe in heouenliche iwaket. *c* **1430** LYDG. *Min. Poems* (Percy Soc.) 90 Hateful of herte he was to sobrenesse, Cherisshyng surfaytes wacche and gloteny.

II. Action of watching or observing.

6. a. The action or an act of watching or observing with continuous attention; a continued look-out, as of a sentinel or guard. Chiefly in phrases, †***to make watch, to keep (a, the) watch, to set a watch.***

1375 BARBOUR *Bruce* IX. 318 He.. has the castell tan, Throu falt of vach, vith litill payn. **1377** LANGL. *P. Pl.* B. IX. 17 Ac þe constable of þat castel þat kepeth al þe wacche, Is a wyse kniȝte with-al, sire Inwitte he hatte. *c* **1440** *Promp. Parv.* 520/1 Wetche, for enmees, *excubie*. *c* **1450** *Merlin* IV. 76 Therfore a-ray youre oste and your barons, and comaunde hem to make gode wacche to diffende hem-self. *Ibid.* xx. 318 And the[i] drinke and ete ech day and trouble so theire braynes that thei sette litill wacche in theire hoste. **1486** CTESS. OXFORD in *Paston Lett.* III. 328, I.. streitly chargie you that ye.. endevore your self that suche wetche or other meanes be used and hadde in the poorts, and creks, and othre places.. to the letting of his seid purpose. **1538** ELYOT *Dict.*, *Excubiæ*,.. watche, as well by daye as by nyghte. **1549** *Chron. Grey Friars* (Camden) 64 That day begane agayne the washe at every gatt in London of the comeneres in harnes with weppyns. **1560** DAUS tr. *Sleidane's Comm.* 120 They kepe so good watche, that nothing can escape them. **1568** GRAFTON *Chron.* II. 650 The Magistrates and gouernours caused great watches to be kept, and good order to be obserued. **1582** N. LICHEFIELD tr. *Castanheda's Conq. E. Ind.* I. vii. 18 The Generall.. determined to enter into the Harbour of Monsambicke,.. appointing also there shoulde be great watch, for preuention of the Moores. **1594** SHAKS. *Rich. III*, V. iii, 54 *Rich.* Good Norfolke, hye thee to thy charge, Vse carefull Watch, chuse trusty Centinels. **1625** BACON *Ess.*, *Love* (Arb.) 445 Loue can finde entrance, not only into an open Heart; but also into a Heart well fortified; if watch be not well kept. **1670** RAY *Prov.* 28 Good watch prevents misfortune. *a* **1700** EVELYN *Diary* an. 1625, I well remember the strict watches and examinations upon the ways as we passed. **1798** SOPHIA LEE *Canterb. T.*, *Young Lady's T.* II. 238 [He] had a strict watch kept on the wanderings of the melancholy Lenox. **1827** KEBLE *Chr. Yr.*, *Advent Sunday* iv, Even so, heart-searching Lord,.. Thou keepest silent watch from thy triumphal throne. **1835** JAMES *Gipsy* ii, 'Keep a good watch, my boys,' he said, ..'There is danger stirring abroad.' **1842** DICKENS *Amer. Notes* xvi, Many an eager eye glanced up to where the Look-out on the mast kept watch for Holyhead. **1867** SWINBURNE *Ess. & Stud.* (1875) 159 The look in it as of bright bewildered eyes with tears not theirs and alien wonder in the watch of them. **1886** C. SCHOLL *Phraseol. Dict.* II. 834, I kept a watch on that man all the time he was on the premises. **1901** *Munsey's Mag.* XXIV. 515/2 He kept watch of you even after the money was stolen.

transf. **1804** CAMPBELL *Soldier's Dream* 2 The night-cloud had lowered, And the sentinel stars set their watch in the sky.

b. The duty, post or office of watchman or sentinel. *Obs.* exc. in Bible phrase ***to stand upon one's watch.***

1535 COVERDALE *Neh.* vii. 3 Whyle they are yet stondinge in the watch, the dores shall be shut and barred. And there were certayne citesyns of Ierusalem appoynted to be watch-men, euery one in his watch. **1550** *S'hampton Crt. Leet Rec.* (1905) I. i. 15 Wherfore yt ys comaunded that every man paye his watches for the welthe and Savegard of the towne as [etc.]. **1581** A. HALL *Iliad* VII. 132 They to their supper do departe, some to the watch do hye, And some their tyred limmes to reste on couches downe do lye. **1604** SHAKS. *Oth.* II. iii. 12 Welcome Iago: we must to the Watch. *Ibid.* v. ii. 326 There is besides, in Rodorigo's Letter, How he vpbraides Iago, that he made him Braue me vpon the Watch. **1605** —— *Macb.* V. v. 33 As I did stand my watch vpon the Hill I look'd toward Byrnane, and anon me thought The Wood began to moue. **1611** BIBLE *Hab.* ii. 1, I will stand vpon my watch, and set mee vpon the towre, and will watch to see what he will say vnto me.

c. Surveillance *over* a person, either for his protection or with hostile intent.

1611 BIBLE *Job* vii. 12 Am I a sea, or a whale, that thou settest a watch ouer me? **1776** *Trial of Nundocomar* 23/2, I do not put a watch over him; how can I tell who has seen him. **1782** MISS BURNEY *Cecilia* III. viii, We shall be able to keep a better watch over her. **1827** SCOTT *Highl. Widow* v, Impatient of the watch which was placed over her. **1885** BIBLE (R.V.) *1 Sam.* xxvi. 15 Wherefore then hast thou not kept watch over thy lord the king?

d. ***on, upon (the) watch***: on the look out, exercising vigilance. Const. *for, to* with *inf.*

1719 DE FOE *Crusoe* I. (Globe) 203, I resolv'd to put my self upon the Watch to see them when they came to Shore. **1775** A. BURNABY *Trav. N. Amer.* 28 *note*, The bald-eagle, which is generally upon the watch, instantly pursues [the fishing-hawk]. **1797** JANE AUSTEN *Sense & Sensib.* xxvi, Wherever they went she was evidently always on the watch. **1848** DICKENS *Dombey* xxv, The.. door.. opened when he knocked—for Rob was on the watch. **1849** MACAULAY *Hist. Eng.* ii. I. 182 He must be always on the watch for the indications of a coming reaction. **1875** JOWETT *Plato* (ed. 2) III. 237 We should not have been on the watch to keep one another from doing wrong.

†**e.** Watchfulness, vigilance. *Obs.*

14.. LYDG. *Lyke thyn Audience* 28 in *Pol. Rel. & Love Poems* (1903) 48 [Hunt game] with bowe and arow in honde Mawgre the wache of fosters and parkerris. **1450–1530** *Myrr. our Ladye* II. 241 Thoughe she ordeyned wyth all watche and dylygence her thoughtes wordes & dedes to the worshyp of god yet she [etc.]. **1465** *Paston Lett.* II. 214 Maketh gode wache be tyme.

personified. *c* **1412** HOCCLEVE *De Reg. Princ.* 76 Agayn my luste, Wach profrid his seruise, And I admittid hym in heuy wyse.

7. a. ***watch and ward***: the action of 'watching and warding' (see WATCH *v.* 6 b, 10, WATCHING *vbl. sb.* 1 c); the performance of the duty of a watchman or sentinel, esp. as a feudal obligation. Now only (as often in earlier times) a rhetorical and more emphatic synonym of *watch* in sense 6; also *fig.*

It has often been supposed that in this phrase *watch* refers to service by night and *ward* to service by day, but this seems to be merely an unsupported inference from the etymology.

1390 GOWER *Conf.* II. 202 Thei.. maken thanne warde and wacche, Wher thei the profit mihten cacche. *c* **1425** in *Black Bk. Admir.* (Rolls) I. 284 That every man be obeissant to his capitene to kepe his wacche and warde. **1471** CAXTON *Recuyell* (Sommer) 94 He doth yow to wete that ye do kepe yow wyth good wacche and warde. **1523** BERNERS *Froiss.* I. ccccxxxiii. 308 Thus they stode styll kepynge watche and warde, redy at their defence. **1576** GASCOIGNE *Philomene* (Arb.) 87 But I which spend, the darke and dreadful night, In watch and ward, when those birds take their rest, Forpine my selfe. **1596** SPENSER *F.Q.* I. iii. 9 Still, when she slept, he kept both watch and ward. **1630** *R. Johnson's Kingd. & Commw.* 137 As for their Watch and Ward, it goes by course, as in the City of Embden, and divers other in those low countries. **1687** *Declar. Dubl.* 8 Dec. in *Lond. Gaz.* No. 2222/3 We do hereby further Require.. that the Laws of this Realm concerning the keeping of Watch and Ward, and for raising the Hue-and-Cry be duly observed. **1780** BURKE *Sp. Bristol* 60 But let government.. comprehend the whole in its justice, and restrain the suspicious by its vigilance; let it keep watch and ward;.. and then it will be as safe as ever God and nature intended it should be. **1817** COLERIDGE *Biog. Lit.* I. x. 191 At least let us not be lulled into such a notion of our entire security, as not to keep watch and ward, even on our best feelings. **1848** DICKENS *Dombey* xi, Mrs. Pipchin had kept watch and ward over little Paul and his sister for nearly twelve months. **1859** —— *T. Two Cities* II. iii, The jury.. were not agreed... My Lord.. signified his pleasure that they should retire under watch and ward, and retired himself. **1868** *Local Act 31 & 32 Vict.* c. lix. Preamble, Whereas the Power of Watch and Ward within the University and City of Oxford has heretofore been customarily exercised during the Night by the Chancellor, Masters, and Scholars of the University of Oxford, and during the Day by the Mayor, Aldermen, and Citizens of the City of Oxford. **1873** BLACK *Pr. Thule* xvii. 267 The necessity of keeping some watch and ward over his tongue. **1906** S. J. REID *Life & Lett. Ld. Durham* xviii. II. 32 Along the southern line of the Russian frontiers it was necessary to keep military watch and ward against the predatory incursions of Tartar tribes.

†**b.** in *plural. Obs. rare.*

1398 TREVISA *Barth. De P.R.* IX. xxv. (1495) 362 By watches and wardes of knyghtes the nighte is departed in foure, bi foure partes and orders of watches. **1511** *Guylforde's Pilgr.* (Camden) 10 Arragonse.. is the strongest towne of walles, towres, bulwerkes, watches, and wardes that euer I sawe in all my lyfe.

†**c.** = 8 b. *Obs.*

1566 *S'hampton Crt. Leet Rec.* (1905) I. I. 41 Item that non put eny catall Into the comyn who is not a howseholder and paye watche and warde vpon payne to furfet for evere tyme so offendinge 2/-.

†**8. a.** The action of keeping guard and maintaining order in the streets, esp. during the night, performed by a picked body of the community. Phrase, *to keep watch. Obs.*

1442 *Extracts Aberd. Reg.* (1844) I. 8 And ony waicheman that slepis in the nyght, or removis fra the waiche quhile the son rise, sal pay vi d. to the seriandes. **1532** *Cov. Leet Bk.* 712 All Constables within the Citie & suburbes of the same shalbe discharged fromehensforth of the Comen watche in this Citie & also of all paymentes & charges of the same. **1534** in W. H. Turner *Select. Rec. Oxford* 128 In the night wach to be kept by the Univ. no freman.. should.. be vexed.. by the wach. **1549** *Chron. Grey Friars* (Camden) 65 That nyght was the comyneres of London was dyscharged of ther waching at alle the gattes of London in harnes, and to wache no more but the comyne wache as a nyttes in every warde as it hath bene acostomyd before. **1878** J. DAVIDSON *Inverurie*

iv. 138 A watch to be kept by sixteen persons every night, and two sentinels in every steeple by day.

†**b.** A payment or tax for the upkeep of watchmen. *Obs.*

1430 in *10th Rep. Hist. MSS. Comm.* App. v. 294 No Maire..shal pardon and forgyve amercements of brede, ale, wacche and affrayes. **1467** in *Eng. Gilds* (1870) 390 That then he pay taske, tallage, knyghtenspence, wacches, and other charges wᵗyn the warde that he comyth furst in to the seid cite by. **1506** *Ord. Crysten Men* (W. de W.) IV. ix. 192 To paye taxes watches subsydes, or passages agayne theyr wyll.

†**9.** A lying in wait, an ambush; hence an insidious design or plot. Phrases, ***to lay watch***, to place an ambush, ***to lie at, in, watch*** (for). *Obs.*

c **1400** *Destr. Troy* 5585 Bot the ffreikes were ferd of hor fre shippes, ffor to caire by the coste, & knew not the waches. **1432–50** tr. *Higden* (Rolls) I. 195 Helle..fleenge the wacches of here steppe moder [L. *fugiens insidias novercales*]. **1483** CAXTON *Golden Leg.* 430/2 Kepyng hym self ryght curyously fro the prychyng sawtes and watche of the world. **1533** BELLENDEN *Livy* v. (S.T.S.) II. 207 Þai..began to drede sum hid watche and tressoun [L. *insidias vereri*]. **1535** COVERDALE *1 Macc.* xi. 68 And beholde, the hoostes of the Heithen met them in the felde, & layed watch for them in the mountaynes. **1545** in Leadam *Court Requests* (Selden Soc.) 183 Defendauntes..leyd at divers tymes watch to take the corne off the said complaynaunt. **1548** CRANMER *Catech.* 190 b, For if we shuld not much forbeare and forgyue one another,..we shoulde neuer haue measure nor ende of chiding, scoldynge, laying in watche one of another [etc.]. **1549** *Compl. Scot.* xi. 87 Thai lay at the vatch [*printed* vacht], lyik the ald subtil doggis. **1555** *Instit. Gentl.* E vij, Manius.. was..abhorred of hys own soldiers, euen so muche as they tooke hym in a watche, and set hym vpon an Asse backe hys fete bounde vnder the bely of the Asse [etc.]. **1653** WALTON *Angler* iii. 91 He [the trout] gets him into swifter and swifter streams, and there lies at the watch for any flie or Minow that comes neer to him.

10. a. One who watches; a look-out man; †a spy.

1375 BARBOUR *Bruce* VI. 44 Bot he, that had his vachis ay On ilk syde, of thar cummyng, Lang or thai com, had vittering. *Ibid.* XIX. 442 Bot the lord dowglas, that ay-quhar Set out wachis heir and thar [Gat] wit of thair enbuschement. *c* **1475** *Rauf Coilȝear* 276 The King buskit him sone, with scant of Squyary Wachis and Wardroparis all war away. **1483** CAXTON *G. de la Tour* cxxiii. lv, By the false watches & bacbyters whiche ben neuer cessyng to talke of som euylle rather than of somme good. **1820** IRVING *Sketch Bk.* I. ii. 16 Suddenly the watch gave the alarm of 'a sail ahead!'

b. *Cricket.* A fieldsman; also, a fielding position or station. (***Winchester College.***)

1836 *New Sporting Mag.* Oct. 360 The fielding of the 'Wykehamist watches' was very different from years gone by. **1843** [F. GALE] *Pract. Hints Cricket* Frontisp., The 'watches' are placed more behind the wicket, since the introduction of Round Bowling, than they were formerly. **1871** F. GALE *Echoes fr. Old Cricket Fields* 27 What I call an all-round player is a man who will go to any watch he is told, long or short, except wicket-keeper.

11. One who watches, or those who watch, for purposes of guarding and protecting life and property, and the like; *esp.* before the introduction of the New Police, a watchman or body of watchmen, who patrolled and guarded the streets of a town, proclaimed the hour, etc.

1539 *Cov. Leet Bk.* 738 That fromehensfurthe the seriauntes that shall warne the comen watche of this Citie shall furst begyn to warne the said watche at seynt Margettes Chappell. **1571** *Rec. Burgh Lanark* (1893) 63 The cunsall ordanis the fouir balleis to deill the toun in fouir, and ilke ane of thame nychtly rasave the wache, and put nychtly sufecent wyches to the port. **1596** SHAKS. *1 Hen. IV*, II. iv. 536 *Hostesse.* The Sherife and all the Watch are at the doore: they are come to search the House, shall I let them in? **1599** —— *Much Ado* III. v. 49 *Dog.* One word sir, our watch sir haue indeede comprehended two aspitious persons. **1607** T. D. & G. WILKINS *Jests* 10 A yong man, being taken by a watch in the day time, for an idle fellow, was by a Constable brought before one of the Sheriffes of London, [etc.]. **1670–1** MARVELL *Corr.* Wks. (Grosart) II. 376 On Munday morning at two a'clock, some persons reported to be of great quality,..set upon the watch and killd a poore beadle. **1681** OTWAY *Soldier's Fort.* v. (1687) 61 *Enter Constable and Watch. Const...* I and my Watch going my morning Rounds, and finding your door open, made bold to enter to see there were no danger. **1703** *Lond. Gaz.* No. 3901/2 A Watch which was posted near that Place..came to his Assistance. **1751** F. COVENTRY *Pompey the Little* I. xiii. 114 Gentlemen, answered the Watch, we are no Rascals, but Servants of His Majesty King George. **1812** *Murphy Delany's Feast* 12 Hullo! what's all this noise about? To the watch-house you must go, sir. Phelim struck the watch across the nose, And cried out no, no, no, sir. **1838** *Bentley's Misc.* III. 51 From such neighbours the Cheap could not escape. The watch was generally scanty and always idle, and in the depth of winter the streets were without lights, save [etc.]. **1841** DICKENS *Barn. Rudge* xvi, Then there was the watch with staff and lanthorn, crying the hour, and the kind of weather. **1845** D. JERROLD *St. Giles* i, The woman, with a piercing shriek, called the watch; but the watch.. answered not.

12. A sentinel; also, the body of soldiers constituting the guard of a camp, town, gate of a town, etc. ? *Obs.* exc. *Hist.*

13.. *E.E. Allit. P.* B. 1205 Bot er þay at-wappe ne moȝt þe wach wyth-oute, Hiȝe skelt was þe askry þe skewes anvnder. **1375** BARBOUR *Bruce* IX. 375 Thai herd no vachis spek no cry. *Ibid.* XVII. 481 Thai set gud wachis to thar wall. *c* **1380** *Sir Ferumb.* 5185 Þan was þar non of al þe wacche þat ys herte ne by-gan to cacche. *a* **1400–50** *Wars Alex.* 5215 Sone þe wacchis on þe wallis þam wiȝtly ascryes, Qua þai ware & of quethen & quat was þar errande. *c* **1425** WYNTOUN *Cron.* IV. lv. 1177 (Wemyss), And that ȝit Brynnyus wonnyng had Had nocht the guss sic craking maid That walknyt the wache sodanely. *c* **1500** *Three Kings' Sons* 123 The ladies and gentilwomen..were not wele assured when they herd the belle of the wacche, for the comyng of the Turke. **1500–20** DUNBAR *Poems* xlii. 33 Langour wes weche vpoun the wall, That nevir sleipit bot evir wouke. **1539** BIBLE (Cranmer) *Matt.* xxvii. 65 Pylate sayde vnto them: Ye haue the watch [Gr. ἔχετε κουστωδίαν]; go your waye, make it as sure as ye can. **1598** BARRET *Theor. Warres* II. i. 19, It is also his [the Sergeant's] office to set & remoue the watches. **1611** BIBLE *Matt.* xxviii. 11 Behold, some of the watch came into the citie, and shewed vnto the chiefe Priests all the things that were done. *a* **1670** SPALDING *Troub. Chas. I* (Bannatyne Club) II. 321 Sir Johne Hurry..gois throw the marques of Montrois watches, saying, he wes the lord Gordoun's man. *c* **1672** *Verney Mem.* (1907) II. 345 They told me they were the watch sent to stop all Passengers. **1825** SCOTT *Betrothed* xx, 'Guarine,' he added, addressing his squire, 'let the watch be posted, and do thou remain within the tent.' **1844** TALFOURD *Athen. Captive* III. iii, The watch presently will be removed.

13. In the early 18th c., the designation of certain companies of irregular troops in the Highlands. ***Black Watch***, a name given (from the dark-coloured tartan worn by them) to some of these companies raised *c* 1729–30, and afterwards, 1739–40, embodied as the 42nd Regiment, which still retains the name.

1739 LOVAT in W. Fraser *Chiefs of Grant* (1883) II. 380 My dear Frank..is not to stay any time in what you call the Black Watch. I think it is a right name to us, for we are represented very black to our Generall. **1822** D. STEWART *Sk. Highlanders* I. 223 This corps, which has been so well known for nearly eighty years under the appellation of the 42nd Highland Regiment..was originally known by the name of the *Reicudan Du*, or Black Watch. This was an appellation given to the Independent Companies of which the regiment was formed. It arose from the colour of their dress. **1900** LD. ROBERTS *Dispatch* in *Daily News* 10 May 4/7 The Black Watch distinguished themselves, and were very skilfully led. **1913** N. MUNRO *New Road* iii. (1914) 35 The Highland Watches were considered in some quarters dubious servants of the King.

14. A hill serving as a look-out station. *Sc.* (? *Obs.* exc. in local names.)

17.. PENNECUIK *Wks.* (1815) 50 (E.D.D.) Hills are variously named, according to their magnitude; as..Tor, Watch, Rig. **1806** FORSYTH *Beauties Scot.* III. 114 There are hills in the same parish, called watches, where persons sat in order to give notice on the first approach of an enemy.

†**15.** Something to catch the eye, a bait to catch the attention of a hawk. *Obs.*

c **1450** *Bk. Hawking* in *Rel. Ant.* I. 293 And thou wolt take a goshawke, let his wach be a colvour; and yf he falle not there to, put a rabbett.

†**16.** A signal. *Obs.*

1578 H. WOTTON *Courtlie Controv.* 247 The Englishe lordes hauing giuen the princesse Virginia a watch to linger behinde and step aside [orig. *ayans par vn signal fait escarter de la compagnie la Princesse V.*].

III. Nautical uses.

17. a. [Developed from sense 4.] That period of time for which each of the divisions of a ship's company (called 'watches': see 18) alternately remains on deck; usually four hours, with the exception of the dog-watches (see DOG-WATCH). (One's) ***watch below, off***, the time one is off duty. ***to be off the watch***: to be off duty.

1585 T. WASHINGTON tr. *Nicholay's Voy.* I. ii. 2 We about the first watch sayled straight towards the port of Carry. *a* **1624** in Capt. J. Smith *Hist. Virginia* I. Wks. I. 340 When we had run 30. leagues we had 40. fadom, then 70. then 100. After 2. or 3. watches more we were in 24. fadoms. **1634** BRERETON *Trav.* (Chetham Soc.) 4 As the master of the ship conceived we ran seven leagues in a watch, in four hours. **1697** *Lond. Gaz.* No. 3317/4 In a Watch and a half..they gained so much of us, that we saw no probability of coming up with them. **1781** COWPER *Retirem.* 434 He that on the mainmast head While morning kindles with a windy red, Begins a long look-out for distant land, Nor quits, till ev'ning watch, his giddy stand. **1848** W. A. ROSS *Yacht Voy. Norway*, etc. II. 256 The sailors who were below and off the watch, rose as we entered. **1850** H. MELVILLE *White Jacket* I. xxi. 128 At eight o'clock in the morning your watch-below comes round, and you are not liable to duty until noon. **1867** SMYTH *Sailor's Work-bk, Watch*,..the word is also applied to the time during which the watch remains on deck, usually four hours, with the exception of the dog-watches. **1898** KIPLING *Fleet in Being* i. 4, I counted seven speeds in one watch, ranging from eight knots to seventeen. **1914** *Glasgow Herald* 26 Aug. 8 The master was having his watch off, and was lying down amidships.

b. A sailor's turn or period of duty.

1725 DE FOE *Voy. round World* (1840) 44 They were a part of the men whose watch it was. **1833** HT. MARTINEAU *Loom & Lugger* I. iii. 26 He stood as fair a chance as a brighter man ..of sustaining his six hours' watch to the satisfaction of his officer.

transf. **1908** *Daily Chron.* 10 Apr. 1/5 This afternoon a batch of telegraphists due on duty refused to attend. The batch then on duty declared that they would go out on strike when their watch ended.

18. a. That part, usually one half, of the officers and crew, who together attend to the working of a vessel during a 'watch' (see 17). The usual two divisions, ***port*** (†***larboard***) and ***starboard watches***, are sometimes again divided into two, making four in all.

1626 CAPT. J. SMITH *Accid. Yng. Seamen* 790 The Corporall is to see to the setting and releeuing the watch. **1627** —— *Sea Gram.* xiii. 61 Watch be vigilant to keepe your berth to windward. **1628** DIGBY *Voy. Mediterr.* (Camden) 14 It was all that both the watches could do together to take about the sailes. **1699** T. ALLISON *Voy. Archangel* 103 We set our Sprit-Sail too, but all the Watch, which were ten Men, were two hours in getting it loose. **1743** BULKELEY & CUMMINS *Voy. S. Seas* 8, I was Officer of the Watch (tho' I was Gunner of the Ship, I had the Charge of a Watch during the whole Voyage). **1769** FALCONER *Dict. Marine* (1780) s.v., *To set the Watch*, is to appoint one division of the crew to enter upon the duty of the watch; as at eight o'clock in the evening. Hence it is equivalent to *mounting the guard* in the army. **1820** SCORESBY *Acc. Arctic Reg.* II. 235 Each watch consists of two boats' crews. **1836** MARRYAT *Midsh. Easy* xxvi, The watch was called as soon as the sails were trimmed. **1840** R. H. DANA *Bef. Mast* xiv. 33 Instead of having a watch on deck and a watch below, as at sea, all hands are at work together. **1913** M. ROBERTS *Salt of Sea* vii. 181 'Any man would scorn to be Tyser's sister's son,' said the starboard watch. *Ibid.*, 'The grub's horrid,' said both watches.

b. ***watch and watch***, the arrangement by which the two halves of a ship's crew take duty alternately every four hours.

1780 *Mirror* No. 97 'Business,' cried the Captain, 'is not oratory business? and why cannot they set to it watch and watch, as we do at sea?' **1813** SOUTHEY *Nelson* I. 22 He was stationed in the foretop at watch and watch. **1829** MARRYAT *F. Mildmay* xii, They were either mast-headed, or put watch and watch. **1850** H. MELVILLE *White Jacket* I. xxi. 128 In a man-of-war at sea, the sailors have watch and watch; that is, through every twenty-four hours they are on and off duty every four hours. **1867** SMYTH *Sailor's Word-bk., Watch and Watch*, the arrangement of the crew in two watches.

transf. **1889** 'MARK TWAIN' *Yankee at Crt. Arthur* xl, Well, he stood watch-and-watch with me, right straight through, for three days and nights, till the child was out of danger.

IV. A timepiece.

†**19.** An alarm-clock, or an alarum attached to a clock. *Obs.*

The sense in the first example is doubtful, as the Latin rendering is omitted; but on etymological grounds it seems likely that the sense 'alarum' is the oldest of the senses of this branch. With the form *wecche* in quot. 1440 cf. WECCHE *v.* (trans.) to awaken.

c **1440** *Promp. Parv.* 520/1 Wecche, of a clokke. **1542** in *Archæol. Jrnl.* XVIII. 142 Item oone Clocke... Item oone Larum or Watch of iron, the case being likewise iron gilt with two plumettes of led.

20. †**a.** A dial or clock-face; the circle of figures on a dial. *Obs.*

1588 GREENE *Perimedes* G 2 b, Restlesse the clocke that chimes hir fast a sleepe, Disquiet thoughts the minits of her watch. **1593** SHAKS. *Rich. II*, v. v. 52 For now hath Time made me his numbring clocke; My Thoughts, are minutes; and with Sighes they iarre, Their watches on vnto mine eyes, the outward Watch, Whereto my finger, like a Dialls point, Is pointing still, in cleansing them from teares. **1672** in *Lostwithiel Rec.* (Hist. MSS. Comm., *Var. Collect.* 1901) I. 335 For mending the clock there, and for making a watch or dyall uppon the tower of the said Borough.

b. The going-part of a clock. ? *Obs.*

1696 W. DERHAM *Artif. Clock-m.* i. 3 The parts of a Movement, which I shall consider, are the Watch, and Clock. The Watch-part of a Movement is that which serveth to the measuring the hours. In which the first thing I shall consider is the Ballance. **1816** J. SMITH *Panorama Sci. & Art* I. 376 The profile of the watch or going part of a clock is shewn by fig. 1, pl. VI.

21. a. A small time-piece; orig. one with a spring-driven movement, and of a size to be carried in the pocket; now also freq., a wrist-watch (spring- or battery-driven).

The occasional occurrence of the term ***pocket-watch*** (see quot. 1705 below) suggests that the word was sometimes applied to spring-driven clocks of larger size. From the beginning of the 17th c. 'watches' (from the context clearly pocket watches) are often spoken of as striking.

1588 SHAKS. *L.L.L.* III. i. 194 A woman that is like a Germane Cloake, Still a repairing: euer out of frame, And neuer going a right, being a Watch: But being watcht, that it may still goe right. **1590** R. HARVEY *Plain Perc.* 24 Surrender vp thy watch though it were gold. **1592** GREENE *Conny Catching* III. E 2 b, He reported his freend had lost a watch of golde: shewing how closely his freende wore it in his bosome. **1610** SHAKS. *Temp.* II. i. 12 Looke, hee's winding up the watch of his wit, By and by it will strike. **1625** B. JONSON *Staple of N.* I. i, (*He drawes foorth his watch, and sets it on the table.*) 't strikes! One, two, Three, foure, fiue, six. Inough, inough, deare watch. *c* **1633** in *Verney Mem.* (1907) I. 147 The gold watch sett with Turkies. **1651** JER. TAYLOR *Holy Dying* i. §3 (1676) 22 While he told the sands of his hour-glass, or the throbs and little beatings of his Watch. **1652** in *10th Rep. Hist. MSS. Comm.* App. I. 38 A verie prettie vatche of an agat, with ane case of silver. *c* **1657** in *Verney Mem.* (1907) II. 135 A plain sillvor woch. .. I have it merely to know how the time goes away. **1662** J. DAVIES tr. *Olearius' Voy. Ambass.* 270 A gilt brass Candlestick, that had thirty branches, having a striking Watch within the Body of it. **1662** S. P. *Acc. Latitude-men* 16 There are also imperfect Clocks called Watches that do not strike, but onely have a Dyall with a hand turning round. **1688** R. STAPLEY *Diary* in *Sussex Archæol. Collect.* II. 113 July 12th, bought..a silver-cased watch, wᶜʰ cost me 3 *li*... This watch shewes yᵉ hour of yᵉ day, yᵉ day of yᵉ month, yᵉ months of yᵉ year, yᵉ age of yᵉ moon, and yᵉ ebbing and flowing of yᵉ water; and will goe 30 hours with once winding up. **1705** HICKERINGILL *Priest-cr.* IV. (1721) 210 Pocket your Watch, and Watch your Pockets. **1705** W. DERHAM in *Lett. Lit. Men* (Camden) 317 Whether the vacuum affected the going of a pocket-watch. **1706** PHILLIPS (ed. Kersey), *Watch*,..a Pocket-clock for the measuring of Time. **1751** F. COVENTRY *Pompey the Little* I. iv. 37 Lady Tempest, looking at her Watch, declared it was time to be going. **1784** JOHNSON *Let. to Sastres* 21 Aug., Dictionaries are like watches, the worst is better than none, and the best cannot be expected to go quite true. **1837** HEBERT *Engin. & Mech. Encycl.* I. 683 The essential difference between clocks and watches consists in the nature of the regulator employed; which in clocks is the pendulum, and in watches the balance wheel. **1840** DICKENS *Old C. Shop* xlvi, The doctor..drew out his watch, and felt her pulse. **1879** THOMSON & TAIT *Nat. Phil.* I. I. §414 A Clock is primarily an instrument which, by means of a train of wheels, records the number of vibrations executed by a pendulum; a Chronometer or Watch performs the same duty for the oscillations of a flat spiral spring.

b. Applied to a pocket time-piece regulated otherwise than by a balance-wheel and hair-spring.

1666 in Birch *Hist. Royal Soc.* (1756) II. 83 April 18. Mr. Hooke produced a new kind of watch, the motion of which was regulated by a load-stone, the balance of it being a rod of steel. **1667** SPRAT *Hist. Royal Soc.* 247 Several new kinds of Pendulum Watches for the Pocket, wherein the motion is regulated, by Springs, or Weights, or Loadstones, or Flies moving very exactly regular. **1696** W. DERHAM *Artif. Clock-m.* viii. 98 Of the Invention of those Pocket-Watches, commonly called Pendulum Watches.

c. A chronometer as used on board ship.

1778 R. WADDINGTON *Sea Officer's Comp.* 7 Suppose the alt. of the sun taken at 8h. 12' A.M. by the watch. **1794** J. H. MOORE *Pract. Navig.* (ed. 10) 216 Suppose a ship at sea in lat. 47° 34' N. by account, at 9H. 55M. 30S. by watch. **1816** TUCKEY *Narr. Exped. R. Zaire* ii. (1818) 51 Our chronometers gave the longitude of the north end of Prince's island 7°... The same watch makes the N.W. point of St. Thomas in 6° 31', [etc.].

d. *nonce-use.* A mechanism with rotating hands or pointers which move at any fixed ratio of speed.

1882 MINCHIN *Unipl. Kinem.* 95 *AB* and *AC* may then be simply two hands of a 'Watch' whose mechanism is at *A*, such that the angle turned through by the hand *AC* is always three times the angle turned through by the hand.

e. ***silly*** (or ***crazy***) ***as a two-bob watch***: extremely stupid, mad. *Austral. slang.*

1954 P. GLADWIN *Long Beat Home* 72 There now, I clean forgot. I'm getting silly as a two-bob watch. **1963** L. GLASSOP *Rats in New Guinea* 192 Crazy as a two-bob watch. Should have reported it, corporal. **1972** J. DE HOOG *Skid Row Dossier* 75 'Don't buy him a beer, Johnny, he's silly as a two bob watch', someone advised as he tapped me on the shoulder.

22. A trial-piece of glass, pottery, copper, etc. put in a furnace and taken out again, to enable the workman to judge of the degree of heating and the condition of the material operated on.

[App. a mistranslation of F. *montre*, in this application used in the sense of show-piece (from *montrer* to show), but commonly meaning a watch (timepiece).]

1606 PEACHAM *Art of Drawing* 69 Lay with every bed of your wrought and drawn glass one of the said pieces, which are called watches. **1839** URE *Dict. Arts* 330 A small proof of copper, of the form of a watch-case, and therefore called *montre*, is taken out from time to time. *Ibid.* 1016 Pyrometric balls of red clay.. are employed in the English potteries to ascertain the temperature of the glaze kilns... The glazer provides himself at each round with a stock of these ball watches.

23. *U.S.* (See quot.)

1891 *Century Dict.*, *Watch* 9. pl. A name of the trumpet-leaf, *Sarracenia flava*, probably alluding to the resemblance of the flowers to watches.

†**V. 24.** Cant. ***his, her, my watch***: = Himself, herself, myself. *Obs.*

c **1530** COPLAND *Hye Way Spyttel Hous* in Hazl. *E.P.P.* IV. 69 The patryng coue in the darkman cace Docked the dell for a coper meke, His watch shall feng a prounces nobchete. **1567** HARMAN *Caveat* (1869) 61 Thys harlot.. had an vpright man or two alwayes attendinge on her watche (whyche is on her parson). *Ibid.* 86 That is beneshyp to our watche. **1612** DEKKER *O per se O* O 1 b, I met a Dell, I viewde her well, she was benship to my watch.

VI. 25. *dial.* = WAKE *sb.*^{2} 6.

1892 *Pictorial World* 23 Apr. 733/2 They are feeding in one of the little pieces of open water—'watches' they are called—where the springs are strong, and the fowl keep the water moving.

VII. *attrib.* and *Comb.*

26. simple attrib. (sense 6) ***watch temple***; (sense 21), as ***watch-back, -band, -barrel*** (BARREL 5 b), ***bow*** (*sb.*^{1} 11 a), ***cock*** (*sb.*^{1} 16), ***-dial*** (*sb.*^{1} 4), ***-face, -holder, -key*** (also *attrib.*), ***-movement*** (3 b), ***pendant*** (*sb.* 11), ***pendulum-wire, pillar*** (*sb.* 8), ***-strap.***

1894 A. H. CHURCH *J. Wedgwood* x. 76 *Watch-backs,.. for which Wedgwood employed with success his beautiful jasper paste. **1924** *Sears, Roebuck Catal.* 410/1 *Watch-band, woven wire. For watches. **1970** N. ARMSTRONG et al. *First on Moon* iii. 64, I found the little card.. and stuck it under his watchband. **1858** SIMMONDS *Dict. Trade*, *Watch-barrel. **1884** F. J. BRITTEN *Watch & Clockm.* 284 **Watch Bow*, the round ring of a watch case to which the guard is attached. **1899** —— *Old Clocks & Watches* 346 **Watch Cocks.* The first of the cocks or brackets used to support one end of the balance staff were probably quite plain. **1875** KNIGHT *Dict. Mech.* s.v., *Watch-dials are usually made of thin sheet copper [etc.]. **1899** F. J. BRITTEN *Old Clocks & Watches* 120 Decoration in enamel is sometimes to be found on watch dials.. produced during the early part of the seventeenth century. **1893** *Scribner's Mag.* June 725/1 He felt for his matches and struck one to look at his *watch-face. **1915** KIPLING *Diversity of Creatures* (1917) 410 Your watch also [is] in the coralline *watch-holder. **1773** *Pennsylv. Gaz.* 16 June, Suppl. 2/2 [Advt.] Steel and brass *watch keys. **1840** HOOD *Up Rhine* 110 A.. watch-key in the shape of a pistol. **1723** *Lond. Gaz.* No. 6189/4 *Watch Key-maker. **1795** J. AIKIN *Manchester* 311 They make *watch-movements. **1884** F. J. BRITTEN *Watch & Clockm.* 284 *Watch Movement*, the plates with the wheels and pinions composing the train. *Ibid.* 285 **Watch Pendant*, the little neck of metal connecting the bow to the band of a watch case. **1849** NOAD *Electricity* (ed. 3) 65 The finest flattened steel, sold at the watchmakers' tool shops, under the name of *watch pendulum-wire. **1899** F. J. BRITTEN *Old Clocks & Watches* 348 *Watch Pillars.. are now universally made of a plain cylindrical form. **1925** *Watchmaker, Jeweler, Silversmith & Optician* LI. 138 (Advt.), The finest range of *watch straps. **1977** P. THEROUX *Consul's File* 126 The woman [was] covered with welts the shape of watch-straps. **1921** D. H. LAWRENCE *Sea & Sardinia* ii. 66 Venus of the aborigines, from her *watch-temple looking at Africa.

27. Special combs.: **watch-alarm** (see quot.); **watch-ball**, a ball of clay used to test the temperature of a glaze kiln (see sense 22 above); †**watch-birth** *nonce-wd.*, ? a literary work brought to birth by watching; **watch-boat**, a boat on patrol duty; **watch bracelet**, a bracelet fitted with a small watch; **watch-candle**, a candle used for night-watching, a watching candle; **watch cap** (see quot. 1911); **watch-care** *U.S.*, watchful care; **watch-chain**, a metal chain used as a watch-guard; hence **watch-chained** *a.*; **watch-charm** *U.S.*, a small ornament that may hang from a watch-chain; **watch-cloak, -coat**, a thick, heavy cloak or coat worn by seamen, soldiers, or watchmen when on duty in bad weather; †**watch-cobbler**, ? a mender of watches; **watch committee** *Hist.*, the committee of a county borough council which dealt with all matters pertaining to the policing and public lighting of the borough; **watch-fire**, a fire maintained during the night as a signal, or for the use of a sentinel, party or person on watch; **watch-free** *a.*, free from the duty of watching or keeping guard; †**watch George**, ? a George (GEORGE 3) in the form of a watch; **watch-guard**, a chain, cord, ribbon, or the like used to secure a watch when it is worn on the person; **watch-gun**, †(*a*) a spring gun used as guard against trespassers; (*b*) *Naut.* (see quot. 1815); **watch hand**, each of the hands of a watch; also *attrib.* in ***watch-hand rotation***, rotation from left to right like that of the hands of a watch; **watch-header** *U.S.*, the officer in charge of a watch; **watch hill** (see quot. 1895); **watch-hook**, a hook for fastening a watch to the dress; †**watch hour**, the hour for sounding the watch; **watch jeweller**, a workman who fits the jewels in the pivot-holes of watches; **watch-jobber**, a mender of watches, esp. as a watchmaker's employé; **watch-keeper**, one who keeps watch or serves as a member of a watch on board ship; an officer in charge of a watch; also in gen. use, one who keeps watch or acts as a look-out; hence **watch-keeping** *sb.* and *a.*; †**watch-knoll (-know)** *Sc.* = sense 14; cf. *watch-hill*; **watch lamp**, an apparatus for illuminating the face of a watch at night; **watch-lining** = *watch-paper*; **watch-list**, a list of items or names which require close surveillance, esp. for legal or political reasons; †**watch-mail, -meal** *Sc.*, 'a duty imposed for maintaining a garrison' (Jam.); **watch mark** *Naut.*, a mark worn on the sleeve, indicating the watch to which the wearer belongs; †**watch-master** (see quot.); **watch-mastiff**, a mastiff kept as a watch dog; **watch-mate**, a fellow-member of a ship's watch; †**watch-meal** (see *watch-mail*); †**watch money**, a sum of money paid for watching; **watch-nick** (see quot.); **watch-night**, (*a*) originally a religious service extending over midnight held monthly by Wesleyan Methodists; in later use a service held (by Methodists and others) on New Year's eve, lasting until midnight; also, the night upon which the service is held; (*b*) *W. Afr.*, a night-watchman; **watch-officer**, an officer who takes his turn as the officer in charge of the watch; **watch-oil**, a highly refined lubricating oil used for watches and clocks; **watch-paper**, a disc of paper, silk, or other material, inscribed or painted with an ornamental design, a picture, rhyme, or other device, inserted as a lining or pad in the outer case of an old-fashioned watch; **watch-part** = *watch train*; **watch-peal**, a warning peal (of a bell); **watch-peel** (see PEEL *sb.*^{1} 4); **watch-pocket**, a small pocket in a garment for carrying a watch; also, a pocket or pouch at the head of a bed, to hold a person's watch at night; **watch point**, a watching station; **watch pole**, a watchman's pole or staff; **watch-post** *Mil.*, a position at which a body of soldiers, a sentinel or watchman, is stationed on watch; also, a body of guards; **watch rate**, a rate levied by a municipal borough to defray the expenses of watching; **watch-riband, -ribbon**, a watch-guard in the form of a riband; **watch room**, a room from or within which a watch is kept; **watch round** = ROUND *sb.*^{1} 14; **watch-seal** = SEAL *sb.*^{2} 3 f; **watch-setting** *Mil.*, the posting of the watch; **watch-spring**, the mainspring of a watch; also (without article) as a material; also *attrib.*; **watch-stand**, †(*a*) a look-out position for a sentinel or watchman; (*b*) a small case or stand in or upon which a watch may be placed so that its face may be seen; †**watch-star** = GUARD *sb.* 12; **watch-string**, a watch-guard of cord; **watch-tackle** *Naut.*, a TACKLE (*sb.* 3) by means of which the watch can perform various operations without the help of additional men; **watch train**, the set of wheels and pinions which drive the hands of a clock, as distinguished from the striking train; **watch-wheel**, the balance wheel of the 'watch-work' of a clock; also *Comb.*; **watch-woman**, (*a*) a woman who 'watches' in a sick room or attends a sick person; (*b*) a woman who performs the duties of a night watchman; (*c*) a woman who keeps vigil (*nonce-use*); †**watch-wright**, a watchmaker. Also WATCH-BELL, WATCH-BILL, WATCH-BOX, WATCH-CASE, WATCH-CLOCK, WATCH-DOG, WATCH-GLASS, etc.

1875 KNIGHT *Dict. Mech.*, **Watch-alarm*, an instrument with going works to sound an alarm at a specified period. **1839** URE *Dict. Arts* 1016 The *watch-balls of these first rounds have generally not so deep a colour as if they were tried in a furnace three or four months old. **1606** SYLVESTER *Du Bartas* II. iv. *Magnif.* 1197 Th' eternall *Watch-births of thy [*sc.* Solomon's] sacred Wit [*i.e.* his three books: Fr. *De ton diuin esprit les veilles eternelles*]. **1789** T. ANBURY *Trav. Amer.* I. 303 We are now within sight of the enemy, and their *watch-boats are continually rowing about. **1892** C. R. B. BARRETT *Essex* iii. 50 The *Henrietta* [pinnace] was at that time [*c* 1664] acting as watch-boat, and there are many references to its 'staying' boats that had used trawls. **1910** *Times* 13 Oct. 14/3 He was hailed by an Icelandic watchboat. The watchboat interrupted their fishing, and finally steamed alongside. **1896** *Godey's Mag.* Apr. 449/1 The *watch bracelet, with its setting of substantial leather, is a convenient adjunct to the cycler. **1601** HOLLAND *Pliny* XVI. xxxvii. I. 485 Rushes.. the pith where-of.. maketh wieke for *watch-candles, and funerall lights. **1605** BACON *Adv. Learn.* I. iv. §6 For were it not better for a man in a faire roome, to set vp one great light,.. than to goe about with a small watch candle into euerie corner? *a* **1711** KEN *Anodynes* Poet. Wks. 1721 III. 421 As in the Night I restless lie, I the Watch-Candle keep in Eye. **1911** WEBSTER, **Watch cap*, a knitted close-fitting navy blue cap worn by enlisted men in the United States navy in cold or storm. **1966** T. PYNCHON *Crying of Lot 49* v. 114 He opened his door and found an aged bum with a knitted watch cap on his head. **1977** J. F. FIXX *Compl. Bk. Running* xii. 139 What I've found best is a simple wool hat, the kind sailors call a watch cap. **1984** *New Yorker* 31 Dec. 64/3 Bearded young fishermen, with ponytails coming out from beneath their knitted watch caps. **1845** *Indiana Mag. Hist.* (1927) XXIII. 152 Very much.. depends on the.. preachers and leaders, who have the after *watch-care of the persons that are brought into the church. **1896** *Paterson Mag.* (U.S.) VI. 253/1 The years of watch-care which she had given to the child left in her charge. **1908** D. S. MACKAY *Relig. of Threshold* i. 27 The faith of this man lays hold of God's watch-care in these two extremes of the day. **1739** *Act 12 Geo. II*, c. 26 §13 For assaying.. Gold Hooks for *Watch Chains, ten Pence apiece. **1796** MME. D'ARBLAY *Camilla* I. 249 Sir Sedley smiled, and played with his watch chain. **1837** DICKENS *Sk. Boz, Parl. Sk.*, The.. immensely long waistcoat, and silver watch-chain dangling below it. **1944** BLUNDEN *Cricket Country* i. 12 One or two *watch-chained elders. **1976** 'R. GORDON' *Doctor on Job* xi. 93 Frock-coated and gold watch-chained. **1898** H. S. CANFIELD *Maid of Frontier* 15 [How's] the little baby I gave the *watch-charm to? **1929** W. FAULKNER *Sound & Fury* 99 Father brought back a watch-charm from the Saint Louis Fair. **1979** *Arizona Daily Star* 1 Apr. C4/2 His uniform number and watch-charm size aren't the only distinctive things. **1814** SCOTT *Diary* 18 Aug. in *Lockhart* (1837) III. vi. 207 Duff and I sit upon deck, like two great bears, wrapt in *watch-cloaks. **1825** —— *Betrothed* xiv, Enveloping himself in his long *chappe*, or military watch-cloak, he [the Norman soldier] withdrew. ? **1704** in Alice M. Earle *Two Cent. Costume Amer.* (1903) II. 407 A White Cape-cloth *Watch-coat. **1719** DE FOE *Crusoe* I. (Globe) 135 There were also several thick Watch-Coats of the Seamens,.. but they were too hot to wear. **1827** E. MACKENZIE *Newcastle* II. 726 Each watchman is provided with a warm watch-coat, a lanthorn, a rattle. **1848** DICKENS *Dombey* xlviii, The Captain.. laid her down, and covered her with a great watch-coat. **1756** TOLDERVY *Hist. 2 Orphans* I. 177 'I'll warrant ye (said a shrewd lawyer, though not Foxer) this Roebuck left his colours for no good.' 'Good! ha,' cried a great greasy *watch-cobler, ''tis my belief that he was reduced for cowardice.' **1835** *Act 5 & 6 Will. IV*, c. 76 §76 The Council.. shall.. appoint.. a sufficient Number of their own Body, who, together with the Mayor.. shall be and be called the *Watch Committee for such Borough. **1884** *Encycl. Brit.* XVII. 28/1 The mayor.. is *ex officio* a magistrate for the borough and a member of the watch committee. **1801** SCOTT *Glenfinlas* xxxix, And by the *watch-fire's glimmering light, .. was seen An huntress maid. **1814** BYRON *Corsair* I. ii, Such were the notes that from the Pirate's isle Around the kindling watch-fire rang the while. **1867** LADY HERBERT *Cradle L.* viii. 215 Watch-fires were lit round the encampment. **1581** STYWARD *Martial Discipl.* I. 30 The which.. except in great extremitie shall be *watch free. **1614** in *Archæologia* XLII. 350 Item a *watche George. **1834** DICKENS *Sk. Boz, Steam Excurs.*, Miss Emily Taunton was making a *watch-guard. **1839** —— *Nickleby* ii, The dark-complexioned men who wear large rings and heavy watch-guards. **1768** *Ann. Reg.* 106 A maid-servant at Paddington was accidentally shot by a *watch-gun, which was usually set by the family as a defence against rogues. **1772** *Regul. H.M. Service at Sea* 9 Captains are forbid to fire the Watch-Gun in any Port.. unless there be at least Five of H.M. Ships in Company. **1798** NELSON in Nicolas *Disp.* (1845) III. 132 The Marquis fired a shot from his morning-gun into the Town... I fire no watch-gun. **1815** *Falconer's Dict. Marine* (ed. Burney), *Watch-Gun*, the gun which is fired on board ships of war at the setting of the watch in the evening, and relieving it in the morning. **1773** *Pennsylv. Gaz.* 16 June, Suppl. 2/2 [Advt.] Clock and *watch hands. **1882** MINCHIN *Unipl. Kinem.* 36 An observer.. sees.. every point in the body rotated about him in a sense opposite to that of watch-hand rotation. *Ibid.* 222. **1887** GOODE *Fisheries of U.S.* V. ii. 229 (Cent.) The divisions of the crew are known as the starboard and larboard watches, commanded respectively by the first and second mates or the second and third mates, who are known as *watch-headers. **1560** in J. Scott *Berwick-upon-Tweed* (1888) 448 Any man that cometh to the *watch hill and is by the officers to watch. **1895** *Lakeland Gloss.* Suppl., *Watch Hill*, the hill from which the outlook was kept against border freebooters; hence now frequent as Border place-name. **1698** *Lond. Gaz.* No. 3376/4 A Diamond *Watch-Hook..was lost the 17th instant. *c* **1500** MEDWALL *Nature* (Brandl) 43 Who taught the cok hys *watche howres to obserue. **1884** F. J. BRITTEN *Watch & Clockm.* 102 *Watch jewellers use a glass with double lenses half an inch in diameter. **1895** *Daily Chron.* 28 Aug. 8/4 *Watch Jobber (Really good) wanted. **1900** F. T. BULLEN *With Christ at Sea* xi. 210 The second mate.. combined in himself the various offices of bosun, sailmaker, and *watchkeeper. **1920** *Times Lit. Suppl.* 13 May 298/4 He exchanged his duties as a watch-keeper in an ironclad for service in the Cockatrice. **1981** J. R. L. ANDERSON *Death in High Latitude* ix. 141 We must have someone on watch... And the watchkeeper must have a rifle. **1946** C. S. FORESTER *Lord Hornblower* iv. 32 Nine years as a captain had not eradicated the habits acquired during a dozen years as a *watchkeeping officer. **1977** *Proc. R. Soc. Med.* LXX. 485/2 A sailor reported recurrent unilateral swelling after watchkeeping. **1645** in J. Wilson *Annals of Hawick* (1850) 65 [A burgess charged with not being present at the riding of the common] confessit he was at the *Watch-Know. [They] assoilzied him of the penalty and fine. **1823** J. BADCOCK *Dom. Amusem.* 203 Contrivance for a *Watch Lamp..which will show the Hour of the Night, without trouble to a person lying in bed. **1857** DICKENS *Dorrit* I. xxx, An old silk *watch-lining, worked with beads! **1974** P. GORE-BOOTH *With Great Truth & Respect* 238 There had been three categories of control, namely embargo, quantitative restriction and a '*watch-list'. **1982** 'J. PENN' *Notice of Death* xix. 178 The Watch List..a list the officials have at ports of entry, of people who are wanted for one thing or another. **1710** FOUNTAINHALL *Decis.* (1761) II. 552 Others more probably conjecture from its name given to it by Skeen, *voce* Pension ..of the *watch-meal of Kilpatrick, that it was for the sustenance of the garrison of Dumbarton. *Ibid.*, When this *watch-mail was constitute. **1860** STUART *Seaman's Catech.* (1862) 83 It is now a general rule through-out the navy to have '*watch marks' on the sleeve of the frock. **1585** HIGINS *Junius' Nomencl.* 479/2 *Tesserarius*,..the *watchmaister, or the sargeant that giueth the charge or watchword to the souldiers. **1778** W. PEARCE *Haunts of Shakespeare* 13 Or drowsy *watch-mastiff that bays the sharp wind. **1631** L. FOX *N.-W. Fox* (1635) 174 That no man shall..make any doubt thereof, eyther..at his Messe or to his *Watch-mate. **1840** R. H. DANA *Bef. Mast* xvi, About midnight we were waked up by our two watch-mates. **1898** F. T. BULLEN *Cruise of 'Cachalot'* xiv. 162 All my watchmates were.. waiting to be taken on board again. **1628** *Toke* (Kent) *Estate Acc.* (MS.) fol. 125 *Watch money. *c* **1750** in W. Alexander *Notes & Sk. 18th Cent.* (1877) 66 There is paid in black mail or watch money, openly, or privately, £5000. **1897** P. WARUNG *Tales Old Régimes* 122 Bunt..owned a *watch-nick—a tiny saw filed out of the tempered steel of a watch-spring. **1742** WESLEY *Jrnl.* 9 Apr., We had the first *watch-night in London. We commonly choose for this Solemn Service the Friday night nearest the full moon. **1835** *Court Mag.* VI. 70/2 A methodist, she always goes to their chapel on New Year's-eve—or the 'Watch Night', as they call it. **1883** *Pall Mall Gaz.* 10 July 10/1 A man..was charged with ..annoying the Salvation Army at a 'watch-night' service. **1953** G. M. DURRELL *Overloaded Ark* vi. 113, I engaged what in the Cameroons is known as Watchnight... There were two reasons for engaging a night watchman: the first.. to wake me up. The second..was that he patrolled the edge of the compound..for driver ant columns. **1975** J. WYLLIE *Butterfly Flood* (1977) xxxi. 148 The watch night. Where is the watch night?.. The nightwatchman was lying in his reclining chair. **1898** KIPLING *Fleet in Being* ii. 29 On a third-class cruiser, he [the Sub] is a *watch-officer. **1870** PREECE *Telegraphy* 249 Only good *watch-oil should be employed. **1777** in *Phil. Trans.* LXVII. 335 A *watch-paper ..on which there are some very fine hair strokes of a graver. **1818** HAZLITT *Eng. Poets* vii. (1870) 170 Nor did he cut out poetry as we cut out watch-papers. **1858** O. W. HOLMES *Autocrat* ix. (1903) 208 He..opened the watch, and handed me the loose outside case without a word.—The watch-paper had been pink once... Two little birds, a flower [etc.]. **1908** [MISS E. FOWLER] *Betw. Trent & Ancholme* 21 He wrote minutely the Creed and the Lord's Prayer on watch-papers. **1696** W. D[ERHAM] *Artif. Clock-m.* i. 3 The *Watch-part of a Movement is that which serveth to the measuring the hours. **1656** HEYLIN *Surv. France* 12 The Protestants, of this Bell [rung at the procession of the host] ..use it as a warning or *watch-peal to avoid that street through which they hear it coming. **1882** A. GEIKIE *Geol. Sk.* i. 7 *Watch-peels, castles, and towers. **1831** M. WHALLEY *Let.* 15 Feb. in J. Constable *Corr.* (1962) I. 260 Thanks for..a pair of tastefully & beautifully made *watch pockets. **1837** DICKENS *Pickw.* xxxvii, Consulting a copper time-piece which dwelt at the bottom of a deep watch-pocket, and was raised to the surface by means of a black string. **1845** D. JERROLD *St. Giles* xxi, [The] pistols..he attempted to place in the watch-pocket at the head of the bed. **1893** J. WATSON *Conf. Poacher* 167 When a constable, then a second, and a third, were all tearing down upon me from *watch points, where they had been in hiding. **1712** STEELE *Spect.* No. 358 ¶1 A Gentleman that has several Wounds in the Head by *Watch Poles. **1852** GROTE *Greece* II. lxxii. IX. 298 The occupation of Æolis by the Lacedæmonian general was a sort of *watch-post. **1887** BOWEN *Æneid* III. 238 Signal Misenus gives from his watch-post set on the steep. **1888** E. GERARD *Land beyond Forest* II. xxxviii. 144 On the extreme frontier of Transylvania, however, he left behind him a portion of his army, to serve as watch-post. **1835** *Act 5 & 6 Will. IV*, c. 76 §92 Provided that in every Case in which before the passing this Act any Rate might be levied in any Borough..for the Purpose of watching..it shall be lawful for the Council of such Borough to levy a *Watch Rate. **1860** SMILES *Self Help* 114 Flaxman..was on one occasion selected by the ratepayers to collect the watch-rate for the parish of St. Anne. **1832** *Chambers's Edin. Jrnl.* I. 82/2 Having changed the wear..of a silk *watch-riband for a chain. **1834** MARRYAT *P. Simple* iii, The captain gave a youngster five dozen the other day for wearing a scarlet watch-riband. **1804** BYRON *Let.* 29 Aug. (1973) I. 51 Do not overlook my *watch ribbon, and purse as I wish to Carry them with me. **1827** DISRAELI *Vivian Grey* III. v. vii. 131 Here are Eau de Cologne, violet soap, and watch-ribbons. **1850** *Ann. Sci. Discovery* 73 On the top of the structure [*sc.* a lighthouse] is the *watch-room, and lantern, or light-room. **1883** 'MARK TWAIN' *Life on Mississippi* 338 One of the two establishments where the Government keeps and watches corpses until the doctors decide that they are permanently dead... A wire led to a bell in a watch-room yonder..where a watchman sits always alert. **1943** *Gloss. Terms Telecomm.* (*B.S.I.*) 85 *Watch room*, the room, at the fire station, which is continuously staffed and contains the alarm-recording apparatus, call-bell keys and telephonic intercommunicating equipment. **1977** *Stornoway Gaz.* 27 Aug. 1/4 The Commission also want to renovate the existing harbour watchroom to provide welfare facilities for dock workers, a new watchroom, and public toilets. **1979** N. WALLINGTON *Fireman!* iii. 37, I saw..the watchroom into which came all the emergency calls. **1828–43** TYTLER *Hist. Scot.* (1864) I. 133 Spalding.. determined, on the night when it was his turn to take his part in the *watch rounds, to assist the enemy in an escalade. **1798** SOPHIA LEE *Canterb. T.*, *Young Lady's T.* II. 151 The *watch-seals..of the Marquis. **1840** CARLYLE *Heroes* v. (1841) 293 He does not 'engrave *Truth* on his watch-seal'. **1811** *Regul. & Orders Army* 101 After which no Trumpet is to sound, or Drum to beat, in the Garrison, except at *Watch-setting and Tattoo. **1844** *Ibid.* 259 The Trumpet is to sound for Watch-setting, and the Tattoo is to beat at Eight o'clock. **1920** *Daily Tel.* 21 Mar. 10/7 The ceremony of playing 'Retreat' on watch-setting is observed all over the Empire wherever an infantry battalion is quartered. **1760** in *Phil. Trans.* LI. 829, I cut off several slips from different leaves, each of which I placed between two bits of *watch-spring. **1815** J. SMITH *Panorama Sci. & Art* II. 375 Thin plates..rolled up in the manner of a watch-spring. **1837** DICKENS *Pickw.* liv, The fat boy returned, slumbering as peaceably in his dickey, over the stones, as if it had been a down bed on watch-springs. **1843** HOLTZAPFFEL *Turning* I. 250 Watch springs are hammered out of round steel wire of suitable diameter, until they fill the gage for width. **1897** *Daily News* 1 June 7/4 The watch-spring steel is manufactured at Sheffield. **1610** HEALEY *St. Aug. Citie of God* III. xii. 121 In time of warre, or suspition, the watchmen placed bundels of drye small sticks, vpon their high *watch-stands [L. *in editis speculis*]. **1858** SIMMONDS *Dict. Trade*, *Watch-stand*, a mantel-piece or toilet rest or support for a watch. **1588** ASHLEY *Wagenar's Mariners Mirr.* B 2 b, If the said *watch stars stand South southwest. [Cf. *supra*, 'those Guardes or watches of *Vrsa minor*'.] **1773** *Pennsylv. Gaz.* 16 June, Suppl. 2/2 [Advt.] Silver and steel watch chains,..silk *watch strings. **1789** *Trifler* No. xxxiii. 427 A gentleman of the present age has seldom more taste than he can..lavish away in the choice of a watch-string. **1840** R. H. DANA *Bef. Mast.* xxv, By..clapping *watch-tackles upon all the sheets and halyards, we managed to hold our own. **1838** *Penny Cycl.* XII. 299/1 The one..gives motion to the train of wheels called the going or *watch train; the other to the striking train of wheels. **1894** F. J. BRITTEN *Former Watch & Clockm.* 210 The 'going' or 'watch' train, that drives the hands. **1568** *Ludlow Churchw. Acc.* (Camden) 132 For the mendinge of the staye of the *wache while..jd. **1569** *Ibid.* 136 For the mending of the watchwhele of the clock. **1688** HOLME *Armoury* III. 362/1 The Second..is termed the Ballance Wheel of a Clock... Some call it the Wauch Wheel, or Motion Wheel. **1813** *Examiner* 5 Apr. 219/1 R. Payne,.. watch-wheel-maker. **1638** G. DANIEL *Eclog* i. 170 Thy verse may creepe To Chimneyes, or *watch-women till they sleepe. **1829** *Good's Study Med.* (ed. 3) IV. 96 The mischievous fondness of her nearest relations has since removed this faithful watchwoman [female attendant]. **1836** LONGF. *Life* (1891) I. 245 At Brunnen there is no watchman, but a watchwoman. **1674** N. FAIRFAX *Bulk & Selv.* 75 The *Watch-wrights craft being not only the Ape of Nature, but the very Tool, still in her hand.

watch (wɒtʃ), *v.* Pa. t. and pa. pple. **watched** (wɒtʃt). Forms: 1 *Northumb.* **wæcca (woæca)**, pa. t. **-wæhte**, *WS.* only in pr. pple. **wæccende**, 2–5 **wecche**, 4–7 **wach(e**, 4–5 *Sc.* **vach**, (? **wauch**), 4–6 **wacche**, 5–6 **weche**, **watche**, 6– **watch**. [OE. *wæcc-*, a doublet of *wacian* WAKE *v.* (weak), repr. WGer. **wakǣjan* (OHG. *wahhên*); in WS. only in pr. pple. *wæccende*, the forms belonging to *wacian* being used for the other parts of the vb.; in Northumbrian the type *wæcc-* is alone recorded. For the Teut. and Indogermanic cognates see WAKE *v.*]

I. Intransitive uses.

†**1. a.** To be or remain awake. *Obs.*

a **1000** *Rituale Eccles. Dunelm.* (Surtees) 28 *Sive vigilemus sive dormiamus*, Sva hvoeðer we woæca *vel* we slepa. *a* **1000** *Riddles* xl[i]. 8 Heht me wæccende wunian longe, þæt ic ne slepe siþþan æfre. *c* **1430** LYDG. *Min. Poems* (Percy Soc.) 169 He..Slepithe on the day and wacchith al the nyght. **1430–40** —— *Bochas* v. vii. (1554) 128 Fyrst the liddes of his eyen twayne, They cut them of.. That he not should slepe in prison, But euer watche with paine intollerable. **1590** BARROUGH *Meth. Phisick* I. xv. (1639) 23 If the sick watch overmuch, then you must apply such things as provoke sleep. **1641** W. CARTWRIGHT *Lady Errant* II. ii, *Pan.* Wee'l keep you, As they doe Hawkes— *Cos.* Watching untill you leave Your wildness. **1658** tr. *Lemnius' Secret Mirac. Nat.* III. viii. 211 Hence grew the Proverb, when men have passed a troublesome nights rest..they say, We have had Saint John Baptist's night: That is, we have not taken any sleep, but watcht all night.

†**b.** To keep awake intentionally. *Obs.*

c **1000** *Rule of Chrodegang* xiv, Eadiȝe beoð þa þeowan, þe heora hlaford, þonne he cymð, hi wæccende fint. *c* **1450** *Cov. Myst.*, *Betray. Christ* 18 Petyr, with thi ffelawys here xalt thou abyde, And weche tyl I come ageyn. *c* **1475** *Partenay* 5375 Where it behouith to wacche nightes thre Without Any sompnolent slepe to be. **1602** VAUGHAN *Direct. Health* in *Babees Bk.* 252 Watch not too long after supper, but depart within two hours to bed. **1650** H. BROOKE *Conserv. Health* 180 The Phlegmatick and Fat should Watch much. **1667** MILTON *P.L.* I. 332 As when men wont to watch On duty, sleeping found by whom they dread, Rouse and bestir themselves ere well awake.

c. Of certain flowers: To remain unclosed (during certain hours of the day).

1812 *New Bot. Gard.* I. 51 The flowers [of *Anthericum ramosum*] watch from seven in the morning to three or four in the afternoon.

d. *to watch up*: to sit up at night. *rare.*

1852 THACKERAY *Esmond* III. v, Esmond had seen this gentleman..toiling to give bread to a great family, and watching up many a long winter night to keep the wolf from his door.

e. To remain awake *with* a sick person or at his bedside, for the purpose of rendering help or comfort.

1691 TILSON in *Baxter's Certainty Worlds Spirits* 148 Between One and Two-a-Clock in the Morning she fell into a Trance. One Widow Turner, who watched with her that Night, says, that [etc.]. *a* **1700** EVELYN *Diary* 6 Mar. 1670, I watched late with him [a brother on his deathbed] this night. **1843** MRS. BROWNING *To Flush* vii, This dog watched beside a bed..Where no sunbeam broke the gloom Round the sick and dreary.

2. a. To remain awake for purposes of devotion; to keep vigil.

971 *Blickl. Hom.* 137 Heo wæs wæccende dæȝes ond nihtes. *c* **1450** CAPGRAVE *St. Gilbert* (1910) 121 Aftyr sche had wecchid in deuoute prayeres al a nyte sche went hom hol fro both sores. **1526** *Pilgr. Perf.* (W. de W. 1531) 13 He was tempted moost suttelly, he watched, he fasted, he prayed moost besyly. **1570–1** *Rec. Burgh Lanark* (1893) 54 Item, for candill to wyche in the kirk, ij s. **1712** P. METCALFE *Life S. Winefride* (1917) 18 She watch'd whole Nights in the Church, either kneeling or prostrate before the Altar or [etc.]. **1756–9** A. BUTLER *Lives Saints*, *S. Peter Damian*, Peter watched long before the signal for matins, and after with the rest. **1865** SWINBURNE *Chastelard* III. i. 90 Fair sir, Give me this hour to watch with and say prayers. **1913** W. K. L. CLARKE *Basil* vi. 89 To fast or watch more than the rest is self-will and vain-glory.

b. quasi-*trans.* with complement. *to watch in*: to keep vigil to greet (the New Year).

1828 ADAM CLARKE in *Life* (1840) 454 Mother was not strong enough to watch-in the New Year.

3. a. To be on the alert, to be vigilant; to be on one's guard against danger or surprise.

a **1225** *St. Marher.* 15 Ah þeo þet stalewurþe beoð ant starke to ȝein me [*sc.* Satan], swa þet heo ham wið me ant mine wrenches wecchinde ham werien, so uuel me puncheð þrof þet [etc.]. **1595** SHAKS. *John* IV. i. 5 Be heedfull: hence and watch. **1658** J. OWEN *Temptation* ii. 30 To watch is as much as to be on our guard, to take heed, to consider all waies, and meanes whereby an enemy may approach to us. **1675** —— *Indwelling Sin* viii. (1732) 81 It [*sc.* sin] adds in its workings, Deceit unto Power. The Efficacy of that must needs be great, and is carefully to be watched against. **1770** GOLDSM. *Des. Vill.* 166 But in his duty prompt at every call, He watched and wept, he prayed and felt for all. **1818** SCOTT *Rob Roy* xxvi, I wad advise ony friends o' mine to gree wi' Rob; for, watch as they like, and do what they like, they are sair apt to be harried when the lang nights come on.

†**b.** To attend diligently to a duty. Const. *upon.* Cf. WAIT *v.*[1] 14 d. *Obs.*

1608 WILLET *Hexapla Exod.* 673 With all their heart and endeuour they should watch vpon their office.

4. a. To be on the look out; to keep a person or thing in sight, so as to be aware of any movement or change.

1375 BARBOUR *Bruce* VI. 87 His twa men bad he..Ga to thair feris to rest and ly; For he vald vach thar com to se. **1547** *Bk. Marchauntes* e j, They haue a .C. eyes euer open to watch as the cat for the mous. **1560** DAUS tr. *Sleidane's Comm.* 45 b, The Byshoppe, whiche as the master of a shyppe sitteth watching at the Healme [L. *qui tanquam gubernator nauis in specula sedeat intentus*]. **1607** CHAPMAN *Bussy d'Ambois* v. iii, Sit vp to night, and watch. **1765** FOOTE *Commissary* II. 41 Watch, Simon, that nobody comes up whilst he is here. **1839** T. T. STODDART *Songs & P.* 40 Quickly lead, Where the roving trout Watches round an eddy, With his eager snout Pointed up and ready. **1845** BROWNING *Lost Leader* 14 Shakespeare was of us, Milton was for us, Burns, Shelley, were with us,—they watch from their graves! **1848** THACKERAY *Van. Fair* xxii, Did you ever see a dun, my dear; or a bailiff and his man? Two of the abominable wretches watched all last week at the green-grocer's opposite. **1860** TYNDALL *Glac.* II. xi. 290, I was to watch, and call out the direction in which he was to run.

b. With indirect question.

1375 BARBOUR *Bruce* VI. 62, I will ga vach all preuely, Giff I heir oucht of thar cummyng. **1390** GOWER *Conf.* I. 163 That made him forto waite and wacche Be alle weies how it ferde. *a* **1533** BERNERS *Huon* lxxxiii. 262 We..layde our busshement in a lytell wood a .ii. legees fro this cyte, to watch whan my brother Huon shold passe by that way. **1586** WHITNEY *Choice Emblems* 3 The Crocodile, by whome th' Ægyptians watche, Howe farre that yeare shall mightie Nilus flowe, For theire shee likes to laie her egges and hatche. **1878** TENNYSON *Revenge* xi, But they dared not touch us again, for they fear'd that we still could sting, So they watch'd what the end would be. **1888** *Glasgow Weekly Mail* 11 Aug. 5/1 It will behove the people..to watch how the Government may endeavour to pave the way for this change.

c. To be on the watch for opportunities *to do* something.

1375 BARBOUR *Bruce* XVII. 930 Bot dede, that vachis ay to mar With all hyr mycht waik and vorthy, Had at his worschip gret invy. **1471** CAXTON *Recuyell* (Sommer) 327 The Inhumanyte and terrybilite of the habitans and Indwellars, that allway wacche and wayte to do euyll and desplaysir to alle the world. **1697** DRYDEN *Virg.*, *Georg.* II. 776 The Groom..stript for Wrestling, smears his Limbs with Oyl, And watches with a Trip his Foe to foil.

d. To be on the watch *for* (something expected).

1831 SCOTT *Cast. Dang.* v, The wonderful turns of fate which have attended this fortress, are sufficient to warrant any one to watch for what seem the peculiar indications of the will of Heaven. **1864** TROLLOPE *Small Ho. Allington* xxvii, But I can see you when you watch for the postman.

e. ***to watch after*** (a person): to follow with one's looks, watch the movements of. *rare.*

1850 THACKERAY *Pendennis* lix, You should have seen Fanny Bolton's eyes watching after the dove-coloured young lady! **1852** —— *Esmond* II. x, Then he had seen her but for two days, and fled. Now he beheld her day after day, and when she was at Court watched after her.

f. Cricket. ***to watch out***: = FIELD *v.* 5.

1786 G. WHITE in *Life & Lett.* (1901) II. 160 Tom bats, his grand-mother bowls, and his great grand-mother watches out!! **1875** *Baily's Mag.* Apr. 403 So narrow is the ground, that long-leg and cover point respectively are quite out of sight, watching out on the hill-side. **1901** *Winch. Coll. Notions, Watch out*, to field at nets for cricket.

g. ***to watch out*** (*colloq.*, orig. *U.S.*): to look out, to be on one's guard.

1845 J. J. HOOPER *Some Adventures Simon Suggs* ix. 115 He determined therefore to 'watch out' and keep himself 'whole' in a pecuniary point of view if possible. *a* **1888** J. W. RILEY *Little Orphant Annie* iv, You better mind yer parents, ..Er the gobble-uns 'll git you Ef you Don't Watch Out! **1895** S. CRANE *Red Badge* i, You watch out, Henry, an' take good care of yerself in this here fighting business. **1909** J. MASEFIELD *Tragedy of Nan* I. 21 You better watch out she don't tread a thy corns. **1918** in *Times Lit. Supp.* 11 July 325/4 The new chantey on Monday morning's route march was a thing to watch out for. **1957** R. LAWLER *Summer of 17th Doll* I. i. 19 If you don't watch out, you're gunna start hating the poor bloke before he even gets here.

†**h.** ***to watch in***: to watch a television programme. *Obs.*

1928 *Daily News* 17 Dec. 6/4 (*heading*) Pictures by Wireless. Where to 'watch-in' this week.

5. watch over——. To exercise protecting care over; to keep in constant view in order to preserve from harm or error.

1526 *Pilgr. Perf.* (W. de W. 1531) 247 b, As heerdmen euer watchynge ouer the flocke of our lorde Jesu. **1655** JER. TAYLOR *Golden Grove, Agenda, Sunday* 65 Watch over thy self, counsel thy self,..and judge thy self impartially. **1712** ADDISON *Spect.* No. 289 ⁋2 That Providence which watches over all its Works. **1781** GIBBON *Decl. & F.* xxxi. III. 233 But there is a Providence (such at least was the opinion of the historian Procopius) that watches over innocence and folly. **1816** J. WILSON *City of Plague* II. ii. 216 From heaven fair beings come at night To watch o'er mortals while they sleep. **1875** JOWETT *Plato* (ed. 2) V. 404 The eye of the rulers is required always to watch over the young. **1879** LUBBOCK *Sci. Lect.* v. 166 We cannot put Stonehenge or the Wansdyke into a museum—all the more reason why we should watch over them where they are. **1899** MARG. BENSON & GOURLAY *Temple of Mut* i. 11 A flock of goats, watched over by an Arab girl.

6. a. To fulfil the duty of a watchman, sentinel, or guard.

1375 BARBOUR *Bruce* x. 572 Vp to the wall I sall ȝow bring, Gif god vs kepis fra persaving Of thame that wachis on the wall. *c* **1475** *Rauf Coilȝear* 407 Him behouit neidlingis to watche on the wald. **1538** ELYOT *Dict., Excubo*, to watche, as they whiche in battaylle, or in the garde of a pryncis personne doo. **1540** HOBY in *Lett. Suppress. Monasteries* (Camden) 284 Besydes that hit did cost me money to persons ffor a long tyme nyghtly to weche and to take hede lest any thyng shuld to be mysordered there. **1576** *S'hampton Crt. Leet Rec.* (1905) I. I. 131 That every householder..should watche in proper person or at the least provide a good honest and able watcheman for the more suertie and save garde of the towne. **1623** in Rymer *Fœdera* (1707) XVII. 529 The Lord Mayor shall cause certain Persons to watch at the Gates, and other like places in the Suburbs where Flesh may be brought, to view and search and to intercept the same. **1662** J. DAVIES tr. *Olearius' Voy. Ambass.* 84 Great Lords and rich Merchants have a Guard in their Courts, who watch all night. *a* **1700** EVELYN *Diary* 6 Aug. 1641, I watched on a horne worke neere our quarters. **1791** MRS. RADCLIFFE *Rom. Forest* ii, Peter was ordered to watch at the door.

† quasi-*trans.* with complement. *nonce use.*

1659 *Nicholas Papers* (Camden) IV. 192 Yᵉ army men are almost watched off theire legs.

†**b.** ***to watch and ward***: to keep 'watch and ward'. Also *fig.* (For the transitive use see 10.)

1583 BABINGTON *Command.* x. (1590) 444 No more quench you the fire by withdrawing yᵉ wood, than assuredly you stay the course of wicked conceits, when you watch and ward well ouer your senses. **1590** SPENSER *F.Q.* II. viii. 2 They for vs fight, they watch and dewly ward, And their bright Squadrons round about vs plant. **1601** W. PARRY *Trav. Sir A. Sherley* 6 Either party lived watching and warding. **1620** *Shuttleworths' Acc.* (Chetham Soc.) 242 To a man, watchinge and wardinge at Burneley faire, iiijᵈ. **1681** W. ROBERTSON *Phraseol. Gen.* (1693) 1296 To watch and ward, *excubare.* **1693** *Urquhart's Rabelais* III. Prol. 4 Every one did watch and ward, and not one was exempted from carrying the Basket.

c. Of a sailor: To be on duty during a watch.

1799 NELSON in Nicolas *Disp.* (1844) I. 5, I was placed in the Seahorse of 20 guns, with Captain Farmer, and watched in the foretop. **1820** SCORESBY *Acc. Arctic Reg.* II. 235 Each man watches four hours, and rests eight.

†**7.** *Hunting.* Of an otter: To retreat into its lair. *Obs.* Cf. 17.

1677 N. COX *Gentl. Recreat.* I. (ed. 2) 10 An Otter Watcheth. **1686** BLOME *Gentl. Recreat.* II. 76 A Fox Kennelleth, a Badger Eartheth, an Otter Watcheth, a Boar Coucheth.

8. *Naut.* †**a.** Of the timbers of a ship: ? To work loose. *Obs.* **b.** Of a buoy: To float on the surface of the water.

1633–4 *Admir. Ct. Exam.* 50, 21 Jan. (MS.), Whilest she was at sea the beames did watch and worke too and froe. **1805** *Naval Chron.* XIII. 328 The Pilots..swept for and weighed (as no buoys watched) the four anchors. **1865** GOSSE *Land & Sea* 84 All the buoys had not yet 'watched' but there was a tremendous sea running.

II. Transitive uses.

†**9. a.** To keep under surveillance (a prisoner, a besieged army) in order to prevent escape or rescue; to set an armed watch upon (a place, road, passage). *Obs.*

c **1330** R. BRUNNE *Chron. Wace* (Rolls) 5086 He dide sette in wardes seers Knyghte to wachem [*v.r.* waite], & squiers. *c* **1375** *Cursor M.* 16893 (Fairf.) And for that skylle lette wacche hym [*sc.* Jesus in the tomb] Thre dais we you pray. *a* **1400** *Sqr. lowe Degre* 997 Than he watched your Chambre bryght, With men of armes hardy and wyght, For to take that squyer. ? *a* **1400** *Morte Arth.* 1613 That they be weisely wachede and in warde holdene. *c* **1470** HENRY *Wallace* III. 70 In a schaw..Thai lugyt thaim..To wache the way als besyly as thai mycht. *Ibid.* v. 239 Schyr Jhone Butler, to wache the furdis rycht, Out fra his men of Wallace had a sicht. **1568** GRAFTON *Chron.* II. 712 They should be kept, and with such vigilant persons continually watched. **1579** HAKE *Newes out of Powles* (1872) B ij b, This Nummus nowe ..Is straightly watchte, and hardly kept with men of each degree.

b. To guard (a dead body, goods).

1450 LOMNER *Let.* 5 May in *Paston Lett.* I. 125 And the shreue of Kent doth weche the body. **1587** *Acc. Mary Q. Scots* (Camden) 60 And for ij men hired to watch the plate at Ware and Peterborowe, iiij nights, vj s. viij d. **1697** DRYDEN *Æneis* XI. 45 Acœtes watch'd the Corps. **1823** 'JON BEE' *Dict. Turf* s.v. *Wake*, He, also, 'died one day,' so they say, and his ever-faithful groom watched the body during the night. **1884** 'MARK TWAIN' *Huck. Finn* xxvii, I peeped through a crack of the dining-room door, and see the men that was watching the corpse all sound asleep on their chairs. **1886** C. SCHOLL *Phraseol. Dict.* II. 834 The goods were watched all night by a watchman.

†**10. a.** To guard against attack; to provide with a body of guards or armed watchmen; to serve as a guard to. Also ***to watch and ward*** (cf. 6 b).

1375 BARBOUR *Bruce* xv. 128 Bot for the trewis he lefit noucht Wachis till set to the castele; Ilk nycht he gert men wach it wele. ? *a* **1400** *Morte Arth.* 547 He wylle werraye i-wysse, be ware ȝif the lykes, Wage many wyghtemene, and wache thy marches. *Ibid.* 613 Thane yschewes þe emperour ..Arayede with his Romaynes..Sexty geauntes be-fore,.. With weches and warlaws to wacchene his tentys. *c* **1450** *Merlin* xi. 166 Than thei leged and pight teyntes and pavilouns, and hem rested, and lete the hoste be wacched. **1451** *Paston Lett.* I. 199 Gonnor was wetched at Felbrygge Halle with xl. persones of the Lady Felbryggs tenaunts. **1549–62** STERNHOLD & H. *Ps.* cxxvii. 1 Likewise in vaine men vndertake, Cities and holdes to watch and ward. **1607** TOPSELL *Four-f. Beasts* 207 The King of Indians was watched with foure and twenty Elephants. **1819** SCOTT *Noble Moringer* x, Wilt thou receive this weighty trust when I am o'er the sea? To watch and ward my castle strong, and to protect my land.

†**b.** *refl.* To guard oneself. *Obs.*

1375 BARBOUR *Bruce* I. 520 For thar is nothir duk ne baroun,..That euir may wauch hym with tresoune!

11. To keep (a person or thing) in view in order to observe any actions, movements, or changes that may occur.

a. with obj. a person (or animal). Sometimes implying the intent to attack or capture.

1590 SHAKS. *Mids. N.* II. i. 177 Hauing once this iuyce Ile watch Titania, when she is asleepe, And drop the liquor of it in her eyes. **1650** *Hamilton Papers* (Camden) 255 Evre since I came hether I have bine so narowly wached by the severe Christans that I could not answer your letter before now. **1675** *Charac. Town-Gallant* (1872) 2 He watches Wenches just as Tumblers do Rabbits. **1821** SCOTT *Kenilw.* viii, Here has been my hang-dog kinsman watching you as close as ever cat watched a mouse. **1831** JAMES *Phil. Augustus* v, He became aware that he was watched by a party of men, whose appearance had nothing in it very consolatory to the journeyer of those days. **1840** DICKENS *Old C. Shop* ix, She would take her station here, at dusk, and watch the people as they passed up and down the street. **1850** TENNYSON *In Mem.* lxxxv, I watch thee from the quiet shore; Thy spirit up to mine can reach. **1902** BUCHAN *Watcher by Threshold* 81, I had not gone twenty yards..ere I knew I was watched. **1917** *Eng. Hist. Rev.* Oct. 495 To divide them [the Marches] between the Nevilles and the Percies, setting each to watch the other.

b. with obj. a thing.

c **1515** *Cocke Lorell's B.* 12 One kepte yᵉ compas, and watched yᵉ our glasse. **1645** STAPYLTON tr. *Musæus* C 2, On her high turret Hero watcht the flame, And as stiffe gales from any quarter came, Still screen'd it with the sacred robe she wore. **1798** COLERIDGE *Anc. Mar.* IV. 278 Within the shadow of the ship I watched their rich attire; Blue, glossy green, and velvet black, They coiled and swam. **1834** DICKENS *Sk. Boz, Boarding-ho.* i, 'You don't think it's at all an out-of-the-way affair then?' asked Mr. Septimus Hicks, who had watched the countenance of Tibbs in mute astonishment. **1886** RUSKIN *Præterita* I. iv. 124 But before everything, at this time, came my pleasure in merely watching the sea. **1900** G. C. BRODRICK *Mem. & Impr.* 293 There we lay, surrounded by twenty or thirty ships..all assembled on the same errand, vainly watching the heavens. **1908** [MISS E. FOWLER] *Betw. Trent & Ancholme* 361 We have watched the red and blue Harvest-waggons.

c. with obj. a process or course of events.

1593 SHAKS. *Rich. II*, III. iii. 73 Thus long haue we stood To watch the fearefull bending of thy knee. **1655** WALTON *Angler* x. (1661) 173 Watch their going forth of their holes and returning. **1827** FARADAY *Chem. Manip.* xix. (1842) 500 By this arrangement..the operations..are more conveniently watched. **1831** JAMES *Phil. Augustus* iii, While the hermit held the arm from which the blood was just beginning to flow, she..anxiously watched the returning animation. **1849** MACAULAY *Hist. Eng.* v. I. 662 It was remarked by those who watched their deportment that they had come back from the carnage of Taunton in a fierce and excited state.

d. with adv. or phrase as complement.

1660 *Nicholas Papers* (Camden) IV. 237 [He] was there discourd by..Colonel Eubank and watcht to his lodging. **1840** THACKERAY *Shabby-genteel Story* v, Many a time had she..painted herself as Helen, tying a sash round her knight's cuirass, and watching him forth to battle. **1844** DICKENS *Mart. Chuzz.* xiii, Didn't I watch him into Codger's commercial boarding-house, and watch him out, and watch him home to his hotel. **1848** —— *Dombey* viii, Then he would turn his head, and watch the child away, and say [etc.]. **1849** C. BRONTE *Shirley* xxxiii, He watched her down: he watched her in: himself shut the door: he knew she was safe. **1876** GEO. ELIOT *Deronda* xvii, He looked out for a perfectly solitary spot where he..could watch out the light of sunset.

e. with accus. and inf. (without *to*) or pres. pple.

1848 MRS. GASKELL *Mary Barton* xxxi, Mary watched the boatman leave the house. **1859** THACKERAY *Virgin.* xvii, Lady Maria..scarcely lifted up her head from her embroidery, to watch the aunt retreating. **1859** FITZGERALD *Omar* xxxvi, For in the Market-place, one Dusk of Day, I watch'd the Potter thumping his wet Clay. **1860** TYNDALL *Glac.* I. xxv. 183 Lying upon my back, I watched the clouds forming. **1896** HOUSMAN *Shropshire Lad* lxii, They put arsenic in his meat And stared aghast to watch him eat. **1908** [MISS E. FOWLER] *Betw. Trent & Ancholme* 41 We used to watch the small bees going in and out of a hole in the wall.

12. a. To keep in mental view; to keep oneself informed about (a course of events, etc.).

1675 DRYDEN *Aurengz.* III. (1676) 36 No hour of pleasure should pass empty by, Youth should watch joys, and shoot 'em as they flie. **1677** EARL ESSEX in *Essex Papers* (Camden) II. 117 Hee parted here with great professions of friend-ship ..yet however I would be glad you did a little watch his proceedings. **1797** GODWIN *Enquirer* I. vi. 41 We must watch their minutest actions. **1838** THIRLWALL *Greece* xliv. V. 357 We cannot believe that he..would willingly have foregone the opportunity of watching the proceedings of his colleagues. **1843** R. J. GRAVES *Syst. Clin. Med.* ix. 99 The cerebral symptoms should be always watched with the most unremitting and anxious attention. **1849** MACAULAY *Hist. Eng.* v. I. 535 The war which was then raging in Hungary.. was watched by all Europe with interest almost as great as that which the Crusades had excited five hundred years earlier. **1868** E. EDWARDS *Ralegh* I. v. 78 The natural jealousy of the Spaniards watched every naval enterprise of Englishmen. **1871** DALE *Commandm.* viii. 204 Merchants watch the rise and fall of the markets in remote countries. **1886** RUSKIN *Præterita* II. i. 25 [My father] watched with some anxiety the use I should make of this first command of money. **1897** J. L. ALLEN *Choir Invisible* xxiii. 347 She had never ceased to watch his career as part of her very life.

b. To be on the alert to avail oneself of (opportunities, advantages); to be vigilant to choose (one's time for action); †to look out for, wait expectantly for (some coming event).

1578 H. WOTTON *Courtlie Controv.* 97 Ponifre gaue a golden fee vnto his olde attorney, who watching hir time, employed all hir wicked inuentions which she had by long vse..collected. *c* **1590** MARLOWE & NASHE *Dido* III. ii. 824 O no, God wot, I cannot watch my time, Nor quit good turnes with double fee downe told. **1592** KYD *Sol. & Pers.* I. ii. 30, I, watch you vauntages? **1617** MORYSON *Itin.* I. 228 But it is the custome, that he that hath once payed the tribute may any time after enter this Church without paying any thing, if he can watch the opportunity of other Christians entering the same. **1639** J. CLARKE *Parœm.* 237 He that meanes to make a good market of his ware, must watch an opportunity to open his shop. **1642** J. TAYLOR (Water P.) *Life Walker* A 2 b, Walker stood watching the Kings comming by. **1763** COLMAN *Jealous Wife* III. 54 Did not She watch her Opportunity and come to You just as I went out? **1821** SCOTT *Kenilw.* xxvii, It was thus that he met not Wayland, who was impatiently watching his arrival. **1837** DICKENS *Pickw.* ii, Mr. Winkle eagerly watched his opportunity: it was not long wanting. **1886** C. SCHOLL *Phraseol. Dict.* II. 834 You must watch your opportunity to sell the goods... Watch the best opportunity for selling.

c. Of a barrister: To attend the trial of (a case) in order to note any point that may arise to affect the interests of a client who is not a party in the litigation, and to raise objections to any questions or evidence that may be inadmissible as compromising the client.

1890 M. WILLIAMS *Leaves* I. 87 Serjeant Ballantine's clerk ..came up and asked me whether, as his chief was absent, I would watch a case that was about to be argued.

d. To exercise care, caution, or restraint about (something). ***to watch one's step***: see STEP *sb.* 10 b.

1837 H. MARTINEAU *Society in Amer.* I. II. 187 The valetudinarians of the place..watch their own and each others' weight. **1958** 'CASTLE' & HAILEY *Flight into Danger* i. 23 You'd better watch that waistline, Pete. **1963** 'W. HAGGARD' *High Wire* iv. 40 Rex said deliberately: 'I have to watch champagne.' 'Really? But this one won't damage you.' **1969** G. CROUDACE *Blackadder* iv. 32 Pauline ate nothing but a small, lightly-grilled steak and a lettuce leaf; it was obvious that she had to watch her weight. **1976** M. MACHLIN *Pipeline* lvii. 573 Just watch your mouth... A man died here tonight. **1981** G. MARKSTEIN *Ultimate Issue* 26 It was a comparatively shabby office... Euram Marketing gave a distinct impression of watching the pennies.

e. ***to watch it***: to be careful. Freq. as imp. (as a threat or warning). *colloq.*

1916 'TAFFRAIL' *Pincher Martin* vi. 100 'Don't yer go lendin' money to any other blokes wot ain't fit to be trusted.' 'I'll watch it.' **1943** K. TENNANT *Ride on Stranger* xviii. 203 You're not getting any younger yourself, kid. You want to watch it. **1954** W. FAULKNER *Fable* 334 'All right,' the corporal said. 'Watch it now.' **1966** 'W. COOPER' *Mem. New Man* II. iv. 144, I replied in the proletarian vernacular of the times. 'Watch it!' **1978** D. BLOODWORTH *Crosstalk* xxii. 170 We really do have to watch it a bit. Thank God we're officially engaged.

13. a. To exercise protecting vigilance over; to tend (a flock).

1526 TINDALE *Luke* ii. 8 There were..shepherds.. watching their flocke by nyght. **1667** MILTON *P.L.* IX. 156 Man he made..and, O indignitie! Subjected to his service Angel wings, And flaming Ministers to watch and tend Thir earthie Charge. **1700** TATE *Suppl. to New Vers. Ps.* 8 While Shepherds watch'd their Flocks by Night. **1848** LONGF. *Resignation* 1 There is no flock, however watched and tended, But one dead lamb is there!

b. To sit up beside (a sick person) in order to render help; to keep watch beside (a dead body).

1526 *Pilgr. Perf.* (W. de W. 1531) 20 b, I am the soule of hym that thou watched the last nyght. **1590** *Aldeburgh Rec.* in *N. & Q.* 12th Ser. VII. 504/1 P[ai]d to Durrants wyfe for watchinge of Father profet,..iiid. *a* **1592** *Greenes Vision* Wks. (Grosart) XII. 233 Tomkins..saw hee was in his bed, ..watcht by his mother and his wife.

†**14.** To do (a person a good or bad turn); to contrive (mischief). *Obs.*

App. a substitute for WAIT *v.*[2], suggested by the synonymity of WAIT *v.*[1] and *watch*.

a **1586** SIDNEY *Ps.* XVII. viii, Yet their high hartes looke so low As how to watch our overthrow. **1586** W. WEBBE *Eng. Poetrie* (Arb.) 56 Which iniury though he meanes to doo me in myrth, yet I hope he wyll make me some suffycient recompence, or els I shall goe neere to watch hym the like or a worse turne. **1639** J. CLARKE *Parœm.* 173 Harme watch harme catch. *Ibid.* 209 I'le watch you a good turne. **1705** HICKERINGILL *Priest-cr.* 16 But look to't, Harm watch, harm catch: If you will needs bite and devour one another, take heed that ye be not consumed one of another.

15. To provide (a town) with watchmen. In *passive*, to be policed *by* a specified body of men.

1806 J. CARR *Stranger in Ireland* 52 At night the city is admirably watched and patroled. Most of the watchmen are armed with muskets, others with a pike [etc.]. **1834** *Picture of Liverpool* 47 The Commissioners for Watching and Lighting the town. **1909** *Rep. H.M. Inspectors of Constabulary* 45 The municipal boroughs of Maidenhead and Newbury are watched by the county constabulary.

16. *Falconry.* To prevent (a hawk) from sleeping, in order to tame it.

c **1575** *Perf. Bk. Kepinge Sparhawkes* (1886) 16 Note, neuer wache sorehawke for then you take her stomake awaye, the rye cometh on so fast, & so hurt her. **1596** SHAKS. *Tam. Shr.* IV. i. 198 Another way I haue to man my Haggard, To make her come, and know her Keepers call: That is, to watch her, as we watch these Kites. **1604** —— *Oth.* III. iii. 23 My Lord shall neuer rest, Ile watch him tame, and talke him out of patience. **1606** —— *Tr. & Cr.* III. ii. 43 What are you gone againe, you must be watcht ere you be made tame, must you? **1689** *Selden's Table-Talk* 31 Lecturers..preach the People tame (as a man watches a Hawk) and then they do what they list with them.

17. *Hunting.* To track (an otter) into its lair.

1576 TURBERV. *Venerie* 241 We watch and vent an Otter. **1686** BLOME *Gentl. Recreat.* II. 76 Terms for Lodging and Dislodging of Beasts... Watch and Vent the Otter. **1688** [see VENT *v.* 17 b].

watcha ('wɒtʃə), repr. a colloq. or vulgar pronunciation of *what do* (or *are* or *have*) *you*? Similarly **watcher**. See WHATCHA.

1926 D. L. SAYERS *Clouds of Witness* vi. 134 Hullo! Watcher mean, nap? I had got hold of a most important train of thought. **1966** R. PETRIE *Dead Loss* xiv. 108 Watcha gonna do, Jeff? You can't leave her here. **1967** E. & M. A. RADFORD *No Reason for Murder* xxiii. 167 Watcher want with Waddy? **1969** in Halpert & Story *Christmas Mumming in Newfoundland* 95 Watcha got there, Uncle?

watcha, var. WOTCHER *int.*

watchable ('wɒtʃəb(ə)l), *a.* [f. WATCH *v.* + -ABLE.] That may be watched; *spec.*, that may be watched with pleasure or profit at the theatre or cinema, or on television.

1611 COTGR., *Guettable*, watchable; subiect vnto watching, and warding. **1933** *Punch* 11 Jan. 51/2 There were two other dancing items: Messrs. Lee, Lee, Lee and Lee, who were very watchable and possessed in their pianist an accomplished clown; and Mr. Jerry Cole. **1970** *Daily Tel.* 12 Oct. 11 That rather unfortunate category among television documentaries—worthy but not terribly watchable. **1972** *Ibid.* 22 Nov. 15/2 He was also needed..to have the stage dressed in something more watchable than brown paper and dustsheets. **1978** *Chicago* June 130/1 Schlafly..was named one of the most influential and watchable women in America in two national polls taken in 1977. **1983** *Times* 26 Oct. 18/1 A very watchable programme.

Hence ˌ**watcha'bility**.

1966 *Guardian* 29 Mar. 10/3 For sheer watchability, the Liberals have just about won. **1975** *Daily Tel.* 10 Apr. 16/5 If watchability is part of the business of TV documentary,.. then 'The Fight Against Slavery'..is surely a winner.

watch-bell. *Obs.* exc. *arch.* [WATCH *sb.*]

1. A bell upon which the half-hourly periods in each watch are struck on board ship.

1497 *Naval Acc. Hen. VII* (1896) 287 Wache Belles..ij. **1815** *Falconer's Dict. Marine* (ed. Burney), *Watch-Bell*, in ships of war, a large bell hung to the beam of the forecastle, ..; it is struck when the half-hour-glass is run out, to make known the time or division of the watch. **1888** F. M. CRAWFORD *With the Immortals* xiv. II. 212 Come, weary mariners!..Worn out with waking when the watch-bell tolls —Here is the land you seek!

2. A bell rung at the setting and relief of a military watch or to sound an alarm on the approach of an enemy.

1560 in J. Scott *Berwick-upon-Tweed* (1888) 448 If there be any person that maketh any affraie at any of the gates of the said towne or at the watch hill at such tyme..as the watch bell is ringing or the watch is setting or afterwards that night untill the watch bell be discharged in the morninge. *a* **1674** MILTON *Hist. Moscovia* iii. Wks. 1851 VIII. 486 The Land of Mugalla..hath many Castles..with Towers..; and on the Gates Alarum-Bells or Watch-Bells.

b. *transf.* and *fig.*

1614 T. TYMME (*title*), A Silver Watch-Bell. The Sound whereof is able..to winne the most profane worldling..to become a true Christian. **1678** *Yng. Man's Call.* 118 Then shalt thou hear..the last trumpet... Oh how loath will the sinner be, to rise at the ringing of this watch-bell!

3. A bell used by a military or municipal watchman; also a bell rung to summon the watch.

1560 ROLLAND *Seven Sages* 78 In the meane time the watches bell thay rang. Than said the Knicht..Heir ȝe not now how that the watche bell rings. **1599** HAKLUYT *Voy.* II. II. 74 Some [of the garrison] keepe about the prison with lanterns and watch-bels answering one another fiue times euery night. **1660** in *Sir R. Sadler's St. Papers* (1809) III. 359 In the Bayliff's Chamber... One watch-bell.

†**watch-bill**[1]. *Obs.* [f. WATCH *sb.* + BILL *sb.*[1]] A watchman's bill or halberd.

1665 *Depos. Cast. York* (Surtees) 128 He had slaine a monster with one watch bill or broome hooke. **1688** *Ibid.* 284 One James Turpin, who was one of the watch,.. endeavoured to putt out the fire with his watchbill. ? *c* **1830** A. WILSON in Axon *Folk Song Lancs.* (1870) 36 There's snakes an' watchbills, just loike poikes.

watch-bill[2]. *Naut.* [f. WATCH *sb.* + BILL *sb.*[3]] (See quot. 1815.)

1813 *Niles' Weekly Reg.* 10 July 304/1 The Shannon had a crew of 376 picked men by her watch-bill. **1815** *Falconer's Dict. Marine* (ed. Burney), *Watch-Bill*, a list of the petty officers, seamen, and marines, of a ship of war, which.. points out the station of each man, and what watch he belongs to. **1875** BEDFORD *Sailor's Pocket Bk.* i. (ed. 2) 18 This abbreviated table is sufficiently compact to allow of its being copied into the watch-bill.

'watch-box. [WATCH *sb.*]

1. A small structure to shelter a person on watch.

1699 DAMPIER *Voy.* II. II. 14 About three or four Leagues Westward of Selam is another Watch-Box on a High Tree. **1890** *Daily News* 8 Jan. 3/1 Escapes are being placed in position as fast as they can be turned out. With 50 watch-boxes at 8*ol.* a piece, these escapes will cost 4,000*l.*

b. A small wooden shelter resembling a sentry-box but furnished with a seat and half-door, used by a municipal watchman. *Obs.* (latterly *Austral.*).

1811 *Ann. Reg.* 44 A female, about three years and a half old..was left in a watch-box, near her home. **1837** DICKENS *Pickw.* xiv, The floor of a watch-box. **1845** D. JERROLD *St. Giles* i. (1851) 2 She drew up at a watch-box, and addressed herself to the..man within. **1890** 'R. BOLDREWOOD' *Col. Reformer* xii, It was lucky Mr. Jedwood had not commenced life at Garrandilla in a watch-box, as he most certainly would have continued the use of that highly compressed apartment.

c. A policeman's shelter.

1905 *Daily Chron.* 10 July 5/4 On the south side of Parliament Hill Fields is a little square chalet, which is used by the County Council police... The watch-box, as it is called, was locked.

†**2.** ? = WATCH-CASE 2. *Obs.*

1656 in Atkins & Overall *Acc. Company of Clockm.* (1881) 232 It is ordered..that..there be noe more of that Mettle wrought in the fashion of Watch Boxes or Cases. **1739** *Act 12 Geo. II*, c. 26 §13 For assaying, trying and marking Gold Watch Cases or Gold Watch Boxes, ten Pence apiece.

'watch-case.

†**1.** ? A place in which one must keep watch.

1597 SHAKS. *2 Hen. IV*, III. i. 17 O thou dull God [*sc.* Sleep], why lyest thou with the vilde, In loathsome Beds, and leau'st the Kingly Couch, A Watch-case, or a common Larum-Bell?

2. A hinged case or cover of an old-fashioned watch, enclosing the watch proper; now, the metal cover enclosing the works of a watch.

1681 GREW *Musæum* IV. §iii. 369 Made of fine Silver-studded Work, as in Watch-Cases. **1697–8** *Foreign Post* 3–7 Jan. 2/2 A Gold Engrav'd Watch-Case lined with Scarlet Satten. **1789** MRS. PIOZZI *Journ. France*, etc. I. 78 Every.. compartment chased, like our old-fashioned watch-cases. **1857** DICKENS *Dorrit* II. xxx, She took the watch-case in her hand. **1899** F. J. BRITTEN *Old Clocks & Watches* 123 A very finely enamelled watch case, illustrating the early life of Christ.

b. *attrib.* and *Comb.*

1671 *Lond. Gaz.* No. 538/4 If any one can give notice of him to his Master..a Watch-case maker. **1773** *Pennsylv. Gaz.* 16 June, Suppl. 2/2 [Advt.] Watch-case stakes and hammers.

3. A small case or bag at the head of a bed for holding a watch at night; a watch-pocket.

1891 *Century Dict.*

†**watch-clock.** *Obs.*

1. a. ? A time-piece actuated by a spring. **b.** ? A clock with a dial indicating minutes and seconds. Also ***watch pendulum clock***.

1592 DEE *Compend. Rehearsall* in *Chetham Misc.* (1851) I. 29 An excellent watch-clock,..by which clock the tyme might sensibly be measured in the seconds of an houre. **1633** T. JAMES *Voy.* Q b, A Watch-clocke, of sixe inches Diameter: and another lesser Watch. **1650** TRAPP *Comm. Exod.* xxxv. 32 A certain artificer set a watch-clock upon a ring that Charls the Fifth wore upon his finger. **1671** FLAMSTEED in Rigaud *Corr. Sci. Men* (1841) II. 118, I spoke and wrote to my kinsman about a watch clock. *Ibid.* 121, I wrote by my coz. Wilson about procuring me a watch pendulum clock.

2. An alarm clock. Cf. WATCH *sb.* 19.

1598 SYLVESTER *Du Bartas* II. i. IV. *Handie Crafts* 94 Pourfull Need (Arts ancient Dame and Keeper, The early watch-clock [Fr. *resveille-matin*] of the sloathfull sleeper).

'watch-cry. [WATCH *sb.*] The periodical cry of a watchman; *fig.* a motto, phrase, or word that is constantly reiterated by a party or the advocate of a cause, to call attention to some principle deemed of supreme importance. Cf. WATCH-WORD.

1882 FARRAR *Early Chr.* II. 87 Every day shows us how easy it is, first to turn any expression into a watchcry, then to empty it of all significance [etc.]. **1893** *Tablet* 4 Mar. 320 Their watch-cry will be order, propriety and economy. *a* **1894** STEVENSON *In South Seas* II. ii. (1908) 153 From shore the cheerful watch-cry of cocks rang out at intervals.

'watch-dog, *sb.* **a.** A dog kept to guard a house, property, etc., and give warning of the approach of intruders.

1610 SHAKS. *Temp.* I. ii. 383 Harke, harke, bowgh wawgh: the watch-Dogges barke, bowgh-wawgh. **1770** GOLDSM. *Des. Vill.* 121 The watch-dog's voice that bayed the whispering wind. **1818** BYRON *Juan* I. cxxiii, 'Tis sweet to hear the watch-dog's honest bark Bay deep-mouth'd welcome as we draw near home. **1876** BANCROFT *Hist. U.S.* III. xv. 235 The baying of a watch-dog alarmed the village. **1894** FENN *In Alpine Valley* I. 120 The old man is as fierce as a watch-dog.

b. *fig.* and in fig. context, esp. denoting a commission or other group appointed as a safeguard against abuses by the authorities (in government, foreign policy, etc.), business interests, etc.

1845 MAURICE *Moral Philos.* in *Encycl. Metrop.* II. 595/1 Now we feel the necessity for a set of guardians or watch-dogs of the state. **1885** LOWELL *Democr.* etc. (1887) 114 Formerly the duty of a librarian was considered too much that of a watch-dog, to keep people as much as possible away from the books. **1910** LD. ROSEBERY *Chatham* xvi. 339 The Chancellor acted as his watch-dog in front of the Treasury. **1985** *Which?* Feb. 58/1 Our regular checks over the years (and those of other 'watchdogs' such as Trading Standards Officers) have consistently revealed a depressingly low standard of workmanship in garages. **1985** *Times* 31 May 13/7 Although climbing may be the most non-bureaucratic of sports it does need a watchdog guarding its interests.

c. quasi-*adj.* Characteristic of a watch-dog.

1862 HELPS *Organiz. Daily Life* 32 He was not a very skilful person in deciding upon difficult questions; but he had a sort of watch-dog carefulness. **1873** [see *scrub-woman* s.v. SCRUB *v.*[1] 6]. **1947** *Toronto Daily Tribune* 21 Dec. 12/1 [Vishinsky] spoke.., raking the United States for.. proposing that the assembly send a semi-permanent UN 'watchdog' commission. **1960** *Daily Tel.* 22 Aug. 1/1 He demanded the dispatch to his country of a United Nations watch-dog force. **1969** *Listener* 3 July 5/1 The watchdog function of the press depends..on the effects of publicity on a politician's own colleagues and opponents. **1977** *Time* 30 May 51/2 Last March the International Trade Commission, a six-member watchdog group appointed by the President, recommended an increase in the tariffs on Japanese sets from 5% to 25%. **1984** *Daily Tel.* 9 Oct. 8/2 The Post Office was accused yesterday by its consumer watchdog body of putting profit before service to customers.

'watchdog, *v.* [f. the sb.] *trans.* To attend, follow, or guard (a person); to maintain surveillance over (an activity, situation, etc.). Hence **'watchdogging** *vbl. sb.*

1902 C. J. C. HYNE *Mr. Horrocks, Purser* 70 There seems to be a whole regiment of ragamuffins on board here watchdogging her. **1962** *Punch* 20 June 933/1 The rigours of public watchdogging. **1964** R. F. FICCHI *Electrical Interference* ii. 9 The only way the system problem can be resolved is to have a completely formalized program to 'watch dog' the problem through to its solution. **1968** *Economist* 13 July 17/1 The job of watchdogging the constitution is second nature to Tories. **1977** M. HERR *Dispatches* 191 We [*sc.* war correspondents] were..there to watchdog the day. **1980** A. SKINNER *Mind's Eye* xiv. 196 Three more..went down with the strange attacks, and he and Holbrook watchdogged them through.

watched ('wɒtʃt), *ppl. a.* [f. WATCH *v.* + -ED[1].] Kept under close observation. †Also, of a hawk, that is kept awake (see WATCH *v.* 16).

1566 T. NUCE *Studley's Agamemnon* Upon the same 4 Hys request was suche: How that, to paynfull laboured stuffe my mynd I wolde annex: And do but as his watched worke, whych he doth here contex Deserues. **1627** E. F. *Hist. Edw. II* (1680) 84 [The Scots] in a watch'd opportunity set upon the tail of his Army. **1650** B. *Discolliminium* 34 Most that are out of the Army will ere long be as gentle as any watch'd Hawke. **1901** *Wide World Mag.* VI. 421/2 How to get Diaz out of the watched room was a very awkward problem indeed.

absol. **1901** J. H. MCCARTHY *If I were King* iv, Suddenly, when the tension of watcher and watched was keenest, there came a mighty crashing at the door.

b. *Proverb.*

1848 MRS. GASKELL *Mary Barton* xxxi, What's the use of watching? A watched pot never boils.

watched, variant of WATCHET.

watcher ('wɒtʃə(r)), *sb.* [f. WATCH *v.* + -ER[1].] One who watches or keeps watch.

a. *gen.* Often const. *of*, also *over*.

1572 HULOET (ed. Higins), Watcher, *insidiator, insidiosus.* **1611** B. JONSON *Catiline* III i, That will Antonius make his care..And watch the watcher. **1812** *Examiner* 24 Aug. 544/1 You heard the watchers exclaim—'Put up the lights.' **1817**

KEATS *Sonn.* xi, Then felt I like some watcher of the skies When a new planet swims into his ken. **1848** DICKENS *Dombey* xlii, The smooth, sleek watcher of his slightest look and tone. **1859** TENNYSON *Vivien* 556 Sir Valence.. Whose kinsman left him watcher o'er his wife And two fair babes. **1885** *Manch. Exam.* 29 May 5/3 Nothing is at present divulged to the public; but the eyes of interested watchers cannot be altogether closed.

b. said of the eye. *poet.*

1591 SHAKS. *Two Gent.* II. iv. 135 Loue hath chas'd sleepe from my enthralled eyes, And made them watchers of mine owne hearts sorrow. **1824** HOOD *Two Swans* 108 On his doubtful face Gleam his unwearied eyes, red watchers of the place. **1847** TENNYSON *Princess* IV. 306 To an eye like mine A lidless watcher of the public weal, Last night, their mask was patent.

c. One who keeps awake at night. Also ***night watcher***.

1509 BARCLAY *Ship of Fools* (1874) I. 296 Of nyght watchers and beters of the stretes playnge by nyght on instrumentes and vsynge lyke Folyes whan tyme is to rest. **1605** SHAKS. *Macb.* II. ii. 71 Get on your Night-Gowne, least occasion call vs, And shew vs to be Watchers. **1861** FANE & LYTTON *Tannhäuser* 78 She kneel'd, A faded watcher through the weary night,.. In deep, perpetual prayer for him she loved. **1867** LADY HERBERT *Cradle L.* iv. 117 There two figures are kneeling, motionless and absorbed in prayer. .. Still the two watchers kneel on.

d. One who watches by a sick bed, or by the dead.

c **1555** *Life Bp. Fisher* (E.E.T.S.) 127 Whervpon two of the watchers tooke it [the dead body] vpon a halbert betweene them. **1764** *Low Life* 9 Women, called Watchers, in Hospitals, taking the Advantage of their Patients being asleep, to pick their Pockets. **1847** TENNYSON *Princess* v. 59 And at her head a follower of the camp.. Sat watching like a watcher by the dead. **1849** C. BRONTË *Shirley* xxv, Then the watcher approaches the patient's pillow. **1885** *Lancet* 4 Apr. 630/1 Then there are the 'watchers', who belong to the Jewish community, and combine the office of a nurse with certain religious functions.

e. One who is occupied in watching; a watchman, guard, sentry, or the like. Also with defining word, as ***river-watcher***, NIGHT-WATCHER.

1525 BERNERS *Froiss.* II. xlix. 61 b, On yͤ mountaynes & hylles costyng the see.. were set watche men & watchers in dyuers maners. **1838** *Bentley's Misc.* III. 274 An inspection was immediately carried on with an earnestness worthy of two watchers at a night-telegraph during a time of war. **1838** DICKENS *Nickleby* xxii, The heavy footfall of the official watcher of the night. **1884** *Manch. Exam.* 10 Oct. 5/1 A river watcher.. and two boys.. lost their lives by the capsizing of a boat. **1896** H. G. WELLS *Wheels of Chance* xvii, There are detectives of an inferior description—watchers. **1897** CROCKETT *Lads' Love* xix. 203 The gamekeepers and water-bailiffs—the 'watchers' as they were called. **1904** *Times* 31 Mar. 9/4 Davies had first been an office-boy and was now a watcher.

f. as the title of a class of angels or of angels generally; tr. Aramaic *ʿīr*, one who is wakeful.

1535 COVERDALE *Dan.* iv. 13 And beholde, a watcher (euen an holy angel) came downe from heauen. **1576** A. G[ILBY] *Test. 12 Patriarchs* (1581) 11 For by such meanes were yͤ Watchers deceiued before the floud. *a* **1711** KEN *Psyche* Poet. Wks. 1721 IV. 312 They Watchers are, and with obsequious Wing Leave Heav'n for Earth, God's Messages to bring. **1801** W. TAYLOR in *Monthly Mag.* XI. 20 (tr. *Bk. Enoch*) All were afraid, even the watchers of the host. **1846** KEBLE *Lyra Innoc.* (ed. 3) 26 And by those features,.. Heaven's keen-eyed Watchers haply mete What mortals holy deem. *a* **1908** C. BIGG *Orig. Christianity* viii. 83 Six angels build the Tower: they are the Archangels, the First Created, the Watchers of Enoch.

†**g.** *Astr.* (*pl.*) = GUARD *sb.* 12, WARDEN *sb.*¹ 1 b.

1588 ASHLEY *Wagenar's Mariners Mirr.* B 2 b, When those Guardes or watchers of *Vrsa minor* being mounted higher. *Ibid.*, The Guards or watchers are to be placed in this Instrument exactly opposite to their due place.

h. With preceding *sb.* in objective relation, freq. hyphenated: an expert student or one who follows the affairs of (a particular person, country, or institution). *colloq.* (orig. *U.S.*).

1966 *N.Y. Times* 27 Dec. 10/3 That was the major question of the 'China watchers' as Mao observed his birthday without public fanfare yesterday. **1971** *N.Y. Post* 20 Dec. 40 The Nixon-watchers.. would construe Kissinger's return to Cambridge as a potential calamity. **1972** *Jrnl. Linguistics* VIII. I. 125 MIT-watchers have lately been puzzled by a division within the movement. **1974** *Guardian* 26 Mar. 16/1 As one experienced Brussels-watcher put it yesterday, Mr Peart has discovered how flexible the Treaty of Accession can be. **1974** Kremlin-watcher [see KREMLIN]. **1975** *Times* 19 June 14/8 The meeting.. achieved a level of futility which left even hardened EEC watchers groggy. **1976** *New Yorker* 8 Mar. 27/3 When Confucius first came under attack, professional China-watchers speculated that the criticism had allegorical overtones. **1978** *Guardian Weekly* 23 Apr. 17/3 A veteran Shah-watcher said, 'He realises the extent of present and future problems.'

†**i.** ***watcher-in***. A television viewer. Cf. WATCH *v.* 4 h. *Obs.*

1928 *Daily News* 17 Dec. 6/4 Watchers in will be able to judge for themselves the value of picture transmissions during this week.

watcher *int.*: see WATCHA.

watchet (ˈwɒtʃɪt), *sb.* and *a.* *Obs.* or *arch.* Forms: [? 2 waschet] 4 waget(t, vachet, 4–7 wachet(t, 5 waycett, 6 wattchett, watchit, -eth, watchshide, wattshode, wetshode, 6–7 watched, watchett, 7 watcht, wetched, -et, 6– watchet. [App. a. OF. (north-eastern) *wachet*, occurring A.D. 1420 (*une heuke.. foree de wachet*, a cloak lined with 'watchet'; it is not clear whether this means a particular fabric or a colour); an earlier instance, spelt *waschet*, occurs in quot. 1198 below; the use of the OF. word in an Anglo-Latin context at that date does not prove that it had already been adopted into English. It is possible that *waschet*, *wachet* may be a dim. of the word which is found once (spelt *wasce*) in a Douay document of 1262; Godefr. explains this as 'sorte d'étoffe', but the interpretation is not certain from the context. The Central OF. *gasche*, recorded once (1448), for some kind of appendage or ornament of a shoe, would correspond formally, but if Godefr. is right in rendering it 'buckle' the connexion is out of the question.

It is tempting to compare mod. Walloon *waiss* royal blue (which Diez would connect with OF. *guesde* WOAD); a dim. formation on a word of this meaning might have been used to denote a lighter shade of the colour. But the phonological possibility of such a derivation of *wachet* is very doubtful.]

A. *sb.* **1.** A light blue colour; cloth or garments of this colour.

[**1198–9** *Curia Regis Roll 8 B* m. 2 (P.R.O.) Ei abstulit .I. scapelarium de Waschet.] *c* **1386** CHAUCER *Miller's T.* 135 Yclad he was ful smal and proprely Al in a kirtel of a lyght waget [*v.rr.* wagett, vachet, wachet(t]. **1407** *Will A. Rymour* (Somerset Ho.) Togam meam de Wachett. **1538** ELYOT *Dict.*, *Scutulatus*, is a colour, I suppose a wachet [**1548** watchet]. **1551–2** *Act 5 & 6 Edw. VI* c. 6 §23 Clothe or Clothes.. of anye other color or colors then.. skarlett redd crymsen.. asewer wattchett [etc.]. **1588** LAMBARD *Eiren.* App. Yy v, Tres vlnas panni lanei, coloris veneti (vocati Anglice Watchet). **1591** LYLY *Endimion* v. ii, Whose teeth shal be so pure a watchet, that they shall staine the truest Turkis. **1601** HOLLAND *Pliny* IX. xxxvi. I. 258 So sullen and melancholie a colour, enclining to a blew or watchet [L. *color austerus in glauco*]. **1610** —— *Camden's Brit.* (1637) 133 The Saxons there in watchet clad, we see [tr. Sidonius Apollinaris: *Istic Saxona cærulum videmus*]. **1616** W. BROWNE *Brit. Past.* II. iii. 392 Here see we watchet deep'ned with a blewe. **1631** TOWNSHEND *Albions Triumph* 17 A garment of watchet. **1865** T. TAYLOR *Ballads & Songs Brittany* 13 What gown.. were't best to wear,—My gown of grain, or of watchet fair?

¶ App. misunderstood. (*Jaune garance* = madder yellow.)

1530 PALSGR. 287/1 Watchet colour, *jaune garance*.

2. A fly used by anglers; an artificial fly made to imitate this. Also ***watchet fly***.

1799 G. SMITH *Laboratory* II. 302 Pale or sky-blue watchet. It is a small fly, and appears on the water on a cold day. *Ibid.* 303 Yellow-watchet. Body, water-rat's fur, [etc.]. **1828** CARR *Craven Gloss.*, *Watchet*, the name of a fly among Craven anglers, because it is of a watchet colour, or pale blue. **1829** *Glover's Hist. Derby* I. 177 Yellow watchet fly.

B. *adj.* Light blue, sky-blue.

1496 *Nottingham Rec.* III. 296 A ȝarde of waycett carssey. **1503** *Priv. Purse Exp. Eliz. York* (1830) 96, x payre of wachet hosyn. **1578** LYTE *Dodoens* II. lv. 216 The flowers.. are of a watcheth or pale blewe colour. **1589** HAKLUYT *Voy.* 282 The mariners being all apparelled in Watchet or skie coloured clothe. **1598** *Inventory* in Greg *Henslowe Papers* (1907) 121 Item, j wattshode tafitie dublet for a boye. **1604** MARSTON & WEBSTER *Malcontent* III. i. (2nd Q.) E 2 b, Sea-water greene sutes, ash-color cloakes, wetchet stockings. **1647** R. STAPYLTON *Juvenal* 242 Who wonders at the Germans watchet eyes? [L. *Caerula quis stupuit Germani lumina?*]. **1657** R. LIGON *Barbadoes* (1673) 12 She wore buskins of wetched Silk, deck'd with Silver lace. **1742** COLLINS *The Manners* 68 Or him whom Seine's blue nymphs deplore In watchet weeds on Gallia's shore. **1887** ASHBY-STERRY *Lazy Minstr.* (1892) 186 Watchet eyes As sweet as early summer skies! **1893** J. DAVIDSON *Fleet St. Eclogues* 37 Wood-violets of watchet hue.

b. prefixed to *blue* as a qualifying term.

1536 *Stories & Proph. Scripture* F v, Betwene euery bell a pomegarnade of purpoure,.. of russed reade, of wetshode blew and of vermillion. **1665** HOOKE *Microgr.* 49 And the rest of the line of a Watchet blew. **1871** M. COLLINS *Mrq. & Merch.* I. iv. 127 Her hair was a light soft brown, her eyes a watchet blue.

†**c.** sometimes app. used to denote a green or greenish colour.

This meaning is uncertain exc. in quot. 1658.

a **1613** J. DENNYS *Secr. Angling* II. xxii. C 6 b, Marke what a line he hath,.. Of Bucephall, or Bayards strongest hayre Twisted with greene or watched silke among. **1635** SWAN *Spec. M.* v. §2 (1643) 93 In stead of a blew, [comets are sometimes] of a watchet or greenish colour. *a* **1658** CLEVELAND *Poems* (1659) 161 Tethys in a Gown Of sea-green watchet.

d. *Comb.*, as ***watchet-coloured***, ***-hued*** adjs.

1609 *Shuttleworths' Acc.* (Chetham Soc.) 183 Four yards of watchet coloured ribin. **1764** H. WALPOLE *Otranto* v, She lies in the watchet-coloured chamber. **1821** SCOTT *Kenilw.* xxx, A watchet-coloured silken mantle. **1895** J. DAVIDSON *Fleet St. Eclogues* Ser. II. 25 Convolvuluses.. Pallid or watchet-hued.

watchful (ˈwɒtʃfʊl), *a.* [f. WATCH *sb.* + -FUL.]

1. Wakeful, sleepless; accustomed to keeping awake. Of time: Passed in wakefulness. *arch.*

1548 UDALL etc. *Erasm. Par. John* xiv. 22–28 Of men obliuious he shal make you of good remembrance,.. of sleapyshe sluggardes vigilant and watchefull. **1577** KENDALL *Flowers Epigr.* 44 Of the Peacok... Then Iuno took his [*sc.* Argus'] watchfull eyes, and brauely by and by, She plast them in my traine. **1591** SHAKS. *Two Gent.* I. i. 31 To be in loue; where.. one fading moments mirth [is bought] With twenty watchfull, weary, tedious nights. **1594** —— *Rich. III*, v. iii. 115 To thee I do commend my watchfull soule, Ere I let fall the windowes of mine eyes. **1601** —— *Jul. C.* II. i. 98 What watchfull Cares doe interpose themselues Betwixt your Eyes, and Night? **1640** J. GOWER *Ovid's Festiv.* I. 14 The cock by night to Nights black Queen they slay, Because his watchfull bill doth wake the day. **1697** DRYDEN *Virg. Georg.* I. 395 Till the watchful Cock awakes the Day, She sings to drive the tedious Hours away. **1805** *Med. Jrnl.* XIV. 274 To alleviate the fever and watchful nights, effervescing draughts.. were administered. **1878** J. P. HOPPS *Rel. & Moral Lect.* xii. 38 Nearly all reformers.. have had to spend watchful nights and laborious days.

2. Of persons or animals, their dispositions or faculties: Engaged in or accustomed to watching or close observation; vigilant.

1601 R. JOHNSON *Kingd. & Commw.* (1603) 81 No more watchfull.. in their campe, then if they were safely intrenched in an ale house. **1605** SHAKS. *Macb.* v. viii. 67 Our exil'd Friends.. That fled the Snares of watchfull Tyranny. **1633** P. FLETCHER *Purple Isl.* XI. xxvii, The watchfull'st sight no difference could descrie. **1664** in *Verney Mem.* (1904) II. 212 A little yealping Dogg that were watchfull & angry were much more usefull to you. **1697** DRYDEN *Æneis* v. 585 His Hand, and watchful Eye keep even pace. **1711** STEELE *Spect.* No. 118 ¶ 1 If it had not been for that watchful Animal her Confident. **1797** MRS. RADCLIFFE *Italian* i, They had remained watchful and still for a considerable time. **1814** SCOTT *Lord of Isles* IV. xii, The galley ploughs no more the sea. Lest, rounding wild Cantyre, they meet The southern foemen's watchful fleet. **1827** KEBLE *Chr. Yr.*, *St. Barnabas* ii, 'Twixt Prayer and watchful Love his heart dividing. **1882** MRS. A. EDWARDES *Ball-room Repent.* I. 76 With a watchful mamma and governess in chaperonage.

b. Const. *about*, *against*, *for*, *of*, *over*; also with inf. of purpose.

Cf. the constructions of WATCH *v.*; *watchful of* corresponds to the transitive constructions.

1621 QUARLES *Hadassa* v. E 3, But she was watchfull of her lips and wise, Disclosing not her kindred, or alyes. **1666** *Extr. St. P. rel. Friend* III. (1912) 259 They are very carefull and watchfull to finde out and prevent all disturbances of that kinde. **1718** *Free-thinker* No. 60. 34 They grew watchful over their New Dominion. **1748** RICHARDSON *Clarissa* (1811) I. 244 We are to live on at this rate (are we?) vexed by you, and continually watchful about you. **1769** WASHINGTON *Let. to G. Mason* 5 Apr., Writ. 1834 II. 352 Selfish, designing men,.. watchful of every turn, that can assist their lucrative views. **1827** LYTTON *Pelham* ii, No one could be.. more watchful to gratify others. **1899** 'G. G.' *Winkles* i. 16 Watchful for such casualties, Posh caught hold of him in an instant.

3. Of actions, care, etc.: Characterized by vigilance.

1582 STANYHURST *Æneis* II. (Arb.) 69 Thee Greeks with custodye watchful, Warded thee towngats. **1609** HOLLAND *Amm. Marcell.* XXII. xv. 213 This beast.. with most watchfull care looketh about him to see the coasts cleere and all at rest, and [etc.]. **1623** J. TAYLOR (Water P.) *Discov. by Sea* B 3, God,.. of his boundlesse bounty, immense power, and eternall eye of watchfull prouidence releeues, guards, and conserues him. **1796** MME. D'ARBLAY *Camilla* IV. 302, I should.. have claimed the continuance of.. your watchful counsel. **1842** HAWTHORNE *Amer. Note-bks.* (1868) II. 90 A hound, crouching down with head erect, as if keeping watchful guard while the master of the mansion was away. **1886** RUSKIN *Præterita* II. vi. 219 My really watchful delineation.. had a quite unusual power of directing the attention of the general crowd to points of beauty.. to which [etc.].

4. Of places, duties, employments: In which one must be on the watch. ? *Obs.*

1590 SPENSER *F.Q.* I. ix. 41 The souldier may not moue from watchfull sted. **1596** *Edw. III*, III. i. 63, I haue discride, my Lord, As I was busie in my watchfull charge, The proud Armado of king Edwards ships. **1703** ROWE *Fair Penit.* I. i, That Country which he long had serv'd In watchful Councils, and in Winter Camps. **1831** SCOTT *Cast. Dang.* viii, Twelve months' service, of a nature the most watchful and unpleasant.

Hence **ˈwatchfully** *adv.*

1538 ELYOT *Dict.*, *Vigilanter*, watchefully, dylygently. **1579** TOMSON *Calvin's Serm. Tim.* 269/2 He that preacheth must.. indeuour to draw the whole flocke, to the obedience of God, to haue them walke in feare and humblenesse, and watchfully. **1660** BOYLE *New Exp. Phys.-Mech.* xvii. 116 If this Experiment were very watchfully try'd. **1752** WARBURTON *Serm.* xi. Wks. 1788 V. 178 Amongst the various Societies of Christians, there are some, in which the holy Ordinances are more regularly administred.. and Christian Liberty more watchfully protected. *a* **1822** SHELLEY *On Future St.* Pr. Wks. 1888 II. 181 Let us.. watchfully establish a discrimination between words and thoughts. **1857** RUSKIN *Pol. Econ. Art* 10 Keeping your embroidery watchfully from the moth. **1870** DICKENS *E. Drood* viii, Neville has made his remark in a watchfully advancing, and yet furtive and shy manner. **1920** *Conquest* Apr. 263/2 One of the fishermen rows the craft, the other hangs watchfully over the side.

watchfulness (ˈwɒtʃfʊlnɪs). [f. WATCHFUL *a.* + -NESS.]

1. Wakefulness, inability to sleep. *Obs.* exc. *Path.*

1596 SPENSER *F.Q.* v. vi. 34 Thus she all night wore out in watchfulnesse, Ne suffred slouthfull sleepe her eye-lids to oppresse. **1615** MARKHAM *Eng. Housw.* II. i. 10 If any of the family be troubled with too much watchfulnesse, so that they cannot by any meanes take rest. **1655** CULPEPPER etc. *Riverius* I. xi. 40 If after bleeding there comes watchfulness, the Humors will be again inflamed. **1758** *Phil. Trans.* L. 683 Pains.. attended with vomiting, anxiety, and great watchfulness. **1843** R. J. GRAVES *Syst. Clin. Med.* xi. 121 Early and decided determination to the brain, producing delirium, watchfulness, coma. **1876** W. ROBERTS *Urin. & Renal Dis.* III. x. (ed. 3) 537 The tumour.. spread in all directions, causing great pain and watchfulness.

2. The quality or state of being watchful or attentively observant; vigilance.

1611 B. JONSON *Catiline* IV. vii. Chorus M 1, And call their diligence, deceipt;.. Their watchfulnesse, but lying in waite. **1644** DIGBY *Nat. Soul* iv. §6. 390 The watchfulnesse and recalling of our thoughts backe to their enioyned worke, when they breake loose and runne astray. **1756** *Phil. Trans.* L. 22 By care and watchfulness the violence of the symptoms were kept under. **1815** SCOTT *Guy M.* xviii, He.. has, at different times, made eulogiums upon the watchfulness and ferocity of his dogs. **1821** LAMB *Elia, Imperf. Sympathies*, A Quaker.. knows that his syllables are weighed—and how far a consciousness of this particular watchfulness.. has a tendency to produce indirect answers, .. might be illustrated [etc.]. **1847** JAMES *Convict* ix, With a quiet, cat-like watchfulness, Filmer remarked everything which passed between Eda Brandon and Charles Dudley. **1879** in *Cassell's Techn. Educ.* I. 285/1 This plan, however, requires constant care and watchfulness, which it is difficult at all times to ensure.

b. const. *of, over*; also with inf. of purpose.

1624 DONNE *Devot.* Med. xiv. (ed. 2) 319 How busie, and perplexed a Cobwebb, is the Happinesse of Man here, that must bee made vp with a Watchfulnesse, to lay hold vpon Occasion. **1725** WATTS *Logic* II. iii. §3 (1726) 203 The Cure of these Prejudices is attain'd by a constant Jealousy of ourselves, and Watchfulness over our Passions. **1853** DICKENS *Bleak Ho.* xiv, His watchfulness of my guardian was incessant. He rarely removed his eyes from his face. **1860** RUSKIN *Unto this Last* i. §9 In protective watchfulness of his master's interest and credit, or in joyful readiness to seize unexpected.. occasions of help. **1868** A. DUFF *True Nobility* 73 As the causes of it [irresolution] came to be detected, there was inward watchfulness over their operation.

'watch-glass. [WATCH *sb.*]

†**1.** A sand-glass or hour-glass used to measure the time of keeping watch, esp. on board ship. Also in fig. context. *Obs.*

1637 RUTHERFORD *Lett.* cclxxvi. (1891) 534 Time and tide carry us upon another life, and there is daily less and less oil in our lamps, and less and less sand in our watch-glass. **1701** TUTTELL & MOXON *Math. Instr.* 22 Watch-glass.. used at Sea, to shift or change their Watches. **1769** FALCONER *Dict. Marine* (1780), *Watch-glasses*, a name given to the glasses employed to measure the period of the watch or divide it into any number of equal parts.. so that the several stations therein may be regularly kept and relieved.

2. A thin piece of glass, usually concavo-convex in form, fitted into the case of a watch over the dial-plate.

1773 *Pennsylv. Gaz.* 16 June, Suppl. 2/2 [Advt.] Watch glasses. **1831** BREWSTER *Optics* i. 4 A concave speculum is one which is hollow like the inside of a watch-glass. **1894** F. J. BRITTEN *Former Clock & Watchm.* 64 Watch glasses seem to have been introduced about 1600.

attrib. **1859** J. R. GREENE *Protozoa* vii. 66 In Ophryoglena flavicans a remarkable body termed the 'watch-glasslike organ' has been recently observed by Lieberkühn.

b. as a receptacle for small objects or portions of material to be subjected to scientific observation.

1757 *Phil. Trans.* L. 286 Pieces of these should be cut off while they are in the sea water, and placed in watch-glasses full of the same. **1818** ACCUM *Chem. Tests* 97 A small evaporating basin, or watch glass. **1880** L. S. BEALE *How to work with Microscope* (ed. 5) 54 Watch Glasses of various sizes should be kept by every observer. **1888** RUTLEY *Rock-Forming Min.* 24 A watch-glass standing in a pill-box lid.

Hence **'watch-glassful.**

1830 SIR J. HERSCHEL *Disc. Study Nat. Philos.* II. vi. §182 (1851) 172 We almost forget that these great masses are made up of watch-glassfuls.

'watch-house. [WATCH *sb.*]

1. A house in which a watch or guard is stationed.

1482 *Cely Papers* (Camden) 111 [You] woll hawe yowre wull howssyd in yowre wull howsse be the est wache howsse. **1530** PALSGR. 287/1 Watche howse, *lieu de guayet.* **1599** HAKLUYT *Voy.* II. I. 108 Vpon the walles euery night doe watch fifteene men in watch houses, for euery watch house fiue men. **1629** *Aldeburgh Rec.* in *N. & Q.* 12th Ser. VIII. 426/1 To John Cooke in p[aymen]t for a wache house set up at the beacon.. 01 00 00. **1739** LABELYE *Short Acc. Piers Westm. Bridge* 70 Useful Buildings, such as.. Watch-houses, &c. **1775** ROMANS *Hist. Florida* App. 72 You will see .. a watch-house (nick-named a fort) on St. Rosa Island. **1871** L. STEPHEN *Playgr. Eur.* (1894) iii. 72 Four of these [summits].. stand like watch-houses on the edge of the cliffs. **1880** A. MCKAY *Hist. Kilmarnock* (ed. 4) 17 One of these loop-holed recesses [in Dean Castle] had been perhaps used as a watch-house in times of emergency. **1881** E. INGERSOLL *Oyster-Industry* 249 *Watch-house*, a shanty built on the shore, or near the planted oyster-beds, from which they may be guarded (Massachusetts).

2. A house used as a station for municipal night-watchmen, in which the chief constable of the night sits to receive and detain in custody till the morning any disorderly persons brought in by the watchmen. (Latterly only in use outside the U.K.)

1716 GAY *Trivia* II. 491 Where statues breath'd, the works of Phidias' hands, A wooden pump, or lonely watch-house stands. **1731–2** *Norwich Mercury* 11–18 Mar. 1/2 Several of the Footmen and Chairmen were carried to St. James's Watch-house, and Yesterday Morning were examined before Justice Lambert. **1774** *Ann. Reg.* 123 The mob pulled down the watch-house, and rescued the prisoners. **1835** *Act 5 & 6 Will. IV*, c. 76 §78 To deliver any Person so apprehended into the Custody of the Constable.. at the nearest Watch-house. **1842** DICKENS *Amer. Notes* vi, Here are The Tombs once more. The city watch-house is a part of the building. **1845** D. JERROLD *St. Giles* i, The watchmen bore the mother to the watch-house. **1876** EMERSON *Lett. & Social Aims* i. 40 This unwritten play in fifty acts, composed by the dullest snorer on the floor of the watch-house. **1919** *Melbourne Argus* 1 Sept. 6 Detectives.. arrested George Whitney.. and locked him up at the City Watchhouse.

attrib. **1711** *Lond. Gaz.* No. 4890/3 The Unicorn over-against the Watch-house Door. **1859** K. CORNWALLIS *Panorama New World* I. 87 Inside there were several detectives and two watchhouse keepers at the books.

watching ('wɒtʃɪŋ), *vbl. sb.* [-ING¹.]

1. The action of the verb WATCH in various senses. *lit.* and *fig.*

c **1375** *Sc. Leg. Saints* xiii. (*Mark*) 131 The bischapis.. gret wechyne mad besyly, to tak sancte marke, for invy. **1479–81** *Rec. St. Mary at Hill* (1905) 99 Item, payd to the Clerke and paris for mete and drynke, for wecchynge of the Sepulcre [etc.] xxiij d. *a* **1529** SKELTON *Bouge of Court* 352 His hede was heuy for watchynge ouer nyghte. **1530** *Extracts Aberd. Reg.* (1844) I. 136 For the wetching and keping of this gude tovne baitht be nicht and day. **1593** SHAKS. *Rich. II*, II. i. 78 For sleeping England long time haue I watcht, Watching breeds leannesse. *a* **1670** SPALDING *Troub. Chas. I* (Bannatyne Club) I. 120 The marquess wondering at the watching of his lodgeing. *a* **1700** EVELYN *Diary* 4 Feb. 1685, Tired indeede as he was with griefe and watching. **1777** SHERIDAN *Trip to Scarb.* v. i, Of all modes of suspense, the watching for a loitering mistress is the worst. **1830** *Act 11 Geo. IV*, c. 27 §1 To make Provision for the lighting and watching of the several Parishes in England and Wales. **1849** MACAULAY *Hist. Eng.* iv. I. 444 The king had been exhausted by long watching and by many violent emotions. He now retired to rest. **1903** MRS. DE LA PASTURE *Cornelius* xvi. 183 She is very far from strong, and requires a deal of watching over. **1911** WACE *Prophecy Jew. & Chr.* ix. 172 He taught His disciples and ourselves to live in a constant state of watching for the complete and final revelation of that kingdom.

b. An act or instance of this.

c **1400** *Sc. Trojan War* (Horstm.) II. 614 Gregeois, yharnande with mayne & mude The wachingis [*v.r.* vachingis] for to execute Of þare fraudfull gyle but delay. **1526** *Pilgr. Perf.* (W. de W. 1531) 247 b, This honour that the chrysten people rendreth to theyr lorde.. is compared to a custody or watchynge. **1533** BELLENDEN *Livy* v. xxiii. (S.T.S.) II. 225 The romanis in þe capitoll war sowpit & oursett with continuall statiouns & watchingis. **1599** SHAKS. *Much Ado* II. i. 387 *Leonato.* My Lord, I am for you, though it cost mee ten nights watchings. **1641** W. CARTWRIGHT *Lady Errant* I. ii, Hard watchings and rough Guards Fill and make up the field. **1669** STILLINGFL. *Serm.* ix. (1673) 167 Their frequent watchings, fastings, hunger and thirst. **1704** NELSON *Fest. & Fasts* II. v. (1739) 501 It was celebrated.. with solemn Watchings. **1793** MARTYN *Lang. Bot.* s.v. *Vigiliæ*, These Vigiliæ or Watchings are performed at determined hours of the day, when plants open, expand, and shut their flowers daily. **1798** SOPHIA LEE *Canterb. T., Young Lady's T.* II. 194 Hours were past by the tender, agitated Emily, in anxious watchings. **1865** GOSSE *Land & Sea* (1874) 80 They had to wait for the successive 'watching' of each buoy, as its first appearance on the surface is technically termed. **1890** STEVENSON *In South Seas* II. vi. (1900) 198 It is the dead man's kindred and next friends who thus deprecate his fury with nocturnal watchings.

c. Sc. ***watching and warding***: see WATCH *v.* 6 b and 10.

1579 *Reg. Privy Council Scot.* III. 217 Subject to all taxationis, wacheing, warding, and utheris impositionis liand upoun the said burgh. **1600** *Reg. Mag. Sig. Scot.* 378/1 Quod omnes in dicto burgo manentes.. auxilia ferrent cum burgensibus ad lie watching, wairding, [etc.]. **1711** E. WARD *Vulgus Brit.* VIII. 95 For Watching, Warding, and Trainbanding, Tho' Customs of an ancient standing. **1765–8** ERSKINE *Inst. Law Scot.* II. iv. §8 This service of watching and warding.. is due by the burgesses within the .. territory of the borough. **1805** FORSYTH *Beauties Scot.* I. 106 The citizens [of Edinburgh] performed a species of personal service for defence of the town, called watching and warding. **1838** W. BELL *Dict. Law Scot.* 117 The *reddendo* (now merely nominal) of watching and warding.

2. The state or condition of being awake, wakefulness; often, wakefulness from disinclination or incapacity for sleep; an instance of this.

c **1550** H. LLOYD *Treas. Health* viii. C viii, Agaynst to much watchynges... The Sygnes. That he can not slepe after his accustomyd fashyon. **1608** TOPSELL *Serpents* 250 Yea and after a man hath recouered his health, yet is he neuerthelesse disquieted by much watching for a long time after. **1669** E. MAYNWARING *Preserv. Health* 90 The Life of Man.. spends its whole course in these two different states, Sleep and Watching: the one appointed for Rest and Ease, the other for Action and Labour. **1672** WISEMAN *Treat. Wounds* II. ii. 8 The Bullet not having been drawn out,.. occasioned great pain with Inflammation, great heat and watchings. **1799** UNDERWOOD *Dis. Childhood* (ed. 4) I. 61 Watching, or want of sleep is frequently a symptom of the foregoing complaints. **1860** MAYNE *Expos. Lex.*, *Pervigilium*, term for disinclination to sleep; watching.

†**3.** = WATCH *sb.* 1 b. *Obs.*$^{-1}$

1688 HOLME *Armory* II. xii. 311/1 A Watching of Nightingales.

4. *attrib.* and *Comb.*, as ***watching-hole, -place***; **watching brief**, a brief instructing counsel to 'watch' a case; also *fig.*; **watching candle**, a candle used at the 'watching' of a shrine or of a corpse; also *transf.*; †**watching-chamber**, (*a*) ? a guard-room adjoining a royal apartment; (*b*) a room adjoining a shrine, to be occupied by a watcher; †**watching lamp**, cf. *watching-candle*; **watching-rate** = *watch-rate.*

1886 *Daily News* 17 July 2/1 *Watching' briefs are held by the Attorney General.. and Sir H. James, Q.C. for Sir Charles Dilke. **1905** H. G. WELLS *Kipps* III. i. §4 Ann held a watching brief for herself. **1526** *Will of T. Stow* in *Beauties of Eng. & W.* X. III. 261 Item to have on every aultar a *wacchyng candle burning from vi of the clocke tyll it be past seven. *a* **1592** *Greenes Vision* D 4, The Mother and the daughter sette vppe a watching Candle, and sat verie mannerlie by a good fier, looking when [he] should wake. **1634** S. R. *Noble Soldier* IV. ii, Beauty was turn'd into a watching Candle that went out stinking. **1533** in W. H. St. J. Hope *Windsor Castle* (1913) I. 253 [A] Galary betwene the Kynges halle and hys *watching chambre. *Ibid.* I. 255 The Quenes watchyng chambre. **1856** *Builder* 14 June 325/3 The Watching Chamber on the north side of the Saint's Chapel [St. Albans], wherein a monk was posted as a guard of honour to the shrine. **1862** R. J. KING *Eastern Cathedr.* 22 (Oxford) The watching chamber which, here as elsewhere, adjoined the shrine for the protection of the gold and jewels which enriched it. **1850** R. G. CUMMING *Hunter's Life S. Africa* (1902) 76/1, I accordingly ordered the usual *watching-hole to be constructed. **1597** *1st Pt. Ret. fr. Parnass.* I. i. 77 If they have lived by a *watchinge lampe, Prysinge each minute of a flyinge houre. **1848** THACKERAY *Van. Fair* xiii, Sambo.. saw the little girl.. jump up from her *watching-place in the window. **1835** DICKENS *Sk. Boz, Parish* iv, *Watching-rates, lighting-rates, paving-rates.

watching ('wɒtʃɪŋ), *ppl. a.* [-ING².] That watches; observant, vigilant, unsleeping.

Beowulf 1268 Se æt Heorote fand wæccendne wer wiʒes bidan. *c* **1000** *Eccl. Inst.* in Thorpe *Anc. Laws* (1840) II. 400 Þæt ʒe mid wæccendre ʒymen ʒehycgen. *a* **1586** SIDNEY *Ps.* XVII. ix, Up, Lord.. And bring to naught those watching pawes. *c* **1680** R. FLEMING *Fulfilling Script.* II. vi. (1726) 315 A watching providence over the church. **1728** RAMSAY *Falling of a Slate* v, But watching sylphs flew round, To guard dear Madie from all skaith. **1848** DICKENS *Dombey* xlvii, He.. kept his watching eyes that way. **1902** *Daily Chron.* 24 July 5/2 Hence the interesting spectacle of a class rivalry has not been presented to a watching nation.

Hence **'watchingly** *adv. rare*$^{-0}$.

1552 HULOET, Watchyngelye, *uigilanter.*

watchit, obs. form of WATCHET.

'watchless, *a.* [f. WATCH *sb.* + -LESS.]

1. a. Keeping no watch. **b.** Unwatched, unguarded.

1622 GATAKER *Spirituall Watch* (ed. 2) 124 There is great difference betweene the watchfull and the watchlesse Christian. **1721** CIBBER *Perolla* I. i, How cam'st thou first to set Thy watchless Eyes upon this fatal Wretch. **1842** *Proc. Berw. Nat. Club* II. 8 The hills are covered with flocks of sheep.. browsing watchless, because they know no danger. **1852** ROCK *Ch. of Fathers* III. I. 199 If.. it happen with them, in some watchless moment, that they stumble.

2. Of a night: Not broken into watches; having no wakeful intervals.

1850 BLACKIE *Æschylus* I. 27 To their hearts' content They live, and through the watchless night prolong Sound slumbers.

'watchlessness. [f. WATCHLESS *a.* + -NESS.] Lack of watchfulness.

1691 J. B[ARDWOOD] *Hearts-ease* (ed. 2) 33 Another common Cause, is our own Watchlessness and Carelessness. **1854** *Tait's Mag.* XXI. 564 To say nothing of the watchlessness of our Admiral in the Black Sea.

'watch-light. [WATCH *sb.*]

1. = NIGHT-LIGHT 2 b, esp. in the form of a slow-burning candle with a rush wick.

1628 *Digby's Private Mem.* (1827) 67 After she was in bed .. she read it by the help of the watch-light which stood burning by her. **1695** CONGREVE *Love for L.* III. xiii, Nurse, let me have a Watch-Light. **1715** ADDISON *Drummer* II. i, Item, a dozen Pound of Watch-Lights for the Use of the Servants. *a* **1732** GAY *Story of Apparition* 88 Swift retir'd the maid, The watch-lights burn, tuckt warm in bed was laid The hardy stranger. **1775** G. WHITE *Selborne, To Barrington* 1 Nov., These rushes give a good clear light. Watch-lights (coated with tallow), it is true, shed a dismal one, 'darkness visible'. **1823** J. BADCOCK *Dom. Amusem.* 204 Luminous Bottle, or Watch-light. *c* **1865** LETHEBY in J. Wylde *Circ. Sci.* I. 94/2 The rushes are peeled on three sides for the best light, and on two only for watch-lights.

2. A light carried by a watchman.

1855 BROWNING *Andrea del Sarto* 209 See, it is settled dusk now; there's a star; Morello's gone, the watch-lights show the wall.

'watchmaker.

1. One whose trade it is to make watches.

1630 CAPT. J. SMITH *True Trav.* 35 Gold-smiths.. and Watch-makers. *a* **1672** WILKINS *Disc. New Planet* II. (1684) 152 We allow every Watch-maker so much wisdom, as not to put any Motion in his Instrument, which is superfluous. **1710** BERKELEY *Princ. Hum. Knowl.* I. §62 Those Actions of the Watchmaker, whereby he makes the Movements and rightly adjusts them. **1758** JOHNSON *Idler* No. 26 ¶8 My first mistress was wife of a working watch-maker. **1832** G. DOWNES *Lett. Cont. Countries* I. 261 Geneva... We have been a full fortnight in this paradise of watchmakers.

b. attrib. uses of possessive, as ***watch-maker's file, glass, lens***, etc.; **watchmaker's cramp**, a form of cramp affecting watchmakers.

1683 MOXON *Mech. Exerc., Printing* xii. ¶1 Small and Fine Files (commonly called Watch-makers Files). **1875** KNIGHT *Dict. Mech.* 2734 *Watchmaker's Glass*, a double convex lens set in a tubular socket, adapted to be held to the eye by the contraction of the orbital muscles. **1888** RUTLEY *Rock-Forming Min.* 3 A watch-maker's lens, held in the eye. **1899** *Syd. Soc. Lex.*, Watchmaker's cramp.

2. *slang.* (See quot.)

1859 *Hotten's Slang Dict.*, *Watchmaker*, a pickpocket, or stealer of watches.

'watchmaking, *vbl. sb.* The making of watches.

1729 MANDEVILLE *Fab. Bees* (1733) II. 336 Watch-making .. is come to a higher degree of perfection, than it would.. if [etc.]. **1879** *Encycl. Brit.* X. 148/2 Watchmaking was already carried to a high degree of perfection, under the influence of Charles Cusin, who had settled in the town [Geneva] in 1587.

attrib. **1871** CARLYLE in *Mrs. Carlyle's Lett.* II. 219 An innocent, good lad, who has learned the watchmaking business.

watchman (ˈwɒtʃmən). Pl. **watchmen**. [f. WATCH *sb.* + MAN *sb.*]

1. A member of a military guard, a sentinel or sentry; a look-out posted to give warning of the approach of danger, etc. *Obs.* in technical use.

Now *rare* exc. in reminiscences from the Bible.

a **1400–50** *Wars Alex.* 5164 Be he þe pauylion a-prochid it past with-in euen, And sone þe wacche-men with-out quen þai him þare sawe, þai tuke him. *c* **1400** *Destr. Troy* 11156 All the burgh is full bigge, ouer the brode wallis, Wacchemen for to wale, wacches to kepe. *c* **1470** HENRY *Wallace* IV. 225 The wachman was hewy fallen on sleipe; The bryg was doun. **1526** TINDALE *Matt.* xxvii. 66 They went and made the sepulcre sure with watchemen, and sealed the stone. **1535** COVERDALE *Isa.* xxi. 11 One of Seir cried vnto me: 'watchman what hast thou espied by night?' [1611 Watch-man, what of the night?] —— *Ps.* cxxvi. 1 Excepte the Lorde kepe the cite, the watchman waketh but in vayne. **1544** *Acc. Ld. High Treas. Scot.* VIII. 305 Item, the xxj day of Julii, deliverrit to the wachemen of the castell of Edinburght xxij s. **1606** SHAKS. *Ant. & Cl.* IV. iii. 18 *Enter a Company of Soldiours.* 1 *Sol*... Walke, let's see if other Watchmen Do heare what we do? **1625** K. LONG tr. *Barclay's Argenis* II. xx. 134 He goes to the walls, as with charge in the Kings name to the Watchmen, through all the watch-towers, that they should not..breake up the watch. **1680** DRYDEN *Span. Friar* I. i, Our Watchmen, from the Tow'rs, with longing Eyes Expect his swift Arrival. **1864** SKEAT tr. *Uhland's Poems* 203 So listen, ye youthful heroes, Mine excellent watchmen three; Here tender young girls may enter. **1913** J. H. MORRISON *On Trail of Pioneers* xvii. 82 Every day the watchman climbed the tower, and gazed down the Cawnpore road for some sign of the relieving force.

b. *transf.* and *fig.*

a **1500** *Bernard. de cura rei fam.* etc. II. 110 þe wouff salbe wachmane and kep mony wayis. **1612** SIR J. DIGBYE in *10th Rep. Hist. MSS. Comm.* App. I. 579 Yt is fitt for us that stande as Watchemen to give warning one unto another.. upon..all seeming dangers. **1655** WALTON *Angler* x. (1661) 175 And in the morning..visit the water-side (but not too near) for they have a Watch-man. **1738** WESLEY *Ps.* CXXI. ii, Rest in Him, securely rest; Thy Watchman never sleeps. **1860** PUSEY *Min. Proph.* 346 Nothing now hinders the visitation, which the watchmen, or prophets, had so long foreseen and forewarned of.

attrib. **1859** H. KINGSLEY *G. Hamlyn* xxvi, Sending the watchman cockatoo screaming aloft to alarm the flock.

†**c.** *pl.* Body-guard. *Obs.*

a **1483** *Liber Niger* in *Househ. Ord.* (1790) 38 Yeomen of the Crowne... These were called the King's Wachemen.

†**2.** A scout, spy. *Obs.*

a **1533** BERNERS *Huon* clxv. 652 Whyles they were thus deuysynge together, the wache men came abought, whome the kyng had sent thether to spye and knowe if Peter..dyd sende to those prisoners any comforte or ayde.

†**3.** One who keeps vigil, a watcher; one who watches over or guards a person or thing, a guardian (*of* something). *Obs.*

14.. LYDG. *Lyke thyn Audience* 53 (Camb. MS.) in *Pol. Rel. & L. Poems* (1903) 51 With wachemen wake, with sloggy folkes slepe. **1447** BOKENAM *Seyntys, Agnes* 295 More-ouyr goddys sone..To me is..A wecheman eek neuer slepyng. **1591** SHAKS. *1 Hen. VI*, III. i. 66 Vnckles of Gloster, and of Winchester, The speciall Watch-men of our English Weale. **1596** J. MELVILL *Autob. & Diary* (Wodrow Soc.) 362 The Watchmen and fathfull Pastours of the Kirk of Scotland. **1628** A. LEIGHTON *Appeal to Parlt.* 124 Removing the Dogges that should keepe and the watchmen that should watch the Flockes: so that they are left a prey to the Wolves and Foxes.

†**b.** Applied to angels. Cf. WATCHER f. *Obs.*

1552 LATIMER *Serm.* 25 Dec. (1584) 270 b, We are not bound to call vppon the aungels when wee heare that they serue vs, but rather to geue God thankes in them that he hath vouchsafed to set such watchmen about vs. **1560** BIBLE (Geneva) *Dan.* iv. 13 Beholde, a watcheman and an holy one came downe from heauen. **1613** PURCHAS *Pilgrimage* I. vii. 31 And the Watch-men (so he [Scaliger] calleth the Angels out of *Dan.* 4) lusted and went astray after them.

†**4.** One of a body of men formerly appointed to keep watch and ward in all towns from sunset to sunrise; later, a constable of the watch who, before the Police Act of 1839, patrolled the streets by night to safeguard life and property. *Obs.*

14.. *Leges Quatuor Burgorum* c. 81, in *Sc. Acts* I. 349 Of ilke house..in þe quhilk þer wonnys ony þat in þe tym of wakyng aw of resoun to cum furth þar sal ane wachman be haldyn to cum furth quhen þat þe wakstaff gais fra dure to dure quha sal..gang til his wache [etc.]. *c* **1440** *Gesta Rom.* xxv. 93 (MS. Harl.) Plebeius..ordeynid for a lawe, that wacchemen shulde eche nyght go about þe cete, & visite eche house, þat þere was no misgouernayle þere in. *Ibid.* 95 In tyme of the nyght, when wacchemen come blowyng hir hornes. **1599** SHAKS. *Much Ado* III. iii. 42 Why you speake like an ancient and most quiet watchman, for I can-not see how sleeping should offend. **1618** J. TAYLOR (Water P.) *Pennyles Pilgr.* B 4 b, A Watchmans bill, or a Welch-hooke falles not halfe so heauy vpon a man. **1681** OTWAY *Soldier's Fort.* v. (1687) 61 *Watchmen at the door.* Almost 4 a Clock and a dark cloudy morning. **1749** FIELDING *Tom Jones* x. ii, Now thieves and ruffians are awake, and honest watchmen fast asleep. **1765** GOLDSM. *Ess.* v. ¶4 The watch-man had gone twelve; my companions had all stolen off. **1785** COWPER *Task* II. 654 [She who] at the watchman's lantern borrowing light, Finds a cold bed her only comfort left. **1810** *Sporting Mag.* XXXV. 39 With the assistance of a watchman and some passengers, conveyed them to the watchhouse. **1849** MACAULAY *Hist. Eng.* ii. I. 251 When Monmouth arrived in London at midnight, the watchmen were ordered by the magistrates to proclaim the joyful event through the streets of the city. **1865** DICKENS *Mut. Fr.* I. v, A face..that had just as much play of expression as a watchman's rattle.

attrib. **1853** DICKENS *Bleak Ho.* xi, The policeman considers him [*sc.* the beadle] an imbecile civilian, a remnant of the barbarous watchmen-times.

5. A man employed to guard private property, a building, etc. while the owner, tenant, or workpeople are away, esp. during the night.

1600 J. PORY tr. *Leo's Africa* III. 136 These shops are garded in the night season by certaine hired and armed watchmen. **1875** KNIGHT *Dict. Mech.*, Watchman's Time-detector. **1876** 'MARK TWAIN' *Tom Sawyer* xv, He..walked boldly on board the boat, for he knew she was tenant-less, except that there was a watchman, who always turned in and slept like a graven image.

6. The dor-beetle, *Geotrupes stercorarius*.

1864–5 J. G. WOOD *Homes without H.* viii. (1868) 155 The common Dor Beetle (*Geotrupes vulgaris*) sometimes called the Watchman or Clock. **1883** —— in *Good Words* Dec. 763/1 The Dor or Watchman Beetle.

7. *Typog.* (See quot.)

1888 JACOBI *Printers' Vocab.*, *Watchman*, a little flag of paper placed *pro tem.* in matter as composed, which serves to indicate the position of a footnote.

Hence **ˈwatchmanly** *a. nonce-wd.*, belonging to or characteristic of a watchman. †**ˈwatchmanship**, the office or function of a watchman.

a **1603** J. RAYNOLDS *Obadiah* iii. (1613) 35 Not content to bee watchmen in Jerusalem, but they must haue a watch-manship in Caesarea too. **1837** *New Monthly Mag.* LI. 116 Have they..taken away from ye that childish and yet watch-manly toy, the rattle?

†**ˈwatchment.** *Obs. rare*⁻¹. [f. WATCH *v.* + -MENT.] A task of watching.

1740 RICHARDSON *Pamela* I. 203 However said she, all is well now; because my *Watchments* are now over, by my Master's Direction... Why, Mrs. Jewkes, said I, is all this fishing about for something,..if there be an end of your *Watchments*, as you call them?

watch-out. [f. vbl. phr. *watch out*: see WATCH *v.* 4 g.] The action of watching or looking out for something.

1884 'MARK TWAIN' *Huck. Finn* iv, I never tried to do anything, but just poked along low-spirited and on the watch-out.

watchshide, obs. form of WATCHET.

watcht, variant of WATCHED *ppl. a.*

watch-tower. [WATCH *sb.*]

1. A tower or station from which observation is kept of the approach of danger; a look-out station.

1544 in Rymer *Foedera* (1713) XV. 52 Huberdyn was Slaine with a halfe Haache out of the Wache Tour, as he and his Men went to vue the same. **1578–9** *Reg. Privy Council Scot.* III. 81 The wache toure upoun Trailtrow,..mon be mendit of the litill diffaceing the Englische army maid of it. **1616** CHAPMAN tr. *Musæus* C 4, A Tower, that Sestian Hero once did make Her Watch-Tower. **1699** DAMPIER *Voy.* II. II. 13 West from Rio de la Gartos, there is a Look-out or Watch-tower, called Selam. **1794** MRS. RADCLIFFE *Myst. Udolpho* xliii, To the left..was seen a ruined watch-tower, standing on a point of rock near the sea. **1813** SCOTT *Trierm.* I. xiii, Upon the watch-tower's airy round No warder stood his horn to sound. **1829** W. IRVING *Granada* (1850) 21 Every peak had its atalaya or watchtower, ready to make its fire by night or to send up its column of smoke by day, a signal of invasion. **1852** GROTE *Greece* II. lxxvii. X. 197 The besieged, detecting from their watch-towers the negligence of the guards, chose a favorable opportunity and made a vigorous sally. **1869** TOZER *Highl. Turkey* I. 361 This place..was the watch-tower that commanded the passes of the Scardus.

b. *fig.*

1561 T. NORTON *Calvin's Inst.* III. xxii. (1634) 458 We must needs come to that lesser people, which Paul in another place said to have been foreknowne to God: not in such sort as these men imagine, to foreknow out of an idle watch-toure the things that hee worketh not: but [etc.]. **1571** GOLDING *Calvin on Ps.* lix. 10 David mounted up intoo the watch tower of fayth, from whence he loketh downe without feare. **1639** ROUSE *Heav. Univ.* ix. (1702) 122 Then stand on thy watch-tower and hear what he teacheth thee. **1768–74** TUCKER *Lt. Nat.* (1834) II. 19 The true philosopher.. considers himself as placed upon some watch tower, there to sit a careful spectator of the earth. **1821** SHELLEY *Adonais* xiv, Morning sought Her eastern watch-tower. **1912** E. RUSSELL *Maitland of Lethington* iii. 72 Knox clung to St. Giles; he could have no better watch-tower.

c. *transf.* (See quot.)

1864–5 J. G. WOOD *Homes without H.* vi. (1868) 113 To enable the spider to see objects in its front a sort of little turret rises from the cephalothorax and on its summit are placed the eyes. Naturalists familiarly call this projection the 'watch-tower'.

†**2.** A pharos or lighthouse. *Obs.*

1601 HOLLAND *Pliny* XXXVI. xii. II. 578 The use of this watch-tower, is to shew light as a lanthorne, and give direction in the night season to ships, for to enter the haven, and where they shall avoid barrs and shelves. **1632** LITHGOW *Trav.* VII. 324 For the commodity of Saylers the ..King builded a watch-towre of white Marble. **1757** W. WILKIE *Epigoniad* VI. 186 As when a watch tower's light, Seen thro' the gloom of some tempestuous night, Glads the wet mariner. **1804** W. L. BOWLES *Spir. Discov.* II. 233 Strangers..whose bark Has foundered nigh, where the red watch-tower glares Through darkness.

watchword (ˈwɒtʃwɜːd). [WATCH *sb.*]

1. *Mil.* A word or short phrase used as a password. *Obs.* in technical use.

c **1400** *Destr. Troy* 6056 Bisé was the buerne... The ost out of angur & auntur to were, Wacche wordes to wale, þat weghis might know. *a* **1513** FABYAN *Chron.* v. lxxxix. (1811) 66 Hengiste beynge mynded to execute his former purposed treason, shewyd his watche worde, by reason wherof anon the Brytons were slayne as shepe amonge woluys. **1538** ELYOT *Dict.*, *Tessera*,..a watch worde or priuie token gyuen to souldiours. **1560** in J. Scott *Berwick-upon-Tweed* (1888) 448 Any man that cometh to the watch hill and is by the officers to watch and thereupon hath the watchword given him. *c* **1592** in *Eng. Hist. Rev.* (1898) XIII. 513 Et les ditz comons auoient entre eux vne wacheworde en Englishe with whome haldes you et le respons fust with Kinge Richarde and the true comons. **1657** *North's Plutarch, Addit. Lives* 45 (Tamberlain) Every evening the watch word was distributed, and each man was to repair to his Quarters.

†**b.** = PAROLE *sb.* 2. *Obs.*

1760 *Cautions & Adv. to Officers of Army* 132 At the Delivery of the Report you are to return the Parole, or Watch-Word, to the Commanding Officer by whispering it in his Ear.

†**c.** The call of a sentinel on his rounds. *Obs.*

1615 G. SANDYS *Trav.* I. 13 Since when, a watch-word euery minute of the night goeth about the wals, to testifie their vigilancie. **1756** R. ROGERS *Jrnls.* (1769) 18 We were so near the enemy as to hear their centry's watch-word. **1797** MRS. RADCLIFFE *Italian* xxvi, I have heard only the watch-word of the sentinels.

†**2.** A preconcerted signal to begin an attack.

1550 LYNNE *Carion's Cron.* 256 b, And then about midnight the watche worde was geuen that euery man shoulde be ready with his weapon. **1555** EDEN *Decades* (Arb.) 178 The kynge..came foorth..with a great bande of armed men cryinge in maner of a larome..Guazzauara, Guazzauara, which..is as it weare a watch worde to giue thonset. **1560** DAUS tr. *Sleidane's Comm.* 452 As a token or watche worde, they cried that the Frenchemen were vp in harnesse. **1583** STOCKER *Civ. Warres Lowe C.* IV. 57 b, The Enemie discharged three Cannons for the Watch word, that the horsemen might get together. **1589** GREENE *Menaphon* (Arb.) 85 Democles seeing his time,..gaue the watchword, and the ambush leapt out. **1630** *R. Johnson's Kingd. & Commw.* 370 The common watchword was the tolling of the Bels to Even-song. **1834** JAMES *J. Marston Hall* ix, The name acted as a watchword, and the moment it was pronounced, a well-directed volley of stones was let fly.

†**b.** *transf.*

1593 SHAKS. *Lucr.* 370 Which giues the watch word to his hand ful soon, To draw the clowd that hides the siluer Moon. **1594** PLAT *Jewell-ho.* III. 90 Take heed..of a false backe to the..furnace, hauing a loose bricke..that may bee taken awaie in an other Roome by a false Sinon that attendeth onely the Alchimistes hemme, or some other suchlike watch-worde. **1680** H. MORE *Apocal. Apoc.* Pref. 25 The Witnesses are already risen in the late Reformation ..that no watch-word may be taken to any Tumults from any such Indication of Time. **1793** [JOHNSON] *Consid. Coal in Scot.* 25 Colliers..in the west country..have some watch-word, by sending round of which they can lay the whole collieries in the country idle.

3. A password used among members of the same sect, society, etc. ? *Obs.* exc. *arch.*

1534 MORE *Comf. agst. Trib.* II. Wks. 1170/1 After their holy watcheworde spoken on both the sydes, after the maner vsed in that place, the one toke the other by the tip of the finger..thorow the grate. **1696** WHISTON *Theory of Earth* II. (1722) 214 A certain Watchword out of 500 pitch'd upon among certain Conspirators. **1809** SYD. SMITH *Wks.* (1859) I. 168/2 Classical quotations are the watchwords of scholars, by which they distinguish each other from the ignorant and the illiterate. **1891** FARRAR *Darkn. & Dawn* li, They meet in the most secret places, and have their watchwords.

b. A word or phrase used as embodying the guiding principle or rule of action of a party or individual.

1738 *Gentl. Mag.* VIII. 292/2 Now I cannot help being of Opinion, that all the former Watch-words, were better chosen than theirs. **1780** COWPER *Table-T.* 322 When the rude rabble's watch-word was—destroy, And blazing London seem'd a second Troy. **1832** TENNYSON *Love thou thy Land* 28 Nor deal in watch-words overmuch. **1844** MACAULAY *Ess.*, *Chatham* (1897) 760 The watchwords of the new government were prerogative and purity. **1875** STUBBS *Const. Hist.* I. x. 307 Again in A.D. 1127 his name was made the watch-word of a renewed struggle. **1876** F. HARRISON *Choice of Bks.* (1886) 7 Our stately Milton said in a passage which is one of the watchwords of the English race, 'as good almost kill a man as kill a good book.'

†**4.** A cautionary word or speech; also, a premonitory sign, a warning event. *Obs.*

c **1475** *Plumpton Corr.* (Camden) 33, I took that for a watche word for medling betwixt lords. **1542** UDALL *Erasm. Apoph.* 124 b, Geuyng a preatie watche woord that best were vtterly to abstein from matrimonie. **1573** G. HARVEY *Letter-bk.* (Camden) 19 He gave me this watchwurd in his own Chamber that it miht be thai ment to make me weri of the Hous. **1584** [A. MUNDAY] (*title*), A Watch-woord to Englande To beware of traytours and tretcherous practises [etc.]. *a* **1639** SPOTTISWOOD *Hist. Ch. Scot.* IV. (1655) 197 The Ambassadours had a watchword given them, not to see nor salute him. **1642** FULLER *Holy & Prof. St.* V. xix. 436 To welcome the Duke..he was entertain'd with prodigies..; as if Nature..made her hand to swerve, that she might shoot a warning-piece to these countreys, and give them a watch-word of the future calamities they were to expect. *a* **1761** [S. HALIBURTON & HEPBURN] *Mem. Magopico* V. (ed. 2) 19 An arch wench..had smelled a rat about Magopico, and had given her lady a watch-word.

†**b.** *to set a watchword upon*: to utter a caveat against. *Obs.*

a **1586** SIDNEY *Apol. Poetrie* (1595) I, S. Paule himselfe, (who yet for the credite of Poets) alledgeth twise two Poets, & one of them by the name of a Prophet, setteth a watch-word vpon Philosophy, indeede vpon the abuse.

watchwork (ˈwɒtʃwɜːk). [WATCH *sb.*] That part of the movement of a timepiece which is concerned with the measuring of the hours, as distinguished from the 'clockwork' or striking part; also, the 'works' or parts composing the movement of a watch.

1667 SPRAT *Hist. Royal-Soc.* 247 Three new wayes of Pendulums for Clocks, and several wayes of applying the motion of the Watch-work to them. **1674** HOOKE *Animadv. Hevelius* 68 To effect which motion of the Table and Instrument, a Watch-work is fitted to the Axis, so as to make it move round in the same time, with a diurnal revolution of the Earth. **1675** J. S. *Horol. Dial.* I. vii. 28 Tis always commendable to see Clock or Watch-work, move thus brisk and lively. **1773** *Pennsylv. Gaz.* 16 June, Suppl. 2/2 [Advt.] Silver watches..cast watch-work, [etc.]. **1825** J. NICHOLSON *Oper. Mech.* 489 Clock-work, properly so called ..in contradistinction to that part of the movement of a clock or watch..which is termed *watch-work*. **1848** *Proc. Soc. Antiquaries Lond.* 271 Facio, a native of Geneva,..is said to have first invented the application of jewels to watchwork.

b. *transf.* and *fig.*

1825 T. HOOK *Sayings* Ser. II. *Man of Many Fr.* I. 181 A shew-woman—like Madam Catharina, with watchwork under her hoop! **1844** *Blackw. Mag.* LVI. 530 The whole machinery and watchwork of pauperism. **1845** CLOUGH *Poems, New Sinai* v, Heaven's A Mécanique Céleste! And heart and mind of human kind A watch-work as the rest!

wate, obs. f. WAIT *sb.*; obs. or dial. f. WAIT *v.*[1]

wate, obs. form of WET.

wate, var. WHAT[2], WHATE *sb. Obs.*, fortune.

wate, Sc. form of *wot*: see WIT *v.*

wate, obs. pa. t. of WITE *v.*, to blame.

watel, obs. form of WATTLE *sb.* and *v.*

water ('wɔːtə(r)), *sb.* Forms: 1–3 **wæter**, 2–5 **weter**, 3 *Orm.* **waterr**, (*pl.* **wattress**), 3–5 **watre**, 4 *Sc.* **valtir**, **vatter**, **vatyr**, (*pl.* **wateren**), 4–5 **watere**, **wattre**, **watur**, **-yr**, 4–6 **watir**, 4, 6 *Sc.* **vattir**, 4–7 chiefly *Sc.* **watter**, **-ir**, 4–7 *Sc.* **walter**, 5 **vatur**, **wature**, **-yre**, **wadyr**, *Sc.* **wattyr**, 5–6 *Sc.* **waltir**, **vater**, 6 **watier**, *Sc.* **wattar**, **valter**, 8–9 *Anglo-Ir.* **wather**, 9 *dial.* **wawter**, **waiter**, **wetter**, 2– **water**. [Com. Teut.: OE. *wæter* neut. corresponds to OFris. *watar*, *watir*, *weter*, etc., OS. *watar* (MLG., LG., Du. *water*), OHG. *wazzar*, *wazar* (MHG. *wazzer*, mod.G. *wasser*):—OTeut. **watar-*; a parallel formation with *n* instead of *r* occurs in Goth. *watō* neut. (genit. *watins*), ON. *vatn* neut. (Norw. *vatn*, Sw. *vatten*, Da. *vand*). The Indogermanic root **wod-* (Teut. **wat-*) occurs in OSl., Russ. *voda* water; the ablaut-variant **wēd-* (Teut. **wǣt-*) is represented in WET *a.*; the ablaut-variant **ud-* (Teut. **ut-*) is found more widely: cf. Skr. *udán*, Gr. ὕδωρ (genit. ὕδατος:—**udn̥tos*), Lith. *undū̃* (also *vandū̃*), OPrussian *unds*, *undo*, Umbrian *utur*, water, L. *unda* wave; also the derivatives with the sense 'water-animal' (see OTTER).]

I. The liquid of which seas, lakes, and rivers are composed, and which falls as rain and issues from springs. When pure, it is transparent, colourless (except as seen in large quantity, when it has a blue tint), tasteless, and inodorous.

Popular language recognizes kinds of 'water' that have not all these negative properties; but (even apart from any scientific knowledge) it has usually been more or less clearly understood that these are really mixtures of water with other substances.

1. a. *gen.*

*c*897 ÆLFRED *Gregory's Past. C.* 309 Onsend Ladzarus, ðætte he ȝewæte his ytemestan finger on wættre. *c* **1050** *Suppl. Ælfric's Gloss.* 177/30, 31 *Aqua*, wæter. *Limpha*, hluttor wæter. *c* **1200** ORMIN 14038 Crist badd tatt teȝȝ sholldenn gan & fillenn þeȝȝre fetless Wiþþ waterr. **1551** T. WILSON *Logic* F ij, Water is made whot, here we see that it chaunceth to water (contrary to her nature) to be warme, and therefore it is called chaunceable. **1625** N. CARPENTER *Geogr. Del.* I. I. (1635) 9 Water being no other than a thin and fluid body,—must needs require a hard and solid body, whereon to support it selfe. **1752** HUME *Polit. Disc.* v. (ed. 2) 83 All water, wherever it communicates, remains always at a level. **1756** BURKE *Subl. & B.* IV. xxi, Water, when simple, is insipid, inodorous, colourless, and smooth. **1798** COLERIDGE *Anc. Mar.* II. 121 Water, water, every where, Nor any drop to drink. **1813** SIR H. DAVY *Agric. Chem.* (1814) i. 16 Water is raised from the ocean diffused through the air and poured down upon the soil. **1816** J. SMITH *Panorama Sci. & Art* II. 145 Water will pass through the pores of gold rather than suffer compression, and appears to be nearly inelastic. **1850** TENNYSON *In Mem.* lviii, As drop by drop the water falls In vaults and catacombs.

b. With various qualifying words, denoting kinds of water distinguished by their properties or origin: see ICE-WATER, RAIN-WATER, RIVER-WATER, SALT WATER, SEA-WATER, SNOW-WATER, SPRING-WATER, SWEET WATER; COLD WATER, HOT WATER, WARM WATER; also FRESH *a.* 5, HARD *a.* 14 a, SOFT *a.* 25 a.

c. Considered as antagonistic to fire.

1390 GOWER *Conf.* I. 266 For as the water of a welle Of fyr abateth the malice, Riht so [etc.]. **1546** J. HEYWOOD *Prov.* (1867) 10 Foule water as soone as fayre, will quenche hot fyre. **1593** SHAKS. *Rich. II*, III. iii. 56 Me thinkes King Richard and my selfe should meet With no lesse terror then the Elements Of Fire and Water, when their thundring smoake At meeting teares the cloudie Cheekes of Heauen. **1879** *Encycl. Brit.* IX. 235/2 In coping with fires, water is the great agent employed.

fig. **1682** BUNYAN *Greatn. Soul* (1691) 3 This kind of Language tends to cast Water upon weak and beginning Desires.

d. As supplied for domestic needs, esp. as conveyed by a channel or conduit from the source, and distributed through pipes to the houses of a district. Phrases, ***to cut off, turn on the water***.

1535 COVERDALE *2 Kings* xx. 20 The pole and water condyte, wherby he conueyed water in to the cite. **1596** HARINGTON *Metam. Ajax* H 2 b, At Shaftsburie, where water is deerest of anie towne I know. **1653** J. NICOLL *Diary* (Bannatyne Club) 105 Lytill watter could be fund, bot the pepill of Edinburgh wer forcit to bring thair watter from far. **1835** DICKENS *Sk. Boz, Parish* i, The turn-cock having turned on the water. **1836** *Ibid.*, *Shops & Tenants*, At last the company's man came to cut off the water.

e. As used for motive power.

1698 FLOYER *Asthma* (1717) To Rdr. p. xxv, Like a Mill which stands still for want of Water.

f. In various similative and figurative phrases, many of which are of biblical origin: see, e.g., Gen. xlix. 4, Jos. vii. 5, 2 Sam. xiv. 14, Ps. lxxix. 3. ***to write on*** or ***in water*** [= L. *in aqua scribere*, Gr. γράφειν εἰς ὕδωρ]: to fail to leave abiding record of (something). (To spend money) ***like water***: profusely, recklessly. † ***to put water in*** (a person's) ***worts***: to make things unpleasant for him. † ***water in one's shoes***: something disagreeable. † ***to hold out water, to bear water***: = 'to hold water' (*fig.*): see HOLD *v.* 32. † ***where the water sticks*** [after L. *hæret aqua*]: where discussion comes to a standstill. ***water over the dam*** or ***under the bridge*** (***dyke, mill*** and varr.): past events which it is unprofitable to revive or discuss; a way of saying 'a long time has passed'.

971 *Blickl. Hom.* 237 Maneȝa tintreȝa hie þe onbringað.. swa þætte þin blod flewþ ofer eorðan swa swa wæter. *c* **1385** CHAUCER *L.G.W.* 852 The blood out of the wounde as brode sterte As water, whan the conduit broken is. **1544** ASCHAM *Toxoph.* I. (Arb.) 28, I found my good bowe..as weake as water. **1546** HEYWOOD *Prov.* I. xi. (1867) 32 It is, to geue him, as muche almes or neede As cast water in tems. **1579** GOSSON *Apol. Sch. Abuse* (Arb.) 64 They haue..threatned highly, too put water in my woortes, whensoeuer they catche me. **1604** SHAKS. *Oth.* v. ii. 134 She was false as water. **1608** DEKKER *Lanth. & Candle-light* viii. G 5, Yet they haue a tricke (like water cut with a swoord) to come together instantly and easily againe. **1611** BEAUM. & FL. *Philaster* v. iii, All your better deeds Shall be in water writ, but this in Marble. **1612** *Pasquil's Night-Cap* (1877) 38 No, this deuice too much in vse is growne, And will not hold out water to the last. **1613** SHAKS. *Hen. VIII*, IV. ii. 46 Mens euill manners liue in Brasse, their Vertues We write in Water. **1655** BRAMHALL *Def. True Liberty* 20 This is the very question where the water sticks between us [*sc.* between Hobbes and Bramhall]. **1697** TRYON *Way to Health* vi. 98 Though it be a vulgar Proverb—*As weak as Water.* **1704** N. N. tr. *Boccalini's Advts. fr. Parnass.* I. 59 But I must beg leave to tell you, this Excuse will not bear Water. **1728** W. SMITH *Univ. College* 185 And upon that Fear and Conviction that his Cause could not bear Water. *a* **1734** R. NORTH *Life Ld. Kpr. Guilford* (1742) 151 They caressed his Lordship very much as a new Comer,..and talked about a Time to dine with him; all which (as they say) was Water in his Shoes. **1824** *Compl. Hist. Murder Mr. Weare* 231 The organ of destructiveness was not at all prominent or developed. This was 'water in the shoes' of the phrenologists. **1831** S. WARREN *Diary Late Physic.* xxii. (1832) II. 247 He [a cabin-boy] was frequently flogged..till the blood ran down his back like water. **1859** DICKENS, etc. *Haunted Ho.* v. 24/1 The sweat poured off my face like water. **1865** KINGSLEY *Herew.* xx (end), And the hearts of all the French were turned to water; and the land had peace from its tyrants for many days. **1871** —— *Lett.* etc. (1877) II. 368 All else is a 'paralogism' and runs off them like water off a duck's back. **1898** S. J. WEYMAN *Shrewsbury* xiii. 116 Though at one time my heart was water when I thought of betraying him, at another it glowed with rage and loathing. **1913** *Wireless World* I. 34/1 Much water has flowed under London Bridge since those days. **1914** KIPLING *Let.* 15 Sept. in Ld. Birkenhead *Rudyard Kipling* (1978) xviii. 279 Your articles..are a little too remote..but of course—much water, or shall we say much blood, has flowed under the bridges since they were written. **1920** GALSWORTHY *In Chancery* I. i. 5 It was a startling remark—showing in a flash what a lot of water had run under bridges since the death of Aunt Ann in '88. **1940** *Nation* (N.Y.) 16 Mar. 364 Last year's results are water under the mill. **1940** *Amer. Guardian* 11 Oct. 1 All that is water over the dam. **1955** C. S. FORESTER *Good Shepherd* 91 He should not have brought the men to battle stations at all. .. But that was water over the dam; no time for regrets at present. **1964** E. F. BECKENBACH *Appl. Combinatorial Math.* x. 292 But these fees are water under the bridge, for we have paid them and they will never be returned to us. **1969** 'W. HAGGARD' *Doubtful Disciple* xi. 116 'Where did he get it?' 'From Seyer, I think—we can't escape that. But that's water over the dam by now.' **1976** *Glasgow Herald* 26 Nov. 5/4 Does he look back in anger as a result of his wartime experiences? 'Not now—perhaps a little to start with. But a lot of water has gone under the dyke since then.' **1977** J. THOMSON *Case Closed* iii. 43 It's been quite a time since we last met. Water under the bridge, as they say. **1981** *Encounter* Oct. 7 You don't want to let any of that business bother you... Water under the bridge. Just accept the fact, file it away.

2. a. As a drink, as satisfying thirst, or as necessary aliment for animals and plants. Also *fig.* (chiefly in biblical uses) applied to what satisfies spiritual needs or desires; cf. WATER OF LIFE.

bread and water (also in Shaks. † ***bran and water***), the type of extreme hard fare, as of a prisoner or a penitent.

*c*950 *Lindisf. Gosp.* John iv. 13 Eȝhuelc seðe ȝedrincað of ðæm uætre þæt ic sello him ne ðyrsteð in æcnisse. *a* **1000** *Colloq. Ælfric* in Wr.-Wülcker 102 Hwæt drincst þu? Eala, ȝif ic hæbbe, oþþe wæter ȝif ic næbbe ealu. *a* **1200** *Vices & Virtues* 43 Leuere him [*sc.* Daniel] was..ðat water to drinken ðanne..ðe gode wines. *c* **1200** ORMIN 3212 Hiss drinnch wass waterr aȝȝ occ aȝȝ, Hiss mete wilde rotess. *c* **1250** *Gen. & Ex.* 1246 Ðor ȝhe gan fremen ysmael Wið watres drinc and bredes mel. **1573–80** TUSSER *Husb.* (1878) 81 Howse calfe, and go sockle it twise in a day, and after a while, set it water and hay. **1580** *Memoriall W. Lambe* C iij b, Whose daily custome it was to meditate vpon a Praier booke, called The Conduit of Comfort,..that with the water thereof his soule..might be refreshed. **1588** SHAKS. *L.L.L.* I. i. 303 You shall fast a Weeke with Branne and water. **1603** —— *Meas. for M.* IV. iii. 159, I am faine to dine and sup with water and bran. **1611** BIBLE *Isa.* xli. 17. **1656** R. SHORT *Drinking Water* 68 Why then should we (like so many Don Quixotes) change our national drink for water? **1731** MILLER *Gard. Dict.* s.v. *Guidonia*, During the Winter-season they should have but little Water. **1749** SMOLLETT *Gil Blas* I. xii, To regale myself still with my bread and water, and the sight of a silent turnkey. **1759** R. BROWN *Compl. Farmer* 13 Give the horse a ball in his water. **1842** LOUDON *Suburb. Horticult.* 386 When plants are ripening their fruit, a diminished supply of water increases the flavour. **1844** H. STEPHENS *Bk. Farm* III. 833 One essential requisite in all pasture-fields is an abundant supply of water for stock to drink. **1865** MRS. WHITNEY *Gayworthys* xxxvi, She fell back, trembling, against her chair. Mr. Brinley brought her hastily some water. **1921** E. L. MASTERS *Mitch Miller* xiv. 113 After that they..put him in a dark room and kept him on bread and water for a day.

b. Contrasted with wine, as inferior in strength or pleasantness.

a **1300** *Cursor M.* 21295 þe stile o matheu, water it was, And win þe letter o lucas. **1842** TENNYSON *Locksley Hall* 152 Woman is the lesser man, and all thy passions, match'd with mine, Are as moonlight unto sunlight, and as water unto wine.

c. ***water bewitched*** (colloq.): used derisively for excessively diluted liquor; now chiefly, very weak tea.

1678 RAY *Prov.* (ed. 2) 84 Water betwitch't, i.e. very thin beer. **1694** [see BEWITCHED]. **1699** T. BROWN *L'Estrange's Colloq. of Erasm.* Add. v. 53 The Broth was nothing in the world but Water bewitched [L. *mera aqua*], if it deserved so good a Name. **1731–8** SWIFT *Pol. Conversat.* i. 24 Your Ladyship is very sparing of your Tea: I protest, the last I took, was no more than Water bewitch'd. *a* **1825** FORBY *Voc. E. Anglia*, *Water-bewitched*, weak tea, coffee, punch, &c.

fig. **1845** CARLYLE *Cromwell* Introd. ii. I. 25 Another Book of Noble's..is of much more stupid character; nearly meaningless indeed; mere water bewitched.

3. a. As used for dilution of liquors.

1382 WYCLIF *Isa.* i. 22 Thi syluer is turned in to dros; thi wyn is mengd with water. **1731–8** SWIFT *Pol. Conversat.* ii. 165 *Lady Smart.* I was told, ours [*sc.* ale] was very strong. *Sir John.* Ay, Madam, strong of the Water. **1837** DICKENS *Pickw.* xxxviii, Mr. Benjamin Allen..produced..a black bottle half full of brandy. 'You don't take water, of course?' said Bob Sawyer.

fig. **1860** LD. ACTON in Gasquet *Acton & Circle* (1906) 149, I am afraid you will think I have poured a good deal of water into your wine in 'Tyrol' and 'Syria'.

b. In phrasal combinations denoting liquors diluted with water, as ***brandy-and-water***, ***gin-and-water***, ***rum-and-water***, ***whisky-and-water***, ***wine-and-water***: see the first words; also MILK-AND-WATER. Hence jocularly in nonce-combinations.

1812 H. C. ROBINSON *Jrnl.* 13 May in E. J. Morley *Blake, Coleridge, Wordsworth, Lamb, Etc.* (1922) 50 Bar. Field called Wilson '*Wordsworth & Water*'. **1882** MRS. OLIPHANT *Lit. Hist. Eng.* I. 168 The weak Addison-and-water of the 'Mirror' and the 'Lounger'. **1899** *Daily News* 13 Mar. 7/1 He once heard a University sermon described as of the Bible and water order.

c. *fig.* (*Stock Exchange.*) Fictitious capital created by the 'watering' or 'diluting' of the stock of a trading company. See WATER *v.* 7 e.

1883 *Nation* (N.Y.) 8 Nov. 384/2 The Committee does not produce any evidence to show that it is the dread of 'water' which is now keeping the foreign investor out of Wall Street. **1894** *Daily News* 12 July 5/5 The stock of the Company has been watered three times over, and the Company has not only been able to pay the regular dividends on the water and all, but [etc.].

4. a. As used for washing, steeping, boiling, etc.

c **1000** *Ags. Gosp.* Matt. xxvii. 24 Ða ȝeseah pilatus þæt hyt naht ne fremode..þa ȝenam he wæter & þwoh hys handa. *a* **1300** *Cursor M.* 20212 Scho..wessh hir suet bodi in water. *c* **1375** *Sc. Leg. Saints* xviii. (*Egipciane*) 1424, & with his teris wysche þam sone as quha with vattir suld þam don. *c* **1400** *Rule St. Benet* (prose) liii. 35 þ abbesse sal giue þe gestis water til þaire hende. *c* **1430** *Two Cookery-bks.* 13 Take Vele, Kyde, or Henne, an boyle hem in fayre Water, or ellys in freysshe brothe. **1577** B. GOOGE *Heresbach's Husb.* I. 35 b, Lupines..being sodden and layd in water..feedeth Oxen in Winter very well. **1605** SHAKS. *Macb.* II. ii. 46 Goe get some Water, And wash this filthie Witnesse from your Hand. **1706** E. WARD *Wooden World Diss.* (1708) 15 So incredibly extravagant is he sometimes, as to wash his Cabin with fresh Water, when the Ship's Company want it to allay the burning Heat of their salt Victuals. **1828** SCOTT *F.M. Perth*, *Chron. Canongate* Ser. II. Introd., These are the stains;.. neither water nor any thing else will ever remove them from that spot.

b. Each of the quantities of water used successively in a gradual process of washing.

a **1225** *Ancr. R.* 324 Wule a weob beon, et one cherre, mid one watere wel ibleched..? **1684** J. S. *Profit & Pleas. United* 149 Feeding him [your hawk] upon the flesh of Rooks, washed in two waters. *a* **1777** in *Jrnl. Friends' Hist. Soc.* (1914) Oct. 187 Take half a pound of sagoe, and wash it well in 3 or 4 hot waters. **1856** KANE *Arctic Expl.* II. ix. 94 Butter

..my own invention, melted from salt beef and washed in many waters. 1875 F. J. Bird *Dyer's Hand-bk.* 33 Wash in two waters and dry.

c. in references to baptism.

c 1000 *Ags. Gosp.* Matt. iii. 11 Ic eow fulliȝe on wætere to dædbote. a 1300 *Cursor M.* 19976 Qua mai for-bede Water at baptim. 1387 [see COLD WATER b.]. 1567 *Gude & Godlie B.* (S.T.S.) 14 Quhen Goddis word with watter Junit be, Throw Faith, to gif vs lyfe Eternallie. 1597 Hooker *Eccl. Pol.* v. lx. §1 Why are we taught that with water God doth purifie and clense his Church?

5. Water of a mineral spring or a collection of mineral springs used medicinally for bathing or for drinking, or both. Often plural (cf. L. *aquæ*) preceded by *the* or the name of a place. *to go to the waters* (? obs.): to visit a 'watering-place' for remedial treatment.

1542-3 *Act 34 & 35 Hen. VIII.* c. 8 Divers honest persones..whome God hathe endued with the knowledge of the nature kinde and operacion of certeyne herbes rotes and waters. 1561 Gresham in Burgon *Life* (1839) I. 122 Sir John a Leye ys not yett come from the water of Spawe. 1563 Fulke *Meteors* iv. (1571) 57 b, Of whote bathes. Some waters that are generated and flowe out of vaynes of brymstone, are sensybly warme, and some very whott... These waters being also drying by nature, are wholsome for many infyrmities. 1641 in *Verney Mem.* (1907) I. 207 Waters have twice donn her good and Spaw water is better than the best waters in England. 1652 J. French *York-sh. Spaw* 85, I approve not of taking the waters too fast. 1676 Lady Chaworth in *12th Rep. Hist. MSS. Comm.* App. v. 29 Lady Portsmouth continues sicke, and some say she will try the French ayre, others the Bath watters. 1712 Steele *Spect.* No. 284 ¶4 Though I have drunk the Waters, and am told I ought not to use my Eyes so much, I cannot forbear writing to you. 1720 Wilcocks in Ellis *Orig. Lett.* Ser. ii. IV. 321 Since the kings return from the waters, which agreed very well with him, we have had [etc.]. 1775 Sheridan *St. Patrick's Day* i. i, She was such a hand at making foreign waters! for Seltzer, Pyrmont, Islington, or Chalybeate, she never had her equal. 1788 Jefferson *Writ.* (1859) II. 453 He has obtained leave to go to the waters. 1837 Dickens *Pickw.* xxxv, Most welcome to Ba-ath, sir. It is long—very long, Mr. Pickwick, since you drank the waters. 1854 Surtees *Handley Cr.* iii. (1901) I. 19 It was well known their waters were immeasurably inferior to what *they* enjoyed, not only in sulphuretted hydrogen, but also in iodine and potash. 1879 *St. George's Hosp. Rep.* IX. 579 She was ordered simply a wine-glass of Orezza water after breakfast every morning.

6. a. Water regarded as collected in seas, lakes, ponds, etc., or as flowing in rivers or streams.

Often with definite article, as denoting a particular portion of water referred to. Also, the aqueous part of the earth's surface as a region inhabited by its own characteristic forms of life, in contradistinction to the land and the air.

For *piece, sheet of water*, see PIECE *sb.* 3, SHEET *sb.*[1] 8 a.

a 1100 *Gerefa* in *Anglia* IX. 259 Ðe on wuda, ȝe on wætere, ȝe on felda, ȝe on falde. c 1175 *Lamb. Hom.* 79 Þe uisces iþe wetere and fuȝeles iþe lufte. c 1250 *Gen. & Ex.* 2968 And aaron held up his hond, to ðe water and ðe more lond. a 1300 *Cursor M.* 399 Þe fiss to watur, als we find, Þe fuxol be-taght he to Þe wynd. 1377 Langl. *P. Pl.* B. xvi. 189 Alle þat lyf hath a londe & a watre. 1473 *Rental Bk. Cupar-Angus* (1879) I. 178 Tha sal gif al possibil cure and laubour til hald furth the watter with makyn of perys..and plantation of willeis. 1503 Dunbar *Thistle & Rose* 66 Dame Nature gaif ane inhibitioun thair To ferss Neptunus, and Eolus the bawld, Nocht to perturb the wattir nor the air. 1573-80 Tusser *Husb.* (1878) 117 Wash sheepe (for the better) where water doth run. 1605 Shaks. *Macb.* i. iii. 79 The Earth hath bubbles, as the Water ha's. 1781 Cowper *Task* iii. 382 But wisdom is a pearl with most success Sought in still water. 1830 Tennyson *Arab. Nts.* 30 Deep inlay Of braided blooms unmown, which crept Adown to where the water slept. 1849 Macaulay *Hist. Eng.* ix. II. 481 The water in the bay was as even as glass. 1867 Ansted *Phys. Geog.* 125 Owing to the position of the land, we have the water divided into two unequal parts, the Pacific Ocean and the Atlantic canal.

b. The plural is often used instead of the sing. esp. with reference to flowing water or to water moving in waves.

For the pl. cf. F. *eaux*, L. *aquæ*, Gr. ὕδατα.

c 1000 *Ags. Gosp.* Matt. xiv. 28 Dryhten, ȝyf þu hyt eart, hat me cuman to þe ofer þas wæteru. a 1300 *Cursor M.* 380 Þe watters al he cald þe see. 13.. *E.E. Allit. P.* B. 437 Þen he wakened a wynde on watterez to blowe. c 1374 Chaucer *Boeth.* v. met. i. (1868) 152 Sone aftre þe same ryueres tigris and eufrates vnioygnen and departen hire watres. 1535 Coverdale *Ps.* lxxvii. 19 Thy waye was in the see, and thy pathes in the great waters. 1610 Shaks. *Temp.* i. ii. 1 If by your Art (my dearest father) you haue Put the wild waters in this Rore, allay them. 1684 J. Peter *Relat. Siege Vienna* 55 About this time the Waters of the Danube swelled so high as to break down the Bridge which the Enemy had made. 1697 Dryden *Æneis* ix. 152 Old Tyber roar'd; and raising up his Head, Call'd back his Waters to their Oozy Bed. a 1774 Goldsm. *Hist. Greece* II. 174 A river not so remarkable for the breadth of its channel, as for the beauty of its waters. 1798 Coleridge *Anc. Mar.* v. 324 Like waters shot from some high crag, The lightning fell with never a jag, A river steep and wide. 1803-6 Wordsw. *Ode, Intim. Immort.* 171 And see the Children sport upon the shore, And hear the mighty waters rolling evermore. 1842 Borrow *Bible in Sp.* xxiv, Waters sounded, nightingales sang. 1862 Longf. *Wayside Inn* i. Prel. 260 The cataract hurled Its headlong waters from the height. 1891 Farrar *Darkn. & Dawn* xiii, They..had been baptised in the waters of their native river.

c. In figurative context. (See also TROUBLED *a.* 1, FISH *v.*[1] 1 c, OIL *sb.*[1] 3 e.)

deep waters (after Ps. lxix. 2, 14), grave distresses and anxieties; also, difficult or dangerous affairs; now usu. in phr. ***in deep water(s)***.

1535 Coverdale *Ps.* lxviii [lxix]. 2, I am come in to depe waters [so also 1611]. *Ibid.* 14. 1628 A. Leighton *Appeal to Parlt.* 19 Therfore she loves to fish in troubled Waters. 1662 Stillingfl. *Orig. Sacræ* i. iii. §8 Joseph Scaliger who hath troubled the waters so much concerning the particular circumstances of this translation, yet fully agrees that it was done in the time of Ptolomæus Philadelphus. c 1720 De Foe *Mem. Cavalier* (1840) 20 The Cardinal..was..not on very good terms with the queen, but willing to keep smooth water there. 1861 T. Hughes *Tom Brown at Oxford* I. v. 83 Tom felt greatly relieved, as he was beginning to find himself in rather deep water. 1867 Trollope *Last Chron. Barset* I. xxxiv. 294 Once he had been very nearly in deep water because Mrs. Proudie had taken it in dudgeon that a certain young rector, who had been left a widower, had a very pretty governess for his children. 1893 Stevenson *Catriona* iii, These are deep waters... Be cautious and think twice. 1902 W. Adamson *Life Joseph Parker* 204 An unwonted interest was created by Dr. Parker's visit. The usually quiet ecclesiastical waters were stirred. 1933 N. Coward *Design for Living* ii. ii. 62 Our lives are diametrically opposed to ordinary social conventions; and it's no use grabbing at those conventions to hold us up when we find we're in deep water. 1950 D. Lessing *Grass is Singing* viii. 157 He stubbornly went his own way, feeling as if she had encouraged him to swim in deep waters beyond his strength, and then left him to his own devices.

d. *pl.* The maritime tract belonging to a particular nation; the seas and oceans in a particular quarter of the globe.

1659 in *Rec. Convent. Burghs Scot.* (1878) III. 487 Who.. went aboard of tuo Dutch wessellis lying near Inchkeyth, being within our watteris. 1920 *Round Table* Dec. 89 The Alliance..freed us from the necessity of keeping more than a skeleton force in eastern waters in order to defend the Dominions and India.

e. *Hunting, Steeplechasing*, etc. Streams or ditches which a horse is required to leap.

1860 Ld. W. Lennox *Pict. Sporting Life* I. 328 You will find him [a horse] a splendid fencer, I never saw the like of him at timber or water; no gate or brook will stop him. 1869 Whyte-Melville *Songs & Verses* 87 Hunters so limber at water and timber Now on the causeway are fain to be led. 1879 *Punch* 13 Dec. 267 I've never tried this horse at water.

f. slang. ***to make a hole in the water***: to commit suicide by drowning.

1853 Dickens *Bleak Ho.* xlvi, Why I don't go and make a hole in the water I don't know. 1865 —— *Mut. Fr.* i. iii, This is the drunken old chap..wot had offered..to make a hole in the water for a quartern of rum stood aforehand, and kept to his word for the first and last time in his life.

†g. *pl.* Pictorial representations of tracts of water. *Obs.*

1747 Francis tr. *Horace, Art P.* 34 *note*, It is chiefly in this View, that Ruisdale's Waters, and Claude Lorrain's Skies are so admirable.

7. In phrases relating to navigation.

a. ***by water***: by ship or boat on the sea or a lake or river or canal. (In OE. = 7 b.)

c 1100 *O.E. Chron.* (MS. D) an. 1016, þa ȝewende se here to Lundenne, & þa buruh utan ymbesæton, & hyre stearclice onfeaht, æȝðær ȝe be wætere ȝe be lande. c 1380 Wyclif *Wks.* (1880) 25 þei traueilen nyȝt & day, bi watir & lond, in cold & in hete. c 1386 Chaucer *Prol.* 400 If þat he faught, and hadde the hyer hond, By water he sente hem hoom to euery lond. 1478 W. Paston, Jr. in *P. Lett.* (1897) III. 237 And if it lyke yow that I may come with Alwedyr be watyr. 1547-8 in Feuillerat *Revels Edw. VI* (1914) 29 The Caring by water to and from grenwy[ch]. 1606 *Arraignm. Late Traitors* (1872) 6 They went from the tower by water, and came to Westminster. 1661 Pr. Rupert in *11th Rep. Hist. MSS. Comm.* App. v. 8 My goods goe by Ratisbon, soe by land to Wurtzbourg, and from thence by water the rest of the journey. 1771 Smollett *Humph. Cl.* 4 July (1815) 219 In going down the river, by water, he was by mistake put on board of another vessel under sail. 1809 W. Irving *Knickerb.* vii. xi. (1849) 437 The hostile ships prepared for an assault by water. 1864 T. S. Williams & Simmonds *Engl. Commerc. Corresp.* 116 You will please to receive the said goods, and forward them to us by water. 1886 C. Scholl *Phraseol. Dict.* II. 834 Conveyance is, in this case, cheaper by water than by rail.

b. ***on or upon (the) water*** (ME. † *a wætere*): on the sea, in naval employments or enterprises. Also, *to be on the water*, to be in course of transport by sea.

c 1205 Lay. 562, I seih his broðer ferden hu heo iuaren weren a wætere & a londe. 1412-20 Lydg. *Troy Bk.* iv. 1997 So þat victorie, worship, and honour,..To be reported on water & on lond, Reserued ben hooly to ȝoure hond. 1758 J. Blake *Mar. Syst.* 28 Great numbers of men..are employed in the coasting trade, or otherwise upon the water. 1914 *Daily News* 6 Aug. 5 There is a very large quantity [of tea] on the water on its way from the East. 1914 *Scotsman* 24 Aug. 4/2 Germany has to-day another enemy in the field and on the water.

c. In expressions like ***across, over, on this side the water, to cross the water***, the reference is most commonly to the sea.

The Jacobite toast, 'the king over the water', meaning the Pretender, was expressed by passing the glass of wine over the water decanter when drinking the health of 'the king'.

1662 Chas. II in Cartwright *Madame* (Henrietta of Orleans) (1893) 128 People on this side the watter love there profit as well as they do every where else. 1680 Alsop *Mischief of Impos.* v. 31 We may be Schismaticks here in England, when, if we cross the water, we shall be none. 1749 Fielding *Tom Jones* vii. iv, From these meals she retired about five minutes after the other servants, having only stayed to drink the king over the water. 1765 *Museum Rust.* IV. 234 As your work is in such high reputation on this side of the water, it is a matter of great surprise to me, that you should not have many correspondents amongst such of our Irish gentlemen as are improving their estates. 1842 Dickens *Amer. Notes* xviii, Those partial readers of my former books, across the Water, who met me with an open hand. 1901 *Essex Weekly News* 15 Mar. 3/3 At Chelmsford the mare would fetch £4 because it was going across the water to be made into meat extract. 1905 H. G. Wells *Kipps* ii. i. §1 Coote remarked that the sea was good for crossing, and asked Kipps if he had been over the water much. 1914 *Q. Rev.* Apr. 318 The world, as we on our side of the water mainly know it.

d. In London the above phrases are often used with reference to the Thames. Similarly (*to go*) ***on the water***.

1600 *Essex Reb. Exam.* (MS.) in *Shaks. Cent. Praise* (1879) 35 They went all together to the Globe over the water wher the L. Chamberlens men vse to play. 1731-8 Swift *Pol. Conversat.* i. 46, I promis'd to go this Evening to Hyde-Park on the Water; but I protest, I'm half afraid. 1753 Jane Collier *Art Torment.* i. i. (1811) 35 To..go upon the water with you. 1836 Dickens *Sk. Boz, Shops & Tenants*, It is on the Surrey side of the water—a little distance beyond the Marsh-gate. 1853 —— *Bleak Ho.* xxi, The theatre over, Mr. George comes across the water again, and makes his way to that curious region lying about the Haymarket and Leicester Square. 1887 T. A. Trollope *What I remember* I. 218, I used to be a good deal upon the water either alone or accompanied by a single friend with a pair of sculls.

8. ***to take (the) water.***

a. Of an animal or waterfowl, also of a person: To enter the sea, a lake or river, and begin to swim. **b.** To embark, take ship; in 17-18th c. chiefly, †to take a boat on the Thames (*obs.*). **c.** *U.S.* 'To abandon one's position' (Thornton). **d.** Of a ship: To be launched.

1580 H. Smith in Hakluyt *Voy.* (1589) 468 This day.. there came a great white beare downe to the water side, and tooke the water of his owne accord. 1607 Topsell *Four-f. Beasts* 149 The sence of smelling is so quicke in these [Sluthhounds], that they can follow the footesteps of theeus,.. and if the theef take the water, they cast in themselues also. a 1676 Hale *Prim. Orig. Man.* ii. vii. (1677) 202 As to the Water-Fowls, the difficulty is less, for they can and do supply the weariness of a long flight by taking Water. 1804 Charlotte Smith *Conversat.* etc. I. 27 If I was on horseback on my filly Truffle, and the dogs were to take water,.. why I should no more mind plunging in directly [etc.]. 1878 *Scribner's Monthly* XV. 765/1, I heard a splash and saw a deer take the water 300 yards or so above me. 1891 *New Review* Aug. 167, I..lay to to see it take the water, as its evident intention was to cross to the mainland.

b. 1548 Patten *Exped. Scot.* D iij b, This thus apointed, my lorde Admirall rode back to take the water agayne. 1650 Trapp *Comm. Num.* xxxii. 23 Taking water, with purpose to sail into Flanders. 1689 Luttrell *Brief Rel.* (1857) I. 524 A gentleman taking water the 18th, when he came near London bridge, pull'd a written paper out of his pocket. 1708 *Constit. Watermen's Co.* 81 None plying the Long-Ferry shall ply one about to take Water with another, except, &c. a 1754 Carte *Hist. Eng.* IV. 50 Stukely agreeing to go with him, they took water: but were seized in the way to Gravesend. 1793 *Regal Rambler* 91 He took water at the Temple-stairs. 1821 Scott *Kenilw.* xv, For see, the Queen's barge lies at the stairs, as if her Majesty were about to take water. 1889 Mrs. Oliphant *Poor Gentl.* I. vi. 93 The boating parties that 'took the water' there.

c. 1858 J. G. Baldwin *Flush Times* 275 'If it please your honor, I believe I will take water' (a common expression, signifying that the person using it would take a nonsuit). 1859 Bartlett *Dict. Amer.* (ed. 2) 470 To Take Water. To run away, make off. A Western expression, doubtless borrowed from sportsmen. 1891 C. Roberts *Adrift Amer.* 200 The fellow, who was really a coward, though nearly twice as big as myself, took water at once.

d. 1901 *Scotsman* 7 Mar. 5/6 Launch of the cruiser Kent. .. The vessel took the water without a hitch.

9. a. Quantity or depth of water, as sufficient or insufficient for navigation. ***to draw*** (so much) ***water***: see DRAW *v.* 13.

1546 J. Heywood *Prov.* ii. viii. (1867) 73 There was no more water than the ship drew. 1580 H. Smith in Hakluyt *Voy.* (1589) 469 There was not water for the boate betweene Vaigats and the other side: finding no more water, there was no other way but to goe backe as we came in. 1584 R. Norman tr. *Safegard of Sailers* 7 Item, from the north Buie to the Nese, keepe the north Buie with Memelicke, as far as you can see, till you bring those two steeples or towers into one, and then you shall haue water enough. 1716 *Lond. Gaz.* No. 5416/1 There not being Water enough, she was not launched. 1791 Smeaton *Edystone L.* §86 A clear passage to the South, with a sufficiency of water for the craft at low water. 1791 R. Mylne *2nd Rep. Thames* 10 Good Water from thence to Moulsford. 1793 —— *Rep. Thames* 35 There is a pretty good water all the way to Datchet Bridge. And from Datchet Bridge, there is a fine navigable water all the way to New-Lock-Shoal.

b. With prefixed adj., a particular state of the tide: see HIGH WATER, LOW WATER. †***full water*** = full tide.

c 1420 ? Lydg. *Assembly of Gods* 110 Where as I shuld haue fyllyd dykes depe At a full watyr I might nat thedyr crepe Before my seon came to retorne ayeyne. 1603 *Reg. Mag. Sig. Scot.* 490/2 Cum potestate colligendi lie wraik et wair fra the full sey to the low watter.

10. a. Water received into a boat or ship through a leak, or by the breaking of the waves over the side. ***to make water*** [= F. *faire eau*, It. *far acqua*, G. *wasser machen*]: (of a ship or boat) to leak, or to admit or 'ship' water over the side, through a port, etc. Also, ***to take (in) water*** in the same sense. † ***to make foul water*** (obs.): see FOUL *a.* 4.

c 1386 Chaucer *Pars. T.* 363 The same harm dooth som tyme the smale dropes of water, that entren thurgh a litel creuace in to the thurrok, and in the botme of the shipe. a 1553 Udall *Royster D.* iii. ii. 16 It liked hir as well, to tell you no lies, As water in hir shyppe, or salt cast in hir eies. 1555 Eden *Decades* (Arb.) 77 The vytayles corrupted by taking water at the riftes euyll closed. *Ibid.* 260 One of theyr shyppes leaked and toke water very sore. 1748 *Anson's Voy.* i. iii. 24 The ship made so much water, that with four pumps and bailing he could not free her. 1799 *Hull Advertiser* 13 July 1/4 St. Anna, leaky: made 20 inches of water in an hour. 1825 *New Monthly Mag.* XV. 74 We found by the well that she [*sc.* a ship] made no water. 1884 *Law Times* 10 May 26/2

She was then found to be making five inches of water per hour. **1890** W. F. RAE *Maygrove* I. iv. 61 The carpenter sounded the well and found that she was making water fast. **1892** *Idler* Apr. 320 The feebleness..of her stroke.. prevented the boat from taking much water.

† **b.** ***to take (in) water*** (fig.): ? to have a flaw or weak place. *Obs.*

1590 NASHE *Pasquil's Apol.* D 2 b, The rest of his reasons haue taken water, and are rotten before they come to shore. **1640** BP. HALL *Episc.* II. xx. 202 All the rest are easily freed; St. Jerome and St. Ambrose in the opinion of some seem to take in water.

11. As an enveloping or covering medium. In various phrases.

a. ***under water***: below the surface of water; (of land) flooded, submerged. Hence *fig.* unsuccessful in life; also (Sc.) in debt. Also Sc. † ***within water***, in the same sense.

1529 *Registr. Aberdon.* (Maitland Club) I. 396 To sustene ..mend and uphald..þe brig forsaid..als weill within wattar as abuf. **1598** FLORIO, *Sott'acqua*, vnder-water, secretlie, out of sight, in hugger mugger. **1660** BOYLE *New Exper. Spring of Air* 363 Cornelius Drebell..is affirm'd..to have contriv'd for the late Learned King James, a Vessel to go under Water. **1708** *Lond. Gaz.* No. 4453/2 Our Governor has put all the Country between Bruges and Newport under Water. **1759** JOHNSON *Idler* No. 49 ¶5 The country was under water. **1816** SCOTT *Old Mort.* xlii, And then he got favour, and Lord Evandale's head was under water. **1827** FARADAY *Chem. Manip.* xxiv. (1842) 628 Close the tube by the finger,..then open its aperture by removing the finger under water. **1839** LOCKHART *Ballantyne-humbug handled* 113 Mr. James [Ballantyne]..was..many thousands under water at the smash. **1914** D. CHRISTIE *30 Yrs. in Moukden* vi. 50 Besides the submerged villages, a large part of the suburbs of Moukden was under water.

b. ***above water***: above the surface of the water. Also *fig.*, esp. in ***to keep one's head above water***, to avoid ruin by a continued struggle.

1662 J. DAVIES tr. *Olearius' Voy. Ambass.* 35 To save all but our Carpenter, who was lost for want of having fasten'd on somewhat that might have kept him above water. **1705** COLLIER *Ess. Mor. Subj.* III. *Pain* 11 Unless a Man can reconcile himself to Suffering, and keep his Spirits above Water, 'tis in vain to pretend to Principles. **1742** FIELDING *J. Andrews* III. xiii, There are many who, I fancy, believe that..my pockets..are lined with bank-bills; but I assure you, you are all mistaken... If I can hold my head above water it is all I can. **1809** MALKIN *Gil Blas* v. i. ¶7 To carry me discreetly through the world, and keep my head above water. **1864** TROLLOPE *Small Ho. Allington* xxv, Modern Lotharios—men who were holding their heads well above water, although it was known that they had played this lady false, and brought that other one to death's door. **1885** *Field* 3 Oct. 502/2 A number of struggling men [agriculturists], who have managed to keep above water during the bad seasons, must now go under.

† **c.** ***to lay in water, to lay a-water***: to make of no effect or value; to dissipate. *Obs.*

c **1394** *P. Pl. Crede* 782 But now þe harlottes han hid thilke rewle, And, for the loue of oure lorde haue leyd hire in water. **1401** *Pol. Poems* (Rolls) II. 43 But, Jak, thouȝ thi questions semen to thee wyse, ȝit liȝtly a lewid man maye leyen hem a water. **1579** GOSSON *Sch. Abuse* (Arb.) 21 Either Apollo must haue played the Bonesetter, or euery occupation beene laide a water. **1583** GOLDING *Calvin on Deut.* xcv. 579 If I lende him money nowe, it is layde a water, I loose a whole yeares occupying of it. **1592** LYLY *Midas* IV. iv, All his expeditions for warres are laid in water.

† **d.** ***(to swim) between two waters*** [= F. (*nager*) *entre deux eaux*]: midway between the surface and the bottom; *fig.* keeping an impartial or a temporizing attitude between two parties. *Obs.*

1579 TOMSON *Calvin's Serm. Tim.* 791/2 How many are there that will swim betwixt two waters, and play the indifferent men, which wuld haue a Gospel betwixt both? **1603** D. CARLETON in *Crt. & Times Jas. I* (1848) I. 28 The king held himself upright betwixt two waters. **1660** F. BROOKE tr. *Le Blanc's Trav.* 3 Sliding the Anchor on one side betwixt two waters.

12. A body of water on the surface of the earth.

a. *gen.* A body or collection of standing or flowing water, irrespective of size; a sea, lake, river, etc.

a **1100** in Kemble *Cod. Dipl.* IV. 204 Mid wateren and mid moren. **1297** R. GLOUC. (Rolls) 19 Wateres he [*sc.* Engelond] haþ ek inouȝ, ac at uore alle oþere þre Out of þe londe in to þe se, armes as þei it be..Severne & temese; homber is þet þridde. *a* **1300** *Cursor M.* 5918 All þe waters on þis land Wex son in to blod red. *c* **1400** MAUNDEV. xiv. (1839) 126 And he schal so passe the Wature, that ys cleped the Brace of seynt George, that ys an Arm of the See. **1542** BOORDE *Dyetary* x. (1870) 253 Standynge waters, the whiche be refresshed with a fresshe spryng, is commendable. **1580** in *Lanc. & Cheshire Wills* (Chetham Soc.) I. 72, I have maid a lease of my capitall and chieffe messuages in lyttle Mearley [etc.]..with th'..waters, ffisshings, moores [etc.]..to Rauffe Tetlowe. **1604** E. G[RIMSTONE] *D'Acosta's Hist. Indies* II. ii. 84 This region is wonderfully scorched and drie; and so by consequence, hath neither waters nor pastures. *a* **1633** G. HERBERT *Outlandish Prov.* 434 Who letts his wife goe to every feast, and his horse drinke at every water, shall neither have good wife nor good horse. **169.** LOCKE *Educ.* §7 Horace..assures us, he was wont in the Winter Season to bathe himself in cold Water. But perhaps Italy will be thought much warmer than England, and the chilness of their Waters not to come near ours in Winter. **1757** [BURKE] *Europ. Settlem. Amer.* VII. xxi. II. 235 Though the winters are sharp,..yet they are seldom severe enough to freeze any considerable water. **1828** DUPPA *Trav. Italy*, etc. 195 This whirlpool [Charybdis] is an agitated water, from seventy to ninety fathoms in depth, circling in quick eddies. **1836** HUGH MURRAY, etc. *China* (Edinb. Cab. Libr.) I. i. 29 Along the lower course of both these magnificent waters [the Hohang-ho and Yang-tse-kiang]. **1843** *Penny Cycl.* XXVII. 789/2 *Zizania aquatica*, Canadian Wild Rice,..is common in all the waters of North America from Canada to Florida. **1850** R. G. CUMMING *Hunter's Life S. Afr.* (ed. 2) I. 279, I inquired of the guides if they would lead me to waters in that direction. They all shouted that that was the desert, and that no man ever found water there. **1850** TENNYSON *In Mem.* lxvii, In thy place of rest By that broad water of the west. **1885** *Riverside Nat. Hist.* (1888) II. 251 They frequent almost every variety of water, from the briny lakes of Utah and California to the clearest mountain-streams of our northern territories. **1898** *Edin. Rev.* Jan. 192 Hundreds of the swallow family may sometimes be seen together, hawking for flies over the London waters on a fine April morning.

b. A sheet of water, a lake, pool. Cf. the proper names Derwentwater, Wastwater, Ullswater, Hawes Water, etc. in n.w. England.

c **1250** *Gen. & Ex.* 749 Nov ist a water of loðlic ble, Men callið it ðe dede se. *a* **1300** *Cursor M.* 13760 A water þar es wit-in þair thede þat es cald piscene in þair lede. *c* **1380** WYCLIF *Serm.* Sel. Wks. I. 301 Crist wandride bi þe water of Galile. *c* **1386** CHAUCER *Pars. T.* (Harl.) 841 Seint Iohan saith þat aduoutris schuln be in helle in watir [*Ellesm.* in a stank; F. *estanc*; L. *stagnum*] brennyng of fuyr and of brimston. **1641** J. JACKSON *True Evang. T.* III. 209 The other is two pots floting upon a pond, or surface of a water with this word, If we knock together, we sink together. **1655** WALTON *Angler* xiii. (1661) 197 The river Dee..springs in Merionnithshire, and as it runs toward Chester, it runs through Pemble-Mere, which is a large water. **1756** AMORY *Buncle* (1770) I. 204 A water on the top of a hill, which stood at the other end of the lake. **1799** A. YOUNG *Agric. Lincoln* 27 A large lawn, a water half a mile long, a very handsome bridge over it. **1842** TENNYSON *Morte d'Arth.* 12 On one side lay the Ocean, and on one Lay a great water, and the moon was full. **1896** HOUSMAN *Shropshire Lad* xli, And like a skylit water stood The bluebells in the azured wood.

c. A stream, river. In early use often ***the water of*** (prefixed to the name of a river). Now chiefly *Sc.* and *north.*; often in the names of small rivers, as Water of Esk, Water of Leith, Allan Water, Moffat Water.

In MHG. and in early and dial. mod.G. *wasser* is used for 'river', often in apposition with the proper name. The frequent use in Coverdale's Bible (where 1611 has 'riuer') is prob. due to the influence of Luther's version.

c **1290** *S. Eng. Leg.*, *John Baptist* 85 Toward þe watere of Jordan. **1297** R. GLOUC. (Rolls) 7654 þer hii gonne abide Bi tuene þe water of trente & of ouse al so. *Ibid.* 8850 Bituene tueye wateres he rerde redinge [*i.e.* built Reading Abbey]. **1303** R. BRUNNE *Handl. Synne* 10528 þys batayle was, þurgh here boþe assent, Besyde a watyr, men calle Trent. **13..** *E.E. Allit. P.* A. 107, I wan to a water by schore þat scherez. **1375** BARBOUR *Bruce* VII. 5 The kyng..held doun toward a vale, Quhar throu the vod a vattir ran. **1387** TREVISA *Higden* (Rolls) VI. 449 A monke..fil doun of a brigge into a water, and was i-stufled. **1390** GOWER *Conf.* II. 102 A stille water ..Which hihte of Lethes the rivere. **1423** *Cov. Leet Bk.* 46 From the watur of Schirburn, þat rennyth to Whitley vnto Hethesale. **1423** in *Reg. Mag. Sig. Scot.* 1430, 30/2 Our fisching of the vater of Anand in al placis and be the see sid. *c* **1450** *Brut* II. 427 The Erle of Armynacke with the dolfynys meyne..mette with the Duke of Clarence and his meyne by this watir of Leyre. **1532** CRANMER *Let. to Hen. VIII* in *Misc. Writ.* (Parker Soc.) II. 233 Passaw, Lyntz, and other places adjoining to the waters of Enus and Danubius. **1535** COVERDALE *Ps.* cxxxvi[i]. 1 By the waters [1611 rivers] of Babilon we sat downe and wepte. —— *Tobit* vi. 1 Ye first night they abode by the water of Tigris [Luther *bei dem Wasser Tigris*]. **1560** DAUS tr. *Sleidane's Comm.* 427 The king went up the water of Some. **1563-87** FOXE *A. & M.* (1596) 1891/2 He answered that I was gone ouer a water. **1598** *Reg. Mag. Sig. Scot.* 355/1 As the said burne rynnis north in the watter callit Dewquhilliegach. **1687** A. LOVELL tr. *Thevenot's Trav.* II. 47 Near to this Town, runs a Water that passes under a Bridge of five Arches. **1721** in W. Macfarlane *Geogr. Collect.* (S.H.S.) I. 44 Thorow this Parish runs the River Eugie Eastward, the Inhabitants there call it the water of Strichen. **1728** CHAMBERS *Cycl.* s.v. *River*, We must not omit here a water in Germany, which is ordinarily supposed to change iron into copper. **1761** MRS. F. SHERIDAN *Sidney Bidulph* III. 184 He was drowned in crossing a deep water on horse back. **1793** HERON *Observ. Journ. W. Scot.* I. 13 Within a little [we] found ourselves crossing the water of Leith. **1865** GEIKIE *Scen. & Geol. Scot.* i. 18 Streams, intermediate in size between brooks and rivers, are known in Scotland as 'waters'.

† **d.** *Sc.* and *north.* The banks of a river; the inhabitants of the district bordering on a river. (*Eng. Dial. Dict.*)

a **1800** *Jamie Telfer* xxv. in Child *Ballads* V. 250/2 Gar warn the water [cf. xxiv, water-side], braid and wide, And warn the Curreers i the skaw. *a* **1859** *Denham Tracts* (1892) I. 313 The Coquet Water. The Northumbrians use the above expression in a peculiar sense; signifying thereby the district of the country immediately adjoining the river bearing that name.

13. † **a.** *sing.* A flood. *Obs.* **b.** *pl.* Floods: esp. in phrase ***the waters are out.***

c **1250** *Gen. & Ex.* 592 Ðo was ilc on wer[l]de slaȝen, ðo gunnen ðe wateres hem wið-draȝen. **1470-85** MALORY *Arthur* I. xiii. 52 Ther blewe a grete wynde & blewe doun her castels and her townes, and after that cam a water and bare hit al awey. **1523** SURREY in *St. Papers Hen. VIII*, IV. 44 By reason of the greate waters that was rysen with this rayne that fell thies 3 dayes paste. *a* **1552** LELAND *Itin.* IV. II. 191 a, Leaving Ottemor on the right Hand, that if the Waters had not beene up had beene the next waye. **1617** MORYSON *Itin.* II. 74 Some were drowned passing the waters then very high. **1624** WALTER *Diary* (Camden) 77 The great army of Spinola before Breda,..was removed by God him self, who sent a great water and drowned his trenches, by means whereof he was enforced to remove. **1743** MRS. E. MONTAGU *Corr.* (1906) I. 141 We were met..by a Messenger..to tell us the waters were out at Burroughbridge, and that we could not pass them. *Ibid.* 142, I..agreed to go on to the place he mentioned, and then send a messenger to see if the waters had fallen. **1853** DICKENS *Bleak Ho.* ii, The waters are out in Lincolnshire... The adjacent low-lying ground, for half a mile in breadth, is a stagnant river.

† **14.** *Astr.* The portion of the constellation Aquarius which is figured as a stream of water. [= L. *Aqua*, Gr. Ὕδωρ.] *Obs.*

1551 RECORDE *Cast. Knowl.* (1556) 267 Besyde these 22 starres, there are other 19, whiche in their dyuers and croked position doo make a forme of a Ryuer, and are called the Water whiche Aquarye sheddeth.

II. 15. The substance of which the liquid 'water' is one form among several; now known to be a chemical compound of two volumes of hydrogen and one of oxygen (formula H_2O); in ancient speculation regarded as one of the four, and in pre-scientific chemistry as one of the five elements of which all bodies are composed.

971 *Blickl. Hom.* 35 Ure lichoma wæs ȝesceapen of feower ȝesceaftum, of eorðan, & of fyre, & of wætere, & of lyfte. *a* **1300** [see EARTH *sb.*[1] 14]. **1390** GOWER *Conf.* III. 92 Above therthe the kepth his bounde The water, which is the secounde Of elementz. **1500-20** DUNBAR *Poems* x. 13 Fyre, erd, air, and watter cleir. **1549** *Compl. Scot.* v. 33 This material varld that is maid of the four elementis, of the eird, the vattir, the ayr, ande the fyir. **1669** W. SIMPSON *Hydrol. Chymica* 258 The like happens in all Vegetables, for Water is the material Principle of Vegetables. **1704** J. HARRIS *Lex. Techn.* I, *Water*, which the Chymists call *Phlegm*, is the 4th of the 5 Chimical Principles, and one of the Passive ones. **1732** A. STEWART in *Phil. Trans.* XXXVII. 330, I think the word (Spirits) was an unhappy Choice [to designate the nervous fluid]..And the simple Qualities of a pure and perfectly defecated elementary Water, will better suit all that our Senses can discover of it. **1812-16** PLAYFAIR *Nat. Philos.* (1819) I. 235 On the different quantities of heat..united to the substance which we call water, depends its existence in the state of a solid, a liquid, or an elastic fluid. **1881** SIR W. ARMSTRONG in *Nature* 8 Sept. 450/2 Water, being oxidised hydrogen, must be placed in the same category as the earths.

III. A liquid resembling (and usually containing) water.

16. a. An aqueous decoction, infusion, or tincture, used medicinally or as a cosmetic or a perfume.

13.. *S. Eng. Leg.* (MS. Bodl. 779) in *Archiv Stud. neu. Spr.* LXXXII. 311 Lechis also of flourus wateris makeþ I-lome & oþer þingus þat þer-to by-come. *c* **1386** CHAUCER *Can. Yeom.* 906 What is Magnasia..? It is a water that is maad, I seye, Of elementes foure. **1523-34** FITZHERB. *Husb.* § 46 There be dyuers waters, & other medicyns, that wolde mende hym [*sc.* a blind sheep]. *a* **1533** BERNERS *Golden Bk. M. Aurel.* (1546) I ij b, He wold washe his handes with very well smellyng waters. **1599-1600** in Nichols *Progr. Q. Eliz.* (1823) III. 458 By Mr. William Goodres, two glasses of pretyous water. **1600** SURFLET *Country Farm* III. lxxi. 600 A water vsed amongst the Ladies of the Court, to keepe a faire white and fresh in their faces: Take a white pigeon, a pinte of goats milke [etc.]. **1617** J. TAYLOR (Water P.) *Three Wks. Observ.* D 3 b, Viols, Gallipots, Glasses, Boxes..where-in.. were Waters, Oyles, Vnguents, [etc.]. **1654** WHITLOCK *Zootomia* 57 Can cure all Diseases, from Aries, head and face, to Pisces, the Feet, with a Water and a Powder. **1662** J. DAVIES tr. *Olearius' Voy. Ambass.* 298 They take Tobacco, and drink of a certain black water, which they call Cahwa [= coffee]. **1824** MISS L. M. HAWKINS *Annaline* I. 255 When the pain was violent they spread light linen dipped in aromatic water over her throbbing temples. **1871** GARROD *Mat. Med.* (ed. 3) 4 The waters of pharmacy consist of water holding in solution very small quantities of oils or other volatile principles.

b. With defining word, applied to liquid preparations of various kinds.

For illustration of the diversity of application, see COLOGNE-*water*, LAVENDER WATER, ORANGE-FLOWER-*water*, ROSE-WATER; BARLEY-WATER, † CHICKEN-*water*; BARYTA-*water*, GUM-*water*, LIME-WATER; LITHIA-*water*, POTASS *water*, SODA-WATER.

c **1407** LYDG. *Reson & Sens.* 5737 Of tast also and of flauour It was swetter than watir rose A man in helthe to dyspose. *a* **1425** tr. *Arderne's Treat. Fistula* etc. 82 þis is called watre of alum... And þis watre mundifieþ in coldand, bot watre of sulphur mundifieþ in hetyng or chaufand. *a* **1440** *Sir Degrev.* 1393 With..Watyr of everrose clere, They wesche ryȝth thare. **1477** NORTON *Ord. Alch.* v. in *Ashm.* (1652) 77 As Water of Litharge. **1502** *Priv. Purse Exp. Eliz. York* (1830) 8 A present of watier of rooses. **1819** J. G. CHILDREN *Chem. Anal.* 426 If water of baryta be added to a solution of silicated potassa, the silica and baryta fall down in combination. **1836-41** BRANDE *Chem.* (ed. 5) 75 He ..observed the rapidity with which baryta-water absorbs carbonic acid from the air. **1844** HOBLYN *Dict. Med.* (ed. 2), *Mastic Water.* A remedy employed by the Albanian physicians in infantile diarrhœa; it is simply water which has been boiled along with mastic.

† **c.** A distilled alcoholic liquor, = STRONG WATER 2, † HOT WATER 2. Also ***burning water*** (= med.L. *aqua ardens*, F. *eau ardente*), alcohol.

1460-70 *Bk. Quinte Essence* 6 Haue biside ȝou a uessel.. fillid ful of the beste brennynge watir þat ȝe may fynde. **1471** RIPLEY *Comp. Alch.* v. xxiv. in *Ashm.* (1652) 154 What Salts, what Powders, what Oyles, and waters fort. **1624** CAPT. J. SMITH *Virginia* v. 174 Some hauing some good and comfortable waters, fetched them and dranke one to another. **1789-96** MORSE *Amer. Geog.* II. 116 Rum, brandy, and other distilled waters.

† **d.** Contextually for STRONG WATER 1 = AQUAFORTIS. Also ***corrosive water***, any strong acid.

1609 J. DAVIES (Heref.) *Holy Rood* (Grosart) 4/1 Vpon the Crosse (as on a Touch) we may Trie our Soules value whether great, or small: If there, it (washt with Water-Strong) doth stay, We may be sure its most Angelicall. **1691** RAY *Creation* I. (1704) 31 Aquafortis or the like corrosive Waters. **1736** T. ATKINSON *Conf. Painter & Engraver* 23 But the general Way [of Etching] is, to work the Offskip tenderly, letting the Water [called 'aqua fortis' above] bite but a little, and then [etc.].

17. a. Used to denote various watery liquids found in the human or animal body, either normally or in disease. † *to run on a water*, to discharge a watery liquid.

1533 ELYOT *Cast. Helthe* (1541) 83 b, Whan they [children] waxe elder, than be they greved with..wormes of the bealy, waters, swellynges under the chynne; &c. **1580** BLUNDEVIL *Curing Horses Dis.* cxli. 61 b, Of the Crowne scab... The cronets will be alwaies mattering, and run on a water. **1643** J. STEER tr. *Exp. Chyrurg.* iii. 7 Pustles doe arise, in the which is contained cleere and white water. **1801** *Monthly Mag.* Feb. 40/2 The immediate cause of her death was found to be an accumulation of water on the chest. **1860** MAYNE *Expos. Lex.* s.v. *Cotunnius*, *Water of Cotunnius*, a peculiar fluid found within the membrane lining the vestibule and semi-circular canals of the internal ear.

b. ***water on*** (or †*in*) ***the brain, in the head***: hydrocephalus; cf. G. *wasser im hirn, im kopf* (*haben*). ***water on the knee***: an excessive accumulation of fluid in the knee joint.

c **1790** in *Jrnl. Friends Hist. Soc.* (1918) 79 The D[ea]r Lamb was..taken of by a short illness of, the docter thaught Water on its Brain. **1806** *Med. Jrnl.* XV. 133 The water in the brain was not, I believe, the immediate cause of death. **1852** J. SAVORY *Dom. Med.* (ed. 4) 261 Water in the head is almost peculiar to infants, and chiefly to those of a scrofulous or rickety habit. **1861** WHYTE MELVILLE *Good for N.* iii, Some people thought he had gout in the stomach, others vowed it was water on the brain. **1890** A. JAMES *Diary* 7 Nov. (1965) 151 They [*sc.* the English] call water on the knee, fluid on the joint. **1902** W. S. CHURCHILL *Let.* 9 Oct. in R. S. Churchill *Winston S. Churchill* (1969) II. Compan. I. 167 He is laid up with Water on the Knee. **1976** *Liverpool Echo* 6 Dec. 1/8 A lone Canadian sailor spent 17 days at sea clinging to his capsized trimaran before he was rescued suffering only from water on the knee.

c. The fluid contained in the amniotic cavity (*liquor amnii*); now usually *plural*. The effusion of this fluid from the womb, which precedes the exclusion of the fœtus, is popularly denoted by the expression 'the waters have broken'.

1688 *Depos. Birth Pr. Wales* 20 Whilst her Majesty was sitting trembling, her Water broke. **1754–64** SMELLIE *Midwifery* II. 425 When the membranes broke, a large quantity of waters were discharged. **1880** J. E. BURTON *Midwifery* 27 The 'waters'..are a whitish, muddy-looking liquid, the quantity of which greatly varies.

d. Tears. (So often in the Bible: see the concordances.)

1362 LANGL. *P. Pl.* A. v. 44 And made William to weope watur with his eȝen. **1390** GOWER *Conf.* I. 115 Ther was no wiht, if he hem syhe, Fro water mihte kepe his yhe. *c* **1400** *Destr. Troy* 7171 Care hade the kyng for Cassibilon his son, ..Full tendurly with teris tynt myche watur. *c* **1470** *Golagros & Gaw.* 1131 The watter wet his chekis. **1562** J. HEYWOOD *Prov. & Epigr.* (1867) 217 His eyes ran a water. **1563–83** FOXE *A. & M.* 1215/1 With that the water stoode in Marbeckes eyes, why weepest thou quoth the Gentleman? **1622** in Foster *Eng. Factories Ind.* (1908) II. 52 [It] made the watter roune doune my checks to looke one them. **1840** DICKENS *Old C. Shop* vi, A dexterous rap on the nose with the key, which brought the water into his eyes.

e. Saliva; now only, flow of saliva provoked by appetite. † *to set* (a person's) ***teeth on water*** = 'to make his mouth water' (see MOUTH *sb.* 2 c, WATER *v.* 12).

1598 FLORIO, *Tutto in sapore*, louing earnestly, euen till ones teeth run a water. **1601** HOLLAND *Pliny* XXXIII. xi. II. 481 Their rich plate set their enemies teeth on water. **1655** tr. *Com. Hist. Francion* III. 74 He delighted it seemed, to eate that which was good, and rare before us, purposely to set our teeth on water. **1661** LOVELL *Hist. Anim. & Min.* 56 The water comming from the pallat mixed with honey and salt, rubbed on the head, &c. helpeth. **1685** H. MORE *Illustr. Daniel* 334 Those fat and fair Objects that make Mens mouths run a-water so. **1830** COBBETT *Hist. Geo. IV*, vi. §334 He has seen them flopping their jaws, the water running out of their mouths; and has seen them go through all the motions of devouring. **187.** W. S. GILBERT *'Bab' Ballads, Etiquette* 26 For the thought of Peter's oysters brought the water to his mouth.

†f. ***all on a water***: covered with sweat. *Obs.*

1530 PALSGR. 562/1 He hath gestylled my horse in the stabyll tyll he hath made hym all on a water [*tant quil la mys tout en eaue*].

g. The liquid of oysters.

c **1430** *Two Cookery-bks.* 13 Take grete Oystrys,..; an take þe water of þe Oystrys, & ale, an brede y-straynid.

18. *esp.* Urine. ***to make water*** [= F. *faire de l'eau*]: to urinate. ***to pass water*** (PASS *v.* 50): to void urine (usually with reference to obstruction or the absence of it). ***to hold*** (*one's*) ***water***: to retain urine.

1375 BARBOUR *Bruce* XIII. 603 He leit thame nocht haf sic lasier As anys wattir for to ma. **1432–50** tr. *Higden* (Rolls) I. 359 Mony men of that cuntre vse to make water and to send furthe theire vryne syttenge. **1535** COVERDALE *2 Kings* ix. 8 And I wyl rote out from Achab, euen him that maketh water agaynst the wall. **1577** KENDALL *Flowers Epigr.* 46 The drinke his bladder burdened so, That he must let his water goe. **1580** HESTER tr. *Fioravanti's Disc. Chirurg.* 19 To helpe those that can-not hold their water. **1584** B. R. tr. *Herodotus* II. 97 b, Hys syght shoulde eftsoones bee restored agayne, if in case hee washed hys eyes in the water of a Woman, whych [etc.]. **1591** SHAKS. *Two Gent.* IV. iv. 41. **1607** TOPSELL *Four-f. Beasts* 754 The nature of the wolfe both in making his water, as also in voyding his excrements is like vnto a Dogs. **1626** BACON *Sylva* §998 The Wound must be at first Washed cleane, with White Wine, or the Parties owne Water. **1719** D'URFEY *Pills* III. 31 Come ye broken Maids that..can never hold your Water. **1786** in J. Howard *Lazarettos* (1789) 195 No prisoner..shall..make water against any part of the building, under the penalty of forfeiting for each offence..four-pence. **1801** *Med. Jrnl.* V. 409 Has been in this state three months; makes only three-quarters of a pint of water in 24 hours. **1860** FLOR. NIGHTINGALE *Notes on Nursing* 199 She will know the shiver which betrays the formation of matter—that which shows the unconscious patient's desire to pass water—that which precedes fever. **1884** THOMPSON *Tumours of Bladder* 35 Case 34... Last four years much difficulty and pain in passing water;..Now passes water about every hour, day and night. **1885** BIBLE (R.V.) *2 Kings* xviii. 27 To drink their own water with you. **1897** *Allbutt's Syst. Med.* IV. 281 The quantity of water voided by a healthy adult in 24 hours is from 40 to 50 ounces.

b. In references (at one time very common) to the inspection of a patient's urine as a means of diagnosis. (Cf. WATER-DOCTOR.) Phrases, *to* †*cast* (CAST *v.* 40), † *look*, † *look in* (a person's) *water*.

1377 LANGL. *P. Pl.* B. II. 224 Thanne loured leches and lettres þei sent, þat he shole wonye with hem wateres to loke. *c* **1440** *Alphabet of Tales* 41 A leche felid his powce & lukid his watir, bod he cuthe fynde no sekenes in hym. *c* **1530** *Beauty & Gd. Prop. Women* (facs.) C j, I haue shewid thy water to thy phesycyon. **1535** JOYE *Apol. Tindale* (Arb.) 22 But I wyll not be his Phisicion and decerne his water at this tyme. **1546** J. HEYWOOD *Prov.* I. xi. (1867) 33 By my faith you come to looke in my water. And for my comfort..Ye would, by my purs, geue me a purgacion. **1550** CROWLEY *Last Trumpet* 826 And shewe by what right thou maist take Two pence for the sight of water, When thou knowest not therbi to make The sick man one farthinge better. **1562** *Child-Marr.* (1897) 75 Sir Roberte sawe this respondentes water; & told hym he might be easilie holpen, & gave hym a drinke. **1597** SHAKS. *2 Hen. IV*, I. ii. 2 *Fal.*.. What saies the Doct. to my water? *Pag.* He said sir, the water it selfe was a good healthy water; but for the party that ow'd it, he might haue more diseases then he knew for. **1600** ROWLANDS *Lett. Humours Blood* vi, Heele looke vnto your water well enough. **1614** JACKSON *Creed* III. 299 But what if some forreiner should of set purpose send a dead-mans water to trie this grand-Phisitions skill. **1625** HART *Anat. Ur.* I. ii. 28 They haue bene with them who haue told them wonders by the water. **1642** FULLER *Holy St.* II. ii. 53 The good Physician..trusteth not the single witnesse of the water if better testimony may be had. *a* **1709** J. LISTER *Autobiog.* (1842) 43 The day after that I sent my water to a physician, who sent me word he could make no judgment of my case. **1712** ADDISON *Spect.* No. 505 ¶7, I can interpret their Dreams by seeing their Water. **1784** *Morn. Chron.* 21 Apr. 1/3 Advt., Miss Mollitor..flatters herself that by seeing the water of the patient to tell if there be a cure or not.

†c. In fig. phrases, ***to attend, watch*** (a person's) ***waters*** [= G. *einem das wasser besehen*], to scrutinize his conduct rigorously. *Obs.*

1700 T. BROWN *Amusem. Ser. & Com.* iii. Wks. 1720 III. 36, I..judged he had been whipping it in with the Gentlewomen before mentioned, tho' 'twas not convenient to tell him so, lest his Wife should watch his Waters more narrowly than she had done. **1706** E. WARD *Wooden World Diss.* (1708) 9 What can we expect less in the succeeding Year, than that his great Proxy, the first Lieutenant, attend his Waters purely to prevent an Interregnum? **1709** MRS. MANLEY *Secr. Mem.* 151 Her Brother..was gone abroad..when this Rogue..courted her, or else he had never got his Will of her; he would have watch'd his Waters for him to some purpose.

19. Applied to vegetable juices.

1585 HIGINS *Junius' Nomencl.* 142/2 *Lachryma*,..the water, moysture, or dropping of a tree that turneth to gumme. **1585** T. WASHINGTON tr. *Nicholay's Voy.* I. viii. 8 b, Another frute..melteth in ones mouth, giuing a water as it were sugred. **1589** BIGGES *Summarie Drake's W. Ind. Voy.* 14 And within this white of the [cochos] nut lyeth a water, which is whitish and very cleere, to the quantitie of halfe a pint or thereabouts. **1697** DAMPIER *Voy.* I. 292 While the Nut [*sc.* coco-nut] is growing, all the inside is full of this Water, without any Kernel. **1842** ANNE PRATT *Pict. Catech. Bot.* v. 79 [In the pitcher plant] the liquid is a clear water, very pleasant and refreshing to the palate.

IV. Appearances resembling water.

20. a. The transparency and lustre characteristic of a diamond or a pearl. The three highest grades of quality in diamonds were formerly known as the ***first, second,*** and ***third water***; the phrase ***of the first water*** survives in popular use as a designation of the finest quality, often applied to jewels generally.

[The equivalent use is found in all the mod. Rom. and Teut. langs.; it may have come from Arabic, where this sense of *mā'*, water, is a particular application of the sense 'lustre, splendour' (e.g. of a sword).]

1607 SHAKS. *Timon* I. i. 18 *Jew.* And have a Iewel heere... *Mer.* 'Tis a good forme. *Jewel.* And rich: heere is a Water looke ye. **1608** —— *Per.* III. ii. 102. **1611** COTGR., s.v. *Eau*, *Perle de belle eau*, of a faire luster, or water. *Ibid.* s.v. *Esclat*, *Diamond de bon esclat*,..a dyamond of a good luster, or water. **1622** MALYNES *Anc. Law Merch.* 75 The best waters are whitish, inclining to the blew, which maketh the best illustration and play, as some call it. **1667** *Phil. Trans.* II. 429 If it [the Diamond] have no good water, or have a Bleb or Flaw, the Carat will not be worth but from 10 to 30 Crowns. **1675** R. VAUGHAN *Coin & Coinage* 241 Value of Pearls. East India Yellow water. 1 Carrat 00 07 s. 6 d. *Ibid.* 242 A later Valuation..of the best Silver water. **1676** *Lond. Gaz.* No. 1057/4 Lost.., one single Rose Diamond set in a Ring close shankt, and enameled with blew, a fair spread Stone clean and good water. **1678** *Ibid.* No. 1330/4 A Table stone, cut in India, perfect square, of the Second water, weighing 5 grains full. **1698** FRYER *Acc. E. India & Persia* 213 The Diamond that is Sandy, or hath any Foulness in it, or is of a Blue, Brown, or Yellow Water, is not worth half the Price of a perfect Stone of a White Water. **1718** LADY M. W. MONTAGU *Let. to C'tess of Mar* 10 Mar., A vest..of purple cloth, straight to her shape, and thick set, on each side..with pearls of the best water. **1727** A. HAMILTON *New Acc. E. Indies* II. xlv. 148 They have small Diamonds, but their Waters being inclined to be yellow, are not so much in Esteem as those of Golcondah. **1732** FIELDING *Miser* v. iii, I defy any jeweller in town to show you their equals; they are, I think, the finest water I ever saw. **1753** *Chambers' Cycl.* Suppl. s.v. *Diamond*, The first water in Diamonds means the greatest purity and perfection of their complexion, which ought to be that of the clearest drop of water. When Diamonds fall short of this perfection, they are said to be of the second or third water, &c. till the stone may be properly called a coloured one. **1832** G. R. PORTER *Porcelain & Gl.* 220 Some artists have even given to this [*sc.* paste in imitation of the diamond] a very considerable play of light, or, as it is technically termed, water. **1835** DICKENS *Sk. Boz, Parish* ii, He..wore a brilliant of the first water on the fourth finger of his left hand. **1910** LD. ROSEBERY *Chatham* i. 4 When Rondet, the royal jeweller, came from Paris to receive it [*sc.* a diamond], he criticised the water of the stone.

b. fig. ***of the first*** (occas. ***purest, rarest, finest***) etc. ***water***: originally (with implied comparison to a jewel), of the highest excellence or purity; now only following a personal designation (often of reproach) with the sense 'out-and-out', 'thorough-paced'. [Similarly in Fr.]

1775 *London Mag.* Nov. 556/2 She has an eye of that quick and brilliant water, that it penetrates and darts through the person it looks on. **1824** DIBDIN *Libr. Comp.* 587 Ascham is a thorough-bred philologist, and of the purest water. **1825** T. HOOK *Sayings* Ser. II. *Man of Many Fr.* (Colburn) 95 He was certain her family were by no means of 'the first water'. **1826** SCOTT *Jrnl.* 6 Dec., He was a..swindler of the first water. **1836–7** SIR W. HAMILTON *Metaph.* (1870) II. xxix. 201 Gassendi himself, who is justly represented by Mr. Stewart as a sensationalist of the purest water. **1854** H. MILLER *Sch. & Schm.* xvi. (1858) 360 Cousin William..had a heart of the finest water. **1869** *Eng. Mech.* 17 Dec. 329/3 All this may seem like paradoxism of the first water. **1883** T. WATTS in *19th Cent.* Mar. 422 His wit, though not abundant and not of 'the rarest water' was quite unique. **1905** W. B. BOULTON *Gainsborough* 194 He..assumed the airs of a beau and lady-killer of the first water.

21. (See quot.) Cf. WATERED *ppl. a.* 5. [So G. *wasser*, F. *eau.*]

1721 BAILEY, *Water* (among Dyers), a certain Lustre imitating Waves, set on Silks, Mohairs, &c.

V. 22. a. = WATER-COLOUR. **b.** *pl.* Water-colour paintings. *colloq.* (Cf. OIL *sb.*[1] 4, 4 b.)

1787 *Exhib. R. Acad.* 17 Portraits of the Princess Royal, and Princess Augusta, in water. **1877** *Paper Hanger* etc. 142 The best work for picture and looking-glass frames is done in water. **1909** *Daily Chron.* 4 June 5/5, I want you to paint as many pictures as you can, oils or waters, just as you like.

VI. 23. The lap of one shingle in roofing.

1703 R. NEVE *City & C. Purchaser* 242 They commonly make 3 Waters, (as they phrase it,) that is, they commonly hang 3 shingles in heighth, in the length of one; so that if the Shingles are 12 Inches long, they are laid at 4 Inches Gage.

VII. *attrib.* and *Comb.*

24. Simple attributive uses. **a.** Designating vessels in which water is held or kept, as ***water-bail, -bowl, -bucket, -cruet,*** †***-fetles, -flask, -gourd, -jar, -jug, -sack,*** †***-say, -scoop,*** †***-skeet, -skin,*** †***-stean, tank, -tin, -trough, -tub,*** †***-tun, -vat, -vessel.*** See also WATER-BOTTLE, -GLASS, etc.

c **1000** *Ags. Gosp.* John ii. 6 Ðar wæron soðlice aset syx stænene wæter-fatu. *c* **1200** ORMIN 14411 Þa sexe waterrfetless, Þatt stodenn wiþþ þatt waterr þær. *c* **1386** CHAUCER *Can. Yeom. Prol. & T.* 681 And in the water vessel he it caste. **1387** TREVISA *Higden* VI. 183 In a water stene [L. *in hydria aquatica*]. **1391** *Earl Derby's Exp.* (Camden) 74 Pro portagio de watertonnes vsque manerium Episcopi. **1420** in *For. Acc. 3 Hen. VI* G/2, j Waterbaille..vj Water-scoupes. **1459–60** *Durham Acc. Rolls* (Surtees) 152 Cum opere carpentr. fact. circa molendinum de Shyncliff et leȝ Watertrowe. **1477–9** *Rec. St. Mary at Hill* (1905) 82 For a watir payle, iij d. **1487–8** *Durham Acc. Rolls* (Surtees) 651 Pro i fatt et i watersay. **1533** *MS. Rawlinson D.* 776 fol. 136 b, ij flatt hooppis..for the water Tubbe. **1552** *Inv. Ch. Goods York* etc. (Surtees) 66, ij water bokettes of latyne. **1556** WITHALS *Dict.* (1562) 47 b/2 A water tankerd, *cadus aquarius.* **1592** NASHE *P. Penilesse* E 3 b, The water-tankard wil keepe vnder the insurrection of their shoulders. **1613** W. BROWNE *Brit. Past.* I. ii. (1616) 31 And for the Maid that had perform'd each thing, She in the Water-paile bad leaue a Ring. **1615** E. S. *Britain's Buss* B, Two water-skeits, to wet the sailes. **1667** in Pettus *Fodinæ Reg.* (1670) 35 One new large Water-wheel with Water-troughs. **1773** *Exhib. R. Acad.* 30 A horse tied to a water-trough, in a Farm-yard. **1779** in *Dict. Amer. Eng.* (1944) IV. 2452/2, 2 water jugs. **1807** R. SOUTHEY *Lett. from England* I. xiv. 161 A compact kind of chest holds the bason, the soap, the tooth brush, and water glass... The water-jug and water-bottle stand below. **1821** Water-skin [see GIRBA]. **1834** MARRYAT *P. Simple* xli, I..set my first lieutenant to work getting in the ballast and water-tanks. **1842** DICKENS *Amer. Notes* ii, The water-jug is plunging and leaping like a lively dolphin. **1853** J. D. H. DALE *Cerem. Roman Rite* 93 The Subdeacon elevates a little the water-cruet towards the Bishop. **1855** *Poultry Chron.* II. 432 The price charged for these pens..will be 6s. 6d. each, complete, with wooden bottom, water tin, and separate cloth. **1864** J. A. GRANT *Walk across Afr.* 430 Here there is a bend in the Nile, and we were able to fill all our water-sacks afresh. **1867** LADY HERBERT *Cradle L.* i. 8 Picturesque water-carriers with their water-skins. **1869** BROWNING *Ring & Bk.* IX. 63 Clouted shoon, staff, scrip and water-gourd. **1886** RUSKIN *Præterita* I. iii. 106, I went head foremost into the large water-tub kept for the garden. **1894** *Outing* June 172 Four or five rough-looking men..were clustered about the water-tank. **1920** Water-tin [see SOUVENIR *v.* 3]. **1922** JOYCE *Ulysses* 491 A man..passes..hugging a full waterjugjar. **1926** D. H. LAWRENCE *David* xiv. 106 Here is the pouch and the water-flask. **1935** C. WINCHESTER *Railway Wonders of World* II. 933 There are eleven sets of water-troughs on the West Coast main line between Euston and Glasgow. **1960** J. R. ACKERLEY *We think the World of You* 89 On the floor was Evie's water-bowl and the vegetable remains of her dinner of yesterday. **1967** O. RUHEN in *Coast to Coast 1965–6* 193, I threw down my swag near the water-tank. **1970** J. H. B. PEEL *Country Talk* vi. 111 Water-troughs in far fields were tepid. 1974 D. Sears *Lark in Clear Air* i. 20 We stopped at every gopher-hole and water-tank and badger-hill. 1979 M. McMullen *But Nellie was so Nice* (1981) i. i. 12 She..filled Titania's water bowl, gave jealous George an extra stroking.

b. Pertaining to the storage or distribution of water in considerable quantities; as ***water-ditch, -lock, †-place, -room, -stank, -station, -well; water-meter, †-purveyance, -service, -storage, -supply.***

a 1300 *Cursor M.* 11677 Vr water purueance es gan, And in þis wildernes es nan. 1473 *Rental Bk. Cupar-Angus* (1879) I. 189 Water-stankis..of sic depnes that ged eyls and fyscis ..ma be..kepit. 1670 Blount *Glossogr.* (ed. 3), *Water-lock*, a watering place fenced with walls, rails, or bars, &c. 1703 Dampier *Voy.* III. i. 88 The Governor very kindly sent an Officer to clear the Water-place for my Men. 1735 in *Trans. Cumberld. & Westm. Antiq. Soc.* (N.S.) XX. 172 Taking water for the use of their families out of the water ditch in the said meadow. 1809 Kendall *Trav.* II. xlvi. 132 The water is led by troughs into a range of vats or rooms, distinguished by the name of water-rooms. 1815 *Pocklington Canal Act* 4 Pens for water, water-stanks, dams. 1840 H. S. Tanner *Canals & Rail Roads U.S.* 263 *Water stations*, places where locomotives obtain their supplies of water. 1848 W. W. Lloyd in *Numism. Chron.* XI. 114 The local water-service. 1849 J. Simon *City Medical Rep.* No. 1, in E. R. Pike *Human Documents of Victorian Golden Age* (1967) 280 It may be doubted, too, whether..the tenants' water supply can be pronounced good. 1858 Simmonds *Dict. Trade*, *Water-meter*, an instrument for registering the supply of water. 1872 *Routledge's Ev. Boy's Ann.* July 500/2 A terrible year of water-famine. 1885 *Weekly Notes* 28 Mar. 67/2 The house had become uninhabitable through failure of the water-supply. 1890 A. R. Wallace *Darwinism* 23 The absence of rivers or water-storage. 1907 *Q. Rev.* Oct. 391 Where the water-rights of villages and small towns are.. threatened. 1921 *Review of Reviews* Aug. 157/2 Hardships of desert travelling, when great gulfs of distance lie between one water well and another. 1976 *Billings* (Montana) *Gaz.* 30 June 5-D/1 (Advt.), Water well drilling.

c. Used for the carriage or transport of water, as ***water barge, boat, ship, tender, truck; water animal, mule.***

1727 A. Hamilton *New Acc. E. Ind.* I. xxviii. 346 He built some Water Boats,..and, by these Boats furnished the Garison with good Water. 1805 Collingwood 18 Oct. in Nicolas *Disp. Nelson* (1846) VII. 127 *note*, I shall be glad to see the Water-Ships as many of the Fleet are getting low. 1898 *Daily News* 3 May 8/3 The baggage and water animals. 1900 *Ibid.* 17 Mar. 7/4 Indians, with their plucky and clever little water-mules, were ordered right up into the firing line. 1918 *Qua Iboe Mission Quarterly* Feb. 121/2 Water-barges to replenish our tanks were soon alongside. 1957 G. V. Blackstone *Hist. Brit. Fire Service* xxv. 443 The evolution of the water tender from the mobile dam unit produced to deal with the water shortages at air-raid fires. 1958 P. Scott *Mark of Warrior* ii. 122 The water truck rendezvoused. Most of the chaps' bottles were empty. 1976 *Billings* (Montana) *Gaz.* 6 July 8-A/2 The county water truck was dispatched at 4.09 p.m... The truck was refilled with water, before the fire was controlled. 1978 *Dumfries Courier* 13 Oct. 17/4 Two water tenders from Dumfries brought the blaze under control.

d. Designating a channel in which water runs, or any contrivance for facilitating or regulating its flow, as ***water-channel, -cock, †-conduct, -conduit, -cut, -cutting; -dam, -gutter, -main, -port, -sewer, -squirt, -tap, †-trunk, †-wising.*** See also watercourse, -furrow, etc.

a 1300 *Cursor M.* 11942 Þe water wissing can he ditt þat water to þe lak broght. *c* 1450 *Godstow Reg.* 44 A plase to make an hede of her water cundit. 1535 Coverdale *Nahum* ii. 6 The water portes [1611 the gates of the rivers; Luther *die Thore der Wasser*] shal be opened and the kinges palace shall fall. 1577–87 Holinshed *Chron.* III. 1186/1 Not forgetting to make a water-conduit for the ease of washing. 1596 Dalrymple tr. *Leslie's Hist. Soc.* (S.T.S.) I. 42 Thay lay in the furdes and waterdames. 1598 R. Bernard tr. *Terence, Phormio* iv. iv. (1607) 432 A snake fel from the tyles through the water gutter. 1600 J. Pory tr. *Leo's Africa* (1896) II. 402 So soone as the said water-conduct was derived unto the Towne, he caused it to be divided. 1662 Atwell *Faithf. Surveyor* 95 The water-squirt which will throw a whole hogs-head of water to the top of a house at once. 1764 *Museum Rust.* II. 234 To bestow a watering on my fields, by means of water-trunks, immediately after my first crop of hay is got off. 1803 W. Tatham *Rep. Impediments Thames* 71 At this place there is a water-main which crosses over to the Middlesex shore. 1833 Loudon *Encycl. Archit.* §16 A water-cock and wash-hand-basin. 1846 *Comic Almanack* (1870) 91 The comic water-plug offers a capital medium for illustrating the leading principles in hydrostatics and hydraulic. 1862 E. Hodder *Memories N.Z. Life* 117 We were glad to..lie down closely together in one of the dry water-cuttings. 1880 J. Dunbar *Pract. Papermaker* 47 Connect the other end of the pipe to the nearest water-tap. 1883 W. C. Russell *Sailors' Lang.*, *Water-ports*, openings in a ship's bulwarks to free the deck of water. 1902 Cornish *Naturalist Thames* 9 Down every ditch, runnel, and water-cut, the turbid waters were hurrying. 1914 *Blackw. Mag.* Dec. 780/1 Fields of young wheat and barley intersected by water-channels.

e. Designating a machine which is worked or driven by water, a part of a machine in which water is heated, a contrivance for drawing or circulating water, and the like; as ***water-back, -barrel, -bellows, -blast, -box, -chamber, †-corn-mill, -drum, -feed, -gin, †-grist-mill, †-motion, -motor, -trap, -trompe, -turbine, -whim.***

1580 *Durham Wills* (Surtees) II. 32 All my interest in the water corne mylne and farmehold in Kirklawe. 1660 R. Dacres *Elem. Water-drawing* Pref., The innumerable shapes, and various forms and fashions of Water-Gins. 1661 [T. Powell] *Hum. Industry* 35 De Aquaticis Machinis, Of Water Motions. 1725 in *Lancs. & Cheshire Wills* (Chetham Soc.) I. 178 A wattercorn Milln called Accorinton Milln. 1763 in Smiles *Engineers* (1861) I. 359 *note*, At the mouth of the cavern is erected a water-bellows. 1786 T. Jefferson *Writ.* (1859) II. 12 A water-grist mill for grinding the corn of the neighborhood. 1819 Rees *Cycl.*, *Water-Bellows*,..a machine used to blow air into a furnace, by the action of a column of water falling through a vertical tube. 1824 R. Stuart *Hist. Steam Engine* 47 The pipe, i, connects the air-chamber, a, with the inner water-chamber, *a*. 1833 T. Sopwith *Mining Distr. Alston Moor* 131 The water blast.. consists of a wooden pipe placed in a shaft, and down which a stream of water is kept running, while a quantity of fresh air is carried with it. 1839 De la Beche *Rep. Geol. Cornwall*, etc. xv. 572 Water-whims..are seldom employed in western Cornwall. 1875 J. H. Collins *Metal Mining* 122 Sent down by means of a fan blower, steam jet, turbine, or a water-trompe. 1875 Knight *Dict. Mech.*, *Water-back*, a permanent reservoir at the back of a stove or range, to utilize the heat of the fire in keeping a supply of hot water. *Ibid.*, *Water-barrel* (Mining), a large wrought-iron barrel with a self-acting valve in the bottom, used in drawing water where there are no pumps. 1876 *Encycl. Brit.* IV. 688/1 In this machine there are two water-boxes. *Ibid.* 468/1 It is from the drying up of the fluid in water-traps that uninhabited houses are so frequently offensive. 1877 Wood *Nature's Teach.* 463 The Water Turbine. 1881 *Encycl. Brit.* XII. 520/1 Water motors may be divided into water-pressure engines, water wheels, and turbines. 1884 Lock *Workshop Rec.* Ser. iii. 388/1 The draught is sometimes kept up by.. a water-drum, an apparatus which sucks in air by means of the friction of a jet of water. 1914 *Chambers's Jrnl.* May 334/2 The..lamp..works automatically, the water-feed to the carbide being drop by drop.

f. Designating implements or contrivances used in or on the water, as ***water-cord, -dress, -staff, -stang.***

c 1570 *Durham Depos.* (Surtees) 263 The said William Sander..dyd..smite at this deponent with a water staff, suche as fishermen hangs ther nett upon. 1866 in Bompas *Life Buckland* viii. (1886) 163 My water-dress put on, the nets and cans, &c. packed, we started in a carriage. 1878 *Cumberld. Gloss.*, *Watter stang*, a pole fixed across a stream in lieu of a bridge or fence. 1904 Gallichan *Fishing Spain* 73 A fifty-yard length of water-cord that I had in the bag.

g. Designating (*a*) a water-tight contrivance, as ***water-joint, -packer***; (*b*) a body of water which makes a vessel air-tight or gas-tight, as ***water-lute, -luting, -seal.***

1837 *Civil Engin. & Arch. Jrnl.* I. 12/1 Both surfaces..fit into each other, and form a perfectly secure water-joint. 1841 S. Clegg *Treat. Coal-Gas* 111 This arch-pipe is made of thin plate-iron, sealed at each end by a water-joint. 1844 H. Stephens *Bk. Farm* II. 206 The shallow water-luting, formed by the marginal groove. 1877 G. E. Waring *Sanitary Conditions City & Country Houses* 31 These gases ..have..the power of passing almost unretarded and unchanged through the water-seal traps. *Ibid.* 36 The water-seal is a trap in more senses than one. 1881 Raymond *Mining Gloss.*, *Water-packer*, a water-tight packing of leather between the pipe and the walls of a bore-hole. 1884 *Century Mag.* Dec. 259/1 The trap..depends for its efficiency on the permanence of its water-seal. 1917 *Chamb. Jrnl.* Dec. 831/2 A water-seal renders the joint air-tight.

h. Designating substances which harden under water and so become impervious to it, as ***water-cement, -lime, -mortar.*** Cf. hydraulic *a.* 3.

1793 Smeaton *Edystone L.* §198 The hardening of water-mortar. *Ibid.* §212 A proper Water-Cement. *Ibid.*, A very competent Water Lime. 1847 G. A. Smeaton *Builder's Man.* 34 The Roman is the most valuable of all water-cements. 1868 *Rep. U.S. Commissioner Agric.* (1869) 377 The making of hydraulic cements, (water-limes,) mastics, &c.

i. Prepared with water, as ***water-size, -starch.*** Of articles of diet: Prepared with water (instead e.g. of milk); mixed or diluted with water; as ***water-biscuit, -broo*** (Sc.), ***-brose*** (Sc.), ***-broth, -cider, -fritters, -kail*** (Sc.), ***†-meat, -pap, -porridge, -pottage, -saps*** (Sc.; see sop *sb.*[1]), ***-tansey; -toast.*** Also water-gruel, -ice[1].

13.. *S.E. Leg.* (MS. Bodl. 779) in *Archiv Stud. neu. Spr.* LXXXII. 335 A lytil water-potage he ete. *c* 1480 Henryson *Wolf & Lamb* 140 To leif vpon dry breid and watter caill. 1572 *Satir. Poems Reform.* xxxiii. 262 Glaid to get Peis breid and watter Caill. *c* 1610 *Women Saints* 26 But to her self being sicke, she was still rigorous, hardlie admitting a little wine, with her water-meates. 1630 Dekker *2nd Pt. Honest Wh.* D 1 b, As arrant a whore as euer stiffned tiffany neck-cloathes in water-starch. *a* 1648 Digby *Closet Opened* (1669) 120 Doctor Harvey's pleasant Water-cider, whereof he used to drink much. 1683 J. Reid *Scots Gard.* (1907) 172 Leaving the dreg behind (the which may go among the pressings for water-cyder). 1747 Mrs. Glasse *Cookery* ix. 81 Water Fritters. *Ibid.* 104 A Water Tansey. 1786 Burns *To J. Smith* xxiv, I'll sit down o'er my scanty meal, Be't water-brose, or muslin-kail, Wi chearfu' face. 1789 W. Buchan *Dom. Med.* (1790) 17 It will then be proper to give it..a little of some food that is easy of digestion, as water-pap, milk-pottage. 1797 *Encycl. Brit.* (ed. 3) VII. 739/2 A water-size..prepared by boiling cuttings of parchment or white leather in water. 1816 Scott *Old Mort.* xiv, We got some water-broo and bannocks. 1816 —— *Bl. Dwarf* vi, 'All clear away, with the water-saps and panada,' returned the unabashed convalescent. 1838 A. Langton *Jrnl.* in *Gentlewoman Upper Canada* (1950) 80 This morning the same party assembled to tea, coffee, and water porridge—a great favourite with most of the backwoodsmen. 1843 *Ainsworth's Mag.* V. 60 My dinner was pudding or pastry, and if these failed, there was a substitute known by the name of *water-toast*... A slice of bread was toasted, and dipped..in boiling water, and then buttered and sugared. 1848 Geo. Eliot *Let.* 8 Mar. (1954) I. 255 The sympathy in Ireland seems at present only of the water toast kind. 1854 Surtees *Handley Cr.* xxxix. (1901) II. 30 Mr. Jorrocks..had looked in vain for a water-biscuit. 1947 W. de la Mare *Coll. Stories for Children* 61 A bowl of water-porridge, using up for it the last pinch of meal.

j. Pertaining to water as a beverage, or as a (teetotal) article of diet, as ***†water-day, -diet, -doctrine, †-drink, -time***; relating to the use of water in medical treatment, as ***water-dressing, -patient, strapping***; also water-cure.

c 1000 *Vercelli MS.* 112 b, in Napier *O.E. Lexicogr.* 67 & sæde eac þæt man mid wæter-drinces sylene mihte him mycele ælmessan ʒedon. *c* 1200 Ormin 14482 Alls iff þu drunnke waterr drinnch Ut off þe firrste fetless. 14.. in Aungier *Syon* (1840) 393 On water dayes sche schal ordeyne for bonnes or newe brede, water grewel, albreys, [etc.]. 1842 R. T. Claridge *Hydropathy* 282 Directly he commenced this water diet, all his complaints disappeared one by one. 1846 Lytton *Conf. Water-patient* 17 The regular life which water-patients lead. *Ibid.* 68 Water-dressings are found the best poultice to an inflamed member. 1854 Thackeray *Leech's Pict.* Wks. 1900 XIII. 484 George..has taken to the water-doctrine, as all the world knows. 1857 Dunglison *Med. Lex.*, *Water-dressing*, the treatment of wounds and ulcers by the application of water. It generally consists in dipping folds of lint in water, and placing them on the part. .. *Water strapping* or *wet strapping* means the treatment of ulcers,..&c., with strips of linen or cotton saturated with water. 1925 R. Graves *Welchman's Hose* 9 Our feeding and our water-time, Our breeding and our slaughter-time.

k. Pertaining to water as a physiographical feature or factor, as ***water-action, †-brim, -depths, -drainage, -edge, -flow, †-ground, -land, -point, †-rim, -scene, -shore, -strand, -view.***

In many of these combinations the first element is equivalent to the genitive *water's*, and in early and dial. examples the sense may often be 'pertaining to the specified "water"' (*i.e.* lake, river, etc.: see senses 12 a, b, c).

c 1220 *Bestiary* 365 Alle þe oðre cumen mide, and..beren him of ðat water grund up to ðe lond al heil and sund. *a* 1300 *Cursor M.* 4779 Jacob yode walcand be þe nile; He sagh a-pon þe watur reme Caf flettand dunward [with] þe strem. 13.. *Metr. Hom.* (Vernon MS.) in *Archiv Stud. neu. Spr.* LVII. 289 Þis hermyt sat by a water brimme. 1390 Gower *Conf.* I. 81 Whan the blake wynter nyht..Bederked hath the water Stronde. 1589 Fleming *Virg. Bucol.* v. 15 Watershores and banks (bedasht) and beaten with the flouds. 1792 A. Young *Trav. France* (1794) I. 17 The water-scenes from the town itself..are delicious. 1799 Robertson *Agric. Perth* 454 Chains of lakes, finely wooded down to the water-edge. 1811 W. H. Marshall *Rev. Rep. to Board Agric. from Eastern Dept. Eng.* 10 The term *Water-Lands* may be deemed a solecism. But when it represents lands that have not only been formed by water, but are liable to be annihilated, and their place reoccupied, by the same element —it is surely allowable as a *Technical Term*, to convey a joint idea of 'Fens' and 'Marshes'. 1813 Southey *Nelson* I. 19 It could not be possible to get the boats to the water edge before the fourteenth. 1826 Cobbett *Rur. Rides* (1885) II. 247 To those who like water-scenes..it is the prettiest spot ..in all England. 1830 Lyell *Princ. Geol.* I. 175 The water drainage of the country. 1854 'Grace Greenwood' *Haps & Mishaps* 10 Seaforth Hall, an elegant seaside residence.. Here I saw a pleasant water-view. 1856 Kane *Arctic Expl.* II. xv. 158 A striated face, whose scratches still indicated the line of water-flow. *Ibid.* App. ii. 309 The coast-ice..had been completely destroyed by thaw and water-action. 1865 *Lond. Rev.* 30 Dec. 686/2 As the fisher saw the buried city in the waterdepths. 1901 *Scotsman* 4 Mar. 10/1 The streams, being small, with a rapid descent from very high land, are subject to much fluctuation of waterflow. 1946 U. Krige *Way Out* xv. 194 They were taken by the Germans at the water-point. 1954 J. R. R. Tolkien *Two Towers* iv. 79 The Entwives..saw the..green herbs in the waterlands in summer. 1964 J. Hillaby *Journey to Jade Sea* 167 The Balessa Kulal, a famous water-point farther down the *lugga*.

l. Consisting of, holding or containing, formed or caused by, water; as ***water-blowball, †water-breath, -breeze, -brook, -chasm, -cloud, -column, †-draught, -drip, -fence, -flow, -foam, -fount, -gush, -leak, -mist, -passage, †-plash, -race, -ring, -ripple, -run, -slide, -song, -sphere, -spray, -spread, †-sprinkle, -stripe*** (Sc.), ***-surface, -swirl, -talk, †-vein, -wash, -wear, -world.***

a 1300 *Cursor M.* 5620 In þis kist þe barn sco did. Quen it spird was wit þe lid,..Sco laid it on þe water fame. *c* 1390 *St. Michael* 629 Alle huy [*sc.* rain, snow, mist, etc.] comiez of water-breth þat þe sonne drauȝth up. 1529 *Conventual Lease, Yorks.* 1190 (P.R.O.), Asmoch grounde..as to make a sufficient dame apon to gedir water and water draught to the said dame. 1531 *Nottingham Rec.* III. 370 The water-wessh bytwen Samon Pasture and Trentt. 1535 Coverdale *Ps.* xli[i]. 1 Like as the hert desyreth the water brokes. 1585 Higins *Junius' Nomencl.* 401/2 *Torrens*,..a water plash. 1596 Spenser *F.Q.* iv. iii. 25 From the same the fierie sparkles flasht, As fast as water-sprinkles gainst a rocke are dasht. 1601 *Reg. Mag. Sig. Scot.* 418/2 Ane watter strype quhilk rynnis at the north syde of the said mure. 1610 Holland *Camden's Brit.* i. 532 A fairer towne than a man would looke to finde..among such slabbes and water-plashes. *c* 1611 Chapman *Iliad* xxi. 241 As a man that finds a water vaine. 1634 Brereton *Trav.* (Chetham Soc.) 61 The channel or water-passage leading from Amsterdam to Utrecht. 1707 Mortimer *Husb.* (1721) II. 202 Their Gardens lie all open, where Prospects may be had, and Water-fences can be made. 1771 *Ann. Reg.* 90/2 For.. filling up upwards of 200 yards of the said water-race. 1813 Scott *Trierm.* iii. xxviii, When, lo! a plashing sound he hears, A gladsome signal that he nears Some frolic water-run. 1818 Byron *Ch. Har.* iv. xviii, A fairy city..Rising like water-columns from the sea. 1818 Keats *Endym.* iii. 101 Thou hast sent A moon-beam to the deep, deep water-world, To find Endymion. *c* 1820 S. Rogers *Italy* (1839) 77 Those Porches passed, thro' which the water-breeze Plays. 1852 Wiggins *Embanking* 94 Such water-fences and drains must..be drawn all around the inlane. *c* 1865 G. M. Hopkins *Poems* (1967) 122 When lily-yellow is the west. Say, o'er it hangs a water-cloud And ravell'd into strings of rain. **1869** BLACKMORE *Lorna D.* xix, I came to remember the steepness and the slippery nature of the water-slide. **1869** R. B. SMYTH *Gold Fields Victoria* 548 Table showing the Length of Water-races constructed. **1869** *Bradshaw's Railway Man.* XXI. 242 The dock..measures 600 feet in length and 300 in width, giving an area of water surface of upwards of four acres. **1876** 'MARK TWAIN' *Tom Sawyer* xxxiii. 260 It was the treasure-box..occupying a snug little cavern, along with..some..rubbish well-soaked with the water-drip. **1879** PRESCOTT *Sp. Telephone* 48 A stone dropped into a pond, throws off a succession of circular undulations or water rings. **1884** *Leisure Hour* June 344/2 One of the finest of the many picturesque water-chasms of Norway. **1887** E. D. MORGAN in *Proc. R. Geogr. Soc.* IX. 214 Lake Koko-nor, a magnificent water-spread 10,800 feet above the sea. **1887** *Essex Weekly News* 11 Mar. 7/1 A small brick archway..which crosses a waterflow known as the Puddle Dyke. **1888** G. M. HOPKINS *Poems* (1967) 198 All in froth and water-blowballs. **1904** W. DE LA MARE *Henry Brocken* vi. 59 Ears that have heard only..dismal water-songs, and the yelp and quarrel and night-voice of unseen hosts in the forests. **1905** A. R. WALLACE *My Life* I. 250 Perpendicular rocks with no sign of water-wear. **1916** BLUNDEN *Pastorals* 30 Mocked by the white wings of the water-swirl. **1920** J. MASEFIELD *Enslaved* 34 The melancholy water-drip alone Broke silence near me. **1921** W. DE LA MARE *Veil* 32 Ice on the waterbrooks their clear chimes dumbing. **1922** JOYCE *Ulysses* 698 A rockery with waterspray. **1928** BLUNDEN *Undertones of War* ix. 98 Ahead, the German front line could not be clearly seen, the water-mist and the smoke veiling it. **1928** E. SITWELL *Five Poems* 4 The water-ripples like mosaics gold. **1935** W. STEVENS in *Southern Rev.* I. 80 The statue stood in stars like water-spheres. *a* **1944** K. DOUGLAS *Alamein to Zem Zem* (1946) 52 Few Crusader tanks would run for more than two days in action without developing either an oil-leak or a water-leak. **1952** L. MACNEICE *Ten Burnt Offerings* x. 60 The water-talk ends; the scrawl on the sky Smudges and fades. **1954** J. BETJEMAN *Few Late Chrysanthemums* 66 Back into what a water-world Of waving weed and waiting claws? **1955** E. POUND *Classic Anthol.* II. 113 Naught stands higher than mount, Nor is hollow deeper than water-fount. *a* **1957** R. CAMPBELL *Coll. Poems* (1960) III. 19 Amidst dead calms collapsing water-gushes, And distances cascading to the deeps. **1961** K. REISZ *Technique Film Editing* (ed. 9) ii. 137 Tiny bugs skim over the water-surface. **1967** *Jane's Surface Skimmer Systems 1967–68* 14/1 The vehicle has been used primarily for testing over land, water and ice, to investigate ..seaworthiness, water spray problems, [etc.]. **1977** *Daily Tel.* 9 July 12 Lands where hearts desire the waterbrooks and wells are of crucial importance. **1984** A. C. & A. DUXBURY *Introd. World's Oceans* iv. 120 Water molecules arrange themselves at any water surface to form a weak elastic membrane.

m. Situated or built on or beside water, as ***water-beacon, -brae, -bridge, -castle, -door, -doorway, -frontage, †-stable, -stair(s), -steps, †-tack.*** Also WATER-FRONT.

1445 in Parker *Dom. Archit.* (1859) III. 79 At Shene the water-brigge. **1603** *Reg. Mag. Sig. Scot.* 499/1 Lie girs of the watter bray. **1608** MACHIN *Dumb Knt.* I. B 3, Why Orators wiues shortly will bee knowne like images on water staires, euer in one wetherbeaten suite. **1623** *North Riding Rec.* (N.S.) II. 10 None ys to repare any water Beakon but such as is subject to the Admiralld Court. **1670** MILTON *Hist. Eng.* VI. 255 A third excursion they [*sc.* the Danes] made,..and.. return'd..like wild Beasts or rather Sea-monsters to thir Water-stables. **1751** LABELYE *Westm. Bridge* 18 Every Pier, Abutments, and Water-Stairs. **1837** HT. MARTINEAU *Soc. Amer.* II. 23 The land is divided into long, narrow strips, that each lot may have a water frontage. **1899** R. BARR *C'tess Tekla* iii. 37 The boatman..propelled the skiff through the water-doorway. *Ibid.* vi. 68 Bid him instantly to take you in his boat to the water-steps of the Palace. **1903** KIPLING *Five Nations, Explorer* 51, I..Counted leagues of water-frontage through the axe-ripe woods that screen 'em. **1906** CROCKETT *White Plumes Navarre* xviii. 133 Cautiously..Madame Granier had peered through the thick *grille* of the water-door before admitting the Professor. **1920** T. S. ELIOT *Ara Vos Prec* 15 Princess Volupine extends A meagre, blue-nailed, phthisic hand to climb the waterstair.

n. Performed, conducted, taking place, on or in the water; as ***water-ballet, -excursion, -fight, -life, -motion, -music, -pageant, -song, -sonnet, -sports,*** etc.

1607 T. D. & G. WILKINS *Jests* 11 [He] demanded.. wherefore all those Barges (like so many Water-pageants) were caryed vp and downe so gaylie with Flags and Streamers? **1634** W. WOOD *New Eng. Prosp.* (1865) 22 Seeing the Beares take water, an Indian will leape after him, where they goe to water cuffs for bloody noses. **1670** MILTON *Hist. Eng.* II. 35 In such a various, and floating water-fight as was to be expected. *a* **1700** EVELYN *Diary* 10 Nov. 1644, Refresh'd with water-musiq, aviaries, and other rarities. *Ibid.* 29 Oct. 1662, I saw the Lord Maior passe in his water triumph to Westminster. **1749** H. WALPOLE *Let. to Mann* 17 May, A concert of water-music. **1801** STRUTT *Sports & Pastimes* III. i. 92 A representation of the water quintain..is given upon the tenth plate. **1817** KIRBY & SP. *Entomol.* xxii. II. 295, I shall not now enlarge on all these kinds of water-motion. **1835** DICKENS *Sk. Boz, River,* We have been on water excursions out of number. **1865** W. WHITE *East. Eng.* I. 86 About a dozen yachts have already arrived in readiness for the morrow's 'water frolic', which is a term much used by Norfolkians to signify a regatta. **1886** *Daily News* 20 Dec. 5/6 A small landscape dotted about with figures representing a water-picnic. **1888** Water-music [see PADDLING *vbl. sb.*[2]]. **1888** L. A. SMITH *Music of Waters* 83 The verses and tune of this water-song..follow. **1892** Water-pageant [see BARGEMASTER]. **1894** H. DRUMMOND *Ascent Man* 106 At one time there was nothing else in the world but water-life. **1920** L. & N. SHEFFIELD *Swimming Simplified* viii. 150 Water sports afford a varied source of amusements. **1940** L. MACNEICE *Last Ditch* 9 And as the twilight filtered on the heather Water-music filled the air. **1944** BLUNDEN *Shells by Stream* 7 Trilling still with finch or lark Or water-sonnet. **1948** T. WILDER *Ides of March* II. 143 When the water-ballet was ended, Caesar's party rose to go in search of the Queen. **1968** Water ballet [see SYNCHRONIZED *ppl. a.*]. **1976** *National Observer* (U.S.) 30 Oct. 3/3 We enjoy water sports. **1976** *Evening Post* (Nottingham) 15 Dec. 1 Mr Michael Hammond said he had not received a reply from the County Council to an offer of assistance in organising a water pageant on the day of the Queen's visit. **1979** *Tucson Mag.* Apr. 57/1 There are.. dance exercises, water ballet classes, separate massage facilities and other services. **1980** *Early Music* Jan. 50/1 It seems likely that Weiss, Buffardin, and Hebenstreit provided 'water music' for the royal couple on the barge.

o. Pertaining to transit or transport by water, as ***water-communication, -highway, -route, -traction.***

1785 J. PHILLIPS *Treat. Inland Nav.* p. vi, Inland districts ..which had no opportunity..of a water-communication. **1816** TUCKEY *Narr. Exped. R. Zaire* iv. (1818) 159 It [Banza Congo] has no water communication with the Zaire. **1868** RUSKIN *Arrows of Chace* (1880) II. 199 The carriage..may ..be done by water-traction and sailing vessels. **1886** *Pop. Sci. Monthly* Mar. 586 (Cass. Suppl.) The water-route is free to all. **1898** F. I. ANTROBUS tr. *Pastor's Hist. Popes* VI. 230 *note,* The improvement of the water-highway on the Tiber and the Anio.

p. Living or occupied on the water; faring by water; as ***water-guide, -people, -police.*** Also, found on the water, as ***water-brother, -stray, -wayfarer.***

1552 HULOET, Waterguide, *conuector.* *a* **1676** HALE *De jure maris* v. in Hargrave *Tracts* (1787) 23 His [the water-baillie's] business was, to look to the king's rights, as his wrecks, his flotsam, jetsam, water-strays, royal fishes. *c* **1826** POLLOK in D. Pollok *Life* (1843) 300 The Baijus—wandering water-gipsies on the eastern seas. **1848** *Sinks of Lond.* 129 *Water pads,* fellows who rob ships. **1893** LADY BURTON *Life Sir R. F. Burton* II. 60 Hasan Hammad..is now sergeant to the water-police. **1897** HINDE *Congo Arabs* 157 The Waginia, who are the water-people, and do all the transport on the river. **1923** D. H. LAWRENCE *Birds, Beasts & Flowers* 99 Fishes..Outsiders. Water-wayfarers. **1965** AUDEN *About House* (1966) 16, I should like To be to my water-brethren as a spell Of fine weather.

q. Designating fabulous beings that live in, or have rule over, water; as ***water-deity, -demon, -devil, -elf, -fairy, -fay, -fiend, -ghost, -goblin, -god, -kelpie, -king, -nixie, -shape, -spirit, -sprite, -wraith.*** Also WATER-HORSE, -NYMPH.

a **1625** FLETCHER *Chances* IV. ii, Get me a conjurer, One that can raise a water Devil. **1702** ADDISON *Dial. Medals* II. Wks. 1766 III. 105 We see abundance of Water-Deities on other Medals. **1742** R. FORBES *Jrnl. to Portsmouth* (1755) 30 You wou'd hae taen me for a water-wreath, or some gruous ghaist. **1785** BURNS *Addr. Deil* 69 Then water-kelpies haunt the foord, By your direction. **17..** LOGAN in Ritson *Sc. Songs* (1794) I. 155 Thrice did the water-wraith ascend, And gave a doleful groan thro' Yarrow. **1798** COLERIDGE *Anc. Mar.* 155 As if it dodged a water-sprite, It plunged and tacked and veered. **1819** J. R. DRAKE *Culprit Fay* xv, He banned the water-goblins' spite. **1819** SCOTT *Ivanhoe* xxv, A water-fiend hath possessed the fair Saxon. **1825** —— *Betrothed* xxxi, The statue of a water-god bending over his urn. **1859** GEO. ELIOT *Adam Bede* xxii, Water-nixies, and such lovely things without souls. **1869** RUSKIN *Q. of Air* i. §12 Myriads of other water spirits, of whom Nereus is the chief. **1871** TYLOR *Prim. Cult.* xv. II. 191 In Australia, special water-demons infest pools and watering-places. **1878** O. WILDE *Ravenna* 5 And down the river, like a flame of blue, Keen as an arrow flies the water-king. **1916** BLUNDEN *Pastorals* 32 That you shall come upon the water-fays. **1925** —— *English Poems* 90 The water-shapes steal towards his gonging drone. **1928** *Oxford Poetry* 10 Many strong men had passed the ford, nor known the presence of that jeering water-ghost Denying their true conquest of the stream.

†r. Occas. used to designate freshwater, as opposed to saltwater, objects; as ***water-fish, -land, -sand.*** (Cf. sense 12 c.)

c **1440** *Pallad. on Husb.* I. 267 Sum grauel or sum watir lond kest vndir [L. *Aliquid etiam terrae dulcis vel arenae subjiciendum est*]. *Ibid.* 438 And feede in hit thy water-fissh & eel [L. *anguillas sane piscesque fluviales*]. **1683** J. REID *Scots Gard.* (1907) 41 If you are forced to use sea or water-sand.

25. Objective: **a.** with vbl. sbs. and pres. pples., as ***water-blowing, †-commanding, -divining, -dowsing, -drawing, †-fetching, †-flinging, -holding, -loving, -raising, †-receiving, -retaining, -selling, -yielding;*** also with *sbs.* and *adjs.*, as ***water-retention, -retentive.***

c **1440** *Promp. Parv.* 456/2 Synke, for water receyvynge, *exceptorium.* **1570** DEE *Math. Pref.* cj, Then, may you, of Ships water drawing, diuersly, in the Sea and in fresh water, haue pleasant consideration. **1660** [R. DACRES] (*title*) The Elements of Water-drawing, or a Compendious abstract of all sorts and kinds of Water-Machins. **1660** MARQ. WORCESTER in Dircks *Life* (1865) 223 That..I may put in practice the greatest gift of invention..(I mean my water-commanding engine). **1670** EACHARD *Cont. Clergy* 16 Bed-making, chamber-sweeping, and water-fetching were doubtless great preservatives against too much vain philosophy. **1695** D. TURNER *Apol. Chyrurg.* 130 Every water-flinging Piss-prophet boasts himself a great Doctor. **1824** MORIER *Hajji Baba* ix, With the money I had gained in water selling, I found myself well off. **1839** URE *Dict. Arts* 824 The trompe, or water-blowing engine. **1841** P. CUNNINGHAM *Hints Austral. Emigrants* title-p., Explanatory Descriptions of the Water-raising Wheels and Modes of irrigating Land in Egypt,..&c. **1851** MAYNE REID *Scalp-Hunters* vi. 48 The water-drawing, wood-hewing pueblos. **1854** A. ADAMS, etc. *Man. Nat. Hist.* 180 Water-loving Beetles (*Philhydridæ*). **1877** HUXLEY *Physiogr.* 32 A great drain was thrown upon the water-yielding power of the strata. **1898** K. L. PARKER in Murdoch & Drake-Brockman *Austral. Short Stories* (1951) 2 We thought you..would.. know of a goolahgool, or water-holding tree. **1909** O. LODGE *Survival of Man* ix. 128 Just as people occasionally seem able to become cognisant of facts or events by means ordinarily closed to them,—a phenomenon which appears akin to the water-dowsing faculty and to the 'homing' instincts of animals,—so sometimes they can write poetry or solve problems beyond their normal capacity. **1913** W. OWEN *Let.* 13 Nov. (1967) 211 What it costs to make a Scout. For instance:..Belt..Staff (Water-divining, extra). **1930** T. S. ELIOT tr. *St-J. Perse's Anabasis* 63 Consecration of stones perfectly round, water-dowsing in dead places. **1936** *Discovery* Jan. 24/1 They [*sc.* the soils] are all highly permeable and with a small water-retaining capacity. **1946** *Nature* 13 July 58/1 The lower part of the profile consists.. either of re-cemented chalk or compact sand, both of which are very water-retentive. **1952** L. MACNEICE *Ten Burnt Offerings* IV. i. 38 A sage whose water-divining mind Will twitch to the smallest drop. **1958** *Yearbk. Agric. 1957* (U.S. Dept. Agric.) 770/2 *Water retention,* the physical property of soil that is based on surface force action and that makes it necessary to do work in order to remove water from soil pores and from soil surface. **1969** G. BECKER in Krishna & Weesner *Biol. Termites* I. xi. 367 The water content of the soil should be slightly below its water-holding capacity. **1973** D. ROBERTSON *Survive Savage Sea* II. 73 The unpalatable, brackish water could be administered rectally in the form of water retention enemas. **1979** *Arizona Daily Star* 5 Aug. (Advt. Section) 4/1 Applicant should have at least 3 years experience in the design of hydraulic, water-retaining structures.

b. with agent-nouns, as ***water-drawer, -fearer, -haunter, -lover, -tender, †-searcher, -seller, -supplier.***

1552 HULOET, Water sercher, *aquilex.* **1562** TURNER *Bathes* 16 Smal byrdes..that are of easy digestion. But water-haunters must ye not touche. **1576** FLEMING tr. *Caius' Dogs* iv. (1880) 29 This kinde of dogge is also called, In latine *Aquarius* in Englishe a water drawer. And these be of the greater..sort drawing water out of wells and deepe pittes, by a wheele which [etc.]. **1842** T. W. HARRIS *Insects Injurious to Vegetation* 11 The water-lovers (Hydrophilidæ) ..act the useful part of scavengers. **1867** MORRIS *Jason* XVII. 264 A marble step..Well worn by many a water-drawer's feet. **1884** *Bookseller* 5 Mar. 262/2 Householders, who have grievances against their local water suppliers. **1884** *U.S. Navy Exec. Ord.* 31 Dec., New ratings are hereby established as follows: boiler maker, water tenders, oilers. *a* **1885** G. M. HOPKINS *Poems* (1967) 192 Fallers in dreadful frothpits, waterfearers wild. **1907** MRS. FR. CAMPBELL *Shepherd Stars* 70 A water-seller ringing his brass bell. **1922** JOYCE *Ulysses* 655 Bloom, waterlover, drawer of water. **1948** H. C. NICHOLS *Voice at Sea* x. 145 This water-tender, or boss stoker as he was sometimes called, was the devil himself.

c. in names of machines, implements, or natural agencies, as ***†water-chafer, -conductor, -feeder, †-forcer, -heater, -holder, -regulator.***

1457 *Will of Poole* (Somerset Ho.), Menne Wat'chafer. **1610** HOLLAND *Camden's Brit.* I. 475 The Citizens conveighed water out of the river through pipes by an artificiall instrument or water-forcer. **1825** J. NICHOLSON *Oper. Mech.* 332 The water-regulator consists of a large cistern, in which another of less area and capacity is inverted. **1839** URE *Dict. Arts* 972 No water-feeder of any magnitude should present itself till the shaft had been sunk 100 fathoms. **1843** *Zoologist* I. 14 A leaden water-conductor at the top of our house. **1853** KANE *Grinnell Exp.* xix. (1856) 142 A rugged little water-feeder, formed by the melting snows, sent down a stream of foam. **1880** H. C. ST. JOHN *Wild Coasts Nipon* 225 The great tanks are more like small natural lakes than artificially constructed water-holders.

26. Instrumental: **a.** with pa. pples., as ***water-beaten, †-bollen, -cooled, -cut, -eaten, -filled, -girt, †-gyved, -hidden, -inwoven, †-loaden, -locked, -marrowed, †-mingled, †-mixed, -pillared, -rolled, -rounded, -saturated, -sealed, -shafted, -smoothed, -sodden, -sorted, -sprinkled, -tempered, -walled, -wattled, -whipped, -wound;*** also with *adjs.*, as ***water-dispersible, -poor, -rich.*** Also WATER-BOUND, -LOGGED, -SOAKED, -WASHED, -WORN, etc.

c **1440** Watertemprid [see UNEVENLY *adv.* 3]. **1555** WATREMAN *Fardle Facions* I. vi. 103 Euery body layes him downe dronckarde-like to reste his water bolne bealy. **1593** NASHE *Christs T.* P 1, The nectarized *Aqua cœlestis* of water-mingled blood, sluced from Christs side. **1595** SHAKS. *John* II. i. 27 England hedg'd in with the maine, That Water-walled Bulwarke. **1598** SYLVESTER *Du Bartas* II. i. IV. *Handie-Crafts* 776 A sable, water-loaden Sky. **1602** CAREW *Cornwall* II. 106 b, While thus they can nor liue nor dye, Nor water-gieu'd, escape away. **1605** SYLVESTER *Du Bartas* II. iii. III. *Law* 589 The pure and plenteous Floud Of his most precious Water-mixèd Bloud. **1672** DR. WILD *Let.* 6 Wellcome as the Dove to the Water-beaten Ark. **1789** J. WILLIAMS *Min. Kingd.* II. 205 The balls and glebes always appear water-rounded. **1800** HURDIS *Fav. Village* 81 Forlorn and water-lock'd stands the lone mill. **1841** H. MILLER *O.R. Sandst.* v. 110 A huge water-rolled boulder of granitic gneiss. **1843** THACKERAY *Irish Sk.-bk.* xv, A great, wide,..water-whipped square lies before the..window. **1855** MOTLEY *Dutch Rep.* II. i. (1866) 132 The blood of a world-wide traffic was daily coursing through the thousand arteries of that water-in-woven territory. **1871** TENNYSON *Last Tourn.* 253 Quiet as any water-sodden log. **1876** G. M. HOPKINS *Poems* (1967) 65 And mazy sands all water-wattled. **1883** FR. M. PEARD *Contrad.* xvi, The old water-eaten and green stones of beautiful palaces. **1886** *Standard* 4 Jan. 6/5 The Kelso..is waterfilled, in all holds. **1905** J. B. BURY *St. Patrick* vii. 134 The water-girt promontory which is washed on the west by Lake Kilglass. **1911** MRS. H. WARD *Case Richard Meynell* I. vi. 120 The narrow strip of land between the pond and the new channel made a little waterlocked kingdom of its own for the cottage. **1922** J. A. DUNN *Man Trap* iv. 49 Most of the young men nowadays are water-marrowed pups. **1924** G. A. BURLS *Cost of Power Production by Internal-Combustion Engines* iv. 23 A gas-holder of the familiar inverted water-sealed type. **1925** E. SITWELL *Troy Park* 19 A water-hidden sound. **1927** V. WOOLF in *Forum* May 704 Her cowardice; her mean, water-sprinkled blood. **1928** 'BRENT OF BIN BIN' *Up Country* xix. 325 The water running on to the water-smoothed stones. **1935** L. MACNEICE *Poems* 21 Set these against your water-shafted air of amethyst and moonstone, the horses' feet like bells of hair. **1939** J. Steinbeck *Grapes of Wrath* i. 1 In the water-cut gullies the earth dusted down in dry little streams. **1939** Dylan Thomas *Map of Love* 6 Down the stacked sea and water-pillared shade. **1946** *Nature* 6 July 14/1 For an ordered system, the expansion on wetting is lateral for a water-rich system, and perpendicular for a water-poor system. *Ibid.* 9 Nov. 675/1 The extent of development obtained is related to the type and throughput of solvent, which is normally 10 ml. of water-saturated ether per strip. **1946** Dylan Thomas *Deaths & Entrances* 63 Turns the moon-chained and water-wound Metropolis of fishes. **1959** *Times* 30 Nov. 18/7 Water-dispersible powders. **1959** A. H. McLintock *Descr. Atlas N.Z.* 36 Soils derived from fine volcanic ash and watersorted derivatives. **1978** J. M. Brown in *Further Perspectives Organic Chem.* (CIBA) 149 The selective terminal addition to squalene in water-rich solvents. **1979** *Amer. Jrnl. Trop. Med. & Hygiene* XXVIII. 1014/2 The Department of Health of the Philippine government..has campaigned since 1950 for the installation of cheap water-sealed toilets.

b. with pres. pples., as †*water-flowing*, *-rippling*, †*-standing*; with vbl. sbs., as *water-dripping*, *-planing*, *-rolling*, *-seasoning*, *-spinning*, *-steeping*, *-wasting*.

1593 Shaks. *3 Hen. VI*, iv. viii. 43 My mercie [hath] dry'd their water-flowing teares. *Ibid.* v. vi. 40 Many an old mans sighe, and many a Widdowes, And many an Orphans water-standing-eye. **1595** *Locrine* iv. iii. 28 And from the Lee with water-flowing pipes The moisture is deriu'd into this arch. **1751** Bankton *Inst. Law Scot.* I. 681 If, by the water-wasting, the ground is worn away, where the dam was formerly. **1754** *Dict. Arts & Sci.* II. s.v. *Japanning*, Rub the work over with a wet rag till it is rendered as smooth as possible; this work is called water-planing. **1766** *Complete Farmer* s.v. *Walk*, In order to make them more firm, it will be necessary to give them three or four water-rollings, that is, they should be rolled when it rains very fast; this will cause the gravel to bind. **1823** P. Nicholson *Pract. Builder* 263 Amongst wheelwrights, the water-seasoning [of timber] is of special regard. **1825** J. Nicholson *Oper. Mech.* 386 Water-spinning differs both from the mule and jenny spinning. *Ibid.* 401 The..process of dew-retting or water-steeping. **1922** T. S. Eliot *Waste Land* (1923) 33 The hermit-thrush..Its 'water-dripping song' is justly celebrated. **1924** E. Sitwell *Sleeping Beauty* xx. 77 A lady sang through water-rippling leaves. **1927** —— *Rustic Elegies* 76 And the trees' vast waterfalls Echoed this water-dripping song like flashing bright bird-calls.

27. Locative, with agent-nouns and vbl. sbs., as *water-diver*, *farer*, †*-skirmisher*; *water-building*, *-dwelling*, *-faring*, *-hunting*. Also *water-dwelling*, *-haunting*, *-growing*, *-living*, *-standing* ppl. adjs.; *water-gifted* adj.

1570 Drant *Serm.* F v b, The Italians be most wittie, the Spanyardes best water skirmigers. **1625** Purchas *Pilgrims* II. Table s.v., Cunning Water-diuers. **1674** Petty *Disc. Dupl. Proportion* 117 Water-Divers who the lower they go, do find their stock of Air more and more to shrink. **1756–7** tr. *Keysler's Trav.* (1760) I. 86 Three leagues from Munich lies..Starenberg, where the court sometimes takes the particular diversion of water-hunting. **1793** Smeaton *Edystone L.* §185 *note*, Mortar for water building. **1864** J. C. Atkinson *Stanton Grange* 160 Their haunts are always among water-growing weeds of some sort. **1865** Lubbock *Preh. Times* 122 The curious habit of water-dwelling. *a* **1882** Emerson *Poet* in *Compl. Wks.* (1883) IX. iii. 309 Methought like water-haunting birds Divers or dippers were his words. **1889** Doughty *Friesland Meres* 277 The waterfarers on this much-frequented river. **1913** E. H. Barker *Wayfaring in France, Auvergne to Bay of Biscay* 254, I decided on a little water-faring up the stream. **1919** H. G. Wells *Outl. Hist.* 12/1 Water-living creatures which are always under water, wave the freely exposed gills by which they breathe in the water. **1934** Webster, Water-dwelling. **1936** *Discovery* Jan. 7/2 South American water-dwelling frogs. **1937** *Ibid.* Aug. 252/1 The larger water-haunting birds. **1942** W. Faulkner *Go down, Moses* 340 The planters ..had wrested from the impenetrable water-standing cane and cypress..cotton patches which..became fields and then plantations. **1960** T. Hughes *Lupercal* 46 Four-legged yet water-gifted.

28. Similative, as *water-grey*, *-green*, *-white* adjs. (and sbs.); *water-chilly*, *-clear*, *-cold*, *-dark*, *-eager*, *-flowing*, *-precious*, †*weak*, adjs.

1612 J. Davies (Heref.) *Muse's Sacrif.* (Grosart) 10/1 If lustie now, forth-with [I] am water-weake. **1877** Raymond *Statist. Mines & Mining* 22 Illuminating-oil..of water-white and odorless qualities. **1884** *Girl's Own Paper* 30 Aug. 762/3 A large range of colour..primrose, water-green, beige. **1893** *Daily News* 16 June 6/1 A coat of water-green satin. **1893** Saltus *Sapphira* xii. 146 A sky of dead rose and water-green. **1900** Mary E. Coleridge *Non Sequitur* 33 The mournful water-gray eyes. **1910** W. de la Mare *Three Mulla-Mulgars* xxi. 275 An odd little water-clear song. **1923** D. H. Lawrence *Birds, Beasts & Flowers* 94 Water-eager eyes. **1923** Water-precious [see *red-gold* s.v. red *a.* 13]. **1924** E. Sitwell *Sleeping Beauty* 27 'Midst brightly perfumed water-flowing Eighteenth-century silks. **1925** —— *Troy Park* 59 A flaxen lily Water-chilly. **1928** —— *Five Poems* 3 That cloud of gold, Its kernel, crackling amber water-cold. **1945** —— *Song of Cold* 11 One of the Dead who lay Beneath the earth, like the water-dark, the water-thin Effigy of Osiris. **1961** R. D. Baker *Essent. Path.* xix. 527 The adenoma has a yellowish or gray, soft cut surface... Microscopically it is composed of chief cells, although occasionally of the so-called 'water-clear' cells.

29. Special comb.: **water authority**, a municipal body administering a system of water supply; **water-ballast**, cisterns filled with water, placed in the hold of a vessel to serve as ballast; **water-baptism**, baptism with water, in contradistinction to baptism with the Holy Spirit; **water-bar**, (*a*) in *Road-making*, a ridge on a road, intended to prevent the accumulation of surface water; (*b*) a tubular bar of a fire-grate, to contain water, communicating with a system of hot-water pipes for warming a building; in quot. *attrib.*; **water-barometer**, a barometer in which the pressure of the atmosphere is measured by the height of a column of water, not of mercury as in the usual form of the instrument; **water-base** *a.*, having water as the main ingredient; **water-based** *a.*, (*a*) operating from ships; (*b*) = *water-base*; †**water-bedrip**, a bedrip at which the reapers were supplied with no other drink than water at meals; **water body**, a body of water forming a physiographical feature, as a sea, reservoir, etc.; **water-bomber** *Canad.*, an aircraft used for extinguishing forest fires by dropping water on them; hence **water-bomb** *v. trans.*; so **water-bombing** *vbl. sb.*; **water-bow** *poet.* (*a*) a rainbow; (*b*) a jet of water issuing so as to form an arch; **water-boy**, (*a*) a boy employed at the riverside; †(*b*) the constellation Aquarius; (*c*) *pl.* rain-clouds (*vulgar*); (*d*) chiefly *U.S.*, a boy or man who carries or takes round drinking water; †**water-breach**, (*a*) app. used for *water-bank* (? some error); (*b*) an irruption of water; **water-breaker**[1] (see quot. 1823); **water-breaker**[2], a keg or cask for holding water (see breaker[2]); **water-breather**, any animal capable of breathing in water (by means of gills); so **water-breathing** *ppl. a.*; **water-bridge**, a fire-bridge which also forms part of the water-space of a boiler, = water-table 4 (Knight *Dict. Mech.* 1875); **water-bus**, a motor-boat or steamer carrying paying passengers as part of a scheduled service; †**water-camlet** (see camlet *sb.* b); **water-candlestick** (? *obs.*), a vertical tube filled with water, to hold a floating piece of wax candle; **water cannon**, a device for shooting a jet of water at high pressure, esp. to disperse crowds, etc.; **water-cell**, (*a*) each of the cells in the walls of the stomach of the camel, in which water is stored; (*b*) an interstice in ice, in which water is occluded; **water-chute** = water-shoot 4; †**water-claw** = dew-claw 1; **water clerk**, an employee of a ship's chandler; †**water-cloth**, ? a dish-cloth; **water-company**, a commercial association for the purpose of supplying water (conducted through pipes) to the inhabitants of a town or district; **water content**, (amount of) water contained in some material; **water-cool** *v. trans.*, to cool (an engine, etc.) by circulating water; hence **water-cooling** *vbl. sb.* and *ppl. a.*; so **water-cooled** *ppl. a.*; **water-cooler**, a vessel or container in which water is kept cool; *spec. U.S.*, a tank of cooled drinking water in a place of work; †**water-corn** *Sc.*, 'the grain paid by farmers for upholding the dams and races of mills' (Jam.); †**water-court** = *court of the watercourse* (see watercourse 1 c); **water cushion**, a depth of water that acts to lessen the impact or force of something; **water-deck** *Mil.*, a piece of painted canvas to cover the saddle, bridle, and girths of a cavalry horse; †**water-dial**, a clepsydra; **water-diviner** = water-finder; †**water-dock** = wet-dock; **water drive** *Oil Industry*, the use of water to force oil out of a reservoir rock; **water drum**, a drum containing water, or placed in water, and played as a musical instrument; **water-dust**, water in the form of extremely fine particles, as in clouds and spray [? suggested by G. *wasserdunst*]; †**water-egg**, an infecund egg (cf. *wind-egg*); **water-engineering**, the construction of reservoirs, embankments, aqueducts, and the like; **water-eynd** *dial.* [ande *sb.*], see quot. 1884; †**water-fare**, a ferry; **water-farm**, a place where pisciculture is carried on; so **water-farming**, (*a*) pisciculture; (*b*) cultivation of plants growing in water; **water-flint** *dial.* (see quot. 1868); **water-foot** *Sc.*, the mouth of a stream; 'used also as the name of a village or town at the mouth of a river' (Jam.); **water fountain**, a drinking fountain; **water-frame**, Arkwright's spinning-machine, which was worked by water-power; †**water-free** *a.*, secure from damage by water; **water-funk** *colloq.*, a person who is afraid to go in the water; **water-gap** (see gap *sb.*[1] 5 b); **water-garden**, (*a*) a garden for aquatic plants, an aquarium; (*b*) see quot. 1902; hence **water-gardening**; †**water-gavel** (see quot. 1706); **water-gilder**, one who practises water-gilding; **water-gilding**, the process of gilding metal surfaces by applying liquid amalgam, the mercury being afterwards removed by evaporation; similarly **water-gilt** *a.*; **water-globe** = water-ball[1]; †**water-glue**, a name for isinglass, ? as being waterproof; **water-gold**, the liquid amalgam used in water-gilding; also (*poet. nonce-use*) applied to the 'liquid' golden radiance of morning sunshine; **water-guard**, (*a*) a body of men employed by the Custom House to watch ships in order to prevent smuggling; (*b*) *U.S.* (see quot. 1868); †**water-gun**, a gun in which the projectile is propelled by pressure of water; **water-haul** *U.S.*, 'a haul of the net which catches no fish; *fig.* fruitless effort' (Webster 1911); **water-heck**, **-hedge** *dial.*, the barred frame hung across a stream at a shallow part to prevent the passage of cattle along the shallow; **water-ickle** *dial.*, a stalactite; **water-inch** (see quot.); **water injection**, (*a*) *Oil Industry*, the forcing of water into a reservoir formation, esp. as a technique of secondary recovery (cf. water-flooding *vbl. sb.*); (*b*) *Aeronaut.*, the injection of water into the cylinders of a piston engine with the fuel, to cool the charge, or into the air intake of a jet engine, to cool the air, so as to increase engine efficiency in either case; **water-insoluble** *a.*, insoluble in water; **water intoxication** *Med.*, a condition resulting from the intake of too much water, leading progressively to drowsiness and unsteadiness, confusion, convulsions, coma, and death; so **water-intoxicated** *a.*; **water-jack**, (*a*) *Sc.* a roasting-jack turned by a current of water; (*b*) *dial.* a waterman; **water-jacket**, a casing containing water, placed about something to prevent its becoming unduly heated or chilled; also *attrib.*; hence **water-jacketed** *ppl. a.*, **water-jacketing**; **water-jet**, a stream of water discharged from a small orifice; a fountain; also *attrib.* **water-jet propeller** (see quot. 1843); **water-jump**, a place where a horse is required to leap a stream or ditch; **water-keeper**, one who guards a tract of water against poachers; cf. gamekeeper; †**water-keeping** *Sc.*, the guarding of a tract of water against poachers; †**water-kin**, **-kind**, the nature of water; **water-laid** *a.*, (*a*) *Naut.* of a rope (see quot. 1857); (*b*) *Geol.* of strata, deposited by water; **water-lain** *a. Geol.* = *water-laid* (*b*); †**water-language**, the rough language of watermen (cf. *water-wit*); †**water-leasow**, a water-meadow; **water-leave**, permission to navigate a watercourse belonging to another (cf. way-leave); †**water-lot** *U.S.*, a lot of ground covered with water, but capable of being filled in and converted into building land; **water-lungs** *pl.*, the branches of the cloaca of holothurians, by some supposed to have respiratory functions; †**water-manikin**, some kind of sailing-boat; **water mass** *Oceanogr.*, a large body of sea water that remains distinguished by its temperature and salinity from surrounding water; **water-mead** = water-meadow; **water-monarch** *nonce-wd.*, a designation applied (*a*) to Neptune; (*b*) to a great fish; **water-monger**, †(*a*) a contemptuous designation for a water-caster; (*b*) a vendor of water; †**water-nail**, ? a nail that will bear exposure to water without rusting; **water-organ**, the hydraulicon or hydraulic organ (hydraulic A. 2); **water-oven**, an oven surrounded by a chamber filled with hot water or steam; **water park**, a recreational area comprising stretches of fresh water that may be used for boating, etc.; **water-party**, a pleasure-party making an excursion on the water; †**water-piece**, ? a piece of leather damaged by water in the process of manufacture; **water-pillow** (cf. *water-bed*); **water-pistol**, a weapon constructed to discharge a sudden jet of water or corrosive liquid; **water-plate**, a receptacle for hot water to be placed under a dinner-plate in order to keep the food warm; **water-pocket**, (*a*) a compartment in a steam-boiler containing a portion of the water; (*b*) a natural cavity in which water falls or collects; †**water-poet**, the title adopted by the writer John Taylor, who was a waterman on the Thames; hence *gen.* a writer of doggerel verse; †**water-poise**, a hydrometer; **water-polo**, a game played by teams of swimmers, usu. in a rectangular pool with goal-posts, using a ball similar to a football; **water-pore** *Bot.* and *Zool.*, a pore through which water is discharged; †**water-pourer**, the constellation Aquarius; **water-power**, the power of moving or falling water employed to drive machinery; *concr.* a fall or flow of water which can be thus utilized; **water-press**, a hydrostatic press; **water-pressure**, hydraulic pressure, so **water-pressure engine** (see quot.

1829); **water-privilege** *U.S.* (*a*) 'the right to use water, esp. the right to use running water to turn machinery'; (*b*) 'a stream or body of water capable of being utilized in driving machinery' (*Cent. Dict.*); †**water-rack** (see quot. 1679); **water-ram** = RAM *sb.*[1] 5 a; **water-rate**, a rate or tax levied by a municipality or a water-company for the supply of water; **water-rent** = prec.; **water-repellent** *a.*, not easily penetrated by water though porous; *sb.*, an agent conferring this property; so **water-repellency**; **water-resistant** *a.*, waterproof or water-repellent; so **water-resistance**; **water resources**, natural sources of water available for man's use; freq. *attrib.* (in *sing.* or *pl.*); **water-rights** (also in *sing.*), the right to the use of water in a tract of land (cf. *water-privilege* (*a*)); †**water-rimer**, the 'water-poet' Taylor; †**water-room**, space to move about in the water; **water-sail**, (*a*) a small sail sometimes set under a lower studding-sail and reaching nearly to the water; (*b*) a sail lowered into the water to act as a sea anchor; **water-screw**, a water-elevator on the principle of the Archimedean screw; also *attrib.* in ***water-screw-pump***; **water-shaft**, (*a*) *Coal Mining*, etc., a shaft sunk to receive the water from an adjoining (coal-)shaft; (*b*) *Salt-making* (see quot.); †**water-shake**, a seismic disturbance of the water; **water-shaken** *a.*, (of land) saturated with water; †**water shard**, a deepened channel made by banking up the sides of a stream; **water-shear, -shier** *Sc.*, a water-parting; †**water-shedder** *Astr.* = sense 14; **water silk**, watered silk (see WATERED *ppl. a.* 5); a garment of this material; also *fig.*; **water-sill** (see quot.); **water-sink**, (*a*) = SINK *sb.*[1] 1 c; (*b*) a swallow-hole or pot-hole; **water-sky** (see quot. 1823); **water-slang**, the slang of rowing-men; **water-smoke** = *water-eynd*; **water-sneak** *slang* (see quot. 1812); **water-softener**, an apparatus for making hard water soft by chemical means; also, a chemical used for this purpose; hence **water-softening** *vbl. sb.* and *ppl. a.*; **water-soluble** *a.*, soluble in water; so **water-solubility**; **water-space**, that part of a steam-boiler which lies below the steam-space, and holds the water to be evaporated; †**water-spelling**, hydromancy; **water-spinel**, a colourless variety of spinel; **water-splash**, a shallow stream or ford crossing a road; †**water-sponge** *Sc.*, an ordinary sponge for washing; **water-spot** *v. intr.*, of fabric: to be liable to show permanently any mark made on it by a drop of water; hence **water-spotting** *vbl. sb.*, the condition of showing such a mark; **water sprout** = WATER-SHOOT 1; **water-stain**, (*a*) a stain made on a surface by contact with water; (*b*) (see quot. 1940); **water-stead** *dial.*, the bed or course of a stream; a convenient spot on the bank of a stream where cattle can go to drink (*Eng. Dial. Dict.*); **water-stock**, shares in a water-company; **water-stoma** (pl. **-stomata**) = *water-pore* (Bot.); **water-stop**, †(*a*) = STOP *sb.*[2] 8 a; (*b*) a place where a traveller or a train may stop for water; (*c*) a sealant to prevent water from leaking through joints (see quot. 1951); **water-streak** = WATER-LINE 2; **water-system**, (*a*) an assemblage of connected rivers and streams; a main stream and its tributaries, considered as a unity; (*b*) = *water-vascular system*; †**water-tabby** = TABBY *sb.* 1; **water-tathe** *v.* (see TATHE *v.* 1); **water taxi**, a small boat used for casual passenger traffic on rivers, canals, etc.; **water-telescope**, an instrument for observing objects under water; **water-thermometer**, a thermometer filled with water instead of mercury, devised by Dalton for ascertaining the precise degree of temperature at which water attains its maximum density; **water-thief** *poet.*, a pirate; **water toothpick** = *water-pick* (see WATER PIK); **water-torture**, a form of torture in which the victim is made to endure an incessant drip of water on the head (see also quot. 1928); also *fig.*; **water-tower**, (*a*) a tower serving as a reservoir to deliver water at a required head; (*b*) a long iron tube, carried vertically on a wheeled frame, for discharging water to extinguish fires in the upper stories of buildings; **water-treader**, †(*a*) *poet.* a ship; (*b*) one who treads water (TREAD *v.* 7); **water treatment**, (*a*) = WATER-CURE; (*b*) = *water torture* above; **water-tube**, (*a*) one of a set of tubular organs which open upon the exterior of certain invertebrates and are supposed to have an excretory function; (*b*) each of the tubes carrying water through a water-tube boiler; **water-tube boiler**, a form of boiler in which the water circulates through tubes exposed to the gases of combustion; †**water-twig** = WATER-SHOOT 1; **water tunnel** (see quot. 1969); **water-twist**, cotton yarn spun on a water-frame; **water-vapour**, the invisible aqueous vapour present in the atmosphere; **water-vascular** *a. Zool.*, pertaining to water-vessels (see next); **water-vessel** *Zool.*, one of a system of vessels in which water circulates, in certain Invertebrata; **water-wag**, a kind of small boat used at Dublin; **water-wagon**, (*a*) orig. *U.S.* = WATER-CART *sb.* (*Cent. Dict.* Suppl.); also *slang* (see quot. 1904); cf. WAGON, WAGGON *sb.* 11 b; (*b*) a kind of cumulus (see quots.); †**water-wan** [WANE *sb.*[1]], lack of water; †**water-want** *a. nonce-wd.*, that can endure privation of water; **water-watcher**, a water-bailiff; **water-wet**, moisture of herbage due to saturation by rain; **water-wit**, the rough wit of watermen; **water-woman**, a woman who acts as a waterman; **water-wood**, timber which grows near water; **water-worship**, religious adoration paid to rivers or other bodies of water; so **water-worshipper**; †**water-wrack**, refuse left by a destructive flood.

1878 D. KEMP *Man. Yacht Sailing* 377 **Water Ballast*, water carried in tanks or breakers as ballast. **1885** J. RUNCIMAN *Skippers & Shellbacks* 238 Bitterly repented having come out with nothing but his water-ballast. **1901** *Scotsman* 14 Mar. 6/8 The boat..has a water ballast tank. **1673** BUNYAN (*title*) Differences in Judgment about *Water-Baptism, No Bar to Communion. *a* **1716** BLACKALL *Wks.* (1723) I. 212 That thus, and no otherwise the Apostles..did admit into the Christian Church all that were receiv'd thereinto, i.e. by the Water-Baptism, is evident. *a* **1879** E. BACKHOUSE *Ch. Hist.* xi. (1884) 122 There were other sects who rejected both water-baptism and the Eucharist. **1868** *Rep. U.S. Commissioner Agric.* (1869) 360 On such road provide low *water bars across the road at intervals of thirty to forty feet. *Ibid.* 362 Water Bars. The purpose of the bar is to cast the surface water from the road to the side or sides before it has accumulated in such amount as to cut the ruts into gullies. **1884** *Health Exhib. Catal.* 124/2 Weeks's Tubular Waterbar Open Fire Grate. **1773** W. EMERSON *Princ. Mech.* (ed. 3) 243 AF a *water barometer. **1866** A. STEINMETZ *Weathercasts* 143 The water barometer at the Royal Society's rooms gave more than 13 inches (13·386) rise and fall for every inch of the mercurial column. **1949** *Sci. Digest* Dec. 93 *Water-base paints have been in use for years, but in the past they could not be washed without coming off. **1975** *McGraw-Hill Yearbk. Sci. & Technol.* 300/2 Because of the cost of oil-base drilling fluids.., research is continuing so that water-base drilling fluids that can provide the properties needed..can be developed. **1955** *Sci. News Let.* 15 Jan. 37/2 The new big swept-wing plane ..was described as a 'truly *water-based aircraft' capable of operating in high waves and marginal sea conditions. **1981** *Sci. Amer.* Aug. 85/1 Oil-based graphites tend to give off fumes, and so the latest trend in the forging industry is toward the use of water-based graphites. *c* **1360** in *Mélanges Charles Bémont* (1913) 83 Nullum potum habebit eo die nisi aquam, et idcirco dicitur **waterbedrip*. **1897** *Water body [see *sheet-flood* s.v. SHEET *sb.*[1] 12 b]. **1974** R. H. BRITTON in R. Goodier *Natural Environment of Shetland* 123 The most abundant type of standing waterbody on Shetland, (accounting for 27·4% of the total), is a dystrophic loch of area less than 1 hectare. **1975** *Sci. Amer.* June 88/1 (Advt.), There are many excellent shots of the planes in action, 2 of which are shown here *water-bombing the blaze. **1961** *Canada Month* 6 Oct. 42/3 The Grove and Tsus fires.. could have been kept small if *water bombers and helicopters had been available from the beginning. **1975** *Globe & Mail* (Toronto) 20 Aug. 8/6 He said 40 ministry firefighters, another force of 48 junior rangers,..a ministry water bomber and commercial aircraft..are all being used. **1959** *Time* (Canada ed.) 17 Aug. 13/3 Ontario has a new gadget that makes *water-bombing more efficient than ever: snorkel-like water intakes on tanks attached to the aircraft floats that enable the planes to load up as they taxi along lake surfaces. **1827** G. DARLEY *Sylvia* 16 With their varied colours blending Hues to shame the *water-bow. **1855** BROWNING *Cleon* 252 They praise a fountain in my garden here Wherein a Naiad sends the water-bow Thin from her tube. **1640** J. GOWER *Ovid's Festiv.* I. 19 Sol leaving Capricorn, His race-horse to the *Water-boy doth turn. **1722** *Applebee's Weekly Jrnl.* 22 Sept. 2471/1 Mr. Lear landed at King's-Arms Stairs, and put on the Water Boy's Cap, the better to disguise himself. **1859** *Harper's Mag.* Apr. 712/1 The 'water-boy' in his first round found me standing by the stove. **1895** *Westm. Gaz.* 7 Sept. 2/1 There were some waterboys out, an' we wanted to get down afore there were any downfall. **1903** *Congress. Directory* 116 He assisted himself in securing an education by working as a 'water boy' on the railroad. **1965** J. A. MICHENER *Source* (1966) 408 Trumpeters, drummers, waterboys and cooks followed in a compact nest, protected by many soldiers, and not until this stupendous preamble had passed did the actual fighting men appear. **1972** J. MOSEDALE *Football* viii. 106 Hubbard was convinced that Dobie was illegally sending in plays by arranging cups on the water tray. He kicked over the tray every time the water boy came on the field. **1979** P. THEROUX *Old Patagonian Express* xii. 185 Praising the quarterback, mocking the water-boy. **1398** TREVISA *Barth. De P.R.* XVII. cxxvi. (1495) 686 And the places wherin suche Papirio Russhes growe is as marreys and moores by meedes and *water breches [L. *aquarum ripis*]. **1669** HOLDER *Elem. Speech* 5 Bells serve to proclaim a scare-fire, and (in some places) Water-breaches. **1823** P. NICHOLSON *Pract. Builder* 302 *Water-breakers,..being the extremities of the piers which meet and divide the water in its course. **1900** *Westm. Gaz.* 27 Dec. 5/2 The commander..had life-belts sent adrift for every man, and six out of the seven were successful in being caught, but the seventh man secured himself to a water-breaker. **1851** WOODWARD *Mollusca* I. (1880) 25 Stale water is so inimical to the *water-breathers, that [etc.]. **1883** *Fisheries Exhib. Catal.* (ed. 4) 99 All crustacea are water breathers. **1861** P. P. CARPENTER in *Rep. Smithsonian Inst.* 1860, 223 The..*Water-breathing Prosobranchs. **1929** A. P. HERBERT in *Times* 16 Nov. 8/1 Let no one tell us that the Londoner 'does not want' the *water-bus. There was not much evidence that he wanted the Tubes..before he got them. **1940** *Economist* 21 Sept. 368/2 The waterbus service, which London Transport has been running..between Westminster and Woolwich and Greenwich, has won a popularity... It is an emergency experiment that may survive both air-raids and the war itself. **1981** T. HOLME *Funeral of Gondolas* i. 9 The Rialto Bridge humped regally over the Grand Canal... A water-bus..churned water in mid-stream. ? **1592** *Greene's Vision, Descr. Sir Geff. Chawcer*, A Sleeuelesse Iacket large and wide..Of *water Chamlet did he weare. **1823** J. BADCOCK *Dom. Amusem.* 203 The pillar..is made hollow, for the purpose of receiving a *water candlestick of an inch diameter. **1964** L. DEIGHTON *Funeral in Berlin* xlii. 251 An American M.P. shouted, 'You want a goddam *water-cannon to wash you across the sidewalk, fella?' **1982** *Listener* 23 & 30 Dec. 5/3 People had begun to take to the streets, defying martial law, tear-gas, water-cannon and bullets. **1859** *Todd's Cycl. Anat.* V. 507/1 The beautiful provision of *water-cells in the walls of the paunch or first cavity of the stomach [of a camel]. **1860** TYNDALL *Glac.* I. xix. 136 Reduced..to a mere skeleton of ice, with water-cells between its walls. **1899** *Westm. Gaz.* 8 May 7/2 The lake has been enlarged, and a switchback railway and a *water chute promise rounds of delight. **1901** *Scotsman* 8 Mar. 6/7 A waterchute is rapidly rising into form in the river Kelvin. **1611** COTGR., *Controngle*, the Deaw-claw, or *water-claw of dogs. **1898** *Barbados Freight Rep.* in F. Holm-Petersen *Fra Sejl til Diesel* (1951) I. 335 Our *Water Clerk will meet the Vessels on their entering the bay. **1973** P. THEROUX *Saint Jack* xiii. 156, I knew my job as a water-clerk..and pored over the shipping pages of the *Straits Times*. **1411** *Nottingham Rec.* II. 86, j. *watre-cloth. **1813** *Examiner* 24 May 325/2 The street being broken up by a *Water Company. **1877** HUXLEY *Physiogr.* 28 An independent source of water was supplied by the great water-companies. **1946** *Nature* 21 Dec. 899/2 Vitamin-like substances..in cells with assumed *water-contents of 80 per cent. **1957** G. E. HUTCHINSON *Treat. Limnol.* I. iv. 222 The water content of the major part of the lithosphere..is unknown. **1969** Water content [see *water-holding*, sense 25 a above]. **1909** WEBSTER, *Water-cool v.t. **1915** W. E. DOMMETT *Submarine Vessels* v. 50 Due to the high temperatures, it is necessary to not only water-cool the cylinder, but also to cool the piston. **1971** *Physics Bull.* July 401/2 The essential difference..is well illustrated in this example by the need to water-cool the measuring head because of high levels of radiant heat. **1905** *Westm. Gaz.* 23 May 4/2 A 12-h.p. *water-cooled Lanchester car. **1984** B. FRANCIS *AA Car Duffer's Guide* 63/1 Modern water-cooled systems incorporate a thermostat. **1984** *Mining Jrnl.* 4 May 297 China has also expressed interest in Japan's PNC heavy water moderated, light water-cooled advanced thermal reactor. **1846** *Catholic Herald* (Philadelphia) 30 Aug. 272/4 Refrigerators, *water coolers, and filterers. **1899** JESSE L. WILLIAMS *Stolen Story*, etc. 34 He..stepped up to the water-cooler and filled a glass. **1955** R. P. JHABVALA *To whom she Will* xxiii. 168 An earthenware water-cooler. **1969** *Canad. Antiques Collector* Aug. 6/1 (Advt.), Salt glazed water cooler with incised blue decoration... Each side has riderless horse. **1978** *Amer. Speech* LIII. 5 Slang..is inexact and meaningless, but these are characteristics it shares with much of standard English, as fifteen minutes at a water cooler or a political rally will show. **1910** R. FERRIS *How it Flies* x. 198 To keep the cylinder cool enough to be serviceable, two methods are in use: the air-cooling system and the *water-cooling system. **1934** *Physical Rev.* XLV. 608/1 At 3,000,000 volts, ion currents of $\frac{1}{3}$ microampere are readily obtainable and it is probable that water-cooling of the accelerators and the bombarded targets will result in considerably larger utilizable currents. **1985** *Dirt Bike* Mar. 39/2 They wanted watercooling for reasons of reliability. **1600** *Reg. Mag. Sig. Scot.* 354/2 Duas nonas partes molendini..cum multuris, sequelis, *lie knaifschippis, lie *watter coirnes*, &c. **1814** *Mill of Inveramsay* 3 (Jam.), 1 boll of water-corn, being small corn, yearly, for each of the said three ploughs, for manufacturing and upholding the dams and water-gangs. **1482** in *Charters* etc. *Edin.* (1871) 169 All vthir custumys and priuilegis..with thare *watir courtis attaichiamentis vnlawes and dewiteis. **1591** in R. P. Cruden *Hist. Gravesend* (1842) 203 Paid..for wine given to my Lords' men when the Water Court was kept 0 0 8. **1907** H. BROWN *Irrigation* vi. 120 A pressure due to $6\frac{3}{4}$ feet head of water, of which 3 feet is balanced by the *water cushion on the floor. **1955** S. LELIAVSKY *Irrigation & Hydraulic Design* I. ii. 270 Finally, we must mention the method of scour prevention which in earlier times was known as the 'stilling pool' or the 'water cushion', and which is now described.. as the 'cistern'. **1972** L. M. HARRIS *Introd. Deepwater Floating Drilling Operations* xvi. 169 The larger the water cushion [in a well], the larger the surface pressures required to unload it. **1844** *Queen's Regul. Army* 74 The supply of Corn Sacks, and *Water Decks to the Cavalry. **1875** J. GRANT *One of 'Six Hundred'* xxii. 169, I also wish the corps to be supplied with water-decks. **1653** *Van Etten's Math. Recreat.* 170 Vitruvius writes of another manner of *water-Dyal more difficult. **1758** E. STONE *Bion's Math. Instrum.* Suppl. 309 The Instruments for measuring Time, are Sun-Dials, Water-Dials, Sand-Dials [etc.]. **1896** *Weekly Times* 24 Jan. 72/2 Lately two '*water-diviners'..visited the well, and both predicted that water would be found at certain indicated spots. **1902** CORNISH *Naturalist Thames* 59 At the Agricultural Show, the water-diviner sits installed. *a* **1700** EVELYN *Diary* 19 July 1661, We tried our Diving Bell or engine in the *water-dock at Deptford. **1938** H. S. GIBSON in A. E. Dunstan et al. *Sci. of Petroleum* I. XI. 538/1 The employment of the *water drive as a process has received considerable attention. **1973** C. J. MAY in Hobson & Pohl *Mod. Petroleum Technol.* (ed. 4) v. 165 When recovery was mostly by water drive, the percentage extraction varied from 24 to 78, and the recovery per acre-foot of sand from 242 to 1165 brl. **1923** C. M. BARBEAU *Indian Days in Canad. Rockies* 120 A deep sound from the seer's lodge startled the people, a sound like that of a large *water drum. **1955** M. BARBEAU *Tree of Dreams* 95 The thumping of water drums at times startled the bleak places, now covered with a mantle of snow. **1970** P. OLIVER *Savannah Syncopators* 106 Outstanding xylophone orchestras, *kora*, water-drum, harp and harp-lute. **1973** A. H. WHITEFORD *North Amer. Indian*

Arts 103 The Iroquois also made water drums with plugs to change the level of the water and the tone of the drum. 1873 Tyndall Forms of Water 4 When the vapour mingles with the cold air..it ceases to be vapour. Every bit of steam shrinks, when chilled, to a much more minute particle of water. The liquid particles thus produced form a kind of *water-dust of exceeding fineness, which floats in the air, and is called a cloud. 1884 Lock Workshop Receipts Ser. III. 257/2 Small pieces..are very well hardened in water-dust finely distributed by means of a stream of air or steam. 1577 B. Googe Heresbach's Husb. IV. 169 Theodorus calleth them *water Egges [L. urina ova], whereof there neuer commeth any thing. 1908 W. M. Ramsay Luke the Physician v. 191 Irrigation has never ceased and is still practised in certain districts, so that the essential principles of *water-engineering have not been wholly forgotten. 1883 G. C. Davies Norfolk Broads xxxv. 266 The '*water-eynd' or sea-smoke,..covers the marsh with a dense watery vapour. 1884 Chamb. Jrnl. 3 May 275/2 Another peculiar and uncomfortable phenomenon of the marshes is the water-eynd or sea-smoke, which, rolling up from the ocean, covers the whole landscape with a dense watery vapour. 1610 Holland Camden's Brit. I. 534 Sometimes there was a Ferry or *Water-fare here. 1868 Peard Water-farm. ii. 12 Though many of our *water-farms have to be created, a large number require only to be improved. Ibid. (title) Practical *Water-farming. 1889 Harper's Mag. May 859/1 A few miles away, the native lotus grows luxuriantly, a relic, it is believed, of Indian water-farming. 1868 Thurnam in Archæologia XLII. 208 The third flat-stone is a quartzose boulder of the kind known as '*water flints' in this part of Somersetshire. 1786 Burns Holy Fair xvi, Peebles, frae the *water-fit, Ascends the holy rostrum. 1946 M. C. Self Horseman's Encycl. 429 Automatic *water fountains are most useful for the stable. 1975 'E. Lathen' By Hook or by Crook xxi. 194 A salt-tablet dispenser beside every water fountain. 1825 J. Nicholson Oper. Mech. 387 In the *water-frame the spindles are moved by an up-right pulley. 1642 Fuller Holy & Prof. St. III. IV. 159 'Tis a tale what Josephus writes of the two pillars set up by the sonnes of Seth in Syria, the one of brick, fire-proof; the other of stone, *water-free. 1899 Kipling Stalky iii. 89 You spoke to Beetle yourself, didn't you? Something about not bathing, and being a *water-funk? 1835 R. M. Bird Hawks i. (1856) 4 The highway to the neighbouring *water-gap..ran through the estate. 1883 Science I. 325/2 Transverse valleys or water-gaps. 1891 Hardwicke's Sci.-Gossip XXVII. 19 Fresh-Water Aquaria, [Reviewed]..A well-written description of these *water-gardens and vivaria. 1899 S. R. Hole Our Gardens x. 214 Where there are pools of water..you may have the beautiful Water Garden. 1902 Cornish Naturalist Thames 176 A recent addition to the country house is the 'water garden', in which a running brook is the centre and motif of the subsidiary ornaments of flowers, ferns, trees, shrubs, and mosses. 1915 Edin. Rev. July 111 The Dutch gardens, like those of Spain, were themselves water-gardens. 1938 F. Perry Water Gardening p. ix, When I first took an interest in *water gardening the dearth of literature upon the subject was the cause of much disappointment. 1982 B. Chatto Damp Garden vi. 98 Water gardening on the landscaping scale is quite a different affair from the marginal plantings. 1231 in Blount Law Dict. (1691) s.v., Redditum..quem homines eorundem Huberti & Margariæ de Manerio suo de Elmour nobis reddere solebant singulis annis per manum Balivi nostri de Menstre-Worth, nomine *Watergavel. 1706 Phillips (ed. Kersey), Water-Gavel, a Rent paid in old Times for fishing in, or other Benefit received from some River, or Water. 1799 G. Smith Laboratory I. 72 The amalgam of gold with mercury ..is used principally by the workmen, in gilding in water-gold, termed *water-gilders. 1897 Allbutt's Syst. Med. II. 931 Until lately water-gilders made use of mercury for depositing gold on metallic surfaces. 1783 Trans. Soc. Arts I. 320 An Apparatus to prevent the ill effects of Mercury in *Water Gilding. c1820 Philos. Recreat. 151 Water-gilding upon Silver. 1855 G. Gore Pract. Chem. 72 The following solutions have been used for gilding by the simple immersion, or 'water-gilding' process. 1883 Mollett Dict. Art & Archæol. 343 Water-gilding, gilding with a thin coat of amalgam. a1776 Duchess of Northumberland Diary in Country Life (1974) 7 Feb. 251/3 The *Water Gilt Locks.. were made at Birmingham. 1898 Westm. Gaz. 28 Oct. 4/2 A Processional cross... The materials employed are silver, water-gilt, carbuncles, green onyx, and enamel. 1897 A. Hartshorne Old Engl. Glasses 60 The mediaeval ourinals —alike the retorts of the alchemist and the *water-globes for the poor Flemish flax-thread spinners..and the lace-makers weaving the subtle webs..of Brussels, Mechlin, or Valenciennes. 1590 Sir J. Smythe Disc. Conc. Weapons 19b, A kinde of *waterglewe to resist wet and moysture. 1678 Evelyn Pomona (ed. 3) 407 As you augment the Proportion of Ising-glass or Water-glew, so it will become more limpid and clear. 1725 Bradley's Family Dict. s.v. Glue, The Fish which is made use of to make Water-glue is very large. 1686 Lond. Gaz. No. 2114/4 Lost.., a large black Boar Skin, lined with new Canvas, with four brass Claws gilt, with *Water-gold. 1839–41 Lane Arab. Nts. III. 220, I command thee to build for me, during this night, a lofty palace, and to decorate it with water-gold. 1855 Browning Old Pict. Florence i, Where, white and wide And washed by the morning's water-gold, Florence lay out on the mountain side. 1646 Jrnls. Ho. Comm. V. 22/2 [A Lords' ordinance] concerning the *Water Guards. 1812 J. Smyth Pract. Customs 1 On the arrival of a Vessel from foreign parts, within the limits of a British Port, it is the duty of the Tide-surveyor, or the Officer who superintends the Water-guard, to proceed on board. 1828 Blackw. Mag. XXIV. 552 A powerful preventive water-guard was placed here. 1868 B. J. Lossing Hudson 351 The 'water-guard' was an aquatic corps, in the pay of the revolutionary government. 1646 Sir T. Browne Pseud. Ep. II. v. 89 There are wayes to discharge a bullet..without any powder at all, as is done by *water and windegunnes. 1871 Congressional Globe 17 Feb. 1356/1 It occurred to me..[that] the gentleman from California had made what fishermen call a '*waterhaul'. [Laughter.] It surely must not have been what he expected. 1882 Critic (Washington) 23 Feb. (Thornton) Ostensibly I went to testify as an expert in the Star-route cases, but I did not testify. You know that was another water-haul. 1639–40 Q. Sess. Rec. (N. Riding Rec. Soc.) IV. 161 Indenture of Conveyance..Together with all and singular wayes, *water-hedges, trees, ditches, fences, etc. 1802 R. Warner Tour Northern Counties I. 161 Those pendant spiral masses called *water-icles or stalactites. 1824 Carr Craven Gloss., Water-icles, stalactites. 1855 Ogilvie Suppl., *Water-inch, the quantity of water flowing in one minute through a circular opening one inch in diameter, whose centre is one and one twelfth inches below a constant surface. 1940 Jrnl. R. Aeronaut. Soc. XLIV. 590 Will *water injection become practical? 1943 Oil & Gas Jrnl. 11 Nov. 230/2 Because an adequate low-cost water supply was available at Midway, the economic possibilities of experimental water injection were clear. 1947 Shell Aviation News No. 106. 21/1 If required water injection apparatus can be included to give additional power for take-off. 1970 M. Smith Aviation Fuels ix. 62 By means of water injection, heat is taken away from the cylinders, pistons and exhaust valves, and removed out of harm's way by the steam so formed, which discharges from the exhaust system. 1982 Water injection [see water-flooding vbl. sb.]. 1946 Nature 16 Nov. 709/2 The black, *water-insoluble pigment. 1937 Amer. Jrnl. Physiol. CXIX. 557 The serum sodium and chloride levels are low in the *water intoxicated animal. 1922 Physiol. Rev. II. 158 (heading) The effects of excessive ingestion: *water intoxication. 1974 Passmore & Robson Compan. Med. Stud. III. xlix. 8/2 Water intoxication should be considered in any patient with unexplained cerebral dysfunction, particularly if the individual has recently undergone an operation. 1869 Eng. Mech. 17 Dec. 324/2 In Scotland..they [sc. turbines] are employed for driving what are called *water-jacks for roasting meat. 1886 R. C. Leslie Sea-painter's Log i. 26 Becoming first the privileged helper of some waterjack. 1869 Tanner Clin. Med. (ed. 2) 62 The vessel is surrounded with a *water-jacket, so as to prevent the chloroform getting too cold to afford the requisite amount of vapour to the air passing over it. 1877 Raymond Statist. Mines & Mining 181 The water-jacket furnace..was built with a view to avoid these costly repairs, but has proved an economical failure thus far. 1898 Kipling Fleet in Being ii. 19 Three Maxims adorned the low nettings. Their water-jackets were filled up from an innocent tin-pot before the game began. It looked like slaking the thirst of devils. 1898 Allbutt's Syst. Med. V. 453 The whole [coagulometer] is surrounded by a water-jacket. 1877 Raymond Statist. Mines & Mining 3 The roasting is effected in a peculiar *water-jacketed furnace or kiln, with a removable bottom. 1907 Motor Boat 19 Sept. 191/2 This is a frequent trouble with paraffin motors,..The cure is to fit a snifter valve to each cylinder to allow a water drip; this, combined with efficient *water-jacketing, should do away with the trouble. 1832 G. Downes Lett. Cont. Countries I. 298 The Temple of Apollo, as another chamber is designated, contains a *water-jet. 1843 Artizan I. 220/1 Water-jet Propellers. A curious mode of propelling steam ships has been invented by Mr. Ruthven, who proposes to give a better direction to the propelling power by forcing jets of water through nozzles placed below the water-line. 1894 W. H. White Nav. Archit. (ed. 3) 585 The Water-jet Propeller. 1875 S. Sidney Bk. Horse xx. 431 A big *water-jump. 1883 Mrs. E. Kennard Right Sort xx, Take a good firm hold of his head, and set King Olaf just as fast as you please at the water-jump. He'll clear it by yards. 1898 J. Macmanus Bend of Road 118 The *wather-keeper..was shot be the poochers on the Dhrowes river. 1920 D. H. Lawrence Women in Love xiv. 202 He called at the water-keeper's cottage and took the key of the sluice. 1420 in Reg. Mag. Sig. Scot. 1430, 30/1 The forsaid lord has grantit to.. Michel the office of *watter keping and the office of chamerlanry of Ananderdale. 1423 Ibid. 30/2. c1200 Ormin Ded. 193 Forr þatt he wollde uss *waterrkinn Till ure fulluhht hallȝhenn. Ibid. 18087 Forr Latin boc seȝȝþ þatt Ennon Bitacneþþ *waterrkinde. 1857 C. Richardson Instruct. Swimming 51 The cord should be well twisted, or what sailors call '*waterlaid'. 1888 E. Clodd Story Creation iv. 29 The study of the erupted, fire-fused, and water-laid rocks. 1895 Nation (N.Y.) 19 Dec. 451/1 The association of basic igneous rocks with the water-laid gravels. 1959 New Biol. XXIX. 14 Any given bed of *water-lain rock is usually formed of relatively uniform particles; wind-deposited sands show a similar sorting. 1977 A. Hallam Planet Earth 55/1 The word 'dune' is often thought to refer only to those forms built by wind, but it is now used equally for water-lain structures. 1721 Amherst Terræ Fil. No. 1, 2 The famous saturnalian feasts among the Romans, at which every scullion..had liberty to tell his master his own... 'Twas all *water-language as these times and no exceptions were to be taken. 1858 Act 21 & 22 Vict. c. 44 § 19 As also all Wayleaves or *Waterleaves, Canals, [etc.]. c1440 Promp. Parv. 518/1 *Water lesu, aquagium. 1777 Maryland Jrnl. 4 Nov. (Thornton) A *Water Lot of Ground, on Fell's Point. 1857 Putnam's Monthly Mag. Feb. 170/2 He had become a merchant of note, a man of water-lots and steam-boats, and shares in desirable sites at the head of navigation. 1877 Revised Statutes Ontario I. 261 marg., Sales and appropriations of water lots declared to be legal. 1877 Encycl. Brit. VII. 639/2 Two, or more rarely four or five, branched processes of the cloaca, the respiratory trees or *water-lungs, are ordinarily present. 1884 F. J. Bell in Proc. Zool. Soc. 254 The so-called water-lungs extend forwards to the anterior end of the body. 1794 Stedman Surinam (1813) II. 403 Sail boats called *water-manakins. 1912 Murray & Hjort Depths of Ocean v. 261 From a study of the distribution of salinity and temperature the average direction of the drift of the *water-masses may be deduced. 1976 Nature 19 Feb. 606/2 No influx of the Atlantic watermass into northeast Icelandic waters was observed in June 1975. 1840 T. A. Trollope Summer in Brittany I. 381 A pretty walk along the valley, which is occupied by a succession of *water-meads. 1818 Keats Endym. III. 917 Meantime a glorious revelry began Before the *Water-Monarch. 1847 Stoddart Angler's Comp. 250 Give me.. the rush of some veteran water-monarch. 1623 Hart Arraignm. Ur. I. ii. 9 Empirickes, *water-mongers, and peticoat-physitians. 1845 Ford Handbk. Spain I. 72 While in particular stations water-mongers in wholesale have a shed. 1403 in Compotus Rolls Obedientiaries St. Swithun's, Winch. (1892) 425 In xlij bordis ad idem emptis viijs. ixd. In cc *Waturnailes ad idem emptis xijd. 1481–90 Howard Househ. Bks. (Roxb.) 211 Item, fur dore nayle, and watter nayle, iiij. c. and qrtr. ij. s. ix. d. ob. 1647 A. Ross Mystag. Poet. xvi. (1675) 384 One of those musical instruments of old called Hydraula, we may call them *water-organs. 1649 Ogilby Virgil, Bucolicks vii. (1684) 30 note, The Motion of Water maketh Musick, as we see in Water-Organs. 1852 Seidel Organ 13 The invention of the water-organ by.. Ctesibius, of Alexandria. 1857 Miller Elem. Chem., Org. 6 By exposing it to a temperature of from 212° to 250° in a *water oven or box of sheet copper. 1884 Health Exhib. Catal. 111/1 Fitted with a patent water-oven, for keeping food hot. 1928 Observer 15 July 12 In the north-eastern workmen's district of Floridsdorf,..a new '*water-park' has just been opened. It..includes two ponds, connected by canals, so that some kind of 'little Venice' has been created. 1972 Daily Tel. 4 Sept. 8 A national water park that would include the Norfolk Broads and the Fens is being planned. 1790 Mrs. P. L. Powys Passages fr. Diaries (1899) 248 August 21st.—Mrs. Williams' *water-party. 1798 W. Windham Diary (1866) 397 June 6th.—Water party to Greenwich. 1834 Disraeli Let. in Monypenny Life (1910) I. 251, I had promised to join a water party in Sir Frank's yacht. 1840 Dickens Sk. Yng. Couples 29 There was a great water-party made up to go to Twickenham and dine. 1687 Proclam. 29 Apr. in Lond. Gaz. No. 2240/2 We have Prohibited, and do hereby Prohibit the Exportation of all Linnen Rags, Glovers Clippings, Parchment Shreds, Calves Pates, and *Waterpieces. 1905 Daily Chron. 29 Nov. 1/7 A burglar who is said to have carried a '*water pistol' and to have thrown or fired some ammonia into the eyes of a householder is under remand at Woolwich. 1747 Gentl. Mag. XVII. 37/2 In chaffing-dish, tho' most of late Prefer the cleanlier *water-plate. 1822 Lamb Elia, Distant Corresp., This kind of dish..requires to be served up hot; or sent off in water-plates, that your friend may have it almost as warm as yourself. 1890 Century Mag. Apr. 916/2 We lunch by a *water-pocket that was filled by a storm 2 months ago. 1891 Pall Mall Gaz. 12 Jan. 7/1 The boiler consists of a cylindrical upper part..6 ft. long, and two lower prismatic water pockets also about 6 ft. in length. 1904 Daily Chron. 19 July 5/3 [Four persons] were crossing the Argentière Glacier to-day, when a water pocket burst, and the whole party were hurled against the rocks by the rush of water. 1679 Alsop Melius Inquir. I. i. 40 Your common Hackney Versifiers or *Water-Poets. 1660 R. Dacres Elem. Water-drawing 24 By which better appeared the vanity of the *water poyse. 1667 Phil. Trans. II. 496 The Sea..was.. much more Salt, the further we went; as I tryed by a Water-poise of Glass, with Quicksilver at the one end. 1772 T. Percival Ess. (1777) I. 342 Dr Hoffman, by means of a glass waterpoise divided by lines, examined hydrostatically several different kinds of water. 1884 *Water polo [see polo 2]. 1888 Field 25 Aug. 277/3 Water Polo Inter-Club Championship. 1919 W. T. Grenfell Labrador Doctor iii. 61 Our water polo games were also a great feature here, the water being warm. 1923 T. Sachs Compl. Swimmer (ed. 2) 151 Water polo differs from other games, not only in the irrelevancy of its name, but also in being a game that was made to order. 1980 Guinness Bk. Records 334/2 Water Polo was developed in England as 'Water Soccer' in 1869. 1884 Bower & Scott De Bary's Phaner. 45 Two varieties of stoma may be distinguished, which may briefly be termed air pores (or stomata), and *water-pores. 1888 Rolleston & Jackson Anim. Life 575 (Crinoidea) Water-pores, or short tubular canals with a median ciliated dilatation, open into the coelome from the exterior. 1565 B. Googe tr. Palingenius' Zodiac XI. QQj, The *Waterpourer, and..the Fishes two that flote. 1573 W. Bourne Regim. Sea (1580) 59b, The names of the Starres..Goates taile. Water pourers leg. 1817 M. Birkbeck Notes Journey Amer. 119 Water-mills, or, in defect of *water-power, steam-mills rise on the nearest navigable stream. 1836 Mrs. C. P. Traill Backw. Canada 89 There is great water-power, both as regards the river and the fine broad creek. a1861 T. Winthrop Life in Open Air (1863) 24 Far down, at some water-power nearest the reach of tide, a boom checks the march of this formidable body. 1871 C. Marshall Canadian Dominion 42 The saw-mills are built where a great water-power can be obtained. 1825 J. Nicholson Oper. Mech. 292 The hydrostatic or *water-press. 1849 J. Glynn Constr. Cranes 48 A self-acting crane..has been erected on the quay at Newcastle-on-Tyne... It is worked by *water pressure. 1829 Nat. Philos., Hydraulics iii. (U.K.S.) 29 What is called the *Water-pressure Engine, being, in fact, a steam-engine, worked by water instead of steam. 1839 Ure Dict. Arts 969 The engines at present employed in the drainage of coal-mines are:—1. The water-wheel, and water-pressure engine. 1853 Glynn Power Water 98 The first water-pressure engine used in England was erected..in the year 1765. 1804 New Hampshire Probate Rec. (1916) III. 755 We set off to Deborah Shackford,..the *Water Privilege belonging to said Estate. 1812 Mass. Spy 9 Sept. 3/5 To be Sold! A Water Privilege in Wrentham. 1822 Ibid. 31 July (Thornton) Valuable Mills and Water Privileges. 1849 Thoreau Week Concord Riv. Tuesday 230 Some of the finest water privileges in the country still unimproved on the former stream. 1877 Raymond Statist. Mines & Mining 243 Just below this lode..Armstrong & Co. have located an admirable mill-site and water-privilege. 1879 F. R. Stockton Rudder Grange i, I then went to a well belonging to a cottage near by where we had arranged for water-privileges, and filled two buckets with delicious water. 1679 J. Goodman Penit. Pard. I. iv. (1713) 114 We count the *Water-rack a very severe torture, to have that element forced down a man's throat, till all the vessels of his body are stretched and tympanized. 1806 tr. Mongolfier in Nicholson's Jrnl. Nat. Philos. XIV. 103 The following is the description of a *water-ram. 1829 Nat. Philos., Hydraulics ii. (U.K.S.) 20 The Water Ram or Bélier Hydraulique, as it was called by its inventor, M. Montgolfier, of Paris. 1877 Wood Nature's Teach., Usef. Arts x. 435 The water-ram with its globular valve. 1837 Dickens Pickw. xxvii, 'What d'ye think it [the money] was all for?'.. 'For the shepherd's *water-rate, Sammy.' 1839 —— Nickleby xiv, Having an uncle who collected a water-rate. 1802 R. Warner Tour N. Counties II. 285 Only 110 l. is received from the *water-rents of the houses to which the element is conducted. 1942 Chem. Abstr. XXXVI. 8428/1 (Index), *Water repellency. (See also Waterproofness.) 1955 Industr. & Engin. Chem. Sept. 1980/1 Some [finishes] add functional qualities, such as water repellency and shrink resistance. 1972 McGraw-Hill Yearbk. Sci. & Technol. 217/2 Water birds..were generally regarded as having attained perfection in water repellency. 1922 Encycl. Brit. XXX. 59/1 The surface of the dope should be *water-repellent. 1952 R. A. Pingree in H. C. Speel Textile Chemicals & Auxiliaries xx. 408 An acetate rayon fabric may tolerate a water repellent which is unacceptable to either viscose rayon or cotton. 1974 P. de Vries Glory of Hummingbird (1975) xv. 231 Testing a line of water-repellent trenchcoats. 1980 Gohl & Vilensky Textile Sci. vii. 132 Water repellent finishes can be divided into two categories: 1. water-proof finishes... 2. water resistant finishes which delay the absorption and penetration of water and..allow a degree of permeability to air. **1935** C. ELLIS *Chem. Synthetic Resins* I. xxxi. 656 A variation of this method, designed to improve the *water-resistance of the resins. **1966** *McGraw-Hill Encycl. Sci. & Technol.* XIII. 541/1 Linseed oil..was used to impart water- and weather-resistance. **1934** WEBSTER, *Water-resistant. **1946** *Nature* 19 Oct. 562/2 The water-proofing of soft fibre boards, surface treatment with a paraffin wax emulsion giving a water-resistant surface. **1971** C. BONINGTON *Annapurna South Face* 243 For high-altitude work it is not essential that it [*sc.* a garment] should be waterproof, but it needs to be water-resistant. **1980** Water-resistant [see *water-repellent* adj. and sb. above]. **1913** W. MCCULLOH *Conservation of Water* v. 99 The work done by the State of New York toward the..conservation of her *water resources is an exemplification of what may be done by..other states. **1971** P. GRESSWELL *Environment* 218 Twenty-nine River Authorities..are responsible for husbanding the water resources of entire river basins, from springs and streams to final exit into the sea. **1976** *National Observer* (U.S.) 10 Apr. 1/3 A water-resources engineer with the World Bank. **1980** *Jrnl. R. Soc. Arts* Feb. 129/2 Workshops dealt with subjects ranging from water resource management to human resource management. **1793** *Columbian Museum* (Philadelphia) Jan. 16 The purchase of the land, including the farm buildings..and *water rights, &c. would probably be at fifteen dollars per acre. **1891** R. WALLACE *Rural Econ. Austral. & N.Z.* xiii. 213 The question of water-right is also one urgently demanding legislation in Victoria. **1920** W. H. MALLOCK *Mem. Life & Lit.* xii. 175 He would..have had to buy from the neighbouring peasants certain way-leaves and water-rights. **1950** *N.Y. Times* 20 Apr. 1/3 He also said that bill threatened their water rights. *a* **1637** B. JONSON *Discov.* (1640) 97 Nay, if it were put to the question of the *Water-rimers workes, against Spencers; I doubt not, but they would find more Suffrages. **1653** WALTON *Angler* viii. 162 The Carp, if he have *water room and good feed, will grow to a very great bigness and length. **1675** H. TEONGE *Diary* (1825) 36 We have made a sayle for the starne of the ship, called a *water sayle. **1794** *Rigging & Seamanship* I. 127 *Sloop's Water-Sail*..It is ocasionally spread under the boom of the main-sail in fair winds. **1883** *Man. Seamanship for Boys* 38 A watersail sets under the spanker-boom end. **1925** A. B. ARMITAGE *Cadet to Commodore* 15 We dropped down on the tide, aided by a large watersail over the stern, to Garden Reach. **1933** P. MITCHELL *Deep Water* 201 [At Calcutta] the mud pilot..brought with him a water sail, like a small royal with the foot weighted and a rope fastened to each corner; this was lowered over the stern into the water. **1655** MARQ. WORCESTER *Cent. Inv.* §55 A double *Water-scrue, the innermost to mount the water, and the outermost for it to descend. **1773** W. EMERSON *Princ. Mech.* (ed. 3) 228 Archimedes's water screw. **1823** P. NICHOLSON *Pract. Builder* 409 The Water Screw Pump. **1708** J. C. *Compl. Collier* (1845) 21 Water which rises at the Coal-Shaft, may run into this *Water or half Shaft, to be drawn there by Horses or Water Wheels. **1869** R. B. SMYTH *Gold Fields Victoria* 625 *Water-shaft*, the drainage-shaft, usually the deepest shaft in a mine. **1886** *Cheshire Gloss.*, *Water-shaft*, salt-making term. A shaft sunk to collect the fresh water near the main shaft. **1577** HOLINSHED *Chron.* II. 1039/2 On the Saterday after,..[1382], earely in the morning, chaunced an other earthquake, or as some write, a *watershake, beeyng so vehemente, that it made the Shippes in the hauens to beate one againste an other, [etc.]. **1581** ANDRESON *Serm. at Paules Crosse* 101 That vniuersall Earthquake, and like watershake, whiche draue vs into present feare. **1805** R. W. DICKSON *Pract. Agric.* I. 537 On a red greet, and *water-shaken soil. **1810** J. BAILEY *Agric. Durham* 9 A moist soft loam..known by the..epithet of 'water shaken'. **1470** *Stat. Rolls Irel. 10 Edw. IV* c. 19 Repaireröunt le dit Gourge..come necessite requiert lessauntz..en la miente del file del auaunt dit ewe xxiiij. pees en laiour appelle le Kynges shard aultrement appelle le *Watersharde. *Ibid.*, Watirshard. **1844** *Zoologist* II. 421 A line running from Loch Spey to Loch Monar, the course of which is regulated by the *water-shears between the east and west coasts. **1847** *Blackw. Mag.* LXII. 162 The water-shier between the Spey and the Dee. **1546** *Gassar's Prognost.* c iij b, The cloudy sterre that is in the beginning of yᵉ *Water sheder of the Waterer [L. *apud initium effusionis aquæ Aquarii*]. **1769** A. MENZIES *Rep. to Commissioners for Annexed Estates* (1973) 83 There is not only soil but climate to fight against, as it lies within half a mile of the *water shire of Scotland. **1852** QUEEN VICTORIA *Jrnl.* 10 Sept. (1980) 74, I wore a white bonnet, a grey *water silk, and..my plaid scarf over my shoulder. **1926** *Glasgow Herald* 1 Apr. 8/4 The copies are bound in magnificent leather volumes with sheets of water-silks. **1953** C. DAY LEWIS *Italian Visit* iv. 47 Rosetted oxen move..The loose-kneed watersilk gait of Priestesses vowed to Love. **1839** URE *Dict. Arts* 748 The overlying *Watersill or sandstone. **1894** *Northumbld. Gloss.*, *Water-sill*, a bed of fine-grained sandstone lying immediately below the great limestone in the south-west of Northumberland. **1798** *Hull Advertiser* 13 Oct. 1/2 An excellent kitchen and scullery, in which there is a pipe for water, a *water sink, with other conveniences. **1890** *Nature* 27 Nov. 93 The water which flows out of Malham Tarn and disappears down a 'water-sink' to the south of the tarn is the stream which emerges at Malham Cove. **1908** *Blackw. Mag.* July 93/2 In this white pavement are found all the famous water-sinks that feed the streams far below. **1823** SCORESBY *Jrnl. Whale Fish.* 472 **Water-sky*, a dark appearance of the atmosphere, near the horizon, indicating clear water below it. **1881** tr. *Nordenskiöld's Voy. 'Vega'* I. x. 518 A blue water-sky was still visible out to sea, indicating that open water was to be found there. **1860** W. W. READE *Liberty Hall* I. v. 77 He listened to their semi-nautical oaths,..and their *water-slang with veneration. **1847** TENNYSON *Princess* VII. 198 Spill Their thousand wreaths of dangling *water-smoke. *a* **1903** 'MERRIMAN' *Last Hope* viii, Through the dazzling white of that which is known on these [Suffolk] coasts as the water-smoke the sky shone a cloudless blue. **1812** J. H. VAUX *Flash Dict.*, **Water-sneak*, robbing ships or vessels on a navigable river or canal, by getting on board unperceived, generally in the night. The water-sneak is lately made a capital offence. **1906** *Engineering* 21 Dec. 834/2 In this combined grease-eliminator and make-up-*water-softener there is, we understand, very little matter precipitated. **1930** L. MUNDAY *Mounty's Wife* xvii. 207 This has since been all changed owing to the installation of water softeners. **1974** *Encycl. Brit. Micropædia* X. 575/2 Water softeners usually consist of zeolite or an ion-exchange resin in a tank connected directly into the water system. **1974** *Trade Names Dict.* I. 85/1 Calgonite—Water softener. **1909** *Cent. Dict.* Suppl. 1435/3 Other types of *water-softening machines employ the same general principles. **1929** A. R. MARTIN *Water Softening: Base-Exchange or Zeolite Process* 6 The base-exchange process for water softening should be considered in relation to the quality of the water to be softened. **1964** N. G. CLARK *Mod. Org. Chem.* xii. 249 It [*sc.* ethylene diamine] is used as a solvent, and as an intermediate for agricultural chemicals and 'water-softening' agents. **1979** *Jrnl. R. Soc. Arts* Dec. 59/1 Presumably *water-solubility is the property which militates against the accumulation of sizeable deposits of potash (and soda) at, or near, the Earth's surface. **1922** *Water-soluble [see *fat-soluble* adj. s.v. FAT *sb.*² 6 c]. **1978** *N.Y. Times* 30 Mar. C7/4 Keep feeding lettuce with a weak application of water-soluble plant foot. **1849** J. GLYNN *Constr. Cranes* 56 The *water-space round the ram being full three-fourths of an inch. **1587** GOLDING *De Mornay* xxii. (1592) 333 Varro reporteth..that Numa vsed *Waterspelling, and had communication with Diuels. **1883** *Encycl. Brit.* XVI. 386 *Chloro-spinel*, grass-green with a yellowish white streak... **Water-spinel* colourless; from Ceylon. **1835** DICKENS *Let.* 18 Dec. (1965) I. 109 Our driver ..ingeniously drove the party into a '*water-splash'. **1844** —— *Mart. Chuz.* xxxvi, Yoho! down the pebbly dip, and through the merry water-splash, and up at a canter to the level road again. **1886** *Bicycling News* 1 Oct., Last Saturday, two riders on a tandem tricycle attempted to rush through Shepperton 'water splash'. **1902** C. G. HARPER *Holyhead Road* I. 229 The old road goes over what used to be a water-splash in the deep hollow. **1497** *Acc. Ld. High Treas. Scot.* I. 377 Item, that samyn day, in Cambuskynneth, for *water spowngis to the King, iij s. iiij d. **1508** DUNBAR *Tua Mariit Wemen* 437, I haif a water spunge for wa, within my wyde clokis, Than wring I it full wylely, and wetis my chekis. **1612** *Sc. Bk. Rates* in *Halyburton's Ledger* (1867) 292 Watter spounges for chirurgeans. **1950** *N.Z. Jrnl. Agric.* Feb. 193/2 Delustred acetate rayons also *water spot very readily; therefore,..they should never be sprinkled with water and ironed directly, or glazed patches which are difficult to remove will be formed. **1964** *McCall's Sewing* viii. 118/1 Test a scrap of your fabric first to be sure that it does not water-spot. *Ibid.* 118/2 Press [silk] with..a piece of tissue paper next to the fabric to prevent *water-spotting. **1944** U. P. HEDRICK *Fruits for Home Garden* vi. 51 Such shoots are called suckers, or *water-sprouts, and numbers of them are deleterious. **1976** *Yankee* Apr. 137/2 Thinning out old watersprouts and suckers will promote better fruiting. **1913** E. F. BENSON *Thorley Weir* i. 26 There was something so completely satisfying and suitable in this rough river-dress that he would not have added any embellishment to it, nor have expunged a single *water-stain or sun-bleach. **1940** *Chambers's Techn. Dict.* 901/2 *Water stain*.., a stain for wood, consisting of colouring matter dissolved in water. **1966** A. W. LEWIS *Gloss. Woodworking Terms* 114 *Water stain*, colouring matter or dyes dissolved in water and used to stain wood to the required shade. **1972** *Gloss. Terms Timber (B.S.I.)* 16 *Water stain*, discoloration caused by water coming into contact with the surface of the converted timber. **1775** J. WATSON *Halifax* 548 **Waterstead*, the Bed or Course of a river or brook. **1867** SMYTH *Sailor's Word-bk.*, *Water-stead*, an old name for the bed of a river. **187.** E. WAUGH *Tufts of Heather, Hermit Cobbler* iv, He fell..into th' wayterstid at th' back o' th' house. **1894** *Westm. Gaz.* 10 Apr. 2/3 (letter signed) A Radical Owner of *Water Stock. **1903** *Daily Chron.* 24 Nov. 4/3 Water stocks fell on the decision in regard to the New River dividends. **1884** BOWER & SCOTT *De Bary's Phaner.* 50 Other stomata..which may be called **Water-stomata* or *-pores*. **1585** *water stop [see STOP *sb.*² 8 a]. **1759** STERNE *Tr. Shandy* II. i, The great sluice or water-stop, where the English were terribly exposed to the shot..of St. Roch. **1912** *Chambers's Jrnl.* Apr. 220/2 The towns that cluster about these desert 'water-stops'. **1945** F. H. HUBBARD *Railroad Avenue* ii. 9 Consolidation engines have enormous tenders, but the water stops on Casey's division were far apart, and the water in his tank often would drop rather low if the engine were hauling a heavy train. **1951** *Archit. Rev.* CX. 345 (Advt.), The problem of making watertight expansion joints in flat concrete roofs can be solved by the use of Expandite rubber waterstops. These waterstops were developed in the first place for sealing joints in hydraulic structures and are widely used by hydraulic engineers. **1968** *Punch* 18 Dec. 873/1 My wife keeps urging me to diversify into coolants, sealants, waterstops, mastics and corrosion inhibitors. **1797** S. JAMES *Voy.* 38 The leak was above *water streak. **1833** *Penny Cycl.* I. 436/2 North America possesses an extensive *water-system on the Pacific slope. **1859** H. KINGSLEY *G. Hamlyn* xix, Having crossed the valley of the Belloury,..I had come on to the water system of another main river. **1704** SWIFT *Tale of Tub* ii. 59 What is..the Sea, but a Wastcoat of *Water-Tabby? **1928** *Observer* 8 Apr. 6 A Budapest company has just been granted permission..to place *water-taxis for hire on the Danube. **1974** LD. MANCROFT *Chinaman in Bath* xxxix. 182 The water-taxis which could do so much to ease London's traffic problems. **1978** *New York* 3 Apr. 12/1 (Advt.), Water taxis across our incredibly blue waters to other islands. **1877** WOOD *Nature's Teach., Optics* ii. 292 An instrument..called the *Water-Telescope. **1883** *Fisheries Exhib. Catal.* 360 Water Telescope, from Bohuslän. **1799** J. DALTON in *Mem. Lit. & Phil. Soc. Manch.* V. II. 374 For this purpose I took a thermometer tube..and filled it with pure water..From repeated trials agreeing in the result, I find, that the *water thermometer is at the lowest point of the scale it is capable of, that is, water is of the greatest density at 42° ½ of the mercurial thermometer. **1596** SHAKS. *Merch. V.* I. iii. 24 There be land rats, and water rats, *water theeues, and land theeues, I meane Pyrats. **1870** MORRIS *Earthly Par.* III. IV. 304 A Tyrrhenian water-thief. **1976** *National Observer* (U.S.) 3 July 13/6 (Advt.), Portable *water toothpick for travel and the office. **1928** G. B. SHAW *Intelligent Woman's Guide Socialism* lxxxi. 415 The *water torture of the Inquisition, in which the fluid was poured down the victims' throats until they were bloated to death. **1946** 'R. WEST' *Train of Powder* (1955) 8 Nuremberg..was also the water-torture, boredom falling drop by drop on the same spot on the soul. **1974** L. DEIGHTON *Spy Story* x. 105 What am I supposed to do, give them the water torture? **1976** *Times* 30 Aug. 8/5 Any individual..is worn down by the Chinese water torture of daily stress. **1983** *Daily Tel.* 12 May 4/8 A former county sheriff..and three former deputies were charged in Houston with using water torture to extract confessions from prisoners. **1887** SIR R. H. ROBERTS *In the Shires* iii. 37 In rear of the observatory a large *water-tower raised its head. **1887** *Sci. Amer.* 22 Jan. 53/2 The fall of a stand pipe or water tower, at Sheepshead Bay. **1898** 'MERRIMAN' *Roden's Corner* vi. 56 To the north of the waterworks..the curious may find to-day a few low buildings clustering round a water-tower. **1916** A. B. REEVE *Poisoned Pen* iii. 61 Four engines, two hook-and-ladders, a water-tower, the battalion chief and a deputy are hurrying to that fire. **1615** CHAPMAN *Odyss.* XIV. 477 When the *water-treader [ποντοπόρος νηῦς], farre away Had left the Land. **1855** *Gentl. Mag.* June 582 Mr. Buckingham, the once renowned boy water-treader of Flushing. **1862** M. D. COLT *Went to Kansas* 197 The homeopathic physician was called to see her yesterday, so she is under his treatment, while I have the privilege of giving her all the *water treatment I choose. **1966** 'G. BLACK' *You want to die, Johnny?* x. 180 That character who had apologised to himself for using the water treatment on Lee Wat. *a* **1877** KNIGHT *Dict. Mech.* III. 2646/2 When the fire passes *through* the tubes, they are properly flues. The term is, however, applied to pipes, whether *water-tubes or fire-tubes, below a certain diameter. **1888** ROLLESTON & JACKSON *Anim. Life* 575 (Crinoidea) Ciliated branched water-tubes depend from the ring and origins of the radial vessels and open into the coelome. **1971** B. SCHARF *Engin. & its Lang.* xiv. 204 In forced circulation boilers there is no need for the boiler drum to be above the water tubes. **1875** KNIGHT *Dict. Mech.*, *Water-tube Boiler. **1894** *Westm. Gaz.* 18 Oct. 8/2 The *Ardent*..is fitted with the Thornycroft water-tube boilers. **1963** *Times* 24 May (Suppl.) p. iv/7 It had 64 Babcock and Wilcox watertube boilers and eight sets of turbines coupled to three-phase 33⅓-cycle alternators generating at 11,000 volts. **1940** H. E. BAUGHMAN *Aviation Dict.* 187/2 **Water Tunnel*, a device similar to a wind tunnel, but using water as the fluid in which models are tested. **1965** *New Scientist* 5 Aug. 333/2 The commissioning..of the..outdoor test tank, and the impending completion of a flume (water tunnel), equips Hovercraft Development Limited with an entire range of skirt-testing apparatus. **1969** *Gloss. Aeronaut. & Astronaut. Terms (B.S.I.)* IV. 18 *Water tunnel*, an apparatus for producing a controlled stream of water or other liquid for fluid dynamic experiments. **1601** HOLLAND *Pliny* XVII. xiii. I. 515 The shoots and suckers that put out at the root, as also other *water-twigs. **1819** *Encycl. Brit.* Suppl. III. 395/1 The yarn produced by this mode of spinning is called *Water Twist. **1839** URE *Dict. Arts* 366 Fig. 347 is a diagram of Arkwright's original water-frame spinning machine, called afterwards the water-twist frame. **1844** G. DODD *Textile Manuf.* i. 33 The name 'water-twist' arose from the circumstance that..Arkwright's [machine] was worked by a water-wheel. **1878** BLAKELY *Dict. Commerc. Inform.*, *Water-twist*, a kind of cotton-twist, of which there are common, seconds, and best seconds. **1880** GEIKIE *Phys. Geog.* ii. 44 By the term *water-vapour, or aqueous-vapour, is meant the invisible steam always present in the air. **1908** *Westm. Gaz.* 31 Jan. 2/1 The latest statement by Sir William Huggins on the existence of water-vapour on Mars is that there is no conclusive proof. **1870** ROLLESTON *Anim. Life* p. lxxxvi, [In other Mollusca] a multi-ramified *water-vascular system appears to spread itself throughout the body, without becoming directly continuous with the blood-vessels. **1885** *Riverside Nat. Hist.* (1888) I. p. xx, In the jelly-fishes the stomach opens into four or more water-vascular canals or passages. **1867** J. HOGG *Microsc.* II. iii. 562 There remains..the ambulacral vessels of the Echinodermata. These are frequently termed '*water-vessels'. **1894** T. B. MIDDLETON in *Yachting* (Badm. Libr.) II. 146 '*Water wags' and 'Mermaids' of Dublin Bay. **1894** *Field* 9 June 838/1 Match for Waterwags, for a cup presented by the Dublin and Wicklow Railway Company. **1815** T. FORSTER *Atmos. Phenom.* 59 Some of these little cumuli..flying along rapidly between the showers, are..called by the vulgar *water waggons. **1844** H. STEPHENS *Bk. Farm* I. 251 The ominous scud is the usual harbinger of the rain-cloud, and is therefore commonly called 'messengers', 'carriers' or 'water-waggons'. **1904** (*Amer.*) *Dialect Notes* II. 402 'To be on the water wagon', to abstain from hard drinks. N.Y. **1927** *Daily Express* 3 Feb. 5/2 'Have a drink,' said Roger.., but Red stayed his hand at the decanter. 'Water-wagon?' asked Roger, surprised. **1928** G. B. SHAW *Intelligent Woman's Guide Socialism* lxxix. 397 The vast majority of modern drinkers..do not miss the extra efficiency they would enjoy on the water wagon. **1934** *Bulletin* (Sydney) 23 May 41/2 Excuse Harrie drinking soft stuff... He's on the water-waggon at present. **1971** R. DENTRY *Encounter at Kharmel* xii. 216 What, no grog? Are you supposed to be on the water waggon, skip? **13..** *Cursor M.* 6389 (Gött.) Þar þai had mekil *watir wan. **1598** SYLVESTER *Du Bartas* II. ii. I. *Ark* 413 The Camell *water-want [Fr. *souffre-soif*]. **1862** *Ann. Reg.* 27 The wilful murder of Edward Atkinson, *water-watcher. **1888** BARRIE *Auld Licht Idylls* (1892) 58 'Water-watchers,' as the bailiffs were sometimes called. **1778** [W. MARSHALL] *Minutes Agric.* 32 Nov. 1775, If possible, mix it perfectly full of sap, but perfectly free from *water-wet. **1804** A. HUNTER *Georg. Ess.* VI. 229 The clover..should be perfectly free from water-wet. **1767** S. PATERSON *Another Trav.* I. 102 That vile ribaldry called *water-wit. **1863** HAWTHORNE *Our Old Home, Up Thames* II. 143 The old rough water-wit for which the Thames used to be so celebrated. **1731** *Flying Post* 28 Jan. 2/2 A *Water-Woman was found suddenly dead, and..it was thought she was strangled. **1762** GOLDSM. *Ess., Fem. Warriors*, The water-women of Plymouth. **1600** SURFLET *Country Farm* VII. xv. 824 The other sort of *water woode is the willow. **1750** W. ELLIS *Mod. Husbandm.* II. ii. 139 (E.D.D.) An alder, a withy, a willow or other water-wood hedge. **1871** TYLOR *Prim. Cult.* xv. II. 192 Africa displays well the rites of *water-worship. *Ibid.* xvi. II. 248 Savage *water-worshippers. **1598** SYLVESTER *Du Bartas* II. i. *Eden* 401 When pale Phlegm, or saffron-colour'd Choler, ..print upon our Understanding's Tables; That, *Water-wracks; this other, flamefull Fables. **1658** *Melrose Regality Rec.* (S.H.S.) I. 174 Quhen tymber treis or onie uther fewall or watter wrak cumes doune the river and lands there. **1834** PRINGLE *Afr. Sk.* ii. 151 The remains of water-wrack.. afforded striking proof that at certain seasons this diminutive rill becomes a mighty..flood.

30. Prefixed to names of animals to denote species inhabiting the water, as ***water-animal, -bat, -beast, -beetle, -bird, -butterfly, -coot, -eel, -finch, -frog, -gnat, †-hydra, -insect, -louse, -raven, -reptile, -shrew(-mouse), -shrimp, -snail, -toad.*** Also **water-adder**, any aquatic serpent resembling an adder; **water-antelope** = WATERBUCK; **water-ask** *dial.*, a newt; **water-beetle**, a beetle of the group *Hydradephaga*; **water-blackbird**, the dipper, *Cinclus aquaticus*; **water-boa**, the anaconda; **water-boatman**, a water-bug of either of the families *Notonectidæ* or *Corixidæ* (*Corisidæ*); **water-buffalo** = *water-cow*; **water-bug**, (*a*) any heteropterous insect of aquatic habit; (*b*) *U.S.* the cockroach, *Blatta orientalis*; **water-bull**, a legendary amphibious animal resembling a bull; **water-cavy** = *water-hog*; **water-chat**, a bird of the South American group *Fluvicolinæ*; **water-cow**, (*a*) the common domestic Indian buffalo, *Bos bubalus* or *Bubalus buffelus*; (*b*) a legendary amphibious animal resembling a cow; cf. *water-bull*; **water-crake**, †(*a*) the water-ouzel or dipper, *Cinclus aquaticus*; (*b*) the spotted crake, *Porzana maruetta*; (*c*) the water-rail, *Rallus aquaticus*; **water-creeper, -cricket**, the larva of the stone-fly; **water-crow**, (*a*) the dipper, *Cinclus aquaticus*; (*b*) the coot, *Fulica atra*; (*c*) *southern U.S.* the snakebird, *Plotus anhinga*; **water-deer**, a small Chinese musk-deer, *Hydropotes inermis*; **water-devil**, (*a*) the larva of the great water-beetle, *Hydrophilus piceus* (Ogilvie 1850); (*b*) *U.S.* 'the dobson or hellgrammite' (*Cent. Dict.*); **water-doe**, a female waterbuck; **water-eagle** (see quot.); **water-eft** = *water-newt*; **water-flea**, any of the small crustaceans that hop like fleas; **water-hog**, the capybara; **water-junket**, an alleged name for the sandpiper; **water-lawyer** *jocular*, a shark; **water-leech** = LEECH *sb.*[2] 1; **water-lizard**, a newt or other lizard-like animal inhabiting the water; **water-mite** = *water-tick*; **water-moccasin** *U.S.* a venomous aquatic pit viper, *Agkistrodon piscivorus*, found in the southern United States; also, one of several harmless water snakes resembling *A. piscivorus*; = *cotton-mouth* s.v. COTTON *sb.*[1] 10 and MOCCASIN 3; **water mongoose**, a dark brown mongoose, *Atilax paludinosus*, found in marshes and near rivers in central and southern Africa; **water monitor** = *Nile monitor* s.v. NILE; **water-moth**, a caddis-fly; **water-newt**, an aquatic newt, a triton; **water-opossum** = YAPOCK; **water-ouzel** (see OUZEL 2c); **water-ox** = *water-cow*; †**water-parrot**, some microscopic insect; **water-pheasant**, (*a*) the pheasant-tailed jacana, *Hydrophasianus chirurgus*; (*b*) the pintail duck; (*c*) the goosander, *Mergus merganser*; **water-piet** (see PIET 1b); **water-pipit**, *Anthus aquaticus*; **water-puppy** = WATER-DOG 3b; **water-rabbit** *U.S.*, the swamp-hare of the Mississippi valley, *Lepus aquaticus*; **water-rattle, -rattler**, the diamond rattlesnake, *Crotalus adamanteus*; **water-rattle-snake**, an incorrect name for the water-viper; **water-salamander** (see SALAMANDER 1b); **water-scorpion**, an aquatic bug of the family *Nepidæ*; **water-skater** = *water-strider* below; †**water-softling** (see quot.); **water-strider** = *pond-skater* s.v. POND *sb.* 4; **water-thrush**, (*a*) the water-ouzel or dipper; (*b*) a bird of the American genus *Seiurus*; **water-tick** = WATER-SPIDER; **water-tiger**, a beetle of the genus *Dytiscus* or family *Dytiscidæ*; **water tortoise**, an aquatic tortoise of the family Pelomedusidæ, native to Africa or South America, esp. *Pelomedusa subrufa*; **water-viper**, any poisonous aquatic snake, esp. *Ancistrodon piscivorus*; **water-weasel** [= G. *wasserwiesel*], an otter; **water-wolf** [cf. G. *wasserwolf*], a rapacious aquatic animal; in quots. applied to the pike [cf. L. *lupus*] and the otter.

1398 TREVISA *Barth. De P.R.* XVIII. ix. (1495) 759 *Water adders dwelle in brymmes of waters. **14..** *Nom.* in Wr.-Wülcker 705/37 *Hic idrus*, a watyrnedyre. **1691** RAY *Creation* I. (1692) 62 Fishes and other *Water-Animals cannot abide without the use of it [*sc.* air]. **1875** W. H. DRUMMOND *Large Game S. & S.E. Afr.* 367 The *water-antelope (*Kobus ellipsiprymnus*). **1820** *Marmaiden of Clyde* xviii. in *Edin. Mag.* VI. 423 The *water-asks, sae cauld and saft, Crawl'd ower the glittie flure. **1892** JANE BARLOW *Irish Idylls* v. 114 She's not the fool, anyway, to be dhrinkin' out o' wather-pools thick wid them black wather-asks, that 'ud lep down your throath as soon as look at you. **1681** GREW *Musæum* I. §iv. i. 54 Barlæus mentions a *Water-Bat, which the Natives of Brasile call Guacucua. **1398** TREVISA *Barth. De P.R.* v. xxxv. (1495) 147 Some *water beestes doon brethe as the dolphyn. *c* **1440** *Promp. Parv.* 372/2 Otur, watyr beest, *lutricius*. **1668** CHARLETON *Onomast.* 46 *Hydrocantharus*, the *Water-beetle. **1771** *Phil. Trans.* LXI. 316 The *dytisci* or water-beetles. **1826** KIRBY & SP. *Entomol.* IV. xlv. 254 The common water-beetle (*Dytiscus marginalis*). *c* **1440** *Promp. Parv.* 127/1 Doppar, or dydoppar, *watyr byrde, *mergulus*. **1803** LEYDEN *Scenes Infancy* II. xxii, The water-birds..Oft rouse the peasant from his tranquil dream. **1917** *Blackw. Mag.* Nov. 645/2 Large water-birds rose from the river. **1678** RAY *Willughby's Ornith.* II. xv. 235 It is as big, or a little bigger than a *Water-Blackbird, or Crake. **1802** SHAW *Gen. Zool.* III. 345 *Water Boa. *Boa Enydris.* **1863** BATES *Nat. Amazons* iii. (1864) 60 The hideous Sucurujú, or water boa (Eunectes Murinus), which sometimes attacks man. **1871** KINGSLEY *At Last* xiii, The Huillia, Anaconda, or Water-boa, bears only a few large round spots. **1815** KIRBY & SP. *Entomol.* iv. (1818) I. 109 The *water boatman, (*Notonecta glauca*, L.) an insect related to the *Cimicidæ*..made me suffer still more severely. **1910** G. H. CARPENTER in *Encycl. Brit.* XIII. 261/1 The *Notonectidæ*, or 'water-boatmen'... By means of the oar-like hind-legs they swim actively through the water with the ventral surface upwards. **1894** *Outing* XXIV. 438/1 A rude wooden plow,..drawn by the clumsy Asiatic or *water buffalo. **1750** GLANDVILLE in W. Ellis *Mod. Husb.* IV. II. 71 Of *Water-bugs.—I have made Observations on Bugs of different Kinds in stagnate Waters. **1778** J. CARVER *Trav. N. Amer.* xviii. 493 The Water Bug.. has many legs, by means of which it passes over the surface of the water with such incredible swiftness that [etc.]. **1816** KIRBY & SP. *Entomol.* xviii. (1818) II. 364 The common water-bug (*Gerris lacustris*, Latr.), though it never goes under water, will sometimes swim upon the surface. **1868** LOUISA M. ALCOTT *Little Women* xii, Fred..did his best to upset both [the other boats] by paddling about in a wherry like a disturbed water-bug. **1901** LEE BACON *Houseboat on Nile* 38 Why did we want hedgehogs on a dahabéah? Nothing more or less than that they are supposed to eat water-bugs. **1726–31** WALDRON *Descr. Isle of Man* (1865) 43 The *water-bull. **1815** SCOTT *Let. to Morritt* 22 Dec., The persuasion of the solitary shepherds who approach its [a lake's] banks, is, that it is tenanted by a very large amphibious animal called by them a water-bull. **1901** RHYS *Celtic Folklore* I. iv. 284 The water-bull or *tarroo ushtey*, as he is called in Manx,..is described as a sort of bull disporting himself about the pools and swamps. **1668** CHARLETON *Onomast.* 39 *Perla*..the Dragon-Fly, or Adders-Boult, and *Water-Butterflies. **1681** GREW *Musæum* I. §vii. i. 157 Water-Butterfly, because they most frequent Rivers and watry places. **1885** *Riverside Nat. Hist.* (1888) V. 82 The gigantic *Water Cavy, or Capybara. **1837** SWAINSON *Nat. Hist. Birds* II. 5 The *water-chats (*Fluvicolinæ*), which seem to connect the tyrant shrikes to the flycatching family. **1852** D. M. MOIR *Poet. Wks.* II. 155 On the lakelet blue, the *water-coot Oar'd forth with her sable young. **1827** SCOTT *Jrnl.* 23 Nov., A set of his kinsmen, ..believing that the fabulous *Water Cow inhabited a small lake near his house, resolved to drag the monster into day. **1895** *Antiquary* July 217 A water-cow is said to inhabit St. Mary's Loch near Yarrow. **1678** RAY *Willughby's Ornith.* II. vii. 149 The Water-Ouzel or *Water-Crake: Merula aquatica. **1802** MONTAGU *Ornith. Dict.*, Ouzel-Water... Provincial, Water Crake. **1811** COL. HAWKER *Diary* (1893) I. 35, I knocked down 15 snipes and 2 water crakes. **1837** KIRKBRIDE *Northern Angler* 35 The Stone Fly..is bred from an insect, found under large stones in the river, called the water cricket, or *creeper. *c* **1711** PETIVER *Gazophyl.* VII. Tab. 70 *Water Cricket,..This is a slow creeping Insect found at the bottom of Ponds amongst the Weeds. **1855** KINGSLEY *Glaucus* (1878) 207 The most interesting of all the tribes of the Naiads..are the little water-cricket. **1398** TREVISA *Barth. De P.R.* XII. xl. (1495) 156 Some fowles haue galles pryuely hydde in a gutte as culuours or douues and *water crowes and swallowes. **1544** TURNER *Avium Præcip.* B 3, Morpetenses..cornicem uocant aquaticum [*marg.* a water craw]. **1661** LOVELL *Hist. Anim. & Min.* 146 The Water Crow..the skinne of which is used to be worne upon the stomach causing concoction. **1804** BEWICK *Brit. Birds* II. 16 Water Ouzel. Water Crow, Dipper, or Water Piot. **1882** *Proc. Berwick. Nat. Club* IX. 504 Of the Thrush family, the Dipper or Watercrow frequented all the streams. **1877–82** *Cassell's Nat. Hist.* III. 63 The Chinese *Water Deer. *Hydropotes inermis.* **1850** R. G. CUMMING *Hunter's Life S. Afr.* (1902) 121/2 A troop of beautiful *water does. **1891** *Century Dict.*, *Water eagle, the fish hawk or osprey. (Rare.) **1895** RIDER HAGGARD *Heart of World* xxv. (1899) 340 Here and there a human corpse, over which already the water-eagles began to gather. **1447** BOWER *Fordun's Scotichron.* XIV. xxxi. (1759) II. 376 Als sikir for to hald as a *water eeil. **1768** G. WHITE *Selborne, To Pennant* 27 July, The *water-eft has not, that I can discern, the least appearance of any gills. *a* **1400** *Nominale* (Skeat) 793 *Freseie et pynceuole*, Nytcrowe and *watirfynche. **1585** HIGINS *Junius' Nomencl.* 74/2 *Pulex aquaticus*,..a *water flea. **1752** J. HILL *Hist. Anim.* 52 The smooth short-horned Dytiscus ..is called by some Pulex aquaticus, the water Flea. **1866** E. C. RYE *Brit. Beetles* 66 The *Gyrini*, commonly known as 'water-fleas', 'whirlwigs', or 'whirligigs'. *a* **1050** *Chrodegang's Rule* (Napier) 96 *Wæterfrocgan hwilon hi ma ȝesihð of wætere, & swaþeah secað to fullicum morseohtrum. **1561** DAUS tr. *Bullinger on Apoc.* (1573) 225b, They play the waterfrogs, singyng croake croake. **1655** WALTON *Angler* xx. (1661) 242 Lebault allows Water-frogs to be good meat..if they be fat. **1731** CATESBY *Nat. Hist. Carolina* II. 70 The Water-Frog. **1877** WOOD *Nature's Teach., Usef. Arts* xiii. 467 The common *Water-gnat (Gerris), which may be seen in almost any piece of fresh water. **1774** GOLDSM. *Nat. Hist.* III. 191 The Capibara resembles an hog of about two years old,..some naturalists have called it the *Water-hog. **1865** TYLOR *Early Hist. Man.* x. 291 He had loaded his stomach with water-hog. **1717** PARNELL *Battle Frogs & Mice* I. 110 Lo! from the deep a *Water-Hydra rose. **1706** PHILLIPS (ed. Kersey), *Notonecta*, certain *water Insects, not much unlike small Beetles. **1774** GOLDSM. *Nat. Hist.* VI. 166 Whether it be that they [gold and silver fish] feed on the water-insects, too minute for our observation, or [etc.]. **1852** MACGILLIVRAY *Brit. Birds* IV. 351 *Actitis Hypoleucos.* The White-breasted Weet-weet. Common Sandpiper. Willywicket. *Water Junket. Fiddler. **1794** *Sporting Mag.* III. 50 A *water-lawyer, or, in plainer terms a shark was caught last month near Workington. **1382** WYCLIF *Prov.* xxx. 15 *Water lechis two ben doȝtris, seiende, Bring on, bring on. *c* **1460** J. RUSSELL *Bk. Nurture* 874 His shon or slyppers [to be] as browne as is þe waturleche. **1608** TOPSELL *Serpents* 212 Of the Nevte or *Water Lizard. **1646** SIR T. BROWNE *Pseud. Ep.* III. xiv. 139 Such an humidity is observed in Newtes, or water-Lizards. **1885** *Riverside Nat. Hist.* (1888) III. 429 The family of water-lizards, the Varanidæ. **1750** GLANDVILLE in W. Ellis *Mod. Husb.* IV. II. 71 Of *Water-lice.—I have often seen these, in stagnate Waters... They are very swift in Motion. **1774** GOLDSM. *Nat. Hist.* VII. 246 The wood-louse, the water-louse, and the scorpion never acquire wings. **1750** GLANDVILLE in W. Ellis *Mod. Husb.* IV. II. 72 Of *Water-maggots, or Grubs.—I have seen various kinds of these in stagnate Waters. **1816** KIRBY & SP. *Entomol.* xxiii. (1818) II. 365 The little *water-mites (*Hydrachna*) may be seen in every pool..working their little legs with great rapidity. **1821** T. NUTTALL *Jrnl. Trav. Arkansa* ix. 216 The other frequents water, and is called the *water-mocksin. **1842, 1853** [see MOCCASIN 3]. **1884** 'MARK TWAIN' *Huck. Finn* xviii. 169 If you'll come down into de swamp I'll show you a whole stack of water-moccasins. **1931** [see COPPERHEAD 1b]. **1976** *National Observer* (U.S.) 7 Aug. 8/5 Most of his patients have been bitten by one of the three pit vipers—rattlesnakes, copperhead moccasins, or water moccasins. **1919** F. W. FITZSIMONS *Nat. Hist. S. Afr.: Mammals* II. 26 The *Water Mungoose is common throughout South Africa, and extends north as far as the Equator. **1971** *Stand. Encycl. S. Afr.* III. 246/2 The marsh or water mongoose..inhabits thick vegetation along river-banks and marshes over the greater part of Africa south of the Sahara. **1947** J. STEVENSON-HAMILTON *Wild Life S. Afr.* xxxv. 316 *Varanus niloticus*, or the *water monitor, is found in reeds and rocks, close to the water's edge. **1974** M. HASTINGS *Dragon Island* v. 47 The water monitor can grow to more than seven feet. **1668** CHARLETON *Onomast.* 58 *Tinea aquatica*, the *Water-Moth. **1854** A. ADAMS, etc. *Man. Nat. Hist.* 216 The Water-Moths and their larvæ are well known to the angler as bait, under the names of Caddice-Flies and Caddice-Worms. *Ibid.* 219 Water-Moths (Phryganeidæ). **1668** CHARLETON *Onomast.* 26 *Lacerta Venenata aquatica*, the *Water Newt or Evet. **1768** G. WHITE *Selborne, To Pennant* 18 June, The *salamandra aquatica* of Ray (the water-newt or eft) will frequently bite at the angler's bait. **1858** WOOD *Common Obj. Country* iv. (1860) 48 Two species of these creatures are found in this country, the common Water-Newt and the Smooth Newt. **1846** WATERHOUSE *Mammalia* I. 533 The Yapock, or *Water-Opossum. **1863** W. C. BALDWIN *Afr. Hunting* viii. 356, I had selected eight of my best *water-oxen. **1884** *Littell's Living Age* CLXI. No. 2077. 88 Water-oxen turned up their noses at us. **1771** *Phil. Trans.* LXI. 242 The *water parrot..is represented..as hermaphrodite. **1781–2** T. JEFFERSON *Notes Virginia* (1787) 118 (List of birds) *Water-pheasant. **1815** *Sporting Mag.* XLV. 256 A water pheasant, a bird not very common, was shot..near Lewes. **1900** POLLOK & THOM *Sports Burma* ii. 34 The water-fowl..are very numerous, but none of them are worth mentioning excepting the water-pheasant. **1881** DRESSER *List European Birds* 13 *Anthus spinotella*, *Water-Pipit. **1896** A. G. BUTLER *Brit. Birds* I. 205 The Water-Pipit. *Anthus spipoletta*, Linn. **1859** BARTLETT *Dict. Amer.* (ed. 2), *Water-Dogs*,..; sometimes called *Water-puppies and Ground-puppies. **1876** *Forest & Stream* 20 July VI. 385/3 The water puppy (*Menobranchus lateralis*) inhabits the lake [Erie]. **1864** WEBSTER, *Water-rabbit. **1877–82** *Cassell's Nat. Hist.* IV. 317 The *water-rattle..abounds in East Florida, the Gulf States, and Mexico. **1736** MORTIMER in *Phil. Trans.* XXXIX. 254 This Sort is commonly called in Carolina, the *Water Rattle-Snake, not that it hath a Rattle, but from the Likeness of its Colour, and its Bite being as mortal. **1601** HOLLAND *Pliny* XI. xxxvii. I. 332 Some reasonlesse creatures ..are by nature bald, as..certaine *water Ravens [L. *corvi aquatici*]. **1825** SCOTT *Betrothed* xxiii, Watching for such small fish or *water-reptiles as might chance to pass by its lonely station. **1681** GREW *Musæum* I. §vii. iii. 176 The *Water-Scorpion..may be easily known by its pointed Tail. **1753** *Chambers' Cycl.* Suppl. s.v. *Scorpion*, Water Scorpion, *scorpio palustris*,..is a very thin and light little creature, yet is but a very slow mover. **1826** KIRBY & SP. *Entomol.* IV. xxxviii. 55 The water-scorpion tribe. **1861** HULME tr. *Moquin-Tandon* II. IV. i. 226 The Grey Nepa (Nepa Cinerea, Linn.), commonly called Water Scorpion or Water Spider. **1769** G. WHITE *Selborne, To Pennant* 8 Dec., De Buffon, I know, has described the *water shrew-mouse; but still I am pleased to find you have discovered it in Lincolnshire. **1770** PENNANT *Brit. Zool. Illustr.* IV. 83 Water Shrew-mouse. **1771** —— *Syn. Quadrupeds* 308 Water Shrew. **1860** GOSSE *Rom. Nat. Hist.* 215 Almost the tiniest of all quadrupeds, the water-shrew. **1750** GLANDVILLE in W. Ellis *Mod. Husb.* IV. II. 72 Of the *Water-shrimp.—I have seen a Sort of Insect, in stagnate Waters, to swim on his Side in a swift Motion, almost in Shape like a Sea-shrimp, very transparent. **1883** G. C. DAVIES *Norfolk Broads* iii. 21 The water-shrimp is the favourite bait for them [perch]. **1941** STEINBECK & RICKETTS *Sea of Cortez* xvi. 164 We had sat beside the little pool and watched..the *water-skaters. **1977** *Country Life* 26 May 1394/3 All you had to do was brush aside the green weed and the spider-like 'water skaters' and bow down to slake your thirst. **1562** TURNER *Herbal* II. 52 Made lyke a litle *water snayle or a crooked rammis horne. **1655** MOUFET & BENNET *Health's Improv.* xii. 109 Water-rails..feed upon water-snails and water-flies. **1835–6** *Todd's Cycl. Anat.* I. 626/1 Examining the young of the viviparous water-snail. **1656** W. DU GARD tr. *Comenius' Gate Lat. Unl.* §158. 47 There are also Sea-spiders, having neither bloud, nor fat, nor prickles (they call them *Water-softlings). **1952** J. CLEGG *Freshwater Life Brit. Isles* 197 The Pond Skaters or *Water Striders.. are larger creatures. **1973** Water-strider [see *pond-skater*]. **1668** CHARLETON *Onomast.* 108 Trynga..the *Water-Thrush. **1808–13** A. WILSON & BONAPARTE *Amer. Ornith.* (1831) II. 125 Turdus Aquaticus, Wilson. Water Thrush. **1872** COUES *Key N. Amer. Birds* 106 *Seiurus noveboracensis.* Water Thrush. *Ibid.*, *S. ludovicianus.* Large-billed Water Thrush. **1864** WEBSTER, *Water-tick. **1870** P. M. DUNCAN *Blanchard's Transf. Insects* 436 The *Hydrachnidæ*, or water ticks or mites. **1889** MARY E. BAMFORD *Up & Down Brooks* 59 Those beetles known as the *Water-tigers, or Dytiscidæ. **1750** GLANDVILLE in W. Ellis *Mod. Husb.* IV. II. 69, I have seen a *Water-toad to ride a Carp till he has starved it to Death. **1774** GOLDSM. *Nat. Hist.* VII. 106 Of this animal there are several varieties; such as the Water and the Land Toad... The water toad is not so large as the other. **1835** A. SMITH *Diary* 11 Mar. (1939) I. 309 Water has been getting more scarce every year. They eat the *water tortoise. **1935** *Discovery* Nov. 330/2 Water tortoises..lay basking on the lily pads. **1974** *Stand. Encycl. S. Afr.* X. 527/1 In Southern

Africa there are both land and water tortoises. **1736** MORTIMER *Nat. Hist. Carolina* in *Phil. Trans.* XXXIX. 254 *Vipera Aquatica*: The *Water Viper. **1611** COTGR. s.v. *Belette*, An Otter, or *water Weesill. **1674** tr. *Scheffer's Lapland* 140 There are found water-weezels, red and white, chiefly in the pools near the Sea. **1834** MEDWIN *Angler in Wales* II. 162 No animal is so hard-biting as an otter.. None but a very *varmint* dog..will face one of these water-weazels a second time. **1606** S. GARDINER *Bk. Angling* 26 Sanguinarie souldiers, the Pike and *water-wolues of the Ocean of this worlde. **1865** KINGSLEY *Herew.* xxix. *note*, Innumerable eels, great water-wolves and pickerel perches [etc.]. **1907** *Athenæum* 10 Aug. 158/2 The poor otter, against which, as the 'water-wolf', ruthless war is waged.

31. In combinations denoting vegetable growths that live in water, as ***water-frond***, ***-fruit***, ***-herb***, ***-herbage***, ***-plant***, ***shrub***; also prefixed to plant-names to designate species or varieties that live in water (or, sometimes, that contain or emit water), as ***water-avens***, ***-chickweed***, ***-crowfoot***, ***-figwort***, ***gladiole***, ***-gladiolus***, ***-orchid***, ***-palm***, ***-ranunculus***, ***-reed***, ***-rush***, ***-speedwell***, ***-tupelo***. Also **† water agrimony** (see AGRIMONY 2 c); **water-aloe** = WATER-SOLDIER; **water-apple**, the sweet-sop, *Anona squamosa*; **water archer** (see ARCHER 6); **water-ash**, any of several North American ash trees, esp. *Fraxinus caroliniana*; also = *box elder* s.v. BOX *sb.*[1] 3 b; **water-bean**, the Egyptian water-lily, *Nelumbium speciosum*; **water-beech**, (*a*) the American plane-tree, *Platanus occidentalis*; (*b*) the American hornbeam, *Carpinus caroliniana*; **water-betony**, = *water-figwort*; **water-blinks** (see BLINKS 2); **water-blob** *dial.*, a name for the marsh-marigold and similar plants; **water-blossom** = WATER-BLOOM 2; **water-buttercup** (see BUTTERCUP 2); **water-caltrop** (see CALTROP 3); **water-cat's-tail** = CAT'S-TAIL 2 b; **water-chestnut**, the saligot; **† water dragon**, *Calla palustris*; **water-dropwort** (see DROPWORT 2); **water-elder**, the guelder rose; **water-elm**, = PLANER-TREE; **water-feather (-foil)** = *water-violet*; **water-fern** (see OSMUND[2] 2); **water flag** (see FLAG *sb.* 1 b); **water-flannel**, a fresh-water alga, *Conferva crispa*, the matted filaments of which resemble flannel; **water germander** (see GERMANDER); **water gillyflower** = *water-violet*; **water gum**, a name for various trees of the Australian genera *Tristania* and *Callistemon*; **water-gut**, an alga, *Ulva enteromorpha*, which when floating resembles the intestines of an animal; **water-hemlock** (see HEMLOCK *sb.* 1 c); **water-hemp** (see HEMP *sb.* 5); **water-horehound** (see HOREHOUND 1 b); **water hyacinth**, an aquatic herb, *Eichhornia crassipes*, of the family Pontederiaceæ, native to tropical America and bearing large blue flowers; **water-hyssop** (see quot.); **water-lemon**, the edible fruit of a species of passion-flower, *Passiflora laurifolia*; **water-lentil** (see LENTIL 1 b); **water-lettuce**, the tropical duckweed, *Pistia Stratiotes*; **water-locust**, a species of locust-tree, *Gleditschia monosperma*, growing in watery or swampy ground; **† water-mango** (see MANGO 3); **water maple** = *red maple* (see MAPLE 1 b and *red maple* s.v. RED *a.* 17 d); **water-milfoil** (see MILFOIL 2); **water-moss**, a moss of the aquatic genus *Fontinalis*; **water-net**, a fresh-water alga, *Hydrodictyon utriculare*; **water-nut** = *water-chestnut*; **water-oats** = *wild rice* (RICE *sb.*[2] 4); **water-pennywort** (see PENNYWORT 2); **water-pimpernel** (see PIMPERNEL 3 b); **water-plantain** (see PLANTAIN[1] 2); **water-purpie** *Sc.*, brooklime, *Veronica Beccabunga*; **water-purslane** (see PURSLANE 2); **water-radish** (see quots.); **water-rice** = *wild-rice*, RICE *sb.*[2] 4; **† water-rose** = WATER-LILY; **water sallow** (see quot.); **† water-shield**, a plant of the sub-order *Cabombaceæ*, having shield-like leaves; **water-smartweed**, the American plant *Polygonum acre*; **water-sorrel** (see SORREL *sb.*[1] 1 b); **water-starwort** (also **-star**, **-stargrass**) (see STARWORT 3); **water-target** = *water-shield*; **water-torch**, the reed-mace, *Typha latifolia*; **water-trefoil**, the bogbean or buckbean; **water-violet** [= G. *wasserveil*, *-viole*], the feather-foil, *Hottonia palustris*; **water-withe**, **-withy**, *Vitis caribæa* of the W. Indies; **water-yarrow** = *water-violet*.

1731 MILLER *Gard. Dict.* s.v. *Aloides*, Aloides;.. Stratiotes foliis Aloes semine longo... The *Water-Aloe, or Fresh-Water Soldier. **1855** ANNE PRATT *Flower. Pl.* V. 192 *Stratiotes aloides* (Water-Soldier)..is often called Water Aloe. **1696** SLOANE *Catal. Plant. Jamaica* 205 *Water-Apple, or Sweet-Apple. **1760** J. LEE *Introd. Bot.* App. 305 Apple, Water, *Annona*. **1709** J. LAWSON *New Voy. Carolina* 93 The *Water-Ash is brittle. **1717** *Petiveriana* III. 185 Water-Ash. Is brittle, the Bark is Food for the Bevers. **1819** E. DANA *Geogr. Sk.* 171 The soil is..thickly covered with timber; such as various species of oak and water ash. **1958** G. A. PETRIDES *Field Guide to Trees & Shrubs* 35 Water Ash... A small tree of southern swamps. **1777** LIGHTFOOT *Flora Scot.* I. 274 Geum..rivale. Red *Water Avens. **1832** LYTTON *Eugene Aram* I. vi, The common enchanter's night-shade, the silver weed, and the water-aven [*sic*]. **1883** *Longman's Mag.* July 308 The marshy water-avens has exactly the same dusky purplish-yellow tint as the marshy comarum. **1846** LINDLEY *Veg. Kingd.* 414 *Nelumbiaceæ*. *Water Beans. **1850** OGILVIE, Water-bean. **1770** J. R. FORSTER tr. *Kalm's Trav. N. Amer.* I. 67 *Platanus occidentalis*, the *water-beech. **1852** MORFIT *Tanning & Currying* (1853) 93 It takes the name of buttonwood, sycamore, plane-tree, and water-beech, according to locality. **1578** LYTE *Dodoens* I. xxxi. 44 Called..in English Broune wurte, and *Water Betony. **1782** W. CURTIS *Browntail Moth* 6 Others..as the *Phalæna Verbasci*, or Water Betony Moth, which appears to be equally fond of the Mullein and Water Betony. **1860** MAYNE *Expos. Lex.*, Water betony. **1821** CLARE *Vill. Minstrel* I. 77 And sigh with anxious, eager dream, For *water-blobs amid the stream. **1884** W. PHILLIPS in *Trans. Shropshire Archæol. Soc.* VII. 285 Though the appearance of the '*water-blossom' has often been observed and examined, very little is known of the causes from which it originates. **1906** *Rep. Brit. Assoc. Adv. Sci.* 759 *Microcystis roseopersicinus*..formed a striking pink 'water blossom'. **1870** *Blackw. Mag.* Oct. 469/2 Those long sweeping rushy stalks which bear the pretty white blossom called the *water-buttercup. **1597** GERARDE *Herbal* II. cclxxxiv. 676 *Water Caltrops hath long slender stalkes, growing vp and rising from the bottome of the water. **1681** GREW *Musæum* II. §iii. ii. 232 The Water-Caltrop. *Tribulus aquaticus*. **1658** ROWLAND tr. *Moufet's Theat. Ins.* I. xiv. 969 The eyes are black, as the horns are also, which are swoln like *water-cats-tails. **1854** A. ADAMS etc. *Man. Nat. Hist.* 402 The *Water-Chesnut (*Trapa natans*). **1870** *Pharmaceut. Jrnl.* 13 Aug. 125/1 The name of 'water chestnuts' has been applied to the fruits of several species of *Trapa*. **1760** J. LEE *Introd. Bot.* 271 Callitriche, Star-Headed *Water-Chickweed. *c* **1550** LLOYD *Treas. Health* I 5, *Watercrowfote stamped wyth crommes of bread and a plaster made thereof taketh awaie the heate of the stomake. **1902** CORNISH *Naturalist Thames* 14 In the shallows grow water-crowfoot, with waving green hair under water. **1578** LYTE *Dodoens* III. vi. 322 *Dracunculus palustris*,..in Englishe, *water Dragon or Marshe Dragon. **1597** GERARDE *Herbal* III. lxxii. 1237 *Sambuca palustris*, the *water Elder, groweth by running streames and water courses. **1650** [W. HOWE] *Phytol. Brit.* 108 Sambucus aquatica..Water Elder. **1838** LOUDON *Arboretum* II. 1039 Viburnum Opulus. The Guelder Rose..Marsh Elder, Rose Elder, Water Elder. **1820** J. C. GILLELAND *Ohio & Mississippi Pilot* 257 *Water elm in marshes, generally in the rear of rich bottoms. **1903** 'O. HENRY' in *McClure's Mag.* Dec. 144/1 [I] noticed a rabbit-hawk sitting on a dead limb in a water-elm. **1930**, **1976** Water elm [see PLANER-TREE]. **1818** T. NUTTALL *Genera N. Amer. Pl.* I. 120 *Hottonia*..*Water-feather. **1860** MAYNE *Expos. Lex.*, **Water-Figwort, Greater*, common name for the *Scrophularia aquatica*. **1849** BALFOUR *Man. Bot.* §1129 *Conferva crispa*, called *Water-flannel. **1898** H. G. WELLS *War of Worlds* II. vi. 242 Its swiftly-growing and Titanic *water-fronds speedily choked both these rivers. **1930** T. S. ELIOT tr. *St.-J. Perse's Anabasis* 65 Eaters of insects, of *water fruits. **1578** LYTE *Dodoens* I. lxxi. 106 The second [kind of floating weed is called]..in English *Water Gillofer. **1597** GERARDE *Herbal* II. cclxxxvi. 679 Water Gilloflower, or Water Violet, is thought to be colde and drie. *Ibid.* I. xxi. 27 *Water Gladiole groweth in standing pooles, motes, and water ditches. **1760** J. LEE *Introd. Bot.* 270 Butomus. Flowering Rush, or *Water Gladiolus. **1847** LEICHHARDT *Jrnl.* xii. 387 Long hollows surrounded with drooping tea-trees and the white *water-gums. **1898** MORRIS *Austral English* 181 Various other trees not of the genus Eucalyptus are also sometimes popularly called *Gums*, such as..Broad leaved Water Gum, *Tristania suaveolens*, Smith; Water Gum, *Callistemon lanceolatus*, De C.; *Tristania laurina*, *T. neriifolia*, R. Br. *c* **1440** *Promp. Parv.* 36/1 Byllerne, *watyr herbe, *berula*. **1870** HOOKER *Stud. Flora* p. x, Nymphæaceæ..Water-herbs; flowers showy. **1844** *Zoologist* II. 499 Then speedily appeared a crop of *water-herbage. **1897** H. J. WEBBER in *Bull. U.S. Dept. Agric.: Bot.* XVIII. 13 The *water hyacinth is becoming a serious menace to navigation. **1927** E. THOMPSON *Indian Day* xiv. 111 A colony of water hyacinth had rooted itself.. where deep water still remained. **1979** *London Rev. Bks.* 25 Oct. 5/3 In this closing scene, the water hyacinths proceed towards the sea. **1864** GRISEBACH *Flora W. Ind. Isl.* 788 *Water-hyssop, *Herpestis Monnieria*. **1785** MARTYN *Lett. Bot.* xxvii. (1794) 426 Another sort, called *Water Lemon in the West Indies, has an agreeable acid flavor in the pulp of the fruit. **1864** GRISEBACH *Flora W. Ind. Isl.* 788 Water-lemon. *Passiflora laurifolia* and *maliformis*. **1866** *Treas. Bot.* 897/1 *Pistia Stratiotes*... Its common West Indian name, *Water Lettuce. **1883** *Century Mag.* July 383/1 The saw-grass, water-lettuce, bonnets, or other aquatic plants which border the fresh-water streams and lakes of Florida. **1817** W. DARBY *Geogr. Descr. Louisiana* 354 *Gleditsia monosperma*. *Water locust. **1803** A. ELLICOTT *Jrnl.* x. 284 *Water maple..is met with as high as the Wabash. **1822** J. FLINT *Lett. Amer.* 131 Dr. Drake..has stated the usual time of the flowering of the water-maple at a month later. **1822** J. WOODS *Two Yrs.' Resid. Illinois* 93 Beech, the prevailing timber, except on the banks of the river; there mostly sycamore, water-maple, and willows. **1912** I. S. COBB *Back Home* 137 [The] walk..[was] shaded well all the way by water maples. **1760** J. LEE *Introd. Bot.* App. 319 *Moss, Water, *Fontinalis*. **1774** GOLDSM. *Nat. Hist., Earth* xvii. I. 287 The vast increase of water-moss, which flourishes upon marshy grounds. **1849** BALFOUR *Man. Bot.* §1129 *Hydrodictyon utriculatum*, *Water-net, has the appearance of a green net. **1904** *Nature* 25 Aug. 396/2 This is likely to be an exaggerated Chinese account of the now well-known water-net (*Hydrodictyon utriculatum* Roth.). **1617** MORYSON *Itin.* III. 83 When the cloth is taken away, they have set before them..*waternuts (which I did see onely in Saxony) and a loafe of bread cut into shives. **1665** LOVELL *Herball* (ed. 2) 464 Water nut, see Saligot. **1819** D. B. WARDEN *Acc. United States* II. 538 *Water oats, or wild rice (*Zizania aquatica*) grows in the soft marshes of the eastern parts [of Louisiana]. **1889** P. H. EMERSON *Engl. Idyls* 160 The water-soldier (Stratiotes aloides), called *water-orchids in parts of England. **1895** RIDER HAGGARD *Heart of World* xxiii. (1899) 312 We beached our boat behind the shelter of some dwarf *water-palms three furlongs below the village. **1768** PENNANT *Brit. Zool.* II. 344 The bittern..builds its nest with the leaves of *water plants on some dry clump among the reeds. **1882** VINES tr. *Sachs' Bot.* 693 What was said.. on the changes which take place in the air contained in the cavities of water-plants, applies in general also to that of land-plants. **1808** JAMIESON, *Water-purpie. **1818** SCOTT *Br. Lamm.* xviii, Cresses or water-purpie, and a bit ait-cake, can serve the Master for breakfast as weel as Caleb. **1827** —— *Chron. Canongate* v, I propose also to have..a sort of green-grocer's stall erected in front of my ironmongery wares, garlanding the rusty memorials of ancient times, with cresses, cabbages, leeks, and water purpy. **1753** *Chambers' Cycl.* Suppl. *App.*, *Water radish, the name by which several species of Sisymbrium are sometimes called. **1866** *Treas. Bot.* 955/1 Water Radish. *Nasturtium amphibium*. **1867** H. MACMILLAN *Bible Teach.* vii. (1870) 147 The common *water ranunculus, whose white flowers cover the surface of many of our quiet rivulets in June. **1825** SCOTT *Talism.* xiii, 'By my crown of lilies, and my sceptre of a specially good *water-reed,' said Nectabanus, 'your Majesty is mistaken.' **1871** ROSSETTI *Poems, Staff & Scrip* vii, Like water-reeds the poise Of her soft body, dainty thin. **1548** TURNER *Names Herbes* (E.D.S.) 56 Nymphea..is called in english *water Roses, & some wyth the Potecaries cal it nenufar. **1601** HOLLAND *Pliny* XXVI. x. II. 256 Of Water-rose, otherwise called Nenuphar. **1826** KIRBY & SP. *Entomol.* III. xxix. 94 The eggs..are inserted in the stem of a *water-rush (*Scirpus*) or other aquatic plant. **1841** *Penny Cycl.* XX. 359/2 *Salix aquatica*, *water sallow... This is also a British species. **1846** LINDLEY *Veg. Kingd.* 412 *Cabombaceæ*, *Watershields. **1849** BALFOUR *Man. Bot.* §749 *Cabombaceæ*, the Watershield Family. **1398** TREVISA *Barth. De P.R.* XVII. xxxi. (Bodl. MS.), Reede gode to many maner vse & amonge *water shrobbes reede is beste. **1784** J. TWAMLEY *Dairying* 117 Water-wort, Water-hemlock, or *Water-skeleton, is esteemed a fatal poison to Horses. **1874** A. GRAY *Man. Bot.* (ed. 5) 416 *Polygonum acre*..(*Water Smartweed). **1777** JACOB *Catal. Plants* 120 *Veronica scutellata*, Narrow leaved *Water Speedwell, or Brooklime. **1806** GALPINE *Brit. Bot.* §9 Veronica anagallis, Water Speedwell. **1858** A. IRVINE *Handbk. Brit. Plants* 49 The earliest Water-speedwell is the Common Brooklime (*Veronica Beccabunga*). **1818** T. NUTTALL *Genera N. Amer. Pl.* I. 3 *Callitriche*..*Water-star. **1854** THOREAU *Walden* ix. (1886) 178 A lily, yellow or white..and perhaps a *water-target or two. **1578** LYTE *Dodoens* IV. liii. 513 *Typha palustris*,..*Water Torche. **1707** MORTIMER *Husb.* 144 In Hampshire they sell *Water-Trefoil as dear as Hops, and say that it doth upon all accounts as well. **1789** W. BUCHAN *Dom. Med.* (1790) 391 The water-trefoil is likewise of great use in this complaint [rheumatism]. **1597** GERARDE *Herbal* II. cclxxxvi. 678 *Water Violet hath long and great iagged leaues, verie finely cut or rent like Yarrowe, but smaller. **1728** BRADLEY *Dict. Bot.* s.v. *Violet*, Water-Violets, in Latin, viola aquatica. **1785** MARTYN *Lett. Bot.* xvi. (1794) 177 Water Violet has a salver-shaped corolla not fringed. **1866** *Treas. Bot.* 1218/2 Water Violet, *Hottonia palustris*. *Ibid.* 1229/1 *Water-withe. **1855** H. G. DALTON *Hist. Brit. Guiana* II. 206 Water vine, or *water withy. **1597** GERARDE *Herbal* II. cclxxxvi. 678 Water Milfoile, or *water Yarrow.

32. *Med.* Designating specific ailments, eruptions, etc., as ***† water-bladder***, ***-blister***, ***† -farcin***, ***-garget***, ***-murrain***, ***† -pang***; **water-blebs**, pemphigus; **water-brash**, pyrosis; **water-canker**, a form of stomatitis; **water-pox**, chicken-pox; **water-stroke** (see quots.); **† water-wheal**, a watery blister.

1587 MASCALL *Bk. Cattell* III. (1596) 243 Some sheepe will haue a *water bladder vnder their chin,..shepeheards haue no other common remedy but to lance it alitle, and then to tar it. **1818–20** E. THOMPSON *Cullen's Nosol. Meth.* (ed. 3) 328 Pompholyx; *Water Blebs. **1822–7** GOOD *Study Med.* (1829) V. 617 Water-blebs. **1895** KIPLING *2nd Jungle Bk., Red Dog* 201 Here would be a heaving mound, like a *water-blister in a whirlpool. **1900** J. HUTCHINSON *Archives Surg.* XI. 259 Vesications ('water-blisters' was the patient's term) broke out. **1802** REECE *Med. Guide* (1850) 531 *Water-brash ..is very prevalent in Scotland and Ireland. **1822–7** GOOD *Study Med.* (1829) I. 165 In the colloquial tongue of England, it is called *black-water*; in that of Scotland, *water-brash*, and *water-qualm*. **1597** P. LOWE *Disc. Chyrurg.* v. xxxiii. (1634) 200 Those Pustules and Ulcers which oftentimes possesse the upper part of the mouth and gums, are named by the Greekes *Apthe*,..in vulgar the *Water Canker. **1877** F. T. ROBERTS *Handbk. Med.* (ed. 3) I. 291 Water Canker is a very rare, but dangerous form of stomatitis. **1728** CHAMBERS *Cycl.* s.v. *Dropsy*, The *Ascites*, or *Water-Dropsy of the Abdomen, is..what we particularly call the Dropsy. **1706** PHILLIPS (ed. Kersey), *Farcin* or **Water-Farcin*, a Swelling under a Horse's Belly and Chaps, caus'd by his Feeding in Low Watery Grounds. **1868** *Rep. U.S. Commissioner Agric.* (1869) 41 A disease called '*water garget' has been slightly prevalent in Merrimack County. **1708** KERSEY, **Water-Murrain*, a Disease in black Cattel. **1633** FORD *'Tis Pity* III. iii, Am I at these yeeres ignorant, what the meaning's of Quames, and *Waterpangs be? **1822–7** GOOD *Study Med.* (1829) III. 61 *Water-pox. *Ibid.* II. 409 In the language of..Dr. Golis *wasserschlag*, or *water-stroke, from its violence. **1899** *Syd. Soc. Lex.*, *Water stroke*, a term for *Meningitis*, whether primary or secondary, when the effusion of fluid forms very rapidly. **1530** PALSGR. 287/1 *Water whele in ones hande, *bubette*.

† 33. Prefixed to certain designations of measures of capacity, to denote the larger measures used for goods sold on board ship (see WATER-MEASURE), as ***water bushel***, ***firlot***, ***peck***; also ***water met*** = WATER-MEASURE. A related use seems to exist in ***water-fother*** (quot. 1300), but the sense is obscure.

1300 *Memoranda K.R. 27 & 28 Edw. I.* m. 32 b, Recognouerunt..se teneri Waltero de Langetone..in lxx. carratis plumbi videlicet Waterfother. **15..** *Burgh Rec. Edin.* (1869) I. 14 The watter mett of Leyth sett to Jhone Dow for ij merks. **1546** *Reg. Privy Council Scot.* I. 30 That na ry be sauld dearer nor XXV s the boll and the quhete for XL s the boll watter mete. **1551** *Burgh Rec. Edin.* II. 155

The prouest baillies and counsale ordanis that Jhone Dalmahoy thair seriand and officer of the port and heavin of Leyth in all tymes cuming keip the mesouris callit the watter metts of salt, rye, quheitt and beir and siclyke. **1555** *Sc. Acts Mary* (1814) II. 496/2 Except the watter met to remane according to the vse of the cuntrie. **1615** E. S. *Britain's Buss* in Arber *Eng. Garner* III. 632 A Water Bushel (that is, five pecks) of Spanish salt, will salt a barrel of herrings. **1630** *Aldeburgh Rec.* in *N. & Q.* 12th Ser. VIII. 427/1 Paid for Iron worke for 4 water busshells..00 16 00. **1655** in *Rec. Convent. Burghs Scot.* (1878) III. 402 The water firlot for bear and oattis. **1801** *Farmer's Mag.* Jan. 102 Potatoes.. from 1s. 2d. to 1s. 4d. per water peck, which is a measure of about fourteen Scots pints.

water (ˈwɔːtə(r)), *v.* Inflected **watered, watering.** Forms: 1 **wæterian, watrian, wætriȝan,** 2 **wettrien, watrien,** 3 **wattren** (*Orm.* **-enn**), **wattre, (wattur),** 3–5, 7 *Sc.* **watter,** 4 **watere, weteri, watrin, watre,** 4–5 **wetery, wateren,** 5 **watron, watir,** 4– **water.** *Pa. pple.* 4 **y-wetered, i-watred, y-watert.** [OE. *wæterian* (also *ȝe-*), f. *wæter* WATER *sb.* Cf. MHG. *wezzern*, mod.G. *wässern* (dial. *wassern*), MLG. *wateren, weteren*, mod.LG. *watern, wätern*, Du. *wateren*.]

I. Transitive uses.

1. a. To give a drink of water to (an animal, esp. a horse on a journey); also, to take (cattle) to the water to drink.

c **1000** ÆLFRIC *Gen.* xix. 3 Hiȝ awylton þone stan of þam pitte and hi heora orf þær wæterodon. *c* **1175** *Lamb. Hom.* 9 A! hwa is þet mei þet hors wectrien [*read* wettrien] þe him self nule drinken? *c* **1250** *Gen. & Ex.* 2745 Ðor he comen water to feten, And for to wattren here sep. *a* **1300** *Cursor M.* 5685 Þai com to wattur þar þair fee. *c* **1350** *Will. Palerne* 3234 Þat men miȝt legge him [a horse] mete & wateren atte wille. **1480** *Cov. Leet Bk.* 459 The people of this Citie..euer haue vsed tyll nowe late to watter theire horses at the seid pole. **1523–34** FITZHERB. *Husb.* §85 Broken wynded.. cometh of rennynge or rydynge ouer moche, and specially shortely after he is watred. *a* **1658** FORD, etc. *Witch Edmonton* III. i, Get my horse dress'd: give him Oats; but water him not till I come. **1729** P. WALKDEN *Diary* (1866) 62, I..then foddered and watered our Seed heifer. **1858** R. S. SURTEES *Ask Mamma* lxxvii. 336 He pulled up..to get his mare watered and fed. **1891** 'R. BOLDREWOOD' *Sydney-side Sax.* i, The beasts to be fed and watered. **1908** *Animal Management* (War Office) 289 It has been said that if a desert camel is frequently watered he loses his power of abstinence for long periods.

absol. **1643** TRAPP *Comm. Gen.* xxvi. 15 They deprived themselves of the benefit of those wells, so that Isaac might not water at them. **1730** W. BURDON *Gentl. Pocket-Farrier* 26 Ever make it a standing Rule to water on the Way before you arrive at the baiting Place. **1842** DICKENS *Amer. Notes* xiv, We often stop to water at a roadside inn.

b. *fig.* and in fig. context.

1597 SPENSER *Sheph. Cal.* Nov. 30 Nay, better learne of hem, that learned bee, And han be watered at the Muses well. **1606** SHAKS. *Tr. & Cr.* III. iii. 314 Would the Fountaine of your minde were cleere againe, that I might water an Asse at it. **1611** —— *Cymb.* II. iii. 23 And Phœbus gins arise, His Steeds to water at those Springs on chalic'd Flowres that lyes. **1654** SIR A. JOHNSTON (Ld. Wariston) *Diary* (S.H.S.) II. 267 God's consolations..ar a fountayne, ..and they ar tuyse a mercy in wattering ourselves and inaibling us to watter uthers. **1898** MEREDITH *Napoleon* v. *Odes* 27 For even a hope in chained desire The vision of it watered thirst.

†**c.** In the name of a children's game. *Obs.*

1760–72 H. BROOKE *Fool of Qual.* (1809) II. 27 One fault brought me into another after it, like Water my chickens, come clock.

2. To furnish with a supply of water. **a.** To supply water to (a company on a journey, an army on the march).

c **1000** *Ags. Ps.* lxxvii. 18 [15] He slat stan on westene & wæterode hiȝ [*a* **1300** *E.E. Psalter*, watred am. **1382** WYCLIF, watride hem]. **1632** LITHGOW *Trav.* VII. 301 He payed fiue Sultans of gold for Watering all vs and the Beasts. **1898** *Daily News* 8 Mar. 3/2 In a campaign like this, where we shall always have the river beside us, the water-bottle is almost superfluity... It should be easy to water troops at fixed intervals.

b. To furnish (a ship, fleet, boat) with a supply of fresh water.

1589 BIGGES *Summarie Drake's W. Ind. Voy.* 42 After three dayes spent in watering our ships we departed. **1620** in Foster *Eng. Factories Ind.* (1906) 215 Shee waighed [into the] road, and was by them watered, cawked, and supplied with [etc.]. **1748** *Anson's Voy.* I. v. 42 Our next employment was wooding and watering our squadron. **1793** NELSON in Nicolas *Disp.* (ed. 2) I. 322 Lord Hood has gone to water the Fleet. **1844** MRS. HOUSTON *Yacht Voy. Texas* II. 252 Our last act and deed before we left Galveston, was watering and victualling the Dolphin. **1855** KINGSLEY *Westw. Ho!* xiii, He seized the town..and watered his ship triumphantly at the enemy's wells.

c. To supply (an engine) with water.

1870 in Schele de Vere *Americanisms* (1872) 359, I question if it be wise in running a railroad to water anything but the engine. **1898** HAMBLEN *Gen. Manager's Story* xiv. 234 The awkward attempts of the new men to get the few remaining dead engines watered and fired-up.

3. a. To supply water as aliment to (a plant, crop, etc.), esp. by pouring or sprinkling with a watering-can, hose, or the like; to pour or sprinkle water on (soil) to promote the growth of plants (or occas. for other purposes: see e.g. quot. 1699). Also const. *in*.

c **897** ÆLFRED *Gregory's Past. C.* xl. 293 Sumu treowu he watrode [*Cotton* watrade], to ðæm ðæt hie ðy suiður sceolden weaxan. *c* **1000** ÆLFRIC *Hom.* I. 304 Se man ðe plantað treowa oððe wyrta, swa lange he hi wæterað oðþæt hi beoð ciðfæste. *c* **1200** ORMIN 13864 All swa summ erþe wattredd iss þurrh reȝȝn & dæw off heffne. *a* **1300** *Cursor M.* 21304 Þe first he tils þe feild to sede, þe toiþer he saus efter þe sede, þe thrid it harus..þe ferth it watters. **1382** WYCLIF *Ecclus.* xxiv. 42, I seide, I shal watrin the gardyn of my plauntingus. *c* **1440** *Promp. Parv.* 518/2 Watron', herbys (or other lyke, *P.*), *irrigo, rigo, humecto.* **1526** *Pilgr. Perf.* (W. de W. 1531) 108 b, Be tender ouer them as ye wolde be ouer a noble & precyous plant.., attendyng it, watrynge it diligently. **1585–7** *Acc. Mary Q. Scots* (Camden) 17 Richarde Garrett and John Smyth, for mindinge and wateringe the garden, xij s. ij d. **1601** HOLLAND *Pliny* XII. i. I. 358 They came to be so highly esteemed, that for to make them grow the better, men would be at the cost to water them with wine. **1662** GERBIER *Princ.* 33 They are Watered with a Gardeners Watering-Pot. **1667** MILTON *P.L.* XI. 279 Who now shall reare ye to the Sun, or ranke Your Tribes, and water from th' ambrosial Fount? **1699** MEAGER *New Art Garden.* 130 To destroy Worms and other Insects,..water your Gravel-Walks with water wherein Tobacco stalks have been boiled. **1707** MORTIMER *Husb.* (1721) II. 56 Strew the Seeds pretty thick, ..keeping of them well water'd every Evening, except when the Season waters them. **1796** C. MARSHALL *Gardening* xx. (1813) 404 Water, if dry weather, new planted trees, shrubs, and flowers. **1853** DICKENS *Bleak Ho.* xxxvii, After we had finished helping the gardener in watering his flowers. **1885** G. NICHOLSON *Illustr. Dict. Gardening* I. 217/2 The plants [*sc.* Brussels sprouts]..should be watered-in when planted. **1917** M. SWAYNE *In Mesopotamia* xi. 161 The swiftness with which seeds grow when properly watered is uncanny. **1958** *Listener* 21 Aug. 275/2 By taking off well-ripened shoots.. and placing three shoots in three-inch pots..watering them in..and keeping them perfectly airtight and shaded, I have got a good percentage to root. **1982** *Times* 22 May 9/4, I always like to water-in my lawn fertilizers.

absol. **1855** DELAMER *Kitch. Gard.* (1861) 22 If May should be very dry, I am obliged to water. **1857** HUGHES *Tom Brown* II. viii, The ground was at last chosen [for the cricket match], and two men set to work upon it to water and roll.

b. *fig.* (See also 5 c.)

c **1200** ORMIN 13848 To wattrenn & to dæwwenn swa þurrh beȝȝske & sallte tæress þatt herrte, þat..Iss.. forrclungenn. **1340** *Ayenb.* 131 Þis trau [of mildenesse] is yzet bezide þe welle of godes drede huer-of hit is echedaye y-wetered ine wyntre and ine zomere. **1534** MORE *Comf. agst. Trib.* III. xxi. S viij b, God..instructeth oure reason.. not onelye to receyue them [the spiritual affections] as engendred and planted in our soule, but also in suche wyse water them with wyse aduertisement of godly counsayle. **1607** SHAKS. *Cor.* v. vi. 23, I rais'd him..: who being so heighten'd, He watered his new Plants with dewes of Flattery, Seducing so my Friends. **1672–5** COMBER *Comp. Temple* (1702) 289 The Apostles..planted this Faith..and watred it with their blood. **1820** SHELLEY *Witch of Atlas* 27 Wordsworth informs us he was nineteen years Considering and retouching Peter Bell; Watering his laurels with the killing tears Of slow, dull care. **1874** ABP. BENSON in A. C. Benson *Life* (1899) I. xi. 373 You have now to water the good seed you have sown with your prayers. **1876** GRANT *One of Six Hundred* lii. 437, I resolved to return thankfully..home, to water my laurels among the..grassy glens of my native place.

absol. **1382** WYCLIF *1 Cor.* iii. 6, I plauntide, Apollo watride, or moystide, but God ȝaf encresynge. **1846** MRS. A. MARSH *Father Darcy* II. ii. 43 Their blood hath watered and we shall reap.

c. To supply (land, crops) with water by flooding or by means of irrigation-channels; to irrigate.

1555 EDEN *Decades* (Arb.) 159 They founde manye fayre gardeyns and pleasaunte fyeldes watered with trenshes distrybuted in marueylous order. **1577** B. GOOGE *Heresbach's Husb.* I. 45 b, Some, where they may ouerflowe it [grass], doo water it a day before they cut it. **1687** A. LOVELL tr. *Thevenot's Trav.* III. 26 The Corn-land is never watered, because the Dew that falls plentifully in the Mornings, is sufficient for it. **1791** *Rep. Commrs. Thames-Isis Navig.* 26 A Hatch Gate..is drawn much in Short-water Time; to water the Meadows. **1799** A. YOUNG *Agric. Lincoln* 275 He set to work, and built sluices, formed carrier trenches and drains; and thus watered 50 acres. **1801** *Farmer's Mag.* Aug. 268 To the person who shall, in a country where irrigation is not generally in practice, water the greatest number of acres.

†**d.** *slang.* To give free entertainment to; to 'treat'. *Obs. rare.*

1742 P. YORKE *Let.* 15 Dec., in G. Harris *Life Ld. Hardwicke* (1847) II. vii. 43 Charles is watering the Quorum of Bennet, ten miles round; or, to speak less quaintly, is treating away at Cambridge.

4. a. Of a river, etc.: To supply water to (vegetation, land). Now chiefly passive.

c **1000** ÆLFRIC *Gen.* ii. 6 Ac an wyll asprang of þære eorðan wætriende ealre þære eorðan bradnysse. *Ibid.* ii. 10 And þæt flod eode of stowe þære winsumnisse to wætrienne neorxena wang. **1387** TREVISA *Higden* I. 133 Nilus ouer-floweþ and watereþ al þe lond of Egipte. *c* **1440** CAPGRAVE *St. Kath.* v. 1905 In stede of blood mylke ran at hir nekke... It ran so plenteuously it wattered al the ground That lay abouten hir. O most merueylous welle! **1555** EDEN *Decades* (Arb.) 133 Ryuers..wherwith al suche trees as are planted on the stiepe or foote of the mountaynes..are watered. **1590** E. WEBBE *Trav.* (Arb.) 22 All the grounde throughout the lande of Egipt is continually watred by the water which..is turned into the cuntries round about. **1632** LITHGOW *Trav.* I. 25 This Prouince is mainely watered through the middle with stately Po. **1735** JOHNSON *Lobo's Abyssinia, Descr.* x. 102 It [the Nile] then waters the kingdoms of Amhara, Olaca, [etc.]. **1756–7** tr. *Keysler's Trav.* (1760) IV. 345 The road lies through a delightful valley, which is watered by the Isse or Itch. **1784** COWPER *Task* VI. 930 Stillest streams Oft water fairest meadows. **1820** SCOTT *Ivanhoe* i, In that pleasant district of merry England which is watered by the river Don. **1853** NEWMAN *Hist. Sk.* (1873) II. I. ii. 63 Sogdiana is watered by a number of great rivers. **1901** SLADEN *In Sicily* I. II. xix. 271 That rocky plateau..could.. be converted into an almost impregnable fortress... It is splendidly watered.

fig. **1671** MILTON *P.R.* IV. 277 Socrates..from whose mouth issu'd forth Mellifluous streams that water'd all the schools Of Academics old and new. **1788** COWPER *Negro's Compl.* 19 Sighs must fan it, tears must water, Sweat of ours must dress the soil.

†**b.** Of water, a river, etc.: To surround or bound (a city, fort). Chiefly *pass.* also with *about*.

c **1400** *Destr. Troy* 319 Hit was þe souerayne Citie of the Soyle euer,..Well wallit for werre, watrit aboute. **1572** T. TWYNE tr. *Dionysius' Surv. World* E vij, On the one side runneth Corus, an other Choaspes,..rising out of the Riuer Indus, and watering the cittie Susa. **1589** IVE *Fortif.* 25 Neither, if the Fort do stand well watered, need the face of the Curtin to be raised..higher then three or foure foote aboue the water. **1601** R. JOHNSON *Kingd. & Commw.* 36 As for the Continent he [the King of Spain] is absolute lord of all that sea coast which watereth Florida, Noua Hispania, Iucatan, [etc.]. **1631** WEEVER *Anc. Funeral Mon.* 597, I saw the remaines of a Monasterie, pleasantly watered about with seuerall streames. **1753** HANWAY *Trav.* VII. xcviii. (1762) I. 457 It [the city] is watered by the Leina.

5. a. *to water* (something) *with one's tears*: to make wet or moist with copious and continued weeping; to shed tears upon or over. Chiefly *hyperbolical* or *fig. Obs. or arch.*

a **1200** *Vices & Virtues* 147 He [ðe prophete] sade: Ich scal watrien min bedd mid mine teares. **1382** WYCLIF *Ps.* vi. 7 With my teres my bedding I shal watrin. **1535** COVERDALE *Luke* vii. 38 She..beganne to water his fete with teares. **1634** HEYWOOD *Maidenh. well lost* I. B 2 b, Each step I treade I'le water with a teare. **1667** MILTON *P.L.* x. 1090 What better can we do, then..there confess Humbly our faults, and pardon beg, with tears Watering the ground. **1675** J. OWEN *Indwelling Sin* viii. (1732) 93 If it teach us to water a free Pardon with Tears,..it is Divine. **1760–72** H. BROOKE *Fool of Qual.* (1809) III. 113 [He] plentifully watered the ground with his tears as he passed. *Ibid.* 119 Often have we watered the good man's memory with our tears. **1779** *Mirror* No. 44. ¶8 La Roche threw his arms round his neck, and watered it with his tears. **1832** TENNYSON *Œnone* 230 Hath he not sworn his love a thousand times..Seal'd it with kisses? water'd it with tears?

†**b.** Said of the tears. *Obs.*

1606 SHAKS. *Ant. & Cl.* I. ii. 177 And indeed the teares liue in an Onion, that should water this sorrow. **1782** MISS BURNEY *Cecilia* VII. viii, 'No, hate me not,' said Mrs. Delvile, kissing from her cheeks the tears that watered them.

†**c.** Phrases. *to water one's eyes*, also jocularly *to water one's plants*: to shed tears, to weep. *Obs.*

c **1400** *Destr. Troy* 8039 Bresaid..With myche weping & waile, waterid hir ene. *c* **1460** *Towneley Myst.* xxii. 331 For sorow I water both myn eeyn. *a* **1562** G. CAVENDISH *Wolsey* (1893) 129 Whiche words caused my Lord of Wyltshere to water his eyes. **1587** TURBERV. *Trag. Tales* 125 b, Which when Symona had beheld, She watred straight her eyes. **1542** UDALL *Erasm. Apoph.* 266 When he read the chronicle of Alexander the greate, he could not forbeare to water his plantes [L. *non tenuit lachrymas*]. **1590** LODGE *Rosalynde* (1592) O 2, Water not thy plants, Phoebe, for I do pity thy plaints, nor seek not to discouer thy loues in teares. **1600** HOLLAND *Livy* XXX. xv. 750 Masanissa, whiles he heard these words..began to water his plants [L. *lacrimæ obortæ*]. **1724** SWIFT *Acc. Wood's Exec.* Misc. (1735) V. 314 *Bodice-maker.* I'll lace his Sides. *Gardener.* I'll make him water his Plants. **1828** CARR *Craven Gloss.* (ed. 2) s.v. *Plants*, 'To water one's plants,' to shed tears.

†**6. a.** To soak in or with water, to steep in a liquor; also, to soften by soaking, macerate. *Obs.*

1398 TREVISA *Barth. De P.R.* XVII. lxiv. (1495) 641 One sayth that beenes grow the sooner..yf they ben watryd in pysse thre dayes or they be sowen. *c* **1430** *Two Cookery-bks.* 43, Nym Milwel or lenge, þat is wel y-wateryd. *c* **1440** *Pallad. on Husb.* I. 795 With ficchis flour ywattrid wel biforn, Let modle al this seed. **1483** *Act 1 Ric. III.* c. 8. §1 No person..shall sell..any Manner Woollen Cloths, called Broad Cloths, unless the same Cloth be before fully watered. **1542** BOORDE *Dyetary* iii. (1870) 236 Also, nygh to the place let nother flaxe nor hempe be watered. **1556** WITHALS *Dict.* (1562) 47 *Macero*, to water fisshe or flesshe. **1577** B. GOOGE *Heresbach's Husb.* I. 10 b, A Hopper..serueth to conuey downe the Malt, after it is watred vnto the hearecloth, where it is dryed. **1611** in *Trans. Exeter Dioc. Archit. Soc.* Ser. II. (1867) I. 399 Item to a man to water the reed,..1 s. **1655** WALTON *Angler* I. xxi. (1661) 246 Which is so much of the strength of the Line lost for want of first watering it, and then re-twisting it. **1675** HANNAH WOOLLEY *Gentlew. Comp.* 123 Lay them [collars of brawn] a-soaking in fair water; be sure that they be watered two days before you bind them up.

†**b.** *to water out*: to free from salt by soaking in water. *Obs.*

1683 PETTUS *Fleta Min.* v. viii. 338 When the Salt is to be put over the Ashes,..it must be well watered out [orig. G. *ausswässern*] that the red bottom may not be very salty.

†**c.** To wash down (solid food) with liquor.

1630 J. TAYLOR (Water P.) *Great Eater of Kent* Wks. I. 144/2 Indeed he is no drunkard,..for one Pinte of Beere or Ale is enough to wash downe a Hog, or water a Sheepe with him.

d. To sprinkle or drench (a road, pavement, etc.) with water, in order to lay the dust.

1662 J. DAVIES tr. *Olearius' Voy. Ambass.* 260 Their Inhabitants had water'd the Streets, which being not pav'd, ..the dust had otherwise..annoy'd us. **1835** DICKENS *Sk. Boz, Streets—Morning*, The apprentice, who pauses every other minute from his task of sweeping out the shop and watering the pavement in front of it. **1861** MRS. H. WOOD *East Lynne* III. xxii, Afy, lifting her capacious dress, for the streets had just been watered, minced off. **1872** SCHELE DE VERE *Americanisms* 359 As American railroads are..liable, in sandy regions, to be enveloped in unbearable clouds of dust, track sprinklers are frequently employed to water them. **1885** *Law Rep.* 14 *Q.B.D.* 891 He was directed by the inspector..to water certain streets.

e. *Mil.* To pour shell-fire upon. Said also of shell-fire. [So Fr. *arroser*, G. *bewässern*.]

1915 J. BUCHAN *Nelson's Hist. War* III. xxi. 89 Thereupon von Hindenburg attempted to 'prepare' a passage by a great bombardment—high angle shell fire which should 'water' the enemy's position. *Ibid.* VII. lii. 106 The Germans were closing in on both sides and 'watering' the whole hinterland with their fire.

f. To sprinkle or drench (a material) with water in order to moisten it or with a solution to impregnate it. Also with *down*.

1474 *Coventry Leet Bk.* 397 Nother that he water nother chaunge no mannes corne to geve hym the wers for the better. **1786** in J. Lloyd *Old South Wales Iron Works* (1906) 35 To take..Water issuing from the said veins of Coal for the purpose of watering their Coaks and Coakyards at Pendarren Furnace. **1815** J. SMITH *Panorama Sci. & Art* II. 562 The cloth is exposed for a few days to the open air in the field, and frequently watered, to remove every trace of the acids. **1836** *Penny Cycl.* V. 408/1 [Brick] The clay and ashes thus mixed together are 'watered down', by water being thrown over them with a wooden scoop. **1839** URE *Dict. Arts* 1255 Spreading them [tobacco leaves] in a heap upon a stone pavement, watering each layer in succession, with a solution..called sauce. **1868** *Rep. U.S. Commissioner Agric.* (1869) 441 In hot weather the [milk] can is covered with a textile wrapper which is watered with a fine sprinkler before the train starts.

g. To saturate (the clothing or) the clothing of (a person) with moisture.

1754 A. MURPHY *Gray's Inn Jrnl.* No. 71 ¶3 Producing a Squirt, he began to let fly at me in such a Manner, that I was soon pretty well watered from Head to Foot. **1844** KINGLAKE *Eothen* xviii, A plenteous sweat burst through my skin, and watered my clothes through and through.

h. To put water into. (See quots.)

1867 SMYTH *Sailor's Word-bk.*, *Water his hole.* A saying used when the cable is up and down, to encourage the men to heave heartily, and raise the shank of the anchor so that the water may get down by the shank, and relieve the anchor of the superincumbent mud. **1878** *E. Schiller's Technol. Dict.* s.v., To Water a vessel on the stocks (Ship-b.) *Ein Schiff wässern oder vollpumpen. Abreuver un bâtiment.*

i. To treat hydropathically. ? *nonce-use.*

1854 KEBLE in J. T. Coleridge *Mem.* (1869) 376 He is being watered at Malvern, I hope successfully.

j. Phrase. ***to water one's clay***, to take liquid refreshment. (Cf. phrases in CLAY *sb.* 4 b.)

1769 GOLDSM. *Ess.* v, Old women should water their clay a little now and then; and now to your story.

7. To add water to as a diluent or solvent, thereby increasing the bulk and reducing the strength.

a. To dilute (wine, strong liquor, milk, tea) with water.

1387 TREVISA *Higden* VI. 255 He wolde drynke a litel wyne i-watred [*v.r.* ywatert]. **1398** —— *Barth. De P.R.* XVII. clxxxv. (1495) 725 Redde wyne that is full red as blood is moost stronge and nedyth therefore to be ryghte wel watred. **1605** ERONDELLE *Fr. Gard.* M I b, If I make any mixture, I do be-wine yᵉ water, and not water yᵉ wine. **1850** H. MELVILLE *White Jacket* I. xliii. 278 He pronounces his grog basely watered. **1865** VISCT. MILTON & W. B. CHEADLE *N.-W. Passage by Land* v. (1867) 73 We..sent off to him a very small quantity [of rum] well watered. **1865** G. MACDONALD *Alec Forbes* viii, They sold milk. And if any customer had accused her of watering it, Mrs. Bruce's best answer would have been [etc.]. **1897** BRAM STOKER *Dracula* xxi. (1912) 301 It was like tea after the teapot had been watered. **1902** SNAITH *Wayfarers* xvi, Tea twice watered with a good deal of sugar in it.

b. *fig.*

1871 RUSKIN *Fors Clav.* vii. 15 The knowledge made up for sale is apt to be watered and dusted. **1887** LOWELL *Old Eng. Dramatists* (1892) 91 But it is not true that the sense is expanded, if by that we are to understand that Chapman watered his thought to make it fill up. **1906** *Times Lit. Suppl.* 2 Nov. 370/2 The book is full of quotations... Indeed much of it is just these writers watered.

c. water down. (*a*) *lit.* To reduce the strength of (liquor) by dilution. (*b*) To weaken the force or strength of (language) by addition or alteration. (*c*) To reduce in efficacy or potency.

(*a*) *Mod.* This whisky is very much watered down.

(*b*) **1850** *Edin. Rev.* July 179 One or two of the recent translations.., while adhering closely to the sense, and, in some degree, to the form of the original, may yet be fairly accused of watering down Æschylus. **1856** J. W. WARTER in *Lett. Southey* Pref. 8 As to Southey's opinions, my business, in the selection of these letters, was, clearly, not to water them down,..but rather to leave them patent to the world in their undisguised reality. **1889** *Spectator* 9 Nov. 623/2 The Bishop would have done better not to water down his manly protest against the overstrained moralists. **1899** J. A. DOYLE in *Eng. Hist. Rev.* July 597 They watered down their political sentiments to the standard which they supposed would suit their hearers.

(*c*) **1879** FROUDE *Cæsar* iii. 29 Still less had the Roman citizens an inclination to share their privileges with Samnites and Etruscans, and see the value of their votes watered down. **1919** W. CROOKE in *Man* XIX. 23 In some cases the ordeal has been so watered down that the risk to life or limb is merely nominal.

†**d.** *U.S. slang.* To pack (a jury). *Obs.*

1792 J. BELKNAP *Hist. New-Hampshire* III. 256 In the administration of justice, frequent complaints were made of partiality... The practice of watering the jury was familiarly known to those persons who had business in the Law.

e. *Comm.* To increase in nominal amount (the stock or capital of a trading company) by the creation of fictitious stock. Also with *up*.

1870 *Tribune* (N.Y.) 17 Dec., in Schele de Vere *Americanisms* (1872) 359 In two years the capitals of twenty-eight Northern railroads have been watered to the extent of nearly two hundred millions. **1883** *Pall Mall Gaz.* 5 July 5/1 The new capital was raised at heavy premiums, and therefore does not 'water' the original shares strictly speaking. **1883** *Manch. Guard.* 15 Oct. 5/5 The decision.. gives unlimited encouragement to the entirely vicious practice of 'watering' stock. **1899** *Westm. Gaz.* 6 Apr. 3/1 Considering the vast extent to which capital has been 'watered up' in transfer to joint-stock companies.

†**8.** = WASH *v.* 9 c. Also ***to water over.*** *lit.* and *fig. Obs. rare.*

1637 RUTHERFORD *Let. to J. Gordon* Lett. (1664) 248 Yet all these are but like gold in clink and colour and watered brass and base mettall. **1637** —— *Let. to Lady Kenmure* 17 June, Since I must have chains, He would put golden chains on me, watered over with many consolations.

9. a. To produce a moiré or wavy lustrous finish on (silk or other textile fabrics) by sprinkling them with water and passing them through a calender. Cf. WATERED *ppl. a.* 5.

c **1450** *Mait. Club Misc.* III. 199 Ane claith of bukram watteryt with letteris of gold. **1603** KNOLLES *Hist. Turkes* (1621) 1326 Five pieces of silke, five of damaske, five of silke watered. **1684** *Patent Office* No. 241 A new way of Beautifying severall Sorts of Cloath..and thereby Watering, Damasking and Flowering the same. **1708** *Brit. Apollo* No. 80. 2/2 No two pieces were ever water'd alike. **1745** R. POCOCKE *Descr. East* II. I. viii. 125 These things [silks and cottons] are watered, which very much adds to their beauty. **1791** W. HAMILTON *Berthollet's Dyeing* I. I. III. x. 295 The calender, under which stuffs are passed to water them. **1837** HOOD *Drinking Song* ii, We water roads, horses, silks, ribands, bank-paper.

†**b.** To represent (a material) as watered in painting. *Obs. rare*⁻¹.

1733 *School of Miniature* 29 When you would water a Stuff of any sort, you must wave it with lighter or darker Colours, according as what you are upon is Light or Shade.

†**c.** *transf.* To give a specious appearance to (defective or inferior goods). Also in fig. context.

1646 W. JENKYN *Reformation's Remora* 18 Rotten stuffs will not be vendible without watering, nor rotten courses without excuses. **1663** J. SPENCER *Prodigies* (1665) 68 The pretty Allegories and Allusions of which Discourse (but the watering of weak and worthless stuff) might possibly shew not unhandsomly in an Oration, but are too airy and thin for a Sermon.

10. *Lumber-trade.* To put (logs) into the water for transport.

1877 *Lumberman's Gaz.* 24 May, There have been 257,000,000 feet of logs watered on the various branches of the Muskegon.

II. Intransitive uses.

11. a. Of the eyes: To fill and run with moisture; to shed water, to flow with tears.

13.. *Guy Warw.* (A) 5023 Her eyȝen watred for gladnesse. **1362** LANGL. *P. Pl.* A. VII. 162 Hongur..wrong him so be þe wombe þat boþe his eȝen watreden. *c* **1400** *Beryn* 579 He had such a pose, That both his eyen waterid. *c* **1460** *Vrbanitatis* 57 in *Babees Bk.*, To depe in þy cuppe þou may not synke.. Leste þy eyen water þere by. **1508** DUNBAR *Tua Mariit Wemen* 439 With that wateris myn ene, and welteris doune teris. **1573** L. LLOYD *Pilgr. Princes* 26 We reade that the eies did water to see him, the eares allured to heare him. **1590** SHAKS. *Mids. N.* III. i. 200 Good master Mustard seede... I promise you, your kindred hath made my eyes water ere now. **1593** —— *3 Hen. VI* I. iv. 82 And if thine eyes can water for his death, I giue thee this to drie thy Cheekes withall. **1697** *Verdicts conc. Virgil & Homer* iv. 12 His Eyes water and shed some drops of Tears. **1796** MORSE *Amer. Geog.* II. 72 When a person walks out in that severe weather, the cold makes the eyes water. **1848** DICKENS *Dombey* xlix, The smoke of the pipe..got into the Captain's eyes, and made them blink and water. **1893** STEVENSON *Catriona* iv, His eye watered and sparkled, and before he sat down I observed him to sway back and forth. No doubt, he had been supping liberally. **1897** *Allbutt's Syst. Med.* II. 102 The eyes water, the sclerotic is injected.

b. Of a person: To secrete and shed tears (†*with eye* or *at the eyes*). Also, of tears, to gather in the eyes. *rare.*

14.. *Voc.* in Wr.-Wülcker 593/14 *Lippo*, to watery with ye. **1821** CLARE *Vill. Minstr.* II. 91 Her tears stood watering in her eye. **1848** DICKENS *Dombey* xxvi, The Major sat gurgling in the throat and watering at the eyes.

12. a. Of the mouth: To secrete abundant saliva in the anticipation of appetizing food or delicacies. Similarly of the teeth (*obs.* exc. *Sc.* ?); also rarely of †the 'chops', †the lips. (See also MOUTH *sb.* 2 c, TOOTH *sb.* 8 g.)

1530 PALSGR. 772/2 My tethe waters to se yonder fayre appels. **1555** EDEN *Decades* (Arb.) 181 These craftie foxes [*sc.* cannibals]..beganne to swalowe theyr spettle as their mouthes watered for greedines of theyr pray. **1592** LYLY *Gallathea* v. i, My teeth still watred with hungar. **1611** CORYAT *Crudities* 298, I obserued passing faire Citrens, which made my mouth euen water vpon them. *a* **1612** HARINGTON *Epigr.* II. xiii. (1618) E 3 b, If one names a Iax, your lips doe water. **1628** *Mad Pranks Robin Goodfellow* (Percy Soc.) 29 A great posset was brought forth: at this Robin Goodfellowes teeth did water. **1639** J. CLARKE *Paræm.* 39 He sees no green cheese but his mouth waters after it. **1657** H. CROWCH *Welsh Traveller* 6 The apples did so lovely looke,..No delaies now could her brook, her shops did so much water. **1768–74** TUCKER *Lt. Nat.* (1834) II. 137 The sight of company sitting down before a plentiful meal will presently make the mouth water to be doing the like. **1771** FIELDING *Intrig. Chambermaid* I. v. Wks. II. 349 *Let.* He is this day to give a grand entertainment... *Rak.* My chops begin to water. **1850** C. BRONTE *Wuthering Heights* i, The canine mother..was sneaking wolfishly to the back of my legs,..her white teeth watering for a snatch. **1854** SURTEES *Handley Cr.* li. (1901) II. 80 All the delicacies of the season in short, that make one's mouth water to write. **1876** RUSKIN *Hortus Inclusus* (1887) 42 My mouth's watering so for that Thwaite Currant jelly, you can't think. **1886** *Encycl. Brit.* XX. 57/2 The dog's mouth waters only at the sight of food, but the gourmand's mouth will also water at the thought of it. **1899** G. GREIG *Logie o' Buchan* ii. 29 Here she pointed to the apples, while Jockie's eyes sparkled and his teeth watered.

b. *fig.*

a **1575** tr. *Pol. Verg. Eng. Hist.* (Camden No. 29) 303 There teethe watering at other men's goods. **1603** HOLLAND *Plutarch's Mor.* 503 His teeth..watred after this treasure. **1608** SHAKS. *Per.* IV. ii. 108 There was a Spaniards mouth watred, and he went to bed to her verie description. **1670** G. H. *Hist. Cardinals* III. II. 256 Whose teeth water'd at the Papacy. **1720** DE FOE *Hist. D. Campbell* iv. 68 [She would] bribe him..to write down the Name of a Young Scotch Peer ..that her Mouth watered after. **1841** S. WARREN *Ten Thou.* I. viii, Huckaback, smiling..and chinking some money in his trowsers pocket. Titmouse heard it, and (as the phrase is) his teeth watered. **1883** E. PENNELL-ELMHIRST *Cream Leicestersh.* 424 Every mouth watering at the sight of the sweet country.

13. Of a ship, ship's company, etc.: To take on board a store of fresh water.

1557 W. TOWRSON in Hakluyt *Voy.* (1589) 113 Wee tolde them that we had not watered. **1611** W. ADAMS *Let.* in Rundall *Mem. Japon* (Hakl. Soc.) 19 But, for refreshing of our men we waited, watering and taking in of wood. **1666** *Lond. Gaz.* No. 97/3 The Armada is certainly come into Cadiz, some say to water. **1748** *Anson's Voy.* I. v. 45 The French..usually wooded and watered in Bon Port. *Ibid.* I. ix. 91 A commodious place for ships to wood and water at. **1787** J. WHITE *Jrnl. Voy. N.S. Wales* (1790) 13 We..gained permission to water, and procure such refreshments as the island [Teneriffe] afforded. **1839** MARRYAT *Phant. Ship* xxi, The Utrecht..watered, and proceeded on her voyage. **1898** P. MANSON *Trop. Dis.* xviii. 306 The recurrence of epidemics of dysentery in the crews of ships which have watered at polluted sources.

14. To drink water; to obtain water to drink.

1607 DEKKER & WEBSTER *Westward Hoe* II. i. C, By Hipocrene I sweare, (which was a certain Well where all the Muses watered). **1646** SIR T. BROWNE *Pseud. Ep.* I. iv. 13 When some young Thessalians on horsebacke were beheld a farre off, while their horses watered,..they were conceived ..to be but one animall. **1839** LADY LYTTON *Cheveley* (ed. 2) III. ii. 54 In the back-ground of the picture cattle were watering in a lake. **1890** 'R. BOLDREWOOD' *Col. Reformer* xix, In the event of a dry season..the cattle habitually watering there would..betake themselves to the 'frontage'.

15. To undergo hydropathic treatment. (Cf. WATERER 5, WATERING *vbl. sb.* 12.)

1868 A. DAWSON *Rambling Recoll.* 42 He annually watered at Pitcaithly to ward off rheumatism.

16. To urinate. *rare.*

1626 B. JONSON *Staple of N.* IV. i, What shal's doe with our selues, while the women water? and the Fidlers eat? **1717** PRIOR *Alma* II. 500 Pleas'd with her Punch, the Gallant Soul First drank, then water'd in the Bowl. **1966** M. CATTO *Bird on Wing* i. 15 He went into the lav. The Major could hear him watering.

17. Of a retriever: To take to the water.

1885 *Bazaar Exch. & M.* 30 Mar. 1260/1 Handsome retriever bitch,..will water and retrieve well.

waterage ('wɔːtərɪdʒ). Also 8 **-idge.** [f. WATER *sb.* + -AGE.] Conveyance or transport by water; the charge made or the money paid for this. Also *attrib.*

1688 in Gutch *Collect. Cur.* II. 378 To Mr. Ince for Coach-hire, Waterage, Porterage, and other petty Expences. **1703** in *Jrnl. Derbysh. Archæol. Soc.* (1881) III. 45 Payd for carrage, Wateridge & Porter to helpe into ye vessells with the Marble. **1766** W. GORDON *Gen. Counting-ho.* 280 Pays for..waterage abroad. **1815** *Falconer's Dict. Marine* (ed. Burney), *Waterage*, money paid for carriage of goods and merchandise, &c. by water. **1829** *Examiner* 282/1 The carriage and waterage was paid at the coach-office, and, on the parcel arriving on board, the waterage-money..was charged again. **1861** MAYHEW *Lond. Labour* III. 239 'Waterage' costs the [coal] whipper an average of 6*d.* a-week. .. 'Waterage' means the conveyance from the vessels to the shore. **1867** SMYTH *Sailor's Word-bk.*, *Waterage*, the charge for using shore-boats.

'water-bag.

1. a. A bag of skin or leather used for holding or carrying water, esp. one used in Eastern countries for transporting and distributing water.

1638 SIR T. HERBERT *Trav.* II. (ed. 2) 242 Having soak't their hussinees or water baggs, the wine bottles are then emptied. **1659–60** *Knaresb. Wills* (Surtees) II. 245, 1 pair of water bags. **1779** *Louth Corporation Acc.* (1891) 67 Pd. to John Jeffery for him to get a pair of new Water Bags..10s. 6d. **1850** R. G. CUMMING *Hunter's Life S. Afr.* (1902) 87/1 This skin..is used by the natives for making water-bags, in which they convey supplies of water from the nearest vley or fountain..to the village. **1895** ANNE C. WILSON *5 Yrs. in India* 262 The water-carrier, with his water-bag of goat-skin slung over his left shoulder.

b. *Austral.* A bag, freq. of canvas, used for carrying water, esp. on journeys in dry areas.

1892 [see SHIRALEE]. **1903** 'T. COLLINS' *Such is Life* (1937) i. 47 Helping myself to a drink from the water-bag under the rear of Thompson's wagon. **1944** *Living off Land* iii. 57 Don't carry a reserve supply of water in a waterbag; evaporation alone can dry it all up in a few hours in hot weather. **1969** P. A. SMITH *Folklore Austral. Railwaymen* 19 The water was no good. We'd bring it out in boiling buckets and then fill the gang's water bags.

†**2.** *Her.* In pl. form = WATER-BOUGET 2. *Obs.*

1688 HOLME *Armoury* III. 295/2 He beareth Or, a Water Bowget, Sable. This is the form of the Bowget in ancient times, and was called a Water Budget, or Water Baggs.

3. (See quot. 1859.)

1836 *Penny Cycl.* VI. 189/1 The..free communication which subsists between the water-bag and rumen in the camel tribe. **1859** T. S. COBBOLD *Ruminantia* in *Todd's Cycl. Anat.* V. 536/2 The second stomachal viscus..other-wise called the reticulum, bonnet, or water-bag..is of much smaller dimensions than the paunch, and forms a sort of cul-de-sac between it and the third cavity.

4. 'An india-rubber bag for holding hot water for local application' (*Syd. Soc. Lex.* 1899).
1895 in *Funk's Stand. Dict.*

† **ˈwater-ˌbailage.** *Obs.* Also 8–9 -bail(l)iage. A duty or tax levied on all goods brought into or carried out of the Port of London.
1669 Pepys *Diary* 20 Jan., Heard at the Council-board the City.. debate upon the business of water-baylage—a tax demanded upon all goods, by the City, imported and exported. **1680** *Lond. Gaz.* No. 1490/3 His Majesty having been graciously pleased to release a Judgment obtained upon a *Quo Warranto*, against the City of London, concerning the Duty of Water-Bailage (which is a considerable Revenue to the City). **1753** [see bailage]. **1854** *Fraser's Mag.* XLIX. 564 The groundage of corn is a duty of 6*d.* on every vessel with corn on board entering the port; and the water-bailliage is a duty of one farthing per quarter on all corn so imported.

† **water-bailie.** *Obs.*
1. = water-bailiff 1.
1434 *Acts Privy Counc.* (1835) IV. 197 Officium de Water-baily de Plymmouth. **1544** in *Lett. & Papers Hen. VIII*, XIX. ii. 175 Personages to remain here at Boulloyn.. Edw. Brown, water-bailly, [and others]. **1587** *Reg. Mag. Sig. Scot.* 450/2 Ballivus marinus (watter baillie) Edinburgi aut Lethe. **1600** *Maldon* (Essex) *Documents* Bundle 162, fol. 4, xliiii s. by them receyved of William Gylman, water baylie, for tolls, yssues, and profitts.
2. = water-bailiff 2.
1395 *Early Chanc. Proc.* 3/30 in *Sel. Cases Chancery* (Selden Soc.) 14 Pur quel trespas le dit Andrew se Compleyna.. del Waterbaille de Quenehithe ei come le leye et vsage del ewe demendent. **1467** *Dunfermline Reg.* (Bannatyne Club) 359 [They] sall.. set owre þare nettis.. quhare þai lykis.. ay quhill þe kingis water bal3e mak revlis in þe watire. **1493–4** *Rec. St. Mary at Hill* 197 Item, spentt at the settyng of þe clarkes wages at þe waterbaylyis, ij d. **1518** *Star Chamber Cases* (Selden Soc.) II. 152 To the waterbailly a gowne of iiij brode yardes and an half at v^{s}. **1603** Stow *Surv.* 539 The Sworde bearer, Common hunt, Water Bayly, common Crier,.. &c. **1667** Hale *De Jure Maris* v. in Hargrave *Coll. Tracts* (1787) I. 23 The office of a water-baillie or scrutator is a bare ministerial officer, which the king doth or may appoint in those rivers or places that are in his franchise... And his business was, to look to the king's rights, as his wrecks, his flotsan, jetsan, water-strays, royal fishes. **1691** T. H[ale] *Acc. New Invent.* p. xcvi, The Lord Mayor as Water-bayly and Conservator of the River of Thames. *Ibid.* p. cv, The Lord Mayor's deputy Water-bayly or Sub-Conservators. *c* **1710** Celia Fiennes *Diary* (1888) 245 Ye Lord Major.. attended by all his officers ye sword bearer and water Baily very well dress'd.
b. = water-bailiff 2 b. Now *Sc.*
So † **water-bailiery** *Sc.*, the jurisdiction of a water-bailie.
1593 in *Rec. Convent. Burghs Scot.* (1870) I. 410 The watter bailliery of thair hevin and portt of Pettycure.

ˈwater-ˌbailiff.
†**1.** An officer in various port towns, charged with the enforcement of shipping regulations, the searching of vessels, and the collection of customs. *Obs.*
14.. *Contin. Brut* 583 [Song on Siege of Calais] Remembres eke on Goby, the watir-bailiffes dog, How he scarmysshed with you twyes vpon the day, And among you, on þe sandes, made many a fray. **1450** *Rolls of Parlt.* V. 200/1 Divers Waterbaillifs, Sercheours, Countrollers of the serche. **1467–8** *Stat. Roll Irel. 7 & 8 Edw. IV*, c. 15 Vne officer appelle le Water baillief de dalkey. **1485** *Rolls of Parlt.* VI. 352/2 The Office of Water Bailliff of oure Towne of Gloucestre. **1577–87** Holinshed *Chron.* III. 1203/1 William Robinson esquier, waterbailife of the towne of Newhauen. **1635** *Maldon* (Essex) *Borough Deeds* Bundle 80, fol. 1 Receaved of Francis Tunbridge, water bayliffe of the said burrough, for the tolls, customes, yssues, and profitts of measurage, poundage, and bulkage. **1700** *Pennsylv. Arch.* I. 140 Coll. Qu. sends home a Coppy of the Comm^{ion} to the Water-bailif. **1731** *Act 4 Geo. II*, c. 19 Whereas it is necessary for the better and more orderly Government of the said Port [Ilfracombe], that a Water Bailiff should be appointed, with Power to require all Ships and Vessels to ballast, anchor, and moor in a proper Manner, and regular Places, and that no Ballast be thrown into the said Harbour [[etc.]. **1764** *Phil. Trans.* LIV. 83 When the tide had hardly begun to flow,.. it was observed, by the water-bailif of the City [Bristol].. to rise very suddenly to almost high-water mark. **1871** Kingsley *At Last* vi, He is now coast-guardman, water-bailiff,.. and indeed practical viceroy of the island.
†**b.** An inferior officer of the custom-house, employed to search vessels. *Obs.*
1771 R. Cumberland *West Indian* i. v, The whole tribe of custom-house extortioners, boat-men, tide-waiters and water-bailiffs.
2. An official responsible for the enforcement of bye-laws relating to fishing-waters.
In the City of London, the office was said to be vested in the Lord Mayor, the titular 'water-bailiff' being regarded as his deputy. For the use in the Isle of Man, see quots. 1873 and 1883.
1667 Hale *De Jure Maris* v. in Hargrave *Coll. Tracts* (1787) I. 23 Those Commissions, that have been granted in common rivers, commonly called commissions of conservancy or water-bailiffs. **1677** *Lond. Gaz.* No. 1172/4 His Majesty having been pleased.. to Grant unto Roger Killigrew Esq; the place of Water Bayliff, to have the oversight of the River of Thames, between Staines and Cyrencester. **1697** *Ibid.* No. 3341/2 The City Banner born by the Water-Bayliff. **1720** Strype *Stow's Surv.* II. v. xxviii. 381/1 The Water Bailiff is the Lord Maior's Deputy, or Sub-conservator.. and every fisherman.. every Year upon St. Paul's Day, must appear before the said Water Bailiff at the Chappel of Guild-Hall, to enter their Names into his Register Book. **1759** *Universal Chron.* 17–24 Mar. 91/1 Wednesday night last Thomas Hayward, Esq., Water-Bailiff, with his assistants, seized three drag-nets in the Medway. **1873** J. Lewis *Digest of Census 1871* 203 The Council [of the Isle of Man] consists of the Lord Bishop of the Diocese, the attorney-general, the clerk of the rolls, the two deemsters, the receiver-general, the water-bailiff or admiralty judge, the archdeacon, and the vicar-general. **1883** *Encycl. Brit.* XV. 452 [Isle of Man.] The herring fishery, and the boats employed in it, are placed under the charge of the water-bailiff, who holds courts to redress grievances and enforce the regulations of the fishery.
b. A river-policeman employed to prevent poaching and arrest offenders against the bye-laws.
1860 G. H. K[ingsley] in F. Galton *Vac. Tour.* 161 Without water-bailiffs, who must be paid, how many salmon would there be left for anybody? **1868** Peard *Water-farm.* ix. 99 On the Severn the water-bailiffs are furnished with a .... summary of the law they have to enforce. **1897** Crockett *Lad's Love* xix, Nor did the gamekeepers and water-bailiffs——the 'watchers'—as they were called—trouble their heads much about sleepy Rab.
†**3.** An officer of the Warden of the Marches: see quot. *Obs.*
1592 in *Archaeologia* XXII. 168 There is belonging to either warden a Water-bayliffe... Theire office is to keepe the entrance of all men without lycense out of either March.

ˈwater-ˌbalance.
†**1.** An appliance, consisting of a scale-beam caused to oscillate by the fall of a stream of water, forming part of a machine for raising water for irrigation purposes. *Obs.*
There is some doubt whether the appliance described by Darwin was ever in practical use.
1800 E. Darwin *Phytologia* xi. Pl. VI, After a time the water balance *q r s* closes the cocks now open, and opens their antagonists.
2. A machine for raising loads to a height, consisting of two cars with water-vessels attached, connected by a chain passing over a pulley, so that the empty car is made to descend by the weight of water in its vessel, thus hoisting up the loaded car.
1875 J. H. Collins *Metal Mining* 84 The Water-Balance.——In many of the open works on the northern side of the great coal basin of South Wales, water-balance machines are largely used for winding purposes. **1886** J. Barrowman *Sc. Mining Terms* 71 *Water-balance*, an arrangement by which a descending tank of water raises mineral in a shaft by a rope passed over a pulley. **1901** *Westm. Gaz.* 16 Feb. 6/2 Hastings Town Council has resolved to construct a water-balance lift to hoist visitors to the breezy heights of East Hill.
3. *Aeronautics.* (See quot.)
1903 *Daily News* 21 Sept. 4/6 The other chief new point in the construction is the water-balance, which will maintain the machine in a horizontal position.. as the airship swings round into the wind.
4. (Written as two words.) Equilibrium between water intake and water loss.
1922 *Physiol. Rev.* II. 158 In diabetes insipidus, the water balance is set at a level higher than normal. **1957** G. E. Hutchinson *Treat. Limnol.* I. iv. 228 (*heading*) Water balance of the hydrosphere and of continental surfaces. **1974** Passmore & Robson *Compan. Med. Stud.* III. xlix. 9/2 The driving force of thirst normally ensures the minimum daily intake of water needed to maintain water balance.

ˈwater-ball.
1. A globe of glass filled with water, used to collect and throw the rays of light upon an object.
1665 Hooke *Microgr.* 53. *Ibid.* 181 The Eggs of Silk-worms.. afford a pretty Object for a Microscope.. especially if.. the light of a window be cast or collected on it by a deep Convex-glass, or Water-ball.
2. *hour water-ball* [after *hour-glass*], a contrivance for measuring time by the rising and sinking of a ball in water.
1655 Marq. Worcester *Cent. Inv.* Index, An Hour Water-ball.
3. (See quots.)
1696 R. H. *Sch. Recreat.* 30 A Fire that will burn in the Water, or Water Ball. **1799** G. Smith *Laboratory* I. 43 Water-balls, or globes, made of wood, which swim and burn upon the water.

† **water-bank.** *Obs.* A bank of a river; also, the sea-shore.
1382 Wyclif *Acts* xxvii. 39 Thei biheelden sum hauene hauynge a water banke, into which thei thou3ten.. for to caste the schipp. *c* **1400** *Destr. Troy* 4239 For many a Troyen sen thei stonde Armed wel opon the londe, To put hem fro the water bankes. *c* **1425** *St. Christina* vii. in *Anglia* VIII. 122 þe preste.. come and stood vpoun þe watir-banke. **1470–85** Malory *Arthur* iv. vi. 125 Thenne were they ware of the herte that lay on a grete water banke, and a brachet bytynge on his throte. **1546** *Yorks. Chantry Surv.* (Surtees) 56 The yerly reparacions of the waterbanke. *a* **1578** Lindesay (Pitscottie) *Chron. Scot.* (S.T.S.) I. 76 Wtheris.. war cruellie slaine wpoun the watter bankis. **1706** Phillips (ed. Kersey), *Sinus*,.. the running or hollowness of Water-banks.
fig. **1533** tr. *Erasm. Expos. Commune Creed* U ij b, Swearyng.. is very cosyn and nere to synne, and it is no good trustyng to this daungerous waterbanke.

† **waterbarge.** *Obs.* In 7 -berge. [f. water *sb.* + ***berge*, **barge*, of obscure origin, but app. identical with the first element of barge-board, -couple, -course. Cf. dial. '*Barge, bairge*, the outer edge of a gable' (*Eng. Dial. Dict.*).] A slab placed along the edge of a roof to afford protection from rain. Hence † **waterbarge** *v.* (Sc. *-bairge*), to furnish with 'waterbarges'.
1558 *Abstr. Protocols Town Clerks Glasgow* (1896) II. 58 The said Cuthtbert to riguell and wattirbairge the saidis Johne C. and to halde hym wattirfast. **1603** G. Owen *Pembrokeshire* (1892) 79 This stonne is Easilie hewed and searveth in buildinges to make wyndowes,.. Coinestones, waterberges, and wynd berges or any other hewen worke.

ˈwater-bath.
1. *Chem.* A vessel containing boiling water or water heated to a given temperature in or over which preparations are placed in suitable vessels to be digested, evaporated or dried.
1824 *Chem. Recreat.* 226 *Bath* (*Water*) A vessel of boiling water, in which other vessels containing water are to be placed. **1874** Garrod & Baxter *Mat. Med.* 70 The liquid is decanted from the precipitated oxide; the latter is then washed with distilled water, and dried on a water-bath. **1888** Rutley *Rock-Forming Min.* 6 It.. has the great advantage of not crystallizing out when cooling after concentration upon the water-bath.
2. = bain-marie.
1833 Loudon *Encycl. Archit.* §593 [In] A Design for a Cottage Kitchen Grate... Fig. 526 shows the top of the water-bath, with holes at one end for inserting saucepans. **1891** *Century Dict.*
3. A bath composed of water as distinguished from a vapour-bath.
1891 *Century Dict.* **1909** *Westm. Gaz.* 4 Feb. 9/2 Equipment.. for the treatment of nervous diseases, in the shape of water-baths, electrical appliances, [etc.].

ˈwater-bear. [bear *sb.*^{1}]
†**1.** = sea-bear 3. *Obs.*
1706 Phillips (ed. Kersey), *Water-Bears*, a sort of Bears in Spitsberg, or North-East Greenland, that live by what they catch in the Sea.
2. A sloth-animalcule.
1852 A. Pritchard *Infusorial Animal.* (new ed.) 685 They are very sluggish in their movements, and are commonly known under the name of 'little water bears'. **1861** H. J. Slack *Marv. Pond-life* 23 Last in the list we have the *Tardigrada*, 'Slow-steppers,' or Water Bears, queer little creatures, something like new-born puppies, with a double allowance of imperfect feet. **1889** [see sloth *sb.*^{1} 5].

ˈwater-ˌbearer.
1. One who carries water; *spec.* one whose employment is to carry water from a spring, well, or river for domestic use. *Obs.* exc. in descriptions of Eastern countries.
1382 Wyclif *Neh.* iii. 26 Gabonites, water bereris forsothe dwelten in Ofel a3en the 3ate of watris at the est. **1466** *Mann. & Househ. Exp.* (Roxb.) 437 Item, owynge to the waterberere for berynge of water, vj.d. **1524–5** *Rec. St. Mary at Hill* (1904) 328 Receued at the Maryage of chappell, the waturberer, vj d. **1549** Latimer *Serm. Ploughers* (Arb.) 28 Yf there be neuer a wyse man, make a water bearer, a tinker,.. a page, comptroller of the mynte. **1598** B. Jonson *Ev. Man in Hum.* i. iii, *Mat.* Lie in a water-bearers house, a gentleman of his note? weil ile tell him my mind. **1698** Fryer *Acc. E. India & P.* 9 Their Head-geer a Clout rowled up like our Water-Bearers. **1877** F. Burnaby *Through Asia Minor* I. xx. 229 The gusts [of wind] were a source of.. inconvenience to the water-bearers; their hands being occupied with the pitchers.
2. *Astr.* = Aquarius.
1594 Blundevil *Exerc.*, *Cosmogr.* i. xxiv. (1597) 158 The eleaueneth Signe called Aquarius, that is to saye, the water bearer contayning two and fourtie starres. **1868** Lockyer *Guillemin's Heavens* (ed. 3) 328 Near the horizon towards the east are perceived the constellations of the Waterbearer and the Goat.
So **ˈwater-ˌbearing** *vbl. sb.*, the action of carrying water as a water-bearer (sense 1).
1481–90 *Howard Househ. Bks.* (Roxb.) 355 Item, the same day, for Waterberynge xij. d.

ˈwater-ˌbearing, *a.* **a.** Of a country: Producing water; not arid. **b.** *Geol.* Of a stratum, bed: Through which water percolates.
1859 H. Kingsley *G. Hamlyn* xlii, The little sienite peak, the last symptom of a water-bearing country, has disappeared behind us. **1862** *Rep. Directors E. Ind. Railway Co.* 23 The large well has been completed, a water-bearing stratum having been reached. **1877** Huxley *Physiogr.* 33 The liquid with which the water-bearing bed is charged. **1890** *Hardwicke's Science-Gossip* XXVI. 249 The sand-stones and pebble beds are noted for their water-bearing characteristics.

ˈwater-bed.
1. A bed on board ship as distinguished from one ashore. *nonce-use.*
1615 Sandys *Trav.* 27 To his house I repaired, with hope of some refreshment after my wearisome voyage: but he then from home, I was forced to returne to my water-bed.
2. A stratum through which water percolates.
1791 Smeaton *Edystone L.* §328 When sunk into, deep enough to pierce the water bed. **1886** A. Winchell *Walks Geol. Field* 32 There are districts where waterbeds may be traced for one or two miles.
3. a. A water-tight mattress filled with water, serving as a bed (orig. for an invalid).
1844 A. N. Brown *Let.* 28 Nov. in *Church Missionary Soc. Archives*: *New Zealand Mission* (MS.), Our kind Bishop had him removed to his House the day he was taken ill and planned a water bed to place him on. *c* **1848** J. R. Planché *Extravaganzas* (1879) III. 294 And something like the sort o' bed That Dr Arnolt designates a water bed. **1853** Mrs. Gaskell *Ruth* vii, Water-beds coming by the carrier, and a doctor from London coming down to-morrow. **1862** Sala *Seven Sons* III. i. 5 Who so hale and strong but he may find

the water-bed a luxury? **1899** *Allbutt's Syst. Med.* VI. 720 The severest cases require a water-bed.

b. A plastic mattress filled with water, designed as an alternative to a conventional bed. Also *fig.*

1970 *Time* 7 Sept. 42 His efforts to improve it led him [*sc.* C. P. Hall] to a much splashier creation... It is the water bed. **1971** *Guardian* 5 Oct. 10/1 The water-bed is simply an ultra-sonically welded vinyl bag filled..with around 150 gallons of water, and contained in a wooden frame which rests on the floor or can be raised to conventional bed height. **1977** *Time Out* 21 Jan. 43 (*caption*) 'The Odyssey', a soft, billowing water-bed of a piece that's performed at the Albert Hall on Tuesday by no less than ten keyboard players plus tympani and vocals. **1978** J. IRVING *World according to Garp* xi. 205 Garp slumps back on the water bed,..the bed rolls like a small sea. **1984** *Listener* 19 July 17/4 (Advt.), For couples who want to get away together..4 poster beds, water beds—with whirlpool bath en suite.

4. *Anat.* The cavity between the arachnoidea and pia mater containing cerebrospinal fluid, upon which the brain rests.

1899 *Allbutt's Syst. Med.* VI. 435 In the circle of Willis, where the arteries lie on a yielding water-bed, the subarachnoid space. *Ibid.* VII. 536 A constant secretion of watery fluid into the ventricles is kept up, in order to maintain the water-bed on which the brain rests.

water-bloom ('wɔːtəbluːm). [f. WATER *sb.* + BLOOM *sb.*[1]] **1.** A flower living in water. *poet. rare.*

1820 SHELLEY *Sensit. Pl.* III. 42 The water-blooms under the rivulet Fell from the stalks on which they were set.

2. [tr. G. *wasserblüte.*] (See quot. 1957.) Cf. RED-WATER 4.

1927, 1948 [see BREAKING *vbl. sb.* 2c]. **1957** *New Biol.* XXIII. 86 'Water-bloom'..describes the discoloration of the waters of ponds and lakes, sometimes slow-flowing rivers and occasionally vast areas of the sea by a superabundance of free-floating, microscopic, plant and, in rare cases, animal life. **1963** [see PERIDINIAN].

'water-board.

†**1.** A board to throw off water; a gutter, louver-board, or the like. *Obs.*

1417 *For. Acc. 8 Hen. V* D/2 In diuersis peciis Maeremii Bordis vocatis Waynescotbordis Waterbordis Shipbordis Englisshbordis [etc.]. **1477–9** *Rec. St. Mary at Hill* (1904) 85 To a Carpynter, for his labour, a principall post & a watir borde, xx d. **1585** HIGINS *Junius' Nomencl.* 210/2 *Deliquiæ*, ..water boords, or weather bordes: gutters whereinto the house eaues doe drop.

b. (See quot.)

1815 *Falconer's Dict. Marine* (ed. Burney), *Water-Boards* or Weather-Boards of a boat, are large boards used to keep out the waves or spray of the sea.

†**2.** A sideboard upon which the water to be served at a meal was placed. *Obs.*

1474 in *Househ. Ord.* (1790) *32 If any man come to late to mattyns..he shall sytt at the water boarde, and have nothinge unto his dynner but breade and water.

3. (Written *Water Board.*) An administrative body having control of the supply of water to a town or district.

1902 *Daily Chron.* 18 Jan. 6/1 The full title of Mr. Long's promised measure is 'A Bill for establishing a Water Board to manage the supply of water within London and certain adjoining districts'.

‖**waterbok** ('wɔːtəbɒk). Also 9 -boc, -bock; and see WATER-BUCK. [a. Du. *waterbok*, f. *water* WATER *sb.* + *bok* (see BUCK *sb.*[1] 1 e).] = WATER-BUCK.

1835 A. SMITH *Diary* 20 Sept. (1940) II. 240 The flesh coarse-grained and exactly like the flesh of the waterbok. *c* **1850** *Nat. Encycl.* I. 813 The other, a waterboc, was found in Karagŭé. **1863** SPEKE *Discov. Nile* iii. 36 'The bags' we made counted two brindled gnū, four water-boc, one pallah-boc, and one pig. **1873** ELLEN B. FREWER tr. *Schweinfurth's Hrt. Africa* v. (1878) 160 These antelopes belonged to the Waterboks (*Antilope ellipsiprymna*)... The hair of this species of Waterbock is extremely long and soft. **1885** *Riverside Nat. Hist.* (1888) V. 336 The Water-bok of South Africa (*Kobus ellipsiprymnus*), which extends through Central Africa up to Abyssinia, where it is known as the Méhedéhet.

'water-boot[1]. = BOOTS[2].

1665–76 RAY *Flora* 133 The double Marsh-marigold is no other than that we commonly call the Water-Boot. **1846** [ANNE PRATT] *Wild Flowers of Year* 27 The marsh marigold (*Caltha palustris*) is well known in villages as the water-blob and water-boot.

'water-boot[2]. [BOOT *sb.*[3]] A kind of jackboot designed for the use of those who have to stand or walk in water.

1813 COL. HAWKER *Diary* (1893) I. 88, I tramped in water boots to the town of Christchurch. **1883** *Fisheries Exhib. Catal.* 62 Water Boots of all lengths. **1887** BARING-GOULD *Gaverocks* x, Last time I went up tiffening in my water-boots; I'm to go in pumps, that is what she means.

'water-borne, *a.* [BORNE *ppl. a.*]

1. Of a boat: Supported by the water so as to be clear of the ground or bottom upon which it has rested; afloat.

1608 *Relat. Trav. W. Bush* E2b, Into which River he passed with his wheeles, vntill he was water-borne. **1644** MANWAYRING *Sea-mans Dict.* 114 When a ship is even just of the ground that she floates, then she is water-borne. **1790** BEATSON *Nav. & Mil. Mem.* II. 254 Launches..were employed in carrying out warps to drag the ships through the mud, as soon as they should be water-borne. **1896** *Strand Mag.* XII. 322/1 The available width for launching is limited, and ships, as a rule, must be pulled up as soon as they are water-borne or completely afloat.

b. *transf.* Said of a living body or an inanimate object.

1886 R. C. LESLIE *Sea Painter's Log* i. 13 Redshanks, godwits, knots, and other waders can move as fast or faster just waterborne in shallow pools..than they can run. **1886** *Manch. Courier* 14 Dec. 8/5 He thought most of the [capsized lifeboat] men were water-borne. **1897** KIPLING *Capt. Cour.* iii. 73 In a dory the weight of a cod is water-borne till the last minute.

2. Of goods: **a.** Carried or transported by water; conveyed by ship or boat. Hence of traffic, commerce.

1702 LUTTRELL *Brief Rel.* V. 158 This day they [the commons]..past the bill for measuring waterborn fruit. **1711** *Lond. Gaz.* No. 4818/1 Duties upon Coals to be Water-born, and carried Coast-wise. **1790** *Act 30 Geo. III*, c. 55 §17 Butter..to be..water-borne, from the said Market, shall be viewed. **1800** COLQUHOUN *Comm. Thames* xi. 331 Fruit and Vegetables, water-borne on the Thames. **1871** *Daily News* 19 May, Scarcely one-third of the fish brought to Billingsgate is waterborne. **1916** *Blackw. Mag.* July 35/2 The orders were to avoid all collisions with the enemy as long as he made no attempt to interrupt our water-borne traffic. **1916** *Edin. Rev.* July 180 Sailing directions are as old as water-borne commerce.

b. Put aboard a vessel for shipment.

1558–9 GRESHAM in Burgon *Life* (1839) I. 258 To understand perfectly at the customers' hands, at the same day, whether all the cloths and kerseys be entryed and shipped and water-borne. And being once all water-borne, then to make a stay of all the fleete. **1662** *Act 14 Chas. II*, c. 11 §7 If any Wharfinger..shall Ship off or suffer to be Water-born at or from any of theire said Wharfs..any Goods..prohibited..such Wharfinger..shall..pay the Summe of One hundred pounds. **1859** in *Merc. Marine Mag.* (1860) VII. 7 Goods thus shipped, or water-borne to be shipped.

3. Of disease: Communicated or propagated by the use of contaminated drinking-water.

1892 *Daily News* 24 Nov. 2/1 Any waterborne epidemic. **1894** *Pop. Sci. Monthly* XLIV. 558 That leads to the dissemination of water-borne diseases.

water bottle.

1. A vessel of leather or skin used in certain countries, esp. by water-bearers or water-carriers, to convey water for domestic use.

1591 PERCIVALL *Sp. Dict.*, *Zanges, zagues*, water bottle, *Lagena, vterculus.* **1914** *Daily News* 9 Mar. 6 A little tip-tapping burros..with panniers holding water-bottles, came round to the doors [in Valparaiso].

2. A bottle to hold drinking water. **a.** One placed on the table for use at meals or in a bedroom.

1825 T. HOOK *Sayings* Ser. II. *Passion & Princ.* vi, The washing-stand [was] soapless, the ewer and water-bottle empty. **1835** DICKENS *Sk. Boz, Thoughts about People*, If he can get it [the newspaper] while he is at dinner, he eats with much greater zest; balancing it against the water-bottle. **1847** C. BRONTË *Jane Eyre* xx, He held out the tiny glass, and I half filled it from the water bottle on the wash-stand.

b. A kind of flask used by soldiers and travellers.

1889 RIDER HAGGARD *Allan's Wife* vi, By an afterthought, we filled our water-bottles. **1898** *Daily News* 8 Mar, 3/2 [The soldiers] will have to carry nothing but their rifles—not even their water bottles.

3. *nonce-use.* A bottle filled with water.

1766 SMOLLETT *Trav.* xiii. I. 224 He places them [the cut carnations] in water-bottles,..and they will continue fresh and unfaded, the best part of a month.

4. = *hot-water bottle* s.v. HOT WATER 1 b.

1840 J. ROMILLY *Diary* 31 Dec. (1967) 207 Lodge burnt his leg with a water bottle & laid up. **1905** S. WEYMAN *Starvecrow Farm* xxv. 230 That was not the day of bedroom fires, or rubber water-bottles. **1929** W. FAULKNER *Sound & Fury* 334 Dilsey reached the top of the stairs and took the water bottle. 'I'll fix hit in a minute... I gwine build de fire myself.'

†**water-bouge.** *Obs.* [Cf. the earlier WATER BULGE.] = WATER-BOUGET. (In quots. *Her.*)

c **1449** *Pol. Poems* (Rolls) II. 223 The Water-Bowge and the Wyne-Botelle, With the Vetturlockes cheyne bene fast. **1550** in *Rep. MSS. Ld. Middleton* (1911) 482 Two stampes of the water boudge for vessell. A brande of the water boudge to marke cattell. **1572** [see BOUGE *sb.*[1] 1 b.].

water bouget. *Obs.* exc. *Her.*

†**1.** A skin or leather bag formerly used to carry water, usually carried in pairs either slung across a stick over the shoulder or across the back of a horse.

a **1566** R. EDWARDS *Damon & Pithias* (1571) Fj b, These are no hose, but watter bougets,..Good for none, but suche as haue no buttockes. **1632** [see 2].

2. *Her.* = BOUGET.

1632 GUILLIM *Heraldry* IV. xviii. (ed. 2) 354 The Water-bowgets, which in ancient times were vsed to carry and conserue in the Campe that vsefull element of Water. **1688, 1859** [see BOUGET]. **1864** BOUTELL *Her. Hist. & Pop.* xiii. 115 The lining is semée of small water-bougets, sable. **1894** *Parker's Gloss. Her.*, *Water-bouget*, a yoke with two large skins appended to it, formerly used for the conveyance of water to an army.

'water-bough. *Obs.* exc. *dial.* (See quots. 1618, 1699 and cf. WATER-SHOOTS.)

1387 TREVISA *Higden* V. 263 As water bowes beeþ i-kutte and i-hewe of treen. **1398** —— *Barth. De P.R.* XVII. ii. (1495) 604 Yf water bowes and superfluyte ben pared of: the tree bereth the beter and the more fruyte. **1523–34** FITZHERB. *Husb.* §129 Cut away all the water-bowes, and the small bowes, that the pryncipall bowes may haue the more sap. **1591** GREENE *Farew. Follie* Wks. (Grosart) IX. 259 As the fairest Cedar hath his water boughes,..and the sweetest rose his prickle: so in a crowne is hidden far more care than content. **1618** W. LAWSON *New Orchard & Garden* xi. (1623) 38 Water boughes, or vndergrowth, are such boughes as grow low vnder others and are by them ouergrowne, ouershadowed, dropped on, and pinde for want of plentie of sap. **1699** MEAGER *New Art Gard.* 46 Take the Water-boughs away, which are those on the Standards that are shaded, and dropt upon, remaining smooth and naked without Buds. **1871** KINGSLEY *At Last* xi, The stem rises, without a fork, for sixty feet or more, and rolls out at the top into a head very like that of an elm trimmed up, and like an elm too in its lateral water-boughs.

'water-bound, *a.* [BOUND *ppl. a.*[2]]

†**1.** *Allusive nonce-use.* Unable to shed tears.

Perh. merely coined to match the corresponding use of *wind-bound* in the context. But it is possible that sense 2 was current in Fuller's time.

1646 FULLER *Wounded Consc.* (1647) 62 And though thou beest water-bound, be not wind-bound also, sigh, where thou canst not sob.

2. Confined or detained by floods. Cf. WIND-BOUND *a.*

1862 *New York Tribune* 30 Apr. 1/3 While water-bound, it [a foraging party] was attacked by guerrillas.

3. Of clay: ? Impervious to water. ? *Obs.*

1710 HILMAN *Tusser Rediv.* Oct. (1744) 136 Yet in some Years it [the clay] is very apt to be Water-bound and Steely.

4. Of macadam roads: Solidified by rolling and watering.

1909 *Westm. Gaz.* 30 Aug. 2/1 Where water is scarce..for the re-coating of a water-bound road. **1919** *Glasgow Her.* 24 June 4 Mr. Drummond has no hesitation in calling for the abolition of the long-established water-bound macadam.

'water-break.

†**1.** An irruption of water: = *water-breach* (WATER *sb.* 20). *Obs.*

1513 DOUGLAS *Æneis* II. vi. 15 Quhen the burne on spait hurlis doun the bank, Othir throw a water brek, or spait of fluide.

2. Broken water, a piece of broken water.

1806 WORDSW. *Misc. Sonn.* II. xxxi. 5 Brook!..whom the curious Painter doth pursue Through rocky passes,..And tracks thee dancing down thy water-breaks. **1835** —— *To May* 75 Streams..Gurgling in foamy water-break, Loitering in glassy pool. **1850** CLOUGH *Dipsychus* II. iv. 94 The dashing stream Stays not to pick his steps among the rocks, Or let his water-breaks be chronicled. **1855** TENNYSON *Brook* 61 And here and there a foamy flake Upon me, as I travel With many a silvery waterbreak Above the golden gravel. **1899** STOPF. A. BROOKE in L. P. Jacks *Life & Lett.* (1917) II. v. xxv. 512 The gay stream, which..runs from one foaming water-break to another.

3. A breakwater. ? *nonce-use.*

1875 tr. *Comte de Paris' Hist. Civ. War America* I. 448 This island..stretches in front of the entrance of Pensacola Bay; and at the extremity of this natural waterbreak stands Fort Pickens.

'water-buck. [Anglicized form of Du. WATERBOK: see BUCK *sb.*[1] 1 e.] A species of antelope, *Cobus ellipsiprymnus*, found in watered districts in central South Africa; an animal of this species which is marked with a characteristic white ring round the buttocks. Sometimes applied to other species, as the SING-SING (*C. defassa*).

1839 W. C. HARRIS *Wild Sports S. Afr.* 186 A water buck ..is about the size of an ass and of somewhat browner colour. **1850** R. G. CUMMING *Hunter's Life S. Afr.* (1902) 120/2, I..rode up to the banks of the river with my dogs to seek for water-buck. **1876** T. E. BUCKLEY in *Proc. Zool. Soc.* 284 Cobus ellipsiprymnus. (The Waterbuck.) A common species, extending from the Zulu country through the east of Equatorial Africa into Abyssinia... It seems never to be found far from water, through which it does not hesitate to go when alarmed. **1910** ROOSEVELT *Afr. Game Trails* ix. 215 Kermit killed a waterbuck of a kind new to us—the sing-sing. *Ibid.* x. 227, I spent a couple of days trying for sing-sing waterbuck on the edge of the papyrus.

attrib. **1863** W. C. BALDWIN *Afr. Hunting* iii. 87, I had two good chances at buffaloes,..one at a waterbuck ram. *Ibid.* v. 125 A waterbuck skin. **1910** ROOSEVELT *Afr. Game Trails* x. 228, I killed a fine waterbuck cow at a hundred yards.

'water-budge. Also 7 -bugge. †**a.** = WATER-BOUGET. *Obs.* **b.** *dial.* A cask on wheels, to serve as a water-cart.

1541 *Rutland MSS.* (1905) IV. 310 For ij halters for the water budgis, ij d. for shoyng of the water budges horse, vj d. **1603** STOW *Surv.* 349 Stephen Bugge Gent. his Armes be three water bugges, 1419. **1897** MRS. COMYNS CARR *Cottage Folk* 3 The stubble-field where her comrades [*sc.* hoppers in Sussex] were laughing and chattering around the water-budge that had been drawn up in its midst.

water budget. = WATER BOUGET. †**a.** *gen. Obs.* **b.** *Her. rare.*

a. 1591 PERCIVALL *Sp. Dict.*, *Odre*, a water budget, a bottle. **1706** J. STEVENS *Span. Eng. Dict.*, *Zangés*, a Water-budget to carry Water in. **1836** *Beckford's Vathek* 12 Is it not enough to have transformed a prince..into a water budget? [F. *une outre*; 1786 *reads* one of those leather barrels, which *etc.*] Perceivest thou not, that I may perish by drinking to excess?

b. 1562 LEGH *Armory* 176b, He beareth Sanguine, a Gorge, Argent. Though this seme vnlikely to be a water budget, yet hath it long time been so taken, and so blazed. **1880** *Encycl. Brit.* XI. 704/1 The Water Budget or bucket is an early charge identified with the names of Ros and Rose.

†**water bulge.** *Obs. rare*$^{-1}$. = WATER-BOUGE.

c **1230** [see BULGE 1].

Waterbury ('wɔːtəbərɪ). The name of a town in Connecticut, U.S.A., used *attrib.* or *absol.* to designate a low-priced watch or clock of a type manufactured there.

1884 *Official Gaz.* (U.S. Patent Office) 6 May 526/1 *The Waterbury Watch Company*, Waterbury, Conn. Application filed July 21, 1883. 'The words "*The Waterbury*".' **1887** KIPLING *Plain Tales from Hills* (1888) 73 Platte, .. being poor, had a Waterbury watch and a plain leather guard. **1890** B. HALL *Turnover Club* 16 The Reporter drew from its resting place the Waterbury chronometer. **1893** SOMERVILLE & 'ROSS' *Vine Country* vi. 105 My cousin with some trouble disinterred the Waterbury. **1908** *Sears, Roebuck Catal.* 348/1 Our new eight-day Waterbury Clock. *c* **1909** D. H. LAWRENCE *Collier's Friday Night* (1934) iii. 76 He .. takes a Waterbury watch with a brass chain from the wall beside the book-case. **1920** F. E. GREEN *Hist. Eng. Agricultural Labourer 1870–1920* IV. 93 He turned up .. on Sunday with a fashionable billycock, a walking stick and a Waterbury. **1939** JOYCE *Finnegans Wake* 290 O Shee who then (4.32 M.P., .. according to all three doctors waterburies) [etc.]. **1963** C. MACKENZIE *My Life & Times* II. 42, I kept surreptitiously looking at my ten-and-sixpenny Waterbury watch.

'water-butt. A large open-headed cask set up on end to receive the rain-water from a roof.

1833 LOUDON *Encycl. Archit.* §448 Water-butt and stand. **1835** DICKENS *Sk. Boz, Early Coaches*, The water is 'coming in' in every area, the pipes have burst, the water-butts are running over. **1849** C. BRONTE *Shirley* xxxii, A woman as round and big as our largest water-butt. **1873** MISS THACKERAY *Wks.* (1891) I. 70 George jumped out of window on to the water-butt, to see what was the matter.

b. A contemptuous epithet for a teetotaller.

1898 *Daily News* 4 May 6/6 Scoffing comrades couldn't call *him* a waterbutt or a milksop.

'water-can.

1. A portable vessel (in mod. use, of tin-plate or other metal) for holding or conveying water.

c **1375** *Sc. Leg. Saints* xxii. (*Laurence*) 361 With þat he brocht a vatir-cane, & laurens hyme baptist þane. *a* **1400** *Nominale* (Skeat) 485 Lauour basyn et poot ewer And watur-canne. **1687** SHADWELL *Juvenal, Sat.* x. 100 Mechanicks soon from that so Worship't face Forge little Platters, and small water Cans [L. *urceolos*]. **1858** SIMMONDS *Dict. Trade, Water-can*, a tin vessel for holding water for a dressing-room.

b. *Astr.*

1870 PROCTOR *Other Worlds* xii. 287 The two streams from the Water-can of Aquarius.

2. The yellow water-lily, *Nuphar lutea*, so called from the shape of the seed-vessels. Also the white water-lily, *Nymphæa alba*.

1622 DRAYTON *Poly-olb* xx. 135 With Water-cans againe, some [Nymphs] wantonly them dight, Whose larger leafe and flower, gaue wonderfull delight. **1630** —— *Muses Elizium* (1892) 18 Water-cans and King-cups ranck. **1796** WITHERING *Brit. Plants* (ed. 3) II. 489 *Nymphæa lutea*... Yellow Water Lilly, or Watercan. *Ibid.*, *N. alba*... Water-lily, Water-can.

'water-ˌcarriage.

1. Conveyance or transportation of people, goods, etc. by water.

1536 *MS. Rawl. D.* 780 fol. 74 For the water carriage of xj loodes iiij fote of the sayd tymbre. **1548–9** in Feuillerat *Revels Edw. VI* (1914) 39 For the water caryage of hangynges ffrom the blake ffryers to the courte at westminster. *a* **1687** PETTY *Polit. Arith.* i. (1691) 10 Conveniencies for Shipping and Water-Carriage. **1726** LEONI *Alberti's Archit.* I. 4 b, The easy bringing in .. of Necessaries, both by Land Carriage and Water Carriage. **1823** SCOTT *Quentin D.* xix, The Maes, .. traversing the city in various directions, offered to every quarter the commercial facilities of water-carriage. *c* **1875** FLOR. NIGHTINGALE in *Contemp. Rev.* (1914) Apr. 514 Is not water-carriage generally the cheapest, the working expenses being so exceedingly small?

b. Carrying away (of sewage) by water.

1873 B. LATHAM *Sanitary Engin.* 39 When a complete system of sewerage is intended to be carried out, and water-carriage is to be used for the removal of all the refuse and fæcal matter usually transported by sewers. **1876** *Jrnl. Soc. Arts* 9 June 728/1 Mr. Richard Monson asked .. if he considered it a better plan to store sewage at every dwelling than to remove it directly by means of water-carriage. *Ibid.*, It was impossible at the present moment to say whether the old prevailing system in this country was better or worse than the water-carriage system.

2. Means or facilities for transporting by water.

1727 ARBUTHNOT *Tables Anc. Coins* etc. 228 Ptolomy Philadelphus .. open'd the Water-carriage from Alexandria to the Indies, by establishing Staples on the Canals of the Nile. **1744** BERKELEY *Siris* §25 The timber, by its remoteness from water carriage, is of small value. **1857** LIVINGSTONE *Trav.* xxix. 594 The great object of my journey being to secure water carriage. **1893** D. J. RANKIN *Zambesi Basin* xii. 205 There is naturally nothing which tends so rapidly and effectually to develop commerce and civilisation as that offered by good water-carriage.

†**b.** *collectively.* Vessels, boats. *Obs.*

1727 ARBUTHNOT *Tables Anc. Coins* etc. 215 The most brittle Water-carriage was used among the Egyptians, who, as Strabo saith, would sail sometimes in Boats made of Earthen-ware.

3. *dial.* A channel for carrying off water.

1794 T. DAVIS *Agric. Wilts* 37 The manager of the mead .. begins cleaning out the main drain, then the main carriage, and then proceeds to .. make good all the water carriages that the cattle have trodden down. **1819** REES *Cycl.*, VI. R 3, s.v. *Canal*, A cut or water-carriage may be taken out of the summit's level, and carried on along the side of the hill with a proper fall. **1898** MISS YONGE *Keble's Parishes* vi. 71 He .. took his revenge by a flying leap over a broad 'water carriage,' leaving them to follow as they could.

'water-ˌcarrier.

1. One who transports goods, etc. by water, not by land or railway. In quot. 1764, a barge-master.

1764 [J. BURTON] *Pres. St. Navig. Thames* 14 These Water-carriers .. look upon themselves as Masters and Lords of the River; .. refusing Carriage of Goods, but on their own Terms, [etc.]. **1881** *Chicago Times* 17 June, The railroads, in their anxiety to secure employment for their idle rolling-stock, will bid against the water-carriers. **1892** *Daily News* 4 Aug. 3/4 Their [*sc.* the railway company's] carrying traffic in wool .. had suffered .. through the competition of a combination of water carriers.

2. A man (or animal) that carries water; *esp.* in oriental countries, the person who supplies an establishment or a number of troops with water.

1787 tr. *Volney's Trav. Syria & Egypt* (1788) I. 256 *note*, At Cairo, it is observed, that the water-carriers, continually wet with the fresh water they carry in skins upon their backs, are never subject to the plague. **1824** MORIER *Hajji Baba* ix, The muleteer .. recommended me strongly to become a *saka*, or water-carrier. **1855** *Poultry Chron.* III. 374 These bees are water-carriers. **1882** F. M. CRAWFORD *Mr. Isaacs* xi. 231, I told him to send a *bhisti*, a water-carrier, with his leathern bucket. **1899** *Atlantic Monthly* LXXXIII. 760/1 Some of the burros were water carriers, with great earthen jars swung in pairs against their panting sides.

3. Something that carries water.

a. A tank or other vessel for carrying water. (See also quot. 1875.)

1854 *Hull Improv. Act* 36 A sufficient number of .. water-carriers, trucks, water-carts. **1875** KNIGHT *Dict. Mech.*, *Water-carrier*, a form of water-elevator in which the bucket lifted from the well or cistern is transported on wires to the house at a considerable distance.

b. *dial.* An open channel for water, esp. in an irrigated meadow.

1879 JEFFERIES *Wild Life* 373 The wild duck .. swim in the water-carriers in the great irrigated meadows.

c. *dial.* A rain-cloud.

a **1887** JEFFERIES *Field & Hedgerow* (1889) 16 The water-carriers, harnessed to the south and west winds, drilling the long rows of rain like seeds into the earth.

'water-cart, *sb.* A cart, usually a barrel or tank on wheels, carrying water; chiefly, an apparatus of this kind intended for watering the streets, the receptacle being fitted with an arrangement by which the water escapes through a number of small holes as the vehicle goes along.

1707–21 MORTIMER *Husb.*, (J.) A gentleman .. watered St. foin .. with a water-cart. **1789** *Trans. Soc. Arts* II. 49 A barrel cart, or what is commonly called a water-cart. **1801** *Farmer's Mag.* Aug. 278 Some superior managers even supply them [*sc.* sheep] regularly with water, in long narrow troughs, led by means of a water-cart, while in the fold on dry hay. **1818** SCOTT *Hrt. Midl.* i, Performing the part of three water-carts for the benefit of their dusty roads. **1875** RUSKIN *Fors Clav.* V. 56 During the filling of the water-cart, through its leathern pipe, from the dripping iron post at the pavement edge. **1914** *Daily News* 20 Aug. 6 A half battalion .. marched up, hoisted their machine guns and watercart aboard, [etc.].

b. *Comb.*, esp. in jocular allusions to weeping.

1837 DICKENS *Pickw.* xvi, Come, come, .. blow this 'ere water-cart bis'ness. *Ibid.* xlv, I'm wery much mistaken if that 'ere Jingle worn't a-doin' somethin' in the water-cart way! *a* **1839** HOOD *Ode to St. Swithin* 59 Why task yourself to lay the dust in streets, As if there were no Water-Cart contractors.

'water-cart, *v.* [f. the sb.] **a.** *trans.* To provide with water-carts. **b.** *intr.* To weep. *slang.*

1851 DICKENS in *Househ. Words* 2 Aug. 433/1 The great metropolis is .. so much more water-carted .. than it usually is. **1920** W. DE MORGAN *Old Man's Youth* (1921) xxix. 282 She makes believe she knew Gromp, and I know she didn't. She'd watercart.

'water-cask. A cask to contain water; † in 17th c. *collectively*. On board ship, the common receptacle of drinking-water.

1613 J. SARIS *Voy. Japan* (Hakl. Soc.) 31 The Coopers provided themselues of rotans for water caske, which make excellen hoopes. **1699** DAMPIER *Voy.* II. I. 152, I received an order from Captain ——to .. put all my Cargo into her; as also all my Water-cask. **1725** DE FOE *Voy. round World* (1840) 86 We had filled our water-casks and taken in what fresh provisions we could get. **1829** MARRYAT *F. Mildmay* xi, I .. ran to the water-cask. **1862** G. T. LLOYD *30 Yrs. Tasmania* i. 3 We arrived at Bona Vista .. in order to replenish our odoriferous water-casks and exhausted hen-coops.

†**water-caster.** *Obs.*

1. One who practises inspection of patients' urine as a means of diagnosis: in early use sometimes depreciatively applied to the medical profession generally; latterly, used as equivalent to 'quack'. Cf. CAST *v.* 40.

1603 DEKKER *Wonderf. Yr.* D 3, Hipocrates, Auicen, Paracelsus, .. with all their succeeding rabble of Doctors and Water-casters. **1609** —— *Ravens Alm.* Wks. (Grosart) IV. 193 Let some skilfull-water-caster toot vpon your vrinell. **1627** J. TAYLOR (Water P.) *Armado* A 5, The fare of Quacksaluers, Mountebanckes, Ratcatching Watercasters. **1675** E. W[ILSON] *Spadacrene Dunelm.* 63 Oppilation or Obstruction, a noted hard word amongst our Water-casters, those pedantick pretenders to Science. **1804** *Med. Jrnl.* XII. 213 The country people have long been deceived by water casters, as they are denominated. **1828** CARR *Craven Gloss. fig.* **1681** T. FLATMAN *Heraclitus Ridens* No. 3 (1713) I. 13, I am just running to a State Water-caster, to resolve me a Horary Question.

2. ? A workman employed to sprinkle water.

1610 *Assessm. Wages* in *Eng. Hist. Rev.* (1898) XIII. 524 A water Caster, v[d]. A caster of stone Clay or marle, v[d].

'water-cat.

†**1.** ? A kind of firework. Also *attrib. Obs.*

1799 G. SMITH *Laboratory* I. 22 Taking two measures for each lay of water-cat-charge, and a little corn powder between each. *Ibid.* 24 Charges for water-cats.

2. A book-name of a variety of otter (see quot.).

1889 *Century Dict.*, *Water-cat*, the nair, or Oriental otter *Lutra nair*, translating a Mahratta name.

†**water-chain.** *Obs.* A chain formerly inserted between the bit and the leather rein of a bridle, to prevent the leather from being rotted by the water when the horse drinks.

1598 FLORIO, *Siciliana*, the water-cheine of a bit. **1611** SPEED *Hist. Gr. Brit.* VII. xlv. §13. 371 The remembrance of which field is retained vnto this day, by certaine small Hilles there remaining, whence haue beene digged the bones of men, Armour, and the water-chaines of horse-bridles.

'water-clock[1]. [CLOCK *sb.*[1]] An instrument actuated by water for the measurement of time. Applied, e.g. to the CLEPSYDRA of the ancients, and to inventions of Sir Isaac Newton and others.

1601 HOLLAND *Pliny* VII. lx. I. 191 This manner of Horologe or water-clocke, hee dedicated in the end within house. **1634** J. B[ATE] *Myst. Nat. & Art* 39 A Water-Clock, or a Glasse shewing the houre of the day. **1723** E. STONE tr. *Bion's Math. Instrum.* VIII. vii. (1758) 253 Of the Construction of a Water-Clock. This Clock is composed of a Metalline well soldered Cylinder, .. wherein is a certain Quantity of prepared water, and several little Cells, which communicate with each other by Holes near the Circumference. **1727** STUKELEY in Turnor *Grantham* (1806) 177 Sir Isaac's water clock .. resembled pretty much our common clocks... There was a dial plate at top with figures of the hours. The index was turned by a piece of wood, which either fell or rose by water dropping. **1825** FOSBROKE *Encycl. Antiq.* 347 *Water-clock*, A new kind was invented in Italy about the middle of the seventeenth century. A cylinder, divided into several small cells, was suspended .. in a frame, in which the hours' distances, found by trial, were marked out. As the water flowed from one cell to another, it changed very slowly the centre of gravity of the cylinder, and put it in motion. **1855** J. H. NEWMAN *Callista* vi. (1856) 47 Here the rushing of the water-clock which measured time in the neighbouring square ceased, signifying thereby that the night was getting on. **1894** BOASE *Register Exeter Coll.* (O.H.S.) p. lxxxix, [16th c.] Logic lectures were given from 6 to 7 in the morning, .. The time was reckoned by a waterclock.

†**water-clock[2].** *Obs.* [CLOCK *sb.*[3]] An aquatic beetle.

1634 MOUFET *Theat. Ins.* I. xxiii. 164 Scarabei aquatici .. quos .. Germani *Wasser kafers*, Angli, Waterclocks appellant. **1681** GREW *Musæum* I. §vii. ii. 171 The Great English Waterclock. *Hydrocantharus major Anglicus*.

'water-ˌcloset. A closet or small room fitted up to serve as a privy, and furnished with water-supply to flush the pan and discharge its contents into a waste-pipe below. Often abbreviated W.C.

Sometimes applied to the pan and the connected apparatus for flushing and discharge; also, loosely, to any kind of privy.

1755 *Connoisseur* No. 100 It was always my office .. to attend him in the water-closet when he took a cathartic. **1760** H. WALPOLE *Let. to G. Montagu* 25 Oct., A little after seven, he went into the water-closet. **1819** SCOTT in *Lockhart* IV. 248, I am happy to learn it has that useful English comfort, a water-closet. **1823** P. NICHOLSON *Pract. Builder* 409 The different parts of water-closets are made in a similar way, and sold to the plumber. **1825** FOSBROKE *Encycl. Antiq.* 348 Water-closet. That of the palace of the Cæsars is adorned with marble, arabesques and mosaicks. **1877** H. ROBINSON & MELLISS *Purif. Water-carried Sewage* 1 Water-closets do not add very much to the volume of sewage.

attrib. **1844** H. STEPHENS *Bk. Farm* I. 218 Fine water-closet latch, with snibbing-bolt. **1873** B. LATHAM *Sanitary Engin.* 39 A district in which the water-closet system is intended only to be partially adopted.

Hence **'water-ˌcloseted,** *a.* [-ED[2]], fitted or provided with water-closets.

1876 *Jrnl. Soc. Arts* 9 June 725/2 A town .. well water-closeted and containing no manufactories.

'water-ˌcolour.

†**1.** The colour of water, blue, greyish-blue. *Obs.*

c **1425** *MS. Digby* 233 fol. 224/2 Loke þat .. þe mennes clothing by coloured with venet colour þat is water coloure. **1580** HOLLYBAND *Treas. Fr. Tong, Coleur d'azur & d'eaue*, azure, or water colour, skie colour.

2. A pigment for which water and not oil is used as a solvent. Usually in *plural*. Also *fig.*

1596 SHAKS. *1 Hen. IV*, V. i. 80 And neuer yet did Insurrection want Such water-colours, to impaint his cause. **1634** J. B[ATE] *Myst. Nat.* 120 Painting may be performed either with water colours or with oyle colours. **1637** SUCKLING *Aglaura* II. i, The loud talking crowd Will think it all but water colours Laid on for a time. **1674** GREW *Anat. Plants, Anat. Trunks* (1682) 138 Smaller Pictures in Water-Colours. **1749** CHESTERF. *Let. to Son* 2 Oct., It is all one to me, whether in enamel or in water colours, provided it is but very like you. **1765** *Phil. Trans.* LVIII. 187 It would be a cheap and usefull water-colour. **1807** MRS. GRANT *Lett. fr. Mountains* I. (ed. 2) Pref. p. viii, It is for such minds as these to distinguish the durable pencil of truth from the water-colours of fiction. **1817** J. EVANS *Excurs. Windsor* etc. 168 A most beautiful drawing in water colours. **1859** DICKENS *T. Two Cities* II. vi, Lucie's..work-table and box of water-colours. **1903** M. A. STEIN *Sand-Buried Ruins of Khotan* xviii. (1904) 271 The thin layer of water-colour with which they are painted has suffered much.

3. A picture painted with water-colours.

1854 ROSSETTI in *Atlantic Monthly* (1896) May 589/2, I shall make him a small water-colour in exchange. **1882** BESANT *All Sorts* xxvi. (1898) 183 It was a pleasant sunny room,..nor..was it hung with immense pictures of game and fruit, but with light and bright water-colours. **1899** CROCKETT *Kit Kennedy* 399 There was Landhaven itself, glittering in the morning light, a water-colour in white and red, as the wet tiles took the sun, and the warmth beneath melted the thin snow.

4. The art or method of painting with water-colours.

1843 RUSKIN *Mod. Paint.* I. II. I. vii. §19 The more specific study of mountains seems to have coincided with the more dexterous practice of water-colour. **1909** C. J. HOLMES *Picture-making* 170 In water colour proper the washes of colour are laid directly on the paper, usually over a faint pencil outline.

5. *attrib.*, as ***water-colour cake, drawing, exhibition, painting.***

1698 T. FROGER *Voy.* 112 A great many fine Water-colour Paintings, that are brought hither from Rome. **1811** JANE AUSTEN *Let.* 25 Apr. (1952) 275 Henry has been to the Watercolour Exhibition, which open'd on Monday. **1824** J. ARROWSMITH *Let.* 19 June in J. Constable *Corr.* (1966) IV. 184, I by this post write to give directions to be sent to me with my watercolour drawings. **1839** HOOD *Literary & Lit.* 52 Men that deal in water-colour cakes. **1856** MISS YONGE *Daisy Chain* II. iii, A very pretty drawing..which had been in the water-colour exhibition. **1862** W. SANDBY *R. Acad.* I. 103 The founder of the English school of water-colour painting. **1876** S. REDGRAVE *Catal. Water-Col. Paintings* 15 When water colour drawing..emerged from mere Indian ink or other monochrome tint. **1880** MISS BRADDON *Just as I am* vii, Water-colour drawings on the wall.

Hence **ˈwater-colour** *v. intr.*, to paint with water-colours; **water-colouring** *ppl. a.*

1855 D. G. ROSSETTI *Let.* 23 Jan. (1965) I. 239, I have been water-colouring again, somewhat against the grain. **1928** R. FRY *Let.* 4 Apr. (1972) II. 621 It was a dismal audience of retired colonel water-colourists and their water-colouring daughters. **1935** A. HUXLEY *Lett.* (1969) 393 Are you oiling or water-colouring or gouaching?

ˈwater-ˌcoloured, *a.*

1. Painted or executed in water-colours.

1773 *Gentl. Mag.* XLIII. 584 A very large and curiously drawn water-coloured chart. **1832** G. DOWNES *Lett. Cont. Countries* I. 165 His cabinet is hung with twenty water-coloured or opaque drawings. **1863** MISS BRADDON *Aurora Floyd* iii, The walls ordinarily covered with French prints and water-coloured sporting-sketches.

2. Of the colour of water. *rare.*

1705 BEVERLY *Virginia* II. iv. (1722) 112 The other [sort of cherry]..is Water-colour'd within. **1797** *Encycl. Brit.* (ed. 3) XII. 138 When polished, the fragments [of granite] appear as if set or inlaid in a fine pellucid or water-coloured matter. *a* **1941** V. WOOLF *Haunted House* (1943) 91 Water-coloured rings set in pearls.

ˈwater-ˌcolourist. [f. WATER-COLOUR + -IST.] One who paints in water-colours.

1850 in OGILVIE. **1870** *Daily News* 2 Dec., The old water-colourists dwell in a medium of perpetual beeswing. **1874** R. TYRWHITT *Sketch. Club* 20 If you have any very patient, keen and skilful water-colourist among you.

ˈwatercourse.

1. A stream of water, a river or brook; also an artificial channel for the conveyance of water.

1510 in Glasscock *Rec. St. Michael's, Bp.'s Stortford* (1882) 31 Item of Rychard wood for a watercorse, jd. **1550** W. HUNNIS *Ps.* vi. (1583) 3 Nor in the deepe, and water course, That passeth vnder ground. **1611** BIBLE *Isa.* xliv. 4 They shall spring vp..as willowes by the water courses. **1724** *Act 11 Geo. I*, c. 11 §7 To cleanse any Ditch or Water-course adjoyning to the said Roads. **1846** *J. Baxter's Libr. Pract. Agric.* I. 229 My own ditches or watercourses are four feet wide. **1849** LAYARD *Nineveh & Rem.* I. vii. 175 Water-courses, once carrying fertility to many gardens, were now empty and dry. **1865** GEIKIE *Scen. & Geol. Scot.* i. 7 Water-courses, from the tiniest runnel up to the ample river.

attrib. **1869** BOUTELL *Arms & Armour* iv. 60 In its form, one of these shields is an elongated and convex oblong, somewhat resembling a hollowed water-course tile.

fig. **1570** T. NORTON tr. *Nowell's Catech.* 68 b, From the spring hed of his diuine liberalitie as it were by certaine guiding of water courses, God conueyeth his benefites to vs by the handes of men.

b. in legal use (see quot. 1848).

1576 in W. H. Turner *Select. Rec. Oxford* (1880) 385 The dyche, tearmed to be a water course,..hath bene stopped. **1626** WHITLOCK, J. in Bulstrode *Rep.* III. (1659) 340 A Water course doth not begin by prescription, nor yet by assent, but the same doth begin *ex jure naturæ*, having taken this course naturally, and cannot be averted. **1681** STAIR *Inst. Law Scot.* I. xvii. §12. 345 Without such a Servitude, Water may not be altered or diverted from its course, as was found, where the Water-course was the March betwixt the Heretors. **1725** *Mod. Rep.* (1769) II. 274 For suppose a man hath a water-course running through his ground, and his neighbour diverts it, this is no trespass. **1832** *Act 2 & 3 Will. IV*, c. 71 §2 No Claim which may be lawfully made..to any Water-course, or the Use of any Water, to be enjoyed [etc.]. **1848** WHARTON *Law Lex.*, *Watercourse*, a species of incorporeal hereditament, being a right which one has to the benefit of the flow of a river or stream, such right commonly referring to a stream passing through one's land.

†**c.** ***Court of the Watercourse*** (see quot.). *Obs.*

1698–9 *Act 11 Will. III* c. 21. §14 Any Right..claimed.. for the holding a certaine Court within the said Mannor [of Gravesend] called Curia Cursus Aquæ or The Court of the Watercourse for the better Government of Barges Boats and Vessells useing the Ferry or Passage from the Towne of Gravesend to London.

2. The bed or channel of a river or stream.

1566 *S'hampton Crt. Leet Rec.* (1905) I. I. 36 We present owen symones hathe not mendyd the watter cowrse of hys close by goslen lane. **1679–88** *Moneys Secr. Serv. Chas. II & Jas. II* (Camden) 88 To scowre the ditches and water-courses at Hampton Court, to keep the fowle there. **1725** DE FOE *Voy. round World* (1840) 265 He presently threw out the water, with the sand [etc.]..into the ordinary water-course. **1830** LYELL *Princ. Geol.* I. 401 A want of relation in the position of alluvial beds to the existing watercourses may be no test of the high antiquity of such deposits. **1871** L. STEPHEN *Playgr. Eur.* (1894) x. 248 Reaching the valley..by the left bank of the stream, or rather watercourse.

†**3.** ? The flow of water. *Obs.*—[0]

1552 HULOET, Water course, *agmen, inis,* (?) *quia aqua habet impetum.*

†**4.** The fairway or width of water-surface under a bridge. *Obs. rare.*

1735 J. PRICE *Stone Br. Thames* 3 The Space of the Water, or Water-course, will be 600 Feet between the Piers.

†**5.** *Anat.* **a.** = AQUEDUCT 3. **b.** The hypogastrium. *Obs.*

1615 CROOKE *Body of Man* 222 In the lower belly.. because this is easily dilated as the burthen increaseth, and in the lower part of it called the watercourse or *Hypogastrium. Ibid.* VIII. xiv. (1631) 581 The watercourse or darke hole betwixt the Mamillary processe and appendix called Styloides.

ˈwater-ˌcracker.

1. A kind of firework. ? *Obs.*

1799 G. SMITH *Laboratory* I. 22 The water-crackers, or divers are commonly rammed..in cases.

2. A Prince Rupert's drop.

1887 *Sci. Amer.* 19 Mar. 181/1 In this way I have taken a water cracker, as they [Prince Rupert drops] are called in the factory, several feet long, and broken it four or five times.

†**3.** *U.S.* A water-biscuit. *Obs.*

1825 *Missouri Intelligencer* 4 June 3/4 Ward and Parker have just received for sale at their grocery and liquor store molasses, water crackers, [etc.]. **1891** in *Century Dict.* **1899** S. T. RORER *Bread & Bread Making* 57 It [*sc.* the dough] may be rolled out into very thin sheets, cut into square crackers, pricked with a fork, baked in a moderate oven, producing what are called Virginia biscuits or water crackers.

ˈwater-craft.

1. Skill in water-matters.

1566 *Act 8 Eliz.* c. 13 §1 To foresee the good Encrease and Mayntenaunce of Shypps and of all kinde of Men traded and browght upp by Water Crafte moost meete for her Majesties Marine Service. **1888** DOUGHTY *Trav. Arabia Deserta* I. 544, I saw Beduins swimming there, and wondered at this watercraft in men of the dry deserts. **1904** R. J. FARRER *Garden Asia* 255 Their tact in water-craft is our sole protection from drowning.

2. A vessel that plies on the water; such vessels collectively.

1618 J. TAYLOR (Water P.) *Penniless Pilgr.* F 2, All the Shippes, Carackes,..Barkes, and Water-craftes, that are now..in the world. **1868** B. J. LOSSING *The Hudson* 203 A broad and beautiful bay, at all times animated with a variety of water-craft. **1916** R. CULLUM *Men who wrought* iv, The object lying upon the table..was a ten-foot model of a strange-looking water craft.

ˈwater-crane.

1. An apparatus for supplying water from an elevated tank (now esp. to the tender of a locomotive).

1658 T. WILLSFORD *Nat. Secrets* 156 From hence it is, that the Air in Water-cranes and pumps being sucked out, the waters..are forced to rise. **1875** KNIGHT *Dict. Mech.*, *Water-crane*, a goose-neck apparatus for supplying water from an elevated tank to the tender of a locomotive engine.

2. A crane worked by hydraulic power.

1849 J. GLYNN *Constr. Cranes* 112 The Water Cranes shown..are Two Self-Acting Machines.

ˈwater-cress. [Cf. MLG., MDu. *waterkerse*, G. *wasserkresse*.]

1. The hardy perennial, *Nasturtium officinale* (N.O. *Cruciferæ*), found in abundance near springs and in small running streams, and now widely cultivated for use as a salad. Also applied to other species of *Nasturtium*.

Often in *plural*, esp. as denoting an article of food; in the 17th and 18th c. the sing. is hardly found.

a. *sing.*

a **1400–50** *Stockh. Med. MS.* p. 209 Watercresse, *nascorium gallicanum.* *a* **1425** tr. *Arderne's Treat. Fistula*, etc. (1910) 76 Þise bene herbez necessary to þe werk of clistry, *scilicet* Violette, maluez,..watercresse. **1597** GERARDE *Herbal* II. xvii. 201 Water Cresse being boiled in wine [etc.]..is verie good against the scuruie. **1599** A. M. tr. *Gabelhouer's Bk. Physicke* 75/2 To make sownde Teeth. Take Watercresse, and rubbe the same with wine, and heerwith washe your mouth often times. **1796** WITHERING *Brit. Plants* (ed. 3) III. 581 Sisymbrium sylvestre,.. Creeping Water Cress. **1800** E. DARWIN *Phytol.* xi. 269 In the winter months the rise of springs may be detected by the presence of aquatic plants, as of water-cress. **1881** F. G. HEATH *My Garden Wild* xiii. 216, I grew in my stream, some Watercress, whose pinnate leaves are so frequently eaten. **1902** CORNISH *Naturalist Thames* 124 The artificial culture of water-cress is comparatively modern.

b. *pl.*

13.. *K. Alis.* 5767 Withinne grene and mychel weed, Waterkressen and heighe reed. *c* **1400** *Lanfranc's Cirurg.* 352 Seþe malue, paritorie, violet, watircressen in watir & lete þe patient sitte þeron anoon to þe nauele. *c* **1450** *Alphita* (Anecd. Oxon.) 165 Senacio, narstucium aquaticum idem, ..watercresses. **1528** PAYNELL *Reg. Sanit. Salerni* (1541) 85 Watercresses doth cure tothe ache. **1590** LODGE *Euphues Golden Legacie* (1592) O 2, My Loues shall growe vp as the water Cresses, slowly, but with a deepe roote. **1611** *Shuttleworths' Acc.* (Chetham Soc.) 196 Given to a man which gott the watercresses and brooke lime, vj[d]. **1725** *Bradley's Family Dict.* s.v. *Cress*, Water-Cresses have a sharp and biting Taste. **1799** SOUTHEY *Cross Roads* 8 There were water-cresses growing, And pleasant was the water's flowing. **1834** DICKENS *Sk. Boz, Boarding-ho.* ii, Tibbs.. began eating water-cresses like a Nebuchadnezzar. **1851–61** MAYHEW *Lond. Labour* I. 145/1 The first coster-cry heard of a morning in the London streets is that of 'Fresh wo-orter-creases'. **1860** LONGF. *Wayside Inn, Saga K. Olaf* vii. 24 He loved..his brook with its water-cresses.

2. Applied (chiefly as book-names) to some other cruciferous plants, esp. *Cardamine amara*, *C. pratensis*, and *Helioscadium nodiflorum*.

a **1400–50** *Stockh. Med. MS.* p. 167 Watercresse, *Apium ranarum.* **1538** TURNER *Libellus*, Cresses, water, *Cardamine.* **1548** —— *Names of Herbes* (E.D.S.) 47 Lauer or Sion is called of some englishe men Bellragges, of other some yealowe watercresses. **1578** LYTE *Dodoens* v. lx. 625 The seconde kinde is called..in Englishe, the lesser Watercresse, and Coccow flowers. **1597** GERARDE *Herbal* II. xviii. 201 There be sixe kindes of wilde herbes numbered among the water Cresse which followe in order. **1866** *Treas. Bot.* 347 Cress, American Water. *Cardamine rotundifolia.*

3. *attrib.* and *Comb.* as ***water-cress-bed, -gatherer, -growing*** vbl. sb., ***sandwich, soup***; **water-cress green**, a particular shade of green.

1906 *Daily Chron.* 21 Aug. 7/6 Extensive *watercress beds. **1902** CORNISH *Naturalist Thames* 125 A notice warning off the poor *water-cress gatherer. **1884** *Daily News* 27 Oct. 2/1 A costume of this in *watercress green is made. **1902** CORNISH *Naturalist Thames* 124 *Water-cress growing is an increasing business in the Thames Valley. **1911** W. J. LOCKE *Glory of Clementina Wing* xxi. 310 He picked up from a plate a little three-cornered *water-cress sandwich. **1978** P. MOYES *Who is Simon Warwick?* xii. 143 Tea had been laid out..silver teapot and milk jug, wafer-thin watercress sandwiches. **1858** SIMMONDS *Dict. Trade*, *Water-cress seller. **1923** W. G. R. FRANCILLON *Good Cookery* (ed. 2) 102 (*heading*) *Watercress soup. **1980** *Redbook* Oct. 234/1, I am intent on the food—water cress soup and a salad of butter lettuce.

Hence **ˈwatercressed**, **ˈwatercressy** *adjs.* (*nonce-wds.*), containing or abounding in water-cress.

1828 WILSON in *Blackw. Mag.* XXIV. 284 Over all the water-cressy and puddocky ditches. **1845** TALFOURD *Vac. Tourists* I. 91 We walked on besides a little water-cressed stream.

ˈwater-cure. [CURE *sb.*[1] 5 b; after G. *wasserkur.*]

1. A method or course of medical treatment by means of water.

1842 [see CURE *sb.*[1] 5 b]. **1843** ABDY *Water Cure* 112 To suppose, that the water cure will have as fair a trial in England as vaccination has had in Germany. **1845** *Murray's Hand-bk. Continent* (ed. 5) 428, 36 m. beyond Landeck..is the Water Cure establishment of Vincent Priessnitz at Gräfenberg. **1857** *Putnam's Monthly Mag.* Mar. 244/1 We sallied out to climb the long hill—half way up which, shone the white-washed walls of the great Silesian Water-cure.

2. In the Philippines, torture by forcing a person to drink large quantities of water in a short time.

1902 'MARK TWAIN' in *N. Amer. Rev.* May 623 The torturing of Filipinos by the awful 'water-cure'..to make them confess. **1976** *New Yorker* 3 May 96/2 The Civil Liberties Union of the Philippines..accused the police and the military of employing 'water cures' and electric shocks as well as beatings with clubs.

Hence **ˈwater-ˌcurer, -ˌcuring.**

1849 MRS. CARLYLE *Lett.* (1883) II. 46 This shall be the last of my water-curing for the present. **1900** *Daily News* 20 Sept. 4/6 The late Pastor Kneip, the Bavarian water-curer.

ˈwater-dock. [DOCK *sb.*[1]; cf. OE. *éa-docce* lit. river-dock, EDOCKE.] A name for various aquatic species of *Rumex*; formerly also applied to other broad-leaved water-plants.

c **1450** *Alphita* (Anecd. Oxon.) 94 *Lappacium aquaticum, uel lappacium maius*, angl. waterdokke uel edokke. **1538** ELYOT *Dict.*, *Hydrolapathon*, water dockes. **1597** GERARDE *Herbal* II. lxxviii. 312 Of water Dockes. *c* **1710** PETIVER *Cat. Ray's Eng. Herbal* Tab. ii, Great Water Dock. **1882** JEFFERIES *Bevis* III. 194 Great water-docks at the margin with leaves almost a yard long.

attrib. **1496** *Bk. St. Albans, Fishing* i j, In Iuyll take..the water docke leyf worme & the hornet worme togyder. **1757** A. COOPER *Distiller* III. lxx. (1760) 270 Of the Water-Dock-Root, five Ounces. **1807** W. ROSCOE *Butterfly's Ball* (1838) 20 A Mushroom their Table, and on it was laid A Water-dock Leaf, which a Table-cloth made.

ˈwater-ˌdoctor.

a. = WATER-CASTER 1. **b.** = HYDROPATHIST.

1801 *Sporting Mag.* XVII. 8 Mrs. Mayersbatch, widow of the celebrated Water-Doctor of that name. **1846** LYTTON *Conf. Water-patient* 43 The peculiar 'crisis', sought for so vehemently by the German water-doctors. **1848** DUNGLISON *Med. Lex.* (ed. 7), *Uromantia*.., the art of divining diseases by simple inspection of the urine... One professing to be able to do this is called *Uromantes.* Vulgarly, a water doctor. **1849** E. FITZGERALD *Lett.* (1889) I. 198 Some one told me that he was gone or going to the Water Doctor at Malvern.

ˈwater-dog.

1. a. A dog bred for or trained to the water; esp. one trained to retrieve waterfowl. Formerly as a specific name, the barbet or poodle imported from the continent. **b.** Any kind of dog that swims well, and is habituated to or not shy of the water.

13.. *K. Alis.* 5771 Bristled hy weren as hogges, And slynken as water-dogges. **1505** *Acc. Ld. High Treas. Scot.* II. 475 For ane corsbow and ane water-dog to the King, vj li. **1600** DARRELL *Detect. Harsnet's Discov.* 130 They..wold neuer haue indured him to haue chopt at his face, as a water-dogge at a duck. **1621** G. MARKHAM *Hunger's Prevent.* xi. 67 Not any amongst vs is so simple that he cannot say when hee seeth him, This is a Water-Dogge, or a Dogge bred for the Water. **1677** N. COX *Gentl. Recreat.* III. (ed. 2) 49 How to train a Water-dog. **1762–71** H. WALPOLE *Vertue's Anecd. Paint.* (1786) IV. 145 She has done a picture of fowls, a water-dog and a heron. **1824** BEWICK *Quadrupeds* (ed. 8) 360 The Large Rough Water Dog..*Le Grand Barbet*, Buff. **1837** T. BELL *Brit. Quadrupeds* 226 The Water-Dog must not be confounded with the Water-Spaniel, from which indeed it differs considerably in size and in proportions. **1867** 'STONEHENGE' *Dogs of Brit. Isl.* 45 Though excellent water dogs,..we have had to complain of their impetuous rush into pond or river. **1876** *Field* 13 May 537/2 It was proposed to have trials of performing dogs, sheepdogs and water dogs.

2. A man thoroughly at home either on or in the water. **a.** A sailor. **b.** A good swimmer.

1674 WYCHERLEY *Plain Dealer* I. i, *2 Sail.*..when I welcom'd him ashore, he gave me a box on the ear, and call'd me fawning Water-dog? **1840** R. H. DANA *Two Yrs. bef. Mast* xiii. (1854) 57 They [*sc.* Sandwich Islanders] are complete water-dogs, and therefore very good in boating. **1878** JOAQUIN MILLER *Songs of Italy* 29 Brave old water-dogs wed to the sea. **1867** S. W. BAKER *Nile Trib.* v. 95 These two Arab water-dogs were up to their necks in the river, screaming out directions to each other. **1878** TRELAWNY *Rec. Shelley*, etc. I. 154, I was the only water-dog of our band; neither Percy nor Captain Roberts nor the mate could swim.

3. A name for various animals.

a. The otter. *Obs.* exc. *W. Afr.*

1576 A. FLEMING tr. *Caius' Dogs* II. 19 Both Ælianus and Ælius, call the Beauer, Κῦνα [*sic*] ποτάμιον, a water dogge, or a dogge fishe. **1655** WALTON *Angler* ii. (1661) 49 There is brave hunting this Water-dog in Cornwall. *c* **1856** DENHAM *Tracts* (1892) I. 87 In Ireland the country people call the otter the Devil's water-dog. **1960** M. MACDONALD in G. Maxwell *Ring of Bright Water* xii. 164 A Senior African joined the group. 'This be the piccin of water-dog,' he intoned.

b. *U.S.* One of the various species of salamanders, *esp.* the hellbender or the mud-puppy.

1859 BARTLETT *Dict. Amer.* (ed. 2). **1882** *Amer. Naturalist* Feb. 140 The Menopoma, here [Pa.] called 'alligator' and 'water-dog'.

c. *U.S.* ? A variety of DOGFISH.

1892 A. E. LEE *Hist. Columbus* (Ohio) I. 299 Suckers, catfish, gars and waterdogs were also taken [in the Scioto River].

d. The water-rat or water-vole, *Arvicola amphibius.*

1876 SMILES *Sc. Nat.* i, The burn itself had plenty of water-dogs, or water-rats, along its banks.

4. A small dark floating cloud supposed to indicate rain. (Cf. DOG *sb.* 10 c.)

a **1825** FORBY *Voc. E. Anglia.* **1910** *Spectator* 3 Sept. 342/1 Other English names for various perceptible forms of vapour in the sky are 'water-dogs', 'sun-galls' [etc.].

†**5.** *Angling.* A device for disentangling a hook.

1688 HOLME *Armoury* III. 103/2 A Water-Dog, is a round peece of Lead like a Ring: It is to unloose the Hookes if they be fastned at the bottom.

†**waterdome.** *Obs.*⁻⁰ [*dome* = DOOM *sb.*] An alleged archaic term for ordeal by water.

1681 BLOUNT *Glossogr.* (ed. 5), *Waterdome*, the antient trial by Water.

ˈwater-ˌdrinker.

1. A drinker of water, one who drinks water in preference to wine or other liquors; now usually *spec.* a total abstainer.

c **1440** *Promp. Parv.* 518/2 Water drynkare, *aquebibus.* **1546** J. HEYWOOD *Prov.* II. v. (1867) 59 A falser water drinker there liueth not. **1599** B. JONSON *Cynthia's Rev.* I. iv. 1 What! the wel-dieted Amorphus become a water-drinker? **1638** T. WHITAKER *Blood of Grape* 31 When as water or small-beere-drinkers look like Apes rather then men. **1765** STERNE *Tr. Shandy* VIII. v, A water-drinker, provided he is a professed one, and does it without fraud or covin, is precisely in the same predicament. **1815** WORDSW. *Poems* Pref. ad fin., Though myself a water-drinker, I cannot resist the pleasure of transcribing what follows. **1882** F. M. CRAWFORD *Mr. Isaacs* 7 A water-drinker in India is always a phenomenon.

†**b.** In the early Christian Church, an epithet applied to those who in the celebration of the Sacrament used water instead of wine. *Obs.*

1562 [T. COOPER] *Answ. Def. Truth* viii. 59 Cyprian wrate against those that were called Aquarij, waterdrinkers.

2. One who drinks the 'waters' at a spa.

1707 JOS. BROWNE (*title*), An Account of the Wonderful Cures Perform'd by the Cold Baths, With Advice to the Water Drinkers at Tunbridge, Hampstead,..and all the other Chalibeate Spaws. **1837** DICKENS *Pickw.* xxxvi, A golden inscription [in the pump-room], to which all the water-drinkers should attend. **1889** GRETTON *Memory's Harkback* 188 It was great fun to see the troop of water-drinkers in the early morning marching up and down..each with an empty wine-glass in hand, which from time to time they got replenished, according to the dose of mineral water prescribed for them.

ˈwater-ˌdrinking, *vbl. sb.*

1. The action or an act of drinking water.

1698 FLOYER *Asthma* (1717) 191 Much Water-drinking is injurious to the Old. **1774** FOOTE *Cozeners* Prol., I am no fish, save me from water-drinking! **1896** *Allbutt's Syst. Med.* I. 410 Water-drinking is certainly beneficial between meals.

2. Drinking mineral waters at a spa.

1697 FLOYER *Enq. Baths* Pref. c4b, By Water-drinking, and Bathing at Buxton, I have procured to my self better Health. **1789** PILKINGTON *View Derbysh.* I. 230 In many cases much advantage has been gained by the administration of medicines in conjunction with the course of water-drinking.

attrib. **1789** CHARLOTTE SMITH *Ethelinde* (1814) I. 106 Sometimes people of a certain style make acquaintance at water-drinking places.

ˈwater-ˌdrinking, *a.* That drinks water and abstains from stronger liquors.

1638–48 G. DANIEL *Eclog.* iii. 284 Let me rather pine Witles and water-drinking, then love wine. **1736** BERKELEY *Discourse* Wks. III. 415 Supply the water-drinking savage with strong liquor, and he shall be drunk for several days. **1771** FOOTE *Maid of B.* I. Wks. 1799 II. 209 That..water-drinking, mirth-marring, amorous old hunks. **1805** WORDSW. *Waggoner* i. 60 A simple water-drinking Bard. **1854** SURTEES *Handley Cr.* iv, The hungry water-drinking guests.

ˈwater-drop.

1. A drop or globule of water. Usually *pl.*

1593 SHAKS. *Rich. II*, IV. i. 262 Oh, that I were a Mockerie, King of Snow, Standing before the Sunne of Bullingbrooke To melt my selfe away in Water-drops. **1606** —— *Tr. & Cr.* III. ii. 193 When water drops haue worne the Stones of Troy. **1821** BYRON *Cain* II. i. 17 There will come An hour, when toss'd upon some water-drops, A man shall say to a man, 'Believe in me, And walk the waters'. **1825** SCOTT *Talism.* xx, The devil a water-drop he gets here... We will teach the light-footed old infidel to be a good Christian, and drink wine of Cyprus. **1866** G. MACDONALD *Ann. Q. Neighb.* iii, The water-wheel, mossy and green with ancient waterdrops.

Comb. **1899** tr. *R. von Jaksch's Clin. Diagn.* vi. (ed. 4) 211 The small shiny water-drop-like bodies.

2. A tear, tear-drop.

1605 SHAKS. *Lear* II. iv. 280 Let not womens weapons, water drops, Staine my mans cheekes. **1818** BYRON *Ch. Har.* iv. cxvi, Egeria!.. The mosses of thy fountain still are sprinkled With thine Elysian water-drops. **1825** NEAL *Bro. Jonathan* II. 149 The large water-drop stood upon his lashes.

3. *Sc.* = EAVESDRIP, STILLICIDE 2.

1818 SCOTT *Hrt. Midl.* xxvii, This is a' about a servitude of water-drap. *Ibid.*, We are obligated to receive the natural water-drap of the superior tenement.

watere, obs. form of WATER *v.*

†**ˈwatered,** *a. Obs.* [f. WATER *sb.* + -ED².] In parasynthetic derivatives, said of a jewel: Characterized by 'water' (of a specified quality).

a **1637** B. JONSON *Execr. Vulcan*, etc. (1640) G2b, A stocke, To graft the greene Emrald on, Or any better water'd Stone. **1704** *Lond. Gaz.* No. 3990/4 The Brilliant very clean and white watered.

watered (ˈwɔːtəd), *ppl. a.* [f. WATER *v.* + -ED¹.]

†**1.** Of the eyes: Filled or running with watery matter or with tears. *Obs.*

a **1400** *Stockholm Med. MS.* i. 80 in *Anglia* XVIII. 297 For wattryd eyne & to grety. **1578** H. WOTTON *Courtlie Controv.* 67 Bending hir watered eyes and woful hart with ioyned hands vnto the heauens, she prayed [etc.]. **1593** DELONEY *Garland Good Will* F1b, Let not offence be found in this, To give my Lord a parting kiss With watr'd eyes.

2. a. Soaked or steeped in water.

c **1430** *Two Cookery-bks.* 26 Take Soundys of watteryd Stokkefysshe, an caste þer-to. **1681** COLVIL *Whigs Supplic.* II. (1741) 113 Our throats cut, Down which we watered Meal of Oats put.

†**b.** Of the cheeks: Wet with tears. *Obs.*

1571 DK. NORFOLK in *14th Rep. Hist. MSS. Comm.* App. IV. 574 Prayinge..with an overwhelminge harte and watered cheekes. **1597** HOOKER *Eccl. Pol.* v. xlii. §2 [They] could not..but with bleeding harts and with watred cheekes be-hold a person of so great place and worth constrayned to indure so foule indignities.

c. Of a road: Soaked or sprinkled with water to lay the dust, etc.

1853 DICKENS *Bleak Ho.* xix, A shop with a sun-blind, and a watered pavement..is a sanctuary. **1896** J. DAVIDSON *Fleet St. Eclogues* Ser. II. 48 The odour stale Of watered streets.

3. a. Of a garden, land: Kept moist by pouring or sprinkling water.

1535 COVERDALE *Jer.* xxxi. 12 Their conscience shalbe as a well watred garden. [**1611** BIBLE *Ibid.*, Their soule shall be as a watered garden.] **1552** HULOET, Watered as a field, or gardein, *rigatus.*.. Watred with dew, *rosidus.* **1654** C. WASE *Gratius' Cyneget.* A3b, But the poore Alaband in his water'd yard Plants grounds of hemp. **1826** SHERER *Notes & Refl. Ramble Germany* 180 The plain is wooded as though it were a forest, and yet you know it to be a watered garden.

b. Of a country, locality: Furnished or supplied with rivers or streams of water. Often with adv., as ***well-, best-watered.*** Of a road: Having streams of water near-by, convenient for travellers.

1798 BLOOMFIELD *Farmer's Boy, Spring* 38 Where noble Grafton spreads his rich domains, Round Euston's water'd vale, and sloping plains. *a* **1859** MACAULAY *Hist. Eng.* xxiii. V. 95 That well watered garden of olives and mulberry trees which spreads many miles on every side of the great white temple of Milan. **1859** H. KINGSLEY *G. Hamlyn* xxv, I should say it was the best watered..piece of country yet discovered in New Holland. **1893** SELOUS *Trav. S.E. Africa* 14, I took the best watered of the roads leading to the Marico river. **1895** *Daily News* 22 Oct. 2/1 [Australian Advt.] Good and watered roads pass through the properties.

c. Of meadow land: Subject to periodical flooding. (Cf. WATER-MEADOW.)

1733 TULL *Horse-Hoeing Husb.* xi. 111 Water, when it runs off very soon, is Beneficial, as is seen in water'd Meadows. **1774** *Pennsylv. Gaz.* 10 Aug., Suppl. 2/2 About 7 acres of watered meadow. **1789** T. WRIGHT *Meth. Watering Meadows* (1790) 6 The farmer who occupies fifty acres of this watered land. **1826** COBBETT *Rur. Rides* (1830) 398 Here are watered meadows nearest to the river on both sides; then the gardens, the houses, and the cornfields. **1842** J. AITON *Domest. Econ.* (1857) 181 Watered meadow, even to the extent of one acre, is a perfect treasure at the manse. **1884** *West. Morn. News* 30 Aug. 1/6 Twenty-four acres of watered meadow.

4. a. Of wine or strong liquor, milk, etc.: Diluted with water. Now usu. as ***watered-down***; cf. 4 b below.

1552 HULOET, Watered, or whereunto water is put, *aquatus.* **1642** HOWELL *For. Trav.* (Arb.) 32 Go to their Diet, the one drinkes Watered Wine, the other Wine watered. **1873** O. W. HOLMES *Addr. Opening Fifth Avenue Theatre* 127 Dealers in watered milk. **1905** H. G. WELLS *Kipps* I. ii. §2 A supper of bread and cheese and watered beer awaited him downstairs. **1976** P. CAVE *High Flying Birds* iv. 51 He matched Lorna glass for glass, chucking the stuff down as though it was watered-down Coke. **1978** A. GILCHRIST *Cod Wars* ii. 7 A watered-down beer, unworthy of the name, is legally sold.

b. *fig.* Weakened in character or force by alteration or addition. Now usu. ***watered-down.***

1889 'MARK TWAIN' *Connecticut Yankee* iv. 55 Everybody took in all this bosh..and never smiled or seemed to notice that there was any discrepancy between these watered statistics and me. **1897** F. HARRISON in *Daily News* 2 Jan. 3/5 A watered orthodoxy and a timid ecclesiasticism. **1898** *Westm. Gaz.* 27 July 8/1 The religious and the profane alike are..anxious to know if the revised Decalogue..is to be only a watered-down version of the Mosaic Tables. **1921** G. C. FIELD *Moral Theory* xii. 153 It is only in a watered-down form that it [*sc.* love] can be extended..to the whole of humanity.

c. Of the capital of a trading company: Diluted, increased in nominal amount by the issue of stock or shares for which no consideration has been received. Cf. WATER *v.* 7 e.

1899 *Westm. Gaz.* 7 Mar. 5/1 Deduct from that £1,250,000 of watered capital. **1904** *Edin. Rev.* Jan. 72 The Company had to pay a dividend on watered capital.

5. a. Of silk or other textile: Having a wavy lustrous damask-like pattern or finish. (Cf. WATER *v.* 9.)

? **1595** *Q. Eliz. & Levant Co.* (1904) 87 Waltered and un-waltered Chamblletts. **1646** *Mem. Rokeby* (Surtees) 9 For watered tabba when my lady was at Yorke 6 l. 9 s. 9 d. **1649** *Bury Wills* (Camden) 220 My watered grogerin gowne. **1665** HOOKE *Microgr.* 8 Of watered Silks, or Stuffs. **1714** *Fr. Bk. Rates* 365 Camlets watered and not watered. **1823** RUTTER *Fonthill* 43 The hangings of crimson cloth and watered moreen are handsome. **1841** S. WARREN *Ten Thou.* I. viii, Over his waistcoat he wore..a broad black watered riband, to which was attached his eyeglass. **1860** GEO. ELIOT *Mill on Floss* II. i, That watered-silk she had on cost a pretty penny. **1893** LIDDON *Life Pusey* I. i. 5 She commonly wore a watered-silk dress.

b. Similarly of steel = DAMASCENED b.

1839 URE *Dict. Arts*, etc. 384 The watered design of the true Damascus scymitar. **1880** W. EGERTON *Handbk. Ind. Arms, India Museum* 98 Dagger; 'Kris'; watered blade. **1883** F. POLLOCK in *Proc. Roy. Instit.* X. 386 The damasked or 'watered' appearance of the blades which are most highly esteemed in the East.

†**6.** *Her.* Having water of a specified tincture. *Obs.*

1780 EDMONDSON *Heraldry* II. Alph. Arms, *Powell* [Oxfordshire]..three wells az. watered ar.

ˈwater-ˌengine.

†**1.** An engine for pumping water to extinguish fire; a fire-engine. *Obs.*

1677 SIR C. WYCHE in *Essex Papers* (Camden) II. 128 The water Engines which are used here when fires happen. **1711** in *Pall Mall Gaz.* (1887) 19 Sept. 14/1 John Oates..is directed by his Lordship to assist with Two Water-Engines on the first Notice that shall be given him, when any Fire breaks out. **1802** ACERBI *Trav.* I. 212 The town has three water-engines. **1864** TROLLOPE *Small Ho. at Allington* II. xi. 113 Calling for the police when there is a row in the house is like summoning the water-engines when the soot is on fire in the kitchen chimney.

2. An engine to raise water; a water pumping engine.

1685 *Phil. Trans.* XV. 1254 A Letter, subscribed W. Tenon, concerning Dr. Papin's new Water-Engine. **1691** WOOD *Ath. Oxon.* II. 340 Edward Ford..made the great water Engine..for the serving the Inhabitants of the Strand. **1712** J. JAMES tr. *Le Blond's Gardening* 191 You must have Recourse to Water-Engines, which raise it from the Bottom of Wells, into receiving Cisterns. **1811** J. T. in *Risdon's Surv. Devon* Introd. 20 Mines..which..have some of the most..powerful water engines. **1886** J. BARROWMAN *Sc. Mining Terms* 71 *Water-engine*, an engine used exclusively for pumping water.

3. An engine driven by water power or by which water power is applied.

1858 LARDNER *Hand-bk. Nat. Phil.* 146 Water-engine... Hydraulic wheels..are by far the most common expedients by which water power is applied.

So **water-engineer**, †(*a*) an official charged with the management of municipal fire-engines; (*b*) an official charged with the management of the water-supply of a district.

1711 in *Pall Mall Gaz.* (1887) 19 Sept. 14/1 The Lord Mayor, to prevent the Calamities that may happen by Fire, has Ordered Publick Notice to be given, That John Oates, Water-Ingineer to the Honourable City of Dublin [etc.]. **1937** *Discovery* Feb. 60/2 Mr Walters, a leading water engineer.

waterer (ˈwɔːtərə(r)). [f. WATER *v.* + -ER[1].]

1. a. One who waters plants, crops, etc. *lit.* and *fig.*

In 17th c. religious literature somewhat common in allusions to 1 Cor. iii. 7, 8.

1549 COVERDALE, etc. *Erasm. Par. 1 Cor.* iii. 6–7 Yf the husband manne be of thys dysapoynted, nothyng in maner preuayleth, the gardiner, nor yet the waterer. **1602** CAREW *Cornwall* I. 80 This ill weed,..maugre the warmers and waterers, hath by her Maiesties gracious breath beene euer parched vp. **1607** [R. PARKER] *Schol. Disc. agst. Antichr.* II. v. 2 The Magistrate must be a remoouer, or reviver of the Ceremonies controversed: a weeder or a waterer of them. **1621** R. JOHNSON *Way to Glory* 23 The very titles that the holy Ghost doth giue them [*sc.* gospellers] in Scripture,..as ..Waterers, Builders, Stewards, [etc.]. **1703** J. FREAME *Test.* in C. Marshal *Sion's Trav.* (1704) b v b, He was both a Planter, as well as a Waterer in God's Vineyard. **1842** LOUDON *Suburban Hort.* 387 Watering plants in pots requires much more consideration on the part of the waterer than watering in free soil.

†**b.** One who practises irrigation. *Obs. rare.*

1789 T. WRIGHT *Meth. Watering Meadows* (1790) 22 This method..is..taught by a systematical waterer in Staffordshire.

†**2.** = AQUARIUS. *Obs. rare*[−1].

1546 *Gassar's Prognost.* b v, In y[e] signe Aquari or waterer.

3. One who is sent ashore to obtain a supply of fresh water for a ship's company.

1773 HAWKESWORTH *Voy.* III. 498 Having..sent the boat away, [he] set out to join the waterers by land. **1777** G. FORSTER *Voy. round World* I. 127 Sail-makers, coopers, waterers, and wood-cutters. **1781** *Gentl. Mag.* LI. 278 The Indians still continuing troublesome, and attacking the waterers with stones at the well.

4. One who supplies animals with drinking water.

1844 DICKENS *Mart. Chuz.* xxxi, He was a mere waterer of horses. **1888** DOUGHTY *Trav. Arabia Deserta* I. 27 The shift of waterers was sent out..to seek a cattle pool some miles lower in the valley.

†**5.** A visitor at a spa or watering-place. *Obs.*

1776 S. J. PRATT *Pupil of Pleas.* (1777) I. 59 My wife says, he understands to a nicety, what, some of the waterers [at 'Buxton bath'] call, the etiquette of dress.

6. A container used for supplying water to animals or plants.

1891 in *Century Dict.* **1958** *Times Lit. Suppl.* 21 Nov. p. xii/5 Would you make a plant waterer or a..pea-shooter? **1960** *Farmer & Stockbreeder* 19 Jan. (Suppl.) 31/3 With deep litter, the use of a droppings pit and waterers over it [*sc.* in a poultry house] are a further help. **1970** *Jrnl. Gen. Psychol.* Oct. 240 The food cups and waterers [for the rats] were replaced with clean containers. **1981** *Farmstead Mag.* Winter 85 (Advt.), Includes choosing proper breeds [of rabbits], housing, feeders, waterers, feeding and diets, rabbit management, disease prevention, marketing.

waterfall (ˈwɔːtəfɔːl). [f. WATER *sb.* + FALL *sb.*; OE. had *wætergefeall.* Cf. G. *wasserfall, -gefäll(e,* ON. *vatnfall.*]

1. A more or less perpendicular descent of water from a height over a ledge of rock or precipice; a cascade, cataract.

998 *Crawford Charters* (1895) 21 Æfter heafdon to þam wætergefeal æfter streame. [**1372** in *Shropsh. Arch. Soc. Trans.* Ser. III. IV. 225 Johannes de Watrefal.] **14..** *Newminster Cartul.* (Surtees) 63 Sicud Derestrete vadit inter Filton et Toland usque ad Waterfal, et a Waterfal per Slade. **1421** *Inquisition* in Hutchinson *Durham* (1787) II. 381 Villa de Langley & le waterfall. **1617** MORYSON *Itin.* I. 21 This River hath foure great water fals. **1725** DE FOE *Voy. round World* (1840) 343 A noise..as of a mighty cataract or waterfall. **1838** LYTTON *Leila* I. iii, The silver tinkling of waterfalls chimed melodiously within the gardens. **1860** TYNDALL *Glac.* I. vii. 50 The ice cascade..appeared..like the foam of a waterfall.

transf. **1889** STEVENSON *Master of Ballantrae* ix. 252 When ..we lay becalmed..in a gasping heat, which was presently exchanged for a surprising waterfall of rain.

Comb. **1867** MACGREGOR *'Rob Roy' in Baltic* 123 Numerous wheels, with waterfall spray rising slowly in the morning air.

2. Such an inclination of the ground as will facilitate the fall or drainage of water.

1522 in *Exch. Rolls Scot.* XV. 601 Terras Thome Haithry ..ex parte occidentali et in longitudine caude ascendendo prope caput montis et le waterfaw earundem. **1590** *Reg. Mag. Sig. Scot.* 611/2 The saidis landis of Schoirthoip streikand south as the hill or wattir fall thairof gais to the landis of Dalgleis. **1603** *Ibid.* 506/2 Passing as the water fall upoun the braaheid gangis [to] the merchis of Brume-hous. **1766** *Complete Farmer* s.v. *Flax*, But in some parts of the country, a sufficiency of water and water-fall is not to be met with. **1859** R. F. BURTON *Centr. Afr.* in *Jrnl. Geog. Soc.* XXIX. 73 Caused by want of waterfall, its only efficient remedy would be [etc.].

†**3.** A swift stream tumbling in a rocky bed, a rapid. *Obs.*

1697 DRYDEN *Virg. Georg.* I. 366 To fire the Brambles, snare the Birds, and steep In wholsom Water-falls the woolly Sheep. **1726** LEONI *Alberti's Archit.* II. 122/1 You may level a Torrent or Water-fall by laying a barrier across the Stream. **1748** *Anson's Voy.* II. viii. 218 The complicated beauties which occurred in this extraordinary water-fall.

4. *Coal-mining.* A special 'head' of water to be turned down a pit-shaft when needed.

1797 J. CURR *Coal Viewer* 33 A stream of water with a waterfall of about half the depth of the pit is necessary, if any business of consequence must be done. **1860** *Ure's Dict. Arts* (ed. 5) III. 957 This distribution was often fraught with such danger, that a torrent of water had to be kept in readiness, under the name of the waterfall, to be let down to extinguish the fire in a moment. **1867** W. W. SMYTH *Coal & Coal-mining* 209 The waterfall, formed by turning a special stream into the downcast shaft, or by allowing the pump-cisterns to run over, is a useful auxiliary, especially for driving in air after an accident.

5. A neckcloth, scarf, or tie with long pendant ends. ? *Obs.*

1848 J. H. NEWMAN *Let.* 3 Sept. (1962) XII. 268 He.. looks a striking man in his Jesuit dress, though what his cut may be with a French coat and satin waterfall I can't tell. **1861** HUGHES *Tom Brown at Oxf.* xxvi, Benjamin, the Jew money-lender,..dressed in a gaudy figured satin waist-coat and waterfall. **1914** *Lit. Digest* 22 Aug. 328/2 A waterfall.. is, in addition, a scarf or necktie with long drooping ends, or a chignon with pendent curls.

6. A chignon; also, a wave of hair falling down the neck below the chignon or net. (Orig. *U.S.*)

1859 C. C. RICHARDS *Village Life in Amer.* (1912) 119, I wore my new waterfall for the first time. **1866** MRS. WHITNEY *Leslie Goldthwaite* iii, The brown silk net..had given way all at once into a great hole under the waterfall, and the soft hair would fret itself through. **1875** *Spectator* (Melbourne) 22 May 27/2 The young lady that affects waterfalls, the Grecian bend, or the kangaroo hop. **1890** *Daily News* 1 Sept. 5/3 Human hair..goes through long processes of purification before it is made up into the wigs, chignons, waterfalls, &c.

7. In a woman's garment, a fall of material or attached decoration (orig. with reference to bustles).

1886 *Girl's Own Paper* 27 Feb. 339/3 Patterns already issued:—polonaise with waterfall back. **1925** *Dialect Notes* V. 346 *Waterfall, n.*, a form of bustle for hanging the dress round the body. **1950** *New Yorker* 25 Mar. 84/2 What she calls 'waterfalls'—cascades of bustle drapery—add interest to the backs of all types of clothes. **1970** *Trafford Spring & Summer Catal.* 4 The dress is fully lined, and a waterfall frill, edged with dainty braid, tops a gently flared skirt. **1981** *Times* 30 July 2/8 The Queen's coat and dress, with its waterfall of pleated crêpe de chine.

8. *Ceramics.* A stream of glaze material used for application to the upper surfaces of tiles (see quot. 1964). Freq. *attrib.*

1961 *Brit. Ceramics Abstracts* 197 Methods of glazing wall-tiles... The second part [deals] with the 'waterfall' process of glazing. **1964** A. E. DODD *Dict. Ceramics* 308 *Waterfall process*, a method for the application of glaze materials to a ceramic body by mechanically conveying the ware through a continuously flowing (recirculated) vertical stream of the glaze suspension. The process is used in the glazing of wall tiles. **1967** M. CHANDLER *Ceramics in Mod. World* iii. 99 (*caption*) Tiles to be glazed on one side only are conveyed mechanically..through a waterfall of glaze slip that covers only their upper surfaces and edges. **1973** C. W. PARMELEE *Ceramic Glazes* (ed. 3) v. 149 Each color is dried between applications and the final station applies the glaze by waterfall. *Ibid.*, Tiles are placed on a conveyor.. and passed under the waterfall machine.

Hence as *v. intr.*, to tumble or cascade in the manner of a waterfall; *trans.*, to cover with a stream of running liquid; so **ˈwaterfalled** *a.*, having a waterfall (also *fig.*); **ˈwaterfalling** *ppl. a.* and *vbl. sb.*

1944 G. BARKER *Eros in Dogma* 34 Who has not seen, over The waterfalling hair at the shoulder of Life, Death from his own face staring out of a glass? **1957** J. FRAME *Owls do Cry* (1958) xxxviii. 171 Gaping idiot mouth waterfalled with slobber. **1967** M. CHANDLER *Ceramics in Mod. World* iii. 99 Spray that misses the articles goes onto a wall at the back of the booth that is continuously 'waterfalled'. *Ibid.* (caption) 'Waterfalling' of wall tiles. **1968** B. HINES *Kestrel for Knave* 128 One boy posed Eros-like, and allowed a jet of water to play into his palm and waterfall out on to the tiles of the drying area. **1976** *Shooting Times & Country Mag.* 16–22 Dec. 26/2 The exotic venue was..the 1,036 acre Wild Life Park at Cricket St Thomas with the waterfalled Bedpool Lakes reposing in the partly wooded valley below. **1980** J. GARDNER *Garden of Weapons* II. iv. 154 The rope ladder.. dislodged, waterfalling on to the balcony.

ˈwater-fast, *a. Sc.* = WATERTIGHT.

1550 *Abstr. Protocols Town Clerks Glasgow* (1894) I. 19 To keip the bwyth wattir fast with haile tymmyr, lofting, and flure. *a* **1568** *Satir. Poems Reform.* xlvi. 16 To pomp als oft as ȝe may haill, ȝeill nevir hald hir watter-fast. **1574** *Burgh Rec. Glasgow* (1876) 20 For helping to repair the said kirk and haldyng of it wattirfast. **1898** LD. E. HAMILTON *Mawkin of Flow* xviii. 254 The shieling's well biggit and as waterfast as a sowen-tub.

ˈwater-ˌfinder. [Cf. G. *wasserfinder.*] One who finds subterranean springs or supplies of water by means of a divining-rod; a dowser.

1883 *Harper's Mag.* Oct. 708/2 He has added the.. profession of water-finder. **1902** *Nature* 30 Jan. 304/2 The employment of a dowser or 'water-finder' is suggested.

So **ˈwater-ˌfinding** *vbl. sb.* Also *attrib.*

1883 *Harper's Mag.* Oct. 708/2, I spent many hours sauntering about with the water-finding fork in my hands. **1899** A. LANG in *Daily News* 10 July 8/2 Hegel believed in the water-finding faculty. **1906** *Times* 27 Sept. 13/2 A number of letters on water-finding were published in *The Times* during the winter of 1904–5.

ˈwater-flag. The yellow flag or flower-de-luce, *Iris Pseudacorus.*

1578 LYTE *Dodoens* II. xli. 199 The wilde yellow Iris is nowe called..in Englishe..Wilde flagges, water flagges, and Lauers. **1650** [W. HOWE] *Phytol. Brit.* 2 Yellow water flower-de-luce, water flagges, Seggs. **1808** SCOTT *Marmion* VI. xxxvii, And shepherd boys repair To seek the water-flag and rush. **1842** TENNYSON *Morte d'Arth.* 63 The many-knotted waterflags, That whistled stiff and dry about the marge. **1847** C. BRONTË *Jane Eyre* xxi, A group of reeds and water-flags.

ˈwater-flood. [OE. *wæterflód*: see WATER *sb.* and FLOOD *sb.* Cf. MHG. *wazzervluot* (mod.G. *wasserflut*), MLG. *watarvlôt*, ON. *vatnsflóð.*]

1. A moving flood or overflowing of water, a tempestuous sea.

c **893** ÆLFRED *Oros.* I. vi. 36 On þæs Ambictiones tide wurdon swa mycele wæterflod ȝeond ealle world. **1535** COVERDALE *Ps.* xxix. 10 The Lorde stilleth [1539 BIBLE sitteth aboue] the water floude. **1571** GOLDING *Calvin on Ps.* lxix. 20. 261 They see the ungodly rush uppon them without staye, and too rage like a waterflud. *a* **1593** MARLOWE *Ovid's Elegies* II. x. 14 Why addst thou..to the vast deepe sea fresh water floods? **1871** MACDUFF *Mem. Patmos* xx. 273 Not like the abrupt and sweeping waterflood, but rather like the silent dew as it distills imperceptibly on blade and flower. **1902** *Monthly Rev.* Aug. 171 Her hair was all about him like a water-flood; her kisses on his brow.

†**2.** *collectively.* Water as opposed to land. *Obs.*

c **1200** ORMIN 17567 O lifft, o land, o waterrflod, Wiþ fele kinne shaffte. **1390** GOWER *Conf.* III. 92 For riht as veines ben of blod In man, riht so the water flod Therthe of his cours makth ful of veines.

3. A body or mass of water in flood.

c **1435** *Torr. Portugal* 1872 A Grype..A way..bare her yong son Ouer a water fflood, Over in to a wyldernes There seynt Antony ermet was. **1864** SWINBURNE *Atalanta* 1380 O that I now, I too were By deep wells and water-floods. **1917** O. WILDRIDGE *Captains & Co.* ix. 108 And now, as the tug drew near, there trailed across the intervening strip of water-flood a snatch of 'Auld Lang Syne'.

4. *Oil Industry.* Water-flooding; an instance of this. Freq. *attrib.*

1928 *Trans. AIME Petroleum Div.* LXXVII. 334, I was interested..to see what the pumping problem would be if it was later decided to mine a water-flood property. **1946** *Producers Monthly* Dec. 20/1 Throughout the water flood, measurements were taken of the pressure distribution. **1977** *Offshore Engineer* Apr. 20/1 (Advt.), In waterflood and other really tough uses, the McEvoy Super Mudwonder proves better than valves B or C, or any other competitor.

ˈwater-flooding, *vbl. sb. Oil Industry.* [f. WATER *sb.* + FLOODING *vbl. sb.*] The injection of water into a reservoir rock through wells drilled for the purpose, in order to force oil into neighbouring production wells.

1928 *Trans. AIME Petroleum Div.* LXXVII. 391 Of some value in water-flooding are water analyses and..data of sand conditions. **1938** H. S. GIBSON in A. E. Dunstan et al. *Sci. of Petroleum* I. XI. 535/1 In the Bradford field of Pennsylvania..water flooding as a production practice was legalized in 1921. **1940** [see SECONDARY *a.* 5k]. **1961** *Economist* 2 Dec. 956/1 The.. water..will be injected around the flanks of the [oil] field, and not in the centre as in most 'waterflooding' projects. **1982** D. R. SKINNER *Introd. Petroleum Production* II. i. 2 The first methods of secondary recovery utilized gas injection and a primitive form of water injection—saltwater disposal. Later, water injection or secondary waterflooding became the dominant form of secondary recovery.

ˈwater-ˌflower. A flower growing in water; the representation of such a flower in metal, in embroidery, etc.

1480 *Wardr. Acc. Edw. IV* (1830) 115 Old spanges and water floures of silver. **1509** *Will* in *Archæologia* LXVI. 313 Item ij. aulter clothes Crymsen velwett vpon velwet sett w[t] water flowres. *Ibid.* 340 Itm a vestyment of blue velvett thorfreis of crymsyn cloth of gold enbroderid w[t] water floures. **1599** BRETON *Will of Wit* (Grosart) 37/2, I must learne to make a waterflower, in an old ragge, good enough for a sampler for mee. *c* **1830** MRS. HEMANS *Streams* 4 Ye [streams] that are born of the valleys deep, With the water-flowers on your breast asleep.

ˈwater-fly. [FLY *sb.*[1]] A fly that frequents water and the water-side.

1606 SHAKS. *Ant. & Cl.* v. ii. 60 Rather on Nylus mudde Lay me starke-naked, and let the water-Flies Blow me into abhorring. **1655** MOUFET & BENNET *Health's Improv.* xii. 109 Water-rails..feed upon water-snails and water-flies. **1774** GOLDSM. *Nat. Hist.* VII. 359 The Common Water-Flie..is by some called the Notonecta. **1818** KEATS *Endym.* II. 135 Quick waterflies and gnats were sporting still. **1828** DAVY *Salmonia* 53 Even in December and January there are a few small gnats or water flies on the water. **1910** *Encycl. Brit.* II. 28/1 The matching of the fly with the insect on the water is a matter of much nicety, for the water-flies are of many shades and colours.

fig. **1602** SHAKS. *Ham.* v. ii. 84 Dost know this waterflie? **1606** —— *Tr. & Cr.* v. i. 38 Ah how the poore world is pestred with such water-flies, diminutiues of Nature.

Waterford (ˈwɔːtəfəd). The name of a city in the south-east of Ireland, used *attrib.* and *absol.* to designate glassware first manufactured there in the eighteenth and nineteenth centuries, esp. drinking glasses and chandeliers.

1783 *Dublin Evening Post* 4 Oct. in M. S. D. Westropp *Irish Glass* (1920) iii. 69 Waterford Glass House. George and William Penrose having established an extensive glass manufacture in this city, their friends and the public may be supplied with all kinds of plain and cut flint glass. **1852** J. F. MAGUIRE *Industrial Movement in Ireland* 102 The Waterford glass-house was in active work up to the year 1845, and had earned the highest reputation for its glass throughout the country. **1898** *Sale Catal.* in *Country Life* (1974) 26 Sept. 854/2 Waterford and Cork cut glass. **1917**

W. J. Locke *Red Planet* xxi. 269 A precious old Waterford claret jug. **1936** M. Kennedy *Together & Apart* III. 211 Come and look at this glass... It's Waterford. **1940** J. Cary *Charley is my Darling* lx. 324 A magnificent seven-branch candlestick of Waterford glass. **1964** Mrs. L. B. Johnson *White House Diary* 25 Apr. (1970) 125, I described the Savonnerie rug, the Waterford chandelier. **1977** *Daily Colonist* (Victoria, B.C.) 26 Oct. 7/3 (Advt.), Waterford crystal, a treasure hunter's delight, now on..sale. **1978** J. Carroll *Mortal Friends* I. ii. 22 The few pieces of Waterford in the village had been loaned and were out, filled with jams and preserves.

waterfowl ('wɔːtəfaʊl). [f. water *sb.* + fowl *sb.*; cf. OHG. *wazzarvogel* (mod.G. *wasser-*), Du. *watervogel*.] Any bird that frequents the water, or inhabits the margin of lakes, rivers, seas, etc.; in mod. use chiefly applied to the larger kinds of swimming birds, esp. those which are regarded as game. Often *collect. sing.* for *pl.*

a **1300** *Cursor M.* 398 Þe fifte dai.. On watur fuxol and fiss he wroght. *c* **1381** Chaucer *Parl. Foules* 327 But watir foule sate lowest in the dale. *Ibid.* 554 The watir foules. **1398** Trevisa *Barth. De P.R.* v. xxix. (1495) 140 Water foules haue bytwene theyr toes and clawes as it were a skynne. **1433** Lydg. *S. Edmund* II. 162 Al watir foul and foul upon the lond. **1538** Elyot *Dict.*, *Querquedula*, a waterfowle callyd a teale. *a* **1593** Marlowe & Nashe *Dido* IV. v. 1382 Where thou shalt see.. White Swannes, and many louely water fowles. **1610** Holland *Camden's Brit.* (1637) 499 Great store of young water-fowle. **1798** Coleridge *Parl. Oscill.* 29 You know that water-fowl that cries, Quack! Quack!? **1843** Marryat *M. Violet* xliv, The water-fowls are plentiful, such as swans, geese, ducks. **1870** Bryant *Iliad* II. 564 As when water-fowl of many tribes—Geese, cranes and long-necked swans—disport themselves.

attrib. **1903** *Amer. Sportsman's Libr. IV.* (title) *The Water-Fowl Family.*

Hence **waterfowler** *U.S.*, a hunter of wildfowl; **waterfowling** *U.S.*, the hunting of wildfowl.

1976 *National Observer* (U.S.) 27 Nov. 14/4 The appeal of hunting for even old men was best described by a 68-year-old friend and lifelong waterfowler who shared a blind with me at Izembek several years ago. **1980** *Outdoor Life* (U.S.) (Northeast ed.) Oct. 80/3 Top-quality decoys are more important in puddler hunting than any other kind of waterfowling.

'water-front. Orig. *U.S.*

1. Land or buildings abutting on a river, a lake, the sea, etc.; the frontage of a town on the water-side.

1856 Emerson *Eng. Traits* iii. 47 A people so skilful and sufficient in economizing water-front by docks, warehouses, and lighters. **1883** *Harper's Mag.* May 813/2 The water-front is lined with shipping. **1896** Howells *Impressions & Exp.* 256 The ugliness is.. that of all city water-fronts. **1897** Kipling *Capt. Cour.* x. 230 Boat-builders, and coopers, and all the mixed population of the water-front.

attrib. **1918** *Punch* 27 Mar. 206/1 In many a sailors' drinking-place and water-front saloon.

2. 'A water-heater set in the front of a stove' (Webster 1911).

'water-ˌfurrow, *sb.* [Cf. G. *wasserfurche*.] A deep furrow made for conducting water from the ground and keeping it dry.

854 in Birch *Cartul. Sax.* II. 78 On þa weter furh innan smalan broc. *c* **1440** *Promp. Parv.* 213/1 Gryppe, or a gryppel, where water rennythe a-way in a londe, or water forowe, *aratiuncula*. *Ibid.* 518/1 Waterforowe [*v.rr.* -foore, -fore], in londe, *elicus, sulcus*. **1482** *Cov. Leet Bk.* 510 Strecchyng down be a watir-fforough where some-tyme was a diche & a heye vnto þe watir of Shirburn. **1483** *Cath. Angl.* 410/2 A Watir fure, *elix*. *a* **1677** T. Manton *Serm.* Ps. cxix. 23 (1725) I. 111 As Husbandmen when their ground is overflowed by waters, make Ditches and Water-furrows to carry it away. **1710** Hilman *Tusser Rediv.* Mar. (1744) 32 [Standing water must be] drain'd off with Water-Furrows. **1812** Sir J. Sinclair *Syst. Husb. Scot.* I. 49 Unless the water collected from the different 'buts' or 'ridges', can easily get away, it will be to no purpose to facilitate its passage from these.. by 'water-furrows', or small cuts made by the plough or spade. **1842** Sproule *Agric.* (ed. 2) 70 These open furrows serve, likewise, for drains to carry off the surface-water, and being cleared out after the seed is sown, they are termed water-furrows.

attrib. **1812** Sir J. Sinclair *Syst. Husb. Scot.* I. 146 The 40 ridges will require 79 turnings of the sower and harrows, and 41 turnings of the water-fur plough.

'water-ˌfurrow, *v.* [f. prec.] *trans.* To make water-furrows in (land). Hence **'water-ˌfurrowing** *vbl. sb.*

1523–34 Fitzherb. *Husb.* §13 If a drye season come before Candelmasse.. it [*sc.* the ridged fallow] wolde be caste downe and waterforowed bytwene the landes. **1557** Tusser *100 Points Husb.* xxii. (1878) 223 The sede being sowne, water-forow thy ground. **1560** Pilkington *Aggeus* G iv b, Let hym.. water, hedge, and waterforow, or what other thyng so euer he can deuise to make the ground fruitfull. **1662** Atwell *Faithf. Surveyor* 91 It follows now to speak of those that must be done either chiefly by the spade, or onely the spade. Chiefly by the spade, called water-furrowing. **1707** Mortimer *Husb.* Kal., October.. Well Water-furrow, and Drain new sown Corn Land. **1743** in R. Maxwell *Sel. Trans. Agric. Scot.* 41 Plow up the Land and water-fur it. **1812** Sir J. Sinclair *Syst. Husb. Scot.* I. 207 In preparing land for a crop, water-furrowing is a very important operation. **1813** Vancouver *Agric. Devon* 140 The furrows [should be] struck out with a plough,.. and the field left gripped and water-furrowed. **1902** *Daily Chron.* 3 Feb. 7/5 The cost of producing wheat.. is per acre about as follows:—Twelve carts of manure at 5s. per cart, £3;.. water-furrowing, 1s.

'water-gall. Also 9 *dial.* -gull. [f. water *sb.* + gall *sb.*²: = G. *wassergalle* in various senses, also MLG. *watergalle* in sense 2.]

†**1.** A boggy tract in a field. *Obs.*

1285 *Yorks. Deeds* (Yorks. Archæol. Soc.) II. 198 *note*, Cum toto prato suo falcabili, ut in capitibus, herbagiis, ranis, et watergallis. **1664** Evelyn *Sylva* xviii. 38 The Alder is of all other the most faithful lover of watery and boggy places, and those most despis'd weeping parts, or water-galls of Forests.

2. A secondary or imperfectly-formed rainbow; also applied to various other phenomena in the clouds that are believed to portend rain. Now *dial.*: cf. weathergall.

1594 Shaks. *Lucr.* 1588 And round about her teare-distained eye Blew circles stream'd, like Rain-bows in the skie. These watergalls in her dim Element, Foretell new stormes. *a* **1676** Hale *Prim. Orig. Man.* (1677) 16 As the Water-gall is the Image, Shadow, or weak Representation of the Rain-bow. **1744** H. Walpole *Let. to Mann* 29 June, False good news are always produced by true good, like the watergall by the rainbow. **1769** Falconer *Dict. Marine* II. (1780), *Oeil de bouc*, water-gall, or weather-gall.

†**3.** A watery bubble in the liver of swine. [So G. *wassergalle* 1587.] *Obs.*

1607 Topsell *Four-f. Beasts* 685 Sometimes there appeare [in swine] certaine blathers in the liuer of water, which are called water-gals.

4. ? A flaw in a material or a manufactured article caused by the settling of water in a particular spot. (Implied in watergalled *a.*). [Cf. G. *wassergalle*, flaw in marble.]

Hence **'water-galled** *a.*, having water-galls (see 4).

1839 Ure *Dict. Arts* 934 The greatest difficulty formerly experienced in the paper manufacture upon the continuous system of Fourdrinier, was to remove the moisture from the pulp, and condense it with sufficient rapidity, so as to prevent its becoming what is called water-galled.

†**'watergang.** *Obs.* Also 3 -gong. [f. water *sb.* + gang *sb.*¹ Cf. ON. *vatn(a)gang-r* flood, (M)Du. *watergang* watercourse, G. *wassergang* flow of water, watercourse.]

1. A flood.

c **1250** *Gen. & Ex.* 662 Nembrot gat hise feres red, for ðat he hadde of water dred, To maken a tur, wel heȝ & strong, Of tigel and ter, for water-gong.

2. A watercourse, esp. an artificial watercourse, a mill-leat or the like.

? *a* **1200** In Dugdale *Monast.* (1661) II. 920/2 Omnibus baillivis de Besintone.. Robertus de Curci salutem: mando vobis.. quatinus justicietis meos homines de Snargate, ut faciant wallas & watergangas & clausuras wallarum. **1209** ['The word watergangs occurs.. in an inedited charter of La Capelle' (*Archæologia* 1893, Ser. II. III. 295 note)]. **1322** in *Muniments Magd. Coll. Oxf.* (1882) 145. **1433** *Sc. Acts Jas. I* (1814) II. 22/2 Þat þe breif vndirwrittyn haf courss quhil þe next parliament alanerly of wattir gangis þat is to say of milne leidis & of nane vthir thingis. **1509** *Reg. Mag. Sig. Scot.* 702/2 Le Wattirgang, aque sive torrentis de Grenelaw. *Ibid.* 703/1 Le Wattirgang dict. molendini. **1601** *Ibid.* 391/2 Passand south up the auld rin or watergang of the Teillburne. **1754** T. Gardner *Hist. Dunwich* 96 In the year 1740 the men of Dunwich were digging a Trench near their Old-Port, cross the Beach, to make a Watergang to drain their Marshes.

3. *Sc. Law.* (See quot.)

1681 Stair *Inst. Law Scot.* I. xvii. §12. 345 A Watergang is a Servitude, of conveying Water thorow the servient Ground for the use of the Dominant.

'water-gas.

1. A gas made by forcing steam over incandescent carbon; used as fuel, and when carburetted as an illuminator.

1851 *Mechanic's Mag.* LIV. 129 (*Heading of article.*) Water gas. *Ibid.* LV. 24 The generation of water gas free from carbonic acid is a problem of great importance. **1897** *Allbutt's Syst. Med.* II. 960 So serious have been the consequences of the inhalation of 'water gas' that some English public bodies have been obliged to do away with it.

2. Water in the form of vapour.

1881 Judd *Volcanoes* 22 The whole mass passes at once into the condition of steam or water-gas. **1882** C. P. Smith in *Nature* 5 Oct. 551/2 If a meteorological spectroscope can .. show the.. fact of watery vapour being in the atmosphere, it may also.. be able to quantify.. the proportions of such aërial supply of water-gas at different times.

'water-gate¹. [gate *sb.*¹]

†**1.** A sluice or floodgate. *Obs.*

1408 in *Eng. Hist. Rev.* (1899) XIV. 517 Les spowtes lignea ducentia aquam a dicto Watergate usque dictam rotam. **1458–9** *Memorials of Fountains* (Surtees) III. 58 Pro factura le Wateryattes per Th. bute in fontans fell. ij s. **1577** *Reg. Mag. Sig. Scot.* 748/2 The syd of the puill foranent the watter yet of the Hauch of Dalkeith. **1585** Higins *Junius' Nomencl.* 391/1 *Emissarium*,.. a floud gate: a watergate: a sluce: a waire. **1755** Johnson, *Sluice*,.. a watergate; a floodgate.

b. *transf.* and *fig.*

1390 Gower *Conf.* I. 302 After that withinne a throwe He reyneth and the watergates Undoth. *Ibid.* I. 312 Fro hevene out of the watergates The reyni Storm fell down algates. *c* **1440** *Jacob's Well* 217 Þe v. watyr-gatys of ȝoure pytt arn ȝoure v. bodyly wyttes, as crisostom seyth... Þise ben þe v. watyr-gatys, þe fyve entrees wherby watyr of curse & wose of synne entryn aȝen in-to þi pytt of lystys, but þei be stoppyd. **1606** Sylvester *Du Bartas* II. iv. II. *Magnif.* 1241 If, with ten-fold chain, Thy hand hath lockt the Water-gates of Rain. **1719** D'Urfey *Pills* II. 25 To open well her Water-gate, and best supply her Mill.

2. A gate (of a town, a castle, etc.) giving access to the water-side.

c **1380** *Sir Ferumb.* 4651 Þan was þar a geant ful of pryde, And openede þe water-gate wyde, Ys name was enfachoun. *a* **1400** *Sir Perc.* 918 In at a watur-ȝate, Ther men vytayled by bate That castel with cornes. **1577–87** Holinshed *Chron.* III. 1135/2 The curteine betwixt the watergate and the soldiers prison on the wall. **1624** Middleton *Game at Chess* III. i. 50 Pack up my plate and goods, and steal away By night at water-gate. **1679** Prance *Narr. Popish Plot* 9 The Watergate (as they call it, that is the furthermost Gate or Passage going down out of the Strand to the Waterside) of Sommerset-House. **1722** De Foe *Col. Jack* (1840) 225 Two .. regiments.. kept possession of the water-gate.. of the town. **1867** Morris *Jason* VII. 123 She came down to a gilded water-gate, Which with a golden key she opened straight. **1911** G. M. Trevelyan *Garibaldi & Making of Italy* vii. 165 On the same evening the last of the Bourbons and his queen were leaving the Palace of Naples by the water-gate and taking ship for Gaeta.

b. A gate through which supplies of water are brought.

1535 Coverdale *Neh.* viii. 3 In the strete that is before the Watergate.

3. A place through which water-traffic passes.

1893 F. Adams *New Egypt* 90 It is strange.. to find that a short passage up a series of rapids has brought you.. among a people almost as different from the people.. of Egypt... This water-gate is an absolute division, ethnologically as well as geologically. **1907** A. J. Phillips (*title*) Gravesend: the Water-gate of London.

'water-gate². *north.* and *Sc.* [gate *sb.*²]

1. A channel for water, a watercourse.

1368–9 *Durham Acc. Rolls* (Surtees) 575 In exp. factis pro uno Watergat pro minera de Raynton, 8*li.* 17*s.* 4*d.* **1408** *Durham Acc. Roll* in *Eng. Hist. Rev.* XIV. 517 Soluta.. laborariis, operantibus et facientibus unum Watergate extendentem de Heribourne usque dictum forgeum. **1417** *Engl. Misc.* (Surtees) 13 And bryng of his coste the water-gate overthwarte at the ende of the same newe house. **1447** *Script. tres* (Surtees) App. p. cccxiii, Alsa the said John [etc.] sall.. labour and wyn a watergate for wynnyng of cole in the same colepit. **1668** *Yorks. Deeds* (Yorks. Arch. Soc., Rec. Ser.) II. 115 To carry a sufficient sough and water-gate through the demised ground. *a* **1800** *Jamie Telfer* xii. in Child *Ballads* V. 250/1 Now Jamie is up the water-gate, Een as fast as he can drie.

2. *Sc.* 'An act of voiding urine' (Jam.). Hence in fig. phrase (cf. water *sb.* 18 c).

1721 J. Kelly *Sc. Prov.* 396 I'll watch your Watergate. That is, I'll watch for an Advantage over you.

'Watergate³. The name of a building in Washington D.C., containing the national headquarters of the Democratic Party, which was burgled on 17 June 1972 by persons connected with the Republican administration; used *attrib.* and *absol.* with reference to this event and the circumstances leading to the resignation of President R. M. Nixon in 1974. Also *transf.*, denoting a political or commercial scandal on a large scale.

The element *-gate* has been used in recent times, preceded by the name of a relevant person, etc., to denote an actual or alleged scandal usually of a political or commercial kind: see -gate.

1972 *New Republic* 19 Aug. 4 The very name, 'the Watergate caper', tells how funny it is. **1972** *Time* 28 Aug. 20 By coming down hard on Mitchell, the Democrats hope they can make Watergate a devasting—and durable—campaign issue. **1973** *Freedom* 2 June 1/2 Anything the Americans do we can do better. We have produced our own miniature Watergate plus two new magic ingredients—sex and drugs. **1973** 'H. Pentecost' *Beautiful Dead* (1975) III. i. 141 That's the way it goes in any kind of criminal conspiracy to hide the truth. It's like a Watergate. More and more people become involved, more and more crimes are committed to hide an initial truth. **1974** E. Ambler *Dr. Frigo* II. 101 A Central American Watergate you want now? **1974** *Times* 27 July 15/7 Your reviewer.. sums up the current Chichester production of *Oedipus Tyrannus* as a 'Theban Watergate drama'... Watergate conspiracies were .. frequent in the history of classical Greece. **1976** *Washington Post* 26 Jan. A 2/6 'The news has been inundated by a financial Watergate of leaked disclosures of troubled banks and bank holding companies,' said Reuss. **1977** M. Edelman *Political Lang.* viii. 150 Watergate, the Pentagon Papers, and revelations of the deception of Congress by officials of the executive branch and by intelligence agencies have made us sensitive to lying in high places. **1980** J. Melville *Chrysanthemum Chain* 175 What about a Watergate style investigation? **1982** M. Russell *Rainblast* xiii. 125 The damage is done. Fleet Street gets the signal and .. everyone's sniffing the stench of another Watergate.

Hence as *v. intr.* (and *trans.*), to take part in political conspiracy or in activities directly or indirectly associated with Watergate, as the use of hidden listening devices, concealment of corrupt activities, suppression of evidence, etc. Hence **'Watergater; 'Watergating** *vbl. sb.*

1973 *Birmingham* (Alabama) *Post-Herald* 28 Apr. A-4/3 In the political machinery of the future we may hear of a political party 'Watergating' another party. *Ibid.* A-4/4 They will be asking the voters to remember 'Watergate', for the GOP's might be Watergating again. **1973** *Black Panther* 12 May 2/3 The issue is not how high *up* Watergate goes. The issue is how far *down* watergating goes. The bug on our telephones, and yours, is the issue. *Ibid.* 21 July 2/3 (*heading*) David Hilliard, victim of Watergaters. **1974** N. Freeling *Dressing of Diamond* 20 'And if you try to keep something from the press they're apt to be vengeful.' 'You mean Watergating.' 'Right... It's easily concluded that an effort is being made to cover something, for personal or political considerations.' **1975** G. SEYMOUR *Harry's Game* vi. 91 Not much eavesdropping in here. Need to Watergate the place. **1976** *Publishers Weekly* 1 Mar. 9/1 'When I [*sc.* Archibald Cox] was Watergating, for instance' (this appears to be a coinage of his own, but he rolls it off the tongue as if it were common usage). **1976** *Times Lit. Suppl.* 2 July 815/2 His followers perform experiments that are sadistic, pointless, and repetitive, and are given to watergating the evidence ('Not that there was anything *wrong* on those tapes'). **1979** *N.Y. Rev. Bks.* 8 Feb. 10/4 Perhaps what Jerry Ford should have done on the day he pardoned Nixon was to pardon all the Watergaters and all the Vietnam resisters in one controversially magnanimous act.

'water-gauge, -gage. (See quots.)

1706 PHILLIPS (ed. Kersey), *Water-gage*..an Instrument to gage or measure the Quantity or Depth of any Water. **1844** H. STEPHENS *Bk. Farm* II. 316 When the boiler is observed to have got a sufficient supply—which is indicated by a float water-gauge—the discharge from the pump is turned off. **1886** J. BARROWMAN *Sc. Mining Terms* 71 *Water-gauge*, a U-shaped glass tube for measuring the difference of pressure between the intake and return air; an indicator showing the quantity of water in a steam boiler; a notched board for measuring flow of water.

attrib. **1883** W. C. RUSSELL *Sailors' Lang.*, *Water-gauge cocks*, small cocks placed in front of a marine boiler, by opening which the height of the water in the boiler is ascertained.

[**water-gauge, -gage,** explained in many Dicts. to mean 'a sea-wall or bank to restrain the current and overflowing of the water', is a spurious word, evolved from the false reading *watergaugia*, *-iis*, *-iorum* for *watergangia*, etc. (= WATERGANG 2) in the 1597 edition of a Romney charter of 1252.

The explanation was given in Spelman's *Glossarium* (1664), whence it was copied in the *Dictionarium Rusticum* (1704), followed by Phillips (ed. Kersey, 1706) and later Dicts.]

'water-glass.

1. A water-clock or clepsydra.

1661 [T. POWELL] *Hum. Industry* 4 The Nasican Scipio was the first that brought the use of Water-glasses amongst them, and distinguished the hours of day and night. **1665** THEAKER *Light to Longitude* To Rdr., The measuring of Distances betwixt any two Meridians by Pendulums, Sand-glasses, Water-glasses, &c. **1800** *Asiatic Ann. Reg.* Suppl. Chron. 147/1 Machinery of this kind was previously unknown in Siam, time being generally measured by water-glasses. **1862** GROTE *Greece* II. lxvii. VI. 74 With full notice to defendants and full time of defence measured by the water-glass [*ed.* 1850 clock].

†**2.** A surface of water serving as a mirror. *nonce-use.*

1610 J. DAVIES (Heref.) *Panegyr.* in *R. Vaughan's Water-Workes* B2b, Such is this Water-glasse, wherein these Times Do see how to adorne their Meades in Greene.

†**3.** A glass finger-bowl. *Obs.*

1766 SMOLLETT *Trav.* I. v. 66, I know of no custom more beastly than that of using water-glasses, in which polite company spirit, and squirt, and spue the filthy scourings of their gums, under the eyes of each other. **1776** TWISS *Tour Ireland* 37 The filthy custom of using water-glasses after meals is as common as in England..no well-bred persons touch their victuals with their fingers, and consequently such ablutions ought to be unnecessary. **1784** COWPER *Let. W. Unwin* 5 Apr., Your mother..begs you will buy for her eight blue, deep blue, water glasses.

4. A glass vessel to contain water; esp. such a vessel intended for keeping plants in water.

1612 *Sc. Bk. Rates* in *Halyburton's Ledger* (1867) 309 Watter glasses the dozen, xl s. **1824** LOUDON *Green-house Comp.* I. 10 Wherever a few plants in pots, or bulbs in water-glasses, are kept in a room, the same objection may be raised. **1849** *Florist* 46 A Hyacinth removed from the water-glass should have its roots nicely arranged in good sandy soil. **1852** THACKERAY *Esmond* III. v, 'Is the Queen dead?' cries out Bolingbroke, seizing on a water-glass.

5. An instrument for making observations beneath the surface of water, consisting of a bucket with a glass bottom; a water-telescope.

1848 JOHNS *Week at Lizard* 75 The fishermen say, that they can..descry, with the help of their water-glasses, pieces of cannon lying at the bottom. **1881** E. INGERSOLL *Oyster Industry* 249 *Water-glass*, a bucket with a partial glass bottom, through which the position of sponges is sought. (Florida reefs.) **1902** A. ALCOCK *Naturalist in Ind. Seas* 49 A water-glass..is a wooden funnel, with a window of good plate-glass in the broad end and a pair of handles about halfway up.

6. An aqueous solution of silicate of soda or potash (or of both), which solidifies when exposed to the air. It is used for many purposes, e.g. as a vehicle for fresco-painting, as a paint for rendering material incombustible, for pickling eggs, etc.

1859 *Ecclesiologist* XX. 283 Water-glass seems likely to offer a substitute for enamel. **1867** BRANDE & COX *Dict. Sci.* etc., *Waterglass*..is a soluble alkaline silicate, a liquified flint, made by boiling silica in an alkali. **1880** *Times* 25 Dec. 5/6 What is designated 'Herr Windsperger's fire-extinguishing solution', which is an aqueous solution of silicate of soda, the substance commonly known under the name of 'water-glass'. **1907** *Westm. Gaz.* 14 May 2/1, I have just bought eleven score of new-laid eggs..and put them down in water-glass to use all through the time when eggs are dear.

b. *attrib.*

1862 *Catal. Internat. Exhib., Brit.* II. No. 5916 The three pictures..are painted—that in the centre panel..in oil, the two in the side panels in fresco, in the water-glass or sterochromic method. **1862** *Lond. Society* 258 The new picture is commonly designated a fresco. It is really a water-glass painting. **1883** R. HALDANE *Workshop Rec.* Ser. II. 295/1 The water-glass paint..is liable to be washed away when exposed to rain. **1905** W. HOLMAN HUNT *Pre-Raph.* II. 332 Silica or water-glass painting was substituted for Maclise's 'Waterloo'..the two water-glass paintings.

'water-grass. A name applied to various grasses and grass-like plants growing in the water; also *dial.* (Warw.) to 'various species of *Equisetum*' (Britten & Holland).

The application to the pond-weed (*Potamogeton*) in quot. 1585 may possibly be an error.

1585 HIGINS *Junius' Nomencl.* 134/1 *Potamogeton, fontinalis*,..pondweede or wotergrasse. **1597** GERARDE *Herbal* I. x. 12 *Gramen aquaticum.* Water grasse, or as we may terme it, Water burre grasse. *Ibid.* xi. 13 The place and time in which they growe, differeth not from the other Water grasses. **1765** *Museum Rust.* IV. 128 Our flote fescue is a water-grass, and cannot be made hay of, at least without being dragged from out of the water. **1848** SCHOMBURGK *Hist. Barbados* 585 Panicum spectabile..Scotch Grass. Water Grass. **1856** OLMSTED *Slave States* 69 Broad, silent pools, around the edges of which remained a skirt of ice, held there by bushes and long, broken water-grasses. **1875** MELLISS *St. Helena* 342 Juncus capensis, Thunb.—Spreading Water Grass, or Rush. **1869** BLACKMORE *Lorna D.* vii, Blades of last year's water-grass, trembling in the quiet places.

¶**b.** Anglo-Irish perversion of WATER-CRESS.

1726 THRELKELD *Synopsis Stirp. Hibern.*, *Nasturtium aquaticum supinum*,..Water-cresses... It is called about the Street by the abusive Name of Water-grass. **1880** *Antrim & Down Gloss.*

†**water-grave.** *Obs.* [See GRAVE *sb.*[3] and *sb.*[4]] A water-bailiff. In quot. 1617 ? repr. G. *wassergraf.*

1479 *Hexham Priory, Black Bk.* (Surtees) II. 73 Et ale-graves, watere-graves, et iiij juratos. **1617** MORYSON *Itin.* III. 280 Water-Graves (overseeing Lakes and Rivers for Swannes, fishing and other like things) are offices given at the Princes pleasure and not proper to any Familie.

'water-,gruel.

1. Thin gruel made with water instead of milk.

14.. *Rules & Const. Nuns Syon* lvi. in Aungier *Syon* (1840) 393 On water dayes sche schal ordeyne for bonnes or newe brede, water grewel. **1589** R. HARVEY *Pl. Perc.* Ded., Like a whelp that had scalded his mouth with lapping vp hotte water Grewell. **1667** WOOD *Life* (O.H.S.) II. 100, 5s. for currans and raisons, oatmell, sugar, and pruans, to make water gruell. **1705** E. WARD *Hudibras Rediv.* IV. 8 So have I seen..A sick Man sipping Water-Gruel. **1782** MISS BURNEY *Cecilia* IX. iv, Breakfast on water-gruel. **1818** SCOTT *Hrt. Midl.* xli, She was glad to acquiesce, and even to go to bed, and drink water-gruel. **1852** J. SAVORY *Dom. Med.* (ed. 4) 310 Water Gruel. Put a large spoonful of oatmeal, or fine Indian meal, by degrees into a pint of water, and when smooth, boil it.

attrib. **1871** A. MEADOWS *Midwifery* (ed. 2) 170 The old-fashioned tea and water-gruel system has, it is to be hoped, long since ceased to be.

†**2.** *fig.* as the type of what is insipid. Chiefly *attrib.* (quasi-*adj.*), namby-pamby, characterless.

c **1613** MIDDLETON *No Wit like Woman's* II. iii, Though he [a wooer] have thousands, And come with a poor Water-gruel spirit,..he shall ne'r speed. **1703** MOTTEUX *Prol. to Farquhar's Inconstant* 14 Your scenes of love, so flowing, soft, and chaste, Are water-gruel, without salt or taste. **1753** FOOTE *Englishm. in Paris* I. i, Their water-gruel jaws sunk in a thicket of curls, appear for all the world like a lark in a soup-dish! **1768–74** TUCKER *Lt. Nat.* (1834) II. 430 Had I continued it [fasting] till this time, I believe my chapters would have dissolved into a water-gruel style. **1784** R. BAGE *Barham Downs* II. 129 A pretty, sweet, smiling, flexible, insipid, water-gruel girl. **1811** MISS L. M. HAWKINS *C'tess & Gertr.* I. 76 His wife, a mere water-gruel character.

Hence †**water-gruellish** *a.*

1812 SARAH LADY LYTTELTON *Let.* 28 Apr. *Corr.* v. (1912) 132, I was of the greatest use in putting in a *water-gruellish* sort of observation every now and then, just to fill up the pauses.

'water-,hammer.

1. An instrument used to illustrate the fact that in a vacuum liquids and solids fall at the same rate. It consists of a hermetically sealed tube exhausted of air and partly filled with water. When the tube is quickly reversed, the water falls on the end with a noise like that of a hammer.

1805 *Nicholson's Jrnl. Nat. Philos.* (8°) XI. 217 The water-hammer. This instrument, which is made and sold by the glass-blowers and barometer-makers, consists of [etc.]. **1870** TYNDALL *Heat* iv. §131. (ed. 4) 112 One effect of the withdrawal of the elastic buffer [i.e. the air] is, that the water falls with the sound of a solid body, and hence this instrument is called the water hammer.

attrib. **1881** TYNDALL *Floating Matter of Air* iii. 147 A number of hermetically-sealed tubes charged with the same infusion..have maintained for more than a year..their water-hammer sound.

2. *Hydraulics.* The concussion or sound of concussion of water in a pipe when its flow is suddenly stopped, or when live steam is admitted.

1891 *Century Dict.* **1910** *Encycl. Brit.* XIV. 67/1 [Hydraulics] If in a pipe through which water is flowing a sluice is suddenly closed so as to arrest the forward movement of the water, there is a rise of pressure... This action is termed water hammer or water ram. **1919** *Blackw. Mag.* Feb. 183/2 There came a bubbling roar from the vent..and then the clang of a heavy 'water-hammer' in the pipe as the tank filled.

b. Path. ***water-hammer pulse***, a jerky pulse with a full expansion, followed by a sudden collapse.

1899 *Allbutt's Syst. Med.* VI. 388 The well-known 'water-hammer pulse' or 'pulse of unfilled arteries' of aortic regurgitation.

3. *Surg.* A metal hammer heated in boiling water, used to produce a blister by gently striking the skin.

1891 *Century Dict.* **1911** WEBSTER.

'water-head.

1. The head or source of a stream; the land adjoining the source of a stream.

1567 in *6th Rep. Hist. MSS. Comm.* 642/2 Ane new gift..of all and haill the four merk land and the half of the watter-heid. **1900** *Daily News* 26 Jan. 3/1 We descended the hill, and, passing by the waterhead his father so loved in the old days of his carriage tours, we drove to the church. **1901** *Scotsman* 16 Sept. 10/5 The men o' the waterheads surround Philógar in grim array.

2. = HEAD *sb.*[1] 17.

1856 OLMSTED *Slave States* 7 The celery trenches are arranged in concentric circles, the water-head being in the center. **1914** *Lond. Q. Rev.* Oct. 227 Only about one-fifteenth of the total length of the dam, or 500 feet, will be exposed to the maximum water-head of 85 feet.

'water-hen.

1. Any of the various ralline birds, esp. the MOOR-HEN, *Gallinula chloropus.*

a **1529** SKELTON *P. Sparowe* 453 The dyuendop to slepe; The water-hen to wepe. **1544** TURNER *Avium Præcip.* I 6, *Τρύγγας*, trynga, Anglice a water hen, or a mot hen. **1621** [see DIDAPPER]. **1675** HOBBES *Odyss.* v. 316 And now in figure of a Water-hen, She sat upon the Raft and to him spake. **1678** RAY *Willughby's Ornith.* III. II. i. 312 Section I. Cloven-footed Birds that swim in the Water... Chap. I. Of Water-hens or More-hens in general. **1765** STERNE *Tr. Shandy* VIII. xxxiv, Thou must..carefully abstain..from peacocks, cranes, coots, didappers and water-hens. **1844** HOOD *Haunted Ho.* I. 54 The coot was swimming in the reedy pond, Beside the water-hen. **1867** MORRIS *Jason* XV. 130 So still she stood, that the quick water-hen Noted her not. **1885** LADY BRASSEY *The Trades* 118 The specimens included..rails, water-hens, [etc.].

b. ***water-hen hackle***, an artificial fly made of the hackle feathers of the water-hen.

1837 KIRKBRIDE *Northern Angler* 31 The Water-hen Hackle..is an excellent trout-fly.

†**2.** ***purple water-hen***: = PORPHYRIO. *Obs.*

1678 RAY *Willughby's Ornith.* III. II. iii. 318 Of the Porphyrio, or purple Water-hen. **1743** G. EDWARDS *Nat. Hist. Birds* II. 87 The Purple Water-Hen.

3. The American coot, *Pulica americana. local U.S.* (Mass.)

1891 *Century Dict.*

4. *East Indian.* (See quot.)

1873 E. BALFOUR *Cycl. India* (ed. 2) V. s.v. *Water hen.* The Indian water hen, *Parra Sinensis*,..is met with in the north of India, running over the leaves of the lotus.

'water-hole.

1. a. A hole or depression in which water collects, a pond or pool; a reservoir.

1679 in Picton *L'pool Munic. Rec.* (1883) I. 315 Wee order that..two dangerous water holes close by the foote waye neere Richard Jones house on the heath, bee filled upp. *a* **1774** FERGUSSON *Mut. Compl. Plainstanes & Causey* 126 O' three shillings Scottish souk him, Or in the water-hole sair douk him. **1817** OXLEY *Jrnls. Two Exped. N.S. Wales* (1820) 154 At the eighth mile we came upon a small water-hole, which our poor horses soon emptied. **1843** MARRYAT *M. Violet* xxi, We..encamped by the side of a small water-hole, formed by a hollow in the prairie. **1875** *Spectator* (Melbourne) 20 June 94/1 A bottomless waterhole, about 300 feet wide, exists at Maryvale homestead, Gipps Land. **1903** KIPLING *Five Nations* 57 Tracked me by the camps I'd quitted—used the water-holes I'd hollowed.

b. A cavity in the bed of a river, esp., as in Colonial use, one that retains water when the river itself is dry.

1792 OSBALDISTONE *Brit. Sportsman* 369 Grope to, or tickle, among fishers, signifies putting ones hand into water-holes where fish lie. **1848** WESTGARTH *Australia Felix* 19 The courses of all the rivers, with scarcely any exception, exhibit a series of ponds or water-holes. **1867** E. P. RAMSAY in *Ibis* III. 413 The Musk-Duck frequents alike the lakes, lagoons, rivers, and even the creeks and water-holes. **1890** *Goldfields of Victoria* 26 The dry weather has reduced Boggy Creek to a mere string of water-holes.

†**2.** *Naut.* A hole to allow the escape of water (see quot.). *Obs. rare.*

1794 *Rigging & Seamanship* I. 117 A water-hole, from 4 to 6 inches in diameter, is made in the second cloth from each leech [in Spritsail Course].

3. *Astr.* The part of the radio spectrum between 1420 MHz (at which hydrogen atoms radiate) and about 1660 MHz (at which hydroxyl radicals radiate). [So called because hydrogen and hydroxyl are the constituents of water.]

1976 *Sci. News* 28 Feb. 132 Between the hydrogen and hydroxyl (OH) bands..lies the 'water hole',..which..offers a frequency less drowned in deep-space static. **1979** *Daily Tel.* 10 Nov. 11/1 Scientists have argued that..the radio water-hole will be the most logical communications medium for intelligences across the universe.

Hence **'water-holing**, the operation of trenching between the plants in the cultivation of coffee.

1880 *Spons' Encycl. Industr. Arts* etc. II. 698 A third operation is called 'trenching', or 'waterholing'. The trenches are made across the slope, and may be either open or closed.

'water-horse.

†**1.** The hippopotamus. *Obs.*

1398, 1572, 1600 [see HIPPOPOTAMUS]. **1601** HOLLAND *Pliny* IX. xii. I. 242 Some [water beasts] have a skin over them, and the same hairie, as the Seales and Water-horses [L. *hippopotami*]. *a* **1642** SIR W. MONSON *Naval Tracts* IV. (1704) 425/2 In the Lake of Zembre..there are Water-Horses, and Water-Oxen.

2. A fabled water-spirit appearing in the form of a horse. Cf. KELPIE[1].

1800 LEYDEN *Tour Highlands* (1903) 13 The people of the vale had been a good deal alarmed by the appearance of that unaccountable being the water-horse (*Each Uisge*). **1807** HOGG *Mountain Bard, Mess John* lxiii. *note*, In some places of the Highlands of Scotland, the inhabitants are still in continual terror of an imaginary being, called The Water Horse. **1893** S. O. ADDY *Hall of Waltheof* 85 A fabulous water-goblin mostly appearing in the shape of a gray water-horse. **1903** *Bradford Antiq.* July 343 A water-horse or sprite that demands at least one life annually.

3. (See quot. 1792.) *Newfoundland.*

1777 G. CARTWRIGHT *Jrnl. Labrador* (1792) II. 242 Fourteen quintals of fish were washed, the water-horse was carried out, and the green fish were spread. **1792** *Ibid.* III. p. x, *Water-horse*, newly washed codfish, which are laid upon each other to drain before they are spread to dry. **1966** A. R. SCAMMELL *My Newfoundland* 49 The Blanchard women were spreading out green, waterhorse fish.

'water-house.

†**1.** A building in which water is raised from a river or well into a 'conduit-head' or reservoir to be conveyed by means of conduits or pipes for domestic use. *Obs.*

1681 T. DINELEY *Tour Irel.* in *Trans. Kilkenny Arch. Soc.* Ser. II. IV. 105 A delightful Water house adjoining to the Bowling Green, which with an Engine of Curious Artifice by the help of one horse furnisheth all the offices of the Castle with that necessary Element. This Water house hath a pleasant Summer banqueting room. **1691** J. GIBSON in *Archæologia* XII. 187 And yet they have no water but what is forced from a deep well into a waterhouse, whence they are furnished by pipes at pleasure. **1697** DE FOE *Ess. Projects* 24 The Water-houses for supplying of the City of London with Water. **1726** LEONI *Alberti's Archit.* II. 113 Water-houses or Conduit-heads for the reception of the public water. **1790** *Act 30 Geo. III c.* 21 §1 To make, erect, construct, repair, and maintain all such..Water Houses, Reservoirs,..Water Wheels..for raising, forcing, and conveying a sufficient Quantity of Water from the said River Wenson into..the said City [of Norwich].

2. ? A fanciful name for a boat or canoe. *rare.*

c **1610** BEAUM. & FL. *Scornf. Lady* I. i, The thing by her commanded, is to see Dovers dreadful cliffe, passing in a poor Water-house. **1634** W. WOOD *New Eng. Prosp.* (1865) 48 There be more Cannowes in this towne than in all the whole Patent; every household having a water-house or two. **1878** STEVENSON *Inland Voy.* 178 The canal, coming to its last lock, began to discharge its water-houses on the Oise.

Waterhouse-Friderichsen ('wɔːtəhaʊs-'friːdərɪksən). *Path.* The names of Rupert *Waterhouse* (1873–1958), English physician, and Carl *Friderichsen* (b. 1886), Danish physician, used *attrib.* to designate a fulminating meningococcal septicæmia with hæmorrhagic destruction of the adrenal cortex that occurs chiefly in children and is fatal within hours if not promptly treated.

1936 *Jrnl. Amer. Med. Assoc.* 16 May 1715/2 The disease now known as the Waterhouse-Friderichsen syndrome was recognised as an entity by Little in 1901. **1974** J. D. MAYNARD in R. M. Kirk et al. *Surgery* xii. 256 Precipitating factors [of adrenal insufficiency] are septicaemia, meningococcal meningitis (Waterhouse Friderichsen syndrome..), severe abdominal trauma, [etc.].

'water-ice.

1. A confection of water and sugar, flavoured and frozen.

1818 *Edin. Rev.* XXX. 15 Its granular spongy texture.. has..the appearance of congealed syrup, or what the confectioners call *water-ice.* **1844** T. MASTERS (*title*), The Ice Book,..with..the most approved recipes for making superior water-ices and ice-creams.

2. 'Massive ice formed by the direct freezing of water, and not by the compacting of snow' (W. 1911).

1882 GEIKIE *Text-bk. Geol.* II. II. vi. 111 Water-ice is formed, 1st, by the freezing of the surface... 2nd, by the freezing of the layer of water lying on the bottom.

†**'watered,** *ppl. a. Obs. nonce-wd.* [f. WATERY *a.* + -ED.] Made watery.

1562 Watried [see UNDADE *a.*]. **1572** BOSSEWELL *Armorie* II. 123 The Towers deuyded watried, and in their propre colour.

waterily ('wɔːtərɪlɪ), *adv.* [f. WATERY *a* + -LY[2].] In a watery manner.

1897 CROCKETT *Lads' Love* xi, I smiled waterily. **1901** OXENHAM *Giant Circumstance* xxiii, His black eyes smouldered waterily.

wateriness ('wɔːtərɪnɪs). [f. WATERY *a.* + -NESS.]

†**1.** *concr.* Watery constituent or element; aqueous matter contained in or diffused through a liquid or solid. *Obs.*

1398 TREVISA *Barth. De P.R.* XVII. clxxxiv. (1495) 725 Whyte wyne is more moyst than blacke bycause of clerenesse and watrynesse that hath maystry therin. *Ibid.* XIX. lvx. 901 Mylke is the better and more holsom yf the moost deale of watrynesse is consumpte and wastyd. *c* **1425** tr. *Arderne's Treat. Fistula* etc. 30 Take þe Iuse of þe herbes ..medled wiþ..hony..and boile tham so long vnto þat þe watrynes of þe Iuyse be somewhat þikned. **1558** WARDE tr. *Alexis' Secrets* (1580) I. VI. 99 The moysture or watrinesse of the saied quicke siluer distilleth out in a vapoure. **1678** R. R[USSELL] tr. *Geber* II. I. IV. v. 94 It is expedient to remove from things to be sublimed the Wateriness only with a very small Fire.

†**b.** Watery secretion. *Obs.*

c **1425** tr. *Arderne's Treat. Fistula* etc. 39 And superflue watrenes swette out fro þe place þat was wonte for to file many lynnen cloþes putte atwix. **1543** TRAHERON *Vigo's Chirurg.* II. i. 48 b, Let ye heade be epithemed in the place wher the aquositie or watrines is. **1605** TIMME *Quersit.* I. xvii. 94 It..dryeth up the tears and wateriness of the eyes.

2. The state of being watery; watery quality or nature.

1624 GATAKER *Transubst.* 186 Mere juglers and impostors, that..seeke to..maske with great wordes the naked watrinesse of their Baptisme. **1904** *Elizabeth in Rügen* iv. 95 [Bathers] meeting you on this common ground of wateriness.

3. Superfluity of water as a constituent, connoting poorness, thinness, insipidity. **a.** of the blood.

1544 PHAER *Regim. Lyfe* (1553) H vij, If suche fluxe.. happen of the watrines of bloud, giue her to drink..hony of roses [etc.]. **1897** *Allbutt's Syst. Med.* IV. 18 Mere wateriness of blood..does not cause an increased flow of bile.

b. of an article of food.

1859 R. F. BURTON *Centr. Afr.* in *Jrnl. Geog. Soc.* XXIX. 243 They attempt to remedy the wateriness of the fish by exposing it spitted to a slow fire. **1870** MISS BROUGHTON *Red as Rose* I. 37 But what hero..can stand..the burning of his soup, or the wateriness of his potatoes.

c. *fig.* of literary style, composition, etc.

1830 *Blackw. Mag.* XXVIII. 587 The general haziness and wateriness of all his disquisitions. **1872** RUSKIN *Fors Clav.* xiv. 20 But as to the simplicity—or, shall we say wateriness,—of the style, I can answer you more confidently.

4. The state of being saturated with water.

1820 L. HUNT *Indicator* No. 21 (1822) I. 164 The sudden missing of one's dry senses,—the deaf plunge and bubbling, and wrapping up in heavy wateriness. **1832** —— *Poems, Hero & Leander* I. 120 Then rising, with a sudden-ceasing sound Of wateriness, he stood on the firm ground. **1841** —— *Seer* (1864) 25 [The fly in a tea cup] then stops, and sinks down, saturated and overborne with wateriness.

5. Lachrymal moistness.

1859 SALA *Gaslight & Daylight* ii. 17 A wateriness in the eye, and a huskiness in the throat.

watering ('wɔːtərɪŋ), *vbl. sb.* [f. WATER *v.* + -ING[1].] **I.** The action of the verb WATER.

†**1.** The action of carrying water. *Obs.*

c **1000** ÆLFRIC *Hom.* II. 222 Þæt Israhela folc ȝeðafode þæt sume ða hæðenan on heora ðeowte leofodon, to wudunge and to wæterunge on ðam widȝillan lande. *a* **1300** [see *watering vessel* in 21].

2. The action (or an act) of pouring or sprinkling water on plants, crops, or the soil.

c **1000** ÆLFRIC *Hom.* I. 304 Syððan hi [*sc.* ða wyrta] growende beoð he ȝeswycð þære wæterunge. *c* **1425** *Found. St. Bartholomew's* II. Prol. ii. (1886) 79 As it were a plante what yt is wele y rotyd, the ofte wateryng of hym cesith. *c* **1440** *Pallad. on Husb.* IV. 140 And yeue hem [the plants] in the hete a wateringe. **1573–80** TUSSER *Husb.* (1878) 101 Now set doo aske watering with pot or with dish. **1786** ABERCROMBIE *Gard. Assist.* 63 Light waterings when the earth is dry. **1858** GLENNY *Gard. Every-day Bk.* 166/2 Indiscriminate watering would ruin half the plants.

fig. *a* **1633** G. HERBERT *Outlandish Prov.* (1640) 581 Folly growes without watering.

3. The action (or an act) of soaking or steeping in water or of impregnating with a liquor.

1398 TREVISA *Barth. De P.R.* XVII. xcv. (1495) 662 Some legumina..ben made swete and sauouri wyth good watryng. **1557** HAKLUYT *Voy.* (1599) I. 298 [An overseer] to foresee that neither the yarne be burnt in tarring, nor the hempe rotted in the watering. **1699** T. ALLISON *Voy. Archangel* 30, I caused the Fish that hung overboard for watering, to be hauled in. *Ibid.* 49 The night past we lost 13 pieces of Beef, as they hung a watering. **1827** STEUART *Planter's Guide* (1828) 499 The liquid is to be drawn off in stablepails, and poured leisurely over the heap. As soon as it has..got two complete waterings, it is to be turned and thoroughly mixed.

4. An inundation, flooding, or irrigation.

1594 R. ASHLEY tr. *Loys le Roy* 36 b, And much profitable to those which dwell neere it, by the waterings and other commodities which they receiue of it. **1604** E. G[RIMSTONE] *D'Acosta's Hist. Indies* III. xxii. 187 (*bis*) The which doth grow in very hote vallies, where there are waterings. **1799** A. YOUNG *Agric. Lincoln* 276 The river..has on its banks a range of low ground, highly capable of watering at a very small expence; but not one acre done.

5. The application of water to a road, etc. in order to lay the dust.

1673 *Humours Town* 120 All the Wat'ring scarce being able to lay the Dust the Horses and Coaches raise. **1885** *Law Rep.* 14 *Q.B.D.* 891 The defendants employed inspectors to superintend the watering of their streets.

6. a. The action of giving drinking-water to cattle, horses, etc.; also, the action (of an animal) of going to the water to drink.

c **1440** *Promp. Parv.* 518/1 Watrynge, or ȝevynge drynke to beestys, *adaquacio.* **1577** B. GOOGE *Heresbach's Husb.* III. 120 It is good also to obserue due times for his feeding, his watering, and his trauayle. **1611** BIBLE *Luke* xiii. 15 Doeth not each one of you on the Sabbath loose his oxe or his asse from the stall, and leade him away to watering? **1697** DRYDEN *Æneis* XI. 747 Thus..The wanton Courser..seeks his wat'ring in the well known Flood, To quench his Thirst. **1859** GEO. ELIOT *Adam Bede* xx, The horses were being led out to watering. **1908** *Animal Management* (War Office) 277 Somali camels..are accustomed to go several days without watering.

†**b.** *transf.* (A person's) act of drinking. *Obs.*

1596 SHAKS. *1 Hen. IV*, II. iv. 17 When you breath in your watering, then they [*sc.* ale-drawers] cry hem, and bid you play it off.

†**c.** A light refreshment between meals. *Obs.*

a **1625** FLETCHER *Elder Bro.* I. ii, He..dines with Tully, takes his watering with the Muses, sups with Livy.

7. *Scots Law.* (See quot.)

1681 STAIR *Inst. Law Scot.* I. xvii. §11. 345 Watering is a Servitude of taking water, proper to one Ground for the use of another, whether it be for the Cattel of the dominant Ground, which is most ordinary, or for other uses thereof.

8. The action of procuring fresh water for a ship.

1613 J. SARIS *Voy. Japan* (Hakl. Soc.) 68 The 29th we made an ende of watring, hauing taken in 36 Tonnes, and good store of Wood. **1745** P. THOMAS *Jrnl. Anson's Voy.* 9 Building a Tent, to shelter the People who were to be employ'd in Watering. **1914** *Blackw. Mag.* Apr. 493/1 On Friday 11th, his watering completed.., Herbert was out again and cruising..along the north coast of Jamaica.

9. The action or process of giving a 'watered' appearance to the surface of a material. Cf. 20.

1665 HOOKE *Microgr.* 9 The surfaces of those threads that run the long way, are by the Mechanical process of watering, creas'd or angled in another kind of posture then they were by the weaving. **1823** J. BADCOCK *Dom. Amusem.* 140 Moiré Watering, by other Methods. **1839** URE *Dict. Arts* 1280 Watering of stuffs (Moirage, Fr.); is a process to which silk and other textile fabrics are subjected. **1841** H. WILKINSON *Engines of War* 200 The *Jowher*, or watering, of the genuine Damascus blades, I conceive to have been originally produced by two principal causes: first, [etc.]. **1859** *Abridg. Specif. Patents Paper* etc. II. 23 Fabrics..for ornamenting walls. An effect called 'watering' may be produced by pressing and 'bruising' two thicknesses..together between heated rollers. **1887** F. POLLOCK in *Encycl. Brit.* XXII. 803/2 The 'damascening' and 'watering' of choice Persian and Indian arms.

10. Dilution with water.

1888 *Pall Mall Gaz.* 16 July 12/1 Indian and Ceylon teas ..are stronger and stand more watering. **1892** J. M. WALSH *Tea* 133 In the milk business the most prevalent Sophistications are watering and skimming. **1896** CONAN DOYLE *Rodney Stone* v, Six drops to the half-pint seems a sinful watering of grog.

fig. **1889** *Spectator* 14 Dec. 848 But is not a great deal of that broadening [of their faith] a watering down of the authority of Christianity to pure humanism?

11. Dilution of the capital of a trading company.

1884 *Christian World* 13 Mar. 193/5 Nor has the management ever been charged with any watering of stock. **1893** *Nation* (N.Y.) 27 Apr. 307/3 While doubling the partnership value is legitimate, doubling the shares of a corporation without payment for them is 'watering'.

12. The action of 'taking the waters'.

1765 G. WILLIAMS in Jesse *Selwyn & Contemp.* (1843) I. 403, I shall have completed my watering [at Brighthelmstone] by the Sunday following.

13. Running (of the eyes); †filling with tears.

c **1400** *Destr. Troy* 2167 Thus carpes the kyng to his clene childur, With weping and wo, wateryng of ene, Sobbyng and sikyng. **1585** HIGINS *Junius' Nomencl.* 428/1 *Delachrymatio*,..the watering of the eyes. **1608** TOPSELL *Serpents* 274 A droppe of two thereof dropped into the eyes, cureth the dropping or watering of them. **1684** J. S. *Profit & Pleas. United* 22 If your Cattel are trobld with a Feavour or Ague, you shall discover it by the watering of their eyes. **1879** *St. George's Hosp. Rep.* IX. 483 There was some watering of and photophobia in the left [eye].

14. Salivation of the teeth, mouth, or 'chops', induced by the thought or anticipation of appetizing food.

1601 HOLLAND *Pliny* XII. i. I. 357 He..brought over with him drie Figs and Raisons: the first fruits also as it were of Oile and Wine for a tast, to set their teeth a watering. **1692** R. L'ESTRANGE *Fables* xiii. 13 A Certain Fox spy'd out a Raven upon a Tree with a Morsel in his mouth, that set his Chops a watering. **1708** *Brit. Apollo* No. 26. 3/1 Which.. will..keep your hungry Chops from Wat'ring. **1897** *Allbutt's Syst. Med.* III. 283 A form of salivation, which in its exaggeration resembles 'the watering of the chops' of a healthy appetite, is..'water brash'.

fig. **1690** DRYDEN *Amphitryon* I. ii, You keep such a billing and colling here, to set ones Mouth a watring. **1691** LOCKE *Money* Wks. 1727 II. 37 Those who contend for four *per Cent.* have found out a way to set Mens Mouths a watering for Money at that rate.

II. Concrete senses.

†**15. a.** A place where horses and cattle are taken to drink. Chiefly as in b. *Obs.*

1578 H. WOTTON *Courtlie Controv.* 305 Saying he woulde neither eate nor drinke, but with the Gentleman his man, who scarcely had caried his horse so far as to the watering.

†**b.** *St. Thomas* (*a, of*) *Watering*(*s*: the name of a place two miles from London on the pilgrims' road to Canterbury, near to a brook at which horses were watered. Until the 17th c. it

was the place of public executions for Surrey; hence often in allusive use (cf. TYBURN). *Obs.*
c **1386** CHAUCER *Prol.* 826 And forth we riden, a litel moore than paas Vn to the wateryng of Seint Thomas. c **1420** *Brut* 380 And so þe King and his prysoners passyd forth by ham, til he come vnto Seint Thomas watryng. **1532** [G. WALKER] *Dice Play* (Vele) D v b, You thinke they come home by Tiburne, or S. Thomas of Watrings, and so they do in dede. **1561** *New Enterl. Q. Hester* 542, I pray god they may spede, Euen as honestly, As he that from stelyng, goth to sent thomas watryng in his yong age. **1615** J. TAYLOR (Water P.) *Cast over Water* Wks. (1630) II. 162/1 He at S. Thomas Wat'rings may goe swing. **1630** B. JONSON *New Inn* I. iii, To which, if he apply him, He may..come to read a lecture Vpon Aquinas at S. Thomas a Waterings, And so goe forth a Laureat in hempe circle!

†**c.** Supply of water for cattle. *Obs. rare.*
1773 *Boston Gaz.* 5 Apr. 4/2 Said Farm..contains near Ninety Acres of Land which abounds with excellent Watering, Pasturing, Mowing, [etc.].

†**16.** A well, spring, or other place where water is obtained for domestic use. *Obs.*
1600 FAIRFAX *Tasso* I. lxxxix, Cedron, Bethsaida, and each watring els Empoison'd he, both fountains, springs and wels. **1613** PURCHAS *Pilgrimage* II. xiv. 159 Their washing is with great scrupulosity, in a common watering or in priuate cesternes, or fountaines.

†**17.** A place where vessels obtain a supply of fresh water. *Obs.*
1582 N. LICHEFIELD tr. *Castanheda's Conq. E. Ind.* I. iii. 8 The Captaine Generall..came to the Watering of Saynt Blaze, which is three score leagues beyonde the Cape. **1682** *Lond. Gaz.* No. 1756/1 The best Water, and the most commodious Watering of any place upon this Coast.

†**18.** Water for irrigation. *Obs.*
1600 SURFLET *Country Farm* II. liv. 380 But that such watering may be conueighed in best sort for their growth, it must be prouided and brought by some lowe conduct. **1707** *Curios. Husb. & Gard.* 51 The Rain or other Waterings dissolve the Salts of the Earth.

19. A ditch for draining a marsh; ? the tract drained by such a ditch.
1790 *Phil. Trans.* LXXX. 128 *note*, A manuscript map [of Romney Marsh]..where the names and boundaries of the waterings..are very distinctly expressed. **1877** L. J. JENNINGS *Field Paths* i. 4 It is necessary to keep much to the right..for the 'waterings' are wide and numerous, and it is very easy to lose..time..on these marshes [of Winchelsea and Rye].

20. The wavy, variegated appearance given to silk, metal, etc. = MOIRÉ 2. Cf. 9.
1670 G. H. *Hist. Cardinals* I. III. 77 When others [Cardinals] had their Caps of Red, they had theirs of water'd Chamblet, and when others wore their Purple, theirs was without watering. **1825** J. NICHOLSON *Oper. Mech.* 727 Metallic Watering, or for Blanc Moire. **1860** *Ure's Dict. Arts* etc. (ed. 5) III. 195 The bold waterings..depend not only on the quality of the silk, but greatly on the way in which they are folded when subjected to the enormous pressure in watering.

III. 21. *attrib.* and *Comb.*, as ***watering-bucket, -party, -pit, -pond, -pool, -tank, -time, -trough, tub, -vessel.***
1875 KNIGHT *Dict. Mech.*, **Watering-bucket.* In the United States service the regulation bucket is made of solid leather. **1850** R. G. CUMMING *Hunter's Life S. Afr.* (1902) 98/1 When the natives had constructed a number of water-bags..a *watering party was despatched with these. **1591** PERCIVALL *Sp. Dict.*, *Abreuadero*, a poole, a *watering pit. **1870** N. F. HELE *Aldeburgh* vii. 76 Near the *watering pond I observed a hawk of this species. **1539** *MSS. Dk. Rutland* (Hist. MSS. Comm.) IV. 294 The *wateryng powles in the parke. **1844** H. STEPHENS *Bk. Farm* III. 833 The proper construction of a watering-pool is sadly misunderstood in this country. **1697** DRYDEN *Virg. Past.* VII. 14 Your lowing Heyfars, of their own accord, At *wat'ring time will seek the neighb'ring Ford. **1611** BIBLE *Gen.* xxx. 38 He set the rods ..before the flockes in the gutters in the *watering troughes when the flocks came to drinke. **1908** *Animal Management* (War Office) 129 Watering troughs should be of sufficient height to prevent restless animals pawing over the rim. **1790** *Act 31 Geo. III c.* 17 §20 Provided always, That previous to any..*Watering Tub or Trough, Pump, Stall, or other Projection, being taken down,..Notice..shall be given. a **1300** *Cursor M.* 15189 A man þar yow sal mete, A *watrin vescel in his hand.

22. Special comb.: **watering-bridle**, a bridle with a snaffle-bit, used chiefly when taking a horse to be watered; also *attrib.*; **watering-call** *Mil.* (see quot.); **watering-can** = WATERING-POT 1; †**watering cap**, a cavalryman's fatigue cap; **watering-cart** = WATER-CART *sb.*; **watering hole**, (*a*) = WATER-HOLE 1 a; (*b*) *slang*, a place where refreshment (esp. alcohol) is available, as a bar, hotel, etc. (see also quot. 1972); †**watering-house**, an inn or public house where stage coachmen and hackney coachmen may obtain water for their horses and refreshment for themselves; †**watering man** = WATERMAN 4; **watering order** *Mil.*, the order in which cavalry are drawn up when going to water their horses; **watering-pan** = WATERING-POT; †**watering saddle**, a saddle used by cavalry when riding their horses to water; **watering slip**, a causeway sloping down into a river, for watering cattle, etc.; **watering snaffle**, cf. *watering-bridle*; **watering stone**, ? a water-trough or a fountain; †**watering-table** = WATER-TABLE 1.
1502 *Acc. Ld. High Treas. Scot.* II. 347 Item, for tua small *watering bridillis in Jedworth, ij s. **1680** *Lond. Gaz.* No. 1583/4 A watering bridle and snaffle. **1875** KNIGHT *Dict. Mech.* 383/2 Watering bridle-bits or snaffles. **1853** STOCQUELER *Mil. Encycl.*, **Watering-Call*, a trumpet sounding, on which the cavalry assemble to water their horses. **1692** SIR J. FOULIS *Acc. Bk.* (S.H.S.) 147 For a whyt iron *watering kan to ye yard, 2 0 0. **1839** URE *Dict. Arts* etc. 1143 Introducing..the strong lye of crude soda, through the rose spout of a watering-can. **1851** *B'ham & Midl. Gardeners' Mag.* May 70 As the plants now cover the tops of the pots,..there will be a greatly increased demand for the watering-can. **1836** SOUTHEY *Cowper's Wks.* VII. 265 He was returning..from an evening drill of the regiment of volunteer cavalry,..being dressed accordingly in a flannel jacket, with a *watering cap. **1764** *Museum Rust.* II. 73 A *watering-cart, not unlike those with which the roads near London are watered. **1919** *Glasgow Herald* 21 Apr. 7 Watering carts, conducted by Indian soldiers, are also spraying the roads. **1882** NARES *Seamanship* (ed. 6) 146 Appoint a place for washing clothes clear of the *watering hole. **1972** B. RODGERS *Queens' Vernacular* 209 *Watering hole [spot]* (Brit gay sl), neighborhood cruising locale, usually a park grounds or a bar. **1975** *Telegraph* (Brisbane) 30 Oct. 35/5 The Jindalee Hotel..is a great watering hole. **1981** J. BARNETT *Firing Squad* viii. 77 'I always visit a watering hole on the way home... Cheers.' Palmer took a slow drink. **1984** *Gainesville* (Florida) *Sun* 30 Mar. 1D/5 In a simpler time, players and fans mingled at local watering holes, drinking beers together and becoming friends. **1801** tr. *Gabrielle's Mysterious Husb.* II. 240 The numerous *watering-houses upon the Kentish road, where postillions and stage coachmen generally refresh their horses. **1836** DICKENS *Sk. Boz, Streets—Night*, Watermen..who have been..rushing about for the last two hours, retire to their watering-houses. **1815** *Sporting Mag.* XLV. 185 The Inspectors are to see that all the *watering men wear their badges or numbers. **1892** *Daily News* 28 Sept. 3/5 The regiment..quitted the Spital Barracks early in the morning in *watering order. **1904** A. GRIFFITHS *50 Yrs. Public Service* x. 130 The hours for 'watering order', feeding, cleaning, exercising, and cleaning down. **1827** STEUART *Planter's Guide* 316 Gardeners usually recommend, that all artificial waterings should be performed with the *Watering-pan, as more accurately imitating the genial rains. **1681** *Lond. Gaz.* No. 1606/4 There was also taken away, a *watering Saddle. **1776** G. SEMPLE *Building in Water* 3 Coach, Coach-man and two Horses..were swept down to the *Watering-slip. **1624** in *Athenæum* (1908) 16 May 605/1 For 2 *watering snaffles, iiis. iiiid. **1835–40** *J. M. Wilson's Tales Borders* (1851) VII. 254 In my wanderings, I had entered King's Park by the eastern stile, at the *watering-stone. **1609** in *Lismore Papers* Ser. II. (1887) I. 132, xij stone lights with there *watering tables.

watering ('wɔːtərɪŋ), *ppl. a.* [f. WATER *v.* + -ING[2].] That waters.

1. a. Of eyes: Discharging watery fluid; running.
a **1400–50** *Stockh. Med. MS.* 127 For wattiryngе eyne. c **1450** *M.E. Med. Bk.* (Heinrich) 67 Take a rede cowle leef, ..and ley hit in to þe watrynge eyen. **1551** TURNER *Herbal* I. A v b, Wormwode..heleth the watering sores in the corner of the eyes. **1849** LYTTON *K. Arthur* II. lxxxii, 'And now checkmate!' the wretched sire exclaims, With watering eyes.

b. Of the teeth, mouth: Secreting saliva profusely in anticipation of appetizing food. Also *fig.*
1630 J. LANE *Contn. Squire's T.* x. 542 But now to tell theire Daintie, roial, fare,..of march pane stuff, which wateringe teeth soone boordes [etc.]. **1789** WOLCOT (P. Pindar) *Expost. Ode* I. ii, Ye sharp State-mousers, with your watering jaws. **1848** DICKENS *Dombey* xlviii, Diogenes..had been eyeing his intended breakfast with a watering mouth. **1869** C. GIBBON *Robin Gray* xi, Those who knew about James Falcon gave their watering mouths a wry twist.

2. In transitive sense: Irrigating.
1844 MRS. BROWNING *Drama of Exile* 553, I feel a music which comes straight from Heaven, As tender as a watering dew.

Hence '**wateringly** *adv.*
1621 LADY M. WROTH *Urania* 364 No more able are wee to giue birth to so high desires, then to looke on the Sunne, without hauing..our eyes cast wateringly for presumptuous gazing. **1967** P. WHITE in *Coast to Coast 1965–6* 227 She.. gasped, looking wateringly at the bundle.

'**watering-place.** [WATERING *vbl. sb.*]

1. A place in a river or lake where animals are brought to obtain water: also a pool or trough prepared for the use of cattle and horses.
c **1440** *Promp. Parv.* 518/2 Watrynge place, where beestys byn wateryd..*adaquarium.* **1478** BOTONER *Itin.* (1778) 168 Ultra le Weere et le wateryng place. **1558** *Nottingham Rec.* IV. 119 For maykyng of wattryng places in the Cowpasture. **1769** *Aclome Inclos. Act* 6 Such ground as the said Commissioners may set out for any common watering place or places. **1816** SCOTT *Old Mort.* xxxix, The by-path.. brought him..to the brink of the Clyde, at a spot marked with the feet of horses, who were conducted to it as a watering-place. **1819** *Rees' Cycl.* VI. R 4, s.v. *Canal*, Watering places for cattle are generally directed to be made, especially where the fields have been deprived of their old ones by the cutting of their canal. **1890** 'R. BOLDREWOOD' *Col. Reformer* xx, One of the best watering-places..on the run.

2. a. A place where a ship's company goes to fill the ship's casks with fresh water.
1613 J. SARIS *Voy. Japan* (Hakl. Soc.) 3 The 16th we anchored at the watering place called Tinga Jaua, being 14 leagues from Bantam. **1720** DE FOE *Capt. Singleton* xii. (1840) 209 We sent the..boats..to the watering-place. **1815** *Falconer's Dict. Marine* (ed. Burney), *Watering-Place*, a situation where boats can load with fresh water for the use of ships. **1919** *Eng. Hist. Rev.* July 283 St. Helena..the chief remaining watering-place on the direct route between the Comoros and home waters.

b. *gen.* A place where a supply of water can be obtained.
1621 in Foster *Eng. Factories Ind.* (1906) 288 Wee had all sortes of refreshments untill certayne Portingalls..forbid and defended the watering-place. **1856** STANLEY *Sinai & Pal.* vii. (1858) 287 It [the Jordan] is still the 'Sheriat-el-Khebir' the 'great watering-place' of the Bedouin tribes. **1908** *Parish Councils* 15 At Gaydon (Warwickshire) the parish council was given a good supply of water... The parish council of Humshaugh..has bought the freehold of a small piece of land,..so as to secure for ever a public watering place.

3. a. A resort of fashionable or holiday visitants, either for drinking or bathing in the waters of a mineral spring, or for sea-bathing.
1757 FOOTE *Author* I. Wks. 1799 I. 137 Tunbridge, Bristol, and the other watering places. **1806–7** J. BERESFORD *Miseries Hum. Life* xiv. §33 A Watering Place does not want the help of the sea to make it execrable; the inland Spa is not a jot behind the Fishing-town in the article of tortures. **1822** W. IRVING *Life & Lett.* (1864) II. 80, I shall..go to a watering-place on the continent. **1855** MACAULAY *Hist. Eng.* xvi. III. 652 Teignmouth, now a gay watering place consisting of twelve hundred houses. **1891** HARDY *Tess* lvi, In a quarter of an hour the news..spread through every street and villa of the popular watering-place. **1899** *Allbutt's Syst. Med.* VII. 461 The treatment for gout—including in one case a visit to Aix-les-Bains and other European 'watering places'.

b. *attrib.*
1817 JANE AUSTEN *Sanditon* vi, in *Minor Works* (1954) 389 The very quietest part of a Watering-place Day. **1837** HT. MARTINEAU *Soc. Amer.* III. 93 Such watering-place manners as I saw at Rockaway are considered and called vulgar on the spot. **1842** LOVER *Handy Andy* xlviii, The Honourable Sackville Scatterbrain,..fortunately for himself, had knocked up a watering-place match. **1854** SURTEES *Handley Cr.* ii. (1901) I. 15 A watering-place public, ever ready for excitement, soon divided the place into Swizzleites and Melloites. **1890** GUNTER *Miss Nobody* viii. (1891) 88 The long round of watering-place dissipations.

'**watering-pot.** [WATERING *vbl. sb.*]

1. A portable vessel for watering plants; now usually of tinned iron, and furnished with a long tubular spout, often ending with a rose for scattering the water.
1580 HOLLYBAND *Treas. Fr. Tong*, *Vne Chantepleure*, a garden pot, a watering pot, the toppe of a Cesterne. **1620** I. C. *Two Merry Milk-maids* I. ii. B 4 What, doe you weepe Brother? *Dor.* Like a Watring-Pot; he wud make an excellent Fountaine in the midst of a Garden. **1633** G. HERBERT *Temple*, *Affliction* 'Broken in pieces' ii, As wat'ring pots give flowers their lives. **1660** BOYLE *New Exp. Phys.-Mech.* xxxiii. 247 A Gardiner's Watering Pot shap'd conically, or like a Sugar-Loaf. **1752** *Phil. Trans.* XLVII. 546 The Duke then took one of his silver watering-pots, which was two feet and an half high. **1842** LOUDON *Suburban Hort.* 499 After which the whole of the hillocks should be watered, from a watering-pot with the rose on. **1915** 'Q' (Quiller-Couch) *Nicky-Nan* xiii. 165 She set down her watering-pot.

2. *Zool.* A mollusc of the genus *Aspergillum*, so named from the shape of its shell. Also *attrib.* as ***watering-pot group, shell.***
1815 BURROW *Elem. Conchol.* 206 *Serpula Aquaria*, Watering-Pot. **1861** P. P. CARPENTER in *Rep. Smithsonian Instit.* 1860, 249 The Watering-pots or Aspergillum group. At first sight a 'Watering-pot shell' would not be supposed to have any connection with ordinary bivalves. **1864–5** WOOD *Homes without H.* v. 106 The Watering-pot Shell (Aspergillum) is well known to conchologists. **1885** *Riverside Nat. Hist.* (1888) I. 283 The most noticeable species is the 'watering pot' *Aspergillum vaginiferum*... This species comes from the Red Sea.

'**waterish,** *a.* [f. WATER *sb.* + -ISH[1]. (Sweet gives an OE. *wæterisc*, of which no example seems to be known.)]

†**1.** Composed of water; of the nature of water, aqueous. *Obs.*
1530 PALSGR. 302 *Eaueux*, wateryshe or watry. **1577** GRANGE *Golden Aphrod.* etc. S j b, In time the watrishe droppes, we see doth perce the stone.

2. a. Resembling water in appearance or sensible properties.
1583 STUBBES *Anat. Abus.* II. (1882) 37 The shoomaker liquoreth his leather with waterish liquor. **1612** WOODALL *Surg. Mate* Wks. (1653) 82 Pellitory roots..chewed, bring forth much waterish flegme. **1622** BANISTER *Treat. Eyes* I. iv. A 8, Concerning the humours whereof the eye is made: the first called *aqueus*, that is, the waterish humor. a **1722** LISLE *Husb.* (1757) 299 The waterish part of the cream comes away first. **1748** tr. *Vegetius Renatus' Distemper Horses* 70 The Humour will be thin, waterish and cold.

†**b.** As a designation of colour: Light grey, pale blue. Also ***waterish-blue.*** *Obs.*
1556 WITHALS *Dict.* (1562) 36 b/1 Watrish colour, *aquileus.* **1576** NEWTON *Lemnie's Complex.* II. ii. 100 Some [flowers] of a sadde or darke greene, some watrishe, blunkette, gray. a **1608** DEE *Relat. Spir.* I. (1659) 355 The waters of the Triangles, are somewhat like a watrish blew. **1631** WIDDOWES *Nat. Philos.* 27 The Hiacinth is of waterish colour. **1684** J. S. *Profit & Pleas. United* 167 To take the Fish, the pale waterish coloured haire is the best to deceive them if the stream be clear.

†**3.** Native to or inhabiting the water, aquatic.
1579 G. HARVEY *Letter.-bk.* (Camden) 84 There be innumerable legions of waterishe and earthlye sprytes. **1617** MORYSON *Itin.* II. 46 Waterish foule, plentie of fish, and generally all meates with the common sort alwaies vnsalted .., doe most preiudice the health. **1717** PARNELL *Battle Frogs & Mice* I. 75 But me, nor Stalks, nor watrish Herbs delight.

†**4.** Relating to or concerned with water. *Obs.*

1635 SWAN *Spec. M.* (1670) 70 In the Earthy dry Signs, they produce barrenness, by reason of drought; in Waterish Signs barrenness also, by reason of too much wet.

5. a. Containing excess of water. Of liquids: Dilute, thin, poor. Of solids: Loose in texture, not firm or compact.

1542 BOORDE *Dyetary* xxi. (1870) 284 Peares..doth increase fatnes, ingenderyng waterysshe blod. 1577 B. GOOGE *Heresbach's Husb.* III. 146 All milke that is milked in spring-time, is watrisher then the milke of sommer. 1604 SHAKS. *Oth.* III. iii. 15 Or feede vpon such nice and waterish diet. 1650 NORGATE *Miniatura* (1919) 22 Remember..that the Carnation in your great pencill be rather thin and waterish than too thick and clamy. 1665-6 *Phil. Trans.* I. 35 It was of a loose watrish contexture. 1675 J. LOVE *Clavis Med.* 25 Small beer is waterish. *a* 1722 LISLE *Husb.* (1757) 128 The kirnels [of the nuts]..become waterish, and in a manner tasteless. 1745 ELIZA HEYWOOD *Female Spect.* XVII. (1748) III. 258 What fruits the orchards yielded were tasteless, waterish, and insipid. 1865 SWINBURNE *Poems & Ballads, Anactoria* 38 Moist with waterish wine. 1879 J. TODHUNTER *Alcestis* 116 My blood Is waterish all with tears, and leaves me weak.

b. *fig.*

1549 COVERDALE etc. *Erasm. Par. Rom.* v. 1-5 In steade of the watryshe letter of the lawe gyuen vnto vs as a gage. *c* 1555 HARPSFIELD *Divorce Hen. VIII* (Camden) 96 It is but a waterish cold argument to say there be so many..forbidd. 1614 D. DYKE *Myst. Self-Deceiv.* 302 The memory [is] slippery and waterish to receiue and retaine any good impressions. 1644 MILTON *Divorce* To Parlt. (ed. 2) A 3, Out of a waterish and queasy conscience. 1823 *New Monthly Mag.* IX. 206/1 The waterish comedy of the 'Belle's Stratagem'.

c. Of a taste: Characteristic of what contains excess of water.

1587 TURBERV. *Trag. T., Epit.* etc. 187 b, Of watrish taste the flesh, not firme like English biefe. 1601 HOLLAND *Pliny* XV. xxviii. I. 449 Plums have a waterish tast. 1653 WALTON *Angler* ii. 58 It takes away the watrish taste which the Chub or Chevin has.

†6. Having a predominance of water in the constitution. Also, of disease, characterized by accumulation of water in some part of the body. *Obs.*

1591 SAVILE *Tacitus, Hist.* II. xxxii. 72 The Germans.. hauing foggy and waterish bodies. 1639 G. PLATTES *Discov. Infin. Treas.* x. 69 Some few Sheepe of the most waterish, and flegmaticke constitution, may be caught with this disease. 1634 T. JOHNSON tr. *A. Paré's Chirurg. Wks.* VII. xviii. 270 Of the cure of a flatulent and waterish Tumor. 1660 INGELO *Bentiv. & Ur.* II. (1682) 18 A hot Fever, a watrish Dropsie, a pining Hectic. 1661 LOVELL *Hist. Anim. & Min.* 117 Their Lungs are very phlegmatick and waterish.

†7. Of eyes: Somewhat watery, disposed to run.

1561 B. GOOGE tr. *Palingenius' Zodiac* VI. Q v, For many.. on the sonne do alwaies loke with watrish winking eies.

Comb. 1702 *Lond. Gaz.* No. 3789/4 A very little Man,.. somewhat thick Lipp'd, watrish Eyed.

8. Of weather, air, mist: Charged with water, watery.

1650 VENNER *Via Recta* (ed. 4) 281 This moneth [February] is commonly very raw and waterish. 1669 WORLIDGE *Syst. Agric.* (1681) 295 If small watrish Clouds appear on the tops of hills, Rain follows. 1670 MILTON *Hist. Eng.* v. 235 In that Fenny and watrish air. 1849 C. BRONTE *Shirley* xxi, A dim but not chill or waterish haze slept blue on the hills. 1864 SWINBURNE *Atalanta* 1292 The waterish air Hissed.

9. Of light or of luminous bodies: Dimmed by watery vapour.

1607 MIDDLETON *Michaelmas Term* IV. iii. 45 Like a hanging moon a little waterish awhile. 1769 *Phil. Trans.* LIX. 314 The disturbance on the Sun's limb [was] so undulatory, pointed, ill-defined, waterish. 1797 *Encycl. Brit.* (ed. 3) II. 439/1 A very narrow waterish penumbra appeared round Venus. 1845 TALFOURD *Vac. Rambles* I. 196 The second walk, agreably perplexed by the waterish moonlight.

10. Of ground: Damp, wet.

1562 TURNER *Herbal* II. 7 Gentian..growethe..in shadowe and waterishe places. 1665-6 *Phil. Trans.* I. 328 Rice prospers most in waterish grounds. 1832 J. P. KENNEDY *Swallow Barn* I. xxvii. 283 His constitution resembles that waterish gravelly soil you see sometimes around a spring.

†11. Juicy, succulent. *Obs.*

1591 A. W. *Bk. Cookrye* 32 b, Take..v. or vj. well watrishe Apples, pare them [etc.]. 1648 GAGE *West Ind.* 87 Excellent fruits,..so waterish that they even melt like snow in the mouth.

Hence **'waterishly** *adv.*; **'waterishness.**

1532 HERVET *Xenoph. Househ.* 50 He also muste..turne vp so downe and styrre the grounde, that the soorenes and the rawe watrisshenes of hit may be warmed and well dryed vp. 1571 GOLDING *Calvin on Ps.* lxiii. 4. 238 More coldly and watrishly do others expound it. *a* 1603 T. CARTWRIGHT *Confut. Rhem. N.T.* (1618) 244 The weaknes and watrishnes of your argument. 1659 H. MORE *Immort. Soul* II. xi. 231 Overmuch Coolness, or Waterishness in the Head. 1872 MISS BRADDON *Rob. Ainsleigh* iii, You and my late master's nephew are like as—I'll not say two drops of water, for there is little waterishness in your dispositions.

'water-knot. [KNOT *sb.*[1]] A kind of knot used in joining together the several portions of a fishing line (see quot. 1847).

a 1450 *Fysshynge w. Angle* (1883) 12, 13 Thenne must ye knytte theym togyder wyth a water knotte... And bycause that ye sholde knowe bothe the water knotte & also the duchys knotte: loo theym here in figure caste vnto the lykenesse of the draughte. 1662 R. VENABLES *Exper. Angler* iv. 51 With a Water-knot (in which you must make both the links to fasten) tye them so that [etc.]. 1795 HUTTON *Math. Dict.* s.v. *Knot*, A Fisher's knot, or Water knot. 1847 STODDART *Angler's Comp.* 44 The Water Knot, Single and Double..is completed, simply by laying the ends of the two threads, links, or strands, required to be joined, alongside of each other; then, doubling the one round the forefinger of the right hand and passing one of the links and its corresponding end through the loop thus formed, draw all tight. 1885 H. CHOLMONDELEY-PENNELL *Fishing* (Badm.) I. 38 What is known as the single fisherman's knot (sometimes called 'water knot').

†'waterlade. *Obs.* [f. WATER *sb.* + LADE *sb.*[2]] A channel for water, an aqueduct.

[*c* 1050 *Voc.* in Wr.-Wülcker 339/4 *Aqueductum* [= *-uum*, genit. pl.], wætergelada.] *a* 1300 *Cursor M.* 11936 Lakes seuen he made o clai, And til ilkan a fur he made þat suld be þaim to watur lade, þat water moght rin fra and till, Vte of þe flum al atte will. *Ibid.* 12019. 1421 *Cov. Leet Bk.* 28 þat euery deister of this Cite, that hath a waturlad ouer the comyn Ryver, schall pay to the Chamburlayns of this Cite euery yer xij d. 1610 HOLLAND *Camden's Brit.* I. 747 The channells were not skoured..but the water-lades stopped up either through negligence, or depopulation.

†'waterlag. *Obs.* [? Short for next.] An epithet of abuse.

a 1529 SKELTON *Sp. Parrot* 88 Moryshe myne owne shelfe, the costermonger sayth; Fate, fate, fate, ye Irysh waterlag.

†water-lagger. *Obs.* [? f. LAG *v.*[3] + -ER[1].] = WATER-LEADER.

1519 HORMAN *Vulg.* 222 b, There is rysen a fray amonge the water laggers [L. *amphorarios*]. *c* 1520 A. BARCLAY tr. *Sallust's Jugurth* xxviii. 39 He commaunded..that the pages, waterlaggers, and scolyons shuld nat come nere the army, nor folowe the same [*ne lixæ sequerentur exercitum*].

'Waterlander. [f. *Waterland*, a district in North Holland + -ER.] (See quots.)

1860 *Chamb. Encycl.* I. 219/1 This cause divided the body, as early as 1554, into the Mild and the Strict Mennonites. The first are known by the title of Waterländers. 1883 *Encycl. Brit.* XVI. 12/2 The Waterlanders in North Holland, who held the least strict doctrine of excommunication.

So **'Waterlandian.** [-IAN.]

1765 A. MACLAINE *Mosheim's Eccl. Hist.* (1768) V. 49 The more moderate..Anabaptists are composed of certain inhabitants of Waterland, Flanders, Friesland, and Germany, who..commonly pass under the denomination of Waterlandians. 1839 *Penny Cycl.* XV. 96/2 The followers of Menno very soon split into two sects, the Flemings and the Waterlandians, so called from the countries in which they arose.

attrib. 1765 A. MACLAINE *Mosheim's Eccl. Hist.* (1768) V. 50 One of these Waterlandian sects was divided, in the year 1664, into two factions.

'Waterlandish, *a.* *nonce-wd.* [-ISH[1]] Characteristic of the theologian Daniel Waterland (1683–1740).

1762 STERNE *Tr. Shandy* VI. xi, This sermon upon the jewish dispensation—I don't like it at all;—Though I own there is a world of *water-landish* knowledge in it,—but 'tis all tritical, and most tritically put together.

'water-lane.

1. *dial.* A green lane with a stream running along it.

1872 *Daily News* 24 Oct., Anything analogous to the leaping Chine of the Isle of Wight, the Guernsey Waterlane, or those noisy streamlets which abound in the hilly districts of Ireland. *a* 1876 M. COLLINS *Pen Sk.* (1879) I. 173 The cool water-lanes of Guernsey. 1891 [D. JORDAN & MRS. J. A. OWEN] *Ann. Fishing Village* xi. 104 It was a water-lane—a public way for any cart-horse or cow that the owners might think fit to take there—as wide as an ordinary road.

2. A narrow passage of open water, e.g. between masses of reeds or between lines of shipping.

1883 G. C. DAVIES *Norf. Broads* ii. 15 We cross the Broad and the river, and enter a narrow water-lane between the reeds. 1898 KIPLING *Fleet in Being* i. 2 A consort was coming up a waterlane, between two lines of shipping, just behind us.

†water-lapper. *Obs.* One who 'lappeth of the water with his tongue' (*Judges* vii. 5).

1652 URQUHART *Jewel* Wks. (1834) 278 No less miraculous acts were expected and promised..then those of Gideon with his water-lappers. 1676 W. ROW *Contn. Blair's Autob.* x. (1848) 163 Captain Ellis' company..were all water lappers, Judges vii. 5-7, and bible bearers.

'water-lead (-liːd). [LEAD *sb.*[2]] **a.** A mill-lead. **b.** An open channel through an ice-field.

1641 *Reg. Mag. Sig. Scot.* 371/2 Lie watter-leidis &c. 1802 G. V. SAMPSON *Statist. Surv. Londonderry* 341 On the return, the [salmon] fry are killed in great numbers, in passing through the water-leads, by the mill-wheels of the bleach-greens. 1853 KANE *Grinnell Exp.* xvii. (1856) 130 But to seaward, open water-leads gladden us in every direction.

†water-leader. *Obs.*

1. One who carts water for sale.

[? *c* 1250 *Cal. Ancient Deeds* A 7319, Grant by Adgarus.. of Stebehee to John le Waterladere of Estsmedhefeld of 1 *a.* land between land of Richard son of Geoffrey le Waterladere (etc.).] 1307 *Exch. K.R. Eccl. Doc.* 2/50 lf. 6 Terram Reginaldi Kempe le Waterledere. 1350 in Riley *Memorials* (1868) 254 [The carters, called] waterleders [shall take for the cart, from Douuegate to Chepe, 1½ d.]. 14.. *Nom.* in Wr.-Wülcker 697/23 *Hic aquaductor*, a waterleder. 1415 in *York Myst.* (1885) Introd. p. xxiv, Waterleders [join with the 'Cukes' in presenting a play]. 1503 in R. Davies *Extr. Munic. Rec. York* (1843) 239 *note*, The cookes shall yerely geddir pagiaunt silver of the waterleders and sandeleders toward the supportacion and charge of bryngyng furth of the pagiaunt of the same cookes. 1600 *Chester Plays* Banes 75 The good symple water-leaders and drawers of deey, see that your Arke in all poyntes be prepared.

2. In Irish iron-works (see quot.).

1645-52 BOATE *Ireland's Nat. Hist.* xvii. 134 Water-leaders, or Water-course-keepers, to steer the Water-courses, and to look to them constantly.

'water-leaf.

1. Any plant of the genus *Hydrophyllum.*

1760 J. LEE *Introd. Bot.* App. 331 Water-leaf, *Hydrophyllum.*

2. *Arch.* An ornament used in sculptured capitals, supposed to be a conventionalized representation of the leaf of some aquatic plant.

1851 RUSKIN *Stones Ven.* I. xxvii. §29 Where the Byzantines use the acanthus, the Lombards use the Persepolitan water-leaf. *a* 1878 SIR G. SCOTT *Lect. Archit.* (1879) I. 120 Most of [the capitals] are of the simple water-leaf form so prevalent in the north of England. 1912 F. BOND *Cathedrals* 90 The voluted water-leaf of the capitals [in the Galilee at Durham].

3. (See quots.)

1854 C. TOMLINSON *Obj. Art-Manuf., Paper* 25 When dry, it is complete paper, but of the kind called waterleaf, which will absorb liquids too freely, and therefore cannot be written on. 1855 HERRING *Paper & Paper Making* 64 First, we have what is termed the water-leaf, or the condition in which the paper appears after being pressed between the felts—this is the first stage. 1863 *Technologist* III. 393 The transformation of water-leaf, or unsized paper, into a material in exact resemblance to parchment, is one of the chemical facts of the last few years.

waterless ('wɔːtəlɪs), *a.* [OE. *waterléas* = Du. *waterloos*, OHG. *wazzerlôs* (mod.G. *wasserlos*); see WATER *sb.* and -LESS.] **a.** Destitute of water; containing no water; unsupplied with water.

c 950 *Lindisf. Gosp.* Luke xi. 24 *Per loca inaquosa*, ðerh stowa wæterleasa. *c* 1000 ÆLFRIC *Gen.* xxxvii. 24 [Hiȝ] dydon hine on ðone wæter-leasan pytt. *a* 1300 *Cursor M.* 4156 In þis wast i wat a pite, Dri and waterles es it. *a* 1300 *E.E. Psalter* cvi. 35 He set..in out-gang of watres land water-les [L. *sine aqua*]. *c* 1386 CHAUCER *Prol.* 180 A monk, whan he is recchelees Is likned til a fissh þat is waterlees. *c* 1400 *Sege Jerusalem* (E.E.T.S.) 44 þoȝ ȝe wantede wynne ȝe noȝt o droppe. *c* 1400 *Master of Game* (MS. Digby 182) xii, And shortly þe houndes vnclene holde and vnclene kept, or longe waterles, hath communlych þe maniewe. 1526 TINDALE *Luke* xi. 24 When the vnclene sprete is gone out of a man, he walketh through waterlesse places sekynge reest. 1577 KENDALL *Flowers Epigr.* 42 b, Can seas be waterles and drie? can hilles be dales without? 1643 TRAPP *Gen.* l. 21 To requite your kindness, that consulted to starve me, in the waterless pit. 1828 DUPPA *Trav. Italy*, etc. 176 Here and there a little waterless fountain completes the design. 1854 SURTEES *Handley Cr.* lix. (1901) II. 140 A half-buttered muffin mounts a waterless slop-basin; a dirty egg accompanies some toasted wedges of bread. 1893 SELOUS *Trav. S.E. Africa* 18 Through this seventy miles of waterless country. 1902 *Times* 24 Nov. 5/2 The long waterless marches are beginning to have their effect upon the camels.

b. *waterless pit*: in the 17th c. often *fig.* with allusion to *Zech.* ix. 11.

1616 J. B. *Serm.* 25 And they will deliuer thy soule..from the water-lesse pits. 1675 T. BROOKS *Golden Key* Wks. 1867 V. 350 The Babylonish captivity..was that waterless pit,.. out of which they were delivered by virtue of the blood of the covenant. 1690 C. NESSE *Old & New Test.* I. 197 The prison of this waterless or comfortless pit.

c. Of processes, apparatus, etc.: employing or needing no water.

1930 *Engineering* 6 June 742/3 One advantage of the waterless gasholder was found to be the absence of a succession of sudden increases and decreases in pressure. 1951 *Good Housek. Home Encycl.* 313/2 The waterless cooker consists of a fairly deep aluminium pan, which is divided into compartments. 1971 *British Printer* Aug. 80/2 The need to maintain a critical ink-water balance..may be overcome by the development of waterless offset-litho.

Hence **'waterlessness.**

1888 *Sat. Rev.* 10 Nov. 563/1 His preconceived opinion of the waterlessness of this country.

'water-,level.

1. A levelling instrument in which water is used instead of alcohol (see quot. 1880).

1563 SHUTE *Archit.* B ij b, Geometrie teacheth vs the order of rules, Compasses, Squiers, Quadrantes, and Iuste water-leueles with manie other knowlaiges. 1674 R. HOOKE *Animadv. Hevelius* 61 This is done by the help of a Water-Level. 1723 E. STONE tr. *Bion's Math. Instrum.* v. i. (1758) 134 The first of these Instruments is a Water-Level, composed of a round Tube of Brass, or other solid Matter, about 3 Feet long [etc.]... This Level, altho' very simple, is very commodious for levelling short Distances. 1880 L. D'A. JACKSON *Aid Surv.-Pract.* 146 The water level..is also an appliance for rough levelling within short distances... It consists of a horizontal tube about two feet long terminated by two bottle-shaped ends, in which water will stand level and thus afford a horizontal line of sight.

2. *Mining.* A road driven on the strike of a seam to carry off water.

1698 *Phil. Trans.* XX. 368 It is only a Spring which rises in a Coal-Drift (or Water-Level made for the draining of the Cannel Coal-Pits). 1836 *Hull & Selby Rlwy. Act* 43 Airways, headways, gateways, or water-levels through the mines. 1886 J. BARROWMAN *Sc. Mining Terms* 71.

3. The plane below which the rock or soil is saturated with water; the situation of this plane. Also *attrib.*

1839 URE *Dict. Arts* 960 To whatever depth a coal-mine is drained of its water, from that depth it is worked, up to the rise of the water-level line. *Ibid.* 974 The miner..is guided in his line of direction entirely by the water-level. **1882** GEIKIE *Text-bk. Geol.* III. II. ii. §2. 345 In most districts rocks are permeated with water below a certain limit termed the water-level.

4. The horizontal surface of still water. Also the (higher or lower) position of the surface of water.

1860 MAURY *Phys. Geog. Sea* (Low) xii. 297 Thus we might have a sea whose level would be much further below the water-level of the ocean than is the Dead Sea. **1862** SMILES *Engineers* III. iii. 26 When the water-level in the pit was lowered, and the suction became incomplete [etc.]. **1878** D. KEMP *Man. Yacht Sailing* 377 A straight line from the fore side of the stem to the aft side of the stern-post at the water level. **1895** J. J. RAVEN *Hist. Suffolk* 39 The salting mound just above the present average water-level in Herringfleet. **1917** L. EINSTEIN *Inside Constantinople* v. 212 The crew.. succeeded in raising the stern [of the submarine] to the water-level, whence all scrambled out.

'water-,lily. The common name for many aquatic plants with large flowers, belonging to the N.O. *Nymphæaceæ*. In British use chiefly applied to the white water-lily, *Nymphæa alba*, and the yellow water-lily, *Nuphar lutea*. The Australian (blue) water-lily is *Nymphæa gigantea*.

1549 *Compl. Scot.* vi. (1872) 67, I sau the vattir lille, quhilk is ane remeid contrar gomoria. **1578** LYTE *Dodoens* II. xxviii. 180 There be two kindes of water Lyllies.. the yellow, and the white. **1597** GERARDE *Herbal* II. cclxxxii. 672 The white water Lillie or Nenuphar, hath great round leaues, in shape of a buckler. **1652** CULPEPPER *Eng. Phys.* 120 The white Water-Lilly hath very large, round and thick dark green leaves. **1760** J. LEE *Introd. Bot.* App. 317 Lily, Lesser Yellow Water, with fringed Flowers, *Menyanthes*. **1788** COWPER (*title*) The Dog and the Water-Lily. **1818** BYRON *Ch. Har.* IV. lxvii, While, chance, some scattered water-lily sails Down where the shallower wave still tells its bubbling tales. **1820** SHELLEY *Sensit. Pl.* 45 Broad water lilies lay tremulously. **1861** TENNYSON in Ld. Tennyson *Mem.* (1897) I. 471 The Isle of Wight is like a water-lily on a blue lake. **1882** *Garden* 11 Nov. 421/1 There is the giant blue Water Lily of Australia.

b. Applied to aquatic plants of other orders. The 'water lily' of New Zealand is *Ranunculus lyallii*.

1653 WALTON *Angler* ii. 40 Look down at the bottom of the hil, there in that Meadow, chequered with water Lillies and Lady-smocks. **1882** H. FRIEND *Devonsh. Plant-n.*, Water Lily, *Iris Pseudacorus*. **1886** *Cheshire Gloss.*, *Water Lily*, the arum lily, *Calla palustris*. **1893** *Wiltshire Gloss.*, Water-lily (1) *Caltha palustris*. (2) *Ranunculus aquatitis*.

'water-line.

†**1.** A rope of some kind. *Obs.*

1626 CAPT. J. SMITH *Accid. Yng. Seamen* 14 The brest ropes are now out of vse, the water line is [*i.e.*, in use].

2. *Naut.* The line of floatation of a ship; the line supposed to be described on the hull by the surface of the water when a ship is afloat. Often (= LOAD-WATER-LINE) the proper line of floatation when the ship is fully laden. *light water-line*: the line of floatation of a ship without cargo.

a **1625** *Nomenclator Navalis* (Harl. MS. 2301). **1627** CAPT. J. SMITH *Sea Gram.* ix. 45 The water line is that Bend or place she should swim in when she is loaded. **1664** EVELYN *Sylva* iv. 20 Elm is.. proper for Water-works, Mills, Pipes, Pumps, Ship-planks beneath the Water-line. **1691** T. H[ALE] *Acc. New Invent.* 122 The Horizontal Section at the water line. *Ibid.* 125 Our second Water-line, which I call the sailing-line. **1773** EMERSON *Princ. Mechanics* (ed. 3) 236 Let *Dd AcC* be the water-line or horizontal section of the water and the hull of a ship. **1805** *Shipwright's Vade-M.* 141 *Water Lines* or *Lines of Floatation*. Those horizontal lines, supposed to be described by the surface of the water on the bottom of a ship, and which are exhibited at certain depths upon the sheer-draught. Of these, the most particular are those denominated the Light Water Line and the Load Water Line. **1837** *Civil Engin. & Arch. Jrnl.* l. 13/1 Her length on the water-line 230 feet. **1882** 'OUIDA' *Maremma* I. 151 Brigs laden to the water-line with cargo and steering straight for Africa. **1889** WELCH *Text Bk. Naval Archit.* i. 8 The line in which the surface of the water cuts the surface of the ship when floating in any position is called the water line for that position. **1892** *Century Mag.* May 23/2 The outlets are below the water-line of the boat.

b. *attrib.* as in *water-line armour, belt, length.*

1868 *Rep. Munitions War* 270 There is a water-line belt of the same thickness (4½ inch plating). **1884** *Pall Mall Gaz.* 25 Sept. 1/2 The water-line armour tends to save the ship from sinking... To leave two-thirds the length of the ship without this water-line armoured belt is a most awfully risky experiment. **1892** *Century Mag.* May 25/1 Which thus gained advantage over square-sterned boats of equal water-line length.

3. *Shipbuilding.* Any one of certain structural lines of a ship, parallel with the surface of the water, which represent the contour of the hull at various heights above the keel, and collectively determine the exterior form of the vessel.

1750 BLANCKLEY *Nav. Expositor*, *Water Line*, is that which goes round the Ship at the Surface of the Water, and shews the true Shape of her Body. **1797** *Encycl. Brit.* (ed. 3) XVII. 399/1 In ships that draw more water abaft than afore, the water lines will not be parallel to the keel. **1830** HEDDERWICK *Mar. Archit.* 186 Having the diagonals drawn on the body-plan, next draw in the water-lines. The water-lines and transoms are commonly drawn first on the sheer-plan, and transferred to the body-plan. **1851-4** *C. Tomlinson's Cycl. Usef. Arts* (1867) II. 506 The principal lines employed in constructing a draught... Water lines, which in the sheer plan are straight lines drawn parallel to the surface of the water, and in the half-breadth plan they show the form of the ship by the successive breadths marked at heights corresponding with the water lines in the sheer plan... The upper water line in the half-breadth plan is the line of flotation. **1878** D. KEMP *Man. Yacht Sailing* 377 *Water Line*, a horizontal plane passing through a vessel longitudinally. A line shown in the half-breadth plan of a ship drawing.

b. *attrib.*, as in *water-line pattern, plan, model.*

1867 EMERSON *May-day* 205 What god is this imperial Heat?.. Doth it bear hidden in its heart Water-line patterns of all art, All figures, organs, hues, and graces? **1867** SMYTH *Sailor's Word-bk.*, *Water-line model*. The same as *key-model*. **1875** KNIGHT *Dict. Mech.*, *Water-line Model*, a model formed by board shaped according to the draft-lines on the paper, and laid upon each other to form a solid model.

4. The weather-mark or stain on a wall showing where a roof formerly terminated against the wall.

1886 WILLIS & CLARK *Cambridge* II. 148 A new roof was constructed, the pitch of which was regulated by the water-line on the eastern face of the tower.

5. = WATER-LEVEL 3. (See quot. 1897.)

1849 DEMPSEY *Drainage Districts & Lands* 70 Districts lying below the level of the adjacent river, or so little above it that drains of adequate capacity must have their beds below the water-line, necessarily require artificial means of discharging the drainage waters. **1869** R. B. SMYTH *Gold Fields Victoria* 625 *Water-line*, the line in any reef where water is struck in the various shafts. **1890** *Nature* 27 Nov. 94/2 The absence of water passing into the ground for a long period naturally leads to a lowering of the free ground water-line. **1897** RIDEAL *Water & Purif.* 84 The 'line of saturation', or water-line, is the level at which the water stands, and to which it will rise in wells, in any water-bearing stratum.

6. The outline of a coast.

1791 W. GILPIN *Forest Scenery* II. 159 The water-line of the island appears to more advantage. Among many smaller indentations of the coast, the bays of Totland, and Newtown, are considerable. **1853** KANE *Grinnell Exped.* xlvi. (1856) 423 The water-line was toothed with fangs of broken ice, which scraped against the beach as the tides rose and fell.

7. A linear watermark in paper.

1847 DE MORGAN *Arithm. Bks.* Introd. p. xiii, It is supposed.. that the waterlines are perpendicular in folio, octavo, and decimo-octavo books, and horizontal in quarto and duo-decimo. **1858** *Sotheby's Principia Typogr.* III. 32 In the identification of the manufacture of paper, two very important points must be observed: First, the space between the divisional water-lines caused by the thicker upright wires of the sieve and secondly, [etc.]. *Ibid.* 86 Remarkably thick and spongy paper, having been much sized; the upright water-lines scarcely visible.

Hence **'waterlined** *a.*, of paper, marked with water-lines. **'waterliner**, a shot that hits a vessel on the water-line.

1898 KIPLING *Fleet in Being* ii. 21 Oh, good shot! That was a water-liner... That was the Marines' three-pounder.

waterlog ('wɔːtəlɒg), *v.* [app. f. WATER *sb.* + LOG *v.*[1]

Cf. LOG *v.*[1] 3 a, where the only example cited is:—**1751** SMOLLETT *Per. Pic.* lxxxvi, Several feet of under-water logging in her hold. In this passage 19th c. editors have altered *logging* into *lodging*; this is doubtless wrong, but the sense of 'logging' is somewhat obscure. The likeliest view seems to be that it is an absolute use of a transitive sense, 'to reduce (a ship) to the condition of a log': cf. quot. 1622 under LOG *sb.*[1] 1 b, 'Having lost all her mastes, and being no other than a logge in the sea'.

The finite verb is not recognized in previous Eng. dictionaries, which give only *waterlogged* ppl. adj.]

1. *trans.* To render (a ship, etc.) unmanageable by flooding with water: see WATERLOGGED *ppl. a.* Also *intr.* for *pass.*

1779 FORREST *Voy. N. Guinea* 101 The Borneo carried too much sail, just before she foundered; and took in a sea forward, which water-logged her. **1780** in Laughton & Heddon *Great Storms* (1927) v. 109 The ship began to waterlog. **1809** *Naval Chron.* XXII. 57 A sudden leak.. water-logged her. **1854** H. MILLER *Sch. & Schm.* (1858) 17 The fearful wave had waterlogged the Friendship from bow to stern. **1901** *Munsey's Mag.* XXV. 345/1 A tremendous sea broke on board,.. opened her hatches, and waterlogged her.

2. To saturate with water so as to render inert. Also *intr.* for *pass.*

1870 R. W. P. BIRCH *Disposal Town Sewage* 6 This last-mentioned method of applying sewage to land.. waterlogs the earth. **1878** RAMSAY *Phys. Geog.* ix. (ed. 5) 137 Beds of coal are not the result of woody matter drifted into, and waterlogged in, lake hollows, by rivers. **1950** *N.Z. Jrnl. Agric.* Mar. 224/1 Heavy soils which waterlog in wet spells should be avoided, as the plants will not tolerate 'wet feet' for long.

3. *fig.*

1868 M. PATTISON *Academ. Org.* ii. 29 This alteration added to the assembly about 100 members—and waterlogged Congregation at one stroke. **1904** *Daily Chron.* 24 Mar. 4/5 No scheme of purchase.. can do otherwise than waterlog the State telephone department with a large amount of unproductive capital.

Hence **'water-logging** *vbl. sb.* Also **'water-logger.** (For the sense cf. WATERLOGGED 3 b.)

1897 *Allbutt's Syst. Med.* IV. 321 Pulmonary œdema in renal diseases is not always a mere accompaniment of general water-logging. **1905** *Westm. Gaz.* 5 Oct. 2/2 Whereas a few years ago only two [butter-making] companies were engaged in water-logging, there were now over 100. *Ibid.* 2/3 It was his business to cater for the honest trading classes and not for fraudulent water-loggers [in butter-making]. **1906** *Macm. Mag.* June 609 There are four main divisions under which adulteration might be classed:—(1) milk-blending, (2) water-logging, [etc.].

waterlogged ('wɔːtəlɒgd), *ppl. a.* [f. prec. + -ED[1]. (The form *water-lodged* in Lescallier *Vocab. des Termes de Marine Anglois et François*, Paris 1777, and in *Encycl. Brit.* 1797, is an ill-advised attempt at correction of *water-logged* in Falconer's Dict.)]

1. Of a ship, boat: Flooded with water by leakage or overflow so as to become impaired in buoyancy, heavy, and unmanageable.

1769-76 FALCONER *Dict. Marine*, *Water-logged*, the state of a ship when, by receiving a great quantity of water into her hold, by leaking, &c. she has become heavy and inactive upon the sea, so as to yield without resistance to the efforts of every wave rushing over her decks. **1797** S. JAMES *Narr. Voyage* 135 The vessel being nearly water-logged, every high sea washed over her. **1817** OXLEY *Jrnls. Two Exped. N.S. Wales* (1820) 145 Our little bark was however completely water logged. **1826** SOUTHEY *Vind. Eccl. Angl.* 478 The Virgin visibly conveyed the water-logged ship over the breakers safely to the shore. **1847** H. MILLER *First Impr. Eng.* ii. (1857) 18 As if becalmed in its voyage, a water-logged hulk, that failed to press on towards its port of destination. **1865** PARKMAN *Huguenots* iii. (1875) 40 The gale subsided.. and.. the crazy, water-logged vessel again bore slowly toward France. **1912** 'G. A. BIRMINGHAM' *Inviolable Sanctuary* v, He climbed over the dredger.. and dropped from her into a small waterlogged punt.

b. *transf.*

1840 HOOD *Up Rhine* 61 You will be glad to hear that we have escaped undrowned from that water-logged country called Holland. **1848** THOREAU *Maine Woods* (1894) 7 That other [house] with a waterlogged look, as if it were still airing and drying its basement.

c. *fig.* and in fig. context.

1795 BURKE *Regic. Peace* iv. Sel. Wks. (1892) 350 Tumbling from the Gallick coast, the victorious tenth wave shall.. poop the shattered, weather-beaten, leaky, water-logged vessel [*sc.* the Government]. **1837** CARLYLE *Fr. Rev.* II. VI. vi, A poor water-logged Legislature can pronounce nothing. **1867** LOWELL *Percival* Pr. Wks. 1890 II. 141 His mind drifts, too waterlogged to answer the helm.

2. Of floating bodies: Saturated with water so as to be deprived of buoyancy.

1832 LYELL *Princ. Geol.* II. 241 When timber is drifted down by a river, it is often arrested by lakes, and becoming water-logged it may sink. **1851** MANTELL *Petrifactions* iv. §2. 370 After death.. the body was thus suspended with the belly uppermost, till it became water-logged, and buried in the silt. **1882** E. O'DONOVAN *Merv Oasis* I. 315 Water-logged tree trunks clung among the roots projecting into the sluggish stream.

3. Suffering from, deteriorated or rendered unserviceable by, excessive saturation with water.

1829 *Bone Manure, Rep. Doncast. Comm.* 8 A gravelly soil may embrace.. the waterlogged yellow clay. **1839** URE *Dict. Arts*, etc. 969 In the course of years, however, many water-logged fissures come to be cut by the workings. **1858** GLENNY *Gardener's Everyday Bk.* 208/1 All the plants throughout the house should be often examined to see that none are pot-bound, or water-logged. **1893** *Outing* XXII. 150/1 A cyclist cannot extract enjoyment from a water-logged day. **1895** *Daily News* 24 June 8/5 They have completed arrangements for borrowing £100,000 to be spent in draining waterlogged mines. **1897** *Allbutt's Syst. Med.* IV. 613 The arterial pressure falls at last.. and in spite of free perspiration the tissues become water-logged. **1897** MARY KINGSLEY *W. Africa* 607, I.. began to fear that the rotten water-logged earth we were on might give way.

b. Of butter: Containing an excess of water.

1906 *Macm. Mag.* June 608 A large quantity of water-logged, milk-blended butter was being manufactured for the purpose of being sold fraudulently.

Hence **waterloggedness.**

1854 THOREAU *Walden* iv. Writ. 1918 II. 198.

Waterloo (,wɔːtə'luː). The name given to the battle fought outside the village of Waterloo, near Brussels, on June 18, 1815, in which Napoleon was decisively and finally defeated. Hence **a.** (with *a, his*): Something which is a 'settler'; a decisive and final contest; chiefly in the phrase *to meet one's Waterloo*.

1816 BYRON *To Moore* 5 Dec., It [Armenian] is.. a Waterloo of an Alphabet. **1842** J. AITON *Domest. Econ.* (1857) 68 If there must be a Waterloo, let it be a conflict for all the minister's rights, so that he may never require to go to law in his lifetime again. **1859** W. PHILLIPS *Lesson of Hour* 11 Every man meets his Waterloo at last. **1887** *Times* (weekly ed.) 24 June 9/3 He will have fought and lost his Waterloo. **1905** A. CONAN DOYLE *Return of Sherlock Holmes* 356 We have not yet met our Waterloo, Watson, but this is our Marengo. **1961** C. MCCULLERS *Clock without Hands* iii. 67, I felt right then and there I had met my Waterloo. **1982** *Times* 20 Oct. 19/6 The main fount of the economic nightmare now engulfing the world has met with its Waterloo.

b. The name of a bright blue tint (see quots.).

1823 MOORE *Country Dance & Quadrille* 84 Eyes of blue (Eyes of that bright, victorious tint, Which English maids call 'Waterloo'). **1871** MRS. H. WOOD *Dene Hollow* xxxviii, The frock.. was of that dark bright blue colour called Waterloo, after the somewhat recent battle of Waterloo.

c. *attrib.*: **Waterloo ball**, a frivolous entertainment preceding a serious occurrence (with reference to a ball given in Brussels by the Duchess of Richmond on the eve of the Battle of Waterloo); †**Waterloo bang-up**, = *Waterloo cracker*; **Waterloo blue** (cf. b. above); **Waterloo church** (see quots. 1938, 1961); **Waterloo cracker**, a kind of firework (cf. CRACKER 6); **Waterloo Cup**, in Coursing, a race held annually at Altcar, near Liverpool; †**Waterloo fly**, an artificial fly with blue wings; † **Waterloo helmet** (see quot.).

1954 P. TOYNBEE *Friends Apart* xi. 132, I now see these dances as a succession of *Waterloo Balls, a rapturously gay company, rapturously doomed. **1968** *Listener* 11 July 44/3 Is it a Waterloo Ball we are invited to watch, a permanent party on the eve of great events? **1826** HONE *Every-day Bk.* II. 1310 His companion cracks a *Waterloo bang-up in their faces. **1858** MISS SEWELL *Ursula* vii, There she was.. dressed out in a bright blue silk dress,—what is called a *Waterloo blue. **1938** B. F. L. CLARKE *Church Builders of 19th C.* ii. 24 In 1828 the Church Building Society was incorporated by Parliament. The same Act abolished Church Briefs... The churches built as the result of the Act were officially known as the Commissioners' Churches; the general public called them *Waterloo Churches. **1961** M. H. PORT *Six Hundred New Churches* ii. 28 The popular misnomer, 'Waterloo Churches', became applied to those built with the aid of the first parliamentary grant. [*Note*] The term is sometimes applied only to the four churches built in the old parish of Lambeth (St John, Waterloo Bridge Road; St Luke, Norwood; St Mark, Kennington; St Matthew, Brixton). This may originate from St John's having been commonly termed..'Waterloo Church', which refers, of course, to its site. **1972** N. PEVSNER *Some Archit. Writers 19th c.* v. 29 This was the heyday of the Greek Revival and the so-called Waterloo churches. **1833** CARLYLE *Sart. Res.* in *Fraser's Mag.* Nov. 583/2 What vehicle of that sort have we, except *Fraser's Magazine*? A vehicle all strewed (figuratively speaking) with the maddest *Waterloo-Crackers. **1851** MAYHEW *Lond. Labour* I. 430/1, I took 15s... for waterloo crackers and ball crackers (the common trade names), 'waterloo' being the 'pulling crackers'. **1878** STEVENSON *Inland Voy.* 72 The child was letting off Waterloo crackers all over the floor. **1836** *Bell's Life* 20 Mar. 3/5 **Waterloo Cup*, eight dogs... Deciding course.—Melanie beat Unicus, and won the Cup. **1898** [see STAKE *sb.*[2] 3]. **1939** R. GODDEN *Black Narcissus* xx. 182 Call in your mad dog, Clo. Is it the Waterloo Cup you've entered it for? **1983** *Times* 3 Mar. 3/2 More than 300 demonstrators yesterday disrupted the second day of the Waterloo Cup hare coursing meeting in Lydiate Field, Lancashire. **1837** KIRKBRIDE *Northern Angler* 61 The *Waterloo Fly. **1887** *Pall Mall Budget* 27 Jan. 16/1 The uniform of the Old Life Guards includes a *Waterloo helmet, with crest and plume at the side.

'waterly, *adv. rare.* [f. WATER *sb.* + -LY[2].] After the manner of water.

1918 D. H. LAWRENCE *New Poems* 62 You undine-clear and pearly, soullessly cool And waterly The pool for my limbs to fathom.

† **waterlyngke.** *Obs.* [f. WATER *sb.* + *lyngke* = LEMEKE. Cf. BROOKLIME and WELLINK.]

a **1400-50** *Stockh. Med. MS.* p. 186 Waterlyngke: *fabria minor*.

† **water-mail[1].** *Sc. Obs.* [MAIL *sb.*[2]] A rent charged upon a piece of water.

1455 *Sc. Acts Jas. II* (1814) II. 42/2 þe lordschippe of Abernethy with þe watter malys of Inuerness. **1488** *Reg. Mag. Sig. Scot.* 381/1 Dicto duci hereditarie pertinentem de magnis custumis et aquarum firmis nuncupatis le Water Malez burgi de Aberdene. **1500** *Exch. Rolls Scot.* XI. 266 *note*, The yerlie pensioun gevin to hir of the custumez and water malis of oure said burrowis. *c* **1550** *Registr. Aberdon.* (Maitland Club) II. 212 [Dedit] xx s. de custumis Abirdonensibus videlicet de ly vatir malis.

† **water-mail[2].** *Sc. Obs.* [The second element is obscure; possibly the word may be an incorrect Sc. reading of WATER-MOLE.] Some kind of fur. Also *attrib.*

1489 *Acc. Ld. High Treas. Scot.* I. 136 Item, for watermayllis to lyne the saim gowne. **1512** *Ibid.* IV. 215 Item, put in ane stomok of the Quenis of blak satin, sex wattermaill skynnis. **1517** *Caldwell Papers* (Maitl. Club) I. 57 Ane goun of tanny, lynit with wattermalis.

waterman ('wɔːtəmən). [Cf. G. *wassermann* (in various senses), WFris. *wetterman*, Sw. dial. *vattenmann* (= sense 5).]

† **1.** A seaman, mariner. *Obs.*

?*a* **1400** *Morte Arth.* 741 Wyghtly one the wale thay wye vp thaire ankers, By wytt of the watyre-mene of the wale ythez. **1549** *Maldon (Essex) Liber B.* 136b, John Boyes of Maldon did bye of John Marteyn of Bradwell, Waterman, oon hunderith & syxe bussells of oysters. **1550** COVERDALE *Spir. Perle* xxii. 165 Lyke as a waterman wyll neuer let out hys sayle so farre, but that he may sone pull it in agayn. **1638** G. PLATTES *Discov. Inf. Treas.* (1639) 44 This all Fishers and watermen can tell, for that they finde the water deepest in the loosest earth, and ebbest where it is most compacted and firme: for Mountaines and Vallies at land, are depths and shallowes at Sea. *a* **1651** SIR J. SKEFFINGTON *Heroe of Lorenzo* (1652) 79 Cæsar..when he was fain to encourage his faint-hearted waterman in a storm, by saying, Be not afraid, for so thou wrong'st the fortunes of Cæsar. **1682** WHELER *Journ. Greece* 301 Our Greek refused absolutely to go further with us unless by water. For he was a kind of Water-man, and was not of their faith, that had rather trust God Almighty by Land than by Sea.

2. A man working on a boat or among boats, *esp.* a boatman (as the licensed wherry-man of London) who plies for hire on a river, etc.

1458 *Forman's Monumt. Christ's Hosp., Abingdon* 41 Ther loved hem a ladde was a water man longe; He helpe stop the streme til the werke were a fore. *a* **1513** FABYAN *Chron.* VII. (1811) 628 This mayer fyrste of all mayers brake that auncient..custome, and was rowed thyther by water; for ye which ye watermen made of hym a roundell or songe to his great prayse. **1580** HOLLYBAND *Treas. Fr. Tong, Payer le port*,..to pay the waterman his fare. **1583** MELBANCKE *Philotimus* P j b, And so imitate the waterman whiche lookethe one waye, and roweth another. *a* **1603** BACON *To Ld. Essex* Wks. 1730 IV. 486 And to her Majesty no other reason, but the reason of a waterman; I am her first man of those who serve in counsel of law? **1610** HOLLAND *Camden's Brit.* I. (1637) 389 The Inhabitants whereof [of Henley on Thames] be for the most part Watermen, who make their chiefest gaine by carrying downe in their Barges wood and Corne to London. **1672** in *Verney Mem.* (1907) II. 304 Seamen and Watermen are daily impressed,..to supply the shipps. **1697** VANBRUGH *Relapse* I. ii, Come, pay the Waterman, and take the Portmantle. **1773** C. BURNEY *Pres. St. Mus. Germany* (1775) II. 21 The boat moved so very slow, there being only one waterman, that it frequently seemed to stand still. **1824** *Friendship's Offering* 220 Rates of Watermen. From London Bridge. **1834** *John Bull* 27 July 238/3 The contest among the watermen of Putney for a purse of sovereigns..took place on Wednesday. **1835** DICKENS *Sk. Boz, River*, Groups of watermen are assembled at the different stairs. **1860** W. W. READE *Liberty Hall* I. v. 95 The watermen on the [college] barge shove them off by pushing against the stroke oars extended. **1913** *Q. Rev.* Apr. 388 One of the bullets struck a waterman in the Queen's barge.

b. ***waterman's knot*** = WATER-KNOT.

1871 *Routledge's Ev. Boy's Ann.* May 297 The Waterman's Knot..may be used. **1875** in KNIGHT *Dict. Mech.*

c. *colloq.* One having a (good) knowledge of boating, etc.

1912 'GUY THORNE' *Gt. Acceptance* i. 13 It is not to be understood that he was in any way a milksop. He was a good waterman upon the river, and at a time when young men of position did not indulge in cricket, football, [etc.]..he was yet a fearless, skilful rider.

d. *slang.* (See quot.)

1860 *Hotten's Slang Dict.* (ed. 2), *Waterman*, a light blue silk handkerchief. The Oxford and Cambridge boats' crews always wear these—light blue for Cambridge, and a darker shade for Oxford.

† **3.** = AQUARIUS. *Obs.* Cf. WATERBEARER 2.

1565 B. GOOGE tr. *Palingenius' Zodiac* XI. QQj, But airy are these three, the Scales, the Waterman, the Twinnes. **1590** T. HOOD *Use Celestial Globe* 35b, The 11. [constellation] is *Aquarius*, the Waterman, which hath 42. starres.

4. A man employed in the supply or distribution of water; *e.g.* a water-carrier, a turncock or fireman, a man engaged in the irrigation of water-meadows, or in pumping.

1705 *Lond. Gaz.* No. 4140/4 They [*sc.* the Fire-Insurance Co.] only Employ..their own Watermen. **1776** G. SEMPLE *Building in Water* 46 At low Water I set all the Drudge and Water-men to that Corner. **1789** T. WRIGHT *Meth. Watering Meadows* (1790) 11 Two of our most skilful watermen were sent for to lay out a meadow of seven acres. **1794** T. DAVIS *Agric. Wilts* 33 The water is thrown over as much of the meadow as it will cover well at a time, which the watermen call a 'Pitch of work'. **1875** BEDFORD *Sailor's Pocket Bk.* vii. (ed. 2) 250 Each half company providing 2 woodmen, 2 watermen. **1877** L. PALMA DI CESNOLA *Cyprus* 141 A sort of wicker yoke, which is put on the back of a donkey ridden by the water-man. **1880** D. C. DAVIES *Metallif. Min.* 425 *Water Men*, men employed in the extraction of water, especially with the rag and chain pump. **1912** MAX PEMBERTON *War & Woman* III. i. 174 Kensington, Paddington, and Hampstead were frozen out. .. Weary water-men plugged the mains.

b. *esp.* An attendant at cab- or coach-stands, whose primary function was to water the horses.

1764 *Low Life* 69 Hackney-Coachmen..are sleeping in Night-Cellars, while the Watermen (as they are termed) are watering their Horses. **1831** *Ann. Reg.* 321 Thomas Taverner, waterman to the coach-stand. **1835** DICKENS *Sk. Boz, Hackney-coach Stands*, The waterman darts from the pump, seizes the horses by their respective bridles, and drags them, and the coach too, round to the house, shouting all the time for the coachman at the very top..of his voice. **1841** S. WARREN *Ten Thou.* I. ii, It ended in a regular set-to between two watermen attached to the adjoining coach-stand. **1908** E. V. LUCAS *Over Bemerton's* iv. (1921) 37 The waterman tends the cab rank and incidentally runs errands for the neighbourhood. London is rich in such wastrels.

5. An imaginary being living in or under water, a water-demon, a merman.

1833 KEIGHTLEY *Fairy Mythol.* II. 72, I am a Christian woman as well as you; and I was carried off by a water-man, who changed me. **1873** W. S. GILBERT *More 'Bab' Ballads, Capt. & Mermaids* 43.

† **6.** In certain nonce-uses. **a.** One who uses water instead of wine in the Eucharist. **b.** A Baptist. *Obs.*

1577 tr. *Bullinger's Decades* (1592) 1070 These watermen, that is to saie, they that vse water onely, in celebrating the Lords supper, are iustly condemned. **1657** J. WATTS *Scribe* etc. I. 109 If you..have been new dipt by some of the watermen, and have been re-baptised Iohn.

7. *colloq.* A water-colour artist.

1888 *Pall Mall Gaz.* 29 Oct. 11/2 The collection of water colours..including among its contributors many of the best living 'water-men'.

8. *Comb.* as ***waterman-like*** adj.

1623 BP. HALL *Gt. Impostor* Wks. (1625) 504 The Will (in both respects) Water-man-like lookes forward, and rowes backward. **1885** *Manch. Exam.* 30 Mar. 3/1 It was a moot point whether the Oxford or the Cambridge crew went through it..with the more watermanlike ease.

Hence **'watermanship,** the art of a waterman; skill in rowing or managing boats, etc.

1882 *Daily News* 18 Jan. 2/1 His weight..combined with good watermanship, fairly points to the conclusion that he will eventually prove to be one of the best oarsmen in this year's crew. **1890** *Pall Mall Gaz.* 27 Aug. 2/1 A 'Varsity crew, carefully coached and with a fine knowledge of watermanship. **1894** R. C. LESLIE *Waterbiog.* Pref., What may be called the seamanship of large racing craft, and the watermanship of smaller ones, is usually left to their skipper and crew. **1902** BUCHAN *Watcher by Threshold* 126 A canvas skiff which it took good watermanship to sit.

attrib. **1900** G. SWIFT *Somerley* 106 This..is a very obvious bit of watermanship information.

'water-mark, watermark, *sb.* [MARK *sb.*[1] Cf. G. *wassermarke* in various senses.]

† **1.** *Sc.* A boundary mark indicating the line of separation between the waters of different rivers (belonging to different proprietors). *Obs.*

1632 *Reg. Mag. Sig. Scot.* 652/2 Cum signis fluvialibus lie water markis intra aquas de Done et Loquhell. **1637** *Ibid.* 266/2 Cum molendino, maneriei loco, signis fluvialibus lie water-merkis inter aquas de Done et Loquhell.

2. The line (whether actually marked or not) forming the limit to which the tide, or the water of a river, well, flood, etc., has risen or usually rises. Cf. HIGH-WATER MARK, LOW-WATER MARK.

1678 DRYDEN *All for Love* I. i, Men and Beasts Were born above the tops of Trees, that grew On th' utmost Margin of the Water-mark. **1751** *Act 24 Geo. II*, c. 8, §16 Till the Water is sunk below the Watermark. *c* **1820** S. ROGERS *Italy, Gondola* 79 Those hundred Isles..That rise abruptly from the water-mark. **1889** *Hardwicke's Sci.-Gossip* XXV. 125 Plunging through the sand we hope to find something on the water-mark.

fig. **1896** E. AUGUSTA KING *Ital. Highways* 62 The water-mark above which it is undesirable that any woman's knowledge shall rise.

3. A mark left by a flood.

1822 J. FLINT *Lett. fr. Amer.* 122 A watermark on the beach showed that the Ohio had lately risen to the height of fourteen or fifteen feet. **1883** G. C. DAVIES *Norfolk Broads* ii. 14 Bright green reeds eight feet high, with a yellow water-mark on their lower stems.

4. The line showing the draught of a ship.

1764 [J. BURTON] *Pres. St. Navig. Thames* 36 The Gauger should first affix on the Side the Water-mark of 3 Feet Draught. **1858** SIMMONDS *Dict. Trade, Water-mark*,..the float-line or sinking depth of a ship. **1883** W. C. RUSSELL *Sailors' Lang., Water-marks*, the figures on a ship's stern showing the depth of water she draws.

5. a. A distinguishing mark or device impressed in the substance of a sheet of paper during manufacture, usually barely noticeable except when the sheet is held against strong light.

So G. *wassermarke* (1785); the more common word is now *wasserzeichen (zeichen* sign). The name was prob. given because the water-mark, being less opaque than the rest of the paper, had the appearance of having been produced by the action of water.

1708 HEARNE *Collect.* 11 Mar. (O.H.S.) II. 98 Has sent specimens of old paper (for water-marks &c.). **1779** *Gentl. Mag.* XLIX. 374/1 He [Mathison] had discovered a method of counterfeiting the water-mark of the bank paper. **1787** FENN *Orig. Lett.* I. Pref. p. xxi. *note*, The paper-marks are those figures formed by wires, on the sieve at the bottom of the mould in which the paper is made, and are impressed on it in its pulpy state... They are often called the water-marks. **1870** E. PEACOCK *Ralf Skirl.* II. 237 It showed a water-mark of a lion standing upright. **1913** F. W. CORNISH *Jane Austen* x. 226 As the water-marks in the original manuscript are 1803 and 1804 it could not have been written before that time.

b. The metal design from which the impression is made.

1854 C. TOMLINSON *Obj. Art-Manuf., Paper* 22 The singular names of the older kinds of paper appear to have some connection with the devices formed in them by the water-marks. Water-marks are ornamental figures in wire or thin brass, sewn upon the wires of the mould, and like those wires, they leave an impression, by rendering the paper where it lies on them, thinner and more translucent.

6. ***watermark disease***, a disease of the cricket-bat willow, *Salix alba* var. *cœrulea*, caused by the bacterium *Erwinia salicis* and producing dying-back in the crown of the tree and stains in the wood.

1924 W. R. DAY in *Oxf. Forestry Mem.* III. (*title*) The watermark disease of the cricket-bat willow. **1950** *Q. Jrnl. Forestry* XLIV. 106 Watermark disease of the cricket bat willow..spreads rapidly both upwards and downwards in the wood vessels. **1976** *Eastern Even. News* (Norwich) 9 Dec. 15/4 This was to cut the cost of services for an inspector on 'watermark disease' of willow trees.

'water-mark, *v.* [f. prec. sb.]

1. *trans.* To mark or stamp with a watermark.

1866: see WATER-MARKED *ppl. a.* **1889** W. LOCKHART in *Athenæum* 16 Mar. 345/1 The Chinese..for a long time past have had the art of water-marking paper. **1895** *Westm. Gaz.* 30 Apr. 7/2 A number of forged Bank of France notes were submitted, watermarked 1,000 francs.

2. To embody as a watermark.

1889 *Century Mag.* Nov. 94/2 The volumes..are without the final refinement of the recurring title water-marked in the lower margins of the page.

Hence **'water-marked** *ppl. a.*; **'water-marking** *vbl. sb.* (also *attrib.*).

1866 ROGERS *Agric. & Prices* I. 644 Wired and water-marked paper is found soon afterwards [*c*1350]. **1896** *Daily News* 4 June 7/7 The method of watermarking must not be forgotten. **1897** *Ibid.* 10 July 8/3 All the dies and water-marking plates are here designed, and made for the Bank Notes, Postal Orders,..and other papers requiring a water-mark. **1913** *Q. Rev.* Apr. 401 All these have been tried, and, with the exception of the water-marking, wholly given up.

'water-,meadow. A meadow periodically overflowed by a stream. Also *attrib.*

1733 TULL *Horse-Hoeing Husb.* xiv. 187 This Thrash'd Hay..has been found more nourishing to Horses, than course Water-Meadow Hay. *a* **1789** WIMPEY in T. Wright *Meth. Watering Meadows* (1790) 25 A water-meadow is laid out in arched lands similar to the segment of a circle. **1801** *Farmer's Mag.* Aug. 254 Water-meadows also, should never be ploughed. **1834** *Brit. Husb.* I. 529 The advantages arising from water-meadows are too well known to require elucidation. **1853** DICKENS *Bleak Ho.* xlviii, On the river where the water-meadows are fresh and green. **1868** MORRIS *Earthly Par., Man born to be King* 1511 Fair with golden sheaves,..Gay with the water-meadows green. **1879** *Cassell's Techn. Educ.* I. 19/2 As a preparatory step in the formation of water-meadows, it is often considered advisable to under-drain the field.

ˈwater-ˌmeasure. A kind of measurement formerly used for coal, salt, fruit, etc., sold on board vessels in port or in the river.

The bushel of water-measure seems to have been originally the ordinary bushel heaped; the statute of 1495 ordained that it should contain five pecks of striked measure, thus exceeding the ordinary bushel by one-fourth. A 'water-measure' exceeding the standard measure in a much larger proportion seems to have been used for coal shipped from northern ports: see quot. 1708, and cf. quot. 1851 under CHALDRON 2.

1465 *Paston Lett.* Suppl. (1901) 93, I may selle here for vj s. viij d. a quarter clene fixed after Royston mesure, which is lesse thanne the water mesure of London. **1495** *Act 11 Hen. VII* c. 4 §3 Provided alwey that this Acte shall not extend to any persone selling or byeng by watermesure.. And..that the seid Watermesure within the Shippes borde shall onely conteyn v pekkis after the seid standard rased and streken. **1499** *Maldon* (Essex) *Court-rolls* Bundle 58. No. 6 Emerunt salt ad portum per mensuram vocat. le water mesur et extra navem vendiderunt per le land mesur in prejudicium legiorum domini Regis. Ideo quilibet eorum in misericordia XL*d*. **1581** *S'hampton Crt. Leet Rec.* (1905) 215 It is ordeynid that none should buye either salt, onions, aples or such lyke vppon the water but by water measure & like wize to sell beeinge once landed & sellerid or housed but by land measure. **1640** *Act 16 Chas. I.* c. 19 §6 Such measure as is comonly called Water measure in any Ports Maritine [*sic*] Townes or other places shall be still used and continued as formerly the same hath beene. [Recited and repealed **1670** *Act 22 Chas. II* c. 8 §1.] *a* **1661** FULLER *Worthies, Devon* (1662) 247 William Alford..of Bediford carried on his back for a Wager, four Bushels, Salt-water-measure [*read* four Bushels Salt, water-measure]. **1702** *Act 1 Anne* Stat. 1, c. 15(9) §1 Whereas Apples and Pears are frequently Sold by Measure, commonly called Water Measure, the Contents whereof are very Uncertain... Be it therefore Enacted..That the Measure, commonly called Water Measure, shall be Round, and in Diameter Eighteen Inches and an half within the Hoop, and Eight Inches Deep, and no more, and so in Proportion for any greater or lesser Measure: And that every Measure, commonly called Water Measure, by which Apples and Pears are Sold, shall be heaped as usually. **1708** J. C. *Compl. Collier* (1845) 17 Water, or New-Castle or Sunderland Measure,..is generally reckoned double the Measure of a London Chaldron, or more. **1708** *Constit. Watermen's Co.* xlii, It is agreed and order'd, that all Lightermen selling Coals, shall sell Pool-measure, commonly call'd Water-measure; That is to say, One and Twenty Chaldron to the Score. **1815** *Falconer's Dict. Marine* (ed. Burney), *Water-Measure*. Salt, sea-coal, &c. while on board vessels in the pool or river, are measured with the corn bushel heaped up; or else five striked pecks are allowed to the bushel. This is called water-measure, and it exceeds Winchester measure by about three gallons in the bushel.

ˈwater-ˌmeasurer. [transl. of *Hydrometra*, f. Gr. ὑδρο-, ὕδωρ water + μέτρ-ον measure.] A book-name for insects of the family *Hydrometridæ* (typical genus *Hydrometra*).

1854 A. ADAMS etc. *Man. Nat. Hist.* 243 Water-measurers (Hydrometridæ). Head generally as broad as thorax, [etc.]. **1871** STAVELEY *Brit. Insects* 319 The..Hydrometridæ, or the water-measurers, may be known at once by their very slender figure, and their habit of skimming upon the surface of the water. **1890** *Hardwicke's Sci.-Gossip* XXVI. 28/2 Great 'water-measurers' (*Gerris lacustris*) were running about in a jerky manner, on the surface of the water.

ˈwater-ˌmelon. [So called from the abundance of watery juice. Cf. F. *melon d'eau*.] A kind of gourd, *Citrullus vulgaris* (formerly *Cucumis Citrullus*). (Applied both to the plant and its fruit.)

1615 R. COCKS *Diary* (Hakl. Soc.) I. 47 A present of 10 water millons. *Ibid.*, 10 water millans. **1666** J. DAVIES *Hist. Caribby Isl.* 66 There grows in these Countries another kind of Melons..call'd Water-Melons, because they are full of a sugar'd water, intermingled with their meat. **1762** MILLS *Syst. Pract. Husb.* I. 153, I design to try liquorice-roots, barley, Cape-Breton wheat, cotton, indigo-seed, wood for dying, and the water melon. **1883** *Fisheries Exhib. Catal.* 270 Two Water-melons used for buoying lines. **1887** MOLONEY *Forestry W. Afr.* 360 Water Melon... Commonly cultivated in all warm countries of the world for its fleshy edible fruit.

attrib. **1832** S. A. FERRALL *Ramble Amer.* 298 Here I—slipped out at the side door into the water-melon patch.

ˈwater-mill.

1. A corn-mill whose machinery is driven by water. Also *attrib.*

c **1425** *St. Christina* vii. in *Anglia* VIII. 122 She wente streight vprighte on þe watir-mylne whele. **1464** *Rolls of Parlt.* V. 529/1 A water Milne..with the ponde of the same Milne. **1484** *Paston Lett.* III. 311 Tweyn water melles, wher off iche was letyn ffor x. marke be yer. **1535** *Aldeburgh Rec.* in *N. & Q.* 12th Ser. VII. 402/2 Pd to Hille for xix Lodes cariedge of watermill gravell into the marshe xiis viiid. **1585** HIGINS *Junius' Nomencl.* 216/1 *Tympanum*,..the water mill wheele that taketh and deliuereth water in turning. **1635** BP. J. WILLIAMS *Articles Enq. Linc.* C 3, Whether have you in your parish any water-mills,..which have been suffered to grinde or go upon the sabbath-day in prayer-time. **1726** SWIFT *Gulliver* II. i, The sound of his voice pierced my ears like that of a water-mill. **1842** BISCHOFF *Woollen Manuf.* II. 167 The north of Germany is deficient both in coals and water mills. **1873** B. STEWART *Conserv. Energy* ii. 26 Let us compare together a watermill driven by a head of water, and a windmill driven by the wind.

2. A water-wheel or a machine driven by a water-wheel.

1580 HOLLYBAND *Treas. Fr. Tong, Martinet*, a water mill causing to rise the great hammer in the forge. **1617** MORYSON *Itin.* I. 9 The beere of Torge is much esteemed through all Misen, whereof they sell such quantity abroad, as ten water-mils besides wind-mils, scarcely serve the towne for this purpose. **1796** MORSE *Amer. Geog.* II. 233 Large water-mills are erected for spinning silk, wool, and thread.

So **water-miller**, the owner or manager of a water-mill.

a **1530** J. HEYWOOD *Weather* (Brandl) 443 Here entreth the water myller. *Ibid.* 446 We water myllers be nothynge in regarde. **1664** *Instr. Jury-Men Spalding* 23 Flood-gates..in a more peculiar manner, belong to the Water-Miller. **1909** E. DANIELS in *Cambr. Mod. Hist.* VI. xx. 714 Arnold, a water-miller in the neighbourhood of Züllichau in the Neumark. **1977** *New Scientist* 14 Apr. 84/1 Water millers in the 1970s can reasonably claim to be the oppressed and persecuted class among a wide range of water users.

ˈwater-mint. Any aquatic plant of the labiate genus *Mentha*; chiefly the Bergamot Mint (*Mentha aquatica*) or the Brook-mint (*M. hirsuta*).

In the 17th c. *water-mint* and *water-cress* were sometimes treated as synonyms; it is not clear which of these names was used incorrectly.

1542 ELYOT *Dict., Sisymbrium*,..water mynte. **1548** TURNER *Names of Herbes* 74 Sisymbrium hortense is called in englishe, baume Mynte, or water Mynte. **1585** HIGINS *Junius' Nomencl.* 136/1 *Sisymbrium, offic. balsamita*,..water mints. **1597** GERARDE *Herbal* II. ccxvii. 555 Of Horse Mint or Water Mint. 1 *Mentha aquatica*. Water mint. 2 *Sisymbria Mentha* Sweete Water Mint. *Ibid.*, Water Mint is a kinde of wilde Mint. **1607** TOPSELL *Four-f. Beasts* 540 The hearbe called water-minte, or water Cresses,..anointed vpon the..wounds which come by the venemous teeth of a Shrew, will very effectually cure the paine thereof. **1626** BACON *Sylva* §518 As wee see that Water-Mint turneth into Field Mint; And the Colewort into Rape by Neglect, &c. **1758** BORLASE *Nat. Hist. Cornw.* 230 Water-mint of a spicey smell. **1819** KEATS *Song of Four Faeries* 34 'Mid water-mint and cresses dim. **1899** BRIDGES *New Poems, Idle Flowers* 11 With Comfrey, Watermint, Loose-strife and Meadowsweet.

ˈwater-mole. [MOLE *sb.*²]

† **1.** The water-vole, *Arvicola amphibius*. *Obs.*

1770 PENNANT *Zool.* IV. 84, I imagine it [the water shrew-mouse] is the same which the inhabitants of Sutherland name the water mole.

2. *Austral.* The ornithorhynchus or duck-bill.

1815 in Oxley *Jrnls. Two Exped. N.S. Wales* (1820) 367 The very curious animal called the water mole (ornithorhynchus paradoxus) is seen in great numbers. **1885** *Riverside Nat. Hist.* (1888) V. 11 The Water-mole or Duck-mole of the Australian colonists.

ˈwater-mouse.

1. The water-vole, *Arvicola amphibius*.

c **1475** *Pict. Voc.* in Wr.-Wülcker 760/11 *Hic gurrex* [read *surrex* = *sorex*], a watermowse. **1601** HOLLAND *Pliny* II. ciii. I. 45 In Stymphalis of Arcadia, there breed..little water-myce [L. *aquatiles musculi*], or small Limpins. **1653** WALTON *Angler* v. 127 If the night be dark..he [the trout] lies boldly neer the top of the water, watching the motion of any Frog or Water-mouse, or Rat betwixt him and the skie. **1707** MORTIMER *Husb.* 227 Bitterns, Herons,..Water-Rats, Water-Mice, Otters, &c. are very great Enemies to Fish. **1819** *Edin. Mag.* June 505 *Arvicola aquatica*. Water Campagnol..E. Water Rat. S. Water Mouse, or Ratten.

2. *Austral.* A rodent of the genus *Hydromys* or the family *Hydromyidæ*.

c **1880** Sooty water-mouse [see SOOTY *a.* 1 c].

ˈwater-mouth. *Sc.* The mouth of a river.

1588 *Reg. Mag. Sig. Scot.* 506/1 Inter le watter-mouth aque de I. et locum de Halgrene. *a* **1670** SPALDING *Troub. Chas. I* (Bannatyne Club) I. 49 Thir haill four ships brake louse..and were driven out at the watter mouth..throw the violence and speat of the watter. **1760** *Inform. Dk. Gordon* v. *Earls Murray & Fife* 3 The Marquis and his successors fished with their tugnet in the Haven, and water mouth. *Ibid.* 5 What is the boundary..that circumscribes the water-mouth, or *ostium fluminis*, and separates it from the river? **1808** JAMIESON. **1824–7** MOIR *Mansie Wauch* xviii. (1828) 259 In case the French should land at the water-mouth.

ˈwater-nymph.

1. A nymph inhabiting or presiding over water; a naiad.

1390 GOWER *Conf.* II. 167 And ek sche, as thei understonde, The water Nimphes hath in honde To leden at hire oghne heste. **1567** GOLDING *Ovid's Met.* VI. 419, I askt him whether that the Altar wee did see Belonged to the Waternymphes, or Faunes, or other God Peculiar to the place. **1579** SPENSER *Sheph. Cal.* Nov. 143 The water Nymphs..Now balefull boughes of Cypres aduance. **1680** OTWAY *Ovid's Epist. Phædra to Hippolytus* 174 So may the Water-Nymphs in Heat of Day, Though thou their Sex despise, thy Thirst allay. **1712** ADDISON *Spect.* No. 351 ¶5 The changing of the Trojan Fleet into Water-Nymphs, which is the most violent Machine in the whole Æneid. **1821** SCOTT *Pirate* xvi, The Nereids and Water-nymphs..displayed, as usual, a little more taste and ornament than was to be seen amongst their male attendants. **1900** *Catal. Sculpt. Parthen. Brit. Mus.* 37 This gap may have been filled by a crouching Water Nymph, associated with the River-god.

b. *transf.* and *fig.*

1664 H. MORE *Myst. Iniq.* 306 It is a Pseudo-prophetick Polity that has spred through the whole Territories of the Empire, a Water-Nymph whose skirts are so large, that she has sat floting upon the whole Imperial Ocean for these many Ages. **1751** F. COVENTRY *Pompey the Little* I. xi. 96 This delicate Fisherwoman..carried him [a dog] one Evening to a certain Coffee-house..where the Lady behind the Bar..prevailed on the gentle Water-Nymph to surrender him for a Dram of Brandy.

2. A water-lily of the genus *Nymphæa*.

1866 *Treas. Bot.*, Water-nymph, *Nymphæa*.

ˈwater-oak. A hard coarse-grained oak, *Quercus aquatica* or *nigra*, of the southern U.S. Also, the pin-oak, *Q. palustris*. Also applied to certain Australian trees of the genera *Casuarina* and *Callistemon*.

1717 *Petiveriana* III. 207 Water Oak. Is an Evergreen, growing in Swamps, Fresh-water Ponds, and by River Sides. **1796** H. HUNTER tr. *St. Pierre's Study Nat.* (1799) II. 165 The water-oak, and the willow-leafed oak, rise to no great height. **1819** D. B. WARDEN *Acc. United States* I. 174 Water oak, *Quercus aquatica*. **1887** G. W. CABLE *Grande Pointe* ii. in *Century Mag.* Mar. 662/1 Sweet-gums, water-oaks, magnolias. **1890** 'R. BOLDREWOOD' *Miner's Right* xvii. 166 Strange shadows gliding..amid the dark-leaved water-oaks.

Water of Ayr. The name of the river (now more commonly known simply as Ayr) at the mouth of which the town of Ayr stands. Used *attrib.* in ***Water of Ayr stone***, a kind of stone found on the banks of the Ayr, used for whetstones and also for polishing.

1805 FORSYTH *Beauties Scot.* II. 467 Upon the banks of the water of Air, a species of white stone is found, which is well known over all Scotland by the name of the water of Air stone. **1881** *Encycl. Brit.* XII. 135 Among hones of less importance in general use may be noted..Water of Ayr stone, Scotch stone, or snake stone, used for tools and for polishing marble and copperplates. **1884** F. J. BRITTEN *Watch & Clockm.* 86 Finish by laying an even and straight grain across the brass with blue or water of Ayr stone.

water of life.

1. *fig.* A drink which gives life or immortality to the drinker.

1382 WYCLIF *Rev.* xxii. 17 And he that wole, take freely the watir of lijf. **1688** BUNYAN (*title*) The Water of Life, or a Discourse shewing the Richness and Glory of the Grace and Spirit of the Gospel. **1867** KINGSLEY *Water of Life* i. 4 The East..was haunted by dreams of a Water of Life, a Fount of Perpetual Youth, a Cup of Immortality.

2. A name for brandy or whisky; rendering med.L. *aqua vitæ* (see AQUA-VITÆ), F. *eau-de-vie* (see EAU), Gael., Ir. *uisge-beatha* (see USQUEBAUGH, WHISKY). *rare* (only as transl.).

1576 G. BAKER tr. *Gesner's Jewell Health* 11 b, The infusions..are done eyther in simple water,..or in water of lyfe. **1822** J. WILSON *Lights & Shadows of Sc. Life* 372 The shepherds..were collected together (not without a quech of the mountain-dew, or water of life) in a large shed.

† **wateˈrologer.** *Obs. rare.* [See WATER *sb.* 18 b and -LOGER.] A contemptuous term for one who diagnoses a disease by inspection of the patient's urine. So † **wateˈrology**, the art of doing this.

1654 WHITLOCK *Zootom.* 47 That Waterologer in Dr. Harts Anatomy of Urines, that sent his Patient word that he was sick of a blinde Ague. *Ibid.* 66, I shall insist somewhat on the Cheat of Waterologie (a word though new, yet easily to be understood, thanks to another Cheat that rhimeth to it) and therefore I shall use it still, to signifie this divining by Urines. **1678** *Quacks Academy* 6 You must either pretend to be Waterologers, or Ass-trologers, or Piss-prophets, or Starr-Wizards. **1786** R. HEATHCOTE *Sylva* (1788) 239 A waterologer, poring mysteriously over an Urinal.

ˈwater-ˌordeal. (See quot. 1701.)

[**1656** BLOUNT *Glossogr.* s.v. *Ordeal*, There were of this, four sorts... The third, was hot water-Ordeal, by putting his arms up to the elbows in seething water, &c. The fourth was cold water-Ordeal, like the late used trial of Witches.] **1701** W. KENNETT *Cowel's Interpr.* s.v., This [purgation] was commonly by Fire-Ordeal, or by Water-Ordeal, and this latter was either by hot water, or by cold water. The purgation by hot water was for the Party accus'd to thrust his hands or feet into scalding water, on presumption that his Innocence would receive no harm. That by cold water, was for the Defendant to be cast into a Pond or River (as they now pretend to try Witches) whether he would sink or swim. **1754** *Stow's Surv. Lond.* (ed. Strype) v. xxx. II. 559/1 They still continue also to try Witches by Water-Ordeal, and believe..that a Witch cannot sink in the Water. **1769** BLACKSTONE *Comm.* IV. xxvii. 337. **1888** H. C. LEA *Hist. Inquisition* I. 65 Several of them purged themselves by the water-ordeal.

ˈwater-ˌparsley.

1. A name for *Sium latifolium* (water-parsnip), *Apium graveolens* (wild celery), or other aquatic umbellifers.

1562 TURNER *Herbal* II. (1568) 32 Syon is..so lyke Selino or Apio..that som haue taken it for Elioselino, and haue named it waterpersely. Whiche name were good to be receyued..that the herbe myght ye better ther by be knowen, then bi ye name of belragges. **1578** LYTE *Dodoens* v. xlvii. 610 Of water Parsly.. There is founde in this Countrie two kyndes of this herbe, one great, the other smal. *Ibid.* 611 (headings of figures) *Lauer Crateuæ*, Great water Parsely. *Lauer minus*, Small water Parsely. **1597** GERARDE *Herbal* II. ccclxxxi. 862 Smallage..is called..in English March Marish Parsley, and *Apium aquatile*, or water Parsley; but *Hydroselinum*, or *Sium maius*, is the true water Parsley. **1611** COTGR., *Berle*, the great water Parsenip, great water Parsely; called also, Belders, and Bell-rags. **1891** [D. JORDAN & MRS. J. A. OWEN] *Ann. Fishing Village* xi. 105 Water-cress and a thick growing plant they called water-parsley.

2. The tropical American herb *Richardsonia scabra* (white ipecacuanha, Mexican clover).

1891 *Century Dict.*

'water-ˌparsnip. Name for the aquatic umbelliferous plants of the genus *Sium*, esp. *S. latifolium*; also applied to *Helosciadium nodiflorum* (sometimes classed as *Sium nodiflorum*).

1597 GERARDE *Herbal* II. xvii. 199 Great water Parsnepe.. is described to haue leaues of a pleasant sauour. *Ibid.* 200 [figure] *Sium maius*, Great water Parsnep. **1671** SALMON *Syn. Med.* III. xxii. 432 Sium,.. Water-parsnep. **1770** *Ann. Reg.* 118/1 Three children of a poor cottager in Ireland having eaten of the herb Daho or Water-parsnep, two of them died. **1785** MARTYN *Lett. Bot.* xvii. (1794) 229 The Creeping Water Parsnep, *Sium nodiflorum* Lin. **1861** S. THOMSON *Wild Fl.* III. (ed. 4) 234 The siums, or water-parsnips, are.. not uncommon.

'water-ˌparting. = WATERSHED 1. (See quot. 1877.)

1859 R. F. BURTON *Centr. Afr.* in *Jrnl. Geog. Soc.* XXIX. 26 A similar expanse of stony ridges and uplands forming the great western waterparting. **1877** HUXLEY *Physiogr.* 18 To avoid this double use of the word 'watershed' the term 'water-parting' has been introduced as the English equivalent of the German *Wasserscheide*. **1901** *Q. Rev.* July 16 The water-parting between the systems of Lake Chad, the Niger, and the Congo.

'water-ˌpepper. [Cf. G. *wasserpfeffer* (from 16th c.).]

1. The acrid plant *Polygonum Hydropiper* or smartweed. In Lyte also ***water-pepperwort***.

1538 TURNER *Libellus, Eupatorium*, water peper. **1578** LYTE *Dodoens* V. lxvii. 632 This herbe is called in English, Water pepper, or Water-pepperwurt, and of some Curagie. **1635** SWAN *Spec. Mundi* VI. iv. (1643) 253 Arsmart, or water Pepper, groweth almost in every waterish plash. **1866** *Treas. Bot.* 915/1.

2. A book-name for the N.O. *Elatinaceæ*.

1830 LINDLEY *Introd. Nat. Syst. Bot.* 159 Elatineæ. The Water-Pepper Tribe. **1846** —— *Veg. Kingd.* 480 Elatinaceæ.—Water-Peppers.

Water Pik ('wɔːtə pɪk). Also **Water-Pik, water-pick.** A device for cleaning the teeth by directing a jet of water at them.

Water Pik is a proprietary name in the U.S.

1963 *Official Gaz.* (U.S. Patent Office) 15 Oct. TM 109 Aqua-Tec Corporation, Fort Collins, Colo. Filed Dec. 14, 1962. *Water Pik.* For readily portable oral hygiene appliance utilizing a pulsed jet of water for massaging the gums and cleaning spaces adjacent to the teeth. First use Oct. 14, 1961. **1971** *Consumer Rep.* June 387/2 Many people incorrectly use the term *Water Pik* as a generic name for dental irrigators, but there are a number of other brands on the market. Our project included 11 electric irrigators (of which three were *Water Pik*). **1971** *Better Homes & Gardens* Nov. 136/2 To use the oral irrigating device, place water in the reservoir, hold the water pick in the mouth and turn the pick on. **1978** G. GREENE *Human Factor* I. iii. 44 He turned on his electric water-pick.. 'Amusing little gadget, that of yours... I suppose it really is better than an ordinary toothbrush?' **1978** J. UPDIKE *Coup* (1979) ii. 78 Her new possessions—..mechanical beauty aids, a hair-blower and a Water-Pik—were overwhelming the little pisé-walled room.

Hence **'water-pick** *v. trans.*

1976 P. DICKSON *Electronic Battlefield* i. 10 Frank was brushing and water-picking his teeth.

'water-pipe.

1. A pipe through which water is conducted.

14.. *Voc.* in Wr.-Wülcker 666/37 *Hec idraulis*, waterpype. **14..** *Nominale* Ibid. 738/12 *Hic idraicus*, a wadyrpype. **1585** HIGINS *Junius' Nomencl.* 392/1 *Euripi*,.. water pipes of smaller size, so made, as that ye water therin mounteth aloft. **1694** *Lond. Gaz.* No. 3026/3 The Inhabitants of Paris.. are to pay 50 Crowns for every Water-Pipe. **1707** MORTIMER *Husb.* 363 The Wood for Piles, Pumps, Hop-poles, Water-pipes. **1812** H. & J. SMITH *Rej. Addr., Tale Drury Lane* 165 Still o'er his head,.. His whizzing water-pipe he waived. **1836** DICKENS *Sk. Boz, Vauxhall Gardens*, The fountain that had sparkled so showily by lamp-light, presented very much the appearance of a water-pipe that had burst. **1869** MOZLEY *Lett.* (1885) 308 The workmen were laying down water-pipes in the hall as we entered.

2. *transf.* †**a.** (See remarks under WATERSPOUT *sb.* 3). *Obs.* **b.** An underground spring or flow of water. *poet.*

1539 BIBLE *Ps.* xlii. 8 One depe calleth another because of ye noyse of thy water pipes. **1832** TENNYSON *Dream Fair Wom.* liii, Single I grew, like some green plant, whose root Creeps to the garden water-pipes beneath, Feeding the flower.

†**c.** A name for a kind of stalactite. *Obs.*

1681 [see STALACTITES].

3. A hookah, narghile, or kalian.

1824 MORIER *Hajji Baba* viii, Ali Katir.. had just lighted his water pipe. **1882** O'DONOVAN *Merv Oasis* I. 330 We saw the white-robed elders (smoking their water-pipes) seated on either side the entry.

'water-pit. [See PIT *sb.*[1] 2.] †**a.** A well or hole sunk in the ground to procure water. *Obs.* **b.** A pit in which water is stored.

c **1000** ÆLFRIC *Exod.* vii. 24 Ealle þa Egiptiscan dulfon wæterpyttas neah þam flode. **1387** TREVISA *Higden* III. 401 þey come in fere unto a deep water pitte [*v.r.* put; L. *ad quendam aquosum puteum et profundum*]. **1800** *Hull Advertiser* 16 Aug. 1/2 The tan-yard comprises 2 large water pits.

c. = WATER-HOLE 1 b. *poet.*

1920 BLUNDEN *Waggoner* 19 The great pike lies.. Watching the waterpit sheer-shelving dark.

'water-ˌpitcher.

1. A pitcher for holding water.

1538 ELYOT *Dict.*, *Vrceolus*, a lytell water pitchar. *a* **1593** MARLOWE *Ovid's Eleg.* I. x. 6 Such as Amimone through the drie fields strayed When on her head a water pitcher laied. **1816** SCOTT *Old Mort.* xxxvii, The child set down her water pitcher. **1846** *Union Mag.* I. 626 Carpet-brooms and water-pitchers. **1893** F. ADAMS *New Egypt* 96 Out from the village come a half-dozen women with the earthen water-pitchers balanced sidewise on their heads.

2. A book-name for pitcher-plants of the N.O. *Sarraceniaceæ*.

1846-50 A. WOOD *Class-bk. Bot.* 155 Order X. Sarraceniaceæ.—Water Pitchers. **1858** BAIRD *Cycl. Nat. Sci.*, *Sarraceniaceæ*, the Water Pitcher or Side-saddle family.

'water-plane.

1. A canal constructed on a level, without locks.

1861 SMILES *Engineers* V. vi. I. 386 We find him [*sc* Brindley] contriving a water-plane for the Duke's collieries.

2. *Ship-building.* A plane passing through a vessel when afloat, on a level with the surface of the water.

1889 WELCH *Text Bk. Naval Archit.* i. 8 The line in which the surface of the water cuts the surface of the ship.. is called the *water line*.., the area enclosed by that line being the *water plane area*.

†**3.** An aeroplane constructed so as to be capable of rising from, alighting upon, and travelling on the water. *Obs.* Cf. SEAPLANE.

1912 *Q. Rev.* July 248 With this [float] Curtiss' water-plane was the first to quit the sea under its own power. **1913** *Daily Mail* 3 Apr., A waterplane is a sea-going aeroplane. **1913** *Times* 14 May 5/6 Mr. Howard Wright.. was attempting to rise from the sea on a waterplane at Cowes yesterday afternoon when the machine capsized.

'water-ˌplantain.

1. The plant *Alisma Plantago*, with leaves somewhat like those of the plantain, growing in ditches and by the river-side. Also as a name for the genus.

1538 ELYOT *Dict.* Add., *Alisma*,.. water plantayne. **1578** LYTE *Dodoens* I. lxvi. 96 Water Plantayne is a fayre herbe, with large greene leaues. **1785** MARTYN *Lett. Bot.* xviii. (1794) 254 The Water Plantains... Great Water Plantain, *Alisma Plantago*. **1858** A. IRVINE *Brit. Plants* 291 *Alisma*, Linn. Water-Plantain... *A. Plantago*. Greater Water-Plantain. **1894** J. DAVIDSON *Ballads & Songs* 122 Water-plantain, rosy vagrant, Flings his garland on the wave.

2. Applied to other aquatic plants: see quots.

1864 GRISEBACH *Flora W. Ind. Isl.* 788 Water-plantain, *Echinodorus cordifolius*. **1866** *Treas. Bot.* s.v. *Plantain*, Water Plantain of Jamaica, *Pontederia azurea*.

'water-pool. A pool of water (large or small).

13.. *St. Cristofore* 839 in Horstm. *Altengl. Leg.* (1881) 464 Me hase thoghte þis fyre als cole Als I had lyggene in a water polle. **1535** COVERDALE *1 Macc.* ix. 33 Ionathas and Symon his brother.. pitched their tentes by the water pole of Asphar. **1598** R. BERNARD tr. *Terence, Adelph.* IV. ii. (1607) 304 At the very waterpoole [*apud ipsum lacum*] there is a hand-mill. **1849** CARLYLE *New Lett.* (1904) II. 72 Eternal Silence of the mountains and their melancholy water-pools. **1882** MISS BRADDON *Mt. Royal* I. iv. 115 Her little hand trembled as it touched Angus Hamleigh's, when he led her across a craggy bit of path, or over a tiny water-pool. **1913** *Blackw. Mag.* Nov. 592/1 We stopped to ask the latest news of tribes and water-pools.

'water-pot.

1. A vessel, usually of earthenware, for holding water.

1382 WYCLIF *John* iv. 28 Therfore the womman lefte the watir pott [Vulg. *hydriam*]. *c* **1386** CHAUCER *Clerk's T.* 234 And she set doun hir water pot anon Biside the thresshfold. **1390** GOWER *Conf.* I. 302 The waterpot sche hente alofte.. And al the water on his hed Sche pourede oute. **1488** *Acc. Ld. High Treas. Scot.* I. 86 Item, a water pot of siluer. **1526** TINDALE *John* ii. 6. **1530** PALSGR. 287/1 Water potte for a table, *aiguiere*. **1555** EDEN *Decades* (Arb.) 160 They founde here also sundry kyndes of waterpottes made of earthe of dyuers colours. **1612** in *10th Rep. Hist. MSS. Comm.* App. I. 599, 6 greate silver water-potts. *a* **1700** EVELYN *Diary* 16 Nov. 1643, A morsel of one of the water-pots in which our Saviour did his first miracle. **1702** *Post Man* 6-8 Aug. 2/1 Stoln.. out of the House of his Grace the Duke of Schomberg, a Silver Oval Shaving-dish, a Silver Water Pot, and a Silver Box for a Wash-ball. **1839** URE *Dict. Arts* 1029, I have.. seen an English moulder expert enough to make 25 waterpots a day. **1867** FREEMAN *Norm. Conq.* (1877) I. v. 302 Striking down the choicest warriors of England with the staves on which they bore their waterpots.

b. *Astr.* The portion of the zodiacal constellation Aquarius which is figured as a vase or urn.

1546 *Gassar's Prognost.* b iij, Wherin at night Mercuri also shall sette after the Sunne with bright *Hidria* or water pott. *Ibid.* b iv b, The sunne settyng wyth *Alphard*, ye bright water pott. **1590** T. HOOD *Use Celestial Globe* 13 The Waterpot, v. *Vrna*. **1841** EMERSON *Ess.* Ser. I. i. (1848) 2 As crabs, goats, scorpions, the balance, and the waterpot lose their meanness when hung as signs in the zodiac, so [etc.].

c. *Her.* (See quots.)

1688 [see FONTAL B. 2]. **1828-40** BERRY *Encycl. Her.* I. Gloss., *Water-Pot*, a fontal, called, also, a *scatebra*, out of which naiads and river-gods are represented as pouring the waters or rivers over which they are fabled to preside.

2. = WATERING-POT 1.

1530 PALSGR. 287/1 Water potte for a gardyne, *arrousouer*. **1605** SHAKS. *Lear* IV. vi. 200 Why, this would make a man, a man of Salt To vse his eyes for Garden water-pots. **1649** JER. TAYLOR *Gt. Exemp.* I. Ad. Sect. 7. 110 Private Devotions, and secret offices of Religion, are like refreshing of a Garden with the distilling and petty drops of a Waterpot. **1712** J. JAMES tr. *Le Blond's Gardening* 168 For Places near at hand, Gardeners make use of Water-Pots. **1828-32** WEBSTER, *Water-pot*, a vessel.. for sprinkling water on cloth in bleaching, or on plants, etc. *c* **1890** STEVENSON *In South Seas* I. x. (1900) 83 He.. was to be seen all day, with spade and water-pot, in his childlike eagerness, actually running between the borders.

fig. **1583** MELBANCKE *Philotimus* L iij, Here is a drie Tale (quoth Parmenio).. and well deserues a water potte.

3. A chamber-pot. ? *Sc.*

1850, 1883 OGILVIE.

4. *Zool.* = WATERING-POT 2.

1815 S. BROOKES *Introd. Conchol.* 157 Water Pot, *Serpula Penis*.

waterproof ('wɔːtəpruːf), *a.* and *sb.* [See PROOF *a.* 1 b.] **A.** *adj.* Impervious to water; capable of resisting the deleterious action of water.

1736 *Gentl. Mag.* VI. 732/1 The everlasting Mountains would be Water-Proof. **1802** W. JESSOP in *Minutes Comm. Surrey Iron Rlwy.* 7 Oct., Quarries of Limestone at Merstham, apparently superior in Quality for Water-Proof Lime to either that of Guildford or Dorking. **1815** J. SMITH *Panorama Sci. & Art* II. 823 To render Boots and Shoes waterproof. **1816** *Sporting Mag.* XLVIII. 192 Joseph Egg's Water Proof Gun. **1836** W. IRVING *Astoria* (1849) 337 These hats were nearly waterproof, and extremely durable. **1871** MRS. BROOKFIELD *Influence* II. 30 The Miss Shaws, in neat waterproof travelling suits. **1877** HUXLEY *Physiogr.* 29 Not a drop of water can reach it as long as the waterproof roof remain sound. **1920** *Conquest* May 311/3 Nowadays the cry is for waterproof roads.

b. *transf.* and *fig.*

1831 TRELAWNY *Adv. Younger Son* III. 330 It.. didn't make a man's inside water-proof, which good Nantz would. **1838** DICKENS *O. Twist* xxxvii, But tears were not the things to find their way to Mr. Bumble's soul; his heart was water-proof. **1854** SURTEES *Handley Cr.* li. (1901) II. 92 Twice Dribbleford Brook comes in the way for those whose ambition is waterproof.

B. *sb.* A fabric or garment rendered impervious to water by treatment with india-rubber or the like.

1799 *Hull Advertiser* 12 Jan. 2/3 Parish's patent water-proof, best superfine. **1875** BEDFORD *Sailor's Pocket Bk.* vii. (ed. 2) 245 Officers.. carry clasp-knife,.. waterproof, haversack. **1877** MAR. M. GRANT *Sun-Maid* i, They were clad in grey waterproof. **1880** HOWELLS *Undiscov. Country* x. 139 The teacher took off her waterproof, the hood of which she had drawn over her head.

'waterproof, *v.* [f. prec. adj.] *trans.* To make waterproof or impervious to water.

1843 *Penny Cycl.* XXVI. 147/1 This.. is the varnish now generally employed in waterproofing the garments well known by the name of Mackintoshes. **1843** *Mech. Mag.* XXXIX. 479 Sylvester's Mode of Waterproofing Walls. **1862** *Jrnl. Soc. Arts* X. 330/2 The oil sheet manufacturers have for more than a century waterproofed linen by layers of oil. **1894** BLACKMORE *Perlycross* xxxv, The Chancel roof which had only been patched up temporarily and water-proofed with thick tarpaulins. **1905** D. WALLACE *Lure Labrador Wild* iii. 53 The tent was.. made of balloon silk and waterproofed.

b. *transf.* and *fig.*

1841 LEVER *O'Malley* lxix. 342 If one did'nt expect to be waterproofed [meaning killed in battle] before morning they really would'nt go out in such weather. **1891** SIR H. MAXWELL in *Blackw. Mag.* Oct. 582/1 Balzac.. was wonderfully waterproofed against despondency by the intense realism of his fancy.

'waterproofed, *ppl. a.* [f. WATERPROOF *v.* and *sb.* + -ED.] Rendered waterproof; provided with, or wearing, a waterproof garment or garments.

1871 SIR S. NORTHCOTE in A. Lang *Life* (1890) II. 25 We started well waterproofed, and got to Suitland about twelve. **1881** MISS BRADDON *Asphodel* I. 251 A party of eager Americans, spectacled, waterproofed. **1883** *Century Mag.* July 378/1 A light.. click reel holding thirty yards of waterproofed and polished fly-line of braided silk.

'waterproofer. [f. WATERPROOF *v.* + -ER[1].]

1. One who makes materials, etc. waterproof.

1858 *Kelly's Directory Lancs.* 1725/2 Waterproofers. **1864** *Leeds Mercury* 20 Sept., India-rubber manufacturer and waterproofer. **1885** LOCK *Workshop Rec.* Ser. IV. 23/1 This recipe is used by woollen-cloth waterproofers. **1890** *Lancet* 22 Feb. 420/2 Waterproofers and lampblack makers.

2. = WATERPROOFING *vbl. sb.* 2 b.

1909 WEBSTER, *Water-proofer*... Also, a waterproofing material, as for roofs. **1923** E. G. BLAKE *Damp Walls* xii. 173 Many of these compounds completely substantiate the claims which are made for them as integral waterproofers by the manufacturers. **1951** *Archit. Rev.* CX. 402/3 To provide a waterproof backing for external tiling Tretol liquid cement waterproofer has been used. **1974** I. H. SEELEY *Building Technol.* iv. 60/1 Colourless waterproofers can make a wall surface water-repellent and less porous, without much change in the appearance.

'waterproofing, *vbl. sb.* [f. WATERPROOF *v.* and *sb.* + -ING[1].]

1. The action or process of making materials, etc. waterproof. Also *attrib.*

1845 G. DODD *Brit. Manuf.* Ser. v. 164 The cap is taken to the 'water-proofing' room. **1852** BRANDE *Dict. Sci.* etc. Suppl., *Waterproofing*.. is most perfectly effected by means of caoutchouc,.. but there are other substances, [etc.]. **1857** MILLER *Elem. Chem.*, *Org.* 509 Gutta percha.. is also largely used as a waterproofing material. **1909** *Westm. Gaz.* 30 Aug. 2/1 The waterproofing of our roads is progressing rapidly.

2. a. The result of this process; the quality of being waterproof. **b.** Material with which a substance is made waterproof.

1882 *Encycl. Brit.* (ed. 9) XIV. 390/1 These materials .. go to give the necessary substance, weight, and waterproofing to the leather. 1897 *Daily News* 17 Mar. 3/6 By this time the flames had got well hold of the roof, which appeared to contain some highly inflammable waterproofing.

'waterproofness. [f. WATERPROOF *a.* + -NESS.] The state or condition of being waterproof.

1934 in WEBSTER. 1943 P. I. SMITH *Synthetic Adhesives* iv. 48 Straight ethyl cellulose cements and ethyl modified adhesives are now being employed... They offer advantages over certain other cellulose thermo-plastic adhesives by reason of their great toughness, waterproofness and heat sealing properties. 1952 *Times* 14 Mar. 6/1 It would then become an offence to describe wrongly such qualities as 'waterproofness' or resistance to fading. 1968 G. MAXWELL *Raven seek thy Brother* xiii. 163 The contact of human hand can remove the 'water-proofness' of a seabird's plumage. 1978 *Detroit Free Press* 16 Apr. E 8/3 The old style boot greases were developed during World War II for government use. Waterproofness of combat boots was the main objective.

'water-pump. A pump for raising water.

1530 PALSGR. 287/1 Water pompe, *aquaticque*. 1824 R. STUART *Hist. Steam Engine* 115 The air-pump barrel is attached to this vessel by the pipe *s*, .. the piston is similar to those usually employed in water-pumps. 1844 H. STEPHENS *Bk. Farm* II. 316 Under this last method, the water-pump is understood to be in constant action. 1878 ABNEY *Photogr.* (1881) 107 The mixed solutions should be filtered, but in this operation great difficulty is often found. The most ready method of effecting it is by the aid of a Bunsen water-pump.

b. jocularly, with ref. to weeping.

1848 THACKERAY *Van. Fair* xxiv, 'Thank you, Dobbin,' he said, rubbing his eyes with his knuckles... The water-pumps were at work again.

So **'water-ˌpumper, 'water-ˌpumping.**

1723 J. CHAMBERLAYNE *Pres. St. Gt. Brit.* (ed. 26) II. [588] Tower of London .. Water-Pumper, Per Diem, 0 0 7. 1909 *Westm. Gaz.* 30 Nov. 5/2 They have also fitted a water-pumping engine in the Turkish Houses of Parliament.

'water-quake. [f. WATER *sb.* + QUAKE *sb.*, after EARTHQUAKE.] A seismic disturbance in the sea.

1577 HOLINSHED *Chron.* II. 1039/2 *marg.*, On the Saturday after .. chaunced an other earthquake, or as some write, a watershake [*marg.*] waterquake. 1610 HOLLAND *Camden's Brit.* I. 500 Wittlesmere doth somtimes in .. faire weather sodainely rise tempestuously, as it were into violent waterquakes. 1755 H. WALPOLE *Let. to Montagu* 25 Nov., There have been lately such earthquakes and waterquakes. 1762 *Gentl. Mag.* XXXII. 291/2 A water-quake was felt at Bergen in Norway. 1862 M. HOPKINS *Hawaii* 419 Earthquakes and waterquakes are also the attendants of these fractures.

'water-rail. [RAIL *sb.*³] A bird, *Rallus aquaticus*, having a general resemblance to the Landrail: native in the temperate portion of the eastern hemisphere.

1655 MOUFET & BENNET *Health's Improv.* xii. 109 Water-rails are preferred in Italy before Thrushes or Quails. 1768 PENNANT *Brit. Zool.* II. 385 The water rail is a bird of a long slender body, with short concave wings. 1829 *Loudon's Mag. Nat. Hist.* I. 289 The water rail has grey wings, spotted with brown; flanks spotted with white; bill, orange underneath. 1883 *Fisheries Exhib. Catal.* (ed. 4) 111 One Case with small Pike and Water Rail.

'water-rat. [Cf. G. *wasserratte, -ratz(e*, MDu. *waterrot* (mod.Du. *-rat*), LG. *waterrötte*.]

1. An aquatic rodent of the family *Muridæ*; in British use, the water-vole, *Arvicola amphibius*, inhabiting the banks of rivers. In the U.S. applied to the MUSK-RAT, and in Australia to the genus *Hydromys*.

1552 HULOET, Water rat, *sorex*. *a*1627 MIDDLETON *Witch* I. i. 45 He .. sticks to small drink like a water-rat. 1629 *Drayner Confirmed* (1647) C 1, There is also an other danger in Banking, procured by a small contemptible Vermine, they be Water-rats, which make their holes in the bank close to the water, [etc.]. 1633 FORD *Broken H.* II. i, Island? prison: .. whom shall we see there? Sea-guls, and Porpiseis, and water-rats? 1752 J. HILL *Hist. Anim.* 518 The water Rat... This is considerably larger than the common rat, and of a different colour; the head is large, and sharp at the extremity. 1768 PENNANT *Brit. Zool.* I. 101 The water-rat never frequents houses. *a*1860 WYNTER *Curios. Civiliz.* 133 The water-rat is a rare animal compared with .. the common brown or Norway rat. 1876 F. G. WATERHOUSE in Harcus *S. Austral.* 282 The curious water-rats or beaver-rats must be mentioned as being purely Australian. 1890 D. DAVIDSON *Mem. Long Life* iv. 95 Herds of cattle swim these flooded rivers like water-rats.

2. *fig.* A water-thief, pirate. Also applied contemptuously to a sailor, boatman, or the like.

1596 SHAKS. *Merch. V.* I. iii. 23 There be land rats, and water rats, water theeues, and land theeues. 1602 ROWLANDS *Greenes Ghost* (1872) 38 To this societie maie be coupled also another fraternity, viz. Water-rats, Watermen I meane, that will be readie and very diligent for anie man, vntil they can get them to their boates, but when [etc.]. 1608 J. DAY *Law Trickes* v. I 2 b, *Lur.* No more a that, neece; y'are a wag. *Em.* Well said, old Water Ratt. *a*1656 R. COX *Actæon & Diana* 36 *Cut.* Where is he, Parnell? *Parn.* Why gone abroad .. to fetch a gang of Saylors, who he vows shal hang thee up at the main Yard... *Cut.* And those same water-rats are Divellish things. 1865 DICKENS *Mut. Fr.* I. xiv, 'A man may speak.' 'And vermin may be silent,' said Eugene. 'Hold your tongue, you water-rat!' 1903 HARDY *Dynasts* I. VI. i, These water-rats [the English] may paddle in their salt slush.

3. ***Grand Order of Water Rats***, a philanthropic show-business society (see quot. 1951). Also *ellipt.*, as ***Water Rats***.

1910 *Era Annual* 47 July .. Memorabilia of Theatrical Events... Water Rats Motor Run to Brighton, 1909. 1935 A. HADDON *Story of Music Hall* xix. 90 Elvin .. founded the Grand Order of Water Rats, which led to the institution of nearly every existing artistes' organisation. 1951 *Oxf. Compan. Theatre* 835/1 *Water Rats, the Grand Order of*, a British association of members of the music-hall profession which originated in 1889 from an up-river (Thames) party to celebrate the successes of the Water Rat, a racing pony. 1956 *Golden Jubilee Bk. Show Business* (Variety Artistes Fed.) 17/3 There is the Grand Order of Water Rats .. also the 'sister' section of the Water Rats—the Lady Ratlings. 1977 T. HEALD *Just Desserts* iii. 56 He .. found a large lavatory decked out in Victorian tiles, original newspaper cartoons .. and a document certifying that Escoffier Savarin Smith was a member of the Grand Order of Water Rats.

'water-ret, *v.* Also corruptly **-rot**: see ROT *v.* 4 c. *trans.* To ret (flax or hemp) by steeping in water: opposed to DEW-RET *v.*

1797 *Encycl. Brit.* (ed. 3) VIII. 404/2 Such hemp as is designed for seed is seldom water-retted. 1797 A. YOUNG *Agric. Suffolk* 121 In a circle of about six miles round Tilnetham, the greater part [of the hemp] is never put into the water at all but is dew-retted... The hemp at market is not worth so much .. as that which hath been water-retted. 1839 URE *Dict. Arts* 489 The diminished value of flax which is much water-retted.

Hence **water-retting** *vbl. sb.* (corruptly *-rotting*: see ROTTING *vbl. sb.* 2).

1794 VANCOUVER *Agric. Cambridge* 218 The practice of water-rotting is generally prefer'd to that of dew-rotting. *a*1825 FORBY *Voc. E. Anglia* s.v. *Retting-pit*, In the fens there are two different modes of retting; dew-retting .. and water-retting, which is laying it in a pond or ditch, covered with turf. 1889 *Encycl. Brit.* (ed. 9) IX. 294/2.

'water-ˌrocket¹. ? *Obs.* [ROCKET *sb.*¹] A name applied to certain aquatic species of *Nasturtium*.

1633 *Gerarde's Herbal* II. x. 248 *Eruca aquatica* Water Rocket. *c*1710, 1753, 1796 [see ROCKET *sb.*²]. 1861 MRS. LANKESTER *Wild Flowers* 33 There are several other species of nasturtium native in England: .. the Water-rocket (N. terrestre).

'water-ˌrocket². [ROCKET *sb.*³]

1. *Pyrotechny.* A rocket constructed to be discharged in the water.

1728 CHAMBERS *Cycl.* s.v. *Rocket*, Method of making a Water-Rocket. 1749 H. WALPOLE *Let. to Mann* 17 May, Then from boats on every side were discharged water-rockets and fires of that kind. 1844 ALB. SMITH *Adv. Mr. Ledbury* i, Like the water-rockets at the Surrey Zoological Gardens.

2. (See quot. 1907.)

1905 A. R. WALLACE *My Life* II. 162 The upper fall, which in its ever-changing vapour-streams and water-rockets is wonderfully beautiful. 1907 V. CORNISH in *Geogr. Jrnl.* Jan. 28 The break-up of a high waterfall into conical masses was described by Livingstone, who compares them to 'small comets.' They have also been called 'water-rockets.'

'water-rot, *v.* *U.S.* [See ROT *v.* 4 c; cf. WATER-RET *v.*] = WATER-RET *v.* So **'water-rotted** *ppl. a.*, **'water-rotting** *vbl. sb.*; hence **'water-rot** *sb.*

1705 *Boston News-Let.* 30 July 2/2 For Hemp Water rotted, .. per Ton, .. Six Pounds. 1759 *Newport* (Rhode Island) *Mercury* 8 May 1/2 Some prefer Water-rotting [for flax]. 1838 H. COLMAN *1st Rep. Agric. Mass.* (Mass. Agric. Survey) 72 The superintendent states that the water-rotted flax of Scotland is much superior to ours, which is dew-rotted. 1843 *Amer. Pioneer* II. 450 The manner of making ropes of linn bark, was to cut the bark in strips .. and water-rot it in the same manner as rotting flax or hemp. 1848 *Rep. U.S. Comm. Patents 1847* 246 It is of great importance in raising flax .. that the water rot and dew rot must be used together to produce a fine white fibre. 1883 R. L. ALLEN *New Amer. Farm Bk.* (rev. ed.) 252 The best plan for water rotting of hemp is in vats under cover, the water in which is kept at an equable temperature.

†water-rug. *Obs. rare*⁻¹. [See RUG *sb.*² 4.] ? A shaggy breed of water-dog.

1605 SHAKS. *Macb.* III. i. 93 Showghes, Water-Rugs, and Demy-Wolues.

water sapphire. [Cf. SAPHIR D'EAU.]

a. A colourless variety of native sapphire (sense 1 b). **b.** A type of clear blue quartz (quot. 1829). **c.** = SAPHIR D'EAU.

1698 [see SAPPHIRE 1 b]. 1727–41 CHAMBERS *Cycl.* s.v., The soft water-sapphires of Bohemia and Silesia are of some account, though far inferior to the oriental ones .. in the brightness of their blue. 1829 *Chapters Phys. Sci.* 171 The blue variety of rock crystal, called *water sapphire*. 1850 ANSTED *Elem. Geol., Min.* etc. §409 It [Iolite] is also called Cordierite and Water sapphire, the latter name being given by jewellers to a variety from Ceylon, which presents different colours in two directions. 1888 *Encycl. Brit.* XVI. 385/2 When perfectly devoid of colour, they are called *Water Sapphires*. 1925, 1936 [see SAPHIR D'EAU]. 1979 HURLBUT & SWITZER *Gemology* xii. 182/2 Iolite is the sapphire-blue gem variety of the mineral known by mineralogists as cordierite... 'Water sapphire', or 'saphir d'eau' are misleading names early applied to the gem.

water-scape¹. *nonce-wd.* [SCAPE *sb.*¹] An escape from drowning.

1665 SIR T. HERBERT *Trav.* (1677) 41 But this and other our Water scapes made that saying of Bias come to mind, *Navigantes nec inter vivos nec inter mortuos esse numerandos.*

'water-scape². Also **waterscape.** [f. WATER *sb.*, after *landscape*.] A piece of scenery consisting of water. Also, a picture of such scenery.

1854 FAIRHOLT *Dict. Terms Art*, *Water-scape*, a term sometimes used to denote sea-views, in contradistinction to *landscapes*. 1860 HOLE *Tour in Ireland* xiii. (1892) 144 The landscape (or waterscape?) was so calm and still. 1886 G. M. HOPKINS *Lett. to R. Bridges* (1935) 240, I may be able some day to let you have a better waterscape from the Dargle or somewhere near Dublin. 1901 *Punch* 21 Sept. 224/1 Peeps of such landscapes and water-scapes as whet the appetite for the entire panorama. 1908 CHESTERTON *All Things Considered* 31 The landscape (or waterscape) of my own romantic town. 1955 R. CHURCH *Over Bridge* i. 4 His aim was to establish a *real* aquarium, with fresh water-scape scenery of .. mosses, rondures, recesses, mournful weeds. 1979 *Sci. Amer.* Nov. 39/1 Good maps show the virgin waterscape, the snow depth, the detail of the complex arteries that bring the water to San Francisco and to Los Angeles.

water-serpent. ? *Obs.*

1. = WATER-SNAKE. Also = SEA-SERPENT.

1530 PALSGR. 287/1 Water serpent, *couleuure deaue*. 1538 ELYOT *Dict.*, *Echidna*, a water serpent. 1756–7 tr. *Keysler's Trav.* (1760) I. 40 Professor Frank, of Frankenau, speaks of a still larger species of water-serpents. 1869 RUSKIN *Q. of Air* i. §2 Hercules killed a water-serpent.

2. The constellation Hydra.

1599 T. HILL *Sch. Skill* 23 The image named the Water Serpent, hath 25. stars. 1669 STURMY *Mariner's Mag.* VI. iii. 128 The Water-Serpent hath 15 Stars.

†3. A plant of the genus *Moringa*. *Obs.*

[1649–51 HERNANDEZ *Nova Plant.* etc. *Mex.* IV. xxv. 119 De Coatli, seu Aqueo serpente (description follows)]. 1659 LOVELL *Herball* 541 Water serpent, *Coatlis, Aqueus serpens.*

watershed¹ ('wɔːtəʃɛd). [f. WATER *sb.* + SHED *sb.*¹

The equivalent G. *wasserscheide* has been in use from the 14th c. As a scientific term, it became common about 1800. The Eng. word, which first appears about the same date, was perh. formed in imitation of the Ger. synonym.]

1. The line separating the waters flowing into different rivers or river basins; a narrow elevated tract of ground between two drainage areas: = WATER-PARTING.

1803 *Prize Ess. Highl. Soc. Scot.* II. 20 Strathcluony .. is a very high inland tract, being the water-shed of the country between the two seas. 1830 LYELL *Princ. Geol.* I. 175 The College, a small stream which flows at a moderate declivity from the eastern water-shed of the Cheviot-Hills. 1845 DARWIN *Voy. Nat.* xix. (1852) 442 The line of Water-shed which divides the inland streams from those on the coast, has a height of 3000 feet. 1850 *Times* 16 Nov. 5/2 In order to satisfy themselves as to the amount of supply furnished by the sources in question, the Board of Health deputed Mr. Rammell to survey the various lines of watershed. 1859 H. KINGSLEY *G. Hamlyn* vi, He was crossing the highest water-shed in the county by an open, low-sided valley. 1863 LYELL *Antiq. Man* xv. 297 We should also remember that the crests or watersheds of the Alps and Jura are about eighty miles apart. 1880 GEIKIE *Phys. Geog.* iv. 257 The water-shed of a country or continent is thus a line which divides the flow of the brooks and rivers on two opposite slopes.

b. *fig.* Also *attrib.*

1878 LONGFELLOW *Kéramos* i. 87 Midnight! the outpost of advancing day! .. The watershed of Time, from which the streams of Yesterday and To-morrow take their way. 1884 R. F. BURTON *Bk. Sword* viii. 150 *note*, Hence, too, the superficial observation that the Afghans .. are Jews because they have the typical Jewish look. The reason is that they are derived from the same ethnic centre, a great watershed of race. 1886 SYMONDS *Renaiss. It., Cath. React.* (1898) VII. 208 A watershed of time between the Renaissance and the Counter-Reformation. 1893 *Nation* (N.Y.) 3 Aug. 87/1 That resolution marks the water-shed of our Revolutionary politics. 1962 *B.B.C. Handbk.* 32 The BBC's Code of Practice on Violence, its new 9.30 p.m. watershed policy, its intention to distinguish those programmes which it thinks unsuitable, and perhaps more important, suitable for children .. show that both sides are aware of the problem. 1973 T. TOBIN *Lett. G. Ade* 2 While a journalist in Chicago, Ade became one of the more astute chroniclers of the daily preoccupations of ordinary people who were living through the 'watershed period'. 1980 *Listener* 29 May 68/3 *On the Town*, which [Gene] Kelly himself describes as a watershed picture, and which opened up the musical to location shooting.

2. *loosely.* **a.** The slope down which the water flows from a water-parting.

1839 MURCHISON *Silur. Syst.* I. xxxvii. 512 To the south-west of Kington the lower beds of the Old Red Sandstone .. have been the sub-aqueous water-shed, down which the coarse detritus has been swept. 1877 HUXLEY *Physiogr.* 18 To avoid all ambiguity it is perhaps best to set aside the original meaning of 'watershed', and employ the term to denote the slope along which the water flows, while the expression 'water-parting' is employed for the summit of this slope.

b. The whole gathering ground of a river system.

1874 E. COUES *Birds N.W.* Introd. p. vii, The Missouri Region, in its broadest sense, as embracing the whole water-shed of that great river and its tributaries. 1880 WEBSTER Suppl., *Water-shed*. 2. The country or basin drained by any stream of water and its tributaries. 1913 WHITE *Catskill Water Supply of N.Y.* 17 The Croton watershed would in a few years be drawn on to its full capacity.

3. [? Associated with SHED *v.*¹ 4 d.] A structure for throwing off water.

1881 R. G. WHITE *Eng. Without & Within* xiv. 319 The great wheel caught my umbrella, which was twisted out of my hand in a twinkling... I picked up my wounded water-shed, and returned with it to Burlington Arcade. 1886 *Trans. R. Inst. Brit. Archit.* II. 79 Nothing indicates the nature of the water-shed. It may have been some description of thatch; but more probably I think of wood shingle. 1898 *Scribner's Mag.* Oct. 503/1 A water-shed to throw the water away from the forecastle hatch was built.

ˈwater-shed². *rare.* [SHED *sb.*²] A shed used as a wash-house.

1859 JEPHSON & REEVE *Brittany* 168 In a water-shed at the end are two women washing.

ˈwatershoot. [f. WATER *sb.* + SHOOT *sb.*]

1. [= Flem. *waterscheute, -schote* (Kilian, De Bo).] A sucker growing from the root, trunk, or main branch of a tree. Cf. WATER-BOUGH.

1585 HIGINS *Junius' Nomencl.* 140/1 *Stolones*,.. water-shootes: young shoots or sciences that growe out of the rootes or sides of the stocke, and proue not. **1601** HOLLAND *Pliny* XVII. xx. I. 525 Those superfluous water-shoots that spring out either from the root or the sides of the tree. **1688** HOLME *Armoury* II. 84/2 The Water shoots, or suckers, are twigs that grow from the roots of trees. **1799** G. SMITH *Laboratory* II. 136 And if any strong wood or water-shoots push from the apricot or peach tree, except they serve to fill up a vacancy, they ought to be taken off. **1953** D. M. WRIGHT *Dwarf Fruit Trees* vi. 53 All that is necessary is the annual cutting out of.. strongly growing 'water shoots'. **1965** *Sunday Mail Mag.* (Brisbane) 26 Sept. 15 Water shoots are strongly growing stems, usually sappy and developing rapidly.

2. †**a.** Outflow of drainage water from land; water carried off by drainage. *Obs.* **b.** A gutter or channel for the overflow of water.

a. **1625** G. MARKHAM *Inrichment Weald Kent* 11 It is good also to draw a crosse or quarter Furrow, and opening the ends of all your land Furrowes into it, to leaue the other ends of your Furrowes stopped, that the water-shoot runne not all the length of the field. **1639** HORN & ROB. *Gate Lang. Unl.* vii, Fens (bogs, marishes) are raising springs or quits, that run not (have no water-shoot). **1707–21** MORTIMER *Husb.* II. 207 The Drips of the Houses, the Water of the declining Walks, and the Water-shoots of other adjacent Lands, which may be reserved in Cisterns or Ponds so as to be of use.

b. **1819** NICHOLSON *Dict. Archit.* 802 *Water Shoot*, a wooden trough for discharging rain water from a building. **1825** *Beverley Lighting Act* ii. 22 A gutter or water-shoot. **1834** BECKFORD *Italy* II. 182 A transparent, gurgling rill, which is conducted through a rustic water-shoot. **1869** BLACKMORE *Lorna D.* x, The bark from the wood-ricks [being] washed down the gutters, and even our water-shoot going brown.

†**3.** A waterfall, cascade. *Obs.*

1738 [G. SMITH] *Cur. Relat.* II. 273 Near the City Hoeicheu flows the River Singan, which has at least 360 Water-shoots falling into it between Rocks and Mountains.

4. An artificial cascade contrived for the amusement or exercise of 'shooting the rapids' in a boat or by swimming. Also *water-chute*: see WATER *sb.* 29.

1900 ELINOR GLYN *Visits Eliz.* 26 In the evening Uncle Geoffrey took us to the Exhibition to go down in the Water Shoot. **1902** *Westm. Gaz.* 21 Oct. 2/1 A water-shoot, a swimming mistress in attendance—yet, all last winter I had the whole thing practically to myself!

†**ˈwatershot,** *sb. Obs.* [f. WATER *sb.* + SHOT *sb.*] A sudden flood.

1567 GOLDING *Ovid's Met.* xv. 294 Deepe valleyes haue by watershotte beene made of leuell ground. **1571** —— *Calvin on Ps.* xviii. 6. 57 That which foloweth of watershots, implyeth as much as if he had sayd hee had bin overwhelmed with violent rage, as if it were with a flud. **1678** in Aubrey *Miscell.* (1696) 10 Within a Year and half after his [my father's] decase, such Charges and Water-scots [1721 Water-schots] came upon this Marsh-land, by the influence of the Sea, that it was never worth one Farthing to me.

ˈwater-shot, *a. rare.* [f. WATER *sb.* + *shot* pa. pple. of SHOOT *v.*] ? Interspersed with streams.

1901 KIPLING *Kim* xiv. 369 Dry upland, hidden salt-lake, age-old timber, and fruitful water-shot valley.

†**water-shot,** *adv. Naut. Obs.* [f. WATER *sb.* + *shot* pa. pple. of SHOOT *v.*] (Moored) so as to lie at an acute angle with the stream.

1627 CAPT. J. SMITH *Sea Gram.* ix. 45 Water shot is to more quartering betwixt both, nether crosse, nor alongst the tide. **1644** MANWAYRING *Sea-mans Dict.* 114 *Water-shot*, is a kind of moreing, that is to lay the Anchors not crosse the tide, nor right up and downe the tide, but (as you would say) betwixt both, that is quartering. **1658–9** *Admir. Crt. Exam.* 72, 10 Jan., The usuall custome of mooreing shipps in the river of Thames at any place above Woollidge is to lay the anchors crosse the tyde and not watershott or right up and downe the river.

†**water-shut.** *Obs.* [? Cf. SHUT *sb.* 2 (But perh. corrupt form of WATERSHOOT.)] ? A pond with walled sides. (? Or = WATERSHOOT 2 b.)

1613–16 W. BROWNE *Brit. Past.* I. iv. 634 A large well squared stone, which he would cut To serue his stile or for some water-shut.

†**water-sick,** *a. Obs. rare.* [Cf. OHG. *wazersioh*, (MHG. *wazzersiech*), MDu. *watersiec*.] Dropsical.

c **1000** *Ags. Gosp.* Luke xiv. 2 Ða wæs þar sum wæter-seoc man [L. *homo quidam hydropicus*] beforan him. **1555** W. TURNER *Spir. Physik* 49 The other kynde of common tokens that the watersyke haue, is an excedyng greate thyrst.

ˈwater-side.

1. The side or brink of water; the bank or margin of the sea, or of a river, stream, or lake.

In dialects or periods in which *a water* means spec. either 'a river' (WATER *sb.* 12 c), or 'a lake' etc. (WATER *sb.* 12 b), this sense remains in the combination. In early use *water-side* was often simply equivalent to *water's side*: cf. quot. *c* 1375, where the rel. pron. refers to *watir* as a separate word.

? *a* **1366** CHAUCER *Rom. Rose* 129 The medewe.. Beet right on the water syde [Fr. *la praerie.. Tres au pié de l'iaue batoit*]. *c* **1375** *Sc. Leg. Saints* xxix. (*Placidas*) 410 Til he com til a watir-syd, þat depe was & wele wyd. *c* **1400** *Destr. Troy* 13466 Oft went þat wegh to the water syde, The Sea for to serche. *c* **1420** *Contn. Brut* 388 Ser Philippe Leiche.. was logged betwene þe watir of Sayne and þe abbey,.. And þe Baron of Carew was loggid on þe watir syde. **1497** *Naval Acc. Hen. VII* (1896) 149 For weying of the same..& careyng of hit to the waterside in Hampton viij^d. **1535** COVERDALE *Ps.* i. 3 Soch a man is like a tre planted by the water syde. **1568** GRAFTON *Chron.* II. 127 At this tyme, the water of the Thames sprang so high that it drowned many houses about the water syde. **1607** DEKKER & WEBSTER *West-w. Hoe* II. iii, At some Tauerne neare the water-side. **1715** *Lond. Gaz.* No. 5353/10 A Large Dye-house at the Waterside.., to be Sold. **1796** MME. D'ARBLAY *Camilla* IX. i, [They] came down in a superb new equipage to the water-side. **1833** TENNYSON *Lady of Shalott* IV. iv, For ere she reach'd upon the tide The first house by the water-side, Singing in her song she died. **1840** *Evid. Hull Docks Comm.* 256 Whose premises were between the High-street and the water-side. **1855** HARE *Cases Chancery* X. 298 The offices of deputy day oyster meters, had.. been the subject of sale and purchase,.. on payment of a fine to the oyster meters in chief, or yeomen of the water-side. **1885** *L'pool Daily Post* 4 Feb. 4/8 Hundreds.. assemble at the dock gates in the hope of obtaining employment at the water-side.

b. *pl.* (*rare.*)

1607 TOPSELL *Four-f. Beasts* 668 When the heat of Summer is about the rising of the Dog-star, we must keepe them [*sc.* swine] altogether by water sides.

c. *attrib.*

1663 in *Geogr. Jrnl.* (1900) XV. 634 Having made fast the blubber to the shore, we have a Waterside-man who stands in a pair of boots, to the middle leg in water, and flaweth such flesh as is not clean cut from the blubber. **1766** W. STORK *Acc. E.-Florida* 56 The variety of swamps, rivulets, and water-side lands. **1831** J. MARCH (*title*) The Jolly Angler; or Waterside Companion. **1838** DICKENS *O. Twist* l, Thronged by the roughest and poorest of waterside-people. **1853** —— *Bleak Ho.* i, The waterside pollutions of a great (and dirty) city. **1883** *Longman's Mag.* July 308 Waterside flies do not seem to care for yellow, and most waterside flowers are therefore pinkish, purplish or white.

2. The side towards the water.

1868 KINGLAKE *Crimea* III. xii. 280 *marg.*, Along its whole front on the water side the place [Sebastopol] was secure without needing troops to defend it.

ˈwatersider. *Austral.* and *N.Z.* [f. WATERSIDE + -ER¹.] A dockside worker.

1914 *Evening Post* (Wellington, N.Z.) 4 Feb. 10 For some time certain sections of watersiders who term themselves loyal men have been making periodic attacks on certain officials of the harbour board. **1925** *Glasgow Herald* 28 Oct. 12 The Entor is berthed at Fremantle under a police guard, with watersiders discharging her. **1949** F. SARGESON *I saw it in my Dream* xiv. 160, I see they're having trouble with those watersiders again. **1969** *Age* (Melbourne) 24 May 3/3 The watersiders' vigilance officer.. went aboard and warned the mate that if the ship sailed she would be declared 'black' in all Australian ports. **1969** *Northern Territory News* 11 July 8/2 Darwin watersiders now officially have a guaranteed minimum wage of $200 a month, but will continue to press for permanent employment with a minimum weekly wage. **1984** *N.Z. Listener* 10–16 Mar. 22/2 There, tattooed watersiders drink away the profits of a crown and anchor session down at the wharves.

ˈwater-ski, *sb.* Also **water ski.** [SKI *sb.*]

1. One of a pair of skis enabling the wearer to skim the surface of water when towed by a motor-boat. Cf. SKI *sb.* 1 c.

1931 *N.Y. Times* 3 May xx. 15/4 In 1928 a young Viennese student and amateur skier named Joseph Krupka, observing a long-legged waterfly racing over the surface of a rain-barrel, conceived the idea of skiing over water as he had done over snow. That night he worked out on paper the construction of a water ski. **1931** *Times Educ. Suppl.* 5 Sept. p. i/3 A schoolmaster.. crossed the Channel.. on a pair of water skis. **1952** D. DODGE *To catch Thief* v. 149 A speedboat roared by... A man and a girl on water skis rode the wake. **1973** L. MEYNELL *Thirteen Trumpeters* iv. 54 I'll lay odds *damage to one pair of water skis* turns up on my bill.

2. *attrib.* (repr. WATER-SKIING *vbl. sb.*).

1931 *N.Y. Times* 3 May xx. 15/4 The 1929 water ski champion, Herr Pribitzer of the water-ski rescue section.. has attained speeds of more than twelve miles an hour. **1955** *Sports Illustr.* 1 Aug. 27 California water-ski clothes show a penchant for dressing to match from trunks to skis. **1960** *Housewife* May 54/1, I left England.. with four pairs of water-skis.. to start a water-ski school. **1981** *Beautiful Brit. Columbia* Spring 44/2 Here you can rent autos, water-ski boats, [etc.].

ˈwater-ski, *v.* Also **water ski.** [f. the sb.] *intr.* To skim over the surface of water on water-skis. Cf. SKI *v.* 1 b.

1953 *Time* 19 Jan. 85/3 Aristotle Socrates Onassis is a Greek-born Argentine who water-skis in the best international circles. **1960** *Sunday Express* 3 July 19/2 What does it cost to water ski? **1971** P. GRESSWELL *Environment* 217 It is not possible to fish and water-ski in the same place. **1979** R. JAFFE *Class Reunion* (1980) II. x. 285 They both liked to water-ski.

ˈwater-skier. Also **water skier.** [f. prec. + -ER¹.] One who water-skis. Cf. SKIER b.

1931 *N.Y. Times* 3 May xx. 15/4 The water skier can carry about sixty pounds additional weight. **1935** *Lit. Digest* 13 Apr. 46/3 Water-skiers who are of championship caliber can hold one ski above the head and swing the free leg back and forth. **1958** X. FIELDING *Corsair Country* vii. 139 He.. would certainly resent its [*sc.* the mole's] present use as a landing-jetty not for galleys but for water-skiers. **1978** P. PORTER *Cost of Seriousness* 34 Up river the water skiers puff and plane.

ˈwater-skiing, *vbl. sb.* Also **water skiing, ski-ing.** [f. as prec. + -ING¹.] The action of the verb, esp. as a sport. Cf. SKI-ING *vbl. sb.* 2.

1931 *N.Y. Times* 3 May xx. 15/4 Water skiing is beginning to eclipse canoeing. **1935** *Lit. Digest* 13 April 46/3 Georges Ducros, European water-skiing champion,.. hopes to popularize his speciality here this summer. **1948** M. MURRAY *King & Corpse* (1949) xix. 214 Water ski-ing at night is a lot more exciting than in the daytime. **1960** *Times* 15 Aug. 12/5 (*heading*) British girl fifth in water-skiing. **1973** 'G. BLACK' *Bitter Tea* ii. 27 Water ski-ing equipment.. including a couple of scuba masks.

ˈwatersmeet. [f. *waters'* gen. pl. of WATER *sb.* + MEET *sb.*; app. first as a place-name (near Exmoor).] A meeting-point of two streams.

1828 T. H. WILLIAMS *Devonshire* II. 17 Below is a part of the river, the general boundary of excursions from Lynmouth, called Waters Meet, a small stream joining the East Lyn, on its left bank... Waters-Meet is accessible by ponies, from Contisbury. **1864** BLACKMORE *Clara Vaughan* xxxiv, The haze that hovers above the watersmeet. **1883** LANG, LEAF & MYERS *Iliad* 78 As when the torrents of winter flow down the mountains to a watersmeet [Gr. ἐς μισγάγκειαν].

ˈwater-snake.

1. Any snake that inhabits or frequents the water. Variously applied *spec.* to snakes of the tropical family *Hydrophidæ*, to certain Indian and American serpents, and, in England, sometimes to the common ringed snake, *Tropidonotus natrix*.

1601 HOLLAND *Pliny* XXIX. iv. II. 358 The goodliest and fairest snakes to see too, are those which live in the water, and are called Hydra, *i.* water-snakes. **1631** CHAPMAN *Cæsar & Pompey* I. i. 19 Looke how against great raines, a standing Poole Of Paddockes, Todes, and water-Snakes put vp Their speckl'd throates aboue the venemous Lake. **1698** FRYER *Acc. E. India & P.* 48 Yet so good is Providence, as to warn us here,.. by Water-Snakes, of our too near approach to the Land. **1768** G. WHITE *Selborne, To Pennant* 18 June, Country people talk much of a water-snake, but, I am pretty sure, without any reason; for the common snake (*coluber natrix*) delights much to sport in the water. **1778** J. CARVER *Trav. N. Amer.* xviii. 486 The Water Snake is much like the Rattle Snake in shape and size, but is not endowed with the same venemous powers, being quite harmless. **1798** COLERIDGE *Anc. Mar.* IV. 273 Beyond the shadow of the ship, I watched the water-snakes. **1836** W. IRVING *Astoria* xvi. I. 265 Aquatic plants, on the broad leaves of which numbers of water snakes.. were basking. **1883** MOLONEY *W. Afr. Fisheries* 43 In West Africa man has competitors as fish destroyers, such as the crocodile, shark,.. water snake, turtle,.. etc.

†**2.** Jocularly applied to a boatman. *Obs.*

1609 DEKKER *Guls Horne-bk.* vi. 31 That dividing of your Fare wil make the poore watersnaks be ready to pul you in peeces to enioy your custome.

3. *Astr.* The Southern constellation Hydrus.

1756 J. FERGUSON *Astron. Expl.* xx. (1757) 234. **1866** PROCTOR *Handbk. Stars* 70.

ˈwater-soak, *v. trans.* 'To soak or fill the interstices [of] with water' (Webster 1828). Chiefly in *passive*. Hence **water-soaked** *ppl. a.*; **water-soaking** *vbl. sb.* **water-soak** *sb. rare*, the state of being water-soaked.

1791 STEEVENS in Boswell *Johnson* an. 1784, The conductors to the wheels, suns, stars, &c. were so thoroughly water-soaked, that it was impossible any part of the exhibition should be made. **1821** J. THOMPSON *Action of Fluid* 7 Suppose a log of water-soaked timber.. balanced on one end.. it would not be found any more floatsome in consequence of its position. **1865** E. BURRITT *Walk to Land's End* 114 The park proper.. was as sour, water-soaked and humpy as any portion of Richmond Park. **1902** *Contemp. Rev.* Oct. 491 We came to regard a condition of permanent water-soak as part of our normal environment. **1909** ELIZ. BANKS *Myst. Frances Farrington* 248 A black velvet hat.. giving evidence of much water-soaking. *Ibid.*, The District Attorney turned to another parcel... Its contents were soiled, water-soaked underwear.

ˈwater-ˌsoaken, *ppl. a.* = WATER-SOAKED.

1783 *Jrnl. Ho. Comm.* XLVII. 372/2 Oak.. frequently becomes so Water-soaken, as scarce ever to dry again. **1791** SMEATON *Edystone L.* § 172, I laid them in a damp place upon a water soaken brick. **1803** MALTHUS *Popul.* I. iii. (1806) 34 A piece of water-soaken wood. *c* **1825** *Houlston Tracts* II. No. 47. 2 'Surely,' said the farmers, as they looked over their.. water-soaken grounds, 'we shall have a fine August.'

†**water-soggen,** *ppl. a. Obs.* [*soggen*, pa. pple. of SOG *v.*] = WATER-SOAKED.

c **1440** *Promp. Parv.* 518/1 Water soggon, *aquosus*.

ˈwater-ˌsoldier. An aquatic plant, *Stratiotes aloides* (N.O. *Hydrocharideæ*), found in the E. of England; it has long sword-like leaves, and flowers resembling plumes of white feathers. Also FRESHWATER *soldier*.

17.. MILLER *Gard. Dict.* (1759), Stratiotes Aloides, Water Soldier. **1889** GEDDES & THOMSON *Evol. Sex* 49 The water-soldier.. bears only female flowers north of 52° lat., and from 50° southwards only male ones.

†**water-sop.** *Obs.* [SOP *sb.*¹]

1. Bread soaked in water. [Cf. G. *wassersuppe*.]

14.. *Nom.* in Wr.-Wülcker 742/6 *Hic ipa*, a watyrsope.

2. Some kind of fruit, prob. = ANCHOVY-PEAR. [Cf. SOP *sb.*¹ 5.]

1716 *Petiveriana* I. 205 Water sop or River-Apple.

water-souchy (-ˈsuːtʃɪ, -ˈsuːʃɪ). Forms: α. 8 -zootje, -zuche, -zouchee, -zoochey, 9 -zootie, -zuchée, -zoutchee; β. 8 -sokey; γ. 8 -soochy, -sutchy, -sousee, 9 -souchee, souchet, 8–9 -suchy, -souchy. [a. Du. *waterzootje*, f. *water* WATER *sb.* + *zootje*, *zoodje* boiling (of fish), dim. of *zode* boiling, related by ablaut to *zieden* SEETHE *v.* A solitary example of MF. *soucié* (a. Du. *zootje*) is given by Godefroy.

The form *sokey* is prob. due to association with SOAK *v.*; the form *souchet* seems to be pseudo-Fr.]

Fish (properly perch) boiled and served in its own liquor.

1731 FIELDING *Grub St. Opera* III. xi, An Irishman loves potatoes;..a Dutchman, waterzuche. **1736** BAILEY *Househ. Dict.* s.v. *Soochy*, A Water Soochy, a Dish of Perch dressed after the Holland fashion. **1737** [G. SMITH] *Cur. Relat.* I. 214, I then order'd a couple of Chickens to be roasted, and a Water Zootje (boild Perch) to be made. **1747** MRS. GLASSE *Cookery* ix. 90 Water-Sokey. **1756** MRS. CALDERWOOD in *Coltness Collect.* (Maitl. Club) 155 A gentleman..desired him to show him the way of dressing a water-sutchy. **1762** *Ann. Reg.* II. 34 His water souchy was borrowed from Marshal d'Auverquerque's table, when he was first in Holland. **1763** *Gentl. Mag.* XXXIII. 221/2 Gentry from London, who come to feast on water sousee [at Dorking]. **1769** PENNANT *Brit. Zool.* III. 212 The Dutch are particularly fond of it [the perch] when made into a dish called Water Souchy. **1769** MRS. RAFFALD *Eng. Housekpr.* (1778) 37 To dress Perch in Water Sokey. **1775** T. BRIDGES *Dutchman* I. vi. 22 Song. *Myn[heer]*. Water Zouchee is a Dish In the foremost Rank of Fish. **1779** WARNER in Jesse *Selwyn & Contemp.* (1844) IV. 290 Pray tell me how you choose to have the perch dressed, in a water-zoochey, or plain boiled. **1826** MARGRAVINE OF ANSPACH *Mem.* II. 282 The Dutch are phlegmatic, from their fondness for water-zooties. **1842** BARHAM *Ingol. Leg.*, *Sir Rupert*, How she Apologised much for their plain water-souchy. **1846** SOYER *Cookery* 135 Flounders, Water Souchet. **1847** DISRAELI *Tancred* II. xv, A fish dinner!..terrines of turtle, pools of water souchee. **1848** W. F. CAMPBELL *Life in Normandy* (1863) II. 1 A very rich variety of water zoutchee. **1848** THACKERAY *Bk. Snobs* xx, Go and reclaim your rights over bowls of water-souchy. **1862** LD. W. LENNOX *Recreat. Sportsm.* II. 206 'Eels stewed, boiled, and spitchcocked,' 'perch water zuchée,' said the waiter, as the tureens and dishes were uncovered. **1863** MISS BRADDON *Aurora Floyd* xvi, A day on which stern business men..rush wildly to the Crown and Sceptre, to cool their overheated systems with water souchy and still hock.

Comb. **1816** GIFFORD *B. Jonson's Wks.* III. 300 Our days have witnessed an attempt to revive the Collegiates—but this was a water-suchy club, merely ridiculous.

b. By Walpole jocularly used for: A sodden mass (said of a ruined hay or corn crop).

1769 H. WALPOLE *Let. to Cole* 26 June, My hay is an absolute water soochy. **1784** —— *Let. to H. S. Conway* 30 June, 'Tis very dear to make nothing but a water-souchy of it [the hay-crop]. **1784** —— *Let. to Earl of Strafford* 7 Sept., It was cruel to behold such expanse of corn everywhere, and yet see it all turned to a water-souchy. **1789** —— *Let. to Miss Mary Berry* 30 June.

Hence (back-formation) **water-zoutch** *v. trans.* To stew (flounders, etc.) in just enough water to cover them. *rare*$^{-1}$.

1846 SMART *Dict.* Suppl., To Zoutch *v.*.. Hence Water-zouched, *a.* **1861** J. BROWN *Horæ Subsec.* Ser. II. 7 Dinners at Lovegrove's with flounders water-zoutched, and iced claret.

ˈwater-ˌspaniel. A variety of spaniel, much used for retrieving water-fowl. Also *attrib.*

1566 EARL OF BEDFORD in Calderwood *Hist. Kirk* (1843) II. 326 One Hickeman..having a water spangell that was verie good. **1570** CAIUS *De Canibus Brit.* 12 Post hunc subsequitur aquaticus, hoc est a Waterspainel. **1576** FLEMING tr. *Caius' Dogs* (1881) 16 Of the Dogge called the water Spaniell, or finder, in Latine *Aquaticus seu inquisitor*. **1588** KYD *Househ. Phil.* Wks. (1901) 267 Good seruants.. obey them..not as a water-spaniel, but as the hand is sturred to obey the mind. **1591** SHAKS. *Two Gent.* III. i. 271 Shee hath more qualities then a Water-Spaniell, which is much in a bare Christian. **1599** NASHE *Lenten Stuffe* G 1 b, Which droue Leander..to play the didopper and ducking water spaniel to swim to her. **1676** DRYDEN *Epil. to 'Man of Mode'* 30 Another's diving Bow he did adore, Which, with a shog, casts all the hair before; Till he with full Decorum brings it back, And rises with a Water Spaniel shake. **1688** *Lond. Gaz.* No. 2381/4 Lost.., a large Water-Spaniel Dog. **1769** G. WHITE *Selborne*, *To Pennant* 2 Jan., If half a dozen gentlemen, furnished with a good strength of water-spaniels, were to beat them [the fens] over for a week, they would certainly find more species. **1821** SCOTT *Pirate* xxx, The puir bairn swam out like a water-spaniel. **1845** YOUATT *Dog* iii. 46 The water-spaniel, although a stouter, is a more docile animal than the land one.

fig. **1616** J. LANE *Contn. Squire's T.* x. 107 Beinge but Videriaes water spanieles.

ˈwater-ˌspider. An aquatic spider of either of the genera *Argyroneta* or *Dolomedes*. In early use applied loosely to insects that move swiftly on the surface of water.

1552 *Elyot's Dict.*, *Tipula*,..a water spider. **1626** BACON *Sylva* §696 The Water-Spider that hath six Legs. **1710** RAY *Hist. Insect.* 71 De Tipula. The Water-Spider. *c* **1711** PETIVER *Gazophyl.* I. Tab. 9 It's much slenderer and less than the common Water-Spider. **1774** GOLDSM. *Nat. Hist.* VII. 263 The Water-spider..resembles the common spider in its appearance, except that its hinder part is made rather in the shape of a nine-pin than a ball. **1854** A. ADAMS etc. *Man. Nat. Hist.* 271 The diving-bell of the Water-Spider (*Argyroneta aquatica*). **1897** *Edin. Rev.* July 174 The water-spider, if but a day old, dives into the water.

†**ˈwaterspike.** *Obs.* Also 6 -spyke, 6–7 -speeke. [SPIKE *sb.*¹: transl. of F. *épi d'eau.*] A plant of the genus *Potamogeton*; pondweed.

1578 [see PONDWEED]. **1585** HIGINS *Junius' Nomencl.* 134/1 *Potamogeton, fontinalis*,..water speeke, pondweede, or wotergrasse. **1601** HOLLAND *Pliny* XXVI. viii. II. 250 Waterspeeke or Pondweed, called in Greek Potamogeton. **1855** ANNE PRATT *Flower. Pl.* V. 329 *Potamogeton natans*.. An old name for this plant was Water spike.

ˈwater-spout, ˈwaterspout, *sb.*

1. A spout, pipe, or nozzle, through which water is discharged; also †a squirt, syringe.

1390 GOWER *Conf.* III. 125 This signe [*sc.* Aquarius] is verraily resembled Lich to a man which halt assembled In eyther hand a water spoute, Wherof the stremes rennen oute. **1585** HIGINS *Junius' Nomencl.* 393/2 *Sipho*, a waterspowt, or a water squirt. **1638** *Cal. Anc. Rec. Dublin* (1892) III. 342 An instrument called a water spoute, which is verie necessarie for quenchinge of any greate fire sodainlie. **1730** A. GORDON *Maffei's Amphith.* 230 Next follows the Cornish,..with a Water-spout. **1751** BANKTON *Inst. Law Scot.* I. 682 One cannot, by his fact or deed, throw the water from his own upon his neighbour's grounds, by water-spouts or otherwise. **1821** PRAED *Gog* Poems 1865 I. 97 The red blood started out Like water from a water-spout. **1841** DICKENS *Barn. Rudge* lxv, Lighted brands came whirling down,..One rolled beneath a wooden bench.. another caught a water-spout. **1848** —— *Dombey* xlii, Mr. Carker..looked down at Mr. Dombey..like a leering face on an old water-spout.

attrib. **1611** SPEED *Hist. Gt. Brit.* IX. xiii. §2 The Maior to attend in his owne person as chiefe Cup-waiter..to serue the King in a Cup of gold with spices, and for his Fees to haue the said Cup, and a Water-spout-pot of gold thereunto belonging. **1881** *Instr. Census Clerks* (1885) 92/2 Spouting Maker. Water Spout Maker.

†**b.** A jet of water from a fountain or from a geyser. *Obs.*

1634 BRERETON *Trav.* (Chetham Soc.) 56 We were then brought down to the water-work, where was a ball tossed and danced two yards high by the strength and force of the water-spout. **1712** J. JAMES tr. *Le Blond's Gardening* 4 Fountains with Water-spouts. **1804** *Naval Chron.* XI. 43 There are several water-spouts of inferior note near the spring of Geyser.

¶**2.** In Ps. xlii. 7 (Bible version) the word is now commonly apprehended as an example of sense 3 below. It was, however, probably intended as a metaphorical use of sense 1; and it seems likely that the meteorological sense 3 arose from recollection of the passage of the psalm.

The Heb. word *ṣinnōr*, here rendered by 'waterspout', occurs elsewhere only in 2 Sam. v. 8, where it has been interpreted 'spout or gutter on a roof': so Vulg. *domatum fistulas* (Wyclif 1382 'the goters of the hows eues,' Douay 'the gutters of the house toppes'); the Bible of 1611 has 'the gutter', and the Revised Version 1881 'the watercourse'. In the psalm, the word is rendered in the LXX. by *καταρράκτης* and in the Vulg. by *cataracta* (Wycl. 'gooteris', Douay 'floud-gates'); the mod. translators from the Heb. essayed to find a literal rendering in accordance with the apparent sense of the word in 2 Sam. v. 8; hence Pagninus has *fistularum* (whence Coverdale by misapprehension renders 'whistles'); the Great Bible (1539) has 'water-pipes'.

1611 BIBLE *Ps.* xlii. 7 Deepe calleth vnto deepe at the noyse of thy water-spouts.

3. *Meteorol.* A gyrating column of mist, spray, and water, produced by the action of a whirlwind on a portion of the sea and the clouds immediately above it.

1738 T. SHAW *Trav.* 362 Water Spouts are more frequent near the Capes of Latikea, Greego, and Carmel than in any other Part of the Mediterranean Sea. **1747** *Scheme Equip. Men of War* 23 Like Monsoons or Water-Spouts, the higher they rise, the more they are contracted. **1787** tr. *Volney's Trav. Syria & Egypt* (1788) I. 340 And hence will result those columns of water known by the name of Typhons and water-spouts. **1815** J. SMITH *Panorama Sci. & Art* II. 51 When a whirlwind happens at sea, or over the surface of water, it forms the phenomenon called a water-spout. **1818** KEATS *Endym.* III. 346 When a dread waterspout had rear'd aloft Its hungry hugeness. **1829** J. RENNIE in *Loudon's Mag. Nat. Hist.* I. 458 Water-spouts make their appearance from the bosom of a heavy cloud,..gradually descending in a point like an inverted cone, sometimes perpendicularly, and sometimes bending, or waved. **1900** G. TYRRELL *Oil & Wine* (1907) 99 After many vain reachings towards one another, sea and sky at last unite in the waterspout.

b. A sudden and violent fall of rain; a cloudburst.

1779 THICKNESSE *Journ. France* (1789) I. 351 The water-spouts which fell into the middle of those narrow streets almost deluged us. **1815** SCOTT *Guy M.* xxiii, Heaps of gravel and stones, which had been swept together when some torrent or water-spout from the neighbouring hills overflowed the marshy ground below. **1827** —— *Highl. Widow* v, This mountain rivulet, suddenly swelled by a water-spout, or thunderstorm, has often been the cause of those accidents, which, [etc.]. **1842** BORROW *Bible in Spain* xxvi, The demons of the clouds..assailed them with water-spouts as they toiled up the steep winding paths of Fuencebadon. **1862** J. SKELTON *Nugæ Crit.* vii. 301 It had begun to rain..a down-pour, a pelt, a water-spout. **1889** GRETTON *Memory's Harkback* 15 A waterspout burst on the hill overhanging the village of Mordiford.

c. *fig.*

1852 J. BRIGHT in G. M. Trevelyan *Life* (1913) 201 'After Lord Derby, the deluge,' says Lord Maidstone... The 'deluge' means Manchester, it is said—a sort of political waterspout which is to sweep away all that Peer and Parson hold dear.

Hence **ˈwaterspout** *v. intr.* (*impers.*), *nonce-wd.*

1892 STEVENSON *Vailima Lett.* (1895) 190 It was water-spouting; we were drenched before we got out of the town.

†**water-spouter.** *Obs.* [SPOUTER.] (See quots.)

a **1700** EVELYN *Diary* 24 Feb. 1651, The water-spouter, who drinking only fountaine water, rendred out of his mouth in severall glasses all sorts of wine and sweete waters, &c. **1816** A. C. HUTCHISON *Pract. Obs. Surg.* (1826) 170 See an account of Blash de Manfré, who died in 1651..and who is styled the 'water spouter'.

ˈwater-spring. A permanent flow of water issuing from the earth: = SPRING *sb.*¹ 2. Also *fig.* Now chiefly in echoes from the Bible.

c **1440** *Jacob's Well* 238 To deluyn ȝoure pyt deppere in lownes tyl ȝe fyndyn a watyr-spryng of grace. **1535** COVERDALE *Ps.* cvi[i]. 33 Which turneth the floudes in to drie londe, and drieth vp the water sprynges. *Ibid.* 35 He maketh the wildernes a standing water, and water sprynges of a drye grounde. **1573–80** TUSSER *Author's Belief*, in *Husb.* (1878) 195 That ioyned brookes to dales, to hilles fresh water springs. **1595** *Locrine* IV. iii, Huge Hidras..which haue drunke vp the flowing water springs. **1607** BP. HALL *Ps.* i. 18 He shall be like the tree, Set by the water-springs. **1766** M. BRUCE *Lochleven* 147 Her pleasing task to tend The flow'rs; to lave them from the water-spring. **1780** VON TROIL *Iceland* 245 Among all the curiosities of Iceland..nothing can be compared to the hot spouting water-springs. **1866** LYTTON *Lost Tales Miletus*, *Secret Way* 12 The cool marge of rush-grown watersprings. **1890** D. DAVIDSON *Mem. Long Life* vi. 146 Friends, whose intercourse had been as refreshing to me as the water-spring to the traveller in the wilderness.

ˈwater-stone. [Cf. G. *wasserstein* in various senses.]

†**1.** A stone basin for holy water. *Obs.*

1379 *Mem. Ripon* (Surtees) III. 98 Le Waterstane pro aqua benedicta in eadem.

†**2.** A kind of 'philosopher's stone'. *Obs. rare*$^{-1}$. So G. *wasserstein* (1709 in Grimm).

1659 J. H[OWELL] (*title*) Paracelsus his Aurora, and Treasure of the Philosophers. As also The Water-Stone of The Wise Men; Describing the matter of and manner how to attain the universal Tincture.

†**3.** (Meaning obscure.) *Obs.*

1703 *Lond. Gaz.* No. 3917/4 The Loading of the Dorothy, ..consisting of Canary Wines, Orchilla, Rosewood, and some few Water-Stones, will be exposed to publick Sale.

4. ? A whetstone used with water and not oil.

So G. *wasserstein*. But cf. WATER-OF-AYR *stone*.

1891 *Daily News* 24 Feb. 2/1, I sharpened the large blade on my water-stone.

5. Some kind of building stone. (See quot.)

1824 G. CHALMERS *Caledonia* III. 54 (Dumfriesshire) There is water-stone, which dresses into a fine polish.

6. A nodule of chalcedony having an internal cavity containing water. [So G. *wasserstein*.]

1867 SELWYN & ULRICH *Phys. Geog.* etc. *Victoria* 71 *note*, The chalcedony of these 'Water Stones' has a hardness above 8, as the sharp edges scratch topaz easily. **1869** R. B. SMYTH *Gold Fields Victoria* 253 A great number of these water stones..were exhibited in the Intercolonial Exhibition.

7. A rock-stratum abounding in water.

1878 ANSTED *Water & Water Supply* 30 Several..springs were found to break out from the water-stones or lower beds of the Keuper.

ˈwater-stream. Now *rare*. [Cf. G. *wasserstrom*, MLG. *waterstrôm*.] A stream or current of water; a river or brook; †a flood.

c **1000** *Ags. Ps.* lxxvii[i]. 44 He wæterstreamas [Vulg. *flumina*] wende to blode. **10..** in Napier *Contrib. OE. Lexicogr.* 67 Ac he [Christ] wolde sylf swa ȝehalȝian ure fulluht mid his halȝan lichaman & ealle wæterstreamas mid his ingange. *c* **1200** *Trin. Coll. Hom.* 177 Ðe water stremes [Vulg. *flumina*, Ps. xciii. 3] on-heueden up here undes. *c* **1200** ORMIN 18092 For all swa se waterstræm Aȝȝ fleteþþ forþ & erneþþ..all swa [etc.]. *c* **1435** *Torr. Portugal* 2032 He led it into his own lond, And told the quene how he it ffond By a water streme. **1535** COVERDALE *Isa.* lix. 19 He shal come as a violent waterstreame, which the wynde of the Lorde hath moued. **1596** SPENSER *F.Q.* VI. i. 21 Like as a water streame, whose swelling sourse Shall drive a Mill, within strong bancks is pent. **1625** T. GODWIN *Moses & Aaron* II. (1641) 78 The Senate..were bound to prepare the wayes to the Cities of Refuge,..and they suffered not any hill or dale to be in the way, nor water-streames, but they made a bridge over it, that nothing might hinder him that fled thither. **1779** THICKNESSE *Journ. France* (1789) I. 351 The roaring of the water-streams was so great, that I very often thought we were upon the margin of some river. **1862** SMILES *Engineers* III. ii. 20 Erecting Lilliputian mills in the little water-streams.

ˈwater-ˌswallow¹. ? *Obs.* [SWALLOW *sb.*¹ Cf. G. *wasserschwalbe*.] A name for the water-wagtail.

1544 TURNER *Avium Præcip.* C 7 b, *Κιγκλος*, *ἡ σεισοπυγίς*, Anglice a water swallow. **1552**, **1668** [see SWALLOW *sb.*¹]. **1611** COTGR., *Batemare*, a wagtayle, or water Swallow. **1658** WILLSFORD *Natures Secr.* 140 The Wagtail, or Water-Swallow. **1706** PHILLIPS (ed. Kersey), *Water-Swallow*, a kind of Bird.

ˈwater-ˌswallow². = SWALLOW *sb.*² 1 b.

1811 in *Marshall's Rev. Rep. Board Agric.*, *Midl.* 83 List of Water-swallows or Holes in the Rocks into which Streams of Water fall and disappear in and near Derbyshire. **1840** HODGSON *Northumb.* II. III. 327/2 *note*, A stratum of limestone full of water-swallow-holes. **1889** *Jrnl. Derbysh. Archæol. Soc.* XI. 34 This valley is entirely drained by 'water-swallows'—natural drains along the bottom, through which the surface-rills sink out of sight.

Hence †**water-swallowed** *a.*, abounding in water-swallows.

1610 FOLKINGHAM *Feudigr.* I. iii. 4 It would be also peruestigated, whether it [*sc.* the earth] be light, loose,.. leane, barren, fertile, water-swallowed, soale-bound.

'water-,table. [See TABLE *sb.* 12 a, 13 b, c.]

1. *Arch.* **a.** The sloping top of a plinth. **b.** A horizontal projecting ledge or moulding sloping on the top, set along the side of a wall so as to throw off the rainfall.

1428 in Heath *Grocers' Comp.* (1869) 5 The walle atte seid west gabilende was maad x fote in heyghte aboue the water table. **1459** in Willis & Clark *Cambr.* (1886) I. 309, iij fotes ..from the gronde leuell to the water tabil..and the said water tabell..alle of freeston. **1482-3** *Acc. Exch. K.R.* 496 No. 25 Pro factura Watertable Garglez et Batilment. **1541** in *Proc. Antiq. Scot.* (1860) III. 161 Fra the sollis of the said queir duris to the vuer pairt of the walter tabill vnder the thak thairof. **1547** in J. R. Boyle *Hedon* (1875) App. 133 Item, for layinge the watter tabyll above the counsell chamer. *a* **1548** [see RAISING-PIECE]. **1548** *Elyot's Dict.*, *Corona*..is also the water table or copyng of a wall. **1617-18** *Hartland Ch. Acc.* in *Rep. Devonsh. Assoc.* XXVII. 60 For putting in water tables of lead. **1707** MORTIMER *Husb.* 297 The Walls of such Edifices ought to be from the Foundation to the first Water-table, three heading course of Brick,..and at every Story a Water-table, or taking in on the inside for the Summers, Girders or Joysts to rest upon. **1833** LOUDON *Encycl. Archit.* §1882 The massive buttress, with its deep weatherings, or water-tables between each graduation or stage of the height. **1878** MᶜVITTIE *Ch. Ch. Cathedral, Dubl.* 66 Weathered in the depth of the buttresses by nine courses of Water-tables.

transf. **1650** BULWER *Anthropomet.* 68 Robbing the Eyes of their natural Pent-house or Water-table, they expose them bare to imbrications.

2. A channel or gutter on each side of a road; 'also, a small hollow made across a road to carry off surplus water' (Elworthy).

1707-21 MORTIMER *Husb.* II. 205 A Water-Table also on each side of the Walk is very good to drain your Walks. **1809** MAVOR *Agric. Berks.* 422 The..roads..are not sufficiently raised in the middle, the water tables are neither regularly made nor with proper outlets towards the ditches. **1817** W. H. MARSHALL *Rev. Rep. Board Agric., South.* 73 *note*, *Water Table* is a west of England term (rather ill chosen) for the draining channel, on the side of a barreled road, to convey away the rain water that may fall upon it. *c* **1830** *Pract. Treat. Roads* 9 in *Libr. Usef. Knowl., Husb.* III, Outlets from the watertables into the ditches cannot be seen in too many places. **1836** W. D. COOPER *Gloss. Sussex*, *Water-table*, a small embankment made across a road, especially on a hill, to carry off the water. **1886** ELWORTHY *W. Somerset Word-bk.* **1906** *Westm. Gaz.* 24 Sept. 4/1 Now that the local authorities have permitted footpaths by the roadside and water-tables to be obliterated.

3. A window-ledge or sill in a ship or railway carriage.

1883 W. C. RUSSELL *Sailors' Lang.*, *Water-tables*, sills to a ship's windows. **1884** STORMONTH, *Water-tables*, in a ship, the sills of the windows in the stern. **1890** *Funk's Stand. Dict.*, *Water-table*, a horizontal board with beveled top, running underneath the windows, the entire length of a [railway] car.

4. = *water-bridge* (see WATER *sb.* 29).

1880 WEBSTER. **1891** *Century Dict.*

5. = WATER-LEVEL 3.

1879 *Cassell's Techn. Educ.* I. 139/2 In other cases it [the water] will not rise to the surface, but form what is known as a 'water-table' one, two, or more feet beneath. **1881** *Encycl. Brit.* XII. 567/1 At varying distances from the surface.. there exists a great subterranean lake or sea, known as the ground-water or water-table.

'water-,tabling. [f. prec. + -ING[1].]

1. *Arch.* Water-tables collectively; a line of water-tables.

1578 *Churchw. Acc. Minchinhampton* in *Archaeologia* (1853) XXXV. 431 For the water tablinge of Anslowes chapele and the bynche of the porche, xvj s. iiij d. **1799** A. YOUNG *Agric. Lincoln* 32, 120 feet of water-tabling. **1893** *Reliquary* Jan. 14 The east and west walls were surmounted by gables. These seem to have been covered with a water-tabling. **1900** *Archæol. Æliana* XXII. 87 The corbels on which rests the water-tabling.

2. The action or process of renovating with sods the side of a ditch where it has become worn away below the roots of a hedge.

1844 H. STEPHENS *Bk. Farm* II. 433 The hedger now resumes his work of water-tabling and scouring ditches. *Ibid.* 562 Of switching, pruning, and water-tabling thorn-hedges.

water-thyme.

†**1.** An (? imaginary) aquatic species of thyme.

1655 WALTON *Angler* vi. (1661) 132 Some think that he [*sc.* the grayling] feeds on Water-Time, and smells so at his first taking out of the water.

2. The American weed *Elodea canadensis* (formerly *Anacharis Alsinastrum*), now common in English waters.

1855 ANNE PRATT *Flower. Pl.* V. 190 The Anacharis is called by the fishermen the Water Thyme.

watertight ('wɔːtətaɪt), *a.* [See TIGHT *a.* 2 a.]

1. a. So closely constructed or fitted that water cannot leak through.

1387 *Charters* etc. *Edin.* (1871) 35 Thekyt abovyn with stane and water thycht. *Ibid.* 36 The qwilke werke the forsaide masounys sal warande watir thicht. **1514** *Lincoln Wills* (1914) I. 61 To keep hyt wyndthyght and waterthyght. **1554** *Extracts Aberd. Reg.* (1844) I. 281 Makand the said tolbuith vattirthicht. **1601** T. MILLES *Customers Accompt* B ij, Her Houses neither Wind-tight, nor Water-tight. **1648** in J. Davidson *Inverurie* (1878) 302 The heritors in all parishes are ordained to keep the kirk wind-fast and water-tight. **1776** in *Trans. Soc. Arts* (1783) I. 232 High-topped water-tight boots. **1793** *Trans. Soc. Arts* V. 202 The joint.. is perfectly water-tight. **1835** MARRYAT *Jacob Faithf.* xl, All the nails in Birmingham won't make this boat water-tight. **1873** B. STEWART *Conserv. Energy* ii. 32 Each of these cylinders is provided with a water-tight piston.

fig. **1647** WARD *Simple Cobler* 33 There is good hope, when peace is setled, people shall dwell more wind-tight and water-tight than formerly. **1892** *Daily News* 12 Jan. 4/7 The most watertight scheme hitherto proposed is undoubtedly Mr. Charles Booth's.

b. ***watertight compartment***: each of the many compartments, with watertight partitions, into which the interior of a large ship is now usually divided for safety. Hence often *fig.*

1858 J. GRANTHAM *Iron Ship-building* 48 Several of these [water-tight bulkheads]..divide the vessel into water-tight compartments. **1888** SIR J. STRACHEY *India* iii. 63 Thus, what has been called 'the policy of watertight compartments' has been applied throughout the Indian army. **1902** J. SMITH *Integr. Script.* vi. (ed. 2) 209 That faith in the Bible..must be kept in a water-tight compartment, jealously excluded from the least contact with criticism.

2. As *sb.* (usu. in *pl.*) Watertight boots.

1867 J. T. THOMSON *Rambles with Philosopher* iii. 14 A shoemaker..beating time with his mallet on the hob-nails of an old *water-tight* that he was repairing. **1880** JEFFERIES *Hodge & M.* xxi. (1890) 303 He..slips his feet into his thick 'water-tights'. **1886** HARDY *Mayor Casterbr.* xxvi, Time-stiffened water-tights reappeared.

Hence **'watertightness.**

1869 SIR E. REED *Shipbuild.* xi. 228 *Watertightness* is usually secured by working angle-irons around the keelsons or stringers in such a manner as to allow the caulking of the joints to be readily performed. **1882** *Athenæum* 6 May 564/3 To have one's representations as to the drainage or water-tightness of one's house neglected. **1889** WELCH *Naval Archit.* vi. 82 The joints being caulked for watertightness.

'water-tree. [Cf. G. *wasserbaum.*]

†**1.** A tree which grows by the water-side or in watery ground. *Obs.*

1600 SURFLET *Country Farm* VII. xiv. 823 There are two sorts of trees in generall: the one is called water trees, or trees delighting to grow in or neere vnto the brinkes of waters. **1612** R. CH. *Olde Thrift newly revived* 51 Will not these trees which you haue tearmed water trees, grow in any other place then in low grounds?

2. A tree which yields a watery juice; applied, e.g. to the pitcher-plant of Sri Lanka, *Nepenthes distillatoria*, the African climbing shrub *Tetracera alnifolia*, and the Australian tree *Hakea leucoptera*.

For *red-water tree* see RED-WATER 3.

1759 B. STILLINGFLEET *Misc. Tracts* (1762) 76 The water-tree in Ceylon produces cylindrical bladders, covered with a lid; into these is secreted a most pure, and refreshing water. **1866** *Treas. Bot.* s.v. *Tetracera*, *T. potatoria* [1874 *T. alnifolia*] is called the Water-tree at Sierra Leone, on account of its climbing stems yielding a good supply of clear water when cut across. **1894** C. D. TYLER in *Geog. Jrnl.* III. 484 The *cetico*, or water-tree [of S. America], is a variety of the *bombax*, or silk-cotton tree. **1898** MORRIS *Austral English*, *Water-tree*, a tree from which water is obtained by tapping the roots, *Hakea leucoptera*, R. Br.

'water-vine. A name for several plants which yield an abundant watery juice. **a.** *Tetracera alnifolia* (or *potatoria*): see prec. 2. **b.** *Phytocrene gigantea*, a tall climbing shrub of Martaban, Burma. **c.** The W. Indian climber *Doliocarpus Calinea.*

1833 *Penny Cycl.* I. 187/1 (art. *Africa*) The water-vine (*Tetracera potatoria*), the stems of which are a sort of vegetable fountain, discharging, when cut across, a cool, limpid, and refreshing fluid. **1846** LINDLEY *Veget. Kingd.* 271 In the province of Martaban, Dr. Wallich found his Water Vine (Phytocrene) whose singular soft and porous wood discharges when wounded a very large quantity of pure and tasteless fluid, which is quite wholesome, and drunk by the natives. **1864** GRISEBACH *Flora W. Ind. Isl.* 788 Water-vine, *Doliocarpus Calinea.* **1871** KINGSLEY *At Last* xi. II. 105 We cut a water-vine, and had a long cool drink.

'water-vole. [See VOLE *sb.*[2]] The common water-rat, *Arvicola amphibius.*

1828 J. FLEMING *Brit. Anim.* 23 Water Vole. **1837** T. BELL *Brit. Quadrupeds* 322 The Water Vole, or, as it is more frequently called, the Water Rat, is found in most parts of Europe. **1869** BLACKMORE *Lorna D.* vii, There never was any sound at all, except of a rocky echo..or the sudden dive of a water-vole.

'water-'wagtail.

1. The common pied wagtail, *Motacilla lugubris.* Also applied, with some distinctive epithet, to other species.

1611 COTGR., *Hausse-queue*, the yellow Water-wagtaile. **1668** CHARLETON *Onomast.* 90 *Motacilla*..the washer, or water-wagtail. *a* **1672** WILLUGHBY *Ornith.* II. xvii. (1676) 171 *Motacilla alba.* The white Water-wagtail. *Ibid.* 172 *Motacilla flava.* The yellow Water-wagtail. **1734** ALBIN *Nat. Hist. Birds* II. 54 The common black and white Water-Wagtail. **1758** G. EDWARDS *Glean. Nat. Hist.* I. 105 The Grey Water-wagtail. **1826** SCOTT *Jrnl.* 14 June, As blithe as a water-wagtail. **1877** MISS A. B. EDWARDS *Up Nile* vi. 138 The sparrows and water-wagtails perch familiarly on the awnings and hop about the deck. **1894** R. B. SHARPE *Handbk. Birds Gt. Brit.* I. 92 The Wagtail of Madagascar, *M. flaviventris*, and the Grey Wagtail of Europe, *M. melanope*, are 'Water' Wagtails, with the colouring of Yellow Wagtails.

†**b.** Applied playfully or derisively to a person.

1694 CROWNE *Married Beau* v. 61 If my old Water-wagtail will only hop about the brinks of Marriage, and never step in, I'll drive him away. **1697** VANBRUGH *Prov. Wife* v. iii, Why now, my pretty Pall; my Goldfinch; my little Watterwagtail—you must know that.

2. *U.S.* = WATER-THRUSH.

1865 J. BURROUGHS *Wake-robin* ii. (1884) 77 The water-wagtail (*Seiurus noveboracensis*)—erroneously called waterthrush. **1872** COUES *Key N. Amer. Birds* 106 *Seiurus noveboracensis.* Water Thrush. Water Wagtail.

'water-wall. [Cf. G. *wasserwall.*]

1. A wall which rises by the side of water; a containing wall beside or around a body of water.

a **1440** *Sir Degrev.* 907 Ther ys a place in the wall, Bytwyne the chaumbur and the hal, Thor ly3the a mychel watur-wal Of fourty feyt brede. **1445-6** *Durham Acc. Rolls* (Surtees) 630 Pro reparacione et emendacione de le Waterwall ac rote exterioris molendini de Scaltoke, 15*s.* **1574** in *Reg. Mag. Sig. Scot.* 1582, 105/2 Necnon edificando lie walterwall cum aist(l)erstanis dicti molendini. **1660** *Melrose Regality Rec.* (S.H.S.) I. 262 [John Mein, mason, sues William Edgar for 4 l. Scots] for beating of the water-wall. **1907** JEAN WEBSTER *Jerry Jr.* ii. 21 Three [girls]..were kneeling on the beach thumping and scrubbing a pile of linen. The grass beyond the water-wall was already white with bleaching sheets.

†**2.** Some plant. *Obs. rare*[−1].

Cf. *penny-wall*, dial. name (Isle of Man) for the wall pennywort (*Eng. Dial. Dict.*).

1607 TOPSELL *Four-f. Beasts* 629 They giue hir the Hearbe Penny-wort or Water-wall to drinke in water.

waterward, -wards ('wɔːtəwɔːd, -wɔːdz), *adv.* [See -WARD, -WARDS.] Toward the water; in earlier use *to (the) waterward(s.* Also †***fra the waterward***, from the direction in which the water lies.

c **1220** *Bestiary* 137 [The adder] walkeð to ðe water-ward, wile ðanne drinken. **13..** *K. Alis.* 3686 To water-ward [*Bodl. MS.* To waterwardes], with sweord egge, Theo othres come at heore rygge. **1418** in *Eng. Misc.* (Surtees) 13 That the water be ledde downe..fra the thrid poste of the house of Dame Alice Plumpton fra the waterward of Use [= Ouse], be a pype of lede closed wyth a loker. **1903** W. S. BLUNT *Golden Odes Arabia* iv. 27 All their will to win there speeding them waterwards.

'water-washed, *pa. pple.* and *ppl. a.* Drenched with water; swept, flushed, or inundated by running water.

1826 J. G. WHITTIER *Exile's Departure* in *Poet. Wks.* (1898) 521/1 The forest-crown'd hill and the water-wash'd strand. **1856** KANE *Arct. Expl.* II. xv. 157 Rounded fragments of water-washed greenstone. **1860** TRISTRAM *Gt. Sahara* v. 89 All these apparently ancient sea-beaches show traces of having been waterwashed only on their north sides. **1883** G. C. DAVIES *Norfolk Broads* ii. 13 The reed-covered water-washed bank.

†**water-washen,** *pa. pple. Obs.* = prec.

c **1400** *Siege of Jerusalem* 788 [He] Made wedes of wolle in wete for to plunge, Water-waschen as þey wer, & on þe walle hengen.

'water-wave, *sb.*

1. *lit.* A wave of water.

c **1560** ? COVERDALE *Treat. Death* I. ix. 35 Like as one water waue foloweth vpon another. **1603** J. DAVIES (Heref.) *Microcosm.* (Grosart) 91/1 Shee stood, as if she stood vpon no ground, But on some water-waue that made her bound. **1610** HOLLAND *Camden's Brit.* I. 529 Bankes formerly raised against the waterwaves then in-rushing. **1834** *Tait's Mag.* I. 340/1 From the engines water-waves are gushing.

2. A seismic wave in the sea.

1877 HUXLEY *Physiogr.* 188 If the centre of disturbance is near the sea, the water-waves may be far more destructive than the earth-waves.

3. A mode of dressing the hair in flattened scallops on the forehead. orig. *U.S.*

1882 *Harper's Mag.* Nov. 877/2 She is pasting down her wetted hair into a semblance of the 'water-waves' of fashionable society. **1895** *Funk's Stand. Dict.* **1911** WEBSTER. **1923** E. F. WYATT *Invis. Gods* I. i. 7 His grandmother..bending over him her water waves and pearl powder. **1958** J. CANNAN *And be a Villain* i. 5 Passing a clean white hand over the water-waves of his naturally fuzzy hair. **1972** *Vogue* June Special 68/2 Hair in sleek water waves, by Jean Louis David, Paris.

Hence **'water-wave** *v. trans.*, to set (hair), with water, in waves; **'water-waved** *ppl. a.*, having a wave-like pattern or changing gloss; also of hair: set, with water, into waves.

1599 T. M[OUFET] *Silkwormes* 3 Last, Easterne wittes from mane of Camels tall Made water-waued stuffe vnseene before. **1841** CATLIN *N. Amer. Ind.* lii. (1844) II. 143 The agates are many of them peculiarly beautiful, most of them water-waved. **1928** A. HUXLEY *Point Counter Point* xxviii. 453 She readjusted a water-waved lock of hair. **1962** E. SNOW *Other Side of River* (1963) lxvii. 513 A little girl with large saucy black eyes and beribboned hair her mother must have water-waved. **1975** J. GORES *Hammet* (1976) xix. 130 Goodie had spent a dollar..to have her blond ringlets water-waved by Georgia.

'water-waving, *vbl. sb.* [f. WATER-WAVE *sb.* + -ING[1].] **1.** The wavy or 'watered' appearance imparted to silk and other fabrics by pressing two pieces together.

1894 J. E. DAVIS *Elem. Mod. Dressmaking* v. 94 Beetled plain linings generally show a marking like a slight water-waving on the surface.

2. A method of waving hair with water.

1925 *Daily Tel.* 13 May 20/5 (Advt.), Wanted, smart man. ..Must be thoroughly competent in perm. waving, Marcel and water waving. **1927** *Daily Express* 30 Nov. 13/3 She can give lessons in water waving, face massage, and chiropody. **1932** [see *finger-waving* vbl. sb. s.v. FINGER *sb.* 15].

†**waterwaw.** [See WOUGH.] A water-wall.
1340 *Durham Acc. Rolls* (Surtees) 540 In sarracione plancorum..pro les Watrewawes molend. Abathie.

'water-way. [Cf. (M)LG. *waterwech* drain, G. *wasserweg* (1) way by water, water as a way, (2) a watercourse.]

†**1.** Used in OE. with uncertain meaning.
Explained by Bosworth-Toller as 'a channel connecting two pieces of water'. This is possible, but in quot. *c* 1000 the lemma means 'paths', and the entry occurs in a group of words meaning 'road' or 'path'. Perh. the sense may be 'a road along which a stream runs' (cf. WATER-LANE).
932 *Charter* in Kemble *Cod. Dipl.* No. 1107 V. 207 Andlang burnan on ðone æwylm; of ðam ewylme andlang wæterweȝes up to strete. **956** *Charter* ibid. No. 1198 V. 374 Andlang burnan on wæterweȝ; of ðan wæterweȝe on wæterhammes. *c* **1000** ÆLFRIC *Gloss.* in Wr.-Wülcker 146/37 *Tramites*, wæterweȝ.

2. A channel for the escape or passage of water.
c **1440** *Promp. Parv.* 518/1 Water wey, *meatus.* **1662** ATWELL *Faithf. Surveyor* 88 If you are to bring it [*sc.* the trench] over some ditch or brook, where the water is lower then your water-way, then must you [etc.]. **1825** J. NICHOLSON *Oper. Mech.* 96 Through the waterway the water presses during the rising tide into a large reservoir. **1844** H. STEPHENS *Bk. Farm* II. 325 If the water is to be carried away by a tunnel, the water-way is arched over and the space above levelled in with earth. **1862** *Rep. Directors E. Ind. Rlwy. Co.* 30, I find that the waterways shown on last year's sections by the different Engineers..are very deficient. **1878** ANSTED *Water & Water Supply* 161 The alluvial bed is wide, but the channel or water-way, except after heavy rain, is small. **1889** RIDER HAGGARD *Allan's Wife* xii, This gully had a water-way at the bottom of it.

3. *Naut.* A long piece of timber, hollowed in the middle, serving to connect the deck of a ship with the side, and to form a channel for carrying off water from the deck by means of the scuppers.
c **1635** CAPT. N. BOTELER *Dialogues about Sea Services* (1685) 149 Water way is that small piece or ledge of timber which lieth on the ship's deck..to keep the water from running down there. **1748** *Anson's Voy.* II. iv. 158 Her water-ways were open and decayed. **1750** BLANCKLEY *Nav. Expositor*, Water ways, is that Strake of Plank on the Flat of each Deck respectively next the Ship's Side, for turning the Water out of the Seams. **1840** R. H. DANA *Bef. Mast* xv. 39 Everything has been moved in the hold, from stem to stern, and from the water-ways to the keelson. **1884** *Law Times* LXXVII. 26/2 A tug towed at her for an hour and a half before she was got off, during that time her decks and waterways were much strained.

4. a. A route for travel or transport by water; a river, canal, or a portion of a sea or lake, viewed as a medium of transit.
1797 G. IMLAY *Topogr. Descr. W. Territory N. Amer.* (ed. 3) 34 Major Willis..found 1300 yards clear water-way between the lower beaches or counter-shores of the banks on both sides of the river. **1832** J. S. MILL *Let.* 24 May in *Wks.* (1963) XII. 99 Yet if such glimpses are numerous, some general tendency shall predominate even in the few furlongs of water-way which they may chance to disclose. **1858** KINGSLEY *Misc.* (1859) I. 167 Pleasant are those hidden waterways. **1869** ROGERS *A. Smith's W.N.* I. I. iii. 20 *note*, When time is no object, the use of a water-way, even though it be artificial, is vastly cheaper than that of any road on land. **1870** YEATS *Nat. Hist. Comm.* 88 The river is the grand waterway for the produce of the Urals and Central Russia. **1904** W. M. RAMSAY *Lett. Seven Ch. Asia* iv. 48 When a waterway is needed, as at Glasgow, we transform a little stream into a navigable river. **1905** LYALL *Life Marq. Dufferin* I. vii. 262 The proposal in the draft treaty, that the waterway of the St. Lawrence should be improved,..was opposed. **1915** A. HURD in *Daily Tel.* 24 Aug. 8/7 The Russians have their main fleet elsewhere,..the defence of this particular waterway [*sc.* the Gulf of Riga] was entrusted to a number of older ships.

b. Distance to be travelled by water.
1883 G. C. DAVIES *Norfolk Broads* ix. 74 The lack of railway and inn accommodation and the length of water-way rendered a cabin necessary.

c. (Right of) access by water.
1883 G. C. DAVIES *Norfolk Broads* xvi. 122 One of the abbots of St. Benedict's once sued the citizens of Norwich for an interference with his right of water-way up to his possessions higher up the river.

d. A track across the water. *nonce-use.*
1865 SWINBURNE *Chastelard* I. ii. 31 Between the sundown and the sea Love watched one hour of love with me; Then down the all-golden water-ways His feet flew after yesterday's.

5. The breadth of a navigable watercourse; esp. the breadth allowed for the watercourse of a canal or the like (exclusive of towpaths, etc.) passing under a bridge or tunnel.
1739 LABELYE *Short Acc. Piers Westm. Bridge* 75 More free Water-way is left for the Stream..than the whole Breadth of the River at the Horse-Ferry. **1753** *Chambers' Cycl.* Suppl. s.v. *Bridge*, These arches give..a water-way of 870 feet. **1776** G. SEMPLE *Building in Water* 16 Total Water-way 755 Feet 5 Inches. **1791** R. MYLNE *and Rep. Thames Navig.* 8 The Water-way..is much contracted by the Bank ..having grown forward, beyond the opening of the Buttment Arch. **1800** TELFORD in Plymley *Agric. Shropsh.* (1803) 301 By this towing-path being hollow below, there is a water-way in the tunnel of ten feet, instead of seven feet. **1838** *Civil Engin. & Arch. Jrnl.* I. 322/1 The Canal Company..demanded..an arch 31 feet wide, 24 for water-way, and 7 for towing path. **1902** *Times* 26 Nov. 16/5 The Thames Conservancy..have made demands in regard to waterway and headway which must render it exceedingly difficult [etc.].

6. An opening for the passage of vessels; a (broader or narrower) course available for navigation; esp. the passage by which vessels enter and leave a harbour, the fairway.
1883 *Manch. Guard.* 18 Oct. 4/7 The Suez Canal Company's engineers have prepared alternative sets of plans for the improvement of the waterway. **1884** J. COLBORNE *With Hicks Pasha* 106 The waterway was considerably reduced in breadth by a large well-cultivated island. **1894** *Law Times Rep.* LXXI. 102/2 The breadth of available waterway depends upon the draught of the vessels navigating it.

7. The full-open passage area in a cock or valve.
1744 DESAGULIERS *Course Exper. Philos.* II. 524 His three Valves (whose Water-way taken together was 48 Inches). **1797** J. CURR *Coal Viewer* 63 Injection cocks with square shanks, 4¼ inches by 1¼ inch water way. **1802** *Nicholson's Jrnl. Nat. Philos.* I. 164 As the sudden stoppage of the descent of the column AB, at the instant when the two plugs were both in the water way, might jar and shake the apparatus, those plugs are made [etc.]. **1825** J. NICHOLSON *Oper. Mech.* 276 The pressure of the incumbent column of water is supported by the plates G G, whose circular edges rest on the brim of the water-way... This piston has every advantage of strength, tightness, and large water-way.

'water-weed. Any aquatic plant with inconspicuous flowers; spec. = WATER-THYME 2.
1842 BROWNING *In a Gondola* 210 Your gondola—let Zorzi wreathe A mesh of water-weeds about Its prow. **1848** SCHOMBURGK *Hist. Barbados* 610 Spigelia anthelmia... Loggerhead Weed, *Hughes*... Water Weed. **1855** ANNE PRATT *Flower. Pl.* V. 185 He found that this water-weed [*sc.* Anacharis] had..accumulated there in great profusion. **1872** OLIVER *Elem. Bot.* II. 257 The 'New Water-weed' (Elodea canadensis), an American plant, was first remarked in Britain in 1817. **1890** BRIDGES *Shorter Poems* II. v. 27 The water-weeds, that..scarce allow a narrow stream to pass. **1914** *Blackw. Mag.* Aug. 211/2 We pass..shikaras laden with wood or hay or water-weed.

'water-wheel.
1. A wheel designed to drive machinery, esp. that of a mill or pump, with water as the motive power.
1408 *Durham Acc. Roll* in *Eng. Hist. Rev.* XIV. 517 Pro cariagio..unius axeltre..pro le Water-whelle. *a* **1530** J. HEYWOOD *Play of Weather* (Brandl) 461 Our floodgate, our myl-poole, our water whele. **1648** WILKINS *Dædalus* xv. 284 For if there were but such a water-wheel made on this instrument [*i.e.* the Archimedean screw], upon which the stream that is carried up, may fall in its descent, it would turn the Screw round. **1759** SMEATON *Exper. Enq.* (1794) 2 Concerning Undershot Water Wheels. **1773** W. EMERSON *Princ. Mech.* (ed. 3) 240 London-bridge water-works. AB the axis of the water-wheel CD. **1830** KATER & LARDNER *Mech.* xiv. 179 In water-wheels, the power is the weight of water contained in buckets at the circumference. **1860** TYNDALL *Glac.* I. iii. 25 At one end was a little water-wheel turned by a brook. **1893** SIR R. BALL *Story of Sun* 242 A water-wheel, turned by Niagara, virtually derives its energy from the transformation of Sunbeams.

2. A wheel for raising water, esp. for irrigation purposes, by means of buckets or boxes fitted on its circumference.
1639 G. PLATTES *Discov. Infin. Treas.* vii. 32 Water wheeles..with wooden bottels which doe fill in the river, and empty themselves above into a trough of wood. **1825** J. NICHOLSON *Oper. Mech.* 230 As the mule..goes round, these horizontal arms..take hold..of those arms which are fixed on the axis of the water-wheel, and keep it in rotation. **1877** MISS A. B. EDWARDS *Up Nile* vi. 140 The water-wheel slowly revolving with its necklace of pots. **1914** *Blackw. Mag.* Oct. 428/1 Waterwheels have to be employed to irrigate the old terraces.

†**3.** A wheel for propelling a boat through the water; a paddle-wheel. *Obs.*
1787 P. MILLER in B. Woodcroft *Steam Navig.* (1848) 29 An account of experiments made by Mr. Miller..in a double vessel..put in motion by his water wheel. **1814** in *Scribner's Mag.* (1887) May 518/2 She is a structure resting upon two boats... The great water-wheel revolves in the space between them. **1822** IMISON *Sci. & Art* I. 226 Some attempts have been made to place the water-wheels, or paddles that drive the vessel, in the middle.

'water-ˌwillow.
†**1.** The purple loosestrife, *Lythrum Salicaria*, or the willow-herb, *Epilobium angustifolium*. (The two plants seem to have been generally confused.)
1585 HIGINS *Junius' Nomencl.* 130/2 *Lysimachium, salicaria*,..willow herbe, or loose strife, waterwillow. **1706** PHILLIPS (ed. Kersey), *Water-Willow*, an Herb otherwise call'd Loose-strife. **1736** AINSWORTH *Dict. Lat.*, *Lysimachia*, willow herb, or loose strife, water willow. Hence **1828–54** in WEBSTER.

2. Applied to *Salix aquatica* and other species.
1850 OGILVIE, *Water-willow*,..the *S*[*alix*] *aquatica*, called also *water-sallow*. **1853** G. JOHNSTON *Nat. Hist. E. Bord.* I. 179 *Salix helix*. Water willow. Common on the margins of our gravel-bedded burns and rivers. **1886** BRITTEN & HOLLAND *Plant-n.*, Water Willow. *Salix rubra*, Hudson.

3. An American plant, *Dianthera americana*, with narrow leaves and purplish flowers, found growing on the borders of streams and ponds.
1856 A. GRAY *Man. Bot.* (1860) 297.

'water-wings, *sb. pl.*
†**1.** Wings having a watered or wavy surface. *nonce-use* [after *water camlet*].
1676 COTTON *Angler* II. viii. 74 The Camlet-Flie, in shape like a moth with fine diapred, or water-wings. [Cf. *water camlet* s.v. CAMLET *sb.* b.]

2. Organs of propulsion in the water.
1835–6 OWEN in *Todd's Cycl. Anat.* I. 294/2 We have already alluded to the use which the Penguin makes of its diminutive anterior extremities as water-wings, or fins.

3. (See quot.)
1841 BREES *Gloss. Civil Engin.* 293 *Water-wings*, the walls erected on the banks of a river next bridges, to secure the foundations from the action of the current; they are usually battered towards the stream, [etc.]. Hence in later Dicts.

4. Inflatable floats which may be fixed to the upper arms of persons learning to swim, in order to give increased buoyancy.
1907 *Yesterday's Shopping* (1969) 323/3 All Water Wings ..support a man as easily as a boy..on just the level at which a person can swim or float comfortably. **1922** WODEHOUSE *Girl on Boat* v. 102 A little undersized shrimp of a fellow with a green face and ears like water-wings. **1948** 'P. WOODRUFF' *Whatever Dies* 151 You could take it, if you would be bold and throw away your water-wings. **1976** 'G. BLACK' *Moon for Killers* iii. 37 Gloria's daughter was.. dressed for the water..with..a pair of water wings.

'water-witch.
1. A witch inhabiting the water.
a **1680** BUTLER *Rem.* (1759) I. 77 A Water-witch with Charms Could sink their Men of War, as easy as Storms. **1877** BLACK *Green Past.* xxxvii. (1878) 297 Presently we found ourselves in a sort of water-witches' paradise. Far below us boiled that hell-cauldron of white smoke [etc.].

2. a. *U.S.* A name for several water-birds noted for their quickness in diving: see quots.
1789 MORSE *Amer. Geog.* (1792) 60 Water-witch. **1859** BARTLETT *Dict. Amer.* (ed. 2), *Dipper*, a small aquatic bird, common throughout the United States, also called the Water-witch and Hell-diver. **1862** COUES & PRENTISS in *Rep. Smithsonian Inst.* 1861, 419 *Podiceps cristatus*..Crested Grebe. 'Water Witch.' *Ibid.*, *Podilymbus podiceps*... 'Dipper.' 'Water Witch.' **1899** C. B. CORY *Birds E. North Amer.* I. 132 *Colymbus auritus* Linn. Horned Grebe. Water Witch.

b. The stormy petrel, *Procellaria pelagica*.
1852 MACGILLIVRAY *Brit. Birds* V. 460.

3. *U.S.* = WATER-FINDER.
1859 BARTLETT *Dict. Amer.* (ed. 2), *Water-Witch.* A person who pretends to have the power of discovering subterranean springs by means of the divining rod. **1883** *Harper's Mag.* Oct. 708/2 Utah..abounds in 'water-witches.' **1890** L. C. DOYLE *Notches* 154 His men had reached a depth of about a hundred and thirty feet without striking water, when there chanced to come along a man known throughout the section as a 'water-witch.'

'water-witching, *vbl. sb.* *U.S.* [f. WATER-WITCH + -ING[1].] = WATER-FINDING *vbl. sb.* Hence **'water-witch** *v. intr. rare* (in quot. *transf.*).
1877 H. RUEDE *Sod-House Days* (1937) 196 Talking with Hoot about digging wells, etc., he told me about one new neighbor, Diegel, who has a firm faith in water witching. **1947** R. BEDICHEK *Adv. with Texas Naturalist* x. 119, I followed for a short distance an immense sow..her nose barely skimming the sand, apparently searching for something. It turned out that she was water-witching..for presently she began rooting. Soon her..snout unearthed a spring of crystal-clear water. **1968** S. E. ROBERTS *Of Us & Oxen* ii. 18 Several homesteaders..had had to dig a number of wells before striking water, even though these wells had been located by 'water-witching'. **1976** *National Observer* (U.S.) 14 Aug. 11/1 One of our neighbors practiced the art of water witching.

'water-withe. A West Indian plant, *Vitis caribæa* (see quot. 1756).
1696 SLOANE *Catal. Plant. Jamaica* 172 Wild Vine or Water-with. **1756** P. BROWNE *Jamaica* 178 Water-withe. The withe of this grape-vine..is so full of juice, that a junk of about 3 feet will yield near a pint of clear tasteless water. **1864** GRISEBACH *Flora W. Ind. Isl.* 788 Water-withe, *Vitis caribæa*.

waterwork ('wɔːtəwɜːk). [f. WATER *sb.* + WORK *sb.* Cf. Du. *waterwerk*, G. *wasserwerk*.]
†**1.** A structure built in the water or serving as a receptacle for water or a defence against the force of water, as a tank, pier, sea-wall, lock, etc. *Obs.*
1443 *Acts Privy Counc.* (1835) V. 283 For þe makyng of þest and west jettys at Caleys for þe weele of þe havene and oþer water werkes in þe same havene. **1540** *Ibid.* VII. 17 Antony Ainger paymaster to the Kinges workmenne of the water workes at Dover. **1577** B. GOOGE *Heresbach's Husb.* II. 106 The wylde Oke serueth also well in water woorkes. **1590** VALLANS *Tale Two Swans* (1744) p. xiii, [At Waltham Abbey] a rare devise they see,..a waterworke: the locke Through which the boates of Ware doe passe with malte. **1629** *Pat. Off.* No. 47. 2 The circular bathes or bathing water-workes above mencioned. *a* **1647** HABINGTON *Surv. Worcs.* (Worcs. Hist. Soc.) I. 29 Mr. William Sandys' waterwourcke on Avon. **1693** MOXON *Mech. Exerc.* (1703) 243 They use it in making of Cisterns to hold Water, and all manner of Water-works. **1707** MORTIMER *Husb.* 326 The knottiest and coarsest [oak] is best for Water-works and Piles. **1765** *Museum Rust.* IV. 380 For properly planting the greatest number of the Small-leaved English Elm, for raising timber, (commonly used for keels of ships and water-works)..a Gold Medal. **1791** SMEATON *Edystone L.* §186 The ancient baths and water-works of the Romans were built with this kind of mortar.
transf. **1596** HARINGTON *Metam. Ajax* H 2 b, Though I called my selfe by metaphor an Admirall for the water workes.

2. †**a.** A system of machinery for raising, conveying, or distributing water. *Obs.*
The 'New Waterwork' referred to in several early quots. was a lofty building erected near Queenhithe in 1594–5 by Bevis Bulmar, containing machinery 'for the conueying and forcing of Thames water to serue in the middle and West parts of the Citie' (Stow *Survey of London*, 1603, p. 364).

1596 SIR J. DAVIES *Epigr.* vi. (*In Titum*), Titus.. Three years togither in this towne hath beene Yet my Lord Chauncellors tombe he hath not seene Nor the New water worke. **1610** B. JONSON *Alchemist* II. i. 76 *Mam.* I'll giue away so much, vnto my man, Shall serue th' whole citie, with preseruatiue, Weekely, each house his dose, and at the rate— *Sur.* As he that built the water-worke, do's with water? *Ibid.* III. iv. 418, I, that was with the griefe Thou took'st for being sess'd at eighteene pence For the water-worke. **1622** J. TAYLOR (Water P.) *Merry-Wherry-Ferry Voy.* Wks. (1630) II. 12/2 Some 10. yeeres since Fresh water there was scant, But with much Cost they haue suppli'd that want; By a most ex'lent Water-worke that's made. **1644** G. PLATTES in *Hartlib's Legacy* (1655) 216 Raise the water by an engine or water-work of the most fit sort for that place and purpose. *a* **1661** FULLER *Worthies, Chester* (1662) 292 John Terer.. erected a seemly waterwork built Steeplewise at the Bridgegate... This since hath served for the conveying of River-water from the Cisterne, in the top of that Work, through Pipes of Lead and Wood, to the Citizens houses. **1663** MARQ. WORCESTER *Cent. Invent.* etc. F 7, The same individual Definition of my Water-work.. I again adventure to present to Your Majesty. **1775** WHITEHURST *Machine Raising Water* in *Phil. Trans.* LXV. 277 The circumstances attending this water-work, require a particular attention.

b. *collect. plural.* (Sometimes construed as sing.) The assemblage of machinery, buildings, and engineering constructions, used for the purpose of supplying a town or neighbourhood with water conveyed and distributed through pipes.

1621 BURTON *Anat. Mel.* II. ii. I. i. (1624) 202 Mr Otho Nicholson, founder of our water works, & elegant Conduit in Oxford. **1691** *Lond. Gaz.* No. 2625/1 An Act for Incorporating the Proprietors of the Water-works in York-Buildings. **1703** *Ibid.* No. 3964/4 The Proprietors concerned in the London-Bridge Water-Works are desired to meet on Wednesday the 10th Instant. **1753** HANWAY *Trav.* (1762) II. I. iv. 21 They have a town house, an exchange, and waterworks, by which the city is supplied from the river. **1818** CRUISE *Digest* (ed. 2) V. 138 Two 36th shares of the King's moiety of the New River waterworks. **1879** *Cassell's Techn. Educ.* I. 226/2 The term water-works is properly applied only to such works as have for their object the collection, supply, and conveyance of water to towns. **1910** *Encycl. Brit.* XIV. 838/2 The municipality owns and operates its water-works.

3. †**a.** Any contrivance for producing a pleasing spectacle by means of water in motion; an ornamental fountain or cascade. Chiefly in plural. *Obs.*

a **1586** SIDNEY *Arcadia* I. xiv. §1 The table was set neere to an excellent water-worke; for by the casting of the water in most cunning maner, it makes (with the shining of the Sunne vpon it) a perfect rainbow. **1649** DAVENANT *Love & Hon.* II. i. 105 Those are the tunes my old widdow prisoner sings With more division than a water work When the maine pipe is halfe stopt. **1680** MORDEN *Geog. Rect., Germany* (1685) 113 In his Palace or Castle of Heidelburg are divers things remarkable, viz. the Grotes and Water-works. *a* **1700** EVELYN *Diary* Aug. 1641 Where, in the upper roomes of the house were divers pretty water-workes, rising 108 foote from the ground. **1702** *Phil. Trans.* XXIII. 1078 There was always a great boyling and flying up of the Water of the Sea, as in a *Jette d'eau*, or Water-work. **1710** ADDISON *Spect.* No. 5 ¶3 There was actually a Project of bringing the New River into the House, to be employed in Jetteaus and Water-works. **1721** *New General Atlas* 219 The Gardens are pleasant and stately, adorn'd with exquisite Water-Works. **1757** MRS. P. L. POWYS *Passages fr. Diaries* (1899) 29 The waterworks.. may be said to be more grand than pleasing,.. particularly the grand cascade, which [etc.]. **1771** SMOLLETT *Humphry Cl.* 4 July (1815) 221, I saw him standing by the wheel, dropping like a water-work, and trembling from head to foot, partly from cold, and partly [etc.]. **1779** J. MOORE *View Soc. Fr.* II. lv. 56 The present Landgrave's grandfather.. formed.. a series of artificial cataracts, cascades, and various kinds of water-works, in the noblest style that can be imagined. **1803** M. WILMOT *Let.* 6 Aug. in *Russ. Jrnls.* (1934) I. 34 The Gardens.. so extensive and so beautiful and the Water works are beyond description. **1842** W. F. TOLMIE *Jrnl.* 7 May (1963) 359 As the great display of waterworks was to take place at 5, I finally decided on remaining.

b. *transf.* Chiefly in jocular references to shedding of tears and (*rare*) to rain.

1647 J. CLEVELAND *Poems* 47 Not Bushells Wells can match a Poets eyes In wanton water-works. **1709** T. ROBINSON *Vindic. Mosaick Syst.* 23 The Veins.. of the Earth being now saturated.. the Subterrene Lymphæducts, or underground Water-works, began to bubble up and play from the Tops and Sides of the Mountains. **1806** J. BERESFORD *Miseries Hum. Life* v. §12 The fire-works put entirely out of countenance by the water-works [*i.e.* the rain]. **1848** THACKERAY *Van. Fair* xiv, 'O Miss B., I never thought to have seen *this* day!' And the waterworks again began to play. **1857** HUGHES *Tom Brown* II. v, Sneaking little brute.. clapping on the water-works just in the hardest place. **1885–6** *F. Leslie's Chatterbox* (N.Y.) 79 Harry could not bear to see Clare cry. 'Hold up!' he cried. 'This will never do. Hullo! no waterworks here, if you please.' **1931** D. L. SAYERS *Five Red Herrings* xvii. 179 'It's not raining.. Better than yesterday.'.. 'Tons better. Really,.. you'd think they'd turned on the water-works yesterday on purpose to spoil my sketching-party.'

c. *pl.* The urinary system. *euphem.*

1902 F. W. MAITLAND *Let.* 6 July (1965) 249, I gather from Albutt that the immediate cause of death was, as A. put it, 'in the water works'. **1922** JOYCE *Ulysses* 355 Cissy.. came back with her tongue out and said uncle said his waterworks were out of order. **1959** E. AMBLER *Passage of Arms* v. 124 Little scotch, lot of soda. Got to keep the old waterworks going in this climate. **1977** W. HILDICK *Loop* xxix. 205 I'd been plagued for a long time.. by—well—let's call it waterworks trouble.

†**4.** A kind of imitation tapestry, painted in size or distemper. *Obs.*

See J. H. Middleton in *Proc. Soc. Antiq.* (1886) 197, where this kind of work is described from extant specimens.

a **1548** HALL *Chron., Hen. VIII*, 28 Goodly tentes of blewe water worke garnyshed wt yelowe & white. **1597** SHAKS. *2 Hen. IV*, II. i. 158 And for thy walles a pretty slight Drollery, of the Storie of the Prodigall, or the Germane hunting in Waterworke, is worth a thousand of these Bed-hangings, and these Fly-bitten Tapistries.

5. In occasional uses: Something done in or on the water, or by means of water; †a pageant exhibited on the water.

1608 *Great Frost* in Arber *Eng. Garner* I. 83 Make me so much beholding to you, as to receive from you the right picture of all these your waterworks; how they began, how they have grown, and in what fashion have continued. **1614** J. TAYLOR (Water P.) (*title*) Taylors Water-worke: or The Scullers Trauels, from Tiber to Thames. **1629** DEKKER *London's Tempe* (Percy Soc.) 43 The first scæne is a water-worke, presented by Oceanus. **1655** W. NICHOLSON *Expos. Catech.* (1663) 171 The Scruple then here is, How water can wash away the spots of sin? To clear it in brief: The truth is, it could not; it is no water-work. **1680** C. NESSE *Ch. Hist.* 291 Such savoury discourse.. for our deliverance from the devils water-works in eighty-eight [*i.e.* the Spanish Armada]. **1902** *Hist. Hawick from 1832*, 140 Usually most of the play [at handball] is in the river, and the 'water work' is the most amusing feature to the onlookers.

6. An operation or a department of labour concerned with hydraulic engineering, irrigation, embanking, drainage, or the like. Chiefly *pl.* Now *rare.*

1564 *Rec. Inverness* (New Spalding Club) I. 117 The prowest baillies and cunsall decernis all watter men to mak thayr partis of thair wattyr wark sufficient betuix the day and dayt heirof and the feist of Andersmes nixt. **1568** in *Sel. Charters Trading Co.* (Selden Soc.) I. 17 Workmasters of great cunning perfectness knowledge and experience in all kind of mineral works and of water works for the draining of all manner of mines. **1571** DIGGES *Pantom.* I. xxxi. Kjb, And heere I thynke it not amisse to gyue you a precepte howe to fynde the diuersitie of these leuelles, wherby yee may exactly resolue sundry questions perteyning to water woorkes, wherein dyuers haue greately erred, obseruyng not this difference. **1610** R. VAUGHAN (*title*) Most approved and long-experienced water-workes. Containing, The manner of Winter and Summer-drowning of Medow and Pasture [etc.]. **1625** K. LONG tr. *Barclay's Argenis* I. xiii. 35 Some famous for Limming; he curious for Architecture; this for Water workes, or any other Art. **1634** J. B[ATE] (*title*) The Mysteryes of Nature and Art. Conteined in foure severall Treatises. The first of Water workes, The second of Fyer workes, The third of Drawing [etc.]. **1638** *Cal. Anc. Rec. Dublin* (1892) III. 345 A sufficient plummer that hath skill in waterworkes, and all other workes belonging to a plummer. **1653** *Van Etten's Math. Recreat.* title-p., Secrets and Experiments in Arithmetick, Geometry,.. Chemistry, Water-works, Fire-works, &c. **1682** LUTTRELL *Brief Rel.* (1857) I. 192 Sir Samuell Moreland, the great engineer in water-works, is gone over to the court of France to shew his skill there. **1848** CLOUGH *Amours de Voy.* iii. 12 Where.. amid cotton and maize peasants their water-works ply.

attrib. **1824** R. STUART *Hist. Steam Engine* 6 The elasticity of the vapour of water.. had now become familiar to water-work artists.

So **'water-,worker.**

1579 FENTON *Guicciard.* VI. (1599) 258 The bottome of the poole, contrarie to the.. opinions of many enginists and water-workers, was found to be higher. **1787** W. H. MARSHALL *Norf.* (1795) II. 391 *Water-workers*, makers of meadow drains and wet ditches.

'water-worm.

1. Any aquatic annelid.

1655 MOUFET & BENNET *Health's Improv.* xi. 100 The Kings-fisher feedeth most upon water-worms, and little fishes. **1681** GREW *Musæum* I. §vii. iii. 177 A Water-Worme. *Lumbricus Aquaticus.* **1797** *Encycl. Brit.* (ed. 3). VIII. 665/2 Animated Horse-Hairs, a term used to express a sort of long and slender water-worm.. by the vulgar supposed to be the hair fallen from a horse's mane into the water.. and there animated by some strange power. **1865** SWINBURNE *Chastelard* v. i. 176 Bred out of Egypt like the water-worm. **1889** *Hardwicke's Sci.-Gossip* XXV. 139 It is not at all uncommon for some Rotifera.. to adhere for a time to larger animals, such as Crustaceæ and water-worms. **1891** M. MURIEL DOWIE *Girl in Karpath.* 56 Water-worms, and newts of every description.

b. *fig.* in derisive use.

1820 BYRON *To Murray* 23 Apr., I hate and abhor that puddle of water-worms [*i.e.* the lake poets] whom you have taken into your troop.

†**2.** Some kind of explosive used under water.

1809 *Naval Chron.* XXII. 203 Fire-devils, water-worms, Shrapnell-shells.

'water-worn, *a.* Worn or corroded by the action of water. Chiefly *Geol.*

1815 BAKEWELL *Introd. Geol.* 10 Water-worn fragments of primary and transition rocks are commonly found in many of the secondary rocks. **1829** J. PHILLIPS *Geol. Yorks.* 49 Fragments of chalk and flint which.. are very little water-worn. **1859** R. F. BURTON *Centr. Afr.* in *Jrnl. Geog. Soc.* XXIX. 33 Bare coralline rocks, smooth and waterworn near the sea, rough and sharp inland. **1888** F. HUME *Mme. Midas* I. Prol., There was a smooth water-worn boulder on the beach.

waterwort ('wɔːtəwɜːt). [WORT *sb.*[1]] A name for several distinct plants. †**a.** In early use identified with MAIDENHAIR (i.e. either *Adiantum Capillus-Veneris* or *Asplenium Trichomanes*, or both). *Obs.* **b.** Any plant of the genus *Elatine.* **c.** Applied by Lindley to plants of the order *Philydraceæ*, native to Australia and Eastern Asia.

a. *c* **1000** *Sax. Leechd.* I. 24 Herba galli tricus þis wæter wyrt. *a* **1400–50** *Stockh. Med. MS.* p. 176 Maydenheer or water-wourt: *capillus virginis.* **1541** *Bk. Properties Herbs* B viij, Capillus veneris. This herbe is called Mayden here or waterworte. **1597** GERARDE *Herbal* Suppl., Waterwort is Maidenhayre. **1607** TOPSELL *Four-f. Beasts* 182 Water-wort with new Lard, applyed to the sore, easeth the same.

b. **1796** WITHERING *Brit. Plants* (ed. 3) II. 387 Elatine Alsinastrum. Water-wort. **1816–20** T. GREEN *Univ. Herbal* I. 489 Elatine Hydropiper; Opposite-leaved Waterwort. *Ibid.*, Elatine Alsinastrum; Whorl-leaved Waterwort. **1848** JOHNS *Week at Lizard* 286 *Elatine hexandra.* Water-wort, a minute succulent plant, with greenish flowers of three petals.

c. **1846** LINDLEY *Veg. Kingd.* 186.

watery ('wɔːtərɪ), *a.* Forms: 1 **wæteriȝ, wætriȝ,** 3, 5 **wateri,** 5 **watiry, wattery, watri, wattry,** 5–6 **watrye,** 5–7 **waterie,** 5–8 **watry,** 6 **waterye,** *Sc.* **wattirrie,** 6–7 **watrie,** 7–9 **wat'ry,** 4– **watery.** [f. WATER *sb.* + -Y. Cf. Du. *waterig*, MLG. *waterich*, OHG. *wazzirig, wezzirig* (MHG. *wazzeric, wezzeric*, mod.G. †*wasserig, wässerig*).]

1. Of land or soil: Full of water; moist, plashy; well-watered.

c **1000** ÆLFRIC *Hom.* II. 402 Rixe weaxst ȝewunelice on wæteriȝum stowum. *c* **1100** *Gloss.* in Wr.-Wülcker 147/6 *Alluvius ager*, wæteriȝ æcer. **1440** *Jacob's Well* 250 þis is a good moyst & a wattery ground for to haue in oure welle be-nethyn. *c* **1440** *Promp. Parv.* 518/1 Watry, or fulle of water, *aquosus, aquilentus.* Watry, or fulle of moysture, *humidus.* **1577** B. GOOGE *Heresbach's Husb.* I. 20 The watrie ground requireth more store of doung, and the drye ground the lesse. *a* **1593** MARLOWE *Ovid's Eleg.* I. xiv. 11 In hilly Idas watry plaines. **1653** WALTON *Angler* ix. 175 Rushes that grow in the water, or watry places. **1680** *Exact Jrnl. Siege Tangier* 11 The third [trench] being very deep and watry,.. a Hundred and twenty four were there killed. **1796** SOUTHEY *Lett. fr. Spain* (1799) 320 In every little watry bottom the frogs croaked out a concert. **1842** HAWTHORNE *Twice-told T.* Ser. II. *Seven Vagabonds*, Some elderly clergyman, long vegetating in a rocky, woody, watery back settlement of New England. **1846** R. E. EGERTON WARBURTON *Hunting Songs* 129 Blackthorns stiff the fields divide With watery ditch on either side.

b. Of clouds: Full of moisture which is ready to fall as rain; rainy. Also of wind, a season, etc.

1377 LANGL. *P. Pl.* B. XVIII. 410 Is no weder warmer þan after watery cloudes. **1555** EDEN *Decades* (Arb.) 133 Vapours.. wherof the watery cloudes are engendred. **1669** WORLIDGE *Syst. Agric.* (1681) 291 At the rising of the Sun, if it appear.. hid in a black watry Cloud, Rain follows. **1743** FRANCIS tr. *Hor., Epodes* x. 19 While watry Winds the bellowing Ocean shake. **1883** G. C. DAVIES *Norfolk Broads* xxxiii. 261 The watery year of 1879.

c. *gen.* Full of water, wet, dripping. *rare.*

1589 GREENE *Menaphon* (Arb.) 23 The Mermaides.. sate .. drying their waterie tresses in the Sunne beames.

d. *transf.* Covered with, permeated by water; set or built in the water; washed by stream or tide.

1593 SHAKS. *Lucr.* 1611 And now this pale Swan in her watrie nest, Begins the sad Dirge of her certaine ending. *a* **1668** DAVENANT *Poems* (1672) 320 The Lark now leaves his watry Nest. **1793** BLAKE *Songs Exp.* Introd. 19 The starry floor, The wat'ry shore. **1878** JOAQUIN MILLER *Songs Italy* 13 Sweet Was the Christmas time in the watery town.

2. Resembling water in consistence; thin, fluid.

c **1000** *Sax. Leechd.* II. 236 ðif se utgang sie windiȝ and wætriȝ and blodiȝ. **1398** TREVISA *Barth. De P.R.* v. xxxvi. (Bodl. MS.), þe herte sometyme quakeþ and þat comeþ of watery moisture. *a* **1425** tr. *Arderne's Treat. Fistula*, etc. 59 Raw fruytez gendreþ watry blode. *c* **1440** *Pallad. on Husb.* IV. 6 For now this vines.. Not wattery but thicke humoures wepe. **1561** T. GALE *Antidot.* II. 15 Boyle them and take two pounde of the Musilage and boyle it with the other thynges vntyll all that is waterye bee consumed. **1626** BACON *Sylva* §30 Quick Siluer, (which is a most Crude and Watry Body). **1787** in *Sixth Rep. Dep. Kpr. Publ. Rec.* II. 177 When the mixture of Oil or Oily Substances with Acetous or Watery Liquors is required. **1842** LOUDON *Suburban Hort.* 283 The mistletoe.. can live on all exogens of which the ascending sap is of a watery consistence. **1899** *Allbutt's Syst. Med.* VII. 815 From the watery conditions of the blood results a transudation of serum.

3. Having the appearance of water; resembling water in colour. Of colour: Pale, looking as if diluted with water.

Said esp. of an overcast condition, betokening rain, of the sky, sun, moon, etc.

c **1407** LYDG. *Reson & Sens.* 1417 Me thought, I sawgh a Reyne-bowe Of blywe and rede and watiry grene. **1585** HIGINS *Junius Nomencl.* 176/2 *Aqueus*,.. a pale white like water, or a waterie colour. *a* **1628** PRESTON *Serm. bef. his Majestie* (1630) 26 The prosperitie of wicked men, like a waterie sun-shine may for a while continue. **1697** DRYDEN *Virg. Georg.* I. 608 But if his Cheeks are swoln with livid blue, He bodes wet Weather by his watery Hue. **1738** GRAY *Tasso* 45 The watery glimmerings of a fainter day. **1808** SCOTT *Marmion* I. Introd. 26 Where yet some faded herbage pines, And yet a watery sunbeam shines. **1821** SHELLEY *Evening at Pisa* 23 A space of watery blue, Which the keen evening star is shining through. **1886** W. J. TUCKER *E. Europe* 401 His eyes were small and of a watery blue.

b. In comb. with an adj. of colour.

1887 PHILLIPS *Brit. Discomyc.* 82 Cup sessile, globose,.. watery-grey;.. Cup.. pale watery-brown, or cinereous. **1913** MRS. STRATTON-PORTER *Laddie* xvii. (1917) 350 A little bit of a man, with watery blue eyes.

4. Of the nature of water.

1477 NORTON *Ord. Alch.* v. in Ashm. (1652) 65 Wann or leady Colour ingendred is Of Waterie and Erthy parts without amisse. **1604** JAS. I *Counterbl. Tobacco* (Arb.) 104 Raynes, Snowes, Deawes, hoare Frostes, and such like waterie Meteors. **1633** G. HERBERT *Temple, Grief* 3 My grief hath need of all the watry things, That nature hath produc'd. *a* **1676** HALE *Prim. Orig. Man.* I. iii. (1677) 76 The Clouds are attracted out of moist and watry, and also earthy Vapours. **1750** G. HUGHES *Barbados* I. 20 The Resistance.. will compel these thin watry Vesicles to coalesce..into Drops. **1787** WINTER *Syst. Husb.* 73 Heat..resolves the watry and oily particles of the earth into vapour. **1876** BRISTOWE *Th. & Pract. Med.* (1878) 817 The watery constituent [of urine]. **1877** HUXLEY *Physiogr.* 67 The watery vapour in the atmosphere.

b. applied to the rainbow. *poet.*

1600 *Wisd. Dr. Dodypoll* I. A 3 b, Looke on the ayre, where with a hundred changes The watry Rain-bow doth imbrace the earth. **1610** SHAKS. *Temp.* IV. i. 71 The Queene o' th Skie, Whose watry Arch, and messenger, am I. **1755** YOUNG *Centaur* ii. Wks. 1757 IV. 145 As if in kindly showers the watry bow had shed all its most celestial colours on it.

†**c.** = AQUEOUS I b. *Obs.*

1615 CROOKE *Body of Man* VIII. ix. (1631) 565 These three humors [of the eye] are called the Watery, the Christalline, and the Glassy. **1699** GID. HARVEY *Van. Philos. & Physick* 169 To preserve the Eye-sight,.. By attenuating the Horny Tunic and the watery Humour.

d. Of a chemical extract, solution, etc.: Made with water, aqueous.

1826 HENRY *Elem. Chem.* II. 545 The watery solution may contain a variety of salts. **1857** MILLER *Elem. Chem., Org.* 528 The formation of the blue colouring matter in watery extracts of the plant. **1863** CURLING *Dis. Rectum* (1876) 45 The watery extract of aloes. **1871** B. STEWART *Heat* §53 Various watery solutions also possess their own points of maximum density. **1889** *Century Dict.* s.v. *Fusion, Aqueous* or *watery fusion*, the melting of certain crystals by heat in their own water of crystallization.

5. Consisting of water. Chiefly *poet.* or *rhet.* of natural features, as the sea and rivers. ***watery way***, a route by which one journeys over water.

1535 COVERDALE *Ps.* lxxvii. 20 He smote the stony rocke, that the watery streames gusshed out. *c* **1586** C'TESS PEMBROKE *Ps.* XLVI. i, Yea soe lett seas withall, In watry hills arise, As may the earthlie hills appall. **1590** SHAKS. *Mids. N.* I. i. 210 When Phœbe doth behold Her siluer visage in the watry glasse. ?**1605** DRAYTON *Poems Lyr. & Past.* Eglog v. E 6, Conuey her prayse to Neptunes watry realme. **1667** MILTON *P.L.* XI. 779 Those few escap't Famin and anguish will at last consume Wandring that watrie Desert. **1678** CUDWORTH *Intell. Syst.* 358 That the gods (or stars)..were at first made out of the ocean—that is out of the watry chaos. **1697** DRYDEN *Virg. Georg.* II. 625 Keels of Ships, that scour the watry Plains. **1715** POPE *Iliad* II. 685 In fourscore Barks they plow the watry Way. **1854** J. S. C. ABBOTT *Napoleon* (1855) I. v. 107 England was mistress of the sea, and she respected no rights of private property upon her watery domain. **1863** BARING-GOULD *Iceland* 189 A quaint peep of the landscape is obtained through a watery arch, spouted from a hollow. **1887** BOWEN *Virg. Æneid* I. 376 Sailing from ancient Troy..o'er many a watery way.

b. ***watery grave***, † ***tomb***: the place in which a person lies drowned. Similarly ***watery death***.

1601 SHAKS. *Twel. N.* V. i. 241 So went he suited to his watery tombe. **1608** —— *Pericles* II. i. 10 Hauing throwne him from your watry graue. **1802** in J. D. Parry *Coast of Sussex* (1833) 72 Last month, a youth of Brighton was rescued from the watery grave, and restored to his father. **1829** LANDOR *Imag. Conv., Chaucer, Boccaccio, & Petrarca* Wks. 1853 I. 416/1 The horrors of a watery grave. **1831** SCOTT *Ct. Robt.* xxix, To exchange..a watery death for one by the more dreadful agency of fire. **1857** *Recoll. Western Texas* 13 O'H—— and another..being unable to swim, soon found a watery grave.

6. Of, belonging to, connected with the water; aquatic. Now *rare*. **a.** of plants and animals that live in or on the water.

1398 TREVISA *Barth. De P.R.* XIII. xxvi. (1495) 456 Fysshe lyckyth therthe and watry herbes and soo gete they meete and nourysshynge. **1586** T. B. *La Primaud. Fr. Acad.* I. 10 Earthie and waterie creatures. **1601** DOLMAN *Ibid.* III. lxii. 286 God hath created them [fish] like watrie birdes, to whom he hath giuen wings agreeable to the element for to sustaine themselues with. **1610** HOLLAND *Camden's Brit.* (1637) 491 Alders, beside other watery Shrubbes. **1626** BACON *Sylva* §656 The Reed or Cane is a Watry Plant, and groweth not but in the Water. **1697** DRYDEN *Virg. Georg.* I. 527 The sev'ral sorts of watry Fowls, That swim the Seas, or haunt the standing Pools. **1725** POPE *Odyss.* v. 64 Wat'ry fowl that seek their fishy food.

b. as an epithet of deities, etc.

1593 SHAKS. *Rich. II*, II. i. 63 Whose rocky shore beates backe the enuious siedge Of watery Neptune. **1595** *Locrine* v. iv. 17 The watrie ladies and the lightfoote fawnes, And all the rabble of the wooddie Nymphs. **1617** J. TAYLOR (Water P.) *Three Wks. Observ.* Ep. Ded. A 4 b, Neptune, Æolus, Tellus, Bacchus, and all the watery, windy, earthly, and drinking Deities. **1697** DRYDEN *Virg. Georg.* I. 43 The watry Virgins for thy Bed shall strive. **1747** GRAY *Ode on Death of Cat* 32 She mew'd to ev'ry watry God. **1801** S. TURNER *Hist. Anglo-Sax.* III. [IV.] ii. II. 39 These watery sovereigns [the sea-kings of the North], who..flourished in the plunder of the sea and its shores. **1803** SIR A. BOSWELL *Spirit of Tintoc* To Rdr., These seem to have had perfect effect on the *watery* spirit Kelpy, but none on the ethereal demons of Tintoc.

c. as an epithet of heavenly bodies, portents, seasons, etc., which are thought to bring rain.

c **1400** tr. *Secreta Secret., Gov. Lordsh.* 86 Whenne þe mone ys yn þe watery tokenynges. *c* **1440** *Astron. Cal.* (MS. Ashm. 391), þis signe is stedfaste septentrional..flewmatik and watri in kinde. *a* **1548** HALL *Chron., Hen. VIII*, 123 b, The sayd writers declared that this yere should be such Eclipses in watery signes, and suche coniunctions that by waters & fluddes many people should perishe. **1594** SHAKS. *Rich. III*, II. ii. 69 That I being gouern'd by the watrie Moone, May send forth plenteous teares to drowne the World. **1611** —— *Wint. T.* I. ii. 1 Nine Changes of the Watry-Starre. **1696** PHILLIPS (ed. 5), *Watry Triplicity*, the Signs so accounted, being cold and moist, are Gemini, Scorpio and Pisces. **1705** ADDISON *Italy, Bolonia* etc. 442 [tr. Claudian]..The Mourning Sisters weep in watry Signs. **1774** BRYANT *Mythol.* II. 341 The constellation of the Hyades..was a watry sign. **1818** J. TAYLOR *Antiq. Cur.* 156 Index, Swithin St., the watery saint. **1901** *Daily Chron.* 15 July 5/1 In France the watery saints' days are those of St. Médard (June 8) and St. Gervais and St. Protais (June 19).

d. *gen.*

watery way, journey, (one's) way or journey over the water: cf. 5.

a **1586** SIDNEY *Arcadia* I. xiv. §1 The table was set neere to an excellent water-worke... There were birds also made so finely, that they did not onely deceiue the sight with their figure, but the hearing with their songs; which the watrie instruments did make their gorge deliuer. **1622** J. TAYLOR (Water P.) *Farew. Tower-Bottles* A 4, When Vpland Tradesmen thus dares take in hand A wat'ry buis'nesse, they not vnderstand. **1697** DRYDEN *Æneis* v. 1 Mean time the Trojan cuts his watry way, Fix'd on his Voyage, thro the curling Sea. **1764** GOLDSM. *Trav.* 289 The firm connected bulwark..Spreads its long arms amidst the watery roar. **1810** SCOTT *Lady of Lake* II. xxvi, Now back they wend their watery way. **1859** DICKENS *Haunted Ho.* i. 7/2 Mr. Beaver.. proved to be an intelligent man, with a world of watery experiences in him. **1881** MISS BRADDON *Asphodel* I. 210 The Rector's wife heard of her niece's watery meanderings and gipsy breakfasts.

7. Of food: Containing too much moisture; tasting too much like water; thin, flavourless.

c **1440** *Pallad. on Husb.* I. 195 Olyuys..With drasty wattry fruyt. **1653** WALTON *Angler* vi. 136 The He Salmon..is more kipper..then the She is; yet she is..as watry and as bad meat. **1846** SOYER *Cookery* 451 Be careful they are not too much done, or they would go in purée and taste watery. **1871** B. TAYLOR *Faust* (1875) I. vi. 102 We're cooking watery soup for beggars.

b. Of a plant or its parts: Containing a large proportion of moisture.

1842 LOUDON *Suburban Hort.* 84 By greatly increasing the perspiration of the leaves and other parts of plants, wind renders them less watery. **1882** *Garden* 20 May 354/2 It rarely happens that we find a single watery shoot in a tree which requires pinchings to maintain the proper balance of the sap.

8. Of the eyes: **a.** Suffused with tears, tearful. Hence *transf.*, of weeping, lamentation, etc.

1447 BOKENAM *Seyntys, Magd.* 1003 Wyth wattry yhe The shypmen he preyid & yaf hem yiftys also. **1588** GREENE *Pandosto* Wks. (Grosart) IV. 264 Pandosto would once a day repaire to the Tombe, and there with watry plaintes bewaile his misfortune. **1591** SPENSER *M. Hubberd* 1362 With fained face, and watrie eyne halfe weeping. *a* **1631** DONNE *Lament. Jer.* iii. 48 With watry rivers doth mine eye oreflow. **1837** LOCKHART *Scott* IV. xi. 356 The Royal Exile surveyed it with a flushed cheek and a watery eye. **1855** THACKERAY *Newcomes* xxvi, Little Rosey and her mother sobbed audibly,..to the surprise of..Miss Honeyman, who had no idea of such watery exhibitions. **1861** DICKENS *Gt. Expect.* vii, Joe's blue eyes turned a little watery.

b. Exuding moisture, as a result of weakness or disease in the lachrymal glands. ***watery eye*** = EPIPHORA I.

c **1460** J. RUSSELL *Bk. Nurture* 282 in *Babees-bk.* 134 Glowtynge ne twynkelynge with youre y3e, ne..watery, wynkynge, ne droppynge, but of sight clere. **1486** *Bk. St. Albans* b ij, An hauke that is broght vp vnder a Bussard or a Puttock: as mony be: hath wateri Eyghen. **1601** HOLLAND *Pliny* XXI. xix. II. 103 But a peculiar vertue they [violets] have besides to stay the running and waterie eyes. **1799** UNDERWOOD *Dis. Childhood* (ed. 4) II. 35 [Ophthalmia] will sometimes degenerate into what is termed the watery eye... There is, however, a case of watery-eye attending older children, in which the discharge is very hot and acrid. **1843** R. J. GRAVES *Syst. Clin. Med.* xxv. 309 His eyes became very red, watery, and intolerant of light.

9. Of the skin, part of the body: Exuding, or suffused with, a humour or moisture resembling water. †Hence in names of diseases, as ***watery mouth, itch; watery head*** = HYDROCEPHALUS. Cf. also 8 b.

a **1425** tr. *Arderne's Treat. Fistula*, etc. 50 þe watry placez I enoynted with ane oyntement made of blak sope, and poudre of sulphur. **1523–34** FITZHERB. *Husb.* §55 Yf the skynne be of ruddy colour and drye, than is he sounde, and if it be pale coloured and watrye, thanne is he rotten. **1697** J. LEWIS *Mem. Dk. Glocester* (1789) 50 The Duke was not the stoutest child, and had been subject to a watry mouth, which now grew better. **1728** CHAMBERS *Cycl.*, *Hydrocephalus*,..a watery Head, or Dropsy in the Head. **1818–20** E. THOMPSON tr. *Cullen's Nosol.* (ed. 3) 331 *Scabies lymphatica*, or watery itch. **1820** GOOD *Nosol.* 490 Scabies.. Vesicularis. Eruption of larger..vesicles filled with a transparent fluid... Watery Itch. **1890** *Retrospect Med.* CII. 172 The brain was watery, the veins turgid.

10. *fig.* Of thought, feeling, literary or artistic composition, persons, etc.: Vapid, washy, poor, thin.

a **1225** *Ancr. R.* 376 þe heorte, þet was wateri, smecchles, and ne uelede no sauur of God. **1605** BACON *Adv. Learn.* I. iv. §2 Then grew the flowing, and watrie vaine of Osorius the Portugall Bishop to be in price. **1673** HICKERINGILL *Greg. F. Greybeard* 183 A loose, flashy, watery memory that will hold no print. **1843** CARLYLE *Past & Pr.* II. ii. (1858) 109 Through the thin watery gossip of our Jocelin, we do get some glimpses of that deep-buried Time. **1851** TENNYSON *Edwin Morris* 128 Slight Sir Robert with his watery smile And educated whisker. **1858** G. MACDONALD *Phantastes* x. (1878) 151 New cataracts of watery melodies. **1875** JOWETT *Plato* (ed. 2) III. 204 Do not tell me that justice is duty..for that sort of watery stuff will not do for me. **1904** M. HEWLETT *Queen's Quair* II. vi. 265 She would calculate as she listened..to what extent she might serve herself yet of this watery fool. **1904** *Times Lit. Suppl.* 1 Apr. 104/1 A watery but harmless story of London society.

11. *Her.* (See quot.)

1486 [see UNDATED *a.* 1]. **1572** [see UNDADIE *a.*]. *c* **1828** BERRY *Encycl. Her.* I. Gloss., *Watery*. This term sometimes occurs, and is used in the same sense as *wavy*, or *undée*.

12. *Comb.* in parasynthetic adjs.

1568 SKEYNE *Pest* (1860) 13 Vrine..first vaterie colourit, thairefter of bilious colour. **1683** *Lond. Gaz.* No. 1805/4 A Sorrel Nag,..watery Eyed. **1785** GROSE *Dict. Vulgar T.*, *Watery headed*, apt to shed tears. **1883** *Harper's Mag.* Apr. 697/1 The..rubicund-visaged watery-eyed driver.

water-zoutch *v.*: see WATER-SOUCHY.

Watford ('wɒtfəd). The name of a town on the N.W. edge of the London conurbation, used with allusion to the view attributed to Londoners that north of the metropolis there is nothing of any significance to English national or cultural life.

1973 G. TALBOT *Ten Seconds from Now* (1974) iii. 37 A man who, until he made the journey from London, thought that woad began at Watford. **1977** *Times* 17 Jan. 13/6 As an Englishman from north of Watford I sometimes suspect that the harmony [in Turkey] is..greater than..between different regional and social sectors in this country. **1980** D. WILLIAMS *Murder for Treasure* ii. 17 'Provincial visitors'.. broadly covered anyone normally domiciled north of Watford. **1983** *Oxford Diocesan Mag.* July 13/2 The urgent need is to unite the country... This does not mean watery consensus politics. It does mean recognising that..Britain does not end at Watford. **1984** *Sunday Tel.* 21 Oct. 9/6 Yorkshire is becoming the most militant county in England. .. There's the rub. The line between North and South is not just drawn at Watford. Scargill is of the South.

wath. *Obs.* exc. *dial.* Also (1 wæð), 5 wadth, wat(t)he, 6 *erron.* warthe, 6– *erron.* warth. [a. ON. *vað* neut. (MSw. *vaþ*, Sw., Da. *vad*) = OE. *wæd* (pl. *wado*), *poet.* the sea, the waves, MLG. *wat* (*wad-*), Du. *wad*, OHG. *wat*:—OTeut. **waðo-m*:—pre-Teut. **wadho-m* = L. *vadum*; cogn. w. WADE *v.*] A ford; a fordable stream.

In quot. *c* 1100 used as the proper name of the river Forth.

[*c* **1100** *O.E. Chron.* (MS. D.) an. 1073 Wyllelm..þæt land on þa sæ healfe mid scypum ymb læi3 & him sylf mid his landfyrde ferde inn ofer þæt Wæð (*Laud MS.* þæt 3ewæd)]. *c* **1450** *St. Cuthbert* (Surtees) 5757 þe watir þat time was farr ebband;..But or he was þe wath all past, The wawes come agayne him fast. *c* **1475** *Pict. Voc.* in Wr.-Wülcker 799/41 *Hoc vadum*, a wadth. **1483** *Cath. Angl.* 410/1 A wathe, *vadum, flustrum*. **1570** LEVINS *Manip.* 38/40 A watthe, foorde, *vadum*. **1583** *Inquis. Sewers Linc.* (1851) 12 That the Township of Burringham in making their warthes or fordes over the aforesaid dytches do not cast in more sand then is needful for passage of their cattell into the Northmoores. **1610** in *N. Riding Rec.* (1884) I. 204 Forasmuch as Skipton bridge..is likely to..become ruinous by..carriages of great burthen,..a ford or wath is there made passable for such purposes. **1674** RAY *N.C. Words* s.v., A Warth; a Waterford. **1691** —— *Gloss. Northanhymb.* s.v., A Wath. Vadum. **1697** DE LA PRYME *Diary* (Surtees) 153 From thence I went over a wath, which tradition says was formerly a great river. **1730** P. WALKDEN *Diary* 4 May (1866) 115 Then came over a corner of Ellhill moor as direct as I could to Wire and over it at a warth. **1825** BROCKETT *N.C. Gloss.*, *Wath, warth*, a water-ford. **1890** R. S. FERGUSON *Hist. Cumbld.* 270 They tried to evade that fortress by taking to the waths over Eden, between Carlisle and the sea. **1894** *Carlisle Patriot* 15 June 7/3 (*Cumbld. Gloss.*) The new bridge over the Kingwater will stand on the site of the wall at the place of the ford or wath.

b. *Comb.*, as ***wath gate*** (GATE *sb.*[2]), ***mouth, way***. Also WATHSTEAD.

1662 DUGDALE *Imbanking & Drayning* 201/1 That the Prior of Haverholme ought to find a certain boat at the Bothe, neer to the Wathe mouthe, for to carry over foot-folk, aswell by night as day. **1876** *Whitby Gloss.* s.v., 'Wath-geeat,' the direction of the ford. **1905** *Eng. Dial. Dict.* s.v., Wath-way, a ford. (East Lincolnshire.)

wath(e: see WAITH *sb.*[1], WHAT, WOTHE.

wather, obs. form of WEATHER, WHETHER.

'wathstead. *dial.* Also 7 warstead. [f. WATH + STEAD *sb.*; cf. Da. *vadested.*] A ford.

1615 *Quarter Sess. Rec.* 9 Jan. in *N. Riding Rec.* (1884) II. 112 [A presentment of] Rob. Spaunton..for digging of a pitt in a wath-stead, called Crooke-holme Wath, whereby men cannot passe. **1691** RAY *N.C. Words* (ed. 2), *Warstead*; used in that sense [i.e. a water-ford]. **1877** *N.W. Linc. Gloss.*, *Wath, Wath-stead*, a ford.

watier, watir, obs. forms of WATER.

†**'watkin.** *Obs.* [f. WAT[2] + -KIN.] A hare.

1585 SHARROCK tr. *Ocland's Notable Battles Eng. Nation* D j b, When as the watchfull grayhound hath a wattkin spied, full faine He springeth on, his pray to get.

Watling-street ('wɒtlɪŋstriːt). Forms: 1 Wæclinga-, Wæxling(g)a-, Wætlinga-, Weatlinga-stræ̆t, 2 Watlingestrate, 3 Watelinge stret, 4 Wat(e)lynge-, 5 Watlyn-, 5 Wadlyng-, Wattelynge-, 6 *Sc.* Vadland-, 6 Watlyng-, 6– Watling-. [OE. *Wæclinga stræ̆t*; the first word, app. the genit. pl. of the name of a (real or imaginary) family or clan, occurs also in *Wæclinga ceaster* ('the Wæclings' city'), the OE. name of the Roman-British Verulamium (now St. Albans), through which the 'Watling-street' passes.

The forms with *tl* for *cl*, which have been universal from the 12th c., are all but non-existent in MSS. of pre-Conquest date; a solitary example is *Wætlinga ceaster* in *OE. Martyrology, St. Alban*, 22 June (MS. Cott. Julius A. x. fol. 112, written *c* 975). The change of *Wæclinga* into *Wætlinga* can hardly be due to the close resemblance of *c* and *t* in OE. script (though many instances of the latter form in modern editions of OE. texts are mere editorial misreadings), because the existence of sense 2 seems to show that the name of the Roman road was preserved in popular and not merely literary tradition. Perhaps the word may have been assimilated to the *Wætlinga* which occurs in the place-name Watlington (Oxon and Norf.).

The Wæclings may have been either an actual family that had obtained possession of the site of Verulamium, or a dynastic family celebrated in Mercian tradition, to whom, as typifying remote antiquity, the road and the city were attributed by popular fancy. It has been suggested that *Wæclinga ceaster* is a corruption of *Werlama ceaster*, an alternative OE. name of Verulamium (*Uæclingacestir siue Uerlamacester*, Bæda *H.E.* I. vii), which is an adoption of the British name in a later form; but the conjecture is untenable.]

1. The English name given in pre-Conquest times to the Roman road running from near London through St. Albans to Wroxeter; by antiquarian writers from the 12th c. onwards extended to Roman roads leading from London to the S.E. and from Wroxeter to the north or west.

The places mentioned in OE. charters as situated on or near the 'Wæclinga-stræt' are: Hampstead; Chalgrave (Beds.); Stowe (Bucks.); Weedon (Northants); Aston (close to Wroxeter): see Birch *Cart. Sax.* Nos. 1309, 659, 986, 792, 1315. According to Henry of Huntingdon (*died* 1154) the Watling-street extended from Canterbury to Chester; according to Robert of Gloucester (*c* 1290) from Dover to Chester; according to Higden (*c* 1340) from Dover to Wroxeter and thence to Cardigan. Modern writers usually assign Dover or Richborough and Chester as the terminal points; but some apply the name Watling-street to the road running northwards from Wroxeter through Lancashire.

c885 *Treaty of Alfred & Guthrum* (MS. 12th c.) in Liebermann *AS. Laws* I. 126 Đonne up on Usan oð Wætlingastræt. **926** *Charter of Æthelstan* in Birch *Cartul. Sax.* II. 335 (Boundaries of Chalgrave, Beds.) Đær se dic sceot in wæclinga stræte, anlanges wæxlinga stræte..æft dice in wæxlingga strate. **a1118** FLORENCE OF WORCESTER *Chron.* an. 1012 (1848) I. 166 In septentrionali plaga Weatlinga-strætæ, id est, strata quam filii Weatlæ regis,.. per Angliam straverunt. **a1154** HEN. HUNTINGDON *Hist. Angl.* I. §7 Tertius [*sc.* callis] est ex transverso a Dorobernia in Cestriam..et vocatur Watlingestrate. **1297** R. GLOUC. (Rolls) 174 From douere in to chestre tilleþ watelinge stret. **c1340** HIGDEN *Polychr.* (Rolls) II. 44 Secunda via principalis dicitur Watlingstrete. **a1552** LELAND *Itin.* (1907) I. 10 Wedon..stondith hard by the famose way, there communely caullid of the people Watheling Strete. **1612** DRAYTON *Poly-olb.* xiii. 312 That Crosse Where those two mightie waies, the Watling and the Fosse, Our Center seeme to cut. (The first doth hold her way, From Douer, to the farth'st of fruitfull Anglesey.) **1725** DE FOE *Tour Gr. Brit.* II. iv. 117 The great antient Road or Way call'd Watling-Street, which comes from London to this Town [Shrewsbury], and goes on from hence to the utmost Coast of Wales.

b. Erroneously applied to other Roman roads.

Leland, e.g., applies the name to the Ermine-street in Lincolnshire, and to several distinct roads in Yorkshire. At the present day the name is very generally given to the road running from York through Corbridge into Scotland.

?**c1500** *Gest of Robyn Hode* ccix. in Child *Ballads* III. 66 'Take thy bowe in thy hande', sayde Robyn,..'And walk vp vnder the Sayles, And to Watlynge-strete'. **a1552** LELAND *Itin.* (1907) I. 32 At the north ende of this village [*sc.* Marton, Lincs.] lyithe the commune way of Watheling Streat to Dancaster. *Ibid.* 39, 43, 44, 98, V. 146. **1767** PERCY *Reliques* (ed. 2) I. 24 *note*, Otterbourn stands near the old Watling street road. **1884** *Encycl. Brit.* XVII. 568 (art. *Northumberland*) The Roman road from London nearly bisects the country, and still goes familiarly under the name of 'the Watling Street'.

c. The name of a street in the City of London, in the 16–17th c. the principal street for drapers' shops.

1569 PRESTON *Cambyses* F 3 b, I beleeue all [the] cloth in Watling street, to make gowns would not serue. **1603** STOW *Surv. Lond.* 84 The Drapers..are seated in Candlewick-streete, and Watheling streete. *Ibid.* 348 Then for Watheling streete, which Leyland calleth Atheling or Noble streete; but since he sheweth no reason why, I rather take it to be so named of the great high way of the same calling... At this present, the inhabitants thereof are wealthy Drapers, retailors of woollen cloathes..more then in any one streete of this citie. **1614** J. COOKE *Greene's Tu Quoque* D 2 b, *Sta.* That I should liue to be a seruing-man..the seruing-man.. weares broad-cloth, and yet dares walke Watling-streete, without any feare of his Draper.

†**2.** The Milky Way, galaxy. *Obs.*

The Milky Way received other popular names from famous highways, esp. pilgrimage routes. In England it was called *Walsingham way*, in Italy *Strada di Roma*. A widespread designation of this kind was *the Way of St. James* (of Compostella); so It. *Via di santo Jacopo* (Dante *Convivio* II. xv), Sp. *Via de Santiago*.

c1384 CHAUCER *H. Fame* II. 431 Se yonder loo the Galoxie ..Somme parfeye Kallen hyt watlynge strete. **1398** TREVISA *Barth. de P.R.* VIII. xxxii. (Tollemache MS.) It semeþ þat þey [*sc.* comets] ben in þat cercle, þat is calde Lacteus, and Galaxia, also Watelynge strete. **c1460** *Towneley Myst.* xxx. 126 *Secundus demon.* let vs go to this dome vp watlyn strete. **c1480** HENRYSON *Orpheus* 71 He..passit to the hevin..To seke his wyf..By wadlyng strete he went but tarying. **1483** *Cath. Angl.* 410/2 Wattelynge strete, *lactea, galaxias, vel galaxia*. **1513** DOUGLAS *Æneis* III. viii. 22 Arthuris huyfe, and Hyades betaiknand rane, Syne Watling streit..and the Charle wane. **1549** *Compl. Scot.* vi. 58 The quhyt circle callit circulus lacteus, the quhilk the marynalis callis vatland streit. **1551** [see MILKY WAY 1]. **1563** FULKE *Meteors* III. (1571) 38 The mylke waye called of some the waye to saint Iames and Watlyng streate. **1590** T. HOOD *Use Celestial Globe* 40 By vs..it is called The milke way: some in sporting manner doe call it Watling streete.

watmol, obs. form of WADMAL.

watna ('wɒtnə), *v. Sc.* [f. *wat* Sc. form of WOT *v.* + NA *adv.*[3]] (I) know not. Hence **watnawhat** *sb.*, a 'don't know what', a nondescript.

1725 RAMSAY *Gent. Sheph.* IV. ii, Sir William's cruel, that wad force his son For watna-whats, sae great a risk to run. **1818** SCOTT *Hrt. Midl.* xvi, He's been a soldier, and he has been a play-actor, and I watna what he has been or hasna been.

watre, obs. form of WATER *sb.* and *v.*

watsail, obs. form of WASSAIL.

watschoed, watshed, obs. forms of WETSHOD.

Watson[1] ('wɒtsən). The name of the doctor who was the stolid, faithful assistant and foil to the detective Sherlock Holmes in the stories of A. Conan Doyle, used allusively of one who acts similarly as a stooge or audience, esp. for a detective.

1927 R. A. KNOX *Three Taps* vi. 52 Watson-work meant that Angela tried to suggest new ideas to her husband under a mask of carefully assumed stupidity. **1946** D. L. SAYERS *Unpopular Opinions* 188 The story is told by the detective's *fidus Achates* or (to use the modern term) his Watson. **1953** WODEHOUSE *Performing Flea* 18, I wonder what an oesteopath does if a patient suddenly comes apart in his hands. ('Quick, Watson, the seccotine!'). **1958** B. HAMILTON *Too Much of Water* x. 228 I've been..a sort of yes-man or Watson to him. **a1976** A. CHRISTIE *Autobiogr.* (1977) v. v. 282, I was..tied to two people: Hercule Poirot and his Watson, Captain Hastings. **1981** CRAIG & CADOGAN *Lady Investigates* ii. 48 Mrs Lucilla Wiggins, the 'Watson' figure in the cases of Mrs Herlock Shomes.

Watson[2] ('wɒtsən). *Austral.* [Allegedly the name of two Australian brothers who were noted betters about the turn of the century: cf. S. J. Baker *Austral. Lang.* (ed. 2, 1966) xii. 273–4.] In catch-phr. ***to bet like the Watsons***: to wager large sums.

1949 L. GLASSOP *Lucky Palmer* 163 Bet well? You bet like the Watsons. **1954** T. RONAN *Vision Splendid* 76 The survey-party is chequed-up to the skies and while they've got it they'll bet like the Watsons. **1967** F. HARDY *Billy Borker yarns Again* 140 I'd bet like the Watsons meself if I had a million quid in the bank.

Watson-Crick (ˌwɒtsən'krɪk). *Biochem.* The names of James D. *Watson* (b. 1928), U.S. biochemist, and Francis H. C. *Crick* (b. 1916), English biochemist, used *attrib.* with reference to the pairing of adenine with thymine (or uracil) and of guanine with cytosine in the two strands of a double helix, described by them in 1953.

1964 G. H. HAGGIS et al. *Introd. Molecular Biol.* ix. 229 The Watson-Crick pairs are purine-pyrimidine pairs. **1966** T. H. JUKES *Molecules & Evolution* i. 5 When cells divide and multiply, this sequence [of bases in DNA] replicates itself enzymatically through the Watson–Crick complementary pairing mechanism. **1976** *Nature* 23 Sept. 289/1 Much of the pairing at the third codon position also involves the normal Watson-Crick base pairs, A–U, and G–C, but for several codon-tRNA interactions, non-Watson-Crick pairs are clearly required.

watsonia (wɒt'səʊnɪə). *Bot.* Also **Watsonia.** [mod.L. (P. Miller *Gardener's Dict.* (ed. 7, 1759) s.v.), f. the name of Sir William *Watson* (1715–87), Scottish naturalist + -IA[1].] A bulbous plant of the genus of this name (family Iridaceæ), native to South Africa and bearing spikes of white, pink, or red flowers similar to gladioli.

1801 *Curtis's Bot. Mag.* XV. 533 (*heading*) Aletris-like Watsonia. **1843** M. EDGEWORTH *Lett. from Eng.* (1971) 595 The most beautiful flowers..Gladiolis and red and white Watsonia. **1902** L. H. BAILEY *Cycl. Amer. Hort.* IV. 1971/1 Great interest has been aroused in Watsonias recently. **1948** A. PATON *Cry, Beloved Country* I. iii. 20 Here..grow the blue agapanthus, the wild watsonia, and the red-hot poker. **1971** P. M. SYNGE *Collins Guide to Bulbs* (ed. 2) 308 All watsonias are easily raised from seed.

Watsonian (wɒt'səʊnɪən), *a.* [f. the surname *Watson* + -IAN.] Of, pertaining to, or characteristic of someone called Watson; *spec.* **a.** J. B. Watson (1878–1958), U.S. behavioural psychologist; **b.** Dr. Watson of the Sherlock Holmes stories (see WATSON[1]).

a. 1923 K. DUNLAP *Old & New Viewpoints in Psychol.* (1925) ii. 54 'Behaviorism' now means the Watsonian view exclusively. **1927** B. RUSSELL *Outl. Philos.* iii. 41 His [*sc.* the ape's] behaviour when he had once realised that one stick could be made by joining the two was scarcely Watsonian. **1928** R. FROST *Let.* 22 June (1964) 188 The logic of religion by nice gradations outside of Catholicism in Protestantism, outside of Protestantism in agnosticism, and finally outside of agnosticism in Watsonian behaviorism. **1960** [see REINFORCEMENT 3 c]. **1968** P. MCKELLAR *Experience & Behav.* viii. 218 The stultifying limitation which Watsonian behaviourism imposed upon psychology. **1983** *Brit. Jrnl. Psychol.* LXXIV. 301 Certain influential modern psychologists have singled out attention as an aspect of cognition that fell early to the Watsonian onslaught.

b. 1940 E. BENTLEY *Those Days* ix. 250 Its [*sc.* the Sherlock Holmes Society's] annual dinners..were followed by discussions on points of Watsonian chronology. **1960** *Encounter* Mar. 66/2 Just one more case of Watsonian blackmail. **1968** *Listener* 4 July 22/1 What the elements of magic in the Holmes stories were, and are, I have never seen analysed. The stilted Watsonian style of sentence structure must be one major element. **1981** CRAIG & CADOGAN *Lady Investigates* i. 32 There is no Watsonian colleague to..assist with her cases.

watstone, obs. form of WHETSTONE.

watt (wɒt). *Physics.* [f. name of James *Watt* (1736–1819), the inventor of the modern steam-engine, and a pioneer in the science of energy.]

a. A unit of activity or power (used chiefly with reference to electricity), corresponding to 10^7 ergs of work per second, to the rate of work represented by a current of one ampere under the pressure of one volt, or to $\frac{1}{746}$ (= ·00134) English horse-power.

1882 SIEMENS in *Rep. Brit. Assoc.*, Presid. Addr. 6 The other unit I would suggest adding to the list is that of power. The power conveyed by a current of an Ampère through the difference of potential of a Volt is the unit consistent with the practical system. It might be appropriately called a Watt, in honour of..James Watt... A Watt, then, expresses the rate of an Ampère multiplied by a Volt, whilst a horse-power is 746 Watts, and a Cheval de Vapeur 735. **1882** *Athenæum* 2 Sept. 310/2 Two of his [Dr. Siemen's] units were unanimously approved—namely, (1) the watt, which is the rate of doing work when a current of one ampere passes through a resistance of one ohm, [etc.]. **1886** THURSTON in *Jrnl. Frankl. Inst.* Oct. 265 It was judged that it might have been driven up to 300,000 watts with safety. **1887** *Rep. Brit. Assoc.* 208 The Watt is defined to be the work done per second by the ampère passing between two points between which the difference of electrical potential is one volt. **1889** *Telegr. Jrnl. & Electr. Rev.* 13 Dec. 665/2 The A type of Sunbeam lamp required only 2 watts per candle-power as compared with $3\frac{1}{2}$ watts for the Edison-Swann lamp.

b. *Comb.*: **watt-hour**, the work done by one watt in one hour; **wattmeter**, an instrument for measuring electric energy; **watt-second**, a unit of energy equal to one joule, being the energy consumed at a rate of one watt during one second; hence (abbreviated as) **wattsec.**

1887 AYRTON *Pract. Electr.* 444 By the employment, however, of a 'wattmeter,' it is possible to measure the watts directly. **1888** *Pall Mall Gaz.* 24 Jan. 11/2 With 4,500 lamps of 16 candle-power,..at a charge of $\frac{1}{2}$*d.* per lamp per hour, or eightpence per Board of Trade unit of 1,000 Watt hours.. the income would be £11,250, irrespective of [etc.]. **1892** J. SWINBURNE in *Min. Proc. Inst. Civ. Engin.* CX. 15 The ordinary wattmeter as used in continuous-current work consists of a fixed and movable coil. **1893** G. KAPP *Dynamos, Alternators, Transformers* ii. 42 This unit [*sc.* the erg] is also inconveniently small, and for practical purposes it is customary to employ a unit 10,000,000 times as great—namely, the 'watt-second' or 'joule'. **1907** E. WILSON & LYDALL *Electr. Traction* I. 379 This can be converted into watt hours per ton mile thus. **1907** *Athenæum* 20 July 74/3 Mr. J. T. Irwin gave a demonstration of the uses of his hot-wire oscillographs and hot-wire wattmeters. **1962** *New Scientist* 18 Jan. 157/1 The term 'wattsec' is..a common one among radio engineers while 'joule' appears to be seldom used in practice. **1981** *Sci. Amer.* Dec. 37/1 A photon with a frequency in the visible region of the electromagnetic spectrum has little energy: less than 10^{-19} joule, or watt-second.

watt(e, obs. ff. WAIT, WAT, WET, WOT *v.*

wattage ('wɒtɪdʒ). [f. WATT + -AGE.] **a.** An amount of electrical power, esp. the operating power of a lamp, appliance, etc., expressed in watts; *colloq.*, electricity, electrical illumination.

1903 *Electr. World & Engineer* 27 June 1095 Dividing the kilowatt-hours mentioned by said number of lamps shows an average per lamp at station of 463·8 watts, deducting from which 9 per cent. for line loss, shows a net wattage per lamp at lamp terminal of 422. **1933** *Times* 5 Dec. (Electricity Supply Suppl.) p. xxiii/1 Employing lamps of comparatively low wattage. **1953** J. CARY *Except the Lord* xviii. 81 The quivering lanterns, the jumping flames..gave an elation to our saturnalia that would not have been kindled by frigid festoons of wattage. **1962** L. DEIGHTON *Ipcress File* xxv. 165 A light of low wattage glowed in the main hall. **1976** A. HOPE *Hi-Fi Handbk.* 29 That's a fairly reasonable minimum wattage rating per channel for a stereo amplifier. **1977** *Time* 21 Nov. 49/1 This Christmas may well burn record wattage. **1984** *Verbatim* Summer 4/2 From the ceiling hang bare light bulbs of such low wattage that the interior is scarcely discernible.

b. *fig.*

1964 *Listener* 10 Dec. 952/1 Peter Cushing's stolip Churchill was thrown in the shade by the high wattage of this acting. **1980** D. FRANCIS *Reflex* xvii. 199 She had a powerful attraction..with the full wattage switched my way.

wattar, obs. Sc. form of WATER.

wattchett, var. WATCHET.

Watteau ('wɒtəʊ, ‖vato). The name of Antoine *Watteau* (1684–1721), a French painter, used *attrib.* in ***Watteau school, Watteau-like*** adj.; also in designations of articles of female costume similar to those represented in Watteau's pictures, as ***Watteau hat***; **Watteau back**, an arrangement of the back of a dress with a broad pleat falling from the neck to the extremity of the skirt without being gathered in at the waist; **Watteau bodice**, a bodice with square opening at the neck and short ruffled sleeves; **Watteau mantle**, a kind of cloak having a Watteau back and other details imitated from Watteau's pictures; **Watteau pleat** (and *ellipt.* Watteau, watteau), the pleat of a Watteau back. Hence **'Watteauish** *a.*, resembling the style of Watteau.

1833 LAMB *Elia* Ser. II. *Barrenness Mod. Art*, This is well, and Watteauish. **1849** THACKERAY *Sk. & Trav.* Wks. 1900 VI. 668 Watteau-like groups in shot silks. **1864** MISS A. B. EDWARDS *Barbara's Hist.* xxvi, The old designs, of a bastard Watteau school, had been lately removed. **1873** *Young Englishwoman* Oct. 490/2, I have made a Princesse dress with a Watteau pleat and flounce of eleven yards of print. **1887** *Brit. Textile Warehouseman* 15 Sept. 70/1 The back fits the figure, but has a full Watteau pleat down the centre, fastened in at the waist, and then flowing in easy folds to the hem. **1891** *Daily News* 12 Dec. 3/1 From the shoulders at the back hung a long Watteau of the richest cut jet. **1899** *Westm. Gaz.* 22 June 3/2 Next week I shall give drawings of an Empire and a Watteau hat. *Ibid.* 23 Nov. 3/1 A heliotrope cashmere tea-gown, made with a Watteau back and a long straight front of silk.

Watteauesque (wɒtəʊ'ɛsk), *a.* [f. WATTEAU + -ESQUE.] Suggestive of or in the style of Watteau.

1925 *Glasgow Herald* 25 Apr. 8/3 Opposite might hang a Watteauesque diversion representing an impossibly light and brilliantly fanciful landscape. **1966** N. MARSH *Black Beech & Honeydew* xi. 256 *Twelfth Night* seemed to work its own miracle... Feste, all frill and Watteauesque stripes, was enchantingly realised. **1974** *Country Life* 7 Feb. 257/1 Throughout the decade 1720–30 Mercier both painted and engraved Watteauesque subjects.

wattel(l, watter: see WATTLE, WATER.

watthe, obs. form of WATH.

†**wattins**, *sb. pl. Obs.* [Cf. F. *ouate*: see WAD *sb.*[1]] ? = *waddings*, WADDING *vbl. sb.* 3.

1690 SIR J. FOULIS *Acc. Bk.* (S.H.S.) 130 To Ja. arbuthnot for silk and wattins to my black coat sleeves, 0 6 6.

wattkin, variant of WATKIN.

wattle ('wɒt(ə)l), *sb.*[1] Forms: 1 watul, *pl.* watla (*North.*), watelas; 4 wattel, 5 wattyl(le, 6 wattill, *Anglo-Irish* vattill (*Sc. pl.* vatlis), 6–7 wattell, 7 wadle, 9 *dial.* waddle, 6– wattle. [OE. *watul* (not found in other Teut. langs.) of uncertain origin, but app. cogn. w. *wætla*, (? *wǽtla*) bandage for a wound (*Sax. Leechdoms* II. 208).

It may possibly represent O.Teut. **waðlo-z* (with irregular treatment of the dental before liquid as in BOTTLE *sb.*[1], BOTTOM *sb.*):—pre-Teut. **wodhlo-s*, f. **wodh-* (: **wedh-*) to intertwine, plait, see weave: WEED *sb.* If so, it may correspond to mod.G. dial. *wadel* brushwood (see Grimm's *Deutsches Wb.* XIII. 2821, s.v. *Wedel.*]

I. 1. a. In *plural* and *collect. sing.* Rods or stakes, interlaced with twigs or branches of trees, used to form fences and the walls and roofs of buildings. Also, rods and branches of trees collected for this purpose.

c **900** *Bæda's Hist.* III. xvi. (1890) 202 And micelne ad ʒesomnade on beamum and on raftrum and on waʒum and on watelum [mistransl. of L. *parietum virgeorum*] and on ðeacon. *c* **950** *Lindisf. Gosp.* Luke v. 19 Astiʒon..onufa hus ðerh ða watla [*c* **1000** *Ags. Gosp.* þurh þa watelas; Vulg. *per tegulas*]. *a* **1000** in Napier *OE. Glosses* ii. 489 *Tegulis*, watelum. *c* **1000** ÆLFRIC *Gloss.* IX. xxvi. (Z) 52/13 *Teges*, watul. **1382** *Durham Halm. Rolls* (Surtees) 175 Habebit meremium..et virg. et wattels, cabul., et ferramenta. **1453–4** *Durham Acc. Rolls* (Surtees) 150, j fothr' de palis et virgis et j fothr' del Wattylle. **1488–9** *Finchale Priory* (Surtees) p. ccclxxxii, Et in adquisitione wattyllis et cariagio straminis et wattyllis iiij^s^. x^d^. **1510** *Galway Archives* in *10th Rep. Hist. MSS. Comm.* App. v. 394 Anny man to bring in wode, troffe, or vattill. **1547–8** *Burgh Rec. Stirling* (1887) 52 And the remanent of the said tenement..standand sufficiently in gret tymmer..and in kaboris, wattillis and stray, thak and devot, sobirly apperand watir ticht. **1563** in *Reg. Mag. Sig. Scot.* 1567, 444/2 Colligere *lie vatlis et fallyne tymmer* de dicta silva pro reparatione et edificatione domorum. **1586** HOOKER *Hist. Irel.* in *Holinshed* II. 12/1 And there they cast a trench, and builded a little castell or hold, with turffes and wattell. **1632** LITHGOW *Trav.* (1906) 374 These Fabrickes are advanced three or foure yardes high,..erected in a singular Frame, of smoake-torne straw ..and Raine-dropping watles. **1633** STAFFORD *Pac. Hib.* III. viii. 313 Having all the day before employed a great partie of men to the Wood..to fetch more wattle, to make Gabions. **1699** DAMPIER *Voy.* II. I. 43 The Walls are either Mud, or Watle bedawbed over. **1834** PRINGLE *Afr. Sk.* vi. 218 Stretching a large tree across it [*sc.* the path]..and fastening it with thongs and wattles at either end. **1836** THIRLWALL *Greece* III. xx. 146 Layers of stiff clay, pressed down close on wattles of reed. **1851–62** D. WILSON *Preh. Ann.* II. IV. i. 189 The earliest British churches were built of wattles. **1867** TENNYSON *Holy Grail* 63 And there he built with wattles from the marsh A little lonely church in days of yore. **1868** MILMAN *St. Paul's* ii. 21 Its growth..from enclosures of wattel and timber to stately buildings of stone. **1886** STEVENSON *Kidnapped* xxiii, The walls were of wattle and covered with moss.

b. wattle and daub (dab): interwoven twigs plastered with clay or mud, as a building material for huts, cottages, etc.; chiefly *attrib.* Also (rarely) ***daub and wattle, mud and wattle.***

1808 T. BATCHELOR *Agric. Bedford* 21 The cottages and barns..are built with wood frame work, and clay plaster upon a kind of hedge work of splints, which is called wattle and dab. **1836** ROSS *Hobart Town Almanack* 66 Wattle and daub. [Instructions for using the branches of the black or the green wattle (see sense 4 below) for this kind of construction.] **1852** W. WICKENDEN *Hunchback's Chest* 311 Strong wattle and daub walls. **1855** DICKENS etc. *Holly-tree Inn* iv. 26/1 Robinson..stood at the door of a considerable erection of wattle-and-dab. **1872–4** JEFFERIES *Toilers of Field* (1892) 183 One wall of the house..was only 'wattle and daub' (i.e., lath and plaster). **1883** OLIVE SCHREINER *Afr. Farm* II. iii, His house was a little square daub-and-wattle building. **1891** KIPLING *City Dreadf. Nt.* 36 There are no houses here—nothing but acres and acres, it seems, of foul wattle-and-dab huts. **1901** *Archæol. Jrnl.* (Instit.) Mar. 68 A light and simple erection of wattle-and-daub. **1913** *Engl. Rev.* Aug. 59, I saw the house, a mud and wattle rancho.

c. *attrib.* and *Comb.*, as ***wattle-canoe, -gate, -wall, -work***; †**wattle-silver**, some kind of feudal impost; **wattle-wood** *W. Indian* (see quot.).

1893 SIR W. W. HUNTER in Skrine *Life* (1901) 424 In the bay, the fishermen use the *wattle-canoes, or curraghs, which their ancestors used at the time of the Roman invasion. **1759** *Universal Chron.* 3–10 Feb. 45/3 The person who committed the robbery, by the help of a short ladder artfully spliced to a *Wattle-gate, set against a closet window, took out a pane of glass, [etc.]. **1263** in *Cal. Inquis. Post Mortem* (1904) I. 173 *Watelselver. **1271** *Ibid.* 253 [Customs called] Mortonefar', Watelselver, Wodelode, [etc.]. **1484** *Anc. Deed* 24 Dec. (P.R.O.) D. 1102 Withe certene Custume siluer to the foresaide Maner perteynyng callid Revesiluer Watel-siluer and Werkesiluer of the Tenauntez of Charletone [near Steyning, Sussex]. **1886** *Athenæum* 24 Apr. 556/3 These were generally huts built of logs or with *wattle-walls. **1864** GRISEBACH *Flora W. Ind. Isl.* 788 *Wattle-wood, *Lætia Thamnia*. **1860** H. MAYHEW *Upper Rhine* vi. 427 A city built out in the water, and surrounded with a thick *wattle-work of piles. **1878** KEARY *Dawn Hist.* ii. 30 The huts were made of wattle-work. **1900** BARING-GOULD *Bk. Dartmoor* 42 The Britons had brought with them their great aptitude for wattle-work.

2. A hurdle. *dial.*

1640 SOMNER *Antiq. Canterb.* 10 The Citizens after much suit to the Monks, prevailed with them..to sell them of their wood to make hurdles or wattles withall, for the defence of their City. **1681** WORLIDGE *Syst. Agric., Dict. Rust.* 334 Wattels also signify spleeted Gates or Hurdles. **1697** in *Sussex Archæol. Collect.* VI. 195 Two wagon Ropes three Rakes 00 04 00 Thirty wattelles 01 10 00. **1805** R. W. DICKSON *Pract. Agric.* II. 674 The flatted hurdle, or what in some districts is termed waddle, is much preferable to the close-rodded or wattled kind. **1822** COBBETT *Rur. Rides* (1885) I. 129 This hazle..furnishes rods wherewith to make fences; but its principal use is, to make wattles for the folding of sheep in the fields. **1857** HUGHES *Tom Brown* I. vii, The scent [in Hares-and-hounds] lies thick right across another meadow and into a ploughed field, where the pace begins to tell; then over a good wattle with a ditch on the other side. **1889** DOR. E. HURST *Horsham* (ed. 2) Gloss. 270 *Wattle*, a hurdle of a particular kind, made by weaving in long thin stems of underwood.

3. a. A wand, rod, stick. *dial.*

1570 LEVINS *Manip.* 38/26 A wattle, rod, *vibex*. **1726** SWIFT *Gulliver* IV. x, I..cut down several oak wattles, about the thickness of a walking-staff, and some larger pieces. [To build a canoe.] **1786** BURNS *Auld Farmer's Salut.* x, Nae whip nor spur, but just a wattle O' saugh or hazle. **1831** LOVER *Leg. & Stor. Irel., Paddy the Piper* 156, I cut a brave long wattle, that I might dhrive the man-ather iv a thief, as she was, without bein' near her at all at all. **1843** J. BALLANTINE *Wee Raggit Laddie* vi, Nae jockey's whup, nor drover's wattle Can frighten thee. **1846** J. KEEGAN *Leg. & Poems* (1907) 395 An old man..tottered with the aid of a long iron-shod wattle which he carried in his withered hand, to the door of a snug-looking public house. **1856** P. KENNEDY *Banks of Boro* xli. (1867) 337 Pat's wattle descended on the upper horizontal line of Charley's thigh.

b. *Comb.*: **wattle-boy** *Anglo-Irish* (see quot.); **wattle-race** *U.S.*, a Western form of 'running the gauntlet' (cf. GANTLOPE).

1832 BARRINGTON *Pers. Sk.* III. xx. 280 His reverence.. was instantly recognised by one of the wattle-boys, as the pikemen were then called. **1839** DUNCAN in *Congr. Globe* Jan., App. 104/2 It would have been like the wattle races I have seen run in the West; he that ran the fastest received the fewest stripes.

II. 4. a. *Australian.* [Originally *wattle-tree*, from the use of the long pliant branches for making wattled fences or wattle-and-daub buildings.] The common name in Australia for indigenous trees of the genus *Acacia*. Also with defining word indicating the particular species, as **black wattle**, *Acacia binervata* and *A. decurrens*; **broad-leaved, golden, green wattle**, *A. pycnantha*; **silver wattle**, *A. dealbata*; but the application of these (and other similar terms) varies according to locality.

The bark of most of these trees is valuable for use in tanning, and they exude a gum resembling gum arabic. The golden yellow flowers are celebrated for their beauty and fragrance.

The acacias were included in the Linnean genus *Mimosa*. Hence in popular use *mimosa* was long current as a synonym of *wattle*, and is still sometimes so used, at least in England. See MIMOSA 1 b.

[*c* **1810**: see *wattle-tree* in d.] **1828** P. CUNNINGHAM *N.S. Wales* I. 201 The acacias are the common wattles of this colony, their bark affording excellent tan. **1832** BISCHOFF *Van Diemen's Land* II. 23 The black and silver wattle..are trees used in housework and furniture. **1859** H. KINGSLEY *G. Hamlyn* xxiii, Fringed with black wattle and light-wood. *Ibid.* xliii, The sarsaparilla still hung in scant purple tufts on the golden wattle. **1863** *Technologist* III. 5 The gum of the black wattle (*Acacia mollissima*, Willd.)..is very inferior to it [*sc.* that of the silver wattle]. **1888** CANDISH *Whispering Voices* 45 And the wattle's yellow bloom Fills pure gales with rich perfume.

b. The flower of the wattle.

1867 A. G. MIDDLETON *Earnest* 132 The maidens were with golden wattles crowned.

c. = *wattle-bark*.

1893 *Advt.* in Morris *Austral Engl.* s.v. *Wattle-bark*, Bark. .. Bundled Black Wattle, superior, £5 to £6 per ton;.. chopped Black Wattle, £5 to £6. 5*s.* per ton. **1911** WEBSTER.

d. *attrib.* and *Comb.*, as ***wattle-bark, -bloom, -blossom, -bough, -cluster, -extract, -flower, -gloom, -gum, -scrub, -tree***; **wattle-gold** *poet.*, the golden-coloured flowers of the wattle.

1828 P. CUNNINGHAM *N.S. Wales* II. 106 The various *wattle-barks are used for tan. **1852** MORFIT *Tanning & Currying* 94 The leather tanned with wattle bark is of excellent quality, but highly coloured. **1890** A. SUTHERLAND *Short Poems* 84 Here, by the *wattle bloom silently laid, Life seems like a rapturous dream. **1896** KIPLING *Seven Seas, Song Engl., England's Answ.* 21 This for the waxen Heath, and that for the Wattle-bloom. **1894** A. ROBERTSON *Nuggets* 62 The honey was coming from the sack as clear as amber and smelling of *wattle-blossom. **1855** DICKENS etc. *Holly-tree Inn* iv. 29/2 Breaking off a small *wattle-bough to whisk the flies from his face. **1852** MUNDY *Antipodes* (1857) 87 A dense scrub of burnt *wattle-bushes about the height of hop-poles. **1889** SHERARD *Daughter of South* 23 Past the plundered *wattle-cluster, Bathed no longer in the lustre, Of its golden rain. **1955** *Times* 30 June 18/2 The price of South African *wattle extract remained the same during 1954 as it was during 1953 and 1952. **1969** T. C. THORSTENSEN *Pract. Leather Technol.* ix. 141 The main source of wattle extract is the *Acacia mollissima*, or Black Wattle. **1900** *Daily News* 9 Oct. 3/1 Something dainty, like the scent of the *wattle flower. **1867** GOODRICH *Angel-Beckoned* 9 Where the *wattle-glooms abound A little way below. **1870** A. L. GORDON *Bush Ballads* Ded. 41 In the Spring, when the *wattle gold trembles, 'Twixt shadow and shine. **1883** KEIGHLEY *Who are You* 54 My wealth has gone like the wattle gold You bound one day on my childish brow. **1863** *Technologist* III. 4 *Wattle Gum, the gum of the Silver Wattle (*Acacia dealbata*, Lindl.). **1865** H. KINGSLEY *Hillyars & Burtons* lii, 'Well! if this don't bang wattle gum', began Gerty. **1859** —— *G. Hamlyn* xxviii, They were passing through a narrow way in a *wattle scrub. *c* **1810** in *Trans. Linnean Soc.* (1827) XV. 328 One of my specimens.. I shot in a green *wattle-tree close to Government House. **1835** in K. Cornwallis *Panorama New World* (1859) I. 402 We observed on a wattle tree..scratches or marks of figures, representing blacks in the act of fighting. **1890** *Melbourne Argus* 10 June 5/2 The tender..for the right to strip the wattle trees growing on the upper portion of the You Yangs.

wattle ('wɒt(ə)l), *sb.*[2] Also 6 wattell(e, 7 waddle, wadle. [Of obscure origin; possibly an altered form of WARTLE (which, however, does not appear so early in our quots.), due to assimilation to prec.

Usually believed to be identical with WATTLE *sb.*[1] On the ground of the reading 'a *watel* ful of nobles' in two closely related MSS. of *Piers Plowman* C (where other MSS. have *walet*) it has been assumed that from the primary sense of 'something intertwined' (see prec.) was developed the sense 'basket', and hence that of 'wallet', which would be a possible source of the senses below. (Cf. Shaks. 'wallets of flesh': see WALLET *sb.*[2]) This explanation is connected with the view that *wallet* is a metathesis of *watel*; but in all probability the reading *watel* in *Piers Plowman* is merely a scribal error for *walet*.]

1. A fleshy lobe (usually bright-coloured) pendent from the head or neck of certain birds, as the domestic fowl, the turkey, the guinea-fowl, etc.

1513 in *Glover's Hist. Derby* (1829) I. App. 61 John Curson..bayryth a Cokatrice displayd, goulls with a hed in hys tayll, hys fette and hys wattelles assur. **1577** B. GOOGE *Heresbach's Husb.* IV. 158 Cockes..theyr wattelles oryent. *Ibid.* 166 b, Ginny Cocks, and Turky Cocks..haue no Coames, but only Wattles. **1611** COTGR. s.v. *Barbe, La barbe d'vn coq*, a Cockes rattles, or waddles. **1653** H. MORE *Antid. Ath.* II. xi. §2 Nor are his [*sc.* the cock's] Comb and his Wattles in vain, for they are an Ornament becoming his Martial Spirit. **1706** PHILLIPS (ed. Kersey), *Wattles*,.. Also the Gills of a Cock, or the red Flesh that hangs under a Turkey's Neck. **1725** *Bradley's Family Dict.* s.v. *Pigeon*, The Leghorn is a Sort of Runt, only distinguished by a little Wattle over his Nostril. **1768** PENNANT *Brit. Zool.* I. 212 Their combs and wattles purple and yellow. **1781** —— *Genera of Birds* 9 On each side of the base of the bill, a red, thin fleshy membrane, or Wattle, of a round form. **1788** J. WHITE *Jrnl. Voy. N.S. Wales* (1790) 144 [The Wattled Bee-eater] Under the eye, on each side, is a kind of wattle, of an orange colour. **1812** CRABBE *Tales* i. 380 From red to blue the [turkey's] pendent wattles turn. **1852** J. BAILY *Fowls* 38 The game cock is of bold carriage;..his face and wattle a beautiful red color. **1854** *Poultry Chron.* II. 90 Cocks. Bright red comb, wattle and face. **1867** BAKER *Nile Trib.* iii. (1872) 45 The only species of guinea-fowl that I have seen in Africa is that with the blue comb and wattles.

b. *transf.* (Cf. GILL *sb.*[1] 3 b.)

1910 'Q' (Quiller-Couch) *Lady Good-for-Nothing* I. xi, Once, it seemed to me, I detected the wattles of your worthy fellow-magistrate. He ought not to strain that neck; you should warn him of the danger.

c. *slang.* (See quots.) ? *Obs. rare*$^{-0}$.

a **1700** B. E. *Dict. Cant. Crew, Wattles*, Ears. **1848** *Sinks of Lond.* 129 *Wattles*, the ears.

2. A flap of skin pendent from the throat or neck of some swine.

1570 LEVINS *Manip.* 38/27 Y^e^ Wattle of a hog, *neuus*. **1611** COTGR., *Goitrons*, Waddles, or wattles; the two little and long excrescences, which hang, teat-like, at either side of the throat of some hogs. *Ibid.*, *Gouytrouz*, Swines wadles. **1879** J. WRIGHTSON *Swine* in *Cassell's Techn. Educ.* IV. 351/2 The 'wattles' or skinny appendages situated upon either side and below the cheek.

b. A similar excrescence on the jaws of sheep or goats. See also quot. 1725 (prob. a mis-use).

1725 *Bradley's Family Dict.* s.v. *Goat*, The Buck or the He-goat ought to have a large Body, thick Legs [etc.],..his Ears should be long and hanging down, and his Chin cover'd with a long Beard, or his Jaws rather have two Wattles or Tufts like a Beard. **1842** BISCHOFF *Woollen Manuf.* II. 330

Four-horned sheep are numerous in several parts, and a few have six horns; their forehead is convex, and there are wattles under the throat. **1859** JEPHSON *Brittany* vi. 81 There were some brown goats, too, with white eyebrows, and wattles hanging down at each side of their necks.

3. A fleshy appendage hanging from the mouths of some fishes; a barb.

1655 WALTON *Angler* xviii. (1661) 231 This Loach is of the shape of the Eele: he had a beard or wattels like a Barbel. **1686** PLOT *Staffordsh.* 240 [A fish] having two small *Cirri* or wattles issuing out of the nose near the mouth. **1836** YARRELL *Brit. Fishes* I. 321 The Barbel is said to have been so called from the barbs or wattles attached about its mouth. **1867** F. FRANCIS *Angling* i. (1880) 50 The barbs or wattles that depend from the sides of the mouth.

4. *Comb.*: (in sense 2) †*wattle-faced*, †*-jawed*. Also **wattle-bird**, (*a*) = *wattle-crow*; (*b*) the wattled or warty-faced bee-eater of Australia, *Anthochæra carunculata* and *A. inauris*; **wattle-crow**, any bird of the genus *Glaucopis* (*G. cinerea* and *G. wilsoni*), inhabiting New Zealand; **wattle honey-eater** = *wattle-bird* (*b*).

1773 *Cook's 2nd Voy.* I. v. (1777) I. 98 The *wattle-bird, so called because it has two wattles under its beak as large as those of a small dunghill cock. **1859–62** SIR J. RICHARDSON etc. *Mus. Nat. Hist.* I. 314 The Long-eared Wattle-bird (*Anthochæra inauris*). *Ibid.* 315 The Short-eared Wattle-bird (*Anthochæra carunculata*)... The Brush Wattle-bird (*Anthochæra mellivora*)... The Lunulated Wattle-bird (*A. lunulata*). **1871** BRACKEN *Behind Tomb* 79 The wattle-bird sings in the leafy plantation. **1837** SWAINSON *Nat. Hist. Birds* II. 265 Subfam. Glaucopinæ. *Wattle Crows. *c* **1600** MIDDLETON *Mayor Quinb.* III. iii, I scorn thee, Thou *wattle-fac'd sing'd Pig. **1862** WOOD *Illustr. Nat. Hist.* II. 222 The Yellow *Wattle Honey-eater (*Anthochæra inauris*). **1630** J. TAYLOR (Water P.) *Gt. Eater Kent* Wks. I. 147/2 Hee is *wattle-iawde, and his eyes are sunke inwarde.

†**'wattle**, *sb.*^{3} *Orkney* and *Shetland*. *Obs.* Forms: 5–7 wattell, 6–7 wattill, vattill, 7–8 watle, 6, 9 *Hist.* wattle. [app. a perversion of Norw. *veitla* (Aasen, Ross), dial. var. of *veitsla*:—ON. *veizla* entertainment, *spec.* 'the reception or entertainment to be given to the Norse king.. or his stewards' (Vigf.); f. *veita* to grant, give, to make (a feast), to show (kindness, etc.): see WAIT *v.*^{2} For the sense of the sb. cf. WAITING *vbl. sb.*^{2}

In a Norwegian charter of 15 Apl. 1412 (*Dipl. Norveg.* II. II. 466), containing a grant by King Erik of land in Shetland, the feudal dues payable by the property are enumerated as 'skat, landskyld, ok *wesel*', with which cf. the 'skat, wattle, and dewties' of quot. 1592 below.]

Originally, the obligation, imposed on landed proprietors in Orkney and Shetland, of giving entertainment to the Foud on his annual journey through the islands for the administration of justice; in later times, a tax for which this obligation was commuted.

1477 *Reg. Mag. Sig. Scot.* 281/1 Cum universis liberatibus,..ad dictas terras..spectantibus, unacum *le Wrak, Wattell, Waithe et Hasewaith*. **1503** in Peterkin *Rentals Orkney* I. (1820) 25 Summa de Wattill of the Ile j last in thre thridis viz cost flesche & fat guid. And the commonis ar all accordit to pay the tua in wattill & the thrid in flesche. **1587** *Reg. Mag. Sig. Scot.* 468/1 Reddendo..105 doleras argenteas pro lie wattill. **1588** *Exchequer Rolls Scot.* X. 391 Selling..1000 cunnyng skynnis, 167 packis vedmell, 105 doleris for vattill, 120 angel nobillis for toill. **1592** in *Reg. Mag. Sig. Scot. 1610*, 118/1 Payand..to me..the yeir maillis, skatt, wattell and dewties contenit in our rentall. **1595** in Peterkin *Rentals Orkney* II. (1820) 83 Thomas Sinclair pays yearly furth of his Wattle of the Bailyerie of Sanday 12 meils bear. **1605** *Shetland Rental* in *Jamieson Suppl.* (1887) 270 Rentall of the wattill as it was in anno 1605... Ska, ij nychtis wattill. Trowoilie & Sandoill, ij nychtis wattill. **1610** *Rec. Earldom Orkney* (S.H.S.) 185 His awin proper land and heretage haldin frielie of the king for payment of scat and wattell and of the teynd therof to the kirk. **1628** in *Proc. Soc. Antiq. Scot.* N.S. VII. 231 Easter Quarff, 1 nyghtis wattill. Summa [for Burray] 4 nyghtis wattill and 6 merkis. **1733** T. GIFFORD *Zetland Isl.* v. (1879) 37 To grant charters to the heritors..holding few of the crown for payment of an annual reddendo, formerly paid, called the *Scat* and *Watle*. **1821** SCOTT *Pirate* xviii, Is it not enough that we must pay *scat* and *wattle*, which were all the public dues under our old Norse government; but must they come over us with king's dues and customs besides? **1840** *New Statist. Acc. Shetland* (1845) 63 The wattle was a tax imposed on every family paid in barley to the foud or bailie.

wattle ('wɒt(ə)l), *v.* Forms: 4 wat(t)ele-n, watle-n, 5 wattyll, 6 wattil, wadle, 6–7 watle, wattel, 7 wattell, 6– wattle. [f. WATTLE *sb.*^{1}]

1. *trans.* To construct (a building, wall, fence, arbour) of rods, posts, or laths interlaced with twigs or flexible branches. Also *rarely* with *up*.

1377 LANGL. *P. Pl.* B. XIX. 323 And there-with Grace bigan to make a good foundement, And watteled [*v.rr.* watelide, watled(e] it and walled it with his peynes and his passioun. **1552** HULOET, Wattle a house, *cratio, iui, ire*, whyche is a maner not vsed but where thacked houses be. **1565** COOPER *Thesaurus*, *Concratitius..paries*..walles wattled with roddes as they vse in the countrey. **1600** HOLLAND *Livy* XXVII. iii. 627 To build..cotages and sheds... These were most of them made of hurdles and bourds, some watteled and wound with reedes [L. *alia arundine texta*]. **1617** MORYSON *Itin.* III. 74 For the meere barbarous Irish either sleepe under the canopy of heaven, or in cabbines watled, and covered with turfe. **1627** in Sir. J. H. Ramsay *Bamff Charters* (1915) 212 Bindis..him..to caber wattell and theik with thak..the hall biggit be him. **1707–21** MORTIMER *Husb.* I. 112 A Hedge wattled standing under a Bog that was five or six Foot above it. **1791** W. GILPIN *Forest Scenery* II. 113 He fixes next on some spreading tree, round the bole of which he wattles a slight circular fence of the dimensions he wants. **1821** CLARE *Vill. Minstrel* II. 24 The arbour he once wattled up is broke. **1832** HT. MARTINEAU *Demerara* i. 12 The walls were merely wattled and smeared with plaster. **1867** C. H. PEARSON *Hist. Eng.* I. 16 The villages were circles of huts hollowed out of the hills or heath, to save wall building, the sides wattled and the roofs thatched.

b. To construct (a sheepfold) with hurdles.

1789 CHARLOTTE SMITH *Ethelinde* IV. 170 The shepherd ..contented himself with staring at them a moment, and then went on with wattling his fold. **1827** CLARE *Sheph. Cal.* 189 Shepherds have wattled pens about.

2. To interlace (boughs, twigs, osiers, etc.) so as to form wattle-work.

1486 *Nottingham Rec.* III. 242 Osyars..to wattyll' betwix piles of þe same Brigges. **1563** T. HILL *Art Garden.* (1593) 7 The Romans vsed to..fence their gardens with stakes and laths, set very thick in order, and with small rods watled in together. **1683** *Brit. Spec.* 121 A Temple or Church..the Walls whereof were on all sides made of Rods, watled or interwoven. **1697** DAMPIER *Voy.* I. 539 The sides and top of the House are filled up with Boughs coursely watled between the poles. **1793** *Trans. Soc. Arts* XI. 296 Fixing stakes..and wattling straw-bands between them. **1805** R. W. DICKSON *Pract. Agric.* I. 110 Pl. xxxiii, The dead materials are wattled in between strong stakes. **1833** LOUDON *Encycl. Archit.* §889 The walls..are frames filled in with studwork, into which branches of furze are thickly wattled. **1855** DICKENS etc. *Holly-tree Inn* iv. 26/1 A building of boughs wattled on stakes, and dabbed over with mud. **1858** RAWLINSON tr. *Herodotus* IV. cxc. III. 169 The dwellings of these people are made of the stems of the asphodel, and of rushes, wattled together. **1871** W. B. LORD & BAINES *Shifts Camp Life* vi. 382 Rattans, osiers, twigs, reeds, or grass are then wattled in in the manner shown in the sketch. **1884** *Weekly Lond. Times* 12 Sept. 18 A framework of oak beams, with mortise holes cut to receive cross beams, through which hazel and birch boughs have been closely wattled.

3. To bind together (posts, laths, etc.) with interlaced osiers, twigs, or flexible branches. Also with *across*.

1602 LD. MOUNTJOY *Let.* in Moryson *Itin.* II. 213 Staked on both sides with pallisades watled. **1697** DAMPIER *Voy.* I. 428 These people make but small low Houses. The sides.. are made of small posts, watled with boughs. **1726** SWIFT *Gulliver* IV. ii, We came to a long kind of building, make of timber stuck in the ground, and wattled across. **1775** JOHNSON *West. Isl.*, *Anoch* 76 The part in which we dined and slept was lined with turf and wattled with twigs, which kept the earth from falling. **1809** A. HENRY *Trav.* 294 The fence was..formed of strong stakes of birch-wood, wattled with smaller branches of the same. **1876** TENNYSON *Harold* V. i. 109, I have seen The trenches dug, the palisades uprear'd And wattled thick with ash and willow-wands. **1882** JEFFERIES *Bevis* II. 268 He proposed to..extend a railing all round and wattle this with willows. **1886** STEVENSON *Kidnapped* xxiii, The trunks of several trees had been wattled across, the intervals strengthened with stakes, and the ground behind this barricade levelled up with earth.

4. To cover or surround with wattle-work. Also with *about*.

1545 ELYOT *Dict.*, *Cratio*, to couer with grates, to wattil. **1577** HARRISON *England* III. xii. 111 b in *Holinshed*, Our hiues are made commonly of Rye straw, and wadled about with bramble quarters. **1615** MARKHAM *Country Content.* I. 14 Which seats [for hounds] would bee either boorded, or watled with stakes and small wands on the sides to hold vp the earth from falling. **1629** HOBBES *Thucyd.* II. 122 They built a Frame of Timber, and watled it about on either side, to serue instead of Walles, to keepe the Earth from falling too much away.

5. To fold (sheep). *dial.*

1908 *Academy* 27 June 920/2 This garden hears the sheep-bells of the flock That browses, wattled, on its further strand.

wattled ('wɒt(ə)ld), *a.* [f. WATTLE *sb.*^{2}] Of a bird: Having wattles or a wattle; in *Heraldry*, having the wattles of a specified tincture distinct from that of the body. Also in parasynthetic formations, as ***blue-wattled***, ***one-wattled***.

1688 HOLME *Armoury* IV. iv. (Roxb.) 298/1 A demy cock with wings displaid Gules, Watled and crested, Or. **1777** PORNY *Elem. Her.* (ed. 3) Dict., *Wattled*.., sometimes used in speaking of a Cock whose Wattles or Gills are of a different Tincture, but *Jollowped* is better. **1782** LATHAM *Gen. Syn. Birds* II. I. 9 Wattled Stare. Pl. xxxvi. Wattled Starlings. **1785** *Ibid.* III. I. 82 Wattled Heron. Size of the Stork... Inhabits Africa. **1788** J. WHITE *Jrnl. Voy. N.S. Wales* (1790) 144 The Wattled Bee-eater..is the size of a missel thrush, [etc.]. **1809** SHAW *Gen. Zool.* VII. 378 Wattled Crow. *Corvus carunculatus*... Said to be a native of New Zealand. *c* **1828** BERRY *Encycl. Her.* I. Gloss. **1849** D. J. BROWNE *Amer. Poultry Yard* (1855) 23 The throat of the female being covered with feathers, instead of being naked and wattled. **1854** *Poultry Chron.* II. 336 A Cock (wattled face) and two Hens. **1862** WOOD *Illustr. Nat. Hist.* II. 220 The Wattled Honey-eater, or Brush Wattle Bird of Australia. **1862** LONGF. *Wayside Inn* Prel. 30 The wattled cocks strut to and fro. **1875–84** A. H. LAYARD *Birds S. Africa* 626 *Grus carunculata*, Gm. Wattled Crane. **1901** *Wide World Mag.* VIII. 150/2 The scrub is full of wild duck, blue-wattled guinea fowl, partridges [etc.]. **1903** *Westm. Gaz.* 5 Jan. 10/1 The 'Zoo' has a new occupant of some importance—the Eastern one-wattled cassowary (*Casuarius aurantiacus*) from German New Guinea.

†**b.** Having folds of flesh. *Obs. rare*$^{-1}$.

1567 GOLDING *Ovid's Met.* IX. (1593) 212, I turning to the shape of bull rebelled against my fo. He stepping to my left side close, did fold his armes about My watled necke [L. *induit ille toris a læva parte lacertos*].

†**c.** ***wattled oval***: an oval ring with projecting knobs. (Holme gives a drawing.) *Obs. rare*$^{-1}$.

1688 HOLME *Armoury* IV. ix. (Roxb.) 383/2 At which coller was hunge the modle of the order on a plate in a wattled ovall a Lilly slipped.

wattled ('wɒt(ə)ld), *ppl. a.* [f. WATTLE *v.* + -ED^1.]

1. Constructed of wattle-work.

1548 *Elyot's Dict.*, *Concratitius*, made of hurdels or suche lyke thynges, watled. **1552** *Ibid.*, *Cratitij parietes*, wattled walles made lyke hurdles, as they vse in the countrey. **1677** in *Verney Mem.* (1907) II. 308 Wattled walls only Daubed over with Mortar. **1712** J. JAMES tr. *Le Blond's Gardening* 124 Make use of wattled Hurdles and Fascines. **1757** DYER *Fleece* I. 361 Nor ope the wattled fence, while balmy morn Lies on the reeking pasture. **1805** R. W. DICKSON *Pract. Agric.* II. 674 The flatted hurdle..is much preferable to the close-rodded or wattled kind, as being much more durable. **1813** RUDGE *Agric. Glouc.* 386 Wattled hurdles, 8*s.* per dozen. **1827** SCOTT *Highl. Widow* v, Awhile she paused at the wattled door. **1834** PRINGLE *Afr. Sk.* vii. 233 His reed hut or wattled cabin generally placed on the side of some narrow ravine. **1836** MRS. C. P. TRAILL *Backw. Canada* 309 The fence is a rude basket or hurdle-work..called by the country folk wattled fence. **1871** *Standard* 12 Apr. 6 The weir is a wattled weir, and had the effect of preventing the passage of fish up the river. **1883** SYMONDS *Ital. Byways* ii. 30 Wattled waggons drawn by oxen.

b. Said of a sheepfold. Chiefly *poet.* in ***wattled cote, pen, fold***.

1634 MILTON *Comus* 344 Might we but hear The folded flocks pen'd in their watled cotes. **1730** THOMSON *Summer* 395 The gather'd flocks Are in the wattled pen innumerous press'd. **1753** T. WATSON *Ode Approach Summer* 99 His wattled cotes the shepherd plants. **1830** TENNYSON *Ode to Memory* 66 The livelong bleat Of the thick-fleeced sheep from wattled folds. **1853** M. ARNOLD *Scholar Gipsy* 2 Go, Shepherd, and untie the wattled cotes. **1886** LOWELL *Democr.* etc. (1887) 193 The wattled fold they were rearing here on the edge of the wilderness.

c. ***wattled daub*** (*rare*) = *wattle and daub* (WATTLE *sb.*^{1} 1 b). ***wattled work*** = *wattle-work* (WATTLE *sb.*^{1} 1 c).

1866 LIVINGSTONE *Last Jrnls.* (1873) I. i. 14 The first hundred yards has 90 square houses of *wattled daub. **1712** J. JAMES tr. *Le Blond's Gardening* 67 Made with Beds of Earth and *Watled-work. *Ibid.* 68 Hurdles, or Watled-work. **1871** W. B. LORD & BAINES *Shifts Camp Life* vi. 382 The manner of making a piece of wattled work for a door, a window shutter, [etc.]. **1878** MACLEAR *Celts* vii. 105 Being erected of stone, instead of the usual wood or wattled work.

d. Of cloth: Made by plaiting. *rare.*

1865 TYLOR *Early Hist. Man.* xiii. 365 The wattled cloth of the Swiss lake dwellings.

2. Of branches, twigs, etc.: Interlaced.

1777 MASON *Engl. Garden* IV. 645 A shed of twisting roots and living moss, With rushes thatch'd, with wattled oziers lin'd, He bids them raise. **1868** MISS YONGE *Cameos* I. xlii. 363 Making a multitude of hurdles of wattled boughs to be laid across the softer places of the bog. **1878** BOSW. SMITH *Carthage* xviii. 338 [The huts] of the Numidians..were made of wattled reeds thatched with straw.

†**b.** Of hair: Tangled. *Obs. rare*$^{-1}$.

1591 SYLVESTER *Du Bartas* I. ii. 1218 Their [*sc.* the wind-gods'] wattled locks gush'd all in Rivers out.

3. Enclosed in a sheepfold, folded.

1898 MEREDITH *Odes Fr. Hist.* 82 And all his host A wattled flock, the foeman's dogs between!

†**'wattle-head.** *Obs. rare.* [? f. WATTLE *sb.*^{1} (sense 1, as designating a weak building-material).] A weak-headed person. So **wattle-headed** *a.*

1613 WITHER *Abuses* I. Sat. i. 127 But he that is with such a humor led I may be bold to terme a watle-head. *Ibid.* Sat. v. 90 Our watle-headed Gallants would but flout At their well tempred passions. **1866** G. A. LAWRENCE *Sans Merci* III. 3 The damsel's father was an easy-going and something 'wattle-headed' elder.

wattless ('wɒtlɪs), *a.* *Electr.* [f. WATT + -LESS.] Of a current, an electromotive force, etc.: Consuming no power.

1902 *Electr. Rev.* 4 Apr. 544/2 The wattless current being taken as positive, when it is in advance of the P.D.

wattling ('wɒtlɪŋ), *vbl. sb.* Also 4–7 wattelyng(e, -ing, 4–6 watlyng(e, -ing(e, 6 wadling. [f. WATTLE *v.* + -ING^1.]

1. The action of the verb WATTLE.

1573–80 TUSSER *Husb.* (1878) 83 To arbor begun, and quick setted about, no poling nor wadling till set be far out. **1633** T. JAMES *Voy.* 60 Our second house was..made for the watteling much after the same manner. **1916** *Contemp. Rev.* July 96 Plaiting, braiding, weaving and wattling, all of which bring into existence very definite rudiments of pattern.

2. *concr.* **a.** An assemblage of rods or laths interlaced with branches, twigs, osiers, or the like, serving as the material of a wattled wall, partition, fence, etc., or as the framework of a 'wattle-and-daub' building. Also, in generalized sense, wattle as a structural material.

1336 *Cal. Docum. Scot.* (1887) III. 349 Item pro amputacione xxiiij carcatarum virgarum pro 'wattelyngs', et pro cariagio earundem de bosco usque castrum. *Ibid.* 351 [similarly but] 'watlyngs'. **1431–40** in Glasscock *Rec. St. Michael's, Bp.'s Stortford* (1882) 8 Et in virgis emptis pro watlyng sprendelles et ligaminibus, xd. ob. *c* **1468** in *Archæologia* (1846) XXXI. 336 On every tarage a tree of gold... The tarage before reherssid, wateled wt gold, wthin the watelinge abowt the said tre, and every of them fylled wt meatis divers. **1545** ELYOT *Dict.*, *Crates*, grates of yron or wood. They be also the watling of a wall or house klayd or thatched. **1598** BARRET *Theor. Warres* V. iii. 131 Watlings, gabbions, and all other things needfull, at batteries, and besieging. **1658** in J. Campbell *Balmerino* (1899) 410 Ane new cupill, cabers, watlings, door-cheeks, half doore. **1699** DAMPIER *Voy.* II. II. 115 The side Walls are Stud or Watling, plaister'd on the inside. **1763** HUME *Hist. Eng.* xxxvii. (1770) IV. 497 The houses [*c* 1560] were nothing but watling, plastered over with clay. **1837** J. E. MURRAY *Summer in Pyrenees* I. 63 A wattling of willow boughs, about eight feet square. **1842** LOUDON *Suburban Hort.* 149 Fig. 66 shows the handle and rim of what is called the Scotch basket. .. Fig. 67 shows the same skeleton, with .. the wattling or woven work commenced. **1909** STACPOOLE *Pools of Silence* xxx, Adams had swung the man aloft and dashed him against the wall with such force, that the wattling gave way and the plaster fell in flakes.

†*transf.* **1567** GOLDING *Ovid's Met.* XII. (1593) 286 He threw an ashen dart Which brake the watling of his ribs [L. *laterum cratem*].

b. Boughs and twigs for use in wattle-work.

1622 F. MARKHAM *Bk. War* III. v. 98 To hew downe boughes and young watlings to make Cabins. **1688** HOLME *Armoury* III. xiv. (Roxb.) 19/2 Thatchers Termes... Watlings iusted of Laths. **1763** 'THEOPHILUS INSULANUS' *Second Sight* 26 Going .. to cut wattling for creels. **1809** tr. *Molina's Hist. Chili* I. 128 The husbandmen .. employ it [a vine] both in making large baskets, and as wattling for their hedges. **1831** JANE PORTER *Sir E. Seaward's Narr.* I. x. 295 To cut the stakes and watlings for the stoccado.

3. *Comb.*

14.. *Master of Game* etc. (MS. Douce 335) fol. 73 Ony smal wode, that is to wete, blatrons, sparres, watlyngroddes, or ony other smal wode.

wattre, wattry, obs. ff. WATER, WATERY.

wattshode, obs. form of WATCHET.

wattur, -yr, watur(e, -yr(e, obs. ff. WATER.

Watusi (wə'tuːsɪ). Also **Watussi, Watutsi.** [Native name.] **1.** The name of a minority racial group in Rwanda and Burundi, probably of Ethiopic or Nilotic origin, which formerly dominated the majority Hutu people; a member of this group. Also *attrib.* or as *adj.* Also called TUTSI.

1899 H. A. NESBITT tr. *P. Kollmann's Victoria Nyanza* ii. 13 None of the large cattle adorned with magnificent horns which we find everywhere else among the Wahuma and Watussi are to be noticed in Uganda. **1937** *John o' London's* 5 Feb. 765/1 The Watussi still preserve certain rites and customs analogous to those which are known to have been operative in Ancient Egypt. **1959** A. MOOREHEAD *No Room in Ark* ii. 66 The Watusi are celebrated hunters, very tall and lithe. **1960** *Guardian* 7 June 4/1 Watutsi pastoralists .. are encircling the Birunga. **1976** D. TOPOLSKI *Muzungu* xv. 227 Noel was a Watutsi and had been adopted at an early age by a farmer from New Zealand.

2. (Also with small initial.) A popular dance of the 1960s. Also as *v. intr.*

1964 *Time* 20 Mar. 62/3 (*caption*) Watutsiing at Whisky à Gogo. *Ibid.*, A pretty eyeful slaps on new records and dances it all by herself. That way, it's called the Watutsi. **1965** [see *hip-swinging* adj. s.v. HIP *sb.*[1] 4 b]. **1966** *Punch* 20 July 116/1 They .. fed on lotus and daiquiri, they frugged and watutsied. **1966** T. PYNCHON *Crying of Lot 49* v. 105 Nefastis had been watching on his TV set a bunch of kids dancing some kind of a Watusi. **1966** H. NIELSON *After Midnight* (1967) xvi. 213 She could teach you to watusi and swim. **1974** *Encycl. Brit. Micropædia* X. 213/3 Dances evolved from the twist, such as the frug, the jerk, and the watusi, were invariably performed by shaking the pelvis. **1979** R. JAFFE *Class Reunion* (1980) II. vi. 244 They danced the frug, the swim, and the watusi.

wau, var. WAW *sb.*[1], wave, WOUGH *dial.*, wall.

wau, var. WAW *sb.*[4] (Hebr. and Arab. letter).

wauble, Sc. form of WOBBLE.

wauch: see WATCH *sb.* and *v.*, WAUGH *a.*, WAUGHT *v.*

waucht, var. WAUGHT *sb.* and *v.*

wauf(f, waufie: see WAFF, WAFFIE.

waugh (wɑf), *a. Sc.* and *north.* Also **wauch, wauf, waff,** etc. [See WALLOW *a.*] Tasteless, insipid; unpleasant to the smell or taste, sickly; faint, weak, etc. (see *Eng. Dial. Dict.*).

1703 THORESBY *Let. to Ray*, *Waugh*, insipid, unsalted, and so unsavory. **1814** [MRS. JOHNSTONE] *Saxon & Gael* III. 189 (Jam.), I think she'll no put owre this night. The wauch earth smell is about her already.

waugh (wɔː), *int.* Also 8 **wa,** 9 **wagh.** [An instinctive exclamation; cf. WOUGH, WHAU.] An exclamation indicating grief, indignation or the like. Chiefly as attributed to N. American Indians etc.

1761 MRS. F. SHERIDAN *Sidney Bidulph* (1796) IV. 92 The other brat .. squalls for it [the toy] directly, Waugh, Sir, it was mine first. **1791** J. LONG *Voy. Ind. Interpr.* 164 *Wa! wa!* or Oh! oh! replied the Savage, but what is the warrior tied up for? **1827** J. F. COOPER *Prairie* I. xvii. 252 A tall Indian .. stood upright, uttering the sententious exclamation, 'Wagh!' **1832** LYTTON *Eugene A.* IV. ix, 'Well, if ever I seed the like!' quoth the corporal; .. 'augh!—waugh!—bother!' **1834** WHITTIER *Mogg Megone* 411 Wagh!—Mogg will have the pale-face's hair. **1846** P. B. ST. JOHN *Enchanted Rock* iv. 89 'Wagh!' escaped from the lips of the Indian girl. **1891** 'R. BOLDREWOOD' *Sydney-side Sax.* vi, Talgai sings out 'Wagh!' and pointed with his chin, like all blacks do.

waugh, variant of WAFF *v.*[3], WAW *sb.*[2]

waugh hawk. ? A perversion or misunderstanding of *ware hawk*: see WARE *v.*[1] 3 b.

1844 THACKERAY *Barry Lyndon* xiii, Waugh hawk, Mr. Barry; don't think .. to stand in my shoes when they are vacant.

Waughian ('wɔːɪən), *a.* [f. the name *Waugh* + -IAN.] Of, pertaining to, or characteristic of the English novelist Evelyn Waugh (1903–66) or his writing.

1960 *Times Lit. Suppl.* 2 Dec. 783/3 Smyth strays into 1960 from some distant Waughian era. **1976** *Ibid.* 1 Oct. 1229/4 Sniping on Firbankian and Waughian lines. **1977** *Time* 19 Dec. 11/1 A country without government? The description immediately calls to mind a Waughian Third World kingdom.

Also **Waughism** ('wɔːɪz(ə)m), (*a*) the ideas or style characteristic of Waugh, or those portrayed in his novels; (*b*) a word or expression characteristic of Waugh.

1934 [see RUSSELLISM]. **1976** A. POWELL *Infants of Spring* x. 167 The sessions he devoted to ragging ('mocking', to use a Waughism ..) were likely to take certain routine forms.

waught (wɑxt), *sb. Sc.* and *north.* Also 9 **waucht, waft.** [f. next vb.] A copious draught. Also *transf.* and *fig.*

1721 RAMSAY *Answ. to Burchet* 2 Thirsting for fame, at the Pierian spring, The poet takes a waught. **1722** —— *Spring & Syke* 11 Ae day, after great waughts of wet. **1788** BURNS *Auld Lang Syne* v, And we'll tak' a right gude-willie waught, For auld lang syne. **1816** SCOTT *Old Mort.* iv, Ye needna stick to gie them a waught o' drink and a bannock. **1882** C. GIBBON *Golden Shaft* xxxii, Sae my father takes up the bottle and took a waft and says he—'Ay, that's rael fine chlorodyne'. **1893** STEVENSON *Catriona* xix. 219, I had a good wacht of milk in by Ratho.

waught (wɑxt), *v. Sc.* Forms: 6 **waucht, wacht, vacht,** 9 **wauch,** 7–9 **waught.** [Of obscure origin; prob. allied to QUAFF, QUAUGHT *vbs.*] *trans.* To drink or quaff in large draughts; to drain (a goblet); also with *out*, *over*. Also *absol.* or *intr.*

1508 DUNBAR *Tua Mariit Wemen* 39 Thay wauchtit at the wicht wyne. **1513** DOUGLAS *Æneis* VII. iii. 90 In flacon and in skull Thai skynk the wyne, and wauchtis coupis full. **1567** *Gude & Godlie B.* (S.T.S.) 26 To wacht gude wyne. **1581** *Satir. Poems Reform.* xliv. 94 Except his coup var vachtit out aluay. **1624** *Extracts Aberd. Reg.* (1848) II. 391 That nane presume .. to wse at any tyme any excessive drinking or scolling, or to vrge thair nichtbouris to waught or scole farder nor thair plesour. **1728** RAMSAY *Archers diverting themselves* 100 How heaty went these healths about! How blythly were they waughted out! *c* **1730** —— *Masque* 193, I waught o'er This flowing glass of .. wine. **1849** W. JAMIE *Stray Effusions* 27 (E.D.D.) Packman billies waught their ale.

Hence '**waughting** *vbl. sb.*

1637–50 ROW *Hist. Kirk* (Wodrow Soc.) 173 Excessive drinking and waughting. **1842** VEDDER *Poems* 78 But now he's a dyvor, wi' birling an' wauchin'.

waughtar, -er, obs. ff. WAFTER *sb.*[1]

waugle-eghed, obs. form of WALL-EYED *a.*

wauk, Sc. var. WAKE *v.*, WALK *v.*[1], *v.*[2]

wauken, Sc. variant of WAKEN *v.*

wauker, Sc. var. WALKER *sb.*[2]

waukrife, variant of WAKERIFE *Sc.*

waul (wɔːl), *sb.* [f. next.] A loud cry or howl.

1856 MEREDITH *Shav. Shagpat* 355 This was followed by .. the waul of Krooz .. and the complainings of Dob.

waul, wawl (wɔːl), *v.* Also 6 *Sc.* **wawill,** 6–7 **wawle,** 6–8 **waule,** 9 *dial.* **whaul, whawl.** [? Echoic; cf. WRAWL *v.*] *intr.* To utter the loud harsh cry characteristic of cats or of new-born babies.

15.. *Poems Gray MS.* v. 19 (S.T.S) 51 Quhat helpis þan to wawill or weip? **1557** PHAER *Æneid.* VII. (1558) S ij b, And figures foule of wolues thei heare for wo to fret and wawle. **1601** *2nd Pt. Return fr. Parnass.* v. iv. 2151 Where cats do waule by day, dogges barke by night. **1605** SHAKS. *Lear* IV. vi. 184 Thou know'st, the first time that we smell the Ayre We wawle, and cry. **1620** MELTON *Astrolog.* 52 Many people in these dayes cannot .. heare a Dogge howle, or a Cat wawle, but instantly they will runne to the Calculator. **1681** T. FLATMAN *Heraclitus Ridens* No. 35 (1713) I. 228 Your Babes of Grace, which waul and cry, because their Mother won't let them scratch her Eyes out. **1774** COLMAN *Man of Business* Prol., His brats .. Brought up on playhouse pap, they waule and cry. **1871** POSTE *Gaius* IV. §§21–25. 420 The plaintiff on three market-days shall stand before the defendant's door and waul [*ed.* 2 1875 wawl].

Hence '**wauling** *vbl. sb.* and *ppl. a.*

a **1530** HEYWOOD *Johan & Tyb* 118 (Brandl), Wylt thou neuer leue this wawlyng? **1543** BALE *Yet a Course* 43 b, Wolde Tolwyn haue bene a good Idoll mayntener with holye water and sensynge, latine Iabberynge and wawlynge, .. he had not bene thus brought forth for an heretyque. **1621** MOLLE *Camerar. Liv. Libr.* v. xv. 380 Without the shameful bawling and wawling of Lawyers and Atturneys. **1648** *Mistris Parliament brought to Bed* 8 There was .. heard terrible thunderings, intermix'd with wawling of Catts, howling of Doggs, and barking of Wolves. *a* **1708** T. WARD *England's Reform.* I. (1710) 121 Like snarling Dog and wawling puss. **1812** G. COLMAN *Lady of Wreck* II. xxi, Around his wawling presence swell A huge Seraglio, stock'd, pell-mell, With black, white, tabby, tortoise-shell. **1861** L. L. NOBLE *Icebergs* 296 Grimalkin answered with a terrible wauling.

waul, waule, obs. forms of WALL *sb.*[1], *v.*[4]

wauld, Sc. form of WIELD *sb.* and *v.*, WOLD.

wauld, Sc. f. *would*: see WILL *v.*

waulk, obs. f. WAKE *v.*; variant of WALK *v.*[2]

waulm(e, variant forms of WALM *sb.*[1], *v.*

wault, variant of WALT *v.*

1611 COTGR., *Verser vn chariot*, to wault, ouerturne, or ouerthrow a chariot; whence the Prouerbe; *Il n'est si bon chartier qui ne verse*; The best that driues, will sometimes wault, a cart.

waulter, -tre, obs. forms of WALTER *v.*[1]

waum(e, variant forms of WALM *sb.*[1]

waumle, obs. form of WAMBLE *v.*

waun(d)s, vulgar or affected pron. of *wounds*, used as a profane oath: see WOUNDS *int.*

waundy: see WOUNDY *a.*

waunt, dial. var. WANT *sb.*[1]; obs. f. WANT *v.*

waunty, obs. form of WANTY.

wauompeg, obs. form of WAMPUMPEAG.

waur: see WAR *a.*, *adv.*, *v.*[2]

waur, variant of WARE *sb.*[1], *sb.*[5], *v.*[2]

waurscaw, corrupt or blundered form of WARESTALL *Sc.*

1533 *Extracts Aberd. Reg.* (1844) I. 451 Ane bukat, ane wavrscaw, ane skayne for the buitht.

wausper: see WAWSPER *Sc.*

waut, dial. form of WALT *v.*, WELT *sb.* and *v.*

wautt, obs. form of VAULT *sb.*[1]

1553–54 in Willis & Clark *Cambridge* (1886) II. 607 With ij wavtts, furth of y[e] chambers, in to y[e] galarye.

wauve, variant of WHAUVE.

wau-wau, variant of WOW-WOW.